KU-275-922

LANGENSCHEIDT'S
POCKET
DICTIONARIES

LANGENSCHEIDT'S POCKET DICTIONARY

OF THE ENGLISH AND GERMAN LANGUAGES

First Part

English-German

by

PROF. EDMUND KLATT
and
DR. DIETRICH ROY

Enlarged and updated edition

HODDER AND STOUGHTON

Contents

Published in the British Commonwealth
by Hodder & Stoughton Limited

The inclusion of any word in this dictionary is not an expression of the publisher's opinion on whether or not such word is a registered trademark or subject to proprietary rights. It should be understood that no definition in this dictionary or the fact of the inclusion of any word herein is to be regarded as affecting the validity of any trademark.

Enlarged and updated edition 1983

Printed in Germany

Preface

For a century now Langenscheidt's Taschenwörterbücher have been an indispensable tool of the language student in Germany. The English-German Taschenwörterbuch has been completely revised and reset six times.

The present 1983 edition (enlarged and updated) retains the long-established merits of the Taschenwörterbuch, while at the same time offering the very latest vocabulary of the eighties. Thousands of neologisms from all fields have been included in the dictionary, making an enlarged edition necessary.

The following brief excursion into a few of these areas gives some indication of the variety and scope of vocabulary covered by the many additions:

Pollution: *acid rain* (saurer Regen), *anti-pollution device* (Abgasentgiftungsanlage), *ecocidal* (umweltzerstörend), *ecocide* (Umweltzerstörung), *ecocrisis* (Umweltkrise)

Politics: *shuttle diplomacy* (Pendeldiplomatie), *urban guerilla* (Stadtguerilla), *nuke* (Atom-, Kernwaffe)

Fashion: *the beautiful people* (Schickeria), *drain-pipe trousers* (Röhrenhosen)

Technology: *digital telephone* (Tastentelefon), *light emitting diode* (Leuchtdiode)

Television: *chat show* (Talk-Show), *phone-in* (Sendung mit Zuschauer- od. Zuhörerbeteiligung)

Work: *time credit* (Zeitguthaben bei gleitender Arbeitszeit), *time debit* (Fehlzeit bei gleitender Arbeitszeit), *bleeper* (Piepser-, Funkrufempfänger), *mom-and-pop store* (Tante-Emma-Laden)

Traffic: *acceleration lane* (Beschleunigungsspur), *metermaid* (Politesse)

Music: *audiophile* (Hi-Fi-Fan), *deejay* (Diskjockey)

Similarly, careful consideration has been given to more general vocabulary such as *computer dating*, *character assassination*, *non-stick*, not forgetting slang and colloquialisms (cf. *aggro*, *dishy*). Among the very recent developments covered in detail in this dictionary are the revised film certificates (cf. p. 672).

The new Taschenwörterbuch has, needless to say, preserved the time-honoured principles which secured its predecessor's reputation as a valuable source of information. The pronunciation of the headwords, given in the International Phonetic Alphabet, and the marking of word divisions make for easier use. American English continues to be well represented. Translations and additional explanations are consistently presented in systematic, readable and economical form; the wealth of information provided in the articles renders this Taschenwörterbuch a highly useful English-German reference work.

Among the nine appendices dealing with a variety of subjects there is an extensive new appendix on punctuation and capitalisation which deserves special mention as a thoroughly reliable and helpful guide on this particular aspect of the English language.

We trust that the English Taschenwörterbuch in this new enlarged edition will appeal to old and new users alike.

LANGENSCHEIDT

Vorwort

Seit 100 Jahren gehören die Taschenwörterbücher von Langenscheidt zum Handwerkszeug des Sprachenlernenden in Deutschland. Sechsmal wurde das englisch-deutsche Taschenwörterbuch vollständig neu bearbeitet, neu gesetzt und wesentlich erweitert.

Die vorliegende erweiterte Neuausgabe 1983 behält die millionenfach bewährte Grundstruktur des Wörterbuches bei – sie bietet aber jetzt dem Benutzer gleichzeitig den modernen Wortschatz der achtziger Jahre. Die aufgenommenen Neuwörter – es sind Tausende aus allen Lebensbereichen – machten wiederum eine Erweiterung dieses Standardwörterbuches notwendig.

Der folgende kleine Streifzug durch einige Fachgebiete gibt eine Vorstellung von der Vielgestaltigkeit dieses neuen Wortschatzes:

Umweltverschmutzung: *acid rain* (saurer Regen), *anti-pollution device* (Abgasentgiftungsanlage), *ecocidal* (umweltzerstörend), *ecocide* (Umweltzerstörung), *ecocrisis* (Umweltkrise)

Politik: *shuttle diplomacy* (Pendeldiplomatie), *urban guerilla* (Stadtguerilla), *nuke* (Atom-, Kernwaffe)

Mode: *the beautiful people* (Schickeria), *drain-pipe trousers* (Röhrenhosen)
Technik: *digital telephone* (Tastentelefon), *light emitting diode* (Leuchtdiode)
Fernsehen: *chat show* (Talk-Show), *phone-in* (Sendung mit Zuschauer- od. Zuhörerbeteiligung)
Arbeitswelt: *time credit* (Zeitguthaben bei gleitender Arbeitszeit), *time debit* (Fehlzeit bei gleitender Arbeitszeit), *bleeper* (Piepser, Funkrufempfänger), *mom-and-pop store* (Tante-Emma-Laden)
Straßenverkehr: *acceleration lane* (Beschleunigungsspur), *metermaid* (Politesse)
Musik: *audiophile* (Hi-Fi-Fan), *deejay* (Diskjockey)

Andere Beispiele mögen die Spannweite der im Bereich der Allgemeinsprache durchgeführten Neuwörter-Arbeit für dieses Wörterbuch zeigen: *computer dating*, *character assassination*, *non-stick*. Auch der Bereich des Slang und der Umgangssprache wurde bei den Neuaufnahmen nicht vernachlässigt (vgl. *aggro*, *dishy*). Neue Entwicklungen wie z. B. die veränderte Kennzeichnung der jugendfreien Filme wurden ausführlich dargestellt (vgl. S. 672).

Selbstverständlich wurden in der vorliegenden Neuausgabe die bewährten Grundsätze beibehalten, denen das englische Taschenwörterbuch seinen Ruf und seinen Nachschlagewert verdankt.

Die Angabe der Aussprache in Internationaler Lautschrift und die Markierung der Silbentrennungsmöglichkeiten erleichtern die Verwendung der englischen Stichwörter. Das amerikanische Englisch ist im Wörterverzeichnis nach wie vor stark vertreten. Alle Übersetzungen und Erläuterungen sind auf engstem Raum übersichtlich dargestellt; ihre Vielzahl macht das vorliegende Taschenwörterbuch zu einem englisch-deutschen Kompendium von hohem Informationswert.

Von den neun Anhängen mit verschiedenster Thematik sei vor allem der umfangreiche neue Anhang „Zeichensetzung und Großschreibung" erwähnt, der den Benutzer auf diesem Gebiet kaum jemals im Stich lassen dürfte.

Wir hoffen, daß das englische Tachenwörterbuch in seiner erweiterten Fassung noch zusätzliche Freunde gewinnen wird.

LANGENSCHEIDT

Guide to the Use of the Dictionary

Hinweise für den Benutzer

1. English Headwords. 1.1 The alphabetical order of the headwords has been observed throughout, including the irregular forms.

1.2 Centred dots or stress marks within a headword indicate syllabification,

e.g. **cul·ti·vat·ed** ... **cul·tiˈva·tion**

1.3 In hyphenated compounds a hyphen coinciding with the end of a line is repeated at the beginning of the next.

1.4 The tilde (**~**, ~) is used to avoid repeating the headword. **1.41** If a headword constitutes the initial element of compounds which immediately follow, it is replaced by a boldfaced tilde (**~**),

e.g. **aft·er** ... **ˈ~·birth** (= afterbirth) ...

1.42 The simple tilde (~) replaces the bold-faced word immediately preceding (which itself may have been formed with the aid of a tilde),

e.g. **dis·tance** ... *at a* ~ ~ at a distance
day ... **ˈ~·light** ... *~-saving time* = daylight-saving time.

1.5 When the initial letter changes from small to capital or vice versa, the usual tilde is replaced by **2** or 2,

e.g. **foot...**: ... **2 Guards** = Foot Guards.

2. Pronunciation. 2.1 The pronunciation of English headwords is given in square brackets by means of the symbols of the International Phonetic Association (see pp. 13 to 15).

2.2 To save space the tilde (~) has been made use of in many places within the phonetic transcription. It

1. Englisches Stichwort. 1.1 Das Wörterverzeichnis ist alphabetisch geordnet und verzeichnet auch die unregelmäßigen Formen an ihrer alphabetischen Stelle.

1.2 Der in den Stichwörtern auf Mitte stehende Punkt bzw. der Betonungsakzent zeigt an, wo das englische Wort getrennt werden kann:
cul·ti·vat·ed ... **cul·tiˈva·tion**

1.3 Fällt bei einem mit Bindestrich zu schreibenden englischen Stichwort der Bindestrich auf das Zeilenende, so wird er am Anfang der folgenden Zeile wiederholt.

1.4 Um die Wiederholung des Stichworts zu vermeiden, wird die Tilde (**~**, ~) verwandt. **1.41** Folgen einem ausgerückten Stichwort weitere Zusammensetzungen mit diesem, so wird es durch die halbfette Tilde (**~**) ersetzt:
aft·er ... **ˈ~·birth** (= afterbirth) ...

1.42 Die magere Tilde (~) ersetzt in Anwendungsbeispielen das unmittelbar vorangehende halbfette Stichwort, das auch selbst mit einer halbfetten Tilde gebildet sein kann:
dis·tance ... *at a* ~ = at a distance
day ... **ˈ~·light** ... *~-saving time* = daylight-saving time.

1.5 Wenn sich der Anfangsbuchstabe eines Stichworts ändert (klein zu groß oder umgekehrt), steht statt der Tilde **2** bzw. 2:
foot...: **2 Guards** = Foot Guards

2. Aussprache. 2.1 Die Aussprache des englischen Stichworts steht in eckigen Klammern und wird durch die Symbole der International Phonetic Association wiedergegeben. (Siehe Seite 13–15.)

2.2 Aus Gründen der Platzersparnis wird in der Lautschriftklammer oft die Tilde (~) verwandt. Sie ersetzt

replaces any part of the preceding complete transcription which remains unchanged,
e.g. **as·so·ci·a·ble** [əˈsəuʃjəbl] ... **asˈso·ci·ate** **1.** [~ʃieit] ... **2.** [~ʃiit] ... **as·so·ci·a·tion** [~siˈeiʃən]

2.3 Words ending in one of the suffixes transcribed on p. 15 are given without transcription, unless they figure as headwords. For their stress marks see p. 14, paragraph C.

3. Subject Labels. The field of knowledge from which an English headword or some of its meanings are taken is indicated by symbols or labels, either in abbreviated form or written out in full. A figurative or abbreviated label placed between the headword and its phonetic transcription refers to all translations. A label preceding an individual translation refers to this translation only.

4. Usage Label. The indication of the level of usage by abbreviations such as F, *sl.*, *lit.*, *poet.*, refers to the English headword. Wherever possible the same level of usage between headword and translation has been aimed at.

5. Grammatical References.

5.1 In the appendix (pp. 663/664) the user will find a list of irregular verbs.

5.2 (*irr.*) following a verb refers the user to this list, where he will find the principal parts of this particular verb.

5.3 A reference such as (*irr. fall*) indicates that the compound verb is conjugated exactly like the primary verb as given in the list of irregular verbs.

5.4 An adjective marked with □ takes the regular adverbial form, i.e. by affixing ...ly to the adjective or by changing ...le into ...ly or ...y into ...ily.

5.5 (*~ally*) means that an adverb is formed by affixing ...ally to the adjective.

5.6 When there is only one adverb

den Teil der Lautschrift, der sich gegenüber der vorhergehenden Vollumschrift nicht verändert:
as·so·ci·a·ble [əˈsəuʃjəbl] ... **asˈso·ci·ate** **1.** [~ʃieit] ... **2.** [~ʃiit] ... **as·so·ci·a·tion** [~siˈeiʃən] ...

2.3 Stichwörter mit einer der auf S. 15 umschriebenen Endungen erhalten keine Aussprachebezeichnung, es sei denn, sie seien ausgerückt. Zum Betonungsakzent siehe S. 14, Abschnitt C.

3. Sachgebiet. Das Sachgebiet, dem ein englisches Stichwort oder einige seiner Bedeutungen angehören, wird durch bildliche Zeichen, Abkürzungen oder ausgeschriebene Hinweise kenntlich gemacht. Steht die bildliche oder abgekürzte Sachgebietsbezeichnung vor der Lautschriftklammer, bezieht sie sich auf alle folgenden Übersetzungen. Steht sie innerhalb des Artikels vor einer Übersetzung, so gilt sie nur für diese.

4. Sprachebene. Die Kennzeichnung der Sprachebene durch Abkürzungen wie F, *sl.*, *lit.*, *poet.* etc. bezieht sich auf das englische Stichwort. Die deutsche Übersetzung wurde möglichst so gewählt, daß sie auf der gleichen Sprachebene wie das Stichwort liegt.

5. Grammatische Hinweise.

5.1 Eine Liste der unregelmäßigen Verben befindet sich im Anhang auf S. 663/664.

5.2 Der Hinweis (*irr.*) bei einem Verb zeigt an, daß es unregelmäßig konjugiert wird und daß seine Stammformen in dieser Liste aufgeführt sind.

5.3 Hinweise wie (*irr. fall*) zeigen an, daß das Stichwort ebenso konjugiert wird wie das in der Liste der unregelmäßigen Verben aufgeführte Grundverb *fall*.

5.4 Das Zeichen □ bei einem Adjektiv bedeutet, daß das Adverb regelmäßig, d. h. durch Anhängung von ...ly oder durch Verwandlung von ...le in ...ly oder ...y in ...ily gebildet wird.

5.5 Der Hinweis (*~ally*) bei einem Adjektiv bedeutet, daß das Adverb durch Anhängung von ...ally gebildet wird.

5.6 Bei Adjektiven, die auf ...ic und

for adjectives ending in both ...ic and ...ical, this is indicated in the following way:

his·tor·ic, his·tor·i·cal □,
i.e. historically is the adverb of both adjectives.

5.7 The indication of the parts of speech (noun, adjective, verb, etc.) has been omitted where it is obvious. In cases of doubt, however, the parts of speech have been indicated.

6. Translations.

6.1 Translations of a headword have been subdivided by Arabic numerals to distinguish the various parts of speech. Words of similar meanings have been subdivided by commas, those with distinct differences in meaning by semicolons.

6.2 Explanatory additions have been printed in italics; thus, for example, a direct object precedes a verb, a subject follows it in parentheses,

e.g. **a·bate** ... *v/t.* ... *Schmerz* lindern; ... *Preis* herabsetzen; ... *v/i.* ... sich legen (*Wind*); fallen (*Preis*) ...

6.3 Prepositions governing an English headword (verb, adjective, noun) are given in both languages,

e.g. **dis·sent** ... **2.** (*from*) anderer Meinung sein (als), nicht übereinstimmen (mit); abweichen (von) ...
dis·qual·i·fy ... unfähig *od.* untauglich machen *od.* erklären (*for* zu) ...

6.4 Where a German preposition may govern the dative or the accusative case, the case is given in parentheses,

e.g. **en·ter** ... eintreten in (*acc.*) ...

7. Illustrative phrases and their translations are given at the end of the respective part of speech (in verb articles at the end of *v/t* und *v/i.* respectively), e.g.

deal[2] ... **1.** Teil *m*; ... *a good* ~ ziemlich viel; *a great* ~ sehr viel; *give a square* ~ *to* gerecht werden (*dat.*); **2.** ...

...ical enden können, wird die Adverbbildung so gekennzeichnet:

his·tor·ic, his·tor·i·cal □,
d. h. historically ist das Adverb zu beiden Adjektivformen.

5.7 Die Kennzeichnung der Wortart (wie Substantiv, Adjektiv etc.) ist unterblieben, wenn sie aus der deutschen Übersetzung eindeutig hervorgeht. Wo Mißverständnisse möglich wären, wird die Wortart angegeben.

6. Deutsche Übersetzung.

6.1 Die Übersetzungen des englischen Stichworts sind durch arabische Ziffern nach Wortarten gegliedert. Innerhalb einer Wortart sind bedeutungsähnliche Wörter durch Komma, Bedeutungsunterschiede durch Semikolon getrennt.

6.2 Erläuternde Zusätze sind kursiv gegeben: bei Verben steht z. B. ein mögliches Objekt vor der Übersetzung, ein Subjekt in Klammern danach:

a·bate ... *v/t.* ... *Schmerz* lindern; ... *Preis* herabsetzen; ... *v/i.* ... sich legen (*Wind*); fallen (*Preis*) ...

6.3 Wird das englische Stichwort (Verb, Adjektiv oder Substantiv) von bestimmten Präpositionen regiert, so werden diese mit den deutschen Entsprechungen, der jeweiligen Bedeutung zugeordnet, angegeben:

dis·sent ... **2.** (*from*) anderer Meinung sein (als), nicht übereinstimmen (mit); abweichen (von) ...
dis·qual·i·fy ... unfähig *od.* untauglich machen *od.* erklären (*for* zu) ...

6.4 Bei deutschen Präpositionen, die den Dativ und den Akkusativ regieren können, wird der Fall in Klammern angegeben:

en·ter ... eintreten in (*acc.*) ...

7. Anwendungsbeispiele und ihre Übersetzungen sind am Ende der jeweiligen Wortart (bzw. bei Verbartikeln am Ende von *v/t.* oder *v/i.*) zusammengefaßt:

deal[2] ... **1.** Teil *m*; ... *a good* ~ ziemlich viel; *a great* ~ sehr viel; *give a square* ~ *to* gerecht werden (*dat.*); **2.** ...

8. Symbols — Bildliche Zeichen

~, ≗, ~, ≗ s. 1.4—1.5, 2.2.

F familiär, *familiar*; Umgangssprache, *colloquial language*.

P populär, ungebildet, *low colloquialism*.

V vulgär, *vulgar*.

† veraltet, *obsolete*.

☆ selten, *rare, little used*.

⚘ Pflanzenkunde, *botany*.

⊕ Handwerk, *handicraft*; Technik, *engineering*.

⚒ Bergbau, *mining*.

⚔ militärisch, *military term*.

⚓ Schiffahrt, *nautical term*.

☤ Handelswesen, *commercial term*.

□ s. 5.4.

🚂 Eisenbahn, *railway, railroad*.

✈ Luftfahrt, *aviation*.

📯 Postwesen, *postal affairs*.

♪ Musik, *musical term*.

⩓ Architektur, *architecture*.

⚡ Elektrotechnik, *electrical engineering*.

⚖ Rechtswissenschaft, *jurisprudence*.

△ Mathematik, *mathematics*.

⚲ Landwirtschaft, *agriculture*.

⚗ Chemie, *chemistry*.

⚕ Medizin, *medicine*.

9. Abbreviations — Abkürzungen

a. *also*, auch.
abbr. *abbreviation*, Abkürzung.
acc. *accusative* (*case*), Akkusativ, 4. Fall.
adj. *adjective*, Adjektiv, Eigenschaftswort.
adv. *adverb*, Adverb, Umstandswort.
allg. allgemein, *commonly*.
Am. *Americanism*, sprachliche Eigenheit aus dem oder (besonders) im amerikanischen Englisch.
anat. *anatomy*, Anatomie, Korperbaulehre.
ast. *astronomy*, Astronomie.
attr. *attributively*, als Attribut od. Beifügung.
biol. *biology*, Biologie.
b.s. *bad sense*, abwertend.
bsd. besonder(s), *particular(ly)*.
cj. *conjunction*, Konjunktion, Bindewort.
co. *comical*, scherzhaft.
coll. *collectively*, als Sammelwort.
comp. *comparative*, Komparativ, Höherstufe.
contp. *contemptuously*, verächtlich.
dat. *dative* (*case*), Dativ, 3. Fall.
eccl. *ecclesiastical*, kirchlich.
e-m, *e-m* einem, *to a* (*an*).
e-n, *e-n* einen, *a, an*.
engl. englisch, *English*.
engS. in engerem Sinne, *specifically*.
e-r, *e-r* einer, *of a* (*an*), *to a* (*an*).
e-s, *e-s* eines, *of a* (*an*).
et., *et.* etwas, *something*.
etc. *et cetera, and so on*, und so weiter.
f *feminine*, weiblich.
fenc. *fencing*, Fechtkunst.
fig. *figuratively*, bildlich, im übertragenen Sinn.
fr. französisch, *French*.
gen. *genitive* (*case*), Genitiv, 2. Fall.
geogr. *geography*, Geographie, Erdkunde.
geol. *geology*, Geologie.
ger. *gerund*, Gerundium.
Ggs. Gegensatz, *antonym*.
gr. *grammar*, Grammatik.
hist. *history*, Geschichte.
hunt. *hunting*, Jagd.
ichth. *ichthyology*, Fischkunde.
inf. *infinitive*, Infinitiv, Nennform.
int. *interjection*, Interjektion, Ausruf.
ir. irisch, *Irish*.
iro. *ironically*, ironisch.
irr. *irregular*, unregelmäßig (s. Hinweise für den Benutzer 5.2–5.3).

j., j-s, j-m, *j.*, *j-s*, *j-m* jemand(es *of*; -em *to*) *somebody*.
konkr. konkret, *concretely*.
lit. *literary*, nur in der Schriftsprache vorkommend.

m *masculine*, männlich.
metall. *metallurgy*, Hüttenwesen.
meteor. *meteorology*, Wetterkunde.
min. *mineralogy*, Gesteinskunde.
m-n meinen, *my*.
mot. *motoring*, Kraftfahrwesen.
mount. *mountaineering*, Bergsteigerei.
m-r meiner, *of or to my*.
mst meistens, *mostly*, *usually*.
myth. *mythology*, Mythologie.

n *neuter*, sächlich.
npr. *proper name*, Eigenname.

od. oder, *or*.
opt. *optics*, Optik.
orn. *ornithology*, Vogelkunde.
o.s. *oneself*, sich.

P. Person, *person*.
paint. *painting*, Malerei.
parl. *parliamentary term*, parlamentarischer Ausdruck.
pharm. *pharmacy*, Arzneimittelwesen.
phls. *philosophy*, Philosophie.
phot. *photography*, Photographie.
phys. *physics*, Physik.
physiol. *physiology*, Physiologie.
pl. *plural*, Plural, Mehrzahl.
poet. *poetry*, Dichtkunst; *poetic*, dichterisch.
pol. *politics*, Politik.
p.p. *past participle*, Partizip Perfekt, Mittelwort der Vergangenheit.
p.pr. *present participle*, Partizip Präsens, Mittelwort der Gegenwart.
pred. *predicatively*, prädikativ, als Aussage gebraucht.
pret. *preterit(e)*, Präteritum, Vergangenheit.
pron. *pronoun*, Pronomen, Fürwort.
prov. *provincialism*, Provinzialismus.
prp. *preposition*, Präposition, Verhältniswort.
psych. *psychology*, Psychologie.
rhet. *rhetoric*, Rhetorik, Redekunst.

S. Sache, *thing*.
s. siehe, man sehe, *see*, *refer to*.
schott. schottisch, *Scots*.
s-e, *s-e* seine, *his*, *once's*.
sg. *singular*, Singular, Einzahl.
sl. *slang*, Slang.
s-m, *s-m* seinem, *to his*, *to one's*.
s-n, *s-n* seinen, *his*, *one's*.
s.o. *someone*, jemand.
s-r, *s-r* seiner } *of his*,
s-s, *s-s* seines } *of one's*.
s.th. *something*, etwas.
su. *substantive*, Hauptwort.
sup. *superlative*, Superlativ, höchste Steigerungsstufe.
surv. *surveying*, Landvermessung.

tel. *telegraphy*, Telegraphie.
teleph. *telephony*, Fernsprechwesen.
thea. *theatre*, Theater.
typ. *typography*, Buchdruck.

u. und, *and*.
unbet. unbetont, *unstressed*.
univ. *university*, Hochschulwesen.

v. von, vom, *of*, *by*, *from*.
v/aux. *auxiliary verb*, Hilfszeitwort.
vb. *verb*, Verb, Zeitwort.
vet. *veterinary medicine*, Tierheilkunde.
v/i. *verb intransitive*, intransitives Verb, nichtzielendes Zeitwort.
v/t. *verb transitive*, transitives Verb, zielendes Zeitwort.

weitS. in weiterem Sinne, *by extension*.

z. B. zum Beispiel, *for instance*.
zo. *zoology*, Zoologie.
zs. zusammen, *together*.
Zssg(n) Zusammensetzung(en), *compound word(s)*.

Key to Pronunciation

A. Vokale und Diphthonge

[ɑː] reines langes a, wie in Vater, kam, Schwan: *far* [fɑː], *father* [ˈfɑːðə].

[ʌ] kommt im Deutschen nicht vor. Kurzes dunkles a, bei dem die Lippen nicht gerundet sind. Vorn und offen gebildet: *butter* [ˈbʌtə], *come* [kʌm], *colour* [ˈkʌlə], *blood* [blʌd], *flourish* [ˈflʌriʃ], *twopence* [ˈtʌpəns].

[æ] heller, ziemlich offener, nicht zu kurzer Laut. Raum zwischen Zunge und Gaumen noch größer als bei ä in Ähre: *fat* [fæt], *man* [mæn].

[ɛə] nicht zu offenes halblanges ä; im Englischen nur vor r, das als ein dem ä nachhallendes ə erscheint: *bare* [bɛə], *pair* [pɛə], *there* [ðɛə].

[ai] Bestandteile: helles, zwischen ɑː und æ liegendes a und schwächeres offenes i. Die Zunge hebt sich halbwegs zur i-Stellung: *I* [ai], *lie* [lai], *dry* [drai].

[au] Bestandteile: helles, zwischen ɑː und æ liegendes a und schwächeres offenes ŭ *house* [haus], *now* [nau].

[e] halboffenes kurzes e, etwas geschlossener als das e in Bett: *bed* [bed], *less* [les].

[ei] halboffenes e, nach i auslautend, indem die Zunge sich halbwegs zur i-Stellung hebt: *date* [deit], *play* [plei], *obey* [əˈbei].

[ə] flüchtiger Gleitlaut, ähnlich dem deutschen, flüchtig gesprochenen e in Gelage: *about* [əˈbaut], *butter* [ˈbʌtə], *connect* [kəˈnekt].

[əu] mit [ə] beginnend und in schwaches u auslautend; keine Rundung der Lippen, kein Heben der Zunge; *note* [nəut], *boat* [bəut], *below* [biˈləu].

[iː] langes i, wie in lieb, Bibel, aber etwas offener einsetzend als im Deutschen; wird in Südengland doppellautig gesprochen, indem sich die Zunge allmählich zur i-Stellung hebt: *scene* [siːn], *sea* [siː], *feet* [fiːt], *ceiling* [ˈsiːliŋ].

[i] kurzes offenes i wie in bin, mit: *big* [big], *city* [ˈsiti].

[iə] halboffenes halblanges i mit nachhallendem ə: *here* [hiə], *hear* [hiə], *inferior* [inˈfiəriə].

[ɔː] offener langer, zwischen a und o schwebender Laut: *fall* [fɔːl], *nought* [nɔːt], *or* [ɔː], *before* [biˈfɔː].

[ɔ] offener kurzer, zwischen a und o schwebender Laut, offener als das o in Motte: *god* [gɔd], *not* [nɔt], *wash* [wɔʃ], *hobby* [ˈhɔbi].

[ɔi] Bestandteile: offenes o und schwächeres offenes i. Die Zunge hebt sich halbwegs zur i-Stellung: *voice* [vɔis], *boy* [bɔi], *annoy* [əˈnɔi].

[əː] im Deutschen fehlender Laut; offenes langes ö, etwa wie gedehnt gesprochens ö in öffnen, Mörder; kein Vorstülpen oder Runden der Lippen, kein Heben der Zunge: *word* [wəːd], *girl* [gəːl], *learn* [ləːn], *murmur* [ˈməːmə].

[uː] langes u wie in Buch, doch ohne Lippenrundung; vielfach diphthongisch als halboffenes langes u mit nachhallendem geschlossenem u: *fool* [fuːl], *shoe* [ʃuː], *you* [juː], *rule* [ruːl], *canoe* [kəˈnuː].

[u] flüchtiges u: *put* [put], *look* [luk], *careful* [ˈkɛəful].

[uə] halboffenes halblanges u mit nachhallendem ə: *poor* [puə], *sure* [ʃuə], *allure* [əˈljuə].

Ganz vereinzelt werden auch die folgenden französischen Nasallaute gebracht: [ɑ̃] wie in frz. *blanc*, [ɔ̃] wie in frz. *bonbon* und [ɛ̃] wie in frz. *vin*.

Die **Länge eines Vokals** wird durch [ː] bezeichnet, z. B. *ask* [ɑːsk], *astir* [əˈstəː].

B. Konsonanten

[r] nur vor Vokalen gesprochen. Völlig verschieden vom deutschen Zungenspitzen- oder Zäpfchen-R. Die Zungenspitze bildet mit der oberen Zahnwulst eine Enge, durch die der Ausatmungsstrom mit Stimmton hindurchgetrieben wird, ohne den Laut zu rollen. Am Ende eines Wortes wird r nur bei Bindung mit dem Anlautvokal des folgenden Wortes gesprochen: *rose* [rəuz], *pride* [praid], *there is* [ðɛərˈiz].

[ʒ] stimmhaftes sch, wie g in Genie, j in Journal: *azure* [ˈæʒə], *jazz* [dʒæz], *jeep* [dʒiːp], *large* [lɑːdʒ].

[ʃ] stimmloses sch, wie im deutschen Schnee, rasch; *shake* [ʃeik], *washing* [ˈwɔʃiŋ], *lash* [læʃ].

[θ] im Deutschen nicht vorhandener stimmloser Lispellaut; durch Anlegen der Zunge an die oberen Schneidezähne hervorgebracht: *thin* [θin], *path* [pɑːθ], *method* [ˈmeθəd].

[ð] derselbe Laut stimmhaft, d h. mit Stimmton: *there* [ðɛə], *breathe* [briːð], *father* [ˈfɑːðə].

[s] stimmloser Zischlaut, entsprechend dem deutschen ß in Spaß, reißen: *see* [siː], *hats* [hæts], *decide* [diˈsaid].

[z] stimmhafter Zischlaut wie im Deutschen sausen: *zeal* [ziːl], *rise* [raiz], *horizon* [həˈraizn].

[x] stimmloser, hinten im Mund gebildeter Reibelaut wie ch in ach: *loch* [lɔx].

[ŋ] wird wie der deutsche Nasenlaut in fangen, singen gebildet: *ring* [riŋ], *singer* [ˈsiŋə].

[ŋk] derselbe Laut mit nachfolgendem k wie im deutschen senken, Wink: *ink* [iŋk], *tinker* [ˈtiŋkə].

[w] flüchtiges, mit Lippe an Lippe gesprochenes w, aus der Mundstellung für u: gebildet: *will* [wil], *swear* [swɛə], *queen* [kwiːn].

[f] stimmloser Lippenlaut wie im Deutschen flott: *fat* [fæt], *tough* [tʌf], *effort* [ˈefət].

[v] stimmhafter Lippenlaut wie im Deutschen Vase, Ventil: *vein* [vein], *velvet* [ˈvelvit].

[j] flüchtiger zwischen j und i schwebender Laut: *onion* [ˈʌnjən], *yes* [jes], *filial* [ˈfiljəl].

C. Betonungsakzent

Die Betonung der englischen Wörter wird durch das Zeichen [ˈ] vor der zu betonenden Silbe angegeben, z. B. *onion* [ˈʌnjən]. Sind zwei Silben eines Wortes mit Betonungsakzent versehen, so sind beide gleichmäßig zu betonen, z. B. *upstairs* [ˈʌpˈstɛəz]; jedoch wird häufig, je nach der Stellung des Wortes im Satzverband oder in nachdrucksvoller Sprache, nur eine der beiden Silben betont: z. B. *upstairs* in „*the upstairs rooms*“ [ði ˈʌpstɛəz ˈrumz] und „*on going upstairs*“ [ɔn ˈgəuiŋ ʌpˈstɛəz].

Bei zusammengesetzten Stichwörtern, deren Bestandteile als selbständige Stichwörter mit Aussprachebezeichnung im Wörterbuch gegeben sind, und bei Stichwörtern, die eine der unter D verzeichneten Endungen besitzen, wird der Betonungsakzent im Stichwort selbst gegeben. Die Betonung erfolgt auch im Stichwort, wenn nur ein Teil der Lautschrift gegeben wird und die Betonung nicht auf der ersten Silbe des durch eine Tilde ersetzten Lautschriftteils liegt, z. B. **adˈministratix** [⁓treitriks]. Liegt diese aber auf der ersten Silbe oder in dem gegebenen Lautschriftteil, dann erfolgt keine Betonungssetzung im Stichwort, sondern diese steht dann in der Klammer, z. B. **accurate** [ˈ⁓rit], **adamantine** [⁓ˈmæntain].

D. Endsilben ohne Lautschrift

Um Raum zu sparen, werden die häufigsten Endungen der englischen Stichwörter im folgenden einmal mit Lautschrift gegeben, dann aber im Wörterverzeichnis ohne Lautumschrift verzeichnet (sofern keine Ausnahmen vorliegen). Die nachstehenden Endungen sind auch dann nicht umschrieben, wenn ihnen ein Konsonant vorausgeht, der in der Lautschrift des vorhergehenden Wortes nicht gegeben war, im Englischen und Deutschen aber dasselbe Lautzeichen aufweist, z. B. -**t**ation, -**r**ing.

-ability [-əbiliti]
-able [-əbl]
-age [-idʒ]
-al [-əl]
-ally [-əli]
-an [-ən]
-ance [-əns]
-ancy [-ənsi]
-ant [-ənt]
-ar [-ə]
-ary [-əri]
-ation [-eiʃən]
-cious [-ʃəs]
-cy [-si]
-dom [-dəm]
-ed [-d; -t; -id]*
-edness [-dnis; -tnis; -idnis]*
-ee [-i:]
-en [-n]
-ence [-əns]
-ent [-ənt]
-er [-ə]
-ery [-əri]
-ess [-is]
-fication [-fikeiʃən]
-ial [-əl]
-ible [-əbl]
-ian [-jən]
-ic(s) [-ik(s)]
-ical [-ikəl]
-ily [-ili]
-iness [-inis]
-ing [-iŋ]
-ish [-iʃ]
-ism [-izəm]
-ist [-ist]
-istic [-istik]
-ite [-ait]
-ity [-iti]
-ive [-iv]
-ization [-aizeiʃən]
-ize [-aiz]
-izing [-aiziŋ]
-less [-lis]
-ly [-li]
-ment(s) [-mənt(s)]
-ness [-nis]
-oid [-ɔid]
-or [-ə]
-ous [-əs]
-ry [-ri]
-ship [-ʃip]
-(s)sion [-ʃən]
-sive [-siv]
-ties [-tiz]
-tion [-ʃən]
-tious [-ʃəs]
-trous [-trəs]
-try [-tri]
-y [-i]

* [-d] nach Vokalen und stimmhaften Konsonanten; [-t] nach stimmlosen Konsonanten; [-id] nach auslautendem d und t.

Über die Aussprache des amerikanischen Englisch vgl. Seite 16.

Das englische Alphabet

a [ei], b [bi:], c [si:], d [di:], e [i:], f [ef], g [dʒi:], h [eitʃ], i [ai], j [dʒei], k [kei], l [el], m [em], n [en], o [əu], p [pi:], q [kju:], r [ɑ:], s [es], t [ti:], u [ju:], v [vi:], w ['dʌblju:], x [eks], y [wai], z [zed].

American Pronunciation

Das amerikanische Englisch (AE) weist in Intonation, Rhythmus und Lautung gegenüber dem britischen Englisch (BE) hauptsächlich folgende Eigenheiten auf:

1. **Intonation:** Das AE zeigt größere Monotonie als das BE; das AE hat einfachere Satzmelodien.
2. **Rhythmus:** Wörter mit zwei oder mehr Silben nach der Haupttonsilbe [ˈˈ] haben im AE einen deutlichen Nebenton [ˈ], den die entsprechenden BE-Wörter nicht oder nur schwächer tragen, z. B. dictionary [AE ˈˈdikʃəˈnɛri = BE ˈdikʃənri], secretary [AE ˈˈsekrəˈtɛri = BE ˈsekrətri]; im AE werden kurze Tonvokale gedehnt (*American drawl*), z. B. capital [AE ˈkæːpətəl = BE ˈkæpitl]; im AE erfährt die unbetonte Silbe (nach einer betonten) eine Abschwächung, die u. a. anlautendes p, t, k zu b, d, g erweicht, z. B. property [AE ˈprɑbərti = BE ˈprɔpəti], united [AE juˈnaidid = BE juːˈnaitid].
3. Allgemein noch auffällige Merkmale der AE-Sprechweise im Vergleich zum BE sind die **Nasalierung** vor und nach nasalem Konsonant [m, n, ŋ] sowie die geschlossenere Aussprache von [-e] und [o-] als erster Bestandteil in Diphthongen, z. B. home [AE hoːm], take [AE teːk].
4. Geschriebenes **r** wird im Auslaut nach Vokal oder zwischen Vokal und Konsonant deutlich (retroflex) gesprochen, z. B. car [AE kɑːr = BE kɑː], care [AE kɛr = BE kɛə], border [AE ˈbɔːrdər = BE ˈbɔːdə].
5. Das **o** [BE ɔ] wird im AE etwa wie das dunkle **a** [AE ɑ] in „h*a*lten" ausgesprochen, z. B. dollar [AE ˈdɑlər = BE ˈdɔlə], college [AE ˈkɑliðʒ = BE ˈkɔlidʒ], lot [AE lɑt = BE lɔt], problem [AE ˈprɑbləm = BE ˈprɔbləm]; in zahlreichen Fällen besteht die [ɑ]- und [ɔ]-Aussprache nebeneinander, wenn auch nicht gleich üblich.
6. Das **a** [BE ɑː] wird im AE zu [æ] oder [æː] in Wörtern vom Typ pass [AE pæ(ː)s = BE pɑːs], answer [AE ˈæ(ː)nsər = BE ˈɑːnsə], dance [AE dæ(ː)ns = BE dɑːns], half [AE hæ(ː)f = BE hɑːf] sowie bei laugh [AE læ(ː)f = BE lɑːf].
7. Das **u** [BE juː] in Haupttonsilben im Inlaut wird im AE zu [uː], z. B. Tuesday [AE ˈtuːzdi = BE ˈtjuːzdi], student [AE ˈstuːdənt = BE ˈstjuːdənt], aber nicht in music [AE, BE = ˈmjuːzik], fuel [AE, BE = ˈfjuːəl].
8. Die Ableitungssilbe **-ile** (BE vorzugsweise [-ail]) wird im AE häufig zu [-əl] oder [-il] verkürzt, z. B. futile [AE ˈfjuːtəl = BE ˈfjuːtail], textile [AE ˈtekstil = BE ˈtekstail]; durchgehende [-əl]- oder [-il]-Lautung besteht nicht.
9. Die Endung **-ization** (BE meist [aiˈzeiʃən]) wird im AE vorzugsweise [əˈzeiʃən] gesprochen, seltener [aiˈzeiʃən]. Diesem Lautungsunterschied steht das Ausspracheverhältnis AE (bevorzugt) [ə] und BE (Standard) [i] nahe, z. B. editor [AE ˈedətər = BE ˈeditə], basket [AE ˈbæ(ː)skət = BE ˈbɑːskit].

A

a [ei; ə], *vor vokalischem Anlaut* **an** [æn; ən] *Artikel*: ein(e); der-, die-, dasselbe; per, pro, je; *they are of an age* sie sind gleichaltrig; *twice a week* zweimal wöchentlich *od.* in der Woche.

A 1 F ['ei 'wʌn] Ia, prima.

a·back [ə'bæk] rückwärts; *taken* ~ überrascht, verblüfft, bestürzt.

ab·a·cus ['æbəkəs], *pl.* **ab·a·ci** ['~sai] Rechenbrett *n*; ⚠ Säulendeckplatte *f*.

a·baft ⚓ [ə'bɑ:ft] **1.** *adv.* nach achtern zu; **2.** *prp.* achter.

a·ban·don [ə'bændən] auf-, preisgeben; im Stich lassen, verlassen; überlassen; *Sport*: aufgeben; ~ *o.s. to* sich hingeben (*dat.*); **a'ban·doned** *adj.* verlassen; verworfen; **a'ban·don·ment** Auf-, Preisgabe *f*; Hingabe *f*; Unbeherrschtheit *f*.

a·base [ə'beis] erniedrigen; demütigen; **a'base·ment** Erniedrigung *f*; Demütigung *f*.

a·bash [ə'bæʃ] beschämen, verlegen machen; *~ed at* fassungslos über (*acc.*); **a'bash·ment** Beschämung *f*, Verlegenheit *f*.

a·bate [ə'beit] *v/t.* verringern, vermindern; *Schmerz* lindern; *Stolz* mäßigen; *Preis* herabsetzen; ⚖ aufheben; *Mißstand* abstellen; *v/i.* abnehmen, nachlassen; sich legen (*Wind*); fallen (*Preis*); **a'bate·ment** Verminderung *f*; *Preis-*, *Steuer-*Nachlaß *m*; Abschaffung *f*; Aufhebung *f*.

ab·at·tis ⚔ [ə'bætis] Verhau *m*, *n*.

ab·at·toir ['æbətwɑ:] Schlachthaus *n*.

ab·ba·cy ['æbəsi] Abtwürde *f*; **'ab·bess** Äbtissin *f*; **ab·bey** ['æbi] Abtei *f*; **ab·bot** ['æbət] Abt *m*.

ab·bre·vi·ate [ə'bri:vieit] (ab-, ver-) kürzen; **ab·bre·vi'a·tion** Abkürzung *f*.

ABC ['eibi:'si:] ABC *n*, Alphabet *n*; alphabetischer (Fahr)Plan *m*; ~ *weapons* ABC-Waffen, atomare, biologische und chemische Waffen *f/pl*.

ab·di·cate ['æbdikeit] *v/i.* abdanken; *v/t. Amt* niederlegen, entsagen (*dat.*); ~ *the throne* abdanken; **ab·di'ca·tion** Verzicht *m*; Abdankung *f*.

ab·do·men ['æbdəmen; ⚕ æb'dəumen] Unterleib *m*, Bauch *m*; **ab·dom·i·nal** [æb'dɔminl] Unterleibs..., Bauch...

ab·duct [æb'dʌkt] entführen; **ab'duc·tion** Entführung *f*.

a·be·ce·dar·i·an [eibi:si:'dεəriən] **1.** alphabetisch (geordnet); **2.** Abc-Schütze *m*.

a·bed [ə'bed] zu *od.* im Bett.

ab·er·ra·tion [æbə'reiʃən] Abweichung *f*; *fig.* Verirrung *f*; *ast. u. phys.* Aberration *f*.

a·bet [ə'bet] anstiften, aufhetzen; *mst aid and* ~ ⚖ Vorschub leisten (*dat.*); **a'bet·ment** Anstiftung *f*, Aufhetzung *f*; Vorschub *m*; **a'bet·tor** Anstifter *m*; (Helfers)Helfer *m*.

a·bey·ance [ə'beiəns] Unentschiedenheit *f*; *in* ~ ⚖ unentschieden, in der Schwebe; herrenlos.

ab·hor [əb'hɔ:] verabscheuen; **ab·hor·rence** [əb'hɔrəns] Abscheu *m* (*of* vor *dat.*, gegen); *hold s.th. in* ~ vor et. Abscheu haben; **ab'hor·rent** □ zuwider, verhaßt (*to dat.*); abstoßend; unvereinbar (*to*, *from* mit).

a·bide [ə'baid] (*irr.*) *v/i.* bleiben; ~ *by* treu bleiben (*dat.*), festhalten an (*dat.*); *v/t.* erwarten; (v)ertragen, aushalten; *I cannot* ~ *him* ich kann ihn nicht ausstehen; **a'bid·ing** □ dauernd.

a·bil·i·ty [ə'biliti] Fähigkeit *f*; *to the best of one's* ~ nach besten Kräften; *abilities pl.* geistige Anlagen *f/pl*.

ab·ject □ ['æbdʒekt] verworfen; gemein; **ab'jec·tion, ab'ject·ness** Verworfenheit *f*; Niedrigkeit *f*.

ab·jure [əb'dʒuə] abschwören; entsagen (*dat.*).

a·blaze [ə'bleiz] in Flammen; (*a. fig.*) lodernd.

a·ble □ ['eibl] fähig, tüchtig, geschickt; *be* ~ imstande *od.* in der Lage sein, können; ~ *to pay* zahlungsfähig; **~-bod·ied** ['~'bɔdid]

körperlich leistungsfähig, kräftig; ⚔ tauglich; ~ *seaman* ⚓ Vollmatrose *m*.
ab·lu·tion [əˈbluːʃən] Waschung *f*.
ab·ne·gate [ˈæbnigeit] ab-, verleugnen; *Anspruch etc.* aufgeben; **abneˈga·tion** Ableugnung *f*; *a. self-~* Selbstverleugnung *f*; Verzicht *m*.
ab·nor·mal □ [æbˈnɔːməl] ungewöhnlich, regelwidrig, abnorm; **abˈnor·mi·ty** Abnormität *f*.
a·board [əˈbɔːd] ⚓ an Bord (*gen.*); *all ~! Am.* 🚂, ✈ *etc.* einsteigen!
a·bode [əˈbəud] **1.** *pret. u. p.p. von abide*; **2.** Aufenhalt *m*; Wohnung *f*, Wohnsitz *m*.
a·bol·ish [əˈbɔliʃ] abschaffen, aufheben; **aˈbol·ish·ment**, **ab·o·li·tion** [æbəuˈliʃən] Abschaffung *f*, Aufhebung *f*; **ab·oˈli·tion·ist** Gegner *m* der Sklaverei.
A-bomb [ˈeibɔm] = *atomic bomb*.
a·bom·i·na·ble □ [əˈbɔminəbl] abscheulich; **aˈbom·i·nate** [~neit] verabscheuen; **a·bom·iˈna·tion** Abscheu *m* (*of* gegen); Greuel *m*.
ab·o·rig·i·nal [æbəˈridʒənl] **1.** □ eingeboren, einheimisch; Ur...; **2.** Ureinwohner *m*; **ab·oˈrig·i·nes** [~dʒiniːz] *pl.* Ureinwohner *m/pl.*, Urbevölkerung *f*.
a·bort [əˈbɔːt] ⚕ eine Fehl- *od.* Frühgeburt haben; *biol.* verkümmern; ~ *a mission* ⚔, *Raumfahrt*: e-e Mission abbrechen; **aˈbor·tion** ⚕ Fehl- *od.* Frühgeburt *f*; Abtreibung *f*; Mißgeburt *f* (*a. fig.*); *fig.* Fehlschlag *m*; *produce ~* abtreiben; **aˈbor·tive** [~tiv] □ vorzeitig; erfolglos, fehlgeschlagen; verkümmert.
a·bound [əˈbaund] reichlich vorhanden sein; Überfluß haben (*in* an *dat.*); ~ *with* wimmeln von.
a·bout [əˈbaut] **1.** *prp.* über (*acc.*); von; um ... herum; bei; im Begriff, dabei; *talk ~ business* über Geschäfte sprechen; *send s.o. ~ his business* j. wegschicken *od.* hinauswerfen *od.* kurz abfertigen; ~ *the house* irgendwo im Haus; *wander ~ the streets* in den Straßen umherwandern; *what are you ~* was macht ihr da?; *I had no money ~ me* ich hatte kein Geld bei mir; *be ~ to do* im Begriff sein zu tun; **2.** *adv.* herum, umher; in der Nähe; auf den Beinen; etwa, ungefähr; ungefähr um, gegen; *travel ~* umher- *od.* herumreisen; *it must be somewhere ~* es muß hier in der Nähe sein; *a long way ~* ein großer Umweg; *bring ~* zustande bringen; *come ~* zustande kommen; *be up and ~* (wieder) auf den Beinen sein; *he is ~ my height* er hat etwa meine Größe; ~ *ten o'clock* gegen 10 Uhr; *right ~!* rechtsum!; ~ *turn!* kehrt!
a·bove [əˈbʌv] **1.** *prp.* über, oberhalb; *fig.* erhaben über; ~ *300* über 300; ~ *all (things)* vor allem; *be ~ s.o. in s.th.* j-m in e-r Sache überlegen sein; *it is ~ me* das ist mir zu hoch; **2.** *adv.* oben; darüber; *over and ~* obendrein; **3.** *adj.* obig; obenerwähnt; *the ~ points* die obenerwähnten Punkte; **4.** *das* Obige; **aˈbove-ˈboard** ehrlich, offen; **aˈbove-ˈground** am Leben.
ab·ra·ca·dab·ra [æbrəkəˈdæbrə] Abrakadabra *n*; Kauderwelsch *n*.
ab·rade [əˈbreid] abschaben, abschleifen, abreiben, abscheuern.
ab·ra·sion [əˈbreiʒən] Abreiben *n*, Abschleifen *n*; Abnutzung *f*; (Haut)Abschürfung *f*; **abˈra·sive** [~siv] ⊕ Schleifmittel *n*.
ab·re·act [æbriˈækt] abreagieren.
a·breast [əˈbrest] nebeneinander; ~ *of od. with* auf der Höhe (*gen.*); *keep ~ of* Schritt halten mit.
a·bridge [əˈbridʒ] (ab-, ver)kürzen; *fig.* beschränken; **aˈbridg(e)·ment** Ab-, Verkürzung *f*; Abriß *m*; Auszug *m*; gekürzte Ausgabe *f e-s Buches*.
a·broad [əˈbrɔːd] im (ins) Ausland; überall(hin); draußen, im Freien; *there is a report ~* es geht das Gerede *od.* Gerücht; *the thing has got ~* die Sache ist ruchbar geworden; *all ~* ganz im Irrtum.
ab·ro·gate [ˈæbrəugeit] abschaffen, aufheben; **ab·roˈga·tion** Abschaffung *f*, Aufhebung *f*.
ab·rupt □ [əˈbrʌpt] jäh; plötzlich, abrupt, unvermittelt; zs.-hanglos; schroff (*Benehmen*); **abˈrupt·ness** Steilheit *f e-s Abhangs*; Plötzlichkeit *f*; Zs.-hanglosigkeit *f*; Schroffheit *f*.
ab·scess ⚕ [ˈæbsis] Abszeß *m*, Geschwür *n*.
ab·scond [əbˈskɔnd] sich heimlich davonmachen, flüchten.
ab·sence [ˈæbsəns] Abwesenheit *f*, Fehlen *n*; Mangel *m* (*of* an *dat.*);

~ *of mind* Geistesabwesenheit *f*, Zerstreutheit *f*.
ab·sent 1. □ [ˈæbsənt] abwesend; fehlend; *fig.* geistesabwesend, zerstreut; **2.** [æbˈsent]: ~ *o.s.* fernbleiben (*from dat.*); **ab·sen·tee** [æbsənˈtiː] Abwesende *m*, *f*; dauernd im Ausland Lebende *m*, *f*; ~ *ballot bsd. Am.* Briefwahl *f*; ~ *voter bsd. Am.* Briefwähler *m*; **ab·senˈtee·ism** Absentismus *m* (*dauerndes Wohnen im Ausland*); *im Betrieb*: unerlaubtes Fernbleiben *n*; Drückebergerei *f*; **ˈab·sent-ˈmind·ed** □ geistesabwesend, zerstreut; **ˈab·sent-ˈmind·ed·ness** Geistesabwesenheit *f*, Zerstreutheit *f*.
ab·sinth [ˈæbsinθ] ⚘ Wermut *m*; Absinth *m*.
ab·so·lute □ [ˈæbsəluːt] absolut (*a.* ⚗, *phys.*, *gr.*); unumschränkt; vollkommen; unvermischt; unbedingt; **ˈab·so·lute·ness** Unumschränktheit *f etc.*; **ab·soˈlu·tion** Lossprechung *f*; **ˈab·so·lut·ism** Absolutismus *m*, unbeschränkte Regierung(sform) *f*.
ab·solve [əbˈzɔlv] frei-, lossprechen; entbinden (*from* von), entheben (*from gen.*).
ab·sorb [əbˈsɔːb] absorbieren, aufsaugen; verschlucken; *fig.* fesseln, ganz in Anspruch nehmen (*Arbeit etc.*); *Wissen* sich aneignen; *Kaufkraft* abschöpfen; ~*ed in* vertieft in (*acc.*); **abˈsorb·ent** aufsaugend(es Mittel *n*); ~ *cotton wool* Verbandwatte *f*.
ab·sorp·tion [əbˈsɔːpʃən] Aufsaugung *f*, Absorption *f*; *fig.* Vertieftsein *n*; Abschöpfung *f der Kaufkraft*.
ab·stain [əbˈstein] sich enthalten (*from gen.*); abstinent leben; ~ (*from voting*) *parl.* sich der Stimme enthalten; **abˈstain·er** *mst total* ~ Abstinenzler *m*.
ab·ste·mi·ous □ [əbˈstiːmjəs] enthaltsam; mäßig; frugal.
ab·sten·tion [æbˈstenʃən] Enthaltung *f* (*from* von); *parl.* Stimmenthaltung *f*.
ab·ster·gent [əbˈstəːdʒənt] reinigend(es Mittel *n*).
ab·sti·nence [ˈæbstinəns] Enthaltsamkeit *f* (*from* von); *total* ~ Abstinenz *f vom Alkohol*; **ˈab·sti·nent** □ enthaltsam.
ab·stract 1. □ [ˈæbstrækt] abstrakt; dunkel, schwer verständlich; **2.** [~] Abriß *m*, Auszug *m*; *a.* ~ *noun gr.* Abstraktum *n*; *in the* ~ rein theoretisch, rein begrifflich; **3.** [æbˈstrækt] *v/t.* abstrahieren; *Geist etc.* ablenken; absondern; entwenden; kurz zs.-fassen; **abˈstract·ed** □ (ab)gesondert; *fig.* zerstreut; **ab·strac·tion** [æbˈstrækʃən] Abstraktion *f*; (abstrakter) Begriff *m*; Entwendung *f*; *fig.* Zerstreutheit *f*; *Kunst*: abstrakte Komposition *f*.
ab·struse □ [æbˈstruːs] *fig.* dunkel, schwerverständlich; tiefgründig; **abˈstruse·ness** Dunkelheit *f etc.*
ab·surd □ [əbˈsəːd] absurd, unsinnig, sinnwidrig; albern; lächerlich; abwegig; **abˈsurd·ist** absurdistisch; **abˈsurd·i·ty** Sinnwidrigkeit *f*, Albernheit *f etc.*
a·bun·dance [əˈbʌndəns] Überfluß *m*; Fülle *f* (*of* von, an *dat.*); Überschwang *m des Herzens*; **aˈbun·dant** □ reichlich; ~ *in* reich an (*dat.*); **aˈbun·dant·ly** vollauf.
a·buse 1. [əˈbjuːs] Mißbrauch *m*, -stand *m*; Beschimpfung *f*; **2.** [~z] mißbrauchen; beschimpfen; † mißhandeln; **aˈbu·sive** □ [~siv] mißbräuchlich; beleidigend, ausfallend; Schimpf...; *be* ~ schimpfen.
a·but [əˈbʌt] angrenzen, -stoßen (*on*, *upon*, *against* an *acc.*); **aˈbut·ment** ⩓ Strebepfeiler *m*; Widerlager *n e-r Brücke*; **aˈbut·ter** Anlieger *m*.
a·bysm [əˈbizəm] *poet.* = *abyss*; **a·bys·mal** □ [əˈbizməl] abgrundtief, bodenlos; **a·byss** [əˈbis] Abgrund *m*, Schlund *m*; Hölle *f*.
Ab·ys·sin·i·an [æbiˈsinjən] abessinisch.
a·ca·cia ⚘ [əˈkeiʃə] Akazie *f*.
ac·a·dem·ic [ækəˈdemik] akademisch; Universitäts...; rein theoretisch; ~ *year* Studienjahr *n*; **ac·aˈdem·i·cal 1.** □ = *academic*; **2.** ~*s pl.* akademische Tracht *f*; **a·cad·e·mi·ci·an** [əkædəˈmiʃən] Akademiemitglied *n*.
a·cad·e·my [əˈkædəmi] Akademie *f*.
a·can·thus [əˈkænθəs] ⚘ Bärenklau *m*; ⩓ Akanthusblatt *n*.
ac·cede [ækˈsiːd]: ~ *to e-m Verein* beitreten; *e-r Meinung etc.* zustimmen; *Amt* antreten; *Thron* be-

steigen.

ac·cel·er·ate [ək'seləreit] beschleunigen; *fig.* ankurbeln; **ac·cel·er'a·tion** Beschleunigung *f*; ~ *lane mot.* Beschleunigungsspur *f*; **ac'cel·er·a·tor** *mot.* Gaspedal *n*.

ac·cent 1. ['æksənt] Akzent *m*; Tonzeichen *n*; Betonung *f*; Ton *m*; Aussprache *f*; **2.** [æk'sent] *v/t.* akzentuieren; betonen (*a. fig.*).

ac·cen·tu·ate [æk'sentjueit] akzentuieren, betonen; **ac·cen·tu'a·tion** Betonung *f*.

ac·cept [ək'sept] *oft* ~ *of* annehmen; ⚕ akzeptieren; übernehmen; hinnehmen; **ac·cept·a'bil·i·ty** Annehmbarkeit *f*; **ac'cept·a·ble** □ annehmbar; angenehm, erwünscht; **ac'cept·ance** Annahme *f*; Übernahme *f*; Hinnahme *f*; (freundliche) Aufnahme *f*; ⚕ Akzept *n*; **ac·cep·ta·tion** [æksep'teiʃən] gebräuchlicher Sinn *m e-s Wortes*; **ac·cept·ed** □ [ək'septid] allgemein anerkannt; **ac'cept·er, ac'cept·or** Annehmer *m*; ⚕ Akzeptant *m*.

ac·cess ['ækses] Zugang *m*, Zutritt *m* (*to* zu); *Wut-, Fieber- etc.* Anfall *m*; *Computer*: Zugriff *m*; *easy of* ~ zugänglich; ~ *road* Zufahrtsstraße *f*; **ac·ces·sa·ry** [ək'sesəri] Mitschuldige *m, f* (*to* an *dat.*), Helfershelfer(in); = *accessory* 2; **ac·ces·si·bil·i·ty** [~si'biliti] Zugänglichkeit *f*; **ac'ces·si·ble** □ [~səbl] zugänglich (*to* für); **ac'ces·sion** Gelangen *n* (*to* zu *e-r Würde*); Antritt *m* (*to e-s Amtes*); Eintritt *m* (*to* in *ein Alter*); Zuwachs *m*; ~ *to the throne* Thronbesteigung *f*; *recent* ~*s pl.* Neuanschaffungen *f/pl.*

ac·ces·so·ry [ək'sesəri] **1.** □ zusätzlich; nebensächlich; Neben...; **2.** Zubehörteil *n*; = *accessary*; *accessories pl.* Zubehör *n*; ~ **shoe** *phot.* Steckschuh *m*.

ac·ci·dence *gr.* ['æksidəns] Formenlehre *f*.

ac·ci·dent ['æksidənt] Zufall *m*; Un(glücks)fall *m*; Nebensache *f*; ~ *insurance* Unfallversicherung *f*; *be killed in an* ~ bei einem Unfall ums Leben kommen, tödlich verunglücken; *by* ~ zufällig; **ac·ci·den·tal** [æksi'dentl] **1.** □ zufällig; nebensächlich; ~ *death* Tod *m* durch Unfall; **2.** Zufällige *n*; Nebensache *f*; ♪ Versetzungszeichen *n*.

ac·claim [ə'kleim] mit Beifall *od.* Jubel begrüßen (als).

ac·cla·ma·tion [æklə'meiʃən] *oft* ~*s pl.* lauter Beifall *m od.* Zuruf *m*; *by* ~ durch Zuruf.

ac·cli·mate *bsd. Am.* [ə'klaimit] = *acclimatize*.

ac·cli·ma·ti·za·tion [əklaimətai'zeiʃən] Akklimatisierung *f*; **ac'cli·ma·tize** (sich) akklimatisieren, (sich) eingewöhnen.

ac·cliv·i·ty [ə'kliviti] Steigung *f*.

ac·com·mo·date [ə'kɔmədeit] anpassen (*to dat.*; an *acc.*); unterbringen; *Streit* schlichten; *Streitende* versöhnen; *j-m* gefällig sein; versorgen (*with* mit); *j-m* aushelfen (*with* mit *Geld*); **ac'com·mo·dat·ing** □ gefällig, entgegenkommend; **ac·com·mo'da·tion** Anpassung *f*; Aushilfe *f*; Bequemlichkeit *f*; Unterbringung *f*, -kunft *f*; Beilegung *f*; Darleh(e)n *n*; ~ *bill* ⚕ Gefälligkeitswechsel *m*; ~ *ladder* ⚓ Fallreep *n*; *seating* ~ Sitzgelegenheit *f*; ~ *train Am.* Personenzug *m*.

ac·com·pa·ni·ment [ə'kʌmpənimənt] Begleitung *f*; Begleiterscheinung *f*; **ac'com·pa·nist** ♪ Begleiter(in); **ac'com·pa·ny** begleiten; *accompanied with* verbunden mit.

ac·com·plice [ə'kɔmplis] Mitschuldige *m, f* (*in* an *dat.*); Komplice *m*.

ac·com·plish [ə'kɔmpliʃ] vollenden, zu Ende führen; zustande bringen; *Absicht etc.* ausführen; **ac'com·plished** vollendet, perfekt; kultiviert; **ac'com·plish·ment** Vollendung *f*; Ausführung *f*; Tat *f*, Leistung *f*; Meisterschaft *f*; *mst* ~*s pl.* Künste *f/pl.*, Talente *n/pl.*

ac·cord [ə'kɔ:d] **1.** Übereinstimmung *f*; Einklang *m*; ⚖ Vergleich *m*; *with one* ~ einstimmig; *of one's own* ~ aus eigenem Antrieb; **2.** *v/i.* übereinstimmen (*with* mit); *v/t.* gewähren, geben, erweisen; **ac'cord·ance** Übereinstimmung *f*; *in* ~ *with* in Übereinstimmung mit, gemäß; **ac'cord·ant** □ (*with, to*) übereinstimmend (mit), gemäß (*dat.*); **ac'cord·ing:** ~ *to* gemäß, laut, entsprechend (*dat.*); ~ *as* je nachdem (wie *od.* ob); **ac'cord·ing·ly** demgemäß; folglich.

ac·cor·di·on ♪ [ə'kɔ:djən] Handharmonika *f*, Akkordeon *n*.

ac·cost [ə'kɔst] *j. bsd. auf der Straße*

ansprechen.

ac·cou·cheur [æku:ˈʃə:] Geburtshelfer *m*; **ac·couˈcheuse** [~z] Hebamme *f*.

ac·count [əˈkaunt] **1.** Rechnung *f*; Berechnung *f von Ausgaben*; Abrechnung *f*; Nota *f*; ☤ Konto *n*; Rechenschaft *f*; Bericht *m*, Darstellung *f*, Erzählung *f*; Geltung *f*; *current* ~ Kontokorrent *n*; *payment on* ~ Abschlag(s)zahlung *f*; *sale for the* ~ Verkauf *m* auf Rechnung; *statement of* ~ Kontoauszug *m*; *of no* ~ ohne Bedeutung; *on no* ~ auf keinen Fall; *on his* ~ um seinetwillen; *on* ~ *of* wegen; *have od. hold an* ~ *with* ein Konto bei (*e-r Bank*) haben; *place to s.o.'s* ~ j-m auf die Rechnung setzen; *take into* ~, *take* ~ *of* in Rechnung *od.* Betracht ziehen; *leave out of* ~ außer acht lassen; *turn to* ~ ausnutzen; *keep* ~*s* die Bücher führen; *call to* ~ zur Rechenschaft ziehen; *give od. render an* ~ *of* Rechenschaft ablegen über (*acc.*); Bericht erstatten über (*acc.*); *et.* erklären; *give a good* ~ *of o.s.* sich bewähren; *make (little)* ~ *of* (wenig) Wert legen auf (*acc.*); **2.** *v/i.* ~ *for* Rechenschaft ablegen über (*acc.*); (sich) erklären; *hunt.* zur Strecke bringen; *be much (little)* ~*ed of* hoch (gering) geachtet sein; *v/t* ansehen als, halten für; ~ *o.s. happy* sich glücklich schätzen; **ac·count·aˈbil·i·ty** Verantwortlichkeit *f*; **acˈcount·a·ble** □ verantwortlich; erklärlich; **acˈcount·an·cy** Rechnungswesen *n*; **acˈcount·ant** Buchhalter *m*; *chartered* ~, *Am. certified public* ~ vereidigter Buchprüfer *m*; **acˈcount·ing** Buchführung *f*.

ac·cou·tred [əˈku:təd] ausgerüstet; **ac·cou·tre·ments** ⚔ [əˈku:təmənts] *pl.* Ausrüstung *f* (*außer Uniform u. Waffen*).

ac·cred·it [əˈkredit] *Gesandten* beglaubigen, akkreditieren; bestätigen; anerkennen; ~ *s.th. to s.o.*, ~ *s.o. with s.th.* j-m et. zuschreiben.

ac·cre·tion [æˈkri:ʃən] Zuwachs *m*.

ac·crue [əˈkru:] erwachsen (*from* aus); zufallen; auflaufen (*Zinsen*).

ac·cu·mu·late [əˈkju:mjuleit] (sich) (an-, auf)häufen, ansammeln; **ac·cu·muˈla·tion** Anhäufung *f*, An...lung *f*; Haufe(n) *m*; **acˈcu·...tive** □ [~lətiv] (sich) an- Anhäufungs...; **acˈcu·mu·lator** ⚡ [~leitə] Akkum...

ac·cu·ra·cy [ˈækjurəsi] G...keit *f*; Richtigkeit *f*; **ac·cu·r...** [ˈ~rit] genau; richtig; sorgfälti...

ac·curs·ed [əˈkə:sid], **ac·c...** [əˈkə:st] verflucht, verwünscht.

ac·cu·sa·tion [ækju:ˈzeiʃən] Anklage *f*, An-, Beschuldigung *f*; **ac·cu·sa·tive** [əˈkju:zətiv] *a.* ~ *case gr.* Akkusativ *m*, 4. Fall *m*; **ac·cu·sa·to·ry** [əˈkju:zətəri] anklagend; **ac·cuse** [əˈkju:z] anklagen, beschuldigen (*of gen.*, wegen; *before, to* bei); *the* ~*d* der (die) Angeklagte; **acˈcus·er** Kläger(in).

ac·cus·tom [əˈkʌstəm] gewöhnen (*to* an *acc.*); **acˈcus·tomed** gewohnt, üblich; gewöhnt (*to* an *acc.*, zu *inf.*); *be* ~ *to doing* (*Am. a. to do*) *s.th.* et. zu tun pflegen.

ace [eis] As *n*; Eins *f auf Würfeln*; *fig.* As *n* (*erfolgreicher Flieger od. Rennfahrer*); ~ *in the hole Am.* F Trumpf *m* in Reserve; *he was within an* ~ *of dying* er wäre um ein Haar gestorben.

a·cer·bi·ty [əˈsə:biti] Herbheit *f*.

ac·e·tate ⚗ [ˈæsitit] Acetat *n*, essigsaures Salz *n*; ~ *rayon* Acetatkunstseide *f*; ~ *silk* Acetatseide *f*; **a·ce·tic** [əˈsi:tik] essigsauer; ~ *acid* Essigsäure *f*; **a·cet·i·fy** [əˈsetifai] säuern; **ac·e·tone** [ˈæsitəun] Azeton *n*; **ac·e·tous** [ˈ~təs] sauer; Essig...; **a·cet·y·lene** [əˈsetili:n] Azetylen *n*.

ache [eik] **1.** schmerzen, weh tun; Schmerzen haben; sich sehnen (*for* nach; *to do* zu tun); **2.** *anhaltende* Schmerzen *m/pl.*

a·chieve [əˈtʃi:v] ausführen; zustande bringen; leisten; erlangen; *Ziel* erreichen; *Erfolg* erzielen; **aˈchieve·ment** Ausführung *f*, Vollendung *f*; *oft* ~*s pl.* Leistung *f*, Errungenschaft *f*; Werk *n*.

ach·ing [ˈeikiŋ] □ schmerzhaft.

ach·ro·mat·ic [ækrəuˈmætik] (~*ally*) achromatisch (*farblos*).

ac·id [ˈæsid] **1.** sauer; ~ *drops pl. Br.* saure Drops *m/pl.*; ~ *rain* ⚗ saurer Regen *m*; **2.** Säure *f*; *sl.* LSD; **ˈ~head** *sl.* LSD-Süchtige *m*, *f*; **a·cid·i·fy** [əˈsidifai] säuern; **aˈcid·i·ty** Säure *f*; **ac·i·do·sis** [æsiˈdəusis] Übersäuerung *f* des Blutes; **ˈac·id-proof** säurefest; **a·cid·u·lant** [əˈsidjulənt] Säuremittel *n*; **aˈcid·u·late** [~leit] säuern; ~*d drops pl.* saure Drops *m/pl.*; **a·cid·u·lous** [əˈsidjuləs] säuerlich.

ac·knowl·edge [ək'nɔlidʒ] anerkennen; zu-, eingestehen; † bestätigen; sich erkenntlich zeigen für; **ac'knowl·edg(e)·ment** Anerkennung *f*; Eingeständnis *n*; *bsd.* † Empfangsbestätigung *f*, -schein *m*.

ac·me ['ækmi] Gipfel *m*; ⚕ Krisis *f*.

ac·ne ⚕ ['ækni] Akne *f* (*Hautausschlag*).

ac·o·nite ⚘ ['ækənait] Eisenhut *m*.

a·corn ⚘ ['eikɔːn] Eichel *f*.

a·cous·tic, a·cous·ti·cal □ [ə'kuːstik(əl)] akustisch; Gehör...; **a'cous·tics** *mst sg.* Akustik *f*.

ac·quaint [ə'kweint] bekannt (*fig. a.* vertraut) machen; *j-m* mitteilen (*with s.th.* et.; *that* daß); *be* ~*ed with* kennen; *become* ~*ed with* kennenlernen; **ac'quaint·ance** Bekanntschaft *f* (*a. konkr.*); Kenntnis *f* (*with gen.*); Bekannte *m*, *f*.

ac·qui·esce [ækwi'es] (*in*) hinnehmen (*acc.*), dulden (*acc.*); einwilligen (in *acc.*); **ac·qui'es·cence** (*in*) Ergebung *f* (in *acc.*); Nachgeben *n*, Nachgiebigkeit *f* (gegenüber); Einwilligung *f* (in); **acqui'es·cent** □ ergeben; fügsam; nachgiebig.

ac·quire [ə'kwaiə] erwerben (*a. fig.*); ~*d taste* anerzogener Geschmack *m*; **ac'quire·ment** Erwerbung *f*; (erworbene) Fertigkeit *f*.

ac·qui·si·tion [ækwi'ziʃən] Erwerbung *f*; Erwerb *m*; Errungenschaft *f*; **ac·quis·i·tive** □ [ə'kwizitiv] auf Erwerb gerichtet; lernbegierig; **ac'quis·i·tive·ness** Gewinnsucht *f*.

ac·quit [ə'kwit] freisprechen (*of* von); ~ *o.s. of Pflicht* erfüllen; ~ *o.s. well* (*ill*) seine Sache gut (schlecht) machen; **ac'quit·tal** Freisprechung *f*; Erfüllung *f e-r Pflicht*; **ac'quit·tance** Tilgung *f*; Quittung *f*.

a·cre ['eikə] Acre *m* (*4047 qm*), Morgen *m*.

ac·rid ['ækrid] scharf, beißend (*a. fig.*).

ac·ri·mo·ni·ous □ [ækri'məunjəs] *fig.* scharf, beißend, bitter; **ac·ri·mo·ny** ['ækriməni] *fig.* Schärfe *f*, Bitterkeit *f*.

ac·ro·bat ['ækrəbæt] Akrobat *m*; **ac·ro·bat·ic** [ækrəu'bætik] (~*ally*) akrobatisch; **ac·ro'bat·ics** *pl.* Akrobatik *f*; ✈ Kunstflug *m*.

a·cross [ə'krɔs] **1.** *adv.* hin-, herüber; (quer) durch; im Durchmesser; drüben; kreuzweise, überkreuz; *come* ~ herüberkommen; *saw* ~ durchsägen; *a lake three miles* ~ ein 3 Meilen breiter See; *with arms* ~ mit verschränkten Armen; **2.** *prp.* (quer) über (*acc.*); (mitten) durch; jenseits (*gen.*), über (*dat.*), auf der anderen Seite von; *run* ~ *the road* über die Straße laufen; ~ *the Channel* über dem Kanal, jenseits des Kanals; *come* ~, *run* ~ stoßen auf (*acc.*); *fig.* ~ *the board* linear; *a 5% wage increase* ~ *the board* eine lineare Lohnerhöhung von 5%.

act [ækt] **1.** *v/i.* handeln; sich benehmen; wirken (*on, upon* auf *acc.*); fungieren (*as* als); funktionieren, gehen; *auf der Bühne* spielen; *fig.* Theater spielen, schauspielern, so tun als ob; ~ (*up*)*on s.o.'s advice* sich nach j-s Rat richten; *v/t. Rolle* spielen (*a. fig.*), *Stück* aufführen; **2.** Handlung *f*, Tat *f*, Werk *n*; *thea.* Aufzug *m*, Akt *m*; *Zirkus*-Nummer *f*; Gesetz *n*, Beschluß *m*; Urkunde *f*, Vertrag *m*; ≈ *of God* höhere Gewalt *f*; ≈*s of the Apostles* Apostelgeschichte *f*; **'act·a·ble** bühnengerecht; **'act·ing 1.** Handeln *n*; *thea.* Spiel(en) *n*; **2.** tätig, amtierend; stellvertretend; geschäftsführend; ~ *partner* † tätiger Teilhaber *m*.

ac·tion ['ækʃən] Handlung *f* (*a. thea.*); Tätigkeit *f*; Verrichtung *f*; Tat *f*; Wirkung *f*; ⚖ Klage *f*, Prozeß *m*; Gang *m* (*Maschine, Pferd*); Gefecht *n*; Vortragsweise *f*; *paint.* Stellung *f*, Haltung *f*; Mechanismus *m* (*Klavier etc.*); ~ *radius* Aktionsradius *m*; *bring an* ~ *against* klagen *od.* Klage erheben gegen; *killed in* ~ gefallen; *take* ~ Schritte unternehmen; **ac·tion·a·ble** ['~ʃnəbl] (ver)klagbar; strafbar.

ac·tiv·ate ['æktiveit] aktivieren, in Betrieb setzen.

ac·tive □ ['æktiv] tätig; handelnd; rührig, geschäftig; wirksam; behend; aktiv; † lebhaft; Aktiv...; ~ **voice** *gr.* Tatform *f*, Aktiv *n*; **ac'tiv·i·ty** (*oft pl.*) Tätigkeit *f*; Betriebsamkeit *f*, Rührigkeit *f*; *bsd.* † Lebhaftigkeit *f*; *in full* ~ in vollem Gange; *intense* ~ Hochbetrieb *m*.

ac·tor ['æktə] Schauspieler *m*; **ac·tress** ['æktris] Schauspielerin *f*.

ac·tu·al □ ['æktʃuəl] wirklich, tatsächlich, eigentlich; gegenwärtig; **ac·tu·al·i·ty** [~'æliti] Wirklichkeit *f*; **ac·tu·al·ly** ['æktʃuəli] tatsächlich; in Wirklichkeit; F eigentlich.
ac·tu·ar·y ['æktjuəri] Versicherungsstatistiker *m*.
ac·tu·ate ['æktjueit] in Gang bringen; *fig*. (an)treiben; **ac·tu'a·tion** Antrieb *m*; Anstoß *m*.
a·cu·men [ə'kju:men] Scharfsinn *m*.
ac·u·punc·ture ['ækjupʌŋktʃə] Akupunktur *f*.
a·cute □ [ə'kju:t] spitz; scharf (*Schmerz, Gehör etc*.); scharfsinnig; fein, klar; schrill (*Ton*); brennend (*Frage*); fühlbar; ⚕ akut, heftig; **a'cute·ness** Schärfe *f*; Akutheit *f*; Scharfsinn *m*.
ad F [æd] = *advertisement*.
ad·age ['ædidʒ] Sprichwort *n*.
ad·a·mant ['ædəmənt] steinhart; *fig*. unerbittlich (*to* gegenüber); **ad·a·man·tine** [~'mæntain] diamanten, Diamant...; *fig*. = *adamant*.
a·dapt [ə'dæpt] anpassen (*to, for dat*.); zurechtmachen; *Text* bearbeiten (*from* nach); *~ed from* frei nach; **a·dapt·a'bil·i·ty** Anpassungsfähigkeit *f*; **a'dapt·a·ble** anpassungsfähig; **ad·ap·ta·tion** [ædæp'teiʃən] Anpassung *f* (*to* an *acc*.); Bearbeitung *f*; **a·dap·ter** [ə'dæptə] *Radio*: Zwischenstecker *m*; **a'dap·tive** anpassungsfähig.
add [æd] *v/t*. hinzufügen, -zählen; erweitern; *~ up* zs.-zählen, addieren; *~ in* einschließen; *v/i*. hinzukommen; *~ up* F Sinn haben; *~ up to et*. ergeben; hinauskommen auf (*acc*.), *et*. bedeuten; *~ to* beitragen zu, vergrößern, vermehren; **'ad·ded** zusätzlich.
ad·den·dum [ə'dendəm], *pl*. **ad'den·da** [~də] Zusatz *m*; Nachtrag *m*.
ad·der ['ædə] Natter *f*.
ad·dict 1. [ə'dikt]: *~ o.s.* sich hin-, ergeben (*to dat*.); **2.** ['ædikt] (*opium etc. ~*) (Opium- *etc*.) Süchtige *m, f*; **ad·dict·ed** [ə'diktid] ergeben (*to dat*.); süchtig (*to* nach), abhängig (*to* von).
add·ing ['ædiŋ] *attr*. Rechen...
ad·di·tion [ə'diʃən] Hinzufügen *n*; Zusatz *m*; An-, Ausbau *m* (*to* zu *od. gen*.); *Am*. parzelliertes Gelän-
[...] Addition *f*; *~ to* Verm[...] au[...] *n*.); *an ~ to the fam*[...] **'di·ti**[...]achs *m*; *in ~* zu-, Zusatz. *~ to* außer, zu; **ad·di·tive** zusätzlich, weiter; Zusatz *m*. [...]; Nach...
ad·dle ['ædl] [...] (Lebensmittel-) (*Verstand etc*.) [...] (*Ei*); *fig*. hohl *u. v/i*.); *Verstand* [...]rderben (*v/t*.
ad·dress [ə'dres] [...]rren. richten (*to* an *acc*.); *Worte etc*. *j*. anreden (*as* als); [...]chen zu; sieren; *a. ~ o.s. to* sich a[...] adressen; *~ o.s. to s.th*. sich an [...]wenchen; **2.** Adresse *f*, Anschrift *f*; Anrede *f*; *parl*. Ansprache *f*; Anstand *m*, Manieren *f/pl*.; Gewandtheit *f*; *give an ~* e-e Rede halten; *pay one's ~es to a lady* e-r Dame den Hof machen; **ad·dress·ee** [ædre'si:] Adressat(in); **ad·dress tag** Kofferanhänger *m*.
ad·duce [ə'dju:s] *Beweis etc*. anführen, beibringen.
ad·e·noids ⚕ ['ædinɔidz] *pl*. adenoide Wucherungen *f/pl*., Polypen *m/pl*. (*im Nasen-Rachenraum*).
ad·ept ['ædept] **1.** erfahren; geschickt (*in* in *dat*.); **2.** Eingeweihte *m, f*; Kenner(in); *be an ~ at* Meister sein in (*dat*.).
ad·e·qua·cy ['ædikwəsi] Angemessenheit *f*; **ad·e·quate** □ ['~kwit] angemessen, entsprechend; aus-, hinreichend.
ad·here [əd'hiə] (*to*) kleben, haften (an *dat*.); *fig*. festhalten (an *dat*.); sich an *e-e Regel etc*. halten; zu *j-m* halten; es halten mit; *e-r Partei etc*. angehören; **ad'her·ence** (*to*) Anhaften *n* (an *dat*.); Festhalten *n* (an *dat*.); Befolgung *f e-r Regel etc*.; Anhänglichkeit *f* (an *acc*.); **ad'her·ent 1.** anhaftend; **2.** Anhänger(in).
ad·he·sion [əd'hi:ʒən] *s. adherence*; *fig*. Einwilligung *f*; *phys*. Adhäsion *f*; *give one's ~ to a plan* sich mit einem Plan einverstanden erklären.
ad·he·sive [əd'hi:siv] **1.** □ anklebend; klebrig; Klebe...; gummiert; *~ plaster, ~ tape* Heftpflaster *n*; **2.** Klebstoff *m*.
a·dieu [ə'dju:] **1.** lebe wohl!; **2.** Lebewohl *n*; *make one's ~(s)* Lebewohl sagen.

ad·i·pose ['ædipəʊ... fett(halt)ig; ~ *tissue* ... n.
... tollen m.
ad·it ['ædit] Zug... Angren-
ad·ja·cen·cy ... Umgebung *f*;
zen *n*; *adjacent* ... [ə...legend (*dat.*),
ad'ja·cent □ ... end (an *acc.*),
anstoßend, benachbart ...
ad·jec·ti·val [...dʒek'taivəl] adjek-
tivisch; **ad·jec·tive** ['ædʒiktiv] Adjektiv *n*, Eigenschaftswort *n*.
ad·join [...dʒɔin] angrenzen an
(*acc.*); **ad'join·ing** angrenzend,
benachbart, Neben...
ad·journ [ə'dʒə:n] aufschieben; (*v/i.*
sich) vertagen; *Sitzungsort* verlegen (*to* nach); **ad'journ·ment**
Aufschub *m*; Vertagung *f*.
ad·judge [ə'dʒʌdʒ] zuerkennen; ⚖ entscheiden; als *et.* erklären; verurteilen (*to* zu).
ad·ju·di·cate [ə'dʒu:dikeit] *s. adjudge*; **ad·ju·di'ca·tion** Zuerkennung *f*; Entscheidung *f*, Urteil *n*.
ad·junct ['ædʒʌŋkt] Nebenumstand *m*; Zusatz *m*; *gr.* Attribut *n*.
ad·ju·ra·tion [ædʒuə'reiʃən] Beschwörung *f*; **ad·jure** [ə'dʒuə] *j.* beschwören, dringend bitten (*to inf.* zu *inf.*).
ad·just [ə'dʒʌst] in Ordnung bringen, berichtigen; anpassen; *Streit* schlichten; *Maße* eichen; *Mechanismus* einstellen; ~ *o.s. to fig.* sich anpassen (*dat.*) *od.* an (*acc.*), sich einfügen in (*acc.*); ~*ing screw* Stellschraube *f*; **ad'just·a·ble** □ ein-, verstellbar; **ad'just·ment** Anordnung *f*; Berichtigung *f*; Einstellung *f*; Einstellvorrichtung *f*; Schlichtung *f*; Eichung *f*; Justieren *n*.
ad·ju·tan·cy ⚔ ['ædʒutənsi] Adjutantur *f*; '**ad·ju·tant** Adjutant *m*.
ad-lib F [æd'lib] improvisieren.
ad·man F ['ædmæn] Werbefachmann *m*; **ad·mass** ['ædmæs] *durch Werbung beeinflußbares* Massenpublikum *n*.
ad·min F ['ædmin] Verwaltung *f*.
ad·min·is·ter [əd'ministə] *v/t.* verwalten; *bsd. Sakramente u. fig.* darreichen, spenden; *Eid* abnehmen; ⚕ verabfolgen; ~ *justice*, ~ *the law* Recht sprechen; ~ *punishment* strafen; *v/i.* beitragen (*to* zu); **ad·min·is'tra·tion** Verwaltung *f*; Handhabung *f*; Darreichung *f*; Regierung *f*; *bsd. Am.* Amtsperiode *f e-s Präsidenten*; ~ *of justice* Rechtspflege *f*, Rechtsprechung *f*; **ad'min·is·tra·tive** [~trətiv] Verwaltungs...; ausführend; **ad'min·is·tra·tor** [~treitə] Verwalter *m*; Nachlaß-, Vermögensverwalter *m*; **ad'min·is·tra·trix** [~treitriks] Verwalterin *f*.
ad·mi·ra·ble □ ['ædmərəbl] bewundernswert, (vor)trefflich.
ad·mi·ral ['ædmərəl] Admiral *m*; ♀ *of the Fleet* Großadmiral *m*; '**ad·mi·ral·ty** Admiralität *f*; *First Lord of the* ♀ (britischer) Marineminister *m*.
ad·mi·ra·tion [ædmə'reiʃən] Bewunderung *f*; Gegenstand *m* der Bewunderung; *she was the* ~ *of all* sie wurde von allen bewundert.
ad·mire [əd'maiə] bewundern; verehren; **ad'mir·er** Bewunderer *m*; Verehrer(in).
ad·mis·si·bil·i·ty [ədmisə'biliti] Zulässigkeit *f*; **ad'mis·si·ble** □ zulässig; zulassungsfähig; **ad'mission** Zulassung *f* (*into, to* zu), Aufnahme *f* (*into, to* in *acc.*); Eintritt(sgeld *n*) *m*; Eingeständnis *n* (*of gen.*; *that* daß).
ad·mit [əd'mit] *v/t.* (her)einlassen (*to, into* in *acc.*), eintreten lassen; aufnehmen (*to* in *acc.*), zulassen (*to* zu); Raum haben für; zugeben; ~ *to the bar* ⚖ *bsd. Am. j.* als Rechtsanwalt zulassen; *v/i.*: ~ *of* gestatten, zulassen; *it* ~*s of no excuse* es läßt sich nicht entschuldigen; **ad'mit·tance** Einlaß *m*, Zutritt *m*; *no* ~! Zutritt verboten!; **ad'mit·ted·ly** zugestandenermaßen.
ad·mix·ture [əd'mikstʃə] Beimischung *f*, Zusatz *m*.
ad·mon·ish [əd'mɔniʃ] ermahnen (*to inf.* zu *inf.*; *that* daß); warnen (*of, against* vor *dat.*; *that* daß); **ad·mo·ni·tion** [ædməu'niʃən] Ermahnung *f*; Warnung *f*; **ad·mon·i·to·ry** □ [əd'mɔnitəri] ermahnend; warnend; Warnungs...
a·do [ə'du:] Getue *n*, Aufheben *n*, Lärm *m*; Mühe *f*; *without much* ~ mir nichts, dir nichts.
a·do·be [ə'dəubi] Luftziegel *m*.
ad·o·les·cence [ædəu'lesns] Adoleszenz *f*, Reifezeit *f*; **ad·o'les·cent** **1.** jugendlich, heranwachsend; **2.** Jugendliche *m, f*.
a·dopt [ə'dɔpt] adoptieren; *fig.* an-

nehmen, sich zu eigen machen; *~ed country* Wahlheimat *f*; **a'dop·tion** Adoption *f*; Annahme *f*; **a'dop·tive** Adoptiv...; **a·dop·tive coun·try** Wahlheimat *f*.

a·dor·a·ble □ [ə'dɔ:rəbl] verehrungswürdig; **ad·o·ra·tion** [ædɔ:'reiʃən] Anbetung *f*; Verehrung *f*; **a·dore** [ə'dɔ:] anbeten (*a. fig.*); innig lieben; **a'dor·er** Anbeter (-in); Verehrer(in).

a·dorn [ə'dɔ:n] schmücken, zieren; **a'dorn·ment** Schmuck *m*; Verzierung *f*.

A·dri·at·ic [eidri'ætik] Adria *f*.

a·drift [ə'drift] ⚓ treibend; *fig.* aufs Geratewohl; *turn s.o.* ~ j. hinauswerfen *od.* verjagen.

a·droit □ [ə'drɔit] gewandt; **a'droit·ness** Gewandtheit *f*.

ad·u·late ['ædjuleit] *j-m* schmeicheln; **ad·u'la·tion** Schmeichelei *f*; **'ad·u·la·tor** Schmeichler *m*; **'ad·u·la·to·ry** schmeichlerisch.

a·dult ['ædʌlt] **1.** erwachsen; **2.** Erwachsene *m, f*; ~ *education* Erwachsenenbildung *f*.

a·dul·ter·ant [ə'dʌltərənt] Verfälschungsmittel *n*; **a'dul·ter·ate** **1.** [~reit] verfälschen; *fig.* verderben; **2.** [~rit] verfälscht; ehebrecherisch; **a·dul·ter·a·tion** [ədʌltə'reiʃən] Verfälschung *f*, Fälschung *f*; **a'dul·ter·a·tor** Verfälscher *m*; **a'dul·ter·er** Ehebrecher *m*; **a'dul·ter·ess** Ehebrecherin *f*; **a'dul·ter·ous** □ ehebrecherisch; **a'dul·ter·y** Ehebruch *m*.

ad·um·brate ['ædʌmbreit] im Umriß darstellen, skizzieren; andeuten; **ad·um'bra·tion** Umriß *m*, Skizze *f*; Andeutung *f*.

ad·vance [əd'vɑ:ns] **1.** *v/i.* vorrücken, -gehen, -dringen; sich nähern; *im Rang* aufrücken; vorankommen; steigen (*Preis*); Fortschritte machen; *v/t.* vorrücken, -schieben; vorverlegen; vorbringen, äußern; vorausbezahlen; vorschießen; (be)fördern; *Preis* erhöhen; beschleunigen; **2.** Vorrücken *n*; ⚔ Vormarsch *m*; Beförderung *f*; Fortschritt *m*; Angebot *n*; Vorschuß *m*; Erhöhung *f des Preises etc.*; *in* ~ im voraus; *be in* ~ *of s.o.* j-m voraus sein; **3.** Vor(aus)...; **ad'vanced** *adj.* vorgeschritten; ~ *in years* in vorgerücktem Alter; ~ *English* Englisch für Fortgeschrittene; **ad'vance·ment** Beförderung *f*; Förderung *f*; Fortschritt *m*.

ad·van·tage [əd'vɑ:ntidʒ] Vorteil *m* (*a. beim Tennis*; *to* für); Überlegenheit *f*; Gewinn *m*; *gain an* ~ *over s.o.* sich e-n Vorteil gegenüber j-m verschaffen; *take* ~ *of* ausnutzen; *j.* übervorteilen; *to* ~ vorteilhaft; *you have the* ~ *of me iro.* ich habe nicht die Ehre, Sie zu kennen; **ad·van·ta·geous** □ [ædvən'teidʒəs] vorteilhaft, günstig.

ad·vent ['ædvənt] (Auf)Kommen *n*; ♀ *eccl.* Advent *m*; **ad·ven·ti·tious** □ [ædven'tiʃəs] zufällig; fremd; Neben...

ad·ven·ture [əd'ventʃə] **1.** Abenteuer *n*, Wagnis *n*; ✝ Spekulationsgeschäft *n*; **2.** (sich) wagen; **ad'ventu·r·er** Abenteurer *m*; Spekulant *m*; **ad'ven·tur·ess** Abenteu(r)erin *f*; **ad'ven·tur·ous** □ abenteuerlich; kühn, verwegen; abenteuer-, unternehmungslustig.

ad·verb ['ædvə:b] Adverb *n*; **ad·ver·bi·al** [əd'və:bjəl] □ adverbial; ~ *phrase* adverbiale Bestimmung *f*.

ad·ver·sar·y ['ædvəsəri] Gegner *m*, Widersacher *m*; **ad·verse** □ ['~və:s] widrig; gegnerisch, feindlich; ungünstig, nachteilig (*to* für); ~ *to* gegen; ~ *balance of trade* ungünstige Handelsbilanz *f*; **ad·ver·si·ty** [əd'və:siti] Widerwärtigkeit *f*; Unglück *n*.

ad·vert [əd'və:t] hinweisen, sich beziehen (*to* auf *acc.*).

ad·ver·tise ['ædvətaiz] ankündigen; annoncieren, inserieren; Reklame machen (für); ~ *for* durch Inserat suchen; **ad·ver·tise·ment** [əd'və:tismənt] Ankündigung *f*, (Zeitungs)Anzeige *f*, Annonce *f*, Inserat *n*; Reklame *f*; **ad·ver·tis·er** ['ædvətaizə] Anzeiger *m*, Anzeigenblatt *n*; Inserent *m*; **'ad·ver·tis·ing** Werbung *f*, Reklame *f*; ~ *agency* Werbeagentur *f*; ~ *campaign* Werbekampagne *f*; ~ *manager* Werbeleiter *m*.

ad·vice [əd'vais] Rat *m*; Ratschlag *m*; Ratschläge *m/pl.*; ✝ Avis *m*; Nachricht *f*, Meldung *f*; *letter of* ~ Avisbrief *m*, Benachrichtigungsschreiben *n*; *on the* ~ *of* auf Anraten von; *take medical* ~ e-n Arzt zu Rate ziehen.

ad·vis·a·ble □ [əd'vaizəbl] ratsam; **ad'vise** *v/t. et.* (an)raten; *j.* beraten; *j-m* raten (*to inf.* zu *inf.*); † benachrichtigen (*of* von, *that* daß), avisieren (*s.o. of s.th.* j-m et.); *v/i.* (sich) beraten (*with* mit); ~ *on* zu *et.* raten; **ad'vised** □ wohlbedacht; **ad'vis·ed·ly** [~idli] mit Bedacht; **ad'vis·er** Ratgeber(in); **ad'vi·so·ry** [~əri] beratend; 2 *Board* Beratungsstelle *f.*

ad·vo·ca·cy ['ædvəkəsi] (*of*) Eintreten *n* (für), Befürwortung *f* (*gen.*); **ad·vo·cate 1.** ['~kit] Advokat *m*, Anwalt *m*; *fig.* Verfechter *m*, Fürsprecher *m*; **2.** ['~keit] verteidigen, verfechten, befürworten, vertreten.

adze ⊕ [ædz] Breitbeil *n.*

Ae·ge·an Sea [i:'dʒi:ən'si:] Ägäisches Meer *n.*

ae·gis ['i:dʒis] *fig.* Ägide *f*, Schutzherrschaft *f.*

Ae·o·li·an [i:'əuljən] äolisch; Äols...

ae·on ['i:ən] Äon *m*; *fig.* Ewigkeit *f.*

a·er·at·ed ['eiəreitid] kohlensauer.

a·e·ri·al ['εəriəl] **1.** □ Luft...; Flieger...; gasförmig; ~ *camera* Luftbildgerät *n*; ~ *survey* Luftbildvermessung *f*; ~ *view* Luftaufnahme *f*; **2.** *Radio, Fernsehen*: Antenne *f.*

a·er·ie ['εəri] Horst *m* (*a. fig.*).

a·er·o... ['εərəu] Luft...; **a·er·o·bat·ics** [~'bætiks] *sg.* Kunstfliegen *n*; **a·er·o·cab** ['εərəkæb] *Am.* F Lufttaxi *n* (*Hubschrauber als Zubringer*); **a·er·o·drome** ['~drəum] Flugplatz *m*, -hafen *m*; **a·er·o·gram** ['~græm] Funkspruch *m*; **a·er·o·lite** ['εərəulait] Meteorstein *m*; **a·er·o·naut** ['εərənɔ:t] Luftschiffer *m*; **a·er·o'nau·tic, a·er·o'nau·ti·cal** □ aeronautisch; Luftfahrt...; **a·er·o'nau·tics** *mst sg.* Luftfahrt *f*; **'a·er·o·plane** Flugzeug *n*; **a·er·o·sol (can)** ['~sɔl] Aerosolzerstäuber *m*; **a·er·o·space in·du·stry** Raumfahrtindustrie *f*; **a·er·o·stat** ['εərəustæt] Luftschiff *n*; Ballon *m*; **a·er·o'stat·ic** aerostatisch.

aes·thete ['i:sθi:t] Ästhet *m*, Schöngeist *m*; **aes·thet·ic, aes·thet·i·cal** □ [i:s'θetik(əl)] ästhetisch; **aes'thet·ics** *sg.* Ästhetik *f.*

a·far [ə'fɑ:] *mst* ~ *off* fern, weit (weg); *from* ~ von fern, weither.

af·fa·bil·i·ty [æfə'biliti] Leutseligkeit *f.*

af·fa·ble □ ['æfəbl] leutselig.

af·fair [ə'fεə] Geschäft *n*; Angelegenheit *f*, Sache *f*; F Sache *f*, Ding *n*; Liebschaft *f*; ~ *of honour* Ehrenhandel *m.*

af·fect [ə'fekt] (ein- *od.* sich aus-) wirken auf (*acc.*); beeinflussen; berühren, betreffen; rühren, ergreifen; *die Gesundheit* angreifen, in Mitleidenschaft ziehen; neigen zu, gern mögen, bevorzugen; vortäuschen, nachahmen; *he* ~*s the freethinker* er spielt den Freigeist; *he* ~*s to sleep* er tut, als ob er schliefe; **af·fec·ta·tion** [æfek'teiʃən] Vorliebe *f* (*of* für); Ziererei *f*, Affektiertheit *f*; Verstellung *f*; **af·fect·ed** □ [ə'fektid] gerührt; befallen (*von Krankheit*); angegriffen (*Augen etc.*); geneigt, gesinnt (*towards s.o.* gegen j.); geziert, affektiert; erheuchelt; **af'fec·tion** Gemütsbewegung *f*, -zustand *m*; (Zu)Neigung *f*, Liebe *f* (*for, towards* zu); Erkrankung *f*; **af'fec·tion·ate** □ [~kʃnit] liebevoll, herzlich; *yours* ~*ly* Dein Dich liebender (*Briefschluß*); **af'fec·tive** ergreifend; affektiv, Affekt...

af·fi·ance [ə'faiəns] **1.** Vertrauen *n* (*in* in *acc.*); **2.** verloben (*to* mit).

af·fi·da·vit [æfi'deivit] *schriftliche* beeidigte Erklärung *f.*

af·fil·i·ate [ə'filieit] *als Mitglied* aufnehmen; angliedern, anschließen (*to dat. od.* an *acc.*); verschmelzen (*with* mit); ⚖ die Vaterschaft *e-s Kindes* zuschreiben (*on, to dat.*); ~*d company* Tochtergesellschaft *f*; **af·fil·i'a·tion** Aufnahme *f* (*als Mitglied etc.*); Angliederung *f.*

af·fin·i·ty [ə'finiti] Verschwägerung *f*; *fig.* (geistige) Verwandtschaft *f*; ⚗ Affinität *f.*

af·firm [ə'fə:m] bejahen, behaupten; bestätigen; **af·fir·ma·tion** [æfə:'meiʃən] Behauptung *f*; Bestätigung *f*; **af·firm·a·tive** □ [ə'fə:mətiv] **1.** bejahend; positiv; **2.** *su.*: *answer in the* ~ bejahen.

af·fix 1. ['æfiks] Anhang *m*; **2.** [ə'fiks] (*to*) anheften (an *acc.*); befestigen (an *dat.*); *Siegel* aufdrücken (auf *acc.*); beifügen (*dat.*); zufügen (zu).

af·flict [ə'flikt] betrüben; quälen; ~*ed with* geplagt von, leidend an (*dat.*); **af'flic·tion** Betrübnis *f*;

Leiden *n*; Pein *f*.

af·flu·ence [ˈæfluəns] Überfluß *m*; Reichtum *m*, Wohlstand *m*; **ˈaf·flu·ent 1.** □ reich (fließend); reich (*in* an *dat.*); ~ *society* Wohlstandsgesellschaft *f*; **2.** Nebenfluß *m*.

af·flux [ˈæflʌks] Zufluß *m*.

af·ford [əˈfɔːd] gewähren; bieten; sich leisten; *I can ~ it* ich kann es mir leisten.

af·for·est [æˈfɔrist] aufforsten; **af·for·estˈa·tion** Aufforstung *f*.

af·fran·chise [əˈfræntʃaiz] befreien.

af·fray [əˈfrei] Schlägerei *f*.

af·front [əˈfrʌnt] **1.** beleidigen; trotzen (*dat.*); **2.** Beleidigung *f*; *put an ~ upon, offer an ~ to j.* beleidigen.

a·fi·cio·na·do [əfisjəˈnɑːdəu] Fan *m*, Liebhaber *m*.

a·field [əˈfiːld] ins Feld; im Feld; (von zu Hause) weg; *far ~* weit weg.

a·fire [əˈfaiə] in Flammen.

a·flame [əˈfleim] in Flammen; *fig.* glühend; *set s.th. ~* et. in Brand stecken *od.* anzünden.

a·float [əˈfləut] ⚓ flott, schwimmend, auf See; in vollem Gange (*Geschäft etc.*); in Umlauf (*Gerücht*); von Wasser bedeckt; *keep ~* sich über Wasser halten; *set ~* flottmachen; *the rumour is ~* das Gerücht geht um.

a·foot [əˈfut] im Gange; zu Fuß; auf den Beinen; in Bewegung.

a·fore ⚓ [əˈfɔː] *s. before*; **aˈfore·men·tioned** [~menʃənd], **aˈfore·named** [~neimd], **aˈfore·said** vorerwähnt, vorgenannt; **aˈfore·thought** vorbedacht.

a·fraid [əˈfreid] besorgt, bange; *be ~ of* sich fürchten *od.* Angst haben vor (*dat.*); *I am ~* es tut mir leid; leider.

a·fresh [əˈfreʃ] von neuem.

Af·ri·can [ˈæfrikən] **1.** afrikanisch; **2.** Afrikaner(in); *bsd. Am. in Zssgn* Neger...; **Af·ri·can·der** [~ˈkændə] Kapholländer *m*.

Af·ri·kaans [æfriˈkɑːns] Kapholländisch *n*, Afrikaans *n*.

Af·ro [ˈæfrəu] 1. afro...; 2. Afro-Frisur *f*.

aft ⚓ [ɑːft] (nach) achtern *od.* hinten.

aft·er [ˈɑːftə] **1.** *adv.* hinterher; nachher, darauf; **2.** *prp. zeitlich*: nach; *räumlich*: nach, hinter (... her); *Maß, Richtschnur*: nach, gemäß; *~ all* nach alledem; schließlich (doch); im Grunde; immerhin; *be ~ s.o.* hinter j-m her sein, j. verfolgen; *time ~ time* immer wieder; *~ having seen him* nachdem ich ihn gesehen hatte; **3.** *cj.* nachdem; **4.** *adj.* später; Nach...; ⚓ Achter...; **ˈ~·birth** ⚕ Nachgeburt *f*; **ˈ~·care** ⚕ Nachbehandlung *f*; **ˈ~·crop** Nachernte *f*; **ˈ~-ˈdin·ner** nach Tisch...; *~ speech* Tischrede *f*; **ˈ~-ef·fect** Nachwirkung *f*; **ˈ~-glow** Abendrot *n*; **ˈ~-hours** *pl.* Zeit *f* nach (Dienst)Schluß; **~·math** [ˈ~mæθ] *fig.* Nachwirkung(en *pl.*) *f*, Folgen *f/pl.*; **ˈ~ˈnoon** Nachmittag *m*; *this ~* heute nachmittag; **ˈ~·pains** *pl.* ⚕ Nachwehen *pl.*

aft·ers F [ˈɑːftəz] *pl.* Nachtisch *m*.

aft·er...: **ˈ~-sales serv·ice** Kundendienst *m*; **ˈ~-sea·son** Nachsaison *f*; **ˈ~-shave** After-shave(-Lotion *f*) *n*; **ˈ~-taste** Nachgeschmack *m*; **ˈ~-thought** nachträglicher Einfall *m*; **ˈ~-treat·ment** Nachkur *f*; **~·wards** [ˈ~wədz] nachher; hinterher; später; nachträglich.

a·gain [əˈgən] wieder, abermals, noch einmal; wiederum; schon wieder; ferner, außerdem; dagegen; *~ and ~, time and ~* immer wieder; *as much (many) ~* noch einmal soviel (so viele); *now and ~* hin und wieder.

a·gainst [əˈgenst] *räumlich*: gegen; *fig.* in Erwartung (*gen.*); *as ~* verglichen mit; *~ the wall* an der Wand; *~ a background* vor *od.* auf e-m Hintergrund; *over ~* gegenüber; *run ~ s.o.* j-m in den Weg laufen.

a·gape [əˈgeip] gaffend, mit offenem Mund.

ag·ate [ˈægət] *min.* Achat *m*; *Am.* Murmel *f*; *Am. typ.* = *ruby*.

a·ga·ve ⚘ [əˈgeivi] Agave *f*.

age [eidʒ] **1.** (Lebens)Alter *n*; Zeit (-alter *n*) *f*; Menschenalter *n*, Generation *f*; *oft ~s pl.* F Ewigkeit *f*; *(old) ~* Greisenalter *n*; *at the ~ of* im Alter von; *in the ~ of Queen Anne* in der *od.* zur Zeit ...; *of ~* mündig; *over ~* zu alt; *under ~* unmündig; *what is his ~?* wie alt ist er?; *when I was your ~* als ich in deinem Alter war; *act od. be your ~!* sei kein Kindskopf!; *come of ~* mündig werden; **2.** alt werden *od.*

machen; ˈ**age-brack·et** Altersgruppe *f*; **aged** [eidʒd] ... Jahre alt; ~ *twenty* 20 Jahre alt; **a·ged** [ˈ~id] alt, betagt, bejahrt; ˈ**age-group** Altersgruppe *f*; ˈ**age·less** zeitlos; ˈ**age--lim·it** Altersgrenze *f*.

a·gen·cy [ˈeidʒənsi] Tätigkeit *f*, Wirkung *f*; Vermittlung *f*; ✝ Agentur *f*, Büro *n*; Dienststelle *f*.

a·gen·da [əˈdʒendə] Tagesordnung *f*.

a·gent [ˈeidʒənt] Handelnde *m*, *f*; Agent *m*; F (Handlungs)Reisende *m*; wirkende Kraft *f*, Agens *n*.

age-old [ˈeidʒəuld] uralt.

age-worn [ˈeidʒwɔːn] altersschwach.

ag·glom·er·ate [əˈglɔməreit] (sich) zs.-ballen; (sich) (an)häufen; **ag·glom·erˈa·tion** Zs.-ballung *f*; Anhäufung *f*.

ag·glu·ti·nate 1. [əˈgluːtineit] zs.-, an-, verkleben; ⚗, *gr.* agglutinieren; 2. [~nit] zs.-geklebt, verbunden; *gr.* agglutiniert; **ag·glu·ti·na·tion** [~ˈneiʃən] Zs.-kleben *n*; ⚗, *gr.* Agglutination *f*; **agˈglu·ti·na·tive** [~nətiv] zs.-klebend; agglutinierend.

ag·gran·dize [əˈgrændaiz] vergrößern; *im Range etc.* erhöhen; **agˈgran·dize·ment** [~dizmənt] Vergrößerung *f*; *fig.* Erhöhung *f*.

ag·gra·vate [ˈægrəveit] erschweren; verschlimmern, verschärfen; F ärgern; **ag·graˈva·tion** Erschwerung *f etc.*; F Verärgerung *f*.

ag·gre·gate 1. [ˈægrigeit] (sich) anhäufen; vereinigen (*to* mit); F sich insgesamt belaufen auf (*acc.*); 2. □ [ˈ~git] gehäuft; gesamt; Gesamt...; 3. [ˈ~git] Anhäufung *f*; Aggregat *n*; *in the* ~ im ganzen; **ag·gre·ga·tion** [~ˈgeiʃən] Anhäufung *f*.

ag·gres·sion [əˈgreʃən] Angriff *m*, Überfall *m*; **ag·gres·sive** □ [əˈgresiv] angreifend; aggressiv, streitlustig, -süchtig; ~ *war* Angriffskrieg *m*; **agˈgres·sive·ness** Aggressivität *f*; **agˈgres·sor** Angreifer *m*.

ag·grieve [əˈgriːv] kränken.

ag·gro *sl.* [ˈægrəu] Aggressivität *f*; Aggression *f*; Ärger *m*.

a·ghast [əˈgɑːst] entgeistert, entsetzt, bestürzt (*at* über *acc.*).

ag·ile □ [ˈædʒail] flink, behend.

a·gil·i·ty [əˈdʒiliti] Behendigkeit *f*.

ag·i·o ✝ [ˈædʒəu] Agio *n*, Aufgeld *n*; **ag·i·o·tage** [ˈædʒətidʒ] Agiotage *f*, Wechsel-, Börsengeschäft *n*.

ag·i·tate [ˈædʒiteit] *v/t.* bewegen, schütteln; *fig.* erregen; erörtern; *v/i.* agitieren (*for* für); **ag·iˈta·tion** Bewegung *f*, Erschütterung *f*; Aufregung *f*, Gärung *f*; Agitation *f*; ˈ**ag·i·ta·tor** Agitator *m*, Aufwiegler *m*, Hetzredner *m*.

a·glow [əˈgləu] glutrot, glühend (*with* von, vor *dat.*).

a·go [əˈgəu]: *a year* ~ vor einem Jahre; *it is a year* ~ es ist ein Jahr her; *long* ~ vor langer Zeit.

a·gog [əˈgɔg] erpicht; gespannt (*for* auf *acc.*).

ag·o·nize [ˈægənaiz] *v/t.* quälen; *v/i.* (mit dem Tode *u. fig.*) ringen; sich quälen; ˈ**ag·o·niz·ing** □ qualvoll.

ag·o·ny [ˈægəni] Qual *f*, Pein *f*; Ringen *n*, Kampf *m*; Todesangst *f*; *a.* ~ *of death, mortal* ~ Todeskampf *m*; ~ *column* F Seufzerspalte *f* (*Zeitung*).

a·grar·i·an [əˈgrɛəriən] 1. Befürworter *m* der Landaufteilung; Agrarier *m*; 2. agrarisch; Agrar...

a·gree [əˈgriː] *v/i.* übereinstimmen; sich vertragen; einwilligen; (*upon, on*) einig werden (über *acc.*), sich einigen (auf *acc.*); übereinkommen, vereinbaren (*that* daß); ~ *with j-m* bekommen *od.* zuträglich sein; ~ *to* zustimmen (*dat.*), eingehen auf (*acc.*); einverstanden sein mit; ~ *to differ* das Streiten aufgeben; *v/t.* ✝ *Bücher etc.* abstimmen; *be* ~*d* (sich) einig sein (*on* über *acc.*; *that* darüber, daß); ~*d!* abgemacht!;

a·gree·a·ble □ [əˈgriəbl] (*to*) angenehm (für); übereinstimmend (mit); F einverstanden (mit); **aˈgree·a·ble·ness** Annehmlichkeit *f*; **a·gree·ment** [əˈgriːmənt] Übereinstimmung *f*; Einklang *m*; Vereinbarung *f*, Überein-, Abkommen *n*; Vertrag *m*; *come to an* ~ e-e Verständigung erzielen; *make an* ~ ein Abkommen treffen.

ag·ri·cul·tur·al [ægriˈkʌltʃərəl] landwirtschaftlich, Ackerbau...; **ag·ri·cul·ture** [ˈ~tʃə] Ackerbau *m*, Landwirtschaft *f*; **ag·riˈcul·tur·ist** [~tʃərist] Landwirt *m*.

a·ground ⚓ [əˈgraund] gestrandet; *run* ~ auflaufen, auf (den) Strand setzen.

a·gue [ˈeigjuː] Wechselfieber *n*; Schüttelfrost *m*; ˈ**a·gu·ish** fieber-

haft, fieb(e)rig.
ah [ɑː] ah!, ach!
a·ha [ɑːˈhɑː] aha!
a·head [əˈhed] vorwärts; voraus; vorn; *straight* ~ geradeaus; ~ *of s.o.* j-m voraus; *go* ~ vorgehen, vorankommen; weitermachen; *go* ~*!* vorwärts!; los!; weiter!
a·hoi, a·hoy ⚓ [əˈhɔi] ho!, ahoi!
aid [eid] **1.** helfen (*dat.*; *in* bei *et.*); fördern; **2.** Hilfe *f*; *by* (*with*) *the* ~ *of* mit Hilfe von *od. gen.*; *in* ~ *of* zur Unterstützung *gen.*; ~*s and appliances* Hilfsmittel *n/pl.*
aide-de-camp ⚔ [ˈeiddəˈkɑ̃ːŋ] Adjutant *m.*
ai·grette [ˈeigret] Federbusch *m.*
ail [eil] *v/i.* kränkeln; *v/t.* schmerzen, weh(e) tun (*dat.*); *what* ~*s him?* was fehlt ihm?
ai·ler·on ✈ [ˈeilərɔn] Querruder *n.*
ail·ing [ˈeiliŋ] leidend, kränklich; ˈ**ail·ment** Leiden *n.*
aim [eim] **1.** *v/i.* zielen (*at* auf *acc.*); ~ *at fig.* abzielen auf, streben nach, bezwecken; ~ *to do bsd. Am.* beabsichtigen *od.* versuchen zu tun, tun wollen; *v/t. Geschütz, Schlag, Gewehr, etc.* richten (*at* auf *acc.*, gegen); **2.** Ziel *n*; *fig.* Zweck *m*, Absicht *f*; *Leistungs-*Soll *n*; *take* ~ zielen; ˈ**aim·less** □ ziellos.
ain't F [eint] = *are not, am not, is not, have not, has not.*
air[1] [ɛə] **1.** Luft *f*; Luftzug *m*, Lüftchen *n*; *by* ~ auf dem Luftwege; *go by* ~ fliegen; *in the open* ~ im Freien; *castles in the* ~ Luftschlösser *n/pl.*; *be in the* ~ in der Luft liegen; ungewiß sein; *on the* ~ im Rundfunk *zu hören*; *go off the* ~ zu senden aufhören; ~ *supply* Luftzufuhr *f*; *take the* ~ frische Luft schöpfen; ✈ aufsteigen; **2.** (aus)lüften, an die Luft bringen; *Wäsche* trocknen; an die Öffentlichkeit bringen; erörtern; zur Schau tragen; ~ *o.s.* an die Luft gehen.
air[2] [~] Miene *f*; Aussehen *n*; *give o.s.* ~*s* vornehm tun; *with an* ~ mit Würde; ~*s and graces* Vornehmtuerei *f.*
air[3] ♪ [~] Weise *f*, Melodie *f*; Arie *f.*
air...: ˈ~**·bag** *mot.* Luftsack *m*; ˈ~**-base** Luftstützpunkt *m*; ˈ~**-bath** Luftbad *n*; ˈ~**-bed** Luftmatratze *f*; ˈ~**-bladder** Schwimmblase *f*; ˈ~**-borne** im Flugzeug befördert; in der Luft (*Flugzeug*); ⚔ Luftlande...; *we are* ~ wir fliegen; ˈ~**-brake** Druckluftbremse *f*; ˈ~**·bus,** ~ **bus** ✈ Airbus *m*; ~ **car·go** Luftfracht *f*; ˈ~**-cham·ber** *biol.* Luftkammer *f*; ⊕ Windkessel *m*; ˈ~**-con·di·tioned** mit Klimaanlage, klimatisiert; ˈ~**-con·di·tion·er** Klimaanlage *f*; ˈ~**-con·di·tion·ing** Klimaanlage *f*; ˈ~**-cooled** luftgekühlt; ˈ~**·craft** Luftfahrzeug(e *pl.*) *n*, Flugzeug(e *pl.*) *n*; ~ *carrier* Flugzeugträger *m*; ˈ~**-cush·ion** Luftkissen *n*; ˈ~**--drop** Abwerfen *n od.* Absetzen *n* aus der Luft; ˈ~**-ex·haust·er** Entlüfter *m*; ˈ~**-field** Flugplatz *m*; ˈ~**--force** Luftwaffe *f*; ˈ~**·frame** Flugzeugzelle *f*; ~ **freight** Luftfracht *f*; Luftfrachtgebühr *f*; ˈ~**-gun** Luftgewehr *n*; ~ **host·ess** Stewardeß *f*, Flugbegleiterin *f.*
air·i·ness [ˈɛərinis] Luftigkeit *f*; Leicht(fert)igkeit *f.*
air·ing [ˈɛəriŋ] Lüften *n*; Spaziergang *m*, -fahrt *f*, -ritt *m*; *give s.th. an* ~ et. lüften; *the room needs an* ~ das Zimmer muß (durch)gelüftet werden; *take an* ~ frische Luft schöpfen.
air...: ˈ~**-jack·et** Schwimmweste *f*; ⊕ Luftmantel *m*; ˈ~**·less** ohne Luft (-zug); dumpf(ig); ~ **let·ter** *Am.* Luftpostleichtbrief *m*, Aerogramm *n*; Luftpostbrief *m*; ˈ~**-lift** Luftbrücke *f* (*Versorgung auf dem Luftwege*); ˈ~**-line** Luftverkehrslinie *f*, -gesellschaft *f*; ˈ~**-lin·er** Verkehrsflugzeug *n*; ˈ~**-mail** Luftpost *f*; ˈ~**-man** Flieger *m*; ˈ~**-meˈchan·ic** Bordmonteur *m*; ˈ~**-mind·ed** flugbegeistert; ˈ~**-pas·sen·ger** Fluggast *m*; ~ **pho·to**(**·graph**) Luftbild *n*; ˈ~**--pipe** ⊕ Luftrohr *n*; ˈ~**·plane** *bsd. Am.* Flugzeug *n*; ˈ~**·pock·et** ✈ Luftloch *n*; ˈ~**-port** Flughafen *m*; ˈ~**-proof** luftdicht; ˈ~**-pump** Luftpumpe *f*; ˈ~**-raid** ⚔ Luftangriff *m*; ~ *precautions pl.* Luftschutz *m*; ~ *shelter* Luftschutzraum *m*; ~ **scout** ⚔ Aufklärungsflugzeug *n*; ˈ~**·ship** Luftschiff *n*; ˈ~**·sick** luftkrank; ˈ~**·strip** Start- u. Landestreifen *m*; ~ **ter·mi·nal** Flughafenabfertigungsgebäude *n*; ˈ~**-tight** luftdicht; ~ *case sl.* todsicherer Fall *m*; ˈ~**-traf·fic con·trol·ler** Fluglotse *m*; ˈ~**-tube** Luftschlauch *m*; ~ **um·brel·la** ⚔ Luftsicherung *f*, Deckung *f* durch die Luftwaffe; ˈ~**·way** Flugstraße *f*;

Luftverkehrsgesellschaft *f*; '~·**wom·an** Fliegerin *f*; '~·**wor·thy** ✈ lufttüchtig.

air·y □ ['ɛəri] luftig; leicht; lebhaft; leichtfertig.

aisle [ail] ⛪ Seitenschiff *n*; Gang *m zwischen Tischreihen etc.*; '~-**sit·ter** *Am.* F Theaterkritiker *m*.

aitch [eitʃ] *Name des englischen* h.

aitch·bone ['eitʃbəun] Lendenstück *n*.

a·jar [ə'dʒɑː] halb offen, angelehnt (*Tür*); *fig.* im Zwiespalt.

a·kim·bo [ə'kimbəu] in die Seite gestemmt (*Arme*).

a·kin [ə'kin] verwandt (*to* mit).

al·a·bas·ter ['æləbɑːstə] **1.** Alabaster *m*; **2.** alabastern.

a·lack † [ə'læk] ach!, o weh!; *~-a-day!* lieber Himmel!

a·lac·ri·ty [ə'lækriti] Munterkeit *f*; Bereitwilligkeit *f*, Eifer *m*.

a·larm [ə'lɑːm] **1.** Alarm *m*, Warnung *f*; Alarmzeichen *n*; Angst *f*, Unruhe *f*; Wecker *m*; *~ pistol* Schreckschußpistole *f*; *give* (*raise, ring, sound*) *the ~* Alarm schlagen; **2.** alarmieren; beunruhigen; **a'larm-bell** Sturmglocke *f*; **a'larm-clock** Wecker *m*; **a'larm·ist 1.** Bangemacher *m*; **2.** beunruhigend.

a·lar·um [ə'lɛərəm] *obs. für alarm*.

a·las [ə'læs] ach!, o weh!, leider!

alb [ælb] Albe *f*, Chorhemd *n*.

Al·ba·ni·an [æl'beinjən] **1.** albanisch; **2.** Albanier(in).

al·ba·tross ['ælbətrɔs] Albatros *m*, Sturmvogel *m*.

al·be·it [ɔːl'biːit] obgleich, obwohl.

al·bi·no *biol.* [æl'biːnəu] Albino *m*.

al·bum ['ælbəm] Album *n*; Schallplattenalbum *n*.

al·bu·men, al·bu·min ⚗ ['ælbjumin] Eiweiß(stoff *m*) *n*; **al·bu·mi·nous** [æl'bjuːminəs] eiweißartig; eiweißhaltig.

al·chem·ic, al·chem·i·cal □ [æl'kemik(əl)] alchimistisch; **al·che·mist** ['ælkimist] Alchimist *m*; '**al·che·my** Alchimie *f*.

al·co·hol ['ælkəhɔl] Alkohol *m*; **al·co'hol·ic 1.** alkoholisch; Alkohol...; 2. Alkoholiker(in); '**al·co·hol·ism** Alkoholvergiftung *f*; **al·co·hol·ize** ['~laiz] alkoholisieren.

al·cove ['ælkəuv] Alkoven *m*; Nische *f*; (Garten)Laube *f*.

al·der ⚘ ['ɔːldə] Erle *f*; Erlen...

al·der·man ['ɔːldəmən] Ratsherr *m*; Stadtrat *m*; **al·der·man·ic** [~'mænik] ratsherrlich; *fig.* würdevoll; **al·der·man·ship** ['~mənʃip] Ratsherrnamt *n*.

ale [eil] Ale *n* (*engl. Bier*).

a·lee ⚓ [ə'liː] leewärts.

a·lem·bic ⚗ [ə'lembik] Destillierkolben *m*.

a·lert [ə'ləːt] **1.** □ wachsam; munter; **2.** Alarmbereitschaft *f*; (Flieger-) Alarm *m*; *on the ~* auf der Hut; in Alarmbereitschaft; **a'lert·ness** Wachsamkeit *f*; Munterkeit *f*.

Al·ex·an·drine [ælig'zændrain] Alexandriner *m* (*12silbiger Vers*).

al·fal·fa ⚘ [æl'fælfə] Luzerne *f*.

al·fres·co [æl'freskəu] im Freien; *~ lunch* Mittagessen *n* im Freien.

al·ga ⚘ ['ælgə], *pl.* **al·gae** ['ældʒiː] Alge *f*.

al·ge·bra ⅍ ['ældʒibrə] Algebra *f*; **al·ge·bra·ic** [~'breiik] algebraisch.

a·li·as ['eiliæs] **1.** alias, sonst (genannt); **2.** angenommener Name *m*, Deckname *m*.

al·i·bi ['ælibai] Alibi *n*; *Am.* F Entschuldigung *f*; Ausrede *f*.

al·ien ['eiljən] **1.** fremd, ausländisch; *fig.* fremd (*to dat.*); **2.** Ausländer (-in); '**al·ien·a·ble** veräußerlich; **al·ien·ate** ['~eit] veräußern; *fig.* entfremden, abspenstig machen (*from dat.*); **al·ien'a·tion** Veräußerung *f*; *fig.* Entfremdung *f*; *~ of mind* Geistesgestörtheit *f*; '**al·ien·ist** Irrenarzt *m*, Psychiater *m*.

a·light[1] [ə'lait] brennend, in Flammen; erhellt.

a·light[2] [~] ab-, aussteigen; ✈ niedergehen, landen; sich niederlassen (*on* auf *acc. od. dat.*).

a·lign [ə'lain] (sich) (aus)richten (*with* nach); *surv.* abstecken; *~ o.s. with* sich anschließen an (*acc.*); **a'lign·ment** Ausrichtung *f*; *surv.* Absteckung(slinie) *f*.

a·like [ə'laik] **1.** *adj.* gleich, ähnlich; **2.** *adv.* gleich; in gleicher Weise; ebenso.

al·i·ment ['ælimənt] Nahrung *f*; **al·i·men·ta·ry** [~'mentəri] nahrhaft; Nahrungs...; Ernährungs...; *~ canal* Verdauungskanal *m*; **al·i·men'ta·tion** Ernährung *f*, Unterhalt *m*.

al·i·mo·ny ⚖ ['æliməni] Unterhalt *m* (*bsd. für geschiedene Ehefrau*).
a·line(·ment) [ə'lain(mənt)] = *align* (*-ment*).
al·i·quant ℞ ['ælikwənt] nicht (*ohne Rest*) aufgehend; **al·i·quot** ['~kwɔt] (*ohne Rest*) aufgehend.
a·live [ə'laiv] lebend, lebendig; munter, lebhaft; in Kraft, wirksam, gültig; (*to*) bewußt (*gen.*), empfänglich (für), Anteil nehmend (an *acc.*); (*with*) voll (von), belebt (von), wimmelnd (von *od.* vor *dat.*); *be* ~ am Leben sein, leben; ⚡ Strom führen; *man* ~! F Menschenskind!; *keep* ~ aufrechterhalten; *look* ~! F beeil dich!, mach schnell!
al·ka·li ⚗ ['ælkəlai] Alkali *n*, Laugensalz *n*; **al·ka·line** ['~lain] alkalisch.
all [ɔ:l] **1.** *adj.* all; ganz; jede(r, -s); ~ *day* (*long*) den ganzen Tag; ~ *kind*(*s*) *of books* allerlei Bücher; *s. above, after*; *for* ~ *that* dessenungeachtet, trotzdem; **2.** alles; alle *pl.*; *my* ~ mein Alles; ~ *of them* sie alle; *not at* ~ durchaus nicht, überhaupt nicht; *for* ~ (*that*) *I care* meinetwegen; *for* ~ *I know* soviel ich weiß; *in* ~ zusammen, insgesamt; **3.** *adv.* ganz, gänzlich, völlig; ~ *at once* auf einmal, plötzlich; ~ *the better* desto besser; ~ *but* beinahe, fast; ~ *in Am.* F fertig, ganz erledigt; ~ *right* (alles) in Ordnung; fertig; ganz recht!; gut!, schön!
all-A·mer·i·can [ɔ:lə'merikən] rein amerikanisch; die ganzen USA vertretend.
al·lay [ə'lei] beruhigen; mildern, lindern; *Durst* stillen.
al·le·ga·tion [æli'geiʃən] *unerwiesene* Behauptung *f*; Aussage *f*; Darstellung *f*; **al·lege** [ə'ledʒ] *Unerwiesenes* behaupten; angeben; **al'leged** angeblich, vermeintlich.
al·le·giance [ə'li:dʒəns] Lehnspflicht *f*; Loyalität *f*; (Untertanen)Treue *f* (*to* zu); *oath of* ~ Treueid *m*, Untertaneneid *m*.
al·le·gor·ic, al·le·gor·i·cal □ [æli'gɔrik(əl)] sinnbildlich, allegorisch; **al·le·go·rize** ['æligəraiz] allegorisch darstellen; '**al·le·go·ry** Allegorie *f*.
al·le·lu·ia [æli'lu:jə] Halleluja *n*.
al·ler·gic [ə'lə:dʒik] (*a. fig.*) □ allergisch (*to* gegen); **al·ler·gy** ⚕ ['ælədʒi] Allergie *f* (*Überempfindlichkeit*).
al·le·vi·ate [ə'li:vieit] erleichtern, lindern; **al·le·vi'a·tion** Erleichterung *f*, Linderung *f*.
al·ley ['æli] Allee *f*; Gäßchen *n*; *bsd. Am.* schmale Zufahrtstraße *f zwischen der Rückseite zweier Häuserreihen*; *s. back*~; Gang *m*; *s. blind* **1**, *skittle-*~; *that is right down his* ~ F das ist etwas für ihn; das ist sein Fall; '**al·ley·way** *Am.* Gasse *f*, schmale Straße *f*.
All Fools' Day ['ɔ:l'fu:lzdei] der 1. April.
al·li·ance [ə'laiəns] Bündnis *n*, Bund *m*; Verwandtschaft *f*; *form an* ~ ein Bündnis schließen.
al·li·ga·tor *zo.* ['æligeitə] Alligator *m*.
all-in ['ɔ:l'in] Gesamt..., alles inbegriffen.
al·lit·er·ate [ə'litəreit] alliterieren; **al·lit·er'a·tion** Alliteration *f*, Stabreim *m*; **al'lit·er·a·tive** [~rətiv] □ alliterierend.
all...: '~-'**mains** ⚡ Allstrom...; '~-'**met·al** Ganzmetall...
al·lo·cate ['æləukeit] zuteilen; anweisen; **al·lo'ca·tion** Zuteilung *f*; Zahlungsanweisung *f*.
al·lo·cu·tion [æləu'kju:ʃən] feierliche Ansprache *f*.
al·lop·a·thist ⚕ [ə'lɔpəθist] Allopath *m*; **al'lop·a·thy** ⚕ Allopathie *f*.
al·lot [ə'lɔt] an-, zuweisen, zuteilen; zugestehen; **al'lot·ment** Zu-, Verteilung *f*; Anteil *m*; Los *n im Leben*; Parzelle *f*; Schrebergarten *m*.
all-out ['ɔ:l'aut] umfassend, total, Groß...; ~ *effort* Anstrengung *f* aller Kräfte.
al·low [ə'lau] erlauben; bewilligen, gewähren; einräumen; ermöglichen; ab-, anrechnen; vergüten; *be* ~*ed to* dürfen, die Erlaubnis haben zu; ~ *for* berücksichtigen, bedenken; in Betracht ziehen; *it* ~*s of no excuse* es läßt sich nicht entschuldigen; **al'low·a·ble** □ erlaubt, zulässig; **al'low·ance 1.** Erlaubnis *f*; Bewilligung *f*; Kost-, Taschengeld *n*, Zuschuß *m*; Rente *f*; Ration *f*; Abzug *m*, Rabatt *m*, Vergütung *f*; Ermäßigung *f*; Nachsicht *f*; ⊕ Toleranz *f*; *make* ~ *for* Nachsicht üben mit *j-m*; *et.*

berücksichtigen; **2.** auf Rationen setzen; *Brot etc.* rationieren.

al·loy 1. ['ælɔi] Legierung *f*; [ə'lɔi] *fig.* Beimischung *f*; **2.** [~] legieren; *fig.* verunedeln; (ver)mischen.

all...: '~-'pur·pose Allzweck..., Universal...; **'~-'red** rein britisch; **'~-'round** allseitig; zu allem brauchbar; ✝ Pauschal...

All Saints' Day ['ɔ:l'seintsdei] Allerheiligen *n* (*1. November*).

All Souls' Day ['ɔ:l'səulzdei] Allerseelen *n* (*2. November*).

all...: '~-'star *Am. Sport u. thea.* aus den besten (Schau)Spielern bestehend; **'~-'time** unerreicht, beispiellos; ~ *high* Höchstleistung *f*, -stand *m*; ~ *low* Tiefststand *m*.

al·lude [ə'lu:d] anspielen (*to* auf *acc.*).

al·lure [ə'ljuə] (an-, ver)locken; **al'lure·ment** Verlockung *f*; Lockmittel *n*; Reiz *m*; **al'lur·ing** □ verlockend.

al·lu·sion [ə'lu:ʒən] Anspielung *f* (*to* auf *acc.*); **al'lu·sive** □ anspielend (*to* auf *acc.*); verblümt.

al·lu·vi·al □ [ə'lu:vjəl] alluvial, angeschwemmt; **al'lu·vi·on** [~vjən] Anschwemmung *f*; **al'lu·vi·um** [~vjəm] Schwemmland *n*, Alluvium *n*.

'all-'weath·er Allwetter...

al·ly 1. [ə'lai] (sich) vereinigen, -binden, -bünden (*to, with* mit); *allied to fig.* verwandt *od.* verbunden mit; **2.** ['ælai] Verbündete *m, f*, Bundesgenosse *m*; *the Allies pl.* die Alliierten *pl.*

al·ma·nac ['ɔ:lmənæk] Almanach *m*.

al·might·i·ness [ɔ:l'maitinis] Allmacht *f*; **al'might·y 1.** □ allmächtig; F mächtig; **2.** ♀ Allmächtige *m*.

al·mond ['ɑ:mənd] Mandel *f*.

al·mon·er ['ɑ:mənə] Krankenhausfürsorger(in); *hist.* Almosenpfleger *m*.

al·most ['ɔ:lməust] fast, beinahe.

alms [ɑ:mz] *sg. u. pl.* Almosen *n*; **'~-bag** Klingelbeutel *m*; **'~-house** Armenhaus *n*.

al·oe ⚘ *u. pharm.* ['æləu] Aloe *f*.

a·loft [ə'lɔft] (hoch) (dr)oben; (nach) oben (⚓ *in der od. die Takelung*).

a·lone [ə'ləun] allein; *let od. leave s.o.* ~ j. in Ruhe lassen; *let it* ~! laß das bleiben!; *let* ~ ... abgesehen von ...; geschweige denn ...

a·long [ə'lɔŋ] **1.** *adv.* weiter, vorwärts, her; mit, bei (sich); *all* ~ die ganze Zeit; ~ *with* zs. mit; *get* ~ *with* vorankommen mit, Fortschritte machen bei; auskommen mit; *get* ~ *with you!* F scher dich weg!; **2.** *prp.* entlang, längs; ~ *here* in dieser Richtung; **a'long·shore** längs der Küste; **a'long'side 1.** ⚓ *adv.* längsseits; Seite an Seite; **2.** *prp. fig.* neben.

a·loof [ə'lu:f] fern; weitab; *keep* ~ (*from*) sich fernhalten (von); *stand* ~ für sich bleiben; **a'loof·ness** Sichfernhalten *n*; Zurückhaltung *f*.

a·loud [ə'laud] laut; hörbar.

alp [ælp] Alp(e) *f*; ♀*s pl.* Alpen *pl.*

al·pac·a [æl'pækə] *zo.* Alpaka *n*; Alpakawolle *f*, -stoff *m*.

al·pen·stock ['ælpinstɔk] Bergstock *m*.

al·pha·bet ['ælfəbit] Alphabet *n*; **al·pha·bet·ic, al·pha·bet·i·cal** □ [~'betik(əl)] alphabetisch.

Al·pine ['ælpain] Alpen...; alpin; **al·pin·ist** ['~pinist] Alpinist(in).

al·read·y [ɔ:l'redi] bereits, schon.

Al·sa·tian [æl'seiʃjən] **1.** elsässisch; **2.** Elsässer(in); *a.* ~ *dog* deutscher Schäferhund *m*.

al·so ['ɔ:lsəu] auch; ferner, außerdem; ~ *ran Rennsport*: ferner liefen; **'al·so-ran** siegloses Pferd *n*; *fig.* Versager *m*, Niete *f*.

al·tar ['ɔ:ltə] Altar *m*; **'~-piece** Altar(blatt *n*, -gemälde *n*) *m*.

al·ter ['ɔ:ltə] (sich) (ver)ändern; ab-, umändern; *Am.* F *Tier* kastrieren; **'al·ter·a·ble** veränderlich; **al·ter'a·tion** Änderung *f* (*to* an *dat.*).

al·ter·cate ['ɔ:ltəkeit] zanken; **alter'ca·tion** Zank *m*, Streit *m*.

al·ter·nate 1. ['ɔ:ltəneit] abwechseln (lassen); *alternating current* ⚡ Wechselstrom *m*; **2.** □ [ɔ:l'tə:nit] abwechselnd; Wechsel...; *on* ~ *days* einen Tag um den andern; **3.** [ɔ:l'tə:nit] *Am.* Stellvertreter *m*; **al·terna·tion** [ɔ:ltə'neiʃən] Abwechslung *f*; Wechsel *m*; **al·ter·na·tive** [ɔ:l'tə:nətiv] **1.** □ einander ausschließend; nur eine Möglichkeit lassend; ⊕ Ausweich...; **2.** Alternative *f*; Wahl *f zwischen zwei Dingen*; Möglichkeit *f*; *I have no* ~ mir bleibt keine Wahl; **al·ter·na·tor** ⚡ ['ɔ:ltəneitə] Wechselstrommaschine *f*.

al·though [ɔːl'ðəu] obwohl, obgleich.
al·tim·e·ter ['æltimiːtə] Höhenmesser *m.*
al·ti·tude ['æltitjuːd] Höhe *f* (*bsd. bei Messungen*); ~ *flight* Höhenflug *m.*
al·to ♪ ['æltəu] Alt(stimme *f*) *m.*
al·to·geth·er [ɔːltə'geðə] **1.** im ganzen (genommen), alles in allem, insgesamt, gänzlich, ganz und gar; **2.** *in the* ~ F pudel-, splitternackt.
al·tru·ism ['æltruizəm] Altruismus *m*, Uneigennützigkeit *f*; '**al·tru·ist** Altruist(in); **al·tru'is·tic** (~*ally*) altruistisch.
al·um ⚗ ['æləm] Alaun *m*; **a·lu·mi·na** [ə'ljuːminə] Tonerde *f*; **al·u·min·i·um** [ælju'minjəm] Aluminium *n*; ~ *acetate* essigsaure Tonerde *f*; **a·lu·mi·nous** [ə'ljuːminəs] alaunartig, -haltig; **a·lu·mi·num** [ə'luːminəm] *Am.* für *aluminium.*
a·lum·na [ə'lʌmnə], *pl.* **a'lum·nae** [~niː] *Am.* ehemalige Schülerin *f od.* Studentin *f*; **a'lum·nus** [~nəs], *pl.* **a'lum·ni** [~nai] *Am.* ehemaliger Schüler *m od.* Student *m.*
al·ve·o·lar [æl'viələ] alveolar; *anat.* Zahn...; *gr.* am Zahndamm artikuliert.
al·ways ['ɔːlweiz] immer, stets.
am [æm; əm] (*irr. be*) bin.
a·mal·gam [ə'mælgəm] Amalgam *n*; **a'mal·gam·ate** [~meit] amalgamieren; (sich) verschmelzen; **a·mal·gam'a·tion** Amalgamierung *f*; Verschmelzung *f*; ✝ Fusion *f.*
a·man·u·en·sis [əmænju'ensis], *pl.* **a·man·u'en·ses** [~siːz] (Schreib-) Gehilfe *m*, Sekretär *m.*
am·a·ranth ⚘ ['æmərænθ] Fuchsschwanz *m.*
a·mass [ə'mæs] an-, aufhäufen.
am·a·teur ['æmətəː] Amateur *m*; Liebhaber *m*; Dilettant *m*; **am·a'teur·ish** dilettantisch.
am·a·tive ['æmətiv], **am·a·to·ry** ['~təri] verliebt; Liebes...; erotisch.
a·maze [ə'meiz] in Staunen setzen, überraschen, verblüffen; **a'mazed** ☐ höchst erstaunt (*at* über *acc.*); **a'maze·ment** Staunen *n*, Verwunderung *f*, Verblüffung *f*; **a'maz·ing** ☐ erstaunlich, verblüffend.
Am·a·zon ['æməzən] Amazone *f*; ♀ Mannweib *n*; **Am·a·zo·ni·an** [~'zəunjən] amazonenhaft.
am·bas·sa·dor [æm'bæsədə] Botschafter *m*, Gesandte *m*; **am·bas·sa·do·ri·al** [~'dɔːriəl] Botschafts..., Gesandtschafts...; **am'bas·sa·dress** [~dris] Botschafterin *f*; Frau *f* e-s Botschafters.
am·ber ['æmbə] **1.** Bernstein *m*; Gelb *n*, gelbes Licht *n* (*Verkehrsampel*); **2.** bernsteinfarben; Bernstein...; **am·ber·gris** ['~griːs] Ambra *f.*
am·bi·dex·trous ☐ ['æmbi'dekstrəs] beidhändig, mit beiden Händen gleich geschickt; *fig.* hinterhältig.
am·bi·ent ['æmbiənt] umgebend, Umgebungs...
am·bi·gu·i·ty [æmbi'gjuːiti] Zwei-, Vieldeutigkeit *f*, Doppelsinn *m*; **am'big·u·ous** [~gjuəs] ☐ zwei-, vieldeutig; doppelsinnig; zweifelhaft.
am·bit ['æmbit] Gebiet *n*, Bereich *m.*
am·bi·tion [æm'biʃən] Ehrgeiz *m*; Streben *n* (*of, for* nach); ~*s pl.* Bestrebungen *f/pl.*; **am'bi·tious** ☐ ehrgeizig; begierig (*of, for* nach).
am·bi·va·lent ['æmbi'veilənt] ambivalent, doppelwertig, zwiespältig.
am·ble ['æmbl] **1.** Paßgang *m*; **2.** im Paßgang gehen *od.* reiten; *fig.* (~ *up* daher)schlendern; '**am·bler** Paßgänger *m*, Zelter *m.*
am·bro·si·a [æm'brəuzjə] Ambrosia *f*, Götterspeise *f*; **am'bro·si·al** ☐ ambrosisch; *fig.* köstlich.
am·bu·lance ['æmbjuləns] Krankenwagen *m*; *attr.* Sanitäts...; ~ *box* Verbandskasten *m*; ~ *station* Sanitätswache *f*, Unfallstation *f*; '**am·bu·lant** ambulant.
am·bu·la·to·ry ['æmbjulətəri] **1.** umherziehend, Wander...; zum Gehen geeignet; beweglich; **2.** Wandelhalle *f*, -gang *m.*
am·bus·cade [æmbəs'keid], **am·bush** ['æmbuʃ] **1.** Hinterhalt *m*; *be od. lie in* ~ *for s.o.* j-m auflauern; **2.** *v/t.* auflauern (*dat.*); aus dem Hinterhalt überfallen; *v/i.* im Hinterhalt liegen.
a·meer [ə'miə] Emir *m.*
a·mel·io·rate [ə'miːljəreit] verbessern; besser werden; **a·mel·io'ra·tion** Verbesserung *f.*

a·men ['ɑ:'men] Amen *n.*
a·me·na·ble □ [ə'mi:nəbl] unterworfen; zugänglich; verantwortlich (*alle*: *to dat.*).
a·mend [ə'mend] *v/t.* verbessern; ⚖ berichtigen; *Gesetz* ergänzen, (ab)ändern; *v/i.* sich bessern; **a'mend·ment** Besserung *f*; ⚖ Berichtigung *f*; *parl.* Zusatz-, Änderungsantrag *m*; *Am.* Zusatzartikel *m* zur Verfassung der USA; **a'mends** *pl.* Ersatz *m*; *make* ~ *for et.* ersetzen, wiedergutmachen.
a·men·i·ty [ə'mi:niti] Annehmlichkeit *f*; Anmut *f*; *amenities pl.* Höflichkeiten *f/pl.*; natürliche Vorzüge *m/pl.*, Reize *m/pl.*
A·mer·i·can [ə'merikən] **1.** amerikanisch; ~ *cloth* Wachstuch *n*; ~ *Legion* Frontkämpferbund *m* der USA; ~ *plan Am. Hotelzimmervermietung mit voller Verpflegung*; **2.** Amerikaner(in); **A'mer·i·can·ism** Amerikanismus *m*; **A·mer·i·can·i'za·tion** Amerikanisierung *f*; **A'mer·i·can·ize** (sich) amerikanisieren.
am·e·thyst *min.* ['æmiθist] Amethyst *m.*
a·mi·a·bil·i·ty [eimjə'biliti] Liebenswürdigkeit *f*; **'a·mi·a·ble** □ liebenswürdig, freundlich.
am·i·ca·ble □ ['æmikəbl] freundschaftlich; gütlich.
a·mid(st) [ə'mid(st)] inmitten (*gen.*); (mitten) unter; mitten in (*dat.*).
a·mid·ships ⚓ [ə'midʃips] mittschiffs.
a·miss [ə'mis] verkehrt; übel; ungelegen; *take* ~ übelnehmen; *it would not be* ~ (*for him*) es würde (ihm) nicht schaden; *what is* ~ *with it?* was ist denn damit los?
am·i·ty ['æmiti] Freundschaft *f.*
am·me·ter ⚡ ['æmitə] Amperemeter *n.*
am·mo·ni·a [ə'məunjə] Ammoniak *n*; *liquid* ~ Salmiakgeist *m*; **am'mo·ni·ac** [~niæk], **am·mo·ni·a·cal** [æməu'naiəkəl] ammoniakalisch; *s. sal.*
am·mon·ite ['æmənait] Ammonshorn *n*, Ammonit *m.*
am·mu·ni·tion ⚔ [æmju'niʃən] Munition *f.*
am·ne·sia ⚕ [æm'ni:zjə] Gedächtnisverlust *m*, Amnesie *f.*
am·nes·ty ['æmnisti] **1.** Amnestie *f* (*Straferlaß*); **2.** begnadigen.
a·m(o)e·ba *zo.* [ə'mi:bə] Amöbe *f.*
a·mok [ə'mɔk] = *amuck.*
a·mong(st) [ə'mʌŋ(st)] (mitten) unter, zwischen; *from* ~ aus ... hervor; *be* ~ gehören zu; *they had two pounds* ~ *them* sie hatten zusammen ...
a·mor·al [ei'mɔrəl] amoralisch.
am·o·rous □ ['æmərəs] verliebt (*of in acc.*); Liebes...; **'am·o·rous·ness** Verliebtheit *f.*
a·mor·phous [ə'mɔ:fəs] *min.* amorph; *fig.* ungestalt; formlos.
am·or·ti·za·tion [əmɔ:ti'zeiʃən] Tilgung *f*, Amortisation *f*; **am'or·tize** [~taiz] amortisieren, tilgen.
a·mount [ə'maunt] **1.** ~ *to* sich belaufen auf (*acc.*), betragen; hinauslaufen auf (*acc.*); **2.** Betrag *m*, (Gesamt)Summe *f*, Höhe *f* (*e-r Summe*); Menge *f*; Bedeutung *f*, Wert *m*; *to the* ~ *of* bis zur *od.* in Höhe von, im Betrage von.
a·mour [ə'muə] Liebschaft *f*; **~-pro·pre** ['æmuə'prɔpr] Selbstachtung *f*; Eitelkeit *f.*
amp ⚡, F [æmp] = *ampere.*
am·pere ⚡ ['æmpɛə] Ampere *n.*
am·phet·a·mine ⚗ [æm'fetəmi:n] Benzedrin *n.*
am·phib·i·an *zo.* [æm'fibiən] **1.** Amphibie *f*; **2.** = **am'phib·i·ous** □ Amphibien...; amphibisch.
am·phi·the·a·tre, *Am.* **am·phi·the·a·ter** ['æmfiθiətə] Amphitheater *n.*
am·ple □ ['æmpl] weit, groß; geräumig; reichlich, mehr als genug; genügend; ausführlich.
am·pli·fi·ca·tion [æmplifi'keiʃən] Erweiterung *f*; *rhet.* weitere Ausführung *f*; *phys.* Verstärkung *f*; **am·pli·fi·er** ['~faiə] *Radio*: Verstärker *m*; **'am·pli·fy** erweitern, ausdehnen; verstärken; weiter ausführen; ausführlich sprechen; *~ing valve* Verstärkerröhre *f*; **am·pli·tude** ['~tju:d] Umfang *m*, Weite *f*, Fülle *f*; *phys.* Amplitude *f* (*Schwingungsweite*).
am·poule ['æmpu:l] Ampulle *f.*
am·pu·tate ⚕ ['æmpjuteit] amputieren, abnehmen; **am·pu'ta·tion** Amputation *f.*
a·muck [ə'mʌk]: *run* ~ Amok laufen; *run* ~ *at od. on od. against*

fig. herfallen über (*acc.*).
am·u·let ['æmjulit] Amulett *n.*
a·muse [ə'mju:z] amüsieren; unterhalten; belustigen, Spaß machen (*dat.*); **a'muse·ment** Unterhaltung *f*; Zeitvertreib *m*; Belustigung *f*; ~ *arcade* Spielhalle *f*; *for* ~ zum Vergnügen; **a'mus·ing** □ amüsant; unterhaltsam.
an [æn, ən] *Artikel*: *s. a.*
an·a·bap·tist [ænə'bæptist] Wiedertäufer *m.*
a·nach·ro·nism [ə'nækrənizəm] Anachronismus *m.*
an·a·con·da *zo.* [ænə'kɔndə] Anakonda *f*; Riesenschlange *f.*
a·n(a)e·mi·a [ə'ni:mjə] Anämie *f*, Blutarmut *f*; **a'n(a)e·mic** blutarm.
an·(a)es·the·si·a [ænis'θi:zjə] Anästhesie *f*, Narkose *f*; **an·(a)es·thet·ic** [~'θetik] **1.** (*~ally*) betäubend, Narkose...; **2.** Betäubungsmittel *n*; **a'n(a)es·the·tist** Anästhesist *m*, Narkosearzt *m*; **a'n(a)es·the·tize** betäuben.
an·a·log·ic, an·a·log·i·cal □ [ænə'lɔdʒik(əl)], **a·nal·o·gous** □ [ə'næləgəs] analog, ähnlich; **a'nal·o·gy** [~dʒi] Ähnlichkeit *f*, Analogie *f.*
an·a·lyse ['ænəlaiz] analysieren; zerlegen; *gr.* zergliedern; untersuchen; **a·nal·y·sis** [ə'næləsis], *pl.* **a'nal·y·ses** [~si:z] Analyse *f*, Zerlegung *f*, Zergliederung *f*; **an·a·lyst** ['ænəlist] Analytiker *m*; *public* ~ Gerichtschemiker *m.*
an·a·lyt·ic, an·a·lyt·i·cal □ [ænə'litik(əl)] analytisch.
an·ar·chic, an·ar·chi·cal □ [æ'nɑ:kik(əl)] gesetzlos; zügellos; **an·ar·chism** ['ænəkizəm] Anarchismus *m*; **'an·arch·ist** Anarchist(in); **'an·arch·y** Anarchie *f*, Gesetzlosigkeit *f*; Zügellosigkeit *f.*
a·nath·e·ma [ə'næθimə] Kirchenbann *m*; **a'nath·e·ma·tize** in den Bann tun; (ver)fluchen.
an·a·tom·i·cal □ [ænə'tɔmikəl] anatomisch; **a·nat·o·mist** [ə'nætəmist] Anatom *m*; **a'nat·o·mize** zergliedern; **a'nat·o·my** Anatomie *f*; Zergliederung *f*, Analyse *f*; F Gerippe *n.*
an·ces·tor ['ænsistə] Stammvater *m*, Vorfahr *m*, Ahn *m*; **an·ces·tral** [~'sestrəl] angestammt; Stamm...; Ahnen...; **an·ces·tress** ['ænsistris] Stammutter *f*, Ahne *f*; **'an·ces·try** Abstammung *f*; Ahnen *m/pl.*
an·chor ⚓ *u. fig.* ['æŋkə] **1.** Anker *m*; *at* ~ vor Anker; **2.** *v/t.* verankern; *v/i.* ankern; vor Anker gehen; **'an·chor·age** Ankerplatz *m.*
an·cho·ret, an·cho·rite ['æŋkəret; '~rait] Einsiedler *m.*
an·chor·man ['æŋkəmən] *Am.* Moderator *m* e-r Nachrichtensendung.
an·cho·vy ['æntʃəvi] An(s)chovis *f*, Sardelle *f.*
an·cient ['einʃənt] **1.** alt, antik; uralt; **2.** *the ~s pl.* die Alten *pl.* (*Griechen und Römer*), die antiken Klassiker *pl.*; **'an·cient·ly** vorzeiten.
an·cil·lar·y [æn'siləri] untergeordnet (*to dat.*), Hilfs..., Neben...; ~ *road* Nebenstraße *f.*
and [ænd, ənd, F ən] und; *thousands ~ thousands* Tausende und aber Tausende; *there are flowers ~ flowers* es gibt mancherlei Blumen; *try ~ take it* versuche es zu nehmen.
and·i·ron ['ændaiən] Feuerbock *m.*
an·ec·do·tal [ænek'dəutl], **an·ec·dot·i·cal** [~'dɔtikəl] anekdotisch; **an·ec·dote** ['ænikdəut] Anekdote *f.*
an·e·mom·e·ter [æni'mɔmitə] Windmesser *m.*
a·nem·o·ne [ə'neməni] Anemone *f.*
an·er·oid ['ænərɔid] *a.* ~ *barometer* Aneroidbarometer *n.*
a·new [ə'nju:] von neuem.
an·gel ['eindʒəl] (*a. fig.*) Engel *m*; finanzkräftiger Hintermann *m*; **an·gel·ic, an·gel·i·cal** □ [æn'dʒelik(əl)] engelgleich, -haft.
an·ge·lus ['ændʒiləs] Angelus(gebet *n*, -läuten *n*) *m.*
an·ger ['æŋgə] **1.** Zorn *m*, Ärger *m* (*at* über *acc.*); **2.** erzürnen, ärgern.
an·gi·na ⚕ [æn'dʒainə] Angina *f*, Halsentzündung *f*; ~ *pectoris* Angina *f* pectoris.
an·gle ['æŋgl] **1.** Winkel *m*, Ecke *f*; *fig.* Gesichtswinkel *m*, Standpunkt *m*; *~-dozer* Planierraupe *f*; *~-iron* Winkeleisen *n*; *~-parking mot.* Parken *n* quer zum Gehweg; *at right ~s* im rechten Winkel; **2.** angeln (*for* nach); **'an·gler** Angler(in).
An·gles ['æŋglz] *pl.* Angeln *pl.*
An·gli·can ['æŋglikən] **1.** anglikanisch, hochkirchlich; *Am. a.* englisch; **2.** Anglikaner(in).

An·gli·cism ['æŋglisizəm] englische Spracheigenheit *f*, Anglizismus *m*.
an·gling ['æŋgliŋ] Angeln *n*.
An·glo-Sax·on ['æŋgləu'sæksən] **1.** Angelsachse *m*; **2.** angelsächsisch.
an·go·ra [æŋ'gɔ:rə] Angorawolle *f*; ~ (*cat*) Angorakatze *f*.
an·gry ['æŋgri] zornig, böse (*with s.o., at s.th.* über, auf *acc.*); ärgerlich; ⚕ böse, schlimm.
an·guish ['æŋgwiʃ] Pein *f*, (Seelen-)Qual *f*, Schmerz *m*.
an·gu·lar □ ['æŋgjulə] wink(e)lig; Winkel...; *fig.* eckig; ~ *point* ⅍ Scheitelpunkt *m*; **an·gu·lar·i·ty** [~'læriti] Winkligkeit *f*; *fig.* Eckigkeit *f*.
an·i·line ⚗ ['ænili:n] Anilin *n*.
an·i·mad·ver·sion [ænimæd'və:ʃən] Verweis *m*, Tadel *m*; **an·i·mad·vert** [~'və:t] tadeln, kritisieren, bekritteln (*on, upon acc.*).
an·i·mal ['æniməl] **1.** Tier *n*; **2.** animalisch; tierisch; Tier...; ~ *home* Tierheim *n*; ~ *kingdom zo.* Tierreich *n*; ~ *lover* Tierfreund *m*; ~ *shelter Am.* Tierheim *n*; ~ *spirits pl.* Lebensgeister *m/pl.*; **an·i·mal·cule** [~'mælkju:l] Tierchen *n*; **an·i·mal·ism** ['~məlizəm] Vertiertheit *f*, Sinnlichkeit *f*.
an·i·mate 1. ['ænimeit] beleben; beseelen; aufmuntern; **2.** ['~mit], *mst* **an·i·mat·ed** ['~meitid] belebt, lebend(ig); *fig.* lebhaft, munter.
an·i·ma·tion [æni'meiʃən] Leben *n* (und Treiben *n*), Lebhaftigkeit *f*, Munterkeit *f*.
an·i·mos·i·ty [æni'mɔsiti], *a.* **an·i·mus** ['æniməs] Feindseligkeit *f*.
an·ise ⚘ ['ænis] Anis *m*; **an·i·seed** ['~si:d] **1.** Anissamen *m*; **2.** Anis...
an·kle ['æŋkl] Fußknöchel *m*.
an·klet ['æŋklit] Fußkettchen *n*; Söckchen *n*.
an·nals ['ænlz] *pl.* Jahrbücher *n/pl.*; historischer Bericht *m*.
an·neal ⊕ [ə'ni:l] *Metall* (aus-)glühen; härten (*a. fig.*).
an·nex 1. [ə'neks] anhängen, beifügen (*to dat.*); annektieren, sich aneignen; (sich) einverleiben; ~ *to Bedingung etc.* knüpfen an (*acc.*); **2.** ['æneks] Anhang *m*, Nachtrag *m*; Nebengebäude *n*; **an·nex'a·tion** Annexion *f*, Aneignung *f*; Einverleibung *f*.
an·ni·hi·late [ə'naiəleit] vernichten; = *annul*; **an·ni·hi'la·tion** Vernichtung *f*; = *annulment*.
an·ni·ver·sa·ry [æni'və:səri] Jahrestag *m*; Jahresfeier *f*.
an·no·tate ['ænəuteit] mit Anmerkungen versehen; kommentieren (*a. on acc.*); **an·no'ta·tion** Kommentieren *n*; Anmerkung *f*.
an·nounce [ə'nauns] ankündigen, bekanntgeben, anzeigen; ansagen; (an)melden; **an'nounce·ment** Ankündigung *f*; Ansage *f*; *Radio*: Durchsage *f*; (An)Meldung *f*; Anzeige *f*; **an'nounc·er** *Radio*: Ansager *m*.
an·noy [ə'nɔi] ärgern; belästigen, stören; schikanieren; **an'noy·ance** Störung *f*; Plage *f*; Ärgernis *n*; **an'noyed** verdrießlich, ärgerlich (*Person*); **an'noy·ing** □ ärgerlich (*Sache*); lästig, störend.
an·nu·al ['ænjuəl] **1.** □ jährlich; Jahres...; *bsd.* ⚘ einjährig; ~ *ring* ⚘ Jahresring *m*; **2.** einjährige Pflanze *f*; Jahrbuch *n*.
an·nu·i·tant [ə'nju:itənt] Leibrentner *m*.
an·nu·i·ty [ə'nju:iti] (Jahres)Rente *f*, Jahreszahlung *f*; *a.* ~ *bond* ⚚ Rentenbrief *m*; *s. life*.
an·nul [ə'nʌl] für ungültig erklären, aufheben, annullieren.
an·nu·lar □ ['ænjulə] ringförmig.
an·nul·ment [ə'nʌlmənt] Aufhebung *f*, Nichtigkeitserklärung *f*.
an·nun·ci·a·tion [ənʌnsi'eiʃən] Verkündigung *f*; **an'nun·ci·a·tor** Klappenkasten *m e-r Klingelanlage etc.*
an·ode ⚡ ['ænəud] Anode *f*, positiver Pol *m*.
an·o·dyne ['ænəudain] schmerzstillend(es Mittel *n*).
a·noint [ə'nɔint] *bsd. eccl.* salben (*a. fig.*); einschmieren.
a·nom·a·lous □ [ə'nɔmələs] anomal, unregelmäßig, regelwidrig; **a'nom·a·ly** Anomalie *f*.
a·non [ə'nɔn] sogleich, sofort; bald; *ever and* ~ immer wieder.
an·o·nym·i·ty [ænə'nimiti] Anonymität *f*; **a·non·y·mous** □ [ə'nɔniməs] anonym, ungenannt.
a·noph·e·les *zo.* [ə'nɔfili:z] Fiebermücke *f*.
an·oth·er [ə'nʌðə] ein anderer; ein zweiter; noch ein; ~ *ten years* weitere zehn Jahre; *tell us* ~! F das glaubst du doch selbst nicht!

an·swer ['ɑːnsə] **1.** *v/t. et.* beantworten, *j-m* antworten; entsprechen (*dat.*); *Zweck* erfüllen; *dem Steuer* gehorchen; *e-r Vorladung* Folge leisten; ~ *the bell od. door* (die Haustür) aufmachen; *v/i.* antworten (*to s.o.* j-m; *to a question* auf e-e Frage); entsprechen (*to dat.*); Erfolg haben, anschlagen; sich lohnen; ~ *back* frech antworten *od.* widersprechen (*bsd. Kinder gegenüber Erwachsenen*); ~ *for* einstehen für, die Folgen tragen von; bürgen für; ~ *to the name of* ... auf den Namen ... hören; **2.** Antwort *f* (*to* auf *acc.*); ♘ Lösung *f*; ⚖ Replik *f*; '**an·swer·a·ble** □ verantwortlich.
ant [ænt] Ameise *f*.
an't [ɑːnt] F = *are not, am not*; *sl. od. prov.* = *is not.*
an·tag·o·nism [æn'tægənizəm] Widerstreit *m* (*between* zwischen *dat.*); Widerstand *m*; Feindschaft *f* (*to* gegen); **an'tag·o·nist** Gegner(in); **an·tag·o'nis·tic** (~*ally*) widerstreitend (*to dat.*); gegnerisch, feindlich (*to* gegen); **an'tag·o·nize** ankämpfen gegen; sich *j-n* zum Feind machen.
ant·arc·tic [ænt'ɑːktik] antarktisch; Südpol...; *the* ♀ die Antarktis; ♀ *Circle* südlicher Polarkreis *m*.
an·te *Am.* ['ænti] *Pokerspiel*: **1.** Einsatz *m*; **2.** *mst* ~ *up v/t. u. v/i.* (ein)setzen; *v/i. fig.* sein Scherflein beitragen.
an·te·ced·ence [ænti'siːdəns] Vortritt *m*, -rang *m*; *ast.* Rückläufigkeit *f*; **an·te'ced·ent 1.** □ vorhergehend; früher (*to* als); **2.** Vorhergehende *n*; *gr.* Beziehungswort *n*; *his* ~*s pl.* sein Vorleben *n*.
an·te·cham·ber ['æntitʃeimbə] Vorzimmer *n*.
an·te·date ['ænti'deit] zurückdatieren; (*zeitlich*) vorangehen (*dat.*).
an·te·di·lu·vi·an ['æntidi'luːvjən] vorsintflutlich(er Mensch *m*).
an·te·lope *zo.* ['æntiləup] Antilope *f*.
an·te me·rid·i·em ['ænti mə'ridiəm] vormittags.
an·te·na·tal [ænti'neitl] *bsd. Br.* **1.** vor der Geburt, pränatal; **2.** Mutterschaftsvorsorgeuntersuchung *f*.
an·ten·na [æn'tenə], *pl.* **an'ten·nae** [~niː] *zo.* Fühler *m*; *Radio, Fernsehen*: Antenne *f*.
an·te·ri·or [æn'tiəriə] vorhergehend; früher (*to* als); vorder.
an·te-room ['æntirum] Vorzimmer *n*.
an·them ['ænθəm] Hymne *f*.
an·ther ⚘ ['ænθə] Staubbeutel *m*.
ant-hill ['ænthil] Ameisenhaufen *m*.
an·thol·o·gy [æn'θɔlədʒi] Anthologie *f*, Gedichtsammlung *f*.
an·thra·cite *min.* ['ænθrəsait] Anthrazit *m*, Glanzkohle *f*; **an·thrax** *vet.* ['ænθræks] Milzbrand *m*.
an·thro·poid ['ænθrəupɔid] **1.** menschenähnlich; **2.** Menschenaffe *m*; **an·thro·po·log·i·cal** [ænθrəpə'lɔdʒikəl] anthropologisch; **an·thro·pol·o·gist** [ænθrə'pɔlədʒist] Anthropologe *m*; **an·thro'pol·o·gy** [~dʒi] Anthropologie *f*, Menschenkunde *f*.
an·ti... ['ænti] *in Zssgn* Gegen...; gegen ... eingestellt; anti..., Anti...
an·ti-air·craft ['ænti'εəkrɑːft] Fliegerabwehr...; ~ *gun* Fliegerabwehrgeschütz *n*.
an·ti·bi·ot·ic ⚕ ['æntibai'ɔtik] Antibiotikum *n*.
an·ti·bod·y ⚕ ['æntibɔdi] Antikörper *m*, Abwehrstoff *m*.
an·tic ['æntik] Posse *f*; ~*s pl.* Mätzchen *n/pl.*; (tolle) Sprünge *m/pl.*
An·ti·christ ['æntikraist] Antichrist *m*.
an·tic·i·pate [æn'tisipeit] vorwegnehmen; zuvorkommen (*dat.*); voraussehen, ahnen; erwarten; im voraus verbrauchen; **an·tic·i'pa·tion** Vorwegnahme *f*; Zuvorkommen *n*; Voraussicht *f*; Erwartung *f*; Vorgefühl *n*; Vorfreude *f*; *payment by* ~ Vorauszahlung *f*; *in* ~ im voraus; **an'tic·i·pa·to·ry** [~peitəri] vorwegnehmend.
an·ti·cler·i·cal ['ænti'klerikəl] □ antiklerikal, kirchenfeindlich.
an·ti·cli·max *rhet. u. fig.* ['ænti'klaimæks] (Ab)Fallen *n*, Abstieg *m*.
an·ti·clock·wise ['ænti'klɔkwaiz] entgegen dem *od.* gegen den Uhrzeigersinn.
an·ti-cor·ro·sive a·gent ['æntikə'rəusiv'eidʒənt] Rostschutzmittel *n*.
an·ti·cy·clone *meteor.* ['ænti'saikləun] Antizyklone *f*, Hoch(druckgebiet) *n*.
an·ti·daz·zle *mot.* ['ænti'dæzl] Blendschutz...; ~ *switch* Abblendumschalter *m*.
an·ti·dote ['æntidəut] Gegengift *n*, -mittel *n* (*against, for, to* gegen).

an·ti-fas·cist ['ænti'fæʃist] **1.** Antifaschist(in); **2.** antifaschistisch.
an·ti-freeze *mot.* ['æntifri:z] Gefrierschutzmittel *n.*
an·ti-fric·tion ['ænti'frikʃən] Reibungsschutz *m*; *attr.* ⊕ Gleit...
an·ti·ha·lo *phot.* ['ænti'heiləu] lichthoffrei.
an·ti-knock *mot.* ['ænti'nɔk] **1.** klopffest; **2.** Antiklopfmittel *n.*
an·ti·mo·ny *min.* ['æntiməni] Antimon *n.*
an·tip·a·thy [æn'tipəθi] Antipathie *f*, Abneigung *f* (*against*, *to* gegen).
an·tip·o·dal □ [æn'tipədl] antipodisch, genau entgegengesetzt; **an·ti·pode** *fig.* ['~pəud] genaues Gegenteil *n*; **an'tip·o·des** [~pədi:z] *pl.* einander gegenüberliegende Seiten *f/pl.* der Erde.
an·ti-pol·lu·tion de·vice ['æntipɔ-'lu:ʃəndi'vais] Abgasentgiftungsanlage *f.*
an·ti·quar·i·an [ænti'kwɛəriən] **1.** □ Altertums...; **2.** Altertumsforscher *m*; **an·ti·quar·y** ['~kwəri] Altertumsforscher *m*; Antiquitätensammler *m*, -händler *m*; **an·ti·quat·ed** ['~kweitid] veraltet, überlebt, altmodisch, antiquiert.
an·tique [æn'ti:k] **1.** □ antik, alt; altmodisch; **2.** Antike *f*; alter Kunstgegenstand *m*; **an·tiq·ui·ty** [~'tikwiti] Altertum *n*; *die* Antike; Vorzeit *f*; *antiquities pl.* Altertümer *n/pl.*; Antiquitäten *f/pl.*
an·ti-rust ['ænti'rʌst] Rostschutz *m.*
an·ti-Sem·ite ['ænti'si:mait] Antisemit(in); **an·ti-Se·mit·ic** ['~si'mitik] antisemitisch; **an·ti-Sem·i·tism** ['~'semitizəm] Antisemitismus *m.*
an·ti·sep·tic [ænti'septik] antiseptisch(es Mittel *n*).
an·ti-skid ['ænti'skid] *mot.* Gleitschutz...; rutschfest.
an·ti·so·cial [ænti'səuʃəl] gesellschaftsfeindlich.
an·ti·tank ⚔ [ænti'tæŋk] Panzerabwehr...
an·tith·e·sis [æn'tiθisis], *pl.* **an'tith·e·ses** [~θisi:z] Gegensatz *m*; **an·ti·thet·ic, an·ti·thet·i·cal** □ [~'θetik(əl)] gegensätzlich.
ant·ler ['æntlə] Sprosse *f am Geweih*; *~s pl.* Geweih *n.*
an·to·nym ['æntəunim] Wort *n* entgegengesetzter Bedeutung.
A num·ber 1 ['ei nʌmbə 'wʌn] *Am.* F *s.* *A 1.*
a·nus ['einəs] After *m.*
an·vil ['ænvil] Amboß *m* (*a. fig.*).
anx·i·e·ty [æŋ'zaiəti] Angst *f*, Besorgnis *f*; *fig.* Sorge *f* (*for* um; *to inf.* zu *inf.*); ⚕ Beklemmung *f*; *~ dream* Angsttraum *m.*
anx·ious □ ['æŋkʃəs] ängstlich, besorgt (*about* um, wegen); bang; begierig, gespannt (*for* auf *acc.*; *to inf.* zu *inf.*); bemüht, bestrebt (*for* um; *to inf.* zu *inf.*); *I am ~ to see him* mir liegt daran, ihn zu sehen.
an·y ['eni] **1.** *pron.* (irgend)einer; einige *pl.*; (irgend)welcher; (irgend) etwas; jeder (beliebige); alle möglichen *pl.*; *not ~* kein; **2.** *adv.* irgend (-wie); **'~·bod·y, '~·one** (irgend) jemand, irgendeiner; jeder; *not ~* niemand; **'~·how** irgendwie; jedenfalls; **'~·thing** (irgend) etwas, alles; *~ but* alles andere als; **'~·way** = *anyhow*; ohnehin; **'~·where** irgendwo(hin); überall.
a·or·ta ⚕ [ei'ɔ:tə] Hauptschlagader *f.*
a·pace [ə'peis] schnell; rasch.
ap·a·nage ['æpənidʒ] *fig.* Attribut *n*, notwendige Begleiterscheinung *f*; Anhang *m*; Erbteil *m.*
a·part [ə'pɑ:t] einzeln; getrennt; für sich; beiseite; *~ from* abgesehen von; *joking ~* Spaß beiseite; *set ~ for* beiseite legen *od.* erübrigen für; bestimmen für.
a·part·heid *pol.* [ə'pɑ:theit] Apartheid *f*, Rassentrennung(spolitik) *f.*
a·part·ment [ə'pɑ:tmənt] Zimmer *n*; *Am.* Mietwohnung *f*; *~s pl.* Wohnung *f*; *~ hotel Am.* Wohnhotel *n mit od. ohne Bedienung*; *~ house Am.* Wohn-, Mietshaus *n.*
ap·a·thet·ic [æpə'θetik] (*~ally*) apathisch; **'ap·a·thy** Apathie *f*; Gleichgültigkeit *f* (*to* gegen).
ape [eip] **1.** Affe *m*; *go ~ Am. sl.* durchdrehen, überschnappen; **2.** nachäffen.
a·peak ⚓ [ə'pi:k] senkrecht.
a·pe·ri·ent [ə'piəriənt] **1.** Abführmittel *n*; **2.** abführend.
ap·er·ture ['æpətjuə] Öffnung *f.*
a·pex ['eipeks], *pl. oft* **ap·i·ces** ['eipisi:z] Spitze *f*; *mst fig.* Gipfel *m.*
aph·o·rism ['æfərizəm] Aphorismus *m*, Maxime *f*; **aph·o'ris·tic** (*~ally*) aphoristisch.
a·pi·ar·y ['eipjəri] Bienenhaus *n*; **a·pi·cul·ture** ['eipikʌltʃə] Bienen-

zucht *f*.
a·piece [ə'pi:s] (für) das Stück; je.
ap·ish □ ['eipiʃ] affig; äffisch.
a·plomb [ə'plɔm] selbstsicheres Auftreten *n*.
a·poc·a·lypse [ə'pɔkəlips] Offenbarung *f*.
A·poc·ry·pha [ə'pɔkrifə] *pl. Bibel*: Apokryphen *n/pl.*; **a'poc·ry·phal** apokryphisch; unecht; zweifelhaft.
ap·o·gee *ast.* ['æpəudʒi:] Erdferne *f*, Apogäum *n*; *fig.* Höhepunkt *m*.
a·pol·o·get·ic [əpɔlə'dʒetik] (*~ally*) verteidigend; rechtfertigend; entschuldigend; *~ letter* Entschuldigungsbrief *m*; **a'pol·o·gist** Verteidiger(in); **a'pol·o·gize** sich entschuldigen (*for* wegen; *to* bei); **a'pol·o·gy** Entschuldigung *f*; Rechtfertigung *f*; Verteidigungsrede *f*; F Notbehelf *m*; *an ~ for a dinner* F ein armseliges Essen; *make an ~* e-e Entschuldigung vorbringen.
ap·o·plec·tic, ap·o·plec·ti·cal □ [æpəu'plektik(əl)] apoplektisch, Schlag(fluß)...; **ap·o·plex·y** ['~pleksi] Schlag(fluß *m*, -anfall) *m*.
a·pos·ta·sy [ə'pɔstəsi] Abtrünnigkeit *f*; **a'pos·tate** [~stit] Apostat *m*, Abtrünnige *m*; **a'pos·ta·tize** [~stətaiz] abfallen (*from* von); abtrünnig werden (*from dat.*).
a·pos·tle [ə'pɔsl] Apostel *m*; **ap·os·tol·ic, ap·os·tol·i·cal** □ [æpəs'tɔlik(əl)] apostolisch.
a·pos·tro·phe [ə'pɔstrəfi] Anrede *f*; Apostroph *m*; **a'pos·tro·phize** anreden, sich wenden an (*acc.*).
a·poth·e·car·y † [ə'pɔθikəri] Apotheker *m*.
a·poth·e·o·sis [əpɔθi'əusis] Vergötterung *f*; Verherrlichung *f*.
ap·pal [ə'pɔ:l] erschrecken; **ap'pall·ing** □ erschreckend, entsetzlich.
ap·pa·ra·tus [æpə'reitəs] Apparat(e *pl.*) *m*, Vorrichtung *f*, Gerät *n*, Anlage *f*; *~ work* Geräteturnen *n*.
ap·par·el [ə'pærəl] **1.** Kleidung *f*; Gewand *n*; **2.** (be)kleiden.
ap·par·ent □ [ə'pærənt] augenscheinlich, offenbar; anscheinend; scheinbar; *s. heir*; **ap·pa·ri·tion** [æpə'riʃən] Erscheinung *f*; Gespenst *n*.
ap·peal [ə'pi:l] **1.** ⚖ appellieren (*to* an *acc.*); sich berufen (*to* auf *e-n Zeugen*); dringend bitten (*to s.o. for s.th.* j. um et.); *~ to* sich wenden an (*acc.*); ansprechen (*acc.*); wirken auf (*acc.*); Anklang finden bei, gefallen, zusagen (*dat.*); *s. country*; **2.** Appellation *f*, Berufung(sklage) *f*; *fig.* Appell *m*, dringende Bitte *f*, Aufruf *m* (*to* an *acc.*); Anrufung *f* (*to gen.*); Wirkung *f*, Anziehungskraft *f*, Reiz *m*; *court of ~* Berufungsinstanz *f*; *lodge od. file an ~* Berufung einlegen (*with* bei); *right of ~* Einspruchsrecht *n*; *~ for mercy* Gnadengesuch *n*; **ap'peal·er** Appellant(in); **ap'peal·ing** □ flehend; ansprechend.
ap·pear [ə'piə] erscheinen (*auch von Büchern u. vor Gericht*); sich zeigen; scheinen, den Anschein haben; *öffentlich* auftreten; **ap'pear·ance** Erscheinen *n*, Auftreten *n*; Äußere *n*, Erscheinung *f*; Anschein *m*; *~s pl.* äußerer Schein *m*; *keep up od. save ~s* den Schein wahren; *make one's ~* in Erscheinung treten, auftreten; *put in an ~* (persönlich) erscheinen; *to od. by all ~s* allem Anschein nach.
ap·pease [ə'pi:z] beruhigen, beschwichtigen, *Hunger etc.* stillen, *Leiden* mildern, *Streit* beilegen; **ap'pease·ment** Beruhigung *f*; Beschwichtigung(spolitik) *f*; *~ policy* Beschwichtigungspolitik *f*.
ap·pel·lant [ə'pelənt] **1.** appellierend; **2.** Appellant(in), Berufungskläger(in); Beschwerdeführer(in); **ap'pel·late** [~lit] Berufungs...; **ap·pel·la·tion** [æpə'leiʃən] Benennung *f*; Name *m*; **ap·pel·la·tive** *gr.* [ə'pelətiv] *a. ~ name* Appellativum *n*, Gattungsname *m*.
ap·pel·lee [æpe'li:] Berufungsbeklagte *m*, *f*.
ap·pend [ə'pend] anhängen; hinzu-, beifügen; **ap'pend·age** Anhang *m*; Anhängsel *n*; Zubehör *n*, *m*; **ap·pen·dec·to·my** [~'dektəmi] Blinddarmoperation *f*; **ap·pen·di·ci·tis** [~di'saitis] Blinddarmentzündung *f*; **ap'pen·dix** [~diks], *pl. a.* **ap'pen·di·ces** [~disi:z] Anhang *m*; *a. vermiform ~ anat.* Wurmfortsatz *m*.
ap·per·tain [æpə'tein] (*to*) (zu)gehören (*dat.*); *fig.* gehören (zu); *j-m* zustehen.
ap·pe·tence, ap·pe·ten·cy ['æpitəns(i)] (*for, after, of*) Verlangen *n* (nach); Instinkt *m* (für).

ap·pe·tite ['æpitait] (*for*) Appetit *m* (auf *acc.*); *fig.* Verlangen *n*, Gelüst *n* (nach); Neigung *f*, Trieb *m* (zu); ~ **sup·pres·sant** [sə'presənt] Appetitzügler *m*.

ap·pe·tiz·er ['æpitaizə] appetitanregendes Mittel *n*; **'ap·pe·tiz·ing** appetitanregend.

ap·plaud [ə'plɔ:d] applaudieren, Beifall spenden (*dat.*); loben.

ap·plause [ə'plɔ:z] Applaus *m*, Beifall *m*.

ap·ple ['æpl] Apfel *m*; *the* ~ *of s.o.'s eye fig.* j-s Augapfel *od.* Liebling; **'~-cart** Apfelkarren *m*; *upset s.o.'s* ~ F j-s Pläne über den Haufen werfen; **'~·jack** *Am.* Apfelschnaps *m*; **'~-'pie** gedeckter Apfelkuchen *m*; *in* ~ *order* F in schönster Ordnung; **'~-pol·ish** *sl.* sich lieb Kind machen bei (*j-m*); **'~'sauce** Apfelmus *n*; *Am. sl.* Schmus *m*; Quatsch *m*.

ap·pli·ance [ə'plaiəns] Vorrichtung *f*; Gerät *n*; Mittel *n*.

ap·pli·ca·bil·i·ty [æplikə'biliti] Anwendbarkeit *f*; **'ap·pli·ca·ble** anwendbar, zutreffend (*to* auf *acc.*); **'ap·pli·cant** Bittsteller(in); Bewerber(in) (*for* um); **ap·pli'ca·tion** (*to*) Auflegung *f*, Anlegen *n e-s Verbandes etc.* (auf *acc.*); Anwendung *f* (auf *acc.*), Verwendung *f* (für); Gebrauch *m* (für); Bedeutung *f* (für); Bitte *f*, Gesuch *n* (*for* um), Antrag *m* (auf *acc.*); Bewerbung *f* (um); Fleiß *m*; (*letter of*) ~ Bewerbungsschreiben *n*; *make an* ~ e-n Antrag stellen.

ap·ply [ə'plai] *v/t.* (*to*) an-, auflegen; anwenden (auf *acc.*); verwenden (für); gebrauchen (zu); *Gedanken etc.* richten (auf *acc.*); ~ *o.s. to* sich verlegen auf (*acc.*); *v/i.* (*to*) passen, sich anwenden lassen, Anwendung finden (auf *acc.*); gelten, zutreffen (für); sich wenden (an *acc.*); sich befleißigen (*gen.*); ~ *for* sich bewerben um; nachsuchen um; *et.* beantragen; *applied sciences pl.* angewandte Naturwissenschaften *f/pl.*

ap·point [ə'pɔint] bestimmen; festsetzen; verabreden; ernennen, bestellen (*s.o. governor* j-n zum ...); berufen (*to* auf *e-n Posten*, in *e-e Stellung*); *well* ~*ed* gut eingerichtet; **ap'point·ment** Festsetzung *f*, Bestimmung *f*; Stelldichein *n*; Verabredung *f*; Ernennung *f*, Bestellung *f*, Berufung *f*; Stelle *f*; ~*s pl.* Ausstattung *f*, Einrichtung *f*; ~ *book* Terminkalender *m*; *by* ~ nach Vereinbarung; *by special* ~ *to* ... Hoflieferant *m* des ...

ap·por·tion [ə'pɔ:ʃən] ver-, zuteilen; **ap'por·tion·ment** *gleichmäßige* Ver-, Zuteilung *f*.

ap·po·site □ ['æpəuzit] (*to*) passend (für), angemessen (*dat.*); treffend; **'ap·po·site·ness** Angemessenheit *f*.

ap·po·si·tion [æpəu'ziʃən] Beifügung *f*.

ap·prais·al [ə'preizəl] (Ab)Schätzung *f*; **ap'praise** abschätzen, taxieren; **ap'praise·ment** Schätzung *f*; Taxwert *m*; **ap'prais·er** Taxator *m*.

ap·pre·ci·a·ble □ [ə'pri:ʃəbl] (ab-) schätzbar; merkbar; **ap'pre·ci·ate** [~ʃieit] *v/t.* schätzen; (hoch)schätzen; richtig einschätzen, würdigen, zu schätzen wissen; anerkennen; dankbar sein für; Gefallen finden an; aufwerten; *v/i.* im Werte steigen; **ap·pre·ci'a·tion** (Wert)Schätzung *f*, Würdigung *f*; Verständnis *n* (*of* für); Einsicht *f*; kritische Besprechung *f*; Dankbarkeit *f*; Aufwertung *f*; **ap·pre·ci·a·tive** □ [ə'pri:ʃjətiv], **ap'pre·ci·a·to·ry** verständnisvoll (*of* für); *be* ~ *of* Verständnis haben für.

ap·pre·hend [æpri'hend] ergreifen, festnehmen; fassen, begreifen; befürchten; **ap·pre·hen·si·ble** □ [~'hensəbl] begreiflich, faßlich; **ap·pre'hen·sion** Ergreifung *f*, Festnahme *f*; Fassungskraft *f*; Auffassung *f*; Begriff *m*; Besorgnis *f*; **ap·pre'hen·sive** □ schnell begreifend (*of acc.*); ängstlich; besorgt (*of s.th., for s.o.* wegen, um; *that* daß).

ap·pren·tice [ə'prentis] **1.** Lehrling *m*; **2.** in die Lehre geben (*to* bei, zu); *be* ~*d to* in der Lehre sein bei; **ap'pren·tice·ship** Lehrzeit *f*; Lehre *f*.

ap·prise [ə'praiz] in Kenntnis setzen, unterrichten (*of* von).

ap·pro ✝ ['æprəu]: *on* ~ zur Ansicht.

ap·proach [ə'prəutʃ] **1.** *v/i.* näherkommen, sich nähern, nahen; *fig.* nahekommen (*to dat.*); *v/t.* sich nähern (*dat.*), herankommen an (*acc.*), *fig.* nahekommen (*dat.*); herangehen *od.* -treten an (*acc.*) (*a. fig.*); sich wenden an (*s.o.* j.);

2. Annäherung *f*, Nahen *n*; *fig.* Herangehen *n*; Versuch *m*; Methode *f*, Weg *m*; Zutritt *m*; Zugang *m*, Auffahrt *f*; *easy (difficult) of* ~ leicht (schwer) zugänglich (*Sache*) *od.* zu erreichen (*Person*); *make* ~*es to s.o.* j-n zu gewinnen versuchen; **ap'proach·a·ble** zugänglich; erreichbar.

ap·pro·ba·tion [æprəu'beiʃən] Billigung *f*, Beifall *m*.

ap·pro·pri·ate 1. [ə'prəuprieit] sich aneignen; verwenden; *parl.* bewilligen (*to, for* zu, für); 2. □ [~priit] (*to*) angemessen (*dat.*); passend, geeignet (für); entsprechend (*dat.*); eigen; **ap·pro·pri·a·tion** [~pri'eiʃən] Aneignung *f*; Verwendung *f*; ♀ *Committee parl.* Bewilligungsausschuß *m*.

ap·prov·a·ble [ə'pru:vəbl] löblich; **ap'prov·al** Billigung *f*, Beifall *m*; *on* ~ zur Ansicht; **ap'prove** *a.* ~ *of* billigen, gutheißen, anerkennen, genehmigen; (~ *o.s.* sich) erweisen (*as* als); **ap'proved** □ bewährt; **ap'prov·er** ⚖ Kronzeuge *m*.

ap·prox·i·mate 1. [ə'prɔksimeit] sich nähern; 2. □ [~mit] annähernd; ungefähr; nahe (*to* bei, an *dat.*); **ap·prox·i·ma·tion** [~'meiʃən] Annäherung *f*; **ap'prox·i·ma·tive** □ [~mətiv] annähernd.

ap·pur·te·nance [ə'pə:tinəns] *mst* ~*s pl.* Zubehör *n, m*.

a·pri·cot ♀ ['eiprikɔt] Aprikose *f*.

A·pril ['eiprəl] April *m*; *make an* ~ *fool of s.o.* j. in den April schicken.

a·pron ['eiprən] Schürze *f*; Schurz (-fell *n*) *m*; ✈ Hallenvorfeld *n*; *thea.* Vorbühne *f*; '**~-string** Schürzenband *n*; *be tied to one's wife's (mother's)* ~*s* unterm Pantoffel stehen (der Mutter am Rockzipfel hängen).

ap·ro·pos ['æprəpəu] angemessen; zur rechten Zeit; ~ *of* in bezug auf (*acc.*); gelegentlich (*gen.*).

apt □ [æpt] geeignet, passend; treffend (*Bemerkung etc.*); begabt; geschickt (*at* in *dat.*); *he is* ~ *to believe it* er wird es wahrscheinlich *od.* wohl glauben; ~ *to* geneigt zu; **ap·ti·tude** ['~titju:d] Neigung *f* (*to* zu); Befähigung *f*, Eignung *f* (*for, to* für, zu); ~ *test* Eignungsprüfung *f*; '**apt·ness** = *aptitude*.

aq·ua·lung ['ækwəlʌŋ] Unterwasser-Atmungsgerät *n*.

aq·ua·ma·rine *min.* [ækwəmə'ri:n] Aquamarin *m*; Aquamarinblau *n*.

aq·ua·plane ['ækwəplein] Gleitbrett *n zum Wellenreiten*; '**aq·ua·plan·ing** *bsd. Br.* Aquaplaning *n*.

aq·ua·relle [ækwə'rel] Aquarell (-malerei *f*) *n*; **aq·ua'rel·list** Aquarellmaler(in).

a·quar·i·um [ə'kwɛəriəm] Aquarium *n*.

A·quar·i·us *ast.* [ə'kwɛəriəs] Wassermann *m*.

a·quat·ic [ə'kwætik] 1. Wasser...; ~ *sports pl.* Wassersport *m*; 2. Wasserpflanze *f*; ~*s pl.* Wassersport *m*.

aq·ua·tint ['ækwətint] Aquatinta *f* (*Tuschmanier*).

aq·ue·duct ['ækwidʌkt] Aquädukt *m*, Wasserleitung *f*; **a·que·ous** □ ['eikwiəs] wässerig.

aq·ui·line ['ækwilain] Adler...; gebogen; ~ *nose* Adlernase *f*.

Ar·ab ['ærəb] Araber(in); Araber *m* (*Pferd*); *street* ♀ *sl.* Straßenjunge *m*; **ar·a·besque** [~'besk] 1. Arabeske *f*; 2. arabeskenhaft; **A·ra·bi·an** [ə'reibjən] 1. arabisch; *The* ~ *Nights* Tausendundeine Nacht; 2. Araber (-in); **Ar·a·bic** ['ærəbik] 1. arabisch; *gum* ♀ Gummiarabikum *n*; 2. Arabisch *n*.

ar·a·ble ['ærəbl] 1. pflügbar; 2. *a.* ~ *land* Ackerland *n*.

ar·bi·ter ['ɑ:bitə] Schiedsrichter *m*; *fig.* Gebieter *m*; **ar·bi·trage** † [ɑ:bi'trɑ:ʒ] Arbitrage *f*; '**ar·bi·tral tri'bu·nal** Schiedsgericht *n*; **ar'bit·ra·ment** Schiedsspruch *m*; '**ar·bi·trar·i·ness** Willkür *f*; Eigenmächtigkeit *f*; '**ar·bi·trar·y** □ willkürlich; eigenmächtig; **ar·bi·trate** ['~treit] entscheiden, schlichten; **ar·bi'tra·tion** Schiedsgerichtsverfahren *n*; Schiedsspruch *m*; Entscheidung *f*; ~ *of exchange* † Wechselarbitrage *f*; '**ar·bi·tra·tor** ⚖ Schiedsrichter *m*; '**ar·bi·tress** Schiedsrichterin *f*; *fig.* Gebieterin *f*.

ar·bor ['ɑ:bə] ⊕ Welle *f*, Spindel *f*; ♀ *Day Am.* Tag *m* des Baumes; **ar·bo·re·al** [ɑ:'bɔ:riəl], **ar'bo·re·ous** Baum...; **ar·bo·res·cent** □ [ɑ:bə'resnt] baumartig.

ar·bour ['ɑ:bə] Laube *f*.

ar·bu·tus ♀ [ɑ:'bju:təs] Erdbeerbaum *m*.

arc *ast.*, ℞ *etc.* [ɑ:k] (⚡ Licht-)

Bogen *m*; **ar·cade** [ɑːˈkeid] Arkade *f*; Bogen-, Laubengang *m*.
ar·ca·num [ɑːˈkeinəm], *pl.* **arˈca·na** [~nə] Geheimnis *n*.
arch¹ [ɑːtʃ] **1.** *bsd.* ⚠ Bogen *m*; Gewölbe *n*; Triumphbogen *m*; ~ *support* Senkfußeinlage *f*; **2.** (sich) wölben; überwölben.
arch² □ [~] schalkhaft, schelmisch; schlau.
arch³ □ [~] erst; schlimmst; Haupt...; Erz...
ar·ch(a)e·o·log·i·cal [ɑːkiəˈlɔdʒikəl] □ archäologisch; **ar·ch(a)e·ol·o·gist** [~ˈɔlədʒist] Archäologe *m*; **ar·ch(a)eˈol·o·gy** Archäologie *f*, Altertumskunde *f*.
ar·cha·ic [ɑːˈkeiik] (*~ally*) altertümlich; **ˈar·cha·ism** Archaismus *m*, veralteter Ausdruck *m*.
arch·an·gel [ˈɑːkeindʒəl] Erzengel [*m*.]
arch·bish·op [ˈɑːtʃˈbiʃəp] Erzbischof *m*; **archˈbish·op·ric** [~rik] Erzbistum *n*.
arch·dea·con [ˈɑːtʃˈdiːkən] Archidiakon *m*.
arch·duch·ess [ˈɑːtʃˈdʌtʃis] Erzherzogin *f*; **ˈarchˈduch·y** Erzherzogtum *n*; **ˈarchˈduke** Erzherzog *m*.
arch·er [ˈɑːtʃə] Bogenschütze *m*; **ˈarch·er·y** Bogenschießen *n*.
ar·che·type [ˈɑːkitaip] Urform *f*, -bild *n*, Archetyp *m*.
arch-fiend [ˈɑːtʃˈfiːnd] Erzfeind *m* (*der Teufel*).
ar·chi·e·pis·co·pal [ɑːkiiˈpiskəpəl] erzbischöflich.
ar·chi·pel·a·go [ɑːkiˈpeligəu] Archipel *m*; Inselmeer *n*; Inselgruppe *f*.
ar·chi·tect [ˈɑːkitekt] Architekt *m*, Baumeister(in), Erbauer(in); Urheber(in), Schöpfer(in); **ar·chi·tec·ton·ic** [~ˈtɔnik] (*~ally*) architektonisch; baulich; *fig.* aufbauend; **ar·chiˈtec·tu·ral** [~tʃərəl] architektonisch; **ˈar·chi·tec·ture** Architektur *f*; Baukunst *f*; Baustil *m*.
ar·chives [ˈɑːkaivz] *pl.* Archiv *n*.
arch·ness [ˈɑːtʃnis] Schalkhaftigkeit *f*, Schelmerei *f*.
arch·way [ˈɑːtʃwei] Triumphbogen *m*.
arc-lamp [ˈɑːklæmp], **ˈarc-light** ⚡ Bogenlampe *f*.
arc·tic [ˈɑːktik] **1.** arktisch, nördlich; Nord..., Polar...; *the* ♀ die Arktis; ♀ *Circle* Nördlicher Polarkreis *m*; ♀ *Ocean* Nördliches Eismeer *n*; **2.** *Am.* wasserdichter, warmer Überschuh *m*.
ar·den·cy [ˈɑːdənsi] Hitze *f*, Glut *f*; Innigkeit *f*; **ˈar·dent** □ *mst fig.* heiß, glühend; *fig.* feurig; eifrig; innig; ~ *spirits pl.* Spirituosen *pl*.
ar·do(u)r [ˈɑːdə] *fig.* Hitze *f*, Glut *f*; Eifer *m*.
ar·du·ous □ [ˈɑːdjuəs] schwierig, mühsam, anstrengend, beschwerlich.
are [ɑː] sind; seid.
a·re·a [ˈɛəriə] Areal *n*; (Boden-) Fläche *f*; Flächeninhalt *m*; Raum *m*, Gegend *f*; Gebiet *n*; Bereich *m*; Kellervorhof *m bei alten engl. Stadthäusern*; ~ *code Am. teleph.* Vorwählnummer *f*; *danger* ~ Gefahrenzone *f*; *goal* ~ *Fußball*: Torraum *m*; *penalty* ~ *Fußball*: Strafraum *m*; *prohibited* ~ Sperrzone *f*.
a·re·na [əˈriːnə] Arena *f*, Kampf-, Schauplatz *m* (*a. fig.*).
aren't F [ɑːnt] = *are not*.
a·rête *mount.* [æˈreit] Grat *m*, Gebirgskamm *m*.
ar·gent [ˈɑːdʒənt] silberfarben, silbern.
Ar·gen·tine [ˈɑːdʒəntain] **1.** argentinisch; **2.** Argentinier(in); *the* ~ Argentinien *n*.
ar·gil [ˈɑːdʒil] Ton(erde *f*) *m*; **ar·gil·la·ceous** [~ˈleiʃəs] tonig; Ton...
ar·gon ⚗ [ˈɑːgɔn] Argon *n*.
Ar·go·naut [ˈɑːgənɔːt] Argonaut *m*; *Am.* Goldsucher *m* in Kalifornien.
ar·gu·a·ble [ˈɑːgjuəbl] diskutabel;
ar·gue [ˈɑːgjuː] *v/t.* erörtern; beweisen; begründen; ausführen, darlegen; vorbringen; einwenden; ~ *s.o. into* j. zu *et.* überreden; ~ *s.o. out of* j. von *et.* abbringen; *v/i.* streiten; Einwendungen machen.
ar·gu·ment [ˈɑːgjumənt] Argument *n*, Beweis(grund) *m*; Beweisführung *f*; Erörterung *f*; Thema *n*; Streit (-frage *f*) *m*; **ar·gu·men·ta·tion** [~menˈteiʃən] Beweisführung *f*; **ar·gu·men·ta·tive** □ [~ˈmentətiv] beweiskräftig; streitlustig.
a·ri·a ♪ [ˈɑːriə] Arie *f*.
ar·id [ˈærid] dürr, trocken, öde (*a. fig.*); **aˈrid·i·ty** Trockenheit *f*.
Ar·ies *ast.* [ˈɛəriːz] Widder *m*.
a·right [əˈrait] recht, richtig.
a·rise [əˈraiz] (*irr.*) *fig.* sich erheben; ent-, erstehen (*from* aus); **a·ris·en** [əˈrizn] *p.p. von arise*.

ar·is·toc·ra·cy [æris'tɔkrəsi] Aristokratie *f* (*a. fig.*); **a·ris·to·crat** ['~təkræt] Aristokrat(in); **a·ris·to·'crat·ic, a·ris·to'crat·i·cal** □ aristokratisch; vornehm.

a·rith·me·tic [ə'riθmətik] Arithmetik *f*, Rechnen *n*; **ar·ith·met·i·cal** □ [æriθ'metikəl] arithmetisch.

ark [ɑːk] *Bibel*: Arche *f* (Noah); ♀ *of the Covenant* Bundeslade *f*.

arm[1] [ɑːm] *allg.* Arm *m*; Armlehne *f*; *within* ~*'s reach* in Reichweite; *keep s.o at* ~*'s length* sich j. vom Leibe halten; *infant in* ~*s* Säugling *m*; *take s.o. to od. in one's* ~*s* j. in die Arme nehmen.

arm[2] [~] **1.** *mst* ~*s pl.* Waffe *f*; *mst* ~*s sg.* Waffengattung *f*; ~*s pl.* Wappen *n*; *s. coat*; ~*s race* Wettrüsten *n*; ~*s reduction* (*talks pl.*) Abrüstung(sgespräche *n/pl.*) *f*; *be* (*all*) *up in* ~*s* in vollem Aufruhr sein; in Harnisch geraten; entrüstet (und zum Streit bereit) sein (*about* über); *take up* ~*s* zu den Waffen greifen; **2.** (sich) (be)waffnen; (aus-)rüsten; ⊕ armieren; *zo.*, ♀ bewehren.

ar·ma·da [ɑː'mɑːdə] Kriegsflotte *f*; *the* (*Invincible*) ♀ die Armada (*1588*).

ar·ma·ment ['ɑːməmənt] (Kriegs-aus)Rüstung *f*; Kriegsmacht *f*; ⚓ Bestückung *f*; *a. naval* ~ Kriegsflotte *f*; ~*s industry* Rüstungsindustrie *f*; ~ *race* Wettrüsten *n*; **ar·ma·ture** ['~tjuə] Rüstung *f*; ⚠, *phys.* Armatur *f*; ⚡ Anker *m*; *zo.*, ♀ Bewehrung *f*.

arm·chair ['ɑːm'tʃɛə] Lehnstuhl *m*, Sessel *m*; *attr.* ~ *politician* Bierbankpolitiker *m*.

armed [ɑːmd] bewaffnet; ~ *forces pl.* Streitkräfte *f/pl.*

...-armed [ɑːmd] ...armig.

Ar·me·ni·an [ɑː'miːnjən] **1.** armenisch; **2.** Armenier(in).

arm·ful ['ɑːmful] Armvoll *m*.

ar·mi·stice ['ɑːmistis] Waffenstillstand *m* (*a. fig.*).

arm·let ['ɑːmlit] Armspange *f*; Armbinde *f als Abzeichen*.

ar·mo·ri·al [ɑː'mɔːriəl] Wappen...

ar·mo(u)r ['ɑːmə] **1.** ⚔ Rüstung *f*, (*a. fig., zo.*) Panzer *m*; Taucheranzug *m*; ⚔ *coll.* Panzerfahrzeuge *n/pl.*; **2.** panzern; ~*ed car* Panzerwagen *m*; ~*ed division* Panzerdivision *f*; ~*ed turret* Panzerturm *m*; **'~-clad, '~-plat·ed** gepanzert; Panzer...; **'ar·mo(u)r·er** Waffenschmied *m*; ⚔, ⚓ Waffenmeister *m*; **'ar·mo(u)r·y** Rüstkammer *f* (*a. fig.*); Zeughaus *n*; *Am.* Waffenfabrik *f*, Rüstungsbetrieb *m*.

arm·pit ['ɑːmpit] Achselhöhle *f*; **'arm-rest** Armlehne *f*.

ar·my ['ɑːmi] Heer *n*, Armee *f*; *fig.* Menge *f*; ~ *chaplain* Militärgeistliche *m*; *s. service*; **'~-corps** Armeekorps *n*; **'~-list** ⚔ Rangliste *f*.

a·ro·ma [ə'rəumə] Aroma *n*; Duft *m*; Würze *f*; **ar·o·mat·ic** [ærəu'mætik] (~*ally*) aromatisch, würzig, wohlriechend, -schmeckend.

a·rose [ə'rəuz] *pret. von arise*.

a·round [ə'raund] **1.** *adv.* rundherum; rundum; *Am.* F hier herum; **2.** *prp.* um ... her(um); *bsd. Am.* F ungefähr, etwa (*bei Zahlenangaben*).

a·rouse [ə'rauz] (auf)wecken; *fig.* aufrütteln; erregen.

ar·rack ['ærək] Arrak *m*.

ar·raign [ə'rein] vor Gericht stellen, anklagen; *fig.* rügen; **ar'raign·ment** Anklage *f*.

ar·range [ə'reindʒ] *v/t.* (an)ordnen, *bsd.* ♪ einrichten; *Tag* festsetzen; *Streit* schlichten; arrangieren, veranstalten; abmachen, vereinbaren; erledigen; *v/i.* Anordnungen *od.* Vorkehrungen treffen (*for* für, zu); sich verständigen; ~ *for s.th. to be there* dafür sorgen, daß et. da ist; **ar'range·ment** Anordnung *f*; Disposition *f*; ♪ Arrangement *n*; Übereinkommen *n*; Abmachung *f*; Vorkehrung *f*; *make one's* ~*s* s-e Dispositionen treffen.

ar·rant □ ['ærənt] völlig, ausgesprochen, komplett, heillos (*Unsinn etc.*); Erz...; ~ *knave* Erzgauner *m*.

ar·ray [ə'rei] **1.** (Schlacht)Ordnung *f*; *fig.* Aufgebot *n*; stattliche Reihe *f*; *poet.* Kleid *n*; **2.** ordnen, aufstellen; aufbieten; kleiden, putzen.

ar·rear [ə'riə] Rückstand *m*; ~*s of rent* rückständige Miete *f*; *be in* ~*s* im Rückstand sein; **ar'rear·age** Restsumme *f*.

ar·rest [ə'rest] **1.** Verhaftung *f*, Festnahme *f*; Haft *f*; Beschlagnahme *f*; Aufhalten *n*, Hemmung *f*; *under* ~ in Haft; **2.** verhaften; beschlagnahmen; an-, aufhalten, hemmen; *Aufmerksamkeit etc.* fesseln.

ar·riv·al [ə'raivəl] Ankunft *f*; Auftreten *n*; Ankömmling *m*; ~*s pl.* angekommene Personen *f/pl.*; ankommende Züge *m/pl. od.* Schiffe *n/pl.*; ✝ Zufuhren *f/pl.*; *attr.* Ankunfts...; **ar'rive** (an)kommen, eintreffen; erscheinen; eintreten (*Ereignis*); ~ *at* erreichen (*acc.*); kommen zu.

ar·ro·gance ['ærəugəns] Anmaßung *f*; Überheblichkeit *f*; Arroganz *f*; **'ar·ro·gant** □ anmaßend; überheblich; arrogant; **ar·ro·gate** ['~-geit] *mst* ~ *to o.s.* sich *et.* anmaßen, *et.* für sich beanspruchen; in Anspruch nehmen (*to* für).

ar·row ['ærəu] Pfeil *m*; *surv.* Markierstab *m*; **'~-head** Pfeilspitze *f*; **'~-root** ⚘ Pfeilwurz(mehl *n*) *f*.

arse V [ɑːs] Arsch *m*.

ar·se·nal ['ɑːsinl] Zeughaus *n*, Arsenal *n*.

ar·se·nic ['ɑːsnik] Arsen(ik) *n*; **ar·sen·i·cal** [ɑː'senikəl] arsen(ik)haltig; Arsen(ik)...

ar·son ⚖ ['ɑːsn] Brandstiftung *f*.

art[1] [ɑːt] Kunst *f*; *engS.* Geschicklichkeit *f*; *fig.* List *f*, Verschlagenheit *f*; Kniff *m*; ~ *critic* Kunstkritiker *m*; ~ *dealer* Kunsthändler *m*; ~*s pl.* Geisteswissenschaften *f/pl.*; *Master of* ⁀*s* (*abbr. M. A.*) Magister *m* der freien Künste; *fine* ~*s die* schönen Künste; *liberal* ~*s die* freien Künste; ~*s and crafts* Kunstgewerbe *n*; *Faculty of* ⁀*s* philosophische Fakultät *f*; ~*s page Zeitung*: Kulturseite *f*.

art[2] † [~] *du* bist.

ar·te·ri·al [ɑː'tiəriəl] Pulsader...; ~ *road* Verkehrsader *f*; Hauptverkehrsstraße *f*; Ausfallstraße *f*; **ar·te·ri·o·scle·ro·sis** [ɑː'tiəriəuskliə'rəusis] Arterienverkalkung *f*; **ar·ter·y** ['ɑːtəri] Arterie *f*, Schlag-, Pulsader *f*; *fig.* Verkehrsader *f*.

Ar·te·sian well [ɑː'tiːzjən'wel] Artesischer Brunnen *m*.

art·ful □ ['ɑːtful] schlau, verschmitzt, listig.

art gal·ler·y ['ɑːt'gæləri] Kunstgalerie *f*.

ar·thrit·ic ⚕ [ɑː'θritik] gichtisch; **ar·thri·tis** [ɑː'θraitis] Gelenkentzündung *f*.

ar·ti·choke ⚘ ['ɑːtitʃəuk] Artischocke *f*.

ar·ti·cle ['ɑːtikl] **1.** Artikel *m* (*Abschnitt e-s Vertrages etc.*; *Aufsatz in e-r Zeitung etc.*; *Handelsware*; *gr. Geschlechtswort*); *fig.* Punkt *m*; ~ *of clothing* Kleidungsstück *n*; ~*s of apprenticeship* Lehrvertrag *m*; ~*s of association* Statuten *n/pl.* e-r Handelsgesellschaft; **2.** *v/t.* in die Lehre geben (*to* bei); förmlich anklagen (*for* wegen); *Klage* vorbringen; ~*ed* in der Lehre (*to* bei).

ar·tic·u·late 1. [ɑː'tikjuleit] deutlich (aus)sprechen; *Knochen* zs.-fügen; gliedern; **2.** □ [~lit] fähig, sich klar auszudrücken; deutlich, klar; gegliedert; **ar'tic·u·lat·ed** [~leitid] gegliedert; artikuliert; ~ *lorry mot.* Sattelschlepper *m*; **ar·tic·u'la·tion** Artikulation *f*, deutliche Aussprache *f*; *anat.* Gelenkfügung *f*, -verbindung *f*; Gliederung *f*.

ar·ti·fact ['ɑːtifækt] Kunstprodukt *n*; von Menschenhand geschaffener Gegenstand *m*.

ar·ti·fice ['ɑːtifis] Kunstgriff *m*, Kniff *m*, List *f*; **ar'tif·i·cer** Handwerker *m*; Urheber *m*; **ar·ti·fi·cial** □ [~'fiʃəl] künstlich; Kunst...; ~ *insemination* künstliche Befruchtung *f*; ~ *respiration* ⚕ künstliche Beatmung *f*; ~ *silk* Kunstseide *f*; ~ *person* ⚖ juristische Person *f*.

ar·til·ler·y [ɑː'tiləri] Artillerie *f*; **ar'til·ler·y·man** [~mən] Artillerist *m*.

ar·ti·san [ɑːti'zæn] Handwerker *m*.

art·ist ['ɑːtist] Künstler(in), *bsd.* Kunstmaler(in); **ar·tiste** [ɑː'tiːst] Artist(in); Künstler(in), Sänger(in), Tänzer(in); **ar·tis·tic, ar·tis·ti·cal** □ [ɑː'tistik(əl)] künstlerisch; Kunst...

art·less □ ['ɑːtlis] ungekünstelt, schlicht; arglos; **'art·less·ness** Schlichtheit *f*; Arglosigkeit *f*.

art·y ['ɑːti] künstlerisch aufgemacht; gewollt bohemienhaft.

Ar·y·an ['ɛəriən] **1.** arisch; **2.** Arier (-in).

as [æz, əz] *adv. u. cj.* (eben)so; während, als (*zeitlich*); da, weil; (wenn) auch; (eben)so wie; wie; (*in der Eigenschaft*) als; wie z. B.; *young* ~ *I am* so jung ich auch bin; *such women* ~ *knew him* jene Frauen, die ihn kannten; ~ *heavy* ~ *lead* (so) schwer wie Blei; ~ *if*, ~ *though* als ob; ~ *for*, ~ *to* was ... betrifft, bezüglich (*gen.*); *so* ~ *to* um ... zu; so ... daß; ~ *good* ~ so gut wie, praktisch; *be* ~ *good* ~ *one's word* sein Versprechen halten; ~ *long* ~ vorausgesetzt daß; solange (wie); ~ *much* gerade *od.* eben das;

I thought ~ *much* das dachte ich mir; ~ *from* (*Datum*) von ... an; ~ *per* laut (*gen.*); ~ *yet* bis jetzt; ~ *it were* gleichsam; ~ *well* ebenfalls, auch.

as·bes·tos [æz'bestɔs] Asbest *m*.

as·cend [ə'send] *v/i.* (auf-, empor-, hinauf)steigen; *zeitlich*: hinaufreichen, zurückgehen (*to* bis zu, bis auf, bis in *acc.*); *v/t.* be-, ersteigen; ~ *a river* e-n Fluß hinauffahren; ~ *the throne* den Thron besteigen; **as'cend·an·cy** (*over*) Überlegenheit *f*, Herrschaft *f* (über *acc.*); Einfluß *m* (auf *acc.*); **as'cend·ant** **1.** aufsteigend; überlegen (*over dat.*); **2.** = *ascendancy*; *ast.* Aufgangspunkt *m*; Vorfahr *m*; *be in the* ~ *fig.* im Kommen sein; **as'cend·en·cy, as'cend·ent** = *ascendancy, ascendant*.

as·cen·sion [ə'senʃən] Aufsteigen *n* (*bsd. ast.*); *the* ♀ (Christi) Himmelfahrt *f*; ♀ *Day* Himmelfahrt(stag *m*) *f*.

as·cent [ə'sent] Aufstieg *m*; Besteigung *f*; Steigung *f*; Anstieg *m*; Aufgang *m*.

as·cer·tain [æsə'tein] ermitteln, feststellen; sich vergewissern; **as·cer'tain·a·ble** □ ermittelbar, feststellbar; **as·cer'tain·ment** Ermitt(e)lung *f*, Feststellung *f*.

as·cet·ic [ə'setik] **1.** (~*ally*) asketisch, mönchisch; **2.** Asket(in); **as'cet·i·cism** [~tisizəm] Askese *f*.

as·cor·bic ac·id [əs'kɔ:bik'æsid] Ascorbinsäure *f*, Vitamin C *n*.

as·crib·a·ble [əs'kraibəbl] zuzuschreiben(d); **as'cribe** (*to*) zuschreiben, beimessen, beilegen (*dat.*), zurückführen (auf *acc.*).

a·sep·tic ⚕ [æ'septik] aseptisch(es Mittel *n*).

ash[1] [æʃ] ♀ Esche *f*; Eschenholz *n*.

ash[2] [~], *mst* **ash·es** ['~ʃiz] *pl.* Asche *f*; *Ash Wednesday* Aschermittwoch *m*.

a·shamed [ə'ʃeimd] beschämt; *be od. feel* ~ *of* sich *e-r Sache od. j-s* schämen; *be* ~ *of o.s.* sich schämen.

ash-can *Am.* ['æʃkæn] Mülleimer *m*.

ash·en[1] ['æʃn] eschen, von Eschenholz.

ash·en[2] [~] Aschen...; aschgrau, aschfahl.

a·shore [ə'ʃɔ:] am *oder* ans Ufer *od.* Land; *run* ~, *be driven* ~ stranden, auflaufen.

ash...: '~**-pan** Aschenkasten *m*; '~**-tray** Aschenbecher *m*, Ascher *m*.

ash...: '~**-tree** ♀ Esche *f*; '~**-wood** Eschenholz *n*.

ash·y ['æʃi] aschig; Aschen...; aschgrau, -fahl.

A·si·at·ic [eiʃi'ætik] **1.** asiatisch; **2.** Asiat(in).

a·side [ə'said] **1.** beiseite (*a. thea*), auf die Seite; abseits; seitwärts; ~ *from Am.* abgesehen von; **2.** *thea.* Aparte *n*.

as·i·nine ['æsinain] Esels...; eselhaft, dumm.

ask [ɑ:sk] *v/t. u. v/i.* fragen, sich erkundigen (*for* nach); bitten; einladen; verlangen, fordern; ~ *the price* nach dem Preis fragen; ~ (*s.o.*) *a question* (j-m) e-e Frage stellen; ~ (*him*) *his name* frage (ihn) nach seinem Namen; ~ *s.th. of s.o.* et. von j-m verlangen; *you are* ~*ing too much* Sie verlangen zuviel; ~ *s.o. for help* j. um Hilfe bitten; ~ *after s.o.* (*s.th.*) nach j-m (et.) fragen; ~ *s.o. to come* j. bitten zu kommen; ~ *s.o. to dinner* j. zum Essen einladen; ~ *s.o. in* j. hereinbitten; *he* ~*ed for it od. for trouble* er wollte es ja so haben; *to be had for the* ~*ing* umsonst zu haben.

a·skance [əs'kæns], **a'skant, as·kew** [əs'kju:] von der Seite, seitwärts; *fig.* schief, scheel.

a·slant [ə'slɑ:nt] schräg, schief.

a·sleep [ə'sli:p] schlafend; in den *od.* im Schlaf; eingeschlafen (*Glied*); *be* ~ schlafen; *fall* ~ einschlafen.

asp[1] *zo.* [æsp] Natter *f*.

asp[2] ♀ [~] Espe *f*.

as·par·a·gus ♀ [əs'pærəgəs] Spargel *m*.

as·pect ['æspekt] Aussehen *n*, Äußere *n*; Anblick *m*; Aussicht *f*, Lage *f*; Aspekt *m* (*a. gr.*), Seite *f*, Gesichtspunkt *m*; *the house has a southern* ~ das Haus liegt nach Süden.

as·pen ['æspən] Espe *f*; Espen...

as·per·gill, as·per·gil·lum *eccl.* ['æspədʒil, ~'dʒiləm] Weihwedel *m*.

as·per·i·ty [æs'periti] Rauheit *f*; Unebenheit *f*; *fig.* Schroffheit *f*.

as·perse [əs'pə:s] besprengen; *fig.* anschwärzen, schlechtmachen; **as·per·sion** Besprengung *f*; *fig.* Verleumdung *f*; Anwurf *m*.

as·phalt ['æsfælt] **1.** Asphalt *m*;

2. asphaltieren.
as·pho·del ⚘ ['æsfədel] Asphodill *m*; *poet.* Narzisse *f*.
as·phyx·i·a [æs'fiksiə] Erstickung(s-tod *m*) *f*; **as'phyx·i·ate** [~eit] ersticken; **as·phyx·i'a·tion** Erstickung *f*.
as·pic ['æspik] Aspik *m*, Sülze *f*.
as·pi·dis·tra ⚘ [æspi'distrə] Aspidistra *f*, Sternschild *n*.
as·pir·ant [əs'paiərənt] Bewerber (-in) (*to, after, for* um); ~ *officer* Offiziersanwärter *m*; **as·pi·rate** ['æspərit] 1. *gr.* aspiriert; 2. *gr.* Hauchlaut *m*; 3. ['~reit] *gr.* aspirieren; ⊕, ⚕ absaugen; **as·pi'ra·tion** Aspiration *f*; Bestrebung *f*; Trachten *n*, Sehnen *n*; ⊕, ⚕ Absaugung *f*; **as'pire** [əs'paiə] streben, trachten (*to, after, at* nach).
as·pi·rin *pharm.* ['æspərin] Aspirin *n*.
as·pir·ing □ [əs'paiəriŋ] hochstrebend.
ass[1] [æs] Esel *m*; *make an ~ of o.s.* sich lächerlich machen.
ass[2] *Am.* V [~] Arsch *m*.
as·sail [ə'seil] angreifen, überfallen (*a. fig.*); befallen (*Zweifel etc.*); *fig.* bestürmen (*with* mit); *Aufgabe* in Angriff nehmen; ~ *s.o. with questions* j. mit Fragen bestürmen; **as'sail·a·ble** angreifbar; **as'sail·ant, as'sail·er** Angreifer(in), Gegner(in).
as·sas·sin [ə'sæsin] (Meuchel)Mörder *m*; **as'sas·si·nate** [~neit] (hinterrücks) ermorden; **as·sas·si'na·tion** Ermordung *f*.
as·sault [ə'sɔ:lt] 1. Angriff *m* (*a. fig., on, upon* auf *acc.*); ⚔ Sturm *m*; ⚖ tätliche Bedrohung *f od.* Beleidigung *f*; *s. battery, indecent*; 2. anfallen; ⚖ tätlich angreifen *od.* beleidigen; ⚔ bestürmen (*a. fig.*).
as·say [ə'sei] 1. (Erz-, Metall)Probe *f*; 2. *v/t.* untersuchen; *v/i. Am.* Edelmetall enthalten.
as·sem·blage [ə'semblidʒ] Ver-, Ansammlung *f*; ⊕ Montage *f*; **as'sem·ble** (sich) versammeln; zs.-berufen; *Truppen* zs.-ziehen; ⊕ montieren; zs.-setzen, zs.-bauen; **as'sem·bler** ⊕ Monteur *m*; **as'sem·bly** Versammlung *f*; Zs.-kunft *f*; Gesellschaft *f*; ⚔ Sammelsignal *n*; ⊕ Montage *f*; *a.* ~ *shop* Montagehalle *f*; ~ *hall* Aula *f*; Montagehalle *f*; ~ *line* Montage-, Fließband *n*, (laufendes) Band *n*; ~ *man pol.* Abgeordnete *m*.
as·sent [ə'sent] 1. Zustimmung *f*; Genehmigung *f*; 2. (*to*) zustimmen (*dat.*), genehmigen; billigen.
as·sert [ə'sə:t] behaupten, erklären; durchsetzen; geltend machen; ~ *s.th. to be true* et. für wahr erklären; **as'ser·tion** Behauptung *f*, Erklärung *f*; Geltendmachung *f*; **as'ser·tive** □ bestimmt, ausdrücklich; positiv; **as'ser·tor** Fürsprecher *m*.
as·sess [ə'ses] besteuern; zur Steuer veranlagen (*in, at* mit); *Steuer etc.* festsetzen (*at* auf *acc.*); **as'sess·a·ble** □ steuerpflichtig; **as'sess·ment** (Ein)Schätzung *f*; (Steuer)Veranlagung *f*; Steuer *f*; **as'ses·sor** Assessor *m*, Beisitzer *m*; Steuereinschätzer *m*.
as·set ['æset] ✝ Aktivposten *m*; *fig.* Gut *n*, Gewinn *m*; ~*s pl.* Vermögen *n*, Konkursmasse *f*; ✝ Aktiva *pl.*; ~*s pl. and liabilities pl.* Aktiva *pl.* und Passiva *pl.*
as·sev·er·ate [ə'sevəreit] beteuern; **as·sev·er'a·tion** Beteuerung *f*.
as·si·du·i·ty [æsi'dju:iti] Emsigkeit *f*; Fleiß *m*; *assiduities pl.* Aufmerksamkeiten *f/pl.*; **as·sid·u·ous** □ [ə'sidjuəs] emsig, fleißig; aufmerksam.
as·sign [ə'sain] 1. an-, zuweisen, zuteilen; festsetzen, bestimmen; zuschreiben; *Grund* angeben; übertragen; 2. ⚖ Rechtsnachfolger *m*; **as'sign·a·ble** □ bestimmbar; nachweisbar; übertragbar; **as·sig·na·tion** [æsig'neiʃən] Verabredung *f*, Stelldichein *n*; *s. assignment*; **as·sign·ee** [æsi'ni:] = *assign* 2; Bevollmächtigte *m, f*; ⚖ Treuhänder *m*; ~ *in bankruptcy* Konkursverwalter *m*; **as·sign·ment** [ə'sainmənt] An-, Zuweisung *f*; *bsd. Am.* Auftrag *m*, Aufgabe *f*; Angabe *f* (*von Gründen*); ⚖ Übertragung *f*, Abtretung *f*; **as·sign·or** [æsi'nɔ:] ⚖ Übertrager(in).
as·sim·i·late [ə'simileit] (*to, with dat.*) ähnlich *od.* gleich machen; (sich) angleichen; aufnehmen, absorbieren; sich aneignen; *physiol.* (sich) assimilieren; **as·sim·i'la·tion** Assimilation *f*, Angleichung *f*.
as·sist [ə'sist] *j-m* beistehen, helfen; *j. od. et.* unterstützen; ~ *at* bei-

wohnen (*dat.*), teilnehmen an (*dat.*); **as'sist·ance** Beistand *m*; Hilfe *f*, Unterstützung *f*; **as'sist·ant 1.** behilflich (*to dat.*); Hilfs...; **2.** Gehilfe *m*, Gehilfin *f*, Hilfskraft *f*, Assistent(in).

as·size ⚖ [ə'saiz] (Schwur)Gerichtssitzung *f*; ~*s pl. periodisches* Geschworenengericht *n*, Assisen *pl.*

as·so·ci·a·ble [ə'səuʃjəbl] vereinbar (*with* mit); **as'so·ci·ate 1.** [~ʃieit] (sich) zugesellen (*with dat.*), (sich) vereinigen; (sich) verbinden; Umgang haben (*with* mit); ~ *in* mit einbeziehen in (*acc.*); **2.** [~ʃiit] verbunden; beigeordnet; Mit...; **3.** [~ʃiit] Genosse *m*; Partner *m*; ✝ Gesellschafter *m*, Teilhaber *m*; außerordentliches Mitglied *n e-r wissenschaftlichen Gesellschaft etc.*; **as·so·ci·a·tion** [~si'eiʃən] Vereinigung *f*, Verbindung *f*, Bund *m*; *wissenschaftliche, Handels- etc.* Gesellschaft *f*; Verband *m*, Verein *m*; *a. mutual* ~ Genossenschaft *f*; Umgang *m*; (Ideen)Assoziation *f*; ~ *football europäischer* Fußball *m*.

as·so·nance ['æsəunəns] Assonanz *f*.

as·sort [ə'sɔːt] *v/t.* sortieren, (passend) zs.-stellen, -bringen; ✝ assortieren; *v/i.* (*with*) übereinstimmen (mit), passen (zu); ~*ed toffees pl.* Bonbonmischung *f*; **as'sort·ment** Sortieren *n*; ✝ Sortiment *n*, Auswahl *f*.

as·suage [ə'sweidʒ] *v/t.* lindern; besänftigen, beschwichtigen; *Hunger etc.* stillen; **as'suage·ment** Linderung *f etc.*

as·sume [ə'sjuːm] annehmen, voraussetzen; *Amt etc.* übernehmen; sich anmaßen; vorgeben; **as'sum·ing** □ anmaßend; **as·sump·tion** [ə'sʌmpʃən] Annahme *f*, Voraussetzung *f*; Übernahme *f*; Anmaßung *f*; ♀ (*Day*) *eccl.* Mariä Himmelfahrt *f*; *on the* ~ *that* in der Annahme, daß; **as'sump·tive** □ angenommen; anmaßend.

as·sur·ance [ə'ʃuərəns] Ver-, Zusicherung *f*; Zuversicht *f*; Sicherheit *f*, Gewißheit *f*; Selbstsicherheit *f*; *b.s.* Dreistigkeit *f*; (*bsd.* Lebens)Versicherung *f*; *life* ~ Lebensversicherung *f*; **as'sure** sichern; sicherstellen; *Leben* versichern; ~ *s.o. of s.th.* j. e-r Sache versichern; j-m et. ver- *od.* zusichern; ~ *o.s.* sich vergewissern; **as'sured 1.** (*adv.* **as'sur·ed·ly** [~ridli]) sicher, gewiß; selbstsicher; *b.s.* dreist; **2.** Versicherte *m, f*; **as'sur·er** [~rə] Versicherte *m, f*; *a.* = **as'sur·or** [~rə] Versicherer *m*.

As·syr·i·an [ə'siriən] **1.** assyrisch; **2.** Assyrer(in); Assyrisch *n*.

as·ter ⚘ ['æstə] Aster *f*; **as·ter·isk** *typ.* ['~risk] Sternchen *n* (*).

as·ter·oid *ast.* ['æstərɔid] Asteroid *m*, kleiner Planet *m*.

a·stern ⚓ [ə'stəːn] achteraus; *of* ~ hinter.

asth·ma ['æsmə] Asthma *n*, Atemnot *f*; **asth·mat·ic** [~'mætik] **1.** *a.* **asth'mat·i·cal** □ asthmatisch; Asthma...; **2.** Asthmatiker(in).

as·tig·mat·ic *opt.* [æstig'mætik] (~*ally*) astigmatisch; **a'stig·ma·tism** [~mətizəm] Astigmatismus *m*.

a·stir [ə'stəː] auf (den Beinen); in Bewegung, rege.

as·ton·ish [əs'tɔniʃ] in Erstaunen setzen; verwundern; befremden; *be* ~*ed* erstaunt *etc.* sein (*at* über *acc.*); **as'ton·ish·ing** □ erstaunlich; **as'ton·ish·ment** Erstaunen *n*; Staunen *n*; Verwunderung *f*.

as·tound [əs'taund] in Staunen setzen; verblüffen.

as·tra·khan [æstrə'kæn] Astrachan *m*, Krimmer *m* (*Pelzart*).

a·stray [əs'trei] vom (rechten) Wege ab (*a. fig.*); irre; *go* ~ sich verlaufen, irregehen.

a·stride [əs'traid] mit gespreizten Beinen; rittlings (*of* auf *dat.*); *ride* ~ im Herrensitz reiten.

as·trin·gent □ ⚕ [əs'trindʒənt] zusammenziehend(es Mittel *n*).

as·tro·dome ✈ ['æstrədəum] Kuppel *f* für astronomische Navigation.

as·trol·o·ger [əs'trɔlədʒə] Astrologe *m*, Sterndeuter *m*; **as·tro·log·i·cal** □ [æstrə'lɔdʒikəl] astrologisch; **as·trol·o·gy** [əs'trɔlədʒi] Astrologie *f*, Sterndeuterei *f*.

as·tro·naut ['æstrəunɔːt] Astronaut *m*, Raumfahrer *m*; **as·tro·nau·tics** [æstrə'nɔːtiks] *mst sg.* Astronautik *f*, Raumfahrtwissenschaft *f*.

as·tron·o·mer [əs'trɔnəmə] Astronom *m*; **as·tro·nom·i·cal** □ [æstrə'nɔmikəl] astronomisch; **as·tron·o·my** [əs'trɔnəmi] Astronomie *f*, Sternkunde *f*; **as·tro·phys·ics** [æstrəu'fiziks] *sg.* Astrophysik *f*.

as·tute □ [əs'tjuːt] scharfsinnig;

schlau; **as'tute·ness** Scharfsinn *m*; Schlauheit *f*.
a·sun·der [ə'sʌndə] auseinander; entzwei.
a·sy·lum [ə'sailəm] Asyl *n*; Irrenanstalt *f*; Heim *n*.
a·sym·me·try [æ'simitri] Asymmetrie *f*, Ungleichmäßigkeit *f*.
at [æt; ət] *prp.* an; auf; aus; bei; für; in; mit; nach; über; um; von; vor; zu; ~ *the door* an *od.* vor der Tür; ~ *my expense* auf meine Kosten; ~ *a ball* auf e-m Ball; *run* ~ *s.o.* auf j. losstürzen; ~ *daybreak* bei Tagesanbruch; ~ *table* bei Tisch; ~ *a low price* zu einem niedrigen Preis; ~ *school* in der Schule; ~ *Stratford* in Stratford; ~ *peace* im Frieden; ~ *the age of* im Alter von; ~ *one blow* mit einem Schlag; ~ *five o'clock* um fünf Uhr; ~ *Christmas* zu Weihnachten.
at·a·vism *biol.* ['ætəvizəm] Atavismus *m*, Rückschlag *m*.
a·tax·y ⚕ [ə'tæksi] Ataxie *f* (*Bewegungsstörung*).
ate [et] *pret. von eat 1.*
a·the·ism ['eiθiizəm] Atheismus *m*, Gottesleugnung *f*; **'a·the·ist** Atheist(in); **a·the'is·tic, a·the'is·ti·cal** □ atheistisch.
A·the·ni·an [ə'θi:njən] **1.** athenisch; **2.** Athener(in).
a·thirst [ə'θə:st] begierig (*for* nach).
ath·lete ['æθli:t] (*bsd.* Leicht)Athlet *m*, Sportler *m*; ~*'s foot* Fußpilz *m*; **ath·let·ic** [æθ'letik], **ath'let·i·cal** □ athletisch; *athletic heart* Sportherz *n*; **ath'let·ics** *pl.* (*bsd.* Leicht-) Athletik *f*.
at-home [ət'həum] Empfangstag *m*.
a·thwart [ə'θwɔ:t] **1.** *prp.* quer über; entgegen (*dat.*); **2.** *adv.* quer, ⚓ dwars; schräg; in die Quere.
a·tilt [ə'tilt] vorgebeugt; kippend.
a·tish·oo *co.* [ə'tiʃu:] hatschi!
At·lan·tic [ət'læntik] **1.** atlantisch; **2.** *a.* ~ *Ocean* Atlantik *m*.
at·las ['ætləs] Atlas *m* (*Buch*).
at·mos·phere ['ætməsfiə] Atmosphäre *f* (*a. fig.*); **at·mos·pher·ic, at·mos·pher·i·cal** □ [~'ferik(əl)] atmosphärisch; Luft...; **at·mos'pher·ics** *pl. Radio*: atmosphärische Störungen *f/pl*.
at·oll *geogr.* ['ætɔl] Atoll *n*.
at·om ['ætəm] Atom *n* (*a. fig.*); ~ *bomb* Atombombe *f*; **a·tom·ic** [ə'tɔmik] atomartig, Atom...; atomistisch; ~ *age* Atomzeitalter *n*; ~ *bomb* Atombombe *f*; ~ *energy* Atomenergie *f*; ~ *fission* Atomspaltung *f*; ~ *nucleus* Atomkern *m*; ~ *pile* Atombatterie *f*; ~ *power* Atomkraft *f*; ~ *research* Atomforschung *f*; ~ *waste* Atommüll *m*; ~ *weight* Atomgewicht *n*; **a'tom·ic-pow·ered** durch Atomkraft betrieben; **at·om·ize** ['ætəumaiz] in Atome auflösen; atomisieren; *Flüssigkeit* zerstäuben; **'at·om·iz·er** Zerstäuber *m* (*Gerät*); **at·o·my** ['ætəmi] Knirps *m*; *bsd. fig.* Skelett *n*, Gerippe *n*.
a·tone [ə'təun]: ~ *for* büßen für *et.*, *et.* sühnen; **a'tone·ment** Buße *f*; Sühne *f*; *the* ♀ *eccl.* das Sühneopfer Christi.
a·ton·ic [æ'tɔnik] atonisch, erschlafft; *gr.* unbetont; **at·o·ny** ['ætəni] Atonie *f*, Erschlaffung *f*.
a·top F [ə'tɔp] oben(auf); ~ *of* oben auf (*dat.*).
a·tro·cious □ [ə'trəuʃəs] scheußlich, gräßlich; **a·troc·i·ty** [ə'trɔsiti] Scheußlichkeit *f*, Gräßlichkeit *f*; Greuel(tat *f*) *m*, Grausamkeit *f*; F Verstoß *m*.
at·ro·phy ['ætrəfi] **1.** Atrophie *f*, Schwund *m*; **2.** atrophieren, verkümmern.
at·tach [ə'tætʃ] *v/t.* (*to*) anheften, -binden (an *acc.*), befestigen (an *dat.*); *Sinn* verknüpfen (mit *e-m Wort*); *Wert, Schuld, Namen, Wichtigkeit* beilegen (*dat.*); ⚖ *j.* verhaften; *et.* beschlagnahmen; ~ *o.s. to* sich anschließen an (*acc.*); ~ *value to* Wert legen auf, halten auf (*acc.*); *v/i.* ~ *to* anhaften (*dat.*), haften an (*dat.*), verbunden sein mit; **at·ta·ché** [ə'tæʃei] Attaché *m*; ~ *case* Aktentasche *f*; **at·tached** [ə'tætʃt]: ~ *to* gehörig zu; *j-m* zugetan, ergeben; ~ *house Am.* Reihenhaus *n*; **at'tach·ment** Befestigung *f*; (*to, for*) Bindung *f* (an *acc.*); Anhänglichkeit *f* (an *acc.*), Neigung *f* (zu); Anhängsel *n* (*to gen.*); ⊕ Zusatzeinrichtung *f*; ⚖ Verhaftung *f*; Beschlagnahme *f*.
at·tack [ə'tæk] **1.** angreifen (*a. fig.*); befallen (*Krankheit*); *Arbeit* in Angriff nehmen; **2.** Angriff *m* (*on* auf *acc.*; *a. fig.*); ⚕ Anfall *m*; Inangriffnahme *f*; *heart* ~ Herzanfall *m*; **at'tack·er** Angreifer *m*.

at·tain [ə'tein] *v/t. Ziel* erreichen, erlangen; erzielen; *v/i.* ~ *to* gelangen zu; erreichen; **at'tain·a·ble** erreichbar; **at'tain·der** ⚖ [~də] Ehrverlust *m*; **at'tain·ment** Erreichung *f*; *fig.* Aneignung *f*; ~*s pl.* Kenntnisse *f/pl.*, Fertigkeiten *f/pl.*
at·tar ['ætə]: ~ *of roses* Rosenöl *n.*
at·tem·per [ə'tempə] mildern, mäßigen; beruhigen; anpassen (*to dat.*).
at·tempt [ə'tempt] **1.** versuchen; ~ *the life of* ein Attentat verüben auf (*acc.*); **2.** Versuch *m* (*to inf.* zu *inf.*; *at* an *dat.*); Attentat *n* (*on od. upon s.o.'s life* auf j.).
at·tend [ə'tend] *v/t.* begleiten; bedienen; *Kranke* pflegen; *ärztlich* behandeln; *j-m* aufwarten; beiwohnen (*dat.*); *Vorlesung etc.* besuchen; *v/i.* merken, achten, hören (*to* auf *acc.*); anwesend sein (*at* bei); ~ *on Kranke* pflegen; bedienen; ~ *to* erledigen; *are you being* ~*ed to?* werden Sie schon bedient?; **at'tend·ance** Begleitung *f*; Aufwartung *f*, Bedienung *f* (*upon* bei); Pflege *f*; *ärztliche* Behandlung *f*; Dienerschaft *f*, Gefolge *n*; (*at*) Anwesenheit *f* (bei); Teilnahme (an *dat.*); Besuch *m* (*gen.*; *bsd. der Schule etc.*); Besucher(zahl *f*) *m/pl.*, Publikum *n*, Zuhörerschaft *f*; *hours of* ~ Dienststunden *f/pl.*; *be in* ~ zu Diensten stehen; *dance* ~ F herumscharwenzeln (*on* um); **at'tend·ant 1.** begleitend (*on, upon acc.*); anwesend (*at* bei); diensttuend (*on* bei); **2.** Diener(in); Begleiter(in); Wärter(in); ⊕ Bedienungsmann *m*; Begleiterscheinung *f* (*on, upon gen.*); ~*s pl.* Dienerschaft *f.*
at·ten·tion [ə'tenʃən] Aufmerksamkeit *f* (*a. fig.*); ~! ⚔ Achtung!; *s. call, give, pay*; **at'ten·tive** □ aufmerksam (*to* auf *acc.*; *fig.* gegen).
at·ten·u·ate [ə'tenjueit] dünn(er) machen, verdünnen; *fig.* vermindern, abschwächen.
at·test [ə'test] bezeugen (*a. fig.*); beglaubigen; bescheinigen; *bsd.* ⚔ vereidigen; **at·tes·ta·tion** [ætes'teiʃən] Bezeugung *f etc.*; Zeugnis *n*; *bsd.* ⚔ Vereidigung *f*; **at·test·er, at·test·or** [ə'testə] Zeuge *m.*
At·tic[1] ['ætik] attisch.
at·tic[2] [~] Dachstube *f*, Mansarde *f*; ~*s pl.* Dachgeschoß *n.*
at·tire *lit.* [ə'taiə] **1.** kleiden; **2.** Gewand *n.*
at·ti·tude ['ætitju:d] Stellung *f*, Haltung *f*; *fig.* Stellungnahme *f*, Einstellung *f* (*to, towards* zu); ✈ Fluglage *f*; *strike an* ~ eine Pose annehmen; ~ *of mind* Geisteshaltung *f*, Einstellung *f*; **at·ti'tu·di·nize** [~dinaiz] sich in Positur setzen; affektiert tun.
at·tor·ney [ə'tə:ni] Bevollmächtigte *m*, Stellvertreter *m*; *Am.* Rechtsanwalt *m*; *letter od. warrant of* ~ Vollmacht(erteilung) *f*; *power of* ~ *erteilte* Vollmacht *f*; ♀ *General* Oberstaats-, Kronanwalt *m*, *Am.* Justizminister *m.*
at·tract [ə'trækt] anziehen, *Aufmerksamkeit* auf sich ziehen, erregen; *fig.* (an)locken, reizen, fesseln; **at'trac·tion** [~kʃən] Anziehung(skraft) *f*; *fig.* Reiz *m*, Attraktion *f*; *thea.* Zugstück *n*, -nummer *f*; **at'trac·tive** □ *mst fig.* anziehend; hübsch, charmant; reizvoll, verlockend, einladend; *thea.* zugkräftig.
at·trib·ut·a·ble [ə'tribjutəbl] zuzuschreiben(d); **at·trib·ute** [ə'tribju:t] bemessen, zuschreiben; zurückführen (*to* auf *acc.*); **at·tri·bute** ['ætribju:t] Attribut *n*, Eigenschaft *f*; Merkmal *n*, (Kenn-)Zeichen *n*; *gr.* Attribut *n*, Beifügung *f*; **at·tri'bu·tion** Zuschreibung *f*; beigelegte Eigenschaft *f*; zuerkanntes Recht *n*; **at·trib·u·tive** *gr.* [ə'tribjutiv] **1.** □ attributiv; **2.** Attribut *n.*
at·tri·tion [ə'triʃən] Abrieb *m*; Abnutzung *f*, ⊕ Verschleiß *m*; Zermürbung *f*; *war of* ~ Zermürbungs-, Abnutzungskrieg *m.*
at·tune [ə'tju:n] ♪ stimmen; ~ *to fig.* abstimmen auf (*acc.*).
au·burn ['ɔ:bən] gold-, nuß-, kastanienbraun.
auc·tion ['ɔ:kʃən] **1.** Auktion *f*, Versteigerung *f*; *sell by* (*Am. at*) ~, *put up for* ~ verauktionieren, versteigern; *sale by* ~ Versteigerung *f*; **2.** *mst* ~ *off* versteigern; **auc·tion·eer** [~'niə] Auktionator *m.*
au·da·cious □ [ɔ:'deiʃəs] kühn, keck, verwegen; *b.s.* dreist, frech, unverschämt; **au·dac·i·ty** [ɔ:'dæsiti] Kühnheit *f*; *b.s.* Dreistigkeit *f*, Frechheit *f*, Unverschämtheit *f.*
au·di·bil·i·ty [ɔ:di'biliti] Hörbar-

keit *f*, Vernehmlichkeit *f*; **au·di·ble** □ ['ɔːdəbl] hörbar, vernehmlich; Hör...
au·di·ence ['ɔːdjəns] Publikum *n*, Zuhörerschaft *f*; Leserkreis *m*; Audienz *f*; Gehör *n*; *give* ~ *to* Gehör schenken (*dat.*).
au·di·o-fre·quen·cy ['ɔːdiəu'friːkwənsi] *Radio*: Tonfrequenz *f*.
au·di·on ['ɔːdiən] *Radio*: Audion *n*, Verstärkerröhre *f*.
au·di·o·phile ['ɔːdiəufail] Hi-Fi-Fan *m*; **au·di·o·typ·ist** [~'taipist] Phonotypistin *f*; **au·di·o-vis·u·al aids** [~'vizjuəl eidz] *pl.* audiovisuelle Lehrmittel *n/pl.*
au·dit ['ɔːdit] **1.** Rechnungsprüfung *f*; **2.** *Rechnungen* prüfen; **au'di·tion** Hörvermögen *n*; *thea.* Vorsprechen *n od.* -singen *n*; **'au·di·tor** *bsd. univ.* Hörer *m*; Rechnungs-, Buchprüfer *m*; **au·di·to·ri·um** [~'tɔːriəm] Auditorium *n*, Hörsaal *m*; *Am.* Festhalle *f* (*für Vorträge, Konzerte, Versammlungen etc.*); **au·di·to·ry** ['~təri] **1.** (Ge)Hör...; **2.** Hörer(schaft *f*) *m/pl.*; = *auditorium.*
au·ger ⊕ ['ɔːgə] *großer* Bohrer *m*.
aught [ɔːt] (irgend) etwas; *for* ~ *I care* meinetwegen; *for* ~ *I know* soviel ich weiß.
aug·ment [ɔːg'ment] *v/t.* vermehren, vergrößern; *v/i.* zunehmen; **aug·men'ta·tion** Vermehrung *f*, -größerung *f*, Zunahme *f*; Zusatz *m*.
au·gur ['ɔːgə] **1.** Augur *m*; **2.** weissagen, prophezeien; ~ *well* (*ill*) ein gutes (schlechtes) Zeichen sein (*for* für); **au·gu·ry** ['ɔːgjuri] Prophezeiung *f*; An-, Vorzeichen *n*; Vorahnung *f*; Vorbedeutung *f*.
Au·gust 1. ['ɔːgəst] *Monat* August *m*; **2.** ♀ □ [ɔː'gʌst] erhaben, hehr; **Augus·tan** [ɔː'gʌstən] augusteisch; klassisch.
auk *orn.* [ɔːk] Alk *m*.
auld lang syne *schott.* ['ɔːldlæŋ'sain] die gute alte Zeit.
aunt [ɑːnt] Tante *f*; ♀ *Sally volkstümliches* Wurfspiel *n*; **aunt·ie, aunt·y** F ['~ti] Tantchen *n*.
au pair [əu'pɛə] Au-pair-Mädchen *n*.
au·ra ['ɔːrə] Aura *f*, Atmosphäre *f*.
au·ral ['ɔːrəl] Ohren...
au·re·ole *eccl.*, *ast.* ['ɔːriəul] Aureole *f*.
au·ri·cle ['ɔːrikl] äußeres Ohr *n*; Herzvorhof *m*; **au·ric·u·la** ♀ [ə'rikjulə] Aurikel *f*; **au·ric·u·lar** □ [ɔː'rikjulə] das Ohr betreffend; Ohr(en)...; Hör...; ~ *confession eccl.* Ohrenbeichte *f*; ~ *witness* Ohrenzeuge *m*.
au·rif·er·ous [ɔː'rifərəs] goldhaltig.
au·rist ['ɔːrist] Ohrenarzt *m*.
au·rochs *zo.* ['ɔːrɔks] Auerochs *m*, Ur *m*.
au·ro·ra [ɔː'rɔːrə] Morgenröte *f*, -dämmerung *f*; ♀ Aurora *f* (*Göttin der Morgenröte*); ~ *borealis* [bɔːri'eilis] Nordlicht *n*; **au'ro·ral** die Morgenröte betreffend.
aus·cul·ta·tion ⚕ [ɔːskəl'teiʃən] Abhorchen *n*.
aus·pice ['ɔːspis] Vorzeichen *n*; ~*s pl.* Auspizien *pl.*, Schutz-, Schirmherrschaft *f*; **aus·pi·cious** □ [~'piʃəs] günstig, glücklich.
Aus·sie F ['ɔzi] **1.** Australier *m*; **2.** australisch.
aus·tere □ [ɔs'tiə] streng; herb; hart, rauh; einfach; scharf (*Geschmack*); **aus·ter·i·ty** [~'teriti] Strenge *f*; Härte *f*; Einfachheit *f*; eingeschränkte Lebensweise *f*; ~ *budget* Sparhaushalt *m*.
aus·tral ['ɔːstrəl] südlich.
Aus·tra·lian [ɔs'treiljən] **1.** australisch; **2.** Australier(in).
Aus·tri·an ['ɔstriən] **1.** österreichisch; **2.** Österreicher(in).
au·tar·ky ['ɔːtɑːki] Autarkie *f* (*wirtschaftliche Unabhängigkeit*).
au·then·tic [ɔː'θentik] (~*ally*) authentisch; zuverlässig; echt; **au'then·ti·cate** [~keit] beglaubigen; verbürgen; als echt erweisen; rechtsgültig machen; **au·then·ti'ca·tion** Legalisierung *f*, Beglaubigung *f*; **au·then'tic·i·ty** [~siti] Authentizität *f*; Glaubwürdigkeit *f*; Echtheit *f*.
au·thor ['ɔːθə] Urheber(in); Autor(-in); Verfasser(in); Schriftsteller(-in); **'au·thor·ess** Autorin *f*, Verfasserin *f*; Schriftstellerin *f*; **au·thor·i·tar·i·an** [ɔːθɔri'tɛəriən] autoritär, Obrigkeits...; **au'thor·i·ta·tive** □ [~tətiv] maßgebend; gebieterisch; zuverlässig (*Bericht*); **au'thor·i·ty** Autorität *f*; (Amts-)Gewalt *f*, Vollmacht *f*, Ermächtigung *f*, Befugnis *f* (*for*, *to inf.* zu *inf.*); Einfluß *m* (*over* auf *acc.*); An-

sehen *n* (*with* bei); Glaubwürdigkeit *f*; Zeugnis *n e-r maßgebenden Person etc.*; Gewährsmann *m*, Quelle *f*, Beleg *m*; Fachmann *m*, Autorität *f*; *mst pl.* Verwaltung *f*, Behörde *f*; *on good ~* aus guter Quelle; *on the ~ of* auf *j-s* Zeugnis hin; *I have it on the ~ of Mr. X* ich habe es von Herrn X; **au·thor·i·za·tion** [ɔ:θərai'zeiʃən] Bevollmächtigung *f*, Ermächtigung *f*; **'au·thor·ize** *j.* autorisieren, bevollmächtigen, ermächtigen, berechtigen; *et.* gutheißen, billigen; **'au·thor·ship** Urheberschaft *f*; Autorschaft *f*; Schriftstellerei *f*.

au·to ['ɔ:təu] Auto(mobil) *n*.

au·to... ['ɔ:təu] auto..., selbst...; Auto..., Selbst...

au·to·bi·og·ra·pher [ɔ:təubai'ɔgrəfə] Autobiograph(in); **au·to·bi·o·graph·ic, au·to·bi·o·graph·i·cal** □ ['~əu'græfik(əl)] autobiographisch; **au·to·bi·og·ra·phy** [~'ɔgrəfi] Auto-, Selbstbiographie *f*.

au·to·bus ['ɔ:təubʌs] Autobus *m*.

au·to·cade *Am.* ['ɔ:təukeid] = *motorcade*.

au·toch·thon [ɔ:'tɔkθən] Autochthone *m* (*Ureinwohner*); **au'toch·tho·nous** autochthon (*ureingesessen*).

au·to·cide ['ɔ:təusaid] tödlicher Autounfall *m*.

au·toc·ra·cy [ɔ:'tɔkrəsi] Autokratie *f*, unumschränkte Herrschaft *f*; **au·to·crat** ['ɔ:təukræt] Autokrat *m*, unumschränkter Herrscher *m*; **au·to'crat·ic, au·to'crat·i·cal** □ autokratisch, despotisch, unumschränkt.

au·tog·e·nous weld·ing ⊕ [ɔ:'tɔdʒənəs'weldiŋ] autogene Schweißung *f*.

au·to·gi·ro ✈ ['ɔ:təu'dʒaiərəu] Autogiro *n*, Tragschrauber *m*.

au·to·graph ['ɔ:təgrɑ:f] **1.** Autogramm *n* (*eigene Handschrift*); **2.** eigenhändig (unter)schreiben; ⊕ autographieren, umdrucken; **au·to·graph·ic** [ɔ:təu'græfik] (*~ally*) autographisch; **au·tog·ra·phy** [ɔ:'tɔgrəfi] Autographie *f*, Umdruck *m*.

au·to·mat ['ɔ:təmæt] Automaten-Restaurant *n*; **au·to·mate** ['~meit] automatisieren; **au·to·mat·ic** [~'mætik] **1.** (*~ally*) automatisch, selbsttätig; unwillkürlich; *~ machine* (Verkaufs)Automat *m*; *~ transmission mot.* Automatik *f*; **2.** *Am.* Selbstladepistole *f*, -gewehr *n*; **au·to'ma·tion** Automation *f*; **au·tom·a·ton** [ɔ:'tɔmətən], *pl. mst* **au'tom·a·ta** [~tə] *fig.* Roboter *m*.

au·to·mo·bile *bsd. Am.* ['ɔ:təməubi:l] Auto(mobil) *n*; **au·to·mo·tive** [ɔ:tə'məutiv] selbstfahrend; Kraftfahrzeug...

au·ton·o·mous [ɔ:'tɔnəməs] autonom (*sich selbst regierend*); **au'ton·o·my** Autonomie *f*, Selbständigkeit *f*.

au·to·pi·lot ['ɔ:təpailət] automatische Steuerung *f*.

au·top·sy ['ɔ:təpsi] Autopsie *f*, Obduktion *f*, Leichenöffnung *f*.

au·to·type ⊕ ['ɔ:təutaip] **1.** Faksimileabdruck *m*; **2.** autotypieren.

au·tumn ['ɔ:təm] Herbst *m*; **au·tum·nal** □ [ɔ:'tʌmnəl] herbstlich; Herbst...

aux·il·ia·ry [ɔ:g'ziljəri] **1.** helfend; Hilfs...; *be ~ to* helfen (*dat.*); **2.** *a. ~ verb gr.* Hilfszeitwort *n*; *auxiliaries pl.* Hilfstruppen *f/pl*.

a·vail [ə'veil] **1.** (*v/t. j-m*) nützen, helfen; *~ o.s. of* sich *e-r Sache* bedienen, *et.* benutzen; **2.** Nutzen *m*; *of no ~* nutzlos; *of what ~ is it?* was nützt es?; **a·vail·a'bil·i·ty** Benutzbar-, Verfügbar-, Gültigkeit *f*; **a'vail·a·ble** □ benutzbar; verfügbar; *pred.* erhältlich, vorhanden, zu haben; gültig (*Fahrkarte etc.*); *make ~* zur Verfügung stellen.

av·a·lanche ['ævəlɑ:nʃ] Lawine *f*.

av·a·rice ['ævəris] Geiz *m*; Habsucht *f*; **av·a'ri·cious** □ geizig; habgierig.

a·vast! ⚓ [ə'vɑ:st] fest!

a·venge [ə'vendʒ] rächen, *et.* ahnden; *~ o.s., be ~d* sich rächen (*on, upon* an *dat.*); *avenging angel* Racheengel *m*; **a'veng·er** Rächer (-in).

av·e·nue ['ævinju:] Allee *f*; Avenue *f*, Prachtstraße *f*; *fig.* Weg *m*, Straße *f*; *~s to success* Wege zum Erfolg.

a·ver [ə'və:] als Tatsache hinstellen, behaupten; ⚖ beweisen.

av·er·age ['ævəridʒ] **1.** Durchschnitt *m*; *general* (*particular*) *~* ⚓ große (besondere *od.* partielle) Havarie *f*; *on an ~* durchschnittlich; **2.** □ durchschnittlich; Durchschnitts...; **3.** durchschnittlich schätzen (*at* auf *acc.*); durchschnittlich betragen, erreichen, arbeiten, verlangen *etc.*

a·ver·ment [ə'vəːmənt] Behauptung *f*; ⚖ Beweis(angebot *n*) *m*.

a·verse □ [ə'vəːs] abgeneigt (*to, from dat.*); widerwillig; **a'verse·ness, a'ver·sion** Widerwille *m*, Abneigung *f* (*to, from, for* gegen); *he is my* ~ er ist mir ein Greuel.

a·vert [ə'vəːt] abwenden (*a. fig.*).

a·vi·ar·y ['eivjəri] Vogelhaus *n*.

a·vi·ate ✈ ['eivieit] fliegen; **a·vi'a·tion** Fliegen *n*; Flugsport *m*, -wesen *n*; Luftfahrt *f*; ~ *ground* Flugplatz *m*; ~ *spirit* Flugbenzin *n*; **'a·vi·a·tor** Flieger *m*.

av·id □ ['ævid] gierig (*of* nach; *for* auf *acc.*); **a·vid·i·ty** [ə'viditi] Gier *f*.

a·vi·on·ics ✈ [eivi'ɔniks] *sg.* Bordelektronik *f*, Avionik *f*.

av·o·ca·do ♀ [ævəu'kɑːdəu] Avocado *f*.

av·o·ca·tion [ævəu'keiʃən] Nebenbeschäftigung *f*.

a·void [ə'vɔid] (ver)meiden; entgehen (*dat.*); *j-m* ausweichen; *Pflicht* umgehen; ⚖ anfechten; aufheben, ungültig machen; **a'void·a·ble** vermeidbar; **a'void·ance** Meiden *n*, Vermeidung *f*; ⚖ Anfechtung *f*; Aufhebung *f*; freie Stelle; ~ *of taxation* Steuerhinterziehung *f*.

av·oir·du·pois † [ævədə'pɔiz] *a.* ~ *weight* Handelsgewicht *n* (*das Pfund zu 16 Unzen*).

a·vouch [ə'vautʃ] verbürgen, bestätigen; = *avow*.

a·vow [ə'vau] bekennen, (ein)gestehen; anerkennen; **a'vow·al** Bekenntnis *n*, (Ein)Geständnis *n*; **a'vow·ed·ly** [~idli] eingestandenermaßen.

a·wait [ə'weit] erwarten (*a. fig.*).

a·wake [ə'weik] **1.** wach, munter; ~ *to* sich *e-r Sache* bewußt; *wide* ~ hellwach, *fig.* schlau, auf der Hut; **2.** (*irr.*) *v/t. mst* **a'wak·en** (auf-, er-)wecken; ~*n s.o. to s.th.* j-m et. zum Bewußtsein bringen; *v/i.* auf-, erwachen; gewahr werden (*to s.th.* et.).

a·ward [ə'wɔːd] **1.** Urteil *n*, Spruch *m*; Zuerkennung *f*; Belohnung *f*; Auszeichnung *f*, Preis *m*; **2.** zuerkennen; *Orden etc.* verleihen.

a·ware [ə'wɛə]: *be* ~ wissen (*of* von *od. acc.*; *that* daß), sich bewußt sein (*of gen.*; *that* daß); *become* ~ *of et.* gewahr werden, merken, sich *e-r Sache* bewußt werden; **a'ware·ness** Bewußtsein *n*.

a·wash ⚓ [ə'wɔʃ] (im Wasser) treibend; unter der Wasseroberfläche.

a·way [ə'wei] weg, hinweg; fort, abwesend; *bei vb. auch* immer weiter, darauflos; *Sport.*: Auswärts...; *2 miles* ~ 2 Meilen entfernt *od.* von hier; *water has boiled* ~ Wasser ist verkocht; *explain* ~ hinwegerklären; ~ *back Am.* F (schon) damals, weit zurück; *right* ~, *straight* ~ sofort; *out and* ~ bei weitem.

awe [ɔː] **1.** Ehrfurcht *f*, Scheu *f* (*of* vor *dat.*); **2.** Ehrfurcht *od.* Furcht einflößen (*dat.*); **'~-in·spir·ing** Ehrfurcht einflößend; **~some** ['~səm] ehrfurchtgebietend; **'~-struck** von Ehrfurcht ergriffen.

aw·ful □ ['ɔːful] ehrfurchtgebietend; furchtbar; F schrecklich, kolossal; **aw·ful·ly** ['ɔːfli] F sehr, furchtbar, schrecklich; *I'm* ~ *sorry* es tut mir furchtbar leid.

a·while [ə'wail] eine Weile.

awk·ward □ ['ɔːkwəd] ungeschickt, unbeholfen, linkisch; umständlich; unangenehm, peinlich; mißlich, fatal; dumm, ungünstig, unpraktisch; *an* ~ *corner* eine dumme Ecke; **'awk·ward·ness** Ungeschicklichkeit *f*, Unbeholfenheit *f*; linkisches Wesen *n*; Unannehmlichkeit *f*.

awl [ɔːl] Ahle *f*, Pfriem *m*.

awn ♀ [ɔːn] Granne *f*.

awn·ing ['ɔːniŋ] Wagendecke *f*, Plane *f*; Markise *f*; ⚓ Sonnensegel *n*.

a·woke [ə'wəuk] *pret. u. pp. von awake* 2.

a·wry [ə'rai] schief; *fig.* verkehrt; *go* ~, *turn* ~ schiefgehen (*Sache*).

ax(e) [æks] **1.** Axt *f*, Beil *n*; *apply the* ~ F Streichungen *od.* Entlassungen vornehmen; *have an* ~ *to grind* eigennützige Zwecke verfolgen; **2.** *v/t.* F *Ausgaben* zs.-streichen; *Beamte etc.* abbauen.

ax·i·om ['æksiəm] Axiom *n* (*Grundsatz*); **ax·i·o·mat·ic** [~siəu'mætik] (~*ally*) axiomatisch, unumstößlich.

ax·is ['æksis], *pl.* **ax·es** ['~siːz] Achse *f* (*a. pol.*).

ax·le ⊕ ['æksl] (Rad)Achse *f*, Welle *f*.
ay(e) [ai] **1.** ja; **2.** Ja *n*; *parl.* Stimme *f* für; *the ~s have it* die Mehrheit ist dafür.
a·zal·ea ⚘ [ə'zeiljə] Azalee *f*.
az·i·muth *ast.* ['æziməθ] Scheitelkreis *m*, Azimut *m*, *n*.
a·zo·ic *geol.* [ə'zəuik] azoisch (*keine Lebewesen enthaltend*).
az·ure ['æʒə] **1.** azurn, azurblau; **2.** Azur(blau *n*) *m*.

B

baa [bɑː] **1.** blöken; **2.** Blöken *n*.
Ba·al ['beiəl] *Gott* Baal *m*; Abgott *m*, Götze *m*.
Bab·bitt ['bæbit] *Am.* Spieß(bürg)er *m*; ♀ *metal* ⊕ Lagerweißmetall *n*.
bab·ble ['bæbl] **1.** stammeln, lallen; (nach)plappern; *Geheimnis* ausplaudern; plätschern (*Bach*); **2.** Gestammel *n*; Geplapper *n*; Geschwätz *n*; '**bab·bler** Schwätzer(in).
babe [beib] *poet.* kleines Kind *n*; Naivling *m*.
Ba·bel ['beibəl] *Bibel:* Babel *n*; ♀ *fig.* (Stimmen)Gewirr *n*.
ba·boon *zo.* [bə'buːn] Pavian *m*.
ba·by ['beibi] **1.** Säugling *m*, Baby *n*, kleines Kind *n*; *Am. sl.* Süße *f* (*Mädchen*); Kindchen *n*; *it's your ~* F das ist dein Bier; *be left holding the ~* F der Dumme sein; 2. Kinder...; Zwerg...; klein; ~ **act:** *mst plead* (*play*) *the ~ Am.* Unreife *f* plädieren (spielen); ~**boom** Geburtenboom *m*; ~ **car** Klein(st)wagen *m*; ~ **car·riage** *Am.* Kinderwagen *m*; '**~-farm·er** j., der Kinder gewerbsmäßig in Pflege nimmt; ~ **grand** ♩ Stutzflügel *m*; **ba·by·hood** ['~hud] Säuglingsalter *n*, frühe Kindheit *f*; '**ba·by·ish** □ kindlich; kindisch.
Bab·y·lo·ni·an [bæbi'ləunjən] **1.** babylonisch; 2. Babylonier(in).
ba·by...: '**~-mind·er** Tagesmutter *f*; '**~-sit·ter** Babysitter *m*, Kinderhüter(in).
bac·cha·nal ['bækənl] = *bacchant*; '**bac·cha·nals** *pl.*, **bac·cha·na·li·a** [~'neiljə] *pl.* Bacchanal *n* (*wüstes Gelage*); **bac·cha'na·li·an** bacchantisch.
bac·chant ['bækənt] Bacchant(in); **bac·chante** [bə'kænti] Bacchantin *f*; **bac'chan·tic** bacchantisch.
bac·cy F ['bæki] Tabak *m*.
bach·e·lor ['bætʃələ] Junggeselle *m*; *univ.* Bakkalaureus *m*; ~ *girl* Junggesellin *f*; **bach·e·lor·hood** ['~hud] Junggesellenstand *m*, -leben *n*.
bac·il·la·ry [bə'siləri] Bazillen...; **ba'cil·lus** [~ləs], *pl.* **ba'cil·li** [~lai] Bazillus *m*.
back [bæk] **1.** Rücken *m* (*von Mensch od. Tier*); Rückenlehne *f*; Rücken *m*, Rückseite *f*; = *full-back*; *have s.o. at one's ~* von j-m unterstützt werden; *behind s.o.'s ~* hinter j-s Rücken; *put one's ~ into s.th.* sich in et. hineinknien; *put od. get od. set s.o.'s ~ up* j. in Wut bringen; *break s.o.'s ~* j. überfordern; *break the ~ of s.th.* das Schlimmste von et. überstehen *od.* schaffen; *be on one's ~* auf der Nase liegen; *with one's ~ to the wall* in Bedrängnis; *at the ~ of* hinter (*dat.*); *on the ~ of that* zu alledem; **2.** *adj.* Hinter..., Rück...; hinter; rückwärtig; entlegen; rückläufig; rückständig; **3.** *adv.* zurück; *go ~ from od. upon one's word* sein Wort nicht halten; **4.** *v/t.* mit e-m Rücken versehen; *a. ~ up j-m* den Rücken decken *od.* stärken, *j-m* beistehen, *j-m* helfen, *j.* unterstützen; hinten anstoßen *od.* grenzen an (*acc.*); zurückbewegen, -schieben, -drücken *etc.*; wetten *od.* setzen auf (*acc.*); auf der Rückseite beschreiben; ⚕ indossieren; ~ *the sails* ⚓ die Segel backholen; ~ *water*, ~ *the oars* rückwärts rudern; ~ *up et.* befürworten; *v/i.* sich rückwärts bewegen, rückwärts fahren, zurückgehen *od.* -fahren; zurücktreten, abspringen (*out of* von *e-m Unternehmen*); ~ *down* F sich zurück-

ziehen (*from* von); ~ **al·ley** *Am.* finstere Seitengasse *f*; '~-'**bench·er** *pol.* Hinterbänkler *m*; '~-**bend** *Turnen*: Brücke *f*; '~-**bite** (*irr. bite*) verleumden; '~·**bone** Rückgrat *n* (*a. fig.*); *to the* ~ *fig.* bis auf die Knochen; '~-**break·ing** anstrengend; '~·**chat** (freche) Widerrede *f*; '~·**cloth** *thea. u. fig.* Hintergrund *m*; '~·**cou·pling** Rückkoppelung *f*; '~·**date** (zu)rückdatieren; ~*d to* rückwirkend ab; '~-'**door** Hintertür *f* (*a. fig.*); '~·**drop** = *backcloth*; ~ **en·trance** Hintereingang *m*; '**back·er** Unterstützer(in); ✝ Indossierer; Hintermann *m*; Wetter(in).

back...: '~·**field** *Sport*: Hinterfeld (-spieler *m*) *n*; '~-'**fire** *mot.* **1.** Frühzündung *f*; **2.** frühzünden; ~ **for·ma·tion** *gr.* Rückbildung *f*; ~-'**gam·mon** Puffspiel *n*; '~·**ground** Hintergrund *m*; Herkunft *f*, Milieu *n*, Bildung *f*; '~-'**hand 1.** Rückhand(schlag *m*) *f*; **2.** Rückhand...; '~-**hand·ed** rückhändig; *fig.* unerwartet; '~-**hand·er** *s. back-hand* **1**; unerwarteter Angriff *m*.

back·ing ['bækiŋ] Unterstützung *f*.

back...: '~·**lash** Rückschlag *m*, Gegenstoß *m*; *white* ~ weißer Gegenstoß *m gegen die Gleichberechtigung der Neger in den USA*; '~·**log** Rückstand *m* (*of* von); Reserve *f* (*of* an); ~ **num·ber** alte Nummer *f* (*e-r Zeitung*); *j. od. et.* Altmodisches *n*; '~-**pack** *Am.* Rucksack *m*; '~'**pack·ing** Rucksacktourismus *m*; ~ **pay** Lohn-, Gehaltsnachzahlung *f*; '~-'**ped·al** rückwärtstreten (*Radfahrer*); ~*ling brake* Rücktrittbremse *f*; '~-**room boy** F Wissenschaftler *m mit Geheimauftrag*; ~ **seat** Rücksitz *m*; *take a* ~ sich im Hintergrund halten; *back-seat driver* Besserwisser *m*; '~'**side** Hinter-, Rückseite *f*; V Hintern *m*; '~·**sight** (Visier)Kimme *f*; '~-**slap·per** *Am.* plump-vertraulicher Mensch *m*; '~'**slide** (*irr. slide*) rückfällig werden; '~'**slid·er** Rückfällige *m, f*; '~'**slid·ing** Rückfall *m*; '~'**stage** (*a. fig.*) hinter den Kulissen; in der Garderobe; '~'**stairs** Hintertreppe *f*; '~·**stitch 1.** Steppstich *m*; **2.** mit Steppstichen nähen; '~·**stop** *Am. Baseball*: Gitter *n hinter dem Fänger*; *Schießstand*: Kugelfang *m*; ~ **street** Seitenstraße *f*; '~-**street a'bor·tion·ist** Engelmacher(in); '~·**stroke** Rückenschwimmen *n*; ~ **talk** *Am.* freche Antworten *f/pl.*; ~ **to back** Rücken an Rücken (gebaut); nacheinander; ~ **to front** verkehrt herum, mit der Rückseite nach vorne; '~-**track** *Am.* F *fig.* e-n Rückzieher machen.

back·ward ['bækwəd] **1.** *adj.* rückwärts gerichtet; Rück(wärts)...; langsam; zurückgeblieben, rückständig; zurückhaltend; **2.** *adv. a.* '**back·wards** rückwärts, zurück; **back·ward'a·tion** ✝ Deport *m*, Kursabschlag *m*; '**back·ward·ness** Rückständigkeit *f*; Langsamkeit *f*; Widerstreben *n*.

back...: '~·**wa·ter** Stauwasser *n*; totes Wasser *n*; '~·**woods** *pl.* weit abgelegene Waldgebiete *n/pl.*; *fig.* Provinz *f*; '~·**woods·man** Hinterwäldler *m*.

ba·con ['beikən] Speck *m*; *save one's* ~ F mit heiler Haut davonkommen; *bring home the* ~ *sl.* es geschafft haben.

bac·te·ri·al □ [bæk'tiəriəl] bakteriell; Bakterien...; **bac·te·ri·o·log·i·cal** □ [~tiəriə'lɔdʒikəl] bakteriologisch; **bac·te·ri·ol·o·gist** [~tiəri'ɔlədʒist] Bakteriologe *m*; **bac'te·ri·um** [~riəm], *pl.* **bac'te·ri·a** [~riə] Bakterie *f*.

bad □ [bæd] schlecht, böse, schlimm, arg; falsch (*Münze*); anstößig (*Wort etc.*); faul (*Schuld*); *not (too)* ~, *not so* ~, *not half* ~ F gar nicht übel; *things are not so* ~ die Sache ist halb so schlimm; *he is* ~*ly off* es geht ihm sehr schlecht; ~*ly wounded* schwerverwundet; *want* ~*ly* dringend brauchen; *in* ~ *with Am.* F in Ungnade bei; *s. worse.*

bade [bæd] *pret. von bid* **1**.

badge [bædʒ] Ab-, Kennzeichen *n*.

badg·er ['bædʒə] **1.** *zo.* Dachs *m*; **2.** hetzen, plagen, belästigen.

bad·lands *Am.* ['bædləndz] *pl.* Ödland *n*, unfruchtbares Land *n*.

bad·min·ton ['bædmintən] Federballspiel *n*, Badminton *n*.

bad·ness ['bædnis] schlechte Beschaffenheit *f*; Schlechtigkeit *f*.

bad-tem·pered ['bæd'tempəd] schlecht gelaunt, mürrisch.

baf·fle ['bæfl] *j.* verwirren, verblüffen; *Plan etc.* vereiteln, durchkreuzen; *they were* ~*d in their attempt* ihr Versuch wurde zunichte gemacht; *it ~s description* es spottet jeder Beschreibung.

bag [bæg] **1.** Tasche *f*, Beutel *m*, Sack *m*; Tüte *f*; *hunt.* Strecke *f*; *~s pl. sl.* Hosen *f/pl.*; *it's in the ~* F das haben wir sicher; *~ and baggage* mit Sack und Pack; *~s of sl.* e-e Menge; **2.** in e-n Beutel *etc.* tun, einsacken; F stibitzen; *hunt.* zur Strecke bringen; (sich) bauschen.

bag·a·telle [bægəˈtel] Kleinigkeit *f*.

bag·gage [ˈbægidʒ] *Am.* (Reise-) Gepäck *n*; ⚔ Troß *m*; *co.* kleines Biest *n*, Fratz *m* (*Mädchen*); **~ al·low·ance** Freigepäck *n*; **~ car** 🚃 *Am.* Gepäckwagen *m*; **ˈ~-check** *Am.* Gepäckschein *m*; **~ (re·)claim** Gepäckausgabe *f am Flughafen*.

bag·ging [ˈbægiŋ] Sack-, Packleinwand *f*.

bag·gy [ˈbægi] ausgebeult (*Hose*); sackartig; bauschig.

bag...: **~·man** [ˈbægmən] F Handlungsreisende *m*; **ˈ~·pipes** *pl.* Dudelsack *m*; **ˈ~-snatch·er** Handtaschenräuber *m*.

bah [bɑː] bah!, pah!

bail[1] [beil] **1.** Bürge *m*; Bürgschaft *f*; Kaution *f*; *admit to ~* ⚖ gegen Bürgschaft freilassen; *be od. go od. stand ~ for* bürgen für *j.*; **2.** bürgen für; *~ out j.* freibürgen; mit dem Fallschirm abspringen.

bail[2] ⚓ [~] ausschöpfen.

bail[3] [~] *Kricket*: Querholz *n*.

bail[4] [~] Henkel *m e-s Eimers etc.*

bail·iff [ˈbeilif] Gerichtsdiener *m*; (Guts)Verwalter *m*; Amtmann *m*.

bail·ment ⚖ [ˈbeilmənt] (vertragliche) Hinterlegung *f einer beweglichen Sache*.

bail·or ⚖ [ˈbeilə] Deponent *m*, Hinterleger *m*.

bairn *schott.* [bɛən] Kind *n*.

bait [beit] **1.** Köder *m*; *fig.* Lockung *f*, Reiz *m*; Rast *f*; *take the ~* (*a. fig.*) anbeißen; **2.** *v/t.* mit e-m Köder versehen; *Pferde unterwegs* füttern; *hunt.* hetzen; *fig.* quälen; reizen; *v/i.* rasten, einkehren.

baize [beiz] (grüner) Fries *m*.

bake [beik] **1.** backen; braten; *Ziegel* brennen; (aus)dörren; *~d potatoes pl.* Folien-, Ofenkartoffeln *f/pl.*; **2.** *Am.* gesellige Zusammenkunft *f*.

ba·ke·lite ⊕ [ˈbeikəlait] Bakelit *n*.

bak·er [ˈbeikə] Bäcker *m*; *~'s dozen* dreizehn; **ˈbak·er·y** Bäckerei *f*; **ˈbak·ing** *a. ~ hot* glühend heiß; **ˈbak·ing-pow·der** Backpulver *n*.

bak·sheesh [ˈbækʃiːʃ] Bakschisch *n* (*Trinkgeld im Orient*).

Ba·la·cla·va [bæləˈklɑːvə]: *~ helmet Hals u. Ohren bedeckende* Wollmütze *f*.

bal·a·lai·ka ♪ [bæləˈlaikə] Balalaika *f* (*dreieckige Gitarre*).

bal·ance [ˈbæləns] **1.** Waage *f*; Gleich-, Übergewicht *n* (*a. fig.*); Ausgeglichenheit *f*, Harmonie *f*; ✝ Bilanz *f*, Saldo *m*, Überschuß *m*; Restbetrag *m*; F Rest *m*, Überbleibsel *n*; *a. ~ wheel* Unruhe *f der Uhr*; *be od. hang in the ~* in der Schwebe sein; *keep* (*lose*) *one's ~* das Gleichgewicht halten (verlieren); *fig.* ruhig bleiben (nervös werden); *throw s.o. off his ~ fig.* j. aus der Fassung bringen; *turn the ~* den Ausschlag geben; *~ of payments* Zahlungsbilanz *f*; *~ of power pol.* Kräftegleichgewicht *n*; *~ of trade* (Außen)Handelsbilanz *f*; *s. strike 2*; **2.** *v/t.* (ab-, er)wägen; im Gleichgewicht halten; ins Gleichgewicht bringen, ausgleichen; ✝ bilanzieren, ausgleichen; saldieren, abschließen; *v/i.* balancieren; sich ausgleichen; **ˈ~-sheet** ✝ Bilanz *f*.

bal·co·ny [ˈbælkəni] Balkon *m* (*a. thea.*); Rang *m*.

bald [bɔːld] kahl; *fig.* nackt; dürftig.

bal·da·chin [ˈbɔːldəkin] Baldachin *m*.

bal·der·dash [ˈbɔːldədæʃ] Geschwätz *n*.

bald...: **ˈ~-head, ˈ~-pate** Kahlkopf *m*; **ˈ~-ˈhead·ed** kahlköpfig; *go ~ into* blindlings hineinrennen in (*acc.*); **ˈbald·ness** Kahlheit *f*.

bale[1] ✝ [beil] Ballen *m*.

bale[2] ⚓ [~] ausschöpfen.

bale·fire [ˈbeilfaiə] Signalfeuer *n*.

bale·ful □ [ˈbeilful] verderblich; unheilvoll.

balk [bɔːk] **1.** (Furchen)Rain *m*; Balken *m*; Hemmnis *n*; **2.** *v/t.* (ver-)hindern; enttäuschen; umgehen; verpassen; stutzig machen; *v/i.* stutzen, scheuen (*at* bei, vor *dat.*).

Bal·kan [ˈbɔːlkən] Balkan...; balkanisch.

ball[1] [bɔːl] **1.** Ball *m*; Kugel *f*; (Hand-, Fuß)Ballen *m*; Knäuel *m*, *n*; Kloß *m*; *Sport*: Wurf *m*; *Am. Baseball*: falscher Wurf *m*; *start* (*keep*) *the ~ rolling* die Sache *od.*

das Gespräch in Gang bringen (halten); *have the ~ at one's feet* die beste Gelegenheit haben; *the ~ is with you* du bist dran; *play ~ Am.* F mitmachen; *be on the ~* auf Draht sein; **2.** (sich) (zs.-)ballen; *~ed up Am. sl.* durcheinander.

ball² [~] Ball *m*, Tanzgesellschaft *f*; *open the ~ fig.* den Reigen eröffnen; *have a ~ fig.* sich köstlich amüsieren.

bal·lad ['bæləd] Ballade *f*; **'~-mon·ger** Bänkelsänger *m*.

ball-and-sock·et ['bɔːlən'sɔkit]: *~ joint* ⊕ Kugelgelenk *n*.

bal·last ['bæləst] **1.** ⚓ Ballast *m* (*a. fig.*); 🚂 Schotter *m*, Bettung *f*; *mental ~* innerer Halt *m*; **2.** mit Ballast beladen; 🚂 beschottern, betten.

ball...: '~-'bear·ing(s *pl.*) ⊕ Kugellager *n*; **'~-boy** *Tennis*: Balljunge *m*; **'~-car·tridge** scharfe Patrone *f*.

bal·let ['bælei] Ballett *n*.

bal·lis·tics [bə'listiks] *mst sg.* Ballistik *f*.

bal·loon [bə'luːn] **1.** Ballon *m*; *~ barrage* Ballonsperre *f*; *~ tire mot.* Ballonreifen *m*; **2.** im Ballon aufsteigen; sich bauschen; *sl. Ball* hoch in die Luft schießen; **bal'loon·ist** Ballonfahrer *m*.

bal·lot ['bælət] **1.** Wahlkugel *f*, -zettel *m*; (geheime) Wahl *f*; **2.** (geheim) abstimmen; *~ for* losen um; **'~-box** Wahlurne *f*.

ball...: ~(-point) pen Kugelschreiber *m*; **'~-room** Ballsaal *m*; *~ dancing* Gesellschaftstanz *m*.

balls V [bɔːlz] *pl.* Eier *n/pl.* (*Hoden*).

bal·ly·hoo F [bæli'huː] **1.** Tamtam *n*, aufdringliche Reklame *f*; **2.** marktschreierisch anpreisen.

bal·ly·rag F ['bæliræg] aufziehen; tyrannisieren.

balm [bɑːm] Balsam *m*; *fig.* Trost *m*.

balm·y □ ['bɑːmi] balsamisch (*a. fig.*); mild.

ba·lo·ney *Am. sl.* [bə'ləuni] Quatsch *m*.

bal·sam ['bɔːlsəm] Balsam *m*; **bal·sam·ic** [~'sæmik] (*~ally*) balsamisch.

Bal·tic ['bɔːltik] **1.** baltisch; *~ Sea* = **2.** Ostsee *f*.

bal·us·ter ['bæləstə] Geländersäule *f*.

bal·us·trade [bæləs'treid] Balustrade *f*, Brüstung *f*; Geländer *n*.

bam·boo [bæm'buː] Bambus *m*.

bam·boo·zle F [bæm'buːzl] beschwindeln (*into ger.* zu *inf.*; *out of* um).

ban ['bæn] **1.** Bann *m*; Ächtung *f*, Acht *f*; (amtliches) Verbot *n*; **2.** verbieten; *~ s.o. from speaking* j-m verbieten zu sprechen.

ba·nal [bə'nɑːl] banal, abgedroschen.

ba·nan·a [bə'nɑːnə] ♆ Banane *f*; *~ split Am.* Eisbecher *m* mit Banane; **ba'na·nas** *sl.* bescheuert (*verrückt*).

band [bænd] **1.** Band *n*; ⊕ Treibriemen *m*; Streifen *m*; Leiste *f*; Bande *f*; Trupp *m*; Gruppe *f*, Schar *f*; ♪ (Musik)Kapelle *f*, Band *f*; **2.** zs.-binden; *~ together* sich zs.-tun, *b.s.* sich zs.-rotten.

band·age ['bændidʒ] **1.** Bandage *f*; Binde *f*; Verband *m*; *first-aid ~* Notverband *m*; **2.** bandagieren; verbinden.

band-aid *Am.* ['bændeid] Heftpflaster *n*.

ban·dan·na [bæn'dɑːnə] buntes Halstuch *n*.

band·box ['bændbɔks] Hutschachtel *f*; *as if one came out of a ~* wie aus dem Ei geschält.

ban·dit ['bændit] Bandit *m*; **'ban·dit·ry** Banditentum *n*.

band-mas·ter ['bændmɑːstə] Kapellmeister *m*.

ban·do·leer [bændəu'liə] Patronengurt *m*.

bands·man ['bændzmən] Orchestermitglied *n*, Musiker *m*; **'band·stand** Musikpavillon *m*; **band wag·on** *Am.* Wagen *m* mit Musikkapelle; *jump on the ~ fig.* sich der erfolgversprechenden Sache anschließen.

ban·dy ['bændi] **1.** *Ball etc.* hin und her werfen; *Worte* wechseln, *Blicke, Schläge etc.* tauschen; **2.** krumm, gekrümmt; **3.** Ochsenkarren *m*; **'~-leg·ged** O-beinig.

bane [bein] Ruin *m*; *the ~ of his life* der Fluch s-s Lebens; **bane·ful** □ ['beinful] verderblich.

bang [bæŋ] **1.** bum(s)!, peng!; **2.** gerade(swegs), genau; **3.** Knall *m*; *go over with a ~ Am.* F ein Bombenerfolg sein; **4.** dröhnend schlagen; knallen; F hauen; *Tür* zuschlagen; F knallen mit *et.*; *sl. Preise* drücken; **'bang·er** Knallkörper *m*; F Klapperkiste *f*; F (Brat)Würstchen *n*; *~s pl. and mash* Würstchen *n/pl.* mit Kartoffelbrei.

ban·gle ['bæŋgl] Arm-, Fußring *m.*
bang-on F [bæŋ'ɔn] ganz genau (richtig).
bangs *Am.* [bæŋz] *pl.* Ponyfrisur *f.*
bang-up *Am. sl.* ['bæŋʌp] Klasse..., prima.
ban·ish ['bæniʃ] verbannen; '**ban·ish·ment** Verbannung *f.*
ban·is·ter ['bænistə] Geländersäule *f*; '**ban·is·ters** *pl.* Treppengeländer *n.*
ban·jo ♪ ['bændʒəu] Banjo *n.*
bank [bæŋk] **1.** Damm *m*, Ufer *n*; Böschung *f*; *Sand-, Wolken- etc.* Bank *f*; ✝ Bank(haus *n*) *f*; Spielbank *f*; ~ *of deposit* Depositenbank *f*; ~ *of issue* Notenbank *f*; **2.** *v/t.* eindämmen; ✝ *Geld* auf die Bank legen; ✈ in die Kurve bringen; *v/i.* Bankgeschäfte machen; ein Bankkonto haben (*with* bei); ✈ in die Kurve gehen, in der Kurve liegen; ~ *on* sich verlassen auf (*acc.*); ~ *up* (sich) aufhäufen; '**bank·a·ble** bankfähig; '**bank-ac·count** Bankkonto *n*; '**bank-bill** Bankwechsel *m*; *Am. s. bank-note*; '**bank·er** Bankier *m*; *Roulette etc.*: Bankhalter *m*; **bank hol·i·day** gesetzlicher Feiertag *m*; '**bank·ing 1.** Bankgeschäft *n*; Bankwesen *n*; ✈ Schräglage *f*; **2.** Bank...; **bank·ing charg·es** *pl.* Bankgebühren *f/pl.*; '**bank·ing-house** Bankhaus *n*; '**bank-note** Banknote *f*, Geldschein *m*; Kassenschein *m*; '**bank-rate** Diskontsatz *m*; **bank·rupt** ['~rʌpt] **1.** Bankrotteur *m*; ~'*s estate* Konkursmasse *f*; **2.** bankrott; *go* ~ Bankrott machen; ~ *in od. of e-r Eigenschaft* bar; **3.** Bankrott machen; **bank·rupt·cy** ['~rəptsi] Bankrott *m*, Konkurs *m*; *declaration of* ~ Bankrotterklärung *f*; ~ *petition* Konkursantrag *m.*
ban·ner ['bænə] **1.** Banner *n*; Fahne *f*; Transparent *n bei politischen Umzügen*; **2.** *Am. in Zssgn* Haupt..., führend.
ban·nock *schott.* ['bænək] Haferbrot *n.*
banns [bænz] *pl.* Aufgebot *n* (*vor der Hochzeit*); *put up the* ~, *publish the* ~ *j-n* aufbieten.
ban·quet ['bæŋkwit] **1.** Bankett *n*, Festmahl *n*, -essen *n*; **2.** festlich bewirten; tafeln; ~*ing hall* Bankettsaal *m*; '**ban·quet·er** Bankettteilnehmer *m.*
ban·shee *schott., ir.* [bæn'ʃi:] Todesfee *f.*
ban·tam ['bæntəm] Zwerghuhn *n*; *fig.* Zwerg *m*; ~ *weight Sport*: Bantamgewicht *n.*
ban·ter ['bæntə] **1.** Neckerei *f*, Hänselei *f*; **2.** necken, hänseln; '**ban·ter·er** Spötter(in), Spaßvogel *m.*
bap·tism ['bæptizəm] Taufe *f*; ~ *of fire* Feuertaufe *f*; **bap·tis·mal** [~'tizməl] Tauf...
bap·tist ['bæptist] Täufer *m*; '**bap·tis·ter·y** Taufkapelle *f*; **bap·tize** [~'taiz] taufen (*a. fig.*).
bar [bɑ:] **1.** Stange *f*; Stab *m*; *metall.* Barren *m*; Riegel *m*; Tafel *f Schokolade*; Schranke *f*, Barriere *f*; Sandbank *f*; *fig.* Hindernis *n*; Streifen *m*, Band *n*; ⚔ Spange *f*; ♪ Takt (-strich) *m*; (Gerichts)Schranke *f*; *fig.* Urteil *n*; Anwaltschaft *f*; Bar *f im Hotel etc.*; *horizontal* ~ Reck *n*; *parallel* ~*s pl.* Barren *m*; *be called to the* ~ ⚖ als Anwalt zugelassen werden; *prisoner at the* ~ Untersuchungsgefangene *m*, *f*; *stand at the* ~ vor Gericht stehen; *behind prison* ~*s* hinter Gittern; **2.** verriegeln; (ver-, ab)sperren; verwehren; einsperren; aufhalten; (ver-) hindern (*from* an *dat.*); ausnehmen, absehen von; ~ *one* außer einem; ~ *out* aussperren.
barb [bɑ:b] *zo.* Bart(faden) *m*; Widerhaken *m*; Fahne *f der Feder*; **barbed** mit Widerhaken versehen; ~ *wire* Stacheldraht *m.*
bar·bar·i·an [bɑ:'bɛəriən] **1.** fremd; barbarisch; grausam; **2.** Barbar *m*; **bar·bar·ic** [~'bærik] (~*ally*) barbarisch; **bar·ba·rism** ['~bərizəm] Barbarismus *m*, Sprachwidrigkeit *f*; Unkultur *f*, Barbarei *f*; **bar·bar·i·ty** [~'bæriti] Barbarei *f*, Unmenschlichkeit *f*; **bar·ba·rize** ['~bəraiz] verrohen lassen; verderben; '**bar·ba·rous** □ barbarisch, unmenschlich, roh; grausam.
bar·be·cue ['bɑ:bikju:] **1.** Grill *m*; Grillparty *f*; Grillfleisch *n*; **2.** grillen, am Spieß braten.
bar·bel *ichth.* ['bɑ:bəl] Barbe *f.*
bar-bell ['bɑ:bel] *Sport*: Kugelhantel *f.*
bar·ber ['bɑ:bə] Barbier *m*; (Herren)Friseur *m*; ~ *shop* Friseurgeschäft *n.*
bar·bi·tu·rate [bɑ:'bitjuərət] Barbi-

turat *n*, Schlaf- *od.* Beruhigungsmittel *n.*

bard [bɑːd] Barde *m*, Sänger *m.*

bare [bɛə] **1.** nackt, bloß; kahl; bar, leer; arm, entblößt (*of* von); *the* ~ *idea* der bloße Gedanke; **2.** entblößen, zeigen; '~**-back**(**ed**) ungesattelt; '~**·faced** □ frech, schamlos; '~**·faced·ness** Frechheit *f*, Schamlosigkeit *f*; '~**·foot** barfuß; '~'**foot·ed** barfüßig; barfuß; '~-'**head·ed** barhäuptig; '**bare·ly** kaum, gerade, knapp; '**bare·ness** Nacktheit *f*, Blöße *f*; Dürftigkeit *f.*

bar·gain ['bɑːgin] **1.** Geschäft *n*; Handel *m*, Kauf *m* (*a. gekaufte Sache*); Vertrag *m*, Abschluß *m*; vorteilhafter Kauf *m*, Gelegenheitskauf *m*; ~ *price* Spottpreis *m*; *a* (*dead*) ~ spottbillig; *it's a* ~! F abgemacht!; *into the* ~ noch dazu, obendrein; *make od. strike a* ~ handelseinig werden, e-n Handel abschließen; *drive a hard* ~ hart feilschen; **2.** handeln, feilschen (*about* um), übereinkommen (*for* über *acc.*; *that* daß); ~ *for* rechnen mit, gefaßt sein auf (*acc.*); erwarten; ~ **basement** Sonderangebotsabteilung *f* im Tiefgeschoß *e-s Kaufhauses*; '**bar·gain·er** Handelnde *m*, *f*; **bar·gain sale** Ausverkauf *m.*

barge [bɑːdʒ] **1.** Flußboot *n*, Lastkahn *m*; ⚓ Barkasse *f*; Hausboot *n*; **2.** F taumeln, torkeln; ~ *in* hereinplatzen; *fig.* sich *auf unwirsche Art* einmischen; **bar'gee, barge·man** ['~mən] Kahnführer *m.*

bar-i·ron ['bɑːaiən] Stabeisen *n.*

bar·i·tone ♪ ['bæritəun] Bariton *m.*

bar·i·um ⚗ ['bɛəriəm] Barium *n.*

bark[1] [bɑːk] **1.** Borke *f*, Rinde *f*; ⊕ Lohe *f*; **2.** abrinden; *Haut* abschürfen.

bark[2] [~] **1.** bellen, kläffen (*a. fig.*); böllern (*Schußwaffe*); ~ *at* anbellen; *be* ~*ing up the wrong tree* F auf dem Holzweg sein; 2. Bellen *n* (F *Husten*) *etc.*

bark[3] [~] ⚓ = *barque*; *poet.* Barke *f.*

bar-keep·er ['bɑːkiːpə] Barbesitzer *m*; Barkellner *m.*

bark·er ['bɑːkə] Kläffer *m* (*a. fig.*); Kundenfänger *m.*

bar·ley ['bɑːli] Gerste *f*; Graupe *f.*

barm [bɑːm] Bärme *f*, Hefe *f.*

bar·maid ['bɑːmeid] Kellnerin *f*, Bardame *f.*

bar·man ['bɑːmən] *s. bartender.*

barm·y ['bɑːmi] hefig; P verdreht.

barn [bɑːn] Scheune *f*; *bsd. Am.* (Vieh)Stall *m.*

bar·na·cle[1] ['bɑːnəkl] *orn.* Bernikelgans *f*; *zo.* Entenmuschel *f*; *fig.* Klette *f* (*nicht abzuschüttelnder Mensch*).

bar·na·cle[2] [~] *vet.* Bremse *f*; ~*s pl.* F Brille *f*, Kneifer *m.*

barn·storm *Am. pol.* ['bɑːnstɔːm] herumreisen u. (Wahl)Reden halten; '**barn·yard** Hof *m zwischen Bauernhaus u. Scheune.*

ba·rom·e·ter [bə'rɔmitə] Barometer *n*; **bar·o·met·ric, bar·o·met·ri·cal** □ [bærəu'metrik(əl)] barometrisch; Barometer...

bar·on ['bærən] Baron *m*, Freiherr *m*; *coal* ~ Kohlenbaron *m*; '**bar·on·ess** Baronin *f*; **bar·on·et** ['~nit] Baronet *m*; **bar·on·et·cy** ['~nitsi] Baronetswürde *f*; **ba·ro·ni·al** [bə'rəunjəl] freiherrlich; **bar·o·ny** ['bærəni] Baronie *f*; Baronswürde *f.*

ba·roque [bə'rɔk] **1.** barock; **2.** Barock *n*, *m.*

barque ⚓ [bɑːk] Bark *f.*

bar·rack ['bærək] **1.** *mst* ~*s pl.* Kaserne *f*; Mietskaserne *f*; **2.** *sl.* anpöbeln.

bar·rage ['bærɑːʒ] Staudamm *m*, Talsperre *f*; *weitS.* Sperre *f*; ⚔ Sperrfeuer *n*; ~ *balloon* Sperrballon *m*; *creeping* ~ ⚔ Feuerwalze *f.*

bar·rel ['bærəl] **1.** Faß *n*, Tonne *f*; (Gewehr)Lauf *m*; (Geschütz)Rohr *n*; ⊕ Trommel *f*; Walze *f*; Rumpf *m e-s Pferdes etc.*; **2.** in Fässer füllen; '**bar·relled** ...läufig (*Gewehr*); '**bar·rel-or·gan** ♪ Drehorgel *f.*

bar·ren □ ['bærən] unfruchtbar; dürr, trocken (*alle a. fig.*); † tot (*Kapital*); '**bar·ren·ness** Unfruchtbarkeit *f.*

bar·ri·cade [bæri'keid] **1.** Barrikade *f*; **2.** verbarrikadieren, verrammeln; sperren.

bar·ri·er ['bæriə] Schranke *f* (*a. fig.*); Barriere *f*, Sperre *f*; Schlagbaum *m*; Hindernis *n*; ~ *cream* schmutzabweisende Hautcreme *f.*

bar·ring F ['bɑːriŋ] ausgenommen, abgesehen von; ~ *a miracle* wenn kein Wunder geschieht.

bar·ris·ter ['bæristə] *a.* ~*-at-law*

(plädierender) Rechtsanwalt *m an den höheren Gerichtshöfen*, Barrister *m*.
bar·row[1] ['bærəu] *s. hand-~, wheel-~*; **~-man** ['~mən] Straßenhändler *m*.
bar·row[2] [~] Hügelgrab *n*, Tumulus *m*.
bar·tend·er ['bɑːtendə] Büfettier *m*, Schankkellner *m*.
bar·ter ['bɑːtə] **1.** Tausch(handel) *m*; ~ *shop* Tauschladen *m*; **2.** tauschen (*for* gegen); Tauschhandel treiben; *b.s.* (ver)schachern; ~ *away a. fig.* verschachern.
bar·y·tone ♪ ['bæritəun] Bariton *m*.
ba·salt ['bæsɔːlt] Basalt *m*; **ba·sal·tic** [bə'sɔːltik] basaltisch; Basalt...
base[1] □ [beis] gemein, niedrig; unedel, unecht, falsch (*Metall etc.*).
base[2] [~] **1.** Basis *f*, Grundfläche *f*, -linie *f*, -lage *f*; Fundament *n*; Fuß *m*, Sockel *m*; ⚗ Base *f*; Stützpunkt *m*; *Sport*: Mal *n*; **2.** *fig.* gründen, stützen, aufbauen (*on, upon* auf *acc.*); ✈ landen; ~ *o.s. on* sich stützen auf (*acc.*); *be ~d (up)on* beruhen auf (*dat.*), sich stützen auf (*acc.*).
base...: '**~·ball** Baseball *m*; '**~-board** Fuß-, Scheuerleiste *f*; '**~-born** von niedriger Abkunft; unehelich; '**~·less** grundlos; '**~-line** Grundlinie *f*; *surv.* Standlinie *f*; '**base·ment** Fundament *n*; Kellergeschoß *n*.
base·ness ['beisnis] Gemeinheit *f etc.* (*s. base*[1]).
bash F [bæʃ] **1.** heftig schlagen; **2.** heftiger Schlag *m*; *have a ~ at s.th.* et. mal probieren.
bash·ful □ ['bæʃful] verschämt, schüchtern.
bas·ic ['beisik] (*~ally*) grundlegend, Grund...; ⚗ basisch; ♀ *English* Basic English *n* (*vereinfachtes Englisch*); ~ *iron* Thomaseisen *n*; ~ *slag* Thomasschlacke *f*; '**bas·ics** *pl. das* Wesentliche.
basil ♀ ['bæzl] Basilienkraut *n*.
ba·sil·i·ca ⛪ [bə'zilikə] Basilika *f*.
bas·i·lisk ['bæzilisk] **1.** Basilisk *m*; **2.** Basilisken...
ba·sin ['beisn] *allg.* Becken *n*; *engS.* Schüssel *f*, Schale *f*; Tal-, Wasser-, Hafenbecken *n*; Innenhafen *m*.
ba·sis ['beisis], *pl.* **ba·ses** ['~siːz] Basis *f*, Grundlage *f*; ⚔, ⚓ Stützpunkt *m*; *take as ~* zugrunde legen.
bask [bɑːsk] sich sonnen (*a. fig.*); sich wärmen.
bas·ket ['bɑːskit] Korb *m*; '**~-ball** Korbball(spiel *n*) *m*; ~ **din·ner**, ~ **sup·per** *Am.* Picknick *n*; '**bas·ket-work** Korbgeflecht *n*.
bass[1] ♪ [beis] Baß *m*.
bass[2] *ichth.* [bæs] Barsch *m*.
bass[3] [~] Bast *m*; Bastmatte *f*.
bas·si·net [bæsi'net] Korbwiege *f*, Stubenwagen *m*.
bas·soon ♪ [bə'suːn, ♪ bə'zuːn] Fagott *n*.
bast [bæst] Bast *m*.
bas·tard ['bæstəd] **1.** □ unehelich; unecht; Bastard...; **2.** Bastard *m*; '**bas·tar·dy** uneheliche Geburt *f*.
baste[1] [beist] *Braten* (mit Fett) begießen; durchprügeln.
baste[2] [~] lose nähen, (an)heften.
bas·ti·na·do [bæsti'neidəu] **1.** Bastonade *f*; **2.** *j-m* die Bastonade geben.
bas·tion ⚔ ['bæstiən] Bastion *f*.
bat[1] [bæt] Fledermaus *f*; *as blind as a ~* stockblind.
bat[2] [~] *Sport*: **1.** Schlagholz *n*, Schläger *m*; Schläger *m* (*Spieler*); *off one's own ~ fig.* selbständig; **2.** (mit dem Schlagholz) schlagen; am Schlagen sein; ~ *for s.o.* für j-n eintreten.
batch [bætʃ] Schub *m Brote*; Stoß *m Briefe etc.*
bate [beit] verringern; *Preis* heruntersetzen; *with ~d breath* mit angehaltenem Atem, gespannt.
Bath[1] [bɑːθ]: ~ *brick* Metallputzstein *m*; ~ *chair* Rollstuhl *m*.
bath[2] [~] **1.** *pl.* **baths** [bɑːðz] Bad *n* (*Wannen-, Licht-, Sonnenbad; Badewasser, -wanne, -zimmer, -ort*); ~ *foam* Schaumbad *n*; **2.** *Kind* baden; ein Bad nehmen.
bathe [beið] **1.** baden; **2.** Bad *n im Freien*.
bath·house ['bɑːθhaus] Badeanstalt *f*; Umkleidekabinen *f/pl.*
bath·ing ['beiðiŋ] Baden *n*, Bad *n*; *attr.* Bade...; '**~-cap** Badekappe *f*; '**~-cos·tume**, '**~-dress** Badeanzug *m*; '**~-hut** Strandkorb *m*; '**~-ma'chine** Badekarren *m*; '**~-suit** Badeanzug *m*; '**~-trunks** *pl.* Badehose *f*.
ba·thos *rhet.* ['beiθɔs] Abgleiten *n* vom Erhabenen ins Niedrige; Niedergang *m*; Gemeinplatz *m*.

bath...: **'~-robe** *Am.* Bademantel *m*; **'~-room** Badezimmer *n*; Toilette *f*; **'~-sheet** Badelaken *n*; **'~-tow·el** Badetuch *n*; **'~-tub** Badewanne *f*.
ba·tik ['bætik] Batik(druck) *m*.
ba·tiste [bæ'ti:st] Batist *m*.
bat·man ['bætmən] Offiziersbursche *m*.
ba·ton ['bætən] *Amts-, Kommando-* Stab *m*; ♪ Taktstock *m*, Stab *m*; (Polizei)Knüppel *m*.
bats·man ['bætsmən] *Kricket etc.*: Schläger *m*.
bat·tal·ion [bə'tæljən] Bataillon *n*.
bat·ten ['bætn] **1.** Latte *f*; Leiste *f*; **2.** (mit Latten) befestigen; sich mästen (*on, upon* mit); ~ *down the hatches* ⚓ die Luken schalken.
bat·ter ['bætə] **1.** *Kricket*: Schläger *m*; *Küche*: Rührteig *m*; **2.** heftig schlagen, zerschlagen; ein-, ver-, zerbeulen; arg mitnehmen; ⚔ bombardieren; *fig.* herunter-, verreißen (*Kritiker etc.*); ~ *down od. in Tür* einschlagen; **'bat·tered** zerschlagen, zertrümmert; abgenutzt; mißhandelt; ~ *babies* mißhandelte Kinder; ~ *wives* mißhandelte (Ehe-) Frauen; **'bat·ter·ing** Belagerungs..., Sturm...; ~ *ram* Sturmbock *m*; **'bat·ter·y** ⚔ Batterie *f*; ⚓ Geschützgruppe *f*; ⚡ Batterie *f*, Akku *m*; *fig.* Satz *m*; ⚖ Realinjurien *f/pl.*; *assault and* ~ tätlicher Angriff *m*; ~-*operated* mit Batteriebetrieb.
bat·tle ['bætl] **1.** Schlacht *f*, Gefecht *n* (*of* bei); ~ *royal* Massenschlägerei *f*; **2.** streiten (*for* um), kämpfen (*against* gegen, *with* mit); **'~-axe** Streitaxt *f*; F Xanthippe *f*.
bat·tle·dore ['bætldɔ:] Federballschläger *m*.
bat·tle-field ['bætlfi:ld], **'bat·tle--ground** Schlachtfeld *n*.
bat·tle·ment ['bætlmənt] Brustwehr *f*; ~*s pl.* Zinnen *f/pl*.
bat·tle-ship ⚔ ['bætlʃip] Schlachtschiff *n*.
bat·tue [bæ'tu:] Treibjagd *f*.
bat·ty *sl.* ['bæti] nicht ganz bei Trost.
bau·ble ['bɔ:bl] Spielzeug *n*, Tand *m*.
baulk [bɔ:k] = *balk*.
baux·ite *min.* ['bɔ:ksait] Bauxit *m*.
Ba·var·i·an [bə'veəriən] **1.** bay(e)risch; **2.** Bayer(in).
baw·bee *schott.* [bɔ:'bi:] = *halfpenny*.
bawd [bɔ:d] Kupplerin *f*; **'bawd·y** unzüchtig, obszön.
bawl [bɔ:l] brüllen; johlen, grölen; *j.* anschreien; ~ *out* auf-, los-, *et.* herausbrüllen; *Am. sl. j.* laut herunterputzen, anschnauzen.
bay[1] [bei] **1.** braun (*Pferd*); **2.** Braune *m, f*.
bay[2] [~] Bai *f*, Bucht *f*; *geol.* Kar *n*; ~ *salt* Seesalz *n*.
bay[3] [~] ⚠ Joch *n*, Fach *n*; Erker *m*; Abteilung *f*; Seitenbahnsteig *m*; *bomb* ~ ✈ Bombenschacht *m*; *sick-*~ ⚓ Schiffslazarett *n*.
bay[4] ⚘ [~] Lorbeer *m*.
bay[5] [~] **1.** bellen, anschlagen (*Hund*); ~ *at* anbellen; **2.** *stand at* ~ sich verzweifelt wehren; *bring to* ~, *keep od. hold at* ~ *Wild* stellen; *turn to* ~ sich stellen (*a. fig.*).
bay·o·net ⚔ ['beiənit] **1.** Bajonett *n*; **2.** mit dem Bajonett niederstoßen; **'~-catch** ⊕ Bajonettverschluß *m*.
bay·ou *Am. geogr.* ['baiu:] sumpfiger Nebenarm *m, bsd. e-s Flusses*.
bay-win·dow ['bei'windəu] Erkerfenster *n*; *Am. sl.* Vorbau *m* (*Bauch*).
ba·zaar [bə'zɑ:] Basar *m*.
ba·zoo·ka ⚔ [bə'zu:kə] Panzerfaust *f*.
be [bi:; bi] (*irr.*) a) sein; *there is od. are* es gibt; *here's to you(r health)!* auf Ihr Wohl!; *here you are again!* da haben wir's wieder!; *as it were* sozusagen; ~ *about* beschäftigt sein mit; im Begriff sein; ~ *after s.o.* hinter j-m her sein, j. verfolgen; ~ *at s.th.* et. vorhaben; ~ *off* fort sein; aus sein; weggehen, aufbrechen; fortkommen; ausverkauft sein; ~ *off with you!* fort mit dir!; ~ *on at s.o.* auf j-m herumhacken; ~ *on to s.th.* et. spitzkriegen; b) *v/aux. mit p.pr. zum Ausdruck von Unvollständigkeit u. Fortdauer*: ~ *reading* beim Lesen sein, gerade lesen; c) *v/aux. mit inf. zum Ausdruck e-r Pflicht, Absicht, Möglichkeit*: *I am to inform you* ich soll Ihnen mitteilen; *it is (not) to be seen* es ist (nicht) zu sehen; *if he were to die* wenn er sterben sollte; d) *v/aux. mit p.p. zur Bildung des Passivs*: werden; *I am asked* ich werde gefragt.
beach [bi:tʃ] **1.** Strand *m*; **2.** ⚓ auf den Strand setzen *od.* ziehen; ~ **ball** Wasserball *m*; **'~·comb·er** lange Welle *f*; Strandgutjäger *m*; *fig.* Nichtstuer *m*;

'~·head ⚔ Brückenkopf *m*.
bea·con ['bi:kən] **1.** Feuerzeichen *n*, Signalfeuer *n*; Leuchtfeuer *n*, Leuchtturm *m*; ⚓ Bake *f*; Blinklicht *n an Zebrastreifen*; *fig.* Fanal *n*; **2.** mit Baken versehen; *fig. j.* führen.
bead [bi:d] **1.** *Glas-, Holz- etc.* Perle *f*; Tropfen *m*; *Visier*-Korn *n*; ~s *pl. a.* Rosenkranz *m*; **2.** *v/t.* mit Perlen besetzen; (wie Perlen) aufreihen; *v/i.* perlen; '**bead·ing** Perlstickerei *f*; △ Perlstab *m*.
bea·dle ['bi:dl] Kirchendiener *m*.
beads·man, beads·wom·an ['bi:dzmən, '~wumən] Armenhäusler(in).
bead·y ['bi:di] perlartig; perlend; klein u. rund (*Augen*).
bea·gle ['bi:gl] kleiner Spürhund *m*.
beak [bi:k] Schnabel *m*; Tülle *f*; **beaked** schnabelförmig; spitz.
beak·er ['bi:kə] Becher(glas *n*) *m*.
beam [bi:m] Balken *m*; Weberbaum *m*; Pflugbaum *m*; Waagebalken *m*; ⚓ Deck(s)balken *m*; *hunt.* Stange *f am Geweih*; (Licht-, Sonnen-) Strahl *m*; Glanz *m*; *Radio*: Leit-, Richtstrahl *m*; *be on (off)* ~ *fig. Person*: richtig- (daneben)liegen; **2.** (aus-) strahlen; '~-'**ends** *pl.*: *the ship is on her* ~ das Schiff hat starke Schlagseite; *on one's* ~ *fig.* (finanziell) am Ende.
bean [bi:n] Bohne *f*; *Am. sl.* Birne *f* (*Kopf*); *full of* ~*s* F lebensprühend; *give s.o.* ~*s sl.* j-m Saures geben (*j. strafen, schelten*); '~-**feast, bean·o** *sl.* ['bi:nəu] Freudenfest *n*.
bear[1] [bɛə] **1.** Bär *m* (*fig. Tölpel*); ⚚ *sl.* Baissier *m*; **2.** ⚚ auf Baisse spekulieren; die Kurse drücken.
bear[2] [~] (*irr.*) *v/t.* tragen; hervorbringen, gebären; *Schwert, Namen* führen; *Liebe etc.* hegen; ertragen, dulden, leiden; zulassen; ~ *away* davon-, wegtragen; ~ *down* überwältigen; ~ *out* unterstützen, bestätigen; ~ *up* stützen, ermutigen; *v/i.* tragen; fruchtbar *od.* trächtig sein; leiden, dulden; ⚓ (*mit adv.*) segeln; ~ *down upon* ⚓ zusteuern auf (*acc.*); ~ *to the right* sich rechts halten; ~ *up* standhalten, fest bleiben; ~ (*up*)*on* einwirken auf (*acc.*); ~ *with* ertragen, Nachsicht haben mit; *bring to* ~ zur Anwendung bringen, einwirken lassen, *Druck etc.* ausüben (*on, upon* auf *acc.*); **bear·a·ble** ['bɛərəbl] erträglich.
beard [biəd] **1.** Bart *m*; ⚘ Granne *f*; **2.** *j-m* entgegentreten, Trotz bieten; *j.* reizen; '**beard·ed** bärtig; '**beard·less** bartlos.
bear·er ['bɛərə] Träger(in); Überbringer(in); ⚚ Inhaber(in), Vorzeiger(in) *e-s Wechsels*.
bear·ing ['bɛəriŋ] Tragen *n*; Ertragen *n*; Haltung *f*; Benehmen *n*; Beziehung *f*, Bezug *m* (*on* auf *acc.*); Tragweite *f*; Richtung *f*; ⚓ Peilung *f*; ~*s pl.* Position *f*; ⊕ Lager *n*; Wappen *n*; *ball* ~*s pl.* ⊕ Kugellager *n*; *beyond all* ~ nicht zu ertragen; *in full* ~ gut tragend (*Baum*); *have no* ~ *on* nichts zu tun haben mit; *lose one's* ~*s* die Orientierung verlieren; *take one's* ~*s* sich orientieren.
bear·ish ['bɛəriʃ] bärenhaft; ⚚ Baisse...
bear·skin ['bɛəskin] Bärenfell(mütze *f*) *n*.
beast [bi:st] Vieh *n*, Tier *n*; *fig. a.* Bestie *f*, Biest *n*; **beast·li·ness** ['~linis] viehisches Wesen *n*; *fig.* Bestialität *f*, Brutalität *f*; '**beast·ly** viehisch, tierisch; bestialisch, brutal; F ekelhaft, scheußlich.
beat [bi:t] **1.** (*irr.*) *v/t. wiederholt* schlagen; gegen *od.* mit *et.* schlagen; *a.* ~ *out Metall* schlagen, hämmern, schmieden; prügeln; besiegen, *Am.* F *j-m* zuvorkommen; übertreffen; *Am.* F beschummeln, betrügen; erschöpfen; F zu schwer *od.* viel sein für; *Pfad* treten; *hunt. Wild* treiben; *Revier* absuchen; ~ *it! Am. sl.* hau ab!; ~ *the band Am.* F wichtig *od.* großartig sein; ~ *one's brains* sich den Kopf zerbrechen; ~ *a retreat* zum Rückzug blasen; den Rückzug antreten; ~ *time* ♪ den Takt schlagen; ~ *one's way* sich durchschlagen; ~ *down* niederschlagen; ⚚ drücken; ~ *up Eier etc.* schlagen; auftreiben; *v/i.* schlagen; ~ *about* (umher)suchen; ~ *about the bush* wie die Katze um den heißen Brei herumgehen; **2.** Schlag *m*; Trommel-, Takt-, Pulsschlag *m*; Runde *f od.* Revier *n e-s Schutzmanns etc.*; *Am.* sensationelle Erstmeldung *f e-r Zeitung*; *fig.* Sphäre *f*, Bereich *m*; *on the* ~ auf Streifendienst; = *beatnik*; **3.** F baff, verblüfft; *dead* ~ todmüde;

ˈ**beat·en** **1.** *p.p. von beat 1*; **2.** *adj.* (aus)getreten (*Weg*); ˈ**beat·er** Schläger *m*; Stößel *m*; Ramme *f*; *hunt.* Treiber *m*.
be·a·tif·ic [biəˈtifik] (glück)selig; seligmachend; ~ *vision* Gottesvision *f*.
be·at·i·fi·ca·tion *eccl.* [bi:ætifiˈkeiʃən] Seligsprechung *f*; **beˈat·i·fy** selig machen, beseligen; *eccl.* selig sprechen.
beat·ing [ˈbi:tiŋ] Schlagen *n*; Schläge *m/pl.*, Prügel *m/pl.*; *give s.o. a good* ~ j-m e-e Tracht Prügel geben.
be·at·i·tude [bi:ˈætitju:d] (Glück-) Seligkeit *f*.
beat·nik [ˈbi:tnik] Beatnik *m*, junger Antikonformist *m* und Bohemien *m*.
beau [bəu], *pl.* **beaux** [~z] Stutzer *m*; Anbeter *m*.
beau·teous *poet.* [ˈbju:tjəs] schön.
beau·ti·cian [bju:ˈtiʃən] Schönheitspfleger(in), Kosmetiker(in).
beau·ti·ful □ [ˈbju:təful] schön; *the* ~ *people pl. bsd. Am.* die Schickeria.
beau·ti·fy [ˈbju:tifai] verschönern.
beau·ty [ˈbju:ti] Schönheit *f* (*a. schöne Frau*); Prachtstück *n*; *Sleeping* ♀ Dornröschen *n*; ~ *parlo(u)r*, ~ *shop* Schönheitssalon *m*; ~ *sleep* Schlaf *m* vor Mitternacht; ~ *spot* Schönheitspflästerchen *n*; schöner Fleck *m Erde*.
bea·ver [ˈbi:və] Biber *m*; Biberpelz *m*; Biber-, Kastorhut *m*.
be·bop ♪ *Am.* [ˈbi:bɔp] Bebop *m*.
be·calm [biˈkɑ:m] beruhigen, stillen; *be* ~*ed* ⚓ in e-e Flaute geraten.
be·came [biˈkeim] *pret. von become.*
be·cause [biˈkɔz] weil, da; ~ *of* wegen.
beck [bek] Wink *m*.
beck·on [ˈbekən] (*j-m* zu)winken.
be·cloud [biˈklaud] umwölken.
be·come [biˈkʌm] (*irr.*) *v/i.* werden (*of* aus); *v/t.* anstehen, (ge)ziemen (*dat.*); sich schicken für; kleiden (*Hut etc.*); **beˈcom·ing** □ passend; schicklich; kleidsam.
bed [bed] **1.** Bett *n* (*a. e-s Flusses etc.*); Lager *n e-s Tieres*; ⚘ Beet *n*; ⊕ Bett(ung *f*) *n*, Unterlage *f*; Flöz *n*; *be brought to* ~ *of* niederkommen mit; ~ *and board* Tisch u. Bett *pl.* (*Ehe*); Unterkunft *f* u. Verpflegung *f*; *take to one's* ~ das Bett hüten; *as you make your* ~ *so you must lie on it* wie man sich bettet, so schläft man; ~ *and breakfast* Übernachtung *f* mit Frühstück; **2.** betten; *Pferd etc.* mit Streu versorgen; ⚘ ~ (*out* aus-) pflanzen.
be·daub [biˈdɔ:b] beschmieren.
be·dazzle [biˈdæzl] blenden; verblenden, -wirren.
bed...: ˈ~**·cham·ber** königliches Schlafgemach *n*; ˈ~**-clothes** *pl.* Bettzeug *n*.
bed·ding [ˈbediŋ] Bettzeug *n*; Streu *f*.
be·deck [biˈdek] zieren, schmücken.
be·dev·il [biˈdevl] be-, verhexen; verhunzen; quälen; **beˈdev·il·ment** Hexensabbat *m*.
be·dew [biˈdju:] betauen; *poet.* benetzen.
bed·fel·low [ˈbedfeləu] Schlafkamerad *m*.
be·dight † [biˈdait] schmücken, aufputzen.
be·dim [biˈdim] trüben.
be·diz·en [biˈdaizn] herausputzen.
bed·lam [ˈbedləm] Tollhaus *n*; **bed·lam·ite** [ˈ~mait] Tollhäusler (-in).
bed-lin·en [ˈbedlinin] Bettwäsche *f*.
Bed·ou·in [ˈbeduin] **1.** Beduine *m*; **2.** Beduinen...
bed-pan [ˈbedpæn] Stechbecken *n*, Bettschüssel *f*.
be·drag·gle [biˈdrægl] *Kleider etc.* beschmutzen; beschmuddeln.
bed...: ˈ~**·rid(·den)** bettlägerig; ˈ~**-ˈrock** *geol.* Grundgebirge *n*; *fig.* Grundlage *f*; ˈ~**·room** Schlafzimmer *n*; ˈ~**·side:** *at the* ~ am (Kranken)Bett; *good* ~ *manner* gute Art, mit Kranken umzugehen; ~ *lamp* Nachttischlampe *f*; ~ *rug* Bettvorleger *m*; ~ *table* Nachttisch *m*; ˈ~**-ˈsit·ter** F, ˈ~**-ˈsit·ting-room** Wohnschlafzimmer *n*; ˈ~**·sore** ⚕ wundgelegene Stelle *f*; ˈ~**·space** (An)Zahl *f* der Betten *in Klinik, Hotel etc.*; ˈ~**·spread** Tagesdecke *f*; ˈ~**-stead** Bettstelle *f*; ˈ~**·tick** Inlett *n*; ˈ~**·time** Schlafenszeit *f*; ~ *reading* Bettlektüre *f*; ~ *story* Gutenachtgeschichte *f*.
bee [bi:] Biene *f* (*a. fig.*); *Am.* nachbarliches Treffen *n*; Wettbewerb *m*; *have a* ~ *in one's bonnet* F eine fixe Idee haben.
beech ⚘ [bi:tʃ] Buche *f*; ˈ~**·nut** Buchecker *f*.
beef [bi:f] **1.** Rind-, Ochsenfleisch *n*; F Muskelkraft *f*; **2.** *Am.* F nörgeln, sich beklagen; ˈ~**·eat·er** Tower-

wächter *m*; **~·steak** ['bi:f'steik] Beefsteak *n*; '**~-'tea** klare Fleischbrühe *f*, Bouillon *f*; '**beef·y** fleischig; kräftig.

bee...: '**~·hive** Bienenkorb *m*, -stock *m*; '**~-keep·er** Bienenzüchter *m*; '**~-keep·ing** Bienenzucht *f*; '**~-line** kürzester Weg *m*; *make a ~ for* schnurstracks losgehen auf (*acc.*).

been [bi:n, bin] *p.p. von be.*

beer [biə] Bier *n*; *~ on tap* Faßbier *n*, Bier *n* vom Faß; *small ~* Dünnbier *n*; F Kleinigkeit *f*; *he thinks no small ~ of himself* er hält sich für wer weiß wen; *~* **can** Bierdose *f*; '**beer·y** F bierselig.

bees·wax ['bi:zwæks] **1.** Bienenwachs *n*; **2.** mit Bienenwachs einreiben *od.* polieren.

beet ⚘ [bi:t] Runkelrübe *f*, Bete *f*; *red ~* rote Rübe *f*; *white ~* Zuckerrübe *f*.

bee·tle[1] ['bi:tl] **1.** Ramme *f*; **2.** rammen, stampfen.

bee·tle[2] [~] Käfer *m*.

bee·tle[3] [~] **1.** überhängend; buschig (*Brauen*); **2.** *v/i.* überhängen.

beet·root ['bi:tru:t] Runkelrübe *f*.

beet-sug·ar ['bi:tʃugə] Rübenzucker *m*.

beeves [bi:vz] *pl. von beef.*

be·fall [bi'fɔ:l] (*irr. fall*) *v/t.* zustoßen, widerfahren (*dat.*); *v/i.* sich ereignen.

be·fit [bi'fit] sich schicken *od.* gehören für; passen (*dat.*); **be'fit·ting** passend, schicklich.

be·fog [bi'fɔg] umnebeln.

be·fool [bi'fu:l] betören.

be·fore [bi'fɔ:] **1.** *adv. Raum*: vorn; voran; *Zeit*: vorher, früher; schon (früher); **2.** *cj.* bevor, ehe, bis; **3.** *prp.* vor; *be ~ one's time* zu früh kommen; *be ~ s.o.* vor j-m liegen; *fig.* j-m vorliegen; *~ long* binnen kurzem, bald; *~ now* schon früher; *the day ~ yesterday* vorgestern; **be'fore·hand** vorher, zuvor; voraus; im voraus.

be·foul [bi'faul] besudeln.

be·friend [bi'frend] *j-m* behilflich sein; sich *j-s* annehmen.

beg [beg] *v/t. et.* erbetteln; erbitten (*of* von); betteln *od.* bitten um *et.*; *j.* bitten (*to do* zu tun); *v/i.* betteln; bitten (*for s.th.* um et.; *of s.o.* j.); betteln gehen; Männchen machen (*Hund*); *I ~ to inform you* ⚕ ich möchte Ihnen mitteilen; *go ~ging fig.* keinen Interessenten finden.

be·gan [bi'gæn] *pret. von begin.*

be·get [bi'get] (*irr.*) (er)zeugen; **be'get·ter** Erzeuger *m*.

beg·gar ['begə] **1.** Bettler(in); F Kerl *m*; **2.** Bettel...; **3.** zum Bettler machen; *fig.* übertreffen; *it ~s all description* es spottet jeder Beschreibung; '**beg·gar·ly** arm(selig); '**beg·gar·y** Bettelarmut *f*; *reduce to ~* an den Bettelstab bringen.

be·gin [bi'gin] (*irr.*) beginnen, anfangen (*at* bei; mit); *~ (up)on s.th.* et. vornehmen; *to ~ with* um damit zu beginnen, zunächst; **be'gin·ner** Anfänger(in); **be'gin·ning** Beginn *m*, Anfang *m*; *from the ~* von Anfang an.

be·gird [bi'gə:d] (*irr. gird*) umgürten; umschließen.

be·gone [bi'gɔn] fort!, pack dich!

be·go·ni·a ⚘ [bi'gəunjə] Begonie *f*.

be·got, be·got·ten [bi'gɔt(n)] *pret. u. p.p. von beget.*

be·grime [bi'graim] besudeln.

be·grudge [bi'grʌdʒ] *j-m et.* mißgönnen *od.* ungern geben.

be·guile [bi'gail] täuschen; betrügen (*of, out of* um); *Zeit* vertreiben, verkürzen; *~ into* verlocken zu.

be·gun [bi'gʌn] *p.p. von begin.*

be·half [bi'hɑ:f]: *on od. in ~ of* im Namen *od.* Auftrag von; um ... (*gen.*) willen; seitens; für.

be·have [bi'heiv] sich benehmen, auftreten; *~ o.s.* sich anständig betragen; **be'hav·io(u)r** [~jə] Benehmen *n*, Betragen *n*; Auftreten *n*; Verhalten *n* (*a. von Sachen*); *be on one's good od. best ~* sich zs.-nehmen; *put s.o. on his best ~* j-m einschärfen, sich gut zu benehmen; **be'hav·io(u)r·al** Verhaltens...; *~ psychology* Verhaltenspsychologie *f*; **be'hav·io(u)r·ism** *psych.* Behaviorismus *m*, Verhaltensforschung *f*.

be·head [bi'hed] enthaupten; **be'head·ing** Enthauptung *f*.

be·hest *poet.* [bi'hest] Geheiß *n*.

be·hind [bi'haind] **1.** *adv.* hinten; dahinter; hinterher; zurück; *be ~ with s.th.* mit et. im Rückstand sein; **2.** *prp.* hinter; *s. time*; **3.** F Hintern *m*; **be'hind·hand** zurück, im Rückstand.

be·hold [bi'həuld] **1.** (*irr. hold*) erblicken, anschauen; **2.** siehe (da)!;

be'hold·en verpflichtet, verbunden; **be'hold·er** Betrachter *m*, Zuschauer *m*.
be·hoof [bi'hu:f]: *to (for, on) (the)* ~ *of* in *j-s* Interesse, um *j-s* willen.
be·hoove *Am.* [bi'hu:v] = *behove*.
be·hove [bi'həuv]: *it* ~*s s.o. to inf.* es ist j-s Pflicht zu *inf.*
beige [beiʒ] **1.** Beige *f* (*Stoff*); **2.** beige(farben).
be·ing ['bi:iŋ] Sein *n*; Dasein *n*; Wesen *n*; *in* ~ lebend; wirklich (vorhanden); *come into* ~ entstehen.
be·la·bo(u)r [bi'leibə] verbleuen.
be·laid [bi'leid] *pret. u. p.p. von belay*.
be·lat·ed [bi'leitid] verspätet.
be·lay [bi'lei] **1.** (*irr.*) ⚓ belegen; festmachen; *mount.* sichern; **2.** *mount.* Sicherung *f*.
belch [beltʃ] **1.** rülpsen; ausspeien; **2.** Rülpsen *n*; Ausbruch *m*.
bel·dam *contp.* ['beldəm] alte Hexe *f*, Vettel *f*.
be·lea·guer [bi'li:gə] belagern.
bel·fry ['belfri] Glockenstuhl *m*; Glockenturm *m*.
Bel·gian ['beldʒən] **1.** belgisch; **2.** Belgier(in).
be·lie [bi'lai] Lügen strafen; *Versprechen* nicht halten.
be·lief [bi'li:f] Glaube *m* (*in* an *acc.*; *that* daß); *the* ♀ das Apostolische Glaubensbekenntnis; *past all* ~ unglaublich; *to the best of my* ~ nach bestem Wissen u. Gewissen.
be·liev·a·ble [bi'li:vəbl] glaubhaft.
be·lieve [bi'li:v] glauben (*in* an *acc.*); ~ *in j-m* vertrauen; an *j. od. et.* glauben; viel halten von; **be'liev·er** Gläubige *m, f*.
be·like † [bi'laik] vielleicht.
Be·li·sha bea·con [bə'li:ʃə'bi:kən] Blinklicht *n an Fußgängerüberwegen*.
be·lit·tle [bi'litl] *fig.* verkleinern.
bell[1] [bel] **1.** Glocke *f* (*a.* ⚘, ⚠), Klingel *f*, Schelle *f*; ♪ Schalltrichter *m einer Trompete*; Taucherglocke *f*; **2.** *v/t.* ~ *the cat* der Katze die Schelle umhängen, die Gefahr auf sich nehmen.
bell[2] [~] röhren (*Hirsch*).
bell·boy *Am.* ['belbɔi] Hotelpage *m*.
belle [bel] Schöne *f*, Schönheit *f*.
belles-let·tres ['bel'letr] *pl.* Belletristik *f*, schöne Literatur *f*.
bell...: '**~-flow·er** Glockenblume *f*; '**~-found·er** Glockengießer *m*; '**~-glass** Glasglocke *f*; '**~·hop** *Am. sl.* Hotelpage *m*.
bel·li·cose ['belikəus] kriegslustig.
bel·lied ['belid] bauchig.
bel·lig·er·ent [bi'lidʒərənt] **1.** kriegführend; **2.** kriegführendes Land *n*.
bel·low ['beləu] **1.** brüllen; **2.** Gebrüll *n*.
bel·lows ['beləuz] *pl.* (*a pair of* ~ ein) Blasebalg *m*; *phot.* Balgen *m*.
bell...: '**~-pull** Klingelzug *m*; '**~-push** Klingelknopf *m*; '**~-weth·er** Leithammel *m* (*a. fig.*).
bel·ly ['beli] **1.** Bauch *m*; Magen *m*; ~ *landing* ✈ Bauchlandung *f*; **2.** (sich) bauchen; (an)schwellen; ~ **but·ton** F (Bauch)Nabel *m*; '**~-flop** Bauchklatscher *m beim Schwimmen*;
bel·ly·ful F ['~ful]: *one's* ~ (mehr als) genug, die Nase voll.
be·long [bi'lɔŋ] (an)gehören; ~ *to* gehören *dat. od.* zu; sich gehören für; *j-m* gebühren; **be'long·ings** *pl.* Habseligkeiten *f/pl.*, Habe *f*; F Angehörigen *pl.*
be·lov·ed [bi'lʌvd] **1.** geliebt; **2.** [*mst* ~vid] Geliebte *m, f*.
be·low [bi'ləu] **1.** *adv.* unten; *poet.* hienieden; **2.** *prp.* unter(halb); ~ *me fig.* unter meiner Würde.
belt [belt] **1.** Gürtel *m*; Gurt *m*; ⚔ Koppel *n*; *fig.* Streifen *m*; Zone *f*, Bezirk *m*; ⊕ Treibriemen *m*; ⚓ Panzergürtel *m*; *hit below the* ~ unfair sein; **2.** umgürten; mit Streifen versehen; ~ *out Am.* F herausschmettern, loslegen (*singen*).
be·moan [bi'məun] betrauern, beklagen.
be·mused [bi'mju:zd] verwirrt; gedankenverloren.
bench [bentʃ] Bank *f*; Richterbank *f*; Gerichtshof *m*; Arbeitstisch *m*, Werkbank *f*; *s. treasury*; '**bench·er** Vorstandsmitglied *n e-r Rechtsanwaltsinnung*.
bend [bend] **1.** Krümmung *f*, Biegung *f*, Bogen *m*, Kurve *f*; ⚓ Seemannsknoten *m*; **2.** (*irr.*) (sich) biegen, (sich) krümmen; *den Bogen* spannen; *Augen etc.* lenken, *Geist etc.* richten (*to, on* auf *acc.*); (sich) beugen (*a. fig.*); sich neigen (*to* vor *dat.*); ⚓ *Segel* anschlagen; *s. bent*[1] *1.*
be·neath [bi'ni:θ] = *below*.
ben·e·dick ['benidik] junger Ehemann *m*; bekehrter Hagestolz *m*.
Ben·e·dic·tine [beni'diktin] Bene-

diktiner *m* (*Mönch*); [~ti:n] (*Likör*).
ben·e·dic·tion *eccl.* [beni'dikʃən] Segen *m*; Segnung *f*.
ben·e·fac·tion [beni'fækʃən] Wohltat *f*; ~*s pl.* Spenden *f/pl.*; **ben·e·fac·tor** ['~tə] Wohltäter *m*; **ben·e·fac·tress** ['~tris] Wohltäterin *f*.
ben·e·fice ['benifis] Pfründe *f*; **be·nef·i·cence** [bi'nefisəns] Wohltätigkeit *f*; **be'nef·i·cent** □ wohltätig.
ben·e·fi·cial □ [beni'fiʃəl] wohltuend; zuträglich, nützlich (*to dat.*); ⚖ nutznießend; ~ *interest* Nutzrecht *n*; **ben·e'fi·ci·ar·y** Nutznießer *m*; Empfänger *m*; Pfründner *m*.
ben·e·fit ['benifit] **1.** Wohltat *f*; Nutzen *m*, Vorteil *m*; Wohltätigkeitsveranstaltung *f*; (Wohlfahrts-) Unterstützung *f*; *for the* ~ *of* zum Besten, zugunsten (*gen.*); **2.** nützen; begünstigen; Nutzen ziehen (*by, from, of* von, aus, durch).
be·nev·o·lence [bi'nevələns] Wohlwollen *n*; Mildherzigkeit *f*; **be'nev·o·lent** □ wohlwollend; gütig, mildherzig; wohltätig; ~ *society* Wohltätigkeitsverein *m*.
Ben·gal [beŋ'gɔ:l] bengalisch; **Ben'gal·i** [~li] **1.** Bengale *m*, Bengalin *f*; Bengalisch *n*; **2.** bengalisch.
be·night·ed [bi'naitid] von der Nacht überfallen; *fig.* umnachtet, unwissend.
be·nign □ [bi'nain] freundlich, gütig; zuträglich; ⚕ gutartig; **be·nig·nant** □ [bi'nignənt] freundlich, gütig; zuträglich; **be'nig·ni·ty** Freundlichkeit *f*, Güte *f*, Milde *f*; Zuträglichkeit *f*.
bent[1] [bent] **1.** *pret. u. p.p. von bend 2*; ~ *on* versessen *od.* erpicht auf (*acc.*); **2.** Hang *m*; Neigung *f*; *to the top of one's* ~ nach Herzenslust.
bent[2] ⚘ [~] Straußgras *n*; Grasland *n*.
be·numb [bi'nʌm] erstarren; lähmen.
ben·zene ⚗ ['benzi:n] Benzol *n*.
ben·zine ⚗ ['benzi:n] Benzin *n*.
be·queath [bi'kwi:ð] vermachen.
be·quest [bi'kwest] Vermächtnis *n*.
be·rate [bi'reit] schelten.
be·reave [bi'ri:v] (*irr.*) berauben; *be* ~*d of* durch den Tod *j-s* beraubt sein; ~*d* hinterblieben; *bereft of hope* der Hoffnung beraubt; **be'reave·ment** *schmerzlicher* Verlust *m*; Trauerfall *m*.
be·reft [bi'reft] *pret. u. p.p. von bereave.*
be·ret ['berei] Baskenmütze *f*.
berg [bə:g] = *iceberg*.
Ber·lin [bə:'lin]: ~ *black* schwarzer Eisenlack *m*; ~ *wool* feine Strickwolle *f*.
ber·ry ['beri] Beere *f*.
berth [bə:θ] **1.** ⚓ Ankergrund *m*; (Schlaf)Koje *f*; *fig.* (gute) Stelle *f*; *give s.o. a wide* ~ e-n großen Bogen um j. machen; **2.** vor Anker legen; *j-m* e-e Koje anweisen; unterbringen.
ber·yl *min.* ['beril] Beryll *m*.
be·seech [bi'si:tʃ] (*irr.*) ersuchen; dringend bitten; anflehen; um *et.* bitten; **be'seech·ing** □ flehend; **be'seech·ing·ly** flehentlich.
be·seem [bi'si:m] sich ziemen für.
be·set [bi'set] (*irr. set*) umgeben; bedrängen; verfolgen; ~*ting sin* Gewohnheitssünde *f*.
be·side [bi'said] **1.** *s.* ~*s 1*; **2.** *prp.* neben (*a. fig.*), (dicht) bei; weitab von; verglichen mit; ~ *o.s.* außer sich (*with* vor *Freude etc.*); ~ *the purpose* unzweckmäßig; ~ *the question* nicht zur Sache gehörig; **be'sides** [~dz] **1.** *adv.* überdies, außerdem; **2.** *prp. fig.* neben, abgesehen von, außer.
be·siege [bi'si:dʒ] belagern; *fig.* bedrängen, bestürmen; **be'sieg·er** Belagerer *m*.
be·slav·er [bi'slævə] begeifern; *fig.* lobhudeln.
be·slob·ber [bi'slɔbə] abküssen.
be·smear [bi'smiə] beschmieren.
be·smirch [bi'smə:tʃ] beschmutzen.
be·som ['bi:zəm] (Reisig)Besen *m*.
be·sot·ted [bi'sɔtid] vernarrt; betrunken.
be·sought [bi'sɔ:t] *pret. u. p.p. von beseech.*
be·spat·ter [bi'spætə] (be)spritzen; *fig.* überhäufen; beschimpfen.
be·speak [bi'spi:k] (*irr.*) vorbestellen; (an)zeigen, verraten.
be·spoke [bi'spəuk] *pret. von bespeak*; ~ *tailor* Maßschneider *m*; **be'spo·ken** *p.p. von bespeak.*
be·sprin·kle [bi'spriŋkl] besprengen.
best [best] **1.** *adj.* best; höchst; größt, meist; ~ *man* Brautführer *m*; *the* ~ *part of* der größte Teil (*gen.*);

all the ~! alles Gute!, viel Glück!; *s. seller*; **2.** *adv.* am besten, aufs beste; **3.** Beste *m, f, n*, Besten *pl.*; *Sunday* ~ Sonntagsanzug *m*; *for the* ~ zum Besten; *to the* ~ *of* ... nach bestem ...; *have od. get the* ~ *of it* am besten dabei wegkommen; *make the* ~ *of* tun, was man kann, mit; *make the* ~ *of a bad job* gute Miene zum bösen Spiel machen; *I made the* ~ *of my way to* ... ich ging möglichst schnell nach ...; *at* ~ bestenfalls, im besten Falle; **4.** *vb.* F übervorteilen.

be·ste(a)d [biˈsted]: *hard* ~ hart bedrängt.

bes·tial □ [ˈbestjəl] tierisch, viehisch, bestialisch; **bes·ti·al·i·ty** [~tiˈæliti] Bestialität *f*; **bes·tial·ize** [ˈ~tjəlaiz] vertieren.

be·stir [biˈstəː]: ~ *o.s.* sich rühren.

be·stow [biˈstəu] geben, schenken, verleihen (*on, upon dat.*); unterbringen; **beˈstow·al, beˈstow·ment** Schenkung *f*, Verleihung *f*.

be·strew [biˈstruː] (*irr. strew*) bestreuen; verstreut liegen auf (*dat.*).

be·stride [biˈstraid] (*irr. stride*) mit gespreizten Beinen auf *e-m Fleck*, über *j-m* stehen; reiten auf (*dat.*).

bet [bet] **1.** Wette *f*; **2.** (*irr.*) wetten; *you* ~ F bestimmt, sicherlich; *I* ~ *you a shilling* ich wette mit dir um 'nen Taler.

be·take [biˈteik] (*irr. take*): ~ *o.s. to* sich begeben nach; *fig.* seine Zuflucht nehmen zu.

be·think [biˈθiŋk] (*irr. think*): ~ *o.s.* sich besinnen (*of* auf *acc.*); ~ *o.s. to inf.* sich in den Kopf setzen zu *inf.*

be·tide [biˈtaid] geschehen; *j-m* zustoßen; *woe* ~ *him!* wehe ihm!

be·times [biˈtaimz] beizeiten.

be·to·ken [biˈtəukən] ankündigen, andeuten; anzeigen.

be·tray [biˈtrei] verraten (*a. fig. offenbaren*); verleiten; **beˈtray·al** Verrat *m*; ~ *of trust* Vertrauensbruch *m*; **beˈtray·er** Verräter(in).

be·troth [biˈtrəuð] verloben (*to* mit); *the* ~*ed* das verlobte Paar; **beˈtroth·al** Verlobung *f*.

bet·ter[1] [ˈbetə] **1.** *adj.* besser; *he is* ~ es geht ihm besser; *get* ~ sich erholen; *for* ~ *or (for) worse* in Freud und Leid (*Trauungsformel*); **2.** Besseres *n*; ~*s pl.* Höherstehenden *pl.*, Vorgesetzten *pl.*; *get the* ~ *of* die Oberhand gewinnen über (*acc.*); überwinden, besiegen; *j-m* den Rang ablaufen; *he is my* ~ er ist mir überlegen; **3.** *adv.* besser; mehr; *be* ~ *off* besser daran sein; *so much the* ~ desto besser; *you had* ~ *go* es wäre besser, wenn du gingest; *I know* ~ ich weiß es besser; *think* ~ *of it* sich eines Besseren besinnen; **4.** *v/t.* (ver-)bessern; ~ *o.s.* sich *im Lohn etc.* verbessern; *v/i.* besser werden, sich verbessern.

bet·ter[2] [~] Wettende *m, f*.

bet·ter·ment [ˈbetəmənt] Verbesserung *f*.

bet·ting [ˈbetiŋ] Wetten *n*; ~ *debt* Wettschuld *f*.

be·tween [biˈtwiːn], *poet. u. prov. a.* **be·twixt** [biˈtwikst] **1.** *adv.* dazwischen; *betwixt and* ~ in der Mitte; halb und halb; *in* ~ dazwischen; *far* ~ weit auseinander; **2.** *prp.* zwischen, unter; ~ *ourselves* unter uns; *they had 5 shillings* ~ *them* sie besaßen zusammen 5 Schilling; **beˈtween-decks** ⚓ Zwischendeck *n*.

bev·el [ˈbevəl] **1.** schräg, schief; **2.** ⊕ Schrägung *f*; Schrägmaß *n*, Schmiege *f*; **3.** *v/t.* abschrägen; *v/i.* schräg verlaufen; ˈ**~-wheel** ⊕ Kegelrad *n*.

bev·er·age [ˈbevəridʒ] Getränk *n*.

bev·y [ˈbevi] Schwarm *m*; Schar *f*.

be·wail [biˈweil] *v/t.* beklagen; *v/i.* wehklagen.

be·ware [biˈwɛə] sich hüten, sich in acht nehmen (*of* vor *dat.*); ~ *of the dog!* Vorsicht, bissiger Hund!

be·wil·der [biˈwildə] irremachen; verwirren, verblüffen; bestürzt machen; **beˈwil·der·ment** Verwirrung *f*; Bestürzung *f*.

be·witch F [biˈwitʃ] bezaubern, *b.s.* behexen; **beˈwitch·ment** Bezauberung *f*; Zauber *m*.

be·yond [biˈjɔnd] **1.** *adv.* darüber hinaus; jenseits; **2.** *prp.* jenseits, über (... hinaus); mehr *od.* weiter als; außer; ~ *endurance* unerträglich; ~ *measure* über die Maßen; ~ *dispute* außer allem Zweifel; ~ *words* unsagbar; *get* ~ *s.o.* j-m über den Kopf wachsen; *go* ~ *one's depth* den Boden verlieren; *it is* ~ *me* es geht über meinen Verstand.

bi... [bai] zwei...

bi·an·nu·al [baiˈænjuəl] halbjährlich.

bi·as [ˈbaiəs] **1.** *adj. u. adv.* schief,

schräg; **2.** Neigung *f*, Hang *m*; Vorurteil *n*; *Schneiderei*: schräger Schnitt *m*; *cut on the* ~ diagonal geschnitten; **3.** (ungünstig) beeinflussen; ~*sed* voreingenommen, befangen.

bib [bib] Lätzchen *n*; Schürzenlatz *m*.

Bi·ble ['baibl] Bibel *f*.

bib·li·cal □ ['biblikəl] biblisch; Bibel...

bib·li·og·ra·pher [bibli'ɔgrəfə] Bibliograph *m*, Verfasser *m* e-r Bibliographie; **bib·li·o·graph·ic, bib·li·o·graph·i·cal** [~əu'græfik(əl)] bibliographisch; **bib·li·og·ra·phy** [~'ɔgrəfi] Bibliographie *f*; **bib·li·o·ma·ni·a** [~əu'meinjə] Bücherleidenschaft *f*; **bib·li·o·ma·ni·ac** [~əu'meiniæk] Büchernarr *m*; **bib·li·o·phile** ['~əufail] Bücherfreund *m*, Bibliophile *m*.

bib·u·lous □ ['bibjuləs] saugfähig; trunksüchtig; feuchtfröhlich.

bi·car·bon·ate ⚗ [bai'kɑ:bənit] Bikarbonat *n*; ~ *of soda* doppeltkohlensaures Natron *n*.

bi·ceps ['baiseps] Bizeps *m* (*Muskel*); *fig.* Kraft *f*.

bick·er ['bikə] (sich) zanken; flackern (*Flamme*); plätschern (*Fluß, Regen*); prasseln (*Schläge*); '**bick·er·ing**(*s pl.*) Gezänk *n*.

bi·cy·cle ['baisikl] **1.** Fahrrad *n*; *folding* ~ Klapprad *n*; *ride a* ~ = **2.** radfahren, radeln.

bid [bid] **1.** (*irr.*) gebieten, befehlen; (*pret. u. p.p. bid*) *Versteigerung*: bieten; *Karten*: melden, reizen; *Gruß* entbieten; ~ *fair to inf.* scheinen zu, versprechen zu *inf.*; ~ *farewell* Lebewohl sagen; ~ *up Preis* hochtreiben; ~ *welcome* willkommen heißen; **2.** *Geld*-Gebot *n*, Angebot *n*; Versuch *m* (*to inf.* zu *inf.*); *to make a* ~ *for* sich bemühen um; *no* ~ *Karten*: ich passe; '**bid·den** *p.p. von bid*; '**bid·der** Bieter(in); *s. high, low*; '**bid·ding** Bieten *n*; Gebot *n*; Geheiß *n*; Einladung *f*.

bide [baid]: ~ *one's time* den rechten Augenblick abwarten.

bi·en·ni·al [bai'eniəl] zweijährig(e Pflanze *f*).

bier [biə] (Toten)Bahre *f*.

bi·fo·cals [bai'fəukəlz] *pl.* Zweistärkenbrille *f*.

bi·fur·cate ['baifə:keit] gabelförmig teilen; sich gabeln; **bi·fur'ca·tion** Gabelung *f*.

big [big] groß; erwachsen; schwanger (*a. fig. with* mit); F wichtig; wichtigtuerisch; ♀ *Apple Spitzname für* New York City; ~ *bang* Urknall *m*; ♀ *Ben Uhrturm des Parlamentsgebäudes in London*; ~ *business* Großunternehmertum *n*; ~ *shot* F hohes Tier *n*; ~ *stick Am.* Macht(entfaltung) *f*; ~ *top* Zirkuszelt *n*, *a. fig.* Zirkus *m*; *the* ♀ *Three* die großen Drei; *talk* ~ den Mund (zu) voll nehmen.

big·a·mous ['bigəməs] bigamisch, in Doppelehe lebend; '**big·a·my** Bigamie *f*, Doppelehe *f*.

bight ⚓ [bait] Bucht *f*; Tauschleife *f*.

big·mouth F ['bigmauθ] Großmaul *n*.

big·ness ['bignis] Größe *f*.

big·ot ['bigət] blinder Anhänger *m* (*to gen.*); Frömmler(in); '**big·ot·ed** blindgläubig, bigott; *fig.* blind ergeben; '**big·ot·ry** Blindgläubigkeit *f*.

big·wig F *co.* ['bigwig] großes *od.* hohes Tier *n*.

bike F [baik] (Fahr)Rad *n*.

bi·lat·er·al □ [bai'lætərəl] zweiseitig.

bil·ber·y ♀ ['bilbəri] Heidelbeere *f*.

bile [bail] Galle *f* (*a. fig.*); ~-*stone* ⚕ Gallenstein *m*.

bilge [bildʒ] ⚓ Kielraum *m*, Bilge *f*, Kimm *f*; *sl.* Quatsch *m*, Mist *m*.

bi·lin·gual [bai'liŋgwəl] zweisprachig.

bil·ious □ ['biljəs] Gallen..., gallig, biliös; *fig.* gallig, gereizt; ~ *colic* ⚕ Gallenkolik *f*.

bilk [bilk] betrügen, prellen.

bill[1] [bil] **1.** Schnabel *m*; Spitze *f am Anker, Zirkel*; Hippe *f*, Gartenmesser *n*; **2.** (sich) schnäbeln.

bill[2] [~] **1.** Rechnung *f*; Gesetzentwurf *m*, Vorlage *f*; Klage-, Rechtsschrift *f*; Schriftstück *n*; *a.* ~ *of exchange* Wechsel *m*; Zettel *m*, Schein *m*; Plakat *n*; *Am.* Banknote *f*; ~ *of fare* Speisekarte *f*; ~ *of health* Gesundheitspaß *m*; ~ *of lading* Seefrachtbrief *m*, Konnossement *n*; ~ *of sale* Sicherungsübereignung *f*; Kaufvertrag *m*; ♀ *of Rights englische* Freiheitsurkunde *f* (*1689*); *Am.* die ersten 10 Zusatzartikel zur Verfassung der USA; **2.** (durch Anschlag) ankündigen *od.*

bekanntmachen; in e-e Liste eintragen; auf die Rechnung setzen; *j-m* e-e Rechnung schicken; *Am.* buchen.

bill·board *Am.* ['bilbɔ:d] Anschlagbrett *n*; Reklamefläche *f*.

bil·let ['bilit] **1.** ⚔ Quartier(zettel *m*) *n*; Unterkunft *f*; (Holz)Scheit *n*; **2.** ⚔ einquartieren (*on* bei, in *dat.*).

bill·fold *Am.* ['bilfəuld] Brieftasche *f für Papiergeld*.

bill·hook ['bilhuk] Hippe *f*, Gartenmesser *n*.

bil·liard ['biljəd] *in Zssgn* Billard...; '**~-cue** Queue *n*; '**bil·liards** *pl. od. sg.* Billard(spiel) *n*.

bil·lion ['biljən] Milliarde *f*; *in England* †: Billion *f*.

bil·low ['biləu] **1.** Welle *f*, Woge *f* (*a. fig.*); **2.** wogen; '**bil·low·y** wellig, wogend.

bill-stick·er ['bilstikə] Plakat-, Zettelankleber *m*.

bil·ly *Am.* ['bili] (Polizei-, Gummi-) Knüppel *m*; '**~-can** Kochtopf *m*; '**~-cock** F Melone *f* (*Hut*); '**~-goat** F Ziegenbock *m*.

bi·met·al·lism ☤ [bai'metəlizəm] Bimetallismus *m* (*Währung mit 2 Metallen*).

bi-mo·tored ['baiməutəd] zweimotorig.

bin [bin] Kasten *m*, Behälter *m*.

bi·na·ry ['bainəri] aus zwei (Einheiten) bestehend; *~ fission biol.* Zellteilung *f*.

bin·au·ral [bain'ɔ:rəl] beide Ohren betreffend; für beide Ohren; zweikanalig, stereo.

bind [baind] (*irr.*) *v/t.* binden; an-, um-, auf-, fest-, verbinden; verpflichten; *Handel* abschließen; *Rock, Saum* einfassen; *Rad* beschlagen; *Bücher* binden; *Sand etc.* fest *od.* hart machen; *~ over* durch Bürgschaft verpflichten; *be bound up with fig.* eng verbunden sein mit; *~ s.o. apprentice to* j. in die Lehre geben bei; *be bound up in fig.* nur leben für, aufgehen in (*dat.*); *s. bound*[1] 2; *v/i.* binden; fest werden; '**bind·er** Binder *m*; Buchbinder *m*; Garbenbinder(in); Binde *f*, Band *n*; '**bind·ing 1.** bindend; verbindlich; **2.** Binden *n*; Einband *m*; *Schilauf*: Bindung *f*; *Schneiderei*: Einfaßband *n*, Einfassung *f*; '**bind·weed** ⚘ Winde *f*; *lesser ~* Ackerwinde *f*.

binge *sl.* [bindʒ] Sauferei *f*, Bierreise *f*.

bin·go ['biŋgəu] (*Art*) Lottospiel *n*.

bin·na·cle ⚓ ['binəkl] Kompaßhaus *n*.

bin·oc·u·lar 1. [bai'nɔkjulə] für zwei Augen; **2.** [bi'nɔkjulə] *mst ~s pl.* Feldstecher *m*, Fern-, Opernglas *n*.

bi·o·chem·i·cal ['baiəu'kemikəl] biochemisch; '**bi·o'chem·ist** Biochemiker *m*; '**bi·o'chem·is·try** Biochemie *f*.

bi·og·ra·pher [bai'ɔgrəfə] Biograph (-in); **bi·o·graph·ic, bi·o·graph·i·cal** □ [~əu'græfik(əl)] biographisch; **bi·og·ra·phy** [~'ɔgrəfi] Biographie *f*, Lebensbeschreibung *f*.

bi·o·log·ic, bi·o·log·i·cal □ [baiəu'lɔdʒik(əl)] biologisch; **bi·ol·o·gist** [~'ɔlədʒist] Biologe *m*; **bi'ol·o·gy** Biologie *f*.

bi·par·ti·san [baipɑ:ti'zæn] Zweiparteien...

bi·par·tite [bai'pɑ:tait] zweiteilig; zweiseitig; doppelt ausgefertigt (*Dokumente*).

bi·ped ['baiped] **1.** zweifüßig; **2.** Zweifüßer *m*.

bi·plane ✈ ['baiplein] Doppeldecker *m*.

birch [bə:tʃ] **1.** ⚘ Birke *f*; (Birken-) Rute *f*; **2.** Birken...; *~ broom* Reisbesen *m*; **3.** mit der Rute züchtigen; '**birch·en** birken; Birken...

bird [bə:d] Vogel *m*; *kill two ~s with one stone* zwei Fliegen mit einer Klappe schlagen; *give the ~ Schauspieler* auszischen, -pfeifen; *a queer ~* ein komischer Vogel (*Mensch*); *for the ~s* für die Katz; *tell a child about the ~s and the bees* ein Kind (sexuell) aufklären; '**~·call** Vogelruf *m*; '**~-fan·ci·er** Vogelliebhaber(in), -züchter(in), -händler(in); **bird·ie** ['bə:di] Vögelchen *n*.

bird...: '**~-lime** Vogelleim *m*; **~ sanc·tu·ar·y** Vogelschutzgebiet *n*; '**~-seed** Vogelfutter *n*; '**bird's-eye view** (Blick *m* aus der) Vogelperspektive *f*; allgemeiner Überblick *m*; '**bird's-nest 1.** Vogelnest *n*; **2.** Vogelnester ausnehmen; *~ soup* Schwalbennestersuppe *f*.

bi·ro ['baiərəu] Kugelschreiber *m*.

birth [bə:θ] Geburt *f*; Ursprung *m*; Entstehung *f*; Herkunft *f*; *new ~* Wiedergeburt *f*; *bring to ~* entstehen lassen, veranlassen; *come to*

~ entstehen, veranlaßt werden; *give ~ to* gebären, zur Welt bringen; *fig.* hervorbringen; **'~-con·trol** Geburtenbeschränkung *f*, -regelung *f*; **'~·day** Geburtstag *m*; *~ honours am offiziellen Geburtstag des britischen Monarchen verliehene Titel*; **'~-mark** Muttermal *n*; **'~-place** Geburtsort *m*, -haus *n*; **'~-rate** Geburtenziffer *f*; **'~·right** (Erst)Geburtsrecht *n*.

bis·cuit ['biskit] **1.** Zwieback *m*; Keks *m* (*n*); Biskuit *n* (*Porzellan*); **2.** hellbraun.

bi·sect ⩕ [bai'sekt] halbieren; **bi'sec·tion** Halbierung *f*.

bish·op ['biʃəp] Bischof *m*; Läufer *m im Schach*; **bish·op·ric** ['~rik] Bistum *n*.

bis·muth ⚗ ['bizməθ] Wismut *n*.

bi·son *zo.* ['baisn] Wisent *m*.

bis·sex·tile [bi'sekstail] **1.** Schalt...; *~ year* = **2.** Schaltjahr *n*.

bit [bit] **1.** Bißchen *n*, Stückchen *n*; (Pferde)Gebiß *n*; ⊕ (Zangen)Maul *n*; Bohrspitze *f*; Schlüsselbart *m*; *Computer*: Bit *n*; *~ by ~* allmählich; stückweise; *a ~ of a coward* ein wenig feige; *take the ~ between one's teeth* durchgehen (*Pferd*); *fig.* aufsässig werden; **2.** aufzäumen; zügeln; **3.** *pret. von bite* 2.

bitch [bitʃ] **1.** Hündin *f*; V Hure *f*; *~ fox* Füchsin *f*; *~ wolf* Wölfin *f*; **2.** verpfuschen.

bite [bait] **1.** Beißen *n*; Biß *m*; Bissen *m*, Happen *m*; Anbeißen *n*; ⊕ Fassen *n*, Haften *n*; **2.** (*irr.*) beißen; brennen (*Pfeffer*); schneiden (*Kälte*); zerfressen (*Rost etc.*); (an-)beißen (*Fisch*); ⊕ fassen (*Anker, Schraube etc.*); *fig.* verletzen; *~ at* schnappen nach; *~ the dust fig.* ins Gras beißen (*sterben*); *~ one's lips* sich auf die Lippen beißen; *~ one's nails* Fingernägel kauen; **'bit·er** Beißer *m*; *the ~ bit* der betrogene Betrüger.

bit·ing □ ['baitiŋ] scharf, beißend.

bit·ten ['bitn] *p.p. von bite* 2; *be ~ fig.* hereingefallen sein; *once ~ twice shy* gebranntes Kind scheut das Feuer.

bit·ter ['bitə] **1.** □ bitter; beißend, streng; *fig.* (v)erbittert; **2.** *halbdunkles, herbes Bier*.

bit·tern *orn.* ['bitən] Rohrdommel *f*.

bit·ter·ness ['bitənis] Bitterkeit *f*, Verbitterung *f*.

bit·ters ['bitəz] *pl.* Bittere *m*, Magenbitter *m*.

bi·tu·men ['bitjumin] Bitumen *n*, Asphalt *m*, Erdpech *n*; **bi·tu·mi·nous** [bi'tju:minəs] bituminös.

bi·valve *zo.* [bai'vælv] zweischalige Muschel *f*.

biv·ou·ac ['bivuæk] **1.** Biwak *n*; **2.** biwakieren.

biz F [biz] Geschäft *n*.

bi·zarre [bi'zɑ:] bizarr.

blab F [blæb] **1.** *a.* **'blab·ber** Schwätzer(in); **2.** (aus)schwatzen.

black [blæk] **1.** □ schwarz; dunkel; finster, düster; *~ cattle* Rind-, Hornvieh *n*; *~ eye* blaues Auge *n*; *s. frost*; *in ~ and white* schwarz auf weiß; *beat s.o. ~ and blue* j. grün u. blau schlagen; *~ in the face* dunkelrot (im Gesicht *vor Wut*); *look ~ at s.o.* j. böse anschauen; **2.** schwärzen; wichsen; *~ out* verdunkeln; **3.** Schwarz *n* (*a. Kleidung*); Schwärze *f*; Schwarze *m*, *f* (*Neger*).

black...: **~·a·moor** ['~əmuə] Neger *m*; **'~·ball** gegen *j.* stimmen; **'~·ber·ry** ⚘ Brombeere *f*; *go ~ing* Brombeeren sammeln; **'~·bird** Amsel *f*; **'~·board** Wandtafel *f*; **'~-coat·ed**: *~ worker* Büroangestellte *m*; **'~·cock** *orn.* Birkhahn *m*; **'~-'cur·rant** schwarze Johannisbeere *f*; **'black·en** *v/t.* schwärzen, schwarz machen; *fig.* anschwärzen; *v/i.* schwarz werden.

black...: **'~·guard** ['blægɑ:d] **1.** Lump *m*, Schuft *m*; **2.** *a.* **'~·guard·ly** □ schuftig, niederträchtig; **3.** *j.* (Lump) schimpfen; **~·head** ⚕ ['blækhed] Mitesser *m*; *~* **ice** Glatteis *n*; **'black·ing** Schuhwichse *f*; **'black·ish** □ schwärzlich.

black...: **'~·jack 1.** *bsd. Am.* Totschläger *m* (*Instrument*); **2.** niederknüppeln; **~·lead** ['~'led] **1.** Reißblei *n*; **2.** mit Reißblei schwärzen; **'~·leg** Betrüger *m*; Streikbrecher *m*; **'~-'let·ter** *typ.* Fraktur *f*; **'~-list** auf die schwarze Liste setzen; **'~·mail 1.** Erpressung(sgeld *n*) *f*; **2.** Geld von *j-m* erpressen; **'~·mail·er** Erpresser *m*; *~* **mar·ket** schwarzer Markt *m*; *~* **mar·ket·eer** Schwarzhändler *m*, Schieber *m*; **'black·ness** Schwärze *f*.

black...: **'~-out** Verdunkelung *f*; Gedächtnisstörung *f*; *thea.* Verlöschen *n* der Lichter; *news ~* Nachrichtensperre *f*; *~* **pud·ding** Blutwurst *f*; ~

sheep *fig.* schwarzes Schaf *n*; '~**smith** Grobschmied *m*; '~**tail** *zo. Am.* Kolumbischer Hirsch *m*; '~**thorn** ⚘ Schwarz-, Schlehdorn *m*; '**black·y** F Schwarze *m, f.*
blad·der ['blædə] (*bsd.* Harn-, Gallen-, Schwimm)Blase *f.*
blade [bleid] Blatt *n*, ⚘ Halm *m*; *Säge-, Ruder-, Schulter- etc.* Blatt *n*; Propellerflügel *m*; Schneide *f*, Klinge *f eines Messers etc.*; '~-**bone** *anat.* Schulterblatt *n.*
blae·ber·ry ['bleibəri] Heidelbeere *f.*
blah F [blɑ:] leeres Gerede *n.*
blam·a·ble □ ['bleiməbl] tadelnswert; schuldhaft.
blame [bleim] **1.** Tadel *m*; Schuld *f*; **2.** tadeln; *be to* ~ *for* schuld sein an (*dat.*); ~ *s.th. on s.o.* die Schuld für et. auf j. schieben.
blame·ful ['bleimful] tadelnswert; '**blame·less** □ untadelig; schuldlos; '**blame·less·ness** Makellosigkeit *f*; '**blame·wor·thy** tadelnswert.
blanch [blɑ:ntʃ] bleichen; erbleichen (lassen); ~ *over* beschönigen.
blanc-mange [blə'mɔnʒ] *Küche*: Flammeri *m.*
bland □ [blænd] mild, sanft; '**blan·dish** schmeicheln (*dat.*), liebkosen; '**blan·dish·ment** Schmeichelei *f.*
blank [blæŋk] **1.** □ blank; leer; unausgefüllt; unbeschrieben; ✝ Blanko...; verdutzt, verblüfft; ~ *cartridge* ⚔ Platzpatrone *f*; *fire* ~ mit Platzpatronen schießen; **2.** Weißes *n*; Leere *f*; leerer Raum *m*; Lücke *f*, freie Stelle *f*; unbeschriebenes Blatt *n*, leeres Formular *n*, Blankett *n*; Niete *f in der Lotterie*; Platzpatrone *f.*
blan·ket ['blæŋkit] **1.** Wolldecke *f*; *engS.* (Bett-, Pferde)Decke *f*; *wet* ~ *fig.* Dämpfer *m*; Spielverderber *m*; Störenfried *m*; **2.** mit e-r Wolldecke zudecken; F unterdrücken, vertuschen; **3.** *Am.* umfassend, Gesamt..., Allgemein..., Pauschal...
blank·ness ['blæŋknis] Weiße *f*, Leere *f*; Verdutztheit *f*; **blank verse** *poet.* Blankvers *m.*
blare [blɛə] schmettern (*Trompete*).
blar·ney ['blɑ:ni] **1.** Schmus *m*, leeres Gerede *n*; Überredungskunst *f*; **2.** *j.* einwickeln; schmeichelhaft reden.
bla·sé ['blɑ:zei] blasiert.
blas·pheme [blæs'fi:m] lästern (*against* über *acc.*); **blas'phem·er** Gotteslästerer *m*; **blas·phe·mous** □ ['blæsfiməs] blasphemisch, gotteslästerlich; '**blas·phe·my** Blasphemie *f*, Gotteslästerung *f.*
blast [blɑ:st] **1.** Windstoß *m*; Ton *m e-s Blasinstruments*; ⊕ Gebläse (-luft *f*) *n*; Luftdruck *m e-r Explosion*; (Spreng)Ladung *f*; ⚘ Mehltau *m*; *at full* ~ mit Volldampf; *in* (*out of*) ~ in (außer) Betrieb (*Hochofen*); ~ *of a trumpet* Trompetenstoß *m*; **2.** (in die Luft) sprengen; zerstören (*a. fig.*); ~ (*it*)! verdammt!; '**blast·ed** verdammt, verflucht; '**blast-fur·nace** ⊕ Hochofen *m*; '**blast·ing** Sprengen *n*; '**blast-off** *Raumfahrt*: Raketenstart *m.*
bla·tant □ ['bleitənt] lärmend; marktschreierisch; *fig.* eklatant.
blath·er *Am.* ['blæðə] **1.** Gewäsch *n*; **2.** schwätzen.
blaze [bleiz] **1.** Flamme(n *pl.*) *f*; Feuer *n*; heller Schein *m*; *fig.* Ausbruch *m*; ~*s pl.* Hölle *f*, Teufel *m*; *go to* ~*s!* zum Teufel mit dir!; *like* ~*s* F wie ein Irrer; **2.** *v/i.* brennen, flammen, lodern; leuchten; ~ *away* F losschießen; *blazing scent* warme Fährte *f*; *v/t. Baum* markieren; ~ *abroad* ausposaunen; ~ *a trail* e-n Pfad markieren; *fig.* e-n Weg bahnen; '**blaz·er** Blazer *m.*
bla·zon ['bleizn] **1.** Wappenkunde *f*; Wappen(schild) *n*; **2.** *Wappen* beschreiben, malen; *fig.* schmücken; verherrlichen; (ver)künden; F ausposaunen; '**bla·zon·ry** Wappenkunde *f*; Zurschaustellung *f*; Schmuck *m.*
bleach [bli:tʃ] bleichen; '**bleach·er** Bleicher(in); ~*s pl. Am.* nichtüberdachte Zuschauerplätze *m/pl. bei Sportveranstaltungen*; '**bleach·ing** Bleichen *n*; '**bleach·ing-pow·der** Bleichpulver *n.*
bleak □ [bli:k] öde, kahl; rauh; *fig.* trüb, freudlos, finster; '**bleak·ness** Öde *f*; Rauheit *f.*
blear [bliə] **1.** trüb (*bsd. Auge*); **2.** trüben; ~-**eyed** ['bliəraid] triefäugig; '**blear·y** trüb.
bleat [bli:t] **1.** Blöken *n*; **2.** blöken.
bleb [bleb] Bläschen *n*, Pustel *f.*
bled [bled] *pret. u. p.p von bleed.*
bleed [bli:d] (*irr.*) *v/i.* bluten; *v/t.*

zur Ader lassen; *fig.* schröpfen; '**bleed·ing** **1.** Bluten *n*; Aderlaß *m*; **2.** *sl.* verflixt.
bleep·er F ['bli:pə] Piepser *m*, Funkrufempfänger *m*.
blem·ish ['blemiʃ] **1.** Fehler *m*; Makel *m*, Schande *f*; **2.** verunstalten; brandmarken.
blench [blentʃ] *v/i.* zurückschrekken; *v/t.* die Augen schließen vor.
blend [blend] **1.** (sich) (ver)mischen; *Tee* mischen; *Wein etc.* verschneiden; *fig.* (miteinander) verschmelzen; ineinander übergehen; **2.** Mischung *f*; ✝ Verschnitt *m*.
blende *min.* [blend] (Zink)Blende *f*.
bless [bles] segnen; preisen; beglücken (*with* mit); ~ *me!*, ~ *my soul!* F meine Güte!, herrje!; ~ *you!* Gesundheit! (*beim Niesen*); **bless·ed** □ [*p.p.* blest; *adj.* 'blesid] glückselig; gesegnet; ~ *event* freudiges Ereignis *n*; **bless·ed·ness** ['blesidnis] Glückseligkeit *f*; *live in single* ~ Junggeselle sein; '**blessing** Segen *m*; Segnung *f*; Wohltat *f*.
blest *poet.* [blest] *s. blessed.*
bleth·er ['bleðə] *s. blather.*
blew [blu:] *pret. von blow*[2] *u. blow*[3] *1.*
blight [blait] **1.** ⚘ Mehltau *m*; *fig.* Gifthauch *m*; **2.** vernichten; '**blight·er** *sl.* Ekel *n* (*Person*); Kerl *m*, Bursche *m*.
Blight·y ⚔ *sl.* ['blaiti] Heimat *f*; *a* ~ *one* ein Heimatschuß *m*.
bli·mey V ['blaimi] verflucht!
blind [blaind] **1.** □ blind (*fig. to* gegen); geheim; nicht erkennbar; ~ *alley* Sackgasse *f*; ~ *corner* unübersichtliche Straßenecke *f*; ~ *flying* ✈ Blindflug *m*; ~ *drunk sl.* betrunken, blau; ~ *spot* blinder Fleck *m*; toter Winkel *m*; *Radio*: Empfangsloch *n*; *turn one's* ~ *eye to s.th.* ein Auge zudrücken bei et.; **2.** Blende *f*; (Fenster)Vorhang *m*, Jalousie *f*, Rouleau *n*; Scheuklappe *f*; *Am.* Versteck *n*; Vorwand *m*; **3.** blenden, blind machen; verblenden (*to* gegen); abblenden.
blind·fold ['blaindfəuld] **1.** blindlings; blind; mit verbundenen Augen; **2.** *j-m* die Augen verbinden; '**blind·ly** *fig.* blindlings; '**blind-man's-'buff** Blindekuhspiel *n*; '**blind·ness** Blindheit *f*; '**blind-worm** *zo.* Blindschleiche *f*.
blink [bliŋk] **1.** Blinzeln *n*; Schimmer *m*; ⚓ Blink *m*; *on the* ~ F defekt, nicht in Ordnung; **2.** *v/i.* blinzeln; zwinkern; blinken; schimmern; *v/t. absichtlich* übersehen; blinzeln mit; '**blink·er** Blinzler *m*; Scheuklappe *f*; '**blink·ing** F verflixt.
blip [blip] *Radar*: Echozeichen *n*.
bliss [blis] Seligkeit *f*, Wonne *f*.
bliss·ful □ ['blisful] glückselig, selig, wonnig; '**bliss·ful·ness** Glückseligkeit *f*, Wonne *f*.
blis·ter ['blistə] **1.** Blase *f* (*auf der Haut, im Lack*); Zugpflaster *n*; **2.** Blasen bilden (auf *dat.*).
blithe □ [blaið], **~·some** ['~səm] *mst poet.* lustig, munter, fröhlich.
blith·er·ing *sl.* ['bliðəriŋ]: ~ *idiot* Vollidiot *m*.
blitz [blits] **1.** Luftangriff *m*; **2.** bombardieren.
bliz·zard ['blizəd] Schneesturm *m*.
bloat [bləut] aufblasen; aufschwellen; *Fische* räuchern; ~*ed* aufgedunsen; *fig.* aufgeblasen; '**bloat·er** Bückling *m*.
blob [blɔb] Tropfen *m*; Klümpchen *n*.
block [blɔk] **1.** Block *m*; Klotz *m*; (Häuser)Block *m*; ⊕ Block *m*, Rolle *f*; Druckstock *m*; Verstopfung *f*, Stockung *f*; *the* ~ der Richtblock; **2.** pressen, formen; verhindern, durchkreuzen; ~ *in* entwerfen, skizzieren; *mst* ~ *up* (ab-, ver)sperren; *Hafen etc.* blockieren; einschließen; ~*ed account* Sperrkonto *n*.
block·ade [blɔ'keid] **1.** Blockade *f*; *run the* ~ die Blockade brechen; **2.** blockieren; einschließen; **block-'ade-run·ner** Blockadebrecher *m*.
block...: '**~·bust·er** *sl.* Luftmine *f*; F Knüller *m*, Wucht *f*, tolle Sache *f*; '**~·head** Dummkopf *m*; '**~·house** Blockhaus *n*; ~ **let·ters** *pl.* Block-, Druckschrift *f*; ~ **of flats** Wohnblock *m*; '**~-sys·tem** 🚂 Block(signal)system *n*.
bloke F [bləuk] Bursche *m*, Kerl *m*.
blond(*e f*) [blɔnd] **1.** blond; **2.** Blondine *f*; *a. blonde-lace* ✝ Blonde *f*, seidene Spitze *f*.
blood [blʌd] Blut *n*; *fig.* Blut *n*, Temperament *n*; Geblüt *n*, Abstammung *f*; *in cold* ~ kalten Blutes, kaltblütig; *s. run 1*; '**~-and-'thunder** sensationell, dramatisch, aufregend; ~ **clot** ⚕ Blutgerinnsel *n*;

'~-cur·dling haarsträubend, entsetzlich; ~ **do·nor** Blutspender(in).
blood·ed ['blʌdid] Vollblut...; ...-blütig.
blood...: '**~-guilt·i·ness** Blutschuld *f*; '**~-heat** Blutwärme *f*, Körpertemperatur *f*; '**~-horse** Vollblutpferd *n*; '**~·hound** Blut-, Schweißhund *m*; '**blood·i·ness** Blutgier *f*; '**blood·less** □ blutlos, -leer (*fig. bleich*; *kraft-, geistlos*); unblutig.
blood...: '**~-let·ting** Aderlaß *m*; '**~-poi·son·ing** ⚕ Blutvergiftung *f*; '**~-pres·sure** Blutdruck *m*; '**~-re·'la·tion** Blutsverwandte *m, f*; ~ **sam·ple** ⚕ Blutprobe *f*; '**~·shed** Blutvergießen *n*; '**~·shot** blutunterlaufen; ~ **sports** *pl.* ‚*blutige*' *Sportarten wie Fuchsjagd, Hahnenkampf etc.*; '**~-suck·er** Blutegel *m*; *fig.* Blutsauger *m*; '**~·thirst·y** blutdürstig; '**~-ves·sel** Blutgefäß *n*; '**blood·y** □ blutig; grausam; P verdammt; '**blood·y-'mind·ed** F stur; boshaft.
bloom [blu:m] **1.** Blüte *f*; *fig.* Blüte(-zeit) *f*; Reif *m*; Flaum *m auf Früchten*; *fig.* Schmelz *m*; *metall.* Luppe *f*; *be in* ~ blühen; **2.** (er-)blühen (*a. fig.*).
bloom·er ['blu:mə] *sl.* Schnitzer *m*; *~s pl.* Schlüpfer *m*.
bloom·ing □ ['blu:miŋ] blühend; P verdammt, verflixt.
blos·som ['blɔsəm] **1.** *bsd. fruchtbildende* Blüte *f*; **2.** blühen; ~ *into* erblühen zu, sich entwickeln zu.
blot [blɔt] **1.** Klecks *m*, Fleck(en) *m*; *fig.* Makel *m*; **2.** beklecksen, beflecken (*a. fig.*); klecksen (*Feder*); (ab)löschen *mit Löschpapier*; *mst* ~ *out Schrift* ausstreichen, *fig.* auslöschen. [Klecks *m*.]
blotch [blɔtʃ] Pustel *f*; Fleck *m*;
blot·ter ['blɔtə] Löscher *m*; *Am.* Protokollbuch *n bsd. der Polizei*.
blot·ting...: '**~-pad** Schreibunterlage *f*; '**~-pa·per** Löschpapier *n*.
blot·to *sl.* ['blɔtəu] besoffen.
blouse [blauz] Bluse *f*.
blow[1] [bləu] Schlag *m*, Stoß *m*; *at one* ~ mit einem Schlag; *come to ~s* handgemein werden.
blow[2] [~] (*irr.*) blühen.
blow[3] [~] **1.** (*irr.*) *v/i.* blasen; wehen; keuchen, schnaufen; geblasen *od.* geweht werden, fliegen; durchbrennen (*Sicherung*); ~ *over* vorüberziehen, -gehen; *fig.* vergessen werden; ~ *up* explodieren, in die Luft fliegen; *v/t.* (weg- *etc.*)blasen, wehen; reißen; ertönen lassen; *Sicherung* durchbrennen lassen; *a.* ~ *up* (in die Luft) sprengen; *Geld* verpulvern, hinauswerfen; *sl. Chancen* vermasseln; ~ *one's nose* sich die Nase putzen, sich schneuzen; ~ *up Reifen* aufpumpen; *Photo* vergrößern; ~ *out one's brains* sich eine Kugel durch den Kopf jagen; *I'll be ~ed if ...* *sl.* zum Teufel, wenn ...; ~ *one's top* F in die Luft gehen; **2.** Blasen *n*, Wehen *n*; *get a* ~ F sich vom Wind durchblasen lassen; '**~-dry** *Haare* fönen; '**blow·er** Bläser *m*; Schieb(e)blech *n am Kamin*.
blow...: '**~·fly** Schmeißfliege *f*; '**~-hole** Luftloch *n*; '**~·lamp** (Benzin)Lötlampe *f*; Schweißbrenner *m*.
blown [bləun] *p.p von blow*[2] *u. blow*[3] *1.*
blow...: '**~-'out** *mot.* Reifenpanne *f*; '**~·pipe** Gebläsebrenner *m*; Schweißbrenner *m*; Blasrohr *n*; '**~·torch** *s. blowlamp*; '**~-up** Explosion *f*; F *fig.* Zornesausbruch *m*, Wutanfall *m*; F *fig.* Krach *m*, Streit *m*; *phot.* (Riesen)Vergrößerung *f*; '**blow·y** windig.
blowz·y ['blauzi] schlampig, ungepflegt u. mit grobem Teint.
blub·ber ['blʌbə] **1.** Walfischspeck *m*; **2.** heulen, weinen.
bludg·eon ['blʌdʒən] **1.** Knüppel *m*; **2.** niederknüppeln; prügeln.
blue [blu:] **1.** □ blau; F trüb, schwermütig; ~ *jokes pl.* unanständige Witze *m/pl.*; **2.** Blau *n*; *pol.* Konservative *m, f*; *out of the* ~ aus heiterem Himmel; **3.** blau färben, blauen.
blue...: ~ **ba·by** ⚕ Blue Baby *n* (*Kind n mit Blausucht durch angeborenen Herzfehler*); '**~·bell** ⚘ Sternhyazinthe *f*; Glockenblume *f*; '**~·ber·ry** ⚘ Blau-, Heidelbeere *f*; '**~·bird** *orn.* amerikanische Singdrossel *f*; '**~-book** *pol.* Blaubuch *n*; '**~·bot·tle** ⚘ Kornblume *f*; *zo.* Schmeißfliege *f*; '**~·jack·et** Blaujacke *f* (*Matrose*); '**~-jay** *orn.* Blauhäher *m*; ~ **jeans** *pl.* Blue jeans *pl.*; ~ **laws** *pl. Am.* strenge (puritanische) Gesetze *n/pl.*; '**blue·ness** Bläue *f*; '**blue-'pen·cil** zensieren, zs.-streichen; '**blue·print** Blaupause *f*; *fig.* Entwurf *m*; **blues** *pl.* Trübsinn *m*; ♪ Blues *m*; '**blue·stock·ing** *fig.* Blaustrumpf *m*.
bluff [blʌf] **1.** □ schroff; steil; derb,

gerade; **2.** Steilufer *n*; Bluff *m*, Irreführung *f*; **3.** bluffen, irreführen.

blu·ish ['blu:iʃ] bläulich.

blun·der ['blʌndə] **1.** Fehler *m*, Schnitzer *m*; **2.** einen Fehler *od.* Schnitzer machen; stolpern; stümpern; verpfuschen; ~ *out* F herausplatzen mit; **blun·der·buss** *hist.* ['blʌndəbʌs] Donnerbüchse *f*; '**blun·der·er**, '**blun·der·head** Stümper *m*.

blunt [blʌnt] **1.** □ stumpf (*a. fig.*); plump, grob, derb; **2.** abstumpfen; '**blunt·ness** Stumpfheit *f*; Grobheit *f*, Plumpheit *f*.

blur [blə:] **1.** Fleck(en) *m*; *fig.* Verschwommenheit *f*, Schleier *m*; **2.** *v/t.* beflecken; verwischen; *Sinn* trüben; ~*red bsd. phot.* verschleiert.

blurb [blə:b] Waschzettel *m*, Klappentext *m*.

blurt [blə:t]: ~ *out* herausplatzen mit.

blush [blʌʃ] **1.** (Scham)Röte *f*; Erröten *n*; flüchtiger Blick *m*; **2.** erröten (*at* über *acc.*); (sich) röten, rot werden; ~ *to inf.* sich schämen zu *inf.*; '**blush·er** Rouge *n*; '**blush·ing** □ schamhaft.

blus·ter ['blʌstə] **1.** Brausen *n*, Toben *n*, Getöse *n*; Prahlerei *f*; **2.** *v/i.* brausen, toben, tosen; prahlen; *v/t. a.* ~ *out* ausstoßen; '**blus·ter·er** Polterer *m*; Prahler *m*.

bo(h) [bəu] hu!, buh!

bo·a *zo.* ['bəuə] Boa *f*.

boar [bɔ:] Eber *m*; *hunt.* Keiler *m*.

board [bɔ:d] **1.** Brett *n*, Bohle *f*; Anschlagbrett *n*; Tafel *f*; Konferenztisch *m*; Ausschuß *m*, Komitee *n*, Kommission *f*; Gremium *n*; Behörde *f*, Amt *n*; Verpflegung *f*; Pappe *f*; *the* ~*s pl. thea.* die Bretter *n/pl.*; *on* ~ an Bord; *on* ~ *a train Am.* in e-m Zug; *go by the* ~*s* über Bord gehen, *fig.* ins Wasser fallen (*Plan etc.*); *above* ~ ehrlich, offen; *sweep the* ~ alles gewinnen; ~ *of governors* Kuratorium *n bsd. e-r Public School*; ♀ *of Trade* Handelsministerium *n*; ~ *and lodging* Unterkunft *f* u. Verpflegung *f*; **2.** *v/t.* dielen, verschalen; beköstigen; *a.* ~ *out* in Kost *od.* Pension geben; ⚓ an Bord *e-s Schiffes* gehen; ⚓ entern; *bsd. Am.* (*Fahr-, Flugzeug*) besteigen; einsteigen in (*acc.*); ~ *up* mit Brettern verschlagen *od.* vernageln; *v/i.* in Kost sein (*with* bei); '**board·er** Kostgänger (-in); Internatsschüler(in).

board·ing ['bɔ:diŋ] Verschalung *f*; Verpflegung *f*; ⚓ Entern *n*; *attr.* Kost...; '~**-axe** ⚓ Enterbeil *n*; '~**-house** Pension *f*, Fremdenheim *n*; '~**-school** Internat(sschule *f*) *n*.

board...: ~ **of di·rec·tors** Aufsichts-, Verwaltungsrat *m*; '~**-room** Sitzungssaal *m*; '~**-walk** *bsd. Am.* Strandpromenade *f aus Holzplanken.*

boast [bəust] **1.** Prahlerei *f*; *fig.* Stolz *m*; **2.** (*of, about*) sich rühmen (*gen.*), prahlen (mit); ~ *s.th.* sich (des Besitzes) e-r Sache rühmen, et. aufzuweisen haben; '**boast·er** Prahler(in); **boast·ful** □ ['~ful] prahlerisch.

boat [bəut] **1.** Boot *n*; Schiff *n*; *burn one's* ~*s* alle Brücken hinter sich abbrechen; *take to the* ~*s* in die Rettungsboote gehen; *be in the same* ~ in der gleichen Lage sein; *s. sauce-*~; **2.** in e-m Boot fahren; '**boat-hook** Bootshaken *m*; '**boat-house** Bootshaus *n*; '**boat·ing** Bootfahrt *f*; '**boat-race** Ruderregatta *f*; **boat-swain** ['bəusn] Bootsmann *m*; '**boat-train** Schiffszug *m*.

bob [bɔb] **1.** Bommel *f*, Quaste *f*; Pendellinse *f*; Ruck *m*; Knicks *m*; (Haar)Schopf *m*; *sl.* Schilling *m*; = ~*bed hair*; **2.** *v/t.* klopfen; stoßen; *Haar* stutzen; ~*bed hair* Bubikopf *m*; *v/i.* springen, tanzen; knicksen; ~ *for* schnappen nach.

bob·bin ['bɔbin] Spule *f* (*a.* ⚡); *Spitzen*-Klöppel *m*; Zugschnur *f*; '~**-lace** Klöppelspitze *f*.

bob·ble *Am.* F ['bɔbl] Schnitzer *m*, Fehler *m*.

bob·by *sl.* ['bɔbi] Polizist *m*; '~**-pin** Haarklemme *f*; '~**-socks** *pl.* Söckchen *n/pl.*; ~**-sox·er** *Am.sl.* ['~sɔksə] Backfisch *m*.

bob·cat *zo.* ['bɔbkæt] Rotluchs *m*.

bob·o·link *orn.* ['bɔbəliŋk] Reisstärling *m*.

bob·sled ['bɔbsled], **bob·sleigh** ['bɔbslei] Bob(sleigh) *m* (*Mannschaftsrennschlitten*).

bob·tail ['bɔbteil] (Pferd *n od.* Hund *m* mit) Stutzschwanz *m*; *the rag-tag and* ~ Krethi u. Plethi *pl.*

bob·white *orn.* ['bɔb'wait] Virginische Wachtel *f*.

bode [bəud] prophezeien (*well* Gu-

tes *n*, *ill* Übles *n*).
bod·ice ['bɔdis] Leibchen *n*, Mieder *n*; Taille *f am Kleid*.
bod·i·ly ['bɔdili] **1.** *adj.* körperlich; ~ *injury* Körperverletzung *f*; **2.** *adv.* ganz u. gar; persönlich.
bod·kin ['bɔdkin] Ahle *f*; Durchziehnadel; Haarnadel *f*; *sit* ~ eingepfercht sitzen.
bod·y ['bɔdi] **1.** Körper *m*, Leib *m*; Rumpf *m*; Leichnam *m*; Person *f*; Körperschaft *f*; Hauptteil *m*; *mot.* Karosserie *f*; (Hut)Stumpen *m*; ⚔ Truppenkörper *m*; *fig.* Masse *f*; *in a* ~ zusammen, geschlossen; **2.** ~ *forth* verkörpern; '**~guard** Leibwache *f*; ~ **o·do(u)r** (*abbr. B.O.*) (unangenehmer) Körpergeruch *m*; ~ **snatch·er** Leichenräuber *m*; '**~work** *mot.* Karosserie *f*.
Boer ['bəuə] **1.** Bure *m*; **2.** Buren..., burisch.
bof·fin *sl.* ['bɔfin] Wissenschaftler *m*, Experte *m*.
bog [bɔg] **1.** Sumpf *m*, Moor *n*; Morast *m*; **2.** im Schlamm versenken; *be od. get* ~*ged down* steckenbleiben.
bog·gle ['bɔgl] stutzen, schwanken, unschlüssig sein; pfuschen.
bog·gy ['bɔgi] sumpfig.
bo·gie ['bəugi] 🚃 Drehschemel *m*; *a.* = *bogy*.
bo·gus ['bəugəs] falsch, Schwindel...
bo·gy ['bəugi] Kobold *m*; Popanz *m*, Schreckgespenst *n*; *the* ~ (*man*) der Schwarze Mann.
Bo·he·mi·an [bəu'hi:mjən] **1.** böhmisch; **2.** Böhme *m*, Böhmin *f*; Zigeuner(in); *fig.* Bohemien *m*.
boil [bɔil] **1.** kochen, sieden (*a. fig.*); (sich) kondensieren; **2.** Sieden *n*; Beule *f*, Geschwür *n*; Furunkel *m*; '**boil·er** Sieder *m*; (Dampf-)Kessel *m*, Boiler *m*; ~ *suit* Overall *m*; '**boil·ing** siedend; Siede...
bois·ter·ous □ ['bɔistərəs] ungestüm; heftig, laut; lärmend; '**bois·ter·ous·ness** Ungestüm *n*.
bold □ [bəuld] kühn, keck; *b.s.* dreist; steil (*Küste*); deutlich; *typ.* fett; *make* (*so*) ~ (*as*) *to do* sich erkühnen zu tun; '**bold·ness** Kühnheit *f etc.*; *b.s.* Dreistigkeit *f*.
bole [bəul] starker Baumstamm *m*.
bo·ler·o [bə'lɛərəu] Bolero *m* (*Tanz*); ['bɔlərəu] Bolero *m* (*Damenjacke*).
boll ⚘ [bəul] Samenkapsel *f*.
bol·lard ['bɔləd] ⚓ Poller *m*; Verkehrsinsellampe *f*.
bo·lo·ney *sl.* [bə'ləuni] Quatsch *m*.
Bol·she·vism ['bɔlʃivizəm] Bolschewismus *m*; '**Bol·she·vist** **1.** Bolschewist(in); **2.** bolschewistisch.
bol·ster ['bəulstə] **1.** Kopfkeil *m*; Unterlage *f* (*a.* ⊕); **2.** *mst* ~ *up* polstern; (unter)stützen.
bolt [bəult] **1.** Bolzen *m*; *Tür-, Schloß- etc.* Riegel *m*; Blitzstrahl *m*; Ausreißen *n*, Durchgehen *n*; ~ *upright* kerzengerade; **2.** *v/t.* verbolzen; verriegeln; F hinunterschlingen; *v/i.* eilen, stürzen; durchgehen (*Pferd u. fig.*); *Am. pol.* abtrünnig werden; sieben; '**bolt·er** Ausreißer(in), Durchgänger(in); Beutelsieb *n*.
bolt·hole ['bəulthəul] Schlupfloch *n*.
bomb [bɔm] **1.** *bsd.* ⚔ Bombe *f*; ~ *alert* Bombenalarm *m*; ~ *disposal squad* Bombenräumkommando *n*; **2.** mit Bomben belegen, bombardieren; *bsd. Am.* F *im Examen* durchrasseln, -fallen; ~*ed out* ausgebombt; ~ *up Flugzeug* mit Bomben beladen.
bom·bard [bɔm'ba:d] beschießen; bombardieren (*a. fig. u. phys.*); **bom'bard·ment** Bombardement *n*; Beschießung *f*, Beschuß *m*.
bom·bast ['bɔmbæst] Bombast *m*, Schwulst *m*; **bom'bas·tic, bom'bas·ti·cal** □ bombastisch, schwülstig.
bomb-bay ['bɔmbei] Bombenschacht *m*.
bombed *sl.* [bɔmd] besoffen; high *durch Drogen*.
bomb·er ✈ ['bɔmə] Bomber *m*.
bomb...: '**~-proof** **1.** bombensicher; **2.** Bunker *m*; '**~shell** *fig.* Bombe *f*; '**~-sight** ⚔ Bombenzielgerät *n*.
bo·nan·za *Am.* F [bəu'nænzə] **1.** *fig.* Goldgrube *f*; **2.** sehr einträglich; Groß...
bon·bon ['bɔnbɔn] Bonbon *m*, *n*.
bond [bɔnd] **1.** Band *n* (*a. fig.*); Fessel *f* (*a. fig.*); Bündnis *n*; Schuldschein *m*; ⚚ Obligation *f*; *in* ~ ⚚ unter Zollverschluß; **2.** verpfänden; ⚚ unter Zollverschluß legen; ~*ed port* Zollhafen *m*; ~*ed warehouse* Zollspeicher *m*; '**bond·age** Leibeigenschaft *f*, Hörigkeit *f*; Knechtschaft *f* (*a. fig.*); '**bond-hold·er** Inhaber *m* von Obligationen; '**bond**(*s*)**·man** Leibeigene

m; ˈ**bond**(**s**)**·wom·an** Leibeigene *f*, Hörige *f*.

bone [bəun] **1.** Knochen *m*, Bein *n*; Gräte *f*; ~*s pl. a.* Gebeine *n/pl.*; Kastagnetten *f/pl.*; Würfel *m/pl.*; ~ *of contention* Zankapfel *m*; *feel in one's* ~*s* in den Knochen spüren; sicher sein; *frozen to the* ~ durchgefroren; *have a* ~ *to pick with* F ein Hühnchen zu rupfen haben mit; *make no* ~*s about* F nicht lange fackeln mit; **2.** ausbeinen, entgräten; *a.* ~ *up* F büffeln, fest lernen; **3.** knöchern; Knochen...; **boned** ...knochig; ˈ**bone-**ˈ**dry** knochentrocken; ˈ**bone-dust** Knochenmehl *n*; ˈ**bone-head** *sl.* Dummkopf *m*; ˈ**bone-**ˈ**i·dle,** ˈ**bone-**ˈ**la·zy** *contp.* stinkfaul; ˈ**bon·er** *Am. sl.* Schnitzer *m*, grober Fehler *m*; ˈ**bone-set·ter** Heilgehilfe *m*; ˈ**bone-shak·er** altes Fahrrad *n*; Klapperkasten *m*.

bon·fire [ˈbɔnfaiə] Freudenfeuer *n*; (Reisig-, Kartoffel- *etc.*) Feuer *n*.

bon·kers *sl.* [ˈbɔŋkəz] verrückt.

bon·net [ˈbɔnit] **1.** Haube *f*, Schute(nhut *m*) *f*; Schottenmütze *f*; ⊕ (Motor)Haube *f*; *Schornstein- etc.* Kappe *f*, Haube *f*; ⚓ Bonnett *n*; **2.** mit e-r Mütze *etc.* bedekken.

bon·ny *bsd. schott.* [ˈbɔni] hübsch; drall; rosig; munter.

bo·nus ⚕ [ˈbəunəs] Prämie *f*; Extradividende *f*; Gratifikation *f*; Gewinnanteil *m*; Zulage *f*.

bon·y [ˈbəuni] knöchern; Knochen...; knochig; grätig.

boo [buː] (nieder)brüllen, (aus)pfeifen.

boob *Am.* [buːb] Simpel *m*, Dummkopf *m*.

boo·by [ˈbuːbi] Tölpel *m* (*a. orn.*); ~ *prize* Trostpreis *m*; ~ *hatch Am. sl.* Klapsmühle *f*; ˈ~**-trap** Minenfalle *f*; grober Scherz *m*.

boog·ie-woog·ie [ˈbuːgiwuːgi] Boogie-Woogie *m*.

boo·hoo F [buːˈhuː] plärren.

book [buk] **1.** Buch *n*; Heft *n*; Liste *f*; Block *m* *Fahrkarten etc.*; *the* ♀ die Bibel; *stand in the* ~*s at* ⚕ zu Buche stehen mit; *be in s.o.'s good* (*bad*) ~*s fig.* bei j-m gut (schlecht) angeschrieben sein; *bring s.o. to* ~ von j-m Rechenschaft verlangen; **2.** buchen; einschreiben, -tragen; *Eintritts-, Fahrkarte* lösen; *e-n Platz etc.* bestellen; *Gepäck* aufgeben; F *j.* vormerken; ~ *through* e-e durchgehende Fahrkarte lösen; ˈ~**·bind·er** Buchbinder *m*; ˈ~**·case** Bücherschrank *m*; ˈ~**-end** Bücherstütze *f*; **book·ie** [ˈbuki] F *Sport*: Buchmacher *m*; ˈ**book·ing-clerk** Schalterbeamte *m*; ˈ**book·ing-of·fice** Fahrkartenausgabe *f*, -schalter *m*; *thea.* Kasse *f*; ˈ**book·ish** □ gelehrt; ˈ**book-keep·er** Buchhalter *m*; ˈ**book-keep·ing** Buchführung *f*; **book·let** [ˈ~lit] Büchlein *n*; Broschüre *f*.

book...: ˈ~**-mak·er** Buchmacher *m*; ˈ~**-mark**(**·er**) Lesezeichen *n*; ~**·mo·bile** *Am.* [ˈ~məuˈbiːl] Wanderbücherei *f*; ˈ~**-plate** Exlibris *n*; ˈ~**·sell·er** Buchhändler *m*; ˈ~**·shop** Buchhandlung *f*; ˈ~**-stall** Bücher(verkaufs)stand *m*; ~ **to·ken** Büchergutschein *m*; ˈ~**-worm** Bücherwurm *m* (*a. fig.*).

boom[1] ⚓ [buːm] Baum *m*; Ausleger *m*; Spiere *f*.

boom[2] [~] **1.** ⚕ Aufschwung *m*, Hochkonjunktur *f*, Hausse *f*; Reklamerummel *m*; ~ *and bust* wirtschaftliches Hoch *n* und Tief *n*; **2.** in die Höhe treiben *od.* gehen; für *et.* Reklame machen.

boom[3] [~] **1.** brummen; brausen; dröhnen; **2.** Donnern *n*.

boom·e·rang [ˈbuːməræŋ] Bumerang *m* (*a. fig.*).

boon[1] [buːn] Gefallen *m*; Segen *m*, Wohltat *f*.

boon[2] [~] freundlich, munter; ~ *companion* Zechkumpan *m*.

boon·docks *Am. sl.* [ˈbuːndɔks] *pl.* die Provinz.

boor *fig.* [buə] Bauer *m*, Lümmel *m*, Flegel *m*.

boor·ish □ [ˈbuəriʃ] bäuerisch, lümmel-, flegelhaft; ˈ**boor·ish·ness** flegelhaftes Wesen *n*.

boost [buːst] heben; in die Höhe treiben; nachhelfen (*dat.*), Auftrieb geben (*dat.*); verstärken (*a.* ⚡); Reklame machen; ~ *business* die Wirtschaft ankurbeln; ˈ**boost·er** Verstärkung *f*, Zusatz *m*; ~ *rocket* Startrakete *f*.

boot[1] [buːt]: *to* ~ obendrein.

boot[2] [~] Stiefel *m*; Kofferraum *m*; *the* ~ *is on the other leg* es ist genau umgekehrt; *get the* ~ *sl.* rausfliegen (*entlassen werden*); *give s.o. the* ~ *sl.* j. rausschmeißen *od.* -werfen (*entlas-*

sen); *put the ~ in sl.* kräftig zutreten; '~**black** *Am.* = *shoeblack*; '**boot·ed** gestiefelt; **boot·ee** ['bu:ti:] *Damen-*Halbstiefel *m.*
booth [bu:ð] (Markt-, Schau)Bude *f*; Wahlzelle *f*; *Am.* Fernsprechzelle *f.*
boot...: '**~·jack** Stiefelknecht *m*; '**~·lace** Schnürsenkel *m*; '**~·leg** *bsd. Am.* illegal (*hergestellt, transportiert, verkauft*); Geheim...; Schmuggel...; '**~·leg·ger** Alkoholschmuggler *m*; *weitS.* Schieber *m.*
boot·less *poet.* ['bu:tlis] nutzlos.
boots [bu:ts] Hausdiener *m* (*Hotel*).
boot-tree ['bu:ttri:] Leisten *m.*
boo·ty ['bu:ti] Beute *f*, Raub *m.*
booze P [bu:z] **1.** saufen; **2.** Sauferei *f*; '**booz·y** P besoffen.
bop [bɔp] = *bebop.*
bo-peep [bəu'pi:p] Guck-guck-Spiel *n.*
bo·rax ⚗ ['bɔ:ræks] Borax *m.*
bor·der ['bɔ:də] **1.** Rand *m*, Bord *m*, Saum *m*; Grenze *f e-s Landes*; Einfassung *f*; Leiste *f*; (Schmal-)Beet *n*, Rabatte *f*; *~ state* Randstaat *m*; **2.** begrenzen, einfassen, besetzen; grenzen (*upon* an *acc.*); '**bor·der·er** Grenzbewohner *m*; '**bor·der·land** *mst fig.* Grenzgebiet *n*; '**bor·der·line 1.** Grenzlinie *f*; **2.** zweifelhaft, an der Grenze, Grenz...
bore[1] [bɔ:] **1.** Bohrloch *n*; Bohrung *f e-r Feuerwaffe*, Seele *f*; Kaliber *n*; *et.* Langweiliges *od.* Stumpfsinniges; langweiliger Mensch *m*; **2.** bohren; langweilen; belästigen, *j-m* lästig sein.
bore[2] [~] Springflut *f.*
bore[3] [~] *pret. von bear*[2].
bo·re·al ['bɔ:riəl] nördlich, Nord...
bore·dom ['bɔ:dəm] Langweiligkeit *f*, Langeweile *f*, Stumpfsinn *m.*
bor·er ['bɔ:rə] Bohrer *m.*
bo·ric ac·id ⚗ ['bɔ:rik'æsid] Borsäure *f.*
bor·ing ['bɔ:riŋ] Bohr...; langweilig.
born [bɔ:n] *p.p. von bear*[2] geboren.
borne [bɔ:n] *p.p. von bear*[2] getragen.
bo·ron ⚗ ['bɔ:rɔn] Bor *n.*
bor·ough ['bʌrə] Stadt *f od.* Stadtteil *m mit Parlamentsvertretung*; *Am. a.* Wahlbezirk *m* von New York City; *municipal ~* Stadtgemeinde *f*; *parliamentary ~* städtischer Wahlkreis *m.*

bor·row ['bɔrəu] borgen, aus-, entleihen; '**bor·row·er** Entleiher(in); Kreditnehmer(in); '**bor·row·ing** Anleihe *f*; *gr.* Lehnwort *n*, -form *f.*
Bor·stal ['bɔ:stl] Besserungsanstalt *f*; *~ training* Fürsorgeerziehung *f.*
bos·cage ['bɔskidʒ] Gebüsch *n.*
bosh F [bɔʃ] Blödsinn *m*, Quatsch *m.*
bos·om ['buzəm] Busen *m*; Brust *f*; *fig.* Schoß *m*, Herz *n*, Inneres *n*; *~-friend* Busenfreund(in).
boss[1] [bɔs] **1.** Buckel *m*, Knopf *m*; Schlußstein *m*; **2.** bossieren, treiben.
boss[2] F [~] **1.** Boß *m*, Chef *m*; (Partei)Bonze *m*; **2.** leiten; *sl.* kommandieren.
boss·y ['bɔsi] gebuckelt; *Am.* F herrisch, tyrannisch.
Bos·ton ['bɔstən] *langsamer Walzer.*
bo·tan·ic, bo·tan·i·cal □ [bə'tænik(əl)] botanisch; Pflanzen...; **bot·a·nist** ['bɔtənist] Botaniker(in); **bot·a·nize** ['~naiz] botanisieren; '**bot·a·ny** Botanik *f.*
botch [bɔtʃ] **1.** Flicken *m*; Flickwerk *n*, -wort *n*; **2.** (zs.-)flicken; verpfuschen; '**botch·er** Flicker(in); *fig. contp.* (Flick)Schuster *m.*
both [bəuθ] beide(s); *~ ... and* sowohl ... als (auch); *~ of them* alle beide.
both·er F ['bɔðə] **1.** Plage *f*; **2.** (sich) plagen, (sich) quälen, (sich) aufregen, (sich) beunruhigen, (sich) Sorgen machen; *~ it!* zum Henker damit!; **both·er'a·tion** F Plage *f*; *~!* zum Henker!; **both·er·some** ['~səm] ärgerlich, lästig.
bot·tle ['bɔtl] **1.** Flasche *f*; Bund *n* (*Heu*); **2.** auf Flaschen ziehen; *~ up* ⚔ einschließen; *fig. Zorn etc.* zurückhalten, unterdrücken; *~d beer* Flaschenbier *n*; *bottling plant* (Flaschen)Abfüllanlage *f*; '**~-green** flaschengrün; '**~-neck** *fig.* Engpaß *m*, Enge *f*; Schwierigkeit *f*; '**~-nose** Schnapsnase *f.*
bot·tom ['bɔtəm] **1.** Boden *m*; Grund *m*; Grundfläche *f*, Sohle *f*, Fuß *m*, Ende *n*; *Stuhl-*Sitz *m*; unterster Platz *m in e-r Reihe etc.*; hinterster Teil *m e-s Gartens etc.*; Ankergrund *m*; Schiffsboden *m*; F Hintern *m*; *fig.* Grund *m der Seele*, Wesen *n*, Kern *m*; *at the ~* am untersten Ende, ganz unten; *fig. a. at ~* im Grunde; *get to the ~ of a matter* e-r Sache auf den

Grund gehen *od.* kommen; *jealousy is at the ~ of it* Eifersucht steckt dahinter; *knock the ~ out of an argument* ein Argument entkräften; **2.** grundlegend, Grund...; letzt; **3.** mit e-m Boden versehen; gründen (*upon* auf *acc.*); ergründen; **'bot·tom·less** bodenlos; **'bot·tom·ry** ⚓ Bodmerei *f.*

bou·doir ['bu:dwɑ:] Boudoir *n.*

bough [bau] Ast *m,* Zweig *m.*

bought [bɔ:t] *pret. u. p.p. von buy.*

bouil·lon ['bu:jɔ̃:ŋ] Kraftbrühe *f,* Bouillon *f.*

boul·der ['bəuldə] Geröllblock *m;* Findlingsblock *m.*

bou·le·vard ['bu:lvɑ:] Boulevard *m.*

bounce [bauns] **1.** *plötzlicher* Sprung *m;* Auf-, Rückprall *m;* F Aufschneiderei *f;* Auftrieb *m,* Schwung *m;* **2.** (hoch)springen; hüpfen; schnellen; F platzen (*Scheck*); F aufschneiden; F auszanken; *~ in* (*out*) hinein- (hinaus)stürmen; *~ s.o. out of s.th.* j. aus et. hinausdrängen; **3.** bums!, plauz!; **'bounc·er** F Mordskerl *m,* -weib *n,* -ding *n; Am. sl.* Rausschmeißer *m;* unverschämte Lüge *f;* **'bounc·ing** F Mords...; stramm, drall.

bound[1] [baund] **1.** *pret. u. p.p. von bind;* **2.** *adj.* verpflichtet; *be ~ to do* tun müssen, sicher tun werden; *I will be ~* ich bürge dafür; *s. bind.*

bound[2] [~] bestimmt, unterwegs (*for* nach).

bound[3] [~] **1.** Grenze *f,* Schranke *f; within the ~s of reason* in den Grenzen der Vernunft; *out of ~s* Zutritt verboten (*to* für); **2.** begrenzen; beschränken.

bound[4] [~] **1.** Sprung *m;* **2.** (hoch-) springen; an-, abprallen.

bound·a·ry ['baundəri] Grenze *f; ~ line* Grenzlinie *f.*

boun·den ['baundən]: *my ~ duty* meine Pflicht u. Schuldigkeit.

bound·less □ ['baundlis] end-, grenzenlos, unbegrenzt.

boun·te·ous □ ['bauntiəs], **boun·ti·ful** □ ['~tiful] freigebig; reichlich.

boun·ty ['baunti] Freigebigkeit *f,* Großmut *f; milde* Gabe *f,* Spende *f bsd. des Königs;* ✝ Prämie *f.*

bou·quet [bu:'kei] Bukett *n;* Strauß *m;* Blume *f des Weines.*

bour·bon ['bə:bən] Bourbon *m* (*amerikanischer Maiswhisky*).

bour·geois[1] ['buəʒwɑ:] **1.** Bourgeois *m;* Spießbürger *m;* **2.** bourgeois; spießbürgerlich.

bour·geois[2] *typ.* [bə:'dʒɔis] Borgis *f.*

bour·geoi·sie [buəʒwɑ:'zi:] Bourgeoisie *f.*

bourn(e) *poet.* [buən] Grenze *f.*

bout [baut] Mal *n; Fecht-*Gang *m; Tanz-*Tour *f; Krankheits-*Anfall *m;* Kraftprobe *f;* Gelage *n.*

bou·tique [bu:'ti:k] Modegeschäft *n.*

bo·vine ['bəuvain] rinderartig; träge, stur, dumm.

bov·ril ['bɔvril] Fleischextrakt *m.*

bov·ver *sl.* ['bɔvə] Schlägerei *f; ~-boots pl. schwere Stiefel, mit denen Rocker aufeinander eintreten.*

bow[1] [bau] **1.** Verbeugung *f;* **2.** *v/i.* sich beugen; sich verbeugen, sich verneigen (*to* vor *dat.*); *~ing acquaintance* bloße Grußbekanntschaft *f; v/t.* biegen; *mst fig.* beugen; *~ s.o. in* (*out*) j. mit tiefen Verbeugungen empfangen (hinausführen).

bow[2] ⚓ [~] Bug *m.*

bow[3] [bəu] **1.** Bogen *m;* Bügel *m; gebundene* Schleife *f,* Knoten *m;* **2.** ♪ den Bogen führen; geigen.

bowd·ler·ize ['baudləraiz] *Text* von anstößigen Stellen reinigen.

bow·els ['bauəlz] *pl.* Eingeweide *n; das* Innere; *fig.* Herz *n.*

bow·er ['bauə] Laube *f; poet.* (Schlaf)Gemach *n;* ⚓ Buganker *m.*

bow·ie-knife ['bəuinaif] langes Jagdmesser *n.*

bow·ing ♪ ['bəuiŋ] Bogenführung *f.*

bowl[1] [bəul] Schale *f,* Napf *m,* Schüssel *f;* Bowle *f; Pfeifen-*Kopf *m;* Höhlung *f e-s Löffels etc.*

bowl[2] [~] **1.** Kugel *f; ~s pl.* Bowlingspiel *n;* **2.** *v/t. Ball etc.* werfen; *~ out* hinauswerfen; *~ over* umwerfen (*a. fig.*); *v/i.* rollen; kegeln.

bow-legged ['bəulegd] O-beinig.

bowl·er ['bəulə] *Kricket:* Werfer *m; a. ~ hat* Melone *f* (*steifer Filzhut*).

bowl-fire ⚡ ['bəulfaiə] Heizsonne *f.*

bow·line ⚓ ['bəulin] Bulin(e) *f.*

bowl·ing ['bəuliŋ] Bowling(spiel) *n; ~ al·ley* Kegelbahn *f; ~ green* Rasenplatz *m* zum Bowlingspiel.

bow...: ~·man ['bəumən] Bogenschütze *m;* **'~·sprit** ⚓ Bugspriet *n;* **'~·string** Bogensehne *f;* **~ tie** Fliege *f,* Schleife *f* (*Querbinder*).

bow-wow! ['bau'wau] wauwau!
box¹ [bɔks] **1.** Buchsbaum *m*; Büchse *f*, Dose *f*; Schachtel *f*, Kiste *f*, Kasten *m*; Koffer *m*; ⊕ Gehäuse *n*; *thea.* Loge *f*; Häuschen *n*; Abteilung *f*; Bank *f der Geschworenen*; *a.* ~ *seat* Kutschbock *m*; Box *f im Pferdestall*; **2.** in Kästen *etc.* tun *od.* einschließen; *a.* ~ *up fig.* einpferchen.
box² [~] **1.** boxen; ~ *s.o.'s ear* j. ohrfeigen; **2.** ~ *on the ear* Ohrfeige *f*; '**~-calf** Boxkalf *n* (*Kalbleder*); '**~car** *bsd. Am.* geschlossener Güterwagen *m*; '**box·er** Boxer *m*.
Box·ing-Day ['bɔksiŋdei] zweiter Weihnachtsfeiertag *m*.
box...: '**~-keep·er** Logenschließer (-in); '**~-num·ber** Chiffre *f* (*in Zeitungsanzeigen*); '**~-of·fice** Theaterkasse *f*.
boy [bɔi] **1.** Junge *m*, junger Mann *m*; Bursche *m* (*a. Diener*); **2.** Knaben...; jung, jugendlich; *~-friend* Freund *m* (*eines Mädchens*); ~ *scout* Pfadfinder *m*.
boy·cott ['bɔikət] **1.** boykottieren; **2.** Boykott *m*.
boy·hood ['bɔihud] Knabenalter *n*, Kindheit *f*.
boy·ish □ ['bɔiiʃ] Knaben..., knaben-, jungenhaft; kindisch.
bra F [brɑː] = *brassière*.
brace [breis] **1.** ⊕ Strebe *f*, Stütze *f*, Anker *m*; Stützbalken *m*; Bohrwinde *f*; Klammer *f*, *a. typ.* Akkolade *f*; *hunt.* Paar *n* (*Wild, Geflügel*); ⚓ Brasse *f*; *~s pl.* Tragbänder *n/pl.*; Hosenträger *m/pl.*; **2.** stützen; versteifen; verankern; (an)spannen; ⚓ brassen; *fig.* stärken, erfrischen.
brace·let ['breislit] Armband *n*.
brac·ing ['breisiŋ] kräftigend, erfrischend (*Klima etc.*).
brack·en ⚘ ['brækən] Farnkraut *n*.
brack·et ['brækit] **1.** ⚠ Kragstein *m*, Konsole *f*; Winkelstütze *f*; *typ.* Klammer *f*; *Leuchter-*, *Gas*-Arm *m*; ⚓ Klampe *f*; *lower income* ~ niedrige Einkommensstufe *f*; **2.** einklammern; *fig.* gleichstellen.
brack·ish ['brækiʃ] brackig, salzig.
bract ⚘ [brækt] Deckblatt *n*.
brad [bræd] Drahtstift *m*.
brae *schott.* [brei] (Ab)Hang *m*.
brag [bræg] **1.** Prahlerei *f*; **2.** prahlen (*of, about* mit).
brag·gart ['brægət] **1.** Prahler *m*; **2.** □ prahlerisch.
Brahm·an ['brɑːmən], *mst* **Brahmin** ['~min] **1.** Brahmane *m*; **2.** brahmanisch.
braid [breid] **1.** *Haar*-Flechte *f*; Borte *f*; Litze *f*; ⚔ Tresse *f*; **2.** flechten; mit Borte *etc.* besetzen.
brail ⚓ [breil] Geitau *n*.
braille [breil] Blindenschrift *f*.
brain [brein] **1.** Gehirn *n*, Hirn *n*; *~s pl. fig.* Kopf *m*, Köpfchen *n*, Verstand *m*; *have s.th. on the* ~ nur Gedanken für etwas haben; *pick od. suck s.o.'s* ~ F j-m die Würmer aus der Nase ziehen, j-s Ideen stehlen; *turn s.o.'s* ~ j. eingebildet machen; **2.** *j-m* den Schädel einschlagen; '**~child** Geistesprodukt *n*; ~ **drain** Abwanderung *f* der Intelligenz; **brained** ...köpfig.
brain...: '**~-fag** geistige Erschöpfung *f*; '**~-fe·ver** Gehirnentzündung *f*; '**~less** hirnlos; *fig.* unbesonnen; '**~-pan** Hirnschale *f*; '**~-storm·ing** Ideen-Konferenz *f*; **brain(s) trust** *Am.* Expertenrat *m*, Beratergruppe *f* (*mst pol.*).
brain...: '**~-twist·er** Denkaufgabe *f*; harte Nuß *f*; '**~wash** e-r Gehirnwäsche unterziehen; '**~-wash·ing** Gehirnwäsche *f*; '**~-wave** F Geistesblitz *m*, genialer Einfall *m*; '**~-work** Kopfarbeit *f*; '**brain·y** gescheit.
braise [breiz] *Küche*: schmoren, dünsten.
brake¹ [breik] Farnkraut *n*; Dikkicht *n*, Unterholz *n*.
brake² [~] **1.** ⊕ Bremse *f* (*a. fig.*); Kremser *m*; Wagen *m zum Einfahren der Pferde*; ~ *fluid mot.* Bremsflüssigkeit *f*; ~ *pedal* Bremspedal *n*; 2. bremsen; **brake(s)·man** 🚂 ['~(s)-mən] Bremser *m*; *Am.* Schaffner *m*; '**brak·ing** Brems...; ~ *distance* Bremsweg *m*.
bram·ble ⚘ ['bræmbl] Brombeerstrauch *m*; '**bram·bly** dornig.
bran [bræn] Kleie *f*.
branch [brɑːntʃ] **1.** Zweig *m*, Ast *m*; Arm *m*; Fach *n*; Dezernat *n*; Linie *f des Stammbaums*; Abkömmling *m*; Teil *m*; *a. local* ~ Zweigstelle *f*, Filiale *f*; Ortsgruppe *f*; *chief of* ~ Dezernent *m*; **2.** *a.* ~ *out* (sich) verzweigen; *a.* ~ *off* abzweigen; '**branch·ing** ⚡ Abzweigung *f*;

ˈ**branch-line** 🚂 Nebenlinie *f*; **branch of·fice** Zweigstelle *f*, Filiale *f*; ˈ**branch·y** zweigig.

brand [brænd] **1.** (Feuer)Brand *m*; ⚘ Brand *m*; Brandzeichen *n*, -mal *n*; *a.* ~*ing iron* Brand-, Brenneisen *n*; Marke *f*; Sorte *f*; Fabrikzeichen *n*; *poet.* Schwert *n*; ~ *name* Markenname *m*; **2.** einbrennen; mit e-m Brandzeichen versehen; brandmarken.

bran·dish [ˈbrændiʃ] schwingen.

bran(d)·new [ˈbræn(d)ˈnjuː] nagelneu.

bran·dy [ˈbrændi] Kognak *m*; Weinbrand *m*; Branntwein *m*; Schnaps *m*; ˈ~**-ball** Kognakbohne *f*.

brant *orn.* [brænt] Wildgans *f*.

brash *contp.* [bræʃ] ungestüm; unverfroren; unüberlegt.

brass [brɑːs] Messing *n*; F (Kupfer-) Geld *n*; *fig.* Unverschämtheit *f*; *the* ~ ♪ die Blechbläser *m/pl.*; ~ *band* Blaskapelle *f*; ~ *hat* ⚔ *sl.* Stabsoffizier *m*, hohes Tier *n*; ~ *knuckles pl. Am.* Schlagring *m*; ~ *tacks pl. sl.* die Hauptsache; *get down to* ~ *tacks* zur Sache kommen.

bras·sard [ˈbræsɑːd] Armbinde *f*.

bras·se·rie [brɑːsəˈriː] Restaurant *n* (mit Bierausschank).

bras·sière [ˈbræsiə] Büstenhalter *m*.

bras·sy [ˈbrɑːsi] messingartig; *fig.* unverschämt.

brat F [bræt] *contp.* Balg *m*, Range *f*.

bra·va·do [brəˈvɑːdəu], *pl.* ~**(e)s** herausforderndes Benehmen *n*.

brave [breiv] **1.** □ brav, tapfer, mutig, kühn; großartig, prächtig; **2.** trotzen; mutig begegnen (*dat.*); **3.** indianischer Krieger *m*; ˈ**brav·er·y** Tapferkeit *f*; Pracht *f*.

bra·vo [ˈbrɑːˈvəu] bravo!

brawl [brɔːl] **1.** Krakeel *m*, Krawall *m*; **2.** krakeelen, Krawall machen, lärmen; zanken; ˈ**brawl·er** Krakeeler(in).

brawn [brɔːn] *Art* Sülze *f*; Muskeln *m/pl.*; *fig.* Muskelkraft *f*; ˈ**brawn·i·ness** Muskelkraft *f*; ˈ**brawn·y** muskulös.

bray[1] [brei] **1.** Eselsschrei *m*; Schmettern *n*, Dröhnen *n*; **2.** schreien (*Esel*); schmettern; dröhnen.

bray[2] [~] (zer)stoßen, kleinreiben.

braze ⊕ [breiz] hartlöten.

bra·zen □ [ˈbreizn] **1.** bronzen; metallisch; *a.* ~*-faced* unverschämt; **2.** ~ *it out* es kaltschnäuzig durchstehen; ˈ**bra·zen·ness** Unverschämtheit *f*.

bra·zier [ˈbreizjə] Kupferschmied *m*; Kohlenpfanne *f*.

Bra·zil·ian [brəˈziljən] **1.** brasil(ian)isch; **2.** Brasili(an)er(in).

Bra·zil-nut [brəˈzil ˈnʌt] Paranuß *f*.

breach [briːtʃ] **1.** Bruch *m*; *fig.* Verletzung *f*; ⚔ Bresche *f*; ~ *of contract* Vertragsbruch *m*; ~ *of duty* Verletzung *f* der Amtspflicht; ~ *of peace* Friedensbruch *m*; **2.** eine Bresche schlagen in (*acc.*); durchbrechen.

bread [bred] Brot *n* (*a. Lebensunterhalt*); ~ *and butter* Butterbrot *n*; *take the* ~ *out of s.o.'s mouth* j-m sein Brot nehmen; *know which side one's* ~ *is buttered* s-n Vorteil (er)kennen; ˈ~**-bas·ket** Brotkorb *m*; ˈ~**-crumb 1.** Brotkrume *f*; **2.** panieren; ˈ~**-fruit** ⚘ Brotfrucht *f*; ˈ~**-grains** *pl.* Brotgetreide *n*; ˈ~**-line** Schlange *f* von Bedürftigen (*an die Lebensmittel verteilt werden*).

breadth [bredθ] Breite *f*, Weite *f*; Bahn *f* (*Stoff*); *fig.* Größe *f*; Großzügigkeit *f*.

bread-win·ner [ˈbredwinə] Ernährer *m e-r Familie.*

break [breik] **1.** Bruch *m*; Lücke *f*; Pause *f*, Unterbrechung *f*; Wechsel *m*, Umschwung *m*; *typ.* Absatz *m*; ✝ *Am.* (Preis)Rückgang *m*; Kremser *m*; Wagen *m zum Einfahren der Pferde*; Anbruch *m* (*of day* des Tages); *Billard*: Serie *f*; *a bad* ~ F e-e Dummheit *f*; Pech *n*; *a lucky* ~ Glück *n*; *give s.o. a* ~ F j-m e-e Chance geben; **2.** (*irr.*) *v/t.* (zer)brechen; unterbrechen; ⚡ ab-, ausschalten; übertreten; abrichten; *Bank* sprengen; *Brief*, *Tür* erbrechen; zerschlagen; zerreißen; *Stück* abbrechen; *Vorrat* anbrechen; *Nachricht* schonend mitteilen; ✓ umbrechen; ruinieren; ~ *a leg! sl.* Hals- und Beinbruch!; ~ *down* niederbrechen, niederschlagen; ~ *in* einbrechen; abrichten, einfahren, zureiten; gewöhnen (*to* an *acc.*); ~ *up* entzwei-, zerbrechen; auflösen; entlassen; *Schule* schließen; *v/i.* (zer)brechen; bersten; sich brechen (*Wellen*); aus-, losbrechen; anbrechen; aufbrechen; hervorbrechen; umschlagen (*Wetter*); ~ *away* sich losreißen; abfallen; sich zerteilen; ~ *down* zs.-brechen; steckenbleiben; e-e Panne haben; versagen; durchfallen (*beim Examen*); ~ *into a run* sich in Lauf setzen; ~ *up* schließen (*Schule*); *s. a. broken*; ˈ**break·a·ble** zerbrechlich; ˈ**break·age** Zerbrechen *n*; Bruch *m*; Bruchstelle *f*; ˈ**break-down** Zs.-bruch *m*; Maschinenschaden *m*; *mot.* Panne *f*; *nervous* ~ Nervenzusammenbruch *m*; ~ *lorry*, ~ *truck* Abschleppwagen *m*; ~ *service* Pannendienst *m*; ˈ**break·er** Brecher(in) *etc.* (*s. break 2*); ~*s pl.* Brandung *f*.

break...: ~**·fast** [ˈbrekfəst] **1.** Frühstück *n*; ~ *television* Fernsehen *n* am frühen Morgen; *have* ~ = **2.** frühstücken; ~**·neck** [ˈbreiknek] halsbrecherisch; ˈ~**-out** Ausbruch *m*; ˈ~**-through** ⚔ Durchbruch *m*; ˈ~-ˈ**up** Verfall *m*; Auflösung *f*; Schulschluß *m*; (Wetter)Umschlag *m*; ˈ~**·wa·ter** Wellenbrecher *m*.

bream *ichth.* [bri:m] Brassen *m*.

breast [brest] **1.** Brust *f*; Busen *m*; Herz *n*; *make a clean* ~ *of s.th.* et. offen gestehen; **2.** ankämpfen gegen; trotzen (*dat.*); ˈ**breast·ed** ...brüstig.

breast...: ˈ~**-feed** *Säugling* stillen; ˈ~**-pin** Busennadel *f*; ˈ~**·plate** Brustharnisch *m*; ˈ~**-stroke** Brustschwimmen *n*; ˈ~**·work** ⚔ Brustwehr *f*.

breath [breθ] Atem *m*; Atemzug *m*; Hauch *m*; *bad* ~ übler Mundgeruch *m*; *under od. below one's* ~ flüsternd; *out of* ~ atemlos, außer Atem; *waste one's* ~ s-e Worte verschwenden.

breath·a·lys·er [ˈbreθəlaizə] Alkoholtestgerät *n*, ‚Röhrchen' *n*.

breathe [bri:ð] *v/i.* atmen; Atem holen; *fig.* leben; *v/t.* (aus-, ein)atmen; hauchen; leise äußern; verschnaufen lassen; ˈ**breath·er** Atemübung *f*; Atempause *f*; Strapaze *f*.

breath·ing [ˈbri:ðiŋ] **1.** lebenstreu (*Porträt*); **2.** Atmen *n*; Hauch *m*; ˈ~**-space**, ˈ~**-time** (Atem)Pause *f*.

breath·less □ [ˈbreθlis] atemlos; ˈ**breath·less·ness** Atemlosigkeit *f*.

breath-tak·ing [ˈbreθteikiŋ] atemberaubend.

bred [bred] *pret. u. p.p. von breed* [2.]

breech ⊕ [bri:tʃ] Verschluß *m am Gewehr od. Geschütz*; **breech·es** [ˈbritʃiz] *pl.* Knie-, Reithosen *f/pl.*; F Hosen *f/pl.*; *she wears the* ~ sie hat die Hosen an; ˈ**breech·es-buoy** ⚓ Hosenboje *f*; **breech-load·er** [ˈbri:tʃləudə] Hinterlader *m*.

breed [bri:d] **1.** Brut *f*, Zucht *f*; Rasse *f*; Herkunft *f*; Art *f*, Schlag *m*; **2.** (*irr.*) *v/t.* erzeugen; auf-, erziehen; züchten; *v/i.* sich fortpflanzen; sich vermehren; ˈ**breed·er** Erzeuger(in); Züchter(in); *phys.* Brutreaktor *m*; ˈ**breed·ing** Erziehung *f*; Bildung *f*; Zucht *f von Tieren*; ~ *ground* Brutstätte *f*.

breeze[1] [bri:z] **1.** Brise *f*, leichter Wind *m*; F Streit *m*; **2.** ~ *in* F hereingeschneit kommen.

breeze[2] ⊕ [~] Kohlenlösche *f*; ~ *block* Leichtbaustein *m*; ~ *concrete* Leichtbeton *m*.

breez·y [ˈbri:zi] windig, luftig; frisch, flott, lebhaft.

Bren gun ⚔ [ˈbrenˈgʌn] leichtes Maschinengewehr *n*.

brent-goose *orn.* [ˈbrentˈgu:s] Ringelgans *f*.

breth·ren *eccl.* [ˈbreðrin] *pl.* Brüder *m/pl.*

breve [bri:v] Kürzezeichen *n* (*über Vokalen*).

bre·vet ⚔ [ˈbrevit] Brevet *n* (*höherer Rang ohne entsprechenden Sold*); ~ *rank* Titularrang *m*; ~ *major* Hauptmann *m* im Rang e-s Majors.

bre·vi·ar·y *eccl.* [ˈbri:vjəri] Brevier *n*.

brev·i·ty [ˈbreviti] Kürze *f*.

brew [bru:] **1.** *v/t. u. v/i.* brauen; zubereiten; *fig.* anzetteln; *v/i.* sich zs.-brauen, im Anzug sein (*Sturm, Gewitter*); **2.** Gebräu *n*; ˈ**brew·age** *lit.* Gebräu *n*; ˈ**brew·er** Brauer *m*; ˈ**brew·er·y** Brauerei *f*.

bri·ar [ˈbraiə] = *brier*[1] *u. brier*[2].

brib·a·ble [ˈbraibəbl] bestechlich; **bribe 1.** Bestechung(sgeld *n*, -geschenk *n*) *f*; **2.** bestechen, verlocken (*to* zu); ˈ**brib·er** Bestecher(in); ˈ**brib·er·y** Bestechung *f*.

bric-a-brac [ˈbrikəbræk] Nippsachen *f/pl.*

brick [brik] **1.** Back-, Ziegelstein *m*; (Bau)Klotz *m*; *a regular* ~ F ein Prachtkerl *m*; *drop a* ~ F ins Fettnäpfchen treten; *make* ~*s without straw* et. Schwieriges versuchen; **2.** mit Backsteinen mauern; ˈ~**·bat** Ziegelbrocken *m*; ˈ~**-kiln** Ziegelofen *m*; ˈ~**·lay·er** Maurer *m*; ˈ~**-works** *sg.* Ziegelei *f*.

brid·al ['braidl] **1.** □ bräutlich; Braut...; ~ *procession* Brautzug *m*; **2.** *mst poet.* Hochzeit *f*.
bride [braid] Braut *f* (*am Hochzeitstage, oft auch kurz vorher oder nachher*), Neuvermählte *f*; '**~·groom** Bräutigam *m*, Neuvermählte *m*; '**brides·maid** Brautjungfer *f*; **brides·man** ['~zmən] Brautführer *m*; **bride-to-'be** zukünftige Braut *f*.
bride·well ['braidwəl] Arbeitshaus *n*.
bridge[1] [bridʒ] **1.** Brücke *f* (*a.* ⚓); Steg *m* (*der Violine*); **2.** eine Brücke schlagen über (*acc.*); *fig.* überbrücken.
bridge[2] [~] Bridge *n* (*Kartenspiel*).
bridge...: '**~-head** Brückenkopf *m*; '**~-work** Brücke *f* (*Zahnersatz*).
bri·dle ['braidl] **1.** Zaum *m*; Zügel *m*; **2.** *v/t.* (auf)zäumen; zügeln; *v/i. a.* ~ *up* den Kopf aufwerfen; '**~-path,** '**~-road** Reitweg *m*.
bri·doon [bri'du:n] Trense *f*.
brief [bri:f] **1.** □ kurz, knapp, bündig; flüchtig; **2.** Auftrag *m* und schriftliche Instruktion *f* an den plädierenden Anwalt; *weitS.* Mandat *n*; *päpstliches* Breve *n*; ⚔, ✈ Einsatzbesprechung *f*, Befehlsausgabe *f*; *hold a* ~ *for* einstehen für; *take a* ~ ⚖ e-e Sache übernehmen; **3.** ⚖ *Anwalt, a.* ⚔ beauftragen und informieren; '**~-bag,** '**~-case** Aktenmappe *f*; '**brief·ness** Kürze *f*.
bri·er[1] ⚘ ['braiə] Dorn-, Hagebuttenstrauch *m*, wilde Rose *f*.
bri·er[2] [~] *a.* ~ *pipe* Bruyèrepfeife *f*.
brig ⚓ [brig] Brigg *f*.
bri·gade ⚔ [bri'geid] **1.** Brigade *f*; **2.** zu einer Brigade vereinigen; **brig·a·dier** [brigə'diə] Brigadekommandeur *m*, -general *m*.
brig·and ['brigənd] Brigant *m*; '**brig·and·age** Brigantentum *n*; Räuberei *f*.
bright □ [brait] hell, leuchtend, glänzend, klar; blank; heiter; lebhaft; gescheit, klug, aufgeweckt; '**bright·en** *v/t.* auf-, erhellen; polieren; aufheitern; *v/i. a.* ~ *up* sich aufhellen; '**bright·ness** Helligkeit *f*; Glanz *m*, Helle *f*; Klarheit *f*; Heiterkeit *f*; Aufgewecktheit *f*; ~ *control Fernsehen*: Helligkeitsregler *m*.
brill *ichth.* [brill] Glattbutt *m*.
bril·liance, bril·lian·cy ['briljəns(i)] Glanz *m*; *fig.* Intelligenz *f*; '**bril·liant** **1.** □ glänzend, strahlend; prächtig; brillant; ausgezeichnet; hochbegabt; **2.** Brillant *m*.
brim [brim] **1.** Rand *m*; Krempe *f*; **2.** bis zum Rande füllen *od.* voll sein; ~ *over* überfließen (*a. fig.*), über den Rand treten; '**~'ful,** '**~-'full** ganz voll; '**~·less** ohne Rand.
brim·stone ['brimstən] Schwefel *m*; ~ **but·ter·fly** *zo.* Zitronenfalter *m*.
brin·dle(d) ['brindl(d)] scheckig.
brine [brain] **1.** Salzwasser *n*, Sole *f*; *poet.* Meer *n*; **2.** (ein)salzen.
bring [briŋ] (*irr.*) bringen; tragen; *j.* veranlassen; *Klage* erheben; *Grund etc.* vorbringen; ~ *about*, ~ *to pass* zustande bringen, herbeiführen; ~ *along* mitbringen; ~ *down Preise* herabsetzen; ~ *down the house thea.* stürmischen Beifall ernten; ~ *forth* hervorbringen; gebären; ~ *forward* fördern; anführen, zitieren; ✝ übertragen; ~ *home to j.* überzeugen; *j-m et.* klarmachen *od.* nahebringen; ~ *in* (hin)einbringen; *Gewinn* bringen; ~ *in guilty* für schuldig erklären; ~ *off* zustande bringen; durchführen; ~ *on* herbeiführen; ~ *out* in die Gesellschaft einführen; herausbringen, veröffentlichen; vorbringen; ~ *round* wieder zu sich bringen; ~ *s.o. to do* j. dahin bringen, daß er tut; ~ *o.s. to do* es fertigbringen zu tun; ~ *to* ⚓ beidrehen; ~ *s.o. to himself* j. wieder zu sich bringen; ~ *under* unterwerfen; ~ *up* herauf-, *fig.* vorbringen; zur Sprache bringen; auf-, erziehen; erbrechen, ausspeien; innehalten lassen; *bsd.* ⚓ die Reise beenden.
bring·er ['briŋə] Überbringer(in).
brink [briŋk] Rand *m*; '**~·man·ship** Politik *f* des äußersten Risikos.
brin·y ['braini] salzig.
bri·quette [bri'ket] Brikett *n*.
brisk [brisk] **1.** □ lebhaft, munter, lebendig; frisch (drauflosgehend); rasch, flink; belebend, frisch; **2.** *mst* ~ *up* (sich) beleben.
bris·ket ['briskit] Bruststück *n e-s Tieres*.
brisk·ness ['brisknis] Lebhaftigkeit *f*.
bris·tle ['brisl] **1.** Borste *f*; **2.** *oft* ~ *up* (sich) sträuben; hochfahren, zornig *od.* borstig werden (*with* vor *dat.*); ~ *with fig.* starren *od.* strotzen

von; 'bris·tled, 'bris·tly gesträubt; borstig, struppig.
Bri·tan·nic [bri'tænik] britannisch.
Brit·ish ['britiʃ] britisch; *the* ~ *pl.* die Briten *pl.*; '**Brit·ish·er** *bsd. Am.* Einwohner(in) Großbritanniens.
Brit·on *hist., poet.* ['britn] Brite *m.*
brit·tle ['britl] zerbrechlich, spröde; *fig.* reizbar; '**brit·tle·ness** Sprödigkeit *f etc.*
broach [brəutʃ] **1.** Bratspieß *m*; ⊕ Stecheisen *n*; Räumnadel *f*; **2.** *Faß* anzapfen, anstechen; vorbringen; *Thema* anschneiden.
broad □ [brɔːd] breit; weit; hell (*Tag*); deutlich (*Wink etc.*); (zu) frei, derb (*Witz*); allgemein; weitherzig, liberal; breit (*Aussprache*); '~**-axe** ⊕ Breitbeil *n*, Zimmeraxt *f*; '~'**brimmed** breitrandig; '~**·cast** **1.** ✓ breitwürfig; *fig.* weitverbreitet; **2.** (*irr. cast*) *v/t.* ✓ breitwürfig säen; *fig.* weit verbreiten; *Radio*: senden, übertragen; *v/i.* senden; ~*ing station* Rundfunkstation *f*; **3.** Rundfunk(sendung *f*) *m*; '~**·cast·er** Rundfunksprecher(in); '~**·cloth** feiner Wollstoff *m*; '**broad·en** (sich) verbreitern; (sich) erweitern; '**broad'mind·ed** weitherzig, großzügig; '**broad·ness** Plumpheit *f*, Gemeinheit *f der Sprache*.
broad...: '~**·sheet** Flugblatt *n*; '~**·side** ⚓ Breitseite *f* (*a.* ⚔ *u. fig.*); *a.* = *broadsheet*; '~**·sword** Pallasch *m.*
bro·cade [brəu'keid] Brokat *m*; **bro'cad·ed** brokaten, aus Brokat.
broc·co·li ⚘ ['brɔkəli] Brokkoli *pl.*, Spargelkohl *m.*
bro·chure [brəu'ʃjuə] Broschüre *f.*
brogue [brəug] derber Schuh *m*; (*bsd.* irische) Mundart *f.*
broi·der ['brɔidə] = *embroider*.
broil [brɔil] **1.** Lärm *m*, Streit *m*; **2.** auf dem Rost braten; *fig.* in der Sonne braten; *fig.* kochen; ~*ing* glühend heiß; '**broil·er** Bratrost *m*; Brathühnchen *n.*
broke [brəuk] **1.** *pret. von break 2*; **2.** *sl.* pleite, ohne einen Pfennig.
bro·ken ['brəukən] *p.p. von break 2*; ~ *health* zerrüttete Gesundheit *f*; ~ *home* gestörte häusliche Verhältnisse *n/pl.*; ~ *stones pl.* Steinschlag *m*, Schotter *m*; ~ *time* Verdienstausfall *m*; *speak* ~ *English* gebrochen Englisch sprechen; '~**-'heart·ed** mit gebrochenem Herzen; '**bro·ken·ly** gebrochen; mit Unterbrechungen; ruckweise; '**bro·ken-'wind·ed** *vet.* kurzatmig.
bro·ker ['brəukə] Zwangsversteigerer *m*; ⚚ Makler *m*; Agent *m*; '**bro·ker·age** ⚚ Maklergeschäft *n*; Maklergebühr *f.*
bro·king ⚚ ['brəukiŋ] Maklergeschäft *n.*
bro·mide ['brəumaid] ⚗ Bromid *n*; *sl.* Binsenwahrheit *f*; **bro·mine** ⚗ ['~miːn] Brom *n.*
bron·chi·al *anat.* ['brɔŋkjəl] Bronchial...; **bron·chi·tis** ⚕ [brɔŋ'kaitis] Bronchitis *f.*
bron·co ['brɔŋkəu] (halb)wildes Pferd *n*; ~**-bust·er** *sl.* ['~bʌstə] Zureiter *m.*
Bronx cheer *Am.* ['brɔŋks'tʃiə] *verächtliches* Zischen *n.*
bronze [brɔnz] **1.** Bronze *f*; **2.** bronzen, Bronze...; **3.** bronzieren; *fig.* bräunen; ♀ **Age** Bronzezeit *f.*
brooch [brəutʃ] Brosche *f*; Spange *f.*
brood [bruːd] **1.** Brut *f*; Schwarm *m*; *attr.* Zucht..., *z. B.* ~ *hen*, ~ *sow*, *etc.* Zuchthenne *f*, -sau *f etc.*; **2.** brüten (*a. fig.*); nachdenken; '**brood·er** *Am.* Brutkasten *m.*
brook[1] [bruk] Bach *m.*
brook[2] *rhet.* [~] *mst verneint*: *et.* vertragen; *the matter* ~*s no delay* die Sache gestattet keinen Aufschub.
brook·let ['bruklit] Bächlein *n.*
broom ⚘ [bruːm] Ginster *m*; [brum] Besen *m*; ~**·stick** ['brumstik] Besenstiel *m.*
broth [brɔθ] Fleisch-, Kraftbrühe *f.*
broth·el ['brɔθl] Bordell *n.*
broth·er ['brʌðə] Bruder *m*; ~(*s*) *and sister*(*s*) Geschwister *pl.*; ~**·hood** ['~hud] Bruderschaft *f*; '~**-in-law** Schwager *m*; '**broth·er·ly** brüderlich.
brougham ['bruːəm] Brougham *m* (*zweisitziger Wagen*).
brought [brɔːt] *pret. u. p.p. von bring*; ~*-in capital* Geschäftseinlage *f.*
brow [brau] (Augen)Braue *f*; Stirn *f*; Kante *f e-s Steilhanges*; Abhang *m*; Vorsprung *m*; '~**·beat** (*irr. beat*) einschüchtern; tyrannisieren.
brown [braun] **1.** braun; ~ *ale* mildes, dunkles Ale *n*; ~ *bread* Schwarzbrot *n*; ~ *paper* Packpapier *n*; *be in a* ~ *study* in

Gedanken versunken sein; **2.** Braun *n*; **3.** (sich) bräunen; *~ed off sl.* gelangweilt; restlos bedient; **brown·ie** ['~ni] Heinzelmännchen *n*; Pfadfinderin *f* (*8–11 Jahre alt*); '**brown·ish** bräunlich; '**brown·ness** Bräune *f* (*Farbe*); '**brown·stone** *Am.* **1.** rotbrauner Sandstein *m*; **2.** wohlhabend.

browse [brauz] **1.** Grasen *n*; *fig.* Schmökern *n*; **2.** grasen, weiden; *fig.* naschen (*on* von); schmökern.

Bru·in ['bru:in] Braun *m*, Petz *m* (*der Bär*).

bruise [bru:z] **1.** Quetschung *f*, blauer Fleck *m*; **2.** *v/t.* (zer)quetschen; *Malz* schroten; *v/i.* blaue Flecke bekommen; '**bruis·er** *sl.* Boxer *m*.

brunch [brʌntʃ] ausgedehntes, spätes Frühstück *n*.

bru·nette [bru:'net] **1.** Brünette *f*; **2.** brünett.

brunt [brʌnt] Hauptstoß *m*, (volle) Wucht *f*; *das* Schwerste; *bear the ~* die Hauptlast tragen.

brush [brʌʃ] **1.** Bürste *f*; großer Pinsel *m*; Rute *f des Fuchses*; ⚡ Strahlenbündel *n*; Scharmützel *n*; Unterholz *n*, Gestrüpp *n*; *give a ~* abbürsten; *have a ~ with s.o.* mit j-m aneinandergeraten; **2.** *v/t.* (ab-, aus)bürsten, abkehren; streifen (*leicht berühren*); *~ aside fig.* beiseite schieben; *~ away*, *~ off et.* abbürsten; *~ down j.* abbürsten; *~ off j.* abblitzen lassen, abweisen; *~ up* wieder aufbürsten, *fig.* auffrischen; *v/i.* bürsten; *a. ~ away*, *~ off* (davon)stürzen, (davon)eilen; *~ against s.o.* j. streifen; gegen j. laufen; *~ by od. past* vorbeisausen, -rennen (an *dat*); '**~·wood** Gestrüpp *n*, Unterholz *n*.

brusque □ [brusk] brüsk, barsch, schroff.

Brus·sels sprouts ⚘ ['brʌsl'sprauts] *pl.* Rosenkohl *m*.

bru·tal □ ['bru:tl] viehisch; brutal, roh, gemein; **bru·tal·i·ty** [~'tæliti] Brutalität *f*, Roheit *f*; **bru·tal·ize** ['~təlaiz] zum Tier machen; brutal behandeln; **brute 1.** tierisch, viehisch; unvernünftig, dumm; gefühllos, roh; **2.** (unvernünftiges) Vieh *n* (*a. fig. roher Mensch*); F Untier *n*, Scheusal *n*; '**brut·ish** □ = *brute 1*; '**brut·ish·ness** Roheit *f*; Dummheit *f*.

bub·ble ['bʌbl] **1.** Blase *f*; *fig.* Seifenblase *f*; Schwindel *m*; **2.** sieden; sprudeln; *~* **gum** Bubble-Gum *m*, Knallkaugummi *m*; '**bub·bly 1.** sprudelnd, schäumend; **2.** *co.* Schampus *m*, Sekt *m*.

buc·ca·neer [bʌkə'niə] **1.** Seeräuber *m*; **2.** Seeräuberei treiben.

buck [bʌk] **1.** *zo.* (*bsd.* Reh)Bock *m*; Rammler *m* (*Hase*); Stutzer *m*; *Am. sl.* Dollar *m*; *pass the ~* F die Verantwortung von sich abschieben; **2.** bocken; *Am.* F dagegen sein; angehen gegen; *~ up* F sich zs.-reißen; sich beeilen; aufmuntern, in Schwung bringen.

bucket ['bʌkit] **1.** Eimer *m*, Kübel *m*; *a mere drop in the ~* ein Tropfen auf den heißen Stein; **2.** F *Pferd* abjagen; (dahin)rasen; **~·ful** ['~ful] Eimervoll *m*; *~* **seat** *mot.* Schalensitz *m*; '**~-shop** Winkelbörse *f*.

buck·le ['bʌkl] **1.** Schnalle *f*, Spange *f*; **2.** *v/t.* (an-, auf-, um-, zu)schnallen; *v/i.* ⊕ sich (ver)biegen; *~ to a task* sich ernsthaft an eine Aufgabe machen; '**buck·ler** Schild *m*.

buck·ram ['bʌkrəm] Steifleinen *n*; *fig.* Steifheit *f*.

buck...: '**~·shot** *hunt.* Rehposten *m*; '**~·skin** Wildleder *n*; Buckskin *m* (*Stoff*); '**~·wheat** ⚘ Buchweizen *m*.

bud [bʌd] **1.** Knospe *f*, Auge *n*; *fig.* Keim *m*; *Am.* Debütantin *f*; *in ~* in der Knospe; *nip in the ~ fig.* im Keim ersticken; **2.** *v/t.* okulieren; *v/i.* knospen, sprossen; *~ding lawyer etc.* angehender Jurist *m etc.*

Bud·dhism ['budizəm] Buddhismus *m*; '**Bud·dhist** Buddhist(in).

bud·dy *Am.* F ['bʌdi] Kumpel *m*, Kamerad *m*.

budge [bʌdʒ] *v/i.* sich (von der Stelle) rühren; *v/t.* bewegen.

bud·ger·i·gar ['bʌdʒəriga:] Wellensittich *m*.

budg·et ['bʌdʒit] Budget *n*, Staatshaushalt *m*, Haushaltsplan *m*; *mst fig.* Vorrat *m*, Menge *f*; *draft ~* Haushaltsplan *m*; *open the ~* das Budget vorlegen; '**budg·et·ar·y** Budget...

bud·gie F ['bʌdʒi] = *budgerigar*.

buff[1] [bʌf] **1.** Ochsenleder *n*; Lederfarbe *f*; bloße Haut *f*; *in (one's) ~* nackt; **2.** lederfarben, blaßgelb.

buff[2] F [~] Fan *m*, ...narr *m*.

buf·fa·lo *zo.* ['bʌfələu], *pl.* **buf·fa-**

loes ['~z] Büffel *m*.
buff·er ['bʌfə] 🚂 Puffer *m*; *a.* ~ *stop* Prellbock *m*; *old* ~ *sl.* alter Kauz *m*; ~ *state* Pufferstaat *m*.
buf·fet[1] ['bʌfit] **1.** Puff *m*, Stoß *m*, Schlag *m*; **2.** puffen, schlagen; ankämpfen gegen; kämpfen (*with* mit).
buf·fet[2] ['bufei] Büfett *n*; Schanktisch *m*, Theke *f*; Tisch *m* mit Speisen und Getränken; Erfrischungsraum *m*; ~ *car* 🚂 Erfrischungswagen *m*.
buf·foon [bə'fu:n] Possenreißer *m*; **buf'foon·er·y** Possenreißerei *f*; Possen *f/pl*.
bug [bʌg] *zo.* Wanze *f* (*sl. auch Abhörgerät*); *Am.* Käfer *m*, Insekt *n*; Bazillus *m*; *Am. sl.* Defekt *m*, Fehler *m*; *big* ~ *sl.* hohes Tier *n*; **~·a·boo** ['~əbu:], '**~-bear** Schreckbild *n*, Popanz *m*; '**bug·ger** V Sodomit *m*; V Scheißkerl *m*; V Scheißding *n*; P Kerl *m*; *poor* ~! armer Kerl!; **bug·ging de·vice** Abhörgerät *n*; '**bug·gy 1.** verwanzt; **2.** leichter Einspänner *m*.
bu·gle[1] ['bju:gl] Wald-, Signalhorn *n*.
bu·gle[2] [~] schwarze Glasperle *f*.
bu·gler ⚔ ['bju:glə] Hornist *m*.
buhl [bu:l] Einlege-, Boulearbeit *f*.
build [bild] **1.** (*irr.*) bauen; errichten; *fig.* bauen, sich verlassen (*on*, *upon* auf *acc.*); ~ *in* einbauen; ~ *up* ver-, zubauen; *be* ~*ing* im Bau sein; **2.** Bauart *f*; Schnitt *m*; '**build·er** Erbauer *m*, Baumeister *m*, -unternehmer *m*; '**build·ing** Erbauen *n*; Bau *m*, Bauwerk *n*, Gebäude *n*; ~ *contractor* Bauunternehmer *m*; ~ *craftsman* Bauhandwerker *m*; ~ *site* Baustelle *f*; ~ *society* Baugenossenschaft *f*; ~ *trade* Baugewerbe *n*; '**build-up** Aufbau *m*; Reklame *f*.
built [bilt] **1.** *pret. u. p.p. von build* **1**; **2.** *adj.* ...gebaut; von ... Bau(art); '**~-'in** eingebaut, Einbau...; '**~-'up a·re·a** bebautes Gelände *n*.
bulb [bʌlb] ⚘ Zwiebel *f*, Knolle *f*; Kugel *f des Thermometers etc.*; (Glüh)Birne *f*; '**bulb·ous** ⚘ knollig.
Bul·gar ['bʌlgɑ:] Bulgare *m*, Bulgarin *f*; **Bul·gar·i·an** [~'gɛəriən] **1.** bulgarisch; **2.** Bulgare *m*, Bulgarin *f*.
bulge [bʌldʒ] **1.** (Aus)Bauchung *f*; Anschwellung *f*; Beule *f*; Vorsprung *m*; **2.** sich (aus)bauchen; (an-, auf)schwellen; hervorquellen.
bulk [bʌlk] Umfang *m*, Größe *f*; Masse *f*; Hauptteil *m*, -masse *f*; ⚓ Ladung *f*; *in* ~ lose; in großer Menge; ~ *buying* Großeinkauf *m*; ~ *goods pl.* lose Waren *f/pl.*; '**~·head** ⚓ Schott *n*; '**bulk·i·ness** (großer) Umfang *m*; '**bulk·y** (sehr) umfangreich, dick; unhandlich; 🚂 sperrig.
bull[1] [bul] **1.** Bulle *m*, Stier *m*; ✝ *sl.* Haussier *m*; *a* ~ *in a china shop* ein Elefant im Porzellanladen; *take the* ~ *by the horns* den Stier bei den Hörnern packen; ~ *session Am. sl.* Herrengesellschaft *f*; **2.** ✝ *sl.* auf Hausse spekulieren; *die Kurse* treiben.
bull[2] [~] *päpstliche* Bulle *f*.
bull[3] [~] Schnitzer *m*, grober Fehler *m*; *oft Irish* ~ Quatsch *m*, Unsinn *m*.
bull-bait·ing ['bulbeitiŋ] Stierhetze *f*.
bull·dog ['buldɔg] Bulldogge *f*; F *univ.* Helfer *m* des *Proctor*.
bull·doze *Am.* F ['buldəuz] terrorisieren; '**bull·doz·er** Planierraupe *f*, Bulldozer *m*.
bul·let ['bulit] Kugel *f*, Geschoß *n e-r Handfeuerwaffe*.
bul·le·tin ['bulitin] Tagesbericht *m*; Bekanntmachungsblatt *n*; ~ *board Am.* Schwarzes Brett *n* (*für Anschläge*).
bul·let-proof ['bulitpru:f] kugelsicher.
bull...: '**~·fight** Stierkampf *m*; '**~·finch** *orn.* Dompfaff *m*; Hecke *f*; '**~·frog** *zo.* Ochsenfrosch *m*.
bul·lion ['buljən] Gold-, Silberbarren *m*; ungemünztes Gold *n od.* Silber *n*; Gold-, Silberlitze *f*.
bull·ock ['bulək] Ochse *m*.
bull·pen *Am.* ['bul'pen] F *Untersuchungs*-Haftraum *m*; *Baseball*: Platz *m* zum Üben u. Warmlaufen.
bull's-eye ['bulzai] ⚓ Bullauge *n*; *das* Schwarze, Zentrum *n e-r Schießscheibe*; Pfefferminzbonbon *m*; ~ *pane* Butzenscheibe *f*.
bull·shit *bsd. Am.* V ['bulʃit] Scheißdreck *m*; Quatsch *m*.
bully[1] ['buli] **1.** brutaler Kerl *m*, Kameradenschinder *m*; Maulheld *m*; Tyrann *m*; Zuhälter *m*; **2.** lärmend, prahlerisch; *bsd. Am.* F prima (*a. int.*); **3.** einschüchtern; tyrannisieren, schikanieren, piesacken.
bul·ly[2] [~] *a.* ~ *beef* Rinderpökel-

fleisch *n.*
bul·rush ⚘ ['bulrʌʃ] *große* Binse *f.*
bul·wark ['bulwək] *mst fig.* Bollwerk *n*; ⚓ Schanzkleid *n.*
bum[1] V [bʌm] Hintern *m.*
bum[2] *Am.* F [~] **1.** Nichtstuer *m*, Vagabund *m*; *be od. go on the* ~ kaputt sein *od.* gehen; trampen; **2.** nassauern, organisieren; **3.** armselig, schlecht.
bum·ble-bee ['bʌmblbi:] Hummel *f.*
bum·boat ['bʌmbəut] Proviantboot *n.*
bump [bʌmp] **1.** Schlag *m*, Stoß *m*; Beule *f*; *fig.* Sinn *m*, Talent *n* (*of* für, zu); **2.** stoßen; rumpeln, holpern (*Wagen*); *Wettrudern*: überholen; ~ *into s.o.* F j. anrempeln; ~ *into s.th.* F et. rammen, mit et. zs.-stoßen; ~ *off* abmurksen, umlegen.
bump·er ['bʌmpə] volles Glas *n* (*Wein*); F *et.* Riesiges *n*; *mot.* Stoßstange *f*; ~ *crop* Rekordernte *f*; ~ *house thea.* volles Haus *n*; ~ *sticker* Autoaufkleber *m.*
bump·kin ['bʌmpkin] Tölpel *m.*
bump-start *mot.* ['bʌmpsta:t] **1.** Anschieben *n*; **2.** anschieben.
bump·tious □ F ['bʌmpʃəs] aufgeblasen; arrogant.
bump·y ['bʌmpi] holperig; ✈ böig.
bun [bʌn] Rosinenbrötchen *n*; (Haar)Knoten *m.*
bu·na ['bu:nə] Buna *m* (*Kautschuk*).
bunch [bʌntʃ] **1.** Bund *n*, Bündel *n*; Büschel *n*; Haufen *m* (*Menge*); ~ *of flowers* Blumenstrauß *m*; ~ *of grapes* Weintraube *f*; **2.** (zs.-)bündeln; bauschen; '**bunch·y** büschelig; bauschig.
bun·combe ['bʌŋkəm] Blödsinn *m*; Mumpitz *m.*
bun·dle ['bʌndl] **1.** Bündel *n*, Bund *n*; **2.** *v/t. a.* ~ *up* (zs.-)bündeln; ~ *away*, ~ *off* F wegjagen; *v/i.* ~ *off* sich packen.
bung [bʌŋ] **1.** Spund *m*; **2.** (zu-)spunden; ~*ed up* verstopft (*Nase*).
bun·ga·low ['bʌŋgələu] Bungalow *m* (*einstöckiges Haus*).
bung-hole ['bʌŋhəul] Spundloch *n.*
bun·gle ['bʌŋgl] **1.** Pfuscherei *f*; **2.** (ver)pfuschen; '**bun·gler** Pfuscher (-in); '**bun·gling 1.** □ ungeschickt, stümperhaft; **2.** Pfuscherei *f.*
bun·ion ⚕ ['bʌnjən] entzündeter Fußballen *m.*
bunk[1] *sl.* [bʌŋk] Geschwätz *n*, Quatsch *m.*
bunk[2] [~] Schlafkoje *f.*
bunk·er ⚓ ['bʌŋkə] **1.** Bunker *m* (*Kohlenbehälter*); **2.** bunkern; *be* ~*ed fig.* in e-e Klemme geraten.
bun·kum ['bʌŋkəm] = *buncombe.*
bun·ny ['bʌni] Kaninchen *n*; ~ (**girl**) F Häschen *n.*
bun·sen ['bunsn]: ~ *burner* Bunsenbrenner *m.*
bunt *Am.* [bʌnt] *Baseball*: Stoppballschlag *m.*
bun·ting[1] *orn.* ['bʌntiŋ] Ammer *f.*
bun·ting[2] [~] Flaggen(tuch *n*) *f/pl.*
buoy ⚓ [bɔi] **1.** Boje *f*; **2.** *Fahrwasser* betonnen; *mst* ~ *up* schwimmend erhalten; *fig.* aufrechterhalten; emporheben.
buoy·an·cy ['bɔiənsi] Schwimm-, *fig.* Spannkraft *f*; ✈ *u. fig.* Auftrieb *m*; '**buoy·ant** □ schwimmfähig; hebend; *fig.* spannkräftig; *fig.* heiter; ✝ steigend.
bur ⚘ [bə:] Klette *f* (*a. fig.*).
Bur·ber·ry ['bə:bəri] *wasserdichter Stoff od. Mantel.*
bur·bot *ichth.* ['bə:bət] Quappe *f.*
bur·den[1] ['bə:dn] **1.** Last *f*, Bürde *f* (*on* für); ⚖ Auflage *f*; ⚓ Ladung *f*; ⚓ Tragfähigkeit *f*; **2.** beladen; belasten (*a. fig.*).
bur·den[2] [~] Kehrreim *m*, Refrain *m.*
bur·den·some ['bə:dnsəm] lästig; drückend.
bur·dock ⚘ ['bə:dɔk] Klette *f* [(*Pflanze*).]
bu·reau ['bjuərəu], *pl. a.* **bu·reaux** ['~z] Büro *n*, Geschäfts-, Amtszimmer *n*; Schreibpult *n*; *Am.* Kommode *f*; **bu·reauc·ra·cy** [~'rɔkrəsi] Bürokratie *f*; **bu·reau·crat** ['bjuərəukræt] Bürokrat *m*; **bu·reau'crat·ic** (~*ally*) bürokratisch; **bu·reauc·ra·tize** [bjuə'rɔkrətaiz] bürokratisieren.
bu·rette ⚗ [bjuə'ret] Meßröhre *f.*
burg *Am.* F [bə:g] Stadt *f.*
bur·gee ⚓ ['bə:dʒi:] Stander *m.*
bur·geon *lit.* ['bə:dʒən] **1.** Knospe *f*; Keim *m*; **2.** knospen, sprießen.
burg·er *Am.* F ['bə:gə] Hamburger *m.*
bur·gess ['bə:dʒis] stimmberechtigter Bürger *m*; *hist.* Abgeordnete *m.*
burgh *schott.* ['bʌrə] Burgflecken *m*; **bur·gher** *hist.* ['bə:gə] Bürger *m* (*bsd. e-r holländischen od. deutschen Stadt*).
bur·glar ['bə:glə] *nächtlicher* Ein-

brecher *m*; **bur·glar·i·ous** □ [bəː-ˈglɛəriəs] einbrecherisch; **bur·gla·ry** [ˈ~gləri] *nächtlicher* Einbruch (-diebstahl) *m*; ˈ**bur·gle** einbrechen (in *acc.*).

bur·go·mas·ter [ˈbəːgəumɑːstə] Bürgermeister *m* (*e-r holländischen od. flämischen Stadt*).

bur·gun·dy [ˈbəːgəndi] Burgunder *m* (*Wein*).

bur·i·al [ˈberiəl] Begräbnis *n*; ˈ~-**-ground** Begräbnisplatz *m*, Friedhof *m*; ~ **serv·ice** Trauerfeier *f*.

bu·rin ⊕ [ˈbjuərin] Grabstichel *m*.

burke [bəːk] *et.* vertuschen.

burl [bəːl] Noppe *f im Tuch*.

bur·lap [ˈbəːlæp] Sackleinwand *f*.

bur·lesque [bəːˈlesk] **1.** burlesk, possenhaft; **2.** Burleske *f*, *n*, Posse *f*; **3.** burlesk behandeln; parodieren.

bur·ly [ˈbəːli] stämmig, kräftig.

Bur·mese [bəːˈmiːz] **1.** birmanisch; **2.** Birmane *m*, Birmanin *f*; Birmanisch *n*.

burn [bəːn] **1.** Brandwunde *f*; Brandmal *n*; **2.** (*irr.*) *v/t. u. v/i.* (ver-, an)brennen; ˈ**burn·er** Brenner *m*; ˈ**burn·ing** □ brennend, glühend; heiß; Brenn...

bur·nish [ˈbəːniʃ] polieren, glätten; ˈ**bur·nish·er** Polierer(in); Polierstahl *m*.

burnt [bəːnt] *pret. u. p.p. von burn 2*; ~ *almond* gebrannte Mandel *f*; ~ *offering* Brandopfer *n*.

burp *Am. sl.* [bəːp] **1.** Rülpser *m*; **2.** rülpsen, aufstoßen.

burr [bəː] **1.** Schwirrton *m* (*von Maschinen*); Zäpfchen-R *n*; **2.** (das R) guttural aussprechen; ˈ~**-drill** ⚕ Drillbohrer *m*.

bur·ro F [ˈburəu] Packesel *m*.

bur·row [ˈbʌrəu] **1.** Höhle *f*, Bau *m*; **2.** (sich ein)graben; *fig.* sich vergraben; *in Geheimnisse* eindringen.

bur·sar [ˈbəːsə] Quästor *m* (*an Universitäten*); Stipendiat *m*.

bur·sa·ry [ˈbəːsəri] Quästur *f*; Stipendium *n*.

burst [bəːst] **1.** Bersten *n*; Krach *m*; Riß *m*; Bruch *m*; Explosion *f*; *fig.* Ausbruch *m*, Anfall *m*; **2.** (*irr.*) *v/i.* bersten, platzen (*a. fig.*); zerspringen; brechen; ⚘ aufspringen; aufgehen (*Geschwür*); explodieren; ~ *from* sich losreißen von; ~ *forth*, ~ *out* hervorbrechen; ~ *into flame* (*leaf*) aufflammen (-blühen); ~ *into tears* in Tränen ausbrechen; ~ *out laughing* in Gelächter ausbrechen; ~ *upon s.o.* sich j-m plötzlich zeigen; *v/t.* (zer)sprengen.

bur·then ⚓ [ˈbəːðən] = *burden*.

bur·y [ˈberi] begraben, beerdigen; verbergen; vergraben; *be buried in thought* in Gedanken vertieft sein; ˈ**bur·y·ing-ground** Begräbnisplatz *m*.

bus F [bʌs] **1.** (Omni)Bus *m*; *miss the* ~ *sl.* den Anschluß verpassen; ~ *boy Am.* Kellnerlehrling *m*, Pikkolo *m*; **2.** *v/t. u. v/i.* (*Kinder*) mit dem Bus (*in die Schule*) fahren.

bus·by ⚔ [ˈbʌzbi] Bärenmütze *f*.

bush [buʃ] Busch *m*; Gebüsch *n*; ⊕ Buchse *f*; **bush·el** [ˈbuʃl] Scheffel *m* (*36,35 Liter*); große Menge *f*; *hide one's light under a* ~ sein Licht unter den Scheffel stellen; **bush league** *Am. Baseball*: untere Spielklasse *f*; ˈ**bush·man** Buschmann *m*; ˈ**bush-rang·er** Buschklepper *m*, Strauchdieb *m*.

bush·y [ˈbuʃi] buschig.

busi·ness [ˈbiznis] Geschäft *n* (*Unternehmen*); Beschäftigung *f*; Beruf *m*, Gewerbe *n*; Angelegenheit *f*, Sache *f*; Aufgabe *f*; ⚚ Handel *m*; Geschäft(slokal) *n mit allem Zubehör*; ~ *of the day* Tagesordnung *f*; ~ *research* Konjunkturforschung *f*; *on* ~ geschäftlich; *no admittance except on* ~ Zutritt für Unbefugte verboten; *get down to* ~ zur Sache kommen; *have no* ~ *to inf.* nicht befugt sein zu *inf.*; *mind one's own* ~ sich um seine eignen Angelegenheiten kümmern; *send s.o. about his* ~ j. kurz abfertigen; *that's none of his* ~ das geht ihn nichts an; ~ **end** F wesentlicher Teil *m e-r Sache*; ~ **hours** *pl.* Geschäftszeit *f*; ˈ~**-like** kaufmännisch, geschäftsmäßig; sachlich; ˈ~**·man** Geschäftsmann *m*; ~ **tour**, ~ **trip** Geschäftsreise *f*.

bus·ker [ˈbʌskə] Straßenmusikant *m*.

bus·kin [ˈbʌskin] Halbstiefel *m*; *Altertum*: Kothurn *m*.

bus·man [ˈbʌsmən] Busfahrer *m*; ~*'s holiday* im Beruf verbrachter Urlaub *m*; ˈ**bus·sing** *bsd. Am. Beförderung von Schülern mit Bussen in andere Schulen, um Rassenintegration zu erreichen*; ˈ**bus-stop** Bushaltestelle *f*.

bust[1] [bʌst] Büste *f*.

bust[2] *Am.* F [~] Bankrott *m*; Saufpartie *f*.

bus·tard *orn.* ['bʌstəd] Trappe *f*.

bus·tle ['bʌsl] **1.** Geschäftigkeit *f*; geschäftiges Treiben *n*, Getriebe *n*, Hast *f*; Turnüre *f*; **2.** *v/i.* sich tummeln; (umher)wirtschaften; hasten; *v/t.* hetzen, jagen (*a. fig.*); '**bus·tler** rühriger Mensch *m*; '**bus·tling** □ geschäftig, rührig.

bust-up F ['bʌstʌp] Zusammenbruch *m*; Krach *m* (*Streit*).

bus·y ['bizi] **1.** □ beschäftigt (*with* mit); geschäftig, emsig, fleißig, eifrig, tätig (*at* bei, an *dat.*); lebhaft; belebt, verkehrsreich; *teleph.* besetzt; *be* ~ (viel) zu tun haben; ~ *packing* mit Packen beschäftigt; **2.** (*mst* ~ *o.s.* sich) beschäftigen (*with, in, at, about, ger.* mit); '**~-bod·y** G(e)schaftlhuber *m*; '**bus·y·ness** Geschäftigkeit *f*, Emsigkeit *f*.

but [bʌt; bət] **1.** *cj.* aber, jedoch, sondern; *a.* ~ *that* wenn nicht; indessen, nichtsdestoweniger; **2.** *prp.* außer; *the last* ~ *one* der vor- *od.* zweitletzte; *the next* ~ *one* der übernächste; ~ *for* wenn nicht ... gewesen wäre; ohne; **3.** *nach Negation*: der (die *od.* das) nicht; *there is no one* ~ *knows* es gibt niemand, der nicht wüßte; **4.** *adv.* nur; ~ *just* soeben, eben erst; ~ *now* erst jetzt; *all* ~ fast, nahe daran; *nothing* ~ nichts als; *I cannot* ~ *inf.* ich kann nicht umhin zu *inf.*, ich kann nur *inf.*; **5.** Aber *n*, Einwendung *f*.

bu·tane ⚗ ['bju:tein] Butan *n*.

butch·er ['butʃə] **1.** Schlächter *m*, Fleischer *m*, Metzger *m*; *fig.* Mörder *m*; **2.** (*fig.* ab-, hin)schlachten; '**butch·er·y** Schlächterei *f* (*a. fig.*); Schlachthaus *n*; ~ *business* Metzgerhandwerk *n*.

but·ler ['bʌtlə] Butler *m*; Kellermeister *m*.

butt[1] [bʌt] **1.** Stoß *m mit den Hörnern*; *a.* ~ *end* dickes Ende *n e-s Baumes etc.*; Stummel *m*, Kippe *f*; *Gewehr*-Kolben *m*; ⊕ Balkenende *n*; Kugelfang *m*; *the* ~*s pl.* Schießstand *m*; *fig.* (End)Ziel *n*; *fig.* Zielscheibe *f*; **2.** (mit dem Kopf) stoßen; ~ *in* F herein-, hineinplatzen.

butt[2] [~] Stückfaß *n*.

butte *Am. geol.* [bju:t] Restberg *m*.

but·ter ['bʌtə] **1.** Butter *f*; F Schöntuerei *f*, Schmeichelei *f*; *as if* ~ *would not melt in his mouth* als ob er nicht bis drei zählen könnte; **2.** mit Butter bestreichen *od.* anrichten; '**~·cup** Butterblume *f*, Hahnenfuß *m*; '**~-fin·gered** ungeschickt im Gebrauch der Hände, tolpatschig; '**~-fin·gers** *sg.* Tolpatsch *m*; '**~·fly** Schmetterling *m* (*a. fig.*); *have butterflies in one's stomach* ein flaues Gefühl in der Magengegend haben; '**~·milk** Buttermilch *f*; '**but·ter·y** **1.** butter(art)ig; Butter...; **2.** Speisekammer *f*.

but·tock ['bʌtək], *mst* '**but·tocks** *pl.* Hintern *m*.

but·ton ['bʌtn] **1.** Knopf *m*; ⚘ Knospe *f*; ~*s sg.* F Hotelpage *m*; **2.** *oft* ~ *up Kleid* zuknöpfen; einknöpfen, *fig.* verschließen; Knöpfe nähen *od.* anbringen an; '**~·hole** **1.** Knopfloch *n*; Knopflochsträußchen *n*; **2.** Knopflöcher nähen in; *j.* beim Knopf festhalten; '**~-hook** Stiefelknöpfer *m*; '**~·wood** ⚘ Platane *f*.

but·tress ['bʌtris] **1.** Strebepfeiler *m*; *fig.* Stütze *f*; **2.** ~ *up* abstützen; *fig. Argument etc.* unterstützen.

bux·om ['bʌksəm] drall, stramm.

buy [bai] (*irr.*) *v/t.* (an-, ein)kaufen (*from* bei); *fig.* einbringen; erkaufen; *order to* ~ Kaufauftrag *m*; '**buy·er** Käufer(in); Abnehmer(in); Einkäufer(in); '**buy·ing** Kauf...

buzz [bʌz] **1.** Gesumm *n*; Gesurr(e) *n*; Geflüster *n*; ~ *saw Am.* Kreissäge *f*; **2.** *v/i.* summen; surren; ~ *about* herumschwirren, -eilen; *v/t. anderes Flugzeug durch Anfliegen* belästigen; F schmeißen.

buz·zard *orn.* ['bʌzəd] Bussard *m*.

buzz·er ⚡ ['bʌzə] Summer *m*; Sirene *f*.

by [bai] **1.** *prp. Raum*: bei; an, neben; *Richtung*: durch, über, via; an (*dat.*) entlang *od.* vorbei; *Zeit*: an, bei; spätestens bis, bis zu; *Urheberschaft, Ursache*: von, durch (*Passiv*); *Mittel, Werkzeug*: (ver)mittels, durch, mit; *Art u. Weise*: bei; *Schwur*: bei; *Maß*: um, bei; *Richtschnur*: gemäß, bei; *North* ~ *East* Nord zu Ost; *side* ~ *side* Seite an Seite; ~ *day* bei Tage; ~ *now* jetzt (schon); ~ *the time* (*that*) bis; *a play* ~ *Shaw* ein Stück von Shaw; ~ *lamplight* bei Lampenlicht; ~ *the dozen* dutzendweise; ~ *far* bei weitem; *50 feet* ~ *20* fünfzig Fuß lang und zwanzig breit; ~ *half* um die Hälfte; ~ *o.s.* allein; für sich; aus eigner Kraft, aus sich; ~ *land* zu Lande; ~ *rail* per Bahn; *day* ~ *day* Tag für Tag; ~ *twos* zu zweien; **2.** *adv.* dabei; vorbei; beiseite; ~ *and* ~ nächstens, bald; nach und nach; ~ *the* ~ nebenbei bemerkt; *close* ~ dicht dabei; *go* ~ vorbeigehen; ~ *and large* im großen und ganzen; **3.** *adj.* Neben...; Seiten...

bye [bai] *Kricket: Lauf, ohne den Ball geschlagen zu haben; Tennis:* Überzählige *m, f*; *be od. draw a* ~ rasten (müssen).

bye-bye F ['bai'bai] Wiedersehen!; ['baibai] *Kindersprache:* Heia *f* (*Bett*).

by...: '**~-e·lec·tion** Nachwahl *f*; '**~gone 1.** vergangen, früher; **2.** *~s pl.* Vergangene *n*; *let ~s be ~s* laß(t) die Vergangenheit ruhen; '**~-law** Ortsstatut *n*; *~s pl.* Satzung *f*, Statuten *n/pl.*; '**~-line** *Am.* Verfasserangabe *f zu e-m Artikel*; '**~-name** Bei-, Spitzname *m*; '**~-pass 1.** Umgehungsstraße *f*; **2.** umgehen, -fahren; *Verkehr* umleiten; '**~-path** Seitenpfad *m*; '**~-play** *thea.* Nebenhandlung *f*; stummes Spiel *n*; '**~-prod·uct** Nebenprodukt *n*.

byre ['baiə] Kuhstall *m*.

by-road ['bairəud] Seitenweg *m*, -straße *f*.

By·ron·ic [bai'rɔnik] (*~ally*) byronisch.

by...: '**~·stand·er** Zuschauer *m*; '**~-street** Neben-, Seitenstraße *f*; '**~-way** Seiten-, *b.s.* Schleichweg *m*; '**~-word** Sprichwort *n*; Inbegriff *m*; *be a* ~ *for* sprichwörtlich bekannt sein wegen.

By·zan·tine [bi'zæntain] **1.** byzantinisch; **2.** Byzantiner(in).

C

cab [kæb] **1.** Droschke *f*, Mietwagen *m*, Taxi *n*; 🚂 Führerstand *m*; **2.** ~ *it* F mit e-r Droschke *od.* e-m Taxi fahren.

ca·bal [kə'bæl] **1.** Kabale *f* (*Ränke*); Clique *f*; **2.** intrigieren.

cab·a·ret ['kæbərei] Kabarett *n*.

cab·bage ['kæbidʒ] Kohl(kopf) *m*; ~ *butterfly* Kohlweißling *m*; ~ *lettuce* Kopfsalat *m*.

cab·ba·lis·tic, cab·ba·lis·ti·cal □ [kæbə'listik(əl)] kabbalistisch.

cab·by F ['kæbi] Droschkenkutscher *m*, Taxifahrer *m*.

cab·in ['kæbin] **1.** Hütte *f*; ⚓ Kajüte *f*; Kabine *f*; Kammer *f*; **2.** einpferchen; '**~-boy** ⚓ Offiziersbursche *m*; Stewardhelfer *m*; **~ class** ⚓ Kabinenklasse *f*, 2. Klasse *f*; **~ cruis·er** ⚓ Kabinenkreuzer *m*.

cab·i·net ['kæbinit] Kabinett *n*, Ministerrat *m*; Schrank *m*, Vitrine *f*; (Radio)Gehäuse *n*; *phot.* Kabinettformat *n*; ♀ *Council* Kabinettssitzung *f*; '**~-mak·er** Kunsttischler *m*.

ca·ble ['keibl] **1.** ⚓ *u. tel.* Kabel *n*; ⚓ Trosse *f*, Ankertau *n*, -kette *f*; Telegramm *n*; *buried* ~ Erdkabel *n*; **2.** *tel.* telegraphieren, kabeln; '**~-car** Standseilbahn(wagen *m*) *f*; **~·gram** ['~græm] Kabeltelegramm *n*; ~ **re·lease** *phot.* Drahtauslöser *m*; '**~-stitched** mit Kreuzstichstickerei; ~ **tel·e·vi·sion** Kabelfernsehen *n*.

cab·man ['kæbmən] Droschkenkutscher *m*, Taxifahrer *m*.

ca·boo·dle *sl.* [kə'bu:dl]: *the whole* ~ der ganze Kram; die ganze Sippschaft.

ca·boose [kə'bu:s] ⚓ Kombüse *f*; *Am.* 🚂 Eisenbahnerwagen *m am Güterzug*.

cab·ri·o·let *bsd. mot.* [kæbriə'lei] Kabriolett *n*, offener Wagen *m*.

cab-stand ['kæbstænd] (Kraft-) Droschkenhalteplatz *m*, Taxistand *m*.

ca'can·ny ⊕ [kɑ:'kæni] die Arbeitsleistung bremsen.

ca·ca·o [kə'kɑ:əu] Kakaobaum *m*; Kakaobohne *f*.

cache [kæʃ] **1.** unterirdisches Depot *n*; geheimes Lager *n*; **2.** verbergen.
cack·le [ˈkækl] **1.** Gegacker *n*, Geschnatter *n*; *fig.* Geschwätz *n*; **2.** gackern, schnattern; *fig.* schwatzen; ˈ**cack·ler** gackerndes Huhn *n*; *fig.* Schwätzer(in).
ca·coph·o·ny [kæˈkɔfəni] Kakophonie *f* (*Mißklang*).
cac·tus ⚘ [ˈkæktəs] Kaktus *m*.
cad F [kæd] Prolet *m*; übler Charakter *m*.
ca·das·tre [kəˈdæstə] Grundbuch *n*.
ca·dav·er·ous □ [kəˈdævərəs] leichenhaft; leichenblaß.
cad·die [ˈkædi] Golfjunge *m*, Caddie *m*.
cad·dis *zo.* [ˈkædis] Larve *f* der Köcherfliege.
cad·dish F □ [ˈkædiʃ] proletenhaft; gemein, schurkisch.
cad·dy [ˈkædi] Teebüchse *f*; = *caddie*.
ca·dence [ˈkeidəns] ♪ Kadenz *f*; Tonfall *m*; Rhythmus *m*.
ca·det [kəˈdet] Kadett *m*; ~ *corps* Jugendkompanie *f e-r Schule*.
cadge [kædʒ] (er)betteln; schnorren; ˈ**cadg·er** Schmarotzer *m*; Schnorrer *m*.
ca·di [ˈkɑːdi] Kadi *m* (*Richter im Orient*).
cad·mi·um ⚗ [ˈkædmiəm] Kadmium *n*.
cad·re [ˈkɑːdə] Rahmen *m*; ⚔ Kader *m*.
ca·du·cous ⚘ *u. zo.* [kəˈdjuːkəs] abfallend.
cae·cum *anat.* [ˈsiːkəm] Blinddarm *m*.
Cae·sar [ˈsiːzə] Cäsar *m*; **Cae·sar·i·an** [siːˈzɛəriən] cäsarisch.
cae·sar·e·an (**sec·tion**) ⚕ [siːˈzɛəriən ˈsekʃən] Kaiserschnitt *m*.
cae·su·ra [siːˈzjuərə] Zäsur *f*.
ca·fé [ˈkæfei] Café *n*; Restaurant *n*.
caf·e·te·ri·a [kæfiˈtiəriə] Restaurant *n* mit Selbstbedienung.
caf·e·to·ri·um *Am.* [kæfiˈtɔːriəm] Kantinen- und Festsaal *m*.
caf·fe·ine [ˈkæfiːn] Koffein *n*.
cage [keidʒ] **1.** Käfig *m* (*a. fig.*); Kriegsgefangenenlager *n*; ⚒ Förderkorb *m*; **2.** einsperren.
cage·y □ *bsd. Am.* F [ˈkeidʒi] gerissen, raffiniert.
cairn [kɛən] Steinhaufen *m*.
cais·son [kəˈsuːn] ⚔ Munitionswagen *m*; *Wasserbau*: Senkkasten *m*.
cai·tiff [ˈkeitif] Lump *m*, Schurke *m*.
ca·jole [kəˈdʒəul] *j-m* schöntun, schmeicheln; *j.* beschwatzen (*into* zu); **caˈjol·er** Schmeichler(in); **caˈjol·er·y** Schöntuerei *f*; Schmeichelei *f*.
cake [keik] **1.** Kuchen *m*; Stück *n Seife etc.*; ~*s and ale* Lustbarkeit *f*; *a piece of* ~ *sl.* ein Kinderspiel *n*; *like hot* ~*s* wie warme Semmeln; **2.** zs.-backen; überziehen (*with* mit).
cal·a·bash [ˈkæləbæʃ] Kalebasse *f* (*Flaschenkürbis*).
cal·a·mine *min.* [ˈkæləmain] Galmei *m*.
ca·lam·i·tous □ [kəˈlæmitəs] elend; katastrophal; **caˈlam·i·ty** Elend *n*, Unglück *n*, Unheil *n*; Katastrophe *f*; **caˈlam·i·ty-howl·er** Schwarzseher *m*; **caˈlam·i·ty-howl·ing** *bsd. Am.* Schwarzseherei *f*.
cal·car·e·ous [kælˈkɛəriəs] kalkartig, -reich, kalkig; Kalk...
cal·ce·o·la·ri·a ⚘ [kælsiəˈlɛəriə] Pantoffelblume *f*.
cal·ci·fi·ca·tion [kælsifiˈkeiʃən] Verkalkung *f*; **cal·ci·fy** [ˈ~fai] (sich) verkalken; **cal·ci·na·tion** ⚗ [kælsiˈneiʃən] Kalzinierung *f*, Brennen *n*; **cal·cine** ⚗ [ˈkælsain] kalzinieren, brennen; ˈ**cal·cite** *min.* Kalzit *m*; **cal·ci·um** ⚗ [ˈ~siəm] Kalzium *n*; **cal·ci·um car·bide** ⚗ Karbid *n*.
cal·cu·la·ble [ˈkælkjuləbl] berechenbar; **cal·cu·late** [ˈ~leit] *v/t.* kalkulieren; be-, aus-, errechnen; ~*d* berechnet (*for* auf *acc.*); *v/i.* rechnen, vertrauen (*on, upon* auf *acc.*); F *Am.* vermuten; *calculating machine* Rechenmaschine *f*; **calˈcu·la·tion** Kalkulation *f*, Berechnung *f etc.*; ˈ**cal·cu·la·tor** Kalkulator *m*; Rechner *m*; **cal·cu·lus** [ˈ~ləs] ⩚ Differential- u. Integralrechnen *n*; ⚕ Stein *m*.
cal·dron [ˈkɔːldrən] Kessel *m*.
cal·en·dar [ˈkælində] **1.** Kalender *m*; Liste *f*; **2.** registrieren.
cal·en·der ⊕ [~] **1.** Kalander *m*, Tuchpresse *f*; **2.** kalandern, pressen.
cal·ends [ˈkælindz]: *on the Greek* ~ am St. Nimmerleinstag.
calf [kɑːf], *pl.* **calves** [kɑːvz] Kalb *n* (*a. fig.*); *a.* ~*-leather* Kalbleder *n*; Lederband *m*; *anat.* Wade *f*; *in* ~, *with* ~ trächtig; ~ *love* F Jugendliebe *f*; ˈ**~-skin** Kalbfell *n*.

cal·i·brate ⊕ [ˈkælibreit] kalibrieren; **cal·i·bre** [ˈ~bə] Kaliber *n* (*Rohrweite*; *fig. Art*; *Gewicht*).
cal·i·co ✝ [ˈkælikəu] Kaliko *m*, (bedruckter) Kattun *m*.
Cal·i·for·nian [kæliˈfɔːnjən] **1.** kalifornisch; **2.** Kalifornier(in).
ca·liph [ˈkælif] Kalif *m*; **cal·iph·ate** [ˈ~eit] Kalifat *n*.
calk [kɔːk] **1.** (durch)pausen; ⚓ kalfatern (*abdichten*); scharf beschlagen; **2.** Gleitschutzbeschlag *m*, Stollen *m am Hufeisen*; **calk·in** [ˈkælkin] *s. calk* 2.
call [kɔːl] **1.** Ruf *m*; *teleph.* Anruf *m*, Gespräch *n*; *fig.* Ruf *m*, Berufung *f* (*to* in *ein Amt*; auf *e-n Lehrstuhl*); Appell *m*; Signal *n*; *thea.* Hervorruf *m*; Lockruf *m*; (innere) Berufung *f*; Forderung *f*; F Anlaß *m*; *kurzer* Besuch *m*; Nachfrage *f* (*for* nach); Kündigung *f v. Geldern*; ~ *money* ✝ täglich kündbares Geld *n*; *port of* ~ Anlaufhafen *m*; *on* ~ ✝ auf Abruf; *give s.o. a* ~ *teleph.* j. anrufen; **2.** *v/t.* (herbei)rufen; (an)rufen; *Versammlung* (ein)berufen; *Am. Baseball*: *Spiel* abbrechen; *fig.* berufen (*to* in *ein Amt*); nennen; kommen lassen; wecken; *Aufmerksamkeit* lenken (*to* auf *acc.*); *be* ~*ed* heißen; ~ *s.o. names* j. beschimpfen *od.* beleidigen; ~ *s.o. down Am. sl.* j. anpfeifen; ~ *forth* hervorrufen; *Kraft* aufbieten; ~ *in Geld* kündigen, aufrufen; *j.* hinzuziehen; ~ *out Arbeiter* zum Streik auffordern; ~ *over Namen* verlesen; ~ *up* aufrufen; *teleph.* anrufen; *v/i.* rufen; *teleph.* (an)rufen; vorsprechen (*at* an *e-m Ort*; *on s.o.* bei j-m); ~ *at a port* e-n Hafen anlaufen; ~ *for* rufen nach; *thea.* herausrufen; *et.* fordern, verlangen; *j. od. et.* abholen; *to be (left till)* ~*ed for* postlagernd; ~ *on* e-n Besuch machen bei *j-m*; sich an *j.* wenden (*for* wegen); *j.* berufen, auffordern, aufrufen (*to inf.* zu *inf.*); ~ *to j-m* zurufen; ~ *upon s.* ~ *on*; ˈ**call·a·ble** kündbar (*Geld*); ˈ**call-box** Fernsprechzelle *f*; ˈ**call·er** Rufer(in); Besucher(in); *teleph.* Anrufer(in); ˈ**call-girl** Callgirl *n* (*Prostituierte*).
cal·li·graph·ic [kæliˈgræfik] (~*ally*) kalligraphisch; **cal·lig·ra·phy** [kəˈligrəfi] Kalligraphie *f* (*Schönschreibekunst*).
call-in [ˈkɔːlin] Sendung *f* mit Zuschauer- *od.* Zuhörerbeteiligung.
call·ing [ˈkɔːliŋ] Rufen *n*; Berufung *f*; Beruf *m*; ~ *card Am.* Visitenkarte *f*.
cal·li·pers [ˈkælipəz] *pl.* Tasterzirkel *m*.
cal·lis·then·ics [kælisˈθeniks] *mst sg.* Freiübungen *f/pl.*
call-of·fice [ˈkɔːlɔfis] Fernsprechstelle *f*.
cal·los·i·ty [kæˈlɔsiti] Verhärtung *f*, Schwiele *f*; *fig.* Dickfelligkeit *f*; Indifferenz *f*; ˈ**cal·lous** □ schwielig; *fig.* dickfellig, herzlos; indifferent.
cal·low [ˈkæləu] nackt (*ungefiedert*); noch nicht flügge (*fig. unerfahren*).
call-up [ˈkɔːlʌp] Einberufung *f*.
cal·lus [ˈkæləs] Schwiele *f*.
calm [kɑːm] **1.** □ still, ruhig (*a. fig.*); **2.** Stille *f*, Ruhe *f* (*a. fig.*); ⚓ Windstille *f*, Flaute *f*; **3.** (~ *down* sich) beruhigen; besänftigen; ˈ**calmness** Stille *f*; (Gemüts)Ruhe *f*.
Cal·or gas [ˈkæləˈgæs] Propangas *n*.
ca·lor·ic *phys.* [kəˈlɔrik] Wärme *f*; ~*-engine* Heißluftmaschine *f*; **cal·o·rie** *phys.* [ˈkæləri] Kalorie *f*, Wärmeeinheit *f*; **cal·o·rif·ic** [kæləˈrifik] Wärme erzeugend, erhitzend.
cal·trop ⚘ [ˈkæltrəp] Wegedistel *f*.
ca·lum·ni·ate [kəˈlʌmnieit] verleumden; **ca·lum·niˈa·tion** Verleumdung *f*; **caˈlum·ni·a·tor** Verleumder(in); **caˈlum·ni·ous** □ verleumderisch; **cal·um·ny** [ˈkæləmni] Verleumdung *f*.
Cal·va·ry [ˈkælvəri] Kalvarienberg *m*, Kreuzigungsgruppe *f*.
calve [kɑːv] kalben; **calves** [kɑːvz] *pl. von calf*.
Cal·vin·ism [ˈkælvinizəm] Kalvinismus *m*.
ca·lyp·so [kəˈlipsəu] Calypso *m* (*Tanz etc.*).
ca·lyx ⚘ *u. zo.* [ˈkeiliks], *pl.* **cal·y·ces** [ˈ~lisiːz] Kelch *m*.
cam ⊕ [kæm] Nocken *m*, Daumen *m*; ~ *gear* Nockensteuerung *f*.
cam·ber ⊕ [ˈkæmbə] **1.** Wölbung *f*; Krümmung *f*; **2.** wölben.
cam·bric [ˈkeimbrik] Batist *m*.
came [keim] *pret. v. come*.
cam·el *zo. u.* ⚓ [ˈkæməl] Kamel *n*.
ca·mel·li·a ⚘ [kəˈmiːljə] Kamelie *f*.
cam·e·o [ˈkæmiəu] Kamee *f*.
cam·er·a [ˈkæmərə] Kamera *f*, Photoapparat *m*; *in* ~ ⚖ unter Ausschluß der Öffentlichkeit.

cami-knick·ers ['kæmi'nikəz] *pl.* Hemdhose *f.*
cam·i·on ['kæmiən] niedriger LKW *m.*
cam·o·mile ⚘ ['kæməumail] Kamille *f*; ~ *tea* Kamillentee *m.*
cam·ou·flage ⚔ ['kæmuflɑ:ʒ] **1.** Tarnung *f*; **2.** tarnen.
camp [kæmp] **1.** Lager *n*; ⚔ Feldlager *n*; ~ *bed* Feldbett *n*; ~ *chair*, ~ *stool* Feldstuhl *m*; **2.** kampieren, lagern; ~ *out* zelten.
cam·paign [kæm'pein] **1.** Feldzug *m*; *pol. u. fig.* Kampagne *f*, Schlacht *f*; *election* ~ Wahlkampf *m*; **2.** einen Feldzug mitmachen *od.* unternehmen; **cam'paign·er** Feldzugsteilnehmer *m*; *old* ~ F alter Praktikus *m.*
camp·er ['kæmpə] Lager-, Zeltbewohner(in); Camper *m*; Wohnmobil *n.*
cam·phor ['kæmfə] Kampfer *m*; **cam·phor·at·ed** ['~reitid] Kampfer...
camp·ing ['kæmpiŋ] Camping *n*, Zelten *n.*
camp·site ['kæmpsait] Campingplatz *m.*
cam·pus *Am.* ['kæmpəs] Universitätsgelände *n.*
cam·shaft ⊕ ['kæmʃɑ:ft] Nockenwelle *f.*
can[1] [kæn] (*irr.*) *v/aux.* kann *etc.*
can[2] [~] **1.** Kanne *f*; *Am.* (Konserven)Büchse *f*; ~ *opener* Dosenöffner *m*; *carry the* ~ F die Schuld tragen; **2.** *Am.* in Büchsen konservieren, eindosen.
Ca·na·di·an [kə'neidjən] **1.** kanadisch; **2.** Kanadier(in).
ca·nal [kə'næl] Kanal *m*; *anat.* Gang *m*, Röhre *f*; ~*-boat* Lastkahn *m*; **ca·nal·i·za·tion** [kænəlai'zeiʃən] Kanalisation *f*, Kanalbau *m*; '**canal·ize** kanalisieren.
can·a·pé ['kænəpei] Appetithappen *m.*
ca·nard [kæ'nɑ:d] (Zeitungs)Ente *f.*
ca·nar·y [kə'nɛəri] *a.* ~*-bird* Kanarienvogel *m.*
can·cel ['kænsəl] (durch)streichen; entwerten; absagen; ~ *out* (sich) aufheben; ⚖ sich heben; *be* ~*led* ausfallen; **can·cel'la·tion** Streichung *f*; Entwertung *f*; Aufhebung *f*; Absage *f*; ~ *charge*, ~ *fee* Rücktrittsgebühr *f.*
can·cer ['kænsə] ⚕ Krebs *m*; ♋ *ast.* Krebs *m*; '**can·cer·ous** krebsartig.
can·de·la·bra [kændi'lɑ:brə], **can·de'la·brum** [~brəm] Kandelaber *m*, Leuchter *m.*
can·did □ ['kændid] aufrichtig; offen.
can·di·da·cy ['kændidəsi] Kandidatur *f*; **can·di·date** ['kændidit] Kandidat *m* (*for* für), Bewerber *m* (*for* um); **can·di·da·ture** ['~tʃə] Kandidatur *f.*
can·died ['kændid] kandiert; *fig.* schmeichelhaft.
can·dle ['kændl] Licht *n*, Kerze *f*; ~ *power* Lichtstärke *f*; *hold a* ~ *to fig.* herankommen an, den Vergleich aushalten mit; *not worth the* ~ nicht der Mühe wert; *burn the* ~ *at both ends* mit s-n Kräften Raubbau treiben; '~**·light** Kerzenlicht *n*; **Can·dle·mas** *eccl.* ['~məs] Lichtmeß *f*; '**can·dle·stick** Leuchter *m.*
can·dour ['kændə] Unparteilichkeit *f*; Aufrichtigkeit *f*; Offenheit *f.*
can·dy ['kændi] **1.** Kandis(zucker) *m*; *Am.* Süßigkeiten *f/pl.*, Bonbons *m/pl.*; **2.** *v/t.* kandieren; *v/i.* kristallisieren; ~ **floss** Zuckerwatte *f.*
cane [kein] **1.** ⚘ Rohr *n*; Peddigrohr *n*; (Rohr)Stock *m*; **2.** aus Rohr flechten; prügeln; ~ **sug·ar** Rohrzucker *m.*
ca·nine **1.** ['keinain] Hunds..., Hunde...; **2.** ['kænain] *a.* ~ *tooth* Eckzahn *m.*
can·ing ['keiniŋ] Tracht *f* Prügel.
can·is·ter ['kænistə] Blechbüchse *f*; Kanister *m.*
can·ker ['kæŋkə] **1.** ⚕ Krebs *m*; ⚘ Brand *m*; *fig.* Krebsschaden *m*; **2.** anfressen; '**can·kered** *fig.* giftig (*boshaft*); '**can·ker·ous** krebsartig.
can·na·bis ['kænəbis] Hanf *m*; Haschisch *n.*
canned *Am.* [kænd] Büchsen..., eingemacht.
can·ner·y *Am.* ['kænəri] Konservenfabrik *f.*
can·ni·bal ['kænibəl] **1.** Kannibale *m*, Menschenfresser *m*; **2.** kannibalisch; Kannibalen...; '**can·ni·bal·ism** Kannibalismus *m*; '**can·ni·bal·ize** *Auto etc.* ausschlachten.
can·non ['kænən] **1.** ⚔ Kanone *f*; Artillerie *f*; *Billard*: Karambolage *f*; **2.** karambolieren (*fig. against*, *with* mit); **can·non·ade** [~'neid]

Kanonade *f*; ˈ**can·non-ball** Kanonenkugel *f*; ˈ**can·non-fod·der** Kanonenfutter *n*.
can·not [ˈkænɔt] kann nicht.
can·ny □ *schott.* [ˈkæni] vorsichtig; sanft, ruhig.
ca·noe [kəˈnuː] **1.** Kanu *n*; Paddelboot *n*; **2.** paddeln.
can·on [ˈkænən] Kanon *m* (*Regel*; *Richtschnur*; *Gesamtheit echter Schriften*; *Verzeichnis der Heiligen*; *Kettengesang*; *Schriftgrad*); Kanoniker *m*, Domherr *m*; ~ *law* kanonisches Recht *n*, Kirchenrecht *n*.
ca·ñon [ˈkænjən] = *canyon*.
can·on·ess [ˈkænənis] Stiftsdame *f*;
can·on·i·za·tion [~naiˈzeiʃən] Heiligsprechung *f*; ˈ**can·on·ize** heiligsprechen; ˈ**can·on·ry** Kanonikat *n*.
ca·noo·dle *sl.* [kəˈnuːdl] knutschen.
can·o·py [ˈkænəpi] **1.** Baldachin *m* (*a. fig.*); *fig.* Dach *n*; ⚠ Überdachung *f*; ✈ Kabinendach *n*; **2.** (mit einem Baldachin) überdachen.
cant[1] [kænt] **1.** Schrägung *f*; schräge Lage *f*; Stoß *m*, Ruck *m*; **2.** (sich) auf die Seite legen *od.* werfen; kanten; ~ *over* umkippen.
cant[2] [~] **1.** Zunftsprache *f*, *besondere* Ausdrucksweise *f*; Gewäsch *n*; scheinheiliges Gerede *n*; Scheinheiligkeit *f*; *thieves'* ~ Diebessprache *f*; **2.** zunftmäßig *od.* scheinheilig reden.
can't F [kɑːnt] = *cannot*.
Can·tab F [ˈkæntæb] (Student *m*) von Cambridge.
can·ta·loup ⚘ [ˈkæntəluːp] Zuckermelone *f*.
can·tan·ker·ous F □ [kənˈtæŋkərəs] zänkisch, mürrisch; rechthaberisch.
can·teen [kænˈtiːn] ⚔ Feldflasche *f*; *Kasernen-*, *Betriebs- etc.* Kantine *f*; ⚔ Kochgeschirr *n*; *Tafel*-Silberkasten *m*.
can·ter [ˈkæntə] **1.** kurzer Galopp *m*, Kanter *m*; **2.** in kurzem Galopp reiten, kantern.
can·ter·bur·y [ˈkæntəbəri] Notenständer *m*; 𝟐 *bell* ⚘ Glockenblume *f*.
can·thar·i·des ⚕ [kænˈθæridiːz] *pl.*, *mst sg.* Kanthariden *f/pl.* (*spanische Fliegen*).
can·ti·cle [ˈkæntikl] Lobgesang *m*; 𝟐*s pl. Bibel*: *das* Hohelied.
can·ti·le·ver ⚠ [ˈkæntiliːvə] Konsole *f*; freitragender Arm *m*; ~ *bridge* Auslegerbrücke *f*.
can·to [ˈkæntəu] Gesang *m* (*Abteilung e-s Gedichtes*).
can·ton **1.** [ˈkæntɔn] Kanton *m*, Bezirk *m*; **2.** ⚔ [kənˈtuːn] (sich) einquartieren; ˈ**can·ton·ment** ⚔ Quartier *n*, Ortsunterkunft *f*.
can·vas [ˈkænvəs] Segeltuch *n*; Zelt(e *pl.*) *n*; Zeltbahn *f*; *Wagen*-Plane *f*; Segel *n/pl.*; *paint.* Leinwand *f*, *weitS.* Gemälde *n*.
can·vass [~] **1.** (Stimmen)Werbung *f*; *Am. a.* Wahlnachprüfung *f*; **2.** *v/t.* erörtern; *Wahlkreis od. Wähler* bearbeiten (*a. fig.*); *v/i.* (Stimmen, *a.* Kunden) werben; ˈ**can·vass·er** Stimmen-, Kundenwerber(in); *Am. a.* Wahlprüfer *m*.
can·yon [ˈkænjən] Cañon *m*, Felsschlucht *f*.
caou·tchouc [ˈkautʃuk] Kautschuk *m*, *n*.
cap [kæp] **1.** Kappe *f*; Mütze *f*; Haube *f*; *univ.* Barett *n*; ⊕, ⛏ *etc.* Kappe *f*, Haube *f*; ⊕ Aufsatz *m*; Zündhütchen *n*; ~ *and bells* Schellenkappe *f*; ~ *and gown* Barett *n* und Talar *m* (*akademische Tracht*); ~ *in hand fig.* demütig, unterwürfig; *set one's* ~ *at s.o.* nach j-m angeln (*Frau*); **2.** mit einer Kappe *etc.* versehen; *fig.* krönen; F übertreffen, -trumpfen; die Mütze abnehmen (*to s.o.* vor j-m); *be* ~*ped Sport*: in die Nationalmannschaft berufen werden.
ca·pa·bil·i·ty [keipəˈbiliti] *körperliche od. geistige* Fähigkeit *f*; ˈ**ca·pa·ble** □ fähig, imstande (*of* zu); tüchtig.
ca·pa·cious □ [kəˈpeiʃəs] geräumig, umfassend; **ca·pac·i·tate** [kəˈpæsiteit] befähigen; **caˈpac·i·ty** **1.** Inhalt *m*; Kapazität *f*, Aufnahme-, Ladefähigkeit *f*; *geistige* (*od.* ⊕ Leistungs)Fähigkeit *f* (*for ger.* zu *inf.*); *amtliche etc.* Stellung *f*; *disposing* ~ Geschäftsfähigkeit *f*; *full to* ~ voll besetzt; *legal* ~ Rechtsfähigkeit *f*; *in my* ~ *as* in meiner Eigenschaft als; **2.** *attr.* Höchst...; zahlreich; *thea.* voll.
cap-à-pie [kæpəˈpiː] von Kopf bis Fuß.
ca·par·i·son *lit.* [kəˈpærisn] Schabracke *f*; *fig.* Putz *m*.
cape[1] [keip] Kap *n*, Vorgebirge *n*.
cape[2] [~] Cape *n*, Umhang *m*.

caper[1] ⚘ ['keipə] Kaper *f*.
ca·per[2] [~] **1.** Kapriole *f* (*a. fig.* = *toller Streich*), Luftsprung *m*; *cut* *~s* = **2.** Kapriolen *od.* Sprünge machen.
ca·pi·as ⚖ ['keipiæs]: *writ of* ~ Haftbefehl *m*.
cap·il·lar·i·ty *phys.* [kæpi'læriti] Kapillarität *f*; **cap·il·lar·y** [kə'piləri] **1.** Kapillar...; haarfein; **2.** *anat.* Kapillargefäß *n*.
cap·i·tal ['kæpitl] **1.** □ Kapital...; todeswürdig, Todes...; verhängnisvoll; hauptsächlich, Haupt...; vortrefflich, F famos; ~ *crime* Kapitalverbrechen *n*; ~ *punishment* Todesstrafe *f*; **2.** Hauptstadt *f*; Kapital *n*; *a.* ~ *letter typ.* Majuskel *f*, Großbuchstabe *m*; ⩓ Kapitell *n*; ~ **as·sets** *pl.* Anlagevermögen *n*; ~ **gains tax** Kapitalertragssteuer *f*; **cap·i·tal·ism** ['~təlizəm] Kapitalismus *m*; '**cap·i·tal·ist** Kapitalist(in); **cap·i·tal'is·tic** kapitalistisch; **cap·i·tal·i·za·tion** [kəpitəlai'zeiʃən] Kapitalisierung *f*; **cap'i·tal·ize** kapitalisieren; groß schreiben.
cap·i·ta·tion [kæpi'teiʃən] *a.* ~ *tax* Kopfsteuer *f*; Zahlung *f* pro Kopf.
Cap·i·tol ['kæpitl] Kapitol *n* (*Jupitertempel in Rom u. Sitz des Kongresses in Washington*).
ca·pit·u·late [kə'pitjuleit] kapitulieren (*to* vor *dat.*), sich ergeben; **ca·pit·u'la·tion** Kapitulation *f*, Übergabe *f*.
ca·pon ['keipən] Kapaun *m*.
ca·price [kə'pri:s] Kaprice *f*, Laune *f*; ♪ Capriccio *n*; **ca·pri·cious** □ [kə'priʃəs] kapriziös; launisch, launenhaft; **ca'pri·cious·ness** Launenhaftigkeit *f*.
Cap·ri·corn *ast.* ['kæprikɔ:n] Steinbock *m*.
cap·ri·ole ['kæpriəul] Kapriole *f* (*Luftsprung*).
cap·size ⚓ ['kæpsaiz] **1.** *v/i.* kentern; *fig.* sich überschlagen; *v/t.* zum Kentern bringen; **2.** Kentern *n*.
cap·stan ⚓ ['kæpstən] Gangspill *n*.
cap·su·lar ['kæpsjulə] kapselförmig; Kapsel...; **cap·sule** ⚘ *u.* ⚕ ['kæpsju:l] Kapsel *f*.
cap·tain ['kæptin] Führer *m*; Heerführer *m*, Feldherr *m*; *Sport*: Spiel-, Mannschaftsführer *m*; ⚓ Kapitän *m*; ⚔ Hauptmann *m*; ~ *of industry* Industriekapitän *m*; **cap·tain·cy**, **cap·tain·ship** ['~si, '~ʃip] Führung *f*; Kapitäns-, Hauptmannsstelle *f*, -rang *m*.
cap·tion ['kæpʃən] **1.** Überschrift *f*; Titel *m*; *Film*: Untertitel *m*; **2.** *v/t.* *Am.* mit Überschrift *od.* Titel *etc.* versehen.
cap·tious □ ['kæpʃəs] krittelig; spitzfindig.
cap·ti·vate *fig.* ['kæptiveit] gefangennehmen, fesseln; **cap·ti'va·tion** Fesselung *f*; '**cap·tive 1.** gefangen, gefesselt; ~ *balloon* Fesselballon *m*; **2.** Gefangene *m*, *f* (*a. fig.*); **cap·tiv·i·ty** [~'tiviti] Gefangenschaft *f*.
cap·tor ['kæptə] Fänger *m*; ⚓ Kaper *m*; **cap·ture** ['~tʃə] **1.** Eroberung *f*; Gefangennahme *f*; ⚓ Kapern *n*; **2.** (ein)fangen; gefangennehmen; erobern; erbeuten; ⚓ kapern, aufbringen.
Cap·u·chin *eccl.* ['kæpjuʃin] Kapuziner *m*.
car [kɑ:] Auto *n*, Wagen *m*; (Eisenbahn-, Straßenbahn)Wagen *m*; Ballonkorb *m*; Luftschiffgondel *f*; Kabine *f e-s Aufzugs*; ~ *park* Parkplatz *m*; Parkhaus *n*; ~ *pool* Fahrgemeinschaft *f*; Fahrbereitschaft *f*; *~port* überdachter Autoabstellplatz *m*.
car·a·cole ['kærəkəul] *Reitkunst*: **1.** Schwenkung *f*; **2.** schwenken.
ca·rafe [kə'ræf] Karaffe *f*.
car·a·mel ['kærəmel] Karamel *m*; Karamelle *f*.
car·a·pace *zo.* ['kærəpeis] Rückenschild *m*.
car·at ['kærət] Karat *n* (*Gewicht*).
car·a·van ['kærəvæn] Karawane *f*; Wohnwagen *m*; **car·a'van·se·rai** [~sərai] Karawanserei *f*; **car·a·van site** Campingplatz *m* für Wohnwagen.
car·a·way ⚘ ['kærəwei] Kümmel *m*.
car·bide ⚗ ['kɑ:baid] Karbid *n*.
car·bine ['kɑ:bain] Karabiner *m*.
car·bo·hy·drate ⚗ ['kɑ:bəu'haidreit] Kohlehydrat *n*.
car·bol·ic ac·id ⚗ [kɑ:'bɔlik'æsid] Karbolsäure *f*.
car·bon ['kɑ:bən] ⚗ Kohlenstoff *m*; ⚡ Kohlestift *m*; *a.* ~ *paper* Kohlepapier *n*; ~ *copy* Durchschlag *m von Maschinenschrift*; ~ *dioxide* Kohlendioxyd *n*; ~ *monoxide* Kohlenmonoxyd *n*; **car·bo·na·ceous** [~bəu'neiʃəs] kohlenstoffhaltig; **car·bon·ate** ['~bənit] kohlensaures Salz

n; **car·bon·ic** [~ˈbɔnik] Kohlen...; ~ *acid* Kohlensäure *f*; **car·bon·if·er·ous** *geol.* [~bəˈnifərəs] kohleführend (*Schicht*); **car·bon·i·za·tion** [~bənaiˈzeiʃən] Verkohlung *f*; ˈ**car·bon·ize** verkohlen.

car·bo·run·dum [kɑːbəˈrʌndəm] Karborund *n* (*Schleifmittel*).

car·boy [ˈkɑːbɔi] Säureballon *m*.

car·bun·cle [ˈkɑːbʌŋkl] *min.* Karfunkel *m*; ⚕ Karbunkel *m*.

car·bu·ret ⚗ [ˈkɑːbjuret] vergasen; ˈ**car·bu·ret·ter,** *mst* ˈ**car·bu·ret·tor** *mot.* Vergaser *m*.

car·case, *mst* **car·cass** [ˈkɑːkəs] (Tier)Kadaver *m*; *Fleischerei*: Rumpf *m*; *fig.* Gerippe *n*.

car·ci·no·ma ⚕ [kɑːsiˈnəumə] Karzinom *n*, Krebs *m*; **car·cin·o·gen·ic** [~nəˈdʒenik] karzinogen, krebserregend.

card[1] ⊕ [kɑːd] **1.** Wollkratze *f*, Karde *f*; **2.** *Wolle* karden, kämmen.

card[2] [~] Karte *f*; (Post-, Visiten-, Spiel)Karte *f*; *house of ~s* Kartenhaus *n*; *queer ~* F komischer Kauz *m*; *have a ~ up one's sleeve* et. in petto haben.

car·dan ⊕ [ˈkɑːdən]: *~ joint* Kardangelenk *n*; *~ shaft* Kardanwelle *f*.

card...: ˈ**~·board** Kartonpapier *n*; Pappe *f*; *~ box* Pappkarton *m*.

car·di·ac ⚕ [ˈkɑːdiæk] 1. Herz...; *~ arrest* Herzstillstand *m*; *~ stimulant* herzstärkendes Mittel; 2. Herzmittel *n*.

car·di·gan [ˈkɑːdigən] Strickjacke *f*.

car·di·nal □ [ˈkɑːdinl] **1.** Kardinal..., Haupt...; hochrot; *~ number* Grundzahl *f*; **2.** Kardinal *m* (*a. orn.*); **car·di·nal·ate** [ˈ~nəleit] Kardinalswürde *f*.

card...: ˈ**~-in·dex** Kartei *f*; ˈ**~-sharp·er** Falschspieler *m*.

care [kɛə] **1.** Sorge *f*; Sorgfalt *f*, Acht(samkeit) *f*; Obhut *f*, Pflege *f*; *medical ~* ärztliche Behandlung *f*; *~ of the mouth* Mundpflege *f*; *~ of the nails* Nagelpflege *f*; *~ of* (*abbr. c/o*) ... per Adresse, bei ...; *take ~* sich in acht nehmen, achtgeben; *take ~! bsd. Am.* F mach's gut!; *take ~ of* aufpassen *od.* acht(geb)en auf (*acc.*); verantwortlich sein für; *with ~!* Vorsicht! (*Aufschrift*); **2.** Lust *od.* Interesse haben (*to inf.* zu *inf.*); *~ for* sorgen für, sich kümmern um; *mst verneint*: sich etwas machen aus, mögen; *I don't ~ (if I do)!* F meinetwegen!; *I don't ~ what he said* es ist mir egal, was er gesagt hat; *I couldn't ~ less* F es ist mir völlig schnuppe; *well ~d-for* gepflegt.

ca·reen ⚓ [kəˈriːn] kielholen.

ca·reer [kəˈriə] **1.** Karriere *f*; Laufbahn *f*, Beruf *m*; Lauf *m*; *~ diplomat* Berufsdiplomat *m*; **2.** rasen, rennen; **caˈreer·ist** Karrieremacher *m*, Streber *m*.

care·free [ˈkɛəfriː] sorgenfrei, sorglos.

care·ful □ [ˈkɛəful] besorgt (*for* um), achtsam (*of* auf *acc.*); sorgsam, vorsichtig; sorgfältig, gewissenhaft; *be ~ to inf.* darauf bedacht sein zu *inf.*; nicht vergessen zu *inf.*; ˈ**care·ful·ness** Sorgsamkeit *f*; Vorsicht *f*; Sorgfalt *f*.

care·less □ [ˈkɛəlis] sorglos; unbekümmert (*of* um); unsorgfältig, nachlässig; unachtsam; unbedacht, unbesonnen, leichtsinnig, unvorsichtig; ˈ**care·less·ness** Sorglosigkeit *f*; Nachlässigkeit *f*.

ca·ress [kəˈres] **1.** Liebkosung *f*; **2.** liebkosen; *fig.* schmeicheln.

care·tak·er [ˈkɛəteikə] Wärter(in); (Haus)Verwalter(in); *~ government* geschäftsführende Regierung *f*.

care-worn [ˈkɛəwɔːn] abgehärmt.

car·fare *Am.* [ˈkɑːfɛə] Fahrgeld *n*.

car-ferry [ˈkɑːferi] Autofährschiff *n*; *a. car-air-ferry* Autoluftfähre *f*.

car·go ⚓ [ˈkɑːgəu] Ladung *f*, Fracht *f*; *mixed od. general ~* Stückgut *n*; *shifting ~* lose Ladung *f*.

car·i·bou *zo.* [ˈkæribuː] Karibu *m*.

car·i·ca·ture [kærikəˈtjuə] **1.** Karikatur *f*; **2.** karikieren; **car·i·caˈtur·ist** Karikaturist *m*.

car·i·es ⚕ [ˈkɛəriiːz] Karies *f*; Knochenfraß *m*; Zahnfäule *f*.

car·il·lon [kæˈriljən] Glockenspiel *n*.

car·i·ous [ˈkɛəriəs] kariös, angefault.

car·load [ˈkɑːləud] Wagenladung *f*; F Menge *f*.

car·man [ˈkɑːmən] Fuhrmann *m*.

car·mine [ˈkɑːmain] Karmin(rot) *n*.

car·nage [ˈkɑːnidʒ] Blutbad *n*; ˈ**car·nal** □ fleischlich; sinnlich, geschlechtlich; **car·nal·i·ty** [~ˈnæliti] Fleischeslust *f*; Sinnlichkeit *f*; **car·na·tion** [~ˈneiʃən] **1.** Fleischton *m*, Blaßrot *n*; ⚘ Nelke *f*; **2.** blaßrot.

car·ni·val [ˈkɑːnivəl] Karneval *m*,

Fasching *m*.
car·ni·vore [ˈkɑːnivɔː] Fleischfresser *m*; **car·niv·o·rous** [~ˈnivərəs] fleischfressend.
car·ol [ˈkærəl] **1.** Weihnachtslied *n*; **2.** Weihnachtslieder singen.
ca·rot·id *anat.* [kəˈrɔtid] *a.* ~ *artery* Karotis *f* (*Halsschlagader*).
ca·rouse [kəˈrauz] **1.** *a.* **caˈrous·al** (Trink)Gelage *n*; **2.** zechen.
carp[1] [kɑːp] Karpfen *m*.
carp[2] [~] kritteln, nörgeln; ~ *at* kritteln an (*dat.*), bekritteln.
car·pen·ter [ˈkɑːpintə] **1.** Zimmermann *m*; **2.** zimmern; **ˈcar·pen·try** Zimmerhandwerk *n*.
car·pet [ˈkɑːpit] **1.** Teppich *m* (*a. fig.*); *bring on the* ~ aufs Tapet bringen; ~ *dance* zwangloses Tänzchen *n*; **2.** mit e-m Teppich belegen; F zur Rede stellen; **ˈ~-bag** Reisetasche *f*; **ˈ~-bag·ger** politischer Abenteurer *m*; **ˈcar·pet·ing** Teppichstoff *m*.
car·pet...: **ˈ~-ˈknight** Salonlöwe *m*; **ˈ~-sweep·er** Teppichkehrmaschine *f*.
car·riage [ˈkæridʒ] Beförderung *f*, Transport *m*; Fracht *f*; Wagen *m* (*a.* ⊕); Kutsche *f*; ⚔ Lafette *f*; Fuhr-, Frachtlohn *m*; (Körper-)Haltung *f*, Gang *m*; Benehmen *n*; Aus-, Durchführung *f*; ~ *free*, ~ *paid* frachtfrei; **ˈcar·riage·a·ble** befahrbar (*Weg*).
car·riage...: **ˈ~-drive** Anfahrt *f* (*vor e-m Hause*); **ˈ~-way** Fahrbahn *f*; *dual* ~ doppelte Fahrbahn *f*.
car·ri·er [ˈkæriə] Fuhrmann *m*; Spediteur *m*; Träger *m* (*a.* ⚕ = *Keim*); Gepäckträger *m am Fahrrad*; **ˈ~-bag** Trag(e)tasche *f*; **ˈ~-pi·geon** Brieftaube *f*.
car·ri·on [ˈkæriən] **1.** Aas *n*; Unrat *m*; **2.** Aas...
car·rot [ˈkærət] Mohrrübe *f*, Möhre *f*, Karotte *f*; **ˈcar·rot·y** F rot (-blond).
car·ry [ˈkæri] **1.** *v/t. wohin* bringen, führen, tragen, fahren, befördern; (bei sich) haben; *Ansicht* durchsetzen; *Gewinn, Preis* davontragen; *Zahlen* übertragen; *Ernte, Zinsen* tragen; ⚓ *Segel* führen; *Mauer etc.* weiterführen; *Benehmen* fortsetzen; *Antrag, Kandidaten* durchbringen; ⚔ *Festung etc.* erobern; *be carried* angenommen werden, durchgehen (*Antrag*); durchkommen (*Kandidat*); ~ *the day* den Sieg davontragen; ~ *away* wegtragen; fortreißen (*a. fig.*); ~ *everything before one* alles mit sich fortreißen; ~ *forward od. over* † vor-, übertragen; ~ *on* fortsetzen, weiterführen; *Geschäft, Prozeß etc.* betreiben, führen; ~ *out*, ~ *through* durchführen; ~ *out* ⚖ *Strafe* vollstrecken; *v/i.* tragen; *weit etc.* tragen (*Gewehr*); ~ *on* F sich haben; weitermachen; *~ing capacity* Tragfähigkeit *f*; **2.** Trag-, Schußweite *f*; **ˈ~-cot** Babytragtasche *f*.
cart [kɑːt] **1.** Karren *m*; *bsd. in Zssgn*: Wagen *m*; ~ *grease* Wagenschmiere *f*; *put the* ~ *before the horse fig.* das Pferd beim Schwanz aufzäumen; *in the* ~ *sl.* in der Patsche; **2.** karren, fahren; **ˈcart·age** Fahren *n*; Fuhrlohn *m*; Rollgeld *n*.
car·tel [kɑːˈtel] Kartell *n*, Zweckverband *m*; ⚔ (Abkommen *n* über den) Austausch *m* von Gefangenen.
cart·er [ˈkɑːtə] Fuhrmann *m*.
car·ti·lage [ˈkɑːtilidʒ] Knorpel *m*; **car·ti·lag·i·nous** [~ˈlædʒinəs] knorpelig.
cart-load [ˈkɑːtləud] Fuhre *f*.
car·tog·ra·pher [kɑːˈtɔgrəfə] Kartograph *m*; **carˈtog·ra·phy** Kartographie *f*.
car·ton [ˈkɑːtən] Karton *m*; *a* ~ *of cigarettes* e-e Stange *f* Zigaretten.
car·toon [kɑːˈtuːn] **1.** *paint.* Karton *m*; ⊕ Musterzeichnung *f*; Karikatur *f*; Zeichentrickfilm *m*; **2.** karikieren; **carˈtoon·ist** Karikaturist *m*.
car·touche ⚠ [kɑːˈtuːʃ] Kartusche *f*.
car·tridge [ˈkɑːtridʒ] Patrone *f*; (Film)Kassette *f*; **ˈ~-pa·per** Zeichenpapier *n*.
cart-wheel [ˈkɑːtwiːl] Wagenrad *n*; *Am.* Silberdollar *m*; *turn ~s* radschlagen.
cart·wright [ˈkɑːtrait] Stellmacher *m*.
carve [kɑːv] *Fleisch* vorschneiden, zerlegen; (*in*) *Holz* schnitzen; (*in*) *Stein* meißeln; sich *e-n Weg* bahnen; **ˈcarv·er** (Bild)Schnitzer *m*; Vorschneider *m*; Vorlegemesser *n*; *~s pl.* Vorlegebesteck *n*; **ˈcarv·ing** **1.** Schnitzerei *f*; **2.** Schnitz...; Vorlege...
car wash [ˈkɑːwɔʃ] Autowaschanlage *f*.

cas·cade [kæs'keid] Kaskade *f* (*kleiner Wasserfall*).
case[1] [keis] **1.** Behälter *m*; Kiste *f*; Futteral *n*, Etui *n*, Tasche *f*; Gehäuse *n*; Schachtel *f*; Scheide *f*; Kapsel *f*; Fach *n*; Necessaire *n*; *Patronen*-Hülse *f*; *typ.* Setzkasten *m*; **2.** (ein)stecken; ver-, umkleiden (*with* mit).
case[2] [~] Fall *m* (*a.* ⚕, ⚖); ⚕ *a.* Kranke *m*, *f*; *Am.* F komischer Kauz *m*; ⚖ *a.* Rechtsgrund *m*, Schriftsatz *m*; Hauptargument *n*; Sache *f*, Angelegenheit *f*; *a ~ for* gewichtige Gründe für; *make out one's ~* seine Argumente vorbringen; *have a strong ~* das Recht auf seiner Seite haben; *as the ~ may be* je nachdem; *in ~* im Falle, falls, für den Fall, daß; *in any ~* jedenfalls.
case-book ['keisbuk] Patientenbuch *n*.
case-hard·en ⊕ ['keishɑ:dn] hartgießen; *~ed fig.* hartgesotten.
case his·to·ry ['keishistəri] Vorgeschichte *f*; Krankengeschichte *f*.
ca·se·in ⚗ ['keisi:in] Käsestoff *m*.
case·mate ⚔ ['keismeit] Kasematte *f*.
case·ment ['keismənt] Fensterflügel *m*; *~ window* Flügelfenster *n*.
case-shot ⚔ ['keisʃɔt] Kartätsche *f*.
cash [kæʃ] **1.** Bargeld *n*, Kasse *f*; *~ down, for ~* gegen bar; *in ~* bar, netto Kasse; *be in (out of) ~* bei (nicht bei) Kasse sein; *~ and carry* Barzahlung *f* und Selbstabholung *f* (im Großhandel); *~ payment* Barzahlung *f*; *~ on delivery* Lieferung *f* gegen bar; (per) Nachnahme *f*; *~ price* Kassenpreis *m*; *~ register* Registrierkasse *f*; **2.** einkassieren, -lösen; '**~-book** Kassabuch *n*; '**~-cheque** Barscheck *m*; **~ desk** Kasse *f*, Kassentisch *m*; **~ dis·pens·er** Geldautomat *m*; **cash·ier 1.** [kæ'ʃiə] Kassierer(in); 2. [kə'ʃiə] ⚔ kassieren (*entlassen*); **cash·less** ['kæʃlis] bargeldlos.
cash·mere [kæʃ'miə] Kaschmir *m* (*feiner Wollstoff*).
cas·ing ['keisiŋ] Überzug *m*, Gehäuse *n*, Futteral *n*; ⚠ Verkleidung *f*; *~ paper* Packpapier *n*.
ca·si·no [kə'si:nəu] Kasino *n*.
cask [kɑ:sk] Faß *n*.
cas·ket ['kɑ:skit] Kassette *f*, (Schmuck)Kästchen *n*; *Am.* Sarg *m*.
Cas·pi·an Sea ['kæspiən'si:] *das* Kaspische Meer, *der* Kaspisee.
casque [kæsk] Helm *m*.
cas·sa·tion [kæ'seiʃən] Kassation *f*.
cas·sa·va ⚘ [kə'sɑ:və] Maniokstrauch *m*.
cas·se·role ['kæsərəul] Kasserolle *f*, Tiegel *m*.
cas·sette [kæ'set] Film-, Tonbandkassette *f*; **~ deck** Kassettendeck *n*.
cas·si·a ⚘ ['kæsiə] Kassia *f*; *Art* Zimt *m*.
cas·sock ['kæsək] Soutane *f*, Priesterrock *m*.
cas·so·war·y *orn.* ['kæsəwεəri] Kasuar *m*; *New Holland ~* Emu *m*.
cast [kɑ:st] **1.** Wurf *m*; Wurfweite *f*; ⊕ Guß(form *f*) *m*; Abguß *m*, -druck *m*; Schattierung *f*, Anflug *m*; Form *f*, Art *f*, Zuschnitt *m*; ⚓ Auswerfen *n von Senkblei, Netz etc.*; *thea.* (Rollen)Besetzung *f*; ⚕ Aufrechnung *f*; **2.** (*irr.*) *v/t.* (ab-, aus-, hin-, um-, weg)werfen; *zo. Haut etc.* abwerfen; *Zähne etc.* verlieren; *Anker*, *fig. Blick, Licht, Schatten etc.* werfen; verwerfen, ausmustern; gestalten; *Metall* gießen; *a. ~ up* aus-, zs.-rechnen; *thea. Rolle* besetzen; *Rolle* übertragen (*to dat.*); *be ~ in costs* ⚖ zu den Kosten verurteilt werden; *be ~ in a lawsuit* ⚖ e-n Prozeß verlieren; *~ lots (for)* losen (um); *~ in one's lot with s.o.* j-s Los teilen; *~ one's skin* sich häuten; *~ s.th. in s.o.'s teeth* j-m et. vorwerfen; *~ away* wegwerfen; *be ~ away* ⚓ verschlagen werden; *~ down* niederwerfen; *die Augen* niederschlagen; *be ~ down* niedergeschlagen sein; *~ up* aufwerfen; erbrechen; *~ up (accounts)* ⚕ zs.-rechnen; *v/i.* sich gießen lassen; ⊕ sich (ver)werfen; *~ about for* sinnen auf (*acc.*); sich *et.* überlegen; *~ off* ⚓ loswerfen.
cas·ta·net [kæstə'net] Kastagnette *f*.
cast·a·way ['kɑ:stəwei] **1.** verworfen; ⚓ schiffbrüchig; **2.** Verworfene *m*, *f*; Schiffbrüchige *m*, *f* (*a. fig.*), Gestrandete *m*, *f*.
caste [kɑ:st] Kaste *f* (*a. fig.*); *~ feeling* Kastengeist *m*.
cas·tel·lan ['kæstələn] Kastellan *m*;
cas·tel·lat·ed ['kæsteleitid] mit Zinnen (versehen); burgenreich.
cas·ter ['kɑ:stə] = *castor*[2].
cas·ti·gate ['kæstigeit] züchtigen; *fig.* geißeln; **cas·ti'ga·tion** Züchtigung *f*; *fig.* Geißelung *f*.

cast·ing [ˈkɑːstiŋ] **1.** Wurf...; entscheidend (*Stimme*); **2.** Werfen *n etc.*; *~s pl.* Gußwaren *f/pl.*

cast i·ron [ˈkɑːstˈaiən] Gußeisen *n*; **ˈcast-ˈi·ron** gußeisern.

cas·tle [ˈkɑːsl] **1.** Burg *f*, Schloß *n*; *Schach*: Turm *m*; *~s in the air*, *~s in Spain* Luftschlösser *n/pl.*; **2.** *Schach*: rochieren.

cast-off [ˈkɑːstˈɔf] Verstoßene *m, f*; Abgelegte *n*.

cas·tor[1] *pharm.* [ˈkɑːstə]: *~ oil* Rizinusöl *n*.

cas·tor[2] [~] Laufrolle *f unter Möbeln*; (Salz-, Zucker- *etc.*) Streuer *m*; *~ sugar* Streuzucker *m*.

cas·trate [kæsˈtreit] kastrieren; **casˈtra·tion** Kastrierung *f*; Verstümmelung *f*.

cast steel [ˈkɑːstˈstiːl] Gußstahl *m*; **ˈcast-ˈsteel** aus Gußstahl.

cas·u·al □ [ˈkæʒjuəl] zufällig; gelegentlich; beiläufig; F lässig; *~ labourer* Gelegenheitsarbeiter *m*; **ˈcas·u·al·ty** Unfall *m*; *casualties pl.* ⚔ Verluste *m/pl.*

cas·u·ist [ˈkæzjuist] Kasuist *m*; **ˈcas·u·ist·ry** Kasuistik *f*.

cat [kæt] **1.** Katze *f*; *Am. sl.* Jazzfanatiker *m*; *wait for the ~ to jump*, *see which way the ~ jumps* sehen, wie der Hase läuft; *not room to swing a ~* kaum Platz zum Umdrehen; *~ burglar* Fassadenkletterer *m*, Einsteigdieb *m*; **2.** P kotzen.

cat·a·clysm [ˈkætəklizəm] Sintflut *f*; Katastrophe *f*.

cat·a·comb [ˈkætəkuːm] Katakombe *f*.

cat·a·logue, *Am. a.* **cat·a·log** [ˈkætəlɔg] **1.** Katalog *m*; Liste *f*; (*Am. univ.* Vorlesungs)Verzeichnis *n*; **2.** katalogisieren.

ca·tal·y·sis ⚗ [kəˈtælisis], *pl.* **caˈtal·y·ses** [~siːz] Katalyse *f*; **cat·a·lyst** [ˈkætəlist] (*a. fig.*) Katalysator *m*.

cat·a·pult [ˈkætəpʌlt] Schleuder *f*; ✈ Katapult *m, n*.

cat·a·ract [ˈkætərækt] Katarakt *m*, Wasserfall *m*; ⚕ grauer Star *m*.

ca·tarrh [kəˈtɑː] Katarrh *m*; F *bsd.* Schnupfen *m*; **ca·tarrh·al** [kəˈtɑːrəl] katarrhalisch; Schnupfen...

ca·tas·tro·phe [kəˈtæstrəfi] Katastrophe *f*; **cat·a·stroph·ic** [kætəˈstrɔfik] (*~ally*) katastrophal.

ca·taw·ba *Am.* ♀ [kəˈtɔːbə] Catawba-Rebe *f*.

cat·bird *zo.* [ˈkætbəːd] Spottdrossel *f*.

cat bur·glar [ˈkætbəːglə] Einsteigdieb *m*, Fassadenkletterer *m*.

cat·call [ˈkætkɔːl] **1.** *thea. etc.* (gellender) Pfiff *m*; **2.** auspfeifen.

catch [kætʃ] **1.** Fang *m*; Beute *f*, *fig.* Vorteil *m*; ♪ Rundgesang *m*; Kniff *m*; ⊕ Haken *m* (*a. fig. e-r Sache*), Griff *m*, Schnapper *m*, Klinke *f*; *s. ~word*; **2.** (*irr.*) *v/t.* fassen, *oft* F kriegen; fangen, ergreifen; abfassen, ertappen; *Blick etc.* auffangen, erhaschen; *Zug etc.* erreichen; bekommen, erhalten; sich *Krankheit* zuziehen, holen; angesteckt werden (von); *Feuer* fangen; *Atem* anhalten; *Schlag* versetzen, *mit e-m Schlag* treffen; *fig.* erfassen, verstehen; *~ it* F es (*Prügel, Schelte*) kriegen; *~ in the act* auf frischer Tat ertappen; *~ me!* da kannst du lange warten!, das fällt mir nicht ein!; *~ (a) cold* sich erkälten; *~ s.o.'s eye* j-m ins Auge fallen; *~ the Speaker's eye* (*im engl. Parlament*) das Wort erhalten; *~ up* auffangen; F *j.* unterbrechen; einholen; *v/i.* sich verfangen, hängenbleiben; fassen, einschnappen (*Schloß etc.*); *~ at* fassen *od.* greifen nach; *~ on* F Anklang finden; *Am.* kapieren; *~ up with j.* einholen; **ˈ~·all** *Am.* Platz *m od.* Behälter *m* für alles mögliche (*a. fig. u. attr.*); **ˈ~-as-ˈcatch-ˈcan** *Sport*: Freistilringen *n*; **ˈcatch·er** Fänger(in); **ˈcatch·ing** packend; ♪ eingängig; ⚕ ansteckend; **ˈcatch-line** Schlagzeile *f*; **ˈcatch·ment ba·sin** Einzugsgebiet *n e-s Stromes*; Staubecken *n*, -see *m*.

catch...: **ˈ~·pen·ny** ✝ Lock..., Schleuder...; **ˈ~-phrase** Schlagwort *n*; **ˈ~·pole** Büttel *m*; **ˈ~·word** Schlagwort *n*; *thea.*, *typ.* Stichwort *n*; **ˈcatch·y** F *fig.* packend; verfänglich.

cat·e·chism [ˈkætikizəm] Katechismus *m*; **cat·e·chize** [ˈ~kaiz] katechisieren; **cat·e·chu·men** [~ˈkjuːmen] Konfirmand *m*.

cat·e·gor·i·cal □ [kætiˈgɔrikəl] kategorisch; **cat·e·go·ry** [ˈ~gəri] Kategorie *f*, Klasse *f*, Gruppe *f*.

ca·ter [ˈkeitə]: *~ for* Lebensmittel liefern für; *fig.* sorgen für; befriedi-

gen; ˈ**ca·ter·er** (Lebensmittel)Lieferant *m*; Gastwirt *m*, Hotelier *m*; ˈ**ca·ter·ing** Verpflegung *f*.
cat·er·pil·lar [ˈkætəpilə] Raupe *f*.
cat·er·waul [ˈkætəwɔːl] miauen.
cat·fish [ˈkætfiʃ] Katzenfisch *m*, Wels *m*.
cat·gut [ˈkætgʌt] Darmsaite *f*.
ca·thar·sis [kəˈθɑːsis] seelische Läuterung *f*; ⚕ Abführen *n*; **caˈthar·tic** [~tik] reinigend, läuternd.
ca·the·dral [kəˈθiːdrəl] **1.** Dom *m*, Kathedrale *f*; **2.** Dom...
Cath·er·ine-wheel [ˈkæθərinwiːl] △ Fensterrose *f*; *Feuerwerk*: Feuerrad *n*.
cath·e·ter ⚕ [ˈkæθitə] Katheter *m*.
cath·ode ⚡ [ˈkæθəud] **1.** Kathode *f*; **2.** Kathoden...; ~ **ray** Kathodenstrahl *m*.
cath·o·lic [ˈkæθəlik] **1.** (~*ally*) katholisch; **2.** Katholik(in); **ca·thol·i·cism** [kəˈθɔlisizəm] Katholizismus *m*.
cat·kin ⚘ [ˈkætkin] (Blüten)Kätzchen *n*.
cat·like [ˈkætlaik] katzenartig; ˈ**cat·nap** Nickerchen *n*; ˈ**cat·nip** ⚘ Katzenminze *f*.
cat-o'-nine-tails [ˈkætəˈnainteilz] neunschwänzige Katze *f* (*Peitsche*).
cat's...: ~ **eye** Katzenauge *n*; ˈ**~-paw** *fig*. [ˈkætspɔː] (willenloses) Werkzeug *n*.
cat·suit [ˈkætsuːt] Overall *m*, einteiliger Hosenanzug *m*.
cat·tish *fig*. [ˈkætiʃ] falsch, hinterlistig, boshaft.
cat·tle [ˈkætl] Vieh *n*; ˈ**~-breed·ing** Viehzucht *f*; **~·man** [ˈ~mən] Viehzüchter *m*; Viehknecht *m*; ˈ**~-plague** Rinderpest *f*; ˈ**~-rus·tler** *Am*. Viehdieb *m*; ˈ**~-show** Viehschau *f*, -ausstellung *f*.
cat·ty [ˈkæti] = *cattish*.
cat·walk [ˈkætwɔːk] Laufsteg *m*.
Cau·ca·sian [kɔːˈkeizjən] **1.** kaukasisch; **2.** Kaukasier(in).
cau·cus [ˈkɔːkəs] Wahlvorbereitung *f*, -ausschuß *m*; *contp*. Klüngel (-wirtschaft *f*) *m*; *Am. pol*. Parteitagung *f*.
cau·dal [ˈkɔːdl] Schwanz...; **cau·date** [ˈ~deit] geschwänzt.
caught [kɔːt] *pret. u. p.p von catch* [2.]
caul·dron [ˈkɔːldrən] Kessel *m*.
cau·li·flow·er ⚘ [ˈkɔliflauə] Blumenkohl *m*.
caulk ⚓ [kɔːk] kalfatern (*abdichten*); ˈ**caulk·er** Kalfaterer *m*.
caus·al □ [ˈkɔːzəl] kausal, ursächlich; **cau·sal·i·ty** [~ˈzæliti] Kausalität *f*, Ursächlichkeit *f*; ˈ**caus·a·tive** verursachend (*of acc*.); **cause** **1.** Ursache *f*, Grund *m*; ⚖ Klage (-grund *m*) *f*; Prozeß *m*; Angelegenheit *f*, Sache *f*; *make common* ~ *with* gemeinsame Sache machen mit; **2.** verursachen, veranlassen; ˈ**cause·less** □ grundlos.
cause·way [ˈkɔːzwei], *a*. **cau·sey** [ˈ~zei] Damm *m im Sumpfgelände*.
caus·tic [ˈkɔːstik] **1.** Ätzmittel *n*; **2.** (~*ally*) ätzend; *fig*. scharf, beißend.
cau·ter·i·za·tion ⚕ [kɔːtəraiˈzeiʃən] Ausbrennen *n*; ˈ**cau·ter·ize** (aus-) brennen, beizen; ˈ**cau·ter·y** Brenneisen *n*.
cau·tion [ˈkɔːʃən] **1.** Vorsicht *f*; Warnung *f*; *tadelnde* Verwarnung *f*; ⚖ Rechtsbelehrung *f*; F ulkige Nummer *f*; ~ *money* Kaution *f*, Haftsumme *f*; **2.** warnen (*against* vor *dat*.); *tadelnd* verwarnen; ⚖ belehren; **cau·tion·ar·y** [ˈ~ʃnəri] warnend.
cau·tious □ [ˈkɔːʃəs] behutsam, vorsichtig; ˈ**cau·tious·ness** Behutsamkeit *f*, Vorsicht *f*.
cav·al·cade [kævəlˈkeid] Kavalkade *f*, Reiterzug *m*, -trupp *m*.
cav·a·lier [kævəˈliə] **1.** Kavalier *m*; Reiter *m*; **2.** □ hochmütig.
cav·al·ry ⚔ [ˈkævəlri] Kavallerie *f*, Reiterei *f*.
cave [keiv] **1.** Höhle *f*; *attr*. Höhlen...; **2.** ~ *in v/i*. einstürzen; klein beigeben; *v/t*. F einschlagen, -drücken.
ca·ve·at ⚖ [ˈkeiviæt] Einspruch *m*.
cave-dweller [ˈkeivdwelə], **cave-man** [ˈ~mæn] Höhlenmensch *m*.
cav·en·dish [ˈkævəndiʃ] Plattentabak *m*.
cav·ern [ˈkævən] Höhle *f*; ˈ**cav·ern·ous** voller Höhlen; *fig*. hohl.
cav·i·ar(e) [ˈkæviɑː] Kaviar *m*; ~ *to the general* Kaviar fürs Volk.
cav·il [ˈkævil] **1.** Krittelei *f*; **2.** kritteln (*at, about* an *dat*.); ˈ**cav·il·ler** Krittler(in).
cav·i·ty [ˈkæviti] Höhlung *f*, Höhle *f*; Loch *n*.
ca·vort *Am*. F [kəˈvɔːt] sich aufbäumen, umherspringen.
ca·vy [ˈkeivi] Meerschweinchen *n*.

caw [kɔ:] **1.** krächzen; **2.** Krächzen *n.*
cay·enne [kei'en] *a.* ~ *pepper* ['keien] Cayennepfeffer *m.*
cay·man *zo.* ['keimən] Kaiman *m.*
cease [si:s] *v/i.* (*from*) aufhören (mit), ablassen (von); *v/t.* aufhören mit, (⚔ *Feuer*) einstellen; '~-'**fire** ⚔ Feuereinstellung *f*, Waffenruhe *f*; '**cease·less** □ unaufhörlich.
ce·dar ⚘ ['si:də] Zeder(nholz *n*) *f.*
cede [si:d] abtreten, überlassen.
ce·dil·la [si'dilə] Cedille *f.*
ceil [si:l] *Zimmer* mit e-r Decke versehen; *Decke* verschalen; '**ceil·ing** (Zimmer)Decke *f*; ✈ Gipfelhöhe *f*; *fig.* Höchstgrenze *f*; ~ *lighting* Deckenbeleuchtung *f*; ~ *price* Höchstpreis *m.*
cel·an·dine ⚘ ['seləndain] Schell-, Schöllkraut *n.*
cel·a·nese [selə'ni:z] Celanese *f* [(*Kunstseide*).]
cel·e·brate ['selibreit] feiern (*fig.* = *rühmen*); *eccl.* zelebrieren; '**cel·e·brat·ed** gefeiert, berühmt (*for* wegen); **cel·e'bra·tion** Feier *f*; *eccl.* Zelebrierung *f*; *in* ~ *of* zur Feier (*gen.*); '**cel·e·bra·tor** Lobpreiser *m.*
ce·leb·ri·ty [si'lebriti] Berühmtheit *f.*
ce·ler·i·ty [si'leriti] Geschwindigkeit *f.*
cel·er·y ⚘ ['seləri] Sellerie *m, f.*
ce·les·tial □ [si'lestjəl] himmlisch; Himmel(s)...
cel·i·ba·cy ['selibəsi] Zölibat *n, m*, Ehelosigkeit *f*; **cel·i·bate** ['~bit] **1.** unverheiratet; **2.** Junggeselle *m.*
cell [sel] *allg.* Zelle *f*; ⚡ Element *n.*
cel·lar ['selə] **1.** Keller *m*; **2.** einkellern; '**cel·lar·age** Keller(ei *f*) *m/pl.*; Kellermiete *f*; **cel·lar·et** [~'ret] Flaschenständer *m.*
...celled [seld] ...zellig.
cel·list ♪ ['tʃelist] Cellist(in); **cel·lo** ['~ləu] Cello *n.*
cel·lo·phane ['seləufein] Cellophan *n.*
cel·lu·lar ['seljulə] zellig; **cel·lule** ['~ju:l] kleine Zelle *f*; **cel·lu·loid** ['~julɔid] Zelluloid *n*; **cel·lu·lose** ['~juləus] Zellstoff *m*, Zellulose *f.*
Celt [kelt] Kelte *m*, Keltin *f*; '**Celt·ic** keltisch.
ce·ment [si'ment] **1.** Zement *m*; Kitt *m* (*a. fig.*); **2.** zementieren; (ver)kitten (*a. fig.*); **ce·men·ta·tion** [si:men'teiʃən] Zementieren *n*; **ce·ment mix·er** Betonmischmaschine *f.*
cem·e·ter·y ['semitri] Friedhof *m.*
cen·o·taph ['senəutɑ:f] Ehrengrabmal *n.*
cense [sens] beräuchern; '**cen·ser** Weihrauchfaß *n.*
cen·sor ['sensə] **1.** Zensor *m*; **2.** zensieren; **cen·so·ri·ous** □ [sen'sɔ:riəs] kritisch; kritt(e)lig, tadelsüchtig; **cen·sor·ship** ['~səʃip] *amtliche* Zensur *f*; Zensoramt *n.*
cen·sur·a·ble □ ['senʃərəbl] tadelnswert; '**cen·sure** **1.** Tadel *m*; Verweis *m*; **2.** tadeln.
cen·sus ['sensəs] Volkszählung *f*; '~-**pa·per** Erhebungsbogen *m.*
cent [sent] Hundert *n*; *Am.* Cent *m*, $^1/_{100}$ Dollar *m*; *per* ~ Prozent *n.*
cen·taur ['sentɔ:] Kentaur *m.*
cen·tau·ry ⚘ ['sentɔ:ri] Flockenblume *f.*
cen·te·nar·i·an [senti'nɛəriən] **1.** hundertjährig; **2.** Hundertjährige *m, f*; **cen·te·nar·y** [sen'ti:nəri] *s.* *centennial.*
cen·ten·ni·al [sen'tenjəl] hundertjährig(es Jubiläum *n*).
cen·tes·i·mal □ [sen'tesiməl] hundertteilig.
cen·ti... ['senti]: '~·**grade** hundertgradig; *degrees* ~ Grad Celsius; ~ *thermometer* Celsiusthermometer *n*; '~·**gramme** Zentigramm *n*; '~·**me·tre** Zentimeter *n, m*; ~·**pede** *zo.* ['~pi:d] Hundertfüßer *m.*
cen·tral ['sentrəl] **1.** □ zentral (gelegen); Zentral...; Mittel...; bedeutendst, Haupt...; ~ *heating* Zentralheizung *f*; ~ *locking mot.* Zentralverriegelung *f*; ♀ *Powers pl.* Mittelmächte *f/pl.*; ~ *office*, ⚡ ~ *station* Zentrale *f*; **2.** *teleph.* Amt *n*; **cen·tral·i·za·tion** [~lai'zeiʃən] Zentralisation *f*; '**cen·tral·ize** zentralisieren.
cen·tre, *Am.* **cen·ter** ['sentə] **1.** Zentrum *n* (*a.* ⚔, *pol.*), Mittelpunkt *m*, Mitte *f*; ~ *forward Fußball*: Mittelstürmer *m*; ~ *half* Mittelläufer *m*; ~ *of gravity* Schwerpunkt *m*; **2.** zentral; **3.** (sich) konzentrieren; zentralisieren; zentrieren; '~-**bit** ⊕ Zentrumsbohrer *m*; '~-**board** Schwert *n e-s Segelboots.*
cen·tric, **cen·tri·cal** □ ['sentrik(əl)] zentrisch, zentral; **cen·trif·u·gal** □ [sen'trifjugəl] zentrifugal; **cen'trip·e·tal** □ [~pitl] zentripetal.

cen·tu·ple ['sentjupl] **1.** □ hundertfältig; **2.** verhundertfachen.
cen·tu·ri·on [sen'tjuəriən] *Rom*: Zenturio *m.*
cen·tu·ry ['sentʃuri] Jahrhundert *n.*
ce·ram·ic [si'ræmik] keramisch; **ce'ram·ics** *pl.* Keramik *f*, Töpferkunst *f.*
ce·re·al ['siəriəl] **1.** Getreide...; **2.** *mst* ~*s pl.* Getreide(pflanze *f*) *n*; *bsd. Am.* (Frühstücks)Nahrung *f aus Weizen, Mais etc.*
cer·e·bel·lum *anat.* [seri'beləm] Zerebellum *n*, Kleinhirn *n.*
cer·e·bral *anat.* ['seribrəl] Gehirn...
ce·re·brum *anat.* ['seribrəm] Zerebrum *n*, Großhirn *n.*
cere·cloth ['siəklɔθ] Leichentuch *n.*
cer·e·mo·ni·al [seri'məunjəl] **1.** □ *a.* **cer·e'mo·ni·ous** □ zeremoniell; förmlich, formell, feierlich; **2.** Zeremoniell *n*; **cer·e·mo·ny** ['seriməni] Zeremonie *f*; Feierlichkeit *f*; Förmlichkeit(en *pl.*) *f*; *Master of Ceremonies* Zeremonienmeister *m*; Conférencier *m*; *stand on* ~ förmlich sein; *without* ~ ohne Umstände, ohne weiteres.
cert *sl.* [sə:t] todsichere Sache *f.*
cer·tain □ ['sə:tn] sicher, gewiß; zuverlässig; bestimmt (*festgesetzt*); gewisse(r, -s); *for* ~ bestimmt, mit Sicherheit; *make* ~ sich vergewissern; '**cer·tain·ly** sicherlich, selbstverständlich, bestimmt; '**cer·tain·ty** Sicherheit *f*, Gewißheit *f*; Zuverlässigkeit *f.*
cer·tes † ['sə:tiz] sicherlich, gewißlich.
cer·ti·fi·a·ble ['sə:tifaiəbl] nachweisbar; F unzurechnungsfähig.
cer·tif·i·cate **1.** [sə'tifikit] Zeugnis *n*, Schein *m*, Bescheinigung *f*; ~ *of birth* (*death, marriage*) Geburts- (Sterbe-, Heirats)urkunde *f*; ~ *of employment* Beschäftigungsnachweis *m*, Arbeitsbescheinigung *f*; *medical* ~ ärztliches Attest *n*; **2.** [sə'tifikeit] mit e-m Zeugnis versehen, bescheinigen; ~*d* staatlich anerkannt; **cer·ti·fi·ca·tion** [sə:tifi'keiʃən] Bescheinigung *f*; **cer·ti·fy** ['~fai] *et.* bescheinigen; bezeugen; amtlich für geisteskrank erklären; *this is to* ~ hiermit wird bescheinigt; *certified cheque als gedeckt* bestätigter Scheck *m*; *s. accountant*; **cer·ti·tude** ['~tju:d] Gewißheit *f.*
ce·ru·le·an [si'ru:ljən] azur-, tiefblau.
cer·vi·cal [sə:'vaikəl] Hals..., Nak[ken...]
ces·sa·tion [se'seiʃən] Aufhören *n*, Einstellung *f.*
ces·sion ['seʃən] Abtretung *f*, Überlassung *f.*
cess·pit ['sespit], **cess·pool** ['sespu:l] Senkgrube *f.*
ce·ta·cean [si'teiʃjən] **1.** Walfisch *m*; **2.** *a.* **ce'ta·ceous** Wal...
chafe [tʃeif] *v/t.* reiben; wundreiben; aufbringen, erzürnen; *v/i.* sich scheuern (*against* an *dat.*); sich wundreiben; toben, wüten.
chaff [tʃɑ:f] **1.** Spreu *f*; Häcksel *n*; Plunder *m*; F Neckerei *f*; **2.** zu Häcksel schneiden; F necken; '**~-cut·ter** Häckselbank *f.*
chaf·fer ['tʃæfə] feilschen.
chaf·finch ['tʃæfintʃ] Buchfink *m.*
chaf·ing-dish ['tʃeifiŋdiʃ] Wärmeschüssel *f*, -pfanne *f.*
cha·grin ['ʃægrin] **1.** Ärger *m*; **2.** ärgern.
chain [tʃein] **1.** Kette *f*; Reihe *f*; *fig.* Fessel *f*; **2.** (an)ketten; *fig.* fesseln; **~ re·ac·tion** Kettenreaktion *f*; '**~-smoker** Kettenraucher(in); '**~-store** Filialbetrieb *m.*
chair [tʃɛə] **1.** Stuhl *m*; *Am. a.* elektrischer Stuhl *m*; Sitz *m*; *a. professorial* ~ Lehrstuhl *m*; Vorsitz *m*; ~*!* zur Ordnung!; *be in the* ~, *take the* ~ den Vorsitz führen; **2.** zum (zur) Vorsitzenden machen; im Triumph umhertragen; '**~-lift** Sessellift *m*; **~·man** ['~mən] Vorsitzende *m*; Präsident *m*; '**~·man·ship** Vorsitz *m*; '**~·per·son** Vorsitzende *m, f*; '**~·wom·an** Vorsitzende *f*, Präsidentin *f.*
chaise [ʃeiz] Chaise *f*, Halbkutsche *f.*
chal·ice ['tʃælis] (Abendmahls-) Kelch *m.*
chalk [tʃɔ:k] **1.** Kreide *f*; *red* ~ Rötel *m*; *by a long* ~ F bei weitem; **2.** mit Kreide (be)zeichnen; *mst* ~ *up* ankreiden; ~ *out* entwerfen; *fig. Weg* vorzeichnen; '**chalk·y** kreidig.
chal·lenge ['tʃælindʒ] **1.** Herausforderung *f*, Kampfansage *f*; Aufforderung *f*; ⚔ Anruf *m*; *bsd.* ⚖ Ablehnung *f*; ~ *prize Sport*: Wanderpreis *m*; **2.** (*a. fig. Aufmerksamkeit etc.*) herausfordern; anrufen;

ablehnen (*bsd.* ⚖); anzweifeln; ˈ**chal·leng·er** Herausforderer *m.*
cha·lyb·e·ate [kəˈlibiit] stahlhaltig.
cham·ber [ˈtʃeimbə] *parl., zo.,* ⚘, ⊕ Kammer *f*; ~*s pl.* Junggesellenwohnung *f*; Geschäftsräume *m/pl.*; ♀ *of Commerce* Handelskammer *f*; **cham·ber·lain** [ˈ~lin] Kämmerer *m*, Kammerdiener *m*; ˈ**~·maid** Zimmermädchen *n*; ˈ**~-mu·sic** Kammermusik *f*; ˈ**~-pot** Nachtgeschirr *n.*
cham·bray *Am.* [ˈʃæmbrei] bunter Baumwollstoff *m.*
cha·me·le·on *zo.* [kəˈmiːljən] Chamäleon *n.*
cham·fer ⚠ [ˈtʃæmfə] **1.** Auskehlung *f*; **2.** auskehlen.
cham·ois [ˈʃæmwɑː] **1.** *zo.* Gemse *f*; *a.* ~ *leather* Wildleder *n*; **2.** chamois(farben) (*gelblichbraun*).
champ¹ [tʃæmp] (geräuschvoll) kauen, mampfen; *fig.* ungeduldig werden *od.* sein.
champ² F [~] *s. champion 1.*
cham·pagne [ʃæmˈpein] Champagner *m*, Sekt *m.*
cham·paign [ˈtʃæmpein] flaches Land *n.*
cham·pi·on [ˈtʃæmpjən] **1.** Vorkämpfer *m*, Verfechter *m*, Verteidiger *m*; *Sport*: Meister *m*, Sieger *m*; **2.** verteidigen; verfechten, kämpfen für; stützen; **3.** großartig; ˈ**cham·pi·on·ship** Meisterschaft *f.*
chance [tʃɑːns] **1.** Zufall *m*; Schicksal *n*; Glück(sfall *m*) *n*; Chance *f*; Aussicht *f* (*of* auf *acc.*); (günstige) Gelegenheit *f*; Möglichkeit *f*; Wahrscheinlichkeit *f*; *by* ~ zufällig; *take a* ~, *take one's* ~ es darauf ankommen lassen; *take no* ~ nichts riskieren (wollen); **2.** Zufalls..., zufällig; gelegentlich; **3.** *v/i.* (zufällig) geschehen; sich ereignen; *I* ~*d to be there* ich war zufällig da; ~ *upon* stoßen auf (*acc.*); *v/t.* F wagen, es ankommen lassen auf (*acc.*).
chan·cel ⚠ [ˈtʃɑːnsəl] hoher Chor *m*; ˈ**chan·cel·ler·y** (Botschafts-, Konsulats)Kanzlei *f*; ˈ**chan·cel·lor** Kanzler *m*; *s. exchequer*; ˈ**chan·cel·lor·ship** Kanzleramt *n.*
chan·cer·y [ˈtʃɑːnsəri] Kanzleigericht *n*; *in* ~ *fig.* in der Klemme.
chanc·y F [ˈtʃɑːnsi] gewagt.
chan·de·lier [ʃændiˈliə] Lüster *m.*
chan·dler [ˈtʃɑːndlə] Krämer *m*, Händler *m*; ˈ**chan·dler·y** Kramladen *m*; Krämerwaren *f/pl.*
change [tʃeindʒ] **1.** Veränderung *f*, Wechsel *m*, Abwechslung *f*, Umstellung *f*; Tausch *m*; Wechselgeld *n*; Kleingeld *n*; ♀ Börse *f*; *for a* ~ zur Abwechslung; *give* ~ *for* herausgeben auf (*acc.*); **2.** *v/t.* (ver)ändern; um-, verwandeln; (aus)wechseln, (aus-, ver)tauschen (*for* gegen); ~ *over Industrie etc.* umstellen; *I've* ~*d my mind* ich habe es mir anders überlegt; *v/i.* sich ändern, wechseln; sich umziehen; ~ *into second gear mot.* in den 2. Gang schalten; *a.* ~ *trains* umsteigen; **change·aˈbil·i·ty** Veränderlichkeit *f*; ˈ**change·a·ble** □ veränderlich; wankelmütig; launisch; ˈ**change-gear** ⊕ Wechselgetriebe *n*; ˈ**change·less** □ unveränderlich; **change·ling** [ˈ~liŋ] Wechselbalg *m*; ˈ**change-ˈo·ver** Umstellung *f*; ˈ**chang·ing** Wechsel *m*; Veränderung *f*; ⚔ Wachablösung *f.*
chan·nel [ˈtʃænl] **1.** Kanal *m*; Flußbett *n*; Rinne *f*; Furche *f*; Gosse *f*; *Radio, Fernsehen*: Kanal *m*, Programm *n*; *fig.* Weg *m*, Kanal *m*; *by the official* ~*s* auf dem Dienstwege; **2.** furchen; aushöhlen.
chant [tʃɑːnt] **1.** Kirchengesang *m*; *fig.* Singsang *m*; **2.** singen; **chan·ti·cleer** *poet.* [tʃæntiˈkliə] Hahn *m*; **chan·try** *eccl.* [ˈtʃɑːntri] Messe(-kapelle) *f*; **chan·ty** [ˈ~ti] Matrosenlied *n*, Shanty *n.*
cha·os [ˈkeiɔs] Chaos *n*, Durcheinander *n*; **chaˈot·ic** (~*ally*) chaotisch.
chap¹ [tʃæp] **1.** Riß *m*, Sprung *m*; **2.** rissig machen *od.* werden.
chap² [~] Kinnbacken *m* (*bsd. von Tieren*).
chap³ F [~] Bursche *m*, Kerl *m*, Junge *m*; ˈ**~-book** Volksbuch *n.*
chap·el [ˈtʃæpəl] Kapelle *f*; Gottesdienst *m*; *typ.* Betrieb *m*, Betriebsversammlung *f.*
chap·er·on [ˈʃæpərəun] **1.** Anstandsdame *f*; **2.** (als Anstandsdame) begleiten.
chap-fall·en [ˈtʃæpfɔːlən] entmutigt.
chap·lain [ˈtʃæplin] Kaplan *m*; ˈ**chap·lain·cy** Kaplanstelle *f.*

chap·let [ˈtʃæplit] Kranz *m* (*aus Blumen etc.*); *eccl.* Rosenkranz *m*.
chap·man [ˈtʃæpmən] Hausierer *m*.
chap·py □ [ˈtʃæpi] rissig.
chap·ter [ˈtʃæptə] *Buch-*, *Dom-*, *Ordens-*Kapitel *n*; *Am.* Orts-, Untergruppe *f e-r Vereinigung*; *give ~ and verse* genaue Quellen *od.* Belegstellen angeben, genau zitieren.
char[1] *ichth.* [tʃɑː] Saibling *m*, Rotforelle *f*.
char[2] [~] verkohlen.
char[3] [~] **1.** reinemachen, putzen; **2.** = *charwoman*.
char-à-banc [ˈʃærəbæŋ] Gesellschaftswagen *m*, Kremser *m*.
char·ac·ter [ˈkæriktə] Charakter *m*; Merkmal *n*; Schrift(zeichen *n*) *f*; (ausgeprägte) Sinnesart *f*; Art *f*, Beschaffenheit *f*; (ausgeprägte) Persönlichkeit *f*; Figur *f*, Gestalt *f*; F *a.* Original *n*; *thea.*, *Roman*: Person *f*; Rang *m*, Würde *f*; Leumund *m*, (*bsd.* guter) Ruf *m*; Zeugnis *n e-s Angestellten*; *~ assassination* Rufmord *m*; **char·ac·terˈis·tic 1.** (*~ally*) charakteristisch, kennzeichnend, bezeichnend (*of* für); **2.** Kennzeichen *n*, Merkmal *n*, Wesenszug *m*; **char·ac·ter·i·za·tion** [~raiˈzeiʃən] Charakteristik *f*; **ˈchar·ac·ter·ize** charakterisieren; kennzeichnen; schildern.
cha·rade [ʃəˈrɑːd] Scharade *f*, Silbenrätsel *n*.
char·coal [ˈtʃɑːkəul] Holzkohle *f*; **ˈ~-burn·er** Köhler *m*.
chard ♀ [ˈtʃɑːd] Mangold *m*.
chare [tʃɛə] **1.** Hausarbeiten übernehmen, reinemachen (in *od.* bei); **2.** *mst ~s pl.* (tägliche) Hausarbeit *f*, -reinigung *f*.
charge [tʃɑːdʒ] **1.** Ladung *f e-r Feuerwaffe*; *fig.* Last *f*, Belastung *f* (*on* für); Verwahrung *f*, Obhut *f*, Pflege *f*; Pflegebefohlene *m*, *f*, Schützling *m*; Mündel *m*, *f*, *n*; anvertrautes Gut *n*; Amt *n*, Stelle *f*; Auftrag *m*, Befehl *m*; ⚔ Angriff *m*; Ermahnung *f*; ⚖, *eccl.* Belehrung *f*; Beschuldigung *f*, Anklage *f*; ⚒ Beschickung *f*; in Rechnung gestellter Betrag *m*, Preis *m*; Gebühr *f*; Forderung *f*; *~s pl.* Kosten *pl.*, Spesen *pl.*; *be in ~ of* mit *et.* beauftragt sein; für *et.* sorgen; für *et.* verantwortlich sein; *et.* leiten; *be in the ~ of s.o.* in j-s Obhut sein; *take ~ of* die Verantwortung übernehmen für; sich kümmern um (*acc.*); *free of ~* kostenlos; **2.** *v/t. Gewehr etc.* laden; beladen, belasten; beauftragen (*with* mit); *j-m et.* einschärfen, (an)befehlen, auferlegen; ermahnen; beschuldigen, anklagen (*with gen.*); zuschreiben, zur Last legen (*on, upon dat.*); *bsd.* fordern, verlangen (*s.o. a price* e-n Preis von j-m); *Preis*, *Ware* an-, berechnen, in Rechnung stellen (*to dat.*); ⚒ beschicken; *mit der blanken Waffe* angreifen (*a. v/i.*); behaupten; *~ s.o. with the duty of ger.* es j-m zur Pflicht machen zu *inf.*; **ˈcharge·a·ble** □ zu belasten(d) (*with* mit); zur Last fallend, anzurechnen(d) (*to dat.*); zur Last zu legen(d) (*on dat.*); zahlbar; strafbar; **charge ac·count** Kundenkreditkonto *n*.
char·gé d'af·faires *pol.* [ˈʃɑːʒeidæˈfɛə] Geschäftsträger *m*.
charg·er [ˈtʃɑːdʒə] *poet.* Schlachtroß *n*; ⚔ Dienstpferd *n*.
char·i·ot *poet. od. hist.* [ˈtʃæriət] Streit-, Triumphwagen *m*; **char·i·ot·eer** [~ˈtiə] Wagenlenker *m*.
char·i·ta·ble □ [ˈtʃæritəbl] wohltätig, mild(tätig); mild (*nachsichtig*); *~ society* Wohltätigkeitsverein *m*; **ˈchar·i·ta·ble·ness** Mildtätigkeit *f*; Milde *f*.
char·i·ty [ˈtʃæriti] Nächstenliebe *f*; Wohltätigkeit *f*; Güte *f*; Milde *f*, Nachsicht *f*; milde Gabe *f*; Wohlfahrtseinrichtung *f*; *sister of ~* Barmherzige Schwester *f*; *~ begins at home* die Nächstenliebe beginnt zu Hause; **ˈ~-ˈchild** Armenkind *n*; **ˈ~-ˈschool** Armenschule *f*.
cha·ri·va·ri [ˈʃɑːriˈvɑːri] Stimmengewirr *n*; Durcheinander *n*.
char·la·tan [ˈʃɑːlətən] Scharlatan *m*, Marktschreier *m*; **ˈchar·la·tan·ry** Scharlatanerie *f*, Marktschreierei *f*.
char·lock ♀ [ˈtʃɑːlɔk] Ackersenf *m*, Hederich *m*.
char·lotte [ˈʃɑːlət] *Küche*: Apfelpudding *m*.
charm [tʃɑːm] **1.** Zauber *m*; *fig.* Reiz *m*; **2.** bezaubern; *fig.* entzücken; *~ away etc.* weg- *etc.* zaubern; *~ed a.* gefeit (*Leben*); **ˈcharm·er** *fig.* Zauberin *f*, Schöne *f*; **ˈcharm·ing** □ bezaubernd, reizend, entzückend.

char·nel-house [ˈtʃɑːnlhaus] Bein-, Leichenhaus *n*.
chart [tʃɑːt] **1.** ⚓ Seekarte *f*; Tabelle *f*; **2.** auf einer Karte einzeichnen, vermessen.
char·ter [ˈtʃɑːtə] **1.** Urkunde *f*; Freibrief *m* (*a. fig.* = *Vorrecht*); Patent *n*; ⚓ Schiffsmiete *f*, Frachtvertrag *m*; *mst* ~-*party* Chartepartie *f*; **2.** privilegieren, *j-m* e-n Freibrief ausstellen; chartern, mieten; *s. accountant*; ~ **mem·ber** *Am.* Gründungsmitglied *n*.
char·wom·an [ˈtʃɑːwumən] Putz-, Reinemachefrau *f*.
char·y □ [ˈtʃɛəri] (*of*) vorsichtig (in *dat.*); sparsam *od.* zurückhaltend (mit).
chase[1] [tʃeis] **1.** Jagd *f*; Verfolgung *f*; Jagdrevier *n*; gejagtes Wild *n* (*a. fig.*) *od.* Schiff *n*; *beasts of* ~ jagdbares Wild *n*; *give* ~ *to* nachjagen (*dat.*); **2.** jagen, hetzen (*a. fig.*); Jagd machen auf (*acc.*); *j-m* nachjagen; vertreiben, verfolgen.
chase[2] [~] ziselieren.
chase[3] *typ.* [~] Setzrahmen *m*.
chas·er[1] [ˈtʃeisə] Jäger(in); Verfolger(in); ✈ Jagdflugzeug *n*; ⚓ Jagdgeschütz *n*.
chas·er[2] [~] Ziseleur *m*.
chasm [ˈkæzəm] Kluft *f*, Abgrund *m* (*a. fig.*), Spalt *m*; Lücke *f*.
chas·sis *mot.* [ˈʃæsi], *pl.* **chas·sis** [ˈʃæsiz] Fahrgestell *n*.
chaste □ [tʃeist] keusch, rein, unschuldig; schlicht (*Stil*).
chas·ten [ˈtʃeisn] züchtigen; reinigen, läutern; mäßigen.
chas·tise [tʃæsˈtaiz] züchtigen; **chas·tise·ment** [ˈ~tizmənt] Züchtigung *f*.
chas·ti·ty [ˈtʃæstiti] Keuschheit *f*; *fig.* Reinheit *f*.
chas·u·ble *eccl.* [ˈtʃæzjubl] Meßgewand *n*.
chat [tʃæt] **1.** Geplauder *n*, Plauderei *f*; **2.** plaudern.
châ·teau [ˈʃætəu] Schloß *n*, Landhaus *n in Frankreich*.
chat show [ˈtʃætʃəu] Talk-Show *f*.
chat·tels [ˈtʃætlz] *pl. mst goods and* ~ Hab *n* und Gut *n*; Vermögen *n*.
chat·ter [ˈtʃætə] **1.** plappern, schwatzen; schnattern; klappern; **2.** Geplapper *n etc.*; ˈ~**box** F Plaudertasche *f*; ˈ**chat·ter·er** Schwätzer (-in).
chat·ty [ˈtʃæti] gesprächig.
chauf·feur [ˈʃəufə] Chauffeur *m*, Fahrer *m*; **chauf·feuse** [~ˈfəːz] Chauffeurin *f*.
chau·vin·ism [ˈʃəuvinizəm] Chauvinismus *m*; ˈ**chau·vin·ist** Chauvinist(in); **chau·vinˈis·tic** (~*ally*) chauvinistisch.
chaw *sl.* [tʃɔː] kauen; ~ *up Am. sl. mst fig.* fix und fertig machen (*vernichten*); ˈ~-ˈ**ba·con** Bauerntölpel *m*.
cheap □ [tʃiːp] billig; *fig. a.* gemein; *feel* ~ F sich elend fühlen; sich schäbig vorkommen; *hold* ~ niedrig einschätzen; *on the* ~ F billig; *make o.s.* ~ seinen guten Ruf ruinieren; ♀ *Jack* Hausierer *m*; ˈ**cheap·en** (sich) verbilligen; *fig.* herabsetzen; ˈ**cheap·skate** *Am. sl.* Knicker *m*.
cheat [ˈtʃiːt] **1.** Betrug *m*, Schwindel *m*; Betrüger(in); **2.** betrügen, prellen (*[out] of s.th.* um et.); ˈ**cheat·ing** Betrügerei *f*.
check [tʃek] **1.** Schach(stellung *f*) *n*; Hemmnis *n*, Hindernis *n* (*on* für); ⚔ Schlappe *f*; Zwang *m*, Aufsicht *f*; Kontrolle *f*, Untersuchung *f* (*on gen.*); Kontroll-, Garderobe-, Spielmarke *f*; *Am. Gepäck*-Schein *m*; *Am.* ⚚ = *cheque*; *Am.* Rechnung *f im Restaurant*; karierter Stoff *m*; ~ *pattern* Karomuster *n*; *pass od. hand in one's* ~*s Am.* F sterben, abkratzen; *keep s.o. in* ~ j. in Schach halten; **2.** Schach bieten (*dat.*); *Am.* Scheck ausschreiben, einlösen; hemmen, aufhalten, *fig.* zügeln; kontrollieren; nach-, überprüfen; in der Garderobe abgeben; *bsd. Am.* stimmen *nach Kontrolle*; ~ *in Am.* in e-m Hotel absteigen; ~ *out v/i.* ein Hotel verlassen; ausstempeln; *v/t. Am.* überprüfen; ~ *one's baggage Am.* sein Gepäck aufgeben; ~ *up* genau prüfen, nachprüfen, -rechnen, -schlagen; ˈ~**book** *Am.* Scheckbuch *n*; **checked** kariert; ˈ**check·er** Aufsichtsbeamte *m*; ~*s pl. Am.* Damespiel *n*; = *chequer*; ˈ**check·er·board** *Am.* Damebrett *n*; ˈ**check·ered** kariert; ˈ**check-in count·er** Abfertigungsschalter *m*; ˈ**check-in desk** Hotelrezeption *f*; Abfertigungsschalter *m*; ˈ**check·ing** Hemmung *f*; Kontrolle *f*; *attr.* Kontroll...; ˈ**check-in time** ✈ Eincheckzeit *f*; ˈ**check·list** Kontroll-,

Checkliste *f*; ˈ**check-mate 1.** Schachmatt *n*; **2.** matt setzen (*mst fig.*); ˈ**check-out count·er** Kasse *f e-s Supermarkts*; ˈ**check-point** Kontrollpunkt *m*; ˈ**check·room** *Am.* Garderobe *f*; Gepäckaufbewahrung *f*; ˈ**check-up** *Am.* scharfe Kontrolle *f*.
Ched·dar [ˈtʃedə] Cheddarkäse *m*.
cheek [tʃiːk] **1.** Backe *f*, Wange *f*; F Unverschämtheit *f*; ⊕ Backe *f*, Seitenteil *n*; *s. jowl*; **2.** F unverschämt werden gegen; ˈ**cheek-bone** Backenknochen *m*; ˈ**cheek-ed** ...wangig; ˈ**cheek·y** F frech, dreist.
cheep [tʃiːp] piepen.
cheer [tʃiə] **1.** (*engS.* frohe) Stimmung *f*, Fröhlichkeit *f*; Hoch(ruf *m*) *n*; Beifall(sruf) *m*, Hurra *n*; Speisen *f/pl.*, Mahl *n*; *be of good* ~ guter Dinge sein; *three* ~*s!* dreimal hoch!; **2.** *v/t. a.* ~ *up* aufheitern, trösten; mit Beifall begrüßen, *j-m* zujubeln; *a.* ~ *on* anspornen, ermutigen; *v/i.* hoch rufen; jauchzen, jubeln; *a.* ~ *up* Mut fassen; ˈ**cheer-ful** □ heiter, fröhlich; ˈ**cheer·ful-ness,** ˈ**cheer·i·ness** Heiterkeit *f*; ˈ**cheer·ing** Beifallsrufen *n*; **cheer-i·o** [ˈ~riˈəu] F mach's gut!, Tschüs!; prosit!; ˈ**cheer·lead·er** *Am. Sport*: Einpeitscher *m*; ˈ**cheer·less** □ freudlos; ˈ**cheer·y** □ heiter, froh.
cheese [tʃiːz] Käse *m*; *sl. das* einzig Wahre; ˈ~**-cake** Käsekuchen *m*; *sl.* Pin-up-Girl *n*; ˈ~**-cloth** Seihtuch *n*; ˈ~**·mon·ger** Käsehändler *m*; ˈ~**-par·ing 1.** Käserinde *f*; *fig.* Knickerei *f*; **2.** knickerig.
chees·y [ˈtʃiːzi] käsig.
chee·tah *zo.* [ˈtʃiːtə] Jagdleopard *m*.
chef [ʃef] Küchenchef *m*.
chei·ro·man·cy [ˈkaiərəumænsi] Chiromantie *f* (*Handlesekunst*).
chem·i·cal [ˈkemikəl] **1.** □ chemisch; **2.** ˈ**chem·i·cals** *pl.* Chemikalien *pl*.
che·mise [ʃəˈmiːz] *Frauen*-Hemd *n*.
chem·ist [ˈkemist] Chemiker(in); Apotheker(in); Drogist(in); ~*'s shop* Apotheke *f*; Drogerie *f*; ˈ**chem·is·try** Chemie *f*.
chem·i·ty·py ⊕ [ˈkemitaipi] Chemigraphie *f*.
chem·o·ther·a·py ⚕ [kemәuˈθerәpi] Chemotherapie *f*.
cheque ✝ [tʃek] Scheck *m*; *not negotiable* ~, *crossed* ~ Verrechnungsscheck *m*; ~ **ac·count** Girokonto *n*; ˈ~**-book** Scheckbuch *n*.
chequer [ˈtʃekə] **1.** *mst* ~*s pl.* Karomuster *n*; **2.** karieren; ˈ**chequered** kariert; *fig.* bunt.
cher·ish [ˈtʃeriʃ] hegen, pflegen; schätzen; festhalten an (*dat.*).
che·root [ʃəˈruːt] Stumpen *m* (*Zigarre*).
cher·ry [ˈtʃeri] **1.** Kirsche *f*; **2.** Kirsch...; kirschrot; ~ **bran·dy** Kirschlikör *m*.
cher·ub [ˈtʃerəb] Cherub *m*; **che-ru·bic** [~ˈruːbik] engelhaft.
cher·vil ⚘ [ˈtʃəːvil] Kerbel *m*.
chess [tʃes] Schach(spiel) *n*; ˈ~**-board** Schachbrett *n*; ˈ~**·man** Schachfigur *f*.
chest [tʃest] Kiste *f*, Kasten *m*; Truhe *f*; *anat.* Brustkasten *m*; ~ *of drawers* Kommode *f*; ~ *note* Brustton *m*; *get s.th. off one's* ~ sich et. von der Seele schaffen; ˈ**chest·ed** ...brüstig.
ches·ter·field [ˈtʃestəfiːld] einreihiger Mantel *m*; Polstersofa *n*.
chest·nut [ˈtʃesnʌt] **1.** Kastanie *f*; Kastanienbraun *n*; F alter Witz *m*; **2.** kastanienbraun.
chest·y F [ˈtʃesti] tiefsitzend (*Husten*); vollbusig.
che·val-glass [ʃəˈvælglɑːs] Ankleidespiegel *m*.
chev·a·lier [ʃevəˈliə] Ritter *m*.
chev·i·ot [ˈtʃeviət] Cheviot *m* (*Tuchart*).
chev·ron ⚔ [ˈʃevrən] Armwinkel *m*.
chev·y F [ˈtʃevi] **1.** Hetzjagd *f*; Barlaufspiel *n*; **2.** hetzen, jagen.
chew [tʃuː] kauen; sinnen (*on, upon, over* über *acc.*); ~ *the fat od. rag sl.* die Sache durchkauen; ˈ**chew-ing-gum** Kaugummi *m*.
chi·cane [ʃiˈkein] **1.** Schikane *f*; **2.** schikanieren; **chiˈcan·er·y** Schikane *f*; *fig.* Haarspalterei *f*.
chick [tʃik] *s. chicken*.
chick·a·dee *Am. orn.* [ˈtʃikədiː] Meise *f*.
chick·a·ree *Am. zo.* [ˈtʃikəriː] rotes Eichhörnchen *n*.
chick·en [ˈtʃikin] **1.** Hühnchen *n*, Küchlein *n*, Küken *n*; **2.** ~ *out sl.* e-n Rückzieher machen; ˈ~**-farm·er** Geflügelzüchter *m*; ˈ~**-feed** *Am.* Geflügelfutter *n*; *sl.* Pappenstiel *m*; ˈ~**-heart·ed,** ˈ~**-liv·ered** furchtsam,

feige; '~-pox ⚕ Windpocken *f/pl.*; ~ **run,** *Am.* ~ **yard** Hühnerauslauf *m*; '**chick-pea** ⚘ Kichererbse *f*; '**chick·weed** ⚘ Vogelmiere *f*.

chic·o·ry ['tʃikəri] Zichorie *f*.

chid [tʃid] *pret. u. p.p.*, '**chid·den** *p.p. von chide*.

chide *lit.* [tʃaid] (*irr.*) schelten.

chief [tʃi:f] **1.** □ oberst; Ober..., Haupt...; hauptsächlich; ~ *clerk* Bürovorsteher *m*; **2.** Oberhaupt *n*, Haupt *n*, Chef *m*; Häuptling *m*; ...-*in*-~ Ober...; ~ **jus·tice** Oberrichter *m*; *Am.* Vorsitzende *m e-s Bundesgerichts*; ♀ Vorsitzende *m des Supreme Court*; **chief·tain** ['~tən] Häuptling *m*; Anführer *m*.

chif·fon ['ʃifɔn] Chiffon *m* (*Seidenstoff*); **chif·fo·nier** [ʃifə'niə] Chiffonière *f* (*Schrank*).

chil·blain ['tʃilblein] Frostbeule *f*.

child [tʃaild], *pl.* **chil·dren** ['tʃildrən] Kind *n*; *be a good* ~ artig sein; *from a* ~ von Kindheit an; *with* ~ schwanger; ~'*s play fig.* Kinderspiel *n*; '~**·bed** Kindbett *n*; '~**·birth** Niederkunft *f*; '**child·hood** Kindheit *f*; *second* ~ Greisenalter *n*; '**child·ish** □ kindlich; *b.s.* kindisch; '**child·ish·ness** Kindlichkeit *f*; *b.s.* kindisches Wesen *n*; '**child·less** kinderlos; '**child·like** *fig.* kindlich; '**child·mind·er** Tagesmutter *f*; **chil·dren** ['tʃildrən] *pl. von child*; **child wel·fare** Jugendfürsorge *f*.

chil·i *Am.* ⚘ ['tʃili] Paprika(schote *f*) *m*.

Chil·i·an ['tʃiliən] **1.** Chilene *m*, Chilenin *f*; **2.** chilenisch.

chill [tʃil] **1.** *lit.* eisig, frostig; **2.** Frost *m*, Kälte *f* (*a. fig.*); ⚕ Fieberfrost *m*; Erkältung *f*; *take the* ~ *off a liquid* e-e Flüssigkeit anwärmen; **3.** *v/t.* erkalten lassen; erstarren lassen; (*bsd. fig.* ab)kühlen; *metall.* abschrecken; ~*ed meat* Kühlfleisch *n*; *v/i.* erkalten; erstarren; '**chill·ness,** '**chill·i·ness** Kälte *f*; '**chill·y** kalt, frostig, kühl; fröstelnd.

chime [tʃaim] **1.** Glockenspiel *n*; Geläut *n*; *fig.* Einklang *m*; **2.** läuten; *fig.* übereinstimmen, harmonieren; ~ *in* einfallen, -stimmen.

chi·me·ra [kai'miərə] Schimäre *f*, Hirngespinst *n*; **chi·mer·i·cal** □ [~'merikəl] schimärisch, phantastisch.

chim·ney ['tʃimni] Schornstein *m*; Kamin *m* (*a. mount.*); Rauchfang *m*; (Lampen)Zylinder *m*; '~**-piece** Kaminsims *m*; '~**-pot** Schornsteinkappe *f*; F *fig.* Angströhre *f*, Zylinder(hut) *m*; '~**-stalk** Schornsteinkasten *m auf dem Dach*; Fabrikschornstein *m*; '~**-sweep(·er)** Schornsteinfeger *m*.

chimp F [tʃimp] Schimpanse *m*.

chim·pan·zee *zo.* [tʃimpən'zi:] Schimpanse *m*.

chin[1] [tʃin] **1.** Kinn *n*; *take it on the* ~ *Am.* F es standhaft ertragen; *keep one's* ~ *up* F den Nacken steifhalten; **2.** *Am.* e-n Klimmzug machen.

chin[2] *sl.* [~] schwatzen, quasseln.

chi·na ['tʃainə] Porzellan *n*; '♀**·man** Chinese *m*.

chine [tʃain] Rückgrat *n*; *Küche*: Kammstück *n*; Grat *m*, Kamm *m*.

Chi·nese ['tʃai'ni:z] **1.** chinesisch; **2.** Chinese(n *pl.*) *m*, Chinesin *f*; Chinesisch *n*.

chink[1] [tʃiŋk] Ritz *m*, Ritze *f*, Spalt *m*, Spalte *f*.

chink[2] [~] **1.** (*bsd. Geld*-)Klang *m*; **2.** klimpern (*mit Geld*).

chintz [tʃints] Chintz *m*, Möbelkattun *m*.

chin·wag *sl.* ['tʃinwæg] Schwatz *m*.

chip [tʃip] **1.** Schnitzel *n*, Stückchen *n*; Splitter *m*; Span *m*; angeschlagene Stelle *f in Glas etc.*; Spielmarke *f*; *Computer*: Chip *m*; *have a* ~ *on one's shoulder* aggressiv sein; ~*s pl.* Pommes frites *pl.*; **2.** *v/t.* (ab)schnitzeln; an-, abschlagen; abschilfern (*a. v/i.*); *v/i.* abbröckeln; ~ *in* F unterbrechen; sich einmischen; *Am.* F aushelfen; **chip·muck** ['~mʌk], **chip·munk** ['~mʌŋk] nordamerikanisches gestreiftes Eichhörnchen *n*; '**chip-pan** Friteuse *f*; '**chip·py** dürr; F verkatert.

chi·rop·o·dist [ki'rɔpədist] Fußpfleger(in); **chi'rop·o·dy** Fußpflege *f*; **chi·ro·prac·tor** ⚕ [kairəu'præktə] Chiropraktiker *m*.

chirp [tʃə:p] **1.** zirpen; zwitschern; **2.** Gezirp *n*; '**chirp·y** F munter.

chirr [tʃə:] zirpen.

chir·rup ['tʃirəp] **1.** Zwitschern *n*; **2.** zwitschern.

chis·el ['tʃizl] **1.** Meißel *m*; **2.** meißeln; F (be)mogeln; '**chis·el·er** Nassauer *m*.

chit [tʃit] Kindchen *n*; *a* ~ *of a girl*

ein junges Ding *n.*
chit-chat [ˈtʃittʃæt] Geplauder *n.*
chiv·al·rous □ [ˈʃivəlrəs] ritterlich; ˈ**chiv·al·ry** Ritterschaft *f*, Rittertum *n*; Ritterlichkeit *f.*
chive ⚘ [tʃaiv] Schnittlauch *m.*
chiv·y F [ˈtʃivi] = *chevy.*
chlo·ral ⚗ [ˈklɔːrəl] Chloral *n*; **chlo·ride** [ˈ~aid] Chlorverbindung *f*; ~ *of lime* Chlorkalk *m*; **chlo·rin·ate** [ˈ~ineit] *Wasser* chloren; **chlo·rine** [ˈ~iːn] Chlor *n*; **chlo·ro·form** [ˈklɔrəfɔːm] **1.** Chloroform *n*; **2.** chloroformieren; **chlor·o·phyl(l)** [ˈ~əfil] Chlorophyll *n*, Blattgrün *n.*
choc-ice [ˈtʃɔkais] Eis *n* mit Schokoladeüberzug.
chock ⊕ [tʃɔk] **1.** Keil *m*; **2.** festkeilen; ˈ**~-a-ˈblock** verklemmt (*with* mit); ˈ**~-ˈfull** übervoll.
choc·o·late [ˈtʃɔkəlit] Schokolade *f*; ~ *cream* Praliné *n.*
choice [tʃɔis] **1.** Wahl *f*; Auswahl *f*; *have one's* ~ die Wahl haben; *make od. take one's* ~ s-e Wahl treffen; *multiple* ~ Auswahlantwort(form) *f*; **2.** □ auserlesen, vorzüglich; ausgesucht; ~ *fruit* Edelobst *n.*
choir [ˈkwaiə] (Kirchen-, Sänger-) Chor *m*; ˈ**~·mas·ter** Chorleiter *m*; ~ **stalls** *pl.* Chorgestühl *n.*
choke [tʃəuk] **1.** *v/t.* (er)würgen, (*a. v/i.*) ersticken (*a. fig.*); ⊕ würgen (*verengen*); ⚡ (ab)drosseln; *mst* ~ *up* (ver)stopfen; *mst* ~ *down* hinunterwürgen; ~ *off* F abschütteln; abbringen (*from* von); **2.** Erstickungsanfall *m*; ⊕ Würgung *f*; *mot.* Choke *m*, Starterklappe *f*; ~ *coil* ⚡ Drosselspule *f*; ˈ**~-bore** ⊕ (Flinte *f* mit) Würgebohrung *f*; ˈ**~-damp** ⚒ Schwaden *m*; ˈ**chok·er** *co.* steifer Kragen *m*; Krawattenschal *m*; enge Halskette *f*; ˈ**chok·y** erstickend.
chol·er·a ⚕ [ˈkɔlərə] Cholera *f*; ˈ**chol·er·ic** cholerisch, jähzornig.
cho·les·te·rol [kəˈlestərɔl] Cholesterin *n.*
choose [tʃuːz] (*irr.*) (aus)wählen; ~ *to inf.* vorziehen zu *inf.*, lieber wollen; ˈ**choos·y** wählerisch.
chop[1] [tʃɔp] **1.** Hieb *m* (*at* nach); Kotelett *n*; ~*s pl.* Maul *n*, Rachen *m* (*a. fig.*); ⊕ Backen *f/pl.*; ~*s and changes pl.* Wechselfälle *m/pl.*; **2.** *v/t.* hauen, hacken; *oft* ~ *up* zerhacken; austauschen; *v/i.* wechseln; ~ *about* umschlagen (*Wind u. fig.*); ~ *and change* schwanken.
chop[2] ⚓ [~] Marke *f*; *first* ~ erste Sorte *f*; *attr.* erster Güte.
chop-chop *sl.* [ˈtʃɔpˈtʃɔp] schnell.
chop-house [ˈtʃɔphaus] Speisehaus *n*; ˈ**chop·per** Hackmesser *n*; F Hubschrauber *m*; ˈ**chop·ping** Hack...; ˈ**chop·py** unstet; unruhig (*See*); böig (*Wind*); = *chappy*; ˈ**chop·stick** Eßstäbchen *n der Chinesen*; **chop-su·ey** [~ˈsuːi] Chop Suey *n* (*chinesisches Gericht*).
cho·ral □ [ˈkɔːrəl] chormäßig; Chor...; **cho·ral(e)** ♪ [kɔˈrɑːl] Choral *m.*
chord [kɔːd] ♪, *poet. od. fig.* Saite *f*; ⚔ Sehne *f*; ♪ Akkord *m*; *anat.* Strang *m*, Band *n.*
chore *bsd. Am.* [tʃɔː] = *chare* 2.
chor·e·og·ra·phy [kɔriˈɔgrəfi] Choreographie *f.*
chor·ine [ˈkɔːriːn] *s. chorus-girl.*
chor·is·ter [ˈkɔristə] Chorist *m*, Sängerknabe *m*; *Am. a.* Leiter *m* des Kirchenchores.
cho·rus [ˈkɔːrəs] **1.** Chor *m*; Kehrreim *m*; **2.** im Chor singen *od.* sprechen; ˈ**~-girl** Revuegirl *n.*
chose [tʃouz] *pret.*, ˈ**cho·sen** *p.p. von choose.*
chough *orn.* [tʃʌf] Dohle *f.*
chouse F [tʃaus] **1.** Prellerei *f*; **2.** prellen.
chow *Am. sl.* [tʃau] Essen *n.*
chow·der *Am.* [ˈtʃaudə] *Mischgericht aus Fischen, Muscheln etc.*
chrism [ˈkrizəm] Salböl *n*; Ölung *f.*
Christ [kraist] Christus *m*; *for* ~*'s sake!* Herrgott noch mal!
chris·ten [ˈkrisn] taufen; **Chris·ten·dom** [ˈ~dəm] Christenheit *f*; ˈ**chris·ten·ing 1.** Tauf...; **2.** Taufe *f.*
Chris·tian [ˈkristjən] **1.** □ christlich; ~ *name* Vor-, Taufname *m*; ~ *Science* Christliche Wissenschaft *f*, Szientismus *m*; **2.** Christ(in); **Chris·ti·an·i·ty** [~tiˈæniti] Christentum *n*; **Chris·tian·ize** [ˈ~tjənaiz] zum Christentum bekehren.
Christ·mas [ˈkrisməs] **1.** Weihnachten *n*; **2.** Weihnachts...; ~ *Day* erster Weihnachtsfeiertag *m*; ~ *Eve* Heiliger Abend *m*; ~ **bo·nus** Weihnachtsgeld *n*, -gratifikation *f*; ˈ**~-box** Weihnachtsgeschenk *n* (*für Bedienstete*); ˈ**~·tide** Weihnachtszeit *f*; ˈ**~-tree** Weihnachtsbaum *m.*
chro·mat·ic *phys.*, ♪ [krəuˈmætik]

(*~ally*) chromatisch; Farben...; **chro'mat·ics** *pl. u. sg.* Farbenlehre *f.*
chrome ⚗ [krəum] Chrom *n* (*Farbe*); **chro·mi·um** ['~jəm] Chrom *n* (*Metall*); '**chro·mi·um-'plat·ed** verchromt; **chro·mo-lith·o·graph** ['~əu'liθəugrɑ:f] farbiger Steindruck *m.*
chron·ic ['krɔnik] (*~ally*) chronisch (*mst* ⚕), dauernd; P ekelhaft; **chron·i·cle** ['~l] **1.** Chronik *f*; **2.** aufzeichnen; '**chron·i·cler** Chronist *m.*
chron·o·log·i·cal □ [krɔnə'lɔdʒikəl] chronologisch; *~ly* in chronologischer Reihenfolge; **chro·nol·o·gy** [krə'nɔlədʒi] Zeitrechnung *f*; Zeitfolge *f.*
chro·nom·e·ter [krə'nɔmitə] Chronometer *n, m.*
chrys·a·lis ['krisəlis] *Insekten-*Puppe *f.*
chrys·an·the·mum ⚘ [kri'sænθəməm] Chrysantheme *f.*
chub *ichth.* [tʃʌb] Döbel *m*; '**chub·by** F rundlich; dick; pausbäckig; plump (*a. fig.*).
chuck[1] [tʃʌk] **1.** Glucken *n*; *my ~!* mein Täubchen!; **2.** glucken; **3.** put, put! (*Lockruf für Hühner*).
chuck[2] F [~] **1.** schmeißen, werfen; *~ out* 'rausschmeißen; *~ under the chin* unters Kinn fassen; *~ it! sl.* hör auf damit!; **2.** Hinauswurf *m.*
chuck[3] ⊕ [~] (Spann)Futter *n.*
chuck·er-out *sl.* ['tʃʌkər'aut] Rausschmeißer *m.*
chuck·le ['tʃʌkl] in sich hineinlachen.
chug [tʃʌg] tuckern (*Motor etc.*).
chum F [tʃʌm] **1.** (Stuben)Kamerad *m*; Busenfreund *m*; *be great ~s* dicke Freunde sein; **2.** zs.-wohnen.
chump F [tʃʌmp] Holzklotz *m*; dickes Ende *n*; (Dumm)Kopf *m*; *off one's ~* P blödsinnig.
chunk F [tʃʌŋk] Klotz *m*, Runken *m*; '**chunk·y** klotzig, stämmig.
church [tʃə:tʃ] **1.** Kirche *f*; *attr.* Kirch(en)...; *♀ of England* englische Staatskirche *f*; *~ rate* Kirchensteuer *f*; *~ service* Gottesdienst *m*; **2.** *be ~ed* zum ersten Mal wieder in die Kirche gehen (*Wöchnerin*); '**~-go·er** Kirchgänger(in); '**church·ing** Aussegnung *f e-r Wöchnerin*; '**church·man** Mitglied *n* der Kirche; '**church'ward·en** Kirchenvorsteher *m*; Tabakspfeife *f aus Ton*; '**church'yard** Kirchhof *m.*
churl [tʃə:l] Grobian *m*, Flegel *m*; Geizhals *m*, Knicker *m*; '**churl·ish** □ grob, roh, flegelhaft; knickerig.
churn [tʃə:n] **1.** Butterfaß *n*; Milchsammeleimer *m*; **2.** buttern; aufwühlen.
chute [ʃu:t] Stromschnelle *f*; Gleit-, Rutschbahn *f*; Fallschirm *m.*
chut·ney ['tʃʌtni] Chutney *n* (*Gewürz*).
chyle [kail] Chylus *m* (*Milchsaft*).
chyme [kaim] Chymus *m* (*Speisebrei*).
ci·ca·da *zo.* [si'kɑ:də] Zikade *f.*
cic·a·trice ['sikətris] Narbe *f*; **cic·a·tri·za·tion** [~trai'zeiʃən] Vernarbung *f*; '**cic·a·trize** vernarben.
ci·ce·ro·ne [tʃitʃə'rəuni] Cicerone *m*, Fremdenführer *m.*
Cic·e·ro·ni·an [sisə'rəunjən] ciceron(ian)isch.
ci·der ['saidə] Apfelwein *m.*
ci·gar [si'gɑ:] Zigarre *f*; **ci'gar-case** Zigarrentasche *f*; **ci'gar-cut·ter** Zigarrenabschneider *m.*
cig·a·rette [sigə'ret] Zigarette *f*; **cig·a'rette-case** Zigarettenetui *n*; **cig·a'rette-end** Zigarettenstummel *m*; **cig·a'rette-hold·er** Zigarettenspitze *f.*
ci·gar-hold·er [si'gɑ:həuldə] Zigarrenspitze *f*; **ci'gar-tip** *abgeschnittene* Zigarrenspitze *f.*
cil·i·a ['siliə] *pl.* (Augen)Wimpern *f/pl.*; **cil·i·ar·y** ['siliəri] Wimper...
cinch *Am. sl.* [sintʃ] sichere Sache *f.*
cin·cho·na ⚘ [siŋ'kəunə] Chinarindenbaum *m.*
cinc·ture ['siŋktʃə] Gürtel *m*, Gurt [*m.*]
cin·der ['sində] Schlacke *f*; *~s pl.* Asche *f*; **Cin·der·el·la** [~'relə] Aschenbrödel *n*; '**cin·der-track** *Sport*: Aschenbahn *f.*
cin·e-cam·er·a ['sinikæmərə] Filmkamera *f.*
cin·e-film ['sinifilm] Schmalfilm *m.*
cin·e·ma ['sinəmə] Kino *n*; Film *m* (*als Kunstform*); **cin·e·mat·o·graph** [~'mætəgrɑ:f] **1.** Filmprojektor *m*; *attr.* Kino...; **2.** (ver)filmen; **cin·e·mat·o·graph·ic** [~mætə'græfik] (*~ally*) kinematographisch.
cin·er·ar·y ['sinərəri] Aschen...
cin·na·bar ['sinəbɑ:] Zinnober *m.*
cin·na·mon ['sinəmən] Zimt *m*,

Kaneel *m*; Zimtbraun *n*.
cinque [siŋk] Fünf *f auf Würfeln*; ~ **foil** ⚘ Fingerkraut *n*.
ci·pher ['saifə] **1.** Ziffer *f*; Null *f* (*a. fig.*); Geheimschrift *f*, Chiffre *f*; *in* ~ chiffriert; **2.** chiffrieren; (aus-) rechnen.
cir·ca ['sə:kə] um (*vor Jahreszahlen*).
cir·cle ['sə:kl] **1.** Kreis *m*; *Bekannten-*, *Gesellschafts-*, *Wirkungs-*Kreis *m*; Kreislauf *m*; *thea.* Rang *m*; Ring *m*, Reif *m*; **2.** Kreise ziehen; (um)kreisen; *fig.* die Runde machen; **cir·clet** ['~klit] kleiner Kreis *m*; Reif *m*.
circs F [sə:ks] = *circumstances*.
cir·cuit ['sə:kit] Kreislauf *m*; ⚡ Stromkreis *m*; Rundreise *f bsd. der Richter des High Court in der Provinz*; Gerichtsbezirk *m*; ✈ Rundflug *m*; *integrated* ~ ⚡ integrierter Schaltkreis *m*; *short* ~ ⚡ Kurzschluß *m*; ~ *breaker* ⚡ Aus-, Selbstschalter *m*; *make a* ~ *of* e-n Rundgang machen durch; **cir·cu·i·tous** □ [sə:'kju:itəs] weitschweifig; ~ *route* Umweg *m*.
cir·cu·lar ['sə:kjulə] **1.** □ kreisförmig, rund; Kreis...; Rundreise...; ~ *letter* Rundschreiben *n*; ~ *note* Kreditbrief *m*; ~ *railway* Ringbahn *f*; ~ *saw* Kreissäge *f*; ~ *skirt* Glockenrock *m*; **2.** Rundschreiben *n*; Laufzettel *m*; **'cir·cu·lar·ize** durch Rundschreiben benachrichtigen.
cir·cu·late ['sə:kjuleit] *v/i.* umlaufen, zirkulieren; *v/t.* in Umlauf setzen; verbreiten; ✝ *Wechsel* girieren; **'cir·cu·lat·ing:** ~ *decimal* periodischer Dezimalbruch *m*; ~ *library* Leihbücherei *f*; ~ *medium* Tauschmittel *n*; **cir·cu'la·tion** Zirkulation *f*, Kreislauf *m*; *fig.* Umlauf *m*; Verbreitung *f*; *Zeitungs-*Auflage *f*; **cir·cu'la·to·ry** Kreislauf...
cir·cum... ['sə:kəm] (her)um; **cir·cum·cise** ⚕, *eccl.* [~'saiz] beschneiden; **cir·cum·ci·sion** [~'siʒən] Beschneidung *f*; **cir·cum·fer·ence** [sə'kʌmfərəns] (Kreis)Umfang *m*; Peripherie *f*; **cir·cum·flex** ['sə:kəmfleks] *gr.* Zirkumflex *m*; **cir·cum·ja·cent** [~'dʒeisənt] umliegend; **cir·cum·lo·cu·tion** [~lə'kju:ʃən] Umständlichkeit *f*; Weitschweifigkeit *f*; **cir·cum·loc·u·to·ry** [~'lɔkjutəri] weitschweifig; **cir·cum'nav·i·gate** umsegeln; **cir·cum'nav·i·ga·tor** (Welt)Umsegler *m*; **cir·cum·scribe** ⩕ ['~skraib] umschreiben; *fig.* begrenzen; **cir·cum·scrip·tion** ⩕ [~'skripʃən] Umschreibung *f*; *fig.* Begrenzung *f*; Umschrift *f e-r Münze*; **cir·cum·spect** □ ['~spekt] um-, vorsichtig; **cir·cum·spec·tion** [~'spekʃən] Um-, Vorsicht *f*; **cir·cum·stance** ['~stəns] Umstand *m*, Sachverhalt *m*; Einzelheit *f*; Umständlichkeit *f*; ~*s pl.* Verhältnisse *n/pl.*; *in od. under the* ~*s* unter diesen Umständen; **'cir·cum·stanced** in e-r ... Lage; *poorly* ~ in ärmlichen Verhältnissen; **cir·cum·stan·tial** [~'stænʃəl] □ umständlich; ~ *evidence* ⚖ Indizienbeweis *m*; **cir·cum·stan·ti·al·i·ty** ['~stænʃi'æliti] Umständlichkeit *f*; **cir·cum·vent** [~'vent] überlisten; vereiteln.
cir·cus ['sə:kəs] Zirkus *m*; (runder) Platz *m* (*bsd. in Namen*).
cir·rho·sis ⚕ [si'rəusis] Zirrhose *f*.
cir·rus ['sirəs], *pl.* **cir·ri** ['~rai] Zirrus-, Federwolke *f*.
cis·sy ['sisi] = *sissy*.
cis·tern ['sistən] Zisterne *f*; Wasserbehälter *m*, -kasten *m*.
cit·a·del ['sitədl] Zitadelle *f*.
ci·ta·tion [sai'teiʃən] Vorladung *f*; Anführung *f*, Zitat *n*; *Am. öffentliche* Ehrung *f*; **cite** zitieren; vorladen; anführen.
cit·i·zen ['sitizn] Bürger(in); Staatsangehörige *m*, *f*; Städter(in); ⚔ Zivilist *m*; **cit·i·zen·ship** ['~ʃip] Bürgerrecht *n*; Staatsangehörigkeit *f*.
cit·ric ac·id ['sitrik'æsid] Zitronensäure *f*; **cit·ron** ['~rən] Zitrone *f*; **cit·rus** ['~rəs] Zitrusfrucht *f*.
cit·y ['siti] **1.** Stadt *f*; *the* ♀ *London*: die City, die Altstadt; das Geschäftsviertel; **2.** städtisch, Stadt...; ♀ *article* Börsen-, Handelsbericht *m*; ~ *editor Am.* Lokalredakteur *m*; ~ *hall Am.* Rathaus *n*; ~ *manager Am.* Stadtdirektor *m*; ~ *state* Stadtstaat *m*; ~**-'fa·ther** *Am.* Stadtrat *m*; ~*s pl.* Stadtväter *m/pl.*
civ·ic ['sivik] (staats)bürgerlich; Bürger...; städtisch; ~ *rights pl.* bürgerliche Ehrenrechte *n/pl.*; **'civ·ics** *sg.* Staatsbürgerkunde *f*.
civ·il □ ['sivl] bürgerlich, Bürger...; zivil, Zivil...; ⚖ zivilrechtlich; höflich; ~ *defence* Zivilverteidigung *f*, Luftschutz *m*; ~ *war* Bürgerkrieg *m*;

♀ *Servant* Verwaltungsbeamte *m*; ~ *engineering* Hoch- und Tiefbau *m*; ~ *law* bürgerliches Recht *n*; ~ *rights pl.* Bürgerrechte *n/pl.*; ~ *rights activist* Bürgerrechtler *m*; ~ *rights movement* Bürgerrechtsbewegung *f*; ♀ *Service* Verwaltungs-, Staatsdienst *m*, öffentlicher Dienst *m*; **ci·vil·ian** ⚔ [si'viljən] Zivilist *m*; ~ *population* Zivilbevölkerung *f*; **ci'vil·i·ty** Höflichkeit *f*; **civ·i·li·za·tion** [~lai'zeiʃən] Zivilisation *f*, Kultur *f*; **'civ·i·lize** zivilisieren; ~*d nation* Kulturnation *f*.

civ·vies *sl.* ['siviz] *pl.* Zivil(klamotten *f/pl.*) *n*; **'civ·vy street** *sl.* Zivilleben *n*.

clack [klæk] **1.** Geklapper *n*; *fig.* Geplapper *n*, Geschwätz *n*; ⊕ (Ventil-)Klappe *f*; **2.** klappern; *fig.* schwatzen.

clad *lit.* [klæd] *pret. u. p.p von clothe*; *hills* ~ *in verdure poet.* begrünte Hügel *m/pl.*

claim [kleim] **1.** Anspruch *m*; Anrecht *n* (*to* auf *acc.*); Forderung *f*; ⚖ Klagebegehren *n*; ⚒ Mutung *f*; *bsd. Am.* selbstabgestecktes Stück Land *n zum Siedeln*; *lay* ~ *to* Anspruch erheben auf (*acc.*); *put in a* ~ *for* als Eigentum beanspruchen; **2.** beanspruchen, in Anspruch nehmen; fordern; behaupten; sich berufen auf (*acc.*); ~ *to be* sich ausgeben für; **'claim·a·ble** zu beanspruchen(d); **'claim·ant** Beanspruchер *m*; ⚖ Kläger *m*.

clair·voy·ance [klɛə'vɔiəns] Hellsichtigkeit *f* (*a. fig.*); **clair'voy·ant**(**e**) Hellseher(in).

clam *zo.* [klæm] Venusmuschel *f*.

cla·mant *lit.* ['kleimənt] lärmend, laut.

clam·ber ['klæmbə] klimmen, klettern.

clam·mi·ness ['klæminis] feuchte Kälte *f*; **'clam·my** □ feuchtkalt, klamm.

clam·or·ous □ ['klæmərəs] lärmend, schreiend; **'clam·our 1.** Geschrei *n*, Lärm *m*; Tumult *m*; **2.** schreien (*for* nach).

clamp[1] ⊕ [klæmp] **1.** Klammer *f*; Klampe *f*; **2.** verklammern; befestigen.

clamp[2] [~] (Kartoffel- *etc.*)Miete *f*.

clan [klæn] Clan *m*, schottischer Stamm(verband) *m*; *fig.* Sippschaft *f*.

clan·des·tine □ [klæn'destin] heimlich; Geheim...

clang [klæŋ] **1.** Klang *m*, Geklirr *n*; **2.** schallen; klirren (lassen); **clang·or·ous** ['~gərəs] klirrend; gellend; **'clang·o(u)r** = *clang*.

clank [klæŋk] **1.** Gerassel *n*, Geklirr *n*; **2.** rasseln, klirren (mit).

clan·nish ['klæniʃ] Sippen...

clap [klæp] **1.** (Hände)Klatschen *n*; Schlag *m*, Klaps *m*; *sl.* Tripper *m*; **2.** klappen (mit); klatschen (*one's hands* in die Hände); *j-m* Beifall klatschen; *j-m auf die Schulter* klopfen; aufhalsen (*on dat.*); ~ *eyes on s.o.* j. erblicken, sehen; **'~·board** Schalbrett *n*; **'~-net** Schlagnetz *n zum Vogelfang*; **'clap·per** Klapper *f*; Klöppel *m e-r Glocke*; **'clap·trap 1.** Effekthascherei *f*; Klimbim *m*; **2.** auf Beifall berechnet.

clar·et ['klærət] roter Bordeaux *m*; *allg.* Rotwein *m*; Weinrot *n*; *sl.* Blut *n*.

clar·i·fi·ca·tion [klærifi'keiʃən] (Ab)Klärung *f*; **clar·i·fy** ['~fai] *v/t.* (ab)klären; *fig.* klären; *v/i.* sich klären.

clar·i·net [klæri'net], **clar·i·o·net** [~ə'net] Klarinette *f*.

clar·i·on ['klæriən] lauter Ruf *m*.

clar·i·ty ['klæriti] Klarheit *f*.

clash [klæʃ] **1.** Geklirr *n*; Zs.-stoß *m*; Widerstreit *m*; **2.** klirren, rasseln (mit); zs.-stoßen; widerstreiten (*with dat.*).

clasp [klɑːsp] **1.** Haken *m*, Klammer *f*; Schnalle *f*; (*a. Ordens*)Spange *f*; *Buch*-Schloß *n*; *fig.* Umklammerung *f*; Umarmung *f*; Händedruck *m*; **2.** *v/t.* an-, zuhaken; umklammern; umfassen; ergreifen; *die Hände* falten; ~ *s.o.'s hand* j-m die Hand drücken; *v/i.* festhalten; **'~-knife** Klapp-, Taschenmesser *n*.

class [klɑːs] **1.** Klasse *f*; Stand *m*; (Unterrichts)Stunde *f*; Kursus *m*; *Am. univ.* Jahrgang *m*; *attr.* F Klasse...; erstklassig; **2.** (in Klassen) einteilen, einordnen, -reihen; ~ *with* gleichstellen mit; **'~-'con·scious** klassenbewußt; **'~-fel·low** Klassenkamerad *m*, Mitschüler *m*.

clas·sic ['klæsik] **1.** Klassiker *m*; ~*s pl.* die alten Sprachen *f/pl.*; klassische Philologie *f*, Altphilologie *f*; **2.** = **'clas·si·cal** □ klassisch.

clas·si·fi·ca·tion [klæsifi'keiʃən]

Klassifizierung *f*, Einteilung *f*; Rubrik *f*; **clas·si·fied** ['~faid] in Klassen eingeteilt; *pol.* geheim; ~ *ads pl.* Kleinanzeigen *f/pl.*; **clas·si·fy** ['~fai] klassifizieren, (in Klassen) einteilen, einstufen.

class...: '**~-mate** *s. class-fellow*; '**~·room** Klassenzimmer *n*; '**~-strug·gle,** '**~-war·fare** Klassenkampf *m*; '**class·y** F nobel, exklusiv.

clat·ter ['klætə] **1.** Geklapper *n*, Getrappel *n*; Geplapper *n*; **2.** klappern, rasseln (mit); plappern.

clause [klɔ:z] Klausel *f*, Bestimmung *f*; *gr.* Satz *m*; *subordinate* ~ Nebensatz *m*.

claus·tral ['klɔ:strəl] klösterlich.

claus·tro·pho·bi·a *psych.* [klɔ:strə'fəubiə] Klaustrophobie *f*, Platzangst *f*.

clav·i·cle ['klævikl] Schlüsselbein *n*.

claw [klɔ:] **1.** Klaue *f* (*a.* ⊕), Kralle *f*; Pfote *f*; *Krebs*-Schere *f*; **2.** (zer-)kratzen; (um)krallen; **clawed** mit (...) Klauen.

clay [klei] Ton *m*, Lehm *m*; *fig.* Erde *f*, Staub *m*; ~ *pigeon*, ~ *bird* Tontaube *f zum Übungsschießen*; **clay·ey** ['kleii] tonig.

clean [kli:n] **1.** *adj.* □ rein; sauber; *fig.* fehlerfrei; glatt (*Bruch*); geschickt; **2.** *adv.* rein, völlig; **3.** reinigen, säubern (*of* von); sich waschen lassen (*Stoff etc.*); *be ~ed out* F pleite sein; ~ *up* gründlich reinigen; aufräumen; '**~-cut** klar umrissen; '**clean·er** Reiniger *m*; Putzfrau *f*; *mst ~s pl.* (chemische) Reinigung *f*; *send to the ~s* in die Reinigung geben, reinigen lassen; *take s.o. to the ~'s* F j. schröpfen; '**clean·ing** Reinigung *f*; *attr.* Reinigungs...; ~ *woman* Reinemache-, Putzfrau *f*; **clean·li·ness** ['klenlinis] Reinlichkeit *f*; **clean·ly** **1.** *adv.* ['kli:nli] rein *etc.*; **2.** *adj.* ['klenli] reinlich; **clean·ness** ['kli:nnis] Reinheit *f*; Sauberkeit *f*; **cleanse** [klenz] reinigen; säubern; '**cleans·er** Reinigungsmittel *n*; Reinigungsmilch *f od.* -creme *f*.

clean-shav·en ['kli:n'ʃeivən] glattrasiert.

clean-up ['kli:n'ʌp] Aufräumung *f*; *pol.* Säuberungsaktion *f*; *Am. sl.* Profit *m*.

clear [kliə] **1.** □ *mst* klar (*durchsichtig*; *deutlich*; *verständlich*; *scharf* [*Geist etc.*]; *sicher, gewiß*; *einwandfrei*); *oft* hell, rein (*Ton, Licht etc.*); *fig.* rein (*from* von *Verdacht etc.*); frei (*unbehindert*; *of* von); ganz, voll; ✝ rein, netto; ~ *of* frei *od.* fern *od.* los von; *as ~ as day* sonnenklar; *get ~ of* loskommen von; **2.** *in the ~* ⚠ im Lichten; **3.** *v/t. a. ~ up* er-, aufhellen, *fig. a.* aufklären; klären; reinigen, säubern (*of, from* von); *Wald* lichten, roden; *a. ~ away, ~ off* wegräumen; *Hindernis* nehmen; *Rechnung* ins reine bringen, bezahlen; ✝ *s. ~ off*; ✝ (aus-)klarieren, verzollen; ⚖ lossprechen; befreien; rechtfertigen (*from* von); ✝ als Reingewinn erzielen; *~ off* ✝ räumen; *~ a port* aus einem Hafen auslaufen; *~ a ship for action* ein Schiff klar zum Gefecht machen; *~ one's throat* sich räuspern; *v/i. a. ~ up* sich aufhellen; *a. ~ off* sich verziehen (*Wolken etc.*); *~ out* F verschwinden; *~ through e-n Ort* passieren; '**clear·ance** Aufklärung *f*; Freilegung *f*; Räumung *f*; ✝ Abrechnung *f*; ⚓, ✝ Verzollung *f*, Klarierung *f*; Zollschein *m*; ⊕ Spielraum *m*, lichter Raum *m*; *~ sale* Räumungsausverkauf *m*; '**clear-'cut** ganz klar; '**clear·ing** Aufklärung *f etc. s. clear 3*; Rodung *f*, Lichtung *f*, Schneise *f*; ✝ Ab-, Verrechnung *f*; *~ arrangement* Abrechnungsverkehr *m*; *~ bank* Girobank *f*; ♀ *House* Ab-, Verrechnungsstelle *f*; Abrechnungsbörse *f in London*; *~-hospital* Feldlazarett *n*; '**clear·ness** Klarheit *f*, Deutlichkeit *f*; Reinheit *f*.

cleat [kli:t] ⚓ Klampe *f*; Keil *m*; Pflock *m*.

cleav·age ['kli:vidʒ] Spaltung *f* (*a. fig.*); *min.* Spaltbarkeit *f*.

cleave[1] [kli:v] (*irr.*) (sich) spalten; *Wasser, Luft* (zer)teilen; *in a cleft stick* in der Klemme; *cleft palate* ⚕ Wolfsrachen *m*; *show the cloven hoof* sein wahres Gesicht zeigen.

cleave[2] [~] *fig.* festhalten (*to* an *dat.*); treu bleiben (*dat.*); *~ together* zusammenhalten.

cleav·er ['kli:və] Spaltende *m*; Hackmesser *n*.

cleek [kli:k] Haken *m*; Golfstock *m*.

clef ♪ [klef] Schlüssel *m*.

cleft [kleft] **1.** Spalte *f*; Sprung *m* Riß *m*; **2.** *pret. u. p.p. von cleave*[1]

clem·a·tis ⚘ ['klemətis] Waldrebe *f*

Klematis *f*.
clem·en·cy ['klemənsi] Milde *f*; '**clem·ent** □ mild.
clench [klentʃ] *Lippen etc.* fest zs.-pressen; *Zähne* zs.-beißen; *Faust* ballen; festhalten; = *clinch*.
clere·sto·ry ⚠ ['kliəstəri] Lichtgaden *m e-r Kirche*.
cler·gy ['klə:dʒi] Geistlichkeit *f*, Klerus *m*; '**~·man, cler·ic** ['klerik] Geistliche *m*.
cler·i·cal ['klerikəl] **1.** □ geistlich; Schreib(er)...; ~ *error* Schreibfehler *m*; ~ *work* Büroarbeit *f*; **2.** Geistliche *m*; *pol.* Klerikale *m*.
cler·i·hew ['klerihju:] Clerihew *n* (*vierzeiliges witziges Gedicht*).
clerk [klɑ:k] (Büro)Schreiber *m*, Büroangestellte *m*; Sekretär *m*; ☦ kaufmännischer Angestellter *m*, Handlungsgehilfe *m*, Kommis *m*; *bsd. Am.* Verkäufer(in) *im Laden*; *eccl.* Küster *m*.
clev·er □ ['klevə] klug, gescheit; geschickt; ~ **dick** F Besserwisser *m*; '**clev·er·ness** Geschicklichkeit *f*; Klugheit *f*.
clew [klu:] Knäuel *m*, *n*; *s. clue*.
cli·ché ['kli:ʃei] stehende Redensart *f*, übliche Phrase *f*, Schlagwort *n*, Klischee *n*.
click [klik] **1.** Klicken *n*, Knipsen *n*, Ticken *n*, Knacken *n*; ⊕ Sperrhaken *m*, -klinke *f*; **2.** klicken, ticken, knacken; zu-, einschnappen; tadellos klappen; *sl.* sich auf den ersten Blick ineinander verlieben; Glück haben.
cli·ent ['klaiənt] Klient(in); Kunde *m*, Kundin *f*; **cli·en·tèle** [kli:ɑ̃:n'teil] Klientel *f*, Kundschaft *f*.
cliff [klif] Klippe *f*; Felsen *m*; (Steil)Abhang *m*; '**~·hang·er** *bsd. Radio, Fernsehen: Folge eines Mehrteilers, die im spannendsten Moment aufhört*.
cli·mac·ter·ic [klai'mæktərik] **1.** (*~ally*) klimakterisch; **2.** ⚕ Klimakterium *n*; *fig.* Lebenswende *f*, Wendepunkt *m*.
cli·mate ['klaimit] Klima *n*; **cli·mat·ic** [~'mætik] (*~ally*) klimatisch.
cli·max ['klaimæks] **1.** Steigerung *f*; Gipfel *m*, Höhepunkt *m*; **2.** auf e-n Höhepunkt bringen; e-n Höhepunkt erreichen.
climb [klaim] **1.** (er)klettern, (er-)klimmen, (er)steigen; **2.** Kletterei *f*; Kletterpartie *f*; '**climb·er** Kletterer *m*, Bergsteiger(in); *fig.* Streber(in); ⚘ Kletterpflanze *f*; '**climb·ing** Klettern *n*; *attr.* Kletter...; '**climb·ing-i·ron** Steigeisen *n*.
clinch [klintʃ] **1.** ⊕ Vernietung *f*; *fig.* Festhalten *n*; *Boxen*: Umklammerung *f*, Clinch *m*; **2.** *v/t.* um-, vernieten; *Beweis* verstärken, *Handel* festmachen; entscheiden; *s. clench*; *v/i.* festhalten; '**clinch·er** ⊕ Krampe *f*; F treffende Antwort *f*, Trumpf *m*.
cling [kliŋ] (*irr.*) (*to*) festhalten (an *dat.*), sich (an)klammern (an *acc.*); sich (an)schmiegen (an *acc.*); *j-m* anhängen; sich heften *od.* hängen (an *acc.*); '**cling·ing** enganliegend (*Kleid*); anhänglich.
clin·ic ['klinik] Klinik *f*; klinisches Praktikum *n*; '**clin·i·cal** □ klinisch; ~ *thermometer* Fieberthermometer *n*.
clink[1] *sl.* [kliŋk] Kittchen *n*, Gefängnis *n*.
clink[2] [~] **1.** Klingen *n*; Geklirr *n*; **2.** klingen, klirren (lassen); klimpern mit; mit den Gläsern anstoßen; '**clink·er** Klinkerstein *m*; Schlacke *f*; *sl.* Prachtkerl *m*, -stück *n*; '**clin·ker-built** ⚓ klinkergebaut; '**clink·ing** *sl.* fabelhaft, F blendend.
clip[1] [klip] **1.** Schur *f*; *at one ~ Am.* F auf einmal, auf e-n Schlag; **2.** ab-, aus-, beschneiden; *Schafe etc.* scheren; *Silben* verschlucken; *Fahrkarte* lochen; ~ *s.o.'s ear sl.* j-m e-e knallen.
clip[2] [~] **1.** (Büro-, Heft)Klammer *f*; Spange *f*; **2.** zs.-klammern.
clip·per ['klipə] Klipper *m*; ⚓ Schnellsegler *m*; schnelles Pferd *n*; *sl.* Prachtstück *n*; (*a. pair of*) *~s pl.* Haarschneide-, Schermaschine *f*; '**clip·pings** *pl.* Abfälle *m/pl.*; Schnitzel *n/pl.*; *Zeitungs- etc.* Ausschnitte *m/pl.*
clique [kli:k] Clique *f*, Sippschaft *f*.
clit·o·ris *anat.* ['klitəris] Klitoris *f*, Kitzler *m*.
cloak [kləuk] **1.** Umhang *m*, Mantel *m*; *fig.* Deckmantel *m*; **2.** *fig.* bemänteln, verhüllen; '**~-room** Garderobe(nraum *m*) *f*; Toilette *f*; 🚂 Gepäckaufbewahrung *f*.

clob·ber *sl.* [ˈklɔbə] **1.** Klamotten *f/pl.*; **2.** (zs.-)schlagen; *fig.* besiegen.
clock [klɔk] **1.** *Schlag-, Wand-, Turm-*Uhr *f*; Zwickel *m am Strumpf*; *Sport sl.* Stoppuhr *f*; *put the ~ back fig.* die Uhr zurückdrehen; **2.** *v/t. Sport sl. Rennen* mit der Stoppuhr messen; *v/i. ~ in (out) Arbeitszeitkontrolle*: einstempeln (ausstempeln); **ˈ~·face** Zifferblatt *n*; **~ ra·di·o** Radiowecker *m*; **ˈ~·wise** im Uhrzeigersinn; **ˈ~·work** Federwerk *n*; *~ train* Eisenbahn *f* zum Aufziehen; *like ~* wie am Schnürchen.
clod [klɔd] Erdkloß *m*; Klumpen *m*; *a. ~-hopper* (Bauern)Tölpel *m*.
clog [klɔg] **1.** Klotz *m*; *fig.* Hindernis *n*; Holzschuh *m*; Überschuh *m*; **2.** belasten; *fig.* hemmen; (sich) verstopfen; **ˈclog·gy** klumpig.
clois·ter [ˈklɔistə] **1.** Kreuzgang *m*; Kloster *n*; **2.** (in ein Kloster) einschließen.
close 1. [kləuz] Schluß *m*, Ende *n*; Abschluß *m*; [kləus] Einfriedung *f*, Hof *m*; **2.** [kləuz] *v/t.* (ab-, ein-, ver-, zu)schließen; zumachen; beschließen; *~ down Betrieb* schließen, stillegen; *~ one's eyes to* die Augen schließen vor (*dat.*); *v/i.* (sich) schließen; abschließen; enden; zuheilen; handgemein werden (*with* mit); *~ in* hereinbrechen (*Nacht*); kürzer werden (*Tage*); *~ on (prp.)* sich schließen um, umschließen, umfassen; *~ up* ⚔ aufschließen; *closing time Geschäfts- etc.* Schluß *m*, Feierabend *m*; Polizeistunde *f*; **3.** □ [kləus] geschlossen; verborgen; verschwiegen; knapp, eng; eng anliegend (*Kleid etc.*); begrenzt, geschlossen (*Gesellschaft*); nah, eng; bündig (*Stil etc.*); dicht; gedrängt (*Schrift etc.*); schwül, dumpf; knickerig; genau (*Aufmerksamkeit etc.*); eingehend (*Prüfung*); fest (*Griff*); fast gleich (*Wettkampf*); *~ by, ~ to* dicht bei *od.* daneben, ganz in der Nähe; *~ fight, ~ combat, ~ quarters pl.* Handgemenge *n*, Nahkampf *m*; *~ prisoner* streng bewachter Gefangener *m*; *~ season, ~ time hunt.* Schonzeit *f*; *sail ~ to the wind* ⚓ hart am Wind segeln; *fig.* sich hart an der Grenze des Erlaubten bewegen; *a ~ shave* ein knappes Entrinnen; **ˈ~-ˈcropped, ˈ~-ˈcut** kurz geschnitten (*Haar, Gras etc.*).
closed [kləuzd] geschlossen; **~ book** *fig.* Buch *n* mit sieben Siegeln; **~ cir·cuit** geschlossener Stromkreis *m*; **~-cir·cuit tel·e·vi·sion** Fernsehüberwachungsanlage *f*; interne Fernsehanlage *f*; **~ shop** Unternehmen *n* mit Gewerkschaftszwang.
close...: **ˈ~-ˈfist·ed** knickerig; **ˈ~-ˈfit·ting** eng anliegend; **ˈ~-ˈgrained** feinkörnig (*Holz*); **ˈ~-ˈhauled** ⚓ hart am Wind; **ˈ~-ˈknit** eng (zs.-gewachsen) (*Familie, Gemeinschaft*); **ˈ~-ˈmeshed** engmaschig; **ˈclose·ness** Genauigkeit *f*, Geschlossenheit *f etc.* (*s. close 3*).
clos·et [ˈklɔzit] **1.** *bsd. Am.* Abstell-, Vorratsraum *m*; (Wand)Schrank *m*; Kabinett *n*, Geheimzimmer *n*; *s. water-~*; **2.** *be ~ed with* mit *j-m* e-e geheime Beratung haben.
clos·ing [ˈkləuziŋ]: *~ date* Schlußtermin *m*; *~ time* Ladenschluß *m*; Polizeistunde *f*.
close-up [ˈkləusʌp] *Film*: Groß-, Nahaufnahme *f*.
clo·sure [ˈkləuʒə] **1.** Verschluß *m*; *parl.* (Antrag *m* auf) Schluß *m e-r Debatte*; *apply the ~* Schluß der Debatte beantragen; die Debatte schließen; **2.** *Debatte etc.* schließen.
clot [klɔt] **1.** Klümpchen *n*; **2.** zu Klümpchen gerinnen (lassen).
cloth [klɔθ] Stoff *m*, Tuch *n*; Tischtuch *n*; Kleidung *f*, Tracht *f bsd. der Geistlichen*; *the ~* F der geistliche Stand *m*; *lay the ~* den Tisch decken; *bound in ~* in Leinen gebunden; *~ binding* Leinenband *m*.
clothe [kləuð] (*irr.*) (an-, be)kleiden; *fig.* be-, einkleiden.
clothes [kləuðz] *pl.* Kleider *n/pl.*; Kleidung *f*; Anzug *m*; Wäsche *f*; **ˈ~-bas·ket** Waschkorb *m*; **~ hang·er** Kleiderbügel *m*; **~ horse** Wäscheständer *m*; **ˈ~-line** Wäscheleine *f*; **ˈ~-peg** Kleiderhaken *m*; Wäscheklammer *f*; **ˈ~·pin** *bsd. Am.* Wäscheklammer *f*; **ˈ~-press** Kleider-, Wäscheschrank *m*.
cloth·ier [ˈkləuðiə] Tuch-, Kleiderhändler *m*.
cloth·ing [ˈkləuðiŋ] Kleidung *f*.
cloud [klaud] **1.** Wolke *f* (*a. fig.*); dunkler Fleck *m*, Trübung *f*; Schatten *m*; *be under a ~* in Ungnade sein; *in the ~s* geistes-

abwesend; **2.** (sich) be-, umwölken, trüben (*a. fig.*); ~**ed** gewölkt (*Bernstein*); geädert (*Holz etc.*); moiriert (*Seide*); '~**-burst** Wolkenbruch *m*; ~-'**cuck·oo-land** Wolkenkuckucksheim *n*; '**cloud·less** □ wolkenlos; '**cloud·y** □ wolkig; Wolken...; trüb; unklar.

clough [klʌf] Schlucht *f*.

clout [klaut] **1.** F *j-m* e-e Kopfnuß geben; **2.** Flicken *m*, Lappen *m*; F Kopfnuß *f*.

clove[1] [kləuv] (Gewürz)Nelke *f*.

clove[2] [~] (Knoblauch)Zehe *f*.

clove[3] [~] *pret. von* cleave[1]; '**clo·ven 1.** *p.p. von* cleave[1]; **2.** *adj.* gespalten; Spalt...

clo·ver ⚘ ['kləuvə] Klee *m*; *live od. be in* ~ im Wohlstand leben; '~**-leaf** *Autobahn*: Kleeblatt(kreuzung *f*) *n*.

clown [klaun] Hanswurst *m*, Clown *m*; *lit.* Bauer *m*, Tölpel *m*; '**clown·ish** □ bäurisch; plump; clownhaft.

cloy [klɔi] übersättigen, -laden; anekeln.

club [klʌb] **1.** Keule *f*; (Gummi-) Knüppel *m*; Klub *m*, Verein *m*; ~*s pl. Karten*: Treff *n*, Kreuz *n*, Eicheln *f/pl.*; **2.** *v/t.* mit e-r Keule *od.* dem Gewehrkolben schlagen; ~ *together Geld* zs.-legen; *v/i. mst* ~ *together* sich zs.-tun; '**club·a·ble** klub-, gesellschaftsfähig; '**club-'foot** Klumpfuß *m*; '**club-'house** Klub-, Vereinshaus *n*; '**club-'law** Faustrecht *n*.

cluck [klʌk] glucken (*Henne*).

clue *fig.* [klu:] Anhaltspunkt *m*, Fingerzeig *m*, Hinweis *m*.

clump [klʌmp] **1.** Klumpen *m*; (Baum)Gruppe *f*; *mst* ~ *sole* Doppelsohle *f*; **2.** trampeln; zs.-drängen; mit Doppelsohlen versehen; in Gruppen pflanzen.

clum·si·ness ['klʌmzinis] Unbeholfenheit *f etc.*; '**clum·sy** □ unbeholfen, ungeschickt, schwerfällig; plump.

clung [klʌŋ] *pret. u. p.p. von cling.*

clus·ter ['klʌstə] **1.** ⚘ Traube *f*; Büschel *m*, *n*; Haufen *m*, Schwarm *m*, Gruppe *f*; **2.** büschelweise wachsen; (sich) zs.-drängen.

clutch[1] [klʌtʃ] **1.** Griff *m*; ⊕ Kupplung *f*; *in his* ~*es* in seinen Krallen; ~ *pedal mot.* Kupplungspedal *n*; **2.** (er)greifen, packen; greifen (*at* nach).

clutch[2] [~] Gelege *n*, Brut *f*.

clut·ter ['klʌtə] **1.** Wirrwarr *m*, Durcheinander *n*; **2.** ~ *up* durcheinanderbringen, in Unordnung bringen; vollstopfen.

clys·ter ['klistə] Klistier *n*.

co... [kəu] *Wortelement*: mit, gemeinsam, Ko...

coach [kəutʃ] **1.** Kutsche *f*; 🚃 Wagen *m*; Reisebus *m*; *univ.* Einpauker *m*; *Sport*: Trainer *m*; **2.** in e-r Kutsche fahren; (ein)pauken; trainieren; '~**·man** Kutscher *m*; '~**·work** *mot.* Karosserie *f*.

co·ad·ju·tor *bsd. eccl.* [kəu'ædʒutə] Gehilfe *m*, Koadjutor *m*.

co·ag·u·late [kəu'ægjuleit] gerinnen (lassen); **co·ag·u'la·tion** Gerinnen *n*.

coal [kəul] **1.** (Stein)Kohle *f*; *coll.* Kohlen *pl.*; *carry* ~*s to Newcastle* Eulen nach Athen tragen; *haul od. call s.o. over the* ~*s fig.* j-m die Hölle heiß machen; **2.** ⚓ (be-) kohlen; ~*ing station* Kohlenstation *f*; '~**·bed** Kohlenflöz *m*; '~-'**dust** Kohlenstaub *m*.

co·a·lesce [kəuə'les] zs.-wachsen, sich vereinigen; **co·a'les·cence** Zs.-wachsen *n*; Vereinigung *f*.

coal...: '~**-field** Kohlenrevier *n*; '~**-gas** Leuchtgas *n*.

co·a·li·tion [kəuə'liʃən] Verbindung *f*; Bund *m*, Koalition *f*.

coal...: '~**-mine**, '~**-pit** Kohlengrube *f*, -bergwerk *n*; '~**-scut·tle** Kohleneimer *m*.

coarse □ [kɔ:s] grob; *fig.* roh; ungeschliffen; '**coarse·ness** Grob-, Derbheit *f*.

coast [kəust] **1.** Küste *f*; *bsd. Am.* Rodelbahn *f*, (Rodel)Abfahrt *f*; **2.** die Küste entlangfahren; im Freilauf fahren; rodeln; '**coast·al** Küsten...

coast·er ['kəustə] *Am.* Rodelschlitten *m*; ⚓ Küstenfahrer *m*; Untersetzer *m für Gläser*; ~ **brake** *Am.* Rücktrittbremse *f*.

coast-guard ['kəustgɑ:d] Küstenwache *f*; '**coast·ing** Küstenfahrt *f*; Rodeln *n*; ~ *trade* Küstenschiffahrt *f*; '**coast-line** Küste(nlinie) *f*.

coat [kəut] **1.** Jackett *n*, Jacke *f*, Rock *m*; Mantel *m*; Haare *n/pl.*, Pelz *m*, Gefieder *n*; Überzug *m*, Schicht *f*; Anstrich *m*; ~ *of mail*

Panzerhemd *n*; ~ *of arms* Wappen (-schild *m*) *n*; *cut the ~ according to the cloth* sich nach der Decke strecken; *turn one's ~* sein Mäntelchen nach dem Wind hängen; **2.** bedecken; überziehen; anstreichen; '**~-hang·er** Kleiderbügel *m*; '**coat·ing** Überzug *m*, Anstrich *m*; Bewurf *m*; Mantelstoff *m*.

coax [kəuks] schmeicheln (*dat.*); beschwatzen (*into* zu); ~ *s.o. out of s.th.* j-m et. abschwatzen.

cob [kɔb] kleines starkes Pferd *n*; männlicher Schwan *m*; Klumpen *m*; *Am.* Maiskolben *m*; = ~*-nut*.

co·balt *min.* [kəu'bɔ:lt] Kobalt *n*.

cob·ble ['kɔbl] **1.** Kopf-, Pflasterstein *m*; ~*s pl.* = *cob-coal*; **2.** flikken; '**cob·bler** Schuhmacher *m*; Stümper *m*; *eisgekühltes Mischgetränk*; '**cob·ble-stone** Pflasterstein *m*.

cob...: '**~-coal** Nuß-, Stückkohle *f*; '**~-loaf** rundes Brot *n*; '**~-nut** *Art* Haselnuß *f*.

co·bra *zo.* ['kəubrə] Kobra *f*.

cob·web ['kɔbweb] Spinnwebe *f*.

co·caine *pharm.* [kə'kein] Kokain *n*.

coch·i·neal ['kɔtʃini:l] Koschenille *f*.

cock [kɔk] **1.** Hahn *m*; *Vogel-Männchen n*; ⊕ Hahn *m am Faß und Gewehr*; Anführer *m*; *kleiner* Heuhaufen *m*; V Schwanz *m*, Penis *m*; **2.** *oft* ~ *up* aufrichten; *die Ohren* spitzen; *Gewehrhahn* spannen; *den Hut* aufs Ohr setzen; ~ *one's eye* (*at s.o.* j-m zu)zwinkern.

cock·ade [kɔ'keid] Kokarde *f*.

cock-a-doo·dle-doo ['kɔkədu:dl'du:] Kikeriki *n od. m*.

cock-a-hoop ['kɔkə'hu:p] frohlockend.

Cock·aigne [kɔ'kein] Schlaraffenland *n*.

cock-and-bull sto·ry ['kɔkənd'bul'stɔ:ri] Räubergeschichte *f*.

cock·a·too [kɔkə'tu:] Kakadu *m*.

cock-a·trice ['kɔkətrais] Basilisk *m* (*a. fig.*).

cock·boat ⚓ ['kɔkbəut] Jolle *f*.

cock·chaf·er ['kɔktʃeifə] Maikäfer *m*.

cock-crow(·**ing**) ['kɔkkrəu(iŋ)] Hahnenschrei *m*; Tagesanbruch *m*.

cocked hat ['kɔkt'hæt] Zwei-, Dreispitz *m*; *knock into a ~* zu Brei schlagen.

cock·er[1] ['kɔkə]: ~ *up* aufpäppeln.

cock·er[2] [~] Cockerspaniel *m*.

cock·er·el ['kɔkərəl] Hähnchen *n*.

cock...: '**~-eyed** *sl.* schieläugig; *Am.* blau (*betrunken*); '**~-fight**(·**ing**) Hahnenkampf *m*; '**~-'horse** Stekkenpferd *n*.

cock·le[1] ⚘ ['kɔkl] Kornrade *f*.

cock·le[2] [~] **1.** *zo.* Herzmuschel *f*; Falte *f*; *warm od. delight the ~s of one's heart* dem Herzen wohltun; **2.** (sich) kräuseln, falten.

cock·ney ['kɔkni] waschechter Londoner *m*; '**cock·ney·ism** Cockneyausdruck *m*.

cock·pit ['kɔkpit] Kampfplatz *m* für Hähne; ⚓ Raumdeck *n*; ✈ Führerraum *m*, Kanzel *f*.

cock·roach *zo.* ['kɔkrəutʃ] Schabe *f*.

cocks·comb ['kɔkskəum] Hahnenkamm *m* (*a.* ⚘); '**cock-'sure** F absolut sicher; überheblich; '**cock-tail** Cocktail *m* (*Mischgetränk; Früchte*); '**cock-up:** *make a ~ of s.th. sl.* et. verpfuschen; '**cock·y** □ F selbstbewußt; naseweis; frech.

co·co ['kəukəu] Kokospalme *f*.

co·coa ['kəukəu] Kakao *m*.

co·co·nut ['kəukənʌt] Kokosnuß *f*.

co·coon [kə'ku:n] Kokon *m der Seidenraupe*.

cod *ichth.* [kɔd] Kabeljau *m*, Dorsch *m*; *dried ~* Stockfisch *m*; *cured ~* Klippfisch *m*.

cod·dle ['kɔdl] verhätscheln, verwöhnen; ~ *up* aufpäppeln.

code [kəud] **1.** Gesetzbuch *n*; (Ehren)Kodex *m*; Code *m*; Schlüssel *m*; **2.** *tel.* chiffrieren.

co·de·ine ⚗ ['kəudi:n] Kodein *n*.

co·dex ['kəudeks], *pl.* **co·di·ces** ['~disi:z] Kodex *m*, Handschrift *f*.

cod·fish ['kɔdfiʃ] = *cod*.

codg·er F ['kɔdʒə] komischer Kauz *m*.

co·di·ces ['kəudisi:z] *pl. von codex*.

cod·i·cil ['kɔdisil] Kodizill *n*; **cod·i·fi'ca·tion** Kodifikation *f*; **cod·i·fy** ['~fai] kodifizieren.

cod·ling ['kɔdliŋ] ⚘ Kochapfel *m*; *ichth.* junger Kabeljau *m*.

cod-liv·er oil ['kɔdlivər'ɔil] Lebertran *m*.

co-ed *Am.* F ['kəu'ed] Schülerin *f* e-r Koedukationsschule, *allg.* Studentin *f*.

co-ed·u·ca·tion ['kəuedju:'keiʃən] Koedukation *f* (*gemeinsamer Schulbesuch beider Geschlechter*).

co·ef·fi·cient [kəui'fiʃənt] **1.** mit-

wirkend; 2. Koeffizient *m*.
co·erce [kəu'əːs] zwingen; *et.* erzwingen; **co'er·ci·ble** zu (er)zwingen(d); **co'er·cion** [~ʃən] Zwang *m*; Zwangsherrschaft *f*; *under* ~ unter Zwang, in e-r Zwangslage; **co'er·cive** [~siv] □ Zwangs...
co·e·val □ [kəu'iːvəl] gleichzeitig; gleichalterig.
co·ex·ist ['kəuig'zist] gleichzeitig bestehen; **'co·ex'ist·ence** Koexistenz *f*; Nebeneinander *n*; **'co·ex'ist·ent** gleichzeitig (existierend).
cof·fee ['kɔfi] Kaffee *m*; **'~-bean** Kaffeebohne *f*; **'~-grounds** *pl.* Kaffeegrund *m*, -satz *m*; **'~-house** Kaffeehaus *n*; Café *n*; **'~-pot** Kaffeekanne *f*; **'~-room** Speisesaal *m* *e-s Hotels*; **'~-set** Kaffeeservice *n*; **~ shop** Kaffeegeschäft *n*; Kaffeestube *f*, kleines Restaurant *n*; **~ ta·ble** Couchtisch *m*.
cof·fer ['kɔfə] (Geld)Kasten *m*; △ Deckenkassette *f*; ~*s pl.* Schatz (-kammer *f*) *m*, Tresor *m*; *a.* ~*-dam* Senkkasten *m*, Caisson *m*.
cof·fin ['kɔfin] **1.** Sarg *m*; **2.** einsargen.
cog ⊕ [kɔg] *Rad*-Zahn *m*.
co·gen·cy ['kəudʒənsi] zwingende Kraft *f*; **'co·gent** □ zwingend.
cogged ⊕ [kɔgd] gezahnt, Zahn...
cog·i·tate ['kɔdʒiteit] *v/i.* nachdenken; *v/t.* (er)sinnen; **cog·i'ta·tion** Nachdenken *n*.
co·gnac ['kɔnjæk] Kognak *m*.
cog·nate ['kɔgneit] **1.** verwandt; **2.** Blutsverwandte *m*, *f*.
cog·ni·tion [kɔg'niʃən] Erkenntnis *f*.
cog·ni·za·ble ['kɔgnizəbl] erkennbar; ⚖ abzuurteilen(d); **'cog·ni·zance** Kenntnis *f*; Erkenntnis *f* (⚖ *n*); Gerichtsbarkeit *f*, Zuständigkeit *f*; Abzeichen *n*; **'cog·ni·zant** Kenntnis habend (*of* von); zuständig.
cog·no·men [kɔg'nəumen] Zuname *m*; Bei-, Spitzname *m*.
cog-wheel ⊕ ['kɔgwiːl] Zahnrad *n*.
co·hab·it [kəu'hæbit] in wilder Ehe leben; **co·hab·i'ta·tion** wilde Ehe *f*.
co·heir ['kəu'ɛə] Miterbe *m*; **co·heir·ess** ['kəu'ɛəris] Miterbin *f*.
co·here [kəu'hiə] zs.-hängen; **co'her·ence, co'her·en·cy** Zs.-hang *m*; **co'her·ent** □ zs.-hängend; klar, verständlich; **co'her·er** *Radio*: Fritter *m*.
co·he·sion [kəu'hiːʒən] Kohäsion *f*; **co'he·sive** [~siv] (fest) zs.-hängend.
co·hort ['kəuhɔːt] Kohorte *f*; Schar *f*.
coif [kɔif] Haube *f*.
coif·feur [kwaː'fəː] Friseur *m*; **coif·fure** [~'fjuə] **1.** Frisur *f*; **2.** frisieren.
coign of van·tage [kɔinəv'vaːntidʒ] guter Beobachtungsposten *m*.
coil [kɔil] **1.** *oft* ~ *up* aufwickeln; (sich) zs.-rollen; sich winden; **2.** Rolle *f*, Spirale *f*; Wicklung *f*; ⚡ Spule *f*; Windung *f*; ⊕ (Rohr-) Schlange *f*.
coin [kɔin] **1.** Münze *f*, Geldstück *n*; *pay s.o. back in his own* ~ j-m mit gleicher Münze heimzahlen; **2.** prägen (*a. fig.*); münzen; *be* ~*ing money* Geld wie Heu verdienen; **'coin·age** Prägung *f*, Prägen *n* (*a. fig.*); Geld *n*, Münze *f*; Münzsystem *n*; **'coin-box tel·e·phone** Münzfernsprecher *m*.
co·in·cide [kəuin'said] zs.-treffen, -fallen; *fig.* übereinstimmen; **co·in·ci·dence** [kəu'insidəns] Zs.-treffen *n*, -fallen *n*; *fig.* Übereinstimmung *f*; *mere* ~ bloßer Zufall *m*; **co'in·ci·dent** □ zs.-fallend; *fig.* übereinstimmend.
coin·er ['kɔinə] Münzer *m*, Präger *m*; *bsd.* Falschmünzer *m*.
coir ['kɔiə] Kokosbast *m*.
coke [kəuk] **1.** Koks *m* (*a. sl.* = *Kokain*); *Am.* F Coca-Cola *f*; **2.** verkoken.
co·ker·nut ['kəukənʌt] = *coco-nut*.
col·an·der ['kʌləndə] *Küche*: Durchschlag *m*, Sieb *n*.
cold [kəuld] **1.** □ kalt (*a. fig.*); *throw* ~ *water on* die Begeisterung für *et.* dämpfen; *give s.o. the* ~ *shoulder* = ~*-shoulder*; *have* ~ *feet* F kalte Füße (*Angst*) haben; **2.** Kälte *f*, Frost *m*; Erkältung *f*; *oft* ~ *in the head* Schnupfen *m*; *be left in the* ~ vernachlässigt *od.* im Stich gelassen werden; **'~-'blood·ed** kaltblütig (*a. fig.*); **~ cream** Feuchtigkeitscreme *f*; **'~-'heart·ed** kalt-, hartherzig; **'cold·ness** Kälte *f*.
cold...: **'~-shoul·der** *j-m* die kalte Schulter zeigen, *j.* kühl behandeln, links liegen lassen; **~ steel** blanke Waffe *f*; **'~-'stor·age** Kühlhaus (-lagerung *f*) *n*; *attr.* Kühl(haus)...;

'~-'**store** kühl lagern; ~ **war** kalter Krieg *m*.
cole ⚘ [kəul] *mst in Zssgn* Kohl *m*.
cole-seed ⚘ ['kəulsi:d] Rübsamen *m*.
cole·slaw *Am*. ['kəulslɔ:] Krautsalat *m*.
col·ic ⚕ ['kɔlik] Kolik *f*.
col·lab·o·rate [kə'læbəreit] zs.-arbeiten; **col·lab·o'ra·tion** Zs.-, Mitarbeit *f*; *in ~ with* gemeinsam mit; **col·lab·o'ra·tion·ist** *pol*. Kollaborateur *m*; **col'lab·o·ra·tor** Mitarbeiter *m*.
col·lapse [kə'læps] **1.** zs.-, einfallen; zs.-brechen; **2.** Zs.-bruch *m*; **col'laps·i·ble** zs.-klappbar; ~ *boat* Faltboot *n*.
col·lar ['kɔlə] **1.** Kragen *m*; Halsband *n*; Halskette *f*; Kum(me)t *n*; ⊕ Lager *n*, Pfanne *f*; **2.** beim Kragen packen; *Fleisch* zs.-rollen; '~-**bone** Schlüsselbein *n*; '~-**stud** Kragenknopf *m*.
col·late [kɔ'leit] *Texte etc*. vergleichen, kollationieren.
col·lat·er·al [kɔ'lætərəl] **1.** □ parallel laufend; Seiten..., Neben...; indirekt; **2.** Seitenverwandte *m, f*.
col·la·tion [kɔ'leiʃən] Vergleichung *f von Texten*; Imbiß *m*.
col·league ['kɔli:g] Kollege *m*, Kollegin *f*.
col·lect **1.** ['kɔlekt] Kollekte *f* (*Altargebet*); **2.** [kə'lekt] *v/t*. (ein-, auf)sammeln; *Gedanken etc*. sammeln; *Geld* einziehen, einkassieren; abholen; ~ *one's wits* s-e Gedanken sammeln; ~*ing business* Inkassogeschäft *n*; *v/i*. sich (ver)sammeln; ~ **call** *Am. teleph*. R-Gespräch *n*; **col'lect·ed** □ *fig*. gefaßt; **col'lect·ed·ness** *fig*. Fassung *f*; **col'lec·tion** Sammlung *f*; Kollekte *f*; Einziehung *f*, Inkasso *n*; *forcible* ~ Zwangsbeitreibung *f*; **col'lec·tive** gesammelt; Sammel...; Kollektiv...; ~ *bargaining* Tarifverhandlungen *f/pl*.; **col'lec·tive·ly** insgesamt, im ganzen; gemeinschaftlich; **col'lec·tiv·ism** *pol*. Kollektivismus *m*; **col'lec·tiv·ize** in Gemeineigentum überführen, verstaatlichen; **col'lector** Sammler *m*; *Steuer*-Einnehmer *m*, Erheber *m*; 🚂 Fahrkartenabnehmer *m*; ⚡ Stromabnehmer *m*; ~*'s item* Sammler-, Liebhaberstück *n*.
col·leen *ir*. [kɔ'li:n] Mädchen *n*.
col·lege ['kɔlidʒ] College *n* (*Teil e-r Universität*); höhere Schule *f od*. Lehranstalt *f*; Hochschule *f*; Akademie *f*; Kollegium *n*; **col·le·gi·an** [kə'li:dʒjən] Student *m*; höherer Schüler *m*; **col'le·giate** [~dʒiit] Schul..., College...
col·lide [kə'laid] (*with*) kollidieren (mit); zs.-stoßen (mit); *fig*. widerstreiten (*dat*.).
col·lie ['kɔli] Collie *m*, schottischer Schäferhund *m*.
col·lier ['kɔliə] Bergmann *m*; ⚓ Kohlenschiff *n*; **col·lier·y** ['kɔljəri] Kohlenbergwerk *n*.
col·li·sion [kə'liʒən] Kollision *f*; Zs.-stoß *m*; *fig*. Widerstreit *m*.
col·lo·ca·tion [kɔləu'keiʃən] Anordnung *f*.
col·lo·di·on [kə'ləudjən] Kollodium *n*.
col·logue [kə'ləug] sich vertraulich besprechen.
col·lo·qui·al □ [kə'ləukwiəl] umgangssprachlich, familiär; **col'lo·qui·al·ism** Ausdruck *m* der Umgangssprache.
col·lo·quy ['kɔləkwi] Gespräch *n*.
col·lude [kə'lu:d] im heimlichen Einverständnis sein; **col'lu·sion** [~ʒən] heimliches Einverständnis *n*; ⚖ Verdunkelung *f*.
col·ly·wob·bles F ['kɔliwɔblz]: *the* ~ ein flaues Gefühl in der Magengegend.
co·lon ['kəulən] *typ*. Kolon *n*, Doppelpunkt *m*; *anat*. Dickdarm *m*.
colo·nel ⚔ ['kə:nl] Oberst *m*; '**colo·nel·cy** Rang *m* e-s Obersten.
co·lo·ni·al [kə'ləunjəl] Kolonial...; **co'lo·ni·al·ism** *pol*. Kolonialismus *m*; **col·o·nist** ['kɔlənist] Kolonist *m*, Ansiedler *m*; **col·o·ni·za·tion** [kɔlənai'zeiʃən] Kolonisation *f*, Besiedelung *f*; '**col·o·nize** kolonisieren; (sich) ansiedeln; *Land* besiedeln.
col·on·nade [kɔlə'neid] Säulengang *m*, Kolonnade *f*.
col·o·ny ['kɔləni] Kolonie *f*; Siedlung *f*.
col·o·pho·ny [kɔ'lɔfəni] Kolophonium *n*, Geigenharz *n*.
Col·o·ra·do bee·tle [kɔlə'rɑ:dəu'bi:tl] Kartoffelkäfer *m*.
co·los·sal □ [kə'lɔsl] kolossal; **co'los·sus** [~səs] Koloß *m*, Riese *m*.
col·our, *Am*. **col·or** ['kʌlə] **1.** Farbe

f; Gesichts-, Hautfarbe *f*; *fig.* Färbung *f*; Anschein *m*; Vorwand *m*; *~s pl.* ⚔ Fahne *f*, Flagge *f*; *local ~* Lokalkolorit *n*; **2.** *v/t.* färben; anstreichen; kolorieren; *fig.* beschönigen; *v/i.* sich färben; sich verfärben, erröten; **ˈcol·o(u)r·a·ble** □ trügerisch; **col·o(u)rˈa·tion** Färbung *f*; Farbgebung *f*.

col·o(u)r...: **ˈ~-bar** Rassenschranke *f*; **ˈ~-blind** farbenblind; **ˈcol·o(u)red** gefärbt, farbig, bunt; *~ film* Farbfilm *m*; *~ pencil* Farbstift *m*; *~ (wo)man* Farbige *m* (*f*); **ˈcol·o(u)r-fast** farbecht; **col·o(u)r·ful** [ˈ~ful] farbenprächtig, -freudig, bunt; lebhaft; **ˈcol·o(u)r·ing 1.** färbend; *~ book* Malbuch *n*; *~ matter* Farbstoff *m*; **2.** Färbung *f*; Farbgebung *f*, Ton *m*; *fig.* Beschönigung *f*; **ˈcol·o(u)r·ist** Kolorist *m*; **ˈcolo(u)r·less** □ farblos; **col·o(u)r line** *bsd. Am.* Rassenschranke *f*; **col·o(u)r scheme** Farbenzs.-stellung *f*; **col·o(u)r sup·ple·ment** Farbbeilage *f e-r Zeitung*; **col·o(u)r wash** farbige Tünche *f*.

colt [kəult] Hengstfüllen *n*; *fig.* Neuling *m*; **ˈcolts·foot** ⚘ Huflattich *m*.

col·um·bine ⚘ [ˈkɔləmbain] Akelei *f*.

col·umn [ˈkɔləm] Säule *f*; Pfeiler *m*; *typ.* Spalte *f*; ⚔ Kolonne *f*; **co·lum·nar** [kəˈlʌmnə] säulenartig, -förmig; **col·um·nist** [ˈkɔləmnist] *Am.* Kolumnist *m* (*Journalist, für den stets e-e bestimmte Spalte reserviert ist*).

col·za ⚘ [ˈkɔlzə] Raps *m*.

co·ma [ˈkəumə] ⚕ Koma *n*, tiefe Bewußtlosigkeit *f*; ⚘ Schopf *m*, Haarbüschel *n*.

comb [kəum] **1.** Kamm *m* (*a. von Hahn u. Woge*); ⊕ Hechel *f*; *s. curry-~*; *s. honey~*; **2.** *v/t.* kämmen; striegeln; *Flachs* hecheln; *~ out fig.* (aus)sieben; *v/i.* sich brechen (*Welle*).

com·bat [ˈkɔmbət] **1.** Kampf *m*, Streit *m*; *single ~* Zweikampf *m*; **2.** (be)kämpfen; **ˈcom·bat·ant** Kämpfer *m*; **ˈcom·bat·ive** □ streitbar, -süchtig; Kampf...

comb·er [ˈkəumə] ⊕ Krempelmaschine *f*; ⚓ Schaumwelle *f*.

com·bin·a·ble [kəmˈbainəbl] verbindungsfähig; **com·bi·na·tion** [kɔmbiˈneiʃən] Verbindung *f* (*engS.* ⚗); Vereinigung *f*; Zs.-arbeit *f*; *mst ~s pl.* Hemdhose *f*; Motorrad *n* mit Beiwagen; *~ lock* Kombinationsschloß *n* (*mit Zahlen od. Buchstaben*); **com·bine 1.** [kəmˈbain] (sich) verbinden *od.* -einigen; kombinieren; **2.** [ˈkɔmbain] ✝ Ring *m*, Interessengemeinschaft *f*; *a. ~ harvester* Mähdrescher *m*.

com·bus·ti·ble [kəmˈbʌstəbl] **1.** brennbar; leicht entzündbar; **2.** *~s pl.* Brennmaterial *n*; *mot.* Treibstoff *m*; **com·bus·tion** [~ˈbʌstʃən] Verbrennung *f*; *~ engine* Verbrennungsmotor *m*.

come [kʌm] (*irr.*) kommen; *to ~* künftig, kommend; *how ~?* F wieso denn?; *~ about* sich zutragen; zustandekommen; *~ across* auf *j. od. et.* stoßen; *j-m* zufällig begegnen; *~ along* sich beeilen; mitkommen; *~ at* erlangen, erreichen; *j-m od. der Wahrheit etc.* beikommen; *~ by* vorbeikommen; zu *et.* kommen, *et.* bekommen; *~ down* herunterkommen (*a. fig.*); zs.-stürzen; *~ down upon s.o.* j. zurechtweisen; *~ down upon s.o. for £10* von j-m £10 verlangen; *~ down with* herausrücken mit *Geld*; *Am.* F erkranken an; *~ for* abholen; *~ in* hereinkommen; eintreten; ⚓ einlaufen; aufkommen, Mode werden; zur Macht *od.* ins Amt *etc.* kommen; *~ in!* herein!; *~ in for* bekommen; *~ off* davonkommen; abgehen (*Knopf*), ausfallen (*Haare etc.*); stattfinden; gelingen; *~ on* herankommen; wachsen; vorankommen, Fortschritte machen; *~ on!* komm her!; los!; vorwärts!; *~ out* herauskommen; erscheinen; ausfallen; *~ out right* stimmen (*Rechnung*); *~ round* vorbeikommen (*bsd. zu Besuch*); wiederkehren; zu sich kommen; *fig.* einlenken; zustimmen; *~ to adv.* dazukommen; = *~ to o.s.*; ⚓ beidrehen; *prp.* betragen, sich belaufen auf (*acc.*); *~ to o.s. od. to one's senses* wieder zu sich kommen; *~ to anchor* vor Anker gehen; *~ to know* kennenlernen; *~ up* herauf-, heraus-, herankommen; aufgehen, keimen; aufkommen; sich erheben (*Frage*); *~ up against fig.* aufstehen gegen; *~ up for (active) consideration* (ernsthaft) erwogen werden; *~ up to* entsprechen (*dat.*); es *j-m* gleichtun; *Stand, Maß* erreichen; ~ *up with j.* einholen; ~ *upon* stoßen auf (*acc.*); über *j.* kommen (*Gefühl etc.*); überfallen; **~-'at-a·ble** F erreichbar; zugänglich; **'~-back** Wiederkehr *f*, Wiederhochkommen *n*, Comeback *n*; *Am. sl.* schlagfertige Antwort *f*.

co·me·di·an [kəˈmi:djən] Schauspieler(in); Komiker(in); Lustspieldichter *m*.

com·e·dy [ˈkɔmidi] Komödie *f*, Lustspiel *n*.

come·li·ness [ˈkʌmlinis] Anmut *f*; **ˈcome·ly** anmutig, hübsch.

com·er [ˈkʌmə] (An)Kommende *m, f*.

co·mes·ti·ble [kəˈmestibl] *mst* ~*s pl.* Eßware(n *pl.*) *f*.

com·et [ˈkɔmit] Komet *m*.

com·fort [ˈkʌmfət] **1.** Bequemlichkeit *f*, Komfort *m*; Behaglichkeit *f*; Trost *m*; *fig.* Beistand *m*; Labsal *n*, Erquickung *f*; **2.** trösten; erquicken; beleben; **ˈcom·fort·a·ble** □ behaglich; angenehm; bequem, komfortabel; tröstlich; *I am* ~ mir ist behaglich, ich sitze *etc.* bequem; **ˈcom·fort·er** Tröster *m*; wollenes Halstuch *n*; Schnuller *m*; *Am.* Steppdecke *f*; **ˈcom·fort·less** □ unbehaglich; trostlos; **ˈcom·fort sta·tion** *Am.* Bedürfnisanstalt *f*.

com·frey ⚘ [ˈkʌmfri] Schwarzwurz(el) *f*.

com·fy □ F [ˈkʌmfi] = *comfortable*.

com·ic [ˈkɔmik] (~*ally*) komisch; Lustspiel...; *fig. mst* **ˈcom·i·cal** □ lustig, drollig; ~ *journal*, ~ *paper* Witzblatt *n*; **ˈcom·ics** *pl.* Comics *pl.* (*primitive Bildserien*).

Com·in·form [ˈkɔminfɔ:m] *pol.* Kominform *n*.

com·ing [ˈkʌmiŋ] **1.** kommend; künftig; ~, *Sir!* sofort, der Herr!; **2.** Kommen *n*, Ankunft *f*.

Com·in·tern *pol.* [ˈkɔmintə:n] Komintern *f*.

com·i·ty [ˈkɔmiti]: ~ *of nations* gutes Einvernehmen *n* der Nationen.

com·ma [ˈkɔmə] Komma *n*.

com·mand [kəˈmɑ:nd] **1.** Herrschaft *f*, Beherrschung *f* (*a. fig. e-r Sprache etc.*); Befehl *m*; Königlicher Erlaß *m* (*mst Cmd.*); ⚔ Kommando *n* (*in jedem Sinne*); *at od. by* ~ *of* auf Befehl (*gen.*); *have* ~ *of* beherrschen; *be* (*have*) *at* ~ zur Verfügung stehen (haben); *be in* ~ *of* ⚔ befehligen; **2.** befehlen, gebieten; *Truppe*, *Schiff* befehligen, ⚔ kommandieren; verfügen über (*acc.*); beherrschen; ⚔ bestreichen; beherrschen (*überschauen*); **com·man·dant** ⚔ [kɔmənˈdænt] Kommandant *m*, Befehlshaber *m e-r Festung*; **com·man·deer** [~ˈdiə] ⚔ zum Militärdienst zwingen; requirieren; **com·mand·er** ⚔ [kəˈmɑ:ndə] Kommandeur *m*, Befehlshaber *m e-r Truppenabteilung*; ⚓ Fregattenkapitän *m*; *Ordens*-Komtur *m*; **comˈmand·er-in-ˈchief** Oberbefehlshaber *m*; **comˈmand·ing** Herrscher...; beherrschend; *fig.* hervorragend; ~ *point* strategischer Punkt *m*; **comˈmand·ment** Gebot *n*; **com·mand mod·ule** *Raumfahrt*: Kommandokapsel *f*; **comˈman·do** ⚔ [~dəu] Kommando (-truppe *f*) *n*; **com·mand per·form·ance** *thea.* Aufführung *f* auf königlichen Wunsch.

com·mem·o·rate [kəˈmeməreit] gedenken (*gen.*), feiern; erinnern an (*acc.*); **com·mem·oˈra·tion** Gedächtnisfeier *f*; **comˈmem·o·ra·tive** □ [~rətiv] erinnernd (*of* an *acc.*); Gedächtnis..., Erinnerungs...; ~ *issue Briefmarken etc.* Gedenkausgabe *f*.

com·mence [kəˈmens] anfangen, beginnen; ⚖ anhängig machen; **comˈmence·ment** Anfang *m*, Beginn *m*; feierliche Verleihung *f* akademischer Grade.

com·mend [kəˈmend] empfehlen; loben; anvertrauen; ~ *me to ...* F da lobe ich mir ...; **comˈmend·a·ble** □ empfehlenswert; lobenswert; **com·men·da·tion** [kɔmenˈdeiʃən] Empfehlung *f*, Lob *n*; **comˈmend·a·to·ry** [~dətəri] empfehlend; Empfehlungs...

com·men·su·ra·ble □ [kəˈmenʃərəbl] vergleichbar (*with*, *to* mit); **comˈmen·su·rate** □ [~rit] (*with*, *to*) angemessen (*dat.*), entsprechend (*dat.*).

com·ment [ˈkɔmənt] **1.** Kommentar *m*; Erläuterung *f*; An-, Bemerkung *f*; Stellungnahme *f* (*on* zu); Kritik *f*; **2.** (*upon*) erläutern, kommentieren (*acc.*); sich auslassen (über *acc.*); kritische Bemerkungen machen (über *acc.*); **ˈcom·men·tar·y** Kommentar *m*; **com·men-**

ta·tor ['⁓teitə] Kommentator *m*; Erklärer *m*; *Radio*: Berichterstatter *m*.

com·merce ['kɔmə:s] Handel *m*; Verkehr *m*; Umgang *m*; *Chamber of* ♀ Handelskammer *f*; **com·mer·cial** □ [kə'mə:ʃəl] **1.** kaufmännisch; Handels..., Geschäfts...; gewerbsmäßig; ⁓ *traveller* Handlungsreisende *m*; **2.** F = ⁓ *traveller*; *bsd. Am. Radio*: kommerzielle Sendung *f*; **com'mer·cial·ism** Handelsgeist *m*; **com'mer·cial·ize** in den Handel bringen; ein Geschäft machen aus, kommerzialisieren; **com'mer·cial tel·e·vi·sion** kommerzielles Fernsehen *n*.

com·mie F ['kɔmi] Kommunist *m*.

com·min·gle [kɔ'miŋgl] zusammenmischen.

com·mis·er·ate [kə'mizəreit] bemitleiden; **com·mis·er·a·tion** [⁓'reiʃən] Mitleid *n* (*for* mit).

com·mis·sar *pol.* [kɔmi'sɑ:] Kommissar *m*.

com·mis·sar·i·at [kɔmi'sɛəriət] Kommissariat *n*; ⚔ Intendantur *f*; **com·mis·sar·y** ['⁓səri] Kommissar *m*; ⚔ Intendanturbeamte *m*.

com·mis·sion [kə'miʃən] **1.** Auftrag *m*; Übertragung *f von Macht etc.* (*to s.o.* auf j.); Begehung *f e-s Verbrechens*; Provision *f*; Kommission *f*, Ausschuß *m*; (Offiziers)Patent *n*; Bestallung *f*; ⚓ Bereitschaft *f*; ⁓ *sale* Kommissionsverkauf *m*; *on* ⁓ in Kommission; **2.** beauftragen; bevollmächtigen; ⚔ bestallen; ⚓ in Dienst stellen; **com·mis·sion·aire** [⁓'nɛə] Portier *m*; **com'mis·sion·er** Bevollmächtigte *m*, *f*; Beauftragte *m*, *f*; Kommissar *m*.

com·mit [kə'mit] anvertrauen; übergeben, (*parl.* e-r Kommission) überweisen; *Verbrechen etc.* begehen; bloßstellen; ⁓ (*o.s.* sich) festlegen (*to* auf *acc.*); (sich) verpflichten (*to* zu); ⁓ (*to prison*) in Untersuchungshaft nehmen; ⁓ *for trial* zur Aburteilung überweisen; **com'mit·ment** Überweisung *f* (*parl.* an eine Kommission); Verhängung *f* der Haft; Bindung *f*, Verpflichtung *f*; **com'mit·tal** = *commitment*; Verübung *f*, Begehung *f*; ⁓ *order* Haftanordnung *f*; **com'mit·tee** [⁓ti] Komitee *n*, Ausschuß *m*.

com·mode [kə'məud] Kommode *f*; Nachtstuhl *m*; **com'mo·di·ous** □ [⁓djəs] geräumig; **com·mod·i·ty** [kə'mɔditi] Ware *f* (*mst pl.*), Gebrauchsartikel *m*; ⁓ *value* Sachwert *m*.

com·mo·dore ⚓ ['kɔmədɔ:] Kommodore *m*, Geschwaderführer *m*.

com·mon ['kɔmən] **1.** □ (all)gemein; gewöhnlich; gemeinschaftlich, gemeinsam; öffentlich; gemein (*niedrig*); *of* ⁓ *gender gr.* beiderlei Geschlechts; ⁓ *noun* Gattungsname *m*; ♀ *Council* Gemeinderat *m*; *Book of* ♀ *Prayer das* anglikanische Gebetbuch; ⁓ *weal* Gemeinwohl *n*; *in* ⁓ gemeinsam (*with* mit); *in* ⁓ *with fig.* genau wie; **2.** Gemeindewiese *f*; **com·mon·al·ty** ['⁓nlti] *das* gemeine Volk; **'com·mon·er** Bürger *m*, Gemeine *m*, Nichtadlige *m*; Mitglied *n* des Unterhauses.

com·mon...: ⁓ **law** Gewohnheitsrecht *n*; ♀ **Mar·ket** Gemeinsamer Markt *m*; **'⁓·place 1.** Gemeinplatz *m*; **2.** gewöhnlich, alltäglich; Alltags...; abgedroschen; **'⁓-room** Gemeinschaftsraum *m für Studenten, Lehrer od. Dozenten*.

com·mons ['kɔmənz] *pl. das* gemeine Volk; gemeinschaftliche Kost *f*; *short* ⁓ schmale Kost *f*; *mst House of* ♀ Unterhaus *n*.

com·mon...: ⁓ **sense** gesunder Menschenverstand *m*; **'⁓·wealth** Gemeinwesen *n*, Staat *m*; *bsd.* Republik *f*, Freistaat *m*; *the British* ♀ das Commonwealth; *the* ♀ *of Australia* der Australische Staatenbund.

com·mo·tion [kə'məuʃən] Erschütterung *f*; Aufruhr *m*; Aufregung *f*; Aufsehen *n*.

com·mu·nal □ ['kɔmjunl] gemeinschaftlich; Gemeinschafts...; innerhalb der Gemeinde; Kommunal..., Gemeinde...; **com·mu·nal·ize** ['⁓nəlaiz] kommunalisieren; eingemeinden.

com·mune 1. [kə'mju:n] sich vertraulich besprechen, zu Rate gehen; **2.** ['kɔmju:n] Gemeinde *f*, Kommune *f*.

com·mu·ni·ca·bil·i·ty [kəmju:nikə'biliti] Mitteilbarkeit *f*; **com'mu·ni·ca·ble** □ mitteilbar; **com'mu·ni·cant** Kommunikant(in); **com'mu·ni·cate** [⁓keit] *v/t.* mitteilen;

v/i. das Abendmahl nehmen, kommunizieren; in Verbindung stehen, sich in Verbindung setzen (*with* mit); **com·mu·niˈca·tion** Mitteilung *f*; Verständigung *f*; Verbindung *f*; *be in ~ with* in Verbindung stehen mit; *~ cord* 🚃 Notbremse *f*; **comˈmu·ni·ca·tive** □ [~kətiv] mitteilsam, gesprächig; **comˈmu·ni·ca·tor** [~keitə] Mitteilende *m*, *f*; *tel.* Zeichengeber *m*; 🚃 Notbremse *f*.

com·mun·ion [kəmˈjuːnjən] Gemeinschaft *f*; Kirchen-, Glaubensgemeinschaft *f*; *eccl.* Abendmahl *n*.

com·mu·ni·qué [kəˈmjuːnikei] Kommuniqué *n*, amtliche Verlautbarung *f*.

com·mu·nism [ˈkɔmjunizəm] Kommunismus *m*; **ˈcom·mu·nist 1.** Kommunist(in); **2.** = **com·muˈnis·tic** (*~ally*) kommunistisch.

com·mu·nity [kəˈmjuːniti] Gemeinschaft *f*; Gemeinde *f*; Gemeinwesen *n*; *the ~* der Staat; *~ ownership* öffentliches Eigentum *n*; *~ service* Gemeinschaftsdienst *m*; *~ spirit* Gemeinschaftsgeist *m*; *~ of interests* Interessengemeinschaft *f*; **~ cen·tre** Gemeinschaftshaus *n*; **~ chest** *Am.* Wohlfahrtsfonds *m*.

com·mu·nize [ˈkɔmjunaiz] sozialisieren; kommunistisch machen.

com·mut·a·ble [kəˈmjuːtəbl] ablösbar; umwandelbar; **com·mu·ta·tion** [kɔmjuːˈteiʃən] Vertauschung *f*; Umwandlung *f* (*for, into* in *acc.*); Ablösung *f*; Strafmilderung *f*; *~ ticket Am.* Zeitkarte *f*; **com·mu·ta·tive** [kəˈmjuːtətiv] wechselseitig; Tausch...; **com·mu·ta·tor** ⚡ [ˈkɔmjuːteitə] Stromwender *m*; **com·mute** [kəˈmjuːt] (*for, into*) *Verpflichtung* ablösen (durch); *Strafe* (mildernd) umwandeln (in *acc.*); *Zahlung* umwandeln (in *acc.*); *Am.* pendeln, (täglich) hin- u. herfahren; **comˈmut·er** *Am.* Pendler *m*.

com·pact 1. [ˈkɔmpækt] Vertrag *m*; Kompaktpuder *m*; **2.** [kəmˈpækt] dicht, fest; knapp, bündig; **3.** [~] fest verbinden; **comˈpact·ness** Dichtigkeit *f*, Festigkeit *f*.

com·pan·ion [kəmˈpænjən] Gefährte *m*, Gefährtin *f*; Kamerad(in); Gesellschafter(in); ⚕ Kompagnon *m*; ⚓ Kajütskappe *f*; Handbuch *n*; *~ in arms* Waffenbruder *m*; **comˈpan·ion·a·ble** □ gesellig; **comˈpan·ion·ate** [~nit]: *~ marriage* Kameradschaftsehe *f*; **comˈpan·ion·ship** Gesellschaft *f*; Genossenschaft *f*.

com·pa·ny [ˈkʌmpəni] Gesellschaft *f*; ⚕ *u.* ⚔ Kompanie *f*; Handelsgesellschaft *f*; Genossenschaft *f*, Innung *f*; ⚓ Mannschaft *f*; *thea.* Truppe *f*; *be good* (*bad*) *~* ein guter (schlechter) Gesellschafter sein; *bear s.o. ~* j-m Gesellschaft leisten; *have ~* Gäste haben; *keep ~ with* verkehren mit.

com·pa·ra·ble □ [ˈkɔmpərəbl] vergleichbar; **com·par·a·tive** [kəmˈpærətiv] **1.** □ vergleichend; verhältnismäßig; *~ degree* = **2.** *gr.* Komparativ *m*; **comˈpar·a·tive·ly** ziemlich; vergleichsweise; **com·pare** [~ˈpɛə] **1.** *beyond ~, without ~, past ~* unvergleichlich; **2.** *v/t.* vergleichen (*with* mit); gleichstellen (*to* mit); *gr.* steigern; (*as*) *~d with* im Vergleich zu; *v/i.* sich vergleichen (lassen); **com·par·i·son** [~ˈpærisn] Vergleich *m*; *gr.* Steigerung *f*; *in ~ with* im Vergleich zu.

com·part·ment [kəmˈpɑːtmənt] Abteilung *f*; ⚠ Fach *n*, Feld *n*; 🚃 (Wagen)Abteil *n*.

com·pass [ˈkʌmpəs] **1.** Bereich *m*; ♪ Umfang *m*; Kompaß *m*; (*oft pair of*) *~es pl.* Zirkel *m*; **2.** herumgehen um; einschließen; *Zweck* erreichen; planen; anstiften.

com·pas·sion [kəmˈpæʃən] Mitleid *n*, -gefühl *n*; *have ~ on* Mitleid haben mit; **comˈpas·sion·ate** □ [~nit] mitleidig; *on ~ grounds* aus Mitleid.

com·pat·i·bil·i·ty [kəmpætəˈbiliti] Vereinbarkeit *f*, Verträglichkeit *f*; **comˈpat·i·ble** □ vereinbar, verträglich; schicklich, passend.

com·pa·tri·ot [kəmˈpætriət] Landsmann *m*.

com·peer [kɔmˈpiə] (Standes)Genosse *m*, Genossin *f*.

com·pel [kəmˈpel] *j.* zwingen, nötigen; *et.* erzwingen, zu *et.* zwingen.

com·pen·di·ous □ [kəmˈpendiəs] kurz(gefaßt), gedrängt; **comˈpen·di·ous·ness** Kürze *f*, Gedrängtheit *f*.

com·pen·di·um [kəmˈpendiəm] Kompendium *n*, Abriß *m*.

com·pen·sate ['kɔmpenseit] *v/t. j.* entschädigen (*for* für; *with* mit; *by* durch); *et.* ersetzen; ausgleichen; ⊕ kompensieren; *v/i.* ~ *for* Ersatz leisten für, entschädigen für; *et.* ausgleichen, wettmachen; **com·pen'sa·tion** Ersatz *m*; Entschädigung *f*; Ausgleich(ung *f*) *m*; *Am.* Vergütung *f* (= *Gehalt*); ⊕ Kompensation *f*; **com'pen·sa·tive** [~sətiv], **com'pen·sa·to·ry** ausgleichend.

com·père ['kɔmpɛə] **1.** Conférencier *m*; **2.** ansagen (bei).

com·pete [kəm'pi:t] sich (mit)bewerben (*for* um); konkurrieren (*with* mit); ~ *with s.o.* j-m Konkurrenz machen.

com·pe·tence, com·pe·ten·cy ['kɔmpitəns(i)] Kompetenz *f*, Befugnis *f*, Zuständigkeit *f*; Auskommen *n*; '**com·pe·tent** □ hinreichend; (leistungs)fähig; kompetent; fachkundig; berechtigt, zuständig.

com·pe·ti·tion [kɔmpi'tiʃən] Wettbewerb *m*, -streit *m*; ✝ Konkurrenz *f*; *rifle* ~ Preisschießen *n*; **com·pet·i·tive** □ [kəm'petitiv] wetteifernd; Konkurrenz...; **com'pet·i·tor** Mitbewerber(in); Konkurrent(in).

com·pi·la·tion [kɔmpi'leiʃən] Zs.-stellung *f*, Kompilation *f*; **com·pile** [kəm'pail] zs.-tragen, -stellen (*from* aus); sammeln.

com·pla·cence, com·pla·cen·cy [kəm'pleisns(i)] Selbstzufriedenheit *f*; **com'pla·cent** □ selbstzufrieden, selbstgefällig.

com·plain [kəm'plein] (sich be)klagen, sich beschweren (*about*, *of* über *acc.*; *that* daß; *to* bei); reklamieren; **com'plain·ant** Kläger(in); **com'plain·er** Klagende *m*; Beschwerdeführer(in); **com'plaint** Klage *f*, Beschwerde *f*; Reklamation *f*; ⚕ Leiden *n*.

com·plai·sance [kəm'pleizəns] Gefälligkeit *f*; Entgegenkommen *n*; Höflichkeit *f*; **com'plai·sant** □ gefällig; entgegenkommend; höflich.

com·ple·ment ['kɔmplimənt] **1.** Ergänzung *f* (*a. gr.*); volle Anzahl *f od.* Stärke *f*; ⚓ Komplement *n*; **2.** ergänzen; **com·ple'men·tal, com·ple'men·ta·ry** ergänzend (*to acc.*); Ergänzungs...; Komplementär...

com·plete [kəm'pli:t] **1.** □ vollständig, ganz; völlig, vollkommen; **2.** vervollständigen; -kommnen; ergänzen; vollenden, abschließen; **com'plete·ness** Vollständigkeit *f*; **com'ple·tion** Vervollständigung *f*; -kommnung *f*; Vollendung *f*, Abschluß *m*; Erfüllung *f*; Ergänzung *f*.

com·plex ['kɔmpleks] **1.** □ zs.-gesetzt; *fig.* kompliziert, verwickelt; ~ *sentence gr.* Satzgefüge *n*; **2.** Gesamtheit *f*, (*engS. seelischer*) Komplex *m*; **com·plex·ion** [kəm'plekʃən] Aussehen *n*; Charakter *m*, Zug *m*; Gesichtsfarbe *f*, Teint *m*; **com'plex·i·ty** Kompliziert-, Verwickeltheit *f*; Verwick(e)lung *f*.

com·pli·ance [kəm'plaiəns] Einwilligung *f*; Willfährigkeit *f*; Einverständnis *n* (*with* mit); *in* ~ *with* gemäß; **com'pli·ant** □ willfährig; gefällig.

com·pli·cate ['kɔmplikeit] komplizieren, erschweren; '**com·pli·cat·ed** kompliziert, schwierig, verwickelt; **com·pli'ca·tion** Verwick(e)lung *f*; ⚕ Komplikation *f*.

com·plic·i·ty [kəm'plisiti] Mitschuld *f* (*in* an *dat.*).

com·pli·ment 1. ['kɔmplimənt] Kompliment *n*, Lob *n*; Schmeichelei *f*; Gruß *m*; **2.** ['~ment] *v/t.* (*on*) beglückwünschen (zu); *j-m* Komplimente machen (über *acc.*); **com·pli'men·ta·ry** höflich; Höflichkeits...; ~ *dinner* Festessen *n*; ~ *ticket* Freikarte *f*.

com·ply [kəm'plai] sich fügen; nachkommen, entsprechen, willfahren (*with dat.*); einwilligen; ~ *with the rules* die Vorschriften befolgen.

com·po·nent [kəm'pəunənt] **1.** Bestandteil *m*; **2.** e-n Teil bildend; ~ *part* = ~ *1*.

com·port [kəm'pɔ:t] übereinstimmen (*with* mit); ~ *o.s.* sich betragen.

com·pose [kəm'pəuz] zs.-setzen; komponieren, verfassen; schriftstellern; zurechtlegen, ordnen; *Streit* beilegen; *Gemüt* beruhigen; *typ.* setzen; **com'posed**, *adv.* **com'pos·ed·ly** [~zidli] ruhig, gesetzt, gelassen; **com'pos·er** Komponist (-in); Verfasser(in); **com'pos·ing 1.** beruhigend; **2.** Zs.-setzen *n*; Komponieren *n*; Dichten *n*; ~ *machine* Setzmaschine *f*; ~ *room*

Setzerei *f*; **com·pos·ite** ['kɔmpəzit] **1.** zs.-gesetzt; **2.** *konkr.* Zs.-setzung *f*; ⚘ Komposite *f*; **com·po'si·tion** Zs.-setzung *f*; Abfassung *f*; 𝄞, ♪, *paint.* Komposition *f*; (Schrift)Satz *m*; (Schul)Aufsatz *m*; ✝ Vergleich *m*; **com·pos·i·tor** [kəm'pɔzitə] (Schrift)Setzer *m*; **com·post** ['kɔmpɔst] **1.** Kompost *m*; **2.** kompostieren; **com·po·sure** [kəm'pəuʒə] Fassung *f*, Gemütsruhe *f*, Gelassenheit *f*.

com·pote ['kɔmpɔt] Kompott *n*.

com·pound[1] **1.** ['kɔmpaund] zs.-gesetzt; ~ *fracture* ⚕ komplizierter Bruch *m*; ~ *interest* Zinseszinsen *m/pl.*; **2.** [~] Zs.-setzung *f*, Verbindung *f*; *a.* ~ *word gr.* Kompositum *n*; **3.** [kəm'paund] *v/t.* zs.-setzen; *Streit* beilegen; *v/i.* sich einigen; ✝ sich vergleichen, akkordieren (*for* über *acc.*).

com·pound[2] ['kɔmpaund] eingezäuntes Gelände *n*.

com·pre·hend [kɔmpri'hend] umfassen; begreifen, verstehen.

com·pre·hen·si·ble □ [kɔmpri'hensəbl] verständlich; **com·pre'hen·sion** Verständnis *n*; Fassungskraft *f*; Umfang *m*; **com·pre'hen·sive** □ umfassend; ~ *insurance* Vollkaskoversicherung *f*; ~ *school* Gesamtschule *f*; **com·pre'hen·sive·ness** Umfassende *n*.

com·press 1. [kəm'pres] zs.-drücken, -pressen; **2.** ['kɔmpres] ⚕ Kompresse *f*; **com·pressed** [kəm'prest] komprimiert; ~ *air* Preß-, Druckluft *f*; **com'press·i·ble** komprimierbar; **com·pres·sion** [~'preʃən] Zs.-drücken *n*; *phys.* Verdichtung *f*, Kompression *f*; ⊕ Druck *m*; **com'pres·sor** [~sə] ⊕ Kompressor *m*.

com·prise [kəm'praiz] umfassen, einschließen, enthalten.

com·pro·mise ['kɔmprəmaiz] **1.** Kompromiß *n*, *m*; Vergleich *m*; **2.** *v/t.* *Streit* beilegen; bloßstellen, kompromittieren; *v/i.* sich vergleichen, ein(en) Kompromiß schließen (*on* über *acc.*).

comp·trol·ler [kən'trəulə] Rechnungsprüfer *m*.

com·pul·sion [kəm'pʌlʃən] Zwang *m*; **com'pul·sive** [~siv] zwanghaft; **com'pul·so·ry** [~səri] obligatorisch; zwangsmäßig, Zwangs...; Pflicht...; ~ *military service* Wehrpflicht *f*; ~ *subject* Pflichtfach *n*.

com·punc·tion [kəm'pʌŋkʃən] Gewissensbisse *m/pl.*; Reue *f*; Bedenken *n*.

com·put·a·ble [kəm'pju:təbl] berechen-, zählbar; **com·pu·ta·tion** [kɔmpju:'teiʃən] Rechnung *f*; Berechnung *f*; **com·pu'ta·tor** = *computer*; **com·pute** [kəm'pju:t] (be-, er)rechnen; schätzen (*at* auf *acc.*); **com'put·er** Computer *m*; Elektronenrechner *m*; ~-*controlled* computergesteuert; ~ *dating* Heiratsvermittlung *f* mit Hilfe e-s Computers; ~ *science* Informatik *f*.

com·rade ['kɔmrid] Kamerad *m*; Genosse *m*; **'com·rade·ship** Kameradschaft *f*.

con[1] [kɔn] fleißig studieren, auswendig lernen.

con[2] ⚓ [~] *Schiff* leiten, steuern.

con[3] [~] *abbr.* = *contra* wider; *pro and* ~ für und wider; *the pros and* ~*s* die Gründe für und wider.

con[4] *Am. sl.* [~] **1.** *in Zssgn s. confidence man*; **2.** 'reinlegen (*betrügen*).

con·cat·e·nate [kɔn'kætineit] *mst fig.* verketten; **con·cat·e'na·tion** Verkettung *f* (*a. fig.*).

con·cave □ ['kɔn'keiv] konkav; Hohl...; **con·cav·i·ty** [~'kæviti] Konkavität *f*; Höhlung *f*; Hohlrundung *f*.

con·ceal [kən'si:l] verbergen; *fig.* verhehlen, -heimlichen, -schweigen, -bergen (*from s.o.* vor j-m); **con'ceal·ment** Verbergung *f etc.*; Verborgenheit *f*; *a. place of* ~ Versteck *n*.

con·cede [kən'si:d] zugestehen; einräumen; gewähren; nachgeben; **con'ced·ed·ly** zugestandenermaßen.

con·ceit [kən'si:t] Einbildung *f*, Selbstüberschätzung *f*; spitzfindiger Gedanke *m*; übertriebenes sprachliches Bild *n*; *out of* ~ *with* unzufrieden mit; **con'ceit·ed** □ eingebildet, eitel, dünkelhaft; **con'ceit·ed·ness** Dünkel *m*.

con·ceiv·a·ble □ [kən'si:vəbl] denkbar; begreiflich; **con'ceive** *v/i.* empfangen (*schwanger werden*); sich denken (*of acc.*); *v/t.* *Kind* empfangen; sich (aus)denken, sich vorstellen; erdenken, ersinnen; *Abneigung* fassen; ~*d in* ... ausgedrückt

in ... (*dat.*).
con·cen·trate ['kɔnsəntreit] **1.** (sich) zs.-ziehen, (sich) konzentrieren (*a. fig.*); verdichten; ⚗ sättigen; **2.** Konzentrat *n* (*angereicherter Stoff*); **con·cen'tra·tion** Konzentration *f*, Zs.-ziehung *f*, Zs.-fassung *f*; ⚗ Sättigung *f*; ~ *camp* Konzentrationslager *n*; **con'cen·tre, con'cen·ter** [~tə] (sich) konzentrieren, (sich) vereinigen; **con'cen·tric** (~*ally*) konzentrisch.
con·cept ['kɔnsept] Begriff *m*, Vorstellung *f*; **con·cep·tion** [kən'sepʃən] Begreifen *n*; Vorstellung *f*, Begriff *m*, Idee *f*; *biol.* Empfängnis *f*; **con·cep·tu·al** [kən'septjuəl] begrifflich.
con·cern [kən'sə:n] **1.** Angelegenheit *f*, Sache *f*, Anliegen *n*; Interesse *n* (*in* an *dat.*; *for* für); Unruhe *f*, Sorge *f*; Beziehung *f* (*with* zu); ✝ Geschäft *n*, (industrielles) Unternehmen *n*; F Ding *n*; **2.** betreffen, angehen, interessieren; ~ *o.s. with* sich befassen mit; ~ *o.s. about od. for* sich kümmern um; *be* ~*ed* in Betracht kommen; *be* ~*ed that* sich Sorgen darüber machen, daß; *I am* ~*ed to inf.* es kommt mir darauf an zu *inf.*; *be* ~*ed with* sich befassen mit, behandeln; **con'cerned** □ interessiert, beteiligt (*in* an *dat.*); bekümmert, betroffen (*at, about, for* um, wegen); *those* ~ die Beteiligten; **con'cern·ing** *prp.* betreffend, betreffs, in betreff, über, wegen, hinsichtlich.
con·cert 1. ['kɔnsət] Konzert *n*; ['~sə:t] Einverständnis *n*; **2.** [kən'sə:t] ein Einverständnis schaffen, verabreden; *Kräfte* zs.-fassen; **con'cert·ed** gemeinsam, gemeinschaftlich; ♪ mehrstimmig; **con·cer·ti·na** ♪ [kɔnsə'ti:nə] *Art* Ziehharmonika *f*; **con·cer·to** ♪ [kən'ʃtə:təu] (Solo-) Konzert *n*.
con·ces·sion [kən'seʃən] Zugeständnis *n*; Erlaubnis *f*, Genehmigung *f*; zugewiesenes Land *n*; **con·ces·sion·aire** [~'nɛə] Konzessionär *m*.
con·ces·sive □ [kən'sesiv] einräumend.
conch [kɔŋk] *große* Seemuschel *f*.
con·cil·i·ate [kən'silieit] aus-, versöhnen; ausgleichen; in Einklang bringen; *Liebe etc.* gewinnen; **con·cil·i'a·tion** Aus-, Versöhnung *f*; Ausgleich *m*; **con'cil·i·a·tor** Vermittler *m*; **con'cil i·a·to·ry** [~ətəri] versöhnend, vermittelnd; ~ *proposal* Vorschlag *m* zur Güte.
con·cin·ni·ty [kən'siniti] Feinheit *f*, Eleganz *f des Stils*.
con·cise □ [kən'sais] kurz, bündig, knapp; **con'cise·ness** Kürze *f*.
con·clave ['kɔnkleiv] Konklave *n*.
con·clude [kən'klu:d] schließen, beschließen (*beendigen*; *das Ende bilden*); *Brief, Geschäft etc.* abschließen; folgern; beschließen, sich entscheiden (*to inf.* zu *inf.*); *to be* ~*d* Schluß folgt; **con'clud·ing** Schluß...
con·clu·sion [kən'klu:ʒən] Schluß *m*, Ende *n*; Abschluß *m e-s Vertrags etc.*; Schluß *m*, Folgerung *f*; Beschluß *m*; *in* ~ schließlich; *try* ~*s with* sich messen mit; **con'clu·sive** [~siv] □ beweiskräftig, schlüssig; überzeugend; endgültig.
con·coct [kən'kɔkt] zs.-brauen; *fig.* aussinnen, -hecken; **con'coc·tion** Zs.-brauen *n*; Gebräu *n*; *fig.* Erfindung *f*.
con·com·i·tance, con·com·i·tan·cy [kən'kɔmitəns(i)] Zs.-bestehen *n*, Gleichzeitigkeit *f*; **con'com·i·tant 1.** □ begleitend; **2.** begleitender Umstand *m*.
con·cord ['kɔŋkɔ:d] Eintracht *f*; Übereinstimmung *f* (*a. gr.*); ♪ Harmonie *f*, Zs.-klang *m*; **con·cord·ance** [kən'kɔ:dəns] Übereinstimmung *f*; *eccl.* Konkordanz *f*; **con'cord·ant** □ übereinstimmend; einstimmig; ♪ harmonisch; **con'cor·dat** *eccl.* [~dæt] Konkordat *n*.
con·course ['kɔŋkɔ:s] Zusammen-, Auflauf *m*; Menge *f*; *Am.* Bahnhofs-, Schalterhalle *f*.
con·crete 1. □ ['kɔnkri:t] konkret; Beton...; **2.** [~] Beton *m*; *phls., gr.* Konkretum *n*; *in the* ~ im konkreten Falle; **3.** [kən'kri:t] *zu e-r Masse* verbinden; ['kɔnkri:t] betonieren; ~ **noun** *gr.* Konkretum *n*; **con·cre·tion** [kən'kri:ʃən] Zs.-wachsung *f*; Festwerden *n*, Verhärtung *f*.
con·cu·bi·nage [kɔn'kju:binidʒ] Konkubinat *n*; **con·cu·bine** ['kɔŋkjubain] Konkubine *f*.
con·cu·pis·cence [kən'kju:pisəns] Sinnenlust *f*, Begierde *f*; **con'cupis·cent** lüstern; sinnlich.

con·cur [kən'kəː] zs.-treffen, -wirken; übereinstimmen (*with* mit; *in* in *dat.*); mitwirken (*to* zu); **con·cur·rence** [~'kʌrəns] Zusammentreffen *n*; Übereinstimmung *f*; Einverständnis *n*; Mitwirkung *f*; *in ~ with* gemeinschaftlich mit; **con'cur·rent** □ zs.-treffend *etc.* (*s. concur*); gleichzeitig.

con·cus·sion [kən'kʌʃən]: *~ of the brain* Gehirnerschütterung *f*.

con·demn [kən'dem] verdammen; verurteilen (*to* zu) (*a. fig.*); (als untauglich) verwerfen; *Kranke* aufgeben; für verfallen erklären, beschlagnahmen; *his looks ~ him* s-e Augen verraten ihn; *~ed cell* Zelle *f* für die zum Tode Verurteilten; **con'dem·na·ble** [~nəbl] verdammenswert, verwerflich; **con·dem·na·tion** [kɔndem'neiʃən] Verurteilung *f*; Verdammung *f*; Verwerfung *f*; **con·dem·na·to·ry** □ [kən'demnətəri] verurteilend.

con·den·sa·ble [kən'densəbl] verdichtbar; **con·den·sa·tion** [kɔnden'seiʃən] Verdichtung *f*; **con·dense** [kən'dens] (sich) verdichten; ⊕ kondensieren; abkürzen, zs.-drängen; **con'dens·er** Verdichter *m*; ⚡, ⊕ Kondensator *m*.

con·de·scend [kɔndi'send] sich herablassen; geruhen; **con·de'scend·ing** □ herablassend; **con·de'scen·sion** Herablassung *f*.

con·dign □ [kən'dain] angemessen; gehörig.

con·di·ment ['kɔndimənt] Würze *f*.

con·di·tion [kən'diʃən] **1.** Zustand *m*; Stand *m*, Stellung *f*; Bedingung *f*; Kondition *f*; Lage *f*; Befinden *n*; *~s pl.* Verhältnisse *n/pl.*, Umstände *m/pl.*, Lage *f*; *on ~ that* unter der Bedingung, daß; *out of ~* in schlechter Verfassung; **2.** bedingen; ausmachen, vereinbaren; in e-n bestimmten Zustand bringen, regulieren; **con'di·tion·al** □ bedingt (*on, upon* durch); Bedingungs..., Konditional...; *~ (mood) gr.* Konditionalis *m*; **con·di·tion·al·i·ty** [~'næliti] Bedingtheit *f*; **con'di·tion·al·ly** [~əli] bedingungsweise; **con'di·tioned** bedingt; (*mst in Zssgn*) beschaffen; geartet; **con'di·tioned re·flex** *psych.* bedingter Reflex *m*.

con·dole [kən'dəul] kondolieren, sein Beileid bezeigen (*with s.o.* j-m); **con'do·lence** Beileid *n*.

con·do·min·i·um ['kɔndə'miniəm] Kondominium *n* (*gemeinsame Herrschaft*); *Am.* Eigentumswohnung *f*, Haus *n* mit Eigentumswohnungen.

con·do·na·tion [kɔndəu'neiʃən] Verzeihung *f*; **con·done** [kən'dəun] *Vergehen* verzeihen.

con·dor *orn.* ['kɔndɔː] Kondor *m*.

con·duce [kən'djuːs] führen, dienen (*to* zu); **con'du·cive** dienlich, förderlich (*to dat.*).

con·duct 1. ['kɔndʌkt] Führung *f*, Leitung *f*; Verhalten *n*, Betragen *n*; Verwaltung *f*; **2.** [kən'dʌkt] führen, geleiten; durchführen; ♪ dirigieren; verwalten; *Tätigkeit* ausüben; *phys.* leiten; *~ o.s.* sich (auf)führen *od.* benehmen; **con·duct·i·bil·i·ty** [kəndʌkti'biliti] *phys.* Leitfähigkeit *f*; **con'duct·i·ble** [~təbl] *phys.* leitfähig; leitend; **con'duct·ing** Leitungs...; **con'duc·tion** Leitung *f*; **con'duc·tive** □ [~tiv] *phys.* leitend; **con·duc·tiv·i·ty** [kɔndʌk'tiviti] *phys.* Leitfähigkeit *f*; **con·duc·tor** [kən'dʌktə] Führer *m*; Leiter *m* (*a. phys.*); Schaffner *m*; ♪ Dirigent *m*; ⚡ Leiter *m*; Blitzableiter *m*; **con'duc·tress** Schaffnerin *f*.

con·duit ['kɔndit] Leitungsröhre *f*; Kanal *m*; ['~djuit] ⚡ Isolierrohr *n*.

cone [kəun] Kegel *m*; ♀ Zapfen *m*.

co·ney ['kəuni] Kaninchen *n*.

con·fab F ['kɔnfæb] **1.** = **con·fab·u·late** [kən'fæbjuleit] plaudern; **2.** = **con·fab·u'la·tion** Geplauder *n*.

con·fec·tion [kən'fekʃən] *Schneiderei*: Konfektionsartikel *m*; Konfekt *n*; **con·fec·tion·er** [~'fekʃnə] Konditor *m*; **con'fec·tion·er·y** Konfekt *n*; Konditorei *f*; *bsd. Am.* Süßwarengeschäft *n*.

con·fed·er·a·cy [kən'fedərəsi] Bündnis *n*, Bundesgenossenschaft *f*; Komplott *n*; *the* ♀ *Am.* die Konföderation *der 11 Südstaaten 1860 bis 1861*; **con'fed·er·ate 1.** [~rit] verbündet; **2.** [~rit] Bundesgenosse *m*, Verbündete *m*; Mitschuldige *m*; **3.** [~reit] (sich) verbünden; **con·fed·er'a·tion** Bund *m*, Bündnis *n*; Staatenbund *m*.

con·fer [kən'fəː] *v/t.* übertragen,

verleihen, erteilen; *Gunst* erweisen (*alle: on dat.*); *v/i.* sich besprechen, sich beraten, Rücksprache nehmen (*with* mit; *about, upon* über *acc.*); **con·fer·ence** ['kɔnfərəns] Konferenz *f*, Besprechung *f*, Beratung *f*; Verhandlung *f*.

con·fess [kən'fes] bekennen, gestehen; beichten; *eccl. j-m* die Beichte abnehmen; ~ *to* sich bekennen zu; **con'fess·ed·ly** [~sidli] zugestandenermaßen; **con'fes·sion** [~ʃən] Geständnis *n*; Bekenntnis *n*; *eccl.* Beichte *f*; **con'fes·sion·al** [~ʃənl] **1.** konfessionell; **2.** Beichtstuhl *m*; **con'fes·sor** [~sə] Bekenner *m*; *eccl.* Beichtvater *m*.

con·fet·ti [kən'feti:] *pl.* Konfetti *pl.*

con·fi·dant [kɔnfi'dænt] Vertraute *m*; **con·fi'dante** [~] Vertraute *f*.

con·fide [kən'faid] anvertrauen (*to s.o.* j-m); vertrauen, sich verlassen (*in* auf *acc.*).

con·fi·dence ['kɔnfidəns] Vertrauen *n* (*in* auf *acc.*); Zuversicht *f*; Zutrauen *n*; vertrauliche Mitteilung *f*; ~ **game** = *confidence trick*; ~ **man** Schwindler *m*, Hochstapler *m*; ~ **trick** Bauernfängerei *f*; **'con·fi·dent** □ vertrauend (*of* auf *acc.*); vertrauensvoll; überzeugt, zuversichtlich; **con·fi·den·tial** □ [~'denʃəl] vertraulich; vertraut; ~ *clerk* Privatsekretär *m*.

con·fig·u·ra·tion [kənfigju'reiʃən] Gestalt(ung) *f*.

con·fine **1.** ['kɔnfain] *mst* ~*s pl.* Grenze *f*; **2.** [kən'fain] begrenzen; ein-, beschränken (*to* auf *acc.*); einsperren; *be* ~*d to bed* das Bett hüten müssen; *be* ~*d (of)* entbunden werden (von), niederkommen (mit); **con'fine·ment** Einsperrung *f*; Haft *f*; Beschränkung *f*; Entbindung *f*.

con·firm [kən'fə:m] (be)kräftigen; bestätigen; aufrechterhalten; *eccl.* konfirmieren, firmen; **con·fir·ma·tion** [kɔnfə'meiʃən] Bestätigung *f*; Konfirmation *f*, Firmung *f*; **con·firm·a·tive** □ [kən'fə:mətiv], **con'firm·a·to·ry** [~təri] bestätigend; **con'firmed** fest, bestimmt; chronisch (*bsd.* ⚕); unheilbar.

con·fis·cate ['kɔnfiskeit] einziehen, beschlagnahmen, konfiszieren; **con·fis'ca·tion** Beschlagnahme *f*; **con'fis·ca·to·ry** [~kətəri] konfiszierend.

con·fla·gra·tion [kɔnflə'greiʃən] großer Brand *m*, Feuersbrunst *f*.

con·flict **1.** ['kɔnflikt] Konflikt *m*; Zs.-stoß *m*; Kampf *m*, Zwist *m*, Streit *m*; *fig.* Widerstreit *m*; **2.** [kən'flikt] (*with*) sich im Konflikt befinden (mit); nicht übereinstimmen (mit).

con·flu·ence ['kɔnfluəns], **con·flux** ['~flʌks] Zs.-fluß *m*; Zulauf *m*, Zs.-strömen *n von Menschen*; **con·flu·ent** ['~fluənt] **1.** zs.-fließend, zs.-laufend; **2.** Zu-, Nebenfluß *m*.

con·form [kən'fɔ:m] *v/t.* anpassen; *v/i.* ~ *to* sich fügen in (*acc.*), sich richten nach, sich anpassen an (*acc.*); ~ *with* entsprechen (*dat.*); **con'form·a·ble** □ (*to*) übereinstimmend (mit); entsprechend (*dat.*); nachgiebig (*dat.*); **con·for·ma·tion** [kɔnfɔ:'meiʃən] Bau *m*, Gestalt *f*; **con·form·ist** [kən'fɔ:mist] Anhänger *m* der anglikanischen Staatskirche; **con'form·i·ty** Übereinstimmung *f*; *in* ~ *with* in Übereinstimmung *od.* übereinstimmend mit; gemäß.

con·found [kən'faund] vermengen; verwechseln; *j.* verwirren; *et.* vereiteln; ~ *it!* F verdammt!; ~ *you!* F zum Henker mit dir!; **con'found·ed** □ F verdammt.

con·fra·ter·ni·ty [kɔnfrə'tə:niti] Brüderschaft *f*.

con·front [kən'frʌnt] gegenüberstellen (*with dat.*); entgegentreten (*dat.*); entgegensehen (*dat.*); gegenüberstehen, gegenübertreten (*dat.*); *find o.s.* ~*ed with* sich ... (*dat.*) gegenübersehen; **con·fron·ta·tion** [kɔnfrʌn'teiʃən] Gegenüberstellung *f*.

con·fuse [kən'fju:z] vermischen (*a. fig.*); verwechseln; verwirren, durcheinanderbringen; bestürzt machen; **con'fused** □ verwirrt, bestürzt; verworren; **con'fu·sion** [~ʒən] Verwirrung *f*; Bestürzung *f*; Verwechslung *f*; Durcheinander *n*.

con·fut·a·ble [kən'fju:təbl] widerlegbar; **con·fu·ta·tion** [kɔnfju:'teiʃən] Widerlegung *f*; **con·fute** [kən'fju:t] widerlegen.

congé ['kɔ̃:nʒei] Entlassung *f*; *give s.o. his* ~ j. ohne weitere Umstände entlassen.

con·geal [kən'dʒi:l] erstarren (lassen) (*a. fig.*); gefrieren (lassen); gerinnen (lassen); **con'geal·a·ble** gefrier-, gerinnbar.

con·ge·la·tion [kɔndʒi'leiʃən] Gefrieren *n*, Gerinnen *n*; Erstarren *n*.

con·gen·ial □ [kən'dʒi:njəl] (geistes)verwandt, kongenial (*with dat.*); zusagend (*to dat.*); **con·ge·ni·al·i·ty** [~ni'æliti] Geistesverwandtschaft *f*.

con·gen·i·tal [kɔn'dʒenitl] angeboren; **con'gen·i·tal·ly** [~təli] von Geburt an.

con·ger (**eel**) *ichth.* ['kɔŋgə(r'i:l)] Meeraal *m*.

con·gest [kən'dʒest] (⚕ mit Blut) überfüllen; **con'ges·tion** (Blut-) Andrang *m*, Stauung *f*, Überfüllung *f*; ~ *of population* Übervölkerung *f*; *traffic* ~ Verkehrsstockung *f*.

con·glom·er·ate 1. [kən'glɔmərit] zusammengeballt; **2.** [~] Konglomerat *n*, (An)Häufung *f*; **3.** [~reit] (sich) zs.-ballen; **con·glom·er'a·tion** Anhäufung *f*, Konglomerat *n*.

con·grat·u·late [kən'grætjuleit] beglückwünschen; gratulieren (*s.o. on od. upon s.th.* j-m zu et.); **con·grat·u'la·tion** Glückwunsch *m*; **con'grat·u·la·tor** Gratulant *m*; **con'grat·u·la·to·ry** Glückwunsch...

con·gre·gate ['kɔŋgrigeit] (sich) (ver)sammeln; **con·gre'ga·tion** *eccl.* Gemeinde *f*; **con·gre'ga·tion·al** [~ʃənl] kirchengemeindlich; *eccl.* unabhängig.

con·gress ['kɔŋgres] Kongreß *m*; ⁓ *Am. pol.* Kongreß *m* (*Senat u. Repräsentantenhaus*); **con·gres·sion·al** [~'greʃənl] Kongreß...; **'Con·gress·man**, **'Con·gress·wom·an** *Am. pol.* Mitglied *n* des Repräsentantenhauses.

con·gru·ence, con·gru·en·cy ['kɔŋgruəns(i)] = *congruity*; ⩘ Kongruenz *f*; **'con·gru·ent** = *congruous*; ⩘ kongruent; **con·gru·i·ty** [~'gru:iti] Übereinstimmung *f*; Angemessenheit *f*, Geeignetheit *f*; Folgerichtigkeit *f*; **con·gru·ous** □ ['~gruəs] angemessen (*to* für); übereinstimmend (*to, mst with* mit); folgerichtig.

con·ic, con·i·cal □ ['kɔnik(əl)] konisch, kegelförmig; Kegel...; ~ *section* ⩘ Kegelschnitt *m*.

co·ni·fer ['kəunifə] Nadelholzbaum *m*; **co'nif·er·ous** zapfentragend.

con·jec·tur·al □ [kən'dʒektʃərəl] mutmaßlich; **con'jec·ture 1.** Mutmaßung *f*, Vermutung *f*; **2.** mutmaßen, vermuten.

con·join [kən'dʒɔin] (sich) verbinden; **con·joint** ['kɔndʒɔint] verbunden; **'con·joint·ly** gemeinschaftlich.

con·ju·gal □ ['kɔndʒugəl] ehelich; Ehe...; **con·ju·gate 1.** ['~geit] *v/t.* konjugieren; *v/i. biol.* sich paaren (*Zellen*); **2.** ['~git] ⚘ gepaart; **con·ju·ga·tion** [~'geiʃən] Konjugation *f*.

con·junct □ [kən'dʒʌŋkt] verbunden; **con'junc·tion** Verbindung *f*; *ast., gr.* Konjunktion *f*; Zs.-treffen *n*; **con·junc·ti·va** *anat.* [kɔndʒʌŋk'taivə] Bindehaut *f*; **con·junc·tive** [kən'dʒʌŋktiv] verbindend; ~ *mood* Konjunktiv *m*; **con'junc·tive·ly** in Verbindung, zusammen; **con·junc·ti·vi·tis** ⚕ [~'vaitis] Bindehautentzündung *f*; **con'junc·ture** [~tʃə] Zs.-treffen *n* (*von Umständen*); Krise *f*.

con·ju·ra·tion [kɔndʒuə'reiʃən] Beschwörung *f*; **con·jure** [kən'dʒuə] *v/t.* beschwören, inständig bitten; ['kʌndʒə] *v/t.* beschwören, rufen; *et. wohin* zaubern; ~ *up* heraufbeschwören; *v/i.* zaubern; **'con·jur·er, 'con·jur·or** Zauberer *m*, Zauberin *f*; Taschenspieler(in); **'con·jur·ing-trick** Zauberkunststück *n*.

conk F [kɔŋk] versagen, F streiken (*Mechanismus etc.*).

con·ker F ['kɔŋkə] (Roß)Kastanie *f*.

con man F ['kɔnmæn] = *confidence man*.

con·nate ['kɔneit] angeboren; ⚘ *u. anat.* verwachsen; **con·nat·u·ral** [kə'nætʃrəl] gleicher Natur (*to* wie); angeboren.

con·nect [kə'nekt] (sich) verbinden; ⚡ schalten; **con'nect·ed** □ verbunden; zs.-hängend (*Rede etc.*); *be* ~ *with* in Verbindung stehen mit *j-m*, beteiligt sein bei *od.* an *et.* (*dat.*); *be well* ~ gute Beziehungen haben; **con'nect·ing** Verbindungs-...; Binde...; Anschluß...; ~ *rod* Pleuelstange *f*; **con'nec·tion** *s. connexion*; **con'nec·tive** □ verbindend; ~ *tissue anat.* Bindegewebe *n.*

con·nex·ion [kəˈnekʃən] Verbindung *f*; ⚡ Schaltung *f*; *Bahn- etc.* Verbindung *f*, Anschluß *m* (*a.* ⚡); Zs.-hang *m*; Verwandtschaft *f*; Verwandte *m*, *f*; Vereinigung *f von Personen*; ✝ Kundschaft *f*; ~s *pl.* (gute) Beziehungen *f/pl.*

conn·ing-tow·er ⚓ [ˈkɔniŋtauə] Kommandoturm *m.*

con·niv·ance [kəˈnaivəns] stillschweigende Duldung *f* (*at, in, with gen.*); **conˈnive:** ~ *at* ein Auge zudrücken bei, *et.* stillschweigend dulden.

con·nois·seur [kɔnəˈsəː] (*of od. in wine, etc.* Wein- *etc.*) Kenner(in).

con·no·ta·tion [kɔnəuˈteiʃən] Begriffsinhalt *m*; (Neben)Bedeutung *f*; **conˈnote** andeuten, (zugleich) bedeuten.

con·nu·bi·al □ [kəˈnjuːbjəl] ehelich; Ehe...; verheiratet.

con·quer [ˈkɔŋkə] erobern; *fig.* erringen; überwinden; (be)siegen; **ˈcon·quer·or** Eroberer *m*; Sieger *m*; F Entscheidungsspiel *n.*

con·quest [ˈkɔŋkwest] Eroberung *f*; Errungenschaft *f.*

con·san·guin·e·ous [kɔnsæŋˈgwiniəs] blutsverwandt; **con·sanˈguin·i·ty** Blutsverwandtschaft *f.*

con·science [ˈkɔnʃəns] Gewissen *n*; *in all* ~ F wahrhaftig, sicherlich; *have the* ~ *to do* so unverschämt sein zu tun; ~ *money* Reugeld *n*, freiwillige Zahlung *f*; **ˈcon·science-less** gewissenlos.

con·sci·en·tious □ [kɔnʃiˈenʃəs] gewissenhaft; Gewissens...; ~ *objector* Kriegsdienstverweigerer *m* aus Gewissensgründen; **con·sciˈen·tious·ness** Gewissenhaftigkeit *f.*

con·scious □ [ˈkɔnʃəs] bewußt; *be* ~ *of* sich bewußt sein (*gen.*; *that* daß); **ˈcon·scious·ness** Bewußtsein *n.*

con·script ⚔ **1.** [kənˈskript] einberufen; **2.** [ˈkɔnskript] einberufen, eingezogen; **3.** [~] Dienstpflichtige *m*, Rekrut *m*; **con·scrip·tion** ⚔ [kənˈskripʃən] Einberufung *f*; *industrial* ~ Arbeitsverpflichtung *f.*

con·se·crate [ˈkɔnsikreit] weihen, einsegnen; heiligen; widmen; **con·seˈcra·tion** Weihung *f*, Einsegnung *f*; Heiligung *f*; **ˈcon·se·cra·tor** Weihende *m.*

con·sec·u·tive [kənˈsekjutiv] aufeinanderfolgend; fortlaufend (*Nummer*); *gr.* konsekutiv; **conˈsec·u·tive·ly** nacheinander, fortlaufend.

con·sen·sus [kənˈsensəs] allseitige Zu- *od.* Übereinstimmung *f.*

con·sent [kənˈsent] **1.** (*to*) Zustimmung *f* (zu), Einwilligung *f* (in *acc.*); *age of* ~ Mündigkeitsalter *n*; *with one* ~ einstimmig; **2.** (*to*) einwilligen (in *acc.*), zustimmen (*dat.*); **con·sen·tient** [~ˈsenʃənt] zustimmend.

con·se·quence [ˈkɔnsikwəns] Folge *f*, Konsequenz *f*; Wirkung *f*, Einfluß *m* (*to* auf *acc.*); Bedeutung *f* (*to* für); *in* ~ *of* infolge (*gen.*); **ˈcon·se·quent 1.** folgend; *be* ~ *on* die Folge sein von; **2.** Folge(rung) *f*, Schluß *m*; **con·se·quen·tial** □ [~ˈkwenʃəl] (er)folgend (*on, upon* aus); folgerecht; wichtigtuend; **con·se·quent·ly** [ˈ~kwəntli] folglich, daher.

con·ser·va·tion [kɔnsəːˈveiʃən] Erhaltung *f*; **con·serˈva·tion·ist** Umweltschützer *m*; **con·serv·a·tism** [kənˈsəːvətizəm] Konservatismus *m*; **conˈserv·a·tive** □ **1.** erhaltend (*of acc.*); *pol.* konservativ; vorsichtig (*Schätzung*); **2.** Konservative *m*; **conˈser·va·toire** [~twɑː] ♪ Konservatorium *n*; **conˈser·va·tor** Konservator *m*; **conˈserv·a·to·ry** [~tri] Treib-, Gewächshaus *n*; ♪ Konservatorium *n*; **conˈserve** erhalten.

con·sid·er [kənˈsidə] *v/t. geistig* betrachten; erwägen, bedenken; überlegen; beraten; *et.* in Betracht ziehen; Rücksicht nehmen auf (*acc.*); berücksichtigen; ansehen als; halten für, erachten als; meinen, glauben; *v/i.* überlegen; *all things* ~*ed* wenn man alles in Betracht zieht; **conˈsid·er·a·ble** □ ansehnlich, beträchtlich, erheblich; **conˈsid·er·a·bly** bedeutend, ziemlich, (sehr) viel; **conˈsid·er·ate** [~rit] □ rücksichtsvoll; **con·sid·er·a·tion** [~ˈreiʃən] Betrachtung *f*, Erwägung *f*, Überlegung *f*; Rücksicht *f*; Berücksichtigung *f*; wichtiger Umstand *m*; Entschädigung *f*, Vergütung *f*; Entgelt *n*, Gegenleistung *f*; ✝ Prämie *f*; *be under* ~ erwogen werden; in Betracht kommen; *take into* ~ in Erwägung *od.* Betracht ziehen; *money is no ~* auf Geld kommt es nicht an; *on no ~* unter keinen Umständen; **con'sid·er·ing** □ **1.** *prp.* in Anbetracht (*gen.*); **2.** *adv.* F den Umständen entsprechend.

con·sign [kən'sain] übergeben, -liefern; anvertrauen; ⚓ konsignieren; **con·sig·na·tion** [kɔnsai'neiʃən], **con·sign·ment** [kən'sainmənt] (Über)Sendung *f*; ⚓ Konsignation *f*; **con·sign·ee** [kɔnsai'ni:] (Waren)Empfänger *m*; **con·sign·er, con·sign·or** [kən'sainə] (Waren)Absender *m*; Verfrachter *m*.

con·sist [kən'sist] bestehen (*of* aus; *in* in *dat.*); in Einklang stehen (*with* mit); **con'sist·ence, con'sist·en·cy** Festigkeit(sgrad *m*) *f*, Konsistenz *f*, Beschaffenheit *f*; Übereinstimmung *f*; Folgerichtigkeit *f*, Konsequenz *f*; **con'sist·ent** □ übereinstimmend, vereinbar (*with* mit); folgerichtig, konsequent; *~ly a.* durchweg; **con'sis·to·ry** *eccl.* Konsistorium *n*.

con·sol·a·ble [kən'səuləbl] tröstbar, zu trösten(d); **con·so·la·tion** [kɔnsə'leiʃən] Trost *m*; *~ goal Sport*: Ehrentor *n*; **con·sol·a·to·ry** [kən'sɔlətəri] tröstend, Trost...

con·sole 1. [kən'səul] trösten; **2.** ['kɔnsəul] Konsole *f*; △ Krag-, Tragstein *m*; *~ table* Wandtischchen *n*.

con·sol·er [kən'səulə] Tröster(in).

con·sol·i·date [kən'sɔlideit] festigen; *fig.* vereinigen; *Schuld* konsolidieren, fundieren; zs.-legen; *~d annuities = consols*; *℞d Fund* konsolidierter Staatsfonds *m*; **con·sol·i'da·tion** Festigung *f*; Konsolidierung *f*; Vereinigung *f*; Zs.-legung *f*.

con·sols [kən'sɔlz] *pl.* Konsols *m/pl.*, konsolidierte Staatsanleihen *f/pl.*

con·som·mé [kən'sɔmei] klare Fleischbrühe *f*.

con·so·nance ['kɔnsənəns] Konsonanz *f*; Übereinstimmung *f*; **'con·so·nant 1.** □ ♪ konsonierend; übereinstimmend (*with, to* mit); **2.** *gr.* Konsonant *m*.

con·sort 1. ['kɔnsɔ:t] Gemahl(in); Geleitschiff *n*; **2.** [kən'sɔ:t] (*with*) sich gesellen (zu), umgehen (mit); passen (zu).

con·spec·tus [kən'spektəs] Übersicht *f*; Abriß *m*.

con·spic·u·ous □ [kən'spikjuəs] *deutlich* sichtbar; auffallend; *fig.* hervorragend; *be ~ by one's absence* durch Abwesenheit glänzen; *make o.s. ~* sich auffällig benehmen.

con·spir·a·cy [kən'spirəsi] Verschwörung *f*; **con'spir·a·tor** [~tə] Verschwörer *m*; **con'spir·a·tress** Verschwörerin *f*; **con·spire** [kən'spaiə] sich verschwören; zs.-wirken.

con·sta·ble ['kʌnstəbl] Polizist *m*, Schutzmann *m*; **con·stab·u·lar·y** [kən'stæbjuləri] Polizei(truppe) *f*.

con·stan·cy ['kɔnstənsi] Standhaftigkeit *f*; Beständigkeit *f*; Unveränderlichkeit *f*; Bestand *m*, Dauer *f*; **'con·stant 1.** □ konstant, beständig, fest; unveränderlich, gleich; bleibend; fortwährend, dauernd; treu, getreu; **2.** ⚗ Konstante *f*.

con·stel·la·tion *ast.* [kɔnstə'leiʃən] Sternbild *n*.

con·ster·na·tion [kɔnstə:'neiʃən] Bestürzung *f*.

con·sti·pate ⚕ ['kɔnstipeit] verstopfen; **con·sti'pa·tion** ⚕ Verstopfung *f*.

con·stit·u·en·cy [kən'stitjuensi] Wählerschaft *f*; Wahlkreis *m*; F Kunden-, Abonnentenkreis *m*; **con'stit·u·ent 1.** wesentlich; Grund..., Bestand...; konstituierend; **2.** wesentlicher Bestandteil *m*; Wähler *m*; Vollmachtgeber *m* (*a.* ⚓).

con·sti·tute ['kɔnstitju:t] ein-, errichten; einsetzen, ernennen; zs.-setzen, bilden, ausmachen; *~ s.o. judge* j. als Richter einsetzen, *fig.* zum Richter machen; **con·sti'tu·tion** Ein-, Errichtung *f*; Bildung *f*, Zs.-setzung *f*; Konstitution *f*, Körperbau *m*; Verfassung *f*, Konstitution *f*, Satzung *f*; **con·sti'tu·tion·al** [~ʃənl] **1.** □ konstitutionell; körperlich bedingt; natürlich; verfassungsmäßig; *~ law* Verfassungsrecht *n*; **2.** F Spaziergang *m bsd. zur Verdauung*; **con·sti'tu·tion·al·ist** [~ʃnəlist] Anhänger(in) der konstitutionellen Regierungsform; **con·sti·tu·tive** □ ['kɔnstitju:tiv] wesentlich.

con·strain [kən'strein] zwingen; *et.* erzwingen; **con·straint** [~'streint] Zwang *m*; ⚖ Nötigung *f*.

con·strict [kən'strikt] zs.-ziehen, -schnüren; verengen; **con'stric·tion** Zs.-ziehung *f etc.*; **con'stric·tor** *anat.* Schließmuskel *m*; *zo. a. boa* ~ Riesenschlange *f*, Boa *f*.
con·strin·gent [kən'strindʒənt] zs.-ziehend.
con·struct [kən'strʌkt] konstruieren, bauen, errichten; *fig.* bilden, erdenken; **con'struc·tion** Konstruktion *f*; Bau *m*, Gebäude *n*; Auslegung *f*; Sinn *m*; ~ *site* Baustelle *f*; *under* ~ im Bau; **con'struc·tive** aufbauend, schöpferisch, konstruktiv, positiv; Bau..., Konstruktions...; gefolgert, angenommen; **con'struc·tor** Erbauer *m*, Konstrukteur *m*.
con·strue [kən'stru:] *gr.* konstruieren; auslegen, auffassen; Wort für Wort übersetzen.
con·sue·tu·di·nar·y [kɔnswi'tju:dinəri] gewohnheitsmäßig; Gewohnheits...
con·sul ['kɔnsəl] Konsul *m*; ~ *general* Generalkonsul *m*; **con·su·lar** ['kɔnsjulə] konsularisch; Konsular...; **con·su·late** ['~lit] Konsulat *n* (*a. Gebäude*); ~ *general* Generalkonsulat *n*; **con·sul·ship** ['kɔnsəlʃip] Konsulat *n*.
con·sult [kən'sʌlt] *v/t.* konsultieren, um Rat fragen, zu Rate ziehen; befragen; in *e-m Buch* nachschlagen; berücksichtigen; *~ing engineer* technischer Berater *m*; *~ing physician* fachärztlicher Berater *m*; *v/i.* sich beraten; **con'sult·ant** (ärztliche *etc.*) Autorität *f*; **con·sul·ta·tion** [kɔnsəl'teiʃən] Konsultation *f*, Beratung *f*; Rücksprache *f*; Konferenz *f*; ~ *hour* Sprechstunde *f*; **con·sult·a·tive** [kən'sʌltətiv] beratend.
con·sum·a·ble [kən'sju:məbl] verzehrbar; **con'sume** *v/t.* verzehren (*a. fig.*); verbrauchen; vergeuden; zerstören; *v/i.* sich verzehren; **con'sum·er** Konsument *m*, Verbraucher *m*; Abnehmer *m*; ~ *association* Verbraucherverband *m*; ~ *demand* Verbrauchernachfrage *f*; ~ *goods pl.* Verbrauchsgüter *n/pl.*
con·sum·mate **1.** □ [kən'sʌmit] vollendet; **2.** ['kɔnsəmeit] vollenden, vervollständigen; *Ehe* vollziehen; **con·sum·ma·tion** [~'meiʃən] Vollendung *f*; Vollziehung *f*; Ende *n*; *fig.* Ziel *n*.

con·sump·tion [kən'sʌmpʃən] Verbrauch *m*, Konsum *m*; ⚕ Auszehrung *f*, Schwindsucht *f*; **con'sump·tive** □ verzehrend; schwindsüchtig.
con·tact **1.** ['kɔntækt] Berührung *f*; Fühlung(nahme) *f*; ⚡ Kontakt *m*; *make* (*break*) ~ den Kontakt herstellen (unterbrechen); **2.** [kən'tækt] Fühlung nehmen mit; ~ **lens·es** ['kɔntækt'lensiz] *pl.* Haft-, Kontaktschalen *f/pl.*; ~ **print** *phot.* Kontaktabzug *m*.
con·ta·gion ⚕ [kən'teidʒən] Ansteckung *f*; Verseuchung *f*; Seuche *f* (*a. fig.*); **con'ta·gious** □ ansteckend; verseuchend.
con·tain [kən'tein] (ent)halten, (um)fassen; ⚔ *den Feind* festhalten; *fig.* in Schach halten; ~ *o.s.* an sich halten, sich mäßigen; **con'tain·er** Behälter *m*; Container *m*; **con'tain·ment** Festhalten *n etc.*; *pol.* Eindämmung *f*.
con·tam·i·nate [kən'tæmineit] verunreinigen; *fig.* anstecken, vergiften; verseuchen; **con·tam·i'na·tion** Verunreinigung *f etc.*, (radioaktive) Verseuchung *f*; *gr.* Kontamination *f*.
con·temn *lit.* [kən'tem] verachten.
con·tem·plate ['kɔntempleit] *fig.* betrachten; beabsichtigen; **con·tem'pla·tion** Betrachtung *f*; Nachsinnen *n*; *have in* ~ beabsichtigen; **'con·tem·pla·tive** □ nachdenklich; beschaulich.
con·tem·po·ra·ne·ous □ [kəntempə'reinjəs] gleichzeitig; ~ *performance* ⚖ Erfüllung *f* Zug um Zug; **con'tem·po·rar·y** **1.** zeitgenössisch; gleichzeitig; **2.** Zeitgenosse *m*, Zeitgenossin *f*; Altersgenosse *m*, Altersgenossin *f*.
con·tempt [kən'tempt] Verachtung *f*; Verächtlichkeit *f*; ~ *of court* Mißachtung *f* des Gerichts; Nichterscheinen *n* vor Gericht; *hold in* ~ verachten; *in* ~ *of* in Mißachtung (*gen.*); **con'tempt·i·ble** □ verächtlich; zu verachten(d); **con'temp·tu·ous** □ [~tjuəs] geringschätzig (*of* gegen); verachtungsvoll; verächtlich.
con·tend [kən'tend] *v/i.* streiten, ringen (*for* um); *v/t.* behaupten.
con·tent [kən'tent] **1.** zufrieden; *parl.* einverstanden; *not* ~ dagegen;

2. befriedigen, zufriedenstellen; ~ *o.s.* sich begnügen (*with* mit); 3. Zufriedenheit *f*; *to one's heart's* ~ nach Herzenslust; ['kɔntent] Umfang *m*; *innerer* Gehalt *m*; ~*s pl.* Inhalt *m*; *table of* ~*s* Inhaltsverzeichnis *n*; **con·tent·ed** □ [kən'tentid] zufrieden.

con·ten·tion [kən'tenʃən] (Wort-)Streit *m*; Wetteifer *m*; Behauptung *f*; **con'ten·tious** □ streitsüchtig; streitig.

con·tent·ment [kən'tentmənt] Zufriedenheit *f*, Genügsamkeit *f*.

con·test 1. ['kɔntest] Streit *m*; Wettkampf *m*, -bewerb *m*; 2. [kən'test] (be)streiten; anfechten; um *et.* streiten; ~ *a borough* sich um das Mandat e-s Wahlkreises bewerben; ~ *s.o.'s right to do s.th.* j-m das Recht streitig machen, et. zu tun; **con'test·a·ble** bestreit-, anfechtbar, streitig; **con'test·ant** streitende Partei *f*; Herausforderer *m*; **con'test·ed** umstritten.

con·text ['kɔntekst] Zusammenhang *m*, Kontext *m*; **con·tex·tu·al** □ [kən'tekstjuəl] dem Zs.-hang entsprechend; aus dem Zs.-hang sich ergebend; **con'tex·ture** [~tʃə] Gewebe *n*, Bau *m*, Struktur *f*.

con·ti·gu·i·ty [kɔnti'gju:iti] Berührung *f*; Nähe *f*; **con·tig·u·ous** □ [kən'tigjuəs] anstoßend (*to* an *acc.*); benachbart.

con·ti·nence ['kɔntinəns] Enthaltsamkeit *f*; Mäßigung *f*; '**con·ti·nent** 1. □ enthaltsam; mäßig; 2. Kontinent *m*, Erdteil *m*; Festland *n*; **con·ti·nen·tal** [~'nentl] 1. □ kontinental; Kontinental...; ~ *quilt* Federbett *n*; 2. Kontinentaleuropäer(in).

con·tin·gen·cy [kən'tindʒənsi] Zufälligkeit *f*; Zufall *m*; Möglichkeit *f*; unvorhergesehener Fall *m*; **con'tin·gen·cies** *pl.* unvorhergesehene Ausgaben *f/pl.*; **con'tin·gent** 1. □ zufällig; *unter Umständen* möglich (*to* bei), eventuell; ~ *on* abhängig von; 2. ⚔ *Truppen*-Kontingent *n*.

con·tin·u·al □ [kən'tinjuəl] fortwährend, unaufhörlich, dauernd, ständig; **con'tin·u·ance** Fortdauer *f*, Dauer *f*; Bleiben *n*; Anhalten *n*; **con·tin·u'a·tion** Fortsetzung *f*; Fortdauer *f*; ⚖ Prolongation *f*; ~ *school* Fortbildungsschule *f*; **con'tin·ue** [~nju:] *v/t.* fortsetzen; fortführen, verlängern; beibehalten; ~ *reading* weiter lesen; *to be* ~*d* Fortsetzung folgt; *v/i.* sich fortsetzen, fortdauern; (ver)bleiben, beharren; fortfahren; ~ (*in*) *a business* ein Geschäft fortführen; **con·ti·nu·i·ty** [kɔnti'nju:iti] Kontinuität *f*; Stetigkeit *f*; *Film*: Drehbuch *n*; *Radio*: verbindende Worte *n/pl.*; ~ *girl* Skriptgirl *n*; **con·tin·u·ous** □ [kən'tinjuəs] ununterbrochen, fortlaufend, durchgehend; ~ *current* ⚡ Gleichstrom *m*.

con·tort [kən'tɔ:t] verdrehen; verzerren; **con'tor·tion** Verdrehung *f*; Verzerrung *f*; **con'tor·tion·ist** [~ʃnist] Schlangenmensch *m*.

con·tour ['kɔntuə] Umriß *m*, Kontur *f*; ~ **line** *surv.* Höhenschichtlinie *f*; ~ **map** Höhenlinienkarte *f*.

con·tra ['kɔntrə] wider; *per* ~ ⚖ als Gegenleistung.

con·tra·band ['kɔntrəbænd] 1. Schmuggel...; 2. Schmuggelware *f*; Schleichhandel *m*; Konterbande *f*.

con·tra·cep·tion [kɔntrə'sepʃən] Empfängnisverhütung *f*; **con·tra'cep·tive** empfängnisverhütend(es Mittel *n*).

con·tract 1. [kən'trækt] *v/t.* zs.-ziehen; *Gewohnheit* annehmen; *Krankheit* sich zuziehen; *Schulden* machen; *Heirat etc.* (ab)schließen; *v/i.* sich zs.-ziehen, einschrumpfen; e-n Vertrag schließen (*for* auf *acc.*); sich vertraglich verpflichten (*to* zu); ~ *for* (aus)bedingen; ~*ing party* vertragschließende Partei *f*; 2. ['kɔntrækt] Kontrakt *m*, Vertrag *m*; *by* ~ vertraglich; *under* ~ in Auftrag gegeben (*Bau*); **con·tract·ed** □ [kən'træktid] zs.-gezogen *etc.*; *fig.* beschränkt; ~ *form gr.* Kurzform *f*; **con·tract·i'bil·i·ty** Zs.-ziehbarkeit *f*; **con'tract·i·ble** zs.-ziehbar; **con'trac·tile** [~tail] zs.-ziehend; zs.-ziehbar; ✈ einziehbar (*Fahrwerk*); **con'trac·tion** Zs.-ziehung *f*; *gr.* Kurzform *f*; **con'trac·tor** Unternehmer *m* (*for e-s Baues etc.*); Lieferant *m*; *anat.* Schließmuskel *m*; **con'trac·tu·al** [~tjuəl] vertraglich, vertragsmäßig; Vertrags...

con·tra·dict [kɔntrə'dikt] widersprechen (*dat.*); **con·tra'dic·tion** Widerspruch *m*; **con·tra'dic·tious** □ zum Widerspruch neigend;

streitsüchtig; **con·tra'dic·to·ry** [~təri] □ (sich) widersprechend.

con·tra·dis·tinc·tion [kɔntrədis'tiŋkʃən] Gegensatz *m*; **con·tra·dis'tin·guish** [~gwiʃ] unterscheiden.

con·tral·to ♪ [kən'træltəu] **1.** Alt (-stimme *f*) *m*; Altistin *f*; **2.** Alt...

con·trap·tion *sl.* [kən'træpʃən] (komisches) Ding(s) *n*, Apparat *m*.

con·tra·ri·e·ty [kɔntrə'raiəti] Widerspruch *m*; Widrigkeit *f des Wetters etc.*; **con·tra·ri·ly** ['~trərili] entgegen, zuwider; **'con·tra·ri·ness** Gegensätzlichkeit *f*; Widerstand *m*, -spenstigkeit *f*; **con·tra·ri·wise** ['~waiz] entgegengesetzt; umgekehrt; **'con·tra·ry 1.** entgegengesetzt (*a. adv.*); ungünstig, widrig; F [kən'trɛəri] widerspenstig, eigensinnig; ~ *to prp.* zuwider (*dat.*), gegen (*acc.*); entgegen (*dat.*); **2.** Gegenteil *n*; *on the* ~ im Gegenteil; *to the* ~ dagegen.

con·trast 1. ['kɔntrɑ:st] Kontrast *m*, Gegensatz *m*; *in* ~ *to* im Gegensatz zu; *by* ~ als Gegensatz (hierzu); **2.** [kən'trɑ:st] *v/t.* gegenüberstellen; (*with dat.*); vergleichen; sich abheben von; *v/i.* sich unterscheiden, abstechen (*with* von).

con·tra·vene [kɔntrə'vi:n] zuwiderhandeln (*dat.*); übertreten; im Widerspruch stehen zu; bestreiten; **con·tra·ven·tion** [~'venʃən] Zuwiderhandlung *f*; Übertretung *f*; Verstoß *m* (*of* gegen).

con·trib·ute [kən'tribju:t] *v/t.* beitragen, beisteuern; einbringen; *v/i.* beitragen, mitwirken (*to* an *dat.*, bei); **con·tri·bu·tion** [kɔntri'bju:ʃən] Mitwirkung *f*; Beitrag *m*; eingebrachtes Gut *n*; Einlage *f*; ⚔ Kontribution *f*, Kriegssteuer *f*; **con·trib·u·tor** [kən'tribjutə] Beitragende *m*; Mitarbeiter(in) (*to a newspaper* an e-r Zeitung); **con'trib·u·to·ry** beitragend (*to* zu).

con·trite □ ['kɔntrait] zerknirscht, reuevoll; **con·tri·tion** [kən'triʃən] Zerknirschung *f*.

con·triv·ance [kən'traivəns] Erfindung *f*; Plan *m*; Vorrichtung *f*; Kunstgriff *m*; Scharfsinn *m*, Findigkeit *f*; **con'trive** *v/t.* ersinnen; ausdenken; planen; zuwegebringen; *v/i.* fertig werden, auskommen; es möglich machen, es fertigbringen (*to inf.* zu *inf.*); **con'triv·er** Erfinder(in); erfinderischer Kopf *m*; *she is a good* ~ sie ist eine gute Hausfrau.

con·trol [kən'trəul] **1.** Kontrolle *f*, Aufsicht *f*; Überwachung *f*; Beherrschung *f*; Befehl *m*; Zwang *m*; Macht *f*, Gewalt *f*, Herrschaft *f*; (Nach)Prüfung *f*; Zwangsbewirtschaftung *f*, -wirtschaft *f*; ⚖ Verfügungsgewalt *f*; Kontrollvorrichtung *f*, Regler *m*, Steuerung *f*; *attr.* Kontroll...; ~ *surfaces pl.* ✈ Leitwerk *n*; *foreign* ~ Überfremdung *f*; *remote od. distant* ~ Fernsteuerung *f*; ~ *board* ⊕ Schaltbrett *n*; ~ *column* ✈ Steuerknüppel *m*; ~ *desk* Steuer-, Schaltpult *n*; *Fernsehen*: Regiepult *n*; ~ *knob* Bedienungsknopf *m*; ~ *panel mot.* Armaturenbrett *n*; ~ *tower* ✈ Kontrollturm *m*, Tower *m*; ~ *valve Radio*: Steuerröhre *f*; *be in* ~ die Aufsicht führen (*of* über *acc.*); *put s.o. in* ~ j-m die Aufsicht übertragen (*of* über *acc.*); **2.** kontrollieren; einschränken; beaufsichtigen; überwachen; beherrschen; (nach)prüfen; *Waren* bewirtschaften; ⊕ regeln; ✈ steuern; ~*ling interest* maßgebliche Beteiligung *f an e-m Unternehmen*; **con'trol·la·ble** kontrollierbar; lenkbar; **con'trol·ler** Kontrolleur *m*, Aufseher *m*; Leiter *m*, Geschäftsführer *m*; Rechnungsprüfer *m*.

con·tro·ver·sial □ [kɔntrə'və:ʃəl] umstritten; streitsüchtig; polemisch; **con·tro·ver·sy** ['~və:si] Streit *m*; Streitfrage *f*; **con·tro·vert** ['~və:t] bestreiten; *j-m* widersprechen; **con·tro'vert·i·ble** □ bestreitbar.

con·tu·ma·cious □ [kɔntju'meiʃəs] widerspenstig; ⚖ ungehorsam; **con·tu·ma·cy** ['kɔntjuməsi] Widerspenstigkeit *f*; ⚖ absichtliches Nichterscheinen *n*.

con·tu·me·li·ous □ [kɔntju:'mi:ljəs] frech, beleidigend; **con·tu·me·ly** ['kɔntju:mli] Beschimpfung *f*; Schmach *f*.

con·tuse ⚕ [kən'tju:z] quetschen; **con'tu·sion** [~ʒən] Quetschung *f*.

co·nun·drum [kə'nʌndrəm] Scherzrätsel *n*.

con·ur·ba·tion [kɔnə:'beiʃən] Ballungsraum *m*, Gruppe *f* zs.-gewachsener Städte.

con·va·lesce [kɔnvə'les] genesen;

con·va'les·cence Genesung *f*; **con·va'les·cent 1.** □ genesend; Genesungs...; **2.** Genesende *m, f*.
con·vec·tion *phys.* [kən'vekʃən] Fortpflanzung *f*, Übertragung *f*; **con'vec·tor** Konvektor *m* (*Heizkörper*).
con·vene [kən'vi:n] (sich) versammeln; zs.-rufen; *Versammlung* (ein)berufen; ⚖ vorladen.
con·ven·ience [kən'vi:njəns] Bequemlichkeit *f*, Annehmlichkeit *f*; Angemessenheit *f*; Vorteil *m*; Klosett *n*; *at your earliest* ~ möglichst bald; *make a* ~ *of s.o.* j. ausnutzen; *marriage of* ~ Vernunftehe *f*; **con'ven·ient** □ bequem, angenehm; passend (*to, for* für); brauchbar.
con·vent ['kɔnvənt] (*bsd.* Nonnen-) Kloster *n*; **con·ven·ti·cle** [kən'ventikl] Versammlung *f*; Konventikel *n* (*bsd. v. non-conformists*); **con'ven·tion** Versammlung *f*; Konvent *m*; Konvention *f*, Übereinkommen *n*, Vertrag *m*; Herkommen *n*; **con'ven·tion·al** [~ʃənl] vertraglich; herkömmlich, konventionell; ~ *weapons pl.* konventionelle Waffen *f/pl.*; **con'ven·tion·al·ism** [~ʃnəlizəm] Festhalten *n* am Herkömmlichen; *das* Herkömmliche; **con·ven·tion·al·i·ty** [~ʃə'næliti] Herkömmlichkeit *f*; **con'ven·tu·al** [~tjuəl] □ Kloster..., klösterlich.
con·verge [kən'və:dʒ] konvergieren, zs.-laufen (lassen); **con'ver·gence, con'ver·gen·cy** Konvergenz *f*; **con'ver·gent, con'verg·ing** konvergierend.
con·vers·a·ble [kən'və:səbl] umgänglich; gesprächig; **con'ver·sant** (*with*) vertraut (mit); bewandert (in *dat.*); **con·ver·sa·tion** [~və'seiʃən] Gespräch *n*, Unterhaltung *f*; **conver'sa·tion·al** [~ʃənl] Unterhaltungs...; gesprächig; umgangssprachlich; **con·verse 1.** □ ['kɔnvə:s] umgekehrt; **2.** [~] Gespräch *n*; *vertrauter* Umgang *m*; ⅄, *phls.* Kehrsatz *m*; Umkehrung *f*; **3.** [kən'və:s] sich unterhalten (*with* mit); **con'ver·sion** Um-, Verwandlung *f*; ⊕, ⚡ Umformung *f*; *phls.* Umkehrung *f*; *eccl.* Bekehrung *f* (*to* zu); *pol.* Meinungswechsel *m*, Übertritt *m*; ✝ Konvertierung *f*; Umstellung *f e-r Währung, e-s Betriebs etc.*
con·vert 1. ['kɔnvə:t] Bekehrte *m, f*, Konvertit *m*; **2.** [kən'və:t] (sich) um- *od.* verwandeln; ⊕, ⚡ umformen; *eccl.* bekehren; verwenden (*to* zu); *e-n Satz* umkehren; ✝ konvertieren; *Betrieb, Währung etc.* umstellen; große Wohnung in kleinere Wohnungen umbauen, aufteilen; **con'vert·er** Bekehrer(in); ⊕, ⚡ Umformer *m*; **con·vert·i·bil·i·ty** [~ə'biliti] Umwandelbarkeit *f*; ✝ Konvertierbarkeit *f*; **con'vert·i·ble 1.** □ um-, verwandelbar; ✝ konvertierbar; **2.** *mot.* Kabrio (-lett) *n*.
con·vex □ ['kɔn'veks] konvex; **con'vex·i·ty** Konvexheit *f*.
con·vey [kən'vei] befördern, bringen, schaffen, tragen; übermitteln; vermitteln, mitteilen; *phys.* leiten; ausdrücken; sagen; ⚖ übertragen; **con'vey·ance** Transport *m*, Beförderung *f*; Spedition *f*; Übermittlung *f*; Transportmittel *n*; Fuhrwerk *n*; ⚖ Übertragung *f*; ⚡ Leitung *f*; *public* ~ öffentliches Verkehrsmittel *n*; **con'vey·anc·er** Notar *m für Übertragungen von Grundeigentum*; **con'vey·or** ⊕ *a.* ~ *belt* Förderband *n*.
con·vict 1. ['kɔnvikt] Zuchthäusler *m*, Sträfling *m*; **2.** [kən'vikt] überführen (*of gen.*); ⚖ für schuldig erklären (*of gen.*); **con'vic·tion** ⚖ Überführung *f*, Schuldigerklärung *f*, Verurteilung *f*; Überzeugung *f* (*of* von); *previous* ~ Vorstrafe *f*.
con·vince [kən'vins] überzeugen (*of* von); **con'vinc·ing** überzeugend.
con·viv·i·al [kən'viviəl] Fest...; festlich; gesellig; **con·viv·i·al·i·ty** [~'æliti] Geselligkeit *f*; festliche Stimmung *f*.
con·vo·ca·tion [kɔnvəu'keiʃən] Einberufung *f*; Versammlung *f*.
con·voke [kən'vəuk] einberufen.
con·vo·lu·tion [kɔnvə'lu:ʃən] Zs.-wicklung *f*; Windung *f*.
con·vol·vu·lus ⚘ [kən'vɔlvjuləs] Winde *f*.
con·voy ['kɔnvɔi] **1.** Geleit *n*; Geleitzug *m*; (Geleit)Schutz *m*; **2.** geleiten.
con·vulse *fig.* [kən'vʌls] erschüttern; *be* ~*d with laughter* sich biegen vor Lachen; **con'vul·sion** Zuckung *f*, Krampf *m*; ~*s of laughter* Lachkrampf *m*; **con'vul·sive** □ krampfhaft, -artig; konvulsiv.

co·ny ['kəuni] Kaninchen *n.*
coo [ku:] girren, gurren.
cook [kuk] **1.** Koch *m*; Köchin *f*; **2.** kochen; *fig.* zs.-brauen; sich kochen lassen; F *Bericht etc.* zurechtstutzen, frisieren; '**~·book** *Am.* Kochbuch *n*; '**cook·er** Kocher *m*; Kochapfel *m*, -birne *f*; F Erfinder *m*; **~** *hood* Abzugshaube *f über dem Herd*; '**cook·er·y** Kochen *n*; Kochkunst *f*; **~** *book* Kochbuch *n*; '**cook-house** Lagerküche *f*; ⚓ Kombüse *f*; **cook·ie** *Am.* ['~i] Plätzchen *n*; '**cook·ing** Kochen *n*; Küche *f* (*Kochweise*); **cook·y** ['~i] = *cookie*.
cool [ku:l] **1.** □ kühl (*a. Gefühl*), frisch; *fig.* kaltblütig, gelassen; *b. s.* unverfroren; *a* **~** *thousand pounds* F die Kleinigkeit von tausend Pfund; **2.** Kühle *f*; **3.** (sich) abkühlen; *let him* **~** *his heels* laß ihn warten; '**cool·er** (Wein)Kühler *m*; *sl.* Gefängnis(zelle *f*) *n*; '**cool-'head·ed** mit kühlem Kopf, besonnen.
coo·lie ['ku:li] Lastträger *m*, Kuli *m*.
cool·ing ⊕ ['ku:liŋ] Kühlung *f*; *attr.* Kühl...; '**cool·ness** Kühle *f*, Kälte *f* (*a. fig.*); Kaltblütigkeit *f*.
coomb [ku:m] Talmulde *f*.
coon *Am.* F [ku:n] *zo.* Waschbär *m*; Neger *m*; (schlauer) Bursche *m*; *a gone* **~** ein hoffnungsloser Fall *m*; **~** *song* Negerlied *n*.
coop [ku:p] **1.** Hühnerkorb *m*; **2.** **~** *up od. in* einsperren.
co-op F ['kəuɔp] = *co-operative (store)* Konsum *m*.
coop·er ['ku:pə] Böttcher *m*; Küfer *m*; '**coop·er·age** Böttcherei *f*.
co-op·er·ate [kəu'ɔpəreit] mitwirken; zs.-arbeiten; **co-op·er'a·tion** Mitwirkung *f*; Zs.-arbeit *f*; **co-'op·er·a·tive** [~rətiv] **1.** zs.-wirkend; genossenschaftlich; **~** *society* Konsumverein *m*; **~** *store* Konsum(vereinsladen) *m*; **2.** = **~** *store*; **co-'op·er·a·tor** [~reitə] Mitarbeiter *m*; Konsumvereinsmitglied *n*.
co-opt [kəu'ɔpt] hinzuwählen; **co-op'ta·tion** Zuwahl *f*.
co-or·di·nate **1.** □ [kəu'ɔ:dinit] gleich-, beigeordnet; **2.** [~neit] koordinieren, gleichordnen, -schalten; aufeinander einstellen *od.* abstimmen; **co-or·di'na·tion** Gleichordnung *f*, -stellung *f*, -schaltung *f*.
coot [ku:t] Wasserhuhn *n*; F Tölpel *m*; **coot·ie** ⚔ *sl.* ['~i] (Kleider-) Laus *f*.
cop *sl.* [kɔp] **1.** erwischen; **~** *it* es kriegen; **2.** Polyp *m* (*Polizist*); Gefangennahme *f*.
co·pal ['kəupəl] Kopal(harz *n*) *m*.
co·part·ner ['kəu'pɑ:tnə] Teilhaber *m*; '**co'part·ner·ship** Genossenschaft *f*; Teilhaberschaft *f*; Gewinnbeteiligung *f* der Arbeitnehmer.
cope[1] [kəup] **1.** Chorrock *m*; *fig.* Decke *f*; Gewölbe *n des Himmels*; **2.** decken, überwölben.
cope[2] [~]: **~** *with* sich messen mit, fertig werden mit.
Co·per·ni·can [kəu'pə:nikən] kopernikanisch.
cope·stone ['kəupstəun] *mst fig.* Schlußstein *m*.
cop·i·er ['kɔpiə] Kopiergerät *n*.
co-pi·lot [kəu'pailət] Kopilot *m*.
cop·ing ⚠ ['kəupiŋ] (Mauer-) Kappe *f*; '**~-stone** *fig.* Krönung *f*.
co·pi·ous □ ['kəupjəs] reich(lich); weitschweifig; '**co·pi·ous·ness** Fülle *f*; Weitläufigkeit *f*.
cop·per[1] ['kɔpə] **1.** Kupfer *n*; Kupfermünze *f*; Kupfergeld *n*; Kupfergeschirr *n*; **2.** kupfern; Kupfer...; **3.** verkupfern.
cop·per[2] *sl.* [~] Polyp *m* (*Polizist*).
cop·per·as ⚗ ['kɔpərəs] Vitriol *n*.
cop·per...: **~ beech** ⚘ Blutbuche *f*; '**~·plate** Kupferstich(platte *f*) *m*; *like* **~** wie gestochen (*Schrift*); '**~-smith** Kupferschmied *m*.
cop·pice ['kɔpis], **copse** [kɔps] Unterholz *n*, Dickicht *n*.
cop·u·late *zo.* ['kɔpjuleit] sich paaren; **cop·u'la·tion** Paarung *f*; **cop·u·la·tive** ['~lətiv] **1.** verbindend; **2.** *gr.* Kopula *f*, Bindewort *n*.
cop·y ['kɔpi] **1.** Kopie *f*; Nachbildung *f*; Abschrift *f*; Durchschlag *m*; Vorlage *f*; Muster *n*; Exemplar *n e-s Buches*; *Zeitungs*-Nummer *f*; druckfertiges Manuskript *n*; Zeitungsstoff *m*; *fair od. clean* **~** Reinschrift *f*; *rough od. foul* **~** Entwurf *m*, Konzept *n*; **2.** kopieren; abschreiben; nachbilden, nachahmen; **~** *fair* ins reine schreiben; **~***ing stand phot.* Kopierrahmen *m*; '**~-book** (Schön)Schreibheft *n*; '**~-cat** F *contp.* Nachäffer *m*; *ped.* Abschreiber *m*; **~ desk** Redaktionstisch *m*; **~ ed·i·tor** Redakteur *m*; '**~·hold** Lehnbesitz *m*; Lehngut *n*; '**cop·y-**

ing-ink Kopiertinte *f*; '**cop·y·ing-press** Kopierpresse *f*; '**cop·y·ist** Abschreiber *m*; Nachahmer *m*; '**cop·y·right** Verlags-, Urheberrecht *n*, Copyright *n*; *attr.* verlags-, urheberrechtlich; **cop·y writ·er** Werbetexter *m*.
co·quet [kɔ'ket] kokettieren; **co·quet·ry** ['~kitri] Gefallsucht *f*; **co·quette** [~'ket] Kokette *f*; **co'quet·tish** □ kokett.
cor·a·cle ['kɔrəkl] Boot *n* aus überzogenem Weidengeflecht.
cor·al ['kɔrəl] **1.** Koralle *f*; Kinderklapper *f* mit Beißkoralle; **2.** *a.* **cor·al·line** ['~lain] Korallen...; korallenartig, -rot.
cor·bel ⚠ ['kɔ:bəl] Kragstein *m*.
cord [kɔ:d] **1.** Schnur *f*, Strick *m*, Seil *n*; Kabel *n*; Klafter *f Holz*; *fig.* Fessel *f*; *anat.* Strang *m*, Band *n*; = *corduroy*; **2.** (zu)schnüren, binden; '**cord·ed** gerippt (*Stoff*); '**cord·age** Tauwerk *n*.
cor·dial ['kɔ:djəl] **1.** □ herzlich, aufrichtig; herzstärkend; **2.** Herzstärkung *f*; (Magen)Likör *m*; **cor·dial·i·ty** [~di'æliti] Herzlichkeit *f*.
cord-mak·er ['kɔ:dmeikə] Seiler *m*.
cor·don ['kɔ:dn] **1.** ⚠ Mauerkranz *m*; ⚔ Kordon *m*, Postenkette *f*; Polizeikordon *m*; Ordensband *n*; **2.** ~ *off* abriegeln, -sperren (*Polizei*).
cor·do·van ['kɔ:dəvən] Korduan (-leder *n*) *m*.
cor·du·roy ['kɔ:dərɔi] Kord(samt) *m* (*gerippter Stoff*); ~*s pl.* Kordhosen *f/pl.*; ~ *road* Knüppeldamm *m*.
core [kɔ:] **1.** ♀ Kernhaus *n*; *fig.* Innerste *n*; Herz *n*; Kern *m*; Eiterpfropf *m e-s Geschwürs*; ~ *time Arbeitszeit*: Kernzeit *f*; **2.** entkernen; '**cor·er** Fruchtentkerner *m*.
co-re·li·gion·ist ['kəuri'lidʒənist] Glaubensgenosse *m*, Glaubensgenossin *f*.
Co·rin·thi·an [kə'rinθiən] korinthisch.
cork [kɔ:k] **1.** Kork *m*; **2.** (ver-)korken, *fig. a.* ~ *up* verschließen; '**cork·age** Ver-, Entkorken *n*; Korkengeld *n*; '**corked** korkig, nach dem Kork schmeckend; '**cork·er** *sl.* Prachtkerl *m*; prima *od.* pfundige Sache *f*; *das* Entscheidende; '**cork·ing** *Am.* F fabelhaft, prima.
cork...: '**~-jack·et** Schwimmweste *f*; '**~-screw** **1.** Kork(en)zieher *m*; **2.** spiralig; **3.** sich schrauben; '**~-tree** ♀ Korkeiche *f*; '**cork·y** korkig; F lebhaft.
cor·mo·rant *orn.* ['kɔ:mərənt] Scharbe *f*, Kormoran *m*.
corn[1] [kɔ:n] **1.** Korn *n*; Getreide *n*; *a. Indian* ~ *Am.* Mais *m*; *Am. in Zssgn* ~ *bread* Maisbrot *n*; **2.** einpökeln; ~*ed beef* Corned Beef *n*, Büchsenfleisch *n*.
corn[2] ⚕ [~] Hühnerauge *n*.
corn...: '**~-chan·dler** Korn-, Samenhändler *m*; '**~-cob** *Am.* Maiskolben *m*.
cor·ne·a *anat.* ['kɔ:niə] Hornhaut *f des Auges*.
cor·nel ♀ ['kɔ:nəl] Kornelkirsche *f*.
cor·nel·ian *min.* [kɔ:'ni:ljən] Karneol *m*.
cor·ne·ous ['kɔ:niəs] hornartig.
cor·ner ['kɔ:nə] **1.** Ecke *f*, Winkel *m*; Kurve *f*; *fig.* Enge *f*, Klemme *f*; † spekulativer Aufkauf *m*; † (Aufkäufer)Ring *m*; ~ *kick* Eckball *m*; **2.** in die Ecke (*fig.* Enge) treiben; † aufkaufen; '**cor·nered** ...eckig.
corner...: '**~-house** Eckhaus *n*; '**~-stone** Eck-, *fig.* Grundstein *m*.
cor·net ['kɔ:nit] ♪ (kleines) Horn *n*; *Spitz*-Tüte *f*; Schwesternhaube *f*.
corn...: '**~-ex·change** Getreidebörse *f*; '**~-field** Korn-, *Am.* Maisfeld *n*; ~ **flakes** *pl.* Corn-flakes *pl.*; '**~-flour** = *corn-starch*; '**~-flow·er** Kornblume *f*.
cor·nice ['kɔ:nis] ⚠ Karnies *n*, Gesims *n*; *Schnee*-Wächte *f*.
Cor·nish ['kɔ:niʃ] kornisch; aus Cornwall.
corn...: '**~-juice** *Am. sl.* Maisschnaps *m*; ~ **pone** *Am.* Maisbrot *n*; '**~-pop·py** ♀ Klatschmohn *m*; '**~-stalk** Getreidehalm *m*; *Am.* Maisstengel *m*; '**~-starch** *Am.* Maismehl *n*.
cor·nu·co·pi·a *poet.* [kɔ:nju'kəupjə] Füllhorn *n*.
corn·y ['kɔ:ni] kornreich; körnig; *sl.* abgedroschen, altmodisch; *bsd. Am.* ♪ schmalzig (*sehr sentimental*).
co·rol·la ♀ [kə'rɔlə] Blumenkrone *f*;
cor'ol·la·ry Folgesatz *m*; *fig.* Folge *f*.
co·ro·na [kə'rəunə], *pl.* **co'ro·nae** [~ni:] *ast.* Korona *f*; ⚠ Kranzleiste *f*; **co'ro·nal** *anat.* Scheitel..., Stirn...; **cor·o·nar·y** ⚕ ['kɔrənəri]

1. Herzkranz...; ~ *thrombosis* Herzinfarkt *m*; 2. F Herzinfarkt *m*; **cor·o·na·tion** [kɔrəˈneiʃən] Krönung *f*; **ˈcor·o·ner** Leichenbeschauer *m* u. Untersuchungsrichter *m*; **cor·o·net** [ˈ~nit] Adelskrone *f*.

cor·po·ral [ˈkɔːpərəl] **1.** □ körperlich; **2.** ⚔ Korporal *m*; Unteroffizier *m*; **cor·po·rate** [ˈ~rit] □ vereinigt; körperschaftlich; gemeinsam, Gemeinschafts...; ~ *body* juristische Person *f*; **cor·po·ra·tion** [~ˈreiʃən] Korporation *f*, Körperschaft *f*, Zunft *f*; Stadtverwaltung *f*; *Am.* Aktiengesellschaft *f*; F Schmerbauch *m*; ~ *tax* Körperschaftssteuer *f*; **cor·po·ra·tive** [ˈ~rətiv] korporativ; **cor·po·re·al** □ [~ˈpɔːriəl] körperlich; materiell; **cor·po·re·i·ty** [~pəˈriːiti] Körperlichkeit *f*.

corps [kɔː], *pl.* **corps** [kɔːz] Korps *n*.

corpse [kɔːps] Leichnam *m*.

cor·pu·lence, cor·pu·len·cy [ˈkɔːpjuləns(i)] Beleibtheit *f*, Korpulenz *f*; **ˈcor·pu·lent** beleibt, korpulent.

cor·pus [ˈkɔːpəs], *pl.* **cor·po·ra** [ˈ~pərə] Körper *m*; Sammlung *f von Gesetzen etc.*; ♀ *Christi* [ˈkristi] *Day* Fronleichnamstag *m*; **cor·pus·cle** [ˈkɔːpʌsl] Teilchen *n*, Korpuskel *n*.

cor·ral *bsd. Am.* [kɔːˈrɑːl] **1.** Umzäunung *f*, Pferch *m* (*a. fig.*); Wagenburg *f*; **2.** zs.-pferchen, *fig.* einsperren; e-e Wagenburg bilden.

cor·rect [kəˈrekt] **1.** *adj.* □ korrekt, richtig; *be* ~ richtig sein, stimmen; **2.** *v/t.* korrigieren, berichtigen, verbessern; zurechtweisen; strafen; *Mißbrauch* abstellen; ⚗ mildern; **corˈrec·tion** Berichtigung *f*, Verbesserung *f*; Verweis *m*; Strafe *f*; ⚗ Milderung *f*; Korrektur *f*; *house of* ~ Besserungsanstalt *f*, Zuchthaus *n*; *I speak under* ~ ich lasse mich gern korrigieren; **corˈrect·i·tude** [~titjuːd] Korrektheit *f*; **corˈrec·tive 1.** verbessernd; ⚗ mildernd; **2.** Besserungsmittel *n*; **corˈrec·tor** Verbesserer *m*, Berichtiger *m*; *typ.* Korrektor *m*; Milderungsmittel *n*.

cor·re·late [ˈkɔrileit] **1.** in Wechselbeziehung stehen *od.* bringen; **2.** Korrelat *n*; **cor·reˈla·tion** Wechselbeziehung *f*; **cor·rel·a·tive** □ [~ˈrelətiv] in Wechselbeziehung (stehend).

cor·re·spond [kɔrisˈpɔnd] (*with, to*) entsprechen (*dat.*), übereinstimmen (mit); in Briefwechsel stehen, korrespondieren (*with* mit); **cor·reˈspond·ence** Übereinstimmung *f*; Briefwechsel *m*, Korrespondenz *f*; Briefe *m/pl.*; Verbindung *f*; **cor·reˈspond·ent 1.** □ entsprechend; **2.** Briefschreiber(in); Korrespondent(in); Geschäftsfreund *m*; *my* ~*s* Leute, mit denen ich im Briefwechsel stehe; **cor·reˈspond·ing** entsprechend; korrespondierend (*Akademiemitglied*).

cor·ri·dor [ˈkɔridɔː] Korridor *m*; Gang *m*, Flur *m*; ~ *train* D-Zug *m*.

cor·ri·gi·ble □ [ˈkɔridʒəbl] verbesserlich, zu verbessern(d).

cor·rob·o·rant [kəˈrɔbərənt] **1.** stärkend; bestätigend; **2.** Stärkungsmittel *n*; Bestätigung *f*; **corˈrob·o·rate** [~reit] stärken; bestätigen; **cor·rob·oˈra·tion** Bestätigung *f*; **corˈrob·o·ra·tive** [~rətiv] bestätigend.

cor·rode [kəˈrəud] zerfressen, angreifen, korrodieren, wegätzen; **corˈro·dent 1.** ätzend; **2.** Ätzmittel *n*; **corˈro·sion** [~ʒən] Ätzen *n*, Zerfressen *n*; ⊕ Korrosion *f*; Rost *m*; **corˈro·sive** [~siv] **1.** □ zerfressend, ätzend; *fig.* nagend; **2.** Ätzmittel *n*; **corˈro·sive·ness** ätzende Schärfe *f*.

cor·ru·gate [ˈkɔrugeit] runzeln; ⊕ riefen; ~*d cardboard* Wellpappe *f*; ~*d iron* Wellblech *n*.

cor·rupt [kəˈrʌpt] **1.** □ verdorben, faul; verderbt (*a. Text etc.*); bestechlich, bestochen; ~ *practices pl. pol.* Bestechungsmanöver *n/pl.*; **2.** *v/t.* verderben; bestechen; anstecken; *v/i.* (ver)faulen, verderben; **corˈrupt·er** Verderber(in); Bestecher(in); **cor·rupt·i·bil·i·ty** [~təˈbiliti] Verderbbarkeit *f*; Bestechlichkeit *f*; **corˈrupt·i·ble** □ verderblich; bestechlich; **corˈrup·tion** Verderbnis *f*, Verdorbenheit *f* (*a. fig.*); Fäulnis *f*; Verderbtheit *f e-s Textes*; Bestechung *f*; **corˈrup·tive** □ verderbend.

cor·sage [kɔːˈsɑːʒ] Taille *f*, Mieder *n*; *Am.* Ansteckblume(n *pl.*) *f*.

cor·sair [ˈkɔːsɛə] Seeräuber(schiff *n*) *m*, Korsar *m*.

corse [kɔːs] *poet.* = *corpse*.

cors(e)·let [ˈkɔːslit] Brustschild *m*.

cor·set ['kɔːsit] Korsett *n*; '**cor·set·ed** geschnürt.
cor·tège [kɔː'teiʒ] Gefolge *n*; Prozession *f*.
cor·tex ⚘, *zo., anat.* ['kɔːteks], *pl.* **cor·ti·ces** ['~tisiːz] Rinde *f*.
cor·ti·cal ['kɔːtikəl] rindig; *fig.* äußerlich.
co·run·dum *min.* [kə'rʌndəm] Korund *m*.
cor·us·cate ['kɔrəskeit] (auf)blitzen, funkeln.
cor·vette ⚓ [kɔː'vet] Korvette *f*.
cor·vine ['kɔːvain] raben-, krähenartig; Raben...; Krähen...
cosh *sl.* [kɔʃ] **1.** Knüppel *m*, Totschläger *m*; **2.** mit einem Knüppel schlagen; '**~-boy** *sl.* jugendlicher Straßenräuber *m*.
cosh·er ['kɔʃə] (ver)hätscheln.
co-sig·na·to·ry ['kəu'signətəri] **1.** mitunterzeichnend; **2.** Mitunterzeichner *m*.
co·sine ⩘ ['kəusain] Kosinus *m*.
co·si·ness ['kəuzinis] Behaglichkeit *f*.
cos·met·ic [kɔz'metik] **1.** kosmetisch, verschönernd; **2.** Schönheitsmittel *n*; Kosmetik *f*; **cos·me·ti·cian** [kɔzme'tiʃən] Kosmetiker (-in).
cos·mic, cos·mi·cal □ ['kɔzmik(əl)] kosmisch; Welt(en)...; *cosmic rays pl.* kosmische Strahlung *f*.
cos·mo·naut ['kɔzmənɔːt] Weltraumfahrer *m*, Kosmonaut *m*.
cos·mo·pol·i·tan [kɔzməu'pɔlitən], **cos·mop·o·lite** [~'mɔpəlait] **1.** kosmopolitisch; **2.** Weltbürger(in).
cos·mos ['kɔzmɔs] Kosmos *m*, Universum *n*.
Cos·sack ['kɔsæk] Kosak *m*.
cos·set ['kɔsit] **1.** Nesthäkchen *n*; **2.** (ver)hätscheln.
cost [kɔst] **1.** Preis *m*; Kosten *pl.*; Schaden *m*, Nachteil *m*; *~s pl.* Gerichtskosten *pl.*; Spesen *pl.*; *first od. prime ~* Anschaffungskosten *pl.*; *~ of living* Lebenshaltungskosten *pl.*; *at all ~s* um jeden Preis; *to my ~* zu meinem Schaden; *as I know to my ~* wie ich aus eigner Erfahrung weiß; **2.** (*irr.*) kosten; ⚕ die Selbstkosten *e-r Ware etc.* berechnen; *~ dearly* teuer zu stehen kommen.
co-star ['kəustɑː] **1.** e-r der Hauptdarsteller; **2.** e-e der Hauptrollen spielen; *~ring* in e-r der Hauptrollen.
cos·ter F ['kɔstə] = '**~·mon·ger** Höker(in) mit Handwagen.
cost·ing ['kɔstiŋ] Kostenberechnung *f*; Herstellungskosten *pl.*
cos·tive □ ['kɔstiv] hartleibig.
cost·li·ness ['kɔstlinis] Kostspieligkeit *f*; Kostbarkeit *f*; '**cost·ly** kostbar; kostspielig, teuer.
cost-price ⚕ ['kɔstprais] Selbstkosten-, Einkaufspreis *m*.
cos·tume ['kɔstjuːm] Kostüm *n*; Kleidung *f*; Tracht *f*; **cos'tum·i·er** [~miə] Kostümier *m*; Kostümverleiher *m*.
co·sy ['kəuzi] **1.** □ behaglich, gemütlich; **2.** = *tea-cosy*.
cot [kɔt] Feldbett *n*; ⚓ Hängematte *f* mit Rahmen; Kinderbett *n*.
cote [kəut] Stall *m*, Schuppen *m*.
co·te·rie ['kəutəri] Klüngel *m*, Clique *f*; Zirkel *m*, Kreis *m*, Gruppe *f*.
cot·tage ['kɔtidʒ] Hütte *f*; kleines Landhaus *n*, Sommerhaus *n*; *~ cheese* Hüttenkäse *m*; *~ industry* Heimindustrie *f*; *~ piano* Pianino *n*; '**cot·tag·er** Häusler *m*; Hüttenbewohner *m*; *Am.* Sommergast *m*.
cot·ter ⊕ ['kɔtə] Querkeil *m*; Splint *m*.
cot·ton ['kɔtn] **1.** Baumwolle *f*; ⚕ Kattun *m*; *Näh*-Garn *n*; **2.** baumwollen; Baumwoll...; *~ bud* Wattestäbchen *n*; *~ candy Am.* Zuckerwatte *f*; *~ wool* Watte *f*; **3.** F sich vertragen, sympathisieren (*with* mit); sich anschließen (*to s.o.* an j.); *~ on* (*to s.th.*) F (et.) kapieren; *~ to s.th.* sich befreunden mit et.; *~ up* sich anfreunden (*with, to* mit *j-m*); '**~-grass** Wollgras *n*; '**~-seed** ⚘ Baumwollsamen *m*; '**~-wood** ⚘ *e-e* amerikanische Pappel *f*; '**cot·ton·y** baumwollartig.
cot·y·le·don ⚘ [kɔti'liːdən] Keimblatt *n*.
couch [kautʃ] **1.** Lager *n*; Couch *f*, Sofa *n*, Liege *f*; Schicht *f*; **2.** *v/t.* *Lanze* einlegen; *Meinung etc.* ausdrücken; *Schriftsatz etc.* abfassen; *den Star* stechen; *v/i.* sich (nieder-) legen; versteckt liegen; kauern; '**~-grass** ⚘ Quecke *f*.
cou·gar *zo.* ['kuːgə] Kugar *m*, Puma *m*.
cough [kɔf] **1.** Husten *m*; **2.** (aus-) husten; *~ down* durch Husten zum Schweigen bringen; *~ up* aushusten; *sl.* herausrücken mit; *~* **drop** Hu-

stenbonbon *m*, *n*; ~ **mix·ture** Hustensaft *m*.

could [kud] *pret. von can.*

couldn't ['kudnt] = *could not.*

cou·lee *Am.* ['ku:li] (trockenes) Bachbett *n*.

coul·ter ['kəultə] Pflugeisen *n*.

coun·cil ['kaunsl] Rat(sversammlung *f*) *m*; ~ **house** stadteigenes Haus *n* mit niedriger Miete; **coun·ci(l)·lor** ['~silə] Ratsmitglied *n*, Ratsherr *m*, Stadtrat *m*.

coun·sel ['kaunsəl] **1.** Beratung *f*; Rat(schlag) *m*; ⚖ Anwalt *m*; ~ *for the defence* Verteidiger *m*; ~ *for the prosecution* Anklagevertreter *m*; *keep one's (own)* ~ s-e Gedanken für sich behalten; *take* ~ *with* sich Rat holen bei; **2.** *j.* beraten; *j-m* raten (*to* zu); zu *et.* raten; **coun·se(l)·lor** ['~slə] Ratgeber(in); Anwalt *m*; *s. counci(l)lor.*

count[1] [kaunt] **1.** Rechnung *f*; Zahl *f*; ⚖ Anklagepunkt *m*; *Boxen*: Auszählen *n*; *a.* ~*-out parl.* Vertagung *f* wegen Beschlußunfähigkeit; Berücksichtigung *f*, Notiz *f*; *lose* ~ die Übersicht verlieren (*of* über *acc.*); *take no* ~ *of what s.o. says* sich nicht darum kümmern, was j. sagt; **2.** *v/t.* zählen; rechnen; mit(ein)rechnen; *fig.* schätzen, halten für; *be* ~*ed out Boxen*: ausgezählt werden; *v/i.* zählen; rechnen (*fig. on, upon* auf *acc.*); gelten (*for little* wenig).

count[2] [~] *nichtbritischer* Graf *m*.

count·a·ble ['kauntəbl] zählbar.

count-down ['kauntdaun] Startvorbereitungen *f/pl.*, Countdown *m* (*beim Raketenstart*).

coun·te·nance ['kauntinəns] **1.** Gesicht(sausdruck *m*) *n*, Miene *f*; Fassung *f*, (Gemüts)Ruhe *f*; Ermutigung *f*, Unterstützung *f*; *put s.o. out of* ~ j. aus der Fassung bringen; **2.** begünstigen, unterstützen; gutheißen.

count·er[1] ['kauntə] Zähler *m*, Zählapparat *m*; Spielmarke *f*, Zahlpfennig *m*; Laden-, Zahltisch *m*; Schalter *m*.

coun·ter[2] [~] **1.** (*to dat.*) entgegen; zuwider; Gegen...; **2.** Gegenschlag *m* (*to* gegen); **3.** Gegenmaßnahmen treffen; *Boxen*: kontern.

coun·ter·act [kauntə'rækt] zuwiderhandeln (*dat.*); **coun·ter'ac·tion** Gegenwirkung *f*; Widerstand *m*.

coun·ter-at·tack ['kauntərətæk] Gegenangriff *m*.

coun·ter·bal·ance **1.** ['kauntəbæləns] Gegengewicht *n*; **2.** [~'bæləns] das Gegengewicht halten (*dat.*), aufwiegen; ✈ ausgleichen, ausbalancieren.

coun·ter·blast ['kauntəblɑ:st] kräftige Entgegnung *f*.

coun·ter·charge ['kauntətʃɑ:dʒ] Gegenklage *f*.

coun·ter·check ['kauntətʃek] Gegenstoß *m*; Hindernis *n*.

coun·ter-claim ⚖ ['kauntəkleim] Gegenforderung *f*.

coun·ter-clock·wise ['kauntə'klɔkwaiz] entgegen dem Uhrzeigersinn.

coun·ter-cur·rent ['kauntə'kʌrənt] Gegenstrom *m*.

coun·ter-es·pi·o·nage ['kauntərespiə'nɑ:ʒ] Spionageabwehr *f*.

coun·ter·feit ['kauntəfit] **1.** □ nachgemacht; falsch, unecht; verstellt; **2.** Nachahmung *f*; Nachdruck *m*; Fälschung *f*; Falschgeld *n*; **3.** nachmachen; nachdrucken; fälschen; heucheln; sich verstellen; '**coun·ter·feit·er** Nachahmer(in); Fälscher(in); Falschmünzer *m*; Nachdrucker *m*; Heuchler(in).

coun·ter·foil ['kauntəfɔil] Kontrollblatt *n*, -abschnitt *m*.

coun·ter·fort ⚠ ['kauntəfɔ:t] Strebepfeiler *m*.

coun·ter-in·tel·li·gence ⚔ ['kauntərin'telidʒəns] Gegenspionage *f*.

coun·ter-ir·ri·tant ⚕ [kauntər'iritənt] Gegen(reiz)mittel *n*.

coun·ter-jump·er F ['kauntədʒʌmpə] Ladenschwengel *m*.

coun·ter·mand [kauntə'mɑ:nd] **1.** Gegenbefehl *m*; Widerruf *m*; **2.** widerrufen; abbestellen.

coun·ter·march ['kauntəmɑ:tʃ] **1.** Rückmarsch *m*; **2.** zurückmarschieren.

coun·ter·mark ['kauntəmɑ:k] Gegenzeichen *n*.

coun·ter·mine **1.** ['kauntəmain] Gegenmine *f*; **2.** [~'main] Gegenminen legen (gegen) (*a. fig.*).

coun·ter-move ['kauntəmu:v] *fig.* Gegenzug *m*, -maßnahme *f*.

coun·ter-or·der ['kauntərɔ:də] Gegenbefehl *m*.

coun·ter·pane ['kauntəpein] Bett-, Steppdecke *f*.

coun·ter·part ['kauntəpɑ:t] Gegenstück *n*; Duplikat *n*.
coun·ter·point ♪ ['kauntəpɔint] Kontrapunkt *m*.
coun·ter·poise ['kauntəpɔiz] **1.** Gegengewicht *n*; **2.** das Gleichgewicht halten (*dat.*) (*a. fig.*), ausbalancieren.
coun·ter-pro·duc·tive ['kauntəprə'dʌktiv] widersinnig; destruktiv.
coun·ter-rev·o·lu·tion ['kauntərevəlu:ʃən] Konter-, Gegenrevolution *f*.
coun·ter·scarp ⚔ ['kauntəskɑ:p] äußere Grabenböschung *f*.
coun·ter·shaft ⊕ ['kauntəʃɑ:ft] Vorgelegewelle *f*.
coun·ter·sign ['kauntəsain] **1.** Gegenzeichen *n*; ⚔ Losung(swort *n*) *f*; **2.** gegenzeichnen.
coun·ter·sink ⊕ ['kauntəsiŋk] (aus-)fräsen; *Schraubenkopf etc.* versenken.
coun·ter-stroke ['kauntəstrəuk] Gegenstoß *m*.
coun·ter-ten·or ♪ ['kauntə'tenə] Altstimme *f*; Falsettstimme *f*.
coun·ter·vail ['kauntəveil] aufwiegen; ersetzen.
coun·ter·weight ['kauntəweit] Gegengewicht *n* (*to* gegen).
count·ess ['kauntis] Gräfin *f*.
count·ing-house ['kauntiŋhaus] Kontor *n*.
count·less ['kauntlis] zahllos.
coun·tri·fied ['kʌntrifaid] ländlich; bäurisch.
coun·try ['kʌntri] **1.** Land *n*; Gegend *f*; Heimatland *n*; *appeal od. go to the* ~ Neuwahlen ausschreiben; **2.** Land..., ländlich; Lands...; ~ **club** Klubhaus *n* auf dem Land; '~**-dance** englischer Volks-, Reihentanz *m*; ~ **gen·tle·man** Landedelmann *m*; Gutsherr *m*; '~-'**house** Landhaus *n*, -sitz *m*; '~**·man** Landmann *m* (*Bauer*); Landsmann *m*; '~**-side** Land *n im Gegensatz zur Stadt*; Gegend *f*; Land(bevölkerung *f*) *n*; '~**·wom·an** Landfrau *f*; Landsmännin *f*.
coun·ty ['kaunti] Grafschaft *f*, Kreis *m*; ~ **coun·cil** Grafschaftsrat *m*; ~ **seat** *Am.* = ~ **town** Kreisstadt *f*.
coup [ku:] Schlag *m*, Streich *m*; ~ *d'état* Staatsstreich *m*.
cou·pé ['ku:pei] *mot.* Coupé *n*.
cou·ple ['kʌpl] **1.** Paar *n*; Koppel *f*; *a* ~ *of* zwei; F ein paar; **2.** (ver-)koppeln; ⊕ kuppeln; *Radio*: koppeln; (sich) ehelich verbinden; (sich) paaren; ~ *back* rückkoppeln; '**cou·pler** *Radio*: Koppler *m*; '**cou·ple-skat·ing** *Sport*: Paarlaufen *n*; **cou·plet** ['kʌplit] Verspaar *n*.
cou·pling ⊕ ['kʌpliŋ] Kupplung *f*; *Radio*: Kopplung *f*; *attr.* Kupplungs..., Kopplungs...
cou·pon ['ku:pɔn] Coupon *m*; Abschnitt *m*; Bezugschein *m*; Rabattmarke *f*; Abonnement(karte *f*) *n*; Rundreiseheft *n*.
cour·age ['kʌridʒ] Mut *m*, Tapferkeit *f*; *take od. muster up od. pluck up* ~ Mut fassen; **cou·ra·geous** □ [kə'reidʒəs] mutig, beherzt, tapfer.
cour·gette [kuə'ʒet] Zucchini *f*.
cour·i·er ['kuriə] Kurier *m*, (Eil-)Bote *m*; Reiseleiter(in).
course [kɔ:s] **1.** Lauf *m*, Gang *m*; Weg *m*; ⚓ Kurs *m*; ⚓ Fahrt *f*; Richtung *f*; Lebensbahn *f*; Gewohnheit *f*; Wettrennen *n*; Rennbahn *f*; Gang *m* (*Speisen*); Lehrgang *m*, Kursus *m*; *univ.* Vorlesung *f*; Ordnung *f*, Folge *f*; Verfahren *n*; ⚕ (Geld)Kurs *m*; *in due* ~ zur gegebenen *od.* rechten Zeit; *of* ~ natürlich, selbstverständlich; *matter of* ~ Selbstverständlichkeit *f*; ~ *of exchange* Wechselkurs *m*; *stay the* ~ durchhalten; **2.** *v/t.* hetzen; jagen; *v/i.* rennen.
cours·er *poet.* ['kɔ:sə] Renner *m*, schnelles Pferd *n*.
cours·ing ['kɔ:siŋ] Hetzjagd *f*.
court [kɔ:t] **1.** Hof(raum) *m*; Hof *m e-s Fürsten*; Hofgesellschaft *f*; Hof *m*, Aufwartung *f*; Gericht(shof *m*) *n*; *at* ~ bei Hofe; *pay (one's)* ~ *j-m* den Hof machen; **2.** den Hof machen, huldigen (*dat.*); werben um *j.*; *Unheil* heraufbeschwören; '~**-card** Bildkarte *f beim Kartenspiel*; ~ **cir·cu·lar** Hofnachrichten *f/pl.*; '~**-day** Gerichtstag *m*; **cour·te·ous** □ ['kə:tjəs] höflich, artig; **cour·te·san**, *a.* **cour·te·zan** [kɔ:ti'zæn] Kurtisane *f*; **cour·te·sy** ['kə:tisi] Höflichkeit *f*; Gefälligkeit *f*; ~ *call* Anstandsbesuch *m*; ~ *light mot.* Innenleuchte *f*; **court-guide** ['kɔ:tgaid] Verzeichnis *n* der hoffähigen Personen; **court-house** ['kɔ:thaus] Gerichtsgebäude *n*; *Am. a.*

Amtshaus *n e-s Kreises*; **cour·ti·er** ['kɔ:tjə] Höfling *m*; '**court·li·ness** feiner Ton *m*, Höflichkeit *f*; '**court·ly** höfisch; Hof...; höflich, artig.
court...: '**~-'mar·tial** ⚔ **1.** Kriegsgericht *n*; **2.** vor ein Kriegsgericht stellen; '**~-'plas·ter** Heftpflaster *n*; '**~·room** Gerichtssaal *m*; '**~·ship** Werbung *f*; '**~·yard** Hof *m*.
cous·in ['kʌzn] Vetter *m*, Cousin *m*; Base *f*, Cousine *f*; *first ~, ~ german* leiblicher Vetter *m*; **cous·in·hood** ['~hud], '**cous·in·ship** Vetter(n)-schaft *f*; '**cous·in·ly** vetterlich.
cove[1] [kəuv] **1.** Bucht *f*; *fig.* Obdach *n*; ⚠ Wölbung *f*; **2.** überwölben.
cove[2] F [~] Kerl *m*.
cov·e·nant ['kʌvənənt] **1.** ⚖ Vertrag *m*; *Bibel*: Bund *m*; **2.** *v/t.* geloben; (aus)bedingen; *v/i.* übereinkommen (*with s.o. for s.th.* mit j-m um et.).
Cov·en·try ['kɔvəntri]: *send s.o. to ~* j. gesellschaftlich boykottieren.
cov·er ['kʌvə] **1.** Decke *f*; Deckel *m*; Umschlag *m*; Futteral *n*; Hülle *f*; Deckung *f*; Schutz *m*; Dickicht *n*; Deckmantel *m*; Decke *f*, Mantel *m* (*Bereifung*); Gedeck *n*; *a. ~ address* Deckadresse *f*; *~ charge* Kosten *pl.* für das Gedeck; *under separate ~* gesondert, mit getrennter Post; **2.** (be-, zu)decken; einschlagen, -wickeln (*with* in *acc.*); verbergen, verdecken; schützen; durchlaufen, zurücklegen; ✝ decken; *mit Schußwaffe* zielen nach; *Gelände* bestreichen (*Geschütz*); umfassen, einschließen; *fig.* erfassen; *Zeitung*: berichten über (*acc.*), behandeln; *~ed button* bezogener Knopf *m*; *~ed court Tennis*: Halle *f*; *~ed wire* umsponnener Draht *m*; '**cov·er·age** Berichterstattung *f* (*of* über *acc.*); '**cov·er girl** Titelbildschönheit *f*; '**cov·er·ing** Decke *f*; Futteral *n*; *Bett*-Bezug *m*; Überzug *m*; Bekleidung *f*; Bedachung *f*; *floor ~* Fußbodenbelag *m*; **cov·er·let** ['~lit] Bettdecke *f*; **cov·er sto·ry** Titelgeschichte *f*.
cov·ert **1.** ['kʌvət] □ heimlich, versteckt; ⚖ verheiratet; **2.** ['kʌvə] Schutz *m*; Versteck *n*; Dickicht *n*.
cov·er-up ['kʌvərʌp] Vertuschung(smanöver *n*) *f*.
cov·et ['kʌvit] heftig begehren, sich gelüsten lassen nach; '**cov·et·ous** □ (be)gierig, lüstern (*of* nach); habsüchtig; '**cov·et·ous·ness** Gier *f*; Habsucht *f*.
cov·ey ['kʌvi] Volk *n Feldhühner*.
cov·ing ⚠ ['kəuviŋ] Überhang *m*, Vorsprung *m*.
cow[1] [kau] Kuh *f*.
cow[2] [~] einschüchtern, ducken.
cow·ard ['kauəd] **1.** □ feig; **2.** Feigling *m*; **cow·ard·ice** ['~dis], '**cow·ard·li·ness** Feigheit *f*; '**cow·ard·ly** feig(e).
cow·boy ['kaubɔi] Cowboy *m* (*berittener Rinderhirt*); '**cow-catch·er** 🚂 *Am.* Schienenräumer *m*.
cow·er ['kauə] (nieder)kauern; *fig.* sich ducken (*from* vor *dat.*).
cow·herd ['kauhə:d] Kuh-, Rinderhirt *m*; '**cow·hide** **1.** Kuhhaut *f*; Kuh-, Rindsleder *n*; Ochsenziemer *m*; **2.** peitschen; '**cow-house** Kuhstall *m*.
cowl [kaul] Mönchskutte *f*; Kapuze *f*; Schornsteinkappe *f*.
cow...: '**~·man** Melker *m*; *Am.* Viehzüchter *m*; '**~-'pars·ley** ⚘ Wiesenkerbel *m*; '**~-'pars·nip** ⚘ Bärenklau *m*; '**~-pox** Kuhpocken *f/pl.*; '**~-punch·er** *Am.* F Rinderhirt *m*.
cow·rie ['kauri] Kauri(muschel) *f*.
cow...: '**~-shed** Kuhstall *m*; '**~·slip** ⚘ Schlüsselblume *f*.
cox F [kɔks] **1.** = *coxswain*; **2.** steuern.
cox·comb ['kɔkskəum] Narr *m*; Narrenkappe *f*; **cox'comb·i·cal** □ närrisch.
cox·swain ['kɔkswein, ⚓ 'kɔksn] Bootsführer *m*, Steuermann *m*.
coy [kɔi] □ schüchtern; spröde; '**coy·ness** Sprödigkeit *f*.
coy·ote *zo.* ['kɔiəut] Steppenwolf *m*.
coy·pu *zo.* ['kɔipu:] Nutria *f*, Biberratte *f*.
coz·en *lit.* ['kʌzn] prellen; '**coz·en·age** Prellerei *f*.
co·zy ['kəuzi] = *cosy*.
crab[1] [kræb] Krabbe *f*, Taschenkrebs *m*; *ast.* Krebs *m*; ⊕ Winde *f*; Laufkatze *f*; *catch a ~* e-n Krebs fangen (*mit dem Ruder im Wasser steckenbleiben*).
crab[2] [~] **1.** ⚘ Holzapfel *m*; F Querkopf *m*; Meckerer *m*; Tadel *m*; **2.** meckern über; '**crab·bed** □ verdrießlich; herb; verworren, kraus.
crab-louse ['kræblaus] Filzlaus *f*.
crack [kræk] **1.** Knall *m*, Krach *m*;

Riß *m*, Sprung *m*; F derber Schlag *m*; *Sport sl.* Kanone *f*; Versuch *m*; Witz *m*; *in a* ~ im Nu; *have a* ~ *at s.th.* et. versuchen, e-n Versuch mit et. machen; **2.** F erstklassig; **3.** krach!; **4.** *v/t.* (ver)sprengen; knallen mit *et.*; *Nuß* (auf)knacken; *Ei* aufschlagen; ⚗ *Öl* kracken, spalten; ~ *a bottle* e-r Flasche den Hals brechen; ~ *a joke* e-n Witz reißen; ~ *up* F groß herausstellen; *v/i.* platzen, springen, bersten, rissig werden; e-n Sprung bekommen; knallen; umschlagen (*Stimme*); ~ *down on sl.* scharf vorgehen gegen; ~ *a crib sl.* in ein Haus einbrechen; *get* ~*ing* mit der Arbeit anfangen; '**~-brained** verrückt; '**~-down** *sl.* Razzia *f*, Blitzmaßnahme(n *pl.*) *f*; '**cracked** rissig, geborsten; F verrückt; '**cracker** Knallbonbon *m*; Schwärmer *m*; Lüge *f*; *Am.* Keks *m*; Kräcker *m*; Zwieback *m*; Zs.-bruch *m*; '**crack·er-bar·rel** *Am.* F *attr.* Biertisch...; '**crack·er-jack** *Am.* F prima (*Sache od. Person*); '**crack·ers** F verrückt; '**crack-jaw** Zungenbrecher *m*; **crack·le** ['krækl] knattern, knistern; '**crack·ling** *braune* Kruste *f* des Schweinebratens; Geknister *n*; **crack·nel** ['~nl] Brezel *f*; '**crack-pot** F **1.** Spinner *m* (*verrückter Kerl*); **2.** verrückt; '**cracks·man** *sl.* Einbrecher *m*; '**crack-up** Zs.-stoß *m*; ✈ Bruchlandung *f*; '**crack·y** = *cracked*.

cra·dle ['kreidl] **1.** Wiege *f* (*a. fig.*); Kindheit *f*; ⚓ Stapelschlitten *m*; *teleph.* Gabel *f*; **2.** (ein)wiegen.

craft [krɑ:ft] Handwerk *n*, Gewerbe *n* (*a. coll.* = *Handwerker*); Fahrzeug *n*, *coll.* Fahrzeuge *n/pl.*, *bsd.* Schiffe *n/pl.*; Gerissenheit *f*, Raffinesse *f*; *the gentle* ~ die edle Kunst des Angelns; '**craft·i·ness** Verschmitztheit *f*; '**crafts·man** (Kunst)Handwerker *m*; '**crafts-man·ship** handwerkliches Können *n*; '**craft·y** □ gerissen, raffiniert.

crag [kræg] Klippe *f*, Felsspitze *f*; '**crag·gy** felsig; uneben; '**crags-man** Felsgeher *m*, Kletterer *m*.

crake *orn.* [kreik] Schnarre *f*.

cram [kræm] **1.** (voll)stopfen; *Geflügel* mästen, nudeln; (sich) mit Speisen vollstopfen; (ein)pauken; **2.** Einpauken *n*; '**~-'full** vollgestopft; '**cram·mer** Einpauker *m*.

cramp [kræmp] **1.** Krampf *m*; ⊕ Klammer *f*, Krampe *f*; *fig.* Fessel *f*; **2.** ⊕ verklammern; einengen, *fig.* hemmen; '**cramped** verkrampft; krampfhaft; eng, beengt; schwer leserlich; '**cramp-frame** ⊕ Schraubzwinge *f*; '**cramp-i·ron** Eisenklammer *f*.

cram·pon ['kræmpən] Steigeisen *n*.

cran·ber·ry ⚘ ['krænbəri] Preiselbeere *f*.

crane [krein] **1.** Kranich *m*; ⊕ Kran *m*; **2.** (den Hals) vorstrecken, sich (aus)recken; ⊕ hochwinden; ~ *at* zaudern vor (*dat.*); '**crane·fly** *zo.* Schnake *f*; '**crane's-bill** ⚘ Storchschnabel *m*.

cra·ni·um *anat.* ['kreinjəm] Schädel *m*.

crank [kræŋk] **1.** ⊕ verdreht, verbogen; wacklig; ⚓ rank; munter; **2.** Kurbel *f*; Schwengel *m*; Wortspiel *n*; Schrulle *f*, Laune *f*; komischer Kauz *m*, Fanatiker *m*; *starting* ~ *mot.* Andrehkurbel *f*; *fresh air* ~ Frischluftfanatiker *m*; **3.** *v/t.* ~ *off Film* kurbeln; ~ *up mot.* ankurbeln (*a. v/i.*); '**~-case** Kurbelgehäuse *n*; '**crank·i·ness** Verschrobenheit *f*; '**crank-shaft** ⊕ Kurbelwelle *f*; '**crank·y** wacklig; launisch; verschroben, verdreht.

cran·nied ['krænid] rissig; '**cran·ny** Riß *m*, Ritze *f*, Spalt *m*.

crape [kreip] **1.** Krepp *m*, Flor *m*; **2.** kräuseln.

craps *Am.* [kræps] *pl. ein Würfelspiel.*

crap·u·lence ['kræpjuləns] Trunkenheit *f*; F Katzenjammer *m*.

crash[1] [kræʃ] **1.** Krach *m* (*a.* ✝); ✈ Absturz *m*; **2.** krachen; in *od.* auf *et.* fahren, fliegen, fallen, stürzen *etc.*; einstürzen; ✈ abstürzen, Bruch machen; **3.** *Am.* F blitzschnell ausgeführt; ~ *course* Intensivkurs *m*; ~ *diet* radikale Abmagerungskur *f*.

crash[2] [~] grober Drillich *m*.

crash...: '**~-dive** ⚓ **1.** Schnelltauchen *n*; **2.** schnelltauchen; '**~-hel·met** Sturzhelm *m*; '**~-land** ✈ bruchlanden; '**~-land·ing** ✈ Bruchlandung *f*.

crass *lit.* [kræs] derb, kraß.

crate [kreit] Lattenkiste *f für Porzellan, Fahrräder etc.*; *sl.* Kiste *f* (*Flugzeug*).

cra·ter ['kreitə] Krater *m*; (Granat- *etc.*)Trichter *m*.
cra·vat [krə'væt] Krawatte *f*.
crave [kreiv] *v/t*. dringend bitten *od*. flehen um; *v/i*. sich sehnen (*for* nach).
cra·ven ['kreivən] **1.** feig; **2.** Feigling *m*.
crav·ing ['kreiviŋ] heftige Begierde *f*, Sehnsucht *f* (*for* nach).
craw [krɔ:] Kropf *m der Vögel*.
craw·fish ['krɔ:fiʃ] **1.** Krebs *m*; **2.** *Am*. F kneifen, sich drücken.
crawl [krɔ:l] **1.** Kriechen *n*; Kraul *m*; **2.** kriechen; schleichen; wimmeln (*with* von); kribbeln; *Schwimmen*: kraulen; *it makes one's flesh* ~ man bekommt e-e Gänsehaut davon; '**crawl·er** *fig*. Kriecher(in); Gewürm *n*; Laus *f*; Raupenschlepper *m*; ~*s pl*. Krabbelanzug *m*.
cray·fish ['kreifiʃ] Flußkrebs *m*.
cray·on ['kreiən] **1.** Zeichenstift *m*, *bsd*. Farb-, Pastellstift *m*; Pastell (-gemälde) *n*; *blue* ~, *red* ~ Blau-, Rotstift *m*; **2.** zeichnen, skizzieren.
craze [kreiz] Verrücktheit *f* (*for* nach); übertriebene Begeisterung *f*, Fimmel *m* (*for* für); *be the* ~ Mode sein; '**crazed** verrückt (*with* vor *dat*.); '**cra·zi·ness** Verrücktheit *f*; '**cra·zy** □ verrückt (*for*, *about* nach; *with* vor *dat*.); wahnsinnig; wild begeistert; baufällig; zs.-gestückelt, Flicken...; Mosaik...
creak [kri:k] **1.** Knarren *n*; **2.** knarren; '**creak·y** □ knarrend.
cream [kri:m] **1.** Rahm *m*, Sahne *f*; Creme(speise) *f*; *fig*. Creme *f*, Auslese *f*; *das* Beste; *cold* ~ Cold Cream *n*; ~ *of tartar* gereinigter Weinstein *m*; **2.** abrahmen; *fig*. den Rahm abschöpfen von *et*.; mit Sahne vermengen; '**cream·er·y** Molkerei *f*; Milchgeschäft *n*; '**cream·y** sahnig.
crease [kri:s] **1.** Falte *f*, Kniff *m*; Bügelfalte *f*; Eselsohr *n* (*Buch*); *Kricket*: (Mal)Linie *f*; **2.** (sich) falten, (sich) kniffen.
cre·ate [kri:'eit] (er)schaffen; *thea*. kreieren, gestalten; verursachen, hervorrufen; erzeugen; ernennen, machen zu; **cre'a·tion** Schöpfung *f*; Ernennung *f*; **cre'a·tive** schaffend, schöpferisch; **cre'a·tor** Schöpfer *m*; **cre'a·tress** Schöpferin *f*; **crea·ture** ['~tʃə] Geschöpf *n*, Wesen *n*; Kreatur *f* (*a. contp*.); ~ *comforts pl. die* leiblichen Genüsse *m/pl*.
crèche [kreiʃ] Kinderhort *m*.
cre·dence ['kri:dəns] Glaube *m*; *give* ~ *to* Glauben schenken (*dat*.); *letter of* ~ Empfehlungsschreiben *n*; **cre·den·tials** [kri'denʃəlz] *pl*. Beglaubigungsschreiben *n*; schriftliche Unterlagen *f/pl*.
cred·i·bil·i·ty [kredi'biliti] Glaubwürdigkeit *f*; **cred·i·ble** □ ['kredəbl] glaubwürdig; glaubhaft.
cred·it ['kredit] **1.** Glaube *m*; Ruf *m*, Ansehen *n*; Glaubwürdigkeit *f*; Guthaben *n*; ✝ Kredit *n*; ✝ Borg *m*, Kredit *m*; Einfluß *m*; Verdienst *n*, Ehre *f*; *Am*. *Schule*: (Anrechnungs)Punkt *m*; ~ *balance* Guthaben *n*; ~ *card* Kreditkarte *f*; ~ *note* ✝ Gutschriftsanzeige *f*; ~ *rating* Kreditwürdigkeit *f*; *do s.o.* ~ j-m Ehre machen; *get* ~ *for s.th*. et. angerechnet bekommen; *give s.o.* ~ *for s.th*. j-m et. hoch *od*. als Verdienst anrechnen; *put od. place od. pass to s.o.'s* ~ j-m gutschreiben; **2.** *j-m* glauben; *j-m* trauen; ✝ *Summe* kreditieren, gutschreiben; ~ *s.o. with s.th*. j-m et. zutrauen; '**cred·it·a·ble** □ achtbar; ehrenvoll (*to* für); '**cred·i·tor** Gläubiger *m*.
cred·it...: ~ **squeeze** ✝ Kreditrestriktionen *f/pl*.; ~ **ti·tles** *pl*. *die Namen von Regisseur, Produzent etc. im Vorspann e-s Films*.
cre·du·li·ty [kri'dju:liti] Leichtgläubigkeit *f*; **cred·u·lous** □ ['kredjuləs] leichtgläubig.
creed [kri:d] Glaubensbekenntnis *n*.
creek [kri:k] Bucht *f*; *Am*. Bach *m*.
creel [kri:l] Fischkorb *m* aus Weidengeflecht.
creep [kri:p] **1.** (*irr*.) kriechen; *fig*. (sich ein)schleichen; kribbeln; *it makes my flesh* ~ ich bekomme e-e Gänsehaut davon; **2.** Kriechen *n*; ~*s pl*. Schauder *m*, Gruseln *n*; *it gave me the* ~*s* es überlief mich kalt; '**creep·er** Kriecher(in); Kriechtier *n*; ⚘ Schling-, Kletterpflanze *f*; '**creep·y** kriechend; fröstelnd; gruselig.
creese [kri:s] Kris *m* (*malaiischer Dolch*).
cre·mate [kri'meit] *Leichen* verbrennen; **cre'ma·tion** (Leichen-) Verbrennung *f*; **crem·a·to·ri·um** [kremə'tɔ:riəm], *bsd*. *Am*. **cre·ma·to·ry** ['~təri] Krematorium *n*.

cren·el·(l)at·ed ['krenileitid] mit Zinnen *od.* Schießscharten (versehen).
cre·ole ['kri:əul] **1.** Kreole *m*, Kreolin *f*; **2.** kreolisch.
cre·o·sote ⚗ ['kriəsəut] Kreosot *n.*
crêpe [kreip] Krepp *m*; ~ **pa·per** Kreppapier *n*; ~ **rub·ber** Kreppgummi *m.*
crep·i·tate ['krepiteit] knistern; rasseln; **crep·i'ta·tion** Knistern *n*; Knirschen *n*; Rasseln *n.*
crept [krept] *pret. u. p.p von creep.*
cre·pus·cu·lar [kri'pʌskjulə] dämmerig; Dämmerungs...
cres·cen·do ♪ [kri'ʃendəu] Krescendo *n* (*a. fig.*).
cres·cent ['kresnt] **1.** zunehmend; halbmondförmig; **2.** Halbmond *m* (*a. halbmondförmig gebaute Häuserreihe*); Hörnchen *n* (*Gebäck*); ♀ *City Am.* New Orleans.
cress ⚘ [kres] Kresse *f.*
cres·set ['kresit] Leuchtfeuer *n.*
crest [krest] Kamm *m des Hahnes, e-r Woge*; Schopf *m der Vögel*; Mähne *f*; Federbusch *m*; Helm (-busch, -schmuck) *m*; *Berg*-Kamm *m*, Gipfel *m*; *Heraldik*: Helmzier *f*; *family* ~ Familienwappen *n*; '**crest·ed** mit einem Kamm *etc.*; ~ *lark* Haubenlerche *f*; ~ *note-paper* Briefpapier *n* mit Familienwappen; '**crest·fall·en** niedergeschlagen.
cre·ta·ceous [kri'teiʃəs] kreidig.
cre·tin ['kretin] Kretin *m*; '**cre·tin·ous** kretinhaft.
cre·tonne [kre'tɔn] Kretonne *f*, *m* [(*Gewebe*).
cre·vasse [kri'væs] (Gletscher-) Spalte *f*; *Am.* Deichbruch *m.*
crev·ice ['krevis] Riß *m*, Spalte *f.*
crew[1] [kru:] Schar *f*, *b.s.* Bande *f*; Gruppe *f von Arbeitern*; ⚓, ✈ Mannschaft *f*, Besatzung *f.*
crew[2] [~] *pret. von crow* 2.
crew cut ['kru:kʌt] Bürstenhaarschnitt *m.*
crew·el ⚘ ['kru:il] Stickwolle *f.*
crib [krib] **1.** Krippe *f*; Kinderbettstelle *f*; F *Schule*: Klatsche *f*; F Plagiat *n*; *bsd. Am.* Behälter *m für Mais etc.*; *crack a* ~ *sl.* in ein Haus einbrechen; **2.** einsperren; F mausen; F abschreiben; '**crib·bage** Cribbage(karten)spiel *n*; **crib·ble** ['~bl] grobes Sieb *n*; **crib-bit·er** ['kribbaitə] Krippensetzer *m.*
crick [krik] **1.** Krampf *m*; ~ *in the neck* steifer Hals *m*; **2.** verrenken.
crick·et[1] *zo.* ['krikit] Grille *f*, Heimchen *n.*
crick·et[2] [~] **1.** Kricket *n*; *not* ~ F nicht fair; **2.** Kricket spielen; '**crick·et·er** Kricketspieler *m.*
cri·er ['kraiə] Schreier(in); Ausrufer *m.*
crime [kraim] Verbrechen *n.*
Cri·me·an War [krai'miən'wɔ:] Krimkrieg *m.*
crim·i·nal ['kriminl] **1.** verbrecherisch; Kriminal..., Straf...; **2.** Verbrecher(in); **crim·i·nal·i·ty** [~'næliti] Strafbarkeit *f*; Verbrechertum *n*; **crim·i·nate** *lit.* ['~neit] beschuldigen, anklagen; **crim·i'na·tion** *lit.* Beschuldigung *f*, Anklage *f.*
crimp[1] ⚓, ⚔ [krimp] **1.** Werber *m*; **2.** anwerben, pressen.
crimp[2] [~] **1.** kräuseln; **2.** ~ *cut* Krüllschnitt *m* (*Tabak*).
crim·son ['krimzn] **1.** karmesin; **2.** Karmesin(rot) *n*; **3.** *v/t.* karmesinrot färben; *v/i.* rot werden.
cringe [krindʒ] **1.** sich ducken; *fig.* (zu Kreuze) kriechen (*to* vor *dat.*); **2.** *fig.* Kriecherei *f.*
crin·kle ['kriŋkl] **1.** Windung *f*; Falte *f*; **2.** (sich) winden; (sich) falten; *Haar* kräuseln.
crin·o·line ['krinəli:n] Reifrock *m.*
crip·ple ['kripl] **1.** Krüppel *m*; Lahme *m*, *f*; **2.** verkrüppeln; *fig.* lähmen.
cri·sis ['kraisis], *pl.* **cri·ses** ['~si:z] Krisis *f*, Krise *f*, Wende-, Höhepunkt *m.*
crisp [krisp] **1.** kraus; knusperig; frisch (*Luft*); klar (*Kontur, Ton*); lebendig (*Stil*); steif (*Papier*); **2.** (sich) kräuseln; knusperig machen *od.* werden, braun rösten; **3.** *a. potato* ~*s pl.* Kartoffelchips *pl.*
criss·cross ['kriskrɔs] **1.** Kreuzzeichen *n*; Gewirr *n* von Linien; **2.** kreuz und quer (laufend); **3.** (durch)kreuzen.
cri·te·ri·on [krai'tiəriən], *pl.* **cri'te·ri·a** [~ə] Kennzeichen *n*, Prüfstein *m*, Kriterium *n*, Maßstab *m.*
crit·ic ['kritik] Kritiker(in); Kunstrichter(in); Krittler(in); '**crit·i·cal** □ kritisch; bedenklich; *be* ~ *of* kritisch gegenüberstehen (*dat.*); *in* ~ *condition* ⚕ in Lebensgefahr; **crit·i·cism** ['~sizəm] Kritik *f* (*of* an *dat.*); **crit·i·cize** ['~saiz] kriti-

sieren; beurteilen; tadeln; **cri·tique** [kri'ti:k] kritischer Essay *m*; *die* Kritik.

croak [krəuk] **1.** krächzen; quaken; *fig.* unken; F abkratzen (*sterben*); *sl.* abmurksen (*töten*); **2.** Krächzen *n*; Quaken *n*; '**croak·er** *fig.* Schwarzseher *m*, Unke *f*; '**croak·y** □ krächzend.

Cro·at ['krəuət] Kroat(in).

cro·chet ['krəuʃei] **1.** Häkelei *f*; **2.** häkeln.

crock [krɔk] **1.** irdener Topf *m*; Topfscherbe *f*; F Klepper *m* (*altes Pferd*); F Ruine *f* (*kranker Mensch*); F Klapperkasten *m*, alter Schlitten *m* (*Auto*); **2.** *mst* ~ *up sl.* zs.-brechen; '**crock·er·y** Töpferware *f*; Geschirr *n*.

croc·o·dile ['krɔkədail] *zo.* Krokodil *n*; F Zweierreihe *f* von Schulmädchen; ~ *tears pl. fig.* Krokodilstränen *f/pl.*

cro·cus ⚘ ['krəukəs] Krokus *m*.

Croe·sus *fig.* ['kri:səs] Krösus *m* (*Reicher*).

croft ['krɔft] kleines, eingefriedetes Feld *n*; kleiner Bauernhof *m*; '**croft·er** Kleinbauer *m*.

crom·lech ['krɔmlek] Kromlech *m*, druidischer Steinkreis *m*.

crone F [krəun] altes Weib *n*.

cro·ny F ['krəuni] Spezi *m*, Kumpan *m*, alter Freund *m*.

crook [kruk] **1.** Krümmung *f*; Haken *m* (*a. fig.*); Hirtenstab *m*; Krummstab *m*; *sl.* Schieber *m*, Gauner *m*; *on the* ~ auf krummen Wegen; **2.** (sich) krümmen; (sich) (ver)biegen; **crook·ed** [~kt] krumm, gekrümmt; ['~kid] □ *fig.* krumm, bucklig; unehrlich; F ergaunert.

croon [kru:n] summen; schmalzig singen; '**croon·er** sentimentaler Schlagersänger *m*, Schnulzensänger *m*.

crop [krɔp] **1.** Kropf *m*; Peitschenstiel *m*; Reitpeitsche *f*; Ernte *f*, Getreide *n*, Feldfrucht *f*; (Ernte-)Ertrag *m*, *fig.* Ausbeute *f*; kurzer Haarschnitt *m*; Menge *f*; **2.** (ab-, be)schneiden; stutzen; (ab)ernten; (ab)weiden; *Acker* bebauen; (Frucht) tragen; ~ *up* auftauchen; '**~-dust·ing** Sprühen *n des Getreides zur Schädlingsbekämpfung*; '**~-eared** stutzohrig; ~ **fail·ure** Mißernte *f*; '**crop·per** Stutzende *m etc.* (*s. crop* 2); Kropftaube *f*; F schwerer Sturz *m*; (Frucht)Träger *m*; *Am. sl.* Pächter *m*; *come a* ~ F stürzen; *fig.* Pech haben.

cro·quet ['krəukei] **1.** Krocket(spiel) *n*; **2.** krockieren.

cro·quette [krɔ'ket] *Küche*: Krokette *f*.

cro·sier ['krəuʒə] Bischofsstab *m*.

cross [krɔs] **1.** Kreuz *n* (*fig. Leiden*); (Ordens)Kreuz *n*; Kreuzung *f von Rassen*; *sl.* Unehrlichkeit *f*; **2.** □ sich kreuzend; quer (liegend, laufend *etc.*); F ärgerlich, verdrießlich, böse (*with*, *at* auf *acc.*); entgegengesetzt; wechselseitig; Kreuz..., Quer...; widerwärtig; *sl.* unehrlich; **3.** *v/t.* kreuzen, durchstreichen; *fig.* durchkreuzen; überqueren, über (*acc.*) gehen, fahren, setzen; in den Weg kommen (*dat.*); *fig.* in die Quere kommen (*dat.*); ~ **o.s.** sich bekreuzigen; ~ **out** *Wort* ausstreichen; **keep one's fingers ~ed** den Daumen halten; *v/i.* sich kreuzen; ~ *over* hinübergehen; '**~-bar** *Fußball*: Torlatte *f*; '**~-beam** Querbalken *m*; '**~-bench** *parl.* Bank *f* der Parteilosen; '**~·bones** *pl.* zwei gekreuzte Knochen *m/pl.* *unter e-m Totenkopf*; **~-bow** ['krɔsbəu] Armbrust *f*; '**~-breed** (Rassen)Kreuzung *f*, Mischrasse *f*; Mischling *m*; '**~-'bun** Kreuzbrötchen *n*; '**~-'check** überprüfen; die Gegenprobe machen; '**~-'coun·try** querfeldein; Gelände...; Überland...; ~ *skiing* (Ski)Langlauf *m*; '**~-cut saw** Schrotsäge *f*; '**~-ex·am·i'na·tion** Kreuzverhör *n*; '**~-ex'amine** ins Kreuzverhör nehmen; '**~-eyed** schielend; '**~-fer·ti·li'za·tion** ⚘ Kreuzbefruchtung *f*; *fig.* gegenseitige Befruchtung *f*; ~ **fire** Kreuzfeuer *n* (*a. fig.*); '**~-grained** gegen die Faser (geschnitten); *fig.* widerhaarig; '**cross·ing** (Weg-, Schienen)Kreuzung *f*; Übergang *m*; Überfahrt *f*; Hindernis *n*; '**cross-legged** mit übereinandergeschlagenen Beinen; '**cross·ness** Verdrießlichkeit *f*.

cross...: '**~-patch** F übellaunige Person *f*; ~ **pur·pos·es** *pl.* Widerspruch *m*; *be at* ~ einander mißverstehen; das Entgegengesetzte wollen; ~ **ref·er·ence** Querverweis *m*; '**~-road** Querstraße *f*; '~-

-roads *pl. od. sg.* (Straßen)Kreuzung *f*; *fig.* Scheideweg *m*; '**~-'section** Querschnitt *m*; '**~-stitch** Kreuzstich *m*; '**~·talk** witziges Wortgefecht *n*; *teleph.* Nebensprechen *n*; '**~·walk** *Am.* Fußgängerüberweg *m*; '**~·wind** Seitenwind *m*; '**~·wise** kreuzweise; '**~·word puz·zle** Kreuzworträtsel *n*.

crotch [krɔtʃ] Haken *m*; Gabel(ung) *f*; **crotch·et** ['~it] Haken *m*; ♪ Viertelnote *f*; wunderlicher Einfall *m*; '**crotch·et·y** F wunderlich.

cro·ton ⚘ ['krəutən] Kroton *m*.

crouch [krautʃ] **1.** sich ducken (*to* vor *dat.*) (*a. fig.*); **2.** Hockstellung *f*.

croup[1] [kru:p] Kruppe *f des Pferdes*.

croup[2] ⚕ [~] Krup(p) *m* (*Kinderkrankheit*).

crou·pi·er ['kru:piə] Croupier *m*.

crow [krəu] **1.** Krähe *f*; Krähen *n*; *eat ~ Am.* F zu Kreuze kriechen; *have a ~ to pick with* ein Hühnchen zu rupfen haben mit; *in a ~ line, as the ~ flies* schnurgerade, (in der) Luftlinie; **2.** (*irr.*) krähen; *fig.* triumphieren (*over* über *acc.*); '**~-bar** Brecheisen *n*, -stange *f*.

crowd [kraud] **1.** Haufen *m*, Menge *f*; Masse *f* (*a. gemeines Volk*); Gedränge *n*; F Gesellschaft *f*, Bande *f*, Truppe *f*; **2.** (sich) drängen; (über-)füllen, vollstopfen (*with* mit); wimmeln; bedrängen; eilen; *~ out* verdrängen; *~ on sail* ⚓ alle Segel beisetzen; '**crowd·ed** übervölkert, -füllt, -laufen.

crow·foot ⚘ ['krəufut] Hahnenfuß *m*.

crown [kraun] **1.** *mst* Krone *f* (*des Königs; Ehre, Ruhm; Vollendung; Fünfschillingstück; e-s Zahnes*); Kranz *m*; Gipfel *m*; Scheitel *m*; Kopf *m e-s Hutes*; **2.** krönen (*king* zum König; *a. fig.*); *Zahn* überkronen; *to ~ all* zu guter Letzt, zu allem Überfluß; '**crown·ing** *fig.* höchst; letzt; '**crown-jew·els** *pl.* Kronjuwelen *n/pl.*, -schatz *m*.

crow's... [krəuz]: '**~-feet** *pl.* Krähenfüße *m/pl.* (*Fältchen um die Augen*); '**~-nest** ⚓ Krähennest *n* (*Mastkorb*).

cru·cial □ ['kru:ʃəl] entscheidend; kritisch; **cru·ci·ble** ['kru:sibl] Schmelztiegel *m*; *fig.* Feuerprobe *f*; **cru·ci·fix** ['~fiks] Kruzifix *n*; **cru·ci·fix·ion** [~'fikʃən] Kreuzigung *f*; '**cru·ci·form** kreuzförmig; **cru·ci·fy** ['~fai] kreuzigen (*a. fig.*).

crude □ [kru:d] roh (*unbearbeitet; ungekocht; unreif; unverdaut; unfein*); Roh... (*oil, steel etc.*); grell (*Licht etc.*); '**crude·ness, cru·di·ty** ['~diti] roher Zustand *m*; Roheit *f*; Unreife *f* (*a. fig.*).

cru·el □ ['kruəl] grausam; hart; *fig.* blutig; '**cru·el·ty** Grausamkeit *f*.

cru·et ['kru:it] (Essig-, Öl)Fläschchen *n*; '**~-stand** Gewürzständer *m*.

cruise ⚓ [kru:z] **1.** Kreuz-, Vergnügungsfahrt *f*; **2.** kreuzen; *cruising speed* Reisegeschwindigkeit *f*; *~* **mis·sile** ⚔ Marschflugkörper *m*; '**cruis·er** ⚓ Kreuzer *m*; Jacht *f*; Segler *m*; *Am.* Funkstreifenwagen *m*; *~ weight Boxen:* Halbschwergewicht *n*.

crumb [krʌm] **1.** Krume *f*, Brosame *f*; Brocken *m* (*a. fig.*); **2.** *Fleisch* panieren; = **crum·ble** ['~bl] (zer)krümeln, (-)bröckeln; *fig.* zugrunde gehen; '**crum·bling,** '**crum·bly** bröckelig; **crumb·y** ['krʌmi] krumig.

crum·my *sl.* ['krʌmi] mies (*wertlos, schlecht*); *feel ~* sich mies fühlen.

crump *sl.* [krʌmp] Krachen *n*; ⚔ dicker Brocken *m*.

crum·pet ['krʌmpit] *lockerer* Teekuchen *m*; *sl.* Birne *f* (*Kopf*); *be off one's ~* e-e weiche Birne haben.

crum·ple ['krʌmpl] *v/t.* zerknüllen, -knittern; *fig.* vernichten; *v/i.* zerknüllt werden; sich knüllen.

crunch [krʌntʃ] (zer)kauen; zermalmen; knirschen.

crup·per ['krʌpə] Schwanzriemen *m*; Kruppe *f*.

cru·ral *anat.* ['kruərəl] Schenkel...

cru·sade [kru:'seid] **1.** Kreuzzug *m* (*a. fig.*); **2.** e-n Kreuzzug unternehmen; **cru'sad·er** Kreuzfahrer *m*.

crush [krʌʃ] **1.** Druck *m*; Gedränge *n*; F große Gesellschaft *f*; (Frucht-)Saft *m*; *have a ~ sl.* verknallt sein (*on* in); **2.** *v/t.* (zer)quetschen, (-)drükken; zermalmen; *fig.* vernichten; *Flasche* leeren; *~ out fig.* zertreten; *v/i.* zs.-gequetscht werden; sich drängen; *Am. sl.* flirten; *~* **bar·ri·er** Absperrgitter *n*; '**crush·er** Brechmaschine *f*; F *et.* Überwältigendes *n*, Schlag *m*; '**crush-room** *thea.* Foyer *n*.

crust [krʌst] **1.** Kruste *f*, Rinde *f*; *Am. sl.* Frechheit *f*; **2.** ver-, überkrusten; verharschen.
crus·ta·cean *zo.* [krʌsˈteiʃjən] Krusten-, Krebstier *n*.
crust·ed [ˈkrʌstid] abgelagert (*Wein*); eingewurzelt (*Sitte*); ~ *snow* Harsch(schnee) *m*; ˈ**crust·y** □ krustig; mürrisch.
crutch [krʌtʃ] Krücke *f*; **crutched** an Krücken gehend; Krück...
crux [krʌks] *fig.* Kreuz *n*, Haken *m*, harte Nuß *f*.
cry [krai] **1.** Schrei *m*; Geschrei *n*; Ruf *m*; Weinen *n*; Gebell *n*; *a far ~ from ... to* ein weiter Weg von ... bis; *fig.* ein großer Unterschied zwischen ... und; *within ~ (of)* in Rufweite (von); **2.** schreien; (aus-)rufen; weinen; ~ *for* verlangen nach; ~ *off* plötzlich absagen; ~ *out* aufschreien; sich beschweren (*against* über *acc.*); ~ *up* rühmen; *Preise* hochtreiben; ˈ**~-ba·by** kleiner Schreihals *m*; Heulsuse *f*; ˈ**cry·ing** *fig.* himmelschreiend; dringend.
crypt [kript] Krypta *f*, Gruft *f*; ˈ**cryp·tic** verborgen, geheim; **cryp·to-** [ˈ~təu] *Wortelement*: verborgen, geheim, verkappt.
crys·tal [ˈkristl] **1.** Kristall *m*; Kristall(glas) *n*; *bsd. Am.* Uhrglas *n*; **2.** kristallen; kristallklar; ~ **ball** Kristallkugel *f e-s Hellsehers*; ˈ**~-clear** sonnenklar; ˈ**~-gaz·ing** Hellsehen *n*; **crys·tal·line** [ˈ~təlain] kristallen; Kristall...; **crys·tal·liˈza·tion** Kristallisation *f*; ˈ**crys·tal·lize** kristallisieren; *~d* kandiert (*Frucht*).
cub [kʌb] **1.** Junge *n von Bären etc.*; Bengel *m*, Flegel *m*; Anfänger *m*; **2.** (Junge) werfen; ˈ**cub·bing** Jagd *f* auf Jungfüchse.
cu·bage [ˈkju:bidʒ] Kubikinhalt *m*.
cub·by-hole [ˈkʌbihəul] behagliches Kämmerchen *n*.
cube ⚘ [kju:b] **1.** Würfel *m*, Kubus *m*; Kubikzahl *f*; **2.** in die dritte Potenz erheben; ~ *root* Kubikwurzel *f*; ˈ**cu·bic**, ˈ**cu·bi·cal** □ würfelförmig; kubisch; Kubik...
cu·bi·cle [ˈkju:bikl] Schlafkammer *f*.
cu·bit [ˈkju:bit] Elle *f* (*Maß*).
cub·hood [ˈkʌbhud] Flegeljahre *n/pl.*
cuck·old [ˈkʌkəuld] **1.** Hahnrei *m*; **2.** zum Hahnrei machen.
cuck·oo [ˈkuku:] **1.** Kuckuck *m*; **2.** *sl.* plemplem (*verrückt*).
cu·cum·ber [ˈkju:kʌmbə] Gurke *f*; *as cool as a ~ fig.* eiskalt, gelassen.
cu·cur·bit [kjuˈkə:bit] Kürbis *m*.
cud [kʌd] wiedergekäutes Futter *n*; *chew the ~* wiederkäuen; *fig.* überlegen.
cud·dle [ˈkʌdl] **1.** F Liebkosung *f*; **2.** *v/t.* (ver)hätscheln; *v/i.* sich zs.-kuscheln.
cudg·el [ˈkʌdʒəl] **1.** Knüttel *m*; *take up the ~s for* Partei ergreifen für; **2.** (ver)prügeln; ~ *one's brains* sich den Kopf zerbrechen (*about* über *acc.*; *for* um).
cue [kju:] *Billard*-Queue *n*; *bsd. thea.* Stichwort *n*; Wink *m*; *take the ~ from s.o.* sich nach j-m richten.
cuff[1] [kʌf] **1.** (Faust)Schlag *m*; **2.** knuffen, schlagen.
cuff[2] [~] Manschette *f*; Handschelle *f*; (Ärmel-, *Am. a.* Hosen)Aufschlag *m*; ˈ**~-links** *pl.* Manschettenknöpfe *m/pl.*
cui·rass [kwiˈræs] Küraß *m*.
cui·sine [kwi:ˈzi:n] Küche *f* (*Art zu kochen*).
cul-de-sac [ˈkuldəˈsæk] Sackgasse *f*.
cu·li·nar·y [ˈkʌlinəri] kulinarisch.
cull *lit.* [kʌl] auslesen, -suchen; pflücken.
cul·len·der [ˈkʌlində] = *colander.*
culm [kʌlm] Kohlengrus *m*.
cul·mi·nate [ˈkʌlmineit] *ast.* kulminieren; *fig.* gipfeln, den Höhepunkt erreichen; **cul·miˈna·tion** *ast.* Kulmination *f*; *fig.* Höhepunkt *m*.
cu·lottes [kju:ˈlɔts] *pl.* Hosenrock *m*.
cul·pa·bil·i·ty [kʌlpəˈbiliti] Strafbarkeit *f*; ˈ**cul·pa·ble** □ tadelnswert; strafbar; schuldhaft.
cul·prit [ˈkʌlprit] Angeklagte *m*, *f*; Schuldige *m*, *f*, Missetäter(in).
cult [kʌlt] Kult(us) *m*.
cul·ti·va·ble [ˈkʌltivəbl] kulturfähig; ⸙ anbaufähig.
cul·ti·vate [ˈkʌltiveit] kultivieren; urbar machen; an-, bebauen; *fig.* ausbilden; *Fertigkeit* üben, betreiben; *Geschmack etc.* pflegen; ˈ**cul·ti·vat·ed** *fig.* gepflegt, kultiviert, gebildet; **cul·tiˈva·tion** (An-, Acker)Bau *m*; Ausbildung *f*; Übung *f e-r Kunst etc.*; Pflege *f*, Zucht *f*; ˈ**cul·ti·va·tor** Landwirt *m*; Züchter *m*; Kultivator *m* (*Maschine*).
cul·tur·al □ [ˈkʌltʃərəl] kulturell; Kultur...

cul·ture ['kʌltʃə] Kultur *f*; Pflege *f*; Zucht *f*; '**cul·tured** kultiviert; gebildet; '**cul·ture-me·di·um** *biol.* künstlicher Nährboden *m*; '**culture-pearl** Zuchtperle *f*.
cul·vert ['kʌlvət] Abzugskanal *m*.
cum·ber ['kʌmbə] überladen; belasten; **~·some** ['~səm], **cumbrous** □ ['~brəs] beschwerlich, lästig; schwerfällig; ⚘ sperrig, Sperr...
cum·in ⚘ ['kʌmin] Kümmel *m*.
cu·mu·la·tive □ ['kju:mjulətiv] (an-, auf)häufend; kumulativ; Zusatz...; sich steigernd; **cu·mu·lus** ['~ləs], *pl.* **cu·mu·li** ['~lai] Haufenwolke *f*, Kumulus *m*.
cu·ne·i·form ['kju:niifɔ:m] keilförmig; Keil(schrift)...
cun·ning ['kʌniŋ] **1.** □ schlau, listig, verschmitzt; gescheit; *Am.* reizend; **2.** List *f*, Schlauheit *f*.
cunt V [kʌnt] Fotze *f* (*Vagina*).
cup [kʌp] **1.** Becher *m*, Schale *f*, Tasse *f* (*a. als Maß*); Kelch *m* (*a.* ⚘ *u. fig.*); *Sport*: Pokal *m*; **2.** schröpfen; *die Hand* wölben; **~·board** ['kʌbəd] (Speise-, Silber- *etc.*) Schrank *m*; ~ *love fig.* Liebe *f* aus Berechnung; ~ **fi·nal** *Sport*: Pokalendspiel *n*; **~·ful** ['~ful] Tasse *f* (*als Maß*).
Cu·pid ['kju:pid] Cupido *m*, Amor *m*.
cu·pid·i·ty [kju:'piditi] Habgier *f*.
cu·po·la ['kju:pələ] Kuppel *f*; ⚔, ⚓ Panzerturm *m*.
cup·ping-glass ⚕ ['kʌpiŋglɑ:s] Schröpfkopf *m*.
cu·pre·ous *min.* ['kju:priəs] kupfern; **cu·pric** ['~prik] Kupfer...
cup-tie ['kʌptai] *Sport*: Pokalspiel *n*.
cur [kə:] Köter *m*; Schurke *m*, Halunke *m*.
cur·a·bil·i·ty [kjuərə'biliti] Heilbarkeit *f*; '**cur·a·ble** heilbar.
cur·a·çao [kjuərə'səu] Curaçao *m* (*Likör*).
cu·ra·cy ['kjuərəsi] Unterpfarre *f*; **cu·rate** ['~rit] Hilfsgeistliche *m*, Unterpfarrer *m*; **cu·ra·tor** [~'reitə] Kurator *m*.
curb [kə:b] **1.** Kinnkette *f*; Kandare *f*; *fig.* Zaum *m*, Zügel *m*; *a.* ~*stone* steinerne Einfassung *f*; *bsd.* Bordschwelle *f*, Randstein *m*; **2.** an die Kandare nehmen; *fig.* zügeln, im Zaume halten; '**~-'market** *Am. Börse*: Freiverkehr *m*; '**~-roof** Mansardendach *n*.
curd [kə:d] **1.** Quark *m*; **2.** *mst* **cur·dle** ['~dl] gerinnen (lassen).
cure [kjuə] **1.** Kur *f*; Heilmittel *n*; ~ *of souls* Seelsorge *f*; **2.** heilen; einlegen, pökeln; räuchern; *Heu* trocknen; '**~-all** Allheilmittel *n*.
cur·few ['kə:fju:] Abendglocke *f*; -läuten *n*; *pol.* Ausgehverbot *n*.
cu·ri·a *eccl.* ['kjuəriə] Kurie *f*.
cu·rie *phys.* ['kjuəri] Curie *n* (*Maßeinheit der Radioaktivität*).
cu·ri·o ['kjuəriəu] Rarität *f*; **cu·ri·os·i·ty** [~'ɔsiti] Neugier *f*; Rarität *f*, Seltenheit *f*; Seltsamkeit *f*; '**cu·ri·ous** □ neugierig; genau; seltsam, merkwürdig.
curl [kə:l] **1.** *Haar*-Locke *f*; Kräuselung *f*; ~-*paper* Lockenwickel *m aus Papier*; **2.** (sich) kräuseln; (sich) locken; (sich) ringeln; '**curl·er** Lockenwickel *m*.
cur·lew *orn.* ['kə:lju:] Brachvogel *m*.
curl·ing ['kə:liŋ] *Sport*: Eiskegeln *n*; '**~-i·ron**, '**~-tongs** *pl.* Brenneisen *n*, -schere *f*; '**curl·y** gekräuselt; lockig; Locken...
cur·mudg·eon [kə:'mʌdʒən] Geizhals *m*, Knicker *m*.
cur·rant ['kʌrənt] Johannisbeere *f*; *a. dried* ~ Korinthe *f*.
cur·ren·cy ['kʌrənsi] Umlauf *m*, Verbreitung *f*; ✝ Lauffrist *f*; Kurs *m*, Währung *f*; *fig.* Geltung *f*; '**cur·rent** **1.** □ umlaufend; ✝ kursierend, gangbar (*Geld*); allgemein (bekannt); laufend (*Monat, Jahr*); gegenwärtig; ~ *events pl.* Tagesereignisse *n/pl.*; ~ *account* ✝ Girokonto *n*; **2.** Strom *m* (*a.* ⚡); Strömung *f* (*a. fig.*); *Luft*-Zug *m*; ~ *impulse* ⚡ Stromstoß *m*; ~ *junction* elektrischer Anschluß *m*.
cur·ric·u·lum [kə'rikjuləm], *pl.* **cur'ric·u·la** [~lə] Lehr-, Stundenplan *m*; Pensum *n*; ~ **vi·tae** ['vaiti:] Lebenslauf *m*.
cur·ri·er ['kʌriə] Lederzurichter *m*.
cur·rish □ ['kə:riʃ] *fig.* hündisch; bissig.
cur·ry[1] ['kʌri] **1.** Curry *m*, *n*; ~-*powder* Currypulver *n* (*Gewürz*); **2.** mit Curry würzen.
cur·ry[2] [~] *Leder* zurichten; *Pferd* striegeln; *j.* durchprügeln; ~ *favour with* sich einzuschmeicheln versuchen bei; '**~-comb** Striegel *m*.

curse [kə:s] **1.** Fluch *m*; **2.** (ver-)fluchen; strafen (*with* mit); **curs·ed** □ ['kə:sid] verflucht.
cur·sive ['kə:siv] Kursiv...; Schreib-...
cur·so·ry □ ['kə:səri] flüchtig, oberflächlich; kursorisch.
curt □ [kə:t] kurz, knapp; barsch.
cur·tail [kə:'teil] beschneiden (*a. fig.*); *fig.* beschränken; kürzen (*of* um); **cur'tail·ment** Kürzung *f*.
cur·tain ['kə:tn] **1.** Vorhang *m*; Gardine *f*; *fig.* Schleier *m*; ⚔ Zwischenwall *m*; *draw a ~ over s.th. fig.* et. begraben; **2.** verhängen, verschleiern; *~ off* durch e-n Vorhang abtrennen; '**~-call** *thea.* Hervorruf *m* (*e-s Schauspielers*); '**~-fire** ⚔ Sperrfeuer *n*; '**~-lec·ture** F Gardinenpredigt *f*; '**~-rais·er** *thea. u. fig.* Vorspiel *n*.
curt·s(e)y ['kə:tsi] **1.** Knicks *m*; *drop a ~* e-n Knicks machen; **2.** knicksen (*to* vor).
cur·va·ture ['kə:vətʃə] Krümmung *f*; *~ of the spine* Rückgratverkrümmung *f*.
curve [kə:v] **1.** Kurve *f*; Krümmung *f*; *Am. Baseball*: Effetball *m*; **2.** (sich) krümmen; (sich) biegen.
cush·ion ['kuʃən] **1.** Kissen *n*; Polster *n*; *Billard*-Bande *f*; **2.** mit Kissen versehen; polstern; *fig.* unterdrücken; ⊕ abfedern.
cush·y *sl.* ['kuʃi] leicht, bequem.
cusp [kʌsp] Spitze *f*; Scheitelpunkt *m*; Horn *n des Mondes*.
cus·pi·dor *Am.* ['kʌspidɔ:] Spucknapf *m*; Speitüte *f*.
cuss *Am.* F [kʌs] **1.** Nichtsnutz *m*, *co.* Kerl *m*; **2.** fluchen; **cuss·ed** ['kʌsid] verflucht; widerborstig.
cus·tard ['kʌstəd] Eierspeise *f*; '**~-pow·der** Puddingpulver *n*.
cus·to·di·an [kʌs'təudjən] Hüter *m*; Verwalter *m*; Treuhänder *m*; **cus·to·dy** ['~tədi] Haft *f*; (Ob)Hut *f*; Betreuung *f*; Verwaltung *f*; Schutz *m*.
cus·tom ['kʌstəm] Gewohnheit *f*, Brauch *m*; Sitte *f*; ⚖ Gewohnheitsrecht *n*; ✝ Kundschaft *f*; *~s pl.* Zoll *m*; '**cus·tom·ar·y** □ gewöhnlich, üblich; '**cus·tom·er** Kunde *m*, Kundin *f*; F Bursche *m*; '**cus·tom-house** Zollamt *n*; *~ officer* Zollbeamte *m*; '**cus·tom-'made** *Am.* nach Maß gearbeitet; '**cus·toms clear·ance** Zollabfertigung *f*; **customs du·ty** Zoll(gebühr *f*) *m*.
cut [kʌt] **1.** Schnitt *m*; Hieb *m*; Stich *m*; (Schnitt)Wunde *f*; Ab-, Einschnitt *m*; Durchstich *m*; Graben *m*; Beschneidung *f*; Kürzung *f*; Abstrich *m*; Ausschnitt *m*; *mst short-cut* Wegabkürzung *f*; *Holz*-Schnitt *m*; *Kupfer*-Stich *m*; *Kleider*-Schnitt *m*; Schnitte *f*, Scheibe *f von Braten etc.*; *fig.* Schneiden *n* (*Nichtkennenwollen*); ⚡ (Strom-) Sperre *f*; *iro.* Stück(chen) *n* (*verletzende Handlung*); *Karten*-Abheben *n*; *cold ~s pl. Küche*: kalter Aufschnitt *m*; *give s.o. the ~* (*direct*) F j. schneiden; **2.** (*irr.*) *v/t.* schneiden; schnitzen; gravieren; ab-, an-, auf-, aus-, be-, durch-, zer-, zuschneiden; ⚓ kappen; *Karten* abheben; F sich drücken von; *j. beim Begegnen* schneiden; *~ one's finger* sich in den Finger schneiden; *~ teeth* zahnen; *~ a figure* F eine Figur machen; *~ and come again* in Hülle und Fülle; *~ it fine* F es knapp machen, keinen (*zeitlichen*) Spielraum lassen; *~ short j.* unterbrechen; *to ~ a long story short* um es kurz zu sagen; *~ and run* F auskneifen; *~ back* einschränken; *~ down* fällen; *Getreide* mähen; *Umfang* beschneiden; *Preis* drücken; *~ off* abschneiden (*a. fig.*); ausschließen (*from* von); *teleph.* trennen; *~ out* ausschneiden; *Am. Vieh* aussondern *aus der Herde*; *fig. j.* ausstechen; aufhören mit, einstellen; ⚡ ausschalten; *Radio*: abstellen; *be ~ out for* das Zeug zu *e-r Sache* haben; *have one's work ~ out* (*for one*) genug zu tun haben; *~ it out!* *sl.* hör auf!; *~ up* zer-, aufschneiden; zerlegen; *fig.* heruntermachen, -reißen; *v/i. ~ in* sich einschieben; **3.** geschnitten *etc.*; *sl.* betrunken; *~ flowers pl.* Schnittblumen *f/pl.*; *~ glass* geschliffenes Glas *n*, Kristall *n*; *~ and dry od. dried* fix und fertig.
cu·ta·ne·ous [kju:'teinjəs] Haut...
cut-a·way ['kʌtəwei] *a. ~ coat* Cut (-away) *m*.
cut·back ['kʌtbæk] Kürzung *f*; *Film*: Rückblende *f*.
cute □ F [kju:t] klug, schlau; *Am.* F reizend, nett.
cu·ti·cle *anat.*, ⚘ ['kju:tikl] Ober-

haut *f*; ~ *scissors pl.* Hautschere *f*.
cut-in ['kʌtin] *Film*: Zwischentitel *m*.
cut·lass ['kʌtləs] ⚓ Entermesser *n*; Hirschfänger *m*.
cut·ler ['kʌtlə] Messerschmied *m*; '**cut·ler·y** Messerschmiedearbeit *f*; Messerschmiedewaren *f/pl.*; Stahlwaren *f/pl.*; Besteck(e *pl.*) *n*.
cut·let ['kʌtlit] Kotelett *n*; Schnitzel *n*.
cut...: '**~-off** *Am.* Abkürzung *f* (*Straße, Weg*) (*a. attr.*); '**~-out** *mot.* Auspuffklappe *f*; ⚡ Sicherung *f*; Ausschalter *m*; *Am.* Ausschneidebogen *m*, -bild *n*; '**~-price** verbilligt, *im Preis* herabgesetzt; '**~-purse** Taschendieb *m*; '**~-rate** *im Preis* ermäßigt; '**cut·ter** Schneidende *m, f*; Schnitzer *m*; Zuschneider(in); *Film*: Cutter *m*, Schnittmeister *m*; ⚒ Hauer *m*; ⊕ Schneidezeug *n*, -maschine *f*; ⚓ Kutter *m*; *Am.* leichter Schlitten *m*; '**cut-throat 1.** Halsabschneider *m*; Meuchelmörder *m*; **2.** halsabschneiderisch; mörderisch; '**cut·ting 1.** □ schneidend; scharf; ⊕ Schneid..., Fräs...; ~ *edge* Schneide *f*; ~ *nippers pl.* Kneifzange *f*; **2.** Schneiden *n*; 🚂 *etc.* Einschnitt *m*, Durchstich *m*; ⚘ Steckling *m*; *Zeitungs*-Ausschnitt *m*; ~*s pl.* Schnipsel *n/pl.*; ⊕ Schneidspäne *m/pl.*
cut·tle *ichth.* ['kʌtl] = ~-*fish*; '**~-bone** Schale *f* des Tintenfischs; '**~-fish** Tintenfisch *m*.
cy·a·nide ⚗ ['saiənaid] Zyan *n*; ~ *of potassium* Zyankali *n*.
cy·ber·net·ics [saibəː'netiks] *sg.* Kybernetik *f*.
cyc·la·men ⚘ ['sikləmən] Alpenveilchen *n*.
cy·cle ['saikl] **1.** Zyklus *m*; Kreis(-lauf) *m*; Periode *f*; ⊕ Arbeitsgang *m*; ✝ Konjunkturzyklus *m*; Fahrrad *n*; *four-*~ *engine mot.* Viertaktmotor *m*; **2.** radfahren; '**cy·clic,** '**cy·cli·cal** □ zyklisch; ✝ konjunkturell; Konjunktur...; **cy·cling** ['saikliŋ] **1.** Radfahren *n*; **2.** Rad...; '**cy·clist** Radfahrer(in).
cy·clone ['saikləun] Zyklon *m*, Wirbelsturm *m*; **cy·clon·ic** [~'klɔnik] wirbelsturmartig.
cy·clo·pae·di·a [saikləu'piːdjə] Konversationslexikon *n*.
Cy·clo·pean [sai'kləupjən] zyklopisch, riesig.
cy·clo·style ['saikləustail] Vervielfältigungsapparat *m*; **cy·clo·tron** *phys.* ['saiklətrɔn] Zyklotron *n*.
cyg·net ['signit] junger Schwan *m*.
cyl·in·der ['silində] Zylinder *m*, Walze *f*; Trommel *f*; **cy'lin·dric, cy'lin·dri·cal** □ [~drik(əl)] zylindrisch.
cym·bal ♩ ['simbl] Zimbel *f*, Becken *n*.
cyn·ic ['sinik] **1.** *a.* '**cyn·i·cal** □ zynisch, spöttisch; **2.** Zyniker *m*, Spötter *m*; **cyn·i·cism** ['~sizəm] Zynismus *m*.
cy·no·sure *fig.* ['sinəzjuə] Gegenstand *m* der Bewunderung, Mittelpunkt *m* des Interesses.
cy·press ⚘ ['saipris] Zypresse *f*.
Cyp·rian ['sipriən], **Cyp·ri·ot** ['sipriət] **1.** Zypriot(in); **2.** zyprisch.
cyst [sist] Blase *f*; ⚕ Sackgeschwulst *f*, Zyste *f*; '**cyst·ic** Blasen...; **cys·ti·tis** ⚕ [sis'taitis] Blasenentzündung *f*.
Czar [zɑː] Zar *m*.
Czech [tʃek] **1.** Tscheche *m*, Tschechin *f*; **2.** tschechisch.
Czech·o-Slo·vak ['tʃekəu'sləuvæk] **1.** tschechoslowakisch; **2.** Tschechoslowake *m*, Tschechoslowakin *f*.

D

'd F = *had; would*.
dab [dæb] **1.** Klaps *m*; Betupfen *n*; Tupfen *m*, Klecks *m*; *ichth.* Butt *m*; Kenner *m*; *be a* ~ (*hand*) *at s.th.* sich auf et. verstehen; **2.** klapsen; (be-)tupfen; *Farbe etc.* auftragen; *typ.* abklatschen, klischieren.
dab·ble ['dæbl] bespritzen; plät-

schern; (hinein)pfuschen (*in* in *acc.*); sich ein wenig befassen (*in* mit); '**dab·bler** Amateur(in); Pfuscher(in).

dace *ichth.* [deis] *Art* Weißfisch *m.*

dac·tyl *poet.* ['dæktil] Daktylus *m* (*Versfuß*).

dad F [dæd], **dad·dy** F ['~di] Papa *m*, Vati *m.*

dad·dy-long·legs F *zo.* ['dædi'lɔŋlegz] Schnake *f.*

daf·fo·dil ⚘ ['dæfədil] gelbe Narzisse *f*, Osterglocke *f.*

daft F [dɑ:ft] blöde, doof.

dag·ger ['dægə] Dolch *m*; *be at* ~*s drawn* auf Kriegsfuß stehen; *look* ~*s at s.o.* j. mit Blicken durchbohren.

dag·gle ['dægl] beschmuddeln.

da·go *Am. sl.* ['deigəu] *contp.* = *Spanier, Portugiese, Italiener.*

dahl·ia ⚘ ['deiljə] Dahlie *f.*

Dail Eir·eann [dail'ɛərən] Abgeordnetenkammer *f des irischen Parlaments.*

dai·ly ['deili] **1.** täglich; ~ *dozen* F Morgengymnastik *f*; **2.** Tageszeitung *f*; Tag(es)mädchen *n.*

dain·ti·ness ['deintinis] Leckerhaftigkeit *f*; Verwöhntheit *f*; Zartheit *f*, Feinheit *f*; '**dain·ty** □ **1.** lecker, delikat; zart, fein; wählerisch, verwöhnt; **2.** Leckerbissen *m*; Delikatesse *f.*

dair·y ['dɛəri] Molkerei *f*, Milchwirtschaft *f*; Milchgeschäft *n*; ~ **cat·tle** Milchvieh *n*; '**~-farm** Meierei *f*; Molkerei *f* und Käserei *f*; '**~·maid** Milch-, Kuhmagd *f*; '**~·man** Milchhändler *m.*

da·is ['deiis] Estrade *f.*

dai·sy ['deizi] **1.** Gänseblümchen *n*; *push up the daisies* F die Radieschen von unten wachsen sehen (*tot sein*); **2.** F reizend, lieb.

dale [deil] Tal *n.*

dal·li·ance ['dæliəns] Trödelei *f*; Schäkerei *f*; '**dal·ly** schäkern; vertrödeln.

dam[1] [dæm] Mutter *f von Tieren.*

dam[2] [~] **1.** Deich *m*, Damm *m*; Wehr *n*; Talsperre *f*; **2.** (ab)dämmen (*a. fig.*); ~ *in* eindeichen.

dam·age ['dæmidʒ] **1.** Schaden *m*; ~*s pl.* ⚖ Schadenersatz *m*; **2.** (be-)schädigen; '**dam·age·a·ble** leicht zu beschädigen(d).

dam·a·scene ['dæməsi:n] **1.** damaszenisch, Damaszener...; **2.** damaszieren; **dam·ask** ['dæməsk] **1.** Damast *m*; Damaszenerstahl *m*; Rosenrot *n*; **2.** damasten; rosenrot; **3.** *Stahl* damaszieren; *Stoff* damastartig weben.

dame [deim] Dame *f* (*bsd. als Titel*); *sl.* Frau *f*, Mädchen *n.*

damn [dæm] **1.** verdammen; verurteilen; *thea.* ablehnen; ~ *it!* verwünscht!, verdammt!; **2.** Fluch *m*; *fig.* Pfifferling *m*; *I don't care a* ~*!* ich schere mich den Teufel darum!; **dam·na·ble** □ ['dæmnəbl] verdammenswert; abscheulich; **dam'na·tion** Verdammnis *f*, Verdammung *f*; **dam·na·to·ry** □ ['~nətəri] verdammend; **damned** [dæmd] *adj. u. adv.* verdammt (*a.* = *sehr*); **damn·ing** ['dæmiŋ] schwer belastend.

Dam·o·cles ['dæməkli:z]: *sword of* ~ Damoklesschwert *n.*

damp [dæmp] **1.** feucht, dunstig; **2.** Feuchtigkeit *f*, Dunst *m*; *fig.* Gedrücktheit *f*, Lähmung *f*; ⚒ Schwaden *m*; *cast a* ~ *over* e-n Schatten werfen auf (*acc.*); ~ *course* Isolierschicht *f*; **3.** *a.* '**damp·en** an-, befeuchten; *Feuer, Eifer etc.* dämpfen; *fig.* niederdrücken; '**damp·er** Dämpfer *m* (♪ *u. fig.*); Ofenklappe *f*; '**damp·ish** etwas feucht; '**damp--proof** feuchtigkeitsbeständig.

dam·sel † ['dæmzəl] junges Mädchen *n.*

dam·son ⚘ ['dæmzən] Damaszenerpflaume *f*; ~ *cheese* Pflaumenmus *n.*

dance [dɑ:ns] **1.** Tanz *m*; Ball *m*; *lead s.o. a* ~ j-m Scherereien machen; **2.** tanzen (lassen); aufwallen; '**~-band** Tanzkapelle *f*; '**~-hall** Ballsaal *m*; '**~-hos·tess** Taxigirl *n*; '**danc·er** Tänzer(in).

danc·ing ['dɑ:nsiŋ] Tanzen *n*; *attr.* Tanz...; '**~-girl** Tänzerin *f*; '**~--les·son** Tanzstunde *f*; '**~-room** Tanzsaal *m.*

dan·de·li·on ⚘ ['dændilaiən] Löwenzahn *m.*

dan·der *sl.* ['dændə] gereizte Stimmung *f*; *get s.o.'s* ~ *up* j. auf die Palme bringen.

dan·dle ['dændl] *Kind auf den Armen od. Knien* wiegen.

dan·druff ['dændrʌf] Kopfschuppen *f/pl.*

dan·dy ['dændi] **1.** Dandy *m*, Stutzer

m; F prima Sache *f*; **2.** *bsd. Am.* F Klasse, prima, erstklassig; **dan·dy·ish** ['~diiʃ] stutzerhaft; '**dan·dy·ism** stutzerhaftes Wesen *n*.

Dane [dein] Däne *m*, Dänin *f*.

dan·ger ['deindʒə] Gefahr *f*; '**~-list**: *be on the* ~ F in Lebensgefahr sein; **~ mon·ey** Gefahrenzulage *f*; '**dan·ger·ous** □ gefährlich; '**dan·ger--sig·nal** 🚂 Notsignal *n*.

dan·gle ['dæŋgl] baumeln (lassen); schlenkern (mit); *fig.* schwanken; ~ *about, after, round s.o.* j-m nachlaufen; '**dan·gler** Schürzenjäger *m*.

Dan·ish ['deiniʃ] dänisch.

dank [dæŋk] dunstig, feucht.

Da·nu·bi·an [dæ'nju:bjən] Donau...

daph·ne ['dæfni] ⚘ Seidelbast *m*; Lorbeer *m*.

dap·per □ F ['dæpə] nett, fein; behend, gewandt.

dap·ple ['dæpl] sprenkeln, scheckig machen; '**dap·pled** scheckig; gesprenkelt; '**dap·ple-'grey** Apfelschimmel *m*.

dare [dɛə] *v/i.* es wagen, sich (ge-) trauen, sich unterstehen; *I* ~ *say* ich darf wohl sagen; freilich; das glaube ich wohl; *v/t. et.* wagen; *j.* herausfordern; *j-m* trotzen; '**~--dev·il** Draufgänger *m*, Wagehals *m*; '**dar·ing** □ **1.** verwegen, kühn; **2.** Verwegenheit *f*, Kühnheit *f*.

dark [dɑ:k] **1.** □ *mst* dunkel, finster; brünett; schwer verständlich; geheim(nisvoll); trüb(selig); **2.** Dunkel(heit *f*) *n*; *before (after)* ~ vor (nach) Einbruch der Dunkelheit; *leap in the* ~ Sprung *m* ins Ungewisse; ♀ **A·ges** *pl. das* frühe Mittelalter; '**dark·en** (sich) verdunkeln; (sich) verfinstern; *fig.* verdüstern; verwirren; *never* ~ *s.o.'s door* nie mehr j-s Schwelle betreten; **dark horse** Außenseiter *m*; *fig.* unbeschriebenes Blatt *n*; '**dark·ish** schwärzlich; **dark·ling** ['~liŋ] dunkel (werdend); '**dark·ness** Dunkelheit *f*, Finsternis *f*; '**dark·room** Dunkelkammer *f*; **dark·some** ['~səm] *poet.* = *dark 1*; '**dark·y** F Schwarze *m*, *f* (*Neger*).

dar·ling ['dɑ:liŋ] **1.** Liebling *m*; **2.** Lieblings...; geliebt.

darn[1] *sl.* [dɑ:n] = *damn*.

darn[2] [~] **1.** Stopfnaht *f*; Stopfstelle *f*; **2.** stopfen; ausbessern; '**darn·er** Stopfpilz *m*.

darn·ing ['dɑ:niŋ] Stopferei *f*; '**~--cot·ton** Stopfgarn *n*; '**~-nee·dle** Stopfnadel *f*.

dart [dɑ:t] **1.** Wurfspieß *m*, -pfeil *m*, -speer *m*; Satz *m*, Sprung *m*; *~s pl.* Wurfpfeilspiel *n*; **2.** *v/t.* werfen, schleudern; *v/i. fig.* schießen, (sich) stürzen (*at* auf *acc.*).

Dar·win·ism ['dɑ:winizəm] Darwinismus *m*.

dash [dæʃ] **1.** Schlag *m*, (Zs.-)Stoß *m*; Klatschen *n*; *fig.* Schwung *m*; Vorstoß *m*, Ansturm *m* (*for* auf *acc.*); *fig.* Anflug *m*; Prise *f Salz etc.*; Schuß *m Rum etc.*; *Feder-*Strich *m* (*a.* ♪, *tel.*); *typ.* Gedankenstrich *m*; *cut a* ~ eine gute Figur machen; *at a* ~ schnell; **2.** *v/t.* schlagen, werfen, schleudern; *mst* ~ *to pieces* zerschmettern; *Hoffnung* vernichten; (be)spritzen; vermengen; verwirren; ~ *down*, ~ *off Brief etc.* hinhauen; ~ *it! sl.* verdammt!; *v/i.* stoßen, schlagen; stürzen; stürmen; jagen; rasen; ~ *off* davonjagen; ~ *through* durchbrechen, -waten; ~ *up* heranjagen; '**~-board** *mot.* Armaturenbrett *n*; Spritzbrett *n* (*am Pferdewagen*); '**dash·er** F elegante Erscheinung *f*; '**dash·ing** □ schneidig, forsch; F flott, fesch.

das·tard ['dæstəd] heimtückischer Kerl *m*; '**das·tard·ly** heimtückisch; feig.

da·ta ['deitə] *pl., Am. a. sg.* Angaben *f/pl.*; Tatsachen *f/pl.*; Unterlagen *f/pl.*; Daten *n/pl.*; *personal* ~ Personalangaben *f/pl.*; ~ **print·er** Datenschreiber *m*; ~ **pro·cess·ing** Datenverarbeitung *f*; ~ **trans·mis·sion** Datenübertragung *f*.

date[1] [deit] Dattel *f*.

date[2] [~] **1.** Datum *n*; Zeit *f*; ⚖, ✝ Termin *m*; *bsd. Am.* F Verabredung *f*; Freund(in); *make a* ~ sich verabreden; *out of* ~ veraltet, unmodern; *to* ~ bis heute; *up to* ~ zeitgemäß, modern; auf der Höhe (der Zeit); **2.** datieren; *bsd. Am.* F sich verabreden; ~ *back to*, ~ *from* herrühren von, stammen aus, zurückgehen auf; '**~-block** Abreißkalender *m*; '**dat·ed** altmodisch, veraltet, überholt; '**date·less** ohne Datum; '**date-line** Datumsgrenze *f*; '**date--stamp** Datums-, Poststempel *m*.

da·tive ['deitiv] *a.* ~ *case* Dativ *m*.

da·tum ['deitəm] Angabe *f*; Einzelheit *f*; gegebene Größe *f od.* Tatsache *f*.

daub [dɔ:b] **1.** Schmiererei *f*, Sudelei *f*; **2.** (be)schmieren; *paint.* sudeln; **daub·(st)er** ['~(st)ə] Sudler *m*, Farbenkleckser *m*.

daugh·ter ['dɔ:tə] Tochter *f*; ~ *company* Tochtergesellschaft *f*; **~-in-law** ['dɔ:tərinlɔ:] Schwiegertochter *f*; '**daugh·ter·ly** töchterlich.

daunt [dɔ:nt] entmutigen, schrecken; *nothing* ~*ed* unerschrocken; '**~·less** furchtlos, unerschrocken.

dau·phin ['dɔ:fin] Dauphin *m* (*ältester Sohn des französischen Königs*).

dav·en·port ['dævnpɔ:t] Schreibschrank *m*, Sekretär *m*; Doppelbettcouch *f*, Wiener Bank *f*.

dav·it ⚓ ['dævit] Davit *m*, Bootskran *m*.

da·vy¹ ⚒ ['deivi] *a.* ~*-lamp* Sicherheitslampe *f*.

da·vy² *sl.* [~] Eid *m*; *take one's* ~ schwören.

daw *orn.* [dɔ:] Dohle *f*.

daw·dle F ['dɔ:dl] (ver)trödeln; bummeln; '**daw·dler** F Tagedieb *m*; *fig.* Schlafmütze *f*.

dawn [dɔ:n] **1.** Morgendämmerung *f*; *fig.* Anfang *m*, Anbruch *m*, Erwachen *n*; **2.** dämmern, tagen; *it* ~*ed upon him* es wurde ihm langsam klar.

day [dei] Tag *m*; *oft* ~*s pl.* (*bsd.* Lebens)Zeit *f*; Zeiten *pl.*; ~ *off* (dienst)freier Tag *m*; *carry od. win the* ~ den Sieg davontragen; *the other* ~ neulich; *this* ~ *week* heute in acht Tagen; heute vor acht Tagen; *let's call it a* ~ machen wir Schluß für heute!; *have a nice* ~ *Am.* mach's gut!; *pass the time of* ~ *with s.o.* j-m guten Tag sagen; '**~-book** ✝ Journal *n*; '**~-boy** Tagesschüler *m*, Externe *m*; '**~·break** Tagesanbruch *m*; '**~-care cen·ter** *Am.* Kindertagesstätte *f*; '**~-dream** **1.** Wachtraum *m*; **2.** (mit offenen Augen) träumen; '**~-fly** Eintagsfliege *f*; '**~-'la·bo(u)r·er** Tagelöhner *m*; '**~-light** Tageslicht *n*; ~*-saving time* Sommerzeit *f*; *beat the living* ~*s out of s.o.* j. grün und blau schlagen; '**~-long** den ganzen Tag (dauernd); '**~-'nur·se·ry** Kindergarten *m*; '**~-star** Morgenstern *m*; '**~-time** Tageszeit *f*; '**~-to-'day** täglich; dauernd.

daze [deiz] verwirren; betäuben;

dazed benommen.

daz·zle ['dæzl] blenden; ⚓ tarnen.

D-Day ['di:dei] Tag *m* der Invasion (*6. 6. 1944*).

dea·con ['di:kən] Diakon(us) *m*; '**dea·con·ess** Diakonissin *f*; '**dea·con·ry** Diakonat *n*.

dead [ded] **1.** tot, gestorben; unempfindlich (*to* für); öde; still (*Wasser*, ✝); matt (*Farben*, *Gold etc.*); blind (*Fenster etc.*); glanzlos (*Augen*); erloschen (*Feuer*); schal (*Getränk*); tief (*Schlaf*); totliegend (*Kapital etc.*); ⚡ stromlos; völlig, gänzlich; genau; ~ *bargain* spottbillige Ware *f*; *at a* ~ *bargain* zu e-m Spottpreis; ~ *calm* Wind-, *fig.* Totenstille *f*; ~ *centre* genaue Mitte *f*; ~ *centre*, ~ *point* toter Punkt *m*; ~ *heat* totes Rennen *n*; ~ *letter fig.* toter Buchstabe *m* (*nicht mehr beachtetes Gesetz*); unzustellbarer Brief *m*; ~ *load* Leer-, Eigengewicht *n*; ~ *loss* Totalverlust *m*; F Versager *m*; ~ *march* Trauermarsch *m*; ~ *set* entschlossener Angriff *m*; *a* ~ *shot* ein Meisterschütze *m*; ~ *wall* blinde Mauer *f*; ~ *water* stehendes Wasser *n*; Kielwasser *n*; ~ *weight* totes Gewicht *n*; *fig.* schwere Last *f*; ~ *wood* Reisig *n*; *Am.* Plunder *m*; *play* ~ sich totstellen; **2.** *adv.* gänzlich, völlig, total; durchaus; genau, (haar)scharf; ~ *against* gerade *od.* ganz und gar (ent)gegen; ~ *asleep* in tiefem Schlaf; ~ *drunk* total betrunken; ~ *sure* todsicher; ~ *tired* todmüde; **3.** *the* ~ der Tote; die Toten *pl.*; Totenstille *f*; *in the* ~ *of winter* im tiefsten Winter; *in the* ~ *of night* mitten in der Nacht; '**~-a'live** halbtot; zum Sterben langweilig; '**~-'beat** **1.** todmüde; **2.** *Am. sl.* Schnorrer *m*, Herumtreiber *m*; '**dead·en** abstumpfen (*to* gegen); *fig.* (er)töten; (ab)schwächen; dämpfen; ⊕ mattieren.

dead...: ~ **end** Sackgasse *f* (*a. fig.*); '**~-end** ohne Ausgang; *fig.* ausweglos, zu nichts führend; ~ *kids pl.* Straßenkinder *n/pl.*; ~ *street* Sackgasse *f*; '**~-head** blinder Passagier *m*; Freikarteninhaber *m*; '**~-line** *Am.* Sperrlinie *f im Gefängnis*; Schlußtermin *m*; Stichtag *m*; '**~-lock** Stillstand *m*, Stockung *f*; *fig.* toter Punkt *m*; '**dead·ly** tödlich; ~ *pale* totenblaß; ~ *enemy* Todfeind *m*; ~ *sin* Todsünde *f*; '**dead·ness**

Erstarrung *f*; Unempfindlichkeit *f* (*to* gegen); Schalheit *f*, Mattheit *f*; ⚓ Flaute *f*.

dead...: **'~-'net·tle** Taubnessel *f*; **'~-'pan** *Am. sl.* ausdruckslos (*Gesicht*).

deaf □ [def] taub (*to* gegen, für); *~ and dumb* taubstumm; *turn a ~ ear* sich taub stellen (*to* gegen); *~* **aid** F Hörgerät *n*; **'deaf·en** taub machen; betäuben; **'deaf-'mute** Taubstumme *m, f*; **'deaf·ness** Taubheit *f*.

deal¹ [di:l] Brett *n*, Diele *f*; Fichtenholz *n*.

deal² [~] **1.** Teil *m*; Menge *f*; Kartengeben *n*; F Geschäft *n*; *Am. mst b. s.* Abmachung *f*; *a good ~* ziemlich viel; *a great ~* sehr viel; *give a square ~ to* gerecht werden (*dat.*); **2.** (*irr.*) *v/t.* (aus-, ver-, zu-) teilen; *Karten* geben; *e-n Schlag* versetzen (*at s.o.* j-m); *v/i.* handeln (*in* mit *e-r Ware*); verfahren; verkehren; *~ with* sich befassen mit, behandeln; *have ~t with s.o.* fertig sein mit j-m; **'deal·er** Händler *m* (*in* mit *e-r Ware*); Kartengeber *m*; *plain ~* ehrlicher Mensch *m*; *sharp ~* gerissener Kerl *m*; **'deal·ing** *mst ~s pl.* Handlungsweise *f*; Verfahren *n*; Umgang *m*, (*bsd.* Geschäfts)Verkehr *m*.

dealt [delt] *pret. u. p.p. von deal²* 2.

dean [di:n] Dekan *m*; **'dean·er·y** Dekanat *n*.

dear [diə] **1.** □ teuer; lieb; **2.** Liebling *m*; herziges Geschöpf *n*; **3.** F *o(h) ~!, ~ me!* du meine Güte!; ach herrje!; **'dear·ness** Teuerkeit *f*, Wert *m*; **dearth** [də:θ] Teuerung *f*; Mangel *m*; **dear·y** F ['diəri] Liebling *m*, Schatz *m*.

death [deθ] Tod *m*; *~s pl.* Todesfälle *m/pl.*; *~ penalty* Todesstrafe *f*; *tired to ~* todmüde; **'~-bed** Sterbebett *n*; **'~-blow** Todesstreich *m*, -stoß *m*; **'~-du·ty** Erbschaftssteuer *f*; *~* **grant** Sterbegeld *n*; **'~·less** unsterblich; **'~·like** totenähnlich; **'death·ly** tödlich; **'death-rate** Sterblichkeitsziffer *f*; **'death-roll** ⚔ Gefallenenliste *f*; **death row** Todeszellen *f/pl.*; **'death's-head** Totenkopf *m*; **'death-trap** Todesstrecke *f*, -kurve *f etc.*; *fig.* Mausefalle *f*; **'death-war·rant** Todesurteil *n*.

dé·bâ·cle [dei'bɑ:kl] Zs.-bruch *m*, Katastrophe *f*.

de·bar [di'bɑ:] ausschließen (*from* von); *j.* hindern (*from* an *dat.*); *et.* verhindern.

de·bar·ka·tion [di:bɑ:'keiʃən] Ausschiffung *f*.

de·base [di'beis] verschlechtern; erniedrigen; verfälschen; **de'base·ment** Verschlechterung *f etc.*

de·bat·a·ble □ [di'beitəbl] strittig; umstritten; **de'bate 1.** Erörterung *f*, Debatte *f*; **2.** debattieren; erörtern; beraten; überlegen ([*on*] *s.th.* etwas, *with o.s.* bei sich); **de'bat·er** Diskussionsredner *m*; geschickter Disputant *m*.

de·bauch [di'bɔ:tʃ] **1.** Ausschweifung *f*; **2.** verderben; verführen; **deb·au·chee** [debɔ:'tʃi:] Wüstling *m*; **de·bauch·er·y** [di'bɔ:tʃəri] Ausschweifung *f*.

de·ben·ture [di'bentʃə] Schuldschein *m*; Rückzollschein *m*.

de·bil·i·tate [di'biliteit] schwächen; entkräften; **de·bil·i'ta·tion** Schwächung *f*; **de'bil·i·ty** Schwäche *f*.

deb·it ⚓ ['debit] **1.** Debet *n*, Schuld *f*; *to one's ~* zu j-s Lasten; **2.** *j.* belasten; *Summe* zu Lasten schreiben (*against od. to s.o.* j-m).

deb·o·nair [debə'nɛə] heiter, fröhlich.

de·bouch [di'bautʃ] hervorbrechen, -kommen; sich ergießen.

de·bris ['deibri:] Trümmer *n/pl.*, Schutt *m*.

debt [det] Schuld *f*; *active ~* ausstehende Forderung *f*; *~ collector* Schuldeneintreiber *m*; *owe s.o. a ~ of gratitude* j-m Dank schulden; *pay the ~ of nature, pay one's ~ to nature* der Natur s-n Tribut entrichten (*sterben*); **'debt·or** Schuldner(in).

de·bug [di:'bug] ⊕ den Defekt od. Fehler beheben bei; *sl. Raum* entwanzen (*Abhörgeräte entfernen*).

de·bunk F ['di:'bʌŋk] *fig.* vom Podest stoßen, den Nimbus nehmen (*dat.*).

de·bus [di:'bʌs] abladen; aussteigen (lassen).

dé·but ['deibu:] Debüt *n*; **dé·bu·tante** ['debju:tɑ:nt] Debütantin *f*.

dec·ade ['dekəid] Dekade *f*; Jahrzehnt *n*.

de·ca·dence ['dekədəns] Dekadenz *f*, Verfall *m*; **'de·ca·dent** verfallend, morsch, dekadent.

de·caf·fei·nat·ed [di:'kæfineitid] koffeinfrei (*Kaffee*).

dec·a·log(ue) ['dekəlɔg] Dekalog *m*, *die* Zehn Gebote *n/pl.*
de·camp [di'kæmp] aufbrechen; ausreißen, sich aus dem Staube machen; **de'camp·ment** Aufbruch *m.*
de·cant [di'kænt] abgießen; umfüllen; **de'cant·er** Karaffe *f.*
de·cap [di:'kæp] *Bombe etc.* entschärfen.
de·cap·i·tate [di'kæpiteit] enthaupten; *Am.* absägen (*entlassen*); **de·cap·i'ta·tion** Enthauptung *f.*
de·car·bon·ize *mot.* [di:'kɑ:bənaiz] von Verbrennungsrückständen säubern.
de·car·tel·i·za·tion [di:kɑ:təlai'zaiʃən] Entflechtung *f von Kartellen.*
de·cath·lon [di'kæθlɔn] *Sport:* Zehnkampf *m.*
de·cay [di'kei] **1.** Verfall *m*; Fäulnis *f*; Verwesung *f*; **2.** verfallen; *fig.* schwinden; (ver)faulen; verwesen; *~ed with age* altersschwach.
de·cease *bsd.* ⚖ [di'si:s] **1.** Ableben *n*; **2.** sterben; *the ~d* der (die) Verstorbene.
de·ceit [di'si:t] Täuschung *f*; Betrug *m*; **de'ceit·ful** □ [~ful] (be-)trügerisch; hinterlistig; **de'ceit·ful·ness** Hinterlist *f.*
de·ceiv·a·ble [di'si:vəbl] leicht zu betrügen(d); **de'ceive** betrügen; täuschen; verleiten (*into* zu); *be ~d* sich täuschen; **de'ceiv·er** Betrüger(in).
de·cel·er·ate [di:'seləreit] (sich) verlangsamen; **de·cel·er'a·tion** Verlangsamung *f*; *~ lane mot.* Verzögerungsspur *f.*
De·cem·ber [di'sembə] Dezember *m.*
de·cen·cy ['di:snsi] Anstand *m*; **'de·cen·cies** *pl.* Anstandsformen *f/pl.*
de·cen·ni·al [di'senjəl] zehnjährig; **de'cen·ni·um** [~jəm] Dezennium *n*, Jahrzehnt *n.*
de·cent □ ['di:snt] anständig, ordentlich; F annehmbar, nett.
de·cen·tral·i·za·tion [di:sentrəlai'zeiʃən] Dezentralisierung *f*; **de'cen·tral·ize** dezentralisieren.
de·cep·tion [di'sepʃən] Täuschung *f*, Betrug *m*; Trugbild *n*; **de'cep·tive** □ täuschend, (be)trügerisch.
dec·i·bel *phys.* ['desibel] Dezibel *n.*
de·cide [di'said] (sich) entscheiden (*in favour of, on, upon* für); bestimmen; zu dem Schluß kommen; beschließen; sich entschließen; **de'cid·ed** □ entschieden; bestimmt; entschlossen; **de'cid·er** *Sport:* Entscheidungskampf *m.*
de·cid·u·ous ⚘, *zo.* □ [di'sidjuəs] *jährlich* ab-, ausfallend; *~ tree* Laubbaum *m.*
dec·i·mal ['desiməl] **1.** Dezimal...; *~ point* Komma *n* (*in England:* Punkt *m*) *im Dezimalbruch*; *~ system* Dezimalsystem *n*; *go ~* das Dezimalsystem einführen; **2.** Dezimalbruch *m*; **dec·i·mate** ['~meit] dezimieren; **dec·i'ma·tion** Dezimierung *f.*
de·ci·pher [di'saifə] entziffern; entschlüsseln; **de'ci·pher·a·ble** [~rəbl] entzifferbar; **de'ci·pher·ment** Entzifferung *f.*
de·ci·sion [di'siʒən] Entscheidung *f*; ⚖ Urteil *n*; Beschluß *m*; Entschluß *m*; Entschlossenheit *f*; *take a ~* e-e Entscheidung treffen; e-n Entschluß fassen; **de·ci·sive** □ [di'saisiv] entscheidend; ausschlaggebend; entschieden.
de·civ·i·lize [di:'sivilaiz] entzivilisieren.
deck [dek] **1.** ⚓ Deck *n*, Verdeck *n*; *bsd. Am. ein* Spiel *n* Karten; *on ~* auf Deck; *Am.* F bereit, auf dem Posten; **2.** *lit.* zieren, schmücken; ⚓ mit e-m Deck versehen; **'~-chair** Liegestuhl *m*; **'~-hand** ⚓ Matrose *m.*
deck·le-edged ['dekl'edʒd] mit Büttenrand (*Papier*).
de·claim [di'kleim] deklamieren; eifern (*against* gegen).
dec·la·ma·tion [dekləˈmeiʃən] Deklamation *f*; öffentliche Rede *f*; **de·clam·a·to·ry** [di'klæmətəri] deklamatorisch.
de·clar·a·ble [di'klɛərəbl] steuer-, zollpflichtig; **dec·la·ra·tion** [deklə'reiʃən] Erklärung *f*; Zollerklärung *f*; *make a ~* e-e Erklärung abgeben; **de·clar·a·to·ry** [di'klɛərətəri] erklärend; ausdrücklich; **de'clare** *v/t.* erklären, kundtun; behaupten; *Zollpflichtiges* deklarieren; *~ o.s.* sich erklären; *~ off* rückgängig machen; *v/i.* sich erklären, sich aussprechen; *well, I ~!* F na aber!; **de'clared** □ ausgesprochen, erklärt.

de·class·i·fy [ˈdiːˈklæsifai] die Geheimhaltungspflicht aufheben für, *Information* freigeben.
de·clen·sion [diˈklenʃən] Abfall *m* (*Neigung*); Verfall *m*; *gr.* Deklination *f.*
de·clin·a·ble [diˈklainəbl] deklinierbar; **dec·li·na·tion** [dekliˈneiʃən] Neigung *f*; Abweichung *f*; *ast.*, *phys.* Deklination *f*; **de·cline** [diˈklain] **1.** Abnahme *f*; *fig.* Niedergang *m*; Verfall *m*; ⚕ Abzehrung *f*; **2.** *v/t.* neigen, biegen; *gr.* deklinieren; ablehnen; *v/i.* sich neigen; abnehmen; verfallen.
de·cliv·i·ty [diˈkliviti] Abhang *m*; **deˈcliv·i·tous** abschüssig.
de·clutch *mot.* [ˈdiːˈklʌtʃ] auskuppeln.
de·coct [diˈkɔkt] absieden; **deˈcoc·tion** Abkochung *f*; *bsd. pharm.* Dekokt *n.*
de·code *tel.* [ˈdiːˈkəud] entschlüsseln.
dé·colle·té(e) [deiˈkɔltei] dekolletiert.
de·col·o(u)r·ize [diːˈkʌləraiz] entfärben, bleichen.
de·com·pose [diːkəmˈpəuz] zerlegen; (sich) zersetzen; verwesen; **de·com·po·si·tion** [diːkɔmpəˈziʃən] Zerlegung *f etc.*
de·con·tam·i·nate [ˈdiːkənˈtæmineit] entgiften; **ˈde·con·tam·iˈna·tion** Entgiftung *f*; ~ *squad* Entgiftungstrupp *m.*
de·con·trol [ˈdiːkənˈtrəul] **1.** die Zwangswirtschaft aufheben; *Waren*, *Handel* freigeben; **2.** Aufhebung *f* der Zwangswirtschaft.
dé·cor *thea.* [ˈdeikɔː] Bühnenbild *n*, Ausstattung *f.*
dec·o·rate [ˈdekəreit] (ver)zieren; schmücken; *mit e-m Orden* dekorieren; **dec·oˈra·tion** Verzierung *f*; Schmuck *m*; Orden(sauszeichnung *f*) *m*; ♀ *Day Am.* Heldengedenktag *m*; **dec·o·ra·tive** [ˈdekərətiv] Zier..., Schmuck...; **dec·o·ra·tor** [ˈ~reitə] Dekorateur *m*, Maler *m*, Anstreicher *m.*
dec·o·rous □ [ˈdekərəs] anständig.
de·cor·ti·cate [diˈkɔːtikeit] entrinden; abschälen.
de·co·rum [diˈkɔːrəm] Anstand *m.*
de·coy [diˈkɔi] **1.** Entenfang *m*, -falle *f*; *a.* ~ *bird*, ~ *duck* Lockvogel *m* (*a. fig.*); Köder *m*; **2.** ködern, locken.
de·crease **1.** [ˈdiːkriːs] Abnahme *f*; *on the* ~ im Abnehmen (begriffen); **2.** [diːˈkriːs] (sich) vermindern; abnehmen, zurückgehen.
de·cree [diˈkriː] **1.** Dekret *n*, Verordnung *f*, Erlaß *m*; ⚖ Entscheid *m*; Ratschluß *m Gottes*; Fügung *f des Schicksals*; **2.** beschließen; verordnen, verfügen; ~ **ni·si** ⚖ [~ˈnaisai] vorläufiges Scheidungsurteil *n.*
dec·re·ment [ˈdekrimənt] Abnahme *f.*
de·crep·it [diˈkrepit] altersschwach; **deˈcrep·i·tude** [~tjuːd] Altersschwäche *f.*
de·cres·cent [diˈkresnt] abnehmend (*Mond*).
de·cry [diˈkrai] in Verruf bringen; heruntermachen.
dec·u·ple [ˈdekjupl] **1.** zehnfach; **2.** Zehnfache *n*; **3.** verzehnfachen.
ded·i·cate [ˈdedikeit] widmen; (ein-) weihen; **ded·iˈca·tion** Widmung *f*; Zueignung *f*; Hingabe *f*; Einweihung *f*; **ˈded·i·ca·tor** Widmende *m*, *f*; **ded·i·ca·to·ry** [ˈ~kətəri] Widmungs..., Zueignungs...
de·duce [diˈdjuːs] ab-, herleiten; folgern; **deˈduc·i·ble** herleitbar.
de·duct [diˈdʌkt] abziehen; **deˈduc·tion** Abzug *m*; ✝ Rabatt *m*; Schlußfolgerung *f*; **deˈduc·tive** folgernd, deduktiv.
deed [diːd] **1.** Tat *f*; Helden-, Großtat *f*; Urkunde *f*, Dokument *n*; **2.** *Am.* urkundlich übertragen (*to* auf *acc.*).
dee·jay F [ˈdiːdʒei] Diskjockey *m.*
deem [diːm] *v/t.* halten für; *v/i.* denken, urteilen (*of* über *acc.*).
deep [diːp] **1.** □ tief; gründlich; schlau; scharfsinnig; innig; vertieft (*in* in *acc.*); dunkel (*a. fig.*); verborgen; ~ *hit Boxen*: Tiefschlag *m*; *in* ~ *water(s) fig.* in Schwierigkeiten; **2.** Tiefe *f*; *poet.* Meer *n*; **ˈ~-ˈbreath·ing** Atemübungen *f/pl.*; **ˈdeep·en** (sich) vertiefen; dunkler machen *od.* werden (*Farben*); (sich) verstärken (*Kummer etc.*).
deep...: **ˈ~-ˈfreeze** **1.** tiefkühlen; 2. Tiefkühlfach *n*, -truhe *f*; **ˈ~-ˈfro·zen** tiefgefroren, Tiefkühl...; **ˈ~-ˈfry** fritieren; *~ing pan* Friteuse *f*; **ˈ~-ˈlaid** sorgfältig geplant u. geheimgehalten; **ˈdeep·ness** Tiefe *f.*
deep...: **ˈ~-ˈroot·ed** tiefwurzelnd; **ˈ~-sea** Tiefsee...; **ˈ~-ˈseat·ed** tief-

sitzend, tief eingewurzelt; '~-**set** tiefliegend (*Augen*).
deer [diə] Rotwild *n*; Hirsch *m*; Reh *n*; '~-**lick** Salzlecke *f*; '~-**shot** Rehposten *m*; '~-**skin** Hirsch-, Rehleder *n*; '~-**stalk·er** Pirschjäger *m*; '~-**stalk·ing** Pirsch(jagd) *f*.
de-es·ca·late ⚔ [di:'eskəleit] deeskalieren; **de-es·ca'la·tion** Deeskalation *f*.
de·face [di'feis] entstellen, verunstalten; ausstreichen; **de'face·ment** Entstellung *f etc.*
de fac·to [di:'fæktəu] tatsächlich, De-facto-...; de facto.
de·fal·ca·tion [di:fæl'keiʃən] Unterschlagung *f*, Veruntreuung *f*; *das* unterschlagene Geld.
def·a·ma·tion [defə'meiʃən] Verleumdung *f*; **de·fam·a·to·ry** [di'fæmətəri] verleumderisch; Schmäh...; **de·fame** [di'feim] verleumden; verunglimpfen; **de'fam·er** Verleumder(in).
de·fault [di'fɔ:lt] **1.** Nichterscheinen *n vor Gericht*; Säumigkeit *f im Zahlen*; Verzug *m*; *judgement by* ~ ⚖ Versäumnisurteil *n*; *in* ~ *of which* in Ermangelung dessen; widrigenfalls; *make* ~ nicht erscheinen; nicht zahlen; **2.** s-n Verbindlichkeiten nicht nachkommen; im Verzug sein (*with* mit); ⚖ wegen Nichterscheinens verurteilen; **de'fault·er** zum Termin Nichterscheinende *m*, *f*; säumiger Zahler *m*; ⚔ Delinquent *m*.
de·fea·sance [di'fi:zəns] Annullierung *f*.
de·feat [di'fi:t] **1.** Niederlage *f*; Besiegung *f*; Vereitelung *f*; **2.** ⚔ schlagen, besiegen; vereiteln, vernichten; *parl.* zu Fall bringen; **de'feat·ist** Defätist *m*.
def·e·cate ['defikeit] den Darm entleeren, Stuhlgang haben.
de·fect [di'fekt] Mangel *m*; Fehler *m*; **de'fec·tion** Abfall *m* (*from* von); Treubruch *m*; **de'fec·tive** □ mangelhaft; unvollständig (*a. gr.*); schadhaft, fehlerhaft; ermangelnd (*in gen.*); **de'fec·tor** *pol.* Überläufer *m*.
de·fence, *Am.* **de·fense** [di'fens] Verteidigung *f*; Schutzmaßnahme *f*; ~ *mechanism* Abwehrmechanismus *m od.* -maßnahme *f*; ~ *spending* ⚔ Verteidigungsausgaben *f/pl.*; *witness for the* ~ Entlastungszeuge *m*; **de'fence·less** schutzlos, wehrlos; ⚔ unverteidigt.
de·fend [di'fend] verteidigen (*against* gegen); schützen (*from* vor *dat.*); **de'fen·dant** ⚖ Beklagte *m*, *f*; **de'fend·er** Verteidiger(in).
de·fen·si·ble [di'fensəbl] zu verteidigen(d), haltbar; vertretbar; **de'fen·sive 1.** □ verteidigend; Verteidigungs...; Schutz...; **2.** Defensive *f*; *be on the* ~ sich in der Defensive befinden; *act od. stand on the* ~ sich defensiv verhalten.
de·fer[1] [di'fə:] auf-, verschieben; *Am.* ⚔ zurückstellen; ~*red payment*, *payment on* ~*red terms* Ratenzahlung *f*.
de·fer[2] [~] (*to*) sich fügen (in *acc.*); sich beugen (vor *dat.*); nachgeben (*dat.*); **def·er·ence** ['defərəns] Ehrerbietung *f*; Nachgiebigkeit *f*; *in* ~ *to*, *out of* ~ *to* aus Rücksicht gegen; **def·er·en·tial** □ [~'renʃəl] ehrerbietig.
de·fer·ment [di'fə:mənt] Aufschub *m*; *Am.* ⚔ Zurückstellung *f*.
de·fi·ance [di'faiəns] Herausforderung *f*; *bid* ~ *to* Trotz bieten (*dat.*); *in* ~ *of j-m* zum Hohn; **de'fi·ant** □ herausfordernd; trotzig.
de·fi·cien·cy [di'fiʃənsi] Unzulänglichkeit *f*; Mangel *m*; = *deficit*; **de'fi·cient** mangelhaft; unzureichend; *be* ~ *in* Mangel haben an (*dat.*).
def·i·cit ['defisit] Defizit *n*, Fehlbetrag *m*.
de·fi·er [di'faiə] Herausforderer *m*; Verächter *m*.
de·file[1] **1.** ['di:fail] Engpaß *m*, Hohlweg *m*; **2.** [di'fail] defilieren, vorbeiziehen.
de·file[2] [di'fail] beschmutzen, verunreinigen; beflecken, schänden; entweihen; **de'file·ment** Befleckung *f etc.*
de·fin·a·ble [di'fainəbl] bestimm-, erklär-, definierbar; **de'fine** definieren; erklären; genau bestimmen; **def·i·nite** ['definit] □ bestimmt; deutlich; genau; **def·i'ni·tion** Definition *f*; (Begriffs-)Bestimmung *f*; Erklärung *f*; *opt.* Schärfe *f*; **de·fin·i·tive** □ [di'finitiv] bestimmt; entscheidend; endgültig.
de·flate [di'fleit] Luft ablassen aus *Ballon etc.*; die Inflation beseitigen; **de'fla·tion** Entleerung *f*; Deflation *f e-r Währung*; **de'fla·tion·a·ry** Deflations...

de·flect [di'flekt] ablenken; abweichen; **de·flec·tion,** *mst* **de·flex·ion** [di'flekʃən] Ablenkung *f*; Abweichung *f*.
de·flow·er [di:'flauə] entjungfern; *fig.* schänden.
de·fo·li·ate [di:'fəulieit] sich entlauben.
de·form [di'fɔ:m] entstellen, verunstalten; *~ed* verwachsen; **de·for·ma·tion** [di:fɔ:'meiʃən] Entstellung *f*; **de·form·i·ty** [di'fɔ:miti] Häßlichkeit *f*; Auswuchs *m* (*a. fig.*); Mißgestalt *f*.
de·fraud [di'frɔ:d] betrügen (*of* um).
de·fray [di'frei] *Kosten* tragen *od.* bestreiten.
de·freez·er *mot.* [di:'fri:zə] Frostschutzscheibe *f*.
de·frost ['di:'frɔst] entfrosten, ab-, auftauen; **de'frost·er** Entfroster *m*; **de'frost·ing** Entfrosten *n*; *~ rear window mot.* heizbare Heckscheibe *f*.
deft □ [deft] gewandt, flink.
de·funct [di'fʌŋkt] **1.** verstorben; *fig.* veraltet; **2.** Verstorbene *m, f*.
de·fy [di'fai] herausfordern; trotzen, sich widersetzen (*dat.*); mißachten.
de·gen·er·a·cy [di'dʒenərəsi] Entartung *f*; Verkommenheit *f*; **de'gen·er·ate 1.** [*~*reit] aus-, entarten; **2.** □ [*~*rit] entartet; **de·gen·er·a·tion** [*~*'reiʃən] Entartung *f*; **de'gen·er·a·tive** [*~*rətiv] Entartungs...
deg·ra·da·tion [degrə'deiʃən] Degradierung *f*; Absetzung *f*; **de·grade** [di'greid] *v/t.* degradieren; absetzen; herabwürdigen; erniedrigen; demütigen; *fig.* verringern; *v/i.* entarten.
de·gree [di'gri:] Grad *m* (*a. geogr., gr.,* ⚕, *phys., univ.*); Verwandtschaftsgrad *m*; *fig.* Stufe *f*, Schritt *m* (*to* zu); Rang *m*, Stand *m*; *by ~s* allmählich, nach u. nach; *in no ~* in keiner Weise; *in some ~* einigermaßen; *to a ~* F außerordentlich, ziemlich; *take one's ~* sein Abschlußexamen machen.
de·hu·man·ize [di:'hju:mənaiz] entmenschlichen.
de·hy·drate [di:'haidreit] austrocknen; **de'hy·drat·ed** Trocken...; *~ eggs pl.* Trockenei *n*; *~ potatoes pl.* Trockenkartoffeln *f/pl.*; *~ vegetables pl.* Trockengemüse *n*.
de-ice ✈ ['di:'ais] enteisen; **de-'ic·er** Enteisungsanlage *f*.
de·i·fi·ca·tion [di:ifi'keiʃən] Vergötterung *f*; Vergöttlichung *f*; **de·i·fy** ['di:ifai] vergöttern; vergöttlichen.
deign [dein] geruhen; gewähren.
de·ism ['di:izəm] Deismus *m*; **'de·ist** Deist(in); **de'is·tic, de'is·ti·cal** □ deistisch.
de·i·ty ['di:iti] Gottheit *f*.
de·ject [di'dʒekt] entmutigen; **de'ject·ed** □ niedergeschlagen; **de'ject·ed·ness, de'jec·tion** Niedergeschlagenheit *f*.
de ju·re [di:'dʒuəri] rechtmäßig, De-jure-...; de jure.
dek·ko *sl.* ['dekəu] kurzer Blick *m*; *have a ~* mal schauen.
de·lay [di'lei] **1.** Aufschub *m*, Verzug *m*; Verzögerung *f*, Verspätung *f*; **2.** *v/t.* aufschieben; verzögern; aufhalten; hinhalten; *v/i.* zögern; Zeit verlieren; *~ing tactics pl.* Verzögerungstaktik *f*; **de'layed-'ac·tion** Verzögerungs...
de·le *typ.* ['di:li:] **1.** Tilgungszeichen *n*; **2.** tilgen.
de·lec·ta·ble *oft iro.* □ [di'lektəbl] ergötzlich; **de·lec·ta·tion** [di:lek'teiʃən] Ergötzung *f*.
del·e·ga·cy ['deligəsi] Abordnung *f*; **del·e·gate 1.** ['*~*geit] delegieren; abordnen; übertragen (*to s.o.* j-m); **2.** ['*~*git] Abgeordnete *m, f*, Delegierte *m, f*; Referent *m*; **del·e·ga·tion** [*~*'geiʃən] Abordnung *f*; *Am. parl. die* Kongreßabgeordneten *m/pl.* e-s Staates; Überweisung *f*.
de·lete [di'li:t] streichen, tilgen; **del·e·te·ri·ous** □ [deli'tiəriəs] schädlich; **de·le·tion** [di'li:ʃən] Streichung *f*.
delf(t) [delf(t)] Delfter Steingut *n*.
de·lib·er·ate 1. [di'libəreit] *v/t.* überlegen, erwägen; *v/i.* nachdenken; beraten (*on* über *acc.*); **2.** □ [*~*rit] bedachtsam, besonnen; wohlüberlegt; bewußt, absichtlich, vorsätzlich; **de'lib·er·ate·ness** Bedachtsamkeit *f*; **de·lib·er·a·tion** [*~*'reiʃən] Überlegung *f*; Beratung *f*; Bedächtigkeit *f*; **de'lib·er·a·tive** □ [*~*rətiv] überlegend; beratend.
del·i·ca·cy ['delikəsi] Wohlgeschmack *m*; Leckerbissen *m*; Feinheit *f*, Zartheit *f* (*a. fig.*); Schwächlichkeit *f*; Mißlichkeit *f*; Zart-

gefühl *n*, Feinfühligkeit *f*; **del·i·cate** ['~kit] □ schmackhaft; lecker; zart (*a. fig.*); fein; schwach; mißlich, heikel; empfindlich; zartfühlend, feinfühlig; wählerisch, verwöhnt; **del·i·ca·tes·sen** [delikə'tesn] Feinkost(geschäft *n*) *f*.
de·li·cious [di'liʃəs] köstlich.
de·light [di'lait] **1.** Lust *f*, Freude *f*, Wonne *f*, Entzücken *n*; *take* ~ *in* sich ein Vergnügen aus *et.* machen; **2.** entzücken; (sich) erfreuen (*in* an *dat.*); ~ *to inf.* Freude daran finden zu *inf.*; **de'light·ful** □ [~ful] reizend, entzückend.
de·lim·it [di:'limit], **de·lim·i·tate** [di'limiteit] abgrenzen; **de·lim·i·'ta·tion** Abgrenzung *f*.
de·lin·e·ate [di'linieit] entwerfen; zeichnen; schildern; **de·lin·e'a·tion** Entwurf *m*; Schilderung *f*; **de'lin·e·a·tor** Schilderer *m*.
de·lin·quen·cy [di'liŋkwənsi] Vergehen *n*; Kriminalität *f*; Pflichtvergessenheit *f*; **de'lin·quent 1.** straffällig; pflichtvergessen; **2.** Verbrecher(in).
del·i·quesce [deli'kwes] zergehen.
de·lir·i·ous □ [di'liriəs] irre, wahnsinnig; rasend (*with* vor *dat.*); **de'lir·i·ous·ness** Wahnsinn *m*; **de'lir·i·um** [~əm] Delirium *n*, Fieberwahn *m*; Verzückung *f*; ~ *tremens* [~əm 'tri:menz] Säuferwahnsinn *m*.
de·liv·er [di'livə] befreien, retten (*from* von, aus); *a.* ~ *up* über-, ausliefern; *Botschaft* ausrichten; *Meinung* äußern; *Rede etc.* vortragen, halten; ⚕ entbinden (*of* von); *Waren etc.* abgeben, liefern; ✉ zustellen, austragen; *Schlag* führen; *Ball* werfen; **de'liv·er·a·ble** zu (über)liefern(d); **de'liv·er·ance** Befreiung *f*; (Meinungs)Äußerung *f*, Ausführung *f*; **de'liv·er·er** Befreier(in); Überbringer(in); **de'liv·er·y** ⚕ Entbindung *f*; Lieferung *f*, Ablieferung *f*; ✉ Austragen *n*, Zustellung *f*; Übergabe *f e-r Urkunde*; Vortrag *m*; *Kricket*: Wurf *m*; *special* ~ Zustellung *f* durch Eilboten; *on* ~ *of* bei Lieferung von; **de·liv·er·y charge** Zustellgebühr *f*; **de'liv·er·y-note** Lieferschein *m*; **de·liv·er·y room** ⚕ Entbindungssaal *m*, -zimmer *n*; **de'liv·er·y-truck, de'liv·er·y-van** Lieferwagen *m*.
dell [del] kleines Tal *n*.
de·louse ['di:'laus] entlausen; **de'lous·ing cen·tre** Entlausungsanstalt *f*.
del·ta ['deltə] Delta *n*.
de·lude [di'lu:d] täuschen; verleiten (*into* zu).
del·uge ['delju:dʒ] **1.** Überschwemmung *f*; *fig.* Flut *f*; ♀ Sintflut *f*; **2.** überfluten, -schwemmen (*with* mit).
de·lu·sion [di'lu:ʒən] Täuschung *f*, Verblendung *f*; Wahn *m*; **de'lu·sive** [~siv] □, **de'lu·so·ry** [~səri] (be)trügerisch; täuschend.
delve [delv] graben; suchen, forschen.
dem·a·gog·ic, dem·a·gog·i·cal [demə'gɔgik(əl)] demagogisch; **dem·a·gogue** ['~gɔg] Demagoge *m*; **'dem·a·gog·y** Demagogie *f*.
de·mand [di'mɑ:nd] **1.** Verlangen *n*; Forderung *f* (*on* an *acc.*); Bedarf *m* (*for* an *dat.*); ⚚ Nachfrage *f* (*for* nach); ⚖ Rechtsanspruch *m* (*on* an *acc.*); *in* ~ begehrt, gesucht, gefragt; *on* ~ auf Verlangen; **2.** verlangen, fordern (*of* von); erfordern; ⚖ beanspruchen; fragen (nach); ~ **note** Zahlungsaufforderung *f*.
de·mar·cate ['di:mɑ:keit] abgrenzen; **de·mar'ca·tion** Abgrenzung *f*; *mst line of* ~ Demarkations-, Grenzlinie *f*.
dé·marche *pol.* ['deimɑ:ʃ] Démarche *f*, diplomatischer Schritt *m*.
de·mean[1] [di'mi:n] *mst* ~ *o.s.* sich erniedrigen.
de·mean[2] [~]: ~ *o.s.* sich benehmen; **de'mean·o(u)r** Benehmen *n*.
de·ment·ed [di'mentid] wahnsinnig.
de·mer·it [di:'merit] Unwürdigkeit *f*; Mangel *m*, Fehler *m*, Nachteil *m*.
de·mesne [di'mein] (Land-, Grund-) Besitz *m*; Domäne *f*; *fig.* Gebiet *n*.
demi... ['demi] Halb..., halb...
dem·i·god ['demigɔd] Halbgott *m*; **'dem·i·john** große Korbflasche *f*, Glasballon *m*.
de·mil·i·ta·ri·za·tion ['di:militərai'zeiʃən] Entmilitarisierung *f*; **'de'mil·i·ta·rize** entmilitarisieren.
dem·i·mon·daine ['demimɔn'dein] Halbweltdame *f*; **dem·i·monde** ['~'mɔ̃:nd] Halbwelt *f*.
de·mise [di'maiz] **1.** Ableben *n*; *Besitz*-Übertragung *f*; **2.** übertragen; vermachen.
de·mist *mot.* [di:'mist] *Scheiben* be-

schlagfrei machen; **deˈmist·er** Entfroster *m.*

demo F [ˈdeməu] Demonstration *f.*

de·mob *sl.* [di:ˈmɔb] = *demobilize*; **de·mo·bi·li·za·tion** [ˈdi:məubilaiˈzeiʃən] Demobilisierung *f*; **deˈmo·bi·lize** demobilisieren.

de·moc·ra·cy [diˈmɔkrəsi] Demokratie *f*; **dem·o·crat** [ˈdeməkræt] Demokrat(in); **dem·oˈcrat·ic, dem·oˈcrat·i·cal** □ demokratisch; **de·moc·ra·tize** [diˈmɔkrətaiz] demokratisieren.

dé·mo·dé [deiˈməudei] altmodisch.

de·mog·ra·phy [di:ˈmɔgrəfi] Demographie *f.*

de·mol·ish [diˈmɔliʃ] nieder-, abreißen; *fig.* zerstören; herunterreißen; F verputzen (*essen*); **dem·o·li·tion** [deməˈliʃən] Niederreißen *n*; Abbruch *m*; Zerstörung *f.*

de·mon [ˈdi:mən] Dämon *m*, böser Geist *m*; *he is a ~ for work* F er ist von der Arbeit besessen; **de·mo·ni·ac** [diˈməuniæk] **1.** *a.* **de·mo·ni·a·cal** □ [di:məuˈnaiəkəl] dämonisch; teuflisch; **2.** Besessene *m, f*; **de·mon·ic** [di:ˈmɔnik] dämonisch; übernatürlich.

de·mon·stra·ble □ [ˈdemənstrəbl] nachweislich; **dem·on·strate** [ˈ~streit] demonstrieren, zeigen, vorführen, anschaulich darstellen, dartun; beweisen (*from* aus); **dem·onˈstra·tion** Demonstration *f*; anschauliche Darstellung *f*; Beweis *m*; Äußerung *f*, Bezeigung *f von Gefühlen*; *pol.* Kundgebung *f*; ⚔ Scheinmanöver *n*; *~ car mot.* Vorführwagen *m*; **de·mon·stra·tive** [diˈmɔnstrətiv] **1.** □ anschaulich darstellend *od.* zeigend (*of acc.*); überzeugend; demonstrativ; *gr.* hinweisend; ausdrucksvoll; auffällig, überschwenglich; **2.** *gr.* hinweisendes Fürwort *n*; **dem·on·stra·tor** [ˈdemənstreitə] Erklärer *m*; *anat.* Prosektor *m*; *pol.* Demonstrant *m.*

de·mor·al·i·za·tion [dimɔrəlaiˈzeiʃən] Sittenverfall *m*; **deˈmor·al·ize** demoralisiesen; entmutigen.

de·mote *Am.* [di:ˈməut] degradieren; *Schule*: zurückversetzen; **deˈmo·tion** Degradierung *f etc.*

de·mur [diˈmə:] **1.** Einwendung *f*, Widerrede *f*; **2.** Einwendungen erheben (*to* gegen).

de·mure □ [diˈmjuə] ernst, gesetzt; zimperlich; prüde; **deˈmure·ness** Gesetztheit *f*; Zimperlichkeit *f.*

de·mur·rage ⚓, 🚂 [diˈmʌridʒ] Überliegezeit *f*; Liegegeld *n*; **deˈmur·rer** ⚖ Einwand *m.*

den [den] Höhle *f*; Grube *f*; *sl.* Bude *f.*

de·na·tion·al·ize [di:ˈnæʃnəlaiz] reprivatisieren, entstaatlichen.

de·na·ture ⚗ [di:ˈneitʃə] denaturieren.

de·na·zi·fi·ca·tion [ˈdi:nɑ:tsifiˈkeiʃən] Entnazifizierung *f*; **deˈna·zi·fy** [~fai] entnazifizieren.

de·ni·a·ble [diˈnaiəbl] abzuleugnen(d); **deˈni·al** Leugnen *n*; Verleugnung *f*; Verneinung *f*; abschlägige Antwort *f.*

de·ni·er[1] [diˈnaiə] Verneiner(in), Leugner(in); Verweigerer(in).

de·nier[2] [ˈdeniei] Denier *n* (*Feinheitsmaß für Seide und Chemiefasern*).

den·i·grate [ˈdənigreit] (*fig.* an-) schwärzen.

den·im [ˈdenim] Baumwolldrillich *m.*

den·i·zen [ˈdenizn] Bewohner *m.*

de·nom·i·nate [diˈnɔmineit] (be-) nennen; **de·nom·iˈna·tion** Benennung *f*; Klasse *f*; Sekte *f*; Konfession *f*; Nennwert *m*; **de·nom·i·na·tion·al** [~ˈneiʃənl] Sekten..., konfessionell; *~ school* Bekenntnisschule *f*; **deˈnom·i·na·tive** [~nətiv] benennend; **deˈnom·i·na·tor** ✗ [~neitə] Nenner *m*; *common ~* gemeinsamer Nenner *m* (*a. fig.*).

de·no·ta·tion [di:nəuˈteiʃən] Bezeichnung *f*; Bedeutung *f*; **de·no·ta·tive** [diˈnəutətiv] bezeichnend; bedeutend (*of acc.*); **deˈnote** bezeichnen; bedeuten.

de·nounce [diˈnauns] anzeigen, denunzieren; brandmarken, anprangern; *Vertrag* kündigen; **deˈnounce·ment** öffentliche Anklage *f*; Brandmarkung *f.*

dense □ [dens] dicht, dick (*Nebel*); gedrängt; beschränkt, schwer von Begriff; **ˈdense·ness** Dichtigkeit *f*; *fig.* Beschränktheit *f*; **ˈden·si·ty** Dichtigkeit *f*; *phys.* Dichte *f.*

dent [dent] **1.** Beule *f*, Einbeulung *f*; **2.** ver-, einbeulen.

den·tal [ˈdentl] **1.** Zahn...; *~ floss* Zahnseide *f*; *~ surgeon* Zahnarzt *m*; **2.** Dental(laut) *m*; **den·tate** [ˈ~teit] ⚘

gezähnt; **den·ti·frice** ['~tifris] Zahnpulver *n*, -paste *f*; **'den·tist** Zahnarzt *m*; **'den·tist·ry** Zahnheilkunde *f*; **den'ti·tion** Zahnen *n*; **den·ture** ['~tʃə] (künstliches) Gebiß *n*.

den·u·da·tion [di:nju:'deiʃən] Entblößung *f*; *geol.* Abtragung *f*; **de·nude** [di'nju:d] (*of*) entblößen (*gen.*); *fig.* berauben (*gen.*).

de·nun·ci·a·tion [dinʌnsi'eiʃən] Anzeige *f*, Denunziation *f*; Kündigung *f*; **de'nun·ci·a·tor** Denunziant *m*; **de'nun·ci·a·to·ry** [~ətəri] denunzierend; brandmarkend.

de·ny [di'nai] verneinen, leugnen; verleugnen; bestreiten; verweigern, versagen, abschlagen; *j.* abweisen; ~ *o.s. s.th.* sich et. versagen; ~ *o.s.* (*to a visitor*) sich verleugnen lassen.

de·o·dor·ant [di'əudərənt] desodorierendes Mittel *n*; **de'o·dor·ize** geruchlos machen, desodorieren; **de'o·dor·iz·er** desodorierendes Mittel *n*; Luftreiniger *m*.

de·part [di'pɑ:t] *v/i.* abreisen, abfahren, absegeln (*for* nach); F scheiden (*from* von); abstehen, (ab-) weichen, abgehen (*from* von); verscheiden; *the* ~*ed* der *od.* die Verstorbene; die Verstorbenen *pl.*; *v/t.* ~ *this life* aus diesem Leben scheiden; **de'part·ment** Abteilung *f*; Bezirk *m*, Ressort *n*; ✝ Branche *f*; *Am.* Ministerium *n*; ♀ *of Education and Science*, *Am.* ♀ *of Education* Unterrichtsministerium *n*; ♀ *of the Environment* Umweltschutzministerium *n*; *State* ♀ Außenministerium *n*; ~ *store* Kauf-, Warenhaus *n*; **de·part·men·tal** [di:pɑ:t'mentl] Abteilungs...; Fach...; **de·par·ture** [di'pa:tʃə] Abreise *f*, 🚂, ⚓ Abfahrt *f*; Weggang *m*; Abweichung *f*, Abwendung *f* (*from* von); *a new* ~ eine neue Richtung *f*, ein neuer Weg *m*, et. Neues *n*; ~ *lounge* Abflughalle *f*; ~ *platform* Abfahrtsbahnsteig *m*.

de·pend [di'pend] abhängen (*on*, *upon* von); angewiesen sein, sich verlassen (*on*, *upon* auf *acc.*); ⚖ schweben; *it* ~*s* F es kommt (ganz) darauf an; **de'pend·a·ble** zuverlässig; **de'pend·ant** Abhängige *m*, *f*, Diener *m*, Anhänger *m*; (Familien)Angehörige *m*, *f*; **de'pend·ence** Abhängigkeit *f* (*upon* von); Bedingtheit *f* (*on* durch); Vertrauen *n* (*on* auf *acc.*); **de'pend·en·cy** Schutzgebiet *n*; **de'pend·ent 1.** □ (*on*) abhängig (von); angewiesen (auf *acc.*); bedingt (durch); bauend (auf *acc.*); **2.** *s. dependant*.

de·pict [di'pikt] darstellen; schildern.

de·pil·a·to·ry [de'pilətəri] **1.** enthaarend; **2.** Enthaarungsmittel *n*.

de·plane [di:'plein] aus dem Flugzeug aussteigen.

de·plete [di'pli:t] (ent)leeren; *fig.* erschöpfen; **de'ple·tion** Entleerung *f etc.*; **de'ple·tive** entleerend.

de·plor·a·ble □ [di'plɔ:rəbl] beklagenswert; kläglich; jämmerlich; **de'plore** beklagen, bedauern.

de·ploy ⚔ [di'plɔi] (sich) entwickeln, ausschwärmen; **de'ploy·ment** Aufmarsch *m*, Entwickeln *n von Truppen*.

de·po·nent [di'pəunənt] ⚖ vereidigter Zeuge *m*; *gr.* Deponens *n*.

de·pop·u·late [di:'pɔpjuleit] (sich) entvölkern; **de·pop·u'la·tion** Entvölkerung *f*.

de·port [di'pɔ:t] *Ausländer* abschieben; verbannen; ~ *o.s.* sich benehmen; **de·por·ta·tion** [di:pɔ:'teiʃən] Deportation *f*, Verbannung *f*; **de·port'ee** Deportierte *m*, *f*; **de·port·ment** [di'pɔ:tmənt] Verhalten *n*, Benehmen *n*.

de·pos·a·ble [di'pəuzəbl] absetzbar; **de'pose** absetzen; ⚖ (eidlich) aussagen (*to s.th.* et., *that* daß).

de·pos·it [di'pɔzit] **1.** *geol.* Ablagerung *f* (*a.* ⚒), Lager *n*; ☂ Niederschlag *m*; ✝ Depot *n*; *Bank*-Einlage *f*; Pfand *n*; ✝ Anzahlung *f*; Hinterlegung *f*; *attr.* Depositen...; ~ *account* Sparkonto *n*; **2.** (nieder-, ab-, hin)legen; *Geld* einzahlen; hinterlegen, deponieren; (sich) absetzen *od.* -lagern; **de'pos·i·ta·ry** Verwahrer *m*; **dep·o·si·tion** [depə'ziʃən] Ablagerung *f*; eidliche Zeugenaussage *f*; Absetzung *f* (*from* von); *eccl.* Kreuzesabnahme *f*; **de·pos·i·tor** [di'pɔzitə] Hinterleger *m*, Einzahler *m*; **de'pos·i·to·ry** Verwahrungsort *m*; Niederlage *f*; *fig.* Fundgrube *f*.

de·pot ['depəu] Depot *n*; Niederlage *f*; Lager(haus) *n*; Sammelplatz *m*; *Am.* Bahnhof *m*.

dep·ra·va·tion [deprə'veiʃən] = *depravity*; **de·prave** [di'preiv] *sittlich* verderben; **de'praved** *sittlich*

verdorben, verkommen; **de·prav·i·ty** [di'præviti] Verderbtheit *f*.
dep·re·cate ['diprikeit] mißbilligen; ablehnen; verurteilen; **dep·re'ca·tion** Mißbilligung *f*; Ablehnung *f*; **dep·re·ca·to·ry** ['~kətəri] mißbilligend; ablehnend.
de·pre·ci·ate [di'pri:ʃieit] herabsetzen; *fig*. geringschätzen; im Wert *od*. Preis herabsetzen *od*. (*v/i*.) sinken, entwerten; **de·pre·ci'a·tion** Herabsetzung *f*; Geringschätzung *f*; Entwertung *f*; ✝ Abschreibung *f*; **de'pre·ci·a·to·ry** [~ʃjətəri] herabsetzend, geringschätzig.
dep·re·da·tion [depri'deiʃən] Plünderung *f*; *~s pl*. Verheerungen *f/pl*.; **'dep·re·da·tor** Plünderer *m*; **dep·re·da·to·ry** [di'predətəri] verheerend.
de·press [di'pres] niederdrücken; *den Handel* drücken, *Preise* senken, drücken; *Stimme* senken; *fig*. bedrücken; **de'pres·sant** ⚕ Beruhigungsmittel *n*; **de'pressed** *fig*. niedergeschlagen; **de'press·ing** bedrückend, deprimierend; **de·pres·sion** [di'preʃən] Depression *f*; Senkung *f*; Niedergeschlagenheit *f*; ✝ Flaute *f*, Wirtschaftskrise *f*; ⚕ Abspannung *f*; Schwäche *f*; ⊕, *phys*., *ast*. Sinken *n*; *geogr*. Senke *f*; *meteor*. Tief *n*.
dep·ri·va·tion [depri'veiʃən] Beraubung *f*; *eccl*. Amtsenthebung *f*; Verlust *m*; **de·prive** [di'praiv] berauben; *~ s.o. of s.th.* j-m et. nehmen *od*. entziehen; ausschließen (*of* von); *eccl*. absetzen; **de'prived** arm, unterprivilegiert.
depth [depθ] Tiefe *f* (*a. fig*.); *attr*. Tiefen...; *~ bomb*, *~ charge* Unterwasserbombe *f*; *in ~* gründlich, eingehend; *~ of field od. focus phot*. Schärfentiefe *f*, Tiefenschärfe *f*; *go beyond one's ~* den Boden unter den Füßen verlieren; *be out of one's ~ fig*. unsicher sein, schwimmen.
dep·u·ta·tion [depju:'teiʃən] Abordnung *f*; **de·pute** [di'pju:t] abordnen, deputieren; **dep·u·tize** ['depjutaiz] abordnen; *~ for j*. vertreten; **'dep·u·ty 1.** Abgeordnete *m*, *f*; ⚖ Stellvertreter *m*, Beauftragte *m*, *f*; **2.** Vize...; Stellvertreter *m* des ...
de·rac·i·nate [di'ræsineit] entwurzeln.
de·rail 🚂 [di'reil] *v/i*. entgleisen; *v/t*. zum Entgleisen bringen; **de'rail·ment** Entgleisung *f*.
de·range [di'reindʒ] in Unordnung bringen; stören; zerrütten; (*mentally*) *~d* geistesgestört; *a ~d stomach* e-e Magenverstimmung *f*; **de'range·ment** Unordnung *f*; Zerrüttung *f*; Geistesgestörtheit *f*.
de·rate [di:'reit] die Steuern herabsetzen (für *j*.).
de·ra·tion ['di:'ræʃən] freigeben, die Rationierung von ... aufheben.
Der·by ['dɑ:bi] *Sport*: Derby (-rennen) *n*; **'der·by** *Am*. Melone *f* (*steifer Hut*).
der·e·lict ['derilikt] **1.** verlassen, herrenlos; *bsd. Am*. nachlässig, säumig; **2.** herrenloses Gut *n*; Wrack *n*; **der·e'lic·tion** Aufgeben *n*; Verlassen *n*; Vernachlässigung *f*; *~ of duty* Pflichtvergessenheit *f*.
de·ride [di'raid] verlachen, verspotten; **de'rid·er** Spötter(in).
de ri·gueur [dəri'gə:] unerläßlich.
de·ri·sion [di'riʒən] Verspottung *f*; Hohn *m*; Spott *m*; Gespött *n*; **de·ri·sive** □ [di'raisiv], **de'ri·so·ry** [~səri] spöttisch; lächerlich (klein).
de·riv·a·ble □ [di'raivəbl] her-, ableitbar; **der·i·va·tion** [deri'veiʃən] Ableitung *f*; Herkunft *f*, Ursprung *m*; **de·riv·a·tive** [di'rivətiv] **1.** □ abgeleitet; **2.** Ableitung *f* (*Wort etc*.); **de·rive** [di'raiv] ab-, herleiten (*from* von); *Nutzen etc*. ziehen (*from* aus); *~ from*, *be ~d from* stammen von *od*. aus.
der·ma·ti·tis [də:mə'taitis] Dermatitis *f*, Hautentzündung *f*.
der·ma·tol·o·gist [də:mə'tɔlədʒist] Hautarzt *m*, Dermatologe *m*; **der·ma'tol·o·gy** Dermatologie *f*.
der·o·gate ['derəugeit] Abbruch tun (*from dat*.), schmälern (*from acc*.); **der·o'ga·tion** Beeinträchtigung *f* (*from gen*.); Herabwürdigung *f*; **de·rog·a·to·ry** □ [di'rɔgətəri] (*to*) beeinträchtigend (*acc*.); nachteilig (*dat*., für); herabwürdigend (*acc*.).
der·rick ['derik] ⊕ Drehkran *m*; ⚓ Ladebaum *m*; ⚒ Bohrturm *m*.
der·ring-do ['deriŋ'du:] Verwegenheit *f*.
derv [də:v] Dieseltreibstoff *m*.
der·vish ['də:viʃ] Derwisch *m*.
de·sal·i·nate ['di:'sælineit] *Meerwas-*

ser entsalzen; **de·sal·i'na·tion** Entsalzung *f*; ~ *plant* Entsalzungsanlage *f*.

de·scale ['di:'skeil] den Kesselstein entfernen von.

des·cant [dis'kænt] sich verbreiten *od.* auslassen (*upon* über *ein Thema*).

de·scend [di'send] herab-, hinabsteigen, -fließen, herabkommen; absteigen; ⚒ einfahren; fallen, sinken; ✈ niedergehen; ~ (*up*)*on* herfallen über (*acc.*); einfallen in (*acc.*); hereinbrechen über (*acc.*); ~ *to* durch Erbschaft zufallen (*dat.*); sich hergeben zu *et. Niedrigem*; ~ *from, be* ~*ed from* abstammen von; **de'scend·ant** Nachkomme *m*, Abkömmling *m*.

de·scent [di'sent] Herabsteigen *n*; Abstieg *m*; *Fallschirm*-Absprung *m*; ⚒ Einfahrt *f*; Fallen *n*, Sinken *n*; Gefälle *n*; *feindlicher* Einfall *m*, Landung *f*; Abstammung *f*, Geschlecht *n*; Abhang *m*; ⚖ Heimfall *m e-r Erbschaft etc*; *line of* ~ *Skilauf*: Fallinie *f*.

de·scrib·a·ble [dis'kraibəbl] zu beschreiben(d); **de'scribe** beschreiben, schildern.

de·scrip·tion [di'skripʃən] Beschreibung *f*, Schilderung *f*; F Art *f*; **de'scrip·tive** □ beschreibend; darstellend; schildernd.

de·scry [dis'krai] sehen, erspähen; wahrnehmen.

des·e·crate ['desikreit] entweihen, schänden; **des·e'cra·tion** Entweihung *f*, Schändung *f*.

de·seg·re·gate *Am.* ['di:'segrigeit] die Rassenschranke (zwischen Weißen und Negern) aufheben in; **'de·seg·re'ga·tion** Aufhebung *f* der Rassentrennung.

de·sen·si·tize ['di:'sensitaiz] ⚕ desensibilisieren; *phot.* lichtunempfindlich machen.

des·ert[1] ['dezət] **1.** verlassen; wüst, öde; Wüsten...; **2.** Wüste *f*.

de·sert[2] [di'zə:t] *v/t.* verlassen; *fig.* im Stich lassen; untreu werden (*dat.*); *v/i.* ausreißen; desertieren.

de·sert[3] [di'zə:t] *mst* ~*s pl.* Verdienst *n*; verdienter Lohn *m*, verdiente Strafe *f*.

de·sert·er [di'zə:tə] Fahnenflüchtige *m*, Deserteur *m*; **de'ser·tion** Verlassen *n*; ⚖ böswilliges Verlassen *n*; Fahnenflucht *f*; Einsamkeit *f*.

de·serve [di'zə:v] verdienen; sich verdient machen (*of* um); **de'serv·ed·ly** [~vidli] nach Verdienst; **de'serv·ing** verdienend (*of acc.*), würdig (*of gen.*); verdienstvoll.

des·ha·bille ['dezæbi:l] = *dishabille*.

des·ic·cate ['desikeit] (aus)trocknen; **des·ic'ca·tion** Austrocknung *f*; **'des·ic·ca·tor** Trockenapparat *m*.

de·sid·er·ate [di'zidəreit] bedürfen (*gen.*); wünschen; erfordern; **de·sid·er·a·tum** [~'reitəm] Erwünschte *n*; Bedürfnis *n*; Erfordernis *n*.

de·sign [di'zain] **1.** Plan *m*; Entwurf *m*, Riß *m*; *b. s.* Anschlag *m*; Vorhaben *n*, Absicht *f*; Zeichnung *f*, Muster *n*; ⊕ Konstruktion *f*, Ausführung *f*; *by* ~ mit Absicht; *with the* ~ in der Absicht; *protection of* ~*s, copyright in* ~*s* Musterschutz *m*; **2.** ersinnen; zeichnen, entwerfen (*a. fig.*); planen; beabsichtigen; bestimmen (*for* zu); ~*ed to inf.* dazu bestimmt *od.* darauf abgestellt zu *inf.*

des·ig·nate 1. ['dezigneit] bezeichnen (*as* als); ernennen, bestimmen (*for* zu); **2.** ['~nit] *nachgestellt* vorläufig ernannt, designiert; **des·ig·na·tion** [~'neiʃən] Bezeichnung *f*; Bestimmung *f*, Ernennung *f*.

de·sign·ed·ly [di'zainidli] absichtlich; **de'sign·er** (Muster)Zeichner (-in); Konstrukteur *m*; *fig.* Ränkeschmied *m*; **de'sign·ing** ränkevoll.

de·sir·a·bil·i·ty [dizaiərə'biliti] Erwünschtheit *f*; **de'sir·a·ble** □ wünschenswert; angenehm; **de·sire** [di'zaiə] **1.** Wunsch *m*; Verlangen *n* (*for* nach; *to inf.* zu *inf.*); *at s.o.'s* ~ auf j-s Wunsch *etc.*; **2.** verlangen, wünschen; *what do you* ~ *me to do?* was soll ich tun?; **de·sir·ous** □ [di'zaiərəs] begierig (*of* nach; *to do* zu tun).

de·sist [di'zist] abstehen, ablassen (*from* von).

desk [desk] Pult *n*; Schreibtisch *m*; ~ *pad* Schreibtischunterlage *f*.

des·o·late 1. ['desəleit] verwüsten, -heeren; **2.** □ ['~lit] einsam, verlassen; öde; trostlos; **des·o·la·tion** [~'leiʃən] Verwüstung *f*; Einöde *f*; Verlassenheit *f*.

de·spair [dis'pɛə] **1.** Verzweiflung *f*; **2.** verzweifeln (*of* an *dat.*); **de'spair·ing** □ verzweifelt.

des·patch [dis'pætʃ] = *dispatch.*
des·per·a·do [despə'rɑ:dəu] Desperado *m*, Bandit *m*.
des·per·ate □ ['despərit] *adj. u. adv.* verzweifelt; zu allem fähig; hoffnungslos; F schrecklich; **des·per·a·tion** [~'reiʃən] Verzweiflung *f*; Raserei *f*.
des·pi·ca·ble □ ['despikəbl] verächtlich; jämmerlich.
de·spise [dis'paiz] verachten; verschmähen.
de·spite [dis'pait] **1.** Verachtung *f*; Trotz *m*; Bosheit *f*, Tücke *f*; *in ~ of j-m* zum Trotz, trotz; **2.** *prp. a. ~ of* trotz, ungeachtet; **de'spite·ful** □ *poet.* [~ful] boshaft; tückisch.
de·spoil [dis'pɔil] berauben (*of gen.*), plündern; **de'spoil·ment** Beraubung *f*, Plünderung *f*.
de·spond [dis'pɔnd] verzagen, verzweifeln (*of* an *dat.*); **de'spond·en·cy** Verzagtheit *f*; **de'spond·ent** □, **de'spond·ing** □ verzagt, kleinmütig, mutlos.
des·pot ['despɔt] Despot *m*, Tyrann *m*; **des'pot·ic** (*~ally*) despotisch; **des·pot·ism** ['~pətizəm] Despotismus *m*.
des·qua·ma·tion [deskwə'meiʃən] Abschuppung *f der Haut.*
des·sert [di'zə:t] Nachtisch *m*, Dessert *n*; *Am.* (Süß)Speise *f*; *~ powder* Puddingpulver *n*; **des'sert-spoon** Dessertlöffel *m*.
des·ti·na·tion [desti'neiʃən] Bestimmung(sort *m*) *f*; Ziel *n*; **des·tine** ['~tin] bestimmen (*to*, *for* zu); *be ~d to do* tun sollen; **'des·ti·ny** Schicksal *n*; Los *n*; höhere Fügung *f*.
des·ti·tute □ ['destitju:t] mittellos, notleidend; entblößt (*of* von); **des·ti'tu·tion** Mangel *m* (*of* an *dat.*); bittere Not *f*.
de·stroy [dis'trɔi] zerstören, vernichten; töten; unschädlich machen; *~ing angel* Würgeengel *m*; **de'stroy·er** Zerstörer(in), Vernichter(in); ⚓ Zerstörer *m*.
de·struct·i·bil·i·ty [distrʌkti'biliti] Zerstörbarkeit *f*; **de'struct·i·ble** [~təbl] zerstörbar; **de'struc·tion** Zerstörung *f*, Vernichtung *f*; Tötung *f*; Untergang *m*; **de'struc·tive** □ zerstörend; vernichtend (*of*, *to acc.*); zerstörerisch; rein negativ, destruktiv; **de'struc·tive·ness** zerstörende Gewalt *f*; Zerstörungswut *f*; **de'struc·tor** (Müll)Verbrennungsofen *m*.
des·ue·tude [di'sju:itju:d] Ungebräuchlichkeit *f*; *fall into ~* außer Gebrauch kommen.
des·ul·to·ri·ness ['desəltərinis] Planlosigkeit *f*, Sprunghaftigkeit *f*; Oberflächlichkeit *f*; **'des·ul·to·ry** □ unstet, sprunghaft; planlos; oberflächlich.
de·tach [di'tætʃ] losmachen, (los-)trennen, (ab)lösen; absondern; ⚔ (ab)kommandieren; **de'tach·a·ble** abnehm-, abtrenn-, ablösbar; **de'tached** einzeln; freistehend (*Haus*); unbeeinflußt, objektiv (*Urteil*); unbeschwert (*Gemütsart*); **de'tach·ment** Loslösung *f*; Trennung *f*; Absonderung *f*; ⚔ Abteilung *f*; Objektivität *f*; Unbeschwertheit *f*.
de·tail ['di:teil] **1.** Einzelheit *f*; genaue *od.* eingehende Darstellung *f od.* Schilderung *f*; ⚔ Kommando *n* (*Abteilung*); *~s pl.* (nähere) Einzelheiten *f/pl.*, Nähere *n*; *in ~* ausführlich; *go into ~s* auf (die) Einzelheiten eingehen; **2.** genau *od.* eingehend darstellen *od.* schildern *od.* erzählen; ⚔ abkommandieren; **'de·tailed** eingehend, ausführlich.
de·tain [di'tein] zurück-, auf-, abhalten; ⚖ vorenthalten; *j.* in Haft behalten; **de·tain'ee** Häftling *m*; **de'tain·er** Vorenthaltung *f*; ⚖ Haftverlängerungsbefehl *m*.
de·tect [di'tekt] entdecken; (auf-)finden; **de'tect·a·ble** entdeckbar; **de'tec·tion** Ent-, Aufdeckung *f*; **de'tec·tive 1.** Detektiv..., Kriminal...; *~ force* Kriminalpolizei *f*; *~ story*, *~ novel* Kriminalroman *m*; **2.** Geheimpolizist *m*, Detektiv *m*; **de'tec·tor** Aufdecker *m*; Anzeigevorrichtung *f*; *Radio*: Detektor *m*.
de·tent ⊕ [di'tent] Sperrklinke *f*.
dé·tente *pol.* [dei'tɑ̃:t] Entspannung *f*.
de·ten·tion [di'tenʃən] Vorenthaltung *f*; Zurück-, Abhaltung *f*; Haft *f*; *Schule*: Arrest *m*.
de·ter [di'tə:] abschrecken (*from* von).
de·ter·gent [di'tə:dʒənt] **1.** reinigend; **2.** Reinigungsmittel *n*.
de·te·ri·o·rate [di'tiəriəreit] (sich) verschlechtern; an Wert verlieren; entarten; **de·te·ri·o'ra·tion** Verschlechterung *f*; Entartung *f*.

de·ter·ment [diˈtəːmənt] Abschreckungsmittel *n*.

de·ter·mi·na·ble □ [diˈtəːminəbl] bestimmbar; **deˈter·mi·nant 1.** bestimmend; **2.** Bestimmende *n*; **deˈter·mi·nate** □ [~nit] bestimmt; entschieden; festgesetzt; **de·ter·mi·na·tion** [~ˈneiʃən] Bestimmung *f*; Entschlossenheit *f*, Bestimmtheit *f*; Entscheidung *f*; Entschluß *m*; **deˈter·mi·na·tive** [~nətiv] bestimmend; einschränkend; entscheidend; **deˈter·mine** *v/t.* bestimmen; entscheiden; veranlassen (*to inf.* zu *inf.*); *bsd.* ⚖ *Strafe* festsetzen; beendigen; *be* ~*d* entschlossen sein; *v/i.* sich entschließen (*on* zu *et.*; *to inf.*, *on ger.* zu *inf.*); **deˈter·mined** entschlossen; **deˈter·min·er** *gr.* Bestimmungswort *n*.

de·ter·rent [diˈterənt] **1.** abschreckend; **2.** Abschreckungsmittel *n*; *nuclear* ~ *pol.* atomare Abschreckung *f*.

de·test [diˈtest] verabscheuen; **deˈtest·a·ble** □ abscheulich; **de·tes·ta·tion** [diːtesˈteiʃən] Verabscheuung *f*; Abscheu *m* (*of* vor *dat.*); *he is my* ~ er ist mir ein Greuel.

de·throne [diˈθrəun] entthronen; **deˈthrone·ment** Entthronung *f*.

det·o·nate [ˈdetəuneit] detonieren, explodieren (lassen); **ˈdet·o·nat·ing** Knall..., Zünd...; ~ *cap* Zündhütchen *n*; **det·oˈna·tion** Detonation *f*; Explosion *f*; Knall *m*; **ˈdet·o·na·tor** 🚂 Knallsignal *n*; ⚔ Zünder *m*; Sprengkapsel *f*.

de·tour [ˈdiːtuə], **dé·tour** [ˈdeituə] Umweg *m*; Umleitung *f*.

de·tract [diˈtrækt]: ~ *from s.th.* et. beeinträchtigen, schmälern; **deˈtrac·tion** Verleumdung *f*; Herabsetzung *f*; **deˈtrac·tive** verleumderisch; **deˈtrac·tor** Verleumder *m*.

de·train [diːˈtrein] *v/t. Truppen* ausladen; *v/i.* aussteigen.

de·trib·al·i·za·tion [diːtraibəlaiˈzeiʃən] Auflösung *f* des Stammesverbands; **deˈtrib·al·ize** aus dem Stammesverband herauslösen.

det·ri·ment [ˈdetrimənt] Nachteil *m*, Schaden *m* (*to* für); **det·ri·men·tal** □ [~ˈmentl] schädlich, nachteilig (*to* für).

de·tri·tus *geol.* [diˈtraitəs] Geröll *n*.

de·tune [diˈtjuːn] *Radio*: verstimmen.

deuce [djuːs] Zwei *f im Spiel*; *Tennis*: Einstand *m*; F Teufel *m*; *the* ~! zum Teufel!; (*the*) ~ *a one* nicht einer; **deu·ced** F [djuːst] verteufelt.

de·val·u·ate [ˈdiːˈvæljueit] abwerten; **de·val·u·a·tion** [diːvæljuˈeiʃən] Abwertung *f*; **de·val·ue** [ˈdiːˈvæljuː] abwerten.

dev·as·tate [ˈdevəsteit] verwüsten, verheeren; **ˈdev·as·tat·ing** verheerend; vernichtend (*Kritik*); umwerfend (*Aussehen*, *Charme etc.*); **dev·asˈta·tion** Verwüstung *f*, Verheerung *f*.

de·vel·op [diˈveləp] (sich) entwickeln; (sich) entfalten; (sich) erweitern; *phot.* entwickeln; *Baugelände* erschließen; ausbauen; *Am.* (sich) zeigen, bekannt werden; **deˈvel·op·er** *phot.* Entwickler *m*; **deˈvel·op·ing** *phot.* Entwickeln *n*; *attr.* Entwicklungs...; **deˈvel·op·ment** Entwicklung *f*, Entfaltung *f*; Erweiterung *f*; Ausbau *m*.

de·vi·ate [ˈdiːvieit] abweichen (*from* von); **de·viˈa·tion** Abweichung *f*; Ablenkung *f der Magnetnadel*; **de·viˈa·tion·ism** *pol.* Abweichen *n* von der Parteilinie; **de·viˈa·tion·ist** *pol.* Abweichler *m*.

de·vice [diˈvais] Plan *m*; Einfall *m*; Kunstgriff *m*, Kniff *m*; Erfindung *f*; Vorrichtung *f*; Muster *n*; Wappenbild *n*, Wahlspruch *m*; *leave s.o. to his own* ~*s* j. sich selbst überlassen.

dev·il [ˈdevl] **1.** Teufel *m* (*a. fig.*); Teufelskerl *m*; ⚖ Hilfsanwalt *m*; *fig.* Handlanger *m*; Laufbursche *m*; ⊕ Wolf *m*; *Küche*: gepfeffertes Gericht *n*; *the* ~! zum Teufel!; *between the* ~ *and the deep sea* in der Klemme; **2.** *v/t.* stark gepfeffert braten; ⊕ *im Wolf* zerkleinern; *Am.* plagen, quälen; *v/i.* als Hilfsanwalt arbeiten; **ˈdev·il·ish** □ teuflisch; F verteufelt; **ˈdev·il-may-ˈcare** sorglos; verwegen; **ˈdev·il·ment** Teufelei *f*, Unfug *m*, Dummheiten *f/pl.*; **ˈdev·il·(t)ry** Teufelei *f*; Teufelskunst *f*.

de·vi·ous □ [ˈdiːvjəs] abgelegen; abwegig (*a. fig.*); unredlich; ~ *step* Fehltritt *m*.

de·vis·a·ble [diˈvaizəbl] erdenkbar; **deˈvise 1.** ⚖ Vermachen *n*; Vermächtnis *n*; **2.** erdenken, ersinnen; ⚖ vermachen; **dev·i·see** ⚖ [deviˈziː] Vermächtnisnehmer *m*; **de-**

vis·er [di'vaizə] Erfinder(in); **de·vi·sor** ⚖ [devi'zɔ:] Erblasser *m.*
de·vi·tal·ize [di:'vaitəlaiz] die Lebenskraft nehmen (*dat.*); entkräften.
de·void [di'vɔid] (*of*) bar (*gen.*), ohne, ...los.
dev·o·lu·tion [di:və'lu:ʃən] ⚖ Heimfall *m*; *parl.* Überweisung *f*; Verlauf *m*; *biol.* Entartung *f*; **de·volve** [di'vɔlv] (*upon, to*) *v/t.* abwälzen (auf *acc.*); *j-m* übertragen; *v/i.* übergehen (auf *acc.*); zufallen (*dat.*).
de·vote [di'vəut] weihen, widmen; hingeben; **de'vot·ed** □ ergeben; zärtlich; **dev·o·tee** [devəu'ti:] Verehrer(in); Frömmler(in); **de·vo·tion** [di'vəuʃən] Ergebenheit *f* (*to s.o.* für j.); Hingabe *f*, Hingebung *f* (an *acc.*); Frömmigkeit *f*; ~*s pl.* Andacht *f*; **de'vo·tion·al** □ [~ʃənl] andächtig, fromm.
de·vour [di'vauə] verschlingen (*a. fig.*); ~*ed with* verzehrt von *Neugier etc.*; **de'vour·ing** □ verzehrend.
de·vout □ [di'vaut] andächtig, fromm; innig; **de'vout·ness** Frömmigkeit *f etc.*
dew [dju:] **1.** Tau *m*; **2.** tauen; '**~-drop** Tautropfen *m*; '**~·lap** Wamme *f e-s Rindes*; '**dew-pond** Tau(sammel)teich *m*; '**dew·y** tauig, betaut; taufrisch.
dex·ter ['dekstə] recht, rechts (-seitig).
dex·ter·i·ty [deks'teriti] Gewandtheit *f*; **dex·ter·ous** □ ['~tərəs] gewandt, flink, geschickt.
di·a·be·tes [daiə'bi:ti:z] Zuckerkrankheit *f*, Diabetes *m*; **di·a·bet·ic** [~'betik] 1. Diabetiker(in), Zuckerkranke *m, f*; 2. diabetisch, zuckerkrank; Diabetiker...
di·a·bol·ic, di·a·bol·i·cal □ [daiə'bɔlik(əl)] teuflisch.
di·a·dem ['daiədem] Diadem *n.*
di·ag·nose ['daiəgnəuz] diagnostizieren, erkennen; **di·ag'no·sis** [~sis], *pl.* **di·ag'no·ses** [~si:z] Diagnose *f.*
di·ag·o·nal [dai'ægənl] **1.** □ diagonal; **2.** Diagonale *f*; Diagonal *m*, schräggeripptes Gewebe *n.*
di·a·gram ['daiəgræm] Diagramm *n*; graphische Darstellung *f*; Schema *n*, Plan *m*; **di·a·gram·mat·ic** [daiəgrə'mætik] (~*ally*) schematisch.
di·al ['daiəl] **1.** Sonnenuhr *f*; Zifferblatt *n*; Skala *f*; *teleph.* Wähl(er)scheibe *f*; *Radio*: Skalenscheibe *f*; ~ *light* Skalenbeleuchtung *f*; **2.** *teleph.* wählen.
di·a·lect ['daiəlekt] Mundart *f*, Dialekt *m*; **di·a'lec·tic, di·a'lec·ti·cal** □ dialektisch; **di·a'lec·tic(s)** *sg.* Dialektik *f.*
di·a·logue, *Am. a.* **di·a·log** ['daiəlɔg] Dialog *m*, Gespräch *n*; ~ *track Film*: Sprechband *n.*
di·al...: '**~-sys·tem** *teleph.* Wählsystem *n*; '**~-tone** *teleph.* Amtszeichen *n.*
di·am·e·ter [dai'æmitə] Durchmesser *m.*
di·a·met·ri·cal □ [daiə'metrikəl] diametrisch; diametral *od.* genau entgegengesetzt.
di·a·mond ['daiəmənd] **1.** Diament *m*; Rhombus *m*; *Am. Baseball*: Spielfeld *n*; *Karten*: Karo *n*; ~ *cut* ~ Wurst wider Wurst; *he is a rough* ~ er hat e-e rauhe Schale, aber e-n guten Kern; **2.** Diamant(en)...; Karo...; kariert; rautenförmig; '**~-'cut·ter** Diamentenschleifer *m*; ~ **wed·ding** diamantene Hochzeit *f.*
di·a·pa·son ♪ [daiə'peisn] Zs.-klang *m*; Tonfülle *f*; Mensur *f der Orgel*; *Stimm*-Umfang *m* (*a. fig.*).
di·a·per ['daiəpə] **1.** rautenförmig gemusterte Leinwand *f*; *Am.* Windel *f*; **2.** *Stoff* rautenförmig mustern; *Am. Baby* trockenlegen.
di·aph·a·nous [dai'æfənəs] durchscheinend.
di·a·phragm ['daiəfræm] Zwerchfell *n*; ⊕ Scheidewand *f*; *opt.* Blende *f*; *teleph.* Membran(e) *f.*
di·a·rist ['daiərist] Tagebuchschreiber(in); '**di·a·rize** Tagebuch führen.
di·ar·rhoe·a ⚕ [daiə'riə] Durchfall *m.*
di·a·ry ['daiəri] Tagebuch *n*; Taschenkalender *m.*
Di·as·po·ra [dai'æspərə] Diaspora *f*, (christliche *od.* jüdische) religiöse Minderheit *f.*
di·a·ther·my ⚕ ['daiəθə:mi] Diathermie *f.*
di·a·tribe ['daiətraib] Schmähschrift *f*; Schmähung *f.*
dib·ble ['dibl] **1.** Pflanz-, Setzstock *m*; **2.** *Pflanzen* stecken.
dibs *sl.* [dibz] *pl.* Moneten *pl.*
dice [dais] **1.** *pl. von die*[2] Würfel *m/pl.*;

no ~ *Am.* F nichts zu machen; 2. würfeln; in Würfel schneiden; '~-**box** Würfelbecher *m*; '**dic·er** Würfelspieler(in); **dic·ey** F ['daisi] prekär, heikel.
di·chot·o·my [dai'kɔtəmi] (Zwei)Teilung *f*, Dichotomie *f*.
dick[1] *Am. sl.* [dik] Detektiv *m*, Kriminalbeamte *m*.
dick[2] *sl.* [~] Erklärung *f*; *take one's* ~ schwören.
dick·ens F ['dikinz] Teufel *m*.
dick·er *Am.* ['dikə] (ver)schachern, feilschen.
dick·(e)y ['diki] **1.** *sl.* schlecht, schlimm, mau; **2.** F Notsitz *m*; Hemdenbrust *f*; *a.* ~*-bird* Piepvögelchen *n*.
dic·tate 1. ['dikteit] Diktat *n*, Vorschrift *f*; Gebot *n*; **2.** [dik'teit] diktieren; *fig.* vorschreiben; **dic'ta·tion** Diktat *n* (*Diktieren*; *Niederschrift*); = *dictate 1*; **dic'ta·tor** Diktator *m*; **dic·ta·to·ri·al** □ [diktə'tɔ:riəl] diktatorisch; **dic·ta·tor·ship** [dik'teitəʃip] Diktatur *f*.
dic·tion ['dikʃən] Ausdruck(sweise *f*) *m*, Diktion *f*, Stil *m*; **dic·tion·ar·y** ['~ri] Wörterbuch *n*.
dict·um ['diktəm], *pl.* **dic·ta** ['~tə] (Aus)Spruch *m*; geflügeltes Wort *n*.
did [did] *pret. von do*.
di·dac·tic [di'dæktik] (~*ally*) didaktisch, (be)lehrend; Lehr...
did·dle *sl.* ['didl] übers Ohr hauen, betrügen.
didn't ['didnt] = *did not*; *s. do*.
die[1] [dai] (*p.pr. dying*) sterben, umkommen (*of* an *dat.*, *from* vor *dat.*); untergehen; absterben; F schmachten, sich sehnen (*for* nach; *to inf.* danach, zu *inf.*); ~ *away* ersterben, sich legen (*Wind*); verklingen (*Ton*); sich verlieren (*Farbe*); verlöschen (*Licht*); ~ *down* ersterben; (dahin-)schwinden; erlöschen; ~ *off* absterben; ~ *out* aussterben; ~ *hard* ein zähes Leben haben; nicht tot zu kriegen sein; *never say* ~! nur nicht verzweifeln!
die[2] [~], *pl.* **dice** [dais] Würfel *m*; *pl.* **dies** [daiz] ⊕ Preßform *f*, Gesenk *n*; *Münz*-Stempel *m*; Kubus *m*; *lower* ~ Matrize *f*; *upper* ~ Patrize *f*; *as straight as a* ~ kerzengerade; *the* ~ *is cast* die Würfel sind gefallen.
die...: '~**-a'way** schmachtend; '~**-cast·ing** ⊕ Spritzguß *m*; '~**-hard** Unentwegte *m*, Reaktionär *m*.
di·e·lec·tric [daii'lektrik] dielektrisch.
Die·sel en·gine ['di:zl'endʒin] Dieselmotor *m*.
die-sink·er ['daisiŋkə] Stempelschneider *m*; Werkzeugmacher *m*.
die-stock ⊕ ['daistɔk] Schneidkluppe *f*.
di·et[1] ['daiət] **1.** Diät *f*; Nahrung *f*, Ernährung *f*, Kost *f*; *be (put) on a* ~ diät leben (müssen); **2.** *v/t.* Diät vorschreiben (*dat.*); beköstigen; *v/i.* diät leben.
di·et[2] [~] Reichstag *m* (*hist.*); Parlament *n* in bestimmten Ländern.
di·e·tar·y ['daiətəri] **1.** Diätregel *f*; Ration *f*; **2.** diätetisch; **di·e·tet·ics** [daii'tetiks] *sg.* Diätkunde *f*; **di·e·ti·cian, di·e·ti·tian** [~'tiʃən] Diätspezialist *m*.
dif·fer ['difə] sich unterscheiden; andrer Meinung sein (*with*, *from* als); abweichen (*from* von); *they agreed to* ~ sie gaben es auf, einander zu überzeugen; **dif·fer·ence** ['difrəns] Unterschied *m*, Verschiedenheit *f*; ⅍ *u.* ⚚ Differenz *f*; Meinungsverschiedenheit *f*; Streit(igkeit *f*) *m*; *split the* ~ auf halbem Wege einander entgegenkommen; '**dif·fer·ent** □ verschieden (*from*, *to* von); anders, andere(r, -s) (*from* als); **dif·fer·en·ti·a** [difə'renʃiə] charakteristisches Merkmal *n*; **dif·fer'en·tial** [~əl] **1.** unterscheidend; Differential...; ~ *calculus* Differentialrechnung *f*; **2.** *mot.* Differential-, Ausgleichsgetriebe *n*; **dif·fer'en·ti·ate** [~ʃieit] (sich) unterscheiden; **dif·fer·en·ti'a·tion** Differenzierung *f*.
dif·fi·cult □ ['difikəlt] schwierig (*a. Charakter etc.*); schwer; beschwerlich; '**dif·fi·cul·ty** Schwierigkeit *f*; *difficulties pl. a.* Verlegenheit *f* (*for* um).
dif·fi·dence ['difidəns] Mangel *m* an Selbstvertrauen, Schüchternheit *f*; '**dif·fi·dent** □ ohne Selbstvertrauen, schüchtern.
dif·fract *phys.* [di'frækt] *Licht* beugen.
dif·frac·tion *phys.* [di'frækʃən] Diffraktion *f*, Beugung *f*.
dif·fuse 1. [di'fju:z] *fig.* verbreiten; ⚗ (sich) durchdringen; **2.** □ [~s]

weitverbreitet, zerstreut, diffus (*bsd. Licht*); weitschweifig, breit; **dif'fused** [~zd] zerstreut (*Licht*); **dif'fu·sion** [~ʒən] Verbreitung *f*; ⚗, *phys.* Durchdringung *f*; **dif-'fu·sive** □ [~siv] sich verbreitend; weitschweifig.

dig [dig] **1.** (*irr.*) (um-, aus)graben; wühlen (in *dat.*); F stoßen, puffen; ~ *for* graben nach; ~ *in* (sich) eingraben, schuften; ~ *into* sich vergraben in (*acc.*); ~ *up* ausgraben; **2.** Ausgrabungsstelle *f*, Grabung *f*; F Stoß *m*, Puff *m*; ~*s pl.* F Bude *f*, Einzelzimmer *n*.

di·gest 1. [di'dʒest] ordnen; verdauen (*a. fig.* = *überdenken*; *verwinden*); *v/i.* verdaut werden; **2.** ['daidʒest] Abriß *m*, Übersicht *f*; Auslese *f*, -wahl *f*; ⚖ Gesetzessammlung *f*; **di·gest·i·bil·i·ty** [didʒestə'biliti] Verdaulichkeit *f*; **di-'gest·i·ble** verdaulich; **di'ges·tion** Verdauung *f*; **di'ges·tive** Verdauungsmittel *n*.

dig·ger ['digə] (*bsd.* Gold)Gräber *m*; *sl.* Australier *m*; **dig·gings** F ['~-giŋz] *pl.* Bude *f* (*Wohnung*); *Am.* Goldmine(n *pl.*) *f*.

dig·it ['didʒit] Finger(breite *f*) *m*; ⅍ Ziffer *f*; Stelle *f*; **'dig·it·al** Finger...; Digital...; ~ *telephone* Tastentelefon *n*.

dig·ni·fied ['dignifaid] würdevoll; würdig; **dig·ni·fy** ['~fai] Würde verleihen (*dat.*); (be)ehren; *fig.* adeln; hochtrabend benennen.

dig·ni·tar·y *bsd. eccl.* ['dignitəri] Würdenträger *m*; **'dig·ni·ty** Würde *f*; *stand (up)on one's* ~ formell sein.

di·graph *gr.* ['daigrɑːf] Digraph *m* (*2 Buchstaben, die e-n Laut bilden*).

di·gress [dai'gres] abschweifen; **di-'gres·sion** Abschweifung *f*; **di-'gres·sive** □ abschweifend.

dike[1] [daik] 1. Deich *m*; Damm *m*; Graben *m*; 2. eindeichen; eindämmen.

dike[2] *sl.* [~] Lesbe *f*, Lesbierin *f*.

di·lap·i·date [di'læpideit] verfallen (lassen); **di'lap·i·dat·ed** verfallen, baufällig; schäbig; **di·lap·i'da·tion** Verfall *m*; Baufälligkeit *f*.

di·lat·a·bil·i·ty *phys.* [daileitə'biliti] (Aus)Dehnungsvermögen *n*; **di-'lat·a·ble** (aus)dehnbar; **dil·a'ta·tion** Ausdehnung *f*, Erweiterung *f*; **di'late** (sich) ausdehnen; *Augen, Nüstern* weit öffnen; ~ *upon* sich weitläufig über *et.* verbreiten; **di-'la·tion** = *dilatation*; **dil·a·to·ri·ness** ['dilətərinis] Saumseligkeit *f*; **'dil·a·to·ry** □ aufschiebend, hinhaltend, saumselig.

di·lem·ma [di'lemə] Dilemma *n*; *fig.* Verlegenheit *f*, Klemme *f*.

dil·et·tan·te, *pl.* **dil·et·tan·ti** [dili-'tænti, *pl.* ~'tæntiː] Dilettant(in).

dil·i·gence ['dilidʒəns] Fleiß *m*; **'dil·i·gent** □ fleißig, emsig.

dill ⚘ [dil] Dill *m*.

dil·ly-dal·ly F ['dilidæli] (die Zeit ver)trödeln.

dil·u·ent ['diljuənt] verdünnend(es Mittel *n*); **di·lute** [dai'ljuːt] **1.** (mit Wasser) verdünnen; *fig.* verwässern; **2.** verdünnt; *fig.* verwässert; **di'lu·tion** Verdünnung *f*; *fig.* Verwässerung *f*.

di·lu·vi·al [dai'luːvjəl], **di'lu·vi·an** *geol.* diluvial.

dim [dim] **1.** □ trüb; dunkel; matt; F schwer von Begriff; **2.** (sich) verdunkeln; *mot., Film*: abblenden; (sich) trüben, matt werden.

dime *Am.* [daim] Zehncentstück *n*; ~ *novel* Groschenroman *m*; ~ *store* Einheitspreisgeschäft *n*.

di·men·sion [di'menʃən] Dimension *f*, Abmessung *f*; ~*s pl. a.* Ausmaß *n*.

di·min·ish [di'miniʃ] (sich) vermindern *od.* -ringern *od.* -jüngen; abnehmen; **dim·i·nu·tion** [dimi-'njuːʃən] Verminderung *f*; Abnahme *f* (*in* an *dat.*); ⚠ Verjüngung *f*; **di'min·u·tive** [~njutiv] **1.** □ *gr.* verkleinernd; winzig; **2.** Verkleinerungsform *f*, Diminutiv *n*.

dim·mer ['dimə] Abblendvorrichtung *f*.

dim·ness ['dimnis] Dunkelheit *f*; Mattheit *f*.

dim·ple ['dimpl] **1.** Grübchen *n*; **2.** Grübchen bekommen; (sich) kräuseln; **'dim·pled** mit Grübchen.

din [din] **1.** Getöse *n*, Lärm *m*; **2.** (durch Lärm) betäuben; lärmen; dröhnen; ~ *s.th. into s.o.('s ears)* j-m dauernd et. (vor)predigen.

dine [dain] (zu Mittag) essen; bewirten; (Mittagsgäste) fassen (*Saal*); ~ *out* zum Essen ausgehen; **'din·er** Speisende *m, f*; (Mittags)Gast *m*;

🚃 *bsd. Am.* Speisewagen *m*; '**diner-'out** j., der (oft) auswärts ißt; **di·nette** [dai'net] Eßnische *f in der Küche*.
ding [diŋ] klingen; beständig wiederholen; **~-dong** ['~'dɔŋ] **1.** bim bam; **2.** Klingklang *m*; **3.** unentschieden (*Rennen*); heiß (*Kampf*).
din·gey, din·ghy ['diŋgi] Dingi *n* (*kleines Boot*); *rubber ~* Schlauchboot *n*.
din·gle ['diŋgl] Waldschlucht *f*.
din·gus *Am. sl.* ['diŋgəs] Dingsbums *n*.
din·gy □ ['dindʒi] schmutzig; schmierig; schmuddelig; schäbig.
din·ing... ['dainiŋ]: '**~-'al·cove** Eßnische *f*; '**~-car** 🚃 Speisewagen *m*; '**~-room** Eß-, Speisezimmer *n*; **~ table** Eßtisch *m*.
dink·ey *Am.* ['diŋki] *kleine* Rangierlok *f*.
dink·y F ['diŋki] niedlich; nett.
din·ner ['dinə] Hauptmahlzeit *f* (*Mittag- oder Abendessen*); Festessen *n*; '**~-jack·et** Smoking *m*; '**~-pail** *Am.* Essenträger *m* (*Gerät*); '**~-par·ty** Tischgesellschaft *f*; '**~-serv·ice,** '**~-set** Tafelgeschirr *n*.
di·no·saur *zo.* ['dainəusɔː] Dinosaurier *m*.
dint [dint] **1.** Strieme *f*, Beule *f*; *by ~ of* kraft, vermöge (*gen.*); **2.** ver-, einbeulen.
di·o·ce·san *eccl.* [dai'ɔsisən] **1.** Diözesan...; **2.** Diözesanbischof *m*; **di·o·cese** ['daiəsis] Diözese *f*.
di·ode ⚡ ['daiəud] Diode *f*; *light--emitting ~* Leuchtdiode *f*.
di·op·tric *opt.* [dai'ɔptrik] **1.** dioptrisch; **2.** Dioptrie *f* (*Lichtbrechungseinheit*).
di·ox·ide ⚗ [dai'ɔksaid] Dioxyd *n*.
dip [dip] **1.** *v/t.* (ein)tauchen; senken, ⚓ *Flagge* dippen; *Stoff* (auf-) färben; schöpfen (*out of, from* aus); *mot.* abblenden; *v/i.* (unter)tauchen, untersinken; sich neigen; sich senken; *geol.* einfallen; *~ into* in *den Geldbeutel* greifen; e-n flüchtigen Blick werfen in (*acc.*); **2.** Eintauchen *n*; Desinfektionsbad *n für Schafe*; F kurzes Bad *n*; Senkung *f*, Neigung *f*; Dippen *n der Flagge*; *have a ~, take a ~* kurz baden gehen.
diph·the·ri·a [dif'θiəriə] Diphtherie *f*.
diph·thong ['difθɔŋ] Diphthong *m*, Doppellaut *m*.
di·plo·ma [di'pləumə] Diplom *n*; **di'plo·ma·cy** Diplomatie *f*; Verhandlungsgeschick *n*; **di'plo·maed** [~məd] diplomiert; Diplom...; **dip·lo·mat** ['dipləmæt] Diplomat(in); **dip·lo'mat·ic, dip·lo'mat·i·cal** □ diplomatisch; **dip·lo'mat·ics** *sg.* Diplomatik *f*; **di·plo·ma·tist** [di'pləumətist] Diplomat(in).
dip·per ['dipə] Schöpfkelle *f*; *Am. Big* ♀ *ast. der* Große Bär; '**dip·py** *sl.* verrückt.
dip·so·ma·ni·a [dipsəu'meinjə] Trunksucht *f*; **dip·so'ma·ni·ac** [~niæk] Trunksüchtige *m, f*.
dip-stick ['dipstik] (*bsd. mot.* Öl-) Meßstab *m*.
dip-switch *mot.* ['dipswitʃ] Abblendschalter *m*.
dire ['daiə] gräßlich, schrecklich.
di·rect [di'rekt] **1.** □ direkt; gerade; unmittelbar; offen, aufrichtig; deutlich; glatt, genau; *~ current* Gleichstrom *m*; *~ dial(l)ing teleph.* Durchwahl *f*; *~ hit* Volltreffer *m*; *~ speech* direkte Rede *f*; *~ tax* direkte Steuer *f*; *~ train* durchgehender Zug *m*; **2.** *adv.* geradeswegs; = *~ly 1*; **3.** richten (*to, towards, at* nach, auf *acc.*, gegen); lenken, steuern; leiten, führen, anordnen; *j.* anweisen; *j.* weisen (*to* nach; an *j.*); *Brief* adressieren; *~ to* zuleiten (*dat.*); **di'rec·tion** Richtung *f*; Gegend *f*; Lenkung *f*; Leitung *f*, Führung *f*; Anordnung *f*; Anweisung *f*; Adresse *f*; Direktion *f*, Vorstand *m*; **di'rec·tion·al** [~ʃənl] *Radio*: Peil..., Richt...; **di'rec·tion--find·er** *Radio*: (Funk)Peiler *m*; Peil(funk)empfänger *m*; **di'rec·tion--find·ing** *Radio*: Funkortung *f*; *attr.* (Funk)Peil...; *~ set* Peilgerät *n*; *~ station* Funkpeilstelle *f*; **di'rec·tion in·di·ca·tor** *mot.* Fahrtrichtungsanzeiger *m*; ✈ Kursweiser *m*; **di'rec·tive** richtungweisend; leitend; anweisend; **di'rect·ly 1.** *adv.* unmittelbar; sofort, gleich; **2.** *cj.* sobald (als); **di'rect·ness** gerade Richtung *f*; *fig.* Geradheit *f*.
di·rec·tor [di'rektə] Direktor *m*; *Film*: Regisseur *m*; Mitglied *n* des Aufsichtsrats; *board of ~s* Aufsichtsrat *m*; **di'rec·to·rate** [~rit] Direktorium *n*, Direktion *f*; *a.* **di'rec·tor·ship** Direktorat *n*; **di'rec·to·ry** Adreßbuch *n*; *telephone ~*

Telefonbuch; ~ *enquiries pl.*, *Am.* ~ *assistance* Telefonauskunft *f*.
di·rec·tress [di'rektris] Vorsteherin *f*, Direktorin *f*.
dire·ful □ ['daiəful] schrecklich.
dirge [dəːdʒ] Grabgesang *m*; Klage (-lied *n*) *f*.
dir·i·gi·ble ['diridʒəbl] **1.** lenkbar; **2.** lenkbares Luftschiff *n*.
dirk [dəːk] **1.** Dolchmesser *n*; **2.** erdolchen.
dirt [dəːt] Schmutz *m*; *fig. contp.* Dreck *m*; (lockere) Erde *f*; *treat s.o. like* ~ j. wie den letzten Dreck behandeln; *fling od. throw* ~ *at s.o.* j. mit Schmutz bewerfen; '**~-'cheap** F spottbillig; ~ **road** *Am.* unbefestigte Straße *f*; '**~-track** *Sport*: Aschenbahn *f*; '**dirt·y 1.** □ schmutzig (*a. fig.*); **2.** beschmutzen; besudeln.
dis·a·bil·i·ty [disə'biliti] Unvermögen *n*; (Dienst-, Rechts)Unfähigkeit *f*.
dis·a·ble [dis'eibl] (*bsd.* dienst-, kampf)unfähig *od.* unbrauchbar machen; **dis'a·bled** dienst-, kampfunfähig; invalide, körperbehindert; kriegsversehrt, -beschädigt; **dis'a·ble·ment** Invalidität *f*; Kampfunfähigkeit *f*.
dis·a·buse [disə'bjuːz] e-s Bessern belehren (*of* über *acc.*).
dis·ac·cord [disə'kɔːd] nicht übereinstimmen (*with* mit).
dis·ac·cus·tom ['disə'kʌstəm]: ~ *s.o. to s.th.* j-m et. abgewöhnen.
dis·ad·van·tage [disəd'vaːntidʒ] Nachteil *m*; Schaden *m*; *sell to* ~ mit Verlust verkaufen; **dis·ad·van·ta·geous** □ [disædvaːn'teidʒəs] nachteilig, ungünstig.
dis·af·fect·ed □ [disə'fektid] (*to, towards*) abgeneigt (gegen); unzufrieden (mit); **dis·af'fec·tion** Abneigung *f*; Unzufriedenheit *f*.
dis·af·firm ⚖ [disə'fəːm] umstoßen.
dis·af·for·est [disə'fɔrist] abholzen.
dis·a·gree [disə'griː] nicht übereinstimmen, nicht einverstanden sein (*with* mit); uneinig sein (*on* über *acc.*); *Antrag etc.* ablehnen (*to, with acc.*); nicht bekommen (*with s.o.* j-m); **dis·a·gree·a·ble** □ [~'griəbl] unangenehm (*a. fig.*); **dis·a·gree·ment** [~'griːmənt] Verschiedenheit *f*; Unstimmigkeit *f*; Meinungsverschiedenheit *f*; Verstimmung *f*.

dis·al·low ['disə'lau] nicht erlauben; ablehnen; nicht gelten lassen.
dis·ap·pear [disə'piə] verschwinden; **dis·ap·pear·ance** [~'piərəns] Verschwinden *n*.
dis·ap·point [disə'pɔint] enttäuschen; vereiteln; *j.* im Stich lassen; **dis·ap'point·ment** Enttäuschung *f*; Vereitelung *f*; ~ *in love* unglückliche Liebe *f*.
dis·ap·pro·ba·tion [disæprəu'beiʃən] Mißbilligung *f*.
dis·ap·prov·al [disə'pruːvl] Mißbilligung *f*; **dis·ap'prove** mißbilligen (*of et.*).
dis·arm [dis'ɑːm] *v/t.* entwaffnen (*a. fig.*); *v/i.* abrüsten; **dis'ar·ma·ment** Entwaffnung *f*; Abrüstung *f*.
dis·ar·range ['disə'reindʒ] in Unordnung bringen, verwirren; **dis·ar'range·ment** Verwirrung *f*, Unordnung *f*.
dis·ar·ray ['disə'rei] **1.** Unordnung *f*; **2.** in Unordnung bringen.
dis·as·sem·bly ⊕ [disə'sembli] Auseinandernehmen *n*.
dis·as·ter [di'zɑːstə] Unglück(sfall *m*) *n*, Unheil *n*, Katastrophe *f*; ~ *relief* Katastrophenhilfe *f*; **dis'as·trous** □ unheilvoll, unglücklich; verheerend, katastrophal.
dis·a·vow ['disə'vau] (ab)leugnen; nicht gutheißen; **dis·a'vow·al** Ableugnung *f*; Nichtanerkennung *f*.
dis·band [dis'bænd] *Truppen* entlassen; (sich) auflösen; **dis'band·ment** Auflösung *f*.
dis·bar [dis'bɑː] vom Anwaltsamt ausschließen.
dis·be·lief ['disbi'liːf] Unglaube *m*, Zweifel *m* (*in* an *dat.*); **dis·be·lieve** ['disbi'liːv] nicht glauben, bezweifeln; '**dis·be'liev·er** Ungläubige *m*, *f*, Zweifler(in).
dis·bud [dis'bʌd] überschüssige Knospen entfernen von.
dis·bur·den [dis'bəːdn] entlasten; befreien (*of* von *e-r Last*); *Herz* erleichtern; entladen (*a. fig.*).
dis·burse [dis'bəːs] auszahlen; verauslagen; **dis'burse·ment** Auszahlung *f*; Verauslagung *f*.
disc [disk] = *disk*.
dis·card 1. [dis'kɑːd] *Karten* weglegen, abwerfen; *Kleid, Vorurteil etc.* ablegen; aufgeben; entlassen; **2.** ['diskɑːd] *Karten*: Abwerfen *n*; *bsd. Am.* Abfall(haufen) *m*.

dis·cern [di'sə:n] unterscheiden; erkennen; wahrnehmen; beurteilen; **dis'cern·i·ble** □ unterscheidbar; erkennbar; sichtbar; **dis'cern·ing** **1.** □ kritisch, scharfsichtig; **2.** Einsicht *f*; Scharfblick *m*; **dis'cern·ment** Einsicht *f*; Scharfsinn *m*.

dis·charge [dis'tʃɑ:dʒ] **1.** *v/t*. ent-, ab-, ausladen; ⚓ löschen; ⚡ entladen; entlasten, entbinden; abfeuern; verwalten, *Amt* versehen; *Pflicht etc*. erfüllen; *Zorn etc*. auslassen; ausströmen lassen; *Schuld* abtragen, tilgen; *Rechnung* quittieren; *Wechsel* einlösen; entlassen, abdanken; freisprechen; *v/i*. sich entladen; sich ergießen; eitern; **2.** Entladung *f* (*a*. ⚡); ⚓ Löschen *n*; Abfeuern *n*; Salve *f*; Ausströmen *n*; Ausfluß *m*, Eiter(ung *f*) *m*; Entlassung *f*; Entlastung *f*; Bezahlung *f*; Quittung *f*; Verwaltung *f*; Erfüllung *f e-r Pflicht*; **dis'charg·er** Entlader *m* (*a. phys*.).

dis·ci·ple [di'saipl] Schüler *m*; Jünger *m*; **dis'ci·ple·ship** Jüngerschaft *f*.

dis·ci·pli·nar·i·an [disipli'nɛəriən] strenger Lehrer *m od*. Vorgesetzter *m*; *he is a poor* ~ er kann keine Disziplin halten; **'dis·ci·pli·nar·y** erzieherisch; disziplinar, Disziplinar...; **'dis·ci·pline** **1.** Disziplin *f*, Zucht *f*; Erziehung *f*; (Studien-)Fach *n*, Wissenschaft *f*; Züchtigung *f*; **2.** an Disziplin gewöhnen; erziehen; schulen; strafen.

dis·claim [dis'kleim] (ab)leugnen; ablehnen; verzichten auf (*acc*.); **dis'claim·er** Verzicht(leistung *f*) *m*; Dementi *n*.

dis·close [dis'kləuz] aufdecken; erschließen, offenbaren, eröffnen, enthüllen; **dis'clo·sure** [~ʒə] Enthüllung *f etc*.

dis·col·o(u)r [dis'kʌlə] (sich) verfärben; **dis·col·o(u)r'a·tion** Verfärbung *f*.

dis·com·fit [dis'kʌmfit] *in die Flucht* schlagen; vereiteln; aus der Fassung bringen; **dis'com·fi·ture** [~tʃə] Niederlage *f*; Verwirrung *f*; Vereitelung *f*.

dis·com·fort [dis'kʌmfət] **1.** Unbehagen *n*; **2.** *j-m* Unbehagen verursachen.

dis·com·pose [diskəm'pəuz] beunruhigen; **dis·com'po·sure** [~ʒə] Beunruhigung *f*, Erregung *f*.

dis·con·cert [diskən'sə:t] aus der Fassung bringen; vereiteln.

dis·con·nect ['diskə'nekt] trennen (*from, with* von); ⊕ abstellen; auskuppeln; ⚡ Netzstecker ziehen; **'dis·con'nect·ed** □ zs.-hanglos; **'dis·con'nec·tion** Trennung *f*; ⊕ Auskuppelung *f etc*.

dis·con·so·late □ [dis'kɔnsəlit] untröstlich.

dis·con·tent ['diskən'tent] **1.** ✝ = ~*ed*; **2.** Unzufriedenheit *f*; **'dis·con'tent·ed** □ mißvergnügt, unzufrieden.

dis·con·tin·u·ance [diskən'tinjuəns] Unterbrechung *f*; Aufhören *n*, Aufgabe *f*; **'dis·con'tin·ue** [~nju:] aufgeben, aufhören mit; *Zeitung* abbestellen; **'dis·con'tin·u·ous** □ [~njuəs] unzusammenhängend, mit Unterbrechungen, unterbrochen.

dis·cord ['diskɔ:d], **dis'cord·ance** Uneinigkeit *f*; ♪ Mißklang *m*; **dis'cord·ant** □ verschieden, abweichend (*to, from, with* von); uneinig; ♪ mißtönend, -klingend.

dis·co·theque ['diskəutek] Diskothek *f*.

dis·count ['diskaunt] **1.** ✝ Diskont *m*, Skonto *m*; Abzug *m* (*a. fig*.), Rabatt *m*; ~ *store* Discountladen *m*; *at a* ~ unter Pari; *fig*. nicht gefragt; **2.** ✝ diskontieren; abrechnen, abziehen (*a. fig*.); *fig*. absehen von; *Nachricht* mit Vorsicht aufnehmen; beeinträchtigen; **dis'count·a·ble** diskontierbar; **dis'coun·te·nance** [~tinəns] (offen) mißbilligen; entmutigen.

dis·cour·age [dis'kʌridʒ] entmutigen; *j*. abschrecken (*from* von); abschrecken von *et*.; **dis'cour·age·ment** Entmutigung *f*; Schwierigkeit *f*.

dis·course [dis'kɔ:s] **1.** Rede *f*; Abhandlung *f*; Predigt *f*; **2.** (*on, upon, about*) reden, sprechen (über *acc*.); e-n Vortrag halten (über *acc*.), *et*. abhandeln.

dis·cour·te·ous □ [dis'kə:tjəs] unhöflich; **dis'cour·te·sy** [~tisi] Unhöflichkeit *f*.

dis·cov·er [dis'kʌvə] entdecken; ausfindig machen; **dis'cov·er·a·ble** □ entdeckbar, auffindbar; ersichtlich; **dis'cov·er·er** Entdecker(in); **dis'cov·er·y** Entdeckung *f*.

dis·cred·it [dis'kredit] **1.** schlechter

Ruf *m*, Mißkredit *m*; Unglaubwürdigkeit *f*; **2.** nicht glauben; diskreditieren, in Mißkredit bringen; **dis'cred·it·a·ble** □ entehrend, schimpflich (*to* für).

dis·creet □ [dis'kri:t] besonnen, vorsichtig; klug; verschwiegen; diskret, taktvoll.

dis·crep·an·cy [dis'krepənsi] Verschiedenheit *f*, Widerspruch *m*, Diskrepanz *f*; Unstimmigkeit *f*; Zwiespalt *m*.

dis·crete □ [dis'kri:t] abgesondert, getrennt.

dis·cre·tion [dis'kreʃən] Besonnenheit *f*, Klugheit *f*; Diskretion *f*, Takt(gefühl *n*) *m*; Verschwiegenheit *f*; Verfügungsfreiheit *f*, Belieben *n*; *banker's* ~ Bankgeheimnis *n*; *at one's* ~ nach *od.* in j-s Belieben; *age od. years of* ~ Strafmündigkeit *f* (*14 Jahre*); *surrender at* ~ sich auf Gnade und Ungnade ergeben; **dis'cre·tion·ar·y** [~ʃnəri] willkürlich; unumschränkt.

dis·crim·i·nate [dis'krimineit] unterscheiden; ~ *against* benachteiligen; **dis'crim·i·nat·ing** □ unterscheidend; scharfsinnig; urteilsfähig; **dis·crim·i'na·tion** Unterscheidung *f*; unterschiedliche (*bsd.* nachteilige) Behandlung *f*; Urteilskraft *f*; *reverse* ~ Bevorzugung *f* von Farbigen auf Kosten der Weißen; **dis'crim·i·na·tive** [~nətiv] □ diskriminierend; **dis'crim·i·na·to·ry law** Ausnahmegesetz *n*.

dis·cur·sive □ [dis'kə:siv] weitschweifig; sprunghaft, abschweifend; *phls.* schließend; Urteils...

dis·cus ['diskəs] *Sport*: Diskus *m*.

dis·cuss [dis'kʌs] diskutieren, erörtern, besprechen; untersuchen; *co. Essen od. Getränk* sich zu Gemüte führen; **dis'cuss·i·ble** diskutabel; **dis'cus·sion** Diskussion *f*, Erörterung *f*, Aussprache *f*.

dis·dain [dis'dein] **1.** Geringschätzung *f*, Verachtung *f*; **2.** geringschätzen, verachten; verschmähen; **dis'dain·ful** □ [~ful] verachtend (*of acc.*); geringschätzig.

dis·ease [di'zi:z] Krankheit *f*; Leiden *n*; **dis'eased** krank.

dis·em·bark ['disim'bɑ:k] ausschiffen, landen, an Land gehen; **dis·em·bar·ka·tion** [disəmbɑ:'keiʃən] Ausschiffung *f*.

dis·em·bar·rass ['disim'bærəs] frei-, losmachen (*of* von).

dis·em·bod·y [disim'bɔdi] entkörpern; *Truppen* auflösen.

dis·em·bogue [disim'bəug] (sich) ergießen.

dis·em·bow·el [disim'bauəl] ausweiden.

dis·em·broil [disim'brɔil] entwirren.

dis·en·chant ['disin'tʃɑ:nt] desillusionieren, ernüchtern.

dis·en·cum·ber ['disin'kʌmbə] entlasten, freimachen (*of*, *from*, von).

dis·en·gage ['disin'geidʒ] (sich) freimachen, (sich) lösen; ⊕ loskuppeln; ausschalten; **'dis·en'gaged** frei; **'dis·en'gage·ment** Freimachung *f*; Ungebundenheit *f*; Entlobung *f*.

dis·en·tan·gle ['disin'tæŋgl] entwirren; *fig.* freimachen (*from* von); **'dis·en'tan·gle·ment** Entwirrung *f*.

dis·en·tomb [disin'tu:m] ausgraben.

dis·e·qui·lib·ri·um ['disekwi'libriəm] Unausgeglichenheit *f*.

dis·es·tab·lish ['disis'tæbliʃ] *Kirche* entstaatlichen; **dis·es'tab·lish·ment** Entstaatlichung *f*.

dis·fa·vo(u)r ['dis'feivə] **1.** Mißfallen *n*, Ungnade *f*, Unwillen *m*; **2.** nicht mögen; ungnädig behandeln; mißbilligen.

dis·fig·ure [dis'figə] entstellen, verunstalten; **dis'fig·ure·ment** Entstellung *f*.

dis·fran·chise ['dis'fræntʃaiz] *j-m* das Wahlrecht *od. e-r Stadt* die bürgerlichen Freiheiten nehmen; **dis·fran·chise·ment** [dis'fræntʃizmənt] Entziehung *f* des Wahl- *od.* Bürgerrechts.

dis·frock [dis'frɔk] *j-m* das Priesteramt entziehen.

dis·gorge [dis'gɔ:dʒ] ausspeien; von sich geben; wieder herausgeben; *a.* ~ *o.s.* sich ergießen.

dis·grace [dis'greis] **1.** Ungnade *f*; Schande *f*; **2.** in Ungnade fallen lassen; *j.* entehren, schänden; *be* ~*d* in Ungnade fallen; **dis'grace·ful** □ [~ful] schimpflich; schändlich.

dis·grun·tled [dis'grʌntld] verdrossen (*at* über *acc.*).

dis·guise [dis'gaiz] **1.** verkleiden; *Stimme* verstellen; verhehlen; **2.** Verkleidung *f*; Verstellung *f*; Maske *f*; *blessing in* ~ Glück im Unglück.

dis·gust [dis'gʌst] **1.** (*at, for*) Ekel *m*, Abscheu *m*, *f* (vor *dat.*); Widerwille *m* (gegen); **2.** anekeln; *~ed with* angewidert durch; **dis'gust·ing** □ ekelhaft, widerwärtig.
dish [diʃ] **1.** Schüssel *f*, Platte *f*; Gericht *n* (*Speise*); *the ~es pl.* das Geschirr; *standing ~ fig.* ständiges Thema *n*; **2.** anrichten; *mst ~ up* auftischen (*a. fig.*); *sl. j.* erledigen; hereinlegen; *et.* vermasseln.
dis·ha·bille [disæ'bi:l] Negligé *n*; *in ~* nachlässig gekleidet; im Negligé.
dis·har·mo·ny [dis'hɑ:məni] Mißklang *m*, Disharmonie *f*.
dish-cloth ['diʃklɔθ] Geschirrspültuch *n*.
dis·heart·en [dis'hɑ:tn] entmutigen.
di·shev·el(l)ed [di'ʃevəld] zerzaust (*Haar*); *fig.* liederlich.
dis·hon·est □ [dis'ɔnist] unehrlich, unredlich; **dis'hon·est·y** Unredlichkeit *f*.
dis·hon·o(u)r [dis'ɔnə] **1.** Unehre *f*, Schande *f*; **2.** entehren; schänden; Schande machen (*dat.*); *Wechsel* nicht honorieren; **dis'hon·o(u)r·a·ble** □ entehrend, schimpflich; ehrlos; *~ discharge* ⚔ unehrenhafte Entlassung *f*.
dish...: '**~-pan** *Am.* Spülschüssel *f*; '**~·rag** *Am.* = *dish-cloth*; '**~-wash·er** Tellerwäscher *m*; Geschirrspülmaschine *f*; '**~-wa·ter** Spülwasser *n*.
dish·y F ['diʃi] attraktiv, (sexuell) anziehend.
dis·il·lu·sion [disi'lu:ʒən] **1.** Ernüchterung *f*, Enttäuschung *f*; **2.** ernüchtern, enttäuschen; **dis·il'lu·sion·ment** = *disillusion 1*.
dis·in·cen·tive [disin'sentiv] Entmutigung *f*.
dis·in·cli·na·tion [disinkli'neiʃən] Abneigung *f* (*for, to* gegen); **dis·in·cline** ['~'klain] abgeneigt machen; '**dis·in'clined** abgeneigt (*for, to* gegen).
dis·in·fect [disin'fekt] desinfizieren; **dis·in'fect·ant** Desinfektionsmittel *n*; **dis·in'fec·tion** Desinfektion *f*.
dis·in·fla·tion [disin'fleiʃən] Rückgang *m* der Inflation.
dis·in·gen·u·ous □ [disin'dʒenjuəs] unaufrichtig; falsch.
dis·in·her·it ['disin'herit] enterben; **dis·in'her·it·ance** Enterbung *f*.
dis·in·te·grate [dis'intigreit] (sich) (in seine Bestandteile) auflösen; (sich) zersetzen; aufschließen; **dis·in·te'gra·tion** Auflösung *f etc.*
dis·in·ter ['disin'tə:] wieder ausgraben.
dis·in·ter·est·ed □ [dis'intristid] uneigennützig, selbstlos.
dis·join [dis'dʒɔin] trennen; **dis·joint** [~'dʒɔint] in Unordnung bringen; (ab)trennen; auseinandernehmen; **dis'joint·ed** unzusammenhängend (*Rede*).
dis·junc·tion [dis'dʒʌŋkʃən] Trennung *f*; **dis'junc·tive** □ [~tiv] trennend; *gr.* disjunktiv.
disk [disk] Scheibe *f*; Platte *f*; Schallplatte *f*; **~ brake** *mot.* Scheibenbremse *f*; **~ clutch** *mot.* Scheibenkupplung *f*; '**~-har·row** Scheibenegge *f*; **~ jock·ey** *sl.* Ansager *m* e-r Schallplattensendung.
dis·like [dis'laik] **1.** Abneigung *f*; Widerwille *m* (*for, of, to* gegen); **2.** nicht mögen, nicht lieben, nicht leiden können; *~d* unbeliebt.
dis·lo·cate ['disləukeit] aus den Fugen bringen; verrücken; verrenken; verlagern; *fig.* verwirren; **dis·lo'ca·tion** Verrenkung *f*; Verlagerung *f*; Verlegung *f* (*bsd.* ⚔); *geol.* Verwerfung *f*; *fig.* Verwirrung *f*.
dis·lodge [dis'lɔdʒ] vertreiben, verjagen; umquartieren.
dis·loy·al □ ['dis'lɔiəl] treulos; '**dis'loy·al·ty** Treulosigkeit *f*.
dis·mal ['dizməl] **1.** □ *fig.* trüb (-selig), traurig, düster; öde; trostlos, elend; schaurig; **2.** *the ~s pl.* F der Trübsinn.
dis·man·tle [dis'mæntl] abbrechen, niederreißen; *Festung* schleifen; ⚓ abtakeln; *Haus* (aus)räumen; *Mechanismus etc.* auseinandernehmen; *Industriewerk* demontieren; **dis'man·tling** Demontage *f*.
dis·mast ⚓ [dis'mɑ:st] entmasten.
dis·may [dis'mei] **1.** Furcht *f*, Schrecken *m*, Bestürzung *f*; **2.** *v/t.* erschrecken.
dis·mem·ber [dis'membə] zergliedern, zerstückeln; **dis'mem·ber·ment** Zergliederung *f*, -stückelung *f*.
dis·miss [dis'mis] *v/t.* entlassen, wegschicken; abtun (*as* als); ablehnen; *Thema etc.* fallen lassen; ⚖ abweisen; *be ~ed the service* aus dem Dienst entlassen werden; *v/i.*

⚔ wegtreten; **dis'miss·al** Entlassung *f*; Aufgabe *f*; ⚖ Abweisung *f*.
dis·mount ['dis'maunt] *v/t.* vom Pferde werfen; *Geschütz* demontieren; ⊕ abmontieren, auseinandernehmen; *v/i.* absteigen.
dis·o·be·di·ence [disə'bi:djəns] Ungehorsam *m*; **dis·o'be·di·ent** □ ungehorsam (*to* gegen); **'dis·o'bey** nicht gehorchen (*dat.*), ungehorsam sein (gegen).
dis·o·blige ['disə'blaidʒ] ungefällig sein gegen; kränken; **'dis·o'blig·ing** □ ungefällig; unhöflich; **'dis·o'blig·ing·ness** Ungefälligkeit *f*.
dis·or·der [dis'ɔ:də] **1.** Unordnung *f*; Aufruhr *m*, Unruhe *f*; ⚕ Störung *f*, Krankheit *f*; *mental* ~ Geistesstörung *f*; **2.** in Unordnung bringen; stören; zerrütten; **dis'or·dered** □ unordentlich; verdorben (*Magen*); zerrüttet; **dis'or·der·ly** unordentlich; ordnungswidrig; unruhig, aufrührerisch; liederlich.
dis·or·gan·i·za·tion [disɔ:gənai'zeiʃən] Auflösung *f*, Zerrüttung *f*; **dis'or·gan·ize** zerrütten; in Unordnung bringen.
dis·or·i·en·tate [dis'ɔ:rienteit] irremachen; *he was* ~*d* er hatte die Orientierung verloren.
dis·own [dis'əun] nicht anerkennen, verleugnen; ablehnen.
dis·par·age [dis'pæridʒ] verächtlich machen, verunglimpfen, herabsetzen; **dis'par·age·ment** Herabsetzung *f*, Verunglimpfung *f*; Schande *f*; **dis'par·ag·ing** □ verächtlich.
dis·pa·rate ['dispərit] **1.** □ ungleichartig, (ganz) verschieden; **2.** ~*s pl.* unvereinbare Dinge *n/pl.*; **dis·par·i·ty** [dis'pæriti] Ungleichheit *f*.
dis·part [dis'pɑ:t] (sich) trennen; (sich) spalten; ⊕ kalibrieren.
dis·pas·sion·ate □ [dis'pæʃnit] leidenschaftslos; gelassen; unparteiisch.
dis·patch [dis'pætʃ] **1.** (schnelle) Erledigung *f*; (schnelle) Absendung *f*, Abfertigung *f*; Versand *m*; Eile *f*; Depesche *f*; *mentioned in* ~*es* im Kriegsbericht rühmend erwähnt; *happy* ~ Harakiri *n*; **2.** (schnell) abmachen, erledigen (*a.* = *töten*); abfertigen; absenden; **dis'patch-box** Dokumententasche *f*; **dis'patch-goods** *pl.* Eilgut *n*; **dis'patch note** 🛈 Begleitschein *m*; **dis'patch-rid·er** ⚔ Meldereiter *m*, -fahrer *m*.
dis·pel [dis'pel] vertreiben, zerstreuen (*a. fig.*).
dis·pen·sa·ble [dis'pensəbl] erläßlich; entbehrlich; **dis'pen·sa·ry** Apotheke *f*; Ambulanz *f für Unbemittelte*; **dis·pen·sa·tion** [dispen'seiʃən] Austeilung *f*; Dispensation *f*, Befreiung *f* (*with* von); *göttliche* Fügung *f*.
dis·pense [dis'pens] *v/t.* austeilen, spenden; *Recht* sprechen; *Arzneien* nach Vorschrift bereiten und ausgeben; ~ *from* befreien *od.* entbinden von; *e-r Arbeit etc.* entheben; *v/i.* ~ *with et.* unnötig machen; fertig werden ohne, verzichten auf (*acc.*); **dis'pens·er** Austeiler(in); Apotheker(in).
dis·per·sal [dis'pə:səl] = *dispersion*; **dis'perse** (sich) zerstreuen; verstreuen, -breiten; auseinandergehen; **dis'per·sion** Zerstreuung *f* (*a. opt.*); Streuung *f*; Verbreitung *f*; ♀ *eccl.* Diaspora *f*.
dis·pir·it [di'spirit] entmutigen; **dis'pir·it·ed** □ mutlos.
dis·place [dis'pleis] verrücken, verschieben; absetzen; ersetzen; verdrängen; ~*d person* Verschleppte *m*, *f*; **dis'place·ment** Verrückung *f* *etc.*; Ersatz *m*; (*bsd.* Wasser)Verdrängung *f*.
dis·play [dis'plei] **1.** Entfaltung *f*; Aufwand *m*; Schaustellung *f*; (Schaufenster)Auslage *f*; Prunk *m*; **2.** entfalten, an den Tag legen; zur Schau stellen; ausstellen, -breiten; zeigen; hervorheben; ~ **case** Vitrine *f*, Schaukasten *m*; ~ **stand** Verkaufsständer *m*.
dis·please [dis'pli:z] *j-m* mißfallen; *fig.* verletzen; **dis'pleased** □ ungehalten (*at, with* über *acc.*); **dis'pleas·ing** □ mißfällig, unangenehm; **dis·pleas·ure** [~'pleʒə] Mißfallen *n*, -vergnügen *n*; Verdruß *m* (*at, over* über *acc.*).
dis·port [dis'pɔ:t]: ~ *o.s.* sich (lustig) tummeln, herumtollen.
dis·pos·a·ble [dis'pəuzəbl] verfügbar; **dis'pos·al** Anordnung *f*; Verfügung(srecht *n*) *f* (*of* über *acc.*); Beseitigung *f*; Veräußerung *f*, Verkauf *m*; Übergabe *f*; *at one's* ~ zu j-s Verfügung; **dis'pose** *v/t.* (an-)

ordnen, einrichten, verteilen; geneigt machen, veranlassen (*for* zu *et.*, *to inf.* zu *inf.*); *v/i.* ~ *of* verfügen über (*acc.*); erledigen; verwenden; gebrauchen; veräußern; vermachen; unterbringen, versorgen; beseitigen; verzehren; **dis'posed** □ geneigt (*for*, *to* zu); ...gesinnt; *well* (*ill*) ~ *towards s.o.* j-m wohl-(übel)gesinnt; **dis·po·si·tion** [~pə'ziʃən] Disposition *f*; Anordnung *f*; *fig.* Neigung *f*, Hang *m*; Sinnesart *f*; Verfügung *f* (*of* über *acc.*); *make* ~*s* Anordnungen treffen.

dis·pos·sess ['dispə'zes] (*of*) vertreiben (aus); berauben (*gen.*); *j.* enteignen; *fig.* freimachen (von); **dis·pos·ses·sion** [~'seʃən] Vertreibung *f etc.*

dis·praise [dis'preiz] **1.** Tadel *m*; **2.** tadeln; geringschätzen.

dis·proof ['dis'pru:f] Widerlegung *f*.

dis·pro·por·tion [disprə'pɔ:ʃən] Mißverhältnis *n*; **dis·pro'por·tion·ate** □ [~ʃnit] unverhältnismäßig, unproportioniert, ungleichmäßig; **dis·pro'por·tion·ate·ness** Mißverhältnis *n*; **'dis·pro'por·tioned** [~ʃənd] = *disproportionate*.

dis·prove [dis'pru:v] widerlegen.

dis·pu·ta·ble [dis'pju:təbl] strittig, fraglich; **dis'pu·tant** Disputant *m*; **dis·pu'ta·tion** Disputation *f*; **dis·pu'ta·tious** □ streitsüchtig; **dis'pute 1.** Streit(igkeit *f*) *m*; Auseinandersetzung *f*; Rechtsstreit *m*; *in* ~ streitig; *beyond* (*all*) ~, *past* ~ unstreitig, zweifellos; **2.** *v/t.* bestreiten, anfechten, in Zweifel ziehen; streiten um, streitig machen; *v/i.* streiten (*about* um).

dis·qual·i·fi·ca·tion [diskwɔlifi'keiʃən] Unfähig-, Untauglichkeit(serklärung) *f*; *Sport*: Ausschluß *m*, Disqualifikation *f*; Nachteil *m*; **dis'qual·i·fy** [~fai] unfähig *od.* untauglich machen *od.* erklären (*for* zu); *Sport*: ausschließen, disqualifizieren.

dis·qui·et [dis'kwaiət] **1.** Unruhe *f*, Sorge *f*; **2.** beunruhigen; **dis'qui·et·ing** beunruhigend; **dis·qui·e·tude** [~'kwaiitju:d] Unruhe *f*.

dis·qui·si·tion [diskwi'ziʃən] Untersuchung *f*; Abhandlung *f* (*on* über *acc.*).

dis·re·gard ['disri'gɑ:d] **1.** Nicht(be)achtung *f*, Mißachtung *f*; **2.** unbeachtet lassen; mißachten, nicht beachten.

dis·rel·ish [dis'reliʃ] **1.** Ekel *m*; Widerwille *m* (*for* gegen); **2.** Widerwillen haben gegen.

dis·re·pair ['disri'pεə] Baufälligkeit *f*; *fall into* ~ in Verfall geraten.

dis·rep·u·ta·ble □ [dis'repjutəbl] schimpflich; verrufen; **dis·re·pute** ['~ri'pju:t] übler Ruf *m*; Schande *f*.

dis·re·spect ['disris'pekt] Nichtachtung *f*; Respektlosigkeit *f*; **dis·re'spect·ful** [~ful] □ respektlos; unhöflich.

dis·robe ['dis'rəub] (sich) entkleiden.

dis·root [dis'ru:t] entwurzeln.

dis·rupt [dis'rʌpt] zerreißen; spalten; **dis'rup·tion** Zerbrechen *n*; Spaltung *f*, Zusammenbruch *m*; **dis'rup·tive** störend.

dis·sat·is·fac·tion ['dissætis'fækʃən] Unzufriedenheit *f*; **dis·sat·is·fac·to·ry** ['~'fæktəri] unbefriedigend; **'dis'sat·is·fied** [~faid] unzufrieden; **'dis'sat·is·fy** [~fai] nicht befriedigen; unzufrieden machen; *j-m* mißfallen.

dis·sect [di'sekt] zerlegen; *anat.* sezieren; *fig.* zergliedern; **dis'sec·tion** Zerlegung *f*; *anat.* Sektion *f*; *fig.* Zergliederung *f*.

dis·sem·ble [di'sembl] *v/t.* verhehlen, verbergen; nicht beachten; *v/i.* sich verstellen, heucheln.

dis·sem·i·nate [di'semineit] ausstreuen; verbreiten; **dis·sem·i'na·tion** Ausstreuung *f etc.*

dis·sen·sion [di'senʃən] Zwietracht *f*, Streit *m*, Uneinigkeit *f*.

dis·sent [di'sent] **1.** abweichende Meinung *f*; Nichtzugehörigkeit *f* zur Landeskirche; **2.** (*from*) anderer Meinung sein (als), nicht übereinstimmen (mit); abweichen (von); nicht der Landeskirche angehören; **dis'sent·er** Andersdenkende *m, f*; Dissenter *m*, nicht der Landeskirche Angehörende *m, f*; **dis'sen·tient** [~ʃiənt] **1.** andersdenkend; **2.** Andersdenkende *m, f*.

dis·ser·ta·tion [disə:'teiʃən] Abhandlung *f*, Dissertation *f* (*on* über *acc.*).

dis·serv·ice ['dis'sə:vis] (*to*) schlechter Dienst *m* (an *dat.*); Nachteil *m* (für).

dis·sev·er [dis'sevə] (zer)teilen, trennen; **dis'sev·er·ance, dis'sev·er·ment** Trennung *f*.

dis·si·dence ['disidəns] Uneinigkeit *f*; **'dis·si·dent 1.** uneinig; **2.** Andersdenkende *m*, *f*; Dissident(in) (*bes. pol.*, *eccl.*).

dis·sim·i·lar □ ['di'similə] unähnlich (*to*, *from dat.*); verschieden (*to* von); **dis·sim·i·lar·i·ty** [~'læriti] Unähnlichkeit *f*; Verschiedenheit *f* (*to* von).

dis·sim·u·late [di'simjuleit] = *dissemble*; **dis·sim·u'lation** Verstellung *f*, Heuchelei *f*.

dis·si·pate ['disipeit] (sich) zerstreuen; verschwenden; ein ausschweifendes Leben führen; **'dis·si·pat·ed** ausschweifend, zügellos; **dis·si'pa·tion** Zerstreuung *f*; Verschwendung *f*; ausschweifendes Leben *n*.

dis·so·ci·ate [di'səuʃieit] trennen; zersetzen; ~ *o.s.* sich distanzieren, abrücken (*from* von); **dis·so·ci·a·tion** [~si'eiʃən] Trennung *f etc.*; *psych.* Bewußtseinsspaltung *f*.

dis·sol·u·bil·i·ty [disɔlju'biliti] Auflösbarkeit *f*; Trennbarkeit *f*; **dis'sol·u·ble** [~jubl] (auf)lösbar; trennbar.

dis·so·lute □ ['disəlu:t] liederlich, ausschweifend; **dis·so'lu·tion** Auflösung *f*; Zerstörung *f*; Tod *m*.

dis·solv·a·ble [di'zɔlvəbl] (auf)lösbar; **dis'solve 1.** *v/t.* auflösen (*a. fig.*); lösen; schmelzen; *v/i.* sich auflösen; *fig.* vergehen; **2.** *Am. Film*: *langsames* Überblenden *n*; **dis'solv·ent 1.** (auf)lösend; zersetzend; **2.** Lösungsmittel *n*.

dis·so·nance ['disənəns] ♪ Mißklang *m*; Uneinigkeit *f*; **'dis·so·nant** ♪ mißtönend; *fig.* abweichend (*from*, *to* von).

dis·suade [di'sweid] *j-m* abraten (*from* von); **dis'sua·sion** [~ʒən] Abraten *n*; **dis'sua·sive** [~siv] □ abratend.

dis·taff ['distɑ:f] Spinnrocken *m*; *fig. das* Reich der Frau; ~ *side* weibliche Linie *f e-r Familie.*

dis·tance ['distəns] **1.** Abstand *m*, Entfernung *f* (*örtlich*, *zeitlich*, *fig.*); Ferne *f*; Strecke *f*; Zurückhaltung *f*; *at a* ~ von weitem; in e-r gewissen Entfernung; weit weg; *in the* ~ in der Ferne; *a great* ~ *away* weit weg; *striking* ~ Wirkungsweite *f*; *keep one's* ~ Abstand halten; *keep s.o. at a* ~ j-m gegenüber reserviert sein; **2.** hinter sich lassen (*a. fig.*); **'dis·tant** □ entfernt; fern; zurückhaltend; Fern...; ~ *control* Fernsteuerung *f*; ~ *relative* entfernter Verwandter *m*.

dis·taste ['dis'teist] Widerwille *m* (*for* vor *od.* gegen); *fig.* Abneigung *f* (*for* gegen); **dis'taste·ful** □ [~ful] widerwärtig; ärgerlich.

dis·tem·per[1] [dis'tempə] **1.** Temperamalerei *f*, -farbe *f*; **2.** mit Temperafarben (an)malen; streichen.

dis·tem·per[2] [~] Krankheit *f* (*bsd. von Tieren*); (Hunde)Staupe *f*; *politische* Unruhe *f*; **dis'tem·pered** zerrüttet; krank.

dis·tend [dis'tend] (sich) ausdehnen; (auf)blähen; (sich) weiten; **dis'ten·sion** Ausdehnung *f*.

dis·tich ['distik] Distichon *n* (*Verspaar*).

dis·til(l) [dis'til] herabtröpfeln (lassen); ⚗ destillieren (*a. fig.*), ausziehen; *Branntwein* brennen; **dis·til·late** ['~lit] Destillat *n*; **dis·til·la·tion** [~'leiʃən] Destillierung *f*; **dis'till·er** Branntweinbrenner *m*, Destillateur *m*; **dis'till·er·y** Branntweinbrennerei *f*.

dis·tinct □ [dis'tiŋkt] verschieden; getrennt; deutlich, klar; **dis'tinc·tion** Unterscheidung *f*; Unterschied *m*; Auszeichnung *f*; Rang *m*, Würde *f*; Absonderung *f*; *das* Individuelle; *draw a* ~ *between* e-n Unterschied machen zwischen; *have the* ~ *of ger.* den Vorzug haben zu *inf.*; **dis'tinc·tive** □ unterscheidend, besonder; apart; kennzeichnend, bezeichnend (*of* für); **dis'tinct·ness** Verschiedenheit *f*; Deutlichkeit *f*.

dis·tin·guish [dis'tiŋgwiʃ] unterscheiden; auszeichnen; **dis'tin·guish·a·ble** unterscheidbar; **dis'tin·guished** berühmt, ausgezeichnet, hervorragend; vornehm.

dis·tort [dis'tɔ:t] verdrehen (*a. fig.*); verzerren, -ziehen; ~*ing mirror* Zerrspiegel *m*; **dis'tor·tion** (Wort-)Verdrehung *f*; Verzerrung *f*.

dis·tract [dis'trækt] ablenken, zerstreuen; beunruhigen; verwirren; verrückt machen; **dis'tract·ed** □ verwirrt; von Sinnen, außer sich

(*with* vor *dat.*); **dis'tract·ing** □ wahnsinnig machend; **dis'trac·tion** Zerstreutheit *f*; Verwirrung *f*; Raserei *f*, Wahnsinn *m*; Zerstreuung *f*.
dis·train [dis'trein] pfänden (*on, upon acc.*); **dis'train·a·ble** pfändbar; **dis·traint** [~'treint] Pfändung *f*.
dis·traught [dis'trɔːt] verstört, verwirrt, bestürzt.
dis·tress [dis'tres] **1.** Qual *f*; Elend *n*, Not *f*, Bedrängnis *f*; Erschöpfung *f*; = *distraint*; ~ *rocket* ⚓ Notsignal *n*; **2.** in Not bringen; quälen; erschöpfen; **dis'tressed** notleidend; bedrängt; bekümmert (*for* um); ~ *area* Notstandsgebiet *n*; **dis'tress·ful** □ [~ful] *lit.* qualvoll; gequält, unglücklich; **dis'tress·ing** □ qualvoll; erschütternd.
dis·trib·ut·a·ble [dis'tribjutəbl] verteilbar; **dis'trib·ute** [~juːt] verteilen (*among* unter *acc.*, *to* an *acc.*); *Ware* vertreiben; einteilen; verbreiten; *typ. Schrift* ablegen; **dis·tri'bu·tion** Verteilung *f*; *Waren-*Vertrieb *m*; *Film-*Verleih *m*; Verbreitung *f*; Einteilung *f*; **dis'trib·u·tive** aus-, zu-, verteilend; *gr.* distributiv; **dis'trib·u·tive·ly** im einzelnen, gesondert; **dis'trib·u·tor** Verteiler *m* (*bsd.* ⊕); ✝ Vertreiber *m*, Vertriebsstelle *f*; *Film-*Verleiher *m*.
dis·trict ['distrikt] Distrikt *m*, Bezirk *m*, Kreis *m*; Landstrich *m*, Gegend *f*; ~ *council* Bezirksregierung *f*; ~ *court Am.* Bezirksgericht *n*; ~ *manager* Bezirksleiter *m*.
dis·trust [dis'trʌst] **1.** Mißtrauen *n*, Argwohn *m* (*of* gegen); **2.** mißtrauen (*dat.*); **dis'trust·ful** □ [~ful] mißtrauisch; ~ (*of o.s.*) schüchtern.
dis·turb [dis'təːb] beunruhigen; stören; verwirren; **dis'turb·ance** Störung *f*; Unruhe *f*; Aufruhr *m*; ~ *of the peace* ⚖ öffentliche Ruhestörung *f*; **dis'turbed** geistig gestört; verhaltensgestört; **dis'turb·er** Störenfried *m*, Unruhestifter *m*.
dis·un·ion ['dis'juːnjən] Trennung *f*; Uneinigkeit *f*; **dis·u·nite** ['~'nait] (sich) trennen; (sich) entzweien; **dis·u·ni·ty** [dis'juːniti] Uneinigkeit *f*.
dis·use 1. ['dis'juːs] Nichtgebrauch *m*; *fall into* ~ außer Gebrauch kommen; **2.** ['dis'juːz] nicht mehr gebrauchen.
di·syl·lab·ic ['disi'læbik] (~*ally*) zweisilbig; **di·syl·la·ble** [di'siləbl] zweisilbiges Wort *n*.
ditch [ditʃ] **1.** Graben *m*; *die in the last* ~ bis zum letzten Blutstropfen kämpfen; **2.** *v/t.* mit Gräben versehen; in den Graben fahren; *v/i.* graben, Gräben machen *od.* ausbessern; *Am. sl.* im Stich lassen; notlanden auf dem Wasser; **'ditch·er** Grabbagger *m*.
dith·er F ['diðə] bibbern (*zittern*); zaudern, schwanken.
dith·y·ramb ['diθiræmb] Dithyrambe *f*; begeistertes Lob *n*.
dit·to ['ditəu] dito, desgleichen; (*suit of*) ~*s* Anzug *m* aus gleichem Stoff.
dit·ty ['diti] Liedchen *n*.
di·ur·nal □ [dai'əːnl] täglich.
di·va·gate *fig.* ['daivəgeit] abschweifen.
di·va·ga·tion [daivə'geiʃən] Abschweifung *f*.
di·van [di'væn] Diwan *m*; ~**-bed** [*oft* 'daivænbed] Bettcouch *f*, Liege *f*.
di·var·i·cate [dai'værikeit] sich gabeln; abzweigen.
dive [daiv] **1.** (unter)tauchen; *vom Sprungbrett* springen; ✈ e-n Sturzflug machen; F sich ducken; stürzen; ~ *into* tief eindringen in (*acc.*); in (*acc.*) hineinlangen; **2.** *Schwimmen*: Springen *n*; (Kopf)Sprung *m* (*a. fig.*); Sturzflug *m*; Kellerlokal *n*; *Am.* F Kaschemme *f*; **'~-bomb** im Sturzflug bombardieren; **'div·er** Taucher *m*; Kunstspringer(in).
di·verge [dai'vəːdʒ] divergieren, auseinanderlaufen; abweichen; **di'ver·gence, di'ver·gen·cy** Divergenz *f*; Abweichung *f*; **di'ver·gent** □ divergierend; (voneinander) abweichend.
di·vers ['daivəːz] mehrere.
di·verse □ [dai'vəːs] *dem Wesen nach* verschieden; ungleich(artig); mannigfaltig; **di·ver·si·fi·ca·tion** [~fi'keiʃən] Veränderung *f*, Abwechslung *f*; **di'ver·si·fy** [~fai] verschieden machen; Abwechslung bringen in (*acc.*); **di·ver·sion** [dai'vəːʃən] Ablenkung *f*; Ablenkungsmanöver *n*; Zerstreuung *f*, Zeitvertreib *m*; Umleitung *f*; **di'ver·sion·a·ry** ⚔ Ablenkungs...;

di'ver·si·ty [~siti] Verschiedenheit *f*; Mannigfaltigkeit *f*.
di·vert [dai'vəːt] ablenken; *j.* zerstreuen; unterhalten; *Verkehr* umleiten.
di·vest [dai'vest] entkleiden; *fig.* berauben; ~ *o.s. of* verzichten auf (*acc.*); **di'vest·ment** Entkleidung *f*; Beraubung *f*.
di·vide [di'vaid] **1.** *v/t.* *oft* ~ *up* teilen; trennen; verteilen (*among* unter *acc.*); einteilen; entzweien; ⅌ dividieren (*by* durch); ~ *the house parl.* das Haus abstimmen lassen; *v/i.* sich teilen *etc.*; ⅌ teilbar sein (*by* durch); aufgehen (*into* in); *parl.* abstimmen; **2.** Wasserscheide *f*; **div·i·dend** ['dividend] ✝ Dividende *f*, Gewinnanteil *m*; ⅌ Dividend *m*; '**div·i·dend-war·rant** ✝ Dividendenschein *m*; **di·vid·er** [di'vaidə] *Am. mot.* Mittelstreifen *m*; ~*s pl.* Stechzirkel *m*; **di'vid·ing** Trennungs...; ~ *ridge* Wasserscheide *f*.
div·i·na·tion [divi'neiʃən] Weissagung *f*; Ahnung *f*; **di·vine** [di'vain] **1.** □ göttlich (*a. fig.*); ~ *service* Gottesdienst *m*; **2.** Geistliche *m*; **3.** weissagen; ahnen; **di'vin·er** Wahrsager(in); Rutengänger(in).
div·ing ['daiviŋ] *Schwimmen*: Kunstspringen *n*; *attr.* Taucher...; '**~-bell** Taucherglocke *f*; '**~-board** Sprungbrett *n*; '**~-dress**, '**~-suit** Taucheranzug *m*.
di·vin·ing-rod [di'vainiŋrɔd] Wünschelrute *f*; **di·vin·i·ty** [di'viniti] Gottheit *f*; Göttlichkeit *f*; Theologie *f*.
di·vis·i·bil·i·ty [divizi'biliti] Teilbarkeit *f*; **di'vis·i·ble** □ [~zəbl] teilbar; **di'vi·sion** [~ʒən] (Ein-, Ver)Teilung *f*; Spaltung *f*, Uneinigkeit *f*; Trennung(slinie) *f*; Teil *m*, Abteilung *f*; Bezirk *m*; ⚔, ⅌ Division *f*; *parl.* Hammelsprung *m*; ~ *bell* Abstimmungsglocke *f*; ~ *of labo(u)r* Arbeitsteilung *f*; **di'vi·sion·al** [~ʒənl] (Ab)Teilungs...; ⚔ Divisions...; **di·vi·sive** [di'vaisiv] auf Trennung abzielend; **di'vi·sor** ⅌ [~zə] Teiler *m*, Divisor *m*.
di·vorce [di'vɔːs] **1.** (Ehe)Scheidung *f*; *fig.* Scheidung *f*, Trennung *f*; **2.** *Ehe* scheiden (*a. fig.*); sich scheiden lassen von; **di·vor·cee** [diːvɔː'siː] Geschiedene *m*, *f*; **di·vorc·er** [di'vɔːsə] der die Ehescheidung veranlassende Teil.
di·vulge [dai'vʌldʒ] ausplaudern; verbreiten, bekanntmachen.
dix·ie ⚔ *sl.* ['diksi] Kochgeschirr *n*; Feldkessel *m*; ♀ *Am.* die Südstaaten *pl.*; ♀*crat Am. pol. opponierender* Südstaatendemokrat *m*.
diz·zi·ness ['dizinis] Schwindel *m*; '**diz·zy 1.** □ schwind(e)lig (*Person*); Schwindel erregend (*Sache*); verwirrt; ~ *spell* Schwindelanfall *m*; 2. schwindelig machen.
do [duː] (*irr.*) (*s. a. done*) **1.** *v/t.* tun, machen; an-, verfertigen; ausführen, vollbringen; *Strecke* zurücklegen; (fertig)machen; verrichten; (zu)bereiten, kochen; *e-n Gefallen etc.* erweisen; *Rolle, Stück* spielen; F übers Ohr hauen, prellen; ~ *London* F London besichtigen; ~ *s.o.* F j. versorgen, beköstigen; *what is to be done?* was ist zu tun *od.* zu machen?; ~ *the polite, etc.* den Höflichen *etc.* spielen; *have done reading* fertig sein mit Lesen; ~ *a room* ein Zimmer aufräumen; ~ (*over*) *again* noch einmal machen; ~ *down* F unterkriegen; ~ *in* F um die Ecke bringen; ~ *into* übersetzen, -tragen in; ~ *out* ausfegen; ~ *over mit Farbe etc.* überstreichen, -ziehen; ~ *up* zs.-legen; instandsetzen, reparieren, renovieren; einpacken; F kaputt machen (*gänzlich ermüden*); **2.** *v/i.* tun, handeln; sich benehmen; sich befinden; dem Zweck entsprechen, genügen; tauglich sein, passen; *that will* ~ das genügt; *that won't* ~ das geht nicht; das reicht nicht; *how* ~ *you* ~? guten Tag!, Wie geht's?; ~ *well* s-e Sache gut machen; gute Geschäfte machen; gut fahren; ~ *badly* schlechte Geschäfte machen; *have done!* hör auf!; ~ *away with* abschaffen; ~ *for j-m* den Haushalt führen; ~ *with* auskommen mit; *I could* ~ *with* ... ich könnte ... brauchen *od.* vertragen; *have done with* fertig sein mit, erledigt haben; ~ *without* fertig werden ohne, entbehren können, verzichten auf (*acc.*); **3.** *v/aux. Frage*: ~ *you know him* kennen Sie ihn?; *Verneinung mit not*: *I* ~ *not know him* ich kenne ihn nicht; *emphatisch*,

verstärkend: *I ~ feel better* ich fühle mich wirklich besser; *~ come and see me* besuche mich doch einmal; *~ be quick* beeile dich doch; *für ein vorausgegangenes Verb*: *~ you like London — I do* gefällt Ihnen London? — Ja; *you write better than I ~* Sie schreiben besser als ich; *I take a bath every day. — So ~ I* ich nehme täglich ein Bad. — Ich auch; **4.** F Schwindel *m*; große Sache *f*, Fest *n*, Party *f*.
doc F [dɔk] = *doctor*.
doc·ile ['dəusail] gelehrig; fügsam; **do·cil·i·ty** [~'siliti] Gelehrigkeit *f*; Fügsamkeit *f*.
dock[1] [dɔk] stutzen; *fig*. kürzen (*of* um).
dock[2] ⚘ [~] Ampfer *m*.
dock[3] [~] **1.** ⚓ Dock *n*; Hafenbecken *n*; *bsd. Am.* Kai *m*, Pier *m*, *f*; ⚖ Anklagebank *f*; *dry ~*, *graving ~* Trockendock *n*; *floating ~* Schwimmdock *n*; *wet ~* Schleusenhafen *m*; **2.** ⚓ docken; *Raumfahrt*: ankoppeln; '**~-dues** *pl*. Dock-, Hafengebühren *f/pl*.; '**dock·er** Dock-, Hafenarbeiter *m*.
dock·et ['dɔkit] **1.** Aktenschwanz *m*; Inhaltsvermerk *m*; Bestellschein *m*; Etikett *n*; Adreßzettel *m*; Gerichtskalender *m*; **2.** mit Aktenschwanz *etc*. versehen.
dock·yard ['dɔkjɑːd] Werft *f*.
doc·tor ['dɔktə] **1.** Doktor *m*; Arzt *m*; *~'s certificate* ärztliche Bescheinigung *f*, ärztliches Attest *n*; **2.** F verarzten; zurechtflicken; (*a. ~ up* zurecht)doktern (*fälschen*); **doc·tor·ate** ['~rit] Doktorwürde *f*.
doc·tri·naire [dɔktri'nɛə] **1.** Doktrinär *m*, Prinzipienreiter *m*; **2.** doktrinär, schulmeisterlich; **doc·tri·nal** □ [~'trainl] die Lehre betreffend, lehrmäßig; **doc·trine** ['~trin] Lehre *f*, Doktrin *f*; Dogma *n*.
doc·u·ment 1. ['dɔkjumənt] Dokument *n*, Urkunde *f*, Schriftstück *n*; *travel ~s pl*. Reiseunterlagen *f/pl*.; **2.** ['~ment] beurkunden; mit Urkunden versehen *od*. belegen, dokumentieren; **doc·u'men·ta·ry 1.** □ urkundlich; *~ film* = **2.** Kultur-, Dokumentarfilm *m*; **doc·u·men'ta·tion** Benutzung *f* von Urkunden.
dod·der ['dɔdə] **1.** ⚘ Flachsseide *f*; **2.** schlottern, schwanken.
dodge [dɔdʒ] **1.** Sprung *m* zur Seite; Schlich *m*, Kniff *m*, Winkelzug *m*; **2.** *v/t*. ausweichen (*dat*.); zum besten haben; *v/i*. ausweichen, zur Seite springen; sich drücken vor; Winkelzüge machen; schlüpfen; **dod·gem** F ['dɔdʒəm] Autoskooter *m auf dem Jahrmarkt*; '**dodg·er** Schieber(in); *Am*. Hand-, Reklamezettel *m*; *Am*. Maisbrot *n*, -kuchen *m*; **dodg·y** F ['dɔdʒi] vertrackt; riskant; nicht einwandfrei.
do·do *orn*. ['dəudəu] Dodo *m* (*ausgestorben*).
doe [dəu] Hindin *f*; Reh *n*; Häsin *f*.
do·er ['duːə] Täter(in), Handelnde *m*, *f*.
does [dʌz] *er*, *sie*, *es* tut (*s. do*).
doe·skin ['dəuskin] Rehleder *n*; Doeskin *n* (*Gewebe*).
doesn't F ['dʌznt] = *does not* (*s. do*).
dog [dɔg] **1.** Hund *m*; Rüde *m* (*männlicher Hund od. Fuchs*); ⊕ Feuerbock *m*; Haken *m*, Klammer *f*; Klaue *f*; ⚒ Förderwagen *m*; F Kerl *m*; *Am*. F Angabe *f* (*Prahlerei*); *go to the ~s* vor die Hunde gehen, auf den Hund kommen; **2.** sich an *j-s* Fersen heften, *j-m* nachspüren; '**~-bis·cuit** Hundekuchen *m*; '**~-cart** leichter Jagdwagen *m*; '**~-cheap** spottbillig; '**~-col·lar** Hundehalsband *n*; F *hoher, steifer Kragen e-s Geistlichen*; '**~-days** *pl*. Hundstage *m/pl*.
doge [dəudʒ] Doge *m*.
dog...: '**~-eared** = *dog's-eared*; '**~-fight** F Luftkampf *m*; '**~·fish** *zo*. Hundshai *m*.
dog·ged □ ['dɔgid] verbissen.
dog·ger·el ['dɔgərəl] *a. ~ rhymes pl*. Knüttelverse *m/pl*.
dog·gie ['dɔgi] = *doggy*; '**~-bag** *Restaurant*: *Beutel zum Mitnehmen von Essensresten*.
dog·gish ['dɔgiʃ] hündisch; knurrig; **dog·go** *sl*. ['dɔgəu]: *lie ~* sich nicht rühren; '**dog·gy 1.** Hündchen *n*; **2.** hundefreundlich; Hunde...; *Am*. F *äußerlich* aufgemacht; '**dog-'Lat·in** Küchenlatein *n*; '**~-like** hündisch.
do·gie *Am*. ['dəugi] *mutterloses* Kälbchen *n*.
dog·ma ['dɔgmə] Dogma *n*, Lehr-, Glaubenssatz *m*; Glaubenslehre *f*; **dog·mat·ic, dog·mat·i·cal** □ [~'mætik(əl)] dogmatisch, lehrhaft; bestimmt; selbstherrlich; **dog'mat·ics** *sg*. Dogmatik *f*; **dog·ma-**

tism ['~mətizəm] Bestimmtheit *f*, Selbstherrlichkeit *f*; Dogmatismus *m*; '**dog·ma·tist** Dogmatiker *m*; dreister Behaupter *m*; **dog·ma·tize** ['~mətaiz] seine Meinung als maßgeblich hinstellen.

dog's-bod·y *sl.* ['dɔgzbɔdi] Sklave *m*, Arbeitstier *n*, Kuli *m*; '**dog's-ear** Eselsohr *n im Buch*; '**dog's-eared** mit Eselsohren.

dog...: '**~-'tired** hundemüde; '**~-tooth** ⚠ Zahnornament *n*; '**~-trot** leichter Trab *m*; '**~-watch** ⚓ Spaltwache *f*, Plattfuß *m*; '**~-wood** ⚘ Hartriegel *m*.

doi·ly ['dɔili] Tellerdeckchen *n*.

do·ing ['du:iŋ] **1.** *p.pr. von do* **1**; *nothing ~* nichts zu machen; ✝ kein Geschäft; **2.** Tun *n*, Tat *f*; *~s pl.* Dinge *n/pl.*, Begebenheiten *f/pl.*; Treiben *n*; Betragen *n*.

doit [dɔit] Deut *m*, Heller *m*.

do-it-your·self ['du:itjɔ:'self] 1. Do-it-yourself *n*, Selbstanfertigen *n*; 2. Bastler..., Hobby...

dol·drums ['dɔldrəmz] *pl.* Niedergeschlagenheit *f*; ⚓ Kalmen(zone *f*) *f/pl.*

dole [dəul] **1.** (milde) Spende *f*; F Arbeitslosenunterstützung *f*; *be od. go on the ~* stempeln gehen; **2.** *mst ~ out* verteilen.

dole·ful □ ['dəulful] trübselig, traurig; '**dole·ful·ness** Traurigkeit *f*, Trübseligkeit *f*; Kummer *m*.

doll [dɔl] **1.** Puppe *f* (*a. fig.*); **2.** *~ up* F sich aufdonnern.

dol·lar ['dɔlə] Dollar *m*.

dol·lop F ['dɔləp] Klumpen *m*.

doll·y ['dɔli] Püppchen *n*; Transportkarren *m*; Kamerawagen *m*.

dol·o·mite *min.* ['dɔləmait] Dolomit *m*.

dol·o(u)r *mst poet., co.* ['dəulə] Leid *n*, Schmerz *m*; **dol·o·rous** ['dɔlərəs] schmerzhaft; trübselig, traurig.

dol·phin *ichth.* ['dɔlfin] Delphin *m*.

dolt [dəult] Tölpel *m*; '**dolt·ish** □ tölpelhaft.

do·main [dəu'mein] Domäne *f*; *fig.* Gebiet *n*, Bereich *m*.

dome [dəum] Dom *m*; Kuppel *f*; ⊕ Deckel *m*; **domed** gewölbt.

Domes·day Book ['du:mzdei'buk] Reichsgrundbuch *n Englands*.

do·mes·tic [dəu'mestik] **1.** (*~ally*) häuslich; Haus..., Privat...; inländisch; einheimisch; Innen...; zahm; *~ animal* Haustier *n*; *~ appliance* Haushaltsgerät *n*; *~ bliss* häusliches Glück *n*; *~ coal* Hausbrandkohle *f*; *~ flight* Inlandsflug *m*; *~ science* Hauswirtschaftskunde *f*; **2.** *a. ~ servant* Hausangestellte *f*; *~s pl.* Haushaltsartikel *m/pl.*; **do'mes·ti·cate** [~keit] häuslich *od.* heimisch machen; zähmen; **do·mes·ti'ca·tion** Eingewöhnung *f*; Zähmung *f*; **do·mes·tic·i·ty** [~'tisiti] Häuslichkeit *f*.

dom·i·cile ['dɔmisail] **1.** *bsd.* ⚖ Wohnsitz *m*; Zahlungsort *m*; **2.** ✝ *Wechsel* domizilieren; '**dom·i·ciled** ansässig, wohnhaft; **dom·i·cil·i·ar·y** [~'siljəri] Haus...; *~ visit* Haussuchung *f*; ⚕ Hausbesuch *m*.

dom·i·nance ['dɔminəns] Herrschaft *f*; '**dom·i·nant** **1.** (vor-)herrschend; emporragend; **2.** ♪ Dominante *f*; **dom·i·nate** ['~neit] (be)herrschen; **dom·i'na·tion** Herrschaft *f*; '**dom·i·na·tor** Herrscher *m*; **dom·i·neer** [dɔmi'niə] (despotisch) herrschen; *~ over* tyrannisieren; **dom·i'neer·ing** □ tyrannisch, herrisch; überheblich.

do·min·i·cal [də'minikəl] Sonntags...; *~ prayer* Vaterunser *n*.

Do·min·i·can [də'minikən] Dominikaner *m*.

do·min·ion [də'minjən] Herrschaft *f*; *oft ~s pl.* Gebiet *n* (*a. fig.*); ♀ Dominion *n* (*im Brit. Commonwealth*).

dom·i·no ['dɔminəu] Domino *m*; Maskenkostüm *n*; **dom·i·noes** ['~z] *pl.* Domino(spiel) *n*.

don[1] *univ.* [dɔn] Universitätslehrer *m*.

don[2] [~] *Kleidungsstück* anziehen.

do·nate *Am.* [dəu'neit] schenken; spenden; **do'na·tion, don·a·tive** ['~nətiv] Schenkung *f*, Stiftung *f*; Gabe *f*.

done [dʌn] **1.** *p.p. von do*; *be ~ oft* geschehen; **2.** *adj.* abgemacht; *a. ~ up* erschöpft; fertig; *well ~* gar gekocht; durchgebraten; *he is ~ for* es ist aus mit ihm; **3.** *int.* abgemacht!

do·nee ⚖ [dəu'ni:] Beschenkte *m, f*.

don·jon ['dɔndʒən] Bergfried *m*.

don·key ['dɔŋki] Esel *m*; *attr.* Hilfs...; '**~-en·gine** Hilfsmotor *m*; Rangierlokomotive; '**~-work** Idiotenarbeit *f*.

don·na ['dɔnə] Dame *f*, Frau *f*; Donna *f*.
do·nor ['dəunə] Schenker *m*, (Blut-) Spender *m*; Geber *m*.
do-noth·ing F ['du:nʌθiŋ] **1.** Faulenzer(in); **2.** faul.
don't [dəunt] **1.** = *do not*; *~!* nicht (doch)!; **2.** Verbot *n*.
doo·dle ['du:dl] **1.** gekritzelte Figur *f*; **2.** Männchen malen, kritzeln.
doom [du:m] **1.** *mst b. s.* Schicksal *n*, Verhängnis *n*; Jüngstes Gericht *n*; **2.** verurteilen, verdammen; **dooms·day** ['du:mzdei] Jüngster Tag *m*.
door [dɔ:] Tür *f*, Tor *n*; *next ~ (to)* nebenan; *fig.* nicht weit (von); *two ~s off* zwei Häuser weiter; *(with)in ~s* zu Hause; *out of ~s* im Freien, draußen; *show s.o. the ~* j-m die Tür weisen; *turn out of ~s* hinauswerfen; *lay s.th. to od. at s.o.'s ~* j-m et. zur Last legen; **'~-bell** Türklingel *f*; **'~-case, '~-frame** Türrahmen *m*; **'~-han·dle** Türgriff *m*; **'~-keep·er, '~·man** Pförtner *m*, Portier *m*; **'~-mat** Fußabstreifer *m*; **'~-nail** Türnagel *m*; *dead as a ~* mausetot; **'~-post** Türpfosten *m*; **'~-plate** Türschild *n*; **'~-step** Haustürstufe *f*; Türschwelle *f*; **'~·way** Türöffnung *f*, -eingang *m*; Torweg *m*; **'~·yard** *Am.* Vorhof *m*, -garten *m*.
dope [dəup] **1.** Schmiere *f*; *bsd.* ✈ Lack *m*, Firnis *m*; Nervenreizmittel *n*; Rauschgift *n*; *Am. sl.* Geheimtip *m*, -information(en *pl.*) *f*; Tölpel *m*, Depp *m*; Schwindel *m*; **2.** lackieren, firnissen; *Sport*: dopen, künstlich anreizen, aufpulvern; *Am. sl.* herauskriegen, -tüfteln; **'dope·y** *Am. sl.* doof, belämmert.
Dor·ic ['dɔrik] dorisch; *~ order* dorische Säulenordnung *f*.
dorm F [dɔ:m] = *dormitory*.
dor·mant ['dɔ:mənt] *mst fig.* schlafend, ruhend; latent; unbenutzt, tot; *~ partner* stiller Teilhaber *m*.
dor·mer(-win·dow) ['dɔ:mə('windəu)] Dachfenster *n*.
dor·mi·to·ry ['dɔ:mitri] Schlafsaal *m*; *bsd. Am.* Studentenwohnheim *n*; *~* **town** Schlafstadt *f*.
dor·mouse ['dɔ:maus], *pl.* **dor·mice** ['dɔ:mais] Haselmaus *f*.
dor·sal □ ['dɔ:səl] dorsal, am Rükken; Rücken...
do·ry ⚓ ['dɔ:ri] Dory *n*, flaches Boot *n*.
dose [dəus] **1.** Dosis *f*, Portion *f*; **2.** *a. ~ with* eine Dosis geben (*dat.*); *Wein etc.* verfälschen.
doss *sl.* [dɔs] **1.** Klappe *f*, Flohkiste *f in e-r Penne*; **2.** *~ (down)* pennen, sich hinhauen; **'doss·er** *sl.* Penner *m*.
doss-house *sl.* ['dɔshaus] Penne *f* (*Herberge*).
dos·si·er ['dɔsiei] Dossier *m*, *n*, Akten(bündel *n*) *f/pl.*
dost † [dʌst, dəst] *du* tust (*s. do*).
dot [dɔt] **1.** Punkt *m*, Tüpfelchen *n*; Fleck *m*; Knirps *m*; *on the ~* mit dem Glockenschlag; **2.** punktieren, tüpfeln; *a. ~ about fig.* verstreuen; hier und da hinsetzen *od.* -stellen; über *e-e Fläche* verstreut sein; *~ted with* übersät mit.
dot·age ['dəutidʒ] Altersschwachsinn *m*; Affenliebe *f*; **do·tard** ['~təd] kindischer Greis *m*; alter Narr *m*; **dote** [dəut] kindisch sein, faseln; vernarrt sein (*on, upon* in *acc.*).
doth † [dʌθ, dəθ] *er, sie, es* tut (*s. do*).
dot·ing ['dəutiŋ] □ kindisch; vernarrt (*on* in *acc.*).
dot·ty *sl.* ['dɔti] verdreht, verrückt.
dou·ble □ ['dʌbl] **1.** doppelt; gepaart; zu zweien; gekrümmt; zweideutig; falsch; gefüllt (*Blume*); **2.** Doppelte *n*; Doppelgänger(in); Ebenbild *n*; Haken *m e-s Flußlaufs, Hasen*; *Tennis*: Doppel(spiel) *n*; ⚔ Laufschritt *m*; Winkelzug *m*; **3.** *v/t.* verdoppeln; *a. ~ up* zs.-legen, -falten; *die Faust* ballen; um *et.* herumgehen, *et.* umfahren, -segeln; *~d up* zs.-gekrümmt; *be ~d up with* sich biegen *od.* krümmen vor *Schmerzen etc.* *v/i.* sich verdoppeln; *a. ~ back* e-n Haken schlagen (*Hase*); ⚔ Laufschritt machen; *Karten*: Kontra geben; *~ up* sich krümmen *od.* biegen; sich falten *od.* rollen lassen; **'~-bar·relled** doppelläufig, Doppel... (*Gewehr*); *fig.* zweideutig; *~ name* Doppelname *m*; **'~-'bass** ♪ Kontrabaß *m*; **'~-bed·ded** mit Doppelbett *od.* zwei Betten; **'~-'bend** S-Kurve *f*; **'~-'breast·ed** zweireihig (*Jackett*); **'~-'check** noch einmal (nach-, über)prüfen; **'~-**

-'**cross** *sl.* *Partner* betrügen; '~-'**deal·er** Achselträger *m*, Betrüger *m*; '~-'**deal·ing** Doppelzüngigkeit *f*; '~-'**deck·er** Doppeldecker *m* (*Autobus*, *Schiff*), *Am.* F doppeltes Sandwich *n*; '~-'**dyed** *fig.* eingefleischt; '~-'**edged** zweischneidig (*a. fig.*); '~-'**en·try** ✝ doppelte Buchführung *f*; '~-**faced** unaufrichtig; '~-'**fea·ture** *Am.* Doppelprogramm *n im Kino*; '~-'**glaz·ing** (Fenster *n* mit) Doppelverglasung *f*; '~-'**head·er** *Am. Baseball*: Doppelspiel *n*; '~-'**joint·ed** mit Gummigelenken; '~-'**line** 🚂 Doppelgleis *n*; '**dou·ble·ness** Doppelte *n*; *fig.* Zweideutigkeit *f*, Falschheit *f*; '**dou·ble-'park** *Am.* in zweiter Reihe parken; '**dou·ble-'quick** ⚔ (im) Geschwindschritt *m*.

dou·blet ['dʌblit] Dublette *f*; Doppel-, Nebenform *f*, -stück *n*; *hist.* Wams *n*, Jacke *f*; ~**s** *pl.* Pasch *m beim Würfeln.*

dou·ble...: ~ **take** F Spätzündung *f*; '~-**talk** doppelzüngiges Gerede *n*; '~-**time** *sl.* übers Ohr hauen; '~-'**track** zweigleisig.

doub·ling ['dʌbliŋ] Verdoppelung *f*; Falte *f*; Umsegelung *f*; '**doub·ly** doppelt.

doubt [daut] **1.** *v/i.* zweifeln; Bedenken tragen; *v/t.* bezweifeln; mißtrauen (*dat.*); **2.** Zweifel *m*; Ungewißheit *f*; Bedenken *n*; *no* ~ ohne Zweifel, zweifellos; '**doubt·er** Zweifler(in); **doubt·ful** □ ['~ful] zweifelhaft (*unschlüssig*; *ungewiß*; *verdächtig*); *be* ~ im Zweifel sein; '**doubt·ful·ness** Zweifelhaftigkeit *f*; '**doubt·less** ohne Zweifel, zweifellos.

douche [du:ʃ] **1.** Dusche *f*; ⚕ Irrigator *m*; **2.** duschen; spülen.

dough [dəu] Teig *m*; *sl.* Moneten *pl.*; '~·**boy** *Am.* F Landser *m*; '~·**nut** Krapfen *m*, (Berliner) Pfannkuchen *m*.

dough·ty *co.* ['dauti] mannhaft, beherzt.

dough·y ['dəui] teigig (*a. fig.*); klitschig, nicht durchgebacken.

dour *schott.* ['duə] starr; stur; streng.

douse [daus] *s. dowse.*

dove [dʌv] Taube *f*; *fig.* Täubchen *n*; '~-**col·o(u)red** taubengrau; ~-**cot(e)** ['~kɔt] Taubenschlag *m*; '~·**tail** ⊕ **1.** Schwalbenschwanz *m*; **2.** *v/t.* verschwalben; *v/i. fig.* genau zs.-passen.

dow·a·ger ['dauədʒə] Witwe *f* (*von Stande*).

dow·dy F ['daudi] **1.** unelegant (gekleidet); schlampig; **2.** Schlampe *f*.

dow·el ⊕ ['dauəl] Dübel *m*, Holzpflock *m*.

dow·er ['dauə] **1.** Wittum *n*; *mst fig.* Mitgift *f*; **2.** ausstatten.

down[1] [daun] Daune *f*; Flaum *m*.

down[2] [~] = *dune*; ~*s pl.* kahles Hügelland *n*, Höhenrücken *m*.

down[3] [~] **1.** *adv.* nieder; her-, hinunter, -ab; abwärts; unten; ~ *and out fig.* erledigt, kaputt; *be* ~ gefallen sein (*Preis*); *be* ~ *upon* F über *j-n* herfallen; streng sein mit; ~ *in the country* auf dem Lande; ~ *under* F in Australien; **2.** *prp.* her-, hinab, her-, hinunter; ~ *the river* flußabwärts; ~ (*the*) *wind* mit dem Wind; **3.** *int.* nieder!; **4.** *adj.* ~ *train* Zug *m* von London nach außerhalb; **5.** F *v/t.* niederwerfen; herunterholen; ~ *tools* die Arbeit niederlegen; **6.** *s. up 4*; '~-**and-'out** Pennbruder *m*, Penner *m*; '~·**cast** niedergeschlagen; '~-'**draft**, '~-'**draught** Fallstrom *m*, Abwind *m*; ~-'**East·er** *Am.* Neuengländer *m bsd. aus Maine*; '~·**fall** Fall *m*, Sturz *m*; Verfall *m*; '~·**grade** niedriger einstufen; '~-'**heart·ed** niedergeschlagen; gedrückt; '~-'**hill** 1. bergab; 2. abschüssig; ~ **payment** Anzahlung *f*; '~·**pour** Regenguß *m*; '~·**right** □ 1. *adv.* geradezu, durchaus, völlig; 2. *adj.* offen, ehrlich; plump (*Benehmen*); richtig, glatt (*Lüge*, *Unsinn etc.*); '~·**right·ness** Geradheit *f*, Offenheit *f*.

Down's syn·drome ⚕ ['dauns 'sindrəum] Down-Syndrom *n*, Mongolismus *m*.

down...: '~'**stairs** 1. unten *im Hause*; die Treppe hinunter, nach unten; 2. unten befindlich, untere(r, -s); '~-'**stream** stromabwärts (gelegen *od.* gerichtet); '~·**stroke** Grundstrich *m beim Schreiben*; ⊕ Kolbenniedergang *m*; ~-**to-'earth** nüchtern, realistisch; '~-'**town** *bsd. Am.* Hauptgeschäftsviertel *n*; '~·**trod·den** unterdrückt; ~·**ward** ['~wəd] 1. sich senkend, abschüssig (*a. fig.*); 2. *a.* ~*s* abwärts; '~·**wash** ✈ Abwind *m*.

down·y ['dauni] flaumig; *sl.* gerissen (*schlau*).

dow·ry ['dauəri] Mitgift *f* (*a. fig.*).

dowse ['dauz] **1.** gießen über (*acc.*);

begießen; auslöschen; **2.** mit der Wünschelrute suchen; **'dows·er** Rutengänger(in); **'dows·ing-rod** Wünschelrute *f.*

doze [dəuz] **1.** schlummern, (*~ away* ver)dösen; **2.** Schläfchen *n.*

doz·en ['dʌzn] Dutzend *n*; *talk nineteen to the ~* wie ein Wasserfall reden.

doz·y ['dəuzi] schläfrig; F schwer von Begriff.

drab [dræb] **1.** gelblichgrau; *fig.* eintönig; **2.** Gelblichgrau *n*; graugelber Stoff *m*; *fig.* Eintönigkeit *f*; Schlampe *f*; Hure *f*, Dirne *f.*

drachm [dræm] Drachme *f* (*Gewicht*); = **drach·ma** ['drækmə] Drachme *f* (*Münze*).

draff [dræf] Bodensatz *m*; Abhub *m.*

draft [drɑ:ft] **1.** Entwurf *m*, Konzept *n*, Skizze *f*; ✝ Tratte *f*; Abhebung *f*; ⚔ (Sonder)Kommando *n*; Einberufung *f*; = *draught*; *~ agreement* Vertragsentwurf *m*; **2.** entwerfen; aufsetzen, abfassen; ⚔ abkommandieren; *Am.* einziehen, einberufen; **draft'ee** ⚔ *Am.* Dienstpflichtige *m*; **'drafts·man** (technischer) Zeichner *m*; Verfasser *m*, Entwerfer *m.*

drag [dræg] **1.** Schleppnetz *n*; Schleife *f für Lasten*; Egge *f*; Hemmschuh *m* (*a. fig.*); Blockwagen *m für Holz etc.*; *von e-m Mann getragene* Frauenkleidung *f*; **2.** *v/t.* schleppen, schleifen, ziehen, zerren; ⚒ eggen; *Rad* hemmen; = *dredge* 2; *~ along* mitschleppen; *~ out Leben* hinschleppen; *~ one's feet* sich Zeit lassen, es nicht eilig haben; *~ up a child* ein Kind lieblos u. ohne Erziehung aufwachsen lassen; *v/i.* (sich) schleppen, schleifen; (mit einem Schleppnetz) fischen (*for* nach); ✝ flau gehen; *~* **art·ist** *männlicher Entertainer, der in Frauenkleidern auftritt.*

drag·gle ['drægl] durch den Schmutz ziehen; **'~-tail** Schlampe *f.*

drag·o·man ['drægəumən] Dolmetscher *m*, Dragoman *m.*

drag·on ['drægən] Drache *m*; **'~-fly** Wasserjungfer *f*, Libelle *f.*

dra·goon [drə'gu:n] **1.** Dragoner *m*; *fig.* Rohling *m*; **2.** zwingen (*into ger.* zu *inf.*).

drain [drein] **1.** Abfluß *m*, Abzug(sgraben *m*, -rohr *n*) *m*; Rinne *f*; F Schluck *m*, Tropfen *m*; Inanspruchnahme *f* (*on gen.*); *~s pl.* Kanalisation *f*; **2.** *v/t.* entwässern, drainieren, trockenlegen; *Glas* leeren; *a. ~ off* abziehen, -leiten; verzehren; berauben (*of gen.*); *v/i.* ablaufen; **'drain·age** Abfluß *m*; Kanalisation *f*; Entwässerung(sanlage) *f*; **'drain·ing 1.** Abzugs...; **2.** Trockenlegung *f*; *~s pl.* Abzugsröhren *f/pl.*; **'drain·ing-board** Ablaufbrett *n*; **'drain-pipe** Abflußrohr *n*; *~ trousers pl.* F Röhrenhose(n *pl.*) *f.*

drake [dreik] Enterich *m.*

dram [dræm] Drachme *f* (*Gewicht*); Schluck *m*; Schnaps *m.*

dra·ma ['drɑ:mə] Drama *n*, Schauspiel *n*; **dra·mat·ic** [drə'mætik] (*~ally*) dramatisch; Theater...; **dra'mat·ics** *mst sg.* Theater *n*; **dram·a·tist** ['dræmətist] Dramatiker *m*; **dram·a·tis per·so·nae** ['drɑ:mətis pə:'səunai] *pl. die* Personen *f/pl.* der Handlung; **dram·a·tize** ['dræmətaiz] dramatisieren; **dram·a·tur·gy** ['~tə:dʒi] Dramaturgie *f.*

drank [dræŋk] *pret. von drink* 2.

drape [dreip] drapieren, behängen; in Falten ordnen; **'drap·er** Tuchhändler *m*; **'dra·per·y** Tuchhandel *m*; Tuchwaren *f/pl.*; Draperie *f*; Faltenwurf *m.*

dras·tic ['dræstik] (*~ally*) drastisch.

draught [drɑ:ft] Zug *m* (*Ziehen*; *Fischzug*; *Zugluft*; *Schluck*); ⚓ Tiefgang *m*; *~s pl.* Damespiel *n*; *s. draft*; *~ beer* Faßbier *n*; *at a ~* auf einen Zug; **'~-board** Damebrett *n*; **'~-horse** Zugpferd *n*; **'draughts·man** Damestein *m*; = *draftsman*; **'draught·y** zugig.

draw [drɔ:] **1.** (*irr.*) ziehen; an-, auf-, ein-, zuziehen; sich zs.-ziehen; in die Länge ziehen, dehnen; nach sich ziehen; herausziehen, -locken; entnehmen; *Geld* abheben; *Ware etc.* beziehen; anlocken, anziehen; abzapfen; ausfischen; *Geflügel* ausnehmen; *Zinsen* bringen; zeichnen; entwerfen; *Urkunde* abfassen; *Kampf etc.* unentschieden lassen; unentschieden spielen; ⚓ Tiefgang von ... haben; *e-n Seufzer* ausstoßen; *Luft* schöpfen; *~ away* wegnehmen, entwenden; *~ down* senken; *~ forth* hervorziehen; *~ near* heranrücken, sich nähern; *~ on* herbeiführen, veranlassen; ~ *out* in die Länge ziehen; *j.* ausholen; ~ *up* aufsetzen, ab-, verfassen; entwerfen; *Truppen etc.* aufstellen; vorfahren; halten; ~ *(up)on* ✝ (e-n Wechsel) ziehen auf (*acc.*); *fig.* in Anspruch nehmen, angreifen; **2.** Zug *m* (*Ziehen*); *Lotterie*: Ziehung *f*; Los *n*; *Sport*: unentschiedenes Spiel *n*; F Zugkraft *f*, -stück *n*, -artikel *m*; F Anzapfung *f*; '**~back** Beeinträchtigung *f* (*from gen.*); Nachteil *m*, Schattenseite *f*; Hindernis *n*; ✝ Rückzoll *m*; *Am.* Rückzahlung *f*; '**~bridge** Zugbrücke *f*; **draw'ee** ✝ Bezogene *m*; Trassat *m*; '**draw·er** Ziehende *m*; Zeichner *m*; ✝ Aussteller *m*, Trassant *m*; [*mst* drɔː] Schublade *f*; (*pair of*) ~*s pl.* Unterhose *f*; Schlüpfer *m*; *mst chest of* ~*s* Kommode *f*.

draw·ing ['drɔːiŋ] Ziehen *n*; Zeichnen *n*; Ziehung *f* (*Lotterie*); Zeichnung *f*; ✝ Trassierung *f*; *out of* ~ verzeichnet; ~ *instruments pl.* Reißzeug *n*; '**~-ac'count** Girokonto *n*; '**~-board** Zeichen-, Reißbrett *n*; '**~-pen** Reißfeder *f*; '**~-pin** Reißzwecke *f*; '**~-room** Gesellschaftszimmer *n*, Salon *m*; *bei Hofe*: großer Empfang *m*.

drawl [drɔːl] **1.** *a.* ~ *out* gedehnt *od.* schleppend sprechen; **2.** gedehnte Sprechweise *f*.

drawn [drɔːn] **1.** *p.p. von draw 1*; **2.** *adj.* unentschieden; verzerrt.

draw-well ['drɔːwel] Ziehbrunnen *m*.

dray [drei] *a.* ~*-cart* Roll-, *bsd.* Bierwagen *m*; '**~man** Roll-, Bierkutscher *m*.

dread [dred] **1.** Furcht *f*; Schrecken *m*; **2.** (sich) fürchten (vor), Angst haben (vor); **dread·ful** □ ['~ful] **1.** schrecklich; furchtbar; schauerlich; **2.** *penny* ~ billiger Schauerroman *m*; **dread·nought** ['~nɔːt] dicker Flaus(ch) *m*; ⚓ Schlachtschiff *n*.

dream [driːm] **1.** Traum *m*; **2.** (*irr.*) träumen (*of* von); ~ *away* verträumen; '**dream·er** Träumer(in); '**dream-land** Traumwelt *f*; '**dream-like** traumhaft; '**dream--read·er** Traumdeuter(in); **dreamt** [dremt] *pret. u. p.p von dream 2*; '**dream·y** □ träumerisch; verträumt; traumhaft.

drear *poet.* [driə] = *dreary*.

drear·i·ness ['driərinis] Traurigkeit *f*; Öde *f*; '**drear·y** □ traurig; öde; düster; langweilig.

dredge[1] [dredʒ] **1.** Schleppnetz *n*; Bagger(maschine *f*) *m*; **2.** *a.* ~ *up*, ~ *out* (mit dem Schleppnetz) fischen; (aus)baggern.

dredge[2] [~] (be)streuen.

dredg·er[1] ['dredʒə] Schleppnetzfischer *m*; Bagger(maschine *f*) *m*.

dredg·er[2] [~] (Mehl)Streubüchse *f*.

dregs [dregz] *pl.* Bodensatz *m*, Hefe *f*; Abschaum *m*; *drink od. drain to the* ~ bis zur Neige leeren.

drench [drentʃ] **1.** Arzneitrank *m*; (Regen)Guß *m*; **2.** *e-m Tier* Arznei einflößen; durchnässen, *fig.* baden; '**drench·er** F (Regen)Guß *m*.

dress [dres] **1.** (Damen)Kleid *n*; Kleidung *f*; *fig.* Gewand *n*; *full* ~ Gala *f*; **2.** an-, ein-, zurichten; ⚔ (sich) richten; zurechtmachen; (sich) anziehen *od.* ankleiden; putzen; dekorieren; *Wunde* verbinden; *Weinstock* beschneiden; frisieren; ⚘ düngen; ~ *s.o. down* j. ausschimpfen; j. durchprügeln; ~ *it thea.* Kostümprobe abhalten; ~ *up* sich herausputzen; sich verkleiden; '**~-'cir·cle** *thea.* erster Rang *m*; '**~-'coat** Frack *m*; '**dress·er** Anrichter(in); Ankleider(in); Assistenzarzt *m*; Dekorateur *m*; Anrichte *f*; *Am.* Frisierkommode *f*; Küchenschrank *m*.

dress·ing ['dresiŋ] An-, Zurichten *n*; Ankleiden *n*; Behandeln *n e-r Wunde*; Verband *m*; Appretur *f*; *Küche*: Zutat *f*; ⚘ Dünger *m*; Tracht *f* Prügel; ~*s pl.* Verbandzeug *n*; ~ *down* Standpauke *f*; '**~--case** Reisenecessaire *n*; Verbandskasten *m*; '**~-glass** Toilettenspiegel *m*; '**~-gown** Morgenrock *m*; '**~--jack·et** Frisiermantel *m*; **~ room** Umkleidezimmer *n*; Garderobe *f*; '**~-ta·ble** Frisierkommode *f*.

dress...: '**~mak·er** (Damen)Schneiderin *f*; '**~-pa·rade** Modenschau *f*; ⚔ Parade *f* in Galauniform; **~ re·hears·al** Generalprobe *f*; '**~-shield** Schweißblatt *n*; '**~-'shirt** Frackhemd *n*; '**~-'suit** Frackanzug *m*; '**dress·y** F putzsüchtig; geschniegelt; modisch.

drew [druː] *pret. von draw 1*.

drib·ble ['dribl] tröpfeln, träufeln (lassen); geifern, sabbern; *Fußball*:

dribbeln.

drib·let ['driblit] Kleinigkeit *f*.

dribs and drabs F ['dribzən'dræbz] *pl.*: *in* ~ kleckerweise.

dried [draid] Dörr...; Trocken...; ~ *fruit* Dörrobst *n*.

dri·er ['draiə] Trockner *m*, Trockenapparat *m*; Trockenmittel *n*.

drift [drift] **1.** (Dahin)Treiben *n*; ⚓ Drift *f*, Abtrift *f*; *fig.* Lauf *m*; *fig.* Hang *m*, Neigung *f*; Zweck *m*; Inhalt *m*, Sinn *m*; Gestöber *n* (*Schnee*); Guß *m* (*Regen*); (Schnee-, Sand)Wehe *f*; *geol.* Geschiebe *n*; ⚒ Strecke *f*; **2.** *v/t.* (zs.-)treiben, (zs.-)wehen; *v/i.* getrieben werden, (dahin)treiben; sich anhäufen; '**drift·er** Mensch *m* ohne Ziele; '**drift-ice** Treibeis *n*; '**drift-net** Treibnetz *n*; '**drift-wood** Treibholz *n*.

drill[1] [dril] **1.** Drillbohrer *m*; Furche *f*; ✓ Drill-, Sämaschine *f*; ⚔ Exerzieren *n*, Übung *f*, Drill *m* (*a. fig.*); ~ *ground* Exerzierplatz *m*; **2.** drillen, bohren; ⚔ (ein)exerzieren (*a. fig.*); einüben; ✓ in Rillen säen.

drill[2], **drill·ing** [dril, '~iŋ] Drillich *m*.

drink [driŋk] **1.** Trank *m*, Trunk *m*; (geistiges) Getränk *n*; *in* ~ betrunken; **2.** (*irr.*) trinken; ~ *s.o.'s health* auf j-s Wohl *od.* Gesundheit trinken; ~ *away* vertrinken; ~ *in* einsaugen; ~ *to* trinken auf (*acc.*); ~ *off od. out od. up* austrinken; aufsaugen; '**drink·a·ble** trinkbar; '**drink·er** Trinker *m*; Säufer *m*.

drink·ing ['driŋkiŋ] Trinken *n*, Zechen *n*; '~**-bout** Trinkgelage *n*; '~**-foun·tain** Trinkbrunnen *m*; '~**-song** Trinklied *n*; '~**-wa·ter** Trinkwasser *n*.

drip [drip] **1.** Tröpfeln *n*; Traufe *f*; F ⚕ Tropf *m* (*Infusionsapparat, Infusion*); F *Person*: Flasche *f*, Waschlappen *m*; *be on the* ~ F ⚕ am Tropf hängen; **2.** tröpfeln (lassen); triefen; ~*ping wet* triefnaß; '~-'**dry shirt** bügelfreies Hemd *n*; '**drip·ping** Bratenfett *n*; ~*s pl.* herabtröpfelnde Flüssigkeit *f*; ~ *pan* Fettpfanne *f*.

drive [draiv] **1.** (Spazier)Fahrt *f*; Auffahrt *f*, Fahrweg *m*; *Tennis etc.*: Treibschlag *m*, Flachball *m*; *mot.* Antrieb *m*; *fig.* (Auf)Trieb *m*, Schwung *m*; Drang *m* (*for* nach); Unternehmen *n*, Bewegung *f*, Feldzug *m*, Rummel *m*, Treiben *n*; Treibjagd *f*; *Am.* Sammelaktion *f*; **2.** (*irr.*) *v/t.* (an-, ein)treiben; *Geschäft* betreiben; fahren, lenken; zwingen (*to, into* zu); *oft* ~ *away* vertreiben; *v/i.* treiben (*a.* ⚓ *u. hunt.*); *im Wagen* fahren; eilen, jagen; ~ *at s.th.* hinzielen auf et.; et. wollen; ~ *on* weiterfahren; ~ *up to* vorfahren bei.

drive-in *Am.* ['draivin] **1.** *mst attr.* Auto...; ~ *cinema* Autokino *n*; **2.** Autokino *n*; Autorestaurant *n*.

driv·el ['drivl] **1.** geifern; faseln; **2.** Geifer *m*; Faselei *f*.

driv·en ['drivn] *p.p. von drive* 2.

driv·er ['draivə] Treiber *m*; Fahrer *m*, Chauffeur *m*; 🚂 Führer *m*; † Kutscher *m*; ⊕ Mitnehmer *m*; Treibrad *n*; '**drive·way** *Am.* Fahrweg *m*; Einfahrt *f*.

driv·ing ['draiviŋ] Treiben *n etc.*; *attr.* Treib...; Antriebs...; Fahr...; '~**-belt** Treibriemen *m*; ~ **force** treibende Kraft *f*; '~**-gear** Triebwerk *n*; ~ **in·struc·tor** Fahrlehrer *m*; ~ **li·cence** Führerschein *m*; ~ **mir·ror** Rückspiegel *m*; ~ **school** Fahrschule *f*; '~**-wheel** Treibrad *n*.

driz·zle ['drizl] **1.** Sprühregen *m*; **2.** sprühen, nieseln; '**drizz·ly** regnerisch.

droll [drəul] (*adv. drolly*) drollig; '**droll·er·y** Drolligkeit *f*.

drom·e·dar·y *zo.* ['drʌmədəri] Dromedar *n*.

drone[1] [drəun] **1.** *zo.* Drohne *f*; *fig.* Faulenzer *m*; **2.** faulenzen.

drone[2] [~] **1.** Summen *n*, Dröhnen *n*; ♪ Baßpfeife *f*; **2.** summen; dröhnen.

drool [dru:l] **1.** sabbern; **2.** *Am.* F dummes Geschwätz *n*.

droop [dru:p] *v/t.* sinken lassen; *v/i.* schlaff (herab)hängen; den Kopf hängen lassen; (ver)welken; schwinden; '**droop·ing** □ matt; mutlos.

drop [drɔp] **1.** Tropfen *m*; Drops *m*, Fruchtbonbon *m*; Sinken *n*, Fall *m*; Falltür *f*; *thea.* Vorhang *m*; *get od. have the* ~ *on Am.* überlegen sein (*dat.*), zuvorkommen (*dat.*); ~ *light* Hängelicht *n*; *in* ~*s*, ~ *by* ~ tropfenweise (*a. fig.*); **2.** *v/t.* tropfen lassen; herunterlassen; *Anker* (aus-) werfen; *Bomben* abwerfen; *Brief* einwerfen; *Tränen etc.* vergießen;

Gegenstand, Wort, Thema etc. fallen lassen; *Fahrgast* absetzen; *Gesicht, Stimme* senken; *Knicks* machen; ~ *s.o. a few lines* j-m ein paar Zeilen schreiben; ~ *it!* F laß das!; *v/i.* tröpfeln, lecken (*Faß*); (herab)fallen; aufhören; um-, hinsinken; sterben; ~ *behind* zurückbleiben; ~ *in* unerwartet kommen *od.* vorsprechen (*at, on, upon* bei); ~ *off* allmählich fortgehen; einschlafen; abfallen; ~ *out* aus-, wegfallen; nicht mehr mitmachen; sich wegstehlen; ~ **ac·tion pen·cil** Druckbleistift *m*; **drop·let** ['drɔplit] Tröpfchen *n*; '**drop-out** Aussteiger *m*; Studienabbrecher *m*; '**drop·ping** Tröpfeln *n*; ~*s pl.* Mist *m*; '**drop-scene** *thea.* Vorhang *m*; Schluß(szene *f*) *m*.

drop·si·cal □ ['drɔpsikəl] wassersüchtig; '**drop·sy** Wassersucht *f*.

dross [drɔs] Schlacke *f*; Unrat *m*.

drought [draut], **drouth** [drauθ] Trockenheit *f*, Dürre *f*; '**drought·y**, '**drouth·y** trocken, dürr.

drove [drəuv] **1.** Trift *f Rinder*; Herde *f* (*a. fig.*); **2.** *pret. von drive* 2; '**dro·ver** Viehtreiber *m*, -händler *m*.

drown [draun] *v/t.* ertränken; überschwemmen; *fig.* übertäuben; übertönen; ersticken; *be* ~*ed* ertrinken; *v/i.* ertrinken.

drowse [drauz] schlummern, schläfrig sein *od.* machen; '**drow·si·ness** Schläfrigkeit *f*; '**drow·sy** schläfrig; einschläfernd.

drub [drʌb] (ver)prügeln; trommeln auf (*dat.*); '**drub·bing** Tracht *f* Prügel.

drudge [drʌdʒ] **1.** *fig.* Sklave *m*, Packesel *m*, Kuli *m*; **2.** sich (ab-)placken; '**drudg·er·y** Plackerei *f*.

drug [drʌg] **1.** Droge *f*, Arznei (-mittel *n*) *f*, Medikament *n*; Rauschgift *n*; ~ *on the market* unverkäufliche Ware *f*; ~ *abuse* Drogenmißbrauch *m*; **2.** mit (schädlichen) Zutaten versetzen; viel Arznei eingeben (*dat.*); Rauschgifte *od.* Schlafmittel geben (*dat.*) *od.* nehmen; '**drug·gist** Drogist *m*; Apotheker *m*; **drug push·er** Dealer *m*; '**drug·store** *Am.* Drugstore *m*; **drug traf·fic(k·ing)** Drogenhandel *m*.

dru·id *hist.* ['dru:id] Druide *m*.

drum [drʌm] **1.** Trommel *f* (*a.* ⊕); *anat.* Trommelhöhle *f*; **2.** trommeln; '~**·fire** ⚔ Trommelfeuer *n*; '~**·head** Trommelfell *n*; ~ *court-martial* ⚔ Standgericht *n*; '~-'**ma·jor** ⚔ Tambourmajor *m*; '**drum·mer** Trommler *m*; *bsd. Am.* F Handlungsreisende *m*, Vertreter *m*; '**drum·stick** Trommelstock *m*; Unterschenkel *m von Geflügel*.

drunk [drʌŋk] **1.** *p.p von drink 2*; **2.** *pred.* (be)trunken; *get* ~ sich betrinken; **drunk·ard** ['~əd] Trinker *m*, Trunkenbold *m*; '**drunk·en** *attr.* (be)trunken; trunksüchtig; ~ *driving* Trunkenheit *f* am Steuer; '**drunk·en·ness** Trunkenheit *f*; Trunksucht *f*.

drupe ⚘ [dru:p] Steinfrucht *f*.

dry [drai] **1.** □ *allg.* trocken; dürr; uninteressant, nüchtern; kühl; derb (*Witz*); herb (*Wein*); nicht milchend (*Kuh*); F durstig; F antialkoholisch; ~ *cell* Trockenelement *n*; ~ *goods pl.* F *Am.* Kurzwaren *f/pl.*; **2.** *Am.* F Alkoholgegner *m*; **3.** (ab-)trocknen; dörren; ~ *up* austrocknen; verdunsten; ~ *up!* F sei still!

dry·ad ['draiəd] Waldnymphe *f*.

dry...: ~ **bat·ter·y** Trockenbatterie *f*; ~ **bulb ther·mom·e·ter** *das trockene Thermometer e-s Psychrometers*; ~ **cell** ⚡ Trockenelement *n*; '~-'**clean** chemisch reinigen; '~-'**clean·ing** chemische Reinigung *f*.

dry·er ['draiə] = *drier*.

dry...: ~ **goods** *pl. Am.* Textilien *pl.*; ~ **mount·ing** *phot.* Trockenklebung *f*; '~-'**nurse** **1.** Kinderfrau *f*; **2.** bemuttern; betreuen; '~-'**rot** Trockenfäule *f*; *fig.* Verfall *m*; '~'**shod** trockenen Fußes; '~-'**wall·ing** Trockenmauern *n*.

du·al □ ['dju:əl] zweifach, doppelt; Doppel...; ~-*income family* Doppelverdiener *m/pl.*; '**du·al·ism** Dualismus *m*.

dub [dʌb] zum Ritter schlagen; titulieren; ernennen zu; *Leder* (ein-)fetten; *Film etc.* synchronisieren; '**dub·bing** Lederfett *n*.

du·bi·e·ty [dju:'baiəti] Fragwürdigkeit *f*; zweifelhafte Sache *f*.

du·bi·ous □ ['dju:bjəs] zweifelhaft; *be* ~ im Zweifel sein (*of, about, over* über *acc.*); '**du·bi·ous·ness** Ungewißheit *f*.

du·cal ['dju:kəl] herzoglich.

duc·at ['dʌkət] Dukaten *m*.

duch·ess ['dʌtʃis] Herzogin *f*.

duch·y ['dʌtʃi] Herzogtum *n*.
duck[1] [dʌk] Ente *f*; *Am. sl.* Kerl *m*.
duck[2] [~] **1.** Verbeugung *f*; Neigen *n* des Kopfes; Ducken *n*; **2.** (unter-) tauchen; (sich) ducken; *Am. j-m* ausweichen, F sich verziehen.
duck[3] F [~] Liebling *m*, Püppchen *n*.
duck[4] [~] (Segel)Leinen *n*.
duck...: '**~-bill** *zo.* Schnabeltier *n*; '**~-boards** *pl.* Lattenrost *m*.
duck·ling ['dʌkliŋ] Entchen *n*.
duck·weed ⚘ ['dʌkwi:d] Wasserlinse *f*.
duck·y F ['dʌki] **1.** = duck[3]; **2.** lieb, nett.
duct [dʌkt] Gang *m*; Röhre *f*.
duc·tile □ ['dʌktail] dehnbar; fügsam; geschmeidig; **duc·til·i·ty** [~'tiliti] Dehnbarkeit *f*.
dud *sl.* [dʌd] **1.** Blindgänger *m*; *fig.* Versager *m*; ~*s pl.* Lumpen *m/pl.* (*Kleider*); **2.** verfehlt; falsch.
dude *Am.* [dju:d] Geck *m*; ~ ranch Vergnügungsfarm *f für Feriengäste aus der Großstadt.*
dudg·eon ['dʌdʒən] Groll *m*; in high ~ kochend vor Wut.
due [dju:] **1.** schuldig; gebührend; angemessen; gehörig; fällig; in ~ time zur rechten *od.* gegebenen Zeit; the train is ~ at ... der Zug ist fällig *od.* kommt an um ...; in ~ course zu seiner Zeit; be ~ to *j-m* gebühren; zu verdanken sein; herrühren *od.* kommen von; be ~ to *inf.* sollen; müssen; *Am.* im Begriff sein zu; fall ~ ✝ fällig werden; ~ date Fälligkeitstermin *m*; **2.** *adv.* ⚓ gerade; ~ east genau nach Osten; **3.** Gebührende *n*, Schuldigkeit *f*; Recht *n*, Anspruch *m*; Lohn *m*; *mst* ~*s pl.* Abgabe(n *pl.*) *f*, Gebühr(en *pl.*) *f*; (Mitglieds)Beitrag *m*.
du·el ['dju:əl] **1.** Duell *n*, Zweikampf *m*; **2.** sich duellieren; '**du·el·list** Duellant *m*.
du·et(·to) [dju:'et(əu)] Duett *n*.
duf·fel ['dʌfəl] Düffel *m*, grober Wollstoff *m*; ~-bag Matchbeutel *m*, -sack *m*; ~ coat Dufflecoat *m*.
duff·er F ['dʌfə] Dummkopf *m*.
duf·fle ['dʌfəl] = duffel.
dug [dʌg] **1.** *pret. u. p.p. von dig*; **2.** Zitze *f*; '**~-out** ⚔ Unterstand *m*; Einbaum *m*; *sl.* wiedereingestellter Offizier *m*; *Am. Baseball*: überdachte Spielerbank *f*.
duke [dju:k] Herzog *m*; '**duke·dom** Herzogtum *n*; Herzogswürde *f*.
dul·cet ['dʌlsit] wohlklingend, lieblich; '**dul·ci·mer** ♪ ['~simə] Hackbrett *n*, Zimbel *f*.
dull [dʌl] **1.** □ dumm; träg, schwerfällig; stumpfsinnig; matt (*Auge, Farbe etc.*); schwach (*Gehör*); langweilig, fad(e); teilnahmslos; stumpf; dumpf (*Schmerz, Kopf*); trüb (*z.B. Wetter*); flau (*Handel*); ⚓ windstill; **2.** stumpf machen; *fig.* abstumpfen; (sich) trüben; **dull·ard** ['~əd] Dummkopf *m*; '**dull·ness** Stumpfsinn *m*; Dummheit *f*; Schwerfälligkeit *f*; Mattheit *f*; Langweiligkeit *f*; Teilnahmslosigkeit *f*; Trübheit *f*; Flauheit *f*.
du·ly ['dju:li] *s.* due; gehörig; ordnungsgemäß; richtig; pünktlich.
dumb □ [dʌm] stumm; sprachlos *vor Staunen etc.*; *Am.* F doof, blöd; deaf and ~ taubstumm; *s.* show 2; strike ~ die Sprache verschlagen; '**~-bell** Hantel *f*; *Am. sl.* Dussel *m*; **~'found** F zum Schweigen bringen; ~ed sprachlos; '**dumb·ness** Stummheit *f*; '**dumb-'wait·er** Drehtisch *m*; *Am.* Speiseaufzug *m*.
dum·my ['dʌmi] Attrappe *f*; *fig.* Kulisse *f*; Schein *m*, Schwindel *m*; *fig.* Strohmann *m*; Statist *m*; (Kleider)Puppe *f*; Schnuller *m*; *attr.* Schein...; Schwindel...; ~ whist Whist *n* mit Strohmann.
dump [dʌmp] **1.** auskippen; *Schutt etc.* abladen; *Last* abwerfen (*a. fig.*); *Waren* zu Schleuderpreisen ausführen; hinplumpsen; **2.** Klumpen *m*; Plumps *m*; Abfall-, Schutthaufen *m*; Schuttabladestelle *f*; ⚔ Munitionslager *n*; = ~ing; '**dump·ing** ✝ Schleuderausfuhr *f*, Dumping *n*; '**dump·ing-ground** (Schutt)Abladeplatz *m*; '**dump·ling** Kloß *m*; F Dickerchen *n*, Mops *m*; '**dumps** F *pl.*: (down) in the ~ niedergeschlagen, verdrießlich; '**dump·y** untersetzt.
dun[1] [dʌn] **1.** fahl(braun); falb; **2.** Falbe *m* (*Pferd*).
dun[2] [~] **1.** ungestümer Mahner *m od.* Gläubiger *m*; **2.** mahnen, drängen; ~ning letter Mahnbrief *m*.
dunce [dʌns], **dun·der·head** ['dʌndəhed] Dummkopf *m*.
dune [dju:n] Düne *f*; ~ **bug·gy** *mot.* Strandbuggy *m*.
dung [dʌŋ] **1.** Mist *m*, Dung *m*;

2. düngen.
dun·ga·rees [dʌŋgə'ri:z] *pl.* Overall *m aus grobem Kattun.*
dun·geon ['dʌndʒən] Kerker *m,* Verlies *n.*
dung·hill ['dʌŋhil] Misthaufen *m.*
dunk [dʌŋk] (ein)tunken.
du·o ['dju:əu] Duett *n.*
du·o·dec·i·mal [dju:əu'desiməl] zwölfteilig; Duodezimal...; **du·o·'dec·i·mo** [~məu] *typ.* Duodez *n*; *fig.* Knirps *m.*
du·o·de·nal *anat.* [dju:əu'di:nl] Zwölffingerdarm...; **du·o'de·num** [~nəm] Zwölffingerdarm *m.*
dupe [dju:p] **1.** Gimpel *m,* Angeführte *m, f*; **2.** anführen, täuschen; **'dup·er·y** Prellerei *f.*
du·plex ['dju:pleks] **1.** Doppel...; *tel.* Gegensprech..., Duplex...; **2.** *Am.* Zweifamilienhaus *n*; ~ *apartment Am.* Maison(n)ette *f* (*zweistöckige Wohnung*).
du·pli·cate 1. ['dju:plikit] doppelt; **2.** ['~kit] Duplikat *n,* Doppel *n*; *in* ~ doppelt; **3.** ['~keit] verdoppeln; doppelt ausfertigen; **du·pli'ca·tion** Verdoppelung *f*;' **du·pli·ca·tor** Vervielfältigungsapparat *m*; **du·plic·i·ty** [dju:'plisiti] Zweiheit *f*; Doppelzüngigkeit *f.*
du·ra·bil·i·ty [djuərə'biliti] Dauerhaftigkeit *f*; **'du·ra·ble** □ dauerhaft; **'dur·ance** † Haft *f*; **du·ra·tion** [~'reiʃən] Dauer *f.*
du·ress ⚖ [djuə'res] Zwang *m,* Nötigung *f*; Freiheitsberaubung *f.*
du·ring ['djuəriŋ] *prp.* während.
durst [də:st] *pret. von dare.*
dusk [dʌsk] Halbdunkel *n,* (Abend-)Dämmerung *f*; **'dusk·y** □ dämmerig, düster (*a. fig.*); dunkel; schwärzlich.
dust [dʌst] **1.** Staub *m*; **2.** abstauben; bestreuen; **'~-bin** Mülleimer *m*; ~ *liner* Müllbeutel *m*; **'~-bowl** *Am.* Sandstaub- *u.* Dürregebiet *n im Westen der USA*; **'~-cart** Müllwagen *m*; **'~-cloak, '~-coat** Staubmantel *m*; **'dust·er** Staublappen *m,* -wedel *m*; *Am.* Staubmantel *m*; **'dust·i·ness** Staubigkeit *f*; **'dust·ing** *sl.* Tracht *f* Prügel; **'dust-'jack·et** *Am.* Schutzumschlag *m e-s Buches*; **'dust·man** Müllabfuhrmann *m*; Sandmann *m*; **'dust·pan** Müllschaufel *f*; **dust trap** Staubfänger *m*; **'dust-'up** Lärm *m,* Tumult *m*; **'dust·y** □ staubig.
Dutch [dʌtʃ] **1.** holländisch; *hist. u. Am. sl.* deutsch; *go* ~ (*with s.o.*) (mit j-m) die Kosten teilen; **2.** Holländisch *n*; *the* ~ *pl.* die Holländer *pl.*; *double* ~ Kauderwelsch *n*; ~ **auc·tion** (Auktion *f* mit) Abschlag *m*; ~ **courage** angetrunkener Mut *m*; **'~·man** Holländer *m*; *hist. u. Am. sl.* Deutsche *m*; **'~·wom·an** Holländerin *f.*
du·te·ous ['dju:tjəs] = *dutiful*; **du·ti·a·ble** ['~tjəbl] zoll-, steuerpflichtig; **du·ti·ful** □ ['~tiful] pflichtbewußt; gehorsam; ehrerbietig.
du·ty ['dju:ti] Pflicht *f,* Schuldigkeit *f* (*to* gegenüber *dat.*); Ehrerbietung *f*; Abgabe *f,* Zoll *m*; Dienst *m*; *on* ~ im Dienst; *off* ~ dienstfrei; ~ *call* Anstandsbesuch *m*; *in* ~ *bound* pflichtschuldig; *do* ~ *for* vertreten; *fig.* dienen als; **'~-'free** zollfrei.
du·vet ['dju:vei] Federbett *n.*
dwarf [dwɔ:f] **1.** Zwerg *m*; **2.** in der Entwicklung hindern; klein erscheinen lassen; verkleinern; *~ed* verkümmert; **'dwarf·ish** □ zwerghaft; **'dwarf·ish·ness** Winzigkeit *f.*
dwell [dwel] (*irr.*) wohnen; verweilen (*on, upon* bei); ~ (*up*)*on* bestehen auf; **'dwell·er** Bewohner *m*; **'dwell·ing** Wohnung *f*; **'dwelling-house** Wohnhaus *n*; **'dwelling-place** Wohnsitz *m.*
dwelt [dwelt] *pret. u. p.p. von dwell.*
dwin·dle ['dwindl] (dahin)schwinden, abnehmen; zs.-schrumpfen; **'dwin·dling** Schwund *m.*
dye [dai] **1.** Farbe *f*; *of deepest* ~ *fig.* schlimmster Art; **2.** färben; **'dy·er** Färber *m*; **'dye-stuff** Färbemittel *n*; Farbstoff *m*; **'dye-works** *pl., oft sg.* Färberei *f.*
dy·ing □ ['daiiŋ] (*s. die*[1]) **1.** sterbend; Sterbe...; *lie* ~ im Sterben liegen; **2.** Sterben *n etc.*
dyke [daik] = *dike*[1] *u.* [2].
dy·nam·ic [dai'næmik] **1.** *a.* **dy'nam·i·cal** □ dynamisch, kraftgeladen; **2.** Triebkraft *f*; **dy'nam·ics** *mst sg.* Dynamik *f*; **dy·na·mite** ['dainəmait] **1.** Dynamit *n*; **2.** mit Dynamit sprengen; **'dy·na·mit·er** Sprengstoffattentäter *m*; **dy·na·mo** ['~məu] Dynamomaschine *f.*
dy·nas·tic [di'næstik] (*~ally*) dynastisch; **dy·nas·ty** ['dinəsti] Dynastie *f,* Herrscherhaus *n.*
dyne *phys.* [dain] Dyn *n* (*Krafteinheit*).

dys·en·ter·y ⚕ [ˈdisntri] Ruhr *f*.
dys·lex·i·a [disˈleksiə] Dyslexie *f*, Buchstabenblindheit *f*; **dysˈlex·ic** **1.** buchstabenblind; **2.** an Dyslexie Leidende *m*, *f*.

dys·pep·sia ⚕ [disˈpepsiə] Verdauungsstörung *f*; **dysˈpep·tic** [~tik] **1.** (*~ally*) an Verdauungsstörung leidend, magenkrank; **2.** Magenkranke *m*, *f*.

E

each [i:tʃ] jede(r, -s); ~ *other* einander, sich; *they cost a shilling* ~ sie kosten je einen Schilling.
ea·ger □ [ˈi:gə] (be)gierig (*about, after, for* auf *acc.*, nach), gespannt; *fig.* eifrig; heftig (*Begierde*); **ˈea·ger·ness** Begierde *f*; Eifer *m*.
ea·gle [ˈi:gl] Adler *m*; Zehndollarstück *n*; **ˈ~-ˈeyed** scharfsichtig; **ea·glet** [ˈ~lit] junger Adler *m*.
ea·gre [ˈeigə] Springflut *f*.
ear[1] [iə] Ähre *f*.
ear[2] [~] Ohr *n*, Gehör *n*; Öhr *n*, Henkel *m*; *be all ~s* ganz Ohr sein; *fall on deaf ~s fig.* auf taube Ohren stoßen; *keep an ~ to the ground bsd. Am.* aufpassen, was die Leute sagen *od.* denken; *up to the ~s fig.* bis über die Ohren *in Arbeit*; *play by ~* nach dem Gehör spielen; *set by the ~s* gegeneinander aufhetzen; **~-ache** [ˈiəreik] Ohrenschmerz(en *pl.*) *m*; **~-deaf·en·ing** [ˈ~defniŋ] ohrenbetäubend; **ˈ~-drum** Trommelfell *n*.
earl [ə:l] *britischer* Graf *m*; ℒ *Marshal* Oberzeremonienmeister *m*; **ˈearl·dom** Grafenstand *m*.
ear·li·ness [ˈə:linis] Frühzeitigkeit *f*.
ear·lobe [ˈiələub] Ohrläppchen *n*.
ear·ly [ˈə:li] früh(zeitig); Früh...; Anfangs...; erst; bald(ig); ~ *bird fig.* Frühaufsteher *m*; *the ~ bird catches the worm* Morgenstund hat Gold im Mund; ~ *closing* früher Ladenschluß *m*; *it's ~ closing (day) today* heute haben die Geschäfte nachmittags zu; ~ *life* Jugendzeit *f*; ~ *warning system* ⚔ Frühwarnsystem *n*; *as ~ as* schon in (*dat.*); *earlier on* früher.
ear-mark [ˈiəma:k] **1.** Ohrenzeichen *n bei Tieren*; *fig.* Kennzeichen *n*; **2.** an den Ohren zeichnen; *fig.* (kenn)zeichnen; *für e-n Zweck* bereitlegen, bestimmen.
ear·muffs [ˈiəmʌfs] *pl.* Ohrenschützer *m/pl.*
earn [ə:n] verdienen; erwerben; einbringen (*for dat.*); *~ed income* Arbeitseinkommen *n*.
ear·nest[1] [ˈə:nist] *a.* *~-money* Handgeld *n*, Anzahlung *f*; Pfand *n*; *fig.* Vorgeschmack *m*, Probe *f*; Beweis *m*.
ear·nest[2] [~] **1.** □ ernst; eifrig; ernstlich; aufrichtig; ernstgemeint; **2.** Ernst *m*; *be in ~* es ernst meinen; **ˈear·nest·ness** Ernst(lichkeit *f*) *m*; Eifer *m*.
earn·ings [ˈə:niŋz] *pl.* Verdienst *m*, Lohn *m*, Einkommen *n*; *gross ~ pl.* Bruttoeinkommen *n*.
ear...: **ˈ~-phones** *pl. Radio*: Kopfhörer *m*; **ˈ~·piece** *teleph.* Hörmuschel *f*; **ˈ~-pierc·ing** ohrenzerreißend; **ˈ~-plug** Wattepfropf *m*; **ˈ~-ring** Ohrring *m*; **ˈ~·shot** Hörweite *f*; **ˈ~-split·ting** ohrenzerreißend.
earth [ə:θ] **1.** Erde *f*; Land *n*; Boden *m*; *Fuchs- etc.* Bau *m*; *a.* *~-connection Radio*: Erdung *f*, Erdschluß *m*; **2.** *v/t.* ⚡ erden; ~ *up* mit Erde bedecken, anhäufeln; **ˈearth·en** irden; **ˈearth·en·ware** **1.** Töpferware *f*, Steingut *n*; **2.** irden; **ˈearth·ing** ⚡ Erdung *f*; **ˈearth·li·ness** *das* Irdische; Weltlichkeit *f*; **ˈearth·ly** irdisch; F denkbar; *no ~ ...* gar kein ...; **ˈearth·quake** Erdbeben *n*; **ˈearth-worm** Regenwurm *m*; *fig.* Erdenwurm *m*; **ˈearth·y** erdig; irdisch; *fig.* sinnlich, roh.
ear...: **ˈ~-trum·pet** Hörrohr *n*; **ˈ~-wax** Ohrenschmalz *n*; **ˈ~·wig** Ohrwurm *m*.
ease [i:z] **1.** Gemütlichkeit *f*, Bequemlichkeit *f*, Behagen *n*; Ruhe *f*; Gemächlichkeit *f*; Erleichterung *f*; Ungezwungenheit *f*; Leichtigkeit *f*;

at ~ bequem, behaglich, zwanglos, ungezwungen; *be od. feel at one's* ~ sich wohlfühlen; *ill at* ~ unbehaglich; *stand at* ~! ⚔ rührt euch!; *take one's* ~ es sich bequem machen; *with* ~ mit Leichtigkeit; *live at* ~ in guten Verhältnissen leben; **2.** erleichtern; *Schmerz* lindern; beruhigen; bequem(er) machen; lockern, *Tau etc.* nachlassen; befreien (*of* von); sich entspannen (*Lage*); ~ *nature* ein Bedürfnis verrichten, sich erleichtern; **ease·ful** □ ['~ful] behaglich; beruhigend; müßig.

ea·sel ['i:zl] Staffelei *f*.

eas·i·ly ['i:zili] leicht, mit Leichtigkeit; sicher, bei weitem; **'eas·i·ness** Bequemlichkeit *f*, Gemächlichkeit *f*; Leichtigkeit *f*; Ungezwungenheit *f*; ~ *of belief* Leichtgläubigkeit *f*.

east [i:st] **1.** Ost(en *m*); Orient *m*; *the* ♀ *Am.* die Oststaaten *pl. der USA*; **2.** Ost...; östlich; ostwärts; **'~·bound** in Richtung Osten fahrend.

East·er ['i:stə] Ostern *n od. pl.*; *attr.* Oster...; ~ egg Osterei *n*.

east·er·ly ['i:stəli] östlich; Ost...; nach Osten; **east·ern** ['~tən] = *easterly*; orientalisch; **'east·ern·er** Ostländer(in); Orientale *m*, Orientalin *f*; ♀ *Am.* Oststaatler(in); **east·ern·most** ['~məust] östlichst.

East In·di·a·man ⚓ *hist.* [i:st'indjəmən] Ostindienfahrer *m* (*Schiff*).

east·ing ⚓ ['i:stiŋ] zurückgelegter östlicher Kurs *m*; Ostrichtung *f*.

east·ward(s) ['i:stwəd(z)] ostwärts.

eas·y ['i:zi] **1.** □ leicht; bequem, behaglich; frei von Schmerzen; unbesorgt, ruhig; willig; ungezwungen; bequem (*Kleid*); ✝ flau, lustlos; *in* ~ *circumstances* wohlhabend; *on* ~ *street* in guten Verhältnissen; *on* ~ *terms* ✝ zu günstigen Bedingungen; *make o.s.* ~ es sich bequem machen; *take it* ~ sich Zeit lassen; es sich leicht machen; *take it* ~! nur keine Aufregung!; sachte!; **2.** kurze Pause *f*; **'~-'chair** Lehnstuhl *m*, Klubsessel *m*; **'~-go·ing** *fig.* bequem, lässig; leichtlebig.

eat [i:t] **1.** (*irr.*) *v/t.* essen; fressen; zerfressen; verzehren; ~ *up* aufessen; auffressen; verzehren (*a. fig.*); *v/i.* essen; schmecken; ~ *out* im Restaurant essen; **2.** ~*s pl. Am. sl.* Essen *n*, Eßwaren *f/pl.*; **'eat·a·ble** eßbar; **'eat·a·bles** *pl.* Eßwaren *f/pl.*; **'eat·en** *p.p. von eat 1*; **'eat·er** Esser(in); *be a great (poor)* ~ ein starker (schwacher) Esser sein; **'eat·ing** Essen *n*; **eat·ing ap·ple** Speiseapfel *m*; **'eat·ing--house** Speisehaus *n*.

eau-de-Co·logne ['əudəkə'ləun] Kölnischwasser *n*.

eaves [i:vz] *pl.* Dachvorsprung *m*, Dachüberstand *m*; Traufe *f*; **'~-drop** (er)lauschen; horchen; **'~-drop·per** Horcher(in).

ebb [eb] **1.** Ebbe *f*; *fig.* Abnahme *f*; Verfall *m*; *at a low* ~ heruntergekommen; **2.** verebben; *fig.* abnehmen, sinken; **'~-'tide** Ebbe *f* (*a. fig.*).

eb·on *poet.* ['ebən] aus Ebenholz; schwarz wie Ebenholz; **eb·on·ite** ['~nait] Hartgummi *m*; **'eb·on·y** Ebenholz *n*.

e·bri·e·ty [i:'braiəti] Trunkenheit *f*.

e·bul·li·ent [i'bʌljənt] überschäumend, -schwenglich; *fig.* sprudelnd (*with* vor); **eb·ul·li·tion** [ebə'liʃən] Überschäumen *n*; Aufbrausen *n*.

ec·cen·tric [ik'sentrik] **1.** *a.* **ec'cen·tri·cal** □ exzentrisch; *fig.* überspannt; **2.** ⊕ Exzentrik *f*; Sonderling *m*; **ec·cen·tric·i·ty** [eksen'trisiti] Exzentrizität *f*; *fig.* Überspanntheit *f*.

ec·cle·si·as·tic [ikli:zi'æstik] Geistliche *m*; **ec·cle·si'as·ti·cal** □ geistlich, kirchlich.

ech·e·lon ⚔ ['eʃələn] **1.** Staffel(aufstellung) *f*; **2.** staffeln.

e·chi·nus *zo.* [e'kainəs] Seeigel *m*.

ech·o ['ekəu] **1.** Echo *n*; **2.** widerhallen; *Ton* zurückwerfen; *fig.* echoen, nachsprechen; **'~-sound·er** Echolot *n*.

e·clat ['eiklɑ:] Eklat *m*; allgemeiner Beifall *m*; glänzender Erfolg *m*.

ec·lec·tic [ek'lektik] **1.** eklektisch, auswählend; **2.** Eklektiker *m*; **ec'lec·ti·cism** [~sizəm] Eklektizismus *m*.

e·clipse [i'klips] **1.** Verfinsterung *f*; Verdunkelung *f* (*a. fig.*); Finsternis *f* (*a. fig.*); *in* ~ im Sinken; **2.** (sich) verfinstern, verdunkeln (*a. fig.*); **e'clip·tic** *ast.* [~tik] Ekliptik *f*, Sonnenbahn *f*.

ec·logue ['eklɔg] Ekloge *f*, Hirtengedicht *n*.
e·co·cid·al [i:kəu'saidl] umweltzerstörend; **e·co·cide** ['~said] Umweltzerstörung *f*; **'e·co·cri·sis** Umweltkrise *f*.
e·col·o·gist [i:'kɔlədʒist] Umweltschutzexperte *m*; **e'col·o·gy** Ökologie *f*; ~ *movement* Umweltschutzbewegung *f*.
e·co·nom·ic [i:kə'nɔmik], **e·co'nom·i·cal** □ ökonomisch, haushälterisch; (volks- *etc.*) wirtschaftlich; sparsam; Wirtschafts...; *economic aid* Wirtschaftshilfe *f*; *economic growth* Wirtschaftswachstum *n*; *economic summit* Wirtschaftsgipfel *m*; **e·co'nom·ics** *sg.* Nationalökonomie *f*, Volkswirtschaft(slehre) *f*; **e·con·o·mist** [i:'kɔnəmist] Haushälter *m*; Volkswirt *m*; **e'con·o·mize** sparsam wirtschaften mit; (ein)sparen (*in, on* an *dat.*, *with* mit); **e'con·o·my** Haushaltung *f*, Wirtschaft *f*; Wirtschaftlichkeit *f*, Sparsamkeit *f*; Einsparung *f*; System *n*; *economies pl.* Ersparnisse *f/pl.*; Sparmaßnahmen *f/pl.*; *political* ~ Volkswirtschaft(slehre) *f*; ~ *class Touristik*: Touristenklasse *f*; ~ *drive* Sparmaßnahmen *f/pl.*, -aktion *f*; ~ *size* Sparpackung *f*.
e·co·sys·tem ['ikəusistəm] Ökosystem *n*.
ec·sta·size ['ekstəsaiz] außer sich bringen (*od. v/i.* geraten), verzücken; **'ec·sta·sy** Ekstase *f*, Verzückung *f*; *go into* ~ in Verzückung geraten; **ec·stat·ic** [eks'tætik] (~*ally*) verzückt; ~ *fit* Verzückung *f*.
e·cu·men·i·cal [i:kju:'menikl] ökumenisch.
ec·ze·ma ⚕ ['eksimə] Ekzem *n*, Ausschlag *m*.
e·da·cious [i'deiʃəs] gefräßig.
ed·dy ['edi] **1.** Wirbel *m*, Strudel *m*; **2.** wirbeln, strudeln.
e·den·tate *zo.* [i'denteit] zahnlos.
edge [edʒ] **1.** Schneide *f*, Schärfe *f*; Rand *m*; (scharfe) Kante *f*; *Tisch*-Ecke *f*; Rand *m*, Saum *m*; Grat *m*; *Buch*-Schnitt *m*; Schärfe *f*, Heftigkeit *f*; *be on* ~ nervös sein; *have the* ~ *on s.o. sl.* j-m über sein; *put an* ~ *on* schärfen; *lay on* ~ hochkantig legen; *set s.o.'s teeth on* ~ j-m auf die Nerven gehen; **2.** schärfen; (um)säumen, einfassen; (sich) schieben *od.* drängen; rücken;
edged scharf; ...schneidig; ...kantig.
edge...: **'~·less** stumpf; **'~-tool** Schneidewerkzeug *n*; **'~·ways, ~·wise** ['~waiz] seitwärts; von der Seite; *get a word in* ~ zu Wort kommen.
edg·ing ['edʒiŋ] Schärfen *n*; Rand *m*, Borte *f*, Einfassung *f*, Besatz *m*; **'~-shears** *pl.* Grasschere *f*.
edg·y ['edʒi] scharf; F kratzbürstig, nervös.
ed·i·ble ['edibl] eßbar; **'ed·i·bles** *pl.* Eßwaren *f/pl.*
e·dict ['i:dikt] Edikt *n*, Verordnung *f*.
ed·i·fi·ca·tion *fig.* [edifi'keiʃən] Erbauung *f*; **ed·i·fice** ['~fis] Gebäude *n* (*a. fig.*); **ed·i·fy** *fig.* ['~fai] erbauen; **'ed·i·fy·ing** □ erbaulich.
ed·it ['edit] *Text* herausgeben, redigieren; *Zeitung* als Herausgeber leiten; **'ed·it·ing ta·ble** *Film*: Schneidetisch *m*; **e·di·tion** [i'diʃən] Ausgabe *f e-s Buches*; Auflage *f*; **ed·i·tor** ['editə] Herausgeber *m*; Schriftleiter *m*, Chefredakteur *m*; *letters pl. to the* ~ Leserbriefe *m/pl.*; **ed·i·to·ri·al** [~'tɔ:riəl] **1.** Redaktions...; ~ *office* Redaktion *f* (*Büro*); ~ *staff* Redaktion *f* (*Personal*); **2.** Leitartikel *m*; **ed·i·torship** ['~təʃip] Schriftleitung *f*, Redaktion *f*; Amt *n* e-s Herausgebers.
ed·u·cate ['edju:keit] erziehen; unterrichten, (aus)bilden; **ed·u'ca·tion** Erziehung *f*; Ausbildung *f*; Bildung *f*; Erziehungs-, Schulwesen *n*; *Ministry of* ♀ Unterrichtsministerium *n*; **ed·u·ca·tion·al** □ [~'keiʃənl], **ed·u·ca·tive** ['~kətiv] erzieherisch; Erziehungs...; Bildungs...; erziehlich; *educational film* Lehrfilm *m*; *educational policy* Bildungspolitik *f*; **ed·u·ca·tion(·al)-ist** [~'keiʃn(əl)ist] Pädagoge *m*, Schulmann *m*; **'ed·u·ca·tor** Erzieher *m*.
e·duce [i'dju:s] entwickeln; *fig.* ableiten; ⚗ darstellen.
e·duc·tion [i'dʌkʃən] Entwicklung *f*; Ableitung *f*; ⊕ Abzug *m*; **e'duc·tion-pipe** Abzugsröhre *f*.
eel [i:l] Aal *m*.
e'en [i:n] = *even*.
e'er [ɛə] = *ever*.
ee·rie, ee·ry ['iəri] unheimlich.
ef·face [i'feis] auslöschen; *fig.* tilgen; *fig.* in den Schatten stellen;

ef'face·a·ble auslöschbar; **ef'face·ment** Auslöschung *f*; Tilgung *f*.
ef·fect [i'fekt] **1.** Wirkung *f*; Folge *f*; Inhalt *m*; Eindruck *m*, Effekt *m*; ⚖ Rechtswirksamkeit *f*; ⊕ Effekt *m*, Leistung *f*; **~s** *pl.* Effekten *pl.*; Habseligkeiten *f/pl.*; † Guthaben *n*; *bring to* ~, *carry into* ~ verwirklichen, bewerkstelligen; *take* ~, *be of* ~ Wirkung haben (*on* auf *acc.*); in Kraft treten; *of no* ~ vergeblich; *in* ~ in der Tat; in Kraft; *to the* ~ des Inhalts; *to this* ~ in diesem Sinn; **2.** bewirken, ausführen; *be* ~*ed* erfolgen; **ef'fec·tive 1.** □ wirkend; (⚖ rechts)wirksam; effekt-, wirkungs-, eindrucksvoll; ⚔, ⚓ dienst-, kampffähig; wirklich vorhanden; ⊕ nutzbar; ~ *capacity* ⊕ Nutzleistung *f*; ~ *date* Tag *m* des Inkrafttretens; ~ *range* Wirkungsbereich *m*; ~ *use* Einsatz *m*; **2.** ⚔ *mst* ~*s pl.* Effektivbestand *m*; **ef'fec·tive·ness** Wirksamkeit *f*; **ef'fec·tu·al** [~tʃuəl] wirksam, kräftig; **ef'fec·tu·ate** [~tjueit] bewerkstelligen.
ef·fem·i·na·cy [i'feminəsi] Verweichlichung *f*; **ef'fem·i·nate** [~nit] □ verweichlicht; weibisch.
ef·fer·vesce [efə'ves] (auf)brausen, (auf)schäumen; *fig.* überschäumen; **ef·fer'ves·cence** Aufbrausen *n etc.*; **ef·fer'ves·cent** sprudelnd, schäumend; ~ *powder* Brausepulver *n*.
ef·fete [e'fi:t] verbraucht; entkräftet.
ef·fi·ca·cious □ [efi'keiʃəs] wirksam; **ef·fi·ca·cy** ['~kəsi] Wirksamkeit *f*, Kraft *f*.
ef·fi·cien·cy [i'fiʃənsi] Leistungsfähigkeit *f*, Tüchtigkeit *f*; ⊕ Wirkungsgrad *m*; (Nutz)Leistung *f*; Wirksamkeit *f*; ~ *expert* Rationalisierungsfachmann *m*; **ef'fi·cient** □ wirksam; leistungsfähig, tüchtig.
ef·fi·gy ['efidʒi] Bild(nis) *n*; *burn s.o. in* ~ j. in effigie *od.* im Bild verbrennen.
ef·flo·resce [eflɔ:'res] ⚘ (auf)blühen (*a. fig.*); ⚗ beschlagen, auswittern; **ef·flo'res·cence** Blütezeit *f*; ⚗ Beschlag *m*; **ef·flo'res·cent** beschlagend, auswitternd.
ef·flu·ence ['efluəns] Ausfließen *n*, Ausfluß *m*; **'ef·flu·ent 1.** ausfließend; **2.** Ausfluß *m*.
ef·flux ['eflʌks] Ausströmen *n*; Ausfluß *m*.
ef·fort ['efət] Anstrengung *f*, Bemühung *f* (*at* um); Mühe *f*; F Leistung *f*; **'ef·fort·less** □ mühelos.
ef·fron·ter·y [i'frʌntəri] Frechheit *f*, Unverschämtheit *f*.
ef·ful·gence [e'fʌldʒəns] Glanz *m*; **ef'ful·gent** □ strahlend, glänzend.
ef·fuse [e'fju:z] aus-, vergießen; **ef·fu·sion** [i'fju:ʒən] Ausgießung *f*; Erguß *m* (*a. fig.*); **ef'fu·sive** □ [~siv] überschwenglich; **ef'fu·sive·ness** Überschwenglichkeit *f*.
eft *zo.* [eft] Sumpfeidechse *f*.
egg[1] [eg] *mst* ~ *on* drängen, auf-, anreizen, anstacheln.
egg[2] [~] Ei *n*; *in the* ~ im Anfangsstadium; *bad* ~ F schlechter Kerl *m*; *put all one's* ~*s in one basket* alles auf eine Karte setzen; *as sure as* ~*s is* ~*s* F todsicher; **'~-cup** Eierbecher *m*; **'~-flip** Eierflip *m*; **'~-head** Intellektuelle *m*; **'~-nog** = *egg-flip*; **'~-plant** ⚘ Aubergine *f*, Eierfrucht *f*; **'~-shell** Eierschale *f*; **'~-whisk** Schneebesen *m*.
eg·lan·tine ⚘ ['egləntain] Heckenrose *f*.
e·go ['egəu] *das* Ich; **e·go·cen·tric** [~'sentrik] egozentrisch; **'e·go·ism** Egoismus *m*, Selbstsucht *f*; **'e·go·ist** Egoist(in); **e·go'is·tic, e·go'is·ti·cal** □ egoistisch, selbstsüchtig; **e·go·tism** ['~tizəm] Selbstgefälligkeit *f*, Eigendünkel *m*; **'e·go·tist** Egotist *m*, selbstgefälliger Mensch *m*; **e·go'tis·tic, e·go'tis·ti·cal** □ nur von sich redend; selbstgefällig.
e·gre·gious *iro.* □ [i'gri:dʒəs] großartig; ungeheuer, unerhört.
e·gress ['i:gres] Ausgang *m*; Ausfluß *m*; *fig.* Ausweg *m*.
e·gret ['i:gret] *orn.* kleiner weißer Reiher *m*; Federbusch *m*.
E·gyp·tian [i'dʒipʃən] **1.** ägyptisch; **2.** Ägypter(in).
eh [ei] wie?; nicht wahr?; ei!; sieh da!
ei·der ['aidə] *a.* ~*-duck orn.* Eiderente *f*; ~ *down* Eiderdaunen *f/pl.*; Daunendecke *f*.
eight [eit] **1.** acht; **2.** Acht *f*; ⚓ Achter *m*; *behind the* ~ *ball Am.* in der (die) Klemme; **eight·een** ['ei'ti:n] achtzehn; **'eight'eenth** [~θ] achtzehnt; **'eight·fold** achtfach; **eighth** [eitθ] **1.** achte(r, -s); **2.** Achtel *n*; **'eighth·ly** achtens;

eight-'hour day Achtstundentag *m*; **eight·i·eth** ['~iiθ] achtzigste(r, -s); '**eight·some** [~səm] schottischer Tanz *m für 8 Tänzer*; '**eight·y** achtzig.
eis·tedd·fod [ais'teðvɔd] wallisisches Sängerfest *n*, Eisteddfod *n*.
ei·ther ['aiðə] **1.** *adj. u. pron.* einer *von beiden*; beide; jeder *von zweien*; **2.** *cj.* ~ ... *or* entweder ... oder; *not* (...) ~ auch nicht.
e·jac·u·late [i'dʒækjuleit] *Worte* ausstoßen; **e·jac·u'la·tion** Ausruf *m*; Stoßgebet *n*; Ausstoßen *n*.
e·ject [iː'dʒekt] ausstoßen; vertreiben (*from* von); ausweisen; *e-s Amtes* entsetzen; **e'jec·tion** Ausstoßung *f*, Vertreibung *f*; Ausweisung *f*; **e'ject·ment** ⚖ Vertreibung *f*; **e'jec·tor** ⊕ Auswerfer *m*; ~*-seat* ✈ Schleudersitz *m*.
eke [iːk]: ~ *out* ergänzen; verlängern (*with* durch); sich mit *et.* durchhelfen; ~ *out a miserable existence* sich kümmerlich durchschlagen.
el *Am.* F [el] = *elevated railroad*.
e·lab·o·rate 1. ☐ [i'læbərit] sorgfältig ausgearbeitet; kunstvoll; vollendet; kompliziert; reich verziert; **2.** [~reit] sorgfältig ausarbeiten; herausarbeiten; **e'lab·o·rate·ness** [~ritnis], **e·lab·o·ra·tion** [~'reiʃən] sorgfältige Ausarbeitung *f*.
e·lapse [i'læps] verfließen, -streichen.
e·las·tic [i'læstik] **1.** (~*ally*) elastisch, dehnbar (*a. fig.*); geschmeidig; spannkräftig; **2.** Gummiband *n*; **e·las·tic·i·ty** [elæs'tisiti] Elastizität *f*, Dehnbarkeit *f*; *fig.* Spannkraft *f*.
e·late [i'leit] (er)heben, ermutigen, froh erregen; stolz machen; **e'lat·ed** in gehobener Stimmung, freudig erregt (*at* über *acc.*; *with* durch); **e'la·tion** gehobene Stimmung *f*.
el·bow ['elbəu] **1.** Ellbogen *m*; Krümmung *f*, Biegung *f*; ⊕ Knie *n*, Winkel *m*; *at one's* ~ nahe, bei der Hand; *out at* ~*s* am Ellbogen zerrissen; *fig.* heruntergekommen; **2.** mit dem Ellbogen (weg)stoßen; ~ *one's way through* sich durchdrängen; ~ *out* verdrängen; '~**-'chair** Lehnstuhl *m*; '~**-grease** F Armschmalz *n* (*Kraftanstrengung*); '~**-room** Spielraum *m*.
eld·er[1] ['eldə] **1.** älter; ~ *statesman* Politiker *m* (*mst im Ruhestand*), der (*inoffiziell*) als Berater tätig ist; *fig.* großer alter Mann *m e-r Berufsgruppe*; **2.** der *od.* die Ältere; (Kirchen)Älteste *m*; *my* ~*s pl.* ältere Leute als ich.
el·der[2] ⚘ [~] Holunder *m*; '~**·ber·ry** Holunderbeere *f*.
eld·er·ly ['eldəli] ältlich; älter.
eld·est ['eldist] ältest; *the* ~ *born* der Erstgeborene.
e·lect [i'lekt] **1.** (aus)gewählt; *eccl.* auserwählt; *bride* ~ Verlobte *f*; **2.** (aus-, er)wählen; (er)wählen; *eccl.* auserwählen; vorziehen, sich entschließen (*to do* zu tun); **3.** *the* ~ *pl. eccl.* die Auserwählten *pl.*; **e'lec·tion** Wahl *f*; ~ *address*, ~ *speech* Wahlrede *f*; **e·lec·tion·eer** [~ʃə'niə] Wahlpropaganda machen; **e·lec·tion'eer·ing** Wahlpropaganda *f*; **e'lec·tive 1.** ☐ wählend; gewählt; Wahl...; *Am.* fakultativ; **2.** *Am.* Wahlfach *n*; **e'lec·tive·ly** durch Wahl; **e'lec·tor** Wähler *m*; *Am.* Wahlmann *m*; *hist.* Kurfürst *m*; **e'lec·tor·al** Wahl..., Wähler...; kurfürstlich; ~ *address* Wahlrede *f*; ~ *campaign* Wahlkampf *m*, -kampagne *f*; ~ *college Am.* Wahlmänner *m/pl.*; ~ *roll* Wählerliste *f*; **e'lec·tor·ate** [~tərit] Wähler(schaft *f*) *m/pl.*; Kurwürde *f*; Kurfürstentum *n*; **e'lec·tress** *hist.* Kurfürstin *f*; Wählerin *f*.
e·lec·tric [i'lektrik], **e'lec·tri·cal** ☐ elektrisch; Elektro...; *fig.* elektrisierend, faszinierend; **e'lec·tri·cal en·gi·neer** Elektrotechniker *m*.
e·lec·tric...: ~ **blue** stahlblau; ~ **chair** elektrischer Stuhl *m für Hinrichtungen*; ~ **eel** Zitteraal *m*; ~ **eye** Photozelle *f*; ~ **fence** Elektrozaun *m*.
e·lec·tri·cian [ilek'triʃən] Elektriker *m*, Elektrotechniker *m*; **e·lec'tric·i·ty** [~siti] Elektrizität *f*; **e·lec·tri·fi'ca·tion** Elektrifizierung *f*; **e'lec·tri·fy** [~fai], **e'lec·trize** elektrifizieren; elektrisieren (*a. fig.*); begeistern.
e·lec·tro [i'lektrəu] Elektro...; **e'lec·tro·cute** [~trəkjuːt] auf dem elektrischen Stuhl hinrichten; durch elektrischen Strom töten; **e·lec·tro'cu·tion** Hinrichtung *f od.* Tod *m* durch elektrischen Strom; **e'lec·trode** [~trəud] Elektrode *f*; **e'lec·tro-dy'nam·ics** *mst sg.* Elektrodynamik *f*; **e·lec·tro·lier** [~'liə] elektrischer Kronleuchter *m*; **e'lec·tro·lyse** [~laiz] elektrisch

zersetzen; **e·lec·trol·y·sis** [ilek'trɔlisis] Elektrolyse *f*; **e·lec·tro·lyte** [i'lektrəulait] Elektrolyt *m*; **e·lec·tro·lyt·ic** [~'litik] elektrolytisch; **e'lec·tro'mag·net** Elektromagnet *m*; **e'lec·tro'met·al·lur·gy** Elektrometallurgie *f*; **e'lec·tro'mo·tive** elektromotorisch; **e'lec·tro'mo·tor** Elektromotor *m*.

e·lec·tron [i'lektrɔn] Elektron *n*; *attr.* Elektronen...; **e·lec'tron·ic** Elektronen...; ~ *data processing* elektronische Datenverarbeitung *f*; **e·lec'tron·ics** *sg.* Elektronenphysik *f*, Elektronik *f*.

e·lec·tro·plate [i'lektrəupleit] **1.** galvanisch versilbern; **2.** galvanisch versilberte Gegenstände *m/pl.*; **e'lec·tro·type** galvanischer Druck *m*; Elektrotype *f*.

el·ee·mos·y·nar·y [elii:'mɔsinəri] Almosen..., Wohltätigkeits...

el·e·gance ['eligəns] Eleganz *f*, Vornehmheit *f*, Gepflegtheit *f*, Anmut *f*; **'el·e·gant** □ elegant, vornehm, gepflegt; anmutig; geschmackvoll; *Am.* erstklassig.

el·e·gi·ac [eli'dʒaiək] **1.** elegisch; **2.** elegischer Vers *m*.

el·e·gy ['elidʒi] Elegie *f* (*Klagelied*).

el·e·ment ['elimənt] Element *n*, Urstoff *m*; (Grund)Bestandteil *m*; (Lebens)Element *n*; ⚡ Element *n*; Umstand *m*; Naturkraft *f*; *fig.* Körnchen *n*; ~*s pl.* Anfangsgründe *m/pl.*; **el·e·men·tal** [~'mentl] □ elementar; gewaltig; wesentlich; **el·e'men·ta·ry** □ elementar, einfach; Anfangs...; ~ *school* Volks-, Grundschule *f*; *elementaries pl.* Anfangsgründe *m/pl.*, Elemente *n/pl.*

el·e·phant ['elifənt] Elefant *m*; *white* ~ nutzloses Wertstück *n*; **el·e·phan·tine** [~'fæntain] Elefanten...; elefantenhaft; plump.

el·e·vate ['eliveit] erhöhen; *fig.* erheben; **'el·e·vat·ed 1.** hoch, erhaben; F angeheitert; ~ *railroad* = **2.** *Am.* F Hochbahn *f*; **el·e'va·tion** Erhebung *f*, Erhöhung *f* (*a. fig.*); Höhe *f*; Erhabenheit *f*; Hoheit *f*; *ast.* Höhe *f*; ⊕ Aufriß *m*; **'el·e·va·tor** ⊕ Hebe-, Förderwerk *n*, Aufzug *m*; *Am.* Fahrstuhl *m*; ✈ Höhenruder *n*; (*grain*) ~ *Am.* Getreidespeicher *m*; *bucket* ~ ⊕ Becherwerk *n*; ~ *shaft Am.* Aufzugschacht *m*.

e·lev·en [i'levn] **1.** elf; **2.** Elf *f*; ~**-'plus ex·am·i·na·tion** Aufnahmeprüfung *f* in die höhere Schule; **e'lev·en·ses** F [~ziz] kleiner Imbiß *m um ca. 11 Uhr*, zweites Frühstück *n*; **e'lev·enth** [~θ] elfte(r, -s); *at the* ~ *hour* in letzter Minute.

elf [elf], *pl.* **elves** [elvs] Elf(e *f*) *m*, Kobold *m*; Zwerg *m*; **elf·in** ['~in] elfisch; Elfen...; **'elf·ish** elfengleich; boshaft.

e·lic·it [i'lisit] hervorlocken, herausholen.

e·lide *gr.* [i'laid] elidieren, auslassen.

el·i·gi·bil·i·ty [elidʒə'biliti] Eignung *f*; Vorzug *m*; **'el·i·gi·ble** □ geeignet, annehmbar; passend; akzeptabel, in Frage kommend; (teilnahme)berechtigt.

e·lim·i·nate [i'limineit] aussondern, ausscheiden (*bsd.* ⚗, 𝔄, ⚕); ausmerzen; **e·lim·i'na·tion** Aussonderung *f*; Ausscheidung *f*.

e·li·sion *gr.* [i'liʒən] Elision *f*, Auslassung *f*.

é·lite [ei'li:t] Elite *f*, Auslese *f*; Oberschicht *f*.

é·lit·ist [ei'li:tist] elitär.

e·lix·ir [i'liksə] Elixier *n*.

E·liz·a·be·than [ilizə'bi:θən] **1.** elisabethanisch; **2.** Elisabethaner(in).

elk *zo.* [elk] Elch *m*.

ell *hist.* [el] Elle *f*.

el·lipse 𝔄 [i'lips] Ellipse *f*; **el'lipsis** [~sis], *pl.* **el'lip·ses** *gr.* [~si:z], Ellipse *f*, Auslassung *f*; **el'lip·tic, el'lip·ti·cal** □ [~tik(əl)] elliptisch.

elm ⚘ [elm] Ulme *f*, Rüster *f*.

el·o·cu·tion [elə'kju:ʃən] Vortrag(skunst *f*, -sweise *f*) *m*; **el·o'cu·tion·ar·y** [~ʃnəri] rednerisch; **el·o'cu·tion·ist** Vortragskünstler *m*; Sprecherzieher *m*.

e·lon·gate ['i:lɔŋgeit] verlängern; **e·lon'ga·tion** Verlängerung *f*; *ast.* Elongation *f*, Winkelabstand *m*.

e·lope [i'ləup] (dem Gatten) entlaufen, durchgehen; **e'lope·ment** Entlaufen *n*.

el·o·quence ['eləukwəns] Beredsamkeit *f*; **'el·o·quent** □ beredt, redegewandt.

else [els] sonst, andere(r, -s), weiter; *all* ~ alles andere; *anyone* ~ irgendein anderer; *what* ~? was sonst?; *or* ~ oder aber; **'else'where** anderswo(hin).

e·lu·ci·date [iˈluːsideit] aufklären, erläutern; **e·lu·ci'da·tion** Aufklärung *f*, Erläuterung *f*; **e'lu·ci·da·to·ry** aufklärend, erläuternd.
e·lude [iˈluːd] geschickt umgehen; ausweichen, sich entziehen (*dat.*).
e·lu·sion [iˈluːʒən] Umgehung *f*; Ausflucht *f*; Ausweichen *n*; **e'lu·sive** [~siv] nicht zu fassen(d); **e'lu·sive·ness** (listiges) Ausweichen *n*; **e'lu·so·ry** trügerisch.
elves [elvz] *pl. von elf.*
E·lys·ian [iˈliziən] elysisch, himmlisch; **E'lys·ium** [~iəm] Elysium *n*.
em [em] *typ.* Geviert *n*.
e·ma·ci·ate [iˈmeiʃieit] abzehren, ausmergeln; **e·ma·ci·a·tion** [imeisiˈeiʃən] Abzehrung *f*.
em·a·nate [ˈeməneit] ausströmen; ausgehen (*from* von); **em·a'na·tion** Ausströmung *f*; *fig.* Ausstrahlung *f*; *phys.* Emanation *f*.
e·man·ci·pate [iˈmænsipeit] emanzipieren, befreien; **e·man·ci'pa·tion** Emanzipation *f*, Befreiung *f*; **e'man·ci·pa·tor** Befreier *m*.
e·mas·cu·late **1.** [iˈmæskjuleit] entmannen; verweichlichen; *Text* verstümmeln; **2.** [~lit] entmannt; weibisch; **e·mas·cu·la·tion** [~ˈleiʃən] Entmannung *f*; Verweichlichung *f*; *Text*-Verstümmelung *f*.
em·balm [imˈbɑːm] (ein)balsamieren; vor Vergessenheit bewahren; *be ~ed in* fortleben in (*dat.*); **em'balm·ment** Einbalsamierung *f*.
em·bank [imˈbæŋk] eindämmen; **em'bank·ment** Eindämmung *f*; Deich *m*; (Bahn)Damm *m*; Uferstraße *f*, Kai *m*.
em·bar·go [emˈbɑːgəu] **1.** Embargo *n*; (Hafen-, Handels)Sperre *f*, Beschlagnahme *f*; **2.** *Hafen, Handel* sperren; *Schiff etc.* beschlagnahmen.
em·bark [imˈbɑːk] (sich) einschiffen, verladen (*for* nach); *Geld* anlegen; sich einlassen (*in, on, upon* in, auf *acc.*); **em·bar·ka·tion** [embɑːˈkeiʃən] Einschiffung *f*, Verladung *f*.
em·bar·rass [imˈbærəs] (be)hindern; verwirren, in Verlegenheit bringen; in e-e unangenehme Lage bringen; erschweren, verwickeln; *~ed* verlegen, betreten; in (Geld-)Verlegenheit; **em'bar·rass·ing** □ unangenehm; unbequem; peinlich; **em'bar·rass·ment** (Geld)Verlegenheit *f*; Verwirrung *f*; Schwierigkeit *f*.
em·bas·sy [ˈembəsi] Botschaft *f*; Gesandtschaft *f*.
em·bat·tle [imˈbætl] in Schlachtordnung aufstellen; mit Zinnen versehen.
em·bed [imˈbed] (ein)betten, lagern.
em·bel·lish [imˈbeliʃ] verschönern; *Geschichte* ausschmücken; **em'bel·lish·ment** Verschönerung *f*; Schmuck *m*; Ausschmückung *f*.
em·ber-days [ˈembədeiz] *pl.* Quatember *m* (*die vier Fastenzeiten*).
em·bers [ˈembəz] *pl.* glühende Asche *f*; *fig.* Funken *m/pl.*
em·bez·zle [imˈbezl] veruntreuen, unterschlagen; **em'bez·zle·ment** Veruntreuung *f*, Unterschlagung *f*; **em'bez·zler** Veruntreuer *m*.
em·bit·ter [imˈbitə] verbittern; verschlimmern; erbittern.
em·bla·zon [imˈbleizən] mit e-m Wappenbild bemalen; *fig.* verherrlichen; **em'bla·zon·ry** Wappenmalerei *f*.
em·blem [ˈembləm] Sinnbild *n*, Emblem *n*, Symbol *n*; Wahrzeichen *n*; **em·blem·at·ic, em·blem·at·i·cal** □ [embliˈmætik(əl)] sinnbildlich, symbolisch.
em·bod·i·ment [imˈbɔdimənt] Verkörperung *f*; **em'bod·y** verkörpern; vereinigen; *Land* einverleiben (*in dat.*).
em·bold·en [imˈbəuldən] ermutigen.
em·bo·lism ⚕ [ˈembəlizəm] Embolie *f*.
em·bos·om [imˈbuzəm] ins Herz schließen; *~ed with* umgeben von.
em·boss [imˈbɔs] bossieren; *mit dem Hammer* treiben; **em'bossed** getrieben, erhaben gearbeitet; *~ note-paper* geprägtes Briefpapier *n*.
em·bow·el [imˈbauəl] ausweiden.
em·brace [imˈbreis] **1.** (sich) umarmen; umschließen; umfassen, einschließen; *Gelegenheit, Beruf* ergreifen; *Angebot* annehmen; in sich aufnehmen; **2.** Umarmung *f*.
em·bra·sure [imˈbreiʒə] Leibung *f*; Schießscharte *f*.
em·bro·cate [ˈembrəukeit] einreiben; **em·bro'ca·tion** Einreibung *f*, Liniment *n*.
em·broi·der [imˈbrɔidə] sticken; *fig.* ausschmücken; **em'broi·der·y**

Stickerei *f*; *fig.* Ausschmückung *f*.
em·broil [imˈbrɔil] (in Streit) verwickeln; verwirren; **emˈbroil·ment** Verwirrung *f*.
em·bry·o [ˈembriəu] Embryo *m*, Fruchtkeim *m*; *in* ~ im Werden; **em·bry·on·ic** [~ˈɔnik] embryonal, (noch) unentwickelt (*a. fig.*).
em·bus [imˈbʌs] (auf Kraftfahrzeuge) verladen *od.* steigen.
em·cee F [emˈsiː] Conférencier *m*.
e·mend [iːˈmend] *Text* verbessern, korrigieren; **e·menˈda·tion** Verbesserung *f*; **ˈe·men·da·tor** (Text-) Verbesserer *m*; **eˈmend·a·to·ry** [~dətəri] verbessernd.
em·er·ald [ˈemərəld] **1.** Smaragd *m*; **2.** smaragdgrün.
e·merge [iˈməːdʒ] auftauchen (*a. fig.*); zum Vorschein kommen; hervorgehen (als; *from* aus); sich erheben (*into* zu); sich ergeben *od.* zeigen; **eˈmer·gence** Auftauchen *n*.
e·mer·gen·cy [iˈməːdʒənsi] unerwartetes Ereignis *n*; Notfall *m*; dringende Not *f*; ~ **brake** Notbremse *f*; ~ **call** Notruf *m*; ~ **decree** Notverordnung *f*; ~ **ex·it** Notausgang *m*; ~ **land·ing** ✈ Notlandung *f*; ~ **man** *Sport*: Ersatzmann *m*; ~ **num·ber** Notruf(nummer *f*) *m*; ~ **serv·ice** Notdienst *m*.
e·mer·gent [iˈməːdʒənt] auftauchend, entstehend; ~ *countries pl.* junge Staaten *m/pl.*, Entwicklungsländer *n/pl.*
e·mer·sion [iˈməːʃən] Auftauchen *n*; *ast.* Austritt *m*.
em·er·y [ˈeməri] Schmirgel *m*; ~ **board** Sandblattnagelfeile *f*; **ˈ~-cloth** Schmirgelleinen *n*; **ˈ~-pa·per** Schmirgelpapier *n*.
e·met·ic [iˈmetik] **1.** erbrechenerregend; Brech...; **2.** Brechmittel *n*.
em·i·grant [ˈemigrənt] **1.** auswandernd; **2.** Auswanderer *m*; **em·i·grate** [ˈ~greit] auswandern; **em·iˈgra·tion** Auswanderung *f*; **em·i·gra·to·ry** [ˈ~greitəri] Auswanderungs...
em·i·nence [ˈeminəns] Anhöhe *f*; Auszeichnung *f*, Ruhm *m*; hohe Stellung *f*; ♀ Eminenz *f* (*Titel*); **ˈem·i·nent** □ *fig.* ausgezeichnet (*in*, *for* durch), bedeutend, hervorragend; **ˈem·i·nent·ly** in hohem Maße, ganz besonders.
e·mir [eˈmiə] Emir *m*; **e·mir·ate** [eˈmiərit] Emirat *n*.
em·is·sar·y [ˈemisəri] Sendbote *m*, Emissär *m*; **e·mis·sion** [iˈmiʃən] Aussenden *n*; *phys.* Ausströmen *n*; *fig.* Ausfluß *m*; ⚕ Emission *f*.
e·mit [iˈmit] von sich geben; aussenden, -strömen; ⚕ ausgeben, in Umlauf setzen.
e·mol·u·ment [iˈmɔljumənt] Vergütung *f*; ~*s pl.* Einkünfte *pl.*, Bezüge *pl.*
e·mo·tion [iˈməuʃən] (Gemüts-) Bewegung *f*; Gefühl(sregung *f*) *n*; Erregung *f*; Rührung *f*; **eˈmo·tion·al** [~ʃənl] □ gefühlsmäßig; Gefühls...; gefühlvoll, gefühlsbetont, emotional; **e·mo·tion·al·i·ty** [~ʃəˈnæliti] gefühlvolles Wesen *n*; **eˈmo·tion·less** gefühllos, kühl; **eˈmo·tive** gefühlsmäßig.
em·pan·el [imˈpænl] in die (*bsd.* Geschworenen)Liste eintragen.
em·pa·thy *psych.* [ˈempəθi] Einfühlung(svermögen *n*) *f*.
em·per·or [ˈempərə] Kaiser *m*.
em·pha·sis [ˈemfəsis], *pl.* **em·pha·ses** [ˈ~siːz] Nachdruck *m*, Betonung *f*, Ton *m*; **em·pha·size** [ˈ~saiz] nachdrücklich betonen; hervorheben; **em·phat·ic** [imˈfætik] (~*ally*) nachdrücklich; ausgesprochen; *be* ~ *that* betonen, daß.
em·pire [ˈempaiə] (Kaiser)Reich *n*; Herrschaft *f*; *the British* ♀ das britische Weltreich.
em·pir·ic [emˈpirik] **1.** Empiriker *m*; Quacksalber *m*; **2.** *mst* **emˈpir·i·cal** □ erfahrungsmäßig, empirisch; quacksalberisch; **emˈpir·i·cism** [~sizəm] Empirismus *m*; **emˈpir·i·cist** Empiriker *m*.
em·place·ment ⚔ [imˈpleismənt] Instellungbringen *n*; Geschützstand *m*.
em·plane [imˈplein] in ein Flugzeug steigen *od.* verladen.
em·ploy [imˈplɔi] **1.** beschäftigen, anstellen; an-, verwenden, gebrauchen; **2.** Dienst(e *pl.*) *m*, Beschäftigung *f*; *in the* ~ *of* angestellt bei; **em·ploy·é** *m*, **em·ploy·ée** *f* [ɔmˈplɔiei], **em·ploy·ee** [emplɔiˈiː] Angestellte *m*, *f*; Arbeitnehmer(in); **em·ploy·er** [imˈplɔiə] Arbeitgeber *m*, Dienstherr *m*; ⚕ Auftraggeber *m*; **emˈploy·ment** Beschäftigung *f*; Geschäft *n*; Beruf *m*, (An)Stellung *f*, Arbeit *f*; ~ *agency* Stellenvermitt-

lungsbüro *n*; *place of* ~ Arbeitsstätte *f*; ♀ *Exchange* Arbeitsamt *n*.
em·po·ri·um [em'pɔːriəm] Handels-, Umschlagplatz *m*; Warenhaus *n*; Laden *m*.
em·pow·er [im'pauə] ermächtigen; befähigen.
em·press ['empris] Kaiserin *f*.
emp·ti·ness ['emptinis] Leere *f*, Leerheit *f*; Hohlheit *f*; '**emp·ty** 1. □ leer; *fig.* hohl; F hungrig; 2. (sich) (aus-, ent)leeren; sich ergießen; 3. leerer Behälter *m*; *empties pl.* ✝ Leergut *n*; '**emp·ty-'hand·ed** mit leeren Händen.
em·pur·ple [im'pəːpl] purpurrot färben.
e·mu *orn.* ['iːmjuː] Emu *m*, Kasuar *m*.
em·u·late ['emjuleit] wetteifern mit; nacheifern, es gleichtun (*dat.*); **em·u'la·tion** Wetteifer *m*; **em·u·la·tive** ['~lətiv] nacheifernd (*of dat.*); **em·u·la·tor** ['~leitə] Nacheiferer *m*; '**em·u·lous** □ (*of*) nacheifernd (*dat.*); eifersüchtig (auf *acc.*).
e·mul·sion ⚗ [i'mʌlʃən] Emulsion *f*.
en·a·ble [i'neibl] befähigen, in den Stand setzen, es *j-m* ermöglichen (*to inf.* zu *inf.*); ermächtigen.
en·act [i'nækt] verfügen, verordnen; *Gesetz* erlassen; *thea.* spielen; *be* ~*ed* sich abspielen; **en'act·ment** gesetzliche Verfügung *f*; Erlassen *n e-s Gesetzes*.
en·am·el [i'næməl] 1. Email(le *f*) *n*, (*bsd.* Zahn)Schmelz *m*; Glasur *f*; 2. emaillieren; glasieren; *poet.* (bunt) schmücken.
en·am·o(u)r [i'næmə] verliebt machen; *be* ~*ed of* verliebt sein in (*acc.*).
en·cage [in'keidʒ] einsperren.
en·camp ⚔ [in'kæmp] (sich) lagern, das Lager aufschlagen; **en'camp·ment** Lager(n) *n*.
en·case [in'keis] einschließen; umgeben; (um)hüllen; **en'case·ment** Gehäuse *n*; Hülle *f*.
en·cash·ment ✝ [in'kæʃmənt] Inkasso *n*, Einkassierung *f*.
en·caus·tic [en'kɔːstik] 1. enkaustisch; 2. Enkaustik *f* (*antike Maltechnik*).
en·ceph·a·li·tis ⚕ [enkefə'laitis] Gehirnentzündung *f*, Enzephalitis *f*.
en·chain [in'tʃein] anketten; fesseln.
en·chant [in'tʃɑːnt] bezaubern; *fig.* entzücken; **en'chant·er** Zauberer *m*; **en'chant·ing** bezaubernd; **en'chant·ment** Ver-, Bezauberung *f*; Zauber *m*; **en'chant·ress** Zauberin *f*.
en·chase [in'tʃeis] ziselieren; *Edelstein* fassen; *fig.* schmücken.
en·ci·pher [in'saifə] verschlüsseln, chiffrieren.
en·cir·cle [in'səːkl] einkreisen; umfassen, -geben; **en'cir·cle·ment** Umfassung *f*; *pol.* Einkreisung *f*.
en·close [in'kləuz] einzäunen; einfassen; einschließen; beilegen, beifügen; **en'clo·sure** [~ʒə] Einzäunung *f*; eingehegtes Grundstück *n*; Bei-, Anlage *f zu e-m Brief*.
en·code [in'kəud] = *encipher*.
en·co·mi·ast [en'kəumiæst] Lobredner *m*; **en'co·mi·um** [~mjəm] Lobrede *f*.
en·com·pass [in'kʌmpəs] umgeben.
en·core [ɔŋ'kɔː] 1. noch einmal!; da capo!; 2. *v/i.* da capo rufen; *v/t.* nochmals verlangen; *j.* um e-e Zugabe bitten; 3. Dakaporuf *m*; Wiederholung *f*; Zugabe *f*.
en·coun·ter [in'kauntə] 1. Zs.-treffen *n*; Begegnung *f*; Gefecht *n*; 2. (plötzlich) begegnen (*dat.*), treffen; entgegentreten (*dat.*); auf *Schwierigkeiten etc.* stoßen, mit *j-m* zs.-stoßen.
en·cour·age [in'kʌridʒ] ermutigen, unterstützen, fördern; **en'cour·age·ment** Ermutigung *f*; Unterstützung *f*, Förderung *f*; **en'cour·ag·er** Förderer *m*.
en·croach [in'krəutʃ] eingreifen, -dringen (*on, upon* in *acc.*); beeinträchtigen (*on acc.*); ~ *upon s.o.'s kindness* j-s Güte mißbrauchen; **en'croach·ment** Ein-, Übergriff *m* (*on, upon* in, auf *acc.*).
en·crust [in'krʌst] (sich) überkrusten; ⊕ inkrustieren.
en·cum·ber [in'kʌmbə] belasten; beladen; beschweren; (be)hindern, versperren; **en'cum·brance** Last *f*; *fig.* Hindernis *n*; Hypothekenschuld *f*; Schuldenlast *f*; *without* ~ ohne (Familien)Anhang.
en·cyc·li·cal *eccl.* [en'siklikəl] (päpstliche) Enzyklika *f*.
en·cy·clo·p(a)e·di·a [ensaikləu'piːdjə] Enzyklopädie *f*, Konversationslexikon *n*; **en·cy·clo'p(a)e·dic**

enzyklopädisch.

end [end] **1.** Ende *n*; Ziel *n*, (End-)Zweck *m*; Folge *f*; Endchen *n*; *be at an ~* zu Ende sein; *no ~ of* unendlich viel(e), unzählige, sehr groß *etc.*; *have s.th. at one's fingers' ~s* et. beherrschen; *in the ~* am Ende, auf die Dauer; *on ~* aufrecht; hintereinander; ununterbrochen; *stand on ~* zu Berge stehen; *to the ~ that* damit; *to no ~* vergebens; *to this ~* zu dem Zweck; *come to an ~* zu Ende gehen; *go off the deep ~ fig.* in die Luft gehen; *make an ~ of, put an ~ to e-r Sache* ein Ende machen; *make both ~s meet* (mit dem Geld) gerade auskommen, sich nach der Decke strecken; **2.** enden, beend(ig)en.

en·dan·ger [in'deindʒə] gefährden.

en·dear [in'diə] teuer machen; **en'dear·ing** reizend; zärtlich; **en'dear·ment** Liebkosung *f*, Zärtlichkeit *f*.

en·deav·o(u)r [in'devə] **1.** Bestreben *n*, Bemühen *n*, Bemühung *f*, Anstrengung *f*; **2.** sich bemühen, bestrebt sein; streben (*after* nach).

en·dem·ic ⚕ [en'demik] **1.** *a.* **en'dem·i·cal** □ endemisch; einheimisch; **2.** endemische Krankheit *f*.

end·ing ['endiŋ] Ende *n*; Schluß *m*; *gr.* Endung *f*.

en·dive ⚘ ['endiv] Endivie *f*.

end·less □ ['endlis] endlos, unendlich; ⊕ ohne Ende.

end-of-term [endəv'tə:m] Semesterabschluß...; *~ exam* Semesterabschlußprüfung *f*.

en·dorse [in'dɔ:s] ✝ indossieren, girieren, überweisen; mit e-m Vermerk (*on* auf der Rückseite *e-r Urkunde*) versehen; gutheißen; beipflichten (*dat.*); *endorsing ink* Stempelfarbe *f*; **en·dor·see** [endɔ:'si:] Indossat *m*; **en·dorse·ment** [in'dɔ:smənt] Aufschrift *f*; Bestätigung *f*; ✝ Indossament *n*, Giro *n*; **en'dors·er** Indossant *m*, Girant *m*.

en·do·sperm ⚘ ['endəuspə:m] Endosperm *n*, Nährgewebe *n des Samens*.

en·dow [in'dau] ausstatten, begaben; *Kirche etc.* dotieren; **en'dow·ment** Ausstattung *f*, Stiftung *f*, Dotation *f*; Begabung *f*; *~ policy* Lebensversicherung *f* mit Rentenwahlrecht.

en·due *mst fig.* [in'dju:] bekleiden, versehen, ausstatten (*with* mit).

en·dur·a·ble [in'djuərəbl] erträglich; **en'dur·ance** Dauer *f*; Ertragen *n*, Aushalten *n*; Ausdauer *f*; Geduld *f*; *past ~* unerträglich; *~ flight* Dauerflug *m*; *~ run* Dauerlauf *m*; **en'dure** (aus)dauern; aushalten; ertragen; **en'dur·ing** dauernd, dauerhaft.

end·way(s) ['endwei(z)], **end·wise** ['~waiz] mit dem Ende nach vorn; gerade, aufrecht.

en·e·ma ⚕ ['enimə] Einlauf *m*; Klistierspritze *f*.

en·e·my ['enimi] **1.** Feind *m*; *the* 2 der Teufel, der böse Feind; **2.** feindlich.

en·er·get·ic [enə'dʒetik] (*~ally*) energisch, tatkräftig; wirksam; **'en·er·gize** ⚡ erregen; **'en·er·gy** Energie *f*, Kraft *f* (*a. phys.*); Willens-, Tatkraft *f*; Wirksamkeit *f*; Nachdruck *m*; *~ crisis* Energiekrise *f*; **'en·er·gy-sav·ing** energiesparend.

en·er·vate ['enə:veit] entnerven, schwächen; **en·er'va·tion** Entnervung *f*, Schwächung *f*; Schwäche *f*.

en·fee·ble [in'fi:bl] schwächen; **en'fee·ble·ment** Schwächung *f*.

en·feoff [in'fef] belehnen; **en'feoff·ment** Belehnung *f*; Lehnsbrief *m*.

en·fi·lade ⚔ [enfi'leid] **1.** Längsbestreichung *f*; **2.** bestreichen.

en·fold [in'fəuld] einhüllen; umfassen.

en·force [in'fɔ:s] erzwingen (*upon s.o.* von j-m); durchsetzen (*upon s.o.* bei j-m); aufzwingen (*upon s.o.* j-m); bestehen auf (*dat.*); zur Geltung bringen, durchführen; **en'force·a·ble** erzwingbar; vollstreckbar; **en'force·ment** Erzwingung *f*; Geltendmachung *f*; Durchführung *f*.

en·fran·chise [in'fræntʃaiz] das Wahlrecht verleihen (*dat.*); *Sklaven* befreien; **en'fran·chise·ment** [~tʃizmənt] Verleihung *f* des Wahlrechts; Freilassung *f*.

en·gage [in'geidʒ] *v/t.* ein-, anstellen; verpflichten; mieten; in Anspruch nehmen; ⚔ angreifen; *be ~d* verlobt sein (*to* mit); beschäftigt sein (*in* mit); besetzt sein; *~ the clutch* einkuppeln; *v/i.* sich verpflichten, versprechen, garantieren;

sich beschäftigen (*in* mit); ⚔ angreifen; ⊕ greifen (*Zahnräder*); **en·gaged sig·nal** *od.* **tone** *teleph.* Besetztzeichen *n*; **en'gage·ment** Verpflichtung *f*; Verlobung *f*; Verabredung *f*; Stellung *f*, Beschäftigung *f*; ⚔ Gefecht *n*, Kampf *m*; ⊕ Einrücken *n e-s Ganges etc.*; **en·gage·ment ring** Verlobungsring *m*.

en·gag·ing *fig.* □ [in'geidʒiŋ] gewinnend, einnehmend.

en·gen·der *fig.* [in'dʒendə] erzeugen, hervorbringen, -rufen.

en·gine ['endʒin] Maschine *f*, Motor *m*; 🚂 Lokomotive *f*; Feuerspritze *f*; *fig.* Mittel *n*, Werkzeug *n*; **'en·gined** ...motorig; **'en·gine-driv·er** Lokomotivführer *m*.

en·gi·neer [endʒi'niə] **1.** Ingenieur *m*, Techniker *m*; Maschinenbauer *m*; ⚔ Pionier *m*; ⚓ Maschinist *m*; *Am.* Lokomotivführer *m*; **2.** Ingenieur sein; bauen; F deichseln; **en·gi'neer·ing** Maschinenbau *m*; Ingenieurwesen *n*; F Manipulation *f*; *attr.* technisch; Ingenieur...

en·gine...: **'~-fit·ter** Maschinenschlosser *m*; **'~·man** Maschinist *m*; Lokomotivführer *m*.

en·gird [in'gə:d] (*irr. gird*) umgürten; *fig.* umgeben.

Eng·lish ['iŋgliʃ] **1.** englisch; **2.** Englisch *n*; *the* ~ *pl.* die Engländer *pl.*; *in plain* ~ *fig.* unverblümt; *the Queen's* (*King's*) ~ korrektes Englisch *n*; **'~·man** Engländer *m*; **'~·wom·an** Engländerin *f*.

en·gorge [in'gɔ:dʒ] gierig verschlingen; überfüllen.

en·graft [in'grɑ:ft] pfropfen; *fig.* einprägen (in *dat.*); (ein)pfropfen (*into* in *acc.*); aufpfropfen (*on dat.*).

en·grain [in'grein] tief färben; *fig.* (unauslöschlich) einprägen; **en'grained** eingefleischt, unverbesserlich; eingewurzelt.

en·grave [in'greiv] gravieren, stechen; einmeißeln; *fig.* einprägen; **en'grav·er** Graveur *m*, Stecher *m*; ~ *on copper* Kupferstecher *m*; **en'grav·ing** Gravieren *n etc.*; (Kupfer-, Stahl)Stich *m*; Holzschnitt *m*.

en·gross [in'grəus] an sich ziehen; ganz in Anspruch nehmen; ins reine schreiben; *Unterhaltung* völlig an sich reißen; *~ed in* vertieft in, beschäftigt mit; *~ing* fesselnd; *~ing hand* Kanzleischrift *f*; **en'gross·ment** Anhäufung *f von Besitz*; Inanspruchnahme *f* (*of, with* durch); Urkunde *f*.

en·gulf [in'gʌlf] *fig.* verschlingen (*Abgrund*); (in e-n Abgrund) stürzen.

en·hance [in'hɑ:ns] steigern, vergrößern, erhöhen; **en'hance·ment** Steigerung *f*, Vergrößerung *f*, Erhöhung *f*.

e·nig·ma [i'nigmə] Rätsel *n*; **e·nig·mat·ic, e·nig·mat·i·cal** □ [enig'mætik(əl)] rätselhaft.

en·join [in'dʒɔin] auferlegen, anbefehlen (*on, upon s.o.* j-m).

en·joy [in'dʒɔi] sich erfreuen an (*dat.*), sich freuen über (*acc.*); Gefallen finden an (*dat.*), Freude haben an (*dat.*); genießen; *did you ~ it?* hat es Ihnen gefallen?; *~ o.s.* sich gut unterhalten *od.* amüsieren; *I ~ my dinner* es schmeckt mir; **en'joy·a·ble** genußreich, erfreulich; angenehm; **en'joy·ment** Genuß *m*, Vergnügen *n*, Freude *f*.

en·kin·dle [in'kindl] entzünden, entflammen (*a. fig.*).

en·lace [in'leis] umschlingen.

en·large [in'lɑ:dʒ] *v/t.* erweitern, ausdehnen; vergrößern (*a. phot.*); *v/i.* sich erweitern *etc.*; *fig.* sich verbreiten (*on, upon* über *acc.*); **en'large·ment** Erweiterung *f*, Ausdehnung *f*; Vergrößerung *f*; **en'larg·er** *phot.* Vergrößerungsgerät *n*.

en·light·en [in'laitn] *fig.* erleuchten; *j.* aufklären, belehren; **en'light·en·ment** Aufklärung *f*.

en·list [in'list] *v/t. Soldaten* anwerben; gewinnen (*in* für); *~ed man* ⚔ Soldat *m*; *v/i.* sich anwerben lassen, sich freiwillig melden; *~ in* eintreten für; **en'list·ment** ⚔ (An-)Werbung *f*; *fig.* Gewinnung *f*.

en·liv·en [in'laivn] beleben; *fig.* ankurbeln.

en·mesh [in'meʃ] umgarnen.

en·mi·ty ['enmiti] Feindschaft *f*.

en·no·ble [i'nəubl] adeln (*a. fig.*); veredeln.

e·nor·mi·ty [i'nɔ:miti] Ungeheuerlichkeit *f*; **e'nor·mous** □ ungeheuer, gewaltig, riesig.

e·nough [i'nʌf] genug; *sure ~!* freilich!, gewiß!; *well ~* recht wohl; ziemlich gut; *be kind ~ to inf.* so

freundlich sein zu *inf.*
en·plane [in'plein] = *emplane.*
en·quire [in'kwaiə] = *inquire.*
en·rage [in'reidʒ] wütend machen; **en'raged** wütend (*at* über *acc.*).
en·rap·ture [in'ræptʃə] entzücken.
en·rich [in'ritʃ] bereichern; anreichern; verzieren; **en'rich·ment** Bereicherung *f*; Verzierung *f*.
en·rol(l) [in'rəul] *in e-e Liste* eintragen; ⚔ anwerben; *in e-n Verein etc.* aufnehmen; protokollieren; aufzeichnen; ~ (o.s.) sich einschreiben lassen; sich anwerben lassen; **en'rol(l)·ment** Eintragung *f etc.*; Verzeichnis *n*; Stärke *f*, Schüler-, Studenten-, Teilnehmerzahl *f*.
en route [ɑ̃:n'ru:t] unterwegs.
en·san·guined [in'sæŋgwind] blutbefleckt.
en·sconce [in'skɔns] verbergen; *mst* ~ *o.s.* F es sich bequem machen.
en·sem·ble [ɑ̃:n'sɑ̃:mbl] Gesamteindruck *m*; *thea.*, ♪ Ensemble *n*; *Kleider*: Komplet *n*, Ensemble *n*.
en·shrine [in'ʃrain] einschließen, (als Heiligtum) verwahren.
en·shroud [in'ʃraud] einhüllen.
en·sign ['ensain] Fahne *f*, Flagge *f*; Abzeichen *n*; ⚓ *Am.* ['ensn] Leutnant *m* zur See.
en·si·lage ['ensilidʒ] **1.** Silospeicherung *f*, -futter *n*; **2.** = **en·sile** [in'sail] in e-m Silo einlagern.
en·slave [in'sleiv] zum Sklaven machen (*to gen.*); versklaven, knechten; **en'slave·ment** Versklavung *f*, Knechtung *f*; **en'slav·er** Unterjocher *m* (*bsd. fig.*).
en·snare [in'snɛə] in e-r Schlinge fangen; *fig.* verführen.
en·sue [in'sju:] folgen, sich ergeben (*from, on* aus); (nach)folgen.
en·sure [in'ʃuə] sichern, sicherstellen (*against, from* gegen); garantieren.
en·tab·la·ture ⚠ [en'tæblətʃə] Säulengebälk *n*.
en·tail [in'teil] **1.** zur Folge haben, mit sich bringen; als unveräußerliches Gut vererben; **2.** (Übertragung *f* als) unveräußerliches Gut *n*.
en·tan·gle [in'tæŋgl] (in ein Netz *etc.*) verwickeln (*a. fig.*); *fig.* verstricken; verworren machen; **en'tan·gle·ment** Verwicklung *f*; ⚔ *Draht*-Verhau *m*.
en·tente [ɑ̃:n'tɑ̃:nt] Bündnis *n*.
en·ter ['entə] *v/t.* (ein)treten in (*acc.*); betreten; einsteigen, -fahren *etc.* in (*acc.*); eindringen in (*acc.*); in *die Debatte* eingreifen; hineinbringen; einschreiben, eintragen, ✈ buchen; *Protest* einbringen; einstellen, aufnehmen; melden; *Tier* abrichten; *it* ~*ed his head* es kam ihm in den Sinn; ~ *s.o. at school* j. zur Schule anmelden; ~ *up* ✈ buchen; *v/i.* eintreten; sich einschreiben; *Sport*: melden, nennen (*for* zu); aufgenommen werden; ~ *Macbeth thea.* Macbeth tritt auf; ~ *into* hineingehen, hereinkommen *etc.* in (*acc.*); *Unterhaltung etc.* anfangen; *fig.* eingehen auf *e-n Vorschlag*; *fig. Bündnis etc.* eingehen; *Thema* anschneiden; ~ (*up*)*on* betreten; eintreten in *ein Amt, Lebensjahr*; sich einlassen auf *ein Unternehmen, Thema etc.*; ⚖ Besitz *e-r Sache* antreten.
en·ter·ic ⚕ [en'terik] Darm...; **en·ter·i·tis** [~tə'raitis] Darmkatarrh *m*.
en·ter·prise ['entəpraiz] Unternehmung *f*, -nehmen *n*; Betrieb *m*; Unternehmertum *n*; Unternehmungsgeist *m*, -lust *f*; *private* ~ freie Wirtschaft *f*; **'en·ter·pris·ing** □ unternehmend; unternehmungslustig; kühn.
en·ter·tain [entə'tein] unterhalten; bewirten; in Erwägung ziehen; *Meinung etc.* hegen; eingehen auf (*acc.*); *they* ~ *a great deal* sie geben oft Gesellschaften; ~ *s.o. to supper* j. zum Abendessen einladen; **enter'tain·er** Gastgeber *m*, Wirt *m*; Unterhaltungskünstler *m*; **en·ter'tain·ing** □ unterhaltend, amüsant; **en·ter'tain·ment** Unterhaltung *f*; Aufnahme *f*, Bewirtung *f*; Fest *n*, Gesellschaft *f*; ~ *tax* Vergnügungssteuer *f*.
en·thral(l) [in'θrɔ:l] *fig.* bezaubern, fesseln.
en·throne [in'θrəun] auf den Thron setzen; **en'throne·ment, en·thron·i·za·tion** [enθrəunai'zeiʃən] Einsetzung *f* (als Herrscher).
en·thuse F [in'θju:z]: ~ *over* schwärmen von, sich begeistern für.
en·thu·si·asm [in'θju:ziæzəm] Begeisterung *f*; **en'thu·si·ast** [~æst] Schwärmer(in) (*for, of* für); **en·thu·si'as·tic** (~*ally*) begeistert (*at, about* von).
en·tice [in'tais] (ver)locken; **en-**

ˈ**tice·ment** Verlockung *f*, Reiz *m*; **enˈtic·er** Verführer(in); **enˈtic·ing** □ verführerisch, verlockend.

en·tire □ [inˈtaiə] ganz, unversehrt; vollständig; ungeteilt, voll; vollzählig; nicht kastriert (*Pferd etc.*); **enˈtire·ly** völlig, durchaus; lediglich; **enˈtire·ness** Vollständigkeit *f*; Unversehrtheit *f*; **enˈtire·ty** Gesamtheit *f*.

en·ti·tle [inˈtaitl] betiteln; berechtigen (*to* zu); *be* ~*d to* Anspruch haben auf (*acc.*).

en·ti·ty [ˈentiti] Wesen(heit *f*) *n*; Dasein *n*; *legal* ~ juristische Person *f*.

en·tomb [inˈtuːm] begraben; **enˈtomb·ment** Begräbnis *n*.

en·to·mol·o·gy *zo.* [entəˈmɔlədʒi] Insektenkunde *f*.

entr'acte *thea.* [ˈɔntrækt] Zwischenspiel *n*.

en·trails [ˈentreilz] *pl.* Eingeweide *n/pl.*; Innere *n*.

en·train ⚔ [inˈtrein] in e-n Eisenbahnzug verladen *od.* steigen.

en·trance[1] [ˈentrəns] Ein-, Zutritt *m*; Einfahrt *f*, Eingang *m*, Einzug *m*; Antritt *m* (*into od. upon office* des Amtes); Eintrittsgeld *n*; *thea.* Auftritt *m*; Einlaß *m*; Eingang *m*, *Hafen*-Einfahrt *f*.

en·trance[2] [inˈtrɑːns] entzücken, hinreißen.

en·trance... [ˈentrəns]: ~ **ex·am·i·na·tion** Aufnahmeprüfung *f*; ~ **fee**, ~ **mon·ey** Eintritt(sgeld *n*) *m*.

en·trant [ˈentrənt] (neu) Eintretende *m*; *Sport*: Teilnehmer *m*.

en·trap [inˈtræp] (ein)fangen; bestricken; verleiten (*into, to* zu).

en·treat [inˈtriːt] (inständig) bitten, ersuchen; *et.* erbitten (*of* von); **enˈtreat·y** (dringende) Bitte *f*, Gesuch *n*.

en·trée [ˈɔntrei] Zutritt *m*; Entrée *n*, Zwischengericht *n*.

en·trench [inˈtrentʃ] ⚔ verschanzen; *fig.* einwurzeln; **enˈtrench·ment** Verschanzung *f*.

en·tre·pre·neur [ɔntrəprəˈnəː] Unternehmer *m*; **en·tre·pre·neur·i·al** [~ˈnəːriəl] Unternehmer...

en·trust [inˈtrʌst] anvertrauen (*s.th. to s.o.* j-m et.); betrauen (*s.o. with s.th.* j. mit et.).

en·try [ˈentri] Eintritt *m*; Eingang *m*, Einzug *m*; ⚖ Besitzantritt *m* (*on, upon gen.*); Eintragung *f*, Notiz *f*; Zolldeklaration *f*; *gebuchter* Posten *m*; Eingang *m von Geldern etc.*; *Sport*: Nennung(sliste) *f*, Meldung *f*; Eingang(stür *f etc.*) *m*; ~ *permit* Einreisegenehmigung *f*; ~ *visa* Einreisevisum *n*; *make an* ~ *of s.th.* et. buchen; *book-keeping by double (single)* ~ doppelte (einfache) Buchführung *f*; ˈ~**·phone** Sprechanlage *f*.

en·twine [inˈtwain], **en·twist** [inˈtwist] (um)winden; verflechten.

e·nu·mer·ate [iˈnjuːməreit] aufzählen; **e·nu·merˈa·tion** Aufzählung *f*.

e·nun·ci·ate [iˈnʌnsieit] verkünden; *Lehrsatz etc.* aufstellen; aussprechen; **e·nun·ciˈa·tion** Aufstellung *f*; Aussprache *f*; Ausdrucksweise *f*.

en·vel·op [inˈveləp] einhüllen; einwickeln; umhüllen, -geben; ⚔ einkreisen; **en·ve·lope** [ˈenvələup], *Am. a.* **en·vel·op** [inˈveləp] Briefumschlag *m*; (Ballon)Hülle *f*; **en·vel·op·ment** [inˈveləpmənt] Umhüllung *f*.

en·ven·om [inˈvenəm] vergiften; *fig. a.* verschärfen.

en·vi·a·ble □ [ˈenviəbl] beneidenswert; ˈ**en·vi·er** Neider(in); ˈ**en·vi·ous** □ neidisch (*of* auf *acc.*).

en·vi·ron [inˈvaiərən] umringen, umgeben; **enˈvi·ron·ment** Umgebung *f e-r Person*; **en·vi·ron·men·tal** [~ˈmentl] Umwelt...; **en·vi·ronˈmen·tal·ist** [~təlist] Umweltschützer *m*; **en·vi·rons** [ˈenvirənz] *pl.* Umgebung *f e-r Stadt*.

en·vis·age [inˈvizidʒ] *e-r Gefahr* ins Auge sehen; *Ziel* ins Auge fassen; sich *et.* vorstellen, betrachten.

en·vi·sion [inˈviʒən] sich *et.* vorstellen.

en·voy[1] [ˈenvɔi] Gesandte *m*; Bote *m*.

en·voy[2] [~] Schlußstrophe *f*.

en·vy [ˈenvi] **1.** Neid *m* (*of s.o.* auf j.; *of od. at s.th.* über, auf et.); *his car is the* ~ *of his friends* um s-n Wagen beneiden ihn s-e Freunde; **2.** beneiden (*s.o. s.th.* j. um et.).

en·wrap [inˈræp] einwickeln, -hüllen.

en·zyme *biol.* [ˈenzaim] Enzym *n*.

e·on [ˈiːən] = *aeon*.

ep·au·let(te) [ˈepəulet] Epaulette *f*, Achsel-, Schulterstück *n*.

e·pergne [iˈpəːn] Tafelaufsatz *m*.
e·phem·er·a *zo.* [iˈfemərə], **eˈphem·er·on** [~rɔn] *pl. a.* **eˈphem·er·a** [~rə] Eintagsfliege *f*; **eˈphem·er·al** kurzlebig; vergänglich.
ep·ic [ˈepik] **1.** □ episch; **2.** Epos *n*.
ep·i·cure [ˈepikjuə] Feinschmecker *m*, Genießer *m*, Epikureer *m*; **ep·i·cu·re·an** [~ˈriːən] **1.** genußsüchtig, epikureisch; **2.** = *epicure*.
ep·i·dem·ic [epiˈdemik] **1.** (*~ally*) epidemisch, seuchenartig; *~ disease* = **2.** Seuche *f*, Epidemie *f*.
ep·i·der·mis *anat.* [epiˈdəːmis] Oberhaut *f*.
ep·i·di·a·scope [epiˈdaiəskəup] Epidiaskop *n*, Bildwerfer *m*.
ep·i·gram [ˈepigræm] Epigramm *n*; **ep·i·gram·mat·ic, ep·i·gram·mat·i·cal** □ [~grəˈmætik(əl)] epigrammatisch.
ep·i·lep·sy ⚕ [ˈepilepsi] Epilepsie *f*; **ep·iˈlep·tic** ⚕ **1.** epileptisch; **2.** Epileptiker(in).
ep·i·logue [ˈepilɔg] Nachwort *n*.
E·piph·a·ny [iˈpifəni] Dreikönigsfest *n*, -tag *m*.
e·pis·co·pa·cy [iˈpiskəpəsi] bischöfliche Verfassung *f*; **eˈpis·co·pal** bischöflich; **e·pis·co·pa·li·an** [~kəuˈpeiljən] Anhänger *m* der Episkopalkirche; **eˈpis·co·pate** [~kəupit] Episkopat *n*, Bischofswürde *f*; Bistum *n*.
ep·i·sode [ˈepisəud] Episode *f*; Ereignis *n*; **ep·i·sod·ic, ep·i·sod·i·cal** □ [~ˈsɔdik(əl)] episodisch.
e·pis·tle [iˈpisl] Epistel *f*, Sendschreiben *n*; **eˈpis·to·lar·y** [~tələri] brieflich; Brief...
ep·i·taph [ˈepitɑːf] Grabschrift *f*.
ep·i·thet [ˈepiθet] Beiwort *n*; Beiname *m*; Attribut *n*; Epitheton *n*.
e·pit·o·me [iˈpitəmi] Auszug *m*, Abriß *m*; Inhaltsangabe *f*; **eˈpit·o·mize** e-n Auszug machen *od.* geben von; (zs.-)drängen.
ep·och [ˈiːpɔk] Epoche *f*; **ˈ~-mak·ing** epochemachend.
ep·o·xy [iˈpɔksi] Epoxyd *n*.
Ep·som salts [ˈepsəmˈsɔːlts] *pl.* Bittersalz *n*.
eq·ua·bil·i·ty [ekwəˈbiliti] Gleichförmigkeit *f*; Gleichmut *m*; **ˈeq·ua·ble** □ gleichförmig, -mäßig; *fig.* gleichmütig.
e·qual [ˈiːkwəl] **1.** □ gleich, gleichmäßig, -förmig; gleichberechtigt; angemessen; ebenbürtig; *~ to* fähig zu; gewachsen (*dat.*); *~ opportunities pl.* Chancengleichheit *f*; *~ rights pl.* Gleichberechtigung *f*; **2.** Gleiche *m*; *my ~s pl.* meinesgleichen; **3.** gleichen, gleichkommen (*dat.*); *not to be ~led* seinesgleichen nicht haben;
e·qual·i·ty [iːˈkwɔliti] Gleichheit *f*; Gleichberechtigung *f*; **e·qual·i·za·tion** [iːkwəlaiˈzeiʃən] Gleichmachung *f*; Ausgleich *m*; **ˈe·qual·ize** *v/t.* gleichmachen (*to, with dat.*); *v/i. Sport*: ausgleichen; **ˈe·qual·iz·er** *Sport*: Ausgleich(stor *n*) *m*.
e·qua·nim·i·ty [ekwəˈnimiti] Gleichmut *m*.
e·quate [iˈkweit] gleichsetzen, -stellen (*to, with dat.*); **eˈqua·tion** Ausgleich *m*; ⅄ Gleichung *f*; **eˈqua·tor** Äquator *m*; **e·qua·to·ri·al** □ [ekwəˈtɔːriəl] äquatorial.
eq·uer·ry [iˈkweri] Stallmeister *m*.
e·ques·tri·an [iˈkwestriən] **1.** Reit..., Reiter...; **2.** (Kunst)Reiter *m*.
e·qui·dis·tant [ˈiːkwiˈdistənt] gleich weit entfernt.
e·qui·lat·er·al □ [ˈiːkwiˈlætərəl] gleichseitig.
e·qui·li·brate [iːkwiˈlaibreit] *v/t.* ins Gleichgewicht bringen; im Gleichgewicht halten; *v/i.* im Gleichgewicht sein; **e·quil·i·brist** [iːˈkwilibrist] Seiltänzer *m*; **e·quiˈlib·ri·um** [~əm] Gleichgewicht *n*; Ausgleich *m*.
e·quine *zo.* [ˈiːkwain] pferdeartig; Pferde...
e·qui·noc·tial [iːkwiˈnɔkʃəl] Äquinoktial...; **e·qui·nox** [ˈ~nɔks] Tagundnachtgleiche *f*.
e·quip [iˈkwip] ausrüsten; ausstatten; einrichten; **eq·ui·page** [ˈekwipidʒ] Ausrüstung *f*; Equipage *f*, Kutsche *f*; **e·quip·ment** [iˈkwipmənt] Ausrüstung *f*, -stattung *f*; Einrichtung *f*; Gerätschaften *f/pl.*; *fig.* Rüstzeug *n*.
e·qui·poise [ˈekwipɔiz] **1.** Gleichgewicht *n*; Gegengewicht *n*; **2.** aufwiegen; im Gleichgewicht halten.
eq·ui·ta·ble □ [ˈekwitəbl] billig, gerecht; **ˈeq·ui·ty** Billigkeit *f*; ⚖ Billigkeitsrecht *n*; *equities pl.* Aktien *f/pl.*
e·quiv·a·lence [iˈkwivələns] Gleichwertigkeit *f*; **eˈquiv·a·lent 1.** gleichwertig; gleichbedeutend (*to* mit); **2.** Äquivalent *n*, Gegenwert *m*;

Gegenstück *n*, *genaue* Entsprechung *f*.
e·quiv·o·cal □ [i'kwivəkəl] zweideutig, zweifelhaft; **e'quiv·o·calness** Zweideutigkeit *f*; **e'quiv·o·cate** [~keit] zweideutig reden; **e·quiv·o'ca·tion** Zweideutigkeit *f*; Wortverdrehung *f*.
eq·ui·voque, eq·ui·voke ['ekwivəuk] Wortspiel *n*; Zweideutigkeit *f*.
e·ra ['iərə] Ära *f*, Zeitrechnung *f*; Zeitalter *n*.
e·rad·i·cate [i'rædikeit] ausrotten; **e·rad·i'ca·tion** Ausrottung *f*.
e·rase [i'reiz] auskratzen; ausradieren, -streichen; auslöschen (*a. fig.*); **e'ras·er** Radiermesser *n*, -gummi *m*; **e'ra·sure** [~ʒə] Ausradieren *n*; radierte Stelle *f*.
ere *poet.* [εə] **1.** *cj.* ehe, bevor; **2.** *prp.* vor; ~ *this* schon früher; ~ *long* bald; ~ *now* vormals.
e·rect [i'rekt] **1.** □ aufrecht; zu Berge stehend (*Haare*); **2.** aufrichten; *Denkmal etc.* errichten; *Theorie etc.* aufstellen; **e'rect·ing** Montage *f*; **e'rec·tion** Auf-, Errichtung *f*; Gebäude *n*; **e'rectness** Geradheit *f*, aufrechte Haltung *f*; **e'rec·tor** Errichter *m*, Erbauer *m*.
er·e·mite ['erimait] Einsiedler *m*; **er·e·mit·ic** [~'mitik] einsiedlerisch.
erg *phys.* [ə:g] Erg *n* (*Arbeitseinheit*).
er·go·nom·ics [ə:gəu'nɔmiks] *sg.* Ergonomie *f*, Arbeitswissenschaft *f*.
er·got ⚘ ['ə:gət] Mutterkorn *n*.
er·mine ['ə:min] *zo.* Hermelin *n*; Hermelin(pelz) *m*; *fig.* Richterwürde *f*.
e·rode [i'rəud] zer-, wegfressen; erodieren.
e·rog·e·nous [i'rɔdʒinəs] erogen.
e·ro·sion [i'rəuʒən] Zerfressung *f*, ⚕, *geol.* Erosion *f*; **e'ro·sive** [~siv] zerfressend.
e·rot·ic [i'rɔtik] **1.** erotisch; **2.** erotisches Gedicht *n*; **e'rot·i·cism** [~sizəm] Erotik *f*.
err [ə:] (sich) irren; fehlen, sündigen.
er·rand ['erənd] Botengang *m*, Auftrag *m*; *fool's* ~ Metzgergang *m*, vergebliches Bemühen *n*; *go (on)* ~*s* Botengänge machen; **'~-boy** Laufbursche *m*.
er·rant □ ['erənt] irrend; *s. knight-*~; **'er·rant·ry** Umherschweifen *n*; Irrfahrt *f e-s Ritters*.
er·rat·ic [i'rætik] (~*ally*) wandernd; regellos; unberechenbar; ~ *fever* Wechselfieber *n*; **er·ra·tum** [e'rɑ:təm], *pl.* **er'ra·ta** [~tə] Druckfehler *m*.
er·ro·ne·ous □ [i'rəunjəs] irrig.
er·ror ['erə] Irrtum *m*, Fehler *m*; ~ *of judgement* Fehlschluß *m*; ~ *rate* Fehlerquote *f*; ~*s excepted* Irrtümer vorbehalten.
Erse [ə:s] **1.** gälisch; irisch; **2.** Gälisch *n*; Irisch *n*.
erst·while ['ə:stwail] früher, ehedem; ehemalig.
e·ruc·ta·tion [i:rʌk'teiʃən] Aufstoßen *n*, Rülpsen *n*; Ausbruch *m*.
er·u·dite □ ['eru:dait] gelehrt; **er·u·di·tion** [~'diʃən] Gelehrsamkeit *f*.
e·rupt [i'rʌpt] ausbrechen (*Vulkan*); durchbrechen (*Zähne*); **e'rup·tion** Ausbruch *m e-s Vulkans* (*a. fig.*); ⚕ Hautausschlag *m*; **e'rup·tive** ausbrechend; eruptiv; Eruptiv...
er·y·sip·e·las ⚕ [eri'sipiləs] Erysipel *n*, (Wund)Rose *f*.
es·ca·late ⚔ *u. fig.* ['eskəleit] *v/t.* eskalieren, steigern; *v/i.* sich steigern; in die Höhe schnellen (*Preise etc.*); **es·ca'la·tion** Eskalation *f*, Steigerung *f*.
es·ca·la·tor ['eskəleitə] Rolltreppe *f*.
es·ca·lope ['eskələup] Schnitzel *n*.
es·ca·pade [eskə'peid] toller Streich *m*, Eskapade *f*; *fig.* Seitensprung *m*; **es·cape** [is'keip] **1.** *v/t.* entschlüpfen, entgehen (*dat.*); umgehen; *j-m* entfallen; *v/i.* entkommen, entrinnen (*from dat.*); ausbrechen; entweichen (*Gas etc.*); **2.** Entrinnen *n*, Flucht *f*; Rettung *f*; Entweichen *n*; (Mittel *n* der) Entspannung *f*; *attr.* Abfluß...; Auslaß...; ~ *artist* Entfesselungskünstler *m*; ~ *hatch* Notluke *f*, -ausstieg *m*; *have a narrow* ~ mit knapper Not davon- *od.* entkommen; **es·ca·pee** [eskei'pi:] Ausbrecher *m*, Flüchtling *m*; **es·cape·ment** ⊕ [is'keipmənt] Hemmung *f an der Uhr*; **es'cap·ism** Eskapismus *m*, Wirklichkeitsflucht *f*; **es'cap·ist** 1. j., der die Wirklichkeit flieht; 2. Illusions...
es·carp [is'kɑ:p] **1.** *a.* **es'carpment** Böschung *f*, Abdachung *f*; **2.** böschen, abdachen.
es·cheat ⚖ [is'tʃi:t] **1.** Heimfall *m*

an den Staat etc.; **2.** *v/i.* heimfallen; *v/t.* konfiszieren.
es·chew [is'tʃu:] scheuen, (ver-)meiden.
es·cort 1. ['eskɔ:t] Eskorte *f*; Geleit *n* (*a. fig.*); Begleitung *f*; **2.** [is'kɔ:t] eskortieren, geleiten.
es·cri·toire [eskri:'twɑ:] Schreibpult *n*.
es·cu·lent ['eskjulənt] **1.** eßbar; **2.** Nahrungsmittel *n*.
es·cutch·eon [is'kʌtʃən] Wappenschild *m, n*; Namenschild *n*.
Es·ki·mo ['eskiməu] Eskimo *m*.
e·soph·a·gus [i:'sɔfəgəs] = *oesophagus*.
es·o·ter·ic [esəu'terik] esoterisch, nur für Eingeweihte.
es·pal·ier ✓ [is'pæljə] Spalier *n*; Spalierbaum *m*.
es·pe·cial [is'peʃəl] besonder; vorzüglich; **es'pe·cial·ly** besonders.
Es·per·an·to [espə'ræntəu] Esperanto *n*.
es·pi·al [is'paiəl] Spähen *n*.
es·pi·o·nage [espiə'nɑ:ʒ] Spionage *f*.
es·pla·nade [esplə'neid] Esplanade *f*; Promenade *f*.
es·pous·al [is'pauzəl] Eintreten *n* (*of* für); **es'pouse** heiraten; sich *e-r Sache* annehmen.
es·pres·so [es'presəu] Espresso *m* (*Kaffee*); ~ **bar,** ~ **ca·fé** Espresso (-bar *f*) *n*.
es·py [is'pai] erspähen, erblicken.
es·quire [is'kwaiə] Landedelmann *m*, Gutsbesitzer *m*; *auf Briefen*: *John Smith Esq.* Herrn John Smith.
es·say 1. [e'sei] versuchen; probieren; **2.** ['esei] Versuch *m* (*at* mit), Probe *f*; Aufsatz *m*, kurze Abhandlung *f*, Essay *m*; **'es·say·ist** Essayist *m*.
es·sence ['esns] Geist *m*, Wesen *n* *e-r Sache*; Extrakt *m*; Essenz *f*;
es·sen·tial [i'senʃəl] **1.** □ (*to*) wesentlich (für); wichtig (für); ~ *likeness* Wesensgleichheit *f*; ~ *oil* ätherisches Öl *n*; **2.** *das* Wesentliche, Hauptsache *f*; Grundzug *m*; **es'sen·tial·ly** im Grunde genommen.
es·tab·lish [is'tæbliʃ] festsetzen; errichten, gründen; einrichten, -führen; *Beamten etc.* einsetzen; *Kinder* versorgen; nachweisen; ~ *o.s.* sich niederlassen *od.* etablieren; ≈*ed Church* Staatskirche *f*; ~*ed merchant* selbständiger Kaufmann *m*;
es'tab·lish·ment Festsetzung *f*; Gründung *f*; Er-, Einrichtung *f*; (*bsd. großer*) Haushalt *m*; Anstalt *f*; Firma *f*; *das* Establishment, *die* herrschenden Kreise *m/pl.*; ⚔, ⚓ *Mannschafts*-Bestand *m*; *military* ~ stehendes Heer *n*.
es·tate [is'teit] Grundstück *n*; Landsitz *m*; Grundbesitz *m*, Gut *n*; Besitz *m*, Vermögen *n*; (Konkurs-)Masse *f*, Nachlaß *m*; Stand *m*, Klasse *f*; *family* ~ Familienbesitz *m*; *personal* ~ bewegliches Eigentum *n*; *real* ~ Liegenschaften *f/pl.*; *housing* ~ Wohnsiedlung *f*; *industrial* ~ Industriegebiet *n*; ~ **a·gent** Grundstücks-, Häusermakler *m*; ~ **car** Kombiwagen *m*; ~ **du·ty** Nachlaßsteuer *f*.
es·teem [is'ti:m] **1.** Achtung *f*, Ansehen *n* (*with* bei); **2.** (hoch)achten, (hoch)schätzen; erachten für.
es·ter ⚗ ['estə] Ester *m*.
es·thet·ic [i:s'θetik] = *aesthetic*.
Es·tho·ni·an [es'təunjən] **1.** Este *m*, Estin *f*; Estländisch *n*; **2.** estnisch.
es·ti·ma·ble ['estiməbl] achtens-, schätzenswert.
es·ti·mate 1. ['estimeit] (ab)schätzen; veranschlagen (*at* auf *acc.*); **2.** ['~mit] Schätzung *f*; (Vor)Anschlag *m*, Überschlag *m*; *the* ≈*s pl. parl.* der Haushaltsplan, das Budget; **es·ti·ma·tion** [~'meiʃən] Schätzung *f*; Urteil *n*, Meinung *f*; Achtung *f*; **'es·ti·ma·tor** Abschätzer *m*.
es·trade [es'trɑ:d] Estrade *f*, erhöhter Platz *m*.
es·trange [is'treindʒ] entfremden (*from s.o.* j-m); ~*d couple* getrennt lebendes Ehepaar *n*; **es'trangement** Entfremdung *f*.
es·tro·gen *biol.* ['estrədʒen] Östrogen *n*.
es·tu·ar·y ['estjuəri] Trichtermündung *f*.
et·cet·er·as [it'setrəz] *pl.* Kleinigkeiten *f/pl.*
etch [etʃ] ätzen, radieren; **'etch·ing** Radierung *f*; Kupferstich *m*.
e·ter·nal □ [i:'tə:nl] immerwährend, unaufhörlich, ewig; **e'ter·nal·ize** [~nəlaiz] verewigen; **e'ter·ni·ty** Ewigkeit *f*; **e'ter·nize** [~naiz] verewigen.
e·ther ['i:θə] Äther *m* (*a.* ⚗);
e·the·re·al □ [i:'θiəriəl] ätherisch (*a. fig.*); **'e·ther·ize** mit Äther be-

täuben, narkotisieren.

eth·i·cal □ ['eθikəl] sittlich, ethisch; **'eth·ics** *mst sg.* Sittenlehre *f*, Ethik *f*.

E·thi·o·pi·an [i:θi'əupjən] **1.** äthiopisch; **2.** Äthiopier(in).

eth·nic ['eθnik] ethnisch, völkisch; ~ *joke* Witz *m* auf Kosten e-r bestimmten Volksgruppe.

eth·nog·ra·phy [eθ'nɔgrəfi] Ethnographie *f*, (beschreibende) Völkerkunde *f*; **eth'nol·o·gy** [~lədʒi] Ethnologie *f*, (vergleichende) Völkerkunde *f*.

eth·yl ⚗ ['eθil; ⚗ 'i:θail] Äthyl *n*; **eth·yl·ene** ['eθili:n] Äthylen *n*, Kohlenwasserstoffgas *n*.

e·ti·o·late ['i:tiəuleit] etiolieren, *durch Lichtmangel* bleichen, vergeilen; *fig.* schwächen.

e·ti·ol·o·gy ⚕ [i:ti'ɔlədʒi] Ätiologie *f*, Ursachenforschung *f*.

et·i·quette ['etiket] Etikette *f*.

E·ton crop ['i:tn'krɔp] Herrenschnitt *m* (*Damenfrisur*).

E·trus·can [i'trʌskən] **1.** etruskisch; **2.** Etrusker(in); Etruskisch *n*.

et·y·mo·log·i·cal □ [etimə'lɔdʒikl] etymologisch; **et·y·mol·o·gy** [~'mɔlədʒi] Etymologie *f*, Wortableitung *f*.

eu·ca·lyp·tus ⚘ [ju:kə'liptəs] Eukalyptus *m*.

Eu·cha·rist ['ju:kərist] Abendmahl *n*.

Eu·clid ⩘ ['ju:klid] euklidische Geometrie *f*.

eu·gen·ic [ju:'dʒenik] (~*ally*) eugenisch; **eu'gen·ics** *sg.* Eugenik *f*, Erbgesundheitslehre *f*.

eu·lo·gist ['ju:lədʒist] Lobredner *m*; **eu·lo·gize** ['~dʒaiz] loben; **eu·lo·gy** ['~dʒi] Lob(rede *f*) *n*.

eu·nuch ['ju:nək] Eunuch *m*.

eu·phe·mism ['ju:fimizəm] Euphemismus *m*, beschönigender Ausdruck *m*; **eu·phe'mis·tic, eu·phe'mis·ti·cal** □ beschönigend.

eu·phon·ic, eu·phon·i·cal □ [ju:'fɔnik(əl)] wohlklingend; **eu·pho·ny** ['ju:fəni] Wohlklang *m*.

eu·phor·ia [ju:'fɔ:riə] Euphorie *f*, Wohlbefinden *n*.

eu·phu·ism ['ju:fju:izəm] gezierte Ausdrucksweise *f*, Schwulst *m*.

Eur·a·sian [juə'reiʒjən] **1.** Eurasier (-in); **2.** eurasisch.

eu·re·ka [juə'ri:kə] heureka (*ich hab's gefunden*).

Eu·ro·cheque ['juərətʃek] Euroscheck *m*; **Eu·ro'com·mu·nism** Eurokommunismus *m*; **Eu·ro·crat** ['~kræt] Eurokrat *m*.

Eu·ro·pe·an [juərə'pi:ən] **1.** europäisch; ~ *Commission* Europäische Kommission *f*; ~ *Community* Europäische Gemeinschaft *f*; ~ *Court of Justice* Europäischer Gerichtshof *m*; ~ *Parliament* Europaparlament *n*; **2.** Europäer(in).

Eu·ro–pol·i·tics ['juərəpɔlitiks] *sg. od. pl.* Europapolitik *f*.

Eu·ro·vi·sion [juərə'viʒən] europäische Fernsehringsendung *f*, Eurovision *f*.

eu·tha·na·si·a [ju:θə'neizjə] Euthanasie *f* (*leichter Tod*; *Sterbehilfe*).

e·vac·u·ate [i'vækjueit] entleeren; evakuieren; *Land etc.* räumen; *Bewohner* aussiedeln; ⚕ abführen; **e·vac·u'a·tion** Entleerung *f*; Evakuierung *f*; **e·vac·u'ee** Evakuierte *m, f*.

e·vade [i'veid] (geschickt) ausweichen (*dat.*); umgehen, sich drücken um.

e·val·u·ate *bsd.* ⩘ [i'væljueit] zahlenmäßig bestimmen, auswerten; berechnen; **e·val·u'a·tion** Auswertung *f*; Berechnung *f*.

ev·a·nesce [i:və'nes] (ver)schwinden; **ev·a'nes·cence** (Dahin-) Schwinden *n*; **ev·a'nes·cent** □ (ver)schwindend.

e·van·gel·ic, e·van·gel·i·cal □ [i:væn'dʒelik(əl)] evangelisch; **e·van·ge·list** [i'vændʒilist] Evangelist *m*; **e'van·ge·lize** *j-m* das Evangelium predigen; bekehren.

e·vap·o·rate [i'væpəreit] verdunsten, verdampfen (lassen); *fig.* verschwinden, sich verflüchtigen; ~*ed milk* Kondensmilch *f*; **e·vap·o'ra·tion** Verdunstung *f*, Verdampfung *f*.

e·va·sion [i'veiʒən] Umgehung *f*; Ausflucht *f*; **e'va·sive** □ [~siv] ausweichend (*of dat.*); *be ~ fig.* ausweichen.

eve [i:v] Vorabend *m*; Vortag *m*; *poet.* Abend *m*; *on the ~ of* unmittelbar vor (*dat.*), am Vorabend (*gen.*).

e·ven[1] ['i:vən] **1.** *adj.* □ eben, gerade, gleich; gleichmäßig, -förmig; ausgeglichen; ruhig; glatt; gerade

(*Zahl*); unparteiisch; *make* ~ *with the ground* dem Boden gleichmachen; *be* ~ *with s.o.* mit j-m quitt sein; *get* ~ *with s.o. fig.* mit j-m abrechnen; *odd or* ~ gerade oder ungerade; *of* ~ *date* ⚕ gleichen Datums; *break* ~ F ohne Gewinn u. Verlust abschließen; **2.** *adv.* gerade, eben; selbst, sogar, auch; *vor comp.* noch; *not* ~ nicht einmal; ~ *though*, ~ *if* selbst wenn, wenn auch; **3.** ebnen, glätten; gleichstellen (*to dat.*).

e·ven² *poet.* [~] Abend *m.*

e·ven-hand·ed [ˈiːvənˈhændid] unparteiisch.

eve·ning [ˈiːvniŋ] Abend *m*; ~ *class* Abendkurs *m*; ~ *dress* Gesellschaftsanzug *m*, Frack *m*, Smoking *m*; Abendkleid *n*.

e·ven·ness [ˈiːvənnis] Ebenheit *f*; Geradheit *f*; Gleichmäßigkeit *f*; Unparteilichkeit *f*; Seelenruhe *f*.

e·ven·song [ˈiːvənsɔŋ] Abendgottesdienst *m*.

e·vent [iˈvent] Ereignis *n*, Vorfall *m*, Begebenheit *f*; *fig.* Ausgang *m*; sportliche Veranstaltung *f*; (Programm)Nummer *f*; *athletic* ~*s pl.* Leichtathletikwettkämpfe *m/pl.*; *table of* ~*s* Festprogramm *n*; *at all* ~*s* auf alle Fälle; *in any* ~ sowieso; *in the* ~ *of* im Falle (*gen.*).

e·ven-tem·pered [ˈiːvəntempəd] ausgeglichen; gelassen.

e·vent·ful [iˈventful] ereignisreich.

e·ven·tide *poet.* [ˈiːvəntaid] Abend *m*.

e·ven·tu·al □ [iˈventʃuəl] etwaig, möglich; schließlich; ~*ly* am Ende; schließlich, endlich; **e·ven·tu·al·i·ty** [~tjuˈæliti] Möglichkeit *f*; **eˈven·tu·ate** [~tjueit] endigen; die Folge sein.

ev·er [ˈevə] je, jemals; immer, immer wieder; ~ *so* noch so (sehr); *as soon as* ~ *I can* sobald ich nur irgend kann; ~ *after*, ~ *since* von der Zeit an; ~ *and anon* von Zeit zu Zeit; *for* ~, *for* ~ *and* ~, *for* ~ *and a day* für immer, auf ewig; *liberty for* ~*!* es lebe die Freiheit!; ~ *so much* F recht viel; *for* ~ *so much* um alles in der Welt; *I wonder who* ~ ich möchte wissen, wer nur ...; *the best* ~ F der beste, den es je gegeben hat; *yours* ~ stets Dein ... (*Briefschluß*); ˈ~**·glade** *Am.* sumpfiges Grasland *n*; ˈ~**·green 1.** immergrün; **2.** immergrüne Pflanze *f*; ~ˈ**last·ing 1.** □ ewig; dauerhaft **2.** Ewigkeit *f*; ⚘ Immortelle *f*; ˈ~ˈ**more** immerfort; stets.

ev·er·y [ˈevri] jede(r, -s); alle(s); ~ *bit as much* genau so viel; ~ *now and then* dann und wann; ~ *one of them* jeder von ihnen, alle ausnahmslos; ~ *other day* einen Tag um den andern; jeden zweiten Tag; ~ *twenty years* alle zwanzig Jahre; *her* ~ *movement* jede ihrer Bewegungen; ˈ~**·bod·y** jeder(mann); ˈ~**·day** Alltags...; ˈ~**·one** jeder (-mann); ˈ~**·thing** alles; ˈ~**·way** in jeder Hinsicht; ˈ~**·where** überall.

e·vict [iˈvikt] exmittieren; ausweisen; **eˈvic·tion** Exmittierung *f*; Ausweisung *f*; ~ *order* Räumungsbefehl *m*.

ev·i·dence [ˈevidəns] **1.** Beweis (-stück *n*, -material *n*) *m*, Befund *m*; ⚖ Zeugnis *n*; Zeuge *m*; *in* ~ als Beweis; deutlich sichtbar, zu sehen; *furnish* ~ *of*, *be* ~ *of et.* beweisen; *give* ~, *bear* ~ Zeugnis ablegen (*of* von; *for* für; *against* gegen); **2.** beweisen; zeigen; ˈ**ev·i·dent** □ augenscheinlich, offenbar, -sichtlich, klar; **ev·i·den·tial** □ [~ˈdenʃəl] als Beweis dienend.

e·vil [ˈiːvl] **1.** □ übel, schlimm; schlecht; *moralisch mst* böse; *the* ~ *eye* der böse Blick; *the* ♀ *One* der Böse (*Teufel*); **2.** Übel *n*, Böse *n*; ˈ~-ˈ**do·er** Übeltäter(in); ˈ~-ˈ**mind·ed** übelgesinnt, boshaft.

e·vince [iˈvins] zeigen, bekunden.

e·vis·cer·ate [iˈvisəreit] ausweiden.

ev·o·ca·tion [evəuˈkeiʃən] (Geister-) Beschwörung *f*; **e·voc·a·tive** [iˈvɔkətiv] beschwörend, wachrufend.

e·voke [iˈvəuk] (herauf)beschwören, wachrufen; hervorrufen.

ev·o·lu·tion [iːvəˈluːʃən] Entwicklung *f*; ⅌ Wurzelziehen *n*; ⚔ Entfaltung *f* e-r Formation; **ev·oˈlu·tion·a·ry** [~ʃnəri] Entwicklungs..., Evolutions...

e·volve [iˈvɔlv] (sich) entfalten, (sich) entwickeln; herausarbeiten.

ewe [juː] Mutterschaf *n*.

ew·er [ˈjuːə] Wasserkanne *f*, -krug *m*.

ex [eks] **1.** ⚕ ab *Fabrik etc.*; *Börse*: ohne; aus; **2.** *vor su.* ehemalig, früher; *ex-minister* Ex-Minister *m.*

ex·ac·er·bate [eks'æsə:beit] verschlimmern; verschärfen; erbittern.

ex·act [ig'zækt] **1.** □ genau; pünktlich; tatsächlich; **2.** *Zahlung* eintreiben; fordern; **ex'act·ing** streng, genau; anspruchsvoll; **ex'ac·tion** Eintreibung *f*; (ungebührliche) Forderung *f*; Erpressung *f*; **ex'act·i·tude** [~titju:d] Genauigkeit *f*; Pünktlichkeit *f*; **ex'act·ly** genau; *Antwort*: ganz recht; *not* ~ nicht gerade; **ex'act·ness** = *exactitude.*

ex·ag·ger·ate [ig'zædʒəreit] übertreiben; **ex·ag·ger'a·tion** Übertreibung *f.*

ex·alt [ig'zɔ:lt] erhöhen, erheben; verherrlichen, in den höchsten Tönen loben; **ex·al·ta·tion** [egzɔ:l'teiʃən] Erhöhung *f*, Erhebung *f*; Höhe *f*; Verzücktheit *f*; **ex·alt·ed** [ig'zɔ:ltid] erhaben, hoch; verzückt.

ex·am *Schul-sl.* [ig'zæm] Examen *n.*

ex·am·i·na·tion [igzæmi'neiʃən] Examen *n*, Prüfung *f*; Untersuchung *f*; Vernehmung *f*; **ex'am·ine** untersuchen (*a.* ~ *into s.th.* et.); prüfen, examinieren; verhören; **ex·am·i'nee** Prüfling *m*; **ex'am·in·er** Prüfer *m*; Untersucher *m*; **ex'am·in·ing bod·y** Prüfungsausschuß *m.*

ex·am·ple [ig'zɑ:mpl] Beispiel *n*; Vorbild *n*, Muster *n*; *beyond* ~ beispiellos; *for* ~ zum Beispiel; *make an* ~ *of* ein Exempel statuieren an *j-m*; *set an* ~ ein Beispiel geben.

ex·as·per·ate [ig'zɑ:spəreit] erbittern; (ver)ärgern; (auf)reizen; verschlimmern; **ex·as·per'a·tion** Erbitterung *f*, Ärger *m* (*of* über *acc.*).

ex·ca·vate ['ekskəveit] ausgraben, -heben, -schachten; **ex·ca'va·tion** Ausgrabung *f etc.*; Höhle *f*; **'ex·ca·va·tor** Trockenbagger *m*; Erdarbeiter *m.*

ex·ceed [ik'si:d] überschreiten, hinausgehen über (*acc.*); übertreffen (*in* an, in *dat.*); zu weit gehen; **ex'ceed·ing** übermäßig; **ex'ceed·ing·ly** außerordentlich, überaus.

ex·cel [ik'sel] *v/t.* übertreffen; *v/i.* sich auszeichnen (*in, at* in *dat.*); **ex·cel·lence** ['eksələns] Vortrefflichkeit *f*; hervorragende Leistung *f*; Vorzug *m*; **'Ex·cel·len·cy** Exzellenz *f* (*Titel*); **'ex·cel·lent** □ vortrefflich, ausgezeichnet, hervorragend.

ex·cept [ik'sept] **1.** ausnehmen, -schließen; Einwendungen machen; *present company* ~*ed* die Anwesenden ausgenommen; **2.** *cj.* außer, es sei denn, daß; **3.** *prp.* ausgenommen, außer; ~ *for* abgesehen von; **ex'cept·ing** *prp.* ausgenommen; **ex'cep·tion** Ausnahme *f*; Einwendung *f* (*to* gegen); *take* ~ *to* Anstoß nehmen an (*dat.*); **ex'cep·tion·a·ble** [~ʃnəbl] anstößig; **ex'cep·tion·al** außergewöhnlich; **ex'cep·tion·al·ly** ausnahmsweise.

ex·cerpt 1. [ek'sə:pt] *Schriftstelle* ausziehen, exzerpieren (*from* aus); **2.** ['eksə:pt] Auszug *m*, Exzerpt *n* (*from* aus).

ex·cess [ik'ses] Übermaß *n*; Überschuß *m*; Unmäßigkeit *f*, Ausschweifung *f*, Exzeß *m*; *attr.* Mehr...; *in* ~ *of* mehr als; *carry to* ~ *et.* übertreiben; ~ *charge* zusätzliche Gebühr *f*; ~ *fare* Zuschlag *m*; ~ *luggage* Übergewicht *n* (*Gepäck*); ~ *postage* Nachgebühr *f*; ~ *profit* Mehrgewinn *m*; **ex'ces·sive** □ übermäßig, übertrieben.

ex·change [iks'tʃeindʒ] **1.** (aus-, ein-, um)tauschen (*for* gegen); (aus-, um)wechseln; wert sein (*for acc.*); **2.** (Aus-, Um)Tausch *m*; (*bsd.* Geld)Wechsel *m*; *a. bill of* ~ Wechsel *m*; *a.* ♀ Börse *f*; Fernsprechamt *n*; *a. foreign* ~*s pl.* Devisen *f/pl.*; *in* ~ *for* (als Entgelt) für, gegen; *account of* ~ Wechselkonto *n*; ~ *control* Devisenbewirtschaftung *f*; ~ *list* Kurszettel *m*; *par of* ~ Wechselpari *n*; (*rate of*) ~ Wechselkurs *m*; ~ *student* Austauschstudent(in); **ex'change·a·ble** austauschbar (*for* gegen); ~ *value* Tauschwert *m.*

ex·cheq·uer [iks'tʃekə] Schatzamt *n*; Staatskasse *f*; *Chancellor of the* ♀ *britischer* Schatzkanzler *m*, Finanzminister *m*; ~ *bond* Schatzanweisung *f.*

ex·cise[1] [ek'saiz] **1.** indirekte Steuer *f*, Verbrauchssteuer *f*; **2.** besteuern.

ex·cise[2] [~] (her)ausschneiden; **ex·ci·sion** [ek'siʒən] Ausschneidung *f.*

ex·cit·a·bil·i·ty [iksaitə'biliti] Reizbarkeit *f*; **ex'cit·a·ble** reizbar; **ex·cit·ant** ['eksitənt] Reizmittel *n*; **ex·ci·ta·tion** [~'teiʃən] An-, Er-

regung *f*; Reizung *f*; **ex·cite** [ik'sait] erregen; anregen; reizen; *~d* aufgeregt; *get ~d* sich aufregen; **ex'cite·ment** Auf-, Erregung *f*; Anreizung *f*; **ex'cit·er** Erreger *m*; Reizmittel *n*; **ex'cit·ing** aufregend; erregend; spannend.
ex·claim [iks'kleim] ausrufen; eifern (*against* gegen).
ex·cla·ma·tion [ekskləˈmeiʃən] Ausruf(ung *f*) *m*; *~s pl.* Geschrei *n*; *note of ~, point of ~, ~ mark* Ausrufezeichen *n*; **ex·clam·a·to·ry** □ [~'klæmətəri] Ausrufe...; eifernd.
ex·clude [iks'klu:d] ausschließen.
ex·clu·sion [iks'klu:ʒən] Ausschließung *f*, Ausschluß *m*; *to the ~ of* unter Ausschluß (*gen.*); **ex'clu·sive** □ [~siv] ausschließend (*of acc.*); ausschließlich; sich abschließend, exklusiv; *~ of* ohne; *be mutually ~* einander ausschließen.
ex·cog·i·tate [eks'kɔdʒiteit] ausdenken, -hecken; **ex·cog·i'ta·tion** Ausdenken *n*, Erfindung *f*.
ex·com·mu·ni·cate [ekskə'mju:nikeit] exkommunizieren; **'ex·com·mu·ni'ca·tion** Kirchenbann *m*, Exkommunikation *f*.
ex·con·vict ['eks'kɔnvikt] ehemaliger Häftling *m*.
ex·co·ri·ate [eks'kɔ:rieit] die Haut abziehen (*dat.*); *Haut* wund reiben; *fig.* heftig kritisieren.
ex·cre·ment ['ekskrimənt] Exkrement *n*, Kot *m*.
ex·cres·cence [iks'kresns] Auswuchs *m*; **ex'cres·cent** auswachsend; überflüssig.
ex·crete [eks'kri:t] absondern, ausscheiden; **ex'cre·tion** Absonderung *f etc.*; **ex'cre·tive, ex'cre·to·ry** [~təri] Absonderungs... *etc.*
ex·cru·ci·ate [iks'kru:ʃieit] martern, quälen; **ex'cru·ci·at·ing** □ qualvoll.
ex·cul·pate ['ekskʌlpeit] entschuldigen; rechtfertigen; freisprechen (*from* von); **ex·cul'pa·tion** Entschuldigung *f etc.*
ex·cur·sion [iks'kə:ʃən] Ausflug *m*; Abstecher *m*; *~ train* Sonderzug *m*; **ex'cur·sion·ist** [~ʃnist] Ausflügler *m*.
ex·cur·sive □ [eks'kə:siv] abschweifend.
ex·cus·a·ble □ [iks'kju:zəbl] entschuldbar; **ex'cuse 1.** entschuldigen; *~ s.o. s.th.* j-m et. erlassen; *be ~d from s.th.* et. erlassen bekommen; *~ me* entschuldigen Sie bitte; **2.** [iks'kju:s] Entschuldigung *f*.
ex-di·rec·to·ry [eksdi'rektəri] nicht im Telefonbuch stehend.
ex·e·at ['eksiæt] *Schule etc.*: Urlaub *m*.
ex·e·cra·ble □ ['eksikrəbl] abscheulich; **ex·e·crate** ['~kreit] verwünschen; verabscheuen; **ex·e'cra·tion** Verwünschung *f*; Abscheu *m*.
ex·e·cu·tant ♪ [ig'zekjutənt] Vortragende *m, f*; **ex·e·cute** ['eksikju:t] ausführen, vollziehen; ♪ vortragen; hinrichten; ⚖ vollziehen, rechtsgültig machen; *Testament* vollstrecken; **ex·e'cu·tion** Aus-, Durchführung *f*, Vollziehung *f*; Ausfertigung *f e-r Urkunde*; Vollstreckung *f e-s Testaments*; Zwangsvollstreckung *f*; Hinrichtung *f*; ♪ Vortrag *m*; Technik *f*; *a man of ~* ein tatkräftiger Mensch *m*; *take out an ~ against j.* auspfänden lassen; *do ~* Wirkung tun; *put od. carry a plan into ~* e-n Plan ausführen *od.* verwirklichen; **ex·e·cu·tion·er** [~'kju:ʃnə] Scharfrichter *m*; **ex·ec·u·tive** [ig'zekjutiv] **1.** □ ausübend, vollziehend; *~ committee* Vorstand *m*; *~ editor* Chefredakteur *m*; *~ suite* Vorstandsetage *f*; **2.** vollziehende Gewalt *f*, Exekutive *f*; Organ(e *pl.*) *n e-s Verbandes etc.*; *Am. Staats*-Präsident *m*; ✝ leitender Angestellter *m*; Geschäftsführer *m*; **ex'ec·u·tor** (Testaments)Vollstrecker *m*; **ex'ec·u·to·ry** vollziehend; Ausführungs...; ⚖ Vollstreckungs...; **ex'ec·u·trix** [~triks] (Testaments)Vollstreckerin *f*.
ex·e·ge·sis [eksi'dʒi:sis] Exegese *f*, Auslegung *f bsd. der Bibel.*
ex·em·plar [ig'zemplə] Muster *n*; **ex'em·pla·ri·ness** Musterhaftigkeit *f*; **ex'em·pla·ry** vorbildlich; Muster...; exemplarisch.
ex·em·pli·fi·ca·tion [igzemplifi'keiʃən] Erläuterung *f durch Beispiele*; Veranschaulichung *f*; ⚖ Abschrift *f*; **ex'em·pli·fy** [~fai] durch Beispiele belegen; veranschaulichen; ⚖ e-e beglaubigte Abschrift machen von.
ex·empt [ig'zempt] **1.** befreit, frei (*from* von); bevorrechtet; **2.** aus-

nehmen, befreien (*from* von); **ex'emp·tion** Befreiung *f*, Freiheit *f* (*from* von).
ex·e·quies ['eksikwiz] *pl.* Leichenbegängnis *n*.
ex·er·cise ['eksəsaiz] **1.** Übung *f*; Ausübung *f e-r Kunst*; körperliche Bewegung *f*, Leibesübung *f*; Übungsarbeit *f*; *take* ~ sich Bewegung machen; ~*s pl. Am.* Feierlichkeit(en *pl.*) *f*; ⚔ Manöver *n*; **2.** *v/t. Körper etc.* üben; *Macht etc.* ausüben; Bewegung machen (*dat.*); exerzieren; beunruhigen; *v/i.* üben; sich Bewegung machen; ~ **book** (Schul)Heft *n*; **'ex·er·cis·er** Trainingsgerät *n*.
ex·ert [ig'zəːt] anwenden; *Einfluß etc.* ausüben; ~ *o.s.* sich anstrengen *od.* bemühen; **ex'er·tion** Ausübung *f*; Anstrengung *f*, Bemühung *f*.
ex·e·unt *thea.* ['eksiʌnt] (sie gehen) ab.
ex·fo·li·ate [eks'fəulieit] (sich) abblättern.
ex·ha·la·tion [ekshə'leiʃən] Ausdünstung *f*, -atmung *f*; Dunst *m*; Ausbruch *m*; **ex·hale** [~'heil] ausdünsten, -atmen; *Leben etc.* aushauchen; *Gefühlen* Luft machen.
ex·haust [ig'zɔːst] **1.** erschöpfen (*a. fig.*); entleeren (*of gen.*); *Luft* auspumpen; **2.** ⊕ Abgas *n*, -dampf *m*; Auspuff *m*; ~ *box* Auspufftopf *m*; ~ *fumes pl.* Abgase *n/pl.*; ~ *pipe* Auspuffrohr *n*; **ex'haust·ed** erschöpft (*a. fig.*); vergriffen (*Auflage*); **ex'haust·i·ble** erschöpflich; **ex'haust·ing** □ anstrengend, mühselig; ⊕ Auspump...; **ex'haus·tion** [~tʃən] Erschöpfung *f*; **ex'haus·tive** □ = *exhausting*; erschöpfend.
ex·hib·it [ig'zibit] **1.** ausstellen; zeigen, darlegen, an den Tag legen, aufweisen; vorführen; ⚖ vorlegen; **2.** Ausstellungsstück *n*; Eingabe *f*; Beweisstück *n*; *on* ~ ausgestellt; **ex·hi·bi·tion** [eksi'biʃən] Ausstellung *f*; Darlegung *f*; Zurschaustellung *f*, Vorführung *f*; Stipendium *n*; *make an* ~ *of o.s.* sich zum Gespött machen; *on* ~ ausgestellt; **ex·hi'bi·tion·er** [~ʃnə] Stipendiat *m*; **ex·hi'bi·tion·ism** *psych.* Exhibitionismus *m*; **ex·hi'bi·tion·ist** Exhibitionist *m*.
ex·hil·a·rate [ig'ziləreit] erheitern; **ex·hil·a'ra·tion** Erheiterung *f*.
ex·hort [ig'zɔːt] ermahnen; **ex·hor·ta·tion** [egzɔː'teiʃən] Ermahnung *f*.
ex·hu·ma·tion [ekshjuː'meiʃən] Exhumierung *f*; **ex'hume** *Leiche* exhumieren.
ex·i·gence, ex·i·gen·cy ['eksidʒəns (-i)] dringende Not *f*, kritische Lage *f*; Erfordernis *n*; **'ex·i·gent** dringlich; anspruchsvoll; *be* ~ *of* erfordern.
ex·ig·u·ous [eg'zigjuəs] klein, dürftig, gering.
ex·ile ['eksail] **1.** Verbannung *f*, Exil *n*; Verbannte *m, f*; **2.** verbannen (*from* aus, von).
ex·ist [ig'zist] existieren, dasein, vorhanden sein; leben; bestehen; **ex'ist·ence** Existenz *f*, Dasein *n*, Vorhandensein *n*; Leben *n*; *be in* ~ existieren, bestehen; *in* ~ = **ex'ist·ent** vorhanden; lebend; **ex·is·ten·tial·ism** *phls.* [egzis'tenʃəlizəm] Existenzphilosophie *f*.
ex·it ['eksit] **1.** Abgang *m*; Tod *m*; Ausgang *m*; *make one's* ~ abtreten; ~ *permit* Ausreisegenehmigung *f*; ~ *visa* Ausreisevisum *n*; **2.** *thea.* (geht) ab.
ex·o·dus ['eksədəs] Auszug *m aus Ägypten*; *fig.* Aus-, Abwanderung *f*, Massenflucht *f*; ♀ Exodus *m*, Zweites Buch *n* Mose.
ex of·fi·ci·o [eksə'fiʃiəu] amtlich; von Amts wegen.
ex·on·er·ate [ig'zɔnəreit] *fig.* entlasten, entbinden, befreien (*from* von); rechtfertigen; **ex·on·er'a·tion** Entlastung *f*, Befreiung *f*.
ex·or·bi·tance, ex·or·bi·tan·cy [ig'zɔːbitəns(i)] Übermaß *n*; **ex'or·bi·tant** □ maßlos, übermäßig.
ex·or·cism ['eksɔːsizəm] Geisterbeschwörung *f*; **'ex·or·cist** Geisterbeschwörer *m*; **ex·or·cize** ['~saiz] *Geister* beschwören, bannen, austreiben (*from* aus); befreien (*of* von).
ex·ot·ic [ig'zɔtik] ausländisch; exotisch; fremdländisch.
ex·pand [iks'pænd] (sich) ausbreiten; (sich) ausdehnen; (sich) erweitern (*into* zu); größer machen *od.* werden; *Abkürzungen* (voll) ausschreiben; freundlich *od.* heiter werden; **ex'pand·er** Expander *m*; **ex·panse** [iks'pæns] Ausdehnung *f*; Weite *f*; Breite *f*; weite Fläche *f*; **ex·pan·si·bil·i·ty** [~sə'biliti] Ausdehnbarkeit *f*; **ex'pan·si·ble** aus-

dehnbar; **ex'pan·sion** Ausdehnung *f*; *pol.* Expansion *f*; Weite *f*, Raum *m*; **ex'pan·sive** □ Expansions...; ausdehnungsfähig; ausgedehnt, weit; *fig.* mitteilsam; **ex'pan·sive·ness** Ausdehnungsfähigkeit *f*; Weite *f*, Breite *f*; Mitteilsamkeit *f*.

ex·pa·ti·ate [eks'peiʃieit] sich weitläufig auslassen (*on* über *acc.*); **ex·pa·ti'a·tion** weitläufige Erörterung *f*; Gerede *n*.

ex·pa·tri·ate [eks'pætrieit] **1.** ausbürgern; ~ *o.s.* auswandern; **2.** im Ausland Lebende *m, f*; **ex·pa·tri'a·tion** Ausbürgerung *f*.

ex·pect [iks'pekt] erwarten (*of, from et.* von *j-m*); F annehmen, denken, vermuten, glauben; **ex'pect·an·cy** Erwartung *f*; Anwartschaft *f*; **ex'pect·ant 1.** erwartend (*of acc.*); *be* ~ ein Kind erwarten; ~ *mother* werdende Mutter *f*; **2.** Anwärter *m*; **ex·pec·ta·tion** [ekspek'teiʃən] Erwartung *f*; Aussicht *f*; Wahrscheinlichkeit *f*; *contrary to* ~ wider Erwarten; *beyond* ~ über Erwarten; *on od. in* ~ *of* in Erwartung (*gen.*); ~ *of life* Lebenserwartung *f*; **ex'pect·ing** = *expectant*.

ex·pec·to·rate [eks'pektəreit] aushusten, -werfen (*Schleim etc.*); **ex·pec·to'ra·tion** Auswurf *m*.

ex·pe·di·ence, ex·pe·di·en·cy [iks'pi:djəns(i)] Zweckmäßigkeit *f etc.*; *schlaue* Berechnung *f*; **ex'pe·di·ent 1.** □ zweckmäßig, ratsam; nützlich; berechnend; **2.** (Hilfs)Mittel *n*; (Not)Behelf *m*; **ex·pe·dite** ['ekspidait] beschleunigen; (be)fördern; ausführen; **ex·pe·di·tion** [~'diʃən] Eile *f*; ⚔ Feldzug *m*; (Forschungs-)Reise *f*, Fahrt *f*, Expedition *f*; Unternehmung *f*; **ex·pe'di·tion·ar·y** [~ʃnəri] Expeditions...; **ex·pe'di·tious** □ schnell, geschwind, eilig, flink.

ex·pel [iks'pel] (hin)ausstoßen; vertreiben, -jagen (*from* von, aus); ausschließen; ~ *from school* von der Schule verweisen.

ex·pend [iks'pend] *Geld* ausgeben; *Mühe, Zeit* auf-, verwenden (*on, in* auf *acc.*); verbrauchen; **ex'pend·a·ble** verwend-, verbrauchbar; Verbrauchs...; **ex'pend·i·ture** [~ditʃə] Verausgabung *f*, Ausgabe *f*; Aufwand *m* (*of* an); Verbrauch *m*; Aufwendungen *f/pl.*, Ausgaben *f/pl.*;

ex·pense [iks'pens] Ausgabe *f*; (Kosten)Aufwand *m*; Kosten *pl.*; ~*s pl.* Unkosten *pl.*, Auslagen *f/pl.*; *at my* ~ auf meine Kosten; *at the* ~ *of* auf Kosten (*gen.*); *at any* ~ um jeden Preis; *at great* ~ mit großen Kosten; *go to the* ~ *of* Geld ausgeben für; *put s.o. to great* ~ j. viel Geld kosten, j-m große Unkosten verursachen; **ex'pense ac·count** Spesenrechnung *f*; **ex'pen·sive** □ kostspielig, teuer.

ex·pe·ri·ence [iks'piəriəns] **1.** Erfahrung *f*; Erlebnis *n*; **2.** erfahren, erleben; *Verlust etc.* erleiden; **ex'pe·ri·enced** erfahren, erprobt.

ex·per·i·ment 1. [iks'perimənt] Versuch *m*, Experiment *n*; **2.** [~ment] experimentieren, Versuche anstellen (*on, with* mit); **ex·pe·ri·men·tal** □ [eksperi'mentl] Experimental...; Versuchs...; erfahrungsmäßig; **ex·per·i·men'ta·tion** Experimentieren *n*; **ex·per·i·ment·er** [iks'perimentə] Experimentierer (-in).

ex·pert ['ekspə:t] **1.** □ [*pred.* eks'pə:t] erfahren, geschickt (*at, in* in *dat.*); (sach)kundig, fachmännisch, Fach...; Sachverständigen...; ~ *advice* Rat *m* e-s Fachmanns; ~ *opinion* (Sachverständigen)Gutachten *n*; **2.** Fachmann *m*; Sachverständige *m, f* (*at, in* in *dat.*); Sachbearbeiter(in); Experte *m*; **ex·per·tise** [~'ti:z] (Sachverständigen)Gutachten *n*; Sachkenntnis *f*; **'ex·pert·ness** Erfahrenheit *f*.

ex·pi·a·ble ['ekspiəbl] sühnbar; **ex·pi·ate** ['~pieit] büßen; sühnen; **ex·pi'a·tion** Sühnung *f*; Sühne *f*; **ex·pi·a·to·ry** ['~piətəri] sühnend (*of acc.*); Sühn...

ex·pi·ra·tion [ekspaiə'reiʃən] Ausatmung *f*; Ablauf *m*, Ende *n*; *at the time of* ~ ⚕ zur Verfallzeit; **ex·pir·a·to·ry** [iks'paiərətəri] Ausatmungs...; **ex'pire** ausatmen; sterben, verscheiden; ablaufen (*Zeit, Vertrag etc.*); ⚕ verfallen, fällig werden; erlöschen (*Feuer, Anspruch etc.*); **ex'pi·ry** Ablauf *m*.

ex·plain [iks'plein] *v/t.* erklären, erläutern; verständlich machen; *Gründe* auseinandersetzen; *v/i.* e-e Erklärung abgeben; ~ *away* wegdiskutieren; **ex'plain·a·ble** erklärbar.

ex·pla·na·tion [eksplə'neiʃən] Erklärung *f*; Erläuterung *f*; **ex·plan·a·to·ry** □ [iks'plænətəri] erklärend.
ex·ple·tive [eks'pli:tiv] **1.** □ ausfüllend; **2.** Füll-, Flickwort *n*; Fluch *m*; Lückenbüßer *m*.
ex·pli·ca·ble ['eksplikəbl] erklärlich; **ex·pli·cate** ['~keit] erklären; *Begriff* entwickeln.
ex·plic·it □ [iks'plisit] ausdrücklich, deutlich; bestimmt; *fig.* offen.
ex·plode [iks'pləud] explodieren (lassen); ausbrechen; platzen (*with* vor); *Theorie* widerlegen; über den Haufen werfen; bloßstellen; **ex'plod·ed view** ⊕ Darstellung *f* in auseinandergezogener Anordnung.
ex·ploit 1. [iks'plɔit] ausbeuten, -nutzen; **2.** ['eksplɔit] Heldentat *f*; **ex·ploi'ta·tion** Ausbeutung *f*, Ausnutzung *f*; Auswertung *f*; *a.* ~ *of soil* Raubbau *m*.
ex·plo·ra·tion [eksplɔ:'reiʃən] Erforschung *f*; **ex'plor·a·to·ry** [~rətəri] Erforschungs...; **ex·plore** [iks'plɔ:] erforschen; untersuchen; **ex'plor·er** (Er)Forscher *m*; Forschungsreisende *m*.
ex·plo·sion [iks'pləuʒən] Explosion *f*; Ausbruch *m*; **ex'plo·sive** [~siv] **1.** □ explosiv; Knall...; **2.** Sprengstoff *m*; *gr.* Verschlußlaut *m*.
ex·po·nent [eks'pəunənt] ⩕ Exponent *m*; Erklärer *m*; Vertreter *m*.
ex·port 1. [eks'pɔ:t] ausführen, exportieren; **2.** ['ekspɔ:t] Ausfuhr (-artikel *m*) *f*, Export *m*; ~*s pl.* Gesamtausfuhr *f*; Exportgüter *n/pl.*; **ex'port·a·ble** ausführbar; **ex·por'ta·tion** Ausfuhr *f*, Export *m*; **ex'port·er** Exporteur *m*.
ex·po·sé [eks'pəuzei] Exposé *n*.
ex·pose [iks'pəuz] aussetzen; *phot.* belichten; ausstellen; enthüllen, entlarven; bloßstellen; **ex·po·si·tion** [ekspəu'ziʃən] Ausstellung *f*; Darstellung *f*, Erklärung *f*; **ex'pos·i·tor** Ausleger *m*, Erklärer *m*.
ex·pos·tu·late [iks'pɔstjuleit] protestieren; ~ *with s.o.* j-m Vorhaltungen machen; **ex·pos·tu'la·tion** Vorhaltung *f*; **ex'pos·tu·la·to·ry** [~lətəri] mahnend.
ex·po·sure [iks'pəuʒə] Aussetzen *n*; Ausgesetztsein *n*; Aufdeckung *f*; Enthüllung *f*, Entlarvung *f*; *phot.* Belichtung *f*; Bild *n*; Lage *f e-s Hauses*; ~ *meter* Belichtungsmesser *m*; *death from* ~ Tod *m* durch Erfrieren.
ex·pound [iks'paund] erklären, auslegen.
ex·press [iks'pres] **1.** □ ausdrücklich, deutlich; Expreß..., Eil...; ~ *company Am.* Transportfirma *f*; ~ *highway* Schnell(verkehrs)straße *f*; ~ *parcel* Eilpaket *n*; **2.** Eilbote *m*; *a.* ~ *train* Schnellzug *m*; *by* ~ = **3.** *adv.* durch Eilboten; als Eilgut; **4.** *Gedanken etc.* äußern, ausdrücken, zum Ausdruck bringen; bezeigen, an den Tag legen; auspressen; *be* ~*ed* zum Ausdruck kommen; **ex'press·i·ble** ausdrückbar; **ex·pres·sion** [~'preʃən] Ausdruck *m* (*Sprache*, *Gesicht*, ♪, *paint.*, ⩕); **ex'pres·sion·ism** *Kunst*: Expressionismus *m*; **ex'pres·sion·less** ausdruckslos; **ex'pres·sive** □ ausdrückend (*of acc.*); ausdrucksvoll; **ex'press·ly** ausdrücklich, eigens; **ex'press·way** *Am.* Autobahn *f*.
ex·pro·pri·ate [eks'prəuprieit] enteignen (*s.th.* et.; *s.o.* j.; *s.o. from s.th.* j-m et.); **ex·pro·pri'a·tion** Enteignung *f*.
ex·pul·sion [iks'pʌlʃən] Vertreibung *f*; **ex'pul·sive** (aus)treibend.
ex·punge [eks'pʌndʒ] tilgen, streichen.
ex·pur·gate ['ekspə:geit] *von Anstößigem* reinigen, säubern; *Anstößiges* ausmerzen; **ex·pur'ga·tion** Reinigung *f etc.*; **ex'pur·ga·to·ry** [~gətəri] reinigend *etc.*
ex·qui·site □ ['ekskwizit] auserlesen, vorzüglich, köstlich; fein (*Gehör etc.*); heftig, scharf, groß; **'ex·qui·site·ness** Vorzüglichkeit *f*; Feinheit *f*; Feinfühligkeit *f*; Heftigkeit *f*.
ex-serv·ice·man ⚔ ['eks'sə:vismən] ehemaliger (Front)Soldat *m*.
ex·tant [eks'tænt] (noch) vorhanden.
ex·tem·po·ra·ne·ous □ [ekstempə'reinjəs], **ex·tem·po·rar·y** [iks'tempərəri], **ex·tem·po·re** [eks'tempəri] aus dem Stegreif (vorgetragen); **ex·tem·po·rize** [iks'tempəraiz] aus dem Stegreif reden, vortragen; **ex'tem·po·riz·er** Stegreifredner *m*, -dichter *m*, -spieler *m*, Improvisateur *m*.
ex·tend [iks'tend] *v/t.* ausdehnen; *Hand etc.* ausstrecken; *Gebiet etc.* erweitern; *Frist etc.* verlängern; *Linie*, *Draht* ziehen; fortsetzen; *fig.* ausbauen; *Kurzschrift* übertragen;

Gunst etc. erweisen, *Hilfe* gewähren, *Einladung* aussprechen; ⚔ (aus)schwärmen lassen; *Sport*: alles herausholen aus; *he was fully* ~*ed* er gab sein Letztes her; ~*ed order* Schützenlinie *f*; *v/i.* sich erstrecken, reichen (*to* bis); **ex'tend·ed** ausgedehnt, ausgestreckt, verlängert.

ex·ten·si·bil·i·ty [ikstensə'biliti] Ausdehnbarkeit *f*; **ex'ten·si·ble** ausdehnbar; **ex'ten·sion** Ausdehnung *f*; Erweiterung *f* (*a. gr.*); Verlängerung *f*; Aus-, Anbau *m*; *teleph.* Nebenanschluß *m*; ~ *cord* ⚡ Verlängerungsschnur *f*; ~ *ladder* Ausziehleiter *f*; *University* ♀ Volkshochschule *f*; **ex'ten·sive** □ ausgedehnt, umfassend; **ex'ten·sive·ness** Ausdehnung *f*, Umfang *m*, Weite *f*.

ex·tent [iks'tent] Ausdehnung *f*, Weite *f*, Größe *f*, Umfang *m*; Grad *m*, Maß *n*; *to the* ~ *of* bis zum Betrage von; *to a certain* ~ gewissermaßen, bis zu e-m gewissen Grade; *to a great* ~ in hohem Maße; *to some* ~ einigermaßen; *to that* ~ so weit; *grant* ~ *for* stunden.

ex·ten·u·ate [eks'tenjueit] abschwächen, mildern, beschönigen; **ex·ten·u'a·tion** Abschwächung *f etc.*

ex·te·ri·or [eks'tiəriə] **1.** □ äußerlich; Außen...; außerhalb (*to gen.*); **2.** Äußere *n*; *Film*: Außenaufnahme *f*.

ex·ter·mi·nate [iks'təmineit] ausrotten, vertilgen; **ex·ter·mi'na·tion** Ausrottung *f*; **ex'ter·mi·na·tor** Vertilger *m*.

ex·ter·nal [eks'tə:nl] **1.** □ äußere (-r, -s), äußerlich; außerhalb (*to gen.*) befindlich; Außen...; **2.** ~*s pl.* Äußere *n*; *fig.* Äußerlichkeiten *f/pl.*

ex·ter·ri·to·ri·al ['eksteri'tɔ:riəl] exterritorial, den Landesgesetzen nicht unterworfen.

ex·tinct [iks'tiŋkt] erloschen (*a. fig.*); ausgestorben; **ex'tinc·tion** (Aus-, Er)Löschen *n* (*a. fig.*); Aussterben *n*.

ex·tin·guish [iks'tiŋgwiʃ] auslöschen, zum Erlöschen bringen; *fig.* in den Schatten stellen; vernichten; *Amt* abschaffen; *Schuld* löschen; *Gegner* zum Schweigen bringen; **ex'tin·guish·er** = *fire-*~.

ex·tir·pate ['ekstə:peit] ausrotten; ⚕ ausschneiden; **ex·tir'pa·tion** Ausrottung *f*; ⚕ Extirpation *f*.

ex·tol [iks'təul] erheben, preisen; ~ *s.o. to the skies fig.* j. in den Himmel heben.

ex·tort [iks'tɔ:t] erpressen (*from* von); abnötigen (*from dat.*); **ex'tor·tion** Erpressung *f*; **ex'tor·tion·ate** [~ʃnit] erpresserisch; **ex'tor·tion·er** Erpresser *m*; Wucherer *m*.

ex·tra ['ekstrə] **1.** Extra...; außer...; Neben...; zusätzlich; besondere(r, -s), Sonder...; ~ *pay* Zulage *f*; ~ *time Sport*: Verlängerung *f*; **2.** *adv.* besonders; außerdem; **3.** *et.* Zusätzliches *n*; Zuschlag *m*; Extrablatt *n*; *thea.*, *Film*: Statist(in).

ex·tract 1. ['ekstrækt] Auszug *m* (*a.* ⚗); Ausschnitt *m*; Extrakt *m*; **2.** [iks'trækt] (heraus)ziehen; *Text*, ⚗ ausziehen; ⅍ *Wurzel* ziehen; *Geständnis*, *Geld etc.* herauslocken; ab-, herleiten (*from* von); **ex'trac·tion** (Heraus)Ziehen *n*; Herkunft *f*.

ex·tra·cur·ric·u·lar ['ekstrəkə'rikjulə] außerhalb des Lehrplans.

ex·tra·dit·a·ble ['ekstrədaitəbl] auslieferbar; **'ex·tra·dite** *Verbrecher* ausliefern (lassen); **ex·tra·di·tion** [~'diʃən] Auslieferung *f*.

ex·tra...: **'~·ju'di·cial** außergerichtlich; **'~'mar·i·tal** außerehelich; **'~'mu·ral** außerhalb der Mauern *od.* der Universität; ~ *student* Gasthörer (-in).

ex·tra·ne·ous [eks'treinjəs] unwesentlich (*to* für); fremd.

ex·traor·di·nar·y [iks'trɔ:dnri] außerordentlich, -gewöhnlich; besonder, Sonder..., Extra...; ungewöhnlich; *envoy* ~ bevollmächtigter Gesandter *m*.

ex·trap·o·late [ek'stræpəuleit] extrapolieren.

ex·tra·sen·so·ry per·cep·tion *psych.* ['ekstrə'sensəri pə'sepʃən] anomale Fähigkeit *f* der Sinneswahrnehmung.

ex·tra·ter·res·tri·al ['extrəti'restriəl] außerirdisch.

ex·tra·ter·ri·to·ri·al ['ekstrəteri'tɔ:riəl] = *exterritorial*.

ex·trav·a·gance [iks'trævigəns] Übertriebenheit *f*; Überspanntheit *f*; Verstiegenheit *f*; Verschwendung *f*, Extravaganz *f*; **ex'trav·a·gant** □ übertrieben, -spannt; verstiegen; verschwenderisch, extravagant; **ex·trav·a·gan·za** *thea.*

[ekstrævə'gænzə] Ausstattungsstück *n*.

ex·treme [iks'tri:m] **1.** □ äußerst; größt, höchst; sehr groß *od.* hoch; sehr streng; außergewöhnlich; ~ *unction eccl.* letzte Ölung *f*; **2.** Äußerste *n*; Extrem *n*; *der* höchste Grad; äußerste Maßnahme *f*; *go to* ~*s* äußerste Maßnahmen ergreifen; *in the* ~ äußerst; **ex'trem·ist** Radikale *m*; **ex·trem·i·ty** [~'tremiti] Äußerste *n*; äußerste Verlegenheit *f*; höchste Not *f*; äußerste Maßnahme *f*; **ex'trem·i·ties** [~z] *pl.* Gliedmaßen *pl.*

ex·tri·cate ['ekstrikeit] herauswinden, -ziehen; befreien; ⚗ entwickeln; **ex·tri'ca·tion** Befreiung *f*; Entwicklung *f*.

ex·trin·sic [eks'trinsik] (~*ally*) äußerlich, nicht gehörend (*to* zu).

ex·tro·vert ['ekstrəuvə:t] extravertierter Typ *m*, nur auf die Außenwelt eingestellter Mensch *m*.

ex·trude [eks'tru:d] ausstoßen; verdrängen.

ex·u·ber·ance [ig'zju:bərəns] Überfluß *m*, Fülle *f*; Überschwenglichkeit *f*; **ex'u·ber·ant** reichlich; üppig (wuchernd); übermäßig; überschwenglich.

ex·u·da·tion [eksju:'deiʃən] Ausschwitzung *f*; **ex·ude** [ig'zju:d] ausschwitzen; absondern.

ex·ult [ig'zʌlt] frohlocken (*at od. in s.th.* über et.); triumphieren (*over s.o.* über j.); **ex'ult·ant** frohlockend; **ex·ul·ta·tion** [egzʌl'teiʃən] Frohlocken *n*.

eye [ai] **1.** Auge *n* (*a. fig. u.* ⚘); Blick *m*; Öhr *n*; Öse *f*; *have an* ~ *for* Sinn haben für; *my* ~*s! sl.* au Backe!; *it's all my* ~*! sl.* Quatsch!; *make* ~*s at s.o.* j-m verliebte Blicke zuwerfen; *up to the* ~*s in work* bis über die Ohren in Arbeit; *mind your* ~*!* (sei) vorsichtig!; *with an* ~ *to* mit Rücksicht auf (*acc.*); mit der Absicht zu; **2.** ansehen, betrachten, beäugen; *mit Erstaunen etc.* mustern; '**~·ball** Augapfel *m*; '**~·brow** Augenbraue *f*; '**~-catch·er** Blickfang *m*; **eyed** [aid] ...äugig.

eye...: '**~-glass** Augenglas *n*; Okular *n*; (*pair of*) ~*es pl.* Kneifer *m*, Zwicker *m*; Brille *f*; '**~·hole** Augenhöhle *f*; Guckloch *n*; '**~·lash** Augenwimper *f*; **eye·let** ['~lit] Schnürloch *n*; Guckloch *n*; Öse *f*.

eye...: '**~·lid** Augenlid *n*; '**~-o·pen·er** überraschende Aufklärung *f*; '**~-piece** *opt.* Okular *n*; '**~-shad·ow** Lidschatten *m*; '**~·shot** Sehweite *f*; '**~·sight** Augen(licht *n*) *pl.*, Gesicht *n*; Sehkraft *f*; '**~·sore** *fig.* Dorn *m* im Auge; unschöner Anblick *m*; '**~-tooth** Augenzahn *m*; '**~-wash** *sl.* Schwindel *m*, Betrug *m*; '**~-'wit·ness** Augenzeuge *m*, -zeugin *f*.

ey·rie, ey·ry ['aiəri] = *aerie*.

F

Fa·bian ['feibjən] vorsichtig, zögernd; ~ *policy* Verzögerungspolitik *f*.

fa·ble ['feibl] Fabel *f*; Mythen *f/pl.*, Legenden *f/pl.*; Unwahrheit *f*, Lüge *f*.

fab·ric ['fæbrik] Bau *m*, Gebäude *n*; Gefüge *n*, Struktur *f*; Gewebe *n*, Stoff *m*; **fab·ri·cate** ['~keit] fabrizieren (*mst fig.*: *erdichten*; *fälschen*); **fab·ri'ca·tion** Fabrikation *f*; Erfindung *f*, Fälschung *f*; '**fab·ri·ca·tor** Verfertiger *m*; Erfinder *m von Lügen*; Fälscher *m*.

fab·u·list ['fæbjulist] Fabeldichter *m*; '**fab·u·lous** □ legendär; sagen-, fabelhaft.

fa·çade ⚠ [fə'sɑ:d] Fassade *f*.

face [feis] **1.** Gesicht *n*; Miene *f*; Anblick *m*; *fig.* Stirn *f*, Unverschämtheit *f*; Oberfläche *f*, Fläche *f*; Vorderseite *f*; rechte Seite *f von Tuch*; Zifferblatt *n*; *in* (*the*) ~ *of* angesichts (*gen.*); trotz (*gen.*); ~ *to* ~ *with* Auge in Auge mit; *save one's* ~ das Gesicht wahren; *lose* ~ das Gesicht verlieren; *on the* ~ *of it* auf den ersten Blick; *set one's* ~ *against* sich gegen *et.* stemmen; **2.** *v/t.* ins Gesicht sehen (*dat.*), ansehen; gegenüberliegen, gegenüberstehen (*dat.*); unter die Augen treten (*dat.*); ins Auge sehen (*dat.*); (hinaus)gehen auf (*acc.*) (*Fenster etc.*); die Stirn bieten (*dat.*); *Kleid etc.* einfassen, besetzen (*with* mit); *Wand* bekleiden; *be* ~*d with* sich ... (*dat.*) gegenübersehen; *v/i.* ~ *about* sich umdrehen; *left* ~*!* ⚔ links um!; *about* ~*!* kehrt!; ~ **card** *Karten*: Bildkarte *f*; '~**-cloth** Waschlappen *m*; **faced** mit e-m ... Gesicht; '**face-down** *Am.* Machtprobe *f*; '**face·less** *fig.* anonym, undefinierbar; '**face-lift·ing** *Kosmetik*: Gesichtsstraffung *f*; *fig.* Verschönerung *f*; '**fac·er** Schlag *m* ins Gesicht; plötzliche Schwierigkeit *f*.

fac·et ⊕ ['fæsit] Facette *f*; '**fac·et·ed** facettiert.

fa·ce·tious □ [fə'si:ʃəs] witzig, drollig, spaßhaft.

face val·ue ['feis'vælju:] ✝ Nennwert *m*; *fig. das* Äußere; *take s.th. at its* ~ et. für bare Münze nehmen.

fa·ci·a ['feiʃə] = *fascia*.

fa·cial ['feiʃəl] **1.** Gesichts...; **2.** Gesichtsmassage *f*.

fac·ile ['fæsail] leicht; gewandt; gefällig; nachgiebig; **fa·cil·i·tate** [fə'siliteit] erleichtern, fördern; **fa·cil·i'ta·tion** Erleichterung *f*, Förderung *f*; **fa'cil·i·ty** Leichtigkeit *f*; Gewandtheit *f*; *facilities pl.* Möglichkeiten *f/pl.*; Gelegenheiten *f/pl.*; Einrichtungen *f/pl.*; Anlagen *f/pl.*

fac·ing ['feisiŋ] ⊕ Verkleidung *f*; ⚔ Wendung *f*; ~*s pl.* Besatz *m*.

fac·sim·i·le [fæk'simili] Faksimile *n*, treue Nachbildung *f*.

fact [fækt] Tatsache *f*; Wirklichkeit *f*; Wahrheit *f*; Tat *f*; ~*s pl.* (*of the case*) Tatbestand *m*; *after* (*before*) *the* ~ nach (vor) begangener Tat; *in* (*point of*) ~, *as a matter of* ~ in der Tat, tatsächlich; *know for a* ~ bestimmt wissen; '~**-find·ing** zur Feststellung des Sachverhalts (dienend).

fac·tion ['fækʃən] Splitterpartei *f*; Clique *f*, Klüngel *m*; Uneinigkeit *f*; '**fac·tion·ist** Parteigänger *m*.

fac·tious □ ['fækʃəs] parteisüchtig; aufrührerisch; '**fac·tious·ness** Parteisucht *f*.

fac·ti·tious □ [fæk'tiʃəs] nachgemacht, künstlich.

fac·tor ['fæktə] ⚖ Faktor *m*; *fig.* Umstand *m*, Moment *n*, Faktor *m*; Agent *m*, Vertreter *m*; Verwalter *m*; '**fac·to·ry** Fabrik *f*.

fac·to·tum [fæk'təutəm] Faktotum *n*, Mädchen *n* für alles.

facts of life [fæktsəv'laif] *pl.*: *tell s.o. about the* ~ j. sexuell aufklären.

fac·tu·al ['fæktʃuəl] Tatsachen...; sachlich.

fac·ul·ty ['fækəlti] Fähigkeit *f*; Kraft *f*; *fig.* Gabe *f*; Gewandtheit *f*; ⚖ Vorrecht *n*; *univ.* Fakultät *f*.

fad F [fæd] Liebhaberei *f*, Steckenpferd *n*; Laune *f*, Mode *f*; '**fad·dish**, '**fad·dy** launisch; schrullig; '**fad·dist** Fex *m*; Sonderling *m*.

fade [feid] (ver)welken (lassen); verblassen; verschießen; schwinden; verklingen; *Radio*: schwinden; ~ *away*, ~ *out* dahinschwinden; ~ *in* einblenden; ~ *out* ausblenden; '**fade·less** licht-, farbecht; '**fad·ing 1.** □ vergänglich; **2.** *Radio*: (Ton)Schwund *m*, Fading *n*.

fae·ces *physiol.* ['fi:si:z] *pl.* Kot *m*.

faer·ie, **faer·y** ['feiəri] Feen-, Märchenland *n*.

fag F [fæg] **1.** Plackerei *f*; Erschöpfung *f*; *Schüler, der e-m älteren Dienste leisten muß*; *fig.* Packesel *m*; *sl.* Zigarette *f*; **2.** *v/i.* sich placken; *e-m älteren Schüler Dienste* leisten; *v/t.* erschöpfen, mürbe machen; '~-'**end** F (letzter, schäbiger) Rest *m*; Stummel *m*, Kippe *f*.

fag·ot, **fag·got** ['fægət] Reisigbündel *n*; ⊕ Bündel *n* Stahlstäbe; Frikadelle *f*; *Am.* F Schwule *m*.

Fahr·en·heit ['færənhait]: ~ *thermometer* Fahrenheitthermometer *n*.

fail [feil] **1.** *v/i.* versagen, mißlingen, fehlschlagen; versiegen (*Quelle*); stocken, versagen (*Stimme*); nachlassen, abnehmen, schwächer werden (*Kraft etc.*); unterlassen; ermangeln (*in gen.*); bankrott machen; durchfallen (*Kandidat*); *he* ~*ed to do od. in doing* es mißlang ihm zu tun; *he cannot* ~ *to inf.* er muß (einfach) *inf.*; *v/t.* im Stich lassen, verlassen; verfehlen, versäumen; durchfallen lassen; *his heart* ~*ed him* ihm sank der Mut; **2.** *su.*: *without* ~ unfehlbar, ganz gewiß; '**fail·ing 1.** Mangel *m*,

Fehler *m*, Schwäche *f*; **2.** *prp.* in Ermangelung (*gen.*); ~ *which* widrigenfalls; **fail·ure** ['~jə] Fehlen *n*, Ausbleiben *n*; Fehlschlag(en *n*) *m*; Mißlingen *n*; Mißerfolg *m*; Versagen *n*; Verfall *m*; Zs.-bruch *m*; Versäumnis *n*; Bankrott *m*; Versager *m* (*Person*).

fain *poet.* [fein] gern.

faint [feint] **1.** □ schwach, matt; zaghaft; undeutlich; **2.** schwach werden; in Ohnmacht fallen, ohnmächtig werden (*with* vor); **3.** Ohnmacht *f*; '**~-'heart·ed** □ verzagt; '**~-'heart·ed·ness** Kleinmut *m*; '**faint·ness** Schwäche *f*, Mattigkeit *f*.

fair[1] [fɛə] **1.** *adj.* gerecht, ehrlich, anständig, fair; recht u. billig; ganz gut, ordentlich; schön (*Wetter*), günstig (*Wind*); reichlich, beträchtlich; blond, hellhäutig; freundlich, höflich; sauber, in Reinschrift; schön (*Frau*); ~ *name* guter Name; *the* ~ *sex* das schöne Geschlecht; **2.** *adv.* gerecht, ehrlich, anständig, fair; in Reinschrift; direkt; *write s.th. out* ~ et. ins reine schreiben; ~ *in the face* mitten ins Gesicht.

fair[2] [~] (Jahr)Markt *m*, Messe *f*; '**~·ground** Rummelplatz *m*.

fair-haired ['fɛə'hɛəd] blond.

fair·ly ['fɛəli] *s. fair*[1]; erträglich, leidlich; ziemlich; völlig, gänzlich; '**fair·ness** Schönheit *f*; Blondheit *f*; Gerechtigkeit *f*; Redlichkeit *f*; Billigkeit *f*; '**fair-'spo·ken** höflich; '**fair·way** ⚓ Fahrwasser *n*; '**fair-weath·er friend** Freund *m* im Glück.

fair·y ['fɛəri] **1.** feenhaft; Feen...; Zauber...; **2.** Fee *f*; Zauberin *f*; Elf(e *f*) *m*; '**Fair·y·land** Feen-, Märchenland *n*; '**fair·y·like** feenhaft; '**fair·y-tale** Märchen *n*.

faith [feiθ] Glaube(n) *m*; Vertrauen *n*; Treue *f*, Redlichkeit *f*; *gegebenes* Wort *n*; *have* ~ *in s.th.* an et. glauben; *in good* ~ in gutem Glauben; '**~-cure** = *faith-healing*; **faith·ful** □ ['~ful] treu; gewissenhaft, ehrlich; zuverlässig; wahrheitsgetreu; *the* ~ *pl.* die Gläubigen *pl.*; *yours* ~*ly* ... Ihr ergebener ...; hochachtungsvoll ...; '**faith·ful·ness** Treue *f*; Ehrlichkeit *f*; '**faith-heal·ing** Gesundbeten *n*; '**faith·less** □ treulos; ungläubig; '**faith·less·ness** Treulosigkeit *f*.

fake *sl.* [feik] **1.** Schwindel *m*; Fälschung *f*; *Am. a.* '**fak·er** Schwindler *m*; **2.** *a.* ~ *up* zurechtmachen, fälschen.

fal·con ['fɔːlkən] Falke *m*; '**fal·con·er** Falkner *m*; '**fal·con·ry** Falkenbeize *f*; Falknerei *f*.

fall [fɔːl] **1.** Fall(en *n*) *m*; Sturz *m*; Verfall *m*; Einsturz *m*; (Blätter-, Schnee- *etc.*) Fall *m*; *bsd. Am.* Herbst *m*; Sinken *n der Preise etc.*, Kurssturz *m*, Baisse *f*; Fällen *n von Holz*; Gefälle *n*; *mst* ~*s pl.* Wasserfall *m*; Senkung *f*, Abhang *m*; ⚓ Fall *n*; *the* ♀ (*of Man*) der Sündenfall *m*; *have a* ~ fallen, stürzen; **2.** (*irr.*) fallen; ab-, einfallen; abnehmen; sinken (*Mut etc.*); heruntergehen (*Preise*); *fig.* (herab-) stürzen; sich legen (*Wind*); (*mit Prädikatsnomen*) werden; *in e-n Zustand* verfallen; geworfen werden (*Tiere*); münden (*into* in *acc.*); *his countenance fell* er machte ein langes Gesicht; ~ *asleep* einschlafen; ~ *away* schwinden; abfallen; ~ *back* zurückweichen; ~ *back (up)on* zurückkommen auf (*acc.*); ~ *behind* zurückbleiben (*in* mit); ~ *between two stools* sich zwischen zwei Stühle setzen; ~ *down* niederfallen; einstürzen; F Pech haben; ~ *due* fällig werden; ~ *for* F hereinfallen auf (*acc.*), auf den Leim gehen; ~ *from* abfallen von; ~ *ill od. sick* krank werden; ~ *in* einfallen; ⚔ (sich) formieren, antreten; ablaufen (*Pacht etc.*); fällig werden (*Schuld etc.*); ~ *in with* stoßen auf (*acc.*); übereinstimmen mit *e-r Ansicht*; ~ *in love with* sich verlieben in (*acc.*); ~ *into* verfallen in; geraten in (*acc.*); ~ *into line with* übereinstimmen mit, sich *j-m* anschließen; ~ *off* abfallen (*a. fig.*, *from* von); nachlassen; ~ *on* (*prp.*) über *j.* herfallen; ~ *out* zanken; sich zerstreiten (*with* mit); sich zutragen; ⚔ wegtreten; ~ *short* knapp werden (*of* an *dat.*); ~ *short of* nicht erreichen, zurückbleiben hinter (*dat.*); ~ *to* zufallen (*Tür*); zugreifen (*beim Essen*); anfangen, sich machen an (*acc.*); ~ *under* unter *e-e Zahl etc.* fallen.

fal·la·cious □ [fə'leiʃəs] trügerisch; irreführend; irrig.

fal·la·cy ['fæləsi] Trugschluß *m*; Irrtum *m*; Täuschung *f*.
fall·en ['fɔ:lən] *p.p. von fall 2.*
fall guy *Am. sl.* ['fɔ:l'gai] *der* Lackierte, *der* Dumme.
fal·li·bil·i·ty [fæli'biliti] Fehlbarkeit *f*; **fal·li·ble** □ ['fæləbl] fehlbar.
fall·ing ['fɔ:liŋ] Fallen *n*; ~ **off** Abfall *m*; Abnahme *f*; ~ **sick·ness** Fallsucht *f*; ~ **star** Sternschnuppe *f*.
fall·out ['fɔ:laut] Fallout *m*, radioaktiver Niederschlag *m*.
fal·low ['fæləu] **1.** *zo.* falb; ✓ brach (-liegend); **2.** Brachland *n*; '**~-deer** *zo.* Damwild *n*; '**fal·low·ness** Brachliegen *n*.
false □ [fɔ:ls] falsch, unwahr; unrichtig; treulos (*to* gegen); unecht; Fehl...; ~ *imprisonment* Freiheitsberaubung *f*; ~ *key* Nachschlüssel *m*; *play s.o.* ~ falsches Spiel mit j-m treiben; **false·hood** ['~hud] Falschheit *f*; Unwahrheit *f*, Lüge *f*; '**false·ness** Falschheit *f der Gesinnung*; Verrat *m*; **false teeth** [fɔ:ls 'ti:θ] *künstliches* Gebiß *n*.
fal·set·to ♪ [fɔ:l'setəu] Fistelstimme *f*, Falsett *n*.
fal·si·fi·ca·tion ['fɔ:lsifi'keiʃən] Verfälschung *f*; Fälschung *f*; **fal·si·fi·er** ['~faiə] Fälscher(in); **fal·si·fy** ['~fai] (ver)fälschen; als falsch nachweisen; **fal·si·ty** ['~ti] Falschheit *f*, Unrichtigkeit *f*.
fal·ter ['fɔ:ltə] schwanken; *fig.* stokken (*Ton, Stimme*); stammeln; *fig.* zaudern.
fame [feim] Ruf *m*, Ruhm *m*; **famed** berühmt (*for* wegen).
fa·mil·iar [fə'miljə] **1.** □ vertraut (*to dat.*); intim; bekannt (*with* mit); gewohnt; ungezwungen, vertraulich, familiär; *be* ~ *with* gut kennen; **2.** Vertraute *m*; **fa·mil·i·ar·i·ty** [~li'æriti] Vertrautheit *f*; *familiarities pl.* (plumpe) Vertraulichkeit *f*; **fa·mil·iar·i·za·tion** [~ljərai'zeiʃən] Gewöhnung *f* (*with* an *acc.*); **fa'mil·iar·ize** vertraut machen, bekannt machen.
fam·i·ly ['fæmili] **1.** Familie *f*; **2.** Familien..., Haus...; *in the* ~ *way* F in anderen Umständen; ~ *allowance* Kinderzulage *f*; ~ *doctor* Hausarzt *m*; ~ *man* Hausvater *m*; ~ *planning* Familienplanung *f*; ~ *tree* Stammbaum *m*.
fam·ine ['fæmin] Hungersnot *f*; Mangel *m* (*of* an *dat.*); Not *f*.
fam·ish ['fæmiʃ] aushungern; verhungern (lassen); darben.
fa·mous □ ['feiməs] berühmt (*for* wegen); F famos, ausgezeichnet.
fan[1] [fæn] **1.** Fächer *m*; Ventilator *m*; ⚓ (Schrauben)Flügel *m*; **2.** (an-) fächeln; an-, *fig.* entfachen; ~ *out* ⚔ ausschwärmen.
fan[2] F [~] *Sport- etc.* Fanatiker *m*, Liebhaber *m*, Fan *m*; *Radio*: Bastler *m*; ...narr *m*, ...fex *m*.
fa·nat·ic [fə'nætik] **1.** *a.* **fa'nat·i·cal** □ fanatisch; **2.** Fanatiker(in), Eiferer *m*; **fa'nat·i·cism** [~sizəm] Fanatismus *m*.
fan belt *mot.* ['fænbelt] Keilriemen *m*.
fan·ci·er ['fænsiə] *Vogel- etc.* Liebhaber(in); Züchter(in).
fan·ci·ful □ ['fænsiful] phantastisch; '**fan·ci·ful·ness** Phantasterei *f*.
fan·cy ['fænsi] **1.** *spielerische* Phantasie *f*; Einbildung(skraft) *f*; Schrulle *f*; Neigung *f*, Vorliebe *f*; Liebhaberei *f*; *the* ~ die (*Sport-, Tier- etc.*)Liebhaberwelt *f*; *take a* ~ *to* Gefallen finden an (*dat.*), e-e Neigung fassen zu; **2.** Phantasie...; Liebhaber...; Luxus...; Mode...; ~ *apron* Tändelschürze *f*; ~ *articles pl.* Modeartikel *m/pl.*; ~ *dress* Maskenkostüm *n*; ~*-dress ball* Maskenball *m*; ~ *fair Art* Wohltätigkeitsbasar *m*; ~ *goods pl.* Galanteriewaren *f/pl.*; ~ *man sl.* Zuhälter *m*; ~ *price* Liebhaberpreis *m*, Phantasiepreis *m*; **3.** sich einbilden, sich vorstellen; Gefallen finden an (*dat.*), gern haben; (aus Liebhaberei) züchten; *just* ~*!* denken Sie nur!; '**~-'free** frei und ungebunden; '**~-work** feine Handarbeit *f*, Stickerei *f*.
fane *poet.* [fein] Tempel *m*.
fan·fare ['fænfεə] Fanfare *f*; Tusch *m*; **fan·fa·ron·ade** [~færə'nɑ:d] Großsprecherei *f*, Prahlerei *f*.
fang [fæŋ] Fangzahn *m*; Giftzahn *m*; Zahnwurzel *f*; ⊕ Klaue *f*; Dorn *m*.
fan·ner ⊕ ['fænə] Gebläse *n*.
fan·tail *zo.* ['fænteil] Pfauentaube *f*.
fan·ta·sia ♪ [fæn'teizjə] Phantasie *f*; **fan·tas·tic** [~'tæstik] (*~ally*) phantastisch; **fan·ta·sy** ['~təsi] Phantasie *f*, Einbildung *f*, Hirngespinst *n*.

far [fɑ:] *adj.* fern, entfernt; weit; *adv.* fern; weit; (sehr) viel; ~ *better* weit *od.* viel besser; ~ *the best* weitaus der beste; *as* ~ *as* bis; *by* ~ bei weitem; ~ *from ger.* weit davon entfernt zu *inf.*; *in so* ~ *as* insofern als; ~ *and near,* ~ *and wide* weit u. breit; **~-a·way** ['fɑ:rəwei] weit entfernt, fern.

farce *thea.* [fɑ:s] Posse *f*, Farce *f*, Schwank *m*; **far·ci·cal** □ ['~sikəl] possenhaft.

fare [fɛə] **1.** Fahrgeld *n*; Fahrgast *m*; Verpflegung *f*, Kost *f*; **2.** *j-m* (er)gehen; *gut* leben; *how did you* ~? wie ist es Ihnen ergangen?; ~ *well!* lebe(n Sie) wohl!; ~ *stage* Teilstrecke *f*; '**~'well 1.** lebe(n Sie) wohl!; **2.** Abschied *m*, Lebewohl *n*; **3.** Abschieds...; ~ *party* Abschiedsfeier *f*.

far... [fɑ:]: '**~-'fetched** *fig.* weithergeholt, gesucht; '**~-'flung** weit (ausgedehnt); *fig.* weitgespannt; **~ gone** F fertig (*todkrank, betrunken etc.*).

far·i·na·ceous [færi'neiʃəs] mehlig; stärkehaltig.

farm [fɑ:m] **1.** Bauernhof *m*, -gut *n*, Gehöft *n*, Farm *f*; Züchterei *f*; *chicken* ~ Hühnerfarm *f*; **2.** pachten; *a.* ~ *out* verpachten, *Land* bewirtschaften, bebauen; *Kinder* in (bezahlte) Pflege nehmen; '**farm·er** Landwirt *m*, Bauer *m*; Pächter *m*; '**farm·hand** Landarbeiter(in); '**farm-house** Bauern-, Gutshaus *n*; '**farm·ing 1.** Acker...; landwirtschaftlich; Land...; **2.** Landwirtschaft *f*; **farm·stead** ['~sted] Bauernhof *m*, Gehöft *n*; '**farm·yard** Wirtschaftshof *m e-s Bauernguts*.

far·o ['fɛərəu] Pharo *n* (*Kartenspiel*).

far-off ['fɑ:r'ɔ:f] entfernt, fern, abgelegen.

far-out *sl.* [fɑ:r'aut] toll, super.

far·ra·go [fə'rɑ:gəu] Mischmasch *m*.

far-reach·ing ['fɑ:'ri:tʃiŋ] weitreichend.

far·ri·er ['færiə] Hufschmied *m*.

far·row ['færəu] **1.** Wurf *m* Ferkel; **2.** (Ferkel) werfen, ferkeln.

far-see·ing ['fɑ:'si:iŋ], '**far-'sight·ed** *fig.* weitblickend.

fart V [fɑ:t] **1.** Furz *m*; **2.** furzen.

far·ther ['fɑ:ðə], **far·thest** ['~ðist] *comp. u. sup. von far.*

far·thing ['fɑ:ðiŋ] Farthing *m* (¼ *Penny*; *abgeschafft seit 1961*); *not worth a* ~ keinen (roten) Heller wert.

fas·ci·a *mot.* ['feiʃə] Armaturenbrett *n*.

fas·ci·nate ['fæsineit] bezaubern, faszinieren; **fas·ci'na·tion** Bezauberung *f*; Zauber *m*, Reiz *m*, Faszination *f*.

fas·cine [fæ'si:n] Faschine *f* (*Reisigbündel*).

Fas·cism *pol.* ['fæʃizəm] Faschismus *m*; '**fas·cist** Faschist(in); **fa'scis·tic** (*~ally*) faschistisch.

fash·ion ['fæʃən] **1.** Mode *f*; Art *f*, Weise *f*; feine Lebensart *f*; Form *f*; Schnitt *m*; *rank and* ~ *die* vornehme Welt; *in* (*out of*) ~ (un)modern; *set the* ~ tonangebend sein; **2.** gestalten, formen; *Kleid* machen; **fash·ion·a·ble** □ ['fæʃnəbl] Mode-...; modern, elegant; fein; '**fash·ion·a·ble·ness** Modernität *f*, *das* Moderne, Eleganz *f*; '**fash·ion-pa'rade** Mode(n)schau *f*; '**fash·ion-plate** Modebild *n*.

fast¹ [fɑ:st] fest (*a. Schlaf etc.*); schnell; *phot.* lichtstark; treu (*Freund*); waschecht (*Farbe*); leichtlebig, flott; ~ *to light* lichtecht; ~ *breeder phys.* schneller Brüter *m*; ~ *food* Schnellgerichte *n/pl.*; ~ *train* Schnellzug *m*; *my watch is* ~ meine Uhr geht vor.

fast² [~] **1.** Fasten *n*; **2.** fasten.

fast...: '**~·back** *mot.* (Wagen *m* mit) Fließheck *n*; '**~-day** Fasttag *m*.

fas·ten ['fɑ:sn] *v/t.* befestigen (*to* an *dat.*); anheften, -hängen (*to* an *acc.*); festmachen; fest zumachen; zubinden; *Augen etc.* heften (*on, upon* auf *acc.*); *v/i.* schließen (*Tür*); ~ *upon fig.* sich heften *od.* klammern an (*acc.*); '**fas·ten·er** Befestiger *m*; Verschluß *m*; Musterklammer *f*; *a.* '**fas·ten·ing** Schließe *f*; *patent* ~ Druckknopf *m am Kleid*.

fast-food re·stau·rant ['fɑ:stfu:d 'restərɔ̃:ŋ] Schnellgaststätte *f*.

fas·tid·i·ous □ [fəs'tidiəs] anspruchsvoll, heikel, eigen (*im Essen*), wählerisch, verwöhnt; **fas'tid·i·ous·ness** wählerisches Wesen *n*, Verwöhntheit *f*.

fast·ness ['fɑ:stnis] Festigkeit *f*; Schnelligkeit *f*; Leichtlebigkeit *f*;

⚔ Feste *f*, fester Platz *m*.

fat [fæt] **1.** □ fett (*a. Boden*); dick; fettig; **2.** Fett *n*; *live on the ~ of the land* in Saus und Braus leben; *the ~ is in the fire* der Teufel ist los; **3.** fett machen *od.* werden; mästen.

fa·tal □ [ˈfeitl] verhängnisvoll (*to* für); Schicksals...; tödlich; *~ accident* tödlicher Unfall *m*; **fa·tal·ism** [ˈ~təlizm] Fatalismus *m* (*Glaube an ein vorherbestimmtes Schicksal*); ˈ**fa·tal·ist** Fatalist(in); **fa·tal·i·ty** [fəˈtæliti] Verhängnis *n*; *das* Verhängnisvolle; Tödlichkeit *f*; Unglücks-, Todesfall *m*.

fate [feit] Schicksal *n*; Verhängnis *n*; Verderben *n*; *the* ♀*s pl.* die Parzen *f/pl.*; ˈ**fat·ed** vom Schicksal verhängt; dem Schicksal verfallen; **fate·ful** □ [ˈ~ful] verhängnisvoll, schicksalhaft.

fa·ther [ˈfɑːðə] **1.** Vater *m*; **2.** der Urheber sein von; die Vater- *od.* Urheberschaft von ... anerkennen; die Vaterschaft von (*Kind*) *od.* Urheberschaft von (*et.*) *j-m* zuschreiben; *to ~ an article on s.o.* j. als Autor e-s Artikels hinstellen; **fa·ther·hood** [ˈ~hud] Vaterschaft *f*; ˈ**fa·ther-in-law** Schwiegervater *m*; ˈ**fa·ther·land** Vaterland *n*; ˈ**fa·ther·less** vaterlos; ˈ**fa·ther·ly** väterlich.

fath·om [ˈfæðəm] **1.** Klafter *f* (*Maß*); ⚓ Faden *m*; **2.** sondieren; ⚓ loten; *fig.* ergründen; ˈ**fath·om·less** unergründlich.

fa·tigue [fəˈtiːg] **1.** Ermüdung *f*; Strapaze *f*; ⚔ Arbeitsdienst *m*; *~s pl.* ⚔ Arbeitsanzug *m*; **2.** ermüden; strapazieren; **faˈtigue-par·ty** ⚔ Arbeitskommando *n*.

fat·ling [ˈfætliŋ] junges Mastvieh *n*; ˈ**fat·ness** Fettigkeit *f*; Fettheit *f*; ˈ**fat·ten** fett machen *od.* werden; mästen; *Boden* düngen; ˈ**fat·ty** **1.** fettig; Fett...; *~ degeneration* Verfettung *f*; **2.** F Dickerchen *n*.

fa·tu·i·ty [fəˈtjuːiti] Albernheit *f*; **fat·u·ous** □ [ˈfætjuəs] albern.

fau·cet *bsd. Am.* [ˈfɔːsit] (Zapf-)Hahn *m*.

faugh [fɔː] pfui!

fault [fɔːlt] Fehler *m* (*a. Tennis*); Defekt *m* (*a.* ⚡, ⊕); ⊕ Störung *f*; Vergehen *n*, Versehen *n*; Schuld *f*; *geol.* Verwerfung *f*; *find ~ with* et. auszusetzen haben an (*dat.*); *be at ~* auf falscher Fährte sein; *to a ~ fig.* übermäßig, zu (sehr); ˈ**~-find·er** Besserwisser *m*, Nörgler *m*; ˈ**~-find·ing** **1.** krittelnd, nörgelnd; **2.** Nörgelei *f*, Krittelei *f*; ˈ**fault·i·ness** Fehlerhaftigkeit *f*; ˈ**fault·less** □ fehlerfrei, tadellos; ˈ**faults·man** *teleph.* Störungssucher *m*; ˈ**fault·y** □ fehlerhaft, mangelhaft.

faun [fɔːn] Faun *m*.

faun·a [ˈfɔːnə] Fauna *f*, Tierwelt *f*.

fa·vo(u)r [ˈfeivə] **1.** Gunst(bezeigung) *f*; Gefallen *m*; Begünstigung *f*; Bandschleife *f als Abzeichen*; *in ~ of* zugunsten von *od. gen.*; *I am (not) in ~ of it* ich bin (nicht) dafür; *under ~ of night* unter dem Schutz der Nacht; *do s.o. a ~* j-m e-n Gefallen tun; **2.** begünstigen; beehren (*with* mit); *j-m* nachgeraten, -schlagen; **fa·vo(u)r·a·ble** □ [ˈ~vərəbl] (*to*) günstig (für); gewogen (*dat.*); vorteilhaft (für); ˈ**fa·vo(u)r·a·ble·ness** Gunst *f*; **fa·vo(u)red** [ˈ~vəd] begünstigt; *most-~ nation clause* Meistbegünstigungsklausel *f*; **fa·vo(u)r·ite** [ˈ~vərit] **1.** Lieblings-...; **2.** Günstling *m*; Liebling *m*; *Sport*: Favorit *m*; ˈ**fa·vo(u)r·it·ism** Günstlingswirtschaft *f*; Favoritentum *n*.

fawn[1] [fɔːn] **1.** *zo.* (Dam)Kitz *n*; Rehbraun *n*; **2.** (Kitze) setzen.

fawn[2] [~] schwänzeln (*Hund*); *fig.* kriechen (*upon* vor *dat.*); ˈ**fawn·er** Kriecher *m*; ˈ**fawn·ing** kriecherisch.

fay *poet.* [fei] Fee *f*.

faze *bsd. Am.* F [feiz] *j.* durcheinanderbringen.

fe·al·ty [ˈfiːəlti] (Lehns)Treue *f*.

fear [fiə] **1.** Furcht *f* (*of* vor *dat.*); Befürchtung *f*; Grund *m* zur Furcht; *through od. from ~ of* aus Angst vor (*dat.*); *for ~ of doing* um nicht zu tun; *in ~ of one's life* um sein Leben besorgt; **2.** (be)fürchten; scheuen; sich fürchten (vor *dat.*); Angst haben; **fear·ful** □ [ˈ~ful] furchtsam (*of* vor *dat.*); furchtbar; *be ~ that* Angst haben, daß; ˈ**fear·ful·ness** Furchtsamkeit *f*; Furchtbarkeit *f*; ˈ**fear·less** □ furchtlos (*of* vor *dat.*); ˈ**fear·less·ness** Furchtlosigkeit *f*.

fea·si·bil·i·ty [fiːzəˈbiliti] Durchführbarkeit *f*; ˈ**fea·si·ble** durch-, ausführbar.

feast [fi:st] **1.** Fest *n*; Feiertag *m*; Festmahl *n*, Schmaus *m*; **2.** *v/t.* festlich bewirten; ~ *one's eyes on* seine Augen weiden an (*dat.*); *v/i.* sich ergötzen (*upon* an *dat.*); schmausen (*on* von).

feat [fi:t] (Helden)Tat *f*; Kunststück *n*; Leistung *f*.

feath·er ['feðə] **1.** Feder *f*; *a.* ~*s pl.* Gefieder *n*; *show the white* ~ F sich feige zeigen; *that is a* ~ *in his cap* er kann sich et. darauf zugute tun; *in high* ~ in gehobener Stimmung; **2.** mit Federn versehen *od.* schmücken; ⚓ *die Riemen* platt werfen; ~ *one's nest* sich warm betten; '**~-bed 1.** (*Feder*)Unterbett *n*; **2.** verwöhnen, verpäppeln; *j-m* das Leben leicht machen (*z. B. durch Subventionen*); '**~-brained,** '**~-head·ed** unbesonnen; albern; '**feath·ered** be-, gefiedert; '**feath·er-edge** ⊕ scharfe Kante *f*; '**feath·er·ing** Gefieder *n*; Federbesatz *m*; '**feath·er·stitch** *Stickerei*: Grätenstich *m*; '**feath·er-weight** *Boxen*: Federgewicht *n*; '**feath·er·y** feder(art)ig; federleicht.

fea·ture ['fi:tʃə] **1.** (Gesichts-, Grund-, Haupt-, Charakter)Zug *m*; Gesichtsteil *m*; (charakteristisches) Merkmal *n*, Besonderheit *f*; Hauptfilm *m*; *Radio*: Feature *n*; *Am.* Bericht *m*, Artikel *m*; ~*s pl.* Gesicht *n*; Gepräge *n*; Charakter *m*; **2.** kennzeichnen; sich auszeichnen durch; groß aufziehen; *Film*: (in der Hauptrolle) darstellen, gestalten; die Hauptrolle spielen in (*dat.*); *a film featuring N. N.* ein Film mit N. N. in der Hauptrolle; ~ **film** Haupt-, Spielfilm *m*; '**fea·ture·less** ohne besondere Züge; eintönig.

feb·ri·fuge ['febrifju:dʒ] Fiebermittel *n*.

fe·brile ['fi:brail] fieberhaft.

Feb·ru·ar·y ['februəri] Februar *m*.

feck·less ['feklis] unfähig.

fe·cun·date ['fi:kəndeit] befruchten; **fe·cun'da·tion** Befruchtung *f*; **fe·cun·di·ty** [fi'kʌnditi] Fruchtbarkeit *f*.

fed [fed] *pret. u. p.p. von feed 2.*

Fed *Am.* F [fed] = *Federal Reserve Board.*

fed·er·al ['fedərəl] Bundes...; ♀ *Reserve Board Am.* Zentralbankrat *m*; '**fed·er·al·ism** Föderalismus *m*; '**fed·er·al·ist** Föderalist *m*; '**fed·er·al·ize** (sich) verbünden; (sich) zu einem Staatenbund vereinigen; **fed·er·ate 1.** ['~reit] (sich) zu einem Bunde vereinigen; **2.** ['~rit] verbündet; Bundes...; **fed·er·a·tion** [~'reiʃən] (Staaten)Bund *m*, Föderation *f*; *beruflicher etc.* Verband *m*; **fed·er·a·tive** ['~rətiv] föderativ.

fee [fi:] **1.** Gebühr *f*; Schulgeld *n*; Honorar *n*; Gehalt *n*; Trinkgeld *n*; Entgelt *n*; Lohn *m*; Lehen *n*; Besitz *m*; ~ *simple* Eigengut *n*; **2.** bezahlen; honorieren; *j-m* ein Trinkgeld geben.

fee·ble□ ['fi:bl] schwach; '**~-'mind·ed** geistesschwach; '**fee·ble·ness** Schwäche *f*.

feed [fi:d] **1.** Futter *n*; Nahrung *f*; F Mahlzeit *f*; Futterration *f*; Fütterung *f*; ⊕ Vorschub *m*; ⊕ Zuführung *f*, Speisung *f*, (*a.* ⚔) Ladung *f*; *attr.* Speise...; **2.** (*irr.*) *v/t.* füttern; speisen, (er)nähren; *Auge* weiden (*with* an *dat.*); *Hoffnung etc.* nähren; als Nahrung dienen (*dat.*); *Maschine* speisen; *Material etc.* zuführen; ~ *o.s.* selbst *od.* alleine essen; ~ *off od. down* abweiden; ~ *up* mästen; *be fed up with et. od. j.* satt haben; *well fed* wohlgenährt; *v/i.* fressen; essen, leben, sich nähren (*upon* von); '**~·back 1.** *Radio*: Rückkoppelung *f*; **2.** rückkoppeln; '**feed·er** Fütterer *m*; *Am.* Viehmäster *m*; Esser(in); Fresser(in); Saugflasche *f*; (Kinder)Lätzchen *n*; ⊕ Zuführungsvorrichtung *f*, Speiseleitung *f*; Zuflußgraben *m*; '**feed·er line** 🚂 Zubringerlinie *f*; '**feed·er road** Zubringer(straße *f*) *m*; '**feed·ing** Fütterung *f*; Mästung *f*; Fressen *n*, Essen *n*; *attr.* Futter...; ⊕ Speise...; *high* ~ Wohlleben *n*; ~ *crane* 🚂 Wasserkran *m*; '**feed·ing-bottle** Saugflasche *f*; '**feed·ing-stuff** Futtermittel *n*.

feel [fi:l] **1.** (*irr.*) *v/t.* fühlen; befühlen; empfinden, spüren; glauben; halten für; ⚔ erkunden; *v/i.* fühlen, empfinden; sich fühlen (*P.*); sich anfühlen (*S.*); ~ *bad about s.th.* et. bedauern; ~ *cold* frieren; *I* ~ *like doing* ich habe Lust zu tun, ich möchte am liebsten tun; ~ *for* mit *j-m* fühlen; nach *et.* fühlen;

2. Gefühl(ssinn *m*) *n*; Empfindung *f*; ˈ**feel·er** Fühler *m* (*a. fig.*); *zo.* Fühlhorn *n*; ⚔ Kundschafter *m*; ˈ**feel·ing 1.** □ fühlend; gefühlvoll; mitfühlend; tief empfunden, lebhaft; **2.** Gefühl *n*; Meinung *f*; Erregung *f*; *good* ~ Entgegenkommen *n*.
feet [fiːt] *pl. von foot.*
feign [fein] heucheln; ~ *illness* Krankheit vortäuschen; ~ *to do* vorgeben zu tun; ~ *o.s. mad* sich wahnsinnig stellen; **feigned** vorgeblich; Schein...; **feign·ed·ly** [ˈ~idli] zum Schein.
feint [feint] **1.** Verstellung *f*; Finte *f* (*a.* ⚔); **2.** ein Täuschungsmanöver machen.
feld·spar *min.* [ˈfeldspɑː] Feldspat *m*.
fe·lic·i·tate [fiˈlisiteit] beglückwünschen (*on* zu); **fe·lic·iˈta·tion** Glückwunsch *m*; **feˈlic·i·tous** □ glücklich (gewählt), treffend; **feˈlic·i·ty** Glück(seligkeit *f*) *n*; glücklicher Einfall *m*.
fe·line [ˈfiːlain] katzenartig, Katzen...
fell[1] [fel] **1.** *pret. von fall 2*; **2.** niederschlagen; fällen; umsäumen.
fell[2] *poet.* [~] grausam, grimmig.
fell[3] [~] Fell *n*; (Haar)Schopf *m*.
fel·loe [ˈfeləu] (Rad)Felge *f*.
fel·low [ˈfeləu] Gefährte *m*, Gefährtin *f*, Kamerad(in); Gleiche *m*, *f u. n*; Gegenstück *n*; *univ.* Fellow *m*, Mitglied *n e-s College*; F Kerl *m*, Bursche *m*, Mensch *m*; *attr.* Mit...; Neben...; *a* ~ F eine(r), man; *old* ~ F alter Junge *m*; *the* ~ *of a glove* der andere Handschuh; *be* ~*s* zs.-gehören; *he has not his* ~ er hat nicht seinesgleichen; ˈ~-ˈ**be·ings** *pl.* Mitmenschen *m/pl.*; ˈ~-ˈ**cit·i·zen** Mitbürger *m*; ˈ~-ˈ**coun·try·man** Landsmann *m*; ˈ~-ˈ**crea·ture** Mitgeschöpf *n*; Mitmensch *m*; ˈ~-ˈ**feel·ing** Mitgefühl *n*; ˈ~-ˈ**pas·sen·ger** Mitreisende *m*, *f*; ˈ~**ship** Gemeinschaft *f*; Gesellschaft *f*; *a. good* ~ Kameradschaft *f*; Mitgliedschaft *f*; *univ.* Stelle *f od.* Einkommen *n* e-s Fellows; ~ **sol·dier** (Kriegs-) Kamerad *m*; ˈ~-ˈ**stu·dent** Studienkamerad *m*; ˈ~-ˈ**trav·el·ler** Mitreisende *m*, *f*; *pol.* Mitläufer *m*.
fel·ly [ˈfeli] (Rad)Felge *f*.
fel·on [ˈfelən] ⚖ Verbrecher *m*; ⚕ Nagelgeschwür *n*; **fe·lo·ni·ous** □ ⚖ [fiˈləunjəs] verbrecherisch; mit böser Absicht; **fel·o·ny** ⚖ [ˈfeləni] Kapitalverbrechen *n*.
fel·spar [ˈfelspɑː] = *feldspar*.
felt[1] [felt] *pret. u. p.p. von feel 1.*
felt[2] [~] **1.** Filz *m*; **2.** (be)filzen; (sich) verfilzen; ~**-tip**(**ped**) **pen** [ˈ~tip(t) pen] Filzstift *m*.
fe·male [ˈfiːmeil] **1.** weiblich; ~ *child* Mädchen *n*; ~ *screw* Schraubenmutter *f*; **2.** Weib *n*; Weibchen *n von Tieren*.
fem·i·nine □ [ˈfeminin] weiblich (*a. gr.*); *contp.* weibisch; **fem·iˈnin·i·ty** Weiblichkeit *f*; weibliches *od. contp.* weibisches Wesen *n*; ˈ**fem·i·nism** Frauenrechtlertum *n*; ˈ**fem·i·nist** Frauenrechtler(in); **fem·i·nize** [ˈ~naiz] weiblich (*contp.* weibisch) machen *od.* werden.
fe·mur *anat.* [ˈfiːmə] Oberschenkelknochen *m*.
fen [fen] Fenn *n*, Moor *n*; Marsch *f*.
fence [fens] **1.** Einzäunung *f*, Hecke *f*, Zaun *m*, Staket *n*; Hürde *f*; Fechtkunst *f*; *sl.* Hehler(nest *n*) *m*; *sit on the* ~ abwarten; **2.** *v/t. a.* ~ *in* einhegen, ein-, umzäunen; schützen (*from* vor *dat.*); *v/i.* fechten; *fig.* ausweichen (*with dat.*); *Sport*: e-e Hürde nehmen; *sl.* hehlen; ˈ**fence·less** offen; schutzlos.
fenc·ing [ˈfensiŋ] Einhegung *f*, -fried(ig)ung *f*; Zaunmaterial *n*; Fechten *n*; *attr.* Fecht...; ˈ~**-foil** Florett *n*; ˈ~**-mas·ter** Fechtmeister *m*.
fend [fend]: ~ *off* abwehren; ~ *for* sorgen für; ˈ**fend·er** Schutzvorrichtung *f*; Schutzblech *n*; Kamingitter *n*, -vorsetzer *m*; Stoßfänger *m*, Puffer *m*; ⚓ Fender *m*.
Fe·ni·an [ˈfiːnjən] **1.** fenisch; **2.** Fenier *m* (*Mitglied e-r irischen Unabhängigkeitspartei in USA*).
fen·nel ⚘ [ˈfenl] Fenchel *m*.
fen·ny [ˈfeni] moorig; Moor...
feoff [fef] Leh(e)n *n*; **feoff·ee** [feˈfiː] Belehnte *m*; ˈ**feoff·ment** Belehnung *f*; **feof·for** [feˈfɔː] Lehnsherr *m*.
fer·ment 1. [ˈfəːmənt] Gärung(smittel *n*) *f*; Ferment *n*; **2.** [fəːˈment] gären; in Gärung bringen (*a. fig.*); **ferˈment·a·ble** gärungsfähig; **fer·menˈta·tion** Gärung *f* (*a. fig.*); Unruhe *f*; **ferˈment·a-**

tive [~tətiv] Gärung erregend.
fern ⚘ [fəːn] Farn(kraut *n*) *m*.
fe·ro·cious □ [fəˈrəuʃəs] wild; grausam; **fe·roc·i·ty** [fəˈrɔsiti] Wildheit *f*; Grausamkeit *f*.
fer·ret [ˈferit] **1.** *zo.* Frettchen *n*; *fig.* Spürhund *m*; **2.** *hunt.* frettieren; (umher)stöbern; ~ *out* aufstöbern; herausjagen; aufspüren.
fer·ric ⚗ [ˈferik] Eisen...; **fer·rif·er·ous** [feˈrifərəs], **fer·ru·gi·nous** [feˈruːdʒinəs] eisenhaltig; **fer·ro-con·crete** ⊕ [ˈferəuˈkɔŋkriːt] Eisenbeton *m*; **fer·rous** ⚗ [ˈferəs] Eisen...
fer·rule [ˈferuːl] Zwinge *f*.
fer·ry [ˈferi] **1.** Fähre *f*; **2.** übersetzen; ˈ**~-boat** Fährboot *n*, Fähre *f*; ˈ**fer·ry·man** Fährmann *m*.
fer·tile □ [ˈfəːtail] fruchtbar; reich (*of, in* an *dat.*) (*a. fig.*); **fer·til·i·ty** [fəːˈtiliti] Fruchtbarkeit *f* (*a. fig.*); **fer·ti·li·za·tion** [~laiˈzeiʃən] Befruchtung *f*; (künstliche) Düngung *f*; ˈ**fer·ti·lize** fruchtbar machen; *bsd. biol.* befruchten; düngen; ˈ**fer·ti·liz·er** Düngemittel *n*, (Kunst-)Dünger *m*.
fer·ule [ˈferuːl] Lineal *n zur Züchtigung*; *fig.* Rute *f*.
fer·ven·cy [ˈfəːvənsi] *mst fig.* Glut *f*; Inbrunst *f*; ˈ**fer·vent** □ heiß; *fig.* inbrünstig, glühend.
fer·vid □ [ˈfəːvid] = *fervent*.
fer·vo(u)r [ˈfəːvə] Glut *f*; Inbrunst *f*.
fes·tal □ [ˈfestl] festlich.
fes·ter [ˈfestə] **1.** eitern (lassen); verfaulen; **2.** Geschwür *n*.
fes·ti·val [ˈfestəvəl] Fest *n*; Feier *f*; Festspiele *n/pl.*; **fes·tive** □ [ˈ~tiv] festlich; **fesˈtiv·i·ty** Festlichkeit *f*; festliche Stimmung *f*.
fes·toon [fesˈtuːn] **1.** Girlande *f*; **2.** mit Girlanden schmücken.
fetch [fetʃ] holen; *Preis* erzielen, bringen; F reizen, fesseln; F *Schlag* versetzen; *Seufzer* ausstoßen; ~ *and carry for s.o.* j-s Diener sein; ~ *up Verlust* einholen; ausspeien; zum Stehen kommen; ˈ**fetch·ing** F □ bezaubernd, reizend.
fête [feit] **1.** Fest(lichkeit *f*) *n*; *a.* ~*-day* Namenstag *m*; **2.** feiern.
fet·id □ [ˈfetid] stinkend.
fe·tish [ˈfiːtiʃ] Fetisch *m* (*a. fig.*).
fet·lock [ˈfetlɔk] Köte *f*, Fesse (-gelenk *n*) *f des Pferdes*.
fet·ter [ˈfetə] **1.** Fessel *f*; **2.** fesseln; *fig.* zügeln.
fet·tle [ˈfetl] Form *f*, Verfassung *f*; *in fine* ~ in Form.
feud [fjuːd] Fehde *f*; Leh(e)n *n*; **feu·dal** □ [ˈ~dl] lehnbar; Lehns...; **feu·dal·ism** [ˈ~dəlizəm] Lehnswesen *n*, Feudalismus *m*; **feu·dal·i·ty** [~ˈdæliti] Lehnbarkeit *f*; Lehnsverfassung *f*; **feu·da·to·ry** [ˈ~dətəri] **1.** lehnspflichtig; **2.** Lehnsmann *m*.
fe·ver [ˈfiːvə] Fieber *n*; *fig.* Erregung *f*; ˈ**fe·vered** *bsd. fig.* fiebernd; ˈ**fe·ver·ish** □ fieberig; *fig.* fieberhaft, aufgeregt.
few [fjuː] wenige; *a* ~ einige, ein paar; *quite a* ~, *a good* ~ e-e ganze Menge; *the* ~ die Minderheit.
fi·an·cé(e *f*) [fiˈɑ̃ːnsei] Verlobte *m, f*.
fi·as·co [fiˈæskəu] Reinfall *m*, Mißerfolg *m*, Fiasko *n*.
fi·at [ˈfaiæt] Machtspruch *m*, Befehl *m*; ~ *money Am.* Papiergeld *n* (*ohne Deckung*).
fib F [fib] **1.** Flunkerei *f*, Schwindelei *f*; **2.** schwindeln, flunkern; ˈ**fib·ber** Flunkerer *m*.
fi·bre [ˈfaibə] Fiber *f*, Faser *f*; Struktur *f*; Charakter(eigenschaft *f*) *m*; ˈ**~board** Hartfaserplatte *f*; ˈ**~glass** Glaswolle *f*; **fi·brin** [ˈ~brin] Fibrin *n*, Blutfaserstoff *m*; ˈ**fi·brous** □ faserig; ~ *material* Spinnstoff *m*.
fib·u·la *anat.* [ˈfibjulə] Wadenbein *n*.
fick·le [ˈfikl] wankelmütig; unbeständig; ˈ**fick·le·ness** Wankelmut *m*; Unbeständigkeit *f*.
fic·tion [ˈfikʃən] Erdichtung *f*; ⚖ Fiktion *f*; Roman-, Unterhaltungsliteratur *f*, erzählende Literatur *f*; **fic·tion·al** □ [ˈ~ʃənl] erdichtet; Roman...
fic·ti·tious □ [fikˈtiʃəs] unecht; erdichtet, erfunden, fiktiv; (nur) angenommen; Roman...; ˈ**fic·tive** unecht, erfunden.
fid·dle [ˈfidl] **1.** Geige *f*, Fiedel *f*; **2.** *v/i.* fiedeln; tändeln; *v/t. sl. Steuererklärung etc.* frisieren; ~ *away* vergeuden; **fid·dle·de·dee** [ˈ~diˈdiː] Unsinn *m*; **fid·dle-fad·dle** F [ˈ~fædl] **1.** Lappalie *f*; ~! Unsinn!; **2.** vertrödeln; ˈ**fid·dler** Geiger(in); Spielmann *m*; *sl.* Steuerhinterzieher *m*; ˈ**fid·dle·stick** Geigenbogen *m*; ~*s!* dummes Zeug!; ˈ**fid·dling** läppisch, trivial.

fi·del·i·ty [fi'deliti] Treue *f* (*to* zu, gegen); Genauigkeit *f*.
fidg·et F ['fidʒit] **1.** *oft* *~s pl.* nervöse Unruhe *f*; Zappelphilipp *m*; *have the ~s* kein Sitzfleisch haben; **2.** nervös machen *od.* sein; (umher)zappeln; '**fidg·et·y** nervös, unruhig, kribbelig.
fi·du·ci·ar·y [fi'dju:ʃjəri] **1.** anvertraut; Vertrauens...; ✝ ungedeckt; **2.** Verwahrer *m*, Treuhänder *m*.
fie [fai] pfui!
fief [fi:f] Leh(e)n *n*.
field [fi:ld] **1.** Feld *n*; Wiese *f*; Schlachtfeld *n*; Spielfeld *n*, Spielplatz *m*; Arbeitsfeld *n*, Gebiet *n*; Bereich *m*; *Sport*: Feld *n*, Teilnehmer *m/pl.*; Besetzung *f*; *hold the ~* das Feld behaupten; *take the ~* ins Feld rücken; **2.** *Kricket*: *Ball* fangen u. zurückgeben; Fänger sein; '**~-day** ⚔ Felddienstübung *f*; Parade *f*; *fig.* großer Tag *m*; *Am.* (Schul)Sportfest *n*; *Am.* Exkursionstag *m*; '**field·er** *Kricket*: Fänger *m*.
field...: **~ e·vents** *pl.* Sprung- u. Wurfwettkämpfe *m/pl.*; '**~·fare** Wacholderdrossel *f*; '**~-glass·es** *pl.* Feldstecher *m*; '**~-gun** ⚔ Feldgeschütz *n*; '**~-'hos·pi·tal** ⚔ Feldlazarett *n*; '**~-'mar·shal** Feldmarschall *m*; '**~-of·fi·cer** Stabsoffizier *m*; '**~-sports** *pl.* Jagen *n* u. Fischen *n*; '**~·work** praktische Arbeit *f*; Außendienst *m*.
fiend [fi:nd] böser Feind *m*, Teufel *m*; Unhold *m*; *Frischluft- etc.* Fanatiker *m*; '**fiend·ish** □ teuflisch, boshaft.
fierce □ [fiəs] wild; grimmig; hitzig; heftig; '**fierce·ness** Wildheit *f*; Grimm *m*; Ungestüm *n*.
fi·er·i·ness ['faiərinis] Hitze *f*, Feuer *n*; '**fi·er·y** □ feurig, glühend; hitzig; feuergefährlich; Feuer...
fife [faif] **1.** Querpfeife *f*; **2.** auf der Querpfeife blasen; '**fif·er** Pfeifer *m*.
fif·teen ['fif'ti:n] fünfzehn; '**fif-'teenth** [~θ] fünfzehnte(r, -s);
fifth [fifθ] **1.** fünfte(r, -s); **2.** Fünftel *n*; **fifth col·umn** *pol.* Fünfte Kolonne *f*; '**fifth·ly** fünftens;
fif·ti·eth ['~tiiθ] **1.** fünfzigste(r, -s); **2.** Fünfzigstel *n*; '**fif·ty** fünfzig; '**fif·ty-'fif·ty** F zu gleichen Teilen, halb und halb; *go ~* halbe halbe machen.
fig¹ [fig] Feige *f*; *a ~ for ...!* zum Teufel mit ...!; *I don't care a ~ for him* ich mache mir gar nichts aus ihm.
fig² [~] **1.** F Zustand *m*, Form *f*; *in full ~* in vollem Wichs; **2.** *~ out* F herausputzen.
fight [fait] **1.** Kampf *m*; Faustkampf *m*; Schlägerei *f*; Kampflust *f*, -geist *m*; Gefecht *n*; *make a ~ for* kämpfen für *od.* um; *put up a good ~* sich wacker schlagen; *show ~* sich zur Wehr setzen; **2.** (*irr.*) *v/t.* bekämpfen, sich schlagen mit, kämpfen mit *od.* gegen; verfechten; erkämpfen; ⚔ (im Kampf) führen; *~ off* abwehren; *~ one's way* sich durchschlagen; *v/i.* sich schlagen, kämpfen, fechten; *~ against s.th.* et. bekämpfen, gegen et. ankämpfen; *~ back* zurückschlagen; *~ shy of j-m* aus dem Wege gehen; '**fight·er** Kämpfer *m*, Fechter *m*, Streiter *m*; ⚔ Jagdflugzeug *n*; *~ pilot* Jagdflieger *m*; '**fight·ing** Kampf *m*, Gefecht *n*; *attr.* Kampf...; *~ chance* Erfolgschance *f bei großer Anstrengung*.
fig·ment ['figmənt] reine Erfindung *f*.
fig-tree ['figtri:] Feigenbaum *m*.
fig·u·rant(e *f*) ['figjurənt; (~'rɑ̃:nt)] Ballettänzer(in); Statist(in).
fig·u·ra·tion [figju'reiʃən] Gestaltung *f*; **fig·ur·a·tive** □ ['~rətiv] bildlich, figürlich, übertragen; bilderreich.
fig·ure ['figə] **1.** Figur *f* (*a.* ♞), Gestalt *f*; Zahl *f*, Ziffer *f*; Preis *m*; *~ of speech* Redefigur *f*, bildlicher Ausdruck *m*; *what's the ~?* was kostet es?; *at a high ~* zu e-m hohen Preis; *be good at ~s* gut im Rechnen sein; **2.** *v/t.* abbilden, darstellen; *a. ~ to o.s.* sich et. vorstellen; mit Zahlen bezeichnen; *~ up od. out* berechnen; *~ out* sich *et.* ausmalen *od.* ausdenken; verstehen; *v/i.* erscheinen, e-e Rolle spielen (*as* als); *~ on Am. et.* überdenken, rechnen auf *od.* mit; *~ out at* sich beziffern auf (*acc.*); '**~-head** ⚓ Galionsfigur *f*; *fig.* Aushängeschild *n*; '**~-skat·ing** Eiskunstlauf *m*.
fig·u·rine ['figjuri:n] Statuette *f*.
fil·a·ment ['filəmənt] Faden *m*, Faser *f*; ⚘ Staubfaden *m*; ⚡ Glüh-, Heizfaden *m*.

fil·a·ture [ˈfilətʃə] Seidenspinnerei *f*.
fil·bert ⚘ [ˈfilbə:t] Haselnuß *f*.
filch [filtʃ] stibitzen (*from dat.*).
file[1] [fail] **1.** Akte *f*, Ordner *m*; Reihe *f*; ⚔ Rotte *f*; *on* ~ bei den Akten; aktenkundig; **2.** *v/t.* aufreihen; *Briefe etc.* einordnen; zu den Akten nehmen, ablegen; *Klage etc.* einreichen; *v/i.* ⚔ hintereinander marschieren; ~ *in* (*out*) hintereinander hereinkommen (hinausgehen).
file[2] [~] **1.** Feile *f*; **2.** feilen.
fil·i·al □ [ˈfiljəl] kindlich, Kindes...; **fil·i·a·tion** [filiˈeiʃən] Kindschaft *f*; Abstammung *f*; Abzweigung *f*, Zweig *m*.
fil·i·bus·ter [ˈfilibʌstə] **1.** *Am.* Obstruktion(spolitiker *m*) *f*; **2.** *Am.* Obstruktion treiben.
fil·i·gree [ˈfiligri:] Filigran(arbeit *f*) *n*.
fil·ing cab·i·net [ˈfailiŋkæbinit] Aktenschrank *m*.
fil·ings [ˈfailiŋz] *pl.* Feilspäne *m/pl.*
fill [fil] **1.** (sich) füllen; voll werden; an-, aus-, erfüllen; (voll)stopfen; *Zahn* plombieren; *Stelle etc.* bekleiden, einnehmen, ausfüllen, innehaben; *Am.* Auftrag ausführen; ~ *in Lücke, Scheck etc.* ausfüllen; einsetzen; ~ *out* sich füllen; stärker werden; ~ *up* ausfüllen; zuschütten; sich füllen; **2.** Fülle *f*, Genüge *f*; Füllung *f*; *eat* (*drink*) *one's* ~ sich satt essen (trinken) (*of* an *dat.*).
fill·er [ˈfilə] Füller *m*; Trichter *m*.
fil·let [ˈfilit] **1.** Haarband *n*; Lendenbraten *m*, Filet *n*; Roulade *f*; Band *n*, Leiste *f* (*bsd.* △); *tel.* Papierstreifen *m*; **2.** mit e-m Haarband *etc.* schmücken.
fill·ing [ˈfiliŋ] Füllung *f*; ~ **sta·tion** *Am.* Tankstelle *f*.
fil·lip [ˈfilip] **1.** Schnippchen *n mit dem Finger*; Nasenstüber *m*; Anregung *f*; **2.** einen Nasenstüber geben (*dat.*); antreiben.
fil·ly [ˈfili] (Stuten)Füllen *n*; *fig.* wilde Hummel *f*.
film [film] Häutchen *n*; Schicht *f*, Überzug *m*; Membran(e) *f*; *Zahn- etc.* Belag *m*; *phot. u. thea.* Film *m*; Trübung *f des Auges*; Nebelschleier *m*; Fädchen *n*; *take od. shoot a* ~ e-n Film drehen; **2.** (sich) mit einem Häutchen überziehen; verschleiern; (ver)filmen; ˈ**film·y** □ häutig; trüb; hauchdünn.
fil·ter [ˈfiltə] **1.** Filter *m*; **2.** filtrieren; durchsickern; ~ *in mot.* sich einordnen; ˈ**fil·ter·ing** Filtrier...; ˈ**fil·ter tip** Filtermundstück *n e-r Zigarette*.
filth [filθ] Schmutz *m*; *bsd. fig.* Unflat *m*; ˈ**filth·y** □ schmutzig; unflätig.
fil·trate [ˈfiltreit] filtrieren; **filˈtra·tion** Filtrierung *f*.
fin [fin] Flosse *f* (*sl. Hand*); ✈ Steuerflosse *f*; *mot.* Kühlrippe *f*.
fi·nal [ˈfainl] **1.** □ letzt, endlich; schließlich; End...; endgültig, entscheidend; *gr.* Absichts...; **2.** *a.* ~*s pl.* Schlußprüfung *f*; *Sport*: Schlußrunde *f*; **fi·na·le** [fiˈnɑ:li] Finale *n*, Schluß(satz *m*, -szene *f*) *m*; **fi·nal·ist** [ˈfainəlist] *Sport*: Schlußrundenteilnehmer *m*; **fi·nal·i·ty** [~ˈnæliti] Endgültigkeit *f*; **fi·nal·ize** [ˈ~nəlaiz] abschließen; endgültige Form geben (*dat.*); **fi·nal whis·tle** *Sport*: Schluß-, Abpfiff *m*.
fi·nance [faiˈnæns] **1.** Finanzwesen *n*; ~*s pl.* Finanzen *pl.*, Vermögenslage *f*; **2.** *v/t.* finanzieren; *v/i.* Geldgeschäfte machen; **fiˈnan·cial** □ [~ʃəl] finanziell; ~ *year* Rechnungs-, Geschäftsjahr *n*; **fiˈnan·cier** [~siə] Finanzier *m*; Geldgeber *m*.
finch *orn.* [fintʃ] Fink *m*.
find [faind] **1.** (*irr.*) finden; (an)treffen; auf-, herausfinden; ⚖ *schuldig etc.* befinden, erklären; liefern, stellen; versorgen (*in* mit); ~ *o.s.* sich (be)finden; seine Fähigkeiten erkennen; *all found* freie Station; ~ *out* herausfinden; ertappen; *I cannot* ~ *it in my heart* ich kann es nicht übers Herz bringen; **2.** Fund *m*; ˈ**find·er** Finder(in); *opt.* Sucher *m*; ˈ**find·ing** Entdeckung *f*; *a.* ~*s pl.* Befund *m*; ⚖ Wahrspruch *m*, Urteil *n*.
fine[1] □ [fain] **1.** schön; fein; verfeinert; rein; spitz, dünn, scharf; geziert; vornehm; *you are a* ~ *fellow! iro.* du bist mir ein sauberer Kerl!; ~ *arts pl.* schöne Künste *f/pl.*; **2.** *adv.* gut, bestens; *cut* ~ *Preis, Zeit* zu knapp berechnen; **3.** *meteor.* Schönwetter *n*; **4.** (sich) klären (*bsd. Bier*); ~ *away*, ~ *down*, ~ *off* abschleifen; zuspitzen.
fine[2] [~] **1.** Geldstrafe *f*; Abstandssumme *f*; *in* ~ kurzum; **2.** zu e-r Geldstrafe verurteilen; ~ *s.o. 5 sh.* j. zu 5 Schilling Geldstrafe verur-

teilen.
fine-draw [ˈfainˈdrɔː] kunststopfen.
fine·ness [ˈfainnis] Feinheit *f etc.* (*s. fine*[1]); Feingehalt *m*; Reinheit *f*.
fin·er·y [ˈfainəri] Glanz *m*; Putz *m*, Staat *m*; ⊕ Frischofen *m*.
fi·nesse [fiˈnes] Finesse *f*, Schlauheit *f*, Spitzfindigkeit *f*.
fin·ger [ˈfiŋgə] **1.** Finger *m*; *have a ~ in the pie* die Hand im Spiel haben; *s. end 1*; **2.** befingern, betasten, (herum)fingern an (*dat.*); ♪ mit Fingersatz versehen; spielen; üben; **ˈ~-al·pha·bet** Fingeralphabet *n*; **ˈ~-board** ♪ Griffbrett *n*; **ˈ~-bowl** Fingerschale *f*; **ˈfin·gered** ...fingerig; **ˈfin·ger·ing** Betasten *n*; ♪ Fingersatz *m*; Strumpfwolle *f*.
fin·ger...: **ˈ~-lan·guage** Zeichensprache *f*; **ˈ~-mark** Fingerabdruck *m*; **ˈ~-nail** Fingernagel *m*; **ˈ~-plate** Türschoner *m*; **ˈ~-post** Wegweiser *m*; **ˈ~-print 1.** Fingerabdruck *m*; **2.** *j-s* Fingerabdruck nehmen; **ˈ~-stall** Fingerling *m*.
fin·i·cal □ [ˈfinikəl], **fin·ick·ing** [ˈ~iŋ], **ˈfin·ick·y** geziert; wählerisch; knifflig; pedantisch.
fin·ish [ˈfiniʃ] **1.** *v/t.* beenden, vollenden; fertigstellen; abschließen; *a. ~ off, ~ up* vervollkommnen; ⊕ fertig(bearbeit)en; ⊕ appretieren; aufhören mit; erledigen; *~ed goods pl.* Fertigwaren *f/pl.*; *~ing line Sport*: Ziel(linie *f*) *n*; *~ing touch* letzter Schliff *m*; *v/i.* enden, aufhören; *have ~ed* fertig sein; **2.** Vollendung *f*, letzte Hand *f*; Schluß *m*; Entscheidung *f*; ⊕ Appretur *f*; *Sport*: Ziel *n*; **ˈfin·ish·er** Fertigsteller *m*; ⊕ Appretierer *m*; entscheidender Schlag *m*.
fi·nite □ [ˈfainait] endlich, begrenzt; *~ verb gr.* Verbum *n* finitum; **ˈfi·nite·ness** Endlichkeit *f*.
fink *Am. sl.* [fiŋk] Streikbrecher *m*.
Finn [fin] Finne *m*, Finnin *f*.
Finn·ish [ˈfiniʃ] **1.** finnisch; **2.** Finnisch *n*.
fin·ny [ˈfini] mit Flossen (versehen).
fiord [fjɔːd] Fjord *m*.
fir [fəː] (Weiß)Tanne *f*; *Scotch ~* Föhre *f*, Kiefer *f*; **ˈ~-cone** Tannenzapfen *m*.
fire [ˈfaiə] **1.** Feuer *n*, Brand *m*; Glanz *m*; Glut *f*, Heftigkeit *f*; *on ~* in Feuer, in Brand, in Flammen; *come under ~ from s.o. fig.* in j-s Schußlinie geraten; *lay a ~* ein Feuer anlegen; *set ~ to* in Brand stecken, anzünden; **2.** *v/t.* an-, entzünden; *fig.* anfeuern; *a. ~ off* abfeuern; *Ziegel etc.* brennen; röten; F rausschmeißen (*entlassen*); *~ up* anfeuern, -heizen; *v/i.* Feuer fangen (*a. fig.*); feuern (*at, upon* auf *acc*); sich röten; *~ away!* F schieß los!; *~ up* auffahren (*at* über *acc.*); **ˈ~-a·larm** Feuermelder *m*; **ˈ~-arms** *pl.* Schuß-, Feuerwaffen *f/pl.*; **ˈ~-ball** Meteor *m*; Feuerball *m e-r Atomexplosion*; **ˈ~-bomb** Brandbombe *f*; **ˈ~-box** ⊕ Feuerbüchse *f*; **ˈ~-brand** Feuerbrand *m*; *fig.* Aufwiegler *m*; **ˈ~-break** Schneise *f*; Brandmauer *f*; **ˈ~-brick** feuerfester Stein *m*; **ˈ~-bri·gade** Feuerwehr *f*; **ˈ~·bug** *Am.* F Brandstifter *m*; **ˈ~·clay** feuerfester Ton *m*; **ˈ~-con·trol** ⚔ Feuerleitung *f*; **ˈ~-crack·er** Frosch *m* (*Feuerwerkskörper*); **ˈ~-damp** ⚒ schlagendes Wetter *n*; **ˈ~-de·part·ment** *Am.* Feuerwehr *f*; **ˈ~-dog** Feuerbock *m*; **ˈ~·door** Feuerschutztür *f*; **~ drill** Feuerlöschübung *f*; **ˈ~-eat·er** Raufbold *m*, Kampfhahn *m*; **ˈ~-en·gine** ⊕ (Feuer)Spritze *f*; **ˈ~-es·cape** Rettungsgerät *n*, -tuch *n*, -leiter *f*; Nottreppe *f*; **ˈ~-ex·tin·guish·er** Feuerlöscher *m*; **ˈ~-fight·er** Brandschützer *m*, Feuerwehrmann *m bsd. bei Waldbränden u. im Krieg*; **ˈ~-fly** Leuchtkäfer *m*; **ˈ~-guard** Kamingitter *n*; Brandwache *f*; **ˈ~-in·sur·ance** Feuerversicherung *f*; **ˈ~-i·rons** *pl.* Kamingerät *n*; **ˈ~-light·er** Kohlenanzünder *m*; **ˈ~·man** Feuerwehrmann *m*; Heizer *m*; **ˈ~-of·fice** Feuerversicherungsanstalt *f*; **ˈ~-place** Feuerstelle *f*; Feuerherd *m*; Kamin *m*; **ˈ~-pow·er** ⚔ Feuerkraft *f*; **ˈ~-plug** Hydrant *m*; **ˈ~·proof** feuerfest; **ˈ~-rais·ing** Brandstiftung *f*; **ˈ~-screen** Ofenschirm *m*; **ˈ~·side 1.** Kamin *m*; Häuslichkeit *f*; **2.** häuslich; **ˈ~-sta·tion** Feuerwache *f*; **ˈ~·wood** Brennholz *n*; **ˈ~·work**(s *pl. fig.*) Feuerwerk *n*.
fir·ing [ˈfaiəriŋ] Heizung *f*; Feuerung *f*; ⚔ Feuern *n*; **ˈ~-line** ⚔ vorderster Graben *m*; **ˈ~-par·ty, ~ squad** ⚔ Exekutionskommando *n*.
fir·kin [ˈfəːkin] Viertelfaß *n*; (Butter- *etc.*)Fäßchen *n*.
firm [fəːm] **1.** □ fest; derb; standhaft; entschlossen; **2.** Firma *f*.
fir·ma·ment [ˈfəːməmənt] Firma-

ment *n*, Himmelsgewölbe *n*.
firm·ness ['fə:mnis] Festigkeit *f*, Entschlossenheit *f*.
first [fə:st] **1.** *adj.* erste(r, -s); beste(r, -s); *at ~ hand* aus erster Hand, direkt; *at ~ sight* auf den ersten Blick; *~ strike* ⚔ Erstangriff *m*; **2.** *adv.* erstens; zuerst; *at ~* zuerst, anfangs; *~ of all* an erster Stelle; zu allererst; *~ and last* alles in allem; **3.** Erste *m, f u. n*; *~ of exchange* ✝ Primawechsel *m*; *from the ~* von Anfang an; *go ~* vorangehen; 🚂 erster Klasse fahren; *~* **aid** ⚕ Erste Hilfe *f*; '**~-'aid box** Verbandkasten *m*; '**~-'aid post** Unfallstation *f*; '**~-born** erstgeboren; *~* **class** 1. Klasse *f* (*e-s Verkehrsmittels*); '**~-'class** erstklassig, prima; '**~-fruits** *pl.* Erstlinge *m/pl.*; Erstlingswerk *n*; '**~-'hand** aus erster Hand, direkt; '**first·ly** erstlich; erstens.
first...: *~* **name** Vorname *m*; Beiname *m*; *~* **pa·pers** *pl. Am. vorläufige* Einbürgerungspapiere *n/pl.*; '**~-'rate** ersten Ranges; = *first-class*; '**~-time vot·er** *pol.* Erstwähler(in).
firth [fə:θ] Förde *f*; (Flut)Mündung *f*.
fis·cal ['fiskəl] fiskalisch; Finanz...
fish [fiʃ] **1.** Fisch *m*; *coll.* Fische *m/pl.*; 🚂 (Schienen)Lasche *f*; F Kerl *m*; *odd ~* komischer Kauz *m*; *have other ~ to fry* Wichtigeres zu tun haben; *a pretty kettle of ~* ein hübsches Durcheinander *n*; **2.** fischen; angeln; haschen (*for* nach); 🚂 verlaschen; *~ out* herausholen; *~ in troubled waters* im trüben fischen; '**~-bone** Gräte *f*; '**~·cake** Fischfrikadelle *f*.
fish·er ['fiʃə], **fish·er·man** ['~mən] Fischer *m*; '**fish·er·y** Fischerei *f*.
fish...: '**~-eye lens** *phot.* Fischauge *n*, *extremes* Weitwinkelobjektiv *n*; *~* **fin·ger** Fischstäbchen *n*; **~-hatch·er·y** ['fiʃhætʃəri] Fischzuchtanstalt *f*.
fish-hook ['fiʃhuk] Angelhaken *m*.
fish·ing ['fiʃiŋ] Fischen *n*, Angeln *n*; '**~-boat** Fischerboot *n*; '**~-line** Angelschnur *f*; '**~-rod** Angelrute *f*; '**~-tack·le** Angelgerät *n*.
fish...: '**~-liv·er oil** Lebertran *m*; '**~·mon·ger** Fischhändler *m*; *~* **stick** *Am.* Fischstäbchen *n*; '**~·wife** Fischweib *n*; '**fish·y** fisch(art)ig; fischreich; trüb (*Auge*); F verdächtig, faul.
fis·sile ['fisail] spaltbar.
fis·sion ['fiʃən] Spaltung *f*; *s. atomic*; **fis·sure** ['fiʃə] **1.** Spalt *m*, Riß *m*; **2.** spalten.
fist [fist] Faust *f*; F Klaue *f* (*Hand*; *Handschrift*); **fist·i·cuffs** ['~ikʌfs] *pl.* Faustschläge *m/pl.*
fis·tu·la ⚕ ['fistjulə] Fistel *f*.
fit[1] [fit] **1.** □ geeignet, passend (*for* für); schicklich, tauglich; fähig; *Sport*: in (guter) Form, auf der Höhe, fit; bereit (*to* zu); *it is not ~* es ziemt sich nicht; *~ as a fiddle* quietschvergnügt; kerngesund; **2.** *v/t.* passen für *od. dat.*; anpassen, passend machen; befähigen; geeignet machen (*for, to* für, zu); ⊕ *a. ~ in* einpassen; *a. ~ on* anprobieren; versehen, ausstatten (*with* mit); *~ out* ausrüsten; *~ up* einrichten, ausstatten; montieren; *v/i.* passen; sich eignen; sich schicken *od.* gehören; sitzen (*Kleid*); **3.** Sitz *m e-s Kleides*; *it is a bad ~* es sitzt schlecht.
fit[2] [~] Anfall *m*; Ausbruch *m e-r Krankheit*; Anwandlung *f*; *by ~s and starts* ruckweise; dann und wann; *give s.o. a ~* j. hochbringen; j-m e-n Schock versetzen.
fitch·ew *zo.* ['fitʃu:] Iltis *m*.
fit·ful □ ['fitful] ruck-, krampfartig; *fig.* unstet, unregelmäßig, launenhaft; '**fit·ment** Einrichtungsgegenstand *m*; *~s pl.* Einrichtung *f*; '**fit·ness** Schicklichkeit *f*; Tauglichkeit *f*, Eignung *f*; *~ trail Am.* Trimmpfad *m*; '**fit-out** Ausstattung *f*; '**fit·ted** ausgestattet (*with* mit); *~ carpet* Teppichboden *m*; *~ cupboard* Einbauschrank *m*; *~ sheet* Spannbettuch *n*; '**fit·ter** Monteur *m*; Einrichter *m*; Installateur *m*; Zuschneider *m*; '**fit·ting 1.** □ passend, geeignet, angemessen; schicklich; **2.** Montage *f*; Anprobe *f*; *~s pl.* Einrichtung *f e-s Hauses etc.*; Armaturen *f/pl.*; Beleuchtungskörper *m/pl.*; '**fit-up** F provisorische Bühne *f*; *a. ~ company* Wanderbühne *f*.
five [faiv] **1.** fünf; **2.** Fünf *f*; *~s sg.* Wandball(spiel *n*) *m*; '**five·fold** fünffach; **fiv·er** F ['~və] Fünfpfundnote *f*.
fix [fiks] **1.** befestigen, anheften; *phot. etc., j. mit den Augen* fixieren; *Augen etc.* heften, richten (*on* auf *acc.*); fesseln; fest werden lassen; aufstellen, unterbringen; bestimmen, festsetzen; anberaumen; *bsd. Am.* F (her)richten, *Bett etc.* ma-

chen; ~ *o.s.* sich niederlassen; ~ *up* in Ordnung bringen, arrangieren; unterbringen; *v/i.* fest werden; ~ *on* sich entschließen für; **2.** F Klemme *f*, Patsche *f*, Verlegenheit *f*; **fix'a·tion** Fixierung *f*; **fix·a·tive** ['~ətiv], **fix·a·ture** ['~ətʃə] Fixiermittel *n*; **fixed** fest (*a.* ⚗); bestimmt (*Summe etc.*); starr (*Blick*); **fixed i·de·a** *psych.* fixe Idee *f*; **'fixed-'in·ter·est** festverzinslich; **fix·ed·ly** ['fiksidli] bestimmt; ständig; starr; **'fix·ed·ness** Festigkeit *f* (*a. fig.*); **fixed star** Fixstern *m*; **'fix·er** *phot.* Fixierbad *n*; **'fix·ing** Befestigen *n etc.*; ~*s pl. Am.* Zubehör *n*, Extraausrüstung *f*, -sachen *f/pl.*; Garnierung *f*; **'fix·i·ty** Festigkeit *f*; **fix·ture** ['~tʃə] fest angebrachtes Zubehörteil *n*, feste Anlage *f*; Inventarstück *n* (*a. fig. Person*); *Sport*: *zeitlich festgesetzte* Veranstaltung *f*; ~*s pl.* Einrichtungsstücke *n/pl.*, festes Inventar *n*, Zubehör *n*; *lighting* ~ Beleuchtungskörper *m*.

fizz [fiz] **1.** zischen, sprudeln; **2.** Zischen *n*; F Schampus *m* (*Sekt*); **fiz·zle** ['fizl] **1.** zischen, sprühen; *mst* ~ *out* verpuffen; mißglücken; **2.** Zischen *n*; Fiasko *n*, Pleite *f*; **'fiz·zy** sprudelnd, mit Kohlensäure (versetzt).

flab·ber·gast F ['flæbəgɑːst] verblüffen; *be* ~*ed* baff *od.* platt sein.

flab·by □ ['flæbi] schlaff, schlapp.

flac·cid □ ['flæksid] schlaff, schlapp.

flag[1] [flæg] **1.** Flagge *f*; Fahne *f*; Fähnchen *n*; *black* ~ Seeräuberflagge *f*; ~ *of convenience* billige Flagge *f*; **2.** beflaggen; durch Flaggen signalisieren.

flag[2] [~] **1.** Fliese *f*; **2.** mit Fliesen belegen.

flag[3] ⚘ [~] Schwertlilie *f*.

flag[4] [~] ermatten; mutlos werden.

flag-cap·tain ⚓ ['flæg'kæptin] Kommandant *m* e-s Flaggschiffs.

flag-day ['flægdei] Opfertag *m*; *Am. Flag Day* Tag *m* des Sternenbanners (*14. Juni*).

flag·el·lant ['flædʒilənt] Flagellant *m*; **flag·el·late** ['~dʒeleit] geißeln; **flag·el'la·tion** Geißelung *f*.

flag·eo·let ♪ [flædʒəu'let] Flageolett *n*.

fla·gi·tious □ [flə'dʒiʃəs] abscheulich, schändlich, kriminell.

flag·on ['flægən] (Deckel)Kanne *f*; Bocksbeutel *m*.

flag·post ['flægpəust] Fahnenstange *f*.

fla·grant □ ['fleigrənt] abscheulich; berüchtigt; offenkundig.

flag...: '~**-ship** Flaggschiff *n*; '~**-staff** Fahnenstange *f*, -mast *m*; ⚓ Flaggenstock *m*; '~**-stone** (Stein-)Fliese *f*.

flail ⚒ [fleil] Dreschflegel *m*.

flair [flɛə] Spürsinn *m*, feine Nase *f*.

flake [fleik] **1.** Flocke *f*; Schicht *f*; **2.** (sich) flocken; abblättern; **'flak·y** flockig, schuppig.

flam F [flæm] Schwindel *m*, fauler Zauber *m*.

flam·beau ['flæmbəu] Fackel *f*.

flam·boy·ant [flæm'bɔiənt] farbenprächtig; pompös; auffallend.

flame [fleim] **1.** Flamme *f*, Feuer *n*; *fig.* Hitze *f*, Leidenschaft *f*; Geliebte *m*, *f*; **2.** flammen, lodern (*a. fig.*); ~ *out*, ~ *up* aufflammen; **'flam·ing** flammend, glühend, zündend (*a. fig.*).

fla·min·go *orn.* [flə'miŋgəu] Flamingo *m*.

flam·ma·ble (*bsd. Am.*) ['flæməbl] feuergefährlich.

flan [flæn] Obstkuchen *m*.

flange ⊕ [flændʒ] Flansch *m*.

flank [flæŋk] **1.** Flanke *f*; Weiche *f der Tiere*; **2.** flankieren.

flan·nel ['flænl] Flanell *m*; Waschlappen *m*; **flan·nel·ette** [~'et] Baumwollflanell *m*; **'flan·nels** *pl.* Flanellunterwäsche *f*, -anzug *m*, -hose *f*.

flap [flæp] **1.** (Ohr)Läppchen *n*; Rockschoß *m*; *Hut*-Krempe *f*; Klappe *f*; Lasche *f*; Klaps *m*; (Flügel)Schlag *m*; F nervöse Aufregung *f*; *be* (*get*) *in a* ~ aus dem Häuschen sein (geraten); **2.** *v/t.* klatschen(d schlagen), klapsen (mit); *v/i.* lose herabhängen; flattern; **'flap-jack** Pfannkuchen *m*; **'flap·per** Flosse *f*; Fliegenklatsche *f*; Klapper *f*; *sl.* Backfisch *m*; = *flap 1.*

flare [flɛə] **1.** flackern; sich nach außen erweitern, sich bauschen; ~ *up* aufflammen; *fig.* aufbrausen; **2.** flackerndes Licht *n*; Lichtsignal *n*, Leuchtkugel *f*; '~**-'up** Aufflackern *n*; *fig.* Aufbrausen *n*.

flash [flæʃ] **1.** aufgedonnert; unecht, falsch; Gauner...; **2.** Blitz *m*; *fig.* Aufblitzen *n*, Auflodern *n*; *bsd.*

Am. Zeitung: kurze Meldung *f*; *in a* ~ im Nu, sofort; ~ *of wit* Geistesblitz *m*; ~ *in the pan* Schlag *m* ins Wasser; **3.** blitzen; aufblitzen, auflodern (lassen); *Licht, Blick etc.* werfen; flitzen; funken, telegraphieren; *it* ~*ed on me* mir kam plötzlich der Gedanke; '**~-back** *Film*: Rückblende *f*; '**~·bulb** *phot.* Blitzlicht(lampe *f*) *n*; '**~·cube** *phot.* Blitzwürfel *m*.

flash·er ['flæʃə] *mot.* Lichthupe *f*; F Exhibitionist *m*.

flash...: '**~·gun** *phot.* Blitzgerät *n*; '**~-light** *phot.* Blitzlicht *n*; Blinklicht *n*; *bsd. Am.* Taschenlampe *f*; '**~-point** Flammpunkt *m*; '**flash·y** □ auffallend; aufdringlich, grell.

flask [flɑːsk] Taschen-, Reiseflasche *f*; ⚗ Kolben *m*.

flat [flæt] **1.** □ flach, platt; schal, matt; ✝ flau; klar; glatt (*Lüge etc.*); ♪ um e-n Halbton erniedrigt (*Note*); *Börse*: ohne Zinsenberechnung; ~ *price* Einheitspreis *m*; *fall* ~ danebengehen; *sing* ~ zu tief singen; **2.** Fläche *f*, Ebene *f*; Flachland *n*; Untiefe *f*; flache Seite *f e-s Schwertes*; (Etagen-, Miet)Wohnung *f*; ⚓ Prahm *m*; ♪ B *n*; F Schwachkopf *m*, Simpel *m*; *mot. sl.* Plattfuß *m* (*luftleerer Reifen*); '**~-boat** ⚓ Prahm *m*; '**~-foot** Plattfuß *m*; *Am. sl.* Polyp *m* (*Polizist*); '**~-'foot·ed** plattfüßig; *Am.* F geradeheraus, kompromißlos; '**~·i·ron** Bügeleisen *n*; **flat·let** ['~lit] kleine Wohnung *f*; '**flat·ness** Flachheit *f*; *fig.* Plattheit *f*; ✝ Flauheit *f*; **flat out** F **1.** *adv.* auf Hochtouren; *work* ~ mit Volldampf arbeiten; **2.** *adj.* abgeschlafft (*total erschöpft*); '**flat·ten** (sich) ab-, verflachen; ~ *out* flach *od.* eben werden; *Flugzeug* abfangen.

flat·ter ['flætə] schmeicheln (*dat.*); '**flat·ter·er** Schmeichler(in); '**flat·ter·ing** schmeichelhaft; '**flat·ter·y** Schmeichelei *f*.

flat·u·lence, flat·u·len·cy ['flætjuləns(i)] Blähung *f*; Aufgeblähtheit *f*; '**flat·u·lent** □ blähend; aufgebläht.

flaunt [flɔːnt] prunken (mit); offen zeigen; prangen.

flau·tist ['flɔːtist] Flötist(in).

fla·vo(u)r ['fleivə] **1.** Geschmack *m*; Aroma *n*; Blume *f des Weines*; *fig.* Beigeschmack *m*; Würze *f*; **2.** würzen; '**fla·vo(u)red** mit ...geschmack; '**fla·vo(u)r·ing** Gewürz *n*; '**fla·vo(u)r·less** geschmacklos, fad.

flaw [flɔː] **1.** Sprung *m*, Riß *m*; Fleck *m*; (⚖ Form-, ⊕ Fabrikations)Fehler *m*; Makel *m*, Defekt *m*; ⚓ Bö *f*; **2.** zerbrechen; *fig.* beschädigen; '**flaw·less** □ ohne Sprünge *etc.*; fehler-, makellos.

flax ⚘ [flæks] Flachs *m*, Lein *m*; '**flax·en**, '**flax·y** flachsen; flachsfarben, -blond.

flay [flei] die Haut abziehen (*dat.*), schinden; *fig. j-m* das Fell über die Ohren ziehen; '**flay·er** Schinder *m*.

flea [fliː] Floh *m*; '**~·bane** ⚘ Flohkraut *n*; '**~-bite** Flohstich *m*; *fig.* Bagatelle *f*, kleine Unannehmlichkeit *f*; '**~·pit** F Flohkino *n*.

fleck [flek] **1.** Fleck *m*; **2.** sprenkeln.

flec·tion ['flekʃən] *s. flexion.*

fled [fled] *pret. u. p.p. von flee.*

fledge [fledʒ] *v/i.* flügge werden; *v/t.* befiedern; **fledg(e)·ling** ['~liŋ] Küken *n* (*a. fig.*); Grünschnabel *m*.

flee [fliː] (*irr.*) fliehen (*from* von; vor *dat.*); *a.* ~ *from* meiden.

fleece [fliːs] **1.** Vlies *n*; Schäfchenwolke *f*; **2.** scheren; prellen, schröpfen (*of* um); '**fleec·y** wollig, flockig.

fleer [fliə] **1.** Hohn(lachen *n*) *m*; **2.** höhnen, hohnlachen (*at* über *acc.*).

fleet [fliːt] **1.** □ *poet.* schnell; flüchtig; **2.** Flotte *f*; (Wagen)Park *m*; ♀ *Street* die (Londoner) Presse *f*; **3.** dahineilen; fliehen; '**fleet·ing** □ flüchtig, vergänglich.

Flem·ing ['flemiŋ] Flame *m*, Flamin *f*; '**Flem·ish 1.** flämisch; **2.** Flämisch *n*.

flesh [fleʃ] **1.** (Muskel)Fleisch *n*; Fruchtfleisch *n*; *fig.* Fleisch(eslust *f*) *n*; *make s.o.'s* ~ *creep* j. gruselig machen; **2.** Blut kosten lassen (*a. fig.*); '**~-brush** Frottierbürste *f*; '**flesh·ings** *pl.* fleischfarbenes Trikot *n*; '**flesh·ly** fleischlich; sinnlich; irdisch; '**flesh·y** fleischig; fett.

flew [fluː] *pret. von fly*[1] *2.*

flex ⚡ [fleks] Litze *f*; Kabel *n*; **flex·i·bil·i·ty** [~ə'biliti] Biegsamkeit *f* (*a. fig.*); '**flex·i·ble** □ biegsam; lenksam; anpassungsfähig, flexibel; ~ *working hours pl.* gleitende Arbeitszeit *f*; **flex·ion** ['flekʃən] Biegung *f*; *gr.* Flexion *f*, Beugung *f*; **flex·or**

[ˈ⁓ksə] Beugemuskel *m*; **flex·ure** [ˈflekʃə] Biegung *f*, Krümmung *f*.
flib·ber·ti·gib·bet [ˈflibətiˈdʒibit] Klatschbase *f*; Irrwisch *m*.
flick [flik] **1.** schnippen; schnellen (*at* nach); **2.** leichter Hieb *m od.* Schlag *m*.
flick·er [ˈflikə] **1.** flackern; flattern; flimmern; **2.** Flackern *n etc.*; *Am.* Buntspecht *m*.
flick-knife [ˈfliknaif] Schnappmesser *n*.
fli·er [ˈflaiə] *s. flyer*.
flight [flait] Flucht *f*; Flug *m* (*a. fig.*); Schwarm *m*; ✈, ⚔ Kette *f*; *a.* ⁓ *of stairs* Treppe(nflucht) *f*; *put to* ⁓ in die Flucht schlagen; *take (to)* ⁓ die Flucht ergreifen; ⁓ **bag** Schultertasche *f*; ˈ**⁓-comˈmand·er** Flugkapitän *m*; ˈ**⁓-deck** ⚓ Flugdeck *n*; ⁓ **desk** Flugschalter *m*; ⁓ **en·gi·neer** Bordmechaniker *m*; ˈ**⁓-lieuˈten·ant** Fliegerhauptmann *m*; ⁓ **re·cord·er** Flugschreiber *m*; ˈ**flight·y** □ flüchtig, fahrig; leichtsinnig; flatterhaft.
flim·sy [ˈflimzi] **1.** dünn, locker; nichtig, schwach; fadenscheinig (*Entschuldigung*); **2.** Durchschlagpapier *n*; *sl.* Banknote *f*; Telegramm *n*.
flinch [flintʃ] zurückweichen, -schrecken (*from* vor *dat.*); zucken.
fling [fliŋ] **1.** Wurf *m*; Schlag *m des Pferdes*; *fig.* Hieb *m* (*at* gegen); *have one's* ⁓ sich austoben; *have a* ⁓ *at* sich versuchen an (*dat.*); sich lustig machen über (*acc.*), *j.* verhöhnen; **2.** (*irr.*) *v/i.* eilen, stürzen; ausschlagen (*Pferd*); *a.* ⁓ *out fig.* toben; *v/t.* werfen, schleudern; ⁓ *o.s.* sich stürzen; ⁓ *away* wegwerfen; verschleudern; fahren lassen; ⁓ *forth* herausschleudern, ausstoßen; ⁓ *open* aufreißen.
flint [flint] Kiesel *m*; Feuerstein *m*; ˈ**flint·y** kieselhaltig; *fig.* hart.
flip [flip] **1.** Klaps *m*; Ruck *m*; ✈ *sl.* Vergnügungsflug *m*, Spritztour *f*; Flip *m* (*alkoholisches Heißgetränk*); **2.** schnippen; knipsen; klapsen; (umher)flitzen.
flip-flap [ˈflipflæp] Purzelbaum *m*; Luftschaukel *f*.
flip-flop [ˈflipflɔp] Gummilatsche *f*.
flip·pan·cy [ˈflipənsi] Leichtfertigkeit *f etc.*; ˈ**flip·pant** □ leichtfertig; schnippisch; frivol.
flip·per [ˈflipə] Flosse *f e-r Schildkröte etc.*; Schwimmflosse *f*.
flip side F [ˈflipsaid] B-Seite *f* einer Single.
flirt [flə:t] **1.** Ruck *m*; Kokette *f*; Weiberheld *m*, Filou *m*; **2.** flirten, kokettieren; = *flip* 2; **flirˈta·tion** Liebelei *f*, Flirt(en *n*) *m*; **flirˈta·tious** kokett.
flit [flit] huschen, flitzen; wandern; umziehen.
flitch [flitʃ] Speckseite *f*.
flit·ter [ˈflitə] flattern.
fliv·ver *Am.* F [ˈflivə] **1.** Nuckelpinne *f* (*billiges Auto*); **2.** mißlingen.
float [fləut] **1.** Schwimmer *m an Angel, Netz u.* ⊕; Floß *n*; *thea.* Rampenlicht *n*; Plattformwagen *m*; Fest(zugs)wagen *m*; **2.** *v/t.* überfluten (*mst fig.*); flößen; tragen (*Wasser*); *Schiff* flott machen, *fig.* in Gang bringen; † gründen; verbreiten; *v/i.* obenauf schwimmen, treiben; schweben; umlaufen; ˈ**float·a·ble** schwimmfähig, flößbar; ˈ**float·age** Schwimmkraft *f*; **floatˈa·tion** *s. flotation*; ˈ**float·ing** schwimmend, treibend; schwebend (*Schuld*); ⁓ *bridge* Schiffbrücke *f*; ⁓ *capital* Umlaufskapital *n*; ⁓ *ice* Treibeis *n*; ⁓ *kidney* Wanderniere *f*; ⁓ *light* Feuerschiff *n*; ⁓ *rate* flexibler Wechselkurs *m*; ⁓ *voter pol.* Wechselwähler *m*; ˈ**float-plane** Schwimmerflugzeug *n*.
flock[1] [flɔk] **1.** Herde *f* (*a. fig.*); Schar *f*, Haufe(n) *m*; Flug *m Vögel*; **2.** sich scharen; zs.-strömen.
flock[2] [⁓] (*bsd.* Woll)Flocke *f*.
floe [fləu] schwimmendes Eisfeld *n*; Eisscholle *f*.
flog [flɔg] peitschen; prügeln; ⁓ *a dead horse* seine Mühe verschwenden, sich umsonst anstrengen; ˈ**flog·ging** Prügeln *n*; Prügelstrafe *f*.
flood [flʌd] **1.** *a.* ⁓*-tide* Flut *f*; Überschwemmung *f*; Hochwasser *n*; *the* ♀ die Sintflut; **2.** überfluten, -schwemmen; ˈ**⁓-dis·as·ter** Hochwasserkatastrophe *f*; ˈ**⁓-gate** Schleusentor *n*; ˈ**⁓·light 1.** Scheinwerfer-, Flutlicht *n*; **2.** (mit Scheinwerfern) anstrahlen.
floor [flɔ:] **1.** (Fuß)Boden *m*; Stockwerk *n*; ⛏ Tenne *f*; *parl.* Sitzungssaal *m*; *sl.* Börse *f*; ⁓ *leader Am.* Fraktionsvorsitzende *m*; ⁓ *price*

Mindestpreis *m*; ~ *show Tanz- etc.* Darbietung(en *pl.*) *f in Nachtklubs etc.*; *hold the* ~ *parl.* e-e Rede halten; *be kept on the* ~ zur Debatte stehen; *take the* ~ das Wort ergreifen; **2.** mit e-m Boden versehen, dielen; zu Boden schlagen; verblüffen; '**~-cloth** Aufwisch-, Putzlappen *m*; '**floor·er** zu Boden werfender Schlag *m*; '**floor·ing** Dielung *f*; Fußboden(belag) *m*; '**floor-lamp** Stehlampe *f*; **floor man·ag·er** *Kaufhaus*: Abteilungsleiter; *Fernsehen*: Aufnahmeleiter *m*; **floor show** Varieté-Darbietungen *f/pl. im Nachtklub od. Restaurant*; '**floor-walk·er** *Am.* Aufsicht *f im Kaufhaus*; '**floor-wax** Bohnerwachs *n*.

floo·zy *Am. sl.* ['flu:zi] Flittchen *n*.

flop F [flɔp] **1.** (mit den Flügeln) schlagen; (hin)plumpsen (lassen); baumeln; *Krempe* herunterschlagen; *sl.* versagen; **2.** Plumps *m*; Reinfall *m*; Versager *m*; ~ *house Am. sl.* Penne *f*; **3.** plumps; '**flop·py** schlapp; schludrig.

flo·ra ['flɔ:rə] Flora *f*, Pflanzenwelt *f*; '**flo·ral** Blüten...; Blumen...; ~ *design* Blumenmuster *n*.

flo·res·cence [flɔ:'resns] Blüte(zeit) *f*.

flor·id □ ['flɔrid] blühend; *fig.* blumig; überladen; '**flor·id·ness** lebhafte Farbe *f*; blumiger Stil *m*; Überladenheit *f*.

flor·in ['flɔrin] Gulden *m*; Zweischillingstück *n*.

flo·rist ['flɔrist] Blumenhändler *m*, -züchter *m*.

floss [flɔs] Kokonseide *f*; ~ *silk* Florettseide *f*; '**floss·y** florettseiden.

flo·ta·tion [fləu'teiʃən] Schwimmen *n*; Schweben *n*; Ingangbringen *n*; ✝ Gründung *f*.

flo·til·la ⚓ [fləu'tilə] Flottille *f*.

flot·sam ⚓ ['flɔtsəm] (treibendes) Wrackgut *n*.

flounce[1] [flauns] **1.** Volant *m*, Falbel *f*; **2.** mit Falbeln *etc.* besetzen.

flounce[2] [~] stürzen, stürmen; plumpsen; hopsen; zappeln.

floun·der[1] *ichth.* ['flaundə] Flunder *f*.

floun·der[2] [~] sich (ab)mühen, sich quälen; sich mühsam bewegen.

flour ['flauə] **1.** feines Mehl *n*; **2.** mit Mehl bestreuen.

flour·ish ['flʌriʃ] **1.** Schnörkel *m*; *Rede*-Floskel *f*; Schwingen *n*; ♪ Verzierung *f*; Trompetenstoß *m*, Tusch *m*; **2.** *v/i.* blühen, gedeihen; seine Blütezeit haben; leben; Schnörkel *etc.* machen; *v/t. Schwert etc.* schwingen; *Fahne* schwenken.

flout [flaut] *v/t.* verspotten; ignorieren; *v/i.* spotten (*at* über *acc.*).

flow [fləu] **1.** Fluß *m*; Erguß *m*; Schwall *m*; Überfluß *m*; Flut *f*; ~ *of spirits* heitere Laune *f*; **2.** fließen, fluten, strömen; überfließen (*with* von); wallen (*Haar etc.*); hereinkommen, steigen (*Flut*); ~ *from* herrühren von; ~ **chart** *Datenverarbeitung*: Flußdiagramm *n*.

flow·er ['flauə] **1.** Blume *f*; Blüte *f* (*fig. Auslese*); Zierde *f*; *say it with* ~*s* durch die Blume sprechen; **2.** blühen; **flow·er·et** ['~rit] Blümchen *n*; (Blumenkohl)Röschen *n*; '**flow·er·i·ness** Blumenreichtum *m* (*a. fig.*); '**flow·er-pot** Blumentopf *m*; '**flow·er·y** blumig.

flown [fləun] *p.p. v. fly*[1] 2.

flu F [flu:] = *influenza*.

flub·dub *Am. sl.* ['flʌbdʌb] Geschwätz *n*.

fluc·tu·ate ['flʌktjueit] schwanken; fluktuieren; **fluc·tu'a·tion** Schwanken *n*; ~*s pl.* Schwankungen *f/pl.*

flue [flu:] Kaminrohr *n*; Heizrohr *n*; (Feuerungs)Zug *m*; Rauchfang *m*; Staubflocke(n *pl.*) *f*; = *flu*.

flu·en·cy ['flu:ənsi] Fluß *m der Rede*, Geläufigkeit *f*; '**flu·ent** □ fließend, geläufig (*Rede*).

fluff [flʌf] **1.** Flaum *m*; Staub-, Federflocke *f*; *fig.* Schnitzer *m*, Fehler *m*; **2.** *Kissen* aufschütteln; *Federn* aufplustern (*Vogel*); '**fluff·y** flaumig; locker, flockig; *sl.* angeheitert.

flu·id ['flu:id] **1.** flüssig; *fig.* nicht fixiert; **2.** *konkr.* Flüssigkeit *f*; **flu'id·i·ty** Flüssigkeit *f* (*Zustand*).

fluke [flu:k] Ankerschaufel *f*; F Dusel *m* (*Glück*).

flume [flu:m] Kanal *m*.

flum·mer·y ['flʌməri] *Küche*: Flammeri *m*; fades Geschwätz *n*.

flum·mox F ['flʌməks] verblüffen, verwirren.

flung [flʌŋ] *pret. u. p.p. von fling 2.*

flunk *Am.* F [flʌŋk] durchfallen *im Examen*, durchfallen lassen; sich drücken.

flunk·(e)y [ˈflʌŋki] Lakai *m*; Bedientenseele *f*; ˈ**flunk·ey·ism** Lakaienwesen *n*.
flu·o·res·cence *phys.* [fluəˈresns] Fluoreszenz *f*; **flu·or**ˈ**es·cent** fluoreszierend; ~ *lamp* Leuchtstofflampe *f*.
flur·ry [ˈflʌri] **1.** Nervosität *f*, Unwirschheit *f*; Bö *f*; (Schnee)Schauer *m*; **2.** nervös *od.* unwirsch machen.
flush [flʌʃ] **1.** ⊕ in gleicher Ebene; reichlich; (über)voll; **2.** Erröten *n*; Übermut *m*, Rausch *m*; Fülle *f*; Wachstum *n*; *fig.* Blüte *f*; Spülung *f*; *Karten*: Flöte *f*; **3.** über-, durchfluten; (aus)spülen; strömen; sprießen (lassen); erröten (lassen); übermütig machen; aufjagen.
flus·ter [ˈflʌstə] **1.** Aufregung *f*; **2.** *v/t.* durcheinanderbringen, aufregen, nervös machen; *v/i.* aufgeregt *od.* nervös sein.
flute [flu:t] **1.** ♪ Flöte *f*; ⚠ *Säulen*-Auskehlung *f*; *Plissee- etc.* Falte *f*; **2.** (auf der) Flöte spielen; *fig.* flöten; auskehlen, riefeln; fälteln; ˈ**flut·ist** Flötist(in).
flut·ter [ˈflʌtə] **1.** Flattern *n*; Erregung *f*, Unruhe *f*; F Spekulation *f*; *have a* ~ sein Glück (*im Spiel etc.*) probieren; **2.** *v/t.* flattern lassen; aufregen; *v/i.* flattern; zittern; sich unruhig hin- u. herbewegen.
flux [flʌks] *fig.* Fluß *m*, Strom *m*; ⚕ Ausfluß *m*; beständiger Wechsel *m*; ~ *and reflux* Flut *f* und Ebbe *f*.
fly[1] [flai] **1.** Fliege *f*; Flug *m*; *Am. Baseball*: hochgeschlagener Ball *m*; Droschke *f*; Unruh *f der Uhr*; *flies pl. thea.* Soffitten *f/pl.*; **2.** (*irr.*) fliegen (lassen); eilen, entfliehen (*Zeit*); eilen, stürzen; *Flugzeug* fliegen; *Flagge* hissen; = *flee*; ~ *the Channel* über den Kanal fliegen; ~ *high* hoch hinauswollen; ~ *at* herfallen über (*acc.*); ~ *in the face of* sich nicht scheren um; trotzen (*dat.*); ~ *into a passion od. rage* in Zorn geraten; ~ *off* davonfliegen; ~ *blind od. on instruments* blindfliegen; ~ *out at* ausfällig werden gegen; ~ *open* auffliegen (*Tür*); *send s.o.* ~*ing* j. fortjagen.
fly[2] *sl.* [~] auf Draht; mit allen Wassern gewaschen.
fly...: ˈ**~-blow 1.** Fliegenschmutz *m*; **2.** Eier ablegen (auf); *fig.* beschmutzen; ˈ**~-blown** fliegenbeschmutzt; *fig.* schmutzig; wenig vertrauenerweckend; ˈ**~-catch·er** Fliegenfänger *m*; *orn.* Fliegenschnäpper *m*.
fly·er [ˈflaiə] Flieger *m* (*bsd.* ✈); Renner *m*; Sprung *m* mit Anlauf; Flüchtling *m*; *take a* ~ *Am.* F Vermögen riskieren; ~*s pl.* ⚠ Freitreppe *f*.
fly-flap [ˈflaiflæp] Fliegenklatsche *f*.
fly·ing [ˈflaiiŋ] fliegend; schnell; Flug...; ~ *boat* Flugboot *n*; ~ *buttress* ⚠ Strebebogen *m*; ~ *deck* Landedeck *n*; ~ *field* Flugplatz *m*; ~ *jump* Sprung *m* mit Anlauf; ~ *machine* Flugzeug *n*; ~ *school* Fliegerschule *f*; ~ *squad* Überfallkommando *n*; ~ *start* fliegender Start *m*; ~ *visit* flüchtiger Besuch *m*; ˈ**~-of·fi·cer** Oberleutnant *m* der RAF.
fly...: ˈ**~-leaf** *typ.* Vorsatzblatt *n*; ˈ**~-o·ver** (Straßen)Überführung *f*; ✈ = ˈ**~-past** Luftparade *f*; ˈ**~-sheet** *Camping etc.*: Überzelt *n*; ˈ**~-weight** *Boxen*: Fliegengewicht *n*; ˈ**~-wheel** Schwungrad *n*.
foal [fəul] **1.** Fohlen *n*; *in* ~, *with* ~ trächtig **2.** fohlen.
foam [fəum] **1.** Schaum *m*; **2.** schäumen; ˈ**~-rub·ber** Schaumgummi *n*, *m*; ˈ**foam·y** schaumig.
fob[1] [fɔb] Uhrtasche *f in der Hose*; Chatelaine *f* (*Uhranhänger*).
fob[2] [~]: ~ *off fig. j.* abspeisen (*with* mit); *et.* aufschwatzen (*on dat.*).
fo·cal [ˈfəukəl] den Brennpunkt betreffend, fokal; ~ *length*, ~ *distance phot.* Brennweite *f*; ~*-plane shutter phot.* Schlitzverschluß *m*.
fo'c'sle [ˈfəuksl] = *forecastle*.
fo·cus [ˈfəukəs] **1.** *pl. a.* **fo·ci** [ˈfəusai] Brennpunkt *m*; *fig. a.* Herd *m*, Mittel-, Schwerpunkt *m*; **2.** (sich) im Brennpunkt vereinigen; *opt.* einstellen (*a. fig.*); *Aufmerksamkeit* konzentrieren (*on*, *upon* auf *acc.*); ˈ**fo·cus·(s)ing screen** *phot.* Mattscheibe *f*.
fod·der [ˈfɔdə] **1.** (Trocken)Futter *n*; **2.** füttern.
foe *poet.* [fəu] Feind *m*, Gegner *m*; ˈ**~·man** † Feind *m*.
foe·tus ⚕ [ˈfi:təs] Fötus *m*, Leibesfrucht *f*.
fog [fɔg] **1.** (dichter) Nebel *m*; *fig.* Umnebelung *f*; *phot.* Schleier *m*; **2.** *mst fig.* umnebeln; *phot.* ver-

schleiern; '~-**bank** Nebelbank *f*; '~-**bound** ⚓ durch Nebel behindert.

fo·gey F ['fəugi]: *old* ~ komischer alter Kauz *m*.

fog·gy □ ['fɔgi] neb(e)lig; *fig.* nebelhaft; '**fog-horn** Nebelhorn *n*; '**fog-sig·nal** 🚂 Nebelsignal *n*.

fo·gy *Am.* ['fəugi] = *fogey*.

foi·ble *fig.* ['fɔibl] Schwäche *f*, schwache Seite *f*.

foil[1] [fɔil] Folie *f*; Spiegelbelag *m*; *fig.* Hintergrund *m*.

foil[2] [~] **1.** vereiteln; durchkreuzen; *j-m* e-n Strich durch die Rechnung machen; **2.** *fenc.* Florett *n*.

foist [fɔist]: ~ *s.th.* (*off*) *on s.o.* j-m et. andrehen *od.* aufschwatzen.

fold[1] [fəuld] **1.** Schafhürde *f*; *fig.* Herde *f*; **2.** einpferchen.

fold[2] [~] **1.** Falte *f*; Falz *m*, Kniff *m*, Bruch *m*; **2.** ...fach, ...fältig; **3.** *v/t.* falten; falzen; kniffen; *Arme* kreuzen; *a.* ~ *up* einwickeln; ~ *down* umkniffen; ~ *in one's arms* in die Arme schließen; ~ *up* zs.-legen; *v/i.* sich falten; sich zs.-klappen lassen; *Am.* F eingehen; ~ *up* F zusammenbrechen; Schluß machen; '**fold·er** Mappe *f*, Schnellhefter *m*; Faltprospekt *m*.

fold·ing ['fəuldiŋ] zs.-legbar; Klapp-...; '~-**bed** Feldbett *n*; '~-**boat** Faltboot *n*; '~-**door**(s *pl.*) Flügeltür *f*; '~-**screen** spanische Wand *f*; '~-**seat** Klappsitz *m*.

fo·li·age ['fəuliidʒ] Laub(werk) *n*.

fo·li·o ['fəuliəu] Folio *n*; Foliant *m*; Mappe *f*.

folk [fəuk] *pl.* Leute *pl.*; ~*s pl.* F *m-e etc.* Leute *pl.* (*Angehörige*); '~-**dance** Volkstanz *m*; ~**lore** ['~lɔ:] Volkskunde *f*, -sagen *f/pl.*; Folklore *f*; ~ **mu·sic** Folklore *f*; '~-**song** Volkslied *n*.

fol·low ['fɔləu] folgen (*dat.*); folgen auf (*acc.*); be-, nach-, verfolgen; *s-m Vergnügen, Beruf etc.* nachgehen; *to* ~ hinterher, als Nachspeise; *it* ~*s that* es folgt daraus, daß; ~ *out* weiter verfolgen; ~ *the sea* Seemann sein; ~ *up* (weiter-) verfolgen; '**fol·low·er** Nachfolger (-in); Verfolger(in); Anhänger(in), Gefolgsmann *m*, Jünger *m*; F Verehrer *m* (*e-s Dienstmädchens*); '**fol·low·ing** **1.** Anhängerschaft *f*, Gefolge *n*; *the* ~ das Folgende; **2.** ~ *wind* Rückenwind *m*; '**fol·low-up** weitere Verfolgung *f e-r* Sache; ⚕ Nachbehandlung *f*.

fol·ly ['fɔli] Torheit *f*; Narrheit *f*.

fo·ment [fəu'ment] ⚕ bähen; *j-m* warme Umschläge machen; *Unruhe* stiften *od.* schüren; **fo·men·'ta·tion** Bähung *f*; warmer Umschlag *m*; Anstiftung *f*; **fo'ment·er** *fig.* Anstifter *m*.

fond □ [fɔnd] zärtlich; vernarrt (*of* in *acc.*); töricht, kühn (*Hoffnung etc.*); *be* ~ *of* gern haben, lieben; *be* ~ *of dancing* gern tanzen.

fon·dant ['fɔndənt] Fondant *m*.

fon·dle ['fɔndl] liebkosen; streicheln; (ver)hätscheln.

fond·ness ['fɔndnis] Zärtlichkeit *f*; Vorliebe *f* (*for* für).

font *eccl.* [fɔnt] Taufstein *m*.

food [fu:d] Speise *f*, Nahrung *f* (*a. fig.*); Essen *n*, Beköstigung *f*; Futter *n*; Lebensmittel *n/pl.*, Eßwaren *f/pl.*; ~ **hall** Lebensmittelabteilung *f*; '~-**stuff** Nahrungsmittel *n*.

fool[1] [fu:l] **1.** Narr *m*, Tor *m*, Dummkopf *m*; Betrogene *m*; Hanswurst *m*; *make a* ~ *of s.o.* j. zum besten haben; *make a* ~ *of o.s.* sich lächerlich machen; *I am a* ~ *to him* gegen ihn bin ich ein Waisenknabe; ~*'s paradise* Schlaraffenland *n*; **2.** *Am.* F närrisch, dumm; **3.** *v/t.* narren, aufziehen; zum Narren halten; prellen (*out of* um *et.*); verleiten (*into ger.* zu *inf.*); ~ *away* F vertrödeln; *v/i.* Spaß machen, albern; (herum)spielen; ~ *about* herumalbern; ~ (*a*)*round bsd. Am.* Zeit vertrödeln.

fool[2] [~] Fruchtcreme *f*.

fool·er·y ['fu:ləri] Torheit *f*; '**fool·hard·y** □ tollkühn; '**fool·ish** □ töricht, albern, dumm; '**fool·ish·ness** Torheit *f*; '**fool-proof** ⊕ narrensicher; kinderleicht; **fools·cap** ['fu:lskæp] Kanzleipapier *n*; **fool's-cap** ['fu:lzkæp] Narrenkappe *f*.

foot [fut] **1.** *pl.* **feet** [fi:t] Fuß *m*; Fußende *n*; ⚔ Infanterie *f*; Fuß *m* (= *12 Zoll*); Füßling *m am Strumpf*; *on* ~ zu Fuß; im Gange; *be on one's feet* auf den Beinen sein; *fig.* keine Hilfe brauchen, auf eigenen Füßen stehen; *put one's* ~ *down* fest auftreten; *I have put my* ~ *into it* F ich bin ins Fettnäpfchen getreten; *set* *on* ~ in Gang bringen; *set* ~ *on* betreten; **2.** *v/t.* Füß(ling)e anstrikken an (*acc.*); *mst* ~ *up Rechnung* addieren; ~ *the bill* F die Zeche bezahlen; *v/i.* ~ *it* zu Fuß gehen; tanzen; ˈ**foot·age** Gesamtlänge *f* (*in Fuß*).

foot...: ˈ**~-and-ˈmouth dis·ease** Maul- und Klauenseuche *f*; ˈ**~·ball** Fußball(spiel *n*) *m*; ˈ**~·board** Trittbrett *n*; ˈ**~·boy** *Hotel- etc.* Page *m*; ˈ**~-brake** Fußbremse *f*; ˈ**~-bridge** Steg *m*.

foot·ed [ˈfutid] ...füßig; ˈ**foot·er** F Fußball(spiel *n*) *m*.

foot...: ˈ**~·fall** Tritt *m*, Schritt *m*; ˈ**~-gear** Schuhwerk *n*; ♀ **Guards** *pl.* ⚔ Gardeinfanterie *f*; ˈ**~-hills** *pl.* Vorgebirge *n*; ˈ**~·hold** fester Stand *m*; *fig.* Halt *m*.

foot·ing [ˈfutiŋ] Halt *m*, Stand *m*; Grundlage *f*, Basis *f*; Stellung *f*; fester Fuß *m*; Verhältnis *n*; ⚔ Zustand *m*; Endsumme *f*; *be on a friendly* ~ *with s.o.* ein gutes Verhältnis zu j-m haben; *upon the same* ~ *as* auf gleichem Fuße mit; *get a* ~ festen Fuß fassen; *lose one's* ~ ausgleiten.

foo·tle F [ˈfuːtl] **1.** albern (sein); **2.** Albernheit *f*; Spielerei *f*.

foot·lights *thea.* [ˈfutlaits] *pl.* Rampenlicht(er *pl.*) *n*; Bühne *f*.

foot·ling [ˈfuːtliŋ] läppisch, unbedeutend.

foot...: ˈ**~·loose** ungebunden, unbeschwert; ~ *and fancy-free* frei und ungebunden; ˈ**~·man** Diener *m*, Lakai *m*; ˈ**~-mark** Fußspur *f*; ˈ**~-note** **1.** Fußnote *f*; **2.** mit Fußnoten versehen; ˈ**~·pad** Straßenräuber *m*; ˈ**~-pas·sen·ger** Fußgänger(in); ˈ**~-path** Fußpfad *m*; ˈ**~·print** Fußstapfe *f*, -spur *f*; ˈ**~-race** Wettlauf *m*; ˈ**~-rule** Zollstock *m*.

foot·sie [ˈfutsi]: *play* ~ F fußeln.

foot...: ˈ**~-slog** *sl.* latschen; ˈ**~-sore** fußkrank; ˈ**~·stalk** ♀ Stengel *m*, Stiel *m*; ˈ**~·step** Fußstapfe *f*, Spur *f*; Tritt *m*, Schritt *m*; ˈ**~·stool** Fußbank *f*; ˈ**~·wear** = *foot-gear*; ˈ**~·work** *Sport*: Beinarbeit *f*.

fop [fɔp] Geck *m*, Fatzke *m*; ˈ**fop·per·y** Ziererei *f*, Afferei *f*; ˈ**fop·pish** □ geckenhaft, affig.

for [fɔː; fə; f] **1.** *prp. mst* für; *Sonderfälle*: a) *Zweck, Ziel, Richtung*: zu; nach; *come* ~ *dinner* zum Essen kommen; *the train* ~ *London* der Zug nach London; *it is* ~ *you to decide* es ist an dir zu entscheiden; b) *Wunsch, Erwartung*: *warten, hoffen etc.* auf (*acc.*); *sich sehnen etc.* nach; c) *Grund, Anlaß*: aus, vor (*dat.*), wegen; *were it not* ~ *that* wenn das nicht wäre; *he is a fool* ~ *doing that* er ist töricht, daß er das tut; d) *Zeitdauer*: ~ *three days* drei Tage (lang); auf drei Tage; seit drei Tagen; e) *Entfernung*: *I walked* ~ *a mile* ich ging eine Meile (weit); f) *Austausch*: (an)statt; g) *in der Eigenschaft* als; *I* ~ *one* ich zum Beispiel; ~ *sure!* sicher!, gewiß!; h) *nach adj. vor acc. u. inf.*: *it is good* ~ *us to be here* es ist gut, daß wir hier sind; *the snow was too deep* ~ *them to go on* der Schnee war zu tief, als daß sie weiter gekonnt hätten; **2.** *cj.* denn.

for·age [ˈfɔridʒ] **1.** F(o)urage *f*, Futter *n*; **2.** (nach Futter) suchen.

for·as·much [fərəzˈmʌtʃ]: ~ *as* weil, da, insofern als.

for·ay [ˈfɔrei] räuberischer Einfall *m*.

for·bade [fəˈbæd] *pret. von forbid.*

for·bear[1] [ˈfɔːbɛə] Vorfahr *m*.

for·bear[2] [fɔːˈbɛə] (*irr.*) *v/t.* unterlassen; *v/i.* sich enthalten (*from gen.*); Geduld haben; **forˈbear·ance** Unterlassung *f*; Geduld *f*, Nachsicht *f*.

for·bid [fəˈbid] (*irr.*) verbieten (*s.o. s.th.* j-m et.); hindern; *God* ~*!* Gott behüte!; **forˈbid·den** *p.p. von forbid*; ~ *fruit* verbotene Frucht *f*; **forˈbid·ding** □ abstoßend.

for·bore, for·borne [fɔːˈbɔː(n)] *pret. u. p.p. von forbear*[2].

force [fɔːs] **1.** *mst* Kraft *f*, Stärke *f*, Gewalt *f*; Nachdruck *m*; Gültigkeit *f*; Zwang *m*; Bedeutung *f*; Heer *n*, Truppe *f*; Streitmacht *f*; *the* ~ die Polizei; *armed* ~*s pl.* Streitkräfte *f/pl.*; *by* ~ gewaltsam; *come (put) in* ~ in Kraft treten (setzen); **2.** zwingen, nötigen; erzwingen (*upon* von); aufzwingen, -drängen (*upon dat.*); forcieren, beschleunigen; *Worten, e-r Frau* Gewalt antun; *Schritt* beschleunigen; *Tür etc.* aufbrechen; erstürmen; *Früchte* künstlich reif machen; ~ *back* zurücktreiben; ~ *down* ✈ zum Landen zwingen; ~ *s.o.'s hand* j. zwingen; ~ *on* antreiben; ~ *open* aufbrechen; **forced** (*adv.* **forc·ed·ly** ['~idli]) er-, gezwungen; ~ *loan* Zwangsanleihe *f*; ~ *landing* Notlandung *f*; ~ *march* Eilmarsch *m*; ~ *sale* Zwangsversteigerung *f*; '**force·feed** zwangsernähren; **force·ful** □ ['~ful] kräftig, wirkungsvoll; eindringlich; '**force·meat** *Küche*: gehacktes Füllsel *n*.

for·ceps ⚕ ['fɔ:seps] *sg. u. pl.* Zange *f*.

force-pump ['fɔ:spʌmp] Druckpumpe *f*.

forc·er ⊕ ['fɔ:sə] Kolben *m*.

for·ci·ble □ ['fɔ:səbl] gewaltsam; Zwangs...; eindringlich; wirksam.

forc·ing-house ['fɔ:siŋhaus] Treibhaus *n*.

ford [fɔ:d] **1.** Furt *f*; **2.** durchwaten; '**ford·a·ble** durchwatbar.

fore [fɔ:] **1.** *adv.* vorn; ~ *and aft* ⚓ vorn und hinten; **2.** Vorderteil *m*, *n*; *to the* ~ greifbar, verfügbar, vorhanden; zur Hand; *bring* (*come*) *to the* ~ zum Vorschein bringen (kommen); **3.** *adj.* vorder; Vorder...; '**~·arm**[1] Vorderarm *m*; **~'arm**[2] (sich) wappnen; **~'bode** vorhersagen; ahnen; **~'bod·ing** (böses) Vorzeichen *n*; Ahnung *f*; '**~·cast 1.** (*bsd.* Wetter)Vorhersage *f*; **2.** (*irr. cast*) vorhersehen; voraussagen; '**~·cas·tle** ⚓ ['fəuksl] Vorderdeck *n*; Logis *n*; **~·close** [fɔ:'kləuz] ausschließen (*of* von); *Hypothek* für verfallen erklären; **~'clo·sure** [~ʒə] Verfallserklärung *f*; '**~·court** Vorhof *m*; **~'date** vorausdatieren; **~'doom** im voraus verurteilen *od.* bestimmen; '**~·fa·ther** Vorfahr *m*; '**~·fin·ger** Zeigefinger *m*; '**~·foot** Vorderfuß *m*; '**~·front** Vorderseite *f*; vorderste Reihe *f*; **~'go** (*irr. go*) vorangehen; *~ing* vorhergehend; **~'gone** von vornherein feststehend; ~ *conclusion* Selbstverständlichkeit *f*, ausgemachte Sache *f*; '**~·ground** Vordergrund *m*; '**~·hand** Vorhand *f*; **~·head** ['fɔrid] Stirn *f*.

for·eign ['fɔrin] fremd; ausländisch; auswärtig; ~ *body* Fremdkörper *m*; ~ *affairs pl. pol.* Außenpolitik *f*, auswärtige Angelegenheiten *f/pl.*; ~ *aid* Auslandshilfe *f*; *~-born* im Ausland geboren; ~ *exchange* Devisen *pl.*; '**for·eign·er** Ausländer(in), Fremde *m*, *f*; '**for·eign·ness** Fremdheit *f*.

for·eign...: ♀ **Of·fice** Außenministerium *n*; ~ **pol·i·cy** Außenpolitik *f*; ♀ **Sec·re·tar·y** Außenminister *m*; ~ **trade** Außenhandel *m*.

fore...: **~'judge** im voraus (ver)urteilen; **~'know** (*irr. know*) vorherwissen; '**~'knowl·edge** Vorherwissen *n*, -sehen *n*; **~·land** ['fɔ:lənd] Vorgebirge *n*; '**~·leg** Vorderbein *n*; '**~·lock** Stirnhaar *n*; *take time by the* ~ die Gelegenheit beim Schopfe ergreifen; '**~·man** ⚖ Obmann *m*; Vorarbeiter *m*, (Werk-)Meister *m*; ⚒ Steiger *m*; '**~·mast** ⚓ Fockmast *m*; '**~·most 1.** *adj.* vorderst, erst; **2.** *adv.* zuerst; '**~·name** Vorname *m*; '**~·noon** Vormittag *m*.

fo·ren·sic [fə'rensik] gerichtlich; Gerichts...; ~ *science* Gerichtskriminalistik *f*.

fore...: '**~·or'dain** vorherbestimmen; '**~·paw** Vorderpfote *f*; '**~·play** (sexuelles) Vorspiel *n*; '**~·run·ner** Vorläufer *m*, -bote *m*; **~·sail** ['~seil; ⚓ '~sl] Focksegel *n*; **~'see** (*irr. see*) vorhersehen; **~'see·a·ble** vorauszusehen(d); absehbar (*Zeit*); **~'shad·ow** ankündigen; '**~·shore** (Küsten)Vorland *n*, Strand *m*; **~'short·en** in der Verkürzung zeichnen; '**~·sight** Voraussicht *f*; Vorsorge *f*; Korn *n am Gewehr*; '**~·skin** Vorhaut *f*.

for·est ['fɔrist] **1.** Wald *m* (*a. fig.*), Forst *m*; **2.** beforsten.

fore·stall [fɔ:'stɔ:l] *et.* vereiteln; *j-m* zuvorkommen.

for·est·er ['fɔristə] Förster *m*; Waldarbeiter *m*; '**for·est·ry** Forstwirtschaft *f*; Waldgebiet *n*.

fore...: '**~·taste** Vorgeschmack *m*; **~'tell** (*irr. tell*) voraus-, vorhersagen; vorbedeuten; '**~·thought** Vorbedacht *m*.

for·ev·er [fə'revə] für immer; ständig.

fore...: **~'warn** vorher warnen; '**~·wom·an** Aufseherin *f*; Vorarbeiterin *f*; '**~·word** Vorwort *n*.

for·feit ['fɔ:fit] **1.** verwirkt; **2.** Verwirkung *f*; Strafe *f*, Buße *f*; Pfand *n*; ✝ *u. Sport*: Reugeld *n*; *~s pl.* Pfänderspiel *n*; **3.** verwirken; einbüßen; '**for·feit·a·ble** verwirkbar; **for·fei·ture** ['~tʃə] Verwirkung *f*; Verlust *m*.

for·gath·er [fɔ:'gæðə] zs.-kommen.

for·gave [fə'geiv] *pret. von forgive.*

forge[1] [fɔ:dʒ] **1.** Schmiede *f*;

2. schmieden (*fig. ersinnen*); *Urkunde etc.* fälschen.
forge[2] [~] *mst* ~ *ahead* sich vor(wärts)arbeiten.
forg·er ['fɔːdʒə] Schmied *m*; Fälscher *m*; '**for·ger·y** Fälschung *f*.
for·get [fə'get] (*irr.*) vergessen; vernachlässigen; *I* ~ F ich habe vergessen, ich weiß nicht mehr; **for'get·ful** □ [~ful] vergeßlich; **for'get·ful·ness** Vergeßlichkeit *f*; **for'get-me-not** ⚘ Vergißmeinnicht *n*.
for·give [fə'giv] (*irr.*) vergeben, verzeihen; *Schuld* erlassen; **for'giv·en** *p.p. von forgive*; **for'give·ness** Verzeihung *f*, -gebung *f*; **for'giv·ing** □ versöhnlich; nachsichtig, mild.
for·go [fɔː'gəu] (*irr. go*) verzichten auf (*acc.*); aufgeben.
for·got [fə'gɔt], **for'got·ten** [~tn] *pret. u. p.p. von forget*.
fork [fɔːk] 1. Gabel *f*; Gabelung *f*; 2. (sich) gabeln; ~ *out* F *Geld* herausrücken; **forked** gabelförmig; gegabelt; '**fork-lift** Gabelstapler *m*.
for·lorn [fə'lɔːn] verloren, verlassen; hoffnungslos; hilflos; ~ *hope* aussichtsloses Unternehmen *n*; ⚔ verlorener Posten *m*, Himmelfahrtskommando *n*.
form [fɔːm] **1.** Form *f*; Gestalt *f*; Formalität *f*; Formular *n*; (Schul-)Bank *f*; (Schul)Klasse *f*; Form *f*, Kondition *f*; geistige Verfassung *f*; *in* (*good*) ~ *Sport*: in (guter) Form *od.* Verfassung; *good* (*bad*) ~ gutes (schlechtes) Benehmen *n*; **2.** (sich) formen, (sich) bilden; gestalten; entwerfen, erdenken; ⚔ (sich) aufstellen, formieren; vereinbaren (*into* zu); *Bündnis* schließen; sich *e-e Meinung* bilden.
for·mal □ ['fɔːməl] formal; förmlich; formell; äußerlich, scheinbar; '**for·mal·ism** Formalismus *m*; '**for·mal·ist** Formenmensch *m*; **for·mal·i·ty** [fɔː'mæliti] Förmlichkeit *f*, Formalität *f*; **for·mal·ize** ['fɔːməlaiz] in die richtige Form bringen.
for·mat ['fɔːmæt] Format *n* (*e-s Buches*).
for·ma·tion [fɔː'meiʃən] Bildung *f*, Gestaltung *f*; *bsd.* ⚔ *u. geol.* Formation *f*; ~ *flying* ✈ Fliegen *n* im Verband; **form·a·tive** ['fɔːmətiv] formend, bildend; gestaltend; ~ *years pl.* Entwicklungsjahre *n/pl.*
form·er[1] ⊕ ['fɔːmə] Former *m* (*a. fig.*).
for·mer[2] [~] vorig, früher; ehemalig; vorhererwähnt; erstere(r, -s), jene(r, -s); '**for·mer·ly** ehemals, früher, einst.
for·mic ['fɔːmik]: ~ *acid* Ameisensäure *f*.
for·mi·da·ble □ ['fɔːmidəbl] furchtbar, schrecklich; ungeheuer.
form·less □ ['fɔːmlis] formlos.
For·mo·san [fɔː'məusən] aus Formosa, Formosa...
for·mu·la ['fɔːmjulə], *pl. mst* **for·mu·lae** ['~liː] Formel *f*; ⚕ Rezept *n*; **for·mu·lar·y** ['~ləri] **1.** formelhaft; **2.** Formelbuch *n*; **for·mu·late** ['~leit] formulieren; **for·mu'la·tion** Formulierung *f*.
for·ni·cate ['fɔːnikeit] außerehelichen Geschlechtsverkehr haben, Unzucht treiben; **for·ni'ca·tion** Unzucht *f*.
for·rad·er F ['fɔrədə] (weiter) vorwärts.
for·sake [fə'seik] (*irr.*) aufgeben; verlassen; **for'sak·en** *p.p. von forsake*; **for·sook** [~'suk] *pret. von forsake*.
for·sooth *iro.* [fə'suːθ] wahrlich.
for·swear [fɔː'swɛə] (*irr. swear*) abschwören; ~ *o.s.* falsch schwören; **for'sworn** meineidig.
fort ⚔ [fɔːt] Fort *n*, Festung(swerk *n*) *f*.
forte *fig.* [fɔːt] Stärke *f*, starke Seite *f*.
forth [fɔːθ] *räumlich*: vor(wärts), voran, vorauf; heraus, hinaus, hervor; *in Zeit, Ordnung etc.*: vorwärts, weiter, fort(an); *from this day* ~ von heute an; **~'com·ing** herauskommend, erscheinend; bereit; bevorstehend; F entgegenkommend; *be* ~ zum Vorschein kommen, erscheinen; '**~right** gerade; geradeheraus; '**~'with** sogleich.
for·ti·eth ['fɔːtiiθ] **1.** vierzigste(r, -s); **2.** Vierzigstel *n*.
for·ti·fi·ca·tion [fɔːtifi'keiʃən] Befestigung *f*; ⚔ Festungswerk *n*; **for·ti·fy** [~'fai] ⚔ befestigen; *fig.* (ver)stärken; **for·ti·tude** ['~tjuːd] Seelenstärke *f*; Tapferkeit *f*, Mut *m*.
fort·night ['fɔːtnait] vierzehn Tage; *this day* ~ heute in 14 Tagen; *this* ~ seit 14 Tagen; '**fort·night·ly** vierzehntägig, alle 14 Tage (erscheinend).

for·tress ['fɔːtris] Festung *f*.
for·tu·i·tous □ [fɔː'tjuːitəs] zufällig; **for'tu·i·tous·ness, for'tu·i·ty** Zufälligkeit *f*, Zufall *m*.
for·tu·nate ['fɔːtʃnit] glücklich; **'for·tu·nate·ly** glücklicherweise, zum Glück.
for·tune ['fɔːtʃən] Glück *n*; (zukünftiges) Schicksal *n*; Zufall *m*; Vermögen *n*; ♀ Fortuna *f*; *good* ~ Glück *n*; *bad* ~, *ill* ~ Unglück *n*; *marry a* ~ e-e reiche Partie machen; *tell* ~*s* wahrsagen; **'~-hunt·er** Mitgiftjäger *m*; **'~-tel·ler** Wahrsager(in).
for·ty ['fɔːti] **1.** vierzig; ~*-niner Am.* F *kalifornischer* Goldsucher *m von 1849*; ~ *winks pl.* F Nickerchen *n*; **2.** Vierzig *f*; *the forties* die vierziger Jahre (*e-s Jahrhunderts*); die Vierziger(jahre) (*Alter*).
fo·rum ['fɔːrəm] Forum *n*; Gericht *n*.
for·ward ['fɔːwəd] **1.** *adj.* vorder; bereit(willig); fortschrittlich; vorschnell; vorwitzig, keck; frühzeitig; vorgerückt; ✝ Zeit..., Termin...; ~ *planning* Vorausplanung *f*; **2.** *adv.* vorwärts; nach vorn; ✝ auf Ziel; *from this time* ~ von jetzt an; **3.** *Fußball*: Stürmer *m*; **4.** (be)fördern, beschleunigen; (ab-, ver)senden; *please* ~ ✉ bitte nachsenden; **'for·ward·er** Spediteur *m*.
for·ward·ing ['fɔːwədiŋ] Versand *m*; Spedition *f*; ~ **ad·dress** Nachsendeadresse *f*; ~ **a·gent** Spediteur *m*.
for·ward·ness ['fɔːwədnis] Bereitwilligkeit *f*; Frühreife *f*; Voreiligkeit *f*; Keckheit *f*; **for·wards** ['fɔːwədz] vorwärts.
fosse [fɔs] ⚔ Graben *m*; *anat.* Höhlung *f*, Grube *f*.
fos·sil ['fɔsl] **1.** fossil, versteinert; *fig.* rückständig; **2.** Fossil *n* (*a. fig.*).
fos·ter ['fɔstə] **1.** *fig.* nähren, pflegen; begünstigen; ~ *up* aufziehen; **2.** Pflege...; **'fos·ter·age** Pflege *f*; **'fos·ter-child** Pflegekind *n*; **fos·ter·ling** ['~liŋ] Pflegekind *n*, Schützling *m*.
fought [fɔːt] *pret. u. p.p. von fight* 2.
foul [faul] **1.** □ widerwärtig, ekelhaft; schmutzig(*fig.* = *zotig, gemein*); verschmutzt (*Garten, Gewehr etc.*); schimpfend, Schimpf...; schändlich; unehrlich; falsch, regelwidrig (*Spiel*); ⚓ unklar; faul, verdorben (*Wasser etc.*); übelriechend (*Atem etc.*); schlecht (*Wetter*); widrig (*Wind*); ruchlos (*Tat*); ~ *tongue* böse Zunge *f*, loses Maul *n*; *fall* ~ *of mit dem Gesetz* in Konflikt kommen; ⚓ zs.-stoßen mit; **2.** Zs.-stoß *m*; *Sport*: Foul *n*, Regelverstoß *m*; *through fair and* ~ durch dick u. dünn; **3.** be-, verschmutzen; schmutzig werden; (sich) verwikkeln, hemmen, (ver)sperren; ⚓ ansegeln; **~-mouthed** ['~mauðd], **'~-spo·ken** schmutzige Reden führend.
found[1] [faund] *pret. u. p.p. von find 1.*
found[2] [~] (be)gründen (*a. fig.*); stiften.
found[3] ⊕ [~] schmelzen, gießen.
foun·da·tion [faun'deiʃən] Gründung *f*; Stiftung *f*; Fundament *n*; Grund-, Unterlage *f* (*a. fig.*); ~ **cream** Make-up-Unterlage *f*; ~ **gar·ment** Mieder *n*; **~-stone** Grundstein *m*.
found·er[1] ['faundə] (Be)Gründer(in), Stifter(in); ~ *member* Gründungsmitglied *n*.
found·er[2] ⊕ [~] Schmelzer *m*, Gießer *m*.
found·er[3] [~] *v/i.* ⚓, *fig.* scheitern, untergehen; lahmen (*Pferd*); zs.-fallen; *v/t.* zum Scheitern bringen; lahm machen, zuschanden reiten.
found·ling ['faundliŋ] Findling *m*, Findelkind *n*; ~ **hos·pi·tal** Findelhaus *n*.
found·ress ['faundris] Gründerin *f*.
found·ry ⊕ ['faundri] Gießerei *f*.
fount [faunt] *poet.* Quell(e *f*) *m*; *typ.* [*a.* fɔnt] Schriftguß *m*, -satz *m*.
foun·tain ['fauntin] Quelle *f*; Springbrunnen *m*; ⊕ *Flüssigkeits*-Behälter *m*; **'~-'head** Urquell *m* (*a. fig.*); **'~-pen** Füllfederhalter *m*, Füller *m*.
four [fɔː] 1. vier; 2. Vier *f*; *Sport*: Vierer *m*; **'~-eyes** *sg. iro.* Brillenträger *m*; **'~-'flush·er** *Am. sl.* Blender *m*; Hochstapler *m*; **'~·fold** vierfach; **'~-in-'hand** Vierspänner *m*; **'~-let·ter word** unanständiges Wort *n*; **'~-part** ♪ vierstimmig; **'~·pence** vier Pence; **'~-ply** vierfach (*Sperrholz, Wolle*); **'~-'post·er** Himmelbett *n*; **'~'score** achtzig; **~·some** ['fɔːsəm] *Golf*: Viererspiel *n*; **'~-'square** viereckig; *fig.* unerschütterlich, fest (*to* gegen); **'~-'stroke** *mot.* Viertakt...

four·teen ['fɔ:'ti:n] vierzehn; **'four-'teenth** [~θ] **1.** vierzehnte(r, -s); **2.** Vierzehntel *n*; **fourth** [fɔ:θ] **1.** vierte(r, -s); **2.** Viertel *n*; **'fourth·ly** viertens; **'four-'wheel-er** Droschke *f*.
fowl [faul] **1.** Geflügel *n*; Huhn *n*; Vogel *m*; **2.** Vögel fangen *od.* schießen; **'fowl·er** Vogelsteller *m*, -jäger *m*.
fowl·ing ['fauliŋ] Vogelfang *m*, -jagd *f*; **'~-piece** Vogelflinte *f*.
fowl-run ['faulrʌn] Hühnerhof *m*, Auslauf *m*.
fox [fɔks] **1.** Fuchs *m*; **2.** überlisten; **'~-brush** Fuchsschwanz *m*; **'~-earth** Fuchsbau *m*; **foxed** stockfleckig.
fox...: **'~glove** ⚘ Fingerhut *m*; **'~hole** ⚔ Schützenloch *n*; **'~hound** Hund *m* zur Fuchsjagd; **'~-hunt** Fuchsjagd *f*; **'~-'ter·ri·er** *zo.* Foxterrier *m*; **'~trot** Foxtrott *m* (*Tanz*); **'fox·y** fuchsartig; schlau; fuchsig, fuchsrot; stockfleckig.
foy·er *thea.* ['fɔiei] Foyer *n*, Wandelhalle *f*.
fra·cas ['frækɑ:], *pl.* **~** ['~z] Spektakel *m*.
frac·tion ['frækʃən] ⅍ Bruch *m*; Bruchstück *n*, -teil *m*; *~ line* Bruchstrich *m*; **frac·tion·al** ['~ʃənl] □ gebrochen (*Zahl*); Bruch...
frac·tious ['frækʃəs] reizbar, zanksüchtig, unleidlich.
frac·ture ['fræktʃə] **1.** (*bsd.* Knochen)Bruch *m*; **2.** brechen.
frag·ile ['frædʒail] zerbrechlich; *fig.* gebrechlich; **fra·gil·i·ty** [~'dʒiliti] Zer-, Gebrechlichkeit *f*.
frag·ment ['frægmənt] Bruchstück *n*, Fragment *n*; **'frag·men·tar·y** □ bruchstückhaft, fragmentarisch; in Bruchstücken (vorhanden).
fra·grance ['freigrəns] Wohlgeruch *m*, Duft *m*; **'fra·grant** □ wohlriechend, duftend.
frail[1] [freil] Binsen-, Feigenkorb *m*.
frail[2] □ [~] ge-, zerbrechlich; *bsd. moralisch* schwach; **'frail·ty** *fig.* Schwachheit *f*; Schwäche *f*.
frame [freim] **1.** Rahmen *m*; Gerippe *n*; (Brillen)Gestell *n*; Körper *m*; (An)Ordnung *f*, System *n*; ⚓, ✈ Spant *n*; *phot.* (Einzel)Bild *n* (*e-s Films*); ⚘ Frühbeetkasten *m*; *~ of mind* (Gemüts)Verfassung *f*; **2.** bilden, formen, bauen, machen; entwerfen; (ein)rahmen; sich entwickeln, zu werden versprechen; *a. ~ up sl. j.* mit Absicht fälschlich beschuldigen; **~ aer·i·al** Rahmenantenne *f*; **~ house** Holzhaus *n*; **'fram·er** Gestalter *m*; Rahmenmacher *m*; **'frame-up** *bsd. Am.* F abgekartetes Spiel *n*; **'frame·work** ⊕ Gerippe *n*; ⚠ Fachwerk *n*; Rahmen *m*; *fig.* Bau *m*; System *n*.
franc [fræŋk] Franc *m*; Franken *m*.
fran·chise ⚖ ['fræntʃaiz] Wahlrecht *n*; Bürgerrecht *n*; *bsd. Am.* Konzession *f*.
Fran·cis·can *eccl.* [fræn'siskən] Franziskaner *m*.
Fran·co- ['fræŋkəu] *in Zssgn* französisch.
fran·gi·ble ['frændʒibl] zerbrechlich.
Frank[1] [fræŋk] Franke *m*.
frank[2] [~] **1.** □ frei(mütig), offen; **2.** *Brief* maschinell frankieren.
frank·furt·er ['fræŋkfətə] Frankfurter Würstchen *n*.
frank·in·cense ['fræŋkinsens] Weihrauch *m*.
frank·ing-ma·chine ['fræŋkiŋməʃi:n] Frankiermaschine *f*.
frank·ness ['fræŋknis] Freimut *m*, Offenheit *f*.
fran·tic ['fræntik] (*~ally*) wahnsinnig, rasend (*with* vor); wütend; verzweifelt.
fra·ter·nal □ [frə'tə:nl] brüderlich; **fra'ter·ni·ty** Brüderlichkeit *f*; Brüderschaft *f*; *univ. Am.* Verbindung *f*; **frat·er·ni·za·tion** [frætənai'zeiʃən] Verbrüderung *f*; **'frat·er·nize** sich verbrüdern.
frat·ri·cide ['freitrisaid] Brudermord *m*; Brudermörder *m*.
fraud [frɔ:d] Betrug *m*; F Schwindel *m*; F Schwindler(in); **fraud·u·lence** ['~juləns] Betrügerei *f*; **'fraud·u·lent** □ betrügerisch.
fraught *poet.* [frɔ:t] beladen; voll (*with* von).
fray[1] [frei] (sich) abnutzen; (sich) durchscheuern; ausfransen.
fray[2] [~] Schlägerei *f*, Streit *m*.
fraz·zle *bsd. Am.* F ['fræzl] **1.** Fetzen *m/pl.*; *beat to a ~* in Fetzen hauen; **2.** zerfetzen.
freak [fri:k] **1.** Einfall *m*, Laune *f*; *sl.* Exzentriker *m*, Fanatiker *m*, ...narr *m*; *film ~* Kinonarr *m*; *~ of nature* Laune *f* der Natur; Monstrum *n*; **2.** *~ out sl.* ausflippen; **'freak·ish** □ lau-

nenhaft; abnorm.

freck·le ['frekl] **1.** Sommersprosse *f*; *fig.* Fleckchen *n*; **2.** sommersprossig machen *od.* werden; (sich) sprenkeln; **freck·led** ['~ld] sommersprossig.

free [fri:] **1.** □ *allg.* frei (*from, of* von) (*unabhängig; unbehindert; ungezwungen; unbeschäftigt; offen*); kostenlos, unentgeltlich; freigebig (*of* mit); reichlich; freiwillig; lose; ~ *of debt* schuldenfrei; *he is ~ to inf.* es steht ihm frei zu *inf.*; ~ *and easy* zwanglos; sorglos; *have a ~ hand* freie Hand haben; *give od. allow s.o. a ~ hand* j-m freie Hand lassen; *have one's hands ~ fig.* ungebunden sein; *make ~ with et.* ohne zu fragen benutzen; sich Freiheiten erlauben gegen *j.*; *make ~ of* zur Verfügung stellen; *make s.o. ~ of the city* j. zum Ehrenbürger machen; *set ~* freilassen; **2.** befreien (*from, of* von); freilassen; *et.* freimachen; **~·boot·er** ['~bu:tə] Freibeuter *m*; '**free·dom** Freiheit *f etc.* (*s. free 1*); Freisein *n* (*from* von); Leichtigkeit *f der Auffassung etc.*; freie Benutzung *f*; ~ *of the city* Ehrenbürgerrecht *n*; ~ *of movement* Freizügigkeit *f*; ~ *of speech* Redefreiheit *f*.

free...: ~ en·ter·prise freie Wirtschaft *f*; **~ fight** allgemeine Schlägerei *f*; '**~-for-all** allgemeines Geschrei *n*; = *free fight*; '**~-'hand·ed** freigebig, großzügig; '**~·hold** ⚖ freier Grundbesitz *m*; '**~·hold·er** Grundeigentümer *m*; **~ kick** *Sport*: Freistoß *m*; **~ la·bo(u)r** nichtorganisierte Arbeiter *m/pl.*; '**~-'lance** **1.** freier Journalist *m*; **2.** als freier Journalist arbeiten; '**~-'list** Liste *f* der zollfreien Waren *od.* der Freikartenempfänger; **~ liv·er** Schlemmer *m*; '**~·man** freier Mann *m*; Vollbürger *m*; '**~·ma·son** Freimaurer *m*; '**~·ma·son·ry** Freimaurerei *f*; **~ port** Freihafen *m*; **~ speech** Redefreiheit *f*; '**~-'spo·ken** freimütig; **~ state** Freistaat *m*; '**~-stone** Sandstein *m*; '**~-'think·er** Freidenker(in); '**~-'think·ing**, '**~-thought** **1.** Freidenkerei *f*; **2.** freidenkerisch; **~ trade** Freihandel *m*; '**~-'trad·er** Verfechter *m* des Freihandels; '**~·way** *Am.* Autobahn *f*; '**~-'wheel** **1.** Freilauf *m*; **2.** im Freilauf fahren.

freeze [fri:z] **1.** (*irr.*) *v/i.* (ge)frieren; erstarren; ~ *to death* erfrieren; *v/t.* gefrieren lassen; *Kapital* einfrieren; *Löhne, Preise* stoppen; ~ *out sl. j.* kaltstellen; **2.** Frostperiode *f*; Einfrieren *n*; *wage-~* Lohnstopp *m*; '**~-dry** gefriertrocknen; '**freez·er** Eismaschine *f*; Gefrierautomat *m*, -truhe *f*; 🚃 Kühlwagen *m*; '**freez·ing** □ eisig; ~ *compartment* Tiefkühlfach *n*; ~ *mixture phys.* Kältemischung *f*; ~ *point* Gefrierpunkt *m*.

freight [freit] **1.** Fracht *f*; Frachtgeld *n*; *attr. Am.* Güter...; ~ *out (home)* Hin- (Rück)fracht *f*; **2.** be-, verfrachten; beladen; '**freight·age** = *freight 1*; '**freight-car** 🚃 *Am.* Güterwagen *m*; '**freight·er** ⚓ Frachter *m*; ✈ Transportflugzeug *n*; **freight train** *Am.* Güterzug *m*.

French [frentʃ] **1.** französisch; ~ *beans pl.* grüne Bohnen *f/pl.*; ~ *dressing* Salatsoße *f aus Essig, Öl, Senf u. Gewürzen*; ~ *fried potatoes pl.*, *Am.* ~ *fries pl.* Pommes frites *pl.*; ~ *kiss* Zungenkuß *m*; *take ~ leave* heimlich weggehen; ~ *letter* F Kondom *n*; ~ *windows pl. zweiflügelige* Terrassen-, Balkon-, Verandatür *f*; **2.** Französisch *n*; *the ~ pl.* die Franzosen *pl.*; ~ **horn** ♪ Horn *n*; '**~·man** Franzose *m*; '**~·wom·an** Französin *f*.

fren·zied ['frenzid] wahnsinnig; '**fren·zy** Wahnsinn *m*; Raserei *f*.

fre·quen·cy ['fri:kwənsi] Häufigkeit *f*; ⚡ Frequenz *f*; **~ mod·u·la·tion** ⚡ Frequenzmodulation *f*; **fre·quent** **1.** □ ['~kwənt] häufig; **2.** [fri'kwent] (oft) besuchen; **fre·quen·ta·tion** [fri:kwen'teiʃən] häufiger Besuch *m*; Verkehr *m* (*of* in *dat.*); **fre·quent·er** [fri'kwentə] regelmäßige Besucher(in), Stammgast *m*.

fres·co ['freskəu], *pl.* **fres·co(e)s** ['~z] Fresko(gemälde) *n*.

fresh [freʃ] **1.** □ *allg.* frisch (*noch unverändert; gesund; munter; spannkräftig; kühl; ungesalzen*); neu; unerfahren; *Am. sl.* pampig, frech; *break ~ ground fig.* Neuland betreten; ~ *water* Süßwasser *n*; **2.** *Morgen*-Kühle *f*; Hochwasser *n*; '**fresh·en** frisch machen *od.* werden; auffrischen; **fresh·et** ['~it] *fig.* Flut *f*; '**fresh-fro·zen** tiefgekühlt; '**fresh·man** *univ.* Student *m* im ersten

Jahr; '**fresh·ness** Frische *f*; Neuheit *f*, Unerfahrenheit *f*; '**fresh-wa·ter** Süßwasser...; ~ *college Am.* drittrangiges College *n*.
fret[1] [fret] **1.** Aufregung *f*; Ärger *m*, Verdruß *m*; **2.** zerfressen; (sich) ärgern; (sich) grämen; *Loch* fressen; *Wasser* kräuseln; ~ *away*, ~ *out* aufreiben, verzehren.
fret[2] [~] **1.** ⚠ gebrochener Stab *m*; **2.** gittern; *fig.* bunt machen.
fret[3] [~] ♪ Bund *m*, Griffleiste *f*.
fret·ful □ ['fretful] ärgerlich, verdrießlich, mürrisch; unzufrieden.
fret-saw ['fretsɔ:] Laubsäge *f*.
fret·work ['fretwə:k] (geschnitztes) Gitterwerk *n*; Laubsägearbeit *f*.
Freud·i·an ['frɔidjən] Freudsch; ~ *slip psych.* Freudsche Fehlleistung *f*.
fri·a·bil·i·ty [fraiə'biliti] Bröckligkeit *f*; '**fri·a·ble** bröcklig; zerreibbar.
fri·ar [fraiə] (Bettel)Mönch *m*; '**fri-ar·y** Mönchskloster *n*.
frib·ble ['fribl] **1.** (ver)gammeln, (ver)trödeln; **2.** Tagedieb *m*.
fric·as·see [frikə'si:] **1.** Frikassee *n*; **2.** frikassieren.
fric·tion ['frikʃən] Reibung *f* (*a. fig.*); *attr.* = **fric·tion·al** ['~ʃənl] Reibungs...
Fri·day ['fraidi] Freitag *m*.
fridge F [fridʒ] Kühlschrank *m*.
fried egg [fraid'eg] Spiegelei *n*.
friend [frend] Freund(in); Bekannte *m*, *f*; ♀ Quäker(in); *his* ~*s pl. oft* seine Bekannten *pl.*; *make* ~*s with* sich anfreunden mit; '**friend·less** freundlos; '**friend·li·ness** Freundlichkeit *f*; '**friend·ly** freundschaftlich; freundlich (*a. fig.*); befreundet; ♀ *Society* Versicherungsverein *m* auf Gegenseitigkeit; '**friend·ship** Freundschaft *f*.
frieze [fri:z] Fries *m* (*Stoff u.* ⚠).
frig·ate ⚓ ['frigit] Fregatte *f*.
frig(**e**) F [fridʒ] = *fridge*.
fright [frait] Schreck(en) *m*, Furcht *f*; *fig.* Schreckbild *n*, Vogelscheuche *f*; '**fright·en** erschrecken, in Schrecken versetzen; *be* ~*ed of* F Angst haben vor (*dat.*); **fright·ful** □ ['~ful] schrecklich; '**fright·ful-ness** Schrecklichkeit *f*.
frig·id □ ['fridʒid] kalt, frostig (*a. fig.*); *psych.* frigid; **fri'gid·i·ty** Kälte *f*, Frostigkeit *f*; *psych.* Frigidität *f*.
frill [fril] **1.** Krause *f*, Rüsche *f*; *put on* ~*s* F *fig.* vornehm tun; **2.** kräuseln.
fringe [frindʒ] **1.** Franse *f*; Rand *m*; *a.* ~*s pl.* Ponyfrisur *f*; ~ *benefits pl.* zusätzliche Sozialleistungen *f*/*pl. des Arbeitgebers*; ~ *event* Randveranstaltung *f*; ~ *group* Randgruppe *f*; **2.** mit Fransen besetzen, (um)säumen.
frip·per·y ['fripəri] **1.** Flitterkram *m*, Plunder *m*; **2.** wertlos; Flitter...
Fri·sian ['friziən] **1.** friesisch; **2.** Friese *m*, Friesin *f*; das Friesische.
frisk [frisk] **1.** Hüpfen *n*, Springen *n*; Luftsprung *m*; **2.** hüpfen; *nach Waffen etc.* durchsuchen; '**frisk·i-ness** Munterkeit *f*; '**frisk·y** □ hüpfend; munter, lustig.
frith [friθ] = *firth*.
frit·ter ['fritə] **1.** Pfannkuchen *m*, Krapfen *m*; **2.** ~ *away* verzetteln.
fri·vol ['frivəl] leichtsinnig sein; *Zeit* verplempern; **fri·vol·i·ty** [~'vɔliti] Leichtfertigkeit *f*, Frivolität *f*; **friv·o·lous** □ ['~vələs] nichtig; leichtfertig, leichtsinnig, frivol.
frizz [friz] (sich) kräuseln; *Küche*: brutzeln; **friz·zle** ['~l] *a.* ~ *up* (sich) kräuseln; knusperig braten; brutzeln; '**friz·z**(**l**)**y** kraus, gekräuselt.
fro [frou]: *to and* ~ hin und her, auf und ab.
frock [frɔk] *Mönchs*-Kutte *f*; *Frauen*-Kleid *n*; (Kinder)Röckchen *n*; Kittel *m*; '~-'**coat** Gehrock *m*.
frog [frɔg] Frosch *m*; Schnurverschluß *m e-s Mantels*; 🚂 Herzstück *n e-r Weiche*; ⚔ Säbeltasche *f*; '~-**man** Froschmann *m*, Kampfschwimmer *m*; '~-**march** *Gefangenen* an Armen u. Beinen wegtragen.
frol·ic ['frɔlik] **1.** Fröhlichkeit *f*; lustiger Streich *m*, Scherz *m*; Lustbarkeit *f*; **2.** scherzen, spaßen; **frol-ic·some** □ ['~səm] lustig, fröhlich.
from [frɔm, frəm] von; aus, von ... her; von (... an); seit; (entfernt) von; aus, vor, wegen; nach, gemäß; *defend* ~ schützen vor (*dat.*); *draw* ~ *nature* nach der Natur zeichnen; *hide* ~ verbergen vor (*dat.*); ~ *above* von oben herab; ~ *amidst* mitten aus; ~ *before* aus der Zeit vor.
frond ⚘ [frɔnd] (Farn-, Palm-) Wedel *m*.

front [frʌnt] **1.** Stirn *f*; Vorderseite *f*; ⚔ Front *f*; Hemdbrust *f*; Strandpromenade *f*; Kühnheit *f*, Frechheit *f*; *poet.* Stirn *f*, Gesicht *n*; *in* ~ vorne; *in* ~ *of räumlich* vor; *come to the* ~ *fig.* sich zeigen, hervortreten; **2.** Vorder...; **3.** *a.* ~ *on*, ~ *towards* die Front haben nach; gegenüberstehen, -liegen (*dat.*), gegenübertreten (*dat.*); ˈ**front·age** ▲ Vorderfront *f*; ˈ**fron·tal 1.** Stirn...; Front...; Vorder...; **2.** ▲ Fassade *f*; **front bench** *pol.* vorderste Sitzbänke *f/pl. im Parlament, für führende Mitglieder der Regierung u. der Opposition*; **front bench·er** führendes Fraktionsmitglied *n*; **front door** Haustür *f*; **fron·tier** [ˈ~tiə] **1.** Grenz...; **2.** Grenze *f* (*bsd. hist. Am. Grenze zum Wilden Westen*); ˈ**fron·tiers·man** Grenzbewohner *m*; *fig.* Pionier *m*; **fron·tis·piece** [ˈ~tispiːs] ▲ Vorderseite *f*; *typ.* Titelbild *n*; **front·let** [ˈfrʌntlit] Stirnbinde *f*; **front line** Front(linie) *f*; *be in the* ~ (*a. fig.*) an vorderster Front stehen; **front man** *fig.* Aushängeschild *n*; ˈ**front-page** *Zeitung*: Titelseite *f*; ˈ**front-ˈwheel drive** *mot.* Vorderradantrieb *m*.

frost [frɔst] **1.** Frost *m*; *a. hoar* ~, *white* ~ Reif *m*; F Reinfall *m*; *black* ~ trockener Frost *m*; **2.** (mit Zucker) bestreuen; glasieren; mattieren; durch Frost beschädigen; ~*ed glass* Milchglas *n*; ˈ**~-bite** Erfrierung *f* *e-s Körperteils*; ˈ**frost·bit·ten** erfroren (*Körperteil*); ˈ**frost-bound** gefroren (*Boden*); ˈ**frost·ed** glasiert (*Kuchen*); erfroren (*Pflanzen etc.*); ~ *glass* Mattglas *n*; ˈ**frost·i·ness** Frost *m*, Kälte *f* (*a. fig.*); ˈ**frost·ing** Zuckerguß *m*; ˈ**frost·y** □ frostig, eisig (*a. fig.*); bereift (*fig. ergraut*).

froth [frɔθ] **1.** Schaum *m*; *fig.* Schaumschlägerei *f*; **2.** schäumen; zu Schaum schlagen; ˈ**froth·i·ness** *das* Schaumige; *fig.* Seichtheit *f*; ˈ**froth·y** □ schaumig; *fig.* seicht; schaumschlägerisch.

fro·ward † [ˈfrəuəd] eigensinnig, widerspenstig.

frown [fraun] **1.** Stirnrunzeln *n*; finsterer Blick *m*; **2.** *v/t.* ~ *down* durch finstere Blicke einschüchtern; *v/i.* die Stirn runzeln; finster blikken; ~ *at*, ~ *(up)on* finster ansehen; ablehnen, mißbilligen.

frowst F [fraust] Mief *m* (*schlechte Luft*); ˈ**frowst·y** □, **frowz·y** [ˈfrauzi] moderig, muffig; schlampig; schmutzig.

froze [frəuz] *pret. von freeze 1*; ˈ**fro·zen 1.** *p.p. von freeze 1*; **2.** *adj.* (eis-) kalt; eingefroren (*Kapital etc.*); ~ *assets pl.* festliegendes Kapital *n*; ~ *meat* Gefrierfleisch *n*.

fruc·ti·fi·ca·tion [frʌktifiˈkeiʃən] Befruchtung *f*; **fruc·ti·fy** [ˈ~fai] *v/t.* befruchten; *v/i.* Früchte bringen (*a. fig.*).

fru·gal □ [ˈfruːgəl] genügsam, mäßig; sparsam; einfach, frugal; **fru·gal·i·ty** [~ˈgæliti] Mäßigkeit *f*; Sparsamkeit *f*.

fruit [fruːt] **1.** Frucht *f* (*fig.* = *Erfolg*); *coll.* Früchte *f/pl.*, Obst *n*; **2.** Frucht tragen; ˈ**fruit·age** (Frucht-) Tragen *n*; **frui·ta·ri·an** [fruːˈtɛəriən] Rohköstler(in); ˈ**fruit-cake** englischer Kuchen *m*; ˈ**fruit·er** Fruchtträger *m* (*Baum*); ˈ**fruit·er·er** Obsthändler *m*; **fruit·ful** □ [ˈ~ful] fruchtbar (*a. fig.*); ergiebig; ˈ**fruit·ful·ness** Fruchtbarkeit *f* (*a. fig.*); **fru·i·tion** [fruːˈiʃən] (Voll-) Genuß *m*; Erfüllung *f*, Verwirklichung *f*; **fruit knife** Obstmesser *n*; ˈ**fruit·less** □ unfruchtbar; *fig.* fruchtlos, vergeblich; ˈ**fruit-ma·chine** F Spielautomat *m*; **fruit sal·ad** Obstsalat *m*; ˈ**fruit·y** fruchtig; F deftig, saftig, derb.

frump [frʌmp] *fig.* Vogelscheuche *f*; ˈ**frump·ish**, ˈ**frump·y** altmodisch.

frus·trate [frʌsˈtreit] vereiteln; enttäuschen; **frusˈtra·tion** Vereitelung *f*; Enttäuschung *f*; *psych.* Frustration *f*.

fry [frai] **1.** Gebratene *n*; **2.** Fischbrut *f*; *small* ~ F junges Gemüse *n* (*Kinder*); kleine Leute *pl.*; **3.** braten, backen; *s.* egg; *fried potatoes pl.* Bratkartoffeln *f/pl.*; ˈ**fry·ing-pan** Bratpfanne *f*; *get out of the* ~ *into the fire* vom Regen in die Traufe kommen.

fuch·sia ♀ [ˈfjuːʃə] Fuchsia *f*.

fuck V [fʌk] **1.** ficken; **2.** *int.* verdammte Scheiße!

fud·dle [ˈfʌdl] **1.** (sich) berauschen; **2.** Rausch *m*.

fudge F [fʌdʒ] **1.** zurechtpfuschen; schwindeln; **2.** Fälschung *f*; letzte Meldung *f*; Weichkaramelle *f*; ~! Schwindel!; Unsinn!

fuel ['fjuəl] **1.** Brennmaterial *n*; Betriebs-, *mot.* Kraftstoff *m*; ~ *ga(u)ge mot.* Benzinuhr *f*; ~ *oil* Heizöl *n*; **2.** mit Brennstoff versehen; *mot.* tanken.
fug [fʌg] **1.** Mief *m*; Staubflocken *f/pl.*; **2.** ein Stubenhocker sein.
fu·ga·cious [fju:'geiʃəs] flüchtig, vergänglich.
fu·gi·tive ['fju:dʒitiv] **1.** flüchtig (*a. fig.*); **2.** Flüchtling *m*.
fu·gle·man ['fju:glmæn] (An-, Wort)Führer *m*.
fugue ♪ [fju:g] Fuge *f*.
ful·crum ['fʌlkrəm] Drehpunkt *m*.
ful·fil(l) [ful'fil] erfüllen; vollziehen; **ful'fill·er** Vollbringer(in); **ful'fil(l)·ment** Erfüllung *f*.
ful·gent *poet.* ['fʌldʒənt] glänzend.
full[1] [ful] **1.** □ *allg.* voll; Voll...; vollständig, völlig; reif; reichlich; ausführlich; *at ~ length* ausführlich; *of ~ age* volljährig; ~ *stop gr.* Punkt *m*; ~ *up* besetzt; *house ~ thea.* ausverkauft; **2.** *adv.* völlig, ganz; genau, gerade; recht, sehr; **3.** Fülle *f*; Ganze *n*; Höhepunkt *m*; *in ~* völlig, gänzlich; ausführlich; *pay in ~* voll bezahlen; *to the ~* vollständig, bis ins kleinste.
full[2] ⊕ [~] walken.
full...: '~-'**back** *Fußball*: Verteidiger *m*; '~-'**blood·ed** vollblütig, kräftig; reinrassig; '~-'**blown** voll erblüht; '~'**bod·ied** schwer (*Wein*); ~ **dress** Gesellschaftsanzug *m*; '~-**dress** formell, Gala...; *Am.* ausführlich; ~ *debate* wichtige Debatte *f*; ~ *rehearsal thea.* Generalprobe *f*.
full·er ⊕ ['fulə] Walker *m*.
full...: '~-'**fledged** *orn.* flügge; voll ausgewachsen, fertig; '~-'**grown** ausgewachsen.
full·ing-mill ⊕ ['fuliŋmil] Walkmühle *f*.
full-length ['ful'leŋθ] in Lebensgröße.
ful(l)·ness ['fulnis] Fülle *f*.
full...: '~-'**page** ganzseitig; '~-'**scale** in Lebensgröße, im Maßstab 1 : 1; total, regelrecht; vollständig; '~-'**time** vollbeschäftigt; hauptberuflich (tätig); ganztägig.
ful·ly ['fuli] voll, völlig, gänzlich; ~ *two hours* ganze zwei Stunden; '~-'**fashioned** mit Paßform (*Damenstrümpfe etc.*); '~-'**fledged** flügge (*Vogel, a. fig.*); vollausgebildet, -entwickelt.

ful·mar *orn.* ['fulmə] Fulmar *m*, Eissturmvogel *m*.
ful·mi·nate *fig.* ['fʌlmineit] losdonnern, wettern (*against* gegen); **ful·mi'na·tion** Drohung *f*; Wettern *n*.
ful·some □ ['fulsəm] widerlich.
fum·ble ['fʌmbl] herumtappen, -tasten, -fummeln; '**fum·bler** Tolpatsch *m*.
fume [fju:m] **1.** Dunst *m*, Dampf *m*; Rauch *m*, Qualm *m*; *in a ~* wütend, aufgebracht; **2.** rauchen, dunsten, dampfen; wütend sein.
fu·mi·gate ['fju:migeit] (aus)räuchern, desinfizieren; **fu·mi'ga·tion** (Aus)Räucherung *f*, Desinfektion *f*.
fum·ing □ ['fju:miŋ] aufgebracht, wütend.
fun [fʌn] Scherz *m*, Spaß *m*; *have ~* sich amüsieren; *make ~ of* sich lustig machen über (*acc.*).
func·tion ['fʌŋkʃən] **1.** Funktion *f*; Beruf *m*; Tätigkeit *f*, Wirksamkeit *f*; *physiol.*, ⚗ Funktion *f*; Aufgabe *f*; Feierlichkeit *f*; **2.** funktionieren, arbeiten; **func·tion·al** □ ['~ʃənl] amtlich; ⚗ funktionell; sachlich; **func·tion·ar·y** ['~ʃnəri] Beamte *m*; Funktionär *m*.
fund [fʌnd] **1.** Fonds *m*, Kapital *n*; ~*s pl.* Staatsschulden *f/pl.*, -papiere *n/pl.*; Geld(er *n/pl.*, -mittel *n/pl.*) *n*; Vorrat *m*, Schatz *m*; *in ~s* bei Geld; **2.** *Schuld* fundieren; *Geld* anlegen.
fun·da·men·tal [fʌndə'mentl] **1.** □ grundlegend, -sätzlich; Grund...; **2.** ~*s pl.* Grundlage *f*, -züge *m/pl.*, -begriffe *m/pl.*, -tatsachen *f/pl.*
fu·ner·al ['fju:nərəl] **1.** Beerdigung *f*, Bestattung *f*; **2.** Begräbnis..., Trauer..., Leichen...; ~ *pile* Scheiterhaufen *m*; **fu·ne·re·al** □ [~'niəriəl] Trauer...; düster, traurig.
fun-fair ['fʌnfɛə] Rummelplatz *m*.
fun·gous ['fʌŋgəs] pilz-, schwammartig; **fun·gus** ['~gəs], *pl. mst* **fun·gi** ['~gai] ⚘ Schwamm *m*, Pilz *m*; ⚕ Wucherung *f*.
fu·nic·u·lar [fju:'nikjulə] **1.** Seil...; **2.** *a.* ~ *railway* (Draht)Seilbahn *f*.
funk F [fʌŋk] **1.** Mordsangst *f*; Angsthase *m*; **2.** Angst haben; sich drücken (vor); '**funk·y** F feig(e).
fun·nel ['fʌnl] Trichter *m*; Rauchfang *m*; ⚓, 🚂 Schornstein *m*.
fun·nies *Am.* ['fʌniz] *pl.* = *comics*.

fun·ny □ [ˈfʌni] spaßig, komisch; sonderbar; ˈ~-**bone** Musikantenknochen *m.*
fur [fəː] **1.** Pelz *m*; Belag *m der Zunge*; Kesselstein *m*; ~*s pl.* Pelzwaren *f/pl.*; *make the ~ fly* ein großes Theater machen; **2.** mit Pelz kleiden *od.* besetzen *od.* füttern; Kesselstein ansetzen; ~*red* belegt (*Zunge*).
fur·be·low [ˈfəːbiləu] Falbel *f.*
fur·bish [ˈfəːbiʃ] putzen, polieren.
fur·ca·tion [fəːˈkeiʃən] Gabelung *f.*
fur coat [ˈfəːˈkəut] Pelzmantel *m.*
fu·ri·ous □ [ˈfjuəriəs] wütend; wild, rasend.
furl [fəːl] *Segel* festmachen; *Schirm* einrollen; *Fächer* zs.-klappen; *Vorhang* aufziehen.
fur·long [ˈfəːlɔŋ] Achtelmeile *f.*
fur·lough [ˈfəːləu] **1.** Urlaub *m*; **2.** beurlauben (*bsd.* ⚔).
fur·nace [ˈfəːnis] Schmelz-, Hochofen *m*; (Heiz)Kessel *m*; Feuerung *f.*
fur·nish [ˈfəːniʃ] versehen, ausstatten (*with* mit); *et.* liefern; *Zimmer* möblieren, einrichten; ˈ**fur·nish·er** Lieferant *m*; Möbelhändler *m*; ˈ**fur·nish·ings** *pl.* Einrichtung(sgegenstände *m/pl.*) *f.*
fur·ni·ture [ˈfəːnitʃə] Möbel *n/pl.*, Mobiliar *n*, Einrichtung *f*; Ausstattung *f*; ⊕ Zubehör *n.*
fu·ro·re [fjuəˈrɔːri] Furore *n*; Begeisterung *f*; Aufregung *f.*
fur·ri·er [ˈfʌriə] Kürschner *m*; ˈ**fur·ri·er·y** Kürschnerei *f.*
fur·row [ˈfʌrəu] **1.** Furche *f*; Nut *f*; **2.** furchen; auskehlen.
fur·ry [ˈfəːri] pelzig; Pelz...
fur·ther [ˈfəːðə] **1.** *adj. u. adv.* ferner, weiter; **2.** fördern; ˈ**fur·ther·ance** Förderung *f*, Unterstützung *f*; ˈ**fur·ther·er** Förderer *m*, Förderin *f*; ˈ**fur·ther**ˈ**more** ferner, überdies, außerdem; ˈ**fur·ther·most** weitest, entferntest; am weitesten.
fur·thest [ˈfəːðist] *s. furthermost*; *at (the) ~* spätestens.
fur·tive □ [ˈfəːtiv] verstohlen.
fu·ry [ˈfjuəri] Raserei *f*, Wut *f*; Furie *f.*
furze ⚘ [fəːz] Stechginster *m.*
fuse [fjuːz] **1.** schmelzen; verschmelzen; *als Folge e-s Kurzschlusses* ausgehen (*Licht*); ⚔ mit Zünder versehen; **2.** ⚡ (Schmelz-)Sicherung *f*; ⚔ Zünder *m*; *time-~* Zeitzünder *m.*
fu·se·lage [ˈfjuːzilɑːʒ] (Flugzeug-)Rumpf *m.*
fu·si·bil·i·ty [fjuːzəˈbiliti] Schmelzbarkeit *f*; **fu·si·ble** [ˈfjuːzəbl] schmelzbar.
fu·sil·ier ⚔ [fjuːziˈliə] Füsilier *m.*
fu·sil·lade [fjuːziˈleid] Gewehrfeuer *n.*
fu·sion [ˈfjuːʒən] Schmelzen *n*; Verschmelzung *f*; ~ **bomb** ⚔ Wasserstoffbombe *f.*
fuss F [fʌs] **1.** Lärm *m*; Wesen *n*, Getue *n*; Aufregung *f*; *make a ~ about* sich aufregen über (*acc.*); *make a ~ of s.o.* viel Wesens um j. machen; **2.** viel Aufhebens machen (*about* um, von); hasten; nervös machen, belästigen; ˈ~·**pot** F Umstandskrämer *m*; ˈ**fuss·y** □ F *unnötig* geschäftig, viel Aufhebens machend.
fus·tian ✝ [ˈfʌstiən] Barchent *m*; *fig.* Schwulst *m.*
fust·i·ness [ˈfʌstinis] Modergeruch *m*; ˈ**fust·y** □ muffig; *fig.* verstaubt.
fu·tile □ [ˈfjuːtail] unnütz; wirkungs-, nutzlos; **fu·til·i·ty** [~ˈtiliti] Nichtigkeit *f*, Nutzlosigkeit *f.*
fu·ture [ˈfjuːtʃə] **1.** (zu)künftig; ~ *tense gr.* Futur *n*; **2.** Zukunft *f*; ~*s pl.* ✝ Termingeschäfte *n/pl.*; ˈ**fu·tur·ism** *paint.* Futurismus *m*; **fu·tu·ri·ty** [fjuːˈtjuəriti] Zukunft *f*; zukünftiges Ereignis *n.*
fuzz [fʌz] **1.** feiner Flaum *m*; Fussel *f*; *the ~ sl.* die Bullen *m/pl.*; die Polizei *f*; **2.** fusseln, (zer)fasern; ˈ**fuzz·y** □ fusselig, faserig; kraus; verschwommen, trüb.

G

gab F [gæb] Geschwätz *n*; *the gift of the ~* ein gutes Mundwerk *n*.
gab·ar·dine ['gæbədi:n] Gabardine *m* (*Wollstoff*).
gab·ble ['gæbl] **1.** Geschnatter *n*, Geschwätz *n*; **2.** schnattern, schwatzen; '**gab·bler** Schwätzer (-in); '**gab·by** F geschwätzig.
gab·er·dine ['gæbədi:n] Kaftan *m*; = *gabardine*.
ga·ble ['geibl] Giebel *m*; '**ga·bled** mit Giebel(n); Giebel...
ga·by ['geibi] Trottel *m*.
gad F [gæd]: *~ about* sich herumtreiben; ⚘ wuchern; '**gad·a·bout** F Herumtreiber *m*, Nichtstuer *m*.
gad·fly *zo.* ['gædflai] Bremse *f*.
gadg·et *sl.* ['gædʒit] Dings *n*, Apparat *m*; Kniff *m*, Pfiff *m*; '**gadg·et·ry** *mst contp.* Apparate *m/pl.*, technisches Zubehör.
Gael·ic ['geilik] Gälisch *n*.
gaff [gæf] Fischhaken *m*; ⚓ Gaffel *f*; *sl.* Tingeltangel *n*, *m*; *blow the ~ sl.* alles verraten.
gaffe F [gæf] Dummheit *f* (*Fehler*).
gaf·fer F ['gæfə] Alte *m*; Vorarbeiter *m*.
gag [gæg] **1.** Knebel *m* (*a. fig.*); *parl.* Schluß *m* der Debatte; *thea.* Improvisation *f*; Witz *m*, Trick *m*; Gag *m*; **2.** knebeln; *thea.* improvisieren; *fig.* mundtot machen.
ga·ga *sl.* ['gɑ:gɑ:] senil, verblödet; verrückt.
gage[1] [geidʒ] **1.** Pfand *n*; Fehdehandschuh *m*; **2.** zum Pfand geben.
gage[2] [~] = *gauge*.
gag·gle ['gægl] Schar *f* Gänse; *fig.* Herde *f*.
gai·e·ty ['geiəti] Fröhlichkeit *f*; Lustbarkeit *f*; Heiterkeit *f*.
gai·ly ['geili] *adv. von gay*.
gain [gein] **1.** Gewinn *m* (*bsd.* ✝ *~s pl.*); **2.** *v/t.* gewinnen; erreichen; bekommen; *v/i.* vorgehen (*Uhr*); *~ on* Vorteil erlangen über (*acc.*); *~ in* zunehmen an (*dat.*); '**gain·er** Gewinner(in); **gain·ful** □ ['~ful] einträglich; *~ employment* Erwerbstätigkeit *f*; *~ly occupied* erwerbstätig; '**gain·ings** *pl.* Gewinn *m*, Verdienst *m*.
gain·say *lit.* [gein'sei] (*irr. say*) widersprechen (*dat.*); leugnen.
gainst *poet.* [geinst] = *against*.
gait [geit] Gang(art *f*) *m*; Haltung *f*; Schritt *m*.
gai·ter ['geitə] Gamasche *f*.
gal *Am. sl.* [gæl] Mädel *n*.
ga·la ['gɑ:lə] Fest(lichkeit *f*) *n*.
ga·lac·tic *ast.* [gə'læktik] Milchstraßen...
gal·an·tine ['gælənti:n] Galantine *f* (*Geflügelsülze*).
gal·ax·y ['gæləksi] *ast.* Milchstraße *f*; *fig.* (glänzende) Schar *f*.
gale [geil] Sturm *m* (*a. fig.*); steife Brise *f*.
ga·le·na *min.* [gə'li:nə] Galenit *m*, Bleiglanz *m*.
gall[1] [gɔ:l] Galle *f* (*a. fig.*); *bsd. Am. sl.* Frechheit *f*.
gall[2] ⚘ [~] Gallapfel *m*.
gall[3] [~] **1.** wundgeriebene Stelle *f*, Wolf *m*; *fig.* Pein *f*; **2.** wundreiben; peinigen; reizen, ärgern.
gal·lant ['gælənt] **1.** □ stattlich; tapfer; galant; ritterlich; **2.** Kavalier *m*; *b.s.* Galan *m*, Stutzer *m*; **3.** galant sein; '**gal·lant·ry** Tapferkeit *f*; Galanterie *f*; Liebelei *f*.
gal·leon ⚓ ['gæliən] Galeone *f*.
gal·ler·y ['gæləri] Galerie *f*; Empore *f*; ⚒ Stollen *m*; *play to the ~* den Beifall der Menge suchen.
gal·ley ['gæli] ⚓ Galeere *f*; ⚓ Kombüse *f*; *typ.* Schiff *n*; *~* **proof** Korrekturfahne *f*; '**~-slave** Galeerensklave *m*.
Gal·lic ['gælik] gallisch; *co.* französisch; **Gal·li·can** ['~kən] gallikanisch; **gal·li·cism** ['~sizəm] Gallizismus *m*, französische Spracheigenheit *f*.
gal·li·vant [gæli'vænt] sich herumtreiben.
gall-nut ['gɔ:lnʌt] Gallapfel *m*.
gal·lon ['gælən] Gallone *f* (*4,54 Liter*, *Am. 3,78 Liter*).
gal·lop ['gæləp] **1.** Galopp *m*; **2.** galoppieren (lassen).
gal·lows ['gæləuz] *sg.* Galgen *m*; '**~-bird** Galgenvogel *m*.
Gal·lup poll ['gæləp'pəul] Meinungsumfrage *f*.
ga·lore [gə'lɔ:] in Menge.
ga·losh [gə'lɔʃ] Galosche *f*, Überschuh *m*, Gummischuh *m*.
ga·lumph [gə'lʌmf] (einher)stolzieren.
gal·van·ic [gæl'vænik] (*~ally*) gal-

vanisch; **gal·va·nism** ['gælvənizəm] Galvanismus *m*; '**gal·va·nize** galvanisieren; anfeuern, stimulieren (*into* zu); **gal·va·no·plas·tic** [~nəu'plæstik] galvanoplastisch.
gam·bit ['gæmbit] *Schach*: Gambit *n*; *fig.* Einleitung *f*.
gam·ble ['gæmbl] (um Geld) spielen; **2.** F Glücksspiel *n* (*mst fig.*); '**gam·bler** Spieler(in); '**gam·bling-den**, '**gam·bling-house** Spielhölle *f*.
gam·boge [gæm'bu:ʒ] Gummigutt *n*.
gam·bol ['gæmbəl] **1.** Luftsprung *m*; **2.** (fröhlich) hüpfen, tanzen.
game[1] [geim] **1.** Spiel *n*; Scherz *m*; *b.s.* Schlich *m*; Wild *n*; *beat s.o. at his own ~* j. mit s-n eigenen Waffen schlagen; *play the ~* sich an die Spielregeln halten; *fig.* anständig handeln; *be off one's ~* nicht in Form sein; *make ~ of s.o.* sich über j. lustig machen; **2.** F entschlossen; bereit; *die ~* furchtlos in den Tod gehen; **3.** spielen.
game[2] [~] lahm; verkrüppelt.
game...: '**~-cock** Kampfhahn *m*; '**~·keep·er** Wildhüter *m*; '**~-laws** *pl.* Jagdgesetze *n/pl.*; '**~-li·cence** Jagdschein *m*; '**games-mas·ter** Turnlehrer *m*; **game·ster** ['~stə] Spieler(in); '**gam·ing-house** Spielkasino *n*.
gam·ma rays *phys.* ['gæmə'reiz] *pl.* Gammastrahlen *m/pl.*
gam·mon ['gæmən] (geräucherter) Schinken *m*; F Unsinn *m*, Quatsch *m*.
gam·my F ['gæmi] = *game*[2].
gamp *co.* [gæmp] Regenschirm *m*.
gam·ut ['gæmət] ♪ Tonleiter *f*; *fig.* Skala *f*.
gam·y ['geimi] nach Wild schmekkend; wildreich.
gan·der ['gændə] Gänserich *m*.
gang [gæŋ] **1.** Abteilung *f*, Trupp *m*; Rotte *f*; *b.s.* Bande *f*; **2.** *~ up* sich zs.-rotten *od.* -tun (*against, on* gegen); '**~-board** ⚓ Laufplanke *f*; **gang·er** ['gæŋə] Rottenführer *m*.
gan·gli·on ['gæŋliən] *anat.* Ganglion *n*, Nervenknoten *m*; *fig.* Knotenpunkt *m*.
gang-plank ⚓ ['gæŋplæŋk] Laufplanke *f*.
gan·grene ⚕ ['gæŋgri:n] Gangrän *f*, Brand *m*.
gang·ster *Am.* ['gæŋstə] Gangster *m*, Verbrecher *m*.
gang·way ['gæŋwei] (Durch)Gang *m*; ⚓ Fallreep *n*; ⚓ Laufplanke *f*.
gan·net *orn.* ['gænit] Tölpel *m*.
gan·try ['gæntri] 🚂 Signalbrücke *f*; ⚓ Verladebrücke *f*; Gerüst *n*.
gaol [dʒeil], '**~-bird**, '**gaol·er** *s. jail etc.*
gap [gæp] Lücke *f*; *fig.* Kluft *f*; Spalte *f*; Riß *m*.
gape [geip] **1.** gähnen; klaffen; *~ at* angaffen, -starren; **2.** *the ~s pl.* Schnabelsperre *f*.
ga·rage ['gærɑ:dʒ] **1.** Garage *f*; Autowerkstatt *f*; **2.** *Auto* einstellen.
garb [gɑ:b] **1.** Gewand *n*, Tracht *f*; **2.** kleiden.
gar·bage ['gɑ:bidʒ] Abfall *m*; Schund *m*; *~ can Am.*, *~ pail* Mülleimer *m*; *~ collector Am.* Müllabfuhrmann *m*.
gar·ble ['gɑ:bl] verstümmeln; zustutzen; entstellen.
gar·den ['gɑ:dn] **1.** Garten *m*; *lead s.o. up the ~ path* j. an der Nase herumführen; **2.** Gartenbau treiben; im Garten arbeiten; '**gar·den·er** Gärtner(in).
gar·de·nia ⚘ [gɑ:'di:njə] Gardenie *f*.
gar·den·ing ['gɑ:dniŋ] Gartenarbeit *f*; Gärtnerei *f*; '**gar·den-par·ty** Gartenfest *n*.
gar·gan·tu·an [gɑ:'gæntjuən] gewaltig, ungeheuer.
gar·gle ['gɑ:gl] **1.** gurgeln; **2.** Gurgelwasser *n*.
gar·goyle △ ['gɑ:gɔil] Wasserspeier *m*.
gar·ish □ ['gɛəriʃ] grell, auffallend.
gar·land ['gɑ:lənd] **1.** Kranz *m*; Girlande *f*; **2.** bekränzen.
gar·lic ⚘ ['gɑ:lik] Knoblauch *m*.
gar·ment ['gɑ:mənt] Kleidungsstück *n*; Gewand *n*.
gar·ner ['gɑ:nə] **1.** Kornspeicher *m*; *fig.* Speicher *m*; **2.** aufspeichern.
gar·net *min.* ['gɑ:nit] Granat *m*.
gar·nish ['gɑ:niʃ] garnieren; zieren, schmücken; '**gar·nish·ing** Garnierung *f*.
gar·ret ['gærit] Dachstube *f*.
gar·ri·son ⚔ ['gærisn] **1.** Besatzung *f*; Garnison *f*; **2.** mit einer Besatzung *od.* Garnison belegen; in Garnison legen.
gar·ru·li·ty [gæ'ru:liti] Schwatzhaftigkeit *f*; **gar·ru·lous** □ ['gæruləs] schwatzhaft, geschwätzig.

gar·ter ['gɑːtə] Strumpfband *n*; *Am.* Socken-, Strumpfhalter *m*; *Order of the* ♀ Hosenbandorden *m*.

gas [gæs] **1.** Gas *n*; F leeres Gerede *n*; *Am.* = *gasoline*; *step on the* ~ Gas geben; **2.** vergasen; F faseln; '**~-bag** Gaszelle *f*; F Schwätzer *m*; '**~-brack·et** Gasarm *m*; '**~-burn·er** Gasbrenner *m*; '**~-cham·ber** Gaskammer *f*; '**~-cook·er** Gasherd *m*; '**~-en·gine** Gasmotor *m*; **gas·e·ous** ['geizjəs] gasförmig.

gas...: '**~-fire** Gasofen *m*; '**~-fit·ter** Installateur *m*, Rohrleger *m*; '**~-fit·tings** *pl.* Gasinstallation *f*.

gash [gæʃ] **1.** klaffende Wunde *f*; Hieb *m*; Riß *m*; **2.** tief (ein)schneiden in (*acc.*).

gas·ket ['gæskit] ⚓ Seising *n*; ⊕ Dichtung *f*.

gas...: '**~-light** Gaslicht *n*, Gasbeleuchtung *f*; '**~-mask** Gasmaske *f*; '**~-me·ter** Gasuhr *f*; **gas·o·lene, gas·o·line** *Am. mot.* ['gæsəuliːn] Benzin *n*; **gas·om·e·ter** [gæ'sɔmitə] Gasometer *m*, Gasbehälter *m*; '**gas--oven** Gasbackofen *m*, Gasherd *m*.

gasp [gɑːsp] **1.** Keuchen *n*; schwerer Atemzug *m*; **2.** keuchen; *a.* ~ *for breath* nach Luft schnappen.

gas-pok·er ['gæs'pəukə] Gasanzünder *m*; '**gas-'proof** gassicher; '**gas--range** Gasherd *m*; '**gas-ring** Gasbrenner *m*, -kocher *m*; **gassed** gasvergiftet; **gas sta·tion** *Am.* Tankstelle *f*; '**gas-stove** Gasofen *m*, Gasherd *m*; '**gas·sy** Gas...; geschwätzig; '**gas-tar** Steinkohlenteer *m*.

gas·tric ⚕ ['gæstrik] gastrisch; Magen...; **gas·tri·tis** [gæs'traitis] Magenentzündung *f*, Gastritis *f*.

gas·tron·o·my [gæs'trɔnəmi] Gastronomie *f*, Kochkunst *f*.

gas-works ['gæswəːks] *mst sg.* Gaswerk *n*, -anstalt *f*.

gat *Am. sl.* [gæt] Revolver *m*, Pistole *f*.

gate [geit] Tor *n*; Pforte *f*; Gatter *n*; *fig.* Weg *m*; *Sport*: Besucher(zahl *f*) *m/pl.*; = ~*-money*; Sperre *f*; '**~--crash·er** *sl.* ungebetener Gast *m*; '**~-house** Pförtnerhaus *n*; '**~-keep·er** Pförtner *m*; '**~-leg(ged) ta·ble** Klapptisch *m*; '**~·man** 🚂 Schrankenwärter *m*; '**~-mon·ey** *Sport*: Eintrittsgeld *n*; '**~-post** Tür-, Torpfosten *m*; *between you and me and the* ~ im Vertrauen (gesagt); '**~·way** Torweg *m*, Einfahrt *f*; *fig.* Weg *m*, Tor *n*.

gath·er ['gæðə] **1.** *v/t.* (ein-, ver-)sammeln; ernten; pflücken; schließen (*from* aus); zs.-ziehen; *Schneiderei*: einhalten, ankrausen; *s. information*; ~ *speed* schneller werden; *v/i.* sich (ver)sammeln; sich vergrößern; *a.* ~ *to a head* ⚕ *u. fig.* reifen; **2.** ~*s pl.* (Kräusel)Falten *f/pl.*; '**gath·er·ing** Versammlung *f*; Zs.-kunft *f*; ⚕ Geschwür *n*.

gauche [gəuʃ] linkisch; taktlos; **gau·che·rie** ['~əriː] linkisches *od.* taktloses Benehmen *n*.

gaud·y ['gɔːdi] **1.** □ grell, protzig; **2.** *univ.* jährliches Festmahl *n*.

gauge [geidʒ] **1.** (Normal)Maß *n*; Maßstab *m*; Lehre *f*; 🚂 Spurweite *f*; ⊕ Querschnitt *m*; ⚚ Maschengröße *f bei Strümpfen*; Meßgerät *n*; **2.** eichen; (aus)messen; *fig.* abschätzen; '**gaug·er** Eichmeister *m*.

Gaul [gɔːl] Gallier *m*; *co.* Franzose *m*.

gaunt □ [gɔːnt] hager; finster.

gaunt·let[1] ['gɔːntlit] Stulp-, *fig.* Fehdehandschuh *m*; *throw down* (*pick up, take up*) *the* ~ den Fehdehandschuh hinwerfen (aufnehmen).

gaunt·let[2] [~]: *run the* ~ Spießruten laufen.

gauze [gɔːz] Gaze *f*; *silk* ~ Seidenflor *m*; '**gauz·y** gazeartig.

gave [geiv] *pret. von give 1 u. 2.*

gav·el *Am.* ['gævl] Hammer *m des Versammlungsleiters od. Auktionators.*

gawk F [gɔːk] Tölpel *m*; Schlaks *m*; '**gawk·y** tölpisch; schlaksig.

gay □ [gei] lustig, heiter; bunt, lebhaft, glänzend; ausschweifend; F schwul, homosexuell; *Am. sl.* frech; **gay·e·ty** ['geiəti] = *gaiety*.

gaze [geiz] **1.** starrer *od.* aufmerksamer Blick *m*; **2.** starren; ~ *at*, ~ *on* aufmerksam anblicken; anstarren, -staunen; '**gaz·er** Gaffer(in).

ga·zelle *zo.* [gə'zel] Gazelle *f*.

ga·zette [gə'zet] **1.** (offizielle) Zeitung *f*; *der* Staatsanzeiger; **2.** amtlich bekanntgeben; **gaz·et·teer** [gæzi'tiə] geographisches Lexikon *n*.

gear [giə] **1.** ⊕ Getriebe *n*; *mot.* Gang *m*; Mechanismus *m*; Gerät *n*, Zeug *n*; Ausrüstung *f*; *in* ~ mit eingelegtem Gang; in Betrieb; in Ordnung; *out of* ~ ohne Gang, im Leerlauf; außer Betrieb; nicht in Ordnung; *landing*-~ ✈ Fahrgestell *n*; *steering*-~ ⚓ Ruderanlage *f*; *mot.* Lenkgetriebe *n*; *hunting*-~ Jagdausrüstung *f*; **2.** einschalten; ⊕ greifen; *fig.* abstimmen (*to* auf *acc.*); ~ *up* (*down*) über- (unter)setzen; '**~-box** Getriebe(gehäuse) *n*; '**gear·ing** (Zahnrad)Getriebe *n*; Übersetzung *f*; '**gear-le·ver,** *bsd. Am.* '**gear-shift** Schalthebel *m.*

gee [dʒiː] **1.** *Kindersprache*: Hottehü *n* (*Pferd*); **2.** *Fuhrmannsruf*: hü! hott!; *Am.* so was!; Donnerwetter!

geese [giːs] *pl. von goose.*

Gei·ger ['gaigə]: ~ *counter* Geigerzähler *m.*

gei·sha ['geiʃə] Geisha *f.*

gel·a·tin(e) [dʒelə'tiːn] Gelatine *f*; **ge·lat·i·nize** [dʒi'lætinaiz] gelatinieren; **ge'lat·i·nous** gallertartig.

geld [geld] (*irr.*) *Tier* verschneiden; '**geld·ing** Wallach *m.*

gel·ig·nite ['dʒelignait] Gelatinedynamit *n.*

gelt [gelt] *pret. u. p.p. von geld.*

gem [dʒem] **1.** Edelstein *m*; Gemme *f*; *fig.* Glanzstück *n*; **2.** mit Edelsteinen besetzen *od.* schmücken.

Gem·i·ni *ast.* ['dʒeminai] *pl.* Zwillinge *m/pl.*

gen *sl.* [dʒen] Information *f.*

gen·darme ['ʒɑ̃ndɑːm] Gendarm *m*, Landjäger *m.*

gen·der *gr.* ['dʒendə] Geschlecht *n.*

gene *biol.* [dʒiːn] Gen *n.*

gen·e·a·log·i·cal □ [dʒiːnjə'lɔdʒikəl] genealogisch; Stamm...; ~ *tree* Stammbaum *m*; **gen·e·al·o·gy** [dʒiːni'ælədʒi] Genealogie *f*; Stammbaum *m.*

gen·er·a ['dʒenərə] *pl. von genus.*

gen·er·al ['dʒenərəl] **1.** □ allgemein; gewöhnlich; Haupt..., General...; ~ *an(a)esthetic* ⚕ Vollnarkose *f*; ♀ *Assembly* Generalversammlung *f*; ~ *election* allgemeine Wahlen *f/pl.*; ~ *staff* ⚔ Generalstab *m*; ~ *store* Gemischtwarenhandlung *f*; *as a* ~ *rule, in* ~ im allgemeinen; ~ *knowledge* Allgemeinwissen *n*; **2.** ⚔ General *m*; Feldherr *m*; F *a.* ~ *servant* Mädchen *n* für alles; **gen·er·al·i·ty** [~'ræliti] Allgemeinheit *f*; *die* große Masse; **gen·er·al·i·za·tion** [~rəlai'zeiʃən] Verallgemeinerung *f*; '**gen·er·al·ize** verallgemeinern; '**gen·er·al·ly** im allgemeinen, überhaupt; gewöhnlich; **gen·er·al-'pur·pose** Mehrzweck..., Universal...; '**gen·er·al·ship** Generalsrang *m*; Feldherrnkunst *f*; Leitung *f.*

gen·er·ate ['dʒenəreit] erzeugen (*a. fig.*); '**gen·er·at·ing sta·tion** Kraftwerk *n*; **gen·er'a·tion** (Er-)Zeugung *f*; Generation *f*, Geschlecht *n*; Menschenalter *n*; **gen·er·a·tive** ['~rətiv] zeugend; Zeugungs...; fruchtbar; **gen·er·a·tor** ['~reitə] Erzeuger *m*; ⊕ Generator *m*; *bsd. Am. mot.* Lichtmaschine *f.*

ge·ner·ic [dʒi'nerik] Gattungs...

gen·er·os·i·ty [dʒenə'rɔsiti] Großmut *f*; Großzügigkeit *f*, Freigebigkeit *f*; '**gen·er·ous** □ großmütig; großzügig, freigebig; reichlich; kräftig, voll (*Wein etc.*).

gen·e·sis ['dʒenisis] Entstehung(sgeschichte) *f*; ♀ *Bibel*: Genesis *f*, Erstes Buch *n* Mose; **ge·net·ic** [dʒi'netik] (*~ally*) genetisch; Entstehungs...; ~ *engineering biol.* Genmanipulation *f*; **ge'net·ics** *pl.* Vererbungslehre *f.*

gen·ial □ ['dʒiːnjəl] freundlich; mild (*Klima*); anregend; gemütlich (*Person*); heiter; **ge·ni·al·i·ty** [~ni'æliti] Freundlichkeit *f.*

ge·nie ['dʒiːni] Dschinn *m*, Geist *m* (*in arabischen Märchen*).

ge·ni·i ['dʒiːniai] *pl. von genius.*

gen·i·tals ['dʒenitlz] *pl.* Geschlechtsteile *m/pl.*

gen·i·tive *gr.* ['dʒenitiv] *a.* ~ *case* Genitiv *m.*

gen·ius ['dʒiːnjəs], *pl.* **ge·ni·i** ['~niai] Genius *m*, (Schutz)Geist *m*; *pl.* **gen·ius·es** ['~njəsiz] Genie *n*; Geist *m* (*inneres Wesen*).

genned up *sl.* [dʒend'ʌp] gut informiert (*about* über *acc.*).

gen·o·cide ['dʒenəusaid] Völker-, Rassenmord *m.*

Gen·o·ese [dʒenəu'iːz] **1.** Genuese *m*, Genuesin *f*; **2.** genuesisch.

genre [ʒɑ̃ːŋr] Genre *n*, Stil *m*, Art *f*; *~-painting* Genremalerei *f.*

gent F [dʒent] Herr *m.*

gen·teel □ V *od. iro.* [dʒen'tiːl] vornehm; fein, elegant.

gen·tian ♀ ['dʒenʃiən] Enzian *m.*

gen·tile ['dʒentail] **1.** heidnisch, nichtjüdisch; **2.** Heide *m*, Heidin *f*, Nichtjude *m.*

gen·til·i·ty *mst iro.* [dʒen'tiliti] Vornehmheit *f.*

gen·tle □ ['dʒentl] sanft, mild; fromm, zahm (*Tier*); leise, sacht;

lind (*Lüftchen*); ruhig fließend (*Fluß*); geneigt (*Leser*); vornehm; '**~·folk(s** *pl.*) *die* Vornehmen *pl.*; '**~·man** Herr *m*; Gentleman *m*; *gentlemen!* meine Herren!; '**~-man·like,** '**~·man·ly** gebildet; vornehm; '**~·man's a·gree·ment** Gentleman's Agreement *n*, Kavaliersabkommen *n*; '**gen·tle·ness** Milde *f*, Güte *f*; Sanftheit *f*, -mut *f*; '**gen·tle·wom·an** Dame *f* von Stand.

gen·try ['dʒentri] niederer Adel *m*; gebildete Stände *m/pl.*; *contp.* Leute *pl.*

gen·u·flec·tion, gen·u·flex·ion [dʒenjuː'flekʃən] Kniebeugung *f*.

gen·u·ine □ ['dʒenjuin] echt, wahr; wirklich; aufrichtig, ehrlich.

ge·nus ['dʒiːnəs], *pl.* **gen·er·a** ['dʒenərə] Geschlecht *n*, Gattung *f*.

ge·o·cen·tric [dʒiːəu'sentrik] geozentrisch, mit der Erde als Mittelpunkt.

ge·od·e·sy [dʒiː'ɔdisi] Geodäsie *f*.

ge·og·ra·pher [dʒi'ɔgrəfə] Geograph *m*; **ge·o·graph·ic, ge·o·graph·i·cal** □ [~ə'græfik(əl)] geographisch; **ge·og·ra·phy** [~'ɔgrəfi] Geographie *f*, Erdkunde *f*.

ge·o·log·ic, ge·o·log·i·cal □ [dʒiə'lɔdʒik(əl)] geologisch; **ge·ol·o·gist** [~'ɔlədʒist] Geologe *m*; **ge'ol·o·gy** Geologie *f*.

ge·om·e·ter [dʒi'ɔmitə] Geometer *m*; **ge·o·met·ric, ge·o·met·ri·cal** □ [dʒiə'metrik(əl)] geometrisch; *geometrical progression* geometrische Reihe *f*; **ge·om·e·try** [~'ɔmitri] Geometrie *f*.

ge·o·phys·ics [dʒiːəu'fiziks] *sg.* Geophysik *f*.

ge·o·pol·i·tics [dʒiːəu'pɔlitiks] *sg.* Geopolitik *f*.

geor·gette [dʒɔː'dʒet] Georgette *m*, Seidenkrepp *m*.

ge·ra·ni·um ⚘ [dʒi'reinjəm] Geranie *f*.

ger·i·at·rics ⚕ [dʒeri'ætriks] *pl.* Geriatrie *f*, Lehre *f* von den Alterskrankheiten.

germ [dʒəːm] **1.** Keim *m*; **2.** keimen.

Ger·man[1] ['dʒəːmən] **1.** deutsch; **2.** Deutsche *m*, *f*; Deutsch *n*.

ger·man[2] [~]: *brother etc.* ~ leiblicher Bruder *m etc.*; **ger·mane** [dʒəː'mein] (*to*) verwandt (mit); entsprechend (*dat.*), passend (zu), gehörig (zu).

Ger·man·ic [dʒəː'mænik] germanisch; **Ger·man·ism** ['dʒəːmənizəm] deutsche Spracheigenheit *f*, Germanismus *m*.

germ-car·ri·er ['dʒəːmkæriə] Bazillenträger *m*.

ger·mi·cide ['dʒəːmisaid] keimtötende Substanz *f*.

ger·mi·nal ['dʒəːminl] Keim...; **ger·mi·nate** ['~neit] keimen (lassen); **ger·mi'na·tion** Keimen *n*.

germ...: '**~-proof** keimsicher, -frei; **~ war·fare** ⚔ biologische Kriegführung *f*.

ger·on·tol·o·gy ⚕ [dʒerɔn'tɔlədʒi] Gerontologie *f*, Lehre *f* von den Altersvorgängen.

ger·ry·man·der *pol.* ['dʒerimændə] (Wahl)Schiebung *f*.

ger·und *gr.* ['dʒerənd] Gerundium *n*.

ges·ta·tion [dʒes'teiʃən] Trächtigkeit *f bei Tieren*; Schwangerschaft *f*.

ges·tic·u·late [dʒes'tikjuleit] gestikulieren, Gebärden machen; **ges·tic·u'la·tion** Gebärden *f/pl.*, Gestikulieren *n*.

ges·ture ['dʒestʃə] Geste *f*, Gebärde *f*.

get [get] (*irr.*) **1.** *v/t.* erhalten, bekommen, F kriegen; sich verschaffen; besorgen; holen; bringen; erwerben; verdienen; veranlassen; bewegen; ergreifen, fassen; machen, (veran)lassen; *have got* haben; *you have got to obey* F Sie haben zu gehorchen; ~ *one's hair cut* sich die Haare schneiden lassen; ~ *me the book!* besorge mir das Buch!; ~ *by heart* auswendig lernen; ~ *with child* schwängern; ~ *away* wegbringen; ~ *down* hinunterbringen, -schlucken; aufschreiben; ~ *in* hineinbringen; *Wort, Schlag* anbringen; ~ *s.o. in* j. kommen lassen; ~ *off Kleid* ausziehen; *Ware* loswerden; ~ *on* anziehen; ~ *out* herausbringen, -locken; ~ *over* hinüberbringen; *et.* hinter sich bringen; ~ *through* durchbringen; ~ *up* aufstehen lassen; organisieren; aufmachen; einrichten, herrichten, ausstatten; ~ *up steam* Dampf aufmachen; **2.** *v/i.* gelangen, geraten, kommen; sich begeben, gehen; werden; ~ *ready* sich fertig machen; ~ *about* auf den Beinen sein; herumkommen; die Runde machen (*Gerücht etc.*); ~

abroad unter die Leute kommen; bekannt werden; ~ *ahead* vorwärtskommen; ~ *along* fort-, weiterkommen; ~ *along with* mit *j-m* auskommen; ~ *around to s.th.* zu et. kommen, Zeit finden für et.; ~ *at* (heran-) kommen an (*acc.*); zu *et.* kommen; ~ *away* weg-, davonkommen; sich fortmachen; ~ *away with s.th.* sich et. (ungestraft) leisten können; ~ *by* vorbei-, durchkommen; ~ *down to* sich auseinandersetzen mit; F herangehen an (*acc.*); gelangen zu; ~ *in* einsteigen; ~ *into* hineinkommen *od.* geraten in (*acc.*); ~ *off* davonkommen, entwischen; aus-, absteigen; ⚓ loskommen; ~ *off with s.o.* j. kennenlernen; ~ *on* gelangen auf (*acc.*); vorwärtskommen; aufsitzen, -steigen; ~ *over* hinwegkommen über (*acc.*); ~ *through* durchkommen (*a. teleph.*); ~ *to hear od. know od. learn* erfahren; ~ *up* aufstehen; hinaufsteigen; steigen (*Preise etc.*); **get-at--a·ble** [get'ætəbl] zugänglich; erreichbar; **get-a·way** ['getəwei] *Sport*: Ablauf *m*; Entkommen *n*; ~ *car* Fluchtwagen *m*; *make one's* ~ sich aus dem Staub machen; '**get·ter** Zeuger *m* (*von Pferden*); Gewinner *m*; '**get·ting** Gewinn *m*, Erwerb *m*; '**get-to·geth·er** F Treffen *n*; '**get-up** Aufmachung *f*; *Am.* F Unternehmungsgeist *m*.

gew·gaw ['gju:gɔ:] Spielerei *f*; ~*s pl.* Kinkerlitzchen *n/pl.*

gey·ser ['gaizə] *geogr.* Geysir *m*; ['gi:zə] Boiler *m*, Warmwasserbereiter *m*; (Gas)Badeofen *m*.

ghast·li·ness ['gɑ:stlinis] schreckliches Aussehen *n*; Grausigkeit *f*; '**ghast·ly** gräßlich, grausig; schrecklich, schauderhaft; (toten)bleich; gespenstisch.

gher·kin ['gə:kin] Gewürzgurke *f*.

ghet·to ['getəu] Getto *n*, Judenviertel *n*.

ghost [gəust] Geist *m*, Gespenst *n*; Schatten *m*, Spur *f*; = ~ *writer*; '**ghost·like** geisterhaft; '**ghost·ly** geisterhaft; *eccl.* geistlich; **ghost writ·er** Ghostwriter *m* (*j., der für e-n anderen schreibt*).

ghoul [gu:l] Ghul *m* (*Dämon*); *fig.* Unhold *m*.

gi·ant ['dʒaiənt] **1.** riesig; **2.** Riese *m*; '**gi·ant·ess** Riesin *f*.

gib·ber ['dʒibə] kauderwelschen, schnattern; **gib·ber·ish** ['~riʃ] Kauderwelsch *n*, Geschnatter *n*.

gib·bet ['dʒibit] **1.** Galgen *m*; ⊕ Kranbalken *m*; **2.** aufhängen; *fig.* anprangern.

gib·bon *zo.* ['gibən] Gibbon *m*.

gib·bos·i·ty [gi'bɔsiti] Höcker *m*; Buckel *m*; '**gib·bous** buck(e)lig; gewölbt; dreiviertelvoll (*Mond*).

gibe [dʒaib] **1.** verspotten, aufziehen (*a. at s.o.* j-n); **2.** Spott *m*, Stichelei *f*.

gib·lets ['dʒiblits] *pl.* Gänseklein *n*.

gid·di·ness ['gidinis] Schwindel(gefühl *n*) *m*; Unbeständigkeit *f*; *fig.* Unbesonnenheit *f*, Leichtsinn *m*; '**gid·dy** □ schwind(e)lig; schwindelerregend; *fig.* unbesonnen, leichtfertig, gedankenlos; unbeständig; albern.

gift [gift] **1.** Gabe *f*; Geschenk *n*; Talent *n*; Verleihungsrecht *n*; Schenkung *f*; ~ *box* Geschenkpakkung *f*; *s. horse*; **2.** (be)schenken; '**gift·ed** begabt.

gig [gig] Gig *n* (*Einspänner*); ⚓ Gig *n*.

gi·gan·tic [dʒai'gæntik] (~*ally*) riesenhaft, riesig, gigantisch.

gig·gle ['gigl] **1.** kichern; **2.** Gekicher *n*.

gig·o·lo ['ʒigələu] Gigolo *m*, Eintänzer *m*.

gild [gild] (*irr.*) vergolden; verschönern; ~ *the pill fig.* die bittere Pille versüßen; ~*ed youth* Jeunesse *f* dorée; '**gild·er** Vergolder *m*; '**gild·ing** Vergoldung *f*.

gill[1] [dʒil] Viertelpinte *f*.

gill[2] [gil] *ichth.* Kieme *f*; *fig.* Doppelkinn *n*; ⚘ *Pilz*-Lamelle *f*.

gill[3] [dʒil] Mädchen *n*.

gil·lie ['gili] (Jagd)Helfer *m*, Junge *m*.

gilt [gilt] **1.** *pret. u. p.p. von gild*; **2.** Vergoldung *f*; ~*s pl.* F mündelsichere Wertpapiere *n/pl.*; '**~-edged** mit Goldschnitt; ✝ mündelsicher; ✝ *sl.* hochfein, prima.

gim·bal ['dʒimbəl] *mst* ~*s pl.* Kardanaufhängung *f*.

gim·crack ['dʒimkræk] **1.** Spielerei *f*, Kinkerlitzchen *n*; **2.** wertlos.

gim·let ⊕ ['gimlit] Handbohrer *m*.

gim·mick *Am. sl.* ['gimik] Trick *m*, Dreh *m*.

gin[1] [dʒin] Gin *m* (*Wacholderschnaps*).

gin² [~] **1.** Falle *f*, Schlinge *f*; ⊕ Entkörnungsmaschine *f*; **2.** mit e-r Schlinge fangen; ⊕ entkörnen.
gin·ger [ˈdʒindʒə] **1.** Ingwer *m*; Lebhaftigkeit *f*, Kraft *f*, Schwung *m*, Energie *f*; **2.** ~ *up* ankurbeln, in Schwung bringen; **3.** hellrot, rötlich-gelb; ~ **ale** Ingwer-Limonade *f*; ˈ**~·bread** Leb-, Pfefferkuchen *m*; ~ **group** *pol.* Scharfmacher *m/pl.*; ˈ**gin·ger·ly** *adj. u. adv.* zimperlich; sacht, behutsam; ˈ**gin·ger-nut** Pfeffernuß *f*.
ging·ham [ˈgiŋəm] Gingham *m* (*Baumwollstoff*).
gip·sy [ˈdʒipsi] Zigeuner(in).
gi·raffe *zo.* [dʒiˈrɑːf] Giraffe *f*.
gird¹ [gəːd] **1.** Spott *m*, Stichelei *f*; **2.** höhnen, sticheln (*at* über *acc.*).
gird² [~] (*irr.*) (um)gürten; umgeben.
gird·er ⊕ [ˈgəːdə] Tragbalken *m*; Träger *m*.
gir·dle [ˈgəːdl] **1.** Gurt *m*, Gürtel *m*; Hüfthalter *m*, -gürtel *m*; **2.** umgürten.
girl [gəːl] Mädchen *n*; *~-friend* Freundin *f*; ~ **Fri·day** *Büro*: Mädchen *n* für alles; ♀ **Guide** Pfadfinderin *f*; **girl·hood** [ˈ~hud] Mädchenzeit *f*; Mädchenjahre *n/pl.*; **girl·ie** [ˈ~i] (kleines) Mädchen *n*; ˈ**girl·ish** □ mädchenhaft; ˈ**girl·ish·ness** Mädchenhaftigkeit *f*; **girl scout** *Am.* Pfadfinderin *f*; ˈ**girl·y** *Am.* F mit spärlich bekleideten Mädchen (*Magazin, Varieté etc.*).
Giro [ˈdʒaiərəu]: *the* ~ der Postscheckdienst (*in England*).
girt [gəːt] **1.** *pret. u. p.p. von gird²*; **2.** ⊕ Umfang *m*.
girth [gəːθ] (Sattel)Gurt *m*; Umfang *m*.
gist [dʒist] *das* Wesentliche.
git *sl.* [git] = get.
give [giv] **1.** (*irr.*) *v/t.* geben; ab-, übergeben; her-, hingeben; überlassen; *Lied etc.* zum besten geben, vortragen; schenken; gewähren; *Seufzer etc.* von sich geben; *Resultat* ergeben; ~ *attention to* achtgeben auf (*acc.*); ~ *battle* e-e Schlacht liefern; ~ *birth to* zur Welt bringen; ~ *chase to* verfolgen; ~ *credit to* Glauben schenken (*dat.*); ~ *ear to* Gehör schenken (*dat.*); ~ *one's mind to* sich (*dat.*) widmen; ~ *it to s.o.* es j-m geben (*prügeln; die Meinung sagen*); ~ *away* weggeben, verschenken; F verraten; ~ *away the bride* Brautvater sein; ~ *back* zurückgeben; ~ *forth* von sich geben; herausgeben; ~ *in* eingeben, -reichen; ~ *out* ausgeben; verteilen; bekanntmachen; *Duft etc.* ausströmen; ~ *over* übergeben; aufgeben; ~ *up Geschäft, Recht, Kranke* aufgeben; *j.* ausliefern; ~ *o.s. up* sich ergeben (*to dat.*); **2.** *v/i. mst* ~ *in* nachgeben; weichen; ~ *into*, ~ (*up*)*on* hinausgehen auf (*acc.*) (*Fenster etc.*); ~ *out* zu Ende gehen, aufhören, versiegen; versagen; ~ *over* aufhören; **3.** Nachgeben *n*; Elastizität *f*; ~ **and take** [ˈgivənˈteik] (Meinungs)Austausch *m*; Geben und Nehmen *n*; Kompromiß *m, n*; **~-a·way** [ˈ~əwei] Preisgabe *f*; ~ *show*, ~ *program Radio, Fernsehen*: öffentliches Preisraten *n*; ˈ**giv·en** *p.p. von give 1 u. 2*; ~ *to* ergeben (*dat.*); ~ ... wenn man ... als gegeben ansieht; ˈ**giv·er** Geber(in); ~ *of a bill* Wechselaussteller *m*.
giz·zard *orn.* [ˈgizəd] Muskelmagen *m*; *it sticks in my* ~ es ist mir zuwider.
gla·cé [ˈglæsei] glasiert; kandiert.
gla·ci·al □ [ˈgleisjəl] eisig; Eis...; Gletscher...; ~ *era* Eiszeit *f*; **gla·ci·a·tion** *geol.* [glæsiˈeiʃən] Vereisung *f*, Vergletscherung *f*; **gla·cier** [ˈglæsjə] Gletscher *m*; **gla·cis** [ˈglæsis] Glacis *n*.
glad □ [glæd] froh, erfreut (*of, at* über *acc.*); erfreulich, Freuden...; *give s.o. the* ~ *eye* F j-m schöne Augen machen; ~ *rags pl. sl.* Sonntagsstaat *m*; **glad·den** [ˈ~dn] erfreuen.
glade [gleid] Lichtung *f*; *Am.* sumpfige Niederung *f*.
glad·i·a·tor [ˈglædieitə] Gladiator *m*.
glad·i·o·lus ⚘ [glædiˈəuləs] Gladiole *f*.
glad·ly [ˈglædli] gerne, mit Freuden; ˈ**glad·ness** Freude *f*, Fröhlichkeit *f*; **glad·some** [ˈ~səm] freudig, fröhlich.
Glad·stone [ˈglædstən] *a.* ~ *bag* Handkoffer *m*.
glair [glɛə] **1.** Eiweiß *n*; **2.** mit Eiweiß überziehen.
glam·or·ize [ˈglæməraiz] glanzvoll(er) erscheinen lassen; (übertrieben) verherrlichen; ˈ**glam·or·ous** strahlend (schön), bezaubernd; **glam·our** [ˈ~mə] **1.** Zauber *m*, Glanz

m, Reiz *m*; ~ *girl* Reklameschönheit *f*; 2. bezaubern.

glance [glɑ:ns] **1.** Schimmer *m*, Blitz *m*; flüchtiger Blick *m*; **2.** hinweggleiten (*over* über *acc.*); blitzen; glänzen; ~ *at* flüchtig ansehen; anspielen auf (*acc.*); *mst* ~ *off* abprallen; ~ *over* flüchtig überblicken.

gland *anat.*, ⚘ [glænd] Drüse *f*; **glan·dered** *vet.* ['~dəd] rotzig; **glan·ders** *vet.* ['~dəz] *sg.* Rotz (-krankheit *f*) *m*; **glan·du·lar** ['~djulə] Drüsen...

glare [glɛə] **1.** grelles Licht *n*; wilder, starrer Blick *m*; **2.** grell leuchten; wild blicken; (*at* an)starren; **glar·ing** □ ['~riŋ] grell (leuchtend); *fig.* grell hervortretend, kraß.

glass [glɑ:s] **1.** Glas *n*; Spiegel *m*; Opernglas *n*; Fernglas *n*; Barometer *n*; (*a pair of*) ~*es pl.* (eine) Brille *f*; **2.** gläsern; Glas...; **3.** verglasen; '**~-blow·er** Glasbläser *m*; '**~-case** Vitrine *f*; Schaukasten *m*; '**~-cut·ter** Glasschleifer *m*; Glaserdiamant *m*; **glass-ful** ['~ful] Glas(voll) *n*; '**glass-house** Treibhaus *n*; ⚔ *sl.* Bau *m*; '**glass·i·ness** *das* Glasige, Spiegelglätte *f*; '**glass·ware** Glas (-waren *f/pl.*) *n*; '**glass·y** gläsern; glasig.

glau·co·ma ⚕ [glɔ:'kəumə] Glaukom *n*, grüner Star *m*; '**glau·cous** graugrün.

glaze [gleiz] **1.** Glasur *f*; **2.** *v/t.* verglasen; glasieren; polieren; *v/i.* trübe *od.* glasig werden (*Auge*); ~*d paper* Glanzpapier *n*; ~*d(-in) veranda* Glasveranda *f*; **gla·zier** ['~jə] Glaser *m*; '**glaz·ing** Verglasung *f*; Glasur *f*; '**glaz·y** glasiert; blank; glasig.

gleam [gli:m] **1.** Schimmer *m*, Schein *m*; **2.** schimmern, scheinen.

glean [gli:n] *v/t.* nachlesen, sammeln; *v/i.* Ähren lesen; '**glean·er** Ährenleser(in); *fig.* Sammler(in); '**glean·ings** *pl.* Nachlese *f*.

glebe [gli:b] Pfarrland *n*; *poet.* (Erd)Scholle *f*.

glee [gli:] Fröhlichkeit *f*; mehrstimmiges Lied *n*, Rundgesang *m*; ~ *club* Gesangverein *m*; **glee·ful** □ ['~ful] fröhlich.

glen [glen] Bergschlucht *f*.

glib □ [glib] *fig.* glatt, *bsd.* zungenfertig; '**glib·ness** Zungenfertigkeit *f*.

glide [glaid] **1.** Gleiten *n*; ✈ Gleitflug *m*; *gr.* Gleitlaut *m*; **2.** (dahin-) gleiten (lassen); e-n Gleitflug machen; '**glid·er** Segelflugzeug *n*; ~ *pilot* Segelflieger *m*; '**glid·ing** Gleit-, Segelflug *m*.

glim·mer ['glimə] **1.** Schimmer *m*; *min.* Glimmer *m*; **2.** schimmern.

glimpse [glimps] **1.** flüchtiger Blick *m* (*of* auf *acc.*); Schimmer *m*; flüchtiger Eindruck *m*; **2.** *v/t.* flüchtig erblicken; *v/i.* ~ *at* e-n flüchtigen Blick werfen auf (*acc.*).

glint [glint] **1.** blitzen, glitzern, schimmern; **2.** Lichtschein *m*.

glis·sade *mount.* [gli'sɑ:d] **1.** abfahren; rutschen; **2.** Abfahrt *f*.

glis·ten ['glisn], **glis·ter** † ['glistə], **glit·ter** ['glitə] glitzern, glänzen, funkeln; gleißen; '**glit·ter·ing** glänzend, verlockend; ~ *personality* blendende Erscheinung *f*.

gloam·ing ['gləumiŋ] (Abend-) Dämmerung *f*.

gloat [gləut]: ~ (*up*)*on*, ~ *over* sich weiden an (*dat.*), sich hämisch freuen über (*acc.*).

glob·al ['gləubəl] global, (welt)umfassend; Welt..., Gesamt...; **globe** Kugel *f*; Erdkugel *f*, -ball *m*; Globus *m*; '**globe-fish** *ichth.* Kugelfisch *m*; '**globe-trot·ter** Weltenbummler(in); **glo·bose** ['~bəus], **glob·u·lar** □ ['glɔbjulə] kugelförmig; **glo·bos·i·ty** [gləu'bɔsiti] Kugelform *f*; **glob·ule** ['glɔbju:l] Kügelchen *n*.

gloom [glu:m] **1.** Düsterkeit *f*, Dunkelheit *f*; Schwermut *f*; Trübsinn *m*; **2.** *v/i.* verdrießlich *od.* schwermütig *od.* trüb sein *od.* blicken; *v/t.* verdunkeln, verdüstern; '**gloom·i·ness** Düsternis *f*; Schwermut *f*; '**gloom·y** □ dunkel, düster; schwermütig; verdrießlich.

Glo·ri·a *eccl.* ['glɔ:riə] Gloria *n*.

glo·ri·fi·ca·tion [glɔ:rifi'keiʃən] Verherrlichung *f*; **glo·ri·fy** ['~fai] verherrlichen, verklären; F verschönern, verbessern; '**glo·ri·ous** □ herrlich, köstlich, prächtig; wunderbar; glorreich.

glo·ry ['glɔ:ri] **1.** Ruhm *m*; Glorie *f*, Herrlichkeit *f*, Pracht *f*; Glorienschein *m*; Glanzpunkt *m*; **2.** (*in*) frohlocken (über *acc.*); stolz sein (auf *acc.*).

gloss[1] [glɔs] **1.** Glosse *f*, (erläuternde) Bemerkung *f*; **2.** glossieren; Glossen machen (zu).
gloss[2] [~] **1.** Glanz *m*; **2.** Glanz geben (*dat.*); ~ *over* beschönigen.
glos·sa·ry [ˈglɔsəri] Glossar *n*, Wörterbuch *n*.
gloss·i·ness [ˈglɔsinis] Glanz *m*; ˈ**gloss·y** □ glänzend, blank; ~ *periodical* Illustrierte *f*, *bsd.* Modejournal *n*.
glot·tis *anat.* [ˈglɔtis] Stimmritze *f*.
glove [glʌv] Handschuh *m*; ~ *compartment mot.* Handschuhfach *n*; *s. hand 1*; ˈ**glov·er** Handschuhmacher *m*.
glow [gləu] **1.** Glühen *n*; Glut *f*; **2.** glühen.
glow·er [ˈglauə] finster blicken.
glow-worm [ˈgləuwə:m] Glühwurm *m*.
gloze [gləuz]: ~ *over* beschönigen.
glu·cose [ˈglu:kəus] Traubenzucker *m*.
glue [glu:] **1.** Leim *m*; **2.** leimen; *fig.* (an)drücken, heften (*to* an, auf *acc.*); ˈ**glue·y** klebrig, leimig.
glum □ [glʌm] mürrisch, verdrießlich.
glut [glʌt] **1.** Überfüllung *f*; Übersättigung *f*; Überfülle *f*; **2.** überfüllen; (über)sättigen.
glu·ten [ˈglu:tən] Gluten *n*, Kleber *m*; **glu·ti·nous** □ [ˈ~tinəs] leimig, klebrig.
glut·ton [ˈglʌtn] Schlemmer *m*; Unersättliche *m* (*of, for, at* in *dat.*); *zo.* Vielfraß *m*; ˈ**glut·ton·ous** □ gefräßig; ˈ**glut·ton·y** Gefräßigkeit *f*.
glyc·er·in [ˈglisərin], **glyc·er·ine** [~ˈri:n] Glyzerin *n*.
G-man *Am.* F [ˈdʒi:mæn] FBI-Agent *m*.
gnarl [nɑ:l] Knorren *m*, Ast *m*; **gnarled**, *a.* ˈ**gnarl·y** knorrig.
gnash [næʃ] knirschen (mit).
gnat [næt] (Stech)Mücke *f*.
gnaw [nɔ:] (zer)nagen; (zer)fressen; ˈ**gnaw·er** Nagetier *n*.
gnome [nəum] Erdgeist *m*, Gnom *m*; [ˈnəumi:] Sinnspruch *m*, Gnome *f*; **gnom·ish** [ˈnəumiʃ] gnomenhaft.
go [gəu] **1.** (*irr.*) *allg.* gehen (*s. a. going, gone*); fahren, reisen; werden; reichen, führen (*to* nach); sich wenden, appellieren (*to* an *acc.*); funktionieren, arbeiten, gehen; kommen, gestellt werden; passen, gehen; *in e-m bestimmten Zustand* sein; (über-) gehen (*to* an *acc.*), zuteil werden (*to dat.*); nötig sein (*to* für), dienen; *ungestraft etc.* ausgehen; weg-, abgehen, verkauft werden; ausgegeben werden (*Geld*); aufgegeben werden; nachlassen (*Augenlicht*); umgehen (*Gerücht etc.*); angenommen werden (*Geld*); kaputtgehen, brechen; *mst im p.p.* sterben; verlaufen; lauten; *ein bestimmtes Geräusch* machen; *in der Verlaufsform u. mit nachfolgendem inf. zur Bildung des Futurs*: werden; ~ *bad* verderben; *s. mad*; *s. sick*; *the dog must* ~ der Hund muß weg; *the story* ~*es* man erzählt sich; *here* ~*es! sl.* los!; ~ *it sl.* sich daranmachen, drauflosgehen; ~ *it! sl.* feste!; *as men, etc.* ~ wie Männer *etc.* nun einmal sind; *let* ~ fahren lassen, loslassen; ~ *shares* teilen; ~ *to see*, ~ *and see* besuchen; *just* ~ *and try!* versuch's doch mal!; ~ *about* umher-, umgehen; herangehen an *e-e Arbeit*; ~ *abroad* auf Reisen gehen; ruchbar werden; ~ *ahead* vorwärtsgehen; ~ *at* losgehen auf (*acc.*); ~ *back* zurückgehen; ~ *back from*, F *on Versprechen etc.* rückgängig machen; ~ *behind* untersuchen, nachprüfen; ~ *between* vermitteln (zwischen); ~ *by* vergehen; vorübergehen; sich richten nach; ~ *by the name of* ... unter dem Namen ... gehen; ~ *down* (hin)untergehen; erliegen (*before dat.*); Glauben finden (*with* bei); ~ *for* gehen nach, holen; gelten für; j. angreifen; ~ *for a walk, etc.* e-n Spaziergang *etc.* machen; ~ *in* hineingehen; ~ *in for* sich widmen (*dat.*), sich befassen mit, sich verlegen auf (*acc.*); ~ *in for an examination* e-e Prüfung machen; ~ *into Rechnen*: gehen in (*acc.*); *e-r Frage etc.* auf den Grund gehen; ~ *off* weggehen; abgehen (*Zug, Waren*); losgehen (*Schuß etc.*); vergehen; sich verschlechtern; einschlafen; sterben; ~ *on* vor sich gehen; vorwärts- *od.* weitergehen; fortfahren; ~ *on!* weiter!; ~ *out* ausgehen; abgehen, abtreten; ~ *over* übergehen *zu e-r Partei*; durchgehen, -sehen, prüfen; ~ *through* durchgehen; ausführen; durchmachen; ~ *through with Aufgabe etc.* durchführen; ~ *to* an *j.* gehen *od.*

fallen; sich belaufen auf (*acc.*); ~ *up* hinaufgehen; steigen; entstehen (*Gebäude*); *in Flammen* aufgehen, in die Luft fliegen; zur Universität gehen; ~ *with* passen zu; ~ *without* sich behelfen ohne; entbehren; **2.** F Gang *m*; Mode *f*; Schwung *m*, Schmiß *m*, Schneid *m*; Begeisterung *f*; (unangenehme) Geschichte *f*; Schluck *m*; Happen *m*; ⚕ Anfall *m*; Versuch *m*; *little* ~ *univ. sl.* Vorexamen *n*; *great* ~ Hauptexamen *n*; *on the* ~ auf den Beinen, in Bewegung; im Gange; *it is no* ~ es geht nicht; *is it a* ~? abgemacht?; *in one* ~ auf Anhieb; *have a* ~ *at s.th.* et. in Angriff nehmen, et. versuchen.

goad [gəud] **1.** Stachelstock *m*; *fig.* Stachel *m*; Ansporn *m*; **2.** *fig.* anstacheln.

go-a·head F [ˈgəuəhed] **1.** zielstrebig, rührig; unternehmungslustig; fortschrittlich; **2.** *bsd. Am.* F Unternehmungsgeist *m*, -lust *f*; Erlaubnis *f* zum Weitermachen.

goal [gəul] Mal *n*; Ziel *n* (*a. fig.*); *Fußball*: Tor *n*; **goal·ie** F [ˈgəuli] = ˈ**goal·keep·er** *Fußball*: Torwart *m*; **goal kick** *Fußball*: Abstoß *m*; ˈ**goal-mouth** *Sport*: Torraum *m*; *in the* ~ (unmittelbar) vor dem Tor.

goat [gəut] *zo.* Ziege *f*, Geiß *f*; *get s.o.'s* ~ *sl.* j. hochbringen (*ärgern*); *separate the sheep from the* ~*s fig.* die Schafe von den Böcken scheiden; *play the giddy* ~ sich närrisch benehmen; **goatˈee** Spitzbart *m*; ˈ**goat·ish** ziegenartig; bockig; geil; ˈ**goat·skin** Ziegenleder *n*.

gob [gɔb] V Schleimklumpen *m*; Maul *n*; *Am.* F Blaujacke *f* (*Matrose*); **gob·bet** [ˈgɔbit] Bissen *m*.

gob·ble [ˈgɔbl] *gierig* verschlingen; kollern *wie ein Truthahn*; **gob·ble-dy·gook** *Am. sl.* [ˈgɔbldiguk] Amts-, Berufsjargon *m*, Geschwafel *n*; ˈ**gob·bler** Vielfraß *m*; Truthahn *m*.

go-be·tween [ˈgəubitwiːn] Vermittler(in).

gob·let [ˈgɔblit] Kelchglas *n*; Pokal *m*.

gob·lin [ˈgɔblin] Kobold *m*, Gnom [*m.*]

go-by [ˈgəubai]: *give s.o. the* ~ j. unbeachtet lassen, j. ignorieren.

go-cart [ˈgəukaːt] Laufgestell *n für Kinder*; Sportwagen *m für Kinder*.

god, *eccl.* ♀ [gɔd] Gott *m*; *fig.* Abgott *m*; *the gods pl. thea.* der Olymp; ˈ**god·child** Patenkind *n*; ˈ**god·dess** Göttin *f*; ˈ**god·fa·ther** Pate *m*; ˈ**god·fear·ing** gottesfürchtig; ˈ**god·for·sak·en** gottverlassen; ˈ**god·head** Gottheit *f*; ˈ**god·less** gottlos; ˈ**god·like** gottähnlich; göttlich, erhaben; ˈ**god·li·ness** Frömmigkeit *f*; ˈ**god·ly** gottesfürchtig; fromm; ˈ**god·moth·er** Patin *f*; ˈ**god·par·ent** Pate *m*, Patin *f*; ˈ**god·send** Geschenk *n* des Himmels, Gottesgabe *f*; ˈ**god-ˈspeed:** *bid od. wish s.o.* ~ j-m glückliche Reise wünschen; j-m guten Erfolg wünschen.

go·er [ˈgəuə] Geher(in), Läufer(in).

gof·fer [ˈgəufə] kräuseln, plissieren.

go-get·ter *Am.* F [ˈgəuˈgetə] Draufgänger *m*, Allerweltskerl *m*.

gog·gle [ˈgɔgl] **1.** glotzen; **2.** ~*s pl.* Schutzbrille *f*; ˈ~**-box** *sl.* Glotze *f* (*Fernsehgerät*); ˈ~**-eyed** glotzäugig.

go·ing [ˈgəuiŋ] **1.** gehen; im Gange (befindlich); vorhanden; *be* ~ *to inf.* im Begriff sein zu *inf.*, gleich *od.* bald *tun* wollen *od.* werden; *keep* ~ in Gang halten; *set* ~ in Gang bringen; *a* ~ *concern* ein gutgehendes Geschäft *n*; ~, ~, *gone!* zum ersten, zum zweiten, zum dritten!; **2.** Gehen *n*, Gang *m*; Vorwärtskommen *n*; Straßenzustand *m*; Geschwindigkeit *f*, Leistung *f*; ˈ**go·ings-ˈon** F *pl.* Vorgänge *m/pl.*; Treiben *n*.

goi·tre ⚕ [ˈgɔitə] Kropf *m*; **goi·trous** [ˈgɔitrəs] Kropf...; mit Kropf (behaftet).

go-kart *mot.* [ˈgəukaːt] Go-Kart *m* (*Kleinstrennwagen*).

gold [gəuld] **1.** Gold *n*; **2.** golden; ˈ~**-bear·ing** goldhaltig; ˈ~**·brick** **1.** *fig.* Talmi *n*, Schwindel *m*; **2.** sich drücken; ˈ~**·dig·ger** *Am.* Goldgräber *m*; *sl.* Männerausbeuterin *f*; ˈ**gold·en** *mst fig.* golden, goldgelb; ˈ**gold·en·rod** ⚘ Goldrute *f*.

gold...: ˈ~**·finch** *orn.* Stieglitz *m*; ˈ~**·fish** *ichth.* Goldfisch *m*; ˈ~**·mine** Goldbergwerk *n*; *fig.* Goldgrube *f*; ~ **plate** goldenes Tafelgeschirr *n*; ˈ~**-ˈplat·ed** vergoldet; ˈ~**-rush** Goldrausch *m*; ˈ~**·smith** Goldschmied *m*.

golf [gɔlf] **1.** Golf(spiel) *n*; **2.** Golf spielen; ˈ~**·ball** Golfball *m*; Schreibkopf *m e-r Schreibmaschine*; ~ *typewriter* Kugelkopfschreibmaschine *f*; ˈ~**-club** Golfschläger *m*; Golfklub *m*; ˈ~**-course** = *golf-links*; ˈ**golf·er**

Golfspieler(in); **'golf-links** *pl.* Golfplatz *m.*
gol·li·wog(g) ['gɔliwɔg] Negerpuppe *f*; *fig.* Popanz *m.*
go·losh [gə'lɔʃ] Galosche *f*, Überschuh *m.*
gon·do·la ⚓, ✈ ['gɔndələ] Gondel *f*; **gon·do·lier** [~'liə] Gondoliere *m.*
gone [gɔn] **1.** *p.p. von go*; **2.** *adj.* fort; dahin; F futsch; vergangen; tot; F hoffnungslos; *be ~!, get you ~!* mach, daß du wegkommst!; *~ on s.o. sl.* in j. verknallt; **'gon·er** *sl.* erledigter Mensch *m.*
gong [gɔŋ] Gong *m.*
good [gud] **1.** *allg.* gut; lieb, brav (*Kind*); gültig (*Gesetz*); ⚕ zahlungsfähig; gründlich, gehörig; *the ~ Samaritan* der Barmherzige Samariter; *~ at* geschickt in (*dat.*); *in ~ earnest* in vollem Ernst; **2.** Gute *n*; Wohl *n*, Beste *n*; *~s pl.* Waren *f/pl.*; Güter *n/pl.*; *that's no ~* das nützt nichts; *it is no ~ talking* es ist unnütz zu reden; *for ~* endgültig, für immer; *piece of ~s* F Frauenzimmer *n*, Stück *n*; *~s pl. in process* Halbfabrikate *n/pl.*; **~-bye,** *Am. a.* **~-by 1.** [gud'bai] Lebewohl *n*; **2.** ['gud'bai] Auf Wiedersehen!; Lebewohl!; **'~-for-'noth·ing 1.** nichtsnutzig; **2.** Taugenichts *m*; ♀ **Friday** Karfreitag *m*; **'~'hu·mo(u)red** gutmütig; guter Laune, gutgelaunt; **'good·li·ness** Anmut *f*; **'good-'look·ing** gutaussehend, hübsch; **'good·ly** anmutig, hübsch; *fig.* ansehnlich; tüchtig; **'good·man** † (Haus)Vater *m*; Ehemann *m*; **'good-'na·tured** gutmütig; **'good·ness** Güte *f* (*gute Beschaffenheit*; *Freundlichkeit*); *das* Beste; *in Ausrufen*: mein Gott!, du meine Güte!; *s. gracious*; **goods train** Güterzug *m*; **'good·wife** Hausfrau *f*; **'good'will** Wohlwollen *n*; freundliche Einstellung *f* (*towards* zu); ⚕ Kundschaft *f*; ⚕ Firmenwert *m.*
good·y[1] ['gudi] Bonbon *m.*
good·y[2] [~], *a.* **'good·y-'good·y 1.** prüde; scheinheilig; **2.** Scheinheilige *m, f.*
goo·ey F ['gu:i] klebrig; pappig.
goof F [gu:f] **1.** Trottel *m*; Schnitzer *m*; **2.** *~ (up)* vermasseln, verpatzen; **'goof·y** *sl.* doof, blöde.
goon *Am. sl.* [gu:n] gedungener Raufbold *m bsd. für Streik*; Dummkopf *m.*
goose [gu:s], *pl.* **geese** [gi:s] Gans *f* (*a. fig.*); *cook s.o.'s ~* j-m e-n Strich durch die Rechnung machen; *pl.* **'goos·es** Bügeleisen *n.*
goose·ber·ry ['guzbəri] Stachelbeere *f*; *play ~* F Anstandswauwau spielen.
goose...: **'~-flesh** Gänsehaut *f*; **'~-herd** Gänsehirt(in); **~ pim·ples** *pl. Am.* = *goose-flesh*; **'~-step** Paradeschritt *m*; **'goos·ey, 'goos·ie** F Gänschen *n.*
go·pher *bsd. Am.* ['gəufə] Erdeichhörnchen *n*; *eine* Ratte *f.*
Gor·di·an ['gɔ:djən] gordisch; *~ knot* gordischer Knoten *m.*
gore[1] [gɔ:] (geronnenes) Blut *n.*
gore[2] [~] **1.** Keil *m*, Zwickel *m im Kleid etc.*; **2.** durchbohren, aufspießen.
gorge [gɔ:dʒ] **1.** Kehle *f*, Schlund *m*; enge (Fels)Schlucht *f*; *my ~ rises* mir wird übel (*at* bei, von); **2.** (ver-)schlingen; (sich) vollstopfen.
gor·geous □ ['gɔ:dʒəs] prächtig, glänzend; **'gor·geous·ness** Pracht *f.*
go·rilla *zo.* [gə'rilə] Gorilla *m.*
gor·mand·ize ['gɔ:məndaiz] schlemmen, fressen, prassen.
gorm·less F ['gɔ:mlis] stupid, begriffsstutzig.
gorse ♀ [gɔ:s] Stechginster *m.*
gor·y □ ['gɔ:ri] blutig.
gosh P [gɔʃ] (bei) Gott!, Mensch!
gos·hawk *orn.* ['gɔshɔ:k] Hühnerhabicht *m.*
gos·ling ['gɔzliŋ] Gänschen *n.*
go-slow [gəu'sləu] Bummelstreik *m.*
gos·pel ['gɔspəl] Evangelium *n* (*a. fig.*); **'gos·pel·(l)er** Wanderprediger *m.*
gos·sa·mer ['gɔsəmə] Altweibersommer *m*; feine Gaze *f.*
gos·sip ['gɔsip] **1.** Geschwätz *n*, Klatsch *m*; Plauderei *f*; Klatschbase *f*; *~ column* Klatschspalte *f*; **2.** schwatzen, klatschen.
got [gɔt] *pret. u. p.p. von get.*
Goth [gɔθ] *hist.* Gote *m*; *fig.* Barbar *m*, Wandale *m*; **'Goth·ic** gotisch; *fig.* wandalisch, barbarisch.
got·ten *Am.* ['gɔtn] *p.p. von get.*
gouge [gaudʒ] **1.** ⊕ Hohlmeißel *m*; **2.** *mst ~ out* ausmeißeln; *Am.* F betrügen.
gou·lash ['gu:læʃ] Gulasch *m, n.*
gourd ♀ ['guəd] Kürbis *m.*

gour·mand ['guəmənd] **1.** gefräßig; **2.** Vielfraß *m*.
gour·met ['guəmei] Feinschmecker *m*; ~ *restaurant* Schlemmerlokal *n*.
gout ⚕ [gaut] Gicht *f*; '**gout·y** □ gichtisch; gichtkrank; Gicht...
gov·ern ['gʌvən] *v/t*. regieren (*a. gr.*), verwalten; beherrschen (*a. fig.*); lenken, leiten; *v/i*. herrschen; ~*ing body konkr*. Leitung *f*; '**gov·ern·ess** Erzieherin *f*, Gouvernante *f*; '**gov·ern·ment** Regierung *f*; Leitung *f*; Herrschaft *f* (*of* über *acc.*); Regierung(sform) *f*; Verwaltung *f*; Ministerium *n*; Statthalterschaft *f*; *attr*. Staats...; ~ *spokesman* Regierungssprecher *m*; **gov·ern·men·tal** [~'mentl] Regierungs...; '**gov·er·nor** Gouverneur *m*; Direktor *m*, Präsident *m*, Leiter *m*; Kurator *m*; F Alte *m* (*Vater*; *Chef*); *Anrede*: mein Herr!; ⊕ Regulator *m*; **gov·er·nor gen·er·al** Generalgouverneur *m*; '**gov·er·nor·ship** Gouverneursamt *n*.
gown [gaun] **1.** (Frauen)Kleid *n*; Robe *f*, Talar *m*; **2.** kleiden; '**gowns·man** Student *m*; ⚔ Zivilist *m*.
grab F [græb] **1.** grapsen (*at* nach); an sich reißen, packen, schnappen; **2.** plötzlicher Griff *m*, Graps *m*; ⊕ Greifer *m*; ~-*bag Am*. Glückstopf *m*; '**grab·ber** Habsüchtige *m*, Raffke *m*; Straßenräuber *m*.
grace [greis] **1.** Gnade *f*; Gunst *f*; (Gnaden)Frist *f*, Aufschub *m*; Grazie *f*, Anmut *f*; Anstand *m*; Zier(de) *f*; ~*s pl*. Reize *m/pl.*; ♪ Verzierungen *f/pl.*; ♀*s pl. die* Grazien *f/pl.*; *act of* ~ Gnadenakt *m*; *with* (*a*) *good* (*bad*) ~ bereit-(wider)willig; *Your* ♀ Euer Gnaden; *good* ~*s pl*. Gunst *f*; *period of* ~ Karenzzeit *f*; *s. say 1*; **2.** zieren, schmücken; begünstigen, auszeichnen; **grace·ful** □ ['~ful] anmutig, graziös; höflich; taktvoll; '**grace·ful·ness** Grazie *f*, Anmut *f*; '**grace·less** □ gottlos; schamlos; reizlos.
gra·cious □ ['greiʃəs] gnädig, gütig, huldvoll; *good* ~!, *goodness* ~!, ~ *me!* ach du meine Güte!; '**gra·cious·ness** Gnade *f*.
grack·le *orn*. ['grækl] *ein* Star *m*.
gra·da·tion [grə'deiʃən] Stufengang *m*, Abstufung *f*; *gr*. Ablaut *m*.
grade [greid] **1.** Grad *m*, Rang *m*; Stufe *f*; Qualität *f*; *bsd. Am.* = *gradient*; *Am. Schule*: Klasse *f*, Note *f*; *make the* ~ *Am*. F Erfolg haben; ~ *crossing Am*. schienengleicher Bahnübergang *m*; ~(*d*) *school Am*. Grundschule *f*; **2.** abstufen; einteilen; 🚂 *etc*. planieren; *Vieh* (auf)kreuzen.
gra·di·ent ['greidjənt] 🚂 *etc*. Steigung *f*, Neigung *f*.
grad·u·al □ ['grædʒuəl] stufenweise (fortschreitend), allmählich; '**grad·u·al·ly** nach u. nach; allmählich; **grad·u·ate 1.** ['~djueit] graduieren: mit Gradeinteilung versehen; (sich) abstufen; die Abschlußprüfung machen; promovieren; **2.** ['~dʒuit] Absolvent(in) *e-r Universität etc*., Graduierte *m*, *f*; **grad·u·a·tion** [~dju'eiʃən] Gradeinteilung *f*; Abschlußprüfung *f*; Promotion *f*.
graft[1] [grɑːft] **1.** ✓ Pfropfreis *n*; **2.** ✓ pfropfen (*in*, *upon* auf *acc.*); *fig.*, ⚕ verpflanzen.
graft[2] *Am*. [~] **1.** Bestechung *f*, Korruption *f*, Schiebung(en *pl.*) *f*, Schmiergeld(er *pl.*) *n*; **2.** F Korruptionsgelder einschieben; '**graft·er** F *bsd. pol*. Schieber *m*.
gra·ham ['greiəm]: ~ *bread* Graham-, Weizenschrotbrot *n*.
Grail [greil] *Sage*: Gral *m*.
grain [grein] Korn *n*; Samenkorn *n*; Getreide *n*; Körnchen *n* (*a. fig.*); Gefüge *n*, Struktur *f*; Maserung *f* (*Holz*); Strich *m des Tuches*; *fig*. Natur *f*; Gran *n* (*kleines Gewicht*); *in* ~ echt, gründlich; *dyed in the* ~ in der Wolle gefärbt; *against the* ~ gegen den Strich (*a. fig.*); **grained** in der Wolle gefärbt; gemasert.
gram [græm] = *gramme*.
gra·mer·cy † [grə'məːsi] tausend Dank!
gram·i·na·ceous [greimi'neiʃəs], **gra·min·e·ous** [grei'miniəs] grasartig; Gras...
gram·ma·logue ['græməlɔg] *Kurzschrift*: Sigel *n*, Kürzel *n*.
gram·mar ['græmə] Grammatik *f*; **gram·mar·i·an** [grə'mɛəriən] Grammatiker *m*; '**gram·mar-school** höhere Schule *f*, Gymnasium *n*; *Am. a*. Mittelschule *f*;
gram·mat·i·cal □ [grə'mætikəl] grammati(kali)sch.

gramme [græm] Gramm *n.*
gram·o·phone [ˈgræməfəun] Grammophon *n*; ~ *record* Schallplatte *f.*
gran·a·ry [ˈgrænəri] Kornspeicher *m.*
grand □ [grænd] **1.** *fig.* großartig; erhaben; groß; Groß..., Haupt...; ♀ *Duchess* Großherzogin *f*; ♀ *Duke* Großherzog *m*; ♀ *Old Party Am.* Republikanische Partei *f*; ~ *stand* (Haupt)Tribüne *f*; **2.** *a.* ~ *piano* ♪ Flügel *m*; *Am. sl.* tausend Dollar *m/pl.*; *miniature* ~ Stutzflügel *m*; **gran·dad** F [ˈgrændæd] Opa *m*; **gran·dam(e)** [ˈ~dæm] Mütterchen *n*; ˈ**grand·child** Enkel(in); ˈ**grand-daugh·ter** Enkelin *f*; **gran·dee** [grænˈdiː] *spanischer* Grande *m*; vornehmer Herr *m*; **gran·deur** [ˈgrændʒə] Größe *f*, Hoheit *f*; Erhabenheit *f*, Würde *f*; ˈ**grand-fa·ther** Großvater *m*; ~'*s clock* hohe Standuhr *f.*
gran·dil·o·quence [grænˈdiləkwəns] Redeschwulst *m*; **granˈdil·o·quent** □ hochtrabend, schwülstig.
gran·di·ose □ [ˈgrændiəus] grandios, großartig; pompös.
grand·moth·er [ˈgrændmʌθə], F **grand·ma** [ˈgrænmɑː] Großmutter *f*; **Grand Na·tion·al** *größtes englisches Pferderennen*; ˈ**grand·ness** = *grandeur.*
grand...: ˈ~**·pa** [ˈgrænpɑː] = *grandfather*; ˈ~**-par·ents** *pl.* Großeltern *pl.*; ~**·sire** [ˈ~saiə] † *od. v. Tieren*: Großvater *m*; Ahnherr *m*; ˈ~**·son** Enkel *m*; ˈ~**·stand** Haupttribüne *f.*
grange [greindʒ] Farm *f*; kleiner Gutshof *m*; *Am. Name für* Farmerorganisation *f*; ˈ**grang·er** Farmer *m.*
gran·ite [ˈgrænit] Granit *m*; **gra-nit·ic** [~ˈnitik] granitartig; Granit...
gran·ny F [ˈgræni] Oma *f* (*Großmutter*).
grant [grɑːnt] **1.** Gewährung *f*; Unterstützung *f*, Zuschuß *m*; Stipendium *n*; ⚖ Übertragung *f*; **2.** gewähren; bewilligen; verleihen; zugestehen; ⚖ übertragen; *take for* ~*ed* für selbstverständlich halten; ~*ing this* (*to*) *be so* angenommen, dies wäre so; *God* ~ *...!* Gott gebe ...!; **granˈtee** ⚖ Begünstigte *m*; **grant-in-aid** [ˈgrɑːntinˈeid] Zuschuß *m*, Beihilfe *f*; **grant·or** ⚖ [~ˈtɔː] Verleiher *m.*
gran·u·lar [ˈgrænjulə] körnig; **gran-u·late** [ˈ~leit] (sich) körnen; ˈ**gran-u·lat·ed** körnig, gekörnt; ~ *sugar* Kristallzucker *m*; **gran·uˈla·tion** Körnung *f*; **gran·ule** [ˈ~juːl] Körnchen *n*; **gran·u·lous** [ˈ~juləs] körnig.
grape [greip] Weinbeere *f*, -traube *f*; ˈ~**·fruit** ⚘ Pampelmuse *f*; ˈ~**-shot** ⚔ Kartätsche *f*; ˈ~**-sug·ar** Traubenzucker *m*; ˈ~**-vine** Rebe *f*; *a.* ~ *telegraph* unterirdisches Nachrichtensystem *n*, Flüsterparolen *f/pl.*; *hear s.th. through the* ~ et. gerüchtweise erfahren.
graph [græf] graphische Darstellung *f*; ˈ**graph·ic**, ˈ**graph·i·cal** □ graphisch; Schreib...; anschaulich; *graphic arts pl.* Graphik *f*; **graph-ite** *min.* [ˈ~fait] Graphit *m*; **graph-ol·o·gy** [~ˈfɔlədʒi] Graphologie *f* (*Handschriftendeutung*); **graph paper** Millimeterpapier *n.*
grap·nel ⚓ [ˈgræpnəl] Enterhaken *m*; Dregganker *m.*
grap·ple [ˈgræpl] **1.** ⚓ Enterhaken *m*; ⊕ Greifer *m*; **2.** entern; packen, fassen; ringen; ~ *with* kämpfen mit; in Angriff nehmen.
grasp [grɑːsp] **1.** Griff *m*; Bereich *m*; Beherrschung *f*; Fassungskraft *f*; Begriff *m*; **2.** *v/t.* (er)greifen, packen; begreifen; *v/i.* greifen, streben (*at* nach); ˈ**grasp·ing** □ habsüchtig.
grass [grɑːs] **1.** Gras *n*; Rasen *m*; *sl.* Marihuana *n*; *at* ~ auf der Weide; *fig.* im Urlaub; *send to* ~ = **2.** auf die Weide treiben; ˈ~**·hop·per** Heuschrecke *f*; ˈ~**-ˈplot** Rasenplatz *m*; ~ **roots** *pl. Am. die* landwirtschaftlichen Bezirke *m/pl.*; *die* Landbevölkerung; Grundlage *f*, Quelle *f*; *pol.* Basis *f*; ~ **snake** Ringelnatter *f*; ˈ~**-ˈwid·ow(·er)** Strohwitwe(r *m*) *f*; ˈ**grass·y** grasig, grasreich; grasbewachsen.
grate[1] [greit] (Kamin)Gitter *n*; (Feuer)Rost *m*; *fig.* Herd *m.*
grate[2] [~] *v/t.* raspeln, (zer)reiben; mit *den Zähnen* knirschen; *v/i.* knirschen, knarren; ~ (*up*)*on fig. das Ohr etc.* verletzen.
grate·ful □ [ˈgreitful] dankbar; *von Dingen*: angenehm, willkommen.
grat·er [ˈgreitə] Reibeisen *n.*
grat·i·fi·ca·tion [grætifiˈkeiʃən] Be-

friedigung *f*; Freude *f*; Genuß *m*; **grat·i·fy** ['⁓fai] erfreuen; befriedigen; '**grat·i·fy·ing** erfreulich.
grat·ing ['greitiŋ] 1. □ schrill, unangenehm; 2. Gitter(werk) *n*.
gra·tis ['greitis] umsonst.
grat·i·tude ['grætitju:d] Dankbarkeit *f*.
gra·tu·i·tous □ [grə'tju:itəs] unentgeltlich; freiwillig; mutwillig; grundlos; **gra'tu·i·ty** Abfindung *f*; Gratifikation *f*; Trinkgeld *n*.
gra·va·men ⚖ [grə'veimen] (Haupt)Beschwerdepunkt *m*; *das* Belastende.
grave[1] □ [greiv] ernst; (ge)wichtig; gemessen; gesetzt; feierlich; ⁓ *accent gr.* Gravis *m*.
grave[2] [⁓] 1. Grab *n*; 2. (*irr.*) *mst fig.* (ein)graben; '**⁓-dig·ger** Totengräber *m*.
grav·el ['grævəl] 1. Kies *m*; ⚕ Harngrieß *m*; 2. mit Kies bedecken; F in Verlegenheit bringen, verblüffen; **grav·el·ly** ['grævli] kiesig.
grav·en ['greivən] *p.p von grave*[2] 2.
grav·er ⊕ ['greivə] Grabstichel *m*.
grave...: '**⁓·side:** *at his* ⁓ an seinem Grabe; '**⁓·stone** Grabstein *m*; '**⁓·yard** Kirchhof *m*.
grav·ing dock ⚓ ['greiviŋ'dɔk] Trockendock *n*, Kalfaterdock *n*.
grav·i·tate ['græviteit] (hin)neigen (*towards* zu, nach); **grav·i'ta·tion** Schwerkraft *f*; *fig.* Hang *m*; **grav·i'ta·tion·al** [⁓ʃənl] Schwerkraft..., Anziehungs...; ⁓ *force* Schwerkraft *f*; ⁓ *pull* Anziehungskraft *f*.
grav·i·ty ['græviti] Schwere *f*; Wichtigkeit *f*; Ernst *m*; Feierlichkeit *f*; Schwerkraft *f*; *centre of* ⁓ Schwerpunkt *m*; *specific* ⁓ spezifisches Gewicht *n*.
gra·vy ['greivi] Fleischsaft *m*, Bratensoße *f*; '**⁓-boat** Saucière *f*, Soßenschüssel *f*.
gray *bsd. Am.* [grei] grau; F nicht ganz legal; **gray·ish** *bsd. Am.* ['⁓iʃ] gräulich.
graze [greiz] 1. (ab)weiden; (ab-)grasen; streifen, schrammen; 2. Schramme *f*.
gra·zier ['greizjə] Viehmäster *m*.
grease 1. [gri:z] (ein)fetten, (be-)schmieren; ⁓ *s.o.'s palm fig.* j. schmieren; 2. [gri:s] Fett *n*; Schmiere *f*; '**⁓-cup** ⊕ Schmierbüchse *f*; '**⁓-gun** *mot.* Schmierpresse *f*; '**⁓-proof** fettdicht; ⁓ *paper* Pergamentpapier *n*; **greas·er** *Am. sl.* ['gri:zə] *Schimpfwort für* Mexikaner *m*.
greas·y □ ['gri:zi] fettig; schmierig.
great □ [greit] 1. *allg.* groß (*nach Ausdehnung, Dauer, Zahl, Grad*; *fig.* = *tüchtig*; *geschickt*; *eifrig*; *großmütig*; *bedeutend*; *vornehm*; *mächtig*); Groß...; F großartig; Ur...; *s. deal*[2] *1, many*; 2. *the* ⁓ *pl.* die Großen *m*/*pl.*, die Vornehmen *m*/*pl.*; ⁓*s pl.* Abschlußexamen *n* für B.A. in Oxford; '**⁓·coat** (Winter)Mantel *m*; '**⁓-'grand·child** Urenkel(in); '**⁓-'grand·fa·ther** Urgroßvater *m*; '**great·ly** sehr; '**great·ness** Größe *f*; Stärke *f*.
Gre·cian ['gri:ʃən] griechisch.
greed [gri:d], '**greed·i·ness** Gier(igkeit) *f*; '**greed·y** □ (be)gierig (*of, for* nach); habgierig; gefräßig.
Greek [gri:k] 1. griechisch; 2. Grieche *m*, Griechin *f*; Griechisch *n*; *that is* ⁓ *to me* das sind mir böhmische Dörfer.
green [gri:n] 1. □ grün (*a.* = *unreif*; F *unerfahren*); frisch (*Fisch etc.*); (⊕ fabrik)neu; Grün...; 2. Grün *n*; Jugend(kraft) *f*; Rasen *m*; Wiese *f*; ⁓*s pl.* frisches Gemüse *n*; '**⁓·back** *Am.* Dollarnote *f*; **green·er·y** ['⁓nəri] Grün *n*, Laub *n*.
green...: ⁓ **fin·gers** *pl.* gärtnerische Begabung *f*; '**⁓·gage** ⚘ Reineclaude *f*; '**⁓·gro·cer** Gemüsehändler(in); '**⁓·gro·cer·y** Gemüsehandlung *f*; '**⁓·horn** Grünschnabel *m*; '**⁓·house** Gewächshaus *n*; '**green·ish** grünlich.
Green·land·er ['gri:nləndə] Grönländer(in); **Green·land·man** ['⁓ləndmən] Grönlandfahrer *m*.
green light ['gri:n'lait] grünes Licht *n* (F *fig.* = *Genehmigung*); '**green·ness** Grün *n*; Frische *f*; Unreife *f*.
green...: '**⁓-room** *thea.* Künstlergarderobe *f*; '**⁓·sick·ness** ⚕ Bleichsucht *f*; **⁓·sward** ['⁓swɔ:d] Rasen *m*.
Green·wich ['grinidʒ]: ⁓ *time* Greenwicher Zeit *f*.
green·wood ['gri:nwud] (belaubter) Wald *m*.
greet [gri:t] (be)grüßen; '**greet·ing** Begrüßung *f*; Gruß *m*; ⁓*s card* Glückwunschkarte *f*.
gre·gar·i·ous [gri'gɛəriəs] in Her-

den lebend; gesellig.
gre·nade ⚔ [gri'neid] (Hand-, Gewehr)Granate *f*; **gren·a·dier** [grenə'diə] Grenadier *m*.
grew [gru:] *pret. von grow*.
grey [grei] **1.** □ grau; ♀ *Friar* Franziskaner *m*; **2.** Grau *n*; Grauschimmel *m*; **3.** grau machen *od.* werden; ~ **a·re·a** Grauzone *f*; '~**beard** Graubart *m*, alter Mann *m*.
grey...: '~-'**head·ed** *fig.* altgedient; '~**·hound** Windhund *m*; '**grey·ish** gräulich; **grey mat·ter** *anat.* graue Substanz *f*; *fig.* Grips *m*, Verstand *m*.
grid [grid] *bsd. Radio*: Gitter *n*; *Linien-, Eisenbahn-, Strom- etc.* Netz *n*; *Am. Fußball*: Spielfeld *n*.
grid·dle ['gridl] Backblech *n*.
grid·i·ron ['gridaiən] (Brat)Rost *m*.
grief [gri:f] Gram *m*, Kummer *m*.
griev·ance ['gri:vəns] Beschwerde *f*; Miß-, Übelstand *m*; **grieve** kränken, *j-m* weh tun; sich grämen; '**griev·ous** □ kränkend, schmerzlich; drückend; schlimm; '**griev·ous·ness** *das* Schmerzliche; Druck *m*.
grif·fin ['grifin] *Sage*: Greif *m*.
grig [grig] kleiner Aal *m*; Grille *f*.
grill [gril] **1.** grillen; braten (*a. fig.*); *sl. j.* weichmachen; **2.** Bratrost *m*, Grill *m*; Rostbraten *m*; *a.* ~*-room* Grillroom *m*.
grim □ [grim] grimmig; schrecklich; hart; finster, düster; ~ *facts pl. die* unerbittlichen Tatsachen *f/pl.*; ~ *humour* Galgenhumor *m*.
gri·mace [gri'meis] **1.** Grimasse *f*; **2.** Grimassen machen.
grime [graim] **1.** Schmutz *m*; Ruß *m*; **2.** beschmutzen; '**grim·y** □ schmutzig; rußig. [(*at* über *acc.*).]
grin [grin] **1.** Grinsen *n*; **2.** grinsen
grind [graind] **1.** (*irr.*) *v/t.* (zer)reiben; mahlen; wetzen; schleifen; *Leierkasten etc.* drehen; leiern; *fig.* schinden; *sl.* (ein)pauken; mit *den Zähnen* knirschen; ~ *out* herunterleiern; *v/i.* sich mahlen lassen; sich schinden; *sl.* büffeln; **2.** Schinderei *f*; '**grind·er** Schleifer *m*; Backenzahn *m*; Mahlwerk *n*; Leiermann *m*; *sl.* Einpauker *m*; '**grind·ing** Mahl...; Schleif...; '**grind·stone** Schleif-, Mühlstein *m*; *keep s.o.'s nose to the* ~ *j.* (dauernd) schinden.
grip [grip] **1.** packen, fassen (*a. fig.*); greifen; **2.** Griff *m*; Gewalt *f*; Herrschaft *f* (*of* über *acc.*); ⊕ Greifer *m*; *Am.* = *gripsack*; *get to* ~*s with* sich auseinandersetzen mit.
gripe [graip] **1.** Griff *m*; Gewalt *f*; ~*s pl.* F Bauchgrimmen *n*; *bsd. Am.* Beschwerden *f/pl.* **2.** *v/t.* (er)greifen, packen; drücken, zwicken; *v/i. bsd. Am.* F meckern.
grip·ping ['gripiŋ] fesselnd, spannend.
grip·sack *Am.* ['gripsæk] Handtasche *f*, -köfferchen *n*.
gris·ly ['grizli] gräßlich, schrecklich.
grist [grist] Mahlgut *n*; *bring* ~ *to the mill fig.* Gewinn bringen; *all is* ~ *that comes to his mill* er weiß mit allem et. anzufangen. [knorpelig.]
gris·tle ['grisl] Knorpel *m*; '**gris·tly**
grit [grit] **1.** Schrot(mehl) *n*; Kies *m*; Sand(stein) *m*; *fig.* Mumm *m*; **2.** knirschen (mit); '**grit·ty** sandig.
griz·zle F ['grizl] quengeln; '**griz·zled** = *grizzly 1*; '**griz·zly 1.** grau (-haarig); ~ *bear* = **2.** Graubär *m*.
groan [grəun] **1.** Stöhnen *n*, Seufzen *n*; Ächzen *n*; Murren *n*; **2.** seufzen, stöhnen (*for* nach).
groat [grəut]: *not worth a* ~ keinen Heller wert. [Grütze *f*.]
groats [grəuts] *pl.* (*bsd.* Hafer-)
gro·cer ['grəusə] Lebensmittelhändler *m*; **gro·cer·ies** ['~riz] *pl.* Lebensmittel *n/pl.*; '**gro·cer·y** Lebensmittelgeschäft *n*.
gro·ce·te·ri·a *Am.* [grəusi'tiəriə] Selbstbedienungsladen *m*.
grog [grɔg] Grog *m*; '**grog·gy** betrunken; taumelig; wack(e)lig.
groin [grɔin] **1.** *anat.* Leisten (-gegend *f*) *f/pl.*; ⚠ Grat *m*, Rippe *f*; **2.** mit Kreuzgewölbe bauen.
groom [grum] **1.** Reit-, Stallknecht *m*; = *bridegroom*; **2.** *Pferde* pflegen; *Am. pol. Kandidat* lancieren; *well* ~*ed* gepflegt; elegant; **grooms·man** ['~zmən] Brautführer *m*.
groove [gru:v] **1.** Rinne *f*, Furche *f*, Nut *f*; Rille *f*; *fig.* Gewohnheit *f*, Schablone *f*; ~*s pl.* Züge *m/pl. im Gewehr*; *in the* ~ *fig.* im richtigen Fahrwasser; **2.** nuten, falzen; riefeln; '**groov·y** *Am.* toll, einfach phantastisch.
grope [grəup] (be)tasten; tappen; ~ *one's way* sich vorwärtstasten.
gross [grəus] **1.** □ dick; grob; derb, roh; üppig (*Wachstum*); dick, feist (*Person*); unanständig; ungeheuer-

lich; ⚕ Brutto...; ~ *national product* ⚕ Bruttosozialprodukt *n*; **2.** Gros *n* (*12 Dutzend*); *in the* ~ im ganzen, in Bausch und Bogen; '**gross·ness** Dichtheit *f*; Grobheit *f*; Derbheit *f*, Roheit *f*.

gro·tesque □ [grəu'tesk] grotesk.

grot·to ['grɔtəu], *pl.* '**grot·to(e)s** Grotte *f*.

grouch *Am.* F [grautʃ] **1.** quengeln, meckern; **2.** Meckerei *f*; schlechte Laune *f*; Meckerer *m*; '**grouch·y** queng(e)lig.

ground[1] [graund] *pret. u. p.p. von grind 1*; ~ *glass* Mattglas *n*; *phot.* Mattscheibe *f*.

ground[2] [~] **1.** *mst* Grund *m*, Boden *m*; Gebiet *n*; *Spiel- etc.* Platz *m*; *Jagd*-Revier *n*; *paint.* Grundierung *f*; *Beweg- etc.* Grund *m*; ⚡ Erde *f*, Erdschluß *m*; ~*s pl.* Grundstück *n*, Park(s *pl.*) *m*, Gärten *m/pl.*; *Kaffee*-Satz *m*; Anfangsgründe *m/pl.*; *on the* ~*(s) of* auf Grund (*gen.*); *on the* ~*(s) that* mit der Begründung, daß; *fall to the* ~ hinfallen; *fig.* ins Wasser fallen; *give* ~ zurückweichen; *stand od. hold od. keep one's* ~ sich behaupten; **2.** niederlegen; (be-)gründen; *j-m* die Anfangsgründe beibringen; ⊕ grundieren; ⚡ erden; ⚓ auflaufen (lassen); *be* ~*ed* ✈ Startverbot bekommen; *well* ~*ed* mit guter Grundlage; '**ground·age** ⚓ Hafengebühr *f*, Ankergeld *n*.

ground...: '~**-con·nex·ion** ⚡ Erdung *f*; ~ **crew** = *ground-staff*; ~ **floor** Erdgeschoß *n*; ~ **forc·es** *pl.* ⚔ Bodentruppen *f/pl.*; '~**-'hog** *zo. bsd. Am.* Murmeltier *n*; '~**·less** □ grundlos; **ground·ling** *thea.* ['~liŋ] Gründling *m*, Parterrezuschauer *m*.

ground...: '~**-nut** Erdnuß *f*; '~**-'plan** Grundriß *m*; '~**-rent** Grundpacht *f*.

ground·sel ⚘ ['graunsl] Kreuzkraut *n*.

ground·sheet ['graundʃi:t] *Camping etc.*: Unterlegplane *f*.

grounds·man ['graundzmən] *Sport*: Platzwart *m*.

ground...: ~ **speed** ⚓ Geschwindigkeit *f* über Grund; '~**-staff** ✈ Bodenpersonal *n*; ~ **swell** Dünung *f*; '~**-to-'air mis·sile** ⚔ Boden-Luft-Rakete *f*; '~**-wire** ⚡ Erdleitung *f*; '~**-work** Grundlage *f*, Fundament *n*.

group [gru:p] **1.** Gruppe *f*; Truppe *f*; ~ *dynamics sg.* Gruppendynamik *f*; **2.** (sich) gruppieren.

grouse[1] *orn.* [graus] Schottisches Mohrhuhn *n*.

grouse[2] F [~] meckern, nörgeln.

grove [grəuv] Wäldchen *n*, Hain *m*; Gehölz *n*.

grov·el ['grɔvl] *mst fig.* kriechen; '**grov·el·(l)er** Kriecher(in); '**grov·el·(l)ing 1.** kriechend; kriecherisch niedrig; **2.** Kriecherei *f*.

grow [grəu] (*irr.*) *v/i.* wachsen; werden; ~ *out of* herauswachsen aus; entwachsen (*dat.*); *et.* überwinden; kommen von, entstehen aus; ~ *(up)on s.o.* j-m ans Herz wachsen; ~ *up* heranwachsen, erwachsen werden; *v/t.* anpflanzen, -bauen, ziehen; *Bart* wachsen lassen; '**grow·er** Bauer *m*, Züchter *m*.

growl [graul] **1.** Knurren *n*, Brummen *n*; **2.** knurren, brummen; '**growl·er** *fig.* Brummbär *m*; *Am. sl.* Bierkrug *m*.

grown [grəun] **1.** *p.p. von grow*; **2.** *adj.* erwachsen; bewachsen; '~**-up 1.** erwachsen; **2.** Erwachsene *m, f*; **growth** [grəuθ] Wachstum *n*; (An)wachsen *n*; Entwicklung *f*; Wuchs *m*; Gewächs *n*, Erzeugnis *n*; *of one's own* ~ selbstgezogen.

groyne [grɔin] Buhne *f*.

grub [grʌb] **1.** Raupe *f*, Larve *f*, Made *f*; *contp.* Prolet *m*; *sl.* Futter *n*; **2.** graben (*for* nach); sich abmühen; *sl.* futtern (*essen*); ~ *up* ausjäten, ausroden; *mst* ~ *out* aufstöbern, ausgraben; '**grub·by** schmierig, schmutzig; madig.

grudge [grʌdʒ] **1.** Groll *m*; *bear s.o. a* ~ einen Groll gegen j. hegen; **2.** mißgönnen, neiden; ungern geben *od.* tun *etc.*; ~ *no pains* keine Mühe scheuen; '**grudg·er** Neider *m*; '**grudg·ing·ly** widerwillig, ungern.

gru·el ['gruəl] Haferschleim *m*; *get od. have one's* ~ *sl.* sein Fett kriegen; '**gru·el·(l)ing** zermürbend.

grue·some □ ['gru:səm] grausig, schauerlich.

gruff [grʌf], '**gruff·y** grob, schroff, barsch; mürrisch; rauh.

grum·ble ['grʌmbl] murren, brummen, nörgeln (*at* über *acc.*); (g)rollen (*Donner*); '**grum·bler** *fig.* Brummbär *m*.

grump·y □ F ['grʌmpi] brummig, knurrig.

Grun·dy·ism ['grʌndiizəm] Engstirnigkeit *f*, engstirniger Konfor-

mismus *m*.
grunt [grʌnt] **1.** Grunzen *n*, Grunz-, Knurrlaut *m*; **2.** grunzen; ˈ**grunt·er** Schwein *n*.
guar·an·tee [gærənˈtiː] **1.** Bürgschaftsempfänger *m*; Bürge *m*; = *guaranty*; **2.** bürgen für, garantieren; **guar·an·tor** [~ˈtɔː] Bürge *m*; ˈ**guar·an·ty** Bürgschaft *f*, Garantie *f*; Gewähr(leistung) *f*.
guard [gɑːd] **1.** Wacht *f*; ⚔ Wache *f*; Wächter *m*, Wärter *m*; 🚃 Schaffner *m*; Schutz(vorrichtung *f*) *m*; 2s *pl*. ⚔ Garde *f*; *be on (off) one's* ~ (nicht) auf der Hut sein; *mount* ~ ⚔ auf Wache ziehen; *relieve* ~ ⚔ die Wache ablösen; **2.** *v/t*. bewachen, (be)schützen (*from* vor *dat*.; *against* gegen); (be)hüten; *v/i*. sich hüten (*against* vor *dat*.); ˈ**~-boat** ⚓ Wachboot *n*; ˈ**guard·ed** □ behutsam, vorsichtig; ˈ**guard·house** Wachlokal *n*; Arrestlokal *n*; ˈ**guard·i·an** Hüter *m*, Wächter *m*; ⚖ Vormund *m*; *attr*. Schutz...; ~ *angel* Schutzengel *m*; ~ *of the poor* Armenpfleger(in); ˈ**guard·i·an·ship** Obhut *f*; Vormundschaft *f*; ˈ**guard·rail** Schutzgeländer *n*; **guards·man** ⚔ [ˈgɑːdzmən] Gardist *m*.
gudg·eon [ˈgʌdʒən] *ichth*. Gründling *m*; *fig*. Einfaltspinsel *m*; ⊕ Bolzen *m*.
guer·don *lit*. [ˈgəːdən] **1.** Lohn *m*; **2.** belohnen.
guer(r)·ril·la [gəˈrilə] Partisan *m*, Guerillakämpfer *m*; ~ *war* Kleinkrieg *m*.
guess [ges] **1.** Vermutung *f*; *at a* ~ schätzungsweise; **2.** *v/t*. vermuten; (er)raten; *v/i*. mutmaßen, raten (*at acc*.); *bsd. Am*. denken, meinen, annehmen; ˈ**guess·work** Mutmaßung *f*.
guest [gest] Gast *m*; *paying* ~ zahlender Gast *m*; ˈ**~-house** (Hotel-) Pension *f*, Fremdenheim *n*; ˈ**~-room** Gast-, Fremdenzimmer *n*.
guf·faw [gʌˈfɔː] **1.** schallendes Gelächter *n*; **2.** laut (los)lachen.
guid·a·ble [ˈgaidəbl] lenksam; **guid·ance** [ˈ~dəns] Führung *f*, (An-) Leitung *f*; Orientierung *f*.
guide [gaid] **1.** Führer *m*; *s*. *~-book*; ⊕ Führung *f*; *attr*. Führungs..., Leit...; **2.** leiten, führen; steuern, lenken; *~d missile* ⚔ Fernlenkgeschoß *n*, Rakete *f*; *guiding principle* Leitgedanke *m*; bestimmendes Prinzip *n*; ˈ**~-book** Reiseführer *m*; ~ **dog** Blindenhund *m*; ˈ**~·lines** *pl*. Richtlinien *f/pl*.; ˈ**~-post** Wegweiser *m*; ˈ**~-rope** ✈ Schleppseil *n*.
gui·don ⚔ [ˈgaidən] Standarte *f*.
guild [gild] Gilde *f*, Zunft *f*, Innung *f*; ˈ**guild·er** Gulden *m*; ˈ**Guild**ˈ**hall** Rathaus *n* (*London*).
guile [gail] (Arg)List *f*; **guile·ful** □ [ˈ~ful] arglistig; ˈ**guile·less** □ arglos; ˈ**guile·less·ness** Arglosigkeit *f*.
guil·lo·tine [giləˈtiːn] **1.** Guillotine *f*, Fallbeil *n*; ⊕ Papierschneidemaschine *f*; *pol*. Befristung *f* der Debatte; **2.** hinrichten.
guilt [gilt] Schuld *f*; Strafbarkeit *f*; ˈ**guilt·i·ness** Schuld *f*; ˈ**guilt·less** □ schuldlos (*of* an *dat*.); unkundig (*of gen*.); ˈ**guilt·y** □ schuldig; strafbar; *plead* ~ sich schuldig bekennen.
guin·ea [ˈgini] Guinee *f* (*21 Schilling*); ˈ**~-fowl** Perlhuhn *n*; ˈ**~-pig** Meerschweinchen *n*; *fig*. Versuchskaninchen *n*.
guise [gaiz] *bsd. angenommene* Erscheinung *f*, Gestalt *f*, Maske *f*; Vorwand *m*.
gui·tar ♪ [giˈtɑː] Gitarre *f*.
gulch *Am*. [gʌlʃ] tiefe Schlucht *f*.
gulf [gʌlf] Meerbusen *m*, Golf *m*; Abgrund *m*, Kluft *f* (*a. fig*.); Strudel *m*.
gull[1] *orn*. [gʌl] Möwe *f*.
gull[2] [~] **1.** Trottel *m*, Tölpel *m*; **2.** übertölpeln; verleiten (*into* zu).
gul·let [ˈgʌlit] Speiseröhre *f*; Gurgel *f*, Schlund *m*.
gul·li·bil·i·ty [gʌliˈbiliti] Leichtgläubigkeit *f*; **gul·li·ble** □ [ˈ~ləbl] leichtgläubig.
gul·ly [ˈgʌli] Schlucht *f e-s Gießbachs*; Abzugskanal *m*; Gully *m*, Sinkkasten *m*.
gulp [gʌlp] **1.** Schluck *m*; Schlucken *n*; **2.** (gierig) schlucken.
gum[1] [gʌm] *a*. *~s pl*. Zahnfleisch *n*.
gum[2] [~] **1.** Gummi *n*; Klebstoff *m*; Kaugummi *m*; *~s pl*. *Am*. Gummischuhe *m/pl*.; **2.** gummieren; zukleben.
gum·boil ⚕ [ˈgʌmbɔil] Zahngeschwür *n*.
gum·my [ˈgʌmi] gummiartig; klebrig.
gump·tion F [ˈgʌmpʃən] Grips *m*, Köpfchen *n*; Schwung *m*, Mumm *m*.

gun [gʌn] **1.** Gewehr *n*; Flinte *f*; Büchse *f*; Geschütz *n*, Kanone *f*; *bsd. Am.* Revolver *m*, Pistole *f*; Schütze *m*; *big od. great* ~ F hohes Tier *n* (*wichtige Person*); *stick to one's* ~ festbleiben, nicht nachgeben; **2.** *Am.* auf die Jagd gehen; '**~·boat** ⚓ Kanonenboot *n*; '**~-car·riage** ⚔ Lafette *f*; '**~-cot·ton** Schießbaumwolle *f*; '**~-li·cence** Waffenschein *m*; '**~·man** *bsd. Am.* Gangster *m*, Bandit *m*; '**~-met·al** Rotguß *m*; '**gun·ner** ⚔, ⚓ Kanonier *m*; ✈ Bordschütze *m*; '**gun·ner·y** ⚔ Geschützwesen *n*; Ballistik *f*.

gun·ny ['gʌni] Sackleinwand *f*.

gun...: '**~·pow·der** Schießpulver *n*; ♀ *Plot hist.* Pulververschwörung *f* (*1605*); '**~-room** ⚓ Kadettenmesse *f*; '**~-run·ning** Waffenschmuggel *m*; '**~·shot** Schußweite *f*; Schuß *m*; '**~-shy** schußscheu; '**~·smith** Büchsenmacher *m*; '**~-tur·ret** Geschützturm *m*.

gun·wale ⚓ ['gʌnl] Schandeckel *m*; Dollbord *n*.

gur·gle ['gəːgl] **1.** Gluckern *n*; **2.** gurgeln, gluckern, glucksen.

gush [gʌʃ] **1.** Guß *m*; *fig.* Erguß *m*; **2.** (sich) ergießen, schießen (*from* aus); *fig.* schwärmen; '**gush·er** *fig.* Schwärmer(in); Ölquelle *f*; '**gush·ing** □ überschwenglich, überspannt; '**gush·y** überschwenglich, schwärmerisch.

gus·set ['gʌsit] *Schneiderei*: Zwickel *m*.

gust [gʌst] Windstoß *m*, Bö *f*; Ausbruch *m*, Sturm *m der Leidenschaft*.

gus·ta·to·ry ['gʌstətəri] Geschmacks...

gus·to ['gʌstəu] Geschmack *m* (*for* an *dat.*); Vergnügen *n*.

gus·ty □ ['gʌsti] stürmisch.

gut [gʌt] **1.** Darm *m*; ♪ Darmsaite *f*; ~*s pl.* F Eingeweide *n/pl.*, Bauch *m*; *das* Innere; Durchschlagskraft *f*; Mut *m*; **2.** *Fisch* ausnehmen; *fig.* plündern, ausrauben; ausbrennen; '**gut·less** F feige, ohne Mumm; '**guts·y** F draufgängerisch.

gut·ta-per·cha ['gʌtə'pəːtʃə] Guttapercha *f*.

gut·ter ['gʌtə] **1.** Dachrinne *f*; Gosse *f* (*a. fig.*), Rinnstein *m*; **2.** *v/t.* furchen; auskehlen; *v/i.* rinnen, triefen, tropfen; ~ **press** Schmutzpresse *f*; '**~-snipe** Straßenjunge *m*.

gut·tur·al ['gʌtərəl] **1.** □ Kehl...; kehlig; guttural; **2.** *gr.* Kehllaut *m*.

guy[1] [gai] **1.** F Vogelscheuche *f*; *bsd. Am.* F Kerl *m*, Kumpel *m*; **2.** verulken.

guy[2] [~] Halteseil *n*; ⚓ Gei *f*.

guz·zle ['gʌzl] saufen; fressen.

gym F [dʒim] = *gymnasium, gymnastics.*

gym·kha·na [dʒim'kɑːnə] *Geschicklichkeitswettkampf, Sportfest.*

gym·na·si·um [dʒim'neizjəm] Turnhalle *f*; **gym·nast** ['~næst] Turner(in); **gym'nas·tic** **1.** (~*ally*) gymnastisch; Turn...; ~ *competition* Wetturnen *n*; **2.** ~*s pl.* Turnen *n*, Gymnastik *f*; '**gym-shoes** *pl.* F Turnschuhe *m/pl.*

gyn·ae·col·o·gist [gaini'kɔlədʒist] Gynäkologe *m*, Frauenarzt *m*; **gyn·ae'col·o·gy** Gynäkologie *f*.

gyp [dʒip] Studentendiener *m in Cambridge u. Durham*; Gauner *m*; Gaunerei *f*; *give s.o.* ~ j-m das Leben sauer machen.

gyp·se·ous ['dʒipsiəs] gipsartig.

gyp·sum *min.* ['dʒipsəm] Gips *m*.

gyp·sy *bsd. Am.* ['dʒipsi] = *gipsy.*

gy·rate [dʒaiə'reit] kreisen; wirbeln; **gy'ra·tion** Kreisbewegung *f*; **gy·ra·to·ry** ['~rətəri] Kreis...; Wirbel...

gy·ro-com·pass *phys.* ['dʒaiərəu'kʌmpəs] Kreiselkompaß *m*; **gy·ro·scope** ['gaiərəskəup] Gyroskop *n* (*Kreiselvorrichtung*); **gy·ro·scop·ic sta·bi·liz·er** [gaiərəs'kɔpik'steibilaizə], **gy·ro'sta·bi·liz·er** Schiffskreisel *m*, Stabilisator *m*.

gyve *poet.* [dʒaiv] **1.** ~*s pl.* Fesseln *f/pl.*; **2.** fesseln.

H

h [eitʃ]: *drop one's h's* ohne H *od.* [ungebildet sprechen.
ha [hɑː] ha!
ha·be·as cor·pus ⚖ [ˈheibjəsˈkɔːpəs] *a. writ of* ~ Vorführungsbefehl *m.*
hab·er·dash·er [ˈhæbədæʃə] Kurzwarenhändler *m*; *Am.* Herrenartikelhändler *m*; **ˈhab·er·dash·er·y** Kurzwaren(geschäft *n*) *f/pl.*; *Am.* Herrenartikel *m/pl.*
ha·bil·i·ments [həˈbilimənts] *pl.* Gewand *n*; Kleider *n/pl.*
hab·it [ˈhæbit] **1.** (An)Gewohnheit *f*; Verfassung *f*; Kleid(ung *f*) *n*; *fall od. get into bad* ~*s* schlechte Gewohnheiten annehmen; *get out of a* ~ e-e Gewohnheit ablegen; *get into the* ~ *of smoking* sich das Rauchen angewöhnen; *be in the* ~ *of ger.* pflegen zu *inf.*; **2.** (an)kleiden; **ˈhab·it·a·ble** bewohnbar; **hab·i·tat** ♀, *zo.* [ˈ~tæt] Vorkommen *n*, Stand-, Fundort *m*, Heimat *f*; **hab·iˈta·tion** Wohnen *n*; Wohnung *f.*
ha·bit·u·al □ [həˈbitjuəl] gewohnt, gewöhnlich; Gewohnheits...; **haˈbit·u·ate** [~eit] gewöhnen (*to* an *acc.*); **hab·i·tude** [ˈhæbitjuːd] Gewohnheit *f*; **ha·bit·u·é** [həˈbitjuei] ständiger Besucher *m*, Stammgast *m.*
hack[1] [hæk] **1.** Hieb *m*; Einkerbung *f*; *Fußball*: Tritt *m*; **2.** (zer)hacken; *Fußball*: j. vor das Schienbein treten; ~*ing cough* kurzer, trockener Husten *m.*
hack[2] [~] **1.** Mietpferd *n*; Arbeitsgaul *m* (*a. fig.*); *a.* ~ *writer* literarischer Tagelöhner *m*; Schreiberling *m*; **2.** Miet(s)...; *fig.* abgedroschen; **3.** abnutzen.
hack·le [ˈhækl] **1.** ⊕ Hechel *f*; *orn.* Nackenfeder(n *pl.*) *f*; *get s.o.'s* ~*s up fig.* j. in Wut bringen; **2.** hecheln; zerhacken.
hack·ney [ˈhækni] (Kutsch)Gaul *m*; Klepper *m*; ~ **car·riage,** ~ **coach** Mietsdroschke *f*; **ˈhack·neyed** *fig.* abgedroschen.
hack-saw ⊕ [ˈhæksɔː] Metallsäge *f.*
had [hæd, həd] *pret. u. p.p. von have.*
had·dock *ichth.* [ˈhædək] Schellfisch *m.*
Ha·des [ˈheidiːz] Hades *m*, Unterwelt *f.*
h(a)e·mal [ˈhiːməl] Blut...
h(a)em·a·tite *min.* [ˈhemətait] Roteisenerz *n.*
h(a)e·mo... [ˈhiːməu] Blut...
h(a)e·mo·glo·bin ⚕ [hiːməuˈgləubin] Hämoglobin *n*, roter Blutfarbstoff *m*; **h(a)e·mo·phil·i·a** [~ˈfiliə] Bluterkrankheit *f.*
h(a)em·or·rhage [ˈhemərid͡ʒ] Blutsturz *m*; **h(a)em·or·rhoids** [ˈ~rɔidz] *pl.* Hämorrhoiden *f/pl.*
haft [hɑːft] Heft *n*, Stiel *m.*
hag [hæg] (*mst fig.* alte) Hexe *f.*
hag·gard □ [ˈhægəd] wild, verstört; hager; abgehärmt.
hag·gis [ˈhægis] *schottisches Gericht aus Schafinnereien.*
hag·gle [ˈhægl] feilschen, schachern.
hag·i·ol·o·gy [hægiˈɔləd͡ʒi] Heiligenleben *n/pl.* u. -legenden *f/pl.*
hag·rid·den [ˈhægridn] (vom Alpdruck) gequält.
hah [hɑː] haha!
ha-ha [hɑːˈhɑː] (in e-m Graben versenkter) Grenzzaun *m.*
hail[1] [heil] **1.** Hagel *m*; **2.** *v/i.* hageln; *v/t.* niederhageln lassen.
hail[2] [~] **1.** anrufen; (be)grüßen; ~ *from* stammen aus; **2.** Anruf *m*; ~! Heil!; *within* ~ in Rufweite; *be* ~*-fellow-well-met with* allzu vertraut sein mit *j-m.*
hail·stone [ˈheilstəun] Hagelkorn *n*; **ˈhail·storm** Hagelschauer *m*; *fig.* Schauer *m*, Flut *f.*
hair [hɛə] Haar *n*; *keep your* ~ *on! sl.* immer mit der Ruhe!; *not turn a* ~ ganz gelassen bleiben; ~*'s breadth* = **ˈ~-breadth** Haaresbreite *f*; *by od. within* ~ um Haaresbreite; **ˈ~-cut** Haarschnitt *m*; **ˈ~-do** *Am.* Frisur *f*; **ˈ~·dress·er** (*bsd.* Damen)Friseur *m*; **ˈ~-dri·er** Haartrockner *m*, Fön *m*; **haired** behaart; **ˈhair·i·ness** Haarigkeit *f*, Behaartheit *f.*
hair...: **ˈ~·less** ohne Haare, kahl; **ˈ~·line** Haaransatz *m*; *Schrift*: Haarstrich *m*; **ˈ~·piece** Haarteil *n*; Toupet *n*; **ˈ~·pin** Haarnadel *f*; ~ *bend* Haarnadelkurve *f*; **ˈ~-rais·ing** haarsträubend; ~ **re·stor·er** Haarwuchsmittel *n*; **ˈ~-shirt** härenes Hemd *n*; **ˈ~-split·ting** Haarspalterei *f*; **ˈ~-spring** ⊕ Unruhfeder *f*; **ˈhair·y**

haarig.

ha·la·tion *phot.* [həˈleiʃən] Lichthof *m.*

hal·berd ⚔ [ˈhælbəːd] Hellebarde *f.*

hal·cy·on [ˈhælsiən] **1.** Eisvogel *m*; **2.** still, ruhig, friedlich.

hale [heil] gesund, frisch, rüstig; ~ *and hearty* gesund und munter.

half [hɑːf] **1.** halb; ~ *a crown* eine halbe Krone; *a pound and a* ~ anderthalb Pfund; *not* ~ *sl.* nicht wenig, gehörig, gar nicht schlecht; **2.** *pl.* **halves** [hɑːvz] Hälfte *f*; *Schule*: Halbjahr *n*; ⚖ Partei *f*; *too clever by* ~ viel zu gescheit; *by halves* nur halb; *go halves* teilen; **ˈ~-ˈback** *Fußball*: Läufer *m*; **ˈ~-ˈbaked** *fig.* unfertig; unausgegoren; **ˈ~-bind·ing** Halbfranzband *m*; **ˈ~-blood** Halbblut *n*; **ˈ~-ˈbound** in Halbfranz gebunden; **ˈ~-bred** Halbblut...; **ˈ~-breed** Halbblut *n*; **ˈ~-calf** Halbfranzband *m*; **ˈ~-caste** Halbblut *n*; **ˈ~-ˈcrown** halbe Krone *f* ($2^1/_2$ *Schilling*); **ˈ~-ˈheart·ed** □ lustlos, halbherzig, lau; **ˈ~-ˈhol·i·day** halber Feiertag *m*; freier Nachmittag *m*; **ˈ~-ˈhour 1.** halbe Stunde *f*; **2.** halbstündig, -stündlich; **ˈ~-ˈhour·ly** halbstündlich; **ˈ~-ˈlength** Brustbild *n*; **ˈ~-life (pe·ri·od)** *phys.* Halbwertszeit *f*; **ˈ~-ˈmast:** (*at*) ~ halbmast; **ˈ~-ˈmoon** Halbmond *m*; **ˈ~-ˈmourn·ing** Halbtrauer *f*; **ˈ~-ˈpay** Halbsold *m*: **~·pen·ny** [ˈheipni] halber Penny *m* (= $^1/_2$ p = £ 0.00$^1/_2$); **~-seas-o·ver** F [ˈhɑːfsiːzˈəuvə] angesäuselt; **ˈ~-ˈtime** *Sport*: Halbzeit *f*; **ˈ~-tone proc·ess** ⊕ Rasterverfahren *n*; **ˈ~-track** Halbkettenantrieb *m*, -fahrzeug *n*; **ˈ~-ˈway** auf halbem Wege, halbwegs; ~ *house* Zwischenstation *f*; *fig.* Mittelding *n*; **ˈ~-ˈwit** Schwachkopf *m*; **ˈ~-ˈwit·ted** einfältig, idiotisch.

hal·i·but *ichth.* [ˈhælibət] Heilbutt *m.*

hal·i·to·sis [hæliˈtəusis] übler Mundgeruch *m.*

hall [hɔːl] Halle *f*; Saal *m*; Vorsaal *m*, -raum *m*; Flur *m*, Diele *f*; Herren-, Gutshaus *n*; *univ.* Speisesaal *m*; Mahlzeit *f*; ~ *of residence* (Studenten)Wohnheim *n.*

hal·le·lu·jah [hæliˈluːjə] Halleluja(h) *n.*

hall...: **ˈ~-mark 1.** Feingehaltsstempel *m*; *fig.* Stempel *m* (der Echtheit), Zeichen *n*; **2.** (ab)stempeln; **ˈ~-ˈstand** Flurgarderobe *f.*

hal·lo(a) [həˈləu] hallo!, he!

hal·loo [həˈluː] **1.** hallo!; **2.** Hallo *n*; **3.** *v/i.* (hallo) rufen; *v/t.* anfeuern.

hal·low [ˈhæləu] heiligen, weihen; **Hal·low·mas** [ˈ~mæs] Allerheiligen(fest) *n.*

hal·lu·ci·na·tion [həluːsiˈneiʃən] Halluzination *f*, Sinnestäuschung *f.*

hall·way [ˈhɔːlwei] Diele *f*, Flur *m.*

ha·lo [ˈheiləu] *ast.* Hof *m*; Heiligenschein *m.*

halt [hɔːlt] **1.** Halt *m*; Stillstand *m*; 🚃 Haltestelle *f*; **2.** (an)halten; *mst fig.* hinken; schwanken, zögern; stocken; **3.** lahm.

hal·ter [ˈhɔːltə] Halfter *m*, *n*; Strick *m* (*zum Hängen*).

halve [hɑːv] halbieren; **halves** [~z] *pl. von half 2.*

hal·yard ⚓ [ˈhæljəd] Fall *n.*

ham [hæm] Schenkel *m*; Schinken *m*; *sl.* Funkamateur *m*; *a.* ~ *actor sl.* Schmierenkomödiant *m.*

ham·burg·er *Am.* [ˈhæmbəːgə] Frikadelle *f*; Hamburger *m*, mit Frikadelle belegtes Brötchen *n*; Rinderhack *n.*

ham-fist·ed [ˈhæmˈfistid], **ham-hand·ed** [ˈ~hændid] ungeschickt (mit den Händen).

ham·let [ˈhæmlit] Weiler *m*, Dörfchen *n.*

ham·mer [ˈhæmə] **1.** Hammer *m*; ~ *and tongs* F wild darauflos; **2.** hämmern; behämmern; schlagen; *Börse*: für zahlungsunfähig erklären; ~ *at* eifrig arbeiten an (*dat.*); ~ *out* zurechtschmieden, herausarbeiten.

ham·mock [ˈhæmək] Hängematte *f*; **~ chair** Liegestuhl *m.*

ham·per [ˈhæmpə] **1.** Packkorb *m*; Geschenk-, Freßkorb *m*; **2.** verstricken, verwickeln; behindern, hemmen.

ham·ster *zo.* [ˈhæmstə] Hamster *m.*

ham·string [ˈhæmstriŋ] **1.** *anat.* Kniesehne *f*; **2.** die Kniesehnen zerschneiden (*dat.*); *fig.* lähmen.

hand [hænd] **1.** Hand *f* (*fig.* = *Obhut, Besitz, Gewalt*; *Wirksamkeit*; *Geschicklichkeit*; *Einfluß*); Handschrift *f*; Unterschrift *f*; Handbreit *f*; Seite *f*; *zo.* Vorderfuß *m*; (Uhr)Zeiger *m*; Hilfe *f*; Mann *m*,

Arbeiter *m*, Matrose *m*; Kenner *m*; F Kerl *m*; *Karten*: Handkarten *f/pl.*, Blatt *n*; Spieler *m*; *at* ~ bei der Hand; nahe bevorstehend; *be at* ~ zur Verfügung stehen; *at first* ~ aus erster Hand; *at s.o.'s* ~*s* von seiten j-s; *a good (poor)* ~ *at* (un)geschickt in (*dat.*); ~ *and glove* ein Herz und eine Seele; *bear a* ~ (schnelle) Hilfe leisten, zugreifen; *by* ~ von Hand; durch Boten (*nicht per Post*); *change* ~*s* den Besitzer wechseln; *get out of* ~ außer Kontrolle geraten; *have a* ~ *in* beteiligt sein an (*dat.*); *in* ~ in der Hand; unter Kontrolle; in Arbeit; zur Verfügung; vorliegend; ✝ bar; *lay* ~*s on* Hand an *j.* legen; *lend a* ~ (mit) anfassen, helfen; *off* ~ aus dem Handgelenk *od.* Stegreif; auf der Stelle; ~*s off!* Hände weg!; *on* ~ in Händen; ✝ vorrätig, auf Lager; *bsd. Am.* zur Stelle, bereit; *on one's* ~*s* auf dem Halse; *on all* ~*s* auf *od.* von allen Seiten; *on the one* ~ einerseits; *on the other* ~ andererseits; *have one's* ~ *out* aus der Übung sein; *out of* ~ sogleich; ~ *over fist* spielend; *take a* ~ *at* bei *e-m Spiel* mitspielen; *to (one's)* ~ zur Hand, bereit; ~ *to* ~ Mann gegen Mann; *come to* ~ sich bieten; einlaufen (*Briefe*); *you can feed him out of your* ~ *fig.* er frißt aus der Hand; *get the upper* ~ *of* die Oberhand gewinnen über (*acc.*); *put one's* ~ *to* Hand legen an (*acc.*); *he can turn his* ~ *to anything* er ist zu allem zu gebrauchen; ~*s up!* Hände hoch!; *s. high 1*; **2.** (~ *about, etc.* herum- *etc.*) reichen; aushändigen, übergeben; ~ *down* der Nachwelt überliefern; vererben; ~ *in* einhändigen, abgeben; *Gesuch* einreichen; hineinhelfen; ~ *out* heraushelfen; ~ *over* aushändigen; **'~-bag** Handtasche *f*; **'~-bar·row** Handkarre *f*; Trage *f*; **'~·bill** Flugblatt *n*, Hand-, Reklamezettel *m*; **'~·book** Handbuch *n*; **'~-brake** ⊕ Handbremse *f*; **'~·cart** Handwagen *m*; **'~·clap** Klatschen *n*; **'~·cuff 1.** Handschelle *f*; **2.** *j-m* Handschellen anlegen; **'hand·ed** ...händig; mit ... Händen; **hand·ful** ['~ful] Handvoll *f*; F Plage *f*; F Sorgenkind *n*; **'hand-glass** Handspiegel *m*; Leselupe *f*; **'hand·gun** Faustfeuerwaffe *f*.

hand·i·cap ['hændikæp] **1.** Handikap *n*; Vorgaberennen *n*, -spiel *n*; (Extra)Belastung *f* (*a. fig.*); **2.** (extra) belasten; behindern; *fig. a.* beeinträchtigen; **'hand·i·capped 1.** *the* ~ *pl.* die Behinderten *pl.*; **2.** behindert.

hand·i·craft ['hændikrɑːft] Handwerk *n*; Handfertigkeit *f*; **'hand·i·crafts·man** Handwerker *m*; **'hand·i·ness** Gewandtheit *f*; Handlichkeit *f*; **'hand·i·work** Handarbeit *f*; Werk *n*, Schöpfung *f*.

hand·ker·chief ['hæŋkətʃif] Taschentuch *n*; *dünnes* Halstuch *n*.

han·dle ['hændl] **1.** Griff *m*; Stiel *m*; Kurbel *f*; Henkel *m*; Schwengel *m der Pumpe etc.*; *fig.* Handhabe *f*; F Titel *m*; *fly off the* ~ F platzen vor Wut; **2.** anfassen; handhaben; behandeln; umgehen mit; **'~-bar** Lenkstange *f e-s Fahrrades*; *dropped* ~ *Fahrrad*: Rennlenker *m*.

hand...: **'~·loom** Handwebstuhl *m*; **'~-lug·gage** Handgepäck *n*; **'~-'made** von Hand gemacht; ~ *paper* handgeschöpftes Büttenpapier *n*; **'~-maid(·en)** *fig.* Magd *f*; **'~-me-downs** *Am.* F *pl.* fertige *od.* getragene Kleider *n/pl.*; **'~-or·gan** Drehorgel *f*; **'~-out** F Almosen *n*; Presseerklärung *f*; **'~-rail** Geländer *n*; **'~·saw** Handsäge *f*, Fuchsschwanz *m*; **hand·sel** ['hænsəl] Neujahrsgeschenk *n*; Handgeld *n*; Vorgeschmack *m*; **hand·shake** ['hændʃeik] Händedruck *m*; **hand·some** □ ['hænsəm] ansehnlich, stattlich; schön, hübsch; anständig, nobel.

hand...: **'~·work** Handarbeit *f* (*keine Maschinenarbeit*); **'~·writ·ing** Handschrift *f*; **'hand·y** □ geschickt; handlich; zur Hand, nahe; ~ *man* Gelegenheitsarbeiter *m*; Faktotum *n*.

hang [hæŋ] **1.** (*irr.*) *v/t.* hängen; auf-, einhängen; verhängen (*with* mit); (*pret. u. p.p. mst* ~*ed*) (er-) hängen; hängen lassen; *Tapete* ankleben; *I'll be* ~*ed if* ... F ich lasse mich hängen, wenn ...; ~ *it!* F hol's der Henker!; ~ *fire* auf sich warten lassen; ~ *out* (hin)aushängen; ~ *up* aufhängen; an den Nagel hängen; *fig.* verschieben; *v/i.* hängen (*on* an *dat.*); schweben; sich neigen; ~ *about* herumlungern; sich an *j.* hängen; ~ *back* sich zurückhalten, zögern; ~ *on* sich klammern an (*acc.*); *fig.* hängen an (*dat.*); ~ *up* den (Telefon)Hörer auflegen; ~ *by a hair*, ~ *by a single thread fig.* an einem Haar hängen; *let things go* ~ F sich um nichts kümmern; **2.** Hang *m*; Fall *m e-r Gardine etc.*; F Wesen *n*; *get the* ~ *of s.th.* F den Dreh von et. rauskriegen; *I don't care a* ~ *sl.* es ist mir Wurst.

hang·ar ['hæŋə] Flugzeughalle *f*.

hang·dog ['hæŋdɔg] **1.** Galgenstrick *m*; **2.** Armesünder...

hang·er ['hæŋə] Aufhänger *m*; Hirschfänger *m*; Waldhang *m*; Kesselhaken *m*; '~-'**on** *contp. fig.* Klette *f*, Schmarotzer *m*.

hang-glid·ing ['hæŋglaidiŋ] Drachenfliegen *n*.

hang·ing ['hæŋiŋ] Hänge...; ~ *committee Kunst*: Hängekommission *f*; '**hang·ings** *pl. Wand- etc.* Behang *m*; Tapeten *f/pl.*

hang·man ['hæŋmən] Henker *m*.

hang-nail ⚕ ['hæŋneil] Niednagel *m*.

hang·out F ['hæŋ'aut] Aufenthaltsort *m*, Treffpunkt *m*; Bumslokal *n*.

hang-over ['hæŋəuvə] *sl.* Katzenjammer *m*, Kater *m*; *Am.* Überbleibsel *n*.

hang·up *sl.* ['hæŋʌp] Komplex *m*, Hemmung *f*.

hank [hæŋk] Docke *f*, Strähne *f*.

han·ker ['hæŋkə] sich sehnen, verlangen (*after, for* nach); '**han·ker·ing** Verlangen *n*.

han·kie, han·ky F ['hæŋki] Taschentuch *n*.

han·ky-pan·ky F ['hæŋki'pæŋki] Hokuspokus *m*; Gaunerei *f*.

Han·o·ve·ri·an [hænəu'viəriən] **1.** hannover(i)sch; **2.** Hannoveraner (-in).

Han·sard ['hænsɑ:d] amtlicher Parlamentsbericht *m*.

Hanse [hæns]: *the* ~ *hist.* die Hanse; **Han·se·at·ic** [hænsi'ætik] hanseatisch.

han·sel ['hænsəl] = *handsel*.

han·som ['hænsəm] *a.* ~-*cab* zweirädrige Droschke *f*.

hap ⚒ [hæp] Zufall *m*; Glück *n*; **hap'haz·ard 1.** Zufall *m*; *at* ~ aufs Geratewohl; **2.** zufällig; wahllos; '**hap·less** □ unglücklich; '**hap·ly** † zufällig, vielleicht.

ha'p'orth F ['heipəθ] = *halfpennyworth*.

hap·pen ['hæpən] sich ereignen, geschehen, vorkommen; *he* ~*ed to be at home* er war zufällig zu Hause; ~ *on*, ~ *upon* zufällig treffen auf (*acc.*); ~ *in Am.* F hereingeschneit kommen; '**hap·pen·ing** Ereignis *n*.

hap·pi·ly ['hæpili] glücklicherweise.

hap·pi·ness ['hæpinis] Glück(seligkeit *f*) *n*; Gewandtheit *f im Ausdruck*.

hap·py □ ['hæpi] *allg.* glücklich; glückselig; geschickt, treffend (*Ausdruck*); F angeheitert; '~-**go**-'**luck·y** F unbekümmert.

ha·rangue [hə'ræŋ] **1.** Ansprache *f*, Rede *f*; **2.** *v/t.* feierlich anreden; *v/i.* eine Ansprache halten.

har·ass ['hærəs] fortwährend belästigen, quälen, beunruhigen; '**har·ass·ment** Schikanierung *f*, fortwährende Belästigung *f*.

har·bin·ger ['hɑ:bindʒə] **1.** Vorbote *m*; **2.** ankündigen.

har·bo(u)r ['hɑ:bə] **1.** Hafen *m*; Zufluchtsort *m*; **2.** (be)herbergen; Unterschlupf gewähren (*dat.*); *Rachegedanken etc.* hegen; ankern; '**har·bo(u)r·age** Herberge *f*; Zuflucht *f*; **har·bo(u)r dues** ⚓ *pl.* Hafengebühren *f/pl.*

hard [hɑ:d] **1.** *adj. allg.* hart; schwer, schwierig; kräftig; schwer (zu ertragend), mühselig; streng; abgehärtet, ausdauernd; fleißig; heftig; *gr.* als Verschlußlaut ausgesprochen (*c u. g*); *bsd. Am.* hochprozentig (*von Alkohol*); *the* ~ *facts pl.* die nackten Tatsachen *f/pl.*; ~ *of hearing* schwerhörig; ~ *to deal with* schwer zu behandeln(d), schwierig; *be* ~ (*up*)*on s.o.* j-m hart zusetzen; mit j-m streng sein; *give s.o. a* ~ *time* j-m das Leben schwer machen; **2.** *adv.* heftig, stark; fleißig, tüchtig; mit Mühe, mühselig, schwer; ~ *by* nahe bei; ~ *up* in Not *od.* Verlegenheit (*for* um); *be* ~ *put to it* es sich sauer werden lassen; *ride* ~ scharf reiten; **3.** F Zwangsarbeit *f*; ~*s pl.* Nöte *f/pl.*; ~ **and fast** starr (*Regel*); '~-**back** Buch *n* mit festem Einband; '~-'**bit·ten** verbissen; '~·**board** Preßspanplatte(n *pl.*) *f*; '~-'**boiled** hartgesotten, kaltschnäuzig; *bsd. Am.* gerissen; ~ **cash** Bargeld *n*; klingende Münze *f*; ~ **core** Schotter *m*; *fig.* harter Kern *m*; '~-**cov·er** = *hard-back*; ~ **cur·ren·cy** harte Währung *f*; ~ **drinks** *pl.* harte Getränke *n/pl.* (*stark alkoholisch*); '**hard·en** härten; hart machen *od.* werden; (sich) abhärten; *fig.* (sich) verhärten; † sich festigen (*Preise*); '**hard·en·ing** (Ver-) Härtung *f*; ~ *of the arteries* ⚕ Arterienverkalkung *f*.

hard...: '~-'**fea·tured** mit harten Zügen; '~-'**fist·ed** geizig; ~ **hat** Schutzhelm *m*; *fig.* Bauarbeiter *m*; Melone *f* (*Hut*); *fig.* Reaktionär *m*; '~-'**head·ed** nüchtern *od.* praktisch denkend; '~-'**heart·ed** □ hartherzig.

har·di·hood ['hɑːdihud] Kühnheit *f*; '**har·di·ness** Widerstandsfähigkeit *f*, Härte *f*; ⚔ Kühnheit *f*.

hard·ly ['hɑːdli] kaum; streng; mit Mühe; **hard line** *pol.* harter Kurs *m*; ~*s pl.* F Pech *n*; **hard-'lin·er** *pol.* Verfechter *m* e-s harten Kurses; '**hard-'mouthed** hartmäulig (*Pferd*); '**hard·ness** Härte *f* (*a. fig.*); Strenge *f*; Schwierigkeit *f*; Not *f*.

hard...: '~·**pan** *Am.* harter Boden *m*, *fig.* Grundlage *f*; ~ **sell** aggressive Verkaufsmethode *f*; '~-'**set** in Not; starr; '~·**shell** hartschalig; *fig.* starr; '**hard·ship** Ungemach *n*; Mühsal *f*; Bedrängnis *f*, Not *f*; Härte *f*; **hard shoul·der** *mot.* Standspur *f*; '**hard·ware** Eisenwaren *f/pl.*; *Computer*: Hardware *f*, Maschinenausrüstung *f*; '**hard·wood** Hartholz(baum *m*) *n*; '**hard-work·ing** fleißig.

har·dy □ ['hɑːdi] mutig, kühn; widerstandsfähig, hart; abgehärtet; winterfest (*Pflanze*).

hare [hɛə] Hase *m*; ~ **and hounds** Schnitzeljagd *f*; '~·**bell** Glockenblume *f*; '~-**brained** zerfahren, gedankenlos; '~'**lip** ⚕ Hasenscharte *f*.

ha·rem ['hɛərəm] Harem *m*.

har·i·cot ['hærikəu] Hammelragout *n*; *a.* ~ *bean* weiße Bohne *f*.

hark [hɑːk] horchen (*to* auf *acc.*); ~! horch!; ~ *back hunt.* auf der Fährte zurückgehen; *fig.* zurückkommen (*to* auf *acc.*); '**hark·en** = *hearken*.

har·lot ['hɑːlət] Hure *f*; '**har·lot·ry** Hurerei *f*.

harm [hɑːm] **1.** Schaden *m*; Unrecht *n*, Böse *n*; *out of ~'s way* in Sicherheit; **2.** beschädigen, verletzen; schaden, Leid zufügen (*dat.*); **harm·ful** □ ['~ful] schädlich; '**harm·less** □ arg-, harmlos; unschädlich.

har·mon·ic [hɑː'mɔnik] (~*ally*) harmonisch; **har'mon·i·ca** ♪ [~kə] Mundharmonika *f*; **har·mo·ni·ous** □ [hɑː'məunjəs] harmonisch (*a. fig.*); **har·monize** ['hɑːmənaiz] *v/t.* harmonisieren, in Einklang bringen; *v/i.* harmonieren, übereinstimmen; '**har·mo·ny** Harmonie *f*, Übereinstimmung *f*.

har·ness ['hɑːnis] **1.** Harnisch *m*; *Zug*-Geschirr *n*; *die in ~* in den Sielen sterben; **2.** anschirren; bändigen; *Wasserkraft* nutzbar machen.

harp ♪ [hɑːp] **1.** Harfe *f*; **2.** (auf der) Harfe spielen; ~ *(up)on* herumreiten auf (*dat.*); *be always ~ing on the same string* immer die alte Leier anstimmen; '**harp·er,** '**harp·ist** Harfenist(in); Harfner(in).

har·poon [hɑː'puːn] **1.** Harpune *f*; **2.** harpunieren.

harp·si·chord ♪ ['hɑːpsikɔːd] Cembalo *n*.

har·py ['hɑːpi] *Sage*: Harpyie *f*; *fig.* Blutsauger *m*.

har·ri·dan ['hæridən] alte Vettel *f*.

har·ri·er *hunt.* ['hæriə] Hasenhund *m*.

har·row ⚒ ['hærəu] **1.** Egge *f*; **2.** eggen; *fig.* quälen, martern; ~*ing* erschütternd.

har·ry ['hæri] plündern, verheeren; quälen, martern.

harsh □ [hɑːʃ] rauh; herb; grell (*Ton, Farbe etc.*); hart, streng; schroff; barsch; '**harsh·ness** Rauheit *f*; Herbheit *f*; Strenge *f*.

hart *zo.* [hɑːt] Hirsch *m*; **harts·horn** ⚗ ['hɑːtshɔːn] Hirschhorn *n*.

har·um-scar·um F ['hɛərəm'skɛərəm] **1.** zerfahren, fahrig; leichtsinnig; wild; **2.** Springinsfeld *m*; Wirrkopf *m*.

har·vest ['hɑːvist] **1.** Ernte(zeit) *f*; Ertrag *m*; ~ *festival*, ~ *thanksgiving* Erntedankfest *n*; **2.** ernten; *Ernte* einbringen; '**har·vest·er** Schnitter(in); Mähmaschine *f*; '**har·vest-'home** Erntefest *n*.

has [hæz, həz] *er, sie, es* hat; '~-**been** F Ehemalige *m, f, n*; Gestrige *m, f, n*.

hash[1] [hæʃ] **1.** gehacktes Fleisch *n*; *Am.* F Essen *n*, Fraß *m*; *fig.* Mischmasch *m*; *make a ~ of* F *et.* verpfuschen; *settle s.o.'s ~* F es j-m besorgen; **2.** (zer)hacken.

hash[2] F [~] Hasch(isch) *n*.

hash·ish ['hæʃi:ʃ] Haschisch *n.*
hasp [hɑ:sp] **1.** Haspe *f*; Spange *f*; **2.** zuhaken.
has·sle F ['hæsl] Auseinandersetzung *f*; *fig.* Theater *n*, Zirkus *m.*
has·sock ['hæsək] Grasbüschel *n*, -polster *n*; *eccl.* Kniekissen *n.*
hast † [hæst] *du* hast.
haste [heist] Eile *f*; Hast *f*; *make* ~ (sich be)eilen; *more* ~ *less speed*, *make* ~ *slowly* Eile mit Weile; **has·ten** ['heisn] (sich be)eilen, *j.* antreiben; *et.* beschleunigen; **hast·i·ness** ['heistinis] Hastigkeit *f*, Übereilung *f*; Hitze *f*, Eifer *m*; '**hast·y** □ eilig, hastig; voreilig; hitzig, heftig.
hat [hæt] Hut *m*; *my* ~! *sl.* na, ich danke!; *hang up one's* ~ F sich häuslich niederlassen; *talk through one's* ~ phantasieren, Unsinn reden.
hatch[1] [hætʃ] **1.** Brut *f*, Hecke *f*; Halbtür *f*; ⚓, ✈ Luke *f*; Durchreiche *f*; *under* ~*es* unter Deck; **2.** (aus)brüten (*a. fig.*); aushecken.
hatch[2] [~] schraffieren.
hatch·back *mot.* ['hætʃbæk] (Wagen *m* mit) Heckklappe *f.*
hatch·er·y ['hætʃəri] Brutplatz *m* *bsd. für Fische.*
hatch·et ['hætʃit] Beil *n*; *bury the* ~ das Kriegsbeil begraben; '**~-face** scharfgeschnittenes Gesicht *n.*
hatch·way ⚓ ['hætʃwei] Luke *f.*
hate [heit] **1.** *poet.* Haß *m* (*to, towards* gegen, auf *acc.*); **2.** hassen; nicht mögen; F bedauern; **hate·ful** □ ['~ful] verhaßt; hassenswert; abscheulich; '**hat·er** Hasser(in).
hath † [hæθ] *er, sie, es* hat.
ha·tred ['heitrid] Haß *m*, Groll *m* (*of* gegen).
hat·ter ['hætə] Hutmacher *m*; *as mad as a* ~ völlig verrückt.
haugh·ti·ness ['hɔ:tinis] Stolz *m*; Hochmut *m*; '**haugh·ty** □ stolz; hochmütig.
haul [hɔ:l] **1.** Ziehen *n*; (Fisch)Zug *m*; Fang *m*, Beute *f*; *Am.* Transportweg *m*; *long* ~ (*a. fig.*) weiter Weg *m*; Durststrecke *f*; **2.** ziehen (*at* an *dat.*); ⚓ holen; schleppen; transportieren; ⚒ fördern; umspringen (*Wind*); ⚓ abdrehen; ~ *down one's flag* die Flagge streichen; *fig.* sich geschlagen geben; '**haul·age** Schleppen *n*; Transport (-kosten *pl.*) *m*; ⚒ Förderung *f*; **haul·ier** ['~jə] Transportunternehmer *m.*
haulm [hɔ:m] *Pflanzen*-Stengel *m*; *Bohnen- etc.* Stroh *n.*
haunch [hɔ:ntʃ] Hüfte *f*; Keule *f* *von Wild.*
haunt [hɔ:nt] **1.** Aufenthaltsort *m*; Schlupfwinkel *m*; **2.** oft besuchen; heimsuchen; verfolgen; plagen, beunruhigen; spuken in (*dat.*); *the house is* ~*ed* in dem Hause spukt es; '**haunt·er** häufige Besucher(in), Stammgast *m.*
haut·boy ♪ ['əubɔi] Oboe *f.*
hau·teur [əu'tə:] Hochmut *m.*
Ha·van·a [hə'vænə] *a.* ~ *cigar* Havanna(zigarre) *f.*
have [hæv, həv] **1.** (*irr.*) *v/t.* haben, besitzen; bekommen; *Mahlzeit* einnehmen; lassen; ~ *to do* tun müssen; *I* ~ *my hair cut* ich lasse mir das Haar schneiden; *he had his leg broken* er brach sich das Bein; *I would* ~ *you know* ich möchte, daß Sie wissen; *he will* ~ *it that …* er behauptet, daß …; *I had as well …* es wäre ebenso gut, wenn ich …; *I had better* (*best*) *go* es wäre besser (am besten), wenn ich ginge; *I had rather go* ich möchte lieber gehen; *let s.o.* ~ *it* es j-m besorgen; ~ *about one* bei *od.* an sich haben; ~ *at him!* auf ihn!; ~ *on* anhaben; *fig.* vorhaben; ~ *it out with* sich auseinandersetzen mit; ~ *s.o. up* F j. 'rankriegen (*verklagen*; *for* wegen); **2.** *v/aux.* haben; sein; ~ *come* gekommen sein; **3.** Besitzende *m*; F Schwindel *m*, Betrug *m.*
ha·ven ['heivn] Hafen *m* (*a. fig.*); Zufluchtsort *m.*
have-not ['hævnɔt] Habenichts *m.*
haven't ['hævnt] = *have not.*
hav·er·sack ['hævəsæk] ⚔ Brotbeutel *m*; Rucksack *m.*
hav·ing ['hæviŋ] *oft* ~*s pl.* Habe *f*, Besitz *m.*
hav·oc ['hævək] Verwüstung *f*, Verheerung *f*; *make* ~ *of*, *play* ~ *with* *od. among* verwüsten, verheeren; übel zurichten.
haw[1] ⚘ [hɔ:] Hagebutte *f.*
haw[2] [~] **1.** sich räuspern; stottern; **2.** Räuspern *n.*
Ha·wai·ian [hɑ:'waiiən] **1.** hawaiisch; **2.** Hawaiier(in).
haw·finch *orn.* ['hɔ:fintʃ] Kernbeißer *m.*
haw-haw ['hɔ:'hɔ:] laut lachen.

hawk[1] [hɔːk] **1.** *orn.* Habicht *m* (*a. fig.*); Falke *m*; **2.** Jagd machen (*at* auf *acc.*).
hawk[2] [~] sich räuspern.
hawk[3] [~] verhökern, hausieren mit; **hawk·er** [ˈhɔːkə] Hausierer *m*, Straßenhändler *m*.
hawk-eyed [ˈhɔːkaid] scharfäugig; ˈ**hawk·ing** Falkenbeize *f*.
hawse ⚓ [hɔːz] *a.* ~*-hole* Klüse *f*.
haw·ser ⚓ [ˈhɔːzə] Kabeltau *n*, Trosse *f*.
haw·thorn ⚘ [ˈhɔːθɔːn] Hagedorn *m*.
hay [hei] **1.** Heu *n*; *make* ~ *of* durcheinanderwerfen; **2.** heuen; ˈ**~-box** *a.* ~ *cooker* Kochkiste *f*; ˈ**~·cock** Heuhaufen *m*; ˈ**~·fe·ver** ⚕ Heuschnupfen *m*; ˈ**~·loft** Heuboden *m*; ˈ**~·mak·er** *sl.* K.-o.-Schlag *m*; ˈ**~·rick** = *haycock*; ˈ**~-seed** *bsd. Am.* F Bauerntölpel *m*; ˈ**~·stack** = *haycock*; ˈ**~·wire:** *go* ~ drunter u. drüber gehen, durcheinandergeraten; überschnappen.
haz·ard [ˈhæzəd] **1.** Zufall *m*; Gefahr *f*, Wagnis *n*; Hasard(spiel) *n*; *run a* ~ et. riskieren; **2.** wagen, aufs Spiel setzen; ˈ**haz·ard·ous** □ gewagt, gefährlich.
haze[1] [heiz] Dunst *m*; *fig.* Unklarheit *f*, Verwirrtheit *f*.
haze[2] ⚓ *u. Am.* [~] schinden; schurigeln.
ha·zel [ˈheizl] **1.** ⚘ Hasel(staude) *f*; **2.** nußbraun; ˈ**~-nut** Haselnuß *f*.
ha·zy □ [ˈheizi] dunstig, diesig; *fig.* nebelhaft, verschwommen; unklar; *be* ~ im unklaren sein.
H-bomb ⚔ [ˈeitʃbɔm] H-Bombe *f*, Wasserstoffbombe *f*.
he [hiː; hi] **1.** er; ~ *who* derjenige, welcher; wer; **2.** *in Zssgn*: ...männchen *n*; ...bock *m*, ...hahn *m*.
head [hed] **1.** *allg.* Kopf *m* (*fig. Verstand, Geist, Wille*); Haupt *n*; *nach Zahlwort*: Mann *m* (*pl.*), Stück *n* (*pl.*); *fig.* Haupt *n*, Führer *m*; Leiter(in), Vorsteher(in); Chef *m*; Direktor *m*; Häuptling *m*; *Nagel-, Noten-, Seiten-, Kohl- etc.* Kopf *m*; Kopfende *n e-s Bettes, Tisches etc.*; Kopfseite *f e-r Münze*; Spitze *f e-s Berges, Geschwürs, Zuges etc.*; Schaum *m auf Bier*; *Baum*-Krone *f*; Quelle *f*; *Schiffs*-Vorderteil *n*; Vorgebirge *n*; Kopf(haar *n*) *m*; Geweih *n*; Höhe *f*, Krisis *f e-r Krankheit*; Hauptpunkt *m*; Abschnitt *m*, Kapitel *n*; Rubrik *f*; Posten *m in Rechnungen*; Überschrift *f*; ~ *and shoulders above the rest* allen haushoch überlegen; *bring to a* ~ zur Entscheidung *od.* zum Klappen bringen; *come to a* ~ aufbrechen, eitern (*Geschwür*); sich zuspitzen, zur Entscheidung kommen (*Lage etc.*); *gather* ~ überhandnehmen; zu Kräften kommen; *get it into one's* ~ *that ...* es sich in den Kopf setzen, daß; *keep one's* ~ den Kopf nicht verlieren; ~*(s) or tail(s)?* Zahl oder Wappen?; ~ *over heels* Hals über Kopf; *over* ~ *and ears* bis über die Ohren; *I can't make* ~ *or tail of it* ich kann daraus nicht klug werden; *take the* ~ die Führung übernehmen; **2.** erst; vornehmst; Ober...; Haupt...; **3.** *v/t.* (an)führen; an der Spitze von *et.* stehen, leiten; vorausgehen (*dat.*); mit e-m Kopf versehen; *Kapitel* überschreiben; *Fußball*: köpfen; *be* ~*ed* sich *in e-r Richtung* bewegen; ~ *off* ablenken; *v/i.* ⚓ Kurs halten, zusteuern (*for* auf *acc.*); *Am.* entspringen (*Fluß*); ˈ**head·ache** Kopfweh *n*, -schmerz(en *pl.*) *m* (*a. fig.*); ˈ**head·ach·y** an Kopfweh leidend; Kopfweh verursachend; ˈ**head·band** Stirnband *n*; ˈ**head-boy** Schulsprecher *m*; ˈ**head-dress** Kopfputz *m*, -schmuck *m*; Frisur *f*; ˈ**head·ed** ...köpfig; ˈ**head·er** ⚠ Bindestein *m*; F Kopfsprung *m*; ˈ**head-gear** Kopfbedeckung *f*; Zaumzeug *n*; ˈ**head-girl** Schulsprecherin *f*; ˈ**head-hunt·er** Kopfjäger *m*; ˈ**head·i·ness** Ungestüm *n*; Starrsinn *m*; berauschende Wirkung *f*; ˈ**head·ing** Titelkopf *m*, Rubrik *f*; Überschrift *f*, Titel *m*; Briefkopf *m*; *Sport*: Kopfball *m*; ˈ**head·land** Vorgebirge *n*; ˈ**head·less** kopflos (*a. fig.*); ohne Führer.
head...: ˈ**~·light** *mot.* Scheinwerfer (-licht *n*) *m*; ˈ**~·line** Überschrift *f*; Schlagzeile *f*; ~*s pl. Radio*: *das* Wichtigste in Kürze; *he hits the* ~*s* F er liefert Schlagzeilen; ˈ**~·long 1.** *adj.* ungestüm; unbesonnen, übereilt; **2.** *adv.* kopfüber; ˈ**~ˈman** Vorsteher *m*; Häuptling *m*; Vorarbeiter *m*; ˈ**~ˈmas·ter** Direktor *m e-r Schule*; ˈ**~ˈmis·tress** Direktorin *f*; ˈ**~·most** vorderst; ˈ**~-ˈon**

mit dem Kopf(ende) voran; Frontal...; ~ *collision* Frontalzusammenstoß *m*; '~-**phone** *Radio*: Kopfhörer *m*; '~-**piece** Helm *m*; F Grips *m*, Verstand *m*; *typ*. Titelvignette *f*; '~'**quar·ters** *pl*. ⚔ Hauptquartier *n*; Zentral(stell)e *f*; '~·**rest** Kopfstütze *f*; ~ **re·straint** *mot*. Kopfstütze *f*; '~-**room** lichte Höhe *f*; '~-**set** *Radio*: Kopfhörer *m/pl*.; '**head·ship** Direktorenstelle *f*; '**head·shrink·er** *iro*. Psychiater *m*; Psychoanalytiker *m*; '**heads·man** Scharfrichter *m*.

head...: ~ **start** *Sport*: Vorsprung *m*; '~·**stone** Grabstein *m*; '~·**strong** halsstarrig; '~·**wa·ters** *pl*. Quellgebiet *n*; '~·**way** Fortschritt(e *pl*.) *m*; *make* ~ vorwärtskommen, Fortschritte machen; '~·**wind** Gegenwind *m*; '~·**word** Stichwort *n e-s Wörterbuchs*; '~·**work** Kopfarbeit *f*; '**head·y** □ ungestüm; voreilig; heftig; zu Kopf steigend (*Getränk*).

heal [hi:l] heilen (*of* von); ~ *up* zuheilen; '~-**all** Allheilmittel *n*; '**heal·er** Heilpraktiker *m*; Heilmittel *n*; *time is a great* ~ die Zeit heilt alle Wunden; '**heal·ing** **1.** □ Heil...; heilsam; heilend; **2.** Heilung *f*.

health [helθ] Gesundheit *f* (*a. beim Zutrinken*); *Ministry of* ♀ Gesundheitsministerium *n*; ~ **food**(**s** *pl*.) Reformkost *f*; ~ *shop*, *Am*. ~ *store* Reformhaus *n*; **health·ful** □ ['~ful] gesund; heilsam; **health haz·ard** Gesundheitsrisiko *n*; '**health·i·ness** Gesundheit *f*; '**health-re·sort** Kurort *m*; **health serv·ice** Gesundheitsdienst *m*; '**health·y** □ gesund.

heap [hi:p] **1.** Haufe(n) *m*; F Menge *f*, Masse *f*; *all of a* ~ auf einen Schlag; *struck od. knocked all of a* ~ sprachlos; **2.** *a*. ~ *up* (auf)häufen; überhäufen.

hear [hiə] (*irr*.) hören; erfahren; an-, zuhören; erhören; *Zeugen* verhören; *Lektion* abhören; ~ *s.o. out* j. ausreden lassen; **heard** [hə:d] *pret. u. p.p. von hear*; **hear·er** ['hiərə] Hörer *m*, Zuhörer(in); '**hear·ing** Gehör *n*; Audienz *f*; ⚖ Verhör *n*; öffentliche Informationssitzung *f*, Anhörung *f*; Hörweite *f*; ~ *aid* Hörgerät *n*; **heark·en** ['hɑ:kən] horchen; hören (*to* auf *acc*.); **hear·say** ['hiəsei] Hörensagen *n*.

hearse [hə:s] Leichenwagen *m*.

heart [hɑ:t] *allg*. Herz *n* (*fig*. = *Mut, Erbarmen etc*.); Innere *n*; Wesentlichste *n*, Kern *m*; *Karten*: Herz *n*, Coeur *n*; *a. dear* ~ Liebling *m*, Schatz *m*; ~ *and soul* mit Leib und Seele; *change of* ~ Gesinnungswandel *m*; *at* ~ im Inneren *od*. Herzen; *I have a matter at* ~ et. liegt mir am Herzen; *by* ~ auswendig; *for one's* ~ ums Leben gern; *in good* ~ in gutem Zustand (*Boden*); *in his* ~ (*of* ~*s*) im Grunde seines Herzens; *out of* ~ mutlos; in schlechtem Zustand; *speak from one's* ~ frisch von der Leber weg sprechen; *cross my* ~ Hand aufs Herz!; *cut to the* ~ aufs tiefste verletzen; *with all my* ~ von ganzem Herzen; *lose* ~ den Mut verlieren; *take* ~ sich ein Herz fassen; *take od. lay to* ~ sich *et*. zu Herzen nehmen; '~·**ache** Kummer *m*; '~-**beat** Herzschlag *m*; '~-**break** Herzeleid *n*; '~-**break·ing** □ herzzerbrechend, -zerreißend; '~-**bro·ken** gebrochenen Herzens; '~·**burn** Sodbrennen *n*; '~-**burn·ing** Groll *m*, Neid *m*; '~-**com·plaint**, '~-**dis·ease** Herzleiden *n*; '**heart·ed** ...herzig; '**heart·en** ermutigen, ermuntern; '**heart-fail·ure** Herzversagen *n*; '**heart·felt** innig, tief empfunden.

hearth [hɑ:θ] Herd *m* (*a. fig*.); '~-**rug** Kaminvorleger *m*; '~-**stone** Kaminplatte *f*.

heart·i·ness ['hɑ:tinis] Herzlichkeit *f*; Herzhaftigkeit *f etc*. (*s. hearty*); '**heart·less** □ herzlos; '**heart·rend·ing** herzzerreißend.

heart...: '~'**s·ease** ⚘ Stiefmütterchen *n*; '~-**sick** *fig*. krank im Herzen; verzagt; '~-**strings** *pl. fig*. Herz *n*, innerste Gefühle *n/pl*.; '~·**throb** F Schwarm *m*; ~ **trans·plant** Herzverpflanzung *f*; '~-**whole** nicht verliebt, frei; aufrichtig, herzlich; '**heart·y** **1.** □ herzlich; aufrichtig; gesund; kräftig, herzhaft; ~ *eater* tüchtiger Esser *m*; **2.** ⚓ Matrose *m*; *univ*. Sportler *m*.

heat [hi:t] **1.** *allg*. Hitze *f*; Wärme *f* (*bsd. phys*.); Eifer *m*; Zorn *m*; *Sport*: Gang *m*, einzelner Lauf *m*; Läufigkeit *f von Tieren*; *dead* ~ totes *od*. unentschiedenes Rennen *n*; **2.** heizen; (sich) erhitzen *od*. erwärmen (*a. fig*.); heiß werden; '**heat·ed** □ hitzig; '**heat·er** ⊕ Erhitzer *m*; Ofen *m*; '**heat-flash**

Hitzestrahlung *f e-r Atombomben-explosion.*
heath [hi:θ] Heide *f*; ⚘ Heidekraut *n*; '**~-cock** Birkhahn *m.*
hea·then ['hi:ðən] **1.** Heide *m*, Heidin *f*; **2.** heidnisch; '**hea·then·dom** Heidentum *n*; '**hea·then·ish** □ *mst fig.* heidnisch; roh; '**hea·then·ism** Heidentum *n*; Roheit *f.*
heath·er ⚘ ['heðə] Heide *f*; Heidekraut *n*; '**~-bell** ⚘ Glockenheide *f.*
heat·ing ['hi:tiŋ] Heizung *f*; *attr.* Heiz...; ~ battery Heizbatterie *f*; ~ pad Heizkissen *n.*
heat...: ~ **light·ning** *Am.* Wetterleuchten *n*; '**~-re·sist·ant** hitzebeständig; '**~-stroke** Hitzschlag *m*; ~ **treat·ment** ⚕ Wärmebehandlung *f*; '**~-val·ue** Heizwert *m*; '**~-wave** Hitzewelle *f.*
heave [hi:v] **1.** Heben *n*; Schwellen *n der Brust etc.*; Übelkeit *f*; **2.** (*irr.*) *v/t.* heben, hieven; schwellen; *Seufzer* ausstoßen; ~ the anchor den Anker lichten; ~ down ⚓ kielholen; ~ out auswerfen; *v/i.* sich heben und senken, wogen, schwellen (*Brust, Wellen*); sich übergeben wollen; ~ for breath keuchen; ~ in sight ⚓ in Sicht kommen; ~ to ⚓ beidrehen.
heav·en ['hevn] Himmel *m*; ~s *pl. der* sichtbare Himmel; move ~ and earth Himmel u. Hölle in Bewegung setzen; '**heav·en·ly** himmlisch (*a. fig.*); **heav·en·ward**(s) ['~wəd(z)] himmelwärts.
heav·er ['hi:və] Hebebaum *m*; Ablader *m.*
heav·i·ness ['hevinis] Schwere *f*, Gewicht *n*, Druck *m* (*a. fig.*); Schwerfälligkeit *f*; Schwermut *f.*
heav·y □ ['hevi] *allg.* schwer; schwermütig; schwerfällig; schläfrig; trüb; drückend; heftig (*Regen etc.*); schwer (*Speise*); unwegsam, schmierig (*Straße*); ⚔ schwer(bewaffnet); Schwer...; ~ **cur·rent** ⚡ Starkstrom *m*; '**~-'du·ty** strapazierfähig; Hochleistungs...; '**~-'go·ing** schwierig, anstrengend; '**~-'hand·ed** ungeschickt; '**~-'heart·ed** niedergeschlagen; '**~-'lad·en** schwerbeladen; *fig.* bedrückt; '**~-weight** *Boxen*: Schwergewicht *n.*
heb·dom·a·dal □ [heb'dɔmədl] wöchentlich.
He·bra·ic [hi'breiik] (~ally) hebräisch.
He·brew ['hi:bru:] **1.** hebräisch; **2.** Hebräer *m*; Hebräisch *n.*
hec·a·tomb ['hekətu:m] Hekatombe *f* (*Massenopfer*).
heck·le ['hekl] durch Zwischenfragen in die Enge treiben; '**heck·ler** Zwischenrufer *m*, Störenfried *m.*
hec·tic ⚕ ['hektik] **1.** hektisch (*auszehrend*; *schwindsüchtig*; *sl. fieberhaft erregt*); **2.** hektische Röte *f*; *mst* ~ fever hektisches Fieber *n.*
hec·tor ['hektə] *v/t.* einschüchtern, anmaßend behandeln; *v/i.* großtun, prahlen, renommieren.
hedge [hedʒ] **1.** Hecke *f*; *fig.* Mauer *f*; **2.** *v/t.* einhegen, einzäunen; umgeben; ~ off abzäunen; ~ up sperren; ~ a bet auf beide Möglichkeiten wetten; *v/i.* sich decken; sich nicht festlegen, ausweichen; '**~·hog** *zo.* Igel *m*; *Am.* Stachelschwein *n*; '**~-hop** *sl.* ✈ tieffliegen; '**~·row** Hecke *f*; '**~-spar·row** *orn.* Heckenbraunelle *f.*
heed [hi:d] **1.** Beachtung *f*, Aufmerksamkeit *f*; take ~ of, give *od.* pay ~ to achtgeben auf (*acc.*), beachten; **2.** beachten, achten auf (*acc.*); **heed·ful** □ ['~ful] achtsam (of auf *acc.*); '**heed·less** □ unachtsam; unbekümmert (of um).
hee-haw ['hi:'hɔ:] **1.** Iah *n* (*Eselsschrei*); *fig.* Gewieher *n*; **2.** iahen; *fig.* wiehern (*laut lachen*).
heel[1] ⚓ [hi:l] (sich) auf die Seite legen, überholen, krängen.
heel[2] [~] **1.** Ferse *f*; Hacken *m*, Absatz *m*; letzter Teil *m*, Ende *n*; *bsd. Am. sl.* Lump *m*; ~s *pl.* F Hinterfüße *m/pl. e-s Tiers*; at *od.* on *od.* upon s.o.'s ~s j-m auf den Fersen *folgen*; down at ~ mit schiefgetretenen Absätzen; *fig.* abgerissen, schäbig; schlampig; take to one's ~s, show a clean pair of ~s Fersengeld geben, die Beine in die Hand nehmen; lay s.o. by the ~s j. einsperren; come to ~ bei Fuß gehen (*Hund*); gehorchen; **2.** mit e-m Absatz *etc.* versehen; *a.* ~ out *Fußball*: ausfersen; **heeled** *Am.* F finanzstark; '**heel·er** *Am. sl. pol.* Befehlsempfänger *m.*
heel-tap ['hi:ltæp] Neige *f im Glas*; no ~! ausgetrunken!
heft [heft] **1.** Gewicht *n*; *Am.* F Hauptteil *m*; **2.** (hoch-, an)heben; '**heft·y** F stramm, kräftig.
he·gem·o·ny *pol.* [hi:'geməni] He-

gemonie *f*, Vorherrschaft *f*.
he·goat ['hi:gəut] Ziegenbock *m*.
heif·er ['hefə] Färse *f* (*junge Kuh*).
heigh [hei] hei!, he(da)!; **~-ho** ['~'həu] ach (jeh)!
height [hait] Höhe *f*; Anhöhe *f*; Höhepunkt *m*, höchster Grad *m*; *what is your ~?* wie groß sind Sie?; '**height·en** erhöhen (*a. fig.*), höher machen; vergrößern.
hei·nous □ ['heinəs] abscheulich; verrucht; '**hei·nous·ness** Verruchtheit *f*.
heir [ɛə] Erbe *m*; *be ~ to et.* erben; *~ apparent*, *~ at law* rechtmäßiger Erbe *m*; *~ presumptive* mutmaßlicher Erbe *m*; '**heir·dom** Erbfolge *f*; Erbschaft *f*; '**heir·ess** Erbin *f*; '**heir·less** ohne Erben; **heir·loom** ['~lu:m] Erbstück *n*.
held [held] *pret. u. p.p. von hold 2.*
hel·i·bus *Am.* F ['helibʌs] Hubschrauber *m als Zubringer zum Flugplatz*.
hel·i·cal ['helikəl] spiralen-, schneckenförmig.
hel·i·cop·ter ['helikɔptə] Hubschrauber *m*.
he·li·o... ['hi:liəu] Sonnen..., Helio...; **he·li·o·graph** ['~əugrɑ:f] Heliograph *m*; Spiegeltelegraph *m*; Lichtdruck *m*; **he·li·o·trope** ['heljətrəup] ⚘ Heliotrop *n*, Sonnenwende *f*.
hel·i·pad ['helipæd] Hubschrauberlandeplatz *m*.
hel·i·port ['helipɔ:t] Hubschrauberlandeplatz *m*.
he·li·um ⚗ ['hi:ljəm] Helium *n*.
he·lix ['hi:liks], *pl. mst* **hel·i·ces** ['helisi:z] Schneckenlinie *f*; *zo.*, △ Schnecke *f*; *anat.* Ohrleiste *f*.
hell [hel] Hölle *f*; *attr.* Höllen...; *like ~* höllisch; *oh ~!* verdammt!; *go to ~* zur Hölle fahren; *what the ~ ...?* F was zum Teufel ...?; *a ~ of a noise* ein Höllenlärm *m*; *raise ~* Krach machen; *ride ~ for leather* wie der Teufel reiten; '**~-'bent** *Am. sl.* unweigerlich entschlossen; '**~-cat** *fig.* Hexe *f*.
hel·le·bore ⚘ ['helibɔ:] Nieswurz *f*.
Hel·lene ['heli:n] Hellene *m*, Grieche *m*; **Hel'len·ic** [he'li:nik] hellenisch, griechisch.
hell·ish □ ['heliʃ] höllisch.
hel·lo [he'ləu] hallo!
helm ⚓ [helm] (Steuer)Ruder *n* (*a. fig.*).
hel·met ['helmit] Helm *m*; '**hel·met·ed** behelmt.
helms·man ⚓ ['helmzmən] Steuermann *m*.
hel·ot *hist.* ['helət] Helot *m*; *fig.* Sklave *m*.
help [help] **1.** *allg.* Hilfe *f*, Beistand *m*; (Hilfs)Mittel *n*; (Dienst)Mädchen *n*; *by the ~ of* mit Hilfe (*gen.*); **2.** *v/t.* helfen (*dat.*); abhelfen (*dat.*); unterlassen; *bei Tisch* geben, reichen (*s.th.* et.; *s.o. to s.th.* j-m et.); *~ o.s.* sich bedienen, zulangen; *~ o.s. to s.th.* sich et. nehmen; *I could not ~ laughing* ich konnte nicht umhin zu lachen; *that cannot be ~ed* da läßt sich nichts ändern; *v/i.* helfen, dienen (*to* zu); '**help·er** Helfer(in), Gehilfe *m*, Gehilfin *f*; **help·ful** □ ['~ful] behilflich, hilfreich; nützlich; '**help·ing** (Essens)Portion *f*; '**help·less** □ hilflos; '**help·less·ness** Hilflosigkeit *f*; '**help·mate**, **help·meet** ['~mi:t] Gehilfe *m*, Gehilfin *f*; Gattin *f*.
hel·ter-skel·ter ['heltə'skeltə] holterdiepolter.
helve [helv] Stiel *m*, Griff *m*.
Hel·ve·tian [hel'vi:ʃjən] **1.** helvetisch; Schweizer...; **2.** Helvetier(in).
hem[1] [hem] **1.** *Kleider*-Saum *m*; **2.** säumen; *~ in* einschließen.
hem[2] [~] **1.** sich räuspern; **2.** hm!
he-man *sl.* ['hi:mæn] richtiger Mann *m*.
hem·i·sphere ['hemisfiə] Halbkugel *f*, Hemisphäre *f*.
hem-line ['hemlain] Saum *m e-s Kleides*; *lower* (*raise*) *the ~* das Kleid *etc.* länger (kürzer) machen.
hem·lock ⚘ ['hemlɔk] Schierling *m*; '**~-tree** Schierlingstanne *f*.
he·mo... ['hi:məu] *s. haemo...*
hemp [hemp] Hanf *m*; '**hemp·en** hanfen, hänfen; Hanf...
hem·stitch ['hemstitʃ] **1.** Hohlsaum *m*; **2.** mit Hohlsaum verzieren.
hen [hen] Huhn *n*, Henne *f*; *Vogel*-Weibchen *n*; *~'s egg* Hühnerei *n*.
hen·bane ['henbein] Bilsenkraut *n*.
hence [hens] *oft from ~* von hinnen, weg; hieraus, hiervon; daher, deshalb; von jetzt an; *~!* fort!, hinweg!; *a year ~* heute übers Jahr; '**~'forth**, '**~'for·ward** von nun an, fortan.

hench·man *pol.* ['hentʃmən] Gefolgsmann *m*, Handlanger *m*.
hen...: '**~-coop** Hühnerstall *m*; '**~-party** F Damengesellschaft *f*, Kaffeekränzchen *n*; '**~·pecked** unter dem Pantoffel (stehend); '**~-roost** Hühnerstange *f*.
hep *Am. sl.* [hep]: *be ~ to* kennen, eingeweiht sein in.
he·pat·ic *anat.* [hi'pætik] Leber...
hep·cat *Am. sl.* ['hepkæt] Eingeweihte *m, f*; Jazzfanatiker(in).
hep·ta... ['heptə] Sieben...; **hep·ta·gon** ['~gən] Siebeneck *n*.
her [hə:, hə] sie, ihr; ihr(e).
her·ald ['herəld] **1.** Herold *m*; **2.** (sich) ankündigen; *~ in* einführen; **he·ral·dic** [he'rældik] (*~ally*) heraldisch; **her·ald·ry** ['herəldri] Wappenkunde *f*, Heraldik *f*.
herb [hə:b] Kraut *n*; **her·ba·ceous** [~'beiʃəs] krautartig; '**herb·age** Gras *n*; Weide *f*; ⚖ Weiderecht *n*; '**herb·al 1.** Kräuter...; **2.** Kräuterbuch *n*; '**herb·al·ist** Pflanzenkenner *m*, -sammler *m*; **her·bar·i·um** [~'bɛəriəm] Herbarium *n*; **her·biv·o·rous** [~'bivərəs] pflanzenfressend; **her·bo·rize** ['~bəraiz] botanisieren.
Her·cu·le·an [hə:kju'li:ən] herkulisch, Herkules...
herd [hə:d] **1.** (*bsd.* Rinder)Herde *f* (*a. fig.*); **2.** *v/t. Vieh* hüten; *~ together* zs.-pferchen; *v/i. a. ~ together* in e-r Herde leben; zs.-hausen; '**herd·er,** '**herds·man** Hirt *m*.
here [hiə] hier; hierher; *~'s to ...!* auf das Wohl von ...!
here·a·bout(s) ['hiərəbaut(s)] hierherum; **here·aft·er** [hiər'ɑ:ftə] **1.** künftig; **2.** Zukunft *f*; *das* künftige Leben; '**here'by** hierdurch, hiermit.
he·red·i·ta·ble [hi'reditəbl] vererbbar; **her·e·dit·a·ment** ⚖ [heri'ditəmənt] Erbgut *n*; **he·red·i·tar·y** [hi'reditəri] erblich; Erb...; **he'red·i·ty** Erblichkeit *f*.
here·in ['hiər'in] hierin; **here·of** [hiər'ɔv] hiervon.
her·e·sy ['herəsi] Ketzerei *f*.
her·e·tic ['herətik] **1.** Ketzer(in); **2.** = **he·ret·i·cal** □ [hi'retikəl] ketzerisch.
here·to·fore ['hiətu'fɔ:] bis jetzt; ehemals; **here·up·on** ['hiərə'pɔn] hierauf, darauf; '**here'with** hiermit.
her·it·a·ble ['heritəbl] erbfähig; erblich; '**her·it·age** Erbschaft *f*.
her·maph·ro·dite [hə:'mæfrədait] Zwitter *m*, Hermaphrodit *m*.
her·met·ic, her·met·i·cal □ [hə:'metik(əl)] hermetisch, luftdicht.
her·mit ['hə:mit] Einsiedler *m*; '**her·mit·age** Einsiedelei *f*.
her·ni·a ⚕ ['hə:njə] Bruch *m*; '**her·ni·al** Bruch...
he·ro ['hiərəu], *pl.* **he·roes** ['~rəuz] Held *m*; **he·ro·ic** [hi'rəuik], **he'ro·i·cal** heroisch; heldenmütig, -haft; Helden...
her·o·in *pharm.* ['herəuin] Heroin *n*.
her·o·ine ['herəuin] Heldin *f*; '**her·o·ism** Heldenmut *m*, -tum *n*.
her·on *orn.* ['herən] Reiher *m*; '**her·on·ry** Reiherhorst *m*.
her·ring *ichth.* ['heriŋ] Hering *m*; '**her·ring-bone** Heringsgräte *f*; Fischgrätenmuster *n*; Fischgrätenstich *m*.
hers [hə:z] der (die, das) ihrige; ihr.
her·self [hə:'self] (sie, ihr) selbst; sich.
Hertz·i·an ⚡ ['hə:tsiən]: *~ waves* Hertzsche Wellen *f/pl*.
he's ['hi:z] = *he is*; *he has*.
hes·i·tance, hes·i·tan·cy ['hezitəns(i)] Zaudern *n*, Unschlüssigkeit *f*; **hes·i·tate** ['~teit] zögern, zaudern, unschlüssig sein (*about, over* über *acc.*); Bedenken tragen (*to inf.* zu *inf.*); **hes·i'ta·tion** Zögern *n*, Zaudern *n*; Unschlüssigkeit *f*; Bedenken *n*.
Hes·sian ['hesiən] **1.** hessisch; **2.** Hesse *m*, Hessin *f*; ♀ Rupfen *m*, Sackleinwand *f*.
het·er·o·dox ['hetərəudɔks] heterodox, irrgläubig; '**het·er·o·dox·y** Irrlehre *f*; **het·er·o·dyne** ['~dain] *Radio*: Überlagerungs...; **het·er·o·ge·ne·i·ty** [~dʒi'ni:iti] Anders-, Ungleichartigkeit *f*; **het·er·o·ge·ne·ous** □ ['~rəu'dʒi:njəs] ungleichartig, heterogen.
het up F [het'ʌp] aufgeregt.
hew [hju:] (*irr.*) hauen, hacken; ⊕ behauen; '**hew·er** Hauer *m*; ⚒ Häuer *m*; **hewn** [hju:n] *p.p. von hew*.
hex·a... ['heksə] Sechs...; **hex·a·gon** ['~gən] Sechseck *n*; **hex·ag·o·nal**

□ [hek'sægənl] sechseckig; **hex·am·e·ter** [hek'sæmitə] Hexameter *m.*
hey [hei] ei!; hei!; heda!
hey·day ['heidei] **1.** heisa!; oho!; **2.** *fig.* Höhepunkt *m*; Vollkraft *f*, Blüte *f*; Sturm *m der Leidenschaft.*
hi [hai] he!, heda!; hallo!
hi·a·tus [hai'eitəs] Lücke *f*, Spalt *m*, Kluft *f*; *gr.* Hiatus *m.*
hi·ber·nate ['haibəneit] überwintern; Winterschlaf halten; **hi·ber·'na·tion** Winterschlaf *m.*
hi·bis·cus ⚘ [hi'biskəs] Eibisch *m.*
hic·cup, *a.* **hic·cough** ['hikʌp] **1.** Schlucken *m*, Schluckauf *m*; **2.** schlucken; den Schluckauf haben.
hick F [hik] Bauer(ntölpel) *m*; *attr.* [Bauern...]
hick·o·ry ['hikəri] Hickorynußbaum *m.*
hid [hid] *pret. von hide²*; **hid·den** ['hidn] *p.p. von hide²*.
hide¹ [haid] **1.** Haut *f*, Fell *n*; **2.** F durchprügeln.
hide² [~] (*irr.*) (sich) verbergen, verstecken (*from s.o.* vor j-m); verheimlichen; '**hide-and-'seek** Versteckspiel *n*; *play (at)* ~ Versteck(en) spielen; '**hide·a·way** F Versteck *n.*
hide·bound *fig.* ['haidbaund] engherzig, -stirnig, stur.
hid·e·ous □ ['hidiəs] häßlich; abscheulich, scheußlich; schrecklich, gräßlich; '**hid·e·ous·ness** Scheußlichkeit *f.*
hide·out ['haidaut] Versteck *n.*
hid·ing¹ F ['haidiŋ] Tracht *f* Prügel.
hid·ing² [~] Verbergen *n*; *in* ~ verborgen; versteckt; flüchtig; '**~-place** Versteck *n*; Schlupfwinkel *m.*
hie *poet.* [hai] (*p.pr. hying*) eilen.
hi·er·arch·y ['haiərɑːki] Hierarchie *f*; Priesterherrschaft *f*; Rangordnung *f.*
hi·er·o·glyph ['haiərəuglif] Hieroglyphe *f*; **hi·er·o'glyph·ic**, *a.* **hi·er·o'glyph·i·cal** □ hieroglyphisch; **hi·er·o'glyph·ics** *pl.* Hieroglyphen *f/pl.* (*Bilderschrift*; *fig. Gekritzel*).
hi-fi *Am.* ['hai'fai] = *high fidelity.*
hig·gle·dy-pig·gle·dy ['higldi'pigldi] wirr durcheinander, kunterbunt.
high [hai] **1.** *adj.* □ (*s. a.* ~*ly*) *allg.* hoch; vornehm; erhaben; gut, edel (*Charakter*); stolz; anmaßend; hochtrabend; angegangen (*Fleisch*); extrem; groß, stark, heftig; üppig, flott (*Leben*); Hoch...; Ober...; ~ *and dry* auf dem trocknen; *be on one's* ~ *horse, ride the* ~ *horse* auf dem hohen Roß sitzen; *with a* ~ *hand* arrogant, anmaßend; *in* ~ *spirits* in gehobener Stimmung, guter Laune; *a* ~ *Tory* ein Erzkonservativer *m*; ~ *colo(u)r*, ~ *complexion* rote Gesichtsfarbe *f*; ~ *life die* vornehme Welt; ~ *words pl.* heftige Worte *n/pl.*; ~ *time* höchste Zeit; **2.** *meteor.* Hoch *n*; *Am.* F = *high school*; ~ *and low* hoch und niedrig; *on* ~ in die *od.* der Höhe; **3.** *adv.* hoch; sehr, mächtig; '**~·ball** *Am.* Whisky *m* mit Soda; '**~-born** hochgeboren; '**~-bred** vornehm erzogen; '**~-brow** F **1.** Intellektuelle *m, f*, geistig Anspruchsvolle *m, f*; **2.** betont intellektuell; '**~·chair** Kinderhochstuhl *m*; ♀ **Church** anglikanische Hochkirche *f*; '**~-class** hochwertig; '**~-'col·o(u)red** von lebhafter Farbe; ♀ **Com·mis·sion·er** Hochkommissar *m*; '**~-ex'plo·sive** hochbrisant; Brisanz...; Spreng...; **~-fa·lu·tin(g)** ['~fə'luːtin, '~fə'luːtiŋ] **1.** Schwulst *m*; **2.** schwülstig; '**~-fi'del·i·ty** mit höchster Wiedergabetreue, Hi-Fi; '**~·fli·er** = *highflyer*; '**~-flown** überschwenglich; '**~·fly·er** ehrgeiziger Mensch *m*; '**~-grade** erstklassig; '**~-'hand·ed** anmaßend, willkürlich; '**~-'hat** *sl.* **1.** Snob *m*; **2.** von oben herab behandeln; '**~-'heeled** mit hohen Absätzen; '**~·land·er** Hochländer(in); '**~·lands** *pl.* Hochland *n*; '**~-'lev·el** auf hoher Ebene (*Konferenz etc.*); '**~·light** hervorheben; '**~-lights** *pl. fig.* Höhepunkte *m/pl.*; ~ **liv·ing** Wohlleben *n*; '**high·ly** hoch; höchlich; sehr; *speak* ~ *of s.o.* j. loben; ~ *descended* hochgeboren; '**high-'mind·ed** hochgesinnt; '**high-'necked** hochgeschlossen (*Kleid*); '**high·ness** Höhe *f*; *fig.*, *Titel*: Hoheit *f.*
high...: '**~-'pitched** schrill (*Ton*); steil (*Dach*); '**~-'pow·er:** ~ *station* Großkraftwerk *n*; ~ *radio station* Großfunkstation *f*; '**~-'pow·ered** mächtig, einflußreich (*Person*); '**~-'priced** teuer; '**~-rank·ing** von hohem Rang; ~ *officer* hoher Offizier *m*; '**~·rise:** ~ *flats pl.* Hochhaus *n*; ~ **road** Landstraße *f*;

~ **school** höhere Schule *f*; '~-'**spir·it·ed** lebhaft, kühn; ~ **street** Hauptstraße *f*; '~-'**strung** überempfindlich.

hight *poet. od. co.* [hait] genannt.

high...: ~ **tea** frühes Abendessen *n mit Tee u. Fleisch etc.*; ~ **time** höchste Zeit; '~-'**toned** erhaben; vornehm; ~ **wa·ter** Hochwasser *n*; '~**·way** Landstraße *f*; *fig.* Weg *m*; ~ *code* Straßenverkehrsordnung *f*; '~**·way·man** Straßenräuber *m*.

hi·jack ['haidʒæk] *Flugzeug etc.* entführen; '**hi·jack·er** Gauner *m*, Dieb *m*; (Flugzeug- *etc.*) Entführer *m*; Luftpirat *m*.

hike F [haik] **1.** wandern; **2.** Wanderung *f*; *bsd. Am.* F Anstieg *m*, Erhöhung *f* (*Preis etc.*); '**hik·er** Wanderer *m*.

hi·lar·i·ous □ [hi'lɛəriəs] ausgelassen.

hi·lar·i·ty [hi'læriti] Ausgelassenheit *f*.

Hil·a·ry ['hiləri]: ~ *term* ⚖ *im Januar beginnender Termin*; *univ.* Frühjahrssemester *n*.

hill [hil] Hügel *m*, Berg *m*; ~**·bil·ly** *Am.* F ['~bili] Hinterwäldler *m*; ~ **climb** *mot.* Bergrennen *n*; **hill·ock** ['hilək] kleiner Hügel *m*; '**hill·side** Hang *m*; '**hill-top** Bergspitze *f*; '**hill·y** hügelig.

hilt [hilt] Griff *m* (*bsd. am Degen*); *up to the* ~ bis ans Heft; *fig.* völlig, restlos.

him [him] ihn; ihm; den, dem (-jenigen).

him·self [him'self] (er, ihm, ihn, sich) selbst; sich; *of* ~ von selbst; *by* ~ allein, für sich.

hind[1] [haind] Hirschkuh *f*, Hindin *f*.

hind[2] [~] Hinter...; ~ *leg* Hinterbein *n*; ~ *wheels pl.* Hinterräder *n/pl.*

hind·er[1] ['haində] *adj.* hintere(r, -s); Hinter...

hin·der[2] ['hində] *v/t.* hindern (*from* an *dat.*); hemmen, aufhalten.

hind·most ['haindməust] hinterst, letzt.

hind·quar·ters ['haindkwɔːtəz] *pl.* Hinterteil *n e-s Tieres*.

hin·drance ['hindrəns] Hinderung *f*; Hindernis *n* (*to* für).

hind·sight ['haindsait]: *with* ~ im nachhinein.

Hin·du, *a.* **Hin·doo** ['hin'duː] Hindu *m*.

Hin·du·sta·ni [hindu'stɑːni] hindostanisch.

hinge [hindʒ] **1.** Türangel *f*; Scharnier *n*; *fig.* Angelpunkt *m*; *off the* ~*s* *fig.* aus den Angeln *od.* Fugen; **2.** ~ *upon fig.* abhängen von.

hin·ny ['hini] Maulesel *m*.

hint [hint] **1.** Hinweis *m*, Wink *m*; Anspielung *f*; **2.** andeuten; anspielen (*at* auf *acc.*); zu verstehen geben.

hin·ter·land ['hintəlænd] Hinterland *n*.

hip[1] [hip] Hüfte *f*; *attr.* Hüft...

hip[2] ⚘ [~] Hagebutte *f*.

hip[3] [~]: ~, ~, *hurra(h)!* hipp, hipp, hurra!

hip...: '~**-bath** Sitzbad *n*; '~**-flask** Flachmann *m* (*Reiseflasche*).

hip·po F ['hipəu] = *hippopotamus*.

hip-pock·et ['hippɔkit] Gesäßtasche *f*.

hip·po·pot·a·mus [hipə'pɔtəməs], *pl. a.* **hip·po'pot·a·mi** [~mai] Nil-, Flußpferd *n*.

hip·py ['hipi] *Art beatnik.*

hip-roof ⌂ ['hipruːf] Walmdach *n*.

hip-shot ['hipʃɔt] lendenlahm.

hire ['haiə] **1.** Miete *f*, Entgelt *m*, *n*, Lohn *m*; *on* ~ mietweise; zu vermieten; **2.** mieten; *j.* anstellen; ~ *out* vermieten; '~**-charge** Leihgebühr *f*; **hire·ling** *contp.* ['~liŋ] **1.** Mietling *m*; 2. feil, käuflich; '**hire-'pur·chase** Teilzahlungskauf *m*; *by* ~ auf Raten.

hir·sute ['həːsjuːt] haarig; zottig; struppig; rauh.

his [hiz] sein, seine; der, die, das seinige.

hiss [his] **1.** Zischen *n*; Gezisch *n*; **2.** *v/i.* zischen; zischeln; *v/t. a.* ~ *off* auszischen, -pfeifen.

hist [sːt] st!; still!

his·to·ri·an [his'tɔːriən] Geschichtsschreiber *m*, Historiker *m*; **his·tor·ic, his·tor·i·cal** □ [~'tɔrik(əl)] historisch, geschichtlich; Geschichts...; **his·to·ri·og·ra·pher** [~tɔːri'ɔgrəfə] Geschichtsschreiber *m*; **his·to·ry** ['~təri] Geschichte *f*; Werdegang *m*; Vergangenheit *f*; *make* ~ Geschichte machen.

his·tri·on·ic [histri'ɔnik] Schauspieler...; schauspielerisch.

hit [hit] **1.** Schlag *m*, Stoß *m*; *fig.* (Seiten)Hieb *m*; Glücksfall *m*; Treffer *m*; *thea.*, ♪ Schlager *m*;

2. (*irr.*) schlagen, stoßen; *Ziel, Ton, Ausdruck etc.* treffen; treffen *od.* stoßen auf (*acc.*); *Am.* F ankommen in (*dat.*), erreichen; ~ *s.o. a blow* j-m e-n Schlag versetzen; ~ *at* schlagen nach; ~ *or miss* aufs Geratewohl; ~ *off* F treffend darstellen; ~ *it off with* F sich vertragen mit; ~ *out* um sich schlagen; ~ (*up*)*on* (zufällig) kommen *od.* stoßen *od.* verfallen auf (*acc.*); *he* ~ *his head against a tree* er stieß mit dem Kopf gegen einen Baum; **'~-and-'run driv·er** *mot.* flüchtiger Fahrer *m.*

hitch [hitʃ] 1. Ruck *m*; ⚓ Stich *m*, Knoten *m*; *fig.* Haken *m*, Hindernis *n*, Störung *f*; 2. rücken; (sich) festmachen, -haken; hängenbleiben (*on* an *dat.*); rutschen; ~ *up Hosen* hochziehen; *Kinn etc.* aufwerfen; **'~-hike** F per Anhalter fahren.

hith·er *lit.* ['hiðə] hierher; **hith·er·to** ['~'tuː] bisher; **hith·er·ward**(s) ['~wəd(z)] = *hither.*

hit...: ~ **list** F (*a. fig.*) Abschußliste *f*; **'~·man** *sl.* ['hitmæn] Killer *m.*

hive [haiv] 1. Bienenstock *m*, -korb *m*; Bienenschwarm *m*; *fig.* Schwarm *m*; ~*s pl.* ⚕ Nesselausschlag *m*; 2. *v/t. Bienen* in e-n Stock bringen; ~ *up* aufspeichern; *v/i.* zs.-wohnen.

ho [həu] holla!; heda!; halt!

hoar [hɔː] (alters)grau.

hoard [hɔːd] 1. Vorrat *m*, Schatz *m*; 2. *a.* ~ *up* horten, aufhäufen, sammeln; **'hoard·er** Hamsterer *m.*

hoard·ing ['hɔːdiŋ] Bauzaun *m*; Reklamefläche *f.*

hoar·frost ['hɔː'frɔst] (Rauh)Reif *m.*

hoar·i·ness ['hɔːrinis] Grauheit *f.*

hoarse □ [hɔːs] heiser, rauh; **'hoarse·ness** Heiserkeit *f.*

hoar·y ['hɔːri] (alters)grau.

hoax [həuks] 1. Täuschung *f*, Betrug *m*; Falschmeldung *f*; Schwindel *m*, Manöver *n*; 2. anführen, foppen, zum besten haben.

hob¹ [hɔb] Kamineinsatz *m*; Zielpflock *m bei Wurfspielen.*

hob² [~] = *hobgoblin*; *raise* ~ *bsd. Am.* F die Hölle loslassen, Krach schlagen.

hob·ble ['hɔbl] 1. Hinken *n*, Humpeln *n*; F Klemme *f*, Patsche *f*; 2. *v/i.* humpeln, hinken (*a. fig.*); *v/t.* an den Füßen fesseln.

hob·ble·de·hoy F ['hɔbldi'hɔi] linkischer Bursche *m*, F Schlaks *m.*

hob·by *fig.* ['hɔbi] Steckenpferd *n*, Hobby *n*, Lieblingsbeschäftigung *f*; **'~-horse** Steckenpferd *n*; Schaukelpferd *n*; Karussellpferd *n.*

hob·gob·lin ['hɔbgɔblin] Kobold *m.*

hob·nail ['hɔbneil] Sohlennagel *m.*

hob·nob ['hɔbnɔb] freundschaftlich verkehren; plaudern; zs. eins trinken.

ho·bo *Am. sl.* ['həubəu] Landstreicher *m*, Tippelbruder *m.*

Hob·son's choice *fig.* ['hɔbsnz 'tʃɔis] keine Wahl *f.*

hock¹ [hɔk] 1. *zo.* Hachse *f*; Sprunggelenk *n*; 2. lähmen.

hock² [~] Rheinwein *m.*

hock³ *sl.* [~] 1. Pfand *n*; Loch *n*, Gefängnis *n*; 2. verpfänden; **'~-shop** Pfandleihe *f.*

hock·ey ['hɔki] *Sport*: Hockey *n.*

ho·cus ['həukəs] betrügen; narkotisieren; *e-m Getränk* ein Betäubungsmittel zusetzen; **~-po·cus** ['~'pəukəs] Hokuspokus *m.*

hod [hɔd] Mörteltrog *m.*

hodge-podge ['hɔdʒpɔdʒ] = *hotchpotch.*

hod·man ['hɔdmən] Handlanger *m.*

hoe ⚒ [həu] 1. Hacke *f*; 2. hacken.

hog [hɔg] 1. Schwein *n*; *fig.* Schwein(ehund *m*) *n*; *go the whole* ~ *sl.* aufs Ganze gehen; 2. *v/t. Mähne* stutzen; F gierig an sich reißen; *v/i. mot.* drauflos rasen; **hogged** stark gekrümmt; **'hog·gish** □ schweinisch; gefräßig; **'hog·gish·ness** Schweinerei *f*; Gefräßigkeit *f.*

hog·ma·nay *schott.* ['hɔgmənei] Silvester *n.*

hogs·head ['hɔgzhed] Oxhoft *n* (*etwa 240 Liter*); großes Faß *n*; **'hog·skin** Schweinsleder *n*; **'hog·wash** Schweinetrank *m*; F Gewäsch *n.*

hoi(c)k [hɔik] *Flugzeug* hochreißen.

hoi pol·loi [hɔi'pɔlɔi] *pl.* die große Masse.

hoist [hɔist] 1. Aufzug *m*; 2. hochziehen; *Flagge* hissen.

hoi·ty-toi·ty F ['hɔiti'tɔiti] 1. arrogant, anmaßend; 2. holla!

ho·kum *Am. sl.* ['həukəm] Effekthascherei *f*; Kitsch *m*; Humbug *m.*

hold [həuld] 1. Halten *n*; Halt *m*, Griff *m*; Gewalt *f*, Einfluß *m*; ⚓ Lade-, Frachtraum *m*; *catch, get, lay, take, seize* ~ *of* fassen, ergreifen; Besitz ergreifen von, sich aneignen; *have a ~ of od. on* beherrschen; *keep ~ of* festhalten; **2.** (*irr.*) *v/t. allg.* halten; festhalten; enthalten, fassen; auf-, zurück-, anhalten; *im Gedächtnis* behalten; *Versammlung etc.* abhalten; (inne-) haben, besitzen; *Ansicht* vertreten; *Gedanken etc.* hegen; halten für, schätzen; glauben; behaupten; ⚖ entscheiden (*that* daß); *~ a job down* F fest in e-r Stellung sitzen; *~ one's ground, ~ one's own* sich behaupten, standhalten; *~ the line teleph.* am Apparat bleiben; *~ water* wasserdicht sein; *fig.* stichhaltig sein; *~ off* zurück-, abhalten; ✈ abfangen; *~ on et.* (an s-m Platz fest-) halten; *~ out* ausstrecken; darbieten; *~ over* aufschieben; *~ up* hochhalten; aufrechthalten; (unter-) stützen; *dem Spott etc.* preisgeben; aufhalten; (räuberisch) überfallen; **3.** (*irr.*) *v/i.* (fest)halten; gelten; sich bewähren; standhalten, sich halten; *~ forth* Reden halten, sich auslassen (*on* über *acc.*); *~ good od. true* gelten; sich bestätigen; *~ hard!* F warte(t) mal!; halt!; *~ in* innehalten; an sich halten; *~ off* sich fernhalten; *~ on* ausharren; fortdauern; sich festhalten; *teleph.* am Apparat bleiben; *~ on!* F warte(t) mal!; halt!; *~ to* festhalten an (*dat.*); *~ up* sich (aufrecht) halten; ˈ**hold·all** Reisetasche *f*; ˈ**hold·er** Haltende *m*; Pächter *m*; Halter *m* (*Gerät*); Inhaber(in) (*bsd.* ✝); *~ of shares* Aktienbesitzer *m*; ˈ**hold·fast** Klammer *f*; Haken *m*; Zwinge *f*; ˈ**holding** Halten *n*; Halt *m*; Pachtgut *n*; Besitz *m*; *small ~* Kleingrundbesitz *m*; *~ company* Dachgesellschaft *f*; ˈ**hold·o·ver** *Am.* Überbleibsel *n*, Rest *m*; ˈ**hold-up** bewaffneter Raubüberfall *m*; Stauung *f*, Stokkung *f*.

hole [həul] **1.** Loch *n* (*a. fig.*); Höhle *f*; F *fig.* Klemme *f*; *pick ~s in* bekritteln; **2.** aushöhlen; durchlöchern; *Ball* in ein Loch spielen; ˈ**hole-and-ˈcor·ner** heimlich, hintenherum (geschehen).

hol·i·day [ˈhɔlədi] Feiertag *m*; freier Tag *m*; *~s pl.* Ferien *pl.*, Urlaub *m*; ˈ**~-mak·er** Ferienreisende *m, f*, Urlauber(in).

ho·li·ness [ˈhəulinis] Heiligkeit *f*.

hol·la [ˈhɔlə] **1.** hallo; **2.** hallo rufen.

hol·land [ˈhɔlənd] *a. brown ~* ungebleichte Leinwand *f*; *2s sg.* Wacholderschnaps *m*.

hol·ler *Am.* F [ˈhɔlə] **1.** laut rufen; **2.** Krach *m*.

hol·lo(**a**) [ˈhɔləu] = *holla*.

hol·low [ˈhɔləu] **1.** □ hohl; leer; falsch; **2.** F *adv. a. all ~* völlig; **3.** Höhle *f*, (Aus)Höhlung *f*; *Land-*Senke *f*; ⊕ Rinne *f*; **4.** aushöhlen; ˈ**hol·low·ness** Hohlheit *f*; *fig.* Falschheit *f*.

hol·ly ⚘ [ˈhɔli] Stechpalme *f*.

hol·ly·hock ⚘ [ˈhɔlihɔk] Stockrose *f*.

holm [həum] Holm *m*, Werder *m*; ˈ**~-ˈoak** ⚘ Steineiche *f*.

hol·o·caust [ˈhɔləkɔːst] Massenvernichtung *f*; Brandopfer *n*.

hol·ster [ˈhəulstə] Pistolentasche *f*.

ho·ly [ˈhəuli] **1.** heilig; *2 Thursday* Gründonnerstag *m*; *~ water* Weihwasser *n*; *2 Week* Karwoche *f*; **2.** *~ of holies Bibel: das* Allerheiligste; ˈ**~·stone** ⚓ Scheuerstein *m*.

hom·age [ˈhɔmidʒ] Huldigung *f*; *do od. pay od. render ~* huldigen (*to dat.*).

home [həum] **1.** Heim *n*; Haus *n*, Wohnung *f*; Heimat *f*; Mal *n*, Ziel *n*; *at ~* zu Hause, daheim; *make o.s. at ~* es sich bequem machen; *be not at ~ to anyone* niemanden empfangen; **2.** *adj.* heimisch, häuslich, inländisch; wirkungsvoll, tüchtig (*Schlag etc.*); treffend (*Wahrheit*); *2 Office* Innenministerium *n*; *2 Rule* Selbstregierung *f*; *2 Secretary* Innenminister *m*; *~ trade* Binnenhandel *m*; **3.** *adv.* heim, nach Hause; an die richtige Stelle; gründlich; *be ~* (wieder) zu Hause sein; *bring od. drive s.th. ~ to s.o.* j-m et. klarmachen; j-m et. nachweisen; *come ~* heimkommen; *come ~ to s.o. fig.* j-n nahe berühren; *that comes ~ to you* das geht auf Sie; *hit od. strike ~ fig.* ins Schwarze treffen; **4.** heimkehren; *~* **af·fairs** *pl. pol.* innere Angelegenheiten *f/pl.*; ˈ**~-ˈbrewed** selbstgebraut; ˈ**~-com·ing** Heimkehr *f*; *2* **Coun·ties** *pl. die* Grafschaften *f/pl.* um London; *~* **e·co·ˈnom·ics** *mst sg. Am.* Hauswirtschaftslehre *f*; ˈ**~-felt** tief empfunden; ˈ**~-ˈgrown** einheimisch; *~* **help** Haushaltshilfe *f*; ˈ**home·less** heimatlos; ˈ**home·like** anheimelnd, gemütlich; ˈ**home·li·ness** Hausbackenheit *f*; Anspruchslosigkeit *f*; *Am.* Reizlosigkeit *f*; **ˈhome·ly** □ *fig.* anheimelnd, häuslich; hausbacken; einfach, schlicht; anspruchslos; *Am.* reizlos.

home...: **ˈ~-ˈmade** selbstgemacht, Hausmacher...; **ˈ~·mak·er** Hausfrau *f* (u. Mutter *f*); **ˈ~·sick:** *be* ~ Heimweh haben; **ˈ~·sick·ness** Heimweh *n*; **ˈ~·spun 1.** selbstgesponnen; *fig.* hausbacken; **2.** rauher Wollstoff *m*; **ˈ~·stead** Heimstätte *f*; Gehöft *n*, Anwesen *n*; **~ team** *Sport*: Gastgeber *m/pl.*; **~ truth** unangenehme Wahrheit *f*; **~·ward**(**s**) [ˈ~wəd(z)] heimwärts (gerichtet), Heim...; **ˈ~·work** Hausaufgabe(n *pl.*) *f*, Schularbeiten *f/pl.*; *do one's* ~ Hausaufgaben machen; *fig.* sich gründlich vorbereiten.

hom·i·cide [ˈhɔmisaid] Totschlag *m*; Mord *m*; Totschläger(in).

hom·i·ly [ˈhɔmili] (Lehr)Predigt *f*.

hom·ing [ˈhəumiŋ] Heimkehr *f*; ~ *instinct* Heimkehrvermögen *n*; ~ *pigeon* Brieftaube *f*.

hom·i·ny [ˈhɔmini] Maisbrei *m*.

ho·mo F [ˈhəuməu] Homo *m*.

ho·m(**o**)**e·o·path** [ˈhəumjəupæθ] Homöopath(in); **ho·m**(**o**)**e·oˈpath·ic** (*~ally*) homöopathisch; **ho·m**(**o**)**e·op·a·thist** [~miˈɔpəθist] Homöopath *m*; **ho·m**(**o**)**eˈop·a·thy** Homöopathie *f*.

ho·mo·ge·ne·i·ty [hɔməudʒeˈni:iti] Gleichartigkeit *f*; **ho·mo·ge·ne·ous** □ [~ˈdʒi:njəs] homogen, gleichartig; **ho·mog·en·ized** [hɔˈmɔdʒənaizd] homogenisiert; **hom·o·graph** [ˈhɔməugrɑ:f] Homograph *n* (*Wort mit gleicher Schreibung aber anderer Bedeutung*); **ho·mol·o·gous** [hɔˈmɔləgəs] homolog; **hoˈmol·o·gy** [~dʒi] Übereinstimmung *f*; **hom·o·nym** [ˈhɔmənim] Homonym *n* (*Wort mit gleicher Lautung aber anderer Bedeutung*); **hom·o·phone** [ˈ~fəun] = *homonym*; **ho·mo·sex·u·al** [ˈhəuməuˈseksjuəl] homosexuell.

hom·y F [ˈhəumi] = *homelike*.

hone ⊕ [həun] **1.** Abziehstein *m*; **2.** *Rasiermesser* abziehen.

hon·est □ [ˈɔnist] ehrlich, rechtschaffen; aufrichtig; echt; **ˈhon·es·ty** Rechtschaffenheit *f*, Ehrlichkeit *f etc.*

hon·ey [ˈhʌni] Honig *m*; F Liebling *m*, Süße *f*; **ˈhon·ey-bee** (Honig-)Biene *f*; **ˈhon·ey·comb 1.** (Honig-)Wabe *f*; **2.** durchlöchern; unterminieren; **hon·eyed** [ˈhʌnid] honigsüß; **ˈhon·ey·moon 1.** Flitterwochen *f/pl.*; Hochzeitsreise *f*; **2.** die Flitterwochen verleben; **ˈhon·ey·suck·le** ⚘ Geißblatt *n*.

honk *mot.* [hɔŋk] **1.** Hupenton *m*; **2.** hupen, tuten.

honk·y-tonk *Am. sl.* [ˈhɔŋkitɔŋk] Bumslokal *n*, übles Nachtlokal *n*.

hon·o·rar·i·um [ɔnəˈrɛəriəm] Honorar *n*; **hon·or·ar·y** [ˈɔnərəri] Ehren...; ehrenamtlich.

hon·o(**u**)**r** [ˈɔnə] **1.** Ehre *f*; Achtung *f*; Würde *f*; *fig.* Zierde *f*; *~s pl.* Auszeichnungen *f/pl.*; *~s degree* Honours-Grad *m*; *Your* ♀ Euer Gnaden; *in* ~ *of s.o.* j-m zu Ehren; *do the ~s of the house* die Honneurs machen; **2.** ehren; beehren; ✝ honorieren, einlösen.

hon·o(**u**)**r·a·ble** □ [ˈɔnərəbl] ehrenvoll; redlich; ehrbar; ehrenwert; ~ *discharge* ⚔ ehrenhafte Entlassung *f*; *Right* ♀ Sehr Ehrenwert; *receive* ~ *mention* lobend erwähnt werden; **ˈhon·o**(**u**)**r·a·ble·ness** Ehrenhaftigkeit *f*.

hooch *sl.* [hu:tʃ] Fusel *m*.

hood [hud] Kapuze *f*; *mot.* Verdeck *n*; *Am.* (Motor)Haube *f*; ⊕ Kappe *f*; *univ.* Talarüberwurf *m*; **ˈhood·ed** mit e-r Kapuze *od.* Kappe; *fig.* verhüllt.

hood·lum *Am.* F [ˈhu:dləm] Strolch *m*; Raufbold *m*; Rowdy *m*.

hoo·doo *bsd. Am.* [ˈhu:du:] **1.** Unglücksbringer *m*; Pech *n* (*Unglück*); **2.** Unglück bringen.

hood·wink [ˈhudwiŋk] täuschen.

hoo·ey *Am. sl.* [ˈhu:i] Quatsch *m*.

hoof [hu:f], *pl.* **hoofs** *od.* **hooves** [hu:vz] Huf *m*; Klaue *f*; **ˈ~-beat** Hufschlag *m*; **hoofed** [hu:ft] gehuft, ...hufig.

hook [huk] **1.** (*bsd.* Angel)Haken *m*; Sichel *f*; *~s and eyes* Haken und Ösen; *by* ~ *or by crook* mit allen Mitteln; ~, *line, and sinker* F mit allem Drum und Dran; **2.** *v/t.* (zu-, fest)haken; fangen, angeln (*a. fig.*); *sl.* klauen; ~ *it sl.* abhauen; ~ *up* anhaken; *v/i. a.* ~ *on* sich festhaken.

hook·a(**h**) [ˈhukə] Wasserpfeife *f*.

hooked [hukt] hakenförmig; *sl.* süchtig; **ˈhook·er** ⚓ Huker *m*; *Am. sl.* Nutte *f*; **ˈhook·ey** = *hooky*; **ˈhook-**

-up Bündnis *n*, Übereinkommen *n*; *Radio*: Ringsendung *f*; '**hook·y** **1.** hakig; **2.** *play* ~ *Am. sl.* (die Schule *etc.*) schwänzen.

hoo·li·gan ['hu:ligən] Rowdy *m*.

hoop [hu:p] **1.** *Faß- etc.* Reif(en) *m*; ⊕ Ring *m*; Reifrock *m*; **2.** *Fässer* binden, mit Reifen belegen; '**hoop·er** Küfer *m*, Böttcher *m*.

hoop·ing-cough ['hu:piŋkɔf] Keuchhusten *m*.

hoo·poe *orn.* ['hu:pu:] Wiedehopf *m*.

hoot [hu:t] **1.** Schrei *m*; Geheul *n*; Getute *n*; **2.** *v/i.* heulen; johlen; tuten; *mot.* hupen; *v/t. a.* ~ *at*, ~ *out*, ~ *away* auspfeifen, -zischen; '**hoot·er** Schreier *m*; Sirene *f*, Dampfpfeife *f*; *mot.* Hupe *f*.

Hoov·er ['hu:və] **1.** Staubsauger *m*; **2.** (mit e-m Staubsauger) saugen *od.* reinigen.

hop[1] [hɔp] **1.** ♀ Hopfen *m*; ~*s pl.* Hopfen(früchte *f/pl.*) *m*; ~*-picker* Hopfenpflücker *m*; **2.** *v/t. Bier etc.* hopfen; *v/i.* Hopfen pflücken.

hop[2] [~] **1.** Hopser *m*, Sprung *m*; ✈ Etappe *f*; F (*zwanglose*) Tanzveranstaltung *f*, Tanzerei *f*; **2.** hüpfen, springen (über *acc.*); ~ *it sl.* verduften; ~ *off* ✈ starten.

hope [həup] **1.** Hoffnung *f* (*of* auf *acc.*); *of great* ~*s* vielversprechend; **2.** hoffen (*for* auf *acc.*); ~ *in* vertrauen auf (*acc.*); ~ *against* ~ verzweifelt hoffen; **hope·ful** □ ['~ful] hoffnungsvoll; *be* ~ *that* die Hoffnung haben, daß; '**hope·ful·ly** *bsd. Am.* hoffentlich; '**hope·less** □ hoffnungslos; verzweifelt.

hop-o'-my-thumb ['hɔpəmi'θʌm] Knirps *m*, Dreikäsehoch *m*.

hop·per ['hɔpə] ⊕ Mühlentrichter *m*; Floh *m*; Känguruh *n*.

horde [hɔ:d] Horde *f*.

ho·ri·zon [hə'raizn] Horizont *m*; **hor·i·zon·tal** □ [hɔri'zɔntl] horizontal, waag(e)recht; Horizont...

hor·mone ['hɔ:məun] Hormon *n*.

horn [hɔ:n] Horn *n der Tiere, des Mondes*; *zo.* Fühlhorn *n*; Trinkhorn *n*; Schalltrichter *m*; *mot.* Hupe *f*; *draw in one's* ~*s fig.* sich (*von e-m Unternehmen*) zurückziehen, kein Interesse mehr zeigen; (*stag's*) ~*s pl.* Geweih *n*; ~ *of plenty* Füllhorn *n*; '~**·beam** ♀ Hainbuche *f*; ~**·blende** ['~blend] *min.* Hornblende *f*; **horned** ['~id, *in Zssgn* hɔ:nd] gehörnt; Horn...

hor·net *zo.* ['hɔ:nit] Hornisse *f*.

horn·less ['hɔ:nlis] hornlos; '**horn·pipe** *a. sailor's* ~ *ein* (Seemanns-) Tanz *m*; '**horn·rimmed**: ~ *spectacles pl.* Hornbrille *f*; **horn·swog·gle** *Am. sl.* ['~swɔgl] *j.* (he)reinlegen; '**horn·y** □ hornig; schwielig; *sl.* geil (*Mann*).

ho·rol·o·gy [hɔ'rɔlədʒi] Uhrmacherkunst *f*; **hor·o·scope** ['hɔrəskəup] Horoskop *n*; *cast a* ~ das Horoskop stellen.

hor·ren·dous [hɔ'rendəs] entsetzlich.

hor·ri·ble □ ['hɔrəbl] entsetzlich; scheußlich; **hor·rid** □ ['hɔrid] gräßlich, abscheulich; schrecklich; **hor·rif·ic** [hɔ'rifik] entsetzlich; **hor·ri·fy** ['~fai] erschrecken; entsetzen; **hor·ror** ['hɔrə] Entsetzen *n*, Schauder *m*, Abscheu *f*, *m* (*of* vor *dat.*); Schrecken *m*; Greuel *m*; *chamber of* ~*s* Schreckenskammer *f*; ~ *fiction* (*film*) Gruselroman *m* (-film *m*); '**hor·ror-strick·en** starr vor Entsetzen.

horse [hɔ:s] **1.** Pferd *n*, Roß *n*, Gaul *m*; *coll.* Reiterei *f*; ⊕ Bock *m*, Gestell *n*; *look a gift* ~ *in the mouth fig.* e-m geschenkten Gaul ins Maul schauen; *a* ~ *of another colo(u)r* et. ganz anderes; (*straight*) *from the* ~*'s mouth* aus erster Hand; **2.** bespannen; beritten machen; *j.* auf den Rücken nehmen; '~**·back**: *on* ~ zu Pferd; *go on* ~ reiten; '~**-bean** ♀ Pferdebohne *f*; '~**-box** Pferdetransportwagen *m*; '~**-break·er** Zureiter *m*; ~ **chest·nut** ♀ Roßkastanie *f*; '~**-col·lar** Kum(me)t *n*; '~**-deal·er** Pferdehändler *m*; '~**-flesh** Pferdefleisch *n*; *coll.* Pferde *n/pl.*; '~**-fly** *zo.* Bremse *f*; ♀ **Guards** *pl. englisches* Garde-Kavallerie-Regiment *n*; '~**·hair** Roßhaar *n*; '~**-laugh** F wieherndes Lachen *n*; '~**·man** Reiter *m*; '~**·man·ship** Reitkunst *f*; ~ **op·er·a** *Am. drittklassiger* Wildwestfilm *m*; '~**-play** grober Scherz *m*; '~**-pond** Pferdeschwemme *f*, -tränke *f*; '~**·pow·er** Pferdestärke *f*; '~**-race** Pferderennen *n*; '~**-rad·ish** ♀ Meerrettich *m*; '~**-sense** gesunder Menschenverstand *m*; '~**·shoe** Hufeisen *n*; '~**·whip** Reitgerte *f*; '~**·wom·an** Reiterin *f*.

hors·y [ˈhɔːsi] pferdenärrisch; Pferde..., Reit..., Jockei...
hor·ta·tive □ [ˈhɔːtətiv], **hor·ta·to·ry** [ˈ~təri] ermahnend.
hor·ti·cul·tur·al [hɔːtiˈkʌltʃərəl] Gartenbau...; ˈ**hor·ti·cul·ture** Gartenbau *m*; **hor·tiˈcul·tur·ist** Gartenkünstler *m*.
ho·san·na [həuˈzænə] Hosianna *n*, Loblied *n*.
hose [həuz] **1.** Schlauch *m*; Strumpfhose *f*; *coll.* Strümpfe *m/pl.*; **2.** mit e-m Schlauch (be)sprengen *od.* waschen.
ho·sier [ˈhəuziə] Strumpfwarenhändler *m*; ˈ**ho·sier·y** Strumpfwaren *f/pl.*; Strumpffabrik *f*.
hos·pice [ˈhɔspis] Hospiz *n*.
hos·pi·ta·ble □ [ˈhɔspitəbl] gastfrei, gast(freund)lich; aufgeschlossen (to *dat.*).
hos·pi·tal [ˈhɔspitl] Hospital *n*, Krankenhaus *n*; ⚔ Lazarett *n*; **hos·pi·tal·i·ty** [~ˈtæliti] Gastfreundschaft *f*, Gastlichkeit *f*; **hos·pi·tal·ize** [ˈ~təlaiz] ins Krankenhaus einliefern; stationär behandeln; ˈ**hos·pi·tal-train** ⚔ Lazarettzug *m*.
host[1] [həust] Wirt *m* (*a. zo.*, ⚘); Gastgeber *m*; Gastwirt *m*; *Fernsehen*: Showmaster *m*; reckon without one's ~ die Rechnung ohne den Wirt machen.
host[2] [~] *fig.* Heer *n* (*große Menge*), Unzahl *f*; Schwarm *m*; *Lord of ~s Bibel*: Herr *m* der Heerscharen; *he is a ~ in himself* er leistet so viel wie hundert andere zusammen.
Host[3] *eccl.* [~] Hostie *f*.
hos·tage [ˈhɔstidʒ] Geisel *m, f*.
hos·tel [ˈhɔstəl] Herberge *f*; *univ.* Studenten(wohn)heim *n*; ˈ**hos·tel(l)er** Herbergsbenützer *m*; ˈ**hos·tel·ry** [ˈ~ri] Gasthaus *n*, Herberge *f*.
host·ess [ˈhəustis] Wirtin *f*; Gastgeberin *f*; = air ~.
hos·tile [ˈhɔstail] feindlich (gesinnt); **hos·til·i·ty** [~ˈtiliti] Feindseligkeit *f* (to gegen).
hos·tler [ˈɔslə] Stallknecht *m*.
hot [hɔt] **1.** □ heiß; scharf; beißend; hitzig, heftig; eifrig; warm (*Speise, Fährte*); *Am. sl.* falsch (*Scheck*); gestohlen; radioaktiv; ~ *air* F leeres Geschwätz *n*; *go like ~ cakes* wie warme Semmeln weggehen; ~ *line pol.* heißer Draht *m*; ~ *spot pol.* Krisenherd *m*; ~ *stuff sl.* toller Kerl *m*; tolle *od.* heikle Sache *f*; *get into ~ water* in des Teufels Küche kommen; **2.** *mst ~ up* F heiß machen; ˈ**hot·bed** Mistbeet *n*; *fig.* Pflanz-, Brutstätte *f*; ˈ**hot-ˈblood·ed** heißblütig.
hotch·potch F [ˈhɔtʃpɔtʃ] Mischmasch *m*; Gemüsesuppe *f*.
hot dog F [ˈhɔtˈdɔg] heißes Würstchen *n*.
ho·tel [həuˈtel] Hotel *n*.
hot...: ˈ**~·foot 1.** eiligst; **2.** F eilen; ˈ**~·head** Hitzkopf *m*; ˈ**~·house** Treibhaus *n*; ˈ**hot·ness** Hitze *f*; Schärfe *f*.
hot...: ˈ**~-plate** Heiz-, Kochplatte *f*; ˈ**~-pot** Irish Stew *n*; ˈ**~-press** *Papier* heiß pressen; *Stoff* dekatieren; **~ rod** *mot. Am. sl.* frisiertes altes Auto *n*; **~ shoe** *phot.* Blitz-Mittenkontakt *m*; ˈ**~·spur** Heißsporn *m*, Hitzkopf *m*; **~-ˈwa·ter bot·tle** Wärmflasche *f*.
hough [hɔk] = *hock*[1].
hound [haund] **1.** Jagdhund *m*, *bsd.* Spürhund *m*; *fig.* Hund *m*, Schurke *m*; **2.** jagen, hetzen (*at, on* auf *acc.*).
hour [ˈauə] Stunde *f*; Zeit *f*, Uhr *f*; *~s pl.* Dienst(stunden *f/pl.*) *m*; *eccl.* Stundengebete *n/pl.*; *s. eleventh*; ˈ**~-glass** Sanduhr *f*; ˈ**~-hand** Stundenzeiger *m*; ˈ**hour·ly** stündlich; ständig.
house 1. [haus], *pl.* **hous·es** [ˈhauziz] *allg.* Haus *n* (*a.* ✝, *parl.*, *thea.*); *the* ♀ das Unterhaus *n*; die Börse *f*; *~ and home* Haus und Hof; *keep ~* den Haushalt führen; *on the ~* auf Kosten des Wirts, umsonst; *put one's ~ in order fig.* sein Haus bestellen; **2.** [hauz] *v/t.* ein-, unterbringen; *v/i.* hausen; **~-a·gent** [ˈhauseidʒənt] Häusermakler *m*; **~ ar·rest** Hausarrest *m*; ˈ**~-boat** Hausboot *n*; ˈ**~·break·er** Einbrecher *m bei Tage*; Abbrucharbeiter *m*; ˈ**~-flag** ⚓ Reedereiflagge *f*; ˈ**~-fly** Stubenfliege *f*; ˈ**~·hold** Haushalt *m*; *attr.* Haushalts...; Haus...; *King's ~* königliche Hofhaltung *f*; *~ troops pl.* Gardetruppen *f/pl.*; *~ word* fester *od.* geläufiger Begriff *m*; ˈ**~·hold·er** Haushaltsvorstand *m*, Hausherr *m*; ˈ**~-hunt·ing** F Wohnungssuche *f*; ˈ**~·hus·band** Hausmann *m*; ˈ**~·keep·er** Haushälterin *f*; ˈ**~·keep·ing 1.** Haushaltung *f*; **2.** häuslich; ˈ**~·less** obdachlos; ˈ**~·maid** Hausangestellte *f*; ˈ**~·mas·ter** Internatsleiter

m; ~ **of cards** Kartenhaus *n* (*a. fig.*); ♀ **of God** Gotteshaus *n*; ~ **of ill fame** Freudenhaus *n*; '~**-paint·er** Anstreicher *m*; '~**-phy·si·cian** Krankenhausarzt *m*; '~**·proud:** *be* ~ übertrieben ordentlich sein; e-n Putzfimmel haben; '~**-room** Platz *m* im Haus; *give s.o.* ~ j. in sein Haus aufnehmen; '~**-to-'house** Haus...; ~ *collection* Haussammlung *f*; '~**-top** Dach *n*; *proclaim from the* ~*s* öffentlich verkünden; '~**-train·ed** stubenrein (*Tier*); '~**-warm·ing** Einzugsfeier *f*; ~**·wife** ['~waif] Hausfrau *f*; ['hʌzif] Nähtäschchen *n*; ~**·wife·ly** ['hauswaifli] hausfraulich; Haushaltungs-...; ~**·wif·er·y** ['~wifəri] Haushaltung *f*; '~**·work** Haus(halts)arbeiten *f/pl.*; '~**-wreck·er** *Am.* Abbruchunternehmer *m.*

hous·ing[1] ['hauziŋ] Unterbringung *f*; Wohnung *f*; ~ *conditions pl.* Wohnverhältnisse *n/pl.*; ~ *estate* Wohnsiedlung *f*; ~ *scheme* Wohnungsbauprojekt *n*; ~ *shortage* Wohnungsnot *f*; ~ *subsidy* Wohngeld *n.*

hous·ing[2] [~] Schabracke *f.*

hove [həuv] *pret. u. p.p. von heave* 2.

hov·el ['hɔvəl] Schuppen *m*; Hütte *f.*

hov·er ['hɔvə] schweben; lungern; *fig.* schwanken; ~*ing accent* schwebender Akzent *m*; '~**·craft** Luftkissenfahrzeug *n.*

how [hau] wie; ~ *do you do?* Guten Tag!; ~ *large a room!* was für ein großes Zimmer!; ~ *about ...?* wie steht's mit ...?; ~**·be·it** † F ['~'bi:it] nichtsdestoweniger; ~**-d'ye-do** *sl.* ['~djə'du:] unangenehme Geschichte *f*, Bescherung *f*; ~**'ev·er,** *a.* **how·e'er** [~'ɛə] **1.** *adv.* wie auch (immer); *bei adj. u. adv.*: wenn auch noch so ..., so ... auch; F wie eigentlich?; **2.** *conj.* jedoch, gleichwohl, doch.

how·itz·er ⚔ ['hauitsə] Haubitze *f.*

howl [haul] **1.** heulen, brüllen; **2.** Heulen *n*, Geheul *n*; *Radio*: Pfeifen *n*; '**howl·er** Heuler *m*; *sl.* grober Fehler *m*; '**howl·ing 1.** heulend; F fürchterlich; **2.** Heulen *n.*

how·so·ev·er [hausəu'evə] wie (sehr) auch immer.

hoy [hɔi] **1.** holla!; **2.** ⚓ Leichter *m* (*kleines Küstenfahrzeug*).

hoy·den ['hɔidn] Wildfang *m*, Range *f* (*Mädchen*).

hub [hʌb] (Rad)Nabe *f*; *fig.* Mittel-, Angelpunkt *m.*

hub·ble-bub·ble ['hʌblbʌbl] Geblubber *n*; *Art* Wasserpfeife *f.*

hub·bub ['hʌbʌb] Tumult *m*, Lärm *m.*

hub(·by) F ['hʌb(i)] Männchen *n* (*Ehemann*).

hub·ris ['hju:bris] Hybris *f*, Selbstüberhebung *f.*

huck·a·back ['hʌkəbæk] Drell *m.*

huck·le ['hʌkl] Hüfte *f*; '~**·ber·ry** ⚘ amerikanische Heidelbeere *f*; '~**-bone** Fußknöchel *m*; Hüftknochen *m.*

huck·ster ['hʌkstə] **1.** Höker(in); **2.** (ver)hökern, schachern (mit).

hud·dle ['hʌdl] **1.** *a.* ~ *together* (sich) zs.-drängen, zs.-pressen; ~ (*o.s.*) *up* sich zs.-kauern; **2.** Gewirr *n*, Wirrwarr *m*, Gehudel *n*; *go into a* ~ F Kriegsrat halten.

hue[1] [hju:] Farbe *f*, Färbung *f.*

hue[2] [~]: ~ *and cry* Zetergeschrei *n*; Hetze *f.*

huff [hʌf] **1.** üble Laune *f*; **2.** *v/t.* *grob* anfahren; beleidigen; *e-n Damstein* pusten; *v/i.* wütend werden; schmollen; '**huff·ish** ☐ übelnehmerisch; '**huff·i·ness,** '**huff·ish·ness** Übelnehmerei *f*; Übellaunigkeit *f*; '**huff·y** ☐ übelnehmerisch; F eingeschnappt.

hug [hʌg] **1.** Umarmung *f*; **2.** an sich drücken, umarmen; umklammern; *fig.* festhalten an (*dat.*), hegen; sich dicht am *Lande od. Wege* halten; ~ *o.s.* sich beglückwünschen (*on* zu).

huge ☐ [hju:dʒ] ungeheuer, riesig; '**huge·ness** ungeheure Größe *f.*

hug·ger-mug·ger F ['hʌgəmʌgə] **1.** unordentlich; heimlich; **2.** *v/t.* verheimlichen; *v/i.* Heimlichkeiten haben; **3.** Kuddelmuddel *m.*

Hu·gue·not *hist.* ['hju:gənɔt] Hugenotte *m*, Hugenottin *f.*

hu·la ['hu:lə] Hula(-Hula) *m* (*hawaiischer Tanz*).

hulk ⚓ [hʌlk] Hulk *m, f,* (*abgetakeltes*) altes Schiff *n*; *fig.* Klotz *m*; '**hulk·ing** ungeschlacht, klobig.

hull [hʌl] **1.** ⚘ Schale *f*; Hülse *f*; ⚓ Rumpf *m*; ~ *down* weit entfernt; **2.** enthülsen; schälen; ⚓ in den Schiffsrumpf treffen.

hul·la·ba·loo [hʌləbə'lu:] Spektakel *m*, Lärm *m.*

hul·lo ['hʌ'ləu] hallo (*bsd. teleph.*).
hum [hʌm] **1.** Summen *n*; Brumme(l)n *n*; Gesumm *n*; **2.** hm!; **3.** summen; brumme(l)n; *sl.* stinken; ~ *and haw* verlegen stottern, sich verlegen räuspern; *make things* ~ F Schwung in die Sache bringen.
hu·man ['hju:mən] **1.** □ menschlich; ~*ly* nach menschlichem Ermessen; ~*ly possible* menschenmöglich; ~*ly speaking* nach menschlichen Begriffen; ~ *rights pl.* Menschenrechte *n/pl.*; **2.** F Mensch *m*; **hu·mane** □ [hju:'mein] human, menschenfreundlich; ~ *killer* Schlachtmaske *f*; ~ *learning* humanistische Bildung *f*; **hu·man·ism** ['hju:mənizəm] Humanismus *m*; '**hu·man·ist** Humanist *m*; **hu·man·i·tar·i·an** [hju:mæni'tɛəriən] **1.** Menschenfreund *m*; **2.** menschenfreundlich; **hu'man·i·ty** menschliche Natur *f*; Menschheit *f*; Menschlichkeit *f*, Menschenliebe *f*, Humanität *f*; *the humanities pl.* die antiken Sprachen und Literaturen *f/pl.*; die Geisteswissenschaften *f/pl.*; **hu·man·i·za·tion** [hju:mənai'zeiʃən] Humanisierung *f*; '**hu·man·ize** menschlich *od.* gesittet machen *od.* werden; **hu·man·kind** ['hju:mən'kaind] das Menschengeschlecht, die Menschheit.
hum·ble ['hʌmbl] **1.** □ demütig; bescheiden; niedrig, gering; *my* ~ *self* meine Wenigkeit *f*; *your* ~ *servant* Ihr ergebenster Diener *m*; *eat* ~ *pie* zu Kreuze kriechen, sich demütigen; **2.** erniedrigen; demütigen.
hum·ble-bee ['hʌmblbi:] Hummel *f*.
hum·ble·ness ['hʌmblnis] Demut *f*; Bescheidenheit *f*.
hum·bug ['hʌmbʌg] **1.** Schwindel *m*; Unsinn *m*, Humbug *m*; Schwindler *m*; Pfefferminzbonbon *n*; **2.** prellen, (be)schwindeln.
hum·ding·er *Am. sl.* [hʌm'diŋə] Mordskerl *m*; Mordssache *f*.
hum·drum ['hʌmdrʌm] **1.** eintönig, langweilig; fad; **2.** Alltagseinerlei *n*, Eintönigkeit *f*.
hu·mer·al *anat.* ['hju:mərəl] Schulter...
hu·mid ['hju:mid] feucht, naß; **hu'mid·i·ty** Feuchtigkeit *f*.
hu·mil·i·ate [hju:'milieit] erniedrigen, demütigen; **hu·mil·i'a·tion** Erniedrigung *f*, Demütigung *f*.
hu·mil·i·ty [hju:'militi] Demut *f*.
hum·mer ['hʌmə] Summer *m* (*bsd. teleph.*); *sl.* Betriebmacher *m*.
hum·ming F ['hʌmiŋ] mächtig, gewaltig; '~**-bird** *orn.* Kolibri *m*; '~**-top** Brummkreisel *m*.
hum·mock ['hʌmək] *Erd-*, *Eis-*Buckel *m*; Hügel *m*.
hu·mor·ist ['hju:mərist] Humorist *m*; Spaßmacher *m*, -vogel *m*.
hu·mor·ous □ ['hju:mərəs] humoristisch, humorvoll; spaßig; '**hu·mor·ous·ness** Humor *m*; *das* Spaßige.
hu·mo(u)r ['hju:mə] **1.** Humor *m*; *das* Spaßige; Stimmung *f*, Laune *f*; Körpersaft *m*; *out of* ~ schlecht gelaunt; **2.** *j-m* s-n Willen lassen; eingehen auf (*acc.*); '**hu·mo(u)r·less** humorlos; **hu·mo(u)r·some** □ ['~səm] launisch.
hump [hʌmp] **1.** Höcker *m*, Buckel *m*; *sl.* üble Laune *f*; *give s.o. the* ~ j. verdrießen; **2.** krümmen; ärgern, verdrießen; ~ *o.s. Am. sl.* sich dranhalten; '**hump·back**, '**hump·backed** *s. hunchback*.
humph [mm; hʌmf] hm! (*zum Ausdruck des Zweifels od. der Verachtung*).
Hum·phrey ['hʌmfri]: *dine with Duke* ~ kein Mittagessen haben.
hump·ty-dump·ty F ['hʌmpti'dʌmpti] Dickerchen *n*, Stöpsel *m*.
hump·y ['hʌmpi] bucklig.
hu·mus ['hju:məs] Humus *m*.
hunch [hʌntʃ] **1.** *s. hump*; großes Stück *n*, Runken *m*; *Am.* F Ahnung *f*, Verdacht *m*; **2.** *a.* ~ *out*, ~ *up* krümmen; '**hunch·back** Bucklige *m, f*; '**hunch·backed** bucklig.
hun·dred ['hʌndrəd] **1.** hundert; **2.** Hundert *n*; Hundertschaft *f*; Bezirk *m*; **hun·dred·fold** ['~fəuld] hundertfältig; **hun·dredth** ['~θ] **1.** hundertste; **2.** Hundertstel *n*; '**hun·dred·weight** *englischer* Zentner *m* (*50,8 kg*).
hung [hʌŋ] **1.** *pret. u. p.p. von hang 1*; **2.** *adj.* abgehangen (*Fleisch*).
Hun·gar·i·an [hʌŋ'gɛəriən] **1.** ungarisch; **2.** Ungar(in); Ungarisch *n*.
hun·ger ['hʌŋgə] **1.** Hunger *m* (*a. fig.*; *for* nach); **2.** *v/i.* hungern (*for, after* nach); *v/t.* durch Hunger

zwingen (*into* zu); ~ **strike** Hungerstreik *m*; *go on (a)* ~ in den Hungerstreik treten.
hun·gry □ ['hʌŋgri] hungrig (*for* nach); mager (*Boden*); ~ *work* Arbeit, die hungrig macht.
hunk F [hʌŋk] dickes Stück *n*, Runken *m*; '**hun·kers** *pl.* Hinterbacken *f/pl.*
hunks F [hʌŋks] Geizhals *m*.
hunt [hʌnt] **1.** Jagd *f* (*for* auf *acc.*, *fig.* nach); Jagd(revier *n*) *f*; Jagd(-gesellschaft) *f*; **2.** *v/t.* jagen; *Revier* bejagen; *Hund* hetzen; ~ *out od. up* aufstöbern, -spüren; *v/i.* jagen; Jagd machen (*for, after* auf *acc.*); '**hunter** Jäger *m*; Jagdpferd *n*; '**hunt·ing** **1.** Jagen *n*; Verfolgung *f*; **2.** Jagd...; '**hunt·ing-box** Jagdhütte *f*; '**hunting-ground** Jagdrevier *n*; '**huntress** Jägerin *f*; '**hunts·man** Jäger *m*; Rüdemann *m* (*Meutenführer*).
hur·dle ['hə:dl] Hürde *f* (*a. fig.*); Faschine *f*; '**hur·dler** Hürdenläufer *m*; '**hur·dle-race** Hürdenrennen *n*, -lauf *m*.
hur·dy-gur·dy ['hə:digə:di] Leierkasten *m*.
hurl [hə:l] **1.** Schleudern *n*; **2.** schleudern; *Worte* ausstoßen.
hurl·y-burl·y ['hə:libə:li] Tumult *m*, Aufruhr *m*, Wirrwarr *m*.
hur·ra(h) [hu'rɑ:], **hur·ray** [~'rei] hurra!
hur·ri·cane ['hʌrikən] Hurrikan *m*, Wirbelsturm *m*, Orkan *m*; ~ **lamp** Sturmlaterne *f*.
hur·ried □ ['hʌrid] eilig; übereilt.
hur·ry ['hʌri] **1.** (große) Eile *f*, Hast *f*; *in a* ~ in Eile; *be in a* ~ es eilig haben; *is there any* ~? ist es eilig?; *not ... in a* ~ F nicht so bald, nicht so leicht; **2.** *v/t.* (an)treiben; drängen; hetzen; *et.* beschleunigen; eilig schicken *od.* bringen; ~ *on*, ~ *up* antreiben; beschleunigen; *v/i.* eilen, hasten; *a.* ~ *up* sich beeilen; ~ *over s.th.* et. eilig erledigen; '~-'**scur·ry** **1.** Unruhe *f*, wilde Hast *f*; **2.** in wilder Hast.
hurt [hə:t] **1.** Verletzung *f*; Schaden *m*; **2.** (*irr.*) *v/t.* (*a. fig.*) verletzen; weh tun (*dat.*); schaden (*dat.*); beschädigen; *v/i.* weh tun, schmerzen; F Schaden nehmen; **hurt·ful** □ ['~ful] schädlich (*to* für).
hur·tle ['hə:tl] sausen; fegen; (p)rasseln.
hus·band ['hʌzbənd] **1.** Ehemann *m*, Gatte *m*; **2.** haushalten mit; verwalten; '**hus·band·man** Landwirt *m*; '**hus·band·ry** Landwirtschaft *f*, Ackerbau *m*; *good etc.* ~ gutes *etc.* Wirtschaften *n*.
hush [hʌʃ] **1.** still; **2.** Stille *f*; **3.** *v/t.* zum Schweigen bringen; beruhigen; *Stimme* dämpfen; ~ *up* vertuschen; *v/i.* still sein; '~-'**hush** streng geheim; '~-**mon·ey** Schweigegeld *n*.
husk [hʌsk] **1.** ⚘ Hülse *f*, Schote *f*; Schale *f* (*a. fig.*); **2.** enthülsen; '**husk·i·ness** Heiserkeit *f*, Rauheit *f*.
husk·y[1] ['hʌski] **1.** □ hülsig; trokken; rauh, heiser; F stramm, stämmig, kräftig; **2.** F stämmiger Kerl *m*.
hus·ky[2] [~] Eskimo *m*; Eskimohund *m*.
hus·sar ⚔ [hu'zɑ:] Husar *m*.
hus·sy ['hʌsi] Flittchen *n*; Range *f*.
hus·tings ['hʌstiŋz] *pl.* Wahlkampf *m*.
hus·tle ['hʌsl] **1.** *v/t. im Gedränge* stoßen; drängen, treiben; *v/i.* (sich) drängen; eilen; mit Hochdruck arbeiten, sich dranhalten; **2.** (Hoch-)Betrieb *m*; Getriebe *n*; ~ *and bustle* Gedränge *n* und Gehetze *n*; '**hus·tler** rühriger Mensch *m*.
hut [hʌt] **1.** Hütte *f*; ⚔ Baracke *f*; **2.** in Hütten *od.* Baracken unterbringen *od.* hausen.
hutch [hʌtʃ] Kasten *m*; *bsd. Kaninchen*-Stall *m* (*a. fig.*); Trog *m*.
hut·ment ⚔ ['hʌtmənt] *a.* ~ *camp* Barackenunterkunft *f*, -lager *n*.
huz·za [hu'zɑ:] hussa!, hurra!
huz·zy ['hʌzi] = *hussy*.
hy·a·cinth ⚘ ['haiəsinθ] Hyazinthe *f*.
hy·ae·na *zo.* [hai'i:nə] Hyäne *f*.
hy·brid ['haibrid] **1.** Bastard *m*, Mischling *m*; Kreuzung *f*; **2.** Bastard...; Zwitter...; '**hy·brid·ism** Bastardierung *f*, Kreuzung *f*; **hy-'brid·i·ty** Bastardnatur *f*; '**hy·brid·ize** bastardieren, kreuzen.
hy·dra ['haidrə] Hydra *f* (*vielköpfige Seeschlange der griechischen Mythologie*).
hy·dran·gea ⚘ [hai'dreindʒə] Hortensie *f*.
hy·drant ['haidrənt] Hydrant *m*.
hy·drate ⚗ ['haidreit] **1.** Hydrat *n*; **2.** mit Wasser verbinden.
hy·drau·lic [hai'drɔ:lik] **1.** (~*ally*)

hydraulisch; **2.** ~*s* *sg.* Hydraulik *f.*
hy·dro ['haidrəu] Wasserkuranstalt *f.*
hy·dro... ['haidrəu] Wasser...; **'~-'car·bon** Kohlenwasserstoff *m*; **'~'chlo·ric ac·id** Salzsäure *f*; **'~·dy'nam·ics** *sg.* Hydrodynamik *f*; **'~-e'lec·tric** hydroelektrisch; ~ *generating station* Wasserkraftwerk *n*; **'~·foil** Tragflächenboot *n*; **hy·dro·gen** ⚗ ['haidridʒən] Wasserstoff *m*; **hy·dro·gen·at·ed** [hai'drɔdʒineitid] hydriert; **hy·dro·gen bomb** Wasserstoffbombe *f*; **hy·drog·e·nous** [hai'drɔdʒinəs] wasserstoffhaltig; **hy'drog·ra·phy** [~grəfi] Hydrographie *f*; **hy·dro·path·ic** ['haidrəu'pæθik] **1.** hydropathisch; **2.** *a.* ~ *establishment* (Kalt)Wasserheilanstalt *f*; **hy·drop·a·thy** [hai'drɔpəθi] Wasserheilkunde *f*, -kur *f*.
hy·dro...: ~·pho·bi·a ['haidrəu'fəubjə] Wasserscheu *f*; Tollwut *f*; **'~·plane** (Motor)Gleitboot *n*, Rennboot *n*; Wasserflugzeug *n*; **~·po·nics** [~'pɔnics] *sg.* Wasserkultur *f*; **~'stat·ic 1.** hydrostatisch; ~ *press* hydraulische Presse *f*; **2.** ~*s* *sg.* Hydrostatik *f*.
hy·e·na *zo.* [hai'i:nə] Hyäne *f*.
hy·giene ['haidʒi:n] Hygiene *f*; **hy'gien·ic** (~*ally*) hygienisch; ~*s* *sg.* = *hygiene*.
hy·grom·e·ter [hai'grɔmitə] Feuchtigkeitsmesser *m*.
Hy·men ['haimen] Hymen *m* (*Gott der Ehe*); **hy·me·ne·al** [~'ni:əl] hochzeitlich.
hymn [him] **1.** Hymne *f*; Kirchenlied *n*; **2.** preisen; lobsingen (*dat.*); **hym·nal** ['~nəl] **1.** hymnisch; **2.** *a.* **'hymn-book** Gesangbuch *n*.
hy·per·bo·la ⩘ [hai'pə:bələ] Hyperbel *f*; **hy'per·bo·le** *rhet.* [~bəli] Übertreibung *f*, Hyperbel *f*; **hy·per·bol·ic** ⩘ [~'bɔlik] hyperbolisch; **hy·per'bol·i·cal** □ *rhet.* übertreibend; **hy·per·crit·i·cal** □ ['~'kritikəl] hyperkritisch, allzu scharf; **'hy·per'mar·ket** Verbrauchermarkt *m*; **hy'per·tro·phy** [~trəufi] übermäßiges Wachstum *n*, Hypertrophie *f*.
hy·phen ['haifən] **1.** Bindestrich *m*; **2.** mit Bindestrich schreiben *od.* verbinden; **hy·phen·at·ed** ['~eitid] mit Bindestrich geschrieben; ~ *Americans* *pl.* Bindestrich-, Halb-Amerikaner *m/pl.* (*z. B. German-Americans*).
hyp·no·sis [hip'nəusis], *pl.* **hyp'no·ses** [~si:z] Hypnose *f*.
hyp·not·ic [hip'nɔtik] **1.** (~*ally*) einschläfernd; **2.** Schlafmittel *n*; **hyp·no·tism** ['~nətizəm] Hypnotismus *m*; **'hyp·no·tist** Hypnotiseur *m*; **hyp·no·tize** ['~taiz] hypnotisieren.
hy·po *phot.* ['haipəu] Fixiersalz *n*.
hy·po·chon·dri·a [haipəu'kɔndriə] Schwermut *f*, Hypochondrie *f*; **hy·po'chon·dri·ac** [~driæk] **1.** hypochondrisch; **2.** Hypochonder *m*; **hy·poc·ri·sy** [hi'pɔkrəsi] Heuchelei *f*; **hyp·o·crite** ['hipəkrit] Heuchler (-in); Scheinheilige *m*, *f*; **hyp·o·crit·i·cal** □ [hipəu'kritikəl] heuchlerisch; **hy·po·der·mic** ⚕ [haipəu'də:mik] **1.** subkutan, unter der *od.* die Haut; ~ *injection* = **2.** Einspritzung *f* unter die Haut; **hy·pot·e·nuse** ⩘ [hai'pɔtinju:z] Hypotenuse *f*; **hy'poth·e·car·y** [~θikəri] pfandrechtlich, hypothekarisch; **hy'poth·e·cate** [~θikeit] verpfänden; **hy·po·ther·mi·a** [haipəu'θə:miə] Unterkühlung *f*; **hy·poth·e·sis** [~'pɔθisis], *pl.* **hy·poth·e·ses** [~'pɔθisi:z] Hypothese *f*; **hy·po·thet·ic, hy·po·thet·i·cal** □ [haipəu'θetik(əl)] hypothetisch.
hys·sop ♀ ['hisəp] Ysop *m*.
hys·ter·ec·to·my ⚕ [histə'rektəmi] Hysterektomie *f*.
hys·te·ri·a ⚕ [his'tiəriə] Hysterie *f*; **hys·ter·ic,** *mst* **hys·ter·i·cal** □ [his'terik(əl)] hysterisch; **hys'ter·ics** *pl.* hysterischer Anfall *m*, hysterische Anfälle *m/pl.*; *go into* ~ hysterisch werden.

I

I [ai] ich.

i·am·bic [aiˈæmbik] **1.** iambisch; **2.** *a.* iˈ**am·bus** [~bəs] Jambus *m.*

i·bex *zo.* [ˈaibeks] Steinbock *m.*

i·bi·dem [iˈbaidem] ebenda.

ice [ais] **1.** Eis *n*; (Speise)Eis *n*; *cut no* ~ F nicht von Belang sein; nicht ziehen; *skate on thin* ~ *fig.* sich aufs Glatteis begeben; **2.** gefrieren lassen; *a.* ~ *up* vereisen; *Kuchen* mit Zuckerguß überziehen; in Eis kühlen; ˈ**~-age** Eiszeit *f*; ˈ**~-axe** Eispickel *m*; **~ bag** ⚕ Eisbeutel *m*; **ice·berg** [ˈ~bə:g] Eisberg *m* (*a. fig.*).

ice...: ˈ**~-boat** Eisjacht *f*, Segelschlitten *m*; ˈ**~-bound** eingefroren; ˈ**~-box** Eisschrank *m*; *Am. a.* Kühlschrank *m*; ˈ**~-break·er** ⚓ Eisbrecher *m*; ˈ**~-cap** Eisdecke *f*; ˈ**~-ˈcream** Speiseeis *n*; ˈ**~-cube** Eiswürfel *m.*

iced [aist] eisgekühlt; glasiert.

ice...: ˈ**~-fall** Gletscherbruch *m*, Eiskaskade *f*; ˈ**~-field** (polare) Eisdecke *f*; ˈ**~-floe** Eisscholle *f*; ˈ**~-free** eisfrei; ˈ**~-hock·ey** Eishockey *n*; ˈ**~-house** Eiskeller *m.*

Ice·land·er [ˈaisləndə] Isländer(in); **Ice·lan·dic** [~ˈlændik] Isländisch *n.*

ice...: ˈ**~-lol·ly** Eis *n* am Stiel; ˈ**~-pack** Packeis *n*; ⚕ Eisumschlag *m*; ˈ**~-rink** Eisbahn *f*; ˈ**~-show** Eisrevue *f*; ˈ**~-skate** Schlittschuhlaufen *n.*

ich·thy·ol·o·gy [ikθiˈɔlədʒi] Fischkunde *f.*

i·ci·cle [ˈaisikl] Eiszapfen *m.*

i·ci·ness [ˈaisinis] eisige Kälte *f.*

ic·ing [ˈaisiŋ] Zuckerguß *m*; Vereisung *f*; ~ **sug·ar** Puderzucker *m.*

i·con [ˈaikɔn] Ikone *f.*

i·con·o·clast [aiˈkɔnəuklæst] Bilderstürmer *m.*

i·cy □ [ˈaisi] eisig (*a. fig.*); vereist.

I'd [aid] = *I had*; *I would.*

i·de·a [aiˈdiə] Idee *f*; Begriff *m*, Vorstellung *f*; Gedanke *m*; Meinung *f*; Ahnung *f*; Plan *m*; *form an* ~ *of* sich e-e Vorstellung machen von; **iˈde·al 1.** □ ideell, eingebildet; Gedanken..., Ideen...; vorbildlich, ideal; **2.** Musterbild *n*, Ideal *n*; **iˈde·al·ism** Idealismus *m*; **iˈde·al·ist** Idealist(in); **i·de·alˈis·tic** (*~ally*) idealistisch; **iˈde·al·ize** [~laiz] idealisieren.

i·den·ti·cal □ [aiˈdentikəl] identisch, gleich(bedeutend); **iˈden·ti·cal·ness** = *identity*; **i·den·ti·fiˈca·tion** Identifizierung *f*; Ausweis *m*; ~ *card* = *identity card*; ~ *mark mot.* Kennzeichen *n*; **iˈden·ti·fy** [~fai] identifizieren; gleichsetzen (*with* mit *od. dat.*); (die Persönlichkeit *j-s*, die Gleichheit *od.* Art *e-r Sache*) feststellen; ausweisen; erkennen; **iˈden·ti·kit** [~kit] Phantombild *m*; **iˈden·ti·ty** Identität *f*; Persönlichkeit *f*, Eigenart *f*; ~ *card* Personalausweis *m*, Kennkarte *f*; ~ *disc* ⚔ Erkennungsmarke *f.*

id·e·o·gram [ˈidiəugræm], ˈ**id·e·o·graph** [ˈ~grɑ:f] *gr.* Schriftzeichen *n*, Ideogramm *n.*

id·e·o·log·i·cal □ [aidiəˈlɔdʒikl] ideologisch; **id·e·ol·o·gy** [~ˈɔlədʒi] Ideologie *f*; Begriffslehre *f.*

ides [aidz] *pl. die* Iden *pl.*

id·i·o·cy [ˈidiəsi] Schwach-, Blödsinn *m.*

id·i·om [ˈidiəm] Idiom *n*; Mundart *f*; Spracheigentümlichkeit *f*; idiomatische Wendung *f*, Redewendung *f*; **id·i·o·mat·ic** [~ˈmætik] (*~ally*) idiomatisch; spracheigentümlich.

id·i·o·syn·cra·sy [idiəˈsiŋkrəsi] Idiosynkrasie *f*; persönliche Eigenart *f.*

id·i·ot [ˈidiət] Idiot(in), Schwach-, Blödsinnige *m, f*; **id·i·ot·ic** [idiˈɔtik] (*~ally*) blödsinnig; idiotisch.

i·dle [ˈaidl] **1.** □ müßig; untätig; unbenutzt; träg, faul; unnütz, zwecklos; nichtig, eitel; tot (*Kapital*); ~ *hours pl.* Mußestunden *f/pl.*; **2.** *v/t. mst* ~ *away* vertrödeln, müßig hinbringen; *v/i.* faulenzen; ⊕ leerlaufen; ˈ**i·dle·ness** Muße *f*; Trägheit *f*; Nichtigkeit *f*; ˈ**i·dler** Müßiggänger(in).

i·dol [ˈaidl] Idol *n*, Götzenbild *n*; *fig.* Abgott *m*; **i·dol·a·ter** [aiˈdɔlətə] Götzendiener *m*; blinder Verehrer *m*; **iˈdol·a·tress** Götzendienerin *f etc.*; **iˈdol·a·trous** □ abgöttisch; **iˈdol·a·try** Abgötterei *f*, Götzendienst *m*; Vergötterung *f*; **i·dol·ize** [ˈaidəulaiz] vergöttern.

i·dyll [ˈidil] Idyll(e *f*) *n*; **i·dyl·lic** [aiˈdilik] (*~ally*) idyllisch.

if [if] **1.** wenn, falls; ob; **2.** Wenn *n*; ˈ**if·fy** *Am.* F zweifelhaft.

ig·loo ['iglu:] Iglu *m*, Schneehütte *f*.
ig·ne·ous ['igniəs] feurig.
ig·nit·a·ble [ig'naitəbl] entzündbar; **ig'nite** (sich) entzünden; zünden; ⚗ erhitzen; **ig·ni·tion** [ig'niʃən] Entzündung *f*; *mot.* Zündung *f*; ⚗ Erhitzung *f*; ~ *key mot.* Zündschlüssel *m*.
ig·no·ble □ [ig'nəubl] unedel; niedrig, gemein.
ig·no·min·i·ous □ [ignəu'miniəs] schändlich, schimpflich; **ig·no·min·y** ['ignəmini] Schmach *f*, Schande *f*.
ig·no·ra·mus F [ignə'reiməs] Ignorant(in); Nichtskönner(in); '**ig·no·rance** Unwissenheit *f*; Unkenntnis *f*; '**ig·no·rant** unwissend; unkundig (*of gen.*); **ig·nore** [ig'nɔ:] ignorieren, nicht beachten, übersehen; ⚖ verwerfen.
i·gua·na *zo.* [i'gwa:nə] Leguan *m*.
i·kon ['aikɔn] = *icon*.
i·lex ⚘ ['aileks] Stechpalme *f*.
Il·i·ad ['iliəd] Ilias *f Homers*.
ill [il] **1.** *adj. u. adv.* übel, böse; schlimm, schlecht; krank; *adv.* schwerlich, mit Mühe, kaum; *fall* ~, *be taken* ~ krank werden; *s. ease*; **2.** Übel *n*; Übles *n*, Böses *n*.
I'll [ail] = *I will*.
ill...: '**~-ad'vised** schlecht beraten; unbesonnen, unklug; '**~-af'fect·ed** übelgesinnt (*to dat.*); '**~-'bred** ungebildet, ungezogen, unhöflich; **~ breed·ing** schlechtes Benehmen *n*; '**~-con'di·tioned** in schlechtem Zustand; bösartig; '**~-dis'posed** übelgesinnt (*to dat.*).
il·le·gal □ [i'li:gəl] ungesetzlich, illegal; **il·le·gal·i·ty** [ili:'gæliti] Ungesetzlichkeit *f*.
il·leg·i·ble □ [i'ledʒəbl] unleserlich.
il·le·git·i·ma·cy [ili'dʒitiməsi] Unrechtmäßigkeit *f*; Unehelichkeit *f*; **il·le'git·i·mate** □ [~mit] illegitim; unrechtmäßig; unlogisch; unehelich.
ill...: '**~-'fat·ed** unglücklich; '**~-'fa·vo(u)red** häßlich; '**~-'got·ten** unrechtmäßig erworben; '**~-'hu·mo(u)red** übellaunig.
il·lib·er·al □ [i'libərəl] engstirnig; intolerant; knauserig; **il·lib·er·al·i·ty** [~'ræliti] Engstirnigkeit *f etc.*
il·lic·it □ [i'lisit] unerlaubt; ~ *trade* Schwarzhandel *m*.
il·lim·it·a·ble □ [i'limitəbl] unbegrenzbar, grenzenlos.
il·lit·er·a·cy [i'litərəsi] Unbildung *f*; Analphabetentum *n*; **il'lit·er·ate** [~rit] **1.** ungelehrt, ungebildet; **2.** Analphabet(in).
ill...: '**~-'judged** unklug, unvernünftig; '**~-'man·nered** ungezogen; mit schlechten Umgangsformen; '**~-'na·tured** □ boshaft, bösartig.
ill·ness ['ilnis] Krankheit *f*.
il·log·i·cal □ [i'lɔdʒikəl] unlogisch.
ill...: **~-o·mened** ['il'əumend] von schlechten Vorzeichen begleitet; Unglücks...; '**~-'starred** unglücklich; '**~-'tem·pered** schlecht gelaunt; '**~-'timed** ungelegen, zur Unzeit (geschehend *etc.*); '**~-'treat** mißhandeln.
il·lume *poet.* [i'lju:m] erleuchten (*a. fig.*).
il·lu·mi·nant [i'lju:minənt] **1.** (er-) leuchtend; **2.** Beleuchtungskörper *m*; **il'lu·mi·nate** [~neit] be-, erleuchten (*a. fig.*); erläutern; aufklären; *festlich* illuminieren; bunt ausmalen; *~d advertising* Lichtreklame *f*; **il'lu·mi·nat·ing** Leucht...; *fig.* aufschlußreich; **il·lu·mi'na·tion** Erleuchtung *f*; Illumination *f*; Erläuterung *f*; Aufklärung *f*; **il'lu·mi·na·tive** [~nətiv] erleuchtend; Leucht...; **il'lu·mi·na·tor** Erleuchter *m*; **il'lu·mine** = *illuminate*.
ill-use ['il'ju:z] mißhandeln.
il·lu·sion [i'lu:ʒən] Illusion *f*, Täuschung *f*, Einbildung *f*; **il'lu·sive** □ [~siv], **il'lu·so·ry** □ [~səri] illusorisch, täuschend.
il·lus·trate ['iləstreit] illustrieren; erläutern; veranschaulichen; bebildern; **il·lus'tra·tion** Erläuterung *f*; Illustration *f*; '**il·lus·tra·tive** □ erläuternd; *be ~ of* erläutern; '**il·lus·tra·tor** Erläuterer *m*; Illustrator *m*.
il·lus·tri·ous □ [i'lʌstriəs] berühmt.
ill will ['il'wil] Feindschaft *f*.
I'm [aim] = *I am*.
im·age ['imidʒ] **1.** Bild *n* (*a. rhet.*); Standbild *n*; Ebenbild *n*; Vorstellung *f*; **2.** abbilden; widerspiegeln; anschaulich schildern; '**im·age·ry** Bilder *n/pl.*; Bildersprache *f*, Metaphorik *f*.
im·ag·i·na·ble □ [i'mædʒinəbl]

denkbar; **im'ag·i·nar·y** eingebildet, imaginär; **im·ag·i·na·tion** [~'neiʃən] *schöpferische* Einbildung (-skraft) *f*, Phantasie *f*, Vorstellungskraft *f*, Ideenreichtum *m*; **im'ag·i·na·tive** □ [~nətiv] Einbildungs...; ideen-, einfallsreich; schöpferisch; **im'ag·ine** sich *et.* einbilden, sich *et.* vorstellen, sich *et.* denken.

im·bal·ance [im'bæləns] Unausgeglichenheit *f* (*bsd. der Zahlungsbilanz*).

im·be·cile □ ['imbisi:l] **1.** schwachsinnig; **2.** Schwachsinnige *m*, *f*; **im·be·cil·i·ty** [~'siliti] Schwachsinn *m*.

im·bed [im'bed] = *embed*.

im·bibe [im'baib] einsaugen; *fig.* sich zu eigen machen.

im·bro·glio [im'brəuliəu] Verwirrung *f*.

im·brue [im'bru:] beflecken, benetzen (*in*, *with* mit).

im·bue [im'bju:] (durch)tränken; tief färben; *fig.* erfüllen.

im·i·ta·ble ['imitəbl] nachahmbar; **im·i·tate** ['~teit] nachahmen; nachbilden; ⊕ imitieren; **im·i'ta·tion** Nachahmung *f*; ⊕ Imitation *f*; *attr.* künstlich, Kunst...; ~ *leather* Kunstleder *n*; **im·i·ta·tive** □ ['~tətiv] nachahmend (*of acc.*); ~ *word* lautmalendes Wort *n*; **im·i·ta·tor** ['~teitə] Nachahmer *m*.

im·mac·u·late □ [i'mækjulit] unbefleckt, rein; fehlerlos.

im·ma·nent ['imənənt] immanent, innewohnend.

im·ma·te·ri·al □ [imə'tiəriəl] unkörperlich; unwesentlich (*to* für).

im·ma·ture [imə'tjuə] unreif, unentwickelt; **im·ma'tu·ri·ty** Unreife *f*.

im·meas·ur·a·ble □ [i'meʒərəbl] unermeßlich.

im·me·di·ate □ [i'mi:djət] unmittelbar; unverzüglich, sofortig; **im'me·di·ate·ly** **1.** *adv.* sofort; **2.** *cj.* gleich nachdem.

im·me·mo·ri·al □ [imi'mɔ:riəl] un(vor)denklich; *from time* ~ seit unvordenklichen Zeiten.

im·mense □ [i'mens] unermeßlich; ungeheuer, gewaltig; *sl.* fabelhaft; **im'men·si·ty** Unermeßlichkeit *f*.

im·merse [i'mə:s] (ein-, unter-)tauchen; ~ *o.s. in fig.* sich versenken od. vertiefen in (*acc.*); ~*d in* vertieft in *ein Buch*; verwickelt in *Schulden etc.*; **im'mer·sion** (Ein-, Unter-)Tauchen *n*; Einsinken *n*; *fig.* Versenkung *f*; ~ *heater* Heizspirale *f e-s Boilers*; Tauchsieder *m*.

im·mi·grant ['imigrənt] Einwanderer *m*; **im·mi·grate** ['~greit] *v/i.* einwandern; *v/t.* ansiedeln (*into* in *dat.*); **im·mi'gra·tion** Einwanderung *f*.

im·mi·nence ['iminəns] Bevorstehen *n*, Drohen *n*; **'im·mi·nent** □ bevorstehend, drohend.

im·mit·i·ga·ble □ [i'mitigəbl] nicht zu besänftigen(d); unerbittlich.

im·mo·bile [i'məubail] unbeweglich; **im·mo·bil·i·ty** [~'biliti] Unbeweglichkeit *f*; **im'mo·bi·lize** [~bilaiz] unbeweglich machen; festlegen; *Geld* aus dem Verkehr ziehen.

im·mod·er·ate □ [i'mɔdərit] übermäßig, maßlos; **im'mod·er·ate·ness** Maßlosigkeit *f*.

im·mod·est □ [i'mɔdist] unbescheiden; unanständig; **im'mod·es·ty** Unbescheidenheit *f*; Unanständigkeit *f*.

im·mo·late ['iməuleit] opfern; **im·mo'la·tion** Opferung *f*, Opfer *n*.

im·mor·al □ [i'mɔrəl] unmoralisch, unsittlich; **im·mo·ral·i·ty** [imə'ræliti] Unsittlichkeit *f*.

im·mor·tal [i'mɔ:tl] **1.** □ unsterblich; **2.** Unsterbliche *m*, *f*; **im·mor·tal·i·ty** [~'tæliti] Unsterblichkeit *f*; **im'mor·tal·ize** [~təlaiz] unsterblich machen.

im·mov·a·ble [i'mu:vəbl] **1.** □ unbeweglich; unerschütterlich; **2.** ~*s pl.* Immobilien *pl*.

im·mune [i'mju:n] ⚕ *u. fig.* (*from*) immun, gefeit (gegen); unempfänglich (für); frei (von); **im'mu·ni·ty** Immunität *f*, Freiheit *f* (*from* von *Steuern etc.*); Unempfänglichkeit *f* (*from* für); Vorrecht *n*; **im·mu·nize** ['~naiz] immunisieren.

im·mure [i'mjuə] einkerkern.

im·mu·ta·bil·i·ty [imju:tə'biliti] Unveränderlichkeit *f*; **im'mu·ta·ble** □ unveränderlich.

imp [imp] Teufelchen *n*; Kobold *m*; Schelm *m*, Schlingel *m*.

im·pact ['impækt] (Zs.-)Stoß *m*; Anprall *m*; Einwirkung *f*; *Geschoß-*Aufschlag *m*.

im·pair [imˈpɛə] schwächen; (ver-)mindern; beeinträchtigen.
im·pale [imˈpeil] pfählen; aufspießen.
im·pal·pa·ble □ [imˈpælpəbl] unfühlbar; *fig.* unfaßbar; sehr fein.
im·pan·el [imˈpænl] = *empanel.*
im·part [imˈpɑːt] verleihen; weitergeben; vermitteln; mitteilen.
im·par·tial □ [imˈpɑːʃəl] unparteiisch; **im·par·ti·al·i·ty** [ˈ~ʃiˈæliti] Unparteilichkeit *f*, Objektivität *f*.
im·pass·a·ble □ [imˈpɑːsəbl] ungangbar, unpassierbar.
im·passe [æmˈpɑːs] Sackgasse *f* (*a. fig.*); *fig.* toter Punkt *m*.
im·pas·si·ble □ [imˈpæsibl] unempfindlich, gefühllos (*to* gegen).
im·pas·sion [imˈpæʃən] leidenschaftlich bewegen *od.* erregen; **imˈpas·sioned** leidenschaftlich.
im·pas·sive □ [imˈpæsiv] unempfindlich; teilnahmslos; heiter; **imˈpas·sive·ness** Unempfindlichkeit *f*.
im·pa·tience [imˈpeiʃəns] Ungeduld *f*; Unduldsamkeit *f*; **imˈpa·tient** □ ungeduldig (*at, of* über *acc.*); *be ~ of s.th.* et. nicht ertragen können; *~ for* begierig nach.
im·peach [imˈpiːtʃ] anklagen, beschuldigen (*of, with gen.*); zur Verantwortung ziehen; anfechten, anzweifeln; **imˈpeach·a·ble** anklagbar; anfechtbar; **imˈpeach·ment** Anzweiflung *f*; Anfechtung *f*; öffentliche Anklage *f*.
im·pec·ca·bil·i·ty [impekəˈbiliti] Sündlosigkeit *f*; Makellosigkeit *f*; **imˈpec·ca·ble** □ sündlos; makellos, einwandfrei.
im·pe·cu·ni·ous [impiˈkjuːnjəs] ohne Geld, mittellos.
im·pede [imˈpiːd] (ver)hindern.
im·ped·i·ment [imˈpedimənt] Hindernis *n* (*to* für); *~ in one's speech* Sprachfehler *m*; **im·ped·i·men·ta** ⚔ [~ˈmentə] *pl.* Gepäck *n*, Troß *m*.
im·pel [imˈpel] (an)treiben; **imˈpel·lent 1.** treibend; **2.** Triebkraft *f*.
im·pend [imˈpend] hängen, schweben (*over* über *dat.*); bevorstehen, drohen; **imˈpend·ence** drohende Nähe *f*; **imˈpend·ent, imˈpend·ing** nahe (bevorstehend); drohend.
im·pen·e·tra·bil·i·ty [impenitrəˈbiliti] Undurchdringlichkeit *f* (*a. fig.*); **imˈpen·e·tra·ble** □ undurchdringlich (*to, by* für); *fig.* unergründlich; *fig.* unzugänglich (*to dat.*).
im·pen·i·tence [imˈpenitəns] Unbußfertigkeit *f*, Verstocktheit *f*; **imˈpen·i·tent** □ unbußfertig, verstockt.
im·per·a·tive [imˈperətiv] **1.** □ notwendig, dringend, unbedingt erforderlich; befehlend; gebieterisch; *gr.* imperativisch; *~ mood* = **2.** *gr.* Imperativ *m*.
im·per·cep·ti·ble □ [impəˈseptəbl] unmerklich.
im·per·fect [imˈpəːfikt] **1.** □ unvollkommen; unvollständig; unvollendet; *~ tense* = **2.** *gr.* Imperfekt *n*; **im·per·fec·tion** [~pəˈfekʃən] Unvollkommenheit *f*; *fig.* Schwäche *f*.
im·pe·ri·al [imˈpiəriəl] **1.** □ kaiserlich; Kaiser..., Reichs...; gebietend; großartig; **2.** Fliege *f* (*Bart*); Imperialpapier *n*; **imˈpe·ri·al·ism** Imperialismus *m*, Weltmachtpolitik *f*; **imˈpe·ri·al·ist** Imperialist *m*, Anhänger *m* der Weltmachtpolitik; **im·pe·ri·alˈis·tic** imperialistisch.
im·per·il [imˈperil] gefährden.
im·pe·ri·ous □ [imˈpiəriəs] gebieterisch; anmaßend; dringend.
im·per·ish·a·ble □ [imˈperiʃəbl] unvergänglich.
im·per·ma·nent [imˈpəːmənənt] unbeständig.
im·per·me·a·ble □ [imˈpəːmjəbl] undurchdringlich, -lässig.
im·per·son·al □ [imˈpəːsnl] unpersönlich; **im·per·son·al·i·ty** [~səˈnæliti] Unpersönlichkeit *f*.
im·per·son·ate [imˈpəːsəneit] verkörpern; *thea.* darstellen; **im·per·sonˈa·tion** Verkörperung *f*; *thea.* Darstellung *f*.
im·per·ti·nence [imˈpəːtinəns] Impertinenz *f*, Unverschämtheit *f*, Ungehörigkeit *f*; Nebensächlichkeit *f*; **imˈper·ti·nent** □ impertinent, unverschämt; ungezogen, frech; ungehörig; ⚖ nicht zur Sache gehörig; nebensächlich.
im·per·turb·a·bil·i·ty [ˈimpəːtəːbəˈbiliti] Unerschütterlichkeit *f*; **im·perˈturb·a·ble** □ unerschütterlich.
im·per·vi·ous □ [imˈpəːvjəs] unzugänglich (*to* für) (*a. fig.*); undurchlässig.
im·pe·ti·go ⚕ [impiˈtaigəu] Impe-

tigo *m*, Blasengrind *m*.

im·pet·u·os·i·ty [impetju'ɔsiti] Ungestüm *m*, *n*; **im'pet·u·ous** □ ungestüm, heftig; **im·pe·tus** ['impitəs] Antrieb *m*, Anstoß *m* (*a. fig.*).

im·pi·e·ty [im'paiəti] Gottlosigkeit *f*; Mangel *m* an Ehrfurcht.

im·pinge [im'pindʒ] (ver)stoßen (*on, upon, against* gegen); ~ *on* übergreifen auf (*acc.*); **im'pinge·ment** Stoß *m*, Anprall *m* (*on, upon* gegen); *fig.* Verstoß *m* (gegen).

im·pi·ous □ ['impiəs] gottlos; pietätlos; frevelhaft.

imp·ish □ ['impiʃ] boshaft; schelmisch.

im·pla·ca·bil·i·ty [implækə'biliti] Unversöhnlichkeit *f*; **im'pla·ca·ble** □ unversöhnlich, unerbittlich.

im·plant [im'plɑːnt] *mst fig.* einpflanzen (*in* in *acc.*).

im·plau·si·ble [im'plɔːzəbl] unglaubwürdig.

im·ple·ment 1. ['implimənt] Werkzeug *n*; Gerät *n*; **2.** ['~ment] bewerkstelligen; ausführen; verwirklichen; **im·ple·men'ta·tion** [~men'teiʃən] Ausführung *f*; Verwirklichung *f*.

im·pli·cate ['implikeit] verwickeln, hineinziehen (*in* in *acc.*); mit einbegreifen, in sich schließen; **im·pli'ca·tion** Verwick(e)lung *f*; *stillschweigende* Folgerung *f*; *what are the ~s?* was soll damit gesagt werden?

im·plic·it □ [im'plisit] (stillschweigend) mit eingeschlossen *od.* sich ergebend; unausgesprochen; verblümt; unbedingt, blind (*Glaube etc.*); **im'plic·it·ly** implizite, stillschweigend; unbedingt.

im·plied □ [im'plaid] (stillschweigend) mit inbegriffen; angedeutet.

im·plore [im'plɔː] (an-, er)flehen; flehentlich bitten; **im'plor·ing** □ [~riŋ] flehentlich.

im·ply [im'plai] einschließen, enthalten, in sich schließen; besagen, bedeuten; andeuten; unterstellen; *do you ~ that...?* wollen Sie damit sagen, daß ...?

im·po·lite □ [impə'lait] unhöflich.

im·pol·i·tic □ [im'pɔlitik] unpolitisch, unklug.

im·pon·der·a·ble [im'pɔndərəbl] **1.** unwägbar; **2.** ~*s pl.* unwägbare Dinge *n/pl.*, Imponderabilien *n/pl.*

im·port 1. ['impɔːt] Bedeutung *f*, Sinn *m*; Wichtigkeit *f*; ✝ Einfuhr *f*; ~*s pl.* Einfuhrwaren *f/pl.*; ~ *duty* Einfuhrzoll *m*; **2.** [im'pɔːt] *Waren* einführen; bedeuten; besagen; *j.* betreffen, für *j.* wichtig sein; **im'por·tance** Wichtigkeit *f*; Bedeutung *f*; Einfluß *m*; **im'por·tant** □ wichtig; bedeutend; wichtigtuerisch; **im·por·ta·tion** [~'teiʃən] Einfuhr *f*; Einfuhrwaren *f/pl.*; **im'port·er** Importeur *m*.

im·por·tu·nate □ [im'pɔːtjunit] lästig, zudringlich; **im'por·tune** [~tjuːn] dringend bitten, bestürmen; belästigen; **im·por'tu·ni·ty** Zudringlichkeit *f*.

im·pose [im'pəuz] *v/t.* auf(er)legen, aufbürden, aufdrängen (*on, upon dat.*); *v/i.* ~ *upon j-m* imponieren; *j.* täuschen; *j-s Güte etc.* mißbrauchen; **im'pos·ing** □ imponierend, eindrucksvoll; **im·po·si·tion** [impə'ziʃən] Auflegung *f der Hände*; Beilegung *f e-s Namens*; Auflage *f*, Steuer *f*; *Schule*: Strafarbeit *f*; Betrügerei *f*.

im·pos·si·bil·i·ty [impɔsə'biliti] Unmöglichkeit *f*; **im'pos·si·ble** □ unmöglich.

im·post ['impəust] Abgabe *f*, Steuer *f*; **im·pos·tor** [im'pɔstə] Betrüger *m*; **im'pos·ture** [~tʃə] Betrug *m*.

im·po·tence ['impətəns] Unfähigkeit *f*; Machtlosigkeit *f*; *physiol.* Impotenz *f*; **'im·po·tent** unvermögend, machtlos, schwach; impotent.

im·pound [im'paund] beschlagnahmen; *Vieh* einpferchen.

im·pov·er·ish [im'pɔvəriʃ] arm machen; *Boden* auslaugen.

im·prac·ti·ca·bil·i·ty [impræktikə'biliti] Undurchführbarkeit *f*; Unwegsamkeit *f*; **im'prac·ti·ca·ble** □ undurchführbar; unwegsam.

im·prac·ti·cal [im'præktikəl] unpraktisch; theoretisch; unnütz.

im·pre·cate ['imprikeit] *Böses* herabwünschen (*upon* auf *acc.*); **im·pre'ca·tion** Verwünschung *f*; **im·pre·ca·to·ry** ['~keitəri] Verwünschungs...

im·preg·na·bil·i·ty [impregnə'biliti] Unüberwindlichkeit *f*; **im'preg·na·ble** □ uneinnehmbar; unüberwindlich; **im·preg·nate 1.** ['~neit] schwängern; ⚘ befruchten; ⚗ sättigen, tränken (*a. fig.*); *fig.* durchdringen; ⊕ imprägnieren; **2.** [im'pregnit] geschwängert; durchtränkt; **im·preg·na·tion** [~'neiʃən] Schwängerung *f*; Befruchtung *f*; Sättigung *f*; Imprägnierung *f*.

im·pre·sa·ri·o [impre'sɑːriəu] Impresario *m*, Manager *m*.

im·pre·scrip·ti·ble [impris'kriptəbl] unverjährbar; unveräußerlich.

im·press 1. ['impres] (Ab-, Ein-) Druck *m*; *fig.* Stempel *m*; **2.** [im'pres] eindrücken, prägen (*on s.th. od. s.th. with* auf *acc.*); *Kraft etc.* übertragen (*on, upon* auf *acc.*); *Gedanken etc.* aufzwingen, einprägen (*on dat.*); Eindruck machen auf *j.*, beeindrucken; *j-m* imponieren; ~ *s.o. with s.th.* j. mit et. erfüllen; ⚓ *Matrosen* (zum Dienst) pressen; **im'press·i·ble** eindrucksfähig; **im'pres·sion** [~ʃən] Eindruck *m* (*a. fig.*); *typ.* Abdruck *m*, Abzug *m*; Auflage *f*; *be under the* ~ *that* den Eindruck haben, daß; **im'pres·sion·a·ble** [~ʃnəbl] empfänglich, leicht zu beeindrucken(d), eindrucksfähig; **im'pres·sion·ism** Impressionismus *m*; **im'pres·sion·ist** Impressionist *m*; **im'pres·sion·is·tic** impressionistisch; **im'pres·sive** □ [~siv] eindrucksvoll; **im'press·ment** ⚓ Pressen *n*.

im·print 1. [im'print] aufdrücken, prägen (*on* auf *acc.*); *fig.* einprägen (*on, in dat.*); **2.** ['imprint] Eindruck *m*; Stempel *m* (*a. fig.*); *typ.* Druckvermerk *m*.

im·pris·on [im'prizn] ins Gefängnis werfen, einsperren, -kerkern; **im'pris·on·ment** Einkerkerung *f*; Haft *f*; Gefängnis(strafe *f*) *n*.

im·prob·a·bil·i·ty [imprɔbə'biliti] Unwahrscheinlichkeit *f*; **im'prob·a·ble** □ unwahrscheinlich.

im·pro·bi·ty [im'prəubiti] Unredlichkeit *f*, Unehrlichkeit *f*.

im·promp·tu [im'prɔmptjuː] **1.** ♪ Impromptu *n*; **2.** aus dem Stegreif.

im·prop·er □ [im'prɔpə] ungeeignet, unpassend; unzutreffend, falsch; unanständig; ~ *fraction* Ⱥ unechter Bruch *m*; **im·pro·pri·e·ty** [imprə'praiəti] Ungeeignetheit *f*; Ungehörigkeit *f*; Unrichtigkeit *f*; Unanständigkeit *f*.

im·prov·a·ble □ [im'pruːvəbl] verbesserungsfähig; anbaufähig (*Land*).

im·prove [im'pruːv] *v/t.* verbessern; veredeln; *Gelegenheit etc.* aus-, benutzen; *v/i.* sich (ver)bessern, Fortschritte machen; ~ *upon* vervollkommnen; **im'prove·ment** Verbesserung *f*, Vervollkommnung *f*; (Nutz)Anwendung *f*; Ausnutzung *f*; Fortschritt *m* (*on, upon* gegenüber *dat.*); **im'prov·er** Verbesserer *m*; Volontär *m*.

im·prov·i·dence [im'prɔvidəns] Unbedachtsamkeit *f*; **im'prov·i·dent** □ unbedachtsam; leichtsinnig.

im·pro·vi·sa·tion [imprəvai'zeiʃən] Improvisation *f*; **im·pro·vise** ['~vaiz] improvisieren; '**im·pro·vised** behelfsmäßig; Behelfs...

im·pru·dence [im'pruːdəns] Unklugheit *f*; **im'pru·dent** □ unklug.

im·pu·dence ['impjudəns] Unverschämtheit *f*, Frechheit *f*; '**im·pu·dent** □ unverschämt, frech.

im·pugn [im'pjuːn] anfechten, bestreiten, bezweifeln; **im'pugn·a·ble** anfechtbar.

im·pulse ['impʌls], **im'pul·sion** Impuls *m*, (An)Stoß *m*; *fig.* (An-) Trieb *m*; **im'pul·sive** □ (an)treibend; *fig.* impulsiv, leicht erregbar; rasch (handelnd); **im'pul·sive·ness** Impulsivität *f*.

im·pu·ni·ty [im'pjuːniti] Straflosigkeit *f*; *with* ~ ungestraft.

im·pure □ [im'pjuə] unrein (*a. fig.*); unkeusch; **im'pu·ri·ty** [~riti] Unreinheit *f*; Unkeuschheit *f*.

im·put·a·ble [im'pjuːtəbl] zuzuschreiben(d), beizumessen(d); **im·pu·ta·tion** [~'teiʃən] Beschuldigung *f*; **im'pute** zurechnen, beimessen; zur Last legen.

in [in] **1.** *prp. allg.* in (*dat.*); *engS.*: (~ *the morning, a wound* ~ *the head,* ~ *number,* ~ *size,* ~ *itself, professor* ~ *the university*) an (*dat.*); (~ *a field,* ~ *the street,* ~ *the country,* ~ *search of, blind* ~ *one eye,* ~ *English*) auf (*dat.*); (~ *this manner, trust* ~ *s.o.*) auf (*acc.*); (*bust* ~ *marble, coat* ~ *velvet*) aus; (~ *Shakespeare,* ~ *the daytime,* ~ *crossing the road*) bei; (*engaged* ~ *reading, written* ~ *pencil,* ~ *a word,* ~ *a few words*) mit; (~ *my opinion,* ~ *all probability*) nach; (*rejoice* ~ *s.th.*) über (*acc.*); (~ *the circumstances,* ~ *the reign of, one* ~ *ten*) unter (*dat.*); (*cry out* ~ *alarm*) vor (*dat.*); (*grouped* ~ *tens, speak* ~ *reply,* ~ *s.o.'s defence,*

~ *excuse*, ~ *honour of*) zu; ~ *1969* (im Jahr) 1969; *two days* ~ *three* an zwei von drei Tagen; *there is nothing* ~ *it* es ist nichts daran; F es kommt nichts dabei heraus; *it is not* ~ *her* es liegt ihr nicht; *he hasn't it* ~ *him* er hat nicht das Zeug dazu; ~ *that* ... insofern als, weil; *bei Zeitwörtern der Bewegung u. Veränderung*: in (*acc.*); **2.** *adv.* drin(nen); herein; hinein; *bei Zeitwörtern oft* ein...; *be* ~ drin(nen) sein (*im Zimmer, Haus*); d(a)ran sein (*an der Macht, am Spiel*); *be* ~ *for et.* zu erwarten haben, dran sein bei; *e-e Prüfung etc.* vor sich haben; *be well* ~ *with* F sich gut mit *j-m* stehen; **3.** *adj.* hereinkommend; Innen...; F in, in Mode; **4.** *su.*: *the* ~*s pl. parl.* die Regierungspartei; *the* ~*s and outs pl.* alle Winkel u. Ecken *pl.*; alle Einzelheiten *f/pl.*

in·a·bil·i·ty [inə'biliti] Unfähigkeit *f*, Unvermögen *n*.

in·ac·ces·si·bil·i·ty ['inæksesə'biliti] Unzugänglichkeit *f*; **in·ac'ces·si·ble** □ unzugänglich.

in·ac·cu·ra·cy [in'ækjurəsi] Ungenauigkeit *f*; **in'ac·cu·rate** □ [~rit] ungenau; unrichtig.

in·ac·tion [in'ækʃən] Untätigkeit *f*.

in·ac·tive □ [in'æktiv] untätig, ✝ lustlos; ⚗ unwirksam; **in·ac'tiv·i·ty** Untätig-, Lustlosigkeit *f*.

in·ad·e·qua·cy [in'ædikwəsi] Unangemessenheit *f*; Unzulänglichkeit *f*; **in'ad·e·quate** □ [~kwit] unangemessen; unzulänglich.

in·ad·mis·si·bil·i·ty ['inədmisə'biliti] Unzulässigkeit *f*; **in·ad'mis·si·ble** □ unzulässig.

in·ad·vert·ence, in·ad·vert·en·cy [inəd'və:təns(i)] Unachtsamkeit *f*; Versehen *n*; **in·ad'vert·ent** □ unachtsam; unbeabsichtigt, versehentlich; ~*ly a.* aus Versehen.

in·ad·vis·a·ble □ [inəd'vaizəbl] nicht ratsam, nicht empfehlenswert.

in·al·ien·a·ble □ [in'eiljənəbl] unveräußerlich.

in·al·ter·a·ble □ [in'ɔ:ltərəbl] unveränderlich.

in·am·o·ra·ta *f* [inæmə'rɑ:tə] Geliebte *f*; **in·am·o'ra·to** *m* [~təu] Geliebte *m*, Liebhaber *m*.

in·ane □ [i'nein] *mst fig.* leer; geistlos; albern; fad; unsinnig.

in·an·i·mate □ [in'ænimit] unbeseelt, leblos; *fig.* unbelebt; geistlos, langweilig.

in·a·ni·tion ⚕ [inə'niʃən] Entkräftung *f*.

in·an·i·ty [i'næniti] Leere *f*; Geistlosigkeit *f etc.* (*s. inane*).

in·ap·pli·ca·bil·i·ty ['inæplikə'biliti] Unanwendbarkeit *f*; **in'ap·pli·ca·ble** unanwendbar (*to* auf *acc.*); nicht zu- *od.* betreffend.

in·ap·po·site □ [in'æpəzit] unpassend.

in·ap·pre·ci·a·ble □ [inə'pri:ʃəbl] unmerklich; unbedeutend.

in·ap·pre·hen·si·ble □ [inæpri'hensəbl] unbegreiflich, unfaßbar.

in·ap·proach·a·ble [inə'prəutʃəbl] unnahbar, unzugänglich.

in·ap·pro·pri·ate □ [inə'prəupriit] unangebracht, unpassend.

in·apt □ [in'æpt] ungeeignet, untauglich; ungeschickt; unpassend; **in'apt·i·tude** [~titju:d], **in'apt·ness** Ungeeignetheit *f*; Ungeschicktheit *f etc.*

in·ar·tic·u·late □ [inɑ:'tikjulit] undeutlich; schwer zu verstehen(d); undeutlich sprechend; *zo.* ungegliedert; **in·ar'tic·u·late·ness** Undeutlichkeit *f der Aussprache*.

in·as·much [inəz'mʌtʃ]: ~ *as* da, weil; insofern als.

in·at·ten·tion [inə'tenʃən] Unaufmerksamkeit *f*; **in·at'ten·tive** □ [~tiv] unaufmerksam (*to* gegen).

in·au·di·ble □ [in'ɔ:dəbl] unhörbar.

in·au·gu·ral [i'nɔ:gjurəl] **1.** Antritts...; ~ *lecture* Antrittsvorlesung *f*; **2.** Antrittsrede *f*; **in'au·gu·rate** [~reit] (feierlich) einführen, einweihen; beginnen; **in·au·gu'ra·tion** Einführung *f*, Einweihung *f*; ꝯ *Day Am.* Amtseinführung *f* des neugewählten Präsidenten der USA.

in·aus·pi·cious □ [inɔ:s'piʃəs] ungünstig, unheilvoll.

in·board ⚓ ['inbɔ:d] (b)innenbords.

in·born ['in'bɔ:n] angeboren.

in·bred ['in'bred] angeboren; durch Inzucht erzeugt.

in·breed·ing ['in'bri:diŋ] Inzucht *f*.

in·cal·cul·a·ble □ [in'kælkjuləbl] unberechenbar; unzählig.

in·can·des·cence ['inkæn'desns] Weißglühen *n*, -glut *f*; '**in·can'des·cent** weißglühend; ~ *light* Glühlicht *n*; ~ *mantle* Glühstrumpf *m.*

in·can·ta·tion [inkæn'teiʃən] Beschwörung *f*; Zauberformel *f*.

in·ca·pa·bil·i·ty [inkeipə'biliti] Unfähigkeit *f*, Untüchtigkeit *f*; Untauglichkeit *f*; **in'ca·pa·ble** □ unfähig, ungeeignet (*of* zu); hilflos (*Betrunkener*); **in·ca·pac·i·tate** [inkə'pæsiteit] unfähig machen (*for, from* zu); außer Gefecht setzen; (ver)hindern; **in·ca'pac·i·ty** Unfähigkeit *f* (*for* für, zu).

in·car·cer·ate [in'kɑːsəreit] einkerkern; **in·car·cer'a·tion** Einkerkerung *f*.

in·car·nate 1. [in'kɑːnit] fleischgeworden; *fig.* verkörpert; **2.** ['inkɑːneit] Fleisch werden lassen; *fig.* verkörpern; **in·car'na·tion** Fleischwerdung *f*; *fig.* Verkörperung *f*.

in·case [in'keis] = *encase*.

in·cau·tious □ [in'kɔːʃəs] unvorsichtig; **in'cau·tious·ness** Unvorsichtigkeit *f*.

in·cen·di·ar·y [in'sendjəri] **1.** brandstifterisch; *fig.* aufwieglerisch; ~ (*bomb*) Brandbombe *f*; **2.** Brandstifter *m*; Aufwiegler *m*.

in·cense[1] ['insens] **1.** Weihrauch *m*; **2.** beweihräuchern; durchduften.

in·cense[2] [in'sens] in Wut bringen, aufbringen (*with* über *acc.*).

in·cen·tive [in'sentiv] **1.** anreizend; **2.** Antrieb *m*, Anreiz *m*.

in·cep·tion [in'sepʃən] Anfang *m*; **in'cep·tive** [~tiv] Anfangs...; *gr.* inchoativ (*den Anfang e-r Handlung bezeichnend*).

in·cer·ti·tude [in'səːtitjuːd] Ungewißheit *f*.

in·ces·sant □ [in'sesnt] unaufhörlich; ohne Unterbrechung.

in·cest ['insest] Blutschande *f*, Inzest *m*; **in·ces·tu·ous** □ [in'sestjuəs] blutschänderisch.

inch [intʃ] Zoll *m* (*2,54 cm*); *fig.* bißchen; ~*es pl. a. Körper*-Größe *f*; *by* ~*es* knapp; allmählich; *every* ~ ganz (u. gar); **inched** ...zöllig.

in·cho·a·tive ['inkəueitiv] anfangend; *gr.* inchoativ.

in·ci·dence ['insidəns] Vorkommen *n*, Auftreten *n*; Wirkung *f*, Einfluß *m*; *angle of* ~ Einfallswinkel *m*; **'in·ci·dent 1.** zs.-hängend (*to* mit); vorkommend (*to* bei), eigen (*to dat.*); **2.** Zufall *m*, Vorfall *m*, Zwischenfall *m*; Ereignis *n*; Nebenumstand *m*; *thea.* Zwischenhandlung *f*; **in·ci·den·tal** □ [~'dentl] zufällig, gelegentlich; Neben..., Zwischen...; *be* ~ *to* gehören zu; ~*ly* nebenbei.

in·cin·er·ate [in'sinəreit] *Leiche* einäschern; *Müll* verbrennen; **in·cin·er'a·tion** Einäscherung *f*; **in'cin·er·a·tor** Verbrennungsofen *m*.

in·cip·i·en·cy [in'sipiənsi] Anfang *m*; **in'cip·i·ent** anfangend; Anfangs...

in·cise [in'saiz] einschneiden; einritzen; **in·ci·sion** [~'siʒən] Einschnitt *m*; ⚕ Schnitt *m*; **in·ci·sive** □ [~'saisiv] (ein)schneidend, scharf; treffend; **in·ci·sor** [~'saizə] Schneidezahn *m*.

in·ci·ta·tion [insai'teiʃən] = *incitement*; **in'cite** anspornen, anregen, anstacheln; anstiften; **in'cite·ment** Anstiftung *f*; Anregung *f*; Ansporn *m*, Antrieb *m*.

in·ci·vil·i·ty [insi'viliti] Unhöflichkeit *f*.

in·clem·en·cy [in'klemənsi] Unfreundlichkeit *f*, Rauheit *f des Wetters*; **in'clem·ent** unfreundlich, rauh.

in·cli·na·tion [inkli'neiʃən] Neigung *f* (*a. fig.*); **in·cline** [~'klain] **1.** *v/i.* sich neigen (*a. fig., Tag etc.*); geneigt sein; ~ *to fig.* zu *et.* neigen; dazu neigen, zu *inf.*; *v/t.* neigen; geneigt machen; ~*d plane* schiefe Ebene *f*; **2.** Neigung *f*, Abhang *m*.

in·close [in'kləuz], **in'clos·ure** [~ʒə] = *enclose, enclosure*.

in·clude [in'kluːd] einschließen; enthalten; mit einbeziehen.

in·clu·sion [in'kluːʒən] Einschließung *f*, Einschluß *m*; **in'clu·sive** [~siv] einschließlich; alles inbegriffen; *be* ~ *of* einschließen; ~ *terms pl.* Pauschalpreis *m*.

in·cog F [in'kɔg], **in'cog·ni·to** [~nitəu] **1.** inkognito, unerkannt; anonym; **2.** Inkognito *n*.

in·co·her·ence, in·co·her·en·cy [inkəu'hiərəns(i)] Zs.-hangslosigkeit *f*; Unvereinbarkeit *f*; Inkonsequenz *f*; **in·co'her·ent** □ unzs.-hängend; inkonsequent.

in·com·bus·ti·ble □ [inkəm'bʌstəbl] unverbrennbar.

in·come ['inkʌm] Einkommen *n*; **'in·com·er** Ankömmling *m*; ⚖ Nachfolger *m*; Eindringling *m*; **in·come-tax** ['inkəmtæks] Einkommensteuer *f*.

in·com·ing ['inkʌmiŋ] **1.** Eintritt *m*; *~s pl.* Einkünfte *pl.*; **2.** hereinkommend; neu eintretend.

in·com·men·su·ra·bil·i·ty ['inkəmenʃərə'biliti] Unmeßbarkeit *f*; **in·com'men·su·ra·ble** □ unmeßbar; unvergleichbar; **in·com'men·su·rate** [~rit] in keinem Verhältnis stehend (*with, to* zu); = *incommensurable*.

in·com·mode [inkə'məud] belästigen; stören; **in·com'mo·di·ous** □ [~djəs] unbequem, lästig.

in·com·mu·ni·ca·ble [inkə'mju:nikəbl] □ nicht mitteilbar; **in·com·mu·ni·ca·do** *bsd. Am.* [~'kɑ:dəu] ohne Verbindung mit der Außenwelt; **in·com'mu·ni·ca·tive** □ [~kətiv] nicht mitteilsam, verschlossen.

in·com·mut·a·ble □ [inkə'mju:təbl] unwandelbar.

in·com·pa·ra·ble □ [in'kɔmpərəbl] unvergleichlich.

in·com·pat·i·bil·i·ty ['inkəmpætə'biliti] Unvereinbarkeit *f*; Unverträglichkeit *f*; **in·com'pat·i·ble** □ unvereinbar; unverträglich (*Mensch*).

in·com·pe·tence, in·com·pe·ten·cy [in'kɔmpitəns(i)] Unfähigkeit *f*; Unzulänglichkeit *f*; Inkompetenz *f*, Unzuständigkeit *f*; **in'com·pe·tent** □ untauglich, unfähig; unzuständig, unbefugt.

in·com·plete □ [inkəm'pli:t] unvollständig; unvollkommen.

in·com·pre·hen·si·bil·i·ty [inkɔmprihensə'biliti] Unbegreiflichkeit *f*; **in·com·pre'hen·sible** □ unbegreiflich; **in·com·pre'hen·sion** Nichtverstehen *n*.

in·com·press·i·ble [inkəm'presəbl] nicht zusammendrückbar.

in·con·ceiv·a·ble □ [inkən'si:vəbl] unbegreiflich, unfaßbar.

in·con·clu·sive □ [inkən'klu:siv] nicht überzeugend; ergebnislos; **in·con'clu·sive·ness** Mangel *m* an Beweiskraft.

in·con·gru·i·ty [inkɔŋ'gru:iti] Nichtübereinstimmung *f*; Unangemessenheit *f*; Mißverhältnis *n*; **in'con·gru·ous** □ [~gruəs] nicht übereinstimmend (*with* mit); unangebracht, unpassend; widersinnig, widerspruchsvoll.

in·con·se·quence [in'kɔnsikwəns] Folgewidrigkeit *f*, Inkonsequenz *f*; **in'con·se·quent** □ folgewidrig, inkonsequent; **in·con·se·quen·tial** [~'kwenʃəl] unbedeutend; = *inconsequent*.

in·con·sid·er·a·ble □ [inkən'sidərəbl] unbedeutend; **in·con'sid·er·ate** □ [~rit] unüberlegt, unbesonnen; rücksichtslos (*towards* gegen); **in·con'sid·er·ate·ness** Unüberlegtheit *f*; Rücksichtslosigkeit *f*.

in·con·sist·en·cy [inkən'sistənsi] Unvereinbarkeit *f*; Inkonsequenz *f* (*gen.*); Unstimmigkeit *f*; **in·con'sist·ent** □ unvereinbar; widerspruchsvoll; ungereimt; inkonsequent.

in·con·sol·a·ble □ [inkən'səuləbl] untröstlich.

in·con·spic·u·ous □ [inkən'spikjuəs] unauffällig, unscheinbar.

in·con·stan·cy [in'kɔnstənsi] Unbeständigkeit *f*; **in'con·stant** □ unbeständig; veränderlich.

in·con·test·a·ble □ [inkən'testəbl] unbestreitbar, unstreitig.

in·con·ti·nence [in'kɔntinəns] Unenthaltsamkeit *f*; Ausschweifung *f*; *~ of urine* ⚕ Harnfluß *m*; **in'con·ti·nent** □ unenthaltsam; ausschweifend; *~ly* unverzüglich, sofort.

in·con·tro·vert·i·ble □ ['inkəntrə'və:təbl] unbestreitbar.

in·con·ven·ience [inkən'vi:njəns] **1.** Unbequemlichkeit *f*; Unannehmlichkeit *f*; **2.** belästigen, *j-m* lästig fallen; **in·con'ven·ient** □ unbequem; ungelegen; lästig (*to* für *od. dat.*).

in·con·vert·i·bil·i·ty ['inkənvə:tə'biliti] Unverwandelbarkeit *f*; ✝ Nichtkonvertierbarkeit *f*; **in·con'vert·i·ble** □ unverwandelbar; ✝ nicht umsetzbar, nicht konvertierbar.

in·con·vin·ci·ble □ [inkən'vinsəbl] nicht zu überzeugen(d).

in·cor·po·rate 1. [in'kɔ:pəreit] einverleiben (*into dat.*); (sich) vereinigen, (sich) verbinden; (ver-) mischen; *als Mitglied* aufnehmen; eingemeinden; ⚖ als Körperschaft eintragen; **2.** [in'kɔ:pərit] einverleibt; vereinigt; **in'cor·po·rat·ed** [~reitid] (amtlich) eingetragen; ~

bank Aktienbank *f*; **in·cor·po'ra·tion** Einverleibung *f*; Verbindung *f*; Vermischung *f etc.*

in·cor·po·re·al □ [inkɔːˈpɔːriəl] unkörperlich, nicht stofflich.

in·cor·rect □ [inkəˈrekt] unrichtig; fehlerhaft; falsch; ungehörig; **in·cor'rect·ness** Unrichtigkeit *f*; Fehlerhaftigkeit *f*.

in·cor·ri·gi·bil·i·ty [inkɔridʒəˈbiliti] Unverbesserlichkeit *f*; **in'cor·ri·gi·ble** □ unverbesserlich.

in·cor·rupt·i·bil·i·ty [ˈinkərʌptəˈbiliti] Unverderblichkeit *f*; Unbestechlichkeit *f*; **in·cor'rupt·i·ble** □ unverderblich; unvergänglich; unbestechlich.

in·crease 1. [inˈkriːs] *v/i.* wachsen, zunehmen (*in* an *dat.*); sich verstärken *od.* vergrößern *od.* vermehren; *v/t.* vermehren, vergrößern; verstärken, erhöhen; **2.** [ˈinkriːs] Zunahme *f*; Wachstum *n*, Vergrößerung *f etc.*; Anwachsen *n*; Zuwachs *m*; **in'creas·ing·ly** zunehmend, immer (*mit folgendem comp.*); ~ *difficult* immer schwieriger.

in·cred·i·bil·i·ty [inkrediˈbiliti] Unglaublichkeit *f*; **in'cred·i·ble** □ [~dəbl] unglaublich.

in·cre·du·li·ty [inkriˈdjuːliti] Unglaube *m*; **in·cred·u·lous** □ [inˈkredjuləs] ungläubig, skeptisch.

in·cre·ment [ˈinkrimənt] Zuwachs *m*, Zunahme *f*; Steigerungsbetrag *m*; Wertzuwachs *m*.

in·crim·i·nate [inˈkrimineit] beschuldigen; belasten; **in'crim·i·na·to·ry** [~nətəri] belastend.

in·crust [inˈkrʌst] = *encrust*; **in·crus'ta·tion** Bekrustung *f*; Kruste *f*, Ablagerung *f*; ⊕ Verkleidung *f*, Belag *m*; Kesselstein *m*.

in·cu·bate [ˈinkjubeit] (aus)brüten; **in·cu'ba·tion** Brüten *n*; *biol.*, ⚕ Entwicklungszeit *f*; **'in·cu·ba·tor** Brutapparat *m*; **in·cu·bus** [ˈiŋkjubəs] Alp(druck) *m*.

in·cul·cate [ˈinkʌlkeit] einschärfen (*upon dat.*); **in·cul'ca·tion** Einschärfung *f*.

in·cul·pate [ˈinkʌlpeit] beschuldigen; anklagen; **in·cul'pa·tion** Beschuldigung *f*, Tadel *m*; **in'cul·pa·to·ry** [~pətəri] tadelnd, beschuldigend; Anklage...

in'cum·ben·cy [inˈkʌmbənsi] Obliegenheit *f*; Amtszeit *f*; *eccl.* Pfründenbesitz *m*; **in'cum·bent 1.** aufliegend; obliegend; *be* ~ *on s.o.* j-m obliegen; **2.** *eccl.* Pfründeninhaber *m*.

in·cu·nab·u·la [inkjuːˈnæbjulə] *pl.* Inkunabeln *f/pl.*, Wiegendrucke *m/pl.*

in·cur [inˈkəː] sich *et.* zuziehen; sich *e-r Gefahr etc.* aussetzen; *Schulden* machen; *Verpflichtung* eingehen; *Verlust* erleiden.

in·cur·a·bil·i·ty [inkjuərəˈbiliti] Unheilbarkeit *f*; **in'cur·a·ble 1.** □ unheilbar; **2.** Unheilbare *m, f*.

in·cu·ri·ous □ [inˈkjuəriəs] gleichgültig, uninteressiert.

in·cur·sion [inˈkəːʃən] *feindlicher* Einfall *m*, Raubzug *m*; *fig.* Eingriff *m*.

in·cur·va·tion [inkəːˈveiʃən] Krümmung *f*; **'in'curve** einwärts krümmen, biegen.

in·debt·ed [inˈdetid] verschuldet; *fig.* (zu Dank) verpflichtet; **in'debt·ed·ness** Verschuldung *f*; Verpflichtung *f*; Schulden *f/pl.*

in·de·cen·cy [inˈdiːsnsi] Unanständigkeit *f*; **in'de·cent** □ unanständig; ungebührlich; ⚖ unzüchtig.

in·de·ci·pher·a·ble [indiˈsaifərəbl] unentzifferbar.

in·de·ci·sion [indiˈsiʒən] Unentschlossenheit *f*; **in·de·ci·sive** □ [~ˈsaisiv] nicht entscheidend; unentschieden, schwankend; unbestimmt.

in·de·clin·a·ble *gr.* [indiˈklainəbl] undeklinierbar.

in·dec·o·rous □ [inˈdekərəs] unpassend; ungehörig; **in'dec·o·rous·ness** = **in·de·co·rum** [indiˈkɔːrəm] Ungehörigkeit *f*.

in·deed [inˈdiːd] in der Tat, tatsächlich; wirklich; allerdings; so?; nicht möglich!

in·de·fat·i·ga·ble □ [indiˈfætigəbl] unermüdlich.

in·de·fea·si·ble □ [indiˈfiːzəbl] unverletzlich; unveräußerlich.

in·de·fect·i·ble □ [indiˈfektəbl] unvergänglich; unfehlbar.

in·de·fen·si·ble □ [indiˈfensəbl] unhaltbar.

in·de·fin·a·ble □ [indiˈfainəbl] unbestimmbar, undefinierbar.

in·def·i·nite □ [inˈdefinit] unbestimmt (*a. gr.*); unbeschränkt;

ungenau.

in·del·i·ble □ [in'delibl] unauslöschbar, untilgbar; ~ *ink* Kopiertinte *f*; ~ *pencil* Tintenstift *m*.

in·del·i·ca·cy [in'delikəsi] Unfeinheit *f*; Taktlosigkeit *f*; **in'del·i·cate** □ [~kit] unfein; taktlos.

in·dem·ni·fi·ca·tion [indemnifi'keiʃən] Entschädigung *f*; **in'dem·ni·fy** [~fai] sicherstellen (*from, against* gegen); *j-m* Straflosigkeit zusichern; entschädigen; **in'dem·ni·ty** Sicherstellung *f*; Straflosigkeit *f*; Entschädigung *f*, Schadenersatz *m*.

in·dent 1. [in'dent] einkerben, auszacken; eindrücken; *Zeile* einrücken; ⚖ *Vertrag* mit Doppel ausfertigen; ✝ bestellen (*upon s.o. for s.th.* et. bei j-m); ~*ed coastline* zerklüftete Küste *f*; **2.** ['indent] Einschnitt *m*, Kerbe *f*; Vertiefung *f*; ✝ Auslandsauftrag *m*; ⚔ Requisition *f*; = *indenture*; **in·den'ta·tion** Zähnung *f*; Einschnitt *m*, Auszackung *f*; **in'den·tion** *typ.* Einzug *m*; **in'den·ture** [~tʃə] **1.** Vertrag *m*, Kontrakt *m*; Lehrbrief *m*; (amtliche) Liste *f*; **2.** vertraglich verpflichten.

in·de·pend·ence, in·de·pend·en·cy [indi'pendəns(i)] Unabhängigkeit *f*; Selbständigkeit *f*; hinreichendes Auskommen *n*, Vermögen *n*; *Independence Day Am.* Unabhängigkeitstag *m* (*4. Juli*); **in·de'pend·ent** □ **1.** unabhängig (*of* von); selbständig; ~ *means* eigenes Vermögen *n*; **2.** *pol.* Unabhängige *m*.

in-depth ['indepθ] gründlich.

in·de·scrib·a·ble □ [indis'kraibəbl] unbeschreiblich.

in·de·struct·i·ble □ [indis'trʌktəbl] unzerstörbar.

in·de·ter·mi·na·ble □ [indi'tə:minəbl] unbestimmbar; **in·de'ter·mi·nate** □ [~nit] unbestimmt; **in·de'ter·mi·nate·ness, in·de·ter·mi·na·tion** ['~'neiʃən] Unbestimmtheit *f*.

in·dex ['indeks] **1.** *pl. a.* **in·di·ces** ['indisi:z] Zeiger *m*, Anzeiger *m*; Anzeichen *n*; Zeigefinger *m*; Index *m*, (Inhalts-, Namen-, Sach)Verzeichnis *n*; *eccl.* Verzeichnis *n* der verbotenen Bücher; *A* Exponent *m*, Kennziffer *f*; *a.* ~ *number* Richtzahl *f*; **2.** *Buch* mit e-m Index versehen; ~ **card** Karteikarte *f*; ~ **fin·ger** Zeigefinger *m*; '~-'**linked** dem Lebenshaltungsindex angeglichen; dynamisch.

In·di·a·man ['indjəmən] ⚓ (Ost-)Indienfahrer *m* (*Schiff*).

In·di·an ['indjən] **1.** indisch; indianisch; **2.** Inder(in); *a. Red* ~ Indianer(in); ~ **club** *Turnen*: Keule *f*; ~ **corn** Mais *m*; ~ **file**: *in* ~ im Gänsemarsch; ~ **giv·er** *Am.* F *j., der ein Gegengeschenk erwartet od. ein Geschenk zurückverlangt*; ~ **ink** chinesische Tusche *f*; ~ **pud·ding** *Am.* Maismehlpudding *m*; ~ **sum·mer** Altweiber-, Nachsommer *m*.

India...: ~ **paper** Dünndruckpapier *n*; '♀'**rub·ber** Radiergummi *m*.

in·di·cate ['indikeit] (an)zeigen; hinweisen auf (*acc.*); andeuten; angezeigt erscheinen lassen; **in·di'ca·tion** Anzeige *f*; Anzeichen *n*; Andeutung *f*; **in·dic·a·tive** □ [in'dikətiv] anzeigend (*of acc.*); ~ *mood gr.* Indikativ *m*; **in·di·ca·tor** ['~keitə] Anzeiger *m*; ⊕ Indikator *m*; *tel.* Zeigerapparat *m*; **in'di·ca·to·ry** [~kətəri] (an)zeigend (*of acc.*); Anzeige...

in·di·ces ['indisi:z] *pl. von index.*

in·dict [in'dait] anklagen (*for, on charge of* wegen); **in'dict·a·ble** (an)klagbar; **in'dict·er** Ankläger *m*; **in'dict·ment** Anklage *f*.

in·dif·fer·ence [in'difrəns] Gleichgültigkeit *f* (*to, towards* gegen); **in'dif·fer·ent** □ gleichgültig (*to* gegen); unparteiisch; leidlich, mittelmäßig; (nur) mäßig; unwesentlich; unbedeutend.

in·di·gence ['indidʒəns] Armut *f*.

in·di·gene ['indidʒi:n] Eingeborene *m, f*; **in'dig·e·nous** [~dʒinəs] eingeboren, einheimisch (*to* in *dat.*).

in·di·gent □ ['indidʒənt] arm.

in·di·gest·ed [indi'dʒestid] unverdaut; **in·di'gest·i·ble** □ unverdaulich; **in·di'ges·tion** Verdauungsstörung *f*, Magenverstimmung *f*.

in·dig·nant □ [in'dignənt] entrüstet, empört, ungehalten (*at* über *acc.*); unwillig; **in·dig'na·tion** Entrüstung *f*; Unwille *m* (*with* über *acc.*); ~ *meeting* Protestversammlung *f*; **in'dig·ni·ty** [~niti] unwürdige Behandlung *f*, Demütigung *f*; Beschimpfung *f*.

in·di·go ['indigəu] Indigo *m*; ~ *blue* indigoblau.

in·di·rect □ [indi'rekt] mittelbar, indirekt; nicht direkt; *gr. a.* abhängig.

in·dis·cern·i·ble [indi'sə:nəbl] nicht wahrnehmbar, unmerklich.

in·dis·ci·pline [in'disiplin] Disziplinlosigkeit *f*.

in·dis·creet □ [indis'kri:t] unbesonnen; unachtsam; indiskret, taktlos; **in·dis·cre·tion** [~'kreʃən] Unachtsamkeit *f*; Unbesonnenheit *f*; Indiskretion *f*, Taktlosigkeit *f*.

in·dis·crim·i·nate □ [indis'kriminit] unterschieds-, wahllos; = **in·dis'crim·i·nat·ing** □ [~neitiŋ], **in·dis'crim·i·na·tive** [~nətiv] keinen Unterschied machend; *fig.* blind; **in·dis·crim·i·na·tion** ['~'neiʃən] Wahllosigkeit *f*.

in·dis·pen·sa·ble □ [indis'pensəbl] unentbehrlich, unerläßlich (*Sache*); unabkömmlich (*Person*).

in·dis·pose [indis'pəuz] abgeneigt machen (*towards, from* gegen); untauglich machen (*for s.th., to inf.* für et., zu *inf.*); **in·dis'posed** unpäßlich; (*to*) abgeneigt (gegen), nicht aufgelegt (zu); **in·dis·po·si·tion** [indispə'ziʃən] Abneigung *f* (*to* gegen); Unpäßlichkeit *f*.

in·dis·pu·ta·ble □ ['indis'pju:təbl] unbestreitbar, unstreitig.

in·dis·so·lu·bil·i·ty ['indisɔlju'biliti] Unauflösbarkeit *f* (*a. fig.*); **in·dis·so·lu·ble** □ [~'sɔljubl] unauflösbar; *fig.* unlöslich; untrennbar.

in·dis·tinct □ [indis'tiŋkt] undeutlich; unklar; **in·dis'tinct·ness** Undeutlichkeit *f*; Unklarheit *f*.

in·dis·tin·guish·a·ble □ [indis'tiŋgwiʃəbl] ununterscheidbar.

in·dite [in'dait] *Gedicht etc.* ab-, verfassen; *Schrift* aufsetzen.

in·di·vid·u·al [indi'vidjuəl] **1.** □ persönlich, individuell, charakteristisch; besonder, eigentümlich; Privat...; einzeln; Einzel...; **2.** Individuum *n*, Einzelne *m*; **in·di'vid·u·al·ism** Individualismus *m*; **in·di'vid·u·al·ist** Individualist *m*; **in·di·vid·u·al·i·ty** [~'æliti] Individualität *f*, Einzelpersönlichkeit *f*; **in·di'vid·u·al·ize** [~əlaiz] individualisieren.

in·di·vis·i·bil·i·ty ['indivizi'biliti] Unteilbarkeit *f*; **in·di'vis·i·ble** □ unteilbar.

In·do... ['indəu] Indo...

in·doc·ile [in'dəusail] ungelehrig; unfügsam; **in·do·cil·i·ty** [~'siliti] Ungelehrigkeit *f*.

in·doc·tri·nate [in'dɔktrineit] unterweisen, schulen; durchdringen (*with* mit).

In·do-Eu·ro·pe·an ['indəujuərə'pi:ən] Indogermanisch *n*.

in·do·lence ['indələns] Trägheit *f*, Indolenz *f*; **'in·do·lent** □ indolent, träge, lässig; ⚕ schmerzlos.

in·dom·i·ta·ble □ [in'dɔmitəbl] unbezähmbar.

in·door ['indɔ:] im Hause (befindlich); Haus..., Zimmer..., *Sport*: Hallen...; ~ *aerial* Zimmerantenne *f*; ~ *game* Hallenspiel *n*; ~ *plant* Zimmerpflanze *f*; ~ *swimming-bath* Hallenbad *n*; **'in'doors** zu Hause; im *od.* ins Haus.

in·dorse [in'dɔ:s], **in'dorse·ment**, *etc.* = *endorse, etc.*

in·du·bi·ta·ble □ [in'dju:bitəbl] unzweifelhaft, zweifellos.

in·duce [in'dju:s] veranlassen, *j.* bewegen, dazu bringen, *et.* herbeiführen; ⚡ induzieren; ~*d current* ⚡ Induktionsstrom *m*; **in'duce·ment** Anlaß *m*, Antrieb *m*, Anreiz *m*.

in·duct *eccl.* [in'dʌkt] einführen; **in'duct·ance** ⚡ Induktivität *f*; ~ *coil* Drosselspule *f*; **in'duc·tion** Einführung *f*, Einsetzung *f in Amt, Pfründe*; *phys., phls.* Induktion *f*; **in'duc·tive** □ führend (*to* zu); *phys., phls.* induktiv; Induktions...

in·due [in'dju:] = *endue*.

in·dulge [in'dʌldʒ] nachsichtig sein gegen *j.*, *j-m* nachgeben (*in* in *dat.*); *s-n Wünschen etc.* nachgeben, frönen; ~ *with j.* erfreuen mit; ~ (*o.s.*) *in s.th.* sich et. erlauben *od.* gönnen; sich e-r Sache hin- *od.* ergeben, e-r Sache frönen; **in'dul·gence** Nachsicht *f*; Nachgiebigkeit *f* (*of, in* gegenüber *dat.*); Sichgehenlassen *n*, Zügellosigkeit *f*; Vergünstigung *f*; Stundung *f*; *eccl.* Ablaß *m*; **in'dul·gent** □ nachsichtig, schonend.

in·du·rate ['indjuəreit] (sich) (ver-)härten; **in·du'ra·tion** Verhärtung *f*.

in·dus·tri·al [in'dʌstriəl] **1.** □ gewerbetreibend, gewerblich; industriell; Gewerbe...; Industrie...;

~ *action* Arbeitskampf(maßnahmen *f/pl.*) *m*; ~ *area* Industriebezirk *m*; ~ *disease* Berufskrankheit *f*; ~ *espionage* Werkspionage *f*; ~ *estate* Industriegebiet *n e-r Stadt*; ~ *school* Gewerbeschule *f*; ~ *tribunal* Arbeitsgericht *n*; **2.** = **in'dus·tri·al·ist** Industrielle *m*; **in'dus·tri·al·ize** [~laiz] industrialisieren; **in'dus·tri·ous** □ fleißig, arbeitsam.

in·dus·try ['indəstri] Fleiß *m*, Betriebsamkeit *f*, Emsigkeit *f*; Gewerbe *n*; Industrie *f*; *heavy industries pl.* Schwerindustrie *f*.

in·dwell ['in'dwel] (*irr. dwell*) (be-)wohnen; *fig.* innewohnen (*dat.*).

in·e·bri·ate 1. [i'ni:brieit] betrunken machen; **2.** [~briit] betrunken; **3.** [~briit] Trunkenbold *m*; **in·e·bri'a·tion, in·e·bri·e·ty** [~'braiəti] Trunkenheit *f*.

in·ed·i·ble [in'edibl] ungenießbar.

in·ed·it·ed [in'editid] unveröffentlicht.

in·ef·fa·ble □ [in'efəbl] unaussprechlich.

in·ef·face·a·ble □ [ini'feisəbl] unauslöschlich.

in·ef·fec·tive [ini'fektiv], **in·ef'fec·tu·al** □ [~tʃuəl] unwirksam, fruchtlos; (*bsd.* ⚔ dienst)unfähig.

in·ef·fi·ca·cious □ [inefi'keiʃəs] unwirksam; **in'ef·fi·ca·cy** [~kəsi] Unwirksamkeit *f*, Fruchtlosigkeit *f*.

in·ef·fi·cien·cy [ini'fiʃənsi] (Leistungs)Unfähigkeit *f*; Wirkungslosigkeit *f*; **in·ef'fi·cient** □ unwirksam, wirkungslos; (leistungs-)unfähig.

in·el·e·gance [in'eligəns] Unfeinheit *f*, Geschmacklosigkeit *f*; **in'el·e·gant** □ unelegant, geschmacklos.

in·el·i·gi·bil·i·ty [inelidʒə'biliti] Unwählbarkeit *f*; Ungeeignetheit *f*; **in'el·i·gi·ble** □ nicht wählbar; ungeeignet; *bsd.* ⚔ untauglich.

in·e·luc·ta·ble [ini'lʌktəbl] unentrinnbar.

in·ept □ [i'nept] unpassend; abwegig; albern; **in'ept·i·tude** [~titju:d], **in'ept·ness** Ungeeignetheit *f*; Abwegigkeit *f*; Albernheit *f*.

in·e·qual·i·ty [ini:'kwɔliti] Ungleichheit *f*; Ungleichmäßigkeit *f*; Unebenheit *f*.

in·eq·ui·ta·ble □ [in'ekwitəbl] ungerecht, unbillig; **in'eq·ui·ty** Unbilligkeit *f*, Ungerechtigkeit *f*.

in·e·rad·i·ca·ble □ [ini'rædikəbl] unausrottbar.

in·ert □ [i'nə:t] träge; **in·er·tia** [i'nə:ʃiə], **in'ert·ness** Trägheit *f*.

in·es·cap·a·ble [inis'keipəbl] unentrinnbar; unvermeidlich.

in·es·sen·tial ['ini'senʃəl] unwesentlich (*to* für).

in·es·ti·ma·ble □ [in'estiməbl] unschätzbar.

in·ev·i·ta·ble □ [in'evitəbl] unvermeidlich, nicht zu umgehen(d); **in'ev·i·ta·ble·ness** Unvermeidlichkeit *f*; **in'ev·i·ta·bly** unweigerlich.

in·ex·act □ [inig'zækt] ungenau; **in·ex'act·i·tude** [~titju:d], **in·ex'act·ness** Ungenauigkeit *f*.

in·ex·cus·a·ble □ [iniks'kju:zəbl] unentschuldbar.

in·ex·haust·i·bil·i·ty ['inigzɔ:stə'biliti] Unerschöpflichkeit *f*; **in·ex'haust·i·ble** □ unerschöpflich; unermüdlich.

in·ex·o·ra·bil·i·ty [ineksərə'biliti] Unerbittlichkeit *f*; **in'ex·o·ra·ble** □ unerbittlich.

in·ex·pe·di·en·cy [iniks'pi:djənsi] Unzweckmäßigkeit *f*; **in·ex'pe·di·ent** □ unzweckmäßig, unpassend.

in·ex·pen·sive □ [iniks'pensiv] nicht teuer, billig, preiswert.

in·ex·pe·ri·ence [ineks'piəriəns] Unerfahrenheit *f*; **in·ex'pe·ri·enced** unerfahren.

in·ex·pert □ [in'ekspə:t] unerfahren, ungeübt.

in·ex·pi·a·ble □ [in'ekspiəbl] unsühnbar; unversöhnlich (*Haß etc.*).

in·ex·pli·ca·ble □ [in'eksplikəbl] unerklärlich.

in·ex·press·i·ble □ [iniks'presəbl] unaussprechlich.

in·ex·pres·sive □ [iniks'presiv] ausdruckslos; **in·ex'pres·sive·ness** Ausdruckslosigkeit *f*.

in·ex·tin·guish·able □ [iniks'tiŋgwiʃəbl] unauslöschlich.

in·ex·tri·ca·ble □ [in'ekstrikəbl] unentwirrbar.

in·fal·li·bil·i·ty [infælə'biliti] Unfehlbarkeit *f*; **in'fal·li·ble** □ unfehlbar; untrüglich, sicher.

in·fa·mous □ ['infəməs] ehrlos; schändlich, gemein; verrufen; **'in·fa·my** Ehrlosigkeit *f*; Schande *f*;

Niedertracht *f*.
in·fan·cy ['infənsi] Kindheit *f*; ⚖ Minderjährigkeit *f*; *in its* ~ in den Anfängen; **in·fant** ['infənt] **1.** Säugling *m*; (kleines) Kind *n*; Minderjährige *m, f*; ~ *school* Kindergarten *m*; **2.** kindlich; jugendlich, jung.
in·fan·ta [in'fæntə] Infantin *f*; **in'fan·te** [~ti] Infant *m*.
in·fan·ti·cide [in'fæntisaid] Kindesmord *m*; Kindesmörder(in); **in·fan·tile** ['infəntail] kindlich; Kindes..., Kinder...; *b. s.* kindisch; ~ *paralysis* Kinderlähmung *f*; **in·fan·tine** ['~tain] = *infantile*.
in·fan·try ⚔ ['infəntri] Infanterie *f*; **'in·fan·try·man** Infanterist *m*.
in·fat·u·ate [in'fætjueit] betören, verblenden; ~*d* vernarrt (*with* in *acc.*); **in·fat·u'a·tion** Betörung *f*; Vernarrtheit *f* (*for* in *acc.*).
in·fect [in'fekt] anstecken (*a. fig.*); infizieren, verseuchen, verpesten; *become* ~*ed* sich anstecken; **in'fec·tion** Infektion *f*, Ansteckung *f*; **in'fec·tious** □, **in'fec·tive** [~tiv] ansteckend; Ansteckungs...
in·fe·lic·i·tous [infi'lisitəs] unglücklich; ungeschickt; **in·fe'lic·i·ty** Unglück *n*, Elend *n*; ungeschickter Ausdruck *m*.
in·fer [in'fə:] folgern, schließen (*from* aus); **in'fer·a·ble** zu folgern(d), ableitbar; **in·fer·ence** ['infərəns] Folgerung *f*, Schluß *m*; **in·fer·en·tial** □ [~'renʃəl] folgernd; gefolgert; **in·fer'en·tial·ly** durch Folgerung.
in·fe·ri·or [in'fiəriə] **1.** untere(r, -s); untergeordnet, niedriger; geringer; schwächer (*sämtlich*: *to* als); unterlegen (*to dat.*); minderwertig; **2.** Untere *m, f*, Geringere *m, f*; Untergebene *m, f*; **in·fe·ri·or·i·ty** [~ri'ɔriti] geringerer Wert *m od.* Stand *m*; Unterlegenheit *f*; Minderwertigkeit *f*; ~ *complex* Minderwertigkeitskomplex *m*.
in·fer·nal □ [in'fə:nl] höllisch; Höllen...; F entsetzlich; ~ *machine* Höllenmaschine *f*; **in'fer·no** [~nəu] Inferno *n*, Hölle *f*.
in·fer·tile [in'fə:tail] unfruchtbar; **in·fer·til·i·ty** [~'tiliti] Unfruchtbarkeit *f*.
in·fest [in'fest] heimsuchen; verseuchen, plagen; *fig.* überschwemmen; **in·fes'ta·tion** Heimsuchung *f*; Verseuchung *f*.
in·fi·del ['infidəl] **1.** ungläubig; **2.** Ungläubige *m*; **in·fi·del·i·ty** [~'deliti] Unglaube *m*; Untreue *f* (*to* gegen).
in·field ['infi:ld] *Sport*: inneres Spielfeld *n*, Innenfeld *n*; Innenfeldspieler *m*.
in·fight·ing ['infaitiŋ] *Boxen*: Nahkampf *m*; *fig.* interne Streitereien *f/pl. od.* Machtkämpfe *m/pl.*
in·fil·trate ['infiltreit] *v/t.* durchdringen; durchtränken; durchsickern lassen; *v/i.* durchsickern, eindringen; **in·fil'tra·tion** Infiltration *f*; Durchsickern *n*.
in·fi·nite □ ['infinit] unendlich, endlos, unbegrenzt; ungeheuer; zahllos; **in·fin·i·tes·i·mal** [~'tesiməl] winzig, unendlich klein; **in'fin·i·tive** *gr. a.* ~ *mood* Infinitiv *m*, Grund-, Nennform *f*; **in'fin·i·tude** [~tju:d], **in'fin·i·ty** Unendlichkeit *f*; unendliche Größe *f od.* Menge *f*.
in·firm □ [in'fə:m] kraftlos, schwach; gebrechlich; ~ *of purpose* unentschlossen; **in'fir·ma·ry** Krankenhaus *n*; (Kranken)Revier *n*; **in'fir·mi·ty** Schwäche *f* (*a. fig.*); Gebrechen *n*.
in·fix [in'fiks] hineintreiben; einfügen (*in* in *acc.*); *fig.* einprägen.
in·flame [in'fleim] entflammen (*mst fig.*); (sich) entzünden (*a. fig. u.* ⚕).
in·flam·ma·bil·i·ty [inflæmə'biliti] Entzündlichkeit *f*; **in'flam·ma·ble** **1.** □ entzündlich; feuergefährlich; **2.** ~*s pl.* leicht entzündbare Stoffe *m/pl.*; **in·flam·ma·tion** [inflə'meiʃən] Entzündung *f*; **in·flam·ma·to·ry** [in'flæmətəri] entzündlich; aufrührerisch; hetzerisch; Hetz...
in·flate [in'fleit] aufblasen, aufblähen (*a. fig.*); **in'flat·ed** schwülstig; **in'fla·tion** Aufblähung *f*; ⚕ Inflation *f*; *fig.* Aufgeblasenheit *f*; **in'fla·tion·ar·y** ⚕ [~ʃnəri] inflationistisch; Inflations...; ~ *spiral* Lohn-Preis-Spirale *f*.
in·flect [in'flekt] biegen; *gr.* flektieren; **in'flec·tion** = *inflexion*.
in·flex·i·bil·i·ty [infleksə'biliti] Unbiegsamkeit *f*; *fig.* Unbeugsamkeit *f*; **in'flex·i·ble** □ unbiegsam; *fig.* unbeugsam; **in'flex·ion** [~ʃən] Bie-

gung *f*; *gr.* Flexion *f*, Beugung *f*; Modulation *f der Stimme.*

in·flict [in'flikt] auferlegen; zufügen; aufzwingen; *Hieb* versetzen (*alle*: on, upon s.o. j-m); *Strafe* verhängen (on über *acc.*); **in'flic·tion** Auferlegung *f etc.*; Heimsuchung *f*, Plage *f*.

in-flight ['inflait] während des Fluges.

in·flo·res·cence ⚘ [inflɔ:'resns] Aufblühen *n*; Blütenstand *m.*

in·flow ['infləu] = influx.

in·flu·ence ['influəns] **1.** Einfluß *m* (with bei, on, upon auf *acc.*); (Ein-) Wirkung *f* (on, upon auf *acc.*); **2.** einwirken auf (*acc.*); beeinflussen; **in·flu·en·tial** □ [~'enʃəl] einflußreich.

in·flu·en·za ⚕ [influ'enzə] Grippe *f*.

in·flux ['inflʌks] Einströmen *n*; *fig.* Zufluß *m*, (Zu)Strom *m.*

in·fo F ['infəu] Info *f* (*Information*).

in·fold [in'fəuld] = enfold.

in·form [in'fɔ:m] *v/t.* benachrichtigen, in Kenntnis setzen, unterrichten (of von, about über *acc.*); mitteilen (s.o. of s.th. j-m et.); well ~ed gut unterrichtet; keep s.o. ~ed j. auf dem laufenden halten; *v/i.* anzeigen, denunzieren (against s.o. j.); **in'for·mal** □ formlos, zwanglos; formwidrig; **in·for·mal·i·ty** [~'mæliti] Formlosigkeit *f etc.*; Formfehler *m*; **in'form·ant** [~mənt] (Informations)Quelle *f*; Gewährsmann *m*; = informer; **in·for·ma·tion** [infə'meiʃən] Auskunft *f*; Nachricht *f*, Information *f*; Unterweisung *f*; Kenntnis *f*; ⚖ Anklage *f*; ~ science Informatik *f*; gather ~ Erkundigungen einziehen (about über *acc.*); **in·form·a·tive** [in'fɔ:mətiv] informatorisch; lehrreich; mitteilsam; **in'form·er** *a.* common ~ Denunziant *m*; Spitzel *m.*

in·fra ['infrə] unten; see ~ siehe unten (*in Büchern*).

in·frac·tion [in'frækʃən] Verletzung *f*, Übertretung *f*.

in·fra...: ~ **dig** F ['infrə'dig] unter j-s Würde; '~-'**red** *phys.* infrarot; '~**struc·ture** Infrastruktur *f*, Unterbau *m.*

in·fre·quen·cy [in'fri:kwənsi] Seltenheit *f*; **in'fre·quent** □ selten.

in·fringe [in'frindʒ] *a.* ~ upon *Vertrag etc.* verletzen; *Gesetz* übertreten; **in'fringe·ment** Übertretung *f*; Verletzung *f*.

in·fu·ri·ate [in'fjuərieit] wütend machen.

in·fuse [in'fju:z] einflößen, eingeben (into *dat.*); ⚗, *pharm.* einweichen; *Tee etc.* aufgießen; **in'fu·sion** [~ʒən] Aufguß *m*; *fig.* Einflößung *f*; **in·fu·so·ri·a** *zo.* [~'zɔ:riə] *pl.* Infusorien *n/pl.*; **in·fu'so·ri·al** Infusorien...

in·gath·er·ing ['ingæðəriŋ] Einernten *n*; Sammeln *n.*

in·gen·ious □ [in'dʒi:njəs] geistreich; sinnreich; erfinderisch; raffiniert; **in·ge·nu·i·ty** [indʒi'nju:iti] Scharfsinn *m*; *das* Sinnreiche; **in·gen·u·ous** □ [in'dʒenjuəs] aufrichtig, offen, freimütig; unbefangen.

in·gle ['iŋgl] Kamin(feuer *n*) *m*; '~**nook** Kaminecke *f*.

in·glo·ri·ous □ [in'glɔ:riəs] ruhmlos; unrühmlich, schimpflich.

in·go·ing ['ingəuiŋ] **1.** Hineingehen *n*; Antritt *m*; **2.** (hin)eingehend; (neu) eintretend (*Mieter etc.*).

in·got ['iŋgət] *Gold- etc.* Barren *m*; '~-**steel** Flußstahl *m.*

in·grain ['in'grein] in der Wolle gefärbt; *fig. a.* ~ed eingewurzelt; *von Personen*: eingefleischt.

in·gra·ti·ate [in'greiʃieit]: ~ o.s. sich beliebt machen (with bei); **in·grat·i·tude** [in'grætitju:d] Undankbarkeit *f*.

in·gre·di·ent [in'gri:djənt] Bestandteil *m*; Zutat *f*.

in·gress ['ingres] Eintritt *m*; Zutritt *m.*

in·grow·ing ['ingrəuiŋ] nach innen wachsend, eingewachsen.

in·gui·nal *anat.* ['iŋgwinl] Leisten...

in·gur·gi·tate [in'gə:dʒiteit] hinunterschlingen, -schlucken.

in·hab·it [in'hæbit] bewohnen; **in'hab·it·a·ble** bewohnbar; **in'hab·it·an·cy** Aufenthalt *m*; **in'hab·it·ant** Bewohner(in), Einwohner(in).

in·ha·la·tion [inhə'leiʃən] Einatmung *f*; ⚕ Inhalation *f*; **in·hale** [in'heil] einatmen; ⚕ inhalieren; **in'hal·er** ⚕ Inhalationsapparat *m.*

in·har·mo·ni·ous □ [inha:'məunjəs] unharmonisch.

in·here [in'hiə] anhaften, innewohnen (in in *dat.*); **in'her·ence, in'her·en·cy** [~rəns(i)] Anhaften *n*,

Innewohnen *n*; **in'her·ent** □ anhaftend; innewohnend, angeboren, eigen (*in dat.*).

in·her·it [in'herit] (er)erben; **in'her·it·a·ble** □ erblich, vererbbar; **in'her·it·ance** Erbteil *n*, Erbe *n*; Erbschaft *f*; *biol.* Vererbung *f*; **in'her·i·tor** Erbe *m*; **in'her·i·tress, in'her·i·trix** [~triks] Erbin *f*.

in·hib·it [in'hibit] (ver)hindern; hemmen; verbieten (*s.o. from s.th.* j-m et.); zurückhalten; **in·hi·bi·tion** [~'biʃən] Hemmung *f*; Verbot *n*; **in'hib·i·to·ry** [~təri] hemmend; verbietend; Hemmungs...

in·hos·pi·ta·ble □ [in'hɔspitəbl] ungastlich, unwirtlich; **in·hos·pi·tal·i·ty** ['~'tæliti] Ungastlich-, Unwirtlichkeit *f*.

in·hu·man □ [in'hju:mən] unmenschlich; **in·hu·mane** [~'mein] unmenschlich, grausam; **in·hu·man·i·ty** [~'mæniti] Unmenschlichkeit *f*.

in·hu·ma·tion [inhju:'meiʃən] Beerdigung *f*.

in·hume [in'hju:m] beerdigen.

in·im·i·cal □ [i'nimikəl] feindlich; schädlich.

in·im·i·ta·ble □ [i'nimitəbl] unnachahmlich.

in·iq·ui·tous □ [i'nikwitəs] ungerecht; frevelhaft; **in'iq·ui·ty** Ungerechtigkeit *f*; Schlechtigkeit *f*.

in·i·tial [i'niʃəl] **1.** □ Anfangs...; anfänglich; ~ *payment* Anzahlung *f*; ~ *salary* Anfangsgehalt *n*; **2.** Anfangsbuchstabe *m*; **3.** mit den Anfangsbuchstaben *e-s Namens* versehen; **in·i·ti·ate 1.** [i'niʃiit] eingeweiht (*in* in *acc.*); Eingeweihte *m*; **2.** [~ʃieit] beginnen; anbahnen; *pol.* zuerst beantragen; einführen, einweihen (*into* in *acc.*); **in·i·ti'a·tion** Einleitung *f*; Einführung *f*, Einweihung *f*; *bsd. Am.* ~ *fee* Aufnahmegebühr *f* (*Vereinigung*); **in'i·ti·a·tive** [~ətiv] **1.** einleitend; **2.** Initiative *f*; einleitender Schritt *m*; Entschlußkraft *f*; Unternehmungsgeist *m*; Volksbegehren *n*; *on one's own* ~ aus eigener Initiative; *take the* ~ die Initiative ergreifen; **in'i·ti·a·tor** [~eitə] Initiator *m*, Anreger *m*, Urheber *m*; **in'i·ti·a·to·ry** [~ətəri] einleitend, -weihend.

in·ject [in'dʒekt] einspritzen (*into* in *acc.*); ausspritzen (*with* mit); **in'jec·tion** Einspritzung *f*; ⚕ Injektion *f*.

in·ju·di·cious □ [indʒu:'diʃəs] unverständig, unklug, unüberlegt.

in·junc·tion [in'dʒʌŋkʃən] gerichtliche Verfügung *f*; ausdrücklicher Befehl *m*.

in·jure ['indʒə] (be)schädigen; schaden, Unrecht tun (*dat.*); verletzen; beleidigen, kränken; **in·ju·ri·ous** □ [in'dʒuəriəs] schädlich, nachteilig; ungerecht; beleidigend; **in·ju·ry** ['indʒəri] Unrecht *n*; Schaden *m*; Verletzung *f*; Beleidigung *f*, Kränkung *f*; Schädigung *f*.

in·jus·tice [in'dʒʌstis] Ungerechtigkeit *f*; Unrecht *n*.

ink [iŋk] **1.** Tinte *f*; *mst printer's* ~ Druckerschwärze *f*; *attr.* Tinten...; **2.** (mit Tinte) schwärzen; beklecksen; ~ *in od. over* nach-, ausziehen.

ink·ling ['iŋkliŋ] Andeutung *f*; dunkle *od.* leise Ahnung *f*.

ink...: '**~-pad** Stempelkissen *n*; '**~-pen·cil** Tintenstift *m*; '**~·pot** Tintenfaß *n*; '**~·stand** Schreibzeug *n*; '**ink·y** tintig; Tinten...; tintenschwarz; tintenfleckig.

in·laid ['inleid] eingelegt; Einlege...; ~ *floor* Parkettfußboden *m*.

in·land 1. ['inlənd] binnenländisch, inländisch; Binnen...; im Inland gelegen; ♀ *Revenue* Steuereinnahmen *f/pl.*; **2.** [~] Innere *n* des Landes, Binnenland *n*; **3.** [in'lænd] landeinwärts; **in·land·er** ['inləndə] Binnenländer(in).

in-law ['inlɔ:] angeheiratete Verwandte *m, f*.

in·lay 1. ['in'lei] (*irr. lay*) einlegen; **2.** ['inlei] Einlage *f*; Einlegearbeit *f*.

in·let ['inlet] Meeresarm *m*, Bucht *f*; ⊕ Einlaß *m*, -gang *m*.

in·mate ['inmeit] Insasse *m*, Insassin *f*, Bewohner(in); Hausgenosse *m*, Hausgenossin *f*.

in·most ['inməust] innerst.

inn [in] Gasthof *m*, -haus *n*, Wirtshaus *n*; ♀*s pl. of Court die vier* Rechtsschulen *f/pl. in London.*

in·nards F ['inədz] *pl.* Eingeweide *n*, Innereien *f/pl.*

in·nate □ ['i'neit] angeboren.

in·ner ['inə] inner, inwendig; geheim; ~ *tube* Schlauch *m e-s Reifens*; *the* ~ *man* die Seele, das Innere; *co.* der Magen; **in·ner·most** ['~məust] innerst; geheimst.

in·ner·vate ['inə:veit] Nervenkraft

zuführen (*dat.*), kräftigen.

in·nings ['iniŋz] *sg. Sport*: Dransein *n*; *have one's* ~ am Spiel sein; *fig.* an der Macht sein.

inn·keep·er ['inki:pə] Gastwirt(in).

in·no·cence ['inəsns] Unschuld *f*; Harmlosigkeit *f*; Einfalt *f*; **in·no·cent** ['~snt] **1.** □ unschuldig (*of* an *dat.*); harmlos (*arglos*; *unschädlich*); ~ *of* F ohne; **2.** Unschuldige *m*; Einfältige *m*; Idiot *m*.

in·noc·u·ous □ [i'nɔkjuəs] unschädlich, harmlos.

in·nom·i·nate [i'nɔminit] namenlos, unbenannt.

in·no·vate ['inəuveit] Neuerungen machen; **in·no'va·tion** Neuerung *f*; '**in·no·va·tor** [~tə] Neuerer *m*.

in·nox·ious □ [i'nɔkʃəs] unschädlich.

in·nu·en·do [inju:'endəu] Andeutung *f*, Anspielung *f*, Wink *m*.

in·nu·mer·a·ble □ [i'nju:mərəbl] unzählbar, unzählig.

in·nu·tri·tious [inju:'triʃəs] nicht nahrhaft, ohne Nährwert.

in·ob·serv·ance [inəb'zə:vəns] (*of*) Unachtsamkeit *f* (gegen); Nichtbeachtung *f* (*gen.*).

in·oc·cu·pa·tion ['inɔkju'peiʃən] Beschäftigungslosigkeit *f*.

in·oc·u·late [i'nɔkjuleit] ⚕ *u. fig. j.* impfen (*with* mit, *for* gegen); *et.* einimpfen (*on*, *into dat.*); ⚘ okulieren; **in·oc·u'la·tion** (Ein)Impfung *f*; Okulieren *n*.

in·o·dor·ous [in'əudərəs] geruchlos.

in·of·fen·sive □ [inə'fensiv] harmlos, gutartig; **in·of'fen·sive·ness** Harmlosigkeit *f*.

in·of·fi·cial [inə'fiʃəl] nichtamtlich, inoffiziell.

in·op·er·a·ble ⚕ [in'ɔpərəbl] inoperabel (*Tumor*).

in·op·er·a·tive [in'ɔpərətiv] unwirksam.

in·op·por·tune □ [in'ɔpətju:n] unangebracht, zur Unzeit.

in·or·di·nate □ [i'nɔ:dinit] regellos; übermäßig; zügellos.

in·or·gan·ic [inɔ:'gænik] unorganisch.

in-pa·tient ['inpeiʃənt] Krankenhauspatient *m*, stationärer Patient*m*.

in·put ['input] Input *m*, *a. n*; Energiezufuhr *f*; Einsatz *m*; ⊕, *bsd.* ⚡ Eingangsenergie *f*.

in·quest ⚖ ['inkwest] Untersuchung *f* (*on* über *acc.*); *coroner's* ~ Gerichtsverhandlung *f* zur Feststellung der Todesursache.

in·qui·e·tude [in'kwaiitju:d] Unruhe *f*.

in·quire [in'kwaiə] fragen, sich erkundigen (*about*, *after*, *for* nach; *of* bei *j-m*); ~ *into* untersuchen, erforschen; **in'quir·er** Fragende *m*, *f*, Frager(in); Untersucher(in); **in'quir·ing** □ forschend; **in'quir·y** Erkundigung *f*, An-, Nachfrage *f*; Untersuchung *f*, Nachforschung *f*; Ermittlung *f*; *make inquiries* Erkundigungen einziehen (*of* bei *j-m*; *on*, *about* über *acc.*); **in'quir·y-'of·fice** Auskunft(sbüro *n*) *f*.

in·qui·si·tion [inkwi'ziʃən] Untersuchung *f* (*a.* ⚖); ♀ *hist.* Inquisition *f*; **in'quis·i·tive** □ [~tiv] neugierig; wißbegierig; **in'quis·i·tive·ness** Neugier *f*; Wißbegierde *f*; **in'quis·i·tor** Untersucher *m*; *hist.* Inquisitor *m*; **in·quis·i·to·ri·al** □ [~'tɔ:riəl] inquisitorisch, forschend; aufdringlich fragend; neugierig.

in·road ['inrəud] *feindlicher* Einfall *m*; Ein-, Übergriff *m* (*in*, *on* in, auf *acc.*).

in·rush ['inrʌʃ] Zustrom *m*.

in·sa·lu·bri·ous [insə'lu:briəs] ungesund.

in·sane □ [in'sein] geisteskrank, wahnsinnig; verrückt, unsinnig; ~ *asylum* Irrenanstalt *f*; **in·san·i·tar·y** □ [in'sænitəri] ungesund, unhygienisch; **in'san·i·ty** Wahnsinn *m*.

in·sa·ti·a·bil·i·ty [inseiʃjə'biliti] Unersättlichkeit *f*; **in'sa·ti·a·ble** □, **in'sa·ti·ate** [~ʃiit] unersättlich (*of* nach).

in·scribe [in'skraib] ein-, aufschreiben; beschreiben (*with* mit); beschriften; ✝ eintragen; ⚖ einzeichnen; *fig.* einprägen (*in*, *on dat.*); *Buch* zueignen (*to dat.*); ~*d stock pl.* Namensaktien *f*/*pl*.

in·scrip·tion [in'skripʃən] In-, Aufschrift *f*; ✝ Eintragung *f*.

in·scru·ta·bil·i·ty [inskru:tə'biliti] Unerforschlichkeit *f*; **in'scru·ta·ble** □ unerforschlich, unergründlich.

in·sect ['insekt] Insekt *n*; **in'sec·ti·cide** [~tisaid] Insektengift *n*; **in·sec·tiv·o·rous** [~'tivərəs] insektenfressend.

in·se·cure □ [insiˈkjuə] unsicher; **in·seˈcu·ri·ty** [~riti] Unsicherheit *f*; Ungewißheit *f*.

in·sem·i·nate *biol.* [inˈsemineit] befruchten; *fig.* einpflanzen, einprägen; **in·sem·iˈna·tion** Befruchtung *f*.

in·sen·sate [inˈsenseit] empfindungs-, gefühllos; unvernünftig; **in·sen·si·bil·i·ty** [~səˈbiliti] Unempfindlichkeit *f*; Bewußtlosigkeit *f*; Gleichgültigkeit *f* (of, to gegen); **inˈsen·si·ble** □ unempfindlich (of, to für); bewußtlos; unmerklich; gleichgültig; ~ of *od.* to s.th. sich e-r Sache nicht bewußt; **inˈsen·si·tive** [~sitiv] unempfindlich (to gegen).

in·sen·ti·ent [inˈsenʃənt] empfindungslos.

in·sep·a·ra·bil·i·ty [insepərəˈbiliti] Untrennbarkeit *f etc.*; **inˈsep·a·ra·ble** □ untrennbar; unzertrennlich.

in·sert 1. [inˈsəːt] einsetzen, -führen, -schalten, -fügen; (hinein)stecken; *Münze* einwerfen; *in e-e Zeitung* einrücken, inserieren; **2.** [ˈinsəːt] Bei-, Einlage *f*; **inˈser·tion** Einsetzung *f*, -fügung *f*, -tragung *f*; Einwurf *m e-r Münze*; Anzeige *f*, Inserat *n*.

in·set [ˈinset] Einsatz *m*, -lage *f*; Nebenbild *n*.

in·shore ⚓ [ˈinˈʃɔː] an *od.* nahe der Küste (befindlich); Küsten...

in·side [ˈinˈsaid] **1.** Innenseite *f*; Innere *n* (F *Magen*); turn ~ out umkrempeln; auf den Kopf stellen; **2.** *adj.* inner, inwendig; Innen...; ~ information Einblick *m in interne Dinge*; ~ lane *Sport*: Innenbahn *f*; ~ left *Fußball*: Halblinke *m*; ~ right Halbrechte *m*; **3.** *adv.* im Innern; ~ of F innerhalb; **4.** *prp.* innerhalb; ˈ**in**ˈ**sid·er** Eingeweihte *m*, *f*.

in·sid·i·ous □ [inˈsidiəs] heimtückisch.

in·sight [ˈinsait] Einsicht *f*; ~ into *fig.* Einblick *m* in (*acc.*).

in·sig·ni·a [inˈsigniə] *pl.* Abzeichen *n/pl.*, Insignien *pl.*

in·sig·nif·i·cance, *a.* **in·sig·nif·i·can·cy** [insigˈnifikəns(i)] Bedeutungslosigkeit *f*; **in·sigˈnif·i·cant** bedeutungslos; unbedeutend.

in·sin·cere □ [insinˈsiə] unaufrichtig, falsch; **in·sin·cer·i·ty** [~ˈseriti] Unaufrichtigkeit *f*, Falschheit *f*.

in·sin·u·ate [inˈsinjueit] unbemerkt hineinbringen; zu verstehen geben; andeuten; durchblicken lassen; ~ o.s. into sich einschleichen in (*acc.*); **inˈsin·u·at·ing** □ einschmeichelnd; **in·sin·uˈa·tion** Einschmeichelung *f*; Anspielung *f*, Andeutung *f*; Wink *m*.

in·sip·id □ [inˈsipid] geschmacklos, fad, schal; **in·siˈpid·i·ty** Geschmacklosigkeit *f*; Fadheit *f*, Schalheit *f*.

in·sist [inˈsist]: ~ on, ~ upon bestehen *od.* beharren auf (*dat.*); dringen auf (*acc.*); Gewicht legen auf (*acc.*), halten auf (*acc.*); *et.* betonen; ~ that darauf bestehen, daß; **in**ˈ**sist·ence** Bestehen *n* (on, upon auf *dat.*); Beharrlichkeit *f*; at his ~ auf sein Drängen hin; **inˈsist·ent** □ beharrend (on, upon auf *dat.*); beharrlich; eindringlich.

in·so·bri·e·ty [insəuˈbraiəti] Unmäßigkeit *f*.

in(·)so(·)far as [insəˈfɑːrəz] insofern als.

in·so·la·tion [insəuˈleiʃən] Sonnenbestrahlung *f*; Sonnenstich *m*.

in·sole [ˈinsəul] Brandsohle *f*; Einlegesohle *f*.

in·so·lence [ˈinsələns] Unverschämtheit *f*; ˈ**in·so·lent** □ unverschämt, frech.

in·sol·u·bil·i·ty [insɔljuˈbiliti] Unlöslichkeit *f*; **inˈsol·u·ble** □ [~jubl] unlöslich; unlösbar.

in·sol·ven·cy [inˈsɔlvənsi] Zahlungsunfähigkeit *f*; **inˈsol·vent 1.** zahlungsunfähig; **2.** zahlungsunfähiger Schuldner *m*.

in·som·ni·a [inˈsɔmniə] Schlaflosigkeit *f*.

in·so·much [insəuˈmʌtʃ]: ~ that dermaßen *od.* so sehr, daß.

in·spect [inˈspekt] untersuchen, prüfen, nachsehen; inspizieren; **in**ˈ**spec·tion** Prüfung *f*, Untersuchung *f*; Inspektion *f*; for ~ ✝ zur Ansicht; **inˈspec·tor** Aufsichtsbeamte *m*; (Polizei)Inspektor *m*; **inˈspec·tor·ate** [~tərit] Aufsichtsbehörde *f*.

in·spi·ra·tion [inspəˈreiʃən] Einatmung *f*; Eingebung *f*, Erleuchtung; Inspiration *f*; Begeisterung *f*; **in·spire** [inˈspaiə] einatmen; *Leben* einhauchen (into, in *dat.*); *fig.* ein-

geben (*s.th. in s.o., s.o. with s.th.* j-m et.), erfüllen; *j.* begeistern; **in·spir·it** [in'spirit] beleben; anfeuern.
in·spis·ate [in'spiseit] eindicken, eindampfen.
in·sta·bil·i·ty [instə'biliti] Unstetigkeit *f*; *bsd. fig.* Unbeständigkeit *f*.
in·stall [in'stɔːl] einsetzen (*in* in *ein Amt*); (sich) niederlassen; ⊕ installieren, einbauen, einrichten; **in·stal·la·tion** [instə'leiʃən] Einsetzung *f*, Bestallung *f*; ⊕ Installation *f*, Einrichtung *f*; ⚡ *etc.* Anlage *f*.
in·stal(l)·ment [in'stɔːlmənt] Rate *f*; Abschlagszahlung *f*; (Teil)Lieferung *f*, Faszikel *m* (*e-s Buchs*); Fortsetzung *f*; *by* ~*s* ratenweise; in Fortsetzungen; *payment by* ~*s* Ratenzahlung *f*; ~ **plan** Teilzahlungssystem *n*.
in·stance ['instəns] **1.** dringende Bitte *f*, Ersuchen *n*; Beispiel *n*; (besonderer) Fall *m*; ⚖ Instanz *f*; *for* ~ zum Beispiel; *in the first* ~ erstens; *at the* ~ *of* auf Veranlassung (*gen.*); **2.** *als Beispiel* anführen.
in·stant □ ['instənt] **1.** dringend; unmittelbar, sofortig; gegenwärtig, laufend; ~ *coffee* Pulverkaffee *m*; *on the 10th* ~ am 10. dieses Monats; **2.** Augenblick *m*; *in an* ~, *on the* ~ im Augenblick; augenblicklich; *the* ~ *you call* sobald du rufst; **in·stan·ta·ne·ous** □ [~'teinjəs] augenblicklich, sofortig; gleichzeitig; Augenblicks...; Moment...; **'in·stant·ly** sogleich, sofort.
in·state [in'steit] einsetzen (*in* in *acc.*).
in·stead [in'sted] statt dessen, dafür; ~ *of* anstatt, statt; an Stelle von; ~ *of going* statt zu gehen.
in·step ['instep] Spann *m*, Rist *m*; *be high in the* ~ F die Nase hoch tragen.
in·sti·gate ['instigeit] anstiften; aufhetzen; **in·sti'ga·tion** Anstiftung *f*; *at the* ~ *of* auf Betreiben *gen.*; **'in·sti·ga·tor** Anstifter *m*, Hetzer *m*.
in·stil(l) [in'stil] einträufeln; *fig.* einflößen (*into dat.*); **in·stil'la·tion, in'stil(l)·ment** Einträufeln *n*; Einflößung *f*.
in·stinct 1. ['instiŋkt] Instinkt *m*, (Natur)Trieb *m*; **2.** [in'stiŋkt] erfüllt; ~ *with life* voller Leben; **in'stinc·tive** □ instinkt-, triebmäßig; unwillkürlich, instinktiv.
in·sti·tute ['institjuːt] **1.** (gelehrte) Gesellschaft *f*, Institut *n* (*a. das Gebäude*); **2.** *et.* einsetzen, stiften, gründen, einrichten; an-, verordnen; *j.* einsetzen (*to, into* in *ein Amt*); **in·sti'tu·tion** Einsetzung *f*, Einrichtung *f*; An-, Verordnung *f*; Gesetz *n*, Satzung *f*; Institut(ion *f*) *n*; Gesellschaft *f*; Anstalt *f*; **in·sti'tu·tion·al** [~ʃənl] Instituts..., Anstalts...; ~ *care* Anstaltsfürsorge *f*; **in·sti'tu·tion·al·ize** [~ʃnəlaiz] institutionalisieren; F in eine Anstalt schicken.
in·struct [in'strʌkt] unterrichten, informieren; belehren, unterweisen; *j.* anweisen; **in'struc·tion** Vorschrift *f*, Instruktion *f*; Unterweisung *f*, Belehrung *f*; Merkblatt *n*; Auftrag *m*; **in'struc·tion·al** [~ʃənl] Lehr...; ~ *film* Lehrfilm *m*; **in'struc·tive** □ belehrend; lehrreich; **in'struc·tor** Lehrer *m*; Ausbilder *m*; *Am. univ.* Dozent *m*; **in'struc·tress** Lehrerin *f*.
in·stru·ment ['instrumənt] Instrument *n* (*a.* ♪), Werkzeug *n* (*a. fig.*); Handlanger *m*; ⚖ Urkunde *f*; ~ *board*, ~ *panel mot.*, ✈ Armaturenbrett *n*; *fly on* ~*s* ✈ blindfliegen; **in·stru·men·tal** □ [instru'mentl] als Werkzeug dienend; dienlich, behilflich, förderlich; ♪ Instrumental...; *be* ~ *to* zu *e-m Zweck* beitragen; *be* ~ *in* zu *e-r Tätigkeit* beitragen; **in·stru'men·tal·ist** ♪ [~təlist] Instrumentalist(in); **in·stru·men·tal·i·ty** [~'tæliti] Mitwirkung *f*, Mittel *n*.
in·sub·or·di·nate [insə'bɔːdnit] aufsässig; **in·sub·or·di·na·tion** ['~di'neiʃən] Auflehnung *f*.
in·sub·stan·tial [insəb'stænʃəl] unwirklich.
in·suf·fer·a·ble □ [in'sʌfərəbl] unerträglich, unausstehlich (*arrogant*).
in·suf·fi·cien·cy [insə'fiʃənsi] Unzulänglichkeit *f*; **in·suf'fi·cient** □ unzulänglich, ungenügend.
in·su·lar □ ['insjulə] insular, Insel...; *fig.* beschränkt, engstirnig; **in·su·lar·i·ty** [~'læriti] insulare Lage *f*; *fig.* insulare Beschränktheit *f*; **in·su·late** ['~leit] zur Insel machen; isolieren (*a.* ⚡); **'in·su·lat·ing** Isolier...; ~ *tape* Isolierband *n*; **in·su'la·tion** Absonderung *f*;

Isolierung *f* (*a. phys.*); ˈ**in·su·la·tor** ⚡ Isolator *m*.
in·su·lin ⚕ [ˈinsjulin] Insulin *n*.
in·sult 1. [ˈinsʌlt] Beleidigung *f*; Beschimpfung *f*; **2.** [inˈsʌlt] beleidigen, beschimpfen.
in·su·per·a·bil·i·ty [insjuːpərəˈbiliti] Unüberwindlichkeit *f*; **inˈsu·per·a·ble** □ unüberwindlich.
in·sup·port·a·ble □ [insəˈpɔːtəbl] unerträglich, unausstehlich.
in·sup·press·i·ble [insəˈpresəbl] ununterdrückbar.
in·sur·ance [inˈʃuərəns] Versicherung *f*; *attr.* Versicherungs...; ~ *coverage* Versicherungsschutz *m*; ~ *fraud* Versicherungsbetrug *m*; ~ *performances pl.* Versicherungsleistungen *f/pl.*; ~ **pol·i·cy** Versicherungspolice *f*, -schein *m*; **inˈsur·ant** Versicherungsnehmer *m*; **inˈsure** versichern; **inˈsured** *der od. die* Versicherte; **inˈsur·er** *der* Versicherer.
in·sur·gent [inˈsəːdʒənt] **1.** aufrührerisch; **2.** Aufrührer *m*.
in·sur·mount·a·ble □ [insəːˈmauntəbl] unübersteigbar; *fig.* unüberwindlich.
in·sur·rec·tion [insəˈrekʃən] Aufstand *m*, Empörung *f*; **in·surˈrec·tion·al** [~ʃənl] aufständisch; **in·surˈrec·tion·ist** [~ʃnist] Aufständische *m*.
in·sus·cep·ti·ble [insəˈseptəbl] unempfänglich (*of*, *to* für).
in·tact [inˈtækt] unberührt; unversehrt; intakt; unangetastet.
in·take [ˈinteik] *Wasser- etc.* Einlaß *m*; (Neu)Aufnahme *f*, Zustrom *m*, -fluß *m*; Neuland *n*.
in·tan·gi·bil·i·ty [intændʒəˈbiliti] Unfühlbarkeit *f*; **inˈtan·gi·ble** □ unfühlbar; unfaßbar (*a. fig.*); unantastbar.
in·te·ger [ˈintidʒə] ⅄ ganze Zahl *f*; *das* Ganze; **in·te·gral** [ˈ~grəl] **1.** □ ganz, vollständig; wesentlich; ⅄ Integral...; **2.** ⅄ Integral *n*; **in·te·grant** [ˈ~grənt] integrierend; **in·te·grate** [ˈ~greit] ergänzen; zs.-tun; einfügen (*into*, *in* in *acc.*); integrieren; ~*d circuit* ⚡ integrierter Schaltkreis *m*; **in·teˈgra·tion** *mst pol.* Integration *f*; Eingliederung *f*; **in·teg·ri·ty** [inˈtegriti] Vollständigkeit *f*; Unversehrtheit *f*; Redlichkeit *f*, Integrität *f*.
in·teg·u·ment [inˈtegjumənt] Hülle *f*, Decke *f* (*a.* ⚘, *anat.*).
in·tel·lect [ˈintilekt] Verstand *m*; *konkr. die* Intelligenz; **in·telˈlec·tu·al** [~tjuəl] **1.** □ intellektuell; Verstandes..., geistig; verständig, vernünftig; **2.** Intellektuelle *m*, *f*; **in·tel·lec·tu·al·i·ty** [ˈ~tjuˈæliti] Verstandeskraft *f*.
in·tel·li·gence [inˈtelidʒəns] Intelligenz *f*; Verstand *m*; Einsicht *f*, Verständnis *n*; Nachricht *f*, Auskunft *f*; ~ *department* Nachrichtendienst *m*; **inˈtel·li·genc·er** Nachrichtenagent *m*; Spion *m*.
in·tel·li·gent □ [inˈtelidʒənt] intelligent; klug, gescheit; **in·tel·li·gent·si·a** [~ˈdʒentsiə] Intelligenz *f*, *die* Gebildeten *pl.*; **in·tel·li·gi·bil·i·ty** [~dʒəˈbiliti] Verständlichkeit *f*; **inˈtel·li·gi·ble** □ verständlich (*to* für).
in·tem·per·ance [inˈtempərəns] Unmäßigkeit *f*; Trunksucht *f*; **inˈtem·per·ate** □ [~rit] unmäßig; zügellos; unbeherrscht; trunksüchtig.
in·tend [inˈtend] beabsichtigen, wollen; meinen (*sagen wollen*; *by* mit); ~ *for* bestimmen für *od.* zu; **inˈtend·ant** Verwalter *m*; **inˈtend·ed 1.** absichtlich; verlobt; ~ *husband* Verlobte *m*; **2.** F *der od. die* Zukünftige *od.* Verlobte.
in·tense □ [inˈtens] intensiv; angespannt, angestrengt; stark, heftig; lebhaft (*Farbe*); eindringlich, leidenschaftlich; **inˈtense·ness** Intensität *f*; Anstrengung *f*, Anspannung *f*; Stärke *f*, Heftigkeit *f*; Lebhaftigkeit *f*.
in·ten·si·fi·ca·tion [intensifiˈkeiʃən] Verstärkung *f* (*a. phot.*); **inˈten·si·fy** [~fai] (sich) verstärken *od.* steigern.
in·ten·sion [inˈtenʃən] Anstrengung *f*; Verstärkung *f*; Stärke *f*; **inˈten·si·ty** = *intenseness*; **inˈten·sive** □ = *intense*; verstärkend; Verstärkungs...; ~ *care unit* ⚕ Intensivstation *f*.
in·tent [inˈtent] **1.** □ gespannt; bedacht, erpicht (*on* auf *acc.*); beschäftigt (*on* mit); aufmerksam; **2.** Absicht *f*, Vorhaben *n*; *to all* ~*s and purposes* in jeder Hinsicht; durchaus; *with* ~ *to kill* in der Absicht zu töten; **inˈten·tion** Absicht *f*; Zweck *m*; **inˈten·tion·al** □

[~ʃənl] absichtlich; **in'ten·tioned** ...gesinnt; *well-~* wohlmeinend; **in'tent·ness** gespannte Aufmerksamkeit *f*; Eifer *m*.
in·ter [in'tə:] beerdigen, begraben.
in·ter... ['intə] zwischen; Zwischen...; gegenseitig, einander.
in·ter·act 1. ['intərækt] *thea.* Zwischenakt *m*; 2. [~'ækt] sich gegenseitig beeinflussen; **in·ter'ac·tion** Wechselwirkung *f*.
in·ter·breed ['intə:bri:d] (*irr. breed*) (sich) kreuzen (*Tiere etc.*).
in·ter·ca·lar·y [in'tə:kələri] eingeschaltet; Schalt...; **in'ter·ca·late** [~leit] einschalten; **in·ter·ca'la·tion** Einschaltung *f*.
in·ter·cede [intə:'si:d] sich verwenden, Fürbitte einlegen (*with* bei); **in·ter'ced·er** Fürsprecher(in).
in·ter·cept [intə:'sept] ab-, auffangen; *Nachricht* abhören; hemmen, aufhalten; unterbrechen, abschneiden; **in·ter'cep·tion** Abfangen *n etc.*; **in·ter'cep·tor** Geruchsverschluß *m in Abflußrohren*; ⚔ Abfangjäger *m*.
in·ter·ces·sion [intə'seʃən] Verwendung *f*, Fürbitte *f*; **in·ter·ces·sor** [~'sesə] Vermittler *m*, Fürsprecher *m*; **in·ter'ces·so·ry** fürsprechend.
in·ter·change 1. [intə:'tʃeindʒ] *v/t.* austauschen, -wechseln; *v/i.* abwechseln; 2. ['~'tʃeindʒ] Austausch *m*; Abwechs(e)lung *f*; **in·ter'change·a·ble** austauschbar.
in·ter·com ✈, ⚓ F ['intə:kɔm] (Bord)Sprechanlage *f*.
in·ter·com·mu·ni·cate [intə:kə'mju:nikeit] miteinander in Verbindung stehen; '**in·ter·com·mu·ni'ca·tion** gegenseitige Verbindung *f od.* Verständigung *f*; *~ system* = *intercom*; **in·ter·com'mun·ion** [~njən] wechselseitiger Verkehr *m*.
in·ter·con·nect ['intə:kə'nekt] untereinander verbinden.
in·ter·con·ti·nen·tal ['intə:kɔnti'nentl] interkontinental, von Kontinent zu Kontinent (reichend).
in·ter·course ['intə:kɔ:s] Verkehr *m*, Umgang *m*.
in·ter·de·nom·i·na·tion·al [intədinɔmi'neiʃənl] interkonfessionell.
in·ter·de·pend·ence [intə:di'pendəns] gegenseitige Abhängigkeit *f*; **in·ter·de'pend·ent** voneinander abhängig.
in·ter·dict 1. [intə:'dikt] untersagen, verbieten (*s.th. to s.o.* j-m et.; *s.o. from doing* j-m zu tun); 2. ['intə:dikt], **in·ter'dic·tion** Verbot *n*; Interdikt *n*.
in·ter·est ['intrist] 1. Interesse *n*; Anziehungskraft *f*; Bedeutung *f*; Nutzen *m*; ⚕ Anteil *m*, Beteiligung *f*, Kapital *n*; Zins(en *pl.*) *m*; *~s pl.* Interessenten *m/pl.*, Kreise *m/pl.*; *in the ~ of* zum Nutzen; für; *be of ~ to* von Interesse sein für; *take an ~ in* sich interessieren für; *return a blow with ~* noch heftiger zurückschlagen; *banking ~s pl.* Bankkreise *m/pl.*; 2. *allg.* interessieren; anziehen; angehen; *j-s* Teilnahme erregen (*for s.o.* für j.); *be ~ed in* beteiligt sein *od.* Interesse haben an (*dat.*); *~ o.s. in* sich interessieren für; '**in·ter·est·ed** □ interessiert; beteiligt; eigennützig; '**in·ter·est-free** zinslos; '**in·ter·est·ing** □ interessant, fesselnd, anziehend.
in·ter·face ['intə:feis] Berührungspunkt(e *pl.*) *m*, Wechselbeziehung (-en *pl.*) *f*.
in·ter·fere [intə'fiə] sich einmengen *od.* -mischen (*with* in *acc.*); einschreiten; vermitteln (*in* bei, in *dat.*); stören (*with acc.*); aufeinandertreffen; **in·ter'fer·ence** Einmischung *f*, Eingreifen *n*; Beeinträchtigung *f*; *phys.* Interferenz *f*, Störung *f*.
in·ter·flow [intə'fləu] ineinanderfließen.
in·ter·fuse [intə:'fju:z] (sich) vermischen.
in·ter·im ['intərim] 1. Zwischenzeit *f*; *in the ~* einstweilen; 2. vorläufig; Interims...; *~ report* Zwischenbericht *m*.
in·te·ri·or [in'tiəriə] 1. □ inner; innerlich; Innen...; binnenländisch; *~ decorator* Innenarchitekt *m*; Maler *m*, Tapezierer *m*; 2. Innere *n e-r Sache*; Binnenland *n*; *paint.* Interieur *n*; *phot.* Innenaufnahme *f*; *pol.* innere Angelegenheiten *f/pl.*; *Department of the* ♀ *Am.* Innenministerium *n*.
in·ter·ja·cent [intə:'dʒeisənt] dazwischenliegend.
in·ter·ject [intə:'dʒekt] einschieben, -werfen; **in·ter'jec·tion** Interjektion *f*, Ausruf *m*; **in·ter'jec·tion·al**

□ [ˌʃənl] eingeschoben (*Wort etc.*).
in·ter·lace [intəːˈleis] *v/t.* durchflechten, -weben; *v/i.* sich kreuzen.
in·ter·lard [intəːˈlɑːd] *fig.* spicken.
in·ter·leave [intəːˈliːv] *Buch mit Papier* durchschießen.
in·ter·line [intəːˈlain] zwischen die Zeilen schreiben; *typ.* durchschießen; **in·ter·lin·e·ar** [ˌˈliniə] zwischenzeilig, interlinear; **in·ter·lin·e·a·tion** [ˈˌliniˈeiʃən] Zwischenschreiben *n*; Zwischengeschriebene *n*.
in·ter·link [intəːˈliŋk] miteinander verbinden.
in·ter·lock [intəːˈlɔk] ineinandergreifen; -haken; miteinander verbinden.
in·ter·lo·cu·tion [intəːləuˈkjuːʃən] Unterredung *f*; **in·ter·loc·u·tor** [ˌˈlɔkjutə] Gesprächspartner *m*; **in·terˈloc·u·to·ry** in Gesprächsform; ⚖ Zwischen...
in·ter·lope [intəːˈləup] sich eindrängen; ✝ wilden Handel treiben; **ˈin·ter·lop·er** Eindringling *m*; ✝ wilder Händler *m*.
in·ter·lude [ˈintəːluːd] Zwischenspiel *n*; Zwischenzeit *f*; ~*s of bright weather* zeitweilig schön.
in·ter·mar·riage [intəːˈmæridʒ] Mischehe *f*; **ˈin·terˈmar·ry** untereinander heiraten.
in·ter·med·dle [intəːˈmedl] sich einmischen (*with*, *in* in *acc.*); **in·terˈmed·dler** Eindringling *m*; Unberufene *m, f*.
in·ter·me·di·ar·y [intəːˈmiːdjəri] **1.** dazwischen befindlich; vermittelnd; **2.** Vermittler *m*; ✝ Zwischenhändler *m*; **in·ter·me·di·ate** □ [ˌˈmiːdjət] in der Mitte liegend; Mittel..., Zwischen...; ~ *landing* ✈ Zwischenlandung *f*; ~-*-range ballistic missile* Mittelstrekkenrakete *f*; ~ *school Am.* Mittelschule *f*; ~ *stage* Zwischenstadium *n*; ~ *trade* Zwischenhandel *m*.
in·ter·ment [inˈtəːmənt] Beerdigung *f*.
in·ter·mez·zo [intəːˈmetsəu] Intermezzo *n*, Zwischenspiel *n*.
in·ter·mi·na·ble □ [inˈtəːminəbl] endlos, unendlich.
in·ter·min·gle [intəːˈmiŋgl] (sich) vermischen.
in·ter·mis·sion [intəːˈmiʃən] Aussetzen *n*, Unterbrechung *f*; Pause *f*.
in·ter·mit [intəːˈmit] unterbrechen, (*a. v/i.*) aussetzen; **in·terˈmit·tent 1.** □ aussetzend; ~ *fever* = **2.** ⚕ Wechselfieber *n*; **in·terˈmit·tent·ly** sprunghaft, ruckweise.
in·ter·mix [intəːˈmiks] (sich) vermischen; **in·terˈmix·ture** [ˌtʃə] Mischung *f*; Beimischung *f*.
in·tern¹ [inˈtəːn] internieren.
in·tern² [ˈintəːn] Assistenzarzt *m*.
in·ter·nal □ [inˈtəːnl] inner(lich); inländisch; **~-comˈbus·tion engine** Verbrennungsmotor *m*; **~ rev·e·nue** *Am.* Steueraufkommen *n*.
in·ter·na·tion·al [intəːˈnæʃənl] **1.** □ international; ~ *date line* Datumsgrenze *f*; ~ *departures pl.* Auslandsflüge *m/pl.*; ~ *flight* Auslandsflug *m*; ~ *law* Völkerrecht *n*; ℒ *Monetary Fund* Internationaler Währungsfonds *m*; ~ *player Sport*: Nationalspieler(in); **2.** *pol.* ℒ Internationale *f*; **in·ter·na·tion·al·i·ty** [ˌˈnæliti] Internationalität *f*; **in·terˈna·tion·al·ize** [ˌnəlaiz] für international erklären.
in·terne [ˈintəːn] = *intern²*.
in·ter·ne·cine war [intəːˈniːsainˈwɔː] gegenseitiger Vernichtungskrieg *m*.
in·tern·ee [intəːˈniː] Internierte *m,f*; **inˈtern·ment** Internierung *f*; ~ *camp* Internierungslager *n*.
in·ter·pel·late [inˈtəːpeleit] interpellieren, um Aufschluß ersuchen; **in·ter·pelˈla·tion** Anfrage *f*, Interpellation *f*.
in·ter·phone [ˈintəːfəun] Haustelephon *n*; ✈ *Am.* Bordsprechanlage *f*.
in·ter·plan·e·ta·ry [intəːˈplænitəri] interplanetarisch.
in·ter·play [ˈintəːˈplei] Wechselwirkung *f*.
in·ter·po·late [inˈtəːpəuleit] einschieben; **in·ter·poˈla·tion** Einschaltung *f*, Einschub *m*.
in·ter·pose [intəːˈpəuz] *v/t. Veto* einlegen; *Wort* einwerfen; *v/i.* dazwischentreten, einschreiten; vermitteln; **in·ter·po·si·tion** [intəːpəˈziʃən] Eingreifen *n*; Vermittlung *f*.
in·ter·pret [inˈtəːprit] auslegen, erklären, interpretieren; dolmetschen; darstellen, wiedergeben; **in·ter·preˈta·tion** Auslegung *f*; Interpretation *f*; Darstellung *f*; **inˈter·pre·ta·tive** [ˌtətiv] auslegend (*of acc.*); **inˈter·pret·er** Ausleger(in); Dolmetscher(in); Interpret(in).
in·ter·ra·cial [intəːˈreiʃjəl] zwischen

den Rassen, interrassisch.

in·ter·reg·num [intə'regnəm] Interregnum *n*, Zwischenregierung *f*; Pause *f*.

in·ter·re·la·tion ['intə:ri'leiʃən] Wechselbeziehung *f*.

in·ter·ro·gate [in'terəugeit] (be-, aus)fragen; verhören; **in·ter·ro'ga·tion** (Be-, Aus)Fragen *n*, Verhör(en) *n*; Frage *f*; *note od. mark od. point of* ~ Fragezeichen *n*; **in·ter·rog·a·tive** [intə'rɔgətiv] **1.** □ fragend; Frage...; **2.** *gr.* Fragewort *n*; **in·ter'rog·a·to·ry** [~təri] **1.** fragend; **2.** Frage *f*; Verhör *n*.

in·ter·rupt [intə'rʌpt] unterbrechen; **in·ter'rupt·ed·ly** mit Unterbrechungen; **in·ter'rupt·er** ⚡ Unterbrecher *m*; **in·ter'rup·tion** Unterbrechung *f*.

in·ter·sect [intə:'sekt] durchschneiden; (sich) schneiden; **in·ter'sec·tion** Durchschnitt *m*; Schnittpunkt *m*; 🚂 Kreuzung *f*.

in·ter·space ['intə:'speis] Zwischenraum *m*.

in·ter·sperse [intə:'spə:s] einstreuen; untermengen, durchsetzen (*with* mit).

in·ter·state *Am.* ['intə:'steit] zwischenstaatlich.

in·ter·stel·lar [intə'stelə] interstellar, zwischen den Sternen.

in·ter·stice [in'tə:stis] Zwischenraum *m*; Lücke *f*, Riß *m*, Spalt *m*; **in·ter·sti·tial** □ [~'stiʃəl] in Zwischenräumen; Zwischen...

in·ter·tri·bal [intə:'traibəl] zwischen den Stämmen.

in·ter·twine [intə:'twain], **in·ter·twist** [~'twist] (sich) verflechten.

in·ter·ur·ban [intər'ə:bən] zwischen Städten, zwischenstädtisch.

in·ter·val ['intəvəl] Zwischenraum *m*; (*a.* Zeit)Abstand *m*; Zwischenzeit *f*, Pause *f*; ♪ Intervall *n*.

in·ter·vene [intə:'vi:n] dazwischenkommen, -treten; sich einmischen; einschreiten; intervenieren; vermitteln, dazwischenliegen; **in·ter·ven·tion** [~'venʃən] Dazwischenkommen *n*; Einmischung *f*; Intervention *f*; Vermitt(e)lung *f*; Dazwischenliegen *n*.

in·ter·view ['intəvju:] **1.** Zusammenkunft *f*, Unterredung *f*; *bsd. Zeitung*: Interview *n*, Befragung *f*; 2. interviewen; **in·ter·view·ee** [~'i:] Interviewte *m*; Kandidat *m*; '**in·ter·view·er** Interviewer *m*.

in·ter·weave [intə:'wi:v] (*irr. weave*) verweben (*a. fig.*).

in·tes·ta·cy ⚖ [in'testəsi] Fehlen *n* e-s Testaments; **in'tes·tate** ⚖ [~tit] **1.** ohne Testament; **2.** ohne Testament Verstorbene *m*, *f*.

in·tes·ti·nal *anat.* [in'testinl] Eingeweide..., Darm...; **in'tes·tine** **1.** inner; einheimisch; **2.** Darm *m*; ~*s pl.* Eingeweide *n/pl.*

in·ti·ma·cy ['intiməsi] Intimität *f*, Vertraulichkeit *f*; vertrauter Umgang *m*; **in·ti·mate** **1.** ['~meit] bekanntgeben; mitteilen; zu verstehen geben; **2.** □ ['~mit] vertraut, intim; innig, eng; **3.** ['~mit] Vertraute *m*, *f*; **in·ti·ma·tion** [~'meiʃən] Andeutung *f*, Wink *m*; Ankündigung *f*, Anzeige *f*.

in·tim·i·date [in'timideit] einschüchtern; **in·tim·i'da·tion** Einschüchterung *f*.

in·to ['intu, *vor Konsonant* 'intə] *prp.* in (*acc.*), in ... hinein.

in·tol·er·a·ble □ [in'tɔlərəbl] unerträglich, unausstehlich; **in'tol·er·ance** Unduldsamkeit *f*, Intoleranz *f*; **in'tol·er·ant** □ unduldsam, intolerant.

in·to·na·tion [intəu'neiʃən] Anstimmung *f*; ♪ Tongebung *f*; *gr.* Intonation *f*, Tonfall *m*; **in·to·nate** ['~neit], **in'tone** anstimmen; *mit besonderem Tonfall* aussprechen.

in·tox·i·cant [in'tɔksikənt] **1.** berauschend; **2.** berauschendes Getränk *n*; **in'tox·i·cate** [~keit] berauschen (*a. fig.*); **in·tox·i'ca·tion** Berauschung *f*; Rausch *m* (*a. fig.*).

in·trac·ta·bil·i·ty [intræktə'biliti] Widerspenstigkeit *f*; **in'trac·ta·ble** □ unlenksam, störrisch; schwer zu bändigen(d).

in·tra·mu·ral ['intrə'mjuərəl] innerhalb der Mauern (vorkommend *etc.*).

in·tran·si·gent [in'trænsidʒənt] unversöhnlich.

in·tran·si·tive [in'trænsitiv] **1.** □ intransitiv; **2.** Intransitivum *n*.

in·tra·state *Am.* [intrə'steit] innerstaatlich.

in·tra·u·te·rine ⚕ [intrə'ju:tərain] intrauterin; ~ *device* (Intrauterin)Spirale *f*.

in·tra·ve·nous ⚕ [intrəˈviːnəs] intravenös.
in·trench [inˈtrentʃ], **inˈtrench·ment** = *entrench etc.*
in·tre·pid □ [inˈtrepid] unerschrocken; **in·tre·pid·i·ty** [intriˈpiditi] Unerschrockenheit *f.*
in·tri·ca·cy [ˈintrikəsi] Kompliziertheit *f*; Schwierigkeit *f*; Knifflichkeit *f*; **in·tri·cate** □ [ˈ~kit] verwickelt; kompliziert; verzwickt; schwierig.
in·trigue [inˈtriːg] **1.** Ränkespiel *n*, Intrige *f*; (Liebes)Verhältnis *n*; **2.** *v/i.* Ränke schmieden, intrigieren; ein (Liebes)Verhältnis haben; *v/t.* interessieren; neugierig machen; **inˈtri·guer** Intrigant(in).
in·trin·sic, **in·trin·si·cal** □ [inˈtrinsik(əl)] inner(lich); wirklich, wahr.
in·tro·duce [intrəˈdjuːs] einführen (*a. fig.*); bekannt machen (*to* mit), *Leute* vorstellen; *Buch etc.* einleiten; *Thema* zur Sprache bringen; **in·tro·duc·tion** [~ˈdʌkʃən] Einführung *f*; Einleitung *f*, Vorrede *f*; Vorstellung *f*, Bekanntmachen *n*; *letter of* ~ Empfehlungsschreiben *n*; **in·troˈduc·to·ry** [~təri] einleitend, einführend.
in·tro·spect [intrəuˈspekt] sich (innerlich) prüfen; **in·troˈspec·tion** Selbstprüfung *f*; Selbstbetrachtung *f*, Introspektion *f*; **in·troˈspec·tive** □ [~tiv] beschaulich; introspektiv.
in·tro·vert **1.** [intrəuˈvəːt] einwärts kehren; **2.** [ˈintrəuvəːt] introvertierter *od.* nach innen gekehrter Mensch *m.*
in·trude [inˈtruːd] hineinzwängen; eindringen; (sich) eindrängen (*into* in *acc.*); (sich) aufdrängen (*upon s.o.* j-m); stören (*upon acc.*); **inˈtrud·er** Eindringling *m*; Störenfried *m*; *a.* ~ *aircraft* Störflugzeug *n.*
in·tru·sion [inˈtruːʒən] Eindringen *n*; Auf-, Zudringlichkeit *f.*
in·tru·sive □ [inˈtruːsiv] zudringlich.
in·trust [inˈtrʌst] = *entrust.*
in·tu·it [inˈtjuːit] intuitiv wissen.
in·tu·i·tion [intjuːˈiʃən] unmittelbare Erkenntnis *f*, Intuition *f*; **inˈtu·i·tive** □ [~tiv] intuitiv, unmittelbar erkennend.
in·un·date [ˈinʌndeit] überschwemmen; **in·unˈda·tion** Überschwemmung *f.*
in·ure [iˈnjuə] gewöhnen (*to* an *acc.*); **inˈure·ment** Gewöhnung *f.*
in·u·til·i·ty [injuːˈtiliti] Nutzlosigkeit *f.*
in·vade [inˈveid] eindringen in, einfallen in (*acc.*), *Land* überfallen; *fig.* befallen; *Recht* verletzen; **inˈvad·er** Angreifer *m*; Eindringling *m.*
in·val·id¹ [ˈinvəliːd] **1.** dienstunfähig; kränklich, gebrechlich; **2.** Kranke *m*; ⚔, ⚓ Invalide *m*; **3.** zum Invaliden machen *od.* werden; ⚔, ⚓ als dienstunfähig entlassen.
in·val·id² [inˈvælid] (rechts)ungültig; nichtig; **in·val·i·date** [inˈvælideit] entkräften; ⚖ ungültig machen; **in·val·iˈda·tion** Entkräftung *f*; Ungültigmachen *n*; **in·va·lid·i·ty** [invəˈliditi] Invalidität *f*; Ungültigkeit *f.*
in·val·u·a·ble □ [inˈvæljuəbl] unschätzbar.
in·var·i·a·ble □ [inˈvɛəriəbl] unveränderlich; beständig; **inˈvar·i·a·bly** ausnahmslos, immer, stets.
in·va·sion [inˈveiʒən] Einfall *m*, Angriff *m*, Invasion *f*; Überfall *m*; ⚖ Eingriff *m* (*of* in *acc.*); ⚕ Anfall *m*; **inˈva·sive** [~siv] angreifend; Angriffs...; eingreifend (*of* in *acc.*); zudringlich.
in·vec·tive [inˈvektiv] Schmähung *f*, Schimpfrede *f*, -wort *n.*
in·veigh [inˈvei] schimpfen (*against* über, auf *acc.*), herziehen (*against* über *acc.*).
in·vei·gle [inˈviːgl] verleiten, (ver-) locken (*into* zu); **inˈvei·gle·ment** Lockung *f.*
in·vent [inˈvent] erfinden; ersinnen, erdichten; **inˈven·tion** Erfindung (-sgabe) *f*; Erdichtung *f*, Lüge *f*; **inˈven·tive** □ [~tiv] erfinderisch; **inˈven·tive·ness** Erfindungsgabe *f*; **inˈven·tor** Erfinder(in); **in·ven·to·ry** [ˈinvəntri] **1.** Inventar *n*; Inventur *f*; **2.** inventarisieren.
in·verse □ [ˈinˈvəːs] umgekehrt; **inˈver·sion** Umkehrung *f*; *gr.* Inversion *f.*
in·vert **1.** [inˈvəːt] umkehren; umstellen; ~*ed commas pl.* Anführungszeichen *n/pl.*; ~*ed flight* ✈ Rückenflug *m*; **2.** [ˈinvəːt] Homosexuelle *m*; Lesbierin *f.*
in·ver·te·brate [inˈvəːtibrit] **1.** wir-

bellos; *fig.* rückgrat-, haltlos; **2.** wirbelloses Tier *n*; *fig.* rückgratloser Mensch *m*.

in·vest [in'vest] *v/t.* investieren, anlegen (*in* in *dat.*); bekleiden; ausstatten (*with* mit); umgeben (*with* von); ⚔ belagern; *v/i.* ~ *in* F kaufen, sich zulegen.

in·ves·ti·gate [in'vestigeit] erforschen; untersuchen; nachforschen; *investigating committee* Untersuchungsausschuß *m*; **in·ves·ti'ga·tion** Erforschung *f*; Untersuchung *f*; Nachforschung *f*; **in'ves·ti·ga·tor** [~geitə] Untersuchende *m, f*.

in·ves·ti·ture [in'vestitʃə] Amtseinführung *f*; **in'vest·ment** Kapitalanlage *f*, Investition *f*; ⚔ Einschließung *f*; Amtseinführung *f*; **in'vest·or** Geldgeber *m*.

in·vet·er·a·cy [in'vetərəsi] Unausrottbarkeit *f*, Hartnäckigkeit *f*; **in'vet·er·ate** □ [~rit] eingewurzelt, unausrottbar (*Sache*); eingefleischt (*Person*); hartnäckig.

in·vid·i·ous □ [in'vidiəs] verhaßt, hassenswert; beneidenswert.

in·vig·i·late [in'vidʒileit] die Aufsicht führen (*bei Prüfungen*); **in'vig·i·la·tor** Aufsichtführende *m, f*.

in·vig·or·ate [in'vigəreit] kräftigen, stärken, beleben; **in·vig·or'a·tion** Kräftigung *f*, Stärkung *f*.

in·vin·ci·bil·i·ty [invinsi'biliti] Unüberwindlichkeit *f*; **in'vin·ci·ble** □ unbesiegbar; unüberwindlich.

in·vi·o·la·bil·i·ty [invaiələ'biliti] Unverletzlichkeit *f*; **in'vi·o·la·ble** □ unverletzlich; unverbrüchlich; **in'vi·o·late** [~lit] unverletzt.

in·vis·i·bil·i·ty [invizə'biliti] Unsichtbarkeit *f*; **in'vis·i·ble** □ unsichtbar; ~ *earnings* ✝ unsichtbare Einkünfte *pl.*; ~ *ink* Geheimtinte *f*; ~ *mending* Kunststopfen *n*.

in·vi·ta·tion [invi'teiʃən] Einladung *f*, Aufforderung *f*; **in·vite** [in'vait] einladen; auffordern; herausfordern; (an)locken; *et.* erbitten; **in'vit·ing** einladend, verlockend.

in·vo·ca·tion [invəu'keiʃən] Anrufung *f*; **in·voc·a·to·ry** [in'vɔkətəri] anrufend.

in·voice ✝ ['invɔis] **1.** Faktura *f*, Warenrechnung *f*; **2.** fakturieren, in Rechnung stellen.

in·voke [in'vəuk] *Gott, j-s Rat etc.* anrufen; *Geist* herauf-, *Rache etc.* herabbeschwören.

in·vol·un·tar·y □ [in'vɔləntəri] unfreiwillig; unwillkürlich.

in·vo·lute ['invəlu:t] eingerollt; verwickelt; **in·vo'lu·tion** Einrollung *f*; Verwicklung *f*; & Potenzierung *f*.

in·volve [in'vɔlv] verwickeln, hineinziehen; in sich schließen, enthalten; nach sich ziehen, mit sich bringen; **in'volved** verwickelt, kompliziert; **in'volve·ment** Verwicklung *f*; (*bsd.* Geld)Schwierigkeit *f*.

in·vul·ner·a·bil·i·ty [invʌlnərə'biliti] Unverwundbarkeit *f*; **in'vul·ner·a·ble** □ unverwundbar; *fig.* unanfechtbar.

in·ward ['inwəd] **1.** inner(lich) (*a. fig.*); nach innen gehend; **2.** *adv.* = *inwards*; **3.** *fig.* Innere *n*; ~*s pl.* Eingeweide *n/pl.*; **'in·ward·ly** innerlich (*a. fig.*); **'in·ward·ness** Innere *n*; Innerlichkeit *f*; **in·wards** ['~z] einwärts; nach innen.

i·od·ic ⚗ [ai'ɔdik] Jod...; **i·o·dide** ['aiədaid] Jodid *n*; **i·o·dine** ['~di:n] Jod *n*.

i·o·do·form ⚗ [ai'ɔdəfɔ:m] Jodoform *n*.

i·on *phys.* ['aiən] Ion *n*.

I·o·ni·an [ai'əunjən] **1.** ionisch; **2.** Jonier(in).

I·on·ic[1] [ai'ɔnik] ionisch.

i·oni·c[2] *phys.* [~] Ionen...; **i·on·ize** *phys.* ['aiənaiz] ionisieren.

i·o·ta [ai'əutə] Jota *n*; Körnchen *n*.

I O U ['aiəu'ju:] (= *I owe you*) Schuldschein *m*.

ip·so fac·to ['ipsəu'fæktəu] gerade durch diese Tatsache.

I·ra·ni·an [ai'reinjən] **1.** iranisch; **2.** Iranier(in).

i·ras·ci·bil·i·ty [iræsi'biliti] Reizbarkeit *f*, Jähzorn *m*; **i'ras·ci·ble** □ [~sibl] reizbar, jähzornig.

i·rate [ai'reit] zornig, wütend.

ire *poet.* ['aiə] Zorn *m*.

ire·ful □ ['aiəful] zornig, wütend.

ir·i·des·cence [iri'desns] Schillern *n in Regenbogenfarben*; **ir·i'des·cent** schillernd, irisierend.

i·rid·i·um [ai'ridiəm] Iridium *n* (*Metall*).

i·ris ['aiəris] *anat.* Regenbogenhaut *f*, Iris *f*; ⚘ Schwertlilie *f*; ~ *diaphragm phot.* Irisblende *f*.

I·rish ['aiəriʃ] **1.** irisch, irländisch; **2.** Irisch *n*; *the* ~ *pl.* die Iren *pl.*;

ˈ**I·rish·ism** irische Spracheigenheit *f*; ˈ**I·rish·man** Irländer *m*, Ire *m*; ˈ**I·rish·wom·an** Irländerin *f*, Irin *f*.

irk [əːk] verdrießen.

irk·some □ [ˈəːksəm] lästig, ermüdend.

i·ron [ˈaiən] **1.** Eisen *n* (*a. fig. u. als Werkzeug od. Waffe*); *a. flat-~* Bügeleisen *n*; *~s pl.* Fesseln *f/pl.*; *strike while the ~ is hot fig.* das Eisen schmieden, solange es heiß ist; **2.** eisern (*fig. fest, hart, unerschütterlich*); Eisen...; **3.** plätten, bügeln; in Eisen legen; mit Eisen beschlagen; ˈ**~-bound** eisenbeschlagen; felsig; unbeugsam, hart; ˈ**~·clad 1.** gepanzert; **2.** Panzerschiff *n*; **~ cur·tain** *pol.* eiserner Vorhang *m*; ˈ**i·ron·er** Bügler(in); ˈ**i·ron-found·ry** Eisengießerei *f*; ˈ**i·ron-ˈheart·ed** *fig.* hartherzig.

i·ron·ic, i·ron·i·cal □ [aiˈrɔnik(əl)] ironisch, spöttisch.

i·ron·ing [ˈaiəniŋ] **1.** Bügeln *n*, Plätten *n*; **2.** *in Zssgn* Plätt..., Bügel...; *~-board* Bügelbrett *n*.

i·ron...: ~ lung ⚕ eiserne Lunge *f*; ˈ**~·mas·ter** Eisenhüttenbesitzer *m*; ˈ**~·mon·ger** Eisenwarenhändler *m*; ˈ**~·mon·ger·y** Eisenwarenhandlung *f*; Eisenwaren *f/pl.*; ˈ**~·mould** Rostfleck *m*; ˈ**♀·sides** *pl.* Reiterei *f* Cromwells; ˈ**~·work** schmiedeeiserne Arbeit *f*; ˈ**~·works** ⊕ *mst sg.* Eisenhütte *f*.

i·ro·ny[1] [ˈaiəni] eisenartig, -haltig.

i·ro·ny[2] [ˈaiərəni] Ironie *f*.

ir·ra·di·ance, ir·ra·di·an·cy [iˈreidjəns(i)] Strahlen(glanz *m*) *n*; Erleuchtung *f* (*a. fig.*); **irˈra·di·ant** strahlend (*with* vor *Freude etc.*).

ir·ra·di·ate [iˈreidieit] bestrahlen (*a.* ⚕); *fig.* aufklären; strahlen machen (*with* vor *Freude etc.*); **ir·ra·diˈa·tion** Strahlen *n*; *phys.* Bestrahlung *f*; *fig.* Erleuchtung *f*.

ir·ra·tion·al □ [iˈræʃənl] unvernünftig; vernunftwidrig; 𝔄 irrational; **ir·ra·tion·al·i·ty** [~ˈnæliti] Unvernunft *f*; Vernunftwidrigkeit *f*.

ir·re·claim·a·ble □ [iriˈkleiməbl] unverbesserlich.

ir·rec·og·niz·a·ble □ [iˈrekəgnaizəbl] nicht (wieder)erkennbar.

ir·rec·on·cil·a·ble □ [iˈrekənsailəbl] unversöhnlich; *von Dingen*: unvereinbar.

ir·re·cov·er·a·ble □ [iriˈkʌvərəbl] unersetzlich; unwiederbringlich (verloren).

ir·re·deem·a·ble □ [iriˈdiːməbl] nicht rückkaufbar; nicht tilgbar, unkündbar (*Rente etc.*); nicht einlösbar (*Papiergeld*); unersetzlich; unverbesserlich.

ir·re·duc·i·ble [iriˈdjuːsəbl] nicht reduzierbar; absolut, äußerst; nicht verwandelbar (*into* in *acc.*, *to* zu).

ir·ref·ra·ga·bil·i·ty [irefrəgəˈbiliti] Unwiderlegbarkeit *f etc.*; **irˈref·ra·ga·ble** □ unwiderlegbar, unumstößlich.

ir·ref·u·ta·ble □ [iˈrefjutəbl] unwiderleglich, unwiderlegbar.

ir·reg·u·lar [iˈregjulə] **1.** □ unregelmäßig, regelwidrig, irregulär; unordentlich; ungleichmäßig; **2.** *~s pl.* Freischärler *m/pl.*; **ir·reg·u·lar·i·ty** [~ˈlæriti] Unregelmäßigkeit *f etc.*

ir·rel·a·tive [iˈrelətiv] ohne Beziehung (*to* auf *acc.*, zu).

ir·rel·e·vance, ir·rel·e·van·cy [iˈrelivəns(i)] Belanglosigkeit *f*, Unerheblichkeit *f*; **irˈrel·e·vant** □ nicht zur Sache gehörig; unzutreffend; unerheblich, belanglos (*to* für).

ir·re·li·gion [iriˈlidʒən] Unglaube *m*; Irreligiosität *f*; **ir·reˈli·gious** □ gottlos; irreligiös.

ir·re·me·di·a·ble □ [iriˈmiːdjəbl] unheilbar; unersetzlich.

ir·re·mis·si·ble □ [iriˈmisəbl] unerläßlich, unverzeihlich.

ir·re·mov·a·ble □ [iriˈmuːvəbl] nicht entfernbar; unabsetzbar.

ir·rep·a·ra·ble □ [iˈrepərəbl] nicht wieder gutzumachen(d).

ir·re·place·a·ble [iriˈpleisəbl] unersetzlich.

ir·re·press·i·ble □ [iriˈpresəbl] ununterdrückbar; unbezähmbar.

ir·re·proach·a·ble □ [iriˈprəutʃəbl] einwandfrei, untadelig; **ir·reˈproach·a·ble·ness** Untadel(haft)igkeit *f*.

ir·re·sist·i·bil·i·ty [ˈirizistəˈbiliti] Unwiderstehlichkeit *f*; **ir·reˈsist·i·ble** □ unwiderstehlich.

ir·res·o·lute □ [iˈrezəluːt] unentschlossen, unschlüssig; **irˈres·o·lute·ness, ir·res·oˈlu·tion** Unentschlossenheit *f*.

ir·re·solv·a·ble [iri'zɔlvəbl] unlöslich; nicht auflösbar.
ir·re·spec·tive □ [iri'spektiv] (*of*) rücksichtslos (gegen); ohne Rücksicht (auf *acc.*); unabhängig (von).
ir·re·spon·si·bil·i·ty ['irispɔnsə'biliti] Unverantwortlichkeit *f*; **ir·re·'spon·si·ble** □ unverantwortlich; verantwortungslos.
ir·re·triev·a·ble □ [iri'tri:vəbl] unwiederbringlich, unersetzlich; nicht wieder gutzumachen(d).
ir·rev·er·ence [i'revərəns] Respektlosigkeit *f*; **ir'rev·er·ent** □ respekt-, ehrfurchtslos.
ir·re·vers·i·ble □ [iri'və:səbl] nicht umkehrbar; unwiderruflich.
ir·rev·o·ca·bil·i·ty [irevəkə'biliti] Unwiderruflichkeit *f*; Unabänderlichkeit *f*; **ir'rev·o·ca·ble** □ unwiderruflich; unabänderlich, endgültig (*Urteil etc.*).
ir·ri·gate ['irigeit] bewässern; berieseln; ⚕ spülen; **ir·ri'ga·tion** Bewässerung *f*; Berieselung *f etc.*
ir·ri·ta·bil·i·ty [iritə'biliti] Reizbarkeit *f*; **'ir·ri·ta·ble** □ reizbar; **'ir·ri·tant 1.** aufreizend; **2.** Reizmittel *n*; **ir·ri·tate** ['~teit] reizen; ärgern; **'ir·ri·tat·ing** □ aufreizend; ärgerlich (*Sache*); **ir·ri'ta·tion** Reizung *f*; Gereiztheit *f*, Ärger *m*.
ir·rup·tion [i'rʌpʃən] Einbruch *m* (*mst fig.*); *feindlicher* Einfall *m*; **ir'rup·tive** [~tiv] (her)einbrechend.
is [iz] *er, sie, es* ist (*s. be*).
i·sin·glass ['aiziŋglɑ:s] Fischleim *m*; Hausenblase *f*.
Is·lam ['izlɑ:m] Islam *m*.
is·land ['ailənd] Insel *f* (*a. fig.*); Verkehrsinsel *f*; **'is·land·er** Inselbewohner(in).
isle [ail] *poet. od. in festen Zssgn* Insel *f*; **is·let** ['ailit] Inselchen *n*.
ism *mst contp.* ['izəm] Ismus *m*, Theorie *f*, System *n*.
isn't ['iznt] = *is not.*
i·so... ['aisəu] *in Zssgn* gleich..., iso...
i·so·bar *meteor.* ['aisəubɑ:] Isobare *f*, Linie *f* gleichen Luftdrucks.
i·so·late ['aisəleit] absondern; isolieren; **'i·so·lat·ed** abgeschieden; **i·so'la·tion** Isolierung *f*, Absonderung *f*; *~ ward* Isolierstation *f*; **i·so'la·tion·ist** *Am. pol.* [~ʃnist] Isolationist *m*.
i·so·met·rics [aisəu'metriks] *pl.* isometrische Übungen *f/pl.*
i·sos·ce·les ⩓ [ai'sɔsili:z] gleichschenk(e)lig (*Dreieck*).
i·so·therm *meteor.* ['aisəuθə:m] Isotherme *f*, Linie *f* gleicher Temperatur.
i·so·tope ⚗ ['aisəutəup] Isotop *n*.
i·so·type ['aisəutaip] statistisches Schaubild *n od.* Diagramm *n*.
Is·ra·el·ite ['izriəlait] Israelit(in); **'Is·ra·el·it·ish** israelitisch.
is·sue ['iʃu:] **1.** Herauskommen *n*, -fließen *n*; Abfluß *m*, Abgang *m* (*von Blut*); Ausgang *m*, -weg *m*; (Fluß)Mündung *f*; *mst* ⚖ Nachkommen(schaft *f*) *m/pl.*; *fig.* Ausgang *m*, Ergebnis *n*; ⚖ Streitfrage *f*; Ausgabe *f von Material etc.*, ✝ Emission *f von Banknoten*; Erlaß *m von Befehlen*; Ausgabe *f*, Exemplar *n*; Nummer *f e-r Zeitung*; *~ in fact* Tatsachenfrage *f*; *~ in law* Rechtsfrage *f*; *force an ~* e-e Entscheidung erzwingen; *join* (*the*) *~* (die) Verhandlungen aufnehmen (*on* über *acc.*); *join ~ with s.o.* anderer Meinung sein als j.; *be at ~* uneinig sein; *point at ~* strittiger Punkt *m*; **2.** *v/i.* herauskommen, -fließen; ausgehen, herkommen, entspringen (*from* von, aus); endigen (*in* in *acc.*); *v/t.* aussenden; von sich geben; *Material etc.* ausgeben, ✝ *Banknoten* emittieren; *Befehl* erlassen; *Buch* herausgeben; *j.* beliefern (*with* mit); **'is·sue·less** ohne Nachkommen.
isth·mus ['isməs] Landenge *f*, Isthmus *m*.
it [it] **1.** es; *nach prp.* da... (*z. B. by it* dadurch; *for it* dafür); *how is ~ with ...?* wie steht es mit ...? *s. lord 2, foot 2*; *go ~* F es wagen; *go ~! sl.* los (doch)!, feste!; *we had a very good time of ~* wir haben uns sehr gut amüsiert; **2.** das gewisse Etwas.
I·tal·ian [i'tæljən] **1.** italienisch; **2.** Italiener(in); Italienisch *n*.
i·tal·ics *typ.* [i'tæliks] *pl.* Kursivschrift *f*; **i'tal·i·cize** [~saiz] in Kursive drucken.
itch [itʃ] **1.** ⚕ Krätze *f*; Jucken *n*; dringendes Verlangen *n* (*for* nach; *to inf.* zu *inf.*); **2.** jucken (*fig. begierig sein*); *I ~* es juckt mich; *be ~ing to inf.* darauf brennen zu *inf.*; *have an ~ing palm* raffgierig sein; **'itch·ing** Jucken *n*; *fig.* Gelüste *n*;

ˈ**itch·y** krätzig.
i·tem [ˈaitəm] **1.** desgleichen; **2.** Einzelheit *f*, Punkt *m*; (Rechnungs-) Posten *m*; (Zeitungs)Artikel *m*; **3.** notieren; **i·tem·ize** [ˈ~maiz] einzeln angeben *od.* aufführen.
it·er·ate [ˈitəreit] wiederholen; **it·erˈa·tion** Wiederholung *f*; **it·er·a·tive** □ [ˈitərətiv] (sich) wiederholend.
i·tin·er·ant □ [iˈtinərənt] reisend; umherziehend; Reise..., Wander...; **i·tin·er·ar·y** [aiˈtinərəri] **1.** Reiseroute *f*, -plan *m*; Reisebericht *m*; **2.** Reise...; **i·tin·er·ate** [iˈtinəreit] (umher)reisen.
its [its] sein(er); dessen, deren.
it's F [its] = *it is, it has.*
it·self [itˈself] (es) selbst; sich; *of* ~ von selbst; *in* ~ in sich, an sich; *by* ~ für sich allein, besonders.
I've F [aiv] = *I have.*
i·vied [ˈaivid] mit Efeu bedeckt.
i·vo·ry [ˈaivəri] **1.** Elfenbein *n*; *ivories pl.* F Klaviertasten *f/pl.*; *tickle the ivories* F *iro.* Klavier spielen; **2.** elfenbeinern; Elfenbein...; ~ *tower fig.* Elfenbeinturm *m*.
i·vy ⚘ [ˈaivi] Efeu *m*; ♀ *League Eliteuniversitäten im Osten der USA.*

J

J [dʒei]: ~ *pen* breite (Schreib-) Feder *f*.
jab F [dʒæb] **1.** stechen; stoßen; **2.** Stich *m*, Stoß *m*; *Boxen*: linke Gerade *f*; F Spritze *f*, Injektion *f*.
jab·ber [ˈdʒæbə] **1.** plappern; quasseln; **2.** Geplapper *n*.
jab·ot [ˈʒæbəu] Spitzenbesatz *m*, Jabot *n*.
Jack[1] [dʒæk] Hans *m*; ~ *Frost* der Winter; ~ *and Gill* Hans und Grete; *before one could say* ~ *Robinson* eh man sich's versah.
jack[2] [~] **1.** Hebevorrichtung *f*, *bsd.* Wagenheber *m*; Malkugel *f beim Bowlsspiel*; ⚓ Gösch *f*, kleine Flagge *f*; *Karten*: Bube *m*; **2.** *a.* ~ *up* aufbocken.
jack·al [ˈdʒækɔːl] *zo.* Schakal *m*; *fig.* Handlanger *m*.
jack·a·napes [ˈdʒækəneips] Geck *m*, Affe *m*; Naseweis *m*; Schlingel *m*; ˈ**jack·ass** Esel *m*; *fig.* Dummkopf *m*; ˈ**jack·boots** *pl.* Reiterstiefel *m/pl.*; hohe Wasserstiefel *m/pl.*; ˈ**jack·daw** *orn.* Dohle *f*.
jack·et [ˈdʒækit] Jacke *f*; ⊕ Mantel *m*; Schutzumschlag *m e-s Buches*; *dust s.o.'s* ~ F j-m die Jacke voll hauen; *potatoes in their* ~*s* Pellkartoffeln *f/pl.*
jack...: ˈ~**-in-of·fice** Bürokrat *m*; ˈ~**-in-the-box** Schachtelmännchen *n*; ♀ **Ketch** der Henker; ˈ~**-knife** (großes) Klappmesser *n*; ˈ~**-of-ˈall--trades** Hansdampf *m* in allen Gassen; ˈ~**-of-ˈall-work** Faktotum *n*; ~**-o'-lan·tern** [ˈdʒækəulæntən] Irrlicht *n*; Kürbislaterne *f*; ˈ~**--plane** Schrupphobel *m*; ˈ~**·pot** *Poker*: Einsatz *m*; *hit the* ~ *Am.* F großes Glück haben; ~ **pud·ding** Hanswurst *m*; ~ **tar** Teerjacke *f* (*Matrose*); ˈ~**-tow·el** Rollhandtuch *n*.
Jac·o·bin *hist.* [ˈdʒækəubin] Jakobiner *m*; **Jac·o·bite** *hist.* [ˈ~bait] Jakobit *m*.
jade[1] [dʒeid] **1.** (Schind)Mähre *f*; Klepper *m*; *contp.* Frauenzimmer *n*, Weib *n*; **2.** ermüden, abhetzen.
jade[2] *min.* [~] Jade *m*, Nephrit *m*.
jag [dʒæg] **1.** Zacken *m*; *sl.* Sauferei *f*, Sauftour *f*; **2.** zacken; ˈ**jag·ged** □, ˈ**jag·gy** zackig; gekerbt; *bsd. Am. sl. jagged* voll (*betrunken*).
jag·uar *zo.* [ˈdʒægjuə] Jaguar *m*.
jail [dʒeil] **1.** Gefängnis *n*; Kerker *m*; **2.** ins Gefängnis werfen, einsperren; ˈ~**-bird** Galgenvogel *m*; ˈ~**·break** Ausbruch *m* aus dem Gefängnis.
jail·er [ˈdʒeilə] Gefängniswärter *m*, Kerkermeister *m*.
ja·lop·(p)y *bsd. Am.* F *mot.*, ✈ [dʒəˈlɔpi] Karre *f*, Kiste *f*.
jam[1] [dʒæm] Marmelade *f*.
jam[2] [~] **1.** Gedränge *n*; ⊕ Hemmung *f*; *Radio*: Störung *f*; *traffic* ~ Ver-

kehrsstockung *f*; *be in a ~ sl.* in der Klemme sein; *~ session* improvisiertes Zusammenspielen *n* von Jazzmusikern; **2.** (sich) (fest-, ver-) klemmen; (zs.-)pressen; *Durchgang* versperren; *Radio*: stören; ⊕ stokken; blockieren; *~ the brakes* mit aller Kraft bremsen.

Ja·mai·ca [dʒəˈmeikə] *a. ~ rum* Jamaika-Rum *m.*

jamb [dʒæm] (Tür)Pfosten *m.*

jam·bo·ree [dʒæmbəˈriː] (*bsd.* Pfadfinder)Treffen *n*; *sl.* Lustbarkeit *f.*

jam-jar [ˈdʒæmdʒɑː] Marmeladenglas *n.*

jam·my *sl.* [ˈdʒæmi] Glücks...; *~ fellow* Glückspilz *m* (*Person*).

jam-packed F [ˈdʒæmˈpækt] proppenvoll.

jan·gle [ˈdʒæŋgl] **1.** schrillen (lassen); laut streiten, keifen; **2.** Mißklang *m*; ˈ**jan·gling** mißtönend, schrill.

jan·i·tor [ˈdʒænitə] Portier *m*, Pförtner *m*; *Am.* Hausmeister *m.*

Jan·u·ar·y [ˈdʒænjuəri] Januar *m.*

Jap F [dʒæp] Japaner *m.*

ja·pan [dʒəˈpæn] **1.** Japanlack *m*; Lackmalerei *f*, -arbeit *f*; **2.** *auf japanische Weise* lackieren.

Jap·a·nese [dʒæpəˈniːz] **1.** japanisch; **2.** Japaner(in); Japanisch *n*; *the ~ pl.* die Japaner *pl.*

ja·pan·ner [dʒəˈpænə] Lackierer *m.*

jar[1] [dʒɑː] Krug *m*; Topf *m*; Glas *n.*

jar[2] [~] **1.** Knarren *n*, Mißton *m*; Streit *m*; mißliche Lage *f*; **2.** knarren, schnarren (lassen); unangenehm berühren, beleidigen (*upon acc.*); erzittern (lassen); streiten; *~ with* widerstreiten (*dat.*); nicht harmonieren.

jar·gon [ˈdʒɑːgən] Kauderwelsch *n*; Berufs-, Fachsprache *f*, Jargon *m.*

jas·min(e) ⚘ [ˈdʒæsmin] Jasmin *m.*

jas·per *min.* [ˈdʒæspə] Jaspis *m.*

jaun·dice [ˈdʒɔːndis] ⚕ Gelbsucht *f*; *fig.* Scheelsucht *f*, Neid *m*; ˈ**jaun·diced** gelbsüchtig; *fig.* neidisch.

jaunt [dʒɔːnt] **1.** Ausflug *m*, Spritztour *f*; **2.** e-n Ausflug machen; ˈ**jaun·ti·ness** munteres Wesen *n*; ˈ**jaunt·ing-car** zweirädriger Pferdewagen *m*; ˈ**jaun·ty** □ munter; flott; forsch; keck.

Jav·a·nese [dʒɑːvəˈniːz] **1.** javanisch; **2.** Javaner(in); Javanisch *n*; *the ~ pl.* die Javaner *pl.*

jave·lin [ˈdʒævlin] Wurfspieß *m*; *Sport*: Speer *m*; *throwing the ~* Speerwerfen *n.*

jaw [dʒɔː] **1.** Kinnbacken *m*, Kiefer *m*; P Getratsch *n*; *~s pl.* Rachen *m*; Maul *n*; *Tal- etc.* Enge *f*, Schlund *m*; ⊕ Backen *f/pl. e-r Zange etc.*; F Moralpredigt *f*; **2.** *v/i.* schwatzen; *v/t.* P anschnauzen; e-e Moralpredigt halten (*dat.*); ˈ**~-bone** Kieferknochen *m*; ˈ**~-break·er** F Zungenbrecher *m.*

jay [dʒei] *orn.* Eichelhäher *m*; F Quasselpeter *m*; ˈ**~-walk·er** achtlos die Straße überquerender Fußgänger *m.*

jazz [dʒæz] **1.** Jazz *m*; **2.** F grell, schreiend; **3.** Jazz spielen *od.* tanzen; *~ up* Leben bringen in (*acc.*); ˈ**~-band** Jazzkapelle *f*; ˈ**jaz·zy** = *jazz* 2.

jeal·ous □ [ˈdʒeləs] (*of*) eifersüchtig (auf *acc.*); besorgt (um), eifrig bedacht (auf *acc.*); neidisch (auf *acc.*); ˈ**jeal·ous·y** Eifersucht *f*; Eifersüchtelei *f*; Besorgtheit *f*; Neid *m.*

jean [dʒiːn] Köper *m*; *~s pl.* Arbeitsanzug *m*; Jeans *pl.*, Niethose *f.*

jeep [dʒiːp] Jeep *m*, kleines Mehrzweckfahrzeug *n.*

jeer [dʒiə] **1.** Spott *m*, Spötterei *f*; **2.** *v/i.* höhnen, spotten (*at* über *acc.*); *v/t. j.* verhöhnen; ˈ**jeer·er** Spötter(in); ˈ**jeer·ing** □ spöttisch.

je·june □ [dʒiˈdʒuːn] nüchtern, fad, trocken; dürr (*Boden*).

jell F [dʒel] gelieren; zum Gelieren bringen; *fig.* feste Form geben (*dat.*).

jel·ly [ˈdʒeli] **1.** Gallert(e *f*) *n*; Gelee *n*; **2.** zu Gallert *etc.* machen *od.* werden, gelieren; *~* **ba·by,** *~* **bean** Geleebonbon *m*, *n*; ˈ**~-fish** *zo.* Qualle *f.*

jem·my [ˈdʒemi] Brecheisen *n.*

jen·ny ⊕ [ˈdʒeni] Laufkran *m*; = *spinning-~.*

jeop·ard·ize [ˈdʒepədaiz] aufs Spiel setzen, gefährden; ˈ**jeop·ard·y** Gefahr *f.*

jer·bo·a *zo.* [dʒəːˈbəuə] Wüstenspringmaus *f.*

jer·e·mi·ad [dʒeriˈmaiəd] Klagelied *n*, Jeremiade *f.*

jerk [dʒəːk] **1.** Ruck *m*, Stoß *m*; (Muskel)Zuckung *f*, (-)Krampf *m*; *by ~s* ruckweise; *put a ~ in it sl.* tüchtig ’rangehen; *physical ~s pl.* F Turnen *n*; **2.** rucken *od.* zerren (an *dat.*); ziehen; schnellen; schleudern; *mit adv. od. prp.* reißen; *Fleisch* an der Luft trocknen.

jer·kin ['dʒəːkin] (Leder)Wams *n.*

jerk·wa·ter *Am.* ['dʒəːkwɔːtə] **1.** Nebenbahn *f*; **2.** F klein, unbedeutend; '**jerk·y 1.** □ ruck-, sprungartig; hoppelig, holperig; **2.** *Am. luftgetrocknetes* Rindfleisch *n.*

jer·ry *sl.* ['dʒeri] ⚔ ♀ deutscher Soldat *m*; Nachttopf *m*; '**~-build·er** Bauschwindler *m*; '**~-build·ing** unsolide Bauart *f*; '**~-built** unsolide gebaut; ~ *house* Bruchbude *f*; '**~-can** Benzin-, Wasserkanister *m.*

jer·sey ['dʒəːzi] Wollpullover *m*; wollenes Unterhemd *n*; ♀ *zo.* Jerseyrind *n.*

jes·sa·mine ⚘ ['dʒesəmin] Jasmin *m.*

jest [dʒest] **1.** Scherz *m*, Spaß *m*; **2.** scherzen, spaßen; '**jest·er** Spaßmacher *m*; Hofnarr *m.*

Jes·u·it ['dʒezjuit] Jesuit *m*; **Jes·u·'it·ic, Jes·u·'it·i·cal** □ jesuitisch.

jet[1] *min.* [dʒet] Jett *n*, Pechkohle *f.*

jet[2] [~] **1.** (Wasser-, Gas)Strahl *m*; Strahlrohr *n*; ⊕ Düse *f*; Düsenflugzeug *n*; Düsenmotor *m*; ~ *age* Düsenzeitalter *n*; ~ *propulsion* Düsenantrieb *m*; ~ *set* Jet-set *m*; *~-setter* Angehörige *m, f* des Jet-set; 2. hervorsprudeln.

jet-black ['dʒet'blæk] pechschwarz.

jet...: ~ **en·gine** Düsenmotor *m*; ~ **fight·er** ⚔ Düsenjäger *m*; '**~·lag** Schwierigkeiten *f/pl.* mit der Zeitumstellung *nach langen Flugreisen*; '**~-plane** Düsenflugzeug *n*; '**~-pow·ered** mit Düsenantrieb.

jet·sam ['dʒetsəm] über Bord geworfene Ladung *f*; Strandgut *n*; *flotsam and* ~ *fig.* (menschliches) Strandgut *n.*

jet·ti·son ['dʒetisn] **1.** Überbordwerfen *n*, Notwurf *m*; **2.** über Bord werfen; '**jet·ti·son·a·ble** abwerfbar, Abwurf...

jet·ty ⚓ ['dʒeti] Mole *f*; Pier *m, f.*

Jew [dʒuː] Jude *m*; *attr.* Juden...; *~'s harp* ♪ Maultrommel *f.*

jew·el ['dʒuːəl] **1.** Juwel *n, m* (*a. fig.*), Kleinod *n*; **2.** mit Juwelen schmücken; *Uhr* mit Steinen auslegen; '**jew·el(l)er** Juwelier *m*; '**jew·el·ry,** '**jew·el·ler·y** Juwelen *n/pl.*, Schmuck *m.*

Jew·ess ['dʒuːis] Jüdin *f*; '**Jew·ish** jüdisch; **Jew·ry** ['dʒuəri] Judentum *n*, *die* Juden *pl.*

jib [dʒib] **1.** ⚓ Klüver *m*; ⊕ Kranbalken *m*; *the cut of his* ~ seine äußere Erscheinung; **2.** scheuen, bocken (*Pferd*); *fig.* nicht mehr wollen; ~ *at* keine Lust haben zu; '**jib·ber** scheuendes Pferd *n*; '**jib-'boom** ⚓ Klüverbaum *m*; ~ **door** Tapetentür *f.*

jibe [dʒaib] *Am.* F übereinstimmen; [= *gibe.*]

jif·fy F ['dʒifi] Augenblick *m*; *in a* ~ im Handumdrehen, im Nu, sofort.

jig [dʒig] **1.** Gigue *f* (*Tanz*); ⊕ Einspannvorrichtung *f*; **2.** Gigue tanzen; auf- und abschnellen.

jig·ger ['dʒigə] Floh *m*; Milbe *f*; *Am.* Meßglas *n für Cocktails.*

jig·gered F ['dʒigəd]: *I'm* ~ *if* ... verdammt will ich sein, wenn ...

jig·gle F ['dʒigl] *v/t.* (leicht) rütteln; *v/i.* wackeln, wippen.

jig-saw ['dʒigsɔː] Laubsäge(maschine) *f*; ~ **puz·zle** Zusammensetz-, Puzzlespiel *n.*

jill [dʒil] = *gill*[3].

jilt [dʒilt] **1.** Kokette *f*; **2.** *Liebhaber* versetzen.

Jim *Am. sl.* [dʒim]: ~ *Crow* Nigger *m*; Rassentrennung *f.*

jim-jams *sl.* ['dʒimdʒæmz] *pl.* Säuferwahnsinn *m*; Tatterich *m*; Gruseln *n.*

jim·my ['dʒimi] Brecheisen *n.*

jin·gle ['dʒiŋgl] **1.** Geklingel *n*; Wortgeklingel *n*; **2.** klingeln *od.* klimpern (mit).

jin·go ['dʒiŋgəu] Chauvinist *m*, Hurrapatriot *m*; *by* ~*! sl.* Donnerwetter!; '**jin·go·ism** Chauvinismus *m.*

jinks [dʒiŋks] *pl.*: *mst high* ~ Ausgelassenheit *f.*

jinn [dʒin] = *genie.*

jinx *sl.* [dʒiŋks] Unglücksbringer *m.*

jit·ney *Am. sl.* ['dʒitni] 5-Cent-Stück *n*; billiger Omnibus *m.*

jit·ter F ['dʒitə] **1.** zittern, bibbern; tanzen; **2.** *~s pl. sl.* Nervosität *f*; *have the ~s* nervös sein, den Tatterich haben; **~·bug** ['~bʌg] **1.** *fig.* Nervenbündel *n*; Swingenthusiast (-in); **2.** wild tanzen; '**jit·ter·y** *sl.* ängstlich, nervös.

jiu-jit·su [dʒuː'dʒitsuː] Jiu-Jitsu *n.*

jive *Am. sl.* [dʒaiv] *heiße* Jazzmusik *f*; Jazzjargon *m.*

Job[1] [dʒəub]: *~'s comforter* schlechter Tröster *m*; *~'s post* Hiobsbotschaft *f*.

job[2] [dʒɔb] **1.** (Stück *n*) Arbeit *f*; Sache *f*, Aufgabe *f*; Beruf *m*; Beschäftigung *f*, Stellung *f*, Posten *m*; ✝ Partieware *f*; *contp*. Schiebung *f*; *typ*. Akzidenzarbeit *f*; *by the* ~ stückweise; im Akkord; *make a good* ~ *of it* s-e Sache ordentlich machen; *a bad* ~ eine aussichtslose Sache *od*. Lage; *on the* ~ *training* Ausbildung *f* am Arbeitsplatz; ~ *lot* Gelegenheitskauf *m*, Ramschware *f*; ~ *printer* Akzidenzdrucker *m*; ~ *work* Akkordarbeit *f*; **2.** *v/t*. *Pferd etc*. (ver-)mieten; ✝ vermitteln; *Amt* mißbrauchen; *v/i*. Gelegenheitsarbeit machen; im Akkord arbeiten; Maklergeschäfte machen; Amtsmißbrauch treiben.

job·ber [ˈdʒɔbə] Gelegenheits-, Akkordarbeiter *m*; Makler *m*; Aktienhändler *m*; Schieber *m*; ˈ**job·ber·y** Amtsmißbrauch *m*; *a piece of* ~ e-e Schiebung *f*; ˈ**job·bing** Akkordarbeit *f*; Börsenwucher *m*; *s. jobbery*; ˈ**job–hunt·ing** F Arbeitssuche *f*; ˈ**job·less** arbeitslos; **job mar·ket** Arbeitsmarkt *m*; **job se·cu·ri·ty** Sicherheit *f* des Arbeitsplatzes.

jock·ey [ˈdʒɔki] **1.** Jockei *m*; **2.** prellen, (be)gaunern.

jock·strap [ˈdʒɔkstræp] *Sport*: Suspensorium *n*.

jo·cose □ [dʒəuˈkəus] scherzhaft, lustig; **joˈcose·ness** Scherzhaftigkeit *f*.

joc·u·lar [ˈdʒɔkjulə] scherzhaft; **joc·u·lar·i·ty** [~ˈlæriti] Scherzhaftigkeit *f*.

joc·und □ [ˈdʒɔkənd] lustig, fröhlich, heiter.

Jodh·purs [ˈdʒɔdpuəz] *pl*. Reithose *f*.

Joe [dʒəu]: ~ *Miller* fader Witz *m*, Kalauer *m*.

jog [dʒɔg] **1.** Stoß(en *n*) *m*; Rütteln *n*; Trott *m*; **2.** *v/t*. (an)stoßen, (auf-)rütteln; stoßen an (*acc*.); *v/i*. *mst* ~ *along*, ~ *on* dahinschlendern, -trotten; zuckeln.

jog·ging [ˈdʒɔgiŋ] Trimm-Trab *m*, Trablaufen *n*.

jog·gle [ˈdʒɔgl] **1.** rütteln, (sich) schütteln; ⊕ verzahnen, verschränken; **2.** Rütteln *n*; ⊕ Falz *m*, Nut *f*; Fuge *f*.

jog-trot [ˈdʒɔgˈtrɔt] Trott *m*; *fig*. Schlendrian *m*.

john[1] *Am*. F [dʒɔn] Klo *n*.

John[2] [~]: ~ *Bull* John Bull *m* (*der Engländer*); ~ *Hancock Am*. Friedrich Wilhelm *m* (*Unterschrift*).

join [dʒɔin] **1.** *v/t*. verbinden, zs.-fügen (*to* mit); ⊕ fügen; sich vereinigen mit, sich gesellen zu, stoßen zu, treffen, eintreten in (*acc*.); ~ *battle* den Kampf beginnen; ~ *company* sich anschließen (*with dat*.); ~ *hands* die Hände falten; sich die Hände reichen (*a. fig*.); *v/i*. sich verbinden, sich vereinigen; angrenzen, anstoßen; ~ *in* sich *e-r Sache* anschließen, sich beteiligen an (*dat*.), mitmachen bei; mit einstimmen in (*acc*.); ~ *up* Soldat werden; *I* ~ *with you* ich halte es mit Ihnen; **2.** Verbindung(sstelle) *f*; Naht *f*; Fuge *f*.

join·er [ˈdʒɔinə] Schreiner *m*, Tischler *m*; ˈ**join·er·y** Schreiner-, Tischlerhandwerk *n*, -arbeit *f*.

joint [dʒɔint] **1.** Verbindung *f*, Fuge *f*; Scharnier *n*; Gewinde *n*; *anat*. Gelenk *n*; ⚘ Knoten *m*; Braten *m*, Keule *f*; *Am. sl*. Bumslokal *n*, Spelunke *f*; *put out of* ~ verrenken; *out of* ~ *fig*. aus den Fugen; **2.** □ verbunden, vereint; gemeinsam; Mit...; ~ *heir* Miterbe *m*; ~ *ownership* Miteigentum *n*; ~ *production* Koproduktion *f*; ~ *venture* Gemeinschaftsunternehmen *n*; **3.** zs.-fügen; ⊕ aneinanderpassen; zergliedern, zerlegen; ˈ**joint·ed** gegliedert; mit Gelenken; ~ *doll* Gliederpuppe *f*; **joint stock** Aktienkapital *n*; ˈ**joint--stock com·pa·ny** Aktiengesellschaft *f*; **join·ture** ⚖ [ˈ~tʃə] Wittum *n*.

joist [dʒɔist] Querbalken *m*; Profilträger *m*.

joke [dʒəuk] **1.** Scherz *m*, Spaß *m*, Witz *m*; *practical* ~ Streich *m*, Schabernack *m*; **2.** *v/i*. scherzen, spaßen; schäkern; *v/t*. necken, aufziehen (*about* mit); ˈ**jok·er** Spaßvogel *m*, -macher *m*; *Karten*: Joker *m*; *Am*. versteckte Klausel *f*; ˈ**jok·y** □ scherzhaft, spaßig.

jol·li·fi·ca·tion F [dʒɔlifiˈkeiʃən] Lustbarkeit *f*; ˈ**jol·li·ness**, ˈ**jol·li·ty** Lustigkeit *f*.

jol·ly [ˈdʒɔli] **1.** □ lustig, fröhlich, vergnügt, fidel; F nett, famos; **2.** F *adv*. sehr, riesig, mächtig; **3.** F *j-m* um den Bart gehen.

jol·ly-boat ⚓ [ˈdʒɔlibəut] Jolle *f*.

Jol·ly Rog·er [ˈdʒɔliˈrɔdʒə] Totenkopf-, Piratenflagge *f*.
jolt [dʒəult] **1.** stoßen, rütteln; holpern; **2.** Stoß *m*; Rütteln *n*; ˈ**jolt·y** rüttelnd; holperig.
Jon·a·than [ˈdʒɔnəθən]: *Brother* ~ Bruder *m* Jonathan (*Amerikaner*).
jon·quil ⚘ [ˈdʒɔŋkwil] *e-e* Narzisse *f*.
jo·rum [ˈdʒɔːrəm] großer Humpen *m*; Punsch *m*.
josh *Am. sl.* [dʒɔʃ] **1.** Ulk *m*; **2.** aufziehen, auf die Schippe nehmen.
joss [dʒɔs] chinesisches Idol *n*; ˈ**~-house** chinesischer Tempel *m*; ˈ**~-stick** Räucherstäbchen *n*.
jos·tle [ˈdʒɔsl] **1.** anrennen; (an-)stoßen; (an)rempeln; **2.** Stoß *m*; Zs.-Stoß *m*.
jot [dʒɔt] **1.** Fünkchen *n*, Körnchen *n*; **2.** ~ *down* notieren; ˈ**jot·ter** Notizbuch *n*, -block *m*; ˈ**jot·tings** *pl*. Notizen *f/pl*.
joule [dʒuːl] Joule *n*.
jour·nal [ˈdʒəːnl] Journal *n* (*a.* ✝, ⚓); Tagebuch *n*; Zeitung *f*; Zeitschrift *f*; ⊕ Wellenzapfen *m*; **jour·nal·ese** F [ˌ~nəˈliːz] Zeitungsstil *m*; ˈ**jour·nal·ism** Zeitungswesen *n*, Journalismus *m*; ˈ**jour·nal·ist** Journalist (-in); **jour·nalˈis·tic** (*~ally*) journalistisch; ˈ**jour·nal·ize** ✝ (in das Journal) eintragen.
jour·ney [ˈdʒəːni] **1.** Reise *f*; Fahrt *f*, Tour *f*; **2.** reisen, wandern; ˈ**~·man** Geselle *m*; ˈ**~-work** Tagelöhnerarbeit *f*.
joust [dʒaust] **1.** Turnier *n*; **2.** turnieren.
Jove [dʒəuv] Jupiter *m*; *by* ~! bei Gott!
jo·vi·al □ [ˈdʒəuvjəl] heiter, lustig; gemütlich; **jo·vi·al·i·ty** [ˌ~viˈæliti] Heiterkeit *f*, Frohsinn *m*.
jowl [dʒaul] Backe *f*; *cheek by* ~ dicht nebeneinander.
joy [dʒɔi] Freude *f*; Fröhlichkeit *f*; **joy·ful** □ [ˈ~ful] freudig; erfreut; fröhlich; ˈ**joy·ful·ness** Fröhlichkeit *f*; ˈ**joy·less** □ freudlos; unerfreulich; ˈ**joy·ous** □ freudig, fröhlich; ˈ**joy-ride** *sl.* Spritztour *f od.* Vergnügungsfahrt *f mit e-m gestohlenen Wagen*; ˈ**joy-stick** ✈ *sl.* Steuerknüppel *m*.
ju·bi·lant [ˈdʒuːbilənt] jubilierend, frohlockend; **ju·bi·late** [ˈ~leit] jubeln; **ju·biˈla·tion** Jubel *m*; **ju·bi·lee** [ˈ~liː] Jubiläum *n*.
Ju·da·ism [ˈdʒuːdeiizəm] Judentum *n*.
Ju·das [ˈdʒuːdəs] *fig.* Judas *m*, Verräter *m*; *a.* ♀*-hole* Guckloch *n*.
judge [dʒʌdʒ] **1.** Richter *m*; Schiedsrichter *m*; Beurteiler(in), Kenner (-in), Sachverständige *m*, *f*; **2.** *v/i.* urteilen (*from*, *by* nach; *of* über *acc.*); *v/t.* richten; aburteilen; beurteilen (*by* nach); ansehen als; entscheiden.
judg(e)·ment [ˈdʒʌdʒmənt] Urteil *n*; Urteilsspruch *m*; Urteilskraft *f*, -vermögen *n*; Einsicht *f*; Ansicht *f*, Meinung *f*; *göttliches* (Straf)Gericht *n*; *in my* ~ meiner Meinung nach; *pronounce* ~ für Recht erkennen; *sit in* ~ zu Gericht sitzen; *come to* ~ zur Einsicht kommen; *Day of* ♀, ♀*-Day* Jüngster Tag *m*, Jüngstes Gericht *n*.
judge·ship [ˈdʒʌdʒʃip] Richteramt *n*.
ju·di·ca·ture [ˈdʒuːdikətʃə] Gerichtshof *m*; Rechtspflege *f*; Richteramt *n*; Richter *m/pl*.
ju·di·cial □ [dʒuːˈdiʃəl] gerichtlich; Gerichts…; richterlich; kritisch; unparteiisch; ~ *murder* Justizmord *m*; ~ *system* Gerichtswesen *n*.
ju·di·ci·a·ry [dʒuːˈdiʃiəri] *die* Richterschaft.
ju·di·cious □ [dʒuːˈdiʃəs] verständig, klug; **juˈdi·cious·ness** Einsicht *f*.
ju·do [ˈdʒuːdəu] *Sport*: Judo *n*.
jug [dʒʌg] **1.** Krug *m*, Kanne *f*; *sl.* Loch *n* (*Gefängnis*); **2.** dämpfen; *sl.* einlochen; *~ged hare* Hasenpfeffer *m*.
Jug·ger·naut *fig.* [ˈdʒʌgənɔːt] Moloch *m*, Götze *m*; Popanz *m*.
jug·gins F [ˈdʒʌginz] Trottel *m*.
jug·gle [ˈdʒʌgl] **1.** Trick *m*; Schwindel *m*; **2.** jonglieren (*a. fig.*), Kunststücke machen; *fig.* frisieren, verfälschen; betrügen (*out of* um); ˈ**jug·gler** Jongleur *m*; Taschenspieler(in); ˈ**jug·gler·y** Jonglieren *n*; Taschenspielerei *f*; Betrügerei *f*.
Ju·go·slav [ˈjuːgəuˈslaːv] **1.** Jugoslawe *m*, Jugoslawin *f*; **2.** jugoslawisch.
jug·u·lar *anat.* [ˈdʒʌgjulə] Kehl…; ~ *vein* Halsader *f*; **ju·gu·late** *fig.* [ˈ~leit] abwürgen.
juice [dʒuːs] Saft *m*; *mot. sl.* Sprit *m*, Gas *n*; ⚡ *sl.* Strom *m*; ˈ**juic·i·ness** Saftigkeit *f*; ˈ**juic·y** □ saftig; F

interessant; pikant.

ju·jube ['dʒu:dʒu:b] ⚘ Brustbeere *f*; *pharm.* Brustbonbon *m*, *n*.

ju-jut·su [dʒu:'dʒutsu:] Jiu-Jitsu *n*.

juke-box *Am.* F ['dʒu:kbɔks] Musikautomat *m*.

ju·lep ['dʒu:lep] *süßes* (Arznei)Getränk *n*; *bsd. Am. alkoholisches* Eisgetränk *n*.

Ju·ly [dʒu:'lai] Juli *m*.

jum·ble ['dʒʌmbl] **1.** Durcheinander *n*; **2.** *v/t. a.* ~ *up* durcheinanderwerfen; *v/i.* durcheinanderlaufen; '**~-sale** Wohltätigkeitsbasar *m*.

jum·bo ['dʒʌmbəu], *a.* ~ **jet** Jumbo(-Jet) *m*; '**~-sized** Riesen...

jump [dʒʌmp] **1.** Sprung *m*; sprunghafter Anstieg *m*; ~*s pl.* nervöses Zs.-Fahren *n*; *high* (*long*) ~ Hoch-(Weit)Sprung *m*; *get* (*have*) *the* ~ *on Am.* F zuvorkommen; *give a* ~ e-n Satz machen; zs.-fahren; **2.** *v/i.* springen; stoßen; ~ *at* sich *begierig* stürzen auf (*acc.*); ~ *to conclusions* übereilte Schlüsse ziehen; ~ *on*, ~ *upon* sich auf *j.* stürzen; *fig. j-m* aufs Dach steigen; *v/t.* hinwegspringen *od.* -setzen über (*acc.*); überspringen; springen lassen; mit Gewalt (weg-)nehmen; ~ *the gun Sport*: e-n Fehlstart verursachen; *fig.* verfrüht handeln *od.* reagieren; ~ *the lights* bei Rot über die Kreuzung fahren; ~ *the queue* sich vordrängen; '**jump·er** Springer *m*; Jumper *m*; Matrosenbluse *f*; '**jump·ing-'off** Absprung *m*; '**jump-seat** ✈, *mot.* Klappsitz *m*; '**jump-suit** Overall *m*; '**jump·y** nervös; nervös machend.

junc·tion ['dʒʌŋkʃən] Verbindung *f*; Kreuzung *f*; 🚂 Knotenpunkt *m*; ~ *box* ⚡ Abzweigdose *f*; **junc·ture** ['~tʃə] Verbindungspunkt *m*, -stelle *f*; (kritischer) Zeitpunkt *m*; *at this* ~ bei diesem Stand der Dinge.

June [dʒu:n] Juni *m*.

jun·gle ['dʒʌŋgl] Dschungel *m*.

jun·ior ['dʒu:njə] **1.** jünger (*to* als); Unter...; *Am. univ.* der Unterstufe (angehörend); ~ *high school Am.* Schule mit Klasse 7, 8, 9; ~ *partner* jüngerer Teilhaber *m*, Associé *m*; **2.** Jüngere *m, f an Jahren od. im Amt*; Junior *m*; *Am.* (Ober)Schüler *m od.* Student *m* im 3. Jahr; F Kleine *m*; *he is my* ~ *by four years, he is four years my* ~ er ist vier Jahre jünger als ich; **jun·ior·i·ty** [dʒu:ni'ɔriti] geringeres Alter *n od.* Dienstalter *n*.

ju·ni·per ⚘ ['dʒu:nipə] Wacholder *m*.

junk[1] ⚓ [dʒʌŋk] Dschunke *f*.

junk[2] [~] F Talmi *n*, Plunder *m*, alter Kram *m*; *contp.* Schund *m*, Mist *m*; *sl.* Rauschgift *n*; ~ *mail Am.* Reklamesendung(en *pl.*) *f*.

jun·ket ['dʒʌŋkit] **1.** Sauermilch-, Quarkspeise *f*; *Am.* Party *f*; Picknick *n*; Festessen *n*; Vergnügungsfahrt *f*; **2.** feiern.

junk·ie, junk·y *sl.* ['dʒʌŋki] Drogensüchtige *m, f*.

junk·yard ['djʌŋkjɑ:d] Schrottplatz *m*.

jun·ta ['dʒʌntə] (spanische) Junta *f*; **jun·to** ['~təu] Clique *f*.

ju·rid·i·cal □ [dʒuə'ridikəl] rechtlich, gerichtlich; Rechts...

ju·ris·dic·tion [dʒuəris'dikʃən] Rechtsprechung *f*; Gerichtsbarkeit *f*; Gerichtsbezirk *m*; **ju·ris·pru·dence** ['~pru:dəns] Rechtswissenschaft *f*; '**ju·ris·pru·dent** Rechtsgelehrte *m*, Jurist *m*.

ju·rist ['dʒuərist] Jurist *m*.

ju·ror ⚖ ['dʒuərə] Geschworene *m*.

ju·ry ⚖ ['dʒuəri] Geschworenengericht *n*; Preisgericht *n*, Jury *f*; '**ju·ry-box** Geschworenenbank *f*; '**ju·ry·man** Geschworene *m*.

ju·ry-mast ⚓ ['dʒuərimɑ:st] Notmast *m*.

just [dʒʌst] **1.** *adj.* □ gerecht; rechtschaffen; richtig, wahr; genau; gehörig, recht (*Maß etc.*); ganz; **2.** *adv.* gerade, genau; (so)eben, gerade; gerade noch; nur; ~ *now* eben jetzt, gerade jetzt; ~ *over* (*below*) ... knapp über (unter) ...; *but* ~ eben erst; ~ *let me see!* laß mal sehen!; *it's* ~ *splendid!* es ist einfach glänzend!

jus·tice ['dʒʌstis] Gerechtigkeit *f*, Billigkeit *f*; Richter *m*; Recht *n*; Rechtswesen *n*; Rechtsverfahren *n*; ♀ *of the Peace* Friedensrichter *m*; *court of* ~ Gericht(shof *m*) *n*; *do* ~ *to s.o.* j-m Gerechtigkeit widerfahren lassen; *do o.s.* ~ sein wahres Können zeigen; '**jus·tice·ship** Richteramt *n*.

jus·ti·fi·a·bil·i·ty [dʒʌstifaiə'biliti] Entschuldbarkeit *f*; '**jus·ti·fi·a·ble**

□ zu rechtfertigen(d).
jus·ti·fi·ca·tion [dʒʌstifiˈkeiʃən] Rechtfertigung *f*; **jus·ti·fi·ca·to·ry** [ˈ~təri] rechtfertigend.
jus·ti·fi·er *typ.* [ˈdʒʌstifaiə] Justierer *m*; ˈ**jus·ti·fy** rechtfertigen; *typ.* justieren.
just·ly [ˈdʒʌstli] mit Recht.
just·ness [ˈdʒʌstnis] Gerechtigkeit *f etc.* (*s. just 1*).
jut [dʒʌt] **1.** *a.* ~ *out* hervor-, herausragen, -stehen; vorspringen; **2.** Vorsprung *m.*
Jute[1] [dʒu:t] Jüte *m*, Jütin *f.*
jute[2] ⚘ [~] Jute *f.*
ju·ve·nes·cence [dʒu:viˈnesns] Verjüngung *f*; Jugend *f*; **ju·veˈnes·cent** jugendlich; **ju·ve·nile** [ˈ~nail] **1.** jung, jugendlich; Jugend...; ♀ *Court* Jugendgericht *n*; ~ *delinquency* Jugendkriminalität *f*; ~ *delinquent* jugendlicher Straftäter *m*; **2.** junger Mensch *m*; **ju·ve·nil·i·ty** [~ˈniliti] Jugendlichkeit *f*; Kinderei *f.*
jux·ta·pose [dʒʌkstəˈpəuz] nebeneinanderstellen, vergleichen; **jux·ta·po·si·tion** [~pəˈziʃən] Nebeneinanderstellung *f.*

K

Ka(f)·fir [ˈkæfə] Kaffer *m*; ~*s pl.* ✝ *sl.* Südafrikanische Bergwerksaktien *f/pl.*
kale [keil] (*bsd.* Kraus-, Grün)Kohl *m*; *Am. sl.* Moos *n* (*Geld*).
ka·lei·do·scope *opt.* [kəˈleidəskəup] Kaleidoskop *n.*
kal·ends [ˈkælendz] = *calends.*
kan·ga·roo [kæŋgəˈru:] Känguruh *n.*
ka·o·lin *min.* [ˈkeiəlin] Kaolin *n.*
ka·pok [ˈkeipɔk] Kapok *m.*
ka·put *sl.* [kæˈpu:t] kaputt, erledigt.
ka·yak [ˈkaiæk] Kajak *m*, *n*; Paddelboot *n.*
keck [kek] würgen; sich ekeln (*at* vor).
kedge ⚓ [kedʒ] **1.** Warpanker *m*; **2.** warpen, verholen.
ked·ge·ree [kedʒəˈri:] Reisgericht *n* mit Fisch und Eiern.
keel ⚓ [ki:l] **1.** Kiel *m*; *on an even* ~ gleichlastig; *fig.* gleichmäßig; **2.** ~ *over* kieloben legen *od.* liegen; umschlagen; kentern; ˈ**keel·age** ⚓ Kielgeld *n*; **keeled** ⚘ gekielt; **keel-haul** ⚓ [ˈ~hɔ:l] kielholen; **keel·son** ⚓ [ˈkelsn] Kielschwein *n* (*Kielverstärkung*).
keen[1] □ [ki:n] scharf (*fig. Kälte, Blick, Verstand, Kampf, Kritik, Verhör etc.*); eifrig, begierig; stark, groß (*Appetit etc.*); ~ *on* F scharf *od.* erpicht auf *acc.*; *be* ~ *on hunting* ein leidenschaftlicher Jäger sein.
keen[2] *ir.* [~] Totenklage *f.*
keen-edged [ˈki:nedʒd] scharfgeschliffen; ˈ**keen·ness** Schärfe *f*; Heftigkeit *f*; Scharfsinn *m*, Feinheit *f.*
keep [ki:p] **1.** *Lebens*-Unterhalt *m*; *hist.* Bergfried *m*; *for* ~*s* F für immer, endgültig; zum Behalten; **2.** (*irr.*) *v/t. allg.* halten; behalten; unterhalten (*ernähren*); *in e-m Zustand* (er)halten; *Versprechen, Gesetz, Regel, Feiertag, Richtung, Verabredung etc.* einhalten; *Fest* (ab-) halten, feiern; *Konto* unterhalten; *Buch, Ware etc.* führen; *Bett etc.* hüten; fest-, aufhalten; (bei)behalten; (auf)bewahren; (be)hüten (*from* vor *dat.*); ~ *s.o. company* j-m Gesellschaft leisten; ~ *company with* verkehren mit; ~ *silence* Schweigen bewahren; ~ *one's temper* sich beherrschen; ~ *time* richtig gehen (*Uhr*); ♪, ⚔ Takt, Schritt halten; ~ *watch* aufpassen; ~ *s.o. waiting* j. warten lassen; ~ *away* fernhalten; ~ *down* niederhalten; *Preise* niedrig halten; ~ *s.o. from* j. abhalten von; ~ *s.th. from s.o.* j-m et. vorenthalten; ~ *in* drinbehalten; *Gefühl etc.* zurückhalten; *Schüler* nachsitzen lassen; *Feuer* unterhalten; ~ *in money* mit Geld versehen; ~ *in view* im Auge behalten; ~ *off* abhalten; ~ *on* (bei)behalten; *Kleid* anbehalten, *Hut* aufbehalten; ~ *out* nicht hereinlassen, ausschließen; ~ *up* auf-

rechterhalten; *Mut* bewahren; in Ordnung halten; hindern, zu Bett zu gehen; aufbleiben lassen; *Gespräch* in Gang halten; ~ *it up* (es) durchhalten; **3.** *irr. v/i.* sich halten, bleiben; F sich aufhalten; sich halten (*Früchte etc.*); *mit Partizip*: ~ *doing* immer wieder tun; fortwährend tun; weiter tun; ~ *away* sich fernhalten; ~ *clear of* sich frei halten von; ~ *from* sich fernhalten von; ~ *in with* sich gut stehen mit j-m; ~ *off* sich fernhalten (von); ~ *on* fortfahren, weitermachen; ~ *on talking* fortfahren zu sprechen, weitersprechen; ~ *on at s.o.* j-m ständig zusetzen; ~ *to* sich halten an (*acc.*), bleiben bei, beibehalten; ~ *up* sich aufrecht(er)halten; ~ *up with* Schritt halten mit; ~ *up with the Joneses* es den Nachbarn gleichtun.

keep·er ['ki:pə] Wärter *m*, Wächter *m*; Aufseher *m*; Verwalter *m*; Inhaber *m*; '**keep·ing** Verwahrung *f*, Aufsicht *f*; Obhut *f*; Gewahrsam *m*; Unterhalt *m*; *be in (out of)* ~ *with* (nicht) übereinstimmen mit; **keepsake** ['~seik] Andenken *n* (*Geschenk etc.*).

keg [keg] Fäßchen *n*.

kelp ⚘ [kelp] *ein* Seetang *m*.

kel·son ⚓ ['kelsn] = *keelson*.

ken [ken] Gesichtskreis *m*.

ken·nel[1] ['kenl] Gosse *f*, Rinnstein *m*.

ken·nel[2] [~] Hundehütte *f*, -zwinger *m*.

kept [kept] *pret. u. p.p. von keep 2.*

kerb [kə:b], '**~·stone** = *curb etc.*

ker·chief ['kə:tʃif] (Kopf-, Hals-) Tuch *n*; '**ker·chiefed** verschleiert.

kerf [kə:f] (Ein)Schnitt *m*.

ker·nel ['kə:nl] Kern *m* (*a. fig.*); Hafer-, Mais- *etc.* -korn *n*.

ker·o·sene ['kerəsi:n] Kerosin *n* (*Brennöl*).

kes·trel *orn.* ['kestrəl] Turmfalke *m*.

ketch ⚓ [ketʃ] Ketsch *f* (*Küstensegler*).

ketch·up ['ketʃəp] (Tomaten)Ketchup *m*.

ket·tle ['ketl] Kessel *m*; '**~·drum** ♪ (Kessel)Pauke *f*.

key [ki:] **1.** Schlüssel *m* (*a. fig.*); Schlußstein *m*; ⊕ Keil *m*, Splint *m*; Schraubenschlüssel *m*; Taste *f an Klavier, Schreibmaschine etc.*; Klappe *f e-r Flöte etc.*; ⚡ Taste *f*, Druckknopf *m*; ♪ Tonart *f*; *fig.* Ton *m*; **2.** ~ *up* ♪ stimmen; erhöhen; *fig.* in erhöhte Spannung versetzen; '**~·board** Klaviatur *f*, Tastatur *f*; ~*s pl.* F Tasteninstrumente *n/pl.*; ~ *operator typ.* Maschinensetzer *m*; '**~-bu·gle** ♪ Klappenhorn *n*; '**~·hole** Schlüsselloch *n*; ~ **in·dus·try** Schlüsselindustrie *f*; '**~-man** Schlüsselfigur *f*; '**~·mon·ey** Ablösung *f* (*für e-e Wohnung*); '**~-note** Grundton *m*; ~ **punch** Kartenlocher *m*; ~ **sig·na·ture** ♪ Tonartbezeichnung *f*; '**~·stone** Schlußstein *m*; *fig.* Grundlage *f*.

khak·i ['kɑ:ki] **1.** khaki-, staubfarben; **2.** Khaki (*Farbe*) *n*, (*Stoff*) *m*.

khan[1] [kɑ:n] Khan *m*, *orientalischer* Herrscher *m*.

khan[2] [~] Karawanserei *f*.

kibe [kaib] (offene) Frostbeule *f*.

kib·itz·er *Am.* F ['kibitsə] Kiebitz *m*; Besserwisser *m*.

ki·bosh *sl.* ['kaibɔʃ] Unsinn *m*; *put the ~ on s.o.* es j-m besorgen.

kick [kik] **1.** (Fuß)Tritt *m*; Stoß *m*; Rückschlag *m des Gewehres*; Elan *m*, Schwung *m*; F Nervenkitzel *m*; *fig.* Feuer *n*, Kraft *f*, Prozente *n/pl.*; Fußballspieler *m*; *more ~s than halfpence* mehr Prügel als Lob; *get the ~ sl.* rausfliegen; *get a ~ out of* F Spaß finden an (*dat.*); *do s.th. for ~s* F et. aus Spaß *od.* Jux machen; *it's got a ~ to it* das hat's in sich; **2.** *v/t.* (mit dem Fuß) stoßen *od.* treten; F *Verehrer* abblitzen lassen; *Fußball*: schießen; ~ *the bucket sl.* ins Gras beißen; ~ *downstairs* die Treppe hinunterwerfen; ~ *one's heels* F sich die Beine in den Leib stehen (*warten müssen*); ~ *s.o. around* F j. schlecht behandeln, j. schikanieren; ~ *out* F hinauswerfen; ~ *up a row od. fuss od. dust* F Radau machen; *v/i.* (hinten) ausschlagen; stoßen (*Gewehr*); sich auflehnen *od.* sträuben (*against, at* gegen); ~ *in with Am. sl. Geld* reinbuttern; ~ *off Fußball*: anstoßen; '**kick·back** *bsd. Am.* F Rückzahlung *f*; '**kick·er** Schläger *m* (*Pferd*); Fußballspieler *m*; '**kick-'off** *Fußball*: Anstoß *m*; '**kick·shaw** Leckerei *f*; Kinkerlitzchen *n*; '**kick-start·er** Kickstarter *m* (*am Motorrad*); '**kick-'up** *sl.* Radau *m*, Krach *m*.

kid [kid] **1.** Zicklein *n*; Ziegenleder *n*; *sl.* Kind *n*; **2.** *sl.* foppen, (an-)pflaumen, (ver)kohlen; '**kid·dy** *sl.* Kind *n*; **kid glove** Glacéhandschuh *m* (*a. fig.*); '**kid-glove** sanft, zart.
kid·nap ['kidnæp] *bsd. Kinder* entführen; '**kid·nap·(p)er** Kindesentführer *m*, Kidnapper *m*.
kid·ney ['kidni] *anat.* Niere *f*; F Art *f*, Schlag *m*; ~ *bean* ⚘ weiße Bohne *f*; ~ **ma·chine** ⚕ künstliche Niere *f*.
kike *Am. sl. contp.* [kaik] Jude *m*.
kill [kil] **1.** töten (*a. fig.*), umbringen; schlachten; *fig.* vernichten, morden; erdrücken; *parl.* zu Fall bringen; *fig.* überwältigen; ~ *off* abschlachten; ~ *time* die Zeit totschlagen; **2.** Tötung *f*; Jagdbeute *f*; '**kill·er** Totschläger *m*; Vernichtungsmittel *n*; '**kill·ing 1.** □ mörderisch; unwiderstehlich; F urkomisch; **2.** *Am.* F *finanzieller* Volltreffer *m*; '**kill-joy** Spaßverderber *m*.
kiln [kiln, ⊕ kil] Brenn-, Darrofen *m*; '**~-dry** darren, dörren.
kil·o·cy·cle *phys.* ['kiləusaikl] Kilohertz *n*; **kil·o·gram, kil·o·gramme** ['~græm] Kilogramm *n*; **kil·o·me·ter, kil·o·me·tre** ['kiləumi:tə] Kilometer *n*; **ki·lo·watt** ⚡ ['kiləuwɔt] Kilowatt *n*.
kilt [kilt] **1.** Kilt *m*, Schottenrock *m*; **2.** aufschürzen, plissieren.
ki·mo·no [ki'məunəu] Kimono *m*; kimonoartiger Morgenrock *m*.
kin [kin] **1.** (Bluts)Verwandtschaft *f*; Sippe *f*; *the next of* ~ die nächsten Verwandten; **2.** verwandt (*to* mit).
kind [kaind] **1.** □ gütig, freundlich (*to* zu, gegen); **2.** Art *f*, Sorte *f*; Gattung *f*, Geschlecht *n*; Art und Weise *f*; Natur *f*; *people of all* ~*s* allerhand Leute; *different in* ~ artverschieden; *pay in* ~ in Waren (*fig.* mit gleicher Münze) zahlen; *I* ~ *of expected it* F ich habe es beinahe *od.* so ziemlich erwartet.
kin·der·gar·ten ['kindəga:tn] Kindergarten *m*; ~ *teacher* Kindergärtnerin *f*.
kind·heart·ed ['kaind'ha:tid] gütig, gutherzig.
kin·dle ['kindl] anzünden; (sich) entzünden (*a. fig.*).
kind·li·ness ['kaindlinis] Freundlichkeit *f*, Güte *f*.
kin·dling ['kindliŋ] *a.* ~*s pl.* Holz *n* zum Anfeuern.
kind·ly ['kaindli] *adj.* freundlich (*a. adv.*); günstig (*Klima etc.*).
kind·ness ['kaindnis] Güte *f*, Freundlichkeit *f*; Gefälligkeit *f*.
kin·dred ['kindrid] **1.** verwandt, gleichartig; **2.** Verwandtschaft *f*.
kine † [kain] *pl. von cow*[1].
ki·ne·ma ['kinimə] = *cinema*.
kin·e·mat·o·graph [kaini'mætəugra:f] = *cinematograph*.
ki·net·ic [kai'netik] bewegend; kinetisch; **ki'net·ics** *sg.* Kinetik *f*.
king [kiŋ] König *m* (*a. fig. u. Schach, Kartenspiel*); *fig.* Magnat *m*; ~*'s evil* ⚕ Skrofulose *f*; *turn* ~*'s evidence* gegen seine Komplizen aussagen; '**king·bird** *orn.* Königsvogel *m*; '**king·craft** Herrscherkunst *f*; '**king·cup** ⚘ Butterblume *f*; Sumpfdotterblume *f*; '**king·dom** Königreich *n*; *bsd.* ⚘, *zo.* Reich *n*, Gebiet *n*; *eccl.* Reich *n Gottes*; ~ *come* F das Jenseits; '**king·fish·er** Eisvogel *m*; **king·let** ['~lit] Duodezfürst *m*; '**king·like** königlich; '**king·li·ness** *das* Königliche, königliches Wesen *n*; '**king·ly** königlich; '**king·pin** Achszapfen *m*; *fig.* Hauptperson *f*; '**king·post** ⚠ Giebelbalken *m*; '**king·ship** Königtum *n*; Königswürde *f*; '**king-size** F überlang, übergroß.
kink [kiŋk] **1.** Schleife *f im Tau etc.*; Knoten *m*; *fig.* Schrulle *f*, Fimmel *m*; *Am.* Betriebsfehler *m*; *have a* ~ F e-n Vogel haben; **2.** (sich) verfitzen; knicken; '**kink·y** kraus (*Haar*); verrückt, ausgefallen.
kins·folk ['kinzfəuk] Verwandten *pl.*; '**kin·ship** Verwandtschaft *f*; '**kins·man** Verwandte *m*; '**kins·wom·an** Verwandte *f*.
ki·osk ['ki:ɔsk] Kiosk *m*; Telefonzelle *f*.
kip F [kip] **1.** Schlaf *m*; **2.** pennen.
kip·per ['kipə] **1.** Räucherhering *m*, Bückling *m*; *sl.* Mensch *m*, Kerl *m*; **2.** *Fische* leicht räuchern.
kirk [kə:k] (schottische) Kirche *f*.
kir·tle † ['kə:tl] kurzer Frauenrock *m*; Wams *n*.
kiss [kis] **1.** Kuß *m*; *fig.* leichte Berührung *f*; **2.** (sich) küssen; ~ *the book* die Bibel küssen *beim Schwören*; ~ *the dust* im Staub kriechen

(*sich unterwerfen*); ins Gras beißen; '~-**proof** kußfest.
kit [kit] Ausrüstung *f* (*a.* ⚔ *u. Sport*); Handwerkszeug *n*, Werkzeug *n*; *do-it-yourself* ~ Bausatz *m*, -kasten *m*; '~-**bag** ⚔ Tornister *m*; ⚓ Seesack *m*; Reisetasche *f*.
kitch·en ['kitʃin] Küche *f*; '**kitch·en·er** Küchenherd *m*; **kitch·en·ette** [~'net] Kochnische *f*.
kitch·en...: '~-'**gar·den** Gemüsegarten *m*; '~-**maid** Küchenmädchen *n*; '~-**range** Kochherd *m*; ~ **scales** *pl.* Küchenwaage *f*; ~ **sink** Spüle *f*; ~ *drama* realistisches Sozialdrama *n*.
kite [kait] *orn.* Gabelweihe *f*; *Papier*-Drachen *m*; *fig.* Versuchsballon *m*; ✝ *sl.* Kellerwechsel *m*; ~ *balloon* ⚔ Fesselballon *m*; *fly a* ~ e-n Drachen *od. fig.* Versuchsballon steigen lassen.
kith [kiθ]: ~ *and kin* Freunde und Verwandte *pl.*
kit·ten ['kitn] **1.** Kätzchen *n*; **2.** Junge werfen (*Katze*); **kit·ten·ish** ['kitniʃ] kätzchenhaft.
kit·tle *fig.* ['kitl] kitz(e)lig, heikel.
kit·ty¹ ['kiti] Kätzchen *n*.
kit·ty² [~] (gemeinsame) Kasse *f*.
ki·wi *orn.* ['ki:wi:] Kiwi *m*.
Klan *Am.* [klæn] Ku-Klux-Klan *m*; **Klansman** ['klænzmən] Mitglied *n* des Ku-Klux-Klan.
klax·on *mot.* ['klæksn] Hupe *f*.
klep·to·ma·ni·a [kleptəu'meinjə] Kleptomanie *f* (*krankhafter Stehltrieb*); **klep·to'ma·ni·ac** [~niæk] Kleptomane *m*, Kleptomanin *f*.
knack [næk] Kunstgriff *m*, Kniff *m*, Dreh *m*; Geschicklichkeit *f*.
knack·er ['nækə] Abdecker *m*, Schinder *m*; Abbruchunternehmer *m*; '**knack·ered** *sl.* total geschafft; '**knack·er·y** Abdeckerei *f*.
knag [næg] Knorren *m*.
knap·sack ['næpsæk] Tornister *m*; Rucksack *m*.
knar [nɑ:] Knorren *m*.
knave [neiv] Schurke *m*; *Karten*: Bube *m*; '**knav·er·y** Gaunerei *f*, Schurkenstreich *m*; '**knav·ish** □ schurkisch.
knead [ni:d] kneten; massieren.
knee [ni:] **1.** Knie *n*; ⊕ Kniestück *n*; *bring s.o. to his* ~*s* j. auf die Knie zwingen; *on the* ~*s of the gods* noch ungewiß, im Schoße der Götter; **2.** *Hose* am Knie ausbeulen; '~-**breech·es** *pl.* Kniehose(n *pl.*) *f*; '~-**cap** Kniescheibe *f*; Knieschützer *m*; '~-'**deep** bis an die Knie (reichend); '~-**joint** Kniegelenk *n*;
kneel [ni:l] (*irr.*) knien (*to* vor *dat.*); '**kneel·er** Kniende *m, f*;
'**knee-pan** Kniescheibe *f*.
knell [nel] Totenglocke *f*.
knelt [nelt] *pret. u. p.p. von kneel*.
knew [nju:] *pret. von know 1*.
knick·er·bock·ers ['nikəbɔkəz] *pl.* Knickerbocker *pl.*, Kniehosen *f/pl.*; '**knick·ers** F *pl. Damen*-Schlüpfer *m*; = *knickerbockers*.
knick·knack ['niknæk] Spielerei *f*, Nippsache *f*; ~*s pl.* Kinkerlitzchen *n/pl.*
knife [naif] **1.** *pl.* **knives** [naivz] Messer *n*; *get one's* ~ *into s.o. fig.* j. gefressen haben, j-m übelwollen; **2.** schneiden; (er)stechen; '~-**grind·er** Scherenschleifer *m*.
knight [nait] **1.** Ritter *m*; Springer *m im Schach*; **2.** zum Ritter schlagen, adeln; **knight-er·rant** ['~'erənt] fahrender Ritter *m*; **knight·hood** ['~hud] Rittertum *n*; Ritterschaft *f*; '**knight·li·ness** Ritterlichkeit *f*; '**knight·ly** ritterlich.
knit [nit] (*irr.*) stricken; (ver)knüpfen; (sich) eng verbinden; ~ *the brows* die Stirn runzeln; '**knit·ter** Stricker(in); = *knitting-machine*; '**knit·ting 1.** Stricken *n*; Strickzeug *n*; **2.** Strick...; '**knit·ting-ma·chine** Strickmaschine *f*; '**knit·ting-nee·dle** Stricknadel *f*; '**knit·wear** Strickkleidung *f*, Strick-, Wirkwaren *f/pl.*
knives [naivz] *pl. von knife*.
knob [nɔb] Knopf *m*; Buckel *m*; Brocken *m Kohle etc.*; '**knobbed,** '**knob·by** mit einem Knopf *etc.*; knorrig; '**knob-stick** Knotenstock *m*; Streikbrecher *m*.
knock [nɔk] **1.** Schlag *m*; Anklopfen *n*; *mot.* Klopfen *n*; **2.** *v/i.* klopfen (*a. mot.*); pochen; stoßen; schlagen; ~ *about* F sich herumtreiben; ~ *off sl.* abhauen; Schluß *od.* Feierabend machen; ~ *under* sich ergeben; *v/t.* klopfen, stoßen, schlagen; *Am. sl.* bekritteln, schlechtmachen; ~ *about* herumstoßen, übel zurichten; ~ *down* niederschlagen; zu Boden werfen; *Auktion*: zuschlagen; ⊕ auseinandernehmen; *be* ~*ed down*

überfahren werden; ~ *off* abschlagen; aufhören mit; F zs.-hauen (*schnell erledigen*); *Summe* abziehen; ~ *out Boxen*: k.o. schlagen; ~ *up* (durch Klopfen) wecken; erschöpfen; **~·a·bout** ['~əbaut] **1.** lärmend; unstet; Strapazier... (*Kleidung*); *thea.* Clown..., Radau...; **2.** Radaustück *n*; **'~-'down** niederschmetternd; äußerst (*Preis*); **'knock·er** Klopfende *m*; Türklopfer *m*; *Am. sl.* Kritikaster *m*; *~s pl. sl.* Titten *f/pl.*; **'knock-'kneed** X-beinig; *fig.* hinkend; **'knock-out** *Boxen*: Knockout *m*, K.o. *m*; *sl.* tolle Sache *f od.* Person *f*.

knoll[1] [nəul] kleiner Erdhügel *m*.

knoll[2] [~] (*bsd.* zu Grabe) läuten.

knot [nɔt] **1.** Knoten *m*; Knorren *m*, Ast(knoten) *m*; ⚓ Knoten *m*, Seemeile *f*; ⚘ Knospe *f*; Schleife *f*, (Achsel)Band *n*; Schwierigkeit *f*; **2.** (ver)knoten, (ver)knüpfen (*a. fig.*); *Stirn* runzeln; verwickeln; **'knot·hole** Astloch *n*; **'knot·ti·ness** *das* Knotige; Schwierigkeit *f*; **'knot·ty** knotig, knorrig; *fig.* verwickelt; **'knot·work** Knüpfarbeit *f*.

knout [naut] **1.** Knute *f*; **2.** *j-m* die Knute geben.

know [nəu] **1.** (*irr.*) wissen; kennen; erkennen; erfahren; ~ *French* Französisch können; *come to* ~ erfahren; *get to* ~ kennenlernen; ~ *one's business*, ~ *the ropes*, ~ *a thing or two*, ~ *what's what* sich auskennen, Erfahrung haben; *do you* ~ *how to play chess?* können Sie Schach spielen?; *you ought to* ~ *better than to do that* Sie sollten so klug sein, das nicht zu tun; *I don't* ~ *one from the other* ich kann den einen nicht vom andern unterscheiden; *you* ~ *am Ende des Satzes*: nämlich; **2.** *be in the* ~ F Bescheid wissen (*of* über *acc.*), im Bilde sein; **'know·a·ble** (er)kennbar; **'know-all 1.** allwissend; **2.** Alleswisser *m*; **'know-how** praktische Erfahrung *f*; Know-how *n*; **'know·ing 1.** □ erfahren; klug; schlau; verständnisvoll; wissentlich; F schick; **2.** Wissen *n*; **'know·ing·ly** wissentlich; bewußt, absichtlich; **knowl·edge** ['nɔlidʒ] Kenntnis(se *f/pl.*) *f*; Wissen *n*; *to my* ~ meines Wissens; **'knowl·edge·a·ble** F gut informiert; kenntnisreich, klug; aufgeschlossen; **known** [nəun] *p.p. von know 1*; *come to be* ~ bekannt werden; *make* ~ bekanntmachen; *make o.s.* ~ sich bekannt machen, sich vorstellen.

knuck·le ['nʌkl] **1.** *a.* **'~-bone** Knöchel *m*; Kniestück *n vom Kalb etc.*; **2.** ~ *down*, ~ *under* nachgeben; **'~-dust·er** Schlagring *m*.

ko·a·la *zo.* [kəu'ɑːlə] Koala *m*.

kook *Am. sl.* [kuk] Spinner *m*.

Ko·ran [kɔ'rɑːn] Koran *m*.

Ko·re·an [kə'riən] **1.** Koreaner(in); **2.** koreanisch.

kosh·er ['kəuʃə] **1.** koscher (*Speisen*); F rechtmäßig, in Ordnung; **2.** koscheres Essen *n*.

ko·tow ['kəu'tau] **1.** Kotau *m* (*demütige Ehrenerweisung*); **2.** Kotau machen, *fig.* kriechen (*to* vor *dat.*).

Krem·lin ['kremlin] *der* Kreml.

ku·dos *co.* ['kjuːdɔs] Ruhm *m*.

Ku-Klux-Klan *Am.* ['kjuː'klʌks'klæn] Ku-Klux-Klan *m* (*Geheimbund in den USA*).

L

la ♪ [lɑː] la *n* (*Solmisationssilbe*).

lab F [læb] = *laboratory*.

la·bel ['leibl] **1.** Zettel *m*, Etikett *n*; Aufschrift *f*; Schildchen *n*; Bezeichnung *f*; ⚠ Kranzleiste *f*; **2.** etikettieren, beschriften; ✝ mit Preis auszeichnen; *fig.* abstempeln (*as* als).

la·bi·al ['leibjəl] **1.** Lippen..., labial; **2.** Lippenlaut *m*, Labial *m*.

lab·o·ra·to·ry [lə'bɔrətəri] Laboratorium *n*; ~ *assistant* Laborant(in).

la·bo·ri·ous □ [lə'bɔːriəs] mühsam, -selig, anstrengend; arbeitsam;

schwerfällig (*Stil*).

la·bo(u)r ['leibə] **1.** Arbeit *f*; Mühe *f*, Anstrengung *f*; (Geburts)Wehen *f/pl.*; Arbeiter *m/pl.*, Arbeitskräfte *f/pl.*; Arbeiterschaft *f*; *Ministry of* ♀ Arbeitsministerium *n*; *hard* ~ Zwangsarbeit *f*; **2.** Arbeiter...; Arbeits...; **3.** *v/i.* arbeiten; sich abmühen; sich mühsam (vorwärts-) bewegen; ~ *under* leiden unter (*dat.*), zu kämpfen haben mit; ~ *under a delusion* sich e-r Täuschung hingeben; *v/t.* ausarbeiten; ausführlich eingehen auf (*acc.*); ~ **camp** Arbeitslager *n*; ♀ **Day** Tag *m* der Arbeit; ~ **dis·pute** Arbeitskonflikt *m*; **'la·bo(u)red** schwerfällig, steif (*Stil*); mühsam (*Atem etc.*); **'la·bo(u)r·er** *ungelernter* Arbeiter *m*; **La·bo(u)r Ex·change** Arbeitsamt *n*; **la·bo(u)r force** Belegschaft *f*; **'la·bo(u)r·ing** arbeitend; Arbeits...; ~ *breath* schwerer Atem *m*; **la·bo(u)r·ite** ['~rait] Mitglied *n od.* Anhänger *m* der Labour Party; **La·bour Par·ty** *pol.* Labour Party *f*; **'la·bo(u)r-sav·ing** arbeitssparend; **la·bor un·ion** *Am.* Gewerkschaft *f*.

Lab·ra·dor ['læbrədɔ:]: ~ *dog zo.* Neufundländer *m*.

la·bur·num ⚘ [lə'bə:nəm] Goldregen *m*.

lab·y·rinth ['læbərinθ] Labyrinth *n*; **lab·y'rin·thi·an** [~θiən], *mst* **laby'rin·thine** [~θain] labyrinthisch.

lac [læk] (Gummi)Lack *m*; Lak *n*; *a* ~ *of rupees* 100 000 Rupien.

lace [leis] **1.** Spitze *f*; Borte *f*, Tresse *f*; Schnur *f*; Schnürband *n*; **2.** (zu)schnüren; mit Spitze *etc.* besetzen; *Schnur* durch-, einziehen; *Getränk* mischen, versetzen (*with* mit *Spirituosen*); ~ (*into*) *s.o.* j. verprügeln.

lac·er·ate 1. ['læsəreit] auf-, zerreißen, zerfleischen; *fig.* quälen; **2.** ['~rit] zerrissen; **lac·er·a·tion** [~'reiʃən] Zerreißen *n*; Riß *m*.

lach·es ⚖ ['leitʃiz] Fahrlässigkeit *f*, Versäumnis *n*.

lach·ry·mal ['lækriməl] Tränen...; **lach·ry·mose** ['~məus] weinerlich; tränenreich.

lack [læk] **1.** Fehlen *n*, Mangel *m*; **2.** *v/t.* ermangeln (*gen.*); *he* ~*s money* es fehlt ihm an Geld; *v/i. be* ~*ing* fehlen, mangeln; *he is* ~*ing in courage* es fehlt ihm an Mut.

lack·a·dai·si·cal □ [lækə'deizikəl] gelangweilt, gleichgültig, uninteressiert.

lack·ey ['læki] **1.** Lakai *m* (*a. fig.*); **2.** *j-s* Lakai sein.

lack·ing ['lækiŋ] *s. lack 1.*

lack·land ['læklænd] **1.** ohne Land; besitzlos; **2.** Habenichts *m*; **lack-lus·tre**, *Am.* **lack-lus·ter** ['~lʌstə] glanzlos, matt.

la·con·ic [lə'kɔnik] (~*ally*) lakonisch, wortkarg, kurz u. prägnant.

lac·quer ['lækə] **1.** Lack *m*; **2.** lakkieren; ~*ed* Lack...

lac·quey ['læki] = *lackey*.

la·crosse [lə'krɔs] *Sport*: Lacrosse *n* (*Ballspiel*).

lac·ta·tion [læk'teiʃən] Säugen *n*, Stillen *n*.

lac·tic ['læktik] Milch...; ~ *acid* Milchsäure *f*.

la·cu·na [lə'kju:nə] Lücke *f*.

lac·y ['leisi] spitzenartig; Spitzen...

lad [læd] Bursche *m*, Junge *m*.

lad·der ['lædə] **1.** Leiter *f* (*a. fig.*); ⚓ Strickleiter *f*, *a.* Treppe *f*; Laufmasche *f im Strumpf*; **2.** e-e Laufmasche bekommen; **'~-proof** maschenfest (*Strumpf etc.*).

lad·die ['lædi] Bürschlein *n*.

lade [leid] (*irr.*) = *load*; **'lad·en 1.** *p.p. von lade*; **2.** *adj.* beladen.

la-di-da ['lɑ:di'dɑ:] **1.** Fatzke *m*, Affe *m*; **2.** affig, geckenhaft.

la·ding ['leidiŋ] Ladung *f*, Fracht *f*.

la·dle ['leidl] **1.** Schöpflöffel *m*, Kelle *f*; **2.** ~ *out Suppe* austeilen; *fig.* ver-, austeilen.

la·dy ['leidi] Dame *f*; Lady *f*, Herrin *f*; *Ladies sg.* Damentoilette *f*; *Ladies and Gentlemen!* meine Damen u. Herren!; ♀ *Day* Mariä Verkündigung *f* (*25. März*); ~ *doctor* Ärztin *f*; ~*'s maid* Zofe *f*; ~*'s od. ladies' man* Weiberheld *m*; **'~-bird** Marienkäfer *m*; **'~-in-'waiting** Hofdame *f*; **'~-kill·er** Herzensbrecher *m*; **'~-like** damenhaft; *contp.* weibisch; **'~-love** Geliebte *f*; ~ **of the bed·cham·ber** Hofdame *f*; **'~-ship:** *her* ~ die gnädige Frau; *Your* ♀ gnädige Frau, Euer Gnaden.

lag[1] [læg] **1.** zögern; *a.* ~ *behind* zurückbleiben; **2.** Verzögerung *f*.

lag[2] *sl.* [~] **1.** Zuchthäusler *m*; **2.** ins Zuchthaus bringen.

lag[3] [~] *Wasserrohr etc.* isolieren.

la·ger (beer) ['lɑ:gə('biə)] Lagerbier *n*; ~ *and lime Lagerbier mit e-m Schuß Limonensirup.*
lag·gard ['lægəd] Nachzügler *m*; Trödler *m*, Bummler *m*.
la·goon [lə'gu:n] Lagune *f*.
la·ic ['leiik] **1.** *a.* '**la·i·cal** □ weltlich; Laien...; **2.** Laie *m*; **la·i·cize** ['~saiz] verweltlichen.
laid [leid] *pret. u. p.p. von lay*[4] 2; ~ *up* bettlägerig (*with* infolge).
lain [lein] *p.p. von lie*[2] 2.
lair [lɛə] Lager *n e-s wilden Tieres.*
laird *schott.* [lɛəd] Gutsherr *m*.
la·i·ty ['leiiti] Laien *m/pl.*
lake[1] [leik] See *m*.
lake[2] [~] rote Pigmentfarbe *f*.
lake-dwel·lings ['leikdweliŋz] *pl.* Pfahlbauten *m/pl.*
lam *sl.* [læm] abhauen, verduften; ~ *into s.o.* j. verdreschen, j. vermöbeln.
la·ma ['lɑ:mə] Lama *m*, buddhistischer Mönch *m*; '**la·ma·se·ry** ['~səri] Lamakloster *n*.
lamb [læm] **1.** Lamm *n*; Lammfleisch *n*; **2.** lammen.
lam·baste *sl.* [læm'beist] vermöbeln; zs.-stauchen (*abkanzeln*).
lam·bent ['læmbənt] leckend; züngelnd (*Flamme*); funkelnd, sprühend.
lamb·kin ['læmkin] Lämmchen *n*; '**lamb·like** lammfromm; '**lamb·skin** Lammfell *n*.
lame [leim] **1.** □ lahm (*a. fig.* = *mangelhaft*); **2.** lähmen; '**lame·ness** Lahmheit *f*.
la·ment [lə'ment] **1.** Wehklage *f*; **2.** (be)klagen; trauern (*for* um); **lam·en·ta·ble** □ ['læməntəbl] beklagenswert; kläglich, jämmerlich; **lam·en'ta·tion** Wehklage *f*.
lam·i·na ['læminə], *pl.* **lam·i·nae** ['~ni:] Plättchen *n*; ⚡, ⚘ Lamelle *f*; '**lam·i·nar** in Plättchen; **lam·i·nate** ['~neit] auswalzen; aufspalten; schichten; belegen; ~*d glass* Verbundglas *n*.
lamp [læmp] Lampe *f*; *fig.* Leuchte *f*; '**~·black** Ruß *m*; '**~-chim·ney** Lampenzylinder *m*; '**~·light** Lampenlicht *n*; '**~·light·er** Laternenanzünder *m*; '**~-oil** Petroleum *n*.
lam·poon [læm'pu:n] **1.** Schmähschrift *f*; **2.** schmähen.
lamp-post ['læmppəust] Laternenpfahl *m*.
lam·prey *ichth.* ['læmpri] Neunauge *n*.
lamp·shade ['læmpʃeid] Lampenschirm *m*.
lance [lɑ:ns] **1.** Lanze *f*; Speer *m*; **2.** aufschneiden (*a.* ⚕); '**~-'cor·po·ral** ⚔ Gefreite *m*; **lan·ce·o·late** ⚘ ['lænsiəlit] lanzettförmig; **lanc·er** ⚔ ['lɑ:nsə] Ulan *m*; ~*s pl.* Lanciers *m/pl.* (*englischer Tanz*).
lan·cet ['lɑ:nsit] Lanzette *f*; ~ **arch** △ Spitzbogen *m*; ~ **win·dow** Spitzbogenfenster *n*.
land [lænd] **1.** *das* feste Land; Land *n*; Grund und Boden *m*; Gut *n*, Grundstück *n*; *by* ~ auf dem Landweg; ~*s pl.* Ländereien *f/pl.*; *see how the* ~ *lies* sehen, wie die Sache steht *od.* wie der Hase läuft; **2.** landen; ⚓ löschen; *Hieb* anbringen, versetzen; *Preis* gewinnen; '**~-a·gent** Grundstücksmakler *m*; Gutsverwalter *m*.
lan·dau ['lændɔ:] Landauer *m* (*Pferdewagen*).
land·ed ['lændid] Grund besitzend; Land..., Grund...; ~ *gentry* Landadel *m*.
land...: '**~·fall** ⚓ Landkennung *f*; '**~-forc·es** *pl.* Landstreitkräfte *f/pl.*; '**~-grab·ber** Landraffer *m*; '**~-hold·er** Grundbesitzer(in).
land·ing ['lændiŋ] Landung *f*; Treppenabsatz *m*; Anlegestelle *f*; '**~-craft** ⚓, ⚔ Landungsboot *n*; '**~-field** ✈ Landebahn *f*; '**~-gear** ✈ Fahrgestell *n*; '**~-net** Hamen *m*; '**~-par·ty** ⚔ Landungstrupp *m*; '**~-stage** ⚓ Landungsbrücke *f*; '**~-strip** = *landing-field.*
land·la·dy ['lænleidi] Vermieterin *f*, Wirtin *f*.
land·less ['lændlis] ohne Grundbesitz.
land...: '**~·locked** landumschlossen; '**~·lop·er** Landstreicher *m*; **~·lord** ['lænlɔ:d] Vermieter *m*, Wirt *m*; Haus-, Grundbesitzer *m*; **~-lub·ber** ⚓ *contp.* ['lændlʌbə] Landratte *f*; '**~·mark** *bsd.* ⚓ Landmarke *f*; Grenz-, Markstein *m* (*a. fig.*); Wendepunkt *m*; Wahrzeichen *n*; '**~-own·er** Grundbesitzer(in); '**~-plane** Landflugzeug *n*; **~·scape** ['lænskeip] Landschaft *f*; Landschaftsmalerei *f*; ~ *gardener* Gartenarchitekt *m*; ~ *gardening* Gartenarchitektur *f*; **~·slide** ['lændslaid] Erdrutsch *m* (*a. pol.*); *a Democratic* ~ ein

Erdrutsch zugunsten der Demokraten; '~**·slip** *konkr.* Erdrutsch *m*; ~**s·man** ⚓ ['~zmən] Landratte *f*; '~**-sur·vey·or** Landmesser *m*; '~**-tax** Grundsteuer *f*; ~**·ward** ['~wəd] landwärts (gelegen).
lane [lein] Feldweg *m*; Gasse *f*; Spalier *n*; *mot.* Fahrbahn *f*, Spur *f*.
lang syne *schott.* ['læŋ'sain] längst vergangen(e Zeit *f*).
lan·guage ['læŋgwidʒ] Sprache *f*; Worte *n/pl.*; *bad* ~ häßliche Worte *n/pl.*; *strong* ~ Kraftausdrücke *m/pl.*; ~ **lab·o·ra·to·ry** Sprachlabor *n*.
lan·guid □ ['læŋgwid] matt, schlaff; teilnahmslos; träg (*Strom etc.*); ✝ flau; '**lan·guid·ness** Mattigkeit *f*; Flauheit *f*.
lan·guish ['læŋgwiʃ] matt werden; schmachten (*for* nach); dahinsiechen; ✝ darniederliegen; '**lan·guish·ing** □ schmachtend; ✝ flau.
lan·guor ['læŋgə] Mattigkeit *f*; Schlaffheit *f*; Schmachten *n*; Stille *f*; '**lan·guor·ous** □ matt; schlaff; drückend.
lank □ [læŋk] schmächtig, dünn; schlaff (*Börse*); schlicht, glatt (*Haar*); '**lank·y** □ schlaksig.
lan·o·lin ['lænəuli:n] Lanolin *n*, Wollfett *n*.
lan·tern ['læntən] Laterne *f* (*a.* ⚠); *dark* ~ Blendlaterne *f*; '~**-jawed** hohlwangig; '~**-slide** Dia(positiv) *n*, Lichtbild *n*; ~ *lecture* Lichtbildervortrag *m*.
lan·yard ⚓ ['lænjəd] Taljereep *n*.
lap[1] [læp] **1.** Schoß *m* (*a. fig.*); ⊕ übergreifende Kante *f*; Vorstoß *m*; *Garn*-Windung *f*; *Sport*: Runde *f*; ~ *of hono(u)r Sport*: Ehrenrunde *f*; **2.** übereinanderlegen, umschlagen; (ein)hüllen (*in* in *acc.*).
lap[2] [~] **1.** Lecken *n*; Schluck *m*; Anschlagen *n*, Plätschern *n von Wellen*; **2.** (auf)lecken; schlürfen; verschlingen; plätschern (gegen) (*Wellen*).
lap-dog ['læpdɔg] Schoßhund *m*.
la·pel [lə'pel] Aufschlag *m am Rock*.
lap·i·dar·y ['læpidəri] **1.** Stein...; Lapidar...; **2.** Steinschneider *m*.
lap·is laz·u·li [læpis'læzjulai] Lapislazuli *m*, Lasurstein *m*.
lapse [læps] **1.** Dahingleiten *n*; Verlauf *m der Zeit*; Verfallen *n* (*into* in *acc.*); ⚖ Verfall *m*; Fehltritt *m*, Versehen *n*; **2.** fallen, gleiten; verfließen (*Zeit*); *moralisch* fallen; verfallen (*into* in *acc.*); fehlen; ⚖ verfallen; erlöschen.
lap-strap ✈ ['læpstræp] Beckengurt *m*.
lap·wing *orn.* ['læpwiŋ] Kiebitz *m*.
lar·ce·ny ⚖ ['lɑ:səni] Diebstahl *m*.
larch ⚘ [lɑ:tʃ] Lärche *f*.
lard [lɑ:d] **1.** (Schweine)Schmalz *n*; **2.** spicken (*a. fig.*); '**lard·er** Speisekammer *f*; '**lard·ing-nee·dle,** '**lard·ing-pin** Spicknadel *f*.
large □ [lɑ:dʒ] groß; weit, umfassend; reichlich; weitherzig; flott, schwungvoll; *at* ~ auf freiem Fuße; ausführlich; in seiner *od.* ihrer Gesamtheit, im allgemeinen; wahllos; *talk at* ~ in den Tag hineinreden; *in* ~ im großen; '**large·ly** zum großen Teil, weitgehend; großzügig, reichlich; '**large·ness** Größe *f* (*a. fig.*); Weite *f*; '**large-'mind·ed** weitherzig; '**large-'scale** Groß...; '**large-'sized** groß(formatig).
lar·gess(e) † [lɑ:'dʒes] Freigebigkeit *f*; Schenkung *f*.
lar·go ♪ ['lɑ:gəu] **1.** Largo *n*; **2.** largo, sehr langsam.
lar·i·at *Am.* ['læriət] Lasso *n*, *m*.
lark[1] *orn.* [lɑ:k] Lerche *f*.
lark[2] [~] **1.** Streich *m*, Jux *m*; **2.** tolle Streiche machen; **lark·some** ['səm] = *larky*.
lark·spur ⚘ ['lɑ:kspə:] Rittersporn *m*.
lark·y F ['lɑ:ki] zu Streichen aufgelegt; scherzhaft.
lar·va *zo.* ['lɑ:və], *pl.* **lar·vae** ['~vi:] Larve *f*, Puppe *f*; **lar·val** ['~vəl] Larven...
lar·yn·gi·tis ⚕ [lærin'dʒaitis] Kehlkopfentzündung *f*; **lar·ynx** ['læriŋks] Kehlkopf *m*.
las·civ·ious □ [lə'siviəs] lüstern.
la·ser ['leizə] Laser *m*; ~ *beam* Laserstrahl *m*.
lash [læʃ] **1.** Peitschenschnur *f*; (Peitschen)Hieb *m*; Geißel *f*, Rute *f*; Wimper *f*; *the* ~ Auspeitschen *n*; die Prügelstrafe; **2.** peitschen; peitschen gegen *et.* (*Wogen etc.*); *fig.* geißeln; schlagen (*at* nach); anbinden (*to* an *acc.*); ~ *out* um sich schlagen; ausschlagen (*Pferd*); *fig.* losbrechen; '**lash·er** Wehr *n*; '**lash·ing** Prügel *pl.*; ~*s pl.* F Unmenge *f*.
lass [læs] Mädchen *n*; Liebste *f*; **las·sie** ['læsi] Mädelchen *n*.

las·si·tude ['læsitju:d] Mattigkeit *f*, Abgespanntheit *f*, Desinteresse *n*.
las·so ['læsəu] **1.** Lasso *n*, *m*; **2.** mit dem Lasso fangen.
last[1] [lɑ:st] **1.** *adj.* letzt; vorig; äußerst, höchst; geringst; ~ *but one* vorletzt; ~ *night* gestern abend; **2.** Letzte *m*; Ende *n*; *my* ~ mein letzter Brief *m*; mein Jüngster *m*; *at* ~ zuletzt; schließlich, endlich; *at long* ~ zu guter Letzt; *breathe one's* ~ den letzten Atemzug tun; **3.** *adv.* zuletzt; ~, *but not least* nicht zuletzt.
last[2] [~] dauern, währen; halten (*Farbe etc.*); ausreichen (*Vorräte etc.*); ausdauern (*bei Rennen etc.*).
last[3] [~] *Schuhmacher*-Leisten *m*; *stick to one's* ~ bei s-m Leisten bleiben.
last-ditch [lɑ:st'ditʃ] allerletzt; ~ *attempt* allerletzter (verzweifelter) Versuch *m*.
last·ing ['lɑ:stiŋ] **1.** □ dauerhaft; beständig; **2.** dauerhafter Stoff *m*.
last·ly ['lɑ:stli] zuletzt, schließlich.
latch [lætʃ] **1.** Klinke *f*, Drücker *m*; Schnapp-, Druckschloß *n*; *on the* ~ (nur) eingeklinkt; **2.** ein-, zuklinken, zugehen (*Tür*); '**~-key** Hausschlüssel *m*.
late [leit] spät; zu spät, verspätet; (kürzlich) verstorben, selig; ehemalig; jüngst; *at* (*the*) ~*st* spätestens; *as* ~ *as yesterday* erst *od.* noch gestern; *of* ~ letzthin, neulich; *of* ~ *years* seit einigen Jahren; ~*r on* später; *be* ~ (zu) spät kommen; 🚂 Verspätung haben; *keep* ~ *hours* spät aufbleiben; spät heimkommen; '**~-com·er** Nachzügler *m*.
la·teen ⚓ [lə'ti:n]: ~ *sail* Lateinsegel *n*.
late·ly ['leitli] in letzter Zeit, vor kurzem, unlängst, letzthin, neulich, kürzlich.
la·ten·cy ['leitənsi] Verborgenheit *f*, Gebundenheit *f*, Latenz *f*.
late·ness ['leitnis] Verspätung *f*; späte Zeit *f*.
la·tent □ ['leitənt] verborgen, gebunden (*Wärme etc.*), latent.
lat·er·al □ ['lætərəl] seitlich; Seiten...
la·tex ⚘ ['leiteks] Milchsaft *n bsd.* [*des Gummibaums.*]
lath [lɑ:θ] **1.** Latte *f*; **2.** belatten.
lathe [leið] Drehbank *f*; Lade *f am Webstuhl.*
lath·er ['lɑ:ðə, 'læðə] **1.** (*bsd.* Seifen)Schaum *m*; **2.** *v/t.* einseifen; P verdreschen; *v/i.* schäumen.
Lat·in ['lætin] **1.** lateinisch; **2.** Latein *n*; ~ **A·mer·i·ca** Lateinamerika *n*; '**Lat·in·ism** Latinismus *m*; '**Lat·in·ize** latinisieren; ins Lateinische übersetzen.
lat·i·tude ['lætitju:d] Breite *f* (*a. geogr., ast.*); *fig.* Umfang *m*, Weite *f*; Spielraum *m*; ~*s pl.* Breiten *pl.* (*Gegenden*); **lat·i'tu·di·nal** [~dinl] Breiten...; **lat·i·tu·di·nar·i·an** ['~di'nɛəriən] **1.** frei(sinnig); **2.** Freidenker *m*.
la·trine [lə'tri:n] Latrine *f*.
lat·ter ['lætə] neuer; *der, die, das* letztere; *poet.* später, Spät...; ~ *end* Ende *n*; '**~-day** aus neuester Zeit; ~ *saints eccl. die* Heiligen *pl.* der letzten Tage (*Mormonen*); '**lat·ter·ly** neuerdings.
lat·tice ['lætis] **1.** *a.* ~*-work* Gitter *n*; **2.** (ver)gittern.
Lat·vi·an ['lætviən] **1.** lettisch; **2.** Lette *m*, Lettin *f*; Lettisch *n*.
laud [lɔ:d] loben, preisen; '**laud·a·ble** □ lobenswert, löblich; **lau'da·tion** Lob *n*; **laud·a·to·ry** □ ['~dətəri] lobend, preisend (*of acc.*).
laugh [lɑ:f] **1.** Gelächter *n*, Lachen *n*; *have a* ~ lachen; *raise a* ~ Gelächter erregen; **2.** lachen (*at* über *acc.*); ~ *at s.o.* j. auslachen; ~ *off* lachend hinweggehen über (*acc.*); ~ *out of j.* durch Lachen abbringen von; *you will* ~ *on the wrong side od. on the other side of your mouth od. face* dir wird das Lachen noch vergehen; *he* ~*s best who* ~*s last* wer zuletzt lacht, lacht am besten; *s. sleeve*; '**laugh·a·ble** □ lächerlich; '**laugh·er** Lacher(in); '**laugh·ing** **1.** Lachen *n*; **2.** □ lachend; *it is no* ~ *matter* es ist nicht zum Lachen; '**laugh·ing-gas** Lachgas *n*; '**laugh·ing-stock** Gegenstand *m* des Gelächters; **laugh·ter** ['~tə] Gelächter *n*, Lachen *n*.
launch [lɔ:ntʃ] **1.** ⚓ Stapellauf *m*; Barkasse *f*; Ausflugsdampfer *m*; **2.** *v/t.* vom Stapel lassen; *Boot* aussetzen; schleudern (*a. fig.*); *Schläge* versetzen; *Rakete* starten, abschießen; *fig.* in Gang bringen; lancieren; *v/i.* ~ *out* loslegen; ~ (*out*) *into* sich stürzen in (*acc.*); sich ergehen in (*dat.*); '**launch·ing-**

-pad (Raketen)Abschußrampe *f*; **launch·ing site** (Raketen)Abschußbasis *f*; **'launch·ing-tube** ⚓, ⚔ Torpedorohr *n*.

laun·der ['lɔːndə] waschen (u. bügeln); sich waschen (lassen); **laun·der·ette** [lɔːndə'ret] Selbstbedienungswaschsalon *m*.

laun·dress ['lɔːndris] Wäscherin *f*; **'laun·dry** Waschanstalt *f*; Wäsche *f*; **'laun·dry-man** Wäscher *m*; (Aus)Fahrer *m* einer Wäscherei.

lau·re·ate ['lɔːriit] **1.** lorbeergekrönt; **2.** *the* ♀, *the Poet* ♀ der Hofdichter.

lau·rel ⚘ ['lɔrəl] Lorbeer *m*; *win* ~*s fig.* Lorbeeren ernten; **'lau·relled** lorbeerumkränzt.

lav F [læv] Klo *n*.

la·va ['lɑːvə] Lava *f*.

lav·a·to·ry ['lævətəri] Waschraum *m*; Toilette *f*; *public* ~ Bedürfnisanstalt *f*; ~ *attendant* Toilettenfrau *f*.

lave *mst poet.* [leiv] (sich) waschen, baden; bespülen.

lav·en·der ⚘ ['lævində] Lavendel *m*.

lav·ish ['læviʃ] **1.** □ freigebig, verschwenderisch (*of* mit; *in* in *dat.*); **2.** verschwenden; **'lav·ish·ness** Verschwendung *f*.

law [lɔː] Gesetz *n*; Vorschrift *f*, (*bsd.* Spiel)Regel *f*; ⚖ Gesetze *n/pl.*, Recht *n*; Rechtswissenschaft *f*; Juristenberuf *m*; Gericht(sverfahren) *n*; *at* ~ gesetzlich; *be a* ~ *unto o.s.* sich über Konventionen hinwegsetzen; *go to* ~ vor Gericht gehen; *have the* ~ *of s.o.* j. gerichtlich belangen; *...-in-law* Schwieger...; *necessity knows no* ~ Not kennt kein Gebot; *lay down the* ~ den Ton angeben; *practise* ~ als Rechtsanwalt praktizieren; **'~-a·bid·ing** ⚖ gesetzestreu, friedlich; **'~-break·er** Gesetzesübertreter *m*; **'~-court** Gericht(shof *m*) *n*; **law·ful** □ ['~ful] gesetzlich; rechtmäßig; gültig (*Urkunde etc.*); **'law-giv·er** Gesetzgeber *m*; **'law·less** □ gesetzlos; ungesetzlich; zügellos; **'law-mak·er** Gesetzgeber *m*.

lawn[1] [lɔːn] Batist *m*.

lawn[2] [~] Rasen(platz) *m*; **'~-mow·er** Rasenmäher *m*; **'~-sprin·kler** Rasensprenger *m*; **'~-'ten·nis** (Lawn-)Tennis *n*.

law...: ~ **school** juristische Fakultät *f*; **~suit** ['lɔːsjuːt] Prozeß *m*; **law·yer** ['~jə] Jurist *m*; (Rechts)Anwalt *m*.

lax □ [læks] lax; locker; lose, schlaff (*a. fig.*); lasch, lässig; **lax·a·tive** ['~ətiv] **1.** abführend; **2.** Abführmittel *n*; **'lax·i·ty, lax·ness** Laxheit *f etc.*

lay[1] [lei] *pret. von lie*[2] 2.

lay[2] [~] Ballade *f*; *poet.* Lied *n*.

lay[3] [~] weltlich; Laien...; ~ *preacher* Laienprediger *m*.

lay[4] [~] **1.** Lage *f*, Richtung *f*; *sl.* Unternehmen *n*, Beschäftigung *f*; **2.** (*irr.*) *v/t.* legen; nieder-, umlegen; *Geister* bannen; stellen, setzen; *Tisch* decken; löschen, dämpfen, stillen; besänftigen; vorlegen; *Summe* wetten; *Wette* eingehen; ~ *aside* beiseite legen; aufgeben; ~ *bare* bloßlegen, aufdecken; ~ *before s.o.* j-m vorlegen; ~ *by* beiseite legen; ~ *down* niederlegen; *Hoffnung* aufgeben; *Weg etc.* bauen; *Grundsatz* festlegen, aufstellen; ~ *s.o.* (*fast*) *by the heels* j. dingfest machen; ~ *in* einlagern, sich eindecken mit; ~ *low* niederwerfen; ~ *off* ablegen; (zeitweilig) entlassen; *Am. sl.* aufhören mit *et. od. j.*; ~ *on Farbe* auftragen; *Steuer* auferlegen; *Schläge* versetzen; *Wasserleitung* legen; ~ *it on* (*thick*) *fig.* (dick) auftragen; ~ *open* darlegen; ~ (*o.s.*) *open to s.th.* (sich) e-r Sache aussetzen; ~ *out* ausbreiten, -legen; *Garten, Geld etc.* (gut) anlegen; ~ *o.s. out* sich einrichten (*for* für); ~ *s.o. under an obligation od. a necessity* j. zwingen; ~ *up Geld, Vorräte* hinlegen, aufbewahren; *Kenntnisse* sammeln; *Land* brachliegen lassen; ⚓ auflegen; *be laid up* ans Bett gefesselt sein; ~ *with* belegen mit; *v/i.* (Eier) legen; *a.* ~ *a wager* wetten; ~ *about one* um sich schlagen; ~ *into s.o. sl.* j. verdreschen; ~ (*it*) *on* F zuschlagen.

lay·a·bout *sl.* ['leiəbaut] Strolch *m*, Stromer *m*; **'lay-by** Park-, Rastplatz *m an e-r Fernstraße*.

lay·er 1. ['leiə] Leger *m*; Lage *f*, Schicht *f*; ⚘ Ableger *m*; **2.** ⚘ ['lɛə] absenken.

lay·ette [lei'et] Babyausstattung *f*.

lay-fig·ure ['lei'figə] Gliederpuppe *f*.

lay·man ['leimən] Laie *m*.

lay...: **'~-off** Arbeitsunterbrechung *f*; **'~-out** Anlage *f*; Entwurf *m*;

Aufmachung *f*.
laz·a·ret, *mst* **laz·a·ret·to** [læzə'ret(əu)] Aussätzigenspital *n*.
laze F [leiz] faulenzen, bummeln; '**laz·i·ness** Faulheit *f*; '**la·zy** träg, faul; '**la·zy-bones** Faulpelz *m*.
lea *poet.* [li:] Au(e) *f*, Flur *f*.
leach [li:tʃ] auslaugen; durchsickern lassen.
lead[1] [led] **1.** Blei *n*; ⚓ Lot *n*, Senkblei *n*; *typ.* Durchschuß *m*; ~*s pl.* Bleiplatten *f/pl.*; Bleidach *n*; ~ *pencil* Bleistift *m*; *swing the* ~ *sl.* sich drücken; **2.** verbleien; *typ.* durchschießen.
lead[2] [li:d] **1.** Führung *f*, Leitung *f*; Beispiel *n*; Vorsprung *m*; *thea.* Hauptrolle *f*; Hauptdarsteller(in); *Karten*: Vorhand *f*; ⚡ Leitung *f*; *Hunde*-Leine *f*; Mühlkanal *m*; *it's my* ~ *Karten*: ich spiele aus; *take the* ~ die Leitung übernehmen; vorangehen; ~ *story Zeitung*: Hauptartikel *m*; **2.** (*irr.*) *v/t.* (an)führen, leiten; dazu bringen, bewegen (*to* zu); *Karte* ausspielen; ~ *on* (ver)locken; *v/i.* vorangehen; Anführer sein; ~ *off* den Anfang machen; *Sport*: anspielen; ~ *up to* überleiten zu.
lead·en ['ledn] bleiern (*a. fig.*); Blei...
lead·er ['li:də] (An)Führer(in), Leiter(in); ⚖ erster Anwalt *m*; Erste *m*; Leitpferd *n*; Leitartikel *m*; *Film*: Startband *n*; ⚘ Leit-, Haupttrieb *m*; *anat.* Sehne *f*; **lead·er·ette** [~'ret] *kurzer* Leitartikel *m*; '**lead·er·ship** Führerschaft *f*; Führungsqualitäten *f/pl.*
lead-in ⚡ ['li:din] Antennenzuleitung *f*.
lead·ing ['li:diŋ] **1.** leitend; Leit...; Haupt...; ~ *article* Leitartikel *m*; ⚕ Lockartikel *m*, Schlager *m*; ~ *case* ⚖ Präzedenzfall *m*; ~ *man thea.* Hauptdarsteller *m*, erster Liebhaber *m*; ~ *lady* Hauptdarstellerin *f*, erste Liebhaberin *f*; ~ *question* Suggestivfrage *f*; **2.** Leitung *f*, Führung *f*; '**~-strings** *pl.* Gängelband *n*.
lead... [led]: **~ poi·son·ing** Bleivergiftung *f*; '**~-works** *mst sg.* Bleihütte *f*.
leaf [li:f], *pl.* **leaves** [li:vz] Blatt *n*; *Tür- etc.* Flügel *m*; *Tisch*-Klappe *f*, Platte *f*; *in* ~ belaubt; *come into* ~ ausschlagen, Blätter bekommen; '**leaf·age** Laub(werk) *n*; '**leaf-bud** Blattknospe *f*; '**leaf·less** blätterlos; **leaf·let** ['~lit] Blättchen *n*; Flug-, Merk-, Faltblatt *n*; Prospekt *m*; '**leaf·y** belaubt; Laub...
league[1] [li:g] **1.** Liga *f* (*a. hist. u. Sport*); Bund *m*; ♀ *of Nations* Völkerbund *m*; **2.** (sich) verbünden.
league[2] *mst poet.* [~] Meile *f* (*4,8 km*).
leak [li:k] **1.** Leck *n*, Loch *n*; **2.** leck sein, lecken; tropfen (*Wasserhahn*); ~ *out* auslaufen; *fig.* durchsickern; '**leak·age** Lecken *n*; ⚕ Leckage *f*; *fig.* Verlust *m*; Durchsickern *n*; '**leak·y** leck; undicht.
lean[1] [li:n] **1.** mager; **2.** mageres Fleisch *n*.
lean[2] [~] **1.** (*irr.*) (sich) (an)lehnen (*against* an *acc.*); (sich) stützen (*on, upon* auf *acc.*); (sich) (hin)neigen (*to* zu); **2.** (*fig. a.* '**lean·ing**) Neigung *f*.
lean·ness ['li:nnis] Magerkeit *f*.
leant [lent] *pret. u. p.p. von lean*[2] *1.*
lean-to ['li:ntu:] Anbau *m*.
leap [li:p] **1.** Sprung *m*; *by* ~*s* (*and bounds*) sprunghaft, rapide; **2.** (*irr.*) *v/i.* springen, hüpfen; *fig.* hervorschießen; *he* ~*t at the opportunity* er stürzte sich auf die Gelegenheit; *v/t.* überspringen; '**~-frog 1.** Bockspringen *n*; **2.** bockspringen; **leapt** [lept] *pret. u. p.p. von leap 2*; '**leap-year** Schaltjahr *n*.
learn [lə:n] (*irr.*) lernen; erfahren, hören; V beibringen; ~ *from* ersehen aus; **learn·ed** □ ['~nid] gelehrt; '**learn·er** Anfänger(in); '**learn·ing** Lernen *n*; Gelehrsamkeit *f*; **learnt** [lə:nt] *pret. u. p.p. von learn.*
lease [li:s] **1.** Verpachtung *f*, -mietung *f*; Pacht *f*, Miete *f*; Pacht-, Mietvertrag *m*; *let (out) on* ~ verpachten; *a new* ~ *of life* neues Leben *n*; **2.** (ver)pachten, (-)mieten; '**~·hold 1.** Pacht(ung) *f*; **2.** Pacht...; '**~·hold·er** Pächter *m*.
leash [li:ʃ] **1.** Koppelleine *f*; Koppel *f* (= *3 Hunde etc.*); *hold in* ~ *fig.* im Zaum halten; *strain at the* ~ *fig.* kaum zu halten sein; **2.** koppeln.
least [li:st] **1.** *adj.* kleinst, geringst; wenigst, mindest; **2.** *adv. a.* ~ *of all* am wenigsten; *at (the)* ~ wenigstens; zum mindesten; *at the very* ~ allermindestens; *not in the* ~ nicht im geringsten; *to say the* ~ gelinde

gesagt.

leath·er ['leðə] **1.** Leder *n* (*fig. Haut*); F Leder(ball *m*) *n*; *~s pl.* Lederhosen *f/pl.*; Ledergamaschen *f/pl.*; **2.** ledern; Leder...; **3.** mit Leder beziehen; versohlen (*prügeln*); **leath·er·ette** [~'ret] Kunstleder *n*; **leath·ern** ['leðən] ledern; '**leath·er·neck** ⚔ *Am. sl.* Ledernacken *m*, Marineinfanterist *m*; '**leath·er·y** ledern, zäh.

leave [li:v] **1.** Erlaubnis *f*; *a. ~ of absence* Urlaub *m*; Abschied *m*; *by your ~* mit Verlaub; *take one's ~* Abschied nehmen, (weg)gehen; *take ~ of* sich verabschieden von; *take ~ of one's senses* den Verstand verlieren; **2.** (*irr.*) *v/t.* (ver)lassen; hinterlassen (*vermachen*); zurück-, hinterlassen; übriglassen; überlassen, anheimstellen; *be left* (übrig)bleiben; *~ it at that* es dabei bewenden lassen; *s. call*; *~ behind j.* hinter sich lassen; *Spur etc.* hinterlassen; *et.* stehen *od.* liegen lassen; zurücklassen; *~ off* aufhören (mit); *Gewohnheit* aufgeben; Kleid ablegen; *~ s.o. to himself od. to his own devices* j. sich selbst überlassen; *~ s.o. od. s.th. alone* j. *od.* et. in Ruhe lassen; *be (nicely) left* F (schön) in der Patsche sitzen; *~ go of s.th.* et. loslassen; *v/i.* ablassen; weggehen; abgehen, abreisen (*for* nach).

leav·en ['levn] **1.** Sauerteig *m* (*a. fig.*), Hefe *f*; **2.** säuern; *fig.* durchsetzen; '**leav·en·ing** Gärungsmittel *n*.

leaves [li:vz] *pl. von leaf*; *oft* Laub *n*.

leav·ings ['li:viŋz] *pl.* Überbleibsel *n/pl.*, (Speise)Reste *m/pl.*

lech·er ['letʃə] Wüstling *m*; '**lech·er·ous** wollüstig; '**lech·er·y** Wollust *f*.

lec·tern *eccl.* ['lektə:n] Lese-, Chorpult *n*.

lec·ture ['lektʃə] **1.** Vorlesung *f*, Vortrag *m* (*on* über *acc.*; *to* vor *dat.*); Strafpredigt *f*; *s. curtain*; *read s.o. a ~* j. abkanzeln; *~ room* Hörsaal *m*; Vortragsraum *m*; **2.** *v/i.* Vorlesungen *od.* Vorträge halten, lesen (*on* über *acc.*); *v/t.* abkanzeln; '**lec·tur·er** Vortragende *m*; *univ.* Dozent(in); *eccl.* Hilfsprediger *m*; '**lec·ture·ship** Dozentur *f*; Hilfspredigeramt *n*.

led [led] *pret. u. p.p. von lead*[2] 2.

ledge [ledʒ] Leiste *f*; Sims *m*, *n*; Riff *n*.

ledg·er ['ledʒə] ✝ Hauptbuch *n*; ⊕ Querbalken *m am Gerüst*; *a. ~ line* ♪ Hilfslinie *f*.

lee ⚓ [li:] Lee(seite) *f*.

leech [li:tʃ] *zo.* Blutegel *m*; *fig.* Blutsauger *m*.

leek ⚘ [li:k] Lauch *m*, Porree *m*.

leer [liə] **1.** (lüsterner *od.* finsterer) Seitenblick *m*; **2.** schielen (*at* nach); '**leer·y** □ *sl.* argwöhnisch.

lees [li:z] *pl.* Bodensatz *m*, Hefe *f*.

lee·ward ⚓ ['li:wəd] leewärts.

lee·way ⚓ ['li:wei] Abtrift *f*; *make ~* abtreiben; *fig.* zurückbleiben; *make up ~ fig.* Versäumtes nachholen.

left[1] [left] *pret. u. p.p. von leave* 2.

left[2] [~] **1.** *adj.* linke(r, -s); **2.** *adv.* links; **3.** Linke *f*; '**~-hand** linke(r, -s); mit der linken Hand; *~ drive mot.* Linkssteuerung *f*; '**~-'hand·ed** □ linkshändig; *fig.* linkisch; zur linken Hand (*Ehe*); fragwürdig (*Kompliment*); ⊕ linksgängig.

left·ist *pol.* ['leftist] **1.** linksgerichtet; 2. Linksgerichtete *m*, *f*.

left...: '**~-'lug·gage lock·er** (Gepäck)Schließfach *n*; '**~-'lug·gage of·fice** Gepäckaufbewahrung(sstelle) *f*; '**~·o·vers** *pl.* Speisereste *m/pl.*

left-wing ['left'wiŋ] *pol.* Links..., des linken Flügels.

left·y F *pol.* ['lefti] Linke *m*, *f*.

leg [leg] Bein *n*; *Hammel- etc.* Keule *f*; (Stiefel)Schaft *m*; ⩕ Schenkel *m*; Etappe *f*, Teilstrecke *f bsd. e-r Flugreise*; *give s.o. a ~ up* j-m (hin)aufhelfen; *fig.* j-m unter die Arme greifen; *be on one's last ~s* F auf dem letzten Loch pfeifen; *pull s.o.'s ~* j. auf den Arm nehmen (*hänseln*); *not have a ~ to stand on fig.* der *od.* jeglicher Grundlage entbehren.

leg·a·cy ['legəsi] Vermächtnis *n*; '**~-hunt·er** Erbschleicher(in).

le·gal □ ['li:gəl] gesetzlich, legal; rechtsgültig; rechtlich, juristisch; Rechts...; *~ aid* Rechtshilfe *f*; *~ capacity* Geschäftsfähigkeit *f*; *~ costs pl.* Gerichtskosten *pl.*; *~ dispute* Rechtsstreit *m*; *~ entity* juristische Person *f*; *~ remedy* Rechtsmittel *n*; *~ status* Rechtsstellung *f*; *s. tender*; **le·gal·i·ty** [li:'gæliti] Gesetzlichkeit *f*, Legalität *f*; **le·gal·i·za·tion** [li:gəlai'zeiʃən] Legalisierung *f*; '**le·gal·ize** legalisie-

ren, rechtskräftig machen; beurkunden.
leg·ate ['legit] *päpstlicher* Legat *m.*
leg·a·tee ⚖ [legə'ti:] Vermächtnisnehmer *m,* Erbe *m.*
le·ga·tion [li'geiʃən] Gesandtschaft *f.*
leg-bail ['leg'beil]: *give* ~ Fersengeld geben.
leg·end ['ledʒənd] Legende *f,* Sage *f;* Inschrift *f;* Text *m zu e-r Illustration;* '**leg·end·ar·y** legendär, sagenhaft.
leg·er·de·main ['ledʒədə'mein] Taschenspielerei *f,* Kunststück *n.*
legged [legd] ...beinig; '**leg·gings** *pl.* Gamaschen *f/pl.;* '**leg·gy** langbeinig.
leg·horn [le'gɔ:n] italienischer Strohhut *m;* Leghorn *n (Hühnerrasse).*
leg·i·bil·i·ty [ledʒi'biliti] Leserlichkeit *f;* **leg·i·ble** ['ledʒəbl] □ leserlich.
le·gion ['li:dʒən] Legion *f (a. fig.);* '**le·gion·ar·y 1.** Legions...; **2.** Legionär *m.*
leg·is·late ['ledʒisleit] Gesetze geben *od.* erlassen; **leg·is'la·tion** Gesetzgebung *f;* **leg·is·la·tive** □ ['~lətiv] gesetzgebend; Gesetzgebungs...; **leg·is·la·tor** ['~leitə] Gesetzgeber *m;* **leg·is·la·ture** ['~leitʃə] Legislatur *f,* Gesetzgebung *f;* gesetzgebende Körperschaft *f.*
le·git·i·ma·cy [li'dʒitiməsi] Rechtmäßigkeit *f,* Legitimität *f;* Ehelichkeit *f;* **le'git·i·mate 1.** □ [~mit] legitim, rechtmäßig; berechtigt, zu rechtfertigen(d); ehelich; **2.** [~meit] legitimieren, für rechtmäßig erklären, rechtfertigen; **le·git·i'ma·tion** Legitimierung *f;* Legitimation *f,* Ausweis *m;* **le'git·i·ma·tize** [~mətaiz], **le'git·i·mize** = *legitimate* 2.
leg-room ['legrum] Beinfreiheit *f.*
leg·ume ['legju:m] Hülsenfrucht *f;* **le'gu·mi·nous** [~minəs] Hülsenfrucht...
lei·sure ['leʒə] **1.** Muße *f,* Freizeit *f; be at* ~ Muße haben; *at your* ~ wenn es Ihnen paßt; **2.** müßig; Muße...; ~ **ac·tiv·i·ties** *pl.* Freizeitbeschäftigung(en *pl.*) *f;* '**lei·sured** unbeschäftigt; *the* ~ *classes* die begüterten Klassen; '**lei·sure·ly** *adj. u. adv.* gemächlich; **lei·sure wear** Freizeitkleidung *f.*
lem·on ['lemən] Zitrone *f;* Zitronenbaum *m;* **lem·on·ade** [~'neid] Zitronenlimonade *f;* '**lem·on-'squash** Zitronenwasser *n;* '**lem·on-squeez·er** Zitronenpresse *f.*
lend [lend] *(irr.)* (ver-, aus)leihen; *Hilfe* leisten, gewähren, ~ *a hand* helfen; ~ *o.s. to* sich hergeben zu *(Person);* sich eignen zu *od.* für *(Sache);* ~*ing library* Leihbücherei *f;* '**lend·er** (Ver)Leiher(in); '**Lend-'Lease Act** Leih-Pacht-Gesetz *n (1941).*
length [leŋθ] Länge *f;* Strecke *f;* (Zeit)Dauer *f; at* ~ endlich, zuletzt; *at (great)* ~ (sehr) ausführlich; *go all* ~*s* aufs Ganze gehen; *go (to) great* ~*s* sehr weit gehen; *he goes the* ~ *of saying* er geht so weit zu sagen; '**length·en** (sich) verlängern, (sich) ausdehnen; '**length·ways,** '**length·wise** der Länge nach, längs; '**length·y** □ sehr lang; weitschweifig.
le·ni·ence, le·ni·en·cy ['li:njəns(i)] = *lenity;* '**le·ni·ent** □ mild, nachsichtig; '**len·i·tive** ⚕ **1.** lindernd; **2.** linderndes Mittel *n;* **len·i·ty** ['leniti] Milde *f,* Nachsicht *f.*
lens [lenz] *Glas*-Linse *f; phot.* Objektiv *n;* ~ *system phot.* Optik *f.*
lent[1] [lent] *pret. u. p.p. von lend.*
Lent[2] [~] Fasten *pl.,* Fastenzeit *f.*
Lent·en ['lentən] Fasten..., fastenmäßig.
len·tic·u·lar □ [len'tikjulə] linsenförmig; Linsen...
len·til ⚘ ['lentil] Linse *f.*
Leo *ast.* ['li:əu] Löwe *m.*
leop·ard ['lepəd] Leopard *m.*
le·o·tard ['li:əuta:d] Gymnastikanzug *m.*
lep·er ['lepə] Aussätzige *m, f.*
lep·re·chaun *ir.* ['leprəkɔ:n] Kobold *m.*
lep·ro·sy ⚕ ['leprəsi] Aussatz *m,* Lepra *f;* '**lep·rous** aussätzig.
Les·bian ['lezbiən] Lesbierin *f;* '**Les·bian·ism** weibliche Homosexualität *f.*
lese-maj·es·ty ⚖ ['li:z'mædʒisti] Majestätsbeleidigung *f;* Hochverrat *m.*
le·sion ['li:ʒən] Verletzung *f,* Wunde *f.*
less [les] *adj. u. adv.* kleiner, geringer; weniger *(a.* Ꭿ); *prp.* Ꭿ

minus; ✝ abzüglich; *no ~ than* ebenso gut wie; *no ~ a p. than* kein Geringerer als; *none the ~* dennoch, trotzdem, nichtsdestoweniger.

...less [lis] ...los, un...

les·see [le'si:] Pächter *m*, Mieter *m*.

less·en ['lesn] *v/t.* vermindern, verringern, verkleinern, schmälern (*a. fig.*); *v/i.* kleiner werden, abnehmen.

less·er ['lesə] kleiner; geringer.

les·son ['lesn] Lektion *f*; Aufgabe *f*; (Unterrichts)Stunde *f*; Lehre *f*; *eccl.* Lesung *f*; *~s pl.* Unterricht *m*; *teach s.o. a ~* j-m e-e Lektion erteilen; j-m e-e Lehre sein.

les·sor [le'sɔ:] Verpächter *m*, -mieter *m*.

lest [lest] damit nicht, daß nicht; aus Furcht, daß.

let[1] [let] (*irr.*) *v/t.* lassen, zulassen, gestatten; vermieten, verpachten; *~ alone* nicht anrühren; zufrieden *od.* in Ruhe lassen; *adv.* geschweige denn; *~ be* in Ruhe lassen; *~ down j.* im Stich lassen, versetzen; *~ s.o. down gently* j. glimpflich behandeln; *~ drive at s.o.* auf j. losschlagen *od.* losfeuern; *~ fly* losdrücken; *fig.* vom Stapel lassen; *~ go* loslassen; *Anker* fallen lassen; *~ it go at that* es dabei bewenden lassen; *~ o.s. in for* sich auf *et.* einlassen; *~ into* einweihen in (*acc.*), wissen lassen; *~ loose* loslassen; *~ off* abschießen; *Witz* loslassen; *j.* laufen lassen; *s. steam*; *~ out* hinauslassen; ausplaudern; vermieten; *Arbeit* vergeben; *v/i.* sich vermieten (*at, for* für); *~ on* F es verraten, plaudern; *~ out at* treten, schlagen; *fig.* ausfällig werden gegenüber *j-m*; *~ up* aufhören.

let[2] [~] *a. ~ ball Tennis*: Netzball *m*; *without ~ or hindrance* unbehindert.

let·down F ['letdaun] Enttäuschung *f*.

le·thal □ ['li:θəl] tödlich; Todes...

le·thar·gic, le·thar·gi·cal □ [le'θɑ:dʒik(əl)] lethargisch (*a. fig.*); **leth·ar·gy** ['leθədʒi] Lethargie *f*; Schlafsucht *f*; *fig.* Teilnahmslosigkeit *f*.

Le·the ['li:θi:] Lethe *f* (*Fluß des Vergessens im Hades*).

let·ter ['letə] **1.** Buchstabe *m*; Type *f*; Brief *m*; buchstäblicher Sinn *m*; *~s pl.* Literatur *f*, Wissenschaft *f*; *by ~* brieflich; *man of ~s* Literat *m*; *to the ~* buchstäblich; **2.** mit Buchstaben versehen, zeichnen; *Buch* betiteln; **'~-bal·ance** Briefwaage *f*; **'~-box** Briefkasten *m*; **'~-card** Kartenbrief *m*; **'~-car·ri·er** *Am.* Briefträger *m*; **'~-case** Brieftasche *f*; **'~-cov·er** Briefumschlag *m*; **'let·tered** (literarisch) gebildet; **'let·ter-file** Briefordner *m*; **'let·ter-found·er** Schriftgießer *m*; **let·ter·gram** ['~græm] Brieftelegramm *n*; **'let·ter·head** (gedruckter) Briefkopf *m*; Kopfpapier *n*; **'let·ter·ing** Beschriftung *f*.

let·ter...: **'~·less** ungebildet; **'~-o·pen·er** Brieföffner *m*; **'~-'per·fect** *theat.* rollensicher; **'~·press** *typ.* Druck *m*, Text *m*; *~ printing* Hoch-, Buchdruck *m*; **'~-press** Kopierpresse *f*; **'~-weight** Briefbeschwerer *m*.

let·tuce ⚘ ['letis] (Kopf)Salat *m*.

let·up F ['letʌp] Nachlassen *n*; Unterbrechung *f*.

leu·co... ['lju:kəu] weiß; **leu·co·cyte** ['~sait] weißes Blutkörperchen *n*, Leukozyte *f*; **leu·k(a)e·mi·a** ⚕ [lju:'ki:miə] Leukämie *f*.

le·vant[1] [li'vænt] durchbrennen.

le·vant[2] [~] Levante *f*; **le·vant·ine** ['levəntain] **1.** Levantiner(in); **2.** levantinisch.

lev·ee[1] *hist.* ['levi] Lever *n*, Morgenempfang *m*.

lev·ee[2] *Am.* [~] Ufer-, Schutzdamm *m*.

lev·el ['levl] **1.** waagerecht, eben, gleich; ausgeglichen; *my ~ best* mein möglichstes; *~ crossing* 🚂 schienengleicher Übergang *m*; *~ stress gr.* schwebende Betonung *f*; *~ teaspoon* gestrichener Teelöffel *m*; **2.** ebene Fläche *f*; (gleiche) Höhe *f*, Niveau *n*, Stufe *f*, Stand *m*; Ebene *f*; *fig.* Richtschnur *f*, Maßstab *m*; Wasserwaage *f*, Libelle *f*; *~ of the sea* Meeresspiegel *m*; *on a ~ with* in *od.* auf gleicher Höhe mit (*a. fig.*); *dead ~* gerade Ebene *f*; *fig.* Eintönigkeit *f*; *on the ~* F offen, aufrichtig, fair; **3.** *v/t.* gleichmachen, ebnen; *surv.* nivellieren; *fig.* anpassen; richten, zielen mit (*at* auf *acc.*, nach); *~ with the ground* dem Boden gleichmachen; *~ down* erniedrigen; *~ up* erhöhen; *v/i. ~ at, ~ against* zielen auf (*acc.*); *~ off* heruntergehen (*Preis*); **'~-'head·ed** vernünftig; **'lev·el·(l)er** *surv.* Nivellierer *m*; *fig.* Gleichmacher *m*; **'lev·el-(l)ing** Nivellier...

le·ver ['li:və] **1.** Hebel *m*; Hebestange *f*; **2.** (mit e-m Hebel) bewegen, hebeln; **'le·ver·age** Hebelkraft *f*.

lev·er·et ['levərit] Häschen *n*. [*f*.]

le·ver-watch ['li:vəwɔtʃ] Ankeruhr

le·vi·a·than [li'vaiəθən] Leviathan *m*; Ungetüm *n*.

lev·i·tate ['leviteit] *Spiritismus*: schweben (lassen).

Le·vite ['li:vait] *Bibel*: Levit *m*.

lev·i·ty ['leviti] Leichtfertigkeit *f*.

lev·y ['levi] **1.** Erhebung *f von Steuern*; ⚔ Aushebung *f*; Aufgebot *n*; *capital* ~ Kapitalabgabe *f*; **2.** *Steuern* erheben, auferlegen; *Truppen* ausheben; *Krieg* führen (*on*, *against* gegen); beschlagnahmen; *Beschlagnahme* durchführen.

lewd □ [lu:d] liederlich, unzüchtig; **'lewd·ness** Unzüchtigkeit *f*.

lex·i·cal □ ['leksikəl] lexikalisch.

lex·i·cog·ra·pher [leksi'kɔgrəfə] Lexikograph *m*, Verfasser *m* e-s Wörterbuchs; **lex·i·co·graph·i·cal** □ [~kəu'græfikəl] lexikographisch; **lex·i·cog·ra·phy** [~'kɔgrəfi] Lexikographie *f*; **lex·i·con** ['~kən] *bsd. griechisches od. hebräisches* Wörterbuch *n*.

li·a·bil·i·ty [laiə'biliti] Verantwortlichkeit *f*; ⚖ Haftpflicht *f*; Verpflichtung *f*; Unterworfensein *n*; *fig.* Hang *m*, Neigung *f*; *liabilities pl.* Verbindlichkeiten *f/pl.*, ✝ Passiva *pl.*

li·a·ble □ ['laiəbl] verantwortlich (*for* für); ⚖ haftpflichtig; verpflichtet (*to* zu); unterliegend, ausgesetzt (*to dat.*); in Gefahr (*to inf.* zu *inf.*); neigend (*to* zu); *be* ~ *to* neigen *od.* geneigt sein zu; leicht *et. tun* können; ~ *to duty* zollpflichtig; ~ *to punishment* straffällig, -bar.

li·aise F [li'eiz] Verbindung aufnehmen (*with* mit); als Verbindungsmann fungieren.

li·ai·son [li:'eizɔ̃:ŋ] Liebschaft *f*, Liaison *f*; [li:'eizən] ⚔ Verbindung *f*; Zs.-arbeit *f*; ~ *officer* Verbindungsoffizier *m*.

li·ar ['laiə] Lügner(in).

li·ba·tion [lai'beiʃən] Trankopfer *n*.

li·bel ['laibəl] **1.** Schmähschrift *f*; Verleumdung *f*; Hohn *m* (*on* auf *acc.*); ⚖ Klageschrift *f*; **2.** schmähen; verunglimpfen; ⚖ schriftlich klagen gegen; **'li·bel·(l)ous** □ verleumderisch; Schmäh...

lib·er·al ['libərəl] **1.** □ liberal (*a. pol.*), freigebig, großzügig (*of* mit); reichlich; unbefangen; frei; freisinnig; **2.** Liberale *m*; **'lib·er·al·ism** Liberalismus *m*; **lib·er·al·i·ty** [~'ræliti] Freigebigkeit *f*; Freisinnigkeit *f*; Vorurteilslosigkeit *f*.

lib·er·ate ['libəreit] befreien (*from* von); *Sklaven* freilassen; **lib·er'a·tion** Befreiung *f*; **'lib·er·a·tor** Befreier *m*.

lib·er·tine ['libə:tain] **1.** Wüstling *m*; **2.** liederlich; **lib·er·tin·ism** ['libətinizəm] Liederlichkeit *f*, Zügellosigkeit *f*.

lib·er·ty ['libəti] Freiheit *f*; Vorrecht *n*; *take liberties* sich Freiheiten erlauben; *be at* ~ frei sein; *be at* ~ *to do* tun dürfen; ~ *of conscience* Gewissensfreiheit *f*; ~ *of speech* Redefreiheit *f*; ~ *of the press* Pressefreiheit *f*.

li·bid·i·nous □ [li'bidinəs] wollüstig, unzüchtig; libidinös.

Li·bra *ast.* ['librə] Waage *f*.

li·brar·i·an [lai'brɛəriən] Bibliothekar(in); **li·brar·y** ['laibrəri] Bücherei *f*, Bibliothek *f*.

li·bret·to ♪ [li'bretəu] Libretto *n*, Text(buch *n*) *m*.

lice [lais] *pl. von louse*.

li·cence ['laisəns] Lizenz *f*; Erlaubnis *f*, Genehmigung *f*; Konzession *f*; (*bsd.* dichterische) Freiheit *f*; Zügellosigkeit *f*; *driving* ~ Führerschein *m*; ~ **plate** *mot.* Nummernschild *n*.

li·cense [~] **1.** *bsd. Am.* = *licence*; **2.** lizenzieren, berechtigen, konzessionieren, *et.* genehmigen; *Buch etc.* zensieren; (*fully*) *licensed* mit (voller) Schankerlaubnis; *licensing hours pl.* Ausschankstunden *f/pl.*; **li·cen·see** [~'si:] Lizenznehmer *m*, Konzessionsinhaber *m*; **li·cense plate** *Am.* = *licence plate*; **'li·cens·er** Lizenzgeber *m*; Zensor *m*.

li·cen·ti·ate *univ.* [lai'senʃiit] Lizentiat *m*.

li·cen·tious □ [lai'senʃəs] unzüchtig; ausschweifend.

li·chen ⚘ *u.* ⚕ ['laiken] Flechte *f*.

lich·gate ['litʃgeit] = *lychgate*.

lick [lik] **1.** Lecken *n*; *Am.* Salzlecke *f*; *sl.* Schlag *m*; F Tempo *n*;

2. lecken; belecken; F verdreschen; übertreffen, schlagen; ~ *the dust* im Staub kriechen; fallen; geschlagen werden; ~ *into shape* zurechtbiegen, -stutzen, in die richtige Form bringen; **'lick·er** Lecker *m*; ⊕ Öler *m*; **'lick·er·ish** lecker (-haft); lüstern (*after* nach); **'lick·ing** Lecken *n*; F Dresche *f*; **'lick·spit·tle** Speichellecker *m*.

lic·o·rice ♀ ['likəris] Lakritze *f*.

lid [lid] Deckel *m* (*sl. Hut*); (Augen-) Lid *n*; *put the ~ on it* F das Maß vollmachen.

li·do ['li:dəu] Strandbad *n*.

lie[1] [lai] **1.** Lüge *f*; *give s.o. the ~* j. Lügen strafen; *tell a ~* lügen; *white ~* Notlüge *f*; **2.** lügen.

lie[2] [~] **1.** Lage *f*; *the ~ of the land* die Lage der Dinge, die Sachlage; **2.** (*irr.*) liegen; ⚖ zulässig sein; ~ *by* still-, brachliegen; ~ *down* sich niederlegen; *take it lying down* nicht mucken, es über sich ergehen lassen; *as far as in me ~s* nach Kräften, soweit es in meinen Kräften steht; ~ *in* (*adv.*) in den Wochen liegen; länger liegen bleiben; (*prp.*) liegen in *od.* an (*dat.*); ~ *in wait for j-m* auflauern; ~ *over* ✝ nicht zur Verfallzeit bezahlt werden; aufgeschoben werden; ~ *to* ⚓ beiliegen; ~ *under e-r Sache* unterworfen sein, unterliegen (*dat.*); unter *Verdacht etc.* stehen; ~ *up* ruhen; das Bett hüten; *it ~s with you* es liegt bei dir; *let sleeping dogs ~ fig.* daran rühren wir lieber nicht.

lie-a·bed ['laiəbed] Langschläfer (-in); **lie-'down** Nickerchen *n*, Schläfchen *n*.

lief *lit.* [li:f] gern; **'lief·er** lieber.

liege *hist.* [li:dʒ] **1.** lehnspflichtig; **2.** *a. ~man* Lehnsmann *m*; *a. ~ lord* Lehnsherr *m*.

lie-in [lai'in]: *have a ~* sich gründlich ausschlafen.

li·en ⚖ ['liən] Pfandrecht *n*.

lieu [lju:]: *in ~ of* (an)statt.

lieu·ten·an·cy [lef'tenənsi, ⚓ le'tenənsi] Leutnantsstelle *f*; Statthalterschaft *f*; *die* Leutnants *m/pl.*

lieu·ten·ant [lef'tenənt, ⚓ le'tenənt] Leutnant *m*; Statthalter *m*; Stellvertreter *m*; **'~-'colo·nel** Oberstleutnant *m*; **'~-com'mand·er** Korvettenkapitän *m*; **'~-'gen·er·al** Generalleutnant *m*; **'~-'gov·er·nor** Vizegouverneur *m*.

life [laif], *pl.* **lives** [laivz] Leben *n*; Menschenleben *n*; Lebensbeschreibung *f*; ~ *and limb* Leib u. Leben; *for ~* auf Lebenszeit, lebenslänglich; *for one's ~, for dear ~* ums (liebe) Leben; *to the ~* naturgetreu (*Bild*); ~ *sentence* lebenslängliche Zuchthausstrafe *f*; *have the time of one's ~* die schönste Zeit seines Lebens haben; **'~-an·nu·i·ty** Leibrente *f*; **'~-as·sur·ance** Lebensversicherung *f*; **'~-belt** Rettungsgürtel *m*; **'~-blood** Herzblut *n*; **'~-boat** Rettungsboot *n*; **'~-buoy** Rettungsboje *f*; ~ **ex·pect·an·cy** Lebenserwartung *f*; **'~-giv·ing** lebenspendend; **'~-guard** Leibwache *f*; Rettungsschwimmer *m*, Bademeister *m am Strand*; **'~-'in·ter·est** lebenslängliche Nutznießung *f* (*in* aus); **'~-jack·et** ⚓ Schwimmweste *f*; **'life·less** □ leblos; kraftlos, matt (*a. fig.*); **'life·less·ness** Leblosigkeit *f etc.*; **'life·like** lebenswahr, naturgetreu; **'life-line** Rettungsleine *f*; **'life-long** lebenslänglich; **'life-pre·serv·er** *Am.* Schwimmgürtel *m*; Bleistock *m*, Totschläger *m*.

lif·er *sl.* ['laifə] lebenslängliche Zuchthausstrafe *f*.

life...: **'~-sav·er** *Australien*: Rettungsschwimmer *m*; **'~-'size(d)** lebensgroß; **'~-span** Lebensdauer *f*; Lebenserwartung *f*; **'~-strings** *pl.* Lebensfaden *m*; **'~-time** Lebenszeit *f*; **'~-'work** Lebenswerk *n*.

lift [lift] **1.** Heben *n*, ⊕ Hub *m*; *phys.*, ✈ Auftrieb *m*; *fig.* Erhebung *f*; Aufzug *m*, Fahrstuhl *m*; *give s.o. a ~* j-m helfen; j. (im Auto) mitnehmen; **2.** *v/t.* (*a. fig. Maßnahme etc.* auf)heben; hoch-, anheben; *oft ~ up Augen, Stimme etc.* erheben (*a. fig.*); beseitigen; abnehmen; *sl.* klauen, stehlen; *v/i.* sich heben; **'~-at·tend·ant, '~-boy** Fahrstuhlführer *m*; **'lift·er** *der, die, das* Hebende; Dieb *m*; **'lift·ing** ⊕ Hebe...; Hub...; ~ *power* ✈ Auftrieb *m*; **'lift-off** Start *m*, Abheben *n* (*Hubschrauber, Rakete*).

lig·a·ment *anat.* ['ligəmənt] Band *n*.

lig·a·ture ['ligətʃuə] **1.** Binde *f*; ⚕ Verband *m*; ♪, *typ.* Ligatur *f*; **2.** (ab)binden.

light[1] [lait] **1.** Licht *n* (*a. fig.*);

Fenster *n*; Aspekt *m*, Gesichtspunkt *m*; Feuer *n*; Glanz *m*; *fig.* Leuchte *f*; *~s pl.* Fähigkeiten *f/pl.*; *a box of ~s* eine Schachtel Streichhölzer; *in the ~ of* im Lichte (*gen.*), angesichts (*gen.*); *bring (come) to ~* an den Tag bringen (kommen); *will you give me a ~* darf ich Sie um Feuer bitten; *put a ~ to* anzünden; *see the ~* das Licht der Welt erblicken; *fig.* verstehen, begreifen; **2.** licht, hell; blond; *~ ale* helles, leichtes Ale *n*; **3.** (*irr.*) *v/t. oft ~ up* be-, erleuchten; anzünden; *j-m* leuchten; *v/i. mst ~ up* aufleuchten; *~ out Am. sl. schnell* losziehen, abhauen.

light[2] [~] **1.** □ *adj. u. adv.* leicht (*a. Speisen, Stoffe, Regen, Truppen, Gang, Münzen, Charakter, Kenntnisse etc.*); *~ current* ⚡ Schwachstrom *m*; *~ reading* Unterhaltungslektüre *f*; *make ~ of et.* leicht *od.* auf die leichte Schulter nehmen; **2.** *su.* = *lights*; **3.** *~ on, ~ upon* stoßen auf (*acc.*), geraten an (*acc.*); zufällig kommen zu; sich niederlassen auf (*dat.*) (*Vogel*); fallen auf (*acc.*).

light-col·o(u)red ['laitkʌləd] hell (*Kleid etc.*).

light·en[1] ['laitn] erleuchten, erhellen; sich erhellen; blitzen.

light·en[2] [~] leichter machen *od.* werden, (sich) erleichtern (*a. fig.*).

light·er[1] ['laitə] Anzünder *m*; (Taschen)Feuerzeug *n*.

light·er[2] ⚓ [~] L(e)ichter *m* (*leichtes Entladungsschiff*).

light...: '**~-fin·gered** geschickt; langfingerig, diebisch; '**~-foot·ed** leichtfüßig; flink; '**~-hand·ed** e-e leichte Hand habend; mit leichter Hand (gemacht); *fig.* geschickt in der Menschenführung; '**~-hand·ed·ness** Geschick *n*, leichte Hand *f*; '**~-'head·ed** wirr im Kopfe; leichtsinnig; '**~-'heart·ed** □ leichtherzig; fröhlich; **~-'heav·y·weight** *Sport*: **1.** Halbschwergewichts...; Leichtschwergewichts...; **2.** Halbschwergewichtler *m*; Leichtschwergewichtler *m*; '**~-house** Leuchtturm *m*.

light·ing ['laitiŋ] Beleuchtung *f*; Anzünden *n*; *~ up* Aufblenden *n*.

light·ly ['laitli] *adv.* leicht; leichtsinnig, -fertig; heiter; **light me·ter** *phot.* Belichtungsmesser *m*; **light--'mid·dle·weight** *Sport*: **1.** Halbmittelgewichts...; **2.** Halbmittelgewichtler *m*; '**light'mind·ed** leichtsinnig; '**light·ness** Leichtigkeit *f*; Leichtsinn *m*, -fertigkeit *f*.

light·ning ['laitniŋ] Blitz *m*; *like ~, with ~ speed* blitzschnell; '**~-ar-'rest·er** Blitzschutzsicherung *f*; **~ bug** *Am.* Leuchtkäfer *m*; '**~-con·duc·tor**, '**~-rod** Blitzableiter *m*.

light pen ['laitpen] *Computer*: Lichtgriffel *m*.

lights [laits] *pl.* Lunge *f von Tieren.*

light·ship ['laitʃip] Feuerschiff *n*.

light·some ['laitsəm] anmutig; lustig, fröhlich; leichtfertig.

light-weight ['laitweit] *Sport*: Leichtgewicht *n*.

light-'wel·ter·weight *Sport*: **1.** Halbweltergewichts...; **2.** Halbweltergewichtler *m*.

lig·ne·ous ['ligniəs] holzig; holzartig; **lig·nite** ['lignait] Braunkohle *f*.

lik·a·ble ['laikəbl] liebenswert, sympathisch, angenehm.

like [laik] **1.** *adj. u. adv.* gleich; ähnlich; wie; *~ a man* wie ein Mann; *such ~* dergleichen; *feel ~* F sich aufgelegt fühlen zu *et.*, Lust haben auf *et.*; *s. look*; *something ~ ...* so etwa ...; *~ that* so; *what is he ~?* wie sieht er aus?; wie ist er?; *that's more ~ it* das läßt sich eher hören; **2.** Gleiche *m, f, n*; *~s pl.* Neigungen *f/pl.*; *his ~* seinesgleichen; *the ~* der-, desgleichen; *the ~(s) of* F eine(r) wie, solche wie; **3.** gut leiden können, mögen, gern haben; *~ best* am liebsten haben; *how do you ~ London?* wie gefällt Ihnen London?, wie finden Sie London?; *I should ~ to know* ich möchte wissen.

like·a·ble ['laikəbl] = *likable*.

like·li·hood ['laiklihud] Wahrscheinlichkeit *f*; '**like·ly** wahrscheinlich; geeignet, richtig; aussichtsreich; *as ~ as not* sehr wahrscheinlich; *he is ~ to die* er wird wahrscheinlich sterben.

like-mind·ed ['laik'maindid] gleichgesinnt; '**lik·en** vergleichen (*to* mit); '**like·ness** Ähnlichkeit *f*; Abbild *n*; Gestalt *f*; *have one's ~ taken* sich malen *od.* photographieren lassen; '**like·wise** gleich-, ebenfalls.

lik·ing ['laikiŋ] (*for*) Neigung *f* (für, zu), Gefallen *n* (an *dat.*); *to s.o.'s ~* nach j-s Geschmack.

li·lac ['lailək] **1.** lila; **2.** ⚘ spanischer Flieder *m.*
Lil·li·pu·tian [lili'pju:ʃjən] **1.** Liliputaner *m*; **2.** winzig, liliputanerhaft.
lilt [lilt] **1.** trällern; **2.** rhythmische Weise *f*; Schwung *m.*
lil·y ⚘ ['lili] Lilie *f*; ~ *of the valley* Maiglöckchen *n*; '**~-'liv·ered** feige; '**~-white** schneeweiß.
limb[1] [lim] *Körper*-Glied *n*; ⚘ Ast *m*; F Range *f*; *out on a* ~ F in e-r gefährlichen Lage.
limb[2] *ast.*, ⚘ [~] Rand *m.*
limbed [limd] ...gliederig.
lim·ber[1] ['limbə] **1.** ⚔ Protze *f*; **2.** *mst* ~ *up* aufprotzen.
lim·ber[2] [~] **1.** biegsam, geschmeidig; **2.** ~ *up* (sich) geschmeidig machen, (sich) lockern.
lim·bo ['limbəu] Vorhölle *f*; *sl.* Gefängnis *n*; Rumpelkammer *f*; *fig.* Vergessenheit *f.*
lime[1] [laim] **1.** Kalk *m*; Vogelleim *m*; **2.** mit Kalk düngen; *Rute* leimen (*a. fig.*).
lime[2] ⚘ [~] Linde *f.*
lime[3] ⚘ [~] Limone *f*; '**~-juice** Limonensaft *m.*
lime...: '**~-kiln** Kalkofen *m*; '**~-light** Kalklicht *n*; Bühnenlicht *n*; *fig.* Mittelpunkt *m* des öffentlichen Interesses.
lim·er·ick ['limərik] Limerick *m* (*absurdes Gedicht*).
lime...: '**~·stone** Kalkstein *m*; '**~-tree** ⚘ Linde(nbaum *m*) *f*; '**~-twig** Leimrute *f.*
lim·it ['limit] **1.** Grenze *f*; *in* (*off*) *~s* Zutritt gestattet (verboten) (*to* für); *that is the ~!* F das ist der Gipfel!; das ist (doch) die Höhe!; *go the ~ Am.* F bis zum Äußersten gehen; **2.** begrenzen; beschränken (*to* auf *acc.*); **lim·i'ta·tion** Begrenzung *f*, Beschränkung *f*; *fig.* Grenze *f*; ⚖ Verjährung *f*; '**lim·it·ed 1.** beschränkt, begrenzt (*to* auf *acc.*); ~ (*liability*) *company* Gesellschaft *f* mit beschränkter Haftung; ~ *in time* befristet; **2.** Schnellzug *m*, -bus *m mit Platzkarten*; '**lim·it·less** □ grenzen-, schrankenlos.
limn † [lim] (ab)malen; schildern.
lim·ou·sine ['limu:zi:n] Limousine *f* mit Trennwand *zwischen Fahrer u. Passagieren.*
limp[1] [limp] **1.** hinken (*a. fig.*), humpeln; sich mühsam bewegen; **2.** Hinken *n.*
limp[2] [~] schlaff; weich.
lim·pet ['limpit] *zo.* Napfschnecke *f*; *fig.* j. der sein Amt nicht abgeben will; *fig.* Klette *f*; ~ **mine** ⚓, ⚔ Haftmine *f.*
lim·pid □ ['limpid] klar, durchsichtig, hell, rein; '**lim·pid·ness** Klarheit *f*, Reinheit *f.*
lim·y ['laimi] kalkig.
lin·age ['lainidʒ] Zeilenzahl *f*; Zeilenhonorar *n.*
linch·pin ['lintʃpin] Vorstecker *m am Wagenrad.*
lin·den ⚘ ['lindən] Linde *f.*
line[1] [lain] **1.** Linie *f*; Reihe *f*; Zeile *f*; Vers *m*; Strich *m*; Falte *f*, Furche *f*; (Menschen)Schlange *f*; Folge *f*; Verkehrsgesellschaft *f*; (Eisenbahn-, Autobus-, Schiffahrts)Linie *f*; Strecke *f*; *teleph.* Leitung *f*; Branche *f*, Fach *n*, Sparte *f*; Leine *f*, Schnur *f*; Äquator *m*; Grenze *f*; Richtung *f*; *fig.* Richtschnur *f*; Maßnahme *f*, Methode *f*; ☤ Ware *f*, Artikel *m*, Sorte *f*; ⚔ Linie(ntruppe) *f*; Front *f*; *~s pl.* Richtlinien *f/pl.*, Grundsätze *m/pl.*; Grundlage *f*; *Trau- etc.* Schein *m*; *thea.* Rolle *f*; ~ *of battle* Gefechtslinie *f*; ~ *of business* Geschäftszweig *m*, Fach *n*; ~ *of conduct* Lebensweise *f*; *ship of the* ~ Linienschiff *n*; *hard ~s* hartes Los *n*, Pech *n*; *all down the* ~ auf der ganzen Linie; *in* ~ *with* in Übereinstimmung mit; *that is not in my* ~ das schlägt nicht in mein Fach; *stand in* ~ Schlange stehen; *fall into* ~ *with s.o.* sich j-m anschließen; *draw the* ~ *fig.* nicht mehr mitmachen; *party* ~ *pol.* Parteilinie *f*; *party* ~, *shared* ~ *teleph.* Gemeinschaftsanschluß *m*; *toe the* ~ *pol.* sich der (Partei)Disziplin beugen; *hold the* ~ *tel.* am Apparat bleiben; **2.** *v/t.* liniieren; *fig.* furchen; aufstellen; *Weg etc.* umsäumen, einfassen; ~ *the streets* die Straßen säumen; ~ *out* entwerfen; ~ *through* durchstreichen; *v/i.* ~ *up* sich auf- *od.* anstellen.
line[2] [~] *Kleid etc.* füttern; sich *die Taschen etc.* füllen.
lin·e·age ['liniidʒ] Abstammung *f*; Familie *f*; Stammbaum *m*; **lin·e·al** □ ['~əl] gerade, direkt (*Nach-*

komme etc.); **lin·e·a·ment** ['~əmənt] (Gesichts)Zug *m*; **lin·e·ar** ['~ə] linear, geradlinig; Längen...

line·man ['lainmən] Telegraphenarbeiter *m*, Störungssucher *m*; *Am.* = *linesman*.

lin·en ['linin] **1.** Leinen *n*, Leinwand *f*; Wäsche *f*; *wash one's dirty ~ in public fig.* s-e schmutzige Wäsche vor allen Leuten waschen; **2.** leinen; ~ **bas·ket** Wäschekorb *m*; '~**-clos·et**, '~**-cup·board** Wäscheschrank *m*; '~**-drap·er** Weißwarenhändler *m*, Wäschegeschäft *n*.

lin·er ['lainə] Linienschiff *n*, Passagierdampfer *m*; Verkehrsflugzeug *n*; Zeilenschinder *m*; **lines·man** ['lainzmən] *Sport*: Linienrichter *m*; '**line-up** Reihe *f*; Verbindung *f*; *Sport*: Aufstellung *f*.

ling[1] *ichth.* [liŋ] Leng(fisch) *m*.

ling[2] ⚘ [~] Heidekraut *n*.

lin·ger ['liŋgə] zögern, säumen; (ver)weilen; sich aufhalten (*over, upon* bei); sich hinziehen (*Krankheit*); dahinsiechen (*Kranker*); nachklingen (*Ton*); ~ *at*, ~ *about* sich herumdrücken an *od.* bei (*dat.*).

lin·ge·rie ['læ̃:nʒəri:] Damenunterwäsche *f*.

lin·ger·ing ['liŋgəriŋ] □ zögernd; bleibend; schleichend (*Krankheit etc.*); in Resten vorhanden.

lin·go ['liŋgəu] Kauderwelsch *n*.

lin·gua fran·ca ['liŋgwə'fræŋkə] Verkehrssprache *f*.

lin·gual ['liŋgwəl] Zungen...

lin·guist ['liŋgwist] Linguist(in); Sprachenkenner(in); **lin'guis·tic** (*~ally*) sprachwissenschaftlich, linguistisch; **lin'guis·tics** *sg.* Sprachwissenschaft *f*, Linguistik *f*.

lin·i·ment ⚕ ['linimənt] Liniment *n*, Einreibemittel *n*.

lin·ing ['lainiŋ] Futter *n e-s Kleides*; Besatz *m*; *fig.* Saum *m*; Verkleidung *f e-r Wand etc.*; *every cloud has a silver ~* jedes Unglück hat auch sein Gutes.

link[1] [liŋk] **1.** *Ketten*-Glied *n*, Gelenk *n*; Manschettenknopf *m*; *fig.* Bindeglied *n*, Band *n*; **2.** (sich) verketten, (sich) verbinden.

link[2] *hist.* [~] Fackel *f*.

link·man ['liŋkmən] Fackelträger *m*.

links [liŋks] *pl.* Dünen *f/pl.*; *a. golf-~* Golfplatz *m*.

link·up ['liŋkʌp] Zusammenschluß *m*; *Raumfahrt*: Kopplung *f*.

lin·net *orn.* ['linit] Hänfling *m*.

li·no ['lainəu] = *linoleum*; '~**-cut** Linolschnitt *m*.

li·no·leum [li'nəuljəm] Linoleum *n*.

lin·o·type *typ.* ['lainəutaip] Linotype *f*, Zeilensetz- und -gießmaschine *f*.

lin·seed ['linsi:d] Leinsamen *m*; ~ *oil* Leinöl *n*.

lin·sey-wool·sey ['linzi'wulzi] Halbwollzeug *n*.

lint ⚕ [lint] Scharpie *f*.

lin·tel ⌂ ['lintl] Oberschwelle *f*; Fenstersturz *m*.

li·on ['laiən] Löwe *m* (*a. ast. u. fig.*); *fig.* Größe *f*, Berühmtheit *f*; *the ~'s share* der Löwenanteil; '**li·on·ess** Löwin *f*; '**li·on-heart·ed** tapfer; '~**-hunt·er** *fig.* Prominentenjäger (-in); '**li·on·ize** *j.* als Zelebrität herumreichen, *j.* feiern.

lip [lip] Lippe *f* (*a.* ⚘); Rand *m e-r Tasse, Wunde*; *sl.* Unverschämtheit *f*; *curl one's ~* die Lippen verächtlich schürzen; *none of your ~!* keine Unverschämtheiten!; '~**-read** von den Lippen ablesen; '~**-serv·ice** Lippendienst *m*; '~**·stick** Lippenstift *m*.

liq·ue·fac·tion [likwi'fækʃən] Verflüssigung *f*; **liq·ue·fi·a·ble** ['~faiəbl] schmelzbar; '**liq·ue·fy** (sich) verflüssigen; schmelzen; **liq·ues·cent** [li'kwesnt] sich (leicht) verflüssigend.

li·queur [li'kjuə] Likör *m*.

liq·uid ['likwid] **1.** □ flüssig, fließend; ✝ liquid; klar (*Augen, Luft etc.*); **2.** Flüssigkeit *f*; *gr.* Liquida *f*.

liq·ui·date ['likwideit] ✝ liquidieren; *Schulden* tilgen; **liq·ui'da·tion** Abwicklung *f*, Liquidation *f*; '**liq·ui·da·tor** Liquidator *m*; '**liq·uid·iz·er** Mixer *m*, Mixgerät *n*; Entsafter *m*.

liq·uor ['likə] **1.** Flüssigkeit *f*; Alkohol *m*, alkoholisches Getränk *n*; *in ~, the worse for ~* betrunken; **2.** *a. ~ up sl.* einen heben.

liq·uo·rice ⚘ ['likəris] Lakritze *f*.

li·ra ['liərə], *pl.* **li·re** ['~ri] Lira *f* (*italienische Währungseinheit*).

lisp [lisp] **1.** Lispeln *n*; **2.** lispeln.

lis·som(e) ['lisəm] geschmeidig, wendig.

list[1] [list] **1.** Liste *f*, Verzeichnis *n*;

Rand *m*, Leiste *f*; Webkante *f*; **2.** *v/t.* (in e-e Liste) eintragen; verzeichnen, aufführen; katalogisieren; *v/i.* sich *als Soldat* anwerben lassen.

list[2] ⚓ [~] **1.** Schlagseite *f*; **2.** Schlagseite haben.

list·ed ['listid] unter Denkmalsschutz (stehend).

list·en ['lisn] (*to*) hören, horchen (auf *acc.*); anhören (*acc.*); zuhören (*dat.*); lauschen (*dat.*); folgen (*dat.*); ~ *in teleph.*, *Radio*: (mit)hören; ~ *in to Radio*: hören; **'lis·ten·er** Horcher(in), (Zu)Hörer(in).

lis·ten·ing ['lisniŋ] Horch...; ~ *apparatus* Horchgerät *n*; **'~-post** Horchposten *m*.

list·less □ ['listlis] gleichgültig; lust-, teilnahmslos; **'list·less·ness** Lustlosigkeit *f*.

lists [lists] *pl.* Schranken *f/pl.*, Kampfplatz *m*; *enter the ~s fig.* in die Schranken treten.

lit [lit] **1.** *pret. u. p.p. von light*[1] *3*; **2.** ~ *up sl.* beschwipst.

lit·a·ny *eccl.* ['litəni] Litanei *f*.

li·ter *Am.* ['li:tə] = *litre*.

lit·er·a·cy ['litərəsi] Fähigkeit *f* zu lesen u. zu schreiben; **'lit·er·al 1.** □ Buchstaben...; buchstäblich; am Buchstaben klebend; wörtlich; *fig.* nüchtern, prosaisch; **2.** *a.* ~ *error* Druckfehler *m*; **'lit·er·al·ism, 'lit·er·al·ness** Buchstabenglaube *m*.

lit·er·ar·y □ ['litərəri] literarisch; Literatur...; Schrift..., Buch...; ~ *man* Schriftsteller *m*; literarisch Interessierte *m*; **lit·er·ate** ['~rit] **1.** des Lesens u. Schreibens kundig; gebildet; literarisch; **2.** Gebildete *m*; **lit·e·ra·ti** [litə'rɑ:ti:] *pl.* Literaten *m/pl.*, *die* Gelehrten *m/pl.*; **lit·e'ra·tim** [~tim] buchstäblich; **lit·er·a·ture** ['litəritʃə] Literatur *f*, Schrifttum *n*.

lithe(**·some**) ['laið(səm)] geschmeidig, wendig.

lith·o·graph ['liθəugrɑ:f] **1.** Lithographie *f*, Steindruck *m* (*Bild od. Druck*); **2.** lithographieren; **li·thog·ra·pher** [li'θɔgrəfə] Lithograph *m*; **lith·o·graph·ic** [liθəu'græfik] (*~ally*) lithographisch; **li·thog·ra·phy** [li'θɔgrəfi] Lithographie *f*, Steindruck *m*.

Lith·u·a·ni·an [liθju:'einjən] **1.** litauisch; **2.** Litauer(in); Litauisch *n*.

lit·i·gant ⚖ ['litigənt] **1.** streitend; **2.** (streitende) Partei *f*; **lit·i·gate** ['~geit] prozessieren *od.* streiten (um); **lit·i'ga·tion** Prozeß *m*; **li·ti·gious** □ [li'tidʒəs] streitsüchtig; ⚖ streitig, strittig.

lit·mus ⚗ ['litməs] Lackmus *m*; **'~-pa·per** Lackmuspapier *n*.

li·to·tes *rhet.* ['laitəuti:z] Litotes *f* (*Bejahung durch doppelte Verneinung*).

li·tre ['li:tə] Liter *n*, *m*.

lit·ter ['litə] **1.** Sänfte *f*; Tragbahre *f*; Streu *f*; Abfall *m*; Wust *m*; Unordnung *f*; Wurf *m junger Tiere*; **2.** *Junge* werfen; ~ *down e-m Tier* streuen; ver-, bestreuen; ~ *up Zimmer* in Unordnung bringen; **'~-bas·ket, '~-bin** Abfallkorb *m*; **'~-bug** F *j., der Abfall auf der Straße wegwirft*.

lit·tle ['litl] **1.** *adj.* klein; kurz (*Zeit*); gering(fügig); wenig; kleinlich; *a ~ one* ein Kleines (*Kind*); *a ~ house* ein Häuschen; *my ~ Mary* F mein Magen; *his ~ ways* seine komische Art; ~ *people* Heinzelmännchen *n/pl.*; **2.** *adv.* wenig; *a ~ red* schwachrot; **3.** Wenige *n*, Kleinigkeit *f*; ~ *by ~*, *by ~ and ~* nach und nach; *for a ~* für ein Weilchen; *not a ~* nicht wenig; **'~-go** F *univ.* Vorexamen *n*; **'lit·tle·ness** Kleinheit *f*; Geringfügigkeit *f*; Kleinigkeit *f*.

lit·to·ral ['litərəl] **1.** Küsten...; **2.** Küstengebiet *n*.

lit·ur·gy *eccl.* ['litə:dʒi] Liturgie *f*.

liv·a·ble ['livəbl] F wohnlich (*Haus etc.*); erträglich (*Leben*); *mst ~-with* F umgänglich (*Person*).

live 1. [liv] *allg.* leben; wohnen; fortleben, -dauern, bestehen; sich (er)nähren, leben (*on* von); *Leben* führen; ~ *to see* erleben; ~ *s.th. down* et. durch guten Lebenswandel vergessen machen; ~ *in* (*out*) im (außer) Hause wohnen (*Hausangestellte*); ~ *through* durchmachen, -stehen, überleben; ~ *up to s-m Ruf* gerecht werden, *s-n Grundsätzen* gemäß leben; *Versprechen* halten; ~ *and learn* man lernt nie aus; ~ *and let* ~ leben u. leben lassen; **2.** [laiv] lebendig; richtig; aktuell; glühend, brennend (*Kohle etc.*); ⚔ scharf (*Munition*); ⚡ stromführend; *Radio*: Direkt...; Original...; ~ *wire fig.* energiegeladener Mensch *m*; ~ *broadcast* Direktübertragung *f*;

live·a·ble ['livəbl] *s. livable*; **lived** ...lebig; **live·li·hood** ['laivlihud] Unterhalt *m*; '**live·li·ness** Lebhaftigkeit *f*; **live·long** ['livlɔŋ]: *the ~ day poet.* den lieben langen Tag; **live·ly** ['laivli] lebhaft; lebendig; aufregend; schnell; bewegt; *make things ~ for s.o.* j. in Atem halten, j-m einheizen.
liv·en ['laivn] *mst ~ up* F sich beleben, munter werden.
liv·er¹ ['livə] Lebende *m*; *fast ~* Lebemann *m*; *good ~* Schlemmer *m*.
liv·er² [~] Leber *f*; '**liv·er·ish** F leberleidend; mürrisch.
liv·er·y¹ ['livəri] = *liverish*.
liv·er·y² [~] Livree *f*; (Amts)Tracht *f*; *fig.* Kleid *n*; = *~-stable*; **~ com·pa·ny** (Handels)Zunft *f* der *City of London*; '**~·man** Zunftmitglied *n* der *City of London*; '**~-sta·ble** Mietstall *m*.
lives [laivz] *pl. von life*; '**live-stock** Vieh(bestand *m*) *n*; '**live-weight** Lebendgewicht *n*.
liv·id ['livid] bläulich; fahl; wütend, wild; **li'vid·i·ty** Fahlheit *f*.
liv·ing ['liviŋ] **1.** □ lebend(ig); *the ~ image of* das genaue Ebenbild *gen.*; *the ~ theatre* die Bühne, das Theater (*im Ggs. zu Film u. Fernsehen*); *the ~ pl.* die Lebenden *pl.*; *in ~ memory* seit Menschengedenken; **2.** Leben *n*; Wohnen *n*; Lebensweise *f*; Lebensunterhalt *m*; *eccl.* Pfründe *f*; '**~-room** Wohnzimmer *n*; '**~-space** Lebensraum *m*.
Li·vo·ni·an [li'vəunjən] **1.** livländisch; **2.** Livländer(in).
liz·ard ['lizəd] Eidechse *f*.
Liz·zie *Am. co.* ['lizi] billiges kleines Auto *n*; alte Kiste *f*.
lla·ma ['lɑːmə] Lama(wolle *f*) *n*.
Lloyd's [lɔidz] Lloyd's (*Gemeinschaft von Seeversicherern in London*); *A 1 at ~* erstklassig.
lo † [ləu] siehe!
loach *ichth.* [ləutʃ] Schmerle *f*.
load [ləud] **1.** Last *f* (*a. fig.*); Ladung *f*; ⊕ (Arbeits)Belastung *f*, Leistung *f*; *~s of* F e-e Menge; **2.** *Güter, Gewehr, Kamera etc.* laden; beladen; beschweren (*a. fig.*); *fig.* überhäufen (*with* mit); *den Magen* überladen; *~ test* Belastungsprobe *f*; *~ed* bleibeschwert (*Stock*); *~ed dice pl.* falsche Würfel *m/pl.*; *~ed question* Fangfrage *f*; *~ the dice against s.o. fig.* j. ins Unrecht setzen; j-s Chancen verringern; zu j-s Ungunsten sprechen; '**load·er** (Ver-)Lader *m*; (Gewehr)Lader *m*; '**load·ing** **1.** Lade...; **2.** Laden *n*; Ladung *f*, Fracht *f*; '**load-line** ⚓ Ladelinie *f*; '**load·stone** Magnet(eisenstein) *m*.
loaf¹ [ləuf], *pl.* **loaves** [ləuvz] *Brot-*Laib *m*; *Zucker-*Hut *m*; *Fleisch-*, *Fisch-*Kloß *m*; *sl.* Kopf *m*, Verstand *m*; *use your ~* streng deinen Grips an.
loaf² [~] herumlungern, bummeln; '**loaf·er** Müßiggänger *m*, Faulenzer *m*, Bummler *m*.
loaf-sug·ar ['ləufʃugə] Würfelzucker *m*.
loam [ləum] Lehm *m*, Mutterboden *m*, Ackerkrume *f*; '**loam·y** lehmig.
loan [ləun] **1.** Anleihe *f*, Darlehen *n*; Leihen *n*; Leihgabe *f*; *on ~* leihweise; *ask for the ~ of s.th.* et. leihweise erbitten; *put out to ~* verleihen; **2.** *bsd. Am.* ausleihen; '**~-word** *gr.* Lehnwort *n*.
loath [ləuθ] abgeneigt; *be ~ for s.o. to do s.th.* dagegen sein, daß j. et. tut; *nothing ~* durchaus nicht abgeneigt.
loathe [ləuð] sich ekeln vor (*dat.*); verabscheuen; nicht mögen; '**loath·ing** Ekel *m*; Abscheu *m*; **loath·some** □ ['~səm] ekelhaft; verhaßt; '**loath·some·ness** Ekelhaftigkeit *f*.
loaves [louvz] *pl. von loaf*¹.
lob [lɔb] *Tennis*: **1.** Hochschlag *m*; **2.** *Ball* hochschlagen.
lob·by ['lɔbi] **1.** Vorhalle *f*, Vestibül *n*; *parl.* Wandelgang *m*; *thea.* Foyer *n*; *parl.* Lobby *f*, Interessenvertreter *m/pl.*; **2.** *v/i. parl.* s-n Einfluß geltend machen; *v/t. Gesetz etc.* mit Hilfe der Lobby durchbringen; '**lob·by·ist** *parl.* Lobbyist *m*, Interessenvertreter *m*.
lobe *anat.*, ⚘ [ləub] Lappen *m*; *~ of the ear* Ohrläppchen *n*.
lo·be·lia ⚘ [ləu'biːljə] Lobelie *f*.
lob·ster ['lɔbstə] Hummer *m*.
lo·cal □ ['ləukəl] **1.** örtlich; Orts...; lokal; am Ort befindlich; *s. branch*; *~ an(a)esthetic* örtliche Betäubung *f*; *~ call teleph.* Ortsgespräch *n*; *~ colour* Lokalkolorit *n*; *~ elections pl.* Kommunalwahlen *f/pl.*; *~ government* Gemeindeverwaltung *f*; **2.** *Zeitung*: Lokalnachricht *f*; *a. ~ train* 🚂 Vorortzug *m*; F Wirtshaus *n* (am Ort); *~s pl.*

Ortsbewohner *m/pl.*; **lo·cale** [ləu'kɑːl] Schauplatz *m e-s Ereignisses*; **lo·cal·ism** ['~kəlizəm] Lokalpatriotismus *m*; Provinzialismus *m*; **lo·cal·i·ty** [~'kæliti] Örtlichkeit *f*; Lage *f*; **lo·cal·ize** ['~kəlaiz] lokalisieren.

lo·cate [ləu'keit] *v/t.* versetzen, -legen, unterbringen; ausfindig machen; *Am.* an-, festlegen; *be* ~*d* gelegen sein; wohnen; *v/i.* sich niederlassen; **lo'ca·tion** Standort *m*; Lage *f*; Niederlassung *f*; ⚖ Vermietung *f*; *Am.* Anweisung *f* von Land; angewiesenes Land *n*; Ort *m*; Eingeborenenviertel *n bsd. in Südafrika*; *Film*: Gelände *n* für Außenaufnahmen; *on* ~ auf Außenaufnahme.

loch *schott.* [lɔx] See *m*; Bucht *f*.

lock[1] [lɔk] **1.** *Tür-, Gewehr- etc.* Schloß *n*; Schleuse(nkammer) *f*; ⊕ Sperrvorrichtung *f*; Gedränge *n*, Stauung *f von Wagen*; ~, *stock and barrel* völlig, gänzlich, mit allem Drum u. Dran; **2.** (ver)schließen (*a. fig.*), absperren; ein Schloß haben, sich verschließen lassen; ⊕ blockieren, sperren, greifen; umschließen, umfassen, ineinander verschlingen; ~ *s.th. away* et. wegschließen; ~ *s.o. in* j. einsperren; ~ *s.o. out* j. aussperren; ~ *up* wegschließen; abschließen; einsperren; *in e-e Irrenanstalt* einliefern; *Geld* fest anlegen.

lock[2] [~] Locke *f*; Wolldecke *f*; ~*s pl. co.* Haare *n/pl.*

lock·age ['lɔkidʒ] Schleusengeld *n*; Schleusen(anlage *f*) *f/pl.*; **'lock·er** Schrank *m*, Kasten *m*; *go to Davy Jones's* ~ ertrinken; **lock·et** ['lɔkit] Medaillon *n*.

lock...: **'~-gates** *pl.* Schleusentore *n/pl.*; **'~-jaw** Kaumuskelkrampf *m*; **'~-keep·er** Schleusenwärter *m*; **'~-nut** ⊕ Gegenmutter *f*; **'~-out** Aussperrung *f von Arbeitern*; **'~-smith** Schlosser *m*; **'~-stich** Steppstich *m*; **'~-up 1.** Haftzelle *f*; ✝ zinslose (Kapital)Anlage *f*; **2.** verschließbar.

lo·co *Am. sl.* ['ləukəu] verrückt.

lo·co·mo·tion [ləukə'məuʃən] Fortbewegung(sfähigkeit) *f*; **lo·co·mo·tive** ['~tiv] **1.** (sich) fortbewegend; beweglich; **2.** *a.* ~ *engine* Lokomotive *f*.

lo·cust ['ləukəst] Heuschrecke *f*; *a.* ~*-tree* ⚘ unechte Akazie *f*.

lo·cu·tion [ləu'kjuːʃən] Ausdruck *m*, Redensart *f*.

lode ⚒ [ləud] Erzgang *m*; **'~·star** Leitstern *m* (*a. fig.*); Polarstern *m*; **'~·stone** Magnet(eisenstein) *m*.

lodge [lɔdʒ] **1.** (*bsd.* Jagd)Hütte *f*, Häuschen *n*; (Forst-, Park-, Pförtner)Haus *n*; Portierloge *f*; *Freimaurer*-Loge *f*; **2.** *v/t.* beherbergen, (*bsd.* als Mieter) aufnehmen; unterbringen; *Geld* hinterlegen; *Klage* einreichen; *Kugel* hineinschießen, *Hieb* versetzen; *Korn* umlegen; *v/i.* (*bsd.* zur Miete) wohnen; logieren; steckenbleiben; **'lodge·ment** *s. lodgment*; **'lodg·er** (Unter)Mieter (-in); **'lodg·ing** Unterkunft *f*; ~*s pl.* möbliertes Zimmer *n*; Wohnung *f*; **'lodg·ing-house** Fremdenheim *n*; **'lodg·ment** ⚖ Einreichung *f*; Deponierung *f*; Anhäufung *f*.

lo·ess ['ləuis] Löß *m*.

loft [lɔft] (Dach)Boden *m*; Empore *f*, Chor *m*, *n*; **'loft·i·ness** Höhe *f*, Erhabenheit *f* (*a. fig.*); Hochmut *m*; **'loft·y** □ sehr hoch; erhaben; stolz, hochmütig.

log [lɔg] Klotz *m*; Block *m*; *gefällter* Baumstamm *m*; ⚓ Log *n*; = *log-book*.

lo·gan·ber·ry ⚘ ['ləugənbəri] Loganbeere *f* (*Kreuzung zwischen Brombeere u. Himbeere*).

log·a·rithm A ['lɔgəriθm] Logarithmus *m*.

log...: **'~-book** ⚓ Log-, *mot.* Fahrten-, ✈ Bordbuch *n*; ~ **cab·in** Blockhaus *n*; **logged** (mit Wasser) vollgesogen; **log·ger** ['lɔgə] Holzfäller *m*; **'log·ger·head:** *be at* ~*s* sich in den Haaren liegen.

log·gia ['lɔdʒə] Loggia *f*.

log·ging ['lɔgiŋ] Holzfällen *n*; ~ *camp* Holzfällerlager *n*; **log house, log hut** Blockhaus *n*.

log·ic ['lɔdʒik] Logik *f*; **'log·i·cal** □ logisch; **lo·gi·cian** [ləu'dʒiʃən] Logiker *m*.

lo·gis·tics ⚔ [ləu'dʒistiks] *oft sg.* Logistik *f* (*Nachschubwesen*).

log·roll *bsd. pol.* ['lɔgrəul] (sich gegenseitig) in die Tasche arbeiten; **'log·roll·ing** *pol.* Kuhhandel *m*; *Sport*: Baumstammtreten *n*.

log·wood ['lɔgwud] Kampeseholz *n*.

loin [lɔin] Lende *f*; *Fleischerei*:

Lenden-, Nierenstück *n*; *gird up one's ~s* s-e Lenden gürten, sich reisefertig machen; '**~-cloth** Lendenschurz *m*.

loi·ter ['lɔitə] trödeln, bummeln; (herum)lungern; schlendern; *~ away* vertrödeln; '**loi·ter·er** Trödler(in), Bummler(in); Faulenzer (-in).

loll [lɔl] (sich) lehnen, (sich) hinstrecken, (sich) rekeln; *~ about* herumlungern; *~ out* heraushängen (lassen) (*Zunge*).

lol·li·pop F ['lɔlipɔp] Lutscher *m* (*Bonbon am Stiel*); *~* **man,** *~* **woman** F Schülerlotse *m*, -lotsin *f*.

lol·lop F ['lɔləp] latschen.

lol·ly ['lɔli] F = *lollipop*; *sl.* Mäuse *f/pl.* (*Geld*).

Lom·bard ['lɔmbəd] Lombarde *m*; *~ Street Londoner Geldmarkt*.

Lon·don·er ['lʌndənə] Londoner *m*.

lone [ləun] einsam; *~ wolf* = '**lon·er** Einzelgänger *m*; **lone·li·ness** ['~linis] Einsamkeit *f*; '**lone·ly** □, **lonesome** □ ['~səm] einsam.

long[1] [lɔŋ] **1.** Länge *f*; *before ~* binnen kurzem; *for ~* lange; *take ~* lange brauchen *od.* dauern; *the ~ and the short of it* die ganze Geschichte; **2.** *adj.* lang; langfristig; langsam; *at ~ date* ✝ langfristig; *in the ~ run* am Ende; auf die Dauer; *be ~* lange dauern *od.* brauchen; *take ~ views* weit vorausblicken; **3.** *adv.* lang; lange; *as ~ ago as 1900* schon 1900; *so ~!* bis dann! (*auf Wiedersehen*); *~er* länger; mehr; *no ~er ago than* erst (nach) ...

long[2] [~] sich sehnen (*for* nach).

long...: '**~boat** ⚓ Großboot *n*; **~-bow** ['~bəu] *hist.* Langbogen *m*; *draw the ~ fig.* aufschneiden, übertreiben; '**~-'dated** langfristig; '**~-'dis·tance** Fern..., Weit...; *~ flight* Langstreckenflug *m*; *~ race* Langstreckenlauf *m*; '**~-drawn-'out,** *a.* '**~-'drawn** in die Länge gezogen; lang(atmig); **lon·gev·i·ty** [lɔn'dʒeviti] Langlebigkeit *f*; langes Leben *n*; **long firm** Schwindelfirma *f*; '**long·hair** F konservativer Musiker *m*, Gegner *m* der Swingmusik; Intellektuelle *m, f*; '**long-haired** F betont intellektuell; '**long·hand** *gewöhnliche* Schreibschrift *f*; '**long-'head·ed** *fig.* schlau, klug.

long·ing ['lɔŋiŋ] **1.** □ sehnsüchtig; **2.** Sehnsucht *f*; Verlangen *n*.

long·ish ['lɔŋiʃ] länglich, ziemlich lang.

lon·gi·tude *geogr.* ['lɔndʒitju:d] Länge *f*; **lon·gi'tu·di·nal** □ [~dinl] Längen...; der Länge nach.

long...: *~* **johns** *pl.* F lange Unterhose *f*; *~* **jump** *Sport*: Weitsprung *m*; '**~-'lived** langlebig; '**~-'range** weittragend; auf lange Sicht; ⚔ Fernkampf...; ✈ Langstrecken...; *~* **run:** *in the ~* langfristig (gesehen), auf die Dauer; '**~-shore-man** Hafenarbeiter *m*; '**~-shot** *Film*: Fernaufnahme *f*; '**~-'sight·ed** weitsichtig, -blickend; '**~-'stand·ing** seit langer Zeit bestehend, alt; '**~-'suf·fer·ing 1.** langmütig; **2.** Langmut *f*; '**~-'term** langfristig, Langzeit...; *~ memory* Langzeitgedächtnis *n*; *~* **waves** *pl.* ⚡ Langwellen *f/pl.*; '**~·ways** der Länge nach; '**~-'wind·ed** □ langatmig.

loo[1] [lu:] Lu *n* (*ein Kartenspiel*).

loo[2] F [~] Klo *n* (*Toilette*).

loo·fah ⚘ ['lu:fɑ:] Luffaschwamm *m*.

look [luk] **1.** Blick *m*; *oft ~s pl.* Aussehen *n*; *new ~* neueste Mode *f*; *have a ~ at s.th.* sich et. ansehen; *I don't like the ~ of it* es gefällt mir nicht; **2.** *v/i.* sehen, blicken (*at, on* auf *acc.*, nach); zusehen, *daß od. wie ...*; nachsehen, *wer etc. ...*; *krank etc.* aussehen; *nach e-r Richtung* liegen; *it ~s like rain* es sieht nach Regen aus; *he ~s like winning* es sieht so aus, als ob er gewinnt; *~ about* sich umsehen (*for* nach); *~ after* sehen nach, sich kümmern um; versorgen; nachsehen, -blikken; *~ at* ansehen; *not much to ~ at* nicht sehr ansehnlich; *~ down on* verachten; *~ for* erwarten; suchen; *~ forward to* sich freuen auf (*acc.*); *~ in als Besucher* herein-, hineinschauen (*on* bei); *~ into* prüfen; erforschen; *~ on* zuschauen; betrachten (*as* als); gelegen sein zu, liegen zu, gehen auf (*Zimmer*); *~ out* sich vorsehen, aufpassen; *~ out for* sich umsehen nach; sich in acht nehmen vor (*dat.*); *~ over s.th.* et. genau ansehen *od.* inspizieren; et. durchsehen; et. übersehen; *~ round* sich umsehen; *~ through* durchsehen; durchlesen; herausblicken aus; *~ to* im Auge haben, achtgeben auf (*acc.*); sich verlassen auf (*acc.*); *~ to*

s.o. to inf. von j-m erwarten, daß er ...; ~ *up* aufblicken; steigen (*Aktien*), sich bessern; ~ *(up)on fig.* ansehen, betrachten (*as* als), halten (*as* für); *v/t.* ~ *s.o. in the face* j-m ins Gesicht sehen; ~ *one's age* so alt aussehen, wie man ist; ~ *disdain* verächtlich blicken; ~ *over et.* durchsehen; *j.* mustern; ~ *up et.* nachschlagen; F *j.* aufsuchen.
look-a·like *Am.* ['lukəlaik] Doppelgänger *m.*
look·er-on ['lukər'ɔn] Zuschauer (-in).
look-in ['luk'in] kurzer Besuch *m*; F Chance *f.*
look·ing-glass ['lukiŋglɑːs] Spiegel *m.*
look-out ['luk'aut] Ausguck *m*; Ausblick *m*, -sicht *f* (*a. fig.*); *be on the* ~ Ausschau halten; auf der Hut sein; *that is my* ~ das ist meine Sache; '**look-o·ver** Durchsicht *f*; *give s.th. a* ~ e-n prüfenden Blick auf et. werfen.
loom[1] [luːm] Webstuhl *m.*
loom[2] [~] undeutlich zu sehen sein, sich abzeichnen; ~ *large fig.* von großer Bedeutung sein *od.* scheinen.
loon[1] *schott.* [luːn] Lümmel *m*; Bursche *m*; Dummkopf *m.*
loon[2] *orn.* [~] Taucher *m.*
loon·y *sl.* ['luːni] 1. verrückt, bekloppt; 2. Verrückte *m, f*; ~ **bin** *sl.* Klapsmühle *f.*
loop [luːp] **1.** Schlinge *f*, Schleife *f*, Schlaufe *f*, Öse *f*; ~ *aerial Radio*: Rahmenantenne *f*; **2.** *v/t.* in Schleifen legen; schlingen; ~ *up Kleid, Haar* aufstecken; ~ *the* ~ ✈ e-n Looping drehen; *v/i.* e-e Schleife machen; sich winden; '**~-hole** Guckloch *n*; Schlupfloch *n* (*a. fig.*); ⚔ Schießscharte *f*; Sehschlitz *m*; '**~-line** 🚂 *u. tel.* Schleife *f.*
loose [luːs] **1.** □ *allg.* lose, locker; schlaff; weit; frei; unzs.-hängend; ungenau, nachlässig; liederlich; ~ *connection* ⚡ Wackelkontakt *m*; *at a* ~ *end* beschäftigungslos; *play fast and* ~ *with* Schindluder treiben mit; es nicht so genau nehmen mit; **2.** *v/t. Knoten, Zunge, Schuß* lösen; *a.* ~ *off* aufbinden; *Griff* lockern; ~ *one's hold on s.th.* et. loslassen *od.* fahren lassen; *v/i.* schießen; **3.** *give (a)* ~ *to* freien Lauf lassen (*dat.*); '**~-leaf** Loseblatt...; ~ *book*, ~ *ledger* Loseblattbuch *n*; **loos·en** ['luːsn] (sich) lösen, (sich) lockern; '**loose·ness** Lockerkeit *f*; Ungenauigkeit *f*; Liederlichkeit *f*; ⚕ Durchfall *m.*
loot [luːt] **1.** plündern; erbeuten; **2.** Beute *f.*
lop[1] [lɔp] *Baum* beschneiden; stutzen; *mst* ~ *away*, ~ *off* abhauen.
lop[2] [~] schlaff herunterhängen (lassen).
lope [ləup] **1.** (daher)trotten; **2.** Trott *m*, Lauf *m.*
lop...: '**~-ears** *pl.* Hängeohren *n/pl.*; '**~-'sid·ed** schief; einseitig.
lo·qua·cious [ləu'kweiʃəs] geschwätzig; **lo·quac·i·ty** [ləu'kwæsiti] Schwatzhaftigkeit *f.*
lo·ran ✈ ['lɔːrən] Loran *n*, Fernbereichs-Navigationssystem *n.*
lord [lɔːd] **1.** Herr *m*; Gebieter *m*; Magnat *m*; Lord *m*; *the* 2 der Herr (*Gott*); *my* ~ Mylord, Euer Gnaden; *the* 2*'s Prayer* das Vaterunser; *the* 2*'s Supper* das Abendmahl; (*House of*) 2*s pl.* Oberhaus *n*; **2.** ~ *it* den Herrn spielen; ~ *it over* herrschen über (*acc.*); '**lord·li·ness** Würde *f*; *b.s.* Hochmut *m*; '**lord·ling** Herrchen *n*; '**lord·ly** vornehm, edel; großartig; hochmütig, arrogant; **Lord May·or** Oberbürgermeister *m*; '**lord·ship** Lordschaft *f*, Herrlichkeit *f* (*Titel*).
lore [lɔː] Lehre *f*, Kunde *f.*
lor·gnette [lɔː'njet] Stielbrille *f.*
lor·ry ['lɔri] Last(kraft)wagen *m*, Lkw *m*; 🚂 Lore *f*, Lori *f.*
lose [luːz] (*irr.*) *v/t.* verlieren; einbüßen; vergeuden; *Zug, Gelegenheit* verpassen, versäumen; *j.* um *et.* bringen; *Leiden etc.* loswerden; *Gewicht* abnehmen; ~ *o.s.* sich verlieren; sich verirren; ~ *sight of* aus den Augen verlieren; *v/i.* verlieren, Verlust(e) haben; nachgehen (*Uhr*); '**los·er** Verlierer(in); *come off a* ~ den kürzeren ziehen; '**los·ing** **1.** verlustbringend; Verlust...; **2.** ~*s pl.* Verluste *m/pl.* im Spiel.
loss [lɔs] Verlust *m*; Schaden *m*; *at a* ~ in Verlegenheit; außerstande (*to inf.* zu *inf.*); *be at a* ~ *for words* keine Worte finden; *be at a* ~ *what to say* nicht wissen, was man sagen soll; '**~-lead·er** ✝ Zugartikel *m*, Schlager *m.*
lost [lɔst] *pret. u. p.p. von lose*; *be* ~ verlorengehen; verschwunden sein;

fig. versunken sein; *this won't be ~ on me* das werde ich mir merken; *be ~ upon s.o.* keinen Eindruck machen auf j.; get ~ hau ab!, verduf-te!; '~-'**prop·er·ty of·fice** Fundbüro *n.*

lot [lɔt] **1.** Los *n*; *fig.* Schicksal *n*; Anteil *m*; ✝ Partie *f*; Posten *m*; F Menge *f*, Haufen *m*, Masse *f*; Bauplatz *m*, Parzelle *f*, Stück *n* Land; *Am. Film*: Ateliergelände *n*; *a ~ of people* F eine Menge Leute; *draw ~s* losen (*for* um); *fall to s.o.'s ~* j-m zufallen; *throw in one's ~ with* sich auf Gedeih und Verderb verbinden mit; *he is feeling a ~ better* F er fühlt sich sehr viel wohler; **2.** durch das Los verteilen; zuteilen.

loth [louθ] = *loath.*

lo·tion ['ləuʃən] (Haut-, Schönheits)Wasser *n*, Emulsion *f*.

lot·ter·y ['lɔtəri] Lotterie *f*.

lo·tus ⚘ ['ləutəs] Lotos *m* (*a. Frucht der Sage*); '~-**eater** Lotosesser *m*; Träumer *m*, Genußmensch *m*.

loud □ [laud] laut (*a. adv.*); schreiend; grell; '~-'**hail·er** ⚓ Megaphon *n*; '~·**mouth** Großmaul *n*; '**loud-ness** Lautheit *f*; Lärm *m*; Auffallende *n*; *Radio*: Lautstärke *f*; '**loud--'speak·er** Lautsprecher *m*.

lough *irisch* [lɔk] See *m*; Bucht *f*.

lounge [laundʒ] **1.** sich rekeln; faulenzen, herumlungern; **2.** Bummel *m*; Wohnzimmer *n*, -diele *f*; Gesellschaftsraum *m e-s Hotels*; *thea.* Foyer *n*; Chaiselongue *f*; '~-'**chair** Klubsessel *m*; '~-**liz·ard** *sl.* Salonlöwe *m*; Gigolo *m*; '**loung·er** Faulenzer(in); '**lounge-'suit** Straßenanzug *m*; **lounge suite** Couchgarnitur *f*.

lour ['lauə] finster blicken *od.* aussehen; die Stirn runzeln; **lour·ing** □ ['~riŋ] trüb, finster.

louse 1. [laus], *pl.* **lice** [lais] Laus *f*; **2.** [lauz] lausen; **lous·y** ['lauzi] verlaust; lausig; Lause...; *~ with money sl.* stinkreich.

lout [laut] Tölpel *m*, Lümmel *m*; **lout·ish** tölpelhaft.

lou·vre, *Am.* **lou·ver** ['lu:və] Jalousie *f*.

lov·a·ble □ ['lʌvəbl] liebenswürdig, -wert.

love [lʌv] **1.** Liebe *f* (*of, a. for, to, towards* zu); Liebschaft *f*, Angebetete *f*; Liebling *m* (*als Anrede*); F goldiges Ding *n* (*Person od. Sache*); liebe Grüße *m/pl.*; ♀ Liebesgott *m*; *~s pl.* Amoretten *f/pl.*; *Sport*: nichts, null; *attr.* Liebes...; *a ~ of a book* F ein allerliebstes Buch; *for the ~ of God* um Gottes willen; *play for ~* um nichts spielen; *four (to) ~* vier zu null; *give od. send one's ~ to s.o.* j. freundlichst grüßen lassen; *in ~ with* verliebt in (*acc.*); *fall in ~ with* sich verlieben in; *make ~ to* werben um; *neither for ~ nor money* weder für Geld noch für gute Worte; **2.** lieben; gern haben; *~ to do* gern tun; '~-**af·fair** Liebschaft *f*; '~--**bird** Sperlingspapagei *m*; '~-**child** Kind *n* der Liebe; '**love·less** lieblos; '**love-let·ter** Liebesbrief *m*; '**love·li·ness** Lieblichkeit *f*; '**love-lock** Schmachtlocke *f*; **love·lorn** ['~lɔ:n] unglücklich verliebt; '**love-ly** lieblich; entzückend, reizend; '**love-mak·ing** Lieben *n*; Liebeswerben *n*; '**love-match** Liebesheirat *f*; '**love-phil·tre,** '**love--po·tion** Liebestrank *m*; '**lov·er** Liebhaber *m*; *fig.* Verehrer(in), Liebhaber(in); *~s pl.* Liebende *pl.*; *pair of ~s* Liebespaar *n*; '**love·set** *Sport*: Nullpartie *f*; '**love·sick** liebeskrank; '**love-to·ken** Liebespfand *n*.

lov·ing □ ['lʌviŋ] liebevoll; '~--'**kind·ness** (Herzens)Güte *f*.

low[1] (□ ↖) [ləu] **1.** niedrig; tief; seicht; gering; kärglich; leise; *fig.* niedergeschlagen; schwach (⚕ *Puls etc.*); gemein, erbärmlich, schlecht; *~est bid* Mindestgebot *n*; *in a ~ voice* leise; *be brought ~* gedemütigt werden; *lay ~* niederwerfen; *lie ~* ausgestreckt liegen; sich verborgen halten; **2.** *meteor.* Tief(druckgebiet) *n*; *bsd. Am.* Tiefstand *m*, -punkt *m*.

low[2] [~] **1.** brüllen, muhen (*Rind*); **2.** Brüllen *n*.

low...: '~-'**born** von niedriger Geburt; '~-'**bred** ungebildet, ohne Manieren; '~-**brow 1.** geistig anspruchslos, spießig; **2.** Spießer *m*, Banause *m*; '~-'**browed** mit niederem Eingang, düster (*Gebäude etc.*); = *low-brow 1*; ~ **co·me·di·an** *mst fig.* Hanswurst *m*; ~ **com·e·dy** Posse *f*, Schwank *m*; '~-**cost** preiswert, billig; ~ **coun·try** Tiefland *n*; '~-**down 1.** F niederträchtig, gemein; **2.** *sl. die* eigentliche Wahrheit *f*, *die*

Hintergründe *m/pl.*
low·er[1] ['ləuə] **1.** niedriger *etc.* (*s. low*[1]); nieder(e), unter(e); Unter...; ~ *case typ.* Kleinbuchstaben *m/pl.* **2.** *v/t.* nieder-, herab-, herunterlassen; senken; *die Augen* niederschlagen; erniedrigen; abschwächen; *Preise* herunter-, herabsetzen; ~ *one's voice* leiser sprechen; *v/i.* fallen, sinken.
low·er[2] ['lauə] *s. lour.*
low·er·most ['ləuəməust] niedrigst; am niedrigsten; **low-'in·come** einkommensschwach; **low-'key** unaufdringlich, verhalten; *phot.* in dunklen Tönen gehalten; **'low·land** Tiefland *n*; **'low·land·er** Tieflandbewohner (-in); **Low Lat·in** *gr.* Vulgärlatein *n*; **'low·li·ness** Demut *f*; Niedrigkeit *f*; **'low·ly** *adj. u. adv.* niedrig, tief; gering; demütig, bescheiden, gering; **'low-'necked** tief ausgeschnitten (*Kleid*); **'low·ness** Niedrigkeit *f*; Kärglichkeit *f*; ♪ Tiefe *f*; ~ *of spirits* Niedergeschlagenheit *f*; **'low-'noise** rauscharm; **low pres·sure** ⊕ Nieder-, Unterdruck *m*; *meteor.* Tiefdruck *m*; **'low-'spir·it·ed** niedergeschlagen; **low wa·ter** Niedrigwasser *n*, tiefste Ebbe *f*; *in ~ fig.* knapp bei Kasse.
loy·al □ ['lɔiəl] loyal, treu; **'loy·al·ist** Regierungstreue *m*; **'loy·al·ty** Treue *f*, Loyalität *f*.
loz·enge ['lɔzindʒ] Raute *f*; *pharm.* Pastille *f*; Tablette *f*; (Brust)Bonbon *m, n*.
£.s.d. F ['eles'di:] Geld *n*.
lub·ber ['lʌbə] Tölpel *m*, Stoffel *m*; **'lub·ber·ly** plump, tölpelhaft.
lu·bri·cant ['lu:brikənt] Schmiermittel *n*; **lu·bri·cate** ['~keit] schmieren; **lu·bri'ca·tion** Schmieren *n*, ⊕ Ölung *f*; **'lu·bri·ca·tor** ⊕ Schmierbüchse *f*; **lu'bric·i·ty** [~siti] ⊕ Schmierfähigkeit *f*; *fig.* Schlüpfrigkeit *f*.
lu·cerne ⚘ [lu:'sə:n] Luzerne *f*.
lu·cid □ ['lu:sid] *mst poet.* leuchtend, hell; klar, deutlich; ~ *interval* ⚕ lichter Augenblick *m*; **lu'cid·i·ty, 'lu·cid·ness** Klarheit *f*.
Lu·ci·fer ['lu:sifə] Satan *m*, Luzifer *m*; Morgenstern *m*.
luck [lʌk] Glück(sfall *m*) *n*; Geschick *n*; *good* ~ Glück *n*; *bad* ~, *hard* ~, *ill* ~ Unglück *n*, Pech *n*; *be down on one's* ~ F Pech haben; *worse* ~ unglücklicherweise; **'luck·i·ly** glücklicherweise, zum Glück; **'luck·i·ness** Glück *n*; **'luck·less** unglücklich; **'luck·y** □ glücklich; glückbringend; Glücks...; *be* ~ Glück haben; **'luck·y-bag, 'luck·y-dip** Glücksbeutel *m*.
lu·cra·tive □ ['lu:krətiv] einträglich, lukrativ; **lu·cre** ['lu:kə] Gewinn(sucht *f*) *m*.
lu·cu·bra·tion [lu:kju:'breiʃən] mühsames Studium *n*; *mst ~s pl.* gelehrte Arbeit *f*.
lu·di·crous □ ['lu:dikrəs] lächerlich, albern.
lu·do ['lu:dəu] *Spiel*: Mensch, ärgere dich nicht.
luff ⚓ [lʌf] **1.** Luv *f*; Luvseite *f*; **2.** *a. ~ up* anluven.
lug[1] [lʌg] **1.** zerren, schleppen; ~ *in fig.* an den Haaren herbeiziehen; **2.** Henkel *m*, Öhr *n*.
lug[2] [~] = *lugsail.*
luge [lu:ʒ] **1.** Rodelschlitten *m*; **2.** rodeln.
lug·gage ['lʌgidʒ] Gepäck *n*; **'~-car·ri·er** Gepäckträger *m am Fahrrad*; **'~-of·fice** 🚂 Gepäckschalter *m*; **'~-rack** Gepäcknetz *n*; **'~-tick·et** Gepäckschein *m*; **'~-van** 🚂 Gepäck-, Packwagen *m*.
lug·ger ⚓ ['lʌgə] Logger *m*, Lugger *m*.
lug·sail ⚓ ['lʌgseil, ⚓ 'lʌgsl] Lugger-, Sturmsegel *n*.
lu·gu·bri·ous □ [lu:'gu:briəs] traurig, kläglich, düster, finster.
luke·warm ['lu:kwɔ:m] lau (*a. fig.*); **'luke·warm·ness** Lauheit *f*.
lull [lʌl] **1.** *v/t.* einlullen; beruhigen; *v/i.* sich beruhigen; sich legen (*Wind*); **2.** Ruhepause *f*.
lull·a·by ['lʌləbai] Wiegenlied *n*.
lum·ba·go ⚕ [lʌm'beigəu] Hexenschuß *m*, Lumbago *f*.
lum·ber ['lʌmbə] **1.** Bau-, Nutzholz *n*; Gerümpel *n*, Plunder *m*; **2.** *v/t. a. ~ up* vollstopfen; *v/i.* rumpeln, poltern; sich (dahin)schleppen; **'lum·ber·er, 'lum·ber·man** Holzfäller *m*, -arbeiter *m*; **'lum·ber·ing** schwerfällig; **'lum·ber·jack** Holzfäller *m*; **'lum·ber-mill** Sägewerk *n*; **'lum·ber-room** Rumpelkammer *f*; **'lum·ber-yard** Holzplatz *m*, -lager *n*.
lu·mi·nar·y ['lu:minəri] Himmelskörper *m*; Leuchtkörper *m*; *fig.*

Leuchte *f*, Koryphäe *m*, *f*; **lu·mi·nos·i·ty** [⁓ˈnɔsiti] Helle *f*, Glanz *m*; ˈ**lu·mi·nous** □ leuchtend; Licht...; *fig.* lichtvoll; klar; ⁓ *dial* Leuchtzifferblatt *n*; ⁓ *paint* Leuchtfarbe *f*.

lump [lʌmp] **1.** Klumpen *m*; *fig.* Klotz *m*; Beule *f*; Stück *n* *Zucker etc.*; *in the* ⁓ in Bausch und Bogen; ⁓ *sugar* Würfelzucker *m*; ⁓ *sum* Pauschalsumme *f*; *have a* ⁓ *in the throat fig.* e-n Kloß im Hals haben; **2.** *v/t.* zs.-stecken, -werfen, -fassen (*into, in* zu); *fig.* hinnehmen; *if you don't like it you can* ⁓ *it* du mußt dich damit abfinden; ⁓ *together* in einen Topf werfen; *v/i.* Klumpen bilden; ˈ**lump·ish** schwerfällig; dumm; ˈ**lump·y** □ klumpig; unruhig (*Wasser*).

lu·na·cy [ˈluːnəsi] Irr-, Wahnsinn *m*.

lu·nar [ˈluːnə] Mond...; ⁓ *caustic* ⚗ Höllenstein *m*; ⁓ **mod·ule** Mondfähre *f*.

lu·na·tic [ˈluːnətik] **1.** irr-, wahnsinnig; **2.** Irre *m*, *f*; Wahnsinnige *m*, *f*; Geistesgestörte *m*, *f*; ⁓ **a·sy·lum** Irrenhaus *n*, -anstalt *f*; ⁓ **fringe** *die* Extremen *pl.*, *die* Hundertfünfzigprozentigen *pl.*

lunch [lʌntʃ] **1.** Lunch *m*, Mittagessen *n*; zweites Frühstück *n*; *packed* ⁓ Lunchpaket *n*; 2. zu Mittag essen; *j-m* ein Mittagessen geben; **lunch·eon** [ˈ⁓tʃən] = *lunch 1*; ⁓ *meat* Frühstücksfleisch *n*; ⁓ *voucher* Essensgutschein *m*; ˈ**lunch-hour** Mittagszeit *f*, -pause *f*.

lu·nettes [luːˈnets] *pl.* Taucherbrille *f*.

lung [lʌŋ] Lunge(nflügel *m*) *f*; *the* ⁓*s pl.* die Lunge *f*.

lunge [lʌndʒ] **1.** *fenc.* Ausfall *m*; **2.** *v/i.* ausfallen (*at* gegen); (dahin-) stürmen; *v/t.* stoßen.

lung·er *sl.* [ˈlʌŋə] Lungenkranke *m*, *f*; ˈ**lung-pow·er** Stimmkraft *f*.

lu·pin(e) ⚘ [ˈluːpin] Lupine *f*.

lurch[1] [ləːtʃ] **1.** ⚓ Überholen *n*; *fig.* Taumeln *n*; **2.** ⚓ überholen, schlingern; *fig.* taumeln, torkeln.

lurch[2] [⁓]: *leave in the* ⁓ im Stich lassen.

lurch·er [ˈləːtʃə] Spürhund *m*.

lure [ljuə] **1.** Köder *m*; *fig.* Lockung *f*; **2.** ködern, (an)locken.

lu·rid [ˈljuərid] gespenstisch, unheimlich; düster, finster.

lurk [ləːk] lauern; versteckt liegen; ˈ**lurk·ing-place** Schlupfwinkel *m*.

lus·cious □ [ˈlʌʃəs] köstlich; üppig; sehr süß; *b.s.* süßlich, widerlich; ˈ**lus·cious·ness** Süße *f*; Üppigkeit *f*.

lush [lʌʃ] üppig, saftig (*Pflanze*).

lust *lit.* [lʌst] **1.** (sinnliche) Begierde *f*; Wollust *f*; *fig.* Gier *f*, Sucht *f*; **2.** *I* ⁓ es gelüstet mich (*after, for* nach); **lust·ful** □ [ˈ⁓ful] lüstern.

lust·i·ness [ˈlʌstinis] Rüstigkeit *f*.

lus·tre [ˈlʌstə] Glanz *m*; Lüster *m*, Kronleuchter *m*; ˈ**lus·tre·less** glanzlos.

lus·trous □ [ˈlʌstrəs] glänzend.

lust·y □ [ˈlʌsti] rüstig; *fig.* lebhaft; kräftig.

lu·ta·nist [ˈluːtənist] Lautenspieler (-in), Lautenist(in).

lute[1] ♪ [luːt] Laute *f*.

lute[2] [⁓] **1.** Kitt *m*; **2.** verkitten.

Lu·ther·an [ˈluːθərən] **1.** lutherisch; **2.** Lutheraner(in); ˈ**Lu·ther·an·ism** Luthertum *n*.

lut·ist [ˈluːtist] = *lutanist*.

lux·ate [ˈlʌkseit] verrenken.

lux·u·ri·ance [lʌgˈzjuəriəns] Üppigkeit *f*; **luxˈu·ri·ant** □ üppig; **luxˈu·ri·ate** [⁓rieit] schwelgen (*fig. in* in *dat.*); **luxˈu·ri·ous** □ luxuriös, üppig, verschwenderisch; F feudal; **luxˈu·ri·ous·ness** Verschwendung *f*; **lux·u·ry** [ˈlʌkʃəri] Luxus *m*, Üppigkeit *f*; Luxusartikel *m*; Genußmittel *n*.

ly·ce·um [laiˈsiəm] Vortragsraum *m*; *bsd. Am.* Volkshochschule *f*.

lych·gate [ˈlitʃgeit] überdachtes Friedhofstor *n*.

lye [lai] Lauge *f*.

ly·ing [ˈlaiiŋ] **1.** *p.pr. von lie*[1] *2 u. lie*[2] 2; **2.** *adj.* lügnerisch; ˈ⁓-ˈ**in** Wochenbett *n*; ⁓ *hospital* Entbindungsanstalt *f*, -heim *n*.

lymph [limf] ⚕ Lymphe *f*; *poet.* Quellwasser *n*; **lym·phat·ic** [⁓ˈfætik] **1.** (⁓*ally*) lymphatisch, Lymph...; *fig.* schwerfällig, langsam; **2.** Lymphgefäß *n*.

lynch [lintʃ] lynchen; ˈ⁓**-law** Lynchjustiz *f*.

lynx *zo.* [liŋks] Luchs *m*; ˈ⁓**-eyed** *fig.* luchsäugig, mit Luchsaugen.

lyre [laiə] Lyra *f*, Leier *f*; ˈ⁓**-bird** *orn.* Leierschwanz *m*.

lyr·ic [ˈlirik] **1.** lyrisch; liedhaft;

2. lyrisches Gedicht *n*; ~*s pl.* (Lied-) Text *m* (*bsd. e-s Musicals*); Lyrik *f*; **'lyr·i·cal** □ lyrisch, gefühlvoll; schwärmerisch, begeistert.
ly·sol *pharm.* ['laisɔl] Lysol *n.*

M

ma F [mɑː] Mama *f.*
ma'am [mæm] Majestät *f* (*Anrede für die Königin*); Hoheit *f* (*Anrede für Prinzessinnen*); [məm] F gnä' Frau *f* (*von Dienstboten verwendete Anrede*).
mac F [mæk] = *mackintosh.*
ma·ca·bre [mə'kɑːbr] grausig, makaber; *danse* ~ Totentanz *m.*
mac·ad·am [mə'kædəm] Schotter (-straße *f*) *m*; **mac'ad·am·ize** makadamisieren, beschottern.
mac·a·ro·ni [mækə'rəuni] Makkaroni *pl.*
mac·a·roon [mækə'ruːn] Makrone *f.*
mace[1] [meis] *hist.* Streitkolben *m*; Amtsstab *m.*
mace[2] [~] Muskatblüte *f.*
Mac·e·do·ni·an [mæsi'dəunjən] **1.** Mazedonier(in); **2.** mazedonisch.
mac·er·ate ['mæsəreit] *durch Flüssigkeit* erweichen; auslaugen, ausmergeln; kasteien; **mac·er'a·tion** Einweichung *f etc.*
Mach *phys.* [mæk]: ~ *number* Machsche Zahl *f*, Machzahl *f*; ~ *two* Mach 2 (*doppelte Schallgeschwindigkeit*).
ma·che·te [mə'tʃeiti] Machete *m, f*, Buschmesser *n.*
Mach·i·a·vel·li·an [mækiə'veliən] machiavellistisch.
mach·i·na·tion [mæki'neiʃən] Anschlag *m*; ~*s pl.* Machenschaften *f/pl.*, Ränke *pl.*; **mach·i·na·tor** ['~tə] Ränkeschmied *m*; **ma·chine** [mə'ʃiːn] **1.** Maschine *f*; Maschinerie *f*, Mechanismus *m* (*fig. Organisation*); **2.** maschinell herstellen *od.* (be)arbeiten; **ma'chine-gun** ⚔ Maschinengewehr *n*; **ma'chine-made** maschinell hergestellt; **ma'chin·er·y** Maschinen *f/pl.*; Maschinerie *f*, Mechanismus *m*; **ma'chine-shop** Maschinenhalle *f*; **ma'chine-tool** Werkzeugmaschine *f*; **ma'chine-wash·a·ble** waschmaschinenfest; **ma'chin·ist** Maschinist *m*; Maschinennäherin *f.*
mack F [mæk] = *mackintosh.*
mack·er·el *ichth.* ['mækrəl] Makrele *f.*
mack·i·naw *Am.* ['mækinɔː] Stutzer *m* (*Kleidungsstück*).
mac(k)·in·tosh ['mækintɔʃ] Regenmantel *m.*
mac·ro... ['mækrəu] groß..., lang...; ~**·bi·ot·ic** [~bai'ɔtik] makrobiotisch; ~**·bi'ot·ics** *sg.* Makrobiotik *f*; ~**·cosm** ['~kɔzəm] Makrokosmos *m.*
mad □ [mæd] wahnsinnig, verrückt (*with* vor); *bsd. von Tieren*: toll; *fig.* toll, wild (*on, about, after, for* nach; *at, about* über *acc.*); F wütend, böse; *go* ~ verrückt werden; *drive* ~ verrückt machen.
mad·am ['mædəm] gnädige Frau *f*, gnädiges Fräulein *n* (*Anrede*); *she's a bit of a* ~ F sie kommandiert e-n gerne herum.
Ma·dame ['mædəm] Frau *f* (*vor dem Namen e-r verheirateten Ausländerin*).
mad·cap ['mædkæp] **1.** toll; **2.** Tollkopf *m*; Wildfang *m*; **mad·den** ['mædn] toll *od.* rasend machen; *it is* ~*ing* es ist zum Verrücktwerden.
mad·der ⚘, ⊕ ['mædə] Krapp *m.*
made [meid] *pret. u. p.p. von make 1.*
made(-)to(-)meas·ure ['meidtə'meʒə] maßgeschneidert.
made-up ['meid'ʌp] zurechtgemacht; erfunden; fertig; ~ *clothes pl.* Konfektion *f*; ~ *of* bestehend aus.
mad·house ['mædhaus] Toll-, Irrenhaus *n*; **'mad·man** Wahnsinnige *m*, Irre *m*, Verrückte *m*; **'mad·ness** Wahnsinn *m*; *vet.* Tollwut *f*; Tollheit *f*; *Am.* Wut *f* (*at* über *acc.*).

ma·don·na [mǝ'dɔnǝ] Madonna *f*, Madonnendarstellung *f*; ~ **li·ly** ⚘ weiße Lilie *f*.

mad·ri·gal ♪ ['mædrigǝl] Madrigal *n*.

mad·wom·an ['mædwumǝn] Wahnsinnige *f*.

mael-strom ['meilstrǝum] Mahlstrom *m* (*Strudel*).

ma·es·tro [mɑː'estrǝu] Maestro *m*, Meister *m*.

maf·fick ['mæfik] wild *od.* lärmend feiern.

mag·a·zine [mægǝ'ziːn] Magazin *n*; Vorratsraum *m*; ⚔ Munitionslager *n*; Patronenbehälter *m*; Zeitschrift *f*.

mag·da·len ['mægdǝlin] reuige Sünderin *f*.

ma·gen·ta ⚗ [mǝ'dʒentǝ] Magenta (-rot) *n* (*Färbemittel*).

mag·got ['mægǝt] Made *f*; *fig.* Grille *f*; '**mag·got·y** madig; grillenhaft.

Ma·gi ['meidʒai] *pl. die drei* Weisen *m/pl.* aus dem Morgenlande.

mag·ic ['mædʒik] **1.** *a.* '**mag·i·cal** □ magisch; zauberhaft; Zauber...; **2.** Magie *f*, Zauberei *f*; *fig.* Zauber *m*; **ma·gi·cian** [mǝ'dʒiʃǝn] Zauberer *m*, Magier *m*; **mag·ic lan·tern** Laterna magica *f*.

mag·is·te·ri·al □ [mædʒis'tiǝriǝl] obrigkeitlich; behördlich; maßgebend, autoritativ; *b. s.* herrisch; **mag·is·tra·cy** ['~trǝsi] Richteramt *n*; die Richter *m/pl.*; **mag·is·trate** ['~treit] (Polizei-, Friedens)Richter *m*.

mag·na·nim·i·ty [mægnǝ'nimiti] Großmut *f*; **mag·nan·i·mous** □ [~'nænimǝs] großmütig.

mag·nate ['mægneit] Magnat *m*.

mag·ne·sia ⚗ [mæg'niːʃǝ] Magnesia *f*; **mag'ne·si·um** ⚗ [~zjǝm] Magnesium *n*.

mag·net ['mægnit] Magnet *m*; **mag·net·ic** [~'netik] (*~ally*) magnetisch; ~ *field* Magnetfeld *n*; ~ *pole* Magnetpol *m*; ~ *tape* Tonband *n*; **mag·net·ism** ['~nitizǝm] Magnetismus *m*; *fig.* Anziehungskraft *f e-r Person*; **mag·net·i·za·tion** [~nitai'zeiʃǝn] Magnetisierung *f*; '**mag·net·ize** magnetisieren; '**mag·net·iz·er** Magnetiseur *m*; **mag·ne·to** [mæg'niːtǝu] *mot.* Magnetzünder *m*.

mag·nif·i·cat *eccl.* [mæg'nifikæt] Magnifikat *n*; *fig.* Lobgesang *m*.

mag·nif·i·cence [mæg'nifisns] Pracht *f*, Herrlichkeit *f*; **mag'nif·i·cent** prächtig, prachtvoll, herrlich; **mag·ni·fi·er** ['~faiǝ] Vergrößerungsglas *n*; '**mag·ni·fy** vergrößern (*a. fig.*); *~ing glass* Vergrößerungsglas *n*, Lupe *f*; **mag·nil·o·quence** [mæg'nilǝukwǝns] Großsprecherei *f*; **mag'nil·o·quent** großsprecherisch; **mag·ni·tude** ['~tjuːd] Größe *f*; Wichtigkeit *f*; *star of the first* ~ Stern *m* erster Größe.

mag·no·lia ⚘ [mæg'nǝuljǝ] Magnolie *f*.

mag·pie *orn.* ['mægpai] Elster *f*; *fig.* Klatschbase *f*.

Magyar ['mægjɑː] **1.** Madjar(in); **2.** madjarisch.

mahl·stick *paint.* ['mɔːlstik] Malstock *m*.

ma·hog·a·ny [mǝ'hɔgǝni] Mahagoni(holz) *n*.

maid [meid] *lit.* Mädchen *n*; † Jungfrau *f*; (Dienst)Mädchen *n*; *old* ~ alte Jungfer *f*; ~ *of hono(u)r* Ehren-, Hofdame *f*; *Am. erste* Brautjungfer *f*.

maid·en ['meidn] **1.** *prov. od. co.* = *maid*; **2.** jungfräulich; unverheiratet; *fig.* Jungfern..., Erstlings...; ~ *name* Mädchenname *m e-r Frau*; ~ *speech* Jungfernrede *f*; '**~·hair** ⚘ Frauenhaar *n*; '**~·head** Jungfräulichkeit *f*; '**~·hood** Mädchenjahre *n/pl.*; '**~·like**, '**maid·en·ly** jungfräulich, mädchenhaft; **maid·en voy·age** ⚓ Jungfernfahrt *f*; ✈ Jungfernflug *m*.

maid-of-all-work ['meidǝv'ɔːl-wǝːk] Mädchen *n* für alles; '**maid-serv·ant** Dienstmädchen *n*.

mail[1] *hist.* [meil] (Ketten)Panzer *m*.

mail[2] [~] **1.** Post(dienst *m*) *f*; Post (-sendung) *f*; **2.** *bsd. Am.* aufgeben, mit der Post schicken; *~ing list* Adressenkartei *f*; '**mail·a·ble** *Am.* postversandfähig.

mail...: '**~-bag** Briefträger-, Posttasche *f*; Postsack *m*; '**~-box** *bsd. Am.* Briefkasten *m*; ~ **car·ri·er** *Am.* Briefträger *m*; '**~-coach** Postkutsche *f*; '**~·man** *bsd. Am.* Briefträger *m*; '**~-or·der cat·a·log(ue)** Versandhauskatalog *m*; '**~-or·der firm**, *bsd. Am.* '**~-or·der house** Versandhaus *n*; '**~-train** Postzug *m*.

maim [meim] verstümmeln.

main [mein] **1.** Haupt..., hauptsächlich; ~ *chance* materieller Vorteil *m*; ~ *station teleph.* Hauptanschluß *m*; *by* ~ *force* mit voller Kraft; ~ *plane unit* ✈ Tragwerk *n*; **2.** Hauptrohr *n*, -leitung *f*; Wasserleitung *f*; *poet.* Meer *n*; ~*s pl.* ⚡ (Strom)Netz *n*; ~*s adapter* Netzteil *n e-s Batteriegeräts*; ~*s aerial* Netzantenne *f*; ~*s operated* mit Netzbetrieb; ~*s set* Netzempfänger *m*; *in the* ~ in der Hauptsache, im wesentlichen; *s. might 1*; '~**·land** Festland *n*; '**main·ly** hauptsächlich.

main...: ~**·mast** ['~mɑːst, ⚓ '~məst] Großmast *m*; ~**·sail** ['~seil, ⚓ '~sl] Großsegel *n*; '~**·spring** Uhrfeder *f*; *fig.* Haupttriebfeder *f*; '~**·stay** ⚓ Großstag *n*; *fig.* Hauptstütze *f*; '~**·stream** *fig.* Hauptströmung *f*, -richtung *f*; ℒ **Street** *Am.* Hauptstraße *f*; Kleinstadtbewohner *m/pl.*

main·tain [mein'tein] (aufrecht)erhalten; beibehalten; *Meinung etc.* (unter)stützen; *Familie, Gespräch, Briefwechsel, Weg etc.* unterhalten; *Stellung, Preis etc.* behaupten; ~ *that* behaupten, daß; **main'tain·a·ble** haltbar; **main'tain·er** Versorger(in); Verfechter(in).

main·te·nance ['meintənəns] Erhaltung *f*; Unterhalt *m*; Behauptung *f*; Instandhaltung *f*; ~ *costs pl.* Unterhaltskosten *pl.*

main·top ⚓ ['meintɔp] Großmars *m.*

mai·son·(n)ette [meizə'net] Einfamilienhaus *n*; zweistöckige Mietswohnung *f.*

maize ⚘ [meiz] Mais *m.*

ma·jes·tic [mə'dʒestik] (~*ally*) majestätisch; **maj·es·ty** ['mædʒisti] Majestät *f*; Würde *f*, Hoheit *f.*

ma·jor ['meidʒə] **1.** größer; bedeutend(er), wichtig(er); mündig, volljährig; ♪ Dur *n*; *A* ~ A-Dur *n*; ~ *third* große Terz *f*; ~ *key* Dur-Tonart *f*; ~ *league Am. Baseball*: Oberliga *f* **2.** Major *m*; Mündige *m, f*, Volljährige *m, f*; *hinter Eigennamen*: der Ältere; *phls.* Obersatz *m*; *Am. univ.* Hauptfach *n*; **3.** *Am.* als Hauptfach studieren, sich spezialisieren *auf e-m Gebiet*; '~**-'gen·er·al** Generalmajor *m*; **ma·jor·i·ty** [mə'dʒɔriti] Mehrheit *f*, Majorität *f*; Mehrzahl *f*; Mündigkeit *f*, Volljährigkeit *f*; Majorsstelle *f*, -rang *m*; ~ *decision* Mehrheitsbeschluß *m*; ~ *rule* Mehrheitsregierung *f*; *join the* ~ sich zu seinen Vätern versammeln; *win by a large* ~ mit großer Mehrheit gewinnen; **ma·jor road** Vorfahrtsstraße *f.*

make [meik] **1.** (*irr.*) *v/t. allg.* machen; herstellen, anfertigen, fabrizieren; schaffen; bilden; hervorbringen; (er)bauen; ergeben; (veran)lassen; machen *od.* ernennen zu; gewinnen, verdienen; sich erweisen als, abgeben; *Regel* aufstellen; *Verlust* (er)leiden; *Freundschaft, Frieden* schließen; *e-e Rede* halten; ~ *believe that* so tun als ob, vorgeben zu; ~ *the best of it* das Beste daraus machen, es möglichst gut ausnützen; sich damit abfinden; ~ *capital out of* Kapital schlagen aus; ~ *do with* sich behelfen mit, auskommen mit; ~ *good ein Unrecht etc.* wieder gutmachen; *et.* ersetzen; *Wort* halten; wahr machen; glücklich bewerkstelligen; ~ *it* F es schaffen; ~ *(the) land* ⚓ Land sichten; ~ *or mar s.o.* j-s Glück oder Unglück sein; *do you* ~ *one of us?* machen Sie mit?; ~ *port* ⚓ den Hafen anlaufen; ~ *shift* sich behelfen; ~ *way* vorwärtskommen; ~ *way for* vor *j-m* zurücktreten (*a. fig.*); ~ *into* verarbeiten zu; ~ *out* ausfindig machen; ausmachen, erkennen; verstehen; entziffern; beweisen; zu erkennen geben; hinstellen als; *Rechnung etc.* ausstellen, ausfertigen; vervollständigen; ~ *over* übertragen; ~ *up* ergänzen; vervollständigen; zs.-setzen, -stellen, -bringen *etc.*; bilden, ausmachen; ✝ ausgleichen; *Streit* beilegen; verfertigen; zurechtmachen, schminken; erfinden; = ~ *up for* (*v/i.*); ~ *up one's mind* sich schlüssig werden, sich entschließen (*to inf.* zu *inf.*); sich abfinden (*to, for* mit *et.*); **2.** (*irr.*) *v/i.* sich *in e-r Richtung* bewegen; eintreten (*Flut*); ~ *as if* sich stellen als ob; ~ *after* nachjagen (*dat.*); ~ *against* schaden (*dat.*); sprechen gegen; ~ *at* auf *j.* losgehen; ~ *away* sich davonmachen; ~ *away with* beseitigen; umbringen; *Geld* vertun; ~ *for* zugehen auf (*acc.*); sich aufmachen *od.* begeben nach; sprechen für, fördern; ~ *off* sich fortmachen, verschwinden; ~ *up* sich zurechtmachen, sich schminken; ~ *up for* nach-, aufholen; wieder gutmachen; für *et.* entschädigen; *Verlust* wieder einholen; ~ *up to s.o.* sich an j. heranmachen; sich mit j-m versöhnen; **3.** Mach-, Bauart *f*; Bau *m des Körpers*; Form *f*, Fasson *f*, Schnitt *m*; Fabrikat *n*, Erzeugnis *n*; Marke *f*, Typ *m*; ⚡ Schließen *n e-s Stromkreises*; *of poor* ~ minderwertig; *on the* ~ *sl.* auf Profit *od.* s-n Vorteil aus; **'~-be·lieve 1.** Spiegelfechterei *f*; Schein *m*, Vorwand *m*, Verstellung *f*; **2.** vorgeblich, scheinbar; **'mak·er** Hersteller *m*, Erzeuger *m*; ♀ Schöpfer *m (Gott)*.

make...: '~·shift 1. Notbehelf *m*; **2.** behelfsmäßig; Behelfs..., Not...; **'~-up** Umbruch *m*, typographische Anordnung *f*; *fig.* Beschaffenheit *f*, Charakter *m*, Natur *f*; Schminke *f*, Make-up *n*; **'~·weight** Zugabe *f zum Gewicht*; *fig.* Lückenbüßer *m*.

mak·ing ['meikiŋ] Machen *n etc.*; Herstellung *f*; ~*s pl.* F Verdienst *m*; *in the* ~ im Werden; *that was the* ~ *of him* das machte ihn zu dem, was er ist; *have the* ~*s of* das Zeug haben zu.

mal·a·chite *min.* ['mæləkait] Malachit *m*.

mal·ad·just·ed *psych.* ['mælə'dʒʌstid] s-r Umwelt entfremdet, schlecht angepaßt; **'mal·ad'just·ment** mangelhafte Anpassung *f*.

mal·ad·min·is·tra·tion ['mælədminis'treiʃən] schlechte Verwaltung *f*, Mißwirtschaft *f*.

mal·a·droit ['mælə'drɔit] ungeschickt.

mal·a·dy ['mælədi] Krankheit *f*.

ma·laise [mæ'leiz] Unbehagen *n*, Unwohlsein *n*.

mal·a·prop·ism ['mæləprɔpizəm] Wortverwechslung *f*; **mal·a·pro·pos** ['~'æprəpəu] **1.** *adj.* ungelegen; **2.** *adv.* zur unrechten Zeit; **3.** et. Unangebrachtes *n*.

ma·lar·i·a ⚕ [mə'lɛəriə] Malaria *f*, Sumpffieber *n*; **ma'lar·i·al** malariaverseucht; Malaria...

Ma·lay [mə'lei] **1.** Malaie *m*, Malaiin *f*; **2.** malaiisch.

mal·con·tent ['mælkəntent] **1.** unzufrieden; **2.** Unzufriedene *m*, *f*.

male [meil] **1.** männlich; ~ *chauvinism* Männlichkeitswahn *m*; ~ *child* Knabe *m*; ~ *model* Dressman *m*; ~ *nurse* Krankenpfleger *m*; ~ *screw* Schraube(nspindel) *f*; **2.** Mann *m*; Männchen *n der Tiere*.

mal·e·dic·tion [mæli'dikʃən] Fluch *m*, Verwünschung *f*.

mal·e·fac·tor ['mælifæktə] Übeltäter *m*.

ma·lef·i·cence [mə'lefisns] Schädlichkeit *f*; **ma'lef·i·cent** schädlich.

ma·lev·o·lence [mə'levələns] Böswilligkeit *f*; **ma'lev·o·lent** □ böswillig (*to* gegen).

mal·for·ma·tion ['mælfɔ:'meiʃən] Mißbildung *f*.

mal·func·tion [mæl'fʌŋkʃən] **1.** ⚕ Funktionsstörung *f*; ⊕ Defekt *m*; **2.** defekt sein.

mal·ice ['mælis] Bosheit *f*; Groll *m*; ⚖ böse Absicht *f*; *bear s.o.* ~ e-n Groll *od.* Rachegefühle gegen j. hegen; *with* ~ *aforethought* ⚖ vorsätzlich.

ma·li·cious □ [mə'liʃəs] boshaft, heimtückisch; ⚖ böswillig; **ma'li·cious·ness** Bosheit *f*.

ma·lign [mə'lain] **1.** □ schädlich; ⚕ bösartig; **2.** verleumden, beschimpfen; **ma·lig·nan·cy** [mə'lignənsi] Bosheit *f*; ⚕ Bösartigkeit *f*; **ma'lig·nant** □ **1.** boshaft, böswillig; ⚕ bösartig; **2.** Übelgesinnte *m*; **ma'lig·ni·ty** Bosheit *f*; Schadenfreude *f*; *bsd.* ⚕ Bösartigkeit *f*.

ma·lin·ger [mə'liŋgə] simulieren; **ma'lin·ger·er** Simulant *m*.

mall [mɔ:l] Promenade *f*; Mittelstreifen *m e-r Autobahn*; *Am.* Einkaufszentrum *n*.

mal·lard *orn.* ['mæləd] Stockente *f*.

mal·le·a·ble ['mæliəbl] hämmerbar, verformbar; *fig.* geschmeidig, anpassungsfähig.

mal·let ['mælit] Holzhammer *m*, Schlegel *m*; *Sport*: Schlagholz *n*.

mal·low ⚘ ['mæləu] Malve *f*.

malm·sey ['mɑ:mzi] Malvasier (-wein) *m*.

mal·nu·tri·tion ['mælnju:'triʃən] Unterernährung *f*.

mal·o·dor·ous □ [mæ'ləudərəs] übelriechend.

mal·prac·tice ['mæl'præktis] Übeltat *f*; ⚕ falsche Behandlung *f*; ⚖ Amtsmißbrauch *m*.

malt [mɔ:lt] **1.** Malz *n*; ~ *liquor* gegorener Malztrank *m*, *bsd.* Bier *n*; **2.** malzen; zu Malz machen; mit Malz versetzen.

Mal·tese [ˈmɔːlˈtiːz] **1.** maltesisch; **2.** Malteser(in).
mal·treat [mælˈtriːt] schlecht behandeln; mißhandeln; **malˈtreat·ment** Mißhandlung *f.*
malt·ster [ˈmɔːltstə] Mälzer *m.*
mal·ver·sa·tion [mælvəːˈseiʃən] Veruntreuung *f*; Amtsmißbrauch *m.*
ma·ma, mam·ma [məˈmɑː] Mama *f.*
mam·mal [ˈmæməl] Säugetier *n*; **mam·ma·li·an** [məˈmeiljən] Säugetier...
mam·mon [ˈmæmən] Mammon *m.*
mam·moth [ˈmæməθ] **1.** *zo.* Mammut *n*; **2.** riesig, ungeheuer.
mam·my F [ˈmæmi] Mami *f*; *Am.* farbiges Kindermädchen *n.*
man [mæn, *in Zssgn* ... mən] **1.** *pl.* **men** [men] Mann *m* (*a.* ⚔); Mensch(en *pl.*) *m*; Menschheit *f*; Diener *m*; Untertan *m*; *Schach*: Figur *f*; Damestein *m*; *attr.* männlich; *to a* ~, *to the last* ~ bis auf den letzen Mann; ~ *on leave* ⚔ Urlauber *m*; *be one's own* ~ sein eigener Herr sein; **2.** ⚔, ⚓ bemannen, besetzen; ~ *o.s.* sich ermannen.
man·a·cle [ˈmænəkl] **1.** Handfessel *f*; **2.** fesseln.
man·age [ˈmænidʒ] *v/t.* handhaben; behandeln; *Geschäft etc.* verwalten, führen, leiten; *Menschen, Tiere* leiten, lenken; *j.* herumbringen; mit *j-m* fertig werden; *et.* fertigbringen, möglich machen; ~ *to inf.* es fertigbringen zu *inf.*; *v/i.* die Aufsicht haben, die Geschäfte führen; es schaffen; auskommen, sich behelfen (*with* mit; *without* ohne); **ˈman·age·a·ble** □ handlich; lenksam; **ˈman·age·ment** Handhabung *f*; Verwaltung *f*, Leitung *f*, Direktion *f*, Geschäftsführung *f*; geschickte Behandlung *f*; Kunst (-griff *m*) *f*; **ˈman·ag·er** Verwalter *m*, Leiter *m*, Vorsteher *m*, Direktor *m*, Regisseur *m*, Unternehmer *m*, Impresario *m*, Manager *m*; *departmental* ~ Abteilungsleiter *m*; *good* (*bad*) ~ guter (schlechter) Haushälter *m*; *sales* ~ Verkaufsleiter *m*; **ˈman·ag·er·ess** Leiterin *f*, Vorsteherin *f*, Direktorin *f*; **man·a·ge·ri·al** □ [~əˈdʒiəriəl] geschäftsführend, leitend, Direktions...
man·ag·ing [ˈmænidʒiŋ] geschäftsführend; Betriebs...; sparsam; ~ *clerk* Geschäftsführer *m*, Prokurist *m.*
man-at-arms [ˈmænətˈɑːmz] Gewappnete *m.*
Man·ches·ter [ˈmæntʃistə]: ~ *goods pl.* Baumwollwaren *f/pl.*
Man·chu [mænˈtʃuː], **Man·chu·ri·an** [~ˈtʃuəriən] **1.** mandschurisch; **2.** Mandschu *m*; *das* Mandschurische.
man·da·mus ⚖ [mænˈdeiməs] Befehl *m e-s höheren Gerichtes an ein niederes.*
man·da·rin [ˈmændərin] Mandarin *m*; *das* Mandarinische (*chines. Gebildetensprache*); *a.* **ˈman·da·rine** ⚘ Mandarine *f.*
man·da·tar·y ⚖ [ˈmændətəri] Mandatar *m* (*Bevollmächtigter*); **man·date** [ˈ~deit] **1.** Mandat *n*; Befehl *m*; Auftrag *m*; Vollmacht *f*; **2.** unter ein Mandat stellen; **manˈda·tor** Mandant *m* (*Vollmachterteiler*); **man·da·to·ry** [ˈ~dətəri] **1.** befehlend; *Am.* obligatorisch; **2.** Mandatar(staat) *m.*
man·di·ble *anat.* [ˈmændibl] Kinnbacken *m*, Kiefer *m.*
man·do·lin ♪ [ˈmændəlin] Mandoline *f.*
man·drag·o·ra [mænˈdrægərə], **man·drake** ⚘ [ˈ~dreik] Alraun(e *f*) *m.*
man·drel ⊕ [ˈmændril] Dorn *m.*
man·drill *zo.* [~] Mandrill *m.*
mane [mein] Mähne *f*; **maned** mit einer Mähne.
man-eat·er [ˈmæniːtə] Menschenfresser *m.*
ma·nes [ˈmɑːneiz] *pl.* Manen *pl.* (*Geister der Toten*).
ma·neu·ver [məˈnuːvə] = *manoeuvre.*
man·ful □ [ˈmænful] mannhaft; **ˈman·ful·ness** Mannhaftigkeit *f.*
man·ga·nese ⚗ [mæŋgəˈniːz] Mangan *n*; **man·gan·ic** [~ˈgænik] manganhaltig; Mangan...
mange *vet.* [meindʒ] Räude *f.*
man·gel(-wur·zel) [ˈmæŋgl(ˈwəːzl)] = *mangold.*
man·ger [ˈmeindʒə] Krippe *f*; *dog in the* ~ F Neidhammel *m.*
man·gle[1] [ˈmæŋgl] **1.** Wringmaschine *f*; Wäschemangel *f*; **2.** mange(l)n; wringen.
man·gle[2] [~] zerstückeln, zerflei-

schen; *fig.* verstümmeln; ˈ**mangler** Fleischwolf *m.*

man·go ♀ [ˈmæŋgəu] Mangopflaume *f*; -baum *m.*

man·gold ♀ [ˈmæŋgəld] Mangold *m.*

man·grove ♀ [ˈmæŋgrəuv] Mangrove *f.*

man·gy [ˈmeindʒi] räudig; schäbig.

man...: ˈ**~-han·dle** durch Menschenkraft bewegen; *sl.* rauh anpacken *od.* behandeln; ˈ**~-hat·er** Menschenfeind(in); ˈ**~·hole** ⊕ Mann-, Einsteigloch *n*; ˈ**~·hood** Mannesalter *n*; Männlichkeit *f*; Männer *m/pl.*; Menschentum *n*; ˈ**~-ˈhour** Arbeitsstunde *f* pro Mann.

ma·ni·a [ˈmeinjə] Wahnsinn *m*; Sucht *f*, Manie *f*; *in Zssgn*: ...sucht *f*; ...trieb *m*; ...narrheit *f*; **ma·ni·ac** [ˈ~niæk] **1.** Wahnsinnige *m*; **2.** *a.* **ma·ni·a·cal** □ [məˈnaiəkəl] wahnsinnig.

man·ic-de·pres·sive *psych.* [ˈmænikdiˈpresiv] **1.** manisch-depressiv; **2.** Manisch-Depressive *m, f.*

man·i·cure [ˈmænikjuə] **1.** Maniküre *f*; **2.** maniküren; ˈ**~-case** Maniküreetui *n*; **man·i·cur·ist** [ˈ~rist] Maniküre *f* (*Person*).

man·i·fest [ˈmænifest] **1.** □ offenbar, -kundig, augenscheinlich; **2.** ⚓ Ladungsverzeichnis *n*; **3.** *v/t.* offenbaren; zeigen, kundtun; *v/i.* e-e Kundgebung veranstalten; **man·i·fesˈta·tion** Offenbarung *f*; Kundgebung *f*; **man·iˈfes·to** [~təu] Manifest *n* (*öffentliche Erklärung*).

mani·fold □ [ˈmænifəuld] **1.** mannigfaltig; zahlreich; **2.** vervielfältigen; **3.** ⊕ Rohrverzweigung *f*; *intake* ~ *mot.* Einlaßkrümmer *m*; ~ **writ·er** Vervielfältigungsgerät *n.*

man·i·kin [ˈmænikin] Männlein *n*; Gliederpuppe *f.*

Ma·nil·(l)a [məˈnilə] *a.* ~ *cheroot* Manilazigarre *f*; *a.* ~ *hemp* Manilahanf *m*; ~ *paper* Packpapier *n.*

ma·nip·u·late [məˈnipjuleit] (geschickt) handhaben *od.* behandeln; zurechtmachen; **ma·nip·uˈla·tion** Manipulation *f*, Handhabung *f*, Behandlung *f*, Verfahren *n*; (künstliche) Beeinflussung *f*; Kniff *m*; **maˈnip·u·la·tive** [~lətiv] Handhabungs...; **maˈnip·u·la·tor** [~leitə] Handhaber *m*; *phys.* Manipulator *m.*

man·kind [mænˈkaind] Menschheit *f*; [ˈ~] Männerwelt *f*; ˈ**man-like** = *manly*; *mannish*; ˈ**man·liness** Männlich-, Mannhaftigkeit *f*; ˈ**man·ly** männlich; mannhaft; ˈ**man-ˈmade** künstlich; von Menschen geschaffen; ~ *fibre*, *Am.* ~ *fiber* Kunst-, Chemiefaser *f.*

man·na [ˈmænə] Manna *n, f.*

man·ne·quin [ˈmænikin] Mannequin *n, m*, Vorführdame *f*; ~ *parade* Modenschau *f.*

man·ner [ˈmænə] (Art *f* u.) Weise *f*; Art *f*, Gattung *f*; *paint. etc.* Manier *f*, Stil *m*; ~*s pl.* Manieren *f/pl.*; Umgangsformen *f/pl.*; Benehmen *n*; *no* ~ *of doubt* gar kein Zweifel; *in a* ~ gewissermaßen; *in such a* ~ *that* derartig, daß; ˈ**man·nered** ...gesittet, ...geartet; manieriert, gekünstelt; ˈ**man·ner·ism** Manieriertheit *f*, Künstelei *f*; Manierismus *m*; ˈ**man·ner·li·ness** Manierlichkeit *f*, gute Lebensart *f*; ˈ**man·ner·ly** gesittet, manierlich.

man·nish [ˈmæniʃ] männlich (*Frau*).

ma·noeu·vra·ble, *Am. a.* **ma·neu·ver·a·ble** [məˈnuːvrəbl] manövrierfähig; **maˈnoeu·vre**, *Am. a.* **maˈneu·ver** [~və] **1.** Manöver *n* (*a. fig.*); ~*s pl.* F *fig.* Mätzchen *pl.*; **2.** manövrieren (lassen).

man-of-war [ˈmænəvˈwɔː] Kriegsschiff *n.*

ma·nom·e·ter *phys.*, ⊕ [məˈnɔmitə] Manometer *n*, Druckmesser *m.*

man·or [ˈmænə] (Ritter)Gut *n*; *lord of the* ~ Gutsherr *m*; ˈ**~-house** Herrschaftshaus *n*, Herrensitz *m*; Schloß *n*; **ma·no·ri·al** [məˈnɔːriəl] herrschaftlich; Ritterguts...

man·pow·er [ˈmænpauə] Menschenpotential *n*; Arbeitskräfte *f/pl.*

manse *schott.* [mæns] Pfarrhaus *n.*

man·serv·ant [ˈmænsəːvənt] Diener *m.*

man·sion [ˈmænʃən] herrschaftliches Wohnhaus *n*; ~*s pl.* Häuserblock *m.*

man·slaugh·ter [ˈmænslɔːtə] Totschlag *m*, fahrlässige Tötung *f.*

man·tel·piece [ˈmæntlpiːs], ˈ**man·tel·shelf** Kaminsims *m*, -platte *f.*

man·til·la [mænˈtilə] Mantille *f.*

man·tle [ˈmæntl] **1.** Mantel *m* (*a. anat.*, △, *zo.*); *fig.* Schleier *m*, Hülle *f*; *a. incandescent* ~ Glühstrumpf *m*; **2.** *v/t.* verhüllen; *fig.* bemänteln; ~ *on* überziehen; *v/i.* sich röten (*Gesicht*); ~ *with* sich überziehen mit.

man·trap ['mæntræp] Fußangel *f.*

man·u·al ['mænjuəl] **1.** □ Hand...; mit der Hand (gemacht); ~*ly operated* handgesteuert; ~ *exercises pl.* ⚔ Griffeüben *n*; ~ *training* Werkunterricht *m*; **2.** Handbuch *n*, Leitfaden *m*; Manual *n der Orgel*; *instruction* ~ Bedienungsanleitung(en *pl.*) *f.*

man·u·fac·to·ry [mænju'fæktəri] Fabrik *f.*

man·u·fac·ture [mænju'fæktʃə] **1.** Fabrikation *f*, Herstellung *f*; Fabrikat *n*; **2.** fabrizieren, herstellen; verarbeiten (*into* zu); *fig.* erfinden; ~*d goods pl.* Fabrik-, Fertig-, Manufakturwaren *f/pl.*; **man·u'fac·tur·er** Fabrikant *m*, Hersteller *m*; **man·u'fac·tur·ing** Fabrik...; Gewerbe...; Industrie...

ma·nure [mə'njuə] **1.** Dünger *m*; **2.** düngen.

man·u·script ['mænjuskript] **1.** Manuskript *n*; Handschrift *f*; **2.** handschriftlich.

Manx [mæŋks] **1.** von der Insel Man; **2.** *die* Bewohner *m/pl.* der Insel Man.

man·y ['meni] **1.** viele; ~ *a* manche(r, -s); ~ *a one* manch eine(r, -s); *as* ~ *as* nicht weniger als; *one too* ~ einer zuviel; überflüssig; *be one too* ~ *for s.o.* j-m überlegen sein; **2.** Menge *f*; *a great* ~, *a good* ~ e-e ziemliche Menge, ziemlich viele, sehr viele; '~-'**sid·ed** vielseitig.

map [mæp] **1.** (Land-, *a.* Himmels-) Karte *f*; *off the* ~ F nicht vorhanden *od.* da, erledigt; *on the* ~ F noch vorhanden, da; **2.** aufzeichnen, eintragen; kartographisch erfassen; ~ *out* planen; einteilen.

ma·ple ⚘ ['meipl] Ahorn *m.*

map·per ['mæpə] Kartograph *m.*

ma·quis ['mæki:] *der* Maquis, *die* französische Widerstandsbewegung.

mar [mɑ:] beeinträchtigen; stören, verderben.

mar·a·bou *orn.* ['mærəbu:] Marabu *m.*

mar·a·schi·no [mærə'ski:nəu] Maraschino(likör) *m.*

Mar·a·thon ['mærəθən] *a.* ~ *race* Langstrecken-, Marathonlauf *m.*

ma·raud [mə'rɔ:d] plündern; **ma'raud·er** Plünderer *m*, Marodeur *m.*

mar·ble ['mɑ:bl] **1.** Marmor *m*; Marmorbildwerk *n*; Murmel *f*; **2.** marmorn; *fig.* hart; **3.** marmorieren.

mar·cel [mɑ:'sel] **1.** *a.* ~ *wave* Ondulationswelle *f*; **2.** ondulieren.

March[1] [mɑ:tʃ] März *m.*

march[2] [~] **1.** Marsch *m*; Fortschritt *m*; Gang *m der Ereignisse etc.*; ~ *past* ⚔ Vorbei-, Parademarsch *m*; *steal a* ~ *on s.o.* j-m zuvorkommen; **2.** marschieren (lassen), ziehen; gehen, schreiten; *fig.* vorwärtsschreiten; ~ *off* ⚔ *Gefangene* abführen; ~ *past* vorbeimarschieren.

march[3] [~] **1.** *mst* ~*es pl. hist.* Mark *f*, Grenzgebiet *n*; **2.** grenzen (*with* an *acc.*).

march·ing ['mɑ:tʃiŋ] Marsch...; ~ *order* Marschausrüstung *f*; ~ *orders pl.* Marschbefehl *m*; *in heavy* ~ *order* feldmarschmäßig.

mar·chion·ess ['mɑ:ʃənis] Marquise *f.*

march·pane ['mɑ:tʃpein] Marzipan *n*, *m.*

mare [mɛə] Stute *f*; ~'*s nest fig.* Schwindel *m*; (Zeitungs)Ente *f.*

mar·ga·rine [mɑ:dʒə'ri:n], F *a.* **marge** [mɑ:dʒ] Margarine *f.*

mar·gin ['mɑ:dʒin] Rand *m*; Grenze *f*; Spielraum *m*; *a.* ~ *of profit* Verdienst-, Gewinn-, Handelsspanne *f*, Marge *f*; *safety* ~ Sicherheitsfaktor *m*; '**mar·gin·al** □ am Rande (befindlich); Rand...; ~ *note* Randbemerkung *f.*

mar·grave ['mɑ:greiv] Markgraf *m*; **mar·gra·vine** ['~grəvi:n] Markgräfin *f.*

mar·gue·rite ⚘ [mɑ:gə'ri:t] Gänseblümchen *n*; Marguerite *f.*

Ma·ri·a [mə'raiə]: *Black* ~ F grüne Minna *f.*

mar·i·gold ⚘ ['mærigəuld] Dotterblume *f.*

mar·i·jua·na [mæri'hwɑ:nə] Marihuana *n* (*Rauschgift*).

ma·ri·nade [mæri'neid] **1.** Marinade *f*; marinierter Fisch *m*; **2.** = **ma·ri·nate** [~'neit] marinieren.

ma·rine [mə'ri:n] **1.** See..., Marine...; Schiffs...; **2.** Marineinfanterist *m*; Marine *f*; *paint.* Seestück *n*; *tell that to the* ~*s!* mach das einem anderen weis!; **mar·i-**

ner *poet. od.* ⚖ ['mærinə] Seemann *m.*

mar·i·o·nette [mæriə'net] Mario-nette *f.*

mar·i·tal □ ['mæritl] ehelich, Ehe..., Gatten...; ~ *status* Familienstand *m.*

mar·i·time ['mæritaim] an der See liegend *od.* lebend, See...; Küsten-...; Schiffahrt(s)...; ~ *power* Seemacht *f.*

mar·jo·ram ⚘ ['mɑːdʒərəm] Majoran *m.*

mark[1] [mɑːk] Mark *f* (*Geldstück*).

mark[2] [~] **1.** Marke *f*, Merkmal *n*, Zeichen *n*; ⚕ Preiszettel *m*, Auszeichnung *f an Waren*; Fabrik-, Schutzmarke *f*; (Brand)Mal *n*; Narbe *f*; Kratzer *m*, Fleck(en) *m*; Zeichen *n*, Kreuz *n* (*als Unterschrift*); Norm *f*, Standard *m*; *Schule*: Zensur *f*, Note *f*, Punkt *m*; *Sport*: Startlinie *f*; Ziel *n*; *vet.* Kennung *f*; *a man of* ~ ein Mann von Bedeutung; *up to the* ~ *fig.* auf der Höhe; den Erwartungen entsprechend; *hit the* ~ ins Schwarze treffen; *miss the* ~ vorbeischießen; *beside the* ~, *wide of the* ~ den Kern der Sache verfehlend; unrichtig; **2.** *v/t.* (be)zeichnen; *Waren* auszeichnen; *Stand e-s Spiels* anschreiben; kundtun; kennzeichnen, markieren; beachten, aufpassen auf (*acc.*); sich *et.* merken; ~ *down* (im Preis) herabsetzen; *j.* vormerken; ~ *off* abtrennen; ~ *out* bezeichnen; abstecken; vormerken; ~ *time* ⚔ auf der Stelle treten (*a. fig.*); **3.** *v/i.* achtgeben; ~! Achtung!; **marked** auffallend; merklich; ausgeprägt, markant; **mark·ed·ly** ['mɑːkidli] ausgesprochen; '**mark·er** *Billard*: Markör *m*; Lesezeichen *n.*

mar·ket ['mɑːkit] **1.** Markt *m*; Marktplatz *m*; Handel *m*; Absatz *m von Waren*; *in the* ~ am Markt; *come into the* ~ auf den Markt kommen, zum Verkauf angeboten werden; *play the* ~ *Am. sl.* an der Börse spekulieren; **2.** *v/t.* auf den Markt bringen, verkaufen; *v/i.* auf den Markt gehen; einkaufen; '**mar·ket·a·ble** □ ⚕ marktfähig, -gängig, verkäuflich; **mar·ket·eer** [~'tiə]: *black* ~ Schwarzhändler *m*; '**mar·ket-gar·den** (Gemüse)Gärtnerei *f*; '**mar·ket·ing** Marketing *n*, Absatzpolitik *f*; Marktbesuch *m*; '**mar·ket-place** Marktplatz *m*; **mar·ket re·search** Marktforschung *f*; '**mar·ket-town** Markt(flecken) *m*; '**mar·ket-value** Markt-, Kurswert *m.*

mark·ing ['mɑːkiŋ] Bezeichnung *f*, Markierung *f*; Musterung *f*, Zeichnung *f*; '**~-ink** Wäschetinte *f.*

marks·man ['mɑːksmən] (guter) Schütze *m*; '**marks·man·ship** Schießkunst *f.*

marl [mɑːl] **1.** *min.* Mergel *m*; **2.** ⚒ mergeln.

mar·ma·lade ['mɑːməleid] Orangenmarmelade *f.*

mar·mo·re·al □ *poet. u. rhet.* [mɑː'mɔːriəl] marmorn.

mar·mot *zo.* ['mɑːmət] Murmeltier *n.*

ma·roon[1] [mə'ruːn] kastanienbraun.

ma·roon[2] [~] *auf e-r einsamen Insel* aussetzen.

ma·roon[3] [~] Leuchtrakete *f.*

mar·plot ['mɑːplɔt] Störenfried *m.*

marque ⚓ [mɑːk]: *letter(s pl.) of* ~ Kaperbrief *m.*

mar·quee [mɑː'kiː] (großes) Zelt *n.*

mar·quess, *mst* **mar·quis** ['mɑːkwis] Marquis *m* (*englischer Adelstitel*).

mar·que·try ['mɑːkitri] Einlegearbeit *f.*

mar·riage ['mæridʒ] Heirat *f*, Ehe *f*; Ehestand *m*; Hochzeit *f*; *civil* ~ standesamtliche Trauung *f*; *by* ~ angeheiratet; *related by* ~ verschwägert; *take in* ~ zum Mann (zur Frau) nehmen; '**mar·riage·a·ble** heiratsfähig.

mar·riage...: ~ **ar·ti·cles** *pl.* Ehevertrag *m*; ~ **cer·e·mo·ny** Trauung *f*; ~ **guid·ance** Eheberatung *f*; ~ **lines** *pl.* Trauschein *m*; ~ **por·tion** Mitgift *f.*

mar·ried ['mærid] verheiratet; ehelich; Ehe...; ~ *couple* Ehepaar *n.*

mar·row ['mærəu] Mark *n*; *fig.* Kern *m*, Beste *n*; *vegetable* ~ ⚘ Markkürbis *m*; '**~·bone** Markknochen *m*; **~s** *pl. co.* Knie *n/pl.*; '**mar·row·y** markig.

mar·ry ['mæri] *v/t.* heiraten; verheiraten (*a. fig.*), vermählen (*to* mit); *eccl.* trauen; *v/i. a. get married* (sich ver)heiraten.

marsh [mɑːʃ] **1.** Sumpf *m*, Morast *m*, Marsch *f*; **2.** Sumpf...; ~ *fever*

Sumpffieber *n*; ~ *gas* Sumpfgas *n*.
mar·shal ['mɑ:ʃəl] **1.** Marschall *m*; *hist.* Hofmarschall *m*; Zeremonienmeister *m*, Festordner *m*; *Am.* Bezirkspolizeichef *m*; Leiter *m* der Feuerwehr; **2.** ordnen; führen; zs.-stellen; **mar·shal·ling-yard** ['~ʃliŋjɑ:d] Verschiebebahnhof *m*; '**mar·shal·ship** Marschallamt *n*.
marsh mal·low ['mɑ:ʃmælou] ⚘ Eibisch *m*, Althee *f*; *Art* türkischer Honig *m*; **marsh mar·i·gold** Sumpfdotterblume *f*; '**marsh·y** sumpfig.
mar·su·pi·al *zo.* [mɑ:'sju:pjəl] **1.** Beutel...; Beuteltier...; **2.** Beuteltier *n*.
mart [mɑ:t] Markt *m*; Auktionsraum *m*.
mar·ten *zo.* ['mɑ:tin] Marder *m*.
mar·tial □ ['mɑ:ʃəl] kriegerisch; Kriegs...; ~ *law* Kriegs-, Standrecht *n*; *state of* ~ *law* Belagerungszustand *m*; ~ *music* Militärmusik *f*.
Mar·tian ['mɑ:ʃjən] **1.** Marsbewohner *m*; **2.** Mars...
mar·tin[1] ['mɑ:tin] Mauerschwalbe *f*.
Mar·tin[2] [~]: *St.* ~*'s summer* Altweibersommer *m*.
mar·ti·net [mɑ:ti'net] Zuchtmeister *m*; Leuteschinder *m*.
mar·ti·ni [mɑ:'ti:ni] Martini *m* (*Cocktail*).
Mar·tin·mas ['mɑ:tinməs] Martinstag *m* (*11. November*).
mar·tyr ['mɑ:tə] **1.** Märtyrer(in); **2.** zum Märtyrer machen; (zu Tode) martern; '**mar·tyr·dom** Märtyrertum *n*; '**mar·tyr·ize** quälen; opfern.
mar·vel ['mɑ:vəl] **1.** Wunder *n*; **2.** sich wundern (*at* über *acc.*).
mar·vel·(l)ous □ ['mɑ:vələs] wunderbar, erstaunlich; '**mar·vel·(l)ous·ness** *das* Wunderbare.
Marx·ian ['mɑ:ksjən] **1.** Marxist *m*; **2.** marxistisch; '**Marx·ism** Marxismus *m*; '**Marx·ist** = *Marxian*.
mar·zi·pan [mɑ:zi'pæn] Marzipan *n*, *m*.
mas·ca·ra [mæs'kɑ:rə] Wimperntusche *f*.
mas·cot ['mæskət] Maskottchen *n*, Talisman *m*, Glücksbringer(in); *radiator* ~ *mot.* Kühlerfigur *f*.
mas·cu·line ['mæskjulin] **1.** □ männlich; mannhaft; **2.** *gr.* Maskulinum *n*.
mash [mæʃ] **1.** Gemisch *n*; *Brauerei*: Maische *f*; ⚒ Mengfutter *n*; **2.** mischen; zerdrücken, -quetschen; (ein)maischen; *sl. j-m* den Kopf verdrehen; ~*ed potatoes pl.* Kartoffelbrei *m*; *be* ~*ed on sl.* verschossen (*verliebt*) sein in (*acc.*); '**mash·er** Maischapparat *m*; *sl.* Geck *m*; Schwerenöter *m*, Schürzenjäger *m*.
mash·ie ['mæʃi] Mashie *m* (*Golfschläger*).
mask [mɑ:sk] **1.** Maske *f*; Larve *f*; *s. masque*; **2.** maskieren; *fig.* verbergen, verdecken; tarnen; **masked** maskiert; Masken...; ~ *ball* Maskenball *m*; '**mask·er** Maske *f* (*Person*).
ma·so·chism *psych.* ['mæzəukizəm] Masochismus *m*.
ma·son ['meisn] Steinmetz *m*; Maurer *m*; Freimaurer *m*; **ma·son·ic** [mə'sɔnik] freimaurerisch; **ma·son·ry** ['meisnri] Mauerwerk *n*.
masque [mɑ:sk] Maskenspiel *n*;
mas·quer·ade [mæskə'reid] **1.** Maskenball *m*; Verkleidung *f*, Maskerade *f*; **2.** *fig.* sich maskieren.
mass[1] *eccl.* [mæs] Messe *f*; *High* ♀ Hochamt *n*; *Low* ♀ stille Messe *f*.
mass[2] [~] **1.** Masse *f*; Menge *f*; *the* ~*es pl.* die breite Masse; *in the* ~ im ganzen; **2.** (sich) (an)häufen; (sich) (an)sammeln.
mas·sa·cre ['mæsəkə] **1.** Blutbad *n*, Gemetzel *n*; **2.** niedermetzeln.
mas·sage ['mæsɑ:ʒ] **1.** Massage *f*; ~ (*suction*) *roller* Punktroller *m*; **2.** massieren.
mass com·mu·ni·ca·tions ['mæskəmju:ni'keiʃənz] *pl.* = *mass media*.
mas·seur [mæ'sə:] Masseur *m*;
mas·seuse [mæ'sə:z] Masseuse *f*.
mas·sif ['mæsi:f] (Gebirgs)Massiv *n*.
mas·sive □ ['mæsiv] massiv; schwer; gediegen; mächtig; '**mas·sive·ness** *das* Massive, *das* Schwere; Gediegenheit *f*.
mass...: ~ **me·di·a** *pl.* Massenmedien *n/pl.*; ~ **meet·ing** Massenversammlung *f*, -veranstaltung *f*; '~**-pro·duce** serienmäßig herstellen; ~ **pro·duc·tion** Massen-, Serienproduktion *f*; ~ **so·ci·e·ty** Massengesellschaft *f*.
mas·sy ['mæsi] massig; schwer; derb.
mast[1] ⚓ [mɑ:st] **1.** Mast *m*; **2.** bemasten.

mast[2] [~] Mast(futter *n*) *f*.

mas·ter[1] [ˈmɑːstə] **1.** Meister *m in Handwerk, Kunst etc. u. fig.*; Herr *m* (*a. fig.*); Gebieter *m*; Lehrer *m*; Kapitän *m e-s Handelsschiffs*; *Anrede*: (junger) Herr *m*; *univ.* Rektor *m e-s College*; ♀ *of Arts* Magister *m* Artium; ♀ *of Ceremonies* Conférencier *m*; *be one's own* ~ sein eigener Herr sein; **2.** Meister...; *fig.* leitend, führend; Haupt...; **3.** Herr sein *od.* werden über (*acc.*); *Sprache etc.* meistern, beherrschen.

mas·ter[2] ⚓ [~] ...master *m*; *three-*~ Dreimaster *m*.

mas·ter-at-arms ⚓ [ˈmɑːstərətˈɑːmz] Schiffsprofos *m*; **mas·ter build·er** Baumeister *m*; **mas·ter cop·y** Original *n*; **mas·ter·ful** □ [ˈ~ful] herrisch, gebieterisch; meisterhaft; ˈ**mas·ter-key** Hauptschlüssel *m*; ˈ**mas·ter·less** herrenlos, unbändig; ˈ**mas·ter·ly** meisterhaft.

mas·ter...: ˈ~**·mind** *fig.* der Kopf sein von; ˈ~**·piece** Meisterstück *n*; ˈ~**·ship** Meisterschaft *f*; Herrschaft *f*; Vorsteher-, Lehramt *n*; ˈ~**-stroke** Meister-, Glanzstück *n*; ˈ**mas·ter·y** Herrschaft *f*, Gewalt *f*; Vorrang *m*; Oberhand *f*; Meisterschaft *f*; Beherrschung *f e-r Sprache etc.*

mast-head [ˈmɑːsthed] Mars *m*, Mastkorb *m*.

mas·tic [ˈmæstik] Mastix(harz *n*) *m*.

mas·ti·cate [ˈmæstikeit] kauen; **mas·tiˈca·tion** Kauen *n*.

mas·tiff [ˈmæstif] englische Dogge *f*.

mas·to·don *zo.* [ˈmæstədɔn] Mastodon *n*.

mas·toid ⚕ [ˈmæstɔid] Warzenfortsatz *m hinter der Ohrmuschel*.

mat[1] [mæt] **1.** Matte *f*; Deckchen *n*; Unterlage *f*; **2.** mit Matten belegen; *fig.* bedecken; (sich) verflechten; (sich) verfilzen.

mat[2] ⊕ [~] mattiert, matt.

match[1] [mætʃ] Streichholz *n*.

match[2] [~] **1.** *der od. die od. das* Gleiche *od.* Passende; Partie *f*; Wettspiel *n*, -kampf *m*; Heirat *f*; *be a* ~ *for j-m* gewachsen sein; *meet one's* ~ seinen Meister finden; **2.** *v/t.* passend machen, anpassen; vergleichen (*with* mit); passen zu, entsprechen (*dat.*); et. Gleiches *od.* Passendes finden *od.* geben zu; es aufnehmen mit; *well* ~*ed* zs.-passend; *v/i.* zs.-passen; ~ *with* passen zu; *to* ~ dazu passend.

match-box [ˈmætʃbɔks] Streichholzschachtel *f*.

match·et [ˈmætʃet] = *machete*.

match·less □ [ˈmætʃlis] unvergleichlich, ohnegleichen; ˈ**match-mak·er** Ehestifter(in).

match·wood [ˈmætʃwud] Kleinholz *n*, Splitter *m/pl*.

mate[1] [meit] *Schach*: matt (setzen).

mate[2] [~] **1.** Gefährte *m*, Gefährtin *f*, Genosse *m*, Genossin *f*, Kamerad (-in); Gatte *m*, Gattin *f*; Männchen *n*, Weibchen *n von Tieren*; Gehilfe *m*, Gehilfin *f*; ⚓ Maat *m*; **2.** (sich) verheiraten; *zo.* (sich) paaren; ˈ**mate·less** ohne Gefährten.

ma·ter *sl.* [ˈmeitə] Mutter *f*.

ma·te·ri·al [məˈtiəriəl] **1.** □ materiell; stofflich; körperlich; materialistisch; wesentlich (*to* für); **2.** Material *n*, Stoff *m*; *coll. od.* ~*s pl.* Materialien *n/pl.*; Bestandteile *m/pl.*; *working* ~ Werkstoff *m*; *writing* ~*s pl.* Schreibzeug *n*; **maˈte·ri·al·ism** Materialismus *m*; **maˈte·ri·al·ist** Materialist(in); **ma·te·ri·alˈis·tic** (~*ally*) materialistisch; **ma·te·ri·al·i·ty** [~riˈæliti] Stofflichkeit *f etc.*; **ma·te·ri·al·i·za·tion** [~riəlaiˈzeiʃən] Materialisierung *f*; **maˈte·ri·al·ize** (sich) materialisieren; (sich) verkörperlichen; (sich) verwirklichen.

ma·ter·nal □ [məˈtəːnl] mütterlich; Mutter...; mütterlicherseits; **maˈter·ni·ty** [~niti] Mutterschaft *f*; Mütterlichkeit *f*; *mst* ~ *hospital* Entbindungsanstalt *f*; ~ *benefit* Mutterschaftsgeld *n*; ~ *dress* Umstandskleid *n*; ~ *leave* Mutterschaftsurlaub *m*; ~ *ward* Entbindungsstation *f* (*e-r Klinik*).

mat·ey [ˈmeiti] vertraulich, kameradschaftlich.

math *Am.* F [mæθ] = *maths*.

math·e·mat·i·cal □ [mæθiˈmætikəl] mathematisch; **math·e·ma·ti·cian** [~məˈtiʃən] Mathematiker *m*; **math·e·mat·ics** [~ˈmætiks] *mst sg.* Mathematik *f*.

maths F [mæθs] Mathe *f* (*Mathematik*).

mat·ie [ˈmeiti] Matjeshering *m*.

mat·in [ˈmætin] **1.** *poet.* Morgen..., früh; **2.** ~*s pl. eccl.* Morgengebet *n*; *poet.* Morgenlied *n der Vögel*.

mat·i·née ['mætinei] Nachmittagsvorstellung *f*; Matinee *f*.
mat·ing ['meitiŋ] Paarung *f*; ~ *season* Paarungszeit *f*.
ma·tri·arch ['meitriɑːk] Stammesmutter *f*; '**ma·tri·ar·chy** Matriarchat *n*, Mutterrecht *n*; **ma·tri·cide** ['~said] Muttermord *m*; Muttermörder(in).
ma·tric·u·late [mə'trikjuleit] (sich) immatrikulieren (lassen); **ma·tric·u'la·tion** Immatrikulation *f*.
mat·ri·mo·ni·al □ [mætri'məunjəl] ehelich; Ehe...; **mat·ri·mo·ny** ['~məni] Ehe(stand *m*) *f*.
ma·trix ['meitriks] *fig.* Nährboden *m*; *geol.* Mutterboden *m*; Grundmasse *f*, umgebendes Gestein *n*; ⊕ *a.* ['mætriks] Matrize *f*, Gießform *f*.
ma·tron ['meitrən] Matrone *f*, verheiratete Frau *f*; Hausmutter *f e-s Internats etc.*; Oberin *f in e-m Krankenhaus etc.*; '**ma·tron·ize** bemuttern; '**ma·tron·ly** matronenhaft; *fig.* gesetzt.
mat·ter ['mætə] **1.** Materie *f*, Stoff *m*; ⚕ Eiter *m*; Gegenstand *m*; Inhalt *m*; Ursache *f*; Sache *f*, Angelegenheit *f*, Geschäft *n*; *typ.* Satz *m*; *~s pl.* die Umstände *m/pl.*, die Lage *f*; *postal* ~ Postsachen *f/pl.*; *printed* ~ Drucksache *f*; *in the* ~ *of* hinsichtlich (*gen.*); *what's the* ~*?* was gibt es?; was ist los?; *what's the* ~ *with you?* was fehlt Ihnen?; *no* ~ es hat nichts zu sagen; *no* ~ *who* gleichgültig wer; ~ *of course* Selbstverständlichkeit *f*; *as a* ~ *of course* selbstverständlich; *for that* ~, *for the* ~ *of that* was dies betrifft; ~ *of fact* Tatsache *f*; *as a* ~ *of fact* tatsächlich, in der Tat; in Wirklichkeit; ~ *in hand* vorliegende Sache *f*; *that is a hanging* ~ das kann dich *etc.* den Hals kosten; *no laughing* ~ nichts zum Lachen; **2.** von Bedeutung sein, darauf ankommen (*to* für); ins Gewicht fallen; *they* ~ auf sie kommt es an; *it does not* ~ es macht nichts; '**~-of-'course** selbstverständlich; '**~-of-'fact** tatsächlich; sachlich, nüchtern.
mat·ting ['mætiŋ] Mattenstoff *m*; -belag *m*.
mat·tock ['mætək] (Breit)Hacke *f*.
mat·tress ['mætris] Matratze *f*.
ma·ture [mə'tjuə] **1.** □ reif; reiflich (*Überlegungen etc.*); ⚜ fällig (*Wechsel*); **2.** reifen; zur Reife bringen; ⚜ fällig werden; **ma'tu·ri·ty** Reife *f*; ⚜ Fälligkeit *f*; Verfall(frist *f*) *m*.
ma·tu·ti·nal □ [mætjuː'tainl] morgendlich; Morgen...
maud·lin □ ['mɔːdlin] sentimental, rührselig.
maul [mɔːl] schwer beschädigen; mißhandeln; *fig.* heruntermachen; ~ *about* roh umgehen mit.
maul·stick *paint.* ['mɔːlstik] Malstock *m*.
maun·der ['mɔːndə] ziellos handeln, gammeln; faseln.
Maun·dy Thurs·day ['mɔːndi'θəːzdi] Gründonnerstag *m*.
mau·so·le·um [mɔːsə'liəm] Mausoleum *n*.
mauve [məuv] **1.** Malvenfarbe *f*; **2.** hellviolett.
mav·er·ick *Am.* ['mævərik] herrenloses Vieh *n* ohne Brandzeichen; *pol. u. fig.* Einzelgänger *m*.
maw [mɔː] *Tier*-Magen *m*; Rachen *m*.
mawk·ish □ ['mɔːkiʃ] rührselig, sentimental; '**mawk·ish·ness** Rührseligkeit *f*, Sentimentalität *f*.
maw·worm ['mɔːwəːm] Spulwurm *m*.
max·il·lar·y [mæk'siləri] Kiefer...
max·im ['mæksim] Maxime *f*, Grundsatz *m*; '**max·i·mal** maximal; '**max·i·mize** ⚜, ⊕ maximieren; **max·i·mum** ['~məm] **1.** Maximum *n*, Höchstmaß *n*, -stand *m*, -betrag *m*; **2.** Höchst..., Maximal...; ~ *wages pl.* Spitzenlohn *m*.
May[1] [mei] Mai *m*; ♀ ⚘ Weißdornblüte *f*.
may[2] [~] *v/aux.* (*irr.*) mag, kann, darf.
may·be ['meibiː] vielleicht.
may-bee·tle *zo.* ['meibiːtl], '**may-bug** Maikäfer *m*.
may·day ['meidei] *internationales Funk-Notsignal.*
May Day ['meidei] der 1. Mai.
may·fly *zo.* ['meiflai] Eintagsfliege *f*.
may·hap † ['meihæp] vielleicht.
may·hem ['meihem] *Am.*, ⚖ schwere Körperverletzung *f od.* Verstümmelung *f*; Chaos *n*, Verwüstung *f*.
may·on·naise [meiə'neiz] Mayonnaise *f*.
may·or [mɛə] Bürgermeister *m*; '**may·or·al** bürgermeisterlich;

ˈ**may·or·al·ty** Bürgermeisteramt *n*, -würde *f*; ˈ**may·or·ess** Bürgermeisterin *f*.
may·pole [ˈmeipəul] Maibaum *m*.
maze [meiz] Irrgarten *m*, Labyrinth *n*; *fig. a.* Wirrnis *f*; *be* ~*d*, *be in a* ~ bestürzt *od.* verlegen sein; ˈ**ma·zy** □ labyrinthisch; wirr, verworren.
Mc·Coy *Am. sl.* [məˈkɔi]: *the real* ~ der wahre Jakob, das Richtige.
me [miː, mi] mich; mir; F ich.
mead[1] [miːd] Met *m*.
mead[2] *poet.* [~] = *meadow*.
mead·ow [ˈmedəu] Wiese *f*; ˈ~-ˈ**saf·fron** ⚘ Herbstzeitlose *f*; ˈ**mead·ow·y** wiesenartig, -reich.
mea·ger, mea·gre □ [ˈmiːgə] mager, dürr (*a. fig.*); dürftig; ˈ**mea·ger·ness,** ˈ**mea·gre·ness** Magerkeit *f*; Dürre *f*; Dürftigkeit *f*.
meal[1] [miːl] Mahl *n*; Mahlzeit *f*; ~*s pl. on wheels* Essen *n* auf Rädern.
meal[2] [~] *grobes* Mehl *n*; **meal·ies** [ˈ~iz] *pl. Süd-Afrika*: Mais *m*.
meal·time [ˈmiːltaim] Essenszeit *f*.
meal·y [ˈmiːli] mehlig; ˈ~-**mouthed** duckmäuserig; zimperlich.
mean[1] □ [miːn] gemein, niedrig, gering; armselig; niederträchtig; schäbig; knauserig; kleinlich.
mean[2] [~] **1.** mittel, mittler, mittelmäßig; Durchschnitts...; *in the* ~ *time* = ~*time*; **2.** Mitte *f*; Mittelmäßigkeit *f*; ⚖ Mittel *n*; ~*s pl.* (Geld)Mittel *n/pl.*, Vermögen *n*; (Vermögens)Verhältnisse *n/pl.*; (*a. sg.*) Mittel *n*, Weg *m zu e-m Zweck*, Möglichkeit *f*; *by all* ~*s* jedenfalls; ganz gewiß; *by no* ~*s* keineswegs; *by this* ~*s* hierdurch; *by* ~*s of* mit Hilfe (*gen.*), durch; *by some* ~*s or other* auf irgendeine Weise; ~*s* ˈtest Bedürftigkeitsüberprüfung *f*.
mean[3] [~] (*irr.*) meinen; (ge)denken, beabsichtigen, vorhaben; bestimmen (*for* zu); sagen wollen (*by* mit); bedeuten, heißen; ~ *well* (*ill*) es gut (schlecht) meinen (*by*, *a. to* mit).
me·an·der [miˈændə] **1.** Windung *f*, Krümmung *f*; ~*s pl. a.* Schlängelweg *m*; **2.** sich schlängeln.
mean·ing [ˈmiːniŋ] **1.** □ bedeutsam; *well* ~ wohlmeinend, -wollend; **2.** Sinn *m*, Bedeutung *f*; ⚒ Absicht *f*; ˈ**mean·ing·less** bedeutungslos; sinnlos; ausdruckslos (*Züge*).
mean·ness [ˈmiːnnis] Gemeinheit *f*, Niedrigkeit *f etc.* (*s. mean*[1]).
meant [ment] *pret. u. p.p. von mean*[3].
mean·time [ˈmiːnˈtaim], **mean·while** [ˈmiːnˈwail] mittlerweile, inzwischen, unterdessen.
mea·sles [ˈmiːzlz] *pl.* ⚕ Masern *pl.*; *vet.* Finnen *f/pl.*; *German* ~ Röteln *pl.*; ˈ**mea·sly** finnig; fleckig; *sl.* armselig.
meas·ur·a·ble □ [ˈmeʒərəbl] meßbar.
meas·ure [ˈmeʒə] **1.** Maß *n*; ♪ Takt *m*; Maßnahme *f*, -regel *f*; ~ *of capacity* Hohlmaß *n*; *beyond* ~ über alle Maßen; *in some* ~ gewissermaßen; *in a great* ~ großenteils; *made to* ~ nach Maß gemacht; *for good* ~ gut gemessen; *set* ~*s to* Grenzen setzen (*dat.*); *take s.o.'s* ~ j. taxieren, j. abschätzen; *take* ~*s* Maßnahmen ergreifen; **2.** messen; ab-, aus-, vermessen; *j-m* Maß nehmen (*for* zu); ~ *up Am.* heranreichen (*to* an); ˈ**mea·sure·less** □ unermeßlich; ˈ**meas·ure·ment** (Ab)Messung *f*; Maß *n*; ⚓ Tonnengehalt *m*.
meas·ur·ing [ˈmeʒəriŋ] messend; Meß...
meat [miːt] Fleisch *n* (*a. von Früchten*); † *od. prov.* Speise *f*; *fig.* (innerer) Gehalt *m*; *butcher's* ~ Schlachtfleisch *n*; *cold* ~ kalter Braten *m*; *fresh* ~ Frischfleisch *n*; *preserved* ~ Fleischkonserve *f*; *roast* ~ Braten *m*; ˈ~**ball** Fleischklößchen *n*; ˈ~-**fly** *zo.* Schmeißfliege *f*; ~ **loaf** Hackbraten *m*; ~ **pie** Fleischpastete *f*; ˈ~-**safe** Fliegen-, Speiseschrank *m*; ~ **tea** = *high tea*; ˈ**meat·y** fleischig; *fig.* gehaltvoll.
mec·ca·no [miˈkɑːnəu] Stabilbaukasten *m*.
me·chan·ic [miˈkænik] Handwerker *m*; Mechaniker *m*; **me**ˈ**chan·i·cal** □ mechanisch; Maschinen...; ~ *engineering* Maschinenbau(kunde *f*) *m*; **mech·a·ni·cian** [mekəˈniʃən] Mechaniker *m*; Monteur *m*; **me·chan·ics** [miˈkæniks] *mst sg.* Mechanik *f*.
mech·a·nism [ˈmekənizəm] Mechanismus *m*; ˈ**mech·a·nize** mechanisieren; ⚔ motorisieren.
med·al [ˈmedl] Medaille *f*, Denkmünze *f*; Orden *m*, Auszeichnung *f*;

ˈ**med·al(l)ed** medaillengeschmückt; **me·dal·lion** [miˈdæljən] Medaillon *n*; Schaumünze *f*; **med·al·(l)ist** [ˈmedlist] Medaillenschneider *m*; Münzkenner *m*; Medaillenträger (-in).

med·dle [ˈmedl] (*with, in*) sich einmischen (in *acc.*); sich abgeben (mit); ˈ**med·dler** Eindringling *m*, Unberufene *m*; **med·dle·some** [ˈ~səm] □ zudringlich; vorwitzig.

me·di·a[1] [ˈmiːdjə] *pl. von medium.*

me·di·a[2] [~] *pl.* Medien *n/pl.*

me·di·ae·val [mediˈiːvəl] = *medieval.*

me·di·al □ [ˈmiːdjəl], ˈ**me·di·an** Mittel..., in der Mitte (stehend *od.* befindlich).

me·di·an strip *Am.* [ˈmiːdjənˈstrip] Mittelstreifen *m* (*der Autobahn etc.*).

me·di·ate 1. □ [ˈmiːdiit] mittelbar; **2.** [ˈmiːdieit] vermitteln; **me·diˈa·tion** Vermittlung *f*; ˈ**me·di·a·tor** Vermittler *m*; *eccl.* Mittler *m*; **me·di·a·to·ri·al** □ [~əˈtɔːriəl], **me·di·a·to·ry** [ˈ~ətəri] vermittelnd; Mittler...; **me·di·a·trix** [ˈ~eitriks] Vermittlerin *f*.

med·ic F [ˈmedik] Mediziner(in) (*Medizinstudent, a. Arzt*).

Med·ic·aid *Am.* [ˈmedikeid] Gesundheitsfürsorge *f* für Arme und Arbeitsunfähige.

med·i·cal □ [ˈmedikəl] medizinisch, ärztlich; ~ *board* Gesundheitsbehörde *f*; ~ *certificate* Krankenschein *m*, Attest *n*; ~ *evidence* ärztliches Gutachten *n*; ~ *jurisprudence* Gerichtsmedizin *f*; ~ *man* Arzt *m*, Mediziner *m*; ~ *officer* Amtsarzt *m*; ~ *specialist* Facharzt *m*; ~ *student* Medizinstudent *m*; 2 *Superintendent* Chefarzt *m*; ~ *ward* innere Abteilung *f e-s Krankenhauses*; **meˈdic·a·ment** Heilmittel *n*.

Med·i·care *Am.* [ˈmedikɛə] Gesundheitsfürsorge *f bsd. für ältere Bürger.*

med·i·cate [ˈmedikeit] medizinisch behandeln; mit Arzneistoff versetzen; **med·iˈca·tion** Beimischung *f* von Arzneistoffen; medizinische Behandlung *f*; **med·i·ca·tive** [ˈ~kətiv] heilend.

me·dic·i·nal □ [meˈdisinl] medizinisch; heilend, heilsam; als Arznei (dienend).

med·i·cine [ˈmedsin] Medizin *f*; Arznei *f*; Heilkunde *f*; ˈ**~-ball** *Sport*: Medizinball *m*; ˈ**~-chest** Hausapotheke *f*; ˈ**~-man** Medizinmann *m*.

med·i·co F *co.* [ˈmedikəu] Medikus *m* (*Arzt*).

me·di·e·val □ [mediˈiːvəl] mittelalterlich.

me·di·o·cre [miːdiˈəukə] mittelmäßig; **me·di·oc·ri·ty** [~ˈɔkriti] Mittelmäßigkeit *f*; kleiner Geist *m*.

med·i·tate [ˈmediteit] *v/i.* nachdenken (*on* über *acc.*), überlegen; *v/t.* sinnen auf (*acc.*); erwägen, planen; **med·iˈta·tion** Nachdenken *n*, -sinnen *n*; *innere* Betrachtung *f*; **med·i·ta·tive** □ [ˈ~tətiv] nachdenklich, meditativ.

Med·i·ter·ra·ne·an [meditəˈreinjən] Mittelmeer *n*.

me·di·um [ˈmiːdjəm] **1.** *pl. a.* **me·di·a** [ˈ~djə] Mitte *f*; Mittelweg *m*; Mittel *n*; Vermittlung *f*; vermittelnder Stoff *m*; *phys. u. Spiritismus*: Medium *n*; *biol.* Nährboden *m*; *Lebens*-Element *n*; **2.** mittel, mittlere(r, -s); *Zensur*: genügend; Mittel..., Durchschnitts...; ˈ**~-ˈsized** mittelgroß; **~ wave** *Radio*: Mittelwelle *f*.

med·lar ♀ [ˈmedlə] Mispel *f*.

med·ley [ˈmedli] Gemisch *n*; *contp.* Mischmasch *m*; ♪ Potpourri *n*.

me·dul·la [meˈdʌlə] Mark *n*; **medˈul·lar·y** Mark...; markig.

me·du·sa *zo.* [miˈdjuːzə] Meduse *f*, Qualle *f*.

meed *poet.* [miːd] Lohn *m*.

meek □ [miːk] sanft(mütig); demütig; bescheiden; ˈ**meek·ness** Sanftmut *f*; Demut *f*.

meer·schaum [ˈmiəʃəm] Meerschaum(pfeife *f*) *m*.

meet[1] [miːt] passend; schicklich.

meet[2] [~] **1.** (*irr.*) *v/t.* treffen; begegnen (*dat.*); kennenlernen; abholen *vom Bahnhof etc.*; stoßen auf *den Gegner*; *e-r Meinung etc.* entgegenkommen; *Wunsch, Nachfrage* befriedigen, *e-m Wunsch* gerecht werden, *e-r Verpflichtung* nachkommen; *der Not* steuern; ~ *s.o. half-way fig.* j-m auf halbem Weg entgegenkommen; *come od. go od. run to* ~ *s.o.* j-m entgegenkommen *od.* -gehen *od.* -laufen; *they are well met* sie passen zueinander; ~ *one's death* den Tod finden; ~ *the eye* (*ear*) zu sehen (hören) sein; ~ *s.o.'s eye* j-s Blick erwidern; *v/i.* sich treffen, einander begegnen; feindlich zs.-stoßen, handgemein werden; sich versammeln; ~ *with* stoßen auf (*acc.*); erfahren, erleiden, betroffen werden von; ~ *with an accident* verunglücken; *make both ends* ~ mit seinen Einkünften auskommen, sich einrichten; **2.** *Sport*: (Zs.-) Treffen *n*.

meet·ing ['mi:tiŋ] Begegnung *f*; (Zs.-)Treffen *n*, Zs.-kunft *f*, Versammlung *f*; Sitzung *f*, Tagung *f*; '**~-house** Versammlungshaus *n*; Andachtshaus *n*, Kirche *f bsd. der Quäker*; '**~-place** Sammelplatz *m*.

meg·a·cy·cle ⚡ ['megəsaikl] Megahertz *n*; **meg·a·fog** ['~fɔg] sehr lautes Nebelsignal *n*; **meg·a·lith** ['~liθ] Megalith *m*, großer Steinblock *m*; **meg·a·lo·ma·ni·a** ['~ləu'meinjə] Größenwahn *m*; **meg·a·lop·o·lis** [~'lɔpəlis] Großstadt *f*; Ballungsraum *m*; **meg·a·phone** ['~fəun] Megaphon *n*, Sprachrohr *n*; **meg·a·ton** ['~tʌn] Megatonne *f* (*Sprengwirkung von 1 Million t Trinitrotoluol*).

me·grim ['mi:grim] Migräne *f*; Grille *f*, Schrulle *f*; ~*s pl.* Schwermut *f*.

mel·an·chol·ic [melən'kɔlik] melancholisch; **mel·an·chol·y** ['~kəli] **1.** Melancholie *f*, Schwermut *f*; **2.** melancholisch; schwermütig; düster.

mé·lange [mei'lɑ̃:nʒ] Mischung *f*, Gemisch *n*.

mê·lée ['melei] Handgemenge *n*; Tumult *m*.

mel·io·rate ['mi:ljəreit] (sich) verbessern.

mel·lif·lu·ent [me'lifluənt], *mst* **mel'lif·lu·ous** honigsüß.

mel·low ['meləu] **1.** □ mürbe, reif, weich; *fig.* gereift (*Urteil etc.*); mild; *fig.* weich, sanft, zart (*Ton, Farbe, Licht*); *sl.* angeheitert; **2.** reifen (lassen); weich machen *od.* werden; (sich) mildern; '**mel·low·ness** Reife *f*, Mürbheit *f*; Milde *f*; Sanftheit *f*, Weichheit *f*.

me·lo·di·ous □ [mi'ləudjəs] melodisch, wohlklingend; **me'lo·di·ous·ness** Wohlklang *m*; **mel·o·dist** ['melədist] Liederkomponist *m*, -sänger *m*; '**mel·o·dize** melodisch machen; *Lied etc.* vertonen; **mel·o·dra·ma** ['meləudrɑ:mə] Melodrama *n*; Volksstück *n*; **me·lo·dra'mat·ic** melodramatisch; **mel·o·dy** ['melədi] Melodie *f*; Lied *n*.

mel·on ⚘ ['melən] Melone *f*.

melt [melt] (zer)schmelzen, zergehen (lassen); *fig.* zerfließen; *Gefühl* erweichen; ~ *away* dahinschmelzen; *fig.* (dahin)schwinden; ~ *down* einschmelzen; ~ *into tears* in Tränen zerfließen.

melt·ing □ ['meltiŋ] schmelzend; Schmelz...; *fig.* weich; schmachtend; '**~-point** Schmelzpunkt *m*; '**~-pot** Schmelztiegel *m* (*a. fig.*).

mem·ber ['membə] Mitglied *n*; *parl.* Abgeordnete *m, f*; Glied *n*; *make a* ~ eingliedern (*of* in *acc.*); '**mem·ber·ship** Mitgliedschaft *f*; Mitgliederzahl *f*; ~ *card* Mitgliedsausweis *m*; ~ *fee* Mitgliedsbeitrag *m*.

mem·brane ['membrein] Membran(e) *f*, Häutchen *n*; **mem'bra·nous, mem'bra·ne·ous** [~jəs] häutig.

me·men·to [mi'mentəu] Erinnerungszeichen *n*, Andenken *n*.

mem·o ['meməu] = *memorandum*.

mem·oir ['memwɑ:] Denkschrift *f*; ~*s pl.* Memoiren *n/pl.*; Lebenserinnerungen *f/pl.*

mem·o·ra·ble □ ['memərəbl] denkwürdig.

mem·o·ran·dum [memə'rændəm] Notiz *f*; *pol.* Note *f*, Memorandum *n*; Schriftsatz *m*; (*mst* innerbetriebliche) Mitteilung *f*.

me·mo·ri·al [mi'mɔ:riəl] **1.** Gedächtnis..., Gedenk...; ♀ *Day Am.* Gefallenengedenktag *m* (*30. Mai*); **2.** Denkmal *n*; Denkschrift *f*; Eingabe *f*; Gesuch *n*; **me'mo·ri·al·ist** Bittsteller(in); **me'mo·ri·al·ize** ein Gesuch einreichen bei.

mem·o·rize ['meməraiz] auswendig lernen, memorieren.

mem·o·ry ['meməri] Gedächtnis *n*; Erinnerung(svermögen *n*) *f*; Andenken *n*; *Computer*: Speicher *m*; *commit to* ~ dem Gedächtnis einprägen; *beyond* (*within*) *the* ~ *of man* vor (seit) Menschengedenken; *in* ~ *of* zum Andenken an (*acc.*).

men [men] *pl. von man*; Männer *m/pl.*; Menschen *m/pl.*; Mannschaft *f*.

men·ace ['menəs] **1.** (be)drohen; **2.** Gefahr *f*; Drohung *f*.

me·nag·er·ie [mi'nædʒəri] Menagerie *f.*

mend [mend] **1.** *v/t.* (ver)bessern; ausbessern, flicken; besser machen; *den Schritt* beschleunigen; ~ *the fire* (Kohlen *etc.*) nachlegen; ~ *one's ways* sich *moralisch* bessern; *v/i.* sich bessern; genesen; **2.** Flicken *m*; *on the* ~ auf dem Wege der Besserung.

men·da·cious □ [men'deiʃəs] lügnerisch, verlogen; **men·dac·i·ty** [~'dæsiti] Verlogenheit *f*; Unwahrheit *f.*

mend·er ['mendə] Ausbesserer *m.*

men·di·can·cy ['mendikənsi] Bettelei *f*; '**men·di·cant** **1.** bettelnd; Bettel...; **2.** Bettler *m*; Bettelmönch *m*; **men'dic·i·ty** [~siti] Bettelei *f.*

men·folk F ['menfəuk] *die* Männer *pl.*

men·hir ['menhiə] Druidenstein *m.*

me·ni·al *contp.* ['mi:njəl] **1.** □ knechtisch, niedrig; **2.** Knecht *m*; Lakai *m.*

men·in·gi·tis ⚕ [menin'dʒaitis] Hirnhautentzündung *f*, Meningitis *f.*

men·o·pause ['menəupɔ:z] Wechseljahre *pl*, Menopause *f.*

men·ses ['mensi:z] *pl.* Menses *pl.* (*s. menstruation*); **men·stru·al** ['~struəl] monatlich; Menstruations...; '**men·stru·ate** menstruieren, die Regel haben; **men·stru'a·tion** Menstruation *f*, monatliche Regel *f*, Periode *f.*

men·su·ra·ble ['menʃurəbl] meßbar; **men·su·ra·tion** [~sjuə'reiʃən] Meßkunst *f.*

men·tal □ ['mentl] geistig; Geistes-...; seelisch; ~ *arithmetic* Kopfrechnen *n*; ~ *home*, ~ *hospital* Nervenheilanstalt *f*; ~*ly handicapped* geistig behindert; ~*ly ill* geisteskrank; **men·tal·i·ty** [~'tæliti] Mentalität *f*, Geisteshaltung *f*, Denkart *f.*

men·thol *pharm.* ['menθɔl] Menthol *n.*

men·tion ['menʃən] **1.** Erwähnung *f*; **2.** erwähnen; *don't* ~ *it!* bitte!; *not to* ~ ..., *without* ~*ing* ... ganz zu schweigen von ...; **men·tion·a·ble** ['~ʃnəbl] erwähnenswert.

men·tor ['mentɔ:] Mentor *m.*

men·u ['menju:] Speisenfolge *f*, Menü *n*; Speisekarte *f.*

Meph·is·to·phe·le·an [mefistə'fi:ljən] mephistophelisch, teuflisch.

mer·can·tile ['mə:kəntail] kaufmännisch; Handels...; ~ *marine* Handelsmarine *f.*

mer·ce·nar·y ['mə:sinəri] **1.** □ feil, käuflich; gedungen; gewinnsüchtig; **2.** ⚔ Söldner *m.*

mer·cer ['mə:sə] Seidenwaren-, Stoffhändler *m*; '**mer·cer·y** Seidenwaren *f/pl.*, Stoffe *m/pl.*; Stoffgeschäft *n.*

mer·cer·ize ['mə:səraiz] *Baumwolle* merzerisieren (*veredeln*).

mer·chan·dise ['mə:tʃəndaiz] Ware(n *pl.*) *f.*

mer·chant ['mə:tʃənt] **1.** Kaufmann *m*; *Am.* Kleinhändler *m*, Händler *m*; **2.** Handels..., Kaufmanns...; *law* ~ Handelsrecht *n*; '**mer·chant·a·ble** marktfähig; **mer·chant bank** Handelsbank *f*; '**mer·chant·man, mer·chant ship** Handelsschiff *n*; **mer·chant na·vy** Handelsmarine *f.*

mer·ci·ful □ ['mə:siful] barmherzig; gnädig (*Gott, Strafe*); '**mer·ci·ful·ness** Barmherzigkeit *f*, Gnade *f.*

mer·ci·less □ ['mə:silis] unbarmherzig, erbarmungslos; '**mer·ci·less·ness** Erbarmungslosigkeit *f.*

mer·cu·ri·al [mə:'kjuəriəl] Merkur...; ⚗ Quecksilber...; *fig.* quecksilbrig; unbeständig, launisch.

Mer·cu·ry ['mə:kjuri] Merkur *m*; *fig.* Bote *m*; ♀ ⚗ Quecksilber *n*; ♀ *poisoning* Quecksilbervergiftung *f.*

mer·cy ['mə:si] Barmherzigkeit *f*; Gnade *f*; *be at s.o.'s* ~ in j-s Gewalt sein; *at the* ~ *of the waves* den Wellen preisgegeben; *have* ~ *upon* sich erbarmen (*gen.*); *it is a* ~ *that* ... es ist ein wahrer Segen, daß ...; ~ *killing* Gnadentod *m.*

mere[1] [miə] Teich *m*, Weiher *m.*

mere[2] [~] rein, lauter; bloß; ~(*st*) *nonsense* rein(st)er Unsinn *m*; ~ *words pl.* bloße Worte *n/pl.*; '**mere·ly** nur, rein, bloß, lediglich, allein.

mer·e·tri·cious □ [meri'triʃəs] hurerisch; *fig.* aufdringlich; kitschig.

merge [mə:dʒ] *v/t.* (*in*) verschmelzen (mit); einverleiben (*dat.*); *v/i.* (*in*) verschmelzen (mit), aufgehen (in *dat.*); *Am. mot.* sich (in den Verkehr) einfädeln; '**merg·er** Verschmelzung *f*; ⚜ Fusion *f.*

me·rid·i·an [mə'ridiən] **1.** mittägig; Mittags...; *fig.* höchst; **2.** *geogr.* Meridian *m*; Mittag *m*; *fig.* Gipfel *m*; **me'rid·i·o·nal** □ mittägig, südlich.

me·ringue [mə'ræŋ] Baiser *n*, Meringe *f*.

me·ri·no [mə'ri:nəu] Merinoschaf *n*; Merinowolle *f*; Merino *m* (*Stoff*).

mer·it ['merit] **1.** Verdienst *n*; Wert *m*; Vorzug *m*; Bedeutung *f*; ~*s pl. bsd.* ⚖ Hauptpunkte *m/pl.*, Wesen *n e-r Sache*; *on the* ~*s of the case* nach wesentlichen Gesichtspunkten; *on its (own)* ~*s* für sich allein, an sich; *make a* ~ *of* als Verdienst ansehen; **2.** *fig.* verdienen; **mer·i·to·ri·ous** □ [~'tɔ:riəs] verdienstvoll, lobenswert.

mer·maid ['mə:meid] Seejungfer *f*, Nixe *f*; **mer·man** ['~mæn] Wassermann *m*; Triton *m*.

mer·ri·ment ['merimənt] Lustigkeit *f*; Belustigung *f*, Lustbarkeit *f*.

mer·ry □ ['meri] lustig, fröhlich; scherzhaft, ergötzlich; *make* ~ vergnügt *od.* lustig sein; **~-an·drew** ['~'ændru:] Hanswurst *m*; '**~-go--round** Karussell *n*; '**~-mak·ing** Lustbarkeit *f*, Fest *n*; '**~·thought** Gabelbein *n e-s Huhns*.

me·sa *geogr.* ['meisə] Tafelberg *m*, kleines Plateau *n*.

mé·sal·li·ance [me'zæliəns] Mesalliance *f*, Mißheirat *f*.

me·seems † [mi'si:mz] es scheint mir.

mes·en·ter·y *anat.* ['mesəntəri] Gekröse *n*.

mesh [meʃ] **1.** Masche *f*; *fig. oft* ~*es pl.* Netz *n*; *be in* ~ ⊕ (ineinander-) greifen; **2.** in e-m Netz fangen; ⊕ (ineinander)greifen; **meshed** ...-maschig; '**mesh-work** Netzwerk *n*; Gespinst *n*.

mes·mer·ism ['mezmərizəm] Mesmerismus *m*; '**mes·mer·ize** magnetisieren.

mess¹ [mes] **1.** Wirrwarr *m*; Unordnung *f*, Durcheinander *n*; Schmutz *m*; F Manscherei *f*, P Schweinerei *f*; F Schlamassel *m*; Klemme *f*; *look a* ~ F scheußlich aussehen; *make a* ~ *of* verpfuschen, P versauen; **2.** *v/t. a.* ~ *up* in Unordnung bringen; verpfuschen, verderben; *v/i.* ~ *about* herummanschen, -murksen.

mess² [~] **1.** Gericht *n*, Portion *f*; ⚔ Kasino *n*, Messe *f*; ⚓ Back *f*; **2.** zusammen speisen.

mes·sage ['mesidʒ] Botschaft *f*, Sendung *f*; Meldung *f*, Mitteilung *f*; *get the* ~ F (es) kapieren; *go on a* ~ e-e Besorgung machen; *take a* ~ et. ausrichten.

mes·sen·ger ['mesindʒə] Bote *m*; ~ *boy* Botenjunge *m*, Kurier *m*.

Mes·si·ah *eccl.* [mi'saiə] Messias *m*.

Mes·sieurs, *mst* **Messrs.** ['mesəz] (die) Herren *m/pl.*; Firma *f*.

mess·ing al·low·ance ⚔ ['mesiŋə'lauəns] Verpflegungsgeld *n*.

mess...: '**~-jacket** ⚔ kurze Uniformjacke *f*; '**~·mate** ⚔, ⚓ Tischgenosse *m*; '**~-room** Kasino *n*; '**~--tin** Kochgeschirr *n*.

mes·suage ⚖ ['meswidʒ] Anwesen *n*.

mess-up F ['mesʌp] Durcheinander *n*; Mißverständnis *n*.

mess·y ['mesi] unordentlich, schlampig; schmutzig.

met [met] *pret. u. p.p. von meet² 1.*

met·a·bol·ic [metə'bɔlik] Stoffwechsel...; **me·tab·o·lism** *physiol.* [me'tæbəlizəm] Stoffwechsel *m*.

met·age ['mi:tidʒ] Meß-, Wägegeld *n*.

met·al ['metl] **1.** Metall *n*; *Wegebau*: Beschotterung *f*, Schotter *m*; ~*s pl.* F Schienen *f/pl.*, Geleise *n*; **2.** beschottern; **me·tal·lic** [mi'tælik] (~*ally*) metallisch; Metall...; **met·al·lif·er·ous** [metə'lifərəs] metallhaltig; **met·al·line** ['~lain] metallen; '**met·al·lize** metallisieren; **met·al·log·ra·phy** [~'lɔgrəfi] Metallographie *f*; **met·al·loid** ['~lɔid] **1.** metallartig; **2.** Nichtmetall *n*; **met·al·lur·gic, met·al·lur·gi·cal** □ [~'lə:dʒik(əl)] metallurgisch; **met·al·lur·gy** [me'tælədʒi] Metallurgie *f*, Hüttenkunde *f*.

met·a·mor·phose [metə'mɔ:fəuz] verwandeln, umgestalten; **met·a·'mor·pho·sis** [~fəsis], *pl.* **met·a·'mor·pho·ses** [~fəsi:z] Verwandlung *f*, Metamorphose *f*.

met·a·phor ['metəfə] Metapher *f*, bildlicher Ausdruck *m*; **met·a·phor·ic**, *mst* **met·a·phor·i·cal** □ [~'fɔrik(əl)] bildlich, übertragen, metaphorisch.

met·a·phys·ic [metə'fizik] **1.** *mst* **met·a'phys·i·cal** □ metaphysisch; **2. met·a'phys·ics** *oft sg.* Meta-

physik *f*.
mete [mi:t] messen; *mst ~ out* zumessen.
me·te·or ['mi:tjə] Meteor *m*, *n* (*a. fig.*); **me·te·or·ic** [mi:ti'ɔrik] meteorisch; Meteor...; **me·te·or·ite** ['mi:tjərait] Meteorstein *m*, Meteorit *m*; **me·te·or·o·log·i·cal** □ [mi:tjərə'lɔdʒikəl] meteorologisch; **me·te·or·ol·o·gist** [~'rɔlədʒist] Meteorologe *m*; **me·te·or'ol·o·gy** Meteorologie *f*, Wetterkunde *f*.
me·ter ['mi:tə] Messer *m*, Meßinstrument *n*, Zähler *m*; '**~·maid** *Am.* F Politesse *f*.
me·thinks † [mi'θiŋks] (*pret. methought*) mich dünkt.
meth·od ['meθəd] Methode *f*; Art u. Weise *f*; Verfahren *n*; Ordnung *f*, System *n*; **me·thod·ic**, *mst* **me·thod·i·cal** □ [mi'θɔdik(əl)] methodisch; **Meth·od·ism** *eccl.* ['meθədizəm] Methodismus *m*; '**Meth·od·ist** *eccl.* Methodist *m*; '**meth·od·ize** methodisch ordnen.
me·thought † [mi'θɔ:t] *pret. von methinks.*
meth·yl ⚗ ['meθil] Methyl *n*, **meth·yl·at·ed spir·it** ['meθileitid-'spirit] vergällter Spiritus *m*; **meth·yl·ene** ['meθili:n] Methylen *n*.
me·tic·u·lous □ [mi'tikjuləs] peinlich genau, äußerst gewissenhaft.
me·tre ['mi:tə] Versmaß *n*, Metrum *n*; Meter *n*, *m*.
met·ric ['metrik] (*~ally*) metrisch; *~ system* Dezimalsystem *n*; '**met·ri·cal** □ metrisch; Vers...; messend; Maß...; '**met·rics** *pl. u. sg.* Metrik *f*, Verslehre *f*.
Met·ro F ['metrəu] Metro *f*, Stadtbahn *f*, U-Bahn *f*; '**~·land** F *die* Außenbezirke *m/pl.*, *die* Vororte *m/pl. Londons.*
me·trop·o·lis [mi'trɔpəlis] Hauptstadt *f*, Metropole *f*; **met·ro·pol·i·tan** [metrə'pɔlitən] **1.** hauptstädtisch; *~ Railway* Stadtbahn *f*; **2.** Erzbischof *m*; Metropolit *m*.
met·tle ['metl] Feuereifer *m*, Mut *m*; *be on one's ~* sein Bestes tun; *put s.o. on his ~* j. anspornen, sein möglichstes zu leisten; *a horse full of ~* ein feuriges Pferd *n*; '**met·tled**, **met·tle·some** ['~səm] hitzig, feurig, mutig.
mew[1] *orn.* [mju:] Möwe *f*.
mew[2] [~] **1.** Miau *n*; **2.** miauen.
mew[3] [~] *mst ~ up* einsperren, einschließen.
mewl [mju:l] wimmern, F mauzen.
mews [mju:z] *hist.* königlicher Marstall *m*; Stallung *f*; *daraus entstandene* Garagen *f/pl. od.* Wohnhäuser *n/pl.*
Mex·i·can ['meksikən] **1.** mexikanisch; **2.** Mexikaner(in).
mez·za·nine ['metsəni:n] Zwischenstock *m*, Mezzanin *n*.
mi·aow [mi:'au] **1.** Miau *n*; **2.** miauen.
mi·as·ma [mi'æzmə], *pl. a.* **mi'as·ma·ta** [~tə] schädliche Ausdünstung *f*; Ansteckungsstoff *m*; **mi'as·mal** □ miasmatisch.
miaul [mi'ɔ:l] miauen; mauzen.
mi·ca *min.* ['maikə] Glimmer *m*; **mi·ca·ce·ous** [~'keiʃəs] glimmerartig; Glimmer...
mice [mais] *pl. von mouse.*
Mich·ael·mas ['miklməs] Michaelis(tag *m*) *n* (*29. September*).
mick·ey ['miki] P Betäubungspille *f*; *take the ~ out of s.o.* F j. veräppeln, j. auf den Arm nehmen.
mi·cro... ['maikrəu] klein..., Klein...
mi·crobe ['maikrəub] Mikrobe *f*, Bakterie *f*; **mi'cro·bi·al** [~bjəl] mikrobisch.
mi·cro·cosm ['maikrəukɔzəm] Mikrokosmos *m*; **mi·cro·fiche** ['~fi:ʃ] Mikrofiche *m*; **mi·cro·film** ['~film] **1.** Mikrofilm *m*; **2.** auf Mikrofilm aufnehmen.
mi·crom·e·ter [mai'krɔmitə] Mikrometer *n*, *m*; **mi·cro-or·gan·ism** [maikrəu'ɔ:gənizəm] Mikroorganismus *m*; **mi·cro·phone** ['maikrəfəun] Mikrophon *n*; **mi·cro·pro·ces·sor** [~'prəusesə] Mikroprozessor *m*; **mi·cro·scope** ['~skəup] Mikroskop *n*; **mi·cro·scop·ic**, **mi·cro·scop·i·cal** □ [~s'kɔpik(əl)] mikroskopisch; Mikroskop...; winzig; äußerst genau *od.* fein; **mi·cro·wave** ⚡ ['maikrəuweiv] Mikrowelle *f*, Dezimeterwelle *f*; *~ oven* Mikrowellenherd *m*.
mid [mid] *s. middle* 2; Mitt...; *poet.* = *amid* inmitten *etc.*; *in ~ air* mitten in der Luft; *in ~ winter* mitten im Winter; '**~·day** **1.** Mittag *m*; **2.** mittägig; Mittags...
mid·den ['midn] Misthaufen *m*; Müllgrube *f*.
mid·dle ['midl] **1.** Mitte *f*; Hüften

f/pl.; ~*s pl.* ⚕ Mittelsorte *f*; **2.** mittlere(r, -s); Mittel...; ♀ *Ages pl.* Mittelalter *n*; ~ *America Am.* die amerikanischen Mittelklassen *pl.*; ~ *class*(*es pl.*) Mittelstand *m*; '~-'**aged** von mittlerem Alter; '~-'**class** Mittelstands...; ~ **dis·tance** *paint.* Mittelgrund *m*; ♀ **King·dom** *das* Reich der Mitte; ~ **life** die mittleren Lebensjahre *n/pl.*; '~·**man** Mittelsmann *m*; ⚕ Zwischenhändler *m*; '~·**most** mittelste(r, -s); ~ **name** 2. Vorname *m*; '~-**of-the-**'**road** *pol.* Extreme meidend, gemäßigt; '~-'**sized** mittelgroß; '~-**weight** *Boxen*: Mittelgewicht *n*.

mid·dling ['midliŋ] **1.** *adj.* mittelmäßig; leidlich; Mittel...; Durchschnitts...; **2.** *adv. a.* ~*ly* ziemlich, leidlich; **3.** ~*s pl.* ⚕ Mittelsorte *f*.

mid·dy F ['midi] = *midshipman*.

midge [midʒ] Mücke *f*; **midg·et** ['midʒit] Zwerg *m*, Knirps *m*.

mid·land ['midlənd] **1.** binnenländisch; **2.** *the* ♀*s pl.* Mittelengland *n*; '**mid-**'**morn·ing break** große (Vormittags)Pause *f*; '**mid·most** mittelste(r, -s); '**mid·night 1.** Mitternacht *f*; **2.** mitternächtlich; Mitternachts...; **mid·riff** ['~rif] Zwerchfell *n*; '**mid·ship·man** Seekadett *m*; Leutnant *m* zur See; *Am.* Oberfähnrich *m* zur See; '**mid·ships** ⚓ mittschiffs; **midst** [midst] **1.** Mitte *f*; *in the* ~ *of* inmitten (*gen.*); *in our* ~ (mitten) unter uns; **2.** *prp. poet. s. amidst* inmitten *etc.*; '**mid·stream 1.** Strom-, Flußmitte *f*; **2.** *adv.* in der Flußmitte; '**mid·sum·mer** Sommersonnenwende *f*; Hochsommer *m*; ♀ *Day* Johannistag *m*; '**mid**'**way 1.** halber Weg *m*; *Am.* Schaubudenstraße *f*, Rummelplatz *m*; **2.** *adj.* in der Mitte befindlich; **3.** *adv.* auf halbem Wege; '**mid·wife** Hebamme *f*; **mid·wife·ry** ['~wifəri] Geburtshilfe *f*; '**mid-**'**win·ter** Wintersonnenwende *f*; Mitte *f* des Winters.

mien *lit.* [mi:n] Miene *f*.

miff F [mif] Verstimmung *f*.

might [mait] **1.** Macht *f*, Gewalt *f*, Kraft *f*; *with* ~ *and main* mit aller Gewalt; **2.** *pret. von may*; **might·i·ness** ['~tinis] Macht *f*, Gewalt *f*; '**might·y** □ **1.** *adj.* mächtig, gewaltig; F riesig; **2.** F *adv.* sehr, mächtig.

mi·gnon·ette ⚘ [minjə'net] Reseda *f*.

mi·graine ['mi:grein] Migräne *f*.

mi·grant ['maigrənt] **1.** = *migratory*; **2.** *a.* ~ *bird* Zugvogel *m*.

mi·grate [mai'greit] (fort)ziehen; (aus)wandern; **mi**'**gra·tion** Wanderung *f*; Zug *m*; **mi·gra·to·ry** ['~grətəri] wandernd; Zug...; nomadisch.

mike *sl.* [maik] Mikrophon *n*.

mil [mil] Tausend *n*; $^1/_{1000}$ Zoll *m*.

mil·age ['mailidʒ] = *mileage*.

Mil·an·ese [milə'ni:z] **1.** mailändisch; **2.** Mailänder(in).

milch [miltʃ] milchgebend, melkbar; Milch...; ~ *cow* Milchkuh *f*.

mild □ [maild] mild, sanft; gelind; *to put it* ~*ly* gelinde gesagt.

mil·dew ['mildju:] **1.** Mehltau *m*, Brand *m im Getreide*; Moder-, Stockflecke *m/pl.*; **2.** mit Mehltau überziehen, brandig machen *od.* werden.

mild·ness ['maildnis] Milde *f*.

mile [mail] Meile *f* (*1609,33 m*).

mile·age ['mailidʒ] Laufzeit *f in Meilen*, Meilenstand *m e-s Autos*; Kilometergeld *n*.

mil·er ['mailə] *Sport*: Meilenläufer *m*.

mile·stone ['mailstəun] Meilenstein *m* (*a. fig.*).

mil·foil ⚘ ['milfɔil] Schafgarbe *f*.

mi·lieu ['mi:ljə:] Umwelt *f*, Milieu *n*.

mil·i·tan·cy ['militənsi] Kriegszustand *m*; '**mil·i·tant** □ streitend, kriegführend; kämpferisch, militant, aggressiv; **mil·i·ta·rism** ['~tərizəm] Militarismus *m*; '**mil·i·ta·rist** Militarist *m*; '**mil·i·tar·y 1.** □ militärisch; Kriegs...; ~ *college* Kriegsschule *f*; ♀ *Government* Militärregierung *f*; ~ *map* Generalstabskarte *f*; ~ *service* Militär-, Wehrdienst *m*; 2. *das* Militär *n*; **mil·i·tate** ['~teit]: ~ *in favour of* (*against*) sprechen für (gegen); **mi·li·tia** [mi'liʃə] Miliz *f*, Land-, Bürgerwehr *f*; **mi**'**li·tia·man** Milizsoldat *m*.

milk [milk] **1.** Milch *f*; *the* ~ *of human kindness* die Milch der frommen Denkungsart; *it's no use crying over spilt* ~ geschehen ist geschehen; ~ *and water fig.* Gewäsch *n*; **2.** *v/t.* melken; *fig.* schröpfen; ⚡ *u. tel.* anzapfen; *v/i.* Milch geben;

ˈ**milk-and-ˈwa·ter** weichlich; empfindsam; ˈ**milk-bar** Milchbar *f*; ˈ**milk-churn** Milchkanne *f*; ˈ**milk·er** Melker(in); Milchkuh *f*; **milk float** Milchwagen *m*; ˈ**milking-maˈchine** Melkmaschine *f*.

milk...: ˈ**~·maid** Milch-, Kuhmagd *f*; ˈ**~·man** Milchmann *m*; ˈ**~-pow·der** Milchpulver *n*, Trockenmilch *f*; ˈ**~-ˈshake** Milchmischgetränk *n*; ˈ**~-sop** Weichling *m*; ˈ**~-tooth** Milchzahn *m*; ˈ**~-weed** ⚘ Wolfsmilch *f*; ˈ**~-white** milchweiß; ˈ**milk·y** milchig; Milch...; *fig.* weichlich; ♀ *Way* Milchstraße *f*.

mill[1] [mil] **1.** Mühle *f*; Fabrik *f*; Spinnerei *f*; Prägewerk *n*; *sl.* Keilerei *f*; *go through the ~ fig.* e-e harte Schule durchmachen; **2.** mahlen; ⊕ fräsen; *Geld* prägen; *Münze* rändeln; *Tuch* walken; *Ei* quirlen; (rund)herumlaufen; *sl.* durchwalken.

mill[2] *Am.* [~] ein tausendstel Dollar *m* (= $^1/_{10}$ *cent*).

mill·board [ˈmilbɔːd] starker Pappdeckel *m*; ˈ**mill·dam** Mühlwehr *n*.

mil·le·nar·i·an [miliˈnɛəriən], **mil·len·ni·al** [miˈleniəl] tausendjährig; **mil·le·nar·y** [ˈ~nəri] **1.** aus 1000 (Jahren) bestehend; **2.** Jahrtausend (-feier *f*) *n*; **milˈlen·ni·um** [~niəm] Jahrtausend *n*; *das* Tausendjährige Reich Christi.

mil·le·pede *zo.* [ˈmilipiːd] Tausendfüßer *m*.

mill·er [ˈmilə] Müller *m*; ⊕ Fräsmaschine *f*.

mil·les·i·mal [miˈlesiməl] tausendste(r, -s); tausendfach.

mil·let ⚘ [ˈmilit] Hirse *f*.

mill...: ˈ**~-girl** Fabrik-, *bsd.* Spinnereiarbeiterin *f*; ˈ**~-hand** Fabrikarbeiter *m*.

mil·li·ard [ˈmiljɑːd] Milliarde *f*.

mil·li·gram [ˈmiligræm] Milligramm *n*.

mil·li·me·tre [ˈmilimiːtə] Millimeter *n*.

mil·li·ner [ˈmilinə] Putzmacherin *f*, Modistin *f*; ˈ**mil·li·ner·y** Modewaren(geschäft *n*) *pl*.

mill·ing [ˈmiliŋ] Mahlen *n etc.*; *~ cutter* ⊕ Fräser *m*; *~ machine* Fräsmaschine *f*; *~ product* Mühlen-, Walzprodukt *n*.

mil·lion [ˈmiljən] Million *f*; **mil·lion·aire** [~ˈnɛə] Millionär(in); **mil·lionth** [ˈmiljənθ] **1.** millionste (-r, -s); **2.** Millionstel *n*.

mill...: ˈ**~-pond** Mühlteich *m*; ˈ**~-race** Mühlgerinne *n*; ˈ**~·stone** Mühlstein *m*; *see through a ~* F das Gras wachsen hören; ˈ**~-wheel** Mühlrad *n*; ˈ**~·wright** Mühlenbauer *m*.

mi·lord [miˈlɔːd] Lord *m*; reicher Engländer *m*.

milt[1] [milt] Milch *f der Fische*.

milt[2] ⚕ [~] Milz *f*.

milt·er *ichth.* [ˈmiltə] Milch(n)er *m*.

mime [maim] **1.** Mime *m*; **2.** mimen, spielen.

mim·e·o·graph [ˈmimiəgrɑːf] **1.** Vervielfältigungsgerät *n*; **2.** vervielfältigen.

mi·met·ic [miˈmetik] nachahmend.

mim·ic [ˈmimik] **1.** mimisch, nachahmend; nachgeahmt, Schein...; **2.** Mime *m*, Schauspieler *m*; **3.** nachahmen, nachäffen; ˈ**mim·ic·ry** (possenhafte) Nachahmung *f*; *zo.* Angleichung *f*, Mimikry *f*.

mi·mo·sa ⚘ [miˈməuzə] Mimose *f*.

min·a·ret [ˈminəret] Minarett *n*.

min·a·to·ry [ˈminətəri] drohend.

mince [mins] **1.** *v/t.* zerhacken, kleinschneiden; *he does not ~ matters* er nimmt kein Blatt vor den Mund; *~ one's words* geziert sprechen; *v/i.* sich zieren; **2.** *a. ~d meat* Hackfleisch *n*; ˈ**~·meat** Pastetenfüllung *f* (*Rosinen, Talg, Zucker, Zitrone etc.*) *e-s mince-pie*; *make ~ of* in Stücke reißen; ˈ**~-ˈpie** (mit *mincemeat* gefüllte) Pastete *f*; ˈ**minc·er** Fleischwolf *m*.

minc·ing □ [ˈminsiŋ] affektiert; geziert; ˈ**~-ma·chine** = *mincer*.

mind [maind] **1.** Sinn *m*, Gemüt *n*; Geist *m*, Verstand *m*; Meinung *f*; Absicht *f*; Neigung *f*, Lust *f*, Wille *m*; Gedächtnis *n*; Achtsamkeit *f*, Sorge *f*; *to my ~* meiner Ansicht nach, meines Erachtens; nach meinem Sinn; *~'s eye* geistiges Auge *n*; *out of one's ~, not in one's right ~* von Sinnen; *since time out of ~* seit unvordenklichen Zeiten; *change one's ~* sich anders besinnen; *bear s.th. in ~* (immer) an et. denken; *blow s.o.'s ~* P *fig.* j. umwerfen; *have* (*half*) *a ~ to* (beinahe) Lust haben zu; *have s.th. on one's ~* et. auf dem Herzen haben; *have in ~* im Sinne haben; (*not*) *know one's own ~*

(nicht) wissen, was man will; *make up one's ~* sich entschließen; *make up one's ~ to s.th.* sich mit et. abfinden; *put s.o. in ~ of* j. erinnern an (*acc.*); *speak one's ~* offen s-e Meinung sagen; **2.** merken *od.* achten auf (*acc.*); beachten; sich kümmern um; etwas (einzuwenden) haben gegen, *et.* nicht mögen; *~!* gib acht!; *never ~!* mach dir nichts daraus!; macht nichts!; *~ the step!* Achtung, Stufe!; *I don't ~ (it)* ich habe nichts dagegen; *do you ~ if I smoke?* stört es Sie, wenn ich rauche?; *would you ~ taking off your hat?* würden Sie so freundlich sein, den Hut abzunehmen?; *~ your own business!* kümmern Sie sich um Ihre Angelegenheiten; **'mind-bend·ing, 'mind-blow·ing** F bewußtseinsverändernd, -erweiternd; P irre; **'mind-bog·gling** F unvorstellbar; **'mind·ed** gesonnen, gewillt; ...gesinnt; **'mind·er** Wärter *m*; **mind·ful** ['~ful] (*of*) eingedenk (*gen.*); achtsam (auf *acc.*); **'mind·ful·ness** Achtsamkeit *f*; **'mind·less** □ geistlos, unvernünftig; achtlos; unbekümmert (*of* um), ungeachtet (*of gen.*); **'mind-read·er** Gedankenleser *m*.

mine[1] [main] **1.** der (die, das) meinige; mein; **2.** die Mein(ig)en *pl.*

mine[2] [~] **1.** Bergwerk *n*, Grube *f*; *fig.* Fundgrube *f*; ⚔ Mine *f*; **2.** *v/i.* graben, minieren; *v/t.* graben; ⚒ fördern; ⚔ unterminieren; ⚔ verminen; **~ de·tec·tor** ⚔ Minensuchgerät *n*; **'~·field** ⚔ Minenfeld *n*; ⚒ Grubengelände *n*; **'~·lay·er** ⚓, ⚔ Minenleger *m*; **'min·er** Bergmann *m*; *bsd.* ⚔ Minierer *m*; ⚓ Minenleger *m*; *~s' association* Knappschaft *f*.

min·er·al ['minərəl] **1.** Mineral *n*; *~s pl.*, *~ water* Mineralwasser *n*; **2.** mineralisch; **'min·er·al·ize** vererzen; versteinern; **min·er·al·o·gist** [~'rælədʒist] Mineraloge *m*; **min·er'al·o·gy** Mineralogie *f*.

mine·sweep·er ⚓ ['mainswi:pə] Minensucher *m*.

min·gle ['miŋgl] mischen; vermischen; sich mischen *od.* mengen (*with* unter).

min·gy F ['mindʒi] knickerig.

min·i·a·ture ['minjətʃə] **1.** Miniatur(gemälde *n*) *f*; **2.** in Miniatur; Miniatur...; Klein...; *~ camera* Kleinbildkamera *f*.

min·i·bus ['minibʌs] Klein-, Minibus *m*.

min·i·kin ['minikin] **1.** winzig; geziert; **2.** Knirps *m*.

min·im ['minim] ♪ halbe Note *f*; Tropfen *m* (*kleinste Flüssigkeitsmenge*); Knirps *m*; **'min·i·mize** möglichst klein machen; *fig.* verringern, bagatellisieren; **min·i·mum** ['~məm] **1.** Minimum *n*; Mindestmaß *n*, -stand *m*, -betrag *m*; **2.** Minimal..., Mindest...

min·ing ['mainiŋ] **1.** Berg(bau)...; Gruben...; ⚒ Montan...; ⚔, ⚓ Minen...; **2.** Bergbau *m*.

min·ion ['minjən] Günstling *m*; *fig.* Lakai *m*; *typ.* Kolonelschrift *f*; *~s of the law das* Auge des Gesetzes.

min·i·skirt ['miniskə:t] Minirock *m*.

min·is·ter ['ministə] **1.** Diener *m*; *fig.* Werkzeug *n*; Geistliche *m*, Pfarrer *m*; *pol.* Minister *m*; Gesandte *m*; **2.** *v/t.* darreichen, spenden; *v/i.* dienen, aufwarten; dienen, behilflich sein (*to s.th.* e-r Sache); Gottesdienst halten; **min·is·te·ri·al** □ [~'tiəriəl] *pol.* ministeriell, Ministerial...; Regierungs...; *eccl.* geistlich.

min·is·trant ['ministrənt] **1.** dienend; **2.** *eccl.* Ministrant *m*; **min·is'tra·tion** Dienst *m*, Amt *n* (*bsd. eccl.*); **'min·is·try** geistliches Amt *n*; *pol.* Ministerium *n*; Regierung *f*, Kabinett *n*.

min·i·ver ['minivə] Grauwerk *n*, Feh *n* (*Pelz*).

mink *zo.* [miŋk] Nerz *m*.

min·now *ichth.* ['minəu] Elritze *f*.

mi·nor ['mainə] **1.** kleiner, geringer, weniger bedeutend; Unter...; ♪ Moll...; *A ~* a-Moll *n*; *~ third* kleine Terz *f*; *~ key* Moll-Tonart *f*; **2.** Minderjährige *m*, *f*; *nach Eigennamen*: der Jüngere; *phls.* Untersatz *m*; *Am. univ.* Nebenfach *n*; **mi·nor·i·ty** [mai'nɔriti] Minderheit *f*; Unmündigkeit *f*; *~ government* Minderheitsregierung *f*.

min·ster ['minstə] Münster *n*.

min·strel ['minstrəl] Spielmann *m*, Minnesänger *m*; *~s pl.* Negersänger *m/pl.*; **min·strel·sy** ['~si] Spielmannsdichtung *f*; Spielleute *pl.*

mint[1] ⚘ [mint] Minze *f*; *~ sauce* (saure) Minzsoße *f*.

mint[2] [~] **1.** Münze *f*, Münzstätte *f*; *fig.* Gold-, Fundgrube *f*; *a ~ of money* e-e Menge Geld; **2.** einwandfrei, unbeschädigt (*Buch etc.*);

3. münzen, prägen; '**mint·age** Prägung *f*; geprägtes Geld *n*; Münzgebühr *f*.

min·u·et ♪ [minju'et] Menuett *n*.

mi·nus ['mainəs] **1.** *prp.* weniger; F ohne; **2.** *adj.* negativ; **2.** Minus (-zeichen) *n*; Mangel *m*.

mi·nute[1] [mai'nju:t] □ sehr klein, winzig; unbedeutend; sehr genau, sorgfältig.

min·ute[2] ['minit] **1.** Minute *f*; *fig.* Augenblick *m*; kurzer Entwurf *m*; Notiz *f*; *~s pl.* Protokoll *n*; *in a ~* gleich, sofort; *just a ~!* Moment mal!; *to the ~* auf die Minute; *the ~ (that)* sobald; **2.** protokollieren; entwerfen; aufzeichnen; '**min·ute-hand** Minutenzeiger *m*.

min·ute·ly[1] ['minitli] *adv.* jede Minute.

mi·nute·ly[2] [mai'nju:tli] peinlich genau; **mi'nute·ness** Kleinheit *f*; Genauigkeit *f*.

mi·nu·ti·a [mai'nju:ʃiə], *pl.* **mi'nu·ti·ae** [~ʃii:] Einzelheit *f*.

minx [miŋks] dreistes Mädchen *n*, Racker *m*.

mir·a·cle ['mirəkl] Wunder *n*; *to a ~* wundervoll; *~ play* Mirakel(spiel) *n*; **mi·rac·u·lous** □ [mi'rækjuləs] wunderbar; übernatürlich; **mi'rac·u·lous·ness** *das* Wunderbare.

mi·rage ['mirɑ:ʒ] Luftspiegelung *f*, Fata Morgana *f* (*a. fig.*).

mire ['maiə] **1.** Sumpf *m*, Kot *m*, Schlamm *m*, Dreck *m*; *be in the ~* in der Patsche sitzen; *drag s.o. through the ~* j. in den Schmutz ziehen; **2.** mit Schlamm *od.* Schmutz bedecken; *fig.* j. in Schwierigkeiten bringen; *his car was ~d* sein Auto blieb im Schlamm stecken.

mirk [mə:k] dunkel, düster.

mir·ror ['mirə] **1.** Spiegel *m*; **2.** (wider)spiegeln (*a. fig.*).

mirth [mə:θ] Fröhlichkeit *f*, Freude *f*; **mirth·ful** □ ['~ful] fröhlich; '**mirth·less** □ freudlos.

mir·y ['maiəri] kotig.

mis... [mis] miß..., übel, falsch.

mis·ad·ven·ture ['misəd'ventʃə] Mißgeschick *n*, Unfall *m*.

mis·al·li·ance ['misə'laiəns] Mißheirat *f*, Mesalliance *f*.

mis·an·thrope ['mizənθrəup] Menschenfeind *m*; **mis·an·throp·ic, mis·an·throp·i·cal** □ [~'θrɔpik(əl)] menschenfeindlich; **mis·an·thro·pist** [mi'zænθrəpist] Menschenfeind *m*; **mis'an·thro·py** Menschenhaß *m*.

mis·ap·pli·ca·tion ['misæpli'keiʃən] falsche Anwendung *f*, Mißbrauch *m*; **mis·ap·ply** ['~ə'plai] falsch anwenden, mißbrauchen.

mis·ap·pre·hend ['misæpri'hend] mißverstehen; '**mis·ap·pre'hen·sion** Mißverständnis *n*.

mis·ap·pro·pri·ate ['misə'prəuprieit] sich *et.* widerrechtlich aneignen, unterschlagen, veruntreuen; '**mis·ap·pro·pri'a·tion** widerrechtliche Aneignung *f*, Unterschlagung *f*, Veruntreuung *f*.

mis·be·come ['misbi'kʌm] sich nicht schicken für; '**mis·be'com·ing** unschicklich.

mis·be·got(·ten) ['misbigɔt(n)] unehelich gezeugt; scheußlich.

mis·be·have ['misbi'heiv] sich schlecht benehmen; '**mis·be'hav·io(u)r** [~jə] schlechtes Benehmen *n*.

mis·be·lief ['misbi'li:f] Irrglaube *m*; **mis·be·lieve** ['~'li:v] irrgläubig sein; '**mis·be'liev·er** Irrgläubige *m, f*.

mis·cal·cu·late ['mis'kælkjuleit] falsch (be)rechnen; sich verrechnen; '**mis·cal·cu'la·tion** falsche (Be)Rechnung *f*; Rechenfehler *m*.

mis·call ['mis'kɔ:l] fälschlich nennen.

mis·car·riage [mis'kæridʒ] Mißlingen *n*; Verlust *m von Briefen*; Fehlgeburt *f*; *~ of justice* Fehlspruch *m*; **mis'car·ry** mißlingen, fehlschlagen; verlorengehen (*Brief*); fehlgebären.

mis·cast *thea.* [mis'kɑ:st] (*irr. cast*) *e-m Schauspieler* die falsche Rolle geben; *Stück* fehlbesetzen.

mis·ce·ge·na·tion [misidʒi'neiʃən] Rassenmischung *f*.

mis·cel·la·ne·ous □ [misi'leinjəs] ge-, vermischt; vielseitig; **mis·cel'la·ne·ous·ness** Gemischtheit *f*; Mannigfaltigkeit *f*.

mis·cel·la·ny [mi'seləni] Gemisch *n*; Sammelband *m*; **mis'cel·la·nies** *pl.* vermischte Schriften *f/pl.*

mis·chance [mis'tʃɑ:ns] unglücklicher Zufall *m*; Unfall *m*.

mis·chief ['mistʃif] Schaden *m*, Unheil *n*; Unfug *m*, Mutwille *m*, Übermut *m*; F Racker *m*, Schelm *m*

(*Kind*); *make* ~ *between* Unfrieden stiften zwischen; *get into* ~ Unfug treiben; *what etc. the* ~ ...? was *etc.* zum Teufel ...?; '**~-mak·er** Unheilstifter(in).

mis·chie·vous □ ['mistʃivəs] schädlich; schadenfroh; mutwillig; '**mis·chie·vous·ness** Schädlichkeit *f*; Schadenfreude *f*; Mutwille *m*.

mis·con·ceive ['miskən'si:v] falsch auffassen *od.* verstehen; **mis·con·cep·tion** ['~'sepʃən] falsche Auffassung *f*, Mißverständnis *n*.

mis·con·duct 1. [mis'kɔndʌkt] schlechtes Benehmen *n*; Fehltritt *m*, Ehebruch *m*; schlechte Verwaltung *f*; 2. ['~kən'dʌkt] schlecht verwalten; ~ *o.s.* sich schlecht benehmen; e-n Fehltritt begehen.

mis·con·struc·tion ['miskən'strʌkʃən] Mißdeutung *f*; **mis·con·strue** ['~'stru:] mißdeuten.

mis·count ['mis'kaunt] 1. falsch rechnen *od.* zählen; sich verrechnen; 2. falsche Rechnung *f od.* Zählung *f*.

mis·cre·ant ['miskriənt] 1. Schurke *m*; 2. abscheulich, gemein.

mis·cre·a·ted ['miskri'eitid] monströs, unförmig.

mis·date [mis'deit] 1. falsches Datum *n*; 2. falsch datieren.

mis·deal ['mis'di:l] (*irr. deal*) *Karten*: vergeben.

mis·deed ['mis'di:d] Un-, Missetat *f*.

mis·de·mean·ant ⚖ [misdi'mi:nənt] Übeltäter *m*; **mis·de'mean·o(u)r** ⚖ [~nə] Vergehen *n*.

mis·di·rect ['misdi'rekt] irreleiten; an die falsche Adresse richten; '**mis·di'rec·tion** Irreleitung *f*; falsche Adressierung *f*.

mis·do·ing ['mis'du:iŋ] *mst* ~*s pl.* Vergehen *n*.

mise-en-scène *thea.* ['mi:zɑ̃:n'sein] Inszenierung *f*.

mi·ser ['maizə] Geizhals *m*.

mis·er·a·ble □ ['mizərəbl] elend; unglücklich, erbärmlich; '**mis·er·a·ble·ness** Elend *n*.

mi·ser·ly ['maizəli] geizig, filzig.

mis·er·y ['mizəri] Elend *n*, Not *f*, Trübsal *f*, Jammer *m*; Leid *n*; F Elendsgestalt *f*.

mis·fea·sance ⚖ [mis'fi:zəns] Mißbrauch *m* der Amtsgewalt.

mis·fire ['mis'faiə] 1. Versager *m beim Schießen*; *mot.* Fehlzündung *f*; 2. versagen; fehlzünden; *fig.* danebengehen.

mis·fit ['misfit] schlecht passendes Stück *n* (*Kleid, Stiefel etc.*); Einzelgänger *m*, Eigenbrötler *m*.

mis·for·tune [mis'fɔ:tʃən] Unglück (-sfall *m*) *n*; Mißgeschick *n*.

mis·give [mis'giv] (*irr. give*) Böses ahnen lassen; *my heart misgave me* mir ahnte Böses; **mis'giv·ing** böse Ahnung *f*, Befürchtung *f*.

mis·gov·ern ['mis'gʌvən] schlecht regieren; '**mis'gov·ern·ment** schlechte Regierung *f*.

mis·guide ['mis'gaid] irreleiten; '**mis'guid·ed** irre-, fehlgeleitet.

mis·han·dle ['mis'hændl] mißhandeln; falsch handhaben.

mis·hap ['mishæp] Unfall *m*; Unglück *n*; Mißgeschick *n*; Panne *f*.

mis·hear [mis'hiə] (*irr. hear*) sich verhören; falsch hören.

mish·mash ['miʃmæʃ] Mischmasch *m*.

mis·in·form ['misin'fɔ:m] falsch unterrichten; '**mis·in·for'ma·tion** falscher Bericht *m*, falsche Auskunft *f*.

mis·in·ter·pret ['misin'tə:prit] mißdeuten, falsch auslegen; '**mis·in·ter·pre'ta·tion** falsche Auslegung *f*.

mis·judge ['mis'dʒʌdʒ] falsch (be-) urteilen *od.* einschätzen; sich verschätzen (in); '**mis'judg(e)·ment** falsche Beurteilung *f*; falsches Urteil *n*.

mis·lay [mis'lei] (*irr. lay*) verlegen.

mis·lead [mis'li:d] (*irr. lead*) irreführen; verleiten; **mis'lead·ing** irreführend.

mis·man·age ['mis'mænidʒ] schlecht verwalten; '**mis'man·age·ment** schlechte Verwaltung *f*; Mißwirtschaft *f*.

mis·name ['mis'neim] beschimpfen; fälschlich nennen.

mis·no·mer ['mis'nəumə] falsche Benennung *f od.* Bezeichnung *f*.

mi·sog·a·mist [mi'sɔgəmist] Ehefeind *m*.

mi·sog·y·nist [mai'sɔdʒinist] Weiberfeind *m*; **mi'sog·y·ny** Weiberhaß *m*.

mis·place ['mis'pleis] falsch stellen, verstellen; verlegen; übel anbringen.

mis·print 1. [mis'print] verdrucken;

2. ['mis'print] Druckfehler *m*.
mis·pro·nounce ['misprə'nauns] falsch aussprechen; **mis·pro·nun·ci·a·tion** ['~prənʌnsi'eiʃən] falsche Aussprache *f*.
mis·quo·ta·tion ['miskwəu'teiʃən] falsches Zitat *n*; '**mis'quote** falsch anführen *od*. zitieren.
mis·read ['mis'ri:d] (*irr. read*) falsch lesen *od*. deuten.
mis·rep·re·sent ['misrepri'zent] falsch darstellen, verdrehen; '**mis·rep·re·sen'ta·tion** falsche Darstellung *f*, Verdrehung *f*.
mis·rule ['mis'ru:l] **1.** Unordnung *f*; Tumult *m*; schlechte Regierung *f*; **2.** schlecht regieren.
miss[1] [mis] *mst* ♀ Fräulein *n*; junges Mädchen *n*, Backfisch *m*.
miss[2] [~] **1.** Verlust *m*; Fehlschuß *m*, -stoß *m*, -wurf *m*, -schlag *m*; **2.** *v/t*. (ver)missen; *Weg, Ziel* verfehlen; *Gelegenheit etc.* verpassen, sich entgehen lassen; auslassen; übersehen, -hören; versäumen; ~ *fire* versagen; ~ *one's footing* ausgleiten; ~ *one's hold* fehlgreifen; ~ *out* auslassen; *v/i*. fehlen (*nicht treffen*); fehlgehen; ~ *out on s.th.* et. verpassen.
mis·sal *eccl*. ['misəl] Meßbuch *n*.
mis·shap·en ['mis'ʃeipən] verunstaltet; mißgestaltet.
mis·sile ['misail] (Wurf)Geschoß *n*; Rakete *f*; ~ *site* ⚔ Raketenstellung *f*; *intercontinental ballistic* ~ Interkontinentalrakete *f*.
miss·ing ['misiŋ] fehlend, abwesend; *bsd*. ⚔ vermißt; verschollen; *be* ~ fehlen, vermißt werden.
mis·sion ['miʃən] Sendung *f*; Auftrag *m*; Berufung *f*, Lebensziel *n*; Gesandtschaft *f*; *eccl., pol*. Mission *f*; **mis·sion·ar·y** ['miʃnəri] **1.** Missionar *m*; **2.** Missions...
mis·sis F ['misiz] Frau *f*.
mis·sive ['misiv] Sendschreiben *n*.
mis·spell ['mis'spel] (*irr. spell*) falsch buchstabieren *od*. schreiben.
mis·spend ['mis'spend] (*irr. spend*) falsch verwenden, vergeuden.
mis·state ['mis'steit] falsch angeben; '**mis'state·ment** falsche Angabe *f*.
mis·sus F ['misəz] Frau *f*.
miss·y F ['misi] kleines Fräulein *n*.
mist [mist] **1.** Nebel *m*; *in a* ~ irre, verdutzt; **2.** (um)nebeln; sich trüben; beschlagen.
mis·tak·a·ble [mis'teikəbl] leicht mißzuverstehend *od*. zu verkennend; **mis'take 1.** (*irr. take*) *v/t*. sich irren in (*dat*.), verkennen; falsch auffassen, mißverstehen; verwechseln (*for* mit), fälschlich halten (*for* für); *be* ~*n* sich irren; *v/i*. ⚒ sich irren; **2.** Irrtum *m*; Versehen *n*; Fehler *m*; *by* ~ aus Versehen; *and no* ~ F ganz gewiß; **mis'tak·en** □ irrig, falsch (verstanden); ~ *identity* Personenverwechslung *f*.
mis·ter ['mistə] (*abbr*. **Mr.**) Herr *m*.
mis·time ['mis'taim] zur unrechten Zeit tun *od*. sagen; '**mis'timed** unzeitig.
mist·i·ness ['mistinis] Nebligkeit *f*; *fig*. Unklarheit *f*.
mis·tle·toe ♀ ['misltəu] Mistel *f*.
mis·trans·late ['mistræns'leit] falsch übersetzen; '**mis·trans'la·tion** falsche Übersetzung *f*.
mis·tress ['mistris] Herrin *f*; Hausfrau *f*; Lehrerin *f*; Geliebte *f*, Mätresse *f*; Meisterin *f in e-r Kunst etc*.
mis·tri·al ⚖ ['mis'traiəl] ungültiges Verfahren *n*.
mis·trust ['mis'trʌst] **1.** mißtrauen (*dat*.); **2.** Mißtrauen *n*; '**mis'trust·ful** □ [~ful] mißtrauisch.
mist·y □ ['misti] neb(e)lig; *fig*. unklar.
mis·un·der·stand ['misʌndə'stænd] (*irr. stand*) mißverstehen; '**mis·un·der'stand·ing** Mißverständnis *n*.
mis·us·age [mis'ju:zidʒ] Mißbrauch *m*; Mißhandlung *f*.
mis·use 1. ['mis'ju:z] mißbrauchen; mißhandeln; **2.** ['~'ju:s] Mißbrauch *m*.
mite[1] *zo*. [mait] Milbe *f*.
mite[2] [~] Heller *m*; Scherflein *n*; *a* ~ (*of a child*) ein Wurm *m* (von Kind).
mit·i·gate ['mitigeit] mildern, lindern (*a. fig*.); **mit·i'ga·tion** Milderung *f*, Linderung *f*.
mi·tre, mi·ter ['maitə] **1.** Mitra *f*, Bischofsmütze *f*, -würde *f*; ⊕ Gehrung *f*; **2.** mit der Bischofswürde bekleiden; ⊕ auf Gehrung verbinden; '**mi·tre-wheel** ⊕ Kegelrad *n*.
mitt [mit] Baseball-Handschuh *m*;

F Boxhandschuh *m*; = *mitten*.
mit·ten ['mitn] Fausthandschuh *m*; Halbhandschuh *m* (*ohne Finger*); *Am. sl.* Tatze *f* (*Hand*); *get the* ~ F einen Korb bekommen.
mix [miks] **1.** (sich) (ver)mischen, mengen; ~ *in society* in der Gesellschaft verkehren; ~*ed* gemischt (*fig. zweifelhaft*); ~*ed marriage* Mischehe *f*; ~*ed pickles pl.* Mixed Pickles *pl.* (*Essiggemüse*); ~*ed up* verwirrt, konfus, durcheinander; ~ *up* vermengen; verwechseln; *be* ~*ed up with* in *e-e Angelegenheit* verwickelt sein; ~ *with* verkehren mit; **2.** (back- *od.* kochfertige) Mischung *f*; '**mix·er** Mischer *m*; (Bar)Mixer *m*; *Radio*: Toningenieur *m*; *Küche*: Mixer *m*; *good* (*bad*) ~ (wenig) umgänglicher Mensch *m*; **mix·ture** ['~tʃə] Mischung *f*, Gemisch *n* (*a. fig.*), Mixtur *f*; '**mix-'up** Durcheinander *n*.
miz·en, miz·zen ⚓ ['mizn] Besan *m*; *attr.* Besan..., Kreuz...
miz·zle F ['mizl] nieseln; jammern, klagen; verwirren.
mne·mon·ic [ni:'mɔnik] **1.** (~*ally*) mnemotechnisch; Gedächtnis...; **2. mne'mon·ics** *pl.* Gedächtniskunst *f*.
mo *co. od.* V [məu] = *moment*.
moan [məun] **1.** Stöhnen *n*; **2.** stöhnen.
moat [məut] Burg-, Stadtgraben *m*; '**moat·ed** von e-m Wassergraben umgeben.
mob [mɔb] **1.** Pöbel *m*, Mob *m*; Pöbelhaufen *m*; **2.** anpöbeln; '**mob·bish** pöbelhaft.
mob-cap ['mɔbkæp] Morgenhaube *f*.
mo·bile ['məubail] **1.** beweglich; ⚔ mobil; ~ *home mot.* Wohnmobil *n*; **2.** Mobile *n*; **mo·bil·i·ty** [~'biliti] Beweglichkeit *f*; **mo·bi·li·za·tion** ⚔ [~bilai'zeiʃən] Mobilmachung *f*; '**mo·bi·lize** ⚔ mobil machen.
mob-law ['mɔblɔ:] Lynchjustiz *f*.
mob·oc·ra·cy [mɔ'bɔkrəsi] Pöbelherrschaft *f*; **mob·ster** ['mɔbstə] Bandenmitglied *n*.
moc·ca·sin ['mɔkəsin] weiches Leder *n*; Mokassin *m* (*Schuh*).
mo·cha ['mɔkə] Mokka(kaffee) *m*.
mock [mɔk] **1.** Hohn *m*, Spott *m*; **2.** Schein..., falsch, nachgemacht; ~ *fight* Scheingefecht *n*; **3.** *v/t.* verhöhnen, verspotten; nachmachen; täuschen; vereiteln; *v/i.* spotten (*at* über *acc.*); '**mock·er** Spötter(in); '**mock·er·y** Spötterei *f*, Gespött *n*; Hohn *m*; Äfferei *f*; '**mock-he'ro·ic** komisch-heroisch; '**mock·ing 1.** Gespött *n*; Hohn *m*; **2.** □ spöttisch; '**mock·ing-bird** Spottdrossel *f*.
mock...: '~**-king** Schattenkönig *m*; '~**-'tur·tle soup** falsche Schildkrötensuppe *f*; '~**-up** Nachbildung *f*, Modell *n*.
mod·al □ ['məudl] *bsd. gr.* modal; **mo·dal·i·ty** [~'dæliti] Modalität *f*.
mode [məud] (Art *f* u.) Weise *f*; (Erscheinungs)Form *f*; Sitte *f*, Mode *f*; *gr.* Modus *m*.
mod·el ['mɔdl] **1.** Modell *n*; Muster *n*; *fig.* Vorbild *n*; Vorführdame *f*; *attr.* Muster..., musterhaft, vorbildlich; *act as a* ~ Modell stehen (*to dat.*); ~ *aircraft* Flug(zeug)modell *n*; **2.** modellieren; abformen; *fig.* modeln, bilden (*after, on, upon* nach); **mod·el·(l)er** ['mɔdlə] Modellierer *m*.
mod·er·ate 1. □ ['mɔdərit] mäßig; gemäßigt, mittelmäßig; **2.** ['~reit] (sich) mäßigen, mildern; **mod·er·ate·ness** ['mɔdəritnis] Mäßigkeit *f*; Mittelmäßigkeit *f*; **mod·er·a·tion** [~'reiʃən] Mäßigung *f*; Mäßigkeit *f*; *in* ~ mit Maß; ♀*s pl. univ.* erste öffentliche Prüfung *f in Oxford*; '**mod·er·a·tor** Mittelsmann *m*; *univ.* Examinator *m*; *phys.* Moderator *m*; Diskussionsleiter *m*.
mod·ern ['mɔdən] **1.** modern, neu (-zeitlich); ~ *languages pl.* neuere Sprachen *f/pl.*; **2.** *the* ~*s pl.* die Modernen *pl.*; '**mod·ern·ism** moderne (Geistes)Richtung *f*; '**mod·ern·ist** Modernist *m*, Anhänger *m* der Moderne; **mod·ern'is·tic** modernistisch; **mo·der·ni·ty** [mɔ'də:niti] Modernität *f*; **mod·ern·ize** ['mɔdənaiz] (sich) modernisieren.
mod·est □ ['mɔdist] bescheiden; anständig; anspruchslos; mäßig; '**mod·es·ty** Bescheidenheit *f*.
mod·i·cum ['mɔdikəm] geringe Menge *f*, Wenige *n*, Quentchen *n*.
mod·i·fi·a·ble ['mɔdifaiəbl] änderungsfähig; **mod·i·fi·ca·tion** [~fi'keiʃən] Ab-, Veränderung *f*; Einschränkung *f*; **mod·i·fy** ['~fai] modifizieren, (ab)ändern; *gr.* umlauten; näher bestimmen; einschränken, mildern.

mod·ish ['məudiʃ] modisch, modern.
mo·diste [məu'di:st] Modistin *f*; Damenschneiderin *f*.
mod·u·late ['mɔdjuleit] modulieren; einstellen; *Radio*: (aus)steuern; **mod·u'la·tion** Modulation *f*; '**mod·u·la·tor** Regler *m*; ~ *of tonality Film*: Tonblende *f*; **mod·ule** ['~dju:l] Modul *m* (*a*. △); Maßeinheit *f*; *s. lunar* ~; **mod·u·lus** *phys*. ['~djuləs] Modul *m*.
Mo·gul [məu'gʌl]: *the Great od. Grand* ~ der Großmogul.
mo·hair ['məuhɛə] Angorahaar *n*; Mohair(stoff) *m*.
Mo·ham·med·an [məu'hæmidən] **1.** Mohammedaner(in); **2.** mohammedanisch.
moi·e·ty ['mɔiəti] Hälfte *f*; Teil *m*.
moil [mɔil] sich schinden.
moire [mwɑ:] Moiré *m*, Wasserglanz *m auf Stoffen*; Moiréstoff *m*.
moi·ré ['mwɑ:rei] geflammt (*Stoff*).
moist [mɔist] feucht, naß; **mois·ten** ['mɔisn] *v/t*. an-, befeuchten; *v/i*. feucht werden; **moist·ness** ['mɔistnis], **mois·ture** ['~tʃə] Feuchtigkeit *f*; **mois·tur·ize** ['~tʃəraiz] (*Luft*) befeuchten; (*Haut*) eincremen; '**moist·ur·iz·ing cream** Feuchtigkeitscreme *f*.
moke *sl*. [məuk] Esel *m*.
mo·lar ['məulə] *a*. ~ *tooth* Backenzahn *m*.
mo·las·ses [məu'læsiz] Melasse *f*; Sirup *m*.
mold [məuld], '**mold·board** *etc*. *s*. *mould etc*.
mole[1] *zo*. [məul] Maulwurf *m*.
mole[2] [~] Muttermal *n*.
mole[3] [~] Mole *f*, Hafendamm *m*.
mo·lec·u·lar [məu'lekjulə] Molekular...; **mol·e·cule** *phys*. ['mɔlikju:l] Molekül *n*.
mole·hill ['məulhil] Maulwurfshaufen *m*; *make a mountain out of a* ~ aus e-r Mücke e-n Elefanten machen; '**mole-skin** Maulwurfsfell *n*; Moleskin *m*, Englischleder *n*.
mo·lest [məu'lest] belästigen; **mo·les·ta·tion** [~'teiʃən] Belästigung *f*.
moll F [mɔl] Gangsterbraut *f*; Nutte *f* (*Prostituierte*).
mol·li·fy ['mɔlifai] besänftigen.
mol·lusc *zo*. ['mɔləsk] Molluske *f*, Weichtier *n*; **mol·lus·cous** [mɔ'lʌskəs] molluskenartig, -haft; '**mol·lusk** = *mollusc*.
mol·ly·cod·dle ['mɔlikɔdl] **1.** Weichling *m*, Muttersöhnchen *n*; **2.** verzärteln.
mo·loch ['məulɔk] Moloch *m*.
mol·ten ['məultən] geschmolzen.
mo·lyb·den·um ⚗ [mɔ'libdinəm] Molybdän *n*.
mom *Am*. [mɔm] Mama *f*, Mami *f*; ~-*and-pop store Am*. Tante-Emma-Laden *m*.
mo·ment ['məumənt] Augenblick *m*, Moment *m*; Bedeutung *f*; = ~*um*; *at od. for the* ~ augenblicklich; *to the* ~ pünktlich; genau; '**mo·men·tar·y** □ augenblicklich, vorübergehend; stet, ständig (*Angst etc*.); '**mo·ment·ly** *adv*. jeden Augenblick; **mo·men·tous** □ [məu'mentəs] (ge)wichtig, bedeutend; **mo'mentum** *phys*. [~təm] Moment *n*, Impuls *m*; Triebkraft *f*; *fig*. Wucht *f*, Schwung *m*.
mon·a·chism ['mɔnekizəm] Mönchtum *n*.
mon·ad *phls*. ['mɔnæd] Monade *f*.
mon·arch ['mɔnək] Monarch(in), Herrscher(in); **mo·nar·chic, mo·nar·chi·cal** □ [mɔ'nɑ:kik(əl)] monarchisch; '**mon·arch·ism** ['mɔnəkizəm] Monarchismus *m*; '**mon·arch·ist** Monarchist *m*; '**mon·arch·y** Monarchie *f*.
mon·as·ter·y ['mɔnəstəri] (Mönchs-) Kloster *n*; **mo·nas·tic, mo·nas·ti·cal** □ [mə'næstik(əl)] klösterlich; Mönchs...; **mo'nas·ti·cism** [~sizəm] Mönchtum *n*, mönchisches Leben *n*.
mon·au·ral [mɔn'ɔ:rəl] monaural, nicht stereophon.
Mon·day ['mʌndi] Montag *m*.
mon·e·tar·y ['mʌnitəri] Geld...; ~ *reform* Währungsreform *f*.
mon·ey ['mʌni] Geld *n*; *ready* ~ Bargeld *n*; *out of* ~ nicht bei Kasse; ~ *down* in bar; *get one's* ~*'s worth* et. für sein Geld bekommen; *marry* ~ sich reich verheiraten; *make* ~ Geld verdienen (*by* an *dat*., bei); '**~-box** Sparbüchse *f*; '**~-chang·er** (Geld-) Wechsler *m*; **mon·eyed** ['mʌnid] vermögend; in Geld bestehend.
mon·ey...: '**~-grub·ber** Geldraffer *m*; '**~-lend·er** Geldverleiher *m*; '**~-mar·ket** Geldmarkt *m*; ~ **mat·ters** *pl*. Geldangelegenheiten *f/pl*.; '**~-or·der** Postanweisung *f*; '**~-spin·ner** F (gute) Einnahmequelle *f*.

mon·ger [ˈmʌŋgə] ...händler *m*, ...krämer *m*.

Mon·gol [ˈmɔŋgɔl], **Mon·go·lian** [~ˈgəuljən] **1.** mongolisch; **2.** Mongole *m*, Mongolin *f*.

mon·grel [ˈmʌŋgrəl] **1.** Mischling *m*, Bastard *m*; **2.** Bastard...

mo·ni·tion [məuˈniʃən] Mahnung *f*, Warnung *f*; **mon·i·tor** [ˈmɔnitə] Ermahner *m*; (Klassen)Ordner *m*; ⚓ *Art* Panzerschiff *n*, Monitor *m*; *Radio*: Überwacher *m* der Auslandssendungen; Monitor *m*, Kontrollschirm *m*; ˈ**mon·i·tor·ing:** ~ *device* Überwachungsanlage *f*; ˈ**mon·i·to·ry** ermahnend; warnend; Mahn...

monk [mʌŋk] Mönch *m*; ˈ**monk·er·y** *bsd. contp.* Mönchswesen *n*, Mönchtum *n*.

mon·key [ˈmʌŋki] **1.** Affe *m* (*a. fig.*); ⊕ Rammblock *m*; *sl.* 500 Pfund Sterling; ~*'s allowance sl.* mehr Schläge als Brot; *put s.o.'s* ~ *up* F j. auf die Palme bringen; ~ *business Am sl.* fauler Zauber *m*; **2.** F (herum)albern; ~ *about with* herummurksen an (*dat.*); ˈ**~-en·gine** Rammaschine *f*; ˈ**~-jack·et** ⚓ Munkijacke *f*, Bordjackett *n*. ˈ**~-nut** ⚘ Erdnuß *f*; ˈ**~-puz·zle** ⚘ Schuppentanne *f*; ˈ**~-wrench** ⊕ Engländer *m* (*Schraubenschlüssel*); *throw a* ~ *in s.th. Am. sl.* et. über den Haufen werfen.

monk·hood [ˈmʌŋkhud] Mönchswesen *n*, Mönchtum *n*; ˈ**monk·ish** *mst contp.* mönchisch.

mon·o [ˈmɔnəu] **1.** mono; **2.** F Mono(schall)platte *f*.

mono... [ˈmɔnəu] ein(fach)...; **mo·no·chrome** *paint.* [ˈmɔnəkrəum] **1.** monochrom; **2.** monochrome Malerei *f*; **mon·o·cle** [ˈmɔnɔkl] Monokel *n*; **mo·no·cot·y·le·don** ⚘ [ˈmɔnəukɔtiˈliːdən] Einkeimblättrige *f*; **mo·noc·u·lar** [mɔˈnɔkjulə] einäugig; für ein Auge; **moˈnog·a·my** [~gəmi] Einehe *f*, Monogamie *f*; **mon·o·gram** [ˈmɔnəgræm] Monogramm *n*; **mon·o·graph** [ˈ~grɑːf] Monographie *f*; **mon·o·lith** [ˈmɔnəuliθ] Monolith *m*; **mon·o·lith·ic** [mɔnəuˈliθik] monolithisch; *fig.* gigantisch; **mon·o·logue** [ˈmɔnəlɔg] Monolog *m*, Selbstgespräch *n*; **mon·o·ma·ni·a** [ˈmɔnəuˈmeinjə] fixe Idee *f*, Monomanie *f*; ˈ**mon·oˈma·ni·ac** [~niæk] Monomane *m*, von e-r fixen Idee Besessener *m*; **mon·o·plane** ✈ [ˈmɔnəuplein] Eindecker *m*; **mo·nop·o·list** [məˈnɔpəlist] Monopolist *m*; **moˈnop·o·lize** [~laiz] monopolisieren; *fig.* an sich reißen; **moˈnop·o·ly** Monopol *n* (*of* auf *acc.*); **mon·o·syl·lab·ic** [ˈmɔnəusiˈlæbik] (~*ally*) einsilbig; **mon·o·syl·la·ble** [ˈmɔnəsiləbl] einsilbiges Wort *n*; **mon·o·the·ism** [ˈmɔnəuθiːizəm] Monotheismus *m* (*Glaube an e-n einzigen Gott*); **mon·o·tone** [ˈmɔnətəun] **1.** gleichbleibender Ton *m*; *in* ~ eintönig; **2.** herleiern; **mo·not·o·nous** □ [məˈnɔtnəs] monoton, eintönig, -förmig; **moˈnot·o·ny** Monotonie *f*; Eintönigkeit *f*, -förmigkeit *f*; **Mon·o·type** *typ.* [ˈmɔnəutaip] Monotype *f* (*Setzmaschine für Einzelbuchstaben*); **mon·ox·ide** ⚗ [mɔˈnɔksaid] Monoxyd *n*.

mon·sieur [məˈsjəː] Monsieur *m*, Herr *m*.

mon·soon [mɔnˈsuːn] Monsun *m*.

mon·ster [ˈmɔnstə] Ungeheuer *n* (*a. fig.*); Monstrum *n*, Mißbildung *f*; *attr.* Riesen...

mon·strance *eccl.* [ˈmɔnstrəns] Monstranz *f*.

mon·stros·i·ty [mɔnsˈtrɔsiti] Ungeheuer(lichkeit *f*) *n*; ˈ**mon·strous** □ ungeheuer(lich); gräßlich.

mon·tage [mɔnˈtɑːʒ] *Film-*, *Photo-*Montage *f*.

month [mʌnθ] Monat *m*; *this day* ~ heute in e-m Monat; ˈ**month·ly** **1.** monatlich; ~ *season ticket* Monatskarte *f*; **2.** Monatsschrift *f*.

mon·u·ment [ˈmɔnjumənt] Denkmal *n*; **mon·u·men·tal** □ [~ˈmentl] monumental; Denkmal...; Gedächtnis..., Gedenk...; großartig; riesig.

moo [muː] **1.** muhen; **2.** Muhen *n*.

mooch F [muːtʃ]: ~ *about* herumlungern; herumlatschen.

mood[1] *gr.* [muːd] Modus *m*.

mood[2] [~] Stimmung *f*, Laune *f*.

mood·i·ness [ˈmuːdinis] üble Laune *f*; ˈ**mood·y** □ launisch; schwermütig; übellaunig.

moon [muːn] **1.** Mond *m*; *poet.* Monat *m*; *be over the* ~ überglücklich sein; *cry for the* ~ nach den Sternen greifen; *promise s.o. the* ~ j-m das Blaue vom Himmel (herunter) versprechen; *once in a blue* ~ F alle Jubeljahre einmal; **2.** *mst* ~ *about* F herumdösen;

ˈmoon·beam Mondstrahl *m*; **ˈmoon·less** mondlos; **ˈmoon·light** Mondlicht *n*, -schein *m*; **ˈmoon·light·ing** Nebenbeschäftigung *f*; Schwarzarbeit *f*; **ˈmoon·lit** mondhell.

moon...: **ˈ~·shine** Schwindel *m*, Unsinn *m*; geschmuggelter *od.* schwarz gebrannter Alkohol *m*; **ˈ~·shin·er** *Am.* F Schwarzbrenner *m*; Alkoholschmuggler *m*; **ˈ~·struck** mondsüchtig; **ˈmoon·y** □ Mond...; mondförmig; mondhell; F träumerisch, dösig; *sl.* beschwipst.

Moor[1] [muə] Maure *m*; Mohr *m*.

moor[2] [~] Ödland *n*, *bsd.* Heideland *n*; † *od. prov.* Moor *n*, Sumpf *m*.

moor[3] ⚓ [~] festmachen, (sich) vertäuen; **moor·age** [ˈmuəridʒ] Ankerplatz *m*.

moor·fowl [ˈmuəfaul], **ˈmoor-game** [ˈ~geim] Moorhuhn *n*.

moor·ing-mast [ˈmuəriŋmɑːst] Ankermast *m für Luftschiffe*.

moo·rings ⚓ [ˈmuəriŋz] *pl.* Vertäuungen *f/pl.*; Ankerplatz *m*.

Moor·ish [ˈmuəriʃ] maurisch.

moor·land [ˈmuələnd] Heidemoor *n*.

moose *zo.* [muːs] *a.* *~-deer* amerikanischer Elch *m*.

moot [muːt] **1.** *~ case*, *~ point* Streitpunkt *m*; **2.** diskutieren.

mop [mɔp] **1.** Mop *m*; (Haar)Wust *m*, (Haar)Schopf *m*; **2.** auf-, abwischen; *~ up Feuchtigkeit* auf-, abtrocknen; *sl.* wegschnappen; *sl.* aufräumen mit; *~ the floor with s.o.* j. in Grund u. Boden schlagen.

mope [məup] **1.** Trübsalbläser(in); *the ~s pl.* Trübsinn *m*, das heulende Elend; **2.** *v/i.* Trübsal blasen, den Kopf hängen lassen.

mo·ped [ˈməuped] Moped *n*.

mop·ing □ [ˈməupiŋ], **ˈmop·ish** □ kopfhängerisch, niedergeschlagen; verdrießlich.

mo·raine *geol.* [mɔˈrein] Moräne *f*.

mor·al [ˈmɔrəl] **1.** □ Moral...; moralisch, sittlich (gut); **2.** Moral *f*, Nutzanwendung *f*; *~s pl.* Moral *f*, sittliches Verhalten *n*, Sitten *f/pl.*; **mo·rale** [mɔˈrɑːl] *bsd.* ⚔ Moral *f*, Selbstzucht *f*, innerer Halt *m*; (Arbeits-, Kampf)Geist *m*; **mor·al·ist** [ˈmɔrəlist] Moralist *m*, Sittenlehrer *m*; **mo·ral·i·ty** [məˈræliti] Sittenlehre *f*; Sittlichkeit *f*, Moral *f*; *contp.* Sittenpredigt *f*; *hist. thea.* Moralität *f*; **mor·al·ize** [ˈmɔrəlaiz] *v/i.* moralisieren (*upon* über *acc.*); *v/t.* moralisch machen.

mo·rass [məˈræs] Morast *m*, Sumpf *m*.

mor·bid □ [ˈmɔːbid] krankhaft; **morˈbid·i·ty**, **ˈmor·bid·ness** Krankhaftigkeit *f*; Krankheitsziffer *f*.

mor·dant [ˈmɔːdənt] **1.** beißend; **2.** Beize *f*, Beizmittel *n*.

more [mɔː] **1.** *adj.* mehr; **2.** *adv.* mehr; noch (dazu); wieder; *once ~* noch einmal; *two ~* noch zwei; *so much ~*, *all the ~* um so mehr; *no ~* nicht mehr; *~ and ~* immer mehr; **3.** Mehr *n*.

mo·rel ⚘ [mɔˈrel] Morchel *f*.

mo·rel·lo ⚘ [məˈreləu] *a.* *~ cherry* Morelle *f*, schwarze Sauerweichsel *f*.

more·o·ver [mɔːˈrəuvə] außerdem, überdies, weiter, ferner.

Mo·resque [mɔˈresk] **1.** maurisch; **2.** Arabeske *f*.

mor·ga·nat·ic [mɔːgəˈnætik] (*~ally*) morganatisch, zur linken Hand (getraut).

morgue [mɔːg] Leichenhaus *n*; Archiv *n*.

mor·i·bund [ˈmɔribʌnd] im Sterben (liegend), dem Tode geweiht.

Mor·mon [ˈmɔːmən] Mormone *m*, Mormonin *f*.

morn *poet.* [mɔːn] Morgen *m*.

morn·ing [ˈmɔːniŋ] **1.** Morgen *m*; Vormittag *m*; *in the ~*, *during the ~* am Morgen, morgens; *this ~* heute morgen; *tomorrow ~* morgen früh; **2.** früh; Morgen...; *~* **coat** Cut (-away) *m*; *~* **dress** Besuchsanzug *m*; Stresemann *m*; **ˈ~-ˈglo·ry** ⚘ Prunkwinde *f*; *~* **per·form·ance** Matinee *f*.

Mo·roc·can [məˈrɔkən] marokkanisch.

mo·roc·co [məˈrɔkəu] *a.* *~ leather* Maroquin *m*, Saffian *m*.

mo·ron [ˈmɔːrɔn] Schwachsinnige *m, f*.

mo·rose □ [məˈrəus] mürrisch; **moˈrose·ness** Grämlichkeit *f*.

mor·pheme *gr.* [ˈmɔːfiːm] Morphem *n*.

mor·phi·a [ˈmɔːfjə], **mor·phine** [ˈmɔːfiːn] Morphium *n*.

mor·pho·log·i·cal *biol.*, *gr.* [mɔːfəˈlɔdʒikl] morphologisch, Form...; **mor·phol·o·gy** [~ˈfɔlədʒi] Morphologie *f*, Formenlehre *f*.

mor·row ['mɔrəu] *mst poet.* Morgen *n*, folgende Tag *m*; *the ~ of* der Tag *od.* die Zeit nach.

Morse [mɔ:s] *a. ~ code* Morsealphabet *n.*

mor·sel ['mɔ:səl] Bissen *m*; Bißchen *n*, Stückchen *n.*

mor·tal ['mɔ:tl] **1.** □ sterblich; tödlich; Tod(es)...; menschlich; F fürchterlich, gewaltig; F (zum Sterben) langweilig; **2.** Sterbliche *m, f*; **mor·tal·i·ty** [mɔ:'tæliti] Sterblichkeit *f*; Sterblichkeitsziffer *f.*

mor·tar ['mɔ:tə] **1.** Mörser *m* (*a.* ⚔); Mörtel *m*; **2.** mörteln, mit Mörtel verbinden; '**~-board** Mörtelbrett *n*; *univ.* Barett *n.*

mort·gage ['mɔ:gidʒ] **1.** Verpfändung *f*; Pfandgut *n*, Hypothek *f*; *a. ~-deed* Pfandbrief *m*; **2.** verpfänden; **mort·ga·gee** [mɔ:gə'dʒi:] Hypothekengläubiger *m*; **mort·ga·gor** [~'dʒɔ:] Hypothekenschuldner *m.*

mor·tice ['mɔ:tis] = *mortise.*

mor·ti·cian *Am.* [mɔ:'tiʃən] Leichenbestatter *m.*

mor·ti·fi·ca·tion [mɔ:tifi'keiʃən] ⚕ kalter Brand *m*; Kasteiung *f*; Demütigung *f*; Kränkung *f*; Ärger *m.*

mor·ti·fy ['mɔ:tifai] *v/t.* ertöten; kasteien; demütigen; ärgern, kränken; *v/i.* ⚕ brandig werden.

mor·tise ⊕ ['mɔ:tis] **1.** Zapfenloch *n*, Nut *f*; **2.** mit e-m Zapfen versehen; verzapfen.

mor·tu·ar·y ['mɔ:tjuəri] **1.** Leichen-..., Begräbnis...; **2.** Leichenhalle *f.*

mo·sa·ic[1] [məu'zeiik] Mosaik *n.*

Mo·sa·ic[2] [~] mosaisch.

mo·selle [məu'zel] Moselwein *m.*

Mos·lem ['mɔzlem] **1.** muselmanisch; **2.** Moslem *m*, Muselman *m.*

mosque [mɔsk] Moschee *f.*

mos·qui·to *zo.* [məs'ki:təu], *pl.* **mos'qui·toes** [~z] Stechmücke *f*, Moskito *m*; **mos'qui·to-craft** ⚓ Schnellboot *n*; **mos'qui·to-net** Moskitonetz *n.*

moss [mɔs] ⚘ Moos *n*; (Torf-)Moor *n*; '**moss·i·ness** *das* Moosige; Moosüberzug *m*; '**moss·y** moosig; bemoost.

most [məust] **1.** *adj.* □ meist; größt; *for the ~ part* meistens; **2.** *adv.* meist, am meisten; höchst, äußerst; **3.** das meiste; die meisten; Höchste *n*, Äußerste *n*; *at (the) ~* höchstens; *make the ~ of* möglichst ausnutzen; möglichst gut darstellen.

...most [məust, məst] *Bezeichnung des sup.*

most·ly ['məustli] meistens, größtenteils, hauptsächlich.

mote [məut] (Sonnen)Stäubchen *n*; *the ~ in another's eye* der Splitter im Auge des anderen.

mo·tel [məu'tel] Motel *n.*

mo·tet ♪ [məu'tet] Motette *f.*

moth [mɔθ] Motte *f*; '**~-ball** Mottenkugel *f*; *in ~s fig.* eingemottet; '**~-eat·en** mottenzerfressen.

moth·er ['mʌðə] **1.** Mutter *f*; **2.** hervorbringen; bemuttern; **~ coun·try** Vaterland *n*; Mutterland *n*; **moth·er·hood** ['~hud] Mutterschaft *f*; '**moth·er-in-law** Schwiegermutter *f*; '**moth·er·less** mutterlos; '**moth·er·li·ness** Mütterlichkeit *f*; '**moth·er·ly** mütterlich; '**moth·er-of-'pearl** Perlmutter *f*; **Moth·er's Day** Muttertag *m*; **moth·er ship** Mutterschiff *n*; **moth·er tongue** Muttersprache *f.*

moth-proof ['mɔθpru:f] **1.** mottensicher, -echt; **2.** mottensicher machen; '**moth·y** vermottet.

mo·tif [məu'ti:f] (Leit)Motiv *n.*

mo·tion ['məuʃən] **1.** Bewegung *f*, Gang *m* (*a.* ⊕); *parl.* Antrag *m*; ⚕ Stuhlgang *m*; *bring forward a ~* e-n Antrag stellen; *agree upon a ~* e-n Antrag annehmen; *go through the ~s* et. nachlässig *od.* unaufrichtig tun; *set in ~* in Gang bringen; **2.** *v/t.* durch Gebärden auffordern *od.* andeuten; *j. wohin* winken; *v/i.* winken; '**mo·tion·less** bewegungs-, reglos; **mo·tion of no con·fi·dence** *parl.* Mißtrauensantrag *m*; **mo·tion pic·ture** Film *m*; **mo·tion stud·y** Arbeitsstudie *f.*

mo·ti·vate ['məutiveit] motivieren, begründen; **mo·ti'va·tion** Motivierung *f.*

mo·tive ['məutiv] **1.** Bewegungs..., bewegend; *~ power* Antriebskraft *f*; **2.** Beweggrund *m*, Motiv *n*; **3.** veranlassen; '**mo·tive·less** grundlos.

mo·tiv·i·ty [məu'tiviti] Bewegungskraft *f.*

mot·ley ['mɔtli] (bunt)scheckig.

mo·tor ['məutə] **1.** Motor *m*; treibende Kraft *f*; Automobil *n*; ⚕ Muskel *m*; **2.** motorisch, bewegend; Motor...; Kraft...; Auto...; *~ nerve* motorischer Nerv *m*; **3.** (im) Auto fahren; **'~-as·sist·ed** mit Hilfsmotor; **'~-bi·cy·cle, '~-bike** = *motor-cycle*; **'~-boat** Motorboot *n*; **'~-'bus** Autobus *m*; **~·cade** *Am.* ['~keid] Autokolonne *f*; **'~-car** Auto(mobil) *n*, (Kraft)Wagen *m*; **'~-coach** Reisebus *m*; **'~-cy·cle** Motorrad *n*; **'~-cy·clist** Motorradfahrer *m*; **mo·to·ri·al** [məu'tɔ:riəl] bewegend, Bewegungs..., motorisch; **mo·tor·ing** ['məutəriŋ] Autofahren *n*; **'mo·tor·ist** Auto-, Kraftfahrer(in); **mo·tor·i·za·tion** [~rai'zeiʃən] Motorisierung *f*; **'mo·tor·ize** motorisieren; **'mo·tor--launch** Motorbarkasse *f*; **'mo·tor·less** motorlos.

mo·tor...: '~·man Wagenführer *m*; **'~-plough** Motorpflug *m*; **'~-road, '~·way** Autobahn *f*.

mot·tle ['mɔtl] flecken, sprenkeln; **'mot·tled** gefleckt, gesprenkelt.

mot·to ['mɔtəu], *pl.* **mot·toes** ['~z] Wahl-, Sinnspruch *m*, Motto *n*.

mo(u)ld¹ [məuld] Damm-, Gartenerde *f*; Schimmel *m*, Moder *m*.

mo(u)ld² [~] **1.** (Guß)Form *f* (*a. fig.*); Schablone *f*; Abdruck *m*; Art *f*, Schlag *m*; **2.** formen; gießen (*on, upon* nach *e-m Muster*).

mo(u)ld-board ['məuldbɔ:d] Formbrett *n der Maurer*.

mo(u)ld·er¹ ['məuldə] Former(in), Bildner(in).

mo(u)lder² [~] *a.* ~ *away* zerbröckeln, zerfallen.

mo(u)ld·i·ness ['məuldinis] *das* Schimm(e)lige, Moder *m*.

mo(u)ld·ing ['məuldiŋ] Formen *n*; ⚠ Gesims *n*; Fries *m*; *attr.* Form...; Modellier...

mo(u)ld·y ['məuldi] schimm(e)lig, dumpfig, mod(e)rig.

moult [məult] **1.** Mauser *f*; **2.** (*fig.* sich) mausern; haaren.

mound [maund] Erdwall *m*; *burial-~* Grabhügel *m*.

mount [maunt] **1.** Berg *m* (*poet. außer in geogr. Eigennamen*); Karton *m*, Papier *n zum Aufziehen von Bildern*; Reitpferd *n*; **2.** *v/i.* (empor-)steigen; aufsteigen (*Reiter*); *mst ~ up* anwachsen; *v/t.* be-, ersteigen; *Pferd* besteigen, reiten; beritten machen; montieren; ⊕ beschlagen; *Zeichnung etc.* aufziehen, -kleben; *Edelstein* fassen; *thea.* in Szene setzen; *~ed* beritten; *s. guard 1.*

moun·tain ['mauntin] **1.** Berg *m*; *~s pl.* Gebirge *n*; *make a ~ out of a mole-hill* aus einer Mücke einen Elefanten machen; **2.** Berg..., Gebirgs...; **~ ash** ⚘ Eberesche *f*; **~ chain** Bergkette *f*; **~ dew** F schottischer Whisky *m*; **moun·tain·eer** [~ti'niə] Bergbewohner(in); Bergsteiger(in); **moun·tain'eer·ing** Bergsteigen *n*, Alpinismus *m*; **'moun·tain·ous** bergig, gebirgig; berghoch; **moun·tain range** Gebirgskette *f*; **moun·tain sickness** Berg-, Höhenkrankheit *f*.

moun·te·bank ['mauntibæŋk] Marktschreier *m*, Scharlatan *m*.

mount·ing ⊕ ['mauntiŋ] Montage *f*; Beschlag *m*.

mourn [mɔ:n] (be)trauern; **'mourn·er** Leidtragende *m, f*; *~'s bench Am.* = *anxious bench*; **mourn·ful** □ ['~ful] Trauer...; traurig; **'mourn·ful·ness** Traurigkeit *f*.

mourn·ing ['mɔ:niŋ] **1.** □ trauernd; Trauer...; **2.** Trauer *f*; Trauerkleidung *f*; *national day of ~* Staatstrauertag *m*; **'~-band** Trauerflor *m*; **'~-bor·der, '~-edge** Trauerrand *m*; **'~-pa·per** Briefpapier *n* mit Trauerrand.

mouse 1. [maus], *pl.* **mice** [mais] Maus *f*; **2.** [mauz] mausen; **mous·er** ['mauzə] Mäusefänger *m*; **'mouse-trap** Mausefalle *f*.

mousse [mu:s] gefrorene Schaumspeise *f*.

mous·tache [məs'tɑ:ʃ] Schnurrbart *m*.

mous·y ['mausi] schüchtern, furchtsam (*bsd. Frau*); unscheinbar; braungrau u. glanzlos (*Haar*).

mouth 1. [mauθ], *pl.* **mouths** [mauðz] Mund *m*; Maul *n*; Mündung *f e-s Flusses, e-r Flasche etc.*; Mundstück *n e-s Horns etc.*; Loch *n*, Öffnung *f e-s Ofens, Sackes etc.*; Grimasse *f*; *by word of ~* mündlich; *down in the ~* niedergeschlagen; *laugh on the wrong side of one's ~* jammern; enttäuscht sein; *keep one's ~ shut* den Mund halten, schweigen; **2.** [mauð] mit vollem Munde aussprechen; laut und affektiert reden; in den Mund nehmen; **mouth·ful** ['mauθful] Mundvoll *m*, Happen *m*.

mouth...: '~-or·gan Mundharmonika *f*; **'~·piece** Mundstück *n*; ⊕ Schalltrichter *m*, Sprechmuschel *f*; *fig.* Sprachrohr *n*; **'~-wash** Mundwasser *n*; **'~-wa·ter·ing** leckeraussehend, -riechend.

mov(e)·a·ble ['mu:vəbl] **1.** beweglich; **2.** ~*s pl.* Mobilien *pl.*; '**mov(e)-a·ble·ness** Beweglichkeit *f.*

move [mu:v] **1.** *v/t. allg.* bewegen; in Bewegung setzen; (weg)rücken; antreiben; *Leidenschaft* erregen; *seelisch* rühren, ergreifen; *Antrag* einbringen, beantragen; ~ *on* zum Weitergehen veranlassen; ~ *heaven and earth* Himmel und Hölle in Bewegung setzen; *v/i.* sich (fort-) bewegen; sich regen; sich rühren; aufbrechen, abmarschieren; *Schach etc.*: ziehen; *a.* ~ *house* (um)ziehen (*die Wohnung wechseln*); ~ *for s.th.* et. beantragen; ~ *in* einziehen; ~ *on* weitergehen; ~ *out* ausziehen; **2.** Bewegung *f*; *Schach etc.*: Zug *m*; *fig.* Schritt *m*, Maßnahme *f*; *on the* ~ in Bewegung; *get a* ~ *on* F sich beeilen; *make a* ~ sich (von der Stelle) rühren; die Tafel aufheben; '**movement** Bewegung *f*; ♪ Tempo *n*; ♪ Satz *m*; ⊕ (Geh)Werk *n*; ⚕ Stuhlgang *m*; '**mov·er** Bewegende *m, n*; Anreger(in), Urheber(in); Antragsteller(in); Triebkraft *f.*

mov·ie F ['mu:vi] Film...; Kino...; ~*s pl.* Film *m*; Kino *n.*

mov·ing □ ['mu:viŋ] bewegend; beweglich; *fig.* rührend; ~ *staircase* Rolltreppe *f.*

mow[1] [mau] Heu-, Strohhaufen *m*; [Heuboden *m.*]

mow[2] [məu] (*irr.*) mähen; '**mow·er** Mäher(in), Schnitter(in); Mähmaschine *f*; '**mow·ing** Mähen *n*; Mahd *f*; '**mow·ing-ma·chine** Mähmaschine *f*; **mown** *p.p. von mow*[2].

much [mʌtʃ] *adj.* viel; *adv.* sehr; weit, bei weitem; fast; *as* ~ *more, as* ~ *again* noch einmal soviel; *as* ~ *as* soviel wie; *not so* ~ *as* nicht einmal; *nothing* ~ nichts Bedeutendes; ~ *less* geschweige denn; ~ *as I would like* so gern ich möchte; *I thought as* ~ das dachte ich mir; *make* ~ *of* verstehen; Bedeutung beimessen; viel Wesens machen von; *I am not* ~ *af a dancer* ich bin kein großer Tänzer; (*not*) *up to* ~ (nicht) viel wert; *this od. that* ~ soviel; '**much·ness** F Menge *f*; *much of a* ~ so ziemlich dasselbe.

mu·ci·lage ['mju:silidʒ] (Pflanzen-) Schleim *m*; ⚕ Klebstoff *m*; **mu·ci·lag·i·nous** [~'lædʒinəs] schleimig; klebrig.

muck [mʌk] **1.** Mist *m* (F *a. fig.*); F Dreck *m* (*a. fig.*); *make a* ~ *of s.th.* et. schmutzig machen; et. verpfuschen; **2.** düngen; *mst* ~ *up* beschmutzen; ~ *s.th. up* et. in Unordnung bringen; et. verpfuschen; ~ *about sl.* herumtrödeln; '**muck·er** *sl.* schwerer Sturz *m*; *come od. go a* ~ *bsd. fig.* reinfallen; **muck-rake** ['~reik] **1.** Mistgabel; = ~*r*; **2.** im Schmutz wühlen; '**muck·rak·er** *Am.* Korruptionsschnüffler *m*, Skandalmacher *m*; '**muck·y** schmutzig, dreckig.

mu·cous *physiol.* ['mju:kəs] schleimig; ~ *membrane* Schleimhaut *f.*

mu·cus ['mju:kəs] (Nasen)Schleim *m.*

mud [mʌd] Schlamm *m*; Kot *m*; Schmutz *m*; Lehm *m*; '**mud-bath** Moorbad *n*; '**mud·di·ness** Schlammigkeit *f*; **mud·dle** ['mʌdl] **1.** *v/t.* verwirren, in Unordnung bringen; *a.* ~ *up*, ~ *together* verwechseln, durcheinanderbringen; F benebeln; *v/i.* stümpern; ~ *through* F sich durchwursteln; **2.** Verwirrung *f*; Wirrwarr *m*; F Wurstelei *f*; *get into a* ~ in Schwierigkeiten geraten; '**mud·dle-head·ed** wirrköpfig; '**mud·dy 1.** □ schlammig; trüb (*Wasser etc.*); schmutzig; verworren; **2.** trüben; beschmutzen.

mud...: '~**guard** Kotflügel *m*; '~**lark** F Dreckspatz *m*; '~**-sling·ing** F Beschmutzung *f*, Verleumdung *f.*

muff[1] [mʌf] **1.** F Tolpatsch *m*; Stümper *m*; Stümperei *f*; **2.** (ver-) pfuschen; verpatzen; *Ball* entschlüpfen lassen.

muff[2] [~] Muff *m.*

muf·fin ['mʌfin] Muffin *n* (*heißes Teegebäck*); **muf·fin·eer** [~'niə] Salz-, Zuckerstreuer *m.*

muf·fle ['mʌfl] **1.** ⊕ Muffel *f*; **2.** *oft* ~ *up* ein-, umhüllen; *Stimme etc.* dämpfen; *Ruder* umwickeln; '**muf·fler** Halstuch *n*; Boxhandschuh *m*; ♪ Dämpfer *m*; *mot.* Auspufftopf *m.*

muf·ti ['mʌfti] Mufti *m*; *bsd.* ⚔ Zivilkleidung *f*; *in* ~ in Zivil.

mug [mʌg] **1.** Krug *m*; Becher *m*; *sl.* Schnauze *f*, Fresse *f*, Visage *f*; Trottel *m*; Büffler *m*, Streber *m*; *a* ~*'s game* ein undankbares Geschäft *n*; **2.** überfallen und berauben; '**mug·ging** Raubüberfall *m* auf der

Straße; **mug up** *et.* ochsen.
mug·gy ['mʌgi] schwül.
mug·wort ⚘ ['mʌgwəːt] Beifuß *m.*
mug·wump *Am. iro.* ['mʌgwʌmp] großes Tier *n* (*Person*); *pol.* Unabhängige *m.*
mu·lat·to [mjuː'lætəu] Mulatte *m*, Mulattin *f.*
mul·ber·ry ['mʌlbəri] Maulbeere *f.*
mulch [mʌltʃ] **1.** Torfmull *m*; **2.** mit Torfmull abdecken.
mulct [mʌlkt] **1.** ⚖ Geldstrafe *f*; **2.** mit e-r Geldstrafe belegen; bestrafen (*in* mit); berauben (*of gen.*).
mule [mjuːl] Maultier *n*, -esel *m*; Bastard *m*; sturer Kerl *m*; flache Pantolette *f*; = **'~-jenny** Mule-(spinn)maschine *f*; **mu·le·teer** [~li'tiə] Maultiertreiber *m*; **'mule-track** Saumpfad *m.*
mul·ish □ ['mjuːliʃ] störrisch.
mull[1] ✝ [mʌl] Mull *m.*
mull[2] F [~]: *~ over* hin und her überlegen.
mulled [mʌld]: *~ ale* Warmbier *n*; *~ wine* Glühwein *m.*
mul·le(i)n ⚘ ['mʌlin] Wollkraut *n*, Königskerze *f.*
mul·let *ichth.* ['mʌlit] Meeräsche *f.*
mul·li·gan *Am.* F ['mʌligən] Eintopf *m aus Resten*; **mul·li·ga·taw·ny** [mʌligə'tɔːni] *a. ~ soup* Currysuppe *f.*
mul·li·grubs *sl.* ['mʌligrʌbz] *pl.* Bauchweh *n*; miese Laune *f.*
mul·lion ⚠ ['mʌliən] **1.** Fensterpfosten *m*; **2.** durch Pfosten abteilen.
mul·ti·far·i·ous □ [mʌlti'fɛəriəs] mannigfaltig; **mul·ti·form** ['~fɔːm] vielförmig; **mul·ti·lat·er·al** □ ['~'lætərəl] vielseitig; **mul·ti·mil·lion·aire** ['~miljə'nɛə] Multimillionär *m*; **mul·ti·na·tion·al** [~'næʃənl] multinationaler Konzern *m*; **mul·ti·ple** ['mʌltipl] **1.** vielfach, mannigfaltig; *~ firm*, *~ shop* Firma *f* mit Zweigniederlassungen (in verschiedenen Orten); *~ switchboard* ⚡ Vielfachumschalter *m*; **2.** Vielfache *n*; **mul·ti·plex** ['~pleks] vielfach; **mul·ti·pli·cand** ⚹ [~pli'kænd] Multiplikand(us) *m*; **mul·ti·pli·ca·tion** [~pli'keiʃən] Vervielfältigung *f*, Vermehrung *f*; Multiplikation *f*; *compound* (*simple*) *~* Großes (Kleines) Einmaleins *n*; *~ table* Einmaleins *n*; **mul·ti·plic·i·ty** [~'plisiti] Vielfältigkeit *f*; Menge *f*; **mul·ti·pli·er** [~'plaiə] Multiplikator *m*; Vermehrer (-in); **mul·ti·ply** ['~plai] (sich) vervielfältigen; multiplizieren; sich vermehren; **mul·ti-pur·pose** ['~'pəːpəs] Mehrzweck...; **mul·ti-ra·cial** ['~'reiʃəl] Vielvölker...; **mul·ti·tude** ['~tjuːd] Vielheit *f*, Menge *f*; *der* große Haufe, Pöbel *m*; **mul·ti·tu·di·nous** [~'tjuːdinəs] □ zahlreich; vielfach.
mum[1] [mʌm] **1.** still; **2.** st!, still!; **3.** Mummenschanz treiben; maskiert herumlaufen.
mum[2] F [~] Mama *f.*
mum·ble ['mʌmbl] murmeln; mummeln (*mühsam essen*).
Mum·bo Jum·bo ['mʌmbəu'dʒʌmbəu] Idol *n*; Hokuspokus *m.*
mum·mer *contp.* ['mʌmə] Komödiant *m*; **'mum·mer·y** *contp.* Mummenschanz *m*, Maskerade *f*; Hokuspokus *m.*
mum·mied ['mʌmid] mumienhaft.
mum·mi·fi·ca·tion [mʌmifi'keiʃən] Mumifizierung *f*; **mum·mi·fy** ['~fai] mumifizieren; als Mumie aufbewahren.
mum·my[1] ['mʌmi] Mumie *f*; *beat to a ~* F zu Brei schlagen.
mum·my[2] F [~] Mami *f*, Mutti *f.*
mump [mʌmp] betteln; schmollen; **'mump·ish** verdrießlich; **mumps** [mʌmps] *sg.* ⚕ Ziegenpeter *m*, Mumps *m*; üble Laune *f.*
munch [mʌntʃ] mit vollen Backen kauen, mampfen.
mun·dane □ ['mʌndein] weltlich; Welt...; irdisch.
mu·nic·i·pal □ [mjuː'nisipl] städtisch, Gemeinde..., Stadt...; **mu·nic·i·pal·i·ty** [~'pæliti] Stadtbezirk *m*; *konkr.* Stadtverwaltung *f.*
mu·nif·i·cence [mjuː'nifisns] Freigebigkeit *f*; **mu'nif·i·cent** □ freigebig.
mu·ni·ments ['mjuːnimənts] *pl.* Urkunden *f/pl.*
mu·ni·tion [mjuː'niʃən] **1.** Munitions...; **2.** *~s pl.* Kriegsmaterial *n*, Munition *f.*
mu·ral ['mjuərəl] **1.** Mauer...; **2.** Wandgemälde *n.*
mur·der ['məːdə] **1.** Mord *m*; *get away with* (*blue*) *~* sich alles erlauben können; **2.** (er)morden; *fig.* verhunzen; **'mur·der·er** Mörder *m*; **'mur·der·ess** Mörderin *f*; **'mur·der·ous** □ mörderisch; *fig.* blutig.

mure [mjuə] *mst* ~ *up* einsperren.
mu·ri·at·ic ac·id ⚗ [mjuəri'ætik-'æsid] Salzsäure *f*.
murk·y □ ['mə:ki] dunkel, trübe.
mur·mur ['mə:mə] **1.** Gemurmel *n*; Rauschen *n*; Murren *n*; **2.** murmeln; murren (*against, at* über *acc.*); '**mur·mur·ous** □ murmelnd.
mur·phy *sl.* ['mə:fi] Kartoffel *f*.
mur·rain ['mʌrin] Viehseuche *f*, Maul- und Klauenseuche *f*.
mus·ca·dine ['mʌskədin], **mus·cat** ['~kət], **mus·ca·tel** [~kə'tel] Muskatellerwein *m*, -traube *f*.
mus·cle ['mʌsl] **1.** Muskel *m*; **2.** ~ *in Am. sl.* sich rücksichtslos eindrängen; '**~-bound** mit Muskelkater; *be* ~ Muskelkater haben; **mus·cu·lar** □ ['~kjulə] Muskel...; muskulös.
Muse[1] [mju:z] Muse *f*.
muse[2] [~] (nach)sinnen, grübeln (*on, upon* über *acc.*); '**mus·er** Träumer(in).
mu·se·um [mju:'ziəm] Museum *n*.
mush [mʌʃ] Brei *m*, Mus *n*; *Am.* Polenta *f*, Maisbrei *m*.
mush·room ['mʌʃrum] **1.** Pilz *m*, *bsd.* Champignon *m*; *fig.* Emporkömmling *m*; **2.** Pilz...; *fig.* plötzlich emporgeschossen; **3.** rasch wachsen, zunehmen; ~ *up* in die Höhe schießen; ~ *out* sich rasch ausbreiten; *go ~ing* Pilze sammeln.
mu·sic ['mju:zik] Musik *f* (*a. fig.*), Tonkunst *f*; Musikstück *n*; Noten *f/pl.*; *set to* ~ vertonen; *face the* ~ F die Sache ausbaden; '**mu·si·cal 1.** □ musikalisch; Musik...; wohlklingend; ~ *box* Spieldose *f*; ~ *clock* Spieluhr *f*; ~ *instrument* Musikinstrument *n*; **2.** *a.* ~ *comedy* Musical *n* (*musikalisches Lustspiel*).
mu·sic...: '**~-book** Notenheft *n*; '**~-box** *Am.* Spieldose *f*; '**~-hall** Varieté(theater) *n*.
mu·si·cian [mju:'ziʃən] Musiker (-in); Musikant(in); *be a good* ~ gut spielen; musikalisch sein.
mu·si·col·o·gy [mju:zi'kɔlədʒi] Musikwissenschaft *f*.
mu·sic...: '**~-pa·per** Notenpapier *n*; '**~-stand** Notenständer *m*, -pult *n*; '**~-stool** Klavierstuhl *m*.
musk [mʌsk] Moschus *m*, Bisam *m*; ⚘ Bisampflanze *f*; = '**~-'deer** *zo.* Moschustier *n*.
mus·ket ['mʌskit] Muskete *f*, Flinte *f*; **mus·ket·eer** *hist.* [~'tiə] Musketier *m*; **mus·ket·ry** ⚔ ['~ri] Schießunterricht *m*.
musk...: '**~-rat** *zo.* Bisamratte *f*; '**~-rose** ⚘ Moschusrose *f*; '**musk·y** nach Moschus riechend; Moschus...
Mus·lim ['mʌslim] *s. Moslem*.
mus·lin ✝ ['mʌzlin] Musselin *m*.
mus·quash ['mʌskwɔʃ] Bisamratte *f*; Bisampelz *m*.
muss *bsd. Am.* F [mʌs] **1.** Durcheinander *n*; **2.** in Unordnung bringen.
mus·sel ['mʌsl] (Mies)Muschel *f*.
Mus·sul·man ['mʌslmən] **1.** Muselman(n) *m*; **2.** muselmanisch.
must[1] [mʌst, məst] **1.** *v/aux.* (*irr.*) muß(te) *etc.*; *I* ~ *not* ich darf nicht; **2.** Muß *n*, zwingende Notwendigkeit *f*; *this book is a* ~ dieses Buch muß man lesen.
must[2] [mʌst] Most *m*.
must[3] [~] Schimmel *m*, Moder *m*.
mus·tache *Am.* [məs'tɑ:ʃ], **mus·ta·chio** *Am.* [məs'tɑ:ʃi:əu] *s. moustache*.
mus·tang ['mʌstæŋ] Mustang *m* (*halbwildes Pferd*).
mus·tard ['mʌstəd] Senf *m*; ~ **gas** ⚔ Senfgas *n*, Gelbkreuz *n*; ~ **plaster** ⚕ Senfpflaster *n*.
mus·ter ['mʌstə] **1.** ⚔ Musterung *f*, Parade *f*; *mst* ~ *roll* ⚔ Stammrolle *f*; *fig.* Heerschau *f*, Aufgebot *n*; *pass* ~ *fig.* durchgehen, Zustimmung finden; **2.** *v/t.* ⚔ mustern; aufbieten, -bringen, zs.-bringen (*fig. mst* ~ *up*); ~ *in* einstellen; *v/i.* sich sammeln.
mus·ti·ness ['mʌstinis] Modrig-, Muffigkeit *f*; '**mus·ty** modrig, muffig.
mu·ta·bil·i·ty [mju:tə'biliti] Veränderlichkeit *f*; Wankelmütigkeit *f*; '**mu·ta·ble** □ veränderlich; wankelmütig; **mu·ta·tion** [~'teiʃən] Veränderung *f*; *gr.* Umlaut *m*.
mute [mju:t] **1.** □ stumm; **2.** Stumme *m*; Statist *m*; ♩ Dämpfer *m*; *gr.* Verschlußlaut *m*; **3.** *bsd.* ♩ dämpfen.
mu·ti·late ['mju:tileit] verstümmeln (*a. fig.*); **mu·ti'la·tion** Verstümmelung *f*.
mu·ti·neer [mju:ti'niə] Meuterer *m*; '**mu·ti·nous** □ meuterisch; '**mu·ti·ny 1.** Meuterei *f*; **2.** meutern.
mutt *sl.* [mʌt] Dussel *m*.
mut·ter ['mʌtə] **1.** Gemurmel *n*; **2.** murmeln; murren.

mut·ton ['mʌtn] Hammelfleisch *n*; *leg of* ~ Hammelkeule *f*; ~ **chop** Hammelkotelett *n*; ~*s pl.* Koteletten *pl.* (*Backenbart*).
mu·tu·al □ ['mjuːtʃuəl] gegenseitig, wechselseitig; gemeinsam; *by* ~ *consent* in gegenseitigem Einvernehmen; ~ *insurance* Versicherung *f* auf Gegenseitigkeit; **mu·tu·al·i·ty** [~tju'æliti] Gegenseitigkeit *f*.
muz·zle ['mʌzl] **1.** Maul *n*, Schnauze *f*; Mündung *f e-r Feuerwaffe*; Maulkorb *m*; **2.** e-n Maulkorb anlegen (*dat.*); *fig.* den Mund stopfen (*dat.*); knebeln; '**~-load·er** ⚔ Vorderlader *m*.
muz·zy □ ['mʌzi] stumpfsinnig; wirr, duselig.
my [mai] mein.
my·al·gi·a ⚕ [mai'ældʒiə] Muskelrheumatismus *m*.
my·col·o·gy [mai'kɔlədʒi] Pilzkunde *f*, Mykologie *f*.
my·ope ⚕ ['maiəup] Kurzsichtige *m*, *f*; **my·o·pi·a** [mai'əupjə] Kurzsichtigkeit *f*; **my·op·ic** [~'ɔpik] **1.** (~*ally*) kurzsichtig; **2.** Kurzsichtige *m*, *f*.
myr·i·ad ['miriəd] **1.** Myriade *f*; Unzahl *f*; **2.** unzählig, zahllos.
myr·mi·don ['məːmidən] *contp.* Helfershelfer *m*; Scherge *m*.
myrrh ⚘ [məː] Myrrhe *f*.
myr·tle ⚘ ['məːtl] Myrte *f*.
my·self [mai'self] ich selbst; mir; mich.
mys·te·ri·ous □ [mis'tiəriəs] geheimnisvoll, rätselhaft, mysteriös; **mys'te·ri·ous·ness** *das* Geheimnisvolle.
mys·ter·y ['mistəri] Mysterium *n*; Geheimnis *n*, Rätsel *n*; Geheimlehre *f*; *a.* ~ *play hist.* Mysterienspiel *n*; ~ **mod·el** *mot.* Erlkönig *m*; '**~-ship** U-Bootfalle *f*.
mys·tic ['mistik] **1.** *a.* '**mys·ti·cal** □ mystisch, geheimnisvoll; sinnbildlich; **2.** Mystiker *m*; **mys·ti·cism** ['~sizəm] Mystizismus *m*; **mys·ti·fi·ca·tion** [~fi'keiʃən] Irreführung *f*; **mys·ti·fy** ['~fai] mystifizieren, täuschen, hinters Licht führen; verblüffen.
mys·tique [mis'tiːk] Nimbus *m*; Geheimwissenschaft *f*.
myth [miθ] Mythe *f*, Mythos *m*, Sage *f*; **myth·ic, myth·i·cal** □ ['~ik(əl)] mythisch.
myth·o·log·ic, myth·o·log·i·cal □ [miθə'lɔdʒik(əl)] mythologisch; **my·thol·o·gy** [mi'θɔlədʒi] Mythologie *f*, Sagenkunde *f*.
myx·o·ma·to·sis [miksəumə'təusis] Myxomatose *f* (*Viruskrankheit der Kaninchen*).

N

nab *sl.* [næb] schnappen, erwischen.
na·bob ['neibɔb] Nabob *m*, Krösus *m* (*sehr reicher Mann*).
na·celle ✈ [næ'sel] Motorgehäuse *n*; Motorgondel *f e-s Luftschiffes*.
na·cre ['neikə] Perlmutter *f*; **na·cre·ous** ['~kriəs] perlmutterartig; Perlmutter...
na·dir ['neidiə] *ast.* Nadir *m* (*Fußpunkt*); *fig.* tiefster Stand *m*.
nag[1] F [næg] *kleiner* Klepper *m*.
nag[2] [~] nörgeln, quengeln; bekritteln; quälen; '**nag·ging 1.** Meckerei *f*, Nörgelei *f*; **2.** nörglerisch; *fig.* nagend.
Nai·ad ['naiæd] Najade *f* (*Quellnymphe*).
nail [neil] **1.** (Finger-, Zehen)Nagel *m*; ⊕ Nagel *m*; *zo.* Kralle *f*, Klaue *f*; *fight tooth and* ~ bis zum Äußersten kämpfen; *on the* ~ sofort; *hit the* (*right*) ~ *on the head* den Nagel auf den Kopf treffen; *as hard as* ~*s* eisern, unbarmherzig; fit, in Form; **2.** (an-, fest)nageln; *Augen etc.* heften (*to* auf *acc.*); F abfassen; ~ *down* an-, fest-, zunageln; ~ *s.o. down to fig.* j. festnageln auf (*acc.*); ~ *to the counter et.* als Lüge entlarven; '**~-brush** Nagelbürste *f*; '**~-file** Nagelfeile *f*; '**nail·ing** *sl. oft* ~ *good* fabelhaft; '**nail-scis·sors** *pl.* Nagelschere

f; ˈ**nail-var·nish** Nagellack *m.*

nain·sook [ˈneinsuk] feines Baumwollgewebe *n.*

na·ïve □ [nɑːˈiːv], **na·ive** □ [neiv], unbefangen; ungekünstelt; **na·ïve-te** [nɑːˈiːvtei], **na·ive·ty** [ˈneivti] Naivität *f.*

na·ked □ [ˈneikid] nackt, bloß; kahl; *fig.* unverhüllt; *poet.* schutzlos; ausgesetzt; *the* ~ *eye* das bloße Auge; ˈ**na·ked·ness** Nacktheit *f*, Blöße *f etc.*

nam·by-pam·by [ˈnæmbiˈpæmbi] **1.** abgeschmackt, fad; **2.** Fadheit *f.*

name [neim] **1.** Name *m*; Ruf *m*; bloßes Wort *n*; *of od. by the* ~ *of* ... namens ..., ... mit Namen; *call s.o.* ~*s* j. beschimpfen; *not have a penny to one's* ~ keinen Pfennig besitzen; *know s.o. by* ~ j. dem Namen nach kennen; **2.** (be)nennen; erwähnen; ernennen; ˈ**~-day** Namenstag *m*; ˈ**~-drop·ping** *Wichtigtuerei durch Erwähnung von Prominenten, die man angeblich kennt*; ˈ**name·less** □ namenlos; unbekannt; unbeschreiblich; ˈ**name·ly** (*abbr. viz.*) nämlich; ˈ**name-part** Titelrolle *f*; ˈ**name-plate** Namen-, Tür-, Firmenschild *n*; ˈ**name-sake** Namensvetter *m.*

nan·cy *sl.* [ˈnænsi] Weichling *m*; Homosexuelle *m.*

nan·keen [næŋˈkiːn] Nanking *m* (*Stoff*); ~*s pl.* Nankinghose *f.*

nan·ny [ˈnæni] Kindermädchen *n*; ˈ**~-goat** Ziege *f.*

nap[1] [næp] *Tuch*-Noppe *f*; Haar (-seite *f*) *n des Tuches.*

nap[2] [~] **1.** Schläfchen *n*; *have od. take a* ~ ein Nickerchen machen; **2.** schlummern; *catch s.o.* ~*ping* j-n überrumpeln.

nap[3] [~]: *go* ~ *Karten*: alles auf e-e Karte setzen.

na·palm [ˈneipɑːm]: ~ *bomb* ⚔ Napalmbombe *f.*

nape [neip] *mst* ~ *of the neck* Genick *n.*

naph·tha ⚗ [ˈnæfθə] Naphtha *n, f.*

nap·kin [ˈnæpkin] Serviette *f*; Windel *f*; Monatsbinde *f*; ˈ**~-ring** Serviettenring *m.*

Na·po·le·on·ic [nəpəuliˈɔnik] napoleonisch.

na·poo(h) *sl.* [nɑːˈpuː] aus; futsch, alles alle.

nap·py F [ˈnæpi] Windel *f.*

nar·cis·sism *psych.* [nɑːˈsisizm] Narzißmus *m*; **nar·ciss·us** ⚘ [~ˈsisəs] Narzisse *f.*

nar·co·sis ⚕ [nɑːˈkəusis] Narkose *f.*

nar·cot·ic [nɑːˈkɔtik] **1.** (~*ally*) narkotisch; **2.** Betäubungsmittel *n*; ~*s squad* Rauschgiftdezernat *n*; **nar·co·tize** [ˈnɑːkətaiz] narkotisieren.

nard [nɑːd] Narde(nsalbe) *f.*

nark[1] *sl.* [nɑːk] Polizeispitzel *m.*

nark[2] F [~] verärgern.

nar·rate [næˈreit] erzählen; **narˈra·tion** Erzählung *f*; **nar·ra·tive** [ˈnærətiv] **1.** □ erzählend; **2.** Erzählung *f*; **nar·ra·tor** [næˈreitə] Erzähler *m.*

nar·row [ˈnærəu] **1.** □ eng, schmal, beschränkt; knapp (*Mehrheit, Entkommen*); engherzig; *s. escape*; **2.** ~*s pl.* Engpaß *m*; Meerenge *f*; **3.** *v/t.* verengen; beschränken; ein-, beengen; *Maschen* abnehmen; *v/i.* sich verengen; ˈ**~-ˈchest·ed** eng-, schmalbrüstig; ˈ**~-gauge** 🚂 schmalspurig; ˈ**~-ˈmind·ed** □ engherzig; ˈ**nar·row·ness** Enge *f*; Beschränktheit *f* (*a. fig.*); Engherzigkeit *f.*

nar·whal *zo.* [ˈnɑːwəl] See-Einhorn *n.*

nar·y *Am.* [ˈnɛəri] kein.

na·sal [ˈneizəl] **1.** □ nasal; Nasen...; näselnd; **2.** Nasallaut *m*; **na·sal·i·ty** [~ˈzæliti] Nasalität *f*; **na·sal·ize** [ˈ~zəlaiz] durch die Nase sprechen, näseln; *gr.* nasalieren.

nas·cent [ˈnæsnt] werdend, entstehend, wachsend.

nas·ti·ness [ˈnɑːstinis] Schmutz *m*; Unflätigkeit *f.*

nas·tur·tium ⚘ [nəsˈtəːʃəm] Kapuzinerkresse *f.*

nas·ty [ˈnɑːsti] □ schmutzig; garstig; eklig; widerlich, häßlich; unflätig; ungemütlich.

na·tal [ˈneitl] Geburts...; **na·tal·i·ty** [nəˈtæliti] Geburtenziffer *f.*

na·ta·tion [nəˈteiʃən] Schwimmen *n*; **na·ta·to·ri·al** [nætəˈtɔːriəl] Schwimm...

na·tion [ˈneiʃən] Nation *f*, Volk *n*; *member* ~ Mitgliedstaat *m.*

na·tion·al [ˈnæʃənl] **1.** □ national; Volks..., Staats...; ~ *champion* Landesmeister *m*; **2.** Staatsangehörige *m, f*; **na·tion·al·ism** [ˈnæʃnəlizəm] Nationalismus *m*; ˈ**na·tion·al·ist** **1.** Nationalist(in); **2.** = **na·tion·alˈis·tic** nationalistisch; **na·tion·al·i·ty** [næʃəˈnæliti] Nationalität *f*; Nationalcharakter *m*; Nationalgefühl *n*;

Staatsangehörigkeit *f*; **na·tion·al·i·za·tion** [næʃnəlai'zeiʃən] Verstaatlichung *f*; '**na·tion·al·ize** naturalisieren, einbürgern; verstaatlichen; zu e-r Nation machen.
na·tion·hood ['neiʃənhud] nationale Selbständigkeit *f*; **na·tion-wide** ['~waid] die ganze Nation umfassend.
na·tive ['neitiv] **1.** □ angeboren, natürlich; heimatlich, Heimat...; Landes...; eingeboren; einheimisch (*to* in *dat.*); gediegen (*Metall*); ~ *land* Vaterland *n*; ~ *language* Muttersprache *f*; ~ *speaker* Muttersprachler *m*; **2.** Eingeborene *m, f*; Einheimische *m, f*; einheimisches Tier *n*; einheimische Pflanze *f*; (*bsd.* gezüchtete) britische Auster *f*; *a* ~ *of Ireland* ein gebürtiger Ire *m*; '**~-born** (im Lande) geboren, einheimisch.
na·tiv·i·ty [nə'tiviti] Geburt *f*; Nativität *f*, Horoskop *n*; ♀ **Play** Krippenspiel *n*.
na·tron ⚗ ['neitrən] Natron *n*.
nat·ter F ['nætə] plaudern.
nat·ty □ ['næti] schmuck, nett, fein; flink, geschickt.
na·tu·ral ['nætʃrəl] **1.** □ natürlich; *engS.* angeboren; ungezwungen; unehelich (*Kind*); ~ *disaster* Naturkatastrophe *f*; ~ *gas* Erdgas *n*; ~ *history* Naturgeschichte *f*; ~ *note* ♪ Note *f* ohne Vorzeichen; ~ *philosopher* Naturforscher *m*; ~ *philosophy* Physik *f*, Naturlehre *f*; ~ *resources pl.* Bodenschätze *m/pl.*; ~ *science* Naturkunde *f*; **2.** Idiot(in); ♪ Auflösungszeichen *n*; '**nat·u·ral·ism** Naturalismus *m*; '**nat·u·ral·ist** Naturalist *m*; Naturforscher *m*, -freund *m*; Tierhändler *m*; Präparator *m*; **nat·u·ral·i·za·tion** [~lai'zeiʃən] Naturalisierung *f*; '**nat·u·ral·ize** naturalisieren, einbürgern; ♀, *zo.* eingewöhnen; '**nat·u·ral·ness** Natürlichkeit *f*; **na·tu·ral se·lec·tion** *biol.* natürliche Zuchtwahl *f*.
na·ture ['neitʃə] Natur *f*; *engS.* Beschaffenheit *f*; Art *f*; Wesen(sart *f*) *n*; ~ *reserve* Naturschutzgebiet *n*; ~ *study Schule*: Naturkunde *f*; ~ *trail* Naturlehrpfad *m*; *by* ~ von Natur (aus); '**na·tured** ...geartet, ...artig.
na·tur·ism ['neitʃərizəm] Freikörperkultur *f*; '**na·tur·ist** FKK-Anhänger(in).
naught [nɔ:t] Null *f*; † nichts; *bring* (*come*) *to* ~ zunichte machen (werden); *set at* ~ für nichts achten; **naugh·ti·ness** ['~tinis] Ungezogenheit *f*, Unartigkeit *f*; '**naugh·ty** □ unartig, ungezogen; ungehörig; unanständig.
nau·se·a ['nɔ:sjə] Seekrankheit *f*; Übelkeit *f*; *fig.* Ekel *m*; **nau·se·ate** ['nɔ:sieit] *v/i.* Ekel empfinden (*at* vor *dat.*); *v/t.* verabscheuen; *be* ~*d* sich ekeln; **nau·seous** □ ['nɔ:sjəs] ekelhaft.
nau·ti·cal □ ['nɔ:tikəl] nautisch; See..., Schiffs...; ~ *mile* Seemeile *f*.
naut·i·lus *zo.* ['nɔ:tiləs] Nautilus *m*, Perlboot *n* (*Seetier*).
na·val □ ['neivəl] See..., Schiffs..., Marine...; ~ *architect* Schiffsbauingenieur *m*; ~ *base* Flottenstützpunkt *m*; ~ *staff* Admiralstab *m*.
nave[1] ⚠ [neiv] (Kirchen)Schiff *n*.
nave[2] [~] *Rad*-Nabe *f*.
na·vel ['neivəl] Nabel *m*; *fig.* Mitte *f*; ~ **or·ange** Navelorange *f*.
nav·i·ga·ble □ ['nævigəbl] schiff-, fahrbar; lenkbar (*Luftschiff*); **nav·i·gate** ['~geit] *v/i.* schiffen, (zu Schiff) fahren; *v/t. See etc.* befahren; *Schiff etc.* steuern; **nav·i'ga·tion** Schiffahrt *f*; Navigation *f* (*Schiffsführung*); '**nav·i·ga·tor** Seefahrer *m*; Steuermann *m*; Luftschiffer *m*.
nav·vy ['nævi] Erdarbeiter *m*.
na·vy ['neivi] Marine *f*, Kriegsflotte *f*; '**~-'blue** marineblau.
nay [nei] **1.** † *od. prov.* nein; nein vielmehr; **2.** Nein *n bei Abstimmung*.
Naz·a·rene [næzə'ri:n] Nazarener *m*.
naze [neiz] Landspitze *f*.
Na·zi ['nɑ:tsi] **1.** Nazi *m*; **2.** Nazi..., nazistisch.
neap [ni:p] *a.* ~-*tide* Nippflut *f*; '**neaped:** *be* ~ ⚓ bei Ebbe auf Grund kommen.
Ne·a·pol·i·tan [niə'pɔlitən] **1.** neapolitanisch; **2.** Neapolitaner(in).
near [niə] **1.** *adj.* nahe; gerade (*Weg*); nahe verwandt; vertraut; genau (*z.B. Übersetzung*); knapp (*Entkommen etc.*); knauserig; link *vom Reiter etc.*; ~ *at hand* dicht dabei; ~ *miss* Beinahezusammenstoß *m*; *a* ~ *thing* ein knappes Entkommen; **2.** *adv.* nahe; **3.** *prp.* nahe (*dat.*), nahe bei *od.* an; **4.** sich nähern (*dat.*); **near·by** ['~bai] in der Nähe (gelegen); nah; '**near·ly** nahe; fast, beinahe; genau; *not* ~ bei weitem nicht;

'near·ness Nähe *f*; nahe Verwandtschaft *f*; Genauigkeit *f*; **'near-'sight·ed** kurzsichtig.

neat¹ □ [ni:t] nett, geschmackvoll; zierlich, niedlich; geschickt; ordentlich; sorgfältig; sauber; rein, unverdünnt; pur (*Whisky etc.*); treffend, bündig (*Stil*).

neat² ⚒ [~] Rind(vieh) *n*.

neat·ness ['ni:tnis] Nettigkeit *f*; Sauberkeit *f*; Zierlichkeit *f*.

neat...: '~'s-foot oil Klauenfett *n*; **'~'s-leath·er** Rindsleder *n*; **'~'s-tongue** Rinderzunge *f*.

neb·u·la *ast.* ['nebjulə] Nebel(fleck) *m*; **'neb·u·lar** Nebel(fleck)..., Nebular...; **neb·u·los·i·ty** [~'lɔsiti] Nebligkeit *f*; Nebel *m*; **'neb·u·lous** □ neblig; nebelhaft (*a. fig.*).

ne·ces·sa·ri·ly ['nesisərili] notwendigerweise, unbedingt; **'nec·es·sar·y** □ **1.** notwendig; unvermeidlich; gezwungen; **2.** *mst necessaries pl.* Bedürfnisse *n/pl.*; ✝ Bedarfsartikel *m/pl.*; **ne·ces·si·tate** [ni'sesiteit] *et.* erfordern, notwendig machen; zwingen; **ne'ces·si·tous** bedürftig; **ne'ces·si·ty** Notwendigkeit *f*; Bedürfnis *n*; Zwang *m*; *mst necessities pl.* Not *f*, Armut *f*; *of* ~ notgedrungen; *the bare necessities* (*of life*) das Nötigste zum Leben.

neck [nek] **1.** Hals *m*; Nacken *m*, Genick *n*; Halsstück *n vom Hammel*; *Flaschen- etc.* Hals *m*; Ausschnitt *m* (*Kleid*); *break the* ~ *of a task* das Schwierigste e-r Aufgabe hinter sich bringen; ~ *and* ~ Kopf an Kopf; Seite an Seite; ~ *and crop* F mit Haut und Haaren; ~ *or nothing* F alles oder nichts; auf Leben und Tod; *be up to one's* ~ *in s.th.* bis über die Ohren in et. stecken; *get it in the* ~ *sl.* eins aufs Dach bekommen; *stick one's* ~ *out* einiges riskieren (*et. tun od. sagen, was unangenehme Folgen haben könnte*); **2.** *sl.* sich abknutschen; **'~·band** Halsbund *m*; **'~-cloth** Krawattenschal *m*; **neck·er·chief** ['nekətʃif] Halstuch *n*; **neck·lace** ['~lis], **neck·let** ['~lit] Halskette *f*; **'neck·line** (Hals)Ausschnitt *m* (*e-s Kleides*); **'neck·tie** Krawatte *f*; **'neck·wear** ✝ Krawatten und Kragen *pl*.

ne·crol·o·gy [ne'krɔlədʒi] Totenregister *n*; Nachruf *m*; **nec·ro·man·cy** ['nekrəumænsi] Nekromantie *f*, Schwarze Kunst *f*, Zauberei *f*.

nec·tar ['nektə] Nektar *m*; **nec·tar·ine** ['~rin] *e-e Pfirsichsorte*.

née [nei] *bei Frauennamen*: geborene.

need [ni:d] **1.** Not *f*; Notwendigkeit *f*; Bedürfnis *n* (*for* nach); Mangel *m*; Bedarf *m* (*of* an *dat.*); *one's own* ~*s pl.* Eigenbedarf *m*; *if* ~ *be* nötigenfalls; *be od. stand in* ~ *of* brauchen, benötigen; **2.** nötig haben, brauchen, benötigen; bedürfen (*gen.*); müssen; **need·ful** ['~ful] **1.** □ notwendig; **2.** F *das* Nötige (*bsd. Geld*); **'need·i·ness** Dürftigkeit *f*, Armut *f*.

nee·dle ['ni:dl] **1.** Nadel *f*; Zeiger *m*; **2.** (*mit e-r Nadel*) nähen; *bsd. Am.* irritieren; anstacheln; F *Getränk durch Alkoholzusatz* schärfen; ~ *one's way through* sich durchschlängeln durch; **'~-case** Nadelbüchse *f*; **'~-gun** Zündnadelgewehr *n*.

need·less □ ['ni:dlis] unnötig; **'need·less·ly** unnötig(erweise); **'need·less·ness** Unnötigkeit *f*.

nee·dle...: '~·wom·an Näherin *f*; **'~·work** Handarbeit *f*.

needs [ni:dz] notwendigerweise, notgedrungen, durchaus; **'need·y** □ bedürftig, arm, notleidend.

ne'er [nɛə] = *never*; **~-do-well** ['~du:wel] Tunichtgut *m*.

ne·far·i·ous □ [ni'fɛəriəs] ruchlos, schändlich.

ne·gate [ni'geit] verneinen; **ne'ga·tion** Verneinung *f*; Nichts *n*; **neg·a·tive** ['negətiv] **1.** □ negativ; verneinend; **2.** Verneinung *f*; *phot.* Negativ *n*; **3.** *a. answer in the* ~ verneinen, negieren; ablehnen; widerlegen; unwirksam machen.

neg·lect [ni'glekt] **1.** Vernachlässigung *f*; Nachlässigkeit *f*; Verwahrlosung *f*; **2.** vernachlässigen; *eine Gelegenheit* versäumen; **neg'lect·ful** □ [~ful] nachlässig; achtlos (*of* auf *acc.*).

nég·li·gé, neg·li·gee ['negli:ʒei] Negligé *n* (*Hauskleidung*; *Morgenmantel*).

neg·li·gence ['neglidʒəns] Nach-, ⚖ Fahrlässigkeit *f*; **'neg·li·gent** □ nach-, fahrlässig; ~ *of* gleichgültig gegen.

neg·li·gi·ble ['neglidʒəbl] nebensächlich; geringfügig, unbedeutend.

ne·go·ti·a·bil·i·ty [nigəuʃjə'biliti]

Verkäuflichkeit *f*; **ne'go·ti·a·ble** □ verkäuflich, umsetzbar; börsenfähig; begebbar (*Wechsel*); zu nehmen(d) (*Hindernis*); passierbar (*Straße*); *not* ~ nur zur Verrechnung; **ne'go·ti·ate** [~ʃieit] *v/t.* verhandeln (über *acc.*); zustande bringen; *Hindernis, Kurve* nehmen; bewältigen; *Wechsel* begeben; *v/i.* unterhandeln; **ne'go·ti·at·ing:** ~ *table* Verhandlungstisch *m*; **ne·go·ti'a·tion** Begebung *f e-s Wechsels, e-r Anleihe*; Unterhandlung *f*; Bewältigung *f*; *under* ~ zur Verhandlung stehend; **ne'go·ti·a·tor** Unterhändler *m.*

ne·gress ['ni:gris] Negerin *f*; **ne·gro** ['ni:grəu], *pl.* **ne·groes** ['~z] Neger *m*; **ne·groid** ['ni:grɔid] negroid, negerähnlich.

ne·gus ['ni:gəs] Glühwein *m.*

neigh [nei] **1.** Wiehern *n*; **2.** wiehern.

neigh·bo(u)r ['neibə] **1.** Nachbar(in); Nächste *m, f*; **2.** angrenzen an (*acc.*); **neigh·bo(u)r·hood** ['~hud] Nachbarschaft *f*; Umgebung *f*; *in the* ~ *of* in der Umgebung von; *fig.* F um ... herum; **'neigh·bo(u)r·ing** benachbart, angrenzend; ~ *state* Anlieger-, Nachbarstaat *m*; **'neigh·bo(u)r·li·ness** gutnachbarliches Verhalten *n*; **'neigh·bo(u)r·ly** nachbarlich, freundlich.

nei·ther ['naiðə] **1.** *adj. od. pron.* keiner (von beiden); **2.** *adv.* ~ ... *nor* ... weder ... noch ...; *not* ... ~ auch nicht.

nem·e·sis ['nemisis] Nemesis *f*, strafende Gerechtigkeit *f.*

ne·o·lith·ic [ni:əu'liθik] jungsteinzeitlich, neolithisch.

ne·ol·o·gism [ni:'ɔlədʒizəm] Neologismus *m*, Wortneubildung *f.*

ne·on ['ni:ən] Neon *n*; ~ **light** Neonlicht *n*; ~ **sign** Leuchtreklame *f.*

neph·ew ['nevju:] Neffe *m.*

ne·phri·tis ⚕ [ne'fraitis] Nierenentzündung *f.*

nep·o·tism ['nepətizəm] Nepotismus *m*, Vetternwirtschaft *f.*

Nep·tune ['neptju:n] Neptun *m* (*Meergott*; *Planet*).

Ne·re·id ['niəriid] Nereide *f.*

nerve [nə:v] **1.** Nerv *m*; Sehne *f*; *Blatt*-Rippe *f*; Kraft *f*, Mut *m*; Dreistigkeit *f*; *be all* ~*s* ein Nervenbündel sein; *get on s.o.'s* ~*s* j-m auf die Nerven gehen; *have the* ~ *to do s.th.* es wagen, et. zu tun; *lose one's* ~ den Mut *od.* die Nerven verlieren; **2.** kräftigen; ermutigen (*for* zu); **'~-cell** Nervenzelle *f*; **'~-cen·tre,** *Am.* **'~-cen·ter** Nervenzentrum *n*; **nerved** ⚘ gerippt; ...nervig; **'nerve·less** □ kraftlos; **'nerve-rack·ing** nervenaufreibend.

nerv·ine ⚕ ['nə:vi:n] **1.** nervenstärkend; **2.** nervenstärkendes Mittel *n.*

nerv·ous □ ['nə:vəs] Nerven...; nervig, kräftig; nervös, reizbar; ängstlich; aufgeregt; ~ *breakdown* Nervenzusammenbruch *m*; ~ *system* Nervensystem *n*; **'nerv·ous·ness** Nervosität *f.*

nerv·y *sl.* ['nə:vi] dreist; auf die Nerven gehend; nervös.

nes·ci·ence ['nesiəns] Unwissenheit *f*; **'nes·ci·ent** unwissend (*of* in *dat.*).

ness [nes] Vorgebirge *n.*

nest [nest] **1.** Nest *n* (*a. fig.*); Schlupfwinkel *m*; Satz *m ineinanderpassender Dinge*; **2.** nisten; **'nest·ed** eingenistet; **'nest-egg** Nestei *n*; *fig.* Spar-, Notgroschen *m*; **'nest·er** nistender Vogel *m*; Siedler *m*; **'nes·tle** ['nesl] *v/i.* nisten; sich einnisten; sich (an-) schmiegen (*to* an *acc.*); *v/t.* schmiegen; **nest·ling** ['nestliŋ] Nestling *m.*

net[1] [net] **1.** Netz *n* (*a. fig.*); Tüll *m*, Musselin *m*; ~ *curtains pl.* Stores *m/pl.*; **2.** mit e-m Netz fangen *od.* umgeben (*a. fig.*).

net[2] [~] **1.** netto, rein; Rein...; **2.** netto einbringen.

net·ball ['netbɔ:l] Netzball *m*; *Art* Korbball(spiel *n*) *m.*

neth·er ['neðə] nieder; Unter...; **'~·most** (zu)unterst.

net·ting ['netiŋ] Netzstricken *n*, Filetarbeit *f*; Netzwerk *n.*

net·tle ['netl] **1.** ⚘ Nessel *f*; **2.** ⚒ mit Nesseln brennen; *fig.* ärgern; **'~-rash** ⚕ Nesselfieber *n.*

net·work ['netwə:k] (Straßen-, Kanal- *etc.*)Netz *n*; *Radio*: Sendergruppe *f.*

neu·ral ⚕ ['njuərəl] Nerven...

neu·ral·gia ⚕ [njuə'rældʒə] Nervenschmerz *m*, Neuralgie *f*; **neu·ras·the·ni·a** ⚕ [njuərəs'θi:njə] Neurasthenie *f*, Nervenschwäche *f*; **neu·ras·then·ic** [~'θenik] **1.** neurasthenisch; **2.** Neurastheniker(in); **neu·ri·tis** ⚕ [njuə'raitis] Nervenentzündung *f*; **neu·rol·o·gist** [~'rɔlədʒist] Neurologe *m*; **neu'rol·o·gy** Neurologie *f*; **neu·ro·path·ic** ⚕ [~rəu'pæθik] **1.** nervenleidend; **2.** Nervenleidende *m*; **neu·ro·sis** ⚕ [~'rəusis] Neurose *f*; **neu·rot·ic** [~'rɔtik] **1.** neurotisch; Nerven...; **2.** Neurotiker(in); Nervenmittel *n*.

neu·ter ['nju:tə] **1.** geschlechtslos; *gr.* sächlich; intransitiv; **2.** geschlechtsloses Tier *n*; *gr.* Neutrum *n*.

neu·tral ['nju:trəl] **1.** □ neutral (*a.* ⚘); unparteiisch, parteilos, unbeteiligt; **2.** Neutrale *m*, *f*; Null (-punkt *m*) *f*; Leerlauf(stellung *f*) *m*; **neu·tral·i·ty** [~'træliti] Neutralität *f*; **neu·tral·i·za·tion** [~trəlai'zeiʃən] Neutralisierung *f* (*a.* ⚘); **'neu·tral·ize** neutralisieren (*a.* ⚘); unwirksam machen.

neu·tron *phys.* ['nju:trɔn] Neutron *n*; ~ *bomb* ⚔ Neutronenbombe *f*.

né·vé *mount.* ['nevei] Firn(feld *n*) *m*.

nev·er ['nevə] nie(mals); durchaus nicht, gar nicht; ~ *so* (auch) noch so; *on the* ~-~ *sl.* auf Stottern (*Raten*); *the* ≈-≈ (*Land*) der (australische) Busch; **'nev·er'more** nimmermehr, nie wieder; **nev·er·the·less** [~ðə'les] nichtsdestoweniger.

new [nju:] neu (*a. adv.*); frisch; modern; unerfahren; **'~·born** **1.** neugeboren; **2.** Neugeborene *n*; **'new-'com·er** Ankömmling *m*, Fremde *m*; Neuling *m*; **New Eng·land·er** Neuengländer(in); **new-fan·gled** ['~fæŋgld] neuerungssüchtig; neu(modisch); **new look** neue Mode *f*; neues Äußeres *n*; **'new·ly** neulich, kürzlich, jüngst; neu; **'newly-weds** *pl. die* Neuvermählten *pl.*; **'new·ness** Neuheit *f*; Unerfahrenheit *f*.

news [nju:z] *sg.* Neuigkeit(en *pl.*) *f*, Nachricht(en *pl.*) *f*; *what's the* ~? was gibt's Neues?; *break the* (*bad*) ~ *to s.o.* j-m die (*schlechte*) Nachricht (schonend) beibringen; *he is much in the* ~ F alle Zeitungen schreiben über ihn; **'~-a·gen·cy** Nachrichtenbüro *n*; **'~-a·gent** Zeitungshändler *m*; **'~-boy** Zeitungsausträger *m*; **'~-butch·er** *Am. sl.* Zeitungsverkäufer *m*; **'~·cast** *Radio*: Nachrichten *pl.*; **'~·cast·er** *bsd. Am.* Nachrichtensprecher *m*; ~ **cin·e·ma** Aktualitätenkino *n*; ~ **con·fer·ence** Pressekonferenz *f*; **'~-flash** (eingeblendete) Kurzmeldung *f*; **'~-let·ter** Rundschreiben *n*; ~ **mag·a·zine** Nachrichtenmagazin *n*; **'~-mon·ger** Neuigkeitskrämer *m*; **'~·pa·per** **1.** Zeitung *f*; **2.** Zeitungs...; **'~·print** Zeitungspapier *n*; **'~-read·er** *Br.* Nachrichtensprecher *m*; **'~-reel** *Film*: Wochenschau *f*; **'~-room** Zeitschriftenlesesaal *m*; *Am. Zeitung*: Redaktionsabteilung *f für Nachrichten*; **'~--stall,** *Am.* **'~·stand** Zeitungsstand *m*; **'~-ven·dor** Zeitungsverkäufer *m*; **news·y** ['nju:zi] F voller Nachrichten.

newt *zo.* [nju:t] Wassermolch *m*.

New World ['nju:'wə:ld] *die* Neue Welt (*Amerika*); **'new-world** neuweltlich.

new year ['nju:'jə:] Neujahr *n*; *~'s day* Neujahrstag *m*; *~'s eve* Silvester(abend *m*) *n*; *~'s gift* Neujahrsgeschenk *n*.

next [nekst] **1.** *adj.* nächst; nächst (-folgend); ~ *but one der* übernächste; ~ *door* nebenan; ~ *door to fig.* (schon) beinahe; *the* ~ *of kin* der (*pl.* die) nächste(n) Verwandte(n) *od.* Angehörige(n); ~ *to* nächst (*dat.*); ~ *to nothing* fast gar nichts; *what* ~? was denn noch?; **2.** *adv.* zunächst, gleich darauf, dann; demnächst, nächstens.

nex·us ['neksəs] Verknüpfung *f*, Zusammenhang *m*.

nib [nib] (Schreib)Feder *f aus Stahl od. Gold.*

nib·ble ['nibl] *v/t.* knabbern an (*dat.*); benagen, anknabbern; *v/i.* ~ *at* nagen *od.* knabbern an (*dat.*); *fig.* (herum)kritteln an (*dat.*); *fig.* spielen mit.

nib·lick ['niblik] *ein* Golfschläger *m*.

nice □ [nais] fein (*Beobachtung, Sinn; Urteil; Unterschied; Waage etc.*); wählerisch (*about* in *dat.*); peinlich (genau); heikel; nett; niedlich; hübsch, schön; ~ *and warm* hübsch warm; **'nice·ly** F (sehr) gut; **'nice·ness** Feinheit *f*; Genauigkeit *f*; Nettigkeit *f*; **nice·ty** ['~siti] Feinheit *f*, Schärfe *f*; Genauigkeit *f*; Spitzfindigkeit *f*; *to a* ~ bis aufs Haar; *stand upon niceties* es allzu genau nehmen.

niche [nitʃ] Nische *f*; *fig. der rechte*

Platz.

Nick[1] [nik]: *Old* ~ der Teufel.

nick[2] [~] **1.** Kerbe *f*; *sl.* Kittchen *n*; *in the (very)* ~ *of time* gerade zur rechten Zeit; **2.** (ein)kerben; *sl.* schnappen (*erwischen*).

nick·el ['nikl] **1.** *min.* Nickel *m* (*Am. a. Fünfcentstück*); *~-in-the-slot machine Am.* Warenautomat *m*; **2.** vernickeln.

nick·el·o·de·on *Am.* [nikl'əudjən] Kintopp *n*; Musikautomat *m*.

nick-nack ['niknæk] = *knickknack*.

nick·name ['nikneim] **1.** Spitzname *m*; **2.** e-n Spitznamen geben (*dat.*).

nic·o·tine ['nikəti:n] Nikotin *n*.

nid-nod ['nidnɔd] nicken.

niece [ni:s] Nichte *f*.

niff *sl.* [nif] Mief *m*, Gestank *m*.

niffed F [nift] eingeschnappt (*beleidigt*).

niff·y *sl.* ['nifi] stinkend.

nif·ty *Am.* ['nifti] **1.** elegant; sauber (*hervorragend*); *sl.* stinkend; **2.** treffende Bemerkung *f*.

nig·gard ['nigəd] **1.** Knicker *m*, Geizhals *m*; **2.** □ karg, geizig; '**nig·gard·li·ness** Knickerei *f*, Geiz *m*; '**nig·gard·ly** *adj. u. adv.* geizig, knauserig; karg.

nig·ger F *mst contp.* ['nigə] Nigger *m* (*Neger*); *that's the ~ in the woodpile Am. sl.* da liegt der Hund begraben.

nig·gle ['nigl] (s-e Zeit für Kleinigkeiten ver)trödeln; '**nig·gling** kleinlich; peinlich genau.

nigh † *od. prov.* [nai] = *near*.

night [nait] Nacht *f*; Abend *m*; *by ~, in the ~, at ~* nachts, bei Nacht; *~ out* freier Abend *m*; *make a ~ of it* die Nacht durchmachen; '**~-bell** Nachtglocke *f*; '**~-bird** Nacht(raub)vogel *m*; *fig.* Nachtschwärmer *m*; '**~·cap** Nachtmütze *f*; Schlummertrunk *m*; '**~-club** Nachtlokal *n*; '**~-dress** Damennachthemd *n*; '**~·fall** Einbruch *m* der Nacht; '**~-gown** = *night-dress*; **night·in·gale** *orn.* ['~iŋgeil] Nachtigall *f*; '**night·ly** Nacht..., nächtlich; jede Nacht.

night...: '**~·mare** Alptraum *m*, Alpdruck *m*; böser Traum *m*; '**~-school** Abendschule *f*; '**~·shade** ⚘ Nachtschatten *m*; *deadly ~* Tollkirsche *f*; *~* **shift** Nachtschicht *f*; '**~-shirt** (Herren)Nachthemd *n*; '**~-spot** *Am.* Nachtlokal *n*; '**~·stop** Aufenthalt *m* mit Übernachtung; '**~-stop** e-n Nachtaufenthalt haben; '**~-time** Nacht(zeit) *f*; '**~-walk·er** Nacht-, Schlafwandler(in); '**~-'watch** Nachtwache *f*; '**~-'watch·man** Nachtwächter *m*; '**~·work** Nachtarbeit *f*; '**night·y** F Damen- *od.* Kindernachthemd *n*.

ni·hil·ism ['naiilizəm] Nihilismus *m*; '**ni·hil·ist** Nihilist(in).

nil [nil] *bsd. Sport*: nichts, null.

nim·ble □ ['nimbl] flink, behend, gewandt; '**nim·ble·ness** Behendigkeit *f*; '**nim·ble-'wit·ted** schlagfertig.

nim·bus ['nimbəs] Nimbus *m*, Heiligenschein *m*; Regenwolke *f*.

nim·i·ny-pim·i·ny ['nimini'pimini] zimperlich, geziert.

Nim·rod ['nimrɔd] Nimrod *m* (*großer Jäger*).

nin·com·poop F ['ninkəmpu:p] Einfaltspinsel *m*, Trottel *m*.

nine [nain] **1.** neun; *~ days' wonder* Tagesgespräch *n*; **2.** Neun *f*; *dressed up to the ~s* F aufgedonnert; '**~·fold** neunfach; '**~·pins** *pl.* Kegel *m/pl.*; Kegelspiel *n*; **nine·teen** ['~'ti:n] neunzehn; *talk ~ to the dozen* unaufhörlich reden; '**nine-'teenth** neunzehnte(r, -s); **nine·tieth** ['~tiiθ] **1.** neunzigste(r, -s); **2.** Neunzigstel *n*; '**nine·ty** neunzig.

nin·ny F ['nini] Dummkopf *m*.

ninth [nainθ] **1.** neunte(r, -s); **2.** Neuntel *n*; ♪ None *f*; '**ninth·ly** neuntens.

nip[1] [nip] **1.** Kniff *m*, Kneifen *n*; ⚘ Frostbrand *m*; scharfer Frost *m*; **2.** kneifen, zwicken; schneiden (*Kälte*); *durch Frost* beschädigen, vernichten; *sl.* flitzen, huschen, eilen; *~ in the bud* im Keim ersticken.

nip[2] [~] **1.** Schlückchen *n*; **2.** nippen.

nip·per ['nipə] F Bengel *m*, Stift *m*; Krebsschere *f*; *(a pair of) ~s pl.* (eine) (Kneif)Zange *f*; (ein) Kneifer *m*.

nip·ple ['nipl] Brustwarze *f*; Saughütchen *n*; ⊕ Nippel *m*.

nip·py F ['nipi] **1.** bitter kalt; behende, flink; **2.** Kellnerin *f*.

nir·va·na [niə'vɑ:nə] Nirwana *n*.

Ni·sei *Am.* ['ni'sei] (*a. pl.*) Japaner *m, geboren in den USA*.

Nis·sen hut ['nisn'hʌt] Nissenhütte

f, Wellblechbaracke *f*.
nit [nit] Niß *f* (*Ei der Laus etc.*); '~-**-pick·ing** F pingelig, kleinlich.
ni·trate ⚗ ['naitreit] Nitrat *n*, salpetersaures Salz *n*.
ni·tre, ni·ter ⚗ ['naitə] Salpeter *m*.
ni·tric ac·id ⚗ ['naitrik'æsid] Salpetersäure *f*.
ni·tro·chalk ['nautrəu'tʃɔ:k] *ein* Rasendünger *m*.
ni·tro·gen ⚗ ['naitrədʒən] Stickstoff *m*; **ni·trog·e·nous** [~'trɔdʒinəs] stickstoffhaltig.
ni·tro·glyc·er·ine ⚗ ['naitrəuglisə'ri:n] Nitroglyzerin *n*.
ni·trous ⚗ ['naitrəs] salpetrig.
nit·ty-grit·ty P ['niti'griti]: *get down to the* ~ zum problematischen Teil der Sache kommen.
nit·wit F ['nitwit] Schwachkopf *m*; '**nit·wit·ted** F schwachsinnig.
nix [niks] Nix *m*; **nix·ie** ['~i] Nixe *f*.
no [nəu] **1.** *adj*. kein; *in* ~ *time* im Nu; ~-*claims bonus* Schadenfreiheitsrabatt *m od*. -prämie *f*; ~ *man's land* Niemandsland *n*; ~ *one* keiner, niemand; **2.** *adv*. nein; *beim comp*. nicht; **3.** Nein *n*; *noes pl*. Stimmen *f/pl*. dagegen.
nob[1] *sl*. [nɔb] Dez *m* (*Kopf*); ⊕ Knopf *m*.
nob[2] *sl*. [~] feiner Pinkel *m*.
nob·ble *sl*. ['nɔbl] *j*. (he)rumkriegen; *et*. mopsen (*stehlen*).
nob·by *sl*. ['nɔbi] nobel, schick, schnieke.
No·bel Prize [nəu'bel'praiz] Nobelpreis *m*; *Nobel Peace Prize* Friedensnobelpreis *m*; ~ *winner* Nobelpreisträger(in).
no·bil·i·ar·y [nəu'biliəri] Adels...
no·bil·i·ty [nəu'biliti] Adel *m* (*a. fig*.); Würde *f*.
no·ble ['nəubl] **1.** □ adlig; edel, vornehm; prächtig; vortrefflich; Edel-... (*Gas, Metall etc*.); **2.** Adlige *m, f*; '**~·man** Edelmann *m*, Adlige *m*; '**~-'mind·ed** edelgesinnt; '**no·ble·ness** Adel *m*; Würde *f*; '**no·ble·wom·an** Edelfrau *f*.
no·bod·y ['nəubədi] **1.** niemand; **2.** unbedeutende Persönlichkeit *f*.
nock [nɔk] Kerbe *f*.
noc·tur·nal [nɔk'tə:nl] Nacht...
noc·turne ['nɔktə:n] Nachtszene *f*; ♪ Notturno *n*.
nod [nɔd] **1.** *v/i*. nicken; schlafen; sich neigen; ~*ding acquaintance* oberflächliche Bekanntschaft *f*; ~ *off* einnicken; *v/t*. *Haupt* neigen; ~ *out j*. hinauswinken; **2.** Nicken *n*; Wink *m*.
nod·dle F ['nɔdl] Birne *f* (*Kopf*).
node [nəud] Knoten *m* (*a*. ♀ *u. ast*.); ⚕ Überbein *n*.
nod·u·lar ['nɔdjulə] knotenartig.
nod·ule ['nɔdju:l] Knötchen *n*.
No·el [nəu'el] Weihnacht *f*.
nog [nɔg] Holznagel *m*; Holzblock *m*; **nog·gin** ['nɔgin] kleiner (hölzerner) Krug *m*; '**nog·ging** ⚠ Riegelmauer *f*.
no·how F ['nəuhau] in keiner Weise; nicht in Ordnung.
noil [nɔil] *Tuchmacherei*: Kämmling *m*, Kurzwolle *f*.
noise [nɔiz] **1.** Lärm *m*; Geräusch *n*; Geschrei *n*, Aufsehen *n*; *big* ~ *bsd. Am*. F großes Tier (*Person*) *n*; ~ *abatement* Lärmbekämpfung *f*; ~ *level* Geräusch-, Lärmpegel *m*; **2.** ~ *abroad* in der Öffentlichkeit bekanntmachen; ausschreien.
noise·less □ ['nɔizlis] geräuschlos; '**noise·less·ness** Geräuschlosigkeit *f*.
nois·i·ness ['nɔizinis] Geräusch *n*, Getöse *n*.
noi·some ['nɔisəm] schädlich, ungesund; widerlich; '**noi·some·ness** Schädlichkeit *f*; Ekelhaftigkeit *f*.
nois·y □ ['nɔizi] geräuschvoll, lärmend; aufdringlich (*Farbe*).
no·mad ['nəuməd] Nomade *m*, Nomadin *f*; **no·mad·ic** [~'mædik] (~*ally*) nomadisch; **no·mad·ize** ['~mədaiz] nomadisieren.
nom de plume ['nɔ̃:mdə'plu:m] Pseudonym *n*, Schriftstellername *m*.
no·men·cla·ture [nəu'menklətʃə] Nomenklatur *f*; *systematische* Benennung *f*; Fachsprache *f*; Namensverzeichnis *n*.
nom·i·nal □ ['nɔminl] nominell; (nur) dem Namen nach (vorhanden); namentlich; Namen...; ~ *value* Nennwert *m*; **nom·i·nate** ['~neit] ernennen; zur Wahl vorschlagen; **nom·i'na·tion** Ernennung *f*; Vorschlagsrecht *n*; *in* ~ vorgeschlagen; **nom·i·na·tive** *gr*. ['~nətiv] *a*. ~ *case* Nominativ *m*; **nom·i·na·tor** ['~neitə] Ernenner *m*; **nom·i·nee** [~'ni:] *zu e-m Amt etc*. Vorgeschlagener *m*, Kandidat (-in).

non [nɔn] *in Zssgn*: nicht, un..., Nicht...
non-ac·cept·ance [ˈnɔnəkˈseptəns] Nichtannahme *f*.
non·age [ˈnəunidʒ] Minderjährigkeit *f*.
non·a·ge·nar·i·an [nəunədʒiˈnεəriən] Neunzigjährige *m, f*.
non-ag·gres·sion [ˈnɔnəˈgreʃən]: ~ *pact* Nichtangriffspakt *m*.
non-al·co·hol·ic [ˈnɔnælkəˈhɔlik] alkoholfrei.
non-a·lign·ment *pol*. [nɔnəˈlainmənt] Blockfreiheit *f*.
non-ap·pear·ance ⚖ [ˈnɔnəˈpiərəns] Nichterscheinen *n*.
non-at·tend·ance ⚖ [ˈnɔnəˈtendəns] Ausbleiben *n*, Nichterscheinen *n*.
nonce [nɔns]: *for the* ~ nur für diesen Fall; ~ **word** Ad-hoc-Bildung *f* (*für einen besonderen Fall geprägtes Wort*).
non·cha·lance [ˈnɔnʃələns] Lässigkeit *f*; ˈ**non·cha·lant** □ lässig.
non·com ⚔ F [nɔnˈkɔm] Unteroffizier *m*.
non-com·mis·sioned [ˈnɔnkəˈmiʃənd] nicht bevollmächtigt; ohne Bestallung; ~ *officer* ⚔ Unteroffizier *m*.
non-com·mit·tal [ˈnɔnkəˈmitl] unverbindlich, nichtssagend.
non-com·pli·ance [ˈnɔnkəmˈplaiəns] Zuwiderhandlung *f*, Verstoß *m* (*with* gegen).
non com·pos men·tis ⚖ [nɔnˈkɔmpɔsˈmentis] unzurechnungsfähig.
non-con·duc·tor ⚡ [ˈnɔnkəndʌktə] Nichtleiter *m*.
non·con·form·ist [ˈnɔnkənˈfɔːmist] Dissident(in), Freikirchler(in); **non·conˈform·i·ty** Mangel *m* an Übereinstimmung; *eccl*. Dissidententum *n*.
non-con·ten·tious ⚖ [ˈnɔnkənˈtenʃəs] nicht strittig.
non-de·liv·er·y [ˈnɔndiˈlivəri] Nichtauslieferung *f*, Nichterfüllung *f*.
non-de·nom·i·na·tion·al school [ˈnɔndinəmiˈneiʃənlˈskuːl] Simultanschule *f*.
non·de·script [ˈnɔndiskript] **1.** unbestimmbar; schwer zu beschreibend; **2.** schwer zu beschreibende Person *f*.
none [nʌn] **1.** keine(r, -s); nichts; **2.** keineswegs, gar nicht; ~ *the less* nichtsdestoweniger.
non-en·ti·ty [nɔˈnentiti] Nichtsein *n*; Unding *n*; Nichts *n*; *fig*. Null *f*.
non-es·sen·tial [ˈnɔniˈsenʃəl] **1.** unwesentlich; **2.** Unwesentlichkeit *f*.
non-ex·ist·ence [ˈnɔnigˈzistəns] Nicht(da)sein *n*; ˈ**non·exˈist·ent** nicht vorhanden, nicht existierend.
non-fic·tion [ˈnɔnˈfikʃən] Sachbücher *n/pl*.
non-ha·la·tion *phot*. [ˈnɔnhəˈleiʃən] lichthoffrei.
non-in·ter·fer·ence [ˈnɔnintəˈfiərəns], **non-in·ter·ven·tion** [ˈnɔnintəˈvenʃen] Nichteinmischung *f*.
non-i·ron [ˈnɔnˈaiən] bügelfrei.
non-lad·der·ing [ˈnɔnˈlædəriŋ] maschenfest.
non-mem·ber [ˈnɔnˈmembə]Nichtmitglied *n*.
non-ob·serv·ance [ˈnɔnəbˈzəːvəns] Nichtbeobachtung *f*.
non·pa·reil [nɔnpəˈrel] Unvergleichliche *m, f, n*; *typ*. Nonpareille (-schrift) *f*.
non-par·ti·san [nɔnˈpɑːtizæn] überparteilich.
non-par·ty *pol*. [ˈnɔnˈpɑːti] parteilos.
non-pay·ment [ˈnɔnˈpeimənt] Nichtzahlung *f*.
non-per·form·ance ⚖ [ˈnɔnpəˈfɔːməns] Nichterfüllung *f*.
non·plus [ˈnɔnˈplʌs] **1.** Verlegenheit *f*; *at a* ~ ratlos; **2.** in Verlegenheit bringen; ~*sed* ratlos, verdutzt.
non-pro·lif·er·a·tion [ˈnɔnprəuliˈfəˈreiʃən] Nichtweiterverbreitung *f* (*von Atomwaffen*); ~ *treaty* Atomsperrvertrag *m*.
non-res·i·dent [ˈnɔnˈrezidənt] nicht am Platze wohnend.
non·sense [ˈnɔnsəns] Unsinn *m*; **non·sen·si·cal** □ [~ˈsensikəl] unsinnig, albern.
non-skid [ˈnɔnˈskid] rutschfest, -sicher (*Reifen etc*.).
non-smok·er [ˈnɔnˈsməukə] Nichtraucher *m*.
non·start·er *fig*. [ˈnɔnˈstɑːtə] *Mensch*: Blindgänger *m*; *Idee*, *Plan*: totgeborenes Kind *n*, Rohrkrepierer *m*.
non-stick [ˈnɔnˈstik] mit Antihaftbeschichtung (*Pfanne*).
non-stop [ˈnɔnˈstɔp] 🚂 durchgehend; ✈ ohne Zwischenlandung; Ohnehalt...; Nonstop...
non·such [ˈnʌnsʌtʃ] Unvergleich-

liche *m, f, n.*
non·suit ⚖ ['nɔn'sjuːt] Abweisung *f einer Klage.*
non-U F ['nɔnjuː] unkultiviert.
non-un·ion [nɔn'juːnjən] nicht organisiert (*Arbeiter*).
noo·dle[1] F ['nuːdl] Dummkopf *m.*
noo·dle[2] [~] Nudel *f.*
nook [nuk] Ecke *f*, Winkel *m.*
noon [nuːn] **1.** Mittag *m*; **2.** mittägig; Mittags...; '**~·day**, '**~·tide** = *noon.*
noose [nuːs] **1.** Schlinge *f*; **2.** (mit der Schlinge) fangen; schlingen.
nope *Am.* F [nəup] nein!
nor [nɔː] *nach neither*: noch; *am Satzanfang*: auch nicht; *~ do I* ich auch nicht.
Nor·folk jack·et ['nɔːfək'dʒækit] Herrenjackett *n* mit Gürtel.
norm [nɔːm] Norm *f*; Regel *f*; Muster *n*; Maßstab *m*; '**nor·mal** □ **1.** normal, regelrecht, üblich; ⟂ senkrecht; *~ school* Pädagogische Hochschule *f*; **2.** Normalstand *m*; ⟂ Senkrechte *f*; '**nor·mal·ize** normalisieren; normen.
Nor·man ['nɔːmən] **1.** Normanne *m*; **2.** normannisch.
Norse [nɔːs] **1.** norwegisch; **2.** Norwegisch *n*; '**Norse·man** Nordländer *m*; Norweger *m.*
north [nɔːθ] 1. Nord(en) *m*; 2. nördlich; Nord...; '**~·bound** in Richtung Norden fahrend; '**~-'east** 1. Nordost *m*; 2. *a.* **~-'east·ern** nordöstlich; **north·er·ly** ['~ðəli] nördlich; **northern** ['~ðən] nördlich; Nord...; '**north·ern·er** Nordländer(in); ♀ *Am.* Nordstaatler *m*; '**north·ern-most** nördlichst; **north·ing** ⚓ ['~θiŋ] Weg *m*, *ast.* Distanz *f* nach Nord; '**North·man** Nordländer *m*, Skandinavier *m*; Wikinger *m*; **northward**(**·ly**) ['~wəd(li)] *adj. u. adv.*, **north·wards** ['~wədz] *adv.* nördlich; nordwärts.
north...: '**~-'west 1.** Nordwest *m*; **2.** *a.* '**~-'west·ern**, '**~-'west·er·ly** nordwestlich.
Nor·we·gian [nɔː'wiːdʒən] **1.** norwegisch; **2.** Norweger(in).
nose [nəuz] **1.** Nase *f*; Spitze *f*; Mündung *f e-s Rohres*; Schnauze *f*, Tülle *f*; *cut off one's ~ to spite one's face* sich ins eigene Fleisch schneiden; *pay through the ~* sich übervorteilen lassen, zuviel bezahlen; *poke od. push od. thrust one's ~ into s.th.* s-e Nase in et. (hinein)stecken; *turn one's ~ up at* die Nase rümpfen über; *put s.o.'s ~ out of joint* j-m e-n Strich durch die Rechnung machen; j-m die Freundin *etc.* ausspannen; **2.** *v/t. a. ~ out* riechen, wittern; *~ one's way* vorsichtig fahren; *v/i.* schnüffeln (*after, for* nach); '**~-bag** Futterbeutel *m*; '**~-band** Nasenriemen *m*; '**~-cone** Raketenspitze *f*; **nosed** ...nasig.
nose...: '**~-dive** ✈ Sturzflug *m*; '**~-gay** Blumenstrauß *m*; '**~-heav·y** ✈ kopflastig; '**~-o·ver** ✈ Überschlagen *n beim Landen*; '**~-ring** Nasenring *m.*
nos·ing ⚠ ['nəuziŋ] Ausladung *f*, Kante *f.*
nos·tal·gi·a [nɔs'tældʒiə] Heimweh *n*; Nostalgie *f*, Sehnsucht *f* (*nach et. Vergangenem*); **nos'tal·gic** [~dʒik] Heimweh...; heimwehkrank; nostalgisch, wehmütig.
nos·tril ['nɔstril] Nasenloch *n*, Nüster *f.*
nos·trum ['nɔstrəm] Geheimmittel *n*; Patentlösung *f.*
nos·y ['nəuzi] **1.** duftend; *b. s.* muffig; F neugierig; ♀ *Parker* = **2.** neugieriger Kerl *m.*
not [nɔt] nicht.
no·ta·bil·i·ty [nəutə'biliti] wichtige Persönlichkeit *f*; hervorragende Eigenschaft *f*; '**no·ta·ble 1.** □ bemerkenswert; namhaft; bedeutend; angesehen; hausfraulich tüchtig, fleißig; **2.** angesehene Person *f*, Standesperson *f*; '**no·ta·bly** ganz besonders.
no·tar·i·al □ [nəu'tɛəriəl] Notariats...; notariell (beglaubigt); **no·ta·ry** ['nəutəri] *oft public ~* Notar *m.*
no·ta·tion [nəu'teiʃən] Bezeichnung *f* (*bsd.* ⟂ *u.* ♪); Zeichensystem *n.*
notch [nɔtʃ] **1.** Kerbe *f*, Einschnitt *m*; ⊕ Nut(e) *f*; *Am.* Engpaß *m*, Hohlweg *m*; **2.** einkerben; nuten.
note [nəut] **1.** Zeichen *n*, Merkmal *n*; Brandmal *n*; (Satz)Zeichen *n*; Notiz *f*, Aufzeichnung *f*; Anmerkung *f*; Briefchen *n*; (*bsd.* Schuld-) Schein *m*, Zettel *m*; ♪, *pol.*, ✝ Note *f*; ♪ Taste *f*; Ton *m*; Klang *m*; Bedeutung *f*, Ruf *m*; Beachtung *f*; *take ~s of* sich Notizen machen über (*acc.*); *strike the right ~* den rechten Ton treffen; *strike od. sound a false ~* sich im Ton ver-

greifen; **2.** be(ob)achten; besonders erwähnen; merken, zur Kenntnis nehmen; *a.* ~ *down* notieren, aufschreiben; mit Anmerkungen versehen; *Wechsel* protestieren; '~**book** Notizbuch *n*; Heft *n*; '**not·ed** bekannt, berühmt; berüchtigt (*for* wegen); ~*ly* deutlich; besonders; '**note-pa·per** Briefpapier *n*; '**note-wor·thy** bemerkens-, beachtenswert.

noth·ing ['nʌθiŋ] **1.** nichts; Nichts *n*; Null *f*; *for* ~ umsonst; *good for* ~ untauglich; *bring* (*come*) *to* ~ zunichte machen (werden); *go for* ~ umsonst sein (*Mühe etc.*); *make* ~ *of* sich nichts machen aus; *I can make* ~ *of it* ich kann damit nichts anfangen; *think* ~ *of et.* als normal betrachten; **2.** *adv.* durchaus nicht; '**noth·ing·ness** Nichts *n*; Nichtigkeit *f*.

no·tice ['nəutis] **1.** Notiz *f*, Nachricht *f*, Anzeige *f*; Bekanntmachung *f*; Kenntnis *f*; Kündigung *f*; Warnung *f*; Aufmerksamkeit *f*, Beachtung *f*, Notiz *f*; (Buch-) Besprechung *f*; *at short* ~ kurzfristig; *give* ~ *that* bekanntgeben, daß, *give a week's* ~ j-m acht Tage vorher kündigen; *take* ~ *of* Notiz nehmen von, Beachtung schenken (*dat.*); *until further* ~ bis auf weiteres; *without* ~ fristlos; ~ *of departure* Abmeldung *f*; 2. bemerken, beobachten; feststellen; beachten; erwähnen; F mit Aufmerksamkeit behandeln; *Buch* besprechen; '**no·tice·a·ble** □ wahrnehmbar; bemerkenswert; beachtlich; '**no·tice-board** Anschlagbrett *n*; Schwarzes Brett *n*.

no·ti·fi·a·ble ['nəutifaiəbl] meldepflichtig; **no·ti·fi·ca·tion** [~fi'keiʃən] Anzeige *f*; Meldung *f*; Bekanntmachung *f*; Ankündigung *f*.

no·ti·fy ['nəutifai] *et.* anzeigen, melden; bekanntmachen; *j.* benachrichtigen.

no·tion ['nəuʃən] Begriff *m*, Vorstellung *f*, Idee *f*; Meinung *f*, Ansicht *f*; Absicht *f*; ~*s pl. Am.* Kurzwaren *f/pl.*; *kleine* Gebrauchsartikel *m/pl.*; *have no* ~ *of* keine Ahnung haben von; '**no·tion·al** □ begrifflich; nur in der Vorstellung vorhanden; grillenhaft; ausgefallen.

no·to·ri·e·ty [nəutə'raiəti] Allbekanntheit *f*; allbekannte Sache *f* *od.* Person *f*; **no·to·ri·ous** □ [~'tɔ:riəs] all-, stadt-, weltbekannt; notorisch; *b. s.* berüchtigt (*for* wegen).

not·with·stand·ing [nɔtwiθ'stændiŋ] **1.** *prp.* ungeachtet, trotz (*gen.*); **2.** *adv.* trotzdem, dennoch; **3.** *cj.* ~ *that* obgleich.

nou·gat ['nu:gɑ:] Nougat *m*.

nought *bsd.* ⅌ [nɔ:t] Null *f*, Nichts *n*; *come to* ~ zunichte werden, fehlschlagen.

noun *gr.* [naun] Substantiv *n*, Hauptwort *n*.

nour·ish ['nʌriʃ] (er)nähren; *fig.* nähren, hegen; '**nour·ish·ing** nahrhaft; '**nour·ish·ment** Ernährung *f*, Nahrung(smittel *n*) *f*.

nous [naus] Vernunft *f*; gesunder Menschenverstand *m*.

nov·el ['nɔvəl] **1.** neu; ungewöhnlich; **2.** Roman *m*; *short* ~ = **nov·el·ette** [nɔvə'let] kurzer Roman *m*; '**nov·el·ist** Romanschriftsteller(in), Romancier *m*; **nov·el·ty** ['nɔvəlti] Neuheit *f*.

No·vem·ber [nəu'vembə] November *m*.

nov·ice ['nɔvis] Neuling *m*, Anfänger *m*; *eccl.* Novize *m*, *f*.

no·vi·ci·ate, no·vi·ti·ate [nəu'viʃiit] Lehr(lings)zeit *f*; Noviziat *n*.

now [nau] **1.** nun, jetzt; eben; nun (aber); *by* ~ mittlerweile, jetzt; *just* ~ soeben; *before* ~ schon früher; ~ *and again*, ~ *and then* dann u. wann, hin u. wieder, manchmal; **2.** *cj. a.* ~ *that* nun da; **3.** Jetzt *n*.

now·a·day ['nauədei] heutig; **now·a·days** ['~z] heutzutage.

no·way(s) F ['nəuwei(z)] keineswegs.

no·where ['nəuwɛə] nirgends.

no·wise ['nəuwaiz] keineswegs; in keiner Weise.

nox·ious □ ['nɔkʃəs] schädlich.

noz·zle ['nɔzl] ⊕ Düse *f*; Tülle *f*.

nu·ance [nju:'ɑ̃:ns] Nuance *f*, Schattierung *f*.

nub [nʌb] Knubbe(n *m*) *f*; *Am.* F springende Punkt *m in e-r Sache*.

nu·bile ['nju:bail] heiratsfähig.

nu·cle·ar ['nju:kliə] Kern..., Nuklear..., Atom...; ~ *deterrent* nukleares Abschreckungsmittel *n*; ~ *disintegration* Kernzerfall *m*; ~ *energy*, ~ *power* Kernkraft *f*, -energie *f*; ~ *physics sg.* Kernphysik *f*; ~ *pile* Atomsäule *f*; ~ *power plant* Kernkraftwerk *n*; ~ *research* (Atom)Kernforschung *f*; ~

submarine Atom-U-Boot *n*; ~ *warfare* Atomkrieg *m*; ~ *warhead* Atomsprengkopf *m*; **nu·cle·on** *phys.* ['~kliɔn] Nukleon *n*; **nu·cle·us** ['~kliəs], *pl. a.* **nu·cle·i** ['~kliai] Kern *m*.
nude [nju:d] **1.** nackt; **2.** nackter Körper *m*; *paint.* Akt *m*; *study from the* ~ Aktstudie *f*.
nudge F [nʌdʒ] **1.** *j.* heimlich anstoßen; **2.** Rippenstoß *m*.
nud·ism ['nju:dizəm] Freikörper-, Nacktkultur *f*; '**nud·ist** Anhänger (-in) der Freikörperkultur; ~ *camp*, ~ *colony* FKK-Platz *m*; '**nu·di·ty** Nacktheit *f*; nackte Figur *f*.
nu·ga·to·ry ['nju:gətəri] albern, kindisch; unwirksam.
nug·get ['nʌgit] (*bsd.* Gold)Klumpen *m*.
nui·sance ['nju:sns] Mißstand *m*; Ärgernis *n*; Unfug *m*; *fig.* Last *f*, Plage *f* (*a. Person*); Quälgeist *m*; *what a* ~! wie ärgerlich!; *commit no* ~! dieser Ort darf nicht verunreinigt werden!; *make o.s. od. be a* ~ lästig fallen.
nuke *Am. sl.* [nu:k] Atom-, Kernwaffe *f*; Atom-, Kernkraftwerk *n*.
null [nʌl] ⚖ *u. fig.* nichtig; nichtssagend (*Gesicht*); ~ *and void* null u. nichtig; **nul·li·fi·ca·tion** [nʌlifi'keiʃən] Ungültigkeitserklärung *f*; **nul·li·fy** ['~fai] zunichte machen; aufheben, ungültig machen; '**nul·li·ty** Nichtigkeit *f*, Ungültigkeit *f*; Nichts *n*; *fig.* Null *f*.
numb [nʌm] **1.** starr (*with* vor *Kälte etc.*); taub (*empfindungslos*); **2.** starr *od.* taub machen; ~*ed* erstarrt.
num·ber ['nʌmbə] **1.** Nummer *f*; Zahl *f* (*a. gr.*); Anzahl *f*; Heft *n*, Lieferung *f*, Nummer *f e-s Werkes*; ~*s pl. poet.* Verse *m/pl.*; ♪ Weise(n *pl.*) *f*; *without* ~ zahllos; *in* ~ an der Zahl; **2.** zählen; numerieren; ~ *among*, ~ *in*, ~ *with* rechnen zu *od.* unter (*acc.*); '**num·ber·less** zahllos; **num·ber one** F die eigene Person *f*, das liebe Ich; *look after* ~ den eigenen Vorteil wahren; '**num·ber-plate** *mot.* Nummernschild *n*.
numb·ness ['nʌmnis] Erstarrung *f*, Betäubung *f*; Starr-, Taubheit *f*.
nu·mer·a·ble ['nju:mərəbl] zählbar; '**nu·mer·al 1.** Zahl...; **2.** Zahlzeichen *n*, Ziffer *f*; Zahlwort *n*;
nu·mer'a·tion Zählen *n*; Zählung *f*; Numerierung *f*; '**nu·mer·a·tor** ⅍ Zähler *m e-s Bruches*.
nu·mer·i·cal □ [nju:'merikəl] numerisch, zahlenmäßig; Zahl...
nu·mer·ous □ ['nju:mərəs] zahlreich; '**nu·mer·ous·ness** große Zahl *f*.
nu·mis·mat·ic [nju:miz'mætik] (~*ally*) numismatisch; Münz...; **nu·mis'mat·ics** *mst sg.* Numismatik *f*, Münzkunde *f*; **nu'mis·ma·tist** [~mətist] Numismatiker *m*.
num·skull F ['nʌmskʌl] Dummkopf *m*.
nun [nʌn] Nonne *f*; *orn.* Blaumeise *f*.
nun·ci·a·ture *eccl.* ['nʌnʃjətʃə] Nuntiatur *f*; **nun·ci·o** *eccl.* ['~ʃiəu] Nuntius *m*.
nun·ner·y ['nʌnəri] Nonnenkloster *n*.
nup·tial ['nʌpʃəl] **1.** Hochzeits..., Ehe..., Braut...; **2.** ~*s pl.* Hochzeit *f*.
nurse [nə:s] **1.** Kindermädchen *n*, Säuglingsschwester *f*; *a. wet* ~ Amme *f*; (Kranken)Pflegerin *f*, (Kranken)Schwester *f*; *at* ~ in Pflege; *put out to* ~ in Pflege geben; **2.** stillen, nähren, säugen; auf-, großziehen; pflegen, warten; hätscheln, liebkosen; ~ *a cold* e-e Erkältung auskurieren; '~**-maid** Kindermädchen *n*.
nurs·er·y ['nə:sri] Kinderzimmer *n*; ⚘ Baumschule *f*; *fig.* Pflegestätte *f*; ~ *school* Kindergarten *m*; '~**man** Kunstgärtner *m*; '~**-rhymes** *pl.* Kinderlieder *n/pl.*, -reime *m/pl.*; ~ **slopes** *pl. Ski*: Idiotenhügel *m/pl.*
nurs·ing ['nə:siŋ] Stillen *n*; (Kranken)Pflege *f*; '~**-bot·tle** Saugflasche *f*; '~**-home** Privatklinik *f*.
nurs·ling ['nə:sliŋ] Säugling *m*, Pflegling *m*; Liebling *m*; Hätschelkind *n*.
nur·ture ['nə:tʃə] **1.** Pflege *f*; Erziehung *f*; **2.** *a.* ~ *up* aufziehen; *fig.* nähren.
nut [nʌt] **1.** Nuß *f*; ⊕ (Schrauben-) Mutter *f*; *sl.* Birne *f* (*Kopf*); Verrückte *m*; ~*s pl.* Nußkohle *f*; *that is* ~*s to od. for him sl.* das ist was für ihn; *be* ~*s on sl.* verrückt sein nach; *drive* ~*s sl.* verrückt machen; *go* ~*s sl.* verrückt werden; **2.** *go* ~*ting* in die Nüsse gehen.
nu·ta·tion *ast.* [nju:'teiʃən] Schwanken *n der Erdachse*.
nut·crack·er ['nʌtkrækə], *mst* (*a*

pair of) ~*s pl.* (ein) Nußknacker *m*; '**nut-gall** Gallapfel *m*; **nut·meg** ['~meg] Muskatnuß *f*.
nu·tri·a ['nju:triə] Nutria(fell *n*) *f*.
nu·tri·ent ['nju:triənt] **1.** Ernährungs...; **2.** Nährstoff *m*; '**nu·tri·ment** Nahrung *f*, Futter *n*.
nu·tri·tion [nju:'triʃən] Ernährung *f*; Nahrung *f*; **nu·tri·tion·al** [~'triʃənl] Ernährungs...; ~ *science* Ernährungswissenschaft *f*; **nu'tri·tious** □ nährend, nahrhaft; Ernährungs...; **nu'tri·tious·ness** Nahrhaftigkeit *f*.
nu·tri·tive □ ['nju:tritiv] = *nutritious*.
nut·shell ['nʌtʃel] Nußschale *f*; *in a* ~ in aller Kürze; '**nut·ting** *s. nut* 2; **nut·ty** ['nʌti] nußreich; nußartig; *sl.* verrückt (*on* nach).
nuz·zle ['nʌzl] mit der Schnauze wühlen *od.* stoßen; *a.* ~ *o.s.* sich (an)schmiegen.
ny·lon ['nailən] Nylon *n* (*Kunstfaser*); ~*s pl.* Nylonstrümpfe *m/pl.*
nymph [nimf] Nymphe *f*.

O

o [əu] **1.** oh!; ach!; **2.** (*in Telephonnummern*) Null *f*.
oaf [əuf] Dummkopf *m*; Tölpel *m*; '**oaf·ish** dumm.
oak [əuk] **1.** *su.* Eiche *f*; Eichentür *f*; *s. sport*; **2.** *adj.* eichen; '**~-ap·ple**, '**~-gall** Gallapfel *m*; '**oak·en** *adj.* eichen.
oa·kum ['əukəm] Werg *n*.
oar [ɔ:] **1.** Ruder *n*, Riemen *m*; F Ruderer *m*; *pull a good* ~ ein guter Ruderer sein; *put in one's* ~ F sich einmischen; *rest on one's* ~*s* ausspannen, sich ausruhen; **2.** rudern; **oared** [ɔ:d] mit Rudern; ...rud(e)rig; **oars·man** ['ɔ:zmən] Ruderer *m*; '**oars·man·ship** Gewandtheit *f* im Rudern; '**oars·wom·an** Ruderin *f*.
o·a·sis [əu'eisis], *pl.* **o'a·ses** [~si:z] Oase *f* (*a. fig.*).
oast [əust] Hopfendarre *f*.
oat [əut] *mst* ~*s pl.* Hafer *m*; *feel one's* ~*s Am.* F groß in Form sein; sich wichtig vorkommen; *sow one's wild* ~*s* sich austoben; '**oat·en** Hafer...
oath [əuθ], *pl.* **oaths** [əuðz] Eid *m*; Schwur *m*; *b. s.* Fluch *m*; *administer od. tender an* ~ *to s.o.*, *put s.o. to od. on his* ~ j. schwören lassen; *bind by* ~ eidlich verpflichten; *on* ~ eidlich, unter Eid; *take od. make od. swear an* ~ e-n Eid leisten *od.* ablegen, schwören (*on, to* auf *acc.*).
oat·meal ['əutmi:l] Haferflocken *f/pl.*; -mehl *n*.
ob·du·ra·cy ['ɔbdjurəsi] Verstocktheit *f*; **ob·du·rate** □ ['~rit] verstockt.
o·be·di·ence [ə'bi:djəns] Gehorsam *m*; *in* ~ *to* gemäß (*dat.*), gehorchend (*dat.*); **o'be·di·ent** □ gehorsam.
o·bei·sance [əu'beisəns] Ehrerbietung *f*; Verbeugung *f*; *do od. make od. pay* ~ huldigen.
ob·e·lisk ['ɔbilisk] Obelisk *m*; *typ.* Kreuz(zeichen) *n*.
o·bese □ [əu'bi:s] fettleibig; **o'bese·ness, o'bes·i·ty** Fettleibigkeit *f*.
o·bey [ə'bei] gehorchen (*dat.*); *Befehl etc.* befolgen, Folge leisten (*dat.*).
ob·fus·cate *fig.* ['ɔbfʌskeit] verwirren; verdunkeln.
o·bit·u·ar·y [ə'bitjuəri] **1.** Totenliste *f*; Todesanzeige *f*; Nachruf *m*; **2.** Todes...; ~ *notice* Todesanzeige *f*.
ob·ject 1. ['ɔbdʒikt] Gegenstand *m*; Ziel *n*, *fig.* Zweck *m*; *gr.* Objekt *n*; komische *od.* erbärmliche Sache *f od.* Person *f*; *what an* ~ *you look!* wie komisch du aussiehst!; *salary no* ~ Gehalt Nebensache; **2.** [əb'dʒekt] *v/t.* einwenden (*to* gegen); *v/i.* et. dagegen haben (*to ger.* daß); Einspruch erheben, protestieren (*to* gegen); **~-glass** *opt.* ['ɔbdʒiktglɑ:s] Objektiv *n*.
ob·jec·tion [əb'dʒekʃən] Einwand *m*; *there is no* ~ (*to it*) es ist nichts (dagegen) einzuwenden; **ob'jec-**

tion·a·ble □ [⁓ʃnəbl] nicht einwandfrei; unangenehm.

ob·jec·tive [ɔbˈdʒektiv] **1.** □ objektiv, sachlich; **2.** (⚔ Operations-) Ziel *n*; *opt.* Objektiv *n*; *a.* ⁓ *case gr.* Objektsfall *m*; **obˈjec·tive·ness, ob·jecˈtiv·i·ty** Objektivität *f*, Sachlichkeit *f*.

ob·ject...: ˈ⁓-lens *opt.* Objektiv *n*; **ˈ⁓-less** □ gegenstandslos, zwecklos; **ˈ⁓-les·son** Anschauungsunterricht *m*; *fig.* praktisches Beispiel *n*; **ˈ⁓-teach·ing** Anschauungsunterricht *m*; **ob·jec·tor** [əbˈdʒektə] Gegner *m*; *s. conscientious.*

ob·jur·gate [ˈɔbdʒə:geit] schelten; **ob·jurˈga·tion** Tadel *m*; **obˈjur·ga·to·ry** [⁓gətəri] scheltend.

ob·late □ [ˈɔbleit] (an den Polen) abgeplattet; **ˈob·late·ness** Abplattung *f*.

ob·la·tion [əuˈbleiʃen] Opfer(gabe *f*) *n*.

ob·li·gate *fig.* [ˈɔbligeit] binden, verpflichten; **ob·liˈga·tion** Verpflichtung *f*, Verbindlichkeit *f*; Schuldverschreibung *f*, Obligation *f*; *be under (an)* ⁓ *to s.o.* j-m zu Dank verpflichtet sein; *be under* ⁓ *to inf.* die Verpflichtung haben, zu *inf.*; **ob·lig·a·to·ry** □ [ˈ⁓gətəri] verpflichtend; verbindlich (*on* für).

o·blige [əˈblaidʒ] *v/t.* (zu Dank) verpflichten; nötigen, zwingen; ⁓ *s.o.* j-m e-n Gefallen tun; ⁓ *the company with* die Gesellschaft mit *e-m Lied etc.* erfreuen; *be* ⁓*d* müssen; *much* ⁓*d* sehr verbunden; danke bestens; *v/i.* ⁓ *with a song etc.* F ein Lied *etc.* zum besten geben; *please* ⁓ *with an early reply* um baldige Antwort wird gebeten; **ob·li·gee** [ɔbliˈdʒi:] Gläubiger *m*; **o·blig·ing** □ [əˈblaidʒiŋ] verbindlich, hilfsbereit, gefällig; **oˈblig·ing·ness** Zuvorkommenheit *f*; **ob·li·gor** [ɔbliˈgɔ:] Schuldner *m*.

ob·lique □ [əˈbli:k] schief, schräg; mittelbar, versteckt; unaufrichtig; *gr.* abhängig (*Rede*); ⁓ *case* abhängiger Fall *m*; **obˈlique·ness, ob·liq·ui·ty** [əˈblikwiti] Schiefheit *f*; schiefe Richtung *f*; Verirrung *f*.

ob·lit·er·ate [əˈblitəreit] auslöschen, tilgen (*a. fig.*); *Schrift* ausstreichen; *Briefmarken* entwerten; **ob·lit·erˈa·tion** Auslöschen *n*; Tilgung *f*, Vernichtung *f*.

ob·liv·i·on [əˈbliviən] Vergessen *n*; Vergessenheit *f*; *pol.* Amnestie *f*; *fall od. sink into* ⁓ in Vergessenheit geraten; **obˈliv·i·ous** □ *be* ⁓ *of et.* vergessen; *be* ⁓ *to et.* nicht beachten.

ob·long [ˈɔblɔŋ] **1.** länglich; rechteckig; **2.** Rechteck *n*.

ob·lo·quy [ˈɔbləkwi] Schmähung *f*; Vorwurf *m*; Schande *f*.

ob·nox·ious □ [əbˈnɔkʃəs] anstößig; widerwärtig, verhaßt; **obˈnox·ious·ness** Anstößigkeit *f*; Verhaßtheit *f*.

o·boe ♪ [ˈəubəu] Oboe *f*.

ob·scene □ [ɔbˈsi:n] obszön, unanständig, unzüchtig; zotig; **obˈscen·i·ty** [⁓niti] Obszönität *f*, Unanständigkeit *f*; Zote *f*.

ob·scu·ra·tion [ɔbskjuəˈreiʃən] Verdunkelung *f*; **ob·scure** [əbˈskjuə] **1.** □ dunkel (*a. fig.*); unbekannt, unbedeutend; verborgen; **2.** verdunkeln; verdecken; verbergen; **obˈscu·ri·ty** Dunkelheit *f* (*a. fig.*); Unbekanntheit *f*; Niedrigkeit *f der Geburt*.

ob·se·quies [ˈɔbsikwiz] *pl.* Leichenbegängnis *n*, Trauerfeier *f*.

ob·se·qui·ous □ [əbˈsi:kwiəs] unterwürfig (*to* gegen); knechtisch; **obˈse·qui·ous·ness** Unterwürfigkeit *f*.

ob·serv·a·ble □ [əbˈzə:vəbl] bemerkbar; bemerkenswert; **obˈserv·ance** Befolgung *f*, Einhaltung *f von Gesetzen etc.*; Brauch *m*, Sitte *f*; *eccl.* Observanz *f*; **obˈserv·ant** □ beobachtend (*of acc.*); achtsam, aufmerksam (*of* auf *acc.*); *be* ⁓ *of the rules* die Regeln beachten; **ob·ser·va·tion** [ɔbzə:ˈveiʃən] Beobachtung *f*; Bemerkung *f*; *attr.* Beobachtungs...; Aussichts...; ⁓ *car* 🚂 Aussichtswagen *m*; ⁓ *platform* Aussichtsterrasse *f*; ⁓ *ward* ⚕ Beobachtungsstation *f*; **ob·serv·a·to·ry** [əbˈzə:vətri] Observatorium *n*, Sternwarte *f*; Wetterwarte *f*; **obˈserve** *v/t.* beobachten; *fig.* beachten; *Regel etc.* ein-, innehalten; acht(geb)en auf (*acc.*); bemerken (*wahrnehmen*; *sagen*); *v/i.* sich äußern (*on* über *acc.*); **obˈserv·er** Beobachter(in).

ob·sess [əbˈses] heimsuchen, quälen; ⁓*ed by od. with* besessen von; **ob·ses·sion** [əbˈseʃən] Besessenheit *f*, fixe Idee *f*.

ob·sid·i·an *min.* [ɔbˈsidiən] Obsidian *m*.

ob·so·les·cence [ɔbsəuˈlesns] Ver-

alten *n*; **ob·so'les·cent** veraltend.
ob·so·lete ['ɔbsəli:t] veraltet; altmodisch; *biol.* zurückgeblieben.
ob·sta·cle ['ɔbstəkl] Hindernis *n*; ~ **race** Hindernisrennen *n*.
ob·stet·ric [ɔb'stetrik], **ob'stet·ri·cal** ⚕ Entbindungs..., geburtshilflich; **ob·ste·tri·cian** [~'triʃən] Geburtshelfer *m*; **ob'stet·rics** [~triks] *mst sg.* Geburtshilfe *f*.
ob·sti·na·cy ['ɔbstinəsi] Hartnäckigkeit *f*; Starr-, Eigensinn *m*; **ob·sti·nate** □ ['~nit] halsstarrig; eigensinnig; hartnäckig (*fig. Krankheit*).
ob·strep·er·ous □ [əb'strepərəs] lärmend; ungebärdig.
ob·struct [əb'strʌkt] *v/t.* verstopfen, versperren; hindern; *v/i.* Obstruktion treiben; **ob'struc·tion** Verstopfung *f*; Hemmung *f*; *parl.* Obstruktion *f*; Hindernis *n*; **ob'struc·tive** □ [~tiv] hinderlich (*of* für).
ob·tain [əb'tein] *v/t.* erlangen, erhalten, erreichen, bekommen; *Preis* erzielen; *v/i.* sich erhalten (haben), bestehen; **ob'tain·a·ble** erlangbar; ✝ erhältlich; **ob'tain·ment** Erlangung *f*.
ob·trude [əb'tru:d] (sich) aufdrängen (*on dat.*); **ob'tru·sion** [~ʒən] Aufdrängen *n*; Aufdringlichkeit *f*; **ob'tru·sive** □ [~siv] aufdringlich.
ob·tu·rate ['ɔbtjuəreit] verstopfen; abdichten; '**ob·tu·ra·tor** Abdichtung(smittel *n*) *f*.
ob·tuse □ [əb'tju:s] stumpf (*a.* ⅍ *Winkel*); *fig.* stumpf(sinnig); schwerfällig; **ob'tuse·ness** Stumpfheit *f* (*a. fig.*).
ob·verse ['ɔbvə:s] Vorderseite *f*; Bildseite *f e-r Münze*; *fig.* Gegenstück *n*.
ob·vi·ate *fig.* ['ɔbvieit] begegnen, vorbeugen (*dat.*); aus dem Weg räumen.
ob·vi·ous □ ['ɔbviəs] offensichtlich, augenfällig, einleuchtend, klar; '**ob·vi·ous·ness** Offensichtlichkeit *f*.
oc·ca·sion [ə'keiʒən] **1.** Gelegenheit *f*; Anlaß *m*; Grund *m*; Veranlassung *f*; F (festliches) Ereignis *n*; *on* ~ gelegentlich; *on the* ~ *of* anläßlich (*gen.*); *rise to the* ~ sich der Lage gewachsen zeigen; **2.** verursachen, veranlassen; **oc'ca·sion·al** □ [~ʒənl] gelegentlich; Gelegenheits...; zufällig; **oc'ca·sion·al·ly** [~ʒnəli] gelegentlich, ab u. zu, dann u. wann, manchmal.
oc·ci·dent *poet. u. rhet.* ['ɔksidənt] Westen *m*; Abendland *n*; Okzident *m*; **oc·ci·den·tal** □ [~'dentl] abendländisch, westlich.
oc·cult □ [ɔ'kʌlt] geheim, verborgen; magisch, okkult; **oc·cul'ta·tion** *ast.* Verfinsterung *f*; **oc·cult·ism** ['ɔkəltizəm] Geheimwissenschaft *f*, Okkultismus *m*; '**oc·cult·ist** Okkultist(in); **oc·cult·ness** [ɔ'kʌltnis] Verborgenheit *f*.
oc·cu·pan·cy ['ɔkjupənsi] Besitz (-ergreifung *f*) *m*; Einzug *m* (*of* in *e-e Wohnung*); '**oc·cu·pant** Besitzergreifer(in); Inhaber(in); Bewohner(in); **oc·cu'pa·tion** Besitz(ergreifung *f*) *m*; ⚔ Besetzung *f*; Beruf *m*; Beschäftigung *f*; Zeitvertreib *m*; **oc·cu'pa·tion·al** [~ʃənl] Berufs...; ~ *disease* Berufskrankheit *f*; ~ *hazard* Berufsrisiko *n*; ~ *therapy* Beschäftigungstherapie *f*; **oc·cu·pi·er** ['ɔkjupaiə] *s. occupant*; **oc·cu·py** ['~pai] einnehmen, in Besitz nehmen; ⚔ besetzen; besitzen; *Amt* bekleiden, innehaben; *Raum* einnehmen; *Wohnung* beziehen; bewohnen; *Zeit* in Anspruch nehmen; beschäftigen; ~ *o.s. od. be occupied with od. in* sich beschäftigen mit, arbeiten an (*dat.*).
oc·cur [ə'kə:] vorkommen; sich finden; sich ereignen, geschehen; *it* ~*red to me* es fiel mir ein; **oc·cur·rence** [ə'kʌrəns] Vorkommen *n*; Vorfall *m*, Ereignis *n*, Geschehnis *n*.
o·cean ['əuʃən] Ozean *m*, Meer *n*; ~ *liner* Ozeandampfer *m*; ~ *yacht* Hochseejacht *f*; ~*s of time* F massenhaft Zeit; '~**-go·ing** Übersee...; seetüchtig; **o·ce·an·ic** [əuʃi'ænik] Meeres..., See...
o·chre *min.* ['əukə] Ocker *m*.
o'clock [ə'klɔk] Uhr (*bei Zeitangaben*); *five* ~ fünf Uhr.
oc·ta·gon ['ɔktəgən] Achteck *n*; **oc·tag·o·nal** [ɔk'tægənl] achteckig.
oc·tane ⚗ ['ɔktein] Oktan *n*; ~ *rating mot.* Oktanzahl *f*.
oc·tave ♪ ['ɔktiv] Oktave *f*; **oc·ta·vo** [ɔk'teivəu] Oktav(format *n*, -band *m*) *n*; **oc·tet(te)** [ɔk'tet] ♪ Oktett *n*; *die beiden Quartette e-s Sonetts.*
Oc·to·ber [ɔk'təubə] Oktober *m*.
oc·to·ge·nar·i·an [ɔktəudʒi'nɛəriən] **1.** achtzigjährig; **2.** Achtzigjährige *m*, *f*.

oc·to·pus *zo.* ['ɔktəpəs] Polyp *m* (*a. fig.*).
oc·to·roon [ɔktə'ru:n] Achtelneger (-in).
oc·u·lar □ ['ɔkjulə] Augen...; ~ *demonstration*, ~ *proof* sichtbarer Beweis *m*; '**oc·u·list** Augenarzt *m*.
odd □ [ɔd] ungerade (*Zahl*); einzeln (*Handschuh etc.*), vereinzelt; und einige *od.* etwas darüber; überzählig; gelegentlich, Gelegenheits...; seltsam, sonderbar, merkwürdig, komisch; *40* ~ einige 40; *12 pounds* ~ über 12 Pfund; ~ *jobs pl.* Gelegenheitsarbeiten *f/pl.*; *at* ~ *times* dann und wann; ~ *man out* Übriggebliebene *m*, Überzählige *m*; Außenseiter *m*; *s. odds*; '~**ball** *Am.* F komischer Kauz; '**odd·i·ty** Seltsamkeit *f*; F Original *n* (*Person*); '**odd·ly:** ~ *enough* seltsamerweise; '**odd·ments** *pl.* Überbleibsel *n/pl.*, Reste *m/pl.*; Krimskrams *m*; ✝ Einzelstücke *n/pl.*; **odds** [ɔdz] *pl. oft sg.* (Gewinn)Chancen *f/pl.*; Wahrscheinlichkeit *f*; Vorteil *m*; Vorgabe *f*, Handikap *n*; Verschiedenheit *f*; Unterschied *m*; Streit *m*; *the* ~ *are against you* du bist im Nachteil; *the* ~ *are 3 to 1 in his favour* die Chancen stehen 3 : 1 für ihn; *the* ~ *are that* es ist sehr wahrscheinlich, daß; *be at* ~ *with s.o.* mit j-m im Streit sein; nicht übereinstimmen mit j-m; ~ *and ends* Reste *m/pl.*, Krimskrams *m*; *it makes no* ~ es spielt keine Rolle, es macht nichts aus; *what's the* ~? was tut's?
ode [əud] Ode *f* (*Gedicht*).
o·di·ous □ ['əudjəs] verhaßt, abscheulich; widerlich, ekelhaft; **o·di·um** ['əudjəm] Haß *m*; Vorwurf *m*; Schande *f*; Odium *n*.
o·dom·e·ter *mot.* [o'dɔmitə] Kilometerzähler *m*.
o·don·to·lo·gy ⚕ [ɔdɔn'tɔlədʒi] Zahnheilkunde *f*.
o·dor·if·er·ous □ [əudə'rifərəs], '**o·dor·ous** □ wohlriechend, duftend.
o·do(u)r ['əudə] Geruch *m*; Wohlgeruch *m*, Duft *m*; *fig.* Ruf *m*; '**o·dor·less** geruchlos. [(*a. fig.*).]
O·dys·sey ['ɔdisi] Odyssee *f Homers*
oe·col·o·gy [i:'kɔlədʒi] *s. ecology*.
oec·u·men·i·cal *eccl.* □ [i:kju:'menikəl] ökumenisch.
oe·de·ma ⚕ [i:'di:mə] Ödem *n*.
o'er [əuə] = *over*.
oe·soph·a·gus *anat.* [i:'sɔfəgəs] Speiseröhre *f*.
of [ɔv, *schwache Formen* əv, v] *prp. allg.* von; *Bezeichnung des Genitivs*; *Ort*: bei (*the battle of Quebec*); *räumlicher Abstand*: von (*north of*); *Herkunft*: von, aus (*of good family*); *Trennung, Befreiung*: von (*rid* ~, *cure* ~ *s.th.*); *gen.* (*robbed* ~ *one's purse*); um (*cheat* ~ *s.th.*); *Teil*: von, *gen.* (*the best* ~ *my friends*); *Stoff*: aus, von (*a dress* ~ *silk*); *Eigenschaft*: von, mit (*a man* ~ *honour*, ~ *means*); *Urheber, Art u. Weise*: von; ~ *o.s.* von selbst; *Ursache, Grund*: von, an (*dat.*) (*die* ~); aus (~ *charity*); vor (*dat.*) (*afraid* ~); auf (*acc.*) (*proud* ~); über (*acc.*) (*ashamed* ~); nach (*smell* ~ *roses*); *Beziehung*: hinsichtlich, in betreff (*quick* ~ *eye*); *Ziel*: nach (*desirous* ~); *Thema*: von, über (*acc.*) (*speak* ~ *s.th.*); an (*acc.*) (*think* ~ *s.th.*); *deutsch unausgedrückt*: *Apposition* (*the city* ~ *London*); *Maß* (*a glass* ~ *wine*); *this world* ~ *ours* diese unsere Welt; ~ *an evening* F abends.
off [ɔ:f, ɔf] **1.** *adv. mst in Zssg mit vb*: weg, ab; herunter; aus (*vorbei*); *Raum*: weg (*3 miles* ~); *Zeit*: hin (*3 months* ~); ~ *and on* ab u. an, ab u. zu; hin u. her; *be* ~ fort sein, weg sein; *engS.*: (weg)gehen, (ab-)fahren; weg müssen; zu sein (*Hahn etc.*); aus sein; ausverkauft sein; *be* ~ *with s.o.* mit j-m auseinander sein; *right* ~, *straight* ~ sofort; *have one's shoes etc.* ~ seine *od.* die Schuhe *etc.* aus(gezogen) haben; *well etc.* ~ gut *etc.* daran; **2.** *prp.* von ... (weg, ab, herunter); frei von, ohne; abseits von, unweit (*gen.*), neben; ⚓ auf der Höhe von; *a street* ~ *the Strand* e-e Nebenstraße des Strand; *be* ~ *duty* (dienst)frei haben; *be* ~ *smoking* das Rauchen aufgegeben haben; ~ *the point* nicht zur Sache gehörend; *be* ~ *one's feed sl.* keinen Hunger haben; ~ *one's head sl.* verrückt; **3.** *adj.* entfernt(er); abseits liegend; Seiten..., Neben...; ab(-), los(gegangen); *bei Pferd, Wagen*: rechte(r, -s); arbeits-, dienstfrei; ab, unwohl; nicht frisch; *Kricket*: abseitig; ~ *chance* schwache Möglichkeit *f*; ~ *shade* ✝ Fehlfarbe *f*; **4.** *int.* weg!, fort!, raus!
of·fal ['ɔfəl] Abfall *m*; Schund *m*;

~s pl. Fleischerei: Innereien *f/pl.*
off...: **~beat** F ['ɔf'bi:t] ungewöhnlich, ausgefallen; **'~-chance:** *on the ~* auf die entfernte Möglichkeit hin, auf gut Glück; **~-'col·o(u)r** unwohl; *be od. feel ~* sich unwohl fühlen; unanständig (*Witz etc.*); **'~-day** schlechter Tag; *this is an ~ for me* heute geht mir alles schief.
of·fence [ə'fens] Angriff *m*; Beleidigung *f*, Kränkung *f*; Ärgernis *n*, Anstoß *m*; Verstoß *m*, Vergehen *n*; *no ~!* nichts für ungut!; *give ~* Anstoß *od.* Ärgernis erregen; *take ~* Anstoß nehmen (*at* an *dat.*).
of·fend [ə'fend] *v/t.* beleidigen, verletzen; ärgern; *v/i.* verstoßen, sich vergehen (*against* gegen); **of'fend·er** Übel-, Missetäter(in); Straffällige *m, f*; *first ~* noch nicht Vorbestrafte *m, f*.
of·fense [ə'fens] = *offence*.
of·fen·sive [ə'fensiv] **1.** □ anstößig; widerlich, ekelhaft; Offensiv..., Angriffs...; *~ weapon* Angriffswaffe *f*; **2.** Offensive *f*.
of·fer ['ɔfə] **1.** Angebot *n*, Anerbieten *n*; *~ of marriage* Heiratsantrag *m*; *on ~* zu verkaufen, verkäuflich; **2.** *v/t.* anbieten; *Preis, Möglichkeit etc.* bieten; *Gebet, Opfer* darbringen; versuchen; zeigen; *Widerstand* leisten; *v/i.* sich bieten; **'of·fer·ing** Opfer *n*; Anerbieten *n*, Angebot *n*; Antrag *m*.
of·fer·to·ry *eccl.* ['ɔfətəri] Kollekte *f*.
off-face ['ɔ:f'feis] randlos (*Damenhut*).
off-hand ['ɔ:f'hænd] aus dem Handgelenk *od.* Stegreif, unvorbereitet; ungezwungen, frei, lässig.
of·fice ['ɔfis] Büro *n*, Kontor *n*; Geschäftsstelle *f*; Ministerium *n*; Amt *n*, Pflicht *f*; *~s pl.* Hilfe *f*; *~s pl.* Nebenräume *m/pl. e-s Hauses*; *booking ~* Schalter *m*; *box ~* (Theater-, *etc.*) Kasse *f*; *Divine* ♀ Gottesdienst *m*; **'~-bear·er** Amtsträger *m*; **'~-block** Bürohaus *n*; **'~-boy** Laufbursche *m*; **'~-hours** *pl.* Dienststunden *f/pl.*; Geschäftszeiten *f/pl.*
of·fi·cer ['ɔfisə] Beamte *m*; ⚔ Offizier *m*; **'of·fi·cered:** *~ by* geführt *od.* befehligt von; **of·fice sup·plies** Bürobedarf *m*.
of·fi·cial □ [ə'fiʃəl] **1.** offiziell, amtlich; Amts...; ⚕ = *officinal*; **2.** Beamte *m*; Sachbearbeiter *m*; **of'fi·cial·dom** Beamtentum *n*; Bürokratismus *m*; **of·fi·cial·ese** [~'li:z] Amts-, Behördensprache *f*; **of'fi·cial·ism** = *officialdom*.
of·fi·ci·ate [ə'fiʃieit] amtieren.
of·fic·i·nal [ɔfi'sainl] offizinell, als Arznei (anerkannt).
of·fi·cious □ [ə'fiʃəs] aufdringlich, übereifrig; offiziös, halbamtlich.
off·ing ⚓ ['ɔfiŋ] offene See *f*, Seeraum *m*; *in the ~ fig.* in (Aus)Sicht; **'off·ish** F reserviert, steif.
off...: **~-'key** ♪ falsch; **'~-li·cence** Schankrecht *n* über die Straße; **'~-peak:** *~ charges pl.* verbilligter Tarif *m*; *~ hours pl.* verkehrsschwache Stunden *f/pl.*; **'~-print** Sonderdruck *m*; **~-'put·ting** unangenehm, störend, wenig einladend; unsympathisch (*Person, Wesen*); **'~·scour·ings** *pl.*, **'~·scum** Kehricht *m*; Abschaum *m*; **'~-sea·son** Nebensaison *f*; **'~·set 1.** ⚠ Absatz *m e-r Mauer etc.*; ⊕ Biegung *f e-s Rohrs*; *typ.* Offsetdruck *m*; *s. offshoot*; *s. set-off*; **2.** ausgleichen; **'~·shoot** Sproß *m*; Ausläufer *m*; **'~-shore** küstennah; ablandig (*Wind etc.*); *~ purchases pl. pol.* Off-shore-Käufe *m/pl.*; **'~-'side** *Sport*: abseits; **'~·spring** Abkömmling *m*; Nachkommenschaft *f*; Ergebnis *n*; **~-'stage** hinter den Kulissen; **~-the-'cuff** aus dem Handgelenk *od.* Stegreif; **~-the-'peg** von der Stange; **'~-the-'rec·ord** inoffiziell, vertraulich (*Mitteilung*); **'~-time** Freizeit *f*, freie Zeit *f*; **~-'white** gebrochen weiß.
oft *poet.* [ɔft] oft.
of·ten ['ɔfn] oft(mals), häufig; *as ~ as* jedesmal wenn; *as ~ as not, more ~ than not* sehr oft *od.* häufig; *every so ~* von Zeit zu Zeit; **'of·ten·times, 'oft-times** † oft.
o·gee ⚠ ['əudʒi:] S-Bogen *m*; Kehlleiste *f*.
o·gi·val [əu'dʒaivəl] Spitzbogen...; **'o·give** ⚠ Spitzbogen *m*; Gratrippe *f e-s Gewölbes*.
o·gle ['əugl] liebäugeln (mit).
o·gre ['əugə] Menschenfresser *m* (*im Märchen*); **o·gress** ['əugris] Menschenfresserin *f*.
oh [əu] oh!; ach!
ohm ⚡ [əum] Ohm *n* (*Einheit des Widerstands*).
o·ho [əu'həu] aha!; haha!
oil [ɔil] **1.** Öl *n*; Erdöl *n*, Petroleum *n*; *burn the midnight ~* bis spät in

die Nacht hinein arbeiten; *smell of* ~ nach Schweiß riechen (*Werk*); *pour* ~ *on the flame*(*s*) Öl ins Feuer gießen; *pour* ~ *on the* (*troubled*) *waters* Öl auf die Wogen gießen; *strike* ~ Erdöl finden; *fig.* plötzlich reich werden; *paint in* ~*s* in Öl malen; **2.** ölen; schmieren (*a. fig.*); ~ *s.o.'s palm* j. schmieren; **ˈ~-burn·er** Schiff *n* mit Dieselantrieb; Dieselmotor *m*; Ölofen *m*; **ˈ~-cake** Ölkuchen *m* (*Viehfutter*); **ˈ~-can** Ölkännchen *n*; **ˈ~-change** *mot.* Ölwechsel *m*; **ˈ~-cloth** Linoleum *n*; Wachstuch *n*; **ˈ~-col·o(u)r** Ölfarbe *f*; **ˈ~-dip·stick** *mot.* Ölmeßstab *m*; **ˈoil·er** = *oil-can*; *oil-tanker*; **ˈoil-field** Ölfeld *n*; **oil glut** Ölschwemme *f*; **ˈoil·i·ness** Öligkeit *f* (*a. fig.*); Fettigkeit *f*, Schmierigkeit *f*; **ˈoil-lev·el** *mot.* Ölstand *m*; **ˈoil-man** Ölmann *m*, -händler *m*; Ölproduzent *m*; Farbenhändler *m*; **ˈoil-paint·ing** Ölmalerei *f*; Ölgemälde *n*; **ˈoil-pa·per** Ölpapier *n*; **ˈoil-rig** Bohrinsel *f*; **ˈoil--skin** Ölleinwand *f*; ~*s pl.* Ölzeug *n*; **oil slick** Ölteppich *m*; **ˈoil-tank·er** Öltanker *m*; Tankwagen *m*; **ˈoil-well** Ölquelle *f*; **ˈoil·y** □ ölig (*a. fig.*); fettig, schmierig; *fig.* aalglatt.

oint·ment [ˈɔintmənt] Salbe *f*.

O.K., o·kay [ˈəuˈkei] **1.** richtig, stimmt!; gut, in Ordnung; **2.** annehmen, gutheißen.

old [əuld] alt; altbekannt; althergebracht; erfahren; F oll; *sl.* (*zur Verstärkung*) toll; *the* ~ die Alten; *young and* ~ jung und alt; ~ *age* das Alter; *the* ~ *man* der Alte (*Vater, Gatte, Kapitän*); ~ *man als Anrede*: alter Freund, mein Lieber; *the* ~ *woman* die Alte (*Gattin*); *the* ~ *country* die alte Heimat; *an* ~ *boy* ein ehemaliger Schüler; *a high* ~ *time sl.* e-e tolle Zeit; *the* ~ *one, the* ~ *gentleman,* ~ *Harry od. Scratch* der Teufel; *days of* ~ alte Zeiten; **ˈ~-age** Alters...; ~ *pension* Pension *f*; Rente *f*; ~ *pensioner* Rentner(in); **ˈ~--ˈclothes·man** Trödler *m*; **ˈold·en** † *od. poet.* alt, früher; *in the* ~ *days* in alten *od.* früheren Zeiten.

old...: ˈ~-ˈfash·ioned 1. altmodisch; altväterlich; altklug (*Kind*); mißbilligend (*Blick*); **2.** *Am. ein Cocktail mit Whisky*; **ˈ~-ˈfo·g(e)y·ish** altmodisch, verknöchert; **♀ Glo·ry** Sternenbanner *n*; **ˈold·ish** ältlich; **ˈold-ˈmaid·ish** pingelig; umständlich; altjüngferlich; **old·ster** [ˈ~stə] alter Knabe *m*; **ˈold-time** alt(ertümlich); **ˈold-ˈtim·er** alter Hase *m*; **old wives' tale** Ammenmärchen *n*; **ˈold-ˈwom·an·ish** altweiberhaft; **ˈold-world** altmodisch, altertümlich; altweltlich.

o·le·ag·i·nous [əuliˈædʒinəs] ölig; Öl...

o·le·an·der ♀ [əuliˈændə] Oleander *m*.

ol·fac·to·ry *anat.* [ɔlˈfæktəri] Geruchs...

ol·i·garch·y [ˈɔligɑːki] Oligarchie *f*.

ol·ive [ˈɔliv] ♀ Olive *f*; Olivgrün *n*; **ˈ~-branch** Ölzweig *m*; **ˈ~-tree** Ölbaum *m*.

O·lym·pi·ad [əuˈlimpiæd] Olympiade *f*; **Oˈlym·pi·an** [~piən] olympisch, göttlich; **Oˈlym·pic games** *pl.* Olympische Spiele *n/pl.*

om·buds·man [ˈɔmbudzmən] Ombudsmann *m*.

om·e·let, om·e·lette [ˈɔmlit] Eierkuchen *m*, Omelett *n*.

o·men [ˈəumen] Omen *n*, Vorzeichen *n*, Vorbedeutung *f*.

om·i·nous □ [ˈɔminəs] unheilvoll; ~ *of disaster* unheilverkündend.

o·mis·si·ble [əuˈmisibl] auszulassen(d); **o·mis·sion** [əˈmiʃən] Unterlassung *f*; Aus-, Weglassung *f* (*from* aus); *sin of* ~ Unterlassungssünde *f*.

o·mit [əuˈmit] unterlassen, versäumen (*a. to inf.* zu *inf.*); auslassen, übergehen.

om·ni·bus [ˈɔmnibəs] **1.** † Omnibus *m*; **2.** allumfassend; Sammel...; ~ *volume* Sammelband *m*.

om·nip·o·tence [ɔmˈnipətəns] Allmacht *f*; **omˈnip·o·tent** □ allmächtig.

om·ni·pres·ence [ˈɔmniˈprezəns] Allgegenwart *f*; **ˈom·niˈpres·ent** □ allgegenwärtig.

om·nis·cience [ɔmˈnisiəns] Allwissenheit *f*; **omˈnis·cient** □ allwissend.

om·niv·o·rous [ɔmˈnivərəs] alles fressend *od. fig.* verschlingend.

on [ɔn] **1.** *prp. mst* auf; *engS. festgemacht od. unmittelbar* an (~ *the wall, chain, Thames*); *beschäftigt* bei, an (*be* ~ *the Stock Exchange*); *Richtung, Ziel*: auf ... (los), nach ... (hin) (*march* ~ *London*); *Grund*: auf ...

(hin) (~ *his authority*); *Zeit*: an (~ *Friday*, ~ *the 1st of April*); (gleich) nach, bei (~ *his arrival*); *Thema*: über (*acc.*) (*talk* ~ *a subject*); *siehe die mit on verbundenen Wörter*; *get* ~ *a train bsd. Am.* in e-n Zug einsteigen; *turn one's back* ~ *s.o.* j-m den Rücken kehren; ~ *these conditions* unter diesen Bedingungen; ~ *this model* nach diesem Muster; ~ *hearing it* als ich *etc.* es hörte; **2.** *adv.* darauf; *bsd. Kleidung*: auf (*keep one's hat* ~), an (*have a coat* ~); voran, -aus, -wärts; weiter (*and so* ~); ~ *and* ~ immer weiter; ~ *to* ... auf (*acc.*) ... hinauf *od.* hinaus; *from that day* ~ von dem Tage an; *be* ~ (mit) dabei sein; im Gange sein, vor sich gehen; *thea.* gegeben werden; *what is* ~ *tonight?* Was gibt es heute abend?; d(a)ran (*an der Reihe*) sein; auf sein (*Hahn etc.*); an sein (*Licht, Wasser etc.*); *be a bit* ~ *sl.* e-n Schwips haben (*angetrunken sein*); **3.** *int.* drauf!, ran!

once [wʌns] **1.** *adv.* einmal; einst (-mals); *at* ~ (so)gleich, sofort; zugleich, auf einmal; *all at* ~ auf einmal; ~ *again* noch einmal; ~ *for all* ein für allemal; *for* ~ für diesmal (*ausnahmsweise*); ~ *in a while* dann u. wann; *this* ~ dieses eine Mal; ~ *more* noch einmal; *im Märchen*: ~ *upon a time there was* ... es war einmal ...; **2.** *cj. a.* ~ *that* sobald, wenn erst einmal.

once-o·ver *Am.* F ['wʌnsəuvə] *kurze* Musterung *f.*

on-com·ing ['ɔnkʌmiŋ] **1.** kommend, (heran)nahend; entgegenkommend; ~ *traffic* Gegenverkehr *m*; 2. Nahen *n*, Kommen *n.*

one [wʌn] **1.** ein; einzig; eine(r), ein; eins; man; *his* ~ *care* seine einzige Sorge; ~ *day* eines Tages; ~ *of these days* dieser Tage; ~ *Mr. Miller* ein gewisser Herr Miller; *s. any, every, no*; *take* ~*'s walk* s-n Spaziergang machen; *a large dog and a little* ~ ein großer Hund und ein kleiner; *for* ~ *thing* auf alle Fälle; ~ *and the same* ein und derselbe *etc.*; **2.** Einer *m*, Eins *f*; *the little* ~*s pl.* die Kleinen *n/pl.*, die Kinder *n/pl.*; ~ *another* einander; *at* ~ einig; ~ *by* ~, ~ *after another* einzeln, einer nach dem andern; *it is all* ~ (*to me*) es ist (mir) ganz einerlei; *I for* ~ ich für meinen Teil; ~ *with another* im Durchschnitt; '**~-armed** einarmig; ~ *bandit* Spielautomat *m*; '**~-'eyed** einäugig; *fig.* beschränkt; '**~-'horse** einspännig; *fig. sl.* armselig, zweitrangig; ~ *town* Nest *n*; '**~-i'dea'd** in e-e einzige Idee verrannt; '**one·ness** Einheit *f*; Identität *f*; Einigkeit *f*; '**one-night stand** einmaliger Auftritt *m.*

on·er·ous □ ['ɔnərəs] lästig, beschwerlich.

one...: ~'**self** (man) selbst, sich; *by* ~ aus eigener Kraft, von selbst; allein; '**~-'sid·ed** □ einseitig; '**~-time** einstig; '**~-'track** eingleisig; *have a* ~ *mind* immer nur dasselbe im Kopf haben, monoman sein; **one-'up·man·ship** *die Kunst, allen anderen ständig um eine Nasenlänge voraus zu sein*; '**one-way street** Einbahnstraße *f.*

on·fall ['ɔnfɔ:l] Angriff *m.*

on·go·ings ['ɔngəuiŋz] *pl.* Vorgänge *m/pl.*

on·ion ['ʌnjən] Zwiebel *f*; *off one's* ~ *sl.* übergeschnappt.

on·look·er ['ɔnlukə] Zuschauer(in).

on·ly ['əunli] **1.** *adj.* einzig; **2.** *adv.* nur; bloß; erst; ~ *yesterday* erst gestern; ~ *just* eben erst, gerade, kaum; ~ *think!* denken Sie nur!; **3.** *cj.* ~ (*that*) nur daß.

on·o·mat·o·poe·ia [ɔnəumætəu'pi:ə] Lautmalerei *f.*

on·rush ['ɔnrʌʃ] Ansturm *m.*

on·set ['ɔnset], **on·slaught** ['ɔnslɔ:t] Angriff *m*; *bsd. fig.* Anfall *m*; Anfang *m.*

on·shore [ɔn'ʃɔ:] landwärts; in Küstennähe; an Land.

on·to ['ɔntu, 'ɔntə] auf (*acc.*).

on·tol·o·gy *phls.* [ɔn'tɔlədʒi] Ontologie *f*, Seinslehre *f.*

o·nus *fig.* ['əunəs] (*ohne pl.*) Last *f.*

on·ward ['ɔnwəd] **1.** *adj.* vorwärts-, fortschreitend; **2.** *a.* ~*s adv.* vorwärts, weiter.

on·yx *min.* ['ɔniks] Onyx *m.*

oo·dles *sl.* ['u:dlz] *pl.* Unmengen *f/pl.* (of von).

oof *sl.* [u:f] Moneten *pl.* (*Geld*).

oomph *sl.* [u:mf] *das* (gewisse) Etwas; Verve *f*; Sex Appeal *m.*

ooze [u:z] **1.** Schlamm *m*; Schlick *m*; ⊕ Lohbrühe *f*; **2.** (durch)sickern (lassen); ausströmen, ausschwitzen; ~ *away* schwinden.

oo·zy □ [ˈuːzi] schlammig; feucht.
o·pac·i·ty [əuˈpæsiti] Undurchsichtigkeit *f*; *fig.* Stumpfheit *f*.
o·pal *min.* [ˈəupəl] Opal *m*; **o·pal·es·cent** [~ˈlesnt] opalisierend.
o·paque □ [əuˈpeik] undurchsichtig; *fig.* dunkel; stumpf(sinnig).
ope *poet.* [əup] = *open.*
o·pen [ˈəupən] **1.** □ *allg.* offen; geöffnet, auf; frei (*Feld etc.*); öffentlich; offenstehend, unentschieden; aufrichtig, freimütig; ausgesetzt, zugänglich (*to dat.*); nicht abgeschlossen (*Konto*); aufgeschlossen (*to* gegenüber); mild, frostfrei (*Wetter*); *with ~ arms* begeistert, herzlich; *with ~ hands* großzügig; *the ~ door* die Politik der offenen Tür; *keep ~ house* ein gastfreies *od.* offenes Haus haben; *lay o.s. ~ to* sich (*dat.*) aussetzen; *~ letter* offener Brief *m*; *~ season* Jagd-, Fischzeit *f*; **2.** *in the ~ (air)* im Freien; *come out into the ~ fig.* an die Öffentlichkeit treten; **3.** *v/t.* öffnen, aufmachen; *Buch* aufschlagen; eröffnen (*zugänglich machen*; *beginnen*; *mitteilen*); *Verhandlungen etc.* anknüpfen; *Konto* eröffnen; *~ up* Land erschließen; (*Brunnen*) bohren; (*Straße*) bauen; *v/i.* sich öffnen, sich auftun, aufgehen; aufmachen, öffnen, geöffnet sein (*Laden etc.*); anfangen, beginnen; *~ into* führen in (*acc.*) (*Tür etc.*); *~ on to* hinausgehen auf (*acc.*) (*Fenster etc.*); *~ out* sich ausbreiten; **~-ˈac·cess li·brar·y** Freihandbibliothek *f*; **ˈ~-ˈair** im Freien (stattfindend), Freilicht..., Frei(luft)...; **ˈ~-ˈarmed** herzlich, warm; **ˈ~-ˈend·ed** *fig.* offen, (*bsd.* zeitlich) unbegrenzt; **o·pen·er** [ˈəupnə] (Er)Öffner(in); (Dosen)Öffner *m*; **ˈo·pen-ˈeyed** wach; mit offenen Augen; aufmerksam; überrascht; **ˈo·pen-ˈhand·ed** freigebig, großzügig; **ˈo·pen-ˈheart·ed** offen(herzig), aufrichtig; **o·pen·ing** [ˈəupniŋ] **1.** Öffnung *f* (*a. konkr.*); Eröffnung *f*; Gelegenheit *f*, Aussicht *f*; **2.** Eröffnungs...; *~ night* Eröffnungsvorstellung *f*; *~ time bsd.* *Lokal*: Öffnungszeit *f*; **ˈo·pen-ˈmind·ed** *fig.* aufgeschlossen; **ˈo·pen-ˈmouthed** gierig; verdutzt; **o·pen·ness** [ˈəupnnis] Offenheit *f*; Milde *f des Wetters.*
open...: *~* **or·der** ⚔ geöffnete Ordnung *f*; **ˈ~-ˈplan of·fice** Großraumbüro *n*; *~* **shop** Betrieb *m* ohne Gewerkschaftszwang; 2 **U·ni·ver·si·ty** Fern(seh)universität *f*, *deren Kurse auch ohne entsprechenden Schulabschluß belegt werden können*; *~* **vow·el** offener Vokal *m*; *~* **work** Durchbruchsarbeit *f*.
op·er·a [ˈɔpərə] Oper *f*.
op·e·ra·ble [ˈɔpərəbl] ⚕ operierbar; durchführbar, praktikabel.
opera...: **ˈ~-cloak** Theatermantel *m*; **ˈ~-glass(es** *pl.*) Opernglas *n*; **ˈ~-hat** Klapphut *m*; **ˈ~-house** Opernhaus *n*.
op·er·ate [ˈɔpəreit] *v/t.* (ein)wirken; ⚚, ⚕, ⚔ operieren; *bsd. Am.* in Gang bringen; ⊕ handhaben, bedienen; *Unternehmen* leiten; *v/i.* sich auswirken; *be operating* in Betrieb sein, funktionieren, arbeiten; **op·er·at·ic** [~ˈrætik] opernhaft; *~ singer* Opernsänger(in); **op·er·at·ing** [ˈɔpəreitiŋ] Operations...; *~ expenses pl.* Betriebsunkosten *pl.*; *~ instructions pl.* Bedienungsvorschriften *f/pl.*; *~ theatre* Operationssaal *m mit Zuschauergalerie*; **op·erˈa·tion** Wirkung *f*; Wirksamkeit *f*; Tätigkeit *f*; ⚚ Transaktion *f*; ⚕, ⚔, ⚚ Operation *f*; *be in ~* in Kraft sein; *come into ~* in Kraft treten; **op·erˈa·tion·al** [~ʃənl] Betriebs..., Arbeits...; Operations...; einsatzfähig; **op·er·a·tive** [ˈɔpərətiv] **1.** □ wirksam, tätig; praktisch; ⚕ operativ; **2.** Arbeiter *m*; **op·er·a·tor** [ˈ~reitə] Wirkende *m, f, n*; ⚕ Operateur *m*; *Film*: Vorführer *m*; Telephonist(in); ⊕ Maschinist *m*; ⚚ Spekulant *m*; Unternehmer *m*.
op·er·et·ta [ɔpəˈretə] Operette *f*.
oph·thal·mi·a ⚕ [ɔfˈθælmiə] Augenentzündung *f*; **ophˈthal·mic** Augen...; augenkrank; *~ hospital* Augenklinik *f*.
o·pi·ate *pharm.* [ˈəupiit] **1.** Schlafmittel *n*; **2.** einschläfernd.
o·pine [əuˈpain] meinen; **o·pin·ion** [əˈpinjən] Meinung *f*; Ansicht *f*; Stellungnahme *f*; Gutachten *n*; (gute) Meinung *f*; *the (public) ~* die öffentliche Meinung; *counsel's ~* Rechtsgutachten *n*; *~ poll* Meinungsumfrage *f*; *I am of the ~ that* ich bin der Meinung, daß; *in my ~* meines Erachtens; **oˈpin·ion·at·ed** [~eitid] starr-, eigensinnig.
o·pi·um *pharm.* [ˈəupjəm] Opium *n*.
o·pos·sum *zo.* [əˈpɔsəm] Opossum

n, Beutelratte *f*.
op·po·nent [ə'pəunənt] **1.** Gegner *m*; **2.** gegnerisch.
op·por·tune □ ['ɔpətju:n] günstig; passend; rechtzeitig; '**op·por·tun·ism** Opportunismus *m*; '**op·por·tun·ist** Opportunist(in); **op·por'tu·ni·ty** (günstige) Gelegenheit *f*, Möglichkeit *f*.
op·pose [ə'pəuz] entgegen-, gegenüberstellen; bekämpfen; sich widersetzen (*dat.*); entgegentreten (*dat.*); **op'posed** entgegengesetzt; feindlich; *be* ~ *to* gegen ... sein; **op·po·site** ['ɔpəzit] **1.** □ gegenüberliegend ([*to*] *s.th. dat.*); entgegengesetzt; ~ *number* Gegenspieler(in); Kollege *m*, Kollegin *f*; **2.** *prp. u. adv.* gegenüber; **3.** Gegenteil *n*, -satz *m*; **op·po'si·tion** Gegenüberstehen *n*; Widerstand *m*; (*to* gegen); Gegensatz *m*; Widerspruch *m*, -streit *m*; ⚕ Konkurrenz *f*; *parl. u. ast.* Opposition *f*.
op·press [ə'pres] be-, unter-, niederdrücken; **op·pres·sion** [ə'preʃən] Unterdrückung *f*; Druck *m*; Bedrängnis *f*, Not *f*; Bedrücktheit *f*; **op'pres·sive** □ [~siv] (be)drükkend; gewaltsam; **op'pres·sive·ness** Druck *m*; Schwüle *f*; **op'pres·sor** Unterdrücker *m*.
op·pro·bri·ous □ [ə'prəubriəs] schimpfend, schmähend; **op'pro·bri·um** [~briəm] Schimpf *m*; Schande *f*.
op·pugn [ɔ'pju:n] bestreiten.
opt [ɔpt] optieren (*for* für); **op·ta·tive** *gr.* ['ɔptətiv] Wunschform *f*, Optativ *m*.
op·tic ['ɔptik] Augen..., Seh...; = '**op·ti·cal** □ optisch; **op'ti·cian** [~ʃən] Optiker *m*; '**op·tics** *sg.* Optik *f*.
op·ti·mism ['ɔptimizəm] Optimismus *m*; '**op·ti·mist** Optimist(in); **op·ti'mis·tic** (~*ally*) optimistisch; '**op·ti·mize** optimieren.
op·ti·mum ['ɔptiməm] **1.** Optimum *n*, *das* Beste; **2.** optimal, günstigst, best.
op·tion ['ɔpʃən] Wahl *f*; Wahlfreiheit *f*; ⚕ Vorkaufsrecht *n*, Option *f*; **op·tion·al** □ ['ɔpʃənl] freigestellt, wahlfrei.
op·u·lence ['ɔpjuləns] Reichtum *m*; '**op·u·lent** □ (sehr) reich; üppig, verschwenderisch, opulent.
o·pus ['əupəs] Werk *n*, Opus *n*; *magnum* ~ Hauptwerk *n*.
or [ɔ:] oder; *either* ... ~ entweder ... oder; ~ *else* sonst, wo nicht; *two* ~ *three* zwei bis drei; ~ *so* (*nachgestellt*) ungefähr, etwa.
or·a·cle ['ɔrəkl] Orakel *n*; *work the* ~ F hinter den Kulissen arbeiten; **o·rac·u·lar** [ɔ'rækjulə] orakelhaft (*fig. rätselhaft, dunkel*); Orakel...
o·ral □ ['ɔ:rəl] mündlich; Mund...
o·rang ['ɔ:rəŋ] = *orang-outang*.
or·ange ['ɔrindʒ] **1.** Orange *f*, Apfelsine *f*; Orangenbaum *m*; Orangefarbe *f*; **2.** orange(farben); **or·ange·ade** ['~'eid] Orangenlimonade *f*; **or·ange·ry** ['~əri] Orangerie *f*.
o·rang-ou·tang *zo.* ['ɔ:rəŋ'u:tæŋ] Orang-Utan *m*.
o·ra·tion [ɔ:'reiʃən] *förmliche* Rede *f*; **or·a·tor** ['ɔrətə] Redner *m*; **or·a·tor·i·cal** □ [~'tɔrikəl] rednerisch; **or·a·to·ri·o** ♪ [~'tɔ:riəu] Oratorium *n*; **or·a·to·ry** ['~təri] Redekunst *f*, Beredsamkeit *f*, Rhetorik *f*; *eccl.* Kapelle *f*.
orb [ɔ:b] Ball *m*; *fig.* Himmelskörper *m*; *poet.* Augapfel *m*; **or·bic·u·lar** □ [ɔ:'bikjulə] kugelförmig, rund; **or·bit** ['ɔ:bit] **1.** Planetenbahn *f*; Kreis-, Umlaufbahn *f*; Auge(nhöhle *f*) *n*; **2.** sich in e-r Umlaufbahn bewegen.
or·chard ['ɔ:tʃəd] Obstgarten *m*.
or·ches·tra ♪ ['ɔ:kistrə] Orchester *n*; ~ *pit thea.* Orchesterraum *m*; **or·ches·tral** [ɔ:'kestrəl] Orchester...; **or·ches·trate** ♪ ['ɔ:kistreit] instrumentieren.
or·chid ⚘ ['ɔ:kid] Orchidee *f*; **or·chis** ⚘ ['ɔ:kis] Knabenkraut *n*.
or·dain [ɔ:'dein] an-, verordnen; bestimmen; *Priester* ordinieren.
or·deal [ɔ:'di:l] Gottesurteil *n*; *fig.* Feuerprobe *f*, schwere Prüfung *f*.
or·der ['ɔ:də] **1.** Ordnung *f*; Anordnung *f*; Reihenfolge *f*; Befehl *m*; Regel *f*, Vorschrift *f*; ⚕ Order *f*, Bestellung *f*, Auftrag *m*; Zahlungsanweisung *f*; Klasse *f*, Stand *m*, Rang *m*; Orden *m* (*a. eccl.*); *by* ~ im Auftrag; ~ *of the day* Tagesordnung *f*; ⚔ Tagesbefehl *m*; *take* (*holy*) ~*s* in den geistlichen Stand treten; *put in* ~ in Ordnung bringen; *in* ~ *to* ... um zu ...; *in* ~ *that* damit; *on the* ~*s of* auf Befehl von; *on* ~ ⚕ bestellt; *make to* ~ auf Bestellung anfertigen;

rise to ~ zur Geschäftsordnung sprechen; *standing* ~*s pl. parl.* Geschäftsordnung *f*; **2.** (an)ordnen, einrichten; verordnen; befehlen; ⚕ bestellen, kommen lassen; beordern, schicken; ~ *arms!* Gewehr ab!; ~ *about* herumkommandieren; ~ *down* (*up*) herunter- (herauf)kommen lassen; '**~-book** ⚕ Auftragsbuch *n*; '**or·dered** geordnet; ordentlich; **or·der form** Bestellschein *m*; '**or·der·li·ness** Regelmäßigkeit *f*; Ordnung *f*; Ordentlichkeit *f*; '**or·der·ly 1.** ordentlich; ruhig, gesittet; methodisch; ⚔ diensttuend, Ordonnanz...; ~ *officer* Ordonnanzoffizier *m*, Offizier *m* vom Dienst; ~ *room* Geschäftszimmer *n*; **2.** ⚔ Ordonnanz *f*; Bursche *m*; Krankenpfleger *m*.

or·di·nal ['ɔːdinl] **1.** Ordnungs...; **2.** *a.* ~ *number* Ordnungszahl *f*.

or·di·nance ['ɔːdinəns] Verordnung *f*; vorgeschriebener Brauch *m*.

or·di·nar·y ['ɔːdnri] **1.** □ gewöhnlich, üblich; ~ *debts pl.* ⚕ Buchschulden *f/pl.*; ~ *seaman* Leichtmatrose *m*; *s. share*; **2.** *das* Gewöhnliche; Gasthaus *n*; Tagesgericht *n*; ordentlicher Richter *m*; *in* ~ ordentlich; Leib..., Hof...

or·di·nate ⚹ ['ɔːdnit] Ordinate *f*.

or·di·na·tion [ɔːdi'neiʃən] Ordination *f*, (Priester)Weihe *f*.

ord·nance ⚔, ⚓ ['ɔːdnəns] Artillerie *f*, Geschütze *n/pl.*; Feldzeugwesen *n*; ~ *map* Generalstabskarte *f*; ~ *survey* amtliche Landesvermessung *f*; ~*-survey map* Meßtischblatt *n*.

or·dure ['ɔːdjuə] Kot *m*, Schmutz *m*.

ore [ɔː] Erz *n*; *poet.* Metall *n*.

or·gan ['ɔːgən] ♪ Orgel *f*; Organ *n* (*Körperteil*; *fig. Werkzeug*; *Stimme*; *Partei- etc. Blatt*).

or·gan·die, or·gan·dy ['ɔːgəndi] Organdy *m* (*Baumwollgewebe*).

or·gan-grind·er ['ɔːgəngraində] Leierkastenmann *m*; **or·gan·ic** [ɔː'gænik] (~*ally*) organisch; **or·gan·ism** ['ɔːgənizəm] Organismus *m*; '**or·gan·ist** Organist *m*; **or·gan·i·za·tion** [~nai'zeiʃən] Organisation *f*; Einrichtung *f*; Bau *m*; Verein(igung *f*) *m*; '**or·gan·ize** organisieren, einrichten; '**or·gan·iz·er** Organisator(in).

or·gasm ['ɔːgæzəm] Orgasmus *m*.

or·gy ['ɔːdʒi] Orgie *f*.

o·ri·el ⌂ ['ɔːriəl] Erker *m*.

o·ri·ent 1. ['ɔːriənt] aufgehend; östlich; glänzend (*Perle*); **2.** [~] Osten *m*; Orient *m*, Morgenland *n*; **3.** ['~ent] orientieren; **o·ri·en·tal** [~'entl] **1.** □ östlich; orientalisch; morgenländisch; **2.** Orientale *m*, Orientalin *f*; **o·ri·en·tate** ['ɔːrienteit] orientieren; **o·ri·en'ta·tion** Orientierung *f*.

or·i·fice ['ɔrifis] Mündung *f*, Öffnung *f*.

or·i·gin ['ɔridʒin] Ursprung *m*; Anfang *m*; Herkunft *f*.

o·rig·i·nal [ə'ridʒənl] **1.** □ ursprünglich; originell; Ur...; Original...; ⚕ Stamm...; *s. share*; ~ *capital* Stammkapital *n*; ~ *sin* Erbsünde *f*; **2.** Original *n* (*a. Person*), Urbild *n*, -schrift *f*; **o·rig·i·nal·i·ty** [~'næliti] Originalität *f*; **o·rig·i·nal·ly** [ə'ridʒnəli] originell; ursprünglich, zuerst, anfangs, anfänglich.

o·rig·i·nate [ə'ridʒineit] *v/t.* hervorbringen, schaffen, ins Leben rufen; *v/i.* entstehen (*from*, *in s.th.* aus et.; *with*, *from s.o.* bei j-m, durch j.); **o·rig·i'na·tion** Schaffung *f*, Veranlassung *f*; Entstehung *f*; Ursprung *m*; **o'rig·i·na·tive** □ [~tiv] schöpferisch; **o'rig·i·na·tor** Urheber *m*.

o·ri·ole *orn.* ['ɔːriəul] Goldamsel *f*.

o·ri·son ['ɔrizən] Gebet *n*.

or·mo·lu ['ɔːməuluː] Malergold *n*.

or·na·ment 1. ['ɔːnəmənt] Verzierung *f*, Ornament *n*; *fig.* Zierde *f*; **2.** ['~ment] verzieren; schmücken; **or·na'men·tal** □ ornamental, zierend; schmückend; Zier...; **or·na·men'ta·tion** Ausschmückung *f*, Verzierung *f*.

or·nate □ [ɔː'neit] reich verziert; überladen.

or·ni·tho·log·i·cal □ [ɔːniθə'lɔdʒikl] ornithologisch; **or·ni·thol·o·gist** [~'θɔlədʒist] Ornithologe *m*; **or·ni'thol·o·gy** Ornithologie *f*, Vogelkunde *f*.

o·ro·tund ['ɔrəutʌnd] volltönend; bombastisch.

or·phan ['ɔːfən] **1.** Waise(nkind *n*) *f*; **2.** *a.* ~*ed* verwaist; '**or·phan·age** Waisenhaus *n*.

or·rer·y ['ɔrəri] Planetarium *n*.

or·tho·dox □ ['ɔːθədɔks] orthodox; rechtgläubig; üblich; anerkannt; '**or·tho·dox·y** Rechtgläubigkeit *f*.

or·tho·graph·ic, or·tho·graph·i·cal □ [ɔ:θəu'græfik(əl)] orthographisch; **or·thog·ra·phy** [ɔ:'θɔgrəfi] Rechtschreibung *f*, Orthographie *f*.

or·tho·pae·dic [ɔ:θəu'pi:dik] (*~ally*) orthopädisch; **or·tho'pae·dist** Orthopäde *m*; **'or·tho·pae·dy** Orthopädie *f*.

or·to·lan *orn.* ['ɔ:tələn] Ortolan *m*, Gartenammer *f*.

Os·car ['ɔskə] Oscar *m* (*amerikanischer Filmpreis*).

os·cil·late ['ɔsileit] schwingen; *fig.* schwanken; **os·cil'la·tion** Schwingung *f*; **os·cil·la·to·ry** ['~lətəri] schwingend; **os·cil·lo·graph** [ɔ'siləugrɑ:f] Oszillograph *m*.

os·cu·late *co.* ['ɔskjuleit] (sich) küssen; sich berühren (mit).

o·sier ⚘ ['əuʒə] Korbweide *f*.

os·mo·sis *phys.* [ɔz'məusis] Osmose *f*.

os·prey ['ɔspri] Seeadler *m*; ✝ Reiherfeder *f*.

os·se·ous ['ɔsiəs] Knochen...; knochig; **os·si·fi·ca·tion** [ɔsifi'keiʃən] Verknöcherung *f*; **os·si·fy** ['~fai] verknöchern; **os·su·ar·y** ['ɔsjuəri] Beinhaus *n*.

os·ten·si·ble □ [ɔs'tensəbl] vor-, angeblich; scheinbar.

os·ten·ta·tion [ɔsten'teiʃən] Zurschaustellung *f*; Protzerei *f*; **os·ten'ta·tious** □ ostentativ, prahlend, prahlerisch, großtuerisch.

os·te·ol·o·gy *anat.* [ɔsti'ɔlədʒi] Osteologie *f*, Knochenlehre *f*; **os·te·o·path** ['ɔstiəpæθ] Osteopath *m*.

ost·ler ['ɔslə] Stallknecht *m*.

os·tra·cism ['ɔstrəsizəm] Scherbengericht *n*; Verbannung *f*, Ächtung *f*; **os·tra·cize** ['~saiz] verbannen; ächten.

os·trich *orn.* ['ɔstritʃ] Strauß *m*.

oth·er ['ʌðə] andere(r, -s) (*than, from* als); *the ~ day* neulich; *the ~ morning* neulich morgens; *every ~ day* einen Tag um den andern; *each ~* einander; *somebody or ~* irgendeiner, einer oder der andere; **'~·wise** anders; sonst.

o·ti·ose □ ['əuʃiəus] müßig; zwecklos.

ot·ter *zo.* ['ɔtə] Otter *m*; Otterpelz *m*.

Ot·to·man ['ɔtəumən] **1.** ottomanisch, türkisch; **2.** ♀ Ottomane *f* (*Sofa*).

ought [ɔ:t] **1.** = *aught*; **2.** *v/aux.* (*irr.*) sollte; *I ~ to do it* ich sollte es eigentlich tun; *you ~ to have done it* Sie hätten es tun sollen.

ounce[1] [auns] Unze *f* (= *28,35 g*); *by the ~* nach (dem) Gewicht.

ounce[2] *zo.* [~] Schneeleopard *m*.

our ['auə] unser; **ours** ['auəz] **1.** der (die, das) unsrige; unsere(r, -s); *pred.* unser; **2.** die Unsrigen; **our'selves** wir selbst; uns (selbst).

oust [aust] verdrängen, vertreiben, hinauswerfen; *e-s Amtes* entheben.

out [aut] **1.** *adv.* aus; hinaus, heraus; draußen; außerhalb; (bis) zu Ende (*z.B. hear ~*); *be ~* nicht zu Hause sein; ausgeliehen sein; aus der Mode sein; streiken (*Arbeiter*); aus (= *zu Ende*) sein; aus der Übung sein; heraus sein (*Blüte, neues Buch, Geheimnis, verrenktes Glied etc.*); draußen *od.* F 'raus sein (*nicht mehr an der Macht od. am Spiel*); ungenau *od.* nicht richtig sein; im Irrtum sein; *be ~ for s.th. od. to do s.th. sl.* auf et. aus sein; darauf aus sein, et. zu tun; *she is not ~ yet* sie ist noch nicht in die Gesellschaft eingeführt; *be ~ with* böse sein mit; *~ and ~* durch u. durch; *~ and about* wieder auf den Beinen; *~ and away* bei weitem; *s. elbow*; *have it ~ with s.o.* sich mit j-m aussprechen; sich zs.-raufen; *voyage ~* Ausreise *f*; *way ~* Ausgang *m*; *her day ~* ihr freier Tag; *~ with him!* hinaus mit ihm!; **2.** *typ.* Auslassung *f*, Leiche *f*; *Am.* F Ausweg *m*; *the ~s pl. parl.* die Opposition; *Sport*: die nicht am Schlag befindliche Partei; **3.** auswärtig (*Wettspiel*); ✝ übernormal, Über... (*Größe*); **4.** *prp.* *~ of* aus, aus ... heraus; außerhalb; außer; aus, von; nicht gemäß, zuwider; *s. date, drawing, laugh, money*; **5.** F 'rausschmeißen; *Boxen*: niederschlagen.

out...: ~-and-~ ['autnd'aut] absolut, völlig, Erz...; **'~-and-'out·er** Extremist *m*, Radikale *m*; **'~·back** **1.** entlegen, dünn besiedelt; **2.** die entlegenen Gebiete *n/pl. Australiens*; **~'bal·ance** schwerer wiegen als; **~'bid** (*irr. bid*) überbieten; **'~·board** Außenbord...; **~'brave** an Kühnheit übertreffen; Trotz bieten (*dat.*); **'~·break** Ausbruch *m*; **'~·build·ing** Nebengebäude *n*; **'~·burst** Ausbruch *m*; **'~·cast** **1.** ausgestoßen; **2.** Ausgestoßene *m, f*;

'~·**caste** Kastenlose *m, f,* Ausgestoßene *m, f;* ~'**class** *Sport:* *j-m* weit überlegen sein; *be ~ed* deklassiert werden; '~·**come** Ergebnis *n,* Folge *f;* '~·**crop** Zutagetreten *n; geol.* Schichtenkopf *m;* '~·**cry** Aufschrei *m,* Schrei *m* der Entrüstung; ~-**'dat·ed** (zeitlich) überholt; ~'**dis·tance** überholen, hinter sich lassen; ~'**do** (*irr. do*) übertreffen, -bieten; '~·**door** *adj.,* '~'**doors** *adv.* Außen...; draußen, außer dem Hause (*a. parl.*); im Freien; *outdoor dress* Straßenkleidung *f.*

out·er ['autə] äußer, Außen...; ~ *garments pl.* Oberbekleidung *f;* '~-**most** äußerst.

out...: ~'**face** Trotz bieten (*dat.*); außer Fassung bringen; '~·**fall** Ausfluß *m,* Mündung *f;* '~·**fit** Ausrüstung *f,* Ausstattung *f; Am.* Haufen *m,* Trupp *m,* (Arbeits)Gruppe *f;* '~·**fit·ter** Ausrüstungslieferant *m;* Herrenausstatter *m;* ~'**flank** ⚔ überflügeln; '~·**flow** Ausfluß *m;* ~'**gen·er·al** überlisten; ~'**go 1.** (*irr. go*) schneller gehen als; *fig.* übertreffen; **2.** ['~] Ausgaben *f/pl.;* ~'**go·ing 1.** weg-, abgehend; **2.** Ausgehen *n; ~s pl.* Ausgaben *f/pl.;* ~'**grow** (*irr. grow*) *j-m* über den Kopf wachsen; herauswachsen aus; *fig.* entwachsen (*dat.*); '~·**growth** Schößling *m;* Auswuchs *m;* (natürliche) Folge *f;* Erzeugnis *n;* '~-**house** Nebengebäude *n;* Schuppen *m; Am.* Außenabort *m.*

out·ing ['autiŋ] Ausflug *m,* Tour *f; Rudern u. Pferderennen:* Training *n.*

out...: ~'**land·ish** ausländisch; fremdartig; seltsam (anmutend); unkultiviert; ~'**last** überdauern; '~·**law 1.** Geächtete *m, f,* Verfemte *m, f;* **2.** ächten; '~·**law·ry** Ächtung *f;* Verbrechertum *n;* '~·**lay** *Geld-*Auslage(n *pl.*) *f;* '~·**let** Auslaß *m;* Ausgang *m;* Aus-, Abfluß *m; fig.* Ventil *n;* ⚕ Absatzgebiet *n;* ⚡ Steckdose *f;* '~·**line 1.** Umriß *m;* Überblick *m;* Plan *m,* Skizze *f;* Abriß *m; ~s pl.* Grundzüge *m/pl.;* **2.** umreißen; skizzieren; *~d* scharf abgehoben; ~'**live** überleben; '~-**look** Aussicht *f,* Ausblick *m* (*a. fig.*); Auffassung *f;* Weltanschauung *f;* Standpunkt *m; pol.* Zielsetzung *f;* '~·**ly·ing** entlegen; ~·**ma'noeu·vre** ausmanövrieren; '~'**march** schneller marschieren als; ~'**match** weit übertreffen; ~'**mod·ed** unmodern, überholt, veraltet; '~·**most** äußerst; ~'**num·ber** an Zahl übertreffen; '~-**of-'door(s)** = *outdoor(s);* '~-**of-the-'way** entlegen; *fig.* ausgefallen; '~-**of-'work pay** Erwerbslosenunterstützung *f;* ~'**pace** überholen; '~-**pa·tient** ambulant Behandelte *m, f;* ~'**play** schlagen; '~-**post** Vorposten *m;* '~·**pour·ing** Erguß *m* (*a. fig.*); '~·**put** Produktion *f,* Ertrag *m;* (Produktions-) Leistung *f;* Ausbeute *f;* Ausstoß *m; Computer:* Datenausgabe *f.*

out·rage ['autreidʒ] **1.** Gewalttätigkeit *f;* Gewalttat *f* (*on* gegen); Attentat *n* (*on* auf *acc.*); gröbliche Beleidigung *f* (*on gen.*); **2.** gröblich beleidigen *od.* verletzen; Gewalt antun (*dat.*), schänden; **out'ra·geous** □ abscheulich; heftig; empörend; beschimpfend; zügellos.

out...: ~'**range** an Reichweite übertreffen; ~'**rank** in den Schatten stellen, übertreffen.

ou·tré ['u:trei] outriert, ausgefallen.

out...: ~'**reach** weiter reichen als; '~-**re·lief** Hauspflege *f für Arme;* ~'**ride** (*irr. ride*) schneller reiten als; ⚓ *Sturm* abreiten; '~·**rid·er** Vorreiter *m;* '~·**rig·ger** ⚓ Ausleger (-boot *n*) *m;* ~·**right** [*adj.* 'autrait, *adv.* aut'rait] gerade heraus; gänzlich, völlig, glatt; auf der Stelle; ~'**ri·val** übertreffen, -bieten; ~'**run** (*irr. run*) schneller laufen als; hinausgehen über (*acc.*); '~·**run·ner** Vorreiter *m;* Beipferd *n;* '~·**set** Anfang *m;* Aufbruch *m zur Reise;* ~'**shine** (*irr. shine*) überstrahlen; '~'**side 1.** Äußere *n;* Außenseite *f; fig. das* Äußerste; *at the ~* höchstens; **2.** äußer; Außen...; außenstehend; äußerst (*Preis*); *~ right Sport:* Rechtsaußen *m; ~ left* Linksaußen *m;* **3.** (dr)außen; nach (dr)außen; *~ of* = **4.** *prp.* außerhalb; über ... hinaus; '~'**sid·er** Außenseiter *m,* -stehende *m;* '~·**size** ⚕ Übergröße *f;* '~·**skirts** *pl.* Außenbezirke *m/pl.,* Peripherie *f;* (Stadt)Rand *m;* ~'**smart** *Am.* F übervorteilen; ~'**spoken** □ freimütig; '~'**spread** ausgestreckt, ausgebreitet; ~'**stand·ing** hervorragend (*a. fig.*); hervorstechend, auffallend; ausstehend (*Schuld*); offenstehend (*Frage*);

~ˈ**stay** länger bleiben als; ~ *one's welcome* länger als erwünscht bleiben; ~ˈ**stretched** = *outspread*; ~ˈ**strip** überholen (*a. fig.*); aus dem Felde schlagen, überflügeln; ˈ~**turn** Ertrag *m*; ~ˈ**vie** sich gegenseitig zu überbieten suchen; ~ˈ**vote** überstimmen.

out·ward [ˈautwəd] **1.** äußer, äußerlich; nach (dr)außen gerichtet; **2.** *adv. mst* ˈ**out·wards** auswärts, nach (dr)außen; ˈ**out·ward·ly** äußerlich; an der Oberfläche; ˈ**out·ward·ness** Äußerlichkeit *f*; äußere Form *f*.

out...: ~ˈ**wear** (*irr. wear*) überdauern; abnutzen; erschöpfen; ~ˈ**weigh** überwiegen; ~ˈ**wit** überlisten; ˈ~**work** ⚔ Außenwerk *n*; ⊕ Heimarbeit *f*; ˈ~**work·er** Heimarbeiter(in); ˈ~**worn** erschöpft; *fig.* abgegriffen; überholt.

ou·zel *orn.* [ˈuːzl] Drossel *f*.

o·val [ˈəuvəl] **1.** oval; **2.** Oval *n*.

o·va·ry [ˈəuvəri] *anat.* Eierstock *m*; ⚘ Fruchtknoten *m*.

o·va·tion [əuˈveiʃən] Ovation *f*, Huldigung *f*.

ov·en [ˈʌvn] Backofen *m*; ˈ~**bird** *orn. Am.* Goldkopf-Waldsänger *m*; ~ **cloth** Topflappen *m*; ~ **read·y** bratfertig.

o·ver [ˈəuvə] **1.** *adv.* über; hin-, herüber; drüben; vorbei, vorüber; allzusehr; übermäßig; darüber, mehr; von Anfang bis zu Ende; noch einmal; ~ *and above* neben, zusätzlich zu; (*all*) ~ *again* noch einmal (von vorn); ~ *against* gegenüber (*dat.*); *all* ~ über und über; ganz u. gar; ~ *and* ~ *again* immer wieder; *fifty times* ~ fünfzigmal hintereinander; *get s.th.* ~ (*and done*) *with* et. hinter sich bringen; *read* ~ durchlesen; **2.** *prp.* über; *all* ~ *the town* durch die ganze *od.* in der ganzen Stadt; ~ *night* über Nacht; ~ *a glass of wine* bei e-m Glas Wein; ~ *the way* gegenüber.

o·ver...: ˈ~ˈ**act** übertreiben; ˈ~**all** **1.** Arbeitsanzug *m*, -kittel *m*; Overall *m*; Kittel(schürze *f*) *m*; ~*s pl.* Überziehhosen *f/pl.*; **2.** allumfassend, gesamt, Gesamt...; ~ˈ**arch** überwölben; ~ˈ**awe** einschüchtern; ~ˈ**bal·ance** **1.** Übergewicht *n*, Mehr *n*; **2.** umkippen, das Gleichgewicht verlieren; überwiegen; ~ˈ**bear** (*irr. bear*) überwältigen; ~ˈ**bear·ing** □ anmaßend; ~ˈ**bid** (*irr. bid*) überbieten; ˈ~ˈ**blown** am Verblühen; ˈ~**board** ⚓ über Bord; ˈ~ˈ**brim** überfließen; ~ˈ**bur·den** überladen; ˈ~**cast** **1.** bewölkt; *fig.* traurig; **2.** Bewölkung *f*; ˈ~-ˈ**charge** **1.** überladen; überfordern; **2.** Überladung *f*; Überforderung *f*; ~ˈ**cloud** be-, überwölken, trüben; ˈ~**coat** Mantel *m*; ~ˈ**come** (*irr. come*) überwinden, -wältigen; besiegen; ˈ~-ˈ**con·fi·dent** □ allzu vertrauend (*of* auf *acc.*); zu selbstsicher; vermessen; ~ˈ**crowd** überfüllen; ~ˈ**do** (*irr. do*) zu viel tun; übertreiben, zu weit treiben; zu sehr kochen *od.* braten; überanstrengen; ~**done** [~ˈdʌn] übertrieben; überanstrengt; [ˈ~ˈdʌn] übergar; ˈ~**draft** ✝ überzogener Betrag *m*; ˈ~ˈ**draw** (*irr. draw*) übertreiben; ✝ *Konto* überziehen; ˈ~ˈ**dress** (sich) zu sehr herausputzen; ˈ~**drive** *mot.* Overdrive *m*, Schnellgang *m*; ˈ~ˈ**due** fällig; 🚂, ✝ überfällig; ˈ~ˈ**eat** (*irr. eat*): ~ *o.s.* sich überessen; ˈ~ˈ**es·ti·mate** überschätzen; ˈ~**ex**ˈ**pose** *phot.* überbelichten; ˈ~-**ex**ˈ**po·sure** *phot.* Überbelichtung *f*; ˈ~**fa**ˈ**tigue** **1.** übermüden; **2.** Übermüdung *f*; ˈ~ˈ**feed** (*irr. feed*) überfüttern; ~**flow** **1.** [~ˈfləu] *v/t.* überfluten; *v/i.* überfließen; **2.** [ˈ~fləu] Überfluß *m*; Überschwemmung *f*; Überfüllung *f*; ˈ~**freight** Überfracht *f*; ˈ~**ground** über der Erde (befindlich); ˈ~ˈ**grow** (*irr. grow*) überwuchern; zu sehr wachsen; ˈ~**growth** übermäßiges Wachstum *n*; ˈ~**hand** *Sport*: Überhand...; Hand-über-Hand-...; ~**hang** **1.** [ˈ~ˈhæŋ] (*irr. hang*) *v/t.* über (*acc.*) hängen; *v/i.* überhängen; *fig.* drohen; **2.** [ˈ~hæŋ] Überhang *m*; ~ˈ**haul** überholen (*gründlich nachsehen*; *einholen*); ~**head** **1.** [~ˈhed] *adv.* (dr)oben; **2.** [ˈ~hed] *adj.* ✝ allgemein (*Unkosten*); ~ *railway* Hochbahn *f*; ~ *wire* ⚡ Oberleitung *f*; **3.** [ˈ~hed]: ~*s pl.* ✝ allgemeine Unkosten *pl.*; ~ˈ**hear** (*irr. hear*) be-, erlauschen; zufällig hören; ˈ~ˈ**heat** überhitzen; ˈ~**in**ˈ**dulge** zu nachsichtig sein mit; *e-m Laster*, *e-r Leidenschaft* (übermäßig) frönen; (allzusehr) schwelgen in (*dat.*); ˈ~ˈ**is·sue** zu viel *Banknoten etc.* ausgeben;

'~'**joyed** hocherfreut, entzückt; '~·**kill** ⚔ Overkill *n*; gefährliches Übermaß *n*; '~·**land** Überland...; ~'**lap** *v/t.* übergreifen auf (*acc.*); überragen; überschneiden; *v/i.* ineinandergreifen, überlappen; ~·**lay 1.** [~'lei] (*irr. lay*) belegen; ⊕ überlagern; **2.** ['~lei] Auflage *f*; Deckchen *n*; ~ *mattress* Auflagematratze *f*; '~'**leaf** umseitig; '~'**leap** (*irr. leap*) springen über (*acc.*); ~ *o.s. fig.* über das Ziel hinausschießen; ~·**load 1.** ['~'ləud] überladen; **2.** ['~ləud] Überbelastung *f*; ~'**look** *Fehler etc.* übersehen; überblicken; beaufsichtigen; hinwegsehen über (*acc.*); '~·**lord** Ober(lehns)-herr *m*.

o·ver·ly ['əuvəli] übermäßig; allzu (-sehr).

o·ver...: '~·**man·tel** Kaminaufsatz *m*; ~'**mas·ter** überwältigen; ~'**match** *j-m* weit überlegen sein; '~'**much** zu viel; '~'**night 1.** am Vorabend; über Nacht; **2.** Nacht...; nächtlich; Übernachtungs...; ~ *bag* Reisetasche *f*; ~ *stop* Aufenthalt *m* für eine Nacht; '~·**pass** Überführung *f*; '~'**pay** (*irr. pay*) zu viel bezahlen; ~'**peo·pled** übervölkert; ~'**play** hochspielen, übertreiben; ~ *one's hand Karten*: sich überreizen; *fig.* sich übernehmen, es übertreiben; '~·**plus** Überschuß *m*; ~'**pow·er** überwältigen; '~'**print** überdrucken; '~·**pro'duc·tion** Überproduktion *f*; '~'**rate** überschätzen; ~'**reach** übervorteilen; ~ *o.s.* sich übernehmen; ~·**re'act** übertrieben reagieren (*to* auf *acc.*); ~'**ride** (*irr. ride*) *fig.* sich hinwegsetzen über (*acc.*); umstoßen; ~'**rid·ing** ausschlaggebend; ~'**rule** überstimmen; ⚖ verwerfen; ~'**run** (*irr. run*) überrennen; überziehen; überlaufen; bedecken; *Zeit* überschreiten; *typ.* umbrechen; '~'**sea 1.** *a.* ~*s* überseeisch; Übersee...; ~*s aid* Entwicklungshilfe *f*; **2.** ~*s* in *od.* nach Übersee; '~'**see** (*irr. see*) beaufsichtigen; '~·**se·er** Aufseher *m*; ~'**set** (*irr. set*) umstoßen; *fig.* zerrütten; '~·**sew** (*irr. sew*) überwendlich nähen; ~'**shad·ow** überschatten, verdunkeln; '~·**shoe** Überschuh *m*; '~'**shoot** (*irr. shoot*) über *ein Ziel* hinausschießen; ~ *o.s.* zu weit gehen; '~'**shot** oberschlächtig (*Wasserrad*); '~·**sight** Versehen *n*; '~·**sim·pli·fi'ca·tion** allzu große Vereinfachung *f*; '~'**sleep** (*irr. sleep*) *a.* ~ *o.s.* verschlafen; '~·**sleeve** Ärmelschoner *m*; '~·**spill** (*bsd.* Bevölkerungs)Überschuß *m*; ~'**staffed** überbesetzt; '~'**state** übertreiben; '~'**state·ment** Übertreibung *f*; '~'**step** überschreiten; '~'**stock** überfüllen; ~·**strain 1.** ['~'strein] (sich) überanstrengen; *fig.* übertreiben; **2.** ['~strein] Überanstrengung *f*; ~·**strung** ['~'strʌŋ] überreizt; ['~strʌŋ] kreuzsaitig (*Klavier*); '~·**sub'scribe** *Anleihe* überzeichnen; '~·**sup'ply** Überangebot *n*.

o·vert ['əuvə:t] offen(kundig).

over...: '~'**take** (*irr. take*) einholen; *et.* auf-, nachholen; *j.* überraschen; '~'**tax** zu hoch besteuern; *fig.* überschätzen; übermäßig in Anspruch nehmen; ~·**throw 1.** [~'θrəu] (*irr. throw*) (um)stürzen (*a. fig.*); vernichten, besiegen; **2.** ['~θrəu] Sturz *m*; Vernichtung *f*; ⚔ Niederlage *f*; '~·**time** Überstunden *f/pl.*; '~'**tire** übermüden; '~·**tone** ♪ Oberton *m*; *fig.* Unter-, Zwischenton *m*; '~'**top** überragen; '~·**trump** übertrumpfen.

over·ture ['əuvətjuə] ♪ Ouvertüre *f*, Vorspiel *n*; Vorschlag *m*, Antrag *m*.

o·ver...: ~·**turn 1.** ['~tə:n] Umsturz *m*; **2.** [~'tə:n] umstürzen, -werfen; kentern (lassen); '~'**val·ue** zu hoch einschätzen; überschätzen; ~'**ween·ing** eingebildet; ~·**weight 1.** ['~weit] Übergewicht *n*; **2.** ['~'weit] überladen, -lasten; ~'**whelm** überhäufen, -schütten (*a. fig.*); überwältigen (*a. fig.*); erdrücken; '~'**wise** □ überklug; ~·**work 1.** ['~wə:k] übermäßige Arbeit *f*; Überarbeitung *f*; **2.** [~'wə:k] (*irr. work*) sich überarbeiten; schinden, überanstrengen; '~'**wrought** überarbeitet; überreizt.

o·vi·duct ⚕ ['əuvidʌkt] Eileiter *m*; **o·vi·form** ['~fɔ:m] eiförmig; **o'vip·a·rous** *zo.* [~pərəs] eierlegend; **o·vule** *biol.* ['əuvju:l] Ovulum *n*, kleines Ei *n*; **o·vum** *biol.* ['əuvəm], *pl.* **o·va** ['əuvə] Ovum *n*, Ei(zelle *f*) *n*.

owe [əu] *Geld, Dank etc.* schulden, schuldig sein; verdanken; *Sport*: vorgeben; ~ *s.o. a grudge* Groll gegen j. hegen.

ow·ing ['əuiŋ] schuldig; ~ *to* infolge (*gen.*), wegen (*gen.*), dank (*dat.*); *be* ~ *to* herkommen von, zu verdanken *od.* zuzuschreiben sein

(*dat.*).
owl *orn.* [aul] Eule *f*; **owl·et** [ˈaulit] (junge) Eule *f*; ˈ**owl·ish** □ eulenhaft, -artig.
own [əun] **1.** eigen; wirklich, richtig; einzig, innig geliebt; *my ~ self* ich selbst; *~ brother to s.o.* j-s rechter Bruder; *she makes her ~ clothes* sie näht ihre Kleider selbst; **2.** *my ~* mein Eigentum *n*; meine Angehörigen *pl.*; *a house of one's ~* ein eigenes Haus *n*; *come into one's ~* zu s-m Recht kommen; *get one's ~ back* F sich rächen; sich sein Recht holen; *hold one's ~* standhalten; sich behaupten; *on one's ~* F selbständig; von sich aus, auf eigene Faust; allein; **3.** besitzen; zugeben, zugestehen; anerkennen; sich bekennen (*to* zu); *~ up* (*to*) F bekennen.
own·er [ˈəunə] Eigentümer(in), Inhaber(in); ˈ**~-ˈdriv·er** Herrenfahrer *m*; ˈ**~·less** herrenlos; ˈ**~-ˈoc·cu·pied** vom Eigentümer bewohnt (*Haus*); ˈ**own·er·ship** Eigentum(srecht) *n*, Besitz(recht *n*) *m*.
ox [ɔks], *pl.* **ox·en** [ˈɔksən] Ochs *m*, Ochse *m*; Rind *n*.
ox·al·ic ac·id ⚗ [ɔkˈsælikˈæsid] Oxal-, Kleesäure *f*.
Ox·bridge [ˈɔksbridʒ] (die Universitäten *f/pl.*) Oxford und Cambridge.
ox-cart [ˈɔkskɑːt] Ochsenkarren *m*; **ox·en** [ˈɔksən] *pl. von ox*; ˈ**ox-eye** ⚘ Gänseblümchen *n*.
Ox·ford shoes [ˈɔksfədˈʃuːz] *pl.* Halbschuhe *m/pl.*
ox·i·da·tion ⚗ [ɔksiˈdeiʃən] Oxydation *f*, Oxydierung *f*; **ox·ide** [ˈɔksaid] Oxyd *n*; **ox·i·dize** [ˈɔksidaiz] oxydieren.
ox·lip ⚘ [ˈɔkslip] hohe Schlüsselblume *f*.
Ox·o·ni·an [ɔkˈsəunjən] **1.** Oxforder, Oxford...; **2.** Student *m od.* Absolvent *m* der Universität Oxford.
ox·tail soup [ˈɔksteilˈsuːp] Ochsenschwanzsuppe *f*.
ox·y·a·cet·y·lene [ɔksiəˈsetiliːn] Azetylensauerstoff *m*; *~ torch* Schweißbrenner *m*.
ox·y·gen ⚗ [ˈɔksidʒən] Sauerstoff *m*; **ox·y·gen·ate** [ɔkˈsidʒineit] mit Sauerstoff versetzen *od.* behandeln.
ox·y·hy·dro·gen ⚗ [ˈɔksiˈhaidridʒən] Knallgas *n*.
o·yer ⚖ [ˈɔiə] Verhör *n*.
o·yez [əuˈjes] hört (zu)!; Ruhe!
oys·ter [ˈɔistə] Auster *f*; *attr.* Austern...; ˈ**~-bed** Austernbank *f*.
o·zone ⚗ [ˈəuzəun] Ozon *n*; *~* **lay·er** Ozonschicht *f*; **o·zon·ic** [əuˈzɔnik] ozonhaltig; Ozon...

P

P [piː]: *mind one's Ps and Qs* sich sehr in acht nehmen.
pa F [pɑː] Papa *m*.
pab·u·lum [ˈpæbjuləm] Nahrung *f*.
pace [peis] **1.** Schritt *m* (*a. als Maß*); Gang(art *f*) *m*; Paßgang *m*; Geschwindigkeit *f*, Tempo *n*; *keep ~ with* Schritt halten *od.* mitkommen mit; *put s.o. through his ~s* j. auf Herz u. Nieren prüfen; *set the ~* das Tempo bestimmen, Schrittmacher sein; **2.** *v/t.* abschreiten; *Sport*: Schrittmacher sein für; *v/i.* (einher)schreiten; (im) Paß gehen; **paced 1.** ... schreitend; **2.** *Sport*: mit Schrittmachern; ˈ**pace-mak·er** *Sport*: Schrittmacher *m*; ⚕ Herzschrittmacher *m*; ˈ**pac·er** Schreitende *m*; Fußgänger *m*; = *pace-maker.*
pach·y·derm *zo.* [ˈpækidəːm] Dickhäuter *m*.
pa·cif·ic [pəˈsifik] **1.** (*~ally*) friedlich; *the* ♀ *Ocean* = **2.** *the* ♀ der Pazifik, der Pazifische *od.* Stille Ozean;
pac·i·fi·ca·tion [pæsifiˈkeiʃən] Befriedung *f*; Beruhigung *f*.
pac·i·fi·er [ˈpæsifaiə] Friedensstifter *m*; *Am.* Schnuller *m*; ˈ**pac·i·fism** Pazifismus *m*; ˈ**pac·i·fist** Pazifist(in).
pac·i·fy [ˈpæsifai] besänftigen, beruhigen; *Land* befrieden.
pack [pæk] **1.** Pack *m*, *n*; Packen *m*;

Paket *n*; Ballen *m*; Spiel *n Karten*; Meute *f Hunde*, Rudel *n Wölfe*; Rotte *f*, Bande *f*; Packung *f* (*a.* ⚕); *a.* ~*-ice* Packeis *n*; *a* ~ *of nonsense* lauter Unsinn *m*; **2.** *v/t.* packen; *oft* ~ *up* zs.-, verpacken; einpacken (*a.* ⚕); *a.* ~ *off* fortjagen; parteiisch zs.-setzen; *Am.* F (bei sich) tragen (*als Gepäck, Ausrüstung*); bepacken, vollstopfen; ⊕ dichten; *v/i. a.* ~ *up* packen; sich packen (lassen) (*Ware*); *send s.o.* ~*ing* j. fortjagen; ~ *up* F aufhören; '**pack·age** Pack *m*, Ballen *m*; *bsd. Am.* Paket *n*; Pakkung *f*; Frachtstück *n*; Verpakkung *f*; Verhandlungspaket *n*; ~ *deal* Pauschalangebot *n*; ~ *tour* Pauschalreise *f*; '**pack-an·i·mal** Tragtier *n*; '**pack·er** Packer(in); *Am.* Konservenfabrikant *m*; **pack·et** ['pækit] Paket *n*; Päckchen *n*; Pakkung *f*, Schachtel *f*; *a.* ~*-boat* Postschiff *n*, Paketboot *n*; *catch a* ~ *sl.* schwer verwundet werden; '**pack-horse** Packpferd *n*; Saumtier *n*; *fig.* Packesel *m*.

pack·ing ['pækiŋ] Packen *n*; Verpackung *f*; Packmaterial *n*; ⊕ Dichtung *f*; *attr.* Pack...; '~**-box** 🚂 Stopfbüchse *f*; ~ **house** *Am.* (*bsd.* Fleisch)Konservenfabrik *f*.

pack·thread ['pækθred] Bindfaden *m*, Packzwirn *m*.

pact [pækt] Vertrag *m*, Pakt *m*.

pad[1] *sl.* [pæd] *a.* ~ *it*, ~ *along* tippeln.

pad[2] [~] **1.** Polster *n*; *Sport*: Beinschutz *m*; Schreibblock *m*; Stempelkissen *n*; *hunt.* Pfote *f*; (Abschuß)Rampe *f*; **2.** (aus)polstern; wattieren; ~ *out fig.* auffüllen; ~*ded cell* Gummizelle *f*; '**pad·ding** Auspolstern *n*; Polsterung *f*, Wattierung *f*; *fig.* Lückenbüßer *m*.

pad·dle ['pædl] **1.** Paddel(ruder) *n*; ⚓ (Rad)Schaufel *f*; **2.** rudern, *bsd.* paddeln; planschen; *paddling pool* Planschbecken *n*; ~ *one's own canoe* sich selbst durchschlagen; '~**-box** ⚓ Radkasten *m*; '~**-steam·er** ⚓ Raddampfer *m*; '~**-wheel** Schaufelrad *n*.

pad·dock ['pædək] (Pferde)Koppel *f*; *Sport*: Sattelplatz *m*.

pad·dy[1] ⚘ ['pædi] Reis *m* in Hülsen.

pad·dy[2] F [~] Wutanfall *m*.

pad·dy wag·on *Am.* P ['pædiwægən] Gefangenenwagen *m*, „Grüne Minna" *f*.

pad·lock ['pædlɔk] Vorhängeschloß *n*.

pad·re F ⚔ ['pɑːdri] Kaplan *m*, Geistliche *m*.

pae·an ['piːən] Dank-, Lob-, Freudengesang *m*.

paed·er·as·ty ['pedəræsti] Päderastie *f*, Knabenliebe *f*.

pae·di·a·tri·cian [piːdiə'triʃən] Kinderarzt *m*; **pae·di·at·rics** [~'ætriks] *sg.* Kinderheilkunde *f*.

pa·gan ['peigən] **1.** heidnisch; **2.** Heide *m*, Heidin *f*; '**pa·gan·ism** Heidentum *n*.

page[1] [peidʒ] **1.** Page *m*; Edelknabe *m*; junger Diener *m*; Hotelpage *m*; *Am.* Amtsdiener *m*; **2.** *Am.* (durch e-n Pagen) holen lassen.

page[2] [~] **1.** *Buch*-Seite *f*; *fig.* Blatt *n*; **2.** paginieren.

pag·eant ['pædʒənt] historisches Schau- *od.* Festspiel *n*; festlicher Umzug *m*; '**pag·eant·ry** Prunk *m*, Gepränge *n*.

pag·i·nate ['pædʒineit] *s. page*[2] 2; **pag·i'na·tion** Paginierung *f*.

pa·go·da [pə'gəudə] Pagode *f*.

paid [peid] *pret. u. p.p. von pay* 2.

pail [peil] Eimer *m*.

pail·lasse ['pæliæs] Strohsack *m*.

pain [pein] **1.** Pein *f*, Schmerz *m*; Kummer *m*; Strafe *f*; ~*s pl.* Leiden *n/pl.*; Mühe *f*; Wehen *f/pl.*; *on od. under* ~ *of death* bei Todesstrafe; *be in* ~ leiden; *be a* ~ *in the neck* F e-m auf den Wecker gehen; *be at* ~*s*, *take* ~*s* sich Mühe geben; **2.** *j-m* weh tun, *j.* schmerzen; **pain·ful** □ ['~ful] schmerzhaft, schmerzlich; peinlich; mühevoll; '**pain-kill·er** schmerzstillendes Mittel *n*; '**pain·less** □ schmerzlos; '**pains·tak·ing 1.** □ arbeitsam; sorgfältig; **2.** Sorgfalt *f*.

paint [peint] **1.** Farbe *f*; Schminke *f*; Anstrich *m*; *wet* ~! frisch gestrichen!; **2.** (be)malen; anstreichen; (sich) schminken; *fig.* malen, schildern; ~ *out* übermalen; '~**-box** Malkasten *m*; '~**-brush** Malerpinsel *m*.

paint·er[1] ['peintə] Maler(in).

paint·er[2] ⚓ [~] Fangleine *f*.

paint·ing ['peintiŋ] Malen *n*; Malerei *f*; Gemälde *n*.

paint·work ['peintwəːk] *Auto*: Lack *m*; Anstrich *m*.

pair [pɛə] **1.** Paar *n*; Gespann *n*; Partner *m*; Gegenstück *n*; *a* ~ *of* *scissors* eine Schere *f*; *in* ~*s* paarweise; **2.** (sich) paaren; zs.-passen; *a.* ~ *off* paarweise weggehen; ~ *off with* F heiraten.

pa·ja·mas [pə'dʒɑ:məz] = *pyjamas.*

Pa·kis·ta·ni [pɑ:kis'tɑ:ni] **1.** Pakistaner(in); **2.** pakistanisch.

pal *sl.* [pæl] **1.** Kamerad *m*, Kumpel *m*; **2.** ~ *up with s.o.* sich mit j-m anfreunden.

pal·ace ['pælis] Palast *m.*

pal·ae·o- ['pæliəu] Alt..., Früh..., Ur..., Vor...; **pal·ae·o·lith·ic** [~əu'liθik] altsteinzeitlich; **pal·ae·on·tol·o·gy** [~ɔn'tɔlədʒi] Paläontologie *f.*

pal·at·a·ble □ ['pælətəbl] schmackhaft (*a. fig.*); '**pal·at·a·ble·ness** Schmackhaftigkeit *f.*

pal·a·tal ['pælətl] **1.** Gaumen...; **2.** *gr.* Gaumenlaut *m*, Palatal *m.*

pal·ate ['pælit] Gaumen *m*; Geschmack *m* (*a. fig.*).

pa·la·tial □ [pə'leiʃəl] palastartig.

pa·lat·i·nate [pə'lætinit] Pfalzgrafschaft *f*; *the* ♀ die Pfalz.

pal·a·tine ['pælətain] pfälzisch; Pfalz...; *Count* ♀ Pfalzgraf *m.*

pa·lav·er [pə'lɑ:və] **1.** Unterredung *f*; Geschwätz *n*, Palaver *n*; *sl.* Geschäft *n*; **2.** (be)schwatzen; schmeicheln (*dat.*).

pale[1] [peil] **1.** □ blaß, bleich; fahl; ~ *ale* helles, starkes Ale *n*; **2.** *v/t.* bleich machen, bleichen; *v/i.* bleich werden, (er)bleichen.

pale[2] [~] Pfahl *m*; *die* Grenzen (des Erlaubten).

pale-face ['peilfeis] Bleichgesicht *n.*

pale·ness ['peilnis] Blässe *f.*

pa·le·o- ['pæliəu] *s. palaeo-.*

pal·ette *paint.* ['pælit] Palette *f*; '**~-knife** Streichmesser *n.*

pal·frey ['pɔ:lfri] Zelter *m.*

pal·imp·sest ['pælimpsest] Palimpsest *m, n* (*zweimal beschriebenes Pergament*).

pal·ing ['peiliŋ] Pfahlzaun *m.*

pal·i·sade [pæli'seid] **1.** Palisade *f*; Staket *n*; ~*s pl. Am.* Steilufer *n*; **2.** umpfählen.

pall[1] [pɔ:l] **1.** Bahrtuch *n*; *fig.* Decke *f*, Wolke *f*; **2.** einhüllen.

pall[2] [~] schal werden, den Reiz verlieren (*upon s.o.* für j.).

pal·la·di·um [pə'leidjəm] Palladium *n*; Hort *m*, Schutz *m.*

pall·bear·er ['pɔ:lbɛərə] Sargträger *m.*

pal·let ['pælit] Strohsack *m.*

pal·liasse ['pæliæs] = *paillasse.*

pal·li·ate ['pælieit] bemänteln; beschönigen; lindern; **pal·li'a·tion** Bemäntelung *f*; Beschönigung *f*; Linderung *f*; **pal·li·a·tive** ['~ətiv] **1.** bemäntelnd; lindernd; **2.** Linderungsmittel *n*; *fig.* Bemäntelung *f.*

pal·lid □ ['pælid] blaß; '**pal·lid·ness, pal·lor** ['pælə] Blässe *f.*

pal·ly F ['pæli] freundlich, gesellig; *be* ~ *with s.o.* mit j-m gut Freund sein.

palm [pɑ:m] **1.** Handfläche *f*; Handbreite *f* (*als Maß*); Schaufel *f des Ankers, Hirschgeweihes*; ♣ Palme *f* (*fig. Sieg*); *have an itching* ~ bestechlich sein; **2.** betasten; in der Hand verbergen; ~ *s.th. off upon s.o.* j-m et. andrehen; **pal·mer** ['pɑ:mə] Pilger *m*; '**palm·ist** Handleser(in); '**palm·is·try** Handlesekunst *f*; '**palm-oil** Palmöl *n*; *co.* Schmiergeld(er *pl.*) *n*; **Palm Sunday** Palmsonntag *m*; '**palm-tree** Palme *f*; '**palm·y** glücklich, blühend.

pal·pa·ble ['pælpəbl] □ fühlbar; *fig.* handgreiflich, klar, eindeutig, augenfällig.

pal·pi·tate ['pælpiteit] schlagen, pochen (*Herz*); zittern; **pal·pi'ta·tion** Herzklopfen *n.*

pal·sy ['pɔ:lzi] **1.** Lähmung *f*; *fig.* Ohnmacht *f*; **2.** *fig.* lähmen.

pal·ter ['pɔ:ltə] sein Spiel treiben (*with* mit).

pal·tri·ness ['pɔ:ltrinis] Erbärmlichkeit *f*; '**pal·try** □ erbärmlich; armselig; schäbig; wertlos.

pam·pas ['pæmpəz] *pl. die* Pampas *pl.*

pam·per ['pæmpə] verzärteln.

pam·phlet ['pæmflit] Flugschrift *f*, Broschüre *f*; **pam·phlet·eer** [~'tiə] Pamphletist *m.*

pan [pæn] **1.** Pfanne *f*; Tiegel *m*; **2.** *v/t. Gold etc.* waschen; *Kamera* schwenken; *Am.* F heruntermachen (*scharf kritisieren*); *v/i.* schwenken (*Kamera*); ~ *out* sich bezahlt machen.

pan... [~] all..., gesamt...; All...; Gesamt...; pan..., Pan...

pan·a·ce·a [pænə'siə] Allheilmittel *n.*

pan·cake ['pænkeik] Pfannkuchen *m*; ~ *landing* ✈ Bumslandung *f.*

pan·cre·as ⚕ ['pæŋkriəs] Bauch-

speicheldrüse *f*.
pan·da ['pændə] Panda *m* (*Bärenart*); ~ **car** Streifenwagen *m*.
pan·de·mo·ni·um *fig*. [pændi'məunjəm] Hölle(nlärm *m*) *f*.
pan·der ['pændə] **1.** Vorschub leisten (*to dat*.); kuppeln; **2.** Kuppler (-in).
pane [pein] (Fenster)Scheibe *f*; ⊕ Fach *n*, Feld *n*.
pan·e·gyr·ic [pæni'dʒirik] Lobrede *f*; **pan·e'gyr·ist** Lobredner *m*.
pan·el ['pænl] **1.** Δ Fach *n*, Feld *n*; Füllung *f e-r Tür etc*.; *paint*. Holztafel *f*; Einsatz *m am Kleid*; ⚖ Geschworenenliste *f*; *die* Geschworenen *m/pl*.; Ausschuß *m*; Diskussionsteilnehmer *m/pl*., -redner *m/pl*.; Verzeichnis *n* der Kassenärzte; **2.** täfeln; in Felder einteilen; ~ **dis·cus·sion** Podiumsdiskussion *f*; '~-**doc·tor** Kassenarzt *m*; '**pan·el·ist** Diskussionsteilnehmer *m*; '**pan·el·(l)ing** Täfelung *f*.
pang [pæŋ] plötzlicher Schmerz *m*, Weh *n*; *fig*. Angst *f*, Qual *f*; ~*s pl. of hunger* nagender Hunger *m*.
pan·go·lin *zo*. [pæŋ'gəulin] Schuppentier *n*.
pan·han·dle ['pænhændl] **1.** Pfannenstiel *m*; *Am*. schmaler Fortsatz *m e-s Staatsgebiets*; **2.** *Am*. F betteln; '**pan·han·dler** *Am*. F Bettler *m*.
pan·ic ['pænik] **1.** panisch; **2.** Panik *f*, panischer Schrecken *m*; ~ *buying* Angstkäufe *m/pl*.; **3.** *pret. u. p.p.* '**pan·icked** Angst bekommen; '**pan·ick·y** F beunruhigend; unruhig (*at* über *acc*.); '**pan·ic-·mon·ger** Bangemacher(in); '**pan·ic-strick·en** von panischer Angst erfüllt.
pan·nier ['pæniə] (Trag)Korb *m*.
pan·ni·kin ['pænikin] Kännchen *n*; Pfännchen *n*.
pan·o·ply ['pænəpli] volle Rüstung *f*; *fig*. Anordnung *f*, Reihe *f*.
pan·o·ra·ma [pænə'rɑːmə] Panorama *n*, Rundblick *m*; **pan·o·ram·ic** [~'ræmik] (~*ally*) panoramahaft; umfassend.
pan·sy ['pænzi] ⚘ Stiefmütterchen *n*; *a*. ~-*boy* Weichling *m*; Homosexuelle *m*.
pant [pænt] *v/i*. schnappen (*for breath* nach Luft); keuchen, schnaufen; klopfen (*Herz*); verlangen, lechzen (*for, after* nach); *v/t*. ~ *out* (hervor)keuchen.
pan·ta·loon [pæntə'luːn] Hanswurst *m*; ~*s pl. co. od. Am. für pants*.
pan·tech·ni·con [pæn'teknikən] *a*. ~ *van* Möbelwagen *m*.
pan·the·ism ['pænθiizm] Pantheismus *m*; **pan·the'is·tic** (~*ally*) pantheistisch.
pan·ther *zo*. ['pænθə] Panther *m*.
pant·ies F ['pæntiz] *pl*. Damenschlüpfer *m*; Kinderhöschen *n*.
pan·tile ['pæntail] Dachpfanne *f*.
pan·to F ['pæntəu] = *pantomime*.
pan·to·graph ⊕ ['pæntəugrɑːf] Storchschnabel *m*.
pan·to·mime ['pæntəmaim] Pantomime *f*; revueartiges Märchenspiel *n*; **pan·to·mim·ic** [~'mimik] (~*ally*) pantomimisch.
pan·try ['pæntri] Speise-, Vorratskammer *f*; Geschirr- und Wäschekammer *f*.
pants [pænts] *pl*. Hose *f*; *Am*. Herrenhose *f*; ✝ lange Unterhose *f*.
pant(s) suit ['pæntsuːt] *Am*. Hosenanzug *m*.
pan·ty ['pænti]: ~ **gir·dle** Miederhöschen *n*; ~ **hose** *bsd. Am*. Strumpfhose *f*.
pap [pæp] Brei *m*.
pa·pa [pə'pɑː] Papa *m*.
pa·pa·cy ['peipəsi] Papsttum *n*.
pa·pal □ ['peipəl] päpstlich.
pa·per ['peipə] **1.** Papier *n*; Zeitung *f*; Prüfungsaufgabe *f*; Vortrag *m*, Aufsatz *m*; *a*. ~ *money* Papiergeld *n*; ~*s pl*. (Ausweis)Papiere *n/pl*.; *send in one's* ~*s* zurücktreten; **2.** tapezieren; '~·**back** Taschenbuch *n*, Paperback *n*; ~ **bag** (Papier)Tüte *f*; '~-**chase** Schnitzeljagd *f*; '~-**clip** Büroklammer *f*; ~ **cred·it** ✝ Wechselkredit *m*; ~ **cup** Pappbecher *m*; '~-**fast·en·er** Musterklammer *f*; '~-**hang·er** Tapezierer *m*; '~-**hang·ings** *pl*. Tapeten *f/pl*.; ~ **knife** Brieföffner *m*; '~-**mill** Papierfabrik *f*; ~ **plate** Pappteller *m*; ~ **tape** Lochstreifen *m*; '~'**thin** hauchdünn; '~-**weight** Briefbeschwerer *m*; '**pa·per·y** papierartig, -dünn.
pa·pier mâ·ché ['pæpjei'mɑːʃei] Papiermaché *n*.
pa·pist *contp*. ['peipist] Papist *m*, Katholik *m*.
pap·py ['pæpi] breiig.
pap·ri·ka ['pæprikə] Paprika *m*.
pa·py·rus [pə'paiərəs] Papyrus *m*.

par [pɑ:] ⚕ Nennwert *m*, Pari *n*; *above (below)* ~ über (unter) Pari; *at* ~ zum Nennwert; *be on a* ~ *with* gleich, ebenbürtig sein (*dat.*).

par·a F ['pærə] Fallschirmjäger *m*.

par·a·ble ['pærəbl] Parabel *f*, Gleichnis *n*.

pa·rab·o·la ⅍ [pə'ræbələ] Parabel *f*; **par·a·bol·ic, par·a·bol·i·cal** □ [pærə'bɔlik(əl)] in Gleichnissen; ⅍ parabolisch.

par·a·chute ['pærəʃu:t] Fallschirm *m*; '**par·a·chut·ist** Fallschirmspringer(in).

pa·rade [pə'reid] **1.** ⚔ (Truppen-)Parade *f*; Appell *m*; *eccl.* Prozession *f*; Zurschaustellung *f*; Promenade *f*; (Um)Zug *m*; Modenschau *f*; *programme* ~ *Radio*: Programmvorschau *f*; *make a* ~ *of s.th.* et. zur Schau stellen; **2.** ⚔ antreten (lassen); vorbeimarschieren (lassen); zur Schau stellen; **pa'rade-ground** ⚔ Exerzier-, Paradeplatz *m*.

par·a·digm *gr.* ['pærədaim] Paradigma *n*, (Muster)Beispiel *n*.

par·a·dise ['pærədais] Paradies *n*.

par·a·dis·i·ac [pærə'disiæk] paradiesisch.

par·a·dox ['pærədɔks] Paradox(on) *n*; **par·a'dox·i·cal** □ paradox, widersinnig.

par·af·fin ⚗ ['pærəfin] Paraffin *n*.

par·a·gon ['pærəgən] Vorbild *n*; Muster *n*; Ausbund *m*.

par·a·graph ['pærəgrɑ:f] Absatz *m*, Abschnitt *m*; Paragraph(zeichen *n*) *m*; kurze Zeitungsnotiz *f*.

par·a·keet *orn.* ['pærəki:t] Sittich *m*.

par·al·lel ['pærəlel] **1.** parallel, gleichlaufend; *fig.* entsprechend; **2.** Parallele *f* (*a. fig.*); Breitengrad *m*; Gegenstück *n*; Vergleich *m*; *without (a)* ~ ohnegleichen; **3.** vergleichen; entsprechen; gleichen; parallel laufen (mit); ~ **bars** *pl. Sport*: Barren *m*; '**par·al·lel·ism** Parallelismus *m*; **par·al'lel·o·gram** ⅍ [~ləugræm] Parallelogramm *n*.

par·a·lyse ['pærəlaiz] lähmen; *fig.* unwirksam machen; **pa·ral·y·sis** ⚕ [pə'rælisis] Paralyse *f*, Lähmung *f*; **par·a·lyt·ic** [pærə'litik] **1.** (~*ally*) paralytisch; gelähmt; **2.** Gelähmte *m, f*.

par·a·mil·i·tar·y ['pærə'militəri] halbmilitärisch.

par·a·mount ['pærəmaunt] oberst, höchst, hervorragend, überragend; größer, höher stehend (*to* als).

par·a·mour *rhet.* ['pærəmuə] Geliebte *m, f*; Buhle *m, f*.

par·a·noi·a ⚕ [pærə'nɔiə] Verfolgungswahn *m*; **par·a·noi·ac** [~'nɔiæk] **1.** paranoisch; **2.** Paranoiker *m*; **par·a·noid** ['~nɔid] paranoid.

par·a·pet ['pærəpit] ⚔ Brustwehr *f*; Brüstung *f*; Geländer *n*.

par·a·pher·na·li·a [pærəfə'neiljə] *pl.* Ausrüstung *f*; Zubehör *n, m*; Drum u. Dran *n*.

par·a·phrase ['pærəfreiz] **1.** Paraphrase *f*, Umschreibung *f*; **2.** paraphrasieren, umschreiben.

par·a·ple·gi·a ⚕ [pærə'pli:dʒə] Querschnitt(s)lähmung *f*; **par·a'ple·gic** **1.** querschnitt(s)gelähmt; **2.** Querschnitt(s)gelähmte *m*.

par·a·site ['pærəsait] Parasit *m*, Schmarotzer *m*; **par·a·sit·ic, par·a·sit·i·cal** □ [~'sitik(əl)] schmarotzerhaft, parasitisch.

par·a·sol [pærə'sɔl] Sonnenschirm *m*.

par·a·troop·er ['pærətru:pə] ⚔ Fallschirmjäger *m*; '**par·a·troops** *pl.* Luftlandetruppen *f/pl*.

par·a·ty·phoid ⚕ ['pærə'taifɔid] Paratyphus *m*.

par·boil ['pɑ:bɔil] ankochen; *fig.* braten, schmoren.

par·cel ['pɑ:sl] **1.** Paket *n*, Päckchen *n*; ⚕ Partie *f*; *contp.* Haufe(n) *m*; (Land)Parzelle *f*; **2.** ~ *out* (in Stükke) teilen, *Land* parzellieren; ~ **post** Paketpost *f*.

parch [pɑ:tʃ] rösten, (aus)dörren; ~*ing heat* sengende Hitze *f*.

parch·ment ['pɑ:tʃmənt] Pergament *n*.

pard *sl.* [pɑ:d] Partner *m*.

par·don ['pɑ:dn] **1.** Verzeihung *f*; ⚖ Begnadigung *f*; *eccl.* Ablaß *m*; *I beg your* ~ (ich bitte um) Verzeihung!; wie bitte?; **2.** verzeihen (*s.o.* j-m; *s.th.* et.); *j.* begnadigen; '**par·don·a·ble** □ verzeihlich; '**par·don·er** *hist.* Ablaßkrämer *m*.

pare [pɛə] *Fingernägel etc.* (be-)schneiden; *Äpfel etc.* schälen; ~ *away*, ~ *down fig.* beschneiden.

par·ent ['pɛərənt] **1.** Vater *m*, Mutter *f*; Elternteil *m*; *fig.* Ursache *f*; ~*s pl.* Eltern *pl.*; ~*-teacher association* Elternbeirat *m*; ~*-teacher meeting* Elternabend *m*; **2.** *fig.* Mutter...; Stamm...; Ursprungs...; '**par·ent-**

age Herkunft *f*; Elternschaft *f*; **pa·ren·tal** □ [pə'rentl] elterlich.
pa·ren·the·sis [pə'renθisis], *pl.* **pa'ren·the·ses** [~si:z] Parenthese *f*, Einschaltung *f*; *typ.* (runde) Klammer *f*; **par·en·the·tic, par·en·thet·i·cal** □ [pærən'θetik(əl)] eingeschaltet, beiläufig.
par·ent·hood ['pɛərənthud] Elternschaft *f*; '**par·ent·less** elternlos.
pa·ri·ah ['pæriə] Paria *m*, Rechtlose *m, f*.
pa·ri·e·tal [pə'raiitl] Wand...; ~ *bone anat.* Scheitelbein *n*.
par·ing ['pɛəriŋ] Schälen *n*, Abschneiden *n*; ~*s pl.* Schalen *f/pl.*, Schnipsel *m/pl.*; '**~-knife** ⊕ Schälmesser *n*; Schustermesser *n*.
par·ish ['pæriʃ] **1.** Kirchspiel *n*, Gemeinde *f*; *go on the* ~ der Gemeinde zur Last fallen; **2.** Pfarr...; Gemeinde...; ~ *clerk* Küster *m*; ~ *council* Gemeinderat *m*; ~ *register* Kirchenbuch *n*; **pa·rish·ion·er** [pə'riʃənə] Pfarrkind *n*, Gemeindeglied *n*.
Pa·ri·sian [pə'rizjən] **1.** *adj.* Pariser; **2.** Pariser(in).
par·i·ty ['pæriti] Gleichheit *f*; *Börse*: Parität *f*.
park [pa:k] **1.** Park *m* (*a.* ⚔), Anlagen *f/pl.*; Naturschutzgebiet *n*; *mst car-*~ Parkplatz *m*; ~ *keeper* Parkwächter *m*; **2.** *mot.* parken, abstellen.
par·ka ['pa:kə] Anorak *m*, Schneehemd *n*.
park·ing *mot.* ['pa:kiŋ] Parken *n*; ~ **fee** Parkgebühr *f*; ~ **lot** Parkplatz *m*; ~ **me·ter** Parkuhr *f*; ~ **space** Parkplatz *m*, -lücke *f*; ~ **tick·et** Strafzettel *m für unerlaubtes Parken.*
par·ky *sl.* ['pa:ki] kalt; frisch.
par·lance ['pa:ləns] Ausdrucksweise *f*, Sprache *f*.
par·ley ['pa:li] **1.** Unterhandlung *f*, Konferenz *f*; **2.** *v/i.* unterhandeln; sich besprechen; *v/t.* parlieren (*sprechen*).
par·lia·ment ['pa:ləmənt] Parlament *n*; **par·lia·men·tar·i·an** [~men'tɛəriən] Parlamentarier(in); **par·lia·men·ta·ry** □ [~'mentəri] parlamentarisch; Parlaments...
par·lo(u)r ['pa:lə] Wohnzimmer *n*; Empfangs-, Sprechzimmer *n*; *beauty* ~ *bsd. Am.* Schönheitssalon *m*; ~ *car* 🚃 *Am.* Salonwagen *m*; '**~-maid** Stubenmädchen *n*.

pa·ro·chi·al □ [pə'rəukjəl] parochial; Pfarr...; Gemeinde...; *fig.* engstirnig, beschränkt; ~ *politics pl.* Kirchturmpolitik *f*.
par·o·dist ['pærədist] Parodist(in); '**par·o·dy 1.** Parodie *f*; **2.** parodieren.
pa·role [pə'rəul] **1.** ⚔ Parole *f*, Kennwort *n*; Ehrenwort *n*; *put on* ~ = *3*; **2.** ⚖ mündlich; **3.** ⚖ *bsd. Am.* bedingt freilassen.
par·ox·ysm ['pærəksizəm] Paroxysmus *m*, Anfall *m*.
par·quet ['pa:kei] Parkett(fußboden *m*) *n*; *Am. thea.* Parkett *n*; **par·quet·ed** ['pa:kitid] Parkett...; '**par·quet·ry** Parkett(ierung *f*) *n*.
par·ri·cide ['pærisaid] Vater-, Muttermörder(in); Vater-, Muttermord *m*.
par·rot ['pærət] **1.** *orn.* Papagei *m* (*a. fig.*); **2.** wie ein Papagei (nach-) plappern.
par·ry *fenc.* ['pæri] **1.** Parade *f*; **2.** abwehren, parieren (*a. fig.*).
parse [pa:z] grammatisch zerlegen, analysieren.
Par·see [pa:'si] Parse *m*, Parsin *f*.
par·si·mo·ni·ous □ [pa:si'məunjəs] sparsam, karg; *b.s.* knauserig; **par·si'mo·ni·ous·ness, par·si·mo·ny** ['~məni] Sparsamkeit *f*; Knauserigkeit *f*.
pars·ley ⚘ ['pa:sli] Petersilie *f*.
pars·nip ⚘ ['pa:snip] Pastinake *f*.
par·son ['pa:sn] Pfarrer *m*, Pastor *m*; Geistliche *m*; '**par·son·age** Pfarrei *f*; Pfarrhaus *n*; **par·son's nose** F Bürzel *m von gebratenem od. gekochtem Geflügel.*
part [pa:t] **1.** Teil *m, n*; Stück *n*; Anteil *m* (*of, in* an *dat.*); Seite *f*, Partei *f*; Pflicht *f*, Amt *n*; Rolle *f* (*thea. u. fig.*); Lieferung *f e-s Buches*; ♪ *Einzel*-Stimme *f*; Körperteil *m*; † *geistige* Anlagen *f/pl.*; ~*s pl.* Gegend *f*; ~ *of speech gr.* Wortart *f*; ~ *and parcel of* untrennbar von; *a man of* ~*s* ein fähiger Mensch *m*; *have neither* ~ *nor lot in* nicht das geringste zu tun haben mit; *in foreign* ~*s* im Ausland; *play a* ~ *fig.* schauspielern; *take* ~ *in s.th.* an e-r Sache teilnehmen; *take in good* (*bad*) ~ gut (übel) aufnehmen; *for my* (*own*) ~ was mich betrifft; meinerseits; *for the most* ~ meistenteils; *in* ~ teilweise; Abschlags...; *do one's* ~ das

Seinige tun; *on the* ~ *of* von seiten (*gen.*); *on my* ~ meinerseits; **2.** *adv.* teils, zum Teil; **3.** *v/t.* (zer)teilen; trennen; *Haar* scheiteln; ~ *company* sich trennen (*with* von); *v/i.* sich trennen; scheiden (*from* von); ~ *with* sich trennen von; aufgeben.
par·take [pɑːˈteik] (*irr. take*) teilnehmen, -haben (*in od. of s.th.* an e-r Sache); ~ *of* mitessen *od.* -trinken von; *Mahlzeit* einnehmen; grenzen an (*acc.*); etwas an sich haben von; **parˈtak·er** Teilnehmer(in), -haber (-in) (*of* an *dat.*).
par·terre [pɑːˈtɛə] Ziergarten *m*; *thea.* Parterre *n*.
Par·thian [ˈpɑːθjən] parthisch.
par·tial □ [ˈpɑːʃl] Teil...; teilweise; partiell; parteiisch; eingenommen (*to* von, für); **par·ti·al·i·ty** [pɑːʃiˈæliti] Parteilichkeit *f*; Vorliebe *f* (*to, for* für).
par·tic·i·pant [pɑːˈtisipənt] Teilnehmer(in); **parˈtic·i·pate** [~peit] teilhaben *od.* -nehmen (*in* an *dat.*); **par·tic·iˈpa·tion** Teilnahme *f*; **par·ti·cip·i·al** □ [~ˈsipiəl] *gr.* partizipial; **par·ti·ci·ple** [ˈ~sipl] *gr.* Partizip(ium) *n*, Mittelwort *n*.
par·ti·cle [ˈpɑːtikl] Teilchen *n*; *fig.* Fünkchen *n*; *gr.* Partikel *f*; ~ **phys·ics** *sg.* Elementarteilchen-, Hochenergiephysik *f*.
par·ti-col·oured [ˈpɑːtikʌləd] bunt.
par·tic·u·lar [pəˈtikjulə] **1.** □ *mst* besonder; einzeln; Sonder...; sonderbar; genau, ausführlich; genau, eigen; wählerisch (*in, about, as to* in *dat.*); **2.** Einzelheit *f*; einzelner Punkt *m*, Umstand *m*; ~*s pl.* nähere Umstände *m/pl.*, *das* Nähere; *in* ~ insbesondere; **par·tic·u·lar·i·ty** [~ˈlæriti] Besonderheit *f*; Ausführlichkeit *f*; Eigenheit *f*; **parˈtic·u·lar·ize** [~ləraiz] einzeln *od.* ausführlich angeben; **parˈtic·u·lar·ly** besonders.
part·ing [ˈpɑːtiŋ] **1.** Trennung *f*; Teilung *f*; Abschied *m*; *Haar-*Scheitel *m*; ~ *of the ways bsd. fig.* Scheideweg *m*; **2.** Abschieds..., Scheide...
par·ti·san [pɑːtiˈzæn] **1.** Parteigänger(in); ⚔ Partisan *m*; **2.** Partei...; **par·tiˈsan·ship** Parteigängertum *n*.
par·ti·tion [pɑːˈtiʃən] **1.** Teilung *f*; Scheidewand *f*; Verschlag *m*, Fach *n*; ~ *wall* Zwischenwand *f*, -mauer *f*; **2.** teilen; ~ *off* abteilen, -trennen.
par·ti·tive □ [ˈpɑːtitiv] partitiv.
part·ly [ˈpɑːtli] teilweise, zum Teil.
part·ner [ˈpɑːtnə] **1.** Partner(in), Gefährte *m*, Gefährtin *f*; Tänzer (-in); ⚕ Kompagnon *m*, Teilhaber (-in); Gatte *m*, Gattin *f*; **2.** zs.-bringen; sich zs.-tun mit, zs.-arbeiten mit; **ˈpart·ner·ship** Teilhaberschaft *f*; ⚕ Handelsgesellschaft *f*; Partnerschaft *f*; *enter into* ~ *with* sich assoziieren mit.
part...: **ˈ~-own·er** Miteigentümer (-in); **ˈ~-pay·ment** Teilzahlung *f*.
par·tridge *orn.* [ˈpɑːtridʒ] Rebhuhn *n*.
part...: **ˈ~-song** mehrstimmiges Lied *n*; **ˈ~-time 1.** *adj.* Teilzeit..., Halbtags...; ~ *job* Teilzeitbeschäftigung *f*; **2.** *adv.* halbtags.
par·ty [ˈpɑːti] Partei *f* (*pol.*, ⚖); Parteisystem *n*; ⚔ Trupp *m*, Kommando *n*; Party *f*, Gesellschaft *f*; Gruppe *f*; Teilnehmer *m*, Beteiligte *m*; *co.* Type *f*, Individuum *n*; *s. line*[1] *1*; ~ **lin·er** Linientreue *m*.
par·ve·nu [ˈpɑːvənjuː] Emporkömmling *m*, Parvenu *m*.
pas·chal [ˈpɑːskəl] Passah..., Oster...
pa·sha [ˈpɑːʃə] Pascha *m*.
pass [pɑːs] **1.** Paß *m*, Ausweis *m*; Passierschein *m*; Bestehen *n e-s Examens*; *univ.* gewöhnlicher Grad *m*; Zustand *m*, (kritische) Lage *f*; *Fußball*: Paß *m*; Bestreichung *f*, Strich *m*; *fenc.* Ausfall *m*, Stoß *m*; *sl.* Annäherungsversuch *m*; (Gebirgs)Paß *m*, Durchgang *m*; *Karten*: Passen *n*; *free* ~ Freikarte *f*; *hold the* ~ *fig.* die Stellung halten; **2.** *v/i.* passieren, vorgehen, geschehen; hingenommen werden, hingehen; *Karten*: passen; gehen, kommen, fahren; vorbeigehen, -kommen, -fahren; vorübergehen, vergehen (*Zeit*); sich verwandeln; angenommen werden (*Banknoten*); bekannt sein; vergehen; aussterben; *a.* ~ *away* sterben; verscheiden; durchkommen (*Gesetz*; *Prüfling*); ~ *for* gelten als; ~ *off* vonstatten gehen; ~ *out* F ohnmächtig werden; *come to* ~ geschehen; *bring to* ~ bewirken; **3.** *v/t.* vorbeigehen, -kommen, -fahren an (*dat.*); passieren; kommen *od.* fahren durch; verbringen; reichen, geben; *Bemerkung* machen, von sich geben; *Banknoten* in Um-

lauf bringen; *Gesetz* durchbringen, annehmen; *Prüfling* durchkommen lassen; *Prüfung* bestehen; (hinaus-) gehen über (*acc.*); *Urteil* abgeben; *Meinung* äußern; bewegen; streichen mit; *Ball* zuspielen; *Truppen* vorbeimarschieren lassen; ~ *s.o.* (*s.th.*) *by* j. (et.) übergehen; ~ *off* ablenken von; ~ *s.o.* (*s.th.*) *off as* j. (et.) ausgeben als; ~ *over* übergehen, übersehen; *it* ~*es my comprehension* es geht über m-n Verstand; ~ *one's hand across one's forehead* mit der Hand über die Stirn streichen; ~ *s.th. round s.th.* et. um et. legen; ~ *water* Wasser lassen; ~ *one's word* sein Ehrenwort geben; ˈ**pass·a·ble** passierbar; gangbar, gültig (*Geld*); □ erträglich, leidlich, passabel.

pas·sage [ˈpæsidʒ] Durchgang *m*, -fahrt *f*; Überfahrt *f*; (See-, Flug-) Reise *f*; Durchreise *f*; Korridor *m*, Flur *m*, Gang *m*; Weg *m*; Annahme *f e-s Gesetzes*; ♪ Passage *f*; *Text*-Stelle *f*; ~*s pl.* Beziehungen *f/pl.*; ~ *of od. at arms* Waffengang *m*; *bird of* ~ Zugvogel *m*; ˈ**~·way** Durchgang *m*; Korridor *m*.

pass-book ✝ [ˈpɑːsbuk] Sparbuch *n*.

pas·sé(**e**) [ˈpɑːsei] vergangen, veraltet; verblüht; passé.

pas·sen·ger [ˈpæsindʒə] Passagier *m*, Fahr-, Fluggast *m*, Reisende *m*, *f*; ~ **train** Personenzug *m*.

passe-par·tout [ˈpæspɑːtuː] Passepartout *n* (*Hauptschlüssel*; *phot. Wechselrahmen*).

pass·er-by, *pl.* **pass·ers-by** [ˈpɑːsə(z)ˈbai] Vorübergehende *m*, *f*, Passant(in).

pas·sim [ˈpæsim] passim, an vielen Stellen *e-s Buchs*.

pass·ing [ˈpɑːsiŋ] **1.** Vorbei-, Vorübergehen *n*; Dahinschwinden *n*; Annahme *f e-s Gesetzes*; Hinscheiden *n*; *in* ~ beiläufig; **2.** vorübergehend, flüchtig; ˈ**~-bell** Totenglocke *f*.

pas·sion [ˈpæʃən] Leidenschaft *f* (*Gemütserregung*; *heftige Liebe*; *Liebhaberei*); (Gefühls)Ausbruch *m*; Zorn *m*; ♀ Leiden *n* (Christi), Passion *f*; *be in a* ~ zornig sein; *in* ~ ⚖ im Affekt; ♀ *Week* Karwoche *f*; Woche *f* vor der Karwoche; **pas·sion·ate** □ [ˈ~ʃənit] leidenschaftlich; ˈ**pas·sion-flow·er** ⚘ Passionsblume *f*; ˈ**pas·sion·less** □ leidenschaftslos; ˈ**pas·sion-play** Passionsspiel *n*.

pas·sive □ [ˈpæsiv] passiv (*a. gr.*); teilnahmslos; untätig; ˈ**pas·sive·ness, pas**ˈ**siv·i·ty** Passivität *f*; Teilnahmslosigkeit *f*.

pass-key [ˈpɑːskiː] Hauptschlüssel *m*, Nachschlüssel *m*, Drücker *m*.

Pass·o·ver [ˈpɑːsəuvə] Passah(fest) *n*; Osterlamm *n*.

pass·port [ˈpɑːspɔːt] (Reise)Paß *m*.

pass·word ⚔ [ˈpɑːswəːd] Losung *f*.

past [pɑːst] **1.** *adj.* vergangen; letzt; *gr.* Vergangenheits...; ~ *master* Altmeister *m*; *for some time* ~ seit einiger Zeit; **2.** *adv.* vorbei; *rush* ~ vorbeieilen; **3.** *prp.* nach, über; über ... (*acc.*) hinaus; an (*dat.*) vorbei; *half* ~ *two* halb drei; *it is* ~ *comprehension* es geht über alle Begriffe; ~ *cure* unheilbar; ~ *endurance* unerträglich; ~ *hope* hoffnungslos; *I would not put it* ~ *her* das traue ich ihr glatt zu; **4.** Vergangenheit *f*.

paste [peist] **1.** Teig *m*; Kleister *m*; Paste *f*; unechter Stein *m*; **2.** kleistern, kleben; bekleben; ˈ**~·board** Pappe *f*; *sl.* Karte *f*; *attr.* Papp...; aus Pappe.

pas·tel [pæsˈtel] ⚘ Färberwaid *m*; *paint.* Pastellstift *m*; Pastell(bild) *n*; **pas·tel·(l)ist** [ˈ~təlist] Pastellmaler (-in).

pas·tern *vet.* [ˈpæstəːn] Fessel *f*.

paste-up [ˈpeistʌp] Photomontage *f*; Zs.-stellung *f*.

pas·teur·ize [ˈpæstəraiz] pasteurisieren, keimfrei machen.

pas·tille [ˈpæstəl] Pastille *f*.

pas·time [ˈpɑːstaim] Zeitvertreib *m*, Kurzweil *f*.

pas·tor [ˈpɑːstə] Pastor *m*; Seelsorger *m*; ˈ**pas·to·ral 1.** □ Hirten-...; pastoral; ~ *staff* Krummstab *m*; **2.** Hirtengedicht *n*; Pastorale *n*, *f*; *paint.* Idyll *n*; *eccl.* Hirtenbrief *m*.

pas·try [ˈpeistri] Tortengebäck *n*, Konditorwaren *f/pl.*; Pasteten *f/pl.*; ˈ**~-cook** Pastetenbäcker *m*, Konditor *m*.

pas·tur·age [ˈpɑːstjuridʒ] Weiden *n*; Weide(land *n*) *f*.

pas·ture [ˈpɑːstʃə] **1.** Weide(gras *n*) *f*; Futter *n*; ~ *ground* Weideland *n*; **2.** *v/t.* weiden (*a. v/i.*); abweiden.

past·y 1. [ˈpeisti] teigig; bleich;

2. [ˈpæsti] (Fleisch)Pastete *f*.

pat [pæt] **1.** leichter Schlag *m*, Klaps *m*; Portion *f Butter*; **2.** tätscheln; klopfen; leicht schlagen; **3.** gelegen, gerade recht; bereit, bei der Hand; *stand* ~ festbleiben; *have od. know s.th. (off)* ~ et. aus dem Effeff können.

patch [pætʃ] **1.** Fleck *m*; Flicken *m*; Stück *n* Land; Stelle *f*; ⚕ Pflaster *n*; ⚕ Augenklappe *f*; *Nebel*-Feld *n*; Schönheitspflästerchen *n*; *strike a bad* ~ e-e Pechsträhne haben; ~ *pocket* aufgesetzte Tasche *f*; **2.** flicken; ~ *up* zs.-flicken; *fig.* zs.-stoppeln.

patch·work [ˈpætʃwəːk] Flickwerk *n*; ˈ**patch·y** voller Flicken; *fig.* zs.-gestoppelt; ungleichmäßig.

pate F [peit] Schädel *m*.

pat·ent [ˈpeitənt, ˈpætənt] **1.** offenkundig; patentiert; Patent...; *letters* ~ [ˈpætənt] *pl.* Freibrief *m*; ~ *article* Markenartikel *m*; ~ *leather* Lackleder *n*; **2.** Patent *n*; Privileg(ium) *n*, Freibrief *m*; ~ *pending* ⚖ Patent angemeldet; ~ *agent* Patentanwalt *m*; ~ *office* Patentamt *n*; **3.** patentieren (lassen); **pat·ent·ee** [peitənˈtiː] Patentinhaber *m*.

pa·ter·nal □ [pəˈtəːnl] väterlich; **paˈter·ni·ty** Vaterschaft *f*.

path [pɑːθ], *pl.* **paths** [pɑːðz] Pfad *m*; Weg *m*; *Sport*: Bahn *f*; *cross s.o.'s* ~ j-m über den Weg laufen.

pa·thet·ic [pəˈθetik] (~*ally*) rührend, ergreifend; bemitleidenswert.

path·less [ˈpɑːθlis] unwegsam.

path·o·log·i·cal □ [pæθəˈlɔdʒikəl] pathologisch; **pa·thol·o·gist** [pəˈθɔlədʒist] Pathologe *m*; **paˈthol·o·gy** Krankheitslehre *f*, Pathologie *f*.

pa·thos [ˈpeiθɔs] Pathos *n*.

path·way [ˈpɑːθwei] Pfad *m*, Weg *m*.

path·y *Am.* ⚕ *contp.* [ˈpæθi] Behandlung(sart) *f*.

pa·tience [ˈpeiʃəns] Geduld *f*; Ausdauer *f*; Patience *f (Kartenspiel)*; *be out of* ~ *with, have no* ~ *with* es nicht (mehr) aushalten können mit; ˈ**pa·tient 1.** □ geduldig; *be* ~ *of* ertragen; *fig.* zulassen; **2.** Patient(-in), Kranke *m, f*.

pa·ti·o *Am.* [ˈpætiəu] Innenhof *m*, Patio *m*.

pa·tri·arch [ˈpeitriɑːk] Patriarch *m*; **pa·triˈar·chal** □ patriarchalisch.

pa·tri·cian [pəˈtriʃən] **1.** patrizisch; **2.** Patrizier(in).

pat·ri·cide [ˈpætrisaid] Vatermord *m*; Vatermörder *m*.

pat·ri·mo·ny [ˈpætriməni] väterliches Erbteil *n*.

pa·tri·ot [ˈpætriət] Patriot(in); **pa·tri·ot·eer** [~əˈtiə] Hurrapatriot *m*; **pa·tri·ot·ic** [~ˈɔtik] (~*ally*) patriotisch; **pa·tri·ot·ism** [ˈ~ətizəm] Patriotismus *m*, Vaterlandsliebe *f*.

pa·trol ⚔ [pəˈtrəul] **1.** Patrouille *f*, Streife *f*; Spähtrupp *m*; ~ *wagon Am.* Polizeigefangenenwagen *m*; **2.** (ab)patrouillieren; **~·man** [pəˈtrəulmæn] patrouillierender Polizist *m*; Pannenhelfer *m e-s Automobilclubs*.

pa·tron [ˈpeitrən] Patron *m*, Schutzherr *m*; Schutzheilige *m, f*; Gönner *m*; Kunde *m*; **pa·tron·age** [ˈpætrənidʒ] Gönnerschaft *f*; Kundschaft *f*; Schutz *m*; Patronatsrecht *n*; gönnerhaftes Wesen *n*; **pa·tron·ess** [ˈpeitrənis] Patronin *f etc.* (*s. patron*); **pa·tron·ize** [ˈpætrənaiz] beschützen; begünstigen; Kunde sein bei; gönnerhaft behandeln; ˈ**pa·tron·iz·er** Beschützer(in), Gönner(in).

pat·ter [ˈpætə] **1.** *v/i.* platschen; trappeln; *v/t.* (her)plappern; **2.** Platschen *n*; Getrappel *n*; Geplapper *n*; Jargon *m*, Rotwelsch *n*.

pat·tern [ˈpætən] **1.** Muster *n* (*a. fig.*); Modell *n*; Schablone *f*; Schnittmuster *n*; *fig.* Form *f*; Vorbild *n*; *by* ~ *post* als Muster ohne Wert; **2.** formen (*after, on* nach); mustern; ˈ**~-mak·er** ⊕ Modellbauer *m*.

pat·ty [ˈpæti] Pastetchen *n*.

pau·ci·ty [ˈpɔːsiti] Wenigkeit *f*.

Paul·ine [ˈpɔːlain] paulinisch.

paunch [pɔːntʃ] Wanst *m*; ˈ**paunch·y** dickbauchig.

pau·per [ˈpɔːpə] **1.** Arme *m, f*, Fürsorgeempfänger(in); **2.** Armen...; ˈ**pau·per·ism** Massenarmut *f*; ˈ**pau·per·ize** arm machen.

pause [pɔːz] **1.** Pause *f*, Unterbrechung *f*; ♪ Fermate *f*; *give* ~ *to s.o.* j-m zu denken geben; **2.** pausieren, innehalten; stehen bleiben; verweilen (*upon* bei).

pave [peiv] pflastern; *fig. Weg* bahnen; ˈ**pave·ment** Bürgersteig *m*, Gehweg *m*; Pflaster *n*; ~ *artist* Pflastermaler *m*; ~ *café* Straßencafé *n*.

pa·vil·ion [pəˈviljən] Pavillon *m*;

Zelt *n*; Gartenhaus *n*.
pav·ing-stone ['peiviŋstəun] Pflasterstein *m*.
paw [pɔː] **1.** Pfote *f*, Tatze *f*; **2.** *v/t.* mit den Pfoten berühren *od.* schlagen; F befingern; rauh behandeln; *v/i.* scharren.
pawn[1] [pɔːn] Bauer *m im Schach*; *fig.* (willenloses) Werkzeug *n*.
pawn[2] [~] **1.** Pfand *n*; *in* ~, *at* ~ verpfändet; **2.** verpfänden, versetzen; '**~·bro·ker** Pfandleiher *m*; **pawn'ee** Pfandinhaber(in); '**pawn·er** Verpfänder *m*; '**pawn·shop** Leihhaus *n*; '**pawn-tick·et** Pfandschein *m*.
pay [pei] **1.** Bezahlung *f*; Sold *m*, Lohn *m*; *fig.* Belohnung *f*; **2.** (*irr.*) *v/t.* (be)zahlen; (be)lohnen; sich lohnen *für j.*; *Ehre etc.* erweisen; *Besuch* abstatten; ~ *attention od. heed to* achtgeben auf (*acc.*); ~ *away*, ~ *out* ⚓ *Tau* ablaufen lassen; ~ *down* bar bezahlen; ~ *off j.* bezahlen u. entlassen; *j.* voll auszahlen; ~ *s.o. out for s.th.* j-m et. heimzahlen; ~ *up* voll bezahlen; ~ *one's way* ohne Verlust arbeiten; *put paid to s.th.* F et. erledigen; *v/i.* zahlen; sich lohnen *od.* rentieren; sich bezahlt machen; ~ *for* (für) *et.* bezahlen; (für) *et.* büßen; '**pay·a·ble** zahlbar; fällig; ⚒, ⚕ rentabel; '**pay-as-you-'earn** Lohnsteuerabzug *m*; '**pay-bed** Privatbett *n in e-r Klinik*; '**pay-day** Zahltag *m*; **pay dirt** *Am.* goldhaltige Erde *f*; **pay'ee** ⚕ Zahlungsempfänger *m*; Wechselnehmer *m*; '**pay-en·ve·lope** Lohntüte *f*; '**pay·er** Zahler *m*; ⚕ Trassat *m*, Bezogene *m*; **pay freeze** Lohnstopp *m*; '**pay·ing** lohnend, rentabel; Zahl(ungs)..., Kassen...; ~ *concern* lohnendes Geschäft *n*; **pay·ing-'in slip** Einzahlungsschein *m*; '**pay-load** Nutzlast *f*; '**pay·mas·ter** ⚔, ⚓ Zahlmeister *m*; '**pay·ment** (Be-) Zahlung *f*; Lohn *m*, Sold *m*; Belohnung *f*; *additional* ~ Nachzahlung *f*; *on* ~ *of* gegen Zahlung von.
pay...: '**~-off** Abrechnung *f* (*a. fig.*); *Am.* F Gipfelpunkt *m*; '**~-of·fice** Lohnbüro *n*; '**~-pack·et** Lohntüte *f*; '**~-roll** Lohnliste *f*; '**~·station** *Am.* öffentlicher Fernsprecher *m*.
pea ⚘ [piː] Erbse *f*.
peace [piːs] Friede(n) *m*, Ruhe *f*; *the (King's)* ~ Landfrieden *m*; *be at* ~ in Frieden leben; *break the* ~ die öffentliche Ruhe stören; *keep the* ~ Ruhe halten; '**peace·a·ble** □ friedfertig, -liebend, friedlich; '**peace-break·er** Ruhestörer *m*; **Peace Corps** Friedenstruppe *f*; **peace·ful** □ ['~ful] friedlich; ruhig, ungestört.
peace...: '**~-keep·ing force** Friedenstruppe *f*; '**~·mak·er** Friedensstifter(in); ~ **move·ment** Friedensbewegung *f*; '**~-of·fer·ing** Versöhnungsgeschenk *n*; versöhnliche Geste *f*, Friedenszeichen *n*; ~ **set·tle·ment** Friedensregelung *f*.
peach[1] [piːtʃ] ⚘ Pfirsich(baum) *m*; *sl.* süßer Käfer *m*; *fig.* Gedicht *n*.
peach[2] *sl.* [~]: ~ (*up*)*on Mittäter* verpfeifen; *Schule*: verpetzen.
pea-chick ['piːtʃik] junger Pfau *m*.
peach·y ['piːtʃi] pfirsichähnlich, -farben; *sl.* famos, toll.
pea·cock ['piːkɔk] Pfau(hahn) *m*; Pfauenauge *n* (*Schmetterling*); '**pea-fowl** Pfau *m*; '**pea'hen** Pfauhenne *f*.
pea-jack·et ⚓ ['piːdʒækit] Bordjacke *f*.
peak [piːk] **1.** Spitze *f*; Gipfel *m*; *Mützen*-Schirm *m*; *attr.* Spitzen..., Höchst...; ~ *hour* Hauptverkehrs-, Stoßzeit *f*; ~ *load* Spitzenbelastung *f*; ~ *power etc.* Spitzenleistung *f etc.*; ~ *season* Haupt-, Hochsaison *f*; **2.** F spitz aussehen, kränkeln; **peaked** [piːkt] spitz; ~ *cap* Schirmmütze *f*; '**peak·y** spitz(ig); F spitz (aussehend) (*Gesicht*).
peal [piːl] **1.** Geläut *n*; Glockenspiel *n*; Dröhnen *n*; ~*s pl. of laughter* schallendes Gelächter *n*; **2.** *v/t.* erschallen lassen; laut verkünden; *v/i.* erschallen; dröhnen, krachen.
pea·nut ['pinʌt] Erdnuß *f*; *fig.* Kleinigkeit *f*.
pear ⚘ [pɛə] Birne *f*.
pearl [pəːl] **1.** Perle *f* (*a. fig.*); *typ.* Perlschrift *f*; *attr.* Perl(en)...; **2.** tropfen, perlen; nach Perlmuscheln tauchen; '**pearl·y** perlenartig; perlenreich.
pear-tree ['pɛətriː] Birnbaum *m*.
peas·ant ['pezənt] **1.** Bauer *m*; **2.** bäuerlich; '**peas·ant·ry** Landvolk *n*.
pease [piːz] Erbse(n *pl.*) *f*.
pea-shoot·er ['piːʃuːtə] Blasrohr *n*.
pea soup ['piː'suːp] Erbsensuppe *f*; '**pea-'soup·er** F dicker, gelber Nebel *m*.

peat [pi:t] Torf *m*; **ˈ~-bog** Torfmoor *n*.
peb·ble [ˈpebl] Kiesel(stein) *m*; *Art* Achat *m*; **ˈpeb·bly** kieselig.
pe·can ⚘ [piˈkæn] Pekanhickory *m*.
pec·ca·ble [ˈpekəbl] sündhaft.
peck[1] [pek] Viertelscheffel *m* (*9,087 Liter*); *fig*. Menge *f*.
peck[2] [~] picken, hacken (*at* nach); ~ *at one's food* im Essen umherstochern; **ˈpeck·er** *sl*. Zinken *m* (*Nase*); *keep one's* ~ *up* nicht den Mut verlieren; **ˈpeck·ish** F hungrig.
pec·to·ral [ˈpektərəl] **1.** Brust...; **2.** Brustschild *n*; Brustmittel *n*.
pec·tin [ˈpektin] Pektin *n*.
pec·u·late [ˈpekjuleit] unterschlagen; **pec·uˈla·tion** Unterschlagung *f*; **ˈpec·u·la·tor** Veruntreuer *m*.
pe·cul·iar □ [piˈkju:ljə] eigen(tümlich); besonder; seltsam, merkwürdig; **pe·cu·li·ar·i·ty** [~liˈæriti] Eigenheit *f*; Eigentümlichkeit *f*.
pe·cu·ni·ar·y [piˈkju:njəri] geldlich; Geld...; pekuniär.
ped·a·gog·ic, ped·a·gog·i·cal □ [pedəˈgɔdʒik(əl)] pädagogisch; Erziehungs...; **ped·aˈgog·ics** *mst sg*. Pädagogik *f*; **ped·a·gogue** [ˈ~gɔg] Pädagoge *m*; Lehrer *m*, Schulmann *m*; **ped·a·go·gy** [ˈ~gɔdʒi] Pädagogik *f*.
ped·al [ˈpedl] **1.** Pedal *n*; **2.** Fuß...; **3.** *Radfahren*: fahren, treten; **ˈ~-bin** Treteimer *m*.
ped·ant [ˈpedənt] Pedant(in); **pe·dan·tic** [piˈdæntik] (*~ally*) pedantisch; **ped·ant·ry** [ˈpedəntri] Pedanterie *f*.
ped·dle [ˈpedl] hausieren (mit); tändeln, spielen; **ˈped·dling** geringfügig; **ˈped·dler** *Am*. = *pedlar*.
ped·es·tal [ˈpedistl] Sockel *m* (*a. fig*.); Säulenfuß *m*; **pe·des·tri·an** [piˈdestriən] **1.** Fuß...; zu Fuß; prosaisch, nüchtern; **2.** Fußgänger (-in); ~ *crossing* Fußgängerüberweg *m*.
ped·i·cab [ˈpedikæb] Fahrradrikscha *f*.
ped·i·cure [ˈpedikjuə] Fußpflege *f*; Fußpfleger(in); **ped·i·cur·ist** [ˈ~kjuərist] Fußpfleger(in).
ped·i·gree [ˈpedigri:] **1.** Stammbaum *m*; **2.** *~d* mit Stammbaum; reinrassig.
ped·i·ment ⩓ [ˈpedimənt] (Zier-) Giebel *m*.
ped·lar [ˈpedlə] Hausierer *m*; **ˈped·lar·y** Hausierware *f*.
pe·dom·e·ter [piˈdɔmitə] Schrittmesser *m*.
pee F pinkeln; *go for a* ~ pinkeln gehen.
peek [pi:k] **1.** spähen, gucken, lugen; **2.** flüchtiger Blick *m*; **peek·a·boo** [ˈpi:kəbu:] Guck-Guck-Spiel *n*.
peel [pi:l] **1.** *Zitronen- etc*. Schale *f*; Rinde *f*; **2.** *a*. ~ *off v/t*. (ab)schälen; *Kleid* abstreifen; *v/i*. sich (ab-) schälen; *sl*. sich entblättern (*auskleiden*).
peel·er *sl*. † [ˈpi:lə] Polyp *m* (*Polizist*).
peel·ing [ˈpi:liŋ] *lose* Schale *f*.
peep[1] [pi:p] **1.** Piepen *n*; **2.** piepen.
peep[2] [~] **1.** verstohlener Blick *m*; Anbruch *m des Tages*; **2.** (verstohlen) gucken, lugen; *a*. ~ *out* (hervor)gucken (*a. fig*.); ~ *at* angucken; **ˈpeep·er** Gucker *m* (*sl. Auge*); **ˈpeep-hole** Guckloch *n*; **ˈpeep·ing Tom** Voyeur *m*; **ˈpeep-show** Peep-Show *f*.
peer[1] [piə] spähen, lugen; prüfend blicken; ~ *at* an-, begucken.
peer[2] [~] Gleiche *m*; Pair *m*, Mitglied *n* des Hochadels; **ˈpeer·age** Pairswürde *f*; Pairs *m/pl*.; **ˈpeer·ess** Gemahlin *f* e-s Pairs; **ˈpeer·less** □ unvergleichlich.
peeved F [pi:vd] eingeschnappt.
pee·vish □ [ˈpi:viʃ] verdrießlich, grämlich, mürrisch; **ˈpee·vish·ness** Verdrießlichkeit *f*.
pee·wit [ˈpi:wit] = *pewit*.
peg [peg] **1.** Stöpsel *m*, Dübel *m*, Pflock *m*; *Kleider*-Haken *m*; ♪ Wirbel *m*; *Wäsche*-Klammer *f*; *fig*. Aufhänger *m*; (Zelt)Hering *m*; Whisky *m* mit Soda; *take s.o. down a* ~ *or two* j. demütigen; *be a round* ~ *in a square hole* an der falschen Stelle stehen; **2.** festpflöcken; *a*. ~ *out Grenze* abstecken; *Löhne, Preise* festlegen, halten; ~ *away*, ~ *along* F darauflosarbeiten; ~ *out sl*. abkratzen.
peg-top [ˈpegtop] Kreisel *m*.
peign·oir [ˈpeinwɑ:] Frisiermantel *m*, Morgenrock *m e-r Dame*.
pe·jo·ra·tive [ˈpi:dʒərətiv, piˈdʒɔrətiv] verschlechternd, herabsetzend.
peke F [pi:k] = *pekinese*.
pe·kin·ese [pi:kiˈni:z] Pekinese *m* (*Hund*).
pelf *contp*. [pelf] Mammon *m*.

pel·i·can *orn.* [ˈpelikən] Pelikan *m*; ~ **cross·ing** *mit Ampeln gesicherter Fußgängerüberweg*.
pel·let [ˈpelit] Kügelchen *n*; Pille *f*; Schrotkorn *n*.
pel·li·cle [ˈpelikl] Häutchen *n*.
pell-mell [ˈpelˈmel] **1.** durcheinander; **2.** Durcheinander *n*.
pel·lu·cid [peˈljuːsid] durchsichtig.
Pel·o·pon·ne·sian [peləpəˈniːʃən] peloponnesisch.
pelt[1] [pelt] Fell *n*; ✝ *rohe* Haut *f*.
pelt[2] [~] **1.** *v/t. mit Steinen etc.* bewerfen, bombardieren; *v/i.* niederprasseln (*Regen*); **2.** Wurf *m*, Schlag *m*; Prasseln *n*; *at full* ~ in voller Geschwindigkeit.
pelt·ry [ˈpeltri] Rohpelze *m/pl.*, Rauchwaren *f/pl.*
pel·vis *anat.* [ˈpelvis] Becken *n*.
pem·mi·can [ˈpemikən] Pemmikan *m* (*Dörrfleisch*).
pen[1] [pen] **1.** (Schreib)Feder *f*; Federhalter *m*; **2.** schreiben, abfassen.
pen[2] [~] **1.** Hürde *f*; ⚓ U-Boot-Bunker *m*; *a. play-*~ (Kinder)Ställchen *n*, Laufgitter *n*; **2.** (*irr.*) *oft* ~ *up*, ~ *in* einpferchen.
pe·nal □ [ˈpiːnl] Straf...; strafbar; ~ *code* Strafgesetzbuch *n*; ~ *servitude* Zuchthausstrafe *f*; **pe·nal·ize** [ˈpiːnəlaiz] mit Strafe belegen; *fig.* belasten; *e-m Spieler* e-n Strafpunkt geben; **pen·al·ty** [ˈpenlti] Strafe *f*, Buße *f*; *Sport*: Strafpunkt *m*; ~ *area Fußball*: Strafraum *m*; ~ *goal Fußball*: Elfmetertor *n*; ~ *kick* Strafstoß *m*; ~ *spot Fußball*: Elfmeterpunkt *m*; *under* ~ *of* bei Strafe von.
pen·ance [ˈpenəns] Buße *f*.
pen...: **ˈ~-and-ˈink draw·ing** Federzeichnung *f*.
pence [pens] *pl. von penny*.
pen·chant [ˈpɑ̃ːʃɑ̃] Neigung *f*, Hang *m*, Vorliebe *f*.
pen·cil [ˈpensl] **1.** Bleistift *m*; **2.** zeichnen; (mit Bleistift) anzeichnen *od.* anstreichen; *die Augenbrauen* nachziehen; **ˈ~-case** Federmäppchen *n*; **ˈ~-sharp·en·er** Bleistiftspitzer *m*.
pend·ant [ˈpendənt] Anhänger *m* (*Schmuckstück*); Wimpel *m*; Gegenstück *n*, Pendant *n*.
pend·ent [~] hängend; schwebend.
pend·ing [ˈpendiŋ] **1.** ⚖ schwebend, noch unentschieden; **2.** *prp.* während; bis zu.
pen·du·lous [ˈpendjuləs] frei hängend; pendelnd; **pen·du·lum** [ˈ~ləm] Pendel *n*.
pen·e·tra·bil·i·ty [penitrəˈbiliti] Durchdringbarkeit *f*; **ˈpen·e·tra·ble** □ durchdringbar; **pen·e·tra·li·a** [~ˈtreiljə] Innerste *n*, Allerheiligste *n*; **pen·e·trate** [ˈ~treit] *v/t.* durchdringen (*with* mit); ergründen; durchschauen; eindringen in (*acc.*); *v/i.* eindringen; vordringen (*to* bis zu); **pen·eˈtra·tion** Durch-, Eindringen *n*; Scharfsinn *m*; **pen·e·tra·tive** □ [ˈ~trətiv] durchdringend (*a. fig.*); eindringlich; scharfsinnig; ~ *effect* Durchschlagskraft *f*.
pen-friend [ˈpenfrend] Brieffreund (-in).
pen·guin *orn.* [ˈpeŋgwin] Pinguin *m*.
pen·hold·er [ˈpenhəuldə] Federhalter *m*.
pen·i·cil·lin *pharm.* [peniˈsilin] Penicillin *n*.
pen·in·su·la [piˈninsjulə] Halbinsel *f*; **penˈin·su·lar** Halbinsel...; halbinselförmig.
pe·nis [ˈpiːnis] Penis *m*.
pen·i·tence [ˈpenitəns] Bußfertigkeit *f*, Buße *f*, Reue *f*; **ˈpen·i·tent** **1.** □ reuig, bußfertig; **2.** Bußfertige *m*, *f*; Büßer(in); **pen·i·ten·tial** □ [~ˈtenʃəl] bußfertig; Buß...; **pen·i·ten·tia·ry** [~ˈtenʃəri] Besserungsanstalt *f*; *Am.* Zuchthaus *n*.
pen·knife [ˈpennaif] Taschenmesser *n*.
pen·man [ˈpenmən] Schönschreiber *m*; Schriftsteller *m*; *he is a poor* ~ s-e Schrift ist schlecht; **ˈpen·man·ship** Schreibkunst *f*; Stil *m*.
pen-name [ˈpenneim] Schriftstellername *m*, Pseudonym *n*.
pen·nant [ˈpenənt] ⚓ Wimpel *m*; *bsd. Am.* Siegerwimpel *m*; *fig.* Meisterschaft *f* (*Sport*).
pen·ni·less □ [ˈpenilis] ohne Geld, mittellos, ganz arm.
pen·non [ˈpenən] ⚔ *Lanzen*-Fähnlein *n*; Wimpel *m*.
pen·ny [ˈpeni], *pl. bei Zssgn* **pence** [pens] (englischer) Penny *m* (= *1 p* = *£ 0.01*); *Am.* Centstück *n*; Kleinigkeit *f*; *oft* Groschen *m*; *a pretty* ~ e-e hübsche Summe *f*; *in for a* ~, *in for a pound* wer A sagt, muß auch B sagen; *turn an honest* ~ sich auf ehrliche Weise durchschlagen; ~ *wise and pound foolish*

im Kleinen sparsam, im Großen verschwenderisch; **'~-a-'lin·er** Zeilenschinder *m*; **'~-'dread·ful** Groschenroman *m*; Revolverblatt *n*; **~ pinch·er** Geizhals *m*; **'~·weight** *englisches* Pennygewicht *n* ($1^1/_2$ *Gramm*); **~·worth** ['penəθ] Pennywert *m*, für einen Penny; *a ~ of tobacco* für einen Penny Tabak.

pen...: ~ pal = *pen-friend*; **'~-push·er** F *contp.* Schreiberling *m*.

pen·sion ['penʃən] **1.** Pension *f*, Rente *f*, Ruhegehalt *n*; ['pɑ̃:ŋsiɔ̃:ŋ] Pension *f*, Fremdenheim *n*; **2.** *oft ~ off* pensionieren; **'pen·sion·ar·y, 'pen·sion·er** Ruhegehaltsempfänger(in), Pensionär(in); *contp.* Mietling *m*; **pen·sion scheme** Rentenversicherung *f*.

pen·sive □ ['pensiv] gedankenvoll; nachdenklich; ernst; **'pen·sive·ness** Nachdenklichkeit *f*; Ernst *m*.

pent [pent] *pret. u. p.p. von pen*² *2.*

pen·ta·gon ['pentəgən] Fünfeck *n*; *the* ♀ das Pentagon (*amerikanisches Verteidigungsministerium*); **pen·tag·o·nal** [~'tægənl] fünfeckig.

pen·tath·lon [pen'tæθlɔn] *Sport*: Fünfkampf *m*.

Pen·te·cost ['pentikɔst] Pfingsten *n od. pl.*; **pen·te'cos·tal** pfingstlich; Pfingst...

pent·house ['penthaus] Wetter-, Schutzdach *n*; Dachwohnung *f auf e-m Hochhaus*.

pent-up ['pent'ʌp] aufgestaut (*Zorn etc.*); *~ feelings* aufgestaute Gefühle *n/pl.*

pe·nul·ti·mate [pi'nʌltimit] vorletzt.

pe·num·bra [pi'nʌmbrə] Halbschatten *m*.

pe·nu·ri·ous □ [pi'njuəriəs] geizig; karg; **pe'nu·ri·ous·ness** Geiz *m*; Kargheit *f*.

pen·u·ry ['penjuri] Armut *f*; Mangel *m*.

pe·o·ny ⚘ ['piəni] Pfingstrose *f*.

peo·ple ['pi:pl] **1.** a) *coll.* die Leute *pl.*, man; Volk *n*; *my ~* m-e Angehörigen *pl.*, m-e Familie *f*; b) Volk *n*, Nation *f*; *the ~s pl. of Asia* die Völker *n/pl.* Asiens; **2.** bevölkern.

pep *sl.* [pep] **1.** Schmiß *m*; Schwung *m*; **2.** *~ up* aufmöbeln.

pep·per ['pepə] **1.** Pfeffer *m*; **2.** pfeffern; **'~-box** Pfefferstreuer *m*; **'~-corn** Pfefferkorn *n*; **'~·mint** ⚘ Pfefferminze *f*; Pfefferminz(bonbon) *n*; **~ pot** Pfefferstreuer *m*; **'pep·per·y** □ pfefferig; *fig.* hitzig.

pep...: ~ pill Aufputschtablette *f*; **~ talk** aufmunternde Worte *n/pl.*

pep·tic ['peptik]: *~ ulcer* Magengeschwür *n*.

per [pə:, pə] per, durch, für; laut; je.

per·ad·ven·ture *rhet.* [pərəd'ventʃə] **1.** vielleicht, etwa; **2.** Vielleicht *n*; *beyond ~, without ~* ohne Zweifel.

per·am·bu·late [pə'ræmbjuleit] (durch)wandern; *Grenzen etc.* be-, abgehen; bereisen; **per·am·bu'la·tion** Durchwanderung *f*; Besichtigungsreise *f*; **per·am·bu·la·tor** ['præmbjuleitə] Kinderwagen *m*.

per·cale [pə'keil] Perkal *m* (*Baumwollgewebe*).

per cap·i·ta [pə'kæpitə] pro Kopf; *~ income* Pro-Kopf-Einkommen *n*.

per·ceive [pə'si:v] (be)merken, wahrnehmen; empfinden; erkennen.

per cent, *a.* **per·cent** [pə'sent] Prozent *n*; **per'cent·age** Prozent-, Hundertsatz *m*; Prozente *n/pl.*; *fig.* Teil *m*.

per·cep·ti·ble □ [pə'septəbl] wahrnehmbar; **per'cep·tion** Wahrnehmung(svermögen *n*) *f*; Erkenntnis *f*; Auffassung(skraft) *f*; **per'cep·tive** □ [~tiv] wahrnehmend; Wahrnehmungs...; **per'cep·tive·ness, per·cep'tiv·i·ty** Wahrnehmungsvermögen *n*.

perch¹ *ichth.* [pə:tʃ] Barsch *m*.

perch² [~] **1.** Rute *f* (*Längenmaß* = *5,029 m*); (Sitz)Stange *f für Vögel*; F *fig.* Thron *m*; **2.** (sich) setzen; sitzen; *~ed fig.* thronend, hoch *auf et.* gelegen.

per·chance [pə'tʃɑ:ns] zufällig; vielleicht.

per·cip·i·ent [pə'sipiənt] **1.** wahrnehmend; **2.** Wahrnehmende *m*.

per·co·late ['pə:kəleit] durchtropfen, -sickern (lassen); **'per·co·la·tor** Perkolator *m*, Kaffeemaschine *f*.

per·cus·sion [pə:'kʌʃən] Schlag *m*; Erschütterung *f*; ⚕ Beklopfen *n*; *~ cap* Zündhütchen *n*; *~ instruments pl.* ♪ Schlagzeug *n*; **per'cus·sive** [~siv] Schlag...

per·di·tion [pə:'diʃən] Verderben *n*.

per·e·gri·nate ['perigrineit] (durch-) wandern; **per·e·gri'na·tion** Wanderschaft *f*; Wanderung *f*.

per·emp·to·ri·ness [pəˈremptərinis] Bestimmtheit *f*; *b.s.* rechthaberische Art *f*; **perˈemp·to·ry** □ bestimmt, entschieden; zwingend; *b.s.* rechthaberisch.

per·en·ni·al [pəˈrenjəl] **1.** □ dauernd; immerwährend; ⚘ perennierend; **2.** ⚘ perennierende Pflanze *f*.

per·fect 1. [ˈpəːfikt] □ vollkommen (*a. moralisch*); vollendet, perfekt; gänzlich, völlig; ~ *pitch* ♪ absolutes Gehör; **2.** [~] *a.* ~ *tense gr.* Perfekt *n*; **3.** [pəˈfekt] vervollkommnen; vollenden; **perˈfec·tion** Vervollkommnung *f*, Vollendung *f*, Perfektion *f*; Vollkommenheit *f*; *fig.* Gipfel *m*; **perˈfec·tion·ist** Perfektionist(in) (*a. phls.*).

per·fid·i·ous □ [pəːˈfidiəs] treulos (*to* gegen), verräterisch; **perˈfid·i·ous·ness**, **ˈper·fi·dy** Treulosigkeit *f*, Falschheit *f*.

per·fo·rate [ˈpəːfəreit] durchbohren, durchlöchern; lochen; **per·fo·ˈra·tion** Durchbohrung *f*, Durchlöcherung *f*; Lochung *f*; Loch *n*; **ˈper·fo·ra·tor** Locher *m* (*Gerät*).

per·force [pəˈfɔːs] notgedrungen.

per·form [pəˈfɔːm] verrichten, leisten; durch-, ausführen, vollziehen; *Pflicht etc.* erfüllen; *thea.*, ♪ aufführen, spielen (*a. v/i.*), vortragen; **perˈform·ance** Verrichtung *f*; Erfüllung *f*; *thea.* Aufführung *f*, Vorstellung *f*; Vortrag *m*; ⊕ Leistung *f* (*a. fig.*); Werk *n*, Tat *f*; **perˈform·er** Vollzieher(in); Schauspieler(in); Darsteller(in); Künstler(in); **perˈform·ing** dressiert (*Tier*).

per·fume 1. [ˈpəːfjuːm] Wohlgeruch *m*, Duft *m*; Parfüm *n*; **2.** [pəˈfjuːm] durchduften; parfümieren; **perˈfum·er** Parfümeur *m*; **perˈfum·er·y** Parfümerie *f* (*Geschäft*); Parfümeriewaren *f/pl.*

per·func·to·ry □ [pəˈfʌŋktəri] nachlässig; mechanisch, schablonenhaft; oberflächlich; interesselos.

per·haps [pəˈhæps, præps] vielleicht.

per·i·gee *ast.* [ˈperidʒiː] Erdnähe *f*.

per·il [ˈperil] **1.** Gefahr *f*; *at my* ~ auf meine Gefahr; **2.** gefährden; **ˈper·il·ous** □ gefährlich.

pe·ri·od [ˈpiəriəd] Periode *f*; Zeitabschnitt *m*, -raum *m*, -dauer *f*; *gr.* Punkt *m*; Periode *f*, langer Satz *m*; (Unterrichts)Stunde *f*; ~*s pl.* ⚕ Periode *f*; ~ *furniture* Stilmöbel *n/pl.*; **per·i·od·ic** [~ˈɔdik] periodisch; **pe·riˈod·i·cal 1.** □ periodisch; **2.** Zeitschrift *f*.

per·i·pa·tet·ic [peripəˈtetik] (~*ally*) (umher)wandernd.

pe·riph·er·y [pəˈrifəri] Peripherie *f*.

pe·riph·ra·sis [pəˈrifrəsis], *pl.* **peˈriph·ra·ses** [~siːz] Umschreibung *f*; **per·i·phras·tic** [periˈfræstik] (~*ally*) umschreibend.

per·i·scope ⚓, ⚔ [ˈperiskəup] Periskop *n*, Sehrohr *n*.

per·ish [ˈperiʃ] umkommen, zugrunde gehen; kaputt machen; *be* ~*ed with* umkommen vor *Kälte etc.*; **ˈper·ish·a·ble 1.** □ vergänglich; leicht verderblich (*Eßwaren etc.*); **2.** ~*s pl.* leicht verderbliche Waren *f/pl.*; **ˈper·ish·ing** □ vernichtend, tödlich; F scheußlich.

per·i·style [ˈperistail] Säulengang *m*.

per·i·wig [ˈperiwig] Perücke *f*.

per·i·win·kle[1] ⚘ [ˈperiwiŋkl] Immergrün *n*.

per·i·win·kle[2] *zo.* [~](eßbare) Uferschnecke *f*.

per·jure [ˈpəːdʒə]: ~ *o.s.* falsch schwören; **ˈper·jured** meineidig; **ˈper·jur·er** Meineidige *m*; **ˈper·ju·ry** Meineid *m*.

perk[1] F [pəːk] = *percolate*.

perk[2] F [~] **1.** *mst* ~ *up v/i.* selbstbewußt auftreten, die Nase hoch tragen; sich recken; sich wieder erholen; zu Kräften *od.* in Stimmung kommen; *v/t.* recken, aufrichten; **2.** = ~*y*; **perk·i·ness** [ˈ~inis] Keckheit *f*.

perks F [pəːks] *pl.* = *perquisites*.

perk·y □ [ˈpəːki] keck, dreist; flott, forsch.

perm F [pəːm] **1.** Dauerwelle *f*; **2.** *j-m* Dauerwellen machen.

per·ma·frost [ˈpəːməfrɔst] Dauerfrostboden *m*.

per·ma·nence [ˈpəːmənəns] Dauer *f*, Ständigkeit *f*; **ˈper·ma·nen·cy** *s. permanence*; etwas Bleibendes *n*; Dauerstellung *f*; **ˈper·ma·nent** □ dauernd, bleibend, ständig, anhaltend; dauerhaft; fest, Dauer… (*Stellung*); ~ *wave* Dauerwelle *f*; ~ *way* 🚂 Bahnkörper *m*.

per·me·a·bil·i·ty [pəːmjəˈbiliti] Durchdringbarkeit *f*; **ˈper·me·a·ble** □ durchdringbar, durchlässig (*to* für); **per·me·ate** [ˈ~mieit] *v/t.* durchdringen; *v/i.* eindringen (*into* in *acc.*); sich verbreiten (*among* unter *dat.*).

per·mis·si·ble □ [pə'misəbl] zulässig; **per·mis·sion** [pə'miʃən] Erlaubnis *f*, Genehmigung *f*; **per'mis·sive** □ [~siv] gestattend; ⚖ fakultativ; ~ *society* tabufreie Gesellschaft *f*.

per·mit 1. [pə'mit] *a.* ~ *of* erlauben, gestatten; *weather* ~*ting* bei günstiger Witterung; **2.** ['pə:mit] Erlaubnis *f*, Genehmigung *f*; Erlaubnis-, Passierschein *m*.

per·ni·cious □ [pə:'niʃəs] verderblich; ⚕ perniziös, bösartig.

per·nick·et·y F [pə'nikiti] umständlich, pedantisch; heikel.

per·o·ra·tion [perə'reiʃən] Redeschluß *m*.

per·ox·ide ⚗ [pə'rɔksaid]: ~ *of hydrogen* Wasserstoffsuperoxyd *n*.

per·pen·dic·u·lar [pə:pən'dikjulə] **1.** □ senkrecht; aufrecht; steil; ~ *style* △ englische Spätgotik *f*; **2.** Senkrechte *f*; Perpendikel *n*, *m*.

per·pe·trate ['pə:pitreit] *Verbrechen etc.* begehen, verüben; F *Witz etc.* verbrechen; **per·pe'tra·tion** Verübung *f*; **'per·pe·tra·tor** Täter *m*.

per·pet·u·al □ [pə'petʃuəl] fortwährend, ewig; lebenslänglich; **per'pet·u·ate** [~eit] verewigen; **per·pet·u'a·tion** Verewigung *f*; **per·pe·tu·i·ty** [pə:pi'tju:iti] Ewigkeit *f*; lebenslängliche Rente *f*; *in* ~ auf ewig.

per·plex [pə'pleks] verwirren, verblüffen; verkomplizieren; **per'plexed** □ verwirrt, bestürzt, verdutzt; kompliziert; **per'plex·i·ty** Verwirrung *f*; Verlegenheit *f*; Verworrenheit *f*.

per·qui·sites ['pə:kwizits] *pl.* Nebenverdienst *m*, Sporteln *f/pl.*

per·se·cute ['pə:sikju:t] verfolgen; drangsalieren; **per·se'cu·tion** Verfolgung *f*; Drangsalierung *f*; ~ *mania* Verfolgungswahn *m*; **per·se·cu·tor** ['~tə] Verfolger *m*.

per·se·ver·ance [pə:si'viərəns] Beharrlichkeit *f*, Ausdauer *f*; **per·se·vere** [~'viə] beharren (*in* bei); aushalten (*with* bei); festhalten (*in* an *dat.*); **per·se'ver·ing** □ beharrlich, standhaft.

Per·sian ['pə:ʃən] **1.** persisch; **2.** Perser(in); Persisch *n*.

per·sim·mon ⚘ [pə:'simən] Dattelpflaume *f*, Persimone *f*.

per·sist [pə'sist] beharren, bestehen (*in* auf *dat.*); fortdauern, anhalten; (bestehen) bleiben; **per'sist·ence, per'sist·en·cy** Beharrlichkeit *f*; Fortdauer *f*; **per'sist·ent** □ beharrlich; hartnäckig.

per·son ['pə:sn] Person *f* (*a. gr.*); Persönlichkeit *f*; *thea.* Rolle *f*; Körper *m*; *in* ~ in eigener Person, persönlich; ~-*to*-~ *call teleph.* Voranmeldungsgespräch *n*; **'per·son·a·ble** ansehnlich; **'per·son·age** Persönlichkeit *f*; *thea.* Charakter *m*; **'per·son·al 1.** □ persönlich (*a. gr.*); Personal...; Privat...; eigen; ~ *property od. estate* ⚖ *s. personalty*; **2.** *Zeitung*: Familienanzeige *f*, Persönliches *n*; **per·son·al·i·ty** [pə:sə'næliti] Persönlichkeit *f*; *personalities pl.* persönliche Bemerkungen *f/pl.*; ~ *clash psych.* Persönlichkeitskonflikt *m*; **per·son·al·ty** ['pə:snlti] ⚖ persönliches *od.* bewegliches Eigentum *n*; **per·son·ate** ['~səneit] vor-, darstellen; sich ausgeben für; **per·son'a·tion** Vor-, Darstellung *f*; Verkörperung *f*; **per·son·i·fi·ca·tion** [pə:sɔnifi'keiʃən] Verkörperung *f*; **per·son·i·fy** [pə:'sɔnifai] personifizieren; verkörpern; **per·son·nel** [pə:sə'nel] Personal *n*; Belegschaft *f*.

per·spec·tive [pə'spektiv] **1.** □ perspektivisch; **2.** Perspektive *f*; Ausblick *m*, Fernsicht *f*.

per·spex ['pə:speks] Plexiglas *n*.

per·spi·ca·cious □ [pə:spi'keiʃəs] scharfsichtig, -sinnig; **per·spi·cac·i·ty** [~'kæsiti] Scharfblick *m*, -sinn *m*; **per·spi·cu·i·ty** [~'kjuiti] Klarheit *f*, Deutlichkeit *f*; **per·spic·u·ous** [pə'spikjuəs] □ klar, deutlich.

per·spi·ra·tion [pə:spə'reiʃən] Schwitzen *n*; Schweiß *m*; **perspire** [pəs'paiə] (aus)schwitzen.

per·suade [pə'sweid] überreden, bereden (*to inf.*, *into ger.* zu *inf.*); überzeugen (*of* von; *that* daß); **per'suad·er** *sl.* Überredungsmittel *n*.

per·sua·sion [pə'sweiʒən] Überredung *f*; Überzeugung *f*; Glaube *m*; F *co.* Gattung *f*; *powers pl. of* ~ Überredungskünste *f/pl.*

per·sua·sive □ [pə'sweisiv] überredend, -zeugend; **per'sua·sive·ness** Überzeugungskraft *f*.

pert □ [pə:t] keck, vorlaut, naseweis.

per·tain [pə:'tein] (*to*) gehören (*dat.*

od. zu); sich für *j.* gehören (*geziemen*); betreffen (*acc.*).
per·ti·na·cious □ [pə:ti'neiʃəs] hartnäckig, zäh; **per·ti·nac·i·ty** [~'næsiti] Hartnäckig-, Zähigkeit *f*.
per·ti·nence, per·ti·nen·cy ['pə:tinəns(i)] Sachdienlichkeit *f*, Gemäßheit *f*; **'per·ti·nent** □ sachdienlich, -gemäß; zur Sache gehörig; *be ~ to* Bezug haben auf (*acc.*).
pert·ness ['pə:tnis] Keckheit *f*.
per·turb [pə'tə:b] beunruhigen; stören; **per·tur·ba·tion** [pə:tə:'beiʃən] Beunruhigung *f*; Störung *f*.
pe·ruke [pə'ru:k] Perücke *f*.
pe·rus·al [pə'ru:zəl] sorgfältiges Durchlesen *n*, Durchsicht *f*; Prüfung *f*; **pe'ruse** sorgfältig durchlesen; *fig.* durchgehen, prüfen.
Pe·ru·vi·an [pə'ru:vjən] **1.** peruanisch; *~ bark* ⚘ Chinarinde *f*; **2.** Peruaner(in).
per·vade [pə:'veid] durchdringen, -ziehen, erfüllen; **per'va·sion** [~ʒən] Durchdringung *f*; **per'va·sive** [~siv] durchdringend.
per·verse □ [pə'və:s] verkehrt; ⚕ pervers; eigensinnig, bockig; vertrackt (*Sache*); **per'verse·ness** = *perversity*; **per'ver·sion** Verdrehung *f*; Abkehr *f vom Guten etc.*; **per'ver·si·ty** Verkehrtheit *f*; ⚕ Perversität *f*; Verderbtheit *f*; Eigensinn *m*; **per'ver·sive** verderblich (*of* für).
per·vert 1. [pə'və:t] verdrehen; verführen; **2.** ['pə:və:t] ⚕ perverser Mensch *m*; **per'vert·er** [pə'və:tə] Verdreher(in); Verführer(in).
per·vi·ous ['pə:vjəs] zugänglich (*a. fig.*); durchlässig (*to* für).
pes·ky □ *sl.* ['peski] verflixt.
pes·sa·ry ['pesəri] Scheidenzäpfchen *n*; Pessar *n*, Mutterring *m*.
pes·si·mism ['pesimizəm] Pessimismus *m*; **'pes·si·mist** Pessimist(in), Schwarzseher(in); **pes·si'mis·tic** (*~ally*) pessimistisch.
pest [pest] *fig.* Pest *f*; Plage *f*; Schädling *m*; *~* **con·trol** Schädlingsbekämpfung *f*; **'pes·ter** belästigen; plagen; quälen.
pest·i·cide ['pestisaid] Schädlingsbekämpfungsmittel *n*; **pes'tif·er·ous** □ [~fərəs] krankheitserregend; verderblich; **pes·ti·lence** ['~ləns] Seuche *f*, *bsd.* Pest *f*; **'pes·ti·lent** gefährlich; *co.* verdammt; **pes·ti·len·tial** □ [~'lenʃəl] pestartig; verderbenbringend; verdammt.
pes·tle ['pesl] **1.** Mörserkeule *f*, Stößel *m*; **2.** zerstoßen.
pet[1] [pet] Ärger *m*, üble Laune *f*; *in a ~* übelgelaunt.
pet[2] [~] **1.** zahmes Tier *n*; Liebling *m*, Schoßkind *n*; **2.** Lieblings...; zahm; *~ dog* Schoßhund *m*; *~ name* Kosename *m*; *it is my ~ aversion* es ist mir ein Greuel; **3.** (ver)hätscheln; F knutschen; *petting party* Knutscherei *f*.
pet·al ⚘ ['petl] Blumenblatt *n*.
pe·tard [pe'tɑ:d] Schwärmer *m* (*Feuerwerk*).
pe·ter ['pi:tə]: *~ out* zu Ende gehen; im Sande verlaufen.
pet·i·ole ⚘ ['petiəul] (Blatt)Stiel *m*.
pet·it ['peti] klein, geringfügig; **pe·tite** [pə'ti:t] klein, zierlich (*Frau*).
pe·ti·tion [pi'tiʃən] **1.** Bitte *f*; Bittschrift *f*, Eingabe *f*, Gesuch *n*; *~ in bankruptcy* ⚖ Konkursantrag *m*; *~ for divorce* ⚖ Scheidungsklage *f*; **2.** bitten, ersuchen (*for* um; *to inf.* zu *inf.*); eine Bittschrift *etc.* einreichen (*s.o.* an j.; *for* um); **pe'ti·tion·er** [~ʃnə] Bittsteller(in).
pet·rel *orn.* ['petrəl] Sturmvogel *m*.
pet·ri·fac·tion *geol.* [petri'fækʃən] Versteinerung *f*.
pet·ri·fy ['petrifai] versteinern.
pet·rol *mot.* ['petrəl] Benzin *n*; Treibstoff *m*; *~ bomb* Molotowcocktail *m*; *~ coupon* Benzingutschein *m*; *~ engine* Benzinmotor *m*; *~ station* Tankstelle *f*; *~ tank* Benzintank *m*.
pe·tro·le·um [pi'trəuljəm] Petroleum *n*, Erdöl *n*; *~ jelly* Vaseline *f*.
pe·trol·o·gy *geol.* [pe'trɔlədʒi] Gesteinskunde *f*.
pet·ti·coat ['petikəut] Unterrock *m*; *~ government contp.* Weiberregiment *n*.
pet·ti·fog·ger ['petifɔgə] Winkeladvokat *m*; **'pet·ti·fog·ging** kleinlich, pedantisch.
pet·ti·ness ['petinis] Geringfügigkeit *f*.
pet·tish □ ['petiʃ] launisch, verdrießlich; **'pet·tish·ness** Verdrießlichkeit *f*.
pet·ty □ ['peti] klein, geringfügig; Klein...; *~ bourgeois* Kleinbürger *m*; kleinbürgerlich; *~ bourgeoisie* Klein-

bürgertum *n*; ~ *cash* ✝ kleine Summen *f/pl.*; ~ *officer* ⚓ Maat *m*; ~ *sessions pl.* ⚖ Bagatellgericht *n*.
pet·u·lance ['petjuləns] *s. pettishness*; '**pet·u·lant** *s. pettish*.
pew [pju:] Kirchensitz *m*; -stuhl *m*.
pe·wit *orn.* ['pi:wit] Lachmöwe *f*; Kiebitz *m*.
pew·ter ['pju:tə] Zinn *n*; Zinngefäße *n/pl.*; '**pew·ter·er** Zinngießer *m*.
pha·e·ton *hist.* ['feitn] Phaethon *m* (*Wagen*).
pha·lanx ['fælæŋks] Phalanx *f*.
phan·tasm ['fæntæzəm] Trugbild *n*; **phan·tas·ma·go·ri·a** [~mə'gɔ:riə] Gaukelbild *n*, Phantasmagorie *f*.
phan·tom ['fæntəm] **1.** Phantom *n*, Trugbild *n*; Gespenst *n*; Hirngespinst *n*; **2.** Gespenster...
Phar·i·sa·ic, Phar·i·sa·i·cal □ [færi'seiik(əl)] pharisäisch, scheinheilig.
Phar·i·see ['færisi:] Pharisäer *m*.
phar·ma·ceu·ti·cal □ [fɑ:mə'sju:tikəl] pharmazeutisch; **phar·ma'ceu·tics** *sg.* Pharmazeutik *f*, Arzneimittelkunde *f*; **phar·ma·cist** ['~sist] Pharmazeut *m*, Apotheker *m*; **phar·ma·col·o·gy** [~'kɔlədʒi] Arzneimittellehre *f*; '**phar·ma·cy** Pharmazie *f*; Apotheke *f*.
phar·ynx *anat.* ['færiŋks] Rachenhöhle *f*.
phase [feiz] Phase *f*, (Entwicklungs)Stufe *f*, Stadium *n*; **phased** in Phasen.
pheas·ant *orn.* ['feznt] Fasan *m*; '**pheas·ant·ry** Fasanerie *f*.
phe·nom·e·nal □ [fi'nɔminl] phänomenal; außergewöhnlich; **phe'nom·e·non** [~nən], *pl.* **phe'nom·e·na** [~nə] Phänomen *n*, Erscheinung *f*; *fig.* Wunder *n*.
phew [fju:] puh!
phi·al ['faiəl] Phiole *f*, Fläschchen *n*.
Phi Be·ta Kap·pa *Am.* ['fai 'bi:tə 'kæpə] *e-e* Studentenverbindung *f*.
phi·lan·der [fi'lændə] flirten; **phi'lan·der·er** Schürzenjäger *m*.
phil·an·throp·ic [filən'θrɔpik] (~*ally*) menschenfreundlich; **phi·lan·thro·pist** [fi'lænθrəpist] Menschenfreund(in); **phi'lan·thro·py** Menschenliebe *f*.
phi·lat·e·list [fi'lætəlist] Briefmarkensammler(in); **phi'lat·e·ly** Briefmarkensammeln *n*; Philatelie *f*.
phi·lip·pic [fi'lipik] Philippika *f*, Standpauke *f*, Strafpredigt *f*.
Phi·lis·tine ['filistain] Philister *m* (*a. fig.*).
phil·o·log·i·cal □ [filə'lɔdʒikəl] sprachwissenschaftlich, philologisch; **phi·lol·o·gist** [fi'lɔlədʒist] Philologe *m*, Philologin *f*; Sprachforscher(in); **phi'lol·o·gy** Philologie *f*, Sprachwissenschaft *f*.
phi·los·o·pher [fi'lɔsəfə] Philosoph *m*; ~*s' stone* Stein *m* der Weisen; **phil·o·soph·ic, phil·o·soph·i·cal** [filə'sɔfik(əl)] philosophisch; **phi·los·o·phize** [fi'lɔsəfaiz] philosophieren; **phi'los·o·phy** Philosophie *f*.
phil·tre, phil·ter ['filtə] Liebestrank *m*.
phiz F *co.* [fiz] Visage *f*, Gesicht *n*.
phle·bi·tis ⚕ [fli'baitis] Venenentzündung *f*.
phlegm [flem] Schleim *m*; Phlegma *n*; **phleg·mat·ic** [fleg'mætik] (~*ally*) phlegmatisch.
pho·bi·a ['fəubiə] Phobie *f* (*Angst*).
phoe·be *orn.* ['fi:bi] Tyrannvogel *m*.
Phoe·ni·cian [fi'niʃiən] **1.** phönizisch; **2.** Phönizier(in).
phoe·nix *myth.* ['fi:niks] Phönix *m*.
phone¹ F [fəun] **1.** Telefon *n*; **2.** telefonieren.
phone² [~] (Einzel)Laut *m*.
phone-in ['fəunin] Sendung *f* mit Zuschauer- *od.* Zuhörerbeteiligung.
pho·neme ['fəuni:m] Phonem *n*; **pho'nem·ic** phonemisch.
pho·net·ic [fəu'netik] (~*ally*) phonetisch; ~ *spelling* phonetische Schreibung *f* (*z. B. thru für through*); ~ *transcription* Lautschrift *f*; **pho·ne·ti·cian** [~ni'tiʃən] Phonetiker *m*; **pho·net·ics** [~'netiks] *sg.* Phonetik *f*, Laut(bildungs)lehre *f*.
pho·ney *sl.* ['fəuni] unecht; falsch; Schein...
pho·no·graph *Am.* ['fəunəgrɑ:f] Plattenspieler *m*; Grammophon *n*.
pho·nol·o·gy [fəu'nɔlədʒi] Phonologie *f*, Lautlehre *f*.
pho·ny *Am. sl.* ['fəuni] **1.** Fälschung *f*; Schwindler *m*; **2.** = *phoney*.
phos·phate ⚗ ['fɔsfeit] Phosphat *n*.
phos·pho·resce [fɔsfə'res] phosphoreszieren; **phos·pho'res·cent** phosphoreszierend; **phos·phor·ic** ⚗ [~'fɔrik] Phosphor...; **phos-**

pho·rous ⚗ ['~fərəs] phosphorig; **phos·pho·rus** ⚗ ['~fərəs] Phosphor *m*.

pho·to F ['fəutəu] Photo *n*; '**~·cop·i·er** Photokopiergerät *n*; '**~·cop·y** Photokopie *f*; photokopieren; **~-en'grav·ing** Lichtdruck(verfahren *n*) *m*; '**~-'fin·ish** *Am*. Entscheidung *f* durch Zielphotographie; '**~-flash** Blitzlicht *n*, -lampe *f*; **~·gen·ic** [fəutəu'dʒenik] photogen; **~·gram·me·try** [~'græmitri] Meßbildverfahren *n*.

pho·to·graph ['fəutəgrɑːf] **1.** Photographie *f*, Lichtbild *n*, Aufnahme *f*; *take a ~* e-e Aufnahme machen; **2.** photographieren; **pho·tog·ra·pher** [fə'tɔgrəfə] Photograph(in); **pho·to·graph·ic** [fəutə'græfik] (*~ally*) photographisch; *~ library* Bildarchiv *n*; Photothek *f*; *~ print* Lichtpause *f*; **pho·tog·ra·phy** [fə'tɔgrəfi] Photographie *f*.

pho·to·gra·vure [fəutəgrə'vjuə] Lichtkupferätzung *f*, Kupfertiefdruck *m*; **pho·tom·e·ter** [~'tɔmitə] Belichtungsmesser *m*; **pho·to-play** ['~təplei] Filmdrama *n*; **pho·to·sen·si·tive** ['~təusensətiv] lichtempfindlich; **pho·to·stat** ['~təustæt] Photokopiergerät *n*; Photokopie *f*; **pho·to·te·leg·ra·phy** [~təti'legrəfi] Bildtelegraphie *f*; **pho·to·type** ['~təutaip] Lichtpause *f*.

phrase [freiz] **1.** (Rede)Wendung *f*, Redensart *f*, Ausdruck *m*; Schlagwort *n*; ♪ Satz *m*; **2.** ausdrücken; formulieren; '**~·book** Sprachführer *m*; '**~-mon·ger** Phrasendrescher *m*; **phra·se·ol·o·gy** [~i'ɔlədʒi] Ausdrucksweise *f*; Phraseologie *f*; '**phras·ing** Formulierung *f*.

phre·net·ic [fri'netik] (*~ally*) toll, rasend, frenetisch.

phre·nol·o·gy [fri'nɔlədʒi] Schädellehre *f*.

phthis·i·cal ⚕ ['θaisikəl] schwindsüchtig; **phthi·sis** ['~sis] Schwindsucht *f*.

phut *sl*. [fʌt]: *go ~* futschgehen.

phys·ic F ['fizik] **1.** Arznei *f*; **2.** *j*. verarzten; '**phys·i·cal** □ physisch; körperlich; physikalisch; *~ condition* Gesundheitszustand *m*; *~ culture* Körperpflege *f*; *~ education*, *~ training* Leibeserziehung *f*; **phy·si·cian** [fi'ziʃən] Arzt *m*; **phys·i·cist** ['~sist] Physiker *m*; **phys·ics** ['fiziks] *sg*. Physik *f*.

phys·i·og·no·my [fizi'ɔnəmi] Physiognomie *f*; Gesichtsausdruck *m*; **phys·i·o·log·i·cal** [~ə'lɔdʒikəl] physiologisch; **phys·i·ol·o·gist** [~'ɔlədʒist] Physiologe *m*; **phys·i·'ol·o·gy** Physiologie *f*.

phys·i·o·ther·a·py [fiziəu'θerəpi] Physiotherapie *f*.

phy·sique [fi'ziːk] Körperbau *m*.

pi·an·ist ['piənist] Pianist(in), Klavierspieler(in).

pi·a·no[1] ♪ ['pjɑːnəu] piano.

pi·an·o[2] ['pjænəu] *a*. **pi·an·o·for·te** [~'fɔːti] Klavier *n*; *grand piano* Flügel *m*.

pi·az·za [pi'ætsə] Piazza *f*, (Markt-)Platz *m*; *Am*. große Veranda *f*.

pi·broch ['piːbrɔk] Dudelsackvariationen *f/pl*.

pic·a·resque [pikə'resk] pikaresk; *~ novel* Schelmenroman *m*.

pic·a·yune *Am*. [pikə'juːn] **1.** *mst fig*. Pfennig *m*; Null *f*; Lappalie *f*; **2.** unbedeutend, schäbig.

pic·ca·lil·li [pikə'lili] Piccalilli *pl*. (*scharf eingemachtes, kleingeschnittenes Mischgemüse*).

pic·ca·nin·ny *co*. ['pikənini] **1.** *bsd. Neger*-Kind *n*, Gör *n*; **2.** kindlich.

pick [pik] **1.** Auswahl *f*, -lese *f*; *das Beste*; = *pickaxe*; **2.** auf-, wegnehmen; (*Blumen, Früchte*) pflükken; *in den Zähnen* stochern; *in der Nase* bohren; *Knochen* abnagen; *Schloß* knacken; *Streit* suchen; auswählen, -suchen; (auf)picken; im Essen herumstochern; *~ s.o.'s pocket* j-m die Tasche ausräumen; *~ one's way* vorsichtig gehen; *~ one's words* sich gewählt *od*. vorsichtig ausdrücken; *~ at* herumnörgeln an (*dat*.); *~ off* abnehmen, -machen; abschießen; *~ on* verfallen auf, auswählen; *~ out* auswählen; herausfinden, -suchen, ausfindig machen; *Melodie* nach Gehör spielen; *~ over Früchte etc*. auslesen; *~ up* aufreißen, -brechen; aufnehmen, -heben; sich *e-e Fremdsprache* aneignen; aufgreifen; auflesen; erfassen; auffangen, -schnappen; *j*. (im Auto) mitnehmen; *j*. abholen; *Täter* ergreifen; *Gesundheit* wiedererlangen; gesund werden, sich erholen *~ o.s. up* wieder hochkommen; *~ up speed* auf Touren kommen; *~ up with* kennenlernen; **~-a-back**

['~əbæk] huckepack; '**~·axe** Spitzhacke *f*; '**pick·er** Pflücker(in), Leser(in), Zupfer(in); Pflückmaschine *f*.

pick·er·el *ichth.* ['pikərəl] junger Hecht *m*.

pick·et ['pikit] **1.** Pfahl *m*; Pflock *m*; ⚔ Feldwache *f*; Streikposten *m*; **2.** *v/t.* einpfählen; an e-n Pfahl binden; ⚔ als Feldwache aufstellen; mit Streikposten besetzen; *v/i.* Streikposten stehen.

pick·ing ['pikiŋ] Picken *n*, Pflücken *n etc.* (*s. pick*); Abfall *m*; *mst ~s pl.* (unehrlicher) Nebengewinn *m*.

pick·le ['pikl] **1.** Pökel *m*, Salzlake *f*; Eingepökelte *n*, Pickles *pl.*; F Wildfang *m*; F mißliche Lage *f*; *s. mix*; **2.** (ein)pökeln; *~d herring* Salzhering *m*.

pick...: '**~·lock** Dietrich *m*; Einbrecher *m*; '**~-me-up** F (Magen-) Stärkung *f*; '**~·pock·et** Taschendieb *m*; '**~-up** Ansteigen *n*; Tonabnehmer *m am Plattenspieler*; *a.* *~ in prices* ✝ Hausse *f*; Kleinlieferwagen *m*; Pritschenwagen *m*; Beschleunigung *f*; *sl.* Straßenbekanntschaft *f*; *~ dinner* Essen *n* aus (Fleisch)Resten; '**pick·y** F wählerisch.

pic·nic ['piknik] **1.** Picknick *n*; *fig.* Kinderspiel *n*; **2.** picknicken.

pic·to·ri·al [pik'tɔːriəl] **1.** □ Maler-...; malerisch; illustriert; *~ advertising* Bildreklame *f*; **2.** Illustrierte *f*.

pic·ture ['piktʃə] **1.** Bild *n*, Gemälde *n*; Ebenbild *n*; Verkörperung *f*; *et.* Bildschönes *n*; *~s pl.* F Kino *n*; *put s.o. in the ~* j. ins Bild setzen, j. informieren; **2.** malen; schildern; illustrieren; sich *et.* vorstellen *od.* ausmalen; '**~-book** Bilderbuch *n*; *~* **ed·i·tor** Bildredakteur *m*; '**~-gal·ler·y** Gemäldegalerie *f*; '**~-go·er** Kinobesucher(in); *~* **post·card** Ansichtskarte *f*; *~* **res·o·lu·tion** *Fernsehen*: Bildauflösung *f*.

pic·tur·esque □ [piktʃə'resk] malerisch; **pic·tur'esque·ness** *das* Malerische.

pidg·in ['pidʒin]: *~ English* Pidgin-Englisch *n*; *that's not my ~* F das geht mich nichts an.

pie[1] [pai] Pastete *f*, Obsttorte *f*, -kuchen *m*; *typ.* Zwiebelfische *m/pl.*; *s. finger 1.*

pie[2] *orn.* [~] Elster *f*.

pie·bald ['paibɔːld] gescheckt; buntscheckig.

piece [piːs] **1.** Stück *n* (*a. Teil, Kunstwerk, Münze*); Geschütz *n*; Gewehr *n*; Teil *n e-s Services*; (*Schach- etc.*)Figur *f*; *a ~ of advice* ein Rat *m*; *a ~ of news* e-e Neuigkeit; *~ by ~* eines nach dem anderen; *of a ~* gleichmäßig; *be of a ~ with* im Einklang stehen mit; *give s.o. a ~ of one's mind* j-m gründlich die Meinung sagen; *take to ~s* zerlegen; **2.** *a. ~ up* flicken, ausbessern; *~ together* zs.-stellen, -setzen, -stücken, -flicken; *~ out* ausfüllen; '**~-goods** *pl.* Meterware *f*; '**~·meal** stückweise; '**~-·work** Akkordarbeit *f*.

pied [paid] scheckig, bunt.

pie–eyed ['pai'aid] besoffen.

pie·plant *Am.* ['paiplɑːnt] Rhabarber *m*.

pier [piə] Pfeiler *m*; Wellenbrecher *m*; Pier *m*, *f*, Hafendamm *m*, Mole *f*, Landungsbrücke *f*; '**pier·age** ⚓ Kaigeld *n*.

pierce [piəs] *v/t.* durchbohren; *Ohr* durchdringen; eindringen *in Geheimnisse etc.*; *v/i.* eindringen (*a. fig.*); '**pierc·ing** □ durchdringend (*a. fig.*).

pier-glass ['piəglɑːs] Pfeilerspiegel *m*.

pi·e·tism ['paiətizəm] Pietismus *m*.

pi·e·ty ['paiəti] Frömmigkeit *f*; Pietät *f*.

pif·fle *sl.* ['pifl] **1.** Quatsch *m*; Kitsch *m*; **2.** quatschen.

pig [pig] **1.** Ferkel *n*; Schwein *n*; *metall.* Roheisenbarren *m*, Massel *f*, Mulde *f*; *buy a ~ in a poke* die Katze im Sack kaufen; **2.** ferkeln; F zs.-gepfercht leben.

pi·geon ['pidʒin] Taube *f*; *sl.* Gimpel *m*; '**~-'breast·ed** hühnerbrüstig; '**~-hole 1.** *Brief- etc.* Fach *n*; **2.** in ein Fach legen, aufheben; einordnen; (vorläufig) beiseitelegen; '**pi·geon·ry** Taubenschlag *m*.

pig·ger·y ['pigəri] Schweinezucht *f*.

pig·gish □ ['pigiʃ] schweinisch.

pig·gy ['pigi] **1.** Schweinchen *n*; *~ bank* Sparschwein *n*; **2.** gierig.

pig·head·ed ['pig'hedid] dickköpfig.

pig-i·ron ['pigaiən] Roheisen *n*.

pig·let ['piglit] Ferkel *n*, Schweinchen *n*.
pig·ment ['pigmənt] Pigment *n*.
pig·my ['pigmi] = *pygmy*.
pig...: '**~·nut** Erdnuß *f*; '**~·skin** Schweinsleder *n*; **~·sty** ['~stai] Schweinestall *m*, Koben *m*; '**~·tail** (Haar)Zopf *m*; '**~·wash** Schweinetrank *m*.
pike [paik] ⚔ Pike *f*; Spitze *f*; *ichth.* Hecht *m*; Schlagbaum *m*; gebührenpflichtige Straße *f*; '**pik·er** *Am. sl.* Geizhals *m*; *fig.* kleiner Mann *m*; '**pike·staff**: *as plain as a* ~ sonnenklar.
pil·chard *ichth.* ['piltʃəd] Sardine *f*.
pile[1] [pail] **1.** Haufen *m*; Stoß *m*, Stapel *m*; Scheiterhaufen *m*; großes Gebäude *n*; ⚡ Batterie *f*; *atomic* ~ Atommeiler *m*, Reaktor *m*; **2.** *oft* ~ *up*, ~ *on* auf-, anhäufen, aufschichten; (auf)stapeln, auftürmen.
pile[2] [~] Pfahl *m*.
pile[3] [~] Haar *n*; Noppe *f*; Flor *m des Samtes*.
pile-driv·er ⊕ ['paildraivə] Ramme *f*; '**pile-dwell·ing** Pfahlbau *m*.
piles ⚕ [pailz] *pl.* Hämorrhoiden *f/pl.*
pile-up F ['pailʌp] Massenkarambolage *f*.
pil·fer ['pilfə] stehlen, klauen.
pil·grim ['pilgrim] Pilger *m*, Wallfahrer *m*; ♀ *Fathers pl.* Pilgerväter *m/pl.* (*puritanische Einwanderer nach Amerika*); '**pil·grim·age** Pilgerfahrt *f*.
pill [pil] Pille *f*, Tablette *f*.
pil·lage ['pilidʒ] **1.** Plünderung *f*; **2.** plündern.
pil·lar ['pilə] Pfeiler *m*, Ständer *m*; Säule *f* (*a. fig.*); '**~-box** Briefkasten *m*; '**pil·lared** mit Pfeilern; säulenförmig.
pil·lion ['piljən] Sattelkissen *n*; *mot.* Soziussitz *m*; *ride* ~ auf dem Soziussitz (mit)fahren.
pil·lo·ry ['piləri] **1.** Pranger *m*; *in the* ~ am Pranger; **2.** an den Pranger stellen; *fig.* anprangern.
pil·low ['piləu] **1.** (Kopf)Kissen *n*; ⊕ (Zapfen)Lager *n*; **2.** betten, stützen (*on* auf *acc.*); '**~-case**, '**~-slip** (Kissen)Bezug *m*.
pi·lot ['pailət] **1.** ⚓ Lotse *m*; ✈ Pilot *m*, Flugzeugführer *m*; *fig.* Führer *m*; ~ *instructor* Fluglehrer *m*; ~ *officer* Fliegerleutnant *m*; ~ *pupil* Flugschüler *m*; **2.** Versuchs...; ~ *plant* Versuchsanlage *f*; ~ *project* Versuchs-, Testprojekt *n*; **3.** lotsen, steuern; '**pi·lot·age** Lotsen(geld) *n*; Führung(skunst) *f*; '**pi·lot-bal'loon** Versuchsballon *m*; '**pi·lot-light** Zündflamme *f e-s Gasgeräts*.
pi·men·to [pi'mentəu] Piment *m*, *n*, Nelkenpfeffer *m*.
pimp [pimp] **1.** Kuppler(in), Zuhälter *m*; **2.** kuppeln.
pim·ple ['pimpl] Pickel *m*, Pustel *f*; '**pim·pled**, '**pim·ply** pickelig, finnig.
pin [pin] **1.** (Steck)Nadel *f*; (Krawatten-, Hut- *etc.*)Nadel *f*; Bolzen *m*; Pflock *m*; Kegel *m*; Reißnagel *m*; ♪ Wirbel *m*; ~*s pl. sl.* Stelzen *f/pl.* (*Beine*); **2.** (an)heften; befestigen; *a.* ~ *down sl. fig.* festnageln, fassen; ~ *one's hopes on* seine Hoffnung setzen auf (*acc.*).
pin·a·fore ['pinəfɔː] Lätzchen *n*; Kinder-, Frauenschürze *f*.
pin·ball ma·chine *f* ['pinbɔːlməʃiːn] Flipper *m* (*Spielautomat*).
pin·cers ['pinsəz] *pl.* (*a pair of* ~ eine) Kneifzange *f*.
pinch [pintʃ] **1.** Kniff *m*; Prise *f* (*Tabak etc.*); Druck *m*, Not *f*; *at a* ~ notfalls; **2.** *v/t.* kneifen, zwicken, klemmen; F klauen (*stehlen*); *sl.* kassieren, festnehmen; *be* ~*ed for money* knapp bei Kasse sein; *v/i.* drücken; in Not sein; knausern; **pinched** zs.-gedrückt, schmal; *fig.* zs.-geschnurrt; dünn.
pinch·beck ['pintʃbek] **1.** ⊕ Tombak *m*; Talmi *n* (*a. fig.*); **2.** Talmi...
pinch-hit *Am.* ['pintʃhit] (*irr. hit*) einspringen (*for* für *j.*).
pin·cush·ion ['pinkuʃən] Nadelkissen *n*.
pine[1] ♀ [pain] Kiefer *f*, Föhre *f*.
pine[2] [~] sich abhärmen; sich sehnen, schmachten (*for*, *after* nach); ~ *away* sich verzehren.
pine...: '**~·ap·ple** ♀ Ananas *f*; '**~-cone** Kiefernzapfen *m*; '**pin·er·y** Treibhaus *n* für Ananas; Kiefernpflanzung *f*; '**~-tree** = *pine*[1].
pin-feath·er ['pinfeðə] Stoppelfeder *f*.
ping [piŋ] schwirren, pfeifen.
ping-pong ['piŋpɔŋ] Tischtennis *n*.
pin·ion ['pinjən] **1.** Flügelspitze *f*; *poet.* Schwinge *f*; *a.* ~*-feather* Schwungfeder *f*; ⊕ Ritzel *n* (*An-*

triebsrad); **2.** die Flügel beschneiden (*dat.*); *fig.* fesseln.

pink[1] [piŋk] **1.** ⚘ Nelke *f*; Blaßrot *n*, Rosa *n*; Gipfel *m*, höchster Grad *m*; *in the* ~ *sl.* in bester Verfassung; **2.** rosa(farben).

pink[2] [~] durchstechen; auszacken; ~*ing shears pl.* Zickzackschere *f*.

pink[3] *mot.* [~] klopfen, klingeln.

pink·ish ['piŋkiʃ] blaßrosa.

pin·nace ⚓ ['pinis] Pinasse *f*.

pin·na·cle ['pinəkl] ⚠ Zinne *f*, Spitztürmchen *n*; (Berg)Spitze *f*; *fig.* Gipfel *m*.

pin·nate ⚘ ['pineit] gefiedert.

pi·noc(h)·le *Am.* ['pi:nʌkl] Binokel *n* (*Kartenspiel*).

pin...: '~**·point** genau lokalisieren; *fig.* genau bestimmen; '~**·prick** *fig.* Nadelstich *m*; '~**-stripe** Nadelstreifen *m* (*Stoff*).

pint [paint] Pinte *f* (*0,57 od. Am. 0,47 Liter*).

pin-up ['pinʌp] Pin-up-girl *n*.

pi·o·neer [paiə'niə] **1.** Pionier *m* (*a.* ⚔), Bahnbrecher *m*, Vorkämpfer *m*; **2.** *Weg* bahnen; den Weg bahnen (für).

pi·ous □ ['paiəs] fromm, religiös; pflichtgetreu.

pip[1] [pip] *vet.* Pips *m*; *sl.* miese Laune *f*; *have the* ~ nicht auf dem Damm sein; *it gives me the* ~ es geht mir auf die Nerven.

pip[2] [~] Obstkern *m*; Auge *n auf Würfeln etc.*; ⚔ Stern *m* (*Rangabzeichen*).

pip[3] *sl.* [~] zunichte machen; durchfallen (lassen); abknallen; ~ *out* eingehen (*sterben*).

pip[4] [~] Ton *m* (*Zeitzeichen etc.*).

pipe [paip] **1.** Rohr *n*, Röhre *f*; ♪ (Orgel)Pfeife *f*, Flöte *f*; ⚓ Bootsmannspfeife *f*, -pfiff *m*; Lied *n e-s Vogels*; Luftröhre *f*; (Tabaks)Pfeife *f*; Pipe *f* (*Weinfaß = 470 l*); **2.** pfeifen; quieken; durch Röhren leiten; mit Röhren versehen; *Schneiderei*: paspeln; ~*d music contp.* Musikberieselung *f in Supermärkten etc.*; ~ *one's eye* F weinen; ~ *down* F den Mund halten; ~ *up* F loslegen; '~**·clay 1.** Pfeifenton *m*; **2.** mit Pfeifenton weißen; ~ **dream** Luftschloß *n*; '~**-lay·er** Rohrleger *m*; *Am. pol.* Drahtzieher *m*; '~**·line** Ölleitung *f*, Pipeline *f*; '**pip·er** Pfeifer *m*; *pay the* ~ F die Zeche bezahlen.

pip·ing ['paipiŋ] **1.** pfeifend; schrill (*Stimme*); fröhlich (*Zeit*); ~ *hot* siedend heiß; **2.** Rohrnetz *n*, -system *n*; *coll.* Rohr *n*; *Schneiderei*: Paspel *m*, *f*, Biese *f*; Zuckerguß *m*.

pip·pin ⚘ ['pipin] Pippinapfel *m*.

pip-squeak *sl.* ['pipskwi:k] Knülch *m*, Würstchen *n*.

pi·quan·cy ['pi:kənsi] Pikantheit *f*; '**pi·quant** □ pikant.

pique [pi:k] **1.** Groll *m*; **2.** *Zorn od. Neugier* reizen; ~ *o.s. upon* sich etwas zugute tun auf (*acc.*).

pi·ra·cy ['paiərəsi] Seeräuberei *f*; Raubdruck *m von Büchern*; **pi·rate** ['~rit] **1.** Seeräuber(schiff *n*) *m*; Raubdrucker *m*; *wireless* ~, *radio* ~, ~ *listener* Schwarzhörer(in); ~ *station Radio*: Schwarz-, Piratensender *m*; **2.** unerlaubt nachdrucken; **pi·rat·i·cal** □ [pai'rætikl] (see)räuberisch.

Pis·ces *ast.* ['paisi:z] Fische *m/pl.*

pis·ci·cul·ture ['pisikʌltʃə] Fischzucht *f*.

pish [piʃ] pfui!; pah!

piss V [pis] **1.** Pisse *f*; **2.** (be)pissen; ~ *off!* verdufte!; *be* ~*ed off* die Nase voll haben; **pissed** V besoffen.

pis·ta·chi·o [pi'stɑ:ʃiəu] Pistazie *f*.

pis·til ⚘ ['pistil] Stempel *m*, Griffel *m*; **pis·til·late** ['~lit] mit Stempel(n), weiblich.

pis·tol ['pistl] Pistole *f*.

pis·ton ⊕ ['pistən] Kolben *m*; '~**-rod** Kolbenstange *f*; '~**-stroke** Kolbenhub *m*.

pit [pit] **1.** Grube *f* (*a.* ⚒, *anat.*); 🌱 Miete *f*; *thea.* Parterre *n*; Pockennarbe *f*; (Tier)Falle *f*; *Autorennen*: Box *f*; *Am. Börse*: Maklerstand *m*; *the* ~ die Hölle; **2.** mit Narben bedecken; ~ *against s-e Kraft etc.* messen mit; ~*ted with smallpox* pockennarbig.

pit-a-pat ['pitə'pæt] ticktack.

pitch[1] [pitʃ] **1.** Pech *n*; **2.** (ver-) pichen; ⚓ teeren.

pitch[2] [~] **1.** Stand(platz) *m e-s Straßenhändlers etc.*; ♪ Tonhöhe *f*; Grad *m*, Stufe *f*; Steigung *f*, Neigung *f e-s Daches*; *Kricket*: *Feld zwischen den Dreistäben*; Wurf *m*; ⚓ Stampfen *n*; **2.** *v/t.* werfen; schleudern; *Heu etc.* aufladen; feststecken; *Zelt etc.* aufschlagen, aufstellen; ♪ *Grundton* angeben; ♪ stimmen (*a. fig.*); ~*ed battle*

regelrechte *od.* offene (Feld-) Schlacht *f*; ~ *one's hopes too high* s-e Hoffnungen zu hoch stecken; *v/i.* ⚔ (sich) lagern; fallen; ⚓ stampfen; ~ *upon* verfallen auf (*acc.*); ~ *into* F herfallen über (*acc.*).
pitch...: '**~-and-'toss** Kopf oder Schrift (*Spiel*); '**~-'black,** '**~-'dark** pechschwarz.
pitch·er ['pitʃə] (Ball)Werfer *m*; Krug *m*.
pitch·fork ['pitʃfɔːk] **1.** Heu-, Mistgabel *f*; ♩ Stimmgabel *f*; **2.** mit der Heugabel werfen; zwängen, drängen (*into* in *e-e Lage*).
pitch-pine ⚘ ['pitʃpain] Pechkiefer *f*.
pitch·y ['pitʃi] pechartig.
pit-coal ⚒ ['pitkəul] Steinkohle *f*.
pit·e·ous □ *rhet.* ['pitiəs] traurig; kläglich.
pit·fall ['pitfɔːl] Fallgrube *f*, Falle *f*.
pith [piθ] Mark *n*; *fig.* Kern *m*; Kraft *f*; Gewicht *n*; ~**hel·met** Tropenhelm *m*.
pith·y □ ['piθi] markig, kernig; prägnant, inhaltsreich.
pit·i·a·ble □ ['pitiəbl] erbärmlich.
pit·i·ful □ ['pitiful] mitleidig; mitleiderregend; erbärmlich, jämmerlich, kläglich (*a. contp.*).
pit·i·less □ ['pitilis] unbarmherzig.
pit·man ['pitmən] Bergmann *m*.
pit·tance ['pitəns] Hungerlohn *m*; (kleines) bißchen.
pi·tu·i·tar·y [pi'tjuːitəri] Schleim...; ~ *gland* Hypophyse *f*.
pit·y ['piti] **1.** Mitleid *n* (*on* mit); *for ~'s sake!* um Gottes willen!; *it is a* ~ es ist schade; *it is a thousand pities* es ist jammerschade; **2.** bemitleiden; *I ~ him* er tut mir leid.
piv·ot ['pivət] **1.** ⊕ Zapfen *m*; (Tür)Angel *f*; *fig.* Dreh-, Angelpunkt *m*; ⚔ Flügelmann *m*; **2.** sich drehen (*on, upon* um); **piv·o·tal** ['~tl] den Angelpunkt bildend; Kardinal...
pix·ie ['piksi] Elf *m*, Kobold *m*; Elfe *f*.
pix·i·lat·ed *Am.* F ['piksəleitid] verdreht; irritiert.
pix·y ['piksi] = *pixie*.
pla·ca·bil·i·ty [plækə'biliti] Versöhnlichkeit *f*; '**pla·ca·ble** □ versöhnlich.
pla·card ['plækɑːd] **1.** Plakat *n*, Anschlag *m*; **2.** anschlagen; mit Anschlagzetteln bekleben.
pla·cate [plə'keit] versöhnlich stimmen.
place [pleis] **1.** Platz *m*; Ort *m*; Stadt *f*; Stelle *f*; Stätte *f*; Stellung *f*; Rang *m*; Aufgabe *f*; Anwesen *n*, Haus *n*, Wohnung *f*; ~ *of delivery* Erfüllungsort *m*; ~ *of employment* Arbeitsplatz *m*; *give ~ to j-m* Platz machen; *in* (*out of*) ~ (nicht) am rechten Ort; *fig.* (fehl) am Platz; *in ~ of* anstatt (*gen.*); *in his* ~ an seiner Stelle; *in the first* ~ an erster Stelle; zunächst (einmal); **2.** stellen, legen, setzen; *j.* anstellen; ⚔ *Posten* aufstellen; *Geld* anlegen; *Person* unterbringen (*identifizieren*); *Bestellung* aufgeben, *Auftrag* erteilen; *be ~d Sport:* sich placieren; ~ **mat** Platzdeckchen *n*, Set *n*; '**~-name** Ortsname *m*; '**plac·er** Leger(in); Ordner(in); Preisträger(in).
plac·id □ ['plæsid] mild, sanft; ruhig; **pla'cid·i·ty** Sanftheit *f*; Ruhe *f*.
plack·et ['plækit] Schlitz *m* am [*Damenrock*]
pla·gi·a·rism ['pleidʒjərizəm] Plagiat *n*; '**pla·gi·a·rist** Plagiator *m*, Abschreiber *m*; '**pla·gi·a·rize** abschreiben, plagiieren.
plague [pleig] **1.** Plage *f*; Seuche *f*; Pest *f*; **2.** plagen, quälen; '**~-spot** *mst fig.* Pestbeule *f*.
pla·guy ['pleigi] widerwärtig; F verwünscht, verdammt.
plaice *ichth.* [pleis] Scholle *f*.
plaid [plæd] *schottisches* Plaid (-tuch) *n*.
plain [plein] **1.** □ flach, eben; klar, offenbar; deutlich; rein (*Wahrheit*); einfach, schlicht; unscheinbar (*Gesicht*); offen, ehrlich; unumwunden; einfarbig; ~ *chocolate* bittere Schokolade *f*; ~ *fare* Hausmannskost *f*; ~ *knitting* Rechtsstrickerei *f*; ~ *paper* unliniertes Papier; ~ *sewing* Weißnäherei *f*; **2.** *adv.* klar, deutlich; **3.** Ebene *f*, Fläche *f*; *bsd. Am. attr.* Prärie...; '**~-clothes man** Geheimpolizist *m*; ~**deal·ing** ehrliche Handlungsweise *f*; '**plain·ness** Einfachheit *f*, Offenheit *f*; Klarheit *f*; **plain sail·ing** *fig.* einfache *od.* klare Sache *f*.
plains·man ['pleinzmən] Flachlandbewohner *m*; *Am.* Präriebewohner *m*.
plaint ⚖ [pleint] Klage(schrift) *f*; **plain·tiff** ['~tif] ⚖ Kläger(in); '**plain·tive** □ traurig, klagend.

plait [plæt] **1.** *Haar- etc.* Flechte *f*; Zopf *m*; = *pleat 1*; **2.** flechten; = *pleat 2*.

plan [plæn] **1.** Plan *m*; Entwurf *m*; (Grund)Riß *m*; **2.** e-n Plan entwerfen von *od.* zu; *fig.* planen, vorhaben; *~ned economy* Planwirtschaft *f*; *~ning board* Planungsamt *n*.

plane[1] [plein] **1.** flach, eben; **2.** ⩓ Ebene *f*, Fläche *f*; ✈ Tragfläche *f*; Flugzeug *n*; *fig.* Stufe *f*; ⊕ Hobel *m*; *elevating (depressing) ~s pl.* ✈ Höhen- (Flächen)steuer *n*; **3.** ebnen, glätten; (ab)hobeln; ✈ fliegen; gleiten.

plane[2] ⚘ [~] *a. ~-tree* Platane *f*.

plan·et *ast.* ['plænit] Planet *m*.

plane-ta·ble *surv.* ['pleinteibl] Meßtisch *m*.

plan·e·tar·i·um [plæni'tɛəriəm] Planetarium *n*; **plan·e·tar·y** ['~təri] planetarisch; Planeten...; *fig.* umherirrend.

pla·nim·e·try ⩓ [plæ'nimitri] Planimetrie *f*.

plan·ish ⊕ ['plæniʃ] glätten; polieren.

plank [plæŋk] **1.** Planke *f*, Bohle *f*, Diele *f*, Brett *n*; *Am. parl.* Programmpunkt *m*; **2.** dielen; verschalen; *~ down od. out sl., Am.* F *Geld* auf den Tisch legen; *~* **bed** Pritsche *f im Gefängnis*; '**plank·ing** Verschalung *f*; Planken *f/pl.*

plank·ton *biol.* ['plæŋktən] Plankton *n*.

plant [plɑːnt] **1.** Pflanze *f*; (Betriebs)Anlage *f*; Betriebsmaterial *n*; Fabrik *f*, Werk *n*; *sl.* Falle *f*, Schwindel *m*; **2.** (an-, ein)pflanzen (*a. fig.*); *~ o.s.* sich aufpflanzen, (auf)stellen, (auf)setzen; anlegen, errichten, gründen; ansiedeln; *sl. Schlag* verpassen; *Land* bepflanzen; *Land* besiedeln; *~ s.o. on s.th. sl.* j-m et. andrehen.

plan·tain[1] ⚘ ['plæntin] Wegerich *m*.

plan·tain[2] ⚘ [~] Pisang *m*; Banane *f*.

plan·ta·tion [plæn'teiʃən] Pflanzung *f*; Plantage *f*; Ansiedlung *f*; **plant·er** ['plɑːntə] Pflanzer *m*; Pflanzmaschine *f*; '**plant-louse** Blattlaus *f*.

plaque [plɑːk] (Schmuck)Platte *f*; Agraffe *f*, Schnalle *f*; Gedenktafel *f*; *dental ~* Zahnbelag *m*.

plash [plæʃ] **1.** Platschen *n*; Pfütze *f*; **2.** platsch!; **3.** platschen, plätschern.

plash·y ['plæʃi] pfützig; sumpfig; feucht.

plas·ma *biol.* ['plæzmə] Plasma *n*.

plas·ter ['plɑːstə] **1.** *pharm.* Pflaster *n*; ⊕ Mörtel *m*, Putz *m*; *mst ~ of Paris* Gips *m*; Gipsmörtel *m*, Stuck *m*; *~ cast* Gipsabdruck *m*, -abguß *m*; ⚕ Gipsverband *m*; **2.** bepflastern; (über)tünchen, gipsen; bedecken; '**plas·ter·er** Stukkateur *m*; '**plas·ter·ing** Verputz *m*; Stuck *m*; Gipsen *n*.

plas·tic ['plæstik] **1.** (*~ally*) plastisch; Plastik...; formbar; *~ art* Bildhauerkunst *f*; **2.** Plastik(material) *n*, Kunststoff *m*; **plas·ti·cine** ['~tisiːn] Plastilin *n*; **plas·tic·i·ty** [~'tisiti] Plastizität *f*, Formbarkeit *f*; '**plas·tics** = *plastic 2*.

plat [plæt] *s. plait*; *s. plot*[1].

plate [pleit] **1.** *allg.* Platte *f* (*a. phot., typ.*); *Bild-*Tafel *f*; *Namen-, Tür-*Schild *n*; *Kupfer- etc.* Stich *m*; Silber(geschirr, -besteck) *n*; (Eß-)Teller *m*; Preis *m bei Rennen*; *Am. Baseball*: (Schlag)Mal *n*; *a. dental ~* Gaumenplatte *f*; *Radio*: Anode *f e-r Röhre*; ⊕ Grobblech *n*; **2.** plattieren, versilbern; ⚔, ⚓ panzern.

pla·teau *geogr.* ['plætəu] Hochebene *f*, Plateau *n*.

plate-bas·ket ['pleitbɑːskit] Besteckkorb *m*; **plate·ful** ['~ful] Teller(voll) *m*.

plate...: '**~-glass** Spiegelglas *n*; '**~-lay·er** 🚂 Streckenarbeiter *m*.

plat·en ['plætən] *typ.* Drucktiegel *m*; (Schreibmaschinen)Walze *f*.

plat·er ['pleitə] ⊕ Plattierer *m*; *Sport*: minderwertiges Rennpferd *n*.

plat·form ['plætfɔːm] Plattform *f*; *geogr.* Hochebene *f*; 🚂 Bahnsteig *m*; *Am. bsd.* Plattform *f* am Wagenende; Podium *n*, Rednerbühne *f*; *pol.* Parteiprogramm *n*; *bsd. Am. pol.* Aktionsprogramm *n im Wahlkampf*.

plat·i·num *min.* ['plætinəm] Platin *n*.

plat·i·tude *fig.* ['plætitjuːd] Plattheit *f*.

pla·toon ⚔ [plə'tuːn] Zug *m*.

plat·ter ['plætə] Servierplatte *f*.

plau·dit ['plɔːdit] *mst ~s pl.* Beifallklatschen *n*.

plau·si·bil·i·ty [plɔːzə'biliti] Glaubwürdigkeit *f*; Einnehmende *n*.

plau·si·ble □ ['plɔːzəbl] glaubhaft, einleuchtend, plausibel; einnehmend.

play [plei] **1.** Spiel *n*; *thea.* Schauspiel *n*, (Theater)Stück *n*; Spielerei *f*; ⊕ Spiel *n*, Gang *m*; Spielraum *m* (*a. fig.*); *fair (foul)* ~ (un)ehrliches Spiel *n*; ~ *on words* Wortspiel *n*; *bring into* ~ in Gang *od.* zur Anwendung bringen; *make great* ~ *with* groß angeben mit; **2.** *v/i.* spielen (*a. fig.*); mitspielen; tändeln; ⊕ laufen; ~ *fast and loose with* Schindluder treiben mit; ~ *at cards* Karten spielen; ~ *for time* Zeit zu gewinnen suchen; ~ *up* loslegen; ~ *upon* einwirken auf (*acc.*); *v/t.* spielen (gegen); *thea.* spielen, darstellen; ~ *down fig.* herunterspielen; ~ *off fig.* ausspielen (*against each other* gegeneinander); ~*ed out* erledigt, abgetan; '**~-act·ing** Theaterspielen *n*; *fig.* Schauspielern *n*, Verstellung *f*; '**~·back** Playback *n e-r Tonaufnahme*; '**~-bill** Theaterzettel *m*; '**~-book** *thea.* Textbuch *n*; '**~-boy** Playboy *m*; '**play·er** Spieler (-in); Schauspieler(in); '**play·er-pi·an·o** elektrisches Klavier *n*; '**play·fel·low** Spielkamerad(in); **play·ful** □ ['~ful] spielerisch, scherzhaft; '**play·ful·ness** Mutwille *m*.

play...: '**~·go·er** Theaterbesucher (-in); '**~·ground** Spiel-, Tummelplatz *m*; Schulhof *m*; '**~·house** Schauspielhaus *n*; *Am.* Miniaturhaus *n für Kinder*.

play·ing...: '**~-card** Spielkarte *f*; '**~-field** Sport-, Spielplatz *m*.

play...: '**~·mate** *s. playfellow*; '**~-off** *Sport*: Entscheidungsspiel *n*; '**~·pen** Laufställchen *n*; '**~·thing** Spielzeug *n* (*a. fig.*); '**~·wright** Bühnenautor *m*, Dramatiker *m*.

pla·za ['plɑːzə] (Markt)Platz *m in Spanien*.

plea [pliː] ⚖ Einrede *f*; Ausrede *f*, Vorwand *m*; Befürwortung *f*; Gesuch *n*; Bitte *f*; *make a* ~ Einspruch erheben; *on the* ~ *of od. that* unter dem Vorwand (*gen.*) *od.* daß.

plead [pliːd] *v/i.* vor Gericht reden, plädieren; ~ *for* für *j.* sprechen, bitten; sich einsetzen für; *s. guilty*; *v/t. Sache* vertreten, verteidigen; als Beweis anführen, geltend machen; sich entschuldigen mit; '**plead·a·ble** rechtsgültig; triftig; '**plead·er** ⚖ Sachwalter *m*; Verteidiger *m*; '**plead·ing** ⚖ Schriftsatz *m*; ~*s pl.* Prozeßakten *f/pl.*; Verhandlung(en *pl.*) *f*.

pleas·ant □ ['pleznt] angenehm; vergnüglich; nett; erfreulich; freundlich; '**pleas·ant·ness** Annehmlichkeit *f*; '**pleas·ant·ry** Lustigkeit *f*; Scherz *m*, Spaß *m*.

please [pliːz] *v/i.* gefallen; belieben; *if you* ~ *iro.* stellen Sie sich vor; ~ *come in!* bitte, treten Sie ein!; *v/t. j-m* gefallen, angenehm sein; befriedigen; zufriedenstellen; ~ *yourself* tun Sie, was Ihnen gefällt; *be* ~*d to do* sich freuen, *et.* zu tun; *et.* gerne tun; *be* ~*d with* Vergnügen haben an (*dat.*); **pleased** erfreut, zufrieden.

pleas·ing □ ['pliːziŋ] angenehm, gefällig.

pleas·ur·a·ble □ ['pleʒərəbl] angenehm, vergnüglich.

pleas·ure ['pleʒə] **1.** Vergnügen *n*, Freude *f*; Belieben *n*; *attr.* Vergnügungs...; *at* ~ nach Belieben; *give s.o.* ~ j-m Vergnügen *od.* Freude machen; *take* ~ *in* Vergnügen finden an (*dat.*); **2.** (sich) erfreuen; '**~-ground** (Vergnügungs)Park *m*.

pleat [pliːt] **1.** Plisseefalte *f*; **2.** fälteln, plissieren.

ple·be·ian [pli'biːən] **1.** plebejisch; **2.** Plebejer(in).

pleb·i·scite ['plebisit] Volksentscheid *m*.

pledge [pledʒ] **1.** Pfand *n*; Zutrinken *n*; Gelübde *n*, Gelöbnis *n*, Versprechen *n*; *put in* ~ verpfänden; *take out of* ~ *Pfand* auslösen; **2.** verpfänden; *j-m* zutrinken; *he* ~*d himself* er gelobte; **pledg'ee** Pfandnehmer *m*; '**pledg·er** Verpfänder *m*.

Ple·iad ['plaiəd], *pl.* **Ple·ia·des** ['~diːz] Siebengestirn *n*.

ple·na·ry ['pliːnəri] vollständig; Voll...

plen·i·po·ten·ti·ar·y [plenipəu'tenʃəri] **1.** bevollmächtigt; **2.** Bevollmächtigte *m*.

plen·i·tude ['plenitjuːd] Fülle *f*.

plen·te·ous □ *poet.* ['plentjəs] voll, reichlich; '**plen·te·ous·ness** Fülle *f*.

plen·ti·ful □ ['plentiful] reichlich.

plen·ty ['plenti] **1.** Fülle *f*, Überfluß *m*; ~ *of* viel, eine Menge, reichlich; *horn of* ~ Füllhorn *n*; **2.** F reichlich.

ple·o·nasm ['pliːənæzəm] Pleonasmus *m*.

pleth·o·ra ['pleθərə] Blutandrang *m*;

ple·thor·ic [pleˈθɔrik] (*~ally*) vollblütig; *fig.* dick.
pleu·ri·sy ⚕ [ˈpluərisi] Brustfellentzündung *f.*
pli·a·bil·i·ty [plaiəˈbiliti] Biegsamkeit *f.*
pli·a·ble □ [ˈplaiəbl] biegsam; *fig.* geschmeidig, nachgiebig.
pli·an·cy [ˈplaiənsi] Biegsamkeit *f.*
pli·ant □ [ˈplaiənt] = *pliable.*
pli·ers [ˈplaiəz] *pl.* (*a pair of ~* eine) (Draht-, Kombi)Zange *f.*
plight[1] [plait] **1.** *Ehre, Wort* verpfänden; verloben; **2.** Gelöbnis *n.*
plight[2] [~] Zustand *m*, (Not)Lage *f.*
plim·soll [ˈplimsəl] Turnschuh *m.*
plinth △ [plinθ] Säulenplatte *f.*
plod [plɔd] *a. ~ along, ~ on* sich dahinschleppen; sich plagen, schuften; ˈ**plod·ding** □ arbeitsam; schwerfällig.
plonk F [plɔŋk] billiger Wein *m.*
plop [plɔp] **1.** plumps!; **2.** Plumps *m*; **3.** plumpsen.
plot[1] [plɔt] Stück(chen) *n*, Fleckchen *n Land*; Platz *m*; Parzelle *f.*
plot[2] [~] **1.** Plan *m*; Komplott *n*, Verschwörung *f*, Anschlag *m*; Intrige *f*; Handlung *f e-s Dramas etc.*; **2.** *v/t. a. ~ down* aufzeichnen; *in e-e Landkarte etc.* einzeichnen, -tragen; *b.s.* planen, anzetteln; *v/i.* sich verschwören, intrigieren; ˈ**plot·ter** Anstifter(in); Verschwörer(in).
plough [plau] **1.** Pflug *m*; ⊕ Falzhobel *m*; *univ. sl.* Durchfall *m*; *the* ♀ *ast.* der Große Wagen; **2.** pflügen; furchen (*a. fig.*); *~ back Gewinn* wieder in das Geschäft stecken; *be ~ed univ. sl.* durchfallen; ˈ**~·man** Pflüger *m*; *~'s lunch kaltes Mittagessen, mst aus Brot, Käse u. Bier bestehend*; ˈ**~·share** Pflugschar *f.*
plov·er [ˈplʌvə] *orn.* Regenpfeifer *m*; Strandläufer *m*; F Kiebitz *m.*
plow [plau], ˈ**plow·man** *bsd. Am.* = *plough etc.*
ploy F [plɔi] Masche *f*, Tour *f* (*List*).
pluck [plʌk] **1.** Mut *m*, Schneid *m*; Innereien *f/pl.*; Zug *m*, Ruck *m*; **2.** pflücken; *Vogel* rupfen; zerren, zupfen; reißen (*from* von); *sl. j.* rupfen, ausplündern; *univ. sl.* durchfallen lassen; *~ at* zerren an; *~ up courage* Mut fassen.
pluck·y F □ [ˈplʌki] mutig, schneidig.
plug [plʌg] **1.** Pflock *m*; Dübel *m*; Stöpsel *m*; ⚡ Stecker *m*; *Zahn*-Plombe *f*; Priem *m* (*Tabak*); Klosettspülvorrichtung *f*; *Feuer*-Hydrant *m*; *Am. Radio*: Reklamehinweis *m*; alter Gaul *m*; *~ socket* Steckdose *f*; **2.** *v/t.* zu-, verstopfen; *Zahn* plombieren; stöpseln; *sl. j-m* eins auswischen; *Am.* F *im Rundfunk etc.* Reklame machen für *et.*; *~ in* ⚡ einstöpseln; *v/i. sl.* schuften; ˈ**plug-**ˈ**ug·ly** *Am. sl.* Schläger *m* (*Person*).
plum [plʌm] Pflaume *f*, Zwetsch(g)e *f*; Rosine *f* (*a. fig.* = *das Beste*); *sl.* £ 100 000.
plum·age [ˈpluːmidʒ] Gefieder *n.*
plumb [plʌm] **1.** lotrecht; gerade; richtig; **2.** (Blei)Lot *n*; Senkblei *n*; **3.** *v/t.* lotrecht machen; loten; (*a. fig.*) sondieren; F Rohre legen in (*dat.*); *v/i.* F als Rohrleger arbeiten;
plum·ba·go [~ˈbeigəu] Graphit *m*;
plumb·er [ˈplʌmə] Klempner *m*, Installateur *m*; **plum·bic** [ˈplʌmbik] ⚗ Blei...; **plumb·ing** [ˈ~miŋ] Klempnerarbeit *f*; Rohrleitungen *f/pl.*; ˈ**plumb-line** ⊕ Lotleine *f*, Senkschnur *f*; ˈ**plumb-rule** Lot-, Senkwaage *f.*
plume [pluːm] **1.** *Schmuck*-Feder *f*; Federbusch *m*; **2.** *die Federn* putzen; mit Federn schmücken; *~ o.s. on* sich brüsten mit.
plum·met [ˈplʌmit] (Blei)Lot *n*; Senkblei *n.*
plum·my F [ˈplʌmi] prima.
plump[1] [plʌmp] **1.** drall, prall, mollig, dick; **2.** prall machen *od.* werden.
plump[2] [~] **1.** (schwer) fallen, (hin-) plumpsen (lassen); *parl.* seine Stimme ungeteilt geben (*for dat.*); **2.** Plumps *m*; **3.** F *adv.* plumps; geradewegs; rundweg; **4.** F □ glatt, offen (*Absage etc.*), plump (*Lüge*).
plump·er [ˈplʌmpə] *parl.* ungeteilte Wahlstimme *f*; *sl.* plumpe Lüge *f.*
plump·ness [ˈplʌmpnis] Prallheit *f*, Beleibtheit *f*; F Offenheit *f e-r Antwort etc.*
plum-pud·ding [ˈplʌmˈpudiŋ] Plumpudding *m.*
plum·y [ˈpluːmi] gefiedert; federartig.
plun·der [ˈplʌndə] **1.** Plünderung *f*; Raub *m*, Beute *f*; **2.** plündern; ˈ**plun·der·er** Plünderer *m*; Räuber *m.*

plunge [plʌndʒ] **1.** (Unter)Tauchen *n*; Sturz *m*; (Kopf)Sprung *m*; Ausschlagen *n e-s Pferdes etc.*; *make od. take the* ~ den entscheidenden Schritt tun; **2.** *v/t.* tauchen, stürzen (*into* in *acc.*); *Schwert etc.* stoßen; *v/i.* (unter)tauchen; sich stürzen (*into* in *acc.*); ausschlagen (*Pferd*); ⚓ stampfen.
plung·er [ˈplʌndʒə] (Pumpen)Kolben *m*; *sl.* Spekulant *m*.
plunk [plʌŋk] *v/t. Saite* zupfen; *et.* hinplumpsen lassen, hinwerfen; *v/i.* (hin)plumpsen, fallen.
plu·per·fect *gr.* [ˈpluːˈpəːfikt] Plusquamperfekt(um) *n*.
plu·ral *gr.* [ˈpluərəl] Mehrzahl *f*, Plural *m*; **plu·ral·i·ty** [~ˈræliti] Vielheit *f*, Mehrheit *f*; Mehrzahl *f*; ~ *of wives* Vielweiberei *f*.
plus [plʌs] **1.** *prp.* plus, und; **2.** *adj.* positiv; **3.** Plus *n*; Mehr *n*; **~-fours** F [ˈ~ˈfɔːz] *pl.* Golfhose(n *pl.*) *f*; Knickerbocker *pl.*
plush [plʌʃ] Plüsch *m*.
plush·y [ˈplʌʃi] plüschartig; *sl.* feudal, luxuriös.
plu·toc·ra·cy [pluːˈtɔkrəsi] Plutokratie *f* (*Geldherrschaft*); **plu·to·crat** [ˈ~təukræt] Plutokrat *m*.
plu·to·ni·um ⚗ [pluːˈtəunjəm] Plutonium *n*.
plu·vi·al [ˈpluːviəl], ˈ**plu·vi·ous** regnerisch; Regen...; **plu·vi·om·e·ter** [~ˈɔmitə] Regenmesser *m*.
ply [plai] **1.** Lage *f Tuch od. Holz*; Strähne *f*; *fig.* Neigung *f*, Gewohnheit *f*; **2.** *v/t.* fleißig anwenden, handhaben; *j-m* zusetzen (*mit Fragen etc.*), *j.* überhäufen; ~ *a trade* ein Gewerbe betreiben; *v/i. regelmäßig* fahren *od.* verkehren.
ply-wood [ˈplaiwud] Sperrholz *n*.
pneu·mat·ic [njuːˈmætik] **1.** (~*ally*) Luft...; pneumatisch; ~ *hammer* Preßlufthammer *m*; ~ *tire* Luftreifen *m*; **2.** Luftreifen *m*.
pneu·mo·ni·a ⚕ [njuːˈməunjə] Lungenentzündung *f*.
poach[1] [pəutʃ] wildern.
poach[2] [~] *a.* ~ *up Erde* zertreten, aufwühlen.
poach[3] [~]: ~*ed eggs pl.* verlorene Eier *n/pl.*
poach·er [ˈpəutʃə] Wilddieb *m*.
PO Box [piːˈəubɔks] Postfach *n*.
po·chette [pɔˈʃet] Handtäschchen *n*.
pock ⚕ [pɔk] Pocke *f*, Blatter *f*.
pock·et [ˈpɔkit] **1.** Tasche *f*; *geol.* Nest *n*; Sack *m Wolle, Hopfen*; ✈ *Luft*-Loch *n*; **2.** einstecken (*a. fig.*); *Am. pol. Gesetzesvorlage* nicht unterschreiben, Veto einlegen gegen (*v. Präsidenten*); *Gefühl* unterdrücken; **3.** Taschen...; ~ *lighter* Taschenfeuerzeug *n*; ~ *lamp* Taschenlampe *f*; ˈ**~·book** Notizbuch *n*; Brieftasche *f*; *Am.* Geldbeutel *m*; Damenhandtasche *f*; ~ **cal·cu·la·tor** Taschenrechner *m*; ~ **e·di·tion** Taschenausgabe *f e-s Buches*.
pod [pɔd] **1.** ⚘ Hülse *f*, Schale *f*, Schote *f*; *sl.* Bauch *m*; **2.** Schoten ansetzen; *Erbsen etc.* enthülsen.
po·dag·ra ⚕ [ˈpɔdəgrə] Podagra *n* (*Fußgicht*).
podg·y F [ˈpɔdʒi] quabbelig.
po·di·um [ˈpəudiəm] Podium *n*.
po·em [ˈpəuim] Gedicht *n*.
po·e·sy [ˈpəuizi] Poesie *f*.
po·et [ˈpəuit] Dichter *m*; **po·et·as·ter** [~ˈtæstə] Dichterling *m*; ˈ**po·et·ess** Dichterin *f*; **poˈet·ic, po·et·i·cal** □ [pəuˈetikəl] poetisch, dichterisch; **poˈet·ics** *pl.* Poetik *f*; **po·et·ize** [ˈ~itaiz] dichten; in Verse bringen; ˈ**po·et·ry** Dichtkunst *f*, Poesie *f*; Dichtung *f*, *coll.* Dichtungen *f/pl.*, Gedichte *n/pl.*
poign·an·cy [ˈpɔinənsi] Schärfe *f*; *fig.* Eindringlichkeit *f*; ˈ**poign·ant** □ scharf, beißend; *fig.* eindringlich.
point [pɔint] **1.** Spitze *f*; Pointe *f e-s Witzes etc.*; Landspitze *f*, -vorsprung *m*; *s.* ~-*lace*; Radiernadel *f*; *gr.*, ⅍, *phys. etc.* Punkt *m*; Fleck *m*, Stelle *f*; Stehen *n des Jagdhundes*; (Geweih)Ende *n*; ⚡ Kontakt *m*; ⚓ Kompaßstrich *m*; Auge *n auf Karten, Würfeln*; Grad *m* (*a. ast.*), Stufe *f*; (springender) Punkt *m*, Frage *f*, Sache *f*; Zweck *m*, Sinn *m*; Wirksamkeit *f*, Gewicht *n*; Anliegen *n*; Kernfrage *f*, -punkt *m*; *fig. hervorstechende* Eigenschaft *f*; ~*s pl.* 🚂 Weichen *f/pl.*; ~ *of view* Stand-, Gesichtspunkt *m*; *the* ~ *is that* ... die Sache ist die, daß ...; *there is no* ~ *in ger.* es hat keinen Zweck, zu *inf.*; *make a* ~ *of s.th.* auf et. achten; *make the* ~ *that* die Feststellung machen, daß; *stretch a* ~ fünf gerade sein lassen; *in* ~ *of* in Hinsicht auf (*acc.*); *in* ~ *of fact* tatsächlich; *off od. beyond the* ~ nicht zur Sache (gehörig); *differ on many* ~*s* in vielen

Punkten abweichen; *he was on the ~ of coming* er war im Begriff *od.* nahe daran zu kommen; *win on ~s Boxen*: nach Punkten siegen; *to the ~* zur Sache (gehörig); *stick to the ~* bei der Sache bleiben; **2.** *v/t.* (zu)spitzen; richten, stellen; *oft ~ out* (auf-) zeigen, hinweisen auf (*acc.*); ausführen; punktieren; *~ at Waffe etc.* richten auf (*acc.*); *v/i.* stehen (*Jagdhund*); *~ at* zeigen *od.* weisen auf (*acc.*); *~ to* nach *e-r Richtung* weisen; **'~-'blank** gerade; Kernschuß...; unumwunden; rundweg; *~ shot* Fleckschuß *m*; **'~-du·ty** (*bsd.* Verkehrs)Postendienst *m*; **'point·ed** □ spitz; *fig.* scharf, beißend; **'point·ed·ness** Spitze *f*; Schärfe *f*; **'point·er** Zeiger *m*; Zeigestock *m*; Vorsteh-, Hühnerhund *m*; F Tip *m*; **'point-'lace** genähte Spitzen *f/pl.*; **'point·less** stumpf; witzlos; zwecklos, sinnlos; **'point-po'lice·man** Verkehrspolizist *m*; **'points·man** 🚂 Weichensteller *m*; Verkehrspolizist *m*; **'point-to-'point race** Geländejagdrennen *n.*

poise [pɔiz] **1.** Gleichgewicht *n*; Schwebe *f*; Haltung *f*; Gelassenheit *f*; **2.** *v/t.* im Gleichgewicht halten; ins Gleichgewicht bringen; *Kopf etc. besonders* tragen, halten; *be ~d* = *v/i.* schweben.

poison ['pɔizn] **1.** Gift *n*; *~-pen letter* verleumderischer *od.* obszöner anonymer *Brief*; **2.** vergiften; **'poi·son·er** Vergifter(in); Giftmischer(in); **'poi·son·ous** □ giftig (*a. fig.*); Gift...; F ekelhaft.

poke [pəuk] **1.** Stoß *m*, Puff *m*; **2.** *v/t.* stoßen; *a. ~ up Feuer* schüren; stecken; *~ fun at* sich über *j.* lustig machen; *v/i.* stoßen (*at* nach); stochern; stöbern (*into* in *dat.*).

pok·er[1] ['pəukə] Feuerhaken *m.*

po·ker[2] [~] Poker(spiel) *n*; *~ face fig.* Pokergesicht *n.*

pok·er-work ['pəukəwə:k] Brandmalerei *f.*

pok·y ['pəuki] klein, eng, winzig; schäbig; erbärmlich.

po·lar ['pəulə] polar; Polar...; *~ bear* Eisbär *m*; **po·lar·i·ty** *phys.* [pəu'læriti] Polarität *f*; **po·lar·i·za·tion** *phys.* [~lərai'zeiʃən] Polarisation *f*; *~ filter phot.* Pol(arisations)filter *m*; **'po·lar·ize** *phys.* polarisieren.

Pole[1] [pəul] Pole *m*, Polin *f.*

pole[2] [~] Pol *m* (*geogr., ast., phys., fig.*).

pole[3] [~] **1.** Stange *f*, Mast *m*; Pfosten *m*, Pfahl *m*; Deichsel *f*; (Meß-) Rute *f* (*5,029 Meter*); (Sprung-) Stab *m*; **2.** *Bohnen etc.* stängen; staken; **'~-ax(e)** ⚔ Streitaxt *f*; ⚓ Enterbeil *n*; Schlachtbeil *n*; **'~·cat** *zo.* Iltis *m*; *Am.* Skunk *m*; **~ jump** = *pole vault.*

po·lem·ic [pɔ'lemik] **1.** *a.* **po'lem·i·cal** □ polemisch; feindselig; Streit...; **2.** Polemiker *m*; **po'lem·ics** *pl.* Polemik *f.*

pole-star ['pəulstɑ:] Polarstern *m*; *fig.* Leitstern *m.*

pole-vault ['pəulvɔ:lt] Stabhochsprung *m.*

po·lice [pə'li:s] **1.** Polizei *f*; *two ~* zwei Polizisten *m/pl.*; *~ dossier* polizeiliches Führungszeugnis *n*; *~ force* Polizei *f*, -streitkräfte *f/pl.*; *~ record* Vorstrafen *f/pl.*; **2.** überwachen; **po'lice·man** Polizist *m*; **po'lice-of·fice** Polizeipräsidium *n*; **po'lice-of·fi·cer** Polizeibeamte *m*, Polizist *m*; **po'lice-sta·tion** Polizeiwache *f*; **po'lice-sur'veil·lance** Polizeiaufsicht *f*; **po'lice-trap** Autofalle *f*; **po'lice·wom·an** Polizistin *f*, Polizeibeamtin *f.*

pol·i·cy[1] ['pɔlisi] Politik *f*; (Welt-) Klugheit *f*; geschicktes Verhalten *n.*

pol·i·cy[2] [~] Police *f*; *Am.* Zahlenlotto *n.*

po·li·o(·my·e·li·tis) ['pəuliəu(maiə'laitis)] spinale Kinderlähmung *f.*

Pol·ish[1] ['pəuliʃ] polnisch.

pol·ish[2] ['pɔliʃ] **1.** Politur *f*; Schuhcreme *f*; *fig.* Umgangsformen *f/pl.*, Schliff *m*; **2.** *v/t.* polieren, glätten; bohnern; *fig.* verfeinern; *~ off* verputzen (*essen*); hinhauen (*schnell erledigen*); *~ up* aufpolieren, auffrischen; *v/i.* glänzend werden; **'pol·ish·ing 1.** Politur *f*; **2.** Glanz..., Putz...

po·lite □ [pə'lait] artig, höflich; fein; **po'lite·ness** Höflichkeit *f.*

pol·i·tic □ ['pɔlitik] politisch; schlau, weltklug; *body ~* Staatskörper *m*; **po·lit·i·cal** □ [pə'litikəl] politisch; staatlich; Staats...; *~ science* Politologie *f*; *~ scientist* Politologe *m*, -login *f*; **pol·i·ti·cian** [pɔli'tiʃən] Staatsmann *m*, Politiker *m*; *contp.* Intrigant *m*; **pol·i·tics** ['~tiks] *sg.*

od. pl. Staatswissenschaft *f*, Politik *f*; politische Überzeugung *f*.

pol·i·ty ['pɔliti] Verfassung *f*; Regierung(sform) *f*; Staatswesen *n*.

pol·ka ['pɔlkə] Polka *f*; **~ dot** *Am.* Punktmuster *n auf Stoff*.

poll[1] [pəul] **1.** Wählerliste *f*; Stimmenzählung *f*; Abstimmung *f*; Wahl *f*; Stimmenzahl *f*; Umfrage *f*; *co.* Kopf *m*; *go to the ~s* zur Wahl gehen; **2.** *v/t. Stimmen* erhalten; = *pollard 2*; *v/i.* wählen; *~ for* stimmen für.

poll[2] [pɔl] Papagei *m*.

pol·lard ['pɔləd] **1.** gekappter Baum *m*; hornloses Tier *n*; Kleie(nmehl *n*) *f*; **2.** kappen, stutzen.

poll-book ['pəulbuk] Wählerliste *f*.

pol·len ⚘ ['pɔlin] Blütenstaub *m*; **pol·li·na·tion** [pɔli'neiʃən] Bestäubung *f*.

poll·ing...: **'~-booth** Wahlzelle *f*; **'~-dis·trict** Wahlbezirk *m*; **'~-place** Wahlort *m*; **'~-sta·tion** Wahllokal *n*.

poll·ster ['pəulstə] Meinungsforscher *m*.

poll-tax ['pəultæks] Kopfsteuer *f*.

pol·lut·ant [pə'lu:tənt] Schadstoff *m*.

pol·lute [pə'lu:t] beschmutzen, beflecken (*a. fig.*); entweihen; **pol'lu·tion** Verunreinigung *f*; Umweltverschmutzung *f*; Befleckung *f*; Entweihung *f*.

po·lo ['pəuləu] *Sport*: Polo *n*; **~ neck** Rollkragen(pullover) *m*.

po·lo·ny [pə'ləuni] grobe Zervelatwurst *f*.

pol·troon [pɔl'tru:n] Feigling *m*; **pol'troon·er·y** Feigheit *f*.

po·lyg·a·my [pɔ'ligəmi] Vielweiberei *f*; **pol·y·glot** ['~glɔt] vielsprachig; **pol·y·gon** ['~gən] Vieleck *n*; **po'lyg·o·nal** [~gənl] vieleckig; **pol·y·phon·ic** ♪ [~'fɔnik] polyphon; **pol·yp** *zo.* ['pɔlip], **pol·y·pus** ⚕ ['~pəs] Polyp *m*; **pol·y·sty·rene** [pɔli'staiəri:n] Styropor *n*; **pol·y·syl·lab·ic** ['~si'læbik] vielsilbig; **pol·y·syl·la·ble** ['~siləbl] vielsilbiges Wort *n*; **pol·y·tech·nic** [~'teknik] polytechnisch(e Schule *f*); **pol·y·the·ism** ['~θi:izəm] Polytheismus *m*, Vielgötterei *f*; **pol·y·thene** ['~θi:n] Polyäthylen *n*; *~ bag* Plastiktüte *f*.

po·made [pə'mɑ:d] Pomade *f*.

po·man·der [pəu'mændə] Duftkugel *f*.

pome·gran·ate ⚘ ['pɔmgrænit] Granatapfel *m*.

Pom·er·a·nian [pɔmə'reinjən] **1.** pommer(i)sch; **2.** Pommer(in); *a. ~ dog* Spitz *m*.

pom·mel ['pʌml] **1.** *Degen-, Sattel-, Turm*-Knopf *m*, Knauf *m*; **2.** knuffen, schlagen.

pomp [pɔmp] Pomp *m*, Gepränge *n*.

pompom ['pɔmpɔm] (Flak-) Schnellfeuergeschütz *n*.

pom·pos·i·ty [pɔm'pɔsiti] Prunk *m*; Pomphaftigkeit *f*; **'pomp·ous** □ prunkvoll; hochtrabend; pompös.

ponce *sl.* [pɔns] Zuhälter *m*; *contp.* Schwule *m*; weibischer Kerl *m*.

pon·cho ['pɔntʃəu] Poncho *m*, (Regen)Umhang *m*.

pond [pɔnd] Teich *m*, Weiher *m*.

pon·der ['pɔndə] *v/t.* erwägen, überlegen; *v/i.* nachdenken (*on, over* über *acc.*); **pon·der·a·bil·i·ty** [~rə'biliti] Wägbarkeit *f*; **'pon·der·a·ble** wägbar; **pon·der·os·i·ty** [~'rɔsiti] Schwere *f*, Gewichtigkeit *f*, Schwerfälligkeit *f*; **'pon·der·ous** □ schwer, gewichtig; schwerfällig; **'pon·der·ous·ness** = *ponderosity*.

pone [pəun] Maisbrot *n*.

pong *sl.* [pɔŋ] Gestank *m*, unangenehmer Geruch *m*.

pon·iard ['pɔnjəd] Dolch *m*.

pon·tiff ['pɔntif] Hohepriester *m*; Papst *m*; **pon'tif·i·cal** □ oberpriesterlich; päpstlich; **pon'tif·i·cate** [~kit] Pontifikat *n*.

pon·toon ⚔ [pɔn'tu:n] Ponton *m*; **pon'toon-bridge** Schiffsbrücke *f*.

po·ny ['pəuni] Pony *n*, Pferdchen *n*; *sl.* £ 25; **'~-'en·gine** 🚂 Rangierlokomotive *f*; **'~-tail** Pferdeschwanz *m* (*Frisur*).

pooch *Am. sl.* [pu:tʃ] Köter *m*.

poo·dle ['pu:dl] Pudel *m*.

poof *sl.* [pu:f], *a.* **poof·ter** ['~tə] Schwule *m*.

pooh [pu:] pah!

pooh-pooh [pu:'pu:] geringschätzig behandeln.

pool[1] [pu:l] Teich *m*, Tümpel *m*; Pfütze *f*, Lache *f*; (Schwimm)Bekken *n*.

pool[2] [~] **1.** (Spiel)Einsatz *m*; *Billard*: Poulespiel *n*; ✝ Ring *m*, Kartell *n*; gemeinsame Kasse *f*; *~ room* Billardzimmer *n*; *Am.* Wettannahmestelle *f*; **2.** ✝ zu einem Ring vereinigen; *Gelder* zs.-legen.

pools [pu:lz] Toto *m*, *a. n.*

poop ⚓ [pu:p] **1.** Heck *n*; Achterhütte *f*; **2.** *das Schiff* von hinten treffen (*Woge*).

poor □ [puə] arm; armselig, gering; dürftig, dürr, mager (*Boden*); schlecht (*Ernte*); unruhig, schlecht (*Nacht etc.*); *the* ~ die Armen *pl.*; ~ *me!* ich Armer!; ~ *health* schwache Gesundheit *f*; '**~-box** Armenkasse *f*; '**~-house** Armenhaus *n*; '**~-law** ⚖ Armenrecht *n*; '**poor·ly** **1.** *adj. pred.* unpäßlich; **2.** *adv.* dürftig; *he is* ~ *off* es geht ihm schlecht; '**poor·ness** Armut *f*; Armseligkeit *f*, Dürftigkeit *f*; '**poor-rate** Armensteuer *f*; '**poor-'spir·it·ed** verzagt, feig.

pop[1] [pɔp] **1.** Puff *m*, Knall *m*; F Sprudel *m*; Schampus *m* (*Sekt*); *in* ~ *sl.* verpfändet; **2.** *v/t.* knallen lassen; *Am. Mais* rösten; schnell *wohin* tun, stecken, gießen; ~ *the question to a lady* e-r Dame e-n Heiratsantrag machen; *v/i.* puffen, knallen; *mit adv.* huschen; ~ *in* hereinplatzen; ~ *up* plötzlich auftauchen; **3.** plötzlich; **4.** puff!

pop[2] F [~] **1.** populär, beliebt; **2.** Schlager *m*; volkstümliche Musik *f*.

pop[3] *Am.* F [pɔp] Papa *m*, Papi *m*.

pop-corn *bsd. Am.* ['pɔpkɔ:n] Puffmais *m*.

pope [pəup] Papst *m*; '**pope·dom** Papsttum *n*; '**pop·er·y** *contp.* Papismus *m*.

pop-eyed ['pɔpaid] glotzäugig.

pop·gun ['pɔpgʌn] Knallbüchse *f*.

pop·in·jay ['pɔpindʒei] Geck *m*.

pop·ish □ ['pəupiʃ] papistisch.

pop·lar ⚘ ['pɔplə] Pappel *f*.

pop·lin ['pɔplin] Popelin *m*.

pop·per F ['pɔpə] Druckknopf *m*.

pop·pet ['pɔpit] ⚓ Schlittenständer *m*; ⊕ *Drehbank*-Docke *f*; *s. puppet.*

pop·py ⚘ ['pɔpi] Mohn *m*; '**~·cock** *Am.* F Quatsch *m*.

pop·u·lace ['pɔpjuləs] Pöbel *m*.

pop·u·lar □ ['pɔpjulə] volkstümlich, populär; beliebt; Volks...; ~ *front* Volksfront *f*; **pop·u·lar·i·ty** [~'læriti] Popularität *f*, Volkstümlichkeit *f*, Beliebtheit *f*; **pop·u·lar·ize** ['~ləraiz] popularisieren; volkstümlich machen; gemeinverständlich darstellen; '**pop·u·lar·ly** im Volk(smund).

pop·u·late ['pɔpjuleit] bevölkern; **pop·u'la·tion** Bevölkerung *f*; Einwohnerzahl *f*; ~ *explosion* Bevölkerungsexplosion *f*.

pop·u·lous □ ['pɔpjuləs] volkreich, dicht besiedelt.

por·ce·lain ['pɔ:slin] Porzellan *n*.

porch [pɔ:tʃ] Vorhalle *f*, Portal *n*; überdachter Hauseingang *m*; *Am.* Veranda *f*.

por·cu·pine *zo.* ['pɔ:kjupain] Stachelschwein *n*.

pore[1] [pɔ:] Pore *f*.

pore[2] [~] eifrig studieren (*over acc.*); grübeln, brüten (*over, on, upon* über *dat.*).

pork [pɔ:k] Schweinefleisch *n*; '**~-bar·rel** *Am. sl. politisch berechnete* Geldzuwendung *f der Regierung*; '**~-butch·er** Schweinemetzger *m*; '**pork·er** (Mast-)Schwein *n*; '**pork·y** **1.** F fett, dick; **2.** *Am.* F = *porcupine*.

por·nog·ra·phy [pɔ:'nɔgrəfi] Pornographie *f*, Schmutzliteratur *f*.

po·ros·i·ty [pɔ:'rɔsiti], **po·rous·ness** ['pɔ:rəsnis] Porosität *f*.

po·rous □ ['pɔ:rəs] porös.

por·phy·ry *min.* ['pɔ:firi] Porphyr *m*.

por·poise *ichth.* ['pɔ:pəs] Meerschwein *n*, Tümmler *m*.

por·ridge ['pɔridʒ] Porridge *m*, *n*, Hafer(flocken)brei *m*; **por·rin·ger** ['pɔrindʒə] Suppennapf *m*.

port[1] [pɔ:t] Hafen *m*; ~ *of call* Anlaufhafen *m*; ~ *of destination* Bestimmungshafen *m*; ~ *of trans-shipment* Umschlaghafen *m*.

port[2] ⚓ [~] (Pfort-, Lade)Luke *f*.

port[3] [~] **1.** ⚔ *das Gewehr* schräg vor der Brust halten; **2.** Haltung *f*, Benehmen *n*.

port[4] ⚓ [~] **1.** Backbord *n*; **2.** *das Steuer* links halten.

port[5] [~] Portwein *m*.

port·a·ble ['pɔ:təbl] tragbar; ~ *radio set* Kofferradio *n*; ~ *typewriter* Reiseschreibmaschine *f*.

por·tage ['pɔ:tidʒ] (*bsd.* Trage-)Transport *m*; *s. porterage.*

por·tal ['pɔ:tl] Portal *n*, Haupttor *n*; *fig.* Pforte *f*; '**por·tal-to-'por·tal pay** Lohn *m* für die Zeit zu und von der Arbeitsstätte (*innerhalb der Fabrik etc.*).

port·cul·lis ⚔ [pɔ:t'kʌlis] Fallgatter *n*.

por·tend [pɔ:'tend] vorbedeuten.

por·tent ['pɔːtent] (*bsd.* üble) Vorbedeutung *f*; Vorzeichen *n*; Wunder *n*; **por'ten·tous** □ [~təs] unheilvoll; wunderbar; unheimlich (*a. co.*).

por·ter[1] ['pɔːtə] Pförtner *m*.

por·ter[2] [~] (Gepäck- *etc.*) Träger *m*; Porterbier *n*; '**por·ter·age** Tragen *n*; Trägerlohn *m*; Zustellungsgebühr *f*; '**por·ter-house** Bier-, Speisehaus *n*; *a.* ~ *steak bsd. gutes* Beefsteak *n*.

port·fire ['pɔːtfaiə] Lunte *f*.

port·fo·li·o [pɔːt'fəuljəu] (Akten-)Mappe *f*; (Minister)Portefeuille *n*.

port-hole ⚓ ['pɔːthəul] = *port*[2].

por·ti·co ⚠ ['pɔːtikəu] Säulenhalle *f*.

por·tière ['pɔːtiɛə] Portière *f*, Türvorhang *m*.

por·tion ['pɔːʃən] **1.** Teil *m*; Anteil *m*; Portion *f Essen*; Erbteil *n*; Heiratsgut *n*, Aussteuer *f*; Los *n*, Schicksal *n*; **2.** teilen; ausstatten; '**por·tion·less** ohne Aussteuer.

port·li·ness ['pɔːtlinis] Stattlichkeit *f*, Würde *f*; '**port·ly** stattlich.

port·man·teau [pɔːt'mæntəu] Handkoffer *m*; † Mantelsack *m*; ~ *word gr.* Schachtelwort *n*.

por·trait ['pɔːtrit] Porträt *n*, Bildnis *n*; '**por·trait·ist** Porträtmaler *m*; **por·trai·ture** ['~tʃə] = *portrait*; Porträtmalerei *f*.

por·tray [pɔː'trei] (ab)malen, porträtieren; schildern; **por'tray·al** Porträtieren *n*; Schilderung *f*.

Por·tu·guese [pɔːtju'giːz] **1.** portugiesisch; **2.** Portugiese *m*, Portugiesin *f*; Portugiesisch *n*.

pose [pəuz] **1.** Pose *f*; **2.** (sich) in Positur stellen; auftreten, sich hinstellen (*as* als); *Frage* aufwerfen; '**pos·er** schwierige Frage *f*; Poseur *m*.

posh *sl.* [pɔʃ] schick, pikfein, erstklassig.

po·si·tion [pə'ziʃən] Lage *f*, Stellung *f* (*a. fig.*); Rang *m*; Stand *m*; *fig.* Standpunkt *m*; ⚔, *ast.*, ⚓ Position *f*; ~ *light* Positionslicht *n*; *be in a* ~ *to do* in der Lage sein zu tun.

pos·i·tive ['pɔzətiv] **1.** □ bestimmt, ausdrücklich; positiv; feststehend, sicher; vollkommen; unbedingt; ℞, *phls.*, *phys.*, *phot.*, ⚡ positiv; überzeugt, sicher; rechthaberisch, eigensinnig; **2.** *das* Bestimmte; Positiv (*gr. m*; *phot. n*); '**pos·i·tive·ness** Bestimmtheit *f etc.*

pos·se ['pɔsi] (Polizei- *etc.*)Aufgebot *n*; Haufen *m*, Schar *f*.

pos·sess [pə'zes] besitzen; beherrschen; *fig.* erfüllen (*with* mit); ~*ed* besessen; ~*ed of* im Besitz *e-r Sache*; ~*o.s. of et.* in Besitz nehmen, sich *e-r Sache* bemächtigen; **pos·ses·sion** [pə'zeʃən] Besitz *m*; *fig.* Besessenheit *f*; ~*s pl.* Besitz(tum *n*) *m*; Besitzungen *f/pl.*; Habe *f*, Eigentum *n*; *in* ~ *of* im Besitz *e-r Sache*; **pos'ses·sive** *gr.* [~siv] **1.** □ besitzanzeigend; ~ *case* Genitiv *m*; **2.** besitzanzeigendes Fürwort *n*; Genitiv *m*; **pos'ses·sor** Besitzer *m*; **pos'ses·so·ry** Besitz...

pos·set ['pɔsit] heiße Milch *f* mit Bier *od.* Wein.

pos·si·bil·i·ty [pɔsə'biliti] Möglichkeit *f*; '**pos·si·ble** □ **1.** möglich; **2.** *Sport*: Höchstleistung *f*; '**pos·si·bly** möglicherweise, vielleicht; *if I* ~ *can* wenn ich irgend kann; *how can I* ~ *do it?* wie kann ich es nur *od.* bloß machen?; *I cannot* ~ *do it* ich kann es unmöglich tun.

pos·sum F ['pɔsəm] = *opossum*; *play* ~ krank spielen.

post[1] [pəust] **1.** Pfosten *m*, Pfahl *m*; **2.** *mst* ~ *up Plakat* anschlagen.

post[2] [~] **1.** ⚔, ☤ Posten *m*; ⚔ Standort *m*; Stelle *f*, Amt *n*, Posten *m*; 📯 Post *f* (*Postamt*, *-zustellung*, *-sendung*); Briefpapier *n*; *at one's* ~ ⚔ auf (s-m) Posten; *by* ~ mit der Post; **2.** *v/t. Soldaten etc.* aufstellen, postieren; ☤ eintragen, verbuchen; *oft* ~ *up* ☤ *die Bücher* in Ordnung bringen; zur Post geben; per Post senden; *keep s.o.* ~*ed up* j. auf dem laufenden halten; *v/i.* (dahin)eilen.

post[3] ⚔ [~] Signal *n*; *last* ~ Zapfenstreich *m*.

post·age ['pəustidʒ] Porto *n*, Postgebühr *f*; ~ *due* Nachgebühr *f*; ~ **stamp** Briefmarke *f*.

post·al □ ['pəustəl] **1.** postalisch; Post...; ~ *order* Postanweisung *f*; ♀ *Union* Weltpostverein *m*; **2.** *a.* ~ *card Am.* Postkarte *f*.

post...: '**~card** Postkarte *f*; '**~code** Postleitzahl *f*.

post·date ['pəust'deit] vorausdatieren.

post·er ['pəustə] Plakat *n*, Anschlag *m*; *a. bill-*~ Plakatankleber *m*.

poste res·tante [ˈpəust ˈrestɑ̃ːnt] **1.** postlagernd; **2.** Schalter *m* für postlagernde Sendungen.
pos·te·ri·or F [pɔsˈtiəriə] **1.** □ später (*to* als); hinter; Hinter...; **2.** *a.* ~*s pl.* Hintern *m.*
pos·ter·i·ty [pɔsˈteriti] Nachwelt *f*; Nachkommenschaft *f.*
pos·tern [ˈpəustəːn] Hintertür *f.*
post-free [ˈpəustˈfriː] portofrei.
post-grad·u·ate [ˈpəustˈgrædjuit] **1.** nach beendigter Studienzeit; **2.** Graduierte *m, der s-e Studien fortsetzt*; Doktorand(in).
post-haste [ˈpəustˈheist] eilig(st).
post·hu·mous □ [ˈpɔstjuməs] nachgeboren; hinterlassen; post(h)um.
pos·til·(l)ion [pəsˈtiljən] Postillion *m.*
post...: ˈ**~·man** Briefträger *m*, Postbote *m*; ˈ**~·mark 1.** Poststempel *m*; **2.** abstempeln; ˈ**~·mas·ter** Postamtsvorsteher *m*; ♀ *General* Postminister *m.*
post me·rid·i·em [ˈpəust məˈridiem] nachmittägig; Nachmittags...; **post-mor·tem** [ˈ~ˈmɔːtem] **1.** nach dem Tode; **2.** *a.* ~ *examination* Autopsie *f.*
post...: ˈ**~-of·fice**, *mst* ~ **of·fice** Postamt *n*; *Am. ein Kußspiel*; *general* ~ Hauptpost(amt *n*) *f*; ~ *box* Post(schließ)fach *n*; ~ *engineer* Fernmeldetechniker *m*; ~ *order* Postanweisung *f*; ~ *savings-bank* Postsparkasse *f*; ˈ**~-paid** franko.
post·pone [pəustˈpəun] ver-, aufschieben; *j. od. et.* unterordnen; **postˈpone·ment** Aufschub *m.*
post·pran·di·al □ *co.* [pəustˈprændiəl] nach Tisch (stattfindend).
post·script [ˈpəusskript] Nachschrift *f*, Postskriptum *n.*
pos·tu·lant [ˈpɔstjulənt] Bewerber *m*, Antragsteller *m*; **pos·tu·late 1.** [ˈ~lit] Postulat *n*, Forderung *f*; **2.** [ˈ~leit] fordern; (als gegeben) voraussetzen; **pos·tuˈla·tion** Gesuch *n*; Annahme *f.*
pos·ture [ˈpɔstʃə] **1.** Stellung *f*, Haltung *f des Körpers*; **2.** *v/t.* zurechtstellen; *v/i.* sich zurechtstellen; posieren.
post-war [ˈpəustˈwɔː] Nachkriegs...
po·sy [ˈpəuzi] Motto *n*, Sinnspruch *m*; Blumenstrauß *m.*
pot [pɔt] **1.** Topf *m*; Tiegel *m*; F *Sport*: Silberpokal *m*; *Am. sl.* Marihuana *n*; *a* ~ *of money* F ein Sackvoll *m* Geld; *big* ~ F hohes Tier *n*; **2.** in e-n Topf tun; *Pflanze* eintopfen; *Fleisch* einlegen; F schießen, erlegen.
po·ta·ble [ˈpəutəbl] trinkbar.
pot·ash ⚗ [ˈpɔtæʃ] Pottasche *f.*
po·tas·si·um ⚗ [pəˈtæsjəm] Kalium *n.*
po·ta·tion [pəuˈteiʃən] *mst* ~*s pl.* Trinken *n*, Zecherei *f*; Trunk *m.*
po·ta·to [pəˈteitəu], *pl.* **poˈta·toes** [~z] Kartoffel *f*; ~ **bee·tle** *zo.* Kartoffelkäfer *m*; ~ **chips** *pl. Am.* (Kartoffel)Chips *pl.*; ~ **mash·er** Kartoffelstampfer *m.*
pot...: ˈ**~-bel·ly** Schmerbauch *m*; ˈ**~-boil·er** Brotarbeit *f*; Routinewerk *n*; ˈ**~-boy** Bierkellner *m.*
po·ten·cy [ˈpəutənsi] Macht *f*; Stärke *f*; ˈ**po·tent** □ mächtig; stark; überzeugend; **po·ten·tate** [ˈ~teit] Machthaber *m*, Potentat *m*; **po·ten·tial** [pəuˈtenʃəl] **1.** potentiell; möglich; in der Anlage vorhanden; *phys.* gebunden; **2.** *a.* ~ *mood gr.* Potentialis *m*, Möglichkeitsform *f*; ⚡ Spannung *f*; Leistungsfähigkeit *f*, Potential *n*, Kraftvorrat *m*; **po·ten·ti·al·i·ty** [~ʃiˈæliti] Potentialität *f*; (Entwicklungs)Möglichkeit *f.*
poth·er [ˈpɔðə] **1.** Aufregung *f*; Lärm *m*; **2.** (sich) aufregen.
pot...: ˈ**~-herb** Küchenkraut *n*; ˈ**~-hole** *mot.* Schlagloch *n*; *geol.* Gletschertopf *m*; ˈ**~-hol·er** Höhlenforscher *m*; ˈ**~-hook** Kesselhaken *m*; Schörkel *m*; ~*s pl.* Gekritzel *n*; ˈ**~-house** Kneipe *f.*
po·tion [ˈpəuʃən] (Arznei- *etc.*) Trank *m.*
pot-luck [ˈpɔtˈlʌk]: *take* ~ vorliebnehmen mit dem, was es gibt.
pot·tage [ˈpɔtidʒ] dicke Suppe *f.*
pot·ter[1] [ˈpɔtə]: ~ *about* herumwerkeln, -hantieren; ~ *away* vertrödeln.
pot·ter[2] [~] Töpfer *m*; ~*'s wheel* Töpferscheibe *f*; ˈ**pot·ter·y** Töpferei *f*; Töpferware(n *pl.*) *f.*
pot·ty *sl.* [ˈpɔti] lächerlich, unbedeutend; verrückt.
pouch [pautʃ] **1.** Tasche *f*; Beutel *m* (*a. zo.*); Tabaksbeutel *m*; Patronentasche *f*; **2.** einstecken; (sich) beuteln; **pouched** Beutel...
poul·ter·er [ˈpəultərə] Geflügelhändler *m.*
poul·tice ⚕ [ˈpəultis] Breiumschlag

m, Packung *f*.

poul·try ['pəultri] Geflügel *n*.

pounce [pauns] **1.** Stoß *m*, Sprung *m*; **2.** (herab)stoßen (*Raubvogel*), sich stürzen (*on, upon* auf *acc.*).

pound[1] [paund] Pfund *n* (*abbr. lb.* = *453,6 g*); ~ (*sterling*) Pfund Sterling (*abbr.* £ = *100 pence*).

pound[2] [~] **1.** Pfandstall *m*; Tierasyl *n*; **2.** einpferchen.

pound[3] [~] (zer)stoßen; stampfen; donnern; hämmern, schlagen; *sl. Börse*: drücken; ~ *away* drauflosarbeiten.

pound·age ['paundidʒ] Provision *f od.* Prozentsatz *m* per Pfund.

pound·er ['paundə] ...pfünder *m*.

pour [pɔ:] *v/t.* gießen, schütten; ~ *out Getränk* eingießen; *fig. sein Herz* ausschütten; *v/i.* sich ergießen, strömen; ~ *with rain* in Strömen gießen; *it never rains but it* ~*s fig.* ein Unglück kommt selten allein.

pout [paut] **1.** Schmollen *n*; **2.** *v/t. Lippen* aufwerfen; *v/i.* schmollen; hervorstehen (*Lippen*); '**pout·er** *zo.* Kropftaube *f*.

pov·er·ty ['pɔvəti] Armut *f*; ~ **line** Existenzminimum *n*; '~**-strick·en** verarmt; arm(selig), dürftig.

pow·der ['paudə] **1.** Pulver *n*; Staub *m*; Puder *m*; **2.** pulverisieren; (sich) pudern; bepudern, bestreuen; '~**-box** Puderdose *f*; ~ **keg** *fig.* Pulverfaß *n*; '~**-puff** Puderquaste *f*; ~ **room** Damentoilette *f*; '**pow·der·y** pulverig; überpulvert.

pow·er ['pauə] Kraft *f* (*a.* ⊕, ⚡), Vermögen *n*; Fähigkeit *f*; Macht *f*, Gewalt *f*; ⚖ Vollmacht *f*; ⅌ Potenz *f*; F Masse *f*; *in* ~ an der Macht, im Amt; '~**-cur·rent** Starkstrom *m*; ~ **cut** Stromausfall *m*, -sperre *f*; '~**-dive** ✈ Vollgassturzflug *m*; ~ **fail·ure** Stromausfall *m*; **pow·er·ful** ['~ful] □ mächtig, kräftig; einflußreich; wirksam; '**pow·er--house** = *power-station*; '**pow·er·less** machtlos, kraftlos; **pow·er line** ⚡ Starkstromleitung *f*; **pow·er plant** = *power-station*; **pow·er point** ⚡ Steckdose *f*; **pow·er pol·i·tics** *sg. od. pl.* Machtpolitik *f*; **pow·er saw** Motorsäge *f*; '**pow·er-sta·tion** Kraftwerk *n*; **pow·er steer·ing** *mot.* Servolenkung *f*; **pow·er strug·gle** Machtkampf *m*.

pow·wow ['pauwau] Medizinmann *m*; *Am.* lärmende Versammlung *f*; F Palaver *n*.

pox V [pɔks] Syphilis *f*.

pra(a)m ⚓ [prɑ:m] Prahm *m*.

prac·ti·ca·bil·i·ty [præktikə'biliti] Durchführbarkeit *f*; '**prac·ti·ca·ble** □ tunlich, durch-, ausführbar; gangbar (*Weg*); brauchbar; '**prac·ti·cal** □ praktisch; erfahren, geschickt; tatsächlich, wirklich; eigentlich; sachlich; ~ *joke* Schabernack *m*, Streich *m*; ~ *chemistry* angewandte Chemie *f*; **prac·ti·cal·i·ty** [~'kæliti] *das* Praktische; Sachlichkeit *f*; **prac·ti·cal·ly** ['~kəli] praktisch, so gut wie.

prac·tice ['præktis] **1.** Praxis *f* (*a. des Arztes u. Anwalts*); Übung *f*; Gewohnheit *f*; Brauch *m*; Praktik *f*; *out of* ~ außer Übung; *put into* ~ in die Praxis umsetzen; *sharp* ~ unsaubere Geschäfte *n/pl.*; **2.** *Am.* = *practise*; ~ **am·mu·ni·tion** ⚔ Übungsmunition *f*.

prac·tise [~] *v/t.* in die Praxis umsetzen; *Beruf* ausüben; *Geschäft etc.* betreiben; *et.* auf *e-m Instrument* üben; *j.* schulen; *v/i.* (sich) üben, Übungen machen; *Sport*: trainieren; ♪ üben; praktizieren; ~ *upon j-s Schwäche* ausnutzen; '**prac·tised** geübt (*Person*).

prac·ti·tion·er [præk'tiʃnə] Praktiker *m*; Rechtsanwalt *m*; *a. general* ~ praktischer Arzt *m*.

prae·tor ['pri:tə] *römischer* Prätor *m*.

prag·mat·ic [præg'mætik] (~*ally*) pragmatisch, praktisch, sachlich; geschäftig; vorwitzig; rechthaberisch.

prai·rie *Am.* ['prɛəri] Grasebene *f*; Prärie *f*; ~ *schooner Am.* Planwagen *m der Kolonialzeit*.

praise [preiz] **1.** Preis *m*, Lob *n*; **2.** loben, preisen.

praise·wor·thy ['preizwə:ði] □ lobenswert.

pram F [præm] Kinderwagen *m*.

prance [prɑ:ns] sich bäumen; tänzeln (*Pferd*); paradieren; einherstolzieren.

pran·di·al □ ['prændiəl] auf die Mahlzeit bezüglich; Tafel..., Tisch...

prank [præŋk] **1.** Possen *m*, Streich *m*; **2.** ~ *out* (heraus)putzen.

prate [preit] **1.** Geschwätz *n*;

2. schwatzen, plappern; '**prat·er** Schwätzer(in).
prat·tle ['prætl] = *prate*.
prawn *zo.* [prɔ:n] Steingarnele *f*.
pray [prei] *v/i.* beten (*to* zu; *for* um; für); bitten (*for* um); *v/t. j.* inständig bitten, ersuchen (*for* um); *et.* erbitten; ~ *tell me* bitte sagen Sie mir.
prayer [prɛə] Gebet *n*; Bitte *f*; *oft* ~*s pl.* Andacht *f*; *Lord's* ~ Vaterunser *n*; *Book of Common* ♀ Gebetbuch *n* der anglikanischen Kirche; '~**-book** Gebetbuch *n*.
pre... [pri:, pri] vor(her)...; Vor...; früher.
preach [pri:tʃ] predigen, *Predigt* halten; '**preach·er** Prediger(in); '**preach·ing** Predigen *n*; Lehre *f*; '**preach·ment** Salbaderei *f*.
pre·am·ble [pri:'æmbl] Einleitung *f*, Präambel *f*.
preb·end *eccl.* ['prebənd] Präbende *f*, Pfründe *f*; '**pre·ben·dar·y** Pfründner *m*; Domherr *m*.
pre·car·i·ous □ [pri'kɛəriəs] unsicher, prekär; **pre'car·i·ous·ness** Unsicherheit *f*.
pre·cau·tion [pri'kɔ:ʃən] Vorsicht(smaßregel) *f*; **pre'cau·tion·ar·y** [~ʃnəri] vorbeugend; Warnungs..., Vorsichts...
pre·cede [pri:'si:d] voraus-, vorangehen (*dat.*); *fig.* vorgehen (*dat.*); einführen, -leiten; **pre'ced·ence, pre'ced·en·cy** Vorhergehen *n*; Vortritt *m*, Vorrang *m*; **prec·e·dent** ['presidənt] Präzedenzfall *m*; **pre·ced·ing** [pri:'si:diŋ] vorhergehend.
pre·cen·tor *eccl.* [pri:'sentə] Vorsänger *m*, Kantor *m*.
pre·cept ['pri:sept] Vorschrift *f*, Regel *f*; ⚖ Verordnung *f*; **pre·cep·tor** [pri'septə] Lehrer *m*; **pre'cep·tress** [~tris] Lehrerin *f*.
pre·cinct ['pri:siŋkt] Bezirk *m*; *bsd. Am.* Wahlbezirk *m*, -kreis *m*; ~*s pl.* Nachbarschaft *f*, Umgebung *f*; Bereich *m*; Grenze *f*; *pedestrian* ~ Fußgängerzone *f*.
pre·cious ['preʃəs] **1.** □ kostbar (*a. iro.*); edel (*Steine etc.*); geschraubt, affektiert (*Sprache*); F arg, beträchtlich, schön; **2.** F *adv.* recht, äußerst; '**pre·cious·ness** Kostbarkeit *f*.
prec·i·pice ['presipis] Abgrund *m*;
pre·cip·i·tance, pre·cip·i·tan·cy [pri'sipitəns(i)] Hast *f*, Übereilung *f*; **pre'cip·i·tate 1.** [~teit] (herab)stürzen; ⚗ fällen; beschleunigen; überstürzen; **2.** [~tit] □ hastig, voreilig; übereilt, schleunig; **3.** ⚗ [~tit] Niederschlag *m*; **pre·cip·i·ta·tion** [~'teiʃən] Sturz *m*; Hast *f*; ⚗ Niederschlag(en *n*) *m*; **pre'cip·i·tous** □ steil, jäh, abschüssig.
pré·cis ['preisi:] gedrängte Übersicht *f*, Zs.-fassung *f*.
pre·cise □ [pri'sais] genau; pedantisch; ~*ly!* ganz recht!; **pre'cise·ness** Genauigkeit *f*.
pre·ci·sion [pri'siʒən] Genauigkeit *f*; Präzision *f*; *attr.* Präzisions...
pre·clude [pri'klu:d] ausschließen; vorbeugen (*dat.*); ~ *s.o. from ger.* j. daran hindern, zu *inf.*
pre·co·cious □ [pri'kəuʃəs] frühreif; altklug; **pre'co·cious·ness, pre·coc·i·ty** [pri'kɔsiti] Frühreife *f*.
pre·con·ceive ['pri:kən'si:v] vorher ausdenken; ~*d* vorgefaßt (*Meinung*).
pre·con·cep·tion ['pri:kən'sepʃən] vorgefaßte Meinung *f*.
pre·con·cert·ed ['pri:kən'sə:tid] verabredet; *b. s.* abgekartet.
pre·cur·sor [pri:'kə:sə] Vorläufer *m*, Vorbote *m*; **pre'cur·so·ry** vorausgehend; vorbereitend.
pre·date ['pri:'deit] vordatieren.
pred·a·to·ry ['predətəri] räuberisch.
pre·de·cease ['pri:di'si:s] früher sterben als.
pre·de·ces·sor ['pri:disesə] Vorgänger *m*.
pre·des·ti·nate [pri:'destineit] vorherbestimmen; **pre·des·ti'na·tion** Vorherbestimmung *f*; *eccl.* Gnadenwahl *f*, Prädestination *f*; **pre'destined** auserkoren.
pre·de·ter·mine ['pri:di'tə:min] vorher festsetzen; vorherbestimmen.
pred·i·ca·ble ['predikəbl] aussagbar.
pre·dic·a·ment [pri'dikəmənt] *phls.* Kategorie *f*; (mißliche) Lage *f*.
pred·i·cate 1. ['predikeit] aussagen; **2.** ['~kit] *gr.* Prädikat *n*, Satzaussage *f*; **pred·i·ca·tion** [~'keiʃən] Aussage *f*; **pred·i·ca·tive** [pri'dikətiv] □ aussagend; *gr.* prädikativ.
pre·dict [pri'dikt] vorhersagen; **pre·dic·tion** [~'dikʃən] Prophezeiung *f*, Vorhersage *f*.

pre·di·lec·tion [pri:di'lekʃən] Vorliebe *f* (*for* für).
pre·dis·pose ['pri:dis'pəuz] vorher geneigt *od.* empfänglich machen (*to* für); **pre·dis·po·si·tion** ['~dispə'ziʃən] Geneigtheit *f*; *bsd.* ⚕ Anfälligkeit *f* (*to* für).
pre·dom·i·nance [pri'dɔminəns] Vorherrschen *n*, Vorherrschaft *f*; Übergewicht *n*; Vormacht(stellung) *f*; **pre'dom·i·nant** □ vorherrschend, über-, vorwiegend; **pre'dom·i·nate** [~neit] die Oberhand haben (*over* über *acc.*); vorherrschen.
pre-em·i·nence [pri:'eminəns] Hervorragen *n*; Vorrang *m*; **pre-'em·i·nent** □ hervorragend.
pre-emp·tion [pri:'empʃən] Vorkauf(srecht *n*) *m*; **pre-'emp·tive** [~tiv] Vorkaufs...; präventiv; ~ *first strike* ⚔ Präventivangriff *m*.
preen [pri:n] *das Gefieder* putzen; ~ *o.s. on fig.* sich et. einbilden auf (*acc.*).
pre-en·gage [pri:in'geidʒ] vorher verpflichten *od.* bestellen; **pre-en'gage·ment** frühere Verpflichtung *f*.
pre-ex·ist ['pri:ig'zist] vorher dasein; **'pre-ex'ist·ence** früheres Vorhandensein *n*; **'pre-ex'ist·ent** vorher vorhanden.
pre·fab ['pri:fæb] **1.** zs.-setzbar; Fertig...; **2.** Fertighaus *n*; **'pre'fab·ri·cate** [~rikeit] vorfabrizieren.
pref·ace ['prefis] **1.** Vorrede *f*, -wort *n*, Einleitung *f*; **2.** einleiten.
pref·a·to·ry □ ['prefətəri] einleitend.
pre·fect ['pri:fekt] Präfekt *m*; *Schule*: Vertrauensschüler *m*.
pre·fer [pri'fə:] vorziehen; *Gesuch etc.* vorbringen; *Klage* einreichen (*to* bei); befördern; *s. share* **1**; *I should ~ you not to go* es wäre mir lieber, wenn du nicht gingst; **pref·er·a·ble** □ ['prefərəbl] (*to*) vorzuziehen(d) (*dat.*); vorzüglicher (als); **'pref·er·a·bly** vorzugsweise; lieber; besser; **'pref·er·ence** Vorliebe *f*; *bsd.* ✝ Vorzug *m*; *Zoll*: Meistbegünstigung *f*; *s. share* **1**; **pref·er·en·tial** □ [~'renʃəl] bevorzugt; Vorzugs...; **pref·er'en·tial·ly** vorzugsweise; **pre·fer·ment** [pri'fə:mənt] Beförderung *f*; höheres Amt *n*.
pre·fix 1. ['pri:fiks] Präfix *n*, Vorsilbe *f*; **2.** [pri:'fiks] vorsetzen; vorausgehen lassen.
preg·nan·cy ['pregnənsi] Schwangerschaft *f*; *fig.* Fruchtbarkeit *f*; Bedeutungsreichtum *m*; **'preg·nant** □ schwanger; trächtig (*Tier*); *fig.* fruchtbar, inhaltvoll.
pre-heat ⊕ ['pri:'hi:t] vorwärmen.
pre·hen·sile [pri'hensail] Greif...
pre·his·tor·ic ['pri:his'tɔrik] vorgeschichtlich.
pre-ig·ni·tion *mot.* ['pri:ig'niʃən] Frühzündung *f*.
pre·judge ['pri:'dʒʌdʒ] vorher (ver-)urteilen.
prej·u·dice ['predʒudis] **1.** Voreingenommenheit *f*; Vorurteil *n*; vorgefaßte Meinung *f*; Schaden *m*; *without ~ to* unbeschadet (*gen.*); **2.** einnehmen; benachteiligen; *e-r Sache* Abbruch tun; *~d* (vor)eingenommen.
prej·u·di·cial □ [predʒu'diʃəl] nachteilig, schädlich (*to* für).
prel·a·cy ['preləsi] Prälaten(würde *f*) *m/pl.*
prel·ate ['prelit] Prälat *m*.
pre·lec·tion [pri'lekʃən] Vorlesung *f*; **pre'lec·tor** Vorleser *m*.
pre·lim F [pri'lim] Vorexamen *n*.
pre·lim·i·nar·y [pri'liminəri] **1.** □ vorläufig; einleitend; Vor...; **2.** Einleitung *f*; **pre'lim·i·na·ries** [~riz] *pl.* Vorbereitungen *f/pl.*, Vorverhandlungen *f/pl.*
prel·ude ['prelju:d] **1.** ♪ Vorspiel *n*; Einleitung *f*; **2.** ♪ präludieren; einleiten.
pre·mar·i·tal [pri:'mæritl] vorehelich.
pre·ma·ture □ [premə'tjuə] *fig.* frühreif; vorzeitig; vorschnell; verfrüht; ~ *delivery* Frühgeburt *f*; **pre·ma'ture·ness, pre·ma'tu·ri·ty** [~riti] *fig.* Frühreife *f*; Vorzeitigkeit *f*; Voreiligkeit *f*.
pre·med·i·tate [pri:'mediteit] vorher überlegen; *~d murder* ⚖ vorsätzlicher Mord *m*; **pre·med·i'ta·tion** Vorbedacht *m*.
pre·mi·er ['premjə] **1.** erst; **2.** Premierminister *m*.
prem·ière ['premiɛə] Uraufführung *f*.
pre·mi·er·ship ['premjəʃip] Amt *n od.* Würde *f* des Premierministers.

prem·ise 1. ['premis] Prämisse *f*, Vordersatz *m*; ~*s pl.* (Gebäude *n/pl.* mit) Grundstück *n*, Anwesen *n*; Lokal *n*; *licensed* ~*s pl.* Schankstätte *f*; *on the* ~*s* an Ort und Stelle, im Hause *od.* Lokal; **2. pre·mise** [pri'maiz] vorausschicken.

pre·mi·um ['pri:mjəm] Prämie *f*, Preis *m*; Anzahlung *f*; † Agio *n*; Versicherungsprämie *f*; Lehrgeld *n*; Anzahlung *f auf Mieten*; Super(benzin) *n*; *at a* ~ über pari; sehr gesucht.

pre·mo·ni·tion [pri:mə'niʃən] Warnung *f*; (Vor)Ahnung *f*; **pre·mon·i·to·ry** □ [pri'mɔnitəri] warnend.

pre-na·tal ['pri:'neitl] vor der Geburt (eintretend).

pre·oc·cu·pan·cy *fig.* [pri:'ɔkjupənsi] Vertieftsein *n* (*in* in *acc.*); **pre·oc·cu·pa·tion** [~'peiʃən] vorherige Besitznahme *f*; Vorurteil *n*; Haupttätigkeit *f*; Beschäftigtsein *n* (*with* mit); **pre'oc·cu·pied** [~paid] in Gedanken verloren; **pre'oc·cu·py** [~pai] vorher in Besitz nehmen; ausschließlich beschäftigen; in Anspruch nehmen.

pre·or·dain ['pri:ɔ:'dein] vorher bestimmen.

prep F [prep] = *preparation, preparatory school.*

pre·paid ['pri:'peid] vorausbezahlt; frankiert.

prep·a·ra·tion [prepə'reiʃən] Vorbereitung *f*; Zubereitung *f*; **pre·par·a·tive** [pri'pærətiv] Vorbereitung *f*; **pre'par·a·to·ry** [~təri] □ vorbereitend, Vorbereitungs...; ~ *school* Vorschule *f*; ~ *to* vor (*dat.*).

pre·pare [pri'pɛə] *v/t.* vorbereiten; zurechtmachen, herrichten; *Speise etc.* (zu)bereiten; (aus)rüsten; *v/i.* sich vorbereiten; sich anschicken; **pre'pared** □ bereit; ~ *for* gefaßt auf (*acc.*); **pre'pared·ness** Bereitschaft *f*; Gefaßtsein *n* (*for* auf *acc.*).

pre·pay ['pri:'pei] (*irr. pay*) vorausbezahlen; frankieren; **'pre'pay·ment** Vorausbezahlung *f*; Frankierung *f*.

pre·pense □ [pri'pens] vorbedacht; *with malice* ~ in böswilliger Absicht.

pre·pon·der·ance [pri'pɔndərəns] Übergewicht *n*; **pre'pon·der·ant** □ überwiegend; **pre'pon·der·ate** [~reit] überwiegen.

prep·o·si·tion *gr.* [prepə'ziʃən] Präposition *f*, Verhältniswort *n*; **prep·o'si·tion·al** □ [~ʃənl] präpositional.

pre·pos·sess [pri:pə'zes] günstig stimmen, einnehmen; **pre·pos'sess·ing** □ einnehmend, anziehend; **pre·pos·ses·sion** [~'zeʃən] Voreingenommenheit *f*; Vorurteil *n*.

pre·pos·ter·ous [pri'pɔstərəs] widersinnig, albern; grotesk.

pre·puce *anat.* ['pri:pju:s] Vorhaut *f*.

pre·re·cord·ed [pri:ri'kɔ:did] bespielt (*Musik-, Videokassette*).

pre·req·ui·site ['pri:'rekwizit] Vorbedingung *f*, Voraussetzung *f*.

pre·rog·a·tive [pri'rɔgətiv] Vorrecht *n*, Prärogativ *n*.

pres·age ['presidʒ] **1.** Vorbedeutung *f*; Ahnung *f*; **2.** vorbedeuten; ahnen; prophezeien.

pres·by·ter ['prezbitə] Kirchenälteste *m*; **Pres·by·te·ri·an** [~'tiəriən] **1.** presbyterianisch; **2.** Presbyterianer(in); **pres·by·ter·y** *eccl.* ['~təri] Presbyterium *n*; *katholisches* Pfarrhaus *n*.

pre·sci·ence ['presiəns] Vorherwissen *n*, Voraussicht *f*; **'pre·sci·ent** vorherwissend.

pre·scribe [pris'kraib] *v/t.* vorschreiben; ⚕ verschreiben, verordnen; *v/i.* etwas verschreiben (*for dat.*); ⚖ verjähren.

pre·script ['pri:skript] Vorschrift *f*; **pre·scrip·tion** [pris'kripʃən] Vorschrift *f*, Verordnung *f*; ⚕ Rezept *n*; ⚖ Verjährung *f*; ~ *charge* Rezeptgebühr *f*; **pre'scrip·tive** □ [~tiv] Verjährungs...; verjährt.

pres·ence ['prezns] Gegenwart *f*; Anwesenheit *f*; Vorhandensein *n*; (äußere) Erscheinung *f*; (Geister-)Erscheinung *f*; ~ *of mind* Geistesgegenwart *f*; **'~-cham·ber** Audienzzimmer *n*.

pres·ent[1] ['preznt] **1.** □ gegenwärtig; anwesend, vorhanden; jetzig; heutig; laufend (*Jahr etc.*); vorliegend (*Fall etc.*); ~ *tense gr.* Präsens *n*; ~ *company* die Anwesenden *pl.*; ~ *value* Gegenwartswert *m*; ~! hier!; **2.** Gegenwart *f*; *gr. a.* Präsens *n*; *by the* ~ †, *by these* ~*s* ⚖ hiermit, -durch; *at* ~ jetzt; *for the* ~ für jetzt, einstweilen.

pre·sent[2] [pri'zent] (dar)bieten; darstellen, zeigen; *j.* vorstellen; *Wechsel* vorzeigen; *Kandidaten* vorschlagen; ⚔ präsentieren; (über)reichen;

verleihen; vorlegen; *et.* schenken; *j.* beschenken (*with* mit); ~ *o.s.* sich einfinden; sich melden; ~ *one's compliments to s.o.* sich j-m empfehlen.

pres·ent[3] ['preznt] Geschenk *n*; *make s.o. a* ~ *of s.th.* j-m et. zum Geschenk machen.

pre·sent·a·ble [pri'zentəbl] präsentabel; *is this suit* ~? kann man sich mit diesem Anzug sehen lassen?

pres·en·ta·tion [prezən'teiʃən] Dar-, Vorstellung *f*; Vorschlag(srecht *n*) *m*; Ein-, Überreichung *f*; Schenkung *f*; Vorzeigung *f e-s Wechsels*; ~ *copy* Frei- *od.* Widmungsexemplar *n*.

pres·ent-day ['prezentdei] gegenwärtig, modern, Gegenwarts...

pre·sen·ti·ment [pri'zentimənt] Vorgefühl *n*, Ahnung *f*.

pres·ent·ly ['prezntli] sogleich, bald (darauf), alsbald; *Am.* zur Zeit.

pre·sent·ment [pri'zentmənt] *s. presentation*; ⚖ Anklage *f* von Amts wegen; *thea.* Vorstellung *f*.

pres·er·va·tion [prezə:'veiʃən] Bewahrung *f*, Erhaltung *f*; *in good* ~ gut erhalten; **pre·serv·a·tive** [pri'zə:vətiv] **1.** bewahrend; **2.** Schutz-, Konservierungsmittel *n*.

pre·serve [pri'zə:v] **1.** bewahren, behüten (*from* vor *dat.*); erhalten, konservieren; *Obst etc.* einmachen; *Wild* hegen; (bei)behalten; **2.** *hunt.* *oft* ~*s pl.* Gehege *n* (*a. fig.*); *fig.* Reich *n*; *mst* ~*s pl.* Eingemachte *n*; **pre'serv·er** Bewahrer(in), Retter (-in); Erhalter(in); *hunt.* Heger *m*; Konservierungsmittel *n*; Einkochapparat *m*.

pre·side [pri'zaid] präsidieren, den Vorsitz führen (*over* bei); ~ *over an assembly* e-e Versammlung leiten.

pres·i·den·cy ['prezidənsi] Vorsitz *m*; Oberaufsicht *f*; Präsidentschaft *f*; '**pres·i·dent** Präsident *m*, Vorsitzende *m*; *Am.* ⚕ Direktor *m*; **pres·i·den·tial** [~'denʃəl] Präsidenten...

press [pres] **1.** Druck *m der Hand*; (Wein- *etc.*)Presse *f*; *die* Presse (*Zeitungen*); Druckerei *f*; Verlag *m*; Druck(en *n*) *m*; *a. printing*-~ Drukkerpresse *f*; Menge *f*; *fig.* Druck *m*, Last *f*, Andrang *m*; Schrank *m*; ~ *of sail* ⚓ Segelpreß *m*; **2.** *v/t.* pressen (*a.* ⚔), drücken; auspressen; bügeln; (be)drängen; *fig.* drängen; dringen auf (*acc.*); *Rat etc.* aufdrängen (*on dat.*); belasten, lasten auf (*dat.*); ~ *the button* auf den Knopf drücken; ~ *the point that* besonders betonen, daß; *be* ~*ed for time* es eilig haben; *v/i.* drücken; (sich) drängen; ~ *for* sich eifrig bemühen um; ~ *on* vorwärtsdrängen, weitereilen; ~ *(up)on* eindringen auf (*acc.*); in *j.* dringen; '~**-a·gen·cy** Nachrichtenbüro *n*; ~ **a·gent** Reklameagent *m*; ~ **bar·on** Pressezar *m*; '~**-but·ton** Druckknopf *m*; '~**-cor·rec·tor** *typ.* Korrektor *m*; '~**-cut·ting** Zeitungsausschnitt *m*; '**press·er** Presser *m*; Drucker *m*; '**press-gal·le·ry** Pressetribüne *f*; '**press-gang:** ~ *s.o. into doing s.th.* F j. zu et. zwingen *od.* drängen; '**press·ing 1.** □ pressend; dringend; Preß...; **2.** Plattenpressung *f*; **press lord** Pressezar *m*; '**press·man** Mann *m* der Presse; '**press-mark** Bibliotheksnummer *f e-s Buches*; '**press-stud** Druckknopf *m*; '**press-up** *Sport*: Liegestütz *m*; **pres·sure** ['preʃə] Druck *m* (*a. fig.*); Drang *m*; Drangsal *f*; **pres·sure cook·er** Dampfkochtopf *m*; **pres·sure e·qual·i·za·tion** Druckausgleich *m*; '**pres·sure-ga(u)ge** ⊕ Druckmesser *m*; '**pres·sure-group** *pol.* Interessengruppe *f*; **pres·sur·ize** ['~raiz] unter Druck setzen; '**press-work** *typ.* Druckarbeit *f*.

pres·ti·dig·i·ta·tion ['prestididʒi'teiʃən] Taschenspielerei *f*.

pres·tige [pres'ti:ʒ] Prestige *n*, Ansehen *n*, Geltung *f*; **pres·ti·gious** [~'tidʒəs] renommiert.

pres·to ['prestəu] schnell.

pre-stressed ['pri:'strest]: ~ *concrete* Spannbeton *m*.

pre·sum·a·ble □ [pri'zju:məbl] mutmaßlich, vermutlich; **pre'sume** *v/t. als wahr* annehmen; vermuten, mutmaßen; voraussetzen; *v/i.* vermuten; sich erdreisten, wagen (*to inf.* zu *inf.*); anmaßend sein; ~ *(up)on* pochen auf, ausnutzen, mißbrauchen; **pre'sum·ed·ly** [~idli] mutmaßlich; **pre'sum·ing** □ anmaßend.

pre·sump·tion [pri'zʌmpʃən] Mutmaßung *f*; Wahrscheinlichkeit *f*; Anmaßung *f*, Dünkel *m*; Voraussetzung *f*; **pre'sump·tive** □ [~tiv] mutmaßlich; **pre'sump·tu·ous** □ [~tjuəs] überheblich; vermessen.

pre·sup·pose [pri:sə'pəuz] voraussetzen; **pre·sup·po·si·tion** [pri:sʌpə'ziʃən] Voraussetzung *f.*

pre·tence, *Am.* **pre·tense** [pri'tens] Vortäuschung *f;* Vorwand *m;* Schein *m,* Verstellung *f; false* ~ Vorspiegelung *f* falscher Tatsachen; *make* ~ vorgeben, den Anschein erwecken.

pre·tend [pri'tend] vorgeben; vortäuschen; heucheln; Anspruch erheben (*to* auf *acc.*); ~ *to be ill* so tun, als ob man krank sei; **pre'tend·ed** □ angeblich; **pre'tend·er** Beanspruchер *m;* (Thron)Bewerber *m,* Prätendent *m;* Heuchler *m,* Schauspieler *m.*

pre·ten·sion [pri'tenʃən] Anspruch *m* (*to* auf *acc.*); Anmaßung *f.*

pre·ten·tious [pri'tenʃəs] anmaßend; **pre'ten·tious·ness** Anmaßung *f.*

pret·er·it(**e**) *gr.* ['pretərit] Präteritum *n,* Vergangenheit(sform) *f.*

pre·ter·mis·sion [pri:tə'miʃən] Übergehung *f;* Unterlassung *f.*

pre·ter·nat·u·ral □ [pri:tə'nætʃrəl] außergewöhnlich, abnorm.

pre·text ['pri:tekst] Vorwand *m.*

pret·ti·fy ['pritifai] verniedlichen.

pret·ti·ness ['pritinis] Niedlichkeit *f;* Geziertheit *f des Ausdrucks.*

pret·ty ['priti] **1.** □ hübsch, niedlich; nett; F beträchtlich, schön; *a* ~ *penny* F e-e hübsche Summe, e-e Menge Geld; *my* ~! mein Herzchen!; **2.** *adv.* ziemlich; ganz schön.

pre·vail [pri'veil] die Oberhand haben *od.* gewinnen (*over, against* über *acc.*); sich durchsetzen; (vor-)herrschen; maßgebend *od.* ausschlaggebend sein; ~ (*up*)*on s.o. to do* j. dazu bewegen, *et.* zu tun; **pre'vail·ing** □ (vor)herrschend.

prev·a·lence ['prevələns] Vorherrschen *n,* Verbreitung *f;* **'prev·a·lent** □ vorherrschend, weit verbreitet.

pre·var·i·cate [pri'værikeit] Ausflüchte machen; **pre·var·i'ca·tion** Ausflucht *f.*

pre·vent [pri'vent] *et.* verhüten, verhindern, *e-r Sache* vorbeugen; *j.* hindern (*from* an *dat.*); *j.* abhalten (*from* von); **pre'vent·a·ble** verhütbar; **pre'vent·a·tive** [~tətiv] = *preventive;* **pre'ven·tion** Verhinderung *f;* Verhütung *f;* **pre'ven·tive 1.** □ vorbeugend (*of dat.*); ~ *detention* Sicherheitsverwahrung *f;* ~ *medicine* Präventivmedizin *f;* **2.** Schutzmittel *n* (*of* gegen).

pre·view ['pri:'vju:] Vorschau *f;* Vorbesichtigung *f e-r Ausstellung; thea., Film:* Probeaufführung *f.*

pre·vi·ous □ ['pri:vjəs] vorhergehend; früher; Vor...; F voreilig; ~ *conviction* Vorstrafe *f;* ~ *to* vor (*dat.*); **'pre·vi·ous·ly** vorher, früher.

pre·vi·sion [pri:'viʒən] Voraussicht *f.*

pre-war ['pri:'wɔ:] Vorkriegs...

prey [prei] **1.** Raub *m,* Beute *f; beast* (*bird*) *of* ~ Raubtier *n* (-vogel *m*); *be a* ~ *to* geplagt werden von; **2.** Beute machen; ~ *on,* ~ *upon* rauben, plündern; fressen; *fig.* nagen an (*dat.*).

price [prais] **1.** Preis *m;* Lohn *m; at any* ~ um jeden Preis; **2.** mit Preisen versehen; die Preise festsetzen (für); (ab)schätzen; ~ *s.o. out of the market* j. durch niedrige Preise vom Markt verdrängen; **'price·less** unschätzbar; unbezahlbar; **price range** Preisklasse *f;* **price tag, price tick·et** Preisschild *n;* **'pric·ey** F (ganz schön) teuer.

prick [prik] Stich *m e-s Insekts etc.;* Stachel *m* (*a. fig.*); **2.** *v/t.* (durch-)stechen; prickeln auf *od.* in (*dat.*); *a.* ~ *out* (aus)stechen, lochen, *Muster* punktieren; ~ *out* ⚘ (aus-)pflanzen; ~ *up one's ears* die Ohren spitzen; *v/i.* stechen; prickeln; ~ *up* sich aufrichten, sich recken; **'prick·er** Pfriem *m;* **prick·le** ['~l] Stachel *m,* Dorn *m;* **'prick·ly** stachelig; ~ *heat* ⚕ Hitzpickel *m/pl.;* ~ *pear* ⚘ Feigendistel *f* (*ein Kaktus*).

pric·y ['praisi] = *pricey.*

pride [praid] **1.** Stolz *m;* Genugtuung *f;* Hochmut *m;* Blüte *f,* Höhe *f der Saison etc.;* ~ *of place* Ehrenplatz *m;* Standesdünkel *m; take* (*a*) ~ *in* stolz sein auf (*acc.*); **2.** ~ *o.s.* (*up*)*on* sich brüsten mit, sich etwas einbilden, stolz sein (auf *acc.*), sich rühmen (*gen.*).

priest [pri:st] Priester *m,* Geistliche *m;* **'~craft** Pfaffenlist *f;* **'priest·ess** Priesterin *f;* **priest·hood** ['~hud]

Priesteramt *n*; Priesterschaft *f*; **ˈpriest·ly** priesterlich; **ˈpriest--rid·den** von Priestern beherrscht.

prig [prig] Tugendbold *m*, selbstgerechter Mensch *m*; Pedant *m*; **ˈprig·gish** □ selbstgerecht, -gefällig.

prim □ [prim] steif; spröde, zimperlich.

pri·ma·cy [ˈpraiməsi] Vorrang *m*; **pri·mal** [ˈpraiməl] erst, ursprünglich; wichtigst, Haupt...; **pri·ma·ri·ly** [ˈ~rili] in erster Linie; **ˈpri·ma·ry** □ **1.** ursprünglich; frühest; hauptsächlich; Ur..., Anfangs..., Grund..., Haupt...; Elementar...; höchst (*Wichtigkeit*); ⚡, ⚕ Primär...; **2.** *a.* ~ *meeting Am.* Wahlversammlung *f*; *Am.* (*oft pl.*) Vorwahl *f zur Präsidentenwahl*; *s. share*; **ˈpri·ma·ry school** Volks-, Grundschule *f*; **pri·mate** *eccl.* [ˈ~mit] Primas *m*.

prime [praim] **1.** □ erste(r, -s); Haupt...; vorzüglich(st); erstklassig, prima; ~ *cost* Gestehungs-, Selbstkosten *pl.*; ~ *rate* Eckzins *m*; ♀ *Minister* Premierminister *m*; ~ *number* Primzahl *f*; ~ *time* Hauptsendezeit *f*; **2.** *fig.* Blüte(zeit) *f*; Vollkraft *f*; *das* Beste, Kern *m*; höchste Vollkommenheit *f*; **3.** *v/t.* vorbereiten; *Pumpe* anlassen; instruieren; F vollaufen lassen; *paint.* grundieren.

prim·er[1] [ˈpraimə] Fibel *f*, Elementarbuch *n*; *typ.* [ˈprimə]: *great* ~ Tertia(schrift) *f*; *long* ~ Korpus *f*.

prim·er[2] [ˈpraimə] Grundierer *m*; Zündvorrichtung *f*.

pri·me·val [praiˈmiːvəl] uranfänglich; Ur...

prim·ing [ˈpraimiŋ] *paint.* Grundierung *f*; ⚔ Zündung *f*; Zündmasse *f*; *attr.* Zünd...; Pulver...

prim·i·tive [ˈprimitiv] **1.** □ erst, ursprünglich; Stamm...; Grund...; einfach, primitiv; **2.** *gr.* Stammwort *n*; **ˈprim·i·tive·ness** Ursprünglichkeit *f*; Primitivität *f*.

prim·ness [ˈprimnis] Steifheit *f*; Sprödigkeit *f*; Zimperlichkeit *f*.

pri·mo·gen·i·ture [praiməuˈdʒenitʃə] Erstgeburt(srecht *n*) *f*.

pri·mor·di·al □ [praiˈmɔːdjəl] uranfänglich.

prim·rose ⚘ [ˈprimrəuz] Primel *f*; ~ *path od. way fig.* Rosenpfad *m des Vergnügens*; *take the* ~ *path* das Leben genießen.

prince [prins] Fürst *m*; Prinz *m*; ♀ **Con·sort** Prinzgemahl *m*; **ˈprince·ly** fürstlich; königlich; **prin·cess** [prinˈses, *vor npr.* ˈprinses] Fürstin *f*; Prinzessin *f*.

prin·ci·pal [ˈprinsəpəl] **1.** □ erst, hauptsächlich(st); Haupt...; *gr.* ~ *parts pl.* Stammformen *f/pl. des vb.*; **2.** Hauptperson *f*; Vorsteher *m*; *bsd. Am.* (Schul)Direktor *m*, Rektor *m*; ⚓ Prinzipal *m*, Chef *m*; Auftraggeber *m*; Hauptschuldige *m*; Kapital *n*; **prin·ci·pal·i·ty** [prinsiˈpæliti] Fürstentum *n*.

prin·ci·ple [ˈprinsəpl] Prinzip *n*, Grundsatz *m*; Grund *m*, Ursprung *m*; ⚗ (Grund)Bestandteil *m*; *in* ~ im Prinzip; *on* ~ grundsätzlich, aus Prinzip.

prink F [priŋk] (sich) putzen.

print [print] **1.** Druck *m*; (Fuß-)Spur *f*; (Finger- *etc.*)Abdruck *m*; bedruckter Kattun *m*, Druckstoff *m*; Stich *m*; *phot.* Abzug *m*; *Am.* Zeitungsdrucksache *f*; *out of* ~ vergriffen; *in cold* ~ schwarz auf weiß; **2.** *v/t.* drucken; ab-, auf-, bedrucken; *phot.* kopieren; *fig.* einprägen (*on dat.*); *~ed form* Vordruck *m*; *v/i.* drucken; in Druckbuchstaben schreiben; **ˈprint·er** (Buch)Drucker *m*; *~'s devil* Setzerjunge *m*; *~'s flower* Vignette *f*; *~'s ink* Druckerschwärze *f*.

print·ing [ˈprintiŋ] Druck *m*; Drucken *n*; *phot.* Abziehen *n*, Kopieren *n*; **ˈ~-frame** *phot.* Kopierrahmen *m*; **ˈ~-ink** Druckerschwärze *f*; **ˈ~-of·fice** (Buch-)Druckerei *f*; **ˈ~-press** Druckerpresse *f*.

print-out [ˈprintaut] *Computer*: Ausdruck *m*, Printout *m*.

pri·or [ˈpraiə] **1.** früher, älter (*to* als); **2.** *adv.* ~ *to* vor (*dat.*); **3.** *eccl.* Prior *m*; **ˈpri·or·ess** *eccl.* Priorin *f*; **pri·or·i·ty** [~ˈɔriti] Priorität *f*; Vorrang *m*, Vorzugsrecht *n*; Vorfahrtsrecht *n* (*to, over* vor *dat.*); *give s.th.* ~ et. vorrangig behandeln; *s. share 1*; **pri·o·ry** *eccl.* [ˈ~əri] Priorei *f*.

prism [ˈprizəm] Prisma *n*; ~ *binoculars pl.* Prismen(fern)glas *n*; **pris·mat·ic** [~ˈmætik] (*~ally*) prismatisch.

pris·on [ˈprizn] **1.** Gefängnis *n*; **2.** *poet.* einkerkern; **ˈpris·on·er** Ge-

fangene *m*, *f*, Häftling *m*; ⚖ Angeklagte *m*, *f*; *be a* ~ *to fig.* gefesselt sein an (*acc.*); *take s.o.* ~ j. gefangennehmen; ~*'s bars*, ~*'s base* Barlauf(spiel *n*) *m*. [etepetete.]
pris·sy *Am.* F ['prisi] zimperlich,
pris·tine ['pristain] ursprünglich, urtümlich; unverdorben.
prith·ee † ['priði:] bitte.
pri·va·cy ['praivəsi] Zurückgezogenheit *f*; Privatleben *n*; Heimlichkeit *f*; Geheimhaltung *f*.
pri·vate ['praivit] **1.** □ privat; Privat...; eigen, persönlich; ohne (Regierungs)Amt *od.* Rang; nichtöffentlich; außeramtlich; vertraulich; geheim; ~ *company* offene Handelsgesellschaft *f*; ~ *lessons pl.* Privatunterricht *m*; ~ *member* Parlamentsmitglied *n* ohne Regierungsamt; ~ *theatre* Liebhabertheater *n*; ~ *view* Besichtigung *f* durch geladene Gäste; *at* ~ *sale* unter der Hand; **2.** ⚔ (gewöhnlicher) Soldat *m*; ~*s pl.*, *mst* ~ *parts pl.* Geschlechtsteile *m/pl.*; *in* ~ privatim; im geheimen.
pri·va·teer ⚓ [praivə'tiə] Freibeuter *m*, Kaperschiff *n*; Kaperer *m*; **pri·va'teer·ing** Kaperei *f*; *attr.* Kaper...
pri·va·tion [prai'veiʃən] Mangel *m*, Entbehrung *f*.
pri·va·tive □ ['privətiv] beraubend; verneinend (*a. gr.*).
priv·et ⚘ ['privit] Liguster *m*.
priv·i·lege ['privilidʒ] **1.** Privileg *n*, Vorrecht *n*; **2.** privilegieren, bevorrecht(ig)en.
priv·i·ty ⚖ ['priviti] Mitwisserschaft *f*; Interessengemeinschaft *f*.
priv·y ['privi] **1.** □ ~ *to* eingeweiht in (*acc.*); ⚖ mitbeteiligt an (*dat.*); ♀ *Council* Staatsrat *m*; ♀ *Councillor* Geheimer Rat *m*; ~ *parts pl.* Geschlechtsteile *m/pl.*; ~ *purse* Privatschatulle *f*; ♀ *Seal* Geheimsiegel *n*; *Lord* ♀ *Seal* Geheimsiegelbewahrer *m*; **2.** ⚖ Mitinteressent *m* (*to* an *dat.*); Abtritt *m*, Latrine *f*.
prize[1] [praiz] **1.** Preis *m*, Prämie *f*; ⚓ Beute *f*, Prise *f*; (Lotterie)Gewinn *m*; Vorteil *m*; *first* ~ *Lotterie*: *das* Große Los; **2.** preisgekrönt, Preis...; ⚓ Prisen...; ~ *competition* Preisausschreiben *n*; **3.** (hoch-) schätzen; ⚓ aufbringen, kapern.
prize[2] [~] **1.** *a.* ~ *open* aufbrechen (*öffnen*); **2.** Hebel *m*.
prize...: '~**fight·er** Berufsboxer *m*; '~**-list** Gewinnliste *f*; '~**·man** = *prize-winner*; '~**-ring** *Boxen*: Ring *m*; '~**-winner** Preisträger *m*.
pro[1] [prəu] für; *s. con*[3].
pro[2] F [~] Profi *m*; Professionelle *m*; Nutte *f*.
prob·a·bil·i·ty [prɔbə'biliti] Wahrscheinlichkeit *f*; '**prob·a·ble** □ wahrscheinlich.
pro·bate ⚖ ['prəubit] gerichtliche Testamentsbestätigung *f*.
pro·ba·tion [prə'beiʃən] Probe *f*, Probezeit *f*, *bsd.* ⚖ Bewährungsfrist *f*; ⚖ bedingte Strafaussetzung *f*; ~ *officer* Bewährungshelfer *m*; *on* ~ auf Probe; ⚖ mit Bewährungsfrist; **pro'ba·tion·ar·y:** ~ *period* ⚖ Bewährungsfrist *f*; **pro'ba·tion·er** Probeanwärter(in); Lernschwester *f*; ⚖ Verurteilte *m*, *f* mit Bewährungsfrist.
pro·ba·tive ⚖ ['prəubətiv]: ~ *force* Beweiskraft *f*.
probe [prəub] **1.** ⚕ Sonde *f*; *fig.* Untersuchung *f*; *lunar* ~ Mondsonde *f*; **2.** *a.* ~ *into* sondieren; untersuchen; '~**-scis·sors** *pl.* Wundschere *f*.
prob·i·ty ['prəubiti] Redlichkeit *f*.
prob·lem ['prɔbləm] Problem *n*; schwierige Frage *f*; ♟ Aufgabe *f*; ~ *child* Sorgenkind *n*; *do a* ~ e-e Aufgabe lösen; **prob·lem·at·ic, prob·lem·at·i·cal** □ [~bli'mætik(-əl)] problematisch, zweifelhaft.
pro·bos·cis [prəu'bɔsis] Rüssel *m*.
pro·ce·dur·al [prə'si:dʒərəl] Verfahrens...; **pro'ce·dure** Verfahren *n*; Handlungsweise *f*; Vorgehen *n*.
pro·ceed [prə'si:d] weitergehen (*a. fig.*); fortfahren (*with* mit, in *dat.*); vor sich gehen; vorgehen (*handeln*; ⚖ *against* gegen); *univ.* promovieren; ~ *from* von *od.* aus *et.* kommen; ausgehen von; ~ *on one's journey* s-e Reise fortsetzen; ~ *to* zu *et.* schreiten *od.* übergehen; **pro'ceed·ing** Vorgehen *n*, Verfahren *n*; Handlung *f*; ~*s pl.* ⚖ Verfahren *n*; Verhandlungen *f/pl.*, (Tätigkeits-) Bericht *m e-r Körperschaft etc.*; *take* ~*s against* gerichtlich vorgehen gegen; **pro·ceeds** ['prəusi:dz] *pl.* Einnahmen *f/pl.*, Ertrag *m*, Gewinn *m* (*from* aus).
proc·ess ['prəuses] **1.** Fortschreiten *n*, -gang *m*; Vorgang *m*; Verlauf

m der Zeit; ⚖, ⚗ Prozeß *m*, Verfahren *n*; Arbeitsgang *m*; *anat.*, ⚘ Fortsatz *m*; *in* ~ im Gange; *in* ~ *of construction* im Bau (befindlich); **2.** gerichtlich belangen; ⊕ behandeln, bearbeiten; ~ *into* verarbeiten zu; ~*ed cheese* Käsezubereitung *f*; **'pro·cess·ing** ⊕ Veredelung *f*, Verarbeitung *f*; **pro·ces·sion** [prə'seʃən] Prozession *f*, Umzug *m*; **pro'ces·sion·ar·y** [~ʃnəri] Prozessions...

pro·claim [prə'kleim] proklamieren, öffentlich verkünden; erklären; ausrufen; verraten (als).

proc·la·ma·tion [prɔklə'meiʃən] Proklamation *f*, Verkündung *f*; Bekanntmachung *f*; Erklärung *f*.

pro·cliv·i·ty [prə'kliviti] Neigung *f*; Anlage *f* (*to* zu).

pro·con·sul [prəu'kɔnsəl] Prokonsul *m*.

pro·cras·ti·nate [prəu'kræstineit] zaudern; **pro·cras·ti'na·tion** Zaudern *n*.

pro·cre·ate ['prəukrieit] (er)zeugen; **pro·cre'a·tion** Zeugung *f*; **'pro·cre·a·tive** zeugungsfähig; Zeugungs...

proc·tor ['prɔktə] ⚖ Anwalt *m*, Sachwalter *m*; *univ.* Proktor *m*, Disziplinarbeamte *m*.

pro·cum·bent [prəu'kʌmbənt] (nieder)liegend.

pro·cur·a·ble [prə'kjuərəbl] beschaffbar, erhältlich.

proc·u·ra·tion [prɔkjuə'reiʃən] Stellvertretung *f*; Vollmacht *f*; ✝ Prokura *f*; *by* ~ per Prokura; **'proc·u·ra·tor** Bevollmächtigte *m*.

pro·cure [prə'kjuə] *v/t.* beschaffen; verschaffen, besorgen (*s.o. s.th.*, *s.th. for s.o.* j-m et.); *v/i.* kuppeln; **pro'cure·ment** Beschaffung *f*; Vermittlung *f*; **pro'cur·er** Beschaffer(in); Kuppler(in); **pro'cur·ess** Kupplerin *f*.

prod [prɔd] **1.** Stich *m*; Stoß *m*; *fig.* Ansporn *m*; **2.** stechen; stoßen; *fig.* anstacheln.

prod·i·gal □ ['prɔdigəl] **1.** verschwenderisch (*of* mit); *the* ~ *son* der verlorene Sohn; **2.** Verschwender(in); **prod·i·gal·i·ty** [~'gæliti] Verschwendung *f*.

pro·di·gious □ [prə'didʒəs] erstaunlich, ungeheuer; wunderbar; **prod·i·gy** ['prɔdidʒi] Wunder *n* (*a. fig.*); Ungeheuer *n*; *oft infant* ~ Wunderkind *n*.

prod·uce[1] ['prɔdju:s] (Natur)Erzeugnis(se *pl.*) *n*, Produkt *n*, Ertrag *m*.

pro·duce[2] [prə'dju:s] vorbringen, -führen, -legen, -zeigen; *Zeugen etc.* beibringen; hervorbringen, -holen, -ziehen; *Waren, Früchte etc.* produzieren, erzeugen; herstellen; *Zinsen etc.* (ein)bringen; ⅍ verlängern; *Film etc.* herausbringen; **pro'duc·er** Erzeuger *m*, Hersteller *m*; *Film*: Produzent *m*, Produktionsleiter *m*; *thea.* Regisseur *m*; *Radio*: Spiel-, Sendeleiter *m*; (Gas)Generator *m*; **pro'duc·i·ble** erzeugbar; vorführbar; **pro'duc·ing** Produktions...; Herstellungs...

prod·uct ['prɔdʌkt] Produkt *n* (*a.* ⅍), Erzeugnis *n*; **pro·duc·tion** [prə'dʌkʃən] Hervorbringung *f*; Vorlegung *f*, Beibringung *f*; Produktion *f*, Erzeugung *f*; *thea.* Inszenierung *f*; Erzeugnis *n*, Produkt *n*; ~ **line** Fließband *n*; **pro'duc·tive** □ hervorbringend (*of acc.*); schöpferisch; produktiv, erzeugend; schaffend; ertragreich, ergiebig; fruchtbar; **pro'duc·tive·ness, pro·duc·tiv·i·ty** [prɔdʌk'tiviti] Produktivität *f*.

prof *Am.* F [prɔf] Professor *m*.

prof·a·na·tion [prɔfə'neiʃən] Entweihung *f*; **pro·fane** [prə'fein] **1.** □ profan; weltlich; uneingeweiht; gottlos, lästerlich; **2.** entweihen, profanieren; **pro·fan·i·ty** [~'fæniti] Gott-, Ruchlosigkeit *f*; Fluchen *n*.

pro·fess [prə'fes] bekennen, erklären; sich bekennen zu; *Reue etc.* bekunden; *Beruf* ausüben, betreiben; lehren; **pro'fessed** □ erklärt, ausgesprochen; an-, vorgeblich; Berufs...; **pro'fess·ed·ly** [~sidli] erklärtermaßen.

pro·fes·sion [prə'feʃən] Bekenntnis *n*; Erklärung *f*; Beruf *m*, Stand *m*; **pro'fes·sion·al** [~ʃənl] **1.** □ Berufs..., beruflich; Amts...; berufsmäßig; freiberuflich; ~ *men pl.* Akademiker *m/pl.* **2.** Fachmann *m*; Berufskünstler *m*, -spieler *m etc.*, *bsd. Sport*: Profi *m*, Professional *m*; **pro'fes·sion·al·ism** [~ʃnəlizm] *Sport*: Berufsspielertum *n*.

pro·fes·sor [prə'fesə] Professor *m*; **pro'fes·sor·ship** Professur *f*.

prof·fer ['prɔfə] **1.** anbieten; **2.** Anerbieten *n.*
pro·fi·cien·cy [prə'fiʃənsi] Tüchtigkeit *f*; **pro'fi·cient 1.** □ tüchtig; geübt, bewandert (*in, at* in *dat.*); **2.** Meister *m* (*in* in *dat.*).
pro·file ['prəufail] Profil *n*, Seitenansicht *f*; ⚠ Profil *n*, Durchschnitt *m*; *fig.* Querschnitt *m*; Kurzbiographie *f*.
prof·it ['prɔfit] **1.** Vorteil *m*, Nutzen *m*, Gewinn *m*, Profit *m*, Ertrag *m*; **2.** *v/t. j-m* Nutzen bringen; *v/i.* ~ *by* Nutzen ziehen aus; profitieren von; *Gelegenheit* aus-, benutzen; **prof·it·a'bil·i·ty** Rentabilität *f*; **'prof·it·a·ble** □ nützlich, vorteilhaft, einträglich, gewinnbringend; **'prof·it·a·ble·ness** Nützlichkeit *f*; Einträglichkeit *f*; **prof·it·eer** [~'tiə] **1.** Schiebergeschäfte machen; **2.** Profitmacher *m*, Schieber *m*; *war* ~ Kriegsgewinnler *m*; **prof·it'eer·ing** Schiebergeschäfte *n/pl.*; **'prof·it·less** □ nutzlos; nichts einbringend; **prof·it mar·gin** Gewinnspanne *f*; **prof·it-shar·ing** ['~ʃɛəriŋ] Gewinnbeteiligung *f*.
prof·li·ga·cy ['prɔfligəsi] Liederlichkeit *f*; Verschwendung *f*; **prof·li·gate** ['~git] **1.** □ verworfen; liederlich; verschwenderisch; **2.** liederlicher Mensch *m*.
pro·found □ [prə'faund] tief; tiefgründig, gründlich; *fig.* dunkel; **pro'found·ness, pro·fun·di·ty** [~'fʌnditi] Tiefe *f* (*a. fig.*).
pro·fuse □ [prə'fju:s] verschwenderisch (*in, of* mit); übermäßig, -reich; reich(haltig); **pro'fuse·ness, pro·fu·sion** [~'fju:ʒən] Verschwendung *f*; *fig.* Überfluß *m*.
prog *sl. univ.* [prɔg] Proktor *m*.
pro·gen·i·tor [prəu'dʒenitə] Vorfahr *m*, Ahn *m*; **pro'gen·i·tress** [~tris] Ahne *f*; **prog·e·ny** ['prɔdʒini] Nachkommen(schaft *f*) *m/pl.*; Brut *f*; *fig.* Produkt *n*.
prog·no·sis ⚕ [prɔg'nəusis], *pl.* **prog'no·ses** [~si:z] Prognose *f*.
prog·nos·tic [prəg'nɔstik] **1.** voraussagend (*of acc.*); **2.** Vorzeichen *n*; **prog'nos·ti·cate** [~keit] voraus-, vorhersagen; **prog·nos·ti'ca·tion** Vorhersage *f*.
pro·gram, *mst* **pro·gramme** ['prəugræm] **1.** Programm *n*; *Radio*: *a.* Sendung *f*; **2.** programmieren; **'pro·gram·er,** *mst* **'pro·gram·mer** *Computer*: Programmierer *m*.
prog·ress¹ ['prəugres] Fortschreiten *n*; Vorrücken *n* (*a.* ⚔); Fortgang *m*, Lauf *m*; Weiterentwicklung *f*; Fortschritt(e *pl.*) *m*; Rundreise *f e-s Fürsten*; *in* ~ im Gang.
pro·gress² [prə'gres] fortschreiten, vorankommen, Fortschritte machen; **pro'gres·sion** [~ʃən] Fortschreiten *n*; ♄ Progression *f*; **pro'gres·sion·ist** [~ʃnist], **pro'gress·ist** [~sist] *pol.* Fortschrittler *m*; **pro'gres·sive 1.** □ fortschreitend; zunehmend; progressiv; *pol.* fortschrittlich; ~ *form gr.* Verlaufsform *f*; **2.** *pol.* Fortschrittler *m*.
pro·hib·it [prə'hibit] verbieten (*s.th. et.*; *s.o. from ger.* j-m zu *inf.*); verhindern; **pro·hi·bi·tion** [prəui'biʃən] Verbot *n*; Prohibition *f*, Alkoholverbot *n*; **pro·hi'bi·tion·ist** [~ʃnist] Schutzzöllner *m*; *bsd. Am.* Alkoholgegner *m*; **pro·hib·i·tive** □ [prə'hibitiv] verbietend; Prohibitiv...; unerschwinglich (*Preis*); ~ *duty* Sperrzoll *m*.
proj·ect ['prɔdʒekt] Projekt *n*; Vorhaben *n*, Plan *m*.
pro·ject [prə'dʒekt] *v/t.* planen, entwerfen, projektieren; werfen, schleudern; ♄ projizieren; ~ *o.s. into* sich versetzen in (*acc.*); *v/i.* vorspringen; **pro·jec·tile 1.** ['prɔdʒiktail] Projektil *n*, Geschoß *n*; **2.** [prəu'dʒektail] Wurf...; **pro·jec·tion** [prə'dʒekʃən] Werfen *n*, Wurf *m*; Entwurf *m*; Vortreiben *n*; Fortsatz *m*, Vorsprung *m*; ♄, *ast.*, *phot.* Projektion *f*; Widerspiegelung *f* (*a. fig.*); ~ *room Film*: Vorführraum *m*; **pro'jec·tion·ist** [~ʃnist] Filmvorführer *m*; **pro'jec·tor** Plänemacher *m*; ✝ Gründer *m*; *opt.* Projektionsapparat *m*, Bildwerfer *m*, Projektor *m*.
pro·le·tar·i·an [prəuli'tɛəriən] **1.** proletarisch; **2.** Proletarier(in); **pro·le'tar·i·at,** *mst* **pro·le'tar·i·ate** [~riət] Proletariat *n*.
pro·lif·e·rate [prəu'lifəreit] sich stark vermehren *od.* ausbreiten; *einfache Lebewesen*: sich fortpflanzen; wuchern; **pro·lif·er'a·tion** starke Vermehrung *f od.* Ausbreitung *f*; Fortpflanzung *f*; Wuchern *n*.
pro·lif·ic [prəu'lifik] (~*ally*) fruchtbar; *fig.* reich (*of, in* an *dat.*).

pro·lix □ ['prəuliks] weitschweifig; **pro'lix·i·ty** Weitschweifigkeit *f*.

pro·logue, *Am. a.* **pro·log** ['prəulɔg] Prolog *m*; Einleitung *f*; ~ *to fig.* Auftakt *m od.* Vorspiel *n* zu.

pro·long [prəu'lɔŋ] verlängern; ✝ prolongieren; **pro·lon·ga·tion** [~'geiʃən] Verlängerung *f*.

prom F [prɔm] = *promenade concert*.

prom·e·nade [prɔmi'nɑ:d] **1.** Promenade *f*; Spaziergang *m*; Spazierweg *m*; **2.** promenieren (auf, in *dat.*); spazierenführen; ~ **con·cert** Promenadenkonzert *n*.

prom·i·nence ['prɔminəns] Hervorragen *n* (*a. fig.*); *konkr.* Erhebung *f*, Vorsprung *m*; Berühmtheit *f*; '**prom·i·nent** □ hervorragend (*a. fig.*); *fig.* prominent.

prom·is·cu·i·ty [prɔmis'kju:iti] Verworrenheit *f*; Durcheinander *n*; Wahllosigkeit *f*; Promiskuität *f*; **pro·mis·cu·ous** □ [prə'miskjuəs] unordentlich, verworren; gemeinsam; unterschiedslos.

prom·ise ['prɔmis] **1.** Versprechen *n*; Verheißung *f*; *fig.* Aussicht *f* (*of* auf *acc.*); *of great* ~ vielversprechend; **2.** *v/t.* versprechen; *I* ~ *you* F ich versichere Ihnen; *v/i.* Hoffnungen erwecken; '**prom·is·ing** □ vielversprechend, verheißungsvoll; **prom·is·so·ry** ['~səri] versprechend; ~ *note* ✝ Eigen-, Solawechsel *m*.

prom·on·to·ry ['prɔməntri] Vorgebirge *n*.

pro·mote [prə'məut] *et.* fördern; *j.* befördern; *bsd. Am. Schule*: versetzen; *parl.* unterstützen; ✝ gründen; *bsd. Am. Verkauf durch Werbung* steigern; **pro'mot·er** Förderer *m*; ✝ Gründer *m*; Veranstalter *m von Boxkämpfen etc.*; **pro'mo·tion** Förderung *f*; Beförderung *f*; ✝ Gründung *f*; ~ *prospects pl.* Aufstiegschancen *f/pl.*

prompt [prɔmpt] **1.** □ schnell; bereit(willig); unverzüglich, prompt, umgehend, sofortig; pünktlich; **2.** *adv.* pünktlich; **3.** *j.* (an)treiben, bewegen (*to* zu); *et.* veranlassen; *Gedanken* eingeben; *j-m* vorsagen, einhelfen, *thea.* soufflieren; **4.** ✝ Ziel *n*; *thea.* Stichwort *n*; '**~-box** *thea.* Souffleurkasten *m*; '**prompt·er** Anreger(in); Eingeber(in); *thea.* Souffleur *m*, Souffleuse *f*; **promp·ti·tude** ['~titju:d], '**prompt·ness** Schnelligkeit *f*; Bereitschaft *f*.

pro·mul·gate ['prɔməlgeit] verkünden, verbreiten; **pro·mul'ga·tion** Bekanntmachung *f*, Verbreitung *f*.

prone □ [prəun] mit dem Gesicht nach unten (liegend); hingestreckt; vornüber geneigt; abschüssig; ~ *to fig.* geneigt *od.* neigend zu; anfällig für; '**prone·ness** Neigung *f* (*to* zu).

prong [prɔŋ] Zinke *f e-r Gabel*; Spitze *f*; Heu-, Mistgabel *f*; **pronged** zinkig, zackig.

pro·nom·i·nal □ *gr.* [prəu'nɔminl] pronominal.

pro·noun *gr.* ['prəunaun] Fürwort *n*, Pronomen *n*.

pro·nounce [prə'nauns] *v/t.* aussprechen; verkünden; behaupten; erklären für; *v/i.* sich erklären (*on* über *acc.*); **pro'nounced** □ [*adv.* ~idli] ausgesprochen; entschieden; **pro'nounce·ment** Erklärung *f*.

pro·nounc·ing [prə'naunsiŋ] Aussprache... [gleich.]

pron·to *Am.* F ['prɔntəu] sofort,

pro·nun·ci·a·tion [prənʌnsi'eiʃən] Aussprache *f*.

proof [pru:f] **1.** Beweis *m*; Probe *f*, Versuch *m*; *typ.* Korrekturbogen *m*; *typ., phot.* Probeabzug *m*; ⚗ Normalstärke *f alkoholischer Getränke*; *in* ~ *of* zum *od.* als Beweis (*gen.*); **2.** fest (*against, to* gegen); sicher; undurchlässig; *in Zssgn*: ...fest, ...dicht, ...sicher; *fig.* gefeit (*against* gegen); **3.** undurchlässig machen, wasserdicht machen, imprägnieren; '**~-read** Korrektur lesen; '**~-read·er** *typ.* Korrektor *m*; '**~-sheet** *typ.* Korrekturbogen *m*; '**~-spir·it** ⚗ Normalweingeist *m*.

prop [prɔp] **1.** Stütze *f* (*a. fig.*); Stützbalken *m*; *pit-~s pl.* Grubenhölzer *n/pl.*; **2.** *a.* ~ *up* (unter)stützen.

prop·a·gan·da [prɔpə'gændə] Propaganda *f*; **prop·a'gan·dist** Propagandist(in); **prop·a·gate** ['~geit] (sich) fortpflanzen; *fig.* aus-, verbreiten; **prop·a'ga·tion** Fortpflanzung *f*; Verbreitung *f*; '**prop·a·ga·tor** Fortpflanzer *m*; Verbreiter *m*.

pro·pel [prə'pel] (vorwärts-, an-) treiben; **pro'pel·lant** Treibstoff *m*; **pro'pel·lent** treibende Kraft *f*;

Treibstoff *m*; **pro'pel·ler** Propeller *m*, (Schiffs-, Luft)Schraube *f*; ~ *shaft* Kardanwelle *f*; **pro'pel·ling** Trieb...; ~ *pencil* Drehbleistift *m*.

pro·pen·si·ty [prə'pensiti] Hang *m*, Neigung (*to*, *for* zu).

prop·er □ ['prɔpə] eigen; (*oft nach dem su.*) eigentlich; eigentümlich (*to dat.*); passend, geeignet (*for* für); angemessen; genau; anständig; ordentlich; F richtig; ~ *name* Eigenname *m*; '**prop·er·ty** Eigentum *n*, Besitztum *n*; Vermögen *n*; Eigenschaft *f*; ⚖ Eigentumsrecht *n*; *properties pl. thea.* Requisiten *n/pl.*; '**prop·er·ty-man** *thea.* Requisiteur *m*; '**prop·er·ty-tax** Vermögenssteuer *f*.

proph·e·cy ['prɔfisi] Prophezeiung *f*; **proph·e·sy** ['~sai] prophezeien; weissagen; voraussagen.

proph·et ['prɔfit] Prophet *m*; Vorkämpfer *m*; '**proph·et·ess** Prophetin *f*; **pro·phet·ic**, **pro·phet·i·cal** □ [prə'fetik(əl)] prophetisch.

pro·phy·lac·tic ⚕ [prɔfi'læktik] (~*ally*) vorbeugend(es Mittel *n*).

pro·pin·qui·ty [prə'piŋkwiti] Nähe *f*; nahe Verwandtschaft *f*.

pro·pi·ti·ate [prə'piʃieit] günstig stimmen; versöhnen; **pro·pi·ti'a·tion** Versöhnung *f*; Sühne *f*; **pro'pi·ti·a·tor** [~ʃieitə] Versöhner *m*; **pro'pi·ti·a·to·ry** □ [~ʃiətəri] versöhnend; Sühn(e)...

pro·pi·tious □ [prə'piʃəs] gnädig; günstig; **pro'pi·tious·ness** Gnade *f*; Gunst *f* (*a. des Klimas*).

pro·po·nent [prə'pəunənt] Verfechter *m*, Befürworter *m*.

pro·por·tion [prə'pɔːʃən] **1.** Verhältnis *n*; Gleichmaß *n*; ⚘, ⌂ Proportion *f*; Anteil *m*; Teil *m*; ~*s pl.* (Aus)Maße *n/pl.*; **2.** in ein Verhältnis bringen (*to* zu); **pro'por·tion·al 1.** □ proportional, verhältnismäßig; *s. proportionate*; **2.** ⚘ Proportionale *f*; **pro'por·tion·ate** □ [~ʃnit] angemessen; im richtigen Verhältnis (stehend) (*to* zu); **pro'por·tioned** ...proportioniert.

pro·pos·al [prə'pəuzəl] Vorschlag *m*, (*a.* Heirats)Antrag *m*; Angebot *n*; Plan *m*; **pro'pose** *v/t.* vorschlagen; e-n Toast ausbringen auf (*acc.*); ~ *to o.s.* sich vornehmen; ~ *a motion* e-n Antrag einbringen; *v/i.* beabsichtigen; e-n Heiratsantrag machen (*to j-m*); **pro'pos·er** Antragsteller (-in); **pro·po·si·tion** [prɔpə'ziʃən] Vorschlag *m*, Antrag *m*; Behauptung *f*; *phls.*, ⚘ (Lehr)Satz *m*; Frage *f*, Problem *n*; *sl.* Geschäft *n*; Sache *f*.

pro·pound [prə'paund] *Frage etc.* vorlegen; vorschlagen.

pro·pri·e·tar·y [prə'praiətəri] **1.** e-m Besitzer gehörig; gesetzlich geschützt (*bsd. Arzneimittel*); Besitz(er)...; ~ *name* Markenbezeichnung *f*; **2.** Eigentümer *m/pl.*; **pro'pri·e·tor** Eigentümer *m*, Besitzer *m*; **pro'pri·e·tress** Eigentümerin *f*, Besitzerin *f*; **pro'pri·e·ty** Richtigkeit *f*; Schicklichkeit *f*; *the proprieties pl.* die Anstandsformen *f/pl.*

props F *thea.* [prɔps] *pl.* Requisiten *n/pl.*

pro·pul·sion ⊕ [prə'pʌlʃən] Antrieb *m*; **pro'pul·sive** [~siv] (vorwärts)treibend; Trieb...

pro·rate *Am.* [prəu'reit] anteilmäßig verteilen.

pro·ro·ga·tion *parl.* [prəurə'geiʃən] Vertagung *f*; **pro·rogue** *parl.* [prə'rəug] (sich) vertagen.

pro·sa·ic [prəu'zeiik] (~*ally*) *fig.* prosaisch, nüchtern, trocken.

pro·scribe [prəus'kraib] ächten.

pro·scrip·tion [prəus'kripʃən] Ächtung *f*; Acht *f*; Verbannung *f*.

prose [prəuz] **1.** Prosa *f*; **2.** prosaisch; Prosa...; **3.** langweilig erzählen.

pros·e·cute ['prɔsikjuːt] *e-n Plan etc.* verfolgen; *Gewerbe etc.* betreiben; ⚖ gerichtlich verfolgen, belangen; verklagen (*for* wegen); **pros·e'cu·tion** Verfolgung *f e-s Plans etc.*; Fortsetzung *f*; Betreiben *n e-s Gewerbes etc.*; ⚖ gerichtliche Verfolgung *f*; *witness for the* ~ Belastungszeuge *m*; '**pros·e·cu·tor** ⚖ Kläger *m*; Anklagevertreter *m*; *public* ~ Staatsanwalt *m*.

pros·e·lyte *eccl.* ['prɔsilait] Proselyt(in); **pros·e·lyt·ism** ['~litizəm] Proselytentum *n*; Bekehrungseifer *m*; '**pros·e·lyt·ize** (*v/t. j.* zum) Proselyten machen.

pros·er ['prəuzə] langweiliger Erzähler *m*.

pros·o·dy ['prɔsədi] Verslehre *f*.

pros·pect 1. ['prɔspekt] Aussicht *f* (*a. fig.*); Anblick *m*, Ansicht *f*; ✝ *bsd. Am.* Interessent *m*, möglicher

Kunde *m*; *have in* ~ in Aussicht haben; *hold out a* ~ *of s.th.* et. in Aussicht stellen; **2.** [prəs'pekt] ⚒ schürfen (*for* nach); bohren (*for* nach *Öl*); **pro'spec·tive** □ voraus-blickend; voraussichtlich; ~ *buyer* Kauflustige *m*; **pros'pec·tor** ⚒ Prospektor *m*, Schürfer *m*; Gold-, Ölsucher *m*; **pro'spec·tus** [~təs] (Werbe)Prospekt *m*.

pros·per ['prɔspə] *v/i.* Erfolg haben, gedeihen, florieren, blühen; *v/t.* begünstigen, segnen; **pros·per·i·ty** [~'periti] Gedeihen *n*; Wohlfahrt *f*, -stand *m*; Glück *n*; *fig.* Blüte *f*; **pros·per·ous** □ ['~pərəs] glücklich, gedeihlich; wohlhabend; *fig.* blühend; günstig (*Wind etc.*).

pros·tate ['prɔsteit], *a.* ~ **gland** Prostata *f*, Vorsteherdrüse *f*.

pros·ti·tute ['prɔstitju:t] **1.** Prostituierte *f*, Dirne *f*; **2.** zur Dirne machen; (öffentlich der Schande) preisgeben, feilbieten (*a. fig.*); **pros·ti'tu·tion** Prostitution *f*, gewerbsmäßige Unzucht *f*; Dirnenwesen *n*; *fig.* Entehrung *f*, Schändung *f*.

pros·trate 1. ['prɔstreit] hingestreckt; erschöpft; daniederliegend; demütig; gebrochen; **2.** [prɔs'treit] niederwerfen; *fig.* niederschmettern; entkräften; **pros'tra·tion** Niederwerfung *f*; Fußfall *m*; *fig.* Demütigung *f*; Entkräftung *f*.

pros·y □ *fig.* ['prəuzi] prosaisch; langweilig.

pro·tag·o·nist [prəu'tægənist] *thea.* Träger(in) der Handlung; Hauptfigur *f*; *fig.* Vorkämpfer(in).

pro·tect [prə'tekt] schützen (*from* vor *dat.*); beschützen; † *Wechsel* einlösen; **pro'tec·tion** Schutz *m*; Wirtschaftsschutz *m*, Schutzzoll *m*; **pro'tec·tion·ist 1.** Schutzzöllner *m*; **2.** protektionistisch; **pro'tec·tive** schützend; Schutz...; ~ *custody* Schutzhaft *f*; ~ *duty* Schutzzoll *m*; **pro'tec·tor** Schützer *m* (*a. Vorrichtung*); Schutz-, Schirmherr *m*; *hist.* Protektor *m*; **pro'tec·tor·ate** [~tərit] Protektorat *n*; **pro'tec·to·ry** Fürsorgeanstalt *f*; **pro'tec·tress** Beschützerin *f*, Schutz-, Schirmherrin *f*.

pro·té·gé ['prəuteʒei] Protégé *m*, Schützling *m*.

pro·te·in ⚗ ['prəuti:n] Protein *n* (*Eiweißstoff*).

pro·test 1. ['prəutest] Protest *m*; Ein-, Widerspruch *m*; *in* ~ *against* aus Protest gegen; *enter od. make a* ~ Einspruch erheben; **2.** [prə'test] *v/t.* beteuern; *Wechsel* protestieren; reklamieren; *v/i.* protestieren, sich verwahren, Einspruch erheben (*against* gegen).

Prot·es·tant ['prɔtistənt] **1.** protestantisch; **2.** Protestant(in); **'Prot·es·tant·ism** Protestantismus *m*.

prot·es·ta·tion [prəutes'teiʃən] Beteuerung *f*; Verwahrung *f*.

pro·to·col ['prəutəkɔl] **1.** Protokoll *n*; **2.** protokollieren.

pro·ton *phys.* ['prəutɔn] Proton *n* (*positiv geladenes Elementarteilchen*).

pro·to·plasm *biol.* ['prəutəuplæzəm] Protoplasma *n*.

pro·to·type ['prəutəutaip] Urbild *n*; Prototyp *m*, Modell *n*.

pro·tract [prə'trækt] in die Länge *od.* hinziehen; **pro'trac·tion** Hinziehen *n*; Hinausschieben *n*; **pro'trac·tor** ⩓ Winkelmesser *m*.

pro·trude [prə'tru:d] (sich) (her-)vorstrecken; (her)vorstehen, -treten; **pro'tru·sion** [~ʒən] Vorstrecken *n*; (Her)Vorstehen *n*, -treten *n*.

pro·tu·ber·ance [prə'tju:bərəns] Hervortreten *n*; Auswuchs *m*, Höcker *m*; **pro'tu·ber·ant** hervorstehend.

proud □ [praud] stolz (*of* auf *acc.*; *to inf.* zu *inf.*); ~ *flesh* ⚕ wildes Fleisch *n*; *do s.o.* ~ F j-m große Ehre erweisen.

prov·a·ble □ ['pru:vəbl] be-, nachweisbar; **prove** *v/t.* beweisen; er-, nachweisen; prüfen; erproben; erleben, erfahren; *v/i.* sich herausstellen (als), sich erweisen (als); ausfallen; ~ *true* (*false*) sich (nicht) bestätigen, sich als richtig (falsch) herausstellen; *he has* ~*d to be the heir* es hat sich herausgestellt, daß er der Erbe ist; **prov·en** ['~vən] erwiesen; bewährt.

prov·e·nance ['prɔvinəns] Herkunft *f e-r Sache*.

prov·en·der ['prɔvində] *Vieh*-Futter *n* (F *co. a. von Menschen*).

pro·verb ['prɔvə:b] Sprichwort *n*; *be a* ~ sprichwörtlich *od. b.s.* berüchtigt sein (*for* wegen); **pro·ver·bi·al** □ [prə'və:bjəl] sprichwörtlich.

pro·vide [prəˈvaid] *v/t.* besorgen, beschaffen, liefern; bereitstellen; *j.* versehen, versorgen, ausstatten (*with* mit); ⚖ vorsehen, festsetzen; *~d school* Gemeindeschule *f*; *v/i.* sorgen (*for* für); vorsorgen (*against* gegen; *for* für); *~ for Maßnahmen etc.* vorsehen; *Gelder etc.* bereitstellen; *~d* (*that*) vorausgesetzt, daß; sofern.

prov·i·dence [ˈprɔvidəns] Vorsehung *f*; Voraussicht *f*; Vorsorge *f*; ˈ**prov·i·dent** □ vorausblickend; vorsorglich; haushälterisch; **prov·i·den·tial** □ [~ˈdenʃəl] durch die *göttliche* Vorsehung bewirkt; glücklich.

pro·vid·er [prəˈvaidə] Ernährer *m der Familie*; Lieferant *m*.

prov·ince [ˈprɔvins] Provinz *f*; *fig.* Gebiet *n*, Fach *n*; Amt *n*, Aufgabe *f*.

pro·vin·cial [prəˈvinʃəl] **1.** provinziell; Provinz...; ländlich, kleinstädtisch; **2.** Provinzbewohner(in); *contp.* Provinzler(in); **proˈvin·cial·ism** Provinzialismus *m*; Provinzlertum *n*.

pro·vi·sion [prəˈviʒən] **1.** Beschaffung *f*, Bereitstellung *f*; Vorsorge *f*; ⚖ Bestimmung *f*; Vorkehrung *f*, Maßnahme *f*; Vorrat *m*, Lager *n*; *~s pl.* Proviant *m*, Lebensmittel *n/pl.*; *make ~ for* Vorkehrungen treffen für, sorgen für; *~ merchant* Lebensmittelhändler *m*; **2.** verproviantieren; **proˈvi·sion·al** [~ʒənl] □ vorläufig, provisorisch.

pro·vi·so [prəˈvaizəu] Vorbehalt *m*; Klausel *f*; **proˈvi·so·ry** [~zəri] provisorisch.

Pro·vo [ˈprɔvəu] Mitglied *n* der provisorischen irisch-republikanischen Armee.

prov·o·ca·tion [prɔvəˈkeiʃən] Herausforderung *f*; **pro·voc·a·tive** [prəˈvɔkətiv] **1.** herausfordernd; (auf)reizend (*of* zu); **2.** Reiz(mittel *n*) *m*.

pro·voke [prəˈvəuk] auf-, anreizen; herausfordern, provozieren; hervorrufen; **proˈvok·ing** □ herausfordernd; empörend.

prov·ost [ˈprɔvəst] Leiter *m e-s College*; *schott.* Bürgermeister *m*; ⚔ [prəˈvəu] *~ marshal* Kommandeur *m* der Militärpolizei.

prow ⚓ [prau] Bug *m*, Schiffsschnabel *m*.

prow·ess [ˈprauis] Tapferkeit *f*.

prowl [praul] **1.** *v/i.* umherstreifen; *v/t.* durchstreifen; **2.** Umherstreifen *n*; *~* **car** *Am.* Streifenwagen *m der Polizei*.

prox·i·mate □ [ˈprɔksimit] nächst, unmittelbar; **proxˈim·i·ty** Nähe *f*; **prox·i·mo** [ˈ~məu] ✝ (des) nächsten Monats.

prox·y [ˈprɔksi] Stellvertreter *m*; Stellvertretung *f*; Vollmacht *f*; *by ~* in Vertretung.

prude [pru:d] Prüde *f*, Spröde *f*, Zimperliese *f*.

pru·dence [ˈpru:dəns] Klugheit *f*, Vorsicht *f*; ˈ**pru·dent** □ klug, vorsichtig; **pru·den·tial** □ [~ˈdenʃəl] klug; Klugheits...; vorsichtig.

prud·er·y [ˈpru:dəri] Prüderie *f*, Sprödigkeit *f*, Zimperlichkeit *f*; ˈ**prud·ish** □ prüde, zimperlich.

prune[1] [pru:n] Backpflaume *f*.

prune[2] [~] *Baum* beschneiden (*a. fig.*); *a. ~ away, ~ off* wegschneiden.

prun·ing...: ˈ**~-hook**, ˈ**~-knife** Gartenmesser *n*; ˈ**~-saw** Baumsäge *f*.

pru·ri·ence, pru·ri·en·cy [ˈpruəriəns(i)] Lüsternheit *f*, Laszivität *f*; ˈ**pru·ri·ent** □ geil (*a.* ⚘), lüstern, lasziv.

Prus·sian [ˈprʌʃən] **1.** preußisch; *~ blue* Preußisch-, Berlinerblau *n*; **2.** Preuße *m*, Preußin *f*.

prus·sic ac·id ⚗ [ˈprʌsikˈæsid] Blausäure *f*.

pry[1] [prai] **1.** *~ open* aufbrechen; *~ up* hochheben; **2.** Hebelbewegung *f*.

pry[2] [~] neugierig gucken; *~ into* s-e Nase stecken in (*acc.*); ˈ**pry·ing** □ neugierig.

psalm [sa:m] Psalm *m*; ˈ**psalm·ist** Psalmist *m*; **psal·mo·dy** [ˈsælmədi] Psalmengesang *m*.

Psal·ter [ˈsɔ:ltə] Psalter *m*.

pse·phol·o·gy [pseˈfɔlədʒi] Analyse *f* von Wahlergebnissen *od.* -trends.

pseu·do... [ˈpsju:dəu] Pseudo..., falsch; **pseu·do·nym** [ˈ~dənim] Pseudonym *n*, Deckname *m*; **pseu·don·y·mous** □ [~ˈdɔniməs] pseudonym.

pshaw [pʃɔ:] pah!

pso·ri·a·sis ⚕ [psɔˈraiəsis] Schuppenflechte *f*.

psy·che [ˈsaiki:] Psyche *f*, Seele *f*; Mentalität *f*.

psy·chi·a·trist [saiˈkaiətrist] Psychiater *m*; **psyˈchi·a·try** Psychiatrie *f*.

psy·chic, psy·chi·cal □ [ˈsaikik(əl)]

psychisch, seelisch; '**psy·chics** *sg.* Seelenforschung *f*, -kunde *f*.

psy·cho-a·nal·y·sis [saikəuə'næləsis] Psychoanalyse *f*; **psy·cho-an·a·lyst** [~'ænəlist] Psychoanalytiker (-in).

psy·cho·log·i·cal □ [saikə'lɔdʒikəl] psychologisch; **psy·chol·o·gist** [sai'kɔlədʒist] Psychologe *m*, Psychologin *f*; **psy'chol·o·gy** Psychologie *f* (*Seelenkunde*).

psy·cho·path ['saikəupæθ] Psychopath(in).

psy·cho·sis [sai'kəusis] Psychose *f*, Seelenstörung *f*.

psy·cho·ther·a·py ['saikəu'θerəpi] Psychotherapie *f*.

pto·maine ⚗ ['təumein] Ptomain *n* (*Leichengift*).

pub F [pʌb] Kneipe *f*, Wirtschaft *f*.

pu·ber·ty ['pju:bəti] Geschlechtsreife *f*, Pubertät *f*.

pu·bes·cence [pju:'besns] Geschlechtsreife *f*; **pu'bes·cent** geschlechtsreif werdend; ♀ flaumhaarig.

pub·lic ['pʌblik] **1.** □ öffentlich; staatlich, Staats...; allbekannt; ~ *address system* öffentliche Lautsprecheranlage *f*; ~ *holiday* gesetzlicher Feiertag *m*; ~ *man* Mann *m* der Öffentlichkeit; ~ *spirit* Gemeinsinn *m*; *s. utility*; *works*; **2.** *sg. u. pl.* Publikum *n*; Öffentlichkeit *f*, Welt *f*, Leute *pl.*; Leserschaft *f*; F Kneipe *f*; *in* ~ öffentlich; **pub·li·can** ['~kən] Gastwirt *m*; *hist.* Zöllner *m*; **pub·li·ca·tion** [~'keiʃən] Bekanntmachung *f*; Veröffentlichung *f e-s Werkes*; Verlagswerk *n*; *monthly* ~ Monatsschrift *f*; **pub·lic house** Wirtshaus *n*; **pub·li·cist** ['~sist] Publizist *m*, Tagesschriftsteller *m*; **pub·lic·i·ty** [~'lisiti] Öffentlichkeit *f*; Reklame *f*, Propaganda *f*, Werbung *f*; Publicity *f*; ~ *agent* Werbe-, Reklameagent *m*; **pub·li·cize** ['~saiz] bekanntmachen; werben für.

pub·lic...: ~ **li·bra·ry** Volksbücherei *f*; '~-'**pri·vate** gemischtwirtschaftlich; ~ **re·la·tions** *pl.* Verhältnis *n* zur Öffentlichkeit; Öffentlichkeitsarbeit *f*, Public Relations *pl.*; ~ **school** Public School *f*, Internatsschule *f*; '~-'**spir·it·ed** □ sozial gesinnt.

pub·lish ['pʌbliʃ] bekanntmachen, veröffentlichen; *Buch etc.* herausgeben, verlegen; '**pub·lish·er** Herausgeber *m*, Verleger *m*; *Am.* Besitzer *m* eines Zeitungsverlags; ~*s pl.* Verlag(sanstalt *f*) *m*; '**pub·lish·ing** Herausgabe *f*; Verlag *m*; *attr.* Verlags...; ~ *house* Verlag *m*.

puce [pju:s] braunrot.

puck [pʌk] Puck *m*, Kobold *m*; *Eishockey*: Puck *m*, Scheibe *f*.

puck·a ['pʌkə] echt; solide.

puck·er ['pʌkə] **1.** Bausch *m*; Falte *f*; **2.** *a.* ~ *up* falten; Falten werfen; runzeln.

puck·ish □ ['pʌkiʃ] koboldhaft.

pud·ding ['pudiŋ] Pudding *m*; Süßspeise *f*; Auflauf *m*; Wurst *f*; *black* ~ Blutwurst *f*; '~-**face** Mondgesicht *n*.

pud·dle ['pʌdl] **1.** Pfütze *f*; ⊕ Lehmschlag *m*; **2.** *v/t.* ⊕ mit Lehmschlag dichtmachen; *Stahl* puddeln; zementieren; *v/i.* man(t)schen; '**pud·dler** ⊕ Puddler *m*; '**pud·dling-fur·nace** ⊕ Puddelofen *m*.

pu·den·cy ['pju:dənsi] Verschämtheit *f*; **pu·den·da** [pju:'dendə] *pl.* Schamgegend *f* (*äußere Geschlechtsteile, bsd. e-r Frau*); '**pu·dent** verschämt.

pudg·y F ['pʌdʒi] dicklich.

pueb·lo [pu'ebləu] Pueblo *m*, Dorf *n*.

pu·er·ile □ ['pjuərail] knabenhaft, kindisch; **pu·er·il·i·ty** [~'riliti] Knabenhaftigkeit *f*; Kinderei *f*.

puff [pʌf] **1.** Hauch *m*; Windstoß *m*; Zug *m beim Rauchen*; (Dampf-, Rauch)Wölkchen *n*; *Bäckerei*: Windbeutel *m*; Puffe *f* (*als Besatz etc.*); Puderquaste *f*; (aufdringliche) Reklame *f*; **2.** *v/t.* (von sich) blasen, pusten; *a.* ~ *at Pfeife etc.* paffen; *oft* ~ *out*, ~ *up* aufblasen, -blähen (*a. fig.*); außer Atem bringen; anpreisen; ~ *up Preise* hochtreiben; ~*ed up fig.* aufgeblasen, eingebildet; ~*ed eyes pl.* geschwollene Augen *n/pl.*; ~*ed sleeve* Puffärmel *m*; *v/i.* puffen; pusten, keuchen; '~-**box** Puderdose *f*; '**puff·er** Marktschreier *m*; Preistreiber *m*; '**puff·er·y** Marktschreierei *f*; '**puff·i·ness** Dickheit *f*; '**puff·ing** Marktschreierei *f*; Preistreiberei *f*; **puff paste** Blätterteig *m*; '**puff·y** böig (*Wind*); kurzatmig; geschwollen; dick; bauschig (*Ärmel*).

pug [pʌg], **ˈ~-dog** Mops *m.*
pu·gil·ism [ˈpjuːdʒilizəm] Faustkampf *m*; **ˈpu·gil·ist** Boxer *m.*
pug·na·cious [pʌgˈneiʃəs] kämpferisch; kampflustig; streitsüchtig; **pug·nac·i·ty** [~ˈnæsiti] Kampflust *f*; Streitsucht *f.*
pug-nose [ˈpʌgnəuz] Stupsnase *f.*
puis·ne ⚖ [ˈpjuːni] jünger *an Rang*; Unter...
pu·is·sant [ˈpjuːisnt] mächtig, einflußreich.
puke [pjuːk] (sich) erbrechen.
pule [pjuːl] piepsen; wimmern.
pull [pul] **1.** Zug *m*; Ruck *m*; Anziehung(skraft) *f*; *typ.* Abzug *m*; Ruderfahrt *f*, -partie *f*; Griff *m*, Schwengel *m*; Vorteil *m* (*of* über *acc.*); *sl.* heimlicher Einfluß *m* (*with* auf *acc.*), Beziehungen *f/pl.* (*with* zu); ~ *at the bottle sl.* Zug *m* aus der Flasche; ~ *fastener* Reißverschluß *m*; **2.** *v/t.* ziehen; zerren; rupfen, reißen; zupfen; ziehen *etc.* an (*dat.*); *Obst* pflücken; *Rennsport*: *Pferd* zügeln, pullen; *typ. Fahne* abziehen; ⚓ rudern; ~ *one's weight* sein volles Teil leisten; sich ins Zeug legen; ~ *about* hin- u. herzerren; ~ *down* ab-, niederreißen; ~ *in Ausgaben* kürzen; *sl.* festnehmen; ~ *off* schaffen, zustande bringen; ~ *round* wiederherstellen; ~ *through j.* durchbringen; ~ *o.s. together* sich zs.-nehmen; ~ *up Wagen* anhalten; *v/i.* ziehen (*at* an *dat.*); zerren, reißen; ⚓ rudern, pullen; fahren, sich bewegen; ~ *in* einfahren (*Zug*); ~ *out* her-, hinausfahren; ausscheren; ~ *round* sich erholen; ~ *through* sich erholen; durchkommen; ~ *together* zs.-arbeiten; ~ *up* (an)halten; vorfahren; bremsen; ~ *up with*, ~ *up to* einholen; **ˈpull·er** Zieher *m*, Reißer *m*; Schlager *m*, Zugartikel *m.*
pul·let [ˈpulit] Hühnchen *n.*
pul·ley ⊕ [ˈpuli] Rolle *f*, Flasche *f*; Riemenscheibe *f*; *a. set of* ~*s* Flaschenzug *m.*
pull-in [ˈpulin] = *pull-up.*
Pull·man car 🚃 [ˈpulmənˈkɑː] Pullmanwagen *m* (*Salon- u. Schlafwagen*).
pull...: **ˈ~-out** Zeitschriftenbeilage *f*; ⚔ (Truppen)Abzug *m*; **ˈ~-o·ver** Pullover *m*; **ˈ~-up** Halteplatz *m*, Raststätte *f.*
pul·mo·nar·y *anat.* [ˈpʌlmənəri] Lungen...
pulp [pʌlp] **1.** Brei *m*; *Frucht-*, *Zahn-*Mark *n*; ⊕ Papierbrei *m*, Pulpe *f*; *a.* ~ *magazine Am.* Schundillustrierte *f*; **2.** breiig machen *od.* werden; *Papier* einstampfen.
pul·pit [ˈpulpit] Kanzel *f.*
pulp·y □ [ˈpʌlpi] breiig; fleischig.
pul·sate [pʌlˈseit] pulsieren; pochen, schlagen; **pul·sa·tile** ♪ [ˈ~sətail] Schlag...; **pul·sa·tion** [~ˈseiʃən] Pulsieren *n etc.*; Pulsschlag *m.*
pulse¹ [pʌls] **1.** Puls(schlag) *m*; **2.** pulsieren; pochen, schlagen.
pulse² [~] Hülsenfrüchte *f/pl.*
pul·ver·i·za·tion [pʌlvəraiˈzeiʃən] Pulverisierung *f etc.*; **ˈpul·ver·ize** *v/t.* pulverisieren, zu Staub machen; *fig.* zermalmen; *v/i.* zu Staub werden; **ˈpul·ver·iz·er** Zerstäuber *m.*
pu·ma *zo.* [ˈpjuːmə] Puma *m.*
pum·ice [ˈpʌmis], *a.* ~*-stone* Bimsstein *m.*
pum·mel [ˈpʌml] mit den Fäusten bearbeiten.
pump¹ [pʌmp] **1.** Pumpe *f*; *attr.* Pumpen...; **2.** pumpen; F *j.* ausholen, -horchen; *sl. j.* auspumpen (*erschöpfen*).
pump² [~] Pumps *m* (*Damenschuh*).
pump·kin ⚘ [ˈpʌmpkin] Kürbis *m.*
pump-room [ˈpʌmprum] Trinkhalle *f in Badeorten.*
pun [pʌn] **1.** Wortspiel *n*; **2.** ein Wortspiel machen.
Punch¹ [pʌntʃ] Hanswurst *m*, Kasperle *n*, *m*; ~ *and Judy show* [ˈdʒuːdi] Kasperletheater *n*; *be as pleased as* ~ F sich freuen wie ein Schneekönig.
punch² [~] ⊕ Punze(n *m*) *f*, Locheisen *n*, Locher *m*; Dorn *m*; Lochzange *f*; **2.** punzen, durchbohren, -schlagen; lochen; ~(*ed*) *card* Lochkarte *f.*
punch³ [~] **1.** (Faust)Schlag *m*; F Schlagkraft *f*; *fig.* Energie *f*, Schwung *m*; **2.** knuffen, puffen; *Am. Vieh* treiben, hüten.
punch⁴ [~] Punsch *m.*
punch-drunk [ˈpʌntʃdrʌŋk] *Boxen*: von vielen Schlägen benommen; *fig.* F ganz benommen.
pun·cheon [ˈpʌntʃən] Stützpfosten *m*; Puncheon *n* (*Faß von ca. 320 l*).
punch·er [ˈpʌntʃə] Locheisen *n*, Locher *m*; F Schläger *m*; *Am.*

Cowboy *m*; **'punch·ing-ball** Punchingball *m der Boxer*; **punch line** Pointe *f e-s Witzes*; **'punch-up** F Schlägerei *f*.
punc·til·i·o [pʌŋk'tiliəu] heikler *od.* kitzliger Punkt *m*; = *punctiliousness*; **punc·til·i·ous** [~'tiliəs] peinlich (genau), spitzfindig; förmlich; **punc'til·i·ous·ness** peinliche Genauigkeit *f*; Förmlichkeit *f*.
punc·tu·al □ ['pʌŋktjuəl] pünktlich; **punc·tu·al·i·ty** [~'æliti] Pünktlichkeit *f*.
punc·tu·ate ['pʌŋktjueit] (inter-) punktieren; *fig.* unterbrechen; **punc·tu'a·tion** Interpunktion *f*.
punc·ture ['pʌŋktʃə] **1.** Punktur *f*, Stich *m*; *mot. etc.* Reifenpanne *f*; **2.** (durch)stechen; platzen (*Reifen*).
pun·dit ['pʌndit] Pandit *m*, gelehrter Brahmane *m*; F gelehrtes Haus *n*; Koryphäe *m, f*.
pun·gen·cy ['pʌndʒənsi] Schärfe *f* (*a. fig.*); **'pun·gent** stechend, beißend, scharf.
pun·ish ['pʌniʃ] (be)strafen; *j-m* hart zusetzen; *e-r Speise* tüchtig zusprechen; **'pun·ish·a·ble** □ strafbar; **'pun·ish·er** Bestrafer(in); **'pun·ish·ment** Strafe *f*, Bestrafung *f*; Schaden *m*. [Straf...]
pu·ni·tive ['pju:nitiv] strafend;
punk¹ *Am.* [pʌŋk] **1.** Zunderholz *n*; Zündmasse *f*; F Mist *m*, Käse *m*; **2.** *sl.* miserabel, nichts wert.
punk² [pʌŋk] Anhänger *m* des *punk rock* (*der auch durch schockierende Kleidung auffällt*); ~ **rock** *s. Art pop music mit gesucht schockierender Wirkung*.
pun·ster ['pʌnstə] Wortspielmacher *m*. [kahn *m*; **2.** staken.]
punt¹ ⚓ [pʌnt] **1.** Punt *n*, Stak-
punt² [~] *Spiel*: setzen.
pu·ny □ ['pju:ni] winzig; schwächlich.
pup [pʌp] **1.** = *puppy*; **2.** (Junge) werfen.
pu·pa *zo.* ['pju:pə] Puppe *f*.
pu·pil ['pju:pl] *anat.* Pupille *f*; Schüler(in), Zögling *m*; Mündel *n*; **pu·pil·(l)age** ['~pilidʒ] Schüler-, Lehrjahre *n/pl.*; Unmündigkeit *f*.
pup·pet ['pʌpit] Marionette *f* (*a. fig.*); **'~-show** Marionettentheater *n*, Puppenspiel *n*.
pup·py ['pʌpi] Welpe *m*, junger Hund *m*; *fig.* Laffe *m*, Schnösel *m*.
pur·blind ['pə:blaind] halbblind; *fig.* kurzsichtig.
pur·chase ['pə:tʃəs] **1.** (An-, Ein-) Kauf *m*; Erwerb(ung *f*) *m*; Anschaffung *f*; ⊕ Hebevorrichtung *f*; Halt *m*; *fig.* Ansatzpunkt *m*; *make ~s* Einkäufe machen; *at twenty years' ~* zum Zwanzigfachen des Jahresertrags; *his life is not worth an hour's ~* er hat keine Stunde mehr zu leben; **2.** kaufen; erwerben; *fig.* erkaufen; anschaffen; ⊕ aufwinden; **'pur·chas·er** Käufer(in); Abnehmer(in).
pure □ [pjuə] *allg.* rein; *engS.* lauter; echt; gediegen; theoretisch (*Physik etc.*); **'~-bred** *Am.* reinrassig; **pu·rée** ['pjuərei] pürierte Gemüsesuppe *f*; Püree *n*; **'pure·ness** Reinheit *f*.
pur·ga·tion [pə:'geiʃən] *mst fig.* Reinigung *f*; ⚕ Abführen *n*; **pur·ga·tive** ⚕ ['~gətiv] **1.** abführend; **2.** Abführmittel *n*; **'pur·ga·to·ry** *eccl.* Fegefeuer *n*.
purge [pə:dʒ] **1.** ⚕ Abführmittel *n*; *pol.* Säuberung(saktion) *f*; **2.** *mst fig.* reinigen (*of, from* von); *pol.* säubern; läutern; ⚕ abführen.
pu·ri·fi·ca·tion [pjuərifi'keiʃən] Reinigung *f*; **pu·ri·fi·er** ['~faiə] Reiniger *m* (*bsd. Gerät*); **pu·ri·fy** ['~fai] reinigen (*of, from* von); ⊕ *u. fig.* läutern.
Pu·ri·tan ['pjuəritən] **1.** Puritaner (-in); **2.** puritanisch; **pu·ri·tan·ic** [~'tænik] (*~ally*) puritanisch; **Pu·ri·tan·ism** ['~tənizəm] Puritanismus *m*.
pu·ri·ty ['pjuəriti] Reinheit *f* (*a. fig.*).
purl¹ [pə:l] Golddraht *m*; Zäckchen (-borte *f*) *n*; Häkelkante *f*.
purl² [~] **1.** Murmeln *n des Baches*; **2.** murmeln.
purl·er F ['pə:lə] schwerer Sturz *m*; *come a ~* der Länge nach hinfallen.
pur·lieus ['pə:lju:z] *pl.* Umgebung *f*.
pur·loin [pə:'lɔin] entwenden; **pur'loin·er** Dieb *m*.
pur·ple ['pə:pl] **1.** purpurn, purpurrot; ~ *passage* Glanzstelle *f*; **2.** Purpur *m*; **3.** (sich) purpurn färben; **'pur·plish** purpurartig.
pur·port ['pə:pət] **1.** Sinn *m*; Inhalt *m*; **2.** besagen; beabsichtigen; vorgeben.
pur·pose ['pə:pəs] **1.** Vorsatz *m*; Absicht *f*, Zweck *m*; Wirkung *f*;

Entschlußkraft *f*; *for the* ~ *of* um zu; *on* ~ absichtlich; *to the* ~ zur Sache (gehörig), zweckdienlich; *to no* ~ vergebens, umsonst, sinn-, zwecklos; **2.** vorhaben, beabsichtigen, bezwecken; **~-ˈbuilt** zweckmäßig *od.* für einen bestimmten Zweck gebaut; **pur·pose·ful** □ [ˈ~ful] zweckmäßig; absichtlich; zielbewußt; **ˈpur·pose·less** □ zwecklos; ziellos; **ˈpur·pose·ly** *adv.* vorsätzlich.

purr [pəː] **1.** schnurren (*Katze*); brummen (*Motor*); **2.** Schnurren *n*, Brummen *n*.

purse [pəːs] **1.** Geldbeutel *m*, Börse *f*, Portemonnaie *n*; Geld *n*; Fonds *m*; Geldpreis *m*; *public* ~ Staatssäckel *m*; **2.** *oft* ~ *up Mund* spitzen; *Stirn* runzeln; *Augen* zs.-kneifen; **ˈ~-proud** protzig; **ˈpurs·er** ⚓ Proviant-, Zahlmeister *m*; **ˈpurse--strings:** *hold the* ~ das Geld verwalten.

pur·si·ness [ˈpəːsinis] Kurzatmigkeit *f*.

purs·lane ⚘ [ˈpəːslin] Portulak *m*.

pur·su·ance [pəˈsjuːəns] Verfolgung *f*; *in* ~ *of* zufolge (*dat.*), im Verfolg (*gen.*); **purˈsu·ant** □: ~ *to* zufolge, gemäß, entsprechend.

pur·sue [pəˈsjuː] *v/t.* verfolgen (*a. fig.*); streben nach; *e-m Beruf etc.* nachgehen; fortsetzen; *v/i.* fortfahren; ~ *after j.* verfolgen; **purˈsu·er** Verfolger(in); **pur·suit** [pəˈsjuːt] Verfolgung *f*; Streben *n* (*of* nach); *mst* ~*s pl.* Beschäftigung *f*, Studien *n/pl.*, Arbeiten *f/pl.*; ~ *plane* Jagdflugzeug *n*; **pur·sui·vant** [ˈpəːsivənt] Unterherold *m*; Gefolgsmann *m*.

pur·sy[1] [ˈpəːsi] kurzatmig; fett, dick.

pur·sy[2] [~] zusammengekniffen (*Mund etc.*); faltig; protzig.

pu·ru·lent □ [ˈpjuərulənt] eitrig.

pur·vey [pəːˈvei] *v/t. Lebensmittel* liefern; *v/i.* ~ *for* beliefern, versorgen; **purˈvey·ance** Lieferung *f*; **purˈvey·or** Lieferant *m*; *bsd.* Lebensmittelhändler *m*.

pur·view [ˈpəːvjuː] Wirkungskreis *m*, Bereich *m*; Gesichtskreis *m*.

pus [pʌs] Eiter *m*.

push [puʃ] **1.** (An-, Vor)Stoß *m*; Schub *m*; Druck *m*; Notfall *m*; Energie *f*; Unternehmungsgeist *m*; Elan *m*, Schwung *m*; Anstrengung *f*; *at a* ~ im Notfall; *when it comes to the* ~ wenn es darauf ankommt; *get the* ~ *sl.* 'rausfliegen; *give s.o. the* ~ *sl. j.* 'rausschmeißen; **2.** *v/t.* stoßen, treiben; schieben; drängen; *Knopf* drücken; *fig.* drängen, antreiben; *a.* ~ *through* durchführen; *Anspruch etc.* zur Geltung bringen, durchdrücken; vorwärtsbringen, fördern; ~ *s.th. on s.o.* j-m et. aufdrängen; ~ *one's way* sich durch- *od.* vordrängen; *be* ~*ed for time* (*money*) in Zeit- (Geld)not sein; *v/i.* stoßen; schieben; (sich) drängen; ~ *along*, ~ *on*, ~ *forward* weitermachen, -gehen, -fahren *etc.*; ~ *off* abstoßen (*Boot*); F sich auf den Weg machen; **ˈ~-ball** Push-, Stoßball *m*; **ˈ~-bike** Fahrrad *n*; **ˈ~-button** ⚡ Druckknopf *m*; **ˈ~-chair** (Kinder)Sportwagen *m*; **ˈpush·er** Streber(in); Flugzeug *n* mit Druckschraube; *Am.* 🚂 Hilfslokomotive *f*; **push·ful** □ [ˈ~ful], **ˈpush·ing** □ rührig, strebsam; *b.s.* zudringlich; **ˈpush-off** Anfang *m*; **ˈpush-o·ver** *bsd. Am.* Kinderspiel *n*; leicht zu beeinflussender Mensch *m*; **ˈpush--up** *bsd. Am.* Liegestütz *m*; **ˈpush·y** penetrant, aufdringlich; aggressiv.

pu·sil·la·nim·i·ty [pjuːsiləˈnimiti] Kleinmut *m*; **pu·sil·lan·i·mous** □ [~ˈlæniməs] kleinmütig.

puss [pus] Kätzchen *n*, Katze *f* (*a. fig.* = *Mädchen*); **ˈpuss·y** ⚘ (Weiden)Kätzchen *n*; *a.* ~*-cat* Mieze *f*, Kätzchen *n*; **ˈpuss·y·foot** *Am.* F **1.** Leisetreter *m*, Schleicher *m*; **2.** F leisetreten, sich zurückhalten.

pus·tule ⚕ [ˈpʌstjuːl] Pustel *f*.

put [put] (*irr.*) **1.** *v/t.* setzen, legen, stellen, stecken, tun, machen (*on* auf *acc.*, *to* an *acc.*); *fig. j. wohin* setzen; *den Fall* setzen; *Frage* stellen, vorlegen; werfen, schleudern; ausdrücken, sagen; (ab)schätzen (*at* auf *acc.*); ~ *about Gerücht etc.* verbreiten; ⚓ wenden; *j.* in Verlegenheit bringen; ~ *across sl.* drehen, schaukeln; schmackhaft machen; weismachen; ~ *away* weglegen, -stecken; auf die Seite legen; F in e-e Anstalt bringen; *sl.* verputzen; aufgeben; ~ *back* zurückstellen, -schieben; *Uhr* zurückstellen; *fig.* zurückwerfen; ~ *by*

Geld zurücklegen; beiseite schieben; ~ *down* niederlegen, -setzen, -werfen, -schlagen; absetzen, aussteigen lassen; niederschreiben; j. notieren, vormerken (*for* für); zuschreiben (*to dat.*), schieben (*to* auf *acc.*); schätzen (*at* auf *acc.*), ansehen (*as, for* als); zum Schweigen bringen; unterdrücken; demütigen; *Vorräte* einlagern; ~ *forth Kräfte* aufbieten; *Knospen etc.* treiben; aufbieten; ~ *forward e-e Meinung etc.* vorbringen; *als Kandidat etc.* vorschlagen, aufstellen; *Uhrzeiger* vorstellen; ~ *o.s. forward* sich hervortun; ~ *in* hinein-, hereinst(r)ecken; *Anspruch* erheben, geltend machen; *Gesuch* einreichen; *Urkunde* vorlegen; einsetzen, anstellen; *gutes Wort* einlegen; *Bemerkung* einwerfen; *Schlag* anbringen; F *Zeit* verbringen; ~ *in an hour's work* e-e Stunde arbeiten; ~ *off* auf-, verschieben; vertrösten, abspeisen; ablenken, abbringen; hindern; *fig.* ablegen; ~ *on Kleid* anziehen; *Hut* aufsetzen; *Charakter etc.* annehmen; hinzufügen; ✝ aufschlagen (*to* auf *e-n Preis*); an-, einschalten; vergrößern, verstärken; *Uhr* vorstellen; *Ersatzmann, Sonderzug etc.* einsetzen; *he is* ~*ting it on* er gibt an; ~ *it on thick* dick auftragen; ~ *on airs* sich aufspielen; ~ *on weight* zunehmen; ~ *out* ausmachen, (-)löschen; verrenken; (her)ausstrecken; hinauswerfen; aus der Fassung bringen, durcheinanderbringen, verwirren; *j-m* Ungelegenheiten bereiten; *Kraft* aufbieten; *Arbeit* vergeben, außer Haus geben; *Geld* ausleihen; produzieren; ~ *out of action* außer Gefecht *od.* Betrieb setzen; ~ *over e-m Film etc.* zum Erfolg verhelfen; ~ *o.s. over* Anklang finden; ~ *right* in Ordnung bringen; ~ *through teleph.* verbinden (*to* mit); F durchführen; ~ *s.o. through it* F j. durch die Mühle drehen (*gründlich prüfen*); ~ *to* hinzufügen; *be (hard)* ~ *to it* Schwierigkeiten haben; ~ *to expense j-m* Unkosten machen; ~ *to death* hinrichten; ~ *to the rack od. torture* auf die Folter spannen; ~ *together* zs.-setzen; zs.-zählen; ~ *up* aufstellen *etc.*; errichten, bauen; *Hände* er-, hochheben; *Fahne, Segel* hissen; *Haar* hochstecken; *Waren* anbieten; *Miete* erhöhen; verpacken; *Widerstand* leisten; *Kampf* liefern; (als Kandidaten) vorschlagen; *Geld* beisteuern; wegpacken; *Wild* aufjagen; *Gäste* unterbringen; *Bekanntmachung* anschlagen; *Eheaufgebot* verkünden; ~ *s.o. up to s.th.* j. über et. informieren; j. zu et. anregen *od.* anstiften; **2.** *v/i.*: ~ *off*, ~ *out*, ~ *to sea* ⚓ auslaufen; ~ *in* ⚓ einlaufen; ~ *up at* einkehren, absteigen in (*dat.*); ~ *up for* sich bewerben um; sich als Kandidat aufstellen lassen für; ~ *up with* sich gefallen lassen; sich abfinden mit, hinnehmen.

pu·ta·tive [ˈpjuːtətiv] vermeintlich; mutmaßlich.

put·log ⊕ [ˈpʌtlɔg] Gerüsthebel *m.*

put-on F [ˈputɔn] Mache *f* (*Schau, Täuschung*); *Am.* Spaß *m*; **2.** gemacht (*vorgetäuscht*).

pu·tre·fac·tion [pjuːtriˈfækʃən] Fäulnis *f*; **pu·treˈfac·tive** [~tiv] Fäulnis erregend; faulig.

pu·tre·fy [ˈpjuːtrifai] (ver)faulen.

pu·tres·cence [pjuːˈtresns] Fäulnis *f*; **puˈtres·cent** faulend.

pu·trid □ [ˈpjuːtrid] faul, verdorben; *sl.* scheußlich, saumäßig; **puˈtrid·i·ty** Fäulnis *f.*

putt [pʌt] *Golf*: **1.** putten, leicht schlagen; **2.** Putten *n*, leichter Schlag *m.*

put·tee [ˈpʌti] Wickelgamasche *f.*

putt·er [ˈpʌtə] *Golf*: Putter *m.*

put·ty [ˈpʌti] **1.** *a. glaziers'* ~ Glaserkitt *m*; *a. plasterers'* ~ Kalkkitt *m*; *a. jewellers'* ~ Zinnasche *f*; **2.** kitten.

put-up job [ˈputˈʌpˈdʒɔb] abgekartetes Spiel *n.*

puz·zle [ˈpʌzl] **1.** schwierige Aufgabe *f*, Rätsel *n*; Verlegenheit *f*, Verwirrung *f*; Puzzle-, Geduldspiel *n*; **2.** *v/t.* verwirren, irre machen, in Verlegenheit bringen; *j-m* Kopfzerbrechen machen; ~ *out* austüfteln; ~ *one's brains* = *v/i.* sich den Kopf zerbrechen (*over* über *acc.*); ˈ**~-head·ed** konfus; ˈ**puz·zler** schwierige Frage *f.*

pyg·m(a)e·an [pigˈmiːən] pygmäisch, zwerghaft; **pyg·my** [ˈpigmi] Pygmäe *m*; *fig.* Zwerg *m*; *attr.* Zwerg...; zwerghaft.

py·ja·mas [pə'dʒɑːməz] *pl.* Schlafanzug *m*, Pyjama *m*.
py·lon ['pailən] Hochspannungsmast *m*.
py·lo·rus *anat.* [pai'lɔːrəs] Pförtner *m*.
py·or·rh(o)e·a ⚕ [paiə'riə] Paradentose *f*.
pyr·a·mid ['pirəmid] Pyramide *f*; **py·ram·i·dal** □ [pi'ræmidl] pyramidal.
pyre ['paiə] Scheiterhaufen *m*.
py·ri·tes [pai'raitiːz]: *copper* ~ Kupferkies *m*; *iron* ~ Pyrit *m*, Eisenkies *m*.
py·ro... ['paiərəu] Feuer..., Brand..., Wärme..., Glut...; **py·rog·ra·phy** [pai'rɔgrəfi] Brandmalerei *f*; **py·ro·tech·nic, py·ro·tech·ni·cal** [pairəu'teknik(əl)] pyrotechnisch, Feuerwerks...; **py·ro'tech·nics** *pl.* Feuerwerkerei *f*; *fig.* Feuerwerk *n*; **py·ro'tech·nist** Feuerwerker *m*.
Pyr·rhic vic·to·ry ['pirik'viktəri] Pyrrhussieg *m*.
Py·thag·o·re·an [paiθægə'riːən] **1.** pythagoreisch; **2.** Pythagoreer *m*.
Pyth·i·an ['piθiən] pythisch.
py·thon ['paiθən] Python-, Riesenschlange *f*.
pyx [piks] *eccl.* Monstranz *f*; Büchse *f* mit Probemünzen.

Q

Q-boat ⚓ ['kjuːbəut] U-Bootfalle *f*.
quack[1] [kwæk] **1.** Quaken *n*; **2.** quaken.
quack[2] [~] **1.** Scharlatan *m*; Quacksalber *m*; Kurpfuscher *m*; Marktschreier *m*; **2.** quacksalberisch; Quacksalber...; **3.** quacksalbern (an *dat.*); **quack·er·y** ['~əri] Quacksalberei *f*; Marktschreierei *f*.
quad [kwɔd] = *quadrangle*, *quadrat*, *quadruplet*.
quad·ra·ge·nar·i·an [kwɔdrədʒi'nɛəriən] **1.** vierzigjährig; **2.** Vierzigjährige *m*, *f*.
quad·ran·gle ['kwɔdræŋgl] Viereck *n*; Innenhof *m e-s College*.
quad·rant ['kwɔdrənt] Quadrant *m*; *bsd.* ⩘ Viertelkreis *m*.
quad·ra·phon·ic [kwɔdrə'fɔnik] quadrophon.
quad·rat *typ.* ['kwɔdræt] (großer) Ausschluß *m*; **quad·rat·ic** ⩘ [kwə'drætik] **1.** quadratisch; **2.** quadratische Gleichung *f*; **quad·ra·ture** ['kwɔdrətʃə] Quadratur *f*.
quad·ren·ni·al □ [kwɔ'drenjəl] vierjährig; vierjährlich.
quad·ri·lat·er·al ⩘ [kwɔdri'lætərəl] **1.** vierseitig; **2.** Viereck *n*.
qua·drille [kwə'dril] Quadrille *f*.
quad·ri·par·tite [kwɔdri'pɑːtait] vierteilig; Vierer...
quad·ru·ped ['kwɔdruped] **1.** Vierfüßer *m*; **2.** *a.* **quad·ru·pe·dal** [kwɔ'druːpidl] vierfüßig; **quad·ru·ple** ['kwɔdrupl] **1.** □ vierfach; *a.* ~ *to*, ~ *of* viermal so groß wie; **2.** Vierfache *n*; **3.** (sich) vervierfachen; **quad·ru·plet** ['~plit] Vierling *m*; **quad·ru·pli·cate 1.** [kwɔ'druːplikit] vierfach(e Ausfertigung *f*); **2.** ['~keit] vervierfachen.
quaff [kwɑːf] zechen; ~ *off* in langen Zügen trinken.
quag [kwæg] = ~*mire*; '**quag·gy** sumpfig, moorig; **quag·mire** ['~maiə] Sumpf(land *n*) *m*, Moor *n*.
quail[1] *orn.* [kweil] Wachtel *f*.
quail[2] [~] verzagen; beben.
quaint □ [kweint] anheimelnd; malerisch; putzig; seltsam, wunderlich; '**quaint·ness** Seltsamkeit *f*.
quake [kweik] **1.** beben, zittern (*with*, *for* vor *dat.*); **2.** Erdbeben *n*.
Quak·er ['kweikə] Quäker *m*.
qual·i·fi·ca·tion [kwɔlifi'keiʃən] (erforderliche) Befähigung *f*; Einschränkung *f*; *gr.* nähere Bestimmung *f*; **qual·i·fied** ['~faid] befähigt; geeignet; eingeschränkt; bedingt; **qual·i·fy** ['~fai] *v/t.* befähigen; (be)nennen; *gr.* näher bestimmen; einschränken, mäßigen; mildern; *Getränk* verdünnen; *v/i.* seine Befähigung nachweisen; sich qualifizieren; *qualifying exami-*

nation Eignungsprüfung *f*; **qual·i·ta·tive** □ ['~tətiv] qualitativ; '**qual·i·ty** Eigenschaft *f*, Beschaffenheit *f*; Qualität *f*, Güte *f*; Fähigkeit *f*, Talent *n*; vornehmer Stand *m*.
qualm [kwɑːm] Übelkeit(sanfall *m*) *f*; Zweifel *m*; Bedenken *n*; '**qualm·ish** □ übel, unwohl.
quan·da·ry ['kwɔndəri] verzwickte Lage *f*, Verlegenheit *f*.
quan·go ['kwæŋgəu] *in Großbritannien*: unabhängige Kommission, unabhängiger Ausschuß.
quan·ti·ta·tive □ ['kwɔntitətiv] quantitativ; '**quan·ti·ty** Quantität *f*, Menge *f*; Anzahl *f*; großer Teil *m*; ℞ Größe *f*; (Silben)Zeitmaß *n*; ~ *surveyor* Bausachverständige *m*.
quan·tum ['kwɔntəm] Menge *f*, Größe *f*, Quantum *n*; Anteil *m*; ~ *theory phys.* Quantentheorie *f*.
quar·an·tine ['kwɔrəntiːn] **1.** Quarantäne *f*; **2.** unter Quarantäne stellen.
quar·rel ['kwɔrəl] **1.** Zank *m*, Streit *m*; **2.** (sich) zanken, streiten; **quar·rel·some** ['~səm] □ zänkisch; streitsüchtig.
quar·ry[1] ['kwɔri] **1.** Steinbruch *m*; *fig.* Fundgrube *f*; **2.** *Steine* brechen; *fig.* zs.-tragen; stöbern (*for* nach).
quar·ry[2] [~] (Jagd)Beute *f*.
quar·ry·man ['kwɔrimən] Steinbrucharbeiter *m*.
quart [kwɔːt] Quart *n* (*1,136 l*); *fenc.* [kɑːt] Quart(e) *f*.
quar·ter ['kwɔːtə] **1.** Viertel *n*, vierter Teil *m*; *bsd.* Viertelstunde *f*; Vierteljahr *n*, Quartal *n*; Viertelzentner *m*; *Am.* 25 Cent; Keule *f*, Viertel *n e-s geschlachteten Tieres*; Mondviertel *n*; Stadtviertel *n*, -teil *m*; ⚓ Achterschiff *n*; (Himmels-)Richtung *f*, Gegend *f*; ⚓ Posten *m*; ⚔ Gnade *f*, Pardon *m*; *fig.* Schonung *f*, Nachsicht *f*; *fig.* Stelle *f*, Seite *f*; ~*s pl.* Quartier *n* (*a.* ⚔), Unterkunft *f*; *fig.* Kreise *m/pl.*; *live in close* ~*s* beengt wohnen; *at close* ~*s* dicht aufeinander; *come to close* ~*s* handgemein werden; **2.** vierteln, vierteilen; beherbergen; ⚔ einquartieren; '**~·back** *Am. Sport*: *wichtigster Spieler der Angriffsformation*; '**~-deck** Achterdeck *n*; Offiziere *m/pl.*; '**quar·ter·ly** **1.** vierteljährlich; Vierteljahrs...; **2.** Vierteljahrsschrift *f*; '**quar·ter·mas·ter** ⚔ Quartiermeister *m*; **quar·tern** ['~tən] Viertel(pinte *f*) *n*; Vierpfundbrot *n*; '**quar·ter·staff** Stange *f als Waffe*.
quar·tet(te) ♪ [kwɔː'tet] Quartett *n*.
quar·to ['kwɔːtəu] Quart(format) *n*.
quartz *min.* [kwɔːts] Quarz *m*; **quartz·ite** ['~ait] Quarzit *m*.
quash ⚖ [kwɔʃ] aufheben, verwerfen; unterdrücken.
qua·si ['kwɑːziː] gleichsam, sozusagen; Quasi..., Schein...
qua·ter·na·ry [kwə'təːnəri] aus vier bestehend; *geol.* Quartär...
quat·rain ['kwɔtrein] Vierzeiler *m*.
qua·ver ['kweivə] **1.** Zittern *n*; ♪ Triller *m*; ♪ Achtelnote *f*; **2.** mit zitternder Stimme sprechen *od.* singen; trillern; '**qua·ver·y** zitternd.
quay [kiː] Kai *m*; Uferstraße *f*; **quay·age** ['~idʒ] Kaigeld *n*.
quea·si·ness ['kwiːzinis] Empfindlichkeit *f*; Übelkeit *f*; Ekel *m*; '**quea·sy** □ empfindlich (*Magen, Gewissen*); heikel, mäkelig; ekelhaft; *I feel* ~ mir ist übel.
queen [kwiːn] **1.** Königin *f*; *Schach etc.*: Dame *f*; *sl.* Schwule *m*, Homo *m*; ~ *bee* Bienenkönigin *f*; ~'*s metal* Weißmetall *n*; ~'*s ware* gelbes Steingut *n*; **2.** *Schach*: in e-e Dame verwandeln *od.* verwandelt werden; ~ *it* die Dame spielen; '**queen·like**, '**queen·ly** wie eine Königin, königlich.
queer [kwiə] **1.** sonderbar, seltsam; wunderlich; komisch, unwohl; homosexuell; **2.** ~ *s.o.'s pitch sl.* j-m e-n Strich durch die Rechnung machen; **3.** Homosexuelle *m*.
quell *rhet.* [kwel] bezwingen; unterdrücken.
quench [kwentʃ] *fig. Durst etc.* löschen, stillen, kühlen; *Aufruhr* unterdrücken; *rhet.* (aus)löschen; '**quench·er** F Trunk *m*, Schluck *m*; '**quench·less** □ unauslöschlich.
que·rist ['kwiərist] Fragesteller (-in).
quern [kwəːn] Handmühle *f*.
quer·u·lous □ ['kweruləs] quengelig, mürrisch, verdrossen.
que·ry ['kwiəri] **1.** (*mst abbr. qu.*) bitte!, sage mir; **2.** Frage(zeichen *n*) *f*; **3.** (be)fragen; (be-, an)zweifeln.
quest [kwest] **1.** Suche(n *n*) *f*,

Nachforschen *n*; *in ~ of* auf der Suche nach; **2.** suchen, forschen.

ques·tion ['kwestʃən] **1.** Frage *f*; Problem *n*; Untersuchung *f*; Streitfrage *f*; Zweifel *m*; Sache *f*, Angelegenheit *f*; *~! parl.* zur Sache!; *beyond (all) ~* ohne Frage, fraglos; *in ~* fraglich; *come into ~* in Frage kommen; *call in ~* anzweifeln; *beg the ~* die in Frage gestellte Sache als erwiesen ansehen; *the ~ is ...* es handelt sich darum ...; *that is out of the ~* das steht außer *od.* kommt nicht in Frage; *there is no ~ of od. of ger.* es ist nicht die Rede von *od.* davon, daß; **2.** befragen; bezweifeln; verhören; '**ques·tion·a·ble** □ fraglich, zweifelhaft; bedenklich, fragwürdig; '**ques·tion·a·ble·ness** Zweifelhaftigkeit *f*; Fragwürdigkeit *f*; '**ques·tion·er** Fragende *m*, *f*, Fragesteller(in); **ques·tion mark** Fragezeichen *n*; **ques·tion mas·ter** Moderator *m e-s Quiz*; **ques·tion·naire** [kwestiə'nɛə] Fragebogen *m*; **ques·tion time** *parl.* Fragestunde *f*.

queue [kju:] **1.** Reihe *f von Personen od. Wagen*, Schlange *f*; Zopf *m*; **2.** *mst ~ up* (in e-r Reihe) anstehen, Schlange stehen; '**~-jump·er** j., der sich vordrängelt; *mot.* Kolonnenspringer *m*.

quib·ble ['kwibl] **1.** Wortspiel *n*; Spitzfindigkeit *f*; Ausflucht *f*; **2.** *fig.* ausweichen; witzeln; '**quib·bler** Wortklauber *m*, Sophist *m*.

quick [kwik] **1.** schnell, rasch; voreilig; lebhaft; gescheit; beweglich; lebendig; scharf (*Gehör etc.*); *~ march* ⚔ Eil-, Geschwindmarsch *m*; **2.** lebendes Fleisch *n*; *the ~ pl.* die Lebenden *m/pl.*; *to the ~* (bis) ins Fleisch; *fig.* (bis) ins Herz, tief; *cut s.o. to the ~* j. aufs empfindlichste kränken; **3.** *s. ~ly*; '**~-change ac·tor** Verwandlungskünstler *m*; '**quick·en** *v/t.* beleben; beschleunigen; *v/i.* aufleben; sich regen; '**quick-fir·ing** ⚔ Schnellfeuer...; '**quick-fro·zen** tiefgekühlt; **quick·ie** F ['~i] *auf die Schnelle gemachte Sache*; *have a ~ mst* auf die Schnelle einen trinken; '**quick·lime** ungelöschter Kalk *m*; '**quick·ly** schnell, rasch; '**quick-match** Zündschnur *f*; '**quick-mo·tion pic·ture** *Film*: Zeitrafferaufnahme *f*; '**quick·ness** Lebhaftigkeit *f*; Schnelligkeit *f*; Voreiligkeit *f*; Schärfe *f des Verstandes etc.*

quick...: '**~·sand** Treibsand *m*; '**~·set** ⚘ Setzling *m*; Hagedorn *m*; *a. ~ hedge* lebende Hecke *f*; '**~-'sight·ed** scharfsichtig; '**~·sil·ver** *min.* Quecksilber *n*; '**~·step** Quickstep *m* (*Tanzschritt*); ⚔ Geschwindschritt *m*; '**~-'tem·pered** leicht erregbar, hitzig; '**~-'wit·ted** schlagfertig.

quid[1] [kwid] Priem *m* (*Kautabak*).

quid[2] *sl.* [~] *Pfund Sterling*.

quid·di·ty *phls.* ['kwiditi] Wesen *n e-r Sache*; Spitzfindigkeit *f*.

quid pro quo ['kwid prəu 'kwəu] Gegenleistung *f*; Äquivalent *n*.

qui·es·cence [kwai'esns] Ruhe *f*, Stille *f*; **qui'es·cent** □ ruhend; *fig.* ruhig, still.

qui·et ['kwaiət] **1.** □ ruhig, still; **2.** Ruhe *f*; *on the ~* (*sl.*: *on the q.t.* ['kju:'ti:]) unter der Hand, im stillen; im Vertrauen; **3.** *a. ~ down* (sich) beruhigen; '**qui·et·en** = *quiet 3*; **qui·et·ism** ['kwaiitizəm] *eccl.* Quietismus *m*; '**qui·et·ist** Quietist *m*; **qui·et·ness** ['kwaiətnis], **qui·e·tude** ['kwaiitju:d] Ruhe *f*, Stille *f*.

qui·e·tus [kwai'i:təs] Endquittung *f*; Ende *n*, Tod *m*; Todesstoß *m*.

quill [kwil] **1.** Federkiel *m*; *fig.* Feder *f*; Stachel *m des Igels etc.*; **2.** rund fälteln; '**~-driv·er** Federfuchser *m*; '**quill·ing** Krause *f*, Rüsche *f*; '**quill-pen** Gänsefeder *f zum Schreiben*.

quilt [kwilt] **1.** Steppdecke *f*; **2.** steppen; '**quilt·ing** Steppen *n*; gesteppte Arbeit *f*; Pikee *m*.

quince ⚘ [kwins] Quitte *f*.

qui·nine *pharm.* [kwi'ni:n, *bsd. Am.* 'kwainain] Chinin *n*.

quin·qua·ge·nar·i·an [kwiŋkwədʒi'nɛəriən] **1.** fünfzigjährig; **2.** Fünfzigjährige *m*, *f*.

quin·quen·ni·al □ [kwiŋ'kweniəl] fünfjährig; fünfjährlich.

quins F [kwinz] *pl.* Fünflinge *pl.*

quin·sy ⚕ ['kwinzi] Mandelentzündung *f*.

quin·tal ['kwintl] (Doppel)Zentner *m*.

quint·es·sence [kwin'tesns] Quintessenz *f*, Kern *m*, Inbegriff *m*.

quin·tu·ple ['kwintjupl] **1.** fünffach; **2.** (sich) verfünffachen; **quin-**

tu·plets ['~plits] *pl.* Fünflinge *pl.*
quip [kwip] Stich(elei *f*) *m*; Witz (-wort *n*) *m*; Spitzfindigkeit *f*.
quire ['kwaiə] Buch *n Papier*; *Buchbinderei*: Lage *f*.
quirk [kwəːk] Spitzfindigkeit *f*; Witz(elei *f*) *m*; Kniff *m*; Schnörkel *m*; ⚠ Hohlkehle *f*.
quis·ling ['kwizliŋ] Quisling *m*, Kollaborateur *m*.
quit [kwit] **1.** *v/t.* verlassen; aufgeben, verzichten auf (*acc.*); *Am.* aufhören; vergelten; *Schuld* tilgen; *v/i.* ausziehen (*Mieter*); weggehen; aufhören; **2.** quitt; frei (*of* von), los.
quite [kwait] ganz, gänzlich; recht; durchaus; ~ *a lot* e-e ziemliche *od.* ganze Menge; ~ (*so*)!, ~ *that!* ganz recht!, genau!; ~ *the thing* F große Mode *f*; genau das Richtige.
quits [kwits] quitt (*with* mit); *cry* ~ genug haben.
quit·tance ['kwitəns] Quittung *f*.
quit·ter *Am.* F ['kwitə] Drückeberger *m*.
quiv·er[1] ['kwivə] **1.** Zittern *n*, Beben *n*; **2.** zittern, beben.
quiv·er[2] [~] Köcher *m*.
quix·ot·ic [kwik'sɔtik] donquichotisch, weltfremd, überspannt.
quiz [kwiz] **1.** Prüfung *f*, Test *m*; Quiz *n*, Frage- u. Antwortspiel *n*; belustigter Blick *m*; **2.** (aus)fragen, prüfen; necken, foppen; anstarren, beäugen; '**quiz·zi·cal** □ spöttisch; komisch.
quod *sl.* [kwɔd] Loch *n* (*Gefängnis*).
quoin [kɔin] Ecke *f*; *typ.* Keil *m*.
quoit [kɔit] Wurfring *m*; ~*s pl.* Wurfringspiel *n*.
quon·dam ['kwɔndæm] ehemalig.
quon·set *Am.* ['kwɔnsit] *a.* ~ *hut* Wellblechbaracke *f*.
quo·rum *parl.* ['kwɔːrəm] beschlußfähige Mitgliederzahl *f*; *have a* ~, *form a* ~ beschlußfähig sein.
quo·ta ['kwəutə] Quote *f*, Anteil *m*, Kontingent *n*.
quot·a·ble ['kwəutəbl] zitierbar.
quo·ta·tion [kwəu'teiʃən] Anführung *f*, Zitat *n*; ☤ Preisnotierung *f*; Kostenvoranschlag *m*; *familiar* ~*s pl.* geflügelte Worte *n/pl.*; **quo'ta·tion-marks** *pl.* Anführungszeichen *n/pl.*
quote [kwəut] anführen, zitieren; angeben; ☤ berechnen, notieren (*at* mit).
quoth † [kwəuθ]: ~ *I*, ~ *he* sagte ich, sagte er.
quo·tid·i·an [kwɔ'tidiən] (all)täglich.
quo·tient ⚗ ['kwəuʃənt] Quotient *m*.

R

r [ɑː]: *the three R's* (= *reading, writing, arithmetic*) Lesen *n*, Schreiben *n* u. Rechnen *n*.
rab·bet ⊕ ['ræbit] **1.** Falz *m*, Fuge *f*, Nut *f*; **2.** (ein)falzen, (ein)fügen, fugen.
rab·bi ['ræbai] Rabbiner *m*.
rab·bit ['ræbit] Kaninchen *n*; '**~-fe·ver** Hasenpest *f*.
rab·ble ['ræbl] Pöbel(haufen) *m*; '**~-rous·er** Demagoge *m*; '**~-rous·ing** aufwieglerisch, demagogisch.
rab·id □ ['ræbid] tollwütig (*Tier*); *fig.* wild, rasend, wütend; '**rab·id·ness** Tollheit *f*.
ra·bies *vet.* ['reibiːz] Tollwut *f*.
rac·coon [rə'kuːn] = *racoon*.
race[1] [reis] Geschlecht *n*, Stamm *m*; Volk *n*; Rasse *f*, Schlag *m*.
race[2] [~] Rennen *n*; Lauf *m* (*a. fig.*); Wettlauf *m*, -rennen *n*; Strömung *f*, Strom *m*; ~*s pl.* Pferderennen *n*; **2.** rennen; *weitS.* rasen; um die Wette laufen (mit); rasen mit; *Gesetz* durchpeitschen; *Motor im Leerlauf* hochjagen; '**~-course** Rennbahn *f*, -strecke *f*.
race-ha·tred ['reis'heitrid] Rassenhaß *m*.
race-horse ['reishɔːs] Rennpferd *n*.
rac·er ['reisə] Rennpferd *n*; Rennboot *n*; Rennwagen *m*.
ra·cial ['reiʃəl] Rassen...; ~ *discrimination* Rassendiskriminierung *f*; ~ *equality* Rassengleichheit *f*; ~ *segregation* Rassentrennung *f*; '**ra·cial-**

ism Rassenbewußtsein *n*, -haß *m*.
rac·i·ness ['reisinis] Lebhaftigkeit *f*; Urwüchsigkeit *f*.
rac·ing ['reisiŋ] Rennsport *m*; *attr.* Renn...; ~ *car* Rennwagen *m*.
ra·cism ['reisizəm] Rassismus *m*; '**ra·cist** Rassist *m*.
rack[1] [ræk] **1.** Gerüst *n*, Gestell *n*; Kleiderständer *m*; Gepäcknetz *n*; Raufe *f*, Futtergestell *n*; ⊕ Zahnstange *f*; Folter(bank) *f*; **2.** recken, strecken; foltern, martern, quälen (*a. fig.*); ausnutzen; auf *od.* in das Gestell *etc.* tun; ~ *one's brains* sich den Kopf zermartern.
rack[2] [~] **1.** ziehende Wolkenmasse *f*; **2.** ziehen (*Wolken*).
rack[3] [~]: *go to* ~ *and ruin* ganz und gar zugrunde gehen.
rack[4] [~] *a.* ~ *off Wein* abfüllen.
rack·et[1] ['rækit] *Tennis etc.*: Schläger *m*, Rakett *n*; ~*s pl.* Rakettspiel *n*.
rack·et[2] [~] **1.** Lärm *m*, Krach *m*; *fig.* Getriebe *n*, Trubel *m*; *Am.* F Schwindel(geschäft *n*) *m*; Strapaze *f*, Nervenprobe *f*; *stand the* ~ es durchstehen; die Folgen tragen; **2.** lärmen; sich amüsieren; **rack·et·eer** *bsd. Am. sl.* [~'tiə] Erpresser *m*; **rack·et'eer·ing** *bsd. Am.* Erpresserwesen *n*; '**rack·et·y** ausgelassen.
rack-rail·way ['rækreilwei] Zahnradbahn *f*.
rack-rent ['rækrent] **1.** Wuchermiete *f*, -pacht *f*; **2.** *j-m e-e* Wuchermiete abverlangen.
ra·coon *zo.* [rə'ku:n] Waschbär *m*.
rac·y □ ['reisi] kraftvoll, lebendig; stark; würzig (*Geruch etc.*); urwüchsig.
ra·dar ['reidə] Radar(gerät) *n*; ~ **scan·ner** Radarsuchgerät *n*.
rad·dle ['rædl] 1. Rötel *m*; 2. rot bemalen.
ra·di·al □ ['reidjəl] radial, strahlenförmig; ~ *engine* Sternmotor *m*; ~ *tyre*, *Am.* ~ *tire* Gürtelreifen *m*.
ra·di·ance, ra·di·an·cy ['reidjəns(i)] Strahlen *n*; '**ra·di·ant** □ strahlend, leuchtend (*a. fig.*); Strahlungs...
ra·di·ate 1. ['reidieit] (aus)strahlen; strahlenförmig ausgehen; **2.** ['~it] strahl(enförm)ig; Strahl(en)...; **ra·di'a·tion** (Aus)Strahlung *f*; **ra·di·a·tor** ['~eitə] Heizkörper *m*; *mot.* Kühler *m*.
rad·i·cal ['rædikəl] **1.** □ Wurzel..., Stamm..., Grund...; grundlegend; gründlich; eingewurzelt; radikal (*a. pol.*); ~ *sign* ⅍ Wurzelzeichen *n*; **2.** *gr.* Wurzelbuchstabe *m*, -wort *n*; ⚗ Grundstoff *m*; *bsd. pol.* Radikale *m*; '**rad·i·cal·ism** Radikalismus *m*.
ra·di·o ['reidiəu] **1.** Radio *n*, Rundfunk *m*; Funkspruch *m*; Rundfunk-, Radiogerät *n*; Funkgerät *n*; ~-*car* Funkstreifenwagen *m*; ~ *drama*, ~ *play* Hörspiel *n*; ~ *engineering* Funktechnik *f*; ~ *operator* Funker *m*; ~ *set* Radiogerät *n*; 2. funken; (drahtlos) senden; '~-'**ac·tive** radioaktiv; ~ *waste* radioaktiver Müll *m*, Atom-Müll *m*; '~-**ac'tiv·i·ty** Radioaktivität *f*; ~ **con·tact** Funkkontakt *m*; **ra·di·o·gram** ['~græm] Funktelegramm *n*; Röntgenaufnahme *f*; = **ra·di·o-gram·o·phone** ['~'græməfəun] Musiktruhe *f*, Radiogerät *n* mit Plattenspieler; **ra·di·o·graph** ['~grɑ:f] **1.** Röntgenbild *n*; 2. ein Röntgenbild machen von; **ra·di·og·ra·pher** [reidi'ɔgrəfə] Röntgenassistent *m*; **ra·di'og·ra·phy** Röntgenographie *f*; '**ra·di·o-lo'ca·tion** Funkortung *f*; **ra·di·ol·o·gist** [reidi'ɔlədʒist] Röntgenologe *m*; **ra·di·ol·o·gy** *phys.* [reidi'ɔlədʒi] Strahlenlehre *f*; -forschung *f*, -kunde *f*; Röntgenologie *f*; **ra·di·o-tel·e·gram** ['reidiəu'teligræm] Funktelegramm *n*; '**ra·di·o-'ther·a·py** Strahlen-, Röntgentherapie *f*.
rad·ish ⚘ ['rædiʃ] Rettich *m*; *a. red* ~ Radieschen *n*.
ra·di·um ['reidjəm] Radium *n*.
ra·di·us ['reidjəs], *pl.* **ra·di·i** ['~diai] Radius *m*; ⅍ Halbmesser *m*; *anat.*, *a.* ⊕ Speiche *f*; ⚘ Strahl *m*; *fig.* Umkreis *m*.
raff·ish ['ræfiʃ] liederlich.
raf·fle ['ræfl] **1.** Tombola *f*, Verlosung *f*; **2.** verlosen.
raft [rɑ:ft] **1.** Floß *n*; **2.** flößen; '**raft·er** ⊕ (Dach)Sparren *m*; '**rafts·man** Flößer *m*.
rag[1] [ræg] Lumpen *m*; Fetzen *m*; Lappen *m*; *contp.* Käseblatt *n*.
rag[2] *sl.* [~] **1.** Unfug treiben (mit); *j.* aufziehen; *j.* beschimpfen; herumtollen, Radau machen; **2.** Unfug *m*; Radau *m*.
rag·a·muf·fin ['rægəmʌfin] Lumpenkerl *m*; Gassenjunge *m*.
rag...: '~-**and-'bone man** Lumpensammler *m*; '~-**bag** Lumpensack *m*;

'**~-book** unzerreißbares Bilderbuch *n.*

rage [reidʒ] **1.** Wut *f,* Zorn *m;* Sucht *f,* Gier *f* (*for* nach); Manie *f;* Begeisterung *f,* Ekstase *f; it is all the ~* es ist allgemein Mode, alles ist wild danach; **2.** wüten, rasen, toben.

rag-fair ['rægfɛə] Trödelmarkt *m.*

rag·ged □ ['rægid] rauh; zottig; zackig; unregelmäßig; zerlumpt.

rag·man ['rægmən] Lumpensammler *m.*

ra·gout ['rægu:] Ragout *n.*

rag...: '**~-tag** *mst ~ and bobtail* Pack *n,* Pöbel *m;* Krethi u. Plethi *pl.;* '**~·time** ♪ Ragtime *m* (*Jazzstil*).

raid [reid] **1.** (feindlicher) Überfall *m,* Streifzug *m;* (Luft)Angriff *m;* Razzia *f;* **2.** einbrechen in *acc.,* e-n Überfall machen auf *acc.;* überfallen; plündern; '**raid·er** Stoßtruppteilnehmer *m.*

rail[1] [reil] **1.** *a. ~s pl.* Geländer *n;* Stange *f;* 🚂 Schiene *f; fig.* Eisenbahn *f; ~ strike* Eisenbahnerstreik *m; off the ~s* entgleist; *fig.* in Unordnung; *by ~* per Bahn; 2. *a. ~ in, ~ off* mit e-m Geländer umgeben. [*acc.*).]

rail[2] [~] schimpfen (*at, against* auf

rail[3] *orn.* [~] Ralle *f.*

rail-car ['reilkɑ:] Triebwagen *m.*

rail·ing ['reiliŋ] *a. ~s pl.* Geländer *n,* Gitter *n;* Reling *f;* Staket *n.*

rail·lery ['reiləri] Spötterei *f.*

rail·road *Am.* ['reilrəud] **1.** Eisenbahn *f;* **2.** *Gesetz, Maßnahme* durchpeitschen.

rail·way ['reilwei] Eisenbahn *f;* ~ **car·riage** Eisenbahnwagen *m;* '**~-man** Eisenbahner *m.*

rai·ment *rhet.* ['reimənt] Kleidung *f.*

rain [rein] **1.** Regen *m;* **2.** regnen; **~·bow** ['~bəu] Regenbogen *m;* '**~-coat** *Am.* Regenmantel *m;* '**~-drop** Regentropfen *m;* '**~·fall** Niederschlagsmenge *f;* Regenschauer *m;* **~·ga(u)ge** ['~geidʒ] Regenmesser *m;* '**~-proof 1.** regen-, wasserdicht; **2.** Regenmantel *m;* '**rain·y** □ regnerisch; Regen...; *a ~ day fig.* Notzeiten *f/pl.*

raise [reiz] *oft ~ up* heben; auf-, erheben; auf-, errichten; erhöhen (*a. fig.*); *Geld* aufbringen; *Anleihe* aufnehmen; *Heer* aufstellen; *Steuern, Stimme, Geschrei, Anspruch, Einwand, Frage etc.* erheben; verursachen, hervorrufen; erwecken, erregen, in Bewegung setzen; anstiften, aufwiegeln; *Tiere* züchten; *Pflanzen* ziehen; *Getreide* (an)bauen; *Geister* beschwören; *Belagerung* aufheben; '**rais·er** Züchter *m;* Gründer *m.*

rai·sin ['reizn] Rosine *f.*

ra·ja(h) ['rɑ:dʒə] Radscha *m* (*indischer Fürst*).

rake[1] [reik] **1.** Rechen *m,* Harke *f;* **2.** *v/t.* (glatt-, zs.-)harken; *mst ~ together* zs.-scharren; *a. ~ up, ~ over fig.* durchstöbern; ⚔, ⚓ beharken, (mit Feuer) bestreichen; überblicken; *~ off, ~ away* wegräumen; *v/i.* harken, herumstöbern (*for* nach); '**~-off** *Am. sl.* Schwindelprofit *m.*

rake[2] ⚓ [~] **1.** Hang *m;* **2.** überhängen (lassen).

rake[3] [~] Wüstling *m;* Lebemann *m.*

rak·ish ['reikiʃ] **1.** flott, schnittig; **2.** □ liederlich, ausschweifend; verwegen; salopp.

ral·ly[1] ['ræli] **1.** Sammeln *n;* Tagung *f,* Treffen *n;* Massenversammlung *f;* Erholung *f; Tennis:* Ballwechsel *m; mot.* Rallye *f,* Sternfahrt *f;* **2.** (sich ver)sammeln; sich erholen.

ral·ly[2] [~] *j.* aufziehen, necken.

ram [ræm] **1.** *zo., ast.* Widder *m;* ⚔ *hist.* Sturmbock *m;* ⊕, ⚓ Ramme *f;* **2.** (fest)rammen; ⚓ rammen; *~ up* verrammeln.

ram·ble ['ræmbl] **1.** Streifzug *m;* **2.** umherstreifen; abschweifen; '**ram·bler** Wanderer *m;* ⚘ Kletterrose *f;* '**ram·bling 1.** □ umherschweifend; abschweifend, unstet; weitläufig; unzusammenhängend; **2.** Umherschweifen *n.*

ram·i·fi·ca·tion [ræmifi'keiʃən] Verzweigung *f;* **ram·i·fy** ['~fai] (sich) verzweigen.

ram·jet ['ræmdʒet] *a. ~ engine* Staustrahltriebwerk *n.*

ram·mer ⊕ ['ræmə] Ramme *f.*

ramp[1] *sl.* [ræmp] Schwindel(manöver *n*) *m;* Geldschneiderei *f.*

ramp[2] [~] **1.** Rampe *f;* **2.** sich zum Sprunge erheben; toben; **rampage** *co.* [ræm'peidʒ] **1.** toben, tollen; **2.** *be on the ~* sich austoben; **ramp·an·cy** ['~pənsi] Wuchern *n;* Zügellosigkeit *f;* '**ramp·ant** □ wuchernd; *fig.* zügellos; *Heraldik u.* ⚠ steigend.

ram·part ['ræmpɑ:t] Wall *m* (*a. fig.*).
ram·rod ['ræmrɔd] Ladestock *m*.
ram·shack·le ['ræmʃækl] baufällig, wackelig, klapperig.
ran [ræn] *pret. von run 1.*
ranch [rɑ:ntʃ] Ranch *f*, Viehfarm *f*; '**ranch·er**, '**ranch·man** Rancher *m*, Viehzüchter *m*; Farmer *m*.
ran·cid □ ['rænsid] ranzig; **ran·'cid·i·ty**, '**ran·cid·ness** Ranzigkeit *f*.
ran·cor·ous □ ['ræŋkərəs] voller Groll, boshaft.
ran·co(u)r ['ræŋkə] Groll *m*, Haß *m*.
ran·dom ['rændəm] **1.** *at* ~ aufs Geratewohl, blindlings; **2.** ziel-, wahllos; zufällig; ~ *sample* Stichprobe *f von Waren*; ~ *shot* Schuß *m* ins Blaue.
rand·y F ['rændi] geil.
rang [ræŋ] *pret. von ring² 2.*
range [reindʒ] **1.** Reihe *f*; (Berg-)Kette *f*; ✝ Kollektion *f*; Sortiment *n*; Herd *m*; Raum *m*; Umfang *m*, Bereich *m*; Spielraum *m*; Reichweite *f*; Schuß-, Tragweite *f*; (ausgedehnte) Fläche *f*; Weide- *od.* Jagdgebiet *n*; *take the* ~ die Entfernung schätzen; **2.** *v/t.* (ein)reihen, ordnen; *ein Gebiet etc.* durchstreifen, -laufen; ⚓ längs *et.* fahren; *v/i.* in e-r Reihe *od.* Linie stehen; sich (auf)stellen; (umher)streifen; sich erstrecken, reichen; e-e Reichweite haben (*over* von); ~ *along* entlang fahren; '~-**find·er** Entfernungsmesser *m*; '**rang·er** Förster *m*; Aufseher *m* e-s Parks; ⚔ Nahkampfspezialist *m*; '**rang·y** ausgedehnt; gebirgig; schlank.
rank¹ [ræŋk] **1.** Reihe *f*, Linie *f*; ⚔ Glied *n*; Klasse *f*; Rang *m*, Stand *m*; *the* ~*s pl.*, *the* ~ *and file* die Mannschaften *f/pl.*; *fig.* die große Masse; *join the* ~*s* in das Heer eintreten; *rise from the* ~*s* von der Pike auf dienen; **2.** *v/t.* (ein)reihen, ordnen; rechnen (*with* zu); *v/i.* sich reihen, sich ordnen; gehören, sich rechnen, gerechnet werden (*with* zu; *among* unter *acc.*); e-e Stelle einnehmen, rangieren (*above* über *dat.*; *next to* hinter *dat.*); ~ *as* gelten als.
rank² □ [~] üppig, geil (*Pflanze*); fett (*Boden*); ranzig, stinkend; verderbt; *b.s.* kraß.
rank·er ['ræŋkə] aus dem Mannschaftsstand hervorgegangener Offizier *m*.
ran·kle *fig.* ['ræŋkl] nagen, fressen.
rank·ness ['ræŋknis] Üppigkeit *f des Wachstums*; Ranzigkeit *f*.
ran·sack ['rænsæk] durchwühlen, -stöbern, -suchen; ausrauben.
ran·som ['rænsəm] **1.** Lösegeld *n*; Auslösung *f*; *eccl.* Erlösung *f*; **2.** loskaufen, auslösen; erlösen.
rant [rænt] **1.** Wortschwall *m*, Schwulst *m*; **2.** Phrasen dreschen; mit Pathos vortragen; '**rant·er** Phrasendrescher *m*.
ra·nun·cu·lus ⚘ [rə'nʌŋkjuləs] Ranunkel *f*, Hahnenfuß *m*.
rap¹ [ræp] **1.** Klaps *m*; Klopfen *n*; **2.** schlagen, klopfen (*at* an *acc.*); ~ *s.o.'s fingers od. knuckles fig.* j-m auf die Finger klopfen; ~ *out* herauspoltern.
rap² *fig.* [~] Heller *m*, Deut *m*.
ra·pa·cious □ [rə'peiʃəs] raubgierig; Raub...; habgierig; **ra·pac·i·ty** [rə'pæsiti] Raub-, Habgier *f*.
rape¹ [reip] **1.** Raub *m*; Entführung *f*; ⚖ Notzucht *f*, Vergewaltigung *f*; ~ *and murder* Lustmord *m*; **2.** rauben; vergewaltigen.
rape² ⚘ [~] Raps *m*; '~-**oil** Raps-, Rüböl *n*; '~-**seed** Rübsamen *m*.
rap·id ['ræpid] **1.** □ schnell, rasch, reißend, rapid(e); Schnell...; steil, jäh; *phot.* lichtstark (*Objektiv*); hochempfindlich (*Film*); ~ *fire* Schnellfeuer *n*; **2.** ~*s pl.* Stromschnelle(n *pl.*) *f*; **ra·pid·i·ty** [rə'piditi] Schnelligkeit *f*.
ra·pi·er *fenc.* ['reipjə] Rapier *n*.
rap·ine *rhet.* ['ræpain] Raub *m*.
rap·ist ['reipist] Vergewaltiger *m*.
rap·proche·ment *pol.* [ræ'prɔʃmɑ̃:ŋ] Wiederannäherung *f*.
rapt [ræpt] *fig.* hingerissen, entzückt (*with* vor *dat.*); versunken (*in* in *acc.*).
rap·ture ['ræptʃə] *a.* ~*s pl.* Entzücken *n*; Begeisterung *f*; Taumel *m*; *in* ~*s* entzückt; *go into* ~*s* in Entzücken geraten; '**rap·tur·ous** □ entzückt; leidenschaftlich.
rare¹ □ [rɛə] selten (*a. fig. ungewöhnlich; hervorragend; köstlich*); vereinzelt; *phys. etc.* dünn.
rare² [~] halbgar, blutig (*Fleisch*).
rare·bit ['rɛəbit]: *Welsh* ~ geröstete Käseschnitte *f*.
rar·e·fac·tion *phys.* [rɛəri'fækʃən] Verdünnung *f*; **rar·e·fy** ['~fai]

(sich) verdünnen; verfeinern; 'rare·ness, 'rar·i·ty Seltenheit *f*; Dünnheit *f*; Kostbarkeit *f*.

ras·cal ['rɑːskəl] Schuft *m*, Schurke *m*; Schelm *m*; **ras·cal·i·ty** [~'kæliti] Schurkerei *f*; **ras·cal·ly** *adj. u. adv.* ['~kəli] schuftig; erbärmlich.

rash[1] □ [ræʃ] hastig, vorschnell; unbesonnen; waghalsig.

rash[2] ⚕ [~] Hautausschlag *m*.

rash·er ['ræʃə] Speckschnitte *f*.

rash·ness ['ræʃnis] Voreiligkeit *f*; Unbesonnenheit *f*.

rasp [rɑːsp] **1.** Raspel *f*; **2.** raspeln; *j-m* weh(e) tun; kratzen; krächzen.

rasp·ber·ry ♣ ['rɑːzbəri] Himbeere *f*.

rasp·er ['rɑːspə] Raspler *m*; Kratzeisen *n*.

rasp·ing ['rɑːspiŋ] Raspeln *n*; ~*s pl.* Raspelspäne *m/pl.*

rat [ræt] **1.** *zo.* Ratte *f*; *pol.* Überläufer *m*; *sl.* Streikbrecher *m*; *smell a* ~ Lunte *od.* den Braten riechen; ~*s! sl.* quatsch!; **2.** Ratten fangen; *pol.* überlaufen.

rat·a·ble □ ['reitəbl] steuerpflichtig.

ratch ⊕ [rætʃ] Sperrstange *f*; *Uhrmacherei*: Auslösung *f*.

ratch·et ⊕ ['rætʃit] Sperrklinke *f*; '**~-wheel** Sperrad *n*.

rate[1] [reit] **1.** Verhältnis *n*, Maß *n*, Satz *m*; Rate *f*; Preis *m*, Gebühr *f*; Taxe *f*; (Gemeinde)Abgabe *f*, Steuer *f*; Grad *m*, Rang *m*; *bsd.* ⚓ Klasse *f*; Geschwindigkeit *f*, Gang *m*; *at the* ~ *of* im Verhältnis von; zum Satz von; mit einer Geschwindigkeit von; *at a cheap* ~ ✝ zu billigem Preis; *at any* ~ auf jeden Fall; ~ *of exchange* (Umrechnungs-) Kurs *m*; ~ *of interest* Zinsfuß *m*; ~ *of taxation* Steuersatz *m*; **2.** (ein-) schätzen, taxieren (*at* auf *acc.*); besteuern.

rate[2] [~] *v/t.* ausschelten (*for, about* wegen); *v/i.* schelten (*at* auf, über *acc.*).

rate-pay·er ['reitpeiə] (Gemeinde-) Steuerzahler *m*.

rath·er ['rɑːðə] eher, lieber; vielmehr; besser gesagt; ziemlich; ~! [*a.* 'rɑː'ðəː] F na gewiß!, und ob!; *I had od. would* ~ *do* ich möchte lieber tun; *I* ~ *expected it* ich habe es eigentlich erwartet.

rat·i·fi·ca·tion [rætifi'keiʃən] Bestätigung *f*; **rat·i·fy** ['~fai] bestätigen, ratifizieren.

rat·ing[1] ['reitiŋ] Schätzung *f*; Steuersatz *m*; ⚓ Dienstgrad *m*; ⚓ (Segel)Klasse *f*; Matrose *m*; *Fernsehen*: Einschaltquote *f*.

rat·ing[2] [~] Schelte(n *n*) *f*.

ra·tio ['reiʃiəu] Verhältnis *n*.

ra·tion ['ræʃən] **1.** Ration *f*; Zuteilung *f*; ~ *card* (*book*) Lebensmittelkarte(n *pl.*) *f*; **2.** rationieren; einschränken.

ra·tion·al □ ['ræʃənl] vernunftgemäß; vernünftig, rational (*a.* ⅌); **ra·tion·al·ism** ['ræʃnəlizəm] Rationalismus *m*; '**ra·tion·al·ist** Rationalist *m*; **ra·tion·al·i·ty** [ræʃə'næliti] Vernunft(mäßigkeit) *f*; **ra·tion·al·i·za·tion** [ræʃnəlai'zeiʃən] Rationalisierung *f*; wirtschaftliche Vereinfachung *f*; '**ra·tion·al·ize** rationalisieren; wirtschaftlich vereinfachen.

rat race ['rætreis] sinnlose Hetze *f*; rücksichtsloses Aufstiegsstreben *n*; Prestigesucht *f*.

rat-tat ['ræt'tæt] Pochen *n*.

rat·ten ['rætn] *v/t.* sabotieren; *v/i.* Sabotage treiben; '**rat·ten·ing** Sabotage *f*.

rat·tle ['rætl] **1.** Gerassel *n*; Geklapper *n*; Geplauder *n*, Geplapper *n*; Klapper *f*, Rassel *f*; (Todes)Röcheln *n*; **2.** *v/i.* rasseln, rattern; klappern; plappern; röcheln; *v/t.* rasseln mit; jagen; erschüttern; F nervös machen; ~ *off od. out* her(unter)rasseln, -schnurren; '**~-brain**, '**~-pate** Hohl-, Wirrkopf *m*; '**~-brained**, '**~-pat·ed** hohl-, wirrköpfig; '**rat·tler** Lärmmacher *m*; Schwätzer *m*; *sl.* Mordskerl *m*, -ding *n*; *Am.* F = '**rat·tle·snake** Klapperschlange *f*; '**rat·tle·trap** **1.** klapperig; **2.** Klapperkasten *m* (*Fahrzeug*).

rat·tling □ ['rætliŋ] rasselnd; F lebhaft, schneidig; *adv.* sehr, äußerst; *at a* ~ *pace* in rasendem Tempo.

rat·ty *sl.* ['ræti] nervös, gereizt.

rau·cous □ ['rɔːkəs] heiser, rauh.

rav·age ['rævidʒ] **1.** Verwüstung *f*; **2.** *v/t.* verwüsten, verheeren; *v/i.* Verheerungen anrichten.

rave [reiv] rasen, toben; phantasieren; schwärmen (*about, of* von).

rav·el ['rævəl] *v/t.* verwickeln; *a.* ~ *out* entflechten, auftrennen; *v/i. a.* ~ *out* ausfasern, aufgehen.

ra·ven[1] ['reivn] Rabe *m*.

rav·en² ['rævn] **1.** *s. ravin*; **2.** rauben; gierig sein; verschlingen; **rav·en·ous** □ ['rævənəs] gefräßig; heißhungrig; '**rav·en·ous·ness** Raubgier *f*; Gefräßigkeit *f*; Heißhunger *m*.
rav·in *rhet.* ['rævin] Raubgier *f*; Beute *f*.
ra·vine [rə'vi:n] Schlucht *f*; Hohlweg *m*.
rav·ings ['reiviŋz] *pl.* Delirien *n/pl.*; irres Gerede *n*.
rav·ish ['rævif] entzücken, hinreißen; vergewaltigen; *rhet.* rauben, entreißen; '**rav·ish·er** Schänder *m*; '**rav·ish·ing** □ hinreißend; entzückend; '**rav·ish·ment** Schändung *f*; Entzücken *n*.
raw □ [rɔ:] **1.** roh (*ungekocht*; *unbearbeitet*); Roh...; wund; rauh (*Wetter*); ungeübt, unerfahren; ~ *material* Rohmaterial *n*; *he got a ~ deal sl.* man hat ihm übel mitgespielt; **2.** wunde *od.* empfindliche Stelle *f* (*bsd. fig.*); '**~-boned** hager, knochig; '**~·hide** Rohleder *n*; '**raw·ness** Roheit *f*; Rauhigkeit *f*; Unerfahrenheit *f*.
ray¹ [rei] **1.** Strahl *m* (*a.* ⚘); *fig.* Schimmer *m*; **2.** ausstrahlen.
ray² *ichth.* [~] Rochen *m*.
ray·less ['reilis] strahlenlos.
ray·on ['reiɔn] Kunstseide *f*.
raze [reiz] *Haus etc.* abreißen; *Festung* schleifen; ~ *to the ground* dem Erdboden gleichmachen.
ra·zor ['reizə] Rasiermesser *n*, -apparat *m*; '**~-blade** Rasierklinge *f*; '**~-'edge** *fig. des* Messers Schneide *f*, kritische Lage *f*; '**~-strop** Streichriemen *m*.
razz *Am. sl.* [ræz] aufziehen.
raz·zi·a ['ræziə] Beute-, Raubzug *m*.
raz·zle-daz·zle *sl.* ['ræzldæzl] Durcheinander *n*; Schwindel *m*; Tamtam *n*; Sauftour *f*.
re ⚖, ✝ [ri:] betrifft, bezüglich.
re... [~] wieder...; zurück...; neu...; um...
reach [ri:tʃ] **1.** Ausstrecken *n*; Griff *m*; Reichweite *f*; Fassungskraft *f*, Horizont *m*; Flußabschnitt *m*, -strecke *f*; *beyond ~*, *out of ~* unerreichbar; *within easy ~* leicht erreichbar; **2.** *v/i. a. ~ out* (mit der Hand) reichen, langen, greifen; reichen, sich erstrecken (*to* bis); *v/t.* (hin-, her)reichen, (-)langen; *oft ~ out* ausstrecken; erreichen.
reach-me-downs F ['ri:tʃmi'daunz] *pl.* Kleider *n/pl.* von der Stange.
re·act [ri:'ækt] reagieren (*to* auf *acc.*); (ein)wirken (*on, upon* auf *acc.*); sich auflehnen (*against* gegen).
re·ac·tion [ri'ækʃən] Reaktion *f* (*to* auf *acc.*), Rückwirkung *f* (*upon* auf *acc.*); *pol.* Rückschritt *m*; **re'ac·tion·ar·y** *bsd. pol.* [~ʃnəri] **1.** reaktionär; **2.** Reaktionär *m*.
re·ac·tive □ [ri:'æktiv] rück-, gegenwirkend; **re'ac·tor** *phys.* Reaktor *m*, Umwandlungsanlage *f*.
read 1. [ri:d] (*irr.*) *v/t.* lesen (*a. fig.*); deuten; (an)zeigen (*Thermometer etc.*); ~ *off* ablesen; ~ *out* laut (vor-) lesen; zu Ende lesen; ~ *to s.o.* j-m vorlesen; *v/i.* lesen; studieren; sich *gut etc.* lesen; *so u. so* lauten; **2.** [red] *pret. u. p.p. von 1*; **3.** [red] *adj.* belesen, bewandert (*in* in *dat.*).
read·a·ble □ ['ri:dəbl] lesbar; leserlich; lesenswert.
re-ad·dress ['ri:ə'dres] umadressieren.
read·er ['ri:də] Leser(in); Vorleser (-in); *typ.* Korrektor *m*; *univ.* Dozent *m* (*in* für); Lesebuch *n*; '**read·er·ship** Vorleseramt *n*; *univ.* Dozentenstelle *f*.
read·i·ly ['redili] *adv.* bereit, gleich, leicht; gern; '**read·i·ness** Bereitschaft *f*; Bereitwilligkeit *f*; Schnelligkeit *f*; Raschheit *f*; Fertigkeit *f*; ~ *of mind od. wit* Geistesgegenwart *f*.
read·ing ['ri:diŋ] Lesen *n*; Lesung *f* (*a. parl.*); Stand *m des Thermometers etc.*; Belesenheit *f*; Lektüre *f*; Lesart *f*, Version *f*; Auffassung *f*; *attr.* Lese...; ~ **mat·ter** Lesestoff *m*, Lektüre *f*; '**~-room** Lesesaal *m*, -zimmer *n*.
re·ad·just ['ri:ə'dʒʌst] wieder in Ordnung bringen; wieder anpassen; *pol. etc.* neu orientieren; '**re·ad·'just·ment** Wiederanpassung *f*; Neuordnung *f*.
re·ad·mis·sion ['ri:əd'miʃən] Wiederzulassung *f*.
re·ad·mit ['ri:əd'mit] wieder zulassen; '**re·ad'mit·tance** Wiederzulassung *f*.
read·y ['redi] **1.** *adj.* □ bereit, fertig; bereitwillig, geneigt; schnell bei der Hand; im Begriff (*to inf.* zu *inf.*);

schnell; gewandt (*at, in* in *dat.*); bequem, leicht; gleich zur Hand, nahe; ✝ bar; ⚓ klar; ~ *reckoner* Rechentabelle *f*; ~ *for action* gefechtsbereit; ~ *for take-off* ✈ startbereit; ~ *for use* gebrauchsfertig; ~ *to serve* tafelfertig; *make od. get* ~ (sich) fertig machen; **2.** *adv.* fertig; *readier* schneller; *readiest* am schnellsten; **3.** *su. at the* ~ schußfertig; **'~-'made** fertig, Konfektions... (*Kleidung*); *fig.* schematisch, alltäglich; **'~-to-'wear** Konfektions...

re·af·firm ['riːə'fəːm] nochmals versichern.

re·a·gent ⚗ [riː'eidʒənt] Reagens *n.*

re·al □ [riəl] wirklich, tatsächlich, real; echt; ~ **es·tate** Grundbesitz *m*, Immobilien *f/pl.*

re·a·lign ['riːə'lain] politisch neuordnen; **'re·a'lign·ment** politische Neuordnung *f.*

re·a·lism ['riəlizəm] Realismus *m*; **'re·al·ist 1.** Realist *m*; **2.** = **re·al'is·tic** (*~ally*) realistisch; sachlich; wirklichkeitsnah; **re·al·i·ty** [ri'æliti] Wirklichkeit *f*; **re·al·iz·a·ble** □ ['riəlaizəbl] zu verwirklichen(d); verwertbar; **re·al·i'za·tion** Verwirklichung *f*; Vergegenwärtigung *f*, Erkenntnis *f*; ✝ Verwertung *f*, Realisierung *f*; **'re·al·ize** merken, sich klarmachen, sich im klaren sein über *acc.*, erkennen, sich vergegenwärtigen; verwirklichen, in die Tat umsetzen; ✝ realisieren, zu Geld machen; *Gewinn* erzielen; **'re·al·ly** wirklich, in der Tat.

realm [relm] Königreich *n*; *fig.* Reich *n*; *Peer of the* ~ Mitglied *n* des Oberhauses.

re·al·tor *Am.* ['riəltə] Grundstücksmakler *m*; **'re·al·ty** ⚖ Grundeigentum *n.*

ream[1] [riːm] Ries *n* (*Papier*).

ream[2] ⊕ [~] *Loch* erweitern; ⊕ *mst* ~ *out* nachbohren; **'ream·er** Reibahle *f.*

re·an·i·mate ['riː'ænimeit] wiederbeleben; **'re·an·i'ma·tion** Wiederbelebung *f.*

reap [riːp] *Korn* schneiden; *Feld* mähen; *fig.* ernten; **'reap·er** Schnitter(in); Mähmaschine *f*; **'reap·ing** Ernten *n*; **'reap·ing-hook** Sichel *f*; **'reap·ing-ma·chine** Mähmaschine *f.*

re·ap·pear ['riːə'piə] wieder erscheinen; **'re·ap'pear·ance** Wiedererscheinen *n.*

re·ap·pli·ca·tion ['riːæpli'keiʃən] wiederholte Anwendung *f.*

re·ap·point ['riːə'pɔint] wiederanstellen, -ernennen.

re·ap·prais·al ['riːə'preizəl] Neubeurteilung *f.*

rear[1] [riə] *v/t.* auf-, großziehen; züchten; *rhet.* errichten; *v/i.* sich aufrichten.

rear[2] [~] **1.** Rück-, Hinterseite *f*; Hintergrund *m*; *mot.*, ⚓ Heck *n*; ⚔ Nachhut *f*; hinterer Teil *m*; *at the* ~ *of, in (the)* ~ *of* hinter (*dat.*); *from the* ~ von hinten; **2.** Hinter..., Rück..., Nach...; *~-end collision mot.* Auffahrunfall *m*; *~-view mirror mot.* Rückspiegel *m*; ~ *wheel drive mot.* Hinterradantrieb *m*; ~ *window mot.* Heckscheibe *f*; **'~-'ad·mi·ral** ⚓ Konteradmiral *m*; ~ **ex·it** Hinterausgang *m*; **'~-guard** ⚔ Nachhut *f*; **'~-lamp** *mot.* Schlußlicht *n.*

re-arm ['riː'ɑːm] aufrüsten; **'re-'ar·ma·ment** Aufrüstung *f.*

rear·most ['riəməust] hinterst.

re·ar·range ['riːə'reindʒ] neu ordnen.

rear·ward ['riəwəd] **1.** *adj.* rückwärtig; **2.** *adv. a.* *~s* rückwärts.

re·as·cend ['riːə'send] wieder aufsteigen.

rea·son ['riːzn] **1.** Vernunft *f*; Verstand *m*; Recht *n*, Billigkeit *f*; Ursache *f*, Grund *m*; *by* ~ *of* wegen; *for this* ~ aus diesem Grund; *listen to* ~ Vernunft annehmen; *it stands to* ~ *that ...* es leuchtet ein, daß; **2.** *v/i.* logisch *od.* vernünftig denken; schließen; urteilen; argumentieren; *v/t. a.* ~ *out* durchdenken; ~ *away* wegdisputieren; ~ *s.o. into (out of) s.th.* j-m et. ein- (aus)reden; *~ed* (wohl)durchdacht; **'rea·son·a·ble** □ vernünftig; billig; mäßig; angemessen; leidlich; **'rea·son·a·bly** ziemlich, leidlich; **'rea·son·er** Denker(in); **'rea·son·ing** Urteilen *n*; Schluß *m*; Beweisführung *f*; *attr.* Denk..., Urteils...

re·as·semble ['riːə'sembl] (sich) wieder versammeln.

re·as·sert ['riːə'səːt] wieder behaupten.

re·as·sur·ance [riːə'ʃuərəns] wiederholte Versicherung *f*; Beruhi-

gung *f*; **re·as'sure** wieder versichern; (wieder) beruhigen.
re·a·wak·en [ri:ə'weikən] wieder erwecken; wieder erwachen.
re·bap·tize ['ri:bæp'taiz] wiedertaufen.
re·bate¹ ✝ ['ri:beit] Rabatt *m*, Abzug *m*; Rückzahlung *f*.
re·bate² ⊕ ['ræbit] **1.** Falz *m*, Nut *f*; **2.** (ein)falzen.
reb·el 1. ['rebl] Rebell *m*; Empörer *m*, Aufrührer *m*; **2.** [~] aufrührerisch, rebellisch; *fig.* aufsässig, widerspenstig; **3.** [ri'bel] rebellieren, sich empören, sich auflehnen; **re'bel·lion** [~jən] Aufruhr *m*, -lehnung *f*, Rebellion *f*, Empörung *f*; **re'bel·lious** = *rebel 2.*
re·birth ['ri:'bə:θ] Wiedergeburt *f*.
re·bound [ri'baund] **1.** zurückprallen; **2.** Rückprall *m*, -schlag *m*.
re·buff [ri'bʌf] **1.** Zurück-, Abweisung *f*; **2.** zurück-, abweisen.
re·build ['ri:'bild] (*irr. build*) wieder (auf)bauen.
re·buke [ri'bju:k] **1.** Tadel *m*, Rüge *f*; **2.** tadeln, rügen.
re·bus ['ri:bəs] Rebus *m*, *n*, Bilderrätsel *n*.
re·but [ri'bʌt] zurückweisen; widerlegen; **re'but·tal** Zurückweisung *f*.
re·cal·ci·trant [ri'kælsitrənt] widerspenstig.
re·call [ri'kɔ:l] **1.** Zurückrufung *f*; Abberufung *f*; Widerruf *m*; (Rück-) Erinnerung *f*; *total* ~ absolutes Gedächtnis *n*; *beyond* ~, *past* ~ unwiderruflich; 2. zurückrufen (*fig. to s.o.'s mind* j-m ins Gedächtnis); abberufen; *Ware* abrufen; (sich) erinnern an (*acc.*); *Gefühl* wieder wachrufen; widerrufen; ✝ *Kapital etc.* kündigen; ~ *that* daran erinnern, daß; *until* ~*ed* bis auf Widerruf.
re·cant [ri'kænt] (als irrig) widerrufen; **re·can·ta·tion** [ri:kæn'teiʃən] Widerruf(ung *f*) *m*.
re·cap¹ F ['ri:kæp] = *recapitulate*; *recapitulation*.
re·cap² *Am.* ['ri:'kæp] *Reifen* besohlen.
re·ca·pit·u·late [ri:kə'pitjuleit] kurz wiederholen, zs.-fassen; **'re·ca·pit·u'la·tion** kurze Wiederholung *f*.
re·cap·ture ['ri:'kæptʃə] **1.** Wiedererlangung *f*, -ergreifung *f*; *fig.* Wiederhervorholen *n*; **2.** wiedererlangen; wieder ergreifen; zurückerobern.
re·cast ['ri:kɑ:st] **1.** (*irr. cast*) ⊕ umgießen; umformen, neu gestalten; neu berechnen; *thea.* neu besetzen; **2.** Umformung *f etc.*
re·cede [ri:'si:d] zurücktreten, -weichen; ✝ zurückgehen; *receding* fliehend (*Kinn*, *Stirn*).
re·ceipt [ri'si:t] **1.** Empfang *m e-s Briefes etc.*; Eingang *m von Waren*; ✝ Empfangsschein *m*, Quittung *f*; (Koch)Rezept *n*; ~*s pl.* Einnahmen *f/pl.*; **2.** quittieren.
re·ceiv·a·ble [ri'si:vəbl] annehmbar; ✝ noch zu fordern(d), ausstehend; **re'ceive** *v/t. Besuch*, *Radio etc.* empfangen, erhalten, bekommen; *Eid etc.* abnehmen; *als Gast etc.* aufnehmen; annehmen, anerkennen; *v/i.* empfangen; **re'ceived** anerkannt; allgemein üblich; **re'ceiv·er** Empfänger *m* (*a. tel. u. Radio*); *teleph.* Hörer *m*; *a.* ~ *of stolen goods* Hehler *m*; *Steuer- etc.* Einnehmer *m*; *a. official* ~ ⚖ Masseverwalter *m*; *phys.*, ⚗ Rezipient *m*; **re'ceiv·er·ship** ⚖ Konkursverwaltung *f*; **re'ceiv·ing** Annahme *f*; *Radio*: Empfang *m*; Hehlerei *f*; ~ *set* Rundfunkempfänger *m*.
re·cen·cy ['ri:snsi] Neuheit *f*.
re·cen·sion [ri'senʃən] Durchsicht *f*, Prüfung *f e-s Textes*.
re·cent □ ['ri:snt] neu; frisch; modern; jüngst; *in* ~ *years* in den letzten Jahren; **'re·cent·ly** neulich, kürzlich, vor kurzem, unlängst; **'re·cent·ness** Neuheit *f*.
re·cep·ta·cle [ri'septəkl] Behälter *m*; *a. floral* ~ ⚘ Fruchtboden *m*.
re·cep·tion [ri'sepʃən] Aufnahme *f* (*a. fig.*), (*a.* Radio)Empfang *m*; Annahme *f*; **re'cep·tion·ist** Empfangsdame *f*, -herr *m*; **re'cep·tion-room** Gesellschaftszimmer *n*.
re·cep·tive □ [ri'septiv] empfänglich, aufnahmefähig (*of* für); **re·cep'tiv·i·ty** Empfänglichkeit *f*.
re·cess [ri'ses] **1.** Unterbrechung *f*, Pause *f*; *bsd. parl.* Ferien *pl.*; (entlegener) Winkel *m*; Nische *f*, Vertiefung *f*; ~*es pl. fig.* Tiefe(n *pl.*) *f*; **2.** zurücksetzen; ausbuchten.
re·ces·sion [ri'seʃən] Zurückziehen *n*, -treten *n*; ✝ Konjunkturrückgang *m*, rückläufige Bewegung *f*; **re'ces·sion·al** [~ʃənl] **1.** *eccl.* Schluß...; *parl.* Ferien...; **2.** *eccl.*

Schlußgesang *m*; **re'ces·sive** [~siv] zurücktretend; rezessiv.

re·chris·ten ['ri:'krisn] umtaufen.

re·cid·i·vist [ri'sidivist] Rückfällige *m*.

rec·ipe ['resipi] Rezept *n*; ~ **book** Kochbuch *n*.

re·cip·i·ent [ri'sipiənt] Empfänger (-in).

re·cip·ro·cal [ri'siprəkəl] **1.** wechsel-, gegenseitig; ⚡, *gr.*, *phls.* reziprok; **2.** ⚡ reziproker Wert *m*; **re'cip·ro·cate** [~keit] *v/i.* sich revanchieren, sich erkenntlich zeigen; ⊕ sich hin- und herbewegen; *reciprocating engine* Kolbenmotor *m*; *v/t. Glückwünsche etc.* austauschen, erwidern; **re·cip·ro'ca·tion** Hinundherbewegung *f*; Wechselwirkung *f*; Austausch *m*, Erwiderung *f*; **rec·i·proc·i·ty** [resi'prɔsiti] Gegenseitigkeit *f*.

re·cit·al [ri'saitl] Bericht *m*; Erzählung *f*; ⚖ Darlegung *f* des Sachverhalts; ♪ (Solo)Vortrag *m*, Konzert *n*; **rec·i·ta·tion** [resi'teiʃən] Hersagen *n*; Vortrag *m*, Rezitation *f*; **rec·i·ta·tive** ♪ [~tə'ti:v] **1.** rezitativartig; **2.** Rezitativ *n* (*Sprechgesang*); **re·cite** [ri'sait] vortragen, rezitieren; deklamieren; aufsagen; berichten; **re'cit·er** Vortragskünstler(in); Vortragsbuch *n*.

reck *poet.* [rek] sich kümmern (*of* um), fragen (*of* nach).

reck·less □ ['reklis] unbekümmert (*of* um); rücksichtslos; leichtsinnig, sorglos; **'reck·less·ness** Unbekümmertheit *f*; Rücksichtslosigkeit *f*; Leichtsinn *m*.

reck·on ['rekən] *v/t.* rechnen, zählen; *a.* ~ *for*, ~ *as* schätzen, halten für, ansehen als; ~ *up* zs.-rechnen, -zählen; *v/i.* rechnen; meinen, denken, vermuten; ~ (*up*)*on* rechnen, sich verlassen auf (*acc.*); ~ *with* rechnen mit *Tatsachen etc.*; **reck·on·er** ['reknə] Rechner(in); **'reck·on·ing** Rechnen *n*; (Ab)Rechnung *f*; Berechnung *f*; *be out in od. of one's* ~ *fig.* sich verrechnen *od.* verrechnet haben.

re·claim [ri'kleim] wiedergewinnen; *j.* bessern; bekehren; zähmen; zivilisieren; *Land* urbar machen; ⊕ aus Altmaterial gewinnen; zurückfordern; **re'claim·a·ble** verbesserungsfähig.

rec·la·ma·tion [reklə'meiʃən] Besserung *f*; Urbarmachung *f*; Zurückforderung *f*; Einspruch *m*.

re·cline [ri'klain] (sich) (zurück-) lehnen; ~ *upon fig.* sich stützen auf (*acc.*); **re·clin·ing chair** Lehnstuhl *m*.

re·cluse [ri'klu:s] **1.** zurückgezogen, einsiedlerisch; **2.** Einsiedler(in).

rec·og·ni·tion [rekəg'niʃən] Anerkennung *f*; (Wieder)Erkennen *n*; **rec·og·niz·a·ble** □ ['~naizəbl] erkennbar; **re·cog·ni·zance** ⚖ [ri'kɔgnizəns] schriftliche Verpflichtung *f*; Kaution *f*; **rec·og·nize** ['rekəgnaiz] anerkennen; (wieder-) erkennen; *auf der Straße* grüßen.

re·coil [ri'kɔil] **1.** zurückprallen; **2.** Rückstoß *m*, -lauf *m*.

rec·ol·lect[1] [rekə'lekt] sich erinnern (*gen.*) *od.* an (*acc.*).

re·col·lect[2] ['ri:kə'lekt] wieder sammeln; ~ *o.s.* sich fassen.

rec·ol·lec·tion [rekə'lekʃən] Erinnerung *f* (*of* an *acc.*); Gedächtnis *n*.

re·com·mence ['ri:kə'mens] wieder beginnen.

rec·om·mend [rekə'mend] empfehlen; **rec·om'mend·a·ble** empfehlenswert; **rec·om·men'da·tion** Empfehlung *f*; Vorschlag *m*; **rec·om'mend·a·to·ry** [~dətəri] empfehlend; Empfehlungs...

re·com·mis·sion ['ri:kə'miʃən] wieder an- *od.* einstellen.

re·com·mit ['ri:kə'mit] *parl. an e-n Ausschuß* zurückverweisen; ~ *to prison* wieder verhaften.

rec·om·pense ['rekəmpens] **1.** Belohnung *f*, Vergeltung *f*; Entgelt *n*, Ersatz *m*; **2.** *j. od. et.* belohnen, *et.* vergelten; *j.* entschädigen; *et.* ersetzen, wiedergutmachen.

re·com·pose ['ri:kəm'pəuz] neu zs.-setzen; wieder beruhigen.

rec·on·cil·a·ble ['rekənsailəbl] versöhnbar; vereinbar; **'rec·on·cile** versöhnen; in Einklang bringen (*with*, *to* mit); *Streit* schlichten; ~ *o.s. to* sich aussöhnen mit; sich abfinden mit; **'rec·on·cil·er** Versöhner(in); **rec·on·cil·i·a·tion** [~sili'eiʃən] Versöhnung *f*; Aussöhnung *f*.

re·con·dite □ *fig.* [ri'kɔndait] tief, dunkel; entlegen, ausgefallen.

re·con·di·tion ['ri:kən'diʃən] wieder herrichten; ⊕ überholen.

re·con·nais·sance ['ri'kɔnisəns] ⚔ Aufklärung *f*, Erkundung *f*; *fig.* Übersicht *f*; ~ **car** ⚔ Panzerspähwagen *m*; ~ **flight** ⚔ Aufklärungsflug *m*.

rec·on·noi·ter, rec·on·noi·tre ⚔ [rekə'nɔitə] erkunden, auskundschaften.

re·con·quer ['ri:'kɔŋkə] wiedererobern; **'re'con·quest** [~kwest] Wiedereroberung *f*.

re·con·sid·er ['ri:kən'sidə] wieder erwägen; **'re·con·sid·er'a·tion** nochmalige Erwägung *f*.

re·con·sti·tute ['ri:'kɔnstitju:t] wiederherstellen; **'re·con·sti'tu·tion** Wiederherstellung *f*.

re·con·struct ['ri:kəns'trʌkt] wiederaufbauen; *fig.* rekonstruieren; **'re·con'struc·tion** Wiederaufbau *m*, -herstellung *f*.

re·con·ver·sion ['ri:kən'və:ʃən] Umstellung *f auf Friedensproduktion*; **'re·con'vert** umstellen.

rec·ord[1] ['rekɔ:d] Aufzeichnung *f*; ⚖ Protokoll *n*; Akte *f*; schriftlicher Bericht *m*; Urkunde *f* (*a. fig.*); persönliche Vergangenheit *f*, Ruf *m*, Leumund *m* (*bsd. pol.*); Verzeichnis *n*; Wiedergabe *f*; Schallplatte *f*; *Sport*: Rekord *m*, Höchstleistung *f*; ~ *time* Rekordzeit *f*; *it is on* ~ es steht fest; *place on* ~ schriftlich niederlegen; *beat od. break the* ~ den Rekord brechen; *set up od. establish a* ~ e-n Rekord aufstellen; 2 *Office* Staatsarchiv *n*; *off the* ~ inoffiziell.

re·cord[2] [ri'kɔ:d] auf-, verzeichnen, eintragen; festhalten; *by* ~*ed delivery* ✉ per Einschreiben; **re'cord·er** Registrator *m*; Stadtrichter *m*; Aufnahme-, *bsd.* Tonbandgerät *n*; ♪ Blockflöte *f*; **re'cord·ing** *Radio*: Aufzeichnung *f*, Aufnahme *f*; **'rec·ord-play·er** Plattenspieler *m*.

re·count[1] [ri'kaunt] (eingehend) erzählen.

re-count[2] ['ri:'kaunt] **1.** nachzählen; **2.** Nachzählung *f*.

re·coup [ri'ku:p] *j.* schadlos halten (für); *et.* wieder einbringen.

re·course [ri'kɔ:s] Zuflucht *f*; *have* ~ *to* s-e Zuflucht nehmen zu.

re·cov·er[1] [ri'kʌvə] *v/t.* wiedererlangen, -finden, -gewinnen; wiedererobern; wieder einbringen, wiedergutmachen; *Schulden etc.* eintreiben; *be* ~*ed* wiederhergestellt sein (*Kranker*); *v/i.* sich erholen; wieder zu sich kommen; *a.* ~ *o.s.* sich fangen; ⚖ (*in one's suit* s-n Prozeß) gewinnen.

re-cov·er[2] ['ri:kʌvə] wiederbedekken; *Schirm etc.* neu beziehen.

re·cov·er·a·ble [ri'kʌvərəbl] wiedererlangbar; eintreibbar; wiederherstellbar; **re'cov·er·y** Wiedererlangung *f*; Wiederherstellung *f*; Genesung *f*, Erholung *f*; ~ *vehicle* Abschleppwagen *m*.

rec·re·ant ['rekriənt] **1.** □ feig; abtrünnig; **2.** Feigling *m*; Abtrünnige *m*.

rec·re·ate ['rekrieit] *v/t.* auf-, erfrischen; erquicken; erheitern; *v/i.* *a.* ~ *o.s.* sich erholen; **rec·re'a·tion** Erholung *f*; Erholungspause *f*; Erheiterung *f*; ~ *centre*, *Am.* ~ *center* Freizeitzentrum *n*; ~ *ground* Sport-, Spielplatz *m*; **'rec·re·a·tive** erquickend; erheiternd.

re·crim·i·nate [ri'krimineit] Gegenbeschuldigungen vorbringen; **re·crim·i'na·tion** Gegenbeschuldigung *f*; Gegenklage *f*.

re·cross ['ri:'krɔs] wieder überqueren.

re·cru·desce [ri:kru:'des] wieder aufbrechen (*Wunde*); wieder ausbrechen (*Krankheit*); **re·cru'des·cence** Wiederauf-, Wiederausbrechen *n*.

re·cruit [ri'kru:t] **1.** Rekrut *m*; *fig.* Neuling *m*; **2.** *v/t.* erneuern, ergänzen; rekrutieren; *Rekruten* ausheben, einziehen, anwerben; *Gesundheit* wiederherstellen; *v/i.* sich erholen; ⚔ Rekruten ausheben, werben; **re'cruit·ment** Rekrutierung *f*; Erholung *f*.

rec·tan·gle ['rektæŋgl] Rechteck *n*; **rec'tan·gu·lar** □ [~gjulə] rechteckig, -winklig.

rec·ti·fi·a·ble ['rektifaiəbl] zu berichtigen(d); **rec·ti·fi·ca·tion** [~fi'keiʃən] Berichtigung *f*; Verbesserung *f*; ⚗, ⚗ Rektifikation *f*; **rec·ti·fi·er** ['~faiə] Berichtiger *m*; ⚗ *etc.* Rektifizierer *m*; *Radio*: Gleichrichter *m*; **rec·ti·fy** ['~fai] berichtigen; verbessern; ⚗, ⚗ rektifizieren; ⚡, *Radio*: gleichrichten; **rec·ti·lin·e·al** [rekti'linjəl], **rec·ti'lin·e·ar** □ [~njə] geradlinig; **rec·ti·tude** ['rektitju:d] Geradheit *f*; Redlichkeit *f*, Aufrichtigkeit *f*.

rec·tor [ˈrektə] Pfarrer *m*; *univ.* Rektor *m*; (Schul)Direktor *m*; **rec·tor·ate** [ˈ~rit], ˈ**rec·tor·ship** Rektorat *n*; ˈ**rec·to·ry** Pfarre *f*; Pfarrhaus *n*.

rec·tum *anat.* [ˈrektəm] Mastdarm *m*.

re·cum·bent □ [riˈkʌmbənt] lehnend, liegend; ruhend.

re·cu·per·ate [riˈkjuːpəreit] sich erholen; **re·cu·perˈa·tion** Erholung *f*; **reˈcu·per·a·tive** [~rətiv] wiederherstellend.

re·cur [riˈkəː] *in Gedanken od. Worten* zurückkehren (*to* zu), -kommen (*to* auf *acc.*); wiederkehren, -kommen, sich wieder einstellen (*Gedanke etc.*); (periodisch) wiederkehren; ~ *to s.o.'s mind* j-m wieder ins Gedächtnis kommen, j-m wieder einfallen; ~*ring decimal* periodischer Dezimalbruch *m*; **re·cur·rence** [riˈkʌrəns] Wieder-, Rückkehr *f*; ~ *to* Zurückkommen *n* auf (*acc.*); **reˈcur·rent** □ wiederkehrend; *anat.* rückläufig; ~ *fever* Rückfallfieber *n*.

re·curve [riːˈkəːv] (sich) zurückbiegen.

rec·u·sant [ˈrekjuzənt] widerspenstig.

re·cy·cle [riːˈsaikl] wieder verwerten; **reˈcy·cling** Wiederverwertung *f*, Recycling *n*.

red [red] **1.** rot (*engS. pol.*); ♀ *Cross* Rotes Kreuz *n*; ~ *currant* Johannisbeere *f*; ~ *deer* Rotwild *n*; ~ *ensign* britische Handelsflagge *f*; ~ *heat* Rotglut *f*; ~ *herring* Bückling *m*; *draw a* ~ *herring across the trail* e-n Ablenkungsversuch machen; ~ *lead* Mennige *f*; *paint the town* ~ *sl.* auf die Pauke hauen; **2.** Rot *n*; *bsd. pol.* Rote *m*; *bsd. Am.* F roter Heller *m*; *see* ~ rot sehen, wild werden; *be in the* ~ *Am.* F in Schulden stecken.

re·dact [riˈdækt] abfassen; herausgeben; **reˈdac·tion** Redaktion *f*, Fassung *f*; Neuausgabe *f*.

red·breast [ˈredbrest] *a. robin* ~ Rotkehlchen *n*; ˈ**Red·brick** die Provinzuniversitäten *f/pl.*; ˈ**red·cap** Militärpolizist *m*; *Am.* Gepäckträger *m*; **red·den** [ˈredn] (sich) röten; erröten; ˈ**red·dish** rötlich; **red·dle** [ˈ~l] Rötel *m*.

re·dec·o·rate [ˈriːˈdekəreit] *Zimmer* renovieren (lassen); ˈ**re·dec·oˈra·tion** Renovierung *f*.

re·deem [riˈdiːm] zurück-, loskaufen; aus-, ablösen; *Pfand, Versprechen* einlösen; ✝ amortisieren; büßen, wiedergutmachen; *Zeit* wieder einbringen; ersetzen, entschädigen für; erlösen; bewahren (*from* vor *dat.*); **reˈdeem·a·ble** ablösbar; tilgbar; ✝ kündbar; wiedergutzumachen(d); wiedererlangbar; **Reˈdeem·er** Erlöser *m*, Heiland *m*.

re·de·liv·er [ˈriːdiˈlivə] wieder ab-, ausliefern; wieder befreien.

re·demp·tion [riˈdempʃən] Rückkauf *m*; Auslösung *f*; ✝ Amortisation *f*; Wiedergutmachung *f*; Erlösung *f*; **reˈdemp·tion·er** *hist.* Amerikaeinwanderer *m*, der s-e Überfahrt abdiente; **reˈdemp·tive** erlösend.

re·de·ploy [ˈriːdiˈplɔi] umgruppieren.

re·de·vel·op [ˈriːdiˈveləp] *Haus, Stadtteil* sanieren; ˈ**re·deˈvel·op·ment** Sanierung *f e-s Hauses od. Stadtteils.*

red...: ˈ~**faced** mit rotem Kopf; ˈ~**haired** rothaarig; ˈ~-ˈ**hand·ed:** *catch s.o.* ~ j. auf frischer Tat ertappen; ˈ~**head** Rotschopf *m*; Hitzkopf *m*; ˈ~-ˈ**head·ed** rothaarig; ˈ~-ˈ**hot** rotglühend; *fig.* hitzig.

re·dif·fu·sion [ˈriːdiˈfjuːʒən] Übernahme *f* e-s Radio- *od.* Fernsehprogramms.

Red In·di·an [reˈdindjən] Indianer (-in).

red·in·te·grate [reˈdintigreit] wiederherstellen, erneuern; **red·in·teˈgra·tion** Wiederherstellung *f*.

re·di·rect [ˈriːdiˈrekt] *Brief* umadressieren, nachsenden.

re·dis·count [riːˈdiskaunt] **1.** rediskontieren; **2.** Rediskont(ierung *f*) *m*.

re·dis·cov·er [ˈriːdisˈkʌvə] wieder-entdecken.

re·dis·trib·ute [ˈriːdisˈtribjuːt] neu verteilen.

red-let·ter day [ˈredˈletəˈdei] Fest-, *fig.* Freuden-, Glückstag *m*.

red-light dis·trict [ˈredlaitˈdistrikt] Bordellviertel *n*.

red·ness [ˈrednis] Röte *f*.

re·do [ˈriːˈdu] (*irr. do*) neu machen.

red·o·lence ['redəuləns] Duft *m*; '**red·o·lent** duftend (*of* nach); *be* ~ *of fig.* gemahnen an.

re·dou·ble [ri'dʌbl] (sich) verdoppeln.

re·doubt ⚔ [ri'daut] Redoute *f*; **re'doubt·a·ble** *rhet.* fürchterlich.

re·dound [ri'daund]: ~ *to* beitragen, gereichen, führen zu; ~ (*up*)*on* zurückfallen auf (*acc.*).

re·draft ['ri:'drɑ:ft] **1.** neuer Entwurf *m*; ✝ Rückwechsel *m*; **2.** neu entwerfen.

re·dress [ri'dres] **1.** Abhilfe *f*; Wiedergutmachung *f*; ⚖ Entschädigung *f*; *legal* ~ Rechtshilfe *f*; **2.** abhelfen (*dat.*); wiedergutmachen.

red...: '**~skin** Rothaut *f* (*Indianer*); '**~start** *orn.* Rotschwänzchen *n*; ~ **tape**, **~-tap·ism** ['~'teipizəm] Bürokratismus *m*, Amtsschimmel *m*; '**~-'tap·ist** Bürokrat *m*, Aktenmensch *m*.

re·duce [ri'dju:s] *fig.* zurückführen, bringen (*to* auf, in *acc.*, zu); verwandeln (*to* in *acc.*); verringern, -mindern; verkleinern; einschränken; *Preise* herabsetzen; *fig.* herunterbringen; bezwingen; zwingen (*to* zu); ⚗, ⚗ reduzieren; ⚕ einrenken; ✝ *Konten* abstimmen; F e-e Abmagerungskur machen; ~ *to writing* schriftlich niederlegen; **re'duc·i·ble** zurückführbar, reduzierbar (*to* auf *acc.*); **re·duc·tion** [ri'dʌkʃən] Reduktion *f*; *fig.* Zurückführung *f*; Verwandlung *f*; Herabsetzung *f*, (Preis)Nachlaß *m*, Rabatt *m*; Verminderung *f*; Verkleinerung *f e-s Bildes etc.*; Bezwingung *f*; ⚕ Einrenkung *f*.

re·dun·dance, **re·dun·dan·cy** [ri'dʌndəns(i)] Überfülle *f*, Überfluß *m*; Arbeitslosigkeit *f*; **re'dun·dant** □ überflüssig, -zählig; arbeitslos; übermäßig; üppig; weitschweifig.

re·du·pli·cate [ri'dju:plikeit] verdoppeln; wiederholen; **re·du·pli·'ca·tion** Verdoppelung *f*.

red·wood ['redwud] Rotholz *n*, Redwood *n*.

re·dye ['ri:'dai] (wieder)auffärben.

re·ech·o [ri:'ekəu] widerhallen.

reed [ri:d] Ried *n*, Schilfrohr *n*; Rohrflöte *f*; *the* ~*s pl.* ♪ die Rohrblattinstrumente *n/pl.*

re-ed·it ['ri:'edit] neu herausgeben.

re-ed·u·ca·tion ['ri:edju'keiʃən] Umschulung *f*, Umerziehung *f*.

reed·y ['ri:di] schilfreich; lang aufgeschossen; schrill; piepsend (*Stimme*).

reef[1] [ri:f] (Felsen)Riff *n*.

reef[2] ⚓ [~] **1.** Reff *n*; **2.** reffen.

reef·er[1] ['ri:fə] Seemannsjacke *f*.

reef·er[2] *Am. sl.* [~] Marihuana-Zigarette *f*.

reek [ri:k] **1.** Rauch *m*, Dampf *m*; Dunst *m*; **2.** rauchen, dampfen (*with* von); dunsten, *unangenehm* riechen (*of* nach); '**reek·y** rauchig; dunstig.

reel [ri:l] **1.** Haspel *f*; (Garn-, Film)Rolle *f*, Spule *f*; *schottischer Tanz*; **2.** *v/t.* haspeln; wickeln, spulen; ~ *off* abhaspeln, herunterleiern; *v/i.* wirbeln; schwanken; taumeln.

re-e·lect ['ri:i'lekt] wiederwählen; '**re-e'lec·tion** Wiederwahl *f*.

re-el·i·gi·ble ['ri:'elidʒəbl] wiederwählbar.

re-en·act ['ri:i'nækt] wieder in Kraft setzen; *thea.* neu inszenieren; wiederholen.

re-en·force ['ri:in'fɔ:s] *etc.* = *reinforce etc.*

re-en·gage ['ri:in'geidʒ] *j.* wieder ein-, anstellen.

re-en·list ⚔ ['ri:in'list] wieder eintreten, weiter dienen.

re-en·ter ['ri:'entə] wieder eintreten (in *acc.*); '**re-'ent·er·ing**, **re·en·trant** [ri:'entrənt] einspringend (*Winkel*); '**re-'en·try** *Raumfahrt*: Wiedereintritt *m* in die Erdatmosphäre.

re-es·tab·lish ['ri:is'tæbliʃ] wiederherstellen; '**re-es'tab·lish·ment** Wiederherstellung *f*.

reeve[1] ⚓ [ri:v] einscheren.

reeve[2] [~] Vogt *m*, Statthalter *m*; Aufseher *m*.

re-ex·am·i·na·tion ['ri:igzæmi'neiʃən] nochmalige Prüfung *f*; '**re-ex'am·ine** nochmals prüfen.

re-ex·change ['ri:iks'tʃeindʒ] Rücktausch *m*; ✝ Rückwechsel *m*.

re·fec·tion [ri'fekʃən] Erfrischung *f*; **re'fec·to·ry** [~təri] Refektorium *n*, Speisesaal *m*.

re·fer [ri'fə:]: ~ *to* verweisen, überweisen an (*acc.*); sich beziehen, anspielen auf (*acc.*); sprechen von, erwähnen (*acc.*); gelten für (*od.*

dat.); befragen (*acc.*), nachschlagen in (*dat.*); zurückführen auf (*acc.*), zuschreiben (*dat.*); **re'fer·a·ble:** ~ *to* zu beziehen(d) auf (*acc.*); zuzuschreiben(d) (*dat.*); **ref·er·ee** [refə'ri:] Schiedsrichter *m*; *Boxen*: Ringrichter *m*; *parl. etc.* Referent *m*, Sachbearbeiter *m*; **ref·er·ence** ['refrəns] Referenz *f*, Empfehlung *f*, Zeugnis *n*; Bezugnahme *f*, Verweisung *f* (*to* auf *acc.*); Anspielung *f*; Beziehung *f*; Auskunft(geber *m*) *f*; *in od. with* ~ *to* in betreff, hinsichtlich (*gen.*), in bezug auf (*acc.*); *terms pl. of* ~ Richtlinien *f/pl.*; Zuständigkeitsbereich *m*; *work of* ~, ~ *book* Nachschlagewerk *n*; ~ *library* Handbibliothek *f*; ~ *number* Aktenzeichen *n*; *make* ~ *to* erwähnen; eingehen auf (*acc.*).

ref·er·en·dum [refə'rendəm] Volksentscheid *m*.

re·fill ['ri:fil] **1.** Nachfüllung *f*; Ersatzfüllung *f*, -mine *f*, -batterie *f*; **2.** (sich) wieder füllen, auffüllen.

re·fine [ri'fain] verfeinern, veredeln (*a.* ⊕ *u. fig.*); ⊕ raffinieren, (*a. fig.*) läutern; *v/i.* sich verfeinern *od.* veredeln *od.* läutern; klügeln, tüfteln (*on, upon* an *dat.*); ~ (*up*)*on et.* verfeinern, verbessern; **re'fine·ment** Verfeinerung *f*, Veredlung *f*; Läuterung *f*; Feinheit *f*, Bildung *f*; Klügelei *f*, Spitzfindigkeit *f*; **re'fin·er** Verfeinerer *m*; ⊕ Raffineur *m*; Klügler(in); **re'fin·er·y** ⊕ Raffinerie *f*; *metall.* (Eisen)Hütte *f*.

re·fit ⚓ ['ri:'fit] **1.** *v/t.* ausbessern; neu ausrüsten; *v/i.* ausgebessert werden; **2.** Ausbesserung *f*.

re·flect [ri'flekt] *v/t.* zurückwerfen, reflektieren; zurückstrahlen, widerspiegeln (*a. fig.*); zum Ausdruck bringen; *v/i.* ~ (*up*)*on* nachdenken über (*acc.*); überlegen (*acc.*); sich abfällig äußern über (*acc.*); ein schlechtes Licht werfen auf (*acc.*); **re'flec·tion** Rückstrahlung *f*, Reflexion *f*, (Wider)Spiegelung *f*; Reflex *m*; Spiegelbild *n*; Überlegung *f*; Gedanke *m*; abfällige Bemerkung *f*; Makel *m*; **re'flec·tive** □ reflektierend; nachdenklich; **re'flec·tor** Reflektor *m*; Scheinwerfer *m*; Rückstrahler *m*.

re·flex ['ri:fleks] **1.** zurückgebogen; Reflex...; **2.** Widerschein *m*, (*a. physiol.*) Reflex *m*; ~ **ac·tion** Reflex(-bewegung *f*) *m*; ~ **cam·er·a** Spiegelreflexkamera *f*; **re·flex·ion** [ri'flekʃən] = *reflection*; **re·flex·ive** □ [ri'fleksiv] zurückwirkend; *gr.* reflexiv, rückbezüglich.

ref·lu·ent ['refluənt] zurückflutend.

re·flux ['ri:flʌks] Rückfluß *m*; Ebbe *f*.

re·for·est·a·tion ['ri:fɔris'teiʃən] [Aufforstung *f*.]

re·form[1] [ri'fɔ:m] **1.** Verbesserung *f*, Reform *f*; **2.** verbessern, reformieren; (sich) bessern.

re-form[2] ['ri:'fɔ:m] (sich) neu bilden; ⚔ sich wieder formieren.

ref·or·ma·tion [refə'meiʃən] Umgestaltung *f*; Besserung *f*; ♀ *eccl.* Reformation *f*; **re·form·a·to·ry** [ri'fɔ:mətəri] **1.** bessernd; **2.** Besserungsanstalt *f*; **re'formed** ge-, verbessert; *eccl.* reformiert; **re'form·er** Reformator *m*; **re'form·ist** reformistisch.

re·found ['ri:faund] umgießen.

re·fract [ri'frækt] *Strahlen* brechen; ~*ing telescope* Refraktor *m*; **re'frac·tion** Strahlenbrechung *f*; **re'frac·tive** *opt.* Brechungs...; **re'frac·tor** *opt.* Refraktor *m*; **re'frac·to·ri·ness** Widerspenstigkeit *f*; Hartnäckigkeit *f*; ⚗ Strengflüssigkeit *f*; **re'frac·to·ry** **1.** □ widerspenstig; aufsässig; hartnäckig; ⊕ feuerfest; ⚗ strengflüssig; **2.** ⊕ feuerfester Baustoff *m*.

re·frain[1] [ri'frein] sich enthalten (*from gen.*), unterlassen (*from acc.*).

re·frain[2] [~] Kehrreim *m*, Refrain *m*.

re·fran·gi·ble *phys.* [ri'frændʒəbl] brechbar.

re·fresh [ri'freʃ] (sich) erfrischen; auffrischen; **re'fresh·er** F Erfrischung *f*; *fig.* Auffrischung *f*; ⚖ Nachschuß *m*; ~ *course* Auffrischungs-, Fortbildungskurs *m*; **re'fresh·ment** Erfrischung *f*, Erquickung *f*; ~ *room* Erfrischungsraum *m*.

re·frig·er·ant [ri'fridʒərənt] **1.** kühlend; **2.** Kühlmittel *n*, -trank *m*; **re'frig·er·ate** [~reit] kühlen; **re'frig·er·at·ing** Kühl...; Eis...; **re·frig·er'a·tion** Abkühlung *f*; **re'frig·er·a·tor** Kühlschrank *m*, -raum *m*; ~ *lorry* Kühlwagen *m*.

re·fu·el [ri:'fjuəl] tanken.

ref·uge ['refju:dʒ] Zuflucht(sstätte) *f*; *a. street-*~ Verkehrsinsel *f*;

mount. (Schutz)Hütte *f*; *take ~ in* s-e Zuflucht nehmen zu; **ref·u·gee** [~ˈdʒiː] Flüchtling *m*; *~ camp* Flüchtlingslager *n*.
re·ful·gence [riˈfʌldʒəns] Glanz *m*; **reˈful·gent** □ strahlend.
re·fund 1. [riːˈfʌnd] zurückzahlen; **2.** [ˈriːfʌnd] Rückzahlung *f*.
re·fur·bish [ˈriːˈfəːbiʃ] aufpolieren.
re·fur·nish [ˈriːˈfəːniʃ] neu möblieren.
re·fus·al [riˈfjuːzəl] abschlägige Antwort *f*; Weigerung *f*; Verweigerung *f*; Vorkaufsrecht *n* (*of* auf *acc.*).
re·fuse[1] [riˈfjuːz] *v/t.* abschlagen, verweigern; ab-, zurückweisen, ablehnen; scheuen vor (*dat.*); *v/t.* sich weigern; scheuen (*Pferd*).
ref·use[2] [ˈrefjuːs] Ausschuß *m*; Abfall *m*, Müll *m*; *fig.* Auswurf *m*.
ref·u·ta·ble □ [ˈrefjutəbl] widerlegbar; **ref·uta·tion** [refjuːˈteiʃən] Widerlegung *f*; **re·fute** [riˈfjuːt] widerlegen.
re·gain [riˈgein] wiedergewinnen.
re·gal □ [ˈriːgəl] königlich; Königs...
re·gale [riˈgeil] *v/t.* festlich bewirten; erfreuen; *v/i.* schwelgen (*on* in *dat.*).
re·ga·li·a [riˈgeiljə] *pl.* (Krönungs-) Insignien *pl.*
re·gard [riˈgɑːd] **1.** *fester* Blick *m*; (Hoch)Achtung *f*, Rücksicht *f*; Beziehung *f*; *~s pl.* Grüße *m/pl.*, Empfehlungen *f/pl.*; *have ~ to* Rücksicht nehmen auf (*acc.*); berücksichtigen; sich beziehen auf (*acc.*); *with ~ to* in Hinsicht auf (*acc.*); *with kind ~s* mit herzlichen Grüßen; **2.** ansehen (*as* als); (be)achten; betrachten; betreffen; *as ~s* ... was ... anbetrifft; **reˈgard·ful** □ [~ful] rücksichtsvoll (*of* gegen); **reˈgard·ing** hinsichtlich, betreffs (*gen.*); **reˈgard·less** □ unbekümmert, sorglos; achtlos; *~ of* ohne Rücksicht auf (*acc.*); unbeschadet (*gen.*).
re·gat·ta [riˈgætə] Regatta *f*.
re·gen·cy [ˈriːdʒənsi] Regentschaft *f*.
re·gen·er·ate 1. [riˈdʒenəreit] (sich) erneuern; (sich) regenerieren; (sich) neu bilden; (sich) bessern; **2.** [~rit] wiedergeboren; **re·gen·er·a·tion** [~ˈreiʃən] Erneuerung *f*, *bsd. biol.* Neubildung *f*; *fig.* Wiedergeburt *f*; **reˈgen·er·a·tive** [~rətiv] *Radio*: Rückkoppelungs...
re·gent [ˈriːdʒənt] **1.** herrschend; **2.** Regent *m*; **ˈre·gent·ship** Regentschaft *f*.
reg·i·cide [ˈredʒisaid] Königsmord *m*; Königsmörder *m*.
ré·gime, re·gime [reiˈʒiːm] Regime *n*, Regierungsform *f*; herrschendes System *n*; = *regimen*.
reg·i·men [ˈredʒimen] Diätvorschriften *f/pl.*; Therapie *f*; *gr.* Rektion *f*; = *régime*.
reg·i·ment [ˈredʒimənt] **1.** ⚔ Regiment *n*; *fig.* Schar *f*; **2.** [ˈ~ment] reglementieren; organisieren; **reg·i·men·tal** [~ˈmentl] ⚔ Regiments-...; **reg·i·men·tal·ly** [~ˈmentəli] regimentsweise; **reg·iˈmen·tals** ⚔ *pl.* Uniform *f*; **reg·i·menˈta·tion** Reglementierung *f*; Organisierung *f*.
re·gion [ˈriːdʒən] Gegend *f*, Gebiet *n*, Region *f*; *fig.* Bereich *m*; **re·gion·al** [ˈ~dʒənl] **1.** □ örtlich; Orts...; *Radio*: *~ station* = **2.** Regionalsender *m*.
reg·is·ter [ˈredʒistə] **1.** Register *n*, Verzeichnis *n*; ⊕ Schieber *m*, Ventil *n*; ♪ Register *n*, Stimmumfang *m*; Zählwerk *n*; *cash ~* Registrierkasse *f*; *parish ~* Kirchenbuch *n*; **2.** registrieren *od.* eintragen (lassen); (an)zeigen, auf-, verzeichnen; *Sendung* einschreiben (lassen), *Gepäck* aufgeben, sich *polizeilich* melden; **ˈreg·is·tered** eingetragen; eingeschrieben (*Brief*); gesetzlich geschützt; *~ design* Gebrauchsmuster *n*.
reg·is·trar [redʒisˈtrɑː] Registrator *m*; Standesbeamte *m*; **reg·is·tra·tion** [~ˈtreiʃən] Registrierung *f*, Eintragung *f*; *~ fee* Anmeldegebühr *f*; **ˈreg·is·try** Eintragung *f*; Registratur *f*; Register *n*; *~ office* Standesamt *n*; *servants' ~* Stellenvermittlungsbüro *n*.
reg·nant [ˈregnənt] regierend.
re·gress [ˈriːgres] Rückkehr *f*; *fig.* Rückgang *m*; **re·gres·sion** [riˈgreʃən] Rückkehr *f*; *fig.* Rückgang *m*; *psych.* Regression *f*; **reˈgres·sive** □ [~siv] rückläufig; rückwirkend.
re·gret [riˈgret] **1.** Bedauern *n* (*at* über *acc.*); Schmerz *m*, Trauer *f* (*for* um); **2.** bedauern; bereuen; nachtrauern (*dat.*); *schmerzlich* vermissen; **reˈgret·ful** □ [~ful] be-

dauernd; *~ly* mit Bedauern; **re'gret·ta·ble** □ bedauerlich.

re·group ['riː'gruːp] umgruppieren; **re'group·ment** Umgruppierung *f*.

reg·u·lar ['regjulə] **1.** □ regelmäßig; regelrecht, richtig; ordentlich; pünktlich; ⚔ regulär; *eccl.* Ordens...; **2.** *eccl.* Ordensgeistliche *m*; ⚔ aktiver Soldat *m*; F Stammgast *m*, -kunde *m*; ~ (**gas**) *Am.* Normal(benzin) *n*; **reg·u·lar·i·ty** [~'læriti] Regelmäßigkeit *f*; Richtigkeit *f*, Ordnung *f*.

reg·u·late ['regjuleit] regeln, ordnen; regulieren, stellen; **'reg·u·lat·ing** ⊕ Regulier..., Stell...; **reg·u'la·tion** **1.** Regulierung *f*; Vorschrift *f*, Bestimmung *f*; Verordnung *f*; Regel *f*; *contrary to ~s* ordnungswidrig; **2.** vorschriftsmäßig; ⚔ Kommiß...; **reg·u·la·tive** □ ['~lətiv] regelnd; **reg·u·la·tor** ['~leitə] Regulierer *m*, Ordner *m*; ⊕ Regulator *m* (*a. Uhr*).

re·gur·gi·tate [riː'gəːdʒiteit] *v/t.* wieder ausströmen; *Essen* erbrechen; *v/i.* zurückfließen.

re·ha·bil·i·tate [riːə'biliteit] *Haus* renovieren; *Stadtviertel* sanieren; *ins Berufsleben* wiedereingliedern; rehabilitieren; **'re·ha·bil·i'ta·tion** Sanierung *f*; Wiedereingliederung *f*; Rehabilitierung *f*.

re·hash *fig.* ['riː'hæʃ] **1.** wieder durchkauen *od.* aufwärmen; **2.** Aufguß *m*.

re·hears·al [ri'həːsəl] *thea.*, ♪ Probe *f*; Wiederholung *f*; **re'hearse** *thea.* proben, einstudieren; wiederholen; aufsagen.

re·heat [riː'hiːt] wieder erhitzen.

reign [rein] **1.** Regierung *f*; *fig.* Herrschaft *f*; **2.** herrschen, regieren.

re·im·burse [riːim'bəːs] *j.* entschädigen; *Kosten* (wieder)erstatten; ⚕ decken; **re·im'burse·ment** Wiedererstattung *f*; Dekkung *f*; Entschädigung *f*.

rein [rein] **1.** Zügel *m*; *give ~ to* die Zügel schießen lassen (*dat.*); **2.** ~ *in*, ~ *up*, ~ *back* zügeln.

rein·deer *zo.* ['reindiə] Ren(tier) *n*.

re·in·force [riːin'fɔːs] **1.** verstärken; *~d concrete* ⊕ Stahlbeton *m*; **2.** ⊕ Verstärkung *f*; **re·in'force·ment** Verstärkung *f*; Armierung *f* (*Beton*); *~s pl.* ⚔ Verstärkungen *f/pl*.

re·in·stall ['riːin'stɔːl] wieder einsetzen; **'re·in'stal(l)·ment** Wiedereinsetzung *f*.

re·in·state ['riːin'steit] wieder einsetzen; wieder instandsetzen; **'re·in'state·ment** Wiedereinsetzung *f*; Wiederinstandsetzung *f*.

re·in·sur·ance ['riːn'ʃuərəns] Rückversicherung *f*; **re·in·sure** ['~'ʃuə] rückversichern.

re·in·vest ['riːin'vest] wieder investieren *od.* anlegen.

re·is·sue ['riː'isjuː] **1.** wieder ausgeben; **2.** Wiederausgabe *f*.

re·it·er·ate [riː'itəreit] (dauernd) wiederholen; **re·it·er'a·tion** Wiederholung *f*.

re·ject [ri'dʒekt] ver-, wegwerfen; *als wertlos* ausscheiden; ablehnen, ausschlagen; zurückweisen; **re'jec·tion** Verwerfung *f*; Ablehnung *f*; Zurückweisung *f*; Ausscheidung *f*; *~s pl.* Ausschußwaren *f/pl.*; **re·jec·tor cir·cuit** *Radio*: Sperrkreis *m*.

re·jig ['riː'dʒig] *Fabrik* maschinell neu ausstatten.

re·joice [ri'dʒɔis] *v/t.* erfreuen; *rejoiced at od. by* erfreut über (*acc.*); *v/i.* sich freuen (*at*, *in* über *acc.*); **re'joic·ing** **1.** □ freudig; **2.** *oft ~s pl.* Freude *f*; Freudenfest *n*.

re·join[1] ['riː'dʒɔin] (sich) wieder vereinigen (*to*, *with* mit); wieder zurückkehren zu; *j.* wieder treffen.

re·join[2] [ri'dʒɔin] erwidern; **re'join·der** Erwiderung *f*.

re·ju·ve·nate [ri'dʒuːvineit] verjüngen; **re·ju·ve'na·tion** Verjüngung *f*.

re·kin·dle ['riː'kindl] (sich) wieder entzünden.

re·lapse [ri'læps] **1.** Rückfall *m*; **2.** zurückfallen, rückfällig werden.

re·late [ri'leit] *v/t.* berichten, erzählen; in Verbindung bringen (*to*, *with* mit); *v/i.* sich beziehen (*to* auf *acc.*), betreffen (*to acc.*); **re'lat·ed** verwandt (*to* mit); **re'lat·er** Erzähler(in).

re·la·tion [ri'leiʃən] Bericht *m*; Erzählung *f*; Beziehung *f* (*with* zu); Verhältnis *n* (*to* zu *j-m*); Verwandtschaft *f*; Verwandte *m*, *f*; *in ~ to* in bezug auf (*acc.*); **re'la·tion·ship** Verwandtschaft *f*; Beziehung *f*.

rel·a·tive ['relətiv] **1.** □ sich beziehend, bezüglich (*to gen.*); *gr.*

relativ; bezüglich; verhältnismäßig; entsprechend; jeweilig; **2.** *gr.* Relativpronomen *n*; Verwandte *m, f*; **ˈrel·a·tive·ly** relativ, verhältnismäßig; **rel·aˈtiv·i·ty** Relativität *f*; *theory of ~ phys.* Relativitätstheorie *f*.

re·lax [riˈlæks] *v/t.* lockern; mildern; nachlassen in *e-r Bemühung etc.*; entspannen; *v/i.* nachlassen; ausspannen, -ruhen, sich entspannen; milder *od.* freundlicher werden; **re·laxˈa·tion** Lockerung *f*; Nachlassen *n*; Entspannung *f*, Erholung *f*; **reˈlaxed** entspannt; zwanglos.

re·lay[1] [riˈlei] **1.** frisches Gespann *n*; Ablösung(smannschaft) *f*; [ˈriːˈlei] ⚡ Relais *n*; *Radio*: Übertragung *f*; *~ race Sport*: Staffellauf *m*; *~ team Sport*: Staffel *f*; **2.** *Radio*: übertragen.

re-lay[2] [ˈriːˈlei] (*irr. lay*) *Kabel etc.* neu verlegen.

re·lease [riˈliːs] **1.** Freilassung *f*; *fig.* Befreiung *f*; Freigabe *f*; *Film*: *oft first ~* Uraufführung *f*; ⚖ Verzichtleistung *f*; ⊕, *phot.* Auslöser *m*; *press ~* Pressemitteilung *f*; **2.** frei-, loslassen, erlösen (*from* von); freigeben, entlassen; *Recht* aufgeben, übertragen; *Film* uraufführen; ⊕ auslösen.

rel·e·gate [ˈreligeit] verbannen; verweisen (*to* an *acc.*); *be ~d Sport*: absteigen; **rel·eˈga·tion** Verbannung *f*; Verweisung *f*; *Sport*: Abstieg *m*; *danger of ~ Sport*: Abstiegsgefahr *f*.

re·lent [riˈlent] sich erweichen lassen; **reˈlent·less** □ unbarmherzig.

rel·e·vance, rel·e·van·cy [ˈrelivəns(i)] Erheblichkeit *f*; Bedeutung *f* (*to* für); **ˈrel·e·vant** sachdienlich; zutreffend; wichtig, erheblich (*to* für); entsprechend (*to dat.*).

re·li·a·bil·i·ty [rilaiəˈbiliti] Zuverlässigkeit *f*; **reˈli·a·ble** □ zuverlässig.

re·li·ance [riˈlaiəns] Vertrauen *n*, Zutrauen *n*; Verlaß *m* (*on* auf *acc.*); *fig.* Stütze *f*; **reˈli·ant** vertrauensvoll.

rel·ic [ˈrelik] Überrest *m*, -bleibsel *n*; Reliquie *f*; **rel·ict** [ˈrelikt] Witwe *f*.

re·lief [riˈliːf] Erleichterung *f*; Trost *m*; (angenehme) Unterbrechung *f*; Unterstützung *f*; ⚔ Ablösung *f*; ⚔ Entsatz *m*; Beistand *m*; Hilfe *f*; ⚖ Abhilfe *f*; △ *etc.* Relief *n*, erhabene Arbeit *f*; *be on ~* Unterstützung beziehen; *poor ~* Armenpflege *f*; *~ work* Hilfswerk *n*; *~ works pl.* Notstandsarbeiten *f/pl.*; *stand out in ~ against* sich abheben gegen.

re·lieve [riˈliːv] erleichtern; mildern, lindern; *Arme etc.* unterstützen; ⚔ ablösen; ⚔ entsetzen; ⚖ (ab)helfen (*dat.*); befreien (*of* von); entheben (*of gen.*); hervortreten lassen; (angenehm) unterbrechen; *~ nature, ~ o.s.* s-e Notdurft verrichten.

re·lie·vo [riˈliːvəu] Relief *n*.

re·li·gion [riˈlidʒən] Religion *f*; Ordensleben *n*; *fig.* Ehrensache *f*.

re·li·gious □ [riˈlidʒəs] Religions...; religiös; fromm; *eccl.* Ordens...; gewissenhaft; **reˈli·gious·ness** Religiosität *f*.

re·lin·quish [riˈliŋkwiʃ] aufgeben; verzichten auf (*acc.*); *et.* loslassen; **reˈlin·quish·ment** Aufgeben *n*; Verzicht *m* (*of* auf *acc.*).

rel·i·quar·y [ˈrelikwəri] Reliquienschrein *m*.

rel·ish [ˈreliʃ] **1.** Geschmack *m*; Beigeschmack *m*; *fig.* Kostprobe *f*; Würze *f*; Behagen *n*, Genuß *m*; **2.** *v/t.* gern essen; Geschmack finden an (*dat.*); schmackhaft machen; *did you ~ your dinner?* hat Ihnen das Essen geschmeckt?; *v/i.* schmecken (*of* nach).

re·load [ˈriːˈləud] wieder laden.

re·lo·cate [ˈriːləuˈkeit] *Betrieb, Werk* verlegen; **ˈre·loˈca·tion** Umsiedlung *f*.

re·luc·tance [riˈlʌktəns] Widerstreben *n*; *bsd. phys.* Widerstand *m*; **reˈluc·tant** □ widerstrebend, -willig; zögernd; *be ~ to do* sich sträuben zu tun, ungern tun.

re·ly [riˈlai]: *~ (up)on* sich verlassen auf (*acc.*), bauen *od.* vertrauen auf (*acc.*).

re·main [riˈmein] **1.** (ver)bleiben; zurück-, übrigbleiben; **2.** *~s pl.* Überbleibsel *n/pl.*, -reste *m/pl.*; sterbliche Reste *m/pl.*; **reˈmain·der** [~də] Rest *m*; *Buchhandel*: Restauflage *f*, Remittenden *pl.*; ⚖ Anwartschaft *f*; **reˈmain·ing** übrig, restlich.

re·make 1. (*irr. make*) ['ri:'meik] *bsd. Film* neu machen; **2.** ['ri:meik] Neuverfilmung *f*.

re·mand [ri'ma:nd] **1.** (⚖ in die Untersuchungshaft) zurückschicken; **2.** (Zurücksendung *f* in die) Untersuchungshaft *f*; *be on* ~ sich in Untersuchungshaft befinden; *prisoner on* ~ Untersuchungsgefangene *m, f*; ~ **home** Jugendstrafanstalt *f*.

re·mark [ri'ma:k] **1.** Beachtung *f*; Bemerkung *f*; *pass a* ~ e-e Bemerkung machen; **2.** *v/t.* bemerken (*beobachten*; *äußern*); *v/i.* e-e Bemerkung machen, sich äußern (*upon* über *acc.*); **re'mark·a·ble** □ bemerkenswert; ungewöhnlich; **re'mark·a·ble·ness** Merkwürdigkeit *f*.

re·mar·riage ['ri:'mæridʒ] Wiederverheiratung *f*; **'re'mar·ry** (sich) wieder verheiraten; wieder heiraten.

re·me·di·a·ble □ [ri'mi:djəbl] heil-, abstellbar; **re·me·di·al** □ [ri'mi:djəl] heilend; abhelfend; ~ *teaching* Förderunterricht *m für Lernschwache*.

rem·e·dy ['remidi] **1.** (Heil-, Hilfs-, Gegen-, Rechts)Mittel *n*; (Ab-)Hilfe *f*; **2.** heilen; abhelfen (*dat.*).

re·mem·ber [ri'membə] sich erinnern an (*acc.*); denken an (*acc.*); beherzigen; *im Brief*: *j.* empfehlen; *j.* bedenken (*mit e-m Geschenk*); ~ *me to him!* grüßen Sie ihn von mir!; **re'mem·brance** Erinnerung *f*; Gedächtnis *n*; Andenken *n*; ~*s pl.* Empfehlungen *f/pl.*, Grüße *m/pl.*

re·mil·i·ta·rize ['ri:'militəraiz] remilitarisieren.

re·mind [ri'maind] erinnern (*of* an *acc.*); ~ *me to answer that letter* erinnere mich daran, den Brief zu beantworten; **re'mind·er** Mahnung *f*; Wink *m*.

rem·i·nisce [remi'nis] in Erinnerungen schwelgen; **rem·i·nis·cence** [-'nisns] Erinnerung *f*; **rem·i'nis·cent** □ (sich) erinnernd (*of* an *acc.*); Erinnerungs...; *be* ~ *of* erinnern an (*acc.*).

re·miss □ [ri'mis] schlaff, (nach-)lässig; **re'mis·si·ble** (er)läßlich; **re'mis·sion** Vergebung *f von Sünden*; Erlassung *f von Schulden*; Nachlassen *n*, Abnahme *f*; ~ *of fees* Gebührenerlaß *m*; **re'miss·ness** (Nach)Lässigkeit *f*.

re·mit [ri'mit] *v/t. Sünden* vergeben; *Schuld etc.* erlassen; nachlassen in (*dat.*); abstehen von; überweisen; ⚖ zurückverweisen; übersenden; *v/i.* nachlassen; **re'mit·tance** (*bsd.* Geld)Sendung *f*; Überweisung *f*; ⚕ Wechselsendung *f*, Rimesse *f*; **re·mit'tee** Empfänger *m*; **re'mit·tent** nachlassend, remittierend(es Fieber *n*); **re'mit·ter** (Geld)Sender *m*, ⚕ Remittent *m*.

rem·nant ['remnənt] Überrest *m*; (Stoff)Rest *m*; ~ *sale* Resteverkauf *m*.

re·mod·el ['ri:'mɔdl] umbilden.

re·mon·strance [ri'mɔnstrəns] Vorstellung *f*, Einwendung *f*; **re'mon·strant** Einspruchserhebende *m*; **re·mon·strate** ['remənstreit] Vorstellungen machen (*on* über *acc.*; *with s.o.* j-m); einwenden (*that* daß).

re·morse [ri'mɔ:s] Gewissensbisse *m/pl.*; **re'morse·ful** □ [~ful] reuevoll; **re'morse·less** □ hart(herzig), unbarmherzig.

re·mote □ [ri'məut] fern, entfernt, entlegen, abgelegen; ~ *control* Fernsteuerung *f*; **re'mote·ness** Entfernung *f*, Ferne *f*, Entlegenheit *f*.

re·mount 1. [ri:'maunt] *v/t.* wieder besteigen; ⚔ mit frischen Pferden versehen; neu rahmen; *v/i.* wieder aufsteigen; **2.** ['ri:maunt] frisches Reitpferd *n*; ⚔ Remonte *f*.

re·mov·a·ble [ri'mu:vəbl] abnehmbar; abstellbar (*Übel*); absetzbar; **re'mov·al** [~vəl] Entfernen *n*; Wegräumen *n*; Beseitigung *f*; Umzug *m*; Entlassung *f* (*from office* aus dem Amt); ~ *service* Möbelspedition *f*; ~ *van* Möbelwagen *m*; **re'move 1.** *v/t.* entfernen; wegräumen, -rücken; weg-, abnehmen; beseitigen; entlassen (*from office* aus dem Dienst); *v/i.* (aus-, um-, ver)ziehen; **2.** Entfernung *f*, Abstand *m*; Stufe *f*, Grad *m*; *Schule*: Versetzung *f*; Abteilung *f e-r Klasse*; *get one's* ~ versetzt werden; **re'mov·er** (Möbel)Spediteur *m*.

re·mu·ner·ate [ri'mju:nəreit] (be-)lohnen; entschädigen; **re·mu·ner-**

ˈa·tion Be-, Entlohnung *f*; **re-ˈmu·ner·a·tive** □ [~rətiv] lohnend.
Ren·ais·sance [riˈneisəns] Renaissance *f*.
re·nal *anat*. [ˈri:nl] Nieren...
re·name [ˈri:ˈneim] umbenennen; neu benennen.
re·nas·cence [riˈnæsns] Wiedergeburt *f*; Renaissance *f*; **reˈnas-cent** wieder wachsend.
rend [rend] (*irr*.) (zer)reißen.
ren·der [ˈrendə] wieder-, zurückgeben; *Dienst, Gehorsam etc.* leisten; *Aufmerksamkeit, Ehre etc.* erweisen; *Dank* abstatten; übersetzen (*into* in *acc*.); ♪ vortragen; *künstlerisch* wiedergeben; darstellen, interpretieren; *Grund* angeben; ⚕ *Rechnung* überreichen; übergeben; machen (zu); *Fett* auslassen; **ˈren-der·ing** Wiedergabe *f*; Interpretation *f*; Übersetzung *f etc*.
ren·dez·vous [ˈrɔndivu:] Treffpunkt *m*; Stelldichein *n*.
ren·di·tion [renˈdiʃən] Wiedergabe *f*.
ren·e·gade [ˈrenigeid] Renegat(in), Abtrünnige *m, f*.
re·new [riˈnju:] erneuern; **reˈnew·al** Erneuerung *f*.
ren·net [ˈrenit] Lab *n*.
re·nom·i·nate [ri:ˈnɔmineit] wieder (als Kandidaten) aufstellen.
re·nounce [riˈnauns] *v/t*. entsagen (*dat*.); verzichten auf (*acc*.); verleugnen; *v/i*. *Karten*: nicht bedienen.
ren·o·vate [ˈrenəuveit] erneuern, renovieren; **ren·oˈva·tion** Erneuerung *f*, Renovierung *f*; **ˈren·o·va-tor** (Er)Neuerer *m*.
re·nown [riˈnaun] Ruhm *m*, Ansehen *n*; **reˈnowned** berühmt, namhaft.
rent[1] [rent] **1.** *pret. u. p.p. von rend*; **2.** Riß *m*; Spalte *f*.
rent[2] [~] **1.** Miete *f*; Pacht *f*; **2.** (ver-) mieten, (ver)pachten; vermietet werden; **ˈrent·a·ble** (ver)mietbar; **ˈrent-a-ˈcar (serv·ice)** Autoverleih *m*; **ˈrent·al** (Einkommen *n* aus) Miete *f od.* Pacht *f*; ~ *value* Miet-, Pachtwert *m*; **ˈrent-charge** Erbzins *m*; **ˈrent·er** Mieter *m*, Pächter *m*; Filmverleih(er) *m*; **ˈrent-ˈfree** miet-, pachtfrei; **rent tri·bu·nal** Mieterschiedsgericht *n*.
re·nun·ci·a·tion [rinʌnsiˈeiʃən] Entsagung *f*; Verzicht *m* (*of* auf *acc*.).
re·o·pen [ˈri:ˈəupən] *v/t*. wieder (er)öffnen; *v/i*. (sich) wieder öffnen; wieder beginnen.
re·or·ga·ni·za·tion [ˈri:ɔgənaiˈzeiʃən] Neugestaltung *f*; ⚕ Sanierung *f*; **ˈreˈor·gan·ize** reorganisieren, neugestalten; ⚕ sanieren.
rep[1] [rep] Rips *m* (*Stoff*).
rep[2] *sl*. [~] Wüstling *m*.
rep[3] F [~] Repertoiretheater *n*.
re·pack [ˈri:ˈpæk] umpacken.
re·paint [ˈri:ˈpeint] neu anstreichen.
re·pair[1] [riˈpɛə] **1.** Ausbesserung *f*, Reparatur *f*; ~*s pl*. Instandsetzungsarbeiten *f/pl*.; ~ *shop* Reparaturwerkstatt *f*; *in good* ~ in gutem baulichen Zustand, gut erhalten; *out of* ~ baufällig; **2.** reparieren, ausbessern; erneuern; wiedergutmachen.
re·pair[2] [~]: ~ *to* sich begeben nach.
rep·a·ra·ble [ˈrepərəbl] wiedergutzumachen(d); **rep·aˈra·tion** Ersatz *m*; Entschädigung *f*; *pol*. Wiedergutmachungsleistung *f*; *pol. make* ~*s pol*. Reparationen leisten.
rep·ar·tee [repɑ:ˈti:] schlagfertige Antwort *f*; Schlagfertigkeit *f*; *be good at* ~ schlagfertig sein.
re·par·ti·tion [ˈri:pɑ:ˈtiʃən] (Neu-) Verteilung *f*.
re·pass [ˈri:ˈpɑ:s] *v/i*. zurückgehen; *v/t*. wieder vorbeigehen an (*dat*.).
re·past [riˈpɑ:st] Mahl(zeit *f*) *n*.
re·pa·tri·ate 1. [ri:ˈpætrieit] in die Heimat zurückführen; **2.** [~it] Heimkehrer *m*; **re·pa·tri·a·tion** [ˈ~ˈeiʃən] Rückführung *f* in die Heimat.
re·pay (*irr. pay*) [ri:ˈpei] *et*. zurückzahlen; *fig*. erwidern; *et*. vergelten, lohnen; *j*. entschädigen; [ˈri:ˈpei] nochmals (be)zahlen; **reˈpay·a·ble** rückzahlbar; **reˈpay-ment** Rückzahlung *f*.
re·peal [riˈpi:l] **1.** Aufhebung *f von Gesetzen*; **2.** aufheben, widerrufen.
re·peat [riˈpi:t] **1.** *v/t*. wiederholen; her-, aufsagen; nachliefern; ~ *an order for s.th.* et. nachbestellen; *v/i*. sich wiederholen; repetieren (*Uhr, Gewehr*); aufstoßen (*Essen*); **2.** Wiederholung *f*; *oft* ~ *order* Nachbestellung *f*; ♪ Wiederholungszeichen *n*; **reˈpeat·ed** □ wiederholt; **re-ˈpeat·er** Wiederholer(in); periodischer Dezimalbruch *m*; Repetieruhr *f*, -gewehr *n*; *tel*. Übertrager *m*.

re·pel [ri'pel] zurückstoßen, -treiben, -weisen; *fig.* abstoßen; **re'pel·lent** zurück-, abstoßend.
re·pent [ri'pent] *a.* ~ *of* bereuen.
re·pent·ance [ri'pentəns] Reue *f*; **re'pent·ant** reuig.
re·peo·ple ['ri:'pi:pl] wiederbevölkern.
re·per·cus·sion [ri:pə:'kʌʃən] Rückprall *m*; *fig.* Rückwirkung *f*; Widerhall *m*.
rep·er·toire *thea. etc.* ['repətwɑ:] Repertoire *n*.
rep·er·to·ry ['repətəri] *thea.* Repertoire *n*; *fig.* Fundgrube *f*.
rep·e·ti·tion [repi'tiʃən] Wiederholung *f*; Aufsagen *n*; Stück *n* zum Aufsagen; Nachbildung *f*; ~ *order* ⚕ Nachbestellung *f*.
re·pine [ri'pain] unzufrieden sein, murren (*at* über *acc.*); **re'pin·ing** □ mürrisch, unzufrieden.
re·place [ri'pleis] wieder hinstellen *od.* einsetzen; ersetzen; an *j-s* Stelle treten; **re'place·ment** Ersatz *m*; Vertretung *f*.
re·plant ['ri:'plɑ:nt] umpflanzen.
re·play ['ri:plei] *Sport*: Wiederholungsspiel *n*; *Fernsehen*: Wiederholung *f e-r Spielszene* (in Zeitlupe).
re·plen·ish [ri'pleniʃ] wieder auffüllen; **re'plen·ish·ment** Auffüllung *f*; Ergänzung *f*.
re·plete [ri'pli:t] angefüllt, voll (*with* von); **re'ple·tion** Überfülle *f*.
rep·li·ca ['replikə] *paint. etc.* Nachbildung *f*, Kopie *f*; *fig.* Ab-, Ebenbild *n*.
rep·li·ca·tion [repli'keiʃən] ⚖ Replik *f*; Echo *n*; Nachbildung *f*.
re·ply [ri'plai] **1.** antworten, erwidern (*to* auf *acc.*); **2.** Antwort *f*, Erwiderung *f*; ~ *postcard* Postkarte *f* mit Rückantwort.
re·port [ri'pɔ:t] **1.** Bericht *m* (*on* über *acc.*); Gerücht *n*; *guter* Ruf *m*; Knall *m*; *school* ~ (Schul)Zeugnis *n*; **2.** *v/t.* berichten (über *acc.*), melden; anzeigen; *v/i.* Bericht erstatten, berichten (*on, upon* über *acc.*); sich melden (*to* bei); **re·port·ed speech** *gr.* indirekte Rede; **re'port·er** Berichterstatter(in), Reporter(in).
re·pose [ri'pəuz] **1.** *allg.* Ruhe *f* (*a. fig.*); **2.** *v/t.* ausruhen; (aus-) ruhen lassen; *j-m* Ruhe gewähren; ~ *trust etc. in* Vertrauen *etc.* setzen auf (*acc.*); *v/i. a.* ~ *o.s.* (sich) ausruhen; ruhen, schlafen; beruhen (*on* auf *dat.*); **re·pos·i·to·ry** [ri'pɔzitəri] Verwahrungsort *m*; Niederlage *f*; Warenlager *n*; *fig.* Fundgrube *f*.
rep·re·hend [repri'hend] tadeln; **rep·re'hen·si·ble** □ [~səbl] tadelnswert; **rep·re'hen·sion** Verweis *m*.
rep·re·sent [repri'zent] darstellen; verkörpern; *thea. Stück* aufführen; schildern; bezeichnen (*as* als); angeben (*that* daß); *j-m et.* vorhalten; *j. od. j-s Sache* vertreten; **rep·re·sen'ta·tion** Darstellung *f*; Schilderung *f*; *thea.* Aufführung *f*; Vorstellung *f*, Begriff *m*; ⚖, *pol.* Vertretung *f*; **rep·re'sent·a·tive** □ [~tətiv] **1.** dar-, vorstellend (*of acc.*); vorbildlich, Muster...; (stell)vertretend; repräsentativ; typisch, bezeichnend (*of* für); ~ *government* parlamentarische Regierung *f*; **2.** Vertreter(in); *House of* ⩲*s Am. parl.* Repräsentantenhaus *n*.
re·press [ri'pres] unterdrücken; *psych.* verdrängen; **re'pres·sion** Unterdrückung *f*; Verdrängung *f*; Hemmung *f*; **re'pres·sive** □ unterdrückend.
re·prieve [ri'pri:v] **1.** (Gnaden-) Frist *f*; Aufschub *m*; **2.** *j-m* Aufschub *od.* e-e Gnadenfrist gewähren.
rep·ri·mand ['reprimɑ:nd] **1.** Verweis *m*; **2.** *j-m* e-n Verweis geben.
re·print ['ri:print] **1.** neu drucken; **2.** Neudruck *m*.
re·pris·al [ri'praizəl] Wiedervergeltung, Repressalie *f*.
re·proach [ri'prəutʃ] **1.** Vorwurf *m*; Schande *f*; **2.** vorwerfen (*s.o. with s.th.* j-m et.); *j-m* Vorwürfe machen; ein Vorwurf sein für; **re'proach·ful** □ [~ful] vorwurfsvoll.
rep·ro·bate ['reprəubeit] **1.** verkommen, verderbt; **2.** verkommenes Subjekt *n*; **3.** mißbilligen; verdammen; **rep·ro'ba·tion** Mißbilligung *f*; Verurteilung *f*.
re·pro·cess [ri:'prəuses] *Kernbrennstoffe* wiederaufbereiten; ~*ing plant* Wiederaufbereitungsanlage *f*.
re·pro·duce [ri:prə'dju:s] wiedererzeugen; (sich) fortpflanzen; *Glied* neu bilden; *bildlich etc.* wiedergeben, nachbilden, reproduzieren; **re·pro·duc·tion** [~'dʌkʃən] Wie-

dererzeugung *f* (*a. physiol.*); Fortpflanzung *f*; Nachbildung *f*, Reproduktion *f*; **re·pro'duc·tive** □ sich vermehrend; Fortpflanzungs...

re·proof[1] [ri'pru:f] Vorwurf *m*, Tadel *m*; Verweis *m*.

re·proof[2] ['ri:'pru:f] *Regenmantel etc.* neu imprägnieren.

re·prov·al [ri'pru:vəl] Tadel *m*, Rüge *f*; **re'prove** tadeln, rügen.

rep·tile ['reptail] **1.** Reptil *n*, Kriechtier *n*; *fig.* Kriecher(in); **2.** kriechend.

re·pub·lic [ri'pʌblik] Republik *f*; **re'pub·li·can 1.** republikanisch; **2.** Republikaner(in); **re'pub·li·can·ism** republikanische Gesinnung *f od.* Regierungsform *f*.

re·pub·li·ca·tion ['ri:pʌbli'keiʃən] Wiederveröffentlichung *f*; Neuausgabe *f*.

re·pub·lish ['ri:'pʌbliʃ] wieder veröffentlichen.

re·pu·di·ate [ri'pju:dieit] nicht anerkennen; *als unberechtigt* verwerfen, ab-, zurückweisen; verstoßen; **re·pu·di'a·tion** Verwerfung *f*, Zurückweisung *f*; Nichtanerkennung *f*; Verstoßung *f*.

re·pug·nance [ri'pʌgnəns] Abneigung *f*, Widerwille *m* (*to* gegen); **re'pug·nant** □ abstoßend; widerwärtig.

re·pulse [ri'pʌls] **1.** Zurücktreiben *n*; *fig.* Zurückweisung *f*; **2.** zurücktreiben; *fig.* zurückweisen; **re'pul·sion** *phys.* Abstoßung *f*; *fig.* Widerwille *m*; Abneigung *f*; **re'pul·sive** □ *phys. u. fig.* abstoßend; widerwärtig.

re·pur·chase [ri'pə:tʃəs] **1.** Rückkauf *m*; **2.** zurückkaufen.

rep·u·ta·ble □ ['repjutəbl] achtbar; ehrbar, anständig; **rep·u·ta·tion** [repju:'teiʃən] (*bsd.* guter) Ruf *m*, Ansehen *n*; **re·pute** [ri'pju:t] **1.** Ruf *m*, Ansehen *n*; *by* ~ dem Rufe nach; **2.** halten für; *be* ~*d to be od. as* gelten für; *be well (ill)* ~*d* in gutem (schlechtem) Ruf stehen; **re'put·ed** vermeintlich; angeblich; landesüblich (*Maß etc.*); **re'put·ed·ly** angeblich.

re·quest [ri'kwest] **1.** Gesuch *n*, Bitte *f*; Ersuchen *n*; ⚕ Nachfrage *f*; *at s.o.'s* ~ auf j-s Bitte; *by* ~, *on* ~ auf Wunsch; *in (great)* ~ (sehr) gesucht, begehrt; ~ *stop* Bedarfshaltestelle *f*; (*musical*) ~ *programme* Wunschkonzert *n*; **2.** um *et.* bitten *od.* ersuchen; *j.* bitten (*to inf.* zu *inf.*); *et.* erbitten.

re·qui·em ['rekwiem] Totenmesse *f*, Requiem *n*.

re·quire [ri'kwaiə] *et.* verlangen, fordern (*of* von *j-m*); brauchen, erfordern; ~ (*of*) *s.o. to inf.* j. auffordern zu *inf.*; **re'quired** erforderlich; **re'quire·ment** (*fig.* An)Forderung *f*; Erfordernis *n*.

req·ui·site ['rekwizit] **1.** erforderlich; **2.** Erfordernis *n*; Gebrauchsartikel *m*; *toilet* ~*s pl.* Toilettenartikel *m/pl.*; **req·ui'si·tion 1.** Ersuchen *n*; ⚔ Requisition *f*; **2.** verlangen; ⚔ requirieren, beschlagnahmen; in Anspruch nehmen.

re·quit·al [ri'kwaitl] Vergeltung *f*.

re·quite [ri'kwait] *et. j-m* vergelten; *et.* erwidern.

re-read ['ri:'ri:d] (*irr. read*) nochmals (durch)lesen.

re-re·lease ['ri:ri'li:s] Wiederauflage *f e-r Schallplatte.*

re·run 1. (*irr. run*) ['ri:'rʌn] *Film* wiederaufführen; *Fernsehsendung* wiederholen; **2.** ['ri:rʌn] Wiederaufführung *f*; Wiederholung *f*.

re·sale ['ri:seil] Wiederverkauf *m*; ~ *price* Wiederverkaufspreis *m*.

re·scind [ri'sind] aufheben; zurücktreten von.

re·scis·sion [ri'siʒən] Aufhebung *f*.

re·script ['ri:skript] Erlaß *m*.

res·cue ['reskju:] **1.** Rettung *f*; (⚖ gewaltsame) Befreiung *f*; ~ *operation* Rettungs-, Bergungsaktion *f*; **2.** retten; (⚖ gewaltsam) befreien; **'res·cu·er** Befreier(in); Retter(in).

re·search [ri'sə:tʃ] Forschung *f*; Untersuchung *f*; Nachforschung *f*; ~ *assignment* Forschungsauftrag *m*; **re'search·er** Forscher *m*.

re·seat ['ri:'si:t] (sich) wieder setzen; mit neuen Sitzen versehen.

re·se·da ['residə] Reseda(grün) *n*.

re·sell ['ri:'sel] (*irr. sell*) wieder verkaufen; **'re'sell·er** Wiederverkäufer *m*.

re·sem·blance [ri'zembləns] Ähnlichkeit *f* (*to* mit); *bear* ~ *to* Ähnlichkeit haben mit; **re'sem·ble** [~bl] gleichen, ähneln, ähnlich sein (*dat.*).

re·sent [ri'zent] sich ärgern über (*acc.*); übelnehmen; **re'sent·ful** □

[~ful] empfindlich; grollend; ~ *of* ärgerlich über *od.* auf (*acc.*); **re'sent·ment** Ärger *m*; Verstimmung *f*; Empfindlichkeit *f*, Groll *m*, Unwille *m*.

res·er·va·tion [rezə'veiʃən] Vorbehalt *m*; *Am.* Indianerreservation *f*; Vorbestellung *f*, Reservierung *f von Zimmern etc.*

re·serve [ri'zə:v] **1.** Vorrat *m*; ✝ Rücklage *f*; Reserve *f* (*a. fig.*, ⚔); Zurückhaltung *f*, Verschlossenheit *f*; Vorsicht *f*; Vorbehalt *m*; *Sport*: Ersatzmann *m*; Reservat *n*, Schutzgebiet *n*; *in* ~ in Reserve, vorrätig; *with certain* ~*s* mit gewissen Einschränkungen; **2.** aufbewahren, -sparen, reservieren; vorbehalten; zurückstellen, -legen; *Platz* belegen, vormerken, vorbestellen; **re'served** □ *fig.* zurückhaltend, reserviert.

re·serv·ist ⚔ [ri'zə:vist] Reservist *m*.

res·er·voir ['rezəvwɑ:] Behälter *m für Wasser etc.*; Sammel-, Staubecken *n*; *fig.* Reservoir *n*.

re·set ['ri:'set] (*irr. set*) wieder einfassen; *typ.* neu setzen.

re·set·tle ['ri:'setl] neuordnen; umsiedeln; **'re'set·tle·ment** Neuordnung *f*; Umsiedlung *f*.

re·ship ['ri:'ʃip] wieder verschiffen.

re·shuf·fle ['ri:'ʃʌfl] **1.** umgruppieren; umbilden; **2.** Umgruppierung *f etc.*

re·side [ri'zaid] wohnen; (orts)ansässig sein; ~ *in* innewohnen (*dat.*); liegen in (*dat.*); **res·i·dence** ['rezidəns] Wohnen *n*; Ortsansässigkeit *f*; (Wohn)Sitz *m*; Residenz *f*; (herrschaftliches) Wohnhaus *n*; ~ *permit* Aufenthaltsgenehmigung *f*; **'res·i·dent 1.** wohnhaft; ortsansässig; im Dienstgebäude wohnend (*Lehrer etc.*); **2.** Ortsansässige *m*, Einwohner *m*; Ministerresident *m* (*Gesandter*); **res·i·den·tial** [~'denʃəl] Wohn...; herrschaftlich.

re·sid·u·al [ri'zidjuəl] übrigbleibend; **re'sid·u·ar·y** restlich, übrig (-geblieben); **res·i·due** ['rezidju:] Rest *m*; Rückstand *m*; ⚖ Reinnachlaß *m*; **re·sid·u·um** [ri'zidjuəm] *bsd.* ⚗ Rückstand *m*; Bodensatz *m* (*a. fig.*); 𝔄 Rest *m*.

re·sign [ri'zain] *v/t.* aufgeben, verzichten auf (*acc.*); *Amt* niederlegen; überlassen; ~ *o.s. to* sich ergeben in (*acc.*), sich abfinden mit; *v/i. vom Amt* zurücktreten; resignieren; **res·ig·na·tion** [rezig'neiʃən] Amtsniederlegung *f*, Rücktritt *m*; Ergebung *f*; Entlassungsgesuch *n*; **re·signed** □ [ri'zaind] ergeben, resigniert.

re·sil·i·ence [ri'ziliəns] Elastizität *f*, *fig.* Spannkraft *f*; **re'sil·i·ent** elastisch, *fig.* spannkräftig.

res·in ['rezin] **1.** Harz *n*; **2.** harzen; **'res·in·ous** harzig.

re·sist [ri'zist] widerstehen (*dat.*); sich widersetzen (*dat.*); **re'sist·ance** Widerstand *m* (*a. phys.*, ⚡; *to* gegen); *line of least* ~ Weg *m* des geringsten Widerstands; *attr.* Widerstands...; **re'sist·ant** widerstehend; widerstandsfähig; **re'sis·tor** ⚡ Widerstand *m*.

re·sit 1. ['ri:sit] Wiederholungsprüfung *f*; **2.** ['~'sit] (*irr. sit*) *v/t. Prüfung* wiederholen; *v/i.* die Prüfung wiederholen.

re·sole ['ri:'səul] neu besohlen.

res·o·lute □ ['rezəlu:t] entschlossen; **'res·o·lute·ness** Entschlossenheit *f*.

res·o·lu·tion [rezə'lu:ʃən] *phys.*, 𝔄, ♪ Auflösung *f*; *fig.* Lösung *f*; Entschluß *m*; Entschlossenheit *f*; *parl.* Resolution *f*, Beschluß(fassung *f*) *m*; Entschließung *f*.

re·solv·a·ble [ri'zɔlvəbl] auflösbar.

re·solve [ri'zɔlv] **1.** *v/t.* auflösen (*into* in *acc.*; *a.* ⚗, 𝔄, ♪); *fig. Frage etc.* lösen; *Zweifel etc.* beheben; entscheiden; *the House* ~*s itself into a committee parl.* das Haus konstituiert sich als Ausschuß; *v/i. a.* ~ *o.s.* sich auflösen; beschließen; ~ (*up*)*on* sich entschließen zu; **2.** Entschluß *m*; Beschluß *m*; *lit.* Entschlossenheit *f*; **re'solved** □ entschlossen.

res·o·nance ['reznəns] Resonanz *f*; Nach-, Widerhall *m*; **'res·o·nant** □ nach-, widerhallend; volltönend.

re·sorp·tion *physiol.* [ri'sɔ:pʃən] Aufsaugung *f*, Resorption *f*.

re·sort [ri'zɔ:t] **1.** Zuflucht *f*; Besuch *m*, Zustrom *m*; Aufenthalt(sort) *m*; Erholungsort *m*; *health* ~ Kurort *m*; *seaside* ~ Seebad *n*; *summer* ~ Sommerfrische *f*; *in the last* ~ letzten Endes; **2.** ~ *to* sich begeben zu *od.* nach; *Ort* oft besuchen; seine Zuflucht nehmen zu;

zurückgreifen auf (*acc.*).

re·sound [ri'zaund] widerhallen (lassen) (*with* von).

re·source [ri'sɔ:s] *natürlicher* Reichtum *m*; Hilfsquelle *f*, -mittel *n*; Mittel *n*, Zuflucht *f*; Fähigkeit *f*, sich zu helfen; Findigkeit *f*; Zeitvertreib *m*, Entspannung *f*, Unterhaltung *f*; **re'source·ful** □ [~ful] reich an Hilfsquellen; findig; **re'source·ful·ness** Reichtum *m*; Findigkeit *f*.

re·spect [ris'pekt] **1.** Rücksicht *f* (*to*, *of* auf *acc.*); Hinsicht *f*, Beziehung *f*; Achtung *f*, Ehrerbietung *f* (*for* vor *dat.*); ~*s pl.* Empfehlungen *f/pl.*; *with* ~ *to* in bezug auf (*acc.*), was ... anbetrifft; *in* ~ *of* in Anbetracht (*gen.*); *pay one's* ~*s on s.o.* j-m seine Aufwartung machen; **2.** *v/t.* hochachten; achten, Rücksicht nehmen auf (*acc.*); betreffen; **re·spect·a'bil·i·ty** Achtbarkeit *f*; Ehrbarkeit *f*; Ansehnlichkeit *f*; ⚕ Solidität *f*; *respectabilities pl.* Anstandsregeln *f/pl.*; **re'spect·a·ble** □ achtbar; ehrbar; ansehnlich; achtenswert; anständig; *bsd.* ⚕ solid; **re'spect·ful** □ [~ful] respektvoll; ehrerbietig, höflich; *Yours* ~*ly* hochachtungsvoll; **re'spect·ful·ness** Ehrerbietung *f*; **re'spect·ing** in betreff, hinsichtlich (*gen.*); **re'spec·tive** □ jedem einzeln zukommend; jeweilig; *we went to our* ~ *places* wir gingen jeder an seinen Platz; **re'spec·tive·ly** beziehungsweise, je.

res·pi·ra·tion [respə'reiʃən] Atmung *f*; Atemzug *m*.

res·pi·ra·tor ['respəreitə] Atemfilter *m*; Gasmaske *f*; ⚕ Atemgerät *n*; **re·spir·a·to·ry** [ris'paiərətəri] Atmungs...

re·spire [ris'paiə] atmen; aufatmen.

res·pite ['respait] **1.** ⚖ Frist *f*; Aufschub *m*; Stundung *f*; **2.** *Urteilsvollstreckung* aufschieben; *j-m* e-e Frist gewähren.

re·splend·ence, **re·splend·en·cy** [ris'plendəns(i)] Glanz *m*; *fig.* Pracht *f*; **re'splend·ent** □ glänzend.

re·spond [ri'spɔnd] *bsd. feierlich* antworten, erwidern; ~ *to* reagieren auf (*acc.*), empfänglich sein für; **re'spond·ent** **1.** ⚖ beklagt; ~ *to* empfänglich für; **2.** ⚖ Beklagte *m*, *f*.

re·sponse [ris'pɔns] Antwort *f*, Erwiderung *f*; *fig.* Widerhall *m*, Reaktion *f* (*to* auf *acc.*).

re·spon·si·bil·i·ty [rispɔnsə'biliti] Verantwortlichkeit *f*, Verantwortung *f* (*for*, *of* für); Vertrauenswürdigkeit *f*, ⚕ Zahlungsfähigkeit *f*; **re'spon·si·ble** verantwortlich; verantwortungsvoll (*Amt*); haftbar; vertrauenswürdig, ⚕ zahlungsfähig; *be* ~ *for a. et.* verschulden; schuld sein an (*dat.*); **re'spon·sive** □ antwortend; Antwort...; verständnisvoll; empfänglich (*to* für).

rest[1] [rest] **1.** Ruhe *f*; Rast *f*; Schlaf *m*; *fig.* Tod *m*; Auflage *f*, Stütze *f*; ♪ Pause *f*; *at* ~ in Ruhe, ruhig; **2.** *v/i.* ruhen; rasten; schlafen; (sich) lehnen, sich stützen (*on* auf *acc.*); ~ (*up*)*on fig.* beruhen auf (*dat.*); *it* ~*s with you* es obliegt Ihnen; *v/t.* (aus)ruhen (lassen); stützen (*on*, *upon* auf *acc.*).

rest[2] [~] **1.** Rest *m*; *das* übrige, *die* übrigen; ⚕ Reserve(fonds *m*) *f*; *for the* ~ im übrigen; **2.** *in e-m Zustand* bleiben; ~ *assured* sei versichert.

re·state ['ri:'steit] neu formulieren.

re·stau·rant ['restərɔ̃:ŋ] Restaurant *n*, Gaststätte *f*; '**~-car** Speisewagen *m*.

rest-cure ⚕ ['restkjuə] Liegekur *f*.

rest·ful ['restful] ruhig, geruhsam.

rest-home ['resthəum] Altenheim *n*.

rest·ing-place ['restiŋpleis] Ruheplatz *m*, -stätte *f*.

res·ti·tu·tion [resti'tju:ʃən] Wiederherstellung *f*; Rückerstattung *f*; *make* ~ Ersatz leisten (*of* für).

res·tive □ ['restiv] widerspenstig, störrisch; '**res·tive·ness** Widerspenstigkeit *f*.

rest·less ['restlis] ruhelos; rastlos; unruhig; '**rest·less·ness** Ruhelosigkeit *f*; Rastlosigkeit *f*; Unruhe *f*.

re·stock ['ri:'stɔk] *Vorrat* wieder auffüllen.

res·to·ra·tion [restə'reiʃən] Wiederherstellung *f*; Wiedereinsetzung *f* (*to* in *ein Amt*); Rekonstruktion *f*, Nachbildung *f*; **re·stor·a·tive** □ [ris'tɔrətiv] stärkend(es Mittel *n*).

re·store [ris'tɔ:] wiederherstellen; wiedereinsetzen (*to* in *acc.*); wiedergeben, ersetzen; ~ *s.o. to liberty* j-m die Freiheit schenken; ~ *to health od. life* wieder gesund *od.* lebendig machen; **re'stor·er** Wiederhersteller(in); *hair* ~ Haarwuchsmittel *n.*

re·strain [ris'trein] zurückhalten (*from* von); in Schranken halten; unterdrücken; einsperren; **re'strained** beherrscht; **re·straint** [~'treint] Zurückhaltung *f* (*a. fig.*); Beschränkung *f*, Zwang *m*; Zwangshaft *f*.

re·strict [ris'trikt] be-, einschränken; **re'stric·tion** Be-, Einschränkung *f* (*of, on gen.*); Vorbehalt *m*; Restriktion *f*; **re'stric·tive** □ be-, einschränkend.

rest room *Am.* ['restrum] Toilette *f*.

re·struc·ture ['ri:'strʌktʃə] umstrukturieren.

re·sult [ri'zʌlt] **1.** Ergebnis *n*, Folge *f*, Resultat *n*; **2.** folgen, sich ergeben (*from* aus); ~ *in* hinauslaufen auf (*acc.*), enden in (*dat.*), zur Folge haben; **re'sult·ant 1.** sich ergebend; **2.** ⊕ Resultante *f*.

ré·su·mé ['rezju:mei] Resümee *n*, Zs.-fassung *f*.

re·sume [ri'zju:m] wiedernehmen, -erlangen, -aufnehmen, -anfangen; zs.-fassen; fortfahren; **re·sump·tion** [ri'zʌmpʃən] Zurücknahme *f*; Wiederaufnahme *f*.

re·sur·face ['ri:'sə:fis] *v/t. Straße* mit neuem Belag versehen; *v/i.* wieder auftauchen (*U-Boot*).

re·sur·gence [ri'sə:dʒəns] Wiederemporkommen *n*; **re'sur·gent** sich wiedererhebend, wieder aufkommend.

res·ur·rect [rezə'rekt] wiedererwecken; wiederaufleben lassen; F ausgraben; **res·ur'rec·tion** (Wieder-) Auferstehung *f*; Wiederaufleben *n*; **res·ur'rec·tion·ist** [~ʃnist], **res·ur'rec·tion-man** [~ʃənmən] Leichenräuber *m*.

re·sus·ci·tate [ri'sʌsiteit] *v/t.* wiedererwecken, -beleben; *v/i.* wieder aufleben; **re·sus·ci'ta·tion** Wiedererweckung *f*.

re·tail 1. ['ri:teil] Einzelhandel *m*, Detailgeschäft *n*; *by* ~ im Einzelverkauf; ~ *price* Einzelhandelspreis *m*; **2.** [~] Einzelhandels..., Detail...; **3.** [~] *adv. s. by* ~; **4.** [ri:'teil] *v/t.* im kleinen verkaufen; haarklein (weiter)erzählen; *v/i.* verkauft werden (*at* zu); ~ **book·sell·er** Sortimentsbuchhändler *m*; **re'tail·er** Einzelhändler *m*.

re·tain [ri'tein] behalten (*a. im Gedächtnis*); bewahren; zurück-, festhalten; *Brauch etc.* beibehalten; *Anwalt* nehmen; **re'tain·er** *hist.* Gefolgsmann *m*; *old* ~ altes Faktotum *n*; **re'tain·ing fee** Vorschuß *m für e-n Anwalt.*

re·take ['ri:'teik] (*irr. take*) wiedernehmen.

re·tal·i·ate [ri'tælieit] *v/t. Unrecht* vergelten; *v/i.* sich rächen, Vergeltung üben (*on, upon* an *dat.*); **re·tal·i'a·tion** Vergeltung *f*; **re'tal·i·a·to·ry** [~ətəri] Vergeltungs...

re·tard [ri'tɑ:d] verzögern; aufhalten; verspäten; ~*ed ignition mot.* Spätzündung *f*; *mentally* ~*ed* geistig zurückgeblieben; **re·tar·da·tion** [ri:tɑ:'deiʃən] Verzögerung *f*, -spätung *f*.

retch [retʃ] würgen (*beim Erbrechen*).

re·tell ['ri:'tel] (*irr. tell*) nochmals erzählen, nacherzählen.

re·ten·tion [ri'tenʃən] Zurück-, Behalten *n*; ⚕ Verhaltung *f*; Beibehaltung *f von Sitten*; **re'ten·tive** □ zurück-, behaltend (*of acc.*); gut (*Gedächtnis*).

re·think ['ri:θiŋk] (*irr. think*) neu durchdenken.

ret·i·cence ['retisəns] Verschwiegenheit *f* (*of* in *dat.*); **'ret·i·cent** verschwiegen; schweigsam; zurückhaltend.

ret·i·cle ['retikl] Fadenkreuz *n*.

re·tic·u·late □ [ri'tikjulit], **re'tic·u·lat·ed** □ [~leitid] netzartig; Netz...; **ret·i·cule** ['retikju:l] Damenhandtasche *f*; = *reticle*.

ret·i·na *anat.* ['retinə] Netzhaut *f*.

ret·i·nue ['retinju:] Gefolge *n*.

re·tire [ri'taiə] *v/t.* zurückziehen; in den Ruhestand versetzen, pensionieren; *v/i.* sich zurückziehen; zurück-, abtreten; in den Ruhestand treten; *a.* ~ *to bed* zu Bett gehen; **re'tired** □ zurückgezogen; im Ruhestand (lebend); entlegen (*Ort*); ~ *pay* Pension *f*, Ruhegehalt *n*; **re'tire·ment** Sichzurückziehen *n*; Aus-, Rücktritt *m*; Ruhestand *m*; Zurückgezogenheit *f*; *early* ~ vorzeitiger Ruhestand *m*; **re'tir·ing** □ zurückhaltend; schüchtern; ~ *pension* Ruhegehalt *n*.

re·tort [ri'tɔ:t] **1.** Erwiderung *f*; schlagfertige Antwort *f*; ⚗ Retorte *f*; **2.** *v/t. Beleidigung etc.* zurück-

geben (*on, upon dat.*); *v/i.* (scharf *od.* treffend) erwidern.
re·touch ['riː'tʌtʃ] *et.* überarbeiten; *phot.* retuschieren.
re·trace [ri'treis] zurückverfolgen; ~ *one's steps* zurückgehen.
re·tract [ri'trækt] (sich) zurückziehen; ⊕ einziehen; widerrufen, zurücknehmen; **re'tract·a·ble** einziehbar (✈ *Fahrgestell*); **re·trac'ta·tion** Widerruf *m*; Zurücknahme *f*; **re'trac·tion** Zurückziehen *n.*
re·train ['riː'trein] umschulen.
re·trans·late ['riːtræns'leit] (zu-) rückübersetzen; **'re·trans'la·tion** Rückübersetzung *f.*
re·tread ['riː'tred] **1.** *Reifen* runderneuern; **2.** runderneuerter Reifen *m.*
re·treat [ri'triːt] **1.** Rückzug *m*; Zurückgezogenheit *f*; Zuflucht(sort *m*) *f*; Schlupfwinkel *m*; ⚔ Zapfenstreich *m*; *beat a* ~ *fig.* es aufgeben; **2.** sich zurückziehen; *fig.* zurücktreten.
re·trench [ri'trentʃ] *v/t.* einschränken; kürzen, beschneiden; *Wort etc.* streichen; ⚔ verschanzen; *v/i.* sich einschränken; **re'trench·ment** Kürzung *f*; Einschränkung *f*; ⚔ (innere) Verteidigungsstellung *f.*
re·tri·al ⚖ ['riː'traiəl] Wiederaufnahme(verfahren *n*) *f.*
ret·ri·bu·tion [retri'bjuːʃən] Vergeltung *f*; **re·trib·u·tive** □ [ri'tribjutiv] vergeltend; Vergeltungs...
re·triev·a·ble [ri'triːvəbl] ersetzlich; **re'triev·al** Wiedergewinnung *f*; *beyond* ~, *past* ~ unwiederbringlich (verloren).
re·trieve [ri'triːv] wiederbekommen; wiederherstellen; wiedergutmachen; *hunt.* apportieren; **re'triev·er** *hunt.* Apportierhund *m.*
ret·ro... ['retrəu] (zu)rück...; **~'ac·tive** rückwirkend; **~'cede** zurückgehen; wieder abtreten; **~'ces·sion** Zurückweichen *n*; Wiederabtretung *f*; **~·gra'da·tion** *ast.* rückläufige Bewegung *f*; Zurückgehen *n*; *fig.* Niedergang *m*; **'~·grade** **1.** rückläufig; **2.** zurückgehen (*a. fig.*).
ret·ro·gres·sion [retrəu'greʃən] Rück-, Niedergang *m*; **ret·ro·spect** ['~spekt] Rückblick *m*; *in* ~ rückschauend; **ret·ro'spec·tion** Rückblick *m*; Erinnerung *f*; **ret·ro'spec·tive** □ zurückblickend; rückwirkend; ~ *view* Rückblick *m.*
re·trous·sé [rə'truːsei]: ~ *nose* Stupsnase *f.*
re·try ⚖ ['riː'trai] *Prozeß* wiederaufnehmen; neu verhandeln gegen *j.*
re·turn [ri'təːn] **1.** Rückkehr *f*; Wiederkehr *f*; *parl.* Wiederwahl *f*; *oft* ~*s pl.* Gewinn *m*, Ertrag *m*; (Kapital)Umsatz *m*; ⚕ Rückfall *m*; Rückgabe *f*, -zahlung *f*; Vergeltung *f*; Erwiderung *f*; Gegenleistung *f*; Dank *m*; *amtlicher* Bericht *m*; (Bank)Ausweis *m*; Steuererklärung *f*; △ Seitenflügel *m*; F Rückfahrkarte *f*; ~*s pl.* statistische Aufstellungen *f/pl.*; *many happy* ~*s of the day* herzliche Glückwünsche zum heutigen Tage; *election* ~*s pl.* Wahlergebnis *n*; *in* ~ dafür; *in* ~ *for* (als Gegenleistung) für; *by* ~ (*of post*) postwendend; ~ *match* Rückspiel *n*; ~ *ticket* Rückfahrkarte *f*; ~ *visit* Gegenbesuch *m*; *attr.* Rück...; **2.** *v/i.* zurückkehren; wiederkehren; ~ *to fig.* zurückkehren zu *e-m Thema etc.*; zurückfallen in *e-e Gewohnheit etc.*; *j-m* wieder zufallen; *v/t.* zurückgeben; zurücktun (*to* in *acc.*); zurückzahlen; zurücksenden; *Dank* abstatten; *Rede, Schlag, Gruß, Liebe etc.* erwidern; ⚖ *Urteil* aussprechen; *amtlich* berichten, melden, angeben; *ins Parlament* wählen; *Gewinn* abwerfen; *Karte* nachspielen; ~ *guilty* ⚖ schuldig sprechen; **re'turn·a·ble** zurückzugeben(d); **re'turn·er** Zurücksendende *m*, -zahlende *m*; **re'turn·ing-of·fi·cer** Wahlkommissar *m.*
re·u·ni·fi·ca·tion *pol.* ['riːjuːnifi'keiʃən] Wiedervereinigung *f.*
re·un·ion ['riː'juːnjən] Wiedervereinigung *f*; Treffen *n*, Zs.-kunft *f*;
re·u·nite ['riːjuː'nait] (sich) wieder vereinigen.
rev *mot.* F [rev] **1.** Umdrehung *f*; **2.** (sich) drehen; ~ *up* auf Touren kommen *od.* bringen.
re·val·or·i·za·tion ['riːvælərai'zeiʃən], **re·val·u·a·tion** ['riːvælju'eiʃən] Auf-, Neuwertung *f*; **'re'val·or·ize** [~əraiz], **re·val·ue** ['riː'væljuː] aufwerten, neu bewerten.

re·vamp ⊕ ['ri:'væmp] vorschuhen; *Am.* F aufmöbeln; erneuern.
re·veal [ri'vi:l] enthüllen; offenbaren; zeigen; **re'veal·ing** aufschlußreich.
re·veil·le ⚔ [ri'væli] Reveille *f.*
rev·el ['revl] **1.** Lustbarkeit *f*; lärmende Festlichkeit *f*; Gelage *n*; Rummel *m*; **2.** ausgelassen sein; schwelgen (*in* in *dat.*); sich ergötzen (*in* an *dat.*).
rev·e·la·tion [revi'leiʃən] Enthüllung *f*; Offenbarung *f.*
rev·el·(l)er ['revlə] Feiernde *m, f*; (Nacht)Schwärmer *m*; Zechbruder *m*; **'rev·el·ry** laute Lustbarkeit *f*, Rummel *m*, Orgie *f.*
re·venge [ri'vendʒ] **1.** Rache *f*, Vergeltung *f*; Revanche *f bei Spielen*; **2.** *et., a. j.* rächen (*on, upon* an *dat.*); ~ *o.s. on, be* ~*d on* sich rächen an (*dat.*); **re'venge·ful** □ [~ful] rachsüchtig; **re'venge·ful·ness** Rachsucht *f*; **re'veng·er** Rächer(in).
rev·e·nue ['revinju:] Einkommen *n*; ~*s pl.* Einkünfte *pl.*; ~ *board*, ~ *office* Finanzamt *n*; ~ *cutter* Zollkutter *m*; ~ *officer* Zollbeamte *m*; ~ *stamp* Banderole *f.*
re·ver·ber·ate [ri'və:bəreit] *v/t.* zurückwerfen, -strahlen; *v/i.* zurückstrahlen; widerhallen; **re·ver·ber'a·tion** Zurückwerfen *n*; Widerhall(en *n*) *m*; **re'ver·ber·a·tor** Scheinwerfer *m.*
re·vere [ri'viə] (ver)ehren; **rev·er·ence** ['revərəns] **1.** Verehrung *f*; Ehrfurcht *f*; *Your* ♀ † *od. co.* Euer Ehrwürden; **2.** (ver)ehren; **'rev·er·end 1.** ehrwürdig; *Right* ♀ hochwürdig; **2.** Geistliche *m.*
rev·er·ent □ ['revərənt], **rev·er·en·tial** □ [~'renʃəl] ehrerbietig, ehrfurchtsvoll.
rev·er·ie ['revəri] Träumerei *f.*
re·ver·sal [ri'və:səl] Umkehrung *f*; Umschwung *m*; ⚖ Umstoßung *f*; ⊕ Umsteuerung *f*; **re'verse 1.** Gegenteil *n*; Rück-, Kehrseite *f*; Schlappe *f*; Rückschlag *m*; *in* ~ im umgekehrten Sinne; ⚔ im Rücken; **2.** □ umgekehrt; Rück(wärts)...; ~ (*gear*) *mot.* Rückwärtsgang *m*; ~ *side* linke *Stoff*-Seite *f*; **3.** umkehren, umdrehen; *Urteil etc.* umstoßen; ⊕ umsteuern; **re'vers·i·ble** umkehrbar; umsteuerbar; doppelseitig (*Stoff, Mantel*); **re'vers·ing** ⊕ Umsteuerungs...
re·ver·sion [ri'və:ʃən] Umkehrung *f*; Rückkehr *f*; ⚖ Heimfall *m*; Anwartschaft *f* (*of* auf *acc.*); *biol.* Rückartung *f*; **re'ver·sion·ar·y** ⚖ [~ʃnəri] anwartschaftlich; **re'ver·sion·er** ⚖ [~ʃənə] Anwärter *m.*
re·vert [ri'və:t] umkehren; zurückkommen, -gehen (*to* auf *acc.*); *fig.* zurückfallen (*to* in *acc.*); *biol.* zurückarten (*to* zu); ⚖ heimfallen; *Blick* wenden.
rev·er·y ['reveri] = *reverie.*
re·vet·ment ⊕ [ri'vetmənt] Verkleidung *f*, Futtermauer *f.*
re·view [ri'vju:] **1.** Nachprüfung *f*; ⚔, ⚓ Parade *f*, Truppen-, Flottenschau *f*; Rückblick *m*; Überblick *m*; Besprechung *f*, Rezension *f e-s Buches*; Zeitschrift *f*; *pass s.th. in* ~ et. Revue passieren lassen; *year under* ~ Berichtsjahr *n*; **2.** *v/t.* wieder durchsehen; (über-, nach-) prüfen; zurückblicken auf (*acc.*); überblicken; ⚔, ⚓ besichtigen; *kritisch* besprechen, rezensieren; *v/i.* Rezensionen schreiben; **re'view·er** Rezensent *m*; ~'*s copy* Rezensionsexemplar *n.*
re·vile [ri'vail] schmähen, beschimpfen (*for* wegen).
re·vis·al [ri'vaizl] Revision *f.*
re·vise [ri'vaiz] **1.** *Buch etc.* überarbeiten, durchsehen; überprüfen, revidieren; **2.** *typ.* Korrekturabzug *m*; = *revision*; **re'vis·er** Bearbeiter *m*; *typ.* Korrektor *m.*
re·vi·sion [ri'viʒən] Revision *f*, nochmalige Durchsicht *f*; Überarbeitung *f.*
re·vis·it ['ri:'vizit] wieder besuchen.
re·vi·so·ry [ri'vaizəri] Revisions...
re·vi·tal·ize ['ri:'vaitəlaiz] neu beleben.
re·viv·al [ri'vaivəl] Wiederbelebung *f*; Wiederaufleben *n*, -aufblühen *n*, neue Blüte *f*; Erneuerung *f*; *fig.* Erweckung *f*; **re'vive** *v/t.* wiederbeleben, wieder aufleben lassen; erneuern, wieder einführen; *v/i.* wieder aufleben, -blühen; **re'viv·er** Wiederbeleber(in); Auffrischung(smittel *n*) *f*; **re·viv·i·fy** [ri:'vivifai] wiederbeleben.
rev·o·ca·ble □ ['revəkəbl] widerruflich; **rev·o·ca·tion** [~'keiʃən] Widerruf *m*; Aufhebung *f.*
re·voke [ri'vəuk] *v/t.* widerrufen,

zurücknehmen, einziehen *v/i. Karten*: nicht bedienen.
re·volt [ri'vəult] **1.** Revolte *f*, Empörung *f*, Aufruhr *m*, -stand *m*; **2.** *v/i.* sich empören (*a. fig.*); abfallen (*from* von); *v/t. fig.* empören, abstoßen; **re'volt·ing** abstoßend.
rev·o·lu·tion [revə'lu:ʃən] Umwälzung *f*, Umdrehung *f*; *pol.* Revolution *f*; *~s per minute mot.* Drehzahl *f*; **rev·o'lu·tion·ary** [~ʃnəri] **1.** revolutionär; umwälzend; **2.** *a.* **rev·o'lu·tion·ist** Revolutionär(in); **rev·o'lu·tion·ize** revolutionieren; aufwiegeln; umgestalten; umwälzen.
re·volve [ri'vɔlv] *v/i.* sich drehen (*about, round* um); *v/t.* umdrehen; *fig.* erwägen; **re'volv·er** Revolver *m*; **re'volv·ing** sich drehend; Dreh... (*-tür, -bleistift, -bühne*).
re·vue *thea.* [ri'vju:] Revue *f*; Kabarett *n*.
re·vul·sion [ri'vʌlʃən] *fig.* Umschwung *m*; ⚕ Ableitung *f*; **re'vul·sive** ⚕ [~siv] **1.** □ ableitend; **2.** ableitendes Mittel *n*.
re·ward [ri'wɔ:d] **1.** Belohnung *f*; Lohn *m*; Vergeltung *f*; **2.** belohnen; vergelten.
re·word ['ri:'wə:d] neu formulieren.
re·write ['ri:'rait] (*irr. write*) nochmals *od.* neu schreiben, umschreiben.
rhap·so·dist ['ræpsədist] Rhapsode *m*; **'rhap·so·dize** begeistert reden; **'rhap·so·dy** Rhapsodie *f*; *fig.* Schwärmerei *f*; Wortschwall *m*.
rhe·o·stat ⚡ ['ri:əustæt] Rheostat *m*, Regelwiderstand *m*.
rhet·o·ric ['retərik] Rhetorik *f*; **rhe·tor·i·cal** □ [ri'tɔrikəl] rhetorisch; **rhet·o·ri·cian** [retə'riʃən] guter Redner *m*; *contp.* Phrasendrescher *m*.
rheu·mat·ic ⚕ [ru:'mætik] **1.** (*~ally*) rheumatisch; *~ fever* Gelenkrheumatismus *m*; **2.** Rheumatiker (-in); *~s* F *pl.* = **rheu·ma·tism** ⚕ ['ru:mətizəm] Rheumatismus *m*.
rhi·no¹ *sl.* ['rainəu] Moneten *pl.*
rhi·no² F [~] = **rhi·noc·er·os** *zo.* [rai'nɔsərəs] Rhinozeros *n*, Nashorn *n*.
rhomb, rhom·bus ⩕ ['rɔm(bəs)] Rhombus *m*, Raute *f*.
rhu·barb ⚘ ['ru:bɑ:b] Rhabarber *m*.
rhyme [raim] **1.** Reim *m* (*to* auf *acc.*); Vers *m*; *without ~ or reason* ohne Sinn u. Verstand; **2.** (sich) reimen; **'rhyme·less** □ reimlos; **'rhym·er, rhyme·ster** ['~stə] Verseschmied *m*.
rhythm ['riðəm] Rhythmus *m*; **rhyth·mic, rhyth·mi·cal** □ ['riðmik(əl)] rhythmisch.
Ri·al·to *Am.* [ri'æltəu] Theaterviertel *n e-r Stadt*.
rib [rib] **1.** Rippe *f*; **2.** *Stoff etc.* rippen; *Am. sl.* aufziehen, necken.
rib·ald ['ribəld] **1.** lästerlich; unflätig; **2.** Lästermaul *n*; Zotenreißer *m*; **'rib·ald·ry** Zoten *f/pl.*; derbe Späße *m/pl.*
rib·and ⊕ ['ribənd] Band *n*.
ribbed [ribd] ...rippig.
rib·bon ['ribən] Band *n*; Ordensband *n*; Farbband *n der Schreibmaschine*; Streifen *m*; *~s pl.* Fetzen *m/pl.*; Zügel *m/pl.*; *~ building, ~ development* Bebauung *f* entlang e-r Ausfallstraße; **'rib·boned** bebändert; streifig.
rib cage ['ribkeidʒ] Brustkorb *m*.
rice [rais] Reis *m*; *~ pudding* Milchreis *m*.
rich □ [ritʃ] reich (*in* an *dat.*); reichlich; prächtig, kostbar; ergiebig, fruchtbar; voll (*Ton*); fett, schwer (*Speise*); kräftig (*Wein, Geruch*); satt (*Farbe*); F prächtig, köstlich (*Scherz etc.*); *mot.* fett (*Gemisch*); *the ~ pl.* die Reichen *pl.*; **rich·es** ['~iz] *pl.* Reichtum *m*, Reichtümer *m/pl.*; **'rich·ness** Reichtum *m*; Fülle *f*.
rick¹ ⚒ [rik] **1.** (Heu)Schober *m*; **2.** in Schobern aufsetzen.
rick² [~] = *wrick*.
rick·ets ⚕ ['rikits] *sg. od. pl.* Rachitis *f*; **'rick·et·y** rachitisch; gebrechlich, wackelig.
rick·shaw ['rikʃɔ:] Rikscha *f*.
rid [rid] (*irr.*) befreien, frei machen (*of* von); *get ~ of* loswerden; **'riddance** Befreiung *f*; *he is a good ~* es ist gut, daß man ihn los ist.
rid·den ['ridn] *p.p. von ride* 2; *in Zssgn*: bedrückt *od.* geplagt von ...
rid·dle¹ ['ridl] **1.** Rätsel *n*; **2.** enträtseln; *~ me* rate mal.
rid·dle² [~] **1.** grobes Sieb *n*; **2.** sieben; durchlöchern.
rid·dling □ ['ridliŋ] rätselhaft.
ride [raid] **1.** Ritt *m*; Fahrt *f*; Reitweg *m*; Schneise *f*; *go for a ~* aus-

fahren; -reiten; **2.** (*irr.*) *v/i.* reiten; rittlings sitzen; *bsd. auf dem Fahrrad od. mit e-m öffentlichen Verkehrsmittel* fahren; getragen werden, treiben, *fig.* schweben; ruhen; liegen; ~ *at anchor* vor Anker liegen; ~ *for a fall* wild drauflosreiten; *fig.* ins Unglück rennen; *v/t. ein Pferd etc.* reiten; rittlings sitzen auf (*dat.*); *Land etc.* durchreiten; reiten lassen; ~ *s.o. down* j. niederreiten; j. einholen; ~ (*on*) *a bicycle* radfahren; ~ *out* ⚓ *Sturm* gut überstehen (*a. fig.*); '**rid·er** Reiter(in); Fahrende *m*; Beiblatt *n*; Anhängsel *n*, (Zusatz)Klausel *f*; ⊕ Laufgewicht *n*, Reiter *m*.

ridge [ridʒ] **1.** (Gebirgs)Kamm *m*, Grat *m*; ⚠ First *m*; ↗ Rain *m*; **2.** (sich) furchen; '**~-pole** Firstbalken *m*, -stange *f*.

rid·i·cule ['ridikjuːl] **1.** Hohn *m*, Spott *m*; *hold s.o. up to* ~ j. der Lächerlichkeit preisgeben; **2.** lächerlich machen; bespötteln; **ri'dic·u·lous** [~julǝs] lächerlich; **ri'dic·u·lous·ness** Lächerlichkeit *f*.

rid·ing ['raidiŋ] **1.** Reiten *n*; **2.** Reit...; '**~-breech·es** *pl.* Reithose *f*; '**~-hab·it** Reitkleid *n*.

rife □ [raif] häufig; vorherrschend; ~ *with* voll von.

riff-raff ['rifræf] Gesindel *n*, Pöbel *m*.

ri·fle[1] ['raifl] (aus)plündern.

ri·fle[2] [~] **1.** *gezogenes* Gewehr *n*, Büchse *f*; ~*s pl.* ⚔ Schützen *m/pl.*; **2.** *Gewehrlauf* ziehen; '**~·man** ⚔ Jäger *m*; Schütze *m*; '**~-range** Schießstand *m*; Schußweite *f*.

ri·fling ⊕ ['raifliŋ] Züge *m/pl. im Gewehr.*

rift [rift] Riß *m*, Sprung *m*; Spalte *f*.

rig[1] [rig] **1.** *Markt etc.* manipulieren; **2.** Schwindelmanöver *n*.

rig[2] [~] **1.** ⚓ Takelung *f*, Takelage *f*; F Aufmachung *f*, -zug *m*, Kluft *f*; **2.** auftakeln; ~ *s.o. out* j. versorgen *od.* ausrüsten (*with* mit); j. herausputzen, herrichten, kleiden; ~ *s.th. up* et. (behelfsmäßig) zs.-bauen; et. zs.-basteln; '**rig·ger** ⚓ Takler *m*; ✈ Monteur *m*; '**rig·ging** ⚓ Takelage *f*; ✈ Verspannung *f*.

right [rait] **1.** □ recht; richtig; gesund, wohl; recht (*Ggs. left*); ~ *angle* ⩘ rechter Winkel *m*; *be* ~ recht *od.* richtig sein; recht haben; *be* ~ *to inf.* recht daran tun zu *inf.*; *all* ~*!* alles in Ordnung!; ganz recht!, sehr wohl!; *on the* ~ *side of 50* noch nicht 50 Jahre alt; *get s.th.* ~ et. in Ordnung bringen; et. richtig verstehen; *put od. set* ~ in Ordnung bringen; richtigstellen, berichtigen; **2.** *adv.* recht, richtig; (nach) rechts; gerade; direkt, stracks; ganz (und gar); *in Titeln:* hoch, sehr; ✝ recht (*sehr*); ~ *away* schnurstracks; sogleich; los!; ~ *on* geradeaus, -zu; **3.** Recht *n*, Anspruch *m* (*to* auf *acc.*, *of ger.* darauf zu *inf.*); Rechte *f* (*Hand; Seite, a. parl.*); *Boxen:* Rechte *m*; *the* ~*s of man* die Menschenrechte *n/pl.*; *in* ~ *of his mother* von seiten s-r Mutter; *in one's own* ~ aus eigenem Recht; *the* ~*s and wrongs pl.* der wahre Sachverhalt; *by* ~*(s)* von Rechts wegen; *by* ~ *of* kraft, auf Grund (*gen.*); *set od. put to* ~*s* wieder in Ordnung bringen; *on od. to the* ~ rechts; **4.** *j-m* Rechte verschaffen; *et.* in Ordnung bringen; ⚓ (sich) aufrichten; **~-an·gled** ⩘ ['~'æŋgld] rechtwinklig; '**~-down** regelrecht, ausgemacht; wirklich; **right·eous** □ ['~ʃǝs] gerecht, rechtschaffen; '**right·eous·ness** Rechtschaffenheit *f*; **right·ful** □ ['~ful] recht(mäßig); gerecht; '**right-hand** recht (*Handschuh, Seite*); '**right-'hand·ed** rechtshändig; ⊕ rechtsläufig; '**right·ist** *pol.* **1.** Rechte *m*; **2.** rechtsgerichtet; '**right·ly** richtig; mit Recht; '**right-'mind·ed** rechtschaffen; '**right·ness** Richtigkeit *f*; Rechtlichkeit *f*; **right of way** Wegerecht *n*; Vorfahrt(srecht *n*) *f*; **right wing** *Sport:* Rechtsaußen *m*; *pol.* rechter Flügel *m*; '**right--wing** *pol.* rechtsorientiert, -stehend; **right-'wing·er** *pol.* Rechte *m*; *Sport:* Rechtsaußen *m*.

rig·id □ ['ridʒid] starr; *fig. a.* streng, hart, unbeugsam; **ri'gid·i·ty** Starrheit *f*; Strenge *f*, Härte *f*.

rig·ma·role ['rigmǝrǝul] Geschwätz *n*, Salbaderei *f*.

rig·or ['raigɔː] Fieberfrost *m*; ~ *mortis* ['mɔːtis] Leichenstarre *f*; **rig·or·ous** □ ['rigǝrǝs] streng, rigoros.

rig·o(u)r ['rigǝ] Strenge *f*, Härte *f*; ~*s pl.* Unbilden *pl. des Klimas etc.*

rile F [rail] ärgern, wurmen.
rill *poet.* [ril] Bächlein *n.*
rim [rim] **1.** Felge *f*; Radkranz *m*; Rand *m*; **2.** rändern; einfassen.
rime[1] [raim] Reim *m.*
rime[2] *poet.* [~] Rauhreif *m*; ˈ**rim·y** bereift.
rind [raind] Rinde *f*, Schale *f*; *Speck*-Schwarte *f.*
ring[1] [riŋ] **1.** Ring *m* (*a. Boxring, Manege, Kartell*); Kreis *m*; Buchmacher(stand *m*) *m/pl.*; *make* ~*s round s.o.* F viel schneller sein als j.; **2.** beringen; mit e-m (Nasen)Ring versehen; *mst* ~ *in*, ~ *round*, ~ *about* umringen.
ring[2] [~] **1.** Klang *m*; Geläut(e) *n*; Klingeln *n*; Rufzeichen *n*; Anruf *m*; *give s.o. a* ~ j. anrufen; **2.** (*irr.*) *v/i.* läuten; klingen (*Münze, Stimme, Ohr etc.*); *oft* ~ *out* erschallen (*with* von); ~ *again* widerhallen; ~ *off teleph.* das Gespräch beenden, den Hörer auflegen; *the bell* ~*s* es klingelt; *v/t.* klingen lassen; läuten; ~ *the bell* klingeln; F Erfolg haben; ~ *a bell* F an et. erinnern; ~ *s.o. up* j. *od.* bei j-m anrufen; ˈ**~-bind·er** Ringbuch *n*; ˈ**ring·er** Glöckner *m*; ˈ**ring·ing** □ klingend; laut; ˈ**ring·lead·er** Rädelsführer *m*; **ring·let** [ˈ~lit] (Ringel-)Locke *f*; **ring road** Ringstraße *f*; ˈ**ring·worm** ⚕ Ringelflechte *f.*
rink [riŋk] (*a.* künstliche) Eisbahn *f*; Rollschuhbahn *f.*
rinse [rins] **1.** *oft* ~ *out* (aus)spülen; **2.** = ˈ**rins·ing** Spülen *n*; Spülung *f*; ~*s pl.* Spülicht *n.*
ri·ot [ˈraiət] **1.** Krawall *m*, Tumult *m*; Aufruhr *m*; Orgie *f* (*a. fig.*); *fig.* Bombenerfolg *m*; *run* ~ durchgehen; (sich aus)toben; **2.** Krawall machen, in Aufruhr sein; toben; schwelgen (*in* in *dat.*); ˈ**ri·ot·er** Aufrührer(in); Randalierer *m*; ˈ**ri·ot·ous** □ aufrührerisch; lärmend; liederlich (*Leben*); **ri·ot shield** Schutzschild *m der Polizei*; **ri·ot squad** Bereitschaftspolizei *f*, Überfallkommando *n.*
rip[1] [rip] **1.** Riß *m*; **2.** *v/t. Naht etc.* (auf)trennen; (zer)reißen; ~ *up* aufschlitzen, -reißen; *v/i.* reißen; (dahin)sausen.
rip[2] F [~] Schindmähre *f*; Taugenichts *m.*
ri·par·i·an [raiˈpɛəriən] **1.** Ufer...; **2.** (Ufer)Anlieger *m.*
rip·cord [ˈripkɔːd] Reißleine *f am Fallschirm.*
ripe □ [raip] reif; ˈ**rip·en** reifen; ˈ**ripe·ness** Reife *f.*
rip-off P [ˈripɔf] Wucher *m*, Nepp *m*; Schwindel *m.*
ri·poste [riˈpəust] **1.** *fenc.* Gegenstoß *m*, -hieb *m* (*a. fig.*); **2.** erwidern.
rip·per [ˈripə] Trennmesser *n*, -säge *f*, -maschine *f*; *sl.* Prachtkerl *m*; -stück *n*; ˈ**rip·ping** □ *sl.* fabelhaft, blendend, glänzend.
rip·ple [ˈripl] **1.** kleine Welle *f*; Kräuselung *f*; Geriesel *n*; **2.** (sich) kräuseln; rieseln.
rise [raiz] **1.** (An-, Auf)Steigen *n*; Anwachsen *n*; Anschwellen *n des Wassers, der Stimme*; (Preis-, Gehalts)Erhöhung *f*; *fig.* Aufstieg *m*; ⚒ Aufgang *m der Sonne*; Steigung *f*, Anhöhe *f*; Erhöhung *f* (*a. fig.*); Zuwachs *m*; Ursprung *m*, Anfang *m*; *give* ~ *to* verursachen, hervorrufen; *take* (*one's*) ~ entstehen; entspringen; **2.** (*irr.*) sich erheben, aufstehen; aufbrechen, die Sitzung schließen; in die Höhe gehen, steigen; aufsteigen (*a. fig., Erinnerung etc.*) (*on, upon* vor *j-s Geist etc.*); auferstehen; aufgehen (*Sonne, Samen*); anschwellen, wachsen; sich empören (*against, on* gegen); entspringen (*Fluß*); ~ *to* sich *e-r Lage* gewachsen zeigen; ~ *to the bait* nach dem Köder schnappen; **ris·en** [ˈrizn] *p.p. von rise* 2; ˈ**ris·er** Aufstehende *m*; Steigung *f e-r Stufe*; *early* ~ Frühaufsteher(in).
ris·i·bil·i·ty [riziˈbiliti] Neigung *f* zu lachen; **ris·i·ble** □ [ˈ~ibl] Lach...; zum Lachen aufgelegt.
ris·ing [ˈraiziŋ] **1.** (Auf)Steigen *n*; Steigung *f*; *ast.* Aufgang *m*; Aufbruch *m e-r Versammlung*; Aufstand *m*; **2.** heranwachsend (*Generation*).
risk [risk] **1.** Gefahr *f*, Wagnis *n*; ⚜ Risiko *n*; *at the* ~ *of ger.* auf die Gefahr hin, zu *inf.*; *run the* ~ das Risiko eingehen, Gefahr laufen; **2.** wagen, riskieren, aufs Spiel setzen; ˈ**risk·y** □ gefährlich, gewagt.
ris·sole [ˈrisəul] *Küche*: Frikadelle *f.*
rite [rait] Ritus *m*, *feierlicher* Brauch *m*; **rit·u·al** [ˈritʃuəl] **1.** □ rituell,

feierlich; **2.** Ritual *n.*

ri·val ['raivəl] **1.** Nebenbuhler(in); Rivale *m*, Rivalin *f*; **2.** rivalisierend; ✝ Konkurrenz...; **3.** wetteifern *od.* rivalisieren (mit); '**ri·val·ry** Rivalität *f*; Wetteifer *m.*

rive [raiv] (*irr.*) (sich) spalten.

riv·en ['rivn] *p.p. von rive.*

riv·er ['rivə] Fluß *m*; Strom *m* (*a. fig.*); *sell s.o. down the ~ fig.* j. verraten; '**~-horse** Flußpferd *n*; '**~-po·lice** Wasserschutzpolizei *f*; '**~-side** (Fluß)Ufer *n*; *attr.* am Wasser (gelegen).

riv·et ['rivit] **1.** ⊕ Niet(e *f*) *m*; **2.** (ver)nieten; *fig.* heften (*to* an *acc.*; *on, upon* auf *acc.*); fesseln.

riv·u·let ['rivjulit] Bach *m*, Flüßchen *n.*

roach *ichth.* [rəutʃ] Plötze *f.*

road [rəud] Straße *f* (*a. fig.*), Weg *m*; *Am.* = *railroad*; *mst ~s pl.* ⚓ Reede *f*; *on the ~* unterwegs; *take the ~* aufbrechen; *main ~* Haupt(verkehrs)straße *f*; '**~·bed** Straßenunterbau *m*; 🚂 Bahnkörper *m*; '**~-block** Straßensperre *f*; '**~-hog** *mot.* Verkehrsrowdy *m*; '**~·man** Straßenarbeiter *m*; **~ map** Straßen-, Autokarte *f*; '**~-mend·er** Straßenarbeiter *m*; '**~-race** Straßenrennen *n*; '**~-sense** *mot.* Fahrverstand *m*; '**~·side** Straßenrand *m*; '**~·stead** ⚓ Reede *f*; **road·ster** ['~stə] Roadster *m*, offener Sportwagen *m*; '**road·way** Fahrbahn *f*; **road works** *pl.* Straßenarbeiten *f/pl.*; Baustelle *f auf e-r Straße*; '**road·wor·thi·ness** Verkehrssicherheit *f e-s Autos*; '**road·wor·thy** verkehrssicher (*Auto*).

roam [rəum] *v/i.* umherstreifen, wandern; *v/t.* durchstreifen; '**roam·er** Herumtreiber(in); Wanderer *m.*

roan [rəun] **1.** rötlichgrau; **2.** Rotschimmel *m*; ⊕ Schafleder *n.*

roar [rɔː] **1.** brüllen (*a. fig. überlaut sprechen, lachen*); brausen, tosen, donnern; **2.** Gebrüll *n*; Brausen *n*; Krachen *n*, Getöse *n*; brüllendes Gelächter *n*; **roar·ing** ['~riŋ] **1.** = *roar* 2; **2.** □ brüllend; lärmend; stürmisch; schwunghaft; *be in ~ health* vor Gesundheit strotzen.

roast [rəust] **1.** rösten, braten; backen; *sl. j.* verkohlen (*hänseln*); **2.** geröstet; gebraten; *~ beef* Rinderbraten *m*; *~ meat* Braten *m*; **3.** *rule the ~* das Regiment führen; '**roast·er** Röster *m*; Kaffeeröstmaschine *f*; Spanferkel *n*; '**roast·ing-jack** Bratenwender *m.*

rob [rɔb] (be)rauben; (aus)plündern; '**rob·ber** Räuber *m*; '**rob·ber·y** Raub(überfall) *m*; Räuberei *f.*

robe [rəub] **1.** (Amts)Robe *f*, Talar *m*; Staatskleid *n*; *poet.* Gewand *n*; Kleid *n*; *Am.* Morgenrock *m*; *~s pl.* Amtstracht *f*; *gentlemen of the ~* Juristen *m/pl.*; **2.** kleiden; *j-m* die Robe *etc.* anlegen; *fig.* schmücken.

rob·in *orn.* ['rɔbin] Rotkehlchen *n.*

ro·bot ['rəubɔt] **1.** Roboter *m*; Automat *m*; automatisches Verkehrszeichen *n*; **2.** automatisch, mechanisch.

ro·bust □ [rəu'bʌst] robust, derb, kräftig; widerstandsfähig; **ro'bust·ness** Robustheit *f*, Derbheit *f*, Kraft *f.*

rock¹ [rɔk] Fels(en) *m*; Klippe *f*; Gestein *n*; Zuckerstange *f*; *get down to ~ bottom* der Sache auf den Grund gehen; *~ crystal* Bergkristall *m*; *~ salt* Steinsalz *n.*

rock² [~] *v/t.* schaukeln; (ein)wiegen; rütteln; *fig.* erschüttern; *~ s.o. to sleep* j. in den Schlaf wiegen; *v/i.* schaukeln, (sch)wanken.

rock³ ♪ [~] Rock *m.*

rock-bot·tom F ['rɔk'bɔtəm] allerniedrigst (*Preis*).

rock·er ['rɔkə] *Wiegen- etc.* Kufe *f*; *Am.* Schaukelstuhl *m*; Rocker *m*, Halbstarke *m.*

rock·er·y ['rɔkəri] Steingarten *m.*

rock·et¹ ['rɔkit] **1.** Rakete *f*; *~-launching site* Raketenabschußbasis *f*; *~ plane* Raketenflugzeug *n*; *~ propulsion* Raketenantrieb *m*; **2.** F in die Höhe schießen (*Preise*).

rock·et² ⚘ [~] Rauke *f*, Senfkohl *m*; Nachtviole *f.*

rock·et-pow·ered ['rɔkitpauəd] mit Raketenantrieb; **rock·et·ry** ['~ri] Raketentechnik *f.*

rock...: '**~·fall** Steinschlag *m*; '**~-gar·den** Steingarten *m.*

rock·ing... ['rɔkiŋ]: '**~-chair** Schaukelstuhl *m*; '**~-horse** Schaukelpferd *n.*

rock·y ['rɔki] felsig; Felsen...; F wackelig.

ro·co·co [rəu'kəukəu] Rokoko *n.*

rod [rɔd] Rute *f*; Stab *m*; ⊕ Stange *f*; Meßrute *f* (= $5^1/_2$ *yards*); *Am. sl.*

Pistole *f*; *have a ~ in pickle for s.o.* mit j-m noch ein Hühnchen zu rupfen haben.

rode [rəud] *pret. von ride* 2.

ro·dent ['rəudənt] Nagetier *n*.

ro·de·o *Am.* [rəu'deiəu] Rodeo *m*; Zusammentreiben *n von Vieh*; Cowboy-Turnier *n*.

rod·o·mon·tade [rɔdəmɔn'teid] Aufschneiderei *f*, Prahlerei *f*.

roe[1] [rəu] *a. hard ~* Rogen *m*; *soft ~* Milch *f*.

roe[2] [~] Reh *n*; '**~·buck** Rehbock *m*.

ro·ga·tion *eccl.* [rəu'geiʃən] (Für-)Bitte *f*; *~ Sunday* Sonntag Rogate *m*.

rogue [rəug] Schurke *m*; Schelm *m*, Spitzbube *m*; *~s' gallery* Verbrecheralbum *n*; '**ro·guer·y** Schurkerei *f*; Schelmerei *f*; '**ro·guish** □ schurkisch; schelmisch.

roist·er ['rɔistə] krakeelen; '**roist·er·er** Krakeeler *m*.

role, rôle *thea.* [rəul] Rolle *f* (*a. fig.*).

roll [rəul] **1.** Rolle *f*; ⊕ Walze *f*; Brötchen *n*, Semmel *f*; Rolle *f*, Verzeichnis *n*, Liste *f*; Urkunde *f*; (Donner)Rollen *n*; (Trommel)Wirbel *m*; ⚓ Schlingern *n*; **2.** *v/t.* rollen; wälzen; walzen, strecken; *Zigarette* drehen; rollend (aus-)sprechen; *~ up* aufrollen; einwickeln; *~ed gold* Walzgold *n*, Dublee *n*; *v/i.* rollen (*a. Donner etc.*); sich wälzen; *bsd. ast.* sich drehen; wirbeln (*Trommel*); ⚓ schlingern; *be ~ing in money* im Geld schwimmen; *~ up* vorfahren (*Wagen*); aufkreuzen; *~* **bar** *mot.* Überrollbügel *m*; '**~-call** Namensaufruf *m*, ⚔ Appell *m*; '**roll·er** Rolle *f*, Walze *f*; Sturzwelle *f*; *mst ~ bandage* Rollbinde *f*; *~ coaster Am.* Achterbahn *f*; *~ skate* Rollschuh *m*; *~ towel* Rollhandtuch *n*; '**roll-film** *phot.* Rollfilm *m*.

rol·lick·ing ['rɔlikiŋ] ausgelassen, übermütig.

roll·ing ['rəuliŋ] **1.** rollend; Roll..., Walz...; well(enförm)ig; **2.** Rollen *n*, Walzen *n*; *~ mill* ⊕ Walzwerk *n*; *~ pin* Nudelholz *n*; *~ press typ.* Rotationspresse *f*; '**~-stock** 🚂 rollendes Material *n*.

roll-neck ['rəulnek] Rollkragen *m*.

roll-on ['rəulɔn] *a. ~ belt* Gummischlüpfer *m*, Hüftformer *m*; Deoroller *m*.

roll-top desk ['rəultɔp'desk] Rollpult *n*.

ro·ly-po·ly ['rəuli'pəuli] **1.** Rollkuchen *m*; **2.** rund und dick.

Ro·man ['rəumən] **1.** römisch; **2.** Römer(in); *mst* ♀ *typ.* Antiqua (-schrift) *f*; **~-'Cath·o·lic** *eccl.* **1.** (römisch-)katholisch; **2.** Katholik(in).

ro·mance[1] [rəu'mæns] **1.** (Ritter-, Vers)Roman *m*; Abenteuer-, Liebesroman *m*; Romanze *f* (*a. fig.*); *fig.* Märchen *n*; Romantik *f*; **2.** *fig.* aufschneiden.

Ro·mance[2] [rəu'mæns]: *~ languages pl.* romanische Sprachen *f/pl.*

ro·manc·er [rəu'mænsə] Romanschreiber *m*; Aufschneider *m*.

Ro·man·esque [rəumə'nesk] romanisch(er Baustil *m*).

Ro·man·ic [rəu'mænik] romanisch; *bsd. ~ peoples pl.* Romanen *m/pl.*

ro·man·tic [rəu'mæntik] **1.** (*~ally*) romantisch; **2.** = **ro'man·ti·cist** [~tisist] Romantiker *m*; **ro'man·ti·cism** Romantik *f*.

Ro·ma·ny ['rəuməni] **1.** Zigeuner(in); Zigeunersprache *f*; **2.** Zigeuner...

Rom·ish *mst contp.* ['rəumiʃ] römisch(-katholisch).

romp [rɔmp] **1.** Range *f*, Wildfang *m*; Balgerei *f*; **2.** sich balgen, toben, tollen; '**romp·er**(**s** *pl.*) Spielanzug *m e-s Kindes*.

ron·do ♪ ['rɔndəu] Rondo *n*.

rood [ru:d] Kruzifix *n*; Viertelmorgen *m* (*10,117 Ar*); '**~-loft** ⚠ Chorbühne *f*.

roof [ru:f] **1.** Dach *n*; *~ of the mouth* Gaumen *m*; **2.** *a. ~ over* überdachen; '**roof·ing** **1.** Bedachung *f*; Dachwerk *n*; **2.** Dach...; *~ felt* Dachpappe *f*; **roof rack** *Auto*: Dachgepäckträger *m*; '**roof-tree** Firstbalken *m*.

rook[1] [ruk] **1.** *orn.* Saatkrähe *f*; *fig.* Bauernfänger *m*; **2.** betrügen.

rook[2] [~] *Schach*: Turm *m*.

rook·er·y ['rukəri] Krähenhorst *m*; *fig.* Brutstätte *f*; Nistplatz *m*.

rook·ie *sl.* ['ruki] ⚔ Rekrut *m*; *fig.* Neuling *m*, Anfänger *m*.

room [rum] Raum *m*; Platz *m*; Zimmer *n*; Spielraum *m*, Möglichkeit *f*; *~s pl.* Wohnung *f*; *in my ~* an meiner Stelle; *make ~* Platz machen; **...roomed** ...zimmerig; '**room·er** *bsd. Am.* Untermieter *m*;

ˈ**room·ing-house** *bsd. Am.* Miets-, Logierhaus *n*; ˈ**room-mate** Stubenkamerad *m*; ˈ**room·y** □ geräumig.

roost [ruːst] **1.** Schlafplatz *m e-s Vogels*; Hühnerstange *f*; Hühnerstall *m*; *rule the* ~ F *fig.* Herr im Haus sein; **2.** sich (zum Schlaf) niederhocken; *fig.* übernachten; ˈ**roost·er** Haushahn *m*.

root[1] [ruːt] **1.** Wurzel *f* (*a. fig., anat.*, ♣, *gr.*); ~ *and branch* völlig, mit Stumpf u. Stiel; *take od. strike* ~ Wurzel fassen *od.* schlagen; ~ *idea* Grundgedanke *m*; **2.** (ein)wurzeln; ~ *out* ausrotten; ˈ**root·ed** eingewurzelt; wurzelnd (*in* in *dat.*).

root[2] [~] *v/t. a.* ~ *up* auf-, umwühlen; ~ *out od. up* ausgraben, aufstöbern; *v/i.* wühlen; ~ *for Am. sl.* Stimmung machen für *j.*; ˈ**root·er** *Am. sl.* Schreier *m*, Fanatiker *m für et.*

root·let [ˈruːtlit] Wurzelfaser *f*.

rope [rəup] **1.** Tau *n*, Seil *n*; Strang *m*, Strick *m* (*bsd. zum Hängen*); Schnur *f Perlen etc.*; *on the* ~ am Seil, angeseilt; *be at the end of one's* ~ F mit s-m Latein zu Ende sein; *know the* ~*s* sich auskennen; *learn the* ~*s* sich einarbeiten; *show s.o. the* ~*s* j-m zeigen, wie der Laden läuft; **2.** *v/t.* mit e-m Seil befestigen; *mst* ~ *in*, ~ *off*, ~ *out* absperren; *mount.* anseilen; ~ *down* abseilen; *v/i.* Fäden ziehen (*Sirup etc.*); ˈ~**-danc·er** Seiltänzer(in); ˈ~**-lad·der** Strickleiter *f*; ˈ~**-mak·er** Seiler *m*; ˈ**rop·er·y** Seilerei *f*; ˈ**rope-walk** Seilerbahn *f*; ˈ**rope-way** Seilbahn *f*.

rop·i·ness [ˈrəupinis] Klebrigkeit *f*.

rop·y [ˈrəupi] klebrig, zähflüssig.

ro·sa·ry [ˈrəuzəri] *eccl.* Rosenkranz *m*; Rosengarten *m*, -beet *n*.

rose[1] [rəuz] ♀ Rose *f*; (Gießkannen)Brause *f*; Rosenrot *n*.

rose[2] [~] *pret. von rise* 2.

rose...: ˈ~**·bud** Rosenknospe *f*; *Am.* hübsches Mädchen *n*; Debütantin *f*; ˈ~**-col·o(u)red** rosarot (*a. fig.*); rosig.

ro·se·ate [ˈrəuziit] rosig.

rose·hip ♀ [ˈrəuzhip] Hagebutte *f*.

rose·mar·y ♀ [ˈrəuzməri] Rosmarin *m*.

ro·se·ry [ˈrəuzəri] Rosenbeet *n*.

ro·sette [rəuˈzet] Rosette *f*.

rose...: ~ **win·dow** (Fenster)Rosette *f*; ˈ~**·wood** Rosenholz *n*.

ros·in [ˈrɔzin] **1.** (Geigen)Harz *n*, Kolophonium *n*; **2.** harzen.

ros·ter [ˈrəustə] Dienstplan *m*; Diensttabelle *f*.

ros·trum [ˈrɔstrəm] Rednertribüne *f*.

ros·y □ [ˈrəuzi] rosig.

rot [rɔt] **1.** Fäulnis *f*, Fäule *f*; *sl.* Quatsch *m*; **2.** *v/t.* faulen lassen; *sl. Plan etc.* vermurksen; Quatsch machen mit *j-m*; *v/i.* verfaulen, vermodern.

ro·ta [ˈrəutə] = *roster*.

ro·ta·ry [ˈrəutəri] drehend; Rotations...; ~ *press typ.* Rotations(druck)presse *f*; ~ *pump* Kreiselpumpe *f*; **ro·tate** [rəuˈteit] (sich) drehen, rotieren, (ab)wechseln; **roˈta·tion** Umdrehung *f*; Kreislauf *m*; Abwechs(e)lung *f*; ~ *of crops* ✓ Fruchtfolge *f*, -wechsel *m*; **ro·ta·to·ry** [ˈ~tətəri] *s. rotary*; abwechselnd.

rote [rəut]: *by* ~ auswendig.

ro·tor [ˈrəutə] ⊕ Rotor *m*; ⚡ Läufer *m*; ✈ Rotor *m*, Drehflügel *m des Hubschraubers*.

rot·ten □ [ˈrɔtn] verfault, faul(ig); verderbt, verdorben; modrig; morsch (*alle a. fig.*); *sl.* saumäßig, dreckig; ˈ**rot·ten·ness** Fäulnis *f*; Morschheit *f*.

rot·ter *sl.* [ˈrɔtə] Schweinehund *m*.

ro·tund □ [rəuˈtʌnd] rund; voll (*Stimme*); hochtrabend; **roˈtun·da** △ [~də] Rundbau *m*; **roˈtun·di·ty** Rundheit *f*.

rouge [ruːʒ] **1.** Rouge *n*; Silberputzmittel *n*; **2.** Rouge auflegen (auf).

rough [rʌf] **1.** □ rauh; roh; grob (*alle a. fig.*); holperig; stürmisch; *fig.* ungehobelt; herb (*Wein etc.*); ungefähr (*Schätzung*); ~ *and ready* grob(gearbeitet); (Not)Behelfs...; *fig.* grobschlächtig; ~ *copy* roher Entwurf *m*; ~ *draft* Rohfassung *f*; *cut up* ~ F massiv werden; **2.** Rauhe *n*, Grobe *n*; Lümmel *m*, Strolch *m*; **3.** (an-, auf)rauhen; *Hufeisen* schärfen; ~ *it* sich mühsam durchschlagen; ˈ**rough·age** grobe Nahrung *f*, Grobfutter *n*; ˈ**rough-and-ˈread·y** grob; provisorisch; Behelfs... (*gerade ausreichend für den Zweck*); ˈ**rough-and-ˈtum·ble** **1.** wild, unordentlich; heftig; **2.** Schlägerei *f*; ˈ**rough-cast** **1.** △ Rauhputz *m*; **2.** unfertig; **3.** △ berappen; roh entwerfen; ˈ**rough·en** rauh machen *od.* werden.

rough...: '~-'**hewn** roh behauen; flüchtig; ungehobelt; '**~-house** *sl.* **1.** Radau *m*; Keilerei *f*; **2.** rauhbeinig gegen *j.* sein; Radau machen; '**~-neck** *Am. sl.* Rabauke *m*; '**roughness** Rauheit *f*; Roheit *f*; Grobheit *f*; '**rough-rid·er** Zureiter *m*; verwegener Reiter *m*; '**rough·shod:** *ride ~ over* rücksichtslos behandeln.

rou·lette [ruː'let] Roulett *n.*

Rou·ma·nian [ruː'meinjən] = *Rumanian.*

round [raund] **1.** □ rund (*a. Zahl, Summe*); voll (*Stimme etc.*); flott, scharf (*Gangart*); abgerundet (*Stil*); unverblümt (*Antwort etc.*); derb (*Fluch etc.*); *~ game* Gesellschaftsspiel *n*; *~ hand* Rundschrift *f*; *~ table* Konferenztisch *m*; *~ trip* Rundreise *f*, Hin- und Rückfahrt *f*; **2.** *adv.* rund-, ringsum(her); *a. ~ about* in der Runde; *all ~* ringsum; *fig.* durch die Bank, ohne Unterschied; *all the year ~* das ganze Jahr hindurch; *10 inches ~* 10 Zoll im Umfang; **3.** *prp.* um ... herum; *go ~ the house* im Haus herumgehen; *~ about 2 o'clock* etwa um 2 Uhr; **4.** Rund *n*, Kreis *m*; Rundgang *m*, Runde *f*; Kreislauf *m*; (Leiter-) Sprosse *f*; ♪ Rundgesang *m*, Kanon *m*; Rundtanz *m*; ⚔ Ronde *f*; Lage *f Bier etc.*; ⚔, *a. fig. Lach-, Beifalls-*Salve *f*; *100 ~s* ⚔ 100 Schuß; **5.** *v/t.* runden; herumgehen, -fahren *od.* -segeln um; umfahren, -schiffen; *~ off* abrunden; *~ up* einkreisen; *j.* stellen; *Vieh* zs.-treiben; *v/i.* sich runden; sich umdrehen.

round·a·bout ['raundəbaut] **1.** umschweifig; umwegig; **2.** Umweg *m*; Umschweife *pl.*; Karussell *n*; Kreisverkehr *m.*

roun·del ['raundl] Rondell *n*;

roun·de·ly ['~dilei] Rundgesang *m.*

round·ers ['raundəz] *pl.* Schlagballspiel *n*; '**round·head** *hist.* Rundkopf *m*, Puritaner *m*; '**round·ish** rundlich; '**round·ness** Rundheit *f*; Rundung *f*; Unverblümtheit *f e-r Antwort etc.*; **round rob·in** *von mehreren Leuten unterschriebene* Petition *f*, Denkschrift *f*; **rounds-man** ✝ ['~zmən] Austräger *m*; '**round-ta·ble con·fer·ence** Konferenz *f* am runden Tisch; '**round-the-clock** ununterbrochen, 24-stündig; '**round-up** Einkreisung *f*; Razzia *f*; Zs.-fassung *f*; Zs.-treiben *n.*

roup *vet.* [ruːp] Darre *f der Hühner.*

rouse [rauz] *v/t. a. ~ up* wecken; ermuntern, aufrütteln; *Wild* aufjagen; (auf)reizen; *~ o.s.* sich aufraffen; *v/i.* aufwachen; '**rous·ing** brausend (*Beifall etc.*).

roust·a·bout *Am.* ['raustə'baut] ungelernter (*mst* Hafen)Arbeiter *m.*

rout[1] [raut] Rotte *f*; † große Gesellschaft *f.*

rout[2] [~] **1.** wilde Flucht *f*; Vernichtung *f*; *put to ~* = **2.** vernichtend schlagen.

rout[3] [~] = *root*[2].

route [ruːt, ⚔ *a.* raut] Weg *m*; (Reise)Route *f*; Strecke *f*; ⚔ Marschroute *f*; *en ~* unterwegs; '**~-march** Übungsmarsch *m.*

rou·tine [ruː'tiːn] **1.** Routine *f*; Schablone *f*; **2.** schablonenmäßig; üblich, laufend.

roux [ruː] Mehlschwitze *f*, Einbrenne *f.*

rove [rəuv] umherstreifen, umherwandern; '**rov·er** Wanderer *m*; Herumstreicher *m*; Seeräuber *m*; älterer Pfadfinder *m.*

row[1] [rəu] Reihe *f*; Häuser-, *thea.* Sitzreihe *f*; *~ house Am.* Reihenhaus *n*; *a hard ~ to hoe* e-e schwierige Sache *f.*

row[2] [~] **1.** rudern; **2.** Ruderfahrt *f*, -partie *f.*

row[3] F [rau] **1.** Spektakel *m*; Krawall *m*, Krach *m*; Schlägerei *f*; *what's the ~?* was ist denn los?; **2.** ausschimpfen; zanken (*with* mit).

row·an ♆ ['rauən] Eberesche *f*; '**~ber·ry** Vogelbeere *f.*

row-boat ['rəubəut] Ruderboot *n.*

row·dy ['raudi] **1.** Raufbold *m*, Strolch *m*, Rowdy *m*; **2.** gewalttätig; flegelhaft.

row·el ['rauəl] **1.** Spornrädchen *n*; **2.** spornen.

row·er ['rəuə] Ruderer(in *f*) *m.*

row·ing-boat ['rəuiŋbəut] Ruderboot *n.*

row·lock ['rɔlək] Ruderklampe *f.*

roy·al ['rɔiəl] **1.** □ königlich; prächtig; *~ stag* Kapitalhirsch *m*; **2.** ⚓ Oberbramsegel *n*; '**roy·al·ism** Königstreue *f*; '**roy·al·ist 1.** Royalist *m*, Königstreue *m*; **2.** königstreu; '**roy·al·ty** Königtum *n*, -reich *n*, Königswürde *f*; königliche Persönlichkeit *f*; königliches Vorrecht *n*; vom König verliehenes Verfügungsrecht *n*; Ertragsanteil *m*, Tantieme *f e-s Autors etc.*

rub [rʌb] **1.** Reiben *n*; Schwierigkeit *f*; *fig.* Hieb *m*, Stich *m*; Unannehmlichkeit *f*; *there is the* ~ das ist der Haken; **2.** *v/t.* reiben; (ab-)wischen, scheuern; (wund)scheuern; schleifen; ~ *down* abreiben; *Pferd* striegeln; ~ *in* einreiben; *fig.* betonen, herumreiten auf; ~ *off* abreiben; abschleifen; ~ *out* auslöschen; -radieren; ~ *up* auffrischen; *Farbe etc.* verreiben; *v/i.* sich reiben (*against, on* an *dat.*); ~ *along*, ~ *on*, ~ *through fig.* sich durchschlagen.

rub·ber ['rʌbə] Gummi *n*, *m*; Kautschuk *m*; Radiergummi *m*; Masseur *m*; Wischtuch *n*; ⊕ Polierkissen *n*, -tuch *n*; *Bridge, Whist*: Robber *m*; ~*s pl.* Gummi-, Überschuhe *m/pl.*; *attr.* Gummi...; ~ *check Am. sl.* geplatzter Scheck *m*; ~ *solution* Gummilösung *f*; '~**·neck** *Am. sl.* **1.** Gaffer(in); **2.** sich den Hals verrenken; mithören; ~ **pants** *pl.* Gummihöschen *n für Babys*; ~ **stamp** Gummistempel *m*; *Am.* F *fig.* Nachbeter *m*; '~**-'stamp** automatisch gutheißen.

rub·bish ['rʌbiʃ] Schutt *m*; Abfall *m*; Kehricht *m*; *fig.* Schund *m*; Unsinn *m*; ~ *bin* Abfalleimer *m*; ~ *chute* Müllschlucker *m*; '**rub·bish·y** *fig.* wertlos; unsinnig.

rub·ble ['rʌbl] Schutt *m*.

rube *Am. sl.* [ru:b] Bauernlümmel *m*.

ru·be·fa·cient ⚕ [ru:bi'feiʃjənt] hautrötend.

ru·bi·cund ['ru:bikənd] rötlich, rot.

ru·bric ['ru:brik] Rubrik *f*; *eccl.* liturgische Vorschrift *f*; **ru·bri·cate** ['~keit] rot bezeichnen.

ru·by ['ru:bi] **1.** *min.* Rubin *m*; Rubinrot *n*; *typ.* Pariser Schrift *f*; **2.** rubinrot.

ruck [rʌk] *Rennsport*: *the* ~ das Feld; *the (common)* ~ *fig.* der Haufe(n) *m*.

ruck(·le) ['rʌk(l)] *a.* ~ *up* (sich) falten *od.* zerknittern.

ruck·sack ['ruksæk] Rucksack *m*.

ruc·tion *sl.* ['rʌkʃən] Krawall *m*, Krach *m*.

rud·der ⚓ ['rʌdə] (Steuer)Ruder *n*; ✈ Seitenruder *n*.

rud·di·ness ['rʌdinis] Röte *f*; '**rud·dy** rot, rötlich; frisch (*Gesichtsfarbe*); rotbäckig; *sl.* verflixt.

rude □ [ru:d] unhöflich; unanständig; grob, heftig, unsanft; ungebildet; einfach, kunstlos; robust; roh; '**rude·ness** Unhöflichkeit *f*, Unanständigkeit *f etc.*

ru·di·ment *biol.* ['ru:dimənt] Ansatz *m* (*of* zu *e-m Organ*; *a. fig.*); ~*s pl.* Anfangsgründe *m/pl.*; **ru·di·men·ta·ry** [~'mentəri] rudimentär.

rue[1] ⚘ [ru:] Raute *f*.

rue[2] [~] bereuen, beklagen.

rue·ful □ ['ru:ful] reuig; traurig, kläglich; '**rue·ful·ness** Traurigkeit *f*, Gram *m*.

ruff[1] [rʌf] (Hals-, Papier)Krause *f*.

ruff[2] [~] *Whist*: **1.** Trumpfen *n*; **2.** trumpfen.

ruf·fi·an ['rʌfjən] Rohling *m*; Raufbold *m*; Schurke *m*; '**ruf·fi·an·ly** roh, wüst.

ruf·fle ['rʌfl] **1.** Rüsche *f*, Krause *f*; Kräuseln *n des Wassers*; *fig.* Unruhe *f*; ~ *collar* Rüschenkragen *m*; **2.** *v/t.* kräuseln; zerwühlen, -drücken, -zausen; *fig.* aus der Ruhe bringen; *gute Laune etc.* stören; *v/i.* die Ruhe verlieren.

rug [rʌg] (Woll-, Reise)Decke *f*; Vorleger *m*, Brücke *f* (*kleiner Teppich*).

Rug·by ['rʌgbi] *a.* ~ *football* Rugby *n* (*Ballspiel*).

rug·ged □ ['rʌgid] rauh (*a. fig.*); uneben; zackig; zerklüftet; gefurcht (*Gesicht*); '**rug·ged·ness** Rauheit *f etc.*

rug·ger F ['rʌgə] = *Rugby*.

ru·in ['ru:in] **1.** Ruin *m*, Zs.-bruch *m*; Untergang *m*; Verfall *m*; *mst* ~*s pl.* Ruine(n *pl.*) *f*; *lay in* ~*s* in Trümmer legen; **2.** ruinieren; zugrunde richten; zerstören; verderben; **ru·in'a·tion** Zerstörung *f*; F Verderben *n*, Untergang *m*; '**ru·in·ous** □ ruinenhaft, verfallen; baufällig; verderblich, ruinös.

rule [ru:l] **1.** Regel *f*; *eccl.* Ordensregel *f*; Vorschrift *f*; ⚖ Verfügung *f*; *a. standing* ~ Satzung *f*; Herrschaft *f*; Lineal *n*; ⊕ Zollstock *m*; *as a* ~ in der Regel; ~*(s) of court* Prozeßordnung *f*; ~*(s) of the road* Straßenverkehrsordnung *f*; ~ *of three* ⅍ Regeldetri *f*; ~ *of thumb* Faustregel *f*; *make it a* ~ es sich zur Regel machen; *work to* ~ genau

nach Vorschrift arbeiten (*als Streikmittel*); **2.** *v/t.* regeln; leiten; *a.* ~ *over* beherrschen; entscheiden, verfügen; *Papier* liniieren; ~ *out* ausschließen; *v/i.* herrschen, regieren; ☿ stehen, notieren (*Preise*); **'rul·er** Herrscher(in); Lineal *n*; **'rul·ing 1.** *bsd.* ⚖ Verfügung *f*; **2.** ~ *price* ☿ Tagespreis *m.*
rum[1] [rʌm] Rum *m*; *Am.* Alkohol *m.*
rum[2] *sl.* □ [~] ulkig, komisch.
Ru·ma·nian [ruːˈmeinjən] **1.** rumänisch; **2.** Rumäne *m*, Rumänin *f*; Rumänisch *n.*
rum·ble[1] [ˈrʌmbl] **1.** Rumpeln *n*; Poltern *n*; (G)Rollen *n*; *Am. a.* ~*-seat mot.* Notsitz *m*; *Am.* F Fehde *f* zwischen Gangsterbanden; **2.** rumpeln, rasseln, poltern; grollen (*Donner*).
rum·ble[2] *sl.* [~] *et.* rauskriegen.
rum·bus·tious F [rʌmˈbʌstiəs] ausgelassen, laut und fröhlich, wild.
ru·mi·nant [ˈruːminənt] **1.** wiederkäuend; **2.** Wiederkäuer *m*; **ru·minate** [ˈ~neit] wiederkäuen; *fig.* nachsinnen; **ru·miˈna·tion** Wiederkäuen *n*; Nachdenken *n.*
rum·mage [ˈrʌmidʒ] **1.** Durchsuchung *f*; Ramsch *m*, Ausschuß *m*, Restwaren *f/pl.*; ~ *sale* Wohltätigkeitsbazar *m*; **2.** *v/t.* (durch)suchen, (-)stöbern, (-)wühlen; *v/i.* wühlen.
rum·mer [ˈrʌmə] Römer *m* (*Trinkglas*).
rum·my[1] *sl.* □ [ˈrʌmi] = *rum*[2].
rum·my[2] [~] Rommé *n* (*Kartenspiel*).
ru·mo(u)r [ˈruːmə] **1.** Gerücht *n*; **2.** (als Gerücht) verbreiten; *it is* ~*ed* es geht das Gerücht; **ˈ~-monger** Gerüchteverbreiter *m.*
rump *anat.* [rʌmp] Steiß *m*; *orn.* Bürzel *m*; Rumpf *m*, Rest *m.*
rum·ple [ˈrʌmpl] zerknittern, zerknüllen; *Haar* zerwühlen, (zer)zausen; **ˈrum·pled** zerknittert, zerzaust.
rump·steak [ˈrʌmpsteik] *Küche*: Rumpsteak *n.*
rum·pus F [ˈrʌmpəs] Krawall *m.*
rum-run·ner *Am.* [ˈrʌmrʌnə] Alkoholschmuggler *m.*
run [rʌn] **1.** (*irr.*) *v/i. allg.* laufen (*Mensch, Tier*; *a. Kerze, Gefäß, Augen etc.*; = *fließen*; *verfließen*; *verkehren* [*Zug etc.*]; *im Gang sein*; ⚖ *in Kraft sein*; *thea. gegeben werden*; *sich erstrecken*; *eitern*); rennen (*Mensch, Tier*); eilen; zerlaufen (*Farbe etc.*); umlaufen, -gehen (*Gerücht etc.*); lauten (*Text*); gehen (*Melodie*); sich stellen (*Preis*); ~ *across s.o.* j-m in die Arme laufen; ~ *after* hinter *j-m* herlaufen *od.* -sein; ~ *away* davonlaufen, durchgehen (*a. fig.*); ~ *down* hinunterlaufen; ablaufen (*Uhr etc.*); *fig.* herunterkommen; ~ *dry* aus-, vertrocknen; ~ *for* laufen nach, sich bemühen um; *parl.* kandidieren für; ~ *high* hochgehen; ~ *in* hineinlaufen; *that* ~*s in the blood* (*family*) das liegt im Blut (in der Familie); ~ *into* laufen *od.* rennen in (*acc.*); geraten *od.* (sich) stürzen in (*acc.*); werden zu; ~ *into s.o.* j-m in die Arme laufen; ~ *low* zur Neige gehen; ~ *mad* verrückt werden; ~ *off* weglaufen; ~ *on* fortlaufen, fortgesetzt werden; fortfahren; weiterreden; ~ *out* (hin-) auslaufen; zu Ende gehen; *I have* ~ *out of tobacco* der Tabak ist mir ausgegangen; ~ *over* hinüberlaufen; überlaufen (*Gefäß*); ~ *short* knapp werden, zu Ende gehen; ~ *through* laufen durch; durchmachen, erleben; durchlesen, -gehen; *Vermögen* durchbringen; ~ *to* sich belaufen auf (*acc.*); sich entwickeln zu; F sich *et.* leisten; reichen *od.* langen zu (*Geldmittel*); ~ *up* hinauflaufen; emporschießen; ~ *up to* sich belaufen auf (*acc.*); ~ (*up*)*on* losgehen auf (*acc.*); sich beschäftigen mit, betreffen; ~ *with* triefen von; in *Tränen* schwimmen; **2.** (*irr.*) *v/t. Strecke* durchlaufen; *Rennen* austragen; *Weg* einschlagen; laufen lassen; *Züge etc.* verkehren lassen; *Augen, Hand etc.* gleiten lassen; *Nadel etc.* stecken, stoßen; (vorwärts)treiben; transportieren, fahren, bringen; *Flut* ergießen; *Gold etc.* führen (*Fluß*); *Eisen etc.* schmelzen; *Kugeln* gießen; *Geschäft* betreiben, leiten; *hunt.* verfolgen, hetzen; um die Wette rennen mit; *Waren* schmuggeln; lose nähen, heften; ~ *the blockade* die Blockade brechen; ~ *down* niederrennen, -segeln; abhetzen; *j.* einholen; zur Strecke bringen; *fig.* schlecht machen; herunterwirtschaften; *be* ~ *down* abgearbeitet *od.* erschöpft sein; ~ *errands* Botengänge machen; ~ *hard*

j. bedrängen; ~ *in mot.* einfahren; F einbuchten; ~ *into* hineinstoßen in (*acc.*); hinreißen *od.* bringen zu; fahren an (*acc.*); ~ *off* ablaufen lassen; ~ *out* hinausstoßen, -schieben, -jagen; ~ *over j.* überfahren; *Text* überfliegen; ~ *s.o. through* j. durchbohren; ~ *up Fahne etc.* aufziehen; *Preis* hochtreiben; *Neubau* hochziehen; *Rechnung etc.* auflaufen lassen; **3.** Laufen *n*, Rennen *n*, Lauf *m* (*bsd. im Sport*); Verlauf *m*, Gang *m*, Fortgang *m*; Fahrt *f e-s Schiffes*; Reise *f*, Ausflug *m*; ⚕ Andrang *m*; ⚕ stürmische Nachfrage *f* (*on, upon* nach); *Am.* kleiner Wasserlauf *m*; *bsd. Am.* Laufmasche *f*; ♪ Lauf *m*; *Vieh*-Trift *f*; *Mühle*: Mahlgang *m*; freie Benutzung *f*; Art *f*, Schlag *m*; ⚕ Sorte *f*; *the common* ~ die übliche Art, die große Masse; *have a* ~ *of 20 nights thea.* 20mal nacheinander gegeben werden; *have the* ~ *of s.th.* et. frei zur Verfügung haben; *be in the* ~ *od.* ~*ning bei e-r Wahl* in Frage kommen; *in the long* ~ auf die Dauer, am Ende; *in the short* ~ fürs nächste; *on the* ~ auf den Beinen; auf der Flucht.

run·a·bout *mot.* [ˈrʌnəbaut] kleiner [(Sport)Wagen *m*.]

run·a·way [ˈrʌnəwei] **1.** Ausreißer *m*; Durchgänger *m* (*Pferd*); **2.** entlaufen, -kommen; **3.** flüchtig.

run-down 1. [rʌnˈdaun] heruntergekommen (*Haus etc.*); abgespannt (*Person*); leer (*Batterie*); **2.** F [ˈrʌndaun] (ausführlicher) Bericht *m*.

rune [ru:n] Rune *f*.

rung[1] [rʌŋ] *p.p. von ring*[2] 2.

rung[2] [~] (Leiter)Sprosse *f* (*a. fig.*).

run·ic [ˈru:nik] runisch; Runen...

run-in [ˈrʌnˈin] *Sport*: Einlauf *m*; F Krach *m*, Zs.-stoß *m* (*Streit*).

run·let [ˈrʌnlit], **run·nel** [ˈrʌnl] Rinnsal *n*; Rinnstein *m*.

run·ner [ˈrʌnə] Renner *m*, Läufer *m*; Bote *m*; ⚔ Meldegänger *m*; (Schlitten)Kufe *f*; Schieber *m am Schirm*; ⚘ Ausläufer *m*; *gun*-~ Waffenschmuggler *m*; ˈ**~-ˈup** *Sport*: Zweitbeste *m*.

run·ning [ˈrʌniŋ] **1.** laufend; fließend (*Wasser*); *two days* ~ zwei Tage nacheinander; ~ *hand* Kurrentschrift *f*; ~ *start* fliegender Start *m*; ~ *stitch* Stielstich *m*; **2.** Laufen *n*, Rennen *n*; ˈ**~-board** *mot.*, 🚂 *etc.* Trittbrett *n*; ~ **mate** *Am.* Vizepräsidentschaftskandidat *m*; ~*s pl. Am. Präsidentschaftskandidat und (sein) Vizepräsidentschaftskandidat.*

run-of-the-mill *contp.* [rʌnəvðəˈmil] mittelmäßig, Durchschnitts...

runt [rʌnt] *zo.* Zwergrind *n*; *fig.* Zwerg *m*.

run-up [ˈrʌnʌp] *Sport*: kurzer Probelauf *m*, Anlauf *m*; *fig.* Vorbereitung(szeit) *f*.

run·way [ˈrʌnwei] ✈ Rollbahn *f*; *hunt.* Wechsel *m*; Holzrutsche *f*; ~ *watching* Ansitzjagd *f*.

ru·pee [ru:ˈpi:] Rupie *f*.

rup·ture [ˈrʌptʃə] **1.** Bruch *m* (*a.* ⚕); **2.** brechen; sprengen.

ru·ral □ [ˈruərəl] ländlich; Land...; ˈ**ru·ral·ize** verländlichen.

ruse [ru:z] List *f*, Kniff *m*.

rush[1] ⚘ [rʌʃ] Binse *f*; *fig. mit Verneinung*: Pfifferling *m*, Deut *m*.

rush[2] [~] **1.** Jagen *n*, Hetzen *n*, Stürmen *n*; (An)Sturm *m*; Andrang *m*; Hochbetrieb *m*; ⚕ stürmische Nachfrage *f* (*for* nach); *Wasser- etc.* Flut *f*; ⚡ (Strom)Stoß *m*; ~ *hour(s pl.)* Hauptverkehrszeit *f*; ~ *order* ⚕ eiliger Auftrag *m*; **2.** *v/i.* stürzen, jagen, hetzen, stürmen, schießen, sausen, eilen; ~ *at* sich stürzen auf (*acc.*); ~ *into extremes* ins Extrem verfallen; ~ *into print* et. überstürzt veröffentlichen; *v/t.* jagen, hetzen; drängen; ⚔ *u. fig.* stürmen; *Arbeit etc.* herunterhasten; *sl. j.* neppen (£ 5 um fünf Pfund); ~ *s.o. off his feet* j. überfahren; ~ *through parl.* durchpeitschen; ˈ**rush·ing** □ stürmisch.

rush·y [ˈrʌʃi] binsenbestanden; [Binsen...]

rusk [rʌsk] *Art* Zwieback *m*.

rus·set [ˈrʌsit] **1.** rostbraun; **2.** Rostbraun *n*; grober Stoff *m*.

Rus·sia (**leath·er**) [ˈrʌʃə(ˈleðə)] Juchten(leder) *n*; ˈ**Rus·sian 1.** russisch; **2.** Russe *m*, Russin *f*; Russisch *n*.

rust [rʌst] **1.** Rost *m*; **2.** (ver-, ein-) rosten (lassen) (*a. fig.*).

rus·tic [ˈrʌstik] **1.** (~*ally*) ländlich (*a. fig.*); Land...; *fig.* bäurisch; roh (gearbeitet); **2.** Landmann *m*; **rus·ti·cate** [ˈ~keit] *v/t.* zeitweilig von der Universität verweisen; *v/i.* auf dem Lande leben; **rus·tiˈca·tion** Landleben *n*; *univ.* zeitweilige Verweisung *f*; **rus·tic·i·ty** [~ˈtisiti]

Ländlichkeit *f*; bäurisches Wesen *n*.
rus·tle ['rʌsl] **1.** rascheln (mit *od.* in *dat.*); rauschen; *Am.* F sich ranhalten; *Vieh* stehlen; ~ *up* auftreiben; **2.** Rascheln *n*.
rust...: '~**less** rostfrei; '~-'**proof**, '~-**re'sist·ant** rostbeständig; '**rusty** rostig; eingerostet (*a. fig.*); verschossen (*Stoff*); rostfarben.
rut[1] *hunt.* [rʌt] **1.** Brunft *f*; **2.** brunften.
rut[2] [~] Wagenspur *f*; *bsd. fig.* ausgefahrenes Geleise *n*.
ruth·less □ ['ru:θlis] unbarmherzig; rücksichts-, skrupellos; '**ruth·less-ness** Unbarmherzigkeit *f*; Rücksichts-, Skrupellosigkeit *f*.
rut·ted ['rʌtid] ausgefahren (*Weg*).
rut·ting *hunt.* ['rʌtiŋ] brunftig; Brunft...; ~ *season* Brunftzeit *f*.
rut·ty ['rʌti] ausgefahren (*Weg*).
rye ⚘ [rai] Roggen *m*.

S

sab·bath ['sæbəθ] Sabbat *m*.
sab·bat·i·cal □ [sə'bætikəl] Sabbat...; ~ *year univ.* Ferienjahr *n e-s Professors*.
sa·ble ['seibl] **1.** Zobel(pelz) *m*; Schwarz *n*; **2.** *lit.* schwarz; düster.
sab·o·tage ['sæbətɑ:ʒ] **1.** Sabotage *f*; **2.** sabotieren.
sa·bre ['seibə] **1.** Säbel *m*; **2.** mit dem Säbel niedermachen.
sac *anat., zo.* [sæk] Sack *m*, Beutel *m*.
sac·cha·rin ⚗ ['sækərin] Sacharin *n*; Süßstoff *m*; **sac·cha·rine** ['~rain] Zucker...; Süßstoff...; *fig.* zuckersüß; süßlich.
sac·er·do·tal □ [sæsə'dəutl] priesterlich; Priester...
sack[1] [sæk] **1.** Sack *m*; *Am.* Tüte *f*; Sackkleid *n*; Sakko *m*; *give* (*get*) *the* ~ F entlassen (werden); den Laufpaß geben (bekommen); *hit the* ~ F sich in die Falle hauen; **2.** einsacken; F *j.* rausschmeißen; *j-m* den Laufpaß geben.
sack[2] [~] **1.** Plünderung *f*; **2.** plündern.
sack[3] [~] heller Südwein *m*.
sack·cloth ['sækklɔ:θ], '**sack·ing** Sackleinwand *f*.
sac·ra·ment *eccl.* ['sækrəmənt] Sakrament *n*; **sac·ra·men·tal** □ [~'mentl] sakramental.
sa·cred □ ['seikrid] heilig; geistlich (*Dichtung, Musik*); '**sa·cred·ness** Heiligkeit *f*.
sac·ri·fice ['sækrifais] **1.** Opfer *n*; *at a* ~ ⚕ mit Verlust; **2.** opfern; ⚕ mit Verlust verkaufen.
sac·ri·fi·cial [sækri'fiʃəl] Opfer...; ⚕ Schleuder...
sac·ri·lege ['sækrilidʒ] Kirchenraub *m*, -schändung *f*; Sakrileg *n*; **sac·ri·le·gious** □ [~'lidʒəs] sakrilegisch, frevelhaft.
sa·crist, sac·ris·tan *eccl.* ['sækrist(ən)] Sakristan *m*, Kirchendiener *m*.
sac·ris·ty *eccl.* ['sækristi] Sakristei *f*.
sad □ [sæd] traurig, betrübt; jämmerlich, kläglich; schlimm, arg; dunkel, düster (*Farbe*).
sad·den ['sædn] (sich) betrüben.
sad·dle ['sædl] **1.** Sattel *m*; *break to the* ~ einreiten; **2.** satteln; *fig.* belasten; aufbürden (*upon dat.*); '~-**backed** hohlrückig (*Pferd*); '~-**bag** Satteltasche *f*; '~-**cloth** Satteldecke *f*; '**sad·dler** Sattler *m*; '**sad·dler·y** Sattlerei *f*; Sattelzeug *n*.
sad·ism ['seidizəm] Sadismus *m*; '**sad·ist** Sadist *m*; **sa·dis·tic** [sæ'distik] (~*ally*) sadistisch.
sad·ness ['sædnis] Traurigkeit *f*, Trauer *f*, Schwermut *f*.
sa·fa·ri [sə'fɑ:ri] Safari *f*.
safe [seif] **1.** □ *allg.* sicher; heil, unversehrt; gefahrlos; außer Gefahr; zuverlässig; *to be on the* ~ *side* um ganz sicher zu gehen; **2.** Safe *m*, Geldschrank *m*; Speiseschrank *m*; ~ *deposit* Stahlkammer *f*; '~-**blow-er** *Am.* Geldschrankknacker *m*; ~ **con·duct** freies Geleit *n*; Geleitbrief *m*; '~**guard 1.** Schutz *m*, Sicherung *f*; **2.** sichern; schützen (*against* vor *dat.*); ~*ing duty* Schutz-

zoll *m*; ˈ**safe·ness** Sicherheit *f*.
safe·ty [ˈseifti] Sicherheit *f*; ~ **belt** *mot*. Sicherheitsgurt *m*; ~ **cur·tain** *thea*. eiserner Vorhang *m*; ~ **is·land** Verkehrsinsel *f*; ˈ**~-lock** Sicherheitsschloß *n*; ˈ**~-pin** Sicherheitsnadel *f*; ~ **ra·zor** Rasierapparat *m*; ~ **valve** Sicherheitsventil *n*.
saf·fron [ˈsæfrən] **1.** Safran *m*; Safrangelb *n*; **2.** safrangelb.
sag [sæg] **1.** durchsacken; ⊕ durchhängen; ⚓ (ab)sacken (*a. fig.*); **2.** Durchsacken *n etc.*; ⊕ Durchhang *m*.
sa·ga [ˈsɑːgə] Saga *f* (*Erzählung*).
sa·ga·cious □ [səˈgeiʃəs] scharfsinnig, klug.
sa·gac·i·ty [səˈgæsiti] Scharfsinn *m*.
sag·a·more [ˈsægəmɔː] Indianerhäuptling *m*.
sage[1] [seidʒ] **1.** □ klug, weise; **2.** Weise *m*.
sage[2] ⚘ [~] Salbei *f*.
sage·brush ⚘ [ˈseidʒbrʌʃ] nordamerikanischer Beifuß *m*.
Sa·git·tar·i·us *ast*. [sædʒiˈtɛəriəs] Schütze *m*.
sa·go [ˈseigəu] Sago *m*.
sa·hib [ˈsɑːhib] Herr *m*, Sahib *m*.
said [sed] *pret. u. p.p. von say 1.*
sail [seil] **1.** Segel *n*; Fahrt *f*; Windmühlenflügel *m*; (Segel)Schiff(e *pl.*) *n*; *set* ~ in See stechen; **2.** *v/i.* (ab-)segeln, fahren (*for* nach); *fig.* schweben; *v/t.* befahren; *Schiff* führen; ˈ**~-boat** Segelboot *n*; ˈ**~-cloth** Segeltuch *n*; ˈ**sail·er** Segler *m* (*Schiff*); ˈ**sail·ing-ship,** ˈ**sail·ing-ves·sel** Segelschiff *n*; ˈ**sail·or** Seemann *m*, Matrose *m*; *~'s knot* Schifferknoten *m*; *be a good* (*bad*) ~ (nicht) seefest sein; ˈ**sail-plane** Segelflugzeug *n*.
saint [seint] **1.** Heilige *m, f*; [*vor npr.* snt] Sankt...; **2.** heiligsprechen; ˈ**saint·ed** heilig; selig (*verstorben*); ˈ**saint·li·ness** Heiligkeit *f*; ˈ**saint·ly** *adj*. heilig, fromm.
saith † *od. poet.* [seθ] *3. sg. Präsens von say.*
sake [seik]: *for the* ~ *of* um ... (*gen.*) willen; *for my* ~ meinetwegen, mir zuliebe; *for God's* ~ um Gottes willen.
sal ⚗ [sæl] Salz *n*; ~ *ammoniac* Salmiak *m*; ~ *volatile* Riechsalz *n*.
sal·a·ble [ˈseiləbl] verkäuflich.
sa·la·cious □ [səˈleiʃəs] geil; zotig.
sal·ad [ˈsæləd] Salat *m*; ~ **dress·ing** Salatsoße *f*.
sal·a·man·der [ˈsæləmændə] *zo*. Salamander *m*; Schüreisen *n*.
sa·la·mi [səˈlɑːmiː] Salami(wurst) *f*.
sal·a·ried [ˈsælərid] besoldet; Gehalts...; ˈ**sal·a·ry 1.** Besoldung *f*; Gehalt *n*; **2.** besolden; ˈ**sal·a·ry-earn·er** Gehaltsempfänger *m*.
sale [seil] Verkauf *m*; Absatz *m*; Ausverkauf *m*; Auktion *f*; *for* ~, *on* ~ zum Verkauf, zu verkaufen(d), verkäuflich; *by private* ~ unter der Hand; ˈ**sale·a·ble** verkäuflich, gangbar.
sales... [seilz]: ~ **clerk** *Am*. Verkäufer(in); ~ **com·mis·sion** Verkaufsprovision *f*; ˈ**~·man** Verkäufer *m*; ˈ**~·man·ship** Geschäftstüchtigkeit *f*; ~ **re·sist·ance** Kaufunlust *f*; ˈ**~-wom·an** Verkäuferin *f*.
sa·li·ence [ˈseiljəns] Vorspringen *n*; Vorsprung *m*; ˈ**sa·li·ent 1.** □ vorspringend; *fig*. hervorragend, -tretend; Haupt...; **2.** vorstehende Ecke *f*, Vorsprung *m*; ⚔ (Front)Keil *m*.
sa·line 1. [ˈseilain] salzig; Salz...; **2.** [səˈlain] Saline *f*; ⚕ Salzlösung *f*.
sa·li·va *physiol.* [səˈlaivə] Speichel *m*; **sal·i·var·y** [ˈsælivəri] Speichel...; **sal·iˈva·tion** Speichelfluß *m*.
sal·low[1] ⚘ [ˈsæləu] Salweide *f*.
sal·low[2] [~] blaß; gelblich; ˈ**sal·low·ness** Blässe *f*; gelbliche Farbe *f*.
sal·ly [ˈsæli] **1.** ⚔ Ausbruch *m*; witziger Einfall *m*; **2.** ⚔ *a.* ~ *out* ausbrechen; ~ *forth*, ~ *out* sich aufmachen.
sal·ma·gun·di [sælməˈgʌndi] Ragout *n*; *fig*. Mischmasch *m*.
salm·on [ˈsæmən] **1.** Lachs *m*, Salm *m*; Lachsfarbe *f*; **2.** lachsfarben.
sal·on [ˈsælɔ̃ːŋ] literarischer Salon *m*; Kunstausstellung *f*.
sa·loon [səˈluːn] Salon *m*; (Gesellschafts)Saal *m*; erste Klasse *f auf Schiffen*; *Am*. Kneipe *f*; = **saˈloon-car** 🚃 Salonwagen *m*; *mot*. Limousine *f*.
salt [sɔːlt] **1.** Salz *n* (*a. fig.*); *fig*. Würze *f*; *old* ~ alter Seebär *m*; *with a grain of* ~ cum grano salis, mit Vorbehalt; **2.** salzig; gesalzen (*a. fig.*); Salz...; Pökel...; **3.** (ein)salzen, pökeln; ˈ**~-cel·lar** Salzfäßchen *n*;

ˈ**salt·ed** gesalzen; *sl.* gewiegt, gerieben; ˈ**salt·free** salzlos; **salt·pe·tre** [ˈ~piːtə] Salpeter *m*; ˈ**salt-wa·ter** Salzwasser...; ˈ**salt-works** *sg.* Salzwerk *n*, Saline *f*; ˈ**salt·y** salzig; pikant.

sa·lu·bri·ous □ [səˈluːbriəs] heilsam, gesund; **sa·lu·bri·ty** [səˈluːbriti], **sal·u·tar·i·ness** [ˈsæljutərinis] Heilsamkeit *f*, Bekömmlichkeit *f*; **sal·u·tar·y** □ [ˈsæljutəri] = *salubrious*.

sal·u·ta·tion [sæljuːˈteiʃən] Gruß *m*, Begrüßung *f*; Anrede *f*; **sa·lu·ta·to·ry** [səlˈjuːtətəri] grüßend; Begrüßungs...; **sa·lute** [səˈluːt] **1.** Gruß *m*; *co.* Kuß *m*; ⚔ Salut *m*; **2.** (be)grüßen; ⚔ salutieren.

sal·vage [ˈsælvidʒ] **1.** Bergung *f*; Bergungsgut *n*; Bergegeld *n*; **2.** bergen.

sal·va·tion [sælˈveiʃən] Erlösung *f*; (Seelen)Heil *n*; *fig.* Rettung *f*; ♀ *Army* Heilsarmee *f*; **salˈva·tion·ist** Mitglied *n* der Heilsarmee.

salve[1] [sælv] retten, bergen.

salve[2] [sɑːv] **1.** Salbe *f*; *fig.* Balsam *m*; **2.** *mst fig.* (ein)salben; beruhigen.

sal·ver [ˈsælvə] Präsentierteller *m*.

sal·vo [ˈsælvəu] Vorbehalt *m*; *pl.* **sal·voes** [ˈ~z] ⚔ Salve *f* (*fig.* *Beifall*); ~ *release* ✈ Massenabwurf *m*; **sal·vor** ⚓ [ˈ~və] Berger *m*.

Sa·mar·i·tan [səˈmæritn] **1.** samaritisch; **2.** Samariter(in).

same [seim]: *the* ~ der-, die-, dasselbe; *all the* ~ gleichwohl, dennoch, trotzdem; *it is all the* ~ *to me* es ist mir (ganz) gleich *od.* einerlei; ˈ**same·ness** Gleichheit *f*; Identität *f*; Eintönigkeit *f*.

Sa·mo·an [səˈməuən] **1.** samoanisch; **2.** Samoaner(in).

samp *Am.* [sæmp] grobgemahlener Mais *m*.

sam·ple [ˈsɑːmpl] **1.** *bsd.* ✝ Probe *f*, Muster *n*; Exemplar *n*; **2.** eine Probe zeigen *od.* nehmen von; bemustern; (aus)probieren; ˈ**sampler** Sticktuch *n*; ˈ**sam·pling** Kostprobe *f*.

san·a·tive [ˈsænətiv] heilend, heilsam; **san·a·to·ri·um** [~ˈtɔːriəm] (*bsd.* Lungen)Sanatorium *n*; Luftkurort *m*; **san·a·to·ry** [ˈ~təri] heilsam.

sanc·ti·fi·ca·tion [sæŋktifiˈkeiʃən] Heiligung *f*; Weihung *f*; **sanc·ti·fy** [ˈ~fai] heiligen; weihen; **sanc·ti·mo·ni·ous** □ [~ˈməunjəs] scheinheilig; **sanc·tion** [ˈsæŋkʃən] **1.** Sanktion *f*; Bestätigung *f*; Genehmigung *f*; Zwangsmaßnahme *f*; **2.** bestätigen, gutheißen, genehmigen; **sanc·ti·ty** [ˈ~titi] Heiligkeit *f*; **sanc·tu·ar·y** [ˈ~tjuəri] Heiligtum *n*; *das* Allerheiligste; Asyl *n*, Freistätte *f*; **sanc·tum** [ˈ~təm] Heiligtum *n*; F Privatgemach *n*.

sand [sænd] **1.** Sand *m*; ~*s pl.* Sand (-massen *f/pl.*) *m*; Sandwüste *f*; Sandbank *f*; *his* ~*s are running out* s-e Tage sind gezählt; **2.** mit Sand bestreuen.

san·dal[1] [ˈsændl] Sandale *f*.

san·dal[2] [~], ˈ**~·wood** Sandelholz *n*.

sand...: ˈ**~·bag** Sandsack *m*; ˈ**~·bank** Sandbank *f*; ˈ**~·blast** ⊕ Sandstrahlgebläse *n*; ˈ**~·boy:** *as jolly as a* ~ kreuzfidel; ˈ**~-glass** Sanduhr *f*; ˈ**~-hill** Sanddüne *f*; ˈ**~·pa·per** **1.** Sand-, Schmirgelpapier *n*; **2.** (ab)schmirgeln; ˈ**~-pip·er** *orn.* Flußuferläufer *m*; ˈ**~-pit** Sandkasten *m*; ˈ**~-shoes** Strandschuhe *m/pl.*; ˈ**~-stone** Sandstein *m*.

sand·wich [ˈsænwidʒ] **1.** Sandwich *n*; **2.** *a.* ~ *in* einlegen, -klemmen; ~ **course** *Ausbildung, in der sich Theorie und Praxis abwechseln*; ˈ**~-man** Plakatträger *m*.

sand·y [ˈsændi] sandig; Sand...; sandfarben; strohblond (*Haar*).

sane [sein] geistig gesund *od.* normal; vernünftig (*Antwort etc.*).

San·for·ize [ˈsænfəraiz] *Stoff* sanforisieren (*gegen Einlaufen behandeln*).

sang [sæŋ] *pret. von sing.*

san·gui·nary □ [ˈsæŋgwinəri] blutdürstig; blutig; **san·guine** [ˈ~gwin] sanguinisch, leichtblütig; zuversichtlich; vollblütig; **san·guin·e·ous** [~ˈgwiniəs] Blut...; *s. sanguine.*

san·i·tari·an [sæniˈtɛəriən] Gesundheitsapostel *m*; **san·i·ta·ri·um** [sæniˈtɛəriəm] *Am. für sanatorium*; **san·i·tar·y** □ [ˈ~təri] Gesundheits...; gesundheitlich; ⊕ Sanitär...; ~ *towel* Damenbinde *f*.

san·i·ta·tion [sæniˈteiʃən] Sanierung *f*; Gesundheitspflege *f*; sanitäre Einrichtung *f od.* Anlage *f*; ˈ**san·i·ty** geistige Gesundheit *f*; gesunder Verstand *m*.

sank [sæŋk] *pret. von sink 1.*
sans *lit.* [sænz] ohne.
San·skrit ['sænskrit] Sanskrit *n.*
San·ta Claus [sæntə'klɔːz] Weihnachtsmann *m*, St. Nikolaus *m.*
sap[1] [sæp] ⚘ Saft *m*; *fig.* Lebenskraft *f*, Mark *n*; *sl.* Trottel *m.*
sap[2] [~] **1.** ⚔ Sappe *f*; Laufgraben *m*; Büffler *m*; Büffelei *f*; **2.** *v/i.* sappieren; *sl.* ochsen, büffeln; *v/t.* untergraben (*a. fig.*); unterminieren, schwächen.
sap·id ['sæpid] schmackhaft; **sa·pid·i·ty** [sə'piditi] Schmackhaftigkeit *f.*
sa·pi·ence *mst iro.* ['seipjəns] Weisheit *f*; '**sa·pi·ent** *mst iro.* □ weise.
sap·less ['sæplis] saft-, kraftlos.
sap·ling ['sæpliŋ] junger Baum *m*; *fig.* Grünschnabel *m.*
sap·o·na·ceous ⚗ *od. co.* [sæpəu'neiʃəs] seifig.
sap·per ⚔ ['sæpə] Sappeur *m*; Pionier *m.*
sap·phire *min.* ['sæfaiə] Saphir *m.*
sap·pi·ness ['sæpinis] Saftigkeit *f.*
sap·py ['sæpi] saftig; *fig.* kraftvoll; *sl.* trottelhaft.
Sar·a·cen ['særəsn] Sarazene *m.*
sar·casm ['sɑːkæzəm] bitterer Spott *m*, Sarkasmus *m*; **sar·cas·tic, sar·cas·ti·cal** □ [sɑː'kæstik(əl)] beißend, bissig, sarkastisch.
sar·coph·a·gus, *pl.* **sar'coph·a·gi** [sɑː'kɔfəgəs, ~gai] Sarkophag *m.*
sar·dine *ichth.* [sɑː'diːn] Sardine *f.*
Sar·din·i·an [sɑː'dinjən] **1.** sardinisch; **2.** Sardinier(in).
sar·don·ic [sɑː'dɔnik] (*~ally*) sardonisch, verächtlich, zynisch.
sark·y F ['sɑːki] = *sarcastic.*
sar·to·ri·al [sɑː'tɔːriəl] Schneider...; Kleider...
sash[1] [sæʃ] Fensterrahmen *m e-s Schiebefensters.*
sash[2] [~] Schärpe *f.*
sash-window ['sæʃwindəu] Schiebefenster *n.*
sas·sa·fras ⚘ ['sæsəfræs] Sassafras (-baum) *m.*
sat [sæt] *pret. u. p.p. von sit.*
Sa·tan ['seitən] Satan *m.*
sa·tan·ic [sə'tænik] (*~ally*) satanisch, teuflisch.
satch·el ['sætʃəl] Schulmappe *f.*
sate [seit] = *satiate.*
sa·teen [sæ'tiːn] Satin *m.*
sat·el·lite ['sætəlait] (*a.* künstlicher) Satellit *m*, Trabant *m*; Satellitenstaat *m*; ~ **town** Trabantenstadt *f*; ~ **trans·mis·sion** Satellitenübertragung *f.*
sa·ti·ate ['seiʃieit] (über)sättigen, **sa·ti'a·tion** Sättigung *f*; **sa·ti·e·ty** [sə'taiəti] Sattheit *f*; Überdruß *m.*
sat·in ['sætin] Seidensatin *m*, Atlas *m* (*Stoff*); **sat·i·net(te)** [~'net] Halbatlas *m.*
sat·ire ['sætaiə] Satire *f*; **sa·tir·ic, sa·tir·i·cal** □ [sə'tirik(əl)] satirisch; **sat·i·rist** ['sætərist] Satiriker *m*; '**sat·i·rize** verspotten.
sat·is·fac·tion [sætis'fækʃən] Befriedigung *f*; Genugtuung *f*, Satisfaktion *f*; Zufriedenheit *f*; Sühne *f*; Gewißheit *f.*
sat·is·fac·to·ri·ness [sætis'fæktərinis] *das* Befriedigende; **sat·is'fac·to·ry** □ befriedigend, zufriedenstellend.
sat·is·fied □ ['sætisfaid] zufrieden; überzeugt (*that* daß); **sat·is·fy** ['~fai] *allg.* befriedigen; *e-r Bedingung etc., j-m* genügen; zufriedenstellen; überzeugen (*of* von); *Zweifel* beheben.
sa·trap ['sætrəp] Satrap *m.*
sat·u·rate ⚗ *u. fig.* ['sætʃəreit] sättigen; **sat·u'ra·tion** Sättigung *f*; ~ *point* Sättigungspunkt *m.*
Sat·ur·day ['sætədi] Sonnabend *m*, Samstag *m.*
Sat·urn ['sætən] Saturn *m*; **sat·ur·nine** ['~nain] melancholisch.
sat·yr ['sætə] Satyr *m.*
sauce [sɔːs] **1.** (*oft kalte*) Soße *f*; *Am.* Kompott *n*; *fig.* Würze *f*; F Frechheit *f*; **2.** würzen; F frech werden zu *j-m*; '**~-boat** Soßenschüssel *f*; '**~·pan** Kochtopf *m*; Kasserolle *f*; '**sauc·er** Untertasse *f*; Untersatz *m e-s Blumentopfs.*
sau·ci·ness F ['sɔːsinis] Frechheit *f.*
sau·cy □ F ['sɔːsi] keck, frech; dreist, unverschämt.
sau·na ['sɔːnə] Sauna *f.*
saun·ter ['sɔːntə] **1.** Schlendern *n*; Bummel *m*; **2.** (umher)schlendern; bummeln; '**saun·ter·er** Bummler (-in).
sau·ri·an *zo.* ['sɔːriən] Saurier *m.*
sau·sage ['sɔsidʒ] Wurst *f.*
sau·té ['səutei] sauté, sautiert (*in wenig Fett schnell gebraten*).
sav·age ['sævidʒ] **1.** □ wild; roh, grausam; unbebaut, wüst; F wü-

tend; **2.** Wilde *m*; *fig.* Barbar *m*; **3.** anfallen (*Tier*); **ˈsav·age·ness, ˈsav·age·ry** Wildheit *f*; Barbarei *f*.
sa·van·na(h) [səˈvænə] Savanne *f*.
sav·ant [ˈsævənt] Gelehrte *m*.
save [seiv] **1.** *v/t.* retten; *Schiff etc.* bergen; erlösen; erhalten; bewahren (*from* vor *dat.*); (er)sparen; schonen; *v/i.* sparen; sparsam leben; **2.** *prp. u. cj.* außer, ausgenommen; ~ *for* bis auf (*acc.*); ~ *that* nur daß.
sav·e·loy [ˈsævilɔi] Zervelatwurst *f*.
sav·er [ˈseivə] Retter(in); Sparer(in); sparsames Gerät *n*.
sav·ing [ˈseiviŋ] **1.** □ sparsam; ⚖ ~ *clause* Vorbehalt(sklausel *f*) *m*; **2.** Rettung *f*; ~*s pl.* Ersparnisse *f/pl.*
sav·ings... [ˈseiviŋz]: ~ **ac·count** Sparkonto *n*; **ˈ~-bank** Sparkasse *f*; **ˈ~-de·pos·it** Spareinlage *f*.
sav·io(u)r [ˈseivjə] Retter *m*, Erlöser *m*; *Saviour* Heiland *m*.
sa·vo(u)r [ˈseivə] **1.** Geschmack *m*; *fig.* Beigeschmack *m*; **2.** *v/i. fig.* schmecken, riechen (*of* nach); *v/t. fig.* schmecken *od.* riechen nach; auskosten; **sa·vo(u)r·i·ness** [ˈ~rinis] Wohlgeschmack *m*; Wohlgeruch *m*; **ˈsa·vo(u)r·less** geschmack-, geruchlos.
sa·vo(u)r·y[1] □ [ˈseivəri] schmackhaft; appetitlich; wohlriechend; pikant(e Vor- *od.* Nachspeise *f*).
sa·vo(u)r·y[2] ⚘ [~] Bohnenkraut *n*.
sa·voy [səˈvɔi] Wirsingkohl *m*.
sav·vy *sl.* [ˈsævi] **1.** kapieren; **2.** Grips *m* (*Verstand*).
saw[1] [sɔː] *pret. von* **see**.
saw[2] [~] Spruch *m*, Redensart *f*.
saw[3] [~] **1.** Säge *f*; **2.** (*irr.*) sägen; **ˈ~·dust** Sägespäne *m/pl.*; **ˈ~-horse** Sägebock *m*; **ˈ~-mill** Sägewerk *n*; **sawn** [sɔːn] *p.p. von saw*[3] 2; **saw·yer** [ˈ~jə] Säger *m*.
Sax·on [ˈsæksn] **1.** sächsisch; germanisch; **2.** Sachse *m*, Sächsin *f*.
sax·o·phone ♪ [ˈsæksəfəun] Saxophon *n*; **sax·o·phon·ist** [~ˈsɔfənist] Saxophonist *m*.
say [sei] **1.** (*irr.*) sagen; hersagen; berichten; ~ *grace* das Tischgebet sprechen; ~ *mass* die Messe lesen; *that is to* ~ das heißt; *do you* ~ *so?* meinen Sie wirklich?; *you don't* ~ *so!* was Sie nicht sagen!; *I* ~ sag(en Sie) mal; ich muß schon sagen; *unübersetzt am Anfang der Rede*; *he is said to be ...* es heißt, daß er... ist, er soll ... sein; *no sooner said than done* gesagt, getan; **2.** Rede *f*, Wort *n*; *it is my* ~ *now* jetzt ist die Reihe zu reden an mir; *let him have his* ~ laßt ihn zu Wort kommen; *have a od. some (no)* ~ *in s.th.* etwas (nichts) zu sagen haben bei et.; **ˈsay·ing** Rede *f*; Redensart *f*, Ausspruch *m*; *it goes without* ~ es versteht sich von selbst.
scab [skæb] Schorf *m*; Räude *f*; *sl.* Streikbrecher *m*.
scab·bard [ˈskæbəd] *Säbel*-Scheide *f*.
scab·by □ [ˈskæbi] schorfig; räudig.
sca·bi·es ⚕ [ˈskeibiiːz] Krätze *f*.
sca·bi·ous ⚘ [ˈskeibjəs] Skabiose *f*.
sca·brous [ˈskeibrəs] heikel; anstößig.
scaf·fold [ˈskæfəld] (Bau)Gerüst *n*; Schafott *n*; **ˈscaf·fold·ing** (Bau)Gerüst *n*; Rüstmaterial *n*.
scald [skɔːld] **1.** Verbrühung *f*; **2.** verbrühen; *a.* ~ *out* auskochen; *Milch* abkochen.
scale[1] [skeil] **1.** Schuppe *f*; Kesselstein *m*; Zahnstein *m*; *remove the* ~*s from s.o.'s eyes* j-m die Augen öffnen; **2.** *v/t.* abschuppen, -lösen, -schaben; ⊕ *Kesselstein* abklopfen; *Zähne* vom Zahnstein reinigen; *v/i. oft* ~ *off* sich (ab)schuppen, abblättern.
scale[2] [~] **1.** Waagschale *f*; (*a pair of*) ~*s pl.* (eine) Waage *f*; ~*s pl. ast.* Waage *f*; **2.** wiegen.
scale[3] [~] **1.** Stufenleiter *f*; ♪ Tonleiter *f*; Skala *f*; Gradeinteilung *f*; Maßstab *m*; *fig.* Ausmaß *n*; ~ *model* maßstabgetreues Modell *n*; *on a large* ~ im großen; **2.** ersteigen, erklimmen; ~ *up* (*down*) maßstabgetreu vergrößern (verkleinern).
scaled [skeild] schuppig.
scale·less [ˈskeillis] schuppenlos.
scal·ing-lad·der [ˈskeiliŋlædə] ⚔ Sturmleiter *f*; Feuerleiter *f*.
scal·lion ⚘ [ˈskæljən] Schalotte *f*.
scal·lop [ˈskɔləp] **1.** *zo.* Kammmuschel *f*; Ausbogung *f*; ⊕ Langette *f*; **2.** ausbogen; langettieren.
scalp [skælp] **1.** Kopfhaut *f*; Skalp *m*; **2.** skalpieren.
scal·pel ⚕ [ˈskælpəl] Skalpell *n*.
scal·y [ˈskeili] schuppig; voll Kesselstein.
scamp [skæmp] **1.** Taugenichts *m*; **2.** pfuschen; **ˈscamp·er 1.** (umher-)

tollen; hetzen; **2.** *fig.* Hetzjagd *f*; Galopp(tour *f*) *m*.
scan [skæn] *v/t. Verse* skandieren; absuchen; *fig.* überfliegen; *Fernsehen*: abtasten; *v/i.* sich skandieren lassen.
scan·dal ['skændl] Skandal *m*; Ärgernis *n*; Schande *f*; Klatsch *m*; **'scan·dal·ize** *j-m* Ärgernis geben; *be* ~*d at od. by* Anstoß nehmen an (*dat.*); **'scan·dal-mon·ger** Klatschbase *f*; **scan·dal·ous** □ ['~dələs] skandalös, Ärgernis erregend, anstößig; schimpflich; klatschhaft; **'scan·dal·ous·ness** Anstößigkeit *f etc.*
Scan·di·na·vi·an [skændi'neivjən] **1.** skandinavisch; **2.** Skandinavier (-in).
scant *lit.* [skænt] **1.** knapp, kärglich; **2.** knausern mit, sparen an.
scant·i·ness ['skæntinis] Knappheit *f*; Kärglichkeit *f*.
scant·ling ['skæntliŋ] Sparren *m*; kleines Brett *n*.
scant·y □ ['skænti] knapp; spärlich; kärglich, dürftig.
scape·goat ['skeipgəut] Sündenbock *m*, Prügelknabe *m*.
scape·grace ['skeipgreis] Taugenichts *m*.
scap·u·lar ['skæpjulə] **1.** *anat.* Schulterblatt...; **2.** *eccl.* Skapulier *n*.
scar¹ [skɑː] **1.** Narbe *f*; Schramme *f*; *fig.* (Schand)Fleck *m*, Makel *m*; **2.** *v/t.* schrammen; *v/i.* vernarben.
scar² [~] Klippe *f*; Steilhang *m*.
scar·ab *zo.* ['skærəb] Skarabäus *m*; (Mist)Käfer *m*.
scarce [skɛəs] knapp; rar; selten; Mangel...; *make o.s.* ~ F sich rar machen; **'scarce·ly** kaum; fast nicht; **'scar·ci·ty** Mangel *m*; Knappheit *f* (*of* an *dat.*); Teuerung *f*.
scare [skɛə] **1.** er-, aufschrecken; *a.* ~ *away* verscheuchen; ~*d* verstört; ängstlich; **2.** Panik *f*; **'~·crow** Vogelscheuche *f* (*a. fig.*); Schreckbild *n*; **'~·head** *Am.* große, sensationelle Schlagzeile *f*; **'~·mon·ger** Miesmacher(in).
scarf¹ [skɑːf], *pl. a.* **scarves** [skɑːvz] Schal *m*; Halstuch *n*; Kopftuch *n*; Krawatte *f*; ⚔ Schärpe *f*.
scarf² ⊕ [~] **1.** Laschung *f*, Lasche *f*; **2.** (ver)laschen.
scarf...: **'~-pin** Krawattennadel *f*; **'~-skin** Oberhaut *f*.
scar·i·fi·ca·tion [skɛərifi'keiʃən] ⚕ Einritzung *f*; Verriß *m* (*heftige Kritik*); **scar·i·fy** ['~fai] (ein)ritzen; *fig.* herunter-, verreißen (*Kritiker*); ⚒ lockern.
scar·la·ti·na ⚕ [skɑːlə'tiːnə] Scharlach *m*.
scar·let ['skɑːlit] **1.** Scharlach(rot *n*, -tuch *n*) *m*; **2.** scharlachrot; ~ *fever* ⚕ Scharlach *m*; ~ *runner* ⚘ Feuerbohne *f*.
scarp [skɑːp] **1.** abböschen; ~*ed* steil; **2.** Böschung *f*.
scarred [skɑːd] narbig.
scarves [skɑːvz] *pl. von scarf¹*.
scar·y F ['skɛəri] erschreckend.
scath·ing *fig.* ['skeiðiŋ] vernichtend; verletzend.
scat·ter ['skætə] (sich) zerstreuen; ausstreuen; (sich) verbreiten; bestreuen; ~*ed* verstreut; **'~-brain** Wirrkopf *m*; **'~-brained** wirr, konfus.
scav·enge ['skævindʒ] (die Straßen) kehren; **'scav·en·ger** Straßenkehrer *m*.
sce·nar·i·o [si'nɑːriəu] *Film*: Drehbuch *n*; **sce·nar·ist** ['siːnərist] Drehbuchautor(in).
scene [siːn] Szene *f*; Auftritt *m e-s Dramas* (*a. fig.*); Bühne(nbild *n*) *f*; Schauplatz *m*; ~*s pl.* Kulissen *f/pl.*; **'~-paint·er** Bühnenmaler *m*; **scen·er·y** ['~əri] Szenerie *f*; Bühnenausstattung *f*; Landschaft *f*.
sce·nic, sce·ni·cal □ ['siːnik(əl)] szenisch, Bühnen...; landschaftlich; *scenic railway* Miniaturbahn *f*; *scenic road* landschaftlich schöne Strecke *f*.
scent [sent] **1.** (Wohl)Geruch *m*; Duft *m*; Parfüm *n*; *hunt.* Witterung(svermögen *n*) *f*; *hunt.* Fährte *f*; **2.** wittern; durchduften; parfümieren; **'scent·ed** wohlriechend; **'scent·less** geruchlos.
scep·tic ['skeptik] Skeptiker(in), Zweifler(in); **'scep·ti·cal** □ skeptisch (*about* mit Bezug auf *acc.*), zweiflerisch, zweifelnd; **scep·ti·cism** ['~sizəm] Skeptizismus *m*.
scep·tre ['septə] Zepter *n*.
sched·ule ['ʃedjuːl, *Am.* 'skedʒuːl] **1.** Verzeichnis *n*; Tabelle *f*; ⚖ Anhang *m*; *bsd. Am.* Fahrplan *m*; *on* ~ fahrplanmäßig; **2.** auf-, verzeichnen; festsetzen; ⚖ anhängen (*to dat.*); ~*d for* vorgesehen für;

sched·uled flight ✈ Linienflug *m.*
scheme [ski:m] **1.** Schema *n*; Zs.-stellung *f*; Plan *m*, Entwurf *m*; **2.** *v/t.* planen; *v/i.* Pläne machen; *b.s.* Ränke schmieden; **'schem·er** Plänemacher *m*; Intrigant *m.*
schism ['sizəm] Schisma *n*, Kirchenspaltung *f*; *fig.* Riß *m*; **schis·mat·ic** [siz'mætik] **1.** *a.* **schis'mat·i·cal** □ schismatisch; **2.** Abtrünnige *m*, Schismatiker *m.*
schist *min.* [ʃist] Schiefer *m.*
schi·zo·phre·nia *psych.* [skitsəu'fri:njə] Schizophrenie *f.*
schol·ar ['skɔlə] Gelehrte *m*; *univ.* Stipendiat *m*; † Schüler(in); *he is an apt* ~ er hat e-e gute Auffassungsgabe; **'schol·ar·ly** *adj.* gelehrtenhaft; gelehrt; wissenschaftlich; **'schol·ar·ship** Gelehrsamkeit *f*; Wissenschaftlichkeit *f*; *univ.* Stipendium *n.*
scho·las·tic [skə'læstik] **1.** (*~ally*) scholastisch; schulmäßig; Schul...; **2.** Scholastiker *m*; **scho·las·ti·cism** [skə'læstisizəm] Scholastik *f.*
school[1] [sku:l] = *shoal*[1] *1.*
school[2] [~] **1.** Schule *f* (*a. fig.*); *univ.* Fakultät *f*; Disziplin *f*; Hochschule *f*; *at* ~ auf *od.* in der Schule; *put to* ~ einschulen; **2.** schulen, erziehen; **'~·boy** Schüler *m*; **'~·fel·low** Mitschüler(in); **'~·girl** Schülerin *f*; **'~·house** Schulhaus *n*; **'school·ing** (Schul)Ausbildung *f*; Schulgeld *n.*
school...: **'~-leav·er** Schulabgänger (-in); **'~-leav·ing age** Schulentlassungsalter *n*; **'~·man** Scholastiker *m*; **'~·mas·ter** Lehrer *m* (*bsd. e-r höheren Schule*); **'~·mate** Mitschüler(in); **'~-mis·tress** Lehrerin *f* (*bsd. e-r höheren Schule*); **'~·teach·er** (*bsd.* Volksschul)Lehrer(in).
schoon·er ['sku:nə] ⚓ Schoner *m*; *Am.* großes Bierglas *n*; = *prairie-~.*
sci·at·i·ca ⚕ [sai'ætikə] Ischias *f.*
sci·ence ['saiəns] Wissenschaft *f*; Naturwissenschaft(en *pl.*) *f*; Technik *f*; ~ **fic·tion** Science-fiction *f.*
sci·en·tif·ic [saiən'tifik] (*~ally*) (*engS.* natur)wissenschaftlich; *Sport*: kunstgerecht.
sci·en·tist ['saiəntist] (*bsd.* Natur-) Wissenschaftler *m.*
sci-fi F ['saifai] = *science fiction.*
scim·i·tar ['simitə] Krummsäbel *m.*
scin·til·late ['sintileit] funkeln; **scin·til'la·tion** Funkeln *n.*
sci·on ['saiən] ✓ Pfropfreis *n*; *fig.* Sprößling *m.*
scis·sion ['siʒən] Spalten *n*, Schnitt *m*; **scis·sors** ['sizəz] *pl.* (*a pair of* ~ eine) Schere *f.*
scle·ro·sis ⚕ [skliə'rəusis] Sklerose *f.*
scoff [skɔf] **1.** Spott *m*; **2.** höhnen, spotten (*at* über *acc.*); **'scoff·er** Spötter(in).
scold [skəuld] **1.** zänkisches Weib *n*; **2.** (aus)schelten, schimpfen; **'scold·ing** Schelte(n *n*) *f.*
scol·lop ['skɔləp] = *scallop.*
sconce[1] [skɔns] Wandleuchter *m*; Klavierleuchter *m.*
sconce[2] *univ. sl.* [~] *zu e-r Strafe* verdonnern.
scon(e) [skɔn] Brötchen *n aus Rührteig.*
scoop [sku:p] **1.** Schaufel *f*, Schippe *f*; Schöpfeimer *m*, -kelle *f*; ⚕ Spatel *m*; F Coup *m*, gutes Geschäft *n*; F Exklusivmeldung *f*; **2.** *mst* ~ *out* (aus)schaufeln; aushöhlen; *sl. Gewinn* scheffeln.
scoot·er ['sku:tə] (Kinder)Roller *m*; Motorroller *m*; Schnellboot *n.*
scope [skəup] Bereich *m*; *geistiger* Gesichtskreis *m*, Reichweite *f*; Umfang *m*; Gebiet *n*; Spielraum *m*; *have free* ~ freie Hand haben.
scorch [skɔ:tʃ] *v/t.* versengen, -brennen; *v/t.* F (dahin)rasen; **'scorch·er** F sengend heißer Tag *m*; wilder Fahrer *m*, Raser *m.*
score [skɔ:] **1.** Kerbe *f*; Zeche *f*, Rechnung *f*; 20 Stück; *Sport*: Punktzahl *f*; (Tor)Stand *m*; Grund *m*, Ursache *f*; ♪ Partitur *f*, *weitS.* Musik *f*; *sl.* schlagfertige Entgegnung *f*; *~s of* eine Menge (von), viele; *four* ~ achtzig; *run up ~s* Schulden machen; *on the* ~ *of* wegen; **2.** *v/t.* (ein)kerben; *a.* ~ *up Zeche, Punktzahl u. fig.* anschreiben, verzeichnen; *Sport*: Punkte machen; gewinnen (*a. fig.*); ♪ in Partitur setzen, instrumentieren; *Am.* F *scharfe* Kritik üben an; *v/i.* gerechnet werden; *Sport*: Punkte machen, gewinnen; *Fußball*: ein Tor schießen; *Karten*: zählen; *sl.* Schwein haben; ~ *off s.o.* F j-m e-e Abfuhr erteilen; **'~·board** *Sport*: Anzeigetafel *f*; **'scor·er** Anschreiber(in); *Fußball*: Torschütze *m.*

sco·ri·a, *pl.* **sco·ri·ae** ⊕ ['skɔːriə, '~rii:] Schlacke *f.*

scorn [skɔːn] **1.** Verachtung *f*; Spott *m*; *laugh s.o. to ~* j. verspotten; **2.** verachten; verschmähen, von sich weisen; '**scorn·er** Verächter(in); Spötter(in); **scorn·ful** □ ['~ful] verächtlich.

Scor·pi·o *ast.* ['skɔːpiəu] Skorpion *m.*

scor·pi·on *zo.* ['skɔːpjən] Skorpion *m.*

Scot[1] [skɔt] Schotte *m.*

scot[2] [~]: *pay ~ and lot* sich an den Kosten beteiligen.

Scotch[1] [skɔtʃ] **1.** schottisch; **2.** Schottisch *n*; *the ~ pl.* die Schotten *m/pl.*

scotch[2] [~] (nur) verwunden.

Scotch·man ['skɔtʃmən] Schotte *m.*

scot-free ['skɔt'friː] straflos.

Scots [skɔts] = *Scotch*[1]; '**Scots·man** = *Scotchman.*

Scot·tish ['skɔtiʃ] schottisch (*bsd. in gewählter Sprache u. in Schottland*).

scoun·drel ['skaundrəl] Schurke *m*; '**scoun·drel·ly** *adj.* schurkisch.

scour[1] ['skauə] scheuern; reinigen; sich *ein Bett* graben.

scour[2] [~] *v/i.* eilen; jagen; *~ about* (suchend) umherstreifen; *v/t.* durchstreifen, absuchen.

scourge [skəːdʒ] **1.** Geißel *f* (*a. fig.*); **2.** geißeln.

scout[1] [skaut] **1.** Späher *m*, Kundschafter *m*; ⚓ Aufklärungsfahrzeug *n*; ✈ Aufklärer *m*; *univ.* Aufwärter *m*; *mot.* Mitglied *n* der Straßenwacht; (*Boy*) ♀ Pfadfinder *m*; *~ party* ⚔ Spähtrupp *m*; **2.** (aus-) kundschaften, spähen.

scout[2] [~] verächtlich zurückweisen.

scout·mas·ter ['skautmɑːstə] Pfadfinderführer *m.*

scow ⚓ [skau] Schute *f*, Flachboot *n.*

scowl [skaul] **1.** finsteres Gesicht *n*; **2.** finster blicken.

scrab·ble ['skræbl] (be)kritzeln; scharren; krabbeln.

scrag [skræg] **1.** *fig.* Gerippe *n* (*dürrer Mensch etc.*); *a. ~-end* (*of mutton* Hammel)Hals *m*; **2.** *sl.* (er)würgen; '**scrag·gi·ness** Magerkeit *f*; '**scrag·gy** □ dürr.

scram *sl.* [skræm] verdufte!

scram·ble ['skræmbl] **1.** klettern; sich reißen *od.* balgen (*for* um); *~d eggs pl.* Rührei *n*; **2.** Kletterei *f*; Balgerei *f*, Kampf *m.*

scrap [skræp] **1.** Stückchen *n*, Brokken *m*; (Zeitungs)Ausschnitt *m*, Bild *n zum Einkleben*; Altmaterial *n*; Schrott *m*; *~s pl.* Reste *m/pl.*; *~ of paper* Fetzen *m* Papier (*a. fig.*); **2.** zum alten Eisen werfen; ausrangieren; verschrotten; '**~-book** Sammelalbum *n.*

scrape [skreip] **1.** Kratzen *n*, Scharren *n*; Kratzfuß *m*; Not *f*, Klemme *f*; **2.** *v/t.* schrap(p)en; (ab)schaben; (ab)kratzen; *~ together*, *~ up* zs.-scharren, -kratzen; *~ acquaintance with* sich mit *j-m* anfreunden; *v/i.* kratzen; scharren; Kratzfüße machen; '**scrap·er** Kratzer *m*; Schab-, Kratzeisen *n*, Kratze *f*; '**scrap·ing** Scharren *n*; *~s pl.* Abschabsel *n/pl.*; Zs.-gekratzte *n*; *fig.* Spargroschen *m/pl.*

scrap...: '**~-heap** Abfall-, Schrotthaufen *m*; '**~-i·ron** Alteisen *n*, Schrott *m*; '**scrap·py** □ zs.-gestoppelt; bruchstückartig; '**scrap·yard** Schrottplatz *m.*

scratch [skrætʃ] **1.** Ritz *m*; Riß *m*, Schramme *f*; *Sport*: Startlinie *f*; Gekritzel *n der Feder*; *come up to ~* s-n Mann stellen, durchhalten; *up to ~* auf der Höhe; *start from ~ fig.* von vorne anfangen; **2.** zs.-gewürfelt; *Rennsport*: ohne Vorgabe; **3.** *v/t.* (zer)kratzen; (zer)schrammen; *parl. u. Sport*: streichen; *~ out* auskratzen; ausradieren; ausstreichen; *~ the surface fig.* an der Oberfläche bleiben; *v/i.* kratzen; *Sport*: streichen (*Meldung zurückziehen*); '**scratch·y** kratzig; kritz(e)lig; *Sport*: unausgeglichen.

scrawl [skrɔːl] **1.** kritzeln; **2.** Gekritzel *n.*

scraw·ny *Am.* F ['skrɔːni] dürr.

scream [skriːm] **1.** Schrei *m*; Gekreisch *n*; *he is a ~* F er ist zum Schreien (komisch); **2.** schreien, kreischen; '**scream·ing** □ kreischend; F zum Totlachen, zum Schreien (komisch).

scree [skriː] Geröll(halde *f*) *n.*

screech [skriːtʃ] = *scream*; '**~-owl** *orn.* Käuzchen *n.*

screed [skriːd] Tirade *f*; langatmiges Schreiben *n.*

screen [skriːn] **1.** Wandschirm *m*, spanische Wand *f*; Ofenschirm *m*; Schutzschirm *m*; ⚠ Lettner *m*; *fig.* Schleier *m*; (Film)Leinwand *f*; *der*

Film; Sandsieb *n*; (Fliegen)Gitter *n*; **2.** schirmen; (be)schützen; ⚔ verschleiern, tarnen; auf der Leinwand zeigen; verfilmen; (durch-) sieben; sortieren; *fig.* durchleuchten; **~play** Drehbuch *n*; Fernsehfilm *m*; **~ test** *Film*: Probeaufnahmen *f/pl.*
screev·er ['skri:və] Pflastermaler *m.*
screw [skru:] **1.** Schraube *f* (*a. fig. u.* ⚓); ✈ Propeller *m*, Luftschraube *f*; Tütchen *n Tabak etc.*; *he has a ~ loose* F bei ihm ist e-e Schraube locker; **2.** (fest)schrauben; *fig.* drücken, bedrängen, pressen; ver-, umdrehen; V ficken, vögeln; *~ round* ganz herumdrehen; *~ up* festschrauben; hochschrauben; *~ up one's courage* Mut fassen; **'~·ball** *Am. sl.* Spinner *m*, komischer Kauz *m*; **'~·driv·er** Schraubenzieher *m*; **'~·jack** Wagenheber *m*; **'~-pro'pel·ler** Schiffsschraube *f.*
scrib·ble ['skribl] **1.** Gekritzel *n*; **2.** kritzeln; *~ over* bekritzeln; **'scrib·bler** Schmierer *m*; Skribent *m*; **'scrib·bling-block** Schmierblock *m.*
scribe [skraib] Schreiber *m*; Kopist *m*; *Bibel*: Schriftgelehrte *m.*
scrim [skrim] leichter Leinenstoff *m.*
scrim·mage ['skrimidʒ] Handgemenge *n*; Getümmel *n*; *Rugby*: Gedränge *n.*
scrimp [skrimp], **'scrimp·y** = *skimp etc.*
scrip ⚕ [skrip] Interimsschein(e *pl.*) *m*; Besatzungsgeld *n.*
script [skript] Schrift(art) *f*; Schreibschrift *f*; Manuskript *n*; *Film*: Drehbuch *n*; *~s pl.* (schriftliche) Prüfungsarbeiten *f/pl.*; *~-writer* Rundfunkautor *m.*
Scrip·tur·al ['skriptʃərəl] biblisch; **Scrip·ture** ['~tʃə] *mst the Holy ~s pl.* die Heilige Schrift.
scrof·u·la ⚕ ['skrɔfjulə] Skrofeln *f/pl.*; **'scrof·u·lous** □ skrofulös.
scroll [skrəul] Schriftrolle *f*, Liste *f*; ⚠ Schnecke *f*; Schnörkel *m.*
scro·tum ['skrəutəm] Hodensack *m.*
scrounge F [skraundʒ] organisieren, sich aneignen.
scrub[1] [skrʌb] Gestrüpp *n*, Busch (-werk *n*) *m*; Knirps *m*, Zwerg *m.*
scrub[2] [~] **1.** schrubben, scheuern; **2.** *Am. Sport*: zweite (Spieler-) Garnitur *f.*
scrub·bing-brush ['skrʌbiŋbrʌʃ] Scheuerbürste *f*; Schrubber *m.*
scrub·by ['skrʌbi] struppig; schäbig, armselig.
scruff [skrʌf]: *~ of the neck* Genick *n.*
scrum [skrʌm], **'scrum·mage** = *scrimmage.*
scrump·tious *sl.* ['skrʌmpʃəs] fabelhaft, prima.
scrunch [skrʌntʃ] *v/t.* zermalmen; *v/i.* knirschen.
scrup·le ['skru:pl] **1.** Skrupel *n* (= *20 Gran = 1,296 Gramm*); Skrupel *m*; Zweifel *m*, Bedenken *n*; *make no ~ to do* keine Bedenken haben, zu tun; **2.** Bedenken haben; **scru·pu·lous** □ ['~pjuləs] (allzu) bedenklich (*about in dat.*); gewissenhaft, peinlich; ängstlich.
scru·ti·neer [skru:ti'niə] Wahlprüfer *m*; **'scru·ti·nize** (genau) prüfen; **'scru·ti·ny** Forschen *n*; forschender Blick *m*; genaue (*bsd.* Wahl)Prüfung *f.*
scu·ba ['sku:bə]: *~ diving* Sporttauchen *n.*
scud [skʌd] **1.** (Dahin)Jagen *n*; (dahintreibende) Wolkenfetzen *m/pl.*; Bö *f*; **2.** eilen, jagen; ⚓ lenzen.
scuff [skʌf] schlurfen, schlorren.
scuf·fle ['skʌfl] **1.** Balgerei *f*, Rauferei *f*; **2.** sich balgen, raufen.
scull ⚓ [skʌl] **1.** kurzes Ruder *n*; **2.** rudern, skullen.
scul·ler·y ['skʌləri] Spülküche *f*; *~ maid* Scheuermagd *f*; **scul·lion** † ['skʌljən] Küchenjunge *m.*
sculp·tor ['skʌlptə] Bildhauer *m.*
sculp·ture ['skʌlptʃə] **1.** Plastik *f*, Bildhauerei *f*, Skulptur *f*; **2.** (heraus)meißeln, formen.
scum [skʌm] (*fig.* Ab)Schaum *m.*
scup·per ⚓ ['skʌpə] Speigatt *n.*
scurf [skə:f] (Haut-, *bsd.* Kopf-) Schuppen *f/pl.*; **'scurf·y** □ schuppig.
scur·ril·i·ty [skʌ'riliti] Gemeinheit *f*, Pöbelhaftigkeit *f*, Unflätigkeit *f*; **'scur·ril·ous** gemein, pöbelhaft; unflätig.
scur·ry ['skʌri] **1.** *v/i.* hasten, rennen; *v/t.* jagen; **2.** Hasten *n.*
scur·vy[1] ⚕ ['skə:vi] Skorbut *m.*
scur·vy[2] [~] (hunds)gemein.
scut [skʌt] kurzer Schwanz *m.*
scutch·eon ['skʌtʃən] = *escutcheon.*
scut·tle[1] ['skʌtl] Kohlenbehälter *m.*

scut·tle[2] [~] **1.** ⚓ Springluke *f*; **2.** *Schiff* anbohren, (selbst) versenken.
scut·tle[3] [~] **1.** Drückebergerei *f*; **2.** eilen; *fig.* sich drücken.
scythe ✓ [saið] **1.** Sense *f*; **2.** (ab-)mähen.
sea [si:] See *f*; Meer *n* (*a. fig.*); hohe Welle *f*; *at* ~ auf See; *fig.* ratlos; *by the* ~ am Meer; *go to* ~ zur See gehen; *s. put* 2; **'~board** Küste(ngebiet *n*) *f*; **~ cap·tain** Schiffskapitän *m*; **~ coast** Küste *f*; **'~-dog** alter Seebär *m*; *elisabethanischer* Seeheld *m*; = *seal*[1]; **'~·far·ing** seefahrend; **~food** *Am.* eßbare Meerestiere *n/pl.*; **'~·front** Strand(promenade *f*) *m*; **'~·go·ing** Hochsee..., Ozean...; **'~-gull** (See)Möwe *f*.
seal[1] *zo.* [si:l] Seehund *m*, Robbe *f*.
seal[2] [~] **1.** Siegel *n*, Petschaft *n*; Stempel *m*; Bestätigung *f*, Versicherung *f*; *great* ~, *broad* ~ großes Staatssiegel *n*; **2.** versiegeln; *fig.* besiegeln; ~ *off fig.* abschließen; ~ *up* (fest) verschließen; ⊕ abdichten.
seal·er ['si:lə] Robbenfänger *m*.
sea-lev·el ['si:levl] Meeresspiegel *m*.
seal·ing ['si:liŋ] Robbenfang *m*.
seal·ing-wax ['si:liŋwæks] Siegellack *m*.
seal·skin ['si:lskin] Seehundsfell *n*.
seam [si:m] **1.** Saum *m*, Naht *f*; ⊕ Fuge *f*; *geol.* Flöz *n*; Narbe *f*; *burst at the* ~*s* aus den Nähten platzen (*a. fig.*); **2.** schrammen; furchen.
sea·man ['si:mən] Seemann *m*, Matrose *m*; **'sea·man·ship** Seemannskunst *f*.
sea-mew ['si:mju:] Sturmmöwe *f*.
seam·less □ ['si:mlis] nahtlos.
seam·stress ['semstris] Näherin *f*.
seam·y ['si:mi] narbig; ~ *side fig.* Schattenseite *f*.
sea...: **'~-piece** *paint.* Seestück *n*; **'~·plane** Wasserflugzeug *n*; **'~·port** Seehafen *m*; Hafenstadt *f*; **'~-pow·er** Seemacht *f*.
sear [siə] **1.** dürr, welk; **2.** austrocknen; versengen; ⚕ brennen; *fig.* verhärten.
search [sə:tʃ] **1.** Suchen *n*, Forschen *n* (*for* nach); Unter-, Durchsuchung *f*; *in* ~ *of* auf der Suche nach; **2.** *v/t.* durch-, untersuchen; ⚕ sondieren; *Gewissen etc.* prüfen, erforschen; durchdringen (*Kälte, Geschoß etc.*); ~ *out* ausfindig machen; *v/i.* suchen, forschen (*for* nach); ~ *into* ergründen; **'search·er** (Unter)Sucher *m*; Erforscher *m*; **'search·ing** □ forschend, prüfend (*Blick*); eingehend (*Prüfung etc.*); **'search-light** (Such)Scheinwerfer *m*; **search par·ty** Suchtrupp *m*; **'search-war·rant** ⚖ Haussuchungsbefehl *m*.
sea...: **'~-rov·er** Seeräuber(schiff *n*) *m*; **~-scape** ['si:skeip] *s. sea-piece*; **'~-ser·pent** Seeschlange *f*; **'~-'shore** Seeküste *f*; **'~·sick** seekrank; **'~·sick·ness** Seekrankheit *f*; **'~'side** Strand *m*, Küste *f*; ~ *place*, ~ *resort* Seebad *n*; *go to the* ~ an die See gehen.
sea·son ['si:zn] **1.** Jahreszeit *f*; (rechte) Zeit *f*; Hauptzeit *f*, Saison *f*; F = ~-*ticket*; *height of the* ~ Hochsaison *f*; *in* (*good od. due*) ~ zur rechten Zeit; *cherries are in* ~ jetzt ist die Kirschenzeit; *out of* ~ außer der Zeit; zur Unzeit, ungelegen; *for a* ~ eine Zeitlang; *with the compliments of the* ~ mit den besten Wünschen zum Fest; **2.** *v/t.* reifen (lassen); würzen; abhärten (*to* gegen); *v/i.* ablagern (*Bauholz etc.*); **'sea·son·a·ble** □ zeitgemäß, passend; **sea·son·al** □ ['si:zənl] von der Jahreszeit *od.* (*bsd.* ⚘) Saison abhängig; Saison...; saisonbedingt; **'sea·son·ing** Würze *f*; **'sea·son-tick·et** 🚂 Zeitkarte *f*; *thea.* Abonnement *n*.
seat [si:t] **1.** Sitz *m* (*a. fig.*); Sessel *m*, Stuhl *m*, Bank *f*; (Sitz)Platz *m*; Wohnsitz *m*; Landsitz *m*; Gesäß *n*; Schauplatz *m*; **2.** (hin)setzen; *Würdenträger* einsetzen; fassen, Sitzplätze haben für; mit e-m neuen Sitz versehen; ~ *o.s.* sich setzen; *be* ~*ed* sitzen; sich setzen; s-n Sitz haben (*in* in *dat.*); liegen (*Ort*); **'~-belt** ✈ Sicherheitsgurt *m*; **'seat·ed** sitzend; ...sitzig; **'seat·er** *bsd. mot.*, ✈ ...sitzer *m*.
sea-ur·chin ['si:'ə:tʃin] Seeigel *m*;
sea·ward ['~wəd] *adj.* seewärts gerichtet; *adv. a.* **sea·wards** ['~wədz] seewärts.
sea...: **'~·weed** ⚘ (See)Tang *m*; **'~·wor·thy** seetüchtig.
se·ba·ceous *physiol.* [si'beiʃəs] Fett-..., Talg...
se·cant ⩘ ['si:kənt] **1.** schneidend;

2. Sekante *f*.

séc·a·teur ✓ [sekəˈtəː] *mst (a pair of)* ~*s pl.* (eine) Baumschere *f*.

se·cede [siˈsiːd] sich trennen, sich lossagen, abfallen; **seˈced·er** Abtrünnige *m*.

se·ces·sion [siˈseʃən] Lossagung *f*; Spaltung *f*; Abfall *m*; **seˈces·sion·ist** [~ʃnist] Abtrünnige *m*; Sezessionist *m*.

se·clude [siˈkluːd] abschließen, absondern; **seˈclud·ed** einsam; zurückgezogen; abgelegen; **seˈclu·sion** [~ʒən] Abgeschlossen-, Abgeschiedenheit *f*.

sec·ond[1] [ˈsekənd] **1.** □ zweite(r, -s); nächste(r, -s); geringer (*to* als); *he is* ~ *to none* er steht keinem nach; *on* ~ *thoughts* bei genauerer Überlegung; **2.** Zweite *m*, *f*, *n*; Sekundant *m*; Beistand *m*; Sekunde *f*; ~*s pl.* ✝ zweite Sorte *f*; ~ *of exchange* ✝ Sekundawechsel *m*; **3.** sekundieren, beistehen (*dat.*); unterstützen.

se·cond[2] ⚔ [siˈkɔnd] *Offizier* abkommandieren.

sec·ond·ar·i·ness [ˈsekəndərinis] *das* Sekundäre, Zweitrangigkeit *f*; **ˈsec·ond·ar·y** □ sekundär; in zweiter Linie kommend, untergeordnet; Neben...; Hilfs...; Sekundär...; **sec·ond·ar·y school** höhere Schule *f*; weiterführende Schule *f*; **ˈsec·ond-ˈbest** zweitbest; *come off* ~ F den kürzeren ziehen; **ˈsec·ond-ˈclass** zweitklassig, -rangig; 🚃 zweiter Klasse; **ˈsec·ond·er** Unterstützer *m* (*bsd. parl.*); **sec·ond-hand 1.** [ˈsekəndˈhænd] aus zweiter Hand; *schon* gebraucht; antiquarisch; ~ *bookseller* Antiquar *m*; ~ *bookshoop* Antiquariat *n*; **2.** [ˈsekəndhænd] Sekundenzeiger *m*; **ˈsec·ond·ly** zweitens; **ˈsec·ond-ˈrate** zweiten Ranges; zweitklassig; ✝ ~ *quality* zweite Wahl *f*.

se·cre·cy [ˈsiːkrisi] Heimlichkeit *f*; Verschwiegenheit *f*; **se·cret** [ˈsiːkrit] **1.** □ geheim; Geheim...; verschwiegen; verborgen; ~ *agent* Geheimagent *m*; **2.** Geheimnis *n*; *in* ~ insgeheim; *be in the* ~, *be taken into the* ~ eingeweiht sein.

sec·re·tar·i·at(**e**) [sekrəˈtɛəriət] Sekretariat *n*.

sec·re·tar·y [ˈsekrətri] Schriftführer *m*; Sekretär(in); ♀ *of State* Staatssekretär *m*, Minister *m*; *Am.* Außenminister *m*; **ˈsec·re·tar·y·ship** Sekretariat *n*, Schriftführeramt *n*.

se·crete [siˈkriːt] verbergen; *physiol.* absondern, ausscheiden; **seˈcre·tion** *physiol.* Absonderung *f*, Sekretion *f*; Sekret *n*; **seˈcre·tive** *fig.* verschlossen; geheimtuerisch.

sect [sekt] Sekte *f*; **sec·tar·i·an** [~ˈtɛəriən] **1.** sektiererisch; **2.** Sektierer(in).

sec·tion [ˈsekʃən] ⚕ Sektion *f*, Zerlegung *f*; *mikroskopischer* Schnitt *m*; ⚒ Schnitt *m*; △ Durchschnitt *m*; Teil *m*; Abschnitt *m*, Paragraph *m*; *typ.* Absatz *m*; *s.* ~*-mark*; Sektion *f*, Abteilung *f*; Gruppe *f*; *shopping (residential)* ~ Einkaufs- (Wohn-) viertel *n*; **sec·tion·al** [ˈ~ʃənl] Durchschnitts...; Teil...; Abschnitts...; Abteilungs...; ⊕ zs.-setzbar; partikularistisch, Lokal...; **ˈsec·tion·al·ism** Gruppenegoismus *m*; **ˈsec·tion-mark** Paragraph(enzeichen *n*) *m*.

sec·tor [ˈsektə] (Kreis)Sektor *m*; ⚔ Abschnitt *m*.

sec·u·lar □ [ˈsekjulə] säkular; hundertjährig; weltlich; **sec·u·lar·i·ty** [~ˈlæriti] Weltlichkeit *f*; **sec·u·lar·ize** [ˈ~ləraiz] säkularisieren; *geistliche Güter* einziehen; verweltlichen.

se·cure [siˈkjuə] **1.** □ sicher (*of gen.*; *against, from* vor *dat.*); **2.** sichern; schützen (*from, against* vor *dat.*); *j., et.* sicherstellen; festmachen; sich *et.* sichern *od.* verschaffen; verwahren.

se·cu·ri·ty [siˈkjuəriti] Sicherheit *f*; Sorglosigkeit *f*; Gewißheit *f*; Schutz *m*; Bürgschaft *f*, Kaution *f*; ~ *check* Sicherheitskontrolle *f*; ♀ *Council* Sicherheitsrat *m*; ♀ *Force* Friedenstruppe *f*; *securities pl.* Wertpapiere *n/pl.*; *public securities* Staatspapiere *n/pl.*

se·dan [siˈdæn] Limousine *f*; *a.* ~-*-chair* Sänfte *f*.

se·date □ [siˈdeit] gesetzt; ruhig; **seˈdate·ness** Gesetztheit *f*, Ruhe *f*.

se·da·tion ⚕ [siˈdeiʃən] Beruhigung *f* der Nerven durch Sedativa.

sed·a·tive *mst* ⚕ [ˈsedətiv] **1.** beruhigend; **2.** Beruhigungsmittel *n*.

sed·en·tar·i·ness [ˈsedntərinis] sitzende Lebensweise *f*; Seßhaftigkeit *f*; **ˈsed·en·tar·y** □ sitzend; seßhaft.

sedge ⚘ [sedʒ] Riedgras *n*, Segge *f*.
sed·i·ment [ˈsedimənt] (Boden-) Satz *m*, Niederschlag *m*; *geol.* Ablagerung *f*, Sediment *n*; **sed·i·men·ta·ry** [~ˈmentəri] *geol.* sedimentär; Ablagerungs...
se·di·tion [siˈdiʃən] Aufruhr *m*.
se·di·tious □ [siˈdiʃəs] aufrührerisch.
se·duce [siˈdjuːs] verführen; **seˈduc·er** Verführer(in); **se·duc·tion** [~ˈdʌkʃən] Verführung *f*; **seˈduc·tive** □ verführerisch.
sed·u·lous □ [ˈsedjuləs] emsig.
see[1] [siː] (*irr.*) *v/i.* sehen; *fig.* einsehen; *I* ~ ich verstehe; ~ *about s.th.* sich um et. kümmern; ~ *through s.o. od. s.th.* j. *od.* et. durchschauen; ~ *to* sorgen für, achten auf (*acc.*); ~ *for yourself!* Überzeugen Sie sich selbst!; *v/t.* sehen; ansehen, beobachten; einsehen, begreifen; sorgen (*daß et. geschieht*); *Patienten* besuchen; *Arzt* aufsuchen; ~ *s.th. done* dafür sorgen, daß et. geschieht; *go to* ~ *s.o.* j. besuchen; ~ *s.o. home* j. nach Hause bringen *od.* begleiten; ~ *off Besuch etc.* wegbringen; ~ *out Besuch* hinausbegleiten; *et.* zu Ende erleben; ~ *over s.th.* et. besichtigen; ~ *s.th. through* et. durchhalten *od.* -fechten; ~ *s.o. through* j-m durchhelfen; *live to* ~ erleben.
see[2] [~] (Erz)Bischofssitz *m*; *Holy* ♀ *der* Heilige Stuhl.
seed [siːd] **1.** Same(n) *m*, Saat(gut *n*) *f*; (Obst)Kern *m*; Keim *m* (*a. fig.*); *go od. run to* ~ in Samen schießen; *fig.* herunterkommen; **2.** *v/t.* (be)säen; *Obst* entkernen; *Sport*: *Spieler* setzen; *v/i.* in Samen schießen; ˈ**~·bed** = *seed-plot*; ˈ**seed·i·ness** Schäbigkeit *f*; F Katzenjammer *m*; ˈ**seed·less** kernlos (*Obst*); ˈ**seed·ling** ⚒ Sämling *m*; ˈ**seed-plot** ⚒ Samenbeet *n*; *fig.* Brutstätte *f*; **seeds·man** [ˈ~zmən] Samenhändler *m*; ˈ**seed·y** schäbig; F unwohl, elend.
see·ing [ˈsiːiŋ] **1.** Sehen *n*; *worth* ~ sehenswert; **2.** *cj.* ~ *that* da ja; angesichts der Tatsache, daß.
seek [siːk] (*irr.*) *a.* ~ *after*, ~ *for* suchen (nach); begehren (nach); streben *od.* trachten nach; ˈ**seek·er** Suchende *m, f*; Sucher(in).
seem [siːm] scheinen, erscheinen; ˈ**seem·ing 1.** □ anscheinend; scheinbar; **2.** Anschein *m*; ˈ**seem·li·ness** Anstand *m*, Schicklichkeit *f*; ˈ**seem·ly** geziemend, schicklich.
seen [siːn] *p.p. von* see[1].
seep [siːp] durchsickern, tropfen, lecken; ˈ**seep·age** Durchsickern *n*, Tropfen *n*, Lecken *n*.
seer [ˈsiːə] Seher(in), Prophet(in).
see·saw [ˈsiːsɔː] **1.** Wippen *n*; Wippe *f*, Wippschaukel *f*; **2.** wippen; *fig.* schwanken.
seethe [siːð] sieden, kochen.
seg·ment [ˈsegmənt] Abschnitt *m*; *bsd.* ⩓ Segment *n*.
seg·re·gate [ˈsegrigeit] absondern, trennen; **seg·reˈga·tion** Absonderung *f*; Rassentrennung *f*.
seine [sein] *Fischerei*: Schlagnetz *n*.
sei·sin ⚖ [ˈsiːzin] Besitz *m*.
seis·mic [ˈsaizmik] seismisch.
seis·mo·graph [ˈsaizməgrɑːf] Erdbebenmesser *m*, Seismograph *m*; **seis·mol·o·gy** [~ˈmɔlədʒi] Seismologie *f*, Erdbebenkunde *f*.
seize [siːz] *v/t.* ergreifen, fassen, packen; sich *et.* aneignen, sich *e-r Sache* bemächtigen; mit Beschlag belegen; *mit dem Verstand* erfassen; ⚓ (bei)zeisen; *v/i.* ⊕ sich festfressen; ~ *upon* sich *e-r Sache od. j-s* bemächtigen; ˈ**seiz·ing** Ergreifen *n etc.*; *mst* ~*s pl.* ⚓ Bändsel *n*; **sei·zure** [ˈ~ʒə] Ergreifung *f*; ⚖ Beschlagnahme *f*; ⚕ plötzlicher Anfall *m*.
sel·dom [ˈseldəm] *adv.* selten.
se·lect [siˈlekt] **1.** auswählen, -lesen, -suchen; **2.** auserwählt; erlesen; exklusiv (*Verein etc.*); **seˈlec·tion** Auswahl *f*, -lese *f*; *zo.*, ⚘ Zuchtwahl *f*; *a. musical* ~ Potpourri *n*; **seˈlec·tive** □ auswählend; Auswahl...; *Radio*: trennscharf; **se·lecˈtiv·i·ty** *Radio*: Trennschärfe *f*; **seˈlect·man** *Am.* Stadtrat *m in den Neuenglandstaaten*; **seˈlec·tor** Auswählende *m, f*; *Radio*: Sucher *m*.
self [self] **1.** *pron.* selbst; ✝ *od.* F = *myself etc.*; **2.** *adj.* ⚘ einfarbig; **3.** *pl.* **selves** [selvz] Selbst *n*, Ich *n*; Persönlichkeit *f*; *my poor* ~ meine Wenigkeit; ˈ**~-aˈbase·ment** Selbsterniedrigung *f*; ˈ**~-ˈact·ing** selbsttätig; ˈ**~-adˈhe·sive** selbstklebend; ˈ**~-asˈser·tion** Geltendmachen *n* s-r Meinung, s-s Willens *etc*; ˈ**~-asˈser·tive:** ~ *person* j., der sich

durchzusetzen *od.* zu behaupten versteht; **ˈ~-asˈsur·ance** Selbstbewußtsein *n*; **ˈ~-ˈca·ter·ing** Selbstverpflegungs...; **ˈ~-ˈcen·tred,** *Am.* **ˈ~ˈcen·tered** egozentrisch, ichbezogen; **ˈ~-ˈcol·o(u)red** einfarbig; uni (*Stoff*); **ˈ~-comˈmand** Selbstbeherrschung *f*; **ˈ~-conˈceit** Eigendünkel *m*; **ˈ~-conˈceit·ed** dünkelhaft; **ˈ~-conˈfessed** eingestanden; **ˈ~-ˈcon·fi·dence** Selbstvertrauen *n*; **ˈ~-ˈcon·scious** befangen, gehemmt; **ˈ~-ˈcon·scious·ness** Befangenheit *f*; **ˈ~-conˈtained** (in sich) abgeschlossen; verschlossen (*Charakter*); ~ *country* Selbstversorgerland *n*; ~ *house* Einfamilienhaus *n*; **ˈ~-conˈtrol** Selbstbeherrschung *f*; **ˈ~-deˈfence** Selbstverteidigung *f*; *in* ~ in (der) Notwehr; **ˈ~-deˈni·al** Selbstverleugnung *f*; **ˈ~-de·ter·miˈna·tion** Selbstbestimmung *f*; **ˈ~-ˈed·u·cat·ed:** ~ *person* Autodidakt *m*; **ˈ~-emˈployed** selbständig (*Handwerker etc.*); **ˈ~-ˈev·i·dent** selbstverständlich; **ˈ~-exˈplan·a·to·ry** ohne Erläuterung verständlich; **ˈ~-ˈgov·ern·ment** Selbstverwaltung *f*, Autonomie *f*; **ˈ~-imˈport·ance** Eigendünkel *m*; **ˈ~-imˈport·ant** eingebildet, aufgeblasen; **ˈ~-inˈdul·gent** genießerisch, bequem; **ˈ~-ˈin·ter·est** Eigennutz *m*; **ˈself·ish** □ selbstsüchtig; **ˈself·ishness** Selbstsucht *f*.

self...: **ˈ~-ˈmade** selbstgemacht; ~ *man* j., der durch eigene Kraft et. geworden ist, Selfmademan *m*; **ˈ~-posˈses·sion** Selbstbeherrschung *f*; **ˈ~-pre·serˈva·tion** Selbsterhaltung *f*; **ˈ~-reˈgard** Eigennutz *m*; **ˈ~-reˈli·ance** Selbstsicherheit *f*; **ˈ~-reˈli·ant** selbstsicher; **ˈ~-reˈspect** Selbstachtung *f*; **ˈ~-reˈspect·ing:** *every* ~ *nation* jede Nation, die etwas auf sich hält; **ˈ~-ˈright·eous** selbstgerecht; **ˈ~-ˈsac·ri·fice** Selbstaufopferung *f*; **ˈ~-same** *lit.* ebenderselbe; **ˈ~-ˈseek·ing** eigennützig; **ˈ~-ˈserv·ice res·tau·rant** Selbstbedienungsrestaurant *n*; **ˈ~-ˈstart·er** *mot.* Anlasser *m*; **ˈ~-sufˈfi·cien·cy** Selbstversorgung *f*; Selbstgenügsamkeit *f*; **ˈ~-supˈpli·er** Selbstversorger(in); **ˈ~-supˈport·ing** selbständig; (wirtschaftlich) unabhängig; **ˈ~-ˈwill** Eigenwille *m*; **ˈ~-ˈwilled** eigenwillig.

sell [sel] **1.** (*irr.*) *v/t.* verkaufen (*a. fig.*); *Am.* F anpreisen, beibringen; ~ (*out*) F *j.* reinlegen; ~ *off* † ausverkaufen; ~ *up j.* auspfänden; *v/i.* handeln; sich verkaufen, gehen (*Ware*); ~ *off*, ~ *out* † ausverkaufen; **2.** F Schwindel *m*; Reinfall *m*; **ˈsell·er** Verkäufer *m*; *good etc.* ~ gut *etc.* gehende Ware *f*; **ˈsell·out** F ausverkaufte Veranstaltung *f*; *fig.* Riesenerfolg *m*; Verrat *m*.

selt·zer [ˈseltsə] *a.* ~ *water* Selterswasser *n*.

sel·vage, sel·vedge ⊕ [ˈselvidʒ] Salband *n*, Webekante *f*.

selves [selvz] *pl. von self 3.*

se·man·tics [siˈmæntiks] *sg.* Wortbedeutungslehre *f*, Semantik *f*.

sem·a·phore [ˈseməfɔː] **1.** Zeichentelegraph *m*; ⚔ (*bsd.* Flaggen-) Winken *n*; 🚂 Signalmast *m*; **2.** (*bsd.* durch Winkzeichen) signalisieren.

sem·blance [ˈsembləns] Anschein *m*; Gestalt *f*.

se·men [ˈsiːmən] Samenflüssigkeit *f*.

se·mes·ter *univ.* [siˈmestə] Semester *n*.

sem·i... [ˈsemi] halb...; Halb...; **ˈ~·breve** ♪ ganze Note *f*; **ˈ~·cir·cle** Halbkreis *m*; **ˈ~ˈcir·cu·lar** halbkreisförmig; **ˈ~ˈco·lon** Strichpunkt *m*, Semikolon *n*; **ˈ~·conˈduc·tor** ⚡ Halbleiter *m*; **ˈ~-deˈtached house** Doppelhaus(hälfte *f*) *n*; **ˈ~-ˈfi·nal** *Sport*: Vorschlußrunde *f*; Halbfinale *n*; **ˈ~-man·uˈfac·tured** halbfertig.

sem·i·nal [ˈsiːminl] Samen...; Keim...; *fig.* keimtragend.

sem·i·nar·y [ˈseminəri] (Priester-) Seminar *n*; *fig.* Schule *f*.

sem·i-of·fi·cial [ˈsemiəˈfiʃəl] halbamtlich.

sem·i·pre·cious [ˈsemiˈpreʃəs]: ~ *stone* Halbedelstein *m*.

sem·i·qua·ver ♪ [ˈsemikweivə] Sechzehntel(note *f*) *n*.

Sem·ite [ˈsiːmait] Semit(in); **Se·mit·ic** [siˈmitik] semitisch.

sem·i·tone ♪ [ˈsemitəun] Halbton *m*.

sem·i·vow·el [ˈsemivauəl] Halbvokal *m*.

sem·o·li·na [seməˈliːnə] Grieß *m*.

sempˈstress [ˈsempstris] Näherin *f*.

sen [sen] Sen *m* (*japanische Münze*).

sen·ate [ˈsenit] Senat *m*.

sen·a·tor [ˈsenətə] Senator *m*; **sen·a·to·ri·al** □ [~ˈtɔːriəl] senatorisch.

send [send] (*irr.*) senden, schicken; (*mit adj. od. p.pr.*) machen; *Ball etc.* werfen; *Kugel wohin* schießen; *s. pack 2*; ~ *for* kommen lassen, holen (lassen); ~ *forth* aussenden; von sich geben; *fig.* veröffentlichen; ~ *in* einsenden; einreichen; ~ *in one's name* sich melden lassen; ~ *off* wegschicken; absenden; aussenden; ~ *up* hinaufsenden; *fig.* in die Höhe treiben; ~ *word* mitteilen, Nachricht geben; **ˈsend·er** (Ab)Sender(in); *tel.* Sender *m*; **ˈsend-ˈoff** Abschied(sfeier *f*) *m*.

sen·e·schal [ˈseniʃəl] Seneschall *m*, Majordomus *m*.

se·nile [ˈsiːnail] greisenhaft, senil; **se·nil·i·ty** [siˈniliti] Greisenalter *n*.

sen·ior [ˈsiːnjə] **1.** älter (*to* als); dienstälter; Ober...; ~ *citizens pl.* Senioren *m/pl.*, ältere Mitbürger *m/pl.*; ~ *partner* ⚕ Chef *m*; **2.** Ältere *m*; Dienstältere *m*; Senior *m*; *he is my* ~ *by a year*, *he is a year my* ~ er ist ein Jahr älter als ich; **sen·ior·i·ty** [siːniˈɔriti] höheres (Dienst)Alter *n*.

sen·sa·tion [senˈseiʃən] (Sinnes-) Empfindung *f*, Gefühl *n*; Eindruck *m*; Aufsehen *n*; Sensation *f*; **senˈsa·tion·al** □ [~ʃənl] Empfindungs...; aufregend, sensationell; **senˈsa·tion·al·ism** [~ʃnəlizəm] Effekthascherei *f*, Sensationslust *f*.

sense [sens] **1.** *allg.* Sinn *m* (*of* für); Empfindung *f*, Gefühl *n*; Verstand *m*; Bedeutung *f*; Ansicht *f*; *in* (*out of*) *one's* ~*s* bei (von) Sinnen; *bring s.o. to his* ~*s* j. zur Vernunft bringen; *make* ~ Sinn haben (*Sache*); *talk* ~ vernünftig reden; **2.** spüren.

sense·less □ [ˈsenslis] sinnlos, unsinnig; bewußtlos; gefühllos; **ˈsense·less·ness** Sinnlosigkeit *f*; Bewußt-, Gefühllosigkeit *f*.

sen·si·bil·i·ty [sensiˈbiliti] Sensibilität *f*, Empfindungsvermögen *n*; Empfindlichkeit *f* (*to*, *a. of* für); *sensibilities pl.* Empfindsamkeit *f*, Zartgefühl *n*.

sen·si·ble □ [ˈsensəbl] verständig, vernünftig, klug; empfänglich (*of* für); fühlbar; *be* ~ *of* sich *e-r Sache* bewußt sein; *et.* empfinden; **ˈsen·si·ble·ness** Fühlbarkeit *f*; Vernünftigkeit *f*.

sen·si·tive □ [ˈsensitiv] empfindlich (*to* für); empfindungsfähig; Empfindungs...; feinfühlend; leicht verletzt; *phot.* lichtempfindlich; **ˈsen·si·tive·ness**, **sen·siˈtiv·i·ty** Empfindlichkeit *f* (*to* für).

sen·si·tize *phot.* [ˈsensitaiz] lichtempfindlich machen.

sen·so·ri·al [senˈsɔːriəl], **sen·so·ry** [ˈ~səri] Empfindungs...; Sinnes...; *sensory nerve* Gefühlsnerv *m*.

sen·su·al □ [ˈsensjuəl] sinnlich; **ˈsen·su·al·ism** Sinnlichkeit *f*; **ˈsen·su·al·ist** sinnlicher Mensch *m*; **sen·su·al·i·ty** [~ˈæliti] Sinnlichkeit *f*.

sen·su·ous □ [ˈsensjuəs] sinnlich (*die Sinne betreffend*); sinnenfreudig.

sent [sent] *pret. u. p.p. von send*.

sen·tence [ˈsentəns] **1.** ⚖ Richterspruch *m*, Urteil *n*; *gr.* Satz *m*; *serve one's* ~ s-e Strafe absitzen; *s. life*; **2.** das Urteil fällen über (*acc.*); verurteilen (*to* zu).

sen·ten·tious □ [senˈtenʃəs] sententiös; salbungsvoll; salbaderisch.

sen·tient [ˈsenʃənt] empfindend.

sen·ti·ment [ˈsentimənt] (seelische) Empfindung *f*, Gefühl *n*; Meinung *f*, Ansicht *f*; *s.* ~*ality*; **sen·ti·men·tal** □ [~ˈmentl] empfindsam, gefühlvoll; sentimental, rührselig; ~ *value* Liebhaberwert *m*; **sen·ti·men·tal·ist** [~ˈmentəlist] Gefühlsmensch *m*; **sen·ti·men·tal·i·ty** [~menˈtæliti] Sentimentalität *f*; Empfindsamkeit *f*; Rührseligkeit *f*.

sen·ti·nel [ˈsentinl], **sen·try** [ˈsentri] ⚔ Schildwache *f*, Posten *m*.

sen·try...: **ˈ~-box** Schilderhaus *n*; **ˈ~-go** Postengang *m*.

se·pal ⚘ [ˈsepəl] Kelchblatt *n*.

sep·a·ra·bil·i·ty [sepərəˈbiliti] Trennbarkeit *f*; **ˈsep·a·ra·ble** □ trennbar; **sep·a·rate 1.** □ [ˈseprit] (ab)getrennt, gesondert, besonder, separat, für sich; ~ *property* ⚖ Gütertrennung *f*; **2.** [ˈ~əreit] (sich) trennen; (sich) absondern; (sich) scheiden; **sep·aˈra·tion** Trennung *f*, Scheidung *f*; **sep·a·ra·tist** [ˈ~ərətist] *eccl.* Sektierer *m*; *pol.* Separatist *m*; **sep·a·ra·tor** ⊕ [ˈ~əreitə] Scheider *m*; (Milch-) Zentrifuge *f*.

se·pi·a *paint.* [ˈsiːpjə] Sepia *f*.

sep·sis ⚕ [ˈsepsis] Sepsis *f*, Blutvergiftung *f*.

Sep·tem·ber [sepˈtembə] September *m*.

sep·ten·ni·al □ [sep'tenjəl] siebenjährig.
sep·tic ⚕ ['septik] septisch.
sep·tu·a·ge·nar·i·an [septjuedʒi'nɛəriən] Siebzigjährige *m, f.*
se·pul·chral [si'pʌlkrəl] Grab...; Toten...; *fig.* düster; **sep·ul·chre** ['sepəlkə] **1.** Grab(stätte *f*) *n*; **2.** begraben; **sep·ul·ture** ['~tʃə] Begräbnis *n.*
se·quel ['si:kwəl] Folge *f*; Nachspiel *n*; (Roman)Fortsetzung *f*; *in the ~* in der Folge.
se·quence ['si:kwəns] Aufeinander-, Reihenfolge *f*; *Film*: Szene *f*; *~ of tenses gr.* Zeitenfolge *f*; '**se·quent** aufeinanderfolgend.
se·ques·ter [si'kwestə] *s. sequestrate*; *~ o.s.* sich zurückziehen (*from* von); *~ed* zurückgezogen; einsam.
se·ques·trate ⚖ [si'kwestreit] *Eigentum* einziehen; beschlagnahmen; **se·ques·tra·tion** [si:kwes'treiʃən] Absonderung *f*; ⚖ Beschlagnahme *f*; '**se·ques·tra·tor** ⚖ Zwangsverwalter *m.*
se·quin ['si:kwin] Paillette *f.*
se·quoi·a ⚘ [si'kwɔiə] Mammutbaum *m.*
se·ragl·io [se'ra:liəu] Serail *n.*
ser·aph ['serəf], *pl. a.* **ser·a·phim** ['~fim] Seraph *m*; **se·raph·ic** [se'ræfik] (*~ally*) seraphisch; engelgleich; verzückt.
Serb, Ser·bi·an ['sə:b(jən)] **1.** serbisch; **2.** Serbe *m*, Serbin *f*; Serbisch *n.*
sere *poet.* [siə] dürr, welk.
ser·e·nade [seri'neid] **1.** ♪ Serenade *f*, Ständchen *n*; **2.** ein Ständchen bringen (*dat.*).
se·rene □ [si'ri:n] klar, heiter; ruhig; **se·ren·i·ty** [si'reniti] Heiterkeit *f*; Ruhe *f.*
serf [sə:f] Leibeigene *m, f*, Hörige *m, f*; *fig.* Sklave *m*; '**serf·age**, '**serf·dom** Leibeigenschaft *f.*
serge [sə:dʒ] Serge *f* (*Stoff*).
ser·geant ⚔ ['sa:dʒənt] Feldwebel *m*, Wachtmeister *f*; Polizeisergeant *m*; '**~-'ma·jor** ⚔ Hauptfeldwebel *m.*
se·ri·al □ ['siəriəl] **1.** fortlaufend, reihenweise, Serien...; Fortsetzungs...; *~ly* reihen-, lieferungsweise; **2.** Fortsetzungsroman *m.*
se·ries ['siəri:z] *sg. u. pl.* Reihe *f* (*a.* ℞); Serie *f*; Folge *f*; *biol.* Gruppe *f*; *in ~* ⚡ in Reihe geschaltet.
se·ri·ous □ ['siəriəs] *allg.* ernst (*aufrichtig*; *eifrig*; *schwerwiegend*; *beträchtlich*; *bedenklich*; *gefährlich*); ernsthaft, -lich; *be ~* es im Ernst meinen; '**se·ri·ous·ness** Ernst *m*; Ernsthaftigkeit *f.*
ser·jeant *parl.* ['sa:dʒənt]: *⁓-at-arms* Ordnungsbeamte *m.*
ser·mon ['sə:mən] Predigt *f*; *iro.* Strafpredigt *f*; '**ser·mon·ize** *v/i.* predigen; *v/t.* abkanzeln.
se·rol·o·gy ⚕ [siə'rɔlədʒi] Serologie *f*, (Blut)Serumkunde *f.*
se·rous ['siərəs] serös.
ser·pent ['sə:pənt] Schlange *f*; **ser·pen·tine** ['~tain] **1.** Schlangen...; schlangengleich (*bsd. fig.*); schlangenförmig; gewunden; **2.** *min.* Serpentin *m.*
ser·rate ['serit], **ser·rat·ed** [se'reitid] gezackt; **ser'ra·tion** Auszackung *f.*
ser·ried ['serid] dichtgedrängt.
se·rum ['siərəm] Serum *n* (*physiol. Blutwasser*; ⚕ *Impfstoff*).
serv·ant ['sə:vənt] Diener(in); *a. domestic ~* Dienstbote *m*, Bedienstete *m, f*; '**~-girl** Dienstmädchen *n.*
serve 1. [sə:v] *v/t.* dienen (*dat.*); bedienen (*with* mit); *j-m* aufwarten; *Amt* verwalten; *Speisen* reichen; *a. ~ up Speisen* auftragen; *schlecht etc.* behandeln; helfen, nützen, dienlich sein (*dat.*); *Zweck* erfüllen; *Tennis*: aufschlagen; (*it*) *~s him right* (das) geschieht ihm recht; *s. sentence 1*; *~ out et.* austeilen; F es *j-m* besorgen; *~ a writ on s.o.*, *~ s.o. with a writ* ⚖ j-m e-n Gerichtsbefehl zustellen; *v/i.* dienen (*a.* ⚔); aufwarten, servieren; nützen, passen, zweckmäßig sein; dienen (*as*, *for* als, zu); *~ at table* servieren; **2.** *Tennis*: Aufschlag *m*; '**serv·er** *Tennis*: Aufschläger *m*; *eccl.* Meßdiener *m.*
serv·ice ['sə:vis] **1.** Dienst *m*; Aufwartung *f*; Bedienung *f*; Gefälligkeit *f*; ✝ Dienst *m* am Kunden; *a. divine ~* Gottesdienst *m*; Betrieb *m*; Verkehr *m*; Nutzen *m*; Gang *m von Speisen*; Service *n*, Tafelgerät *n*; ⚓ Bekleidung *f e-s Taues*; ⚖ Zustellung *f*; *Tennis*: Aufschlag *m*; *be at s.o.'s ~* j-m zu Diensten stehen; **2.** betreuen; *j-m* Hilfe

leisten; ⊕ warten, pflegen; ˈ**serv·ice·a·ble** □ dienlich, nützlich; benutzbar, betriebsfähig; strapazierfähig; ˈ**serv·ice·a·ble·ness** Dienlichkeit *f*.

serv·ice...: ~ **ar·e·a** Raststätte *f* mit Tankstelle; ˈ**~-ball** *Tennis*: Aufschlag(ball) *m*; ~ **charge** Bedienung(sgeld *n*) *f*; Bearbeitungsgebühr *f*; ~ **flat** Etagenwohnung *f* mit Bedienung; ˈ**~-line** *Tennis*: Aufschlaglinie *f*; ~ **pipe** ⊕ Zweig-, Anschlußrohr *n*; ~ **sta·tion** Tankstelle *f*; Werkstatt *f*.

ser·vile □ [ˈsəːvail] sklavisch (*a. fig.*); unterwürfig; kriecherisch; **ser·vil·i·ty** [~ˈviliti] Unterwürfigkeit *f*, Kriecherei *f*.

serv·ing [ˈsəːviŋ] Portion *f*.

ser·vi·tude [ˈsəːvitjuːd] Knechtschaft *f*; Sklaverei *f*; ⚖ Servitut *n*; *s. penal*.

ser·vo-brake *mot.* [ˈsəːvəubreik] Servobremse *f*.

ses·a·me ⚘ *u. fig.* [ˈsesəmi] Sesam *m*.

ses·sion [ˈseʃən] (*a.* Gerichts)Sitzung *f*; *be in* ~ tagen; **ses·sion·al** [ˈseʃənl] Sitzungs...

set [set] **1.** (*irr.*) *v/t.* setzen; stellen; legen; zurechtmachen *od.* -stellen, (ein)richten, ordnen; bringen; pflanzen; *Aufgabe*, *Wecker* stellen; *Hund* hetzen (*at*, *on* auf *acc.*); *Messer* abziehen; *Säge* schränken; *Edelstein* fassen; *Zeit* festsetzen; gerinnen *od.* erstarren lassen; *Haar* legen; ⚕ *Knochenbruch* einrichten; ~ *s.o. laughing* j. zum Lachen bringen; ~ *an example* ein Beispiel geben; ~ *the fashion* in der Mode bestimmend sein; ~ *sail* Segel setzen; abfahren; ~ *one's teeth* die Zähne zs.-beißen; ~ *against* gegenüberstellen (*dat.*); *s. apart*; ~ *aside* beiseite setzen; auf die Seite legen, reservieren; *fig.* verwerfen; ~ *at defiance j-m* Trotz bieten; ~ *at ease* beruhigen; ~ *at liberty* in Freiheit setzen; ~ *at rest* beruhigen; *Frage* entscheiden; ~ *store by* Wert legen auf (*acc.*); ~ *down* niedersetzen; absetzen (*aus e-m Wagen etc.*); aufschreiben; zuschreiben (*to s.o.* j-m); ~ *forth* dartun, -legen; ~ *off* hervorheben, -treten lassen; auf-, anrechnen (*against* gegen); ausgleichen; ~ *on* setzen auf (*acc.*); anstiften; ~ *out* auslegen, zeigen; auseinandersetzen, darlegen; pflanzen; ~ *up* auf-, er-, einrichten; *Meinung etc.* aufstellen; *e-n Schrei* ausstoßen; *j-m* aufhelfen; *j.* etablieren; *Geschäft etc.* anfangen; ~ *up in type typ.* setzen; **2.** (*irr.*) *v/i.* untergehen (*Sonne etc.*); gerinnen, fest werden; fließen, laufen (*Flut etc.*); *hunt.* (vor)stehen; sitzen (*Kleid etc.*); ~ *about s.th.* sich an et. machen; ~ *about s.o.* F über j. herfallen; ~ *forth* aufbrechen; ~ *forward* sich auf den Weg machen; ~ *in* beginnen, einsetzen; ~ *off* sich in Bewegung setzen; sich aufmachen, aufbrechen; fahren (*for* nach); ~ (*up*)*on* anfangen; angreifen; ~ *out* abreisen, aufbrechen; *fig.* ausgehen (*from* von); ~ *to* sich daran machen, anfangen; ~ *up* sich niederlassen (*as* als); ~ *up for* sich ausgeben für; sich aufspielen als; **3.** fest; starr, unbeweglich; festgesetzt, bestimmt; regelmäßig; vorgeschrieben; formell; ~ (*up*)*on* versessen auf (*acc.*), entschlossen zu; ~ *with* besetzt mit; ~ *fair Barometer*: beständig; *hard* ~ in großer Not; ~ *piece* Gruppenbild *n*; ~ *speech* wohlüberlegte Rede *f*; **4.** Reihe *f*, Folge *f*, Serie *f*, Sammlung *f*, Satz *m zs.-gehöriger Dinge*; Garnitur *f*; Besteck *n*; Service *n*; (Radio)Gerät *n*; ☤ Kollektion *f*; Gesellschaft *f*; Sippschaft *f*, Rotte *f*; ↗ Setzling *m*; *Tennis*: Satz *m*; Neigung *f*; Richtung *f*; Schnitt *m e-s Kleides etc.*; *poet.* Untergang *m der Sonne*; *thea.* Bühnenausstattung *f*; *make a dead* ~ *at fig.* über *j.* herfallen; es auf *e-n Mann* abgesehen haben (*Frau*).

set·back [ˈsetbæk] *fig.* Rückschlag *m*; △ Mauervorsprung *m*; ˈ**set-down** Dämpfer *m*; ˈ**set-ˈoff** Kontrast *m*; Schmuck *m*; ☤ *u.* ⚖ Gegenrechnung *f*, -forderung *f*; *fig.* Ausgleich *m*; ˈ**set-square** 𝔄 Zeichendreieck *n*.

set·tee [seˈtiː] *kleines* Sofa *n*.

set·ter [ˈsetə] Setzer(in); *hunt.* Setter *m* (*Vorstehhund*).

set the·o·ry 𝔄 Mengenlehre *f*.

set·ting [ˈsetiŋ] Setzen *n etc.* (*s. set 1 u. 2*); Erstarren *n*; Gerinnen *n*; *ast.* Untergang *m*; Richtung *f des Windes etc.*; Fassung *f e-s Edelsteins*; Umgebung *f*, Lage *f*; *thea.*

Ausstattung *f*; *fig.* Umrahmung *f*; ♪ Komposition *f*; ˈ**~-lo·tion** (Haar-) Fixativ *n*.

set·tle [ˈsetl] **1.** Sitzbank *f*; **2.** *v/t.* (fest)setzen; *Kind etc.* versorgen, ausstatten; *j.* etablieren; regeln; *Geschäft* abschließen, abmachen, erledigen; *Frage* entscheiden; *Rechnung* begleichen; ordnen; beruhigen; *Streit* beilegen; *Rente* aussetzen (*on s.o.* j-m); ansiedeln; *Land* besiedeln; *v/i. oft* ~ *down, a.* ~ *o.s.* sich niederlassen; sich ansiedeln; *a.* ~ *in* sich (wohnlich) einrichten; sich setzen (*a. Haus, Boden*); ⚓ wegsacken; nachlassen, sich legen (*Wut etc.*); beständig werden (*Wetter*); sich entschließen (*on* für, zu); sich begnügen (*with* mit); *it is settling for a frost* es wird Frost geben; ~ *down to* sich widmen (*dat.*).

set·tled [ˈsetld] fest, bestimmt; entschieden; beständig (*Wind etc.*); (*auf Rechnung*) bezahlt.

set·tle·ment [ˈsetlmənt] Regelung *f*; Erledigung *f*; Klärung *f*; Schlichtung *f*; Übereinkunft *f*; Niederlassung *f*; (Be)Siedlung *f*; ⚖ (Eigentums)Übertragung *f*; ✝ Ausgleich(ung *f*) *m*; Mission *f*; soziales Hilfswerk *n*.

set·tler [ˈsetlə] Siedler *m*; entscheidender Schlag *m*.

set·tling [ˈsetliŋ] Festsetzung *f etc.* (*s. settle* 2); ✝ Abrechnung *f*.

set...: ˈ**~-**ˈ**to** Kampf *m*; Schlägerei *f*; ˈ**~-up** F Aufbau *m*, Einrichtung *f*.

sev·en [ˈsevn] **1.** sieben; **2.** Sieben *f*; ˈ**sev·en·fold** siebenfach; **sev·en·teen** [ˈ~ˈtiːn] siebzehn; **sev·enth** [ˈsevnθ] **1.** □ siebente(r, -s); **2.** Siebentel *n*; ♪ Septime *f*; **se·ven·ti·eth** [ˈ~tiiθ] siebzigste(r, -s); ˈ**sev·en·ty 1.** siebzig; **2.** Siebzig *f*.

sev·er [ˈsevə] (sich) trennen; (auf-) lösen; zerreißen.

sev·er·al □ [ˈsevrəl] mehrere, verschiedene; einige; einzeln; besonder; getrennt; *joint and* ~ ⚖ solidarisch; ˈ**sev·er·al·ly** besonders, einzeln.

sev·er·ance [ˈsevərəns] Trennung *f*.

se·vere □ [siˈviə] streng; rauh (*Wetter*); hart (*Winter*); scharf (*Tadel*); ernst (*Mühe*); heftig (*Schmerz etc.*); herb (*Stil, Schönheit etc.*); schlimm, schwer (*Unfall, Verlust, Wunde*); **se·ver·i·ty** [siˈveriti] Strenge *f*, Härte *f*; Schwere *f*; Ernst *m*.

sew [səu] (*irr.*) nähen; *Buch* heften; ~ *up* zu-, vernähen.

sew·age [ˈsjuːidʒ] Abwasser *n*; ~ *farm* Rieselfelder *n/pl*.

sew·er[1] [ˈsəuə] Näherin *f*.

sew·er[2] [ˈsjuə] Abwasserkanal *m*; ˈ**sew·er·age** Kanalisation *f*.

sew·ing [ˈsəuiŋ] **1.** Nähen *n*; Näherei *f*; **2.** Näh...

sewn [səun] *p.p. von sew*.

sex [seks] *natürliches* Geschlecht *n*; Sex(ualität *f*) *m*; Geschlechtsverkehr *m*; *attr.* Geschlechts...; ~ *appeal* erotische Anziehungskraft *f*, Sex-Appeal *m*; ~ *education* sexuelle Aufklärung *f*, Sexualerziehung *f*; ~ *object* Lustobjekt *n*.

sex·a·ge·nar·i·an [seksədʒiˈnɛəriən] Sechzigjährige *m, f*; **sex·en·ni·al** □ [sekˈsenjəl] sechsjährig; sechsjährlich; **sex·tant** [ˈsekstənt] Sextant *m*.

sex·ton [ˈsekstən] Küster *m*, *zugleich* Totengräber *m*.

sex·tu·ple [ˈsekstjupl] sechsfach.

sex·u·al □ [ˈseksjuəl] sexuell; Sexual...; geschlechtlich; Geschlechts...; ~ *desire* (geschlechtliche) Begierde *f*; ~ *intercourse* Geschlechtsverkehr *m*; ~ *urge* Geschlechtstrieb *m*; **sex·u·al·i·ty** [~ˈæliti] Sexualität *f*.

sex·y F [ˈseksi] sexy; sexuell anregend; erotisch (*Witz, Buch etc.*).

shab·bi·ness [ˈʃæbinis] Schäbigkeit *f*; ˈ**shab·by** □ schäbig; gemein.

shack *bsd. Am.* [ʃæk] Hütte *f*, Bude *f*.

shack·le [ˈʃækl] **1.** Fessel *f* (*fig. mst* ~*s pl.*); ⚓, ⊕ Schäkel *m* (*Kettenglied*); **2.** fesseln.

shad *ichth.* [ʃæd] Alse *f*.

shade [ʃeid] **1.** Schatten *m*, Dunkel *n* (*a. fig.*); *Lampen- etc.* Schirm *m*; Schattierung *f*; *Am.* Rouleau *n*; *fig.* Spur *f*, Kleinigkeit *f*; **2.** beschatten; verdunkeln (*a. fig.*); *Licht* abschirmen; schützen (*from* gegen *Licht etc.*); *paint.* schattieren; ~ *away*, ~ *off* allmählich übergehen (lassen) (*into* in *acc.*); **shades** *pl.* F Sonnenbrille *f*; ˈ**shad·ing** *paint.* Schattierung *f*; *fig.* Nuance *f*.

shad·ow [ˈʃædəu] **1.** Schatten *m* (*a. fig.*); Phantom *n*; Spur *f*, Kleinigkeit *f*; **2.** beschatten; *mst* ~ *forth*, ~ *out* andeuten; versinnbildlichen; *j.* beschatten, überwachen;

~ **cab·i·net** *pol.* Schattenkabinett *n*; **ˈshad·ow·y** schattig; dunkel; schattenhaft; wesenlos.

shad·y [ˈʃeidi] schattenspendend; schattig; dunkel; F zweifelhaft; *on the ~ side of forty* F über die Vierzig hinaus.

shaft [ʃɑːft] Schaft *m*; Stiel *m*; Pfeil *m* (*a. fig.*); *poet.* Strahl *m*; ⊕ Welle *f*, Spindel *f*; Deichsel *f*; ⚒ Schacht *m*.

shag [ʃæg] Krüllschnitt *m* (*Tabak*).

shag·gy [ˈʃægi] zottig.

sha·green [ʃæˈgriːn] Chagrin(leder) *n*) *m*.

Shah [ʃɑː] Schah *m*.

shake [ʃeik] **1.** (*irr.*) *v/t.* schütteln, rütteln; erschüttern; *~ down* herunterschütteln; *Stroh etc.* hinschütten; zs.-rütteln; *~ hands* sich die Hände geben *od.* schütteln; *~ up Bett* aufschütteln; *fig.* aufrütteln; *v/i.* zittern, beben, wanken, wackeln (*with* vor *dat.*); ♪ trillern; *~ down* sich einleben; **2.** Schütteln *n*; Erschütterung *f*; Beben *n*; ♪ Triller *m*; F Augenblick *m*; *~ of the hand* Händedruck *m*; *no great ~s* F nichts Besonderes; **ˈ~ˈdown** Notlager *n*; *Am. sl.* Erpressung *f*; *~ cruise* ⚓ Probefahrt *f*; **ˈ~-hands** Händedruck *m*; **ˈshak·en 1.** *p.p. von shake 1*; **2.** *adj.* erschüttert; **ˈshak·er** Schüttler(in); Mix-, Mischbecher *m*.

shake-up F [ˈʃeikˈʌp] Aufrüttelung *f*; Umgruppierung *f*.

shak·i·ness [ˈʃeikinis] Wackligkeit *f*; Gebrechlichkeit *f*; **ˈshak·y** □ *mst* wacklig (*a. fig.*); *engS.* (sch)wankend; zitternd, zitterig.

shale *geol.* [ʃeil] Schiefer *m*.

shall [ʃæl] (*irr.*) *v/aux.* soll; werde.

shal·lot ⚘ [ʃəˈlɔt] Schalotte *f*.

shal·low [ˈʃæləu] **1.** seicht; flach; *fig.* oberflächlich; **2.** Untiefe *f*; **3.** (sich) verflachen; **ˈshal·low·ness** Seichtigkeit *f* (*a. fig.*).

shalt † [ʃælt] *du* sollst.

sham [ʃæm] **1.** falsch, unecht; Schein...; **2.** Trug *m*, leerer Schein *m*; Lüge *f*, Täuschung *f*; Schwindler(in); **3.** *v/t.* (er)heucheln, vortäuschen; *v/i.* sich verstellen; simulieren; *~ ill* sich krank stellen.

sham·ble [ˈʃæmbl] watscheln.

sham·bles *fig.* [ˈʃæmblz] *sg.* Schlacht-, Trümmerfeld *n*.

sham·bling □ [ˈʃæmbliŋ] wackelig.

shame [ʃeim] **1.** Scham *f*; Schande *f*; *~!*, *for ~!*, *~ on you!* pfui!, schäme dich!; *cry ~ upon s.o.* pfui über j. rufen; *put to ~* beschämen; **2.** beschämen, schamrot machen; schänden; *j-m* Schande machen.

shame·faced □ [ˈʃeimfeist] schamhaft, schüchtern; **ˈshame·faced·ness** Schamhaftigkeit *f*.

shame·ful □ [ˈʃeimful] schändlich, schmachvoll, beschämend; **ˈshame·ful·ness** Schändlichkeit *f*.

shame·less □ [ˈʃeimlis] schamlos; **ˈshame·less·ness** Schamlosigkeit *f*.

sham·my [ˈʃæmi] Wildleder *n*.

sham·poo [ʃæmˈpuː] **1.** Shampoo *n*, Haarwaschmittel *n*; Haarwäsche *f*; *~ and set Haare*: Waschen *n* und Legen *n*; *have a ~ and set* sich die Haare waschen und legen lassen; **2.** *Haare* schamponieren, waschen.

sham·rock [ˈʃæmrɔk] ⚘ weißer Feldklee *m*; Kleeblatt *n* (*irisches Nationalzeichen*).

shan·dy [ˈʃændi] *Getränk aus Bier und Limonade.*

shang·hai ⚓ *sl.* [ʃæŋˈhai] schanghaien (*gewaltsam heuern*).

shank [ʃæŋk] (Unter)Schenkel *m*; ⚘ Stiel *m*; ⚓ (Anker)Schaft *m*; *go on* ♀*'s mare od. pony* auf Schusters Rappen reiten; **shanked** ...schenkelig.

shan't [ʃɑːnt] = *shall not.*

shan·tung [ʃænˈtʌŋ] Schantungseide *f*.

shan·ty [ˈʃænti] Hütte *f*, Bude *f*; = *chanty.*

shape [ʃeip] **1.** Gestalt *f*, Form *f*; Art *f*; *in bad ~* in schlechtem Zustand; **2.** *v/t.* bilden, formen, gestalten; anpassen (*to dat.*); *~ one's course for* Kurs nehmen auf (*acc.*); *v/i.* sich entwickeln, sich anlassen; **shaped** ...förmig; **ˈshape·less** formlos; unförmig; **ˈshape·li·ness** schöne Form *f*; **ˈshape·ly** wohlgestaltet, hübsch, schön.

share [ʃɛə] **1.** Teil *m*, Anteil *m*; Beitrag *m*, Kontingent *n*; ⚕ Anteilschein *m*, Aktie *f*; ⚒ Kux *m*; *original ~, ordinary ~, primary ~* ⚕ Stammaktie *f*; *preference ~, preferred ~, priority ~* ⚕ Vorzugsaktie *f*; *have a ~ in* teilhaben an (*dat.*); *go ~s* teilen (*with s.o.* mit j-m; *in s.th.* et.); *~ and ~ alike* zu gleichen Teilen; **2.** *v/t.* teilen (*among*

unter *acc.*; *with* mit); teilhaben an (*dat.*); *v/i.* teilhaben (*in* an *dat.*); '**~crop·per** *Am. kleiner* Farmpächter *m*; '**~hold·er** ⚕ Aktionär (-in); '**shar·er** Teiler(in); Teilhaber(in).
shark [ʃɑːk] *ichth.* Hai(fisch) *m*; *fig.* Gauner *m*; *Am. sl.* Kanone *f* (*Experte*).
sharp [ʃɑːp] **1.** □ *allg.* scharf (*a. fig.*); spitz; schneidend, stechend (*Schmerz*); herb (*Wein*); schrill (*Schrei*); hitzig (*Temperament*); schnell, flott; pfiffig, schlau, gewitzt, *b.s.* gerissen; ♪ um e-n halben Ton erhöht; *F* ~ Fis *n*; **2.** *adv.* ♪ (einen halben Ton) zu hoch; F pünktlich; *look* ~! (mach) schnell!; **3.** ♪ Kreuz *n*; durch ein Kreuz erhöhte Note *f*; F Gauner *m*; '**sharp·en** (ver)schärfen; *Bleistift* spitzen; *Appetit* anregen; ♪ erhöhen; '**sharp·en·er** *Messer-*Schärfer *m*; *Bleistift*-Spitzer *m*; '**sharp·er** Gauner *m*; '**sharp-'eyed** scharfsichtig; '**sharp·ness** Schärfe *f* (*a. fig.*); Strenge *f*, Härte *f*; *fig.* Heftigkeit *f e-s Schmerzes*; Scharfsinn *m*; Pfiffigkeit *f*.
sharp...: '**~-'set** hungrig; erpicht (*on* auf *acc.*); '**~shoot·er** Scharfschütze *m*; '**~-'sight·ed** scharfsichtig; '**~-'wit·ted** scharfsinnig.
shat·ter ['ʃætə] zerschmettern, -brechen, -schlagen, -trümmern (*a. fig.*); *Nerven etc.* zerrütten; '**~proof** splitterfrei, -sicher.
shave [ʃeiv] **1.** (*irr.*) *v/t.* rasieren; *bsd. Holz* (ab)schälen; haarscharf vorbeigehen *od.* -fahren *od.* -kommen an (*dat.*); *v/i.* sich rasieren; ~ *through* durchschlüpfen; **2.** Rasieren *n*, Rasur *f*; *have a* ~ sich rasieren (lassen); *by a* ~ um ein Haar; *a close* ~, *a narrow* ~ ein Entkommen *n* mit knapper Not; '**shav·en** *p.p. von shave 1*; *a* ~ *head* ein geschorener Kopf *m*; '**shav·er** Barbier *m*; *young* ~ F Grünschnabel *m*.
Sha·vi·an ['ʃeivjən] Shawsch, charakteristisch für G. B. Shaw.
shav·ing ['ʃeiviŋ] **1.** Rasieren *n*; ~*s pl.* (*bsd.* Hobel)Späne *m/pl.*, Schnitzel *n/pl.*; **2.** Rasier..., Barbier...; ~*-brush* Rasierpinsel *m*; ~ *cream* Rasiercreme *f*; ~ *soap*, ~ *stick* Rasierseife *f*.
shawl [ʃɔːl] Schal *m*, Kopftuch *n*.
shawm ♪ [ʃɔːm] Schalmei *f*.
shay † *od.* F [ʃei] Chaise *f*, Kutsche *f*.
she [ʃiː, ʃi] **1.** sie; **2.** Weib *n*, Sie *f*; **she-...** Weibchen *n von Tieren*.
sheaf [ʃiːf], *pl.* **sheaves** [ʃiːvz] Garbe *f*; Bündel *n*.
shear [ʃiə] **1.** (*irr.*) scheren, abschneiden; *fig.* rupfen; **2.** (*a pair of*) ~*s pl.* (eine) *große* Schere *f*; '**shear·er** (Schaf)Scherer *m*; Schnitter *m*; '**shear·ing** Scheren *n*, Schur *f*; ~*s pl.* Scherwolle *f*.
sheath [ʃiːθ], *pl.* **sheaths** [ʃiːðz] Scheide *f* (*a.* ⚘ *u. anat.*); *zo.* Flügeldecke *f*; **sheathe** [ʃiːð] (in die Scheide) stecken; einhüllen; ⊕ bekleiden, beschlagen; '**sheath·ing** ⊕ Bekleidung *f*, Beschlag *m*.
sheave ⊕ [ʃiːv] Scheibe *f*, Rolle *f*.
sheaves [ʃiːvz] *pl. von sheaf*.
she·bang *Am. sl.* [ʃə'bæŋ] Bruchbude *f*; *the whole* ~ der ganze Laden.
shed[1] [ʃed] (*irr.*) ausgießen; *Blut, Tränen etc.* vergießen; *Licht, Frieden etc.* verbreiten (*upon* über *acc.*); *Blätter, Zähne etc.* abwerfen.
shed[2] [~] Schuppen *m*; Stall *m*; Flugzeughalle *f*.
sheen [ʃiːn] Glanz *m* (*bsd. von Stoffen*); '**sheen·y** glänzend.
sheep [ʃiːp] Schaf *n*; *coll.* Schafe *pl.*; Schafleder *n*; '**~-cot** = *sheep-fold*; '**~-dog** Schäferhund *m*; '**~-fold** Schafhürde *f*; '**sheep·ish** □ blöd(e), einfältig; '**sheep·ish·ness** Blödigkeit *f*.
sheep...: '**~man** *Am.* Schafzüchter *m*; '**~-run** = *sheep-walk*; '**~skin** Schaffell *n*; Schafleder *n*; *Am.* Diplom *n*; '**~-walk** Schafweide *f*.
sheer[1] [ʃiə] *adj. u. adv.* rein, lauter; gänzlich, völlig, glatt; steil; senkrecht; direkt.
sheer[2] [~] **1.** ⚓ gieren, scheren (*vom Kurs abweichen*); ~ *off fig.* sich davonmachen; **2.** ⚓ Ausscheren *n*.
sheet [ʃiːt] **1.** Bett-, Leintuch *n*, Laken *n*; (*Glas-, Metall- etc.*)Platte *f*; Blatt *n*, Bogen *m Papier*; weite Fläche *f* (*von Wasser etc.*); ⚓ Schot(e) *f*; *the rain came down in* ~*s* es regnete in Strömen; ~ *iron* Eisenblech *n*; **2.** einhüllen; '**~-anchor** ⚓ Notanker *m* (*a. fig.*); '**sheet·ing** Leinwand *f* für Betttücher; '**sheet-light·ning** Flächen-

blitz *m*, Wetterleuchten *n*; **sheet mu·sic** Notenblätter *n/pl.*
sheik(h) [ʃeik] Scheich *m.*
shelf [ʃelf], *pl.* **shelves** [ʃelvz] Brett *n*, Regal *n*, Fach *n*, Sims *m*; Riff *n*, Sandbank *f*; *on the* ~ *fig.* ausrangiert, abgetan; *get on the* ~ *fig.* sitzenbleiben (*Mädchen*); ~ **life** Lagerfähigkeit *f.*
shell [ʃel] **1.** Schale *f*, Hülse *f*; Muschel *f*; Schneckenhaus *n*; ⊕ Gehäuse *n*; Gerippe *n e-s Hauses*; ⚔ Bombe *f*, Granate *f*; Renn(ruder)boot *n*; **2.** schälen, enthülsen; ⚔ bombardieren; ~ *out sl. Geld* herausrücken.
shel·lac [ʃəˈlæk] Schellack *m.*
shell-cra·ter [ˈʃelkreitə] Granattrichter *m*; **shelled** [ʃeld] ...schalig.
shell...: ˈ**~-fire** Granatfeuer *n*; ˈ**~-fish** Schalentier *n*; ˈ**~-proof** bombensicher; ˈ**~-shock** Kriegsneurose *f.*
shel·ter [ˈʃeltə] **1.** Schuppen *m*; Schutz-, Obdach *n*; *fig.* Schutz *m*, Schirm *m*; **2.** *v/t.* (be)schützen; (be)schirmen; Zuflucht gewähren (*dat.*); *v/i.* Schutz suchen; ˈ**shel·ter·less** schutzlos.
shelve[1] [ʃelv] mit Brettern *od.* Regalen versehen; auf ein Brett stellen; *fig.* zu den Akten legen; *fig.* außer Dienst stellen; *fig.* beiseite lassen, weglassen; F links liegen lassen.
shelve[2] [~] sich allmählich neigen.
shelves [ʃelvz] *pl. von shelf.*
shelv·ing [ˈʃelviŋ] **1.** Regal(e *pl.*) *n*; **2.** schräg.
she·nan·i·gan *Am.* F [ʃiˈnænigən] Gaunerei *f*; Humbug *m.*
shep·herd [ˈʃepəd] **1.** Schäfer *m*, Hirt *m*; **2.** (be)hüten; leiten, bugsieren; ˈ**shep·herd·ess** Schäferin *f.*
sher·bet [ˈʃəːbət] Sorbett *m*, *n* (*Fruchtgetränk*); Brauselimonade *f.*
sher·iff [ˈʃerif] Sheriff *m.*
sher·ry [ˈʃeri] Sherry *m.*
shew ✎ [ʃəu] = *show.*
shib·bo·leth [ˈʃibəleθ] Erkennungszeichen *n*; Schlagwort *n*; überholte Anschauung *f.*
shield [ʃiːld] **1.** (Schutz)Schild *m*; Wappenschild *m*, *n*; **2.** (be)schirmen, schützen (*from* vor *dat.*, gegen); ˈ**shield·less** schild-, schutzlos.
shift [ʃift] **1.** Veränderung *f*, -schiebung *f*, Wechsel *m*; Notbehelf *m*; List *f*, Kniff *m*; Ausflucht *f*; (Arbeits)Schicht *f*; *make* ~ es möglich machen (*to inf.* zu *inf.*); sich behelfen (*with* mit; *without* ohne); sich durchschlagen; **2.** *v/t.* (ver-, weg)schieben; ⚓ wenden, umlegen; umladen; *Platz, Szene etc.* verlegen, verändern, verlagern; *Betrieb etc.* umstellen (*to* auf *acc.*); *mot. Gang* schalten; *v/i.* den Ort verändern; sich verlagern; umspringen (*Wind*); ⚓ überschießen (*Ballast*); sich behelfen; ~ *for o.s.* für sich sorgen; sich selbst helfen; ˈ**shift·ing** □ veränderlich; ~ *sands pl.* Flugsand *m*; ˈ**shift·less** □ hilflos; *fig.* ungewandt; faul; ˈ**shift·y** □ schlau, verschlagen, gerissen; unzuverlässig.
shil·ling [ˈʃiliŋ] *engl.* Schilling *m*; *cut off with a* ~ enterben.
shil·ly-shal·ly [ˈʃiliʃæli] unentschlossen (sein).
shim·mer [ˈʃimə] flimmern, schimmern.
shin [ʃin] **1.** *a.* ~*-bone* Schienbein *n*; **2.** ~ *up* hinaufklettern.
shin·dy F [ˈʃindi] Radau *m*, Krach *m.*
shine [ʃain] **1.** Schein *m*; Glanz *m*; *give one's shoes a* ~ s-e Schuhe polieren; *rain or* ~ bei jedem Wetter; **2.** (*irr.*) scheinen; leuchten; *fig.* glänzen, strahlen; blank putzen.
shin·gle[1] [ˈʃiŋgl] **1.** Schindel *f*; Herrenschnitt *m* (*Damenfrisur*); *Am.* F (Aushänge)Schild *n*; **2.** mit Schindeln decken; *Haar* kurz schneiden.
shin·gle[2] *coll.* [~] Strandkiesel *m/pl.*; Strand *m.*
shin·gles ⚕ [ˈʃiŋglz] *pl.* Gürtelrose *f.*
shin·gly [ˈʃiŋgli] kies(el)ig, Kies...
shin·y □ [ˈʃaini] blank, glänzend.
ship [ʃip] **1.** Schiff *n*; *Am.* F Flugzeug *n*; ~*'s company* Schiffsbesatzung *f*; **2.** *v/t.* an Bord nehmen *od.* bringen; verschiffen, versenden; (ver)schicken; transportieren; *Matrosen* heuern; ~ *the oars* die Riemen einlegen; ~ *a sea* e-e Sturzsee bekommen; *v/i.* sich anheuern lassen; sich einschiffen; ˈ**~-board:** *on* ~ ⚓ an Bord; ˈ**~-brok·er** Schiffsmakler *m*; -händler *m*; ˈ**~-build·er** Schiffbauer *m*, Schiff-

baumeister *m*; ˈ~-**build·ing** Schiffbau *m*; ˈ~-**ca·nal** Schiffahrtskanal *m*; ˈ~-**chan·dler** Schiffslieferant *m*; ˈ~-**chan·dler·y** Schiffsproviant *m*; ˈ~·**load** Schiffsladung *f*; ˈ**ship·ment** Verschiffung *f*, Verladung *f*; Versand *m*; Schiffsladung *f*; ˈ**ship·own·er** Reeder *m*; ˈ**ship·per** Verschiffer *m*, Verlader *m*.

ship·ping [ˈʃipiŋ] **1.** Verschiffung *f*; Schiffe *n/pl.*, Flotte *f e-s Landes*; **2.** Schiffs...; Verschiffungs..., Verlade...; ˈ~-**a·gent** Reedereivertreter *m*, Schiffsagent *m*; ~ **fore·cast** Seewetterbericht *m*; ˈ~-**of·fice** Heuerbüro *n*.

ship...: ˈ~·**shape** sauber, ordentlich; ˈ~-**way** Helling *f*; ˈ~·**wreck** **1.** Schiffbruch *m*; **2.** scheitern (lassen); *be* ~*ed* Schiffbruch erleiden, scheitern; ˈ~·**wrecked** schiffbrüchig; ˈ~·**wright** Schiffbauer *m*; Schiffszimmermann *m*; ˈ~·**yard** Schiffswerft *f*.

shire [ˈʃaiə, *in Zssgn* ...ʃiə] Grafschaft *f*; ~ *horse* schweres Zugpferd *n*.

shirk [ʃəːk] sich drücken (um *e-e Aufgabe*); ˈ**shirk·er** Drückeberger *m*.

shirt [ʃəːt] Herrenhemd *n*; *a.* ~-*waist Am.* Hemdbluse *f*; *keep one's* ~ *on sl.* sich nicht aufregen; ˈ**shirt·ing** ✝ Hemdenstoff; ˈ**shirt-sleeve** **1.** Hemdsärmel *m*; **2.** hemdsärmelig, informell; ~ *diplomacy bsd. Am.* offene Diplomatie *f*; ˈ**shirt·y** *sl.* aus dem Häuschen, wütend.

shit [ʃit] **1.** V Scheiße *f*; P Shit *n*, Hasch(isch) *n*; **2.** V scheißen.

shiv·er[1] [ˈʃivə] **1.** Splitter *m*; *break to* ~*s* = **2.** *v/t. u. v/i.* zersplittern.

shiv·er[2] [~] **1.** Schauer *m*; *the* ~*s pl.* das Fieber; *it gives me the* ~*s* es läuft mir kalt über den Rücken; **2.** schau(d)ern; (er)zittern; frösteln; ~*ing fit* Fieberschauer *m*, Schüttelfrost *m*; ˈ**shiv·er·y** fröstelnd.

shoal[1] [ʃəul] **1.** Schwarm *m*, Schar *f* (*Fische*; *a. fig.*); **2.** sich scharen.

shoal[2] [~] **1.** Untiefe *f*; **2.** flacher *od.* seichter werden; **3.** = ˈ**shoal·y** seicht, flach.

shock[1] ⸙ [ʃɔk] Garbenhaufen *m*, Mandel *f*.

shock[2] [~] **1.** Stoß *m*; Anstoß *m*, Ärgernis *n*; Erschütterung *f*, Schlag *m*; ⚕ (Nerven)Schock *m*; **2.** *fig.* verletzen, empören, schokkieren, Anstoß erregen bei; *Nervensystem* erschüttern.

shock[3] [~] (*of hair* Haar)Schopf *m*.

shock...: ˈ~-**ab·sorb·er** *mot.* Stoßdämpfer *m*; ˈ~-**bri·gade** Stoßbrigade *f*.

shock·er *sl.* [ˈʃɔkə] Schauerroman *m*.

shock·ing □ [ˈʃɔkiŋ] anstößig; verletzend, empörend; haarsträubend.

shock...: ˈ~·**proof** stoßsicher; ~ **ther·a·py,** ~ **treat·ment** ⚕ Schocktherapie *f*; ~ **wave** Druckwelle *f*; *fig.* Schock *m*, Erschütterung *f*.

shod [ʃɔd] *pret. u. p.p. von shoe* 2.

shod·dy [ˈʃɔdi] **1.** Reißwolle *f*; *fig.* Schund *m*, Kitsch *m*; **2.** unecht, falsch; minderwertig; kitschig.

shoe [ʃuː] **1.** Schuh *m*; Hufeisen *n*; Beschlag *m*; Hemmschuh *m*; **2.** (*irr.*) beschuhen; beschlagen; ˈ~·**black** Schuhputzer *m*; ˈ~·**black·ing** Schuhwichse *f*; ˈ~·**horn** Schuhanzieher *m*; ˈ~-**lace** Schnürsenkel *m*; ˈ~·**mak·er** Schuhmacher *m*; ˈ~-**string** Schnürsenkel *m*; *on a* ~ F mit ein paar Groschen; ˈ~-**tree** Schuhspanner *m*.

shone [ʃɔn] *pret. u. p.p. von shine* 2.

shoo [ʃuː] *Vögel* scheuchen.

shook [ʃuk] *pret. von shake* 1.

shoot [ʃuːt] **1.** *fig.* Schuß *m* (*schnelle Bewegung*); ⸙ Schößling *m*; Jagd *f*; Rutsche *f*; Stromschnelle *f*; **2.** (*irr.*) *v/t.* schießen; abschießen, abfeuern; werfen, stoßen; *Film* aufnehmen, drehen; durchschießen; *fig.* unter *e-r Brücke etc.* hindurch-, über *et.* hinwegschießen; ⸙ treiben; *Riegel* vorschieben; *Müll, Karren* ausschütten; *Faß* schroten; ⚕ (ein)spritzen; *v/i.* schießen (*at* nach); stechen (*Schmerz, Glied*); fliegen, daherschießen; stürzen; fallen; *a.* ~ *forth* sprossen, ausschlagen; ⚓ überschießen (*Ballast*); ~ *ahead* vorwärtsschießen; ~ *ahead of* überholen, hinter sich lassen; ~ *up* emporschnellen; ˈ**shoot·er** Schütze *m*.

shoot·ing [ˈʃuːtiŋ] **1.** Schießen *n*; Schießerei *f*; Jagd *f*; Jagdrecht *n*; *Film*: Dreharbeiten *f/pl.*; **2.** stechend (*Schmerz*); ˈ~-**box** Jagdhäuschen *n*; ˈ~-**brake** Jagdwagen *m*; Kombiwagen *m*; ˈ~-**gal·ler·y**

Schießstand *m*, -bude *f*; '~-**range** Schießplatz *m*; ~ **star** Sternschnuppe *f*; '~-**war** heißer Krieg *m*.
shoot-out F ['ʃu:taut] Schießerei *f*.
shop [ʃɔp] **1.** Laden *m*, Geschäft *n*; Werkstatt *f*, Betrieb *m*; *set up* ~ ein Geschäft eröffnen; *talk* ~ fachsimpeln; **2.** *mst go* ~*ping* einkaufen gehen; '~-**as·sist·ant** Verkäufer(in); ~ **floor** Produktionsstätte *f*; *fig.* Arbeiter *m/pl.* (*Ggs. management*); '~-**keep·er** Ladeninhaber(in); Krämer *m*; '~·**lift·er** Ladendieb *m*; '~·**man** Ladengehilfe *m*; '**shop·per** Käufer (-in); '**shop·ping** Einkaufen *n*; Einkaufs...; ~ *centre*, *Am.* ~ *center* Einkaufszentrum *n*.
shop...: '~-**soiled** angestaubt (*Ware*); '~-'**stew·ard** Betriebsobmann *m der Gewerkschaft*; '~-**walk·er** Aufsichtsherr *m*, -dame *f in großen Geschäften*; '~-'**win·dow** Schaufenster *n*.
shore[1] [ʃɔ:] Küste *f*, Gestade *n*, Ufer *n*; Strand *m*; *on* ~ an Land.
shore[2] [~] **1.** Stütze *f*, Strebe *f*; **2.** ~ *up* (ab)stützen.
shore...: '~·**line** Küstenlinie *f*; '~·**ward** ['~wəd] küstenwärts (gelegen).
shorn [ʃɔ:n] *p.p. von shear 1*; ~ *of e-r Sache* beraubt.
short [ʃɔ:t] **1.** kurz; klein (*Figur*); knapp; mürbe (*Gebäck*); brüchig (*Metall*); kurz angebunden, wortkarg; ⚕ kurzfristig; *s. circuit*; ~ *wave Radio*: Kurzwelle *f*; *in* ~ kurz(um); ~ *of* knapp an (*dat.*), ohne; abgesehen von; *nothing* ~ *of* nichts als; geradezu; ~ *of London* kurz vor London; ~ *of lying* ehe ich lüge; *come od. fall* ~ *of* nicht erreichen, es fehlen lassen an (*dat.*); unter *dat.* bleiben; *cut* ~ plötzlich unterbrechen; *fall od. run* ~ ausgehen (*Vorräte*); *stop* ~ *of* innehalten vor (*dat.*); **2.** *gr.* kurzer Vokal *m*, kurze Silbe *f*; Kurzfilm *m*; ⚡ Kurzschluß *m*; *s. shorts*; ~-*circuit*; '**short·age** Fehlbetrag *m*; Gewichtsverlust *m*, Abgang *m*; Mangel *m*, Knappheit *f*.
short...: '~·**cake** Mürbekuchen *m*; ~-'**change** F *j-m* zu wenig (Wechselgeld) herausgeben; '~-'**cir·cuit** ⚡ kurzschließen; ~-'**com·ing** Unzulänglichkeit *f*; Fehler *m*; Mangel *m*; ~ **cut** Abkürzungsweg *m*; '~-'**dat·ed** ⚕ auf kurze Sicht; '**short·en** *v/t.* ab-, verkürzen; *v/i.* kürzer werden; '**short·en·ing** Backfett *n*.
short...: '~·**fall** Fehlbetrag *m*; '~-**hand** Kurzschrift *f*, Stenographie *f*; ~ *typist* Stenotypistin *f*; '~-'**hand·ed** knapp an Arbeitskräften; ~ **list** Auswahlliste *f*; *be on the* ~ in der engeren Wahl sein; '~-**list** in die engere Wahl ziehen; '~-'**lived** kurzlebig, von kurzer Dauer; '**short·ly** *adv.* kurz; in Kürze, bald; '**short·ness** Kürze *f*; Mangel *m*; **short or·der** *Am.* Schnellgericht *n im Restaurant*; '**short-range** Kurzstrecken..., Nah...; *fig.* kurzfristig.
shorts [ʃɔ:ts] *pl.* Shorts *pl.*, kurze Hose *f*.
short...: '~-'**sight·ed** kurzsichtig; '~-'**tem·pered** aufbrausend, reizbar; '~-**term** kurzfristig; ~ **time** Kurzarbeit *f*; *be on* ~ Kurzarbeit haben; '~-**wave** *Radio*: Kurzwellen...; '~-'**wind·ed** kurzatmig.
shot[1] [ʃɔt] **1.** *pret. u. p.p. von shoot 2*; **2.** *adj.* schillernd (*Seide*).
shot[2] [~] Schuß *m*; Geschoß *n*, Kugel *f*; *a. small* ~ Schrot *n*; *pl. mst* ~ Schrotkorn *n*; Schütze *m*; *Sport*: Stoß *m*, Schlag *m*, Wurf *m*; *phot.*, *Film*: Aufnahme *f*; ⚕ Einspritzung *f*, Spritze *f*; *sl.* Schuß *m Rum etc.*; *have a* ~ *at et.* versuchen; *not by a long* ~ F noch lange nicht; *within* (*out of*) ~ in (außer) Schußweite; *like a* ~ F wie aus der Pistole geschossen; *big* ~ F großes Tier *n*; Bonze *m*; *make a bad* ~ fehlschießen; (*fig. falsch raten*); '~·**gun** Schrotflinte *f*; ~ *marriage Am.* F Mußheirat *f*; '~-**proof** kugelfest; '~-**put** Kugelstoßen *n*.
shot·ten her·ring ['ʃɔtn'heriŋ] Hohlhering *m*.
should [ʃud] *pret. von shall*.
shoul·der ['ʃəuldə] **1.** Schulter *f* (*a. von Tieren*; *fig. Vorsprung*); Achsel *f*; *give s.o. the cold* ~ j. über die Achsel ansehen; *put one's* ~ *to the wheel* sich tüchtig ins Zeug legen; *rub* ~*s with* in Berührung kommen mit; ~ *to* ~ Schulter an Schulter; **2.** auf die Schulter (*fig.* auf sich) nehmen; ⚔ schultern; drängen; ~ *one's way* sich e-n Weg bahnen; '~-**bag** Umhäng(e)tasche *f*; '~-**blade** *anat.* Schulterblatt *n*; '~-**strap** Träger *m am Kleid*; ⚔ Schul-

ter-, Achselstück *n.*
shout [ʃaut] **1.** lauter Schrei *m od.* Ruf *m*; Geschrei *n*; **2.** laut schreien *od.* rufen; jauchzen.
shove [ʃʌv] **1.** Schub *m*, Stoß *m*; **2.** schieben, stoßen.
shov·el [ˈʃʌvl] **1.** Schaufel *f*; **2.** schaufeln; ˈ**~-board** Beilketafel *f*; Beilkespiel *n.*
show [ʃəu] **1.** (*irr.*) *v/t.* zeigen; ausstellen; *Gnade etc.* erweisen; *Gründe* angeben; beweisen; *~ forth* darlegen; *~ in* hereinführen; *~ off* zur Geltung bringen; *~ out* hinausgeleiten; *~ round* herumführen; *~ up* hinaufführen; bloßstellen, entlarven; *v/i. a. ~ up* sich zeigen, erscheinen; zu sehen sein; *~ off* angeben, prahlen, sich aufspielen; **2.** Schau(stellung) *f*; Ausstellung *f*; Auf-, Vorführung *f*; Anschein *m*, Anblick *m*; *sl.* Sache *f*, Geschichte *f*; *~ of hands* Handzeichen *n bei Abstimmungen*; *dumb ~* Pantomime *f*, Gebärdenspiel *n*; *on ~* zu besichtigen; *run the ~ sl.* den Laden schmeißen; **~ busi·ness** Unterhaltungsindustrie *f*; Schaugeschäft *n*; ˈ**~-card** Geschäftsanzeige *f*; ˈ**~-case** Schaukasten *m*, Vitrine *f*; ˈ**~-down** Aufdecken *n* der Karten (*a. fig.*); *fig.* Kraftprobe *f.*
show·er [ˈʃauə] **1.** (Regen-, Hagel-) Schauer *m*; Dusche *f*; *fig.* Fülle *f*, Menge *f*; **2.** herabschütten (*a. fig.*); übergießen, -schütten (*with* mit); sich ergießen; **~-bath** [ˈ~bɑːθ] Brausebad *n*, Dusche *f*; ˈ**show·er·y** regnerisch; Regen...
show·i·ness [ˈʃəuinis] Gepränge *n*; Auffälligkeit *f*; ˈ**show·man** Zirkus-, Varietéunternehmer *m*; j., der sich *od.* et. in Szene zu setzen versteht; ˈ**show·man·ship** Kunst *f*, sich *od.* et. in Szene zu setzen; **shown** [ʃəun] *p.p. von show 1*; ˈ**show·piece** Schau-, Paradestück *n*; ˈ**show-place** Sehenswürdigkeit *f*; ˈ**show-room** Ausstellungsraum *m*; ˈ**show-win·dow** Schaufenster *n*; ˈ**show·y** □ prächtig; prunkhaft; auffällig.
shrank [ʃræŋk] *pret. von shrink.*
shrap·nel ⚔ [ˈʃræpnl] Schrapnell *n.*
shred [ʃred] **1.** Stückchen *n*; Schnitz(el *n*) *m*; Fetzen *m* (*a. fig.*); **2.** (*irr.*) (zer)schnitzeln; zerfetzen; ausfasern; *~ded wheat* fertige Frühstücksnahrung *f* aus Weizen.
shrew [ʃruː] zänkisches Weib *n*; *a. ~-mouse zo.* Spitzmaus *f.*
shrewd □ [ʃruːd] scharfsinnig, klug, schlau; ˈ**shrewd·ness** Scharfsinn *m*, Schlauheit *f.*
shrew·ish □ [ˈʃruːiʃ] zänkisch.
shriek [ʃriːk] **1.** (Angst)Schrei *m*; Gekreisch *n*; *fig.* Pfeifen *n*; **2.** kreischen, schreien.
shrift [ʃrift]: *give s.o. short ~* mit j-m kurzen Prozeß machen, j. kurz abfertigen.
shrike *orn.* [ʃraik] Würger *m.*
shrill [ʃril] **1.** □ schrill, gellend; **2.** schrillen, gellen; schreien.
shrimp *zo.* [ʃrimp] Garnele *f*, Krabbe *f*; *fig.* Knirps *m.*
shrine [ʃrain] (Reliquien)Schrein *m*; Altar *m.*
shrink [ʃriŋk] (*irr.*) *v/i.* (ein-, zs.-) schrumpfen; einlaufen (*Stoff*); sich zurückziehen; *a. ~ back* zurückschrecken (*from, at* vor *dat.*); *v/t.* einschrumpfen lassen; ⊕ Stoff krump(f)en, einlaufen lassen; ˈ**shrink·age** Einlaufen *n*, Zs.-schrumpfen *n*; Schrumpfung *f*; *fig.* Verminderung *f.*
shriv·el [ˈʃrivl] *a. ~ up* einschrumpfen (lassen); *fig.* vergehen (lassen).
shroud[1] [ʃraud] **1.** Leichentuch *n*, Totenhemd *n*; *fig.* Gewand *n*, Umhüllung *f*; **2.** in ein Leichentuch einhüllen; *fig.* hüllen.
shroud[2] ⚓ [~] Want(tau *n*) *f*; *mst ~s pl.* Wanten *f/pl.*
Shrove·tide [ˈʃrəuvtaid] Fastnachtszeit *f*; **Shrove Tues·day** Fastnachtsdienstag *m.*
shrub [ʃrʌb] Staude *f*, Strauch *m*; Busch *m*; ˈ**shrub·ber·y** Strauchpflanzung *f*; Gebüsch *n*; ˈ**shrub·by** strauch(art)ig.
shrug [ʃrʌg] **1.** (die Achseln) zucken; *~ s.th. off* et. abtun; **2.** Achselzucken *n.*
shrunk [ʃrʌŋk] *p.p. von shrink*; ˈ**shrunk·en** *adj.* (ein)geschrumpft; eingefallen (*Wangen*).
shuck *Am.* [ʃʌk] **1.** Hülse *f*, Schote *f*; *~s!* F Quatsch!; **2.** enthülsen, -schoten.
shud·der [ˈʃʌdə] **1.** schaudern; (er-) beben; **2.** Schauder *m*; Erbeben *n.*
shuf·fle [ˈʃʌfl] **1.** *v/t.* schieben; *Karten* mischen; *~ away* wegpraktizieren; *~ off* von sich schieben; abstreifen; *v/i.* schieben,

stoßen; *Karten*: mischen; schlurren, schlurfen; sich herauszureden suchen, Ausflüchte machen; ~ *through one's work* s-e Arbeit flüchtig tun, pfuschen; **2.** Schieben *n*; Mischen *n der Karten*; Schlurfen *n*; *pol.* Umbesetzung *f*; Schiebung *f*; ˈ**shuffler** Mischer *m*; Ausflüchtemacher *m*, Schwindler *m*; ˈ**shuf·fling** □ schleppend (*Gang*); ausweichend; unredlich.

shun [ʃʌn] (ver)meiden.

shunt [ʃʌnt] **1.** 🚂 Rangieren *n*; 🚂 Weiche *f*; ⚡ Nebenschluß *m*; **2.** 🚂 rangieren, verschieben *od.* (*v/i.*) verschoben werden; ⚡ nebenschließen; *fig.* ver-, aufschieben; ˈ**shunt·er** 🚂 Rangierer *m*; ˈ**shunt·ing sta·tion** 🚂 Verschiebe-, Rangierbahnhof *m*.

shut [ʃʌt] (*irr.*) *v/t.* (ver)schließen, zumachen; ~ *one's eyes to* die Augen verschließen vor; ~ *down Betrieb* schließen, stillegen; ~ *in* einschließen; *Finger etc.* einklemmen in (*acc.*); ~ *out* ausschließen; ~ *up* ein-, verschließen; einsperren; ~ *up shop* das Geschäft schließen; *v/i.* sich schließen, zugehen; ~ *up!* F halt den Mund!; ˈ**~·down** Betriebsschließung *f*, Stillegung *f*; ˈ**~·out** *Sport*: Zu-Null-Niederlage *f*; ˈ**shut·ter** Fensterladen *m*; *phot.* Verschluß *m*; ~ *speed phot.* Belichtungszeit *f*; *put up the* ~*s* den Laden dicht machen, schließen; *rolling* ~ Rolladen *m*.

shut·tle [ˈʃʌtl] **1.** Weberschiff *n*; Schiffchen *n der Nähmaschine*; 🚂 *etc.* Pendelverkehr *m*; ~ *diplomacy pol.* Pendeldiplomatie *f*; ~ *service* Pendelverkehr *m*; ~ *train* Pendelzug *m*; **2.** *Verkehr*: pendeln; ˈ**~·cock** Federball(spiel *n*) *m*.

shy[1] [ʃai] **1.** □ scheu; schüchtern; *be od. fight* ~ *of* sich scheuen *od.* hüten vor (*dat.*); **2.** (zurück)scheuen (*at* vor *dat.*).

shy[2] F [~] **1.** werfen; **2.** Wurf *m*; Hieb *m*; *have a* ~ *at* e-n Versuch machen mit.

shy·ness [ˈʃainis] Schüchternheit *f*; Scheu *f*.

shy·ster *bsd. Am. sl.* [ˈʃaistə] gerissener Kerl *m*; Winkeladvokat *m*.

Si·a·mese [saiəˈmiːz] **1.** siamesisch; **2.** Siamese *m*, Siamesin *f*; Siamesisch *n*.

Si·be·ri·an [saiˈbiəriən] **1.** sibirisch; **2.** Sibirier(in).

sib·i·lant [ˈsibilənt] **1.** □ zischend; **2.** *gr.* Zischlaut *m*.

sib·yl [ˈsibil] Sibylle *f*, Seherin *f*; Wahrsagerin *f*; **sibˈyl·line** [~lain] sibyllinisch.

Si·cil·ian [siˈsiljən] **1.** sizilianisch; **2.** Sizilianer(in).

sick [sik] krank (*of* an *dat.*; *with* vor *dat.*); (zum Erbrechen) übel, unwohl; überdrüssig (*of gen.*); *be* ~ *for* sich sehnen nach; *be* ~ *of* genug haben von; *go* ~, *report* ~ sich krank melden; ˈ**~-bay** Lazarett *n*, Krankenrevier *n*; ˈ**~-bed** Krankenbett *n*; ˈ**sick·en** *v/i.* krank werden; kränkeln; ~ *at* sich ekeln vor (*dat.*); ~ *of* (*ger.*) es müde *od.* überdrüssig werden zu (*inf.*); *v/t.* krank machen; anekeln.

sick·le [ˈsikl] Sichel *f*.

sick-leave [ˈsikliːv] Krankheitsurlaub *m*; ˈ**sick·li·ness** Kränklichkeit *f*; Ungesundheit *f des Klimas etc.*; ˈ**sick·ly** kränklich; schwächlich; bleich, blaß; ungesund (*Klima etc.*); widerlich (*Geruch etc.*); matt (*Lächeln etc.*).

sick·ness [ˈsiknis] Krankheit *f*; Übelkeit *f*; ~ **ben·e·fit** Krankengeld *n*.

sick pay [ˈsikˈpei] Krankengeld *n*.

side [said] **1.** *allg.* Seite *f*; Ufer *n*, Rand *m*; Flanke *f e-s Berges*; Partei *f*; ~ *by* ~ Seite an Seite, nebeneinander; *fig.* daneben; *by one's* ~ zur Seite; ~ *by* ~ *with* neben; *at od. by s.o.'s* ~ an j-s Seite; *put on* ~ F angeben; **2.** Seiten...; Neben...; **3.** Partei ergreifen (*with* für); ˈ**~-arms** *pl.* ⚔ Seitengewehre *n/pl.*; ˈ**~·board** Anrichte(tisch *m*) *f*; Sideboard *n*; **~·burns** *Am.* [ˈ~bəːnz] *pl.* Koteletten *n/pl.* (*Backenbart*); ˈ**~-car** *mot.* Beiwagen *m*; ˈ**sid·ed** ...seitig.

side...: ~ **ef·fect** Nebenwirkung *f*; ˈ**~-face** Seitenansicht *f*, Profil *n*; ~ **is·sue** Nebenfrage *f*, Randproblem *n*; ˈ**~-kick** F Kumpel *m*; Gehilfe *m*; ˈ**~-light** Seiten-, *fig.* Streiflicht *n*; ˈ**~-line** 🚂 Nebenbahn *f*; Nebenbeschäftigung *f*; ˈ**~·long** **1.** *adv.* seitwärts; **2.** *adj.* seitlich; Seiten...; *fig.* versteckt (*Lächeln etc.*).

si·de·re·al *ast.* [saiˈdiəriəl] siderisch, Stern(en)...

side...: ˈ**~-road** Seiten-, Nebenstraße

f; '**~-sad·dle** Damensattel *m*; '**~-slip** ✈ seitlich abrutschen; *mot.* schleudern; **sides·man** ['~zmən] Kirchendiener *m*.
side...: '**~-split·ting** zwerchfellerschütternd; '**~-step 1.** Schritt *m* zur Seite; **2.** beiseite treten; *e-r Sache* ausweichen; '**~-street** = *side-road*; '**~-stroke** Seitenschwimmen *n*; '**~-track 1.** 🚂 Nebengleis *n*; **2.** auf ein Nebengleis schieben; *bsd. Am. fig.* zur Seite schieben; '**~-walk** *bsd. Am.* Bürgersteig *m*, Gehweg *m*; **side·ward** ['~wəd] **1.** *adj.* seitlich; **2.** *adv.* = **side·wards** ['~wədz], '**side·ways,** '**side·wise** seitwärts.
sid·ing 🚂 ['saidiŋ] Ausweichstelle *f*; Nebengleis *n*.
si·dle ['saidl] seitwärts *od.* mit der Seite voran gehen.
siege [si:dʒ] Belagerung *f*; *lay ~ to* belagern.
si·er·ra ['siərə] Sierra *f*, Gebirgskette *f*.
sieve [siv] **1.** Sieb *n*; **2.** (durch-) sieben.
sift [sift] sieben; *fig.* sichten; prüfen.
sift·er ['siftə] Sieber(in); Sichter (-in); Sieb *n*.
sigh [sai] **1.** Seufzer *m*; **2.** seufzen; sich sehnen (*for, after* nach).
sight [sait] **1.** Sehvermögen *n*, -kraft *f*; *fig.* Auge *n*; Ansicht *f*, Anblick *m*; Schauspiel *n*; Visier *n am Gewehr*; Sicht *f*; F Masse *f*, Menge *f* (*sehr viel*); *~s pl.* Sehenswürdigkeiten *f/pl.*; *second ~* zweites Gesicht *n*, Hellsehen *n*; *at od. on ~* beim Anblick; ♪ vom Blatt; ⚕ nach Sicht; *catch ~ of* erblicken, zu Gesicht bekommen; *lose ~ of* aus den Augen verlieren; *within ~* in Sicht; *out of ~* aus den Augen; außer Sicht; *take ~* visieren; *not by a long ~* bei weitem nicht; *know by ~* vom Sehen kennen; **2.** *v/t.* sichten; anvisieren; *v/i.* visieren; '**sight·ed** ...sichtig; '**sight·ing-line** Visierlinie *f*; '**sight·less** blind; '**sight·li·ness** Ansehnlich-, Stattlichkeit *f*; '**sight·ly** ansehnlich, stattlich.
sight...: '**~-read** (*irr. read*) ♪ vom Blatt spielen *od.* singen; '**~-see·ing** Besuchen *n* von Sehenswürdigkeiten; '**~-se·er** Tourist(in); '**~-sing·ing** ♪ (Vom)Blattsingen *n*.
sign [sain] **1.** (Kenn-, Vor)Zeichen *n*; Wink *m*; (Aushänge)Schild *n*; *in ~ of* zum Zeichen (*gen.*); **2.** *v/i.* winken, Zeichen geben; *~ on (off) Radio*: (*mit e-r Melodie*) den Beginn (das Ende) e-r Sendung ankündigen; *v/t.* (unter)zeichnen, unterschreiben; *~ on* (*v/i.* sich) vertraglich verpflichten.
sig·nal ['signl] **1.** Signal *n*; Zeichen *n*; *~s pl.* ⚔ Fernmeldetruppe *f*; *busy ~ teleph.* Besetztzeichen *n*; **2.** □ bemerkenswert, außerordentlich; **3.** signalisieren; *j-m* Zeichen geben; melden; anzeigen; '**~-box** 🚂 Stellwerk *n*; **sig·nal·ize** ['~nəlaiz] bemerkenswert machen, auszeichnen; = *signal 3*; '**sig·nal·man** 🚂 Bahnwärter *m*; Funker *m*.
sig·na·to·ry ['signətəri] **1.** Unterzeichner *m*, Signatar *m*; **2.** unterzeichnend; *powers ~ to an agreement* Signatarmächte *f/pl.* e-s Abkommens.
sig·na·ture ['signitʃə] Signatur (*a. typ.*, ♪, ⚕); Unterschrift *f*; *~ tune Radio*: Kennmelodie *f*.
sign·board ['sainbɔ:d] (Aushänge-) Schild *n*; '**sign·er** Unterzeichner (-in).
sig·net ['signit] Siegel *n*; '**~-ring** Siegelring *m*.
sig·nif·i·cance, sig·nif·i·can·cy [sig'nifikəns(i)] Bedeutung *f*; Wichtigkeit *f*; **sig'nif·i·cant** □ bedeutsam; bezeichnend (*of* für); **sig·ni·fi'ca·tion** Bedeutung *f*; **sig'nif·i·ca·tive** [~kətiv] bezeichnend (*of* für); bedeutsam.
sig·ni·fy ['signifai] bezeichnen, andeuten; kundgeben; bedeuten; *it does not ~* es hat nichts auf sich.
si·gnor ['si:njɔ:] Signor *m*, Herr *m*; **si'gnor·a** [~rə] Signora *f*, Frau *f*; **si·gno·ri·na** [~'ri:nə] Signorina *f*, Fräulein *n*.
sign...: '**~-paint·er** Schildermaler *m*; '**~-post** Wegweiser *m*.
si·lage ['sailidʒ] Silofutter *n*.
si·lence ['sailəns] **1.** (Still)Schweigen *n*; Stille *f*, Ruhe *f*; *~!* Ruhe!; *put od. reduce to ~* = **2.** zum Schweigen bringen; '**si·lenc·er** ⊕ Schalldämpfer *m*; *mot.* Auspufftopf *m*.
si·lent □ ['sailənt] still; schweigend; schweigsam; stumm (*Buchstabe*); *~ film* Stummfilm *m*; *~ partner bsd. Am.* ⚕ stiller Teilhaber *m*.
Si·le·sian [sai'li:zjən] **1.** schlesisch; **2.** Schlesier(in).

sil·hou·ette [silu:ˈet] **1.** Silhouette *f*; Schattenriß *m*; **2.** *be ~d against* sich abheben gegen.

sil·i·ca ⚗ [ˈsilikə] Kieselerde *f*; Silikat *n*; **sil·i·cat·ed** [ˈ~keitid] kieselsauer; **siˈli·ceous** [~ʃəs] kieselartig; **sil·i·con** [ˈ~kən] Silizium *n*; **sil·i·cone** [ˈ~kəun] Silikon *n*; **sil·i·co·sis** ⚕ [~ˈkəusis] Staublunge *f*.

silk [silk] **1.** Seide *f*; ⚖ Seidentalar *m*; Kronanwalt *m*; *take ~* Kronanwalt werden; **2.** Seiden...; **silk·en** □ seiden; *s. silky*; **ˈsilk·i·ness** Seidenartigkeit *f*; **ˈsilk--ˈstock·ing** *Am.* vornehm; **ˈ~-worm** Seidenraupe *f*; **ˈsilk·y** □ seid(enart)ig; seidenweich.

sill [sil] Schwelle *f*; Fensterbrett *n*.

sil·li·ness [ˈsilinis] Albernheit *f*.

sil·ly □ [ˈsili] albern, töricht, dumm; *~ season* Sauregurkenzeit *f*.

si·lo [ˈsailəu] Futtersilo *m*.

silt [silt] **1.** Schlamm *m*; **2.** *mst ~ up* verschlammen.

sil·ver [ˈsilvə] **1.** Silber *n* (*a. Silbergeld, -gerät u. fig.*); **2.** silbern; Silber...; **3.** versilbern; silberig *od.* silberweiß werden (lassen); **ˈ~-ˈplate** ⊕ versilbern; **ˈ~·ware** *Am.* Tafelsilber *n*; **ˈsil·ver·y** silberig; silberglänzend; *zo. u.* ⚘ Silber...; silberhell (*Stimme*).

sim·i·lar □ [ˈsimilə] ähnlich, gleich; **sim·i·lar·i·ty** [~ˈlæriti] Ähnlichkeit *f*.

sim·i·le [ˈsimili] Gleichnis *n*.

si·mil·i·tude [siˈmilitju:d] Gestalt *f*; Ebenbild *n*; Gleichnis *n*.

sim·mer [ˈsimə] sieden, brodeln (lassen); *fig.* gären (*Gefühl, Aufstand*); *~ down* ruhig(er) werden.

Si·mon [ˈsaimən] Simon *m*; *the real ~ Pure* F der wahre Jakob; *simple ~* F Einfaltspinsel *m*; **si·mo·ny** [ˈ~ni] Simonie *f*, Ämterkauf *m*.

si·moom *meteor.* [siˈmu:m] Samum *m*.

sim·per [ˈsimpə] **1.** einfältiges Lächeln *n*; **2.** einfältig lächeln.

sim·ple □ [ˈsimpl] einfach; schlicht; einfältig; arglos; **ˈ~-ˈheart·ed, ˈ~-ˈmind·ed** arglos, naiv; **sim·ple·ton** [ˈ~tən] Einfaltspinsel *m*.

sim·plic·i·ty [simˈplisiti] Einfachheit *f*; Klarheit *f*, Schlichtheit *f*; Einfalt *f*; **sim·pli·fi·ca·tion** [~fiˈkeiʃən] Vereinfachung *f*; **sim·pli·fy** [ˈ~fai] vereinfachen.

sim·ply [ˈsimpli] *adv.* einfach *etc.* (*s. simple*); bloß, nur; schlechthin.

sim·u·late [ˈsimjuleit] vortäuschen; (er)heucheln; *j-s* Aussehen annehmen, sich tarnen als; **sim·uˈla·tion** Vortäuschung *f*; Heuchelei *f*; **ˈsim·u·la·tor** Simulator *m*, Übungsgerät *n*.

si·mul·ta·ne·i·ty [siməltəˈniəti] Gleichzeitigkeit *f*.

si·mul·ta·ne·ous □ [siməlˈteinjəs] gleichzeitig; **si·mulˈta·ne·ous·ness** Gleichzeitigkeit *f*.

sin [sin] **1.** Sünde *f*; **2.** sündigen.

since [sins] **1.** *prp.* seit; **2.** *adv.* seitdem; *long ~* schon lange; *how long ~?* seit wann?; *a short time ~* vor kurzem; **3.** *cj.* seit(dem); da (ja), weil.

sin·cere □ [sinˈsiə] aufrichtig; *Yours ~ly* Ihr ergebener; **sin·cer·i·ty** [~ˈseriti] Aufrichtigkeit *f*.

sine 𝔄 [sain] Sinus *m*.

si·ne·cure [ˈsainikjuə] Sinekure *f*, Pfründe *f*.

sin·ew [ˈsinju:] Sehne *f*; *fig. mst ~s pl.* Nerven(kraft *f*) *m/pl.*; Seele *f*; **ˈsin·ew·y** sehnig; nervig, stark.

sin·ful □ [ˈsinful] sündig, sündhaft, böse; **ˈsin·ful·ness** Sündhaftigkeit *f*.

sing [siŋ] (*irr.*) singen (*fig.* = *dichten*); *j., et.* besingen; summen (*Kessel*); klingen (*Ohr*); *~ out* F laut rufen, schreien; *~ small, ~ another song od. tune* kleinlaut werden, klein beigeben.

singe [sindʒ] (ver)sengen.

sing·er [ˈsiŋə] Sänger(in).

sing·ing [ˈsiŋiŋ] Gesang *m*, Singen *n*; *~ bird* Singvogel *m*.

sin·gle [ˈsiŋgl] **1.** □ einzig; einzeln; Einzel...; einfach; ledig, unverheiratet; *~ bill* ✝ Solawechsel *m*; *~ combat* Zweikampf *m*; *bookkeeping by ~ entry* einfache Buchführung *f*; *~ file* Gänsemarsch *m*; **2.** *Tennis*: Einzel(spiel) *n*; einfache Fahrkarte *f*; **3.** *~ out* auswählen, -suchen; **ˈ~-ˈbreast·ed** einreihig (*Jacke etc.*); **ˈ~-ˈen·gin·ed** ✈ einmotorig (*Flugzeug*); **ˈ~-ˈhand·ed** eigenhändig, allein; **ˈ~-ˈheart·ed** □, **ˈ~-ˈmind·ed** □ aufrichtig, grundehrlich; zielstrebig; **ˈ~-ˈline** eingleisig; **ˈsin·gle-ˈseat·er** Einsitzer *m*; **ˈsin·gle-**

stick Stockrapier *n*; **sin·glet** ['siŋglit] Unterhemd *n*; **sin·gle·ton** ['~tən] *Karten*: Singleton *m* (*einzige Karte e-r Farbe*); '**sin·gle-'track** eingleisig; '**sin·gly** einzeln, allein.
sing·song ['siŋsɔŋ] Singsang *m*.
sin·gu·lar ['siŋgjulə] **1.** □ einzigartig, ungewöhnlich; eigenartig; sonderbar; *gr.* singularisch; **2.** *gr.* *a.* ~ *number* Singular *m*, Einzahl *f*; **sin·gu·lar·i·ty** [~'læriti] Einzigartigkeit *f*; Sonderbarkeit *f*.
Sin·ha·lese [siŋhə'li:z] **1.** singhalesisch; **2.** Singhalese *m*, Singhalesin *f*.
sin·is·ter □ ['sinistə] unheilvoll; unheimlich, finster.
sink [siŋk] **1.** (*irr.*) *v/i.* sinken; nieder-, unter-, versinken; sich senken; eindringen (*into* in *acc.*); erliegen (*beneath, under* unter *dat.*); *v/t.* (ver)senken; ⚒ abteufen; *Brunnen* bohren; *Schuld* abtragen; *Geld* festlegen; *et.* weglassen; *Namen, Anspruch* aufgeben; *Streit* beilegen; **2.** Senkgrube *f*; Ausguß *m in Küchen*; *fig.* Pfuhl *m*; '**sink·er** ⚒ Schachtarbeiter *m*; Senkblei *n*; '**sink·ing** Sinken *n etc.*; ⚕ Schwäche(gefühl *n*) *f*; ~ *fund* (Schulden-)Tilgungsfonds *m*.
sin·less ['sinlis] sündenlos, -frei.
sin·ner ['sinə] Sünder(in).
Sinn Fein ['ʃin'fein] Sinn Fein *m* (*irische Partei*).
Sin·o... ['sinəu] chinesisch; China...; Chinesen...
sin·u·os·i·ty [sinju'ɔsiti] Windung *f*, Krümmung *f*; '**sin·u·ous** □ gewunden, krumm (*a. fig.*).
si·nus *anat.* ['sainəs] Nebenhöhle *f*; **si·nus·i·tis** [~'saitis] (Neben)Höhlenentzündung *f*.
Sioux [su:], *pl.* ~ [su:z] Sioux(indianer) *m*.
sip [sip] **1.** Schlückchen *n*; **2.** schlürfen; nippen; langsam trinken.
si·phon ['saifən] **1.** (Saug)Heber *m*, Siphon(flasche *f*) *m*; **2.** saugen.
sir [sə:] Herr *m* (*als Anrede*); ♀ Sir *m* (*Titel e-s baronet od. knight*).
sire ['saiə] *mst poet.* Vater *m*; Vorfahr *m*, Ahnherr *m*; *zo.* Vater(tier *n*) *m*; † Herr *m*, Gebieter *m*.
si·ren ['saiərən] Sirene *f*.
sir·loin ['sə:lɔin] Lendenstück *n*.
sir·rah *contp.* † ['sirə] Bursche *m*.
sir·up ['sirəp] Sirup *m*.
sis F [sis] *Kurzform für sister.*
sis·al ['saisəl] Sisal *m*.
sis·kin *orn.* ['siskin] Zeisig *m*.
sis·sy *Am.* ['sisi] Weichling *m*.
sis·ter ['sistə] Schwester *f*; (Ordens)Schwester *f*; Oberschwester *f im Krankenhaus*; ~ *of charity od. mercy* Barmherzige Schwester *f*; **sis·ter·hood** ['~hud] Schwesternschaft *f*; '**sis·ter-in-law** Schwägerin *f*; '**sis·ter·ly** schwesterlich.
sit [sit] (*irr.*) *v/i.* sitzen; Sitzung halten, tagen; ~ *down* sich setzen; ~*-down strike* Sitzstreik *m*; ~ (*up*)*on* untersuchen; F *j-m* aufs Dach steigen; ~ *up* aufrecht sitzen; aufbleiben; sich aufrichten; *make s.o.* ~ *up* j. aufrütteln; j. aufhorchen lassen; *v/t.* sitzen auf (*dat.*); ~ *a horse well* gut zu Pferde sitzen; ~ *s.th. out* e-r Sache bis zu Ende beiwohnen; ~ *s.o. out* länger bleiben *od.* aushalten als j.
sit·com F ['sitkɔm] Situationskomödie *f*.
site [sait] **1.** Lage *f*; (Bau)Platz *m*; **2.** legen.
sit·ter ['sitə] Sitzende *m, f*; Bruthenne *f*; *sl.* sichere Sache *f*; '**~-'in** Babysitter *m*.
sit·ting ['sitiŋ] Sitzung *f*; *at one* ~ in einem Zug; ~ **duck** *fig.* leichte Beute *f* (*Person*); '**~-room** Wohnzimmer *n*.
sit·u·ate ['sitjueit] *in e-e Lage* versetzen; '**sit·u·at·ed** gelegen; *be* ~ liegen, gelegen sein; *thus* ~ in dieser Lage; **sit·u'a·tion** Lage *f*; Stellung *f*, Stelle *f*.
six [siks] **1.** sechs; **2.** Sechs *f*; *be at ~es and sevens* in Verwirrung sein; '**~·fold** sechsfach; '**~·pence** Sixpence(stück *n*) *m*; **six·teen** ['~'ti:n] sechzehn; **six·teenth** ['~'ti:nθ] **1.** sechzehnte(r, -s); **2.** Sechzehntel *n*; **sixth** [~θ] **1.** sechste(r, -s); **2.** Sechstel *n*; '**sixth·ly** sechstens; **six·ti·eth** ['~tiəθ] sechzigste(r, -s); '**six·ty 1.** sechzig; **2.** Sechzig *f*.
siz·a·ble □ ['saizəbl] ziemlich groß.
size[1] [saiz] **1.** Größe *f*, Umfang *m*; Format *n*; *Schuh- etc.* Nummer *f*; **2.** nach der Größe ordnen; ~ *up* F *j.* abschätzen; **sized** von ... Größe.
size[2] [~] **1.** Leim *m*; **2.** leimen.
size·a·ble □ ['saizəbl] = *sizable*.
siz·zle ['sizl] zischen; knistern; brutzeln; *sizzling hot* glühend heiß.

skate [skeit] **1.** Schlittschuh *m*; *~board* Skateboard *n*, Rollerbrett *n* (*Sportgerät*); *roller-~* Rollschuh *m*; **2.** Schlittschuh *od.* Rollschuh laufen; ˈ**skat·er** Schlittschuh-, Rollschuhläufer(in); ˈ**skat·ing-rink** Eisbahn *f*; Rollschuhbahn *f*.

ske·dad·dle F [skiˈdædl] türmen, ausreißen, abhauen.

skein [skein] Strähne *f Garn etc.*

skel·e·ton [ˈskelitn] **1.** Skelett *n*; Gerippe *n*; Gestell *n e-s Schirms etc.*; *Sport*: Skeleton *m* (*Schlitten*); ⚔ Stammtruppe *f*; *~ in the cupboard* (*Am. closet*) *fig.* dunkler Punkt *m*, streng gehütetes (Familien)Geheimnis *n*; **2.** Skelett...; im Entwurf, skizziert; ⚔ Stamm...; *~ crew* Notbelegschaft *f*, Restmannschaft *f*; *~ key* Nachschlüssel *m*, Dietrich *m*.

skep·tic [ˈskeptik] = *sceptic*.

sketch [sketʃ] **1.** Skizze *f*; Entwurf *m*; Auf-, Umriß *m*; **2.** skizzieren, entwerfen; ˈ**sketch·y** □ skizzenhaft.

skew [skjuː] schief; schräg.

skew·er [ˈskuə] **1.** Speiler *m*, Fleischspieß *m*; **2.** aufspeilern.

ski [skiː] **1.** *pl. a.* ~ Schi *m*, Ski *m*; **2.** Schi *od.* Ski laufen.

skid [skid] **1.** Hemmschuh *m*, Bremsklotz *m*; ✈ (Gleit)Kufe *f*; Rutschen *n*; *mot.* Schleudern *n*; **2.** *v/t.* hemmen; *v/i.* ausrutschen, gleiten; *mot.* schleudern; ✈ abrutschen; ~ **mark** *mot.* Bremsspur *f*; ~ **row** F Pennergegend *f*; *be on ~* Penner sein.

ski·er [ˈskiːə] Schiläufer(in), Skiläufer(in).

skiff ⚓ [skif] Nachen *m*; Skiff *n* (*Rennboot*).

ski·ing [ˈskiːiŋ] Schilauf(en *n*) *m*, Skilauf(en *n*) *m*; ˈ**ski-jump** Skisprung *m*, Schisprung *m*; Sprungschanze *f*; ˈ**ski-jump·ing** Skispringen *n*, Schispringen *n*.

skil·ful □ [ˈskilful] geschickt, gewandt; kundig; ˈ**skil·ful·ness, skill** [skil] Geschicklichkeit *f*, Fertigkeit *f*.

skilled [skild] geschickt; gelernt; *~ worker* Facharbeiter *m*.

skil·let [ˈskilit] Tiegel *m*, Kasserolle *f*.

skill·ful [ˈskilful] *etc. Am. für skilful.*

skim [skim] **1.** *a. ~ off* abschöpfen; *Milch* abrahmen; dahingleiten über (*acc.*); überfliegen (*flüchtig lesen*); *~ through* durchblättern; **2.** *~ milk* Magermilch *f*; ˈ**skim·mer** Schaumlöffel *m*.

skimp [skimp] *j.* knapp halten; sparen (mit *et.*); ˈ**skimp·y** □ knapp, dürftig.

skin [skin] **1.** Haut *f* (*a.* ⚓); Fell *n*; Pelz *m*; *Ballon*-Hülle *f*; Schale *f*, Hülse *f*; *Wein- etc.* Schlauch *m*; *by od. with the ~ of one's teeth* mit knapper Not; *have a thick* (*thin*) *~* ein dickes Fell haben (empfindlich sein); **2.** *v/t.* (ent)häuten; abbalgen; schälen; F betrügen (*of* um); *~ off* F *Strumpf etc.* abstreifen; *keep one's eyes ~ned* F die Augen offenhalten; *v/i. a. ~ over* zuheilen; ˈ**~-ˈdeep** (nur) oberflächlich; ˈ**~-div·ing** Sporttauchen *n*; ˈ**~-flick** *sl.* Sexfilm *m*; ˈ**~-flint** Knicker *m*; ˈ**~-graft·ing** ⚕ Hauttransplantation *f*; ˈ**skin·ner** Kürschner *m*; ˈ**skin·ny** häutig; mager; F knickerig; ˈ**skin·ny-dip** *Am.* F nackt baden.

skint P [skint] pleite, blank.

skin·tight [ˈskintait] hauteng.

skip [skip] **1.** Sprung *m*; ⚒ Förderkorb *m*; **2.** *v/i.* hüpfen, springen; seilhüpfen; *v/t. a. ~ over* überspringen; ˈ**~-jack** Stehaufmännchen *n*; *zo.* Springkäfer *m*.

skip·per[1] [ˈskipə] Hüpfer(in).

skip·per[2] [~] ⚓ Schiffer *m*, Kapitän *m*; F *Sport*: Mannschaftsführer *m*.

skip·ping-rope [ˈskipiŋrəup] Springseil *n*.

skir·mish ⚔ [ˈskəːmiʃ] **1.** Scharmützel *n*; **2.** plänkeln; ˈ**skir·mish·er** Plänkler *m*.

skirt [skəːt] **1.** (Damen)Rock *m*; (Rock-, Hemd)Schoß *m*; *oft ~s pl.* Rand *m*, Saum *m*; **2.** *v/t.* umsäumen; *v/t. u. v/i. a. ~ along* (sich) entlangziehen (an *dat.*); entlangfahren; ˈ**skirt·ing-board** Fuß-, Scheuerleiste *f*.

ski-run [ˈskirʌn] Skipiste *f*.

skit[1] [skit] Stichelei *f*, Hieb *m* (*at* gegen); Satire *f* (*on, upon* auf *acc.*).

skit[2] F [~] Haufen *m*, Masse *f*.

skit·tish □ [ˈskitiʃ] ungebärdig (*bsd. Pferd*); ausgelassen; mutwillig.

skit·tle [ˈskitl] Kegel *m*; *play* (*at*) *~s* Kegel schieben; ˈ**~-al·ley** Kegelbahn *f*.

skive F [skaiv] blaumachen; schwänzen; **'skiv·er** F Drückeberger *m.*
skiv·vy F *contp.* ['skivi] Besen *m* (*Dienstmädchen*).
skul·dug·er·y *Am.* F [skʌl'dʌgəri] Gemeinheit *f*, Schuftigkeit *f*.
skulk [skʌlk] schleichen; sich verstecken; lauern; sich um *et.* drükken; **'skulk·er** Drückeberger *m.*
skull [skʌl] Schädel *m*; ~ *and cross-bones* Totenkopf *m*; *have a thick* ~ dumm sein.
skunk [skʌŋk] *zo.* Stinktier *n*; Skunk *m* (*Pelz*); F Schuft *m.*
sky [skai] *oft skies pl.* Himmel *m*; Himmelsstrich *m*; *praise to the skies fig.* in den Himmel heben; **'~-'blue** himmelblau; **'~·div·ing** *Sport*: Fallschirmspringen *n*; **'~·jack** im Flugzeug entführen; **'~·lark** 1. *orn.* Feldlerche *f*; 2. Ulk treiben; **'~·light** Oberlicht *n*; Dachfenster *n*; **'~·line** Horizont(linie *f*) *m*; Silhouette *f*; **'~·rock·et** F steil ansteigen, emporschnellen; **'~'scrap·er** Wolkenkratzer *m*, Hochhaus *n*; **sky·ward**(**s**) ['~wəd(z)] himmelwärts; **'sky-writ-ing** ✈ Himmelsschrift *f*.
slab [slæb] Platte *f*, Tafel *f*; Scheibe *f*; Streifen *m*; Fliese *f*; ⊕ Holzschwarte *f*.
slack [slæk] 1. schlaff; lose, locker; (nach)lässig; ✝ flau; ~ *water* ⚓ Stillwasser *n*; 2. ⚓ Lose *n* (*loses Tauende*); ✝ Flaute *f*; Kohlengrus *m*; *s.* ~*s*; 3. = ~*en*; = *slake*; F trödeln; **'slack·en** schlaff machen *od.* werden; verringern; *Tau etc.* nachlassen (*a. v/i.*); (sich) lockern; (sich) entspannen; (sich) verlangsamen; **'slack·er** F Drückeberger *m*; Faulenzer *m*; **'slack·ness** Schlaffheit *f etc.*; **slacks** *pl.* Damenhose *f*.
slag [slæg] Schlacke *f*; **'slag·gy** schlackig; **'slag-heap** Schlackenhalde *f*.
slain [slein] *p.p. von slay.*
slake [sleik] *Durst, Kalk* löschen; *Sehnsucht etc.* stillen.
sla·lom ['sleiləm] *Sport*: Slalom *m*, Torlauf *m.*
slam [slæm] 1. Zuschlagen *n*; Knall *m*; *Bridge, Whist*: Schlemm *m*; 2. *Tür etc.* zuschlagen, -knallen; *et. auf den Tisch etc.* knallen.
slan·der ['slɑːndə] 1. Verleumdung *f*; 2. verleumden; **'slan·der·er** Verleumder(in); **'slan·der·ous** □ verleumderisch.
slang [slæŋ] 1. Slang *m*, *n*; Berufssprache *f*; lässige Umgangssprache *f*; 2. *j.* wüst beschimpfen; ~*ing match* wüste gegenseitige Beschimpfungen *f/pl.*; **'slang·y** □ Slang...; vulgär.
slant [slɑːnt] 1. schräge Fläche *f*; Abhang *m*; Neigung *f*; *Am.* F Einstellung *f*; Sicht *f*; 2. *v/t.* schräg legen; *v/i.* schräg liegen, sich neigen; **'slant·ing** □ *adj.*, **'slant·wise** *adv.* schief, schräg.
slap [slæp] 1. Klaps *m*, Schlag *m*; ~ *in the face* Ohrfeige *f* (*a. fig.*); 2. klapsen; schlagen; klatschen; 3. direkt, geradewegs, stracks; **'~-'bang** Knall u. Fall; **'~·dash** hastig, übereilt, ungestüm; *adv. a.* Hals über Kopf; **'~·jack** *Am. Art* Pfannkuchen *m*; **'~·stick** *thea.* (Narren)Pritsche *f*; *a.* ~ *comedy* Posse *f*, Burleske *f*; **'~-up** F piekfein, erstklassig.
slash [slæʃ] 1. Hieb *m*; Schnitt *m*; Schlitz *m in e-m Kleid*; 2. *v/t.* (auf-)schlitzen; einschlagen auf (*acc.*); peitschen; Schlitze machen in (*acc.*); *fig.* geißeln, *Buch etc.* verreißen (*Kritiker*); F *Gehalt* drastisch kürzen; *v/i.* schlagen, hauen (*at* nach); **'slash·ing** □ scharf, vernichtend (*Kritik*).
slat [slæt] Lamelle *f e-r Jalousie.*
slate [sleit] 1. Schiefer *m*; Schiefertafel *f*; *bsd. Am.* Kandidatenliste *f*; *start with a clean* ~ e-n neuen Anfang machen; 2. mit Schiefer dekken; heftig kritisieren; *Am.* F *für e-n Posten* vorschlagen; **'~-'pen·cil** Schieferstift *m*, Griffel *m*; **'slat·er** Schieferdecker *m*; **'slat·ing** heftige Kritik *f*.
slat·tern ['slætəːn] Schlampe *f*; **'slat·tern·ly** schlampig.
slat·y □ ['sleiti] schieferig.
slaugh·ter ['slɔːtə] 1. Schlachten *n von Vieh*; *fig.* Hinschlachten *n*, Morden *n*; Gemetzel *n*, Blutbad *n*; 2. Schlacht...; 3. schlachten; niedermetzeln; **'slaugh·ter·er** Schlächter *m*; Mörder *m*; **'slaugh-ter-house** Schlachthaus *n*; **'slaugh-ter·ous** □ *rhet.* mörderisch.
Slav [slɑːv] 1. Slawe *m*, Slawin *f*; 2. slawisch.
slave [sleiv] 1. Sklave *m*, Sklavin *f* (*a. fig.*); ~ *driver a. fig.* Sklaventreiber *m*; 2. sich placken, schuften.

slav·er[1] ['sleivə] Sklavenschiff *n*; Sklavenhändler *m*.
slav·er[2] ['slævə] **1.** Geifer *m*, Sabber *m*; **2.** (be)geifern, (be)sabbern (*a. fig.*).
slav·er·y ['sleivəri] Sklaverei *f*; Plackerei *f*, Schinderei *f*.
slav·ey *sl.* ['slævi] dienstbarer Geist *m*.
Slav·ic ['slɑːvik] **1.** slawisch; **2.** Slawisch *n*.
slav·ish □ ['sleiviʃ] sklavisch; '**slav·ish·ness** sklavisches Wesen *n*.
slaw [slɔː] Krautsalat *m*.
slay *rhet.* [slei] (*irr.*) erschlagen; töten; '**slay·er** Mörder *m*.
slea·zy ['sliːzi] verschlissen, dünn (*Gewebe*); *fig.* schäbig, heruntergekommen (*Hotel etc.*).
sled [sled] = *sledge*[1].
sledge[1] [sledʒ] **1.** Schlitten *m*; **2.** Schlitten fahren; mit Schlitten befördern.
sledge[2] [~] *a.* ~*-hammer* Schmiedehammer *m*.
sleek [sliːk] **1.** □ glatt, geschmeidig (*Haut etc.*; *a. fig.*); **2.** glätten; '**sleek·ness** Glattheit *f*; Glätte *f*.
sleep [sliːp] **1.** (*irr.*) *v/i.* schlafen; stehen (*Kreisel*); ~ *(up)on od. over et.* beschlafen; *v/t. j.* für die Nacht unterbringen; ~ *away Zeit* verschlafen; ~ *off s-n Rausch etc.* ausschlafen; **2.** Schlaf *m*; *go to* ~ einschlafen; *put to* ~ einschläfern (*Tier schmerzlos töten, a. Person vor Operation narkotisieren*); '**sleep·er** Schläfer(in); 🚂 Schwelle *f*; Schlafwagen *m*; *be a light* ~ e-n leichten Schlaf haben; '**sleep·i·ness** Schläfrigkeit *f*.
sleep·ing ['sliːpiŋ] schlafend; Schlaf...; '~**-bag** Schlafsack *m*; ♀ **Beau·ty** Dornröschen *n*; '~**-car**, '~-'**car·riage** 🚂 Schlafwagen *m*; '~**-draught** Schlaftrunk *m*; ~ **part·ner** ✝ stiller Teilhaber *m*; ~ **pill** Schlaftablette *f*; '~'**sick·ness** Schlafkrankheit *f*.
sleep·less □ ['sliːplis] schlaflos; ruhelos; '**sleep·less·ness** Schlaflosigkeit *f*.
sleep·walk·er ['sliːpwɔːkə] Nachtwandler(in).
sleep·y □ ['sliːpi] schläfrig; verschlafen (*a. Ort*); '~**·head** F *fig.* Schlafmütze *f*.
sleet [sliːt] **1.** Schloßen *f/pl.*, Graupelregen *m*; **2.** graupeln; '**sleet·y** graupelig; Graupel...
sleeve [sliːv] **1.** Ärmel *m*; ⊕ Muffe *f*; *attr.* Muffen...; *have something up one's* ~ etwas in Bereitschaft halten; etwas im Schilde führen; *laugh in one's* ~ sich ins Fäustchen lachen; **2.** Ärmel einsetzen in (*acc.*); **sleeved** ...ärmelig; '**sleeve·less** ärmellos, ohne Ärmel; '**sleeve-link** Manschettenknopf *m*.
sleigh [slei] **1.** (*bsd.* Pferde)Schlitten *m*; **2.** im Schlitten fahren *od.* befördern.
sleight [slait]: ~ *of hand* Taschenspielerei *f*; Kunststück *n*.
slen·der □ ['slendə] schlank, dünn; schmächtig; gering, schwach; dürftig; '**slen·der·ness** Schlankheit *f etc.*
slept [slept] *pret. u. p.p. von sleep 1.*
sleuth [sluːθ], '~**-hound** Blut-, Spürhund *m* (*mst fig. Detektiv*).
slew[1] [sluː] *pret. von slay.*
slew[2] [~] *a.* ~ *round* (sich) drehen.
slice [slais] **1.** Schnitte *f*, Scheibe *f*, Stück *n*; Teil *m*; *Küche*: Wender *m*; Fischheber *m*; **2.** in Scheiben zerschneiden; *a.* ~ *off* (in Scheiben) abschneiden.
slick F [slik] **1.** *adj.* glatt, glitschig; *fig.* raffiniert; **2.** *adv.* direkt, genau; **3.** *a.* ~ *paper Am. sl.* vornehme Zeitschrift *f*; '**slick·er** *Am.* F Regenmantel *m*; gerissener Kerl *m*.
slid [slid] *pret. u. p.p. von slide 1.*
slide [slaid] **1.** (*irr.*) *v/i.* gleiten; rutschen; schlittern; ausgleiten; hineinschlittern (*into* in *acc.*); *let things* ~ die Dinge laufen lassen; *v/t.* gleiten lassen; **2.** Gleiten *n*; Rutsche *f*; ⊕ Schieber *m*; Diapositiv *n*; *a. land* ~ Erdrutsch *m*; '**slid·er** Gleitende *m*; Schieber *m*; '**slide-rule** Rechenschieber *m*.
slid·ing ['slaidiŋ] **1.** Gleiten *n*; **2.** gleitend; Schiebe...; ~ *roof* Schiebedach *n*; ~ *rule* Rechenschieber *m*; ~ *scale* gleitende (Lohn- *od.* Preis)Skala *f*; ~ *seat* Rollsitz *m im Ruderboot*.
slight [slait] **1.** □ schmächtig; schwach; leicht; gering(fügig), unbedeutend; **2.** Nichtachtung *f*, Geringschätzung *f*; **3.** geringschätzig behandeln; unbeachtet lassen; '**slight·ing** □ geringschätzig; '**slight·ly** etwas, ein wenig; '**slight·ness** Dünnheit *f*; Schwäche *f*;

Geringfügigkeit *f*.

slim [slim] **1.** □ schlank; dünn; schmächtig; dürftig; *sl.* schlau, gerissen; **2.** e-e Schlankheitskur machen.

slime [slaim] Schlamm *m*; Schleim [*m*.]

slim·i·ness ['slaiminis] schlammige *od.* schleimige Beschaffenheit *f*.

slim·ness ['slimnis] Schlankheit *f*.

slim·y □ ['slaimi] schlammig; schleimig (*a. fig.*).

sling [sliŋ] **1.** Schleuder *f*; Tragriemen *m*; ✝ Schlinge *f*, Binde *f*; Wurf *m*; **2.** (*irr.*) schleudern; auf-, umhängen; *a.* ~ *up* hochziehen.

slink [sliŋk] (*irr.*) schleichen; sich *wohin* stehlen.

slip [slip] **1.** *v/i.* schlüpfen, gleiten, rutschen; ausgleiten; ausrutschen; *oft* ~ *away* entschlüpfen; sich versehen; *v/t.* schlüpfen *od.* gleiten lassen; loslassen; entschlüpfen, -gleiten (*dat.*); ~ *in Bemerkung* dazwischenwerfen; ~ *into* hineinstecken *od.* -schieben in (*acc.*); ~ *on* (*off*) *Kleid etc.* über-, (ab-) streifen; **2.** (Aus)Gleiten *n*, (Aus-) Rutschen *n*; Fehltritt *m* (*a. fig.*); Versehen *n*; (Flüchtigkeits)Fehler *m*; Verstoß *m*; Streifen *m*; *a.* ~ *of paper* Zettel *m*; ✓ Steckreis *n*; *fig.* Sproß *m*; Unterkleid *n*; ~*s pl. od.* ~*way* ⚓ Helling *f*; (Kissen)Überzug *m*; ~*s pl.* Badehose *f*; *a* ~ *of a girl* ein schmächtiges junges Mädchen *n*; ~ *of the pen* Schreibfehler *m*; *it was a* ~ *of the tongue* ich habe mich (er hat sich) versprochen; *give s.o. the* ~ j-m entwischen; '**~-knot** Laufknoten *m*; Schleife *f*; '**~-on** loser Mantel *m*; '**slip·per** Pantoffel *m*, Hausschuh *m*; '**slip·per·y** □ schlüpfrig; *fig.* aalglatt; '**slip-road** (Autobahn)Einfahrt *f*, (-)Ausfahrt *f*; **slip·shod** ['~ʃɔd] schlampig, nachlässig; **slip·slop** ['~'slɔp] labberiges Zeug *n* (*fig. Gewäsch*); '**slip-stream** ✈ Luftschraubenstrahl *m*, Nachstrom *m*; '**slip-up** F Fehler *m*.

slit [slit] **1.** Schlitz *m*, Spalte *f*; **2.** (*irr.*) (auf-, zer)splittern.

slith·er ['sliðə] schlittern, rutschen; gleiten.

sliv·er ['slivə] Splitter *m*, dünne Scheibe *f*.

slob·ber ['slɔbə] **1.** Sabber *m*; Gesabber *n*; **2.** (be)sabbern; '**slob·ber·y** sabberig; matschig.

sloe ⚘ [sləu] Schlehe *f*; Schwarzdorn *m*.

slog F [slɔg] **1.** hauen; schuften; **2.** Hieb *m*.

slo·gan ['sləugən] *fig.* Schlagwort *n*, Losung *f*; (Werbe)Slogan *m*.

sloop ⚓ [slu:p] Schaluppe *f*.

slop[1] [slɔp] **1.** Pfütze *f*; ~*s pl.* Spülicht *n*; Krankenspeise *f*; **2.** *a.* ~ *over v/t.* verschütten; *v/i.* überlaufen (*a. fig.*).

slop[2] [~]: ~*s pl.* billige Konfektionskleidung *f*; ⚓ Kleidung *f* u. Bettzeug *n*.

slop-ba·sin ['slɔpbeisn] Gefäß *n* für Teereste.

slope [sləup] **1.** (Ab)Hang *m*; Neigung *f*; **2.** *v/t.* schräg *od.* schief machen *od.* legen; neigen; ⊕ abschrägen; ~ *arms!* ⚔ Gewehr über!; *v/i.* schräg verlaufen; abfallen, sich neigen; ~ *off*, *a. do a* ~ *sl.* abhauen, türmen; '**slop·ing** □ schräg.

slop-pail ['slɔppeil] Spül-, Ausgußeimer *m*; '**slop·py** □ naß, schmutzig; wässerig; schlampig; labberig (*Nahrung*); rührselig.

slop-shop ['slɔpʃɔp] Laden *m* mit billiger Konfektionsware.

slosh [slɔʃ] *v/i.* im Matsch herumpatschen; *v/t. sl. j.* verhauen; **sloshed** *sl.* voll, besoffen.

slot [slɔt] *hunt.* Fährte *f*; Schlitz *m am Automaten etc.*; ⊕ Nut *f*.

sloth [sləuθ] Faulheit *f*; *zo.* Faultier *n*; **sloth·ful** □ ['~ful] faul, träg.

slot-ma·chine ['slɔtməʃi:n] (Waren- *od.* Spiel)Automat *m*.

slouch [slautʃ] **1.** faul herumhängen; herumlatschen; **2.** schlaffe Haltung *f*; latschiger Gang *m*; ~ *hat* Schlapphut *m*.

slough[1] [slau] Sumpf(loch *n*) *m*.

slough[2] [slʌf] **1.** *zo.* abgeworfene Haut *f*; ⚕ Schorf *m*; **2.** *v/i.* sich ablösen (*Schorf etc.*); sich häuten (*Schlange etc.*); *v/t. Haut etc.* abwerfen.

slough·y ['slaui] sumpfig.

Slo·vak ['sləuvæk] **1.** Slowake *m*, Slowakin *f*; **2.** = **Slo'va·ki·an** slowakisch.

slov·en ['slʌvn] unordentlicher Mensch *m*; Schlampe *f*; '**slov·en·li·ness** Schlampigkeit *f*; '**slov·en-**

ly liederlich, schlampig.

slow [sləu] **1.** □ langsam (*of* in *dat.*); nachgehend (*Uhr*); schwerfällig; lässig; schleichend (*Fieber*); langweilig; *Sport*: schwer (*die Bewegung hemmend*); *be ~ to do s.th.* nicht schnell et. tun; *my watch is ten minutes ~* meine Uhr geht 10 Minuten nach; **2.** *adv.* langsam; **3.** *oft ~ down, ~ up, ~ off v/t.* verlangsamen; *v/i.* langsam(er) werden *od.* gehen *od.* fahren; '**~-coach** Langweiler *m*; altmodischer Mensch *m*; **~ lane** *mot.* Kriechspur *f*; '**~·match** Lunte *f*; '**~-'mo·tion film** Zeitlupenaufnahme *f*; '**slow·ness** Langsamkeit *f*; **slow train** Bummelzug *m*; '**slow·worm** *zo.* Blindschleiche *f*.

sludge [slʌdʒ] Schlamm *m*; Matsch *m*.

slue [slu:] = *slew*[2].

slug[1] [slʌg] Stück *n* Rohmetall; *typ.* Zeilensatz *m*.

slug[2] *zo.* [~] Wegschnecke *f*.

slug[3] [~] *Am. für slog 1.*

slug·gard ['slʌgəd] Faulenzer(in); '**slug·gish** □ träge, faul.

sluice [slu:s] **1.** Schleuse *f*; **2.** ausströmen (lassen); ausspülen; waschen; '**~-'gate** Schleusentor *n*; '**~-'way** Schleusenkanal *m*.

slum [slʌm] schmutzige Gasse *f*; *~s pl.* Elendsviertel *n*, Slums *pl.*

slum·ber ['slʌmbə] **1.** *a. ~s pl.* Schlummer *m*; **2.** schlummern.

slum·brous, slum·ber·ous □ ['slʌmbrəs, '~bərəs] einschläfernd; schläfrig.

slump [slʌmp] *Börse*: **1.** fallen, stürzen; **2.** (Kurs-, Preis)Sturz *m*; Wirtschaftskrise *f*.

slung [slʌŋ] *pret. u. p.p. von sling 2.*

slunk [slʌŋk] *pret. u. p.p. von slink.*

slur [slə:] **1.** Fleck *m*; *fig.* Tadel *m*, Vorwurf *m*; ♪ Bindezeichen *n*; **2.** *v/t. oft ~ over* hinweggehen über, übergehen; ♪ *Töne* binden; *Silben etc.* verschleifen.

slurp F [slə:p] schlürfen.

slush [slʌʃ] Schlamm *m*; Matsch *m*; Gefühlsduselei *f*; F Kitsch *m*; '**slush·y** matschig; F kitschig.

slut [slʌt] Schlampe *f*; Nutte *f*; '**slut·tish** schlampig.

sly □ [slai] schlau, verschmitzt; hinterlistig, tückisch; *on the ~* heimlich; '**~·boots** F Schlauberger *m*; '**sly·ness** Schläue *f*; Verschmitztheit *f*; Hinterlist *f*.

smack[1] [smæk] **1.** (Bei)Geschmack *m*; Prise *f Salz etc.*; *fig.* Spur *f*; **2.** schmecken (*of* nach); e-n Beigeschmack haben (*of* von).

smack[2] [~] **1.** Schmatz(kuß) *m*; Schlag *m*, Klatsch *m*, Klaps *m*; **2.** klatschen, knallen (mit); schmatzen (mit *den Lippen*); *j-m* e-n Klaps geben; **3.** *int.* klatsch!

smack[3] ⚓ [~] Schmack(e) *f*.

smack·er *Am. sl.* ['smækə] Dollar *m*.

small [smɔ:l] **1.** *allg.* klein; gering, unbedeutend; *fig.* kleinlich; niedrig; wenig; *~ eater* schlechter Esser *m*; *feel ~, look ~* sich gedemütigt fühlen; *the ~ hours pl.* die frühen Morgenstunden *f/pl.*; *in a ~ way* bescheiden; **2.** dünner Teil *m*; *~s pl.* F Leib- und Tischwäsche *f*; *~ of the back anat.* Kreuz *n*; '**~-arms** *pl.* Handfeuerwaffen *f/pl.*; **~ beer** Dünnbier *n*; *think no ~ of o.s.* F sich hübsch was einbilden; *be ~* unbedeutend sein; **~ change** Kleingeld *n*; *fig.* triviale Bemerkungen *f/pl.*; Geplätscher *n*; '**~'hold·er** Kleinbauer *m*; '**~'hold·ing** bäuerlicher Kleinbetrieb *m*; '**small·ish** ziemlich klein; '**small·ness** Kleinheit *f*.

small...: '**~·pox** *pl.* ⚕ Pocken *f/pl.*; **~ print** Kleingedruckte *n*; **~ talk** Plauderei *f*; '**~·time** *Am.* F unbedeutend, drittklassig.

smalt ⊕ [smɔ:lt] Schmalte *f*.

smarm·y F ['smɑ:mi] schmierig (*schmeichelnd*).

smart [smɑ:t] **1.** □ scharf; heftig (*Schmerz, Kampf*); munter, flink; geschickt; gerissen; sauber; schmuck, elegant, fein, adrett, schick; forsch, patent; *~ aleck Am.* Neunmalkluge *m*; **2.** Schmerz *m*; **3.** schmerzen; leiden; *you shall ~ for it* das sollst du büßen; '**smart·en** *mst ~ up* herausputzen; '**smart--mon·ey** Schmerzensgeld *n*; '**smart·ness** Klugheit *f*; Schärfe *f*, Heftigkeit *f*; Gewandtheit *f*; Gerissenheit *f*; Schick *m*, Eleganz *f*.

smash [smæʃ] **1.** *v/t. oft ~ up* zertrümmern, zerschmettern, zerschlagen; *~ in* einschlagen; *fig.* vernichten; schmettern; *v/i.* zerschmettern, *fig.* zs.-brechen; (dahin)stürzen; *oft ~ up* Bankrott machen; **2.** Zerschmettern *n*; Krach *m*; Zs.-bruch *m* (*a.* ✝); *Tennis*: Schmetterball *m*; **'~-and-'grab raid** Schaufenstereinbruch *m*; **'smash·er** *sl.* schwerer Schlag *m*, vernichtende Kritik *f*; **smash hit** F Bombenerfolg *m*; **'smash·ing** F super, toll; **'smash-up** Zs.-stoß *m*; Zs.-bruch *m*.

smat·ter·ing ['smætəriŋ] oberflächliche Kenntnis *f*.

smear [smiə] **1.** beschmieren, bestreichen; einschmieren; *Schrift* verschmieren; *Fett etc.* schmieren (*on* auf *acc.*); *fig.* besudeln, beschmutzen; *~(ing) campaign* Verleumdungskampagne *f*; **2.** Schmiere *f*; Fleck *m*; **~ test** ⚕ Abstrich *m*.

smell [smel] **1.** Geruch *m*; **2.** (*irr.*) riechen (an *dat.*, *a.* *~ at*; *of* nach *et.*); **'smell·ing-salt** Riechsalz *n*; **'smell·y** übelriechend.

smelt[1] [smelt] *pret. u. p.p. von smell* 2.

smelt[2] *ichth.* [~] Stint *m*.

smelt[3] [~] schmelzen; **'smelt·er** Schmelzer *m*; **'smelt·ing-'furnace** Schmelzofen *m*.

smile [smail] **1.** Lächeln *n*; **2.** lächeln (*at* über *acc.*); *~ on*, *~ at j-m* zulächeln.

smirch *rhet.* [smə:tʃ] beschmieren; *fig.* besudeln.

smirk [smə:k] **1.** grinsen; **2.** Grinsen *n*.

smite [smait] (*irr.*) *poet. od. co.* schlagen; vernichten; heimsuchen; *schwer* treffen; quälen (*Gewissen*); *~ upon bsd. fig.* an *das Ohr etc.* schlagen.

smith [smiθ] Schmied *m*.

smith·er·eens F ['smiðə'ri:nz] *pl.* kleine Stücke *n/pl.*, Splitter *m/pl.*, Fetzen *m/pl.*; *smash to ~* in Stücke hauen.

smith·y ['smiði] Schmiede *f*.

smit·ten ['smitn] **1.** *p.p. von smite*; **2.** ergriffen; betroffen; *fig.* hingerissen (*with* von).

smock [smɔk] **1.** fälteln; **2.** *a.* *~-frock* Arbeitskittel *m*, Bluse *f*; **'smock·ing** Smokarbeit *f*.

smog [smɔg] Smog *m*, Gemisch *n* von Nebel und Rauch.

smoke [sməuk] **1.** Rauch *m*; Qualm *m*; ⚔ (Tarn)Nebel *m*; F Rauchen *n e-r Zigarre etc.*; F Zigarre *f*, Zigarette *f*, Tabak *m*; *have a ~* (eine) rauchen; **2.** *v/i.* rauchen; dampfen; *v/t. Tabak* rauchen; (aus)räuchern; ⚔ einnebeln; **'~-bomb** Nebel-, Rauchbombe *f*; **smoked, 'smoke-dried** geräuchert; **'smoke·less** □ rauchlos; **'smok·er** Raucher *m*; Räucherer *m*; 🚃 Raucherwagen *m*, -abteil *n*; **'smoke-screen** ⚔ Rauch-, Nebelvorhang *m*; **'smoke-stack** 🚃 *u.* ⚓ Schornstein *m*.

smok·ing ['sməukiŋ] **1.** Rauchen *n*; *no ~!* Rauchen verboten!; **2.** Rauch(er)...; Räucher...; **'~-compart·ment** 🚃 Raucher(abteil *n*) *m*; **'~-room** Rauchzimmer *n*.

smok·y □ ['sməuki] rauchig; verräuchert.

smol·der *Am.* ['sməuldə] = *smoulder*.

smooth [smu:ð] **1.** □ glatt; *fig.* fließend; sanft, mild; schmeichlerisch; **2.** *oft ~ out*, *~ down* glätten; ebnen (*a. fig.*); plätten; *a. ~ down* mildern; *a. ~ over*, *~ away Schwierigkeit etc.* wegräumen; *~ down* sich glätten; **'smooth·ing 1.** Glätten *n*; **2.** Glätt..., Plätt...; *~ iron* Bügeleisen *n*; *~ plane* Schlichthobel *m*; **'smooth·ness** Glätte *f* (*a. fig.*); **'smooth-tongued** schmeichlerisch.

smote [sməut] *pret. von smite*.

smoth·er ['smʌðə] **1.** Qualm *m*; **2.** *a. ~ up* ersticken (*a. fig.*).

smoul·der ['sməuldə] glimmen, schwelen.

smudge [smʌdʒ] **1.** *v/t.* beschmutzen; (be)schmieren; *v/i.* schmieren; schmutzen; **2.** Schmutzfleck *m*; **'smudg·y** □ schmutzig, schmierig.

smug [smʌg] selbstzufrieden, selbstgefällig.

smug·gle ['smʌgl] schmuggeln; **'smug·gler** Schmuggler(in); **'smug·gling** Schmuggel(ei *f*) *m*.

smut [smʌt] **1.** Schmutz *m*; Ruß(-fleck) *m*; Zoten *f/pl.*; ⚘ *Getreide-Brand m*; **2.** beschmutzen; ⚘ brandig machen.

smutch [smʌtʃ] **1.** schwarz machen; beflecken; **2.** schwarzer Fleck *m*.

smut·ty □ ['smʌti] schmutzig; rußig; zotig, obszön; ⚘ brandig.

snack [snæk] Imbiß *m*; **'~-bar**, **'~-coun·ter** Snackbar *f*, Imbißstube *f*.

snaf·fle[1] ['snæfl] Trense *f*.

snaf·fle[2] *sl.* [~] klauen (*stehlen*).

snaf·fle-bit ['snæflbit] Trensengebiß *n*.

sna·fu *Am. sl.* ⚔ [snæ'fu:] **1.** total drunter und drüber; **2.** tolles Durcheinander *n.*

snag [snæg] Aststumpf *m*; Zahnstumpf *m*, Raffzahn *m*; *fig.* Haken *m* (*Schwierigkeit*); *Am.* Baumstamm *m* *in Flüssen*; **snag·ged** ['~gid], '**snag·gy** ästig; knorrig.

snail *zo.* [sneil] Schnecke *f.*

snake *zo.* [sneik] Schlange *f* (*a. fig.*); '**~-charm·er** Schlangenbeschwörer *m*; '**~-weed** ♀ Natterwurz *f.*

snak·y □ ['sneiki] schlangengleich, -artig; Schlangen...; *fig.* hinterhältig.

snap [snæp] **1.** Schnappen *n*, Biß *m*; Knack(s) *m*, Krach *m*, Knall *m*; *fig.* Schwung *m*, Schmiß *m*; Schnappschloß *n*; *phot.* Schnappschuß *m*; Plätzchen *n*, Keks *m*, *n*; *cold* ~ Kältewelle *f*; **2.** *v/i.* schnappen (*at* nach); zuschnappen (*Schloß*); knacken; (zer)springen, reißen; (*at s.o.* j. an)schnauzen; ~ *into it Am. sl.* mach schnell, Tempo!; ~ *out of it Am. sl.* hör auf damit; komm, komm!; *v/t.* (er)schnappen; (zu)schnappen lassen; *phot.* knipsen; zerknicken, -brechen; ~ *one's fingers at s.o.* mit Verachtung auf j. herabblicken; ~ *out Wort* hervorstoßen; ~ *up et.* wegschnappen; *j.* anschnauzen; *j-m* ins Wort fallen; **3.** knacks!; schwapp!; '**~-drag·on** ♀ Löwenmaul *n*; Rosinenfischen *n aus brennendem Branntwein* (*Spiel*); '**~-fas·ten·er** Druckknopf *m am Kleid*; '**snap·pish** □ bissig, beißend; schnippisch; '**snap·pish·ness** bissiges *od.* schnippisches Wesen *n*; '**snap·py** = *snappish*; F flott, forsch; *make it ~!* F mach mal fix!; '**snap·shot 1.** Schnappschuß *m*, Photo *n*, Momentaufnahme *f*; **2.** Momentaufnahmen machen (von).

snare [snɛə] **1.** Schlinge *f*; **2.** (mit e-r Schlinge) fangen; *fig.* umgarnen.

snarl [snɑ:l] **1.** knurren; murren; verfitzen; **2.** Knurren *n*; Gewirr *n*; '**~-up** Durcheinander *n*; *bsd.* Verkehrschaos *n.*

snatch [snætʃ] **1.** schneller Griff *m*; Ruck *m*; Stückchen *n*; Augenblick *m*; *by ~es* in Absätzen, ruckweise; **2.** schnappen; ergreifen; an sich reißen; nehmen, bekommen; ~ *at* greifen nach; ~ *from s.o.* j-m entreißen.

sneak [sni:k] **1.** *v/i.* (sich *wohin*) schleichen; F petzen; *v/t.* F stibitzen; **2.** Schleicher *m*; F Petzer *m*; '**sneak·ers** *pl.* F leichte Segeltuchschuhe *m/pl.*; '**sneak·ing** □ schleichend; heimlich, still (*Gefühl*); '**sneak-thief** Gelegenheitsdieb *m*; '**sneak·y** F hinterlistig; raffiniert.

sneer [sniə] **1.** Hohnlächeln *n*; Spott *m*; **2.** hohnlächeln; spotten, spötteln (*at* über *acc.*); '**sneer·er** Spötter(in); '**sneer·ing** □ höhnisch.

sneeze [sni:z] **1.** niesen; *not to be ~d at* F nicht zu verachten; **2.** Niesen *n.*

snick·er ['snikə] kichern; wiehern.

sniff [snif] **1.** *v/i.* schnüffeln, schnuppern (*at* an *dat.*); die Nase rümpfen (*at* über *acc.*); *v/t.* riechen; **2.** Schnüffeln *n*; Naserümpfen *n*; Nasevoll *f*; **snif·fles** F ['sniflz] *pl.* Schnupfen *m*; *have the ~* Schnupfen haben; '**sniff·y** F hochnäsig, verächtlich; übelriechend.

snif·ter F ['sniftə] Schnäpschen *n*; *Am.* Kognakschwenker *m.*

snig·ger ['snigə] kichern (*at* über *acc.*).

snip [snip] **1.** Schnitt *m*; Schnippel *m*, Schnipsel *n*; **2.** schnippe(l)n, schnipseln; *Fahrkarte* knipsen.

snipe [snaip] **1.** *orn.* Bekassine *f*, (Sumpf)Schnepfe *f*; *coll.* Schnepfen *pl.*; **2.** ⚔ aus dem Hinterhalt (ab)schießen; '**snip·er** ⚔ Scharf-, *b.s.* Heckenschütze *m.*

snip·pets ['snipits] *pl.* Schnipsel *n/pl.*; *fig.* Bruchstücke *n/pl.*

snitch *sl.* [snitʃ]: ~ *on s.o.* j. verpetzen (*verraten*).

sniv·el ['snivl] aus der Nase triefen; schluchzen; plärren; '**sniv·el·(l)ing** triefnasig; wehleidig; jämmerlich.

snob [snɔb] Großtuer *m*; Snob *m*; '**snob·ber·y** Vornehmtuerei *f*; Snobismus *m*; '**snob·bish** □ vornehm tuend; snobistisch.

snog F [snɔg] knutschen.

snook·er ['snu:kə] **1.** *Art* Billardspiel *n*; **2.** *be ~ed* F in die Enge getrieben sein.

snoop *Am. sl.* [snu:p] **1.** *fig.* (umher-) schnüffeln (*upon* in *dat.*); **2.** Schnüffelei *f*; Schnüffler *m.*

snoot·y F ['snu:ti] hochnäsig.

snooze F [snu:z] **1.** Schläfchen *n*; **2.** dösen; ein Nickerchen machen.

snore [snɔ:] **1.** Schnarchen *n*; **2.** schnarchen.
snor·kel ⚓ [ˈsnɔ:kəl] Schnorchel *m*.
snort [snɔ:t] **1.** Schnauben *n*, Schnaufen *n*; **2.** schnauben, schnaufen.
snot P [snɔt] Rotz *m*; ˈ**snot·ty** P rotzig; *fig.* gemein.
snout [snaut] Schnauze *f*; Rüssel *m*.
snow [snəu] **1.** Schnee *m*; **2.** (be-) schneien; *be ~ed under with fig.* erdrückt werden von; *~ed in od. up* eingeschneit; ˈ**~·ball 1.** Schneeball *m*; **2.** (sich) mit Schneebällen bewerfen; ˈ**~-bound** eingeschneit; ˈ**~-capped,** ˈ**~-clad,** ˈ**~-cov·ered** schneebedeckt; ˈ**~-drift** Schneewehe *f*; ˈ**~·drop** ♀ Schneeglöckchen *n*; ˈ**~·fall** Schneefall *m*; ˈ**~·flake** Schneeflocke *f*; ˈ**~-gog·gles** *pl.* (*a pair of* eine) Schneebrille *f*; ˈ**~-line** Schneegrenze *f*; **~·mo·bile** [ˈ~məbi:l] Motorschlitten *m*, Schneemobil *n*; ˈ**~-plough,** *Am.* ˈ**~·plow** Schneepflug *m*; ˈ**~-shoe** Schneeschuh *m*; ˈ**~·storm** Schneesturm *m*; ˈ**~-ˈwhite** schneeweiß; ˈ**snow·y** □ schneeig; schneebedeckt, beschneit; schneeweiß.
snub [snʌb] **1.** schelten, anfahren; **2.** Verweis *m*; **snub nose** Stupsnase *f*; ˈ**snub-nosed** stupsnasig.
snuff [snʌf] **1.** Schnuppe *f e-r Kerze*; Schnupftabak *m*; *up to ~* F gerissen; *give s.o. ~* F j-m Saures geben; **2.** *a. take ~* schnupfen; *Kerze* putzen; ˈ**~-box** Schnupftabaksdose *f*; ˈ**snuff·ers** *pl.* Lichtputzschere *f*; **snuf·fle** [ˈ~fl] schnüffeln; schnauben; näseln; ˈ**snuff·y** mit Schnupftabak beschmutzt; schnupftabakartig; F *fig.* verschnupft.
snug □ [snʌg] geborgen; behaglich, gemütlich; eng anliegend (*Kleid*); ˈ**snug·ger·y** gemütliches Zimmer *n*, warmes Nest *n*; **snug·gle** [ˈ~gl] *a. ~ up* (sich) schmiegen *od.* kuscheln (*to* an, *in* in *acc.*).
so [səu] so; deshalb; also, so ... denn; *I hope ~* ich hoffe (es); *are you tired? ~ I am* bist du müde? ja; *you are tired, ~ am I* du bist müde, ich auch; *a mile or ~* etwa eine Meile; *~ as to ...* so daß ...; um zu ...; *~ far* bisher; *~ far as I know* soviel ich weiß.
soak [səuk] **1.** *v/t.* einweichen; durchnässen; (durch)tränken; vollsaugen; *sl. j.* schröpfen; *~ up od. in* auf-, einsaugen; *v/i.* weichen; durchsickern (*into, in* in *acc.*); F saufen; **2.** Einweichen *n*; Durchweichung *f*; = ˈ**soak·er** F Regenguß *m*; Sauferei *f*.
so-and-so [ˈsəuənsəu] so und so; *Mr.* 2 Herr *m* Soundso.
soap [səup] **1.** Seife *f*; *soft ~* Schmierseife *f*; **2.** (ein)seifen; ˈ**~-box** Seifenkiste *f*; *fig.* (Redner-) Plattform *f*; *~ orator* Volksredner *m*; *~ race* Seifenkistenrennen *n*; ˈ**~-dish** Seifenschale *f*; ˈ**~-bub·ble** Seifenblase; ˈ**~-op·er·a** *Am.* rührseliges Hör- *od.* Fernsehspiel *n in Fortsetzungen*; ˈ**~-suds** *pl., a. sg.* Seifenlauge *f*; ˈ**soap·y** □ seifig; *fig.* ölig, unterwürfig.
soar [sɔ:] sich erheben; sich aufschwingen (*a. fig.*); schweben; ✈ segelfliegen, gleiten.
sob [sɔb] **1.** Schluchzen *n*; **2.** schluchzen.
so·ber [ˈsəubə] **1.** □ nüchtern (*a. fig. mäßig; sachlich denkend; unauffällig*); **2.** *oft ~ down* ernüchtern; nüchtern werden; ˈ**so·ber·ness, so·bri·e·ty** [~ˈbraiəti] Nüchternheit *f*.
so·bri·quet [ˈsəubrikei] Spitzname *m*.
sob...: *~* **sis·ter** F Briefkastentante *f*; *~* **sto·ry** F rührselige Geschichte *f*; ˈ**~-stuff** F Gefühlsduselei *f*.
so-called [ˈsəuˈkɔ:ld] sogenannt.
soc·cer F [ˈsɔkə] Fußball *m* (*Spiel; im Ggs. zu Rugby*).
so·cia·bil·i·ty [səuʃəˈbiliti] Geselligkeit *f*; ˈ**so·cia·ble** □ **1.** gesellig; Gesellschafts...; gemütlich; **2.** Kremser *m*; Plaudersofa *n*; geselliges Beisammensein *n*.
so·cial [ˈsəuʃəl] **1.** □ gesellschaftlich; gesellig; sozial; Sozial...; *~ activities pl.* gesellschaftliche Veranstaltungen *f/pl.*; *~ insurance* Sozialversicherung *f*; *~ services pl.* Sozialeinrichtungen *f/pl.*; **2.** geselliges Beisammensein *n*; ˈ**so·cial·ism** Sozialismus *m*; ˈ**so·cial·ist 1.** Sozialist(in); **2.** *a.* **so·cial·ˈis·tic** sozialistisch; **so·cial·ite** F [ˈ~lait] Angehörige *m, f* der oberen Zehntausend; ˈ**so·cial·ize** sozialisieren; verstaatlichen; **so·cial se·cu·ri·ty** Sozialhilfe *f*; *be on ~* Sozialhilfe bekommen.

so·ci·e·ty [sə'saiəti] Gesellschaft *f*; Verein *m*, Klub *m*; *secret* ~ Geheimbund *m*.
so·ci·o·log·i·cal □ [sousjə'lɔdʒikəl] soziologisch; **so·ci·ol·o·gist** [~si'ɔlədʒist] Soziologe *m*; **so·ci'ol·o·gy** Sozialwissenschaft *f*, Soziologie *f*.
sock[1] [sɔk] Socke *f*; Einlegesohle *f*.
sock[2] *sl.* [~] **1.** Keile *f*, Senge *f* (*Prügel*); *give s.o.* ~*s* = **2.** *j.* versohlen.
sock·er F ['sɔkə] = *soccer*.
sock·et ['sɔkit] (Augen-, Zahn-) Höhle *f*; (Gelenk)Pfanne *f*; ⊕ Muffe *f*; ⚡ Fassung *f*; Steckdose *f*.
so·cle ['sɔkl] Sockel *m*; Untersatz *m*.
sod [sɔd] **1.** Grasnarbe *f*; Rasen (-stück *n*) *m*; **2.** mit Rasen belegen.
so·da ⚗ ['səudə] Soda *f*; '~**-foun·tain** Siphon *m*; Erfrischungshalle *f*, Eisdiele *f*; '~**-wa·ter** Soda-, Mineralwasser *n*.
sod·den ['sɔdn] durchweicht; teigig (*Brot*); *durch Trinken* verblödet.
so·di·um ⚗ ['səudjəm] Natrium *n*.
so·ev·er [səu'evə] ... auch immer.
so·fa ['səufə] Sofa *n*.
sof·fit △ ['sɔfit] Untersicht *f*, Leibung *f*.
soft [sɔft] **1.** □ *allg.* weich; *engS.* mild; sanft; sacht, leise, leicht; zart, zärtlich; weichlich; F einfältig; ~ *drink* F alkoholfreies Getränk *n*; ~ *furnishings Teppiche, Gardinen, Möbelbezüge etc.*; *a* ~ *thing sl.* e-e ruhige Sache (*einträgliches Geschäft*); *s. soap 1*; **2.** *adv.* weich; **3.** F Trottel *m*; '~-'**boiled** weich (*Ei*).
soft·en ['sɔfn] weich machen (*a. fig.*); (sich) erweichen; mildern; *Ton, Farbe* dämpfen; ⊕ enthärten; '**soft·en·er** Weichmacher *m*; Wasserenthärtungsanlage *f*; **soft-head·ed** ['sɔft'hedid] blöd(e), schwachsinnig; '**soft-'heart·ed** weichherzig, gutmütig; '**soft·ness** Weichheit *f*; Sanftmut *f*; Milde *f*; '**soft-'ped·al** ♪ mit dem Pianopedal spielen; *fig.* abschwächen; '**soft-'saw·der** **1.** *j-m* schmeicheln; **2.** Schmeichelei *f*; '**soft-'soap** *j-m* schmeicheln, um den Bart gehen; '**soft-'spok·en:** *be* ~ eine sanfte Stimme haben; '**soft·ware** *Computer*: Software *f*, Programmausstattung *f*; '**soft·y** F Trottel *m*; Softie *m*.
sog·gy ['sɔgi] durchnäßt, -weicht; feucht.
so·ho ['səu'həu] holla!
soil[1] [sɔil] Boden *m*, Erde *f*.
soil[2] [~] **1.** Fleck *m*; Schmutz *m*; **2.** (be)schmutzen; (be)flecken; '**soil-pipe** Fallrohr *n am Klosett*.
so·journ ['sɔdʒəːn] **1.** Aufenthalt *m*; **2.** sich aufhalten; '**so·journ·er** Fremde *m*, Gast *m*.
sol ♪ [sɔl] Sol *n* (*Solmisationssilbe*).
sol·ace ['sɔləs] **1.** Trost *m*; **2.** trösten.
so·lar ['səulə] Sonnen...; ~ **plex·us** *anat.* ['pleksəs] Solarplexus *m*; *weitS.* Magengrube *f*.
sold [səuld] *pret. u. p.p. von sell 1*.
sol·der ⊕ ['sɔldə] **1.** Lötmetall *n*; **2.** löten; '**sol·der·ing-i·ron** Lötkolben *m*.
sol·dier ['səuldʒə] **1.** Soldat *m*; **2.** Soldat sein; *go* ~*ing* Soldat werden; '**sol·dier·like**, '**sol·dier·ly** soldatisch; Soldaten...; '**sol·dier·ship** soldatische Tüchtigkeit *f*; '**sol·dier·y** Militär *n*; *contp.* Soldateska *f*.
sole[1] □ [səul] alleinig, einzig; ~ *agent* Alleinvertreter *m*.
sole[2] [~] **1.** Sohle *f*; **2.** besohlen.
sole[3] *ichth.* [~] Seezunge *f*.
sol·e·cism ['sɔlisizəm] Sprachschnitzer *m*; Verstoß *m*, Fauxpas *m*.
sol·emn □ ['sɔləm] feierlich; ernst; **so·lem·ni·ty** [sə'lemniti] Feierlichkeit *f*; Steifheit *f*; **sol·em·ni·za·tion** ['sɔləmnai'zeiʃən] Feier *f*; '**sol·em·nize** feiern; feierlich vollziehen.
so·lic·it [sə'lisit] (dringend) bitten (*s.o.* j.; *s.th.* um et.; *s.o. for s.th. od. s.th. of s.o.* j. um et.); ansprechen, belästigen; **so·lic·i'ta·tion** Ansuchen *n*; dringende Bitte *f*; **so'lic·i·tor** ⚖ Anwalt *m*, Rechtsbeistand *m*; *Am.* Agent *m*, Werber *m*; ♀ *General* Kronanwalt *m*; **so'lic·it·ous** □ besorgt, in Sorge (*about, for* um); ~ *of* begierig nach; ~ *to inf.* bestrebt zu *inf.*; **so'lic·i·tude** [~tjuːd] Sorge *f*, Besorgnis *f*; Bemühung *f*.
sol·id ['sɔlid] **1.** □ fest; dauerhaft, haltbar; derb, kräftig; massiv, gediegen; ⅌ körperlich, Raum...; *fig.* gediegen, zuverlässig; *bsd.* ✝ solid; triftig (*Grund*); solidarisch; einmütig, einstimmig; *a* ~ *hour* eine geschlagene *od.* volle Stunde; ~ *geometry* ⅌ Stereometrie *f*; ~ *leather* Kernleder *n*; **2.** (fester) Körper *m*; **sol·i·dar·i·ty** [~'dæriti]

Solidarität *f*; **so'lid·i·fy** [~difai] (sich) verdichten; fest machen *od.* werden; **so'lid·i·ty** Festigkeit *f*, Solidität *f*; Gediegenheit *f*; Zuverlässigkeit *f*; Triftigkeit *f*; **'sol·id-~'state** ⚡ Festkörper..., Halbleiter...

so·lil·o·quize [sə'liləkwaiz] Selbstgespräche führen; **so'lil·o·quy** Selbstgespräch *n*, Monolog *m*.

sol·i·taire [sɔli'tɛə] Solitär *m*, einzeln gefaßter Edelstein *m*; Patience *f* (*Spiel*); **sol·i·tar·y** □ ['~təri] einsam; einzeln; einsiedlerisch; ~ *confinement* Einzelhaft *f*; **sol·i·tude** ['~tju:d] Einsamkeit *f*; Verlassenheit *f*; Öde *f*.

so·lo ['səuləu] ♪ *u. Kartenspiel*: Solo *n*; ✈ Alleinflug *m*; **'so·lo·ist** Solist (-in).

sol·stice ['sɔlstis] Sonnenwende *f*.

sol·u·bil·i·ty [sɔlju'biliti] Löslichkeit *f*; Auflösbarkeit *f*; **sol·u·ble** ['~bl] löslich; (auf)lösbar.

so·lu·tion [sə'lu:ʃən] (Auf)Lösung *f* (*a.* ⚗ *u.* ⚕); ⊕ Gummilösung *f*.

solv·a·ble ['sɔlvəbl] auflösbar; **solve** *Aufgabe, Zweifel etc.* lösen; **sol·ven·cy** ✝ ['~vənsi] Zahlungsfähigkeit *f*; **'sol·vent 1.** (auf)lösend; ✝ zahlungsfähig; **2.** Lösungsmittel *n*.

som·bre, *Am.* **som·ber** □ ['sɔmbə] düster, trübe, dunkel (*a. fig.*).

some [sʌm, səm] **1.** *pron. u. adj.* irgendein; ein gewisser; etwas; einige, manche *pl.*; ~ *bread* (etwas) Brot; ~ *few* einige wenige, ein paar; ~ *20 miles* etwa 20 Meilen; *in* ~ *degree, to* ~ *extent* in gewissem Grade, einigermaßen; *this is* ~ *speech!* das ist mal 'ne Rede!; **2.** *adv.* etwas; *Am.* F prima; **'~·bod·y** jemand; **'~·day** eines Tages; **'~·one** jemand; **'~·how** irgendwie; ~ *or other* so oder so.

som·er·sault ['sʌməsɔ:lt] Salto *m*; Rolle *f*, Purzelbaum *m*; *turn a* ~ e-n Purzelbaum schlagen.

some...: ~·thing ['sʌmθiŋ] (irgend) etwas; *that is* ~ das ist doch etwas; ~ *like* so etwas wie, so ungefähr; **'~·time 1.** einmal, dereinst; **2.** ehemalig; **'~·times** zuweilen, manchmal; **'~·what** etwas, ziemlich; **'~·where** irgendwo(hin); **'~·while** gelegentlich, eine Weile.

som·nam·bu·lism [sɔm'næmbjulizəm] Nachtwandeln *n*; **som'nam·bu·list** Nachtwandler(in).

som·nif·er·ous □ [sɔm'nifərəs] einschläfernd.

som·no·lence ['sɔmnələns] Schläfrigkeit *f*; **'som·no·lent** schläfrig; einschläfernd.

son [sʌn] Sohn *m*.

so·na·ta ♪ [sə'nɑ:tə] Sonate *f*.

song [sɔŋ] Gesang *m*; Lied *n*; Gedicht *n*; *for a mere od. an old* ~ für e-n Pappenstiel; *nothing to make a* ~ *about* F nichts Besonderes; **'~-bird** Singvogel *m*; **'~-book** Liederbuch *n*; **'~-hit** Schlager *m*; **song·ster** ['~stə] Singvogel *m*; Sänger *m*; **song·stress** ['~stris] Sängerin *f*.

son·ic ['sɔnik] Schall...; ~ **bang** Knall *m* beim Durchbrechen der Schallmauer; ~ **bar·ri·er** Schallgrenze *f*, -mauer *f*.

son-in-law, *pl.* **sons-in-law** ['sʌn(z)inlɔ:] Schwiegersohn *m*.

son·net ['sɔnit] Sonett *n*.

son·ny F ['sʌni] Kleiner *m* (*Anrede*).

so·nor·i·ty [sə'nɔriti] Klang-, Tonfülle *f*; **so·no·rous** □ [sə'nɔ:rəs] klangvoll, vollklingend, sonor.

soon [su:n] bald; früh; gern; *as od. so* ~ *as* sobald wie; **'soon·er** eher; früher; lieber; *no* ~ ... *than* kaum ... als; *no* ~ *said than done* gesagt, getan.

soot [sut] **1.** Ruß *m*; **2.** be-, verrußen.

sooth [su:θ]: *in* ~ in Wahrheit, fürwahr; **soothe** [su:ð] beruhigen, besänftigen; mildern; **sooth·say·er** ['su:θseiə] Wahrsager(in).

soot·y □ ['suti] rußig.

sop [sɔp] **1.** eingeweichter Brocken *m*; *fig.* Besänftigungsmittel *n*, Bestechung *f*; **2.** eintunken; durchweichen; ~ *up Wasser* aufnehmen, -wischen.

soph·ism ['sɔfizəm] Sophismus *m*; Trugschluß *m*.

soph·ist ['sɔfist] Sophist *m*; **so·phis·tic, so·phis·ti·cal** □ [sə'fistik(əl)] sophistisch; **so'phis·ti·cate** [~keit] verdrehen; verfälschen; **so'phis·ti·cat·ed** kultiviert, raffiniert; intellektuell; hochgestochen, blasiert; hochentwickelt, kompliziert; **so·phis·ti'ca·tion** Spitzfindigkeit *f*; Verfälschung *f*; Intellektualismus *m*; Kompliziertheit *f*; **soph·ist·ry** ['sɔfistri] Sophisterei *f*, Spitzfindigkeit *f*.

soph·o·more *Am.* ['sɔfəmɔː] Student(in) im zweiten Studienjahr.
so·po·rif·ic [sɔpə'rifik] **1.** (~*ally*) einschläfernd; **2.** Schlafmittel *n.*
sop·ping ['sɔpiŋ] *a.* ~ *wet* patschnaß; '**sop·py** durchweicht; F rührselig; fad.
so·pran·o ♪ [sə'prɑːnəu] Sopran *m.*
sor·cer·er ['sɔːsərə] Zauberer *m*; '**sor·cer·ess** Zauberin *f*; Hexe *f*; '**sor·cer·y** Zauberei *f.*
sor·did □ ['sɔːdid] schmutzig, schäbig (*bsd. fig.*); '**sor·did·ness** Schmutzigkeit *f.*
sore [sɔː] **1.** □ schlimm, entzündet; wund; weh; empfindlich; schmerzend; *fig.* schlimm, arg; ~ *throat* Halsweh *n*, -entzündung *f*; **2.** wunde Stelle *f*, Schaden *m* (*a. fig.*); '**sore·head** *Am.* F mürrischer *od.* enttäuschter Mensch *m*; '**sore·ly** *adv.* heftig; äußerst, sehr; '**sore·ness** Empfindlichkeit *f.*
so·ror·i·ty [sə'rɔriti] Schwesternschaft *f*; *Am. univ.* Studentinnenverbindung *f.*
sor·rel[1] ['sɔrəl] **1.** rötlichbraun (*bsd. Pferd*); **2.** Fuchs *m* (*Pferd*).
sor·rel[2] ⚘ [~] Sauerampfer *m.*
sor·row ['sɔrəu] **1.** Sorge *f*; Kummer *m*, Leid *n*; Trauer *f*; **2.** trauern; sich grämen; **sor·row·ful** □ ['sɔrəful] traurig, betrübt; elend.
sor·ry □ ['sɔri] betrübt, bekümmert; traurig, erbärmlich; (*I am*) (*so*) ~! es tut mir (sehr) leid, (ich) bedaure!; Verzeihung!; *I am* ~ *for him* er tut mir leid; ich bemitleide ihn; *we are* ~ *to say* wir müssen leider sagen; wir bedauern, sagen zu müssen.
sort [sɔːt] **1.** Sorte *f*, Gattung *f*, Art *f*; Weise *f*; *what* ~ *of* was für; *of a* ~, *of* ~*s* so was wie; ~ *of* F gewissermaßen; *out of* ~*s* F unpäßlich; verdrießlich; *a good* ~ ein guter Kerl; (*a*) ~ *of peace* so etwas wie ein Frieden; **2.** sortieren; ⚕ assortieren; aussuchen; ~ *out* (aus-) sondern.
sor·tie ⚔ ['sɔːtiː] Ausfall *m*; ✈ Einsatz *m.*
sot [sɔt] Trunkenbold *m.*
sot·tish □ ['sɔtiʃ] versoffen.
sou [suː] Sou *m* (*französische Münze*); *fig.* Heller *m.*
sou·bri·quet ['suːbrikei] = *sobriquet.*
souf·flé ['suːflei] Soufflé *n*, Auflauf *m.*
sough [sau] **1.** Sausen *n*, Rauschen *n*; **2.** rauschen (*bsd. Wind*).
sought [sɔːt] *pret. u. p.p. von* **seek**; '~-'**aft·er** gesucht, begehrt.
soul [səul] Seele *f* (*a. fig.*); '~-**de·stroy·ing** geisttötend; '**soul·less** □ seelenlos.
sound[1] □ [saund] *allg.* gesund (*a. fig.*); ganz (*unbeschädigt*); vernünftig; tüchtig, gründlich; fest (*Schlaf*); derb (*Schlag etc.*); ⚕ sicher; ⚖ gültig.
sound[2] [~] **1.** Ton *m*, Schall *m*, Laut *m*, Klang *m*; **2.** *v/i.* tönen, klingen; ertönen, erklingen; erschallen; *v/t.* erschallen lassen, ertönen lassen; (aus)sprechen; ~ *the charge* ⚔ zum Angriff blasen.
sound[3] [~] Sund *m*, Meerenge *f*; Fischblase *f.*
sound[4] [~] **1.** ⚕ Sonde *f*; **2.** ⚕ sondieren (*a. fig.*); ⚓ loten; ⚕ abhorchen; ~ *s.o. out* j. ausholen, -horchen.
sound...: ~ **bar·ri·er** Schallmauer *f*; '~-**box** Schalldose *f*; ~ **broad·cast·ing** Tonrundfunk *m*; ~ **ef·fects** *pl.* Klang-, Toneffekte *m/pl.*; '~-**film** Tonfilm *m.*
sound·ing ⚓ ['saundiŋ] Lotung *f*; ~*s pl.* lotbare Wassertiefe *f.*
sound·ing-board ['saundiŋbɔːd] Resonanz-, Schallboden *m.*
sound·less □ ['saundlis] lautlos.
sound·ness ['saundnis] Gesundheit *f* (*a. fig.*).
sound...: '~-**proof**, '~-**tight** schalldicht; '~-**track** *Film*: Tonspur *f*; '~-**wave** Schallwelle *f.*
soup[1] [suːp] Suppe *f.*
soup[2] *Am. sl.* [~] **1.** Pferdestärke *f*; **2.** ~ *up* *Motor* frisieren (*Leistung erhöhen*).
sour ['sauə] **1.** □ sauer; *fig.* bitter; *fig.* sauer(töpfisch), mürrisch; **2.** *v/t.* säuern; *fig.* ver-, erbittern; *v/i.* sauer (*fig.* bitter) werden.
source [sɔːs] Quelle *f*; Ursprung *m*; ~ *language gr.* Ausgangssprache *f.*
sour·ish □ ['sauəriʃ] säuerlich; '**sour·ness** Säure *f*; *fig.* Bitterkeit *f*; '**sour·puss** Miesepeter *m.*
souse [saus] **1.** eintauchen; (mit Wasser) begießen; *Fisch etc.* einlegen, -pökeln; **2.** Plumps *m*; **soused** *sl.* besoffen.
sou·tane *eccl.* [suː'tɑːn] Soutane *f.*

south [sauθ] **1.** Süden *m*; *to the ~ of* südlich von; **2.** Süd...; südlich, südwärts; **'~·bound** in Richtung Süden fahrend.

south-east ['sauθ'iːst] **1.** Südosten *m*; **2.** *a.* **south-'east·ern** südöstlich.

south·er·ly ['sʌðəli], **south·ern** ['~ən] südlich; Süd...; **'south·ern·er** Südländer(in); *Am.* Südstaatler(in).

south·ern·most ['sʌðənməust] südlichst.

south·ing ['sauðiŋ] ⚓ (zurückgelegter) südlicher Kurs *m*; *ast.* Kulmination(szeit) *f*.

south...: **'~·land** Süden *m*; **'~·paw** *Am. Baseball*: Linkshänder *m*; **2 Pole** Südpol *m*.

south·ward(s) ['sauθwəd(z)] *adv.* südwärts, nach Süden.

south...: **'~-'west 1.** Südwesten *m*; **2.** *a.* **~-'west·er·ly, ~-'west·ern** südwestlich; **~-'west·er** Südwestwind *m*; = **sou'west·er** ⚓ [sau'westə] Südwester *m* (*wasserdichter Ölhut*).

sou·ve·nir ['suːvəniə] Andenken *n* (*of* an *acc.*).

sov·er·eign ['sɔvrin] **1.** □ höchst; unübertrefflich; hochwirksam (*Arznei*); unumschränkt, souverän; **2.** Landesherr(in), Herrscher(in), Souverän *m*; Sovereign *m* (*20-Schilling-Stück*); **sov·er·eign·ty** ['~rənti] Oberherrschaft *f*, Landeshoheit *f*, Souveränität *f*.

so·vi·et ['səuviət] Sowjet *m*.

sow¹ [sau] *zo.* Sau *f*, (Mutter-)Schwein *n*; ⊕ Sau *f*, Massel *f*.

sow² [səu] (*irr.*) (aus)säen, ausstreuen; *Land* besäen, bestreuen; **'sow·er** Sämann *m*; Sämaschine *f*; *fig.* Verbreiter(in); **sown** [səun] *p.p. von sow²*.

so·ya ⚘ ['sɔiə] Soja *f*; *~ bean* Sojabohne *f*.

soz·zled *sl.* ['sɔzld] besoffen.

spa [spɑː] Heilbad *n*; Kurort *m*.

space [speis] **1.** Weltraum *m*; Platz *m*; Zwischenraum *m*; Zeitraum *m*; *typ.* Spatium *n*; **2.** *a. ~ out* in Abständen anordnen, verteilen; *typ.* sperren; gesperrt drucken; **'~-craft** Raumschiff *n*; **'~·lab** Weltraumlabor *n*; **~ race** Weltraum-Wettrennen *n*; **'~-ship** Raumschiff *n*; **~ shot** Start *m e-s Satelliten etc.*; **~ shut·tle** Raumfähre *f*; **'~-suit** Raumanzug *m*; **'~-'time** Zeit-Raum *m*, vierte Dimension *f*.

spa·cious □ ['speiʃəs] geräumig; weit, umfassend; **'spa·cious·ness** Weite *f*, Weiträumigkeit *f*.

spade [speid] **1.** Spaten *m*; *call a ~ a ~* das Kind beim rechten Namen nennen; *mst ~s pl. Karten*: Pik *n*, Schippe *f*; **2.** graben; **'~-work** mühevolle Vorarbeit *f*.

spa·ghet·ti [spə'geti] Spaghetti *pl.*

spake † *od. poet.* [speik] *pret. von speak*.

span¹ [spæn] **1.** (*a.* Zeit)Spanne *f*; ⚠ Spannung *f*, Spannweite *f*; *Am.* Gespann *n*; **2.** (um-, über)spannen, überwölben; (aus)messen.

span² [~] *pret. von spin 1.*

span·gle ['spæŋgl] **1.** Flitter *m*; **2.** (mit Flitter) besetzen; *fig.* übersäen.

Span·iard ['spænjəd] Spanier(in).

span·iel ['spænjəl] Spaniel *m*.

Span·ish ['spæniʃ] **1.** spanisch; **2.** Spanisch *n*; *the ~ pl.* die Spanier *pl.*

spank F [spæŋk] **1.** *v/t.* verhauen, -sohlen; *v/t. ~ along* dahineilen; **2.** Klaps *m*, Schlag *m*; **'spank·er** ⚓ Gieksegel *n*; **'spank·ing 1.** □ tüchtig; schnell, scharf; F toll; **2.** F Haue *f*, Tracht *f* Prügel.

span·ner ⊕ ['spænə] Schraubenschlüssel *m*; *throw a ~ into the works fig.* querschießen.

spar¹ [spɑː] ⚓ Spiere *f*; ✈ Holm *m*.

spar² [~] *Boxen*: sparren; Scheinhiebe machen (*at* nach); *fig.* sich streiten; kämpfen (*Hähne*); *~ring partner Boxen*: Sparringspartner *m*.

spar³ *min.* [~] Spat *m*.

spare [spɛə] **1.** □ spärlich, kärglich, sparsam; mager; überzählig; überschüssig; Ersatz...; Reserve...; *~ hours pl.* Mußestunden *f/pl.*; *~ room* Gastzimmer *n*; *~ time* Freizeit *f*; **2.** ⊕ Ersatzteil *n*, *m*; **3.** *v/t.* (ver-)schonen; erübrigen; entbehren; (übrig) haben für; (er)sparen; sparen mit; *enough and to ~* mehr als genug; *v/i.* sparen, sparsam sein; Schonung üben; **'spare·ness** Dürftigkeit *f*; Magerkeit *f*; **spare part** Ersatzteil *n*, *m*; **'spare·rib** *Fleischerei*: Rippe(n)speer *m*, *n*.

spar·ing □ ['spɛəriŋ] sparsam (*in, of* mit); knapp, dürftig; **'spar·ing·ness** Sparsamkeit *f*.

spark[1] [spɑːk] **1.** Funke(n) *m* (*a. fig.*); **2.** *v/i.* Funken sprühen; *v/t.* ~ *s.th. off* et. auslösen.
spark[2] [~] flotter Kerl *m*; Galan *m*.
spark·ing-plug *mot.* [ˈspɑːkiŋplʌg] Zündkerze *f*.
spar·kle [ˈspɑːkl] **1.** Funke(n) *m*; Funkeln *n*; *fig.* sprühendes Wesen *n*; **2.** funkeln; blitzen; sprühen (*Witz*); perlen, moussieren (*Wein*), schäumen; *sparkling wine* Schaumwein *m*; **spar·klet** [ˈ~klit] Fünkchen *n* (*a. fig.*).
spark-plug *mot.* [ˈspɑːkplʌg] Zündkerze *f*.
spar·row *orn.* [ˈspærəu] Sperling *m*, Spatz *m*; ˈ**~-hawk** *orn.* Sperber *m*.
sparse □ [spɑːs] spärlich, dünn.
Spar·tan [ˈspɑːtən] **1.** spartanisch; **2.** Spartaner(in).
spasm ⚕ [ˈspæzəm] Krampf *m* (*a. fig.*); **spas·mod·ic, spas·mod·i·cal** □ [~ˈmɔdik(əl)] krampfhaft, -artig, spasmodisch; *fig.* sprunghaft, unregelmäßig; **spas·tic** [ˈ~tik] 1. (*~ally*) spastisch; 2. Spastiker(in).
spat[1] [spæt] Schaltierlaich *m*.
spat[2] [~] (Schuh)Gamasche *f*.
spat[3] [~] *pret. u. p.p. von spit*[2] 2.
spatch-cock [ˈspætʃkɔk] *Bemerkung etc.* einstreuen, -fügen.
spate [speit] Hochwasser *n*; *fig.* Flut *f*; *be in* ~ Hochwasser führen.
spa·tial □ [ˈspeiʃəl] räumlich, Raum...
spat·ter [ˈspætə] **1.** (be)spritzen; klatschen, prasseln; **2.** Schauer *m* (*a. fig.*).
spat·u·la [ˈspætjulə] Spatel *m*.
spav·in *vet.* [ˈspævin] Spat *m*.
spawn [spɔːn] 1. Laich *m*; *fig. mst contp.* Brut *f*; 2. laichen; *contp.* aushecken; ˈ**spawn·er** Rog(e)ner *m* (*weiblicher Fisch*); ˈ**spawn·ing** 1. Laichen *n*; 2. Laich...; Brut...
spay [spei] *weibliches Tier* sterilisieren.
speak [spiːk] (*irr.*) *v/i.* sprechen; reden; ♪ erklingen; *~ing! teleph.* am Apparat!; *Brown ~ing!* hier Brown!; ~ *out* laut sprechen; offen reden; ~ *to j. od.* mit *j-m* sprechen; ~ *up* kein Blatt vor den Mund nehmen; ~ *up!* (sprich) lauter!; ~ *up against* auftreten gegen; *that ~s well for him* das spricht sehr für ihn; *v/t.* sprechen; *Gedanken etc.* aussprechen, äußern; verkünden; ˈ**~-eas·y** *Am. sl.* Flüsterkneipe *f* (*ohne Konzession*); ˈ**speak·er** Sprecher(in); Redner(in); *parl.* Sprecher *m*, Vorsitzende *m*.
speak·ing [ˈspiːkiŋ] sprechend; sprechend ähnlich (*Bild*); *be on ~ terms with* oberflächlich bekannt sein mit; ˈ**~-trum·pet** Sprachrohr *n*.
spear [spiə] **1.** Speer *m*, Spieß *m*; Lanze *f*; **2.** (auf)spießen; ˈ**~·head** **1.** Speerspitze *f*; *fig.* (Angriffs-)Spitze *f*, Vortrupp *m*; **2.** *Angriff* beginnen.
spec ✝ *sl.* [spek] Spekulation *f*.
spe·cial [ˈspeʃəl] **1.** □ besonder; Sonder...; speziell; extra; Spezial...; ~ *envoy* Sonderbotschafter *m*; **2.** *a.* ~ *constable* Hilfspolizist *m*; *a.* ~ *edition* Sonderausgabe *f*; *a.* ~ *train* Sonderzug *m*; *Am.* Sonderangebot *n* (*in e-m Geschäft*); *Am.* (Tages)Spezialität *f* (*in e-m Restaurant*); ˈ**spe·cial·ist** Spezialist *m*; Fachmann *m*; ⚕ Facharzt *m*; **spe·ci·al·i·ty** [speʃiˈæliti] Besonderheit *f*; Spezialfach *n*; ✝ Spezialität *f*; **spe·cial·i·za·tion** [speʃəlaiˈzeiʃən] Spezialisierung *f*; ˈ**spe·cial·ize** *v/t.* besonders *od.* einzeln anführen; besonders ausbilden; *v/i.* sich spezialisieren (*in* in *dat.*, auf *acc.*), sich besonders verlegen auf (*acc.*); **spe·cial·ty** [ˈ~ti] *s. speciality*; ⚖ besiegelter Vertrag *m*.
spe·cie [ˈspiːʃiː] Metallgeld *n*, Hartgeld *n*; ˈ**spe·cies** *pl. u. sg.* Art *f*, Spezies *f*.
spe·cif·ic [spiˈsifik] **1.** (*~ally*) spezifisch, eigen(tümlich); besonder; bestimmt; ~ *gravity phys.* spezifisches Gewicht *n*; ~ *name* Artname *m*; **2.** ⚕ spezifisches Mittel *n*.
spec·i·fi·ca·tion [spesifiˈkeiʃən] Spezifizierung *f*; ⚖ Patentschrift *f*; *~s pl.* nähere Angaben *f/pl.*; (technische) Beschreibung *f*; **spec·i·fy** [ˈ~fai] spezifizieren, einzeln angeben *od.* (be)nennen.
spec·i·men [ˈspesimin] Probe *f*, Muster *n*, Exemplar *n*.
spe·cious □ [ˈspiːʃəs] *äußerlich* blendend, bestechend; trügerisch; Schein...; ˈ**spe·cious·ness** trügerischer Schein *m*.
speck [spek] **1.** Fleck *m*; Stückchen *n*; **2.** flecken, sprenkeln; **speck·le** [ˈ~kl] **1.** Fleckchen *n*; **2.** *s. speck* 2.

specs F [speks] *pl.* Brille *f.*
spec·ta·cle [ˈspektəkl] Schauspiel *n*; Anblick *m*; (*a pair of*) ~*s pl.* (eine) Brille *f*; ~ *frame* Brillenfassung *f*; ˈ**spec·ta·cled** bebrillt.
spec·tac·u·lar □ [spekˈtækjulə] **1.** eindrucksvoll; auffallend, spektakulär; **2.** *Am.* F Galarevue *f.*
spec·ta·tor [spekˈteitə] Zuschauer *m*; ~ *sport* Zuschauersport *m.*
spec·tral □ [ˈspektrəl] gespenstisch; *opt.* Spektral...; **spec·tre,** *Am.* **spec·ter** [ˈ~tə] Gespenst *n*; **spec·tro·scope** *opt.* [ˈ~trəskəup] Spektroskop *n*; **spec·trum** *opt.* [ˈ~trəm] Spektrum *n.*
spec·u·late [ˈspekjuleit] grübeln, nachsinnen (*on, upon* über *acc.*); † spekulieren; **spec·uˈla·tion** theoretische Betrachtung *f*; Grübelei *f*; † Spekulation *f*; **spec·u·la·tive** □ [ˈ~lətiv] spekulativ, grüblerisch; theoretisch; † spekulierend; **spec·u·la·tor** [ˈ~leitə] Denker *m*; † Spekulant *m.*
spec·u·lum ⚕, *opt.* [ˈspekjuləm] (Metall)Spiegel *m*; Spekulum *n.*
sped [sped] *pret. u. p.p. von speed* 2.
speech [spiːtʃ] Sprache *f*; Rede, Ansprache *f*; *make a* ~ e-e Rede halten; ˈ**~-day** *Schule*: (Jahres-) Schlußfeier *f*; ~ **de·fect** Sprachfehler *m*; **speech·i·fy** *contp.* [ˈ~ifai] viel Worte machen; ˈ**speech·less** □ sprachlos.
speed [spiːd] **1.** Geschwindigkeit *f*; Schnelligkeit *f*; Eile *f*; ⊕ Drehzahl *f*; *phot.* Lichtempfindlichkeit *f*; **2.** (*irr.*) *v/i.* schnell fahren, rasen; ~ *up* (*pret. u. p.p.* ~*ed*) die Geschwindigkeit erhöhen; *v/t. j-m* Glück verleihen; befördern; ~ *up* (*pret. u. p.p.* ~*ed*) beschleunigen; ˈ**~-boat** Rennboot *n*; ˈ**~-cop** motorisierter Verkehrspolizist *m*; ˈ**~-in·di·ca·tor** = *speedometer*; ˈ**~-lim·it** Geschwindigkeitsbegrenzung *f*; **speed·om·e·ter** *mot.* [spiˈdɔmitə] Geschwindigkeitsmesser *m*, Tachometer *n*; **speed trap** Radarfalle *f*; ˈ**speed·way** Motorradrennbahn *f*; *bsd. Am.* Schnellstraße *f*; ˈ**speed·well** ⚘ Ehrenpreis *n, m*; ˈ**speed·y** □ schnell, rasch.
spell[1] [spel] **1.** (Arbeits)Zeit *f*, ⊕ Schicht *f*; Weilchen *n*, Bißchen *n*; Periode *f*; **2.** abwechseln mit *j-m* (*at* bei).
spell[2] [~] **1.** Zauber(spruch) *m*; **2.** (*irr.*) buchstabieren; richtig schreiben; bedeuten; ~ *out* entziffern; ˈ**~·bind·er** *Am.* fesselnder Redner *m*; ˈ**~·bound** *fig.* (fest)gebannt, verzaubert; ˈ**spell·er:** *he is a bad* ~ er kann nicht richtig schreiben.
spell·ing [ˈspeliŋ] Rechtschreibung *f*; ˈ**~-book** Fibel *f.*
spelt[1] [spelt] *pret. u. p.p. von spell*[2] 2.
spelt[2] ⚘ [~] Spelt *m*, Dinkel(weizen) *m.*
spel·ter [ˈspeltə] Zink *n.*
spen·cer [ˈspensə] Spenzer *m* (*Jäckchen*).
spend [spend] (*irr.*) *v/t.* verwenden (*on, upon* für, auf *acc.*); *Geld etc.* ausgeben (*on* für); verbrauchen, *b.s.* verschwenden; *Zeit* verbringen; (*bsd.* ~ *o.s.* sich) erschöpfen; ~ *the night* übernachten; *v/i.* Geld ausgeben; ˈ**spend·er** Verschwender (-in).
spend-thrift [ˈspendθrift] **1.** Verschwender(in); **2.** verschwenderisch.
spent [spent] **1.** *pret. u. p.p. von spend*; **2.** *adj.* erschöpft, entkräftet, matt.
sperm [spəːm] *menschlicher u. tierischer* Same(n) *m*; **sper·ma·ce·ti** [~məˈseti] Walrat *m, n*; **sper·ma·to·zo·on** *biol.* [~ətəuˈzəuɔn] Spermatozoon *n*, Spermium *n.*
spew [spjuː] (sich) erbrechen.
sphere [sfiə] Kugel *f*; Erd-, Himmelskugel *f*; *fig.* Sphäre *f*, (Wirkungs)Kreis *m*; Bereich *m*; Gebiet *n*; **spher·i·cal** □ [ˈsferikəl] sphärisch; kugelförmig.
sphinc·ter *anat.* [ˈsfiŋktə] Schließmuskel *m.*
sphinx [sfiŋks] Sphinx *f* (*a. fig.*).
spice [spais] **1.** Gewürz(e *pl.*) *n*; *fig.* Würze *f*; Beigeschmack *m*; Anflug *m*; **2.** würzen; ~ **rack** Gewürzregal *n*; ˈ**spic·er·y** Gewürze *n/pl.*
spic·i·ness [ˈspaisinis] Würzigkeit *f*; *fig.* Pikantheit *f.*
spick and span [ˈspikənˈspæn] frisch u. sauber; schmuck; funkelnagelneu.
spic·y □ [ˈspaisi] gewürzreich, würzig; *fig.* pikant.
spi·der *zo.* [ˈspaidə] Spinne *f*; ˈ**spi·der·y** spinnengleich.
spiel *Am. sl.* [spiːl] Gequassel *n.*
spiff·y *sl.* [ˈspifi] schick; toll.
spig·ot [ˈspigət] (Faß)Zapfen *m*;

Hahn *m*.
spike [spaik] **1.** Stift *m*; Spitze *f*; Dorn *m*; Stachel *m*; *Sport*: Laufdorn *m*; *mot*. Spike *m*; ⚘ Ähre *f*; **2.** festnageln; ⚔ *Geschütz* vernageln; mit *eisernen* Stacheln versehen; **spike·nard** ['~nɑ:d] Lavendel-, Nardenöl *n*; '**spik·y** □ spitzig.
spill[1] [spil] **1.** (*irr.*) *v/t.* verschütten; *Blut* vergießen; F *Reiter etc.* abwerfen; *weitS.* schleudern; *v/i.* verschüttet werden; überlaufen; **2.** F Sturz *m vom Pferd etc.*
spill[2] [~] Fidibus *m*.
spill·o·ver ['spiləuvə] Bevölkerungsüberschuß *m*.
spill·way ['spilwei] Abflußkanal *m*.
spilt [spilt] *pret. u. p.p. von spill*[1] *1*; *cry over ~ milk* über etwas jammern, was doch nicht zu ändern ist.
spin [spin] **1.** (*irr.*) *v/t.* spinnen (*a. fig.*); wirbeln, (herum)drehen; *Münze* hochwerfen; sich *et.* ausdenken; erzählen; *~ s.th. out* et. in die Länge ziehen; *v/i.* spinnen; *a. ~ round* sich drehen, herumwirbeln; ✈ trudeln; *~ along* dahinsausen; *send s.o.* (*s.th.*) *~ning* j. (et.) schleudern; **2.** Wirbeln *n*, Drehung *f*; Spritztour *f*; ✈ Trudeln *n*.
spin·ach ⚘ ['spinidʒ] Spinat *m*.
spi·nal ['spainl] Rückgrat...; *~ column* Wirbelsäule *f*; *~ cord*, *~ marrow* Rückenmark *n*; *~ curvature* Rückgratverkrümmung *f*.
spin·dle ['spindl] Spindel *f*; '**spindly** spindeldürr.
spin-dri·er ['spindraiə] Wäscheschleuder *f*.
spin-drift ['spindrift] Gischt *m*.
spin-dry ['spin'drai] *Wäsche* schleudern.
spine [spain] Rückgrat *n*; Dorn *m*; (Gebirgs)Grat *m*; (Buch)Rücken *m*; '**spine·less** rückgratlos (*a. fig.*).
spin·et ♪ [spi'net] Spinett *n*.
spin·na·ker ⚓ ['spinəkə] Spinnaker *m*, Dreiecksegel *n*.
spin·ner ['spinə] Spinner(in); Spinnmaschine *f*; **spin·ner·et** *zo.* ['spinəret] Spinndrüse *f*.
spin·ney ['spini] Dickicht *n*.
spin·ning...: **~-jen·ny** ⊕ ['spiniŋ-'dʒeni] Feinspinnmaschine *f*; '**~-mill** Spinnerei *f*; '**~-wheel** Spinnrad *n*.
spin-off ['spinɔf] Nebenprodukt *n*.
spin·ster ['spinstə] unverheiratete Frau *f*; *engS.* alte Jungfer *f*; *nach dem Namen*: ledig.
spin·y ['spaini] dornig.
spi·ra·cle ['spaiərəkl] Luftloch *n*.
spi·rae·a ⚘ [spai'riə] Spierstaude *f*.
spi·ral ['spaiərəl] **1.** □ spiralig; Spiral...; schnecken-, schraubenförmig; **2.** Spirale *f*; *fig.* Wirbel *m*, Welle *f*; **3.** sich spiralförmig bewegen; sich schrauben; wirbeln.
spire ['spaiə] Turmspitze *f*; *Berg-*, *Baum- etc.* Spitze *f*; Spitzturm *m*.
spir·it ['spirit] **1.** *allg.* Geist *m*; Sinn *m*; Temperament *n*, Leben *n*; Mut *m*; Gesinnung *f*; ⚗ Spiritus *m*; Sprit *m*, Benzin *n*; *~s pl.* Stimmung *f*, Laune *f*; geistige Getränke *n/pl.*, Spirituosen *pl.*; *~ of wine* Weingeist *m*; *in* (*high*) *~s* in gehobener Stimmung, gut aufgelegt; *in low ~s* in gedrückter Stimmung, schlecht aufgelegt; **2.** *~ away*, *~ off* verschwinden lassen, wegzaubern; *~ up* aufmuntern.
spir·it·ed □ ['spiritid] geistvoll; lebhaft, lebendig, temperamentvoll; mutig; ...gesinnt; ...gestimmt; '**spir·it·ed·ness** Lebhaftigkeit *f*; Mut *m*.
spir·it·ism ['spiritizəm] Spiritismus *m*; '**spir·it·ist** Spiritist(in).
spir·it·less □ ['spiritlis] geistlos; temperament-, lustlos; mutlos.
spir·it-lev·el ['spiritlevl] Wasserwaage *f*.
spir·it·u·al □ ['spiritjuəl] geistig; geistlich; geistvoll; '**spir·it·u·al·ism** Spiritualismus *m*; Spiritismus *m*; **spir·it·u·al·i·ty** [~'æliti] Geistigkeit *f*; geistige Natur *f*; **spir·it·u·al·ize** ['~əlaiz] ver-, durchgeistigen.
spir·it·u·el(le) [spiritju'el] geistreich, -sprühend.
spir·it·u·ous ['spiritjuəs] alkoholisch.
spirt [spə:t] **1.** (hervor)spritzen, (hervor)schießen (lassen); **2.** (Wasser- *etc.*)Strahl *m*.
spit[1] [spit] **1.** Bratspieß *m*; Landzunge *f*; **2.** aufspießen.
spit[2] [~] **1.** Speichel *m*, Spucke *f*; *be the very ~ of s.o.* F j-m wie aus dem Gesicht geschnitten sein; **2.** (*irr.*) *v/i.* spucken; fauchen (*Katze*); sprühen (*fein regnen*); *~ at* anspucken; *~ upon* bespucken; *v/t.* (*mst ~ out* aus)spucken; *~ it out!* F heraus mit der Sprache!

spit³ [~] Spatenstich *m.*
spite [spait] **1.** Bosheit *f*; Groll *m*; *in ~ of* trotz (*gen.*); **2.** ärgern; kränken.
spite·ful □ ['spaitful] boshaft, gehässig; '**spite·ful·ness** Bosheit *f.*
spit·fire ['spitfaiə] Hitzkopf *m*; Kratzbürste *f.*
spit·tle ['spitl] Speichel *m*, Spucke *f.*
spit·toon [spi'tu:n] Spucknapf *m.*
spiv *sl.* [spiv] Schieber *m.*
splash [splæʃ] **1.** Spritzfleck *m*; P(l)atschen *n*; *make a ~* F Aufsehen erregen; **2.** (be)spritzen; p(l)atschen; planschen; *Farbe etc.* (hin-)klecksen, (auf)klatschen; *~ one's money about sl.* mit Geld um sich werfen; '**~-board** Spritzbrett *n*; '**~·down** Wasserung(sstelle) *f e-s Raumfahrzeugs*; '**splash·y** □ platschend; matschig; klecksig.
splay [splei] **1.** Ausschrägung *f*; **2.** auswärts gebogen; **3.** ausschrägen; ausgeprägt sein; '**~-foot** Spreizfuß *m.*
spleen [spli:n] *anat.* Milz *f*; üble Laune *f*, Ärger *m*; **spleen·ful** ['~ful], '**spleen·y** ärgerlich, launisch.
splen·did □ ['splendid] glänzend, prächtig, herrlich, großartig, wunderbar; **splen·dif·er·ous** F [~'difərəs] = *splendid*; '**splen·do(u)r** Glanz *m*, Pracht *f*, Herrlichkeit *f.*
sple·net·ic [spli'netik] **1.** *a.* **sple'net·i·cal** □ ärgerlich; launisch; **2.** Hypochonder *m.*
splice [splais] **1.** Verspleißung *f*; ⚓ Spleiß *m*; **2.** (ver)spleißen; ⚓ splissen; ⊕ einfalzen; *sl.* verheiraten.
splint ⚕ [splint] **1.** Schiene *f*; **2.** schienen; '**~-bone** *anat.* Wadenbein *n.*
splin·ter ['splintə] **1.** Splitter *m*; **2.** (zer)splittern; '**splin·ter-proof** splittersicher.
split [split] **1.** Spalt *m*, Riß *m*; *fig.* Spaltung *f*; *~s pl.* Grätsche *f*; Spagat *m*; **2.** gespalten; **3.** (*irr.*) *v/t.* (zer)spalten; zerreißen; platzen lassen; (sich) *et.* teilen; *~ hairs* Haarspalterei treiben; *~ one's sides with laughter* sich vor Lachen biegen, sich totlachen; *~ up* aufspalten; platzen; *fig.* sich entzweien; *~ on sl. j.* hochgehen lassen (*verraten*); '**~-'lev·el** △ mit versetzten Ebenen; '**split·ting** sehr heftig; F rasend (schnell).
splotch [splɔtʃ] Fleck *m*, Klecks *m.*
splurge [splə:dʒ] Angabe *f*, Getue *n.*
splut·ter ['splʌtə] *s. sputter*; ✈ kotzen (*Motor*).
spoil [spɔil] **1.** *oft ~s pl.* Beute *f*, Raub *m*; *fig.* Ausbeute *f*; Schutt *m*; **2.** (*irr.*) *v/t.* (be)rauben; plündern; verderben; verwöhnen, *Kind* verziehen; *v/i.* verderben; *~ing for a fight* streitlustig; '**spoil·er** Räuber *m*; Verderber *m*; **spoils·man** *Am. pol.* ['~zmən] Postenjäger *m*; '**spoil--sport** Spielverderber(in); **spoils sys·tem** *Am. pol.* Futterkrippensystem *n.*
spoilt [spɔilt] *pret. u. p.p. von spoil 2.*
spoke¹ [spəuk] *pret. von speak.*
spoke² [~] Speiche *f*; (Leiter-)Sprosse *f*; ⚓ Spake *f.*
spo·ken ['spəukən] *p.p. von speak.*
spokes·man ['spəuksmən] Wortführer *m*, Sprecher *m.*
spo·li·a·tion [spəuli'eiʃən] Beraubung *f*, Plünderung *f.*
spon·dee ['spɔndi:] Spondeus *m.*
sponge [spʌndʒ] **1.** Schwamm *m*; *throw up the ~ Boxen u. fig.* sich geschlagen geben; **2.** *v/t.* mit e-m Schwamm (ab)wischen *od.* reiben; *~ up* aufsaugen; *v/i.* schmarotzen (*on* bei); '**~-bag** Waschbeutel *m*; '**~-'cake** Biskuitkuchen *m*; '**spong·er** Schmarotzer(in).
spon·gi·ness ['spʌndʒinis] Schwammigkeit *f*; '**spon·gy** schwammig; porös.
spon·sor ['spɔnsə] **1.** Taufzeuge *m*, Pate *m*; Bürge *m*; Förderer *m*, Gönner *m*; Auftraggeber *m* für Werbesendung; **2.** Pate stehen bei; aus der Taufe heben; finanzieren; fördern; '**spon·sor·ship** Paten-, Gönnerschaft *f.*
spon·ta·ne·i·ty [spɔntə'ni:iti] Freiwilligkeit *f*; Unmittelbarkeit *f*; Spontaneität *f*; Selbstentstehung *f*, Selbstentwick(e)lung *f*; **spon·ta·ne·ous** □ [~'teinjəs] freiwillig, von selbst (entstanden); Selbst...; spontan; unwillkürlich; unmittelbar; unüberlegt; ⚘ wild wachsend; *~ combustion* Selbstverbrennung *f*; *~ generation* Urzeugung *f.*
spoof *sl.* [spu:f] **1.** *j.* verkohlen; **2.** Mumpitz *m*; Schwindel *m.*
spook [spu:k] Spuk *m*; '**spook·y**

geisterhaft, Spuk...
spool [spu:l] **1.** Spule *f*; **2.** spulen.
spoon [spu:n] **1.** Löffel *m*; *sl.* verliebter Narr *m*; *be ~s on sl.* verschossen sein in *j.*; **2.** löffeln; *sl.* schmusen; **'~-drift** Gischt *m, f*; **'spoon·er·ism** Schüttelreim *m*; **'spoon-fed** *fig.* hochgepäppelt; verhätschelt, verwöhnt; **spoon·ful** ['~ful] Löffel(voll) *m*; **'spoon-meat** (Kinder-, Kranken)Brei *m*; **'spoon·y** □ F verschossen (*on* in *acc.*).
spoor *hunt.* [spuə] Spur *f*, Fährte *f*.
spo·rad·ic [spə'rædik] (*~ally*) sporadisch, verstreut.
spore ⚘ [spɔ:] Spore *f*, Keimkorn *n*.
spor·ran ['spɔrən] Felltasche *f der Schottentracht*.
sport [spɔ:t] **1.** Sport *m*; Spiel *n*; *fig.* Spielball *m*; Unterhaltung *f*; Scherz *m*; *~s pl. allg.* Sport *m*; Sportfest *n*; *a. good ~* feiner Kerl *m*; *make ~ of* sich lustig machen über (*acc.*); **2.** *v/i.* sich belustigen; spielen, scherzen; *v/t.* F protzen mit; *~ one's oak* die Tür verschlossen halten; **'sport·ing** □ Sport...; Jagd...; sportlich; *~ chance* knappe Chance *f*; **'spor·tive** □ lustig; scherzhaft; **'sports-car** *mot.* Sportwagen *m*; **'sports-coat, 'sports-jack·et** Sportsakko *m*; **'sports·man** Sportler *m*; Weidmann *m*; **'sports·man·like** sportlich; anständig, fair; weidmännisch; **'sports·man·ship** Sportlichkeit *f*; *fig.* faires Benehmen *n*; **'sports-wear** Sportkleidung *f*; **'sports·wom·an** Sportlerin *f*.
spot [spɔt] **1.** *allg.* Fleck *m*; Tupfen *m*; Makel *m*; Stelle *f*; Platz *m*; Leberfleck *m*, Pickel *m*; Tropfen *m*; *~s pl.* ⚚ Lokowaren *f/pl.*; *a ~ of* F etwas, ein bißchen; *on the ~* auf der Stelle; sofort, sogleich; *be on the ~* zur Stelle sein; **2.** ⚚ sofort lieferod. zahlbar; Loko...; **3.** *v/t.* (be-)flecken, sprenkeln; ausfindig machen; (genau) erkennen; *v/i.* fleckig werden; F regnen; *~* **check** Stichprobe *f beim Zoll, der Steuer etc.*; **'spot·less** □ fleckenlos; **'spot·less·ness** Unbeflecktheit *f*; **'spot·light** *thea.* Scheinwerfer(licht *n*) *m*; *mot.* Suchscheinwerfer *m*; *in the ~ fig.* im Brennpunkt des Interesses; **'spot·ted** gefleckt, getupft; *~ fever* ⚕ Fleckfieber *n*; **'spot·ter** Beobachter *m* (*bsd. zur Luftraumsicherung*); *Am.* Kontrolleur *m bsd. e-r Verkehrsgesellschaft*; **'spot·ti·ness** Fleckigkeit *f*; **'spot·ty** fleckig, sprenklig.
spouse [spauz] Gatte *m*; Gattin *f*.
spout [spaut] **1.** Tülle *f*, Schnauze *f*; Strahlrohr *n*; ⚠ Wasserspeier *m*; (Wasser)Strahl *m*; **2.** (aus)spritzen; F salbadern.
sprain [sprein] **1.** Verstauchung *f*; **2.** verstauchen.
sprang [spræŋ] *pret. von spring* 2.
sprat *ichth.* [spræt] Sprotte *f*.
sprawl [sprɔ:l] *v/i.* ausgestreckt daliegen, sich rekeln (*a. fig.*); ⚘ wuchern; *fig.* sich ausdehnen; *v/t. ~ out* ausstrecken.
spray[1] [sprei] Zweig(verzierung *f*) *m*.
spray[2] [~] **1.** zerstäubte Flüssigkeit *f*; Sprühregen *m*; Gischt *m*; Spray *m*; = *~er*; **2.** *Flüssigkeit* zerstäuben; *et.* besprühen; spritzen; **'spray·er** Zerstäuber *m* (*Gerät*).
spread [spred] **1.** (*irr.*) *v/t. a. ~ out* ausbreiten; (aus)dehnen; *Gerücht, Krankheit etc.* verbreiten; (be-)decken, belegen, überziehen; *Butter etc.* aufstreichen; *Brot etc.* bestreichen; *~ the table* den Tisch decken; *v/i.* sich aus-, verbreiten; **2.** *~ eagle* fliegender Adler *m als Abzeichen*; **3.** Aus-, Verbreitung *f*; Spannweite *f*; Weite *f*; Fläche *f*; *Am.* Decke *f*; Brotaufstrich *m*; F Festschmaus *m*; **'~-ea·gle** F bombastisch; hurrapatriotisch; **'spread·er** Aus-, Verbreiter(in); **'spread·ing** ausgebreitet, weit.
spree F [spri:] Spaß *m*, Jux *m*; Zechgelage *n*; Orgie *f*; (*Kauf- etc.*)Welle *f*; *go on a ~* e-e Sauftour machen.
sprig [sprig] **1.** Sproß *m*, Reis *n* (*a. fig.*); Zweigverzierung *f*; ⊕ Zwecke *f*, Stift *m*; **2.** mit Stiften befestigen; *~ged* geblümt (*Stoff*).
spright·li·ness ['spraitlinis] Lebendigkeit *f*; **'spright·ly** lebhaft, munter.
spring [spriŋ] **1.** Sprung *m*; Satz *m*; (Sprung)Feder *f*; Feder-, Sprungkraft *f*, Elastizität *f*; Triebfeder *f*; Springquell *m*, Quelle *f*; *fig.* Ursprung *m*; Frühling *m*; **2.** (*irr.*) *v/t.* springen lassen; (zer)sprengen; plötzlich herauskommen mit *et.*; *Wild* aufjagen; *~ a leak* ⚓ leck

werden; ~ *s.th. on s.o.* j. mit et. überraschen; *v/i.* springen; entspringen, entstehen (*from* aus, von); ⚘ sprießen; ~ *up* aufspringen; aufkommen (*Ideen etc.*); aus dem Boden schießen; ~ *into existence* plötzlich entstehen; **'~-'bal·ance** Federwaage *f*; **'~-board** Sprungbrett *n*; **'~-'clean·ing** Frühjahrsputz *m*.
springe *hunt.* [sprindʒ] Schlinge *f*.
spring gun ['spriŋgʌn] Selbstschuß *m*; **'spring·i·ness** Elastizität *f*; **spring mat·tress** Sprungfedermatratze *f*; **spring tide** Springflut *f*; **'spring·tide, 'spring·time** Frühling(szeit *f*) *m*; **'spring·y** □ federnd, elastisch.
sprin·kle ['spriŋkl] *v/t.* (be)streuen; (be)sprengen; *v/i.* sprühen (*Regen*); **'sprin·kler** Berieselungsanlage *f*; Rasensprenger *m*; *eccl.* Weihwedel *m*; **'sprin·kling** Sprühregen *m*; *a* ~ *of fig.* ein wenig, ein paar.
sprint [sprint] *Sport*: **1.** sprinten; spurten; **2.** Sprint *m*; Kurzstreckenlauf *m*; Endspurt *m*; **'sprint·er** Sprinter *m*, Kurzstreckenläufer *m*.
sprit ⚓ [sprit] Spriet *n*.
sprite [sprait] Geist *m*, Kobold *m*.
sprit·sail ⚓ ['spritsl] Sprietsegel *n*.
sprock·et-wheel ⊕ ['sprɔkitwi:l] Kettenrad *n*.
sprout [spraut] **1.** sprießen, wachsen (lassen); **2.** ⚘ Sproß *m*; *a. Brussels* ~*s pl.* Rosenkohl *m*.
spruce[1] □ [spru:s] **1.** schmuck, sauber; **2.** (sich) fein machen.
spruce[2] ⚘ [~] *a.* ~ *fir* Fichte *f*, Rottanne *f*.
sprung [sprʌŋ] *pret.* (↖) *u. p.p. von spring* 2.
spry [sprai] munter, flink.
spud [spʌd] Jätmesser *n*; F Kartoffel *f*.
spume *lit.* [spju:m] Schaum *m*; **'spu·mous, 'spum·y** □ schaumig.
spun [spʌn] *pret. u. p.p. von spin 1.*
spunk [spʌŋk] Zunder *m*; F Feuer *n*, Mumm *m*; **'spunk·y** mutig.
spur [spə:] **1.** Sporn *m* (*a. zo.*, ⚘); *fig.* Ansporn *m*; Vorsprung *m*, Ausläufer *m e-s Berges*; *on the* ~ *of the moment* der Eingebung des Augenblicks folgend; spornstreichs; *put od. set* ~*s to dem Pferd* die Sporen geben; *fig. j.* (an)spornen; *win one's* ~*s* sich die Sporen verdienen; ~ *gear* ⊕ Stirnrad *n*; **2.** *a.* ~ *on* (an)spornen (*a. fig.*); *poet.* sprengen, eilen.
spurge ⚘ [spə:dʒ] Wolfsmilch *f*.
spu·ri·ous □ ['spjuəriəs] unecht, gefälscht; **'spu·ri·ous·ness** Unechtheit *f*.
spurn [spə:n] verschmähen, verächtlich zurückweisen.
spurred [spə:d] gespornt.
spurt [spə:t] **1.** alle s-e Kräfte zs.-nehmen; *Sport*: spurten; *s. spirt*; **2.** plötzliche Anstrengung *f*, Ruck *m*; *Sport*: Spurt *m*; *s. spirt*.
sput·nik ['sputnik] Sputnik *m*, Satellit *m*.
sput·ter ['spʌtə] **1.** Gesprudel *n*; **2.** *v/i.* sprudeln; spritzen; (*at s.o.* j. an)blubbern; *v/t. a.* ~ *out* hervorsprudeln.
spy [spai] **1.** Späher(in); Spion(in); **2.** (er)spähen; erblicken; spionieren; ~ *(up)on s.o.* j-m nachspionieren; **'~·glass** kleines Fernrohr *n*; **'~·hole** Guckloch *n*.
squab [skwɔb] Jungvogel *m*, *bsd.* ungefiederte Taube *f*.
squab·ble ['skwɔbl] **1.** Zank *m*, Zwist *m*, Kabbelei *f*; **2.** (sich) zanken; **'squab·bler** Zänker(in).
squad [skwɔd] Rotte *f*, Trupp *m*; **squad·ron** ['~rən] ⚔ Schwadron *f*; ✈ Staffel *f*; ⚓ Geschwader *n*.
squal·id □ ['skwɔlid] schmutzig, armselig.
squall[1] [skwɔ:l] **1.** Schrei *m*; ~*s pl.* Geschrei *n*; **2.** schreien.
squall[2] ⚓ [~] Bö *f*; **'squall·y** ⚓ böig, stürmisch.
squa·lor ['skwɔlə] Schmutz *m*.
squa·mous ['skweiməs] schuppig.
squan·der ['skwɔndə] verschwenden; **'~'ma·ni·a** Verschwendungssucht *f*.
square [skwɛə] **1.** □ viereckig; quadratisch; senkrecht; im rechten Winkel (*to, with* zu); passend, stimmend; in Ordnung; direkt, unzweideutig, glatt; quitt, gleich (*with* mit); F ehrlich, redlich, offen; *Am.* F altmodisch, spießig; ~ *measure* Flächenmaß *n*; ~ *mile* Quadratmeile *f*; (*take a*) ~ *root* ⩕ Quadratwurzel *f* (ziehen); ~ *sail* ⚓ Rahsegel *n*; **2.** Quadrat *n* (*a. e-r Zahl*); Viereck *n*; Feld *n* (*Schachbrett etc.*); ⚠ Säulenplatte *f*; ⚔ Karree *n*; *öffentlicher* Platz *m*; Winkelmaß *n*; *Am.* F altmodischer Spießer *m*; **3.** *v/t.* viereckig machen; ⩕ qua-

drieren; einrichten (*with* nach), anpassen (*dat.*); ✝ begleichen, ausgleichen; bestechen; *v/i.* (*with*) passen (zu); übereinstimmen (mit); im Einklang stehen (mit); '~-**-'built** vierschrötig; ~ **dance** Quadrille *f*; '~-'**rigged** ⚓ mit Rahen getakelt; '~-**toes** F *sg.* Pedant *m*.

squash[1] [skwɔʃ] **1.** Gedränge *n*; Fruchtsaft *m*; Platsch(en *n*) *m*; Squash *n* (*ein Rakettspiel*); *mst* ~-*hat* Schlapphut *m*; **2.** (zer-, zs.-)quetschen; drücken, pressen; *fig.* erdrücken; F mundtot machen.

squash[2] ⚘ [~] Kürbis *m*.

squat [skwɔt] **1.** kauernd; untersetzt; **2.** hocken, kauern; '**squatter** Hausbesetzer *m*; Siedler *m* ohne Rechtstitel; *Australien*: Schafzüchter *m*.

squaw [skwɔ:] (Indianer)Frau *f*, Squaw *f*.

squawk [skwɔ:k] **1.** kreischen, schreien; **2.** Gekreisch *n*, Geschrei *n*.

squeak [skwi:k] **1.** quieken, quietschen; *sl.* pfeifen, petzen; **2.** Gequieke *n etc.*; *a narrow* ~ F ein knappes Entrinnen *n*; '**squeak·y** □ quiekend *etc.*

squeal [skwi:l] quäken; gell schreien; *s. squeak*.

squeam·ish □ ['skwi:miʃ] empfindlich; mäkelig; Übelkeit empfindend; heikel; penibel; '**squeam·ish·ness** Überempfindlichkeit *f*.

squee·gee ['skwi:'dʒi:] Scheibenreiniger *m* mit Gummilippe; *phot.* Rollenquetscher *m*.

squeez·a·ble ['skwi:zəbl] gefügig.

squeeze [skwi:z] **1.** (sich) drücken, (sich) pressen, (sich) quetschen; auspressen; *fig.* (be)drängen, quälen; **2.** Druck *m* (*a. fig.*); kräftiger Händedruck *m*; Gedränge *n*; '**squeez·er** Presse *f*.

squelch F [skweltʃ] platschen; zermalmen.

squib [skwib] Schwärmer *m*, Frosch *m*; Spottgedicht *n*.

squid *zo.* [skwid] Tintenfisch *m*.

squif·fy *sl.* ['skwifi] beschwipst.

squig·gle F ['skwigl] Schnörkel *m*.

squill ⚘ [skwil] Meerzwiebel *f*.

squint [skwint] **1.** schielen; **2.** Schielen *n*; F flüchtiger *od.* schiefer Blick *m*; '~-**eyed** schielend; *fig.* scheel, böse.

squire ['skwaiə] **1.** Gutsbesitzer *m*; (Land)Junker *m*; *Am.* F (Friedens-)Richter *m*; *hist.* Schildknappe *m*; *co.* Kavalier *m*; Frauenheld *m*; **2.** *e-e Dame* begleiten.

squir(e)·arch·y ['skwaiərɑ:ki] Junkertum *n*; Junkerherrschaft *f*.

squirm F [skwə:m] sich winden.

squir·rel *zo.* ['skwirəl] Eichhörnchen *n*.

squirt [skwə:t] **1.** Spritze *f*; Strahl *m*; F Wichtigtuer *m*; **2.** spritzen.

squish F [skwiʃ] Marmelade *f*.

stab [stæb] **1.** Stich *m*; ~ *in the back fig.* verleumderischer Angriff *m*; **2.** *v/t.* (er)stechen; *v/i.* stechen (*at* nach).

sta·bil·i·ty [stə'biliti] Stabilität *f*; Standfestig-, Beständig-, Stetigkeit *f*; ✈ dynamisches Gleichgewicht *n*.

sta·bi·li·za·tion [steibilai'zeiʃən] Stabilisierung *f*.

sta·bi·lize ['steibilaiz] stabilisieren (*a.* ✈); '**sta·bi·liz·er** ✈, ⚓ Stabilisator *m*.

sta·ble[1] □ ['steibl] stabil; (stand-)fest; dauerhaft; beständig; stetig.

sta·ble[2] [~] **1.** Stall *m*; **2.** einstallen.

sta·bling ['steibliŋ] Stallung *f*.

stac·ca·to ♪ [stə'kɑ:təu] stakkato.

stack [stæk] **1.** ⚒ (Heu-, Stroh-, Getreide)Schober *m*; Stapel *m*, Stoß *m*; Schornsteinreihe *f*; ⚔ Gewehrpyramide *f*; Regal *n*; ~*s pl. bsd. Am.* Hauptmagazin *n e-r Bibliothek*; F Haufen *m*, Menge *f*; *blow one's* ~ F *fig.* in die Luft gehen; **2.** aufstapeln; aufstellen.

sta·di·um ['steidjəm] *Sport*: Stadion *n*, Sportplatz *m*, Kampfbahn *f*.

staff [stɑ:f] **1.** Stab *m*, Stock *m*; Stütze *f*; ⚔ Stab *m*; Personal *n*; Belegschaft *f*; Beamten-, Lehrkörper *m*; ♪ *pl.* **staves** [steivz] Notensystem *n*; **2.** (mit Personal, Beamten *od.* Lehrern) besetzen; ~ **man·a·ger** Personalchef *m*; ~ **room** Lehrerzimmer *n*.

stag [stæg] *zo.* Hirsch *m*; F Herr *m* ohne Dame; ✝ Konzertzeichner *m an der Börse*.

stage [steidʒ] **1.** Bühne *f*, Theater *n*; *fig.* Schauplatz *m*; Stufe *f*, Stadium *n*; Teilstrecke *f*, Etappe *f*; Gerüst *n*, Gestell *n*; *go on the* ~ zur Bühne gehen; **2.** *v/t.* inszenieren; *v/i.* für die Bühne geeignet sein; '**~·box** Proszeniumsloge *f*; '**~-coach** Postkutsche *f*; '**~-craft** dramatisches Talent *n*; Theatererfahrung *f*; **~ di·rec·tion** Bühnenanweisung *f*; **~ fright** Lampenfieber *n*; '**~-hand** Bühnenarbeiter *m*; **~ man·ag·er** Regisseur *m*; '**stag·er:** *old* ~ alter Hase *m*; '**stage-struck** theaterbesessen; **stage ver·sion** Bühnenfassung *f*; '**stag·ey** = *stagy*.

stag·ger ['stægə] **1.** *v/i.* (sch)wanken, taumeln; *fig.* stutzen; *v/t.* wankend machen; ⊕ *u. weitS.* staffeln; **2.** Schwanken *n*, Wanken *n*; ⊕ *u. weitS.* Staffelung *f*; ~*s pl. vet.* Koller *m*; '**stag·ger·ing** *fig.* umwerfend.

stag·nan·cy ['stægnənsi] Stockung *f*; '**stag·nant** □ stehend (*Wasser*); stagnierend; stockend; träg; ✝ still; **stag·nate** [~'neit] stagnieren; stocken; **stag'na·tion** Stockung *f*.

stag-par·ty F ['stægpɑ:ti] Herrengesellschaft *f*.

stag·y □ ['steidʒi] theatralisch.

staid □ [steid] gesetzt, ruhig; '**staid·ness** Gesetztheit *f*.

stain [stein] **1.** Fleck(en) *m* (*a. fig.*); (Holz)Beize *f*; **2.** fleckig machen; *fig.* beflecken, beschmutzen; ⊕ beizen, färben; ~*ed glass* buntes Glas *n*; '**stain·less** □ ungefleckt; *fig.* fleckenlos; ⊕ rostfrei, nichtrostend (*Stahl*).

stair [stɛə] Stufe *f*; ~*s pl.* Treppe *f*, Stiege *f*; '**~-car·pet** Treppenläufer *m*; '**~·case** Treppe(nhaus *n*) *f*; '**~-rod** Läuferstange *f*; '**~·way** = *staircase*.

stake [steik] **1.** Pfahl *m*; Marterpfahl *m*; (Spiel)Einsatz *m* (*a. fig.*); ~*s pl. Pferderennen*: Preis *m*, Einlage *f*; Rennen *n*; *pull up* ~*s Am.* F abhauen; *be at* ~ auf dem Spiele stehen; *place one's* ~ *on* setzen auf (*acc.*); **2.** (um)pfählen; aufs Spiel setzen; *Geld etc.* setzen; ~ *out*, ~ *off* abstecken.

stal·ac·tite ['stæləktait] Stalaktit *m*, hängender Tropfstein *m*; **stal·ag·mite** ['stæləgmait] Stalagmit *m*, stehender Tropfstein *m*.

stale[1] □ [steil] alt (*Ggs. frisch*); schal, abgestanden (*Wasser, Neuigkeit*); altbacken (*Brot*); verbraucht (*Luft, Kraft*); fad (*Geruch*); alt (*Witz*); überanstrengt.

stale[2] [~] **1.** stellen, harnen (*Pferd etc.*); **2.** Harn *m*.

stale·mate ['steil'meit] **1.** *Schach*: Patt *n*; *fig.* Stillstand *m*; **2.** patt setzen; *fig.* zum Stillstand bringen.

stalk[1] [stɔ:k] Stengel *m*, Stiel *m*; Halm *m*.

stalk[2] [~] **1.** *v/i.* einherschreiten; (einher)stolzieren; *hunt.* pirschen; *v/t.* beschleichen; **2.** *hunt.* Pirsch *f*; '**stalk·er** Pirschjäger *m*; '**stalking-horse** *fig.* Deckmantel *m*.

stall [stɔ:l] **1.** (Pferde)Box *f*; (Verkaufs)Stand *m*, Marktbude *f*; *thea.* Sperrsitz *m*; *eccl.* Chorstuhl *m*; **2.** *v/t.* einstallen; ✈ überziehen; *Motor* abwürgen; *v/i. mot.* aussetzen; ✈ durchsacken; *fig.* Ausflüchte machen; '**~-feed·ing** Stallfütterung *f*.

stal·lion ['stæljən] Hengst *m*.

stal·wart ['stɔ:lwət] **1.** □ stramm; handfest; **2.** *pol.* Unentwegte *m*.

sta·men ⚘ ['steimen] Staubfaden *m*, -gefäß *n*; **stam·i·na** ['stæminə] Ausdauer *f*, Widerstandsfähigkeit *f*, Vitalität *f*; **stam·i·nate** ⚘ ['~nit] mit Staubfäden.

stam·mer ['stæmə] **1.** stottern, stammeln; **2.** Stottern *n*; '**stam·mer·er** Stotter(in).

stamp [stæmp] **1.** (Auf)Stampfen *n*; ⊕ Stampfe(r *m*) *f*; Stempel *m* (*a. fig.*); (Brief)Marke *f*; Gepräge *n* (*a. fig.*); Art *f*, Schlag *m*; **2.** *v/t.* stampfen; prägen; stanzen; (ab-)stempeln (*a. fig.*); *Brief* frankieren; ~ *on the memory* dem Gedächtnis einprägen; ~ *out* zertreten; *fig.* niederschlagen; *v/i.* (auf)stampfen; '**~-al·bum** Briefmarkenalbum *n*; '**~-col·lec·tor** Briefmarkensammler *m*; '**~-deal·er** Briefmarkenhändler *m*; '**~-du·ty** Stempelgebühr *f*.

stam·pede [stæm'pi:d] **1.** Panik *f*, wilde Flucht *f*; **2.** durchgehen; in Panik versetzen.

stamp·er ['stæmpə] Stampfer *m*; Stempel *m*; **stamp·ing ground** F Revier *n*; *fig.* Tummelplatz *m*, Treff(-punkt) *m*; '**stamp(·ing)-mill** *metall.* Pochwerk *n*.

stance [stæns] *Golf etc.*: Stellung *f*, Haltung *f*.

stanch [stɑ:ntʃ] **1.** hemmen; stillen; **2.** *adj.* = *staunch 1*; **stan·chion** ['stɑ:nʃən] Stütze *f*, Pfosten *m*.

stand [stænd] **1.** (*irr.*) *v/i. allg.*

stehen; sich befinden; bestehen, beharren; *mst* ~ *still* stillstehen, stehenbleiben; bestehen (bleiben); ~ *against* bestehen gegen, *j-m* widerstehen; ~ *aside* abseits stehen; beiseite treten; ~ *back*, ~ *clear* zurücktreten; ~ *by* dabeistehen, dabei sein; *fig.* (fest) stehen zu; helfen; bereitstehen; ~ *for* sich bewerben um *ein Amt*, kandidieren für *e-n Sitz im Parlament*; bedeuten; eintreten für; vertreten; F sich *et.* gefallen lassen; ~ *in* einspringen (*for* für); ⚓ landwärts anliegen; ~ *in with* sich gut stellen mit; sich mit *j-m* beteiligen (*in* an *dat.*); ~ *off* abstehen; sich entfernt halten; zurücktreten (von); ⚓ seewärts anliegen; ~ *off!* weg da!; ~ *on* (*fig.* be-) stehen auf (*dat.*); ~ *out* hervorstehen; *fig.* deutlich hervortreten, sich abheben (*against* gegen); sich fernhalten; standhalten (*against* gegen); bestehen (*for* auf *dat.*); ⚓ nach See zu liegen; ~ *over für später* stehen *od.* liegen bleiben; *j.* beaufsichtigen; ~ *pat Am.* F stur bleiben; ~ *to* bleiben bei, beharren bei; *s. reason*; ~ *to!* ⚔ an die Gewehre!; ~ *up* aufstehen; sich erheben (*a. fig.*); ~ *up for* eintreten für; ~ *up to* sich zur Wehr setzen gegen; standhalten (*dat.*); ~ *upon* (*fig.* bestehen auf (*dat.*); *v/t.* (hin)stellen; aushalten, (v)ertragen; über sich ergehen lassen; *s. ground*; ~ *s.o. a dinner* F j-m ein Mittagessen spendieren; *s. treat*; **2.** Stand *m*; Standplatz *m*; Bude *f*; Standpunkt *m*; Stellung *f*; Stillstand *m*; Ständer *m*, Gestell *n*; Tribüne *f für Zuschauer*; *bsd. Am.* Zeugenstand *m*; *make a od. one's* ~ *against* standhalten (*dat.*).

stand·ard [ˈstændəd] **1.** Standarte *f*, Fahne *f*; Standard *m*, Norm *f*, Regel *f*, Maßstab *m*; Niveau *n*, Grad *m*; Stufe *f*, Klasse *f der Grundschule*; Münzfuß *m*; Währung *f*; Ständer *m*, Mast *m*; senkrechtes Rohr *n*; ⚘ Hochstamm *m*; ~ *lamp* Stehlampe *f*; ~ *of living* Lebenshaltung *f*, -standard *m*; **2.** maßgebend; Muster..., Normal...; Einheits...; ˈ**~-bear·er** *bsd. fig.* Bannerträger *m*, Vorkämpfer *m*; ˈ**~-ga(u)ge** 🚂 normalspurig; **stand·ard·i·za·tion** [~aiˈzeiʃən] Norm(ier)ung *f*; ˈ**stand·ard·ize** norm(ier)en, festsetzen, vorschreiben; vereinheitlichen.

stand-by [ˈstændbai] Beistand *m*.

stand·ee [stænˈdiː] Stehende *m*; *Am.* Stehplatzinhaber *m*.

stand·er-by [ˈstændəˈbai] Dabeistehende *m*, Zuschauer(in).

stand-in [ˈstændˈin] *Film*: Double *n*.

stand·ing [ˈstændiŋ] **1.** □ stehend; fest; (be)ständig; ~ *jump* Sprung *m* aus dem Stand; ~ *committee pol.* ständiger Ausschuß *m*; ~ *orders pl. parl.* Geschäftsordnung *f*; **2.** Stehen *n*, Stellung *f*, Rang *m*; Ruf *m* (*Ansehen*); Dauer *f*; *of long* ~ alt; ˈ**~-room** Stehplatz *m*.

stand...: ˈ**~-off** *Am.* Unentschieden *n*; Gegengewicht *n*; ˈ**~-ˈoff·ish** zurückhaltend; **~ˈpat·ter** *Am.* F *pol.* sture Konservative *m*; ˈ**~-pipe** Standrohr *n*; ˈ**~·point** Standpunkt *m*; ˈ**~·still** Stillstand *m*; *be at a* ~ stillstehen; *come to a* ~ zum Stehen kommen; ˈ**~-up:** ~ *collar* Stehkragen *m*; ~ *fight* regelrechter Kampf *m*; ~ *supper* kaltes Büfett (*im Stehen eingenommen*).

stank [stæŋk] *pret. von stink* 2.

stan·nic ⚗ [ˈstænik] Zinn...

stan·za [ˈstænzə] Stanze *f*; Strophe *f*.

sta·ple[1] [ˈsteipl] **1.** Haupterzeugnis *n*; *fig.* Hauptgegenstand *m*; Stapel *m* (*Faserwuchs der Wolle etc.*); **2.** Haupt...

sta·ple[2] [~] Haspe *f*, Krampe *f*; Heftklammer *f*.

sta·pler [ˈsteiplə] (Büro)Heftmaschine *f*.

star [stɑː] **1.** *allg.* Stern *m* (*fig.* *Schicksal*); *thea.* Star *m*; ♀*s and Stripes pl. Am.* Sternenbanner *n*; **2.** besternen; *thea.* die Hauptrolle spielen; ~ (*it*) glänzen; *thea.* gastieren; ~*ring* mit ... in der Hauptrolle.

star·board ⚓ [ˈstɑːbəd] **1.** Steuerbord *n*; **2.** *Ruder* steuerbord legen.

starch [stɑːtʃ] **1.** (Wäsche)Stärke *f*; *fig.* Steifheit *f*; ~ *flour* Stärkemehl *n*; **2.** stärken; ~*ed fig.* steif; ˈ**starch·i·ness** Steifheit *f*; ˈ**starch·y** □ steif; stärkehaltig.

star·dom [ˈstɑːdəm] (Star)Ruhm *m*.

stare [stɛə] **1.** Starren *n*; Staunen *n*; starrer Blick *m*; **2.** große Augen machen; (*at* an)starren, (an)staunen.

star·fish *zo.* [ˈstɑːfiʃ] Seestern *m*.

star·ing □ ['stɛəriŋ] starr (*Blick*); auffallend; grell.
stark [stɑːk] starr; völlig; ~ *naked* splitternackt.
star·light ['stɑːlait] Sternenlicht *n.*
star·ling[1] *orn.* ['stɑːliŋ] Star *m.*
star·ling[2] [~] Eisbrecher *m* *e-r Brücke.*
star·lit ['stɑːlit] sternenklar.
star·ry ['stɑːri] gestirnt; Stern(en)...; ~-'**eyed** *fig.* romantisch, wirklichkeitsfremd, verträumt.
star-span·gled ['stɑːspæŋgld] sternenbesät; *Star-Spangled Banner Am.* Sternenbanner *n.*
start [stɑːt] **1.** Auffahren *n*, Stutzen *n*; Ruck *m*; *Sport*: Start *m*; Aufbruch *m*; Anfang *m*; *fig.* Vorsprung *m*; *get the ~ of s.o.* j-m zuvorkommen; *give a ~* zs.-, auffahren; *s. fit*[2]; **2.** *v/i.* aufspringen, auffahren; stutzen (*at* vor *dat.*, bei); *Sport*: starten; abgehen, abfahren; aufbrechen, abreisen, sich aufmachen (*for* nach); *fig. von e-m Gedanken* ausgehen; anfangen (*on* mit *e-r Arbeit*; *doing* zu tun); *to ~ with* zunächst; *v/t.* in Gang bringen; *Maschine* anlassen; *Sport*: starten (lassen); *Wild* aufjagen; *fig.* anfangen; veranlassen (*doing* zu tun); *Geschäft* gründen, errichten; *Frage* aufwerfen.
start·er ['stɑːtə] *Sport*: Starter *m*; Läufer *m*, Rennteilnehmer *m*; *mot.* Anlasser *m.*
start·ing ['stɑːtiŋ] Ausgangs..., Anfangs...; '~-**point** Ausgangspunkt *m*; ~ **sal·a·ry** Anfangsgehalt *n.*
star·tle ['stɑːtl] (er-, auf)schrecken; '**star·tling** □ bestürzend, überraschend, aufsehenerregend.
star·va·tion [stɑː'veiʃən] (Ver-)Hungern *n*, Hungertod *m*; *attr.* Hunger...; **starve** verhungern (lassen); *fig.* verkümmern (lassen); **starve·ling** ['~liŋ] **1.** Hungerleider *m*; *fig.* Kümmerling *m*; **2.** verhungert; *fig.* verkümmert.
state [steit] **1.** Zustand *m*; Stand *m*; Pomp *m*, Staat *m*; *pol. mst* ♀ Staat *m*; ~ *of life* Lebensstellung *f*; ~ *of the art* ⊕ neueste Stand *m* der Technik; *in ~* feierlich; *get into a ~* F sich aufregen; **2.** angeben; darlegen, -stellen; feststellen; melden; *e-e Regel etc.* aufstellen; ~ **a·part·ment** Prunkzimmer *n*; ~ **coach** Staatskarosse *f*; '~**craft** *pol.* Staatskunst *f*; ♀ **De·part·ment** *Am. pol.* Außenministerium *n*; ~ **fu·ner·al** Staatsbegräbnis *n*; '**state·less** staatenlos; '**state·li·ness** Stattlichkeit *f*; Würde *f*; Pracht *f*; '**state·ly** stattlich; prächtig; erhaben; '**state·ment** Angabe *f*; Aussage *f*; Erklärung *f*; Darlegung *f*, Darstellung *f*; Feststellung *f*; Aufstellung *f*, ✝ (*of account* Konto)Auszug *m*; ⊕, ✝ Tarif *m*; **state mourn·ing** Staatstrauer *f*; '**state·room** Prunk-, Staatszimmer *n*; ⚓ Einzelkabine *f*; '**state·side** *Am.* F USA...; *go ~* heimkehren.
states·man ['steitsmən] Staatsmann *m*; '**states·man·like** staatsmännisch; '**states·man·ship** Staatskunst *f*; '**state-'sub·si·dized** staatlich subventioniert.
stat·ic ['stætik] statisch, Ruhe...; '**stat·ics** *pl. od. sg.* Statik *f*; *nur pl. Radio*: atmosphärische Störungen *f/pl.*
sta·tion ['steiʃən] **1.** Stand(ort) *m*; Stelle *f*; Stellung *f*; ⚔, ⚓, 🚂 Station *f*; Bahnhof *m*; (Rundfunk-, Fernseh)Sender *m*; Rang *m*, Stand *m*; ⚒ Beruf *m*, Geschäft *n*; **2.** aufstellen, postieren, stationieren; **sta·tion·ar·y** □ ['~ʃnəri] stillstehend; feststehend, stationär; ~ *engine* Standmotor *m*; '**sta·tion·er** Schreibwarenhändler *m*; ♀*s' Hall* Buchhändlerbörse *f in London*; '**sta·tion·er·y** Schreib- und Papierwaren *f/pl.*; **sta·tion-mas·ter** ['~ʃənmɑːstə] 🚂 Stationsvorsteher *m*; **sta·tion wag·on** *Am. mot.* Kombiwagen *m.*
stat·ism *pol.* ['steitizəm] staatlicher Dirigismus *m*, Planwirtschaft *f*; '**stat·ist** Anhänger *m* der Planwirtschaft.
sta·tis·ti·cal □ [stə'tistikəl] statistisch; **stat·is·ti·cian** [stætis'tiʃən] Statistiker *m*; **sta'tis·tics** *pl.* (*als Wissenschaft sg.*) Statistik *f*; *vital ~* Bevölkerungsstatistik *f*; F weibliche Körpermaße *f/pl.*
stat·u·ar·y ['stætjuəri] **1.** Bildhauer..., Statuen...; **2.** Bildhauerei *f*; Bildhauer *m*; **stat·ue** ['~tjuː] Standbild *n*, Plastik *f*, Statue *f*; **stat·u·esque** □ [~tju'esk] statuenhaft; **stat·u·ette** [~tju'et] Statuette *f.*
stat·ure ['stætʃə] Statur *f*, Wuchs *m*, Gestalt *f.*
sta·tus ['steitəs] Zustand *m*; Stel-

lung *f*, Rang *m*, Stand *m*; Status *m*; ~ *symbol*, *symbol of* ~ Statussymbol *n*.

stat·ute ['stætjuːt] Statut *n*, Satzung *f*; (Landes)Gesetz *n*; '~**-book** Gesetzessammlung *f*; ~ **law** Gesetzesrecht *n*; ~ **mile** Meile *f* (*1,609 km*).

stat·u·to·ry □ ['stætjutəri] gesetzlich.

staunch [stɔːntʃ] **1.** □ fest; zuverlässig, standhaft; treu; **2.** hemmen, stillen.

stave [steiv] **1.** Faßdaube *f*; Strophe *f*; **2.** (*irr.*) *mst* ~ *in* (*dat.*) den Boden einschlagen; ~ *off* abwehren; aufschieben.

staves ♪ [steivz] *pl. von staff 1.*

stay [stei] **1.** ⚓ Stag *n*; Stütztau *n*; *fig.* Stütze *f*; Aufschaub *m*, Frist *f*; Aufenthalt *m*; ~*s pl.* † Korsett *n*; **2.** bleiben; wohnen; (sich) aufhalten; Ausdauer haben; hemmen, (*dat.*) Einhalt gebieten; aufschieben; *Hunger* vorläufig stillen; stützen; ~ *in* zu Hause bleiben; nachsitzen; ~ *for* warten auf (*acc.*); ~ (*for*) *supper* zum Abendessen bleiben; ~ *put* F an Ort und Stelle bleiben; ~ *up* aufbleiben; ~ *the course* (bis zum Ende) durchhalten; ~*ing power* Ausdauer *f*; '~**-at-home** Stubenhocker *m*; '~-'**down strike** Sitzstreik *m der Bergleute*; '**stay·er** *Sport*: Steher *m*; *be a good* ~ Stehvermögen haben.

stead [sted] Stelle *f*, Statt *f*; *in his* ~ an seiner Stelle, statt seiner; *stand s.o. in good* ~ j-m zustatten kommen.

stead·fast □ ['stedfəst] fest, unerschütterlich; standhaft; unverwandt (*Blick*); '**stead·fast·ness** Festigkeit *f*, Standhaftigkeit *f*.

stead·i·ness ['stedinis] Festigkeit *f*.

stead·y ['stedi] **1.** □ (be)ständig; stetig; sicher; fest; ruhig; gleichmäßig; ✈ fest; unerschütterlich; zuverlässig; *go* ~ *with s.o.* mit j-m fest gehen; **2.** stetig *od.* sicher machen *od.* werden; (sich) festigen; stützen; (sich) beruhigen; halten; **3.** *Am.* F feste Freundin *f*.

steak [steik] (Beef)Steak *n*; Fischfilet *n*.

steal [stiːl] **1.** (*irr.*) *v/t.* stehlen (*a. fig.*); ~ *a march on s.o.* j-m zuvorkommen; *v/i.* sich stehlen *od.* schleichen; ~ *into* sich einschleichen in (*acc.*); **2.** *Am.* Korruptionsgeschäft *n*.

stealth [stelθ] Heimlichkeit *f*; *by* ~ heimlich; '**stealth·i·ness** Heimlichkeit *f*; '**stealth·y** □ verstohlen, heimlich.

steam [stiːm] **1.** Dampf *m*; Dunst *m*; *let off* ~ ⊕ Dampf ablassen; *fig.* sich Luft machen; **2.** Dampf...; **3.** *v/i.* dampfen; ~ *up* beschlagen (*Glas*); *v/t.* ausdünsten; mit Dampf behandeln, dämpfen; '~**·boat** Dampfschiff *n*; '~**-boil·er** Dampfkessel *m*; **steamed** beschlagen (*Fenster*); '**steam-en·gine** Dampfmaschine *f*; '**steam·er** ⚓ Dampfer *m*; ⊕ Dämpfer *m*; '**steam·i·ness** Dunstigkeit *f*.

steam...: '~**-roller 1.** Dampfwalze *f*; **2.** *fig.* niederwalzen; '~**·ship** = *steamboat*; ~ **tug** ⚓ Schleppdampfer *m*; '**steam·y** □ dampfig; dampfend; dunstig.

ste·a·rin ⚗ ['stiərin] Stearin *n*.

steed *rhet.* [stiːd] (Streit)Roß *n*.

steel [stiːl] **1.** Stahl *m*; Wetzstahl *m*; **2.** stählern; Stahl...; **3.** (ver)stählen; '~**-clad** stahlgepanzert; ~ **en·grav·ing** Stahlstich *m*; '~-'**plat·ed** gepanzert; '~**-works** *sg.* Stahlwerk *n*; '**steel·y** *mst fig.* stählern; '**steel·yard** Laufgewichtswaage *f*.

steep[1] [stiːp] **1.** steil, jäh; F toll, stark (*unerhört*); **2.** *poet.* jäher Abhang *m*.

steep[2] [~] einweichen; einlegen; eintauchen; tränken; *fig.* versenken (*in* in *acc.*).

steep·en ['stiːpən] steiler machen [*od.* werden.]

stee·ple ['stiːpl] Kirchturm *m*; '~**-chase** Hindernisrennen *n*; '~**·jack** Turm-, Schornsteinarbeiter *m*.

steep·ness ['stiːpnis] Steilheit *f*.

steer[1] [stiə] junger Ochse *m*.

steer[2] [~] steuern; ~ *clear of fig.* vermeiden; '**steer·a·ble** lenkbar.

steer·age ⚓ ['stiəridʒ] Steuerung *f*; Zwischendeck *n*; '~**-way** ⚓ Steuerfähigkeit *f*, -fahrt *f*.

steer·ing... ['stiəriŋ]: ~ **col·umn** *mot.* Lenksäule *f*; '~**-gear** ⚓ Ruderanlage *f*; '~**-wheel** Steuerrad *n*.

steers·man ⚓ ['stiəzmən] Rudergänger *m*.

stein [stain] Maßkrug *m*.

stel·lar ['stelə] Stern(en)...

stem[1] [stem] **1.** (Baum-, Wort-) Stamm *m*; Stiel *m*; Stengel *m*;

2. abstielen; *Am.* (ab)stammen (*from* von).

stem[2] [~] **1.** ⚓ Vordersteven *m*; **2.** *v/t.* sich stemmen *od.* ankämpfen gegen; *v/i. Schilauf*: stemmfahren; *~(ming) turn* Stemmbogen *m.*

stench [stentʃ] Gestank *m.*

sten·cil [ˈstensl] **1.** Schablone *f*; Matrize *f*; **2.** schablonieren; hektographieren.

ste·nog·ra·pher [steˈnɔgrəfə] Stenograph(in); **sten·o·graph·ic** [~nəˈgræfik] (*~ally*) stenographisch; **ste·nog·ra·phy** [~ˈnɔgrəfi] Stenographie *f*, Kurzschrift *f.*

step[1] [step] **1.** Schritt *m*, Tritt *m*; *fig.* (kurze) Strecke *f*; Fußstapfe *f*; (Treppen)Stufe *f*; Trittbrett *n*; (*a pair of*) *~s pl.* (eine) Trittleiter *f*; *in ~ with* in gleichem Schritt mit; *take ~s* Schritte unternehmen; **2.** *v/i.* schreiten; treten, gehen; *~ down* von *e-m Posten* zurücktreten; *~ in fig.* einschreiten; *~ on it! sl.* mach fix!; *~ out* ausschreiten, sich beeilen; *v/t. ~ out, ~ off* abschreiten; *~ up* in die Höhe bringen, ankurbeln.

step[2] [~] *in Zssgn* Stief...; **ˈ~·fa·ther** Stiefvater *m*; **ˈ~·moth·er** Stiefmutter *f.*

steppe [step] Steppe *f.*

step·ping-stone [ˈstepiŋstəun] Trittstein *m*; *fig.* Sprungbrett *n.*

ster·e·o [ˈstiəriəu] **1.** *typ.* Klischee *n*; **2.** ♪ Stereo...

ster·e·o... [ˈstiəriə]: **~·phon·ic** [~ˈfɔnik] stereophonisch, Stereo...; **ˈ~·scope** Stereoskop *n*; **ˈ~·type** **1.** Stereotype *f*; **2.** stereotypieren; *~d* stereotyp.

ster·ile [ˈsterail] steril; unfruchtbar; keimfrei; **ste·ril·i·ty** [~ˈriliti] Unfruchtbarkeit *f*; **ster·il·i·za·tion** [sterilaiˈzeiʃən] Sterilisierung *f*; **ˈster·i·lize** sterilisieren; unfruchtbar machen; entkeimen.

ster·ling [ˈstəːliŋ] vollwertig, echt; gediegen; ✝ Sterling...; *pound ~* Pfund *n* Sterling; **~ a·re·a** Sterlingblock *m.*

stern[1] □ [stəːn] ernst; finster; streng, hart.

stern[2] ⚓ [~] Heck *n*, Spiegel *m.*

stern·ness [ˈstəːnnis] Ernst *m*; Strenge *f.*

stern-post ⚓ [ˈstəːnpəust] Hintersteven *m.*

ster·num *anat.* [ˈstəːnəm] Brustbein *n.*

steth·o·scope ⚕ [ˈsteθəskəup] Stethoskop *n* (*Hörrohr*).

ste·ve·dore ⚓ [ˈstiːvidɔː] Schauermann *m*, Stauer *m.*

stew [stjuː] **1.** schmoren, dämpfen; **2.** Schmorgericht *n*; F Aufregung *f.*

stew·ard [ˈstjuəd] Verwalter *m*; Haushofmeister *m*; ⚓ Steward *m*; (Fest)Ordner *m*; **stew·ard·ess** ⚓, ✈ Stewardeß *f.*

stew...: **ˈ~-pan**, **ˈ~-pot** Schmorpfanne *f*, -topf *m.*

stick[1] [stik] **1.** Stock *m*; Stecken *m*; Stab *m*; (*Besen- etc.*)Stiel *m*; Stange *f Siegellack etc.*; F Klotz *m* (*unbeholfener Mensch*); *~s pl.* Kleinholz *n*; *the ~s pl. Am.* F hinterste Provinz *f*; **2.** ✓ mit Stöcken stützen.

stick[2] [~] (*irr.*) *v/i.* stecken (bleiben); haften; kleben (*to* an *dat.*); *fig.* sich stoßen (*at* an *dat.*); *~ at nothing* vor nichts zurückschrecken; *~ out, ~ up* hervorragen, -stehen; F standhalten; F bestehen (*for* auf *dat.*); *~ to* bleiben bei, festhalten an (*dat.*); *~ up for s.o.* j-m die Stange halten; *v/t.* (ab)stechen; (an)stecken, (an)heften; (an)kleben; F aushalten, ertragen; *~ it on sl.* unverschämte Preise verlangen; *~ out* herausstrecken; *~ it out* F durchhalten, nicht nachgeben; *~ up sl. Bank etc.* überfallen; **ˈstick·er** Klebezettel *m*; **ˈstick·i·ness** Klebrigkeit *f*; **ˈstick·ing-plas·ter** Heftpflaster *n*; **ˈstick-in-the-mud** **1.** rückschrittlich; **2.** Rückschrittler *m*; Spießer *m.*

stick·le [ˈstikl] Partei nehmen; **ˈstick·le·back** *ichth.* Stichling *m*; **ˈstick·ler** Eiferer *m*, Verfechter *m* (*for gen.*).

stick-up [ˈstikʌp] *a. ~ collar* F Stehkragen *m*; *sl.* Raubüberfall *m.*

stick·y □ [ˈstiki] kleb(e)rig; schmierig, schmutzig; zäh; *come to a ~ end sl.* ein schlimmes Ende nehmen; *be ~ about doing* F *et.* ungern tun.

stiff □ [stif] steif; starr; hartnäckig; hart, mühsam; stark (*Getränk*); *be bored ~* F zu Tode gelangweilt sein; *keep a ~ upper lip* die Ohren steifhalten; **ˈstiff·en** (sich) steifen; (sich) versteifen (*bsd.* ✝); erstarren (lassen); *fig.* stärken; **ˈstiff·en·er** steife Einlage *f*; **ˈstiff-ˈnecked** halsstarrig.

sti·fle[1] *vet.* [ˈstaifl] Kniegelenk *n.*

sti·fle[2] [~] ersticken (*a. fig.*).
stig·ma ['stigmə] (Brand-, Schand-) Mal *n*; Stigma *n*; ⚕ Symptom *n*; ⚘ Narbe *f*; **stig·ma·tize** ['~taiz] brandmarken.
stile [stail] Zauntritt *m*, -übergang *m*; ⊕ Seitenpfosten *m e-r Tür etc.*
sti·let·to [sti'letəu] Stilett *n*; ~ *heel* Pfennigabsatz *m*.
still[1] [stil] **1.** *adj.* still; ~ *wine* Stillwein *m*; **2.** Photographie *f* (*im Gegensatz zum Film*); **3.** *adv.* noch immer; *bei comp.* noch; **4.** *cj.* doch, dennoch, trotzdem; **5.** stillen; beruhigen.
still[2] [~] Destillierapparat *m*.
still...: '**~-birth** Totgeburt *f*; '**~-born** totgeboren; '**~-hunt** pirschen; '**~-hunt·ing** Pirschjagd *f*; ~ **life** Stillleben *n*; '**still·ness** Stille *f*, Ruhe *f*.
still-room ['stilrum] Vorratskammer *f*.
still·y *poet.* ['stili] still, ruhig.
stilt [stilt] Stelze *f*; '**stilt·ed** gespreizt, hochtrabend, geschraubt.
stim·u·lant ['stimjulənt] **1.** ⚕ stimulierend; **2.** ⚕ Reizmittel *n*; Genußmittel *n*; Anreiz *m*; **stim·u·late** ['~leit] (an)reizen; anregen; **stim·u'la·tion** Reizung *f*, Antrieb *m*; **stim·u·la·tive** ['~lətiv] (an)reizend; **stim·u·lus** ['~ləs] Antrieb *m* (to zu); Reizmittel *n*.
sting [stiŋ] **1.** Stachel *m von Insekten*; Stich *m*, Biß *m*; *fig.* Schärfe *f*; Antrieb *m*; **2.** (*irr.*) stechen; *fig.* schmerzen; peinigen; (an)treiben; *be stung sl.* geneppt werden (*for* um); '**sting·er** F schmerzhafter Schlag *m*.
stin·gi·ness ['stindʒinis] Geiz *m*; Kargheit *f*.
sting(·ing)-net·tle ⚘ ['stiŋ(iŋ)netl] Brennessel *f*.
stin·gy □ ['stindʒi] geizig; knapp, karg.
stink [stiŋk] **1.** Gestank *m*; **2.** (*irr.*) *v/i.* stinken (*of* nach; *sl. a. fig.*); *v/t.* verstänkern; '**stink·er** F Ekel *n*, ekelhafter Kerl *m*, gemeiner Typ *m*; geharnischter Brief *m*; vertracktes Problem *n*.
stint [stint] **1.** Einschränkung *f*; *zugewiesene* Arbeit *f*; **2.** kargen *od.* knausern mit; einschränken; *j.* knapp halten.
sti·pend ['staipend] Gehalt *n* (*bsd. e-s Pfarrers*); **sti'pen·di·ar·y** [~djəri] **1.** besoldet; **2.** Polizeirichter *m*.
stip·ple *paint.* ['stipl] punktieren.
stip·u·late ['stipjuleit] *a.* ~ *for* zur Bedingung machen, ausbedingen, festsetzen; **stip·u'la·tion** Abmachung *f*; Festsetzung *f*; Klausel *f*, Bedingung *f*.
stir[1] [stə:] **1.** Regung *f*; Bewegung *f*; Rühren *n*; Aufregung *f*; Aufsehen *n*; **2.** *v/t.* (um)rühren, bewegen; (an)schüren; aufregen; ~ *up* aufrühren; reizen, aufhetzen; *v/i.* sich rühren *od.* regen.
stir[2] *sl.* [~] Kittchen *n* (*Gefängnis*).
stir·ring ['stə:riŋ] auf-, erregend; bewegt.
stir·rup ['stirəp] Steigbügel *m*.
stitch [stitʃ] **1.** Stich *m*; Masche *f*; Seitenstechen *n*; *not have a dry* ~ *on one* keinen trockenen Faden am Leibe haben; *a* ~ *in time saves nine* gleich getan ist viel gespart; **2.** nähen; heften; *Buchbinderei*: heften, broschieren.
stoat *zo.* [stəut] Hermelin *n*.
stock [stɔk] **1.** (Baum)Strunk *m*; Pfropfunterlage *f*; Griff *m*, Schaft *m e-s Gerätes*, Kolben *m e-s Gewehrs*; Stamm *m*, Geschlecht *n*, Her-, Abkunft *f*; Roh-, Grundstoff *m*; Suppenstock *m*, (Fleisch-, Gemüse)Brühe *f*; Vorrat *m*, (Waren)Lager *n*; (Wissens)Schatz *m*; *a. live* ~ Vieh(bestand *m*) *n*; *hist.* Halsbinde *f*; ⚘ Levkoje *f*; ✝ (Stamm-, Anleihe)Kapital *n*; ~*s pl.* Effekten *pl.*, Aktien *f/pl.*; Staatspapiere *n/pl.*; ~*s pl.* ⚓ Stapel *m*; ~*s pl. hist.* Stock *m* (*für Gefangene*); *in* (*out of*) ~ (nicht) vorrätig; *take* ~ ✝ Inventur machen; *take* ~ *of fig.* sich klarwerden über (*acc.*), *et.* abschätzen; **2.** auf Lager, vorrätig; Lager...; *bsd. thea.* stehend, ständig; gängig; Standard...; stereotyp; ~ *play* Repertoirestück *n*; **3.** versehen, versorgen; *Waren* führen; vorrätig haben.
stock·ade [stɔ'keid] **1.** Einpfählung *f*, Staket *n*; **2.** einpfählen.
stock...: '**~-breed·er** Viehzüchter *m*; '**~-brok·er** Börsenmakler *m*; '**~-car** Viehwagen *m*; ~ **com·pa·ny** *thea.* ständiges Ensemble *n*; ~ **ex·change** Börse *f*; '**~-farm·er** Viehzüchter *m*; '**~-hold·er** Aktionär *m*.
stock·i·net [stɔki'net] Trikot *n*.

stock·ing ['stɔkiŋ] Strumpf *m.*
stock·ist ☤ ['stɔkist] Lagerhalter *m.*
stock...: '**~-in-'trade** Werk-, Rüstzeug *n*; '**~·job·ber** Börsenmakler *m*; **~ mar·ket** Börse *f*; '**~·pil·ing** (staatliche) Vorratshaltung *f*; '**~-'still** unbeweglich, mäuschenstill; '**~·tak·ing** Inventur *f.*
stock·y ['stɔki] untersetzt, stämmig.
stock·yard ['stɔkjɑ:d] Viehhof *m.*
stodge *sl.* [stɔdʒ] (sich) vollstopfen; '**stodg·y** □ schwer, unverdaulich; *fig.* schwerfällig; langweilig.
sto·gy, sto·gie *Am.* ['stəugi] billige Zigarre *f.*
sto·ic ['stəuik] **1.** stoisch; **2.** Stoiker *m*; '**sto·i·cal** □ *fig.* stoisch; **sto·i·cism** ['~sizəm] Stoizismus *m*; Gleichmut *m*, Gelassenheit *f.*
stoke [stəuk] *Feuer* (an)schüren; heizen, feuern; '**~·hold**, '**~·hole** ⚓ Heizraum *m*; '**stok·er** Heizer *m.*
stole[1] [stəul] Stola *f.*
stole[2] [~] *pret.*, '**sto·len** *p.p. von steal 1.*
stol·id □ ['stɔlid] unerschütterlich, gleichmütig; stur; **sto'lid·i·ty** Unerschütterlichkeit *f*, Gleichmut *m*; Sturheit *f.*
stom·ach ['stʌmək] **1.** Magen *m*; Leib *m*, Bauch *m*; *fig.* Neigung *f*, Lust *f* (*for* zu); **2.** verdauen, -tragen; *fig.* ertragen; '**~-ache** Magen-, Bauchschmerzen *m/pl.*; **sto·mach·ic** [stəu'mækik] **1.** (*~ally*) Magen...; magenstärkend; **2.** magenstärkendes Mittel *n.*
stomp *Am.* [stɔmp] (auf)stampfen.
stone [stəun] **1.** Stein *m*; (Obst-)Kern *m*; *a. precious ~* Edelstein *m*; *Gewichtseinheit von 6,35 kg*; **2.** steinern; Stein...; **3.** steinigen; *Obst* entsteinen; ♀ **Age** *die* Steinzeit; '**~-'blind** stockblind; '**~-'cold** eiskalt; '**~·crop** ⚘ Mauerpfeffer *m.*
stoned *sl.* [stəund] (stink)besoffen; *durch Drogen*: weg.
stone...: '**~-'dead** mausetot; '**~-'deaf** stocktaub; '**~-fruit** ⚘ Steinfrucht *f*; '**~-ma·son** Steinmetz *m*; '**~-pit** Steinbruch *m*; '**~·wall·ing** *Sport*: Mauern *n*; *pol.* Obstruktionspolitik *f*; '**~·ware** Steingut *n*; '**~·work** Steinmetzarbeit *f.*
ston·i·ness ['stəuninis] Härte *f.*
ston·y ['stəuni] steinig; *fig.* steinern; *a. ~-broke sl.* völlig pleite.
stood [stud] *pret. u. p.p. von stand.*
stooge *sl.* [stu:dʒ] **1.** *thea.* Stichwortgeber *m*; *fig.* Handlanger *m*; Prügelknabe *m*; **2.** den Dummen machen.
stool [stu:l] Schemel *m*, Hocker *m*; ⚕ Stuhlgang *m*; ⚘ Wurzelstock *m*; ⚘ Wurzelschößling *m*; '**~-pi·geon** *bsd. Am.* Spitzel *m*, Lockvogel *m.*
stoop [stu:p] **1.** *v/i.* sich bücken; sich erniedrigen *od.* herablassen; krumm gehen; *v/t. Kopf* neigen; **2.** gebeugte Haltung *f*; *Am.* Vorplatz *m*, Veranda *f.*
stop [stɔp] **1.** *v/t.* anhalten; hindern (*from* an *dat.*); aufhören (mit); *a. ~ up* (ver)stopfen; *Zahn* füllen, plombieren; *Weg* versperren; *Scheck* sperren; *Zahlung* einstellen; *Lohn* einbehalten; ♪ *Saite, Ton* greifen; *v/i.* stehenbleiben; aufhören; halten; F bleiben; *~ dead, ~ short* plötzlich *od.* unvermittelt anhalten; *~ at home* F zu Hause bleiben; *~ over* haltmachen, die Reise unterbrechen; *~ up late* F lange aufbleiben; **2.** Halt *m*, Einhalt *m*; Pause *f*; Hemmung *f*; ⊕ Anschlag *m*; Aufhören *n*, Ende *n*; Haltestelle *f*; *mst full ~ gr.* Punkt *m*; ♪ Klappe *f*; ♪ Griff *m*; *gr.* Verschlußlaut *m*; '**~·cock** ⊕ Absperrhahn *m*; '**~·gap** Notbehelf *m*, Lückenbüßer *m*; '**~·light** *Am.* Verkehrsampel *f*; '**~·o·ver** Aufenthalt *m*, Fahrtunterbrechung *f*; ✈ Zwischenlandung *f*; '**stop·page** Verstopfung *f*; (Arbeits-, Betriebs-, Zahlungs-) Einstellung *f*; Sperrung *f*; (Lohn-) Abzug *m*; Aufenthalt *m*; ⊕ Hemmung *f*; Betriebsstörung *f*; (Verkehrs)Stockung *f*; '**stop·per 1.** Stöpsel *m*; ⊕ Hemmer *m*; *~ circuit* ⚡ Sperrkreis *m*; **2.** (zu)stöpseln; '**stopping** Zahnfüllung *f*, Plombe *f*; '**stop-press** (Spalte *f* für) neueste Nachrichten *f/pl.*; '**stop-watch** Stoppuhr *f.*
stor·age ['stɔ:ridʒ] Lagerung *f*, Aufbewahrung *f*; ⚡ Speicherung *f*; Lagergeld *n*; *~ battery* Akkumulator *m.*
store [stɔ:] **1.** Vorrat *m*; *a. ~s pl. fig.* Fülle *f*; Lagerhaus *n*; *Am.* Laden *m*; *~s pl.* Kauf-, Warenhaus *n*; *~s pl.* ⚔, ⚓ Militär-, Schiffsbedarf *m*; *in ~* vorrätig, auf Lager; *be in ~ for* auf *j.* warten; *have in ~ for* bereit halten für; *set od. put great ~*

by Gewicht legen auf (*acc.*); **2.** *a.* ~ *up* (auf)speichern; unterbringen; verstauen; (ein)lagern; versehen, versorgen (*with* mit); ˈ**~·house** Lagerhaus *n*; *mst fig.* Schatzkammer *f*; ˈ**~·keep·er** Lagerverwalter *m*; *Am.* Ladenbesitzer *m*; ˈ**~-room** Vorratskammer *f*.

sto·rey(ed) [ˈstɔːri(d)] *s. story*², *storied*².

sto·ried¹ [ˈstɔːrid] in Geschichten *od.* Sagen gefeiert.

sto·ried² [~] mit ... Stockwerken; [...stöckig.]

stork [stɔːk] Storch *m*.

storm [stɔːm] **1.** Sturm *m* (*a.* ⚔); Gewitter *n*; Unwetter *n*; *take by* ~ im Sturm nehmen; **2.** stürmen (*a.* ⚔); toben, wüten (*at* gegen, über *acc.*); ˈ**storm·y** □ stürmisch; ~ *petrel zo.* Sturmschwalbe; *fig.* Unruhestifter *m*.

sto·ry¹ [ˈstɔːri] Geschichte *f*; Erzählung *f*; Märchen *n*; Darstellung *f*; Handlung *f e-r Dichtung*; F Lüge *f*; *short* ~ Erzählung *f*.

sto·ry² [~] Stock(werk *n*) *m*, Geschoß *n*.

sto·ry-tell·er [ˈstɔːritelə] (Märchen)Erzähler(in); F Lügner(in).

stout [staut] **1.** □ stark, kräftig, stämmig; derb; dick; tapfer; **2.** Starkbier *n*; ˈ**~**ˈ**heart·ed** beherzt; ˈ**stout·ness** Stärke *f*; Mut *m*, Mannhaftigkeit *f*; *Sport*: Ausdauer *f*.

stove [stəuv] **1.** Ofen *m*; Herd *m*; ⚘ Treibhaus *n*; **2.** trocknen; (durch Hitze) desinfizieren; **3.** *pret. u. p.p. von stave 2*; ˈ**~·pipe** Ofenrohr *n*; *Am.* F Zylinder(hut) *m*.

stow [stəu] (ver)stauen, packen; ˈ**stow·age** Stauen *n*, Packen *n*; ⚓ Stauraum *m*; ˈ**stow·a·way** ⚓ blinder Passagier *m*.

stra·bis·mus ⚕ [strəˈbizməs] Schielen *n*.

strad·dle [ˈstrædl] (die Beine) spreizen; rittlings sitzen auf (*dat.*); mit gespreizten Beinen stehen über (*dat.*); ⚔ eingabeln; *Am. fig.* es mit beiden Parteien halten; schwanken.

strafe [strɑːf] (be)strafen; ⚔ bombardieren; ✈ mit Bordwaffen beschießen.

strag·gle [ˈstrægl] verstreut *od.* einzeln liegen; umherstreifen; bummeln; *fig.* abschweifen; ✿ wuchern; ˈ**strag·gler** Umherstreifer *m*; ⚔ Nachzügler *m*; ˈ**strag·gling** □ weitläufig, lose.

straight [streit] **1.** *adj.* gerade; *fig.* aufrichtig, ehrlich; glatt (*Haar*); *Am.* pur, unverdünnt; *Am. pol.* hundertprozentig; *put* ~ in Ordnung bringen; **2.** *Rennsport*: (Ziel-) Gerade *f*; **3.** *adv.* gerade(wegs); geradeaus; direkt; sofort, stracks; ~ *away* sofort; ~ *out* rundheraus; ˈ**straight·en** geademachen *od.* -werden; ~ *out* in Ordnung bringen; entwirren; **straight**ˈ**for·ward** □ gerade; ehrlich, redlich; ˈ**straight·way** sofort, unverzüglich.

strain¹ [strein] **1.** ⊕ (verformende) Spannung *f*, Dehnung *f*; Anspannung *f*, (Über)Anstrengung *f*; starke Inanspruchnahme *f* (*on gen.*); Druck *m* (*on* auf *acc.*); ⚕ Zerrung *f*; Ton *m*; *mst* ~*s pl.* ♪ Weise *f*; Art und Weise *f*; Hang *m* (*of* zu); *put a great* ~ *on* starke Anforderungen stellen an (*acc.*); **2.** *v/t.* (an)spannen; anstrengen (*a. fig.*); überspannen, -anstrengen; ⊕ beanspruchen; ⚕ zerren; durchseihen, -drücken, -pressen; *v/i.* sich spannen; sich anstrengen; sich abmühen (*after* um); zerren (*at* an *dat.*).

strain² [~] Abstammung *f*, Geschlecht *n*; Art *f*.

strain·er [ˈstreinə] Durchschlag *m*; Seihtuch *n*; Filter *m*; Sieb *n*.

strait [streit] **1.** (*in Eigennamen* ♀*s pl.*) Meerenge *f*, Straße *f*; ~*s pl.* Klemme *f*, Not *f*; **2.** ~ *jacket* Zwangsjacke *f*; ˈ**strait·en** beschränken; ~*ed* dürftig; in Not (*for* um); **strait-laced** [ˈ~leist] engherzig, prüde; ˈ**strait·ness** Enge *f*; Beschränktheit *f*; Not *f*.

strand¹ [strænd] **1.** Strand *m*; **2.** *v/t.* auf den Strand setzen; *fig.* stranden lassen; ~*ed* gestrandet (*a. fig.*); *mot.* steckengeblieben; *v/i.* stranden.

strand² [~] Ducht *f e-s Taus*; (Haar)Strähne *f*; *fig.* Ader *f*.

strange □ [streindʒ] fremd (*a. fig.*); seltsam, befremdend, sonderbar, merkwürdig; ˈ**strange·ness** Fremdheit *f*; Seltsamkeit *f*; ˈ**stran·ger** Fremde *m*, Unbekannte *m*; Neuling *m* (*to* in *dat.*).

stran·gle [ˈstræŋgl] erwürgen; *fig.*

unterdrücken; '~·**hold** Würgegriff *m*.
stran·gu·late ⚕ ['stræŋgjuleit] abschnüren; strangulieren, erwürgen; **stran·gu'la·tion** Erwürgung *f*; ⚕ Abschnürung *f*.
strap [stræp] **1.** Riemen *m*; Gurt *m*; Band *n*; **2.** an-, festschnallen; mit Riemen peitschen; '~·**hang·er** F stehender Fahrgast *m*; '**strap·less** trägerlos (*Kleid*); '**strap·ping 1.** drall (*Mädchen*); stramm, stämmig; **2.** ⚕ Heftpflasterverband *m*.
stra·ta ['strɑːtə] *pl. von stratum.*
strat·a·gem ['strætidʒəm] (Kriegs-) List *f*.
stra·te·gic [strə'tiːdʒik] (~*ally*) strategisch; **strat·e·gist** ['strætidʒist] Stratege *m*; '**strat·e·gy** Kriegskunst *f*, Strategie *f*.
strat·i·fy ['strætifai] schichten.
stra·to·cruis·er ✈ ['strætəukruːzə] Stratosphärenflugzeug *n*.
strat·o·sphere *phys.* ['strætəusfiə] Stratosphäre *f*.
stra·tum *geol.* ['strɑːtəm], *pl.* **strata** ['~tə] Schicht *f* (*a. fig.*), Lage *f*.
straw [strɔː] **1.** Stroh *n*; Strohhalm *m* (*a. fig.*); *I don't care a ~* ich mache mir gar nichts daraus; *a man of ~ fig.* ein Strohmann *m*; **2.** Stroh...; *~ vote Am. pol.* Probeabstimmung *f*; '~·**ber·ry** Erdbeere *f*; '**straw·y** strohig.
stray [strei] **1.** irregehen; sich verirren; abirren (*from* von; *a. fig.*); umherschweifen; **2.** *a.* ~*ed* verirrt; vereinzelt; **3.** verirrtes Tier *n*; ~*s pl.* ⚡ atmosphärische Störungen *f/pl.*
streak [striːk] **1.** Strich *m*, Streifen *m*; *fig.* Ader *f*, Spur *f*; kurze Periode *f*; *~ of lightning* Blitzstrahl *m*; **2.** streifen; jagen; '**streak·y** □ streifig; durchwachsen (*Speck etc.*).
stream [striːm] **1.** Wasserlauf *m*; Bach *m*; Strom *m*; Strömung *f*; *Schule*: (Leistungs)Zug *m*; *go with the ~ fig.* mit dem Strom schwimmen; **2.** *v/i.* strömen; überströmen (*Augen*); triefen (*Schirm etc.*); flattern (*Flagge, Haar*); *v/t.* strömen lassen; ausströmen; '**stream·er** Wimpel *m*; (fliegendes) Band *n*; Papierschlange *f*; Lichtstrahl *m beim Nordlicht*; *Zeitung*: Schlagzeile *f*; '**stream·ing** *Schule*: Einteilung *f* in Leistungsgruppen; **stream·let** ['~lit] Bächlein *n*.
stream·line ['striːmlain] **1.** Stromlinie *f*; **2.** stromlinienförmig machen; *fig.* modernisieren.
street [striːt] Straße *f*; *not in the same ~ with* F nicht zu vergleichen mit; '~-**car** *bsd. Am.* Straßenbahnwagen *m*; '~·**walk·er** Straßendirne *f*.
strength [streŋθ] Stärke *f*, Kraft *f* (*a. fig.*); ⚔, ⚓ (Ist)Stärke *f*; *on the ~ of* auf (*acc.*) hin, auf Grund *od.* kraft (*gen.*); '**strength·en** *v/t.* stärken, kräftigen; bestärken; *v/i.* erstarken.
stren·u·ous □ ['strenjuəs] rührig, emsig; eifrig; anstrengend; '**stren·u·ous·ness** Eifer *m*, Emsigkeit *f*.
stress [stres] **1.** Druck *m*; Nachdruck *m*; Betonung *f*; Schwergewicht *n*; Ton *m*; ⊕ Spannung *f*, Beanspruchung *f*; *psych.* Stress *m*; *lay ~ (up)on* Nachdruck legen auf (*acc.*), betonen; **2.** betonen; ⊕ spannen, beanspruchen.
stretch [stretʃ] **1.** *v/t.* strecken; (aus)dehnen; *mst ~ out die Hand etc.* ausstrecken; (an)spannen; *fig.* überspannen; *~ one's legs* sich die Beine vertreten; *v/i.* sich (er)strekken; sich dehnen (lassen) (*into* [bis] zu); *fig.* aufschneiden; *a. ~ one's powers* sich bis zum äußersten anstrengen; **2.** Strecken *n*; Dehnung *f*; Spannung *f*; Anspannung *f*; Übertreibung *f*; Überschreitung *f*; Strecke *f*, Fläche *f*; *at a ~* in e-m Zug, hintereinander, ohne Unterbrechung; *on the ~* (an)gespannt; '**stretch·er** Tragbahre *f*; Streckvorrichtung *f*; Stemmbrett *n im Boot*; '**stretch·er-bear·er** Krankenträger *m*.
strew [struː] (*irr.*) (be)streuen; **strewn** [struːn] *p.p. von strew.*
stri·ate ['straiit], **stri·at·ed** [~'eitid] gerieft.
strick·en ['strikən] ge-, betroffen, befallen, heimgesucht (*with* von); *~ in age* bejahrt.
strict [strikt] streng; genau; *~ly speaking* streng genommen; '**strict·ness** Genauigkeit *f*; Strenge *f*; **stric·ture** ['~tʃə] *oft ~s pl.* kritische Bemerkung *f*, scharfe Kritik *f*; ⚕ Verengung *f*.
strid·den ['stridn] *p.p. von stride 1.*
stride [straid] **1.** (*irr.*) *v/t.* über-, durchschreiten; *v/i. a. ~ out* aus-

schreiten; **2.** (weiter) Schritt *m*; *get into one's* ~ richtig in Schwung kommen.

stri·dent □ [ˈstraidənt] knarrend, kreischend; grell (*Stimme*).

strife *lit.* [straif] Streit *m*, Hader *m*.

strike [straik] **1.** Ausstand *m*, Streik *m*; (Öl-, Erz)Fund *m*; *fig.* Treffer *m*; ⚔ (Luft)Angriff *m auf ein Einzelziel*; *Am. Baseball*: Verlustpunkt *m bei Schlagfehler etc.*; *be on* ~ streiken; *go on* ~ in den Ausstand treten; **2.** (*irr.*) *v/t.* treffen, stoßen; schlagen; prägen; gegen *od.* auf *et.* (*acc.*) schlagen *od.* stoßen; stoßen auf (*acc.*), (auf)finden; *Wort, Flagge, Segel* streichen; *Zelt* abbrechen; *Schlag* führen, tun; *Ton* anschlagen; auffallen (*dat.*); ergreifen; *Handel* abschließen; *Streichholz, Licht* anzünden; *Wurzel* schlagen; *j. blind, sprachlos etc.* machen; *s. attitude*; ~ *a balance* die Bilanz *od.* den Saldo ziehen; ~ *oil* Erdöl finden; F Glück haben; ~ *off* ausstreichen; ~ *out Plan etc.* entwerfen; ausstreichen; ~ *through* durchstreichen; ~ *up* anstimmen; *Freundschaft* schließen; *v/i.* schlagen (*at* nach); ⚓ auf Grund stoßen, auflaufen; ⚓, ⚔ die Flagge streichen; die Arbeit einstellen, streiken; schlagen (*Uhr*); einschlagen (*Blitz*); angehen (*Streichholz*); Wurzel schlagen; *in e-r Richtung* gehen; ~ *home* (richtig, *fig.* empfindlich) treffen; ~ *in* nach innen schlagen; sich einmischen; ~ *into* verfallen in (*acc.*); ~ *up* einsetzen (*Orchester etc.*); ~ *upon the ear* das Ohr treffen; ~ **bal·lot** Urabstimmung *f*; ˈ**~-bound** durch Streik lahmgelegt; ˈ**~-break·er** Streikbrecher *m*; ˈ**~-pay** Streikgeld *n*; ˈ**strik·er** Schläger(in); Streikende *m, f*; ⊕ Schlagbolzen *m*; *Sport*: Stürmer *m*.

strik·ing □ [ˈstraikiŋ] Schlag...; auffallend; eindrucksvoll; treffend; ausständig, streikend.

string [striŋ] **1.** Schnur *f*; Bindfaden *m*; Band *n*; Gängelband *n*; *Am.* F Bedingung *f*; Haken *m*; (Bogen)Sehne *f*; ♀ Faser *f*, (Blatt-)Rippe *f*; ♪ Saite *f*; Reihe *f*, Kette *f*; Schar *f*; ~*s pl.* ♪ Saiteninstrumente *n/pl.*, Streicher *m/pl.*; *harp on the same* ~ auf ein u. derselben Sache herumreiten; *have two* ~*s to one's bow* zwei Eisen im Feuer haben; *pull the* ~*s* der Drahtzieher sein; *there are* ~*s attached to it* F die Sache hat e-n Haken; **2.** (*irr.*) *Bogen* spannen; *Perlen etc.* aufreihen; *Geige etc.* besaiten (*a. fig.*), bespannen; *grüne Bohnen* abziehen; *Am. sl. j.* verkohlen; ~ *up* F aufknüpfen, -hängen; *be strung up* angespannt *od.* erregt sein; ~ **bag** Einkaufsnetz *n*; ~ **band** ♪ Streichorchester *n*; ~ **bean** ♀ grüne Bohne *f*; ~ **cor·re·spon·dent** *Am.* freier Mitarbeiter *m e-r Zeitung*; **stringed** ♪ Saiten...; ...-saitig.

strin·gen·cy [ˈstrindʒənsi] Strenge *f*, Schärfe *f*; bindende *od.* zwingende Kraft *f*; ✝ Knappheit *f*; ˈ**strin·gent** □ streng, scharf; bindend, zwingend; starr, fest; ✝ knapp (*Geld*).

string·er [ˈstriŋə] = *string correspondent.*

string·y [ˈstriŋi] faserig; zäh.

strip [strip] **1.** *v/t.* entkleiden (*a. fig.*; *of gen.*), *j.* ausziehen; *Rinde etc.* abziehen; *fig.* entblößen, berauben (*of gen.*); ⊕ auseinandernehmen; ⚓ abtakeln; *a.* ~ *off Kleid etc.* ausziehen, abstreifen; *v/i.* F sich ausziehen; **2.** *schmaler* Streifen *m*; ~ **car·toon** = *comics.*

stripe [straip] *andersfarbiger* Streifen *m*; ⚔ Tresse *f*; **striped** gestreift.

strip-light·ing [ˈstriplaitiŋ] Neonbeleuchtung *f*.

strip·ling [ˈstripliŋ] Bürschchen *n*.

strip-tease [ˈstripti:z] Striptease *n* (*Entkleidungsnummer*).

strive [straiv] (*irr.*) streben (*after, for* nach), sich bemühen (um); ringen (*against* gegen, *for* um); **striv·en** [ˈstrivn] *p.p. von strive.*

strode [strəud] *pret. von stride* 1.

stroke [strəuk] **1.** Schlag *m*; Streich *m*, Hieb *m*; Stoß *m*; ⚕ Schlaganfall *m*; ⊕ (Kolben)Hub *m*; (Pinsel-, Feder)Strich *m* (*a. fig.*); Schlag *m der Uhr*; *Rudern*: Schlagmann *m*; ~ *of genius* genialer Einfall *m*; ~ *of luck* glücklicher Zufall *m*; **2.** streiche(l)n; *Boot* als Schlagmann rudern.

stroll [strəul] **1.** schlendern, bummeln; spazierengehen; umherziehen; **2.** Bummel *m*; Spaziergang *m*; ˈ**stroll·er** Bummler(in), Spa-

ziergänger(in); *Am.* (Falt)Sportwagen *m.*
strong □ [strɔŋ] *allg.* stark; kräftig, kraftvoll; *fig.* tüchtig; energisch, eifrig; fest (*Überzeugung*); stark (*an Zahl*; *Getränk*, *Geruch*, *Geschmack*); schwer (*Zigarre*, *Speise etc.*); *gr.* stark (*ablautend*); *s. language*; *feel* ~(*ly*) *about* sich aufregen über (*acc.*); s-e besondere Meinung haben über; *be going* ~ F s-n Mann stehen; (noch) rüstig sein; **'~-box** Stahlkassette *f*; **'~-hold** Festung *f*; *fig.* Bollwerk *n*, Hochburg *f*; **'~-'mind·ed** willensstark; **'~-room** Stahlkammer *f*; **'~-'willed** eigenwillig; dickköpfig.
strop [strɔp] **1.** Streichriemen *m*; ⚓ Stropp *n*; **2.** *Messer* abziehen.
stro·phe ['strəufi] Strophe *f.*
strop·py F ['strɔpi] patzig, unwirsch.
strove [strəuv] *pret. von strive.*
struck [strʌk] *pret. u. p.p. von strike 2.*
struc·tur·al □ ['strʌktʃərəl] baulich; Bau...; organisch; strukturell; **'struc·ture** Bau(werk *n*) *m*; Struktur *f*, Gefüge *n*; Gebilde *n.*
strug·gle ['strʌgl] **1.** kämpfen, ringen (*for* um); sich (ab)mühen; sich quälen; sich sträuben; zappeln; **2.** Kampf *m*; Ringen *n* (*for* um); Anstrengung *f*; **'strug·gler** Kämpfer(in).
strum [strʌm] **1.** klimpern; **2.** Geklimper *n.*
strum·pet † ['strʌmpit] Hure *f*, Dirne *f.*
strung [strʌŋ] *pret. u. p.p. von string 2.*
strut [strʌt] **1.** *v/i.* stolzieren; *v/t.* ⊕ verstreben, abstützen; **2.** Stolzieren *n*; ⊕ Strebe(balken *m*) *f*; Stütze *f.*
strych·nine ⚗ ['strikni:n] Strychnin *n.*
stub [stʌb] **1.** (Baum)Stumpf *m*; Stummel *m*; *Am.* Kontrollabschnitt *m*; **2.** *mst* ~ *up* ausroden; *Land* roden; sich *den Fuß* stoßen; ~ *out Zigarette* ausdrücken.
stub·ble ['stʌbl] Stoppel(n *pl.*) *f.*
stub·bly ['stʌbli] stopp(e)lig.
stub·born □ ['stʌbən] eigensinnig; widerspenstig; halsstarrig, stur; hartnäckig (*a. Widerstand*); unerbittlich (*Tatsachen*); **'stub·born-ness** Halsstarrigkeit *f etc.*
stub·by ['stʌbi] stummelhaft.
stuc·co ['stʌkəu] **1.** Stuck *m*; **2.** mit Stuck verzieren, stuckieren.
stuck [stʌk] *pret. u. p.p. von stick*[2]; ~ *on Am.* F verschossen in *j.*; **'~-'up** F hochnäsig.
stud[1] [stʌd] **1.** (Wand)Pfosten *m*; Beschlagnagel *m*, Buckel *m*, Knauf *m*; *herausnehmbarer* Kragenknopf *m*; **2.** beschlagen; besetzen.
stud[2] [~] Gestüt *n*; **'~-book** Gestütbuch *n.*
stud·ding △ ['stʌdiŋ] Fachwerk *n.*
stu·dent ['stju:dənt] Student(in); Studierende *m, f*; Forscher(in); Gelehrte *m, f*; Büchermensch *m*; ~ **hostel** Studentenwohnheim *n*; **'stu-dent·ship** Stipendium *n.*
stud·ied □ ['stʌdid] einstudiert (*Pose*); gesucht (*Stil*); gewollt (*Kränkung*).
stu·di·o ['stju:diəu] Atelier *n*; Studio *n*; *Radio*: Aufnahme-, Senderaum *m*; ~ **couch** Schlafcouch *f.*
stu·di·ous □ ['stju:djəs] fleißig; bedacht (*of* auf *acc.*); bemüht (*to inf.* zu *inf.*); geflissentlich; **'stu·di·ous-ness** Fleiß *m*, Eifer *m*, Beflissenheit *f.*
stud·y ['stʌdi] **1.** Studium *n*; Studier-, Arbeitszimmer *n*; *paint. etc.* Studie *f*; *be in a brown* ~ versunken *od.* geistesabwesend sein; **2.** *v/i.* studieren (*for acc.*); *v/t.* studieren (*a. fig.*); sich *et.* genau ansehen; sich bemühen um; einstudieren.
stuff [stʌf] **1.** Stoff *m*; Zeug *n* (*a. contp.*); † Wollstoff *m*; *fig.* Unsinn *m*; **2.** *v/t.* stopfen (*into* in *acc.*); voll-, ausstopfen; ~ *up* verstopfen; ~*ed shirt Am. sl.* Fatzke *m*; *v/i.* sich vollstopfen; **'stuff·ing** Füllung *f*; ⊕ Polsterung *f*; Füllsel *n*; **'stuff·y** □ dumpf(ig), muffig, stickig (*Luft etc.*); F verschnupft, verärgert; F etepetete.
stul·ti·fi·ca·tion [stʌltifi'keiʃən] Veralberung *f*, Blamage *f*; **stul-ti·fy** ['~fai] lächerlich machen, blamieren; *et.* hinfällig machen.
stum·ble ['stʌmbl] **1.** Stolpern *n*; Versehen *n*; Fehltritt *m*; **2.** stolpern; straucheln (*a. fig.*); ~ *upon* stoßen auf (*acc.*); **'stum·bling--block** *fig.* Stein *m* des Anstoßes.
stump [stʌmp] **1.** Stumpf *m*, Stummel *m*; *Zeichnen*: Wischer *m*;

Kricket: Torstab *m*; F Wahlpropaganda *f*; ~s *pl.* F Stelzen *f/pl.* (*Beine*); *stir one's ~s* F sich beeilen; **2.** *v/t. Kricket*: *Schläger* abwerfen; F verblüffen; *Am.* F herausfordern; ~ *up sl.* berappen (*zahlen*); ~ *the country* als Wahlredner im Land herumziehen; ~*ed for* verlegen um; *v/i.* (daher)stapfen, stelzen; '~-'**or·a·tor** Wahl-, Volksredner *m*; '**stump·y** □ gedrungen (*Körperbau*); plump.

stun [stʌn] betäuben (*a. fig.*); ~*ned fig.* verdutzt, sprachlos.

stung [stʌŋ] *pret. u. p.p. von sting* 2.

stunk [stʌŋk] *pret. u. p.p. von stink* 2.

stun·ner F ['stʌnə] Bombenkerl *m*; Mordsding *n*; '**stun·ning** □ F toll, famos.

stunt[1] F [stʌnt] **1.** Kraft-, Kunststück *n*; (Reklame)Trick *m*; Sensation *f*; Schlager *m*; ✈ Kunstflug *m*; **2.** kunstfliegen.

stunt[2] [~] im Wachstum hindern; '**stunt·ed** verkümmert.

stupe ⚕ [stju:p] **1.** heißer Umschlag *m*; **2.** heiße Umschläge legen auf (*acc.*).

stu·pe·fac·tion [stju:pi'fækʃən] Betäubung *f*; Verblüffung *f*; **stu·pe·fy** ['~fai] *fig.* betäuben; verblüffen; verdummen.

stu·pen·dous □ [stju:'pendəs] erstaunlich.

stu·pid □ ['stju:pid] dumm, einfältig, stumpfsinnig; blöd (*langweilig*); **stu'pid·i·ty** Dummheit *f etc.*

stu·por ['stju:pə] Erstarrung *f*, Betäubung *f*.

stur·di·ness ['stə:dinis] Derbheit *f*; Handfestigkeit *f*; '**stur·dy** derb, kräftig, stark; stämmig; stramm; handfest.

stur·geon *ichth.* ['stə:dʒən] Stör *m*.

stut·ter ['stʌtə] **1.** stottern; **2.** Stottern *n*; '**stut·ter·er** Stotterer *m*.

sty[1] [stai] Schweinestall *m*, Koben *m*.

sty[2] [~] Gerstenkorn *n am Auge*.

style [stail] **1.** Griffel *m* (*a.* ⚘); Stichel *m*; Sonde *f*; Stil *m*; *Schneiderei*: Machart *f*; Betitelung *f*; Zeitrechnung *f*; *in* ~ vornehm; *under the* ~ *of* ... ⚕ unter der Firma ...; **2.** (be)nennen, betiteln.

styl·ish □ ['stailiʃ] stilvoll; stilgerecht, elegant; '**styl·ish·ness** Eleganz *f*.

styl·ist ['stailist] Stilist(in).

sty·lo F ['stailəu], **sty·lo·graph** ['~gra:f] Tintenkuli *m*.

sty·lus ['stailəs] *Plattenspieler*: Nadel *f*.

styp·tic ['stiptik] blutstillend(es Mittel *n*).

sua·sion ['sweiʒən] Überredung *f*.

suave □ [swa:v] verbindlich (*Wesen etc.*); mild (*Wein etc.*); '**suav·i·ty** Verbindlichkeit *f*; Milde *f*.

sub F [sʌb] *abbr. für subordinate* 2; *subscription*; *substitute* 2; *submarine* 2.

sub... [~] *mst* Unter...; unter...; Neben...; Hilfs...; ein wenig ...; fast ...

sub·ac·id ['sʌb'æsid] säuerlich; *fig.* bissig.

sub·al·tern ['sʌbltən] Untergebene *m*; ⚔ Subalternoffizier *m*.

sub·a·tom·ic ['sʌbə'tɔmik] subatomisch, innerhalb des Atoms.

sub·com·mit·tee ['sʌbkəmiti] Unterausschuß *m*.

sub·con·scious □ ['sʌb'kɔnʃəs] unterbewußt.

sub·con·tract [sʌb'kɔntrækt] Nebenvertrag *m*.

sub·cu·ta·ne·ous □ ['sʌbkju:teinjəs] subkutan, unter *od.* die Haut.

sub·deb *Am.* F [sʌb'deb] Backfisch *m*, junges Mädchen *n*.

sub·di·vide [sʌbdi'vaid] (sich) unterteilen; **sub·di·vi·sion** ['~viʒən] Unterteilung *f*; Unterabteilung *f*.

sub·due [səb'dju:] unterwerfen; bezwingen; bändigen; unterdrücken, verdrängen; *Licht etc.* dämpfen.

sub·head(·**ing**) ['sʌbhed(iŋ)] Untertitel *m*.

sub·ja·cent [sʌb'dʒeisənt] darunter *od.* tiefer liegend.

sub·ject ['sʌbdʒikt] **1.** unterworfen (*to dat.*); untergeben, abhängig; *pred.* untertan; unterliegend (*to dat.*); *be* ~ *to* neigen zu; ~ *to a fee od. duty* gebührenpflichtig; **2.** *adv.* ~ *to* vorbehaltlich (*gen.*); ~ *to change without notice* Änderungen vorbehalten; ~ *to this* mit diesem Vorbehalt; **3.** Untertan *m*, Staatsangehörige *m*; *phls., gr.* Subjekt *n*; *a.* ~ *matter* Thema *n*, Gegenstand *m*; ♪ Satz *m*, Thema *n*; *paint.* Sujet *n*; Vorgang *m* (*Akte*); Anlaß *m*; (Lehr-, Studien)Fach *n*; **4.** [səb'dʒekt] unterwerfen; ~ *to e-r Prü-*

fung etc. unterziehen; *e-r Gefahr etc.* aussetzen; ~ **cat·a·logue** Schlagwortkatalog *m*; **sub'jec·tion** Unterwerfung *f*; **sub'jec·tive** □ subjektiv.
sub·join ['sʌb'dʒɔin] noch beifügen.
sub·ju·gate ['sʌbdʒugeit] unterjochen; **sub·ju'ga·tion** Unterjochung *f*.
sub·junc·tive *gr.* [səb'dʒʌŋktiv] *a.* ~ *mood* Konjunktiv *m*.
sub·lease ['sʌb'li:s], **sub·let** ['~'let] (*irr. let*) untervermieten, -verpachten.
sub·li·mate ⚗ **1.** ['sʌblimit] Sublimat *n*; **2.** ['~meit] sublimieren; **sub·li'ma·tion** Sublimierung *f*; **sub·lime** [sə'blaim] **1.** □ erhaben, sublim; großartig; **2.** *the* ~ das Erhabene; **3.** ⚗ sublimieren; *fig.* läutern.
sub·lim·i·nal *psych.* [səb'liminəl] unterschwellig.
sub·lim·i·ty [sə'blimiti] Erhabenheit *f*.
sub-ma·chine gun ['sʌbmə'ʃi:ngʌn] Maschinenpistole *f*.
sub·ma·rine [sʌbmə'ri:n] **1.** unterseeisch; Untersee...; **2.** ⚓ Unterseeboot *n*.
sub·merge [səb'mə:dʒ] untertauchen (*a. v/i.*); überschwemmen; **sub·mers·i·bil·i·ty** [~sə'biliti] Tauchfähigkeit *f*; **sub'mer·sion** Untertauchen *n*; Überschwemmung *f*.
sub·mis·sion [səb'miʃən] Unterwerfung *f* (*to* unter *acc.*); Unterbreitung *f*, Vorlage *f*; **sub'mis·sive** □ unterwürfig.
sub·mit [səb'mit] *v/t.* unterwerfen; anheimstellen; vorlegen, unterbreiten, einreichen; *bsd. parl.* ergebenst bemerken; *v/i. a.* ~ *o.s.* sich unterwerfen *od.* unterordnen (*to dat.*); sich *e-r Operation* unterziehen; *fig.* sich fügen *od.* ergeben (*to* in *acc.*).
sub·nor·mal [səb'nɔ:məl] von unterdurchschnittlicher Intelligenz; schwachsinnig.
sub·or·di·nate **1.** □ [sə'bɔ:dnit] untergeordnet; untergeben; ~ *clause gr.* Nebensatz *m*; **2.** [~] Untergebene *m*; **3.** [sə'bɔ:dineit] unterordnen; **sub·or·di'na·tion** Unterordnung *f* (*to* unter *acc.*).
sub·orn ⚖ [sʌ'bɔ:n] verleiten, anstiften (*to* zu); **sub·or'na·tion** Anstiftung *f*, Verleitung *f*.
sub·p(o)e·na ⚖ [səb'pi:nə] **1.** Vorladung *f*; **2.** vorladen.
sub·scribe [səb'skraib] *Geld* stiften (*to* für); *Summe* zeichnen; *s-n Namen* setzen (*to* unter *acc.*), unterschreiben mit; ~ *to Zeitung etc.* abonnieren; *e-r Meinung* zustimmen, *et.* unterschreiben; **sub'scrib·er** (Unter)Zeichner(in) (*to, for gen.*); Abonnent(in); *teleph.* Teilnehmer(in).
sub·scrip·tion [səb'skripʃən] Unterzeichnung *f etc.*; gezeichnete Summe *f*; Abonnement *n*.
sub·sec·tion ['sʌbsekʃən] Unterabteilung *f*.
sub·se·quence ['sʌbsikwəns] späteres Eintreten *n*; **'sub·se·quent** □ folgend; später (*to* als); ~*ly* hinterher; in der Folge, anschließend.
sub·serve [səb'sə:v] dienen (*dat.*); befördern; **sub'ser·vi·ence** [~vjəns] Dienlichkeit *f*; Unterwürfigkeit *f*; **sub'ser·vi·ent** □ dienlich; dienstbar; unterwürfig.
sub·side [səb'said] sinken, sich senken; sich setzen (*Haus etc.*); sich legen (*nachlassen*); ~ *into* verfallen in (*acc.*); **sub·sid·ence** ['sʌbsidəns] Senkung *f*; Abflauen *n*; **sub·sid·i·ar·y** [səb'sidjəri] **1.** □ Hilfs...; Neben...; als Hilfe dienend (*to* für); *be* ~ *to* ergänzen, unterstützen; **2.** Filiale *f*; *a.* ~ *company* Tochtergesellschaft *f*; **sub·si·dize** ['sʌbsidaiz] mit Geld unterstützen; subventionieren; **'sub·si·dy** Beihilfe *f*, Zuschuß *m*; Subvention *f*.
sub·sist [səb'sist] *v/i.* bestehen; leben (*on* von *e-r Nahrung*; *by* von *e-m Beruf*); *v/t.* er-, unterhalten; **sub'sist·ence** Dasein *n*; (Lebens-)Unterhalt *m*; ~ *wage* Minimallohn *m*.
sub·soil ['sʌbsɔil] Untergrund *m*.
sub·son·ic [sʌb'sɔnik] Unterschall...
sub·stance ['sʌbstəns] Substanz *f*; Wesen *n*; *fig.* Hauptsache *f*; Inhalt *m*; Kern *m*; Wirklichkeit *f*; Stoff *m*; Vermögen *n*.
sub·stan·dard [səb'stændəd] nicht hochsprachlich; unzulänglich (*Qualität*).
sub·stan·tial □ [səb'stænʃəl] wesentlich; wirklich; nahrhaft, kräftig; stark; solid; vermögend; namhaft (*Summe*); **sub·stan·ti·al·i·ty**

[~ʃiˈæliti] Wesenheit *f*; Wirklichkeit *f*; Gediegenheit *f*; Wesentlichkeit *f*.
sub·stan·ti·ate [səbˈstænʃieit] beweisen, begründen, dartun.
sub·stan·ti·val □ *gr.* [sʌbstənˈtaivəl] substantivisch; **sub·stantive** [ˈ~tiv] **1.** □ selbständig; *gr.* substantivisch; wirklich; fest; **2.** *gr.* Substantiv *n*, Hauptwort *n*.
sub·sti·tute [ˈsʌbstitjuːt] **1.** an die Stelle setzen *od.* treten (*for* von); *b.s.* unterschieben (*for* statt); **2.** Stellvertreter *m*; Ersatzmann *m*; Ersatz *m*; **sub·stiˈtu·tion** Einsetzung *f*, *mst b.s.* Unterschiebung *f*; Stellvertretung *f*; Ersatz *m*.
sub·stra·tum [ˈsʌbˈstrɑːtəm] Substrat *n*; Grundlage *f*; ⊕, *geol.* Unterlage *f*; Substanz *f*.
sub·struc·ture [ˈsʌbstrʌktʃə] Unterbau *m*.
sub·ten·ant [ˈsʌbˈtenənt] Untermieter *m*, Unterpächter *m*.
sub·ter·fuge [ˈsʌbtəfjuːdʒ] Ausflucht *f*.
sub·ter·ra·ne·an □ [sʌbtəˈreinjən] unterirdisch.
sub·til·ize [ˈsʌtilaiz] *v/t.* verfeinern; überspitzen; *v/i.* klügeln.
sub·ti·tle [ˈsʌbtaitl] Untertitel *m*.
sub·tle □ [ˈsʌtl] fein(sinnig); subtil scharfsinnig; spitzfindig; ingeniös; ˈ**sub·tle·ty** Feinheit *f*; Spitzfindigkeit *f*.
sub·to·pia [sʌbˈtəupiə] zersiedelte *od.* urbanisierte Landschaft *f*.
sub·tract [səbˈtrækt] abziehen, subtrahieren; **subˈtrac·tion** Abziehen *n*, Subtraktion *f*.
sub·urb [ˈsʌbəːb] Vorstadt *f*, -ort *m*; **sub·ur·ban** [səˈbəːbən] vorstädtisch; Vorstadt..., -ort...; *contp.* spießbürgerlich; **Subˈur·bia** [~bjə] *die* Vorstädte *f/pl.*; *das* Leben in den Vorstädten.
sub·trop·i·cal [ˈsʌbˈtrɔpikəl] subtropisch.
sub·ven·tion [səbˈvenʃən] **1.** Subvention *f*, Zuschuß *m*, Beihilfe *f*; Unterstützung *f*; **2.** subventionieren.
sub·ver·sion [sʌbˈvəːʃən] Umsturz *m*; **subˈver·sive** umstürzend, zerstörend (*of acc.*); subversiv.
sub·vert [sʌbˈvəːt] umstürzen; *Regierung* stürzen; untergraben.
sub·way [ˈsʌbwei] (*bsd.* Fußgänger-) Unterführung *f*; *Am.* Untergrundbahn *f*.
sub-ze·ro [ˈsʌbˈziərəu] unter null Grad, unter dem Gefrierpunkt.
suc·ceed [səkˈsiːd] Erfolg haben (*Person od. Sache*); glücken, gelingen (*Sache*); (nach)folgen (*dat.*); ~ *to* auf *dem Thron* folgen; *Amt* übernehmen; *Gut etc.* erben; *he ~s in ger.* es gelingt ihm, zu *inf.*
suc·cess [səkˈses] Erfolg *m*; glückliches Ergebnis *n*; Glanzleistung *f*; *he was a great* ~ er hatte großen Erfolg; **sucˈcess·ful** □ [~ful] erfolgreich; glücklich; *be* ~ Erfolg *od.* Glück haben; **suc·ces·sion** [~ˈseʃən] (Nach-, Erb-, Reihen)Folge *f*; Nachkommenschaft *f*; ~ *to the throne* Thronfolge *f*; *in* ~ nacheinander; ~ *duty* Erbschaftssteuer *f*; **sucˈces·sive** □ aufeinanderfolgend; **sucˈces·sor** Nachfolger(in); ~ *to the throne* Thronfolger *m*.
suc·cinct □ [səkˈsiŋkt] bündig, kurz.
suc·co·ry ⚘ [ˈsʌkəri] Zichorie *f*.
suc·co(u)r [ˈsʌkə] **1.** Hilfe *f*, Beistand *m*; ⚔ Entsatz *m*; **2.** helfen (*dat.*); beistehen (*dat.*); ⚔ entsetzen.
suc·cu·lence [ˈsʌkjuləns] Saftigkeit *f*; ˈ**suc·cu·lent** □ saftig, wohlschmeckend (*Frucht*); fleischig (*Blatt, Stiel*).
suc·cumb [səˈkʌm] unter-, erliegen.
such [sʌtʃ] **1.** *adj.* solch; derartig; so groß; ~ *a man* ein solcher Mann; *s. another*; *no ~ thing* nichts dergleichen; ~ *as* die, welche; ~ *and* ~ der und der, die und die; ~ *is life* so ist nun mal das Leben; **2.** *pron.* (ein) solch(er, -es), (eine) solche, *pl.* solche; der, die, das; ˈ**suchlike** dergleichen.
suck [sʌk] **1.** (ein)saugen; saugen an (*dat.*); aussaugen; lutschen; ~ *up to Schul-sl.* sich anbiedern *od.* einschmeicheln bei; ~ *s.o.'s brains* j. ausholen; **2.** Saugen *n*; *give* ~ säugen; ˈ**suck·er** Saugorgan *n*; ⊕ Pumpenschuh *m*; ⚘ Wurzelsproß *m*; *Am.* Einfaltspinsel *m*; ˈ**sucking** saugend; Saug...; ~ *pig* Spanferkel *n*; **suck·le** [ˈ~l] säugen, nähren, stillen; ˈ**suck·ling** Säugling *m*.
suc·tion [ˈsʌkʃən] **1.** Saugen *n*; Ansaugen *n*; Sog *m*; **2.** Saug...; ~ *cleaner*, ~ *sweeper* Staubsauger *m*.
sud·den □ [ˈsʌdn] plötzlich; *on a* ~,

(*all*) *of a* ~ (ganz) plötzlich; '**sud·den·ness** Plötzlichkeit *f.*
su·dor·if·ic [sju:də'rifik] schweißtreibend(es Mittel *n*).
suds [sʌdz] *pl.* Seifenlauge *f*; Seifenschaum *m*; '**suds·y** *Am.* schaumig, seifig.
sue [sju:] *v/t.* verklagen; ~ *out* auf dem Rechtsweg erwirken; *v/i.* nachsuchen (*for* um); klagen (*for* auf *acc.*).
suède [sweid] feines Wildleder *n.*
su·et ['sjuit] Nierenfett *n*; Talg *m*; '**su·et·y** talgig.
suf·fer ['sʌfə] *v/i.* leiden (*from* an *dat.*); *v/t.* erdulden, erleiden; dulden, (zu)lassen; '**suf·fer·ance** Duldung *f*; *on* ~ nur geduldet(erweise); '**suf·fer·er** Leidende *m*, *f*; Dulder (-in); '**suf·fer·ing** Leiden *n.*
suf·fice [sə'fais] genügen, (aus-) reichen; ~ *it to say* es sei nur gesagt.
suf·fi·cien·cy [sə'fiʃənsi] Hinlänglichkeit *f*; auskömmliches Vermögen *n*; *a* ~ *of money* genug Geld; **suf'fi·cient** □ genügend, ausreichend, genug; *be* ~ genügen.
suf·fix *gr.* ['sʌfiks] **1.** anhängen; **2.** Nachsilbe *f*, Suffix *n.*
suf·fo·cate ['sʌfəkeit] ersticken; **suf·fo'ca·tion** Erstickung *f*; **suf·fo·ca·tive** □ ['~kətiv] erstickend.
suf·fra·gan *eccl.* ['sʌfrəgən] Weihbischof *m*; '**suf·frage** (Wahl-) Stimme *f*; Abstimmung *f*; Wahl-, Stimmrecht *n*; **suf·fra·gette** [~ə'dʒet] Frauenrechtlerin *f*, Suffragette *f.*
suf·fuse [sə'fju:z] übergießen; überziehen; **suf'fu·sion** [~ʒən] Übergießung *f*; Überzug *m.*
sug·ar ['ʃugə] **1.** Zucker *m*; **2.** zukkern; '**~-ba·sin** Zuckerdose *f*; '**~-beet** Zuckerrübe *f*; '**~-bowl** *Am.* Zuckerdose *f*; '**~-cane** Zuckerrohr *n*; '**~-coat** überzuckern, versüßen; ~ **dad·dy** *älterer, reicher* Liebhaber *m*; '**~-free** ohne Zucker; '**~-loaf** Zuckerhut *m*; '**~-lump** Zuckerwürfel *m*; '**~-plum** Bonbon *m*, *n*; '**~-tongs** *pl.* (*a pair of* eine) Zuckerzange *f*; '**sug·ar·y** zuckerig; zuckersüß.
sug·gest [sə'dʒest] vorschlagen, anregen; nahelegen; vorbringen; *Gedanken* eingeben; andeuten; denken lassen an (*acc.*); **sug'ges·tion** Anregung *f*; Wink *m*, Rat *m*, Vorschlag *m*; Suggestion *f*; Eingebung *f*; Andeutung *f.*
sug·ges·tive □ [sə'dʒestiv] anregend (*of* zu); andeutend (*of acc.*); gehaltvoll; vielsagend; zweideutig (*Witz etc.*); **sug'ges·tive·ness** Gedankenreichtum *m*; Zweideutigkeit *f.*
su·i·cid·al □ [sjui'saidl] selbstmörderisch; **su·i·cide** ['~said] **1.** Selbstmord *m*; Selbstmörder(in); **2.** *Am.* Selbstmord begehen.
suit [sju:t] **1.** (Herren)Anzug *m*; (Damen)Kostüm *n*; Anliegen *n*, Bitte *f*; (Heirats)Antrag *m*; *Karten*: Farbe *f*; ⚖ Prozeß *m*; *follow* ~ Farbe bekennen; dasselbe tun; **2.** *v/t. j-m* passen, zusagen, recht sein, entsprechen, zuträglich sein, bekommen; *j.* kleiden, *j-m* stehen, passen zu (*Kleidungsstück etc.*); ~ *oneself* tun, was e-m beliebt; ~ *s.th. to* et. anpassen (*dat.*); *be* ~*ed* geeignet sein (*for* für), passen (*to* zu); *v/i.* passen; **suit·a'bil·i·ty** Eignung *f*; '**suit·a·ble** □ passend, geeignet (*to, for* für); entsprechend; '**suit·a·ble·ness** = *suitability*; '**suit·case** Handkoffer *m*; **suite** [swi:t] Gefolge *n*; (Reihen)Folge *f*; ♪ Suite *f*; *a.* ~ *of rooms* Zimmerflucht *f*; Garnitur *f*, (Zimmer-) Einrichtung *f*; **suit·ing** ✝ ['sju:tiŋ] Anzugstoff *m*; '**suit·or** Freier *m*; ⚖ Kläger(in), Prozessierende *m*, *f.*
sulk [sʌlk] **1.** *a. be in the* ~*s* schmollen, bocken; **2. sulks** *pl.*, '**sulk·i·ness** üble Laune *f*, Bockigkeit *f*; '**sulk·y 1.** □ verdrießlich; mürrisch, launisch; schmollend, bokkig; **2.** *Sport*: Traberwagen *m*, Sulky *n.*
sul·len □ ['sʌlən] verdrossen, finster, mürrisch; widerspenstig; trotzig; '**sul·len·ness** Verdrießlichkeit *f.*
sul·ly *mst fig.* ['sʌli] beflecken.
sul·pha ['sʌlfə] *pl.* = *sulphonamides.*
sul·phate ⚗ ['sʌlfeit] schwefelsaures Salz *n*, Sulfat *n*; **sul·phide** ⚗ ['~faid] Schwefelverbindung *f*, Sulfid *n.*
sul·pho·na·mides ⚕ [sʌl'fɔnəmaidz] *pl.* Sulfonamide *pl.*
sul·phur ⚗ ['sʌlfə] **1.** Schwefel *m*; **2.** schwefeln; **sul·phu·re·ous** [sʌl'fjuəriəs] schwef(e)lig; **sul·phu-**

ret·ted hy·dro·gen ['~fjuretid-'haidridʒən] Schwefelwasserstoff *m*; **sul·phu·ric** [~'fjuərik] Schwefel...; ~ *acid* Schwefelsäure *f*; '**sul·phu·rize** ⊕ schwefeln, vulkanisieren; **sul·phur·ous** ['~fərəs] Schwefel..., schwefelhaltig.

sul·tan ['sʌltən] Sultan *m*; **sul·tan·a** [sʌl'tɑːnə] Sultanin *f*; [səl-'tɑːnə] Sultanine *f*.

sul·tri·ness ['sʌltrinis] Schwüle *f*; '**sul·try** □ schwül; *fig.* heftig, hitzig.

sum [sʌm] **1.** Summe *f*; Betrag *m*; *fig.* Inbegriff *m*, Inhalt *m*; Rechenaufgabe *f*; *do ~s* rechnen; *in ~* mit e-m Wort; **2.** *mst ~ up* zs.-rechnen, -zählen; *fig.* zs.-fassen, resümieren.

su·mac(h) ⚘ ['suːmæk] Sumach *m*, Färberbaum *m*.

sum·ma·rize ['sʌməraiz] (kurz) zs.-fassen; '**sum·mar·y** **1.** □ summarisch, kurz (zs.-gefaßt); ⚖ Schnell...; **2.** (kurze) Inhaltsangabe *f*, Auszug *m*.

sum·mer[1] ['sʌmə] **1.** Sommer *m*; ~ *resort* Sommerfrische *f*; **2.** den Sommer verbringen; '**~-house** (Garten)Laube *f*.

sum·mer[2] △ [~] Trägerbalken *m*; Oberschwelle *f*.

sum·mer·like ['sʌməlaik], '**sum·mer·ly** sommerlich.

summer...: '**~-school** Ferienkurs *m*; '**~·time** Sommer(szeit *f*) *m*; '**~-'time** Sommerzeit *f* (*um 1 Std. vorgerückt*); '**sum·mer·y** sommerlich.

sum·mit ['sʌmit] Gipfel *m* (*a. fig.*); ~ **con·fe·rence** *pol.* Gipfelkonferenz *f*.

sum·mon ['sʌmən] auffordern; (be)rufen, einberufen; ⚖ vorladen; *fig. mst ~ up* aufbieten; '**sum·mon·er** Bote *m*; **sum·mons** ['~z] Aufforderung *f* (*a.* ⚔ *zur Übergabe*); (gerichtliche) Vorladung *f*.

sump *mot.* [sʌmp] Ölwanne *f*.

sump·ter ['sʌmptə] *a.* '**~-horse**, '**~-mule** † Saumtier *n*.

sump·tu·ar·y ['sʌmptjuəri] Aufwand(s)..., Luxus...

sump·tu·ous □ ['sʌmptjuəs] kostbar, prächtig, luxuriös; '**sump·tu·ous·ness** Pracht *f*.

sun [sʌn] **1.** Sonne *f*; **2.** (sich) sonnen; '**~·baked** von der Sonne getrocknet; '**~-bath** Sonnenbad *n*; '**~-bathe** sonnenbaden; '**~·beam** Sonnenstrahl *m* (*a. fig.*); '**~-blind** Markise *f*; '**~·burn** Sonnenbräune *f*; Sonnenbrand *m*; '**~·burnt** sonn(en)verbrannt.

sun·dae ['sʌndi] Früchte-Eisbecher *m*.

Sun·day ['sʌndi] Sonntag *m*; ~ **school** Sonntagsschule *f*.

sun·der *poet.* ['sʌndə] (sich) trennen.

sun-di·al ['sʌndaiəl] Sonnenuhr *f*.

sun·down ['sʌndaun] Sonnenuntergang *m*; '**sun·down·er** F Dämmerschoppen *m*.

sun·dry ['sʌndri] **1.** verschiedene; **2. sun·dries** *pl. bsd.* ☤ ['~driz] Verschiedenes *n*; Extraausgaben *f/pl.*

sun·flow·er ⚘ ['sʌnflauə] Sonnenblume *f*.

sung [sʌŋ] *pret. u. p.p. von sing.*

sun...: '**~-glass·es** *pl.* (*a pair of* eine) Sonnenbrille *f*; '**~-god** Sonnengott *m*; '**~-hel·met** Tropenhelm *m*.

sunk [sʌŋk] *pret. u. p.p. von sink 1.*

sunk·en ['sʌŋkən] **1.** ⚒ *p.p. von sink 1*; **2.** *adj.* versunken; *fig.* eingefallen (*Wangen etc.*); tiefliegend (*Augen*); ⊕ versenkt.

sun-lamp ['sʌnlæmp] ⚕ künstliche Höhensonne *f*; *Film*: Jupiterlampe *f*.

sun·less ['sʌnlis] sonnen-, lichtlos, dunkel; '**sun·light** Sonnenlicht *n*; '**sun·lit** sonnenbeschienen.

sun·ni·ness ['sʌninis] Sonnigkeit *f* (*a. fig.*); '**sun·ny** □ sonnig (*a. fig.*).

sun...: '**~·rise** Sonnenaufgang *m*; '**~·room** Glasveranda *f*; '**~·set** Sonnenuntergang *m*; '**~·shade** Sonnenschirm *m*; '**~·shine** Sonnenschein *m*; ~ *roof mot.* Schiebedach *n*; '**~·shin·y** sonnig; heiter; '**~-spot** *ast.* Sonnenfleck *m*; '**~-stroke** ⚕ Sonnenstich *m*; '**~-up** Sonnenaufgang *m*.

sup[1] [sʌp] *v/i.* zu Abend essen (*off od. on s.th.* et.).

sup[2] [~] **1.** schlückchenweise trinken, nippen; löffeln; **2.** Schlückchen *n*; *neither bite nor ~* nichts zu essen u. zu trinken.

su·per[1] ['suːpə] **1.** *thea. sl.* Statist (-in); **2.** F erstklassig, super, prima; Riesen...

su·per[2] [~] Über...; über...; Ober..., ober...; Groß...

su·per...: **~·a'bound** im Überfluß vorhanden sein; Überfluß haben (*in, with* an *dat.*); **~·a'bun·dant** □ überreichlich; überschwenglich; **~'add** noch hinzufügen; **~·an·nu·ate** [~'rænjueit] pensionieren; **~d** überaltert; ausgedient; veraltet (*Sache*); **~·an·nu'a·tion** Pensionierung *f*; Ruhegehalt *n*; ~ *fund* Pensionsfonds *m*.

su·perb □ [sju:'pə:b] prächtig; herrlich.

su·per...: **'~·car·go** ⚓ Ladungsaufseher *m*; **'~·charg·er** *mot.* Gebläse *n*, Kompressor *m*; **su·per·cil·i·ous** □ [~'siliəs] hochmütig; **su·per'cil·i·ous·ness** Hochmut *m*; **su·per-'dread·nought** Großkampfschiff *n*; **su·per·er·o·ga·tion** [~rero'geiʃən] Mehrleistung *f*; **su·per·e·rog·a·to·ry** □ [~re'rɔgətəri] über das Pflichtmaß hinausgehend; **su·per·fi·cial** □ [~'fiʃəl] oberflächlich; **su·per·fi·ci·al·i·ty** [~fiʃi'æliti] Oberflächlichkeit *f*; **su·per·fi·ci·es** [~'fiʃi:z] Oberfläche *f*; **'su·per'fine** extrafein; **su·per·flu·i·ty** [~'flu:iti] Überfluß *m* (*of* an *dat.*); **su'per·flu·ous** □ [~fluəs] überflüssig; **su·per'heat** ⊕ überhitzen; **su·per·het** ['~'het] *Radio*: Überlagerungsempfänger *m*, Super(het) *m*.

su·per...: **~'hu·man** □ übermenschlich; **~·im·pose** ['~rim'pəuz] darauf-, darüberlegen; **~·in·duce** ['~rin'dju:s] noch hinzufügen (*on, upon* zu); **~·in·tend** [~rin'tend] die Oberaufsicht haben über (*acc.*); überwachen; **~·in'tend·ence** Oberaufsicht *f*; **~·in'tend·ent** **1.** Leiter *m*, Direktor *m*; (Ober)Aufseher *m*, Inspektor *m*; **2.** aufsichtführend.

su·pe·ri·or [su:'piəriə] **1.** □ ober; höher(stehend); vorgesetzt; besser; hochwertiger; überlegen (*to dat.*); vorzüglich; ~ *officer* höherer Beamter *m od.* Offizier *m*; **2.** Höherstehende *m*, *bsd.* Vorgesetzte *m*; *eccl.* Obere *m*, Superior *m*; *mst lady* ~ Oberin *f*; **su·pe·ri·or·i·ty** [~'ɔriti] Überlegenheit *f*.

su·per·la·tive [su:'pə:lətiv] **1.** □ höchst; überragend; *gr.* superlativisch; **2.** *a.* ~ *degree gr.* Superlativ *m*; **su·per·man** ['su:pəmæn] Übermensch *m*; **'su·per·mar·ket** Supermarkt *m*; **su·per·nal** [su:'pə:nl] überirdisch, himmlisch; **su·per·nat·u·ral** □ [su:pə'nætʃrəl] übernatürlich; **su·per·nu·mer·ar·y** [~'nju:mərəri] **1.** überzählig; **2.** Überzählige *m, f*; *thea.* Statist(in); **'su·per'pose** obenauf legen; überlagern; **'su·per·po'si·tion** Auflagerung *f*; *geol.* Schichtung *f*; **'su·per·pow·er** *pol.* Supermacht *f*; **'su·per'scribe** überschreiben; adressieren; **su·per·scrip·tion** [~'skripʃən] Über-, Aufschrift *f*; **su·per·sede** [~'si:d] ersetzen; verdrängen; absetzen; *fig.* überholen; **su·per'ses·sion** Ersetzung *f*, Ablösung *f*; **su·per·son·ic** *phys.* [~'sɔnik] Überschall...; **su·per·sti·tion** [~'stiʃən] Aberglaube *m*; **su·per·sti·tious** □ [~'stiʃəs] abergläubisch; **su·per·struc·ture** ['~strʌktʃə] Oberbau *m*; **su·per·vene** [~'vi:n] noch hinzukommen (*on, upon* zu); unerwartet eintreten; **su·per·ven·tion** [~'venʃən] Hinzukommen *n*; **su·per·vise** ['~vaiz] beaufsichtigen, überwachen; **su·per·vi·sion** [~'viʒən] (Ober)Aufsicht *f*; Beaufsichtigung *f*, Überwachung *f*; **su·per·vi·sor** ['~vaizə] Aufseher *m*, Inspektor *m*; *univ.* Tutor *m*.

su·pine **1.** *gr.* ['sju:pain] Supinum *n*; **2.** □ [~'pain] auf dem Rücken liegend; zurückgelehnt; lässig, gleichgültig; **su'pine·ness** Lässigkeit *f*, Gleichgültigkeit *f*.

sup·per ['sʌpə] Abendessen *n*; *the* (*Lord's*) ♀ das Heilige Abendmahl.

sup·plant [sə'plɑ:nt] verdrängen; *fig.* ausstechen; ersetzen.

sup·ple ['sʌpl] **1.** □ biegsam, geschmeidig; **2.** geschmeidig machen.

sup·ple·ment **1.** ['sʌplimənt] Supplement *n*, Ergänzung *f*; Nachtrag *m*; (Zeitungs- *etc.*)Beilage *f*; **2.** ['~ment] ergänzen; **sup·ple'men·tal** □, **sup·ple'men·ta·ry** Ergänzungs...; nachträglich; Nachtrags...; ~ *benefit* Sozialhilfe *f*; ~ *order* Nachbestellung *f*.

sup·ple·ness ['sʌplnis] Biegsamkeit *f*; Schmiegsamkeit *f* (*a. fig.*).

sup·pli·ant ['sʌpliənt] **1.** □ demütig bittend, flehend; **2.** Bittsteller(in).

sup·pli·cate ['sʌplikeit] demütig bitten, anflehen; **sup·pli'ca·tion** demütige Bitte *f*; **sup·pli·ca·to·ry** ['~kətəri] flehend; Bitt...

sup·pli·er [sə'plaiə] Versorger(in); ✝ Lieferant(in).

sup·ply [sə'plai] **1.** liefern; *e-m Mangel* abhelfen; *e-e Stelle* ausfüllen, vertreten; ausstatten, versehen, versorgen (*with* mit); ergänzen; **2.** Lieferung *f*; Versorgung *f*; Zufuhr *f*; Menge *f*; Vorrat *m*; Bedarf *m*; ✝ Angebot *n* (*Ggs. demand*); (Stell-) Vertretung *f*; *mst supplies pl.* ✝ Versorgungsgüter *n/pl.*; *parl.* Etat *m*, Budget *n*; ⚔ Nachschub *m*; *in short* ~ knapp, schwer zu haben; *on* ~ in Vertretung; *Committee of* ~ *parl.* Haushaltsausschuß *m*; **sup-'ply-'side:** ~ *economics sg. od. pl. bsd. Am.* angebotsorientierte Wirtschaftspolitik *f*.

sup·port [sə'pɔ:t] **1.** Stütze *f* (*a. fig.*); Hilfe *f*; Fußstütze *f*, Einlage *f*; ⊕ Träger *m*, Halter *m*; Unterstützung *f*; Lebensunterhalt *m*; **2.** (unter)stützen (*a. fig.*); *sich, e-e Familie etc.* unterhalten, ernähren; *Debatte etc.* aufrechterhalten; *e-e Sache* verteidigen; *Meinung, Würde* behaupten; (v)ertragen; *~ing actor* Nebendarsteller *m*; *~ing evidence* ⚖ erhärtendes Beweismaterial *n*; *~ing part* Nebenrolle *f*; *~ing programme Film*: Beiprogramm *n*; **sup'port·a·ble** □ erträglich; aufrechtzuerhalten(d), haltbar; **sup'port·er** Unterstützer(in); Anhänger(in); Helfer(in).

sup·pose [sə'pəuz] annehmen; voraussetzen; vermuten; *he is ~d to do* man erwartet *od.* verlangt von ihm, daß er tut; er soll tun; ~ *od. supposing (that)* ... angenommen (daß) ...; ~ *we go* gehen wir; wie wär's, wenn wir gingen; *he is rich, I* ~ er wird wohl reich sein.

sup·posed □ [sə'pəuzd] vermeintlich; **sup'pos·ed·ly** [~idli] vermutlich.

sup·pos·ing [sə'pəuziŋ] angenommen, falls.

sup·po·si·tion [sʌpə'ziʃən] Voraussetzung *f*; Annahme *f*; Vermutung *f*; **sup·pos·i·ti·tious** □ [səpɔzi'tiʃəs] untergeschoben; **sup'pos·i·to·ry** ⚕ [~təri] Zäpfchen *n*, Suppositorium *n*.

sup·press [sə'pres] unterdrücken; **sup·pres·sion** [sə'preʃən] Unterdrückung *f*; **sup'pres·sive** □ [~siv] unterdrückend; **sup'pres·sor** ⚡ Entstörungselement *n*; *Radio*: Entstörer *m*.

sup·pu·rate ['sʌpjuəreit] eitern; **sup·pu'ra·tion** Eiterung *f*.

su·pra-na·tion·al ['sju:prə'næʃənl] überstaatlich.

su·prem·a·cy [su'preməsi] Obergewalt *f*, -hoheit *f*; Überlegenheit *f*; Vorrang *m*; **su·preme** □ [su:'pri:m] höchst; oberst; Ober...; größt; kritisch (*Zeitpunkt*).

sur·charge [sə:'tʃɑ:dʒ] **1.** überladen; e-n Strafzuschlag erheben von *j-m*; **2.** ['~] Überladung *f*; (Straf)Zuschlag *m*; Strafporto *n*; Überdruck *m auf Briefmarken.*

surd ✗ [sə:d] irrational(e Zahl *f*).

sure □ [ʃuə] *allg.* sicher, gewiß, bestimmt; *to be ~!*, F ~ *enough!*, *Am.* ~*!* sicher(lich)!, natürlich!; *I'm ~ I don't know* ich weiß wirklich nicht; *he is ~ to return* er wird sicher(lich) zurückkommen; *make* ~ sich vergewissern; sich versichern (*of gen.*); **'~-foot·ed** sicher auf den Füßen; **'sure·ly** sicherlich; **'sure·ness** Sicherheit *f*; **'sure·ty** Bürge *m*.

surf [sə:f] Brandung *f*.

sur·face ['sə:fis] **1.** Oberfläche *f*; Fläche(ninhalt *m*) *f*; ✈ Tragfläche *f*; *control* ~ ✈ Steuerfläche *f*; *below the* ~ ⚒ unter Tage; **2.** auftauchen (*U-Boot*); ~ **mail** auf dem Land- und Seeweg beförderte Post *f*; **'~man** 🚂 Streckenarbeiter *m*; **~-to--air** ['~tə'ɛə]: ~ *missile* ⚔ Boden-Luft-Rakete *f*.

surf...: **'~-board** Wellenreiterbrett *n*; **'~-boat** Brandungsboot *n*.

sur·feit ['sə:fit] **1.** Übersättigung *f*, Ekel *m*; **2.** (sich) überladen, -sättigen (*on, fig. with* mit).

surf-rid·ing ['sə:fraidiŋ] *Sport*: Wellenreiten *n*.

surge [sə:dʒ] **1.** Woge *f*; Brandung *f*; **2.** wogen, branden.

sur·geon ['sə:dʒən] Chirurg *m*, Operateur *m*; ⚔ Stabs-, ⚓ Schiffsarzt *m*; **sur·ger·y** ['sə:dʒəri] Chirurgie *f*; chirurgische Behandlung *f*; Sprechzimmer *n*; ~ *hours pl.* Sprechstunden *f/pl*.

sur·gi·cal □ ['sə:dʒikəl] chirurgisch; Operations...

sur·li·ness ['sə:linis] mürrisches Wesen *n*, Unfreundlichkeit *f*; Bärbeißigkeit *f*; **'sur·ly** □ unfreundlich; bärbeißig; zäh (*Boden*).

sur·mise 1. ['sə:maiz] Vermutung *f*; Argwohn *m*; **2.** [sə:'maiz] vermuten; argwöhnen.

sur·mount [sə:'maunt] übersteigen; überragen; *fig.* überwinden; *~ed by od. with* überragt *od.* überdeckt von; **sur'mount·a·ble** übersteigbar, überwindlich.

sur·name ['sə:neim] **1.** Zu-, Nach-, Familienname *m*; **2.** *j-m* den Zunamen ... geben; *~d* mit Zunamen.

sur·pass *fig.* [sə:'pɑ:s] übersteigen, -treffen; *~ed by* überragt von; **sur'pass·ing** □ unübertrefflich, außerordentlich.

sur·plice *eccl.* ['sə:pləs] Chorhemd *n*.

sur·plus ['sə:pləs] **1.** Überschuß *m*, Mehr *n*; **2.** überschüssig; Über...; Mehr...; *~ population* Bevölkerungsüberschuß *m*; **'sur·plus·age** = *surplus 1*; etwas Überflüssiges *n*.

sur·prise [sə'praiz] **1.** Überraschung *f*; ⚔ Überrump(e)lung *f*; *take by ~* überrumpeln; **2.** Überraschungs...; überraschend; **3.** überraschen; ⚔ überrumpeln; **sur'pris·ing** □ überraschend.

sur·re·al·ism [sə'riəlizəm] *Kunst*: Surrealismus *m*; **sur're·al·ist** Surrealist *m*.

sur·ren·der [sə'rendə] **1.** Übergabe *f*, Ergebung *f*; Kapitulation *f*; Aufgeben *n*; **2.** *v/t.* übergeben, ausliefern; *Besitz* aufgeben; *v/i. a. ~ o.s.* sich ergeben.

sur·rep·ti·tious □ [sʌrəp'tiʃəs] erschlichen; heimlich; unecht.

sur·ro·gate ['sʌrogit] Stellvertreter *m bsd. e-s Bischofs.*

sur·round [sə'raund] umgeben; ⚔ umzingeln; **sur'round·ing** umliegend; **sur'round·ings** *pl.* Umgebung *f*; Umwelt *f*.

sur·tax ['sə:tæks] (Einkommen-) Steuerzuschlag *m*.

sur·veil·lance [sə:'veiləns] Überwachung *f*.

sur·vey 1. [sə:'vei] überblicken; besichtigen; mustern; begutachten; *surv.* vermessen; **2.** ['~] Überblick *m* (*a. fig.*); Besichtigung *f*; Gutachten *n*; Umfrage *f*; *surv.* Vermessung *f*, Aufnahme *f*; **sur'vey·or** Aufseher *m*; Inspektor *m*; Land-, Feldmesser *m*, Geometer *m*; Gutachter *m*; *Board of* ♀*s* Baupolizei *f*.

sur·viv·al [sə'vaivəl] Über-, Fortleben *n*; Überbleibsel *n*; **sur'vive** *v/t.* überleben; *v/i.* noch (*od.* fort-) leben; am Leben bleiben; bestehen bleiben; **sur'vi·vor** Überlebende *m, f*.

sus·cep·ti·bil·i·ty [səseptə'biliti] Empfänglichkeit *f* (*to* für); *oft susceptibilities pl.* Empfindlichkeit *f*, empfindliche Stelle *f*; **sus'cep·ti·ble** □, **sus'cep·tive** empfänglich (*to* für); empfindlich (gegen); *be ~ of* zulassen (*Sache*).

sus·pect 1. [səs'pekt] (be)argwöhnen; im Verdacht haben, verdächtigen; zweifeln an (*dat.*); vermuten, befürchten; **2.** ['sʌspekt] Verdächtige *m, f*; **3.** = **sus'pect·ed** verdächtig.

sus·pend [səs'pend] (auf)hängen; aufschieben; unentschieden lassen; *Tätigkeit, Zahlung* einstellen; *Urteil* aussetzen; *Beamten, Gesetz* suspendieren; *Sportler* sperren; *~ed* schwebend; *~ed animation* Scheintod *m*; **sus'pend·er** Strumpf-, Sockenhalter *m*; *~s pl. Am.* Hosenträger *m*.

sus·pense [səs'pens] Ungewißheit *f*; Unentschiedenheit *f*; Spannung *f*; *~ account* ✝ vorläufiges Konto *n*; **sus·pen·sion** [~'penʃən] Aufhängung *f*; Aufschub *m*; Einstellung *f e-r Tätigkeit etc.*; Suspendierung *f*, Amtsenthebung *f*; einstweilige Aufhebung *f e-s Gesetzes*; *Sport*: Sperre *f*; **sus·pen·sion bridge** Hängebrücke *f*; **sus'pen·sive** □ aufschiebend; **sus·pen·so·ry** [~'pensəri] Hänge...; aufschiebend; *~ bandage* ⚕ Suspensorium *n*.

sus·pi·cion [səs'piʃən] Verdacht *m*; Argwohn *m*; Ahnung *f*; *fig.* Spur *f*; **sus'pi·cious** □ argwöhnisch, mißtrauisch; verdächtig; **sus'pi·cious·ness** mißtrauisches Wesen *n od.* Gefühl *n*; Verdächtigkeit *f*.

sus·tain [səs'tein] stützen; *fig.* aufrecht erhalten; aushalten; *Verlust, Schaden* erleiden; ♪ aushalten; ⚖ anerkennen; *thea. e-r Rolle* gerecht werden (*Schauspieler*); **sus'tain·a·ble** haltbar (*Anklage*); **sus'tained** anhaltend; ununterbrochen.

sus·te·nance ['sʌstinəns] (Lebens-) Unterhalt *m*; Nahrung *f*; Nährwert *m*.

sut·ler ⚔ ['sʌtlə] Marketender *m*.

su·ture ['su:tʃə] **1.** ⚘, *anat.*, ⚕ Naht *f*; **2.** nähen.
su·ze·rain ['su:zərein] Oberlehnsherr *m*.
svelte [svelt] schlank (*Frau*).
swab [swɔb] **1.** Aufwischmop *m*; ⚓ Schwabber *m*; ⚕ Tupfer *m*; Abstrich *m*; **2.** *a.* ~ *down* aufwischen; ⚓ schwabbern.
Swa·bi·an ['sweibjən] **1.** Schwabe *m*, Schwäbin *f*; Schwäbisch *n*; **2.** schwäbisch.
swad·dle ['swɔdl] *Baby* wickeln; '**swad·dling-clothes** *pl. mst fig.* Windeln *f/pl.*
swag·ger ['swægə] **1.** (umher)stolzieren; großtun, aufschneiden; **2.** F elegant; **3.** Großtuerei *f*; '~-**cane** ⚔ Ausgehstöckchen *n*.
swain *poet. od.* † [swein] (Bauern-) Bursche *m*; Schäfer *m*; *co.* Liebhaber *m*.
swale *Am.* [sweil] Mulde *f*, Niederung *f*.
swal·low[1] *orn.* ['swɔləu] Schwalbe *f*.
swal·low[2] [~] **1.** Schlund *m*; Schluck *m*; **2.** *v/t.* (*fig. mst* ~ *up*) (hinunter-, ver)schlucken; *fig. Ansicht etc.* begierig aufnehmen; *Behauptung* zurücknehmen; *v/i.* schlucken.
swam [swæm] *pret. von swim 1.*
swamp [swɔmp] **1.** Sumpf *m*, Morast *m*; **2.** überschwemmen (*a. fig.*); ⚓ zum Sinken bringen; *fig.* überhäufen; '**swamp·y** sumpfig.
swan [swɔn] Schwan *m*.
swank *sl.* [swæŋk] **1.** Angabe *f*, Protzerei *f*; **2.** angeben, protzen; '**swank·y** protzig, angeberisch, snobistisch.
swan-neck ['swɔnnek] Schwanenhals *m*; '**swan·ner·y** Schwanenteich *m*; '**swan-song** Schwanengesang *m*.
swap F [swɔp] (ver-, aus)tauschen.
sward [swɔ:d] Rasen *m*.
sware † [swɛə] *pret. von swear.*
swarm[1] [swɔ:m] **1.** Schwarm *m*; Haufe(n) *m*, Gewimmel *n*; **2.** schwärmen; wimmeln (*with* von).
swarm[2] [~]: ~ *up* hochklettern an (*dat.*).
swarth·i·ness ['swɔ:θinis] dunkle Gesichtsfarbe *f*; '**swarth·y** □ schwärzlich; dunkelfarbig, -häutig.
swash [swɔʃ] **1.** *v/i.* plan(t)schen; prahlen; *v/t.* (be)spritzen; **2.** Pla(n)tschen *n*, Klatschen *n des Wassers*; ~·**buck·ler** ['~bʌklə] großmäuliger Draufgänger *m*.
swas·ti·ka ['swɔstikə] Hakenkreuz *n*.
swat [swɔt] **1.** *Fliege etc.* klatschen; **2.** Schlag *m*.
swath ⚒ [swɔ:θ] Schwade(n *m*) *f*.
swathe [sweið] **1.** Wickelband *n*; Binde *f*; *s. swath*; **2.** (ein)wickeln, einhüllen.
sway [swei] **1.** Schaukeln *n*; Wiegen *n*; Einfluß *m*; Macht *f*, Herrschaft *f*; **2.** *v/t.* schaukeln; wiegen; beeinflussen; beherrschen; *v/i.* schaukeln; sich wiegen; schwanken.
swear [swɛə] **1.** (*irr.*) *v/i.* schwören (*by* bei, F auf *j. od. et.*); beschwören (*to s.th.* et.); fluchen (*at* auf *acc.*); *v/t.* (be)schwören; ~ *s.o. in* j. vereidigen; **2.** *a.* ~-*word* F Fluch *m*.
sweat [swet] **1.** Schweiß *m*; *old* ~ *sl.* alter Hase *m*; *by the* ~ *of one's brow* im Schweiße s-s Angesichts; **2.** (*irr.*) *v/i.* schwitzen; *v/t.* (aus-) schwitzen; in Schweiß bringen; *Arbeiter* ausbeuten; ⊕ *Kabel* schweißen; '**sweat·ed** für Hungerlöhne hergestellt; '**sweat·er** Sweater *m*, Pullover *m*; Trainingsjacke *f*; Leuteschinder *m*; '**sweat-shirt** Sweatshirt *n*; Trainingshemd *n*; '**sweat-shop** Ausbeutungsbetrieb *m*; **sweat suit** Trainingsanzug *m*; '**sweat·y** schweißig; verschwitzt.
Swede [swi:d] Schwede *m*, Schwedin *f*; **Swed·ish** ['swi:diʃ] **1.** schwedisch; **2.** Schwedisch *n*.
sweep [swi:p] **1.** (*irr.*) *v/t.* fegen, kehren; *fig.* (*mst mit adv.*) reißen, jagen, treiben; streifen; bestreichen (*a.* ⚔); schleppen, hinter sich herziehen; *v/i.* fegen, kehren; *fig.* (*mst mit adv.*) (dahin)fegen, eilen, stürmen, schießen, sausen; (majestätisch) (dahin)rauschen; sich erstrecken, streichen; *be swept off one's feet fig.* hingerissen sein; **2.** Fegen *n*, Kehren *n*; *fig.* Dahinfegen *n*, Stürmen *n*; Schwung *m*; ♪ Tusch *m*; glänzender Sieg *m*; Schwenkung *f*; Krümmung *f*; Bogen *m*; Fläche *f*; Spielraum *m*, Bereich *m*; Schornsteinfeger *m*; Auffahrt *f vor e-m Hause*; langes Ruder *n*; (Pumpen)Schwengel *m*; *make a clean* ~ (*of*) reinen Tisch machen (mit); hinauswerfen; '**sweep·er** (Straßen)Feger *m*; Kehrmaschine *f*; '**sweep·ing** □

ausgedehnt; umfassend; weitgehend (*Behauptung etc.*); schwungvoll; durchgreifend; ˈ**sweep·ings** *pl.* Kehricht *m*; **sweep·stakes** [ˈ~-steiks] *pl.* (*bsd.* Pferde)Toto *n*.

sweet [swi:t] **1.** □ süß; lieblich, hold; freundlich, lieb(enswürdig); leicht, bequem; frisch; duftend; *have a ~ tooth* ein Leckermaul sein; **2.** Liebling *m*; Süßigkeit *f*, Bonbon *n*; Nachtisch *m*; *~s pl.* Freuden *f/pl.*; ˈ**~·bread** (*bsd.* Kalbs)Bries *n*; ˈ**~-ˈbri·ar** ⚘ Weinrose *f*; ˈ**sweet·en** (ver)süßen; *fig.* angenehm machen; mildern; ˈ**sweet·en·er** Süßstoff *m*; ˈ**sweet·heart** Liebling *m*, Liebchen *n*, Liebste *m*, *f*; Freund(in); ˈ**sweet-ish** süßlich; ˈ**sweet·meat** Bonbon *m*, *n*; kandierte Frucht *f*; ˈ**sweet·ness** Süßigkeit *f*; Lieblichkeit *f*; Annehmlichkeit *f*; Freundlichkeit *f*; Frische *f*; **sweet pea** ⚘ Gartenwicke *f*; ˈ**sweet-shop** Süßwarengeschäft *n*; ˈ**sweet-ˈwil·liam** ⚘ Studentennelke *f*.

swell [swel] **1.** (*irr.*) *v/i.* (an-, auf-) schwellen (*into* zu) (*a. fig.*); sich blähen (*Segel*); sich (aus)bauchen; *v/t.* (an)schwellen lassen; aufblähen; vergrößern, erhöhen; **2.** F flott, elegant; feudal; *sl.* prima; **3.** *bsd.* ♪ Anschwellen *n*; Schwellung *f*, Ausbauchung; ⚓ Dünung *f*; Anhöhe *f*; F feudaler Herr *m*, feudale Dame *f*; ˈ**swell·ing 1.** Anschwellen *n*; Geschwulst *f*; **2.** □ schwellend; schwülstig (*Stil etc.*).

swel·ter [ˈsweltə] sehr heiß sein; vor Hitze umkommen; schwitzen.

swept [swept] *pret. u. p.p. von sweep 1.*

swerve [swəːv] *v/i.* sich seitwärts wenden; abweichen; plötzlich ab- *od.* ausbiegen (*Wagen*); *v/t.* ablenken; *Sport*: *Ball* schneiden.

swift 1. □ schnell, eilig, geschwind, flink; **2.** *orn.* Turmschwalbe *f*; ˈ**swift·ness** Schnelligkeit *f*.

swig F [swig] **1.** (tüchtiger) Schluck *m*; **2.** schlucken; saufen.

swill [swil] **1.** Spülicht *n* (*a. fig.*); Schweinetrank *m*; *contp.* Gesöff *n*; **2.** spülen; saufen.

swim [swim] **1.** (*irr.*) *v/i.* schwimmen; schweben; *my head ~s* mir schwindelt; *v/t.* durchschwimmen; schwimmen lassen; schwemmen; **2.** Schwimmen *n*; *be in the ~* auf dem laufenden *od.* eingeweiht sein; ˈ**swim·mer** Schwimmer(in).

swim·ming [ˈswimiŋ] **1.** Schwimmen *n*; **2.** Schwimm…; ˈ**~-bath** (*bsd.* Hallen)Schwimmbad *n*; ˈ**~-cos·tume** Badeanzug *m*; ˈ**swim-ming·ly** *adv.* leicht, glatt; ˈ**swim-ming-pool** Frei-, Schwimmbad *n*; ˈ**swim-suit** Badeanzug *m*.

swin·dle [ˈswindl] **1.** *v/t.* beschwindeln (*out of* um *et.*); *v/i.* schwindeln; **2.** Schwindel *m*; ˈ**swin·dler** Schwindler(in).

swine *nur rhet., zo. od. fig. contp.* [swain], *pl.* ~ Schwein *n*; ˈ**swine-herd** Schweinehirt *m*.

swing [swiŋ] **1.** (*irr.*) *v/i.* schwingen, schwanken; F baumeln, gehängt werden; (sich) schaukeln; schwenken; sich drehen, ⚓ schwaien; *~ into motion* in Gang kommen; *v/t.* schwingen, (herum)schwenken; schaukeln; **2.** Schwingen *n*; Schwung *m*; Schaukel *f*; freier Lauf *m*; Spielraum *m* (*a. fig.*); ♪ Swing *m*; *Boxen*: Schwinger *m*; *in full ~* in vollem Gange; *go with a ~* Schwung haben; wie am Schnürchen gehen; **3.** Schwing…; **~ bridge** Drehbrücke *f*; **~ door** Drehtür *f*.

swinge·ing □ F [ˈswindʒiŋ] riesig, mächtig.

swing·ing □ [ˈswiŋiŋ] schwingend; Schwing…; schwungvoll.

swin·gle ⊕ [ˈswiŋgl] **1.** *Flachs* schwingen; **2.** Flachsschwinge *f*; ˈ**~·tree** Ortscheit *n*.

swin·ish □ [ˈswainiʃ] schweinisch.

swipe [swaip] **1.** aus vollem Arm schlagen; *sl.* klauen; **2.** kräftiger Schlag *m*; *~s pl.* Dünnbier *n*.

swirl [swəːl] **1.** (herum)wirbeln, strudeln; **2.** Wirbel *m*, Strudel *m*.

swish [swiʃ] **1.** sausen (lassen); zischen (*Sense*); rascheln; peitschen; **2.** Sausen *n etc.*; **3.** F forsch.

Swiss [swis] **1.** schweizerisch, Schweizer; **2.** Schweizer(in); *the ~ pl.* die Schweizer *m/pl.*

switch [switʃ] **1.** Gerte *f*; 🚂 Weiche *f*; ⚡ Schalter *m*; falscher Zopf *m*; **2.** peitschen; 🚂 rangieren; ⚡ (um-) schalten; *fig.* wechseln, überleiten; *~ on (off)* ⚡ ein- (aus)schalten; ˈ**~-back** Berg- und Talbahn *f*; ˈ**~-board** ⚡ Schaltbrett *n*, -tafel *f*; Telefonvermittlung *f*; **~ box** ⚡ Schaltkasten *m*.

swiv·el ⊕ ['swivl] Drehring *m*; Spannschloß *n*; *attr.* Dreh...
swol·len ['swəulən] *p.p. von swell 1.*
swoon [swu:n] **1.** Ohnmacht *f*; **2.** in Ohnmacht fallen.
swoop [swu:p] **1.** ~ *down on od. upon* (herab)stoßen (auf *acc.*) (*Raubvogel*); überfallen; **2.** Stoß *m.*
swop F [swɔp] (ver-, aus)tauschen.
sword F [sɔ:d] Schwert *n*, Degen *m*; Säbel *m*; '**~-cane** Stockdegen *m*; '**~-play** Fechten *n*; *fig.* Wortgefecht *n.*
swords·man ['sɔ:dzmən] Fechter *m*; '**swords·man·ship** Fechtkunst *f.*
swore [swɔ:] *pret. von swear 1.*
sworn [swɔ:n] **1.** *p.p. von swear 1*; **2.** ⚖ gerichtlich vereidigt; ~ *expert* ⚖ gerichtlich vereidigter Sachverständiger *m.*
swot *Schul-sl.* [swɔt] **1.** Paukerei *f*; Streber *m*; **2.** pauken, büffeln.
swum [swʌm] *p.p. von swim 1.*
swung [swʌŋ] *pret. u. p.p. von swing 1.*
syb·a·rite ['sibərait] Weichling *m*, Genüßling *m.*
syc·a·more ⚘ ['sikəmɔ:] Bergahorn *m*; *Am.* Platane *f.*
syc·o·phant ['sikəfənt] Kriecher *m*, Speichellecker *m*, Schmarotzer *m*; **syc·o·phan·tic** [~'fæntik] (*~ally*) kriecherisch.
syl·lab·ic [si'læbik] (*~ally*) silbenmäßig; Silben...; **syl·la·ble** ['siləbl] Silbe *f.*
syl·la·bus ['siləbəs] Auszug *m*, Abriß *m*; (*bsd.* Vorlesungs)Verzeichnis *n*; (*bsd.* Lehr-, Unterrichts)Plan *m.*
syl·lo·gism *phls.* ['silədʒizəm] Syllogismus *m*, Vernunftschluß *m.*
sylph [silf] Sylphe *f*, Luftgeist *m.*
syl·van ['silvən] waldig, Wald...
sym·bi·o·sis *biol.* [simbi'əusis] Symbiose *f* (*Zusammenleben artverschiedener Lebewesen*).
sym·bol ['simbəl] Symbol *n*, Sinnbild *n*; **sym·bol·ic, sym·bol·i·cal** □ [~'bɔlik(l)] symbolisch, sinnbildlich; **sym·bol·ism** ['~bəlizəm] Symbolik *f*; '**sym·bol·ize** sinnbildlich darstellen, symbolisieren, versinnbildlichen.
sym·met·ri·cal □ [si'metrikəl] symmetrisch, ebenmäßig; **sym·me·try** ['simitri] Symmetrie *f*, Ebenmaß *n.*
sym·pa·thet·ic [simpə'θetik] (*~ally*) ein-, mitfühlend; geistesverwandt; sympathisch; sympathetisch (*Nerv, Tinte*); ~ *strike* Sympathiestreik *m*; '**sym·pa·thize** sympathisieren, mitfühlen, empfinden; wohlwollend gegenüberstehen (*with dat.*); übereinstimmen; '**sym·pa·thiz·er** Anhänger(in); **sym·pa·thy** ['~θi] Sympathie *f*, Mitgefühl *n*; (An)Teilnahme *f*; *letter of* ~ Beileidsbrief *m.*
sym·phon·ic ♪ [sim'fɔnik] symphonisch; **sym·pho·ny** ♪ ['~fəni] Symphonie *f.*
sym·po·sium [sim'pəuzjəm] Symposion *n*, Sammlung *f* von Beiträgen.
symp·tom ['simptəm] Symptom *n*, (An)Zeichen *n*; **symp·to·mat·ic** [~'mætik] (*~ally*) symptomatisch; bezeichnend (*of* für).
syn·a·gogue ['sinəgɔg] Synagoge *f.*
sync(h) F [sink] Synchronisation *f*; *out of* ~ nicht synchron, nicht im Einklang.
syn·chro·flash *phot.* ['siŋkrəuflæʃ] Synchronblitzlicht *n.*
syn·chro-mesh gear *mot.* ['siŋkrəumeʃ'giə] Synchrongetriebe *n.*
syn·chro·nism ['siŋkrənizəm] Gleichzeitigkeit *f*; '**syn·chro·nize** *v/i.* gleichzeitig sein, zeitlich zs.-fallen; *v/t.* als gleichzeitig zs.-stellen; *Uhren, Tonfilm* synchronisieren; '**syn·chro·nous** □ gleichzeitig; gleichlaufend.
syn·chro·tron *phys.* ['siŋkrəutrɔn] Synchrotron *n*, Beschleuniger *m.*
syn·co·pate ['siŋkəpeit] verkürzen, synkopieren; **syn·co·pe** ['~pi] Synkope *f.*
syn·dic ['sindik] Syndikus *m*; **syn·di·cate 1.** ['~kit] Syndikat *n*; **2.** ['~keit] zu e-m Syndikat verbinden; '**syn·di·cat·ed** syndikalisiert, in mehreren Zeitungen erscheinend.
syn·od *eccl.* ['sinəd] Synode *f*; **syn·od·al** ['~dəl], **syn·od·ic, syn·od·i·cal** □ *eccl.* [si'nɔdik(l)] synodal.
syn·o·nym ['sinənim] Synonym *n*, sinnverwandtes Wort *n*; **syn·on·y·mous** □ [si'nɔniməs] sinnverwandt.
syn·op·sis [si'nɔpsis], *pl.* **syn'op·ses** [~si:z] *zs.-fassende* Übersicht *f*; Synopse *f.*
syn·op·tic, syn·op·ti·cal □ [si'nɔptik(əl)] synoptisch, übersichtlich.

syn·tac·tic, **syn·tac·ti·cal** □ *gr.* [sin'tæktik(əl)] syntaktisch; **syn·tax** *gr.* ['sintæks] Syntax *f*, Satzlehre *f*.
syn·the·sis ['sinθisis], *pl.* **syn·the·ses** ['~si:z] Synthese *f*, Verbindung *f*; **syn·the·size** ⊕ ['~saiz] künstlich herstellen.
syn·thet·ic, **syn·thet·i·cal** □ [sin'θetik(əl)] synthetisch; künstlich, Kunst...
syn·to·nize ['sintənaiz] *Radio*: abstimmen; '**syn·to·ny** Abstimmung *f*.
syph·i·lis ⚕ ['sifilis] Syphilis *f*.
syph·i·lit·ic ⚕ [sifi'litik] syphilitisch.
sy·phon ['saifən] = *siphon*.
Syr·i·an ['siriən] **1.** syrisch; **2.** Syr(i)er(in).
sy·rin·ga ⚘ [si'riŋgə] Flieder *m*.
syr·inge ['sirindʒ] **1.** Spritze *f*; **2.** (be-, ein-, aus)spritzen.
syr·up ['sirəp] Sirup *m*.
sys·tem ['sistim] System *n*; Organismus *m*, Körper *m*; Plan *m*, Ordnung *f*; **sys·tem·at·ic** [~'mætik] (*~ally*) systematisch, planmäßig; folgerichtig.

T

T [ti:]: *to a ~* F haargenau.
tab [tæb] Streifen *m*; Schildchen *n*, Anhänger *m*; Schlaufe *f*, Aufhänger *m*; (Kartei)Reiter *m*; F Rechnung *f*, Konto *n*; *keep a ~ on*, *keep ~s on* Buch führen über; *fig.* im Auge behalten.
tab·ard ['tæbəd] Heroldsrock *m*.
tab·by ['tæbi], *a.* '**~-cat** getigerte Katze *f*.
tab·er·nac·le ['tæbə:nækl] Tabernakel *n*; Stiftshütte *f*.
ta·ble ['teibl] **1.** Tisch *m*, Tafel *f*; Tisch-, Tafelrunde *f*; Tabelle *f*, Verzeichnis *n*; *Bibel*: Gesetzestafel *f*; *s.* *~-land*; *at ~* bei Tisch; *lay s.th. on the ~ parl.* et. zurückstellen; *turn the ~s* den Spieß umdrehen (*on* gegen); **2.** auf den Tisch legen; tabellarisch anordnen; *parl.* zurückstellen, ruhen lassen.
tab·leau ['tæbləu], *pl.* **tab·leaux** ['tæbləuz] lebendes Bild *n*.
ta·ble...: '**~-cloth** Tischtuch *n*; '**~-land** Tafelland *n*, Hochebene *f*; '**~-lin·en** Tischwäsche *f*.
ta·bles ⅌ ['teiblz] *pl. das* Einmaleins.
ta·ble-spoon ['teiblspu:n] Eßlöffel *m*; '**~·ful** Eßlöffel(voll) *m*.
tab·let ['tæblit] Täfelchen *n*; (Gedenk)Tafel *f*; (Notiz-, Schreib-, Zeichen)Block *m*; Stück *n Seife*; *pharm.* Tablette *f*.
ta·ble...: '**~-talk** Tischgespräch(e *pl.*) *n*; '**~-ten·nis** Tischtennis *n*; '**~-top** Tischplatte *f*; '**~·ware** Geschirr *n* und Besteck *n*; **~ wine** Tisch-, Tafelwein *m*.
tab·loid ['tæblɔid] Revolverblatt *n*.
ta·boo [tə'bu:] **1.** tabu, unantastbar, verboten; **2.** Tabu *n*; Verbot *n*; **3.** verbieten; für tabu erklären.
ta·bor ♪ ['teibə] Tamburin *n*.
tab·u·lar □ ['tæbjulə] tafelförmig, tabellarisch; **tab·u·late** ['~leit] tabellarisch ordnen; **tab·u'la·tion** tabellarische Anordnung *f*.
tac·it □ ['tæsit] stillschweigend; **tac·i·turn** □ ['~tə:n] schweigsam; **tac·i'tur·ni·ty** Schweigsamkeit *f*.
tack [tæk] **1.** Stift *m*, Zwecke *f*; *Näherei*: Heftstich *m*; ⚓ Halse *f*; Gang *m beim Lavieren*; *fig.* Kurs *m*, Weg *m*; ⚓ Essen *n*; *on the wrong ~* auf dem Holzweg; **2.** *v/t.* (an)heften; *fig.* (an)hängen (*to*, *on* an *acc.*); *v/i.* ⚓ wenden, über Stag gehen; *fig.* lavieren.
tack·le ['tækl] **1.** Gerät *n*; ⚓ Takel-, Tauwerk *n*; ⚓ Talje *f*; ⊕ Flaschenzug *m*; **2.** (an)packen; in Angriff nehmen; fertig werden mit; *j.* angehen (*for* um).
tack·y ['tæki] klebrig; *Am.* F schäbig.
tact [tækt] Takt *m*, Feingefühl *n*; **tact·ful** ['~ful] taktvoll.
tac·ti·cal □ ⚔ ['tæktikəl] taktisch; **tac·ti·cian** [~'tiʃən] Taktiker *m*; **tac·tics** ['~iks] *pl.*, *a. sg.* Taktik *f*.
tac·tile ['tæktail] taktil, Tast...
tact·less □ ['tæktlis] taktlos.
tad·pole *zo.* ['tædpəul] Kaulquappe *f*.

taf·fe·ta [ˈtæfitə] Taft *m.*

taf·fy *Am.* [ˈtæfi] = *toffee*; F Schmus *m*, Schmeichelei *f.*

tag [tæg] **1.** (Schnürsenkel)Stift *m*; Schildchen *n*, Etikett *n*; Redensart *f*, Zitat *n*; Zusatz *m*; loses Ende *n*; Fangen *n* (*Kinderspiel*); **2.** etikettieren, auszeichnen; anhängen (*to*, *on to* an *acc.*); ~ *after* hinter (*dat.*) herlaufen; ~ *along* F hinterherlaufen, unaufgefordert mitgehen; ~ *together* aneinanderreihen.

tail [teil] **1.** Schwanz *m*; Schweif *m*; hinteres Ende *n*, Schluß *m*; ~*s pl.* Rückseite *f e-r Münze*; F Frack *m*; *from the ~ of one's eye* aus den Augenwinkeln; *turn ~* davonlaufen; ~*s up* in Hochstimmung; **2.** ~ *after s.o.* j-m nachlaufen; ~ *s.o. Am.* j. beschatten; ~ *off*, ~ *away* abflauen, sich verlieren; zögernd enden; sich auseinanderziehen; **ˈ~·back** *mot.* Rückstau *m*; **ˈ~-board** *mot.* Ladeklappe *f*; **ˈ~-ˈcoat** Frack *m*; **tailed** geschwänzt; **ˈtail-ˈend** hinteres Ende *n*, Schluß *m*; **ˈtail·gate** *mot.* **1.** Heckklappe *f*; **2.** dicht auffahren; **ˈtail·less** schwanzlos; **ˈtail-light** Rück-, Schlußlicht *n.*

tai·lor [ˈteilə] **1.** Schneider *m*; **2.** schneidern; ~*ed suit* Maßanzug *m*; **ˈ~-made** vom Schneider gearbeitet, Schneider...; ~ *costume* Schneiderkostüm *n.*

tail...: **ˈ~·piece** *typ.* Schlußvignette *f*; **ˈ~-spin** ✈ (Ab)Trudeln *n*; **~ wind** Rückenwind *m.*

taint [teint] **1.** Flecken *m*, Makel *m*; Ansteckung *f*; Verderbnis *f*; **2.** *v/t.* beflecken; verderben, vergiften; ⚕ anstecken; *v/i.* verderben.

take [teik] **1.** (*irr.*) *v/t.* nehmen; an-, ab-, auf-, ein-, fest-, hin-, wegnehmen; (weg)bringen; *Speise* (zu sich) nehmen; *Mahlzeit* einnehmen; *Maßnahme*, *Gelegenheit* ergreifen; *Aufgabe etc.* übernehmen; *Eid*, *Gelübde*, *Examen* ablegen; *phot.* aufnehmen; *et. gut etc.* aufnehmen; *Beleidigung* hinnehmen; fassen, ergreifen; *Fisch etc.* fangen; sich *e-e Krankheit* holen; gewinnen; erfordern; brauchen; *gewisse Zeit* dauern; F verstehen; auffassen, auslegen; halten, ansehen (*for* für); *the devil ~ it!* hol's der Teufel!; *I ~ it that* ich nehme an, daß; ~ *breath* verschnaufen; ~ *comfort* sich trösten; ~ *compassion on* Mitleid empfinden mit; sich erbarmen (*gen.*); *s. consideration*; ~ *counsel* beraten; *s. decision*; ~ *a drive* e-e Fahrt machen; *s. effect*; *s. exercise*; ~ *fire* Feuer fangen; ~ *in hand* unternehmen; *s. heart*; ~ *a hedge* über e-e Hecke setzen; ~ *hold of* ergreifen; ~ *it* F es kriegen; *s. liberty*; *s. note*; *s. notice*; ~ *pity on* Mitleid haben mit; ~ *place* stattfinden; spielen (*Handlung*); ~ *s.o.'s place* an j-s Stelle treten; ~ *a rest* (eine) Rast machen; *s. rise*; ~ *a seat* Platz nehmen; ~ *a walk* e-n Spaziergang machen; ~ *my word for it* verlaß dich drauf; ~ *about* herumführen; ~ *along* mitnehmen; ~ *down Gerüst etc.* abnehmen; herunternehmen; einreißen; *j.* demütigen; *j-m* e-n Dämpfer geben; niederschreiben, notieren; ~ *for* halten für, ansehen als; ~ *from j-m* wegnehmen; abziehen von; ~ *in* einnehmen; *Segel* bergen; einnähen, enger machen; *Zeitung* halten; aufnehmen (*als Gast etc.*); *Arbeit* übernehmen; einschließen; verstehen; erfassen, geistig aufnehmen; überblicken; F *j.* 'reinlegen; ~ *off* ab-, wegnehmen; *Kleid* ausziehen, *Hut* absetzen; *Steuer* aufheben; fortführen, wegholen; F nachäffen; *be ~n off* 🚂 nicht mehr verkehren; ~ *on* an-, übernehmen; *Arbeiter etc.* einstellen; *Fahrgäste* zusteigen lassen; ~ *out* heraus-, entnehmen; *Fleck* entfernen; *Kind* spazieren-, ausführen; *Patent etc.* sich geben lassen; *Entscheid etc.* erwirken; *Versicherung* abschließen; ~ *it out of s.o. fig.* j. mitnehmen, j. strapazieren; es j-m austreiben; ~ *over* übernehmen; ~ *to* mitnehmen nach; ~ *to pieces* auseinandernehmen, zerlegen (*a. fig.*); ~ *up* aufnehmen, -heben; *Waffen etc.* ergreifen; sich *e-r Sache* annehmen; *Tätigkeit* aufnehmen; sich befassen mit, sich verlegen auf; *j.* protegieren; aufreißen, -brechen; *Wechsel* akzeptieren; *Aktien* zeichnen; festnehmen, aufgreifen, verhaften; *Raum*, *Zeit* wegnehmen, in Anspruch nehmen; *Wohnsitz* aufschlagen; *j.* unterbrechen, korrigieren; *et.* unterbreiten (*with dat.*); *be ~n up with fig.* angetan sein von; ~ *upon o.s.* auf sich nehmen; **2.** (*irr.*) *v/i.* wirken, ein-, anschlagen; Eindruck machen; gefallen, ziehen (*Theaterstück, Ware etc.*); Feuer fangen; sich *gut etc.* photographieren lassen; ~ *after* j-m nachschlagen; ~ *from* abziehen von; Abbruch tun (*dat.*); ~ *off* abspringen; ✈ aufsteigen; starten; ~ *on* F Anklang finden; ~ *over* die Amtsgewalt übernehmen; ~ *to* sich begeben nach; liebgewinnen; *fig.* sich verlegen auf (*acc.*); Zuflucht nehmen zu; sich zuwenden (*dat.*); sich ergeben (*dat.*); ~ *to ger.* dazu übergehen zu *inf.*; ~ *up* F sich bessern (*Wetter*); ~ *up with* sich anfreunden mit; *that won't* ~ *with me* das verfängt bei mir nicht; **3.** Fang *m*; *Geld*-Einnahme *f*; *Film*: Szene(naufnahme) *f*.

take...: '**~-a·way** 1. zum Mitnehmen (*Essen*); 2. Essen *n* zum Mitnehmen; Restaurant *n* mit Straßenverkauf; '**~-home pay** Nettogehalt *n*, -lohn *m*; '**~-'in** F Reinfall *m*; '**tak·en** *p.p.* *von take*; *be* ~ besetzt sein; *be* ~ *with* entzückt sein von; *be* ~ *ill* krank werden; '**take-off** Nachahmung *f*, Karikatur *f*; Absprung *m*; ✈ Start *m*; '**tak·er** Nehmer(in).

tak·ing ['teikiŋ] **1.** □ F anziehend, fesselnd, einnehmend; **2.** Nehmen *n etc.*; F Aufregung *f*; ~*s pl.* ✝ Einnahmen *f/pl.*

talc *min.* [tælk] Talk *m*; **tal·cum** ['~kəm] = *talc*.

tale [teil] Erzählung *f*, Geschichte *f*; Märchen *n*, Sage *f*; *it tells its own* ~ es spricht für sich selbst; '**~·bear·er** Zuträger(in).

tal·ent ['tælənt] Talent *n*, Begabung *f*, Anlage *f*; '**tal·ent·ed** talentvoll, talentiert, begabt; **tal·ent scout** Talentsucher *m*.

ta·les ⚖ ['teili:z] *pl.* Hilfs-, Ersatzgeschworenen *pl.*

tal·is·man ['tælizmən] Talisman *m*.

talk [tɔ:k] **1.** Gespräch *n*; Unterredung *f*; Plauderei *f*; Vortrag *m*; Geschwätz *n*; *give a* ~ e-n Vortrag halten; *have a* ~ sich unterhalten; **2.** sprechen, reden (von *et.*); plaudern; ~ *to s.o.* F j-m die Meinung sagen; ~ *back* frech antworten; ~ *down* herablassend reden (*to* mit); **talk·a·tive** □ ['~ətiv] gesprächig, geschwätzig, redselig; **talk·ee-talk·ee** F ['tɔ:ki'tɔ:ki] Geschwätz *n*, Kauderwelsch *n*; '**talk·er** Schwätzer(in); Sprechende *m,f*; *he is a good* ~ er kann (gut) reden; **talk·ie** F ['~i] Tonfilm *m*; '**talk·ing** Geplauder *n*; **talk·ing-to** F ['~tu:] Standpauke *f* (*Schelte*).

tall [tɔ:l] groß, lang, hoch (*Mensch, Baum etc.*); F übertrieben, unglaublich; *that's a* ~ *order* F das ist ein bißchen viel verlangt; '**tall·boy** Aufsatzkommode *f*; '**tall·ness** Größe *f*, Länge *f*, Höhe *f*.

tal·low ['tæləu] *ausgelassener* Talg *m*; '**tal·low·y** talgig.

tal·ly ['tæli] **1.** Kerbholz *n*; Gegenstück *n* (*of* zu); Kennzeichen *n*; Kupon *m*; **2.** übereinstimmen.

tal·ly-ho ['tæli'həu] **1.** hallo!; **2.** *hunt.* Weidruf *m*; **3.** hallo rufen.

tal·on *orn.* ['tælən] Kralle *f*, Klaue *f*.

ta·lus[1] ['teiləs] Böschung *f*; *geol.* Schuttkegel *m*.

ta·lus[2] *anat.* [~] Sprungbein *n*.

tam·a·ble ['teiməbl] zähmbar.

tam·a·rind ⚘ ['tæmərind] Tamarinde(nfrucht) *f*.

tam·a·risk ⚘ ['tæmərisk] Tamariske *f*.

tam·bour ['tæmbuə] **1.** Stickrahmen *m*; ⚠ Säulentrommel *f*; **2.** (auf dem Rahmen) sticken; **tam·bou·rine** ♪ [~bə'ri:n] Tamburin *n*.

tame [teim] **1.** □ zahm; folgsam; harmlos; lahm, fad(e); **2.** (be)zähmen, bändigen; '**tame·ness** Zahmheit *f*; '**tam·er** Zähmer(in), Bändiger(in).

Tam·ma·ny *Am.* ['tæməni] New Yorker Demokraten-Vereinigung *f*.

tam-o'-shan·ter [tæmə'ʃæntə] Baskenmütze *f*.

tamp [tæmp] ⚒ *Bohrloch* verdämmen; ⊕ *Lehm etc.* feststampfen.

tam·per ['tæmpə]: ~ *with* sich (unbefugt) zu schaffen machen mit; intrigieren mit *j-m*; *j.* zu bestechen suchen; *Urkunde* fälschen.

tam·pon ⚕ ['tæmpən] Tampon *m*.

tan [tæn] **1.** Lohe *f*; Lohfarbe *f*; (Sonnen)Bräune *f*; **2.** lohfarben; **3.** gerben; bräunen; F *j-m* das Fell gerben (*prügeln*).

tan·dem ['tændəm] Tandem *n*; ~ *connexion* ⚡ Serienschaltung *f*; *in* ~ *with* in Zusammenarbeit mit.

tang[1] [tæŋ] Angel *f*, Heftzapfen *m e-s Messers etc.*; *fig.* besonderer Bei-, Nachgeschmack *m*.

tang[2] [~] **1.** *scharfer* Klang *m*; Schrillen *n*; **2.** *scharf* klingen (lassen); schrillen (lassen).
tan·gent ⩓ ['tændʒənt] Tangente *f*; *go* (*a. fly*) *off at a* ~ vom Thema abkommen; **tan·gen·tial** □ ⩓ [~'dʒenʃəl] Tangential...
tan·ger·ine ⚘ [tændʒə'ri:n] Mandarine *f*.
tan·gi·bil·i·ty [tændʒi'biliti] Fühlbarkeit *f*; **tan·gi·ble** □ ['~dʒəbl] fühlbar, greifbar (*a. fig.*); klar.
tan·gle ['tæŋgl] **1.** Gewirr *n*; Verwicklung *f*; **2.** (sich) verwirren, verwickeln.
tan·go ['tæŋgəu] Tango *m* (*Tanz*).
tank [tæŋk] **1.** Zisterne *f*, Wasserbehälter *m*; ⊕, ⚔ Tank *m*; **2.** tanken; '**tank·age** Fassungsvermögen *n* e-s Tanks.
tank·ard ['tæŋkəd] Kanne *f*, *bsd.* (Bier)Krug *m*.
tank-car 🚂 ['tæŋkkɑ:] Kesselwagen *m*; '**tank·er** Tanker *m*, Tankschiff *n*; '**tank-top** Pullunder *m*.
tan·ner[1] ['tænə] Gerber *m*.
tan·ner[2] *sl.* [~] Sixpence(stück *n*) *pl.*
tan·ner·y ['tænəri] Gerberei *f*.
tan·nic ac·id ⚗ ['tænik'æsid] Gerbsäure *f*.
tan·nin ⚗ ['tænin] Tannin *n*.
tan·noy ['tænɔi] Lautsprecheranlage *f*.
tan·ta·lize ['tæntəlaiz] quälen, peinigen.
tan·ta·mount ['tæntəmaunt] von gleichem Wert (*to* wie); gleichbedeutend (*to* mit).
tan·trum F ['tæntrəm] Rappel *m*, Koller *m*.
tap[1] [tæp] **1.** leichtes Klopfen *n*; **2.** pochen, klopfen; tippen (auf, an, gegen *acc.*).
tap[2] [~] **1.** (Wasser-, Gas-, Zapf-) Hahn *m*; Zapfen *m*; Wasserleitung *f*; F Sorte *f*, Marke *f e-s Getränkes*; ⊕ Gewindebohrer *m*; F *s.* ~-*room*; *on* ~ frisch vom Faß (*Bier*); *fig.* verfügbar; **2.** an-, abzapfen; ~ *the wire(s)* ⚡ Strom stehlen; *teleph.* mithören.
tap-dance ['tæpdɑ:ns] Stepptanz *m*.
tape [teip] schmales Band *n*; *Sport*: Zielband *n*; Tonband *n*; *tel.* Papierstreifen *m*; *red* ~ Bürokratismus *m*; '**~-meas·ure** Bandmaß *n*; **tape re·cord·er** Tonbandgerät *n*; **tape re·cord·ing** Tonbandaufnahme *f*.
ta·per [teipə] **1.** dünne Wachskerze *f*; **2.** *adj.* spitz (zulaufend); schlank (*Finger*); **3.** *v/i.* spitz zulaufen; ~*ing* = ~ 2; *v/t.* zuspitzen.
tap·es·tried ['tæpistrid] gobelingeschmückt; '**tap·es·try** Gobelin *m*, Wandteppich *m*.
tape·worm ['teipwə:m] Bandwurm *m*.
tap·i·o·ca [tæpi'əukə] Tapioka *f*.
ta·pir *zo.* ['teipə] Tapir *m*.
tap·pet ⊕ ['tæpit] Stößel *m*; Daumen *m*, Nocken *m*.
tap-room ['tæprum] Schankstube *f*.
tap-root ⚘ ['tæpru:t] Pfahlwurzel *f*.
taps *Am.* ⚔ [tæps] *pl.* Zapfenstreich *m*.
tap·ster ['tæpstə] Schankkellner *m*.
tap-wa·ter ['tæpwɔ:tə] Leitungswasser *n*.
tar [tɑ:] **1.** Teer *m*; *Jack* ♀ F Teerjacke *f*, Matrose *m*; **2.** teeren.
ta·ran·tu·la *zo.* [tə'ræntjulə] Tarantel *f*.
tar-board ['tɑ:bɔ:d] Teerpappe *f*.
tar·di·ness ['tɑ:dinis] Langsamkeit *f*; '**tar·dy** □ langsam; spät.
tare[1] ⚘ [tɛə] *mst* ~*s pl.* Wicke *f*.
tare[2] ⚚ [~] **1.** Tara *f*; **2.** tarieren.
tar·get ['tɑ:git] (Schieß)Scheibe *f*; *fig.* Ziel(scheibe *f*) *n*; Ziel(leistung *f*) *n*; Soll *n*; ~ *date* ⚚ Stichtag *m*, Termin *m*; ~ *language* Zielsprache *f*; ~ *practice* Scheibenschießen *n*.
tar·iff ['tærif] (*bsd.* Zoll)Tarif *m*.
tar·mac ['tɑ:mæk] Asphalt *m als Straßenbelag*.
tarn [tɑ:n] Bergsee *m*.
tar·nish ['tɑ:niʃ] **1.** *v/t.* ⊕ trüb *od.* blind machen; *fig.* trüben; *v/i.* trüb werden, anlaufen; **2.** Trübung *f*; Belag *m*.
tar·pau·lin [tɑ:'pɔ:lin] ⚓ Persenning *f*; Plane *f*, Wagendecke *f*.
tar·ra·gon ['tærəgən] Estragon *m*.
tar·ry[1] *lit.* ['tæri] säumen, zögern; weilen.
tar·ry[2] ['tɑ:ri] teerig.
tart [tɑ:t] **1.** □ sauer, herb; *fig.* scharf, schroff; **2.** (Obst)Torte *f*; *sl.* Nutte *f*, Dirne *f*.
tar·tan ['tɑ:tən] Tartan *m*; Schottentuch *n*; Schottenmuster *n*; ~ *plaid* Schottenplaid *n*.
Tar·tar[1] ['tɑ:tə] Tatar *m*; *fig.* Hitzkopf *m*; *catch a* ~ an den Unrechten kommen.
tar·tar[2] [~] ⚗ Weinstein *m*; Zahnstein *m*.

task [tɑ:sk] **1.** Aufgabe *f*; *aufgegebene* Arbeit *f*; Tagewerk *n*, Geschäft *n*; *take to* ~ (*for*) zur Rede stellen (wegen); **2.** beschäftigen; in Anspruch nehmen; **task force** ⚔ Kampfgruppe *f für Sonderoperation*; ˈ**task·mas·ter** (strenger) Arbeitgeber *m*; ⊕ Anweiser *m*.

tas·sel [ˈtæsəl] **1.** Troddel *f*, Quaste *f*; **2.** mit Troddeln schmücken.

taste [teist] **1.** Geschmack *m*; (Kost)Probe *f* (*of gen.*, von); Neigung *f*, Lust *f* (*for* zu); *to* ~ nach Belieben; **2.** *v/t.* kosten, schmecken; versuchen; genießen; erleben; *v/i.* kosten (*of* von, *a. acc.*); schmecken (*of* nach); **taste·ful** □ [~ˈful] geschmackvoll.

taste·less □ [ˈteistlis] geschmacklos; ˈ**taste·less·ness** Geschmacklosigkeit *f*.

tas·ter [ˈteistə] (Tee-, Wein- *etc.*) Schmecker *m*, Koster *m*, Prüfer *m*.

tast·y □ F [ˈteisti] schmackhaft.

tat[1] [tæt] *s. tit*[1].

tat[2] [~] Frivolitäten (*Spitzen*) anfertigen.

ta-ta [ˈtæˈtɑ:] F *Kindersprache u. co.* adda (*adieu*).

tat·ter [ˈtætə] **1.** zerfetzen; **2.** ~*s pl.* Fetzen *m/pl.*; **tat·ter·de·mal·ion** [~dəˈmeiljən] zerlumpter Kerl *m*.

tat·tle [ˈtætl] **1.** schwatzen, plaudern; *b.s.* tratschen; **2.** Geschwätz *n*; *b.s.* Tratsch *m*; ˈ**tat·tler** Plauderer(in), Schwätzer(in).

tat·too[1] [təˈtu:] **1.** ⚔ Zapfenstreich *m*; *beat the devil's* ~ *fig.* mit den Fingern trommeln; **2.** *fig.* trommeln.

tat·too[2] [~] **1.** tätowieren; **2.** Tätowierung *f*.

tat·ty F [ˈtæti] schäbig.

taught [tɔ:t] *pret. u. p.p. von teach.*

taunt [tɔ:nt] **1.** Stichelei *f*, Spott *m*; **2.** verhöhnen, spotten; ~ *s.o. with s.th.* j-m et. vorwerfen; ˈ**taunt·ing** □ spöttisch, höhnisch.

Tau·rus *ast.* [ˈtɔ:rəs] Stier *m*.

taut [tɔ:t] ⚓ steif, straff; schmuck; ˈ**taut·en** (sich) straffen.

tau·tol·o·gy [tɔ:ˈtɔlədʒi] Tautologie *f*.

tav·ern [ˈtævən] Schenke *f*, Taverne *f*.

taw[1] ⊕ [tɔ:] weißgerben.

taw[2] [~] Murmel(spiel *n*) *m*, *f*.

taw·dri·ness [ˈtɔ:drinis] Flitterhaftigkeit *f*, Kitsch *m*; ˈ**taw·dry** □ flitterhaft, billig (aufgeputzt); kitschig.

taw·ny [ˈtɔ:ni] lohfarben.

tax [tæks] **1.** Steuer *f*, Abgabe *f* (*on* auf *acc.*); *fig.* Inanspruchnahme *f* (*on, upon gen.*); ~ *allowance* Steuerfreibetrag *m*; ~ *bracket* Steuerklasse *f*; ~ *evasion* Steuerhinterziehung *f*; **2.** besteuern; *fig.* stark in Anspruch nehmen; ⚖ *Kosten* schätzen; auf e-e harte Probe stellen; *j.* zur Rede stellen; mit *j-m* ins Gericht gehen; ~ *s.o. with s.th.* j. e-r Sache beschuldigen; ˈ**tax·a·ble** □ besteuerbar; **taxˈa·tion** Besteuerung *f*; Steuer(n *pl.*) *f*; *bsd.* ⚖ Schätzung *f*; ˈ**tax-col·lec·tor** Steuereinnehmer *m*; ˈ**tax-deˈduct·i·ble** von der Steuer absetzbar; **tax dodg·er** Steuersünder *m*; ˈ**tax-free** steuerfrei; **tax ha·ven** Steuerparadies *n*.

tax·i F [ˈtæksi] **1.** = ˈ**~-cab** Taxi *n*, (Auto)Droschke *f*; **2.** mit e-m Taxi fahren; ✈ rollen; ˈ**~-danc·er** Eintänzer *m*; Taxigirl *n*.

tax·i·der·mist [ˈtæksidə:mist] Tierpräparator *m*.

tax·i...: ˈ**~-driv·er** Taxichauffeur *m*; ˈ**~·me·ter** Taxameter *m* (*Fahrpreisanzeiger*); **~ rank, ~ stand** Taxistand *m*.

tax...: ˈ**~·pay·er** Steuerzahler *m*; **~ re·lief** Steuererleichterung(en *pl.*) *f*; **~ return** Steuererklärung *f*.

tea [ti:] Tee *m*; *high* ~, *meat* ~ frühes Abendbrot *n* mit Tee; ˈ**~·bag** Teebeutel *m*; ˈ**~-break** Teepause *f*; ˈ**~-cad·dy** Teedose *f*.

teach [ti:tʃ] (*irr.*) lehren, unterrichten, *j-m et.* beibringen; ˈ**teach·a·ble** □ gelehrig; lehrbar; ˈ**teach·er** Lehrer(in); ˈ**teach·er-ˈtrain·ing col·lege** Lehrerbildungsanstalt *f*; ˈ**teach-ˈin** (politische) Diskussion *f* (*mst als Großveranstaltung*); ˈ**teach·ing** Unterrichten *n*; ~*s pl. die* Lehren *pl.*

tea...: ˈ**~-co·sy** Teewärmer *m*; ˈ**~·cup** Teetasse *f*; *storm in a* ~ *fig.* Sturm *m* im Wasserglas; ˈ**~-gown** Nachmittagskleid *n*.

teak ⚘ [ti:k] Teakbaum *m*, -holz *n*.

tea-ket·tle [ˈti:ketl] Wasserkessel *m*.

team [ti:m] Team *n*, Arbeitsgruppe *f*; Gespann *n*; *bsd. Sport*: Mannschaft *f*; **~ ef·fort:** *by a* ~ mit gemeinsamen Kräften; **~ spir·it** Gemeinschafts-, Korpsgeist *m*; **team·ster**

['~stə] Gespannführer *m*; *Am.* Lkw-Fahrer *m*; '**team-work** Zusammenarbeit *f*, Teamwork *n* (*a. Sport*); *thea.* Zusammenspiel *n*.

tea·pot ['ti:pɔt] Teekanne *f*.

tear[1] [tɛə] **1.** (*irr.*) *v/t.* zerren, reißen; zerreißen; *Loch* reißen; *v/i.* (zer)reißen; F *mit adv. od. prep.* rasen, stürmen; **2.** Riß *m*; *s. wear.*

tear[2] [tiə] Träne *f*; '**~drop** Träne *f*.

tear·ful □ ['tiəful] tränenreich.

tear-gas ['tiəgæs] Tränengas *n*.

tear·ing *fig.* ['tɛəriŋ] rasend.

tear-jerk·er F ['tiədʒə:kə] Schnulze *f*.

tear·less □ ['tiəlis] tränenlos.

tea·room ['ti:rum] Tearoom *m*, Teestube *f*, Café *n*.

tease [ti:z] **1.** *Wolle etc.* kämmen, zupfen; *Tuch* rauhen; *fig.* necken, hänseln; **2.** Necker *m*; Quälgeist *m*; **tea·sel** ♀ ['ti:zl] Karde(ndistel) *f*; ⊕ Karde *f*, Krempel *f*; '**teas·er** F *fig.* harte Nuß *f*.

tea...: '**~-spoon** Teelöffel *m*; '**~-spoon·ful** Teelöffel(voll) *m*; '**~-strain·er** Teesieb *n*.

teat [ti:t] Zitze *f*, Brustwarze *f*; (Gummi)Sauger *m*.

tea...: '**~-things** *pl.* Teegeschirr *n*; **~ tow·el** Geschirrtuch *n*; '**~-urn** Teemaschine *f*.

tech·nic ['teknik] *a.* ~*s pl. od. sg.* = *technique*; '**tech·ni·cal** □ technisch; gewerblich, Gewerbe... (*Schule etc.*); fachlich, Fach... (*Ausdruck etc.*); **tech·ni·cal·i·ty** [~'kæliti] technische Eigentümlichkeit *f*; Fachausdruck *m*; **tech'ni·cian** [~ʃən] Techniker(in).

tech·ni·col·or ['teknikʌlə] Technikolor...; **2.** Technikolor(verfahren) *n*.

tech·nique [tek'ni:k] Technik *f*; Methode *f*; Art *f* der Ausführung; mechanische Fertigkeit *f*.

tech·no·cra·cy [tek'nɔkrəsi] Technokratie *f*.

tech·nol·o·gy [tek'nɔlədʒi] Technologie *f*; Gewerbekunde *f*; *school of* ~ Technische Hochschule *f*.

tech·y ['tetʃi] = *testy*.

ted·der *Am.* ['tedə] Heuwendemaschine *f*.

ted·dy boy F ['tedibɔi] Halbstarke *m*.

te·di·ous □ ['ti:djəs] langweilig, ermüdend; weitschweifig; '**te·di·ous·ness** Langweiligkeit *f*; Weitschweifigkeit *f*.

te·di·um ['ti:djəm] Lang(e)weile *f*; Langweiligkeit *f*.

tee [ti:] **1.** *Sport*: Mal *n*, Ziel *n*; *Golfspiel*: Abschlagmal *n*; **2.** ~ *off* das Spiel eröffnen.

teem [ti:m] wimmeln; strotzen (*beide*: *with* von).

teen-ag·er ['ti:neidʒə] Jugendliche *m*, *f* von 13 bis 19 Jahren, Teenager *m*.

teens [ti:nz] *pl.* Lebensjahre *n/pl.* von 13 bis 19; *in one's* ~ noch nicht 20 Jahre alt.

tee·ny F ['ti:ni] *Kindersprache*: winzig; **~·bop·per** F *oft contp.* ['~bɔpə] Teenybopper *m* (*nur an Pop und Mode interessierter jüngerer Teenager*).

tee·ter F ['ti:tə] wanken.

teeth [ti:θ] *pl. von tooth.*

teethe [ti:ð] zahnen; *teething troubles pl.* Beschwerden *f/pl.* beim Zahnen.

tee·to·tal [ti:'təutl] abstinent, Abstinenzler...; **tee'to·tal·(l)er** Abstinenzler(in), Antialkoholiker(in).

tee·to·tum ['ti:təu'tʌm] Drehwürfel *m*.

tel·au·to·gram [te'lɔ:təgræm] Bildtelegramm *n*; **tel'aut·o·graph** [~grɑ:f] Bildbriefsender *m*.

tel·e·cast ['telikɑ:st] **1.** Fernsehsendung *f*; **2.** im Fernsehen übertragen.

tel·e·com·mu·ni·ca·tions ['telikəmju:ni'keiʃənz] *pl.* Fernmeldewesen *n*.

tel·e·course *Am.* F ['telikɔ:s] Fernsehlehrgang *m*.

tel·e·gram ['teligræm] Telegramm *n*.

tel·e·graph ['teligrɑ:f] **1.** Telegraph *m*; **2.** Telegraphen...; Telegramm...; **3.** telegraphieren; **tel·e·graph·ic** [~'græfik] (~*ally*) telegraphisch; telegrammäßig (*Stil*); **te·leg·ra·phist** [ti'legrəfist] Telegraphist(in); **te'leg·ra·phy** Telegraphie *f*.

te·lep·a·thy [ti'lepəθi] Telepathie *f*, Gedankenübertragung *f*.

tel·e·phone ['telifəun] **1.** Telephon *n*, Fernsprecher *m*; *by* ~ telephonisch; *be on the* ~ Telephonanschluß haben; am Telefon sein; **2.** telephonieren; *j.* anrufen; '**~-an·swer·ing ma·chine** Anrufbeantworter *m*; **~ booth** Telephonzelle *f*; ~

charg·es *pl.* Telephongebühren *f/pl.*; **tel·e·phon·ic** [~'fɔnik] (*~ally*) telephonisch; Fernsprech...; **te·leph·o·nist** [ti'lefənist] Telephonist(in); **te'leph·o·ny** Fernsprechwesen *n.*

tel·e·pho·to *phot.* ['teli'fəutəu] *a. ~ lens* Teleobjektiv *n.*

tel·e·print·er ['teliprintə] Fernschreiber *m.*

tel·e·scope ['teliskəup] **1.** *opt.* Teleskop *n*, Fernrohr *n*; **2.** (sich) ineinanderschieben; **tel·e·scop·ic** [~'kɔpik] teleskopisch; *~ aerial*, *Am. ~ antenna* Teleskopantenne *f*; *~ sight* Zielfernrohr *n.*

tel·e·typ·er ['teli'taipə] Fernschreiber *m.*

tel·e·vise ['telivaiz] im Fernsehen übertragen; **tel·e·vi·sion** ['~viʒən] Fernsehen *n*; *attr.* Fernseh...; *watch ~* fernsehen; *~ set* Fernsehapparat *m*; **tel·e·vi·sor** ['~vaizə] Fernsehapparat *m.*

tell [tel] (*irr.*) *v/t.* (*bsd. Stimmen*) zählen; sagen, berichten, erzählen, unterscheiden; erkennen; *~ s.o. to do s.th.* j-m sagen, er solle et. tun; j. et. tun heißen; *I have been told* mir ist gesagt worden; *~ off* abzählen; auswählen (*for s.th.* zu et.; *to do* um zu tun); F heruntermachen, abkanzeln; *~ the world sl.* hinausposaunen; *v/i.* erzählen (*of*, *about* von); (aus)plaudern (*on*, *of* über *acc.*); Wirkung tun, sich auswirken; sitzen (*Hieb etc.*); sich geltend machen; **'tell·er** Zähler *m*; Erzähler *m*; Kassierer *m*; **'tell·ing** □ wirkungsvoll; wirksam; **'tell·ing-'off:** *give s.o. a ~* F j. ausschimpfen; **tell·tale** ['~teil] **1.** verräterisch; kennzeichnend; *fig.* sprechend (*Ähnlichkeit*); **2.** Zuträger(in), Klatschbase *f*; ⊕ Anzeiger *m*; *~ clock* Kontrolluhr *f.*

tel·ly F ['teli] Fernsehen *n*; Fernseher *m.*

tel·pher ['telfə] Hängebahn(wagen *m*) *f.*

te·mer·i·ty [ti'meriti] Unbesonnenheit *f*, Verwegenheit *f.*

temp F [temp] Aushilfskraft *f*; *bsd.* Aushilfssekretärin *f.*

tem·per ['tempə] **1.** mäßigen, mildern; ♪ temperieren; *Farbe*, *Kalk* anmachen; *Stahl* anlassen, vergüten; **2.** ⊕ gehörige Mischung *f*; *metall.* Härte(grad *m*) *f*; (Gemüts-) Ruhe *f*, Gleichmut *m*; Temperament *n*, Wesen(sart *f*) *n*, Natur *f*; Stimmung *f*, Laune *f*; Gereiztheit *f*, Wut *f*; *hot ~* Jähzorn *m*; *lose one's ~* wütend werden; **tem·per·a·ment** ['~rəmənt] Temperament *n*, (Gemüts)Art *f*; **tem·per·a·men·tal** □ [~'mentl] anlagebedingt; launisch; **'tem·per·ance** **1.** Mäßigkeit *f*; Enthaltsamkeit *f*; **2.** alkoholfrei (*Gasthaus*); Enthaltsamkeits...; **tem·per·ate** □ ['~rit] gemäßigt; zurückhaltend; maßvoll; mäßig *im Essen etc.*; *~ zone* gemäßigte Zone *f*; **tem·per·a·ture** ['tempritʃə] Temperatur *f*; *have od. run a ~* Fieber haben; **tem·pered** ['tempəd] ...geartet; ...mütig; ...gelaunt; *hot-~* jähzornig.

tem·pest ['tempist] Sturm *m*; Gewitter *n*; **tem·pes·tu·ous** □ [~'pestjuəs] stürmisch; ungestüm.

Tem·plar ['templə] *hist.* Tempelherr *m*; ≗ *univ.* Student *m* der Rechte am Londoner *Temple.*

tem·ple[1] ['templ] Tempel *m*, Kirche *f*; ≗ *Rechtsinstitut u. Rechtskollegien in London.*

tem·ple[2] *anat.* [~] Schläfe *f.*

tem·po ['tempəu] Geschwindigkeit *f*, Tempo *n.*

tem·po·ral □ ['tempərəl] zeitlich, weltlich; **tem·po·ral·i·ties** [~'rælitiz] *pl.* weltliche Güter *n/pl.*; Temporalien *n/pl.*; **tem·po·ra·ri·ness** ['~rərinis] zeitweilige Dauer *f*; **'tem·po·rar·y** □ zeitweilig; vorläufig; vorübergehend; *~ bridge* Notbrücke *f*; *~ work* Gelegenheitsarbeit *f*; **'tem·po·rize** Zeit zu gewinnen suchen; auf Zeit spielen.

tempt [tempt] *j.* versuchen; verleiten; verlocken; *be ~ed* versucht sein; **temp'ta·tion** Versuchung *f*; Reiz *m*; **'tempt·er** Versucher *m*; **'tempt·ing** □ verführerisch; **'tempt·ress** Versucherin *f.*

ten [ten] **1.** zehn; **2.** Zehn *f.*

ten·a·ble ['tenəbl] haltbar (*Theorie etc.*); verliehen (*Amt*).

te·na·cious □ [ti'neiʃəs] zäh; festhaltend (*of* an *dat.*); treu (*Gedächtnis*); *fig.* beharrlich (*of* in *dat.*); **te·nac·i·ty** [ti'næsiti] Zähigkeit *f*; Festhalten *n* (*of* an *dat.*); Treue *f des Gedächtnisses.*

ten·an·cy ['tenənsi] Pachtbesitz *m.*

ten·ant ['tenənt] **1.** Pächter *m*;

Mieter *m*; *fig.* Bewohner *m*, Insasse *m*; ~ *right* Mietrecht *n*; **2.** bewohnen; ˈ**ten·ant·ry** Pächter *m/pl.*; Mieter *m/pl.*

tench *ichth.* [tenʃ] Schleie *f.*

tend[1] [tend] **1.** gerichtet sein (*towards* nach, auf *acc.*), hinstreben (zu); abzielen (*to* auf *acc.*); neigen, den Hang haben (*to* zu); ~ *from* wegstreben von; ~ *upwards* sich nach oben bewegen (*Preise*).

tend[2] [~] *Kranke* pflegen; *Vieh* hüten; *Maschine etc.* bedienen; ˈ**tend·ance** Pflege *f*; Bedienung *f.*

tend·en·cy [ˈtendənsi] Richtung *f*; Neigung *f*; Tendenz *f*; Zweck *m*; **ten·den·tious** [~ˈdenʃəs] tendenziös, zweckbestimmt, einseitig.

ten·der[1] □ [ˈtendə] zart; weich; empfindlich; heikel (*Thema*); zärtlich; schwächlich.

ten·der[2] [~] **1.** (*bsd.* Zahlungs-) Angebot *n*; ✝ (Lieferungs)Angebot *n*, Offerte *f*, Ausschreibung *f*; Kostenanschlag *m*; *legal* ~ gesetzliches Zahlungsmittel *n*; **2.** *v/t.* anbieten; *Entlassung* einreichen; *v/i.* ein Angebot machen.

ten·der[3] [~] Wärter *m*; 🚂, ⚓ Tender *m.*

ten·der·foot *Am.* F [ˈtendəfut] Anfänger *m*, Neuling *m*; ˈ**ten·der·ize** *Fleisch* zart machen; **ten·der·loin** [ˈ~lɔin] *bsd. Am.* Filet *n*; *Am.* berüchtigtes Viertel *n*; ˈ**ten·der·ness** Zartheit *f*; Zärtlichkeit *f.*

ten·don *anat.* [ˈtendən] Flechse *f*, Sehne *f.*

ten·dril ⚘ [ˈtendril] Ranke *f.*

ten·e·ment [ˈtenimənt] Wohnhaus *n*; (*bsd.* Miet)Wohnung *f*; ⚖ *jeder beständige Besitz m*; ~ *house* Mietshaus *n.*

ten·et [ˈti:net] Grund-, Lehrsatz *m.*

ten·fold [ˈtenfəuld] zehnfach.

ten·nis [ˈtenis] Tennis(spiel) *n*; ˈ~**-court** Tennisplatz *m.*

ten·on ⊕ [ˈtenən] Zapfen *m*; ˈ~**-saw** ⊕ Fuchsschwanz *m.*

ten·or [ˈtenə] Fortgang *m*, Verlauf *m*; Inhalt *m*; ♪ Tenor *m.*

tense[1] *gr.* [tens] Zeit(form) *f*, Tempus *n.*

tense[2] □ [~] gespannt (*a. fig.*); straff; ˈ**tense·ness** Gespanntheit *f*; **ten·sile** [ˈtensail] dehnbar; Dehnungs...; ~ *strength* Zugfestigkeit *f*; **ten·sion** [ˈ~ʃən] Spannung *f*; *high* ~ ⚡ Hochspannung *f*; ~ *test* Zerreißprobe *f.*

tent[1] [tent] Zelt *n*; *pitch one's* ~*s* s-e Zelte aufschlagen (*a. fig.*).

tent[2] [~] Tintowein *m.*

ten·ta·cle *zo.* [ˈtentəkl] Fühler *m*; Fangarm *m e-s Polypen.*

ten·ta·tive [ˈtentətiv] **1.** □ versuchend; Versuchs...; ~*ly* versuchsweise; **2.** Versuch *m.*

ten·ter [ˈtentə] Spannrahmen *m*; ˈ~**·hook** Spannhaken *m*; *be on* ~*s fig.* auf die Folter gespannt sein.

tenth [tenθ] **1.** zehnte(r, -s); **2.** Zehntel *n*; ˈ**tenth·ly** zehntens.

tent-peg [ˈtentpeg] Zeltpflock *m*, Hering *m.*

ten·u·ous □ [ˈtenjuəs] dünn; zart; fein; dürftig.

ten·ure [ˈtenjuə] Besitz(art *f*, -dauer *f*, -anspruch *m*) *m*; ~ *of office* Amtszeit *f.*

te·pee [ˈti:pi:] Indianerzelt *n.*

tep·id □ [ˈtepid] lau(warm); **te**ˈ**pid·i·ty**, ˈ**tep·id·ness** Lauheit *f.*

ter·cen·te·nar·y [tə:senˈti:nəri], **ter·cen·ten·ni·al** [~ˈtenjəl] **1.** dreihundertjährig; **2.** Dreihundertjahrfeier *f.*

ter·gi·ver·sa·tion [tə:dʒivə:ˈseiʃən] völlige Kehrtwendung *f*; Ausflucht *f*; Zweideutigkeit.

term [tə:m] **1.** (bestimmte) Zeit *f*, Frist *f*, Termin *m*; Zahltag *m*; Amtszeit *f*; ⚖ Sitzungsperiode *f*; Semester *n*, Quartal *n*, Trimester *n an Universitäten, Schulen*; 𝔄, *phls.* Glied *n*; (Fach)Ausdruck *m*, Wort *n*, Bezeichnung *f*; Begriff *m*; ~*s pl.* Bedingungen *f/pl.*; Honorar *n*; Preise *m/pl.*; Verhältnis *n*, Beziehungen *f/pl.*; *in* ~*s of praise* in lobenden Worten; *be on good* (*bad*) ~*s with* gut (schlecht) *od.* auf gutem (schlechtem) Fuße stehen mit; *come to* ~*s*, *make* ~*s* sich einigen; **2.** (be)nennen; bezeichnen (als).

ter·ma·gant [ˈtə:məgənt] **1.** □ zanksüchtig; **2.** Zankteufel *m* (*Weib*).

ter·mi·na·ble □ [ˈtə:minəbl] begrenzt; befristet; **ter·mi·nal** [ˈ~nl] **1.** □ End..., letzt; (Ab)Schluß...; ⚘ gipfelständig; Termin...; ~*ly* terminweise; **2.** Endstück *n*, -teil *m*; ⚡ Pol *m*; ⚡ Klemme *f*; 🚂 *etc.* Endstation *f*; *Computer*: Terminal *n*; **ter·mi·nate** [ˈ~neit] *v/t.* begrenzen; beendigen; *v/i.* endigen; **ter·mi**ˈ**na·tion** Beendigung *f*; Ende *n*; *gr.* Endung *f.*

ter·mi·nol·o·gy [tə:mi'nɔlədʒi] Terminologie *f*, Fachsprache *f*.
ter·mi·nus ['tə:minəs], *pl.* **ter·mi·ni** ['~nai] Endpunkt *m*; 🚂 Endstation *f*.
ter·mite *zo.* ['tə:mait] Termite *f*.
tern *orn.* [tə:n] Seeschwalbe *f*.
ter·na·ry ['tə:nəri] aus je drei bestehend, dreifältig.
ter·race ['terəs] Terrasse *f*; Häuserreihe *f in Städten*; '**ter·raced** terrassenförmig; flach (*Dach*); ~ *house* Reihenhaus *n*.
ter·rain ['terein] Gelände *n*, Terrain *n*.
ter·ra-cot·ta ['terə'kɔtə] Terrakotta *f*.
ter·res·tri·al □ [ti'restriəl] irdisch; Erd...; *bsd. zo.*, ⚘ Land...
ter·ri·ble □ ['terəbl] schrecklich; '**ter·ri·ble·ness** Schrecklichkeit *f*.
ter·ri·er *zo.* ['teriə] Terrier *m*.
ter·rif·ic [tə'rifik] (*~ally*) fürchterlich, furchtbar, schrecklich; F ungeheuer, großartig, toll; **ter·ri·fy** ['terifai] *v/t.* erschrecken.
ter·ri·to·ri·al [teri'tɔ:riəl] **1.** □ territorial; Land...; Bezirks...; ~ *waters pl.* Hoheitsgewässer *n/pl.*; ♀ *Army*, ♀ *Force* Territorialarmee *f*; **2.** ⚔ Angehöriger *m* der Territorialarmee; **ter·ri·to·ry** ['~təri] Gebiet *n*; Territorium *n*.
ter·ror ['terə] Schrecken *m*, Entsetzen *n*, Furcht *f*; '**ter·ror·ism** Schreckensherrschaft *f*; '**ter·ror·ize** terrorisieren.
ter·ry(-cloth) ['teri(klɔθ)] Frottee *n*, *m*.
terse □ [tə:s] knapp; kurz u. bündig; prägnant; '**terse·ness** Knappheit *f*.
ter·tian ⚕ ['tə:ʃən] dreitägig(es Fieber *n*); '**ter·ti·ar·y** tertiär.
tes·sel·ate ['tesileit] mosaikartig zs.-setzen; *~d pavement* Mosaikfußboden *m*.
test [test] **1.** Probe *f*; Untersuchung *f*; (Eignungs)Prüfung *f*; Test *m*; *fig.* Prüfstein *m*; ⚗ Reagens *n*; *put to the* ~ auf die Probe stellen; **2.** probieren, prüfen, testen.
tes·ta·ceous *zo.* [tes'teiʃəs] hartschalig; Schal...
tes·ta·ment *Bibel*, ⚖ ['testəmənt] Testament *n*; **tes·ta·men·ta·ry** [~'mentəri] testamentarisch.
tes·ta·tor [tes'teitə] Erblasser *m*.
tes·ta·trix [tes'teitriks] Erblasserin *f*.
test...: ~ **ban** (Atombomben)Versuchsverbot *n*; ~ *treaty* Teststoppabkommen *n*; ~ **card** *Fernsehen*: Testbild *n*; ~ **case** Muster-, Schulbeispiel *n*; Präzedenzfall *m*; ~ **drive** *mot.* Probefahrt *f*.
tes·ter[1] ['testə] Betthimmel *m*.
test·er[2] [~] Prüfer *m* (*a. Gerät*).
tes·ti·cle *anat.* ['testikl] Hode *f*.
tes·ti·fi·er ['testifaiə] Zeuge *m*, Zeugin *f* (*to* für); **tes·ti·fy** ['~fai] *v/t.* bezeugen (*a. fig.*); *v/i.* zeugen (*to* für); (als Zeuge) aussagen (*on* über *acc.*).
tes·ti·mo·ni·al [testi'məunjəl] (Führungs)Zeugnis *n*; Zeichen *n* der Anerkennung; **tes·ti·mo·ny** ['~məni] Zeugnis *n* (*Zeugenaussage*; *Beweis*) (*to* für).
tes·ti·ness ['testinis] Gereiztheit *f*.
test...: '**~-match** *Kricket*: internationaler Vergleichskampf *m*; '**~-pa·per** ⚗ Reagenzpapier *n*; '**~-pi·lot** ✈ Testpilot *m*; '**~-print** *phot.* Probeabzug *m*; ~ **run** Probelauf *m e-r Maschine etc.*; '**~-tube** ⚗ Reagenzglas *n*; ~ *baby* ⚕ Retortenbaby *n*.
tes·ty □ ['testi], **tetch·y** □ ['tetʃi] reizbar, gereizt, heftig, kribbelig.
teth·er ['teðə] **1.** Haltestrick *m*; *fig.* Spielraum *m*; *at the end of one's* ~ *fig.* am Ende s-r Kraft; **2.** anbinden.
tet·ra·gon ⚹ ['tetrəgən] Viereck *n*; **te·trag·o·nal** [~'trægənl] viereckig.
tet·ter ⚕ ['tetə] Flechte *f*.
Teu·ton ['tju:tən] Germane *m*, Teutone *m*; **Teu·ton·ic** [~'tɔnik] germanisch, teutonisch.
text [tekst] Text *m*; Bibelstelle *f*; Bibelspruch *m*; '**~·book** Leitfaden *m*, Lehrbuch *n*.
tex·tile ['tekstail] **1.** Textil..., Web...; **2.** *~s pl.* Webwaren *f/pl.*, Textilien *pl.*
tex·tu·al □ ['tekstjuəl] Text...; textlich; textgemäß.
tex·ture ['tekstʃə] Gewebe *n*; Gefüge *n*; Struktur *f*.
tha·lid·o·mide [θə'lidəmaid] Contergan *n*; ~ *baby*, ~ *child* Contergankind *n*.
than [ðæn, ðən] *nach comp.*: als.
thane *hist.* [θein] Than *m*, Lehensmann *m*.
thank [θæŋk] **1.** danken (*dat.*); ~ *you, bei Ablehnung no*, ~ *you* danke;

I will thank you for ich wäre Ihnen dankbar für; ~ *you for nothing iro.* ich danke dafür; **2.** ~*s pl.* Dank *m*; ~*s!* vielen Dank!; danke (schön)!; *give* ~*s* das Tischgebet sprechen; ~*s to* dank (*dat.*); **thank·ful** □ [ˈ~ful] dankbar; ˈ**thank·less** □ undankbar; **thanks·giv·ing** [ˈ~s-giviŋ] Danksagung *f*; Dankfest *n*; ♀ (*Day*) *bsd. Am.* (Ernte)Dankfest *n* (*letzter Donnerstag im November*); ˈ**thank·wor·thy** dankenswert.

that [ðæt, ðət] **1.** *pron.* (*pl. those*) jene(r, -s); der *od.* die *od.* das(jenige); der, die, das, welche(r, -s); *so* ~*'s* ~*!* damit basta!; ... *and* ~ und zwar; *at* ~ zudem, noch dazu; **2.** *cj.* daß; damit; weil.

thatch [θætʃ] **1.** Dachstroh *n*; Strohdach *n*; **2.** mit Stroh decken.

thaw [θɔ:] **1.** Tauwetter *n*; (Auf-)Tauen *n*; **2.** (auf)tauen.

the [ði:; *vor Vokal* ði, *vor Konson.* ðə] **1.** *Artikel*: der, die, das; **2.** *adv.* ~ ... ~ je ... desto, um so.

the·a·tre, *Am.* **the·a·ter** [ˈθiətə] Theater *n*; *fig.* Schauplatz *m*; ⚔ Kriegsschauplatz *m*; ~ *nuclear war bsd. Am.* taktischer Atomkrieg *m*; ~ *nuclear weapons pl. bsd. Am.* taktische Atomwaffen *f/pl.*; ˈ**~-go·er** Theaterbesucher(in); **the·at·ric, the·at·ri·cal** □ [θiˈætrik(əl)] Theater...; bühnenmäßig; theatralisch; **theˈat·ri·cals** *pl.* Theater-, *bsd.* Liebhaberaufführungen *f/pl.*

The·ban [ˈθi:bən] **1.** thebanisch; **2.** Thebaner(in).

thee † *od. lit.* [ði:] dich; dir.

theft [θeft] Diebstahl *m*.

their [ðɛə] ihr(e); **theirs** [~z] der, die, das ihrige *od.* ihre.

the·ism [ˈθi:izəm] Theismus *m*.

them [ðem, ðəm] sie (*acc. pl.*); ihnen.

theme [θi:m] Thema *n* (*a.* ♪); ⚒ Aufgabe *f*, Aufsatz *m*; *gr.* Stamm *m*; ~ **mu·sic** *Film etc.*: Titelmelodie *f*; ~ **song** Hauptmelodie *f e-s Musicals etc.*

them·selves [ðəmˈselvz] sie (*acc. pl.*) selbst; sich selbst.

then [ðen] **1.** *adv.* dann, alsdann; damals; da; *by* ~ bis dahin; inzwischen; *every now and* ~ alle Augenblicke; *there and* ~ sogleich; *now* ~ nun denn; **2.** *cj.* denn, also, folglich; **3.** *adj.* damalig.

thence *lit.* [ðens] daher; von da.

thence·forth [ˈðensˈfɔ:θ], **thence·for·ward** [ˈ~ˈfɔ:wəd] seitdem, von da an.

the·oc·ra·cy [θiˈɔkrəsi] Theokratie *f*; **the·o·crat·ic** [θiəˈkrætik] (~*ally*) theokratisch.

the·o·lo·gi·an [θiəˈləudʒjən] Theologe *m*; **the·o·log·i·cal** □ [~ˈlɔdʒikəl] theologisch; **the·ol·o·gy** [θiˈɔlədʒi] Theologie *f*.

the·o·rem [ˈθiərəm] Lehrsatz *m*; **the·o·ret·ic, the·o·ret·i·cal** □ [~ˈretik(əl)] theoretisch; ˈ**the·o·rist** Theoretiker *m*; ˈ**the·o·rize** theoretisieren; ˈ**the·o·ry** Theorie *f*.

the·os·o·phy [θiˈɔsəfi] Theosophie *f*.

ther·a·peu·tic [θerəˈpju:tik] **1.** therapeutisch; **2.** ~*s mst sg.* Therapeutik *f* (*praktische Heilkunde*); ˈ**ther·a·py** Therapie *f* (*Heilverfahren*); ˈ**ther·a·pist** Therapeut (-in); *mental* ~ Psychotherapeut (-in).

there [ðɛə] **1.** *adv.* da, dort; darin; dorthin; ~ *is*, ~ *are* [ðəˈriz, ðəˈrɑ:] es gibt, es ist, es sind; ~*'s* [ðɛəz] *a good fellow!* so bist du lieb!; sei doch lieb!; ~ *you are!* da hast du es!; **2.** *int.* na!

there...: ˈ**~·a·bout**(**s**) da herum; so ungefähr ...; **~ˈaft·er** danach; ˈ**~ˈby** dadurch, damit; dabei; **~ˈfor** dafür; ˈ**~·fore** darum, deswegen; deshalb, daher; **~ˈfrom** davon; **~ˈin** darin; **~ˈof** davon; dessen, deren; **~ˈon** darauf, dazu; **~ˈto** dazu; ˈ**~·upˈon** darauf(hin); **~ˈwith** damit; **~·withˈal** überdies; damit.

ther·mal □ [ˈθə:məl] **1.** Thermal... (*Bad etc.*); *phys.* Wärme...; ~ *value* Heizwert *m*; **2.** Thermik *f*, Aufwind *m*; ˈ**ther·mic** (~*ally*) thermisch; Hitze...; **therm·i·on·ic** [~ˈɔnik] *Radio*: ~ *valve* Elektronen-, Glühkathodenröhre *f*.

ther·mo-e·lec·tric cou·ple *phys.* [ˈθə:məuiˈlektrikˈkʌpl] Thermoelement *n*; **ther·mom·e·ter** [θəˈmɔmitə] Thermometer *n*; **ther·mo·met·ric, ther·mo·met·ri·cal** □ [θə:məuˈmetrik(əl)] thermometrisch; **ther·mo·pile** *phys.* [ˈ~məupail] Thermosäule *f*; **Ther·mos** [ˈ~mɔs] *a.* ~ *flask*, ~ *bottle* Thermosflasche *f*; **ther·mo·stat** [ˈ~məstæt] Thermostat *m* (*automatischer Wärmeregler*).

the·sau·rus [θiˈsɔːrəs] Thesaurus *m*; Wörterbuch *n*; Sammlung *f*.

these [ðiːz] (*pl. von this*) diese; ~ *three years* seit drei Jahren.

the·sis [ˈθiːsis], *pl.* **the·ses** [ˈ~siːz] Leitsatz *m*, These *f*; Dissertation *f*.

they [ðei] sie (*pl.*); ~ *who* die (-jenigen), welche.

thick [θik] **1.** □ *allg.* dick; dicht (*Nebel, Haar etc.*); trüb (*Flüssigkeit*); legiert (*Suppe*); heiser, belegt (*Stimme*); dumm; *oft as ~ as thieves* F *pred.* dick befreundet; ~ *with* dicht besetzt mit; *that's a bit ~! sl.* das ist ein bißchen stark!; **2.** dickster Teil *m*; *fig.* Brennpunkt *m*; *in the ~ of* mitten in (*dat.*); ˈ**thick·en** *v/t.* dick(er) machen, verdicken; verstärken; *Küche*: legieren; *v/i.* dick(er) *od.* dicht(er) werden; sich verdichten; sich trüben; sich verstärken; **thick·et** [ˈθikit] Dickicht *n*; ˈ**thick-ˈhead·ed** dumm; ˈ**thick-ness** Dicke *f*; Dichtigkeit *f*; Heiserkeit *f*, Belegschaft *f*; ⊕, ⚒ Lage *f*, Schicht *f*; ˈ**thick-ˈset** dicht (gepflanzt); untersetzt; ˈ**thick-ˈskinned** *fig.* dickfellig.

thief [θiːf], *pl.* **thieves** [θiːvz] Dieb (-in); **thieve** [θiːv] stehlen; ˈ**thiev·er·y** Dieberei *f*.

thiev·ish □ [ˈθiːviʃ] diebisch; verstohlen; ˈ**thiev·ish·ness** diebisches Wesen *n*, Spitzbüberei *f*.

thigh [θai] (Ober)Schenkel *m*.

thim·ble [ˈθimbl] Fingerhut *m*; **thim·ble·ful** [ˈ~ful] Fingerhut (-voll) *m*.

thin [θin] **1.** □ *allg.* dünn; leicht; mager; spärlich, dürftig; schwach; fadenscheinig (*bsd. fig.*); *he had a ~ time* F es ging ihm dreckig *od.* miserabel; **2.** *v/t.* verdünnen; *Wald, Schlachtreihe etc.* lichten; *Bevölkerung* dezimieren; *v/i.* dünn werden; abnehmen; sich lichten.

thine † *od. poet.* [ðain] dein; der, die, das deinige *od.* deine.

thing [θiŋ] Ding *n*; Sache *f*; Wesen *n*, Geschöpf *n*; ~*s pl.* Sachen *f/pl.* (*Kleider, Gepäck, Geräte etc.*); die Dinge *n/pl.* (*Umstände*); *such a ~* so etwas; *the ~* F das Richtige; richtig; die Hauptsache *f*; *the ~ is* die Frage ist; *know a ~ or two* F Bescheid wissen, Erfahrung haben; *of all ~s* vor allen Dingen; *~s are going better* es geht jetzt besser; *I don't feel quite the ~* F ich bin nicht so ganz auf Deck.

thing·um(·a)·bob F [ˈθiŋəm(i)bɔb], **thing·um·my** F [ˈ~əmi] Dingsda *m, f, n*.

think [θiŋk] (*irr.*) *v/i.* denken (*of* an *acc.*); nachdenken (*about, over* über *acc.*); sich besinnen (*of* auf *acc.*); meinen, glauben; gedenken (*to inf.* zu *inf.*); *v/t.* denken; sich *et.* denken; halten für; ~ *much etc. of* viel *etc.* halten von; ~ *out* (sich) *et.* ausdenken; ~ *s.th. over* (sich) et. überlegen, über et. nachdenken; ˈ**think·a·ble** denkbar; ˈ**think·er** Denker(in); ˈ**think·ing** denkend; Denk...

thin·ness [ˈθinnis] Dünne *f*.

third [θəːd] **1.** dritte(r, -s); ~ *degree* Folterverhör *n*; **2.** Drittel *n*; ♪ Terz *f*; ˈ**third·ly** drittens; ˈ**third-ˈpar·ty in·sur·ance** Haftpflichtversicherung *f*; ˈ**third-ˈrate** drittklassig.

thirst [θəːst] **1.** Durst *m* (*a. fig.*); **2.** dürsten (*for, after* nach); ˈ**thirst·y** □ durstig (*a. fig.*); dürr (*Boden etc.*); F Durst machend (*Arbeit*).

thir·teen [ˈθəːˈtiːn] dreizehn; ˈ**thir-ˈteenth** [~θ] dreizehnte(r, -s); **thir-ti·eth** [ˈθəːtiiθ] dreißigste(r, -s); ˈ**thir·ty** dreißig; *the thirties pl.* die Dreißigerjahre *pl. des Lebens*; die dreißiger Jahre *pl. e-s Jahrhunderts*.

this [ðis] (*pl. these*) diese(r, -s); ⚒ laufend; *in ~ country* hierzulande; ~ *morning* heute morgen; ~ *day week* heute in acht Tagen.

this·tle ⚘ [ˈθisl] Distel *f*; ˈ**~-down** Distelwolle *f*.

thith·er(·ward) † *od. poet.* [ˈðiðə (-wəd)] dorthin.

tho' [ðəu] = *though*.

thole ⚓ [θəul] Dolle *f*, Ruderpflock *m*; ˈ**~-pin** *fig.* Angelpunkt *m*.

thong [θɔŋ] (Leder-, Peitschen-) Riemen *m*.

tho·rax *anat.* [ˈθɔːræks] Brust(korb *m*, -kasten *m*) *f*, Thorax *m*.

thorn ⚘ [θɔːn] Dorn *m*; ˈ**thorn·y** dornig, stach(e)lig; beschwerlich, dornenvoll.

thor·ough □ [ˈθʌrə] vollkommen; vollständig; vollendet; gründlich;

eingehend; ⁓ly *a.* durchaus; ˈ⁓-ˈbass ♪ Generalbaß *m*; ˈ⁓·**bred** **1.** Vollblut...; gründlich; **2.** Vollblüter *m*; ˈ⁓·**fare** Durchgang *m*, -fahrt *f*; Hauptverkehrsstraße *f*; ˈ⁓·**go·ing** gründlich; tatkräftig; ˈ**thor·ough·ness** Vollständigkeit *f*; Gründlichkeit *f*; ˈ**thor·ough-paced** vollendet; ausgemacht.

those [ðəuz] (*pl. von that 1*) jene, die; diejenigen; *are ⁓ your parents?* sind das Ihre Eltern?

thou †, *Bibel*, *poet.* [ðau] du.

though [ðəu] obgleich, obwohl, wenn auch; zwar; (*mst am Satzende*) aber, doch; freilich; *as ⁓* als ob.

thought [θɔ:t] **1.** *pret. u. p.p. von think*; **2.** Gedanke *m*; (Nach-)Denken *n*; *give ⁓ to* sich Gedanken machen über (*acc.*); *on second ⁓s* nach nochmaliger Überlegung; *take ⁓ for* Sorge tragen für.

thought·ful □ [ˈθɔ:tful] gedankenvoll, nachdenklich; besorgt (*of* um); rücksichtsvoll (*of* gegen); ˈ**thought-ful·ness** Nachdenklichkeit *f*; Rücksichtnahme *f*; Besorgtheit *f*.

thought·less □ [ˈθɔ:tlis] gedankenlos; unbesonnen; rücksichtslos (*of* gegen); ˈ**thought·less·ness** Gedankenlosigkeit *f*; Rücksichtslosigkeit *f*.

thought-read·ing [ˈθɔ:tri:diŋ] Gedankenlesen *n*.

thou·sand [ˈθauzənd] **1.** tausend; **2.** Tausend *n*; **thou·sandth** [ˈ⁓zəntθ] **1.** tausendste(r, -s); **2.** Tausendstel *n*.

Thra·cian [ˈθreiʃjən] **1.** Thrakier (-in); **2.** thrakisch.

thral(l)·dom [ˈθrɔ:ldəm] Knechtschaft *f*.

thrall [θrɔ:l] Sklave *m*.

thrash [θræʃ] *v/t.* (ver)dreschen, (ver)prügeln; F schlagen, besiegen; *v/i.* dreschen; (hin u. her) schlagen; ⚓ sich vorwärtsquälen; = *thresh*; ˈ**thrash·er** = *thresher*; ˈ**thrash-ing** Dresche *f*, Tracht *f* Prügel; = *threshing*.

thread [θred] **1.** Faden *m* (*a. fig.*); Zwirn *m*, Garn *n*; (Schrauben-)Gewinde *n*; **2.** einfädeln; aufreihen; sich durchwinden durch; durchziehen; ˈ⁓·**bare** fadenscheinig (*a. fig.*); ˈ**thread·y** fadenartig; fadendünn.

threat [θret] Drohung *f*; ˈ**threat·en** *v/t. j.* bedrohen, *j-m* drohen; *et.* androhen; *v/i.* drohen; ˈ**threat·en-ing** bedrohlich.

three [θri:] **1.** drei; **2.** Drei *f*; ˈ⁓-ˈ**col·our** Dreifarben...; ˈ⁓·**fold** dreifach; ⁓·**pence** [ˈθrepəns] Dreipence(stück *n*) *m/pl.*; ˈ⁓·**pen·ny** Dreipence...; *fig.* gering; ⁓-**phase cur·rent** ⚡ [ˈθri:feizˈkʌrənt] Drehstrom *m*; ˈ⁓-**piece** dreiteilig; *⁓ suit* dreiteiliger Anzug *m*; *⁓ suite* Sitzgarnitur *f*; ˈ⁓ˈ**score** sechzig.

thresh [θreʃ] *Korn* (aus)dreschen; = *thrash*; *⁓ out fig. Angelegenheit* gründlich erörtern.

thresh·er [ˈθreʃə] Drescher *m*; Dreschmaschine *f*.

thresh·ing [ˈθreʃiŋ] Dreschen *n*; ˈ⁓-**floor** (Dresch)Tenne *f*; ˈ⁓-**ma-chine** Dreschmaschine *f*.

thresh·old [ˈθreʃhəuld] Schwelle *f*.

threw [θru:] *pret. von throw 1.*

thrice ⚔ [θrais] dreimal.

thrift, **thrift·i·ness** [θrift, ˈ⁓inis] Sparsamkeit *f*, Wirtschaftlichkeit *f*; Sparsinn *m*; ˈ**thrift·less** □ verschwenderisch; ˈ**thrift·y** □ sparsam; *poet.* gedeihend.

thrill [θril] **1.** *v/t.* durchdringen, -schauern; *fig.* packen, aufwühlen; aufregen; *v/i.* (er)beben (*with* vor); **2.** Schauer *m*; Beben *n*; aufregendes Erlebnis *n*; Sensation *f*; ˈ**thrill·er** F Reißer *m*, Thriller *m*, Schauerroman *m*, -drama *n*; ˈ**thrill·ing** aufwühlend, packend; aufregend; spannend; sensationell.

thrive [θraiv] (*irr.*) gedeihen, geraten; *fig.* blühen; Glück haben; **thriv·en** [ˈθrivn] *p.p. von thrive*; **thriv·ing** □ [ˈθraiviŋ] gedeihend, blühend, erfolgreich.

thro' [θru:] *abbr. für through.*

throat [θrəut] *allg.* Kehle *f*; Gurgel *f*; Hals *m*; Schlund *m*; *clear one's ⁓* sich räuspern; ˈ**throat·y** □ kehlig; heiser.

throb [θrɔb] **1.** pochen, schlagen, klopfen (*Herz etc.*); pulsieren; **2.** Pochen *n*, Schlagen *n*; Pulsschlag *m*.

throe [θrəu] Schmerz *m*; *⁓s pl.* Geburtswehen *f/pl.* (*mst fig.*).

throm·bo·sis ⚕ [θrɔmˈbəusis] Thrombose *f*.

throne [θrəun] **1.** Thron *m*; **2.** *v/t.* auf den Thron setzen; *v/i.* thronen.

throng [θrɔŋ] **1.** Gedränge *n*; Menge *f*, Schar *f*; **2.** sich drängen (in *dat.*, *a. acc.*); anfüllen mit.
thros·tle *orn.* [ˈθrɔsl] Drossel *f*.
throt·tle [ˈθrɔtl] **1.** erdrosseln; ⊕ (ab)drosseln; **2.** = ˈ**~-valve** ⊕ Drosselklappe *f*.
through [θruː] **1.** durch; **2.** Durchgangs...; durchgehend (*Zug etc.*); ~ **flight** Direktflug *m*; ~ˈ**out 1.** *prp.* überall in (*dat.*); während; ~ *the year* das ganze Jahr hindurch; **2.** durch u. durch, ganz u. gar, durchweg; ˈ**~·way** = *thruway*.
throve [θrəuv] *pret. von thrive*.
throw [θrəu] **1.** (*irr.*) *v/t. allg.* werfen, schleudern; *Wasser* gießen; *Reiter* abwerfen; ⊕ *Seide* zwirnen; *Brücke* schlagen; *Töpferei*: formen, drehen; *Am.* F *Wettspiel, Boxkampf etc.* absichtlich verlieren; ~ *at* werfen nach; ~ *away* wegwerfen; vergeuden; verwerfen; ~ *in* hineinwerfen; *Wort etc.* einwerfen; mit in den Kauf geben; ~ *off* abwerfen; *Kleid etc.*, *Scham* ablegen; ~ *out* (hin)auswerfen; *bsd. parl.* verwerfen; *e-n Wink* geben; ⊕ ausschalten; ~ *over* aufgeben, fallen lassen; ~ *up* in die Höhe werfen; erbrechen; *Amt, Karten etc.* hinwerfen; *s. sponge*; *v/i.* werfen; würfeln; ~ *off* (die Jagd) beginnen; **2.** Wurf *m*; ⊕ (Kolben)Hub *m*; ˈ**~-back** *bsd. biol.* Atavismus *m*; **thrown** [θrəun] *p.p. von throw*; ˈ**throw-**ˈ**off** Aufbruch *m* (zur Jagd); *weitS.* Beginn *m*.
thru *Am.* [θruː] = *through*.
thrum[1] [θrʌm] *Weberei*: Trumm *m*, Saum *m*; Franse *f*; loser Faden *m*, Fussel *f*.
thrum[2] [~] klimpern (auf *dat.*).
thrush[1] *orn.* [θrʌʃ] Drossel *f*.
thrush[2] [~] ⚕ Mundschwamm *m*; *vet.* Strahlfäule *f*.
thrust [θrʌst] **1.** Stoß *m*; ⚔ *u. fig.* Vorstoß *m*; ⊕ Druck *m*, Schub *m*; **2.** (*irr.*) *v/t.* stoßen; ~ *o.s. into* sich drängen in (*acc.*); ~ *out* (her-, hin-) ausstoßen; *Zunge* herausstrecken; ~ *upon s.o.* j-m aufdrängen; *v/i.* stoßen (*at* nach).
thru·way *Am.* [ˈθruːwei] Schnellstraße *f*.
thud [θʌd] **1.** dumpf aufschlagen, bumsen; **2.** dumpfer (Auf)Schlag *m*, Bums *m*, Plumps *m*.
thug [θʌg] (Gewalt)Verbrecher *m*, Gangster *m*; Rowdy *m*.
thumb [θʌm] **1.** Daumen *m*; *Tom* ♀ Däumling *m im Märchen*; **2.** *Buch etc.* abgreifen; ~ *one's nose at s.o.* j-m e-e lange Nase machen; ~ *a lift* per Anhalter fahren; ˈ**~·nail** Daumennagel *m*; ~ *sketch* kleine, flüchtige Skizze *f*; ˈ**~-print** Daumenabdruck *m*; ˈ**~·screw** Daumenschraube *f*; ⊕ Flügelschraube *f*; ˈ**~-stall** Däumling *m* (*Schutzhülle*); ˈ**~·tack** *Am.* Reißnagel *m*.
thump [θʌmp] **1.** Bums *m*; Puff *m*; **2.** *v/t.* bumsen *od.* pochen auf (*acc.*) *od.* gegen; knuffen, puffen; *v/i.* (auf)bumsen; ˈ**thump·er** *sl.* Mordsding *n*; ˈ**thump·ing** *sl.* kolossal.
thun·der [ˈθʌndə] **1.** Donner *m* (*fig. oft* ~*s pl.*); **2.** donnern; ˈ**~·bolt** Blitz *m* (*u.* Donner *m*); ˈ**~·clap** Donnerschlag *m*; ˈ**~·cloud** Gewitterwolke *f*; ˈ**thun·der·er** *myth.* Donnerer *m* (*Jupiter*).
thun·der...: ˈ**~·head** schwere Gewitterwolke(n *pl.*) *f* (*a. fig.*); ˈ**thun·der·ing** *sl.* kolossal; ˈ**thun·der·ous** □ *fig.* donnernd; gewitterschwül; gewaltig; ˈ**thun·der·storm** Gewitter *n*; ˈ**thun·der·struck** wie vom Donner gerührt; ˈ**thun·der·y** gewitterschwül.
Thu·rin·gi·an [θjuəˈrindʒiən] **1.** thüringisch; **2.** Thüringer(in).
Thurs·day [ˈθəːzdi] Donnerstag *m*.
thus [ðʌs] so, auf diese Weise; also, somit.
thwack [θwæk] = *whack*.
thwart [θwɔːt] **1.** durchkreuzen; hintertreiben; *j-m* entgegenarbeiten; **2.** Ducht *f*, Ruderbank *f*.
thy *Bibel, poet.* [ðai] dein(e).
thyme ♀ [taim] Thymian *m*.
thy·roid *anat.* [ˈθairɔid] **1.** Schilddrüsen...; ~ *extract* Schilddrüsenextrakt *m*; ~ *gland* = **2.** Schilddrüse *f*.
thy·self *Bibel, poet.* [ðaiˈself] du selbst; dir, dich (selbst).
ti·ar·a [tiˈɑːrə] Tiara *f* (*Papstkrone*); Stirnreif *m*, Diadem *n*.
tib·i·a *anat.* [ˈtibiə] Schienbein *n*.
tic ⚕ [tik] nervöser (Gesichts)Krampf *m*.
tich F [titʃ] Knirps *m*.
tick[1] *zo.* [tik] Zecke *f*.
tick[2] [~] (Inlett)Überzug *m*.
tick[3] F [~]: *on* ~ auf Pump.

tick[4] [~] **1.** Ticken *n*; F Augenblick *m*; Vermerkhäkchen *n*; *to the* ~ mit dem Glockenschlag; **2.** *v/i.* ticken; ~ *over mot.* leerlaufen; *v/t.* anmerken, anhaken; ~ *off* abhaken; *sl. j.* heruntermachen, zs.-stauchen.

tick·er ['tikə] Börsentelegraph *m*; F Uhr *f*; '**~-tape** *coll.* Luftschlangen *f/pl.*

tick·et ['tikit] **1.** Fahrkarte *f*, -schein *m*; Flugkarte *f*; Eintrittskarte *f*; (Straf)Zettel *m*, (Preis- *etc.*) Schildchen *n*; *pol.* (Wahl-, Kandidaten)Liste *f*; *the* ~ F das Richtige; ~ *of leave* ⚖ Freilassung *f* auf Bewährung; **2.** mit e-m Zettel *etc.* versehen, kennzeichnen; ~ **a·gen·cy** *thea. etc.* Vorverkaufsstelle *f*; *Reisebüro*: Fahrkartenverkaufsstelle *f*; '**~-col·lec·tor** Bahnsteigschaffner *m*; '**~-in·spec·tor** Fahrkartenkontrolleur *m*; '**~-ma·chine** Fahrkartenautomat *m*; '**~-of·fice**, '**~-win·dow** *bsd. Am.* Fahrkartenschalter *m*; '**~-punch** Lochzange *f*.

tick·ing ['tikiŋ] (Inlett)Drell *m*.

tick·le ['tikl] kitzeln (*a. fig.*); '**tick·ler** schwierige Situation *f*; *a.* ~ *coil* Rückkopplungsspule *f*; '**tick·lish** □ kitzlig; heikel.

tid·al □ ['taidl] Gezeiten...; Flut...; ~ *wave* Flutwelle *f* (*a. fig.*).

tid·bit ['tidbit] = *titbit.*

tid·dly-winks ['tidliwiŋks] Floh(hüpf)spiel *n*.

tide [taid] **1.** Gezeit(en *pl.*) *f* (*a. fig.*); (*low* ~) Ebbe und (*high* ~) Flut *f*; *fig.* Strom *m*, Flut *f*; *in Zssgn*: *rechte* Zeit *f*; *turn of the* ~ Flut-, *fig.* Glückswechsel *m*; **2.** mit dem Strom treiben; ~ *over fig.* hinwegkommen *od.* -helfen über (*acc.*).

tide·mark ['taidmɑːk] Flutmarke *f*; *fig. co.* schwarzer Rand *m an der Badewanne od. am Hals.*

ti·di·ness ['taidinis] Sauberkeit *f*.

ti·dings ['taidiŋz] *pl. od. sg.* Neuigkeiten *f/pl.*, Nachrichten *f/pl.*

ti·dy ['taidi] **1.** ordentlich, sauber, reinlich; F ganz schön, beträchtlich (*Summe*); **2.** Behälter *m*; Abfallkorb *m*; **3.** *a.* ~ *up* zurechtmachen; ordnen; *Zimmer etc.* aufräumen, in Ordnung bringen.

tie [tai] **1.** Band *n* (*a. fig.*); Schleife *f*; Halstuch *n*, Krawatte *f*, Schlips *m*; Bindung *f* (*bsd.* ♪); ⚓ Anker *m*; *fig.* Fessel *f*, Verpflichtung *f*; *Sport*: Unentschieden *n*; *parl.* Stimmengleichheit *f*; *Sport*: Entscheidungsspiel *n*; 🚂 *Am.* Schwelle *f*; **2.** *v/t. allg.* binden (*a.* ♪); verbinden; ⚓ verankern; ~ *down fig.* binden (*to* an *e-e Pflicht etc.*); ~ *up* zu-, an-, ver-, zs.-binden; *v/i. Sport*: unentschieden spielen (*with* gegen).

tier [tiə] Reihe *f*; *thea.* Sitzreihe *f*, Rang *m*.

tierce [tiəs] *fenc.*, *Kartenspiel*: Terz *f*.

tie-up ['taiʌp] (Ver)Bindung *f*; ✝ Fusion *f*; Stockung *f*; Stillstand *m*; *bsd. Am.* Streik *m*.

tiff F [tif] **1.** *kleine* Meinungsverschiedenheit *f*; **2.** schmollen.

tif·fin ['tifin] Mittagessen *n*.

ti·ger ['taigə] Tiger *m*; *Am.* F Beifallsgebrüll *n*; *three cheers and a* ~! hoch, hoch, hoch und nochmals hoch!; '**ti·ger·ish** □ *fig.* tigerhaft; Tiger...

tight □ [tait] dicht (*bsd. in Zssgn*); fest *gebaut od. gefügt*; eng; knapp (sitzend) (*Jacke etc.*); straff (*Seil etc.*), prall (*Backen etc.*); knapp (*bsd.* ✝ *Geld*); F beschwipst; *be in a* ~ *place od. corner* F in der Klemme sein; *hold* ~ festhalten; *it is a* ~ *fit* es paßt knapp; '**tight·en** *a.* ~ *up* (sich) zs.-ziehen; *Schraube, Zügel etc.* anziehen; *Gürtel* enger schnallen; *Feder* spannen; (sich) straffen; '**~-'fist·ed** knick(e)rig; '**~-laced** fest geschnürt; engherzig, prüde; '**~-lipped** verschwiegen; verkniffen; '**tight·ness** Festigkeit *f*, Dichtigkeit *f etc.*; '**tight-rope** gespanntes Seil *n*; **tights** [~s] *pl.* Trikot *n der Akrobaten etc.*; Strumpfhose *f*; '**tight·wad** *sl.* Knauser *m*, Knicker *m*.

ti·gress ['taigris] Tigerin *f*.

tile [tail] **1.** (Dach)Ziegel *m*; Kachel *f*; Fliese *f*; *sl.* Deckel *m* (*Hut*); *he has a* ~ *loose sl.* bei ihm ist e-e Schraube locker; **2.** mit Ziegeln *etc.* decken; kacheln; '**~-lay·er**, '**til·er** Dachdecker *m*.

till[1] [til] Laden(tisch)kasse *f*.

till[2] [~] **1.** *prp.* bis (zu); **2.** *cj.* bis.

till[3] ⚒ [~] bestellen, beackern, bebauen; '**till·age** (Land)Bestellung *f*, Beackerung *f*; Ackerbau *m*; Ackerland *n*.

till·er[1] ['tilə] Bauer *m*, Pflüger *m*.

till·er[2] ⚓ [~] Ruderpinne *f*.

tilt[1] [tilt] Plane *f*.

tilt² [~] **1.** Neigung *f*, schiefe Lage *f*; Stoß *m*; Lanzenbrechen *n* (*a. fig.*); *on the* ~ auf der Kippe; (*at*) *full* ~ mit voller Geschwindigkeit; *have a* ~ *at s.o.* mit j-m e-e Lanze brechen; **2.** *v/t.* kippen; *v/i.* kippen; Lanzen brechen (*a. fig.*); stechen (*at* nach); ~ *against* anrennen gegen; ˈ**tilt·ing** Kipp...; Turnier...

tilth [tilθ] Bebauungstiefe *f*; Ackerland *n*.

tim·bal ♪ [ˈtimbəl] (Kessel)Pauke *f*.

tim·ber [ˈtimbə] **1.** (Bau-, Nutz-) Holz *n*; Baum(bestand) *m*; ⚓ Inholz *n*; **2.** zimmern; ~*ed* holzgezimmert; Fachwerk...; bewaldet; ˈ**~-line** Baumgrenze *f*; ˈ**~-work** Gebälk *n*, Holzwerk *n*; ˈ**~-yard** Zimmerplatz *m*.

time [taim] **1.** Zeit *f*; Mal *n*; Takt *m*; Zeitmaß *n*, Tempo *n*; ~! *parl.* Schluß!; ~ *and again* immer wieder; *at* ~*s* zu Zeiten; *at a* ~, *at the same* ~ zugleich; *at one* ~ einstmals; *before one's* ~ verfrüht; *behind one's* ~ verspätet; *behind the* ~*s* hinter der Zeit zurück; *by that* ~ zu der Zeit; bis dahin; unterdessen; *do* ~ F *im Gefängnis* sitzen; *for the* ~ *being* für den Augenblick, einstweilen; zunächst; *have a good* ~ es gut haben; sich amüsieren; *in* (*good*) ~ zur rechten Zeit; *in no* ~ im Nu; *in a month's* ~ nach e-m Monat; *s. mean*² *1*; *on* ~ rechtzeitig; *out of* ~ zur Unzeit; aus dem Takt *od.* Schritt; *beat the* ~ Takt schlagen; *s. keep*; **2.** *v/t.* die Zeit bestimmen für; zeitlich abpassen *od.* einrichten; den richtigen Zeitpunkt wählen für; ♪ den Takt angeben für; *a. take the* ~ *of* die Zeit(dauer) *e-s Rennens etc.* messen; regeln (*to* nach); *Uhr* stellen; *the train is* ~*d to leave at 7* der Zug soll um 7 abfahren; *v/i.* Takt halten (*to* mit); zs.-stimmen (*with* mit); ˈ**~-and-ˈmo·tion stud·y** Zeitstudie *f*; ˈ**~-bar·gain** Termingeschäft *n*; ˈ**~-clock** Stempel-, Stechuhr *f*; ˈ**~-con·sum·ing** zeitraubend; ~ **cred·it** Zeitguthaben *n bei gleitender Arbeitszeit*; ~ **deb·it** Fehlzeit *f bei gleitender Arbeitszeit*; ˈ**~-ex·po·sure** *phot.* Zeitaufnahme *f*; ˈ**~-hono(u)red** altehrwürdig; ˈ**~keep·er** Zeitmesser *m*, *bsd.* Uhr *f*; (Arbeits-) Zeitnehmer *m*; ˈ**~-lag** zeitliche Verzögerung *f*; ˈ**~-ˈlim·it** Befristung *f*; ˈ**time·ly** (recht)zeitig; aktuell, zeitgemäß; ˈ**time·piece** Uhr *f*; ˈ**tim·er** *Sport*: Zeitnehmer *m*; *phot.* Zeitauslöser *m*.

time...: **~-serv·er** [ˈtaimsəːvə] Achselträger *m*, Opportunist *m*; ˈ**~-sheet** Anwesenheitsliste *f*; Stempel-, Kontrollkarte *f*; ˈ**~-sig·nal** *bsd. Radio*: Zeitzeichen *n*; ˈ**~-ta·ble** Terminkalender *m*; 🚃 Fahrplan *m*; *Schule*: Stundenplan *m*.

tim·id □ [ˈtimid] furchtsam, ängstlich; schüchtern; **tiˈmid·i·ty** Furchtsamkeit *f*; Schüchternheit *f*.

tim·ing [ˈtaimiŋ] Wahl *f* des Zeitpunkts.

tim·or·ous □ [ˈtimərəs] = *timid*.

tin [tin] **1.** Zinn *n*; Weißblech *n*; (Blech-, Konserven)Büchse *f*, (-)Dose *f*; *sl.* Piepen *pl.* (*Geld*); **2.** zinnern; Zinn...; Blech...; blechern (*a. fig. contp.*); ~ *solder* Lötzinn *n*; **3.** verzinnen; in Büchsen einmachen, eindosen; ~*ned meat* Dosenfleisch *n*.

tinc·ture [ˈtiŋktʃə] **1.** Farbe *f*; *fig.* Anstrich *m*; *pharm.* Tinktur *f*; **2.** färben, e-n Anstrich geben (*dat.*).

tin·der [ˈtində] Zunder *m*.

tine [tain] Zinke *f*; Zacke *f*; (Geweih)Sprosse *f*.

tin·foil [ˈtinˈfɔil] Stanniol *n*.

ting F [tiŋ] = *tinkle*.

tinge [tindʒ] **1.** Farbe *f*, Färbung *f*; *fig.* Anflug *m*, Spur *f*; **2.** färben; *fig.* e-n Anstrich geben (*dat.*); *be* ~*d with* etwas von ... an sich haben.

tin·gle [ˈtiŋgl] klingen; prickeln, kribbeln; flirren; surren.

tin...: ~ **god** F Götze *m*, Idol *n*; ~ **hat** *sl.* Stahlhelm *m*.

tink·er [ˈtiŋkə] **1.** Kesselflicker *m*; **2.** *v/t.* zs.-flicken; *v/i.* (herum)pfuschen (*at* an *dat.*); (*up* zurechtbasteln.

tin·kle [ˈtiŋkl] **1.** klingeln (mit); **2.** Geklingel *n*.

tin·man [ˈtinmən] Klempner *m*; ˈ**tin·ny** blechern (*Klang*); ˈ**tin-o·pen·er** Dosenöffner *m*; ˈ**tin-plate** Weißblech *n*.

tin·sel [ˈtinsl] **1.** Flitter *m*; Rauschgold *n*; Lametta *f*; *fig.* Flitter(werk *n*) *m*; **2.** Flitter...; flitterhaft; **3.** mit Flitterwerk verzieren.

tint [tint] **1.** *hellgetönte* Farbe *f*; (Farb)Ton *m*, Schattierung *f*;

2. färben; (ab)tönen; *~ed paper* Tonpapier *n.*
tin·tin·nab·u·la·tion ['tintinæbju'leiʃən] Geklingel *n.*
tin·ware ['tinwɛə] Blechwaren *f/pl.*
ti·ny □ ['taini] winzig, klein.
tip [tip] **1.** Spitze *f*; Mundstück *n e-r Zigarette*; Trinkgeld *n*; Tip *m*, Wink *m*, Fingerzeig *m*; leichter Schlag *m od.* Stoß *m*; Schuttabladeplatz *m*; *give s.th. a ~* et. kippen; **2.** *v/t.* mit e-r Spitze versehen; beschlagen; (um)kippen; *j-m* ein Trinkgeld geben; *a. ~ off j-m* e-n Wink geben; *v/i.* (um)kippen; '**~-cart** Kippkarren *m*; '**~-off** Wink *m.*
tip·pet ['tipit] Pelerine *f.*
tip·ple ['tipl] **1.** zechen, picheln; **2.** Getränk *n*; '**tip·pler** Zechbruder *m.*
tip·si·ness ['tipsinis] Trunkenheit *f.*
tip·staff ['tipstɑ:f] Gerichtsdiener *m.*
tip·ster ['tipstə] (Wett)Berater *m.*
tip·sy ['tipsi] angeheitert; wack(e)lig.
tip·toe ['tiptəu] **1.** auf Zehenspitzen gehen; **2.** *on ~* auf Zehenspitzen.
tip·top F ['tip'tɔp] **1.** höchster Punkt *m*; **2.** höchst, vorzüglich; fein.
tip-up seat *thea.* ['tipʌp'si:t] Klappsitz *m.*
ti·rade [tai'reid] Tirade *f*, Wortschwall *m.*
tire¹ ['taiə] (Rad-, Auto)Reifen *m.*
tire² [~] ermüden, müde machen *od.* werden (*of ger.* zu *inf.*).
tired □ ['taiəd] müde (*fig. of gen.*); verbraucht; '**tired·ness** Müdigkeit *f.*
tire·less □ ['taiəlis] unermüdlich.
tire·some □ ['taiəsəm] ermüdend; langweilig, unangenehm, lästig.
ti·ro ['taiərəu] Anfänger *m.*
'tis [tiz] = *it is.*
tis·sue ['tiʃu:] Gewebe *n*; ⚘ (durchwirkter) Schleierstoff *m*; '**~-'pa·per** Seidenpapier *n.*
tit¹ [tit]: *~ for tat* wie du mir, so ich dir; Wurst wider Wurst.
tit² *Am.* [~] = *teat.*
tit³ *orn.* [~] Meise *f.*
Ti·tan ['taitən] Titan(e) *m*; '**Ti·tan·ess** Titanin *f*; **ti·ta·nic** [~'tænik] (*~ally*) titanisch, titanenhaft.
ti·ta·ni·um ⚗ [tai'teinjəm] Titan *n.*
tit·bit ['titbit] Leckerbissen *m.*
titch [titʃ] = *tich.*
tithe [taið] Zehnt(e) *m*; *mst fig.* Zehntel *n.*
tit·il·late ['titileit] kitzeln; **tit·il'la·tion** Kitzel(n *n*) *m.*
tit·i·vate F ['titiveit] (sich) schön- *od.* zurechtmachen.
ti·tle ['taitl] **1.** (Buch-, Ehren)Titel *m*; Überschrift *f*; (*bsd.* Rechts-) Anspruch *m* (*to* auf *acc.*); **2.** betiteln; (be)nennen; *~d bsd.* ad(e)lig; '**~-deed** ⚖ Besitztitel *m*; '**~-holder** *bsd. Sport*: Titelinhaber(in); '**~-page** Titelseite *f*; '**~-role** Titelrolle *f.*
tit·mouse *orn.* ['titmaus], *pl.* **tit·mice** ['~mais] Meise *f.*
ti·trate ⚗ ['titreit] titrieren; **ti'tra·tion** Titrieren *n.*
tits V [tits] *pl.* Titten *f/pl.*
tit·ter ['titə] **1.** kichern; **2.** Kichern *n.*
tit·tle ['titl] Pünktchen *n*; *fig.* Tüttelchen *n*; *to a ~* bis aufs Tüpfelchen; '**~-tat·tle 1.** Schnickschnack *m* (*leeres Geschwätz*); **2.** schnickschnacken.
tit·u·lar □ ['titjulə] Titular...; dem Namen nach.
to [tu:; *im Satz mst* tu, *vor Konsonant* tə] **1.** *zur Bezeichnung des Infinitivs*: zu; **2.** *prp.* zu (*a. adv.*); *Richtung, Ziel*: zu, gegen, nach, an, in, auf; *Vergleich*: gegen; *Gemäßheit*: nach; *Grenze*: bis zu (*od.* an *acc.*, in *acc.*, nach, auf *acc.*); *zeitlich*: bis zu, bis an (*acc.*); *Absicht*: um zu; *Zweck, Ende, Wirkung*: zu, für; *zur Bildung des (betonten) Dativs*: *~ me, ~ you etc.* mir, Ihnen *etc.*; *he gave it ~ his friend* er gab es seinem Freund; *it happened ~ me* es geschah mir; *Beziehung, Zugehörigkeit*: *alive ~ s.th.* empfänglich für et.; *cousin ~* Vetter des *Königs etc. od.* der *Frau N. od.* von *N.*; *heir ~* Erbe des *etc.*; *secretary ~* Sekretär des *etc.*; *Verkürzung e-s Nebensatzes*: *I weep ~ think of it* ich weine, wenn ich daran denke; *here's ~ you!* auf Ihr Wohl!, Prosit!; *~ and fro* hin und her, auf und ab.
toad *zo.* [təud] Kröte *f*; '**~·stool** (größerer Blätter)Pilz *m*; Giftpilz *m.*
toad·y ['təudi] **1.** Speichellecker *m*; **2.** vor *j-m* kriechen *od.* scharwenzeln; '**toad·y·ism** Speichelleckerei *f.*
to-and-fro ['tu:ən'frəu] Kommen *n* und Gehen *n.*
toast [təust] **1.** Toast *m*, geröstetes Brot *n*; Trinkspruch *m*; **2.** toasten, rösten; *fig.* wärmen; trinken auf

(*acc.*); ˈ**toast·er** Toaster *m*, Brotröster *m*.
to·bac·co [təˈbækəu] Tabak *m*; **toˈbac·co·nist** [~kənist] Tabakhändler *m*.
to·bog·gan [təˈbɔgən] **1.** Toboggan *m*; Rodelschlitten *m*; **2.** rodeln.
toc·sin [ˈtɔksin] Sturmglocke *f*.
tod *sl.* [tɔd]: *on one's* ~ ganz allein.
to·day [təˈdei] heute.
tod·dle [ˈtɔdl] watscheln; zotteln; tappen; unsicher gehen; ˈ**tod·dler** Taps *m*, unsicher gehendes Baby *n*.
tod·dy [ˈtɔdi] *Art* Grog *m*.
to-do F [təˈdu:] Lärm *m*, Aufheben *n*.
toe [təu] **1.** Zehe *f*; Spitze *f*; *from top to* ~ von Kopf bis Fuß; *on one's* ~*s fig.* auf Draht; **2.** mit den Zehen berühren; *Schuh* bekappen; ~ *the line Sport*: zum Start antreten; *pol.* sich der Parteidisziplin unterwerfen.
toed [təud] ...zehig.
toff P [tɔf] feiner Pinkel *m* (*Stutzer*).
tof·fee [ˈtɔfi] Sahnebonbon *m*, *n*, Toffee *n*; ˈ~**-nosed** F hochnäsig; aufgeblasen.
tof·fy [ˈtɔfi] = *toffee*.
tog F [tɔg] **1.** anziehen; **2.** *s. togs*.
to·ga [ˈtəugə] Toga *f*.
to·geth·er [təˈgeðə] *örtlich*: zusammen; *zeitlich*: zugleich; nacheinander, ohne Unterbrechung.
tog·gle ⚓ *u.* ⊕ [ˈtɔgl] **1.** Knebel *m*; ~ *switch* ⚡ Kippschalter *m*; **2.** (fest-) knebeln.
togs F [tɔgz] *pl.* Kluft *f* (*Kleidung*).
toil [tɔil] **1.** schwere Arbeit *f*, Mühe *f*, Plackerei *f*; **2.** sich plagen, schwer arbeiten, sich abmühen; sich mühsam bewegen.
toil·er *fig.* [ˈtɔilə] Arbeitspferd *n*.
toi·let [ˈtɔilit] Toilette *f* (*Ankleiden*; *Anzug*; *Kleid*; *Badezimmer*, *Klosett*); *make one's* ~ Toilette machen; ~ **bag** Kulturbeutel *m*; ˈ~**-pa·per** Toilettenpapier *n*; ~ **seat** Toilettensitz *m*, Brille *f*; ˈ~**-set** Toilettengarnitur *f*; ˈ~**-ta·ble** Frisiertoilette *f*.
toils [tɔilz] *pl.* Schlingen *f/pl.*, Netz *n*.
toil·some □ [ˈtɔilsəm] mühsam.
toil-worn [ˈtɔilwɔ:n] abgearbeitet.
to-ing and fro-ing F [ˈtu:iŋənˈfrəuiŋ] Hin und Her *n*.
to·ken [ˈtəukən] Zeichen *n*; Andenken *n*, Geschenk *n*; ~ *money* Ersatz-, Notgeld *n*; ~ *payment* ✝ Pro-forma-Zahlung *f*; ~ *strike* Warnstreik *m*; *in* ~ *of* zum Zeichen (*gen.*).
told [təuld] *pret. u. p.p. von tell*; *all* ~ alles in allem.
tol·er·a·ble □ [ˈtɔlərəbl] erträglich; leidlich; ˈ**tol·er·ance** Duldung *f*; Duldsamkeit *f*, Toleranz *f*; ˈ**tol·er·ant** □ duldsam (*of* gegen); **tol·er·ate** [ˈ~reit] dulden; ertragen; **tol·erˈa·tion** Duldung *f*.
toll[1] [təul] Zoll *m* (*a. fig.*); Wege-, Brücken-, Marktgeld *n*; *fig.* Tribut *m*; ~ *call teleph.* Ferngespräch *n*; ~ *of the road die* Verkehrsopfer *n/pl.*
toll[2] [~] läuten (*bsd. Totenglocke*).
toll...: ˈ~**-bar**, ˈ~**-gate** Schlagbaum *m*; ~ **road** gebührenpflichtige Autostraße *f*, Mautstraße *f*.
tom·a·hawk [ˈtɔməhɔ:k] **1.** Kriegsbeil *n*, Streitaxt *f der Indianer*; **2.** mit der Streitaxt töten *od.* schlagen.
to·ma·to ♀ [təˈmɑ:təu, *Am.* təˈmeitəu], *pl.* **toˈma·toes** Tomate *f*.
tomb [tu:m] Grab(mal) *n*.
tom·boy [ˈtɔmbɔi] Range *f*, Wildfang *m* (*Mädchen*).
tomb·stone [ˈtu:mstəun] Grabstein *m*.
tom·cat [ˈtɔmˈkæt] Kater *m*.
tome [təum] Band *m*, Buch *n*.
tom·fool [ˈtɔmˈfu:l] **1.** Hansnarr *m*; **2.** den Hansnarren spielen; **tomˈfool·er·y** Narretei *f*, Albernheit *f*.
tom·my *sl.* [ˈtɔmi] Tommy *m* (*britischer Soldat*); Fressalien *pl.*; ~ *gun* Maschinenpistole *f*; ~ *rot* richtiger Quatsch *m*.
to·mor·row [təˈmɔrəu] morgen.
tom·tom [ˈtɔmtɔm] Tamtam *n*.
ton [tʌn] Tonne *f* (*Gewichtseinheit*); ~*s pl.* F Massen *f/pl.*
to·nal·i·ty [təuˈnæliti] Tonart *f*; *paint.* Tönung *f*.
tone [təun] **1.** Ton *m beim Sprechen* (*a.* 𝄞, ♪, *paint.*, *fig.*); Klang *m*, Laut *m*; *out of* ~ verstimmt; **2.** *v/t.* e-n Ton *od.* e-e Färbung geben (*dat.*); stimmen; *paint.* abtönen; *phot.* tonen; ~ *down* abschwächen, mildern; *v/i.* stimmen (*with* zu) (*bsd. Farbe*); ~ *down* sich mildern.
tongs [tɔŋz] *pl.* (*a pair of* eine) Zange *f*.
tongue [tʌŋ] *allg.* Zunge *f*; *fig.* Sprache *f*; Landzunge *f*; Zunge *f der Waage etc.*; (Schuh)Lasche *f*;

hold one's ~ den Mund halten; *speak with one's* ~ *in one's cheek* es nicht ernst meinen, unaufrichtig sein; ˈ**tongue·less** ohne Zunge; *fig.* stumm; ˈ**tongue-tied** zungenlahm; *fig.* sprachlos; schweigsam; ˈ**tongue-twist·er** Zungenbrecher *m.*

ton·ic [ˈtɔnik] **1.** (~*ally*) ♪ tonisch; ⚕ tonisch, die Spannkraft erhöhend; stärkend; ~ *chord* ♪ Grundakkord *m*; **2.** ♪ Grundton *m*, Tonika *f*; ⚕ Stärkungsmittel *n*, Tonikum *n.*

to·night [təˈnait] heute abend *od.* nacht.

ton·ing so·lu·tion *phot.* [ˈtəuniŋ səˈlu:ʃən] Tonbad *n.*

ton·nage ⚓ [ˈtʌnidʒ] Tonnengehalt *m*, Tonnage *f*; Lastigkeit *f*; Tonnengeld *n.*

ton·sil *anat.* [ˈtɔnsl] Mandel *f*; **ton·sil·li·tis** [~siˈlaitis] Mandelentzündung *f.*

ton·sure [ˈtɔnʃə] **1.** Tonsur *f*; **2.** tonsurieren, scheren.

ton·y *Am. sl.* [ˈtəuni] schick.

too [tu:] zu, allzu; auch, noch dazu.

took [tuk] *pret. von take.*

tool [tu:l] **1.** Werkzeug *n* (*a. fig.*), Instrument *n*, Gerät *n*; **2.** mit e-m Werkzeug (be)arbeiten; ˈ~**-bag**, ˈ~**-kit** Werkzeugtasche *f*; ~ **shed** Geräteschuppen *m.*

toot [tu:t] **1.** blasen, tuten; **2.** Tuten *n.*

tooth [tu:θ], *pl.* **teeth** [ti:θ] Zahn *m*; ~ *and nail* mit aller Kraft; *cast s.th. in s.o.'s teeth* j-m et. vorwerfen; ˈ~**·ache** Zahnweh *n*; ˈ~**-brush** Zahnbürste *f*; **toothed** mit (...) Zähnen; Zahn...; ˈ**tooth·ing** ⊕ (Ver)Zahnung *f*; ˈ**tooth·less** □ zahnlos; ˈ**tooth-paste** Zahnpasta *f*; ˈ**tooth·pick** Zahnstocher *m.*

tooth·some □ [ˈtu:θsəm] schmackhaft.

too·tle [ˈtu:tl] tuten; dudeln; schwatzen.

top[1] [tɔp] **1.** oberstes Ende *n*; Oberteil *n*; Gipfel *m*, Spitze *f*; Wipfel *m*, Krone *f*; (Haus)Giebel *m*; Kopf *m e-r Seite*; *fig.* Gipfel *m* (*höchster Grad*); Oberfläche *f des Wassers*; (Bett)Himmel *m*; *mot. Am.* Verdeck *n*; ⚓ Mars *m*; Scheitel *m*; Haupt *n*, Erste *m*; Stulpe *f e-s Stiefels*; *at the* ~ obenan; *at the* ~ *of* oben an *od.* auf (*dat.*); *at the* ~ *of one's speed* in höchster Eile; *at the* ~ *of one's voice* aus voller Kehle, so laut man kann; *on* ~ obenauf; dazu noch; *on* ~ *of* oben auf (*dat.*); **2.** ober(er, -e, -es); oberst; Haupt...; *the* ~ *right corner* die rechte obere Ecke; **3.** oben bedecken, krönen; *fig.* übertragen, -treffen; vorangehen in (*dat.*); als erste(r) stehen auf *e-r Liste*; ✂ stutzen, kappen; ~ *up* auffüllen.

top[2] [~] Kreisel *m*; *sleep like a* ~ wie ein Murmeltier schlafen.

to·paz *min.* [ˈtəupæz] Topas *m.*

top...: ˈ~**-ˈboots** *pl.* Stulpenstiefel *m/pl.*; Langschäfter *m/pl.*; ~ **dog** *sl. der* Überlegene, *der* Herr; ~ **earn·er** Spitzenverdiener *m.*

to·pee [ˈtəupi] Tropenhelm *m.*

top·er [ˈtəupə] Zecher *m.*

top...: ˈ~**·flight** F prima, erstklassig; ~**·gal·lant** ⚓ [~ˈgælənt, ⚓ təˈgælənt] **1.** Bram...; **2.** *a.* ~ *sail* Bramsegel *n*; ~ **hat** Zylinderhut *m*; ˈ~**-ˈheav·y** kopflastig; ˈ~**-ˈhole** *sl.* ganz groß (*erstklassig*).

top·ic [ˈtɔpik] Gegenstand *m*, Thema *n*; ˈ**top·i·cal** □ örtlich, lokal (*a.* ⚕); aktuell.

top·knot [ˈtɔpnɔt] Haarknoten *m*; *orn.* Haube *f.*

top·less [ˈtɔplis] oben ohne.

top...: ˈ~**·mast** ⚓ Marsstenge *f*; ˈ~**most** höchst, oberst; ˈ~**-ˈnotch** F prima, erstklassig.

to·pog·ra·pher [təˈpɔgrəfə] Topograph *m*; **top·o·graph·ic, top·o·graph·i·cal** □ [tɔpəˈgræfik(əl)] topographisch; **to·pog·ra·phy** [təˈpɔgrəfi] Topographie *f*, Ortsbeschreibung *f.*

top·per F [ˈtɔpə] Zylinder *m*; ˈ**topping** F prima, toll, fabelhaft.

top·ple [ˈtɔpl] *mst* ~ *over*, ~ *down* (um)kippen, umfallen.

top·sail ⚓ [ˈtɔpsl] Marssegel *n.*

top...: ~ **se·cret** streng geheim; ~ **speed** Höchstgeschwindigkeit *f.*

top·sy·tur·vy □ [ˈtɔpsiˈtə:vi] auf den Kopf gestellt; das Unterste zuoberst; drunter und drüber.

toque [təuk] Toque *f* (*Damenhut*).

tor [tɔ:] Felsturm *m.*

torch [tɔ:tʃ] Fackel *f*; *a. electric* ~ Taschenlampe *f*; ˈ~**·light** Fackelschein *m*; ~ *procession* Fackelzug *m.*

tore [tɔ:] *pret. von tear*[1] *1.*

tor·ment 1. [ˈtɔ:mənt] Qual *f*, Folter *f*, Pein *f*, Marter *f*; **2.** [tɔ:-

ˈment] peinigen, foltern, martern, quälen; **torˈmen·tor** Quälgeist *m*, Folterer *m*, Peiniger *m*.

torn [tɔːn] *p.p. von tear*[1] *1.*

tor·na·do [tɔːˈneidəu], *pl.* **torˈna·does** [˷z] Wirbelsturm *m*, Tornado *m*.

tor·pe·do [tɔːˈpiːdəu], *pl.* **torˈpe·does** [˷z] **1.** ⚓, ✈ Torpedo *m*; *a. toy* ˷ Knallerbse *f*; *a.* ˷*-fish ichth.* Zitterrochen *m*; **2.** ⚓ torpedieren (*a. fig.*); **˷-boat** ⚓ Torpedoboot *n*; **˷-tube** Torpedorohr *n*.

tor·pid □ [ˈtɔːpid] starr, erstarrt; *fig.* stumpf, apathisch; träg, schlaff; **torˈpid·i·ty, ˈtor·pid·ness, tor·por** [ˈtɔːpə] Erstarrung *f*, Betäubung *f*.

torque ⊕ [tɔːk] Drehmoment *n*.

tor·rent [ˈtɔrənt] Sturz-, Gießbach *m*; (reißender) Strom *m* (*a. fig.*); **tor·ren·tial** □ [tɔˈrenʃəl] gießbachartig; Gießbach...; strömend; *fig.* ungestüm.

tor·rid [ˈtɔrid] dörrend; brennend heiß; ˷ *zone* heiße Zone *f*.

tor·sion [ˈtɔːʃən] Drehung *f*; **tor·sion·al** [ˈ˷ʃənl] Drehungs...

tor·so [ˈtɔːsəu] Torso *m*; Rumpf *m*; Bruchstück *n*.

tort ⚖ [tɔːt] Unrecht *n*.

tor·toise *zo.* [ˈtɔːtəs] Schildkröte *f*; **˷-shell** [ˈtɔːtəʃel] Schildpatt *n*.

tor·tu·os·i·ty [tɔːtjuˈɔsiti] Gewundenheit *f*; Windung *f*; **ˈtor·tu·ous** □ gewunden (*a. fig.*); *fig.* krumm.

tor·ture [ˈtɔːtʃə] **1.** Folter *f*, Marter *f*, Tortur *f*, Qual *f*; **2.** foltern, martern; **ˈtor·tur·er** Folterer *m*; Peiniger *m*.

To·ry [ˈtɔːri] **1.** Tory *m* (*engl. Konservativer*); **2.** konservativ; Tory...; **ˈTo·ry·ism** Torytum *n*.

tosh *sl.* [tɔʃ] Quatsch *m*.

toss [tɔs] **1.** Werfen *n*, Wurf *m*; Zurückwerfen *n des Kopfes*; Hochwerfen *n e-r Münze etc.*; *win the* ˷ beim Losen gewinnen; **2.** *v/t. a.* ˷ *about* hin und her werfen; schütteln; (*in Verbindung mit adv.*) werfen; *a.* ˷ *up* hochwerfen; ˷ *off Getränk* hinunterstürzen; *Arbeit* hinhauen; ˷ *the oars* ⚓ die Riemen pieken; *v/i.* sich hin und her werfen; geschüttelt werden; *a.* ˷ *up* losen (*for* um); **ˈ˷-up** Losen *n mit e-r Münze*; *fig.* et. Zweifelhaftes *n*; *it's a* ˷ es ist fraglich.

tot[1] F [tɔt] Knirps *m* (*kleines Kind*); Schlückchen *n*.

tot[2] F [˷] **1.** (Gesamt)Summe *f*; **2.** ˷ *up* zs.-zählen; sich belaufen (*to* auf *acc.*).

to·tal [ˈtəutl] **1.** □ ganz, gänzlich; total; gesamt, Gesamt...; **2.** Gesamtbetrag *m*, -summe *f*; *grand* ˷ Endsumme *f*; **3.** insgesamt betragen, sich belaufen auf (*acc.*); summieren; **to·tal·i·tar·i·an** [˷tæliˈtɛəriən] totalitär; **to·tal·iˈtar·i·an·ism** Totalitarismus *m*; **toˈtal·i·ty** Gesamtheit *f*; Vollständigkeit *f*; **to·tal·i·za·tor** [ˈ˷təlaizeitə] Totalisator *m*; **to·tal·ize** [ˈ˷təlaiz] zs.-zählen.

tote F [təut] (mit sich) schleppen, tragen.

to·tem [ˈtəutəm] Totem *n*; **ˈ˷-pole** Totempfahl *m*.

tot·ter [ˈtɔtə] wanken, wackeln; **ˈtot·ter·ing** □, **ˈtot·ter·y** wack(e)lig.

touch [tʌtʃ] **1.** *v/t.* be-, anrühren; (an)stoßen, stoßen an (*acc.*); betreffen; *fig.* rühren; erreichen; spielen, *Saiten* rühren; *Ton* anschlagen; färben; ˷ *one's hat to s.o.* j. grüßen; ˷ *bottom* auf Grund kommen; *fig.* den Tiefstpunkt erreichen; ˷ *the spot* F gerade das Rechte sein; den Finger auf die Wunde legen; ˷ *s.o. for sl.* j. anbetteln um; *a bit* ˷*ed fig.* ein bißchen verrückt; ˷ *off* skizzieren; *Geschütz* abfeuern; *fig.* auslösen; ˷ *up* auffrischen; *phot.* retuschieren; *v/i.* sich berühren; ˷ *at* ⚓ anlegen bei *od.* in (*dat.*), berühren; ˷ (*up*)*on fig.* berühren; (kurz) erwähnen, betreffen; **2.** Berührung *f*; Gefühl(ssinn *m*) *n*; Anfall *m von Krankheit*; Anflug *m*, Anstrich *m*, Zug *m*; Fertigkeit *f*, Hand *f*; ♪ Anschlag *m*; (Pinsel)Strich *m*; *get in*(*to*) ˷ *with* sich in Verbindung setzen mit; *to the* ˷ beim Anfassen; **ˈ˷-and-ˈgo** **1.** gewagte Sache *f*; *it is* ˷ es steht auf des Messers Schneide; **2.** unsicher; riskant, gewagt; **ˈ˷·down** ✈ Aufsetzen *n*, Landung *f*; **ˈtouch·i·ness** Empfindlichkeit *f*; **ˈtouch·ing** **1.** □ rührend; **2.** *prp.* betreffend, in betreff; **ˈtouch-line** *Fußball*: Seiten-, Marklinie *f*; **ˈtouch·stone** Probierstein *m*; *fig.* Prüfstein *m*; **ˈtouch-type** blindschreiben; **ˈtouch·y** □ empfindlich; heikel; = *testy*.

tough [tʌf] **1.** zäh (*a. fig.*); unnachgiebig; schwer, hart, schwierig (*Arbeit etc.*); grob, brutal, übel; *a ~ customer* F ein übler Bursche *m*; **2.** schwerer Junge *m*; ˈ**tough·en** zäh machen *od.* werden; ˈ**tough·ie** F [ˈtʌfi] = *tough 2*; ˈ**tough·ness** Zähigkeit *f*.

tour [tuə] **1.** (Rund)Reise *f*, Tour (-nee) *f*; *conducted ~* Führung *f*; *~ operator* Reiseveranstalter *m*; **2.** (be)reisen; **tour·ing** [ˈtuəriŋ] Reise..., Touren...; *~ car mot.* Touren-, Reisewagen *m*; ˈ**tour·ism** Tourismus *m*; ˈ**tour·ist** Tourist(in), (Vergnügungs)Reisende *m*; *~ agency*, *~ office*, *~ bureau* Reisebüro *n*; *~ industry* Fremdenindustrie *f*; *~ season* Reisezeit *f*; *~ ticket* Rundreisekarte *f*.

tour·ma·line *min.* [ˈtuəməlin] Turmalin *m*.

tour·na·ment [ˈtuənəmənt], **tour·ney** [ˈ~ni] Turnier *n*.

tour·ni·quet ⚕ [ˈtuənikei] Aderpresse *f*.

tou·sle [ˈtauzl] (zer)zausen.

tout [taut] **1.** Schlepper *m*, (Kunden)Werber *m*; **2.** Kunden werben, schleppen.

tow[1] ⚓ [təu] **1.** Schleppen *n*; Schleppzug *m*; *take in ~* ins Schlepptau nehmen; **2.** (ab)schleppen; treideln; ziehen.

tow[2] [~] Werg *n zum Spinnen*.

tow·age ⚓ [ˈtəuidʒ] Schleppen *n*, Bugsieren *n*; Schleppgebühr *f*.

to·ward(s) [təˈwɔːd(z), tɔːd(z)] gegen; nach ... zu, auf ... (*acc.*) zu; (als Beitrag) zu.

tow-bar *mot.* [ˈtəubɑː] Anhängerkupplung *f*.

tow·el [ˈtauəl] **1.** Handtuch *n*; **2.** abreiben; *sl. j-m* e-e Abreibung geben (*prügeln*); *~* **dis·pens·er** Handtuchautomat *m*; ˈ**~-horse** Handtuchständer *m*; ˈ**~-rack** Handtuchhalter *m*.

tow·er [ˈtauə] **1.** Turm *m*; *fig.* Hort *m*, Bollwerk *n*; **2.** sich (empor)türmen, sich erheben; *~ above mst fig.* überragen; *~* **block** Hochhaus *n*; ˈ**tow·ered** hochgetürmt; ˈ**tow·er·ing** □ turmhoch; *fig.* hoch; rasend (*Wut*).

tow(·ing)... [ˈtəu(iŋ)]: ˈ**~-line** Schlepptau *n*; ˈ**~-path** Treidelpfad *m*.

town [taun] **1.** Stadt *f*; *man about ~* Lebemann *m*; **2.** Stadt...; städtisch; *~* **cen·tre**, *Am.* *~* **cen·ter** Behördenviertel *n*; *~* **clerk** Stadtsyndikus *m*; *~* **coun·cil** Stadtrat *m* (*Versammlung*); *~* **coun·cil·lor** Stadtrat *m* (*Person*); *~* **cri·er** Ausrufer *m*; *~* **hall** Rathaus *n*; ˈ**~-ˈplan·ning** Städtebau *m*, -planung *f*; **~·scape** [ˈ~skeip] Stadtbild *n*.

towns·folk [ˈtaunzfəuk] Stadtleute *pl.*, Städter *m/pl.*

town·ship [ˈtaunʃip] Stadtgemeinde *f*; Stadtgebiet *n*.

towns·man [ˈtaunzmən] Bürger *m*; *univ.* Philister *m*; *fellow ~* Mitbürger *m*; ˈ**towns·people** = *townsfolk*.

tow...: ˈ**~-path** Treidelpfad *m*; ˈ**~-rope** Schlepptau *n*; *~* **truck** *mot.* Abschleppwagen *m*.

tox·ic, tox·i·cal □ [ˈtɔksik(əl)] giftig, toxisch, Gift...; **tox·in** [ˈtɔksin] Toxin *n*, Giftstoff *m*.

toy [tɔi] **1.** Spielzeug *n*; Tand *m*; *~s pl.* Spielwaren *f/pl.*; **2.** Spiel(zeug)-...; Miniatur...; Zwerg...; **3.** spielen (*mst fig.*); ˈ**~-book** Bilderbuch *n*; ˈ**~-box** Spielzeugschachtel *f*; ˈ**~-shop** Spielwarenhandlung *f*.

trace[1] [treis] **1.** Spur *f* (*a. fig.*); Grundriß *m*; **2.** nachspüren (*dat.*); *fig.* verfolgen; auf-, herausfinden, ausfindig machen; *et.* feststellen, nachweisen; (auf)zeichnen; (durch-) pausen; *surv.* abstecken; *~ back et.* zurückverfolgen (*to* bis zu); *~ out* aufspüren.

trace[2] [~] Strang *m*, Zugtau *n*; *kick over the ~s fig.* über die Stränge schlagen.

trace·a·ble □ [ˈtreisəbl] zurückzuverfolgen(d); nachweisbar; **trace el·e·ment** Spurenelement *n*; ˈ**trac·er** *a. ~ ammunition* Leuchtspurmunition *f*; *a. ~ element* Isotopenindikator *m*; ˈ**trac·er·y** △ Maßwerk *n an gotischen Fenstern*.

tra·che·a *anat.* [trəˈkiːə] Luftröhre *f*.

trac·ing [ˈtreisiŋ] Aufzeichnung *f*; Durchpausen *n*; Pauszeichnung *f*; ˈ**~-pa·per** Pauspapier *n*.

track [træk] **1.** Spur *f*; *bsd. Sport*: Bahn *f*; Rennstrecke *f*; Pfad *m*; Geleise *n* (*a.* 🚃); *hunt.* Fährte *f*; ⊕ Raupenkette *f*; *~ events pl.* Lauf (-disziplinen *f/pl.*) *m*; **2.** *v/t.* nachspüren (*dat.*); verfolgen; *~ down*, *~ out* aufspüren; *v/i.* Spur halten; ˈ**~-and-ˈfield sports** *pl.* Leichtathletik *f*; **tracked ve·hi·cle** Raupenfahrzeug *n*; ˈ**track·er** *bsd. hunt.* Spurhalter *m*; Verfolger(in); ˈ**track·ing sta-**

tion *Raumfahrt*: Bodenstation *f*; ˈ**track·less** spur-, pfadlos; ⊕ schienenlos; **track suit** Trainingsanzug *m*.

tract[1] [trækt] Fläche *f*, Strecke *f*, Gegend *f*; *anat*. Trakt *m*.

tract[2] [~] Traktat *m*, *n*, Abhandlung *f*.

trac·ta·bil·i·ty [træktəˈbiliti], ˈ**trac·ta·ble·ness** Lenksamkeit *f*; ˈ**trac·ta·ble** □ lenk-, fügsam.

trac·tion [ˈtrækʃən] Ziehen *n*, Zug *m*; ~ *engine* Zugmaschine *f*; ˈ**trac·tive** Zug...; ˈ**trac·tor** ⊕ Trecker *m*, Zugmaschine *f*, Schlepper *m*, Traktor *m*.

trade [treid] **1.** Handel *m*; Geschäft *n*; Gewerbe *n*; Handwerk *n*; *Am*. Schiebung *f*, Kompensationsgeschäft *n*; *Board of* ♀ Handelsministerium *n*; *the* ♀*s pl*. ⚓ die Passatwinde *m*/*pl*.; *do a good* ~ gute Geschäfte machen; **2.** *v*/*i*. Handel treiben; handeln (*with* mit *j-m*; *in* mit *e-r Ware*); ~ *on* F reisen auf (*acc*.), ausnutzen; *v*/*t*. tauschen (*for* gegen); ~ *s.th. in* et. in Zahlung geben; ~ **cy·cle** Konjunkturzyklus *m*; ˈ**~-fair** ✝ Messe *f*; ~ **mark** Warenzeichen *n*, Schutzmarke *f*; ~ **name** Firmenname *m*; Warenbezeichnung *f*; ~ **price** Händlerpreis *m*; ˈ**trad·er** Händler *m*; Handelsschiff *n*; **trade re·la·tions** *pl*. Handelsbeziehungen *f*/*pl*.; **trade school** Gewerbeschule *f*; **trade se·cret** Geschäfts- *od*. Betriebsgeheimnis *n*; **trade show** Filmvorführung *f* für Verleiher u. Kritiker; **trades·man** [ˈ~zmən] Händler *m*, Geschäftsmann *m*; ˈ**trades·peo·ple** Geschäftsleute *pl*.; **trade un·ion** Gewerkschaft *f*; **trade-ˈun·ion·ism** Gewerkschaftswesen *n*; **trade-ˈun·ion·ist 1.** Gewerkschaftler *m*; **2.** gewerkschaftlich; **trade war** Handelskrieg *m*; **trade wind** ⚓ Passatwind *m*.

trad·ing [ˈtreidiŋ] Handels...

tra·di·tion [trəˈdiʃən] Tradition *f*, Überlieferung *f*; alter Brauch *m*; **traˈdi·tion·al** □ [~ʃənl], **traˈdi·tion·ar·y** [~ʃnəri] □ traditionell, überliefert; herkömmlich.

traf·fic [ˈtræfik] **1.** Verkehr *m*; Handel *m*; **2.** handeln (*in* mit); **traf·fi·ca·tor** [ˈ~keitə] *mot*. Winker *m*; **traf·fic cone** *mot*. Leitkegel *m*; **traf·fic jam** Verkehrsstauung *f*; ˈ**traf·fick·er** Händler *m*, *b.s.* Schacherer *m*; **traf·fic light** Verkehrsampel *f*; **traf·fic news** *pl*. Verkehrsmeldungen *f*/*pl*.; **traf·fic war·den** Politesse *f*.

tra·ge·di·an [trəˈdʒiːdjən] Tragiker *m*; *thea*. Tragöde *m*, Tragödin *f*; **trag·e·dy** [ˈtrædʒidi] Tragödie *f* (*a. fig*.); Trauerspiel *n*.

trag·ic, trag·i·cal □ [ˈtrædʒik(əl)] tragisch (*a. fig*.).

trag·i·com·e·dy [ˈtrædʒiˈkɔmidi] Tragikomödie *f*; ˈ**trag·iˈcom·ic** (*~ally*) tragikomisch.

trail [treil] **1.** *fig*. Schwanz *m*, Schweif *m*; Schleppe *f*; Spur *f*, *hunt*. Fährte *f*; Pfad *m*; ~ *of smoke* Rauchfahne *f*; **2.** *v*/*t*. hinter sich (her)ziehen; auf der Spur verfolgen; *v*/*i*. (sich) schleppen; (sich hin)ziehen; ⚘ kriechen; wehen, flattern; ~ **blaz·er** *Am*. Pistensucher *m*; Bahnbrecher *m*; ˈ**trail·er** (Wohnwagen)Anhänger *m*; ⚘ Kriechpflanze *f*; *Film*: Voranzeige *f*, Vorschau *f*.

train [trein] **1.** (Eisenbahn)Zug *m*; *allg*. Zug *m*; Gefolge *n*; Reihe *f*, Folge *f*, Kette *f*; Schleppe *f am Kleid*; **2.** *v*/*t*. erziehen; schulen; abrichten; ausbilden; einexerzieren; *Sport*: trainieren; *Geschütz* richten; *v*/*i*. (sich) üben; trainieren; *a*. ~ *it* F mit der Eisenbahn fahren; ˈ**~-ac·ci·dent**, ˈ**~-dis·as·ter** Eisenbahnunglück *n*; **trainˈee** in der Ausbildung Begriffene *m*; ˈ**train·er** Ausbilder *m*; Zureiter *m*; Trainer *m*; ˈ**train-ˈfer·ry** Eisenbahnfähre *f*.

train·ing [ˈtreiniŋ] Ausbildung *f*; Übung *f*; *Sport*: Training *n*; *physical* ~ körperliche Ertüchtigung *f*; ˈ**~-col·lege** Lehrerbildungsanstalt *f*; ˈ**~-ship** Schulschiff *n*.

train-oil [ˈtreinɔil] Fischtran *m*.

trait [treit] (Charakter)Zug *m*.

trai·tor [ˈtreitə] Verräter *m* (*to* an *dat*.); ˈ**trai·tor·ous** □ verräterisch.

trai·tress [ˈtreitris] Verräterin *f*.

tra·jec·to·ry *phys*. [ˈtrædʒiktəri] Flugbahn *f*.

tram [træm] ⚒ Förderwagen *m*, Hund *m*; = *~-car*, *~way*; ˈ**~-car** Straßenbahnwagen *m*; ˈ**~-line** Straßenbahnlinie *f*.

tram·mel [ˈtræml] **1.** *Art* Fischnetz *n*; *~s pl. fig*. Fesseln *f*/*pl*.; **2.** fesseln, hemmen.

tramp [træmp] **1.** Getrampel *n*; (schwerer) Tritt *m*; Wanderung *f*; Tramp *m*; Landstreicher *m*; *a.* *~ steamer* Trampschiff *n*; *on the ~* auf der Wanderschaft; **2.** *v/i.* trampeln, treten; (zu Fuß) wandern; *v/t.* durchwandern; **tram·ple** ['~l] (zer)trampeln.

tram·way ['træmwei] Straßenbahn *f*.

trance [trɑːns] Trance *f*, (hypnotischer) Traumzustand *m*; Verzückung *f*.

tran·ny *sl.* ['træni] Kofferradio *n*.

tran·quil □ ['træŋkwil] ruhig; gelassen; **tran'quil·(l)i·ty** Ruhe *f*; Gelassenheit *f*; **tran·quil·i·za·tion** [~lai'zeiʃən] Beruhigung *f*; '**tran·quil·(l)ize** beruhigen; '**tran·quil·(l)i·zer** Beruhigungsmittel *n*, Sedativum *n*.

trans·act [træn'zækt] abwickeln; abmachen; *~ business* Geschäfte machen; **trans'ac·tion** Verrichtung *f*; Geschäft *n*, Transaktion *f*; *~s pl.* (Sitzungs-, Tätigkeits)Bericht(e *pl.*) *m*.

trans·al·pine ['trænz'ælpain] transalpin(isch).

trans·at·lan·tic ['trænzət'læntik] transatlantisch, Transatlantik...

tran·scend [træn'send] überschreiten, -steigen, -treffen; hinausgehen über (*acc.*); **tran'scend·ence, tran'scend·en·cy** Überlegenheit *f*; *phls.* Transzendenz *f*; **tran'scend·ent** □ überragend, vorzüglich; *a.* = **tran·scen·den·tal** □ [~'dentl] ⚘ transzendent; *phls.* transzendental; P phantastisch.

trans·con·ti·nen·tal ['trænzkɔnti'nentl] transkontinental.

tran·scribe [træns'kraib] abschreiben; *Kurzschrift* umschreiben; ♪ umsetzen; *Radio*: aufnehmen.

tran·script ['trænskript] Abschrift *f*; **tran'scrip·tion** Abschreiben *n*; Umschrift *f*; ♪ Umsetzung *f*; *Radio*: Aufnahme *f*.

tran·sept △ ['trænsept] Querschiff *n*.

trans·fer 1. [træns'fəː] *v/t.* übertragen (*bsd.* ⚖, *to* auf *acc.*); versetzen, verlegen (*to* nach; *in*, *into* in *acc.*); *Druck*, *Stich etc.* umdrucken; *v/i.* übertreten; **2.** ['~] Übertragung *f* (*bsd.* ⚖); ✝ Transfer *m*, Überweisung *f*, Versetzung *f*, Verlegung *f*; Abzug *m*, Umdruck *m*; Abziehbild *n*; Umsteiger *m* (*Fahrschein*); **trans'fer·a·ble** übertragbar *etc.*; **trans·fer·ee** ⚖ [~fə'riː] Zessionar *m*, Übernehmer *m*; **trans·fer·ence** ['~fərəns] Übertragung *f*; '**trans·fer fee** Ablösesumme *f für e-n Sportler*; '**trans·fer·or** ⚖ Zedent *m*; **trans·fer-pic·ture** ['~fəːpiktʃə] Abziehbild *n*.

trans·fig·u·ra·tion [trænsfigjuə'reiʃən] Umgestaltung *f*; Verklärung *f*; **trans·fig·ure** [~'figə] umgestalten; verklären.

trans·fix [træns'fiks] durchstecken; *~ed fig.* versteinert, starr (*with* vor *dat.*).

trans·form [træns'fɔːm] umformen; um-, verwandeln; umgestalten; **trans·for·ma·tion** [~fə'meiʃən] Umformung *f*; Um-, Verwandlung *f*; Haarersatz *m*; **trans·form·er** ⚡ [~'fɔːmə] Umformer *m*, Transformator *m*.

trans·fuse [træns'fjuːz] ⚕ *Blut etc.* übertragen (*into* in, auf *acc.*); *fig.* einflößen (*dat.*); *fig.* durchtränken (*with* mit); **trans'fu·sion** [~ʒən] (*bsd.* ⚕ Blut)Übertragung *f*, Transfusion *f*.

trans·gress [træns'gres] *v/t.* überschreiten; übertreten, verletzen; *v/i.* sich vergehen; **trans'gres·sion** Überschreitung *f etc.*; Vergehen *n*; **trans'gres·sor** [~sə] Übertreter *m*.

tran·sience, tran·sien·cy ['trænziəns(i)] Vergänglichkeit *f*.

tran·sient ['trænziənt] **1.** *zeitlich* vorübergehend; vergänglich, flüchtig; **2.** *Am.* Durchreisende *m*.

tran·sis·tor [træn'zistə] Transistor *m*; *~ (radio)* Transistor-, Kofferradio *n*.

trans·it ['trænsit] Durchgang *m*; Durchgangsverkehr *m*; *in ~* unterwegs, auf dem Transport; *~* **camp** Durchgangslager *n*.

tran·si·tion [træn'siʒən] Übergang *m*; **tran'si·tion·al** □ [~ʒənl] Übergangs...; e-n Übergang bildend.

tran·si·tive □ *gr.* ['trænsitiv] transitiv.

tran·si·to·ri·ness ['trænsitərinis] Vergänglichkeit *f*, Flüchtigkeit *f*; '**tran·si·to·ry** □ vergänglich, flüchtig.

trans·lat·a·ble [træns'leitəbl] übersetzbar; **trans'late** *Buch etc.* übersetzen, -tragen; *fig.* umsetzen, -arbeiten (*into* in *acc.*, zu); *Geistliche* versetzen; entrücken; **trans'la·tion** Übersetzung *f etc.*; **trans'la·tor** Übersetzer(in).

trans·lu·cence, **trans·lu·cen·cy** [trænz'lu:sns(i)] Durchscheinen *n*; **trans'lu·cent** durchscheinend; *fig.* hell.

trans·ma·rine [trænzmə'ri:n] überseeisch.

trans·mi·grant ['trænzmigrənt] Durchwanderer *m*; **trans·mi·grate** ['trænzmai'greit] (aus)wandern; *fig.* wandern (*Seele*); **trans·mi'gra·tion** (Aus)Wanderung *f*; ~ *of souls* Seelenwanderung *f*.

trans·mis·si·ble [trænz'misəbl] übertragbar; **trans'mis·sion** Übermittlung *f*, *biol.* Vererbung *f*; *phys.* Fortpflanzung *f*; ⊕ Transmission *f*; *mot.* Getriebe *n*; *Radio*: Übertragung *f*, Sendung *f*.

trans·mit [trænz'mit] übermitteln, -senden; übertragen; *tel.*, *Radio*: senden; *biol.* vererben; *phys.* fortpflanzen; **trans'mit·ter** Übermittler(in); *tel. etc.* Sender *m*; **trans'mit·ting** *Radio*: Sende...; ~ *station* Sendestelle *f*.

trans·mog·ri·fy F [trænz'mɔgrifai] umkrempeln.

trans·mut·a·ble □ [trænz'mju:təbl] umwandelbar; **trans·mu'ta·tion** Um-, Verwandlung *f*; **trans'mute** um-, verwandeln.

trans·o·ce·an·ic ['trænzəuʃi'ænik] überseeisch; Ozean...

tran·som ⚠ ['trænsəm] Querholz *n*; Oberlicht *n*.

trans·par·en·cy [træns'pεərənsi] Durchsichtigkeit *f*; Transparent *n*; Dia(positiv) *n*; **trans'par·ent** □ durchsichtig (*a. fig.*).

tran·spi·ra·tion [trænspi'reiʃən] Ausdünstung *f*; **tran·spire** [~'paiə] ausdünsten, -schwitzen; *fig.* durchsickern, verlauten; V passieren.

trans·plant [træns'plɑ:nt] um-, verpflanzen; **trans·plan'ta·tion** Verpflanzung *f*.

trans·port **1.** [træns'pɔ:t] fortschaffen, befördern, transportieren; *fig.* hinreißen, entzücken; **2.** ['~] Fortschaffen *n*; Beförderung *f*; Transport *m*; Verkehr *m*; Beförderungsmittel *n*; Transportschiff *n*; Entzücken *n*; *Minister of* ♀ Verkehrsminister *m*; *in* ~*s* (*vor Freude od. Wut*) außer sich; **trans'port·a·ble** transportabel; **trans·por'ta·tion** Beförderung *f*, Fortschaffung *f*, Versendung *f*, Transport *m*.

trans·pose [træns'pəuz] versetzen, umstellen; ♪ transponieren; **trans·po·si·tion** [~pə'ziʃən] Umstellung *f*; ♪ Transposition *f*.

trans-ship ⚓, 🚃 [træns'ʃip] umladen.

tran·sub·stan·ti·ate [trænsəb'stænʃieit] stofflich umwandeln; *eccl. Brot u. Wein* verwandeln; '**tran·sub·stan·ti'a·tion** Stoffverwandlung *f*; *eccl.* Transsubstantiation *f*.

trans·ver·sal [trænz'və:səl] **1.** □ quer hindurchgehend; **2.** ⩕ Transversale *f*; '**trans·verse** □ querlaufend; Quer...; ~ *section* Querschnitt *m*; ~ *strength* ⊕ Querbiegefestigkeit *f*.

trap[1] [træp] **1.** Falle *f* (*a. fig.*); Klappe *f*; Wurfmaschine (*bsd. beim Tontaubenschießen*); ⊕ Wasserverschluß *m*; Geruchverschluß *m*; Gig *n* (*leichte Kutsche*); = ~*door*; **2.** (in e-r Falle) fangen, in die Falle locken; *fig.* ertappen; mit Fallen besetzen; ⊕ mit Wasserverschluß versehen.

trap[2] *min.* [~] Trapp *m*.

trap·door ['træp'dɔ:] Falltür *f*; *thea.* Versenkung *f*.

trapes F [treips] latschen.

tra·peze [trə'pi:z] *Zirkus*: Trapez *n*; **tra'pe·zi·um** ⩕ [~zjəm] Trapez *n*; **trap·e·zoid** ⩕ ['træpizɔid] Trapezoid *n*.

trap·per ['træpə] Trapper *m*, Pelzjäger *m*.

trap·pings ['træpiŋz] *pl.* Paradegeschirr *n e-s Pferdes*; Schabracke *f*; *fig.* Schmuck *m*, Putz *m*.

trap·pist *eccl.* ['træpist] Trappist *m*.

trap·py ['træpi] heimtückisch.

traps F [træps] *pl.* Siebensachen *pl.*

trash [træʃ] Abfall *m*; *fig.* Plunder *m*; Unsinn *m*, Blech *n*; Kitsch *m*; ~ **can** *Am.* Mülltonne *f*; '**trash·y** □ wertlos, kitschig.

trau·ma ['trɔ:mə] Trauma *n*; **trau·mat·ic** [~'mætik] traumatisch; ~ *experience psych.* traumatisches Erlebnis *n*; ~ *medicine* Unfallmedizin *f*.

trav·ail † ['træveil] (Geburts-)

Wehen *pl.*

trav·el ['trævl] **1.** *v/i. bsd. weit* reisen (*a.* ✈); *weitS.* sich bewegen; wandern; *v/t.* bereisen, durchwandern; **2.** *das* Reisen; ⊕ Lauf *m*, Bewegung *f*; *~s pl.* Reisen *f/pl.*; ~ **a·gen·cy,** ~ **a·gent's** Reisebüro *n*; ~ **al·low·ance** Reise-, Fahrtkostenzuschuß *m.*

trav·e·la·tor ['trævəleitə] rollender Gehsteig *m* (*Beförderungsband für Fußgänger*); '**trav·el(l)ed** weitgereist; '**trav·el·(l)er** Reisende *m* (*a.* ✈); ⊕ Laufkran *m*, Läufer *m*; *~'s cheque* Reisescheck *m*; '**trav·el·(l)ing** Reise...; ⊕ Lauf...; *~ allowance = travel allowance*; *~ rug* Reisedecke *f*; *~ salesman* Handlungsreisende *m.*

trav·e·log(ue) ['trævəlɔg] Reisebericht *m* (*Lichtbildervortrag*).

trav·erse ['trævə:s] **1.** Durchquerung *f*; *mount.* Quergang *m*; ⚖ Bestreitung *f*; ⚔ Querwall *m*; ⊕ Querstück *n*; **2.** *v/t.* (über-)queren; durchqueren, -ziehen; *fig.* durchkreuzen; ⚖ bestreiten; *Geschütz* (seitwärts) schwenken; *v/i. mount.* queren.

trav·es·ty ['trævisti] **1.** Travestie *f*; Karikatur *f*; Zerrbild *n*; **2.** travestieren (*scherzhaft umgestalten*); verulken.

trawl [trɔ:l] **1.** (Grund)Schleppnetz *n*; **2.** mit dem Schleppnetz fischen; '**trawl·er** Trawler *m.*

tray [trei] (Servier)Brett *n*, Tablett *n*; Ablegekasten *m*, Ablage *f*; *pen-~* Federschale *f.*

treach·er·ous □ ['tretʃərəs] verräterisch, treulos; (heim)tückisch; trügerisch (*Wetter, Gedächtnis etc.*); '**treach·er·ous·ness,** '**treach·er·y** Verrat *m*, Verräterei *f*, Treulosigkeit *f*; Tücke *f.*

trea·cle ['tri:kl] Sirup *m*; Melasse *f*; '**treac·ly** sirupartig; *fig.* zuckersüß.

tread [tred] **1.** (*irr.*) *v/i.* treten (*on, upon* auf *acc.*); einhertreten, schreiten; *v/t.* treten (*a. vom Hahn*); *rhet.* betreten; **2.** Tritt *m*, Schritt *m*; Hahnentritt *m*; Trittstufe *f*; Lauffläche *f e-s Rades etc.*; **trea·dle** ['~dl] **1.** Pedal *n*, Tritt *m*; **2.** treten; '**tread·mill** Tretmühle *f.*

trea·son ['tri:zn] Verrat *m*; '**trea·son·a·ble** □ verräterisch (*bsd. Sache*).

treas·ure ['treʒə] **1.** Schatz *m*, Reichtum *m*; *~s of the soil* Bodenschätze *m/pl.*; *~-house* Schatzkammer *f*; *~ hunt* Schatzsuche *f*; *~ trove* Schatzfund *m*; **2.** *oft ~ up Schätze* sammeln, aufhäufen; *fig.* schätzen; '**treas·ur·er** Schatzmeister *m*, Kassenwart *m.*

treas·ur·y ['treʒəri] Schatzkammer *f*; (*bsd.* Staats)Schatz *m*; ♀ *(Board)*, *Am.* ♀ *Department* Finanzministerium *n*; ♀ **Bench** *parl.* Ministerbank *f*; ~ **bill** Schatzwechsel *m*; ~ **note** Kassenschein *m* (*Papiergeld*).

treat [tri:t] **1.** *v/t.* behandeln; betrachten; *~ s.o. to s.th.* j-m et. spendieren; *~ o.s. to s.th.* sich et. genehmigen; *v/i. ~ of* handeln von, *et.* behandeln; *~ with* unterhandeln mit (*for* über *acc.*); **2.** (Extra-)Vergnügen *n*, Hochgenuß *m*; *school ~* Schulausflug *m*; *it is my ~* F es geht auf meine Rechnung; *stand ~* F (die Zeche) bezahlen; **trea·tise** ['~tiz] Abhandlung *f*; '**treat·ment** Behandlung *f*; '**trea·ty** Vertrag *m*; *be in ~ with* in Unterhandlung stehen mit; *~ port* Vertragshafen *m.*

tre·ble ['trebl] **1.** □ dreifach; ♪ Diskant...; **2.** Dreifache *n*; ♪ Diskant *m*, Sopran *m*; **3.** (sich) verdreifachen; ~ **con·trol** *Radio*: Höhenregler *m.*

tree [tri:] **1.** Baum *m*; *s. family*; *at the top of the ~ fig.* auf der höchsten Stufe; *up a ~* F in der Klemme; **2.** auf e-n Baum treiben; *fig.* in die Enge treiben; '**tree·less** baumlos; '**tree·top** Baumkrone *f*, -wipfel *m.*

tre·foil ['trefɔil] ♀ Klee *m*; ⚠ Kleeblatt *n.*

trek [trek] *Südafrika*: **1.** trecken, (im Ochsenwagen) reisen *od.* ziehen; **2.** Treck *m.*

trel·lis ['trelis] **1.** ↗ Spalier *n*; **2.** vergittern; ↗ am Spalier ziehen.

trem·ble ['trembl] **1.** zittern (*at* bei; *with* vor *dat.*); **2.** Zittern *n.*

tre·men·dous □ [tri'mendəs] schrecklich, furchtbar; F kolossal, riesig, fürchterlich, ungeheuer.

trem·or ['tremə] Zittern *n*, Beben *n.*

trem·u·lous □ ['tremjuləs] zitternd, bebend; '**trem·u·lous·ness** Zittern *n*, Beben *n.*

trench [trentʃ] **1.** Graben *m*; *fig.* Furche *f*; ⚔ Schützengraben *m*;

~ *warfare* Grabenkrieg *m*; **2.** *v/t.* mit Gräben durchziehen; *fig.* durchfurchen; ✓ umgraben; *v/i.* ⚔ Gräben ausheben; ~ *(up)on* eingreifen in *(acc.)*; *fig.* hart grenzen an *(acc.)*; **'trench·ant** □ schneidend, scharf; bündig, markig *(Sprache)*; **trench coat** Wettermantel *m*, Trenchcoat *m*.

trench·er ['trentʃə] Schneidebrett *n*; *fig.* Tafel *f*; ~ **cap** Studentenmütze *f*.

trend [trend] **1.** Richtung *f*; *fig.* Lauf *m*; *fig.* Strömung *f*; Tendenz *f*; **2.** sich erstrecken, laufen; **'~-set·ter** *Mode*: Schrittmacher *m*; **'trend·y** modisch, im Trend; *be* ~ als schick gelten; ‚in' sein; *the trendies pl.* die Schickeria.

tre·pan [tri'pæn] **1.** ⚕ *hist.* Schädelbohrer *m*; **2.** ⚕ trepanieren; ⊕ anfräsen.

trep·i·da·tion [trepi'deiʃən] Zittern *n*, Beben *n*; Bestürzung *f*.

tres·pass ['trespəs] **1.** Vergehen *n*, Übertretung *f*; unbefugtes Betreten *n od.* Verletzen *n fremden Eigentums*; Eingriff *m*; **2.** unbefugt eindringen (*on, upon* in *fremdes Eigentum etc.*); *Zeit etc.* über Gebühr in Anspruch nehmen; **'tres·pass·er** Rechtsverletzer *m*; unbefugter Eindringling *m*; ~*s will be prosecuted* unbefugtes Betreten bei Strafe verboten.

tress [tres] Haarlocke *f*, -flechte *f*.

tres·tle ['tresl] Gestell *n*, Bock *m*; ~ *bridge* Bockbrücke *f*.

trey [trei] Drei *f im Karten- u. Würfelspiel.*

tri·ad ['traiəd] Dreizahl *f*, Triade *f*.

tri·al ['traiəl] Versuch *m* (*of* mit); Probe *f*, Prüfung *f*; *fig.* Prüfung *f*, Plage *f*; ⚖ Verhandlung *f*, Prozeß *m*, (Gerichts)Verfahren *n*; ~ *match* Sichtungsspiel *n*; *on* ~ auf Probe; vor Gericht; *prisoner on* ~ Untersuchungsgefangene *m, f*; ~ *of strength* Kraftprobe *f*; *bring to* ~ vor Gericht bringen; *give s.o. od. s.th. a* ~ es mit j-m *od.* e-r Sache versuchen; *send for* ~ vor Gericht stellen; *stand* ~ sich (vor Gericht) verantworten (*for* wegen); ~ **mar·riage** Ehe *f* auf Probe; ~ **of·fer** Einführungsangebot *n*; ~ **pe·ri·od** Probezeit *f*; ~ **run** Probefahrt *f*.

tri·an·gle ['traiæŋgl] Dreieck *n*; ♪ Triangel *m*; **tri·an·gu·lar** □ [~'æŋgjulə] dreieckig; **tri'an·gu·late** *surv.* [~leit] triangulieren.

trib·al □ ['traibəl] den Stamm betreffend; Stammes...; **tribe** Stamm *m*; Geschlecht *n*; *bsd. contp.* Zunft *f*, Sippe *f*; ⚘, *zo.* Klasse *f*; **tribes·man** ['~zmən] Stammesangehörige *m*, -genosse *m*.

trib·u·la·tion [tribju'leiʃən] Drangsal *f*, Leiden *n*.

tri·bu·nal [tri'bju:nl] Richterstuhl *m*; Gericht(shof *m*) *n*; Tribunal *n* (*a. fig.*); **'trib·une** Tribun *m*; Tribüne *f*.

trib·u·tar·y ['tribjutəri] **1.** □ zinspflichtig; *fig.* helfend; *weitS.* untergeordnet; Neben...; **2.** Tributpflichtige *m*; Nebenfluß *m*; **trib·ute** ['~bju:t] Tribut *m*, Zins *m*; *fig.* Tribut *m*, Zoll *m*; Anerkennung *f*; Hochachtung *f*; Huldigung *f*.

trice[1] [trais]: *in a* ~ im Nu.

trice[2] [~]: ~ *up* aufwinden.

tri·chi·na *zo.* [tri'kainə] Trichine *f*.

trick [trik] **1.** Kniff *m*, Pfiff *m*, List *f*, Trick *m*; Kunstgriff *m*, -stück *n*; Streich *m*, Possen *m*; Eigenheit *f*; *Karten*: Stich *m*; ~ *film* Trickfilm *m*; **2.** betrügen (*out of* um); hereinlegen; verleiten (*into* zu); ~ *out*, ~ *up* herausputzen; **'trick·er, trick·ster** ['~stə] Gauner *m*, Betrüger *m*, Schwindler *m*; **'trick·er·y** Betrügerei *f*; **'trick·ish** □ betrügerisch; verschmitzt.

trick·le ['trikl] **1.** tröpfeln, rieseln; F *fig.* spritzen (*schnell gehen*); **2.** Tröpfeln *n*; Tropfen *m*.

trick·si·ness ['triksinis] Mutwilligkeit *f*; **'trick·sy** □ mutwillig; = **'trick·y** □ verschlagen; F heikel; verzwickt, knifflig, verwickelt, schwierig.

tri·col·o(u)r ['trikələ] Trikolore *f*.

tri·cy·cle ['traisikl] Dreirad *n*.

tri·dent ['traidənt] Dreizack *m*.

tri·en·ni·al □ [trai'enjəl] dreijährig; dreijährlich.

tri·er ['traiə] Untersucher *m*, Prüfer *m*.

tri·fle ['traifl] **1.** Kleinigkeit *f*; Lappalie *f*; *Küche*: Biskuitauflauf *m*; *a* ~ ein bißchen, ein wenig, etwas; **2.** *v/i.* spielen, spaßen, scherzen; *v/t.* ~ *away* vertrödeln, verschwenden; **'tri·fler** oberflächlicher

Mensch *m.*
tri·fling ['traifliŋ] □ geringfügig; unbedeutend.
trig[1] [trig] **1.** hemmen; ~ *up* stützen; **2.** Hemmschuh *m.*
trig[2] [~] schmuck; fest.
trig·ger ['trigə] **1.** Abzug *m am Gewehr*; *phot.* Auslöser *m*; **2.** ~ *off fig.* auslösen; '**~-hap·py** schießwütig; kriegslüstern; *be* ~ (*a. fig.*) gleich losschießen.
trig·o·no·met·ric, trig·o·no·met·ri·cal □ ⩘ [trigənə'metrik(əl)] trigonometrisch; **trig·o·nom·e·try** ⩘ [~'nɔmitri] Trigonometrie *f.*
tri·lat·er·al □ ⩘ ['trai'lætərəl] dreiseitig.
tril·by F ['trilbi] großer Schlapphut *m.*
tri·lin·gual □ ['trai'liŋgwəl] dreisprachig.
trill [tril] **1.** Triller *m*; gerolltes R *n*; **2.** trillern; *bsd.* das R rollen.
tril·lion ['triljən] Trillion *f*; *Am.* Billion *f.*
tril·o·gy ['trilədʒi] Trilogie *f.*
trim [trim] **1.** □ ordentlich; schmuck; gepflegt (*Bart etc.*); **2.** (richtiger) Zustand *m*; Ordnung *f*; ⚓ richtige Lage *f od.* Stellung *f*; (richtige) Verfassung *f*; Putz *m*, Staat *m*; *in* (*out of*) ~ in guter (schlechter) Verfassung; **3.** *v/i.* in Ordnung bringen, zurechtmachen; (*up* heraus)putzen, schmücken; *Kleid etc.* besetzen; *Bart etc.* stutzen; *Hecke etc.* beschneiden; *Lampe* putzen; ✈, ⚓ trimmen (*gleichmäßig verteilen*); *v/i. fig.* schwanken, lavieren; '**trim·mer** Putzer(in); ⚓ Trimmer *m*; *pol.* Achselträger *m*; '**trim·ming** Putzen *n*; *mst* ~*s pl.* Besatz *m*, Garnierung *f*; '**trim·ness** gute Ordnung *f*; gutes Aussehen *n*, Gepflegtheit *f.*
tri·mo·tor ['traiməutə] dreimotoriges Flugzeug *n*; '**tri·mo·tored** dreimotorig.
Trin·i·ty ['triniti] Dreieinigkeit *f.*
trin·ket ['triŋkit] wertloses Schmuckstück *n*; ~*s pl.* Kinkerlitzchen *pl.*
tri·o ♪ ['tri:əu] Trio *n.*
trip [trip] **1.** Reise *f*, Fahrt *f*; Ausflug *m*, Spritztour *f*; Stolpern *n*, Fallen *n*; Fehltritt *m* (*a. fig.*); ~ *of the tongue* Versprechen *n*; **2.** *v/i.* trippeln, tänzeln; stolpern (*over* über *acc.*); e-n Fehltritt tun (*a. fig.*); *fig.* e-n Fehler *od.* Fauxpas machen; *catch s.o.* ~*ping* j. bei e-m Fehler ertappen; *v/t. a.* ~ *up j-m* ein Bein stellen (*a. fig.*).
tri·par·tite ['trai'pɑ:tait] dreiteilig.
tripe [traip] Kaldaunen *f/pl.*, Kutteln *f/pl.*; *sl.* Quatsch *m*, Mist *m.*
tri·phase ['trai'feiz] dreiphasig; ~ *current* ⚡ Drehstrom *m.*
tri·plane ✈ ['traiplein] Dreidecker *m.*
tri·ple □ ['tripl] dreifach; ~ **jump** *Sport*: Dreisprung *m.*
tri·plet ['triplit] Dreiergruppe *f*; *poet.* Dreireim *m*; ♪ Triole *f*; ~*s pl.* Drillinge *m/pl.*
tri·plex ['tripleks] dreifach; ~ *glass* Verbundglas *n.*
trip·li·cate 1. ['triplikit] dreifach; **2.** ['~keit] verdreifachen.
tri·pod ['traipɔd] Dreifuß *m*; *phot.* Stativ *n.*
tri·pos ['traipɔs] letztes Examen *n* für e-n *honours degree in Cambridge.*
trip·per F ['tripə] Ausflügler(in); '**trip·ping 1.** □ flink, flott; **2.** Trippeln *n*; Beinstellen *n.*
trip·tych ['triptik] Triptychon *n*, dreiteiliges Altarbild *n.*
tri·sect [trai'sekt] in drei (gleiche) Teile teilen.
tris·yl·lab·ic ['traisi'læbik] (~*ally*) dreisilbig; '**tri'syl·la·ble** dreisilbiges Wort *n.*
trite □ [trait] abgedroschen, platt.
trit·u·rate ['tritjureit] zerreiben.
tri·umph ['traiəmf] **1.** Triumph *m*, Sieg *m* (*over* über *acc.*) (*a. fig.*); **2.** triumphieren, den Sieg davontragen (*over* über *acc.*) (*a. fig.*); **tri·um·phal** [~'ʌmfəl] Sieges..., Triumph...; ~ *arch* Triumphbogen *m*; ~ *procession* Triumphzug *m*; **tri'um·phant** □ triumphierend, frohlockend.
tri·um·vi·rate [trai'ʌmvirit] Triumvirat *n.*
tri·une ['traiju:n] dreieinig.
triv·et ['trivit] Dreifuß *m zum Kochen*; *as right as a* ~ in schönster Ordnung; pudelwohl.
triv·i·al □ ['triviəl] bedeutungslos; unbedeutend; trivial; gewöhnlich, alltäglich; **triv·i·al·i·ty** [~'æliti]

Belanglosigkeit *f*; Plattheit *f*, Trivialität *f*. [(*Versfuß*).]

tro·chee ['trəukiː] Trochäus *m*

trod [trɔd], *pret.*, '**trod·den** *p.p. von tread 1.*

trog·lo·dyte ['trɔglədait] Höhlenbewohner *m.*

Tro·jan ['trəudʒən] **1.** trojanisch; **2.** Trojaner(in); *work like a* ~ wie ein Pferd arbeiten.

troll[1] [trəul] mit der Schleppangel fischen; (vor sich hin) trällern.

troll[2] [~] Troll *m*, Kobold *m.*

trol·l(e)y ['trɔli] Handwagen *m*, Karren *m*; Draisine *f*; *a. tea-*~ Tee-, Servierwagen *m*; Kontaktrolle *f e-s Oberleitungsfahrzeugs*; *Am.* Straßenbahnwagen *m*; '~**-bus** O(berleitungs)bus *m.*

trol·lop *contp.* ['trɔləp] **1.** Schlampe *f*; Hure *f*; **2.** latschen.

trom·bone ♪ [trɔm'bəun] Posaune *f.*

troop [truːp] **1.** Truppe *f*; Schar *f*, Gruppe *f*, Trupp *m*; ⚔ (Reiter)Zug *m*; ~*s pl.* Truppen *f/pl.*; **2.** sich scharen, sich sammeln; in Scharen ziehen; ~ *away*, ~ *off* abziehen; ~*ing the colour(s)* ⚔ Fahnenparade *f*; '~**-carri·er** ⚓, ✈ Truppentransporter *m*; '**troop·er** Kavallerist *m*; Kavalleriepferd *n*; *swear like a* ~ wie ein Landsknecht fluchen.

trope [trəup] bildlicher Ausdruck *m*, Tropus *m.*

tro·phy ['trəufi] Trophäe *f*, Siegeszeichen *n.*

trop·ic ['trɔpik] Wendekreis *m*; ~*s pl.* Tropen *pl.*; '**trop·ic**, '**trop·i·cal** □ tropisch; Wendekreis...

trot [trɔt] **1.** Trott *m*, Trab *m*; *keep s.o. on the* ~ *fig.* j. in Trab halten; **2.** traben (lassen); trotten; ~ *out* F vorführen; ~ *s.o. round* j. herumführen; j. mitnehmen.

troth † [trəuθ]: *in* ~ meiner Treu, wahrlich; *plight one's* ~ sein Wort verpfänden.

trot·ter ['trɔtə] Traber *m*; ~*s pl.* Hammel-, Schweinsfüße *m/pl. als Speise.*

trou·ble ['trʌbl] **1.** Unruhe *f*; Störung *f* (*a.* ⊕); Kummer *m*, Sorge *f*, Not *f*; Mühe *f*, Beschwerde *f*; Plage *f*; *weitS.* Unannehmlichkeiten *f/pl.*; ~*s pl. pol.* Unruhen *f/pl.*; *be in* ~ in Nöten sein; *ask od. look for* ~ sich (selbst) Schwierigkeiten machen; das Schicksal herausfordern; *take (the)* ~ sich (die) Mühe machen; **2.** *v/t.* stören, beunruhigen, belästigen; quälen, plagen; Mühe machen (*dat.*); ~ *s.o. for* j. bemühen um; *v/i.* F sich bemühen; '~**-mak·er** Unruhestifter *m*; '~**·man**, '~**-shoot·er** *Am.* F Störungssucher *m*; **trou·ble·some** ['~səm] beschwerlich, lästig; '**trou·ble-spot** *pol.* Krisenherd *m*; '**troub·lous** unruhig.

trough [trɔf] (Futter)Trog *m*; Backtrog *m*, Mulde *f*; ~ *of the sea* Wellental *n.*

trounce F [trauns] *j.* verhauen.

troupe [truːp] (Schauspieler-, Zirkus)Truppe *f.*

trou·sered ['trauzəd] behost; **trou·sers** ['~z] *pl.* (*a pair of* eine) (lange) Hose *f*, Hosen *f/pl.*; **trou·ser suit** Hosenanzug *m.*

trous·seau ['truːsəu] Aussteuer *f.*

trout *ichth.* [traut] Forelle *f.*

tro·ver ⚖ ['trəuvə] rechtswidrige Aneignung *f.*

trow † *od. co.* [trau] glauben, meinen.

trow·el ['trauəl] Maurerkelle *f.*

troy (weight) ['trɔi(weit)] Feingewicht *n für Edelmetalle u. -steine.*

tru·an·cy ['truːənsi] (Schul)Schwänzerei *f*; '**tru·ant 1.** müßig, bummelnd; **2.** Schulschwänzer *m*; *fig.* Bummler *m*; *play* ~ die Schule schwänzen; bummeln.

truce [truːs] Waffenstillstand *m*; *political* ~ Burgfriede *m.*

truck[1] [trʌk] (offener) Güterwagen *m*; Last(kraft)wagen *m*, Lkw *m*; Transportkarren *m.*

truck[2] [~] **1.** (ver)tauschen, handeln, (ver)schachern; **2.** Tausch(-handel) *m*; Verkehr *m*; *mst* ~ *system* Naturallohnsystem *n*; ~ *farm Am.* Gemüsegärtnerei *f*; *garden* ~ *Am.* Gemüse *n.*

truck·er *Am.* ['trʌkə] Fernfahrer *m*; Spediteur *m*; Gemüsegärtner *m.*

truck·le[1] ['trʌkl] zu Kreuze kriechen (*to* vor *dat.*).

truck·le[2] [~] *mst* ~*-bed* Unterschiebbett *n.*

truck...: '~**·man** Lkw-Fahrer *m*, Lastwagenfahrer *m*; ~ **stop** *bsd. Am.* Raststätte *f* (*bsd. für Fernfahrer*); ~ **trailer** Lkw-Anhänger *m*; Lastzug *m.*

truc·u·lence, truc·u·len·cy ['trʌkjulǝns(i)] Wildheit *f*; '**truc·u·lent** □ wild, roh; grob; grausam.

trudge [trʌdʒ] wandern; sich (dahin)schleppen, mühsam gehen.

true [truː] (*adv. truly*) wahr; echt, wirklich; treu; wahrheitsgetreu; genau; richtig, (regel)recht; *be ~ of* zutreffen auf (*acc.*), gelten für; *it is ~* gewiß, freilich, zwar, allerdings; *come ~* sich bewahrheiten; *~ to life* (*nature*) lebenstreu (naturgetreu); *prove ~* (sich) bewahrheiten; '**~-'blue** *fig.* **1.** waschecht; treu; **2.** treuer Anhänger *m*; '**~-bred** reinrassig; '**~-love** Lieb(-chen) *n*; '**true·ness** Wahrheit *f*; Treue *f*; Echtheit *f etc.*

truf·fle ⚘ ['trʌfl] Trüffel *f*.

tru·ism ['truːizǝm] Binsenwahrheit *f*.

tru·ly ['truːli] wirklich; wahrhaft; aufrichtig; genau; treu; *Yours ~* Ihr ergebener, Ihre ergebene.

trump [trʌmp] **1.** *Karten*: Trumpf *m*; F feiner Kerl *m*; **2.** (über-)trumpfen, *Karte* stechen; *~ up* erdichten, zs.-schwindeln; '**trump·er·y** **1.** Plunder *m*, Trödel *m*; Kitsch *m*; **2.** lumpig; kitschig.

trum·pet ['trʌmpit] **1.** ♪ Trompete *f*; Schalltrichter *m*; *blow one's own ~ fig.* sein eigenes Lob singen *s. ear-~, speaking-~*; **2.** trompeten; *~ forth fig.* ausposaunen; '**trum·pet·er** Trompeter *m*.

trun·cate ['trʌŋkeit] stutzen; verstümmeln; **trun'ca·tion** Verstümmelung *f*.

trun·cheon ['trʌntʃǝn] (Polizei-, Gummi)Knüppel *m*; Kommandostab *m*.

trun·dle ['trʌndl] **1.** Rolle *f*; **2.** rollen, (sich) wälzen; *Reifen* schlagen.

trunk [trʌŋk] (Baum)Stamm *m*; Rumpf *m*; Rüssel *m des Elefanten*; *großer* Koffer *m*; *s. ~-line*; '**~-call** *teleph.* Ferngespräch *n*; '**~-exchange** *teleph.* Fernamt *n*; '**~-line** 🚂 Hauptlinie *f*; *teleph.* Fernleitung *f*; '**~-road** Fernstraße *f*; **trunks** *pl.* Turnhose *f*; Badehose *f*; Herrenunterhose *f*.

trun·nion ⊕ ['trʌnjǝn] Zapfen *m*.

truss [trʌs] **1.** Bündel *n*, Bund *n*; ⚕ Bruchband *n*; △ Hängewerk *n*, Binder *m*, Gerüst *n*; **2.** (zs.-)binden, zs.-schnüren; △ stützen; '**~-bridge** Fachwerkbrücke *f*.

trust [trʌst] **1.** Vertrauen *n* (*in* auf *acc.*); Glaube *m*; Kredit *m*; Depositum *n*, Pfand *n*; Verwahrung *f*, Obhut *f*; ⚖ Treuhand *f*; ⚖ Treugut *n*; ✝ Ring *m*, Trust *m*; *~ company* Treuhandgesellschaft *f*; *in ~* treuhänderisch, zu treuen Händen; *on ~* auf Treu und Glauben; ✝ auf Kredit; *position of ~* Vertrauensstellung *f*; **2.** *v/t.* (ver)trauen (*dat.*); anvertrauen, übergeben (*s.o. with s.th., s.th. to s.o.* j-m et.); zuversichtlich hoffen; *~ s.o. to do s.th.* j-m zutrauen, daß er et. tut; *v/i.* vertrauen (*in, to* auf *acc.*).

trus·tee [trʌs'tiː] Sach-, Verwalter *m*; ⚖ Pfleger *m*, Treuhänder *m*, Kurator *m*; *~ security, ~ stock* mündelsicheres Papier *n*; **trus'tee·ship** Sachwalterschaft *f*; Treuhänderschaft *f*; Kuratorium *n*.

trust·ful □ ['trʌstful], '**trust·ing** □ vertrauensvoll, zutraulich.

trust·wor·thi·ness ['trʌstwǝːðinis] Vertrauenswürdigkeit *f*; Zuverlässigkeit *f*; '**trust·wor·thy** vertrauenswürdig; zuverlässig; '**trust·y** zuverlässig, treu.

truth [truːθ], *pl.* **truths** [truːðz] Wahrheit *f*; Wirklichkeit *f*; Wahrhaftigkeit *f*; Genauigkeit *f*; *~ to life* Lebenstreue *f*.

truth·ful □ ['truːθful] wahrhaft(ig); '**truth·ful·ness** Wahrhaftigkeit *f*, Wahrheitsliebe *f*.

try [trai] **1.** *v/t.* versuchen; probieren; prüfen (*a. fig.*); ⚖ verhandeln über *et.* (*acc.*) *od.* gegen *j.* (*for* wegen); *j.* vor Gericht stellen; aburteilen; *die Augen etc.* angreifen; *~ on Kleid* anprobieren; *~ it on with s.o.* F es bei j-m probieren; *~ one's hand at* sich versuchen an (*dat.*); *~ out* erproben, ausprobieren; *v/i.* versuchen (*at acc.*); sich bemühen *od.* bewerben (*for* um); **2.** F Versuch *m*; *have a ~* e-n Versuch machen; '**try·ing** □ anstrengend; kritisch; '**try-'on** Anprobe *f*; F Schwindelmanöver *n*; '**try-'out** Erprobung *f*; *Sport*: Ausscheidungsspiel *n*; **try·sail** ⚓ ['traisl] Gaffelsegel *n*.

tryst *schott.* [traist] **1.** Stelldichein *n*; **2.** (sich) verabreden.

Tsar [zɑː] Zar *m*.

T-shirt ['tiːʃǝːt] kurzärmeliges Sporthemd *n*.

…**square** [ˈtiːskwɛə] Reißschiene *f.*

tub [tʌb] **1.** Faß *n*, Zuber *m*; Kübel *m*; Badewanne *f*; F (Wannen)Bad *n*; F *co.* Kahn *m*; *Sport*: Ruderkasten *m*; **2.** *Pflanzen* in Kübel setzen; *Butter* in ein Faß tun; F baden; im Ruderkasten trainieren; ˈ**tub·by** tonnenartig.

tube [tjuːb] Rohr *n*; (*Am. bsd.* Radio)Röhre *f*; Tube *f*; *mot.* (Luft-) Schlauch *m*; Tunnel *m*; F Untergrundbahn *f* (*bsd. in London*).

tu·ber ⚘ [ˈtjuːbə] Knolle *f*; **tu·ber·cle** [ˈ~bəːkl] *anat.*, *zo.* Knötchen *n*; ⚕ Tuberkel *f*; **tu·ber·cu·lo·sis** ⚕ [~bəːkjuˈləusis] Tuberkulose *f*; **tuˈber·cu·lous** ⚕ tuberkulös; **tu·ber·ous** ⚘ [ˈ~bərəs] knollig.

tub·ing [ˈtjuːbiŋ] Röhrenmaterial, -werk *n*.

tub-thump·er [ˈtʌbθʌmpə] Volksredner *m*, Kanzelpauker *m*.

tu·bu·lar □ [ˈtjuːbjulə] röhrenförmig; Röhren…; Rohr…

tuck [tʌk] **1.** Falte *f*; Abnäher *m*; *sl.* Leckereien *f/pl.*; **2.** ab-, aufnähen; ~ in reinhauen, kräftig essen; (*mit adv. od. prp.*) packen, stecken; ~ up aufschürzen, -krempeln; *Beine* unterschlagen; *in e-e Decke etc.* einwickeln.

tuck·er *hist.* [ˈtʌkə] Brusttuch *n*.

tuck…: ˈ**~-in** *sl.* großes Essen *n*; ˈ**~-shop** *sl.* Süßwarengeschäft *n*.

Tues·day [ˈtjuːzdi] Dienstag *m*.

tu·fa *min.* [ˈtjuːfə], **tuff** [tʌf] Tuff (-stein) *m*.

tuft [tʌft] Büschel *n*, Busch *m*; (Haar)Schopf *m*; ˈ**~-hunt·er** gesellschaftlicher Streber *m*, Schmarotzer *m*; ˈ**tuft·y** □ büschelig.

tug [tʌg] **1.** Zug *m*, Ruck *m*; ⚓ Schlepper *m*; *fig.* Anstrengung *f*; ~ of war *Sport u. fig.* Tauziehen *n*; **2.** ziehen, zerren (at an *dat.*); ⚓ schleppen; sich mühen (for um).

tu·i·tion [tjuːˈiʃən] Unterricht *m*; Schulgeld *n*.

tu·lip ⚘ [ˈtjuːlip] Tulpe *f*.

tulle [tjuːl] Tüll *m*.

tum·ble [ˈtʌmbl] **1.** *v/i.* fallen, purzeln; taumeln; sich wälzen; ~ to F kapieren, spitzkriegen; *v/t.* werfen; (um)stürzen; durchwühlen, zerknüllen; **2.** Sturz *m*, Fall *m*; Wirrwarr *m*; ˈ**~·down** baufällig; ˈ**~-ˈdri·er** Wäschetrockner *m*; ˈ**tum·bler** Trinkglas *n*, Becher *m*; ⊕ Zuhaltung *f am Schloß*; *orn.* Tümmler *m*.

tum·brel [ˈtʌmbrəl], **tum·bril** [ˈ~bril] Schutt-, Dungkarren *m*.

tu·mid [ˈtjuːmid] geschwollen; *fig.* schwülstig; **tuˈmid·i·ty** Schwellung *f*; Geschwollenheit *f*.

tum·my F [ˈtʌmi] *Kindersprache*: Bäuchlein *n*, Magen *m*.

tu·mo(u)r ⚕ [ˈtjuːmə] Geschwulst *f*, Tumor *m*.

tu·mult [ˈtjuːmʌlt] Tumult *m*; Lärm *m*; Aufruhr *m* (*a. fig.*); **tuˈmul·tu·ous** □ [~tjuəs] lärmend; stürmisch, ungestüm.

tu·mu·lus [ˈtjuːmjuləs] Grabhügel *m*, Tumulus *m*.

tun [tʌn] Tonne *f*, Faß *n*; Maischbottich *m*.

tu·na *ichth.* [ˈtuːnə] Thunfisch *m*.

tun·dra [ˈtʌndrə] Tundra *f*.

tune [tjuːn] **1.** Melodie *f*, Lied *n*, Weise *f*, Tonstück *n*; ♪ Stimmung *f* (*a. fig.*); in ~ (gut) gestimmt; *fig.* übereinstimmend (with mit); out of ~ verstimmt (*a. fig.*); to the ~ of £ 100 in Höhe von 100 Pfd.; change one's ~ *fig.* andere Saiten aufziehen; **2.** stimmen (*a. fig.*); ~ in *Radio*: einstellen (to auf *acc.*); ~ out *Radio*: ausschalten; ~ up (die Instrumente) stimmen; *fig. Befinden etc.* heben; *mot.* tunen, die Leistung erhöhen; ♪ anstimmen; **tune·ful** □ [ˈ~ful] melodisch; klangvoll; ˈ**tune·less** □ unmelodisch; ˈ**tun·er** ♪ Stimmer *m*; *Radio*: Abstimmvorrichtung *f*.

tung·sten ⚗ [ˈtʌŋstən] Wolfram *m*.

tu·nic [ˈtjuːnik] Tunika *f*; ⚔ Uniformrock *m*; *anat.*, ⚘ Häutchen *n*.

tun·ing…: ˈ**~-coil** *Radio*: Abstimmspule *f*; ˈ**~-fork** ♪ Stimmgabel *f*.

tun·nel [ˈtʌnl] **1.** Tunnel *m*; ⚒ Stollen *m*; **2.** e-n Tunnel bohren (durch).

tun·ny *ichth.* [ˈtʌni] Thunfisch *m*.

tun·y F [ˈtjuːni] melodisch.

tur·ban [ˈtəːbən] Turban *m*.

tur·bid [ˈtəːbid] trüb; dick; verworren; ˈ**tur·bid·ness** Trübheit *f etc.*

tur·bine ⊕ [ˈtəːbin] Turbine *f*; ˈ**~-ˈpow·ered** mit Turbinenantrieb; **tur·bo-jet** [ˈtəːbəuˈdʒet] Strahlturbine *f*; **tur·bo-prop** [ˈ~ˈprɔp] Propellerturbine *f*.

tur·bot *ichth.* [ˈtəːbət] Steinbutt *m*.

tur·bu·lence [ˈtəːbjuləns] Unruhe *f*;

Ungestüm *n*; ˈ**tur·bu·lent** □ unruhig; ungestüm; stürmisch, turbulent.

turd V [tə:d] Haufen *m* Scheiße; Dreckskerl *m*.

tu·reen [təˈri:n] Terrine *f*.

turf [tə:f] **1.** Rasen *m*; Torf *m*; Rennbahn *f*; Rennsport *m*; **2.** mit Rasen belegen; ~ *out sl. j.* 'rausschmeißen; **turf·ite** [ˈ~ait] Rennsportliebhaber *m*; ˈ**turf·y** rasenbedeckt; torfartig; rennsportlich.

tur·gid □ [ˈtə:dʒid] geschwollen, schwülstig (*mst fig.*); **turˈgid·i·ty** Geschwollenheit *f*.

Turk [tə:k] Türke *m*, Türkin *f*; *fig.* Wüterich *m*.

tur·key [ˈtə:ki] **1.** ♀ *carpet* türkischer Teppich *m*; **2.** *orn.* Truthahn *m*, -henne *f*, Pute(r *m*) *f*; *Am. sl. thea.*, *Film*: Pleite *f*, Versager *m* (*schlechtes Stück*).

Turk·ish [ˈtə:kiʃ] türkisch; ~ *bath* türkisches Bad *n*, Schwitzbad *n*; ~ *delight* Geleefrüchte *f/pl.*; ~ *towel* Frottier(hand)tuch *n*.

tur·moil [ˈtə:mɔil] Aufruhr *m*, Unruhe *f*; Getümmel *n*.

turn [tə:n] **1.** *v/t.* drehen; (um-)wenden, umkehren; lenken; richten; verwandeln (*into* in *acc.*); abbringen (*from* von); abhalten, abwehren; übertragen (*into English* ins Englische); formen, bilden; (*a. fig. Verse etc.*) drechseln; schwindlig machen; verrückt machen; *he has* ~*ed 50, he is* ~*ed (of) 50* er ist über 50 Jahre alt; ~ *s.o.'s brain* j-m den Kopf verdrehen; ~ *colour* die Farbe wechseln; ~ *a corner* um eine Ecke biegen; *he can* ~ *his hand to anything* er ist zu allem zu gebrauchen; ~ *tail* F ausreißen; ~ *s.o. against* j. aufhetzen gegen; ~ *aside* abwenden; ~ *away* abwenden; abweisen; wegjagen; ~ *down* umkehren; *Buchseite etc.* umkniffen; *Gas etc.* herunterschrauben, kleinstellen; *Bettdecke etc.* zurückschlagen; *Vorschlag etc.* ablehnen; *j-m* e-n Korb geben; ~ *in* einwärts drehen; F ab-, zurückgeben; ~ *off* ableiten (*a. fig.*); hinauswerfen; wegjagen; ~ *off (on)* ab- (an)drehen, ab- (ein)schalten; ~ *out* auswärts drehen; hinauskehren; *Taschen etc.* umkehren; wegjagen, hinauswerfen, vertreiben; *Fabrikat etc.* herausbringen, produzieren, herstellen; *Gas etc.* ausdrehen; ~ *over* umwenden; *fig.* übertragen; ✝ umsetzen; überlegen; ~ *over a new leaf* ein neues Leben beginnen; ~ *up* nach oben wenden *od.* richten; *Kragen etc.* hochklappen; umwenden; *Spielkarte* aufdecken; *Hose etc.* auf-, umschlagen; *Gas etc.* aufdrehen; ⚒ umpflügen; F *j-m* den Magen umdrehen, zum Erbrechen bringen; *v/i.* sich drehen, sich wenden; sich umdrehen; sich verwandeln (*into* in *acc.*); umschlagen (*Wetter etc.*; *a. fig.*); *Christ, Soldat, grau etc.* werden; *a.* ~ *sour* sauer werden (*Milch*); ~ *about* sich umdrehen; ⚔ kehrt machen; ~ *away* sich abwenden; ~ *back* zurückgehen, -kehren; ~ *in* sich einbiegen; hineingehen, einkehren; F zu Bett gehen; ~ *off* abbiegen; ~ *on* sich drehen um, abhängen von; ~ *out* sich nach außen wenden *od.* kehren; die Arbeit einstellen; ausfallen, ablaufen; (schließlich) werden; sich erweisen als, sich herausstellen als; F *aus dem Bett* aufstehen; aus dem Hause gehen; ⚔ ausrücken; ~ *over* sich umwenden; ~ *round* sich herumdrehen; ~ *to* sich (*dat.*) zuwenden, sich wenden an (*acc.*); sich verwandeln in (*acc.*); werden *od.* gereichen zu; ~ *to* (*adv.*) sich an die Arbeit machen; ~ *up* sich zeigen, auftauchen; ~ *upon* sich drehen um (*a. fig.*); sich wenden *od.* richten gegen; **2.** (Um)Drehung *f*; Krümmung *f*; Serpentine *f*; Wendung *f*, Richtung *f* (*a. fig.*); Neigung *f*, Hang *m* (*for* zu); Wechsel *m*, Veränderung *f*; Gestalt *f*; Beschaffenheit *f*, Art *f*; Spaziergang *m*; Reihe(nfolge) *f*; (Programm)Nummer *f*; F Schreck *m*, Schock *m*; *at every* ~ auf Schritt und Tritt; *by od. in* ~*s* der Reihe nach, abwechselnd; *do s.o. a good (bad)* ~ j-m e-n guten (schlechten) Dienst erweisen; *in* ~ abwechselnd, der Reihe nach; *in my* ~ meinerseits; *it is my* ~ ich bin an der Reihe; *take a* ~ sich ändern; *take a* ~ *at s.th.* et. versuchen; *take a few* ~*s* ein paar Schritte tun; *take one's* ~ et. tun, wenn die Reihe an e-n kommt; *take* ~*s* miteinander abwechseln; *to a* ~ aufs Haar; *a friendly* ~ ein Freundschaftsdienst

...m; *does it serve your ~?* entspricht das Ihren Zwecken?; '**~·a·bout** Kehrt(wendung *f*) *n*; '**~-buck·le** ⊕ Spannschraube *f*; '**~·coat** Abtrünnige *m*; '**turn·down col·lar** Umlegekragen *m*; '**turn·er** Drechsler *m*; Dreher *m*; '**turn·er·y** Drechslerarbeit *f*.

turn·ing ['tə:niŋ] Drechseln *n*; Wendung *f*; Biegung *f*; Straßenecke *f*; (Weg)Abzweigung *f*; Querstraße *f*; *take a ~* um die Ecke biegen; '**~-lathe** ⊕ Drehbank *f*; '**~-point** *fig.* Wendepunkt *m*.

tur·nip ⚘ ['tə:nip] (*bsd.* weiße) Rübe *f*.

turn·key ['tə:nki:] Schließer *m*, Gefangenenwärter *m*; '**turn-off** Abzweigung *f*; Ausfahrt *f e-r Autobahn*; '**turn-'out** Ausstaffierung *f*; Kutsche *f*; Arbeitseinstellung *f*; Versammlung *f*; ✝ Gesamtproduktion *f*; 🚂, ⚓ Ausweichstelle *f*; '**turn·o·ver** ✝ Umsatz *m*; Umgruppierung *f*, Verschiebung *f*; (Apfel- *etc.*)Tasche *f* (*Gebäck*); '**turn·pike** Schlagbaum *m*; *Am.* (gebührenpflichtige) Schnellstraße *f*; '**turn-screw** Schraubenzieher *m*; '**turn·spit** Bratenwender *m*; '**turn·stile** Drehkreuz *n*; '**turn-ta·ble** 🚂 Drehscheibe *f*; Plattenteller *m am Plattenspieler*; '**turn-'up** 1. aufklappbar; 2. Umschlag *m an der Hose*; F Krach *m*; F Keilerei *f*.

tur·pen·tine ⚗ ['tə:pəntain] Terpentin *n*.

tur·pi·tude *lit.* ['tə:pitju:d] Schändlichkeit *f*.

turps F [tə:ps] = *turpentine*.

tur·quoise *min.* ['tə:kwa:z] Türkis *m*.

tur·ret ['tʌrit] Türmchen *n*; ⚔, ⚓ (*mst* drehbarer) Panzerturm *m*; ✈ Kanzel *f*; ⊕ Revolverkopf *m*; *~ lathe* ⊕ Revolverdrehbank *f*; '**tur·ret·ed** mit Türmchen *etc.* besetzt.

tur·tle[1] *zo.* ['tə:tl] Schildkröte *f*; *turn ~* kentern.

tur·tle[2] *orn.* [~] *mst ~-dove* Turteltaube *f*.

tur·tle·neck ['tə:tlnek] Rollkragen (-pullover) *m*.

Tus·can ['tʌskən] 1. toskanisch; 2. Toskaner(in); Toskanisch *n*.

tush [tʌʃ] *int.* pah!

tusk [tʌsk] Fangzahn *m*; Stoßzahn *m des Elefanten etc.*; Hauer *m des Wildschweins*.

tus·sle ['tʌsl] 1. Rauferei *f*, Balgerei *f*; 2. raufen, sich balgen.

tus·sock ['tʌsək] Büschel *n*.

tut [tʌt] ach was!, Unsinn!

tu·te·lage ['tju:tilidʒ] Vormundschaft *f*; Bevormundung *f*.

tu·te·lar·y ['tju:tiləri] schützend; Schutz...

tu·tor ['tju:tə] 1. (Privat-, Haus-) Lehrer *m*; *univ.* Tutor *m*; *Am. univ.* Assistent *m mit Lehrauftrag*; ⚖ Vormund *m*; 2. unterrichten; schulen, erziehen; *fig.* beherrschen; **tu·to·ri·al** [~'tɔ:riəl] 1. Lehrer...; Tutor...; 2. *univ.* Unterrichtsstunde *f* e-s Tutors; **tu·tor·ship** ['~təʃip] (*bsd.* Haus)Lehrerstelle *f* (*of* bei).

tux·e·do *Am.* [tʌk'si:dəu] Smoking *m*.

TV ['ti:'vi:] 1. Fernsehen *n*; Fernsehapparat *m*; 2. Fernseh...

twad·dle ['twɔdl] 1. Geschwätz *n*; 2. schwatzen, quatschen.

twain † [twein] zwei.

twang [twæŋ] 1. Schwirren *n*; *mst nasal ~* näselnde Aussprache *f*; 2. schwirren (lassen), klimpern; näseln.

'twas [twɔz, twəz] = *it was*.

tweak [twi:k] zwicken.

tweed [twi:d] Tweed *m* (*Wollgewebe*).

'tween [twi:n] = *between*.

tween·y ['twi:ni] Aushilfsmädchen *n*.

tweet [twi:t] zwitschern; '**tweet·er** *Radio*: Hochtonlautsprecher *m*.

tweez·ers ['twi:zəs] *pl.* (*a pair of* eine) Haarzange *f*; Pinzette *f*.

twelfth [twelfθ] 1. zwölfte(r, -s); 2. Zwölftel *n*; '**♀-night** Dreikönigsabend *m*.

twelve [twelv] zwölf; **~·fold** ['~fəuld] zwölffach; '**~·month** *ein* Jahr *n*.

twen·ti·eth ['twentiiθ] 1. zwanzigste(r, -s); 2. Zwanzigstel *n*.

twen·ty ['twenti] zwanzig; **~·fold** ['~fəuld] zwanzigfach.

'twere [twə:] = *it were*.

twerp *sl.* [twə:p] Kerl *m*, Knülch *m*.

twice [twais] zweimal; *~ the sum* die doppelte Summe; *~ as much* zweimal *od.* noch einmal soviel.

twid·dle ['twidl] 1. (*v/i.* sich) drehen; mit ... spielen; 2. Schnörkel *m*.

twig[1] [twig] Zweig *m*, Rute *f*.

twig[2] F [~] kapieren, spitzkriegen.

twi·light ['twailait] **1.** Zwielicht *n*; Dämmerung *f* (*a. fig.*); ~ *of the gods* Götterdämmerung *f*; **2.** Dämmer(ungs)...; dämmerig; ~ *sleep* ⚕ Dämmerschlaf *m*.
twill [twil] **1.** Köper *m* (*Gewebe*); **2.** köpern.
'twill [~] = *it will*.
twin [twin] **1.** Zwillings...; doppelt; ~-*engined* ✈ zweimotorig; **2.** Zwilling *m*; ~ **beds** *pl.* zwei Einzelbetten *n/pl.*
twine [twain] **1.** Bindfaden *m*; Schnur *f*; Zwirn *m*; Windung *f*; **2.** *v/t.* zwirnen; zs.-drehen; *fig.* verflechten; schlingen, winden; umwinden, -schlingen, -ranken (*with* mit); *v/i. a.* ~ *o.s.* sich winden *od.* schlingen; sich schlängeln.
twinge [twindʒ] Zwicken *n*; Stechen *n*, Stich *m*; bohrender Schmerz *m*.
twin·kle ['twiŋkl] **1.** funkeln, blitzen; huschen; zwinkern; *in the twinkling of an eye* im Nu; **2.** Funkeln *n etc.*; *in a* ~ im Nu.
twirl [twəːl] **1.** Wirbel *m*; Schnörkel *m*; **2.** wirbeln; drehen; '**twirl·ing-stick** Quirl. *m*.
twirp [twəːp] = *twerp*.
twist [twist] **1.** Drehung *f*; Drall *m*; Windung *f*; Verdrehung *f*; Verdrehtheit *f*; Neigung *f*, Veranlagung *f*; (Gesichts)Verzerrung *f*; Garn *n*; Rollentabak *m*; Kringel *m*, Zopf *m* (*Backwaren*); Tüte *f*; Twist *m* (*Tanz*); **2.** *v/t.* drehen, winden; zs.-drehen; zwirnen; verdrehen; verkrümmen; *Gesicht* verziehen, verzerren; *Ball* anschneiden; *v/i.* sich drehen *od.* winden (*a. fig.*); sich verziehen; '**twist·er** Seiler *m*; Zwirner *m*; *Sport*: (an)geschnittener Ball *m*; *Billard*: Effetstoß *m*; F etwas zum Kopfzerbrechen; *Am.* Tornado *m*.
twit *fig.* [twit] *j.* aufziehen (*with* mit).
twitch [twitʃ] **1.** reißen; zupfen; zwicken; zucken (mit); **2.** Zupfen *n*; Ruck *m*; Zuckung *f*; *vet.* Nasenbremse *f*; = *twinge*.
twit·ter ['twitə] **1.** zwitschern; piepsen; **2.** Gezwitscher *n*; *be in a* ~ zittern, beben.
'twixt [twikst] = *betwixt*.
two [tuː] **1.** zwei; *in* ~ entzwei; *put* ~ *and* ~ *together* sich et. zs.-reimen; seine eignen Schlüsse ziehen; **2.** Zwei *f*; *in* ~*s* zu zweien; '~-**bit** *Am.* F 25-Cent...; *fig.* unbedeutend, Klein...; '~-**edged** zweischneidig; '~-'**faced** falsch, heuchlerisch; ~**fold** ['~fəuld] zweifach; '~-**hand·ed** zweihändig; für zwei Personen; '~-'**job man** Doppelverdiener *m*; ~**·pence** ['tʌpəns] zwei Pence; ~**·pen·ny** ['tʌpni] zwei Pence wert; Zweipenny...; '~-**phase** ⚡ zweiphasig; '~-'**piece** zweiteilig; '~-**ply** zweischäftig (*Tau*); doppelt (*Tuch etc.*); '~-'**seat·er** *mot.* Zweisitzer *m*; '~**·some** F Pärchen *n*, Gespann *n*; *play a* ~ zu zweit spielen; '~-'**step** Twostep *m* (*Tanz*); '~-'**sto·rey** zweistöckig; '~-**stroke** *mot.* Zweitakt...; '~-'**thirds** Zweidrittel...; '~-**time** F *Ehepartner*, *Komplizen etc.* betrügen, hintergehen; '~-**way** ⊕ Zweiweg...; ~ *adapter* ⚡ Doppelstecker *m*; ~ *traffic* Gegenverkehr *m*.
'twould [twud] = *it would*.
ty·coon *Am.* F [tai'kuːn] Industriekapitän *m*, Magnat *m*.
tyke [taik] Köter *m*; Lümmel *m*.
tym·pa·num ['timpənəm] *anat.* Trommelfell *n*; ⚠ Giebelfeld *n*, Tympanon *n*.
type [taip] **1.** Typ(us) *m*; Urbild *n*; Vorbild *n*; Muster *n*; Art *f*; ⊕ Ausführung *f*; Sinnbild *n*; *typ.* Letter *f*, Type *f*, Buchstabe *m*; *in* ~ gesetzt; ~ *area* Satzspiegel *m*; *true to* ~ artecht; *set in* ~ setzen; **2.** = ~*write*; '~**·face** *typ.* Schrift(bild *n*) *f*; '~-**found·er** Schriftgießer *m*; '~-**script** (Schreib)Maschinenschrift *f*; '~-**set·ter** Schriftsetzer *m*; '~**·write** (*irr. write*) mit der Schreibmaschine schreiben; '~**·writer** Schreibmaschine *f*; ~ *face* Schreibmaschinenschrift *f*; ~ *ribbon* Farbband *n*; '~**·writ·ten** maschinengeschrieben.
ty·phoid ⚕ ['taifɔid] **1.** typhös; ~ *fever* = **2.** (Unterleibs)Typhus *m*.
ty·phoon *meteor.* [tai'fuːn] Taifun *m*.
ty·phus ⚕ ['taifəs] Flecktyphus *m*.
typ·i·cal □ ['tipikəl] typisch; (vor-)bildlich; richtig, echt; kennzeichnend, chrakteristisch, bezeichnend (*of* für); **typ·i·fy** ['~fai] typisch sein für; versinnbildlichen.
typ·ing ['taipiŋ] Maschine(n)schreiben *n*; ~ *pool* Schreibzentrale *f*; '**typ·ist** *a. shorthand* ~ Stenotypistin *f*.
ty·pog·ra·pher [tai'pɔgrəfə] Buch-

drucker *m*; **ty·po·graph·ic, ty·po·graph·i·cal** □ [~pə'græfik(əl)] typographisch; Druck...; **ty·pog·ra·phy** [~'pɔgrəfi] Buchdruckerkunst *f*, Typographie *f*.
ty·ran·nic, ty·ran·ni·cal □ [ti'rænik(əl)] tyrannisch; **ty'ran·ni·cide** [~said] Tyrannenmörder *m*; Tyrannenmord *m*; **tyr·an·nize** ['tirənaiz] als Tyrann herrschen; ~ *over* tyrannisieren; **'tyr·an·nous** □ tyrannisch; **'tyr·an·ny** Tyrannei *f*, Gewaltherrschaft *f*.
ty·rant ['taiərənt] Tyrann(in).
tyre ['taiə] *s. tire*[1].
ty·ro ['taiərəu] *s. tiro*.
Tyr·o·lese [tirə'li:z] **1.** Tiroler(in); **2.** tirolisch, Tiroler(...).
Tzar [zɑ:] Zar *m*.

U

u·biq·ui·tous □ [ju:'bikwitəs] allgegenwärtig, überall zu finden(d); **u'biq·ui·ty** Allgegenwart *f*.
U-boat ⚓ ['ju:bəut] *deutsches* U-Boot *n*.
ud·der ['ʌdə] Euter *n*.
ugh [ʌx, uh, ə:h] hu! (*Schreck*); puh! (*Ekel*).
ug·li·fy ['ʌglifai] entstellen.
ug·li·ness ['ʌglinis] Häßlichkeit *f*.
ug·ly □ ['ʌgli] häßlich, garstig; gefährlich, schlimm (*z.B. Wunde*).
U·krain·i·an [ju:'kreinjən] **1.** ukrainisch; **2.** Ukrainer(in).
u·ku·le·le ♪ [ju:kə'leili] Ukulele *n*, Hawaiigitarre *f*.
ul·cer ⚕ ['ʌlsə] Geschwür *n*; Ulkus *m*; (Eiter)Beule *f*; **ul·cer·ate** ['~reit] eitern (lassen); **ul·cer'a·tion** Geschwürbildung *f*; **'ul·cer·ous** geschwürig.
ul·lage ✝ ['ʌlidʒ] Flüssigkeitsverlust *m*, Leckage *f*.
ul·na *anat*. ['ʌlnə], *pl*. **ul·nae** ['~ni:] Elle *f*.
ul·ster ['ʌlstə] Ulster *m* (*Mantel*).
ul·te·ri·or □ [ʌl'tiəriə] jenseitig; *fig*. weiter; anderweitig; tiefer liegend, versteckt; ~ *motive* Hintergedanke *m*.
ul·ti·mate □ ['ʌltimit] letzt; endlich; End...; **'ul·ti·mate·ly** zu guter Letzt.
ul·ti·ma·tum [ʌlti'meitəm], *pl. a.* **ul·ti'ma·ta** [~tə] Ultimatum *n*.
ul·ti·mo ✝ ['ʌltiməu] im letzten Monat, vorigen Monats.
ul·tra ['ʌltrə] übermäßig; Ultra..., ultra...; **'~'fash·ion·a·ble** hypermodern; **'~-high fre·quen·cy** *Radio*: Ultrakurzwelle *f*, Ultrahochfrequenz *f*; **~·ma'rine 1.** überseeisch; **2.** ⚗ *paint*. Ultramarin *n*; **'~'mod·ern** hypermodern; **~·mon·tane** *eccl., pol.* [~'mɔntein] **1.** ultramontan; **2.** Ultramontane *m*; **'~-'red** ultrarot; **'~-'short wave** Ultrakurzwelle *f*; **'~-'son·ic** Überschall...; **'~-'vi·o·let** ultraviolett.
ul·u·late ['ju:ljuleit] heulen.
um·bel ⚘ ['ʌmbəl] Dolde *f*.
um·ber *min., paint.* ['ʌmbə] Umber *m*, Umbra *f* (*brauner Farbstoff*).
um·bil·i·cal □ [ʌm'bilikəl, ⚕ ~'laikəl] Nabel...; ~ *cord* Nabelschnur *f*.
um·brage ['ʌmbridʒ] Anstoß *m* (*Ärger*); *poet*. Schatten *m*; **um·bra·geous** □ [~'breidʒəs] schattig; *fig*. empfindlich.
um·brel·la [ʌm'brelə] Regenschirm *m*; *fig*. Schirm *m*, Schutz *m*; ⚔ Abschirmung *f*; Jagdschutz *m*; ~ **organ·i·za·tion** Dachorganisation *f*; **~-stand** Schirmständer *m*.
um·pire ['ʌmpaiə] **1.** Schiedsrichter *m*; **2.** Schiedsrichter sein.
ump·teen ['ʌmpti:n], **'ump·ty** *sl.* zig, viele, zahlreiche.
un... [ʌn] un...; Un...; ent...; nicht...
'un F [ʌn, ən] = *one*.
un·a·bashed ['ʌnə'bæʃt] unverfroren; unerschrocken.
un·a·bat·ed ['ʌnə'beitid] unvermindert.
un·a·ble ['ʌn'eibl] unfähig, außerstande (*to inf.* zu *inf.*).
un·a·bridged ['ʌnə'bridʒd] unge-

kürzt.

un·ac·cept·a·ble [ˈʌnəkˈseptəbl] unannehmbar.

un·ac·com·mo·dat·ing [ˈʌnəˈkɔmədeitiŋ] nicht entgegenkommend.

un·ac·count·a·ble □ [ˈʌnəˈkauntəbl] unerklärlich; seltsam; nicht zur Rechenschaft verpflichtet.

un·ac·cus·tomed [ˈʌnəˈkʌstəmd] ungewohnt; ungewöhnlich; ~ *to* nicht gewöhnt an (*acc.*).

un·ac·knowl·edged [ˈʌnəkˈnɔlidʒd] nicht anerkannt *od.* zugestanden.

un·ac·quaint·ed [ˈʌnəˈkweintid]: ~ *with* nicht vertraut mit, unkundig *e-r Sache.*

un·a·dorned [ˈʌnəˈdɔ:nd] ungeschmückt.

un·a·dul·ter·at·ed □ [ˈʌnəˈdʌltəreitid] unverfälscht.

un·ad·vis·a·ble □ [ˈʌnədˈvaizəbl] unratsam; ˈ**un·adˈvised** □ [~zd, *adv.* ~zidli] unbedacht; unberaten.

un·af·fect·ed □ [ˈʌnəˈfektid] unberührt; *fig.* ungerührt; ungekünstelt.

un·a·fraid [ˈʌnəˈfreid] furchtlos.

un·aid·ed [ˈʌnˈeidid] ohne Unterstützung; (ganz) allein; unbewaffnet, bloß (*Auge*).

un·al·ien·a·ble [ˈʌnˈeiljənəbl] unveräußerlich.

un·al·loyed [ˈʌnəˈlɔid] unlegiert; *fig.* unvermischt.

un·al·ter·a·ble □ [ʌnˈɔ:ltərəbl] unveränderlich; **unˈal·tered** unverändert.

un·am·big·u·ous □ [ˈʌnæmˈbigjuəs] unzweideutig.

un·am·bi·tious □ [ˈʌnæmˈbiʃəs] ohne Ehrgeiz; anspruchslos.

un·a·me·na·ble [ˈʌnəˈmi:nəbl] unzugänglich.

un-A·mer·i·can [ˈʌnəˈmerikən] unamerikanisch.

un·a·mi·a·ble □ [ˈʌnˈeimjəbl] unliebenswürdig.

u·na·nim·i·ty [ju:nəˈnimiti] Einmütigkeit *f*; **u·nan·i·mous** □ [ju:ˈnæniməs] einmütig, -stimmig.

un·an·nounced [ˈʌnəˈnaunst] unangemeldet.

un·an·swer·a·ble □ [ʌnˈɑ:nsərəbl] unwiderleglich; ˈ**unˈan·swered** unbeantwortet; offen (*Frage*); unerwidert.

un·ap·palled [ˈʌnəˈpɔ:ld] unerschrocken.

un·ap·peal·a·ble ⚖ [ˈʌnəˈpi:ləbl] unanfechtbar.

un·ap·peas·a·ble □ [ˈʌnəˈpi:zəbl] unversöhnlich.

un·ap·proach·a·ble □ [ˈʌnəˈprəutʃəbl] unzugänglich.

un·ap·pro·pri·at·ed [ˈʌnəˈprəuprieitid] nicht verwendet, herrenlos.

un·apt □ [ˈʌnˈæpt] untauglich, ungeeignet; ~ *to inf.* nicht dazu neigend, zu *inf.*; *be* ~ *to learn* nicht leicht lernen.

un·armed [ˈʌnˈɑ:md] unbewaffnet.

un·a·shamed □ [ˈʌnəˈʃeimd; *adv.* ~midli] schamlos.

un·asked [ˈʌnˈɑ:skt] unverlangt; ungebeten.

un·as·sail·a·ble □ [ʌnəˈseiləbl] unangreifbar.

un·as·sist·ed □ [ˈʌnəˈsistid] ohne Hilfe *od.* Unterstützung.

un·as·sum·ing [ˈʌnəˈsju:miŋ] anspruchslos, bescheiden.

un·at·tached [ˈʌnəˈtætʃt] nicht gebunden, nicht organisiert; ungebunden, ledig, frei.

un·at·tain·a·ble □ [ˈʌnəˈteinəbl] unerreichbar.

un·at·tend·ed [ˈʌnəˈtendid] unbegleitet; unbeaufsichtigt.

un·at·trac·tive □ [ʌnəˈtræktiv] wenig anziehend, reizlos; uninteressant.

un·au·thor·ized [ˈʌnˈɔ:θəraizd] unberechtigt, unbefugt.

un·a·vail·a·ble [ˈʌnəˈveiləbl] nicht verfügbar; unbrauchbar; ˈ**un·aˈvail·ing** vergeblich, nutzlos.

un·a·void·a·ble □ [ʌnəˈvɔidəbl] unvermeidlich.

un·a·ware [ˈʌnəˈwɛə] ohne Kenntnis; *be* ~ *of et.* nicht merken; *be* ~ *that* nicht wissen, daß; ˈ**un·aˈwares** unversehens; versehentlich; unvermutet; ohne es zu wissen *od.* zu merken.

un·backed [ˈʌnˈbækt] ohne Unterstützung; ungedeckt (*Scheck*); ~ *horse* Pferd *n*, auf das nicht gesetzt wurde.

un·bag [ˈʌnˈbæg] aus dem Sack holen *od.* lassen.

un·bal·ance [ˈʌnˈbæləns] Unausgeglichenheit *f*; ˈ**unˈbal·anced** nicht im Gleichgewicht befindlich; unausgeglichen; geistesgestört.

un·bap·tized [ˈʌnbæpˈtaizd] ungetauft.

un·bar [ˈʌnˈbɑ:] aufriegeln, -schließen.

un·bear·a·ble □ [ʌnˈbɛərəbl] unerträglich.

un·beat·en [ˈʌnˈbiːtn] ungeschlagen; unbetreten (*Weg*).

un·be·com·ing □ [ˈʌnbiˈkʌmiŋ] unkleidsam; unziemlich, unschicklich (*to od. for s.o.* für j.).

un·be·friend·ed [ˈʌnbiˈfrendid] freundlos; hilflos.

un·be·known [ˈʌnbiˈnəun] unbekannt; ~ *to s.o.* ohne j-s Wissen.

un·be·lief [ˈʌnbiˈliːf] Unglaube *m*, Ungläubigkeit *f*; **un·beˈliev·a·ble** □ unglaublich; ˈ**un·beˈliev·er** Ungläubige *m*, *f*; ˈ**un·beˈliev·ing** □ ungläubig.

un·be·loved [ˈʌnbiˈlʌvd] ungeliebt.

un·bend [ˈʌnˈbend] (*irr. bend*) *v/t.* entspannen (*a. fig.*); ⊕ gerade richten; *v/i.* sich entspannen; freundlich werden, auftauen; ˈ**unˈbend·ing** □ unbiegsam; *fig.* unbeugsam.

un·be·seem·ing □ [ˈʌnbiˈsiːmiŋ] unpassend.

un·bi·as(s)ed □ [ˈʌnˈbaiəst] vorurteilsfrei, unbefangen, unbeeinflußt.

un·bid(·den) [ˈʌnˈbid(n)] ungeheißen, unaufgefordert; ungebeten.

un·bind [ˈʌnˈbaind] (*irr. bind*) losbinden, befreien; lösen.

un·bleached [ˈʌnˈbliːtʃt] ungebleicht.

un·blem·ished [ʌnˈblemiʃt] unbefleckt.

un·blush·ing □ [ʌnˈblʌʃiŋ] nicht errötend; schamlos.

un·bolt [ˈʌnˈbəult] aufriegeln; ˈ**unˈbolt·ed** unverriegelt; ungebeutelt (*Mehl*).

un·born [ˈʌnˈbɔːn] (noch) ungeboren.

un·bos·om [ʌnˈbuzəm] *Gefühl etc.* offenbaren; ~ *o.s.* sich offenbaren, sein Herz ausschütten (*to s.o.* j-m).

un·bound [ˈʌnˈbaund] ungebunden.

un·bound·ed □ [ʌnˈbaundid] unbegrenzt; schrankenlos.

un·bowed *fig.* [ˈʌnˈbaud] ungebeugt, ungebrochen.

un·brace [ˈʌnˈbreis] losmachen; schlaff machen; entspannen.

un·break·a·ble [ˈʌnˈbreikəbl] unzerbrechlich.

un·bri·dled [ʌnˈbraidld] ungezäumt; *fig.* ungezügelt.

un·bro·ken [ˈʌnˈbrəukən] ungebrochen; unversehrt; ununterbrochen; unzugeritten (*Pferd*).

un·buck·le [ˈʌnˈbʌkl] auf-, losschnallen.

un·bur·den [ˈʌnˈbəːdn] *mst fig.* entlasten; *sein Herz* ausschütten.

un·bur·ied [ˈʌnˈberid] unbegraben.

un·burned [ˈʌnˈbəːnd], **un·burnt** [ˈ~ˈbəːnt] unverbrannt; ungebrannt.

un·busi·ness·like [ʌnˈbiznislaik] nicht geschäftsmäßig.

un·but·ton [ˈʌnˈbʌtn] aufknöpfen.

un·called [ˈʌnˈkɔːld] unaufgefordert; ⚕ nicht aufgerufen; **unˈcalled-for** ungerufen; unverlangt (*Sache*); unpassend (*Bemerkung etc.*).

un·can·did □ [ˈʌnˈkændid] unaufrichtig.

un·can·ny □ [ʌnˈkæni] unheimlich.

un·cared-for [ˈʌnˈkɛədfɔː] unbeachtet, vernachlässigt.

un·case [ˈʌnˈkeis] auspacken.

un·ceas·ing □ [ʌnˈsiːsiŋ] unaufhörlich.

un·cer·e·mo·ni·ous □ [ˈʌnseriˈməunjəs] ungezwungen; formlos.

un·cer·tain □ [ʌnˈsəːtn] *allg.* unsicher; ungewiß; unbestimmt; unzuverlässig (*a. Wetter*); *be ~ of e-r Sache* nicht sicher sein; **unˈcer·tain·ty** Unsicherheit *f etc.*

un·chain [ˈʌnˈtʃein] entfesseln.

un·chal·lenge·a·ble [ˈʌnˈtʃælindʒəbl] unanfechtbar; ˈ**unˈchal·lenged** unangefochten.

un·change·a·ble □ [ʌnˈtʃeindʒəbl], **unˈchang·ing** □ unveränderlich, unwandelbar; ˈ**unˈchanged** unverändert.

un·char·i·ta·ble □ [ʌnˈtʃæritəbl] lieblos; unbarmherzig; unfreundlich.

un·charm [ˈʌnˈtʃɑːm] entzaubern.

un·chart·ed [ˈʌnˈtʃɑːtid] unerforscht; auf keiner Landkarte verzeichnet, nicht vermessen.

un·chaste □ [ˈʌnˈtʃeist] unkeusch; **un·chas·ti·ty** [ˈʌnˈtʃæstiti] Unkeuschheit *f*.

un·checked [ˈʌnˈtʃekt] ungehindert.

un·chris·tian □ [ˈʌnˈkristjən] unchristlich.

un·civ·il □ [ˈʌnˈsivl] unhöflich; ˈ**unˈciv·i·lized** [~vilaizd] unzivilisiert.

un·claimed [ˈʌnˈkleimd] nicht beansprucht; unzustellbar (*Brief*).

un·clasp [ˈʌnˈklɑːsp] auf-, los-

haken, -schnallen; aufmachen.
un·clas·si·fied [ˈʌnˈklæsifaid] nicht (ein)geordnet; ⚔ nicht geheim; ~ **road** Landstraße *f*.
un·cle [ˈʌŋkl] Onkel *m*; *sl*. Pfandleiher *m*.
un·clean □ [ˈʌnˈkliːn] unrein (*a. fig.*).
un·clench [ˈʌnˈklentʃ] (sich) öffnen.
un·cloak [ˈʌnˈkləuk] (*j-m*) den Mantel abnehmen; *fig*. enthüllen.
un·close [ˈʌnˈkləuz] (sich) öffnen.
un·clothe [ˈʌnˈkləuð] entkleiden.
un·cloud·ed [ˈʌnˈklaudid] unbewölkt; wolkenlos (*a. fig.*).
un·coil [ˈʌnˈkɔil] (sich) aufrollen.
un·col·lect·ed [ˈʌnkəˈlektid] nicht gesammelt (*a. fig.*).
un·col·o(u)red [ˈʌnˈkʌləd] ungefärbt; *fig*. ungeschminkt.
un-come-at-a·ble F [ˈʌnkʌmˈætəbl] unerreichbar, unzugänglich; schwer erreichbar.
un·come·ly [ˈʌnˈkʌmli] reizlos; unpassend.
un·com·fort·a·ble □ [ʌnˈkʌmfətəbl] unbehaglich, ungemütlich; unangenehm.
un·com·mit·ted [ʌnkəˈmitid] unabhängig, nicht gebunden; *pol*. blockfrei.
un·com·mon □ [ʌnˈkɔmən] (*a.* F *adv.*) ungewöhnlich.
un·com·mu·ni·ca·tive [ˈʌnkəˈmjuːnikətiv] wenig mitteilsam, verschlossen; schweigsam.
un·com·plain·ing □ [ˈʌnkəmˈpleiniŋ] klaglos; ohne Murren; geduldig.
un·com·pro·mis·ing □ [ʌnˈkɔmprəmaiziŋ] kompromißlos; unnachgiebig; *fig*. entschieden.
un·con·cern [ˈʌnkənˈsəːn] Unbekümmertheit *f*; Gleichgültigkeit *f*; **ˈun·conˈcerned** □ [*adv.* ~idli] unbekümmert (*about* um); uninteressiert (*with* an *dat.*); unbeteiligt (*in* an *dat.*).
un·con·di·tion·al □ [ˈʌnkənˈdiʃənl] unbedingt; bedingungslos.
un·con·fined □ [ˈʌnkənˈfaind] unbegrenzt; ungehindert.
un·con·firmed [ˈʌnkənˈfəːmd] unbestätigt; *eccl*. unkonfirmiert.
un·con·gen·ial [ˈʌnkənˈdʒiːnjəl] ungleichartig, unsympathisch.
un·con·nect·ed □ [ˈʌnkəˈnektid] unverbunden.
un·con·quer·a·ble □ [ʌnˈkɔŋkərəbl] unüberwindlich; **ˈunˈcon·quered** unbesiegt, nicht erobert.
un·con·sci·en·tious □ [ˈʌnkɔnʃiˈenʃəs] nicht gewissenhaft, nachlässig.
un·con·scion·a·ble □ [ʌnˈkɔnʃnəbl] gewissenlos; F unverschämt, übermäßig.
un·con·scious □ [ʌnˈkɔnʃəs] **1.** unbewußt; bewußtlos; *be ~ of* nichts ahnen von; **2.** *the ~ psych*. das Unbewußte; **unˈcon·sciousness** Bewußtlosigkeit *f*.
un·con·se·crat·ed [ˈʌnˈkɔnsikreitid] ungeweiht.
un·con·sid·ered [ˈʌnkənˈsidəd] unberücksichtigt; unbedacht.
un·con·sti·tu·tion·al □ [ˈʌnkɔnstiˈtjuːʃənl] verfassungswidrig.
un·con·strained □ [ˈʌnkənˈstreind] ungezwungen.
un·con·test·ed □ [ˈʌnkənˈtestid] unbestritten.
un·con·tra·dict·ed [ˈʌnkɔntrəˈdiktid] unwidersprochen.
un·con·trol·la·ble □ [ʌnkənˈtrəuləbl] unkontrollierbar; unbändig; nicht zu meistern(d); **ˈun·conˈtrolled** unbeaufsichtigt; *fig*. unbeherrscht.
un·con·ven·tion·al □ [ˈʌnkənˈvenʃənl] unkonventionell; ungezwungen.
un·con·vert·ed [ˈʌnkənˈvəːtid] unbekehrt; ✝ nicht konvertiert.
un·con·vinced [ˈʌnkənˈvinst] nicht überzeugt; **ˈun·conˈvinc·ing** nicht überzeugend.
un·cooked [ˈʌnˈkukt] ungekocht, roh.
un·cord [ˈʌnˈkɔːd] auf-, losbinden.
un·cork [ˈʌnˈkɔːk] entkorken.
un·cor·rupt·ed □ [ˈʌnkəˈrʌptid] unverdorben; unbestochen.
un·count·a·ble [ˈʌnˈkauntəbl] unzählbar; **ˈunˈcount·ed** ungezählt.
un·cou·ple [ˈʌnˈkʌpl] los-, auskoppeln.
un·couth □ [ʌnˈkuːθ] grob, ungeschlacht, linkisch; seltsam.
un·cov·er [ʌnˈkʌvə] aufdecken, freilegen; *Körperteil* entblößen.
un·crit·i·cal □ [ˈʌnˈkritikəl] unkritisch.
un·crowned [ˈʌnˈkraund] ungekrönt.
unc·tion [ˈʌŋkʃən] Salbung *f* (*a. fig.*); Salbe *f*; *extreme ~ eccl*. Letzte

Ölung *f*; **unc·tu·ous** □ [ˈʌŋktjuəs] fettig, ölig; *fig.* salbungsvoll.
un·cul·ti·vat·ed [ˈʌnˈkʌltiveitid] unbebaut, unkultiviert; *fig.* ungebildet.
un·cured [ˈʌnˈkjuəd] ungeheilt; ungesalzen, ungepökelt.
un·curl [ˈʌnˈkəːl] (sich) entkräuseln.
un·cut [ˈʌnˈkʌt] ungeschnitten; unbeschnitten; unaufgeschnitten (*Buch*).
un·dam·aged [ˈʌnˈdæmidʒd] unbeschädigt.
un·damped [ˈʌnˈdæmpt] ungedämpft; ungeschwächt.
un·dat·ed [ˈʌnˈdeitid] undatiert.
un·daunt·ed □ [ʌnˈdɔːntid] unerschrocken, kühn, furchtlos.
un·de·ceive [ˈʌndiˈsiːv] *j.* aufklären, *j-m* die Augen öffnen (*of* über *acc.*).
un·de·cid·ed □ [ˈʌndiˈsaidid] unentschieden; unentschlossen.
un·de·ci·pher·a·ble [ˈʌndiˈsaifərəbl] unentzifferbar.
un·de·fend·ed [ˈʌndiˈfendid] unverteidigt.
un·de·filed [ˈʌndiˈfaild] unbefleckt.
un·de·fined □ [ˈʌndiˈfaind, *adv.* ∼nidli] unbegrenzt; unbestimmt.
un·de·mon·stra·tive □ [ˈʌndiˈmɔnstrətiv] zurückhaltend.
un·de·ni·a·ble □ [ʌndiˈnaiəbl] unleugbar, unbestreitbar.
un·de·nom·i·na·tion·al □ [ˈʌndinɔmiˈneiʃənl] konfessionslos; paritätisch; Simultan...
un·der [ˈʌndə] **1.** *adv.* unten; darunter; **2.** *prp.* unter; *from* ∼ ... unter ... hervor; ∼ *sentence of* ⚖ ... zu ... verurteilt; **3.** *in Zssgn*: unter...; Unter...; mangelhaft ...; ˈ∼ˈ**act** *thea.* zu zurückhaltend spielen; ∼ˈ**age** minderjährig, unmündig; ˈ∼ˈ**bid** (*irr. bid*) unterbieten; ˈ∼ˈ**bred** unfein, ungebildet; ˈ∼·**brush** Unterholz *n*, Gesträuch *n*; ˈ∼·**carriage** (Flugzeug)Fahrwerk *n*; *mot.* Fahrgestell *n*; ˈ∼ˈ**charge** *j-m* zu wenig berechnen; ˈ∼·**clothes** *pl.*, ˈ∼·**clothing** Unterbekleidung *f*, -wäsche *f*; ˈ∼·**cov·er** Geheim...; ˈ∼-**cur·rent** Unterströmung *f*; ˈ∼ˈ**cut** *Preise* unterbieten; ˈ∼·**dog** Unterlegene *m*; Unterdrückte *m*; ˈ∼ˈ**done** nicht gar; ˈ∼ˈ**dress** (sich) zu einfach kleiden; ˈ∼·**emˈploy·ment** Unterbeschäftigung *f*; ˈ∼ˈ**es·ti·mate** unterschätzen; ˈ∼-**exˈpose** *phot.* unterbelichten; ˈ∼ˈ**fed** unterernährt; ˈ∼ˈ**feed·ing** Unterernährung *f*; ∼ˈ**foot** unter den Füßen, unter die Füße; ˈ∼·**gar·ments** *pl.* Leibwäsche *f*; ∼ˈ**go** (*irr. go*) erdulden; sich unterziehen (*dat.*); ∼ˈ**grad·u·ate** *univ.* Student(in); ˈ∼**ground** **1.** unterirdisch; Untergrund...; ∼ *movement* Untergrundbewegung *f*; *go* ∼ in den Untergrund gehen; **2.** *a.* ∼ *railway* Untergrundbahn *f*; ˈ∼-**growth** Unterholz *n*; ˈ∼**hand** unter der Hand; heimlich; heimtückisch; ∼ *service Tennis*: Aufschlag *m* aus der Hüfte; ˈ∼ˈ**hung** unter dem Oberkiefer hervorstehend; mit vorstehendem Unterkiefer; ∼·**lay** **1.** [ʌndəˈlei] (*irr. lay*) unterlegen; **2.** [ˈ∼] wasserdichte Unterlage *f*; ˈ∼ˈ**let** (*irr. let*) unterverpachten, -vermieten; unter dem Werte verpachten *od.* vermieten; ∼ˈ**lie** (*irr. lie*) unter *et.* (*dat.*) liegen; *fig.* zugrunde liegen (*dat.*); unterstehen (*dat.*); ∼**line** **1.** [ʌndəˈlain] unterstreichen; **2.** [ˈ∼] Unterstreichung *f*; ˈ∼·**lin·en** Leibwäsche *f*.
un·der·ling [ˈʌndəliŋ] Untergeordnete *m*, Kuli *m*; **un·derˈly·ing** zugrundeliegend; **un·der·manned** [ˈ∼ˈmænd] unterbelegt; **un·derˈmen·tioned** unten erwähnt; **underˈmine** unterminieren; *fig.* untergraben; schwächen, aushöhlen; ˈ**un·der·most** **1.** *adj.* unterst; **2.** *adv.* zuunterst; **un·der·neath** [∼ˈniːθ] **1.** *prp.* unter(halb); **2.** *adv.* unten, unterwärts; darunter; ˈ**un·derˈnour·ished** unterernährt.
un·der...: ˈ∼·**pants** *pl.* Unterhose *f*; ˈ∼·**pass** Unterführung *f*; ˈ∼ˈ**pay** (*irr. pay*) unterbezahlen; ∼ˈ**pin** ⊕ untermauern (*fig.* stützen); ∼ˈ**pinning** ⊕ Untermauerung *f*; Unterbau *m*; ∼ˈ**play** (seine Karten) nicht voll ausspielen; *thea.* (die Rolle) (zu) verhalten spielen; *fig.* sich zurückhalten (in *od.* mit); ˈ∼·**plot** Nebenhandlung *f*; ˈ∼ˈ**print** *phot.* unterkopieren; ˈ∼ˈ**priv·i·leged** benachteiligt, schlechtgestellt; ∼ˈ**rate** unterschätzen; ∼ˈ**score** unterstreichen; ˈ∼-ˈ**sec·re·tar·y** Unterstaatssekretär *m*; ˈ∼ˈ**sell** ✝ (*irr. sell*) *j.* unterbieten; *Ware* verschleudern; ˈ∼ˈ**shoot** (*irr. shoot*): ∼ *the runway* ✈ vor der Landebahn aufkommen; ˈ∼·**shot** unterschlächtig (*Mühlrad*); ˈ∼·**side** Unterseite *f*; ∼ˈ**signed** Unterzeichnete *m*, *f*; ˈ∼-

'**sized** unter Normalgröße, zu klein; '**~'slung** *mot.* Hänge...; *~ frame* Unterzugrahmen *m*; '**~'staffed** unterbesetzt; **~'stand** (*irr. stand*) *allg.* verstehen; sich verstehen auf (*acc.*); (als sicher) annehmen; auffassen; *fig.* hören; sinngemäß ergänzen; *make o.s. understood* sich verständlich machen; *it is understood* es heißt, es verlautet; *that is understood* das ist selbstverständlich; *an understood thing* e-e ausod. abgemachte Sache; **~'stand·a·ble** verständlich; **~'stand·ing 1.** Verstand *m*; Einvernehmen *n*; Verständigung *f*; Vereinbarung *f*, Abkommen *n*, Abmachung *f*; *on the ~ that* unter der Voraussetzung, daß; **2.** verständig; '**~'state** zu gering angeben; unterbewerten; *Tatsache* verkleinern; '**~'state·ment** zu niedrige Angabe *f*; Unterbewertung *f*; Understatement *n*, Untertreibung *f*.

un·der...: '**~·strap·per** = *underling*; '**~·stud·y** *thea.* **1.** Rollenvertreter(in); **2.** einspringen für; **~'take** (*irr. take*) unternehmen; übernehmen; sich verpflichten (*to inf.* zu *inf.*); *~ that* sich dafür verbürgen, daß; '**~·tak·er** Bestattungsinstitut *n*, Leichenbestatter *m*; **~'tak·ing** Unternehmung *f*; Verpflichtung *f*, Zusicherung *f*; ['~teikiŋ] Leichenbestattung *f*; '**~'ten·ant** Untermieter *m*, -pächter *m*; **~-the-'coun·ter** unter der Hand, heimlich; '**~·tone** leiser Ton *m*; Unterton *m*; *in an ~* halblaut; '**~'val·ue** unterschätzen; '**~·wear** Unterkleidung *f*, -wäsche *f*; '**~-weight** Untergewicht *n*; '**~·wood** Unterholz *n*, Gestrüpp *n* (*a. fig.*); '**~·world** Unterwelt *f*; '**~·write** ⚕ (*irr. write*) *Versicherung* abschließen; '**~·wri·ter** Versicherer *m*.

un·de·served □ ['ʌndi'zəːvd] unverdient; '**un·de'serv·ing** unwürdig.

un·de·signed □ ['ʌndi'zaind] unbeabsichtigt, absichtslos.

un·de·sir·a·ble ['ʌndi'zaiərəbl] **1.** □ unerwünscht; **2.** unerwünschte Person *f*.

un·de·terred ['ʌndi'təːd] nicht abgeschreckt.

un·de·vel·oped ['ʌndi'veləpt] unentwickelt; unerschlossen (*Gelände*).

un·de·vi·at·ing □ [ʌn'diːvieitiŋ] unentwegt.

un·dies F ['ʌndiz] *pl.* Damenunterwäsche *f*.

un·di·gest·ed ['ʌndi'dʒestid] unverdaut.

un·dig·ni·fied □ [ʌn'dignifaid] würdelos.

un·di·min·ished ['ʌndi'miniʃt] unvermindert.

un·di·rect·ed ['ʌndi'rektid] führungslos; ungelenkt.

un·dis·cerned □ ['ʌndi'səːnd] unbemerkt; '**un·dis'cern·ing** einsichtslos.

un·dis·charged ['ʌndis'tʃɑːdʒd] (noch) nicht entlastet; unerledigt.

un·dis·ci·plined [ʌn'disiplind] zuchtlos, undiszipliniert; ungeschult.

un·dis·cov·ered ['ʌndis'kʌvəd] unentdeckt.

un·dis·crim·i·nat·ing □ ['ʌndis'krimineitiŋ] unterschiedlos.

un·dis·guised □ ['ʌndis'gaizd] unverkleidet; unverhohlen.

un·dis·posed ['ʌndis'pəuzd] nicht geneigt (*to* zu); nicht vergeben, ⚕ unverkauft.

un·dis·put·ed □ ['ʌndis'pjuːtid] unbestritten.

un·dis·tin·guished ['ʌndis'tiŋgwiʃt] unbedeutend, gewöhnlich.

un·dis·tort·ed ['ʌndis'tɔːtid] unverzerrt.

un·dis·turbed □ ['ʌndis'təːbd] ungestört.

un·di·vid·ed □ ['ʌndi'vaidid] ungeteilt.

un·do ['ʌn'duː] (*irr. do*) aufmachen (*öffnen*); aufknöpfen; (auf)lösen; *j-m* das Kleid aufmachen; auftrennen; ungeschehen machen, aufheben; ⚒ vernichten; '**un'do·ing** Aufmachen *n etc.*; Verderben *n*.

un·do·mes·ti·cat·ed ['ʌndə'mestikeitid] am Haushalt nicht interessiert (*Frau*).

un·done ['ʌn'dʌn] ungetan, ungeschehen *etc.*; erledigt, vernichtet; *he is ~* es ist aus mit ihm; *come ~* auf-, losgehen.

un·doubt·ed □ [ʌn'dautid] unzweifelhaft, zweifellos.

un·dreamt [ʌn'dremt]: *~-of* ungeahnt.

un·dress ['ʌn'dres] **1.** (sich) entkleiden *od.* ausziehen; **2.** Hauskleid *n*; ⚔ Interimsuniform *f*; '**un-**

ˈ**dressed** unbekleidet; nicht ordentlich angezogen; unzugerichtet, nicht zurechtgemacht; unverbunden (*Wunde*); ungegerbt.

un·due [ˈʌnˈdjuː] ungebührlich, unangemessen; übermäßig; unzulässig; ✝ noch nicht fällig.

un·du·late [ˈʌndjuleit] wogen; wallen; wellenförmig verlaufen, wellig sein; ˈ**un·du·lat·ing** □ wogend; well(enförm)ig; **un·duˈla·tion** wellenförmige Bewegung *f*; **un·du·la·to·ry** [ˈ‿lətəri] wellenförmig; Wellen...

un·du·ly [ˈʌnˈdjuːli] *adv. von undue*.

un·du·ti·ful □ [ˈʌnˈdjuːtiful] ungehorsam, pflichtvergessen.

un·dy·ing □ [ʌnˈdaiiŋ] unsterblich, unvergänglich.

un·earned [ˈʌnˈəːnd] nicht aus Arbeit herrührend; *fig.* unverdient; ~ *income* Kapitaleinkommen *n*.

un·earth [ˈʌnˈəːθ] ausgraben; *fig.* auftreiben, -stöbern; **unˈearth·ly** übernatürlich, -irdisch; unheimlich; F unheimlich früh.

un·eas·i·ness [ʌnˈiːzinis] Unruhe *f*; Unbehagen *n*; **unˈeas·y** □ unbehaglich; unruhig, ängstlich (*about* wegen); unsicher.

un·eat·a·ble [ˈʌnˈiːtəbl] ungenießbar.

un·e·co·nom·ic, un·e·co·nom·i·cal □ [ˈʌniːkəˈnɔmik(əl)] unwirtschaftlich.

un·ed·i·fy·ing □ [ˈʌnˈedifaiiŋ] wenig erbaulich *od.* erhebend.

un·ed·u·cat·ed [ˈʌnˈedjukeitid] unerzogen; ungebildet.

un·em·bar·rassed [ˈʌnimˈbærəst] ungehindert; nicht verlegen.

un·e·mo·tion·al □ [ˈʌniˈməuʃənl] leidenschaftslos; passiv; nüchtern.

un·em·ployed [ˈʌnimˈplɔid] **1.** unbeschäftigt; arbeits-, erwerbslos; unbenutzt; **2.** *the* ~ *pl.* die Arbeitslosen *pl.*; ˈ**un·emˈploy·ment** Arbeitslosigkeit *f*; ~ *benefit*, ~ *pay* Arbeitslosenunterstützung *f*.

un·en·cum·bered [ˈʌninˈkʌmbəd] unbelastet.

un·end·ing □ [ʌnˈendiŋ] endlos.

un·en·dowed [ˈʌninˈdaud] nicht ausgestattet (*with* mit).

un·en·dur·a·ble [ˈʌninˈdjuərəbl] unerträglich.

un·en·gaged [ˈʌninˈgeidʒd] frei; nicht gebunden; unbeschäftigt.

un-Eng·lish [ˈʌnˈiŋgliʃ] unenglisch.

un·en·light·ened [ˈʌninˈlaitnd] *fig.* unerleuchtet, nicht aufgeklärt.

un·en·ter·pris·ing [ˈʌnˈentəpraiziŋ] ohne Unternehmungsgeist.

un·en·vi·a·ble □ [ˈʌnˈenviəbl] nicht beneidenswert.

un·e·qual □ [ˈʌnˈiːkwəl] ungleich; nicht gewachsen (*to dat.*); ˈ**un·e·qual(l)ed** unvergleichlich, unerreicht.

un·e·quiv·o·cal □ [ˈʌniˈkwivəkəl] unzweideutig, eindeutig.

un·err·ing □ [ˈʌnˈəːriŋ] unfehlbar.

un·es·sen·tial □ [ˈʌniˈsenʃəl] unwesentlich, -wichtig (*to* für).

un·e·ven □ [ˈʌnˈiːvən] uneben; ungleich(mäßig); unausgeglichen (*Charakter etc.*); ungerade (*Zahl*).

un·e·vent·ful □ [ˈʌniˈventful] ereignislos; *be* ~ ohne Zwischenfälle verlaufen.

un·ex·am·pled [ʌnigˈzɑːmpld] beispiellos.

un·ex·cep·tion·a·ble □ [ʌnikˈsepʃnəbl] untadelig; einwandfrei.

un·ex·cep·tion·al [ˈʌnikˈsepʃənl] (nicht un)gewöhnlich, durchschnittlich.

un·ex·pect·ed □ [ˈʌniksˈpektid] unerwartet.

un·ex·pired [ˈʌniksˈpaiəd] noch nicht abgelaufen.

un·ex·plained [ˈʌniksˈpleind] unerklärt.

un·ex·posed *phot.* [ˈʌniksˈpəuzd] unbelichtet.

un·ex·plored [ˈʌniksˈplɔːd] unerforscht.

un·ex·pressed [ˈʌniksˈprest] unausgesprochen.

un·fad·ing □ [ʌnˈfeidiŋ] nicht welkend; unvergänglich; echt (*Farbe*).

un·fail·ing □ [ʌnˈfeiliŋ] unfehlbar; nie versagend; unerschöpflich; *fig.* treu.

un·fair □ [ˈʌnˈfɛə] unehrlich; unanständig, unfair (*Spiel etc.*); unbillig, ungerecht; ˈ**unˈfair·ness** Unehrlichkeit *f*; Ungerechtigkeit *f etc.*

un·faith·ful □ [ˈʌnˈfeiθful] un(ge)treu, treulos; nicht wortgetreu; ˈ**unˈfaith·ful·ness** Untreue *f*.

un·fal·ter·ing □ [ʌnˈfɔːltəriŋ] nicht schwankend; unentwegt.

un·fa·mil·iar [ˈʌnfəˈmiljə] unbekannt; ungewohnt.

un·fash·ion·a·ble □ [ˈʌnˈfæʃnəbl] unmodern, altmodisch.
un·fas·ten [ˈʌnˈfɑːsn] aufmachen.
un·fath·om·a·ble □ [ʌnˈfæðəməbl] unergründlich.
un·fa·vo(u)r·a·ble □ [ˈʌnˈfeivərəbl] ungünstig.
un·feel·ing □ [ʌnˈfiːliŋ] gefühllos.
un·feigned □ [ʌnˈfeind, *adv.* ~nidli] ungeheuchelt, unverstellt.
un·felt [ˈʌnˈfelt] ungefühlt.
un·fer·ment·ed [ˈʌnfəːˈmentid] unvergoren.
un·fet·ter [ˈʌnˈfetə] entfesseln; **ˈun-ˈfet·tered** *fig.* ungefesselt, frei.
un·fil·i·al □ [ˈʌnˈfiljəl] respektlos, pflichtvergessen (*Kind*).
un·fin·ished [ˈʌnˈfiniʃt] unvollendet; unfertig.
un·fit 1. □ [ˈʌnˈfit] ungeeignet, untauglich, unpassend (*for s.th.* für et.; *to inf.* zu *inf.*); **2.** [ʌnˈfit] untauglich machen; **ˈunˈfit·ness** Untauglichkeit *f*; **unˈfit·ted** ungeeignet; nicht (gut) ausgerüstet.
un·fix [ˈʌnˈfiks] losmachen, lösen; **ˈunˈfixed** unbefestigt.
un·flag·ging □ [ʌnˈflægiŋ] nicht erschlaffend (*Aufmerksamkeit etc.*).
un·flat·ter·ing □ [ˈʌnˈflætəriŋ] nicht schmeichelhaft, ungeschminkt.
un·fledged [ˈʌnˈfledʒd] ungefiedert; (noch) nicht flügge; *fig.* unreif.
un·flick·er·ing [ˈʌnˈflikəriŋ] nicht flackernd; *fig.* beständig.
un·flinch·ing □ [ʌnˈflintʃiŋ] fest entschlossen, unnachgiebig.
un·fly·a·ble [ˈʌnˈflaiəbl]: ~ *weather* ✈ kein Flugwetter.
un·fold [ˈʌnˈfəuld] (sich) entfalten *od.* öffnen; [ʌnˈfəuld] enthüllen.
un·forced □ [ˈʌnˈfɔːst, *adv.* ~sidli] ungezwungen.
un·fore·see·a·ble [ˈʌnfɔːˈsiːəbl] unvorhersehbar.
un·fore·seen [ˈʌnfɔːˈsiːn] unvorhergesehen.
un·for·get·ta·ble □ [ˈʌnfəˈgetəbl] unvergeßlich.
un·for·giv·ing [ˈʌnfəˈgiviŋ] unversöhnlich.
un·for·got, un·for·got·ten [ˈʌnfəˈgɔt(n)] unvergessen.
un·for·ti·fied [ˈʌnˈfɔːtifaid] unbefestigt.
un·for·tu·nate [ʌnˈfɔːtʃnit] **1.** □ unglücklich; unselig; Unglücks...; **2.** Unglückliche *m, f*; **unˈfor·tu·nate·ly** unglücklicherweise, leider.
un·found·ed □ [ˈʌnˈfaundid] unbegründet; grundlos.
un·fre·quent [ʌnˈfriːkwənt] nicht häufig, selten.
un·fre·quent·ed [ˈʌnfriˈkwentid] nicht *od.* wenig besucht; einsam.
un·friend·ed [ˈʌnˈfrendid] freundlos; **ˈunˈfriend·ly** unfreundlich; ungünstig.
un·frock [ˈʌnˈfrɔk] *j-m* das Priesteramt entziehen.
un·fruit·ful □ [ˈʌnˈfruːtful] unfruchtbar.
un·ful·filled [ˈʌnfulˈfild] unerfüllt.
un·furl [ˈʌnˈfəːl] *Fahne, Segel etc.* entfalten, aufrollen.
un·fur·nished [ˈʌnˈfəːniʃt] unmöbliert (*Wohnung*); ~ *with* nicht versehen mit.
un·gain·li·ness [ʌnˈgeinlinis] Unbeholfenheit *f*; **unˈgain·ly** unbeholfen, plump.
un·gal·lant □ [ˈʌnˈgælənt] ungalant (*to* gegen).
un·gat·ed [ˈʌnˈgeitid] unbeschrankt (*Bahnübergang*).
un·gear ⊕ [ˈʌnˈgiə] auskuppeln.
un·gen·er·ous □ [ˈʌnˈdʒenərəs] unedelmütig; nicht freigebig.
un·gen·ial □ [ˈʌnˈdʒiːnjəl] unfreundlich.
un·gen·tle □ [ˈʌnˈdʒentl] unsanft, unzart.
un·gen·tle·man·ly [ʌnˈdʒentlmənli] ungebildet, unfein, ohne Lebensart, e-s Gentleman unwürdig.
un·get-at-able [ˈʌngetˈætəbl] unzugänglich.
un·glazed [ˈʌnˈgleizd] unglasiert; nicht verglast.
un·gloved [ˈʌnˈglʌvd] unbehandschuht.
un·god·li·ness [ʌnˈgɔdlinis] Gottlosigkeit *f*; **unˈgod·ly** □ gottlos; F abscheulich, schrecklich, unmenschlich.
un·gov·ern·a·ble □ [ʌnˈgʌvənəbl] unlenksam; zügellos, unbändig; **ˈunˈgov·erned** unbeherrscht.
un·grace·ful □ [ˈʌnˈgreisful] ungraziös, ohne Anmut; unbeholfen.
un·gra·cious □ [ˈʌnˈgreiʃəs] ungnädig; unfreundlich.
ˈun·gramˈmat·i·cal □ gegen die Regeln der Grammatik verstoßend.
un·grate·ful □ [ʌnˈgreitful] undankbar.

[illegible]d·ed [ʌnˈgraundid] un[illegible]et; ⚡ ungeerdet.
[illegible]dg·ing □ [ˈʌnˈgrʌdʒiŋ] ohne [illegible]en, willig; neidlos.
[illegible]ual *anat.* [ˈʌŋgwəl] Nagel...
un·guard·ed □ [ˈʌnˈgɑːdid] unbewacht; unvorsichtig, unbedacht; ⊕ ungeschützt.
un·guent [ˈʌŋgwənt] Salbe *f.*
un·guid·ed □ [ˈʌnˈgaidid] ungeleitet; führerlos.
un·gu·late [ˈʌŋgjuleit] *a.* ~ *animal* Huftier *n.*
un·hal·lowed [ʌnˈhæləud] unheilig, böse; ungeweiht.
un·ham·pered [ˈʌnˈhæmpəd] ungehindert.
un·hand·some □ [ʌnˈhænsəm] unschön (*a. fig.*).
un·hand·y □ [ʌnˈhændi] ungeschickt; unhandlich (*Sache*); unbeholfen (*Person*).
un·hap·pi·ness [ʌnˈhæpinis] Unglück(seligkeit *f*) *n*; **unˈhap·py** □ unglücklich; un(glück)selig; unpassend.
un·harmed [ˈʌnˈhɑːmd] unversehrt.
un·har·mo·ni·ous □ [ˈʌnhɑːˈməunjəs] unharmonisch.
un·har·ness [ˈʌnˈhɑːnis] abschirren.
un·health·y □ [ʌnˈhelθi] ungesund.
un·heard [ˈʌnˈhəːd] ungehört; **un-heard-of** [ʌnˈhəːdɔv] unerhört.
un·heat·ed [ˈʌnˈhiːtid] ungeheizt.
un·heed·ed [ˈʌnˈhiːdid] unbeachtet; unbewacht; **ˈunˈheed·ing** sorglos, unachtsam.
un·hes·i·tat·ing □ [ʌnˈheziteitiŋ] ohne Zögern; unbedenklich; anstandslos; ~*ly* ohne zu zögern.
un·hin·dered [ˈʌnˈhindəd] ungehindert.
un·hinge [ʌnˈhindʒ] aus den Angeln heben; *fig.* zerrütten.
un·his·tor·ic, un·his·tor·i·cal □ [ˈʌnhisˈtɔrik(əl)] unhistorisch; ungeschichtlich.
un·hitch [ˈʌnˈhitʃ] losmachen; ausspannen.
un·ho·ly [ʌnˈhəuli] unheilig; gottlos; F scheußlich, schrecklich.
un·hon·o(u)red [ˈʌnˈɔnəd] ungeehrt; uneingelöst (*Pfand*, *Scheck*).
un·hook [ˈʌnˈhuk] auf-, aushaken.
un·hoped-for [ʌnˈhauptfɔː] unverhofft.
un·horse [ˈʌnˈhɔːs] aus dem Sattel heben; *Reiter* abwerfen.
un·house [ˈʌnˈhauz] (aus dem Hause) vertreiben; obdachlos machen.
un·hung [ʌnˈhʌŋ] un(auf)gehängt.
un·hurt [ˈʌnˈhəːt] unverletzt.
u·ni·corn [ˈjuːnikɔːn] Einhorn *n.*
un·i·den·ti·fied [ˈʌnaiˈdentifaid] nicht identifizierbar *od.* identifiziert; ~ *flying object* Ufo *n.*
u·ni·fi·ca·tion [juːnifiˈkeiʃən] Vereinigung *f*; Vereinheitlichung *f.*
u·ni·form [ˈjuːnifɔːm] **1.** □ gleichförmig, -mäßig; einheitlich; ~ *price* Einheitspreis *m*; **2.** Dienstkleidung *f*; Uniform *f*; **3.** uniformieren; **u·niˈform·i·ty** Gleichförmigkeit *f*, -mäßigkeit *f.*
u·ni·fy [ˈjuːnifai] verein(ig)en; vereinheitlichen.
u·ni·lat·er·al [ˈjuːniˈlætərəl] einseitig.
un·im·ag·i·na·ble □ [ʌniˈmædʒinəbl] undenkbar; **ˈun·imˈag·i·na·tive** □ [~nətiv] ohne Phantasie, phantasielos, einfallslos.
un·im·paired [ˈʌnimˈpɛəd] unvermindert, ungeschwächt.
un·im·peach·a·ble □ [ʌnimˈpiːtʃəbl] einwandfrei, unanfechtbar.
un·im·ped·ed □ [ˈʌnimˈpiːdid] ungehindert.
un·im·por·tant □ [ˈʌnimˈpɔːtənt] unwichtig.
un·im·proved [ˈʌnimˈpruːvd] nicht kultiviert, unbebaut (*Land*); unverbessert.
un·in·flu·enced [ˈʌnˈinfluənst] unbeeinflußt.
un·in·formed [ˈʌninˈfɔːmd] nicht unterrichtet.
un·in·hab·it·a·ble [ˈʌninˈhæbitəbl] unbewohnbar; **ˈun·inˈhab·it·ed** unbewohnt.
un·in·jured [ˈʌnˈindʒəd] unbeschädigt, unverletzt.
un·in·struct·ed [ˈʌninˈstrʌktid] nicht unterrichtet; nicht instruiert.
un·in·sured [ˈʌninˈʃuəd] unversichert.
un·in·tel·li·gi·bil·i·ty [ˈʌnintelidʒəˈbiliti] Unverständlichkeit *f*; **ˈun·inˈtel·li·gi·ble** □ unverständlich.
un·in·tend·ed □ [ˈʌninˈtendid] unbeabsichtigt.
un·in·ten·tion·al □ [ˈʌninˈtenʃənl] unabsichtlich.
un·in·ter·est·ing □ [ˈʌnˈintristiŋ] uninteressant.
un·in·ter·rupt·ed □ [ˈʌnintəˈrʌptid] ununterbrochen; ~ *working hours*

pl. durchgehende Arbeitszeit *f.*
un·in·vit·ed ['ʌnin'vaitid] un(ein)-geladen; **'un·in'vit·ing** □ wenig einladend.
un·ion ['ju:njən] Vereinigung *f*; (*engS. eheliche*) Verbindung *f*; *pol. etc.* Union *f*, Bund *m*; *univ.* (Debattier)Klub *m*; Einigung *f*; Einigkeit *f*; Verein *m*, Verband *m*; Armenhaus *n*; ⚓ Gösch *f*; ⊕ Rohrverbindung *f*; Gewerkschaft *f*; ~ **dues** *pl.* Gewerkschaftsbeitrag *m*; **'un·ion·ism** *pol. etc.* Unionismus *m*; Gewerkschaftswesen *n*; **'un·ion·ist** *pol. etc.* Anhänger *m* der Union; Gewerkschaftler *m*; **'un·ion·ize** gewerkschaftlich organisieren.
un·ion...: ♀ **Jack** Union Jack *m* (*britische Nationalflagge*); ~ **of·fi·cial** Gewerkschaftsfunktionär *m*; ~ **suit** *Am.* Hemdhose *f.*
u·nique [ju:'ni:k] **1.** □ einzigartig; einmalig; **2.** Unikum *n.*
u·ni·son ♪ *u. fig.* ['ju:nizn] Einklang *m*; *in* ~ unisono (*einstimmig*); **u·nis·o·nous** ♪ [ju:'nisənəs] gleichtönend.
u·nit ['ju:nit] Einheit *f* (*a.* ⚔); ⅍ Einer *m*; ⊕ Anlage *f*; ~ *furniture* Anbaumöbel *pl.*; **U·ni·tar·i·an** [~'tɛəriən] **1.** Unitarier *m*; **2.** unitarisch; **u·ni·tar·y** ['~təri] Einheits...; ⅍ Einer...; **u·nite** [ju:'nait] (sich) vereinigen, verbinden.
u·nit·ed [ju:'naitid] vereinigt, vereint; ♀ **King·dom** *das* Vereinigte Königreich (*Großbritannien u. Nordirland*); ♀ **Na·tions** *pl. die* Vereinten Nationen *pl.*; ♀ **States** *pl. die* Vereinigten Staaten *pl.*
u·ni·ty ['ju:niti] Einheit *f*; Einigkeit *f.*
u·ni·ver·sal □ [ju:ni'və:səl] allgemein; allumfassend; Universal...; Welt...; ~ *heir* Universalerbe *m*; ~ *joint* ⊕ Universalgelenk *n*; ~ *language* Weltsprache *f*; ♀ *Postal Union* Weltpostverein *m*; ~ *suffrage* allgemeines Wahlrecht *n*; **u·ni·ver·sal·i·ty** [~'sæliti] Allgemeinheit *f*; umfassende Bildung *f*, Vielseitigkeit *f*; **u·ni·verse** ['ju:nivə:s] Weltall *n*, Universum *n*; **u·ni'ver·si·ty** Universität *f*; *Open* ♀ Fernuniversität *f* (*in England*).
un·just □ ['ʌn'dʒʌst] ungerecht; **un'jus·ti·fi·a·ble** □ [~tifaiəbl] nicht zu rechtfertigen(d), unverantwortlich.
un·kempt ['ʌn'kempt] ungekämmt; *fig.* ungepflegt, verwahrlost.
un·kind □ [ʌn'kaind] unfreundlich; rücksichtslos.
un·knit *bsd. fig.* ['ʌn'nit] (*irr. knit*) (auf)lösen.
un·knot ['ʌn'nɔt] entknoten; losknüpfen.
un·know·ing □ ['ʌn'nəuiŋ] unwissend; unbewußt; **'un'known** **1.** unbekannt; unbewußt; **2.** *adv.* ~ *to me* ohne mein Wissen; **3.** Unbekannte *m*, *f*; ⅍ Unbekannte *f.*
un·lace ['ʌn'leis] aufschnüren.
un·lade ['ʌn'leid] (*irr. lade*) aus-, entladen; ⚓ löschen.
un·la·dy·like ['ʌn'leidilaik] nicht damenhaft, unfein.
un·laid ['ʌn'leid] ungelegt; ungedeckt (*Tisch*).
un·la·ment·ed ['ʌnlə'mentid] unbeklagt.
un·latch ['ʌn'lætʃ] aufklinken.
un·law·ful □ ['ʌn'lɔ:ful] ungesetzlich; rechtswidrig; *weitS.* unrechtmäßig.
un·learn ['ʌn'lə:n] (*irr. learn*) verlernen; **'un'learn·ed** □ [~nid] ungelehrt, unwissend.
un·leash ['ʌn'li:ʃ] losbinden, *Hund* loskoppeln; *fig.* entfesseln.
un·leav·ened ['ʌn'levnd] ungesäuert.
un·less [ən'les] wenn nicht, außer wenn; es sei denn, daß.
un·let·tered ['ʌn'letəd] ungebildet, unwissend.
un·li·censed ['ʌn'laisənst] unberechtigt, unkonzessioniert.
un·licked *mst fig.* ['ʌn'likt] unbeleckt, unreif; ~ *cub* grüner Junge *m.*
un·like □ ['ʌn'laik] ungleich, unähnlich (*s.o.* j-m), anders als; im Gegensatz zu; **un'like·li·hood** [~hud] Unwahrscheinlichkeit *f*; **un'like·ly** unwahrscheinlich.
un·lim·it·ed [ʌn'limitid] unbegrenzt; unbeschränkt; *fig.* grenzenlos.
un·lined ['ʌn'laind] ungefüttert; unliniiert.
un·liq·ui·dat·ed ['ʌn'likwideitid] unbeglichen, unbezahlt.
un·load ['ʌn'ləud] ent-, ab-, ausladen; *Ladung* löschen; *Börse*: abstoßen.
un·lock ['ʌn'lɔk] aufschließen (*a. fig.*); *Schußwaffe* entsichern; **'un'locked** unverschlossen.
un·looked-for [ʌn'luktfɔ:] uner-

wartet.
un·loose, un·loos·en [ˈʌnˈluːs(n)] lösen, losmachen.
un·lov·a·ble [ˈʌnˈlʌvəbl] nicht liebenswert; ˈ**unˈlove·ly** reizlos, unschön; ˈ**unˈlov·ing** □ lieblos.
un·lucky □ [ʌnˈlʌki] unglücklich.
un·made [ˈʌnˈmeid] ungemacht.
un·make [ˈʌnˈmeik] (*irr. make*) vernichten; rückgängig machen; umbilden; *Herrscher* absetzen.
un·man [ˈʌnˈmæn] entmannen; entmutigen; verrohen (lassen).
un·man·age·a·ble □ [ʌnˈmænidʒəbl] unlenksam, widerspenstig; unhandlich; schwierig (*Lage*).
un·man·ly [ˈʌnˈmænli] unmännlich.
un·manned [ˈʌnˈmænd] unbemannt.
un·man·ner·ly [ʌnˈmænəli] unmanierlich.
un·marked [ˈʌnˈmɑːkt] unbezeichnet; unbemerkt.
un·mar·ried [ˈʌnˈmærid] unverheiratet, ledig.
un·mask [ˈʌnˈmɑːsk] (sich) demaskieren; *fig.* entlarven.
un·matched [ˈʌnˈmætʃt] unerreicht; unvergleichlich.
un·mean·ing □ [ʌnˈmiːniŋ] nichtssagend; **un·meant** [ˈʌnˈment] unbeabsichtigt.
un·meas·ured [ʌnˈmeʒəd] ungemessen; unermeßlich.
un·meet [ˈʌnˈmiːt] ungeeignet, unpassend.
un·men·tion·a·ble [ʌnˈmenʃnəbl] **1.** nicht zu erwähnen(d), unnennbar; **2.** ~*s pl.* F (Unter)Hosen *f/pl.*
un·mer·ci·ful □ [ʌnˈməːsiful] unbarmherzig.
un·mer·it·ed [ˈʌnˈmeritid] unverdient.
un·me·thod·i·cal [ˈʌnmiˈθɔdikəl] unmethodisch.
un·mil·i·tar·y [ˈʌnˈmilitəri] unmilitärisch.
un·mind·ful □ [ʌnˈmaindful] unbedacht(sam); sorglos; ohne Rücksicht (*of* auf *acc.*).
un·mis·tak·a·ble □ [ˈʌnmisˈteikəbl] unverkennbar; unmißverständlich, eindeutig.
un·mit·i·gat·ed [ʌnˈmitigeitid] ungemildert; richtig; *fig.* Erz...
un·mixed [ˈʌnˈmikst] unvermischt.
un·mod·i·fied [ˈʌnˈmɔdifaid] nicht abgeändert.
un·mo·lest·ed [ˈʌnməuˈlestid] unbelästigt.
un·moor [ˈʌnˈmuə] *Schiff* losmachen.
un·mor·al [ˈʌnˈmɔrəl] amoralisch.
un·mort·gaged [ˈʌnˈmɔːgidʒd] unverpfändet.
un·mount·ed [ˈʌnˈmauntid] unberitten; nicht gefaßt (*Stein*); unaufgezogen (*Bild*); unmontiert (*Geschütz*).
un·mourned [ˈʌnˈmɔːnd] unbetrauert.
un·moved □ [ˈʌnˈmuːvd] *mst fig.* unbewegt, ungerührt; **unˈmov·ing** regungslos.
un·mu·si·cal □ [ˈʌnˈmjuːzikəl] unmusikalisch; unmelodisch.
un·muz·zle [ˈʌnˈmʌzl] *e-m Hund* den Maulkorb abnehmen; ~*d* ohne Maulkorb.
un·named [ˈʌnˈneimd] ungenannt.
un·nat·u·ral □ [ʌnˈnætʃrəl] unnatürlich.
un·nav·i·ga·ble [ˈʌnˈnævigəbl] nicht schiffbar.
un·nec·es·sar·y □ [ʌnˈnesisəri] unnötig.
un·neigh·bo(u)r·ly [ˈʌnˈneibəli] nicht gutnachbarlich.
un·nerve [ˈʌnˈnəːv] entnerven.
un·not·ed [ˈʌnˈnəutid] unbemerkt; unbekannt, unberühmt.
un·no·ticed [ˈʌnˈnəutist] unbemerkt.
un·num·bered [ˈʌnˈnʌmbəd] unnumeriert; *poet.* ungezählt.
un·ob·jec·tion·a·ble □ [ˈʌnəbˈdʒekʃnəbl] einwandfrei.
un·ob·serv·ant □ [ˈʌnəbˈzəːvənt] unachtsam (*of* auf *acc.*); ˈ**un·obˈserved** □ unbemerkt.
un·ob·tain·a·ble [ˈʌnəbˈteinəbl] unerreichbar; nicht zu bekommen(d).
un·ob·tru·sive □ [ˈʌnəbˈtruːsiv] unaufdringlich, bescheiden.
un·oc·cu·pied [ˈʌnˈɔkjupaid] unbesetzt; unbewohnt; unbeschäftigt.
un·of·fend·ing [ˈʌnəˈfendiŋ] nicht anstößig, harmlos.
un·of·fi·cial □ [ˈʌnəˈfiʃəl] nichtamtlich, inoffiziell.
un·o·pened [ˈʌnˈəupənd] ungeöffnet.
un·op·posed [ˈʌnəˈpəuzd] ungehindert; ohne Widerstand (zu finden).
un·or·gan·ized [ˈʌnˈɔːgənaizd] unorganisch; unorganisiert.

un·os·ten·ta·tious □ [ˈʌnɔstenˈteiʃəs] anspruchslos; ohne Prunk; unauffällig.
un·owned [ˈʌnˈəund] herrenlos.
un·pack [ˈʌnˈpæk] auspacken.
un·paid [ˈʌnˈpeid] unbezahlt; unbelohnt; ✉ unfrankiert.
un·pal·at·a·ble [ʌnˈpælətəbl] nicht schmackhaft, schlecht (schmekkend); *fig.* widerwärtig.
un·par·al·leled [ʌnˈpærəleld] beispiellos, ohnegleichen.
un·par·don·a·ble □ [ʌnˈpɑːdnəbl] unverzeihlich.
un·par·lia·men·ta·ry □ [ˈʌnpɑːləˈmentəri] unparlamentarisch.
un·pat·ent·ed [ˈʌnˈpeitəntid] unpatentiert.
un·pa·tri·ot·ic [ˈʌnpætriˈɔtik] (*~ally*) unpatriotisch.
un·paved [ˈʌnˈpeivd] ungepflastert.
un·per·ceived □ [ˈʌnpəˈsiːvd] unbemerkt.
un·per·formed [ˈʌnpəˈfɔːmd] unausgeführt.
un·per·plexed [ˈʌnpəˈplekst] nicht verwirrt.
un·per·turbed [ˈʌnpəːˈtəːbd] nicht beunruhigt *od.* verwirrt, ruhig, gelassen, unerschüttert.
un·phil·o·soph·i·cal □ [ˈʌnfiləˈsɔfikəl] unphilosophisch.
un·pick [ˈʌnˈpik] *Naht* (auf)trennen.
un·picked [ˈʌnˈpikt] unsortiert.
un·pin [ˈʌnˈpin] losstecken.
un·pit·ied [ˈʌnˈpitid] unbemitleidet.
un·placed [ˈʌnˈpleist] ohne Platz; *Rennsport*: unplaziert; nichtangestellt.
un·pleas·ant □ [ʌnˈpleznt] unangenehm; unerfreulich; **unˈpleas·ant·ness** Unannehmlichkeit *f.*
un·plumbed [ˈʌnˈplʌmd] unergründlich.
un·po·et·ic, un·po·et·i·cal □ [ˈʌnpəuˈetik(əl)] unpoetisch, prosaisch.
un·po·lished [ˈʌnˈpɔliʃt] unpoliert; *fig.* ungebildet.
un·polled [ˈʌnˈpəuld] nicht in die Wählerliste eingetragen.
un·pol·lut·ed [ˈʌnpəˈluːtid] unbefleckt.
un·pop·u·lar □ [ˈʌnˈpɔpjulə] unpopulär, unbeliebt; **un·pop·u·lar·i·ty** [ˈ~ˈlæriti] Unbeliebtheit *f.*
un·pos·sessed [ˈʌnpəˈzest]: ~ *of s.th.* nicht im Besitz e-r Sache.
un·prac·ti·cal □ [ˈʌnˈpræktikəl] unpraktisch; **ˈunˈprac·ticed, ˈunˈprac·tised** [~tist] ungeübt.
un·prec·e·dent·ed □ [ʌnˈpresidəntid] beispiellos, unerhört; noch nie dagewesen.
un·prej·u·diced □ [ʌnˈpredʒudist] unbefangen, unvoreingenommen.
un·pre·med·i·tat·ed □ [ˈʌnpriˈmediteitid] nicht vorbedacht, unbeabsichtigt; aus dem Stegreif.
un·pre·pared □ [ˈʌnpriˈpɛəd, *adv.* ~ridli] unvorbereitet.
un·pre·pos·sess·ing [ˈʌnpriːpəˈzesiŋ] nicht einnehmend, reizlos.
un·pre·sent·a·ble [ˈʌnpriˈzentəbl] nicht vorzeigbar; nicht salonfähig.
un·pre·tend·ing □ [ˈʌnpriˈtəndiŋ], **ˈun·preˈten·tious** □ anspruchslos, bescheiden.
un·prin·ci·pled [ʌnˈprinsəpld] ohne Grundsätze; gewissenlos.
un·print·a·ble [ˈʌnˈprintəbl] nicht wiederzugeben(d), nicht salonfähig (*Wort*).
un·priv·il·eged *Am.* [ʌnˈprivilidʒd] sozial benachteiligt, arm.
un·pro·duc·tive □ [ˈʌnprəˈdʌktiv] unfruchtbar, unergiebig (*of* an *dat.*); ⚕ unproduktiv.
un·pro·fes·sion·al □ [ˈʌnprəˈfeʃənl] nicht berufsmäßig, berufswidrig.
un·prof·it·a·ble □ [ʌnˈprɔfitəbl] nicht einträglich; nutzlos, unnütz; **unˈprof·it·a·ble·ness** Nutzlosigkeit *f.*
un·prom·is·ing □ [ˈʌnˈprɔmisiŋ] nicht vielversprechend, aussichtslos.
un·prompt·ed [ʌnˈprɔmptid] unbeeinflußt, spontan.
un·pro·nounce·a·ble □ [ˈʌnprəˈnaunsəbl] schwer auszusprechen(d).
un·pro·pi·tious □ [ˈʌnprəˈpiʃəs] ungünstig, ungeeignet.
un·pro·tect·ed □ [ˈʌnprəˈtektid] ungeschützt.
un·proved [ˈʌnˈpruːvd] unerwiesen.
un·pro·vid·ed [ˈʌnprəˈvaidid] nicht versehen (*with* mit); ~ *for* unversorgt, mittellos.
un·pro·voked □ [ˈʌnprəˈvəukt] unprovoziert; ohne Grund.
un·pub·lished [ˈʌnˈpʌbliʃt] unveröffentlicht.
un·punc·tu·al □ [ˈʌnˈpʌŋktjuəl] unpünktlich; **un·punc·tu·al·i·ty** [ˈ~ˈæliti] Unpünktlichkeit *f.*

un·pun·ished ['ʌn'pʌniʃt] ungestraft; *go* ~ straflos ausgehen.
un·qual·i·fied □ [ʌn'kwɔlifaid] ungeeignet, unqualifiziert; unberechtigt; unbeschränkt; F ausgesprochen (*Lügner etc.*).
un·quench·a·ble □ [ʌn'kwentʃəbl] unlöschbar; *fig.* unstillbar.
un·ques·tion·a·ble □ [ʌn'kwestʃənəbl] unfraglich, fraglos; **un'ques·tioned** ungefragt; unbestritten; **un'ques·tion·ing** □ ohne zu fragen; bedingungslos.
un·qui·et [ʌn'kwaiət] unruhig, ruhelos.
un·quote ['ʌn'kwəut] *Zitat* beenden; **un'quot·ed** *Börse*: nicht notiert.
un·rav·el [ʌn'rævəl] (sich) entwirren; enträtseln.
un·read ['ʌn'red] ungelesen; unbelesen (*Person*); **un·read·a·ble** ['ʌn'ri:dəbl] unleserlich; unlesbar.
un·read·i·ness ['ʌn'redinis] mangelnde Bereitschaft *f*; **'un'read·y** □ nicht bereit *od.* fertig; unlustig, zögernd.
un·re·al □ ['ʌn'riəl] unwirklich; **un·re·al·is·tic** ['ʌnriə'listik] wirklichkeitsfremd, unrealistisch; **un·re·al·i·ty** ['~'æliti] Unwirklichkeit *f*; **'un're·al·iz·a·ble** [~əlaizəbl] nicht zu verwirklichen(d), nicht realisierbar; ✝ unverkäuflich.
un·rea·son ['ʌn'ri:zn] Unvernunft *f*; **un'rea·son·a·ble** □ unvernünftig; grundlos; unmäßig.
un·re·claimed ['ʌnri'kleimd] ungebessert; nicht kultiviert, unbebaut (*Land*).
un·rec·og·niz·a·ble □ ['ʌn'rekəgnaizəbl] nicht wiederzuerkennen(d); **'un'rec·og·nized** nicht (an)erkannt.
un·rec·om·pensed ['ʌn'rekəmpenst] unbelohnt.
un·rec·on·ciled ['ʌn'rekənsaild] unversöhnt.
un·re·cord·ed ['ʌnri'kɔ:did] (geschichtlich) nicht aufgezeichnet.
un·re·dee·med □ ['ʌnri'di:md] unerlöst; uneingelöst (*Pfand, Versprechen*); *fig.* ungemildert (*by* durch).
un·re·dressed ['ʌnri'drest] nicht abgestellt (*Mißstand*); ungesühnt.
un·reel ['ʌn'ri:l] (sich) abhaspeln.
un·re·fined ['ʌnri'faind] ungeläutert; *fig.* ungebildet.
un·re·flect·ing □ ['ʌnri'flektiŋ] gedankenlos.
un·re·formed ['ʌnri'fɔ:md] unverbessert; nicht reformiert.
un·re·gard·ed ['ʌnri'gɑ:did] unbeachtet; unberücksichtigt; **'un·re'gard·ful** [~ful] unachtsam (*of* auf *acc.*).
un·reg·is·tered ['ʌn'redʒistəd] unaufgezeichnet; nicht approbiert (*Arzt etc.*); nicht eingeschrieben (*Brief*).
un·re·gret·ted ['ʌnri'gretid] unbeklagt, unbetrauert.
un·re·lat·ed ['ʌnri'leitid] ohne Beziehung (*to* zu).
un·re·lent·ing □ ['ʌnri'lentiŋ] erbarmungslos; unerbittlich.
un·re·li·a·ble ['ʌnri'laiəbl] unzuverlässig.
un·re·lieved □ ['ʌnri'li:vd] ungelindert; nicht unterbrochen, ununterbrochen.
un·re·mit·ting □ [ʌnri'mitiŋ] unablässig, unaufhörlich; unermüdlich.
un·re·mu·ner·a·tive □ ['ʌnri'mju:nərətiv] nicht lohnend.
un·re·pealed ['ʌnri'pi:ld] unwiderrufen.
un·re·pent·ed ['ʌnri'pentid] unbereut.
un·re·pin·ing □ ['ʌnri'painiŋ] klaglos; unverdrossen.
un·re·quit·ed □ ['ʌnri'kwaitid] unerwidert; unbelohnt.
un·re·served □ ['ʌnri'zə:vd, *adv.* ~vidli] rückhaltlos; unbeschränkt; ohne Vorbehalt.
un·re·sist·ing □ ['ʌnri'zistiŋ] widerstandslos.
un·re·spon·sive ['ʌnris'pɔnsiv] unempfänglich (*to* für).
un·rest ['ʌn'rest] Unruhe *f*; **'un'rest·ing** □ rastlos.
un·re·strained □ ['ʌnris'treind] ungehemmt; unbeherrscht; unbeschränkt; ungezwungen.
un·re·strict·ed □ ['ʌnris'triktid] uneingeschränkt.
un·re·vealed ['ʌnri'vi:ld] nicht offenbart.
un·re·ward·ed ['ʌnri'wɔ:did] unbelohnt.
un·rhymed ['ʌn'raimd] ungereimt, reimlos.
un·rid·dle ['ʌnridl] enträtseln.

un·rig ⚓ ['ʌn'rig] abtakeln.
un·right·eous □ [ʌn'raitʃəs] ungerecht; unredlich.
un·rip ['ʌn'rip] auftrennen; aufschlitzen.
un·ripe ['ʌn'raip] unreif.
un·ri·val(l)ed [ʌn'raivəld] unvergleichlich, unerreicht, einzigartig.
un·roll ['ʌn'rəul] auf-, entrollen.
un·roof ['ʌn'ru:f] *Haus* abdecken.
un·rope *mount.* ['ʌn'rəup] (sich) ausseilen.
un·ruf·fled ['ʌn'rʌfld] glatt; unerschüttert; ruhig.
un·ruled ['ʌn'ru:ld] unbeherrscht; unliniiert (*Papier*).
un·rul·y [ʌn'ru:li] ungebärdig, unbändig.
un·sad·dle ['ʌn'sædl] absatteln.
un·safe □ ['ʌn'seif] unsicher.
un·said ['ʌn'sed] ungesagt.
un·sal·a·ried ['ʌn'sælərid] unbezahlt, ehrenamtlich.
un·sal(e)·a·ble ['ʌn'seiləbl] unverkäuflich.
un·salt·ed ['ʌn'sɔ:ltid] ungesalzen.
un·sanc·tioned ['ʌn'sæŋkʃənd] unbestätigt; unerlaubt.
un·san·i·tar·y ['ʌn'sænitəri] unhygienisch.
un·sat·is·fac·to·ry □ ['ʌnsætis'fæktəri] unbefriedigend; unzulänglich; '**un'sat·is·fied** [~faid] unbefriedigt; '**un'sat·is·fy·ing** □ [~faiiŋ] = *unsatisfactory*.
un·sa·vo(u)r·y □ ['ʌn'seivəri] unappetitlich (*a. fig.*), widerwärtig.
un·say ['ʌn'sei] (*irr. say*) zurücknehmen, widerrufen.
un·scathed ['ʌn'skeiðd] unbeschädigt, unversehrt.
un·schooled ['ʌn'sku:ld] ungeschult; unverbildet.
un·sci·en·tif·ic ['ʌnsaiən'tifik] (*~ally*) unwissenschaftlich.
un·screw ['ʌn'skru:] (sich) ab-, los-, aufschrauben.
un·script·ur·al □ ['ʌn'skriptʃərəl] schriftwidrig, nicht biblisch.
un·scru·pu·lous □ [ʌn'skru:pjuləs] bedenkenlos; gewissenlos; skrupellos.
un·seal ['ʌn'si:l] entsiegeln.
un·search·a·ble □ [ʌn'sə:tʃəbl] unerforschlich; unergründlich.
un·sea·son·a·ble □ [ʌn'si:znəbl] unzeitig; *fig.* ungelegen; '**un'sea·soned** nicht abgelagert (*Holz*); *fig.* nicht abgehärtet; ungewürzt.
un·seat ['ʌn'si:t] aus dem Amt entfernen; aus dem Sattel heben, abwerfen; *be ~ed* s-n Sitz *im Parlament* verlieren; (vom Pferd) stürzen.
un·sea·wor·thy ⚓ ['ʌn'si:wə:ði] seeuntüchtig.
un·see·ing *fig.* ['ʌn'si:iŋ] blind.
un·seem·li·ness [ʌn'si:mlinis] Unziemlichkeit *f*; **un'seem·ly** unziemlich, unpassend.
un·seen ['ʌn'si:n] **1.** ungesehen; unsichtbar; **2.** *Schule*: Übersetzung *f* e-s unbekannten Textes; *the ~* die unsichtbare Welt.
un·self·ish □ ['ʌn'selfiʃ] selbstlos, uneigennützig; '**un'self·ish·ness** Selbstlosigkeit *f*.
un·sen·ti·men·tal ['ʌnsenti'mentl] unsentimental.
un·serv·ice·a·ble □ ['ʌn'sə:visəbl] undienlich; unbrauchbar.
un·set·tle ['ʌn'setl] in Unordnung bringen; verwirren; erschüttern; '**un'set·tled** nicht festgesetzt, unbestimmt; unbeständig, schwankend (*a. Wetter*, ⚕ *Markt*); ⚕ unbezahlt; unerledigt (*Frage*); ohne festen Wohnsitz; unbesiedelt (*Land*).
un·sex ['ʌn'seks] entweiben.
un·shack·le ['ʌn'ʃækl] entfesseln.
un·shak(e)·a·ble ['ʌn'ʃeikəbl] unerschütterlich.
un·shak·en ['ʌn'ʃeikən] unerschüttert; unerschütterlich.
un·shape·ly ['ʌn'ʃeipli] ungestalt.
un·shav·en ['ʌn'ʃeivn] unrasiert.
un·sheathe ['ʌn'ʃi:ð] aus der Scheide ziehen.
un·shell ['ʌn'ʃel] (ab)schälen.
un·ship ['ʌn'ʃip] ausschiffen, ausladen; F *fig. j.* ausbooten.
un·shod ['ʌn'ʃɔd] unbeschuht; unbeschlagen (*Pferd*).
un·shorn ['ʌn'ʃɔ:n] ungeschoren.
un·shrink·a·ble ['ʌn'ʃriŋkəbl] nicht einlaufend (*Stoff*); '**un'shrink·ing** □ unverzagt.
un·sight ['ʌn'sait] die Sicht nehmen; **un'sight·ly** häßlich.
un·signed ['ʌn'saind] nicht unterzeichnet.
un·sized[1] ['ʌn'saizd] ungrundiert; ungeleimt (*Papier*).
un·sized[2] [~] nicht nach Größen geordnet; unsortiert.
un·skil(l)·ful □ ['ʌn'skilful] un-

geschickt; ˈ**unˈskilled** ungelernt (*Arbeit, Arbeiter*).
un·skimmed [ˈʌnˈskimd] nicht entrahmt.
un·sleep·ing [ˈʌnˈsli:piŋ] schlaflos.
un·so·cia·ble [ʌnˈsəuʃəbl] ungesellig; **unˈso·cial** ungesellig; unsozial.
un·sold [ˈʌnˈsəuld] unverkauft.
un·sol·der [ˈʌnˈsɔldə] los-, ablöten.
un·sol·dier·ly *adj.* [ˈʌnˈsəuldʒəli] unsoldatisch, unkriegerisch.
un·so·lic·it·ed [ˈʌnsəˈlisitid] unverlangt (*Sache*); unaufgefordert (*Person*).
un·solv·a·ble [ˈʌnˈsɔlvəbl] unlösbar; ˈ**unˈsolved** ungelöst.
un·so·phis·ti·cat·ed [ˈʌnsəˈfistikeitid] unverfälscht; ungekünstelt; unverdorben, unverbildet.
un·sought [ˈʌnˈsɔ:t] ungesucht.
un·sound □ [ˈʌnˈsaund] ungesund; verdorben; wurmstichig; morsch; nicht stichhaltig (*Beweis*); verkehrt; *of ~ mind* geistig nicht gesund; *~ doctrine* Irrlehre *f*.
un·spar·ing □ [ˈʌnˈspɛəriŋ] nicht kargend, freigebig (*of, in* mit); schonungslos, unbarmherzig (*of* gegen).
un·speak·a·ble □ [ʌnˈspi:kəbl] unsagbar; unsäglich.
un·spec·i·fied [ˈʌnˈspesifaid] nicht spezifiziert.
un·spent [ˈʌnˈspent] unverbraucht; unerschöpft.
un·spoiled [ˈʌnˈspɔild], ˈ**unˈspoilt** [~t] unverdorben; unbeschädigt; nicht verzogen (*Kind*).
un·spo·ken [ˈʌnˈspəukən] ungesagt; *~-of* unerwähnt.
un·sport·ing [ˈʌnˈspɔ:tiŋ], **un·sports·man·like** [ˈʌnˈspɔ:tsmənlaik] unsportlich, unfair, unkameradschaftlich; unweidmännisch.
un·spot·ted [ˈʌnˈspɔtid] ungefleckt; *fig.* unbefleckt.
un·sta·ble □ [ˈʌnˈsteibl] nicht (stand)fest; unbeständig; unstet(ig); labil.
un·stained *fig.* [ˈʌnˈsteind] unbefleckt.
un·stamped [ˈʌnˈstæmpt] ungestempelt; ✆ unfrankiert.
un·states·man·like [ˈʌnˈsteitsmənlaik] unstaatsmännisch.
un·stead·y □ [ˈʌnˈstedi] unstet(ig), unsicher; schwankend; unbeständig; unsolid; unregelmäßig.
un·stint·ed [ʌnˈstintid] unverkürzt, unbeschränkt.
un·stitch [ˈʌnˈstitʃ] auftrennen.
un·stop [ˈʌnˈstɔp] durchgängig machen.
un·strained [ˈʌnˈstreind] ungefiltert; *fig.* ungezwungen.
un·strap [ˈʌnˈstræp] los-, abschnallen.
un·stressed [ˈʌnˈstrest] unbetont.
un·string [ˈʌnˈstriŋ] (*irr. string*) *Bogen, Saite* entspannen; *Perlen etc.* abfädeln; **un·strung** [ˈʌnˈstrʌŋ] saitenlos; entspannt; *fig.* abgespannt, nervös, überdreht.
un·stuck [ˈʌnˈstʌk]: *come ~* aufgehen, sich lösen; *sl.* ins Wasser fallen, danebengehen.
un·stud·ied [ˈʌnˈstʌdid] ungesucht, ungekünstelt, natürlich.
un·sub·dued [ˈʌnsəbˈdju:d] unbesiegt, nicht unterjocht.
un·sub·mis·sive □ [ˈʌnsəbˈmisiv] nicht unterwürfig, widerspenstig.
un·sub·stan·tial □ [ˈʌnsəbˈstænʃəl] wesenlos; gegenstandslos; unsolid; gehaltlos; dürftig.
un·suc·cess·ful □ [ˈʌnsəkˈsesful] erfolglos, ohne Erfolg; ˈ**un·sucˈcess·ful·ness** Erfolglosigkeit *f*.
un·suit·a·ble □ [ˈʌnˈsju:təbl] unpassend; unangemessen; ˈ**unˈsuit·ed** ungeeignet (*for, to* für, zu).
un·sul·lied [ˈʌnˈsʌlid] unbefleckt.
un·sup·port·ed [ˈʌnsəˈpɔ:tid] ungestützt; nicht bestätigt; ohne Unterstützung.
un·sure [ˈʌnˈʃuə] unsicher.
un·sur·passed [ˈʌnsə:ˈpɑ:st] unübertroffen.
un·sus·pect·ed [ˈʌnsəsˈpektid] unverdächtig; unvermutet; ˈ**un·susˈpect·ing** nichts ahnend, *pred.* ohne Ahnung (*of* von); arglos.
un·sus·pi·cious □ [ˈʌnsəsˈpiʃəs] nicht argwöhnisch, arglos.
un·swear [ˈʌnˈswɛə] (*irr. swear*) abschwören.
un·swerv·ing □ [ˈʌnˈswə:viŋ] unentwegt.
un·sworn [ˈʌnˈswɔ:n] ungeschworen; unvereidigt (*Zeuge*).
un·tack [ˈʌnˈtæk] losmachen.
un·taint·ed □ [ˈʌnˈteintid] unbefleckt; *fig.* fleckenlos; unverdorben.
un·tam(e)·a·ble [ˈʌnˈteiməbl] unbezähmbar; ˈ**unˈtamed** ungezähmt.

un·tan·gle ['ʌn'tæŋgl] entwirren.
un·tanned ['ʌn'tænd] ungegerbt.
un·tar·nished ['ʌn'tɑ:niʃt] unbefleckt; ungetrübt.
un·tast·ed ['ʌn'teistid] ungekostet.
un·taught ['ʌn'tɔ:t] ungelehrt.
un·taxed ['ʌn'tækst] unbesteuert.
un·teach·a·ble ['ʌn'ti:tʃəbl] unbelehrbar (*Person*); unlehrbar (*Sache*).
un·tem·per·a·men·tal ['ʌntempərə'mentl] temperamentlos.
un·tem·pered ['ʌn'tempəd] ⊕ ungehärtet; ungemildert.
un·ten·a·ble ['ʌn'tenəbl] unhaltbar.
un·ten·ant·ed ['ʌn'tenəntid] unvermietet, unbewohnt.
un·thank·ful □ ['ʌn'θæŋkful] undankbar.
un·think·a·ble [ʌn'θiŋkəbl] undenkbar; **un'think·ing** □ gedankenlos.
un·thought ['ʌn'θɔ:t] unbedacht; ~-*of* unvermutet.
un·thread ['ʌn'θred] ausfädeln; *fig.* sich hindurchfinden durch.
un·thrift·y □ ['ʌn'θrifti] verschwenderisch; nicht gedeihend.
un·ti·dy □ [ʌn'taidi] unordentlich.
un·tie ['ʌn'tai] aufbinden, -knoten, -knüpfen; *Knoten etc.* lösen; *j.* losbinden.
un·til [ən'til] **1.** *prp.* bis; **2.** *cj.* bis (daß); *not* ~ erst wenn *od.* als.
un·tilled ['ʌn'tild] unbebaut (*Acker*).
un·time·ly [ʌn'taimli] unzeitig; vorzeitig; früh(zeitig); ungelegen.
un·tir·ing □ [ʌn'taiəriŋ] unermüdlich.
un·to ['ʌntu] = *to*.
un·told ['ʌn'təuld] unerzählt; ungezählt; unermeßlich, unsäglich.
un·touched ['ʌn'tʌtʃt] unberührt; *fig.* ungerührt; *phot.* unretuschiert.
un·to·ward [ʌn'təuəd] unglücklich; ungünstig; widerspenstig.
un·trained ['ʌn'treind] undressiert; unerzogen; untrainiert.
un·tram·mel(l)ed [ʌn'træməld] ungebunden, ungehindert.
un·trans·fer·a·ble ['ʌntræns'fə:rəbl] nicht übertragbar.
un·trans·lat·a·ble ['ʌntræns'leitəbl] unübersetzbar.
un·trav·el(l)ed ['ʌn'trævld] unbereist; ungereist (*Person*).
un·tried ['ʌn'traid] unversucht; unerprobt; ⚖ ununtersucht (*Fall*); nicht vernommen; nicht abgeurteilt (*Angeklagter*).
un·trimmed ['ʌn'trimd] nicht in Ordnung (gebracht); unbeschnitten (*Haar etc.*); ungeschmückt.
un·trod, un·trod·den ['ʌn'trɔd(n)] unbetreten.
un·trou·bled ['ʌn'trʌbld] ungestört, unbelästigt.
un·true □ ['ʌn'tru:] unwahr; untreu.
un·trust·wor·thy □ ['ʌn'trʌstwə:ði] nicht vertrauenswürdig.
un·truth ['ʌn'tru:θ] Unwahrheit *f.*
un·tu·tored ['ʌn'tju:təd] unerzogen, ungebildet.
un·twine ['ʌn'twain], **un·twist** ['ʌn'twist] *v/t.* aufdrehen; aufflechten; entwirren; *v/i.* aufgehen.
un·used ['ʌn'ju:zd] ungebraucht; ['ʌn'ju:st] nicht gewöhnt (*to* an *acc.*; zu *inf.*); **un·u·su·al** □ [ʌn'ju:ʒuəl] ungewöhnlich; ungewohnt.
un·ut·ter·a·ble □ [ʌn'ʌtərəbl] unaussprechlich.
un·val·ued ['ʌn'vælju:d] nicht (ab-) geschätzt.
un·var·ied [ʌn'vɛərid] unverändert.
un·var·nished ['ʌn'vɑ:niʃt] ungefirnißt; *fig.* ungeschminkt.
un·var·y·ing □ [ʌn'vɛəriiŋ] unveränderlich.
un·veil [ʌn'veil] entschleiern, enthüllen.
un·versed ['ʌn'və:st] unbewandert, unerfahren (*in* in *dat.*).
un·voiced ['ʌn'vɔist] nicht ausgesprochen; stimmlos (*Konsonant*).
un·vouched ['ʌn'vautʃt] *a.* ~-*for* unverbürgt, unbezeugt.
un·want·ed ['ʌn'wɔntid] unerwünscht.
un·war·i·ness [ʌn'wɛərinis] Unbedachtsamkeit *f.*
un·war·like ['ʌn'wɔ:laik] unkriegerisch.
un·war·rant·a·ble □ [ʌn'wɔrəntəbl] unverantwortlich; **'un'war·rant·ed** unberechtigt; unverbürgt.
un·war·y □ ['ʌn'wɛəri] unbedachtsam.
un·washed ['ʌn'wɔʃt] ungewaschen.
un·wa·tered ['ʌn'wɔ:təd] unbewässert; unverwässert (*Milch, Kapital*).
un·wa·ver·ing [ʌn'weivəriŋ] unerschütterlich.
un·wea·ried [ʌn'wiərid], **un·wea·ry·ing** □ [ʌn'wiəriiŋ] unermüdlich.
un·wel·come [ʌn'welkəm] unwillkommen.

un·well [ˈʌnˈwel] unwohl.

un·whole·some [ˈʌnˈhəulsəm] ungesund; schädlich.

un·wield·y □ [ʌnˈwiːldi] unhandlich; ungefüge; sperrig.

un·will·ing □ [ˈʌnˈwiliŋ] un-, widerwillig, abgeneigt; *be ~ to do* nicht tun wollen; *be ~ for s.th. to be done* nicht wollen, daß et. getan wird.

un·wind [ˈʌnˈwaind] (*irr. wind*) auf-, loswickeln; (sich) auf-, abwickeln.

un·wis·dom [ˈʌnˈwizdəm] Unklugheit *f*; **un·wise** □ [ˈʌnˈwaiz] unklug.

un·wished [ʌnˈwiʃt] ungewünscht; *~-for* unerwünscht.

un·wit·ting □ [ʌnˈwitiŋ] unwissentlich; unwillentlich, unbeabsichtigt.

un·wom·an·ly [ʌnˈwumənli] unweiblich.

un·wont·ed □ [ʌnˈwəuntid] ungewohnt; nicht gewöhnt (*to* an *acc.*).

un·work·a·ble [ˈʌnˈwəːkəbl] nicht zu bearbeiten(d); undurchführbar; ⊕ betriebsunfähig.

un·world·ly [ˈʌnˈwəːldli] unweltlich.

un·wor·thy □ [ʌnˈwəːði] unwürdig.

un·wound·ed [ˈʌnˈwuːndid] unverwundet.

un·wrap [ˈʌnˈræp] auswickeln, -packen; aufwickeln.

un·wrin·kle [ˈʌnˈriŋkl] entrunzeln.

un·writ·ten [ˈʌnˈritn] ungeschrieben (*Gesetz*); unbeschrieben (*Seite*).

un·wrought [ˈʌnˈrɔːt] unbearbeitet; roh; Roh...

un·yield·ing □ [ʌnˈjiːldiŋ] unnachgiebig.

un·yoke [ˈʌnˈjəuk] ausspannen.

un·zip [ʌnˈzip] den Reißverschluß aufmachen an.

up [ʌp] **1.** *adv.* (her-, hin)auf; aufwärts, empor; oben, in der Höhe; auf(gestanden); aufgegangen (*Sonne etc.*); abgelaufen (*Zeit*); in Aufregung, in Wallung; nach London *od.* Oxford *od.* Cambridge; *Am. Baseball*: am Schlag; *come ~ to s.o.* auf j. zukommen; *~ and about* wieder auf den Beinen; *be hard ~* in Geldschwierigkeiten *od.* schlecht bei Kasse sein; *~ against a task* einer Aufgabe gegenüber; *~ to* bis an (*acc.*), bis auf (*acc.*); *s. date*[2] *1*; *be ~ to s.th.* e-r Sache gewachsen sein; *fig.* an et. herankommen; et. im Schilde führen; *it is ~ to me to do* es ist meine Sache zu tun; *s. mark 1*; *the time is ~* die Zeit ist um; *what are you ~ to there?* was macht ihr da?; *what's ~ sl.* was ist los?; *~ with* auf gleicher Höhe mit; *it's all ~ with him* es ist aus mit ihm; **2.** *int.* auf!; herauf!; heran!; hoch!; **3.** *prp.* hinauf, auf; *~ the hill* den Berg hinauf, bergan; **4.** *adj. ~ train* Zug *m* nach der Stadt; **5.** *the ~s and downs* das Auf und Ab, die Höhen und Tiefen *des Lebens*; **6.** F (sich) erheben, hochfahren; hochtreiben.

up-and-com·ing *Am.* F [ˈʌpənˈkʌmiŋ] unternehmungslustig; vielversprechend.

up·beat [ˈʌpbiːt] ♪ Auftakt *m*; Anakrusis *f*.

up·braid [ʌpˈbreid] vorwerfen (*s.o. with od. for s.th.* j-m et.).

up·bring·ing [ˈʌpbriŋiŋ] Aufziehen *n*, Aufzucht *f*; Erziehung *f*.

up·build [ˈʌpˈbild] (*irr. build*) aufbauen.

up·cast [ˈʌpkɑːst] Hochwurf *m*; *a. ~ shaft* ⚒ Luftschacht *m*.

up·com·ing *Am.* [ˈʌpkʌmiŋ] bevorstehend, kommend.

up-coun·try [ˈʌpˈkʌntri] landeinwärts (gelegen).

up-cur·rent ✈ [ˈʌpkʌrənt] Aufwind *m*.

up·date **1.** [ʌpˈdeit] auf den neuesten Stand bringen; **2.** [ˈʌpdeit] neuester Bericht *m*.

up·end [ʌpˈend] hochkant stellen.

up·grade **1.** [ˈʌpgreid] Steigung *f*; *on the ~ fig.* im Aufsteigen; **2.** [ʌpˈgreid] höher einstufen, aufwerten.

up·heav·al [ʌpˈhiːvəl] *geol.* Hebung *f*; *fig.* Umwälzung *f*, Umsturz *m*.

up·hill [ˈʌpˈhil] bergan; mühsam.

up·hold [ʌpˈhəuld] (*irr. hold*) aufrecht(er)halten; stützen; **upˈhold·er** *fig.* Stütze *f*, Verteidiger *m*.

up·hol·ster [ʌpˈhəulstə] *Möbel* (auf)polstern; *Zimmer* dekorieren; **upˈhol·ster·er** Tapezierer *m*, Dekorateur *m*, Polsterer *m*; **upˈhol·ster·y** Polstermöbel *n/pl.*; Polsterung *f*, Tapezierarbeit *f*; Zimmerdekoration *f*.

up·keep [ˈʌpkiːp] Instandhaltung(skosten *pl.*) *f*; Unterhalt *m von Personen*.

up·land [ˈʌplənd] **1.** *oft ~s pl.*

Hoch-, Oberland *n*; **2.** Hoch-, Oberland(s)...

up·lift 1. [ʌpˈlift] *fig.* emporheben; **2.** [ˈ~] Erhebung *f*; *fig.* Aufschwung *m*; moralische Unterstützung *f*.

up·most [ˈʌpməust] = *uppermost*.

up·on [əˈpɔn] = *on*.

up·per [ˈʌpə] **1.** ober; Ober...; *the ~ ten (thousand)* die oberen Zehntausend *pl.*; **2.** *mst ~s pl.* Oberleder *n*; F *be (down) on one's ~s* F total pleite *od.* abgebrannt sein; **ˈ~-class** ... der Oberschicht; vornehm; **~ class** (**-es** *pl.*) Oberschicht *f*; **~ crust** Erdkruste *f*; *the ~* F die oberen Zehntausend *pl.*; **ˈ~cut** *Boxen*: Aufwärts-, Kinnhaken *m*; **ˈ~·most** oberst, höchst.

up·pish □ F [ˈʌpiʃ] hochnäsig, eingebildet.

up·pi·ty F [ˈʌpiti] eingebildet; dreist.

up·raise [ʌpˈreiz] erheben.

up·rear [ʌpˈriə] aufrichten.

up·right 1. □ [ˈʌpˈrait] aufrecht (stehend); senkrecht; *fig.* [ˈ~] aufrecht, aufrichtig, gerade; **2.** [ˈ~] Pfosten *m*; Ständer *m*; = **~ pia·no** ♪ Klavier *n*.

up·ris·ing [ʌpˈraiziŋ] Aufstehen *n*; Erhebung *f*, Aufstand *m*.

up·roar *fig.* [ˈʌprɔː] Aufruhr *m*, Tumult *m*; Lärm *m*; Toben *n*; **upˈroar·i·ous** □ lärmend, tobend; tosend (*Beifall etc.*).

up·root [ʌpˈruːt] entwurzeln; (her-) ausreißen.

up·set [ʌpˈset] **1.** (*irr. set*) umwerfen (*a. fig.*); (um)stürzen; außer Fassung *od.* in Unordnung bringen; stören; verwirren; beunruhigen; ⊕ stauchen; *be ~* außer sich sein; **2.** Aufregung *f*, Ärger *m*; *Sport*: Überraschung *f*; *stomach ~* Magenverstimmung *f*; **~ price** Anschlagspreis *m bei Auktionen*.

up·shot [ˈʌpʃɔt] Ausgang *m*, Ende *n*, Ergebnis *n*; *in the ~* am Ende.

up·side *adv.* [ˈʌpsaid]: *~ down* das Oberste zuunterst; *fig.* drunter und drüber; verkehrt; *turn ~ down* auf den Kopf stellen.

up·stage F *fig.* [ˈʌpˈsteidʒ] von oben herab; hochnäsig, eingebildet.

up·stairs [ˈʌpˈsteəz] oben *im Hause*; nach oben.

up·stand·ing [ʌpˈstændiŋ] aufrecht; stramm.

up·start [ˈʌpstɑːt] **1.** Emporkömmling *m*; **2.** emporkommen.

up·state *Am.* [ˈʌpˈsteit] Hinterland *n e-s Staates, bsd. nördlich New York*.

up·stream [ˈʌpˈstriːm] fluß-, stromaufwärts (gelegen, gerichtet).

up·stroke [ˈʌpstrəuk] Aufstrich *m beim Schreiben*.

up·surge [ˈʌpsəːdʒ] Aufwallung *f*.

up·swing [ˈʌpswiŋ] Aufschwung *m*.

up·take [ˈʌpteik] Auffassung(svermögen *n*) *f*; *be slow (quick) in od. on the ~* F e-e lange (kurze) Leitung haben.

up·throw [ˈʌpθrəu] Umwälzung *f*.

up·tight F [ʌpˈtait] verärgert; nervös; steif, förmlich; puritanisch; verklemmt.

up-to-date [ˈʌptəˈdeit] modern, neuzeitlich.

up-to-the-min·ute [ˈʌptəðəˈminit] modernst, allerneu(e)st.

up·town [ˈʌpˈtaun] im *od.* in den oberen Stadtteil; *Am.* im Wohn- *od.* Villenviertel.

up·turn [ʌpˈtəːn] emporrichten; nach oben kehren.

up·ward [ˈʌpwəd] **1.** *adj.* nach oben gerichtet; **2.** *adv.* = **up·wards** [ˈ~z] aufwärts; darüber (hinaus); *~ of* mehr als.

u·ra·ni·um ⚗ [juəˈreinjəm] Uran *n*.

ur·ban [ˈəːbən] städtisch; Stadt...; *~ guerilla* Stadtguerilla *m*; **ur·bane** □ [əːˈbein] höflich; gebildet, urban, weltmännisch; **ur·ban·i·ty** [əːˈbæniti] Höflichkeit *f*; Bildung *f*; **ur·ban·i·za·tion** [əːbənaiˈzeiʃən] Verstädterung *f*; **ˈur·ban·ize** verstädtern.

ur·chin [ˈəːtʃin] Bengel *m*.

u·re·thra *anat.* [juəˈriːθrə] Harnröhre *f*.

urge [əːdʒ] **1.** *oft ~ on j.* drängen, (an)treiben; *fig.* nötigen (*to* zu), dringen in *j.* (*to inf.* zu *inf.*); dringen auf *e-e Sache*; nachdrücklich betonen; geltend machen; *~ s.th. on s.o.* j-m et. eindringlich vorstellen; j-m et. einschärfen; **2.** *innerer* Drang *m*; **ur·gen·cy** [ˈəːdʒənsi] Dringlichkeit *f*; Drängen *n*; **ˈur·gent** □ dringend; dringlich; eilig; *be ~ with s.o. to inf.* in j. dringen zu *inf.*

u·ric ⚗ [ˈjuərik] Harn...

u·ri·nal [ˈjuərinl] Harnglas *n*; Bedürfnisanstalt *f*; **ˈu·ri·nar·y** Harn...; **u·ri·nate** [ˈ~neit] urinieren; **ˈu·rine** Urin *m*, Harn *m*.

urn [əːn] Urne *f*; Kaffee- *od.* Tee-

maschine *f.*
us [ʌs, əs] uns; *all of* ~ wir alle.
us·a·ble ['ju:zəbl] brauch-, verwendbar.
us·age ['ju:zidʒ] Brauch *m*, Gepflogenheit *f*, Usus *m*; Sprachgebrauch *m*; Behandlung *f*, Verwendung *f*, Gebrauch *m*.
us·ance ✝ ['ju:zəns] Wechselfrist *f*, Uso *m*; *bill at* ~ Usowechsel *m*.
use 1. [ju:s] Gebrauch *m*; Benutzung *f*; An-, Verwendung *f*; Gewohnheit *f*, Übung *f*; Brauch *m*; Nutzen *m*; *be of* ~ von Nutzen *od.* nützlich sein; *it is (of) no* ~ *ger. od. to inf.* es ist unnütz *od.* es hat keinen Zweck zu *inf.*; *have no* ~ *for* keine Verwendung haben für; *Am.* F nicht mögen; *put to* ~ nutzbar anwenden; **2.** [ju:z] gebrauchen; benutzen, ver-, anwenden; behandeln; ~ *up* ver-, aufbrauchen; *I* ~*d* ['ju:s(t)] *to do* ich pflegte zu tun, früher tat ich; *used* ['ju:st] *to* gewöhnt an (*acc.*); **use·ful** □ ['ju:sful] brauchbar; nützlich; von Nutzen; ⊕ Nutz...; '**use·ful·ness** Nützlichkeit *f etc.*; '**use·less** □ nutz-, zwecklos, unnütz; unbrauchbar; '**use·less·ness** Nutzlosigkeit *f*; **us·er** ['ju:zə] Benutzer(in).
ush·er ['ʌʃə] **1.** Türhüter *m*, Pförtner *m*; Gerichtsdiener *m*; Platzanweiser *m*; *contp.* Hilfslehrer *m*; **2.** *mst* ~ *in* (hin)einführen, anmelden; *fig.* einleiten; **ush·er·ette** [~'ret] Platzanweiserin *f*.
u·su·al □ ['ju:ʒuəl] gewöhnlich; üblich; gebräuchlich; '**u·su·al·ly** gewöhnlich, normalerweise.
u·su·fruct ⚖ ['ju:sju:frʌkt] Nutznießung *f*; **u·su'fruc·tu·ar·y** [~tjuəri] Nutznießer(in).
u·su·rer ['ju:ʒərə] Wucherer *m*; **u·su·ri·ous** □ [ju:'zjuəriəs] wucherisch; Wucher...
u·surp [ju:'zə:p] sich *et.* widerrechtlich aneignen, an sich reißen; **u·sur'pa·tion** widerrechtliche Aneignung *f*, Usurpation *f*; **u'surp·er** unrechtmäßiger Machthaber *m od.* Besitzer *m*, Usurpator *m*; **u'surp·ing** □ eigenmächtig.
u·su·ry ['ju:ʒuri] Wucher *m*; Wucherzinsen *m/pl.*
u·ten·sil [ju:'tensl] Gerät *n*; Geschirr *n*; ~*s pl.* Utensilien *pl.*
u·ter·ine ['ju:tərain] Gebärmutter...; ~ *brother* Halbbruder *m*; **u·ter·us** *anat.* ['~rəs] Gebärmutter *f*.
u·til·i·tar·i·an [ju:tili'tɛəriən] **1.** Utilitarist *m*, Vertreter *m* des Nützlichkeitsprinzips; **2.** utilitaristisch; **u'til·i·ty 1.** Nützlichkeit *f*, Nutzen *m*; *public* ~ öffentlicher Versorgungsbetrieb *m*; **2.** Gebrauchs..., Einheits... (*Kleidung, Wagen etc.*).
u·ti·li·za·tion [ju:tilai'zeiʃən] Nutzbarmachung *f*, Nutzanwendung *f*; '**u·ti·lize** sich *et.* nutzbar *od.* zunutze machen.
ut·most ['ʌtməust] äußerst.
U·to·pi·an [ju:'təupjən] **1.** utopisch; **2.** Utopist(in), Schwärmer (-in).
ut·ter ['ʌtə] **1.** □ *fig.* äußerst, völlig, gänzlich; ausgesprochen, entschieden; **2.** äußern; *Seufzer etc.* ausstoßen, von sich geben; Falschgeld *etc.* in Umlauf setzen; '**ut·ter·ance** Äußerung *f*, Ausdruck *m*; Aussprache *f*; *give* ~ *to* Ausdruck geben (*dat.*); '**ut·ter·er** Äußernde *m*; Verbreiter(in); '**ut·ter·most** äußerst.
U-turn ['ju:tə:n] Wende *f auf der Straße*; F *fig.* (totale) Kehrtwendung *f*, (völliger) Umschwung *m*.
u·vu·la *anat.* ['ju:vjulə] Zäpfchen *n*; '**u·vu·lar** Zäpfchen...
ux·o·ri·ous [ʌk'sɔ:riəs] treuergeben (*Ehemann*).

V

vac F [væk] = *vacation.*
va·can·cy ['veikənsi] Leere *f* (*a. fig.*); leerer *od.* freier Platz *m*, Lücke *f*; Vakanz *f*, offene Stelle *f*; *gaze into* ~ ins Leere starren; '**va·can·cies** *pl. Zeitung*: Stellenangebote *n/pl.*;

ˈ**va·cant** □ leer (*a. fig.*); frei (*Zeit, Zimmer*); offen (*Stelle*); unbesetzt, vakant (*Amt*); ~ *possession* sofort beziehbar.
va·cate [vəˈkeit, *Am.* ˈveikeit] *Haus* räumen; *Stelle* aufgeben, aus *e-m Amt* scheiden; **vaˈca·tion 1.** (Schul)Ferien *pl.*; Räumung *f*; Niederlegung *f e-s Amtes*; **2.** *Am.* Urlaub machen; **va·ˈca·tion·ist** *Am.* Ferienreisende *m, f.*
vac·ci·nate [ˈvæksineit] impfen; **vac·ciˈna·tion** Impfung *f*; ˈ**vac·ci·na·tor** Impfarzt *m*; **vac·cine** [ˈ~siːn] Impfstoff *m.*
vac·il·late [ˈvæsileit] schwanken; **vac·ilˈla·tion** Schwanken *n.*
va·cu·i·ty [væˈkjuːiti] Leere *f* (*mst fig.*); **vac·u·ous** □ [ˈvækjuəs] *fig.* leer, geistlos; **vac·u·um** [ˈ~əm] **1.** *phys.* Vakuum *n* (*bsd.* luft)leerer Raum *m*; ~ *brake* Unterdruckbremse *f*; ~ *cleaner* Staubsauger *m*; ~ *flask*, ~ *bottle* Thermosflasche *f*; ~-*packed* vakuumverpackt; ~ *tube* Vakuumröhre *f*; **2.** (mit dem Staubsauger) saugen.
va·de-me·cum [ˈveidiˈmiːkəm] Vademekum *n*, Handbuch *n.*
vag·a·bond [ˈvægəbɔnd] **1.** vagabundierend (*a.* ⚡); umherstreifend; Vagabunden...; **2.** Landstreicher *m*, Vagabund *m*; Strolch *m*; ˈ**vag·a·bond·age** Landstreicherei *f.*
va·gar·y [ˈveigəri] wunderlicher Einfall *m*, Laune *f*, Schrulle *f.*
va·gi·na *anat.* [vəˈdʒainə] Scheide *f.*
va·gran·cy [ˈveigrənsi] Landstreicherei *f*; ˈ**va·grant 1.** wandernd; *fig.* unstet; **2.** = *vagabond* 2.
vague □ [veig] vag, unbestimmt; verschwommen, unklar; ˈ**vague·ness** Unbestimmtheit *f.*
vail † *od. poet.* [veil] *Fahne* senken; *Hut* abnehmen.
vain □ [vein] eitel, eingebildet (*of* auf *acc.*); *fig.* eitel, leer; nichtig; vergeblich; *in* ~ vergebens, umsonst; ~**·glo·ri·ous** □ [~ˈglɔːriəs] prahlerisch; ~ˈ**glo·ry** Prahlerei *f.*
val·ance [ˈvæləns] Volant *m.*
vale [veil] *poet. od. in Namen*: Tal *n.*
val·e·dic·tion [væliˈdikʃən] Abschied(sworte *n/pl.*) *m*; **val·eˈdic·to·ry** [~təri] **1.** Abschieds...; **2.** Abschiedsrede *f.*
va·lence ⚗ [ˈveiləns] Wertigkeit *f.*
val·en·tine [ˈvæləntain] Valentinsschatz *m*, -gruß *m* (*am Valentinstag, 14. Februar, erwählt, gesandt*).
va·le·ri·an ⚘ [vəˈliəriən] Baldrian *m.*
val·et [ˈvælit] **1.** (Kammer)Diener *m*; **2.** Diener sein bei *j-m*; *j.* bedienen.
val·e·tu·di·nar·i·an [ˈvælitjuːdiˈnɛəriən] **1.** kränklich; hypochondrisch; **2.** kränklicher Mensch *m*; Hypochonder *m.*
val·iant □ [ˈvæljənt] tapfer.
val·id □ [ˈvælid] triftig, richtig, stichhaltig; (rechts)gültig; *be* ~ gelten; **val·i·date** [ˈ~deit] für gültig erklären; **va·lid·i·ty** [vəˈliditi] Gültigkeit *f*; Triftig-, Richtigkeit *f.*
va·lise [vəˈliːz] Reisetasche *f*; ⚔ Tornister *m.*
val·ley [ˈvæli] Tal *n.*
val·or·i·za·tion [vælǝraiˈzeiʃən] Aufwertung *f*; ˈ**val·or·ize** aufwerten.
val·or·ous □ [ˈvælərəs] tapfer.
val·o(u)r [ˈvælə] Tapferkeit *f.*
val·u·a·ble [ˈvæljuəbl] **1.** □ wertvoll; **2.** ~*s pl.* Wertsachen *f/pl.*
val·u·a·tion [væljuˈeiʃən] Abschätzung *f*; Taxwert *m*; ˈ**val·u·a·tor** Taxator *m*, Schätzer *m.*
val·ue [ˈvæljuː] **1.** Wert *m* (*a. fig.*); Währung *f*, Valuta *f*; *give* (*get*) *good* ~ (*for one's money*) ✝ reell bedienen (bedient werden); ~-*added tax* Mehrwertsteuer *f*; **2.** (ab-) schätzen; werten; *fig.* schätzen, achten; ˈ**val·ued** (hoch)geschätzt; -wertig; **val·ue judg(e)·ment** Werturteil *n*; ˈ**val·ue·less** wertlos; **val·u·er** [ˈvæljuə] (Ab)Schätzer *m*, Taxator *m.*
valve [vælv] Klappe *f* (*a. anat.*, ⚘); Ventil *n*; *Radio*: Röhre *f.*
va·moose *Am. sl.* [væˈmuːs] abhauen; fluchtartig verlassen.
vamp[1] [væmp] **1.** Vorschuh *m*; **2.** vorschuhen; zurechtflicken; ♪ improvisieren.
vamp[2] F [~] **1.** Vamp *m* (*verführerische Frau*); **2.** aussaugen, neppen.
vam·pire [ˈvæmpaiə] Vampir *m.*
van[1] [væn] Möbelwagen *m*; Lieferwagen *m*; 🚃 Packwagen *m*, (geschlossener) Güterwagen *m.*
van[2] ⚔ *od. fig.* [~] Vorhut *f.*
Van·dal [ˈvændəl] *hist.* Vandale *m*; ⁀ *fig.* Vandale *m*, Barbar *m*; ˈ**van·dal·ism** Vandalismus *m*; ˈ**van·dal-**

ize mutwillig zerstören.

van·dyke [væn'daik] Zackenmuster *n*; *attr.* ♀ Van-Dyck-...

vane [vein] Wetterfahne *f*; (Windmühlen-, Propeller)Flügel *m*; *surv.* Visier *n*.

van·guard ⚔ ['vængɑ:d] Vorhut *f*.

va·nil·la ⚘ [və'nilə] Vanille *f*.

van·ish ['væniʃ] (ver)schwinden; ~*ing cream* Tagescreme *f*.

van·i·ty ['væniti] Eitelkeit *f*, Einbildung *f*; Nichtigkeit *f*; Frisiertoilette *f*; ~ *bag* Kosmetiktäschchen *m*.

van·quish ['væŋkwiʃ] besiegen; bezwingen.

van·tage ['vɑ:ntidʒ] *Tennis*: Vorteil *m*; '**~-ground** günstige Stellung *f*.

vap·id □ ['væpid] schal.

va·po(u)r·ize ['veipəraiz] verdampfen, verdunsten (lassen); '**va·po(u)r·iz·er** ⊕ Verdampfer *m*; ⚕ Zerstäuber *m*.

va·por·ous □ ['veipərəs] dunstig; dampfig; *fig.* nebelhaft; duftig (*Gewebe*).

va·po(u)r ['veipə] Dunst *m* (*a. fig.*); Dampf *m*; ~ **bath** Dampfbad *n*; ~ **trail** Kondensstreifen *m e-s Flugzeugs*; '**va·po(u)r·y** = *vaporous*.

var·i·a·bil·i·ty [vɛəriə'biliti] Veränderlichkeit *f*; '**var·i·a·ble** □ veränderlich; '**var·i·ance** Veränderung *f*; Uneinigkeit *f*; *be at* ~ uneinig sein; (sich) widersprechen; *set at* ~ entzweien; '**var·i·ant 1.** abweichend; **2.** Variante *f*; verschiedene Lesart *f*; **var·i'a·tion** Abänderung *f*; Schwankung *f*; Abwechs(e)lung *f*; Abweichung *f*; ♪ Variation *f*.

var·i·cose ⚕ ['værikəus] krampfaderig; ~ *vein* Krampfader *f*.

var·ied □ ['vɛərid] verschieden, verändert, mannigfaltig; **var·i·e·gate** ['~rigeit] bunt gestalten; '**var·i·e·gat·ed** bunt; **var·i·e'ga·tion** Buntheit *f*; **va·ri·e·ty** [və'raiəti] Mannigfaltigkeit *f*, Vielheit *f*, -zahl *f*; Abwechslung *f*; *biol.* Varietät *f*, Spiel-, Abart *f*; *bsd.* ✝ Auswahl *f*; Menge *f*; ~ *show* Varietévorstellung *f*; ~ *theatre* Varietétheater *n*.

va·ri·o·la ⚕ [və'raiələ] Pocken *f/pl.*

var·i·ous □ ['vɛəriəs] verschiedene, mehrere; mannigfaltig; verschiedenartig; wechselvoll.

var·let † ['vɑ:lit] Schurke *m*.

var·mint V, *co.* ['vɑ:mint] *kleiner* Racker *m*.

var·nish ['vɑ:niʃ] **1.** Firnis *m*, Lack *m*; *fig.* (äußerer) Anstrich *m*; **2.** firnissen, lackieren; *fig.* bemänteln, beschönigen.

var·si·ty F ['vɑ:siti] Uni *f*.

var·y ['vɛəri] *v/t.* (ver)ändern; wechseln mit *et.*; *bsd.* ♪ variieren; *v/i.* sich (ver)ändern, wechseln; abweichen, verschieden sein (*from* von).

vas·cu·lar ⚘, *anat.* ['væskjulə] Gefäß...

vase [vɑ:z] Vase *f*.

vas·sal ['væsəl] Vasall *m*; *attr.* Vasallen...; '**vas·sal·age** Vasallentum *n* (*to* gegenüber *dat.*).

vast □ [vɑ:st] ungeheuer, gewaltig, riesig, umfassend, weit; '**vast·ness** ungeheure Größe *f*; Weite *f*.

vat [væt] **1.** *großes* Faß *n*; Bottich *m*; Kufe *f*; (Färber)Küpe *f*; **2.** in ein Faß tun; im Faß behandeln.

vat·ted ['vætid] faßreif (*Wein etc.*).

vaude·ville ['vəudəvil] *Am.* Varieté *n*.

vault[1] [vɔ:lt] **1.** Gewölbe *n*; Wölbung *f*; Stahlkammer *f*; Gruft *f*; **2.** (über)wölben.

vault[2] [~] **1.** *v/i.* springen; *v/t.* springen über (*acc.*); **2.** Sprung *m*.

vault·ing ⚠ ['vɔ:ltiŋ] Gewölbe *n*.

vault·ing-horse ['vɔ:ltiŋhɔ:s] *Turnen*: Pferd *n*.

vaunt *lit.* [vɔ:nt] **1.** (sich) rühmen; **2.** Prahlerei *f*; '**vaunt·ing** □ prahlerisch.

veal [vi:l] Kalbfleisch *n*; *roast* ~ Kalbsbraten *m*.

veer [viə] **1.** (sich) drehen; ~ *round* sich herumdrehen; *fig.* (her)umschwenken; **2.** Schwenkung *f*.

veg F [vedʒ] *mst gekochtes* Gemüse *n*.

veg·e·ta·ble ['vedʒitəbl] **1.** Pflanzen..., pflanzlich; **2.** Pflanze *f*; *mst* ~*s pl.* Gemüse *n*; **veg·e·tar·i·an** [~'tɛəriən] **1.** Vegetarier(in); **2.** vegetarisch; **veg·e·tate** ['~teit] vegetieren; **veg·e'ta·tion** Vegetation *f*; **veg·e·ta·tive** □ ['~tətiv] vegetativ, Wachstums...; wachstumsfördernd.

ve·he·mence ['vi:iməns] Heftigkeit *f*; Gewalt *f*; Ungestüm *n*; Vehemenz *f*; '**ve·he·ment** □ heftig; ungestüm; vehement.

ve·hi·cle ['vi:ikl] Fahrzeug *n*, Beförderungsmittel *n*; *pharm.* Lösemittel *n*; *fig.* Vermittler *m*, Träger *m*; Ausdrucksmittel *n*; **ve·hic·u·lar** □ [vi'hikjulə] Fahrzeug...

veil [veil] **1.** Schleier *m* (*a. phot.*); Hülle *f*; **2.** (sich) verschleiern; *fig.* verhüllen; '**veil·ing** Verschleierung *f* (*bsd. phot.*); ⚕ Schleierstoff *m.*

vein [vein] Ader *f* (*a. fig.*), Vene *f*; Anlage *f*; Neigung *f*; Stimmung *f* (*for* zu); **veined** geädert; '**vein·ing** Äderung *f.*

vel·le·i·ty [ve'li:iti] bloßes Wollen *n*, schwacher Wille *m.*

vel·lum ['veləm] Pergament *n*; *a.* ~ *paper* Velinpapier *n.*

ve·loc·i·pede [vi'lɔsipi:d] *Am.* (Kinder)Dreirad *n*; *hist.* Veloziped *n.*

ve·loc·i·ty [vi'lɔsiti] Geschwindigkeit *f.*

ve·lour(s) [və'luə] Velours *m* (*Samt*).

vel·vet ['velvit] **1.** Samt *m*; *hunt.* Bast *m am neuen Geweih*; **2.** Samt...; samten; **vel·vet·een** [~'ti:n] Baumwollsamt *m*; Manchester *m*; '**vel·vet·y** samtig.

ve·nal ['vi:nl] käuflich, feil; **ve·nal·i·ty** [vi:'næliti] Käuflichkeit *f.*

vend [vend] verkaufen; '**vend·er**, '**vend·or** Verkäufer *m*, Händler *m*; '**vend·i·ble** verkäuflich, gangbar; '**vend·ing ma·chine** (Waren-, Verkaufs)Automat *m.*

ve·neer [vi'niə] **1.** Furnier *n*; *fig.* (äußerer) Anstrich *m*; **2.** furnieren; *fig.* bemänteln.

ven·er·a·ble □ ['venərəbl] ehrwürdig; **ven·er·ate** ['~reit] (ver)ehren; **ven·er'a·tion** Verehrung *f*; '**ven·er·a·tor** Verehrer *m.*

ve·ne·re·al [vi'niəriəl] geschlechtlich; Geschlechts...; ⚕ *a.* venerisch; ~ *disease* Geschlechtskrankheit *f.*

Ve·ne·tian [vi'ni:ʃən] **1.** venetianisch; ~ *blind* (Stab)Jalousie *f*; **2.** Venetianer(in).

venge·ance ['vendʒəns] Rache *f*; *with a* ~ F nicht zu knapp, und wie, ganz gehörig; **venge·ful** □ ['~ful] rachgierig, -süchtig.

ve·ni·al □ ['vi:njəl] verzeihlich; entschuldbar; läßlich (*Sünde*).

ven·i·son ['venzn] Wildbret *n.*

ven·om ['venəm] (*bsd.* Schlangen-)Gift *n*; *fig.* Gift *n*, Gehässigkeit *f*; '**ven·om·ous** □ giftig.

ve·nous ['vi:nəs] Venen...; venös.

vent [vent] **1.** Öffnung *f*; Luft-, Spundloch *n*; Ausweg *m*; Schlitz *m*; *give* ~ *to s-m Zorn etc.* Luft machen; *find* ~ sich Luft machen (*Gefühl*); **2.** *fig.* Luft machen (*dat.*); *Zorn* auslassen (*on* an *dat.*); '**~-hole** Abzugsöffnung *f.*

ven·ti·late ['ventileit] ventilieren, (be-, ent-, durch)lüften; *fig.* erörtern; **ven·ti'la·tion** Ventilation *f*, Lüftung *f*; ⚒ Wetterführung *f*; *fig.* Erörterung *f*; '**ven·ti·la·tor** Ventilator *m.*

ven·tral ['ventrəl] Bauch...

ven·tri·cle *anat.* ['ventrikl] Kammer *f.*

ven·tril·o·quist [ven'triləkwist] Bauchredner *m*; **ven'tril·o·quize** bauchreden.

ven·ture ['ventʃə] **1.** Wagnis *n*; Risiko *n*; gewagtes Unternehmen *n*; Abenteuer *n*; Spekulation(sobjekt *n*) *f*; *at a* ~ auf gut Glück; **2.** *v/t.* wagen, aufs Spiel setzen, riskieren; *v/i.* sich *wohin* wagen; ~ (*up*)*on* sich wagen an (*acc.*); *I* ~ *to say* ich wage zu behaupten; **ven·ture·some** □ ['~səm], '**ven·tur·ous** □ verwegen, kühn.

ven·ue ['venju:] zuständiger Gerichtsort *m*; *fig.* Schauplatz *m*; F Treffpunkt *m.*

ve·ra·cious □ [və'reiʃəs] wahrhaft; **ve·rac·i·ty** [ve'ræsiti] Wahrhaftigkeit *f.*

ve·ran·da(h) [və'rændə] Veranda *f.*

verb *gr.* [və:b] Zeitwort *n*, Verb(um) *n*; '**ver·bal** □ wörtlich; mündlich; Wort...; verbal; '**ver·bal·ize** in Worten ausdrücken; *gr.* in ein Verb verwandeln; **ver·ba·tim** [~'beitim] wörtlich, wortgetreu; **ver·bi·age** ['~biidʒ] Wortschwall *m*; **ver·bose** □ [~'bəus] wortreich; **ver·bos·i·ty** [~'bɔsiti] Wortschwall *m.*

ver·dan·cy ['və:dənsi] Grün *n*; *fig.* Grünheit *f*, Unreife *f*; '**ver·dant** □ grün; *fig.* unerfahren, unreif.

ver·dict ['və:dikt] ⚖ (Urteils-)Spruch *m der Geschworenen*; *fig.* Urteil *n* (*on* über *acc.*); *bring in od. return a* ~ *of guilty* auf schuldig erkennen.

ver·di·gris ['və:digris] Grünspan *m.*

ver·dure ['və:dʒə] Grün *n.*

verge[1] [və:dʒ] (Amts- *etc.*)Stab *m.*

verge[2] [~] **1.** *mst fig.* Rand *m*, Grenze *f*; *on the* ~ *of* am Rande (*gen.*); dicht vor (*dat.*); nahe daran, zu *inf.*;

2. sich (hin)neigen; ~ (*up*)*on* streifen, grenzen an (*acc.*).

ver·ger ['vəːdʒə] Kirchendiener *m*; Amtsstabträger *m*.

ver·i·fi·a·ble ['verifaiəbl] nachweisbar; **ver·i·fi·ca·tion** [~fi'keiʃən] Nachprüfung *f*; Bestätigung *f*; **ver·i·fy** ['~fai] (nach)prüfen, verifizieren; beweisen, belegen; bestätigen; '**ver·i·ly** † wahrlich; **ver·i·si·mil·i·tude** [~si'militjuːd] Wahrscheinlichkeit *f*; **ver·i·ta·ble** □ ['~təbl] wahr(haftig), wirklich; '**ver·i·ty** Wahrheit *f*.

ver·mi·cel·li [vəːmi'seli] Fadennudeln *f/pl.*; **ver·mi·cide** *pharm.* ['~said] Wurmmittel *n*; **ver'mic·u·lar** [~kjulə] wurmartig, -förmig; **ver·mi·form** ['~fɔːm] wurmförmig; Wurm...; **ver·mi·fuge** *pharm.* ['~fjuːdʒ] Wurmmittel *n*.

ver·mil·ion [və'miljən] **1.** Zinnoberrot *n*; **2.** zinnoberrot.

ver·min ['vəːmin] Ungeziefer *n*; *hunt.* Raubzeug *n*; *fig.* Gesindel *n*; '**~-'kill·er** Kammerjäger *m*; '**ver·min·ous** voller Ungeziefer; verlaust.

ver·m(o)uth ['vəːməθ] Wermut *m*.

ver·nac·u·lar □ [və'nækjulə] **1.** einheimisch; Landes...; landes-, muttersprachlich; **2.** Landes-, Muttersprache *f*; Jargon *m*.

ver·nal ['vəːnl] Frühlings...

ver·ni·er ['vəːnjə] ⚒ Gradteiler *m*; ⊕ Fein(ein)steller *m*.

ver·ru·ca [ve'ruːkə] *mst auf der Fußsohle befindliche* Warze *f*.

ver·sa·tile □ ['vəːsətail] wandelbar; wandlungsfähig; beweglich (*Geist*); vielseitig, gewandt; **ver·sa·til·i·ty** [~'tiliti] Wandelbarkeit *f*; Beweglichkeit *f*; Vielseitigkeit *f*.

verse [vəːs] Vers *m*; Strophe *f*; *coll.* Verse *m/pl.*; *weitS.* Dichtung *f*; Poesie *f*; **versed** bewandert, erfahren (*in* in *dat.*).

ver·si·fi·ca·tion [vəːsifi'keiʃən] Verskunst *f*; Versbau *m*; **ver·si·fy** ['~fai] *v/t.* in Verse bringen; *v/i.* Verse machen.

ver·sion ['vəːʃən] Übersetzung *f*; Fassung *f*, Darstellung *f*; Lesart *f*.

ver·so ['vəːsəu] Verso *n*, Rückseite *f e-s Blattes*.

ver·sus *bsd.* ⚖ ['vəːsəs] gegen.

vert F *eccl.* [vəːt] übertreten, konvertieren.

ver·te·bra *anat.* ['vəːtibrə], *pl.* **ver·te·brae** ['~briː] Wirbel *m*; **ver·te·bral** ['~brəl] Wirbel...; **ver·te·brate** ['~brit] **1.** Wirbel...; ~ *animal* = **2.** Wirbeltier *n*.

ver·tex ['vəːteks], *pl. mst* **ver·ti·ces** ['~tisiːz] Scheitel(punkt) *m*; '**ver·ti·cal** □ vertikal, senkrecht; Scheitel...; ~ *take-off aircraft* ✈ Senkrechtstarter *m*.

ver·tig·i·nous □ [vəː'tidʒinəs] schwindlig; schwindelnd (*Höhe*); Schwindel...; **ver·ti·go** ['~tigəu] Schwindel(anfall) *m*.

verve [vəːv] *künstlerische* Begeisterung *f*, Schwung *m*, Verve *f*.

ver·y ['veri] **1.** *adv.* sehr; *the* ~ *best* das allerbeste; **2.** *adj.* wahrhaftig; wirklich; gerade, eben; schon, bloß; *the* ~ *same* ebenderselbe; *in the* ~ *act* auf frischer Tat; gerade dabei; *to the* ~ *bone* bis auf den Knochen; *the* ~ *thing* gerade das; *the* ~ *thought* schon der Gedanke, der bloße Gedanke; *the* ~ *stones* sogar die Steine; *the veriest baby* (selbst) das kleinste Kind; *the veriest rascal* der ärgste *od.* größte Schuft; ~ **high fre·quen·cy** *Radio*: Ultrakurzwelle *f*.

ves·i·ca ['vesikə] Blase *f*; **ves·i·cle** ['~kl] Bläschen *n*.

ves·per ['vespə] *poet.* Abend *m*; ~*s pl. eccl.* Vesper *f*, Abendandacht *f*.

ves·sel ['vesl] Gefäß *n* (*a. anat.*, ♀, *fig.*); ⚓ Fahrzeug *n*, Schiff *n*.

vest [vest] **1.** Unterhemd *n*; † Weste *f*; **2.** *v/t. mst fig. j.* bekleiden (*with* mit); *j.* einsetzen (*in* in *acc.*); *et.* übertragen (*in s.o.* j-m); *v/i.* verliehen werden (*in s.o.* j-m); ~*ed rights pl.* wohlerworbene Rechte *n/pl.*

ves·tal ['vestl] **1.** vestalisch; jungfräulich; **2.** Vestalin *f*.

ves·ti·bule ['vestibjuːl] Vorhof *m* (*a. fig.*); Vorhalle *f*; Hausflur *m*; 🚃 *bsd. Am.* Korridor *m zwischen zwei D-Zug-Wagen*; ~ *train* D-Zug *m*.

ves·tige ['vestidʒ] Spur *f*; **ves'tig·i·al** [~dʒiəl] rudimentär; verkümmert.

vest·ment ['vestmənt] (*bsd.* Amts-) Gewand *n*, Kleid *n*.

vest-pock·et ['vest'pɔkit] Westentaschen..., Klein...

ves·try [ˈvestri] *eccl.* Sakristei *f*; Gemeindevertretung *f*; Gemeindesaal *m*; ˈ**~·man** Gemeindevertreter *m*.
ves·ture *poet.* [ˈvestʃə] **1.** Kleid(er *pl.*) *n*; **2.** kleiden.
vet F [vet] **1.** Tierarzt *m*; *Am.* ⚔ Veteran *m*; **2.** verarzten; *fig.* gründlich prüfen.
vetch ⚘ [vetʃ] Wicke *f*.
vet·er·an [ˈvetərən] **1.** ausgedient; erfahren; **2.** Veteran *m*; ehemaliger Soldat *m*; **~ car** *mot.* Oldtimer *m*, Autoveteran *m*.
vet·er·i·nar·i·an *Am.* [vetəriˈnɛəriən] Tierarzt *m*.
vet·er·i·nar·y [ˈvetərinəri] **1.** tierärztlich; **2.** *a.* **~** *surgeon* Tierarzt *m*.
ve·to [ˈviːtəu] **1.** *pl.* **ve·toes** [ˈ~z] Veto *n*; Einspruch *m*; *put a od. one's* **~** *(up)on* = **2.** sein Veto einlegen gegen.
vex [veks] ärgern; quälen; *bsd.* ⚖ schikanieren; **vexˈa·tion** Verdruß *m*, Ärger *m*; Ärgernis *n*; Schikane *f*; **vexˈa·tious** □ ärgerlich, verdrießlich; schikanös; **vexed** □ ärgerlich (*at s.th., with s.o.* über *acc.*); **~** *question* Streitfrage *f*; ˈ**vex·ing** □ ärgerlich.
vi·a [ˈvaiə] über, via.
vi·a·ble [ˈvaiəbl] lebensfähig.
vi·a·duct [ˈvaiədʌkt] Viadukt *m*, Überführung *f*.
vi·al [ˈvaiəl] Phiole *f*, Fläschchen *n*; Ampulle *f*.
vi·and [ˈvaiənd] *mst* **~s** *pl.* Lebensmittel *n/pl.*
vi·at·i·cum *eccl.* [vaiˈætikəm] Wegzehrung *f*.
vibes [vaibz] *pl.* F Vibraphon *n*; *sl.* Atmosphäre *f*, Wirkung *f*, Ausstrahlung *f*.
vi·brant [ˈvaibrənt] vibrierend; zitternd (*with* vor *dat.*).
vi·bra·phone ♪ [ˈvaibrəfəun] Vibraphon *n*.
vi·brate [vaiˈbreit] vibrieren; schwingen; zittern; **viˈbra·tion** Schwingung *f*, Zittern *n*, Vibrieren *n*, Erschütterung *f*; **viˈbra·tor** Vibrator *m*; **vi·bra·to·ry** [ˈ~brətəri] schwingend; Schwingungs...
vic·ar *eccl.* [ˈvikə] Vikar *m*, (Unter-)Pfarrer *m*; **~** *general* Generalvikar *m*; ˈ**vic·ar·age** Pfarrhaus *n*; **vi·car·i·ous** □ [vaiˈkɛəriəs] stellvertretend.
vice[1] [vais] Laster *n*; Fehler *m*; Unart *f*.
vice[2] ⊕ [~] Schraubstock *m*.
vice[3] [ˈvaisi] *prp.* an Stelle von.
vice[4] [vais] **1.** Vize..., Unter...; **2.** F Stellvertreter *m*; ˈ**~-ˈad·mi·ral** Vizeadmiral *m*; ˈ**~-ˈchair·man** stellvertretender Vorsitzender *m*; Vizepräsident *m*; ˈ**~-ˈchan·cel·lor** Vizekanzler *m*; *univ.* Rektor *m*; ˈ**~-ˈcon·sul** Vizekonsul *m*; **~·ge·rent** [ˈ~ˈdʒerənt] Statthalter *m*, Stellvertreter *m*; ˈ**~-ˈpres·i·dent** Vizepräsident *m*; ˈ**~-ˈre·gal** vizeköniglich; **~·reine** [ˈ~ˈrein] Gemahlin *f* des Vizekönigs; **~·roy** [ˈ~rɔi] Vizekönig *m*.
vi·ce ver·sa [ˈvaisiˈvəːsə] umgekehrt.
vic·i·nage [ˈvisinidʒ], **viˈcin·i·ty** Nachbarschaft *f*; Nähe *f* (*to* bei); *in the* **~** *of 40* um 40 herum.
vi·cious □ [ˈviʃəs] lasterhaft; verwerflich; bösartig (*Tier*); boshaft (*Kritik*); fehlerhaft; **~ cir·cle** Circulus *m* vitiosus, Teufelskreis *m*; **~ spi·ral** *fig.* Schraube *f* ohne Ende.
vi·cis·si·tude [viˈsisitjuːd] Wandel *m*, Wechsel *m*; **~s** *pl.* Wechselfälle *m/pl.*
vic·tim [ˈviktim] Opfer *n*; ˈ**vic·tim·ize** (hin)opfern; *fig. j.* hereinlegen; drangsalieren, verfolgen.
vic·tor [ˈviktə] Sieger *m*; **Vic·to·ri·an** *hist.* [vikˈtɔːriən] Viktorianisch; **vicˈto·ri·ous** □ siegreich; Sieges...; **vic·to·ry** [ˈ~təri] Sieg *m*.
vict·ual [ˈvitl] **1.** (sich) mit Lebensmitteln versehen; **2.** *mst* **~s** *pl.* Lebensmittel *n/pl.*, Proviant *m*; **vict·ual·(l)er** [ˈvitlə] Lebensmittellieferant *m*; *licensed* **~** Schankwirt *m*.
vi·de [ˈvaidiː] siehe!
vi·de·li·cet [viˈdiːliset] (*abbr. viz.*; *lies: namely, that is*) nämlich.
vid·e·o [ˈvidiəu] Fernseh...; Video...; **~ disc** Bildplatte *f*; **~ re·cord·er** Videorecorder *m*; **~ tape** Videoband *n*; *video-tape library* Videothek *f*.
vie [vai] wetteifern.
Vi·en·nese [vieˈniːz] **1.** Wiener(in); **2.** Wiener, wienerisch.
view [vjuː] **1.** Sehen *n*, Sicht *f*, Auge(n *pl.*) *n*, Blick *m*; Besichtigung *f*; Aussicht *f* (*of* auf *acc.*); Anblick *m*; Ansicht *f* (*a. paint., phot.*); Absicht *f*; *fig.* Ansicht *f* (*Meinung*); Anschauung *f*; *at first* **~** auf den

ersten Blick; *in ~* sichtbar, zu sehen; *in ~ of* im Hinblick auf (*acc.*); *fig.* angesichts (*gen.*); *in my ~* in meinen Augen; *on ~* zu besichtigen *od.* sehen; *on the long ~* auf weite Sicht, auf die Dauer; *out of ~* unsichtbar, nicht zu sehen; *with a ~ to ger.*, *with the ~ of ger.* mit *od.* in der Absicht zu *inf.*; zu dem Zweck (*gen.*); im Hinblick auf (*acc.*); *come into ~* sichtbar werden, in Sicht kommen; *have* (*keep*) *in ~* im Auge haben (behalten); **2.** an-, besehen, besichtigen; *geistig* (an)sehen, betrachten; '**view·er** Betrachter(in), (Fernseh-) Zuschauer(in); '**view-find·er** *phot.* Sucher *m*; '**view·less** ohne eigene Meinung; *poet.* unsichtbar; '**~-point** Gesichts-, Standpunkt *m*; '**view·y** □ F schrullig.

vig·il *bsd. eccl.* ['vidʒil] Nachtwache *f*; '**vig·i·lance** Wachsamkeit *f*; *~ committee Am. hist.* Wachkomitee *n*; '**vig·i·lant** □ wachsam; **vig·i·lan·te** *Am.* [~'lænti] Angehörige *m* e-s Wachkomitees.

vi·gnette *typ.*, *phot.* [vi'njet] **1.** Vignette *f*; **2.** vignettieren.

vig·or·ous □ ['vigərəs] kräftig, kraftvoll; energisch; lebhaft; *fig.* nachdrücklich; '**vig·o(u)r** Kraft *f*; Vitalität *f*; Energie *f*; Lebenskraft *f*; *fig.* Nachdruck *m*.

vi·king ['vaikiŋ] **1.** Wiking(er) *m*; **2.** wikingisch, Wikinger...

vile □ [vail] gemein, niedrig, nichtswürdig.

vil·i·fi·ca·tion [vilifi'keiʃən] Verunglimpfung *f*; **vil·i·fy** ['~fai] verunglimpfen, schlechtmachen.

vil·la ['vilə] Villa *f*, Landhaus *n*.

vil·lage ['vilidʒ] Dorf *n*; **~ green** Dorfanger *m*, -wiese *f*; '**vil·lag·er** Dorbewohner(in).

vil·lain ['vilən] Schurke *m*, Schuft *m*, Bösewicht *m* (*a. co.*); '**vil·lain·ous** □ schurkisch, schändlich; F miserabel, scheußlich; '**vil·lain·y** Schurkerei *f*.

vil·lein *hist.* ['vilin] Leibeigene *m, f*.

vim F [vim] Schwung *m*, Schneid *m*.

vin·di·cate ['vindikeit] rechtfertigen (*from* gegen); verteidigen; beanspruchen (*to, for* für); **vin·di'ca·tion** Rechtfertigung *f*; **vin·di·ca·to·ry** □ ['~təri] rechtfertigend; Rechtfertigungs...

vin·dic·tive □ [vin'diktiv] rachsüchtig; nachtragend.

vine ♀ [vain] Wein(stock) *m*, Rebe *f*; Kletterpflanze *f*; '**~-dress·er** Winzer *m*; **vin·e·gar** ['vinigə] **1.** (Wein-) Essig *m*; **2.** mit Essig behandeln; '**vin·e·gar·y** *mst fig.* (essig)sauer; **vine-grow·er** ['vaingrəuə] Weinbauer *m*; '**vine-grow·ing** Weinbau *m*; '**vine-louse** Reblaus *f*; **vine-yard** ['vinjəd] Weinberg *m*.

vi·nous ['vainəs] weinig; Wein...

vin·tage ['vintidʒ] **1.** Weinlese *f*; (Wein)Jahrgang *m*; **2.** klassisch; erlesen; altmodisch; *~ car mot.* Veteran *m*; '**vin·tag·er** Winzer *m*;

vint·ner ['vintnə] Weinhändler *m*.

vi·ol ♪ ['vaiəl] Viole *f*.

vi·o·la[1] ♪ [vi'əulə] Bratsche *f*, Viola *f*.

vi·o·la[2] ♀ ['vaiələ] Viole *f*.

vi·o·la·ble □ ['vaiələbl] verletzbar.

vi·o·late ['vaiəleit] verletzen; *Eid etc.* brechen; *Frau* vergewaltigen (*a. fig.*); *Tempel* schänden; **vi·o'la·tion** Verletzung *f*; (Eid- *etc.*) Bruch *m*; Vergewaltigung *f*; Schändung *f*; '**vi·o·la·tor** Verletzer *m etc.*

vi·o·lence ['vaiələns] Gewalttätigkeit *f*; Gewalttat *f*; Gewaltsamkeit *f*; Heftigkeit *f*, Gewalt *f*; *do od. offer ~ to* Gewalt antun (*dat.*); '**vi·o·lent** □ gewaltsam; gewalttätig; heftig, ungestüm.

vi·o·let ['vaiəlit] **1.** ♀ Veilchen *n*; **2.** veilchenblau, violett, lila.

vi·o·lin ♪ [vaiə'lin] Violine *f*, Geige *f*; '**vi·o·lin·ist** Violinist(in), Geiger (-in).

vi·o·lon·cel·list ♪ [vaiələn'tʃelist] Cellist(in); **vi·o·lon'cel·lo** [~ləu] Cello *n*.

VIP *sl.* ['vi:ai'pi:] hohes Tier *n*.

vi·per *zo.* ['vaipə] Viper *f*, Natter *f* (*a. fig.*); **vi·per·ine** ['~rain], '**vi·per·ous** □ *mst fig.* viperartig; giftig.

vi·ra·go [vi'rɑ:gəu] Zankteufel *m*, Drachen *m*.

vir·gin ['və:dʒin] **1.** Jungfrau *f*; **2.** □ jungfräulich (*fig. unberührt*); *fig. u.* ⊕ Jungfern...; '**vir·gin·al** ['və:dʒinl] **1.** □ jungfräulich; Jungfern-...; **2.** ♪ Virginal *n* (*Spinett*); **Vir·gin·ia** [və'dʒinjə] *a. ~ tobacco* Virginiatabak *m*; *~ creeper* wilder Wein *m*; **Vir'gin·i·an** Virginia...; virginisch; **vir·gin·i·ty** [və:'dʒiniti] Jungfräulichkeit *f*.

Vir·go *ast.* ['və:gəu] Jungfrau *f.*
vir·ile ['virail] männlich; Mannes...; mannhaft; viril; **vi·ril·i·ty** [vi'riliti] Mannesalter *n*; Mannheit *f*; Männlichkeit *f*; Mannhaftigkeit *f.*
vir·tu [və:'tu:]: *article of* ~ Kunstgegenstand *m*; **vir·tu·al** □ ['~tjuəl] dem Wesen nach, eigentlich; '**vir·tu·al·ly** praktisch; **vir·tue** ['~tju:] Tugend *f*; Wirksamkeit *f*; Kraft *f*; Vorzug *m*, Wert *m*; *in od. by* ~ *of* kraft, vermöge (*gen.*); auf Grund von; *make a* ~ *of necessity* aus der Not e-e Tugend machen; **vir·tu·os·i·ty** [və:tju'ɔsiti] Virtuosität *f*; **vir·tu·o·so** [~'əuzəu] *bsd.* ♪ Virtuose *m*; Kunstliebhaber *m*; **vir·tu·ous** □ tugendhaft.
vir·u·lence ['viruləns] Giftigkeit *f*, Virulenz *f*; *fig.* Bösartigkeit *f*; '**vir·u·lent** □ giftig; virulent; *fig.* bösartig.
vi·rus ⚕ ['vaiərəs] Virus *n*; *fig.* Gift *n.*
vi·sa ['vi:zə] **1.** Visum *n*, Sichtvermerk *m*; **2.** *pret. u. p.p.* '**vi·saed** mit e-m Sichtvermerk *od.* Visum versehen.
vis·age *lit.* ['vizidʒ] (An)Gesicht *n.*
vis·cer·a *anat.* ['visərə] Eingeweide *pl.*
vis·cid □ ['visid] = *viscous.*
vis·cose ⚗ ['viskəus] Viskose *f*; ~ *silk* Zellstoffseide *f*; **vis·cos·i·ty** [~'kɔsiti] (Grad *m* der) Zähflüssigkeit *f*, Viskosität *f.*
vis·count ['vaikaunt] Vicomte *m* (*englischer Adelstitel*); '**vis·count·ess** Vicomtesse *f.*
vis·cous □ ['viskəs] zäh-, dickflüssig; klebrig.
vise [vais] *Am.* für *vice*².
vi·sé ['vi:zei] = *visa.*
vis·i·bil·i·ty [vizi'biliti] Sichtbarkeit *f*; Sichtweite *f*; '**vis·i·ble** □ sichtbar; *fig.* (er)sichtlich; *pred.* zu sehen (*Sache*); zu sprechen (*Person*).
vi·sion ['viʒən] Sehvermögen *n*, -kraft *f*; *fig.* Einsicht *f*, Seherblick *m*; Vision *f*, Erscheinung *f*; Traum (-bild *n*) *m* (*a. fig.*); **vi·sion·ar·y** ['~nəri] **1.** phantastisch; **2.** Geisterseher(in); Phantast(in), Träumer (-in).
vis·it ['vizit] **1.** *v/t.* besuchen; besichtigen; *fig.* heimsuchen (*with* mit); *et.* ahnden (*upon* an *j-m*); *v/i.* Besuche machen; ~ *with Am.* sich unterhalten *od.* plaudern mit; **2.** Besuch *m* (*to* bei; *gen.*); '**vis·it·ant** Besuch(er) *m*; *orn.* Strichvogel *m*; **vis·it'a·tion** Besuch *m*; Besichtigung *f*; *fig.* Heimsuchung *f*; **vis·it·a·to·ri·al** [~tə'tɔ:riəl] Besichtigungs...; Aufsichts...; '**vis·it·ing** Besuchs...; ~ *card* Visitenkarte *f*; ~ *professor* Gastprofessor *m*; ~ *team Sport*: Gastmannschaft *f*, *die* Gäste *m/pl.*; '**vis·i·tor** Besuch(er) *m* (*to gen.*); Gast *m*; Inspektor *m*; ~*s' book* Fremden-, Gästebuch *n.*
vi·sor ['vaizə] Helmvisier *n*; Mützenschirm *m*; *mot.* Blendschirm *m.*
vis·ta ['vistə] Durchblick *m*; Rück- *od.* Ausblick *m* (*a. fig.*; *of* auf *acc.*); Allee *f*; Galerie *f*; Reihe *f.*
vis·u·al □ ['vizjuəl] Seh...; Gesichts...; '**vis·u·al·ize** (sich) vor Augen stellen, sich ein Bild machen von.
vi·tal □ ['vaitl] Lebens...; lebenswichtig, wesentlich (*to* für); lebensgefährlich (*Wunde*); ~*s pl.*, ~ *parts pl.* lebenswichtige Organe *n/pl.*, edle Teile *m/pl.*; *s. statistics*; **vi·tal·i·ty** [~'tæliti] Lebenskraft *f*, -fähigkeit *f*; Vitalität *f*; **vi·tal·ize** ['~təlaiz] beleben.
vi·ta·min(e) ['vitəmin] Vitamin *n*; **vi·ta·mi·nized** ['~naizd] (*künstlich*) mit Vitaminen angereichert.
vi·ti·ate ['viʃieit] verderben; beeinträchtigen; hinfällig *od.* ⚖ ungültig machen.
vit·i·cul·ture ['vitikʌltʃə] Weinbau *m.*
vit·re·ous □ ['vitriəs] Glas...; gläsern.
vit·ri·fac·tion [vitri'fækʃən] Verglasung *f*; **vit·ri·fy** ['~fai] verglasen.
vit·ri·ol ⚗ ['vitriəl] Vitriol *n*; **vit·ri·ol·ic** [vitri'ɔlik] Vitriol...; *fig.* ätzend, bissig.
vi·tu·per·ate [vi'tju:pəreit] schelten; schmähen, beschimpfen; **vi·tu·per'a·tion** Schmähung *f*, Beschimpfung *f*; **vi'tu·per·a·tive** □ [~rətiv] schmähend; Schmäh...
vi·va (**vo·ce**) ['vəivə('vəusi)] **1.** mündlich; **2.** mündliche Prüfung *f.*
vi·va·cious □ [vi'veiʃəs] lebhaft, munter; **vi·vac·i·ty** [vi'væsiti] Lebhaftigkeit *f.*
viv·id □ ['vivid] lebhaft, lebendig;

ˈ**viv·id·ness** Lebhaftigkeit *f*.
viv·i·fy [ˈvivifai] (sich) beleben; **viˈvip·a·rous** □ [~pərəs] lebendgebärend; **viv·i·sec·tion** [~ˈsekʃən] Vivisektion *f*.
vix·en [ˈviksn] Füchsin *f*; zänkisches Weib *n*.
viz. [ˈneimli] = *videlicet*.
vi·zier [viˈziə] Wesir *m*.
vi·zor [ˈvaizə] = *visor*.
vo·cab·u·lar·y [vəuˈkæbjuləri] Wörterverzeichnis *n*; Wortschatz *m*, Vokabular *n*.
vo·cal □ [ˈvəukəl] stimmlich; Stimm...; gesprochen; laut; ♪ Vokal..., Gesang...; sprechend; klingend; *gr.* stimmhaft; ~ *c(h)ord* Stimmband *n*; ~ *part* Singstimme *f*; ˈ**vo·cal·ist** Sänger(in); ˈ**vo·cal·ize** (*gr.* stimmhaft) aussprechen; singen; ˈ**vo·cal·ly** *adv.* mittels der Stimme; laut.
vo·ca·tion [vəuˈkeiʃən] *innere* Berufung *f*; Beruf *m*; **voˈca·tion·al** □ [~ʃənl] beruflich; Berufs...; ~ *guidance* Berufsberatung *f*.
voc·a·tive *gr.* [ˈvɔkətiv] Vokativ *m*.
vo·cif·er·ate [vəuˈsifəreit] schreien; laut rufen; brüllen; **vo·cif·erˈa·tion** *a.* ~*s pl.* Geschrei *n*; **voˈcif·er·ous** □ schreiend, laut.
vogue [vəug] Beliebtheit *f*; Mode *f*.
voice [vɔis] **1.** Stimme *f*; *active* (*passive*) ~ *gr.* Aktiv *n* (Passiv *n*); *in* (*good*) ~ (gut) bei Stimme; *give* ~ *to* Ausdruck geben (*dat.*); **2.** äußern, ausdrücken; *gr.* stimmhaft aussprechen; ˈ**~-box** F Kehlkopf *m*; **voiced** *gr.* stimmhaft; *in Zssgn* ...stimmig; ˈ**voice·less** □ *bsd. gr.* stimmlos; stumm.
void [vɔid] **1.** leer; ⚖ nichtig, ungültig; ~ *of* frei von; arm an (*dat.*); ohne; **2.** Leere *f*; Lücke *f*; **3.** entleeren; ungültig machen, aufheben; ˈ**void·ness** Leere *f*.
voile [vɔil] Voile *m*, Schleierstoff *m*.
vol·a·tile [ˈvɔlətail] ⚗ flüchtig (*a. fig.*); flatterhaft; **vol·a·til·i·ty** [~ˈtiliti] Flüchtigkeit *f*; **vol·a·til·ize** [vɔˈlætilaiz] (sich) verflüchtigen.
vol·can·ic [vɔlˈkænik] (~*ally*) vulkanisch; **vol·ca·no** [vɔlˈkeinəu], *pl.* **volˈca·noes** [~z] Vulkan *m*.
vole *zo.* [vəul] Wühlmaus *f*.
vo·li·tion [vəuˈliʃən] Wollen *n*; Wille(nskraft *f*) *m*; *on one's own* ~ aus eigenem Entschluß.
vol·ley [ˈvɔli] **1.** Salve *f*; (Geschoß- *etc.*) Hagel *m*; *fig.* Schwall *m*, Strom *m*; *Tennis*: Volley-, Flugball *m*; **2.** *v/t. mst* ~ *out* e-n Schwall von *Worten etc.* von sich geben; *Ball* volley nehmen; *v/i.* Salven abgeben; sich entladen; *fig.* hageln; dröhnen; ˈ**vol·ley-ball** *Sport*: Volleyball *m*, Flugball *m*.
vol·plane ✈ [ˈvɔlplein] **1.** Gleitflug *m*; **2.** im Gleitflug niedergehen.
volt ⚡ [vəult] Volt *n*; ˈ**volt·age** ⚡ Spannung *f*; **vol·ta·ic** ⚡ [vɔlˈteiik] voltaisch.
volte-face *fig.* [ˈvɔltˈfɑːs] völlige Kehrtwendung *f*.
volt·me·ter ⚡ [ˈvəultmiːtə] Voltmeter *n*, Spannungsmesser *m*.
vol·u·bil·i·ty [vɔljuˈbiliti] Zungenfertigkeit *f*, Redegewandtheit *f*; **vol·u·ble** □ [ˈ~bl] zungenfertig, (rede)gewandt.
vol·ume [ˈvɔljum] Band *m e-s Buches*; *phys. etc.* Volumen *n*; *fig.* Masse *f*, große Menge *f*; (*bsd.* Stimm)Umfang *m*; ~ *of sound Radio*: Lautstärke *f*; ~ *control*, ~ *regulator* Lautstärkeregler *m*; **vo·lu·mi·nous** □ [vəˈljuːminəs] vielbändig; umfangreich; voluminös.
vol·un·tar·y □ [ˈvɔləntəri] **1.** freiwillig; *physiol.* willkürlich; ~ *death* Freitod *m*; **2.** freiwillige Arbeit *f*; ♪ Orgelsolo *n*; **vol·un·teer** [~ˈtiə] **1.** Freiwillige *m*; *attr.* Freiwilligen-...; **2.** *v/i.* freiwillig dienen; sich freiwillig melden; sich erbieten; *v/t.* anbieten; sich *e-e Bemerkung* erlauben.
vo·lup·tu·ar·y [vəˈlʌptjuəri] Genußmensch *m*; Wollüstling *m*.
vo·lup·tu·ous □ [vəˈlʌptʃuəs] wollüstig; üppig; sinnlich; **voˈlup·tu·ous·ness** Wollust *f*; Sinnlichkeit *f*.
vo·lute △ [vəˈljuːt] Volute *f*, Schnecke *f*; **voˈlut·ed** voluten-, schneckenförmig.
vom·it [ˈvɔmit] **1.** (sich) erbrechen; *fig.* (aus)speien, ausstoßen; **2.** Erbrochene *n*; Ausgespiene *n*; Auswurf *m*.
voo·doo [ˈvuːduː] **1.** Wodu *m*, Zauberkult *m*; Hexerei *f*; **2.** behexen.
vo·ra·cious □ [vəˈreiʃəs] gefräßig; gierig; **voˈra·cious·ness, vo·rac·i·ty** [vəˈræsiti] Gefräßigkeit *f*; Gier *f* (*of* nach).
vor·tex [ˈvɔːteks], *pl. mst* **vor·ti·ces**

['~tisi:z] Wirbel *m*, Strudel *m* (*mst fig.*).
vo·ta·ry ['vəutəri] Geweihte *m*; Anhänger(in); Verehrer(in).
vote [vəut] **1.** (Wahl)Stimme *f*; Abstimmung *f*; Stimmrecht *n*; *Abstimmungs*-Beschluß *m*, Votum *n*; ~ *of no confidence* Mißtrauensvotum *n*; *cast a* ~ (s)eine Stimme abgeben; *put to the* ~ zur Abstimmung bringen, abstimmen lassen über; *take a* ~ *on s.th.* über et. abstimmen; **2.** *v/t.* stimmen für; F erklären für; *v/i.* (ab)stimmen; wählen; ~ *for* stimmen für; F für *et.* sein; *et.* vorschlagen; '**vot·er** Stimmberechtigte *m*, *f*; Wähler(in).
vot·ing...: **~-booth** ['vəutiŋbu:ð] Wahlzelle *f*; '**~-box** Wahlurne *f*; '**~-pa·per** Stimmzettel *m*.
vo·tive ['vəutiv] Votiv...; Weih...
vouch [vautʃ] verbürgen; ~ *for* bürgen für; '**vouch·er** Beleg *m*, Unterlage *f*; Gutschein *m*; Zeuge *m*, Gewährsmann *m*; **vouch'safe** *v/t.* gewähren; sich herablassen zu; *v/i.* geruhen.
vow [vau] **1.** Gelübde *n*; (Treu-) Schwur *m*; **2.** *v/t.* geloben.
vow·el ['vauəl] Vokal *m*.
voy·age ['vɔiidʒ] **1.** *längere* (See-, Luft)Reise *f*; **2.** *zur See, in der Luft* reisen, fahren; **voy·ag·er** ['vɔiədʒə] (See)Reisende *m*.
vul·can·ite ['vʌlkənait] Vulkanit *m* (*Hartgummi*); **vul·can·i'za·tion** ⊕ Vulkanisierung *f*; '**vul·can·ize** ⊕ vulkanisieren; *~d fibre* Vulkanfiber *f*.
vul·gar ['vʌlgə] **1.** □ gewöhnlich, gemein, vulgär, pöbelhaft; ~ *tongue* Volkssprache *f*; **2.** *the* ~ der Pöbel; '**vul·gar·ism** vulgärer Ausdruck *m*; **vul·gar·i·ty** [~'gæriti] Gemeinheit *f*; **vul·gar·ize** ['~gəreiz] gemein machen, erniedrigen; populär machen, verbreiten.
vul·ner·a·bil·i·ty [vʌlnərə'biliti] Verwundbarkeit *f etc.*; '**vul·ner·a·ble** □ verwundbar; *fig.* angreifbar; ungeschützt; '**vul·ner·ar·y** **1.** Wund..., Heil...; **2.** Wundmittel *n*.
vul·pine ['vʌlpain] Fuchs...; fuchsartig; *fig.* schlau, listig.
vul·ture *orn.* ['vʌltʃə] Geier *m*; **vul·tur·ine** ['~tʃurain] geierartig.
vy·ing ['vaiiŋ] wetteifernd.

W

wab·ble ['wɔbl] = *wobble*.
wack·y *Am. sl.* ['wæki] verrückt.
wad [wɔd] **1.** (Watte)Bausch *m*; Polster *n*; Pfropf(en) *m*; Banknotenbündel *n*; **2.** wattieren; polstern; zu-, verstopfen; '**wad·ding** Wattierung *f*; Watte *f*.
wad·dle ['wɔdl] watscheln, wackeln.
wade [weid] *v/i.* waten; *fig.* sich hindurcharbeiten; *v/t.* durchwaten; '**wad·er** Watvogel *m*; *~s pl.* Wasserstiefel *m/pl.*
wa·fer ['weifə] Waffel *f*; *a. consecrated* ~ *eccl.* Oblate *f*, Hostie *f*.
waf·fle ['wɔfl] **1.** Waffel *f*; **2.** F quasseln.
waft [wɑ:ft] **1.** wehen, tragen; (ent-) senden; **2.** Hauch *m*.
wag[1] [wæg] **1.** *v/t.* wackeln mit, schütteln; wedeln mit *dem Schwanz*; *v/i.* wackeln; **2.** Schütteln *n*; Wedeln *n*.
wag[2] [~] Spaßvogel *m*, Schalk *m*; *play* ~ *sl.* die Schule schwänzen.
wage [weidʒ] **1.** *Krieg* führen, unternehmen; **2.** *mst ~s pl.* Lohn *m*; ~ **de·mands** *pl.* Lohnforderungen *f/pl.*; ~ **dis·pute** Lohnkampf *m*; **~-earn·er** ['~ə:nə] Lohnempfänger *m*; ~ **in·crease** Lohnerhöhung *f*; ~ **pack·et** Lohntüte *f*; ~ **re·straint** Lohnbeschränkung *f*; '**~-sheet,** '**wag·es-sheet** Lohnliste *f*; **wage slip** Lohnstreifen *m*.
wa·ger *lit.* ['weidʒə] **1.** Wette *f*; **2.** wetten; *Geld* verwetten (*on* für).
wag·ger·y ['wægəri] Schelmerei *f*; Spaß *m*; '**wag·gish** □ schelmisch, schalkhaft.
wag·gle F ['wægl] = *wag*[1] *1*; '**wag-**

gly F wacklig; sich windend.
wag·(g)on ['wægən] (Roll-, Güter-) Wagen *m*; Waggon *m*; Pferdefuhrwerk *n*; *be od. go on the (water)* ~ F nicht trinken; '**wag·(g)on·er** Fuhrmann *m*.
wag·tail *orn.* ['wægteil] Bachstelze *f*.
waif [weif] herrenloses Gut *n*; weggeworfenes Diebesgut *n*; Strandgut *n*; Heimatlose *m, f*; *~s and strays pl.* verwahrloste Kinder *n/pl.*; Reste *m/pl*.
wail [weil] **1.** (Weh)Klagen *n*; **2.** *v/t.* bejammern; *v/i.* (weh)klagen.
wain *poet.* [wein] Wagen *m*; *Charles's* ♀, *the* ♀ *ast.* der Große Wagen.
wain·scot ['weinskət] **1.** Holzverkleidung *f*, (-)Täfelung *f*; **2.** täfeln.
waist [weist] Taille *f*; schmalste Stelle *f*; ⚓ Mitteldeck *n*; '**~-band** Taillen-, Gurtband *n*; **~·coat** ['weiskəut] Weste *f*; **~-deep** ['weist'di:p] bis über die Hüften (reichend; '**waist·ed** tailliert; '**waist-line** Taille *f*.
wait [weit] **1.** *v/i.* warten; *a.* ~ *at* (*Am. on*) *table* bedienen, servieren; ~ *for* warten auf (*acc.*); ~ *(up)on s.o.* j. bedienen; j. besuchen; *keep ~ing* warten lassen; ~ *and see* abwarten; ~ *in line* Schlange stehen; *v/t.* abwarten; mit *dem Essen* warten (*for* auf *j.*); **2.** Warten *n*, Aufenthalt *m*; *~s pl.* Weihnachtssänger *m/pl.*; *have a long* ~ lange warten müssen; *lie in* ~ *for s.o.* j-m auflauern; '**wait·er** Kellner *m*; Tablett *n*.
wait·ing ['weitiŋ] Warten *n*; Dienst *m*; *in* ~ diensttuend; *no* ~ Parken verboten; '**~-maid** Kammermädchen *n*; '**~-room** Wartezimmer *n*, -saal *m*.
wait·ress ['weitris] Kellnerin *f*.
waive [weiv] verzichten auf (*acc.*), aufgeben, ⚖ sich *e-s Rechtes* begeben; '**waiv·er** ⚖ Verzicht *m*.
wake[1] [weik] ⚓ Kielwasser *n* (*a. fig.*); ✈ Luftsog *m*; *fig.* Spur *f*.
wake[2] [~] **1.** (*irr.*) *v/i. a.* ~ *up* aufwachen; *v/t. a.* ~ *up* (auf)wecken; erwecken; *fig.* wachrufen; **2.** Totenwache *f*; Kirmes *f*; **wake·ful** □ ['~ful] wachend; wachsam; schlaflos; '**wak·en** *v/i.* (auf)wachen; *v/i.* (auf)wecken; *fig.* anregen.
wale [weil] *bsd. Am. für weal*[2].
walk [wɔ:k] **1.** *v/i.* (zu Fuß) gehen; spazierengehen; wandern; Schritt gehen; ~ *about* umhergehen, -wandern; ~ *into sl.* herfallen über (*acc.*); ~ *out* F die Arbeit niederlegen, streiken; ~ *out on sl.* im Stich lassen; *v/t.* führen; *Pferd* Schritt gehen lassen; begleiten; spazieren führen; (durch)wandern; umhergehen auf *od.* in (*dat.*); ~ *the hospitals* s-e klinischen Semester machen (*Mediziner*); **2.** (Spazier)Gang *m*; Spazierweg *m*; Schritt *m* (*Gangart*); *go for a* ~ e-n Spaziergang machen, spazierengehen; ~ *of life* Lebensstellung *f*, Beruf *m*; '**~·a·bout:** *go on a* ~ ein Bad in der Menge nehmen (*wichtige Person*); '**walk·er** Fuß-, Spaziergänger(in); *Sport*: Geher *m*; *be a good* ~ gut zu Fuß sein; '**walk·er--on** *thea.* Statist(in).
walk·ie-talk·ie ⚔ ['wɔ:ki'tɔ:ki] tragbares Sprechfunkgerät *n*.
walk·ing ['wɔ:kiŋ] **1.** Spazierengehen *n*, Wandern *n*; *attr.* Spazier...; Wander...; ~ **pa·pers** *pl. Am.* F Entlassung(spapiere *n/pl.*) *f*; Laufpaß *m*; '**~-stick** Spazierstock *m*; '**~-tour** (Fuß)Wanderung *f*.
walk...: '**~-out** *Am.* Ausstand *m*; '**~-over** Kinderspiel *n*, leichter Sieg *m*; '**~-up** ohne Fahrstuhl (*Haus*).
wall [wɔ:l] **1.** Wand *f*; Mauer *f*; *give s.o. the* ~ j-m den Vorrang lassen; *go to the* ~ *fig.* an die Wand gedrückt werden; *~-to-~ carpeting* Teppichboden *m*; **2.** mit Mauern umgeben; (ein-, um)mauern (*mst mit adv.*); *fig.* ein-, abschließen; ~ *up* zumauern.
wal·la·by *zo.* ['wɔləbi] kleines Känguruh *n*.
wal·let ['wɔlit] Brieftasche *f*; Werkzeugtasche *f*; † Ränzel *n*.
wall...: '**~-eye** *vet.* Glasauge *n*; '**~-flow·er** ⚘ Goldlack *m*; *fig.* Mauerblümchen *n*; '**~-fruit** Spalierobst *n*; '**~-map** Wandkarte *f*.
Wal·loon [wɔ'lu:n] **1.** Wallone *m*, Wallonin *f*; Wallonisch *n*; **2.** wallonisch.
wal·lop F ['wɔləp] **1.** *v/i.* brodeln; poltern; *v/t. j.* verdreschen; **2.** kräftiger Schlag *m*, Hieb *m*; *sl.* Bier *n*; '**wal·lop·ing** F riesig.
wal·low ['wɔləu] **1.** sich wälzen; *fig.* schwelgen (*in* in *dat.*); **2.** Sichwälzen *n*; *hunt.* Suhle *f*.
wall...: '**~-pa·per** Tapete *f*; '**~-**

-sock·et ⚡ Steckdose *f*.
wal·nut ⚘ ['wɔːlnʌt] Walnuß(baum *m*) *f*.
wal·rus *zo.* ['wɔːlrəs] Walroß *n*.
waltz [wɔːls] **1.** Walzer *m*; **2.** Walzer tanzen, walzen.
wam·pum ['wɔmpəm] Wampum *n* (*Muschelornament u. Geld der Indianer*); *sl.* Moneten *pl.*
wan □ [wɔn] blaß, bleich, fahl.
wand [wɔnd] Zauberstab *m*; Amtsstab *m*.
wan·der ['wɔndə] wandern; *a.* ~ *about* umherschweifen, -wandern; *fig.* abschweifen (*from* von); irregehen, umherirren; phantasieren; '**wan·der·er** Wanderer(in); '**wan·der·ing 1.** □ wandernd; *fig.* unstet; **2.** ~*s pl.* Wanderung(en *pl.*) *f*, Wanderschaft *f*; (Fieber)Phantasie *f*.
wane [wein] **1.** abnehmen (*Mond*); *fig.* schwinden; **2.** Abnahme *f*; *on the* ~ im Abnehmen *od.* Schwinden.
wan·gle *sl.* ['wæŋgl] schieben, deichseln, drehen, organisieren; '**wan·gler** Schieber *m*.
wan·ness ['wɔnnis] Blässe *f*.
want [wɔnt] **1.** Mangel *m* (*of* an *dat.*); Bedürfnis *n*; Not *f*; *for* ~ *of* aus Mangel an (*dat.*), mangels (*gen.*); **2.** *v/i. be* ~*ing* fehlen; *be* ~*ing in* es fehlen lassen an (*dat.*); *be* ~*ing to* der Lage *etc.* nicht gewachsen sein; *he does not* ~ *for* es mangelt ihm nicht an (*dat.*); *it* ~*s of* es mangelt *od.* fehlt an (*dat.*); *v/t.* bedürfen (*gen.*), nötig haben, brauchen; ermangeln (*gen.*), nicht haben; verlangen; wünschen, (haben) wollen; *it* ~*s s.th.* es fehlt an et.; *he* ~*s energy* es fehlt ihm an Energie; *you* ~ *to be careful* du mußt vorsichtig sein; ~ *s.o. to do* wollen *od.* wünschen, daß j. tut; ~*ed* gesucht; '**~-ad** Kleinanzeige *f*; Stellenangebot *n*, -gesuch *n*.
wan·ton ['wɔntən] **1.** □ wollüstig, geil; üppig; mutwillig; übermütig; **2.** Wollüstling *m*; Dirne *f*; **3.** ⚘ geil wachsen; herumtollen; '**wan·ton·ness** Geilheit *f*; Mutwille *m*.
war [wɔː] **1.** Krieg *m*; *attr.* Kriegs...; *at* ~ im Krieg(szustand); *make* ~ Krieg führen (*upon* gegen); ~ *criminal* Kriegsverbrecher *m*; **2.** *lit.* Krieg führen; *fig.* streiten; einander widerstreiten.
war·ble ['wɔːbl] **1.** trillern; singen (*bsd. Vogel*); **2.** Getriller *n*; '**warbler** Sänger *m*; Singvogel *m*.
war...: '**~-blind·ed** kriegsblind; '**~-cry** Schlachtruf *m*; *fig.* Parole *f*.
ward [wɔːd] **1.** Gewahrsam *m*; Vormundschaft *f*; Mündel *n*; *weitS.* Schützling *m*; *fenc.* Parade *f*; Gefängniszelle *f*; Abteilung *f*, Station *f in e-m Krankenhaus etc.*, Krankenzimmer *n*; (Stadt)Bezirk *m*; ⊕ Einschnitt *m im Schlüsselbart*; Bart *m*; *casual* ~ Obdachlosenasyl *n*; *in* ~ unter Vormundschaft; **2.** ~ *off* abwehren, abwenden; '**ward·en** Aufseher *m*; (Luftschutz)Wart *m*; Herbergsvater *m*; *univ.* Rektor *m*; '**ward·er** (Gefangenen)Wärter *m*, Aufseher *m*; '**ward·robe** Garderobe *f*; Kleiderschrank *m*; ~ *dealer* Kleidertrödler *m*; ~ *trunk* Schrankkoffer *m*; '**ward·room** ⚓ Offiziersmesse *f*; '**ward·ship** Vormundschaft *f*.
ware [wɛə] Ware *f*; Geschirr *n*.
ware·house 1. ['wɛəhaus] (Waren-) Lager *n*; Lagerhaus *n*, Speicher *m*; **2.** ['~hauz] auf Lager bringen, einlagern; **~·man** ['~hausmən] Lagerverwalter *m*; Großhändler *m*; (Möbel)Spediteur *m*; Speicherarbeiter *m*.
war...: '**~·fare** Krieg(führung *f*) *m*; '**~-grave** Soldatengrab *n*; '**~·head** Gefechtskopf *m*.
war·i·ness ['wɛərinis] Vorsicht *f*; Behutsam-, Achtsamkeit *f*.
war·like ['wɔːlaik] kriegerisch; Kriegs...
war-loan ['wɔːləun] Kriegsanleihe *f*.
warm [wɔːm] **1.** □ warm (*a. fig.*); *a.* heiß; *fig.* hitzig; *fig.* glühend; *make things* ~ *for s.o.* j-m die Hölle heiß machen; **2.** F Erwärmung *f*; **3.** *v/t.* (er)wärmen (*a. fig.*); *sl.* vermöbeln (*prügeln*); ~ *up* aufwärmen; *v/i. a.* ~ *up* warm werden, sich erwärmen (*to* für); '**~-'heart·ed** herzlich, warmherzig; '**warm·ing** *sl.* Senge *f* (*Prügel*).
war-mon·ger ['wɔːmʌngə] Kriegstreiber *m*, -hetzer *m*; '**war-mon·ger·ing**, '**war-mon·ger·y** Kriegshetze *f*.
warmth [wɔːmθ] Wärme *f*.
warm-up ['wɔːmʌp] Sichwarmlaufen *n*.
warn [wɔːn] warnen (*of*, *against* vor *dat.*); verwarnen; ermahnen (*to inf.*

zu *inf.*); verständigen (*of* von), aufmerksam machen (*of* auf *acc.*); ˈ**warn·ing** Warnung *f*, Mahnung *f*; Verwarnung *f*; Kündigung *f*; *give* ~ kündigen; *take* ~ *from* sich ein warnendes Beispiel nehmen an (*dat.*).

War Of·fice [ˈwɔːrɔfis] Heeresministerium *n*.

warp [wɔːp] **1.** *Weberei*: Kette *f*; ⚓ Bugsiertau *n*; Verwerfung *f des Holzes*; *fig.* Verkehrtheit *f*; **2.** *v/i.* sich werfen (*Holz*); ⚓ werpen, warpen; *Weberei*: anscheren; *v/t. Holz etc.* werfen, verziehen; ✈ *Tragflächen* verwinden; *Weberei*: anscheren; ⚓ verholen; verzerren, entstellen; *j.* beeinflussen; *j.* abbringen (*from* von).

war-paint [ˈwɔːpeint] Kriegsbemalung *f* (*a. fig.*); *in full* ~ in Gala.

war-path [ˈwɔːpɑːθ] Kriegspfad *m*.

warp·ing ✈ [ˈwɔːpiŋ] Verwindung *f*.

war...: ˈ**~-plane** Kampfflugzeug *n*; ˈ**~-prof·itˈeer** Kriegsgewinnler *m*.

war·rant [ˈwɔrənt] **1.** Vollmacht *f*; Rechtfertigung *f*, Berechtigung *f*; ⚖ (Vollziehungs)Befehl *m*; Berechtigungsschein *m*; Lagerschein *m*; *a.* ~ *of apprehension* Steckbrief *m*; ~ *of arrest* Haftbefehl *m*; **2.** bevollmächtigen; *j.* berechtigen; *et.* rechtfertigen; verbürgen, *bsd.* ✝ garantieren; ˈ**war·rant·a·ble** □ zu rechtfertigen(d), vertretbar; *hunt.* jagdbar (*Hirsch*); ˈ**war·rant·a·bly** *adv.* billigerweise; ˈ**war·rant·ed** garantiert; **war·ranˈtee** ⚖ Sicherheitsempfänger *m*; ˈ**war·rant-offi·cer** ⚓ Deckoffizier *m*; ⚔ Portepeeunteroffizier *m*; **war·ran·tor** ⚖ [ˈ~tɔː] Sicherheitsgeber *m*; ˈ**war·ran·ty** Garantie *f*; Bürgschaft(sschein *m*) *f*; Berechtigung *f*.

war·ren [ˈwɔrən] Kaninchengehege *n*.

war·ri·or [ˈwɔriə] Krieger *m*.

war·ship [ˈwɔːʃip] Kriegsschiff *n*.

wart [wɔːt] Warze *f*; *bsd.* ⚘ Auswuchs *m*; ˈ**wart·y** warzig.

war·time [ˈwɔːtaim] **1.** Kriegszeit(en *pl.*) *f*; **2.** Kriegs...

war·y □ [ˈwɛəri] vorsichtig, behutsam; wachsam.

was [wɔz, wəz] *pret.* von *be*; *im Passiv*: wurde; *he* ~ *to have come* er hätte kommen sollen.

wash [wɔʃ] **1.** *v/t.* waschen; (um-)spülen; *~ed out* verwaschen, ausgeblaßt; F erledigt, fertig; ~ *up* abwaschen, spülen; *v/i.* sich waschen (lassen); waschecht sein (*a. fig.*); spülen, schlagen (*Wellen*); **2.** Waschen *n*; Wäsche *f*; Wellenschlag *m*; ⚓ Kielwasser *n*; ✈ Luftstrudel *m hinter Tragflächen*; Seichtwasser *n*; Schwemmland *n*; Spülwasser *n*; *contp.* Gewäsch *n*; *mouth-~* Mundwasser *n*; *s. white~*; ˈ**wash·a·ble** waschbar; ˈ**wash-and-ˈwear** bügelfrei, pflegeleicht; ˈ**wash-ba·sin** Waschbecken *n*; ˈ**wash-cloth** Waschlappen *m*; ˈ**wash-draw·ing** *Art* Aquarell *n*.

wash·er [ˈwɔʃə] Wäscherin *f*; Waschmaschine *f*; ⊕ Unterlagscheibe *f*, Dichtungsring *m*; ˈ**~-wom·an** Waschfrau *f*, Wäscherin *f*.

wash·ing [ˈwɔʃiŋ] **1.** Waschen *n*; Waschung *f*; Wäsche *f*; *~s pl.* Spülicht *n*; **2.** Wasch...; ˈ**~-ma·chine** Waschmaschine *f*; **~ pow·der** Waschpulver *n*; ˈ**~-silk** Waschseide *f*; **~-ˈup** Geschirrspülen *n*, Abwaschen *n*; ~ *machine* Geschirrspülmaschine *f*.

wash...: ˈ**~-ˈout** *sl.* Versager *m*, Niete *f*; Fiasko *n*; ˈ**~-rag** *bsd. Am.* Waschlappen *m*; ˈ**~-stand** Waschtisch *m*; ˈ**~-tub** Waschbottich *m*; ˈ**wash·y** wässerig (*a. fig.*).

was·n't [wɔznt] = *was not*.

wasp [wɔsp] Wespe *f*; ˈ**wasp·ish** □ gereizt; reizbar, giftig.

was·sail † [ˈwɔseil] Trinkgelage *n*; Würzbier *n*.

wast·age [ˈweistidʒ] Abgang *m*, Verlust *m*; Vergeudung *f*.

waste [weist] **1.** wüst, öde; unbebaut, brach; unfruchtbar; unnütz; ⊕ unbrauchbar; überflüssig; Abfall...; *lay* ~ verwüsten; ~ *paper* Altpapier *n*; **2.** Verschwendung *f*, Vergeudung *f*; Abfall *m*; Einöde *f*, Wüste *f*, *go od. run to* ~ verfallen; **3.** *v/t.* verwüsten, verheeren; verschwenden, vergeuden; verzehren; *v/i.* verschwendet werden; ~ *away* dahinsiechen, verfallen (*Kranker*); **~ dis·pos·al** Müllbeseitigung *f*; *waste-disposal unit* Müllschlucker *m*; **waste·ful** □ [ˈ~ful] verschwenderisch; kostspielig; **waste heat** Abwärme *f*; ˈ**waste·land** Ödland *n*; ˈ**waste-pa·per bas·ket** Papierkorb *m*; ˈ**waste-pipe** Abflußrohr *n*; Fallrohr *n am Klosett*; **waste pro·duct** Abfallprodukt *n*; *biol.* Ausscheidungsstoff *m*; **ˈwast·er** Verschwender(in); = *wastrel*.

wast·rel [ˈweistrəl] Ausschuß(ware *f*) *m*; Taugenichts *m*.

watch [wɔtʃ] **1.** Wache *f* (*a.* ⚓); Taschenuhr *f*; *be on the* ~ *for* achtgeben auf *et.*; **2.** *v/i.* wachen (*with* bei, *over* über *acc.*); ~ *for* warten auf (*acc.*), auflauern (*dat.*); ~ *out* F aufpassen; *v/t.* bewachen; (be-) hüten; beobachten, sehen; achtgeben *od.* aufpassen auf (*acc.*); ~ *one's time* s-e Gelegenheit abpassen; ˈ~**boat** ⚓ Wachtboot *n*; ˈ~**-brace·let** Uhrarmband *n*; ˈ~**-case** Uhrgehäuse *n*; ˈ~**dog** Wachhund *m*; ˈ**watch·er** Wächter *m*; Wärter *m*; **watch·ful** □ [ˈ~ful] wachsam, achtsam.

watch...: ˈ~**-mak·er** Uhrmacher *m*; ˈ~**man** (Nacht)Wächter *m*; ˈ~**-tow·er** Wachtturm *m*; ˈ~**word** Losung *f*, Schlagwort *n*, Parole *f*.

wa·ter [ˈwɔːtə] **1.** Wasser *n*; Gewässer *n*; ~ *supply* Wasserversorgung *f*; Wasserleitung *f*; *high* ~ Hochwasser *n*, Flut *f*; *low* ~ Niedrigwasser *n*, Ebbe *f*; *by* ~ auf dem Wasserweg; *drink od. take the* ~*s* Brunnen trinken; *of the first* ~ vom reinsten Wasser (*a. fig.*); *be in hot* ~ F in der Patsche sitzen; *be in low* ~ F auf dem trocknen sitzen; *hold* ~ *fig.* stichhaltig sein; *make* ~ Wasser lassen; lecken (*Schiff*); **2.** *v/t. Land* bewässern; *Straße* (be)sprengen; *Pflanze* (be)gießen; mit Wasser versorgen; tränken; *oft* ~ *down* verwässern (*a. fig.*); ⊕ moirieren; *v/i.* wässern (*Mund*); tränen (*Augen*); Wasser einnehmen; ✈ wassern; *make s.o.'s mouth* ~ j-m den Mund wässerig machen; ˈ~**-blis·ter** ⚕ Wasserblase *f*; ˈ~**-borne** zu Wasser befördert; ˈ~**-bot·tle** Feldflasche *f*; ~ **butt** Regentonne *f*; ~ **can·non** Wasserwerfer *m*; ˈ~**-cart** Sprengwagen *m*; ˈ~**-clos·et** (Wasser)Klosett *n*; ˈ~**-col·o(u)r** Aquarell *n*; Aquarellmalerei *f*; ~*s pl.* Wasserfarben *f/pl.*; ˈ~**-cool·ing** Wasserkühlung *f*; ˈ~**-course** Wasserlauf *m*; Kanal *m*; Bach-, Flußbett *n*; ˈ~**cress** ♀ Brunnenkresse *f*; ˈ~**fall** Wasserfall *m*; ˈ~**-fowl** *pl.* Wasservögel *m/pl.*; ˈ~**-front** Ufer *n*; *bsd. Am.* städtisches Hafengebiet *n*; ˈ~**ga(u)ge** ⊕ Wasserstandsanzeiger *m*; Pegel *m*; ˈ~**-glass** 🜍 Wasserglas *n*; ˈ~**-hose** Wasserschlauch *m*; ˈ**wa·ter·i·ness** Wässerigkeit *f*.

wa·ter·ing [ˈwɔːtəriŋ] Wässern *n etc.*; ˈ~**-can**, ˈ~**-pot** Gießkanne *f*; ˈ~**-place** Wasserloch *n*; Tränke *f*, Schwemme *f*; Bad(eort *m*) *n*; Seebad *n*.

water...: ˈ~**-jack·et** ⊕ Wasser(kühl)mantel *m*; ˈ~**-lev·el** Wasserspiegel *m*; Wasserstand(slinie *f*) *m*; ⊕ Wasserwaage *f*; ˈ~**-lil·y** ♀ Wasserrose *f*; ˈ~**logged** voll Wasser (gelaufen); ˈ~**-main** Haupt(wasser)rohr *n*; ˈ~**man** Fährmann *m*; Flußschiffer *m*; Bootsführer *m*; Wasserträger *m*; ˈ~**-mark** Wassermarke *f*; Wasserzeichen *n im Papier*; ˈ~**-mel·on** ♀ Wassermelone *f*; ˈ~**-pipe** Wasser(leitungs)rohr *n*; ˈ~**-plane** Wasserflugzeug *n*; ~ **pol·lu·tion** Wasserverschmutzung *f*; ˈ~**-po·lo** Wasserball(spiel *n*) *m*; ˈ~**-pow·er** Wasserkraft *f*; ~ *station* Wasserkraftwerk *n*; ˈ~**proof 1.** wasserdicht; **2.** Regenmantel *m*; **3.** imprägnieren; ˈ~**-reˈpel·lent** wasserabstoßend; ˈ~**-shed** Wasserscheide *f*; *weitS.* Stromgebiet *n*; ˈ~**side 1.** Fluß-, Seeufer *n*; **2.** am Wasser (gelegen); ˈ~**spout** Wasserhose *f*; Abtraufe *f*; ˈ~**-ta·ble** Grundwasserspiegel *m*; ˈ~**tight** wasserdicht; *fig.* eindeutig, unangreifbar; ˈ~**-wave 1.** Wasserwelle *f* (*Frisur*); **2.** Wasserwellen legen; ˈ~**-way** Wasserstraße *f*; Schiffahrtsweg *m*; ˈ~**-wings** *pl.* Schwimmflügel *m/pl.*; ˈ~**works** *pl.*, *a. sg.* Wasserwerk *n*; ˈ**wa·ter·y** wässerig (*a. fig.*).

watt ⚡ [wɔt] Watt *n*.

wat·tle [ˈwɔtl] **1.** Flechtwerk *n*; Hürde *f*; *orn.* Kehllappen *m*; **2.** aus Flechtwerk herstellen.

waul [wɔːl] mauzen, miauen.

wave [weiv] **1.** Welle *f* (*a. phys. u. von Haar*); Woge *f* (*a. fig.*); Schwenken *n*; Winken *n*; **2.** *v/t.* wellig machen; *Haar* wellen; schwingen; schwenken; (*j-m* zu-) winken; ~ *s.o. aside* j. beiseite winken; *v/i.* wogen; wehen, flattern; (~ *to s.o.* j-m zu)winken; ˈ~**-length** ⚡ Wellenlänge *f*; *be on the same* ~ *fig.* auf der gleichen Wellenlänge liegen.

wa·ver [ˈweivə] (sch)wanken (*a.*

fig.); flackern.

wave...: ˈ**~-range** *Radio*: Wellenbereich *m*; ˈ**~-trap** *Radio*: Sperrkreis *m*.

wav·y [ˈweivi] wellig; wogend.

wax[1] [wæks] **1.** Wachs *n*; Siegellack *m*; Ohrenschmalz *n*; Schusterpech *n*; ~ *candle* Wachskerze *f*; ~ *doll* Wachspuppe *f*; **2.** wachsen; bohnern; pichen (*Schuhmacher*).

wax[2] [~] (*irr.*) wachsen, zunehmen (*Mond*); † (*vor adj.*) werden.

wax·en *fig.* [ˈwæksn] wächsern, Wachs...; ˈ**wax·work** Wachsfiguren *f/pl.*; ~*s pl.*, ~ *show* Wachsfigurenkabinett *n*; ˈ**wax·y** □ wachsartig; weich.

way [wei] **1.** *mst* Weg *m*; Straße *f*; Art u. Weise *f*, Methode *f*; *eigene* Art *f*; Stück *n* (*Weg*), Strecke *f*, Entfernung *f*; Richtung *f*; F Gegend *f*; ⚓ Fahrt *f*; *fig.* Hinsicht *f*, Beziehung *f*; Zustand *m*, Verhältnisse *n/pl.*; ⚓ Helling *f*; ~ *in* Eingang *m*; ~ *out* Ausgang *m*; *fig.* Ausweg *m*; ~*s and means* Mittel und Wege *pl. zur Geldbeschaffung*; *right of* ~ ⚖ Wegerecht *n*; *bsd. mot.* Vorfahrt(srecht *n*) *f*; ~ *of life* Lebensweise *f*, -form *f*; *this* ~ hierher, hier entlang; *the wrong* ~ falsch (herum); *in some* ~, *in a* ~ in gewisser Hinsicht; *in no* ~ keineswegs; *go a great* ~ *towards ger.*, *go a long* (*some*) ~ *to inf.* viel (etwas) dazu beitragen zu *inf.*; *by the* ~ im Vorbeigehen; übrigens, nebenbei (bemerkt); *by* ~ *of* durch, (auf dem Weg) über (*acc.*); *by* ~ *of excuse* als Entschuldigung; *on the* ~, *on one's* ~ unterwegs; *out of the* ~ abwegig; ungewöhnlich; *under* ~ im Gange, ⚓ in Fahrt; *give* ~ sich zurückziehen, zurückgehen; *mot.* Vorfahrt lassen (*to dat.*); nachgeben; *fig.* stattgeben (*to dat.*); abgelöst werden (*to* von), übergehen (*to* in); sich hingeben (*to dat.*); *have one's* ~ s-n Willen haben; *if I had my* ~ wenn es nach mir ginge; *have a* ~ *with* umzugehen wissen mit; *lead the* ~ vorangehen; *s. make*; *pay one's* ~ glatt auskommen; sich selbst weiterhelfen; *see one's* ~ *to ger. od. inf.* e-e Möglichkeit für sich sehen, zu *inf.*; **2.** *adv.* (weit) weg; weit; ˈ**~-bill** Beförderungsschein *m*; Frachtbrief *m*; ˈ**~·far·er** Wanderer *m*; **~**ˈ**lay** (*irr. lay*) auflauern (*dat.*); ˈ**~-leave** Wegerecht *n*; ˈ**~·side 1.** Weg-, Straßenrand *m*; *by the* ~ am Wege, an der Straße; **2.** am Wege, an der Straße (befindlich); ~ **sta·tion** *Am.* Zwischenstation *f*; ~ **train** *Am.* Bummelzug *m*.

way·ward □ [ˈweiwəd] starrköpfig, eigensinnig; ˈ**way·ward·ness** Starr-, Eigensinn *m*.

we [wiː, wi] wir.

weak □ [wiːk] *allg.* schwach; schwächlich; dünn (*Getränk*); ˈ**weak·en** *v/t.* schwächen; *v/i.* schwach werden; ˈ**weak·ling** Schwächling *m*; ˈ**weak·ly** schwächlich; ˈ**weak-**ˈ**mind·ed** schwachsinnig; charakterschwach; ˈ**weak·ness** Schwäche *f*.

weal[1] [wiːl] Wohl *n*.

weal[2] [~] Strieme *f*.

wealth [welθ] Wohlstand *m*; Reichtum *m*; *fig.* Fülle *f*; ˈ**wealth·y** □ reich; wohlhabend.

wean [wiːn] *Kind* entwöhnen; *fig.* ~ *s.o. from od. of s.th.* j-m et. abgewöhnen.

weap·on [ˈwepən] Waffe *f*; ˈ**weap·on·less** waffen-, wehrlos.

wear [wɛə] **1.** (*irr.*) *v/t. am Körper* tragen; *ein Lächeln* zur Schau tragen; *ein Gesicht* zeigen; *a.* ~ *away*, ~ *down*, ~ *off*, ~ *out* abnutzen; verbrauchen; *Kleid etc.* abtragen; *Geduld etc.* erschöpfen; ermüden; zermürben; ausnagen; *v/i.* sich *gut etc.* tragen *od.* halten; sich abnutzen *od.* abtragen; ~ *away* abnehmen; vergehen; ~ *off* sich abnutzen *od.* abtragen; *fig.* sich verlieren; ~ *on* vergehen (*Zeit*); ~ *out* sich abnutzen *od.* abtragen; sich erschöpfen; **2.** Tragen *n*; Gebrauch *m*; Abnutzung *f*, Verschleiß *m*; *gentlemen's* ~ Herrenbekleidung *f*; *for hard* ~ zum Strapazieren, strapazierfähig; *s. worse 1*; *there is plenty of* ~ *in it yet* es läßt sich noch gut tragen; ˈ**wear·a·ble** tragbar; zu tragen(d); **wear and tear** Verschleiß *m*; ˈ**wear·er** Träger(in) (*e-s Kleidungsstücks*).

wea·ri·ness [ˈwiərinis] Müdigkeit *f*; Ermüdung *f*; *fig.* Überdruß *m*.

wea·ri·some □ [ˈwiərisəm] ermüdend; langweilig.

wea·ry [ˈwiəri] **1.** □ müde (*with* von); *fig.* überdrüssig (*of s.th.* e-r Sache); ermüdend; beschwerlich, anstrengend; **2.** *v/t.* ermüden; langweilen; *Geduld etc.* erschöpfen; *v/i.* müde werden.

wea·sel *zo.* ['wi:zl] Wiesel *n.*

weath·er ['weðə] **1.** Wetter *n*, Witterung *f*; *s. permit*; **2.** ⚓ Luv...; **3.** *v/t.* dem Wetter aussetzen; lüften; ⚓ luvwärts umschiffen; *a.* ~ *out* ⚓ *Sturm* abwettern, *fig.* überstehen; ~*ed* verwittert; *v/i.* verwittern; **~-beat·en** ['~bi:tn] vom Wetter mitgenommen; wetterhart; '**~-board** Wasserschenkel *m*; Schalbrett *n*; '**~-board·ing** Verschalung *f*; '**~-bound** durch schlechtes Wetter behindert; '**~-bu·reau** Wetteramt *n*; '**~-chart** Wetterkarte *f*; '**~-cock** Wetterhahn *m*, -fahne *f*; '**~-fore·cast** Wetterbericht *m*, -vorhersage *f*; '**~-proof,** '**~-tight** wetterfest; '**~-sta·tion** Wetterwarte *f*; '**~-strip** Dichtungsstreifen *m am Fenster etc.*; '**~-vane** Wetterfahne *f*; '**~-worn** verwittert.

weave [wi:v] **1.** (*irr.*) weben; wirken; flechten; *fig.* ersinnen, erfinden; sich schlängeln *od.* winden; **2.** Gewebe *n*, Webart *f*; '**weav·er** Weber *m*; '**weav·ing** Weben *n*, Weberei *f*; *attr.* Web...

wea·zen ['wi:zn] verhutzelt, [schrump(e)lig.]

web [web] Gewebe *n*; Gespinst *n*; *orn.* Schwimmhaut *f*; Gurt *m*; Papierbahn *f*, -rolle *f*; **webbed** mit Schwimmhäuten; '**web·bing** Gurtband *n*; '**web·foot·ed** mit Schwimmfüßen.

wed [wed] heiraten; *fig.* verbinden (*to* mit).

we'd F [wi:d] = *we had*; *we should*; *we would*.

wed·ded ['wedid] ehelich; Ehe...; ~ *to fig.* verhaftet (*dat.*); '**wed·ding** **1.** Hochzeit *f*; **2.** Hochzeits...; Braut...; Trau...; ~ *anniversary* Hochzeitstag *m* (*Jahrestag*); ~ *ring* Ehe-, Trauring *m*.

wedge [wedʒ] **1.** Keil *m*; *the thin end of the* ~ *fig.* der erste kleine Anfang; ~ *heel* Keilabsatz *m am Schuh*; **2.** (ver)keilen; *a.* ~ *in* (hin)einzwängen, einkeilen; '**~-shaped** keilförmig.

wed·lock ['wedlɔk] Ehe *f*; *out of* ~ unehelich.

Wednes·day ['wenzdi] Mittwoch *m*.

wee [wi:] klein, winzig; *a* ~ *bit* ein klein wenig.

weed [wi:d] **1.** Unkraut *n*; F Kraut *n* (*Tabak*); Kümmerling *m*; **2.** jäten; säubern (*of* von); ~ *out* ausmerzen; '**weed·er** Jäter(in); Jätwerkzeug *n*; '**weed-kill·er** Unkrautvertilgungsmittel *n*.

weeds [wi:dz] *pl. mst widow's* ~ Witwenkleidung *f*.

weed·y ['wi:di] voll Unkraut, verkrautet; *fig.* lang aufgeschossen.

week [wi:k] Woche *f*; *this day* ~ heute in acht Tagen; heute vor acht Tagen; '**~-day** Wochentag *m*; '**~-'end** **1.** Wochenende *n*; ~ *ticket* Sonntagsfahrkarte *f*; **2.** das Wochenende verbringen; '**~-'end·er** Wochenendausflügler *m*; '**week·ly** **1.** wöchentlich; **2.** *a.* ~ *paper* Wochenblatt *n*, -(zeit)schrift *f*.

weep [wi:p] (*irr.*) weinen (*for* vor *Freude etc.*; um *j.*); tropfen; nässen; '**weep·er** Weinende *m*; Leidtragende *m*; Trauerflor *m*, -schleier *m*, -schleife *f*; '**weep·ing** **1.** weinend; Trauer...; ~ *willow* ⚘ Trauerweide *f*; **2.** Weinen *n*.

wee·vil ['wi:vil] Rüsselkäfer *m*; Kornwurm *m*.

weft [weft] *Weberei*: Einschlag *m*, Schuß *m*; *poet.* Gewebe *n*.

weigh [wei] **1.** *v/t.* (ab)wiegen; *a.* ~ *up fig.* abwägen (*with, against* gegen); erwägen; ~ *anchor* ⚓ den Anker lichten; ~ *down et.* überwiegen; ~*ed down* niedergebeugt; *v/i.* wiegen (*a. fig.*); *fig.* Gewicht haben, ausschlaggebend sein (*with* bei); ~ *in* (*out*) vor (nach) dem Rennen gewogen werden (*Jockei*); ~ *in with Argumente* vorbringen; ~ (*up*)*on* lasten auf (*dat.*); **2.** *get under* ~ (= *way*) ⚓ unter Segel gehen; '**weigh·a·ble** wägbar; '**weigh·bridge** Brükkenwaage *f*; '**weigh·er** Wäger *m*; Waagemeister *m*; '**weigh·ing-ma·chine** (*bsd.* Brücken-, Tafel-) Waage *f*.

weight [weit] **1.** Gewicht *n* (*a. fig.*); Last *f* (*a. fig.*); *fig.* Bedeutung *f*; Wucht *f*; *carry great* ~ *fig.* großes Gewicht haben, viel gelten; *give short* ~ zu knapp wiegen; *putting the* ~ Kugelstoßen *n*; **2.** beschweren; *fig.* belasten; '**weight·i·ness** Gewichtigkeit *f*; '**weight·y** □ (ge-)wichtig, bedeutend; schwerwiegend; wuchtig.

weir [wiə] Wehr *n*; Fischreuse *f*.

weird [wiəd] Schicksals...; unheimlich; F sonderbar, seltsam.

wel·come ['welkəm] **1.** □ willkommen; *you are ~ to inf.* es steht Ihnen frei zu *inf.*; *you are ~ to it* es steht Ihnen zur Verfügung; (*you are*) *~!* gern geschehen!, bitte sehr!; **2.** Willkomm(en *n*) *m*; **3.** willkommen heißen, bewillkommnen; *fig.* begrüßen.

weld ⊕ [weld] **1.** (zs.-)schweißen (*into* zu); **2.** *a.* *~ing seam* Schweißnaht *f*; '**weld·ing** ⊕ Schweißen *n*; *attr.* Schweiß...; *~ goggles pl.* Schweißbrille *f.*

wel·fare ['welfɛə] Wohlfahrt *f*; *~* **cen·tre** Fürsorgeamt *n*; *~* **state** Wohlfahrtsstaat *m*; *~* **work** Fürsorge *f*, Wohlfahrtspflege *f*; *~* **work·er** Fürsorger(in).

well[1] [wel] **1.** Brunnen *m*; *fig.* Quelle *f*; ⊕ (Senk)Schacht *m*; ⊕ Bohrloch *n*; Treppen-, Aufzugs-, Licht-, Luftschacht *m*; **2.** quellen.

well[2] [~] **1.** *adv.* wohl; gut; ordentlich, tüchtig, gründlich; *s. as*; *~ off* in guten Verhältnissen, wohlhabend; *~ past fifty* weit über fünfzig; **2.** *pred. adj.* wohl, gesund; *I am not ~* mir ist nicht wohl; *that's ~* das ist gut; **3.** *int.* nun!, F na!

we'll F [wi:l] = *we will*; *we shall*.

well...: '**~-ad'vised** wohlbedacht; wohlberaten; '**~-'bal·anced** ausgeglichen; ausgewogen; '**~-'be·ing** Wohl(sein) *n*; '**~-'born** von guter Herkunft; '**~-'bred** wohlerzogen; '**~-de'fined** deutlich, klar umrissen; '**~-dis'posed** wohlgesinnt (*to, towards dat. od.* gegen); '**~-'fa·vo(u)red** gut aussehend; '**~-in'formed** gut unterrichtet.

Wel·ling·tons ['weliŋtənz] *pl.* Langschäfter *m/pl.* (*Stiefel*).

well...: '**~-in'ten·tioned** wohlmeinend; wohlgemeint (*Rat*); '**~-'judged** wohlberechnet; '**~-'knit** festgefügt; **~ known**, '**~-'known** bekannt; **~ made** gutgebaut (*Figur*); '**~-'man·nered** mit guten Manieren; '**~-'marked** deutlich (erkennbar); '**~-nigh** beinahe; '**~-'off** wohlhabend; gut d(a)ran; '**~-'or·dered** wohlgeordnet; **~-read** ['~'red] belesen; *weitS.* gebildet; '**~-'sea·soned** gut gewürzt; '**~-'spok·en:** *be ~* sich gewählt ausdrücken; '**~-'thumbed** abgegriffen (*Buch*); **~ timed** rechtzeitig; zeitlich wohlberechnet; '**~-to-'do** wohlhabend; '**~-'trained** gut ausgebildet; **~ turned** *fig.* gedrechselt; '**~-'wish·er** Gönner *m*, Freund *m*; '**~-'worn** abgetragen; *fig.* abgedroschen.

wel·ly F ['weli] Gummistiefel *m.*

Welsh[1] [welʃ] **1.** walisisch; **2.** Walisisch *n*; *the ~ pl.* die Waliser *m/pl.*

welsh[2] [~] *Rennsport*: *j-m* mit dem Wettgeld durchbrennen; '**welsh·er** Wettbetrüger *m*; *weitS.* Schwindler *m.*

Welsh...: '**~·man** Waliser *m*; **~ rab·bit** überbackene Käseschnitte *f*; '**~·wom·an** Waliserin *f.*

welt [welt] **1.** ⊕ Rahmen *m*, Rand *m e-s Schuhes*; Einfassung *f am Kleid etc.*; Strieme *f*; **2.** *Schuh* auf Rahmen arbeiten; F durchbleuen; *~ed* randgenäht (*Schuh*).

wel·ter ['weltə] **1.** rollen, sich wälzen; *~ in fig.* schwimmen in *s-m Blut etc.*; **2.** Wirrwarr *m*, Durcheinander *n*; '**~-weight** *Boxen*: Weltergewicht *n.*

wen [wen] ⚕ Balggeschwulst *f*; *bsd.* Grützbeutel *m am Kopf*; *fig.* Pfannkuchen *m* (*unverhältnismäßig angewachsene Stadt*).

wench [wentʃ] Mädchen *n*; Dirne *f.*

wend [wend]: *~ one's way* s-n Weg nehmen (*to* nach, zu).

went [went] *pret. von go 1.*

wept [wept] *pret. u. p.p. von weep.*

were [wə:, wə] *pret. von be.*

we're F [wiə] = *we are.*

weren't F [wə:nt] = *were not.*

west [west] **1.** Westen *m*; **2.** West...; westlich; westwärts; *go ~ sl.* hops gehen (*sterben*); '**~·bound** in Richtung Westen fahrend.

west·er·ly ['westəli] westlich.

west·ern ['westən] **1.** westlich; West...; abendländisch; **2.** Wildwestgeschichte *f*, -film *m*, Western *m*; = '**west·ern·er** Westländer(in); *Am.* Weststaatler(in); Abendländer (-in); '**west·ern·most** westlichst.

West In·dian ['west'indjən] **1.** westindisch; **2.** Westindier(in).

west·ing ⚓ ['westiŋ] (zurückgelegter) westlicher Kurs *m*; Westrichtung *f.*

West·pha·li·an [west'feiljən] **1.** westfälisch; **2.** Westfale *m*, Westfälin *f.*

west·ward(s) ['westwəd(z)] westwärts (gelegen).

wet [wet] **1.** naß, feucht; *Am.* den Alkoholhandel gestattend; *s. blanket 1*; ~ *dressing* feuchter Umschlag *m*; ~ *steam* gesättigter Dampf *m*; ~ *through* durchnäßt; **2.** Nässe *f*; Feuchtigkeit *f*; **3.** (*irr.*) nässen, naß machen; anfeuchten, benetzen; F *Geschäft etc.* begießen; ~ *through* durchnässen.

wet·back *Am. sl.* [ˈwetbæk] illegaler Einwanderer *m aus Mexiko*.

weth·er [ˈweðə] Hammel *m*.

wet-nurse [ˈwetnəːs] Amme *f*.

we've F [wiːv] = *we have*.

whack F [wæk] **1.** verhauen; **2.** Schlag *m*, Hieb *m*; voller Anteil *m*; *have od. take a* ~ *at* ’rangehen an (*acc.*); ˈ**whack·er** F Mordsding *n*; ˈ**whack·ing** F **1.** Haue *f* (*Prügel*); 2. kolossal.

whale [weil] Wal *m*; *a* ~ *of* F e-e Riesenmenge; *a* ~ *at* F e-e Kanone in (*dat.*); ˈ**~·bone** Fischbein *n*; ˈ**~-fish·er**, ˈ**~·man**, *mst* ˈ**whal·er** Walfischfänger *m*; ˈ**whale-oil** Tran *m*.

whal·ing [ˈweiliŋ] Walfischfang *m*.

whang F [wæŋ] **1.** Krach *m*, Bums *m*; **2.** krachen, bumsen; hauen.

wharf [wɔːf] **1.** *pl. a.* **wharves** [wɔːvz] Kai *m*, Anlegeplatz *m*; **2.** ausladen, löschen; ˈ**wharf·age** Kaianlage *f*; Kaigeld *n*; **wharf·in·ger** [ˈ~indʒə] Kaimeister *m*.

what [wɔt] **1.** was; das, was; *know* ~*'s* ~ wissen, was los ist; Bescheid wissen; ~ *money I had* was ich an Geld hatte; ... *and* ~ *not* ... und was nicht sonst noch; **2.** was?; wie?; wieviel?; welch(er, -e, -es)?; was für ein(e)?; ~ *about* ...? wie wär's mit ...?, wie steht's mit ...?; ~ *for?* wozu?; ~ *of it?* was ist denn dabei?; ~ *if* ...? wie wäre es, wenn ...?; und wenn nun ...?; ~ *though* ...? was tut's, wenn ...?; *what-d'you-call-him*, ~*'s-his-name* Dingsda *m*, Dingsbums *m*; ~ *next?* was sonst noch?; *iro.* was denn noch alles?; ~ *a blessing!* was für ein Segen!; ~ *impudence!* was für eine Unverschämtheit!; **3.** ~ *with* ... ~ *with* ... teils durch ... teils durch ...; **what·e'er** *poet.* [wɔtˈɛə], **what·ˈev·er** = *whatsoever*; ˈ**what·not** Etagere *f*; **what·so·e'er** *poet.* [wɔtsəuˈɛə], **what·soˈever 1.** was auch (immer); **2.** welche(r, -s) auch (immer); überhaupt.

wheat ♀ [wiːt] Weizen *m*; ˈ**wheat·en** Weizen...

whee·dle [ˈwiːdl] beschwatzen (*into* zu); ~ *s.th. out of s.o.* j-m et. abschwatzen.

wheel [wiːl] **1.** Rad *n*; Steuer *n*; *bsd. Am.* F Fahrrad *n*; Töpferscheibe *f*; Drehung *f*, Kreis *m*; ⚔ Schwenkung *f*; **2.** *v/t.* rollen, fahren, schieben; *v/i.* rollen, sich drehen; sich umwenden; ⚔ schwenken; F radeln; ˈ**~·bar·row** Schubkarren *m*; **~ base** *mot.* Radstand *m*; **~ chair** Rollstuhl *m*; ˈ**wheeled** mit Rädern; ˈ**wheel·er-ˈdeal·er** F Schlitzohr *n*; ˈ**wheel·wright** Stellmacher *m*.

wheeze [wiːz] **1.** schnaufen, keuchen; krächzen; **2.** Schnaufen *n etc.*; *thea. sl.* Witz *m*, Gag *m*; ˈ**wheez·y** □ schnaufend, keuchend.

whelk *zo.* [welk] Wellhornschnecke *f*.

whelp *rhet.* [welp] **1.** Welpe *m*; *allg.* Junge *n*; Balg *m*, *n* (*ungezogenes Kind*); **2.** (Junge) werfen.

when [wen] **1.** wann?; **2.** wenn; als; während *od.* da doch; und da.

whence [wens] woher, von wo.

when·e'er *poet.* [wenˈɛə], **when-(so·)ev·er** [wen(səu)ˈevə] wann (auch) immer; immer *od.* jedesmal wenn; sooft (als).

where [wɛə] wo; wohin; **~·a·bout**, *mst* **~·a·bouts 1.** [ˈwɛərəˈbaut(s)] wo etwa; **2.** [ˈ~] Aufenthalt *m*; Verbleib *m*; **~ˈas** wohingegen, während (doch); ⚖ in Anbetracht dessen, daß; **~ˈat** wobei, worüber, worauf; **~ˈby** wodurch; ˈ**~·fore** weshalb; **~ˈin** worin; **~ˈof** wovon; **~ˈon** worauf; **~·soˈev·er** wo(hin) (auch) immer; **~·upˈon** worauf(hin); **wher·ˈev·er** wo(hin) (auch) immer, überall wo; **whereˈwhith** womit; **where·with·al 1.** [wɛəwiˈðɔːl] womit; **2.** F [ˈ~] Erforderliche *n*; Mittel *n/pl.*

wher·ry [ˈweri] Fährboot *n*; Jolle *f*.

whet [wet] **1.** wetzen, schärfen; anstacheln; **2.** Wetzen *n*, Schärfen *n*; appetitanregendes Mittel *n*.

wheth·er [ˈweðə] ob; ~ *or no* so oder so.

whet·stone [ˈwetstəun] Wetz-, Schleifstein *m*.

whew [hwuː] hui!; hu!

whey [wei] Molke *f*.

which [witʃ] **1.** welche(r, -s)?; **2.** welche(r, -s); der, die, das; *auf den vorhergehenden Satz bezüglich*: was; **~'ev·er** welche(r, -s) (auch) immer.

whiff [wif] **1.** Hauch *m*; Zug *m beim Rauchen*; Zigarillo *n*; **2.** wehen; rauchen, paffen.

Whig [wig] **1.** Whig *m* (*engl. Liberaler*); **2.** Whig...; whiggistisch.

while [wail] **1.** Weile *f*; Zeit *f*; *for a ~* e-e Zeitlang; *worth ~* der Mühe wert; **2.** *mst ~ away Zeit* verbringen; sich *die Zeit* vertreiben; **3.** *a.* **whilst** [wailst] während.

whim [wim] = *whimsy*.

whim·per ['wimpə] **1.** wimmern; winseln; **2.** Wimmern *n*; Winseln *n*.

whim·si·cal □ ['wimzikəl] wunderlich; schrullig; **whim·si·cal·i·ty** [~'kæliti], **whim·si·cal·ness** ['~kəlnis] Wunderlichkeit *f*.

whim·s(e)y ['wimzi] Grille *f*, Laune *f*, Schrulle *f*, Einfall *m*.

whin ⚘ [win] Stechginster *m*.

whine [wain] **1.** winseln; wimmern; heulen; plärren; **2.** Gewinsel *n etc.*

whin·ny ['wini] wiehern.

whip [wip] **1.** *v/t.* peitschen; geißeln (*a. fig.*); *j.* verprügeln; F *j.* schlagen; *j.* übertreffen; *Sahne etc.* schlagen; werfen, schleudern; übernähen, umsäumen; umwickeln; ⚓ betakeln; *mit adv. od. prp.* werfen; reißen; *~ away* wegreißen; *~ from* wegreißen von; *~ in parl.* zs.-trommeln; *~ off* schnell weg- *od.* herunterreißen; entführen; *~ on Kleidungsstück* überwerfen; *~ up* antreiben; aufraffen; *v/i.* springen, rennen, flitzen; **2.** Peitsche *f*; Geißel *f*; *parl.* Einpeitscher *m*; Aufforderungsschreiben *n*; überwendliche Naht *f*; '**~·cord** Peitschenschnur *f*; Whipcord *m* (*Kammgarnstoff*); '**~-'hand** rechte Hand *f des Reiters*; *have the ~ of s.o.* Gewalt über j. haben.

whipped [wipt]: *~ cream* Schlagsahne *f*, -rahm *m*.

whip·per... ['wipə]: '**~-'in** *hunt.* Pikör *m*; *parl.* Einpeitscher *m*; '**~-snap·per** Dreikäsehoch *m*.

whip·pet *zo.* ['wipit] Whippet *m* (*kleiner engl. Rennhund*).

whip·ping ['wipiŋ] Peitschen *n*; Prügel *pl.*; '**~-boy** Prügelknabe *m*; '**~-post** *hist.* Stäupsäule *f*; '**~-top** Kreisel *m*.

whip·poor·will *orn.* ['wippuəwil] Ziegenmelker *m*.

whip-round F ['wipraund]: *have a ~ Geld* zs.-legen.

whip-saw ⊕ ['wipsɔː] *zweihändige* Schrotsäge *f*.

whir [wəː] = *whirr*.

whirl [wəːl] **1.** wirbeln; (sich) drehen; **2.** Wirbel *m*, Strudel *m*; **whirl·i·gig** ['~ligig] Kreisel *m*; Karussell *n*; *fig.* Wirbel *m*; '**whirl·pool** Strudel *m*; '**whirl·wind** Wirbelwind *m*; Windhose *f*.

whirr [wəː] **1.** schwirren (lassen); **2.** Schwirren *n*.

whisk [wisk] **1.** Wisch *m*; Staub-, Fliegenwedel *m*; *Küche*: Schneebesen *m*; Schwung *m*; Husch *m*; **2.** *v/t.* (ab-, weg)wischen, (-)fegen, (-)kehren; schwingen, wirbeln (mit); *Küche*: *Schnee* schlagen; *~ away* schnell wegtun; *v/i.* huschen, flitzen, wischen; '**whis·ker** *zo.* Bart-, Schnurrhaar *n*; *mst* (*a pair of*) *~s pl.* (ein) Backenbart *m*; '**whis·kered** mit Backenbart.

whis·k(e)y ['wiski] Whisky *m*.

whis·per ['wispə] **1.** flüstern, wispern; raunen; **2.** Geflüster *n*; '**whis·per·er** Flüsterer *m*; Zuträger (-in); **whis·per·ing cam·paign** Verleumdungs-, Flüsterkampagne *f*.

whist[1] [wist] pst!, st!

whist[2] [~] Whist *n* (*Kartenspiel*).

whis·tle ['wisl] **1.** pfeifen; **2.** Pfeife *f*; Pfiff *m*; F Kehle *f*; **~ stop** *Am.* Kleinstadt *f*; *pol.* kurzes Auftreten *n e-s Kandidaten im Wahlkampf*.

whit[1] [wit]: *not a ~* nicht ein bißchen, keinen Deut.

Whit[2] [~] Pfingst...; *~ week* Pfingstwoche *f*.

white [wait] **1.** *allg.* weiß; rein; F anständig; Weiß...; *~ coffee* Kaffee *m* mit Milch; *~ meat* helles Fleisch *n von Geflügel, Kalb etc.*; **2.** Weiß(e) *n*; *typ.* Lücke *f*; Weiße *m* (*Rasse*); **~ ant** *zo.* Termite *f*; '**~·bait** *ichth. Art* Weißfisch *m*, Breitling *m*; **~ book** *pol.* Weißbuch *n*; '**~-caps** *pl.* schaumgekrönte Wellen *f/pl.*; '**~-col·lar** geistig, Kopf..., Büro...; *~ crime* Wirtschaftskriminalität *f*; *~ workers pl.* Angestellten *pl.*; '**~-'faced** blaß; '**~-'haired** weißhaarig; **~ heat** Weißglut *f*; '**~-'hot** weißglühend; **~ lie** Höflichkeitslüge *f*; '**~-liv·ered**

feig(e); ~ **man** Weiße *m*; '**whit·en** *v/t.* weiß machen; ⊕ weißen; bleichen; *v/i.* weiß *od.* blaß werden; '**whit·en·er** Tüncher *m*; '**white·ness** Weiße *f*; Blässe *f*; '**whit·en·ing** Schlämmkreide *f*.

white...: ~ **pa·per** *pol.* Weißbuch *n*; ~ **sheet** Büßerhemd *n*; '~**·smith** Klempner *m*; '~**·wash 1.** Tünche *f*; **2.** weißen, tünchen; *fig.* weiß *od.* rein waschen; '~**·wash·er** Tüncher *m*.

whith·er *lit.* ['wiðə] wohin; **whith·er·so'ev·er** *lit.* wohin auch immer.

whit·ing ['waitiŋ] Schlämmkreide *f*; *ichth.* Weißfisch *m*.

whit·ish ['waitiʃ] weißlich.

whit·low ⚕ ['witləu] Nagelgeschwür *n*, Umlauf *m*.

Whit·sun ['witsn] pfingstlich; Pfingst...; ~**·day** ['wit'sʌndi] Pfingst(sonn)tag *m*; ~**·tide** ['witsntaid] Pfingsten *pl*.

whit·tle ['witl] schnitze(l)n, schnippeln; ~ *away* verkleinern; schwächen; ~ *down* beschneiden.

whit·y ['waiti] *bei Farben*: hell...

whiz(z) [wiz] **1.** zischen, sausen; **2.** Zischen *n*, Sausen *n*.

who [hu:] **1.** welch(r, -s); der, die, das; **2.** wer?; *Who's Who?* Wer ist's? (*biographisches Nachschlagewerk*).

whoa [wəu] brr!

who·dun·(n)it *sl.* [hu:'dʌnit] Kriminalroman *m*, -film *m*.

who·ev·er [hu:'evə] wer auch immer.

whole [həul] **1.** □ ganz; heil, unversehrt; † gesund; *made out of* ~ *cloth Am.* F frei erfunden; **2.** Ganze *n*; *the* ~ *of London* ganz London; *the* ~ *of them* sie alle; (*up*)*on the* ~ alles in allem, im ganzen; im allgemeinen; schließlich; '~-'**bound** in Ganzleder (gebunden); '~-'**heart·ed** □ aufrichtig, ehrlich; rückhaltlos; '~-'**hog·ger** *sl.* kompromißloser Anhänger *m*; Hundert(fünfzig)prozentige *m*; '~-'**length** *a.* ~ *portrait* Ganzbild *n*; '~**-meal bread** Vollkorn-, Schrotbrot *n*; '~**·sale 1.** *mst* ~ *trade* Großhandel *m*; **2.** im großen; Großhandels...; Engros...; *fig.* Massen...; ~ *dealer* = '~**·sal·er** Großhändler *m*; **whole·some** □ ['~səm] gesund, bekömmlich; heilsam; '**whole·time** vollbeschäftigt; hauptberuflich (tätig); Ganztags...; '**whole·wheat** Weizenschrot...

who'll F [hu:l] = *who will*; *who shall*.

whol·ly ['həulli] *adv.* ganz, gänzlich.

whom [hu:m, hum] *acc. von who*.

whoop [hu:p] **1.** Schrei *m*, Geschrei *n*; **2.** laut schreien; ~ *it up Am. sl.* Rabatz machen, laut feiern; **whoop·ee** *Am.* F ['wupi:] Freudenfest *n*; *make* ~ auf die Pauke hauen; **whoop·ing-cough** ⚕ ['hu:piŋkɔf] Keuchhusten *m*.

whop *sl.* [wɔp] vertrimmen; '**whop·per** *sl.* Mordskerl *m*, -ding *n*; *bsd.* faustdicke Lüge *f*; '**whop·ping** *sl.* kolossal, mächtig.

whore [hɔ:] Hure *f*.

whorl [wə:l] ⊕ Wirtel *m*; ⚘ Quirl *m*; *zo., anat.* Windung *f*.

whor·tle·ber·ry ⚘ ['wə:tlberi] Heidelbeere *f*; *red* ~ Preiselbeere *f*.

who's F [hu:z] = *who is*.

whose [hu:z] *gen. von who*; **who·so** (**-ev·er**) ['hu:səu; hu:səu'evə] wer auch immer.

why [wai] **1.** warum, weshalb; ~ *so?* wieso?; *that is why* deshalb; **2.** ei!, ja!; (je) nun.

wick [wik] Docht *m*.

wick·ed □ ['wikid] *moralisch* böse, schlimm, gottlos, sündhaft, schlecht; schalkhaft; '**wick·ed·ness** Bosheit *f etc.*

wick·er ['wikə] aus Weide geflochten; Weiden...; Korb...; ~ *basket* Weidenkorb *m*; ~ *chair* Korbstuhl *m*; ~ *furniture* Korbmöbel *pl.*; '~**-work 1.** Flechtwerk *n*; **2.** = *wicker*.

wick·et ['wikit] Pförtchen *n*; *Krikket*: Dreistab *m*, Tor *n*; '~**-keep·er** Torhüter *m*.

wide [waid] *a.* □ *u. adv.* weit; ausgedehnt; weitgehend; umfassend; weitherzig, großzügig; *bei Maßangaben*: breit; weitab, weit entfernt *vom Ziel*; ~ *awake* völlig *od.* hellwach; *3 feet* ~ 3 Fuß breit; ~ *difference* großer Unterschied *m*; '~**-an·gle** *phot.* Weitwinkel...; ~**-a·wake 1.** ['waidə'weik] hellwach; aufmerksam; F hell(e) (*schlau*); **2.** ['~] Kalabreser *m* (*Schlapphut*); '~**-'eyed** mit großen Augen; verwundert; '**wid·en** (sich) erweitern; '**wide·ness** Weite *f*; '**wide-'o·pen** weit geöffnet; *Am. sl.* großzügig, lax *in der Gesetzesdurchführung*;

ˈ**wide·spread** weitverbreitet, ausgedehnt.
wid·ow [ˈwidəu] Witwe *f*; *attr.* Witwen...; ˈ**wid·owed** verwitwet; *fig.* verwaist; ˈ**wid·ow·er** Witwer *m*; **wid·ow·hood** [ˈ~hud] Witwenstand *m*.
width [widθ] Breite *f*, Weite *f*.
wield *lit.* [wi:ld] *Schwert etc.* handhaben, führen; *fig.* ausüben.
wife [waif], *pl.* **wives** [waivz] (Ehe-) Frau *f*; Gattin *f*; Weib *n*; ˈ**wife·ly** frauenhaft, fraulich.
wig [wig] Perücke *f*; **wigged** mit Perücke; ˈ**wig·ging** F Schelte *f*, Anschnauzer *m*.
wig·gle [ˈwigl] wackeln (mit *et.*).
wight † *od. co.* [wait] Wicht *m*, Kerl *m*.
wig·wag F [ˈwigwæg] (durch Flaggen *etc.*) signalisieren.
wig·wam [ˈwigwæm] Wigwam *m*, Indianerhütte *f*, -zelt *n*.
wild [waild] **1.** □ *allg.* wild; *engS.* toll; unbändig; abenteuerlich; planlos; *run* ~ wild (auf)wachsen; ⚘ ins Kraut schießen; *talk* ~ (wild) darauflos reden; ~ *for od. about s.th.* (ganz) wild nach et.; **2.** *mst the* ~*s pl.* die Wildnis; ˈ**wild·cat 1.** *zo.* Wildkatze *f*; *Am.* Schwindelunternehmen *n*; *bsd. Am.* wilde Ölbohrung *f*; **2.** *fig.* wild; Schwindel...; **wil·der·ness** [ˈwildənis] Wildnis *f*, Wüste *f*; Einöde *f*; **wild·fire** [ˈwaildfaiə]: *like* ~ wie ein Lauffeuer; ˈ**wild-goose chase** *fig.* vergebliche Mühe *f*; ˈ**wild·ing** ⚘ Wildling *m*; ˈ**wild·ness** Wildheit *f*.
wile [wail] **1.** List *f*; *mst* ~*s pl.* Tücke *f*; **2.** (ver)locken; ~ *away* = *while* 2.
wil·ful □ [ˈwilful] eigensinnig; vorsätzlich.
wil·i·ness [ˈwailinis] List *f*, Arglist *f*.
will [wil] **1.** Wille *m*; Wunsch *m*; letzter Wille *m*, Testament *n*; *at* ~ nach Belieben; *of one's own free* ~ aus freien Stücken; **2.** (*irr.*) *v/aux.*: *he* ~ *come* er wird kommen; er pflegt zu kommen, er kommt gewöhnlich; *I* ~ *do it* ich will es tun; **3.** *v/t. u. v/i.* wollen; durch Willenskraft zwingen; **willed** mit e-m ... Willen, ...willig.
will·ing □ [ˈwiliŋ] willig, bereit (-willig); *pred.* willens, gewillt (*to inf.* zu *inf.*); *I am* ~ *to believe* ich glaube gern; ˈ**will·ing·ly** bereitwillig, gern; ˈ**will·ing·ness** (Bereit)Willigkeit *f*, Bereitschaft *f*, Geneigtheit *f*.
will-o'-the-wisp [ˈwiləðəwisp] Irrlicht *n*.
wil·low [ˈwiləu] ⚘ Weide *f*; ⊕ Reißwolf *m*; *attr.* Weiden...; ˈ~**-herb** ⚘ Weiderich *m*; ˈ**wil·low·y** weidenbestanden; *fig.* weidengleich; gertenschlank.
will·pow·er [ˈwilpauə] Willenskraft *f*.
wil·ly-nil·ly [ˈwiliˈnili] wohl oder übel.
wilt[1] † [wilt] *du* willst.
wilt[2] [~] *v/i.* (ver)welken; schlaff werden; *v/t.* welk machen; schlaff machen.
Wil·ton car·pet [ˈwiltənˈkɑ:pit] Veloursteppich *m*.
wil·y □ [ˈwaili] schlau, verschmitzt.
wim·ple [ˈwimpl] (Nonnen)Schleier *m*.
win [win] **1.** (*irr.*) *v/t.* gewinnen; erringen; erlangen, erreichen; ⚔ *sl.* organisieren; *j.* dazu bringen (*to inf.* zu *inf.*); ~ *s.o. over j.* für sich gewinnen; *v/i.* gewinnen; siegen; ~ *through to* sich durchringen zu; **2.** *Sport*: Sieg *m*.
wince [wins] **1.** (zs.-)zucken, zs.-fahren; **2.** Zs.-fahren *n*.
winch [wintʃ] Haspel *m*, *f*, Winde *f*; Kurbel *f*.
wind[1] [wind, *poet. a.* waind] **1.** Wind *m*; *fig.* Atem *m*, Luft *f*; ⚕ Blähung *f*; ♪ Blasinstrumente *n/pl.*; *be in the* ~ heimlich im Gange sein; *have a long* ~ e-e gute Lunge haben; *throw to the* ~*s fig.* in den Wind schlagen; *raise the* ~ *sl.* Geld auftreiben; *get od. have the* ~ *up sl.* Schiß kriegen; **2.** *hunt.* wittern; außer Atem bringen; verschnaufen lassen; *be* ~*ed* außer Atem sein.
wind[2] [waind] (*irr.*) *v/t.* winden; wickeln; *Horn* blasen (*pret. u. p.p. a.* ~*ed*); ~ *up* aufwickeln, -winden; *Uhr* aufziehen; *fig.* spannen; *Geschäft* abwickeln; ⚖ liquidieren; abschließen; *v/i. a.* ~ *o.s.*, ~ *one's way* sich winden; sich schlängeln.
wind... [wind]: ˈ~**·bag** *contp.* Windbeutel *m*, Schwätzer *m*; ˈ~**·bound** ⚓ vom Wind zurückgehalten; ˈ~**-break** Windschutz *m*; ˈ~**-cheat·er** Windjacke *f*; ˈ~**·fall** Fallobst *n*; (unverhoffter) Glücksfall *m*; ˈ~**-ga(u)ge** Windstärkemesser *m*;

ˈ**wind·i·ness** Windigkeit *f*; Aufgeblasenheit *f*.
wind·ing [ˈwaindiŋ] **1.** Winden *n*; Windung *f*; ⊕ Wicklung *f*; **2.** □ sich windend; ~ *staircase*, ~ *stairs pl.* Wendeltreppe *f*; ˈ**~-sheet** Leichentuch *n*; ˈ**~-ˈup** Aufziehen *n*; *fig.* Abschluß *m*; Ende *n*; ✝ Liquidation *f*.
wind-in·stru·ment ♪ [ˈwindinstrumənt] Blasinstrument *n*.
wind-jam·mer ⚓ F [ˈwinddʒæmə] Segler *m* (*Segelschiff*); *Am.* Windmacher *m* (*Schwätzer*).
wind·lass ⊕ [ˈwindləs] Winde *f*.
wind·mill [ˈwinmil] Windmühle *f*.
win·dow [ˈwindəu] Fenster *n*; Schaufenster *n*; ˈ**~-dress·ing** Schaufensterdekoration *f*; *fig.* Aufmachung *f*, Mache *f*; ˈ**win·dowed** mit Fenstern.
win·dow...: ~ **en·ve·lope** Fensterbriefumschlag *m*; ˈ**~-frame** Fensterrahmen *m*; ˈ**~-ledge** Fenstersims *n*; ˈ**~-pane** Fensterscheibe *f*; ˈ**~-shade** *Am.* Rouleau *n*; ˈ**~-shopping** Schaufensterbummel *m*; ˈ**~-shut·ter** Fensterladen *m*; ˈ**~·sill** Fensterbrett *n*.
wind... [wind]: ˈ**~·pipe** Luftröhre *f*; ˈ**~·screen**, *Am.* ˈ**~-shield** *mot.* Windschutzscheibe *f*; ~ *wiper* Scheibenwischer *m*; ˈ**~-tun·nel** ✈ Windkanal *m*.
wind·ward [ˈwindwəd] **1.** windwärts; Wind..., Luv...; **2.** Luv(-seite) *f*.
wind·y □ [ˈwindi] windig (*a. fig. inhaltslos*); ⚕ blähend; geschwätzig.
wine [wain] Wein *m*; ˈ**~-grow·er** Weinbauer *m*; ˈ**~-mer·chant** Weinhändler *m*; ˈ**~·press** Kelter *f*; **win·e·ry** *Am.* [ˈwainəri] Weinkellerei *f*; ˈ**wine-vault** Weinkeller *m*.
wing [wiŋ] **1.** Flügel *m* (*a.* ⚔ *u.* ⚠); Schwinge *f*; F *co.* Arm *m*; *mot.* Kotflügel *m*; ✈ Tragfläche *f*; ✈, ⚔ Geschwader *n*; *Fußball*: Außenstürmer *m*; ~*s pl. thea.* Kulissen *f/pl.*; *take* ~ weg-, auffliegen; *be on the* ~ im Flug sein; *fig.* auf dem Sprung sein; **2.** *v/t.* mit Flügeln versehen; *fig.* beflügeln; *Strecke* (durch)fliegen; flügellahm schießen; *v/i.* fliegen; ˈ**~-case**, ˈ**~-sheath** *zo.* Flügeldecke *f*; ˈ**~-chair** Ohrensessel *m*; **winged** geflügelt; Flügel...; ...flügelig; ˈ**wing-span** Flügelspannweite *f*.
wink [wiŋk] **1.** Blinzeln *n*, Zwinkern *n*; *not get a* ~ *of sleep* kein Auge zutun; *tip s.o. the* ~ *sl.* j-m e-n Wink geben; *s. forty*; **2.** blinzeln, zwinkern (mit *et.*); *fig.* blinken; ~ *at* ein Auge zudrücken bei *et.*; *j-m* zublinzeln; ˈ**wink·ing light** *mot.* Blinker *m*.
win·ner [ˈwinə] Gewinner(in); *Sport*: Sieger(in).
win·ning [ˈwiniŋ] **1.** □ einnehmend, gewinnend; **2.** ~*s pl.* Gewinn *m im Spiel*; ˈ**~-post** *Sport*: Ziel(pfosten *m*) *n*.
win·now [ˈwinəu] *Getreide* schwingen, worfeln; *fig.* sondern; sichten.
win·some [ˈwinsəm] gefällig, einnehmend.
win·ter [ˈwintə] **1.** Winter *m*; ~ *sports pl.* Wintersport *m*; **2.** überwintern; **win·ter·ize** [ˈ~təraiz] *Am.* winterfest machen.
win·try [ˈwintri] winterlich; *fig.* frostig.
wipe [waip] **1.** (ab-, auf)wischen; reinigen; (ab)trocknen; ~ *off* abwischen; *Rechnung* bezahlen; ~ *out* auswischen; *fig.* vernichten; *Schande* tilgen; **2.** Abwischen *n*; F Wischer *m* (*Hieb*); ˈ**wip·er** Wischer *m*; Wischtuch *n*.
wire [ˈwaiə] **1.** Draht *m*; Leitung *f*; F Telegramm *n*; *attr.* Draht...; *pull the* ~*s* der Drahtzieher sein; s-e Beziehungen spielen lassen; *s. live* 2; **2.** *v/t.* (ver)drahten; ⚡ (be-)schalten; (*a. v/i.*) *tel.* drahten, telegraphieren; ˈ**~·drawn** spitzfindig; ˈ**~-ga(u)ge** ⊕ Drahtlehre *f*; ˈ**~-haired** drahthaarig; ˈ**wire·less** **1.** □ drahtlos; Funk...; **2.** *a.* ~ *set* Radio(apparat *m*) *n*; *on the* ~ im Rundfunk *od.* Radio; ~ *station* (Rund)Funkstation *f*; **3.** funken; ˈ**wireˈnet·ting** Maschendraht *m*, Drahtgeflecht *n*; ˈ**wire-pull·er** Marionettenspieler(in); *fig.* Drahtzieher *m*; ˈ**wire-tap·ping** *teleph.* Anzapfen *n der Leitung*; Abhören *n*; ˈ**wire-wove** Velin...
wir·ing [ˈwaiəriŋ] Drahtnetz *n*; ⚡ Verdrahtung *f*; Beschaltung *f*; ✈ Verspannung *f*; ~ *diagram* ⚡ Schaltschema *n*; ˈ**wir·y** □ drahtig, sehnig.
wis·dom [ˈwizdəm] Weisheit *f*; Klugheit *f*; ~ *tooth* Weisheitszahn *m*.

wise[1] □ [waiz] weise, verständig; klug; gelehrt; erfahren; ~ *guy Am. sl.* Schlauberger *m*; *put s.o.* ~ j. aufklären (*to*, *on* über *acc.*).
wise[2] † [~] Weise *f*, Art *f*.
wise·a·cre ['waizeikə] Klugtuer(in); '**wise-crack** F **1.** witzige Bemerkung *f*; **2.** witzeln.
wish [wiʃ] **1.** wünschen; wollen; ~ *s.o. joy* (*of*) j-m Glück wünschen (zu); ~ *for* (sich) *et.* wünschen, sich sehnen nach; ~ *well* (*ill*) wohl-(übel)wollen (*to dat.*); **2.** Wunsch *m*; *good* ~*es pl.* (Glück)Wünsche *m/pl.*; **wish·ful** □ ['~ful] voll Verlangen (*to inf.* zu *inf.*); sehnsüchtig; ~ *thinking* Wunschdenken *n*; '**wish(·ing)-bone** Gabelbein *n des Geflügels.*
wish-wash F ['wiʃwɔʃ] labb(e)riges Zeug *n*; '**wish·y-wash·y** F labb(e)rig, saft- u. kraftlos, seicht.
wisp [wisp] Wisch *m*; Strähne *f*; '**wisp·y** dünn, schmächtig; *Haare*: sehr fein.
wist·ful □ ['wistful] gedankenvoll, versonnen; sehnsüchtig.
wit [wit] **1.** Witz *m*; *a.* ~*s pl.* Verstand *m*; witziger Kopf *m*; *be at one's* ~*'s end* mit seiner Weisheit zu Ende sein; *have one's* ~*s about one* seine fünf Sinne beisammen haben; *keep one's* ~*s about one* e-n klaren Kopf behalten; *live by one's* ~*s* sich durchs Leben schlagen; *out of one's* ~*s* von Sinnen; **2.** *to* ~ nämlich, das heißt.
witch [witʃ] Hexe *f*, Zauberin *f*; '**~craft**, '**witch·er·y** Hexerei *f*; '**witch-doc·tor** Medizinmann *m*; **witch hunt** *Am.* politische Diffamierung *f*, Hexenjagd *f*.
with [wið] mit; nebst; bei; von; durch; vor (*dat.*); *nach Verben der Gemütsbewegung*: vor; *it is just so* ~ *me* es geht mir geradeso; ~ *it sl.* auf Draht, schwer auf der Höhe.
with·al † [wi'ðɔ:l] **1.** *adv.* dabei, obendrein; **2.** *prp.* mit.
with·draw [wið'drɔ:] (*irr. draw*) *v/t.* ab-, ent-, zurückziehen; heraus-, zurücknehmen; *Geld* abheben; *v/i.* sich zurückziehen (*from* von); abtreten; **with'draw·al** Ein-, Zurückziehung *f*; *bsd.* ⚔ Rückzug *m*; (Geld)Abhebung *f*; Entzug *m*; ~ *symptoms pl.* ⚕ Entzugserscheinungen *f/pl.*
withe [wiθ] Weidenrute *f*.
with·er ['wiθə] *a.* ~ *up*, ~ *away v/i.* (ver)welken; verdorren; ver-, austrocknen; *fig.* vergehen; *v/t.* welk machen.
with·ers ['wiðəz] *pl.* Widerrist *m*.
with·hold [wið'həuld] (*irr. hold*) zurückhalten (*s.o. from* j. von *et.*); *et.* vorenthalten (*from s.o* j-m);
with'in **1.** *lit. adv.* im Innern, drin(-nen); zu Hause; *from* ~ von innen (her); **2.** *prp.* innerhalb, binnen, in; ~ *doors* im Hause; ~ *a mile of* bis auf eine Meile von; ~ *call*, ~ *sight*, ~ *hearing* in Ruf-, Seh-, Hörweite;
with'out **1.** *lit. adv.* (dr)außen; äußerlich; *from* ~ von außen (her); **2.** *prp.* ohne; *lit.* außerhalb; **with'stand** (*irr. stand*) widerstehen, trotzen; aushalten.
with·y ['wiði] = *withe*.
wit·less □ ['witlis] witzlos; geistlos; gedankenlos.
wit·ness ['witnis] **1.** Zeuge *m*; Zeugin *f*; *bear* ~ Zeugnis ablegen (*to* für; *of* von); *in* ~ *of* zum Zeugnis (*gen.*); *marriage* ~ Trauzeuge *m*; **2.** *v/t.* bezeugen; Zeuge sein von *et.*; erleben; *v/i.* zeugen (*for*, *to* für; *against* gegen); '**~-box**, *Am.* ~ **stand** Zeugenstand *m*.
wit·ti·cism ['witisizəm] Witz *m*; witzige Bemerkung *f*; '**wit·ti·ness** Witzigkeit *f*; '**wit·ting·ly** wissentlich, geflissentlich; '**wit·ty** □ witzig; geistreich.
wives [waivz] *pl. von wife*.
wiz *Am. sl.* [wiz] Genie *n*; **wiz·ard** ['~əd] **1.** Zauberer *m*, Hexenmeister *m*; *fig.* Genie *n*; *financial* ~ Finanzgenie *n*; **2.** *Schul-sl.* prima; '**wiz·ard·ry** (*a. fig.*) Zauberei *f*, Hexerei *f*.
wiz·en(**·ed**) ['wizn(d)] verhutzelt, schrump(e)lig.
wo(**a**) [wəu] brr!
woad ⚘, ⊕ [wəud] (Färber)Waid *m*.
wob·ble ['wɔbl] schwanken; wakkeln; ⊕ flattern.
wo(**e**) *rhet. od. co.* [wəu] Weh *n*, Leid *n*; ~ *is me!* wehe mir!; '**~-be·gone** jammervoll; **wo**(**e**)**·ful** □ *rhet. od. co.* ['~ful] jammervoll, traurig, elend; '**wo**(**e**)**·ful·ness** Elend *n*, Jammer *m*.
wog *sl. contp.* [wɔg] Farbige *m*, *f* (*bsd. Asiat od. Araber*).
woke [wəuk] *pret. u. p.p. von wake*[2] *1*.
wold [wəuld] (hügeliges) Heide-

land *n.*
wolf [wulf], *pl.* **wolves** [wulvz] **1.** *zo.* Wolf *m*; *sl.* Schürzenjäger *m*; *cry* ~ blinden Alarm schlagen; ~ *whistle* bewundernder Pfiff *m e-s Mannes*; *give s.o. a* ~ *whistle e-r attraktiven Frau* nachpfeifen; **2.** F *gierig* verschlingen; ˈ**wolf·ish** □ wölfisch; Wolfs...; F *fig.* gefräßig.
wolf·ram *min.* [ˈwulfrəm] Wolfram *n.*
wolves [wulvz] *pl. von wolf.*
wom·an [ˈwumən], *pl.* **wom·en** [ˈwimin] **1.** Frau *f*; Weib *n*; ~*'s rights pl.* Frauenrechte *n/pl.*; **2.** weiblich; ~ *doctor* Ärztin *f*; ~ *student* Studentin *f*; ~ *suffrage* Frauenstimmrecht *n*; ˈ**wom·an--hat·er** Weiberfeind *m*; **wom·an-hood** [ˈ~hud] (die) Frauen *f/pl.*; Weiblichkeit *f*; *reach* ~ zur Frau heranreifen; ˈ**wom·an·ish** □ weibisch; ˈ**wom·an·kind** Frauen(welt *f*) *f/pl.*; ˈ**wom·an·like** frauenhaft; ˈ**wom·an·ly** weiblich.
womb [wu:m] *anat.* Gebärmutter *f*; Mutterleib *m*; *fig.* Schoß *m.*
wom·en [ˈwimin] *pl. von woman*; ~*'s rights pl.* Frauenrechte *n/pl.*; ~*'s team Sport*: Damenmannschaft *f*; **wom·en·folk**(s) [ˈ~fəuk(s)], ˈ**wom·en·kind** *die* Frauen *f/pl.* (*bsd. e-r Familie*); Weibervolk *n*; **Wom-en's Lib** [lib] Frauenbewegung *f*; **wom·en's lib·ber** F [ˈlibə] Emanze *f.*
won [wʌn] *pret. u. p.p. von win 1.*
won·der [ˈwʌndə] **1.** Wunder(werk) *n*; Verwunderung *f*; *for a* ~ erstaunlicherweise; **2.** sich wundern (*at* über *acc.*); gern wissen mögen, neugierig sein, sich fragen (*whether, if* ob); **won·der·ful** □ [ˈ~ful] wunderbar, -voll, erstaunlich; wunderschön; herrlich; ˈ**won·der·ing** **1.** □ staunend, verwundert; **2.** Verwunderung *f*; ˈ**won·der-land** Märchenland *n*; Wunderland *n*; ˈ**won·der·ment** Verwunderung *f*; ˈ**won·der-struck** von Staunen ergriffen; ˈ**won·der-work·er** Wundertäter(in).
won·drous □ *lit.* [ˈwʌndrəs] wunderbar, erstaunlich.
won·ky *sl.* [ˈwɔŋki] wack(e)lig (*a. fig.*).
won't [wəunt] = *will not.*
wont [wəunt] **1.** *pred.* gewohnt; *be* ~ *to do* zu tun pflegen; **2.** Gewohnheit *f*; ˈ**wont·ed** gewohnt.
woo [wu:] freien; werben um, umwerben (*a. fig.*); locken, drängen (*to* zu).
wood [wud] Wald *m*, Gehölz *n*; Holz *n*; Faß *n*; ♪ Holzblasinstrumente *n/pl.*; ~*s pl. Schisport*: Hölzer *n/pl.*, Bretter *n/pl.*; *touch* ~*!* unberufen!; *out of the* ~ *fig.* über den Berg; *from the* ~ vom Faß; ~·**bine**, *a.* ~·**bind** ⚘ [ˈ~bain(d)] Geißblatt *n*; ˈ~-**carv·ing** Holzschnitzerei *f*; ˈ~·**chuck** *zo.* Waldmurmeltier *n*; ˈ~·**cock** *orn.* Waldschnepfe *f*; ˈ~-**craft** Weidmannskunst *f*; Kenntnis *f* des Waldes; (Geschicklichkeit *f* in der) Holzbearbeitung *f*; ˈ~·**cut** Holzschnitt *m*; ˈ~·**cut·ter** Holzfäller *m*, -hauer *m*; *Kunst*: Holzschneider *m*; ˈ**wood·ed** bewaldet; ˈ**wood·en** hölzern (*a. fig.*); Holz...; ˈ**wood-en-grav·er** *Kunst*: Holzschneider *m*; ˈ**wood-en-grav·ing** Holzschnitt *m* (*Technik u. Bild*); ˈ**wood·i·ness** Waldreichtum *m*; Holzigkeit *f.*
wood...: ˈ~·**land** **1.** Waldung *f*, Waldland *n*; **2.** Wald...; ˈ~·**lark** *orn.* Heidelerche *f*; ˈ~-**louse** *zo.* Rollassel *f*; ˈ~·**man** Förster *m*; Holzfäller *m*; Waldbewohner *m*; ˈ~·**peck·er** *orn.* Specht *m*; ˈ~·**pile** Holzstapel *m*; ˈ~-**pulp** Holzschliff *m*; ˈ~·**ruff** ⚘ Waldmeister *m*; ˈ~-**shav·ings** *pl.* Hobelspäne *m/pl.*; ˈ~·**shed** Holzschuppen *m*; ˈ**woods-man** *Am. für woodman*; ˈ**wood--wind**, *a.* ~ *instruments pl.* ♪ Holzblasinstrumente *n/pl.*; ˈ~-**work** Holzwerk *n* (*bsd.* △); Holzarbeit(en *pl.*) *f*; ˈ~-**work·ing ma-chine** Holzbearbeitungsmaschine *f*; ˈ**wood·y** waldig; Wald...; holzig; Holz...; ˈ**wood·yard** Holzplatz *m.*
woo·er [ˈwu:ə] Freier *m.*
woof [wu:f] *s. weft.*
woof·er ⚡ [ˈwu:fə] Tieftonlautsprecher *m.*
wool [wul] Wolle *f* (*co. Kopfhaar*); *dyed in the* ~ in der Wolle gefärbt; *fig.* waschecht; *pull the* ~ *over s.o.'s eyes* j. hinters Licht führen; *lose one's* ~ F ärgerlich werden; ˈ~-**gath-er·ing** **1.** Geistesabwesenheit *f*, Zerstreutheit *f*; *go* ~ spintisieren; **2.** geistesabwesend; ˈ**wool·(l)en** **1.** wollen; Woll(en)...; **2.** ~*s pl.* Wollsachen *f/pl.*, -kleidung *f*; ˈ**wool-**

(l)y **1.** wollig; Woll...; belegt (*Stimme*); *paint. u. fig.* verschwommen; **2.** *woollies pl.* F Wollsachen *f/pl.*, -kleidung *f.*

wool...: '**~·sack** Wollsack *m* (*Sitz des Lordkanzlers im Oberhaus*); '**~-sta·pler** Wollgroßhändler *m*; '**~-work** Wollstickerei *f.*

Wop *Am. sl.* [wɔp] *eingewanderter Italiener.*

word [wə:d] **1.** *mst* Wort *n*; *engS.* Nachricht *f*; Zusage *f*, Versprechen *n*; ⚔ Losung(swort *n*) *f*; Spruch *m*; *~s pl.* Wörter *n/pl.*; Worte *n/pl.*; *fig.* Wortwechsel *m*; Text *m e-s Liedes*; *by ~ of mouth* mündlich; *eat one's ~s* das Gesagte zurücknehmen; *have a ~ with* mit *j-m* sprechen; *have ~s* sich zanken (*with* mit); *leave ~* Bescheid hinterlassen; *send* (*bring*) *~* Nachricht geben (bringen); *be as good as one's ~* Wort halten; *take s.o. at his ~ j.* beim Wort nehmen; **2.** (in Worten) ausdrücken, (ab)fassen; *~ed as follows* mit folgendem Wortlaut; '**~-book** Wörterbuch *n*, Glossar *n*; Libretto *n*; '**word·i·ness** Wortfülle *f*, -schwall *m*; '**word·ing** Ausdruck *m*; Wortlaut *m*, Fassung *f*; '**word·less** wortlos, stumm; **word or·der** *gr.* Wortstellung *f*; '**word-'per·fect** *thea.* rollensicher; **word pro·ces·sor** *Computer*: Textverarbeitungsanlage *f*; '**word-split·ting** Wortklauberei *f.*

word·y □ ['wə:di] wortreich; Wort...

wore [wɔ:] *pret. von wear 1.*

work [wə:k] **1.** Arbeit *f*; Werk *n*; *~s sg.* Fabrik *f*, Werk *n*; *~s pl.* ⊕ (Uhr-, Feder)Werk *n*; ⚔ Befestigungen *f/pl.*, Festungswerk *n*; *public ~s pl.* öffentliche Bauten *pl.*; *~ of art* Kunstwerk *n*; *at ~* bei der Arbeit; in Tätigkeit, im Gange, im Betrieb; *be in ~* Arbeit haben; *be out of ~* arbeitslos sein; *make sad ~ of* arg wirtschaften mit; *make short ~ of* kurzen Prozeß machen mit; *put out of ~* arbeitslos machen; *set to ~*, *set od. go about one's ~* an die Arbeit gehen; *~s council* Betriebsrat *m*; **2.** (*irr.*) *v/i.* arbeiten (*a. fig. in heftiger Bewegung sein*); funktionieren; wirken; gären; sich *hindurch- etc.* arbeiten; *~ at* arbeiten an (*dat.*); *~ out* sich auswirken; herauskommen (*Summe*); *v/t.* (be)arbeiten; *tüchtig* arbeiten lassen, zur Arbeit anhalten; abnutzen; *Bergwerk etc.* ausbeuten; *Fabrik etc.* betreiben; *Gut etc.* bewirtschaften; in Betrieb *od.* Bewegung setzen, in Gang bringen; *Maschine etc.* bedienen; gären lassen; (hervor)bringen, (be-)wirken; anrichten; *Wagen etc.* führen, lenken; *Summe* ausrechnen, *Aufgabe* lösen; *~ one's way* sich e-n Weg bahnen, sich durcharbeiten; *he is ~ing his way through college* er arbeitet, um sein Studium zu finanzieren; *~ one's will* s-n Willen durchsetzen (*upon* bei); *~ it sl.* es deichseln, es hinkriegen; *~ off* weg-, aufarbeiten; *Energie* abarbeiten; *Gefühl* abreagieren; ✝ abstoßen; *~ out* ausarbeiten; abnutzen; herausbekommen; lösen; ausrechnen; *~ up Geschäft etc.* hochbringen; *Gefühl*, *Nerven* aufpeitschen, -wühlen; verarbeiten (*into* zu); *Thema* aus-, bearbeiten; sich einarbeiten in (*acc.*).

work·a·ble □ ['wə:kəbl] bearbeitungs-, betriebsfähig; aus-, durchführbar; brauchbar, nützlich; '**work·a·day** Alltags...; *fig.* prosaisch; **work·a·hol·ic** F [wə:kə'hɔlik] Arbeitssüchtige *m*; '**work·day** Werktag *m*; '**work·er** Arbeiter(in); Urheber(in); *~s pl.* Belegschaft *f*; **work force** Arbeiterschaft *f*; '**work·house** Armenhaus *n*; *Am.* Besserungsanstalt *f*, Arbeitshaus *n.*

work·ing ['wə:kiŋ] **1.** Bergwerk *n*; Steinbruch *m*; *mst pl.* Funktions-, Arbeits-, Wirkungsweise *f*; **2.** arbeitend; Arbeits...; brauchbar; *~ knowledge* ausreichende Kenntnisse *f/pl.*; *in ~ order* in betriebsfähigem Zustand; **~ cap·i·tal** Betriebskapital *n*; '**~-class** Arbeiter...; **~ day** Werk-, Arbeitstag *m*; **~ draw·ing** ⚠ Werkplan *m*; **~ hours** *pl.* Arbeitszeit *f*; **~ man** Arbeiter *m*; '**~-out** Ausarbeiten *n*, -rechnen *n*; Ausführung *f*; **~ plan** ⚠ Werkplan *m.*

work·man ['wəkmən] Arbeiter *m*; Handwerker *m*; '**~·like** kunstgerecht, geschickt; fachmännisch; '**work·man·ship** Kunstfertigkeit *f*, Geschicklichkeit *f*; Ausführung *f*; Werk *n.*

work...: '**~·out** *Am.* F *mst Sport*: (Konditions)Training *n*; Erprobung *f*; **~ per·mit** Arbeitserlaubnis *f*; '~-**room** Arbeitsraum *m*; '~-**sheet** *Schule*: Arbeitsunterlage *f*; ✝ Rohbilanz *f*; '~-**shop** Werkstatt *f*; '~-**shy** 1. arbeitsscheu; 2. Arbeitsscheue *m*; '~-**wom·an** Arbeiterin *f*.

world [wə:ld] *allg.* Welt *f*; *a* ~ *of* e-e Unmenge (von); *in the* ~ auf der Welt; *what in the* ~? was in aller Welt?; *bring* (*come*) *into the* ~ zur Welt bringen (kommen); *for all the* ~ *like od. as if* genau so wie *od.* als ob; *a* ~ *too wide* viel zu weit; *think the* ~ *of* alles halten von; *man of the* ~ Weltmann *m*; ~ **cham·pi·on** *Sport*: Weltmeister(in); ~ **cham·pi·on·ship** *Sport*: Weltmeisterschaft *f*; ♀ **Cup** Fußballweltmeisterschaften *f/pl.*; ♀ **Fair** Weltausstellung *f*; **world·li·ness** ['~linis] Weltlichkeit *f*; Weltsinn *m*; '**world·ling** Weltkind *n*.

world·ly ['wə:ldli] weltlich; Welt...; irdisch; ~ *innocence* Weltfremdheit *f*; ~ *wisdom* Weltklugheit *f*; '~-'**wise** weltklug.

world...: '~-**pow·er** *pol.* Weltmacht *f*; '~-'**wear·y** lebensmüde; '~-**wide** über die ganze Welt verbreitet; weltweit; weltumspannend; Welt...

worm [wə:m] 1. Wurm *m* (*a. fig.*); ⊕ (Kühl)Schlange *f*; ⊕ Schnecke(ngewinde *n*) *f*; 2. ~ *a secret out of s.o.* j-m ein Geheimnis entlocken; ~ *o.s.* sich schlängeln; *fig.* sich einschleichen (*into* in *acc.*); '~-**drive** ⊕ Schneckenantrieb *m*; '~-**eat·en** wurmstichig (*a. fig.*); '~-**gear** ⊕ Schneckengetriebe *n*; = '~-**wheel** ⊕ Schneckenrad *n*; '~-**wood** Wermut *m*; *fig.* Wermutstropfen *m*, Bitterkeit *f*; '**worm·y** wurmig.

worn [wɔ:n] *p.p. von wear 1*; '~-'**out** abgenutzt; abgetragen; verbraucht (*a. fig.*); müde, matt, erschöpft; abgezehrt; verhärmt.

wor·ri·ment F ['wʌrimənt] Quälerei *f*; **wor·rit** V ['wʌrit] quälen; ärgern; '**wor·ry** 1. (sich) beunruhigen; (sich) ärgern; sich sorgen, sich Sorgen machen; sich aufregen; bedrücken, bekümmern; zerren, (ab-) würgen; plagen, quälen; 2. Unruhe *f*; Sorge *f*; Ärger *m*; Qual *f*, Plage *f*; Quälgeist *m*.

worse [wə:s] 1. schlechter; ärger; schlimmer (*a.* ⚕); (*all*) *the* ~ desto schlimmer; ~ *luck!* leider!; um so schlimmer!; *he is none the* ~ *for it* er ist darum nicht übler dran; *the* ~ *for wear* abgetragen; 2. Schlimmere *n*; *from bad to* ~ vom Regen in die Traufe; '**wor·sen** (sich) verschlechtern *od.* -schlimmern; schädigen.

wor·ship ['wə:ʃip] 1. Verehrung *f*, Anbetung *f*; Gottesdienst *m*; Kult *m*; *Your* ♀ Euer Würden; *place of* ~ Kultstätte *f*; 2. *v/t.* verehren; anbeten; *v/i.* den Gottesdienst besuchen; **wor·ship·ful** □ ['~ful] *in Titeln*: verehrlich; '**wor·ship·(p)er** Verehrer(in), Anbeter(in); Gottesdienstbesucher(in), Kirchgänger (-in).

worst [wə:st] 1. schlechtest; ärgst; schlimmst; 2. *das* Schlimmste; *at* (*the*) ~ schlimmstenfalls; *do your* ~! mach, was du willst!; *get the* ~ *of it* den kürzeren ziehen; *if the* ~ *comes to the* ~ wenn es ganz schlimm kommt; 3. überwältigen, besiegen.

wor·sted ['wustid] Woll-, Kammgarn *n*; Kammgarnstoff *m*.

wort[1] ⚘ [wə:t] ...kraut *n*, ...wurz *f*.

wort[2] [~] (Bier)Würze *f*.

worth [wə:θ] 1. wert; *he is* ~ *a million* er hat e-e Million; ~ *reading* lesenswert; 2. Wert *m*; Würde *f*; **wor·thi·ness** ['wə:ðinis] Würdigkeit *f*; **worth·less** □ ['wə:θlis] wertlos; unwürdig; '**worth-'while** der Mühe wert, lohnend; **wor·thy** □ ['wə:ði] 1. würdig; *oft co.* ehrbar; ~ *of s.th.* e-r Sache würdig *od.* wert; 2. Mann *m* von Verdienst.

would [wud, wəd] *pret. von will*; wollte; würde, möchte, pflegte.

would-be ['wudbi:] an-, vorgeblich, sogenannt; möglich, potentiell; Schein..., Pseudo...; ~ *aggressor* möglicher Angreifer *m*; ~ *buyer* Kauflustige *m*; ~ *painter* Farbenkleckser *m*; ~ *poet* Dichterling *m*; ~ *politician* Kannegießer *m*.

wouldn't ['wudnt] = *would not*.

wound[1] [wu:nd] 1. Wunde *f*, Verwundung *f*, Verletzung *f*; *fig.* Kränkung *f*; 2. verwunden, verletzen (*a. fig.*).

wound[2] [waund] *pret. u. p.p. von* [*wind*[2].]

wove *pret.*, **wo·ven** ['wəuv(ən)] *p.p. von weave 1*.

wow *Am.* [wau] 1. Mensch!; toll!; 2. *thea. sl.* Bombenerfolg *m*; *weitS.* Bombensache *f*.

wrack[1] ⚘ [ræk] Seetang *m*.

wrack[2] [~] = *rack*[3].
wraith [reiθ] Geist *m e-s Sterbenden od. Verstorbenen.*
wran·gle ['ræŋgl] **1.** streiten, (sich) zanken; **2.** Streit *m*, Zank *m*.
wrap [ræp] **1.** *v/t.* wickeln; *oft ~ up* einwickeln; *fig.* einhüllen; *be ~ped up in* gehüllt sein in; *fig.* ganz aufgehen in (*dat.*); *v/i. ~ up* sich einhüllen; **2.** Hülle *f*; *engS.* Decke *f*; Schal *m*; Mantel *m*; '**wrap·per** Hülle *f*, Umschlag *m*; Morgenrock *m*; Deckblatt *n der Zigarre*; *a. postal ~* Streifband *n*; '**wrap·ping** Umhüllung *f*; Verpackung *f*; *~ paper* Einwickel-, Packpapier *n*.
wrath *lit.* [rɔθ] Zorn *m*, Grimm *m*; **wrath·ful** □ ['~ful] zornig, grimmig.
wreak [ri:k] *Rache* üben, *Zorn* auslassen (*upon* an *j-m*).
wreath [ri:θ], *pl.* **wreaths** [ri:ðz] (Blumen)Gewinde *n*; Kranz *m*, Girlande *f*; Ring *m*, Kreis *m*; Schneewehe *f*; **wreathe** [ri:ð] *v/t.* winden; umwinden; *v/i.* sich ringeln.
wreck [rek] **1.** ⚓ Wrack *n* (*a. fig.*); Trümmer *pl.* (*oft fig.*); Schiffbruch *m*; *fig.* Untergang *m*; **2.** zum Scheitern bringen; *Zug* zum Entgleisen bringen; zertrümmern; vernichten; zugrunde richten; *be ~ed* ⚓ scheitern; Schiffbruch erleiden; '**wreck·age** Trümmer *pl.*; Wrackteile *m/pl.*; **wrecked** schiffbrüchig; gestrandet; zerstört, ruiniert; '**wreck·er** ⚓ Bergungsschiff *n*; -arbeiter *m*; Strandräuber *m*; *fig.* Saboteur *m*; *Am.* Abbrucharbeiter *m*; *mot.* Abschleppwagen *m*; '**wreck·ing** Strandraub *m*; *~ company* Abbruchfirma *f*; *~ service mot.* Abschlepp-, Hilfsdienst *m*.
wren *orn.* [ren] Zaunkönig *m*.
wrench [rentʃ] **1.** winden, drehen; reißen; entwinden (*from s.o.* j-m); verdrehen (*a. fig.*); verrenken; *~ open* aufreißen; *~ out* herausreißen; **2.** *drehender* Ruck *m*; Verdrehung *f* (*a. fig.*); Verrenkung *f*; *fig.* (Trennungs)Schmerz *m*; ⊕ Schraubenschlüssel *m*.
wrest [rest] *drehend* reißen; verdrehen; entreißen, abringen (*from s.o.* j-m).
wres·tle ['resl] **1.** *v/i.* ringen; *fig.* kämpfen; *v/t.* ringen mit; **2.** = *wrestling*; '**wres·tler** Ringer(in); '**wres·tling** Ringkampf *m*, Ringen *n*.
wretch [retʃ] Elende *m*; Schuft *m*; *co.* Schelm *m*, Kerl *m*; *poor ~* armer Teufel *m*.
wretch·ed □ ['retʃid] elend, unglücklich; erbärmlich; '**wretch·ed·ness** Elend *n*; Erbärmlichkeit *f*.
wrick [rik] **1.** verdrehen, verrenken; **2.** Verdrehung *f*, -renkung *f*.
wrig·gle ['rigl] (sich) hin und her drehen *od.* bewegen; sich winden *od.* schlängeln *od.* ringeln; *~ out of* sich herauswinden aus.
wright [rait] ...macher *m*, ...bauer *m*.
wring [riŋ] **1.** (*irr.*) Hände ringen; *Wäsche* (aus)wringen; pressen; *Hals* umdrehen; *~ s.th. from s.o.* j-m et. abringen *od.* entreißen; *~ s.o.'s heart* j-m zu Herzen gehen; *~ing wet* klatschnaß; **2.** Wringen *n*; Druck *m*; '**wring·er**, '**wring·ing-ma·chine** Wringmaschine *f*.
wrin·kle[1] ['riŋkl] **1.** Runzel *f*; Falte *f*; **2.** (sich) runzeln; (sich) falten; *~d* runz(e)lig.
wrin·kle[2] F [~] Wink *m*; Kniff *m*; Trick *m*.
wrist [rist] Handgelenk *n*; *~ watch* Armbanduhr *f*; '**wrist·band** Bündchen *n*, (Hemd)Manschette *f*; = **wrist·let** ['~lit] Armband *n*; *Sport*: Handgelenkschützer *m*.
writ [rit] (behördlicher) Erlaß *m*; (gerichtlicher) Befehl *m*; *Holy* ♀ Heilige Schrift *f*; *~ of attachment* ⚖ Haftbefehl *m*; *~ of execution* ⚖ Vollstreckungsbefehl *m*.
write [rait] (*irr.*) *v/t.* schreiben; *Bogen etc.* voll-, beschreiben; *~ down* auf-, niederschreiben; *~ in full* ausschreiben; *~ off Brief etc.* (schnell) herunterschreiben; ⚕ abschreiben; *~ out* aus-, abschreiben; *~ up* ausführlich niederschreiben; ausarbeiten; hervorheben; *fig.* lobend erwähnen, herausstreichen; *ergänzend* nachtragen; *v/i.* schreiben; schriftstellern; *~ for* schriftlich bestellen, kommen lassen; *~ home about fig.* Staat machen mit; '**~-off** ⚕ Abschreibung *f*; *a complete ~* F ein Totalschaden *m*.
writ·er ['raitə] Schreiber(in); Verfasser(in); Autor(in); Schriftsteller (-in); *~ to the signet in Schottland*: Notar *m*; *~'s cramp*, *~'s palsy* Schreibkrampf *m*.
write-up ['raitʌp] Bericht *m*, Besprechung *f* in der Presse.

writhe [raið] sich (*vor Schmerz*) krümmen; *fig.* leiden.
writ·ing ['raitiŋ] Schreiben *n*; Aufsatz *m*; Schrift *f*, Werk *n*; (Hand-) Schrift *f*; Schriftstück *n*; Urkunde *f*; Schreibart *f*, Stil *m*; *attr.* Schreib...; *in* ~ schriftlich; '~**-block** Schreibblock *m*; '~**-case** Schreibmappe *f*; '~**-desk** Schreibtisch *m*; '~**-pad** Schreibblock *m*; '~**-pa·per** Schreibpapier *n*.
writ·ten ['ritn] **1.** *p.p. von write*; **2.** *adj.* schriftlich.
wrong [rɔŋ] **1.** □ unrecht; verkehrt; unrichtig, falsch; *be* ~ unrecht haben, im Irrtum sein, sich irren; in Unordnung sein; falsch gehen (*Uhr*); *go* ~ den Weg verfehlen; daneben-, schiefgehen; *fig.* auf Abwege geraten; *there is something* ~ irgend etwas ist nicht in Ordnung; *what's* ~ *with ...?* F was fehlt denn ... (*dat.*)?; was ist los mit ...?; *on the* ~ *side of sixty* über die 60 hinaus; **2.** Unrecht *n*; Beleidigung *f*; *be in the* ~ im Unrecht sein, unrecht haben; *put s.o. in the* ~ j. ins Unrecht setzen; **3.** unrecht tun (*dat.*); ungerecht behandeln; '~'**do·er** Übel-, Missetäter(in); '~'**do·ing** Übel-, Missetat *f*; **wrong·ful** □ ['~ful] ungerecht; unrechtmäßig; '**wrong'head·ed** verdreht, verschroben; querköpfig; '**wrong-ness** Ungerechtigkeit *f*; Verkehrtheit *f*.
wrote [rəut] *pret. von write*.
wroth *poet. od. co.* [rəuθ] erzürnt.
wrought *lit.* [rɔːt] *pret. u. p.p. von work* 2; '~-'**i·ron 1.** Schmiedeeisen *n*; **2.** schmiedeeisern; '~**-up** erregt.
wrung [rʌŋ] *pret. u. p.p. von wring* 1.
wry □ [rai] schief, krumm, verzerrt.

X

X ⚒ *u. fig.* [eks] X *n* (*unbekannte Größe*).
x-(cer·tif·i·cate) film † ['eks(sə'tifikit)'film] für Jugendliche ab 18 Jahren freigegebener Film *m*.
xen·o·pho·bi·a [zenə'fəubiə] Xenophobie *f*, Fremdenhaß *m*.
Xmas ['krisməs] = *Christmas*.
X-ray ['eks'rei] **1.** ~*s pl.* Röntgenstrahlen *m/pl.*; **2.** Röntgen...; **3.** durchleuchten; röntgen.
X-shaped ['eksʃeipt] x-förmig.
xy·log·ra·phy [zai'lɔgrəfi] Xylographie *f*, Holzschneidekunst *f*.
xy·lo·nite ['zailənait] Zelluloid *n*.
xy·lo·phone ♪ ['zailəfəun] Xylophon *n*.

Y

yacht ⚓ [jɔt] **1.** (Motor)Jacht *f*; Segelboot *n*; **2.** auf e-r Jacht fahren; segeln; '~**-club** Segel-, Jachtklub *m*; '**yacht·er, yachts·man** ['~smən] Jachtsegler *m*; (Sport)Segler *m*; '**yacht·ing** Segelsport *m*; *attr.* Segel...
yah [jɑː] *int.* äh!; puh!; pfui!
ya·hoo [jə'huː] Rohling *m*; Tölpel *m*.
yam ⚘ [jæm] Jamswurzel *f*.
yank[1] [jæŋk] **1.** *v/t.* (weg-, heraus-) reißen; *v/i.* flink hantieren; rührig sein; **2.** Ruck *m*.
Yank[2] *sl.* [~] = *Yankee*.
Yan·kee F ['jæŋki] Yankee *m* (*Nordamerikaner*); ~ *Doodle amerikanisches Volkslied*.
yap [jæp] **1.** kläffen; F quasseln;

2. Gekläff *n*; F Gequassel *n*.
yard[1] [jɑ:d] Yard *n*, *engl.* Elle *f* (= *0,914 m*); ⚓ Rah(e) *f*.
yard[2] [~] Hof *m*; (Bau-, Stapel-) Platz *m*; *Am.* Garten *m* (*um das Haus*); *the* ♀ *Scotland Yard m*; *marshalling* ~, *railway* ~ Rangierbahnhof *m*.
yard...: '**~-arm** ⚓ Rahnock *f*; '**~-man** 🚂 Rangierer *m*; '**~-measure**, '**~·stick** Yardstock *m*, -maß *n*.
yarn [jɑ:n] **1.** Garn *n*; ⚓ Kabelgarn *n*; F Seemannsgarn *n*; abenteuerliche Geschichte *f*; *spin a* ~ ein Seemannsgarn spinnen, e-e Geschichte erzählen; **2.** F (Geschichten) erzählen.
yar·row ♀ ['jærəu] Schafgarbe *f*.
yaw ⚓, ✈ [jɔ:] gieren (*vom Kurs abweichen*).
yawl ⚓ [jɔ:l] Jolle *f*.
yawn [jɔ:n] **1.** gähnen; **2.** Gähnen *n*.
ye † *od. poet. od. co.* [ji:, ji] ihr.
yea † *od. prov.* [jei] **1.** ja; **2.** Ja *n*.
year [jə:] Jahr *n*; ~ *of grace* Jahr *n* des Heils; *he bears his* ~*s well* er ist für sein Alter (noch) recht rüstig; '**year·ling** Jährling *m* (*einjähriges Tier*); '**year-long** einjährig, ein Jahr dauernd; '**year·ly** jährlich.
yearn [jə:n] sich sehnen, verlangen (*for, after* nach; *to inf.* danach, zu *inf.*); '**yearn·ing 1.** Sehnen *n*, Sehnsucht *f*; **2.** □ sehnsüchtig.
yeast [ji:st] Hefe *f*; Schaum *m*, Gischt *m*; '**yeast·y** □ hefig; schaumig; *fig.* gärend; schaumschlägerisch.
yegg(·man) *Am. sl.* ['jeg(mən)] Stromer *m*; Einbrecher *m*, Geldschrankknacker *m*.
yell [jel] **1.** (gellend) schreien; aufschreien; **2.** (gellender) Schrei *m*; anfeuernder Ruf *m*.
yel·low ['jeləu] **1.** gelb; F hasenfüßig (*feig*); *sl.* chauvinistisch; Sensations...; Hetz...; ~ *pages pl.* Gelbe Seiten *f/pl.*, Branchenfernsprechbuch *n*; **2.** Gelb *n*; **3.** (sich) gelb färben; ~*ed* vergilbt; '**~·back** Schmöker *m* (*billiger Roman*); ~ **fe·ver** ⚕ Gelbfieber *n*; '**~-ham·mer** *orn.* Goldammer *f*; '**yel·low·ish** gelblich; **yel·low press** Sensations-, Boulevardpresse *f*.
yelp [jelp] **1.** Gekläff *n*; **2.** kläffen.
yen *Am. sl.* [jen] brennendes Verlangen *n*.
yeo·man ['jəumən] Yeoman *m*, freier Bauer *m*, Freisasse *m*; ~ *of the guard* Leibgardist *m*; '**yeo·man·ry** Freisassen *m/pl.*, freie Bauernschaft *f*; ⚔ berittene Miliz *f*.
yep *Am.* F [jep] ja.
yes [jes] **1.** ja; doch; **2.** Ja *n*; **~-man** *sl.* ['~mæn] Jasager *m*.
yes·ter·day ['jestədi] **1.** gestern; **2.** der gestrige Tag, das Gestern; **yes·ter'year** voriges Jahr *n*.
yet [jet] **1.** *adv.* noch; jetzt noch; bis jetzt; schon; selbst, sogar, *as* ~ bis jetzt; bisher; *not* ~ noch nicht; **2.** *cj.* doch, jedoch, dennoch, gleichwohl, trotzdem.
yew ♀ [ju:] Eibe *f*, Taxus *m*.
Yid·dish ['jidiʃ] Jiddisch *n*.
yield [ji:ld] **1.** *v/t. als Ertrag* hervorbringen, liefern; *Resultat* ergeben; *Gewinn* (ein)bringen, abwerfen; gewähren; übergeben, -lassen; zugestehen; ~ *up the ghost* den Geist aufgeben; *v/i. bsd.* ✓ tragen; sich fügen; weichen, nachgeben (*Person u. Sache*); **2.** Ertrag *m*; Ausbeute *f*; '**yield·ing** □ nachgebend (*Erdreich etc.*); *fig.* nachgiebig.
yip *Am.* F [jip] jaulen.
yob F [jɔb], **yob·bo** F ['jɔbəu] Halbstarke *m*.
yo·del, yo·dle ['jəudl] **1.** Jodler *m*; **2.** jodeln.
yog·hourt, yog·(h)urt ['jɔgət] Joghurt *m*.
yo·gi ['jəugi] Jogi *m*.
yo-ho [jəu'həu] hau ruck!
yoicks *hunt.* [jɔiks] hussa!
yoke [jəuk] **1.** Joch *n* (*a. fig.*); Paar *n* (Ochsen); Schultertrage *f*; **2.** anjochen, anspannen; zs.-jochen, -spannen; *fig.* paaren (*to* mit); '**~-fel·low** (*bsd.* Lebens)Gefährte *m*, (-)Gefährtin *f*.
yo·kel F ['jəukəl] Tölpel *m*.
yolk [jəuk] (Ei)Dotter *m*, Eigelb *n*; Wollfett *n*.
yon † *od. poet.* [jɔn], **yon·der** *lit.* ['jɔndə] **1.** jene(r, -s); jenseitig; **2.** da *od.* dort drüben.
yore [jɔ:]: *of* ~ ehemals, ehedem.
you [ju:, ju] ihr; du, Sie; man.
you'd F [ju:d] = *you had*; *you would*; **you'll** F [ju:l] = *you will*; *you shall*.
young [jʌŋ] **1.** □ jung (*fig. frisch; neu; unerfahren*); *von Kindern a.* klein; Jung...; **2.** Junge(n) *pl.*; *with*

~ trächtig; 'young·ish ziemlich jung; **young·ster** ['~stə] Kind *n*, *bsd.* Junge *m*.

your [jɔ:, jə] euer(e); dein(e), Ihre; **you're** F [juə] = *you are*; **yours** [jɔ:z] der (die, das) eurige, deinige, Ihrige; euer; dein, Ihr; **your'self**, *pl.* **your·selves** [~'selvz] (ihr, du, Sie) selbst; euch, dich, Sie (selbst), sich (selbst).

youth [ju:θ], *pl.* **youths** [ju:ðz] Jugend *f*; Jüngling *m*; junge Leute *pl.*; ~ *hostel* Jugendherberge *f*; *go ~-hostelling* e-e Jugendherbergswanderung machen; in Jugendherbergen übernachten.

youth·ful □ ['ju:θful] jugendlich, jung; Jugend...; '**youth·ful·ness** Jugendlichkeit *f*; Jugend *f*.

you've F [ju:v, juv] = *you have*.

yuc·ca ⚘ ['jʌkə] Yucca *f*, Palmlilie *f*.

Yu·go-Slav ['ju:gəu'sla:v] **1.** Jugoslawe *m*, Jugoslawin *f*; **2.** jugoslawisch.

yule *lit.* [ju:l] Weihnacht *f*; ~ *log* Weihnachts-, Julblock *m im Kamin*; '**~·tide** *lit.* Weihnachtszeit *f*.

yup·pie ['jʌpi] *in Großstädten: junger, karrierebewußter und ausgabefreudiger Mensch (häufig auch bestimmten Modetrends folgend).*

Z

za·ny ['zeini] Dummkopf *m*, Hanswurst *m*.

zeal [zi:l] Eifer *m*; **zeal·ot** ['zelət] Eiferer *m*; *bsd. eccl.* Zelot *m*; '**zeal·ot·ry** blinder Eifer *m*; Zelotismus *m*; '**zeal·ous** □ eifrig; eifrig bedacht (*for* auf *acc.*; *to inf.* darauf zu *inf.*); innig, heiß.

ze·bra *zo.* ['zi:brə] Zebra *n*; ~ **crossing** Zebrastreifen *m*, Fußgängerüberweg *m*.

ze·bu *zo.* ['zi:bu:] Zebu *n*, Buckelochse *m*.

ze·nith ['zeniθ] Zenit *m*; *fig.* Höhepunkt *m*.

zeph·yr ['zefə] Zephir *m*, Westwind *m*; sanfte Brise *f*; ✝ Zephirwolle *f*; Zephirgarn *n*; Sporttrikot *n*.

ze·ro ['ziərəu] **1.** Null *f* (*a. fig.*); Nullpunkt *m* (*a. fig.*); Anfangspunkt *m*; **2.** ~ *in on* ⚔ sich einschießen auf; *fig.* *Thema* herausgreifen; ~ **growth** Nullwachstum *n*; ~ **hour** ⚔ festgelegter Zeitpunkt *m* für eine geplante Operation, Stunde *f* Null; ~ **op·tion** *bsd. Am.* Nullösung *f*.

zest [zest] **1.** Würze *f* (*a. fig.*); Lust *f*, Freude *f* (*for* an *dat.*); Genuß *m*, Behagen *n*; ~ *for life* Lebenshunger *m*; **2.** würzen.

zig·zag ['zigzæg] **1.** Zickzack *m*; **2.** im Zickzack (laufend), zickzackförmig; Zickzack...; **3.** im Zickzack gehen.

zinc [ziŋk] **1.** *min.* Zink *n*; **2.** verzinken.

Zi·on ['zaiən] Zion *m*; '**Zi·on·ism** Zionismus *m*; '**Zi·on·ist** **1.** Zionist (-in); **2.** zionistisch.

zip [zip] **1.** Schwirren *n*; F Schmiß *m*, Schwung *m*; **2.** den Reißverschluß auf- *od.* zumachen von; **zip code** *Am.* Postleitzahl *f*; '**~-fas·ten·er** = *zipper 1*; '**zip·per** **1.** Reißverschluß *m*; **2.** mit Reißverschluß versehen; '**zip·py** F schmissig.

zith·er ♪ ['ziθə] Zither *f*.

zo·di·ac *ast.* ['zəudiæk] Tierkreis *m*; **zo·di·a·cal** [zəu'daiəkəl] Tierkreis...

zon·al □ ['zəunl] zonenförmig; Zonen...; **zone** Zone *f*; Erdgürtel *m*; *fig.* Gürtel *m*; *fig.* Gebiet *n*.

Zoo F [zu:] Zoo *m*.

zo·o·log·i·cal □ [zəuə'lɔdʒikəl] zoologisch; ~ *garden(s pl.)* Zoologischer Garten *m*; **zo·ol·o·gist** [~'ɔlədʒist] Zoologe *m*; **zo'ol·o·gy** Zoologie *f*.

zoom ✈ *sl.* [zu:m] **1.** das Flugzeug hochdrücken; steil (empor)steigen; **2.** plötzliches steiles Steigen *n*; ~ *lens phot.* Gummilinse *f*, Vario-Objektiv *n*, Zoom-Objektiv *n*.

Zu·lu ['zu:lu:] Zulu *m*, Zulufrau *f*; Zulu(sprache *f*) *n*.

zy·mot·ic [zai'mɔtik] ⚗ zymotisch; Gärung erregend; Gärungs...; ⚕ Infektions...

Proper Names with Phonetic Transcriptions and Explanations

A

Ab·er·deen [æbə'di:n] *Stadt in Schottland.*

Ab·(o)u·kir [æbu:'kiə] Abukir *n* (*Hafenstadt in Ägypten*)

A·bra·ham ['eibrəhæm] Abraham *m.*

Ab·ys·sin·i·a [æbi'sinjə] Abessinien *n* (*früherer Name von Äthiopien*).

Ad·am ['ædəm] Adam *m.*

Ad·di·son ['ædisn] *englischer Autor.*

Ad·e·laide ['ædəleid] *weiblicher Vorname; Stadt in Australien.*

A·den ['eidn] *Hauptstadt des Südjemen.*

Ad·i·ron·dack [ædi'rɔndæk] *Gebirgszug in U.S.A.*

Ad·olf ['ædɔlf], **A·dol·phus** [ə'dɔlfəs] Adolf *m.*

A·dri·at·ic (Sea) [eidri'ætik('si:)] *das* Adriatische Meer.

Af·ghan·i·stan [æf'gænistæn] Afghanistan *n.*

Af·ri·ca ['æfrikə] Afrika *n.*

Ag·a·tha ['ægəθə] Agathe *f.*

Aix-la-Cha·pelle ['eikslɑ:ʃæ'pæl] Aachen *n.*

Al·a·bam·a [ælə'bæmə] *Staat der U.S.A.*

A·las·ka [ə'læskə] *Staat der U.S.A.*

Al·ba·ni·a [æl'beinjə] Albanien *n.*

Al·ba·ny ['ɔ:lbəni] *Hauptstadt des Staates New York* (*U.S.A.*).

Al·bert ['ælbət] Albert *m.*

Al·ber·ta [æl'bə:tə] *Provinz in Kanada.*

Al·der·ney ['ɔ:ldəni] *e-e der Kanalinseln.*

Al·ex·an·der [ælig'zɑ:ndə] Alexander *m.*

Al·ex·an·dra [ælig'zɑ:ndrə] Alexandra *f.*

Al·fred ['ælfrid] Alfred *m.*

Al·ger·non ['ældʒənən] *männlicher Vorname.*

Al·ice ['ælis] Alice *f.*

Al·le·ghe·ny ['æligeni] *Fluß u. Gebirge in U.S.A.*

Al·len ['ælin] *männlicher Vorname.*

Al·sace ['ælsæs], **Al·sa·ti·a** [æl'seiʃjə] das Elsaß.

A·me·lia [ə'mi:ljə] Amalie *f.*

A·mer·i·ca [ə'merikə] Amerika *n.*

A·my ['eimi] *weiblicher Vorname.*

An·des ['ændi:z] *pl. die* Anden.

An·dor·ra [æn'dɔrə] Andorra *n.*

An·drew ['ændru:] Andreas *m.*

An·gle·sey ['æŋglsi] *Grafschaft in Wales.*

An·nap·o·lis [ə'næpəlis] *Hauptstadt von Maryland* (*U.S.A.*).

Ann(e) [æn] Anna *f.*

An·tho·ny ['æntəni; 'ænθəni] Anton *m.*

An·til·les [æn'tili:z] *pl. die* Antillen.

An·to·ni·a [æn'təunjə] Antonia *f.*

An·to·ny ['æntəni] Anton *m.*

Ap·en·nines ['æpinainz] *pl. die* Apenninen.

Ap·pa·la·chians [æpə'leitʃjənz] *pl. die* Appalachen.

A·ra·bi·a [ə'reibjə] Arabien *n.*

Ar·chi·bald ['ɑ:tʃibəld] Archibald *m.*

Ar·den ['ɑ:dn] *englischer Familienname.*

Ar·gen·ti·na [ɑ:dʒən'ti:nə], **the Ar·gen·tine** [ði'ɑ:dʒəntain] Argentinien *n.*

Ar·is·tot·le ['æristɔtl] Aristoteles *m.*

Ar·i·zo·na [æri'zəunə] *Staat der U.S.A.*

Ar·kan·sas ['ɑ:kənsɔ:] *Fluß in U.S.A.; Staat der U.S.A.*

Ar·ling·ton ['ɑ:liŋtən] *Nationalfriedhof bei Washington* (*U.S.A.*).

Ar·thur ['ɑ:θə] Art(h)ur *m.*

As·cot ['æskət] *Stadt in England mit berühmter Rennbahn.*

A·sia ['eiʃə] Asien *n*; ~ *Minor* Kleinasien *n.*

Ath·ens ['æθinz] Athen *n.*
At·lan·tic [ət'læntik] *der* Atlantik.
Auck·land ['ɔ:klənd] *Hafenstadt in Neuseeland.*
Aus·ten ['ɔstin] *englische Autorin.*
Aus·tin ['ɔstin] *Hauptstadt von Texas (U.S.A.).*
Aus·tra·lia [ɔs'treiljə] Australien *n.*
Aus·tri·a ['ɔstriə] Österreich *n.*
A·von ['eivən] *Fluß in England.*
Ax·min·ster ['æksminstə] *Stadt in England.*
A·zores [ə'zɔ:z] *pl. die* Azoren.

B

Ba·con ['beikən] *englischer Staatsmann u. Philosoph.*
Ba·den-Pow·ell ['beidn'pəuəl] *Begründer der Pfadfinderbewegung.*
Ba·ha·mas [bə'hɑ:məz] *pl. die* Bahamainseln.
Bald·win ['bɔ:ldwin] *männlicher Vorname; amerikanischer Autor.*
Bâle [bɑ:l] Basel *n.*
Bal·kans ['bɔ:lkənz] *pl. der* Balkan.
Bal·mor·al [bæl'mɔrəl] *Königsschloß in Schottland.*
Bal·ti·more ['bɔ:ltimɔ:] *Hafenstadt in U.S.A.*
Bar·thol·o·mew [bɑ:'θɔləmju:] Bartholomäus *m.*
Bath [bɑ:θ] *Badeort in England.*
Ba·ton Rouge ['bætən'ru:ʒ] *Hauptstadt von Louisiana (U.S.A.).*
Ba·var·ia [bə'vɛəriə] Bayern *n.*
Bea·cons·field ['bi:kənzfi:ld] *Adelstitel Disraelis.*
Beck·y ['beki] *Kurzform von Rebecca.*
Bed·ford ['bedfəd] *Stadt in England; a.* **Bed·ford·shire** ['~ʃiə] *Grafschaft in England.*
Bee·cham ['bi:tʃəm] *englischer Dirigent.*
Bel·fast [bel'fɑ:st] *Hauptstadt von Nordirland.*
Bel·gium ['beldʒəm] Belgien *n.*
Bel·grade [bel'greid] Belgrad *n.*
Bel·gra·vi·a [bel'greivjə] *Stadtteil von London.*
Ben [ben] *Kurzform von Benjamin.*
Ben·e·dict ['benidikt; 'benit] Benedikt *m.*
Ben·gal [beŋ'gɔ:l] Bengalen *n.*
Ben·ja·min ['bendʒəmin] Benjamin *m.*
Ben Ne·vis [ben'nevis] *höchster Berg in Großbritannien.*
Berk·shire ['bɑ:kʃiə] *Grafschaft in England;* ~ *Hills pl. Gebirgszug in Massachusetts (U.S.A.).*
Ber·lin [bə:'lin] Berlin *n.*
Ber·mu·das [bə:'mju:dəz] *pl. die* Bermudainseln.
Ber·nard ['bə:nəd] Bern(h)ard *m.*
Bern(e) [bə:n] Bern *n.*
Bern·stein ['bə:nstain] *amerikanischer Komponist u. Dirigent.*
Ber·tha ['bə:θə] Bertha *f.*
Ber·trand ['bə:trənd] Bertram *m.*
Bess, Bes·sy ['bes(i)], **Bet·s(e)y** ['betsi], **Bet·ty** ['beti] Lieschen *n.*
Bill, Bil·ly ['bil(i)] *Kurzform von William.*
Bir·ken·head ['bə:kənhed] *Industrie- u. Hafenstadt in England.*
Bir·ming·ham ['bə:miŋəm] *Industriestadt in England.*
Bis·kay ['biskei]: *Bay of* ~ *der* Golf von Biskaya.
Blooms·bur·y ['blu:mzbəri] *Künstlerviertel in London.*
Bob [bɔb] *Kurzform von Robert.*
Bo·he·mi·a [bəu'hi:mjə] Böhmen *n.*
Boi·se ['bɔisi] *Hauptstadt von Idaho (U.S.A.).*
Bol·eyn ['bulin]: *Anne* ~ *Mutter Elizabeths I.*
Bo·liv·i·a [bə'liviə] Bolivien *n.*
Bom·bay [bɔm'bei] *Hafenstadt in Indien.*
Bonn [bɔn] *Hauptstadt der Bundesrepublik Deutschland.*
Bos·ton ['bɔstən] *Hauptstadt von Massachusetts (U.S.A.).*
Bourne·mouth ['bɔ:nməθ] *Badeort in England.*
Brad·ford ['brædfəd] *Industriestadt in England.*
Bra·zil [brə'zil] Brasilien *n.*
Breck·nock(·shire) ['breknɔk(ʃiə)] *Grafschaft in Wales.*
Bridg·et ['bridʒit] Brigitte *f.*
Brigh·ton ['braitn] *Badeort in England.*
Bris·tol ['bristl] *Hafenstadt in England.*
Bri·tan·ni·a *poet.* [bri'tænjə] Großbritannien *n.*
Brit·ten ['britn] *englischer Komponist.*
Broad·way ['brɔ:dwei] *Straße in New York (U.S.A.).*
Bron·të ['brɔnti] *Name dreier englischer Autorinnen.*
Brook·lyn ['bruklin] *Stadtteil von New York (U.S.A.).*
Bruges [bru:ʒ] Brügge *n.*

Bruns·wick ['brʌnzwik] Braunschweig *n.*
Brus·sels ['brʌslz] Brüssel *n.*
Bu·cha·rest [bju:kə'rest] Bukarest *n.*
Buck [bʌk] *amerikanische Autorin.*
Buck·ing·ham ['bʌkiŋəm] *Grafschaft in England;* ~ *Palace Königsschloß in London;* **Buck·ing·ham·shire** ['~ʃiə] *s. Buckingham.*
Bu·da·pest ['bju:də'pest] Budapest *n.*
Bud·dha ['budə] Buddha *m.*
Bul·gar·i·a [bʌl'gɛəriə] Bulgarien *n.*
Bur·ma ['bə:mə] Birma *n.*
Burns [bə:nz] *schottischer Dichter.*
By·ron ['baiərən] *englischer Dichter.*

C

Caer·nar·von(·shire) [kə'nɑ:vən (-ʃiə)] *Grafschaft in Wales.*
Cae·sar ['si:zə] (*Julius*) Cäsar *m.*
Cai·ro ['kaiərəu] Kairo *n.*
Cal·cut·ta [kæl'kʌtə] Kalkutta *n.*
Cal·i·for·nia [kæli'fɔ:njə] Kalifornien *n* (*Staat der U.S.A.*).
Cam·bridge ['keimbridʒ] *englische Universitätsstadt; Stadt in U.S.A., Sitz der Harvard-Universität;* **Cam·bridge·shire** ['~ʃiə] *Grafschaft in England.*
Can·a·da ['kænədə] Kanada *n.*
Ca·nar·y Is·lands [kə'nɛəri'ailəndz] *pl. die* Kanarischen Inseln.
Can·ber·ra ['kænbərə] *Hauptstadt von Australien.*
Can·ter·bur·y ['kæntəbəri] *Stadt in England.*
Cape·town ['keiptaun] Kapstadt *n.*
Ca·pote [kə'pəuti] *amerikanischer Autor.*
Car·diff ['kɑ:dif] *Hauptstadt von Wales.*
Car·di·gan(·shire) ['kɑ:digən(ʃiə)] *Grafschaft in Wales.*
Ca·rin·thi·a [kə'rinθiə] Kärnten *n.*
Car·lyle [kɑ:'lail] *englischer Autor.*
Car·mar·then(·shire) [kə'mɑ:ðən (-ʃiə)] *Grafschaft in Wales.*
Car·ne·gie [kɑ:'negi] *amerikanischer Industrieller.*
Car·o·li·na [kærə'lainə]: *North* ~ Nordkarolina *n* (*Staat der U.S.A.*); *South* ~ Südkarolina *n* (*Staat der U.S.A.*).
Car·o·line ['kærəlain] Karoline *f.*
Car·rie ['kæri] *Kurzform von Caroline.*
Cath·er·ine ['kæθərin] Katharina *f.*
Ce·cil ['sesl; 'sisl] *männlicher Vorname.*
Ce·cil·ia [si'siljə], **Cec·i·ly** ['sisili; 'sesili] Cäcilie *f.*
Cey·lon [si'lɔn] Ceylon *n.*
Cham·ber·lain ['tʃeimbəlin] *Name mehrerer britischer Staatsmänner.*
Char·ing Cross ['tʃæriŋ'krɔs] *Stadtteil von London.*
Char·le·magne ['ʃɑ:lə'mein] Karl der Große.
Charles [tʃɑ:lz] Karl *m.*
Charles·ton ['tʃɑ:lstən] *Hauptstadt von West Virginia* (*U.S.A.*).
Char·lotte ['ʃɑ:lət] Charlotte *f.*
Chau·cer ['tʃɔ:sə] *englischer Dichter.*
Chel·sea ['tʃelsi] *Stadtteil von London.*
Chesh·ire ['tʃeʃə] *Grafschaft in England.*
Ches·ter·field ['tʃestəfi:ld] *Industriestadt in England.*
Chev·i·ot Hills ['tʃeviət'hilz] *pl. Grenzgebirge zwischen England u. Schottland.*
Chi·ca·go [ʃi'kɑ:gəu; *Am. a.* ʃi'kɔ:gəu] *Industriestadt in U.S.A.*
Chil·e, Chil·i ['tʃili] Chile *n.*
Chi·na ['tʃainə] China *n.*
Chris·ti·na [kris'ti:nə] Christine *f.*
Chris·to·pher ['kristəfə] Christoph *m.*
Chrys·ler ['kraizlə] *amerikanischer Industrieller.*
Church·ill ['tʃə:tʃil] *britischer Staatsmann.*
Cin·cin·nat·i [sinsi'næti] *Stadt in U.S.A.*
Cis·sie ['sisi] *Kurzform von Cecilia.*
Clar·a ['klɛərə], **Clare** [klɛə] Klara *f.*
Clar·en·don ['klærəndən] *Name mehrerer britischer Staatsmänner.*
Cle·o·pat·ra [kliə'pætrə] Kleopatra *f.*
Cleve·land ['kli:vlənd] *Industrie- u. Hafenstadt in U.S.A.*
Clive [klaiv] *Begründer der britischen Macht in Indien.*
Clyde [klaid] *Fluß in Schottland.*
Cole·ridge ['kəulridʒ] *englischer Dichter.*
Co·logne [kə'ləun] Köln *n.*
Col·o·ra·do [kɔlə'rɑ:dəu] *Name zweier Flüsse u. Staat der U.S.A.*
Co·lum·bi·a [kə'lʌmbiə] *Fluß in U.S.A.; Bundesdistrikt der U.S.A.; Hauptstadt von Südkarolina* (*U.S.A.*).

Con·cord ['kɔŋkɔ:d] *Hauptstadt von New Hampshire (U.S.A.).*
Con·naught ['kɔnɔ:t] *Provinz in Irland.*
Con·nect·i·cut [kə'netikət] *Fluß in U.S.A.; Staat der U.S.A.*
Con·stance ['kɔnstəns] Konstanze *f*; Konstanz *n*; Lake of ~ Bodensee *m.*
Coo·per ['ku:pə] *amerikanischer Autor.*
Co·pen·ha·gen [kəupn'heigən] Kopenhagen *n.*
Cor·dil·le·ras [kɔ:di'ljɛərəz] *pl. die* Kordilleren.
Cor·ne·lia [kɔ:'ni:ljə] Kornelia *f.*
Corn·wall ['kɔ:nwəl] *Grafschaft in England.*
Cov·ent Gar·den ['kɔvənt'gɑ:dn] *die Londoner Oper.*
Cov·en·try ['kɔvəntri] *Industriestadt in England.*
Cri·me·a [krai'miə] *die* Krim.
Crom·well ['krɔmwəl] *englischer Staatsmann.*
Croy·don ['krɔidn] *früherer Flughafen von London.*
Cu·ba ['kju:bə] Kuba *n.*
Cum·ber·land ['kʌmbələnd] *Grafschaft in England.*
Cy·prus ['saiprəs] Zypern *n.*
Czech·o·slo·va·ki·a ['tʃekəusləu'vækiə] die Tschechoslowakei.

D

Da·ko·ta [də'kəutə]: North ~ Norddakota *n (Staat der U.S.A.)*; South ~ Süddakota *n (Staat der U.S.A.).*
Dan·iel ['dænjəl] Daniel *m.*
Dan·ube ['dænju:b] *die* Donau.
Dar·da·nelles [dɑ:də'nelz] *pl. die* Dardanellen.
Dar·jee·ling [dɑ:'dʒi:liŋ] *Stadt in Indien.*
Dart·moor ['dɑ:tmuə] *Bergmassiv in England.*
Dar·win ['dɑ:win] *englischer Naturforscher.*
Da·vid ['deivid] David *m.*
Dee [di:] *Fluß in England.*
De·foe [di'fəu] *englischer Autor.*
Del·a·ware ['deləwɛə] *Fluß in U.S.A.; Staat der U.S.A.*
Den·bigh(·shire) ['denbi(ʃiə)] *Grafschaft in Wales.*
Den·mark ['denmɑ:k] Dänemark *n.*
Den·ver ['denvə] *Hauptstadt von Colorado (U.S.A.).*
Der·by(·shire) ['dɑ:bi(ʃə)] *Grafschaft in England.*
Des Moines [di'mɔin] *Hauptstadt von Iowa (U.S.A.).*
De·troit [də'trɔit] *Industriestadt in U.S.A.*
Dev·on(·shire) ['devn(ʃiə)] *Grafschaft in England.*
Dew·ey ['dju:i] *amerikanischer Philosoph.*
Dick [dik] *Kurzform von* Richard.
Dick·ens ['dikinz] *englischer Autor.*
Dis·rae·li [dis'reili] *britischer Staatsmann.*
Dol·ly ['dɔli] *Kurzform von* Dorothy.
Don·ald ['dɔnld] *männlicher Vorname.*
Don Quix·ote [dɔn'kwiksət] Don Quijote *m.*
Dor·o·the·a [dɔrə'θiə], **Dor·o·thy** ['dɔrəθi] Dorothea *f.*
Dor·set(·shire) ['dɔ:sit(ʃiə)] *Grafschaft in England.*
Dos Pas·sos [dəs'pæsəs] *amerikanischer Autor.*
Doug·las ['dʌgləs] *schottisches Adelsgeschlecht.*
Do·ver ['dəuvə] *Hafenstadt in England; Hauptstadt von Delaware (U.S.A.).*
Down·ing Street ['dauniŋ'stri:t] *Straße in London mit der Amtswohnung des Prime Ministers.*
Drei·ser ['draisə] *amerikanischer Autor.*
Dry·den ['draidn] *englischer Dichter.*
Dub·lin ['dʌblin] *Hauptstadt der Republik Irland.*
Dun·kirk [dʌn'kə:k] Dünkirchen *n.*
Dur·ham ['dʌrəm] *Grafschaft in England.*

E

Ed·die ['edi] *Kurzform von* Edward.
E·den ['i:dn] Eden *n*, das Paradies.
Ed·in·burgh ['edinbərə] Edinburg *n.*
Ed·i·son ['edisn] *amerikanischer Erfinder.*
Ed·ward ['edwəd] Eduard *m.*
E·gypt ['i:dʒipt] Ägypten *n.*
Ei·leen ['aili:n] *weiblicher Vorname.*
Ei·re ['ɛərə] *Name der Republik Irland.*
Ei·sen·how·er ['aizənhauə] *34. Präsident der U.S.A.*
El·ea·nor ['elinə] Eleonore *f.*

E·li·as [iˈlaiəs] Elias *m.*
El·i·nor [ˈelinə] Eleonore *f.*
El·i·ot [ˈeljət] *englische Autorin; englischer Dichter.*
E·liz·a·beth [iˈlizəbəθ] Elisabeth *f.*
Em·er·son [ˈeməsn] *amerikanischer Philosoph.*
Em·i·ly [ˈemili] Emilie *f.*
Eng·land [ˈiŋglənd] England *n.*
E·noch [ˈi:nɔk] *männlicher Vorname.*
Ep·som [ˈepsəm] *Stadt in England mit Pferderennplatz.*
E·rie [ˈiəri]: Lake ~ Eriesee *m* (*e-r der fünf Großen Seen Nordamerikas*).
Er·nest [ˈə:nist] Ernst *m.*
Es·sex [ˈesiks] *Grafschaft in England.*
Eth·el [ˈeθəl] *weiblicher Vorname.*
E·thi·o·pi·a [i:θiˈəupjə] Äthiopien *n.*
E·ton [ˈi:tn] *berühmte Public School.*
Eu·gene [ju:ˈʒein; ˈju:dʒi:n] Eugen *m.*
Eu·ge·ni·a [ju:ˈdʒi:njə] Eugenie *f.*
Eu·rope [ˈjuərəp] Europa *n.*
Eus·tace [ˈju:stəs] *männlicher Vorname.*
Ev·ans [ˈevənz] *englischer Familienname.*
Eve [i:v] Eva *f.*

F

Falk·land Is·lands [ˈfɔ:lkləndˈailəndz] *pl. die* Falklandinseln.
Faulk·ner [ˈfɔ:knə] *amerikanischer Autor.*
Fawkes [fɔ:ks] *Haupt der Pulververschwörung (1605).*
Fe·li·ci·a [fiˈlisiə] *weiblicher Vorname.*
Fe·lix [ˈfiliks] Felix *m.*
Fin·land [ˈfinlənd] Finnland *n.*
Flint·shire [ˈflintʃiə] *Grafschaft in Wales.*
Flor·ence [ˈflɔrəns] Florenz *n*; *weiblicher Vorname.*
Flor·i·da [ˈflɔridə] *Staat der U.S.A.*
Flush·ing [ˈflʌʃiŋ] Vlissingen *n.*
Folke·stone [ˈfəukstən] *Seebad in England.*
Ford [fɔ:d] *amerikanischer Industrieller.*
France [frɑ:ns] Frankreich *n.*
Fran·ces [ˈfrɑ:nsis] Franziska *f.*
Fran·cis [~] Franz *m.*
Frank·fort [ˈfræŋkfət] *Hauptstadt von Kentucky (U.S.A.).*
Frank·lin [ˈfræŋklin] *amerikanischer Staatsmann und Physiker.*
Fred(·dy) [ˈfred(i)] *Kurzform von* Alfred, Frederic(k).
Fred·er·ic(k) [ˈfredrik] Friedrich *m.*
Fry [frai] *englischer Dramatiker.*
Ful·ton [ˈfultən] *amerikanischer Erfinder.*

G

Gains·bor·ough [ˈgeinzbərə] *englischer Maler.*
Gals·wor·thy [ˈgɔ:lzwə:ði] *englischer Autor.*
Gal·ves·ton [ˈgælvistən] *Hafenstadt in U.S.A.*
Gan·ges [ˈgændʒi:z] *der* Ganges.
Ge·ne·va [dʒiˈni:və] Genf *n*; Lake of ~ Genfer See *m.*
Geof·frey [ˈdʒefri] Gottfried *m.*
George [dʒɔ:dʒ] Georg *m.*
Geor·gia [ˈdʒɔ:dʒjə] *Staat der U.S.A.*
Ger·ald [ˈdʒerəld] Gerhard *m.*
Ger·al·dine [ˈdʒerəldi:n; ˈ~dain] *weiblicher Vorname.*
Ger·ma·ny [ˈdʒə:məni] Deutschland *n.*
Gersh·win [ˈgə:ʃwin] *amerikanischer Komponist.*
Ger·trude [ˈgə:tru:d] Gertrud *f.*
Get·tys·burg [ˈgetizbə:g] *Stadt in U.S.A.*
Gha·na [ˈgɑ:nə] *Staat in Afrika.*
Ghent [gent] Gent *n.*
Gi·bral·tar [dʒiˈbrɔ:ltə] Gibraltar *n.*
Giles [dʒailz] Julius *m.*
Gill [dʒil] Julie *f.*
Glad·stone [ˈglædstən] *britischer Staatsmann.*
Gla·mor·gan(·shire) [gləˈmɔ:gən (-ʃiə)] *Grafschaft in Wales.*
Glas·gow [ˈglɑ:sgəu] *Hafenstadt in Schottland.*
Glouces·ter [ˈglɔstə] *Stadt in England*; *a.* **Glouces·ter·shire** [ˈ~ʃiə] *Grafschaft in England.*
Gold·smith [ˈgəuldsmiθ] *englischer Autor.*
Gor·don [ˈgɔ:dn] *englischer Familienname.*
Gra·ham [ˈgreiəm] *englischer Familienname; männlicher Vorname.*
Great Brit·ain [ˈgreitˈbritn] Großbritannien *n.*
Great Di·vide [ˈgreit diˈvaid] *die Rocky Mountains (U.S.A.).*
Greece [gri:s] Griechenland *n.*
Greene [gri:n] *englischer Autor.*
Green·land [ˈgri:nlənd] Grönland *n.*

Green·wich ['grinidʒ] *Vorort von London*; ~ *Village Künstlerviertel von New York (U.S.A.).*

Greg·o·ry ['gregəri] Gregor *m.*

Gri·sons ['gri:zɔ̃:ŋ] Graubünden *n.*

Gros·ve·nor ['grəuvnə] *Straße u. Platz in London.*

Guern·sey ['gə:nzi] *e-e der Kanalinseln.*

Guin·ness ['ginis; gi'nes] *englischer Familienname.*

Guy [gai] Guido *m.*

Gwen·do·len, Gwen·do·lyn ['gwendəlin] *weiblicher Vorname.*

H

Hague [heig]: *the* ~ Den Haag.

Hai·ti ['heiti] Haiti *n.*

Hal·i·fax ['hælifæks] *Name zweier Städte in England u. Kanada.*

Ham·il·ton ['hæmiltən] *englischer Familienname.*

Hamp·shire ['hæmpʃiə] *Grafschaft in England.*

Hamp·stead ['hæmpstid] *Stadtteil von London.*

Han·o·ver ['hænəuvə] Hannover *n.*

Har·ri·et ['hæriət] Henriette *f.*

Har·ris·burg ['hærisbə:g] *Hauptstadt von Pennsylvanien (U.S.A.).*

Har·row ['hærəu] *berühmte Public School.*

Har·ry ['hæri] *Kurzform von* Henry.

Har·vard U·ni·ver·si·ty ['ha:vəd-ju:ni'və:siti] *amerikanische Universität.*

Har·wich ['hæridʒ] *Hafenstadt in England.*

Has·tings ['heistiŋz] *Stadt in England; britischer Staatsmann.*

Ha·wai·i [hə'waii:] *pl. Staat der U.S.A.*

Heb·ri·des ['hebridi:z] *pl. die* Hebriden.

Hel·en ['helin] Helene *f.*

Hel·i·go·land ['heligəulænd] Helgoland *n.*

Hel·sin·ki ['helsiŋki] Helsinki *n.*

Hem·ing·way ['hemiŋwei] *amerikanischer Autor.*

Hen·ley ['henli] *Stadt in England mit berühmter Regattastrecke.*

Hen·ry ['henri] Heinrich *m.*

Her·e·ford(·shire) ['herifəd(ʃiə)] *Grafschaft in England.*

Hert·ford(·shire) ['ha:fəd(ʃiə)] *Grafschaft in England.*

Hi·ma·la·ya [himə'leiə] *der* Himalaya.

Hin·du·stan [hindu'sta:n] Hindustan *n.*

Ho·garth ['həuga:θ] *englischer Maler.*

Hol·born ['həubən] *Stadtteil von London.*

Hol·land ['hɔlənd] Holland *n.*

Hol·ly·wood ['hɔliwud] *Filmstadt in Kalifornien (U.S.A.).*

Home [hju:m]: *Sir Alec Douglas-*~ *britischer Politiker.*

Ho·mer ['həumə] Homer *m.*

Hon·o·lu·lu [hɔnə'lu:lu:] *Hauptstadt von Hawaii (U.S.A.).*

Hoo·ver ['hu:və] *31. Präsident der U.S.A.*

Hous·ton ['hju:stən] *Stadt in U.S.A.*

Hud·son ['hʌdsn] *Fluß in U.S.A., an seiner Mündung New York; englischer Familienname.*

Hugh [hju:] Hugo *m.*

Hull [hʌl] *Hafenstadt in England.*

Hume [hju:m] *englischer Philosoph.*

Hun·ga·ry ['hʌŋgəri] Ungarn *n.*

Hun·ting·don(·shire) ['hʌntiŋdən (-ʃiə)] *Grafschaft in England.*

Hu·ron ['hjuərən]: *Lake* ~ Huronsee *m (e-r der fünf Großen Seen Nordamerikas).*

Hux·ley ['hʌksli] *englischer Biologe; englischer Autor.*

Hyde Park ['haid'pa:k] *Park in London.*

I

Ice·land ['aislənd] Island *n.*

I·da·ho ['aidəhəu] *Staat der U.S.A.*

I·dle·wild ['aidlwaild] *ehemaliger Name von Kennedy Airport.*

Il·li·nois [ili'nɔi] *Fluß in U.S.A.; Staat der U.S.A.*

In·di·a ['indjə] Indien *n.*

In·di·an·a [indi'ænə] *Staat der U.S.A.*

In·di·an O·cean ['indjən'əuʃən] *der* Indische Ozean.

In·dies ['indiz] *pl.*: *the (East, West)* ~ (Ost-, West)Indien *n.*

In·dus ['indəs] *der* Indus.

I·o·wa ['aiəuə] *Staat der U.S.A.*

I·rak, I·raq [i'ra:k] der Irak.

I·ran [i'ra:n] der Iran.

Ire·land ['aiələnd] Irland *n.*

I·rene [ai'ri:ni; 'airi:n] Irene *f.*

Ir·ving ['ə:viŋ] *amerikanischer Autor.*

I·saac ['aizək] Isaak *m.*

Is·a·bel ['izəbel] Isabella *f.*

Is·ra·el ['izreiəl] Israel *n.*

It·a·ly ['itəli] Italien *n.*

J

Jack [dʒæk] Hans *m.*
James [dʒeimz] Jakob *m.*
Jane [dʒein] Johanna *f.*
Ja·net ['dʒænit] Johanna *f.*
Ja·pan [dʒə'pæn] Japan *n.*
Jean [dʒi:n] Johanna *f.*
Jef·fer·son ['dʒefəsn] *3. Präsident der U.S.A., Verfasser der Unabhängigkeitserklärung von 1776; ~ City Hauptstadt von Missouri (U.S.A.).*
Jen·ny ['dʒeni] Hanne *f.*
Jer·e·my ['dʒerimi] *männlicher Vorname.*
Jer·sey ['dʒə:zi] *e-e der Kanalinseln; ~ City Stadt in U.S.A.*
Je·ru·sa·lem [dʒə'ru:sələm] Jerusalem *n.*
Je·sus (**Christ**) ['dʒi:zəs('kraist)] Jesus (Christus) *m.*
Jill [dʒil] Julia *f.*
Jim(**·my**) ['dʒim(i)] *Kurzform von James.*
Joan [dʒəun] Johanna *f.*
Jo(**e**) [dʒəu] *Kurzform von Joseph.*
John [dʒɔn] Johann(es) *m.*
John·ny ['dʒɔni] Hans *m.*
John·son ['dʒɔnsn] *englischer Autor; 36. Präsident der U.S.A.*
Jo·nah ['dʒəunə] *männlicher Vorname.*
Jon·a·than ['dʒɔnəθən] *männlicher Vorname.*
Jon·son ['dʒɔnsn] *englischer Dramatiker.*
Jor·dan ['dʒɔ:dn] Jordanien *n.*
Jo·seph ['dʒəuzif] Joseph *m.*
Josh·u·a ['dʒɔʃwə] *männlicher Vorname.*
Joyce [dʒɔis] *englischer Autor.*
Jul·ia ['dʒu:ljə], **Ju·li·et** ['~jət] Julia *f.*
Jul·ius ['dʒu:ljəs] Julius *m.*
Ju·neau ['dʒu:nəu] *Hauptstadt von Alaska (U.S.A.).*

K

Kan·sas ['kænzəs] *Fluß in U.S.A.; Staat der U.S.A.*
Ka·ra·chi [kə'rɑ:tʃi] *Stadt in Pakistan.*
Kash·mir [kæʃ'miə] Kaschmir *n.*
Kate [keit] *Kurzform von Catherine, Katharine, Katherine, Kathleen.*
Kath·a·rine, Kath·er·ine ['kæθərin] Katharina *f.*
Kath·leen ['kæθli:n] Katharina *f.*
Keats [ki:ts] *englischer Dichter.*
Ken·ne·dy ['kenidi] *35. Präsident der U.S.A.; Cape ~ Landspitze in Florida (U.S.A.), Raketenversuchsgelände; ~ Airport Flughafen von New York (U.S.A.).*
Ken·sing·ton ['kenziŋtən] *Stadtteil von London.*
Kent [kent] *Grafschaft in England.*
Ken·tuck·y [ken'tʌki] *Fluß in U.S.A.; Staat der U.S.A.*
Ken·ya ['kenjə] *Staat in Afrika.*
Kip·ling ['kipliŋ] *englischer Dichter.*
Kit·ty ['kiti] *Kurzform von Catherine.*
Klon·dike ['klɔndaik] *Fluß u. Landschaft in Kanada u. Alaska.*
Ko·re·a [kə'riə] Korea *n.*
Krem·lin ['kremlin] *der* Kreml.
Ku·weit [ku'weit] Kuwait *n.*

L

Lab·ra·dor ['læbrədɔ:] *Halbinsel Nordamerikas.*
Lan·ca·shire ['læŋkəʃiə] *Grafschaft in England.*
Lan·cas·ter ['læŋkəstə] *Name zweier Städte in England u. U.S.A.; s. Lancashire.*
Law·rence ['lɔrəns] Lorenz *m*; *Name zweier englischer Autoren.*
Leb·a·non ['lebənən] *der* Libanon.
Leeds [li:dz] *Industriestadt in England.*
Leg·horn ['leg'hɔ:n] Livorno *n.*
Leices·ter ['lestə] *Stadt in England; a.* **Leices·ter·shire** ['~ʃiə] *Grafschaft in England.*
Le·man ['lemən]: *Lake ~* Genfer See *m.*
Leon·ard ['lenəd] Leonhard *m.*
Les·lie ['lezli] *männlicher Vorname.*
Lew·is ['lu:is] Ludwig *m*; *englischer Dichter; amerikanischer Autor.*
Lin·coln ['liŋkən] *16. Präsident der U.S.A.; Hauptstadt von Nebraska (U.S.A.); Stadt in England; a.* **Lin·coln·shire** ['~ʃiə] *Grafschaft in England.*
Li·o·nel ['laiənl] *männlicher Vorname.*
Lis·bon ['lizbən] Lissabon *n.*
Lit·tle Rock ['litl'rɔk] *Hauptstadt von Arkansas (U.S.A.).*
Liv·er·pool ['livəpu:l] *Industrie- u. Hafenstadt in England.*

Liz·zie [ˈlizi] *Kurzform von Elizabeth.*

Lloyd [lɔid] *männlicher Vorname; englischer Familienname.*

Locke [lɔk] *englischer Philosoph.*

Lon·don [ˈlʌndən] London *n.*

Lor·raine [lɔˈrein] Lothringen *n.*

Los An·ge·les [lɔsˈændʒiliːz; *Am. a.* ~ˈæŋgələs] *Hafenstadt in Kalifornien (U.S.A.).*

Lou·i·sa [luːˈiːzə] Luise *f.*

Lou·i·si·an·a [luːiːziˈænə] *Staat der U.S.A.*

Lu·cerne [luːˈsəːn]: *Lake of* ~ Vierwaldstätter See *m.*

Lu·cius [ˈluːsjəs] *männlicher Vorname.*

Lu·cy [ˈluːsi] Lucie *f.*

Luke [luːk] Lukas *m.*

Lux·em·b(o)urg [ˈlʌksəmbəːg] Luxemburg *n.*

Lyd·i·a [ˈlidiə] Lydia *f.*

M

Mab [mæb] *Feenkönigin.*

Ma·bel [ˈmeibəl] *weiblicher Vorname.*

Ma·cau·lay [məˈkɔːli] *englischer Historiker.*

Mac·ken·zie [məˈkenzi] *Fluß in Kanada.*

Mac·leod [məˈklaud] *britischer Politiker.*

Ma·dei·ra [məˈdiərə] Madeira *n.*

Madge [mædʒ] Margot *f*, Marg(r)it *f.*

Mad·i·son [ˈmædisn] *4. Präsident der U.S.A.; Hauptstadt von Wisconsin (U.S.A.).*

Ma·dras [məˈdrɑːs] *Hafenstadt in Indien.*

Ma·drid [məˈdrid] Madrid *n.*

Mag·da·len [ˈmægdəlin] Magdalene *f.*

Mag·gie [ˈmægi] Margot *f*, Marg(r)it *f.*

Ma·hom·et [məˈhɔmit] Mohammed *m.*

Maine [mein] *Staat der U.S.A.*

Mal·ta [ˈmɔːltə] Malta *n.*

Man·ches·ter [ˈmæntʃistə] *Industriestadt in England.*

Man·hat·tan [mænˈhætən] *Stadtteil von New York (U.S.A.).*

Man·i·to·ba [mæniˈtəubə] *Provinz in Kanada.*

Mar·ga·ret [ˈmɑːgərit] Margarete *f.*

Mark [mɑːk] Markus *m.*

Marl·bor·ough [ˈmɔːlbərə] *englischer General.*

Mar·lowe [ˈmɑːləu] *englischer Dramatiker.*

Mar·tha [ˈmɑːθə] Martha *f.*

Mar·y [ˈmɛəri] Maria *f.*

Mar·y·land [ˈmɛərilænd; *Am.* ˈmerilənd] *Staat der U.S.A.*

Mas·sa·chu·setts [mæsəˈtʃuːsits] *Staat der U.S.A.*

Ma·t(h)il·da [məˈtildə] Mathilde *f.*

Ma(t)·thew [ˈmæθjuː; ˈmeiθjuː] Matthäus *m.*

Maud [mɔːd] *Kurzform von Magdalene, Mat(h)ilda.*

Maugham [mɔːm] *englischer Autor.*

Mau·rice [ˈmɔris] Moritz *m.*

May [mei] *Kurzform von Mary.*

Mel·bourne [ˈmelbən] *Hafenstadt in Australien.*

Mel·ville [ˈmelvil] *amerikanischer Autor.*

Mer·i·on·eth(·shire) [meriˈɔniθ (-ʃiə)] *Grafschaft in Wales.*

Mex·i·co [ˈmeksikəu] Mexiko *n.*

Mi·am·i [maiˈæmi] *Badeort in Florida (U.S.A.).*

Mi·chael [ˈmaikl] Michael *m.*

Mich·i·gan [ˈmiʃigən] *Staat der U.S.A.; Lake* ~ Michigansee *m (e-r der fünf Großen Seen Nordamerikas).*

Mid·dle·sex [ˈmidlseks] *Grafschaft in England.*

Mid·west [ˈmidwest] *der* Mittlere Westen *(U.S.A.).*

Mil·dred [ˈmildrid] *weiblicher Vorname.*

Mil·ton [ˈmiltən] *englischer Dichter.*

Mil·wau·kee [milˈwɔːkiː] *Stadt in U.S.A.*

Min·ne·ap·o·lis [miniˈæpəlis] *Stadt in U.S.A.*

Min·ne·so·ta [miniˈsəutə] *Staat der U.S.A.*

Mis·sis·sip·pi [misiˈsipi] *Fluß in U.S.A.; Staat der U.S.A.*

Mis·sou·ri [miˈzuəri] *Fluß in U.S.A.; Staat der U.S.A.*

Mo·ham·med [məuˈhæmed] Mohammed *m.*

Moll [mɔl] *Kurzform von Mary.*

Mon·a·co [ˈmɔnəkəu] Monaco *n.*

Mon·mouth(·shire) [ˈmɔnməθ(ʃiə)] *Grafschaft in England.*

Mon·roe [mənˈrəu] *5. Präsident der U.S.A.*

Mon·tan·a [mɔnˈtænə] *Staat der U.S.A.*

Mont·gom·er·y [məntˈgʌməri] *britischer Feldmarschall; a.* **Mont·gom·er·y·shire** [~ʃiə] *Grafschaft in Wales.*

Mont·re·al [mɔntriˈɔːl] *Stadt in Kanada.*

Moore [muə] *englischer Bildhauer.*

Mos·cow ['mɔskəu] Moskau *n.*
Mo·selle [məu'zel] *die* Mosel.
Mu·nich ['mju:nik] München *n.*
Mur·ray ['mʌri] *Fluß in Australien.*

N

Nan·cy ['nænsi] Ännchen *n.*
Na·ples ['neiplz] Neapel *n.*
Na·tal [nə'tæl] Natal *n.*
Ne·bras·ka [ni'bræskə] *Staat der U.S.A.*
Nell, Nel·ly ['nel(i)] *Kurzform von Eleanor, Helen.*
Nel·son ['nelsn] *britischer Admiral.*
Ne·pal [ni'pɔ:l] Nepal *n.*
Neth·er·lands ['neðələndz] *pl. die* Niederlande.
Ne·vad·a [ne'vɑ:də] *Staat der U.S.A.*
New Bruns·wick [nju:'brʌnzwik] *Provinz in Kanada.*
New·cas·tle ['nju:kɑ:sl] *Hafenstadt in England.*
New Del·hi [nju:'deli] *Hauptstadt von Indien.*
New Eng·land [nju:'iŋglənd] Neuengland *n.*
New·found·land [nju:fənd'lænd] Neufundland *n.*
New Hamp·shire [nju:'hæmpʃiə] *Staat der U.S.A.*
New Jer·sey [nju:'dʒə:zi] *Staat der U.S.A.*
New Mex·i·co [nju:'meksikəu] Neumexiko *n* (*Staat der U.S.A.*).
New Or·le·ans [nju:'ɔ:liənz] *Hafenstadt in U.S.A.*
New·ton ['nju:tn] *englischer Physiker.*
New York ['nju:'jɔ:k] *Stadt in U.S.A.*; *Staat der U.S.A.*
New Zea·land [nju:'zi:lənd] Neuseeland *n.*
Ni·ag·a·ra [nai'ægərə] *der* Niagara (*Fluß zwischen Erie- u. Ontariosee*).
Nich·o·las ['nikələs] Nikolaus *m.*
Ni·ge·ri·a [nai'dʒiəriə] *Staat in Afrika.*
Nile [nail] *der* Nil.
Nix·on ['niksn] *37. Präsident der U.S.A.*
Nor·folk ['nɔ:fək] *Grafschaft in England*; *Hafenstadt in U.S.A.*
North·amp·ton [nɔ:'θæmptən] *Stadt in England*; *a.* **North·amp·ton·shire** [~ʃiə] *Grafschaft in England.*
North Sea ['nɔ:θ'si:] *die* Nordsee.
North·um·ber·land [nɔ:'θʌmbələnd] *Grafschaft in England.*
Nor·way ['nɔ:wei] Norwegen *n.*
Not·ting·ham ['nɔtiŋəm] *Stadt in England*; *a.* **Not·ting·ham·shire** ['~ʃiə] *Grafschaft in England.*
No·va Sco·tia ['nəuvə'skəuʃə] *Provinz in Kanada.*
Nu·rem·berg ['njuərəmbə:g] Nürnberg *n.*

O

O·ce·an·i·a [əuʃi'einjə] Ozeanien *n.*
O·hi·o [əu'haiəu] *Fluß in U.S.A.*; *Staat der U.S.A.*
O·kla·ho·ma [əuklə'həumə] *Staat der U.S.A.*; ~ *City Hauptstadt von Oklahoma* (*U.S.A.*).
O·ma·ha ['əuməhɑ:] *Stadt in U.S.A.*
O'Neill [əu'ni:l] *amerikanischer Dramatiker.*
On·tar·i·o [ɔn'tɛəriəu] *Provinz in Kanada*; *Lake* ~ Ontariosee *m* (*e-r der fünf Großen Seen Nordamerikas*).
Or·ange ['ɔrindʒ] *der* Oranje.
Or·e·gon ['ɔrigən] *Staat der U.S.A.*
Ork·ney Is·lands ['ɔ:kni'ailəndz] *pl. die* Orkneyinseln.
Or·well ['ɔ:wəl] *englischer Autor.*
Os·borne ['ɔzbən] *englischer Dramatiker.*
Os·lo ['ɔzləu] Oslo *n.*
Ost·end [ɔs'tend] Ostende *n.*
Ot·ta·wa ['ɔtəwə] *Hauptstadt von Kanada.*
Ox·ford ['ɔksfəd] *englische Universitätsstadt*; *a.* **Ox·ford·shire** ['~ʃiə] *Grafschaft in England.*
O·zark Moun·tains ['əuzɑ:k'mauntinz] *pl. Bergmassiv in U.S.A.*

P

Pa·cif·ic [pə'sifik] *der* Pazifik.
Pak·i·stan [pɑ:kis'tɑ:n] Pakistan *n.*
Pall Mall ['pæl'mæl] *Straße in London.*
Palm Beach ['pɑ:m'bi:tʃ] *Badeort in Florida* (*U.S.A.*).
Palm·er·ston ['pɑ:məstən] *britischer Staatsmann.*
Pan·a·ma [pænə'mɑ:] Panama *n.*
Par·is ['pæris] Paris *n.*
Pa·tri·cia [pə'triʃə] *weiblicher Vorname.*
Pat·rick ['pætrik] *männlicher Vorname.*
Paul [pɔ:l] Paul *m.*
Pau·line [pɔ:'li:n; 'pɔ:li:n] Pauline *f.*

Pearl Har·bor ['pə:l'hɑ:bə] *Hafenstadt auf den Hawaiinseln (U.S.A.).*
Peel [pi:l] *britischer Staatsmann.*
Pe·kin ['pi:kin], **Pe·king** ['pi:kiŋ] Peking *n.*
Peg(·gy) ['peg(i)] Margot *f.*
Pem·broke(·shire) ['pembruk(ʃiə)] *Grafschaft in Wales.*
Penn·syl·va·nia [pensil'veinjə] Pennsylvanien *n* (*Staat der U.S.A.*).
Per·cy ['pə:si] *männlicher Vorname.*
Per·sia ['pə:ʃə] Persien *n.*
Pe·ru [pə'ru:] Peru *n.*
Pe·ter ['pi:tə] Peter *m.*
Phil·a·del·phi·a [filə'delfjə] *Stadt in U.S.A.*
Phil·ip ['filip] Philipp *m.*
Phil·ip·pines ['filipi:nz] *pl. die* Philippinen.
Phoe·nix ['fi:niks] *Hauptstadt von Arizona (U.S.A.).*
Pic·ca·dil·ly [pikə'dili] *Straße in London.*
Pin·ter ['pintə] *englischer Dramatiker.*
Pitts·burgh ['pitsbə:g] *Stadt in U.S.A.*
Pla·to ['pleitəu] Plato(n) *m.*
Plym·outh ['pliməθ] *Hafenstadt in England; Stadt in U.S.A.*
Poe [pəu] *amerikanischer Autor.*
Po·land ['pəulənd] Polen *n.*
Pope [pəup] *englischer Dichter.*
Port·land ['pɔ:tlənd] *Name zweier Städte in U.S.A.*
Ports·mouth ['pɔ:tsməθ] *Hafenstadt in England.*
Por·tu·gal ['pɔ:tjugəl] Portugal *n.*
Po·to·mac [pə'təumək] *Fluß in U.S.A.*
Prague [prɑ:g] Prag *n.*
Prus·sia ['prʌʃə] Preußen *n.*
Pul·itz·er ['pulitsə] *amerikanischer Journalist.*
Pun·jab [pʌn'dʒɑ:b] Pandschab *n.*
Pur·cell ['pə:sl] *englischer Komponist.*

Q

Que·bec [kwi'bek] *Stadt u. Provinz in Kanada.*
Queens [kwi:nz] *Stadtteil von New York (U.S.A.).*

R

Ra·chel ['reitʃəl] Rachel *f.*
Rad·nor(·shire) ['rædnə(ʃiə)] *Grafschaft in Wales.*
Ra·leigh ['rɔ:li; 'rɑ:li; 'ræli] *englischer Seefahrer;* ['rɔ:li] *Hauptstadt von Nordkarolina (U.S.A.).*
Ralph [reif; rælf] Ralph *m.*
Rat·is·bon ['rætizbɔn] Regensburg *n.*
Ra·wal·pin·di ['rɔ:lpindi] *Hauptstadt von Pakistan.*
Read·ing ['rediŋ] *Industriestadt in England; Stadt in U.S.A.*
Rea·gan ['reigən] *40. Präsident der U.S.A.*
Reg·i·nald ['redʒinld] Reinhold *m.*
Rey·kja·vik ['reikjəvi:k] Reykjavik *n.*
Reyn·olds ['renldz] *englischer Maler.*
Rhine [rain] *der* Rhein.
Rhode Is·land [rəud'ailənd] *Staat der U.S.A.*
Rhodes [rəudz] Rhodos *n.*
Rho·de·sia [rəu'di:zjə] Rhodesien *n.*
Rich·ard ['ritʃəd] Richard *m*; ~ *the Lionhearted* Richard Löwenherz.
Rich·mond ['ritʃmənd] *Hauptstadt von Virginia (U.S.A.); Stadtteil von London.*
Rob·ert ['rɔbət] Robert *m.*
Rob·in ['rɔbin] *Kurzform von Robert.*
Rock·e·fel·ler ['rɔkifelə] *amerikanischer Industrieller.*
Rock·y Moun·tains ['rɔki'mauntinz] *pl. Gebirge in U.S.A.*
Rog·er ['rɔdʒə; 'rəudʒə] Rüdiger *m.*
Rome [rəum] Rom *n.*
Roo·se·velt ['rəuzəvelt] *Name zweier Präsidenten der U.S.A.*
Rug·by ['rʌgbi] *berühmte Public School.*
Ru·ma·ni·a [ru:'meinjə] Rumänien *n.*
Rus·sell ['rʌsl] *englischer Philosoph.*
Rus·sia ['rʌʃə] Rußland *n.*
Rut·land(·shire) ['rʌtlənd(ʃiə)] *Grafschaft in England.*

S

Sac·ra·men·to [sækrə'mentəu] *Hauptstadt von Kalifornien (U.S.A.).*
Salis·bur·y ['sɔ:lzbəri] *Stadt in England.*
Sal·ly ['sæli] *Kurzform von Sarah.*
Salt Lake Cit·y ['sɔ:lt'leik'siti] *Hauptstadt von Utah (U.S.A.).*
Sam [sæm] *Kurzform von Samuel.*
Sam·u·el ['sæmjuəl] Samuel *m.*
San Fran·cis·co [sænfrən'siskəu] *Hafenstadt in U.S.A.*
Sar·a(h) ['sɛərə] Sarah *f.*

Sas·katch·e·wan [səs'kætʃiwən] *Provinz in Kanada.*
Sax·o·ny ['sæksni] Sachsen *n.*
Scan·di·na·vi·a [skændi'neivjə] Skandinavien *n.*
Sche·nec·ta·dy [ski'nektədi] *Stadt in U.S.A.*
Scot·land ['skɔtlənd] Schottland *n*; ~ *Yard Polizeipräsidium in London.*
Scott [skɔt] *englischer Autor; englischer Polarforscher.*
Se·at·tle [si'ætl] *Hafenstadt in U.S.A.*
Sev·ern ['sevən] *Fluß in England.*
Shake·speare ['ʃeikspiə] *englischer Dichter.*
Shaw [ʃɔ:] *englischer Dramatiker.*
Shef·field ['ʃefi:ld] *Industriestadt in England.*
Shel·ley ['ʃeli] *englischer Dichter.*
Shet·land Is·lands ['ʃetlənd'ailəndz] *pl. die* Shetlandinseln.
Shrop·shire ['ʃrɔpʃiə] *Grafschaft in England.*
Sib·yl ['sibil] Sibylle *f.*
Sic·i·ly ['sisili] Sizilien *n.*
Sid·ney ['sidni] *männlicher Vorname; englischer Familienname.*
Si·le·sia [sai'li:zjə] Schlesien *n.*
Sin·clair ['siŋkl(ɛ)ə] *männlicher Vorname; amerikanischer Autor.*
Sin·ga·pore [siŋgə'pɔ:] Singapur *n.*
Sing-Sing ['siŋsiŋ] *Staatsgefängnis von New York (U.S.A.).*
Snow·don ['snəudn] *Berg in Wales.*
So·fia ['səufjə] Sofia *n.*
Sol·o·mon ['sɔləmən] Salomo(n) *m.*
Som·er·set(·shire) ['sʌməsit(ʃiə)] *Grafschaft in England.*
So·phi·a [səu'faiə] Sophie *f.*
South·amp·ton [sauθ'æmptən] *Hafenstadt in England.*
South·wark ['sʌðək; 'sauθwək] *Stadtteil von London.*
Spain [spein] Spanien *n.*
Staf·ford(·shire) ['stæfəd(ʃiə)] *Grafschaft in England.*
Steele [sti:l] *englischer Autor.*
Stein·beck ['stainbek] *amerikanischer Autor.*
Ste·phen ['sti:vn] Stephan *m.*
Ste·ven·son ['sti:vnsn] *englischer Autor.*
St. Law·rence [snt'lɔ:rəns] *der* St.-Lorenz-Strom.
St. Lou·is [snt'lu:is] *Stadt in U.S.A.*
Stock·holm ['stɔkhəum] Stockholm *n.*
Strat·ford on A·von ['strætfədən-'eivən] *Geburtsort Shakespeares.*
Stu·art [stjuət] *schottisch-englisches Herrschergeschlecht.*
Styr·i·a ['stiriə] die Steiermark.
Su·dan [su:'dɑ:n] *der* Sudan.
Sue [sju:] *Kurzform von Susan.*
Su·ez ['su:iz] Sues *n.*
Suf·folk ['sʌfək] *Grafschaft in England.*
Su·pe·ri·or [sju:'piəriə]: *Lake* ~ Oberer See *m (e-r der fünf Großen Seen Nordamerikas).*
Sur·rey ['sʌri] *Grafschaft in England.*
Su·san ['su:zn] Susanne *f.*
Sus·que·han·na [sʌskwə'hænə] *Fluß in U.S.A.*
Sus·sex ['sʌsiks] *Grafschaft in England.*
Swan·sea ['swɔnzi] *Hafenstadt in Wales.*
Swe·den ['swi:dn] Schweden *n.*
Swift [swift] *englischer Autor.*
Swit·zer·land ['switsələnd] die Schweiz.
Syd·ney ['sidni] *Hafen- u. Industriestadt in Australien.*
Syr·i·a ['siriə] Syrien *n.*

T

Tal·la·has·see [tælə'hæsi] *Hauptstadt von Florida (U.S.A.).*
Ted(·dy) ['ted(i)] *Kurzform von Edward, Theodore.*
Ten·nes·see [tenə'si:] *Fluß in U.S.A.; Staat der U.S.A.*
Ten·ny·son ['tenisn] *englischer Dichter.*
Tex·as ['teksəs] *Staat der U.S.A.*
Thack·er·ay ['θækəri] *englischer Autor.*
Thames [temz] *die* Themse.
The·o·dore ['θiədɔ:] Theodor *m.*
The·re·sa [ti'ri:zə] Therese *f.*
Thom·as ['tɔməs] Thomas *m.*
Tho·reau ['θɔ:rəu] *amerikanischer Philosoph.*
Thu·rin·gi·a [θjuə'rindʒiə] Thüringen *n.*
Tim·o·thy ['timəθi] Timotheus *m.*
Ti·ra·na [ti'rɑ:nə] *Hauptstadt von Albanien.*
To·bi·as [tə'baiəs] Tobias *m.*
To·by ['təubi] *Kurzform von Tobias.*
Tom(·my) ['tɔm(i)] *Kurzform von Thomas.*
To·pe·ka [təu'pi:kə] *Hauptstadt von Kansas (U.S.A.).*
To·ron·to [tə'rɔntəu] *Stadt in Kanada.*

Toyn·bee ['tɔinbi] *englischer Historiker.*
Tra·fal·gar [trə'fælgə] *Vorgebirge bei Gibraltar.*
Trent [trent] *Fluß in England.*
Treves [tri:vz] Trier *n.*
Trol·lope ['trɔləp] *englischer Autor.*
Tru·man ['tru:mən] *33. Präsident der U.S.A.*
Tu·dor ['tju:də] *englisches Herrschergeschlecht.*
Tur·key ['tə:ki] die Türkei.
Tur·ner ['tə:nə] *englischer Maler.*
Tus·ca·ny ['tʌskəni] die Toskana.
Twain [twein] *amerikanischer Autor.*
Ty·rol ['tirəl]: *the* ~ Tirol *n.*

U

Ul·ster ['ʌlstə] *Provinz in Irland.*
U·nit·ed States of A·mer·i·ca [ju:'naitid'steitsəvə'merikə] *die* Vereinigten Staaten von Amerika.
U·tah ['ju:tɑ:] *Staat der U.S.A.*

V

Val·en·tine ['væləntain] Valentin *m*; Valentine *f.*
Van·cou·ver [væn'ku:və] *Hafenstadt in Kanada.*
Vat·i·can ['vætikən] *der* Vatikan.
Vaughan Wil·liams ['vɔ:n'wiljəmz] *englischer Komponist.*
Ven·ice ['venis] Venedig *n.*
Ver·mont [və:'mɔnt] *Staat der U.S.A.*
Vic·to·ri·a [vik'tɔ:riə] Viktoria *f.*
Vi·en·na [vi'enə] Wien *n.*
Vi·et·nam ['vjet'næm] Vietnam *n.*
Vir·gin·ia [və'dʒinjə] Virginien *n* (*Staat der U.S.A.*); West ~ *Staat der U.S.A.*
Vis·tu·la ['vistjulə] *die* Weichsel.
Vosges [vəuʒ] *pl. die* Vogesen.

W

Wales [weilz] Wales *n.*
Wal·lace ['wɔlis] *englischer Autor; amerikanischer Autor.*
Wall Street ['wɔ:l'stri:t] *Finanzzentrum in New York (U.S.A.).*
War·saw ['wɔ:sɔ:] Warschau *n.*
War·wick(·shire) ['wɔrik(ʃiə)] *Grafschaft in England.*
Wash·ing·ton ['wɔʃiŋtən] *1. Präsident der U.S.A.; Staat der U.S.A.; Bundeshauptstadt der U.S.A.*
Wa·ter·loo [wɔ:tə'lu:] *Ort in Belgien.*
Watt [wɔt] *englischer Erfinder.*
Wedg·wood ['wedʒwud] *englischer Keramiker.*
Wel·ling·ton ['weliŋtən] *englischer Feldherr u. Staatsmann; Hauptstadt von Neuseeland.*
West·min·ster ['westminstə] *Stadtteil von London.*
West·mor·land ['westmələnd] *Grafschaft in England.*
White·hall ['wait'hɔ:l] *Straße in London.*
White House ['wait'haus] *das* Weiße Haus (*Amtssitz des Präsidenten der U.S.A.*).
Whit·man ['witmən] *amerikanischer Dichter.*
Wight [wait]: Isle of ~ *Insel vor der Südküste Englands.*
Wilde [waild] *englischer Dichter.*
Wil·der ['waildə] *amerikanischer Autor.*
Will [wil], **Wil·liam** ['wiljəm] Wilhelm *m.*
Wil·son ['wilsn] *britischer Politiker; 28. Präsident der U.S.A.*
Wilt·shire ['wiltʃiə] *Grafschaft in England.*
Wim·ble·don ['wimbldən] *Vorort von London (Tennisturniere).*
Win·ni·peg ['winipeg] *Stadt in Kanada.*
Wis·con·sin [wis'kɔnsin] *Fluß in U.S.A.; Staat der U.S.A.*
Wolfe [wulf] *amerikanischer Autor.*
Woolf [wulf] *englische Autorin.*
Worces·ter ['wustə] *englische Industriestadt; a.* **Worces·ter·shire** ['~ʃiə] *Grafschaft in England.*
Words·worth ['wə:dzwə:θ] *englischer Dichter.*
Wyc·liffe ['wiklif] *englischer Reformator.*
Wy·o·ming [wai'əumiŋ] *Staat der U.S.A.*

Y

Yale U·ni·ver·si·ty ['jeilju:ni'və:siti] *amerikanische Universität.*
Yeats [jeits] *irischer Dichter.*
Yel·low·stone ['jeləustəun] *Fluß in U.S.A.; Nationalpark.*
York [jɔ:k] *Stadt in England; a.* **York·shire** ['~ʃiə] *Grafschaft in England.*
Yo·sem·i·te [jəu'semiti] *Naturschutzgebiet in U.S.A.*
Yu·go·sla·vi·a ['ju:gəu'slɑ:vjə] Jugoslawien *n.*

Z

Zach·a·ri·ah [zækə'raiə], **Zach·a·ry** ['~ri] Zacharias *m.*

British and American Abbreviations

A

a. *acre* Acre *m* (*4046,8* m^2).

A.A. *anti-aircraft* Flugabwehr *f*; *Brit. Automobile Association* Kraftfahrerverband *m*.

A.A.A. *Brit. Amateur Athletic Association* Leichtathletikverband *m*; *Am. American Automobile Association* Amerikanischer Kraftfahrerverband *m*.

A.B. *able-bodied seaman* Vollmatrose; *s. B.A.* (*Bachelor of Arts*).

abbr. *abbreviated* abgekürzt; *abbreviation* Abk., Abkürzung *f*.

A.B.C. *American Broadcasting Company* Amerikanische Rundfunkgesellschaft *f*.

A.B.M. *anti-ballistic missile* Anti-Rakete *f* (*zur Abwehr von Raketen*).

A.C. *alternating current* Wechselstrom *m*.

A/C *account* (*current*) Kontokorrent *n*, Rechnung *f*.

acc(t). *account* Kto., Konto *n*, Rechnung *f*.

A.D. *Anno Domini* (*Lat.* = *in the year of our Lord*) im Jahr des Herrn, n. Chr., nach Christus.

A.D.A. *Brit. Atom Development Administration* Atomforschungsverwaltung *f*.

Adm. *Admiral* Admiral *m*; *Admiralty* Admiralität *f*.

advt. *advertisement* Anzeige *f*, Ankündigung *f*.

AEC *Atomic Energy Commission* Atomenergiekommission *f*.

A.E.F. *American Expeditionary Forces* Amerikanische Streitkräfte *f/pl.* in Übersee.

AFL-CIO *American Federation of Labor & Congress of Industrial Organizations* (*größter amerikanischer Gewerkschaftsverband*).

A.F.N. *American Forces Network* (*Rundfunkanstalt der amerikanischen Streitkräfte*).

Ala. *Alabama*.

Alas. *Alaska*.

Am. *America* Amerika *n*; *American* amerikanisch.

A.M. *amplitude modulation* Mittelwelle *f*; *s. M.A.* (*Master of Arts*).

a.m. *ante meridiem* (*Lat.* = *before noon*) morgens, vormittags.

A.P. *Associated Press* (*amerikanisches Nachrichtenbüro*).

A/P *account purchase* Einkaufsabrechnung *f*.

A.P.O. *Am. Army Post Office* Heerespostamt *n*.

A.R.C. *American Red Cross* Amerikanisches Rotes Kreuz *n*.

Ariz. *Arizona*.

Ark. *Arkansas*.

A.R.P. *air-raid precautions* Luftschutz *m*.

arr. *arrival* Ank., Ankunft *f*.

A/S *account sales* Verkaufsabrechnung *f*.

ASA *American Standards Association* Amerikanische Normungs-Organisation *f*.

av. *average* Durchschnitt *m*; Havarie *f*.

avdp. *avoirdupois* Handelsgewicht *n*.

A.W.O.L. *Am. absent without leave* abwesend ohne Urlaub.

B

b. *born* geb., geboren.

B.A. *Bachelor of Arts* Bakkalaureus *m* der Philosophie; *British Academy* Britische Akademie *f*.

BA *British Airways* (*britische Fluggesellschaft*).

B.A.O.R. *British Army of the Rhine* Britische Rheinarmee *f*.

Bart. *Baronet* Baronet *m*.

B.B.C. *British Broadcasting Corporation* Britische Rundfunkgesellschaft *f*.

bbl. *barrel* Faß *n*.

B.C. *before Christ* v. Chr., vor Christus.

B.D. *Bachelor of Divinity* Bakkalaureus *m* der Theologie.

B.E. *Bachelor of Education* Bakkalaureus *m* der Erziehungswissenschaft; *Bachelor of Engineering* Bakkalaureus *m* der Ingenieurwissenschaft(en).

B/E *Bill of Exchange* Wechsel *m*.

Beds. *Bedfordshire.*

Benelux ['benilʌks] *Belgium, Netherlands, Luxemburg* Benelux, Belgien, Niederlande, Luxemburg (*Zollunion*).

Berks. *Berkshire.*

b/f *brought forward* Übertrag *m*.

B.F.A. *British Football Association* Britischer Fußballverband *m*.

B.F.N. *British Forces Network* (*Sender der britischen Streitkräfte in Deutschland*).

B.I.F. *British Industries Fair* Britische Industriemesse *f*.

B.L. *Bachelor of Law* Bakkalaureus *m* des Rechts.

B/L *bill of lading* (See)Frachtbrief *m*.

bl. *barrel* Faß *n*.

B.Lit. *Bachelor of Literature* Bakkalaureus *m* der Literatur.

bls. *bales* Ballen *m/pl.*; *barrels* Fässer *n/pl.*

B.M. *Bachelor of Medicine* Bakkalaureus *m* der Medizin.

B.M.A. *British Medical Association* Britischer Ärzteverband *m*.

B/O *Branch Office* Zweigstelle *f*, Filiale *f*.

bot. *bottle* Flasche *f*; *bought* gekauft.

B.O.T. *Brit. Board of Trade* Handelsministerium *n*.

B.R. *British Railways* Britische Eisenbahn *f*.

B/R *bills receivable* ausstehende Wechselforderungen *f/pl.*

B.R.C.S. *British Red Cross Society* Britisches Rotes Kreuz *n*.

Br(it). *Britain* Großbritannien *n*; *British* britisch.

Bros. *brothers* Gebr., Gebrüder *pl.* (*in Firmenbezeichnungen*).

B.S. *Bachelor of Science* Bakkalaureus *m* der Naturwissenschaften; *British Standard* Britische Norm *f*.

B/S *bill of sale* Kaufvertrag *m*, Übereignungsurkunde *f*.

B.Sc. *Bachelor of Science* Bakkalaureus *m* der Naturwissenschaften.

B.Sc.Econ. *Bachelor of Economic Science* Bakkalaureus *m* der Wirtschaftswissenschaft(en).

bsh., bu. *bushel* Scheffel *m* (*Brit. 36,36 l, Am. 35,24 l*).

Bucks. *Buckinghamshire.*

B.U.P. *British United Press* (*Nachrichtenbüro*).

bus(h). *bushel(s)* Scheffel *m* (*od. pl.*) (*Brit. 36,36 l, Am. 35,24 l*).

C

C. *Celsius* C Celsius, *centigrade* hundertgradig (*Thermometereinteilung*).

c. *cent(s)* Cent *m* (*od. pl.*) (*amerikanische Münze*); *circa* ca., circa, ungefähr; *cubic* Kubik...

C.A. *chartered account* Frachtrechnung *f*; *Brit. Chartered Accountant* vereidigter Buchprüfer *m*; Wirtschaftsprüfer *m*.

C/A *current account* laufendes Konto *n*.

c.a.d. *cash against documents* Zahlung *f* gegen Aushändigung der Dokumente.

Cal(if). *California.*

Cambs. *Cambridgeshire.*

Can. *Canada* Kanada *n*; *Canadian* kanadisch.

Capt. *Captain* Kapitän *m*, Hauptmann *m*, Rittmeister *m*.

C.B. *cash book* Kassenbuch *n*; *Brit. Companion of the Bath* Ritter *m* des Bathordens.

C/B *cash book* Kassenbuch *n*.

C.B.C. *Canadian Broadcasting Corporation* Kanadische Rundfunkgesellschaft *f*.

C.C. *continuous current* Gleichstrom *m*; *Brit. County Council* Grafschaftsrat *m*.

C.E. *Church of England* Anglikanische Kirche *f*; *Civil Engineer* Bauingenieur *m*.

cert. *certificate* Bescheinigung *f*.

CET *Central European Time* MEZ, mitteleuropäische Zeit *f*.

cf. *confer* vgl., vergleiche.

ch. *chain* (*Länge einer*) Meßkette *f* (*20,12 m*); *chapter* Kap., Kapitel *n*.

Ches. *Cheshire.*

CIA *Am. Central Intelligence Agency* (*US-Geheimdienst*).

C.I.D. *Brit. Criminal Investigation Department* (*Kriminalpolizei*).

c.i.f. *cost, insurance, freight* Kosten, Versicherung und Fracht einbegriffen.

CINC, C. in C. *Commander-in--Chief* Oberkommandierende(r) *m* (*dem Land-, Luft- und Seestreitkräfte unterstehen*).

cl. *class* Klasse *f.*

C.O. *Commanding Officer* Kommandeur *m.*

Co. *Company* Kompanie *f*, Gesellschaft *f*; *county* Grafschaft *f*, Kreis *m.*

c/o *care of* p.A., per Adresse, bei.

C.O.D. *cash* (*Am. a. collect*) *on delivery* Zahlung *f* bei Empfang, gegen Nachnahme.

Col. *Colonel* Oberst *m*; *Colorado.*

Colo. *Colorado.*

Conn. *Connecticut.*

Cons. *Conservative* konservativ.

Corn. *Cornwall.*

Corp. *Corporal* Korporal *m*, Unteroffizier *m.*

C.P. *Canadian Press* (*Nachrichtenbüro*).

cp. *compare* vgl., vergleiche.

C.P.A. *Am. Certified Public Accountant* beeidigter Bücherrevisor *m*; Wirtschaftsprüfer *m.*

ct(s). *cent(s)* Cent *m* (*od. pl.*) (*amerikanische Münze*).

cu(b). *cubic* Kubik...

Cum(b). *Cumberland.*

c.w.o. *cash with order* Barzahlung *f* bei Bestellung.

cwt. *hundredweight* (*etwa 1*) Zentner *m* (*Brit. 50,8 kg, Am. 45,36 kg*).

D

d. (*Lat. denarius*) *penny, pence* (*britische Münze*); *died* gest., gestorben.

D.A. *deposit account* Depositenkonto *n.*

D.A.R. *Daughters of the American Revolution* Töchter *f/pl.* der amerikanischen Revolution (*patriotischer Frauenverband*).

D.B. *Day Book* Tage-, Kassenbuch *n.*

D.C. *direct current* Gleichstrom *m*; *District of Columbia* Distrikt Columbia (*mit der amerikanischen Hauptstadt Washington*).

D.C.L. *Doctor of Civil Law* Dr. jur., Doktor *m* des Zivilrechts.

D.D. *Doctor of Divinity* Dr. theol., Doktor *m* der Theologie.

d-d *damned* verdammt!

DDD *Am. direct distance dialing* Selbstwählferndienst *m.*

DDT *dichloro-diphenyl-trichloroethane* DDT, Dichlordiphenyltrichloräthan *n* (*Insekten- und Seuchenbekämpfungsmittel*).

Del. *Delaware.*

dep. *departure* Abf., Abfahrt *f.*

dept. *department* Abt., Abteilung *f.*

Derby. *Derbyshire.*

Devon. *Devonshire.*

dft. *draft* Tratte *f.*

disc(t). *discount* Diskont *m*, Abzug *m.*

div. *dividend* Dividende *f.*

do. *ditto* do., dito, dgl., desgleichen.

doc. *document* Dokument *n*, Urkunde *f.*

dol. *dollar* Dollar *m.*

Dors. *Dorsetshire.*

doz. *dozen(s)* Dtzd., Dutzend *n* (*od. pl.*).

d/p *documents against payment* Dokumente *n/pl.* gegen Zahlung.

dpt. *department* Abt., Abteilung *f.*

Dr. *debtor* Schuldner *m*; *Doctor* Dr., Doktor *m.*

dr. *dra(ch)m* Dram *n*, Drachme *f* (*1,77 g*); *drawer* Trassant *m.*

d.s., d/s *days after sight* Tage *m/pl.* nach Sicht (*bei Wechseln*).

Dur(h). *Durham.*

D.V. *Deo volente* (*Lat.* = *God willing*) so Gott will.

dwt. *pennyweight* Pennygewicht *n* (*1,5 g*).

dz. *dozen(s)* Dtzd., Dutzend *n* (*od. pl.*).

E

E. *east* O, Ost(en) *m*; *eastern* östlich; *English* englisch.

E. & O.E. *errors and omissions excepted* Irrtümer und Auslassungen vorbehalten.

E.C. *East Central* (London) Mitte-Ost (*Postbezirk*).

ECE *Economic Commission for Europe* Wirtschaftskommission *f* für Europa (*des ECOSOC*).

ECOSOC *Economic and Social Council* Wirtschafts- und Sozialrat *m* (*der U.N.*).

ECSC *European Coal and Steel Community* EGKS, Europäische Gemeinschaft *f* für Kohle und Stahl.

Ed., ed. *edited* h(rs)g., herausgege-

ben; *edition* Aufl., Auflage *f*; *editor* H(rs)g., Herausgeber *m*.
EE., E./E. *errors excepted* Irrtümer vorbehalten.
EEC *European Economic Community* EWG, Europäische Wirtschaftsgemeinschaft *f*.
EFTA *European Free Trade Association* EFTA, Europäische Freihandelsgemeinschaft *f od.* -zone *f*.
e.g. *exempli gratia* (*Lat.* = *for instance*) z.B., zum Beispiel.
ELDO *European Launcher Development Organization* Europäische Trägerraketen-Entwicklungsorganisation *f*.
EMA *European Monetary Agreement* EWA, Europäisches Währungsabkommen *n*.
Enc. *enclosure(s)* Anlage(n *pl.*) *f*.
Eng(l). *England* England *n*; *English* englisch.
E.R.P. *European Recovery Program(me)* Europäisches Wiederaufbauprogramm *n*, Marshall-Plan *m*.
Esq. *Esquire* Wohlgeboren (*in Briefadressen*).
ESRO *European Space-Research Organization* Europäische Weltraumforschungsorganisation *f*.
Ess. *Essex*.
etc., &c. *et cetera, and the rest, and so on* etc., usw., und so weiter.
EUCOM *Am. European Command* Hauptquartier *n* für den Befehlsbereich Europa.
EURATOM *European Atomic Energy Community* Euratom, Europäische Atomgemeinschaft *f*.
exam. *examination* Prüfung *f*.
excl. *exclusive, excluding* ausschl., ausschließlich, ohne.
ex div. *ex dividend* ohne *od.* ausschließlich Dividende.
ex int. *ex interest* ohne *od.* ausschließlich Zinsen.

F

f. *fathom* Faden *m*, Klafter *f, m, n* (*1,83 m*); *feminine* weiblich; *following* folgend; *foot (feet)* Fuß *m* (*od. pl.*) (*30,48 cm*).
F. *Fahrenheit* F, Fahrenheit (*Thermometereinteilung*); *univ. Fellow* Mitglied *n*.
F.A. *Brit. Football Association* Fußballverband *m*.
Fahr. *Fahrenheit* F, Fahrenheit (*Thermometereinteilung*).
F.A.O. *Food and Agriculture Organization* Organisation *f* für Ernährung und Landwirtschaft (*der U.N.*).
f.a.s. *free alongside ship* frei längsseits Schiff.
FBI *Am. Federal Bureau of Investigation* (*Bundeskriminalamt*).
F.B.I. *Federation of British Industries* Britischer Industrieverband *m*.
F.C.C. *Am. Federal Communications Commission* Bundeskommission *f* für das Nachrichtenwesen.
fig. *figure(s)* Abb., Abbildung(en *pl.*) *f*.
Fla. *Florida*.
F.M. *frequency modulation* UKW, Ultrakurzwelle *f*.
fm. *fathom* Faden *m*, Klafter *f, m, n* (*1,83 m*).
F.O. *Brit. Foreign Office* Auswärtiges Amt *n*.
fo. *folio* Folio *n*; Blatt *n*, Seite *f*.
f.o.b. *free on board* frei Schiff.
FOBS *Fractional Orbital Bombardment System* Orbitalraketensystem *n*.
fol. *folio* Folio *n*; Blatt *n*, Seite *f*.
f.o.q. *free on quay* frei Kai.
f.o.r. *free on rail* frei Bahn.
f.o.t. *free on truck* frei Waggon.
f.o.w. *free on waggon* frei Waggon.
F.P. *fire-plug* Hydrant *m*; *freezing-point* Gefrierpunkt *m*.
Fr. *France* Frankreich *n*; *French* französisch.
fr. *franc(s)* Frank(en *pl.*) *m*.
ft. *foot (feet)* Fuß *m* (*od. pl.*) (*30,48 cm*).
FTC *Am. Federal Trade Commission* Bundeshandelskommission *f*.
fur. *furlong* Achtelmeile *f* (*201,17 m*).

G

g. *gauge* Normalmaß *n*; 🚂 Spurweite *f*; *grain* Gran *n* (*0,0648 g*); *gram(me)* g, Gramm *n*; *guinea* Guinee *f* (*21 Shilling*).
G.A. *General Agent* Generalvertreter *m*; *General Assembly* Generalversammlung *f*.
Ga. *Georgia*.
gal. *gallon* Gallone *f* (*Brit. 4,546 l, Am. 3,785 l*).
GATT *General Agreement on Tariffs and Trade* Allgemeines Zoll- und Handelsabkommen *n*.
G.B. *Great Britain* Großbritannien *n*.

G.B.S. *George Bernard Shaw.*
G.C.B. *(Knight) Grand Cross of the Bath* (Ritter *m* des) Großkreuz(es) *n* des Bathordens.
GDR *German Democratic Republic* DDR, Deutsche Demokratische Republik *f.*
Gen. *General* General *m.*
gen. *generally* allgemein.
GFR *German Federal Republic* BRD, Bundesrepublik *f* Deutschland.
G.I. *government issue* von der Regierung ausgegeben, Staatseigentum *n*; *fig. der amerikanische Soldat.*
gi., gl. *gill* Viertelpinte *f* (*Brit. 0,142 l, Am. 0,118 l*).
G.L.C. *Greater London Council* Stadtrat *m* von Groß-London.
Glos. *Gloucestershire.*
G.M.T. *Greenwich mean time* WEZ, westeuropäische Zeit *f.*
gns. *guineas* Guineen *f/pl.* (*s. g.*).
G.O.P. *Am. Grand Old Party* Republikanische Partei *f.*
Gov. *Government* Regierung *f*; *Governor* Gouverneur *m.*
G.P. *general practitioner* praktischer Arzt *m.*
G.P.O. *General Post Office* Hauptpostamt *n.*
gr. *grain* Gran *n* (*0,0648 g*); *gross* brutto; Gros *n* (*12 Dutzend*).
gr.wt. *gross weight* Bruttogewicht *n.*
gs. *guineas* Guineen *f/pl.* (*s. g.*).
Gt.Br. *Great Britain* Großbritannien *n.*
guar. *guaranteed* garantiert.

H

h. *hour(s)* Std., Stunde(n *pl.*) *f*, Uhr (*bei Zeitangaben*).
Hants. *Hampshire.*
H.B.M. *His (Her) Britannic Majesty* Seine (Ihre) Britannische Majestät *f.*
H.C. *Brit. House of Commons* Unterhaus *n.*
H.C.J. *Brit. High Court of Justice* Hoher Gerichtshof *m.*
H.E. *high explosive* hochexplosiv; *His Excellency* Seine Exzellenz *f.*
Heref. *Herefordshire.*
Herts. *Hertfordshire.*
hf. *half* halb.
hhd. *hogshead* Oxhoft *n* (*etwa 240 l*).
H.I. *Hawaiian Islands* Hawaii-Inseln *f/pl.*
H.L. *Brit. House of Lords* Oberhaus *n.*
H.M. *His (Her) Majesty* Seine (Ihre) Majestät *f.*
H.M.S. *His (Her) Majesty's Service* Dienst *m*, ✉ Dienstsache *f*; *His (Her) Majesty's Ship (Steamer)* Seiner (Ihrer) Majestät Schiff *n* (Dampfer *m*).
H.M.S.O. *Brit. His (Her) Majesty's Stationery Office* (*Staatsdruckerei*).
H.O. *Brit. Home Office* Innenministerium *n.*
Hon. *Honorary* ehrenamtlich; *Honourable* Ehrenwert (*Anrede und Titel*).
H.P., h.p. *horse-power* PS, Pferdestärke *f*; *high pressure* Hochdruck *m*; *hire purchase* Abzahlungskauf *m.*
H.Q., Hq. *Headquarters* Stab(squartier *n*) *m*, Hauptquartier *n.*
H.R. *Am. House of Representatives* Repräsentantenhaus *n.*
H.R.H. *His (Her) Royal Highness* Seine (Ihre) Königliche Hoheit *f.*
hrs. *hours* Stunden *f/pl.*
H.T., h.t. *high tension* Hochspannung *f.*
Hunts. *Huntingdonshire.*

I

I. *Idaho* (*Staat der U.S.A.*); *Island, Isle* Insel *f.*
Ia. *Iowa.*
IAAF *International Amateur Athletic Federation* Internationaler Leichtathletikverband *m.*
I.A.T.A. *International Air Transport Association* Internationaler Luftverkehrsverband *m.*
I.B. *Invoice Book* Fakturenbuch *n.*
ib(id). *ibidem* (*Lat.* = *in the same place*) ebd., ebenda.
IBRD *International Bank for Reconstruction and Development* Internationale Bank *f* für Wiederaufbau und Entwicklung, Weltbank *f.*
I.C.A.O. *International Civil Aviation Organization* Internationale Zivilluftfahrt-Organisation *f.*
I.C.B.M. *intercontinental ballistic missile* interkontinentaler ballistischer Flugkörper *m.*
I.C.F.T.U. *International Confederation of Free Trade Unions* Internationaler Bund *m* Freier Gewerkschaften.
ICPC *International Criminal Police*

Commission Interpol, Internationale Kriminalpolizei-Kommission *f*.
ICRC *International Committee of the Red Cross* Internationales Komitee *n* des Roten Kreuzes.
I.D. *Am. Intelligence Department* ⚔ Nachrichtendienst *m*.
id. *idem* (*Lat.* = *the same author od. word*) id., idem, derselbe, dasselbe.
Id(a). *Idaho.*
i.e. *id est* (*Lat.* = *that is to say*) d. h., das heißt.
IFT *International Federation of Translators* Internationaler Bund *m* der Übersetzer.
I.H.P., i.h.p. *indicated horse-power* i. PS, indizierte Pferdestärke *f*.
Ill. *Illinois.*
I.L.O. *International Labo(u)r Organization* Internationale Arbeitsorganisation *f*.
I.M.F. *International Monetary Fund* IWF, Internationaler Währungsfonds *m*.
in. *inch(es)* Zoll *m* (*od. pl.*) (*2,54 cm*).
Inc. *inclosure* Anlage *f*; *Incorporated* (amtlich) eingetragen.
incl. *inclusive, including* einschl., einschließlich.
incog. *incognito* incognito.
Ind. *Indiana.*
inst. *instant* d. M., dieses Monats.
I.O.C. *International Olympic Committee* IOK, Internationales Olympisches Komitee *n*.
I. of M. *Isle of Man* (*englische Insel*).
I. of W. *Isle of Wight* (*englische Insel*).
I.O.U. *I owe you* Schuldschein *m*.
I.P.A. *International Phonetic Association* Weltlautschriftverein *m* (*Internationale Phonetische Gesellschaft*).
I.Q. *intelligence quotient* Intelligenzquotient *m*.
Ir. *Ireland* Irland *n*; *Irish* irisch.
I.R.C. *International Red Cross* IRK, Internationales Rotes Kreuz *n*.
I.R.O. *International Refugee Organization* Internationale Flüchtlingsorganisation *f*.
ISO *International Organization for Standardization* Internationale Organisation *f* für Normung.
I.T.O. *International Trade Organization* Internationale Handelsorganisation *f*.
I.U.S. *International Union of Students* Internationaler Studentenverband *m*.
I.U.S.Y. *International Union of Socialist Youth* Internationale Vereinigung *f* sozialistischer Jugend.
I.V.S.(P.) *International Voluntary Service (for Peace)* Internationaler freiwilliger Hilfsdienst *m* (für den Frieden).
I.W.W. *Industrial Workers of the World* Weltverband *m* der Industriearbeiter.
I.Y.H.F. *International Youth Hostel Federation* Internationaler Jugendherbergsverband *m*.

J

J. *Judge* Richter *m*; *Justice* Justiz *f*; Richter *m*.
J.C. *Jesus Christ* Jesus Christus *m*.
J.I.B. *Brit. Joint Intelligence Bureau* ⚔ Nachrichtendienst *m*.
J.P. *Justice of the Peace* Friedensrichter *m*.
Jr. *junior* (*Lat.* = *the younger*) jr., jun., der Jüngere.
jun(r). *junior* (*Lat.* = *the younger*) jr., jun., der Jüngere.

K

Kan(s). *Kansas.*
K.C. *Brit. Knight Commander* Großoffizier *m* (*eines Ordens*); *King's Counsel* Kronanwalt *m*.
K.C.B. *Brit. Knight Commander of the Bath* Großoffizier *m* des Bathordens.
kg. *kilogram(me)* kg, Kilogramm *n*.
K.K.K. *Ku Klux Klan* (*geheime Terrororganisation in U.S.A.*).
km. *kilometre* km, Kilometer *m, n*.
k.o., KO *knock(ed) out* k.o.; *Boxen*: durch Niederschlag kampfunfähig; *fig.* erledigt.
k.v. *kilovolt* kV, Kilovolt *n*.
k.w. *kilowatt* kW, Kilowatt *n*.
Ky. *Kentucky.*

L

l. *left* links; *line* Zeile *f*, Linie *f*; *link* (*20,12 cm*); *litre* l, Liter *n, m*.
£ *pound sterling* Pfund *n* Sterling.
La. *Louisiana.*
Lancs. *Lancashire.*
lat. *latitude* geographische Breite *f*.

lb. (*Lat. libra*) *pound* Pfund *n* (*Gewicht*).
L.C. *letter of credit* Kreditbrief *m.*
l.c. *loco citato* (*Lat.* = *at the place cited*) a.a.O., am angeführten Ort.
L.C.J. *Brit. Lord Chief Justice* Lordoberrichter *m.*
Leics. *Leicestershire.*
Lincs. *Lincolnshire.*
ll. *lines* Zeilen *f/pl.*, Linien *f/pl.*
LL.D. *legum doctor* (*Lat.* = *Doctor of Laws*) Dr. jur., Doktor *m* der Rechte.
loc.cit. *loco citato* (*Lat.* = *at the place cited*) a.a.O., am angeführten Ort.
lon(g). *longitude* geographische Länge *f.*
LP *long-playing* (*record*) Langspiel (-platte *f*).
L.P. *Brit. Labour Party* Arbeiterpartei *f.*
l.p. *low pressure* Tiefdruck *m.*
L.S.O. *London Symphony Orchestra* Londoner Sinfonieorchester *n.*
L.S.S. *Am. Life Saving Service* Lebensrettungsdienst *m.*
Lt. *Lieutenant* Leutnant *m.*
L.T., l.t. *low tension* Niederspannung *f.*
Lt.-Col. *Lieutenant-Colonel* Oberstleutnant *m.*
Ltd. *Limited* mit beschränkter Haftung.
Lt.-Gen. *Lieutenant-General* Generalleutnant *m.*

M

m *minim* (*Apothekermaß, Brit. 0,0592 ml, Am. 0,0616 ml*).
m. *masculine* männlich; *metre* Meter *n, m*; *mile* Meile *f* (*1609,34 m*); *minute* Min., min, Minute *f.*
M.A. *Master of Arts* Magister *m* der Philosophie; *Military Academy* Militärakademie *f.*
Maj. *Major* Major *m.*
Maj.-Gen. *Major-General* Generalmajor *m.*
Man. *Manitoba.*
Mass. *Massachusetts.*
M.C. *Master of Ceremonies* Zeremonienmeister *m*; *Am.* Conférencier *m*; *Am. Member of Congress* Kongreßmitglied *n.*
M.D. *medicinae doctor* (*Lat.* = *Doctor of Medicine*) Dr. med., Doktor *m* der Medizin.
Md. *Maryland.*
Me. *Maine.*
mg. *milligram(me)* mg, Milligramm *n.*
mi. *mile* Meile *f* (*1609,34 m*).
Mich. *Michigan.*
Middx. *Middlesex.*
Min. *minute* Min., min, Minute *f.*
Minn. *Minnesota.*
Miss. *Mississippi.*
mm. *millimetre* mm, Millimeter *n, m.*
Mo. *Missouri.*
M.O. *money order* Geldanweisung *f.*
Mon. *Monmouthshire.*
Mont. *Montana.*
MP, M.P. *Member of Parliament* Parlamentsabgeordnete(r) *m*; *Military Police* Militärpolizei *f.*
m.p.h. *miles per hour* Stundenmeilen *f/pl.*
Mr. *Mister* Herr *m.*
Mrs. *Mistress* Frau *m.*
Ms (*briefliche*) *Anredeform falls unbekannt, ob Mrs. oder Miss.*
MS. *manuscript* Ms., Manuskript *n.*
M.S. *motorship* Motorschiff *n.*
MSA *Am. Mutual Security Agency* Verwaltung *f* für gemeinsame Sicherheit.
MSS. *manuscripts* Mss., Manuskripte *n/pl.*
mt. *megaton* Mt, Megatonne *f.*
Mt. *Mount* Berg *m.*
Mx. *Middlesex.*

N

N. *north* N, Nord(en) *m*; *northern* nördlich.
n. *noon* Mittag *m.*
N.A.A.F.I. *Navy, Army and Air Force Institutes* (*Marketenderei- und Truppenbetreuungsinstitution der britischen Streitkräfte*).
NASA *Am. National Aeronautics and Space Administration* Nationale Luft- und Raumfahrtbehörde *f.*
NATO *North Atlantic Treaty Organization* Nordatlantikpakt-Organisation *f.*
N.B.C. *Am. National Broadcasting Corporation* Nationale Rundfunkgesellschaft *f.*
N.C. *North Carolina.*
N.C.B. *Brit. National Coal Board* Nationale Kohlenbehörde *f.*
n.d. *no date* ohne Datum.
N.D(ak). *North Dakota.*
N.E. *northeast* NO, Nordost(en) *m*; *northeastern* nordöstlich.

Neb(r). *Nebraska.*
Nev. *Nevada.*
N.F. N/F *no funds* keine Dekkung.
N.H. *New Hampshire.*
N.H.S. *Brit. National Health Service* Nationaler Gesundheitsdienst *m* (*Krankenversicherung*).
N.J. *New Jersey.*
N.M(ex). *New Mexico.*
No. *north* N, Nord(en) *m*; *number* Zahl *f*; *numero* Nr., Nummer *f*.
Norf. *Norfolk.*
Northants. *Northamptonshire.*
Northumb. *Northumberland.*
Notts. *Nottinghamshire.*
n.p. or d. *no place or date* ohne Ort oder Datum.
N.S.P.C.A. *Brit. National Society for the Prevention of Cruelty to Animals* (*Tierschutzverein*).
N.T. *New Testament* Neues Testament *n*.
Nt.wt. *net weight* Nettogewicht *n*.
N.U.M. *Brit. National Union of Mineworkers* Nationale Bergarbeitergewerkschaft *f*.
N.W. *northwest* NW, Nordwest(en) *m*; *northwestern* nordwestlich.
N.Y. *New York* (*Staat der U.S.A.*).
N.Y.C. *New York City* Stadt *f* New York.
N.Z. *New Zealand* Neuseeland *n*.

O

O. *Ohio*; *order* Auftrag *m*.
o/a *on account* für Rechnung von.
O.A.S. *Organization of American States* Organisation *f* amerikanischer Staaten.
ob. *obiit* (*Lat.* = *died*) gest., gestorben.
OECD *Organization for Economic Co-operation and Development* Organisation *f* für wirtschaftliche Zusammenarbeit und Entwicklung.
O.H. *on hand* vorrätig.
O.H.M.S. *On His (Her) Majesty's Service* im Dienst Seiner (Ihrer) Majestät; ✉ Dienstsache *f*.
O.K. (*möglicherweise aus*:) *all correct* in Ordnung.
Okla. *Oklahoma.*
O.N.A. *Overseas News Agency* Überseenachrichtenagentur *f* (*ein amerikanischer Pressedienst*).
O.N.S. *Overseas News Service* Überseenachrichtendienst *m* (*ein britischer Pressedienst*).
o.r. *owner's risk* auf Gefahr des Eigentümers.
Ore(g). *Oregon.*
O.T. *Old Testament* Altes Testament *n*.
Oxon. *Oxfordshire.*
oz. *ounce(s)* Unze(n *pl.*) *f* (*28,35 g*).

P

p *(new) penny, (new) pence.*
Pa. *Pennsylvania.*
p.a. *per annum* (*Lat.* = *yearly*) jährlich.
Panam. *Pan American Airways* Panamerikanische Luftfahrtgesellschaft *f*.
par. *paragraph* Paragraph *m*, Abschnitt *m*.
P.A.Y.E. *Brit. pay as you earn* Lohnsteuerabzug *m*.
P.C. *police constable* Polizist *m*, Schutzmann *m*; *postcard* Postkarte *f*.
p.c. *per cent.* Prozent *n od. pl.*
p/c *price current* Preisliste *f*.
P.D. *Police Department* Polizeibehörde *f*.
p.d. *per diem* (*Lat.* = *by the day*) pro Tag.
P.E.N., PEN Club *Poets, Playwrights, Editors, Essayists, and Novelists* PEN-Club *m* (*internationale Vereinigung von Dichtern, Dramatikern, Redakteuren, Essayisten und Romanschriftstellern*).
Penn(a). *Pennsylvania.*
per pro(c). *per procurationem* (*Lat.* = *by proxy*) pp., ppa., per Prokura.
P.f.c. *Am. private first class* Obergefreite *m*.
Ph.D. *Philosophiae Doctor* (*Lat.* = *Doctor of Philosophy*) Doktor *m* der Philosophie.
pk. *peck* (*9,087 l*).
P./L. *profit and loss* Gewinn *m* und Verlust *m*.
p.m. *post meridiem* (*Lat.* = *after noon*) nachmittags, abends.
P.O. *postal order* Postanweisung *f*; *Post Office* Postamt *n*.
P.O.B. *Post-Office Box* Post(schließ)-fach *n*.
p.o.d. *pay on delivery* Nachnahme *f*.
P.O.O. *post-office order* Postanweisung *f*.
P.O.S.B. *Post-Office Savings Bank* Postsparkasse *f*.

P.O.W. *Prisoner of War* Kriegsgefangene *m.*
p.p. *per procurationem* (*Lat.* = *by proxy*) pp., ppa., per Prokura.
Pref. *Preface* Vorwort *n.*
Pres. *President* Präsident *m.*
Prof. *Professor* Professor *m.*
prox. *proximo* (*Lat.* = *next month*) n. M., nächsten Monats.
P.S. *Passenger Steamer* Passagierdampfer *m*; *postscript* PS, Postskript(um) *n*, Nachschrift *f.*
pt. *pint* Pinte *f* (*Brit. 0,57 l, Am. 0,47 l*).
P.T.A. *Parent-Teacher Association* Eltern-Lehrer-Vereinigung *f.*
Pte. *Private* Soldat *m* (*Dienstgrad*).
P.T.O., p.t.o. *please turn over* b.w., bitte wenden.
Pvt. *Private* Soldat *m* (*Dienstgrad*).
P.W. *Prisoner of War* Kriegsgefangene *m.*
PX *Post Exchange* (*Marketenderei und Verkaufsläden der amerikanischen Streitkräfte*).

Q

q. *query* Anfrage *f.*
Q.C. *Brit. Queen's Counsel* Kronanwalt *m.*
qr. *quarter* (*etwa 1*) Viertelzentner *m.*
qt. *quart* Quart *n* (*etwa 1 l*).
qu. *query* Anfrage *f.*
quot. *quotation* Kurs-, Preisnotierung *f.*
qy. *query* Anfrage *f.*

R

R. *Réaumur* R, Réaumur (*Thermometereinteilung*); *River* Strom *m*, Fluß *m*; *Road* Str., Straße *f.*
r. *right* rechts.
R.A. *Brit. Royal Academy* Königliche Akademie *f.*
R.A.C. *Brit. Royal Automobile Club* Königlicher Automobilklub *m.*
RADWAR *Am. radiological warfare* Atomkriegführung *f.*
R.A.F. *Royal Air Force* Königlich(-Britisch)e Luftwaffe *f.*
R.C. *Red Cross* Rotes Kreuz *n.*
Rd. *Road* Str., Straße *f.*
rd. *rod* Rute *f* (*5,029 m*).
recd. *received* erhalten.
ref(c). (*in*) *reference* (*to*) (mit) Bezug *m* (auf); Empfehlung *f.*
regd. *registered* eingetragen; ✉ eingeschrieben.
reg.tn. *register ton* RT, Registertonne *f.*
resp. *respective(ly)* bzw., beziehungsweise.
ret. *retired* i.R., im Ruhestand, a.D., außer Dienst.
Rev. *Reverend* Ehrwürden.
R.I. *Rhode Island.*
R.L.O. *Brit. Returned Letter Office* Amt *n* für unzustellbare Briefe.
R.N. *Royal Navy* Königlich(-Britisch)e Marine *f.*
R.P. *reply paid* Rückantwort bezahlt.
r.p.m. *revolutions per minute* U/min., Umdrehungen *pl.* pro Minute.
R.R. *Am. railroad* Eisenbahn *f.*
R.S. *Brit. Royal Society* Königliche Gesellschaft *f.*
R.S.V.P. *répondez s'il vous plaît* (*Fr.* = *please reply*) u.A.w.g., um Antwort wird gebeten.
Rt.Hon. *Right Honourable* Sehr Ehrenwert.
Rutl. *Rutlandshire.*
Ry. *Brit. railway* Eisenbahn *f.*

S

S. *south* S, Süd(en) *m*; *southern* südlich.
s. *second* Sek., sek, Sekunde *f*; *shilling* Shilling *m.*
$ *dollar* Dollar *m.*
S.A. *Salvation Army* Heilsarmee *f*; *South Africa* Südafrika *n*; *South America* Südamerika *n.*
SACEUR *Supreme Allied Commander Europe* Oberbefehlshaber *m* der Alliierten Streitkräfte in Europa.
SACLANT *Supreme Allied Commander Atlantic* Oberbefehlshaber *m* der Alliierten Streitkräfte im Atlantik.
Salop. *Shropshire.*
Sask. *Saskatchewan.*
S.B. *Sales Book* Verkaufsbuch *n.*
S.C. *Security Council* Sicherheitsrat *m* (*der U.N.*); *South Carolina.*
S.D(ak). *South Dakota.*
S.E. *southeast* SO, Südost(en) *m*; *southeastern* südöstlich; *Stock Exchange* Börse *f.*
SEATO *South East Asia Treaty Organization* Südostasienpakt-Organisation *f.*

Sec. *Secretary* Sekretär *m*, Minister *m*.
sec. *second* Sek., sek, Sekunde *f*.
sen(r). *senior* (*Lat.* = *the elder*) sen., der Ältere.
S(er)gt. *Sergeant* Feldwebel *m*, Wachtmeister *m*.
sh. *sheet* Blatt *n*; *shilling* Schilling *m*.
SHAPE *Supreme Headquarters Allied Powers Europe* Oberkommando *n* der Alliierten Streitkräfte in Europa.
S.M. *Sergeant-Major* Oberfeldwebel *m*, Oberwachtmeister *m*.
S.N. *shipping note* Frachtannahme-, Ladeschein *m*, Schiffszettel *m*.
Soc. *society* Gesellschaft *f*, Verein *m*.
Som(s). *Somersetshire*.
SOS *SOS* (*internationales Seenotzeichen*).
sov. *sovereign* Sovereign *m* (*britische 20-Schilling-Goldmünze*).
sp.gr. *specific gravity* spezifisches Gewicht *n*.
S.P.Q.R. *small profits, quick returns* kleine Gewinne, große Umsätze.
Sq. *Square* Pl., Platz *m*.
sq. *square* ... Quadrat...
Sr. *senior* (*Lat.* = *the elder*) sen., der Ältere.
S.S. *steamship* Dampfer *m*.
st. *stone* (*6,35 kg*).
St. *Saint* ... St. ..., Sankt ...; *Station* Bhf., Bahnhof *m*; *Street* Str., Straße *f*.
Staffs. *Staffordshire*.
S.T.D. *Brit. subscriber trunk dialling* Selbstwählferndienst *m*.
St. Ex. *Stock Exchange* Börse *f*.
stg. *sterling* Sterling *m* (*britische Währungseinheit*).
sub. *substitute* Ersatz *m*.
Suff. *Suffolk*.
suppl. *supplement* Nachtrag *m*.
Suss. *Sussex*.
S.W. *southwest* SW, Südwest(en) *m*; *southwestern* südwestlich.
Sy. *Surrey*.

T

t. *ton* t, Tonne (*Brit. 1016 kg, Am. 907,18 kg*).
T.B. *tuberculosis* Tb, Tbc, Tuberkulose *f*.
T.C. *Trusteeship Council of the United Nations* Treuhandschaftsrat *m* der Vereinten Nationen.
T.D. *Am. Treasury Department* Finanzministerium *n*.
Tenn. *Tennessee*.
Tex. *Texas*.
tgm. *telegram* Telegramm *n*.
T.G.W.U. *Brit. Transport and General Workers' Union* Transportarbeiterverband *m*.
T.M.O. *telegraph money order* telegraphische Geldanweisung *f*.
TNT *trinitrotoluene* TNT, Trinitrotoluol *n*.
T.O. *Telegraph* (*Telephone*) *Office* Telegraphenamt *n* (Fernsprechamt *n*); *turn-over* Umsatz *m*.
t.o. *turn-over* Umsatz *m*.
T.P.O. *Travelling Post Office* Bahnpost *f*.
T.U. *Trade(s) Union(s)* Gewerkschaft(en *pl.*) *f*.
T.U.C. *Brit. Trade(s) Union Congress* Gewerkschaftsverband *m*.
T.V. *television* Fernsehen *n*; Fernseh...
T.V.A. *Tennessee Valley Authority* Tennesseetal-Behörde *f*.
T.W.A. *Am. Trans World Airlines* (*Luftfahrtgesellschaft*).

U

U.H.F. *ultra-high frequency* UHF, Dezimeterwelle(nbereich *m*) *f*.
U.K. *United Kingdom* Vereinigtes Königreich *n* (*England, Schottland, Wales und Nordirland*).
ult. *ultimo* (*Lat.* = *last day of the month*) ult., ultimo, am Letzten des Monats.
UMW *Am. United Mine Workers* Vereinigte Bergarbeiter *m/pl.* (*Gewerkschaftsverband*).
UN, U.N. *United Nations* Vereinte Nationen *f/pl*.
UNESCO *United Nations Educational, Scientific, and Cultural Organization* Organisation *f* der Vereinten Nationen für Erziehung, Wissenschaft und Kultur.
UNICEF *United Nations International Children's Emergency Fund* Kinderhilfswerk *n* der Vereinten Nationen.
U.N.S.C. *United Nations Security Council* Sicherheitsrat *m* der Vereinten Nationen.
U.P.I. *Am. United Press International* (*Nachrichtenagentur*).
U.S.(A.) *United States (of America)*

US(A), Vereinigte Staaten *m/pl.* (von Amerika).

USAF(E) *United States Air Force (Europe)* Luftwaffe *f* der Vereinigten Staaten (in Europa).

U.S.S.R. *Union of Socialist Soviet Republics* UdSSR, Union *f* der Sozialistischen Sowjetrepubliken.

Ut. *Utah.*

V

v. *verse* V., Vers *m*; *versus* (*Lat.* = *against*) contra, gegen; *vide* (*Lat.* = see) s., siehe.

V *volt* V, Volt *n.*

Va. *Virginia.*

V.A.T. *value-added tax* Mehrwertsteuer *f.*

V.D. *venereal disease* Geschlechtskrankheit *f.*

V.H.F. *very high frequency* UKW, Ultrakurzwelle(nbereich *m*) *f.*

V.I.P. *very important person* hohes Tier *n*, bedeutende Persönlichkeit *f.*

Vis. *viscount(ess)* Vicomte *m* (Vicomtesse *f*).

viz. *videlicet* (*Lat.* = *namely*) nämlich.

vol. *volume* Bd., Band *m.*

vols. *volumes* Bde., Bände *m/pl.*

vs. *versus* (*Lat.* = *against*) contra, gegen.

V.S. *veterinary surgeon* Tierarzt *m.*

V.S.O.P. *very superior old pale* (*Qualitätsbezeichnung für Kognak*).

Vt. *Vermont.*

V.T.O.(L.) *vertical take-off* (*and landing*) (*aircraft*) Senkrechtstart (-er) *m.*

v.v. *vice versa* (*Lat.* = *conversely*) umgekehrt.

W

W *watt* W, Watt *n.*

W. *west* W, West(en) *m*; *western* westlich.

War. *Warwickshire.*

Wash. *Washington.*

W.C. *West Central* (London) Mitte-West (*Postbezirk*); *water-closet* WC, Wasserklosett *n*, Toilette *f.*

WCC *World Council of Churches* Ökumenischer Rat *m* der Kirchen, Weltkirchenrat *m.*

WFPA *World Federation for the Protection of Animals* Welttierschutzverband *m.*

W.F.T.U. *World Federation of Trade Unions* WGB, Weltgewerkschaftsbund *m.*

WHO *World Health Organization* WGO, Weltgesundheitsorganisation *f.*

W.I. *West Indies* Westindien *n.*

Wilts. *Wiltshire.*

Wis. *Wisconsin.*

W/L., w.l. *wave length* Wellenlänge *f.*

W.O.M.A.N. *World Organization of Mothers of All Nations* Weltbund *m* der Mütter aller Nationen.

Worcs. *Worcestershire.*

W.P. *weather permitting* bei günstigem Wetter.

w.p.a. *with particular average* mit Teilschaden.

W.S.R. *World Students' Relief* Internationales Studentenhilfswerk *n.*

W/T *wireless telegraphy* (*telephony*) drahtlose Telegraphie *f* (Telephonie *f*).

wt. *weight* Gewicht *n.*

W.Va. *West Virginia.*

Wyo. *Wyoming.*

X

x-d. *ex dividend* ausschließlich *od.* ohne Dividende.

x-i. *ex interest* ausschließlich *od.* ohne Zinsen.

Xmas *Christmas* Weihnachten *n.*

Xroads *cross roads* Straßenkreuzung *f.*

Xt. *Christ* Christus *m.*

Y

yd. *yard(s)* Elle(n *pl.*) *f* (*91,44 cm*).

YMCA *Young Men's Christian Association* CVJM, Christlicher Verein *m* junger Männer.

Yorks. *Yorkshire.*

yr(s). *year(s)* Jahr(e *pl.*) *n.*

YWCA *Young Women's Christian Association* Christlicher Verein *m* junger Mädchen.

American Orthography

Gegenüber dem britischen Englisch (BE) weist die Rechtschreibung im amerikanischen Englisch (AE) hauptsächlich folgende Eigenheiten auf:

1. Häufige Weglassung des **Bindestrichs,** z. B. newsstand, breakdown, soapbox, coed, cooperate.

2. Wegfall des **u** in der Endung **-our,** z. B. col*or*, hum*or*, hon*or*able, fav*or*.

3. **-er** statt BE **-re** in Endsilben, z. B. cent*er*, fib*er*, theat*er*, aber nicht bei massacre.

4. Verdopplung des Endkonsonanten **l** erfolgt nur, wenn der Hauptakzent auf der Endsilbe liegt, daher z. B. AE counci*l*or, jewe*l*ry, quarre*l*ed, trave*l*ed, woo*l*en; andererseits findet sich im AE enroll(s), fulfill(s), skillful, installment = BE enrol(s), fulfil(s), skilful, instalment.

5. AE **s** statt BE **c,** besonders in der Endsilbe **-ence,** z. B. def*ense*, off*ense*, lic*ense*, aber auch AE practice und practise als Verb.

6. Verbreitet sind Vereinfachungen oder Wegfall fremdsprachlicher Endungen, z. B. dialo*g*(*ue*), prolo*g*(*ue*) catalo*g*(*ue*), progra*m*(*me*).

7. Verbreitet ist ferner die Vereinfachung von **ae** und **oe** zu **e,** z. B. an(*a*)*e*mia, an(*a*)*e*sthesia, subp(*o*)*e*na.

8. Die Endung **-ction** wird statt **-xion** bevorzugt, z. B. conne*ction*, infle*c-tion*.

9. Verbreitet findet sich Konsonantenvereinfachung, z. B. wa*gon*, kidna*p*ed, worshi*p*ed, benefi*t*ed.

10. AE bevorzugt **-o-** statt **-ou-,** z. B. m*o*(*u*)ld, sm*o*(*u*)lder, pl*o*w statt BE plough.

11. Stummes **e** entfällt in Wörtern wie abridg(*e*)ment, judg(*e*)ment, acknowledg(*e*)ment.

12. AE gebraucht die Vorsilbe **in-** statt **en-** häufiger als BE, z. B. *in*close, *in*fold, *in*case.

13. AE bevorzugt die folgende Schreibweise in Einzelfällen: *check* = BE cheque, *hello* = BE hallo, *cozy* = BE cosy, *mustache* = BE moustache, *skeptical* = BE sceptical, *peddler* = BE pedlar, *gray* = BE grey.

14. Neben although, all right, through finden sich die informell-familiären Formen *altho*, *alright*, *thru*.

Numerals

Cardinal Numbers

0 nought, zero, cipher; *teleph.* 0 [əu] *null*
1 one *eins*
2 two *zwei*
3 three *drei*
4 four *vier*
5 five *fünf*
6 six *sechs*
7 seven *sieben*
8 eight *acht*
9 nine *neun*
10 ten *zehn*
11 eleven *elf*
12 twelve *zwölf*
13 thirteen *dreizehn*
14 fourteen *vierzehn*
15 fifteen *fünfzehn*
16 sixteen *sechzehn*
17 seventeen *siebzehn*
18 eighteen *achtzehn*
19 nineteen *neunzehn*
20 twenty *zwanzig*
21 twenty-one *einundzwanzig*
22 twenty-two *zweiundzwanzig*
30 thirty *dreißig*
31 thirty-one *einunddreißig*
40 forty *vierzig*
41 forty-one *einundvierzig*
50 fifty *fünfzig*
51 fifty-one *einundfünfzig*
60 sixty *sechzig*
61 sixty-one *einundsechzig*
70 seventy *siebzig*
71 seventy-one *einundsiebzig*
80 eighty *achtzig*
81 eighty-one *einundachtzig*
90 ninety *neunzig*
91 ninety-one *einundneunzig*
100 a *od.* one hundred *hundert*
101 hundred and one *hundert(und)-eins*
200 two hundred *zweihundert*
300 three hundred *dreihundert*
572 five hundred and seventy-two *fünfhundert(und)zweiundsiebzig*
1000 a *od.* one thousand *(ein)tausend*
1066 ten sixty-six *tausendsechsund-sechzig*
1971 nineteen (hundred and) sev-enty-one *neunzehnhundertein-undsiebzig*
2000 two thousand *zweitausend*
5044 *teleph.* five 0 double four *fünf-zig vierundvierzig*
1 000 000 a *od.* one million *eine Mil-lion*
2 000 000 two million *zwei Millio-nen*
1 000 000 000 a *od.* one milliard, *Am.* billion *eine Milliarde*

Ordinal Numbers

1. first *erste*
2. second *zweite*
3. third *dritte*
4. fourth *vierte*
5. fifth *fünfte*
6. sixth *sechste*
7. seventh *siebente*
8. eighth *achte*
9. ninth *neunte*
10. tenth *zehnte*
11. eleventh *elfte*
12. twelfth *zwölfte*
13. thirteenth *dreizehnte*
14. fourteenth *vierzehnte*
15. fifteenth *fünfzehnte*
16. sixteenth *sechzehnte*
17. seventeenth *siebzehnte*
18. eighteenth *achtzehnte*
19. nineteenth *neunzehnte*
20. twentieth *zwanzigste*
21. twenty-first *einundzwanzigste*
22. twenty-second *zweiundzwanzig-ste*
23. twenty-third *dreiundzwanzigste*

30. thirtieth *dreißigste*
31. thirty-first *einunddreißigste*
40. fortieth *vierzigste*
41. forty-first *einundvierzigste*
50. fiftieth *fünfzigste*
51. fifty-first *einundfünfzigste*
60. sixtieth *sechzigste*
61. sixty-first *einundsechzigste*
70. seventieth *siebzigste*
71. seventy-first *einundsiebzigste*
80. eightieth *achtzigste*
81. eighty-first *einundachtzigste*
90. ninetieth *neunzigste*
100. (one) hundredth *hundertste*
101. hundred and first *hundertunderste*
200. two hundredth *zweihundertste*
300. three hundredth *dreihundertste*
572. five hundred and seventy-second *fünfhundertundzweiundsiebzigste*
1000. (one) thousandth *tausendste*
1950. nineteen hundred and fiftieth *neunzehnhundertfünfzigste*
2000. two thousandth *zweitausendste*
1 000 000. millionth *millionste*
2 000 000. two millionth *zweimillionste*

Fractions and other Numerical Values

$^1/_2$ one *od.* a half *ein halb*
$1^1/_2$ one and a half *anderthalb*
$2^1/_2$ two and a half *zweieinhalb*
$^1/_3$ one *od.* a third *ein Drittel*
$^2/_3$ two thirds *zwei Drittel*
$^1/_4$ one *od.* a quarter, one fourth *ein Viertel*
$^3/_4$ three quarters, three fourths *drei Viertel*
$^1/_5$ one *od.* a fifth *ein Fünftel*
$3^4/_5$ three and four fifths *drei vier Fünftel*
$^5/_8$ five eighths *fünf Achtel*
$^{12}/_{20}$ twelve twentieths *zwölf Zwanzigstel*
$^{75}/_{100}$ seventy-five hundredths *fünfundsiebzig Hundertstel*
.45 point four five *null Komma vier fünf*
2.5 two point five *zwei Komma fünf*

once *einmal*
twice *zweimal*
three (four) times *drei- (vier)mal*
twice as much (many) *zweimal* od. *doppelt so viel(e)*
firstly (secondly, thirdly), in the first (second, third) place *erstens (zweitens, drittens)*
$7 + 8 = 15$ seven and eight are fifteen *sieben und* od. *plus acht ist fünfzehn*
$9 - 4 = 5$ nine less four are five *neun minus* od. *weniger vier ist fünf*
$2 \times 3 = 6$ twice three are *od.* make six *zweimal drei ist sechs*
$20 : 5 = 4$ twenty divided by five make four *zwanzig dividiert* od. *geteilt durch fünf ist vier*

Weights and Measures

1. Längenmaße
Linear Measures

1 inch (in.)
= 2,54 cm

1 foot (ft.)
= 12 inches = 30,48 cm

1 yard (yd.)
= 3 feet = 91,44 cm

2. Wege- und Vermessungsmaße
Distance and Surveyors' Measures

1 link (li., l.)
= 7.92 inches = 20,12 cm

1 rod (rd.), pole *od.* **perch (p.)**
= 25 links = 5,03 m

1 chain (ch.)
= 4 rods = 20,12 m

1 furlong (fur.)
= 10 chains = 201,17 m

1 (statute) mile (mi.)
= 8 furlongs = 1609,34 m

3. Nautische Maße
Nautical Measures

1 fathom (fm.)
= 6 feet = 1,83 m

1 cable('s) length
= 100 fathoms = 183 m
US 120 fathoms = 219 m

1 nautical mile (n. m.)
= 10 cables' length = 1852 m

4. Flächenmaße
Square Measures

1 square inch (sq. in.)
= 6,45 cm²

1 square foot (sq. ft.)
= 144 square inches
= 929,03 cm²

1 square yard (sq. yd.)
= 9 square feet = 0,836 m²

1 square rod (sq. rd.)
= 30.25 square yards = 25,29 m²

1 rood (ro.)
= 40 square rods = 10,12 a

1 acre (a.)
= 4 roods = 40,47 a

1 square mile (sq. mi.)
= 640 acres = 2,59 km²

5. Raummaße
Cubic Measures

1 cubic inch (cu. in.)
= 16,387 cm³

1 cubic foot (cu. ft.)
= 1728 cubic inches
= 0,028 m³

1 cubic yard (cu. yd.)
= 27 cubic feet = 0,765 m³

1 register ton (reg. tn.)
= 100 cubic feet = 2,832 m³

6. Britische Hohlmaße
British Measures of Capacity

Trocken- und Flüssigkeitsmaße
Dry and Liquid Measures

1 British *od.* **Imperial gill (gi., gl.)**
= 0,142 l

1 British *od.* **Imperial pint (pt.)**
= 4 gills = 0,568 l

1 British *od.* **Imperial quart (qt.)**
= 2 Imp. pints = 1,136 l

1 British *od.* **Imp. gallon (Imp. gal.)**
= 4 Imp. quarts = 4,546 l

Trockenmaße
Dry Measures

1 British *od.* **Imperial peck (pk.)**
= 2 Imp. gallons = 9,092 l

1 Brit. *od.* **Imp. bushel (bu., bsh.)**
= 4 Imp. pecks = 36,36 l

1 Brit. *od.* **Imperial quarter (qr.)**
8 Imp. bushels = 290,94 l

Flüssigkeitsmaß
Liquid Measure

1 Brit. *od.* **Imp. barrel (bbl., bl.)**
= 36 Imp. gallons = 1,636 hl

7. Hohlmaße der USA
U.S. Measures of Capacity

Trockenmaße
Dry Measures

1 U.S. dry pint
= 0,550 l

1 U.S. dry quart
= 2 dry pints = 1,1 l

1 U.S. peck
= 8 dry quarts = 8,81 l

1 U.S. bushel (Getreidemaß)
= 4 pecks = 35,24 l

Flüssigkeitsmaße
Liquid Measures

1 U.S. liquid gill
= 0,118 l

1 U.S. liquid pint
= 4 gills = 0,473 l

1 U.S. liquid quart
= 2 liquid pints = 0,946 l

1 U.S. gallon
= 4 liquid quarts = 3,785 l

1 U.S. barrel
= 31 ½ gallons = 119 l

1 U.S. barrel petroleum
= 42 gallons = 158,97 l

8. Apothekermaße
Apothecaries' Fluid Measures

1 minim (min., m.)
= 0,0006 dl

1 fluid drachm, *US* **dram (dr. fl.)**
= 60 minims = 0,0355 dl

1 fluid ounce (oz. fl.)
= 8 fluid dra(ch)ms = 0,284 dl

1 pint (pt.)
= 20 fluid ounces = 0,568 l
US 16 fluid ounces = 0,473 l

9. Handelsgewichte
Avoirdupois Weight

1 grain (gr.)
= 0,0648 g

1 drachm, *US* **dram (dr. av.)**
= 27.34 grains = 1,77 g

1 ounce (oz. av.)
= 16 dra(ch)ms = 28,35 g

1 pound (lb. av.)
= 16 ounces = 0,453 kg

1 stone (st.)
= 14 pounds = 6,35 kg

1 quarter (qr.)
= 28 pounds = 12,7 kg
US 25 pounds = 11,34 kg

1 hundredweight (cwt.)
= 112 pounds = 50,8 kg
(*a.* long hundredweight: cwt. l.)

US 100 pounds = 45,36 kg
(*a.* short hundredweight: cwt. sh.)

1 ton (tn., t.)
= 2240 pounds (= 20 cwt. l.) = 1016 kg (*a.* long ton: tn. l.)

US 2000 pounds (= 20 cwt. sh.) = 907,18 kg (*a.* short ton: tn. sh.)

10. Fein- und Apothekergewichte
Troy and Apothecaries' Weight

1 grain (gr.)
= 0,0648 g

1 scruple (s. ap.)
= 20 grains = 1,296 g

1 pennyweight (dwt.)
= 24 grains = 1,555 g

1 dra(ch)m (dr. t. *od.* **dr. ap.)**
= 3 scruples = 3,888 g

1 ounce (oz. ap.)
= 8 dra(ch)ms = 31,104 g

1 pound (lb. t. *od.* **lb. ap.)**
= 12 ounces = 0,373 kg

Irregular Verbs

Die an erster Stelle stehende Form bezeichnet das Präsens (present tense), nach dem ersten Gedankenstrich steht das Präteritum (past tense), nach dem zweiten das Partizip Perfekt (past participle).

abide - abode - abode
arise - arose - arisen
awake - awoke - awoke, awaked
be (am, is, are) - was (were) - been
bear - bore - borne *getragen*, born *geboren*
beat - beat - beaten, beat
become - became - become
beget - begot - begotten
begin - began - begun
belay - belayed, belaid - belayed, belaid
bend - bent - bent
bereave - bereaved, bereft - bereaved, bereft
beseech - besought - besought
bet - bet, betted - bet, betted
bid - bade, bid - bidden, bid
bind - bound - bound
bite - bit - bitten
bleed - bled - bled
blow - blew - blown
break - broke - broken
breed - bred - bred
bring - brought - brought
build - built - built
burn - burnt, burned - burnt, burned
burst - burst - burst
buy - bought - bought
can - could
cast - cast - cast
catch - caught - caught
chide - chid - chid, chidden
choose - chose - chosen
cleave - clove, cleft - cloven, cleft
cling - clung - clung
clothe - clothed, *lit.* clad - clothed, *lit.* clad
come - came - come
cost - cost - cost
creep - crept - crept
crow - crowed, crew - crowed
cut - cut - cut
dare - dared, durst - dared
deal - dealt - dealt
dig - dug - dug
do - did - done
draw - drew - drawn
dream - dreamt, dreamed - dreamt, dreamed
drink - drank - drunk
drive - drove - driven
dwell - dwelt - dwelt
eat - ate - eaten
fall - fell - fallen
feed - fed - fed
feel - felt - felt
fight - fought - fought
find - found - found
flee - fled - fled
fling - flung - flung
fly - flew - flown
forbear - forbore - forborne
forbid - forbad(e) - forbidden
forget - forgot - forgotten
forgive - forgave - forgiven
forsake - forsook - forsaken
freeze - froze - frozen
geld - gelded, gelt - gelded, gelt
get - got - got, *Am. a.* gotten
gild - gilded, gilt - gilded, gilt
gird - girded, girt - girded, girt
give - gave - given
go - went - gone
grave - graved - graved, graven
grind - ground - ground
grow - grew - grown
hang - hung - hung
have (has) - had - had
hear - heard - heard
heave - heaved, ⚓ hove - heaved, ⚓ hove
hew - hewed - hewed, hewn
hide - hid - hidden, hid
hit - hit - hit
hold - held - held
hurt - hurt - hurt
keep - kept - kept
kneel - knelt, kneeled - knelt, kneeled
knit - knitted, knit - knitted, knit
know - knew - known
lade - laded - laded, laden
lay - laid - laid

lead - led- led
lean - leaned, leant - leaned, leant
leap - leaped, leapt - leaped, leapt
learn - learned, learnt - learned, learnt
leave - left - left
lend - lent - lent
let - let - let
lie - lay - lain
light - lighted, lit - lighted, lit
lose - lost - lost
make - made - made
may - might
mean - meant - meant
meet - met - met
mow - mowed - mowed, mown
must - must
kein Präsens - **ought**
pay - paid - paid
pen - penned, pent - penned, pent
put - put - put
read - read - read
rend - rent - rent
rid - rid - rid
ride - rode - ridden
ring - rang - rung
rise - rose - risen
rive - rived - riven
run - ran - run
saw - sawed - sawn, sawed
say - said - said
see - saw - seen
seek - sought - sought
sell - sold - sold
send - sent - sent
set - set - set
sew - sewed - sewed, sewn
shake - shook - shaken
shall - should
shave - shaved - shaved, (*mst adj.*) shaven
shear - sheared - shorn
shed - shed - shed
shine - shone - shone
shoe - shod - shod
shoot - shot - shot
show - showed - shown
shred - shredded - shredded, shred
shrink - shrank - shrunk
shut - shut - shut
sing - sang - sung
sink - sank - sunk
sit - sat - sat
slay - slew - slain
sleep - slept - slept
slide - slid - slid
sling - slung - slung
slink - slunk - slunk
slit - slit - slit
smell - smelt, smelled - smelt, smelled
smite - smote - smitten
sow - sowed - sown, sowed
speak - spoke - spoken
speed - sped, ⊕ speeded - sped, ⊕ speeded
spell - spelt, spelled - spelt, spelled
spend - spent - spent
spill - spilt, spilled - spilt, spilled
spin - spun, span - spun
spit - spat - spat
split - split - split
spoil - spoiled, spoilt - spoiled, spoilt
spread - spread - spread
spring - sprang - sprung
stand - stood - stood
stave - staved, stove - staved, stove
steal - stole - stolen
stick - stuck - stuck
sting - stung - stung
stink - stunk, stank - stunk
strew - strewed - (have) strewed, (be) strewn
stride - strode - stridden
strike - struck - struck
string - strung - strung
strive - strove - striven
swear - swore - sworn
sweat - sweat, sweated - sweat, sweated
sweep - swept - swept
swell - swelled - swollen
swim - swam - swum
swing - swung - swung
take - took - taken
teach - taught - taught
tear - tore - torn
tell - told - told
think - thought - thought
thrive - throve - thriven
throw - threw - thrown
thrust - thrust - thrust
tread - trod - trodden
wake - woke, waked - waked, woke(n)
wear - wore - worn
weave - wove - woven
weep - wept - wept
wet - wetted, wet - wetted, wet
will - would
win - won - won
wind - wound - wound
work - worked, *bsd.* ⊕ wrought - worked, *bsd.* ⊕ wrought
wring - wrung - wrung
write - wrote - written

Punctuation and Capitalisation

1. Der Punkt

a) Der Punkt steht am Ende eines vollständigen Satzes, wenn dieser nicht in die Form der Frage oder des Ausrufes gekleidet ist.

Three removes are as bad as a fire.

Er beschließt aber auch unvollständige Sätze, also Wortgruppen und Einzelwörter, die anstelle eines Satzes stehen.

All rights reserved.
Have you locked the shed? Certainly.

b) Der Punkt wird meist nach Abkürzungen gesetzt.

gr.; Mon.; pop. 1028.

Im Gegensatz zum Amerikanischen fehlt im britischen Gebrauch der Punkt vielfach hinter *Mr*, *Mrs* und *Dr*.

Mr W. Smith, son of the Rev. J. Smith, ...

Die Zeichen für Pfund Sterling, Pence und Dollar haben keinen Punkt.

She paid £4.12 for her food.
That's 30 p!
He paid $14.15 for his coat.

c) Nach Büchertiteln, Überschriften etc. steht weder ein Punkt noch irgendein anderes Satzzeichen mit Ausnahme unbedingt notwendiger Frage- und Ausrufezeichen.

d) Bei Dezimalstellen bleibt der Punkt auf der Zeile. Ausnahme: Bei Geldbeträgen werden im britischen Englisch Dezimalstellen durch einen zentrierten, von der Zeile abgehobenen Punkt abgetrennt.

10.41 m
£5·30

e) Römische Zahlen zur Bezeichnung von Seiten oder Kapiteln können mit oder ohne Punkt verwendet werden; stehen sie jedoch hinter Eigennamen, wird der Punkt nicht gesetzt.

James I

f) Auslassungen oder Unterbrechungen werden in einem Satz gewöhnlich durch drei gesperrt gedruckte Punkte angezeigt.

Ausnahmen:
Die einzelnen Buchstaben von Abkürzungen zusammengesetzter Namen internationaler Organisationen etc. werden in der Hauptsache ohne Punkt und Abstand voneinander geschrieben.

ILO; UN; UNESCO; USSR; IPA; WHO

Die Symbole der chemischen Elemente erhalten keinen Punkt.
Die Schreibweisen *1st*, *2(n)d*, *3(r)d* etc. gelten nicht als Abkürzungen und bleiben deshalb ohne Punkt.

2. Das Komma

a) Wörter, Wortgruppen und Sätze werden in einer Aufzählung durch Kommas voneinander getrennt. Bei einer Aufzählung von mehr als zwei Gliedern steht das Komma auch, wenn das letzte Glied durch eine Konjunktion (*and* oder *or*) angeschlossen ist.

He entered a small, tidy, well-lighted room.
Horses and cows, goats and sheep, dogs and cats were shown on this agricultural fair.
All the expenses fell on William, John, and Walter.

Bisweilen findet man auch, daß das Komma vor *and* oder *or* ausgelassen wird.

b) Treffen zwei Adjektive zusammen, von denen das zweite mit dem zu bestimmenden Substantiv in engerer Verbindung steht als das erste, so wird kein Komma gesetzt.

His vivid brown eyes.

c) Geraten *etc., or the like, and so on* bei einer Aufzählung in die Endstellung, ohne damit gleichzeitig den Satz zu beenden, folgt ihnen ein Komma, es sei denn, es ergibt sich aus dem Gesamtsatz eine besondere Zeichensetzung.

Any bookshop selling, lending, copying, etc., this book will be prosecuted.

d) Treffen zwei gleiche Wörter oder Wendungen in einem Satzgefüge zusammen, so trennt sie ein Komma. Das gleiche gilt auch für Zahlengruppen.

He who asks, asks not in vain.
In the year 1962, 650 people frequented this place.

e) Wörter oder Wendungen, die einen Gegensatz ausdrücken, werden durch Kommas abgetrennt. Werden solche Einzelwörter jedoch durch eine adversative Konjunktion (*but, yet, though*) eingeleitet, fällt das Komma fort.

Bread, not words, is what we are hoping for.
It was small yet well made.

f) das Komma deutet die Auslassung eines Wortes (oder einer Gruppe von Wörtern) an, das zwei Satzteilen gemeinsam ist, aber nicht wiederholt wird.

Harold failed in French; Hazel, in mathematics.

g) Beziehen sich Adverbien auf einen ganzen Satz und nicht nur auf ein einzelnes Wort, so werden sie durch Komma abgetrennt.

Unfortunately, she could not come to see it.
The affair was something that could, after all, be overlooked.

h) Hinter längere Adverbialbestimmungen, die nicht an gewohnter Stelle stehen, tritt oft ein Komma.

What he was thinking about his neighbour's behaviour, no one will ever know.

i) Werden Wörter wie *however, moreover, therefore, nevertheless, then, indeed, too, now, of course, no doubt, consequently, accordingly* in einen Satz eingefügt, ohne dessen Sinn zu verändern, so daß sie auch weggelassen werden könnten, trennt man sie durch Kommas ab.

He was, as a matter of fact, on his way to the station.
Still, I am not sure whether he was right.

Allerdings lassen einige Schreiber diese Kommas auch aus.
Bei sehr kurzen Sätzen, in denen die Wörter ohnehin nahe dem Verb stehen, ist die Abtrennung nicht nötig.

Consequently he decided to return.

Wenn einige der in dieser Regel aufgeführten Wörter, z. B. *however, indeed, too,* nicht weggelassen werden können, ohne den Sinn zu verändern, steht kein Komma.

However great the difficulties, he never gave in.
The water was too cold.

j) Nach Ausdrücken wie *namely, viz., that is, i.e., as, e.g., etc.*, die nicht eine Aufzählung einführen, sondern eine Erläuterung, steht ein Komma.

There were only three persons present at the meeting: namely, Mr. Kingstone, Mrs. Turner, and Mr. Williams.

k) Anreden, Eigennamen, akademische oder Ehrentitel, auch mehrere hintereinander, werden durch Komma abgetrennt.

I think, my love, we should go now.
Percy J. Grant, M.Sc., D.Sc., President.

Anreden in persönlichen Briefen und die formelhaften Briefschlüsse werden zumeist durch Komma getrennt.

Dear Bob, ... Sincerely yours,

l) Nachgestellte Vornamen in Bibliographien etc. trennt das Komma ab.

Carvell, Edward C. John.

m) das Komma trennt den Monat vom Jahr und untergliedert größere Zahlen von rechts in Dreiergruppen. Im britischen Englisch trennt es auch die einzelnen Glieder einer vollen Adresse.

It was dated 21st July, 1963.
The total number of the inhabitants of the city is 1,236,178.
Mr John Smith,
32, Pelaw Terrace,
London, N. 1.

n) Appositionell, parenthetisch oder auch unabhängig gebrauchte Wörter, Wendungen und Satzglieder werden durch Komma abgetrennt.

The notes were taken by Mr. Gunn, Clerk to the Council.
Her mother, a native of Germany, had preferred Switzerland to her country.
Fiddlesticks, I don't want that.

Besteht jedoch eine enge Gedankenverbindung zwischen dem Substantiv und seiner Apposition, so wird kein Komma gesetzt.

William the Conqueror; the architect Christopher Wren.

o) Hauptsätze, die durch eine nebenordnende Konjunktion verbunden sind, werden durch Komma getrennt. Das Komma entfällt bei sehr kurzen Sätzen und besonders dann, wenn beide Sätze das gleiche Subjekt haben.

He came early, as he had been asked.
She worked hard but she failed.

p) Als allgemeine Regel gilt, daß ein Komma nach einem Satz gesetzt wird, der nicht an gewohnter Stelle steht.

What had happened during those days, he could not remember.

q) Durch ein Komma getrennt werden Adverbialsätze immer, wenn sie dem Hauptsatz vorangehen, und für gewöhnlich, wenn sie an einer anderen Stelle im Satz stehen.

If it is possible, you may be sure that the work will be done.
Try and meet me at six o'clock, when you can make it.

Das Komma kann entfallen, wenn der Adverbialsatz kurz ist und Haupt- und Nebensatz das gleiche Subjekt haben.

But if you want to win a prize you must before all things strive to win it.

Das Komma entfällt auch, wenn es sich um einen kurzen nachgestellten Adverbialsatz handelt oder überhaupt um einen, der keinen Bruch im Verlauf des Satzes verursacht.

I will leave when he turns up.
He is a great deal cleverer than you are.

Ist die Anfügung jedoch unwesentlich, d. h. schließt sie noch eine zusätzliche Begründung oder Einräumung mit *because, since, as, though* an, muß das Komma stehen.

She has bought a new hat, though I doubt if she can afford it.

r) Während ein Subjekt für gewöhnlich nicht von seinem Verb getrennt wird, ist ein Komma zwischen Subjektsatz und Hauptsatz zulässig.

That the man was an ignoramus of the worst sort in this particular field of learning, is something which admits of no dispute.

s) Nicht notwendige Attributsätze, Relativsätze oder Partizipialsätze werden durch Komma abgetrennt.

I had a look at the stadium outside the town, which was only opened last summer.
Walter, feeling ill, went home soon afterwards.

Ein notwendiger Relativsatz dagegen darf nicht durch Komma abgetrennt werden.

The woman who won the swimming championship was given a medal.

t) Objekt- oder notwendige Attributsätze werden in einer Aufzählung durch Komma voneinander, aber nicht vom Hauptsatz getrennt.

He told me that he had lived in England these four months, that he had come to Germany to pass his examination, and that he wanted to return as soon as possible.
It is a house which had been built in 1925, which was damaged during the war, and which was rebuilt ten years ago.

u) Ein Komma trennt absolute Partizipial- und Infinitivkonstruktionen ab.

The visitors having left, normal life returned to the house.
Granted everything which was said in her favour, she cannot be saved.
They were all, to tell you what has happened, taken in by his words.

v) Bei der direkten Rede sowie bei kurzen Zitaten, Fragen und Maximen werden einleitende, eingeschobene oder nachgestellte *he said, she replied* etc. durch Komma abgetrennt.

"Bacchus' blessings are a treasure," says Dryden.
She asked him hurriedly, "What measure do you propose?"

3. Der Strichpunkt

a) Der Strichpunkt steht zwischen gedanklich zusammenhängenden Hauptsätzen.

Speech is silver; silence is golden.

b) Der Strichpunkt trennt die nebengeordneten Sätze in einer Satzverbindung:

ba) besonders vor den als Konjunktionen verwendeten Adverbien wie *accordingly, also, consequently, for, furthermore, hence, however, indeed, moreover, nevertheless, otherwise, so, still, then, therefore, thus, yet.*
You'll have to ask for it; otherwise you won't get it.

bb) wenn ein Gegensatz zwischen den einzelnen Sätzen besteht.

Heaven and earth will pass away; but my words will never pass away. (Matthew 24:35)

bc) wenn die einzelnen Sätze in sich noch durch Kommas unterteilt sind.

The dilapidated houses, apparently deserted years ago, looked grey and dreary; and neither cats nor dogs were straying about, looking for some food.

bd) wenn keine Konjunktion vorhanden ist.

Keep it under your hat; don't tell him anything about it.

c) Der Strichpunkt trennt die Einzelsätze in einer Reihe von Sätzen oder Ausdrücken, besonders wenn ihnen ein Doppelpunkt vorangeht.

It was in 1929: he had been fired; he had run short of money; and he did not know what to do.

d) Der Strichpunkt wird bei Namen- und Adressenlisten gesetzt und trennt Zahlengruppen etc., wenn die Trennung durch das Komma nicht klar genug erscheint.

John Smith, 41, Oxford Rd., Grantchester; William Fairways, 39, North Street, Dunstable.

4. Der Doppelpunkt

a) Der Doppelpunkt steht vor direkten Zitaten oder Fragen.

And then he cited this line from Pope:
The Proper study of mankind is man.

Stehen die Worte, die das Zitat kennzeichnen, an einer anderen Stelle als am Anfang, so wird ein Komma gesetzt.

b) Ein Doppelpunkt geht detaillierten Aufzählungen voran, besonders wenn Wörter oder Wendungen wie *viz., namely, i.e., that is, e.g., for example, for instance* eingesetzt werden könnten oder tatsächlich dastehen.

Some of the most famous of Thomas Hardy's novels are the following: Under the Greenwood Tree, The Mayor of Casterbridge, Tess of the D'Urbervilles, Jude the Obscure.

c) Der Doppelpunkt trennt zwei Aussagen, die nicht durch eine Konjunktion verbunden sind, von denen aber die zweite die erste erweitern oder erklären hilft.

It is a most interesting book: a vivid description of rural life in Elizabethan England.

d) Der Doppelpunkt steht im Amerikanischen nach der Anrede in Geschäftsbriefen oder auch sonst nach Anreden.

Sirs:
Ladies and Gentlemen:

e) Er steht auch zwischen Verhältniszahlen sowie zwischen Kapitel- und Versangaben aus der Bibel.

10:20 = 1:2
St. Luke 6:12—18

Statt eines Punktes findet sich der Doppelpunkt bei Zeitangaben zwischen Stunden und Minuten.

10:35 a.m.

5. Das Ausrufezeichen

a) Das Ausrufezeichen steht nach Ausrufen, ganz gleich, ob diese aus Einzelwörtern, Wendungen oder vollständigen Sätzen bestehen.

Oh! I see what you mean.
I can never understand why he did this!

b) In einer Serie von Ausrufen steht hinter jedem einzelnen Ausruf ein Ausrufezeichen.

Oh, lift me as a wave, a leaf, a cloud!
I fall upon the thorns of life! I bleed!
(Shelley)

c) Ein Ausrufezeichen wird auch gesetzt nach Wendungen oder Sätzen, die einem Wunsch, einem Befehl oder der Ironie und anderen starken Äußerungen Ausdruck verleihen.

"Stop this nonsense!" he shouted at the crowd.
So this is what you want me to believe!

6. Großschreibung

Großschreibung wird angewandt bei:

a) dem ersten Wort eines vollständigen oder unvollständigen Satzes, dem ersten Wort eines Zitates oder einer Verszeile.

Let's get hold of him.
As if you could kill time without injuring eternity.

b) Eigennamen und Wörtern, die als solche gebraucht werden, sowie bei deren Ableitungen im ursprünglichen Sinne.

Elizabeth, Elizabethan
Roman Empire. **Aber:** *roman types.*

c) Namen von Völkern, Rassen, Stämmen und Sprachen und bei von ihnen abgeleiteten Adjektiven.

Italian; Germanic; Apache tribe.

d) Ehrentiteln, akademischen und kirchlichen Titeln und Berufs- und Geschäftstiteln, die mit Eigennamen zusammen gebraucht werden.

Queen Anne; *Dean Swift*; *Treasurer M.J.P. Hough of the Mermaid Company.*

e) offiziellen und Regierungstiteln sowie Adelstiteln.

President; Chancellor; Speaker of the House; Prince Philip.

f) den amtlichen Bezeichnungen nationaler oder internationaler Regierungsgremien oder bei Dokumenten.

The Twentieth Congress; the United Nations; Charter of the United Nations.

g) Substantiven und oft auch Adjektiven, die auf eine Gottheit Bezug nehmen; bei Pronomen und pronominalen Adjektiven, wenn sie nicht dicht vor oder hinter dem Beziehungswort stehen.

God; the Almighty; Allah; Providence; Holy Ghost.
Now, God be thanked who has matched us with His hour . . .

h) Namen von heiligen Schriften, ihren Teilen und Ausgaben sowie bei adjektivischen Ableitungen, die sich ausdrücklich auf diese Schriften beziehen.

Koran; Old Testament.

i) Namen von Glaubensbekenntnissen, kirchlichen Bezeichnungen und Mönchsorden sowie dem Wort *Church*, wenn es auf ein bestimmtes Kirchengebäude gemünzt ist.

Buddhist; Apostles' Creed; order of Our Lady of Mount Carmel; Church of St. David's.

j) Feiertagen, Monaten und Wochentagen.

Ascension Day; February; Wednesday.

k) Namen von Kongressen, Versammlungen und Ausstellungen.

The Potsdam Conference; Congress of Horticultural Organizations; Brussels' World Fair.

l) Namen von Gerichtshöfen, Verträgen, Gesetzen, Erlassen, wichtigen Ereignissen, historischen Epochen und literarischen Perioden etc.

London Court of Appeals; Magna Charta; Napoleonic Wars; Middle Ages; Victorian Age of Literature.

m) Namen von geologischen Zeitaltern, Perioden, Epochen, Formationen etc. sowie bei Namen prähistorischer Zeitalter.

Mesozoic; Cambrian; Upper Triassic; Age of Coal; Bronze Age.

n) geographischen Gattungsnamen, die ein integrierter Bestandteil eines bestimmten Eigennamens sind: *bay, borough, colony, continent, country, district, hemisphere, island, lake, mountain, ocean, pass, peninsula, river, sea;* und in der gleichen Weise: *avenue, boulevard, bridge, park, road, square, street.*

The Cromwell Current; the Southern Hemisphere; the Red Sea; St. Denis Drive.
Aber: *The Pacific coast of the USA; Bavarian mountains.*

Dennoch finden sich solche Begriffe auch in Kleinschreibung, allerdings selten, wenn sie einem Eigennamen vorausgehen. – Werden sie von zwei oder mehreren Eigennamen begleitet, schwankt der Schreibgebrauch zwischen Groß- und Kleinschreibung.

o) politischen Gattungsnamen, die ein integrierter Bestandteil eines bestimmten Eigennamens sind und ein politisches Einteilungsprinzip andeuten: *colony, department, dominion, empire, kingdom, republic, state, territory* etc.

The Holy Roman Empire; the Third Republic.

p) Namen bestimmter geographischer Gliederungen:

The Orient; the Middle East.

q) Himmelsrichtungen, die, geographisch gesehen, einen Teil eines Landes oder der Welt bezeichnen, sowie bei deren adjektivischen und substantivischen Ableitungen.

The Southeast; a Southerner.

r) personifizierten abstrakten Ideen oder toten Gegenständen und bei personifizierten Jahreszeiten.

To Mercy, Pity, Peace and Love
All pray in their distress.
(Blake)

s) allen Wörtern in den Titeln von Büchern, (Monats)Zeitschriften, Essays, Gedichten mit Ausnahme der weniger betonten Präpositionen, Konjunktionen und Artikel; ferner bei akademischen Graden und ihren Abkürzungen.

Shakespeare's Two Gentlemen of Verona;
Journal of the American Language Association;
Doctor of Philosophy (*Ph.D.*).

t) dem Artikel *the*, wenn er zu einem Eigennamen oder Titel gehört oder wenn er Teil eines gesetzlich geschützten Namens ist. Die Großschreibung wird nicht angewandt, wenn im laufenden Text auf Tageszeitungen und Zeitschriften Bezug genommen wird.

The Very Reverend C.T. Curtis;
... was to be found in the Saturday Evening Post.

Film Certificates – GB

U	Universal. Suitable for all ages. *Für alle Altersstufen geeignet.*
PG	Parental Guidance. Some scenes may be unisuitable for young children. *Einige Szenen ungeeignet für Kinder. Erklärung und Orientierung durch Eltern sinnvoll.*
15	No person under 15 years admitted when a "15" film is in the programme. *Nicht freigegeben für Jugendliche unter 15 Jahren.*
18	No person under 18 years admitted when an "18" film is in the programme. *Nicht freigegeben für Jugendliche unter 18 Jahren.*

Film Certificates – USA

G	All ages admitted. General audiences. *Für alle Altersstufen geeignet.*
PG	Parental guidance suggested. Some material may not be suitable for children. *Einige Szenen ungeeignet für Kinder. Erklärung und Orientierung durch Eltern sinnvoll.*
R	Restricted. Under 17 requires accompanying parent or adult guardian. *Für Jugendliche unter 17 Jahren nur in Begleitung eines Erziehungsberechtigten.*
X	No one under 17 admitted. *Nicht freigegeben für Jugendliche unter 17 Jahren.*

LANGENSCHEIDT'S
POCKET
DICTIONARIES

LANGENSCHEIDT'S POCKET DICTIONARY

OF THE ENGLISH AND GERMAN LANGUAGES

Second Part

German-English

by

PROF. EDMUND KLATT
GISELA KLATT
HEINZ MESSINGER

Enlarged and updated edition 1985

HODDER AND STOUGHTON

Contents

This dictionary is also available in a larger type size in the Langenscheidt Standard Dictionary Series.

Published in the British Commonwealth
by Hodder & Stoughton Limited

Enlarged and updated edition 1985

Printed in Germany

Preface

Since it first appeared a hundred years ago, the German-English Pocket Dictionary has been one of Langenscheidt's best-known publications. There have been six completely revised editions of it.

The present 1985 edition (enlarged and updated) offers its users the very latest vocabulary of the eighties. Thousands of neologisms from all fields have been added to this widely-used and popular dictionary.

A few examples may serve to indicate the scope of these new entries, taken from both everyday and specialized fields of vocabulary: *Bioladen*, *Biomasse*, *Digitalaufnahme*, *Genmanipulation*, *Kabelfernsehen*, *Lauschangriff*, *Lichtgriffel*, *Marschflugkörper*, *ökologisches Gleichgewicht*, *Rucksacktourismus*, *saurer Regen*, *Waldsterben*.

Besides the addition of individual words, the basic vocabulary of entire subject-areas, such as data processing, has been taken into consideration. Colloquialisms popular with the younger generation have also been included (e.g. *ich bin total auf Reggae abgefahren* I'm really into Reggae).

It need hardly be said that this new edition has preserved the long-established principles on which the German-English Pocket Dictionary's reputation as a valuable source of information is based. Thus importance continues to be placed on idiomatic phrases (cf. for example the article *sagen*), the inclusion of American English, the precise labelling of stylistic register, phonetic transcription of the German headwords and clear, concise explanations.

The dictionary is supplemented by eight appendices. The lists of proper names and abbreviations have been brought up to date, and a new and undoubtedly welcome addition are the temperature conversion charts. The foreign user will find the German declension and conjugation tables and the comprehensive list of irregular verbs of invaluable help.

The neologisms were compiled by the English editorial department of Langenscheidt and Christian Nekvedavicius.

We have endeavoured in this new enlarged edition of the German-English Pocket Dictionary to do justice to the rapid developments in today's vocabulary and we hope that as a result it will be of benefit to an even wider range of users.

LANGENSCHEIDT

Vorwort

Seit seinem ersten Erscheinen vor 100 Jahren gehört das deutsch-englische Taschenwörterbuch zu den bekanntesten Werken des Langenscheidt-Verlags. Sechsmal wurde es vollständig neu bearbeitet, neu gesetzt und wesentlich erweitert.

Die vorliegende erweiterte Neuausgabe 1985 bietet dem Benutzer den modernen Wortschatz der achtziger Jahre. Tausende von Neuwörtern aus allen Lebensbereichen mußten daher neu aufgenommen werden; das bedingte wiederum eine Erweiterung des Umfangs dieses in Millionen von Exemplaren verbreiteten Standardwörterbuchs.

Einige Stichwort-Beispiele mögen die Spannweite der im Bereich der Allgemeinsprache und Fachsprachen durchgeführten Neuwortarbeit für dieses Wörterbuch verdeutlichen: *Bioladen*, *Biomasse*, *Digitalaufnahme*, *Genmanipulation*, *Kabelfernsehen*, *Lauschangriff*, *Lichtgriffel*, *Marschflugkörper*, *ökologisches Gleichgewicht*, *Rucksacktourismus*, *saurer Regen*, *Waldsterben*.

Neben diesen Einzelwort-Neologismen wurden auch ganze Fachgebiete neu erarbeitet, so die Terminologie der Datenverarbeitung mit ihrem Kernwortschatz. Auch die familiäre Umgangssprache der jungen Generation wurde bei den Neuaufnahmen berücksichtigt (z. B. *ich bin total auf Reggae abgefahren* I'm really into Reggae).

Selbstverständlich wurden in der vorliegenden Neuausgabe die bewährten Grundsätze beibehalten, denen das deutsch-englische Taschenwörterbuch seinen Ruf und seinen Nachschlagewert verdankt: Die Idiomatik (vgl. z. B. das Stichwort *sagen*), die starke Einbeziehung des Amerikanischen Englisch, die genaue Kennzeichnung der Sprachgebrauchsebenen, die Ausspracheangabe für die deutschen Stichwörter und die ausgefeilten Erläuterungen hatten schon immer einen beträchtlichen Anteil an dem hohen Informationswert dieses Wörterbuchs.

Das Wörterbuch enthält acht Anhänge. Die Anhänge „Eigennamen" und „Abkürzungen" wurden auf den neuesten Stand gebracht. Neu aufgenommen und sicherlich willkommen sind die praktischen Temperatur-Umrechnungstabellen. Dem Ausländer werden die Tabellen zur deutschen Deklination und Konjugation und die umfangreiche Liste der unregelmäßigen Verben sicherlich von Nutzen sein.

Der moderne Wortschatz wurde von der Redaktion Anglistik des Verlags und Christian Nekvedavicius erarbeitet. Wir hoffen, mit der vorliegenden erweiterten Neuausgabe der raschen Entwicklung des Wortschatzes Rechnung zu tragen. Möge das deutsch-englische Taschenwörterbuch in dieser erweiterten Fassung noch zusätzliche Freunde gewinnen!

LANGENSCHEIDT

Directions for the Use of the Dictionary

Hinweise für die Benutzung des Wörterbuches

1. Arrangement. Alphabetical order has been maintained throughout the dictionary. Note that the umlaut-forms ä, ö, ü are treated like a, o, u. (Thus "Müll" will be found directly after "Mull" but not under "muell"). ß is treated like ss. The following forms are also listed alphabetically:

a) the irregular forms of comparatives and superlatives;
b) the various forms of pronouns;
c) the principal parts (infinitive, past tense and past participle) of strong and irregular weak verbs.

Proper names and abbreviations are listed separately at the end of the dictionary.

1. Anordnung: Die alphabetische Reihenfolge ist überall beachtet worden. Dabei wurden die Umlautbuchstaben ä, ö, ü wie a, o, u behandelt. („Müll" z. B. suche man hinter „Mull", nicht unter „muell"). ß wird wie ss eingeordnet. An ihrem alphabetischen Platz sind gegeben:

a) die unregelmäßigen Formen des Komparativs und Superlativs;
b) die verschiedenen Formen der Fürwörter;
c) die Stammformen (Grundform, Vergangenheit, Mittelwort der Vergangenheit) der starken und der unregelmäßigen schwachen Verben.

Eigennamen und Abkürzungen sind am Schluß des Bandes in besonderen Verzeichnissen zusammengestellt.

2. Tilde or swung dash as mark of repetition (**~** **♀** ~ ♀). Words belonging to the same group, derivatives or homographs and words with partly identical spelling are frequently combined with the aid of a tilde to save room. The bold-faced tilde stands for the entry word or the part of it preceding the vertical bar (|). In the examples printed in *lightface* type or in the explanations printed in *italics* the simple tilde (~) stands for the bold-faced word immediately preceding, which itself may have been formed with aid of a bold-faced tilde.

When the initial letter changes from a capital to a small letter, or vice-versa, the tilde is replaced by the sign **♀** or ♀.

2. Das **Wiederholungszeichen** oder die **Tilde** (**~** **♀** ~ ♀). Zusammengehörige und verwandte Wörter, sowie Wörter, die ganz oder teilweise im Schriftbild übereinstimmen, sind häufig zum Zwecke der Raumersparnis unter Verwendung der Tilde zu Gruppen vereinigt. Die fette Tilde (**~**) vertritt dabei entweder das ganze Stichwort oder den vor dem Strich (|) stehenden Teil des Stichwortes. Bei den in *Auszeichnungsschrift* gesetzten Redewendungen oder in *Kursivschrift* gesetzten Erläuterungen vertritt die einfache Tilde (~) stets das unmittelbar voraufgegangene Stichwort, das seinerseits wiederum mit Hilfe der fetten Tilde gebildet sein kann.

Wenn sich die Anfangsbuchstaben ändern (groß zu klein oder umgekehrt), steht statt der Tilde das Zeichen: **♀** *od.* ♀.

Examples: **Drama, ~tiker, ♀tisch; duld|en, ♀er, ~sam; essen** (eat), ♀ (eating; food); **Selbst|kostenpreis** etc., **~verlag:** *im ~* published by the author; **fassen:** *e-n Plan ~.*

The tilde (~) may also stand for the part of the entry word that is not repeated in the phonetic transcription; other parts of the word are replaced by a short dash (-): **Origin|al** [origiˈnaːl], **~altreue** [~-ˈnaːl-]; **neutral** [nɔʏˈtraːl], **~iˈsieren** [~trali-].

3. Phonetic transcription (see the remarks at the head of the Key to Pronunciation, page 685) has usually been omitted:

a) in the case of compounds whose constituent elements are independent words which appear in their normal alphabetical position with pronunciation. Examples: Handbuch, Absicht, see Hand and Buch, ab and Sicht;
b) for suffixes (see list on page 688).

4. The **shortened hyphen** [-] is placed in entry words:

a) before a vowel to mark the glottal stop (e.g. beˈ-antworten);
b) between two consonants to indicate that they must be pronounced separately (e.g. Häus-chen, gesinnungs-treu).

5. Inflexion. The number in parentheses following simple words subject to inflexion refers to the corresponding paradigm in the declension and conjugation tables at the end of the book.

In order to save space the number has frequently been omitted:

a) when nouns have the following endings: -ei, -heit, -ion, -keit, -schaft, -ung; these are inflected according to (16); all feminine nouns ending in -in (e.g. Freundin) are inflected according to (16¹);

Beispiele: **Drama, ~tiker, ♀tisch; duld|en, ♀er, ~sam; essen** (eat), ♀ (eating; food); **Selbst|kostenpreis** usw., **~verlag:** *im ~* published by the author; **fassen:** *e-n Plan ~.*

In der Aussprachebezeichnung wird der ausgelassene Teil der phonetischen Umschrift des Stichwortes durch die Tilde (~) wiedergegeben; weitere Wortteile werden durch einen kurzen Strich (-) ersetzt: **Origin|al** [origiˈnaːl], **~altreue** [~ˈnaːl-]; **neutral** [nɔʏˈtraːl], **~iˈsieren** [~trali-].

3. Die **Aussprachebezeichnung** fällt meistens weg bei

a) Wortzusammensetzungen wie Handbuch, Absicht, deren einzelne Bestandteile (Hand und Buch, ab und Sicht) als Grundwörter an alphabetischer Stelle mit Aussprache gegeben sind;
b) häufig wiederkehrenden Nachsilben (s. die Liste Seite 688).

4. Der **verkürzte Bindestrich** [-] steht in Stichwörtern:

a) vor einem Vokal zur Bezeichnung des Knacklautes (z. B. beˈ-antworten);
b) zwischen zwei Konsonanten, um anzuzeigen, daß sie getrennt auszusprechen sind (z. B. Häus-chen, gesinnungs-treu).

5. Deklination und Konjugation. Bei jedem einfachen abwandelbaren Wort steht in runden Klammern eine Ziffer als Hinweis auf das entsprechende Beispiel der Deklinations- und Konjugationstabellen am Schluß des Bandes.

Aus Gründen der Raumersparnis ist die Ziffer häufig weggelassen worden:

a) bei Substantiven mit den Endungen -ei, -heit, -ion, -keit, -schaft, -ung, die nach (16) abgewandelt werden; alle femininen Substantive auf -in (z. B. Freundin) sind abwandelbar nach (16¹);

b) when adjectives act as nouns, e.g. Uneingeweihte *m*, *f*; these are inflected according to (18);
c) when verbs act as nouns (verbal nouns), e.g. Geschehen; all verbal nouns are neuter and are inflected according to (6);
d) when verbs end in -ieren, e.g. radieren; these are inflected according to (25).

The abbreviation (sn) means that the intransitive verb in question forms its perfect with the auxiliary "sein". All other verbs form their perfect with the auxiliary "haben".

Proper names are inflected according to (17) if no other numbers are given.

The abbreviations *sg.* or *pl.* following a noun indicate that these nouns take singular or plural verbs respectively.

b) bei den substantivierten Adjektiven (z. B. Uneingeweihte *m*, *f*); sie werden nach (18) abgewandelt;
c) bei den substantivierten Verben (z. B. Geschehen); sie sind Neutra und abwandelbar nach (6);
d) bei den Verben auf -ieren (z. B. radieren); sie werden nach (25) abgewandelt.

Der Vermerk (sn) bedeutet, daß das betreffende intransitive Verb das Perfekt usw. mit „sein" bildet. Die übrigen Verben werden mit „haben" konjugiert.

Die Eigennamen werden, falls keine andere Ziffer angegeben ist, nach (17) dekliniert.

Die Bezeichnungen *sg.* bzw. *pl.* nach einem Substantiv bedeuten singularische bzw. pluralische Konstruktion der abhängigen Verben.

6. Semantic differences (printed in *italics*) are made clear:

a) by synonyms in parentheses, e.g.: **rein** pure; (*sauber*) clean;
b) by preceding German explanations, e.g.: **Blick** *flüchtiger*: glance; **dämpfen** *Stoß*, *Schall*: deaden; **Abfall** *der Blätter*: fall; *beim Schlachten*: offal;
c) by additions that supply grammatical information and/or illustrate the use of a word but are left untranslated, e.g.: **abkommen** ... *von et.* ~ give up, drop; ~ *von e-r Ansicht* change; *von e-m Thema* digress from;
d) by preceding symbols and abbreviated definitions (see list, pp. 683–684);
e) by giving the opposite of the word in question, e.g.: **Land** (*Ggs. Wasser*) land; (*Ggs. Stadt*) country.

A semicolon separates one given meaning from another essentially different meaning.

6. Bedeutungsunterschiede (in *Kursivschrift*) sind gekennzeichnet:

a) durch sinnverwandte Wörter in runden Klammern, z. B.: **rein** pure; (*sauber*) clean;
b) durch vorgesetzte deutsche Erklärungen, z. B.: **Blick** *flüchtiger*: glance; **dämpfen** *Stoß*, *Schall*: deaden; **Abfall** *der Blätter*: fall; *beim Schlachten*: offal;
c) durch Einschübe, die einen grammatischen oder bedeutungsmäßigen Zusammenhang verdeutlichen sollen, jedoch unübersetzt bleiben, z. B.: **abkommen** ... *von et.* ~ give up, drop; ~ *von e-r Ansicht* change; ~ *von e-m Thema* digress from;
d) durch vorgesetzte bildliche Zeichen und abgekürzte Begriffsbestimmungen (s. Verzeichnis S. 683 u. 684);
e) durch Angabe des Gegensatzes, z. B.: **Land** (*Ggs. Wasser*) land; (*Ggs. Stadt*) country.

Das Semikolon trennt eine gegebene Bedeutung von einer neuen, wesentlich verschiedenen.

Symbols and Abbreviations

Erklärung der Zeichen und Abkürzungen

1. Symbols — Bildliche Zeichen

~, ⚬, ~ v. Directions for Use, p. 680, section 2. s. *Hinweise S. 680, Absatz 2.*

F familiar, colloquial language, *familiär, Umgangssprache.*

P low colloquialism, *populär, Sprache des (einfachen) Volkes.*

V indecent, *unanständig.*

† archaic, *altertümlich.*

☆ rare, little used, *selten.*

🕮 scientific term, *wissenschaftlich.*

⚘ botany, *Pflanzenkunde.*

⊕ handicraft; engineering, *Handwerk, Technik.*

⚒ mining, *Bergbau.*

⚔ military term, *militärisch.*

⚓ nautical (sailors' or watermen's) term, *Schiffahrt.*

☤ commercial term, *Handelswesen.*

🚂 railroad, railway, *Eisenbahn.*

✈ aviation, *Luftfahrt.*

📯 postal affairs, *Postwesen.*

♪ musical term, *Musik.*

△ architecture, *Baukunst.*

⚡ electrical engineering, *Elektrotechnik.*

⚖ jurisprudence, *Rechtswissenschaft.*

∡ mathematics, *Mathematik.*

⚘ farming, *Landwirtschaft.*

⚗ chemistry, *Chemie.*

⚕ medicine, *Heilkunde, Medizin.*

2. Abbreviations — Abkürzungen

a., a. *also*, auch.

abbr. *abbreviation*, Abkürzung.

acc. *accusative (case)*, Akkusativ, 4. Fall.

adj. *adjective*, Adjektiv, Eigenschaftswort.

adv. *adverb*, Adverb, Umstandswort.

allg. allgemein, *commonly.*

Am. *Americanism*, im amerikanischen Englisch gebräuchlicher Ausdruck.

anat. *anatomy*, Anatomie.

art. *article*, Artikel, Geschlechtswort.

ast. *astronomy*, Astronomie.

attr. *attributively*, als Attribut od. Beifügung.

biol. *biology*, Biologie.

Brt. *in British usage only*, nur im britischen Englisch gebräuchlich.

b.s. *bad sense*, in schlechtem Sinne.

bsd. besonders, *particularly.*

cj. *conjunction*, Konjunktion, Bindewort.

co. *comic(al)*, komisch, scherzhaft.

comp. *comparative*, Komparativ.

contp. *contemptuously*, verächtlich.

dat. *dative (case)*, Dativ, 3. Fall.

dem. *demonstrative*, hinweisend.

ea., *ea.* einander, *one another, each other.*

eccl. *ecclesiastical*, kirchlich, geistlich.

e-e eine, *a (an).*

ehm. ehemals, *formerly.*

e-m, *e-m* einem, *to a (an).*

e-n, *e-n* einen, *a (an).*

engS. in engerem Sinne, *more strictly taken.*

e-r, *e-r* einer, *of a (an), to a (an).*

e-s, *e-s* eines, *of a (an).*

et., *et.* etwas, *something.*

etc., *etc.* *et cetera, and others, and so forth*, und so weiter.

f *feminine*, weiblich.
fenc. *fencing*, Fechtkunst.
fig. *figuratively*, figürlich, bildlich.
fr. französisch, *French.*
gen. *genitive* (*case*), Genitiv, 2. Fall.
geogr. *geography*, Erdkunde.
geol. *geology*, Geologie.
ger. *gerund*, Gerundium.
Ggs. Gegensatz, *antonym.*
gr. *grammar*, Grammatik.
h. haben, *have.*
hist. *history*, Geschichte.
hunt. *hunting*, Jagdwesen.
imp. *imperative* (*mood*), Imperativ.
ind. *indicative* (*mood*), Indikativ.
inf. *infinitive* (*mood*), Infinitiv.
int. *interjection*, Empfindungswort, Ausruf.
interr. *interrogative*, fragend.
inv. *invariable*, unveränderlich.
iro. *ironically*, ironisch.
j., j-s, j-m, j-n jemand(es *of*; -em *dat. to*; -en *acc.*) *somebody.*
l. lassen, *let.*
lit. *literary*, nur in der Schriftsprache vorkommend.
m *masculine*, männlich.
m-e meine, *my.*
metall. *metallurgy*, Hüttenwesen.
min. *mineralogy*, Mineralogie.
m-n meinen, *my.*
mot. *motoring*, Kraftfahrwesen.
mount. *mountaineering*, Bergsteigerei.
m-r meiner, *of my*, *to my.*
mst meistens, *mostly*, *usually.*
n *neuter*, sächlich.
nom. *nominative* (*case*), Nominativ, 1. Fall.
o. ohne, *without.*
od. oder, *or.*
opt. *optics*, Optik.
o.s. *oneself*, sich.
P. Person, *person.*
p., *p.* *person*, Person.
paint. *painting*, Malerei.
parl. *parliamentary term*, parlamentarischer Ausdruck.
perf. *perfect*, Perfekt(um), vollendete Gegenwart.
pharm. *pharmacy*, Apothekerkunst.
phls. *philosophy*, Philosophie.
phot. *photography*, Photographie.
phys. *physics*, Physik.
physiol. *physiology*, Physiologie.
pl. *plural*, Mehrzahl.
poet. *poetry*, Dichtkunst.
pol. *politics*, Politik.
p.p. *past participle*, Partizip der Vergangenheit.
p.pr. *present participle*, Partizip der Gegenwart.
pred. *predicative*, prädikativ.
pret. *preterit(e)*, Präteritum, Vergangenheit.
pron. *pronoun*, Pronomen, Fürwort.
prp. *preposition*, Verhältniswort.
prs. *present* (*tense*), Präsens, Gegenwart.
refl. *reflexive*, reflexiv, rückbezüglich.
rel. *relative*, bezüglich.
rhet. *rhetoric*, Rhetorik.
S., *S.* Sache, *thing.*
s., *s.* siehe, man sehe, *see*, *refer to.*
s-e seine, *his*, *one's.*
sg. *singular*, Einzahl.
sl. *slang*, Slang.
s-m seinem, *to his*, *to one's.*
sn sein (Verb), *be.*
s-n seinen, *his*, *one's.*
s-r seiner, s-s seines — *of his*, *of one's.*
su. *substantive*, Hauptwort.
subj. *subjunctive* (*mood*), Konjunktiv.
sup. *superlative*, Superlativ.
surv. *surveying*, Landvermessung.
tel. *telegraphy*, Telegraphie.
teleph. *telephony*, Fernsprechwesen.
th., *th.* *thing*, Ding, Sache.
thea. *theatre*, Theater.
typ. *typography*, Buchdruck.
u., *u.* und, *and.*
univ. *university*, Hochschulwesen, Studentensprache.
usw. und so weiter, *etc. and so forth.*
v. von, vom, *of*, *by*, *from.*
vb. *verb*, Verb(um), Zeitwort.
v/aux. *auxiliary verb*, Hilfszeitwort.
vet. *veterinary art*, Tierheilkunde.
vgl., *vgl.* vergleiche, *compare.*
v/i. *verb intransitive*, intransitives Zeitwort.
v/refl. *verb reflexive*, reflexives Zeitwort.
v/t. *verb transitive*, transitives Zeitwort.
weitS. im weiteren Sinne, *more widely taken.*
z.B. zum Beispiel, *for instance.*
zo. *zoology*, Zoologie.
Zssg(n) Zusammensetzung(en), *compound word(s).*

Key to Pronunciation

The phonetic alphabet used in this German-English dictionary is that of the Association Phonétique Internationale (A. P. I. or I. P. A. = International Phonetic Association).

The length of vowels is indicated by [ː] following the vowel symbol, the stress by [ˈ] preceding the stressed syllable.

The glottal stop [ʔ] is the forced stop between one word or syllable and a following one beginning with a stressed vowel, as in "beobachten" [bəˈʔoːbaxtən].

Symbol	Examples	Nearest English Equivalents	Remarks
	A. Vowels		
a	Mann [man]		short a as in French "carte" or in British English "cast" said quickly
ɑː	Wagen [ˈvɑːgən]	father	long a
e	Edikt [eˈdikt]	bed	
eː	Weg [veːk]		unlike any English sound, though it has a resemblance to the sound in "**day**"
ə	bitte [ˈbitə]	ago	a short sound, that of unaccented e
ɛ	Männer [ˈmɛnər] Geld [gɛlt]	fair	There is no *-er* sound at the end. It is one pure short vowel-sound.
ɛː	wählen [ˈvɛːlən]		same sound, but long
i	Wind [vint]	it	
iː	hier [hiːr]	meet	
ɔ	Ort [ɔrt]	long	
ɔː	Komfort [kɔmˈfɔːr]	draw	
o	Advokat [atvoˈkɑːt]	molest [moˈlest]	
oː	Boot [boːt]		[oː] resembles the English sound in **go** [gou] but without the [u]

Symbol	Examples	Nearest English Equivalents	Remarks
ø:	schön [ʃø:n]		as in French "**feu**". The sound may be acquired by saying [e] through closely rounded lips.
ø	Ödem [ø'de:m]		same sound, but short
œ	öffnen ['œfnən]		as in French "**neuf**". The sound has a resemblance to the English vowel in "**her**". Lips, however, must be well rounded as for ɔ.
u	Mutter ['mutər]	b**oo**k	
u:	Uhr [u:r]	b**oo**t	
y	Glück [glyk]		almost like the French **u** as in **sur**. It may be acquired by saying i through fairly closely rounded lips.
y:	führen ['fy:rən]		same sound, but long

B. Diphthongs

Symbol	Examples	Nearest English Equivalents	Remarks
aɪ	Mai [maɪ]	l**i**ke	
aʊ	Maus [maʊs]	m**ou**se	
ɔʏ	Beute ['bɔʏtə] Läufer ['lɔʏfər]	b**oy**	

C. Consonants

Symbol	Examples	Nearest English Equivalents	Remarks
b	besser ['bɛsər]	**b**etter	
d	du [du:]	**d**ance	
f	finden ['findən] Vater ['fɑ:tər] Philosoph [filo'zo:f]	**f**ind	
g	Gold [gɔlt] Geld [gɛlt]	**g**old	
ʒ	Genie [ʒe'ni:] Journalist [ʒurna'list]	mea**s**ure	
h	Haus [haʊs]	**h**ouse	
ç	Licht [liçt] Mönch [mœnç] lustig ['lustiç]		An approximation to this sound may be acquired by assuming the mouth-configuration for [i] and emitting a strong current of breath.

Symbol	Examples	Nearest English Equivalents	Remarks
x	Loch [lɔx]	Scotch: **loch**	Whereas [ç] is pronounced at the front of the mouth, x is pronounced in the throat.
j	ja [jɑ:]	**y**ear	
k	keck [kɛk] Tag [tɑ:k] Chronist [kro'nɪst] Café [ka'fe:]	**k**ick	
l	lassen ['lasən]	**l**ump	pronounced like English initial "clear l"
m	Maus [maʊs]	**m**ouse	
n	nein [naɪn]	**n**ot	
ŋ	singen ['zɪŋən] trinken ['trɪŋkən]	si**ng**, dri**n**k	
p	Paß [pas] Weib [vaɪp] obgleich [ɔp'glaɪç]	**p**ass	
r	rot [ro:t]	**r**ot	There are two pronunciations: the frontal or lingual **r** and the uvular **r** (the latter unknown in England).
s	Glas [glɑ:s] Masse ['masə] Mast [mast] naß [nas]	mi**ss**	unvoiced when final, doubled, or next to a voiceless consonant
z	Sohn [zo:n] Rose ['ro:zə]	**z**ero	voiced when initial in a word or a syllable
ʃ	Schiff [ʃɪf] Charlotte [ʃar'lɔtə] Spiel [ʃpi:l] Stein [ʃtaɪn]	**sh**op	
t	Tee [te:] Thron [tro:n] Stadt [ʃtat] Bad [bɑ:t] Findling ['fɪntlɪŋ] Wind [vɪnt]	**t**ea	
v	Vase ['vɑ:zə] Winter ['vɪntər]	**v**ast	

ã, ɛ̃, ɔ̃ are nasalized vowels. Examples: Ensemble [ã'sã:bl], Terrain [tɛ'rɛ̃], Bonbon [bɔ̃'bɔ̃].

List of Suffixes

often given without Phonetic Transcription

Suffix	Phonetic Transcription	Examples	Remarks
-bar	-bɑːr	'schein**bar**	
-chen	-çən	'Städt**chen**	
-d	-t	'fesseln**d**	
-de	-də	'Zier**de**	
-ei	-aɪ	Reede'**rei**	
-en	-ən	zer'stör**en**	
-end	-ənt	'ätz**end**	
-er	-ər	Trans'port**er** be'reich**ern**	
-haft	-haft	'zwergen**haft**	
-heit	-haɪt	Be'sonder**heit**	
-ie	-iː	Orange'**rie**	
-ieren	-iːrən	organi'**sieren** salu'**tieren** mystifi'**zieren**	
-ig	-iç	'lust**ig**	but lust**ige** [-igə], lust**iger** [-igər], lust**iges** [-igəs], etc.
-ik	-ik	Belle'trist**ik**	
-in	-in	'Sänger**in**	
-isch	-iʃ	'belg**isch**	
-ist	-ist	Pessi'**mist**	
-keit	-kaɪt	'Männlich**keit**	
-lich	-liç	'sach**lich**	
-losigkeit	-loːziçkaɪt	'Rücksichts**losigkeit**	
-nis	-nis	'Wirr**nis**	
-sal	-zɑːl	'Trüb**sal**	
-sam	-zɑːm	'furcht**sam**	
-schaft	-ʃaft	'Wähler**schaft**	
-ste	-stə	'dreißig**ste**	
-tät	-tɛːt	Morali'**tät**	
-tum	-tuːm	'Wachs**tum**	
-ung	-uŋ	Ge'sinn**ung**	
-ungs-	**-uŋs-**	Ge'sinn**ungs**wechsel	

A

A, a [aː] *n* A, a (*a.* ♪); *fig. das A u. O* the most important thing; *von A bis Z* from A to Z; *wer A sagt, muß auch B sagen* in for a penny, in for a pound; ♪ *A-Dur* A major; *a-Moll* A minor.

à [a] *prp.* ✝ (at) ... each.

Aal [aːl] *m* (3) eel; '**⁀en** *v/refl.* laze (about); '**⁀glatt** slippery (as an eel).

Aar *poet.* [aːr] *m* (3) eagle.

Aas [aːs] *n* (4, *pl. a.* Äser ['ɛːzər] 1[2]) carrion; (*Köder*) bait; P *Schimpfwort*: beast; **⁀en** F ['aːzən] (27): *mit et.* ~ squander; '**~geier** *m* carrion kite; *fig.* vulture.

ab [ap] *adv. u. prp.* off; down; from; *thea.* exit, *pl.* exeunt; *zeitlich*: (*von* ...) *ab* from ... on(wards), *amtlich*: as from, on and after *May 1st, etc.* ~ *und zu* now and then; *weit* ~ far off; ✝ ~ *Berlin, Fabrik, Lager usw.* ex Berlin, factory, store, *etc.*; 🚂 ~ dep. (= departs, departure); ~ *Brüssel* from Brussels; ~ *dort* (to be) delivered at yours; ~ *Unkosten* less charges; *Hut* ~*!* hat(s) off!; *von jetzt* ~ from now on.

abänder|lich ['apˀɛndərliç] alterable; '**~n** alter; change; modify; *parl.* amend; *jur.* commute; '**⁀ung** *f* alteration; modification; amendment; '**⁀ungsantrag** *parl. m* amendment.

'**ab-arbeiten** *Schuld*: work out; *sich* ~ overwork o.s., slave; *abgearbeitet* worn-out.

'**Ab-art** *f* variety; '**⁀en** (sn) degenerate; (*variieren*) vary; '**⁀ig** abnormal; *sexuell*: perverted; '**~ung** *f* degeneration; variation.

'**Abbau** *m* ⊕ dismantling; ⚒ working; *der Preise, des Personals*: reduction, *Am.* cutback; *einzelner Angestellten*: retrenchment, dismissal; ⚗ decomposition; '**⁀en** *v/t. Gebäude usw.*: pull down, *a.* ⊕ dismantle; ⚒ work, mine; *Preise, Personal*: reduce, cut down; *einzelne Angestellte*: retrench, dismiss; ⚗ reduce.

'**abbeißen** bite off.

'**abbeizen** strip.

'**Abbeizmittel** *n* paint stripper.

'**abbekommen** get off; *s-n Teil* (*od.* et.) ~ get (*od.* come in for) one's share; et. ~ (*verletzt werden*) get hurt, *S.*: be damaged.

'**abberuf|en** recall; '**⁀ung** *f* recall.

'**abbestell|en** countermand, cancel (orders for); *Zeitung*: discontinue; '**⁀ung** *f* countermand, cancellation.

'**abbetteln:** *j-m* et. ~ wheedle a th. out of a p.

'**abbiegen** *v/t.* bend off; *fig. e-e Sache*: avert, ward off; *v/i.* (sn) turn off; *Straße*: branch off.

'**Abbild** *n e-r S.*: copy; *e-r P.*: likeness; (*Ebenbild*) image; '**⁀en** represent; model; copy *a th.*; portray *a p.*; '**~ung** *f* representation; picture; illustration; *Computer*: mapping.

'**abbinden** unbind, untie; ⚕ tie up *od.* off; *Zement*: set.

'**Abbitte** *f* apology; ~ *tun* = '**⁀n** *v/t. u. v/i.* apologize (*j-m* et. to a p. for a th.).

'**abblasen** *v/t. Dampf*: blow off; *Angriff*: break off; *fig.* call off, cancel.

'**abblättern** *v/refl. u. v/i.* (sn) shed the leaves; *fig.* flake *od.* peel off.

'**abblend|en** *v/t.* screen (off), dim; *phot.* stop down; *Film, Radio*: fade down; *v/i. mot.* dip the (head)lights; '**⁀licht** *mot. n* dipped (*Am.* dimmed) headlights *pl.*; '**⁀schalter** *mot. m* dip switch; '**⁀vorrichtung** *f im Kino usw.*: dimmer.

'**abblitzen** F (sn) meet with a rebuff (*bei j-m* from a p.); ~ *lassen* rebuff, send *a p.* packing.

'**abbrausen** *v/t.* (*a. sich* ~) shower; *v/i.* F (sn) buzz off.

'**abbrechen** *v/t. u. v/i.* (sn) break off (*a. fig.*); *Haus usw.*: pull down, demolish; *Lager*: break (up); *Zelt*: strike; *kurz* ~ *v/t.* cut short, *v/i.* stop short; *alle Brücken hinter sich* ~ burn one's boats.

'**abbremsen** slow down; *mot.* brake.

'**abbrennen** *v/t. Haus*: burn down;

Feuerwerk: let off; *v/i.* (sn) burn down; *s. abgebrannt.*

'**abbringen** get off, deflect, divert; *fig. j-n ~ von* put a p. off doing (*a th.*), *von e-r Meinung usw.* talk a p. out of; (*abraten*) dissuade from; *s. ausreden*; *von e-m Thema*: lead away from; *vom* (*rechten*) *Wege ~* (*a. fig.*) lead astray; *sich nicht ~ lassen von etwas* abide by (*od.* stick to) a th.; *davon lasse ich mich nicht ~* nothing can change my mind about that.

'**abbröckeln** (sn) crumble away *od.* off; *Kurse, Preise*: crumble.

'**Abbruch** *m* breaking off (*a. fig. von Beziehungen*); *e-s Hauses*: pulling down, demolition; (*Schaden*) damage, injury; *auf ~ verkaufen* sell for the material; *~ tun* (*dat.*) damage, impair, prejudice; *~ erleiden* be impaired; '**~-unternehmer** *m* demolition contractor, wrecker.

'**abbrühen** *Gemüse*: (par)boil; *Geflügel, Schwein*: scald; *s. abgebrüht.*

'**abbuchen** † charge off; (*abschreiben*) write off.

'**abbüß|en** expiate, atone for; *Strafe*: serve; '**2ung** *f* expiation, atonement.

Abc [aːbeˈtseː] *n* ABC, alphabet; **~-Buch** *n* primer, spelling book.

'**abchecken** F (25) tick (*Am.* check) off.

Abc-Schütze *m* (school) beginner.

ABC-Waffen *f/pl.* NBC-weapons.

abdach|en [ˈapdaxən] (25) slant, slope; *sich ~* slope off; '**2ung** *f* slope, declivity.

'**abdämmen** (25) dam up.

'**abdampf|en** (h. *u.* sn) evaporate; F *Zug*: steam off, *Person*: *sl.* beat it; '**2ung** *f* evaporation.

'**abdank|en** resign; *Herrscher*: abdicate; '**2ung** *f* resignation; abdication; retirement.

'**abdecken** uncover; *Dach*: untile; *Haus*: unroof; *Tisch*: clear; ⊕ mask, cover; *phot.* screen off; *Vieh*: flay; *Sport*: *s. decken.*

'**Abdecker** *m* (7) knacker, flayer; **~ei** [~ˈraɪ] *f* knackery, *Am.* boneyard.

'**Abdeckhaube** *f e-s Plattenspielers*: dust cover.

'**abdicht|en** (26) seal (up); *Maschinenteil*: pack; ⚓ ca(u)lk; '**2gummi** *mot. m, n* body rubber; '**2ung** *f* sealing; packing.

'**abdienen** *Schuld*: work out; *s-e Zeit ~* serve one's time.

'**abdrehen** *v/t.* twist off; *Gas usw.*: turn off; ⚡ switch off; *v/i.* ✈, ⚓ turn away, sheer off.

'**abdrosseln** ⊕ throttle (down *fig.*).

'**Abdruck** *m* impression (*a. typ.*), imprint; (*Nachdruck*) reprint; (*Exemplar*) copy; *typ.* (*Probe2*) proof; (*Abguß*) cast; *e-s Petschafts usw.*: stamp; mark; '**2en** print; *wieder ~* reprint.

'**abdrücken** squeeze off; (*abformen*) mo(u)ld; *Gewehr*: pull the trigger of *a gun*, fire; (*umarmen*) hug; *j-m das Herz ~* break a p.'s heart; *sich ~* leave an imprint.

'**abdunkeln** dim; *Farben*: darken.

'**abdüsen** F (27, sn) clear off, take off.

'**ab-ebben** *a. fig.* ebb (away).

Abend [ˈaːbənt] *m* (3^1) evening; night; *des ~s, 2s* in the evening, at night; *s. essen*; *man soll den Tag nicht vor dem ~ loben* don't halloo till you are out of the wood; *es ist noch nicht aller Tage ~* things may take a turn yet.

'**Abend...** *mst* evening ...; '**~-andacht** *f* evening prayer(s *pl.*); '**~-anzug** *m* evening dress; '**~blatt** *n* evening paper; '**~brot** *n*, '**~-essen** *n* evening meal; dinner; supper; '**~dämmerung** *f* dusk; '**2füllend** *Film usw.*: full-length; '**~gesellschaft** *f* (evening) party; '**~gymnasium** *n* night-school; '**~kasse** *f* box-office; '**~kleid** *n* evening dress *od.* gown; '**~kurs**(**us**) *m* evening class(es *pl.*); '**~land** *n* occident; '**~länder**(**in** *f*) *m* Occidental, Westerner; **2ländisch** [ˈ~lɛndiʃ] western, occidental; '**2lich** evening, of (*od.* in) the evening; '**~mahl** *eccl. n the* Holy Communion, *the* Lord's Supper; '**~mahlskelch** *m* Eucharist cup, chalice; '**~rot** *n*, '**~röte** *f* sunset glow; '**~schule** *f* night-school; '**~sonne** *f* setting sun; '**~stern** *m* evening star; '**~toilette** *f* evening dress; '**~zeit** *f* night-time; '**~zeitung** *f s. Abendblatt.*

Abenteuer [ˈaːbəntɔʏər] *n* (7) adventure; '**2lich** adventurous; *fig.* odd, wild, fantastic; '**~lichkeit** *f* adventurousness; *fig.* strangeness, oddity; '**~lust** *f* spirit of adventure; '**~spielplatz** *m* adventure playground.

'**Abenteurer** *m* adventurer; '**~in** *f*

adventuress; '**~leben** *n*: *ein ~ führen* lead an adventurous life.

aber ['a:bər] **1.** *adv.* again; *tausend und ~ tausend* thousands and (*od.* upon) thousands; **2.** *cj.* but; *nun ~* but now; *nein ~!* I say!; *~, ~!* come, come!; *oder ~* otherwise, (or) else; *~ d(enn)och* (but) yet, however; **3.** ♀ *n* but; *er hat immer (ein Wenn und) ein ~* he is always full of "ifs" and "buts".

'**Aber|glaube** *m* superstition; **♀gläubisch** ['~glɔʏbiʃ] superstitious.

aberkenn|en ['apˀɛrkɛnən]: *j-m et. ~* deny a p. a th.; ⚖ deprive a p. of a th.; '**♀ung** *f* denial; ⚖ deprivation.

aber|malig ['a:bərma:liç] repeated; **~mals** ['~s] again, once more.

abernten ['apˀɛrntən] reap.

Aberwitz ['a:bərvits] *m* madness, folly; '**♀ig** crazy, foolish.

abessen ['apˀɛsən] *v/t.* eat clean.

abfackeln ['apfakəln] *Erdgas*: burn off.

abfahren ['apfa:rən] *v/i.* (sn) leave, depart, set out *od.* off, start (*nach* for); *Ski*: descend, run downhill; F *j-n ~ lassen* send a p. packing; *sl. ich bin total auf Reggae abgefahren* F I'm really into Reggae; *v/t. Last*: carry off; (*abnützen*) wear (out); *Strecke*: drive through, cover; patrol; *ihm wurde ein Bein abgefahren* he lost a leg in a motor-accident.

'**Abfahrt** *f* start, departure; ⚓ sailing; *Ski*: downhill (race *od.* run); *bei ~ des Zuges* at traintime; '**~slauf** *m Ski*: downhill race; '**~släufer** *m Ski*: downhiller; '**~(s)zeit** *f* time of departure.

'**Abfall** *m* falling-off; (*Böschung*) slope; *der Blätter*: fall; (*Trennung*) defection, secession (*von* from), desertion (of); *eccl.* apostasy; (*Abnahme*) decrease, *a.* ⚡ drop; *fig.* contrast (*gegen* to, with); (*Unbrauchbares*) (*oft pl.*) waste; (*Müll*) refuse, *bsd. Am.* garbage; (*Schnitzel*) clippings *pl.*; *beim Schlachten*: offal; '**~eimer** *m* dustbin, *Am.* ashcan; '**♀en** (sn) fall off; (*schräg sein*) slope, decline; *pol.* defect, desert; *eccl.* apostatize; ⚡ drop; (*mager werden*) lose flesh; (*übrigbleiben*) be left; *im Vergleich*: compare badly (*gegen* with); (*sich ergeben*) result; *et. fällt dabei für ihn ab* there will be something in it for him; '**♀end** *Gelände*: sloping; '**~haufen** *m* rubbish heap.

'**abfällig** *fig.* disapproving; *Bemerkung*: disparaging; *Kritik*: adverse; *~ über j-n sprechen* speak disparagingly of a p.; *~ urteilen über (acc.)* criticize unfavo(u)rably, run down.

'**Abfall|produkt** *n* waste product; by-product; '**~verwertung** *f* recycling.

'**abfang|en** catch, snatch; *j-n, Brief,* ⚔ *usw.*: intercept; ⊕ *Stöße*: absorb; ⚠, ⚒ prop; *hunt.* stab; ✈ flatten out; *mot.* get under control; '**♀jäger** ⚔ *m* interceptor.

'**abfärben** *v/i.* stain; lose colo(u)r; *~ auf (acc.)* stain; *fig.* rub off on, influence.

'**abfass|en** *Werk*: compose, write, pen; *Vertrag usw.*: draft, *bsd.* ⚖ draw up; *j-n*: catch; '**♀ung** *f* composition; drawing up.

'**ab|faulen** (sn) rot off; '**~federn** ⊕ cushion, spring(-load); suspend; '**~feilen** file off.

'**abfertig|en** dispatch (*a.* 🚂, ✈); *j-n*: attend to, ☤ *a.* serve, *a. weitS.* serve, deal with; (*abweisen*) snub; *j-n kurz ~* send a p. about his business; '**♀ung** *f* dispatch(ing); *Zoll*: clearance; (*Abweisung*) snub; (*Bedienung*) service; '**♀ungsschalter** *m* check-in counter (*od.* desk); '**♀ungsstelle** *f* dispatching office.

'**abfeuern** fire (off), discharge.

'**abfinden** satisfy, pay off, *Gläubiger*: *a.* compound with; *Partner*: buy out; (*entschädigen*) compensate, indemnify; *sich mit s-m Los usw. ~* resign o.s. to one's fate, *etc.*; *sich mit e-r unangenehmen P. od. S. ~* put up with.

Abfindung ['apfinduŋ] *f* settlement, satisfaction; composition (*der Gläubiger* with the creditors); '**~(s-summe)** *f* indemnity.

abflach|en ['~flaxən] flatten (*a. sich*); '**♀ung** *f* flattening; slope.

abflauen ['~flauən] (25; sn) *Wind usw.*: abate; *fig. a.* slacken (off); *Interesse*: flag; ☤ *Kurse*: fall off.

'**abfliegen** *v/i.* (sn) fly off; ✈ start, take off; *v/t.* ✈ patrol, cover.

'**abfließen** (sn) flow off.

'**Abflug** ✈ *m* start, take-off; departure; '**~hafen** *m* departure airport; '**~halle** *f* departure lounge.

ˈ**Abfluß** *m* flowing off, discharge; drain (*a. fig.*); (*~stelle*) outlet; ˈ**~graben** *m* drain(ing-ditch); ˈ**~rohr** *n* waste-pipe; ⊕ drain-pipe.
ˈ**abfordern:** *j-m et.* ~ demand a th. from a p.
ˈ**abformen** mo(u)ld, model.
ˈ**abfragen:** *j-m et.* ~ question a p. about a th.; *e-m Schüler die Grammatik* ~ hear a boy's grammar.
ˈ**abfressen** eat off; *Wild usw.*: browse on, crop, eat bare.
ˈ**abfrieren** (sn) be bitten off by cold.
Abfuhr [ˈapfuːr] *f* (16) removal; F (*Abweisung*) rebuff; *fenc.* disablement; *Sport u. fig.* beating.
ˈ**abführen** *v/t. j-n*: lead off; *ins Gefängnis*: march off; *vom (rechten) Wege* ~ lead astray (*a. fig.*); *Geld*: branch (*od.* draw) off; *v/i.* ⚕ loosen the bowels; ˈ**~d** ⚕ purgative.
ˈ**Abführmittel** ⚕ *n* laxative.
ˈ**Abfüll-anlage** *f* bottling plant.
ˈ**abfüllen** fill; *Bier, Wein*: draw (*od.* rack) off; *in Flaschen*: bottle.
ˈ**abfüttern** feed; ⊕ line.
ˈ**Abgabe** *f* delivery; *der Wahlstimme*: casting, polling; (*bsd. Zoll*) duty; (*Steuer*) tax, *lokale*: rate; *soziale* ~ social contribution; *Sport*: pass; ⚚ sale; *phys.* emission; ⚡ output; ˈ**2nfrei** duty-free; tax-free; **2npflichtig** [ˈ~pfliçtiç] taxable; dutiable.
ˈ**Abgang** *m* departure; *thea.* exit; *aus e-r Stellung*: retirement; *von der Schule*: leaving (school), *mit Erfolg*: graduation; *von Waren*: sale; (*Verlust*) loss, wastage; (*Fehlen*) deficiency, shortage; ⚕ discharge; (*Abfall*) refuse, offal.
abgängig [ˈapgɛŋiç] missing.
ˈ**Abgangs|prüfung** *f* leaving examination; ˈ**~zeugnis** *n* (school-) leaving certificate.
ˈ**Abgase** *n/pl.* exhaust fumes.
ˈ**Abgas|-entgiftungsanlage** *f* anti-pollution device; ˈ**~katalysator** *mot. m* (8) catalytic converter; ˈ**~test** *m* fume emission test; ˈ**~turbolader** *mot. m* (7) turbocharger.
ˈ**abgeben** deliver, hand over (*an acc.*, *bei* to); *Schriftstück*: submit (to), *a. Schulhefte*: hand in; *Ware*: sell; *Erklärung*: make; *Gepäck*: deposit; *Meinung usw.*: give, pass; *e-n Politiker usw.*: make; *Schuß*: fire; *Fußball*: pass (*a. v/i.*); *s. Stimme*; *von et.*: give some of; (*dienen als*) act as; *sich ~ mit et.* occupy o.s. with, deal with; *sich ~ mit j-m* associate with, have dealings with; *können Sie mir e-e Zigarette ~?* can you spare me a cigarette?; *du willst mir nie was ~* you never want to give me anything.
abge|brannt F [ˈapgəbrant] (*ohne Geld*) (stony-)broke; **~brüht** [ˈ~gəbryːt] *fig.* hardened; **~droschen** [ˈ~gədrɔʃən] trite, hackneyed; ˈ**~fahren** [ˈ~gəfaːrən] *Reifen*: worn down, F bald; **~feimt** [ˈ~gəfaɪmt] cunning, crafty; **~griffen** [ˈ~gəgrifən] *Buch*: well-thumbed; *Münze*: worn; *fig.* hackneyed; **~hackt** [ˈ~gəhakt] *fig.* abrupt, disjointed; ˈ**~härtet** *s. abhärten.*
ˈ**abgehen** (sn) go off; *a.* 🚂 *usw.*: leave, depart, start; *Post*: go; (*Amt aufgeben*) retire, resign; *v. e-r Schule*: leave (school), *mit Erfolg*: graduate (*von* from); (*sich ablösen*) come off; *Seitenweg*: branch off; (*fehlen*) be missing; *thea.* make one's exit; ⚕ be discharged; ⚚ *Ware*: sell; *reißend* ~ F sell like hot cakes; ~ *von e-m Vorhaben* drop; ~ *von e-r Meinung* change; ~ *von e-m Thema* digress (*od.* swerve) from; *vom (rechten) Wege* ~ go astray, deviate (*beide a. fig.*); *davon kann ich nicht* ~ I must insist (up)on that; *hiervon geht ... ab* ... must be deducted; *er geht mir sehr ab* I miss him badly; *ihm geht nichts ab* he does not go short of anything; *fig. gut* ~ pass off well; *schlecht* ~ turn out badly; ~ *lassen* forward, dispatch; *sich et. ~ lassen* deny o.s. a th.
abgekämpft [ˈ~gəkɛmpft] worn--out, spent.
ˈ**abgelegen** remote; out of the way.
ˈ**abgelten** *Forderung*: meet, satisfy.
abgemessen [ˈ~gəmɛsən] measured.
abgeneigt [ˈ~gənaɪkt] disinclined *od.* unwilling (*dat.* for *od.* to *a th.*; *zu inf.* to), averse (to); *j-m* ~ ill--disposed towards a p.; ˈ**2heit** *f s. Abneigung.*
abgenutzt [ˈ~gənutst] worn-out.
Abgeordnete [ˈ~gəˀɔrdnətə] *m, f* (18) delegate, deputy; *parl.* Member of Parliament (*abbr.* M.P.), *Am.* representative.
ˈ**abgepackt** *Lebensmittel*: packaged, prepacked.

abgerissen ['~gərisən] (*zerrissen*) torn; (*zerlumpt*) ragged; (*schäbig*) shabby; *Person*: seedy, out-at--elbows; *Sprache, Stil*: abrupt, disjointed.
'**Abgesandte** *m, f* messenger; *pol.* envoy; *geheimer*: emissary.
'**abgeschieden** secluded, retired; (*tot*) defunct, deceased; '**2heit** *f* retirement, seclusion.
'**abgeschlafft** F whacked.
'**abgeschlossen** (*zurückgezogen*) secluded; *Wohnung*: self-contained; *Ausbildung usw.*: complete; '**2heit** *f* seclusion.
abgeschmackt ['~gəʃmakt] insipid, absurd; '**2heit** *f* insipidity, absurdity.
abgesehen ['~gəze:ən]: ~ *von* apart (*Am. a.* aside) from, except for.
'**abgespannt** *fig.* exhausted, run down; '**2heit** *f* exhaustion.
abgestanden ['~gəʃtandən] stale.
abgestorben ['~gəʃtɔrbən] (*erstarrt*) numb; *gänzlich* ~ dead.
abgestumpft ['~gəʃtumpft] blunt (-ed); ⩕ truncated; *fig.* dull(ed), indifferent (*gegen* to).
'**abgewinnen:** *j-m et.* ~ win a th. from (*od.* off) a p.; *e-r S. Geschmack* ~ acquire a taste for a th.
abgewirtschaftet ['~gəvirtʃaftət] run down, finished, ruined.
'**abgewöhnen:** *j-m et.* ~ cure a p. of a th.; make a p. stop *ger.*; *sich et.* ~ leave off, give up.
abgezehrt ['~gətse:rt] emaciated.
'**abgießen** pour off; *in Gips*: cast.
'**Abglanz** *m* reflection; *fig. schwacher* ~ pale reflection, feeble copy.
'**abgleichen** equalize; *Konten*: square; ⚡ trim.
'**abgleiten,** '**abglitschen** (sn) slip off, glide off; *Vorwürfe usw. gleiten von ihm ab* he is deaf to.
'**Abgott** *m* idol.
Abgött|erei [~gœtə'raɪ] *f* idolatry; *mit j-m* ~ *treiben* idolize a p.; '**2isch** idolatrous; ~ *lieben* idolize, adore.
'**abgraben** dig off; *fig. j-m das Wasser* ~ cut the ground from under a p.'s feet.
'**abgrämen:** *sich* ~ grieve, eat one's heart out.
'**abgrasen** graze (off); *fig.* scour.
'**abgrenz|en** mark off; demarcate; (de)limit; *Begriff*: define; '**2ung** *f* delimitation, demarcation; definition.
'**Abgrund** *m* abyss, chasm, precipice; '**2tief** abysmal (*a. fig.*).
'**abgucken** F: *j-m et.* ~ copy a th. from a p.
'**Abguß** *m in Gips usw.*: cast, mo(u)ld.
'**abhaben:** *etwas* ~ *von* have a share of; *den Hut usw.*: have ... off.
'**abhacken** chop (*od.* cut) off; *Worte*: chop; *s. abgehackt.*
abhaken ['apha:kən] (25) unhook; *in e-r Liste*: tick (*od.* check) off.
'**abhalftern** unhalter; *fig.* sack.
'**abhalt|en** *v/t.* hold (*od.* keep) off; *fig.* detain, (*hindern*) keep, restrain, prevent; (*abwehren*) ward off; *Sitzung, Fest usw.*: hold; *Lehrstunde*: give; *Kind*: hold out; *v/i.* ⚓ *vom Lande* ~ bear off; ~ *auf* (*acc.*) head for; '**2ung** *f e-r Versammlung usw.*: holding; *e-s Festes*: celebration; (*Hindernis*) hindrance; *e-e* ~ *haben* be otherwise engaged.
'**abhand|eln:** *j-m etwas vom Preise* ~ beat a p. down in price (*od.* by a sum); *j-m et.* ~ purchase a th. of a p.; (*erörtern*) treat of, discuss; (*erledigen*) deal with; '**2lung** *f* treatise, article, (*Vortrag in e-m gelehrten Verein*) paper; *wissenschaftliche*: *a.* dissertation.
abhanden [~'handən]: ~ *kommen* get lost.
'**Abhang** *m* slope; *jäher*: precipice.
'**abhängen** *v/t.* take off *od.* down; 🚂, ✈ uncouple; *Anhänger*: unhook; *Verfolger usw.*: shake off; *v/i.* ~ *von* depend on.
abhängig ['~hɛŋiç] dependent (*von* on); (*vorbehaltlich*) subject (to); '**2keit** *f* dependence.
'**abhärmen** (*sich*) pine away; *sich* ~ *über* (*acc.*) grieve at, for, over; *abgehärmt* careworn, haggard.
'**abhärt|en** harden (*gegen* against); *gegen Strapazen*: inure (to); '**2ung** *f* hardening; inurement.
'**abhaspeln** reel off (*a. fig.*).
'**abhauen** *v/t.* cut off; *v/i.* (sn) *sl.* make off, *bsd. Am.* beat it.
'**abhäuten** skin, flay.
'**abheb|en** *v/t.* lift (off); *Geld*: (with)draw; *Karten*: cut (*a. v/i.*); *sich vom Hintergrund usw.* ~ contrast (*von* with), stand out (against); *v/i.* ✈ take off, become airborne; '**2ung** *f von Geld*: withdrawal.

ˈ**abheften** file away.
ˈ**abheilen** (sn) heal.
ˈ**abhelfen** *e-r S.*: help, remedy; *e-r Beschwerde, e-m Mißstand, e-r Notlage*: redress; *e-m Mangel* ~ supply a want.
ˈ**abhetzen** drive hard, harass; *Pferd*: override; *sich* ~ tire o.s. out, rush, hurry.
ˈ**Abhilfe** *f* (*vgl. abhelfen*) help; remedy; redress; ~ *schaffen* take remedial measures.
ˈ**abhold** *j-m*: ill-disposed towards; *e-r S.*: averse to.
ˈ**abhol|en** fetch; *P., Brief, Paket*: call (*od.* come) for, pick up, collect; ~ *lassen* send for; *j-n von der Bahn* ~ go to meet a p. at the station; ˈ**2ung** *f* fetching; pick-up; collection.
ˈ**abholzen** (27) *Wald*: cut down.
ˈ**abhorchen** ⚕ auscultate; ⚔ *usw. s. abhören.*
ˈ**Abhör-anlage** *f* bugging system.
ˈ**abhören** (*abfragen*) hear (*e-m Schüler die Aufgabe* a pupil's lesson); *Gespräch*: listen in on, *mit Mikrophon*: bug; *Telephonleitung*: tap.
ˈ**abhör|sicher** *Telephonleitung*: safe from interception; ˈ**2skandal** *m* bugging scandal.
ˈ**ab-irren** (sn) go astray (*a. fig.*).
ˈ**ab-isolieren** *Draht*: strip.
Abitur [abiˈtuːr] *n* (3) school-leaving (*Am.* final) examination at German secondary schools.
Abiturient(in *f*) [~turiˈɛnt(in)] *m* (12) candidate for the matriculation, *Am.* high-school graduate.
abjagen [ˈapjɑːgən] *Pferd*: override, overdrive; *P.*: rush about; *j-m et.* ~ snatch a th. away from a p.
abkanzeln [ˈ~kantsəln] (29) lecture, F tell *a p.* off.
abkarten [ˈ~kartən] (26) plot; *abgekartete Sache* prearranged affair, F put-up job.
ˈ**abkaufen** *j-m*: buy from.
Abkehr [ˈ~keːr] *f* turning away, departure (*von* from); ˈ**2en** **1.** (*abwenden*) turn away (*a. sich*); **2.** sweep (off).
ˈ**abklappern** F *v/t.* scour, F do.
ˈ**abklär|en** clear, clarify; ⚗ filter; *abgeklärt Urteil*: detached, *Charakter*: mellow; ˈ**2ung** *f* clarification; *fig.* detachment of mind.
Abklatsch [ˈ~klatʃ] *m typ.* impression; *fig.* (*schwacher*) ~ (poor) copy.
ˈ**abklemmen** pinch off.
ˈ**abklingen** (sn) fade away; *Krankheit*: ease off; *Wirkung*: wear off.
ˈ**Abklingzeit** *f* fade-out time.
ˈ**abklopfen** *v/t.* beat (*od.* knock) off; ⚕ percuss; (*abstauben*) dust down; *v/i.* ♪ stop the music.
ˈ**abknabbern** nibble off.
ˈ**abknallen** P bump off.
abknappen, abknapsen [ˈ~knap(s)ən] pinch, stint; *sich et.* ~ stint o.s. of a th.
ˈ**abknicken** crack (*od.* snap) off; (*beugen*) bend.
ˈ**abknöpfen** (25) unbutton; F *j-m et.* ~ do a p. out of a th.
abknutschen F (have a) snog with.
ˈ**abkochen** *v/t.* boil; ⚗ decoct; *Milch*: scald; *v/i.* cook out.
ˈ**abkommandieren** ⚔ detach, detail; *Offizier*: second.
ˈ**Abkomme** *m* (13) descendant.
ˈ**abkommen** **1.** (sn) come (*od.* get) away; *beim Schießen*: mark; *vom Wege* ~ lose one's way; *fig. von et.* ~ give up, drop; ~ *von e-r Ansicht* change; ~ *von e-m Thema* digress from; *von e-m Verfahren* ~ depart from; ✈ *s. abheben*; *Sport*: *gut* ~ get a good start; *er kann nicht* ~ *s. abkömmlich*; **2.** 2 *n* (*Vertrag*) agreement, *pol. a.* treaty, convention.
abkömmlich [ˈ~kœmliç]: *er ist nicht* ~ he cannot be spared, he cannot get away.
Abkömmling [ˈ~kœmliŋ] *m* (3) descendant, offspring (*a. pl.*).
ˈ**abkoppeln** uncouple; *fig. sich* ~ *von et.* dissociate o.s. from a th.
ˈ**abkratzen** scratch (*od.* scrape) off; P (*sterben*) *sl.* peg out.
ˈ**abkriegen** *s. abbekommen.*
ˈ**abkühl|en** cool; *sich* ~ cool down; ˈ**2ung** *f* cooling; *fig.* damper.
Abkunft [ˈ~kunft] *f* (14, *o. pl.*) descent; extraction; (*Geburt*) birth.
ˈ**abkürz|en** *v/t.* shorten; *Inhalt, Unterredung*: abridge; *Wort*: abbreviate; *Besuch, Geschichte*: cut short; ⅍ reduce; *v/i.* take a short-cut; ˈ**2ung** *f* abridgment; abbreviation; *des Weges*: short-cut (*a. fig.*); ⅍ reduction; ˈ**2ungsverzeichnis** *n* list of abbreviations; ˈ**2ungszeichen** *n* (sign of) abbreviation; *s. Kürzel.*

'abküssen *j-n*: smother with kisses.
'abladen unload; *Schutt usw.*: dump.
'Abladeplatz *m* unloading point; *für Schutt*: dump(ing-ground).
'Ablage *f* place of deposit; *von Akten*: filing.
'ablager|n *v/t.* deposit; ~ lassen store, season well; *v/i.* (sn) settle; *Wein usw.*: mature; abgelagert *Tabak, Holz*: well-seasoned; **'2ung** *f* maturing; *geol.*, ⚗ deposition, sedimentation, (*Abgelagertes*) deposit, sediment.
Ablaß *eccl.* ['~las] *m* (4[2]) indulgence; **'~brief** *eccl. m* letter of indulgence; **'~ventil** ⊕ *n* drain valve.
'ablassen *v/t.* let off; *Teich usw.*: drain; *Zug usw.*: start; vom Preis ~ take *od.* knock off the price; (*überlassen*) let *a p.* have *a th.*; *käuflich*: sell; *v/i.* leave off (von et. doing a th.), desist (from).
Ablativ *gr.* ['ablati:f] *m* (3[1]) ablative.
'Ablauf *m e-r Frist*: lapse; *e-s Vertrages, e-r Frist*: expiration; *für Wasser usw.*: drain; ⚕ *e-s Wechsels*: maturity; *Sport*: start; nach ~ von at the end of; **'2en** *v/i.* (sn) *Wasser*: run off; *Frist, Vertrag, usw.*: lapse, expire, terminate; ⚕ *Wechsel*: become due; *Sport*: start (*a.* ~ lassen); *Uhr*: run down; ~ lassen *Flüssigkeit*: drain off; *fig. j-n*: snub; *Schiff*: launch; gut *usw.* ~ come to a good, *etc.* end, pass (*od.* go) off well, *etc.*; *v/t. Schuhe*: wear out; sich die Beine ~ run o.s. off one's legs; *s.* Horn, Rang; die Stadt ~ scour the town.
'Ablaut *gr. m* vowel-gradation, ablaut; **'2en** *gr.* change the radical vowel.
'Ableben *n* death, decease.
'ablecken lick off.
'ablegen lay down, off *od.* aside; *Kleidungsstück* (*ausziehen*): put (*od.* take) off; *altes Kleidungsstück, Vorurteil*: discard; *Gewohnheit*: give up, drop; *Akten, Brief*: file; *Bekenntnis, Gelübde*: make; *Eid*: take; *Prüfung*: pass; *Raumfähre*: separate; *s.* Rechenschaft, Probe, Zeugnis; bitte legen Sie ab! take off your coat, please.
Ableger ✓ ['~le:gər] *m* (7) layer, scion (*a. fig. Person*); ⚕ branch.
'ablehn|en *v/t. u. v/i.* decline, refuse; *als unannehmbar, unbrauchbar usw.*: reject; *Gesuch, Angebot usw.*: turn down; (*nicht anerkennen*) disown; (*ungünstig beurteilen*) object to; *parl. Antrag*: defeat; ⚖ *Zeugen usw.*: challenge; *Theaterstück*: condemn; dankend ~ decline with thanks; **'~end** negative; **'2ung** *f* declining, refusal, *Am.* declination; rejection; *parl.* defeat; ⚖ challenge; *thea.* condemnation.
'ableisten *Dienstzeit*: pass, ⚔ serve.
'ableiten *Fluß usw.*: divert; *Wasser*: drain, draw off; ⚡ shunt (off); *gr.*, ⚘, *fig.* derive.
'Ableitung *f* (*vgl.* ableiten) diversion; ⚡ shunt; *gr.*, ⚘ derivation; (*Abgeleitetes*) derivative; (*Folgerung*) deduction; **'~ssilbe** *gr. f* derivative affix.
'ablenk|en turn away, off *od.* aside, *bsd. Aufmerksamkeit*: take off, divert, distract (*a. j-n*); *Auge, Gedanken, bsd. Verdacht*: avert; *phys., opt.* deflect; *Stoß*: parry; **'2ung** *f* turning away *od.* off; averting; diversion, distraction; deflection; **'2ungsmanöver** ⚔ *n* diversion; *fig. a.* red herring.
'ables|en *Obst, Raupen usw.*: gather, pick off; *Rede usw.*: read off; *Skala*: read; **'2ung** ⊕ *f* reading.
'ableugn|en deny, disavow; **'2ung** *f* denial, disavowal.
'Ablichtung *f* photostat.
'abliefern deliver.
'Ablieferung *f* delivery; bei ~ on delivery; **'~ssoll** *n* delivery quota.
'abliegen (sn) lie at a distance; *s.* abgelegen.
'ablohn|en pay off; **'2ung** *f* paying off; (*Entlassung*) dismissal.
'ablösbar *Rente usw.*: redeemable.
'ablöschen extinguish; *Schreibtafel*: clean; *Geschriebenes*: wipe off, *mit Löschpapier*: blot; *Kalk*: slake; *Stahl*: temper.
'ablös|en loosen, detach; ⚔ relieve; *Amtsvorgänger*: supersede; *Schuld*: discharge; *Anleihe*: redeem; sich ~ come off; sich *od.* ea. ~ alternate, relieve one another; **'2esumme** *f Sport*: transfer fee; **'2ung** *f* loosening; detaching; ⚔ relief; supersession; discharge; redemption.
'Abluft *f* waste air.
'ablutschen lick (off).
'abmach|en undo, loosen; *s.* ablösen;

fig. settle, arrange; (*ausbedingen*) stipulate; *abgemacht!* agreed!, all right!, *bsd. Am.* O.K.!; ˈ**2ung** *f* arrangement.
abmager|n [ˈ~maːgərn] (29) (sn) grow lean *od.* thin; *abgemagert* emaciated; ˈ**2ung** *f* emaciation; ˈ**2ungskur** *f* diet; e-e ~ *machen* go on a diet; (*auf* ~ *sein*) be on a diet.
ˈ**abmalen** paint, portray; *fig. a.* depict; *nach Vorlage*: copy.
ˈ**Abmarsch** *m* departure; ˈ**2ieren** (sn) march off, depart.
ˈ**abmeld|en** give notice of *a p.'s* departure; *sein Telephon* ~ have one's telephone disconnected; ˈ**2ung** *f* notice of leaving; (*Bescheinigung*) leaving-certificate.
ˈ**abmess|en** measure (off); *Worte*: weigh; ˈ**2ung** *f* measurement.
ˈ**abmildern** moderate.
ˈ**abmontieren** *Fabrikanlage*: strip, dismantle; *Geschütz, Maschine*: dismount; *Reifen usw.*: remove, detach.
ˈ**abmühen:** *sich* ~ exert o.s., struggle.
ˈ**abmustern** ⚓ *Mannschaft*: pay off.
ˈ**abnagen** gnaw (off).
ˈ**abnäh|en**, ˈ**2er** *m im Kleid*: tuck.
Abnahme [ˈ~naːmə] *f* (15) taking off; (*Verminderung*) decrease, drop; ⚕ amputation; ✝ (*Übernahme*) taking, (*Verkauf*) sale; *des Mondes*: wane; *der Reifen usw.*: removal; *e-s Eides*: administering; *der Tage*: shortening; ⊕ acceptance (test); *des Körpergewichts*: loss of weight; ✝ *bei* ~ *von* ... on orders of ...
ˈ**abnehm|bar** detachable; ˈ**~en** *v/t.* take off *od.* down; (*ablösen*) detach; *teleph. Hörer*: unhook; *Glied*: amputate; *Bart*: shave off; ⚡ *Strom*: collect; (*wegnehmen*) take *a th.* from *a p.*; *Ware*: take (*dat.* from); ⊕ *Material*: accept, (*prüfen*) inspect; *Obst*: gather; *Rechnung*: audit; *j-m e-n Eid* ~ administer an oath to a p.; *Maschen* ~ narrow; *j-m e-e Mühe* ~ relieve a p. of a trouble; *e-e Parade* ~ take (*od.* hold) a review; *j-m ein Versprechen* ~ make a p. promise (a th.); ✝ *j-m zuviel* ~ overcharge a p.; *v/i.* decrease, diminish; (*verfallen*) decline; *Kräfte usw.*: begin to fail, dwindle; *an Körpergewicht*: lose weight, *absichtlich*: reduce; *Mond*: wane; *Tage*: shorten; ˈ**2er(in** *f*) *m* buyer; (*Kunde*) customer, client.
ˈ**Abneigung** *f* aversion, disinclination, dislike (*gegen* to); *natürliche*: antipathy (against, to).
abnorm [apˈnɔrm] abnormal, exceptional, unusual.
Abnormität [~iˈtɛːt] *f* (16) abnormity.
ˈ**abnötigen** (*erpressen*) extort (*dat.* from); *j-m Bewunderung* ~ compel a p.'s admiration.
ˈ**abnutz|en**, ˈ**abnütz|en** (*a. sich* ~) wear out; **2ung** *f* wear (and tear); (*Zermürbung*) attrition.
Abonnement [abɔn(ə)ˈmɑ̃] *n* (11) subscription (*auf acc.* to); **~karte** *f* 🚂 *usw.*: season-ticket, *Am.* commutation ticket; **~vorstellung** *f* subscription performance.
Abonnent(in *f*) *m* [~ˈnɛnt(in)] subscriber (*gen.* to).
abonˈnieren subscribe (*auf acc.* to); *abonniert sein auf e-e Zeitung* take (in).
ˈ**ab·ord|nen** depute, delegate, *Am. a.* deputize; ˈ**2nung** *f* delegation.
ˈ**Ab·ort**[1] *m* (3) (water-)closet, W.C., lavatory, privy, toilet.
Abort[2] ⚕ [aˈbɔrt] *m* (3), **~us** [~us] *m* (*inv.*) abortion.
ˈ**abpachten** rent, lease (*j-m* from a p.).
ˈ**abpassen** measure; fit; *j-n, Gelegenheit*: wait (*od.* watch) for; *zeitlich*: *gut* (*od. schlecht*) ~ time well (*od.* ill).
ˈ**abperlen** (sn) drip off (*von et.* a th.).
ˈ**abpfeifen:** (*das Spiel*) ~ stop the game.
ˈ**Abpfiff** *m Sport*: final whistle.
ˈ**abpflücken** pluck off, gather.
ˈ**abplacken**, ˈ**abplagen:** *sich* ~ toil, drudge; struggle (*mit* with).
abplatten [ˈ~platən] (26) flatten off.
Abprall [ˈ~pral] *m* (3, *o. pl.*) bounce; ˈ**2en** (sn) bounce off (*a. fig.*).
ˈ**abputzen** clean; (*polieren*) polish.
ˈ**abquälen** (*sich*) *arbeitend*: toil, drudge; *seelisch*: worry o.s.
ˈ**abquetschen** squeeze off.
abrackern F [ˈ~rakərn] (29) (*sich*) drudge, slave.
ˈ**abrahmen** *Milch*: skim.
ˈ**abrasieren** shave off; *fig. Gebäude etc.*: raze to the ground.
ˈ**abraten:** *j-m* ([*von*] *et.*) ~ dissuade a p. (from a th.), advise *od.* warn a p. against a th.

ˈ**Abraum** ⚒ *m* (3, *o. pl.*) mining debris.
ˈ**abräumen** clear away, remove; *den Tisch* ~ clear the table.
ˈ**Abraumsalze** *n/pl.* potassium salts.
ˈ**abreagieren** abreact; (*a. sich*) work off (one's feelings *od.* bad temper); *sich* ~ *a.* let off steam.
ˈ**abrechnen** *v/i.* settle (up) (*od.* square) accounts; *v/t.* (*abziehen*) deduct, discount; *Spesen usw.*: account for; ... *abgerechnet* apart from ..., discounting ...
ˈ**Abrechnung** *f* settlement (of accounts); (*Abzug*) deduction, discount; *auf* ~ on account; ~ *halten* balance (*od.* settle) accounts; ˈ**~stag** *m* settling-day; ˈ**~sverkehr** ⚕ *m* clearing (system).
ˈ**Abrede** *f* agreement, stipulation; *in* ~ *stellen* deny; ˈ**2n** *v/i.*: *j-m* (*von et.*) dissuade a p. (from a th.).
ˈ**Abreib|buchstabe** *m* rub-on letter; ˈ**2en** rub off; *Körper*: rub down; ˈ**~ung** *f* rubbing off; ⚕ rub-down; *nasse*: sponge-down; F (*Prügel, Niederlage*) beating.
ˈ**Abreise** *f* departure; ˈ**2n** (sn) depart, start, leave, set out (*nach* for).
ˈ**Abreiß|birne** ⊕ *f* wrecking ball; ˈ**2en** *v/t.* tear off; *Kleider*: wear out; *Gebäude*: pull down; *s. abgerissen*; *v/i.* (sn) break off (*a. fig.*), snap; *Knopf usw.*: come off; *die Arbeit reißt nicht ab* there is no end of work; ˈ**~kalender** *m* tear-off (*Am.* pad) calendar; ˈ~(**notiz**)**block** *m* tear-off pad.
ˈ**abreiten** *v/i.* (sn) ride away; *v/t.* (*zuviel reiten*) override; *Strecke*: ride; ⚔ *Front*: ride down.
ˈ**abrennen:** *sich* ~ run o.s. off one's legs; *s. a. ablaufen.*
ˈ**abricht|en** *Tier*: train; *Pferd*: break in; ⊕ dress; ˈ**2er** *m* trainer; ˈ**2ung** *f* training; breaking-in.
ˈ**abriegeln** (29) *Tür*: bolt, bar; *Straße*: block (off), *durch Polizei*: cordon off; ⚔ seal off.
ˈ**abringen** wrest (*j-m* from a p.).
ˈ**Abriß** *m* (*kurze Darstellung*) summary, epitome, abstract; (*Übersicht*) digest; (*Buch*) compendium; *von Gebäude*: demolition.
ˈ**abrollen** *v/t. u. v/i.* (sn) unroll; uncoil; *v. e-r Rolle*: unwind, unreel; (*wegrollen*) roll off; ⚕ (*v/t.*) cart away; *fig.* (*v/i.*) unfold, pass.
ˈ**abrücken** *v/t. u. v/i.* (sn) move off (*a.* ⚔); remove; *fig. von j-m* ~ dissociate o.s. from.
ˈ**Abruf** *m*: ⚕ *auf* ~ on call; *Geld auf* ~ call money; ˈ**2bar** ready on call; *Computer*: retrievable; ˈ**2en** call off (*a.* ⚕) *od.* away; 🚂 *Zug*: call out; *Computer*: retrieve.
ˈ**abrunden** round (off); *abgerundet Leistung*: well-rounded, finished; *Zahl*: round.
ˈ**abrupfen** pluck off.
ˈ**abrüst|en** *v/t. Gerüst*: take down; *v/i.* ⚔ disarm; ˈ**2ung** ⚔ *f* disarmament, arms reduction; ˈ**2ungskonferenz** *f* disarmament conference; ˈ**2ungsverhandlungen** *f/pl.* disarmament (*od.* arms reduction) talks.
ˈ**abrutschen** (sn) slip off *od.* down; ✈ sideslip.
ˈ**absäbeln** hack off.
absacken [ˈ~zakən] (25, sn) ⚓ sag; ✈ pancake.
ˈ**Absage** *f* cancellation; (*Ablehnung*) refusal; *fig.* repudiation (*an acc.* of); ˈ**2n** cancel, call off; *unerwartet*: cry off (*v/i.*); (*ablehnen*) decline, refuse; (*entsagen*) renounce.
ˈ**absägen** saw off; F *fig.* ax(e).
ˈ**absahnen** F (25) rake in.
ˈ**absatteln** *v/t.* unsaddle.
ˈ**Absatz** *m* stop, pause; ⚕ sale(s *pl.*), market(ing), outlet; *typ.* period, break; (*kurzer Abschnitt*) paragraph; (*Stiefel*2) heel; (*Treppen*2) landing; *in Absätzen* intermittently, at intervals; *guten* (*od. reißenden*) ~ *finden* meet with a ready sale, F sell like hot cakes; ˈ**2fähig** ⚕ marketable; ˈ**~gebiet** ⚕ *n* marketing area; ˈ**~krise** *f* sales crisis; ˈ**~markt** *m* outlet, market; ˈ**~möglichkeit** *f* marketing potentiality; *engS.* outlet; ˈ**~steigerung** *f* sales increase; ˈ**~stockung** *f* stagnation of trade.
ˈ**absaugen** suck off; *Gas*: exhaust; *Teppich usw.*: vacuum.
ˈ**abschab|en** scrape off; *abgeschabt* (*schäbig*) shabby, threadbare; **2sel** [ˈ~ʃa:psəl] *n/pl.* (7) scrapings *pl.*
ˈ**abschaff|en** (25) abolish, do away with; *Gesetz*: abrogate; (*loswerden*) get rid of; *Auto usw.*: give up; ˈ**2ung** *f* abolition; abrogation.
ˈ**abschälen** *s. schälen.*
ˈ**abschalt|en** *v/t.* switch *od.* turn off; ⚡ *Kontakt*: disconnect; *v/i.* F

fig. relax; 'ᘯ**ung** *f* switching off, disconnection.

'**abschätz|en** estimate, value; (*taxieren*) appraise; *bsd. für die Steuer*: assess; '**~ig** disparaging; 'ᘯ**ung** *f* valuation, estimation; appraisal; assessment.

'**Abschaum** *m* scum; *fig. a.* dregs *pl.*

'**abscheiden** *v/t.* separate (*a. Metall*); ⚕ secrete; ⚗ disengage, (*fällen*) precipitate; *v/i.* (sn) depart (*von dieser Welt* this life); *sich* ~ ⚗ be precipitated.

'**abscheren** *s. scheren.*

'**Abscheu** *m* abhorrence, abomination, detestation (*vor dat.* of), disgust (at, for; *gegen* against), horror (of); ~ *haben vor* (*dat.*) abhor, detest, loathe.

'**abscheuern** scour (*od.* scrub) off; (*abnutzen*) wear away *od.* off (*a. sich*); *Haut*: abrade, chafe.

abscheulich [~'ʃɔʏliç] abominable, detestable; ᘯ**keit** *f* abomination.

'**abschicken** send off, dispatch; ✉ post, *Am.* mail.

'**Abschieb|ehaft** ⚖ *f* remand pending deportation; *j-n in* ~ *nehmen* put a p. on remand pending deportation; 'ᘯ**en** *v/t.* shove off; *Ausländer*: deport; ⚔ evacuate; (*loswerden*) get rid of; *v/i.* (sn) F *fig.* push off; '**~ung** ⚖ *f* deportation.

Abschied ['apʃiːt] *m* (3) (*Abreise*) departure; (*~nehmen*) leave-taking, farewell; (*Entlassung*) dismissal; ⚔ discharge, *freiwillig*: resignation; ~ *nehmen* take leave (*von* of), bid farewell (to); ⚔ *s-n* ~ *erhalten* be put on half-pay; *s-n* ~ *nehmen* resign, retire, ⚔ *a.* quit the service; *j-m den* ~ *geben* dismiss (*od.* discharge) a p.; '**~nehmen** *n* leave-taking.

'**Abschieds|besuch** *m* farewell visit; '**~brief** *m* farewell letter; '**~essen** *n* farewell dinner; '**~feier** *f* farewell party; '**~gesuch** *n* resignation; '**~kuß** *m* parting kiss; '**~rede** *f* valedictory (address); '**~schmerz** *m* wrench; '**~szene** *f* farewell scene.

'**abschießen** *Glied*: shoot off; *Schußwaffe*: shoot, fire (off), discharge; *Pfeil*: let fly; *Rakete*: launch; *Wild*: shoot, *j-n*: *a.* pick off; *Flugzeug*: (shoot *od.* bring) down; *fig. s. Vogel*; F *Beamten usw.*: oust.

abschilfern ['~ʃilfərn] (29) peel (*od.* scale) off.

'**ab|schinden** *s. abrackern*; 'ᘯ**schirmdienst** ⚔ *m* counter-intelligence; '**~schirmen** screen; **~schirren** ['~ʃirən] (25) unharness; '**~schlachten** slaughter, butcher.

'**Abschlag** *m Börse*: discount; (*Preisnachlaß*) reduction; *der Preise*: fall in prices; *auf* ~ on account; *Fußball*: goal kick; 'ᘯ**en** *v/t.* beat (*od.* strike) off; *Baum, Kopf*: cut off; *Bitte*: refuse; *Angriff*: repulse; ⊕ take down; *Lager, Zelt*: strike; *Fußball*: (*a. v/i.*) kick off; *Läufer*: leave far behind.

abschlägig ['~ʃlɛːgiç] negative; ~*e Antwort* refusal, denial; ~ *bescheiden* reject, turn down.

'**Abschlagszahlung** *f* part-payment, instal(l)ment.

'**abschleifen** grind off; *fig.* polish, refine; *fig. sich* ~ acquire polish.

'**Abschlepp|dienst** *m* recovery (*Am.* wrecker) service; 'ᘯ**en** drag off; ⚓, *mot.* take in tow, tow off; *sich* ~ struggle under a load; '**~-öse** *f* towing eye; '**~seil** *n* towrope; '**~wagen** *m* break-down lorry, *Am.* wrecker (truck).

'**abschließen** *v/t.* lock (up); (*abdichten*) seal (off); *Angelegenheit*: close, settle; (*vollenden*) complete; *Brief, Rede usw.*: conclude, close; *Rechnung*, ✝ *Bücher*: balance; *Konto*: close; *Vertrag*: conclude, sign; *Versicherung, Verkauf*: effect; (*absondern*) isolate; ✝ *e-n Handel* ~ strike a bargain, close a deal; *e-n Vergleich mit e-m Gläubiger* ~ compound with a creditor; *sich* ~ seclude o.s.; *v/i.* conclude; *mit dem Leben abgeschlossen haben* have done with life; *ich habe mit allem abgeschlossen* I've done with all that; '**~d** concluding; final(ly *adv.*).

'**Abschluß** *m* closing (*a.* ✝ ~ *der Bücher*), settlement; (*Ende*; *a.* ✝ ~ *e-s Geschäfts*) conclusion; (*Geschäft*) deal; (*Verkauf*) sale; '**~prüfung** *f* leaving (*Am.* final) examination.

'**ab|schmelzen** *v/t.* melt off (*a. v/i.* [sn]); '**~schmieren** scribble off; ⊕ grease, lubricate; *v/i.* (sn) ✈ *sl.* crash; 'ᘯ**schmiernippel** *mot. m* grease nipple; 'ᘯ**schmierpresse** *mot.* *f* grease gun; **'~schminken:** *sich* ~ remove one's make-up; F *fig. sich* et. ~ get a th. out of one's head; **'~schmirgeln** *s. schmirgeln*; **'~schnallen** unbuckle.

'abschneiden *v/t.* cut off (*a. fig. Rückzug, Zufuhr usw.*); (*scheren*) clip; *j-m die Ehre* ~ damage a p.'s reputation; *j-m die Möglichkeit* ~ deprive a p. of the chance; *s. Wort*; *v/i. gut, schlecht usw.* ~ come off (*od.* do) well, badly, *etc.*; ♀ *n* (*Leistung*) performance.

'Abschnitt *m* cut; ⩓ segment; ⚔ sector; ⚕ coupon; *im Scheckbuch*: counterfoil, *Am.* stub; *in e-r Schrift*: section, paragraph; *e-r Reise*: leg; (*Zeit*) period.

'ab|schnüren *s. abbinden*; **'~schnurren** rattle off; **'~schöpfen** skim off (*a.* ⚕ *Gewinne*); *Kaufkraft*: absorb; *fig. den Rahm* ~ take the cream off; **~schrägen** ['~ʃrɛ:gən] (25) slope; bevel; **'~schrauben** screw off.

'abschreck|en scare away; *Metall, Eier*: chill; *j-n* ~ *von* deter a p. from; **'~end** deterrent; (*a.* ~ *häßlich*) repulsive; ~*es Beispiel* warning; **'♀ung** *f* deterrence; **'♀ungsmittel** *n* deterrent; **'♀ungs-potential** *n* deterrent potential.

'abschreib|en *v/t.* copy; *Schuld usw., a. fig. j-n*: write off; *Literaturwerk*: *b. s.* plagiarize; *in der Schule*: *b. s.* crib; *v/i.* (*absagen*) send a refusal; **'♀er** *m* copyist; *b. s.* plagiarist; **'♀ung** ⚕ *f* writing-off; write-off; (*Wertminderung*) depreciation; **'♀ungskünstler** F *m* tax fiddler.

'abschreiten pace off; ⚔ *die Front* ~ receive the military hono(u)rs.

'Abschrift *f* copy; *beglaubigte* ~ certified copy; **'♀lich** *adj.* copied; *adv.* by (*od.* as a) copy.

'abschrubben *s. schrubben.*

'abschuften: *sich* ~ drudge.

'abschuppen (*a. sich*) scale (off).

'abschürf|en: *sich die Haut* ~ graze (*od.* chafe) one's skin; **'♀ung** *f* abrasion, graze (*an dat.* on).

'Abschuß *m e-r Schußwaffe*: discharge; *e-r Rakete, e-s Torpedos*: launching; *hunt.* shooting; *e-s Flugzeuges*: downing; *e-s Panzers*: disabling; **'~rampe** *f* launcher, launching pad.

abschüssig ['~ʃysiç] sloping; (*steil*) steep, precipitous.

'ab|schütteln shake off (*a. Verfolger*); *fig. a.* get rid of; **'~schwächen** weaken, diminish (*beide a. sich*); *phot.* reduce; *Sturz*: cushion; *fig.* (*mildern*) mitigate; (*beschönigen*) extenuate; *Ausdruck*: qualify.

'abschweif|en (sn) stray; *fig. a.* digress (*von* from); **'♀ung** *f* digression.

'ab|schwenken *v/i.* (sn) *bsd.* ⚔ wheel off *od.* aside; *fig.* veer off; *v/t.* rinse, wash off; **'~schwören** abjure; (*leugnen*) deny by oath; **'~segeln** (sn) set sail (*nach* for), sail away; **'~segnen** F give one's blessing to.

absehbar ['~ze:ba:r]: *in* ~*er Zeit* in the foreseeable future; *nicht* ~ not to be foreseen.

'absehen *v/t. Gelegenheit*: watch (for); *in der Schule*: crib; *j-m et.* ~ copy a th. from a p.; *Künftiges*: foresee, tell; *es ist kein Ende abzusehen* there is no end in sight; *es abgesehen haben auf* (*acc.*) aim at, have one's eye on; *abgesehen sein auf* (*acc.*) be aimed at; *das war auf mich abgesehen* that was meant for me; *v/i.* ~ *von* refrain from; *s. abgesehen.*

'abseifen (25) soap down.

'abseihen *s. seihen.*

abseilen ['~zaɪlən] (25) (*a. sich*) *mount.* rope down.

'absein F (*erschöpft sein*) be all in.

abseits ['~zaɪts] **1.** *adv.* aside, apart; *Fußball*: offside; ~ *vom Wege* off the road; *fig.* ~ *stehen* stand aloof; **2.** *prp.* (*gen. od. von*) aside from, off; **'♀tor** *n Fußball*: goal scored from an off-side position.

'absend|en send (off), (*bsd.* ⚕) dispatch; (*befördern*) forward; *Brief usw.*: post, *Am.* mail; **'♀er(in** *f*) *m* sender; **'♀ung** *f* sending (off), dispatch(ing).

'absengen singe off.

'Absenker ⚘ *m* (7) layer.

'absetz|bar ⚕ sal(e)able; *Betrag*: deductible; *Beamter*: removable; **'~en** *v/t.* set down, put down, deposit (*a.* ⛏, *a. sich*); *Hut*: put off; *Beamte*: remove; *König*: depose; *Flugzeug*: set down; *Fahrgast*: set down, drop; *Fallschirm-*

truppen: drop; *Betrag*: deduct; *Bucheintrag, Termin*: cancel; *Ware*: dispose of, sell; *typ.* set up (in type); *Wörter*: separate; *von der Tagesordnung, vom Spielplan* ~ take off ...; *sich* ~ ⚔ retreat; *v/i.* break off, stop, pause; F *es wird et.* ~ there will be trouble; ˈ**2ung** *f* deposition; *von Beamten*: removal.

ˈ**absichern** *s. sichern.*

ˈ**Absicht** *f* intention; *a.* ⚖ intent; (*a. böse* ~) design; (*Ziel*) aim, object; *in der* ~ *zu* with intent to, with a view to; ~*en haben auf* (*acc.*) have designs upon; *sich mit der* ~ *tragen, zu inf.* have thoughts of *ger.*; ˈ**2lich** intentional; *adv. a.* on purpose; ˈ**~s-erklärung** *f* declaration of intent.

ˈ**absitzen** *v/i. Reiter*: dismount; *v/t.* sit out; *Strafzeit*: do, serve.

absolut [apzoˈluːt] absolute; ~ *nicht* by no means; **2ion** [~luˈtsjoːn] *f* absolution; **2ismus** [~ˈtismus] *m* absolutism.

Absolv|ent(in *f*) [apzɔlˈvɛnt(in)] *m* (12) school-leaver, *Am.* graduate; **~ˈieren** (*lossprechen*) absolve; *Studien*: complete; *Schule*: get through; *höhere Schule, Hochschule*: graduate from; *Prüfung*: pass.

abˈsonderlich peculiar, odd.

ˈ**absonder|n** separate; *e-n Kranken*: isolate; ⚕ secrete; *sich* ~ seclude o.s.; ˈ**2ung** *f* separation; isolation; seclusion; ⚕ secretion.

absorbieren [~zɔrˈbiːrən] absorb.

ˈ**abspalten** (*a. sich*) split off, separate (*a.* ⚗).

ˈ**abspann|en** *Pferd*: unhitch; ⊕ stay; *s. abgespannt*; ˈ**2ung** *f* (*Erschöpfung*) exhaustion.

ˈ**absparen:** *sich et.* ~ pinch o.s. for a th.

ˈ**abspecken** (25) lose weight.

ˈ**abspeisen** *v/i.* finish dinner; *v/t.* feed; *fig.* fob *a p.* off (*mit leeren Worten* with fair words).

abspenstig [ˈ~ʃpɛnstiç]: ~ *machen* entice away, alienate (*dat.* from); ~ *werden* desert.

ˈ**absperr|en** shut off; *Tür, Haus*: lock; *Straße*: block (off); *durch Polizei*: cordon off; (*abdrehen*) turn off; *Dampf, Strom usw.*: cut off; *sich* ~ shut o.s. off; ˈ**2gitter** *n der Polizei*: crowd barrier; ˈ**2hahn** *m* stop-cock; ˈ**2ung** *f* shutting off; blocking; cordoning off; turning off; cutting off; isolation.

ˈ**abspiegeln** *s. widerspiegeln.*

ˈ**abspielen** ♪ play; *Tonaufnahme*: play back; (*abnützen*) wear out; *sich* ~ *fig.* take place, happen, pass.

ˈ**absplittern** *v/t. u. v/i.* (sn) splinter off.

ˈ**Absprache** *f* arrangement.

ˈ**absprechen:** *j-m et.* ~ deny a p. a th., deprive a p. of a th.; (*regeln*) settle, agree; ˈ**~d** unfavo(u)rable, disparaging, adverse.

ˈ**abspringen** (sn) leap (*od.* jump) off; *mit Fallschirm*: a) jump, parachute, b) *im Notfall*: bail (*od.* bale) out; *Splitter, Glasur usw.*: crack (*od.* chip) off; (*abprallen*) bounce off; ~ (*von e-m Thema*) digress, drop (*a subject*) abruptly; *von e-r Partei usw.*: quit, desert.

ˈ**Absprung** *m* jump; *Sport*: take-off; ˈ**~balken** *m* take-off board.

ˈ**abspulen** wind off, unspool.

ˈ**abspülen** wash off *od.* up; rinse.

ˈ**abstamm|en** (sn): ~ *von* descend from; *gr.* be derived from; ˈ**2ung** *f* descent; birth; *gr.* derivation; *deutscher* ~ of German extraction; ˈ**2ungslehre** *f* theory of evolution.

ˈ**Abstand** *m räumlich, zeitlich, fig.*: distance; (*Zwischenraum*) interval; *fig.* (*Unterschied*) difference; ~ *nehmen von* stand away from, *fig.* refrain *od.* desist from; ~ *halten od. wahren a. fig.* keep one's distance; *mit* ~ *besser* far and away better; *mit* ~ *gewinnen* by a wide margin.

abstatten [ˈ~ʃtatən] make, give; *Besuch*: pay; *Dank*: return, render.

ˈ**abstauben** *v/t.* (25) dust.

ˈ**abstech|en** *v/t.* cut (off); (*töten*) stick, stab; *v/i.* contrast (strongly) (*gegen od. von* with); ˈ**2er** *m* (7) (*Ausflug*) excursion (*a. fig.*), (side-) trip.

ˈ**absteck|en** *Haar*: unpin; *Kleid*: fit, pin; *Grundriß*: trace out; *Gelände*: mark out, *mit Pfählen*: stake out.

ˈ**abstehen** stand at a distance; *Ohren usw.*: stick out; (sn) (*verzichten*) desist (*von* from); (sn) (*schal werden*) get stale; *s. abgestanden*; ˈ**~d** projecting.

ˈ**absteifen** ⊕ stiffen, strut, prop.

ˈ**Absteige** F *f* dosshouse, *Am.* flophouse; ˈ**2n** (sn) descend; *vom Wagen*,

Pferd: alight; *in e-m Wirtshaus*: put up at; *Sport*: go down, be relegated; '**~quartier** *n* (temporary) lodgings; '**~r** *m* (7) *Fußball*: relegated team.

abstell|en put down; ⊕ turn off, stop; *Radio usw.*: switch off; *Telephon*: disconnect; (*parken*) park; ✈ side-track; *Mißstand*: abolish, put an end to; ⚔ detach; *darauf abgestellt sein, zu inf.* be calculated to; '**2gleis** 🚂 *n* siding; '**2tisch** *m* dumb waiter.

'**abstempeln** stamp (*a. fig. als* as).

'**absteppen** stitch, quilt.

'**absterben** (sn) die off; *Glied*: go numb; *Motor*: conk out.

Abstieg ['~ʃti:k] *m* (3) descent; *Sport*: relegation; '**2sbedroht** threatened by relegation.

'**abstimm|en** *v/i.* vote (*über acc.* on); ~ *lassen über* (*acc.*) put to the vote; *v/t. fig.* harmonize (*auf acc.* with), coordinate (with); *zeitlich*: time; ♪, *Radio*: tune (in); ✝ *Bücher*: balance; *Konto*: check off; '**2ung** *f* voting; vote; ballot; tuning; coordination; timing; '**2ungsregler** *m Radio*: tuning control.

abstinen|t [~sti'nɛnt] *allg.* abstemious; *im Alkoholgenuß*: teetotal; **2z** [~ts] *f inv.* (total) abstinence, teetotalism; **2zler** [~tslər] *m* (7), **2zlerin** *f* (16[1]) total abstainer, teetotal(l)er.

'**abstoppen** stop; *Sport*: time, clock.

'**Abstoß** *m Sport*: goal-kick; '**2en** *v/t.* push off; *phys. u. fig.* repel; ⚕ *Gewebe*: reject; *Aktien, Ware*: dispose of; *e-e Schuld*: discharge; (*abnutzen*) wear (away); *sich* ~ get worn; *v/i. Schiff*: push off; *Sport*: make a goal-kick; '**2end** *fig.* repulsive, forbidding; '**~ung** *f* repulsion.

'**abstottern** F pay off bit by bit.

abstrahieren [~stra'hi:rən] abstract.

'**abstrahlen** *Rost etc.*: sandblast; [*Wärme*: emit.]

abstrakt [~'strakt] abstract; **2ion** [~'tsjo:n] *f* abstraction; **2um** *gr.* [~'straktum] *n* abstract noun.

'**abstreichen** *Rechnungsposten usw.*: strike off; (*abhaken*) tick off; *Rasiermesser*: strop; *Schuhe*: wipe; *Schaum usw.*: skim off; *Gebiet*: scour.

'**abstreifen** slip off; *Geweih, Haut*: cast, shed; *fig.* cast off; *Schuhe*: wipe; (*absuchen*) patrol.

'**abstreiten** contest, dispute; *Schuld, Tatsache*: deny.

'**Abstrich** *m beim Schreiben*: down stroke; (*Abzug*) cut; ⚕ *von Mandeln*: swab, *von Gebärmutter*: smear; *e-n ~ machen* take a swab *od.* smear; *fig.* ~*e machen müssen* have to lower one's sights.

abstuf|en ['~ʃtu:fən] (25) (*a. sich*) grad(u)ate; *Farben*: shade off; '**2ung** *f* grad(u)ation; shade.

abstumpfen ['~ʃtumpfən] (25) blunt; ⅍ truncate; *fig. die Sinne*: dull; *Gefühle*: deaden (*a. v/i.*); *sich* ~ get blunted.

'**Absturz** *m* fall, plunge; ✈ crash; (*Abhang*) precipice.

'**abstürzen** (sn) fall *od.* plunge (down); ✈ crash; (*abschüssig sein*) descend steeply.

'**abstützen** △ prop, support.

'**absuchen** search all over, scour, comb; *mit Scheinwerfer, Radar*: sweep, scan.

Absud ['apzu:t] *m* (3) decoction.

absurd [~'zurt] absurd; **2e** [~'zurdə] *n*, **2ität** [~zurdi'tɛ:t] *f* (16) absurdity.

Abszeß [aps'tsɛs] *m* abscess.

Abt [apt] *m* (3[3]) abbot.

'**abtakeln** (29) unrig, dismantle.

'**abtasten** feel; ⚡, *TV* scan; *fig.* probe; *Boxer*: feel out.

'**abtau|en** defrost; '**2vorrichtung** *f* defroster.

Abtei [ap'taɪ] *f* (16) abbey.

Ab'teil 🚂 *n* compartment.

'**abteil|en** divide; *durch e-e Wand*: partition off; '**2ung** *f* division.

Ab'teilung *f e-r Behörde, e-s Kaufhauses*: department; *e-s Krankenhauses*: ward; ⚔ detachment, detail, (*Bataillon*) battalion; *von Arbeitern*: gang; (*Verschlag*) partition; (*Fach*) compartment; (*Abschnitt*) section; **~sleiter** *m* head of department, departmental manager.

'**abtelegraphieren** wire refusal.

'**abtippen** F type out, *Manuskript etc.*: type up.

Äbtissin [ɛp'tisin] *f* (16) abbess.

'**abtön|en** *paint.* tint, tone (down), shade; '**2ung** *f* tint, shading.

'**abtöten** kill (*a. fig. Gefühle*); *Zahnnerv*: deaden.

Abtrag ['~tra:k] *m* (3[3]): ~ *tun* (*dat.*) prejudice, impair, detract from.

'**abtragen** carry off; *Gebäude*: pull down; *Kleid*: wear out; *Schuld*: pay off; (*die Speisen*) ~ clear the table.

abträglich ['~trɛːkliç] detrimental, prejudicial (*dat.* to); *Kritik*: unfavo(u)rable.

'**Abtransport** *m* transportation.

'**abtreib|en** *v/t.* drive off; *Pferd*: jade; (*ein Kind, die Leibesfrucht*) ~ procure abortion; *v/i.* (sn) drift off; '**2ung** *f* ⚕ (⚖ criminal) abortion; *e-e ~ machen lassen* have an abortion; '**2ungsklinik** *f* abortion clinic; '**2ungsparagraph** *m* abortion law(s *pl.*).

'**abtrenn|en** sever; separate; detach; *Genähtes*: rip (off); '**2ung** *f* severance; separation; detachment.

'**abtret|en** *v/t. Schuh*: wear down; *Stufe usw.*: wear out; (*aufgeben*) cede (*a. Gebiet*), *Anspruch*, *Eigentum*: yield, assign, transfer (*alle*: *an acc.* to); *sich die Füße ~* wipe (*od.* scrape) one's shoes; *v/i.* (sn) retire (*vom Amt* from office), resign; *thea.* go off (the stage); '**2er** *m* (7) ⚖ assignor; (*Fußmatte*) doormat; '**2ung** ⚖ *f* cession, transfer.

'**Abtritt** *m* (3) withdrawal; *thea.* exit; *s. Abort*[1].

'**abtrocknen** dry (*sich die Hände* one's hands).

'**abtröpfeln,** '**abtropfen** (sn) drip (*od.* trickle) down *od.* off.

'**Abtropfgestell** *n* dish (*od.* washing-up) rack.

'**abtrudeln** ✈ go into a spin.

abtrünnig ['~tryniç] unfaithful, disloyal; rebellious; *eccl.* apostate; *~ werden s. abfallen*; **2e** ['~gə] *m, f* deserter, renegade; *eccl.* apostate; **2keit** ['~çkaɪt] *f* defection; *eccl.* apostasy.

'**abtun** (*ablegen*) take off, remove; (*töten*) dispatch; (*erledigen*) dispose of, settle; (*von sich weisen*) dismiss (*als untunlich usw.* as); *Gewohnheit*: cast off.

'**abtupfen** mop up; dab (*a.* ⚕).

'**ab-urteilen** try, bring to trial; pass sentence on; *s. verurteilen, aberkennen.*

'**abverdienen** *Schuld*: work off.

'**abverlangen** *s. abfordern.*

'**abwägen** weigh (*a. fig.*).

'**abwälzen** roll off; *fig.* shift (*von sich* from o.s.); *die Schuld von sich ~* clear o.s. of the charge; *die Schuld auf j-n ~* lay the blame on a p.; *die Verantwortung auf e-n anderen ~* shift the responsibility to someone else, F pass the buck to someone else.

'**abwandel|bar** *gr. Hauptwort*: declinable; *Zeitwort*: capable of conjugation; '**~n** modify, vary; *gr.* decline; conjugate.

'**abwander|n** *v/i.* (sn) migrate; drift away; '**2ung** *f* migration; drift; *des Kapitals usw.*: exodus; *von Wissenschaftlern*: brain-drain.

'**Abwandlung** *f* modification; *gr. Hauptwort*: declension; *Zeitwort*: conjugation.

'**Abwärme** *f* waste heat.

'**abwarten** wait (for); *s-e Zeit, e-e Gelegenheit*: bide; *~!* wait and see!; *das bleibt abzuwarten* that remains to be seen; *~de Haltung* wait-and-see attitude.

abwärts ['~vɛrts] down, downward(s); F *mit ihm geht's ~* a) he is going downhill, b) *Greis*: he is on the decline; *damit geht es ~* it is going to the bad; '**2trend** *m* downward trend.

'**Abwasch** *m* (3) washing-up.

'**abwaschen** wash (off); *Geschirr*: wash up; *fig. Schande*: wipe out.

'**Abwaschwasser** *n* dish-water.

'**Abwasser** *n* (7[1]) waste water; sewage; '**~kanal** *m* sewer; '**2n** ✈ take off from water.

'**abwechseln** *v/t. u. v/i.* alternate (*mit ea. od. sich* with each other); (*verschiedenartig sein*) vary (*a. ~ mit den Darbietungen usw.*); *mit j-m ~* take turns with a p.; '**~d** alternate; *adv.* by turns, alternately.

'**Abwechs(e)lung** *f* change; alternation; variation; (*Mannigfaltigkeit*) variety; (*Zerstreuung*) diversion; *~ bringen in* (*acc.*) relieve, liven up; *zur ~* for a change; '**2s-arm** monotonous; '**2sreich** varied; *Leben usw.*: diversified; (*ereignisreich*) eventful; '**2sweise** *adv.* by turns, alternately.

'**Abweg** *m*: *auf ~e geraten* (*führen*) go (lead) astray; **2ig** ['~giç] (*irrig*) erroneous; (*unangebracht*) inept, out of place; (*belanglos*) not to the point, irrelevant.

'**Abwehr** *f* defen|ce, *Am.* -se (*a. Sport*); *e-s Stoßes, e-r Gefahr usw.*: warding off; *e-s Angriffs, e-r Frage*: parrying; (*Verhütung*) prevention; (*Widerstand*) resistance; ⚔ (*~dienst*) counter-espionage service; '**2en** ward off; parry; prevent; *Unglück usw.*: avert; *Angriff*: repulse; *v/i.*

fig. (*ablehnen*) refuse; **'~maßnahme** *f* defence reaction; **'~mechanismus** *m* defence mechanism; **'~re-aktion** *f* defensive reaction (*gegen* to); **'~spieler** *m* defender; **'~stoff** *m biol.* antibody.

'abweich|en *v/i.* (sn) deviate, diverge (*von* from); *fig.* deviate, depart (from), *von der Wahrheit a.*: swerve from; (*verschieden sein*; *in der Meinung*) differ (*von ea.* from one another); vary (*von* from); *Magnetnadel*: decline; **'2ung** *f* deviation, defle|xion, *Am.* -ction; (*Verschiedenheit*) difference; ⚗ divergence; declination; departure (*von e-r Meinung, Regel* from).

'abweis|en reject, refuse; ⚖ dismiss; *Angriff*: repulse; *schroff*: rebuff; (*fortschicken*) turn *a p.* away; **'~end** unfriendly, cool; **'2ung** *f* refusal, rejection; ⚖ dismissal; repulse; rebuff.

'abwend|en turn off; *Unglück*: avert; *sich* ~ turn away (*von* from), *fig. s. abkehren*; **'~ig** *s. abspenstig*; **'2ung** *f* turning off; averting.

'abwerben ⚕ entice away.

'abwerfen cast (*od.* throw) off; *Bomben usw.*: drop; *Reiter*: throw; *Blätter, Geweih, Haut usw.*: shed; *Gewinn*: yield; *Spielkarte*: discard.

'abwert|en devaluate; **'2ung** *f* devaluation.

abwesen|d ['~ve:zənt] absent; *fig.* absent-minded; *die* **2en** those absent; **'2heit** *f* absence; *fig.* absent-mindedness; *durch* ~ *glänzen* be conspicuous by one's absence.

'abwick|eln unroll, wind off; ⚕ *Geschäft*: transact; *Schuld*: liquidate; *Firma*: wind up; (*durchführen*) effect; **'2lung** *f* transaction; winding-up, *Am.* wind-up.

'ab|wiegen weigh out; **'~winken** give a sign of refusal; **'~wirtschaften** *v/i.* get ruined (by mismanagement); **'~wischen** wipe off; **~wracken** ['~vrakən] (25) break up.

Abwurf ['~vurf] *m* dropping.

'abwürgen strangle; *mot.* stall.

'abzahl|en pay off; *in Raten*: pay by instal(l)ments; **'2ung** *f* payment (in full); *in Raten*: payment by (*Am.* on) instal(l)ments; (*Rate*) instal(l)ment; *auf* ~ on the instal(l)ment system (*Am.* plan).

'abzählen *Geld*: count, tell; *Personen usw.*: tell off; *das kann man sich an den Fingern* ~ that's not hard to guess.

'Abzahlungs|geschäft *n* hire-purchase (firm); **'~kauf** *m* hire-purchase.

'abzapfen *Bier usw.*: tap; *Blut*: draw; *j-m Blut* ~ bleed a p.

abzäunen ['~tsɔʏnən] fence off *od.* in.

'Abzehrung *f* emaciation; ⚕ consumption.

'Abzeichen *n* distinguishing mark; *am Anzug usw.*: badge; ✈ marking.

'abzeichnen copy; draw; (*abhaken*) tick off; *sich* ~ appear in outlines; *Gefahr*: loom; *deutlich*: stand out (*gegen den Himmel usw.* against).

'Abziehbild *n* transfer(-picture); ⊕ decalcomania.

'abziehen *v/t.* draw (*od.* pull) off; *Hut*: take off; *Aufmerksamkeit*: divert; *Summe*: deduct, ⚗ subtract; *Bett*: strip; *Bier*: draw; *typ. Bogen*: pull (off); (*vervielfältigen*) mimeograph; *phot.* print; *Bilder*: transfer; *Tier* ~, *e-m Tier das Fell* ~ skin; *Rasiermesser*: strop; (*abhobeln*) plane off; *Schlüssel*: take out; *Wein*: rack (off); *Truppen*: withdraw; *s-e Hand von j-m* ~ withdraw one's support from a p.; *v/i.* (sn) move off, withdraw; *Rauch usw.*: escape; (*schießen*) pull the trigger.

'abzielen: ~ *auf* (*acc.*) aim at.

'abzirkeln (29) measure with compasses; *fig.* be very precise in.

'Abzug *m* withdrawal, departure; *für Wasser usw.*: outlet; *v. Rauch usw.*: escape; *des Gewehrs*: trigger; *e-r Summe*: deduction; (*Rabatt*) rebate, reduction; *phot.* print; *typ.* (galley-)proof; (*Vervielfältigung*) (mimeographed) copy; *nach* ~ *der Kosten* charges deducted; *in* ~ *bringen* deduct.

abzüglich ['~tsy:kliç] *prp.* (*gen. od. acc.*) less, deducting.

'Abzugs|bügel *m am Gewehr usw.*: trigger-guard; **'2fähig** *Betrag*: deductible; **'~haube** *f über dem Herd*: cooker hood; **'~rohr** *n* drain- (*od.* waste-)pipe; escape-pipe.

Abzweig|dose ⚡ ['aptsvaɪk-] *f* distribution (*od.* junction) box; **2en** ['~tsvaɪgən] (25) (*a. sich*) branch off (*a. fig.*); **'2ung** *f* junction, turn-off; ⚡ branch, shunt.

'**abzwicken** nip (*od.* pinch) off.

ach! [ax] ah!, alas!; ~ (*so*)*!* oh (, I see)!; ~ *wo!* not a bit of it!; ~ *was!* nonsense!; *mit* ♀ *u. Krach* barely, by the skin of one's teeth.

Achat [a'xa:t] *m* (3) agate.

'**Achs-antrieb** *mot. m* final drive.

Achse ['aksə] *f* (15) axis; ⊕ axle; *per* ~ ✝ by road, 🚂 by rail; F *auf der* ~ on the move.

Achsel ['aksəl] *f* (15) shoulder; *mit den* ~*n zucken* shrug one's shoulders; *über die* ~ *ansehen* look down upon; *auf die leichte* ~ *nehmen fig.* make light of; '~**höhle** *f* armpit; '~**zucken** *n* shrug (of one's shoulders).

acht[1] [axt] eight; *heute in* ~ *Tagen* today week; *vor* ~ *Tagen* a week ago; *alle* ~ *Tage* every other week.

Acht[2] *f* (16) **1.** (*Obacht*) *außer* ♀ *lassen* disregard; *in* ♀ *nehmen* take care of; *sich in* ♀ *nehmen* take care, beware (*vor dat.* of); **2.** (*Bann*) ban, outlawry; *in die* ~ *erklären* outlaw.

'**achtbar** respectable, reputable; '♀**keit** *f* respectability.

'**achte** eighth.

'**Acht-eck** *n* (3) octagon; '♀**ig** octagonal.

'**Achtel** *n* (7) eighth (part); '~**note** ♪ *f* quaver; '~**takt** ♪ *m* quaver time.

'**achten** (26) *v/t.* respect; (*schätzen*) esteem; *v/i.* ~ *auf* (*acc.*) *s. achtgeben.*

ächten ['ɛçtən] (26) outlaw, proscribe; *gesellschaftlich*: ostracise.

achtens ['axtəns] eighthly.

'**achter**[1] ⚓ aft.

'**Achter**[2] *m* (7) *a. Rudern*: eight; '~**bahn** *f* switchback, *Am.* roller coaster; '~**deck** ⚓ *n* quarterdeck; '♀**lei** of eight kinds; '~**steven** ⚓ *m* stern-post.

achtfach ['~fax] eightfold.

'**achtgeben** pay attention (*auf acc.* to), attend (to); (*sich et. merken*) mark, mind (*auf acc. a th.*); (*sorgen für*) take care (*auf acc.* of; *daß* that); ~ *auf* (*acc.*) (*beobachten*) watch; *gib acht!* look (*Am.* watch) out!

'**achtjährig** eight years old, *attr.* eight-year-old.

'**achtlos** careless, unmindful; '♀**igkeit** *f* carelessness.

'**achtmal** eight times.

'**Achtmi'nutentakt** *teleph. m* eight-minute limit.

'**achtsam** careful, mindful (*auf acc.* of); '♀**keit** *f* carefulness.

'**Acht**|'**stundentag** *m* eight-hour day; ♀**stündig** ['~ʃtyndiç] eight-hour; ♀**tägig** ['~tɛ:giç] lasting a week, a week's *trip, etc.*

Achtung ['axtuŋ] *f* esteem, regard, respect (*vor dat.* for); (*Aufmerksamkeit*) attention; ~*!* look out!, *Am.* watch out!; ⚔ attention!; ~*! Lebensgefahr!* Caution! Danger of death!; ~, *Stufe!* mind the step!; *j-m* ~ *bezeigen* pay respect to a p.; (*j-m*) ~ *einflößen* command (a p.'s) respect; *sich* ~ *verschaffen* make o.s. respected; *alle* ~ (*vor*)*!* hats off (to)! '~**s-erfolg** *m* succès d'estime (*fr.*); '♀**svoll** respectful.

Ächtung ['ɛçtuŋ] *f* proscription.

'**achtzehn** eighteen; '~**te** eighteenth.

achtzig ['axtsiç] eighty; *in den* ~*er Jahren* in the eighties; *j-n auf* ~ *bringen* get a p. hopping mad; ♀**er** ['~gər] *m*, ~**jährig** ['~çjɛ:riç] octogenarian; '~**ste** eightieth.

'**Achtzylinder** *mot. m* eight-cylinder car.

ächzen ['ɛçtsən] (27) groan; ♀ *n* groan(s *pl.*).

Acker ['akər] *m* (7[1]) field, land; (*Boden*) soil; (*Maß*) acre; '~**bau** *m* (3, *o. pl.*) agriculture, farming; '~**bauer** *m* husbandman, farmer; '♀**bautreibend** agricultural; '~**gaul** *m* farm-horse; '~**gerät** *n* agricultural implements *pl.*; '~**land** *n* arable land; *bestelltes*: tilled (*od.* cultivated) land; '♀**n** (29) *v/t. u. v/i.* plough, *Am.* plow, till; *fig.* toil, drudge; '~**salat** ⚘ *m* lamb's lettuce.

Acryl|**farbe** [a'kryl-] *f* acrylic paint; ~**glas** *n* acrylic glass.

ad absurdum [at ap'zurdum]: ~ *führen* reduce to absurdity.

ad acta [at 'akta]: ~ *legen* file away; *fig.* shelve, *Am.* table *a matter.*

Adam ['a:dam] *m*: *den alten* ~ *ausziehen* cast off the old Adam; *nach* ~ *Riese* according to Spoker.

'**Adams**|**apfel** *m anat.* Adam's apple; *im* '~**kostüm** (*n*) in one's buff, sky-clad.

addier|**en** [a'di:rən] add, sum up; ♀**maschine** *f* adding machine.

Addition [adi'tsjo:n] *f* (16) addition.

ade [a'de:] *s. adieu.*

Adel ['a:dəl] *m* (7, *o. pl.*) nobility; *von* ~ *sein* be of noble birth.

ad(e)lig ['ɑ:d(ə)liç] noble, titled; **ꝰe(r)** ['~ligər] *m* nobleman, aristocrat; '**ꝰe** *f* noblewoman; *die ~n pl.* the nobility.
'**adeln** (29) ennoble (*a. fig.*); *Brt.* knight.
'**Adels|krone** *f* coronet; '**~stand** *m* nobility; *Brt.* peerage; *in den ~ erheben* knight.
Ader ['ɑ:dər] *f* (15) vein (*a.* ⚒, ⚘, *im Holz, Marmor usw. u. fig.*); (*Schlag*ꝰ) artery; *zur ~ lassen* bleed; '**~laß** *m* (4^2) blood-letting (*a. fig.*).
ädern ['ɛ:dərn] (29) vein.
adieu [a'djø:] **1.** *int.* farewell, good-by(e); **2.** ꝰ *n* farewell, adieu.
Adjektiv ['atjɛkti:f] *n* (3^1) adjective; **ꝰisch** [~'ti:viʃ] adjectival.
Adjutant [atju'tant] *m* (12) adjutant; *e-s Generals*: aide(-de-camp).
Adler ['ɑ:dlər] *m* (7) eagle; '**~-auge** *n* eagle eye; *~n haben* be eagle-eyed; '**~horst** *m* aerie; '**~nase** *f* aquiline nose.
Admiral [atmi'rɑ:l] *m* (3^1) admiral; **~ität** [~rali'tɛ:t] *f* admiralty; **~stab** [~'rɑ:lʃtɑ:p] *m* naval staff.
adopt|ieren [adɔp'ti:rən] adopt; **ꝰion** [~'tsjo:n] *f* adoption.
Adoptiv... [~'ti:f] adoptive.
Adressat [adrɛ'sɑ:t] *m* (12) addressee; *e-r Warensendung*: consignee; *e-s Wechsels*: drawee; **~engruppe** *f* target group.
A'dreßbuch *n* directory.
Adresse [a'drɛsə] *f* (15) address, direction; *falsche ~* misdirection; *s. per*; *fig. an die falsche ~ geraten* come to the wrong shop, *weitS.* catch a Tartar.
A'dressenkartei *f* mailing list.
A'dreß-etikett *n* address label.
adres'sieren address, direct; ✝ consign; *falsch ~* misdirect.
Adres'siermaschine *f* addressograph.
adrett [a'drɛt] smart.
adsorbieren [atzɔr'bi:rən] ⚗ adsorb.
Advent [at'vɛnt] *m* (3) Advent; **~skranz** *m* Advent wreath; **~(s)zeit** *f* Advent season.
Adverb [at'vɛrp] *n* (8^2) adverb; **ꝰial** [~vɛr'bjɑ:l] adverbial.
Advokat [atvo'kɑ:t] *m* (12) advocate; *s. Anwalt.*
Aerobic [ɛ'rɔbik] *n* (11^1) *Sport*: aerobics *pl.*

aerodynamisch [aerody'nɑ:miʃ] aerodynamic.
Aerogramm ✉ [aero'gram] *n* (3^1) air letter.
Affäre [a'fɛ:rə] *f* (15) (*a. Liebes*ꝰ) affair; *sich aus der ~ ziehen* wriggle out, *gut*: master the situation.
Affe ['afə] *m* (13) ape, *bsd. kleiner*: monkey; ⚔ *sl.* (*Tornister*) pack; F silly ass; F *e-n ~n haben* be drunk.
Affekt [a'fɛkt] *m* (3) emotion, passion; **~handlung** ⚖ *f* act committed in the heat of passion; **ꝰiert** [~'ti:rt] affected; **~iertheit** *f* affectation.
äffen ['ɛfən] *v/t.* (25) ape; (*necken*) mock; (*täuschen*) fool.
'**affen|-artig** simian; F *mit ~er Geschwindigkeit* like a greased lightning; '**ꝰliebe** *f* doting love; '**ꝰschande** F *f* crying shame; '**ꝰtheater** *n fig.* utter farce; *weitS.* crazy business; '**ꝰzahn** F *m*: *der hat e-n ~ drauf!* he's going some lick!
affig ['afiç] F silly.
Äffin ['ɛfin] *f* (16) she-ape, she-monkey.
Afrikan|er [afri'kɑ:nər] *m* (7), **~erin** *f*, **ꝰisch** African.
After *anat.* ['aftər] *m* (7) anus; '**~kritik** *f* pseudo-criticism; '**~mieter(in** *f*) *m* subtenant; '**~rede** *f*, '**ꝰreden** slander.
ägäisch [ɛ:'gɛ:iʃ]: *ꝰes Meer* Aegean Sea.
Agent [a'gɛnt] *m* (12), **~in** *f* (16^1) ✝ *u. pol.* agent; **~enring** *m* spy ring; **~ur** [~'tu:r] *f* (16) agency.
Aggregat [agre'gɑ:t] *n phys.* aggregate; ⊕ set (of machines), unit; **~zustand** *m* (physical) state.
Aggression [agrɛ'sjo:n] *f pol. u. psych.* aggression.
aggressiv [~'si:f] aggressive; **ꝰi'tät** [~sivi'tɛ:t] *f* (16) aggressiveness.
Ägide [ɛ:'gi:də] *f*: *unter der ~* (*gen.*) under the auspices of.
agieren [a'gi:rən] act, function.
agil [a'gi:l] agile.
Agio ['ɑ:ʒio:] *n* (11) agio, premium; **~tage** [~'tɑ:ʒə] *f* stock-jobbing.
Agitation [agita'tsjo:n] *f* agitation.
Agitator [~'tɑ:tɔr] *m* (8^1) agitator.
agitatorisch [~ta'to:riʃ] fomenting, demagogical.
agi'tieren agitate.
Agraffe [a'grafə] *f* (15) brooch, clasp.

A'grar|minister *m* Minister (*Am.* Secretary) of Agriculture; **~staat** *m* agrarian state.

Ägypt|er [ɛ'gyptər] *m* (7), **~erin** *f* (16¹), **⁓isch** Egyptian.

ah! [ɑː] ah!; **äh!** [ɛ(ː)] *Ekel*: ugh!; *stotternd*: er!; **aha!** [a'hɑː] aha!, I see!

A'ha-Erlebnis *n* sudden insight; *Psychologie*: aha-experience.

Ahle ['ɑːle] *f* (15) awl, pricker.

Ahn [ɑːn] *m* (5 *u.* 12) ancestor, forefather (*a.* '**~herr** *m*); '**~e** *f* (15) ancestress (*a.* '**~frau** *f*).

ahnd|en ['ɑːndən] (26) (*rächen*) avenge; (*strafen*) punish; '**⁓ung** *f* revenge; punishment.

ähneln ['ɛːnəln] (26) (*dat.*) be (*od.* look) like, resemble.

ahnen ['ɑːnən] (25) have a presentiment (*Am.* F hunch) of (*od.* that ...); (*erfassen*; *erraten*) divine; (*vorhersehen*) foresee, anticipate; (*spüren*) sense; (*argwöhnen*) suspect; *et. ~ lassen* foreshadow, *weitS.* give an idea of; *nichts ~d s. ahnungslos.*

'**Ahnen|forschung** *f* ancestry research; '**~tafel** *f* genealogical table.

ähnlich ['ɛːnliç] (*dat.*) like, resembling; *bsd. v. Dingen u.* ⩘ similar (to); *j-m ~ sehen* look like a p.; *iro. das sieht ihm ~* that's just like him; '**⁓keit** *f* likeness, resemblance; similarity.

Ahnung ['ɑːnuŋ] *f* presentiment, *Am.* F hunch; *bsd. v. Unheil*: foreboding, misgiving; (*Argwohn*) suspicion; F *keine ~!* no idea!; F *keine ~ haben von* have not the slightest notion (*od.* idea) of; '**⁓slos** unsuspecting; '**⁓svoll** full of misgivings.

Ahorn ['ɑːhɔrn] *m* (3) maple.

Ähre ['ɛːrə] *f* (15) ear; *Blume*: spike; *Gras*: head; *~n lesen* glean.

Ais ♪ ['ɑːˀis] *n* A sharp.

Akademie [akade'miː] *f* (15) academy.

Akademiker [~'deːmikər] *m* (7) (*Studierter*) university-bred man, *Am.* (university) graduate; *im freien Beruf*: professional man; (*Mitglied e-r Akademie*) academician.

aka'demisch academic; *~ gebildet* university-trained *od.* -bred.

Akazie [a'kɑːtsjə] *f* (15) acacia.

akklimatisier|en [aklimati'ziːrən] acclimatize, *Am.* acclimate; *sich ~* become acclimatized; **⁓ung** *f* acclimatization, *Am.* acclimation.

Akkord [a'kɔrt] *m* (3) ♪ chord; ⚕ (*Vereinbarung*) contract; ⚕ (*Vergleich*) composition; *auf ~, im ~* by the piece (*od.* job); **~-arbeit** *f* piece-work; **~-arbeiter(in** *f*) *m* piece-worker.

Ak'kordeon [~deɔn] *n* (11) accordion.

akkor'dieren *v/t.* arrange; *v/i.* agree, compromise (*mit* with; *über acc.* upon); ⚕ arrange, compound (*mit* with; *wegen* for).

Ak'kordlohn *m* piece wages *pl.*

akkredit|ieren [akredi'tiːrən] accredit (*bei* to); ⚕ open a credit for; **⁓iv** [~'tiːf] *n* (3¹) ⚕ letter of credit; *j-m ein ~ eröffnen* open a credit in favo(u)r of a p.

Akku F ['aku] *m* (11), **~mulator** [~mu'lɑːtɔr] *m* (18¹) accumulator, storage battery.

akkurat [~'rɑːt] accurate.

Akkusativ *gr.* ['akuzatiːf] *m* (3¹) accusative (case); '**~objekt** *n* direct object.

Akne ['aknə] ⚕ *f* (15) acne.

Akontozahlung [a'kɔntotsɑːluŋ] *f* payment on account.

Akquisiteur ⚕ [akvizi'tøːr] *m* canvasser, agent.

Akrib|ie [akri'biː] *f* (15, *o. pl.*) scientific precision, meticulosity; **⁓isch** [a'kriːbiʃ] meticulous.

Akrobat [akro'bɑːt] *m* (12), **~in** *f* acrobat; **~ik** *f* acrobatics *pl.*; **⁓isch** acrobatic.

Akt [akt] *m* (3) act(ion); *thea.* act; ⚖, ⚕ *s. Aktenstück*; *paint.* nude; *~ der Verzweiflung* desperate deed.

Akte ['aktə] *f* (15) *s. Aktenstück.*

'**Akten** *pl.* records, papers, deeds, documents; *abgelegte*: files; *Notiz*: *zu den ~* to be filed; *zu den ~ legen s. ad acta*; '**~deckel** *m* folder; '**~klammer** *f* paper-clip; '**⁓kundig** on record; '**~mappe** *f*, '**~tasche** *f* document-case, portfolio, brief-case; '**⁓mäßig** documentary; *~ festlegen* put on record; '**~mensch** *m* red-tapist; '**~notiz** *f* memo (-randum); *sich von et. e-e ~ machen* write a memo about a th.; '**~-ordner** *m* file; '**~stück** *n einzelnes*: document; (*Aktenband*) file; '**~zeichen** *n* reference (*od.* file) number.

Akteur [ak'tø:r] *m* (3[1]) *thea. u. fig.* actor.

Aktie ['aktsjə] *f* (15) share, *Am.* stock; *~n besitzen* hold shares (*Am.* stock); *s-e ~n sind gestiegen* (*a. fig.*) his stock has gone up; '**~nbesitz** *m* (share, *Am.* stock) holdings *pl.*; '**~ngesellschaft** *f* joint-stock company, *Am.* (stock-)corporation; '**~n-inhaber(in** *f*) *m* shareholder, *bsd. Am.* stockholder; '**~nkapital** *n* share capital, *Am.* capital stock; '**~n-unternehmen** *n* joint-stock undertaking.

Aktion [ak'tsjo:n] *f* (16) action; (*Werbungs*2 *usw.*) drive, campaign; *polizeiliche ~* police raid; *in ~ treten* take action; **~är** [~'nɛ:r] *m* (3[1]), **~ärin** *f* (16[1]) *s. Aktieninhaber*; **~sradius** [~'tsjo:nsrɑ:djus] *m* radius of action, range (*a. fig.*).

aktiv [ak'ti:f] active; *Bilanz*: favo(u)rable; ⚔ regular; *~es Wahlrecht* franchise; *~er Wortschatz* using vocabulary.

Aktiv *gr.* ['akti:f] *n* (3[1]) active voice; **~a** ⚕ [~'ti:va] *n/pl.* assets, *Am. a.* resources; **~handel** [~'ti:f-] *m* active trade; 2**ieren** [~ti'vi:rən] activate; **~ist** [~ti'vist] *m* (12) activist; **~kohle** [~'ti:f-] *f* activated carbon; '**~posten** *m* asset; **~-urlaub** [~'ti:f-] *m* sporting holiday.

'**Aktstudie** *f* study from the nude.

aktuell [aktu'ɛl] current, up-to--date, topical, present-day; *Problem usw.*: acute.

Akupunktur [akupuŋk'tu:r] ⚕ *f* (16[2]) acupuncture.

Akust|ik [a'kustik] *f* (16, *o. pl.*) acoustics; 2**isch** acoustic.

akut [a'ku:t] ⚕ *u. fig.* acute.

Akzent [~'tsɛnt] *m* (3) accent; (*Betonung*) *a.* stress.

akzentuieren [~tu'i:rən] accent; *bsd. fig.* accentuate, stress.

Ak'zentverschiebung *f* shift of emphasis.

Akzept [~'tsɛpt] ⚕ *n* (3) acceptance; **~ant** [~'tant] *m* (12) acceptor; 2**ieren** [~'ti:rən] accept; **~ierung** [~'ti:ruŋ] *f* acceptance.

Akzise [~'tsi:zə] *f* (15) excise.

Alabaster [ala'bastər] *m* (7), 2**n** alabaster.

Alarm [a'larm] *m* (3[1]) alarm; *s. Flieger*2; *~ blasen, schlagen* ⚔ sound (*fig.* give) the alarm; **~-anlage** *f* alarm system; 2**bereit** in constant readiness; on the alert; **~bereitschaft** *f*: *in ~* on the alert; **~glocke** *f* alarm-bell; 2**ieren** [~'mi:rən] alarm (*a. fig.*); ⚔, *die Polizei*: alert; **~zone** *f* alert zone; **~zustand** *m* alert; *in den ~ versetzen* put on the alert.

Alaun ⚗ [a'laun] *m* (3[1]) alum; **~-erde** *f* alumina.

albern ['albərn] silly, foolish; '2**heit** *f* foolishness, silliness.

Album ['album] *n* (9 *u.* 11) album.

Alchim|ie [alçi'mi:] *f* (15) alchemy; **~ist** [~'mist] *m* (12) alchemist.

Alge ['algə] *f* (15) seaweed, alga.

Algebra ['algebra] *f* (15, *o. pl.*) algebra.

algebra·isch [~'brɑ:-] algebraic(al).

Alibi ⚖ ['ɑ:libi] *n* (2) alibi.

Aliment [ali'mɛnt] *n, mst ~e n/pl.* (3) alimony.

alkalisch ⚗ [al'kɑ:liʃ] alcaline.

Alkohol ['alkohol] *m* (3[1]) alcohol; '2**frei** non-alcoholic, F *bsd. Am.* soft; *~es Gasthaus* temperance hotel; '**~gehalt** *m* alcoholic strength; **~iker** [~'ho:likər] *m* alcoholic; 2**isch** [~'ho:liʃ] alcoholic; *~es Getränk* alcoholic (*Am.* hard) liquor; 2**i'sieren** alcoholize; '**~mißbrauch** *m* excessive drinking; '**~schmuggler** *m* liquor-smuggler, *Am.* bootlegger; '2**süchtig** alcoholic; '**~test** *m* breathalyzer; *j-n e-m ~ unterziehen* give a p. a breathalyzer; '**~verbot** *n* prohibition; '**~vergiftung** *f* alcoholic poisoning.

Alkoven [al'ko:vən] *m* (16) alcove.

all [al] **1.** *indef. pron.* all; (*jeder*) every; (*jeder beliebige*) any; *sie ~e* all of them; *~e beide* both of them; *~ und jeder* all and sundry; *~es aussteigen!* all change, please!; *auf ~e Fälle* in any case, at all events; *~e Tage* every day; *~es in ~em* on the whole; *vor ~em* above (*od.* first of) all; *~e zwei Minuten* every two minutes; F *hast du sie noch ~e?* have you gone mad?; **2.** *su. das* **All** the universe.

'**all'-abendlich** every evening.

'**allbe'kannt** notorious.

'**alle** all gone, at an end; *Geld*: all spent; *~ machen* finish.

Allee [a'le:] *f* (15) avenue, *schmale*: (tree-lined) walk.

Allegorie [alego'ri:] *f* allegory.

allegorisch [~'go:riʃ] allegoric(al).

allein [a'laın] **1.** *pred. adj.* alone,

(*ohne Hilfe a.*) single-handed, by o.s.; **2.** *adv.* alone, only; (*ausschließlich*) exclusively; **3.** *cj.* only, yet, but, however; **2besitz** *m* exclusive possession; **2-erbe** *m*, **2-erbin** *f* sole (*od.* universal) heir(ess *f*); **2gang** *m Sport*: solo attempt; *fig.* e-n ~ machen go it alone; **2herrschaft** *f* absolute monarchy, autocracy; **2-herrscher(in** *f*) *m* absolute monarch, autocrat; **~ig** (*einzig*) only; (*ausschließlich*) sole, exclusive; **2-inhaber(in** *f*) *m* sole owner; **2sein** *n* loneliness; being alone; **~'seligmachend** *the* true (Glaube faith, Kirche church); **~stehend** *P.*: alone (in the world); (*unverheiratet*) single; *Gebäude usw.*: isolated, detached; **2-unterhalter** *m* (7) solo entertainer; **2verkauf** *m* exclusive sale, monopoly; **2vertreter** ⚘ *m* sole agent *od.* distributor; **2vertretung** *f* sole agency; **2vertrieb** *m* sole distribution.

'alle'mal always, every time; ~! F any time!, ein für ~ once (and) for all.

'allen'falls (*zur Not*) if need be; (*vielleicht*) possibly, perhaps; (*höchstens*) at best.

allenthalben ['alənt'halbən] everywhere.

'aller... ... of all; *bsd. im Titel*: most ...; **'~best** best of all, very best; aufs ~e in the best possible manner; **~'dings** (*dennoch*) nevertheless; (*in der Tat*) indeed; (*auf jeden Fall*) at any rate; (*freilich*) it is true; (*ich muß zugeben*) to be sure; ~! certainly!, *Am.* F sure!; **'~-erst** (*a.* zu ~) first of all; **'~'hand** of all kinds *od.* sorts, various; F das ist ja ~! I say!; **2'heiligen(fest)** *n* All Saints' Day; **2'heiligste** *n* Holy of Holies; **~'höchst** highest of all; **'~höchstens** *adv.* at the very most; **~'lei** *s.* allerhand; miscellaneous; **2'lei** *n* medley; **~'letzt** last of all (*a.* zu ~), very last; **~'liebst** dearest of all; most lovely, sweet; am ~en möchte ich I should like best of all; **~'meist** most; am ~en most(ly); (*besonders*) chiefly; **~'nächst** very next; **~'neu(e)st** the very latest *od.* newest; ~e Ausgabe! (*Zeitung*) latest edition.

Allerg|ie [alɛr'giː] ⚕ *f* (15) allergy; **2isch** [a'lɛrgiʃ] allergic (für, gegen to).

Aller|'seelen *n* All Souls' Day; **2seits** ['~'zaɪts] on all sides; universally; to all (of you); **~-'weltskerl** *m* devil of a fellow; **2wenigst** [~'veːniçst] least of all; **~'werteste** F *m* posterior, rear.

'alle'samt all of them, all together.

'Alles|kleber *m* all-purpose glue; **'~schneider** *m* food slicer.

'allezeit always, at all times.

'All|'gegenwart *f* omnipresence, ubiquity; **'2'gegenwärtig** omnipresent, ubiquitous; **'2ge'mein** general; common; universal; ~e Redensarten *pl.* generalities; im ~en in general, generally; *s.* Wehrpflicht; **'~ge'meinbildung** *f* general education; **'2ge'meingültig** generally accepted; **~ge'meinheit** *f* generality, universality; (*Öffentlichkeit*) general public; **~ge'meinmedizin** *f* general medicine; Arzt für ~ general practitioner; **'2ge'waltig** all-powerful; **~'heilmittel** *n* panacea, cure-all (*a. fig.*).

Allianz [ali'ants] *f* (16) alliance.

alli'-ier|en *v/refl.* ally o.s. (mit to, with); **2te** *m* ally.

'all|'jährlich annual, yearly; *adv. a.* every year; **'2macht** *f* omnipotence; **~'mächtig** omnipotent, almighty; **~mählich** [~'mɛːliç] gradual; *adv. a.* by degrees; **'~-'nächtlich** every night.

Allopath [alo'pɑːt] *m* allopathist; **~ie** [~pa'tiː] *f* allopathy; **2isch** [~'pɑːtiʃ] allopathic.

'Allrad|-antrieb *mot. m* four-wheel drive; **'~lenkung** *f* all-wheel steering.

Allroundman [ɔːl'raʊndmən] *m* all-rounder.

all|seitig ['~zaɪtiç] universal; *Am.* all-round; **'2strom...** *Radio*: AC-DC... (alternating current-direct current); **'2tag(sleben** *n*) *m* everyday life; **~-'täglich** daily; *fig.* everyday, common, trivial; **2'täglichkeit** *f* commonness, triviality; **'2tags...** common(place), everyday; **'~umfassend** all-embracing; **2'wetter...** all-weather; **~'wissend** omniscient; **2-'wissenheit** *f* omniscience; **~'wöchentlich** weekly; **'~zu** (much) too; **~zu'viel** too much, overmuch; ~ ist ungesund enough is as good as a feast; **'2zweck...** all-purpose..., all-duty...

Alm [alm] *f* (16) Alpine pasture, alp.

Almanach ['almanax] *m* (3[1]) almanac.

Almosen ['~mo:zən] *n* (6) alms, charity; '**~büchse** *f* poor-box; '**~-empfänger(in** *f*) *m* pauper.

Alp [alp] *m* (3), '**~drücken** *n* (*haben* have a) nightmare.

Alpen ['alpən] *pl.* Alps; '**~glühen** *n* alp-glow; '**~rose** *f* Alpine rose; '**~veilchen** *n* cyclamen; '**~ver-ein** *m* Alpine Club; '**~vorland** *n* foothills *pl.* of the Alps.

Alphabet [alfa'be:t] *n* (3) alphabet; **≗isch** alphabetical.

alphanumerisch [alfanu'me:riʃ] alphanumeric.

alpin [al'pi:n] Alpine.

Alpi'nis|t(in *f*) *m* Alpinist; **~mus** *m* (16, *o. pl.*) mountaineering.

Alraun ⚘ [al'raun] *m* (3), **~e** *f* (15) mandrake.

als [als] *nach comp.*: than; (*ganz so wie*) as, like; (*in der Eigenschaft* ~) as; (*statt*) for; *nach Negation*: but, except; *zeitlich*: when, as; *s. ob*; ~ *Geschenk* for a present; *er starb* ~ *Bettler* he died a beggar; *schon* ~ *Kind* when only a child; *er bot zu wenig*, ~ *daß ich es hätte annehmen können* he offered too little for me to accept it; **~'bald** immediately, forthwith; **~'dann** then.

also ['alzo:] *adv.* thus, so; *cj.* therefore, consequently; *na* ~! there you are!; *es ist* ~ *wahr?* it is true then?

alt[1] [alt] old; (*Ggs. modern*) ancient, antique; (*Ggs. frisch*) stale; (*schon gebraucht, z. B. Kleider*) second-hand; *~e Sprachen* ancient languages, classics; *wie* ~ *bist du?* how old are you?, what is your age?; *es bleibt alles beim ~en* everything stands as it was.

Alt[2] ♪ *m* (3) alto.

Altan [al'tɑ:n] *m* (3[1]) balcony.

Altar [al'tɑ:r] *m* (3[1] *u.* 3[3]) altar; **~blatt** *n*, **~gemälde** *n* altar-piece.

'**alt|backen** stale; '**≗bau** *m* old building; '**≗bausanierung** *f* redevelopment of old buildings; '**~bekannt** well-known; '**~bewährt** well-tried; '**~deutsch** Old German; **~'-ehrwürdig** time-hono(u)red; '**≗-eisen** *n* scrap iron.

'**Alte** *m* (18) old man; ~ *f* old woman; F *der* ~ (*Vater*) the old man, (*Chef*) the boss; F *m-e* ~ my old lady; *die ~n pl.* the old; *hist.* the ancients; *das* ~ *n* old things *pl.*; *etwas ~s* an old thing; '**~nheim** *n* old people's home, rest-home; '**~npflegeheim** *n* geriatric care cent|re, *Am.* -er; '**~nteil** *n*: *fig. sich aufs* ~ *zurückziehen* retire.

Alter ['altər] *n* (7) age; (*Greisen≗*) old age; (*Dienst≗*) seniority; *im* ~ *von 20 Jahren* at an age of 20 years; *von ≗s her* of old, from ancient times; *er ist in meinem* ~ he is my age; *von mittlerem* ~ middle-aged.

älter ['ɛltər] older; *der ~e Bruder* the elder brother; *e-e ~e Dame* an elderly lady; *er ist* (*3 Jahre*) ~ *als ich* he is my senior (by 3 years); *er sieht* (*20 Jahre*) ~ *aus, als er ist* he looks (20 years) more than his age.

'**altern** (29) (h. *u.* sn) grow old, (*a.* ⊕) age.

alternativ [altɛrna'ti:f] alternative; **≗e** [~'ti:və] *f* (15) alternative.

'**Alters|-erscheinung** *f* symptom of old age; '**~genosse** *m*, '**~genossin** *f* contemporary; '**~grenze** *f* age-limit; *für Beamte*: retirement age; *flexible* ~ flexible retirement age; '**~gründe** *m/pl.*: *aus ~n* for reasons of age; '**~gruppe** *f* age-group (*od.* -bracket); '**~heim** *n* old people's home; '**~klasse** *f* age group; '**~rente** *f* old-age pension; '**≗schwach** decrepit; '**~schwäche** *f* senile decay, decrepitude; '**~sitz** *m*: *s-n* ~ *in Berchtesgaden nehmen* spend one's retirement in Berchtesgaden; '**~stufe** *f* stage of life; *s. Altersklasse*; '**~versorgung** *f* old-age pension (scheme).

'**Altertum** *n* (1[2]) antiquity; '**~sforscher** *m* arch(a)eologist; '**~skunde** *f* arch(a)eology.

altertümlich ['~ty:mliç] ancient, antique; (*veraltet*) archaic, antiquated.

ältest ['ɛltəst] oldest; *in der Reihenfolge*: eldest; '**≗e** *m* elder, senior; *mein ~r* my eldest son.

'**alt|'hergebracht** [~gəbraxt] traditional; time-hono(u)red; '**~hochdeutsch** Old High German.

Altist(in *f*) [al'tist] *m* (12) alto (-singer).

'**alt|jüngferlich** old-maidish; '**~klug** precocious.

ältlich ['ɛltliç] elderly, oldish.

'**Alt|material** *n* junk, scrap; '**~meister** *m* past master; *Sport*:

ex-champion; '~metall *n* scrap metal; '2modisch old-fashioned; '~-öl *n* waste oil; '~papier *n* waste paper; '~philologe *m* classical philologist; '~reifen *m* old tyre (*Am.* tire); '2sprachlich classical; '~stadt *f* old town, city; '~stimme *f* alto (voice); 2väterisch ['~fɛːtəriʃ] *s. altmodisch*; '~warenhändler(in *f*) *m* second-hand dealer; ~'weibersommer *m* Indian summer; (*Sommerfäden*) gossamer.

Alufolie ['ɑːlufoːliə] *f* aluminium (*Am.* aluminum) foil, tin foil.

Aluminium [alu'miːnjum] *n* (9, *o. pl.*) aluminium, *Am.* aluminum.

am [am] = *an dem, s. an.*

amalgamieren ⚗ [amalga'miːrən] amalgamate (*a. fig.*).

Amateur [ama'tøːr] *m* (3[1]) amateur; ~photograph *m* amateur photographer.

Amazone [~'tsoːnə] *f* (15) Amazon.

ambitioniert [ambitsjo'niːrt] ambitious.

Amboß ['ambɔs] *m* (4) anvil.

Ambra ['ambra] *f* (16, *o. pl.*) amber; *graue* ~ ambergris.

ambulan|t [ambu'lant] out-patient (*a. su.* = ~ *behandelter Patient*); ~es *Gewerbe* itinerant trade; 2z [~ts] *f* (16) (*Klinik*) out-patient department; (*Wagen*) ambulance.

Ameise ['ɑːmaɪzə] *f* (15) ant; '~nbär *m* ant-eater; '~-ei *n* ant's egg; '~nhaufen *m* ant-hill; '~nnest *n* ants' nest; '~nplage *f* plague of ants; '~nsäure ⚗ *f* formic acid.

Amen ['ɑːmən] *int. u. n* (16) amen.

Amerikan|er [ameri'kɑːnər] *m* (7), ~erin *f*, 2isch American; 2i'sieren Americanize; ~ismus [~ka'nismus] *m* (16[2]) Americanism.

Amethyst [ame'tʏst] *m* (3) amethyst.

Amme ['amə] *f* (15) nurse, wet-nurse; '~nmärchen *contp. n* old wives' tale.

Ammer *zo.* ['amər] *f* (15) bunting.

Ammoniak ⚗ [amon'jak] *n* (3[1], *o. pl.*) ammonia.

Amnesie [amne'ziː] ⚕ *f* (15) amnesia.

Amnestie [amnɛs'tiː] *f* (15) amnesty, general pardon; 2ren (grant a) pardon.

Amok ['ɑːmɔk] *inv.*: ~ *laufen* (*fahren*) run (drive) amuck; '~fahrt *f* mad ride; '~läufer *m* mad gunman.

Amor ['ɑːmɔr] *m* Cupid.

amorph [a'mɔrf] amorphous.

Amortisation [amɔrtiza'tsjoːn] *f* amortization; *e-r Anleihe*: redemption.

amorti'sier|bar redeemable; ~en amortize; *e-e Anleihe*: redeem.

Ampel ['ampəl] *f* (15) hanging lamp; (*Verkehrs*2) traffic light.

Ampere|meter ⚡ [ãpɛːr'meːtər] *n* ammeter; ~stunde [ã'pɛːr-] *f* ampere-hour.

Ampfer ⚘ ['ampfər] *m* (7) dock.

Amphibie [am'fiːbjə] *f* (15), ~n... amphibian.

Amphitheater [am'fiːteɑːtər] *n* amphithea|tre, *Am.* -ter.

Ampulle [am'pulə] *f* (12) ampoule.

Ampu|tation [amputa'tsjoːn] *f* (16) amputation; 2'tieren amputate; ~'tierte *m* amputee.

Amsel ['amzəl] *f* (15) blackbird.

Amt [amt] *n* (1[2]) office; (*Posten*) post; (*Behörde*) office, board, agency; (*Pflicht*) official duty, function; (*Aufgabe*) task; (*Gerichts*2) court; (*Fernsprech*2) exchange; *s. antreten, auswärtig, bekleiden, entheben, niederlegen*; *von* ~*s wegen* officially, ex officio; 2ieren [~'tiːrən] hold office; *eccl. od. fig.* officiate; ~ *als* act as; ~d acting, *official* in charge; '2lich official; '~mann *m* (1[2]) bailiff.

'Amts... official, of (an) office; '~-antritt *m* entering upon office; '~-arzt *m* public-health officer; '~befugnis *f* authority; '~bereich *m*, '~bezirk *m* jurisdiction; '~blatt *n* official gazette; '~bruder *m* colleague; '~dauer *f* term of office; '~diener *m* usher; '~-eid *m* oath of office; '~enthebung *f* removal from office, dismissal; '~führung *f* administration (of an office); '~geheimnis *n* official secret; '~gericht *n* Inferior Court; '~geschäfte *n/pl.* official duties; '~gewalt *f* official authority; '~handlung *f* official act; '~kollege *pol. m* opposite number; '~miene *f* solemn air; '2müde weary of one's office; '~niederlage *f* resignation; '~richter *m* *etwa*: district judge; '~schimmel *m* red tape; '~stunden *f/pl.* official hours; '~tracht *f* official attire; ⚖, *eccl.* robe; *univ.* gown; '~träger *m* office-holder; '~-überschreitung *f* abuse of authority; '~-unterschla-

gung *f* ⚖ malversation; '**~verletzung** *f* misconduct in office; '**~verwalter** *m* administrator of an office, substitute, deputy; '**~vorgänger** *m* predecessor in office; '**~vormund** *m* public guardian; '**~vorsteher** *m* head official; '**~weg** *m*: *den ~ beschreiten* go through the official channels; *den ~ (nicht) einhalten* (not to) act through the proper channels; '**~zeichen** *n teleph.* dial(ling) tone; '**~zeit** *f* term of office.

Amulett [amu'lɛt] *n* (3) charm.

amüs|ant [amy'zant] amusing; **~ieren** [~'zi:rən] amuse, entertain; *sich ~ (sich die Zeit vertreiben)* amuse o.s.; *(sich gut unterhalten)* enjoy o.s., have a good time.

an [an] *(wo? dat.; wohin? acc.)* **1.** *prp.* at; on, upon; by; against; to; *(bis ~)* as far as, up to; *(etwa)* near(ly); *am Fenster* at *(od.* by) the window; *~ der Themse* on the Thames; *am 1. März* on March 1st; *am Morgen* in the morning; *am Anfang* at the beginning; *~ e-m Orte* in a place; *~ der Grenze* on the frontier; *~ der Hand führen* by the hand; *am Ufer* on the shore; *~ der Wand* on *(od.* against) the wall; *am Leben* alive; *s. Reihe*; *es ist ~ dir, zu sagen, ob ...* it is up to you now to say whether ...; **2.** *adv.* on, onward; up; *von heute ~* from today (onwards); *von nun (od. jetzt) ~* from now on; ⊕ *~-aus* on-off.

Anachronismus [anakro'nismus] *m* (16²) anachronism.

analog [ana'lo:k] analogous.

Analogie [~lo'gi:] *f* (15) analogy.

Ana'logrechner *m Computer*: analogue computer.

Analphabet|(in *f*) [an⁹alfa'be:t] *m* (12) illiterate; **~entum** *n* illiteracy.

Analyse [ana'ly:zə] *f* (15) analysis.

analy'sieren analy|se, *bsd. Am.* -ze.

Analyt|iker [ana'ly:tikər] *m* (6) analyst; **≗isch** analytic(al).

Ananas ['ananas] *f (inv. od.* 14²) pineapple.

Anarchie [anar'çi:] *f* (15) anarchy.

Anar'chis|mus *m* (16²) anarchism; **~t** *m* (12), **~tin** *f* (16¹) anarchist; **≗tisch** anarchic(al).

Anästhesist [anɛste'zist] *m* (12), **~in** *f* (16¹) an(a)esthetist.

Anatom [~'to:m] *m* (12) anatomist.

Anatomie [~to'mi:] *f* (15) anatomy.

anatomisch [~'to:miʃ] anatomical.

'**anbahn|en** pave the way for, initiate; *sich ~* be at hand; *Beziehungen, Verhandlungen usw.*: open (up); '**≗er** *m* initiator.

anbändeln ['~bɛndəln] (29): *~ mit* make up to, pick up with; *(Streit suchen) s. anbinden (v/i.)*.

'**Anbau** ⚒ *m* cultivation; ⚠ annex, extension, *bsd. Am.* addition, *(Flügel)* wing; '**≗en** ⚒ cultivate, grow; ⚠ add, annex *(an [acc.]* to); ⊕ attach; *sich ~* settle; '**~fläche** *f* arable land; area under cultivation.

'**Anbeginn** *m* earliest beginning, outset; *von ~* from the outset.

'**anbehalten** *Kleid usw.*: keep on.

an'bei *im Brief*: enclosed.

'**anbeißen** *v/t.* bite; *v/i.* bite; *fig.* take the bait.

'**anbelangen** concern; *was mich anbelangt* as to *(od.* for) me.

'**anbellen** bark at.

anberaum|en ['~bəraumən] (25) appoint, fix; '**≗ung** *f* appointment.

'**anbet|en** worship, *fig. a.* adore; '**≗er(in** *f*) *m* worship(p)er, adorer, *fig. a.* admirer.

'**Anbetracht:** *in ~ (gen.)* considering, in consideration *(od.* view) of.

'**anbetreffen** *s. anbelangen.*

'**anbetteln** solicit alms of.

Anbetung ['~be:tuŋ] *f* worship, adoration; '**≗swürdig** adorable.

'**anbiedern** (29): *sich ~ mit od. bei* cotton *(od.* F chum) up to.

'**anbiet|en** *v/t.* offer; *sich ~ P.*: offer one's services, *Gelegenheit*: present itself; '**≗er** ✝ *m* (7) supplier.

'**anbinden** *v/t.* bind, tie up; *~ an (acc.)* tie to; *v/i. mit j-m ~* pick a quarrel with, tangle with; *kurz angebunden sein fig.* be curt *od.* short *(gegen* with).

'**anblasen** blow at *od.* upon; *Hochofen*: blow in; F *(rüffeln)* blow up.

'**Anblick** *m (Blick, Aussehen)* look; *(Bild)* sight, view, aspect; *beim ersten ~* at first sight; '**≗en** look at; *flüchtig*: glance at; *(besehen)* view; *(mustern)* eye.

'**an|blinzeln** blink *od.* *(schlau)* wink at; '**~bohren** bore, pierce; '**~braten** roast gently; '**~brechen** *v/t. Vorrat*: break into; *Flasche*: open, crack; *v/i.* (sn) begin; *Tag*: dawn; *Nacht*: come on; '**~brennen** *v/t.* burn; *Zigarre usw.*: light; *v/i.* (sn) kindle, catch fire; *Speise*: burn (*a.* ~ *lassen*).

ˈ**anbringen** (*herbeibringen*) bring in *od.* on; (*befestigen*) fix, attach, mount, fit (*an dat.* to); *Stempel, Unterschrift*: affix (to); *Gründe*: put forward; *e-n Schlag*: bring home; *ein Wort*: put in; *Sohn usw.*: get a place for; ⚕ *Ware*: dispose of, (*losschlagen*) knock off; e-e *Klage* ~ bring an action; e-e *Beschwerde* ~ lodge a complaint; *das ist bei ihm nicht angebracht* that won't do with him; *s. angebracht.*

ˈ**Anbruch** *m* break, beginning; (*bei*) ~ *des Tages* (at) daybreak; (*bei*) ~ *der Nacht* (at) nightfall.

ˈ**anbrüllen** roar at, bawl at.

Andacht [ˈ~daxt] *f* (16) devotion; (*Handlung*) prayers *pl.*, service; *s. verrichten.*

andächtig [ˈ~dɛçtiç] devout; (*bei e-r Andacht anwesend*) devotional; *fig.* rapt, absorbed, religious.

ˈ**andauern** last; continue; *hartnäckig*: persist; ˈ**~d** lasting; continuous; persistent.

ˈ**Andenken** *n* (6) (*Gedächtnis*) memory, (*a. Gegenstand*) remembrance; (*nur Gegenstand*) keepsake; *mitgenommenes*: souvenir (*an acc.* of); *zum ~ an* (*acc.*) in memory of.

ander [ˈandər] (18) other; (*verschieden*) different; (*zweit*) second; (*folgend*) next; (*gegenüberliegend*) opposite; *der ~e Strumpf usw.* the pair to (*od.* the fellow of) this sock, *etc.*; *am ~en Tag* (on) the next day; *e-n Tag um den ~n* every other day; *et. ~es* another thing, something else; *das ist etwas ~es* that is different; *alles ~e* everything else; *alles ~e als* anything but; *kein ~er* no one else (*als* but), *rühmend*: no lesser person (than); *nichts ~es* nothing else; *~er Ansicht sein* differ; *ein ~es Hemd anziehen* change one's shirt; *s. unter* 1; **~erseits** [ˈ~zaɪts] *s. anderseits.*

ändern [ˈɛndərn] (29) (*a. sich*) alter, (*wechseln*) change; *teilweise*: modify; (*verschieden gestalten*) vary; *ich kann es nicht ~* I can't help it; *es läßt sich nicht ~* it cannot be helped.

ˈ**andern|falls** otherwise; ˈ**~teils** on the other hand.

anders [ˈ~s] otherwise; (*verschieden*) differently (*als* from); *bei pron.*: else; *wer ~?* who else?; *er ist ~ als sein Vater* he is unlike (*od.* different from) his father; *ich kann nicht ~, ich muß weinen* I cannot help crying; *~ werden* change; *s. besinnen* 1; ˈ**~denkend** dissenting.

anderseits [ˈ~zaɪts] on the other hand.

ˈ**anders|ge·artet** different; ˈ**~gläubig** of a different faith, heterodox; ˈ**~herum** the other way round; F (*homosexuell*) bent; ˈ**~wo** elsewhere; ˈ**~woher** from elsewhere; ˈ**~wohin** to some other place, elsewhere.

anderthalb [ˈ~thalp] one and a half.

ˈ**Änderung** *f s. ändern*: alteration; change; modification; variation.

ander|wärts [ˈ~vɛrts] elsewhere; ˈ**~weitig** *adj.* other, further; *adv.* in another way *od.* manner.

ˈ**andeuten** indicate; (*anspielen*) hint; (*zu verstehen geben*) give to understand, intimate, imply; (*zu bedenken geben*) suggest; *paint. u. fig.* outline.

ˈ**Andeutung** *f* indication; hint (*a. fig. Spur*); intimation; suggestion; ˈ**2sweise** by way of intimation; in outlines.

ˈ**andichten:** *j-m et.* ~ impute (*od.* attribute) a th. falsely to a p.

ˈ**Andrang** *m* rush, press; (*Zulauf*) concourse; ⚕ congestion.

ˈ**andrehen** *Gas usw.*: turn on; ⚡ *Licht*: switch on; *Motor*: start up; *Schraube usw.*: tighten; F *j-m et.* ~ palm a th. off on a p.

ˈ**androh|en:** *j-m et.* ~ menace (*od.* threaten) a p. with; ˈ**2ung** *f* threat; ⚖ *unter ~ von od. gen.* under penalty of.

aneign|en [ˈ~ˀaɪgnən] (*sich*) appropriate, make one's own; *Gebiet*: annex; *Gewohnheit*: contract; *Kenntnisse*: acquire; *Meinung anderer*: adopt; *widerrechtlich*: usurp; ˈ**2ung** *f* appropriation; acquisition; adoption; usurpation.

an·eiˈnander together; **~geraten** (*in Streit kommen*) clash (*mit* with); (*handgemein werden*) come to blows.

Anekdote [anɛkˈdoːtə] *f* (15) anecdote; **2nhaft** anecdotic(al).

ˈ**an·ekeln** disgust, sicken; *es ekelt mich an* I am disgusted with it, I loathe it.

ˈ**an·empfehlen** recommend.

ˈ**An·erbieten** *n* (6) offer.
ˈ**an·erkannterˈmaßen** admittedly.
ˈ**an·erkenn|en** acknowledge; recognize (*beide*: *als* as); *Anspruch*, *Schuld*: admit; (*lobend* ~) appreciate; (*billigen*) approve; *Kind*: (*nicht* ~ dis)own; accept; *Wechsel*: hono(u)r; *nicht* ~ repudiate; ˈ**~enswert** commendable; ˈ**≈ung** *f* acknowledgment; recognition (*a. pol.*); (*lobende* ~) appreciation; (*Zeichen der Hochachtung*) tribute (*gen.* to); *e-s Wechsels*: acceptance; (*Zulassung*) admission; *in* ~ *gen.* in recognition of.
ˈ**an·erziehen:** *j-m et.* ~ breed a th. into a p.; *anerzogen* acquired.
anfachen [ˈ~faxən] (25) fan (*a. fig.*).
ˈ**anfahr|en** *v/i.* (sn) (*losfahren*) start; *v/t.* (*rammen*) run into, hit, ⚓ run foul of; (*herbeibringen*) carry up, convey to the spot; *fig. j-n*: bellow at; ˈ**≈t** *f* journey; (*Ankunft*) arrival; (*~weg*) approach, *vor e-m Hause*: drive(way *Am.*).
ˈ**Anfall** *m* attack (*a.* ⚕); ⚕ fit; (*Ertrag*) yield; *v. Gewinn, Zinsen*: accrual; (*Menge*) amount, number; ˈ**≈en** *v/t.* (*angreifen*) attack; *v/i.* (sn) result, occur; *Gewinn, Zinsen*: accrue.
anfällig [ˈ~fɛliç] *allg.* susceptible (*für* to); ⚕ prone to disease.
ˈ**Anfang** *m* beginning, start; *förmlich*: commencement; *am, im, zu* ~ *s. anfangs*; *von* ~ *an* from the beginning (*od.* start, outset); ~ *Mai* early in May; *den* ~ *machen* begin, lead off; *in den Anfängen stecken* be in its infancy; ˈ**≈en** begin; start (*mit e-r Arbeit usw.* on; *zu inf. ger.*); commence; (*tun*) do; *was soll ich* ~? what am I to do?; *was wirst du morgen* ~? what are you going to do with yourself tomorrow?; *das hast du schlau angefangen* that was a clever trick.
Anfäng|er(in *f*) [ˈ~fɛŋər] *m* beginner; (*Neuling*) tiro; ˈ**≈lich** *adj.* initial; (*ursprünglich*) original; *adv.* in the beginning.
anfangs [ˈ~faŋs] in the beginning; ˈ**≈...** initial, early; ˈ**≈buchstabe** *m* initial letter; *großer* (*kleiner*) ~ capital (small) letter; ˈ**≈gehalt** *n* starting (*od.* initial) salary; ˈ**≈gründe** *m/pl.* elements, rudiments; ˈ**≈kapital** *n* opening capital; (*Aktien≈*) original stock; ˈ**≈stadium** *n* initial stage; ˈ**≈-unterricht** *m* elementary instruction.
ˈ**anfassen** *v/t.* take hold of, seize, grasp; (*berühren*) touch, handle (*a fig.*); *fig.* approach, tackle; *scharf* ~ handle *a p.* roughly; *sich* (*ea.*) ~ take hands; *v/i.* (*helfen, a. mit* ~) lend a hand.
ˈ**anfaulen** (sn) (begin to) rot; *angefault* partially decayed.
anfecht|bar [ˈ~fɛçtba:r] contestable; ˈ**~en** contest, ⚖ *a.* avoid; *Urteil*: appeal from; *Meinung*: oppose; (*beunruhigen*) trouble; ˈ**≈ung** *f* contestation; appeal (*gen.* from); *eccl.* (*Versuchung*) temptation.
anfeind|en [ˈ~faɪndən] be hostile to; ˈ**≈ung** *f* persecution (*gen.* of), hostility (*gen.* to).
ˈ**anfertig|en** make, manufacture; ˈ**≈ung** *f* making, manufacture.
ˈ**an|feuchten** moisten, wet, damp; ˈ**~feuern** fire (*a. fig.*); *fig.* ginger up; *Sport*: cheer (on); ˈ**~flehen** implore; ˈ**~flicken** patch on (*an acc.* to); ˈ**~fliegen** *v/t. Ziel*: ✈ approach, head for, (*landen*) land at; *angeflogen kommen* come flying.
ˈ**Anflug** *m* approach (flight); *fig.* touch, tinge; ~ *von Bart* down; ˈ**~schneise** *f* approach corridor.
ˈ**anforder|n** demand, claim; call for; ⚔ requisition; ˈ**≈ung** *f* demand, claim; ⚔ requisition; *allen ~en genügen* meet all requirements, *Am.* fill the bill; *den ~en nicht genügen* not to be up to standard; *hohe ~en stellen* be very exacting.
ˈ**Anfrage** *f* inquiry; *parl.* interpellation; ˈ**≈n** *v/i.* ask (*bei j-m* a p.); inquire (*nach* for; *bei j-m nach et.* of a p. about a th.).
ˈ**an|fressen** gnaw; *Metall*: corrode; **~freunden** [ˈ~frɔʏndən]: *sich* ~ become friends; *sich* ~ *mit* make friends with; ˈ**~frieren** (sn) freeze on (*an acc.* to); ˈ**~fügen** join, attach, add, annex (*an acc.* to); ˈ**~fühlen** feel, touch; *sich* ~ feel.
Anfuhr [ˈ~fu:r] *f* (16) conveyance, carriage; (*Zufuhr*) supply.
ˈ**anführ|en** lead; ⚔ *Truppe*: command; (*erwähnen*) mention, state; *einzeln*: specify; *Gründe*: put forward; *Worte, Beispiele*: quote, cite; (*täuschen*) dupe, fool; *zur Entschul-*

digung ~ plead (in excuse); '2**er(in** *f*) *m* leader; (*Rädelsführer*) ringleader.

'**Anführung** *f s. anführen*: lead(ership); allegation; quotation; '**~s-zeichen** *n* quotation mark, inverted comma.

'**anfüllen** fill (up).

'**Angabe** *f* declaration, statement; (*Anweisung*) instruction; (*Auskunft*) information, *pl. a.* data *pl.*; (~ *v. Einzelheiten*) specification; F (*Prahlerei*) showing off; *bewußt falsche* ~ misrepresentation; *besondere* ~*n* particular items; *genauere* (*od. nähere*) ~*n* particulars.

'**angaffen** gape at.

angängig ['~gɛŋiç] possible.

'**angeben** *v/t. Namen, Grund, Tatsachen*: give; *bestimmt*: state; *im einzelnen*: specify; (*erklären*), *engS. Zollware*: declare; (*vorbringen, behaupten*) allege (*daß* that); (*anzeigen*) denounce, inform against; (*vorgeben*) pretend; ✝ *Preis*: quote; *s. Tempo, Ton*; *zu gering* ~ understate; *zu hoch* ~ overstate; *v/i. Kartenspiel*: deal first; *Tennis*: serve; F (*prahlen*) show off, brag (*mit* with).

'**Angeber**|(**in** *f*) *m* informer; F (*Prahler*) show-off; **~ei** [~'raɪ] *f* denunciation; F (*Prahlerei*) *s. Angabe*; '2**isch** F boastful; showy.

'**Angebinde** *n* gift, present.

angeblich ['~ge:pliç] *adj.* pretended, alleged, ostensible; *adv.* pretendedly *usw.*; ~ *ist er* ... he is said (*od.* reputed) to be ...

'**angeboren** innate, inborn; ⚕ congenital.

'**Angebot** *n* offer; *Auktion*: bid; ✝ (*Ggs. Nachfrage*) supply; (*Lieferungs-, Preis-, Zahlungs*2) tender, *Am.* bid.

angebracht ['~gəbraxt] advisable; *gut* ~ appropriate, opportune; *schlecht* ~ inopportune, out of place.

'**angedeihen:** *j-m et.* ~ *lassen* bestow upon a p., grant to a p.

angegossen ['~gəgɔsən]: *wie* ~ *sitzen* fit like a glove.

angeheiratet ['~gəhaɪrɑ:tət]: ~*er Vetter* cousin by marriage.

angeheitert ['~gəhaɪtərt] slightly tipsy, mellow, *Am.* F happy.

'**angehen** *v/i.* (sn) begin; ⚘ begin to take root; (*leidlich sein*) be tolerable; (*zulässig sein*) be admissible; (*schlecht werden*) spoil; *angegangen Fleisch*: tainted; *das geht* (*nicht*) *an* that will (not) do; *v/t. ein Unternehmen, e-n Gegner*: tackle; *fig. j-n* ~ (*betreffen*) concern; *das geht dich nichts an* that is no business of yours; *j-n um et.* ~ apply to (*od.* solicit) a p. for; '**~d** (*werdend*) budding, would-be, future.

'**angehör**|**en** (*dat.*) belong to; *als Mitglied*: *a.* be member of; '**~ig** (*dat.*) belonging to; '2**ige** *m, f* (*Mitglied*) member; (*Unterhaltsberechtigter*) dependant; *s-e* '2**igen** *pl.* his relations, his people, F his folks; *die nächsten* ~ the next of kin.

Angeklagte ['~gəklɑ:ktə] *m, f* defendant.

angeknackst ['~gəknakst] *fig. ich bin etwas* ~ I'm in a bad way.

Angel ['aŋəl] *f* (*Tür*2) hinge; *s. Angelgerät, -rute.*

angelegen: *sich et.* ~ *sein lassen* make a th. one's business; *es sich* ~ *sein lassen, zu inf.* make a point of *ger.*; '2**heit** *f* business, concern, affair, matter; '**~tlich** urgent.

'**Angel**|**gerät** *n* fishing-gear *od.* -tackle; '**~haken** *m* fish(ing)-hook; '2**n** (29) (*a. fig.*) angle, fish (*nach* for); '**~punkt** *m* pivot; *fig.* crucial point; '**~rute** *f* fishing-rod; '**~sachse** *m*, '2**sächsisch** Anglo-Saxon; '**~schein** *m* fishing permit; '**~schnur** *f* fishing-line.

'**angemessen** suitable, appropriate (*dat.* to); (*annehmbar*) reasonable, fair; (*ausreichend*) adequate; '2**heit** *f* suitableness; reasonableness; adequacy.

'**angenehm** pleasant, agreeable; (*behaglich*) comfortable; (*willkommen*) welcome (*alle*: *dat.* to).

'**angenommen** *s. annehmen.*

Anger ['aŋər] *m* (7) meadow; (*Dorf*2) common, (village) green.

ange|**regt** ['~gəre:kt] animated; '**~schlagen** *Boxen*: groggy; *Geschirr*: chipped; 2**schuldigte** ['~ʃuldiçtə] ⚖ *m, f* accused; '**~sehen** respected; esteemed; (*ausgezeichnet*) distinguished; '**~säuselt** F *s. angeheitert.*

'**Angesicht** *n* face; *von* ~ by sight; *von* ~ *zu* ~ face to face; '2**s** (*gen.*) in the presence of, (*a. fig.*) in view of; *fig.* considering.

ange|stammt ['~gəʃtamt] hereditary; innate; **²stellte** ['~ʃtɛltə] *m, f* (salaried) employee; *die ~n* the staff; '**²stelltenversicherung** *f* employees' insurance; '**~strengt** strained, intense; *~ arbeiten* (*nachdenken*) work (think) hard; **~tan** ['~ta:n]: *~* (*gekleidet*) *mit* attired in; *danach ~, zu* apt to; *~ von* pleased with; **~trunken** ['~truŋkən] tipsy; **~wandt** ['~vant] *Kunst, Wissenschaft*: applied; **~wiesen** ['~vi:zən]: *~ sein auf* be dependent (up)on; '**~wöhnen** accustom (*j-m et.* a p. to a th.); *sich das Rauchen usw. ~* get into the habit of smoking *etc.*, take to smoking *etc.*; '**²wohnheit** *f* habit, custom; **~wurzelt** ['~vurtsəlt]: *wie ~ dastehen* stand rooted to the ground.

'**angleich|en** (*a. sich*) assimilate, adjust (*dat.* to); '**²ung** *f* assimilation; adjustment.

Angler ['aŋlər] *m* (7) angler.

'**anglieder|n** (*annektieren*) annex; (*aufnehmen*) affiliate; '**²ung** *f* annexion; affiliation.

Anglist [aŋ'glist] *m* (12) professor (*od.* student) of English, Anglicist.

An'glistik *f* (16) English language and literature, *Am.* English philology.

Anglizismus [aŋgli'zismus] *m* (16²) Anglicism, *Am.* Briticism.

Anglo... ['aŋglo-] Anglo-...

anglotzen ['anglɔtsən] goggle at.

Angorawolle [aŋ'go:ra-] angora wool, mohair.

angreif|bar ['an-] assailable; *fig.* vulnerable; '**~en** (*anfassen*) handle; *Kapital, Vorräte*: draw on, break into; *Aufgabe*: set about, approach, tackle; *feindlich*: assail, attack, charge; ⚕ *j-n, den Körper*: weaken, affect; ⚗ corrode; *Augen, Nerven*: try, strain; *sich rauh ~* feel rough; *angegriffen aussehen* look poorly; '**~end** aggressive, offensive; *körperlich*: trying; '**²er**(**in** *f*) *m* aggressor (*a. pol.*).

'**angrenzen** border, abut (*an acc.* on, upon); '**~d** adjacent, adjoining (*an acc.* to).

'**Angriff** *m* attack (*a. Sport u. fig.*); charge, assault (*auf acc.* on); *in ~ nehmen* start on, tackle; *zum ~ übergehen* take the offensive; '**~skrieg** *m* offensive war; '**²slustig** aggressive; '**~s-punkt** *m* point of attack; ⊕ working point; '**~swaffe** *f* offensive weapon.

'**angrinsen** grin at.

Angst [aŋst] *f* (14¹) anxiety, fear; (*Schreck*) fright; (*große ~*) dread, terror; *~ haben s.* (*sich*) *ängstigen*; *mir ist ²* I am afraid (*vor dat.* of); *² und bange* terribly frightened; *j-m ² machen, j-n in ~ versetzen* alarm *od.* scare a p.; '**~gegner** *m* formidable opponent; '**~hase** *m* coward, *sl.* chicken.

ängstigen ['ɛŋstigən] (25) alarm; *sich ~* be afraid *od.* in fear (*vor dat.* of); be alarmed (*um* about).

'**Angstkäufe** *m/pl.* panic buying.

ängstlich ['ɛŋstliç] anxious, nervous; (*besorgt*) uneasy; (*schüchtern*) timid; (*sorgfältig*) scrupulous; '**²keit** *f* anxiety, nervousness; timidity; scrupulousness.

'**Angst|macher** *m* (7) scaremonger; '**~neurose** *f* anxiety neurosis; '**~röhre** F *f* stove-pipe hat; '**~schweiß** *m* cold sweat; '**²voll** anxious, fearful; '**~zustände** *m/pl.* state of anxiety, *Am. sl.* jitters.

angucken ['an-] look at.

'**angurten** (26): *sich ~* fasten one's seat belt.

'**anhaben** *Kleid*: have on; *sie konnten ihm nichts ~* they could find (*od.* do) nothing against him, they could do him no harm.

'**anhaften** stick, adhere (*dat.* to).

'**anhaken** hook on; *in e-r Liste*: tick off.

'**Anhalt** *m* (*Stütze*) hold, support; *s. ~spunkt*; '**²en** *v/t.* stop; (*hindern*) check; *polizeilich*: arrest, seize; *den Atem ~* hold (*od.* bate) one's breath; *j-n ~ zu et.* keep a p. to a th.; *v/i.* (*andauern*) continue, last; (*stillstehen*) stop, halt; *~ um ein Mädchen* propose to; '**²end** continuous, sustained, lasting; (*beharrlich*) persistant; *~er Fleiß* assiduity; '**~er** *m* (7) hitch-hiker; *per ~ fahren* hitch-hike; '**~s-punkt** *m* clue, *Am. a.* lead.

'**Anhang** *m* appendage; (*Buch usw.*) appendix, supplement; (*Nachtrag*) annex; (*Angehörige*) dependants *pl.*, family; (*Gefolgschaft*) adherents *pl.*, following; '**²en** (*dat.*) adhere (*od.* cling) to.

'**anhäng|en** *v/t.* hang on; (*hinzufügen*) append, affix, add (*an acc.* to); *sich ~* hang on, cling (*an acc.*

to); *fig.* *j-m et.* ~ implicate a p.; *v/i.* *s. anhangen*; **Ser** ['~hɛŋər] *m* (7) adherent, follower (*a.* **Sin** *f*); (*Schmuck*) pendant; *am Koffer usw.*: label, tag; (*~wagen*) trailer; '**Ser-kupplung** *f* trailer coupling, tow-bar; '**Serschaft** *f* following; '**~ig:** ⚖ ~ *sein* be pending; *e-n Prozeß gegen j-n ~ machen* bring an action against; '**~lich** attached (*an acc.* to); affectionate; devoted; '**Slichkeit** *f* attachment (*an acc.* to); '**Ssel** *n* (7) appendage; (*Etikett*) tag.

'**anhauchen** breathe on; *die Finger*: blow; F (*rüffeln*) blow *a p.* up.

'**anhauen** F: *j-n um et.* ~ scrounge a th. off a p.

'**anhäuf|en** heap up; (*a. sich*) accumulate; '**Sung** *f* accumulation; *phys.* aggregation.

'**anheben** *v/t.* lift (up); *fig.* (*a. v/i.*) begin.

'**anheften** fasten, affix (*an acc.* to); (*annähen*) tack, baste, stitch (*an acc.* to); *mit Reißzwecken*: tack on.

'**anheilen** (sn) heal on *od.* up.

anheimeln ['~haɪməln] (29) remind *a p.* of home; '**~d** homelike, hom(e)y, friendly, cosy.

an'heim|fallen (sn): *j-m* ~ fall to, devolve on; **~geben, ~stellen:** *j-m et.* ~ leave to a p.('s discretion); *dem Urteil j-s*: submit to.

anheischig ['~haɪʃiç]: *sich ~ machen* offer, volunteer.

Anhieb ['~hi:p] *m*: F *auf* ~ at the first go; *sagen können*: off the cuff.

'**anhimmeln** (29) *v/t.* idolize.

'**Anhöhe** *f* rise, hill, elevation.

'**anhör|en** listen to, hear; *sich schlecht* ~ sound badly; *man hört ihm den Ausländer an* one can tell by his accent that he is a foreigner; '**Sung** *f* hearing.

Anilin [ani'li:n] *n* (3, *o. pl.*) anilin(e); **~farbe** *f* anilin(e) dye.

animalisch [ani'mɑ:liʃ] animal.

Animateur [anima'tør] *m* (3[1]) *im Ferienclub*: host; **~in** *f* (16[1]) hostess.

animier|en [ani'mi:rən] incite, encourage, stimulate; **Smädchen** *n* hostess.

Animosität [animozi'tɛ:t] *f* animosity.

Anis ⚘ [a'ni:s] *m* (4) anise.

'**ankämpfen:** ~ *gegen* struggle *od.* battle against, combat.

'**Ankauf** *m* buying, purchase; '**Sen** buy, purchase; *sich* ~ settle.

Anker ['aŋkər] *m* (7) ⚓ *u.* ⊕ anchor; ⚡ armature; *vor ~ gehen* cast *od.* drop anchor; *den ~ lichten* weigh anchor; *vor ~ liegen* ride at anchor; '**~boje** *f* anchor buoy; '**~grund** *m* anchorage; '**~kette** *f* chain cable; '**Sn** (29) anchor; '**~platz** *m* berth; '**~tau** *n* cable; '**~uhr** *f* lever watch; '**~wicklung** ⚡ *f* armature winding; '**~winde** *f* capstan.

'**anketten** chain (*an acc.* to).

'**Anklage** *f* accusation, charge; ⚖ *a.* indictment (*wegen* for); *wegen Amtsvergehens*: impeachment; *s. erheben*; *unter ~ stehen* be on trial (*wegen* for); '**~bank** *f*: *auf der* ~ in the dock; '**Sn** accuse (*wegen* of), charge (with); impeach (of, for); indict (for).

'**Ankläger(in** *f*) *m* accuser; *s. Kläger*; *öffentlicher* ~ public prosecutor, *Am. a.* district attorney.

'**Anklage|schrift** *f* (bill of) indictment; '**~vertreter** *m* counsel for the prosecution.

'**anklammern** ⊕ clamp (*an acc.* to); *mit Büroklammer*: clip on; *sich* ~ cling (*an acc.* to).

'**Anklang** *m*: ~ *an* (*acc.*) reminiscence (*od.* suggestion) of; ~ *finden* meet approval *od.* a favo(u)rable response, catch on; ~ *finden bei* appeal to; *keinen ~ finden* fall flat, *sl.* (be a) flop.

'**ankleben** *v/t.* stick on; *mit Leim*: glue on; *mit Kleister*: paste (on); *mit Gummi*: gum on (*alle*: *an acc.* to); *v/i.* (sn) stick (*an dat.* to).

'**Ankleide|kabine** *f* changing cubicle; '**Sn** (*a. sich*) dress; '**~raum** *m* dressing-room.

'**an|klingeln** *teleph.* *j-n*: ring up, give *a p.* a ring; '**~klingen:** ~ *an* (*acc.*) be suggestive of; ~ *lassen* call up; '**~klopfen** knock (*an acc.* at); '**~knipsen** ⚡ switch on.

'**anknüpf|en** *v/t.* tie (*an acc.* to); *fig.* begin, enter into; *Beziehungen*: establish; *wieder* ~ resume; *v/i.* (*an acc.*) link up (with), continue; *Sprecher*: refer to; '**Sungs-punkt** *m* point of contact, starting-point.

'**ankommen** *v/i.* (sn) arrive; ~ *bei e-r Firma* get a job at; *fig.* ~ (*bei j-m*) (*verstanden werden*) go down (with), (*Erfolg haben*) make a hit (with); ~ *auf* (*acc.*) depend (up)on;

bei j-m gut (schlecht) ~ be well (ill) received by; *es darauf* ~ *lassen* run the risk, take a (*od.* one's) chance; *darauf kommt es an* that is the point; *es kommt (ganz) darauf an* it (all) depends; *es kommt nicht darauf an* it is (a matter) of no consequence; *es kommt mir viel darauf an* it is very important to me; *es kommt darauf an, ob* the question is whether; *es kommt mir darauf an, zu inf. od. daß* I am concerned to *inf. od.* that; *es kommt mir nicht auf ... an* I don't mind ...; *v/t.* befall; *es kommt mich hart an* it is hard on me; *es kam mich (mir) die Lust an, zu ...* I felt like *ger.*

Ankömmling ['~kœmliŋ] *m* (3¹) newcomer, arrival.

'**ankoppeln** couple (*an acc.* to); *Raumfähre*: link up (*an acc.* with, to), dock.

'**Ankopplungsmanöver** *n e-r Raumfähre*: link-up manœuvre (*Am.* maneuver).

ankreiden ['~kraɪdən] (26) chalk up (*j-m* against a p.).

'**ankreuzen** tick *od.* check off.

'**ankündig|en** announce; *fig.* herald; '**2ung** *f* announcement.

Ankunft ['~kunft] *f* (14¹) arrival; '**~sflughafen** *m* arrival airport.

'**ankurbeln** *mot.* crank up; *fig.* stimulate, *sl.* pep up; *Produktion usw.*: step up.

'**anlächeln**, '**anlachen** smile at.

'**Anlage** *f* (*Anlegen*) *e-s Gartens usw.*: laying-out; (*Bau*) construction; (*Einbau, Einrichtung*) installation; (*Anordnung*) plan, arrangement, layout; (*Fabrik2*) plant, works *pl. u. sg.*; (*Betriebs2*) equipment, facility; (*Maschinen2 usw.*) plant, unit; (*Hi-Fi-~*) stereo system; (*Garten2*) pleasure-ground, park; (*Fähigkeit*) talent, ability; (*Natur2*) tendency, bent, *a.* ⚕ (pre)disposition; (*Kapital2*) investment; (*zu e-m Schreiben*) enclosure; *öffentliche ~n pl.* public gardens *pl.*; *im Brief*: *in der* ~ enclosed; '**2bedingt** inherent; '**~berater** *m* advisor on investments; '**~beratung** *f* investment advice; '**~kapital** *n* invested capital; '**~papiere** *n/pl.* investment securities; '**~vermögen** *n* capital assets *pl.*

'**anlangen** *v/i.* (sn) arrive; *v/t.* concern, regard; *was ... anlangt* as to (*od.* for) ...

Anlaß ['~las] *m* (4²) occasion; (*Grund*) reason (*zu* for); (*Ursache*) cause (of); *aus ~ gen. s. anläßlich*; *bei diesem* ~ on this occasion; *ohne allen* ~ for no reason at all; *dem ~ entsprechend* to fit the occasion; ~ *geben zu et.* give rise to; *j-m ~ geben zu* give a p. reason for; *et. zum ~ nehmen, zu inf.* take occasion to *inf.*; *allen ~ haben zu* have every reason for.

'**anlass|en** *Kleid usw.*: keep on; ⊕ start; *Wasser usw.*: turn on; *Stahl*: temper; *j-n hart* ~ rebuke sharply; *sich gut* ~ promise well; '**2er** ⊕ *m* (7) starter.

anläßlich ['~lɛsliç] (*gen.*) on the occasion of.

'**anlasten:** *j-m et.* ~ blame a th. on a p.

'**Anlauf** *m* start, run; ✈ *beim Start*: take-off run; *Sport*: run-up; *fig. e-n ~ nehmen* take a run; '**2en** *v/i.* (sn) *Sport*: run up; (*beginnen*) start; *Film*: open; (*in Schwung kommen*) get underway; (*anwachsen*) run up, accumulate; (*sich trüben*) *Metall*: tarnish, *Glas*: (get) dim; ~ *lassen* start; *angelaufen kommen* come running (up); *rot* ~ turn red; *v/t. s. anrennen*; ⚓ *Hafen*: call at; '**~phase** *f* initial phase; '**~schwierigkeiten** *f/pl.* initial problems.

'**Anlaut** *m* initial sound; '**2en:** ~ *mit* begin with.

'**anläuten** *s. anklingeln.*

'**anleg|en** *v/t.* (*an acc.*) put against, to; *Feuerung*: put on; *Garten, Straße usw.*: lay out; (*planen*) design, plan; (*bauen*) construct, set up; (*einrichten*) instal(l); *Geld*: invest; *Konto*: open; *Gewehr*: level (*auf acc.* at); *Hund*: tie up; *Kleid, Schmuck usw.*: put on; *typ.* feed; *Maßstab, Verband*: apply (*an acc.* to); *Vorrat*: lay in; *sich* ~ lean (*an acc.* against); *Feuer ~ an (acc.) od. in (dat.)* set fire to; *Hand ~ (helfen)* lend hands; *es ~ auf (acc.)* aim at, make *it* one's object; *darauf angelegt sein zu inf.* be calculated to; *v/i. Schütze*: (take) aim (*auf acc.* at); ⚓ land; '**2er** ⚜ *m* (7) investor; '**2estelle** ⚓ *f* landing-place; (*Hafendamm*) pier; '**2ung** *f* laying out; setting up; foundation; ⚜ investment; application.

'**anlehnen** (*a. sich*) lean (*an acc.*

against); *Tür*: leave ajar; *fig. sich ~ an (acc.)* take pattern from.

Anleihe ['~laɪə] *f* (15) loan; *s. aufnehmen; eine ~ bei j-m machen* borrow money of a p., *fig.* borrow from a p.

'**anleimen** glue on (*an acc.* to).

'**anleit|en** guide (*zu* to); (*lehren*) instruct (in); '**2ung** *f* guidance; instruction; *s. a. Leitfaden.*

'**anlern|en** teach, train, break in; '**2ling** *m* trainee.

'**anliefern** deliver.

'**anlieg|en 1.** *s. angrenzen; Kleid*: fit well, cling; **2.** 2 *n* (6) request; *fig.* concern; '**~end** adjacent; *Kleid*: tight-fitting; *im Brief*: enclosed; '**2er** *m* abutter; *mot.* local resident; '**2erstaat** *m* neighbo(u)ring state.

'**anlocken** allure, entice, attract.

'**anlöten** solder (*an acc.* to).

'**anlügen:** *j-n ~* tell a p. a lie.

'**anmachen** fasten, fix, attach (*an acc.* to); *Feuer*: make, light; *Licht*: switch on; (*mischen*) mix; *Kalk, Farbe*: temper; *Salat*: dress; F *j-n ~ sexuell*: give a p. the come-on.

'**anmalen** paint.

'**Anmarsch** *m*, '**2ieren** (sn) approach.

anmaß|en ['~mɑːsən] (27): *sich et. ~* usurp, presume; *sich ~ zu tun* pretend to, have the impudence to; '**~end** arrogant; '**2ung** *f* arrogance, presumption.

'**anmeld|en** announce, *a. polizeilich*: notify, report (*bei* to); *sich ~: beim Arzt usw.* make an appointment with, *zur Teilnahme* book for, *Schüler usw.*: enrol(l) for, *Sport*: enter for; *sich ~ lassen als Besucher* have o.s. announced; *s. Patent*; '**~epflichtig** notifiable; '**2eschein** *m* entry-form; '**2ung** *f* announcement, notification, report; booking; enrol(l)ment; entry.

'**anmerk|en** (*anstreichen*) mark; (*aufschreiben*) note down; *j-m et. ~* observe (*od.* notice) a th. in a p.; *sich et. nicht ~ lassen* not to betray a th.; *laß dir nichts ~!* F don't let on!; '**2ung** *f* comment, remark; *schriftlich*: note; *erklärend*: annotation; *Text mit ~en versehen* annotate.

'**anmessen:** *j-m et. ~* measure a p. for; *s. angemessen.*

'**Anmut** *f* (16, *o. pl.*) grace, charm, sweetness; '**2ig** graceful, charming, lovely; *Gegend*: pleasant.

'**annageln** nail on (*an acc.* to).

'**annähen** sew on (*an acc.* to).

annähernd ['~nɛːərnt] approximate, *adv. a.* (*nicht ~* not) nearly.

'**Annäherung** *f* approach; *pol.* rapprochement (*fr.*); *fig.* approximation; '**~sversuche** *m/pl.* approaches *pl.*; *amourös*: advances.

Annahme ['~nɑːmə] *f* (15) acceptance; *e-s Kindes, a. e-s Antrags, e-s Plans*: adoption; *e-s Gesetzes*: passing, *bsd. Am.* passage; (*~stelle*) receiving office; (*Vermutung*) assumption, supposition; *ich habe Grund zu der ~* I have reasons to believe; *in der ~, daß* on the supposition that; '**~schluß** *m Anzeigenwerbung*: deadline; '**~verweigerung** *f* non-acceptance.

Annalen [a'nɑːlən] *f/pl.* annals.

'**annehm|bar** acceptable; *Preis usw.*: reasonable; (*leidlich*) passable; '**~en** accept, take; (*vermuten*) assume, suppose, think, *Am.* guess; *Glauben, Meinung*: embrace; *Gestalt*: assume; *Farbe*: take (on); *Bedienten*: engage; *Schüler usw.*: admit; *Wechsel*: accept; *Gewohnheit*: contract; *Antrag, Kind, Haltung, Meinung*: adopt; *Gesetz*: pass; *sich j-s od. e-r S. ~* take care of; *angenommen, es wäre so* supposing (*od.* suppose) it were so; '**2lichkeit** *f* amenity, agreeableness; *~en pl. des Lebens* comforts *pl.* of life.

anne|ktieren [anɛk'tiːrən] annex; **2xion** [~'ksjoːn] *f* annexation.

Anno ['ano] in the year; *~ dazumal* in the olden times.

Annon|ce [a'nɔ̃sə] *f* (15) advertisement, F ad; **2'cieren** advertise.

annullier|en [anu'liːrən] annul; ✝ *Auftrag*: cancel; **2ung** *f* annulment.

[**~n...** anode ...]

Anode ⚡ [a'noːdə] *f* (15) anode;

'**an-öden** (26) F bore stiff.

anomal ['anomɑːl] anomalous.

anonym [ano'nyːm] anonymous; **2ität** [~nymi'tɛːt] *f* anonymity.

Anorak ['~rak] *m* (11) anorak, parka.

'**an-ordn|en** arrange; *fig.* order, direct; '**2ung** *f* arrangement; *fig.* direction, order; *auf ~ von* by order of; *~en treffen* make dispositions.

'**an-organisch** inorganic.

'**anpacken** *s. anfassen.*

'**anpass|en** fit, adapt (*a. geistig*), *e-r Norm, e-m Zweck*: adjust (*alle*: *dat.* to); *s. anprobieren*; *sich* ~ (*dat.*) adapt o.s. to; adjust to; '**2ung** *f* adaptation; adjustment.

'**anpassungsfähig** adaptable (*an acc.* to); '**2keit** *f* adaptability.

'**anpeilen** take the bearings of, locate.

'**Anpfiff** *m Sport*: whistle; F *e-n* ~ *kriegen* get a ticking-off.

'**anpflanz|en** plant, cultivate; '**2ung** *f* planting; *konkret*: plantation.

'**anpöbeln** molest, mob.

Anprall ['~pral] *m* (3[1]) impact, (*a.* ⚔) shock; '**2en** (sn) bound, strike (*an acc.* against).

anprangern ['~praŋərn] (29) pillory, denounce, brand.

'**anpreis|en** (*empfehlen*) (re)commend; (*loben*) praise; *durch Reklame*: boost, *Am. a.* push; '**2ung** *f* praising; boosting.

'**Anprob|e** *f* try-on, fitting; '**2ieren** try (*od.* fit) on.

'**anpumpen** F: *j-n* ~ *um* touch a p. for.

'**anraten** advise; (*empfehlen*) recommend; 2 *n*: *auf sein* ~ at his suggestion *od.* advice.

'**anrechn|en** charge; (*gutschreiben*) credit; (*abziehen*) deduct; *j-m zuviel* ~ overcharge a p.; *fig. j-m et. hoch* ~ think highly of a p. for a th.; *j-m et. in* '**2ung** (*f*) *bringen* put a th. to a p.'s account.

'**Anrecht** *n* right, title, claim (*auf acc.* to).

'**Anrede** *f* address; *im Brief*: salutation; '**2n** address, speak to.

'**anreg|en** (*berühren*) touch; *geistig, a. physiol.*: stimulate; (*vorschlagen*) suggest; *j-n zu e-m Werk usw.* ~ give a p. the idea of; *s. angeregt*; '**~end** stimulating; '**2ung** *f* stimulation; (*Vorschlag*) suggestion; '**2ungsmittel** *n* stimulant.

anreicher|n ['~raɪçərn] (29) enrich; (*sättigen*) concentrate; '**2ung** *f* enrichment; concentration; '**2ungsanlage** *f für Uran*: enrichment plant.

'**anreihen** join; *sich* ~ (*dat.*) join, rank with; (*sich anstellen*) queue (*Am.* line) up.

'**Anreiz** *m* incentive, stimulus, inducement; '**2en** incite, stimulate; (*verlocken*) induce.

anrempeln ['~rɛmpəln] (29) jostle (*od.* bump) against.

'**anrennen** *v/t. u. v/i.* (sn): ~ *gegen* run against; ⚔ assault; *angerannt kommen* come running (up).

'**anrichte|n** *Speisen*: prepare, dish, dress, serve; *Unheil usw.*: cause, do; *es ist angerichtet* dinner *etc.* is served; '**2(tisch** *m*) *f* (15) sideboard.

anrüchig ['~ryçiç] disreputable.

'**anrücken** (sn) approach.

'**Anruf** *m* call (*a. teleph.*); '**~be-antworter** *teleph. m* (7) telephone answering machine; '**2en** call, shout to; *teleph.* call (up), ring (up), (tele-) phone; *Schiff, Taxi*: hail; ⚔ *v. Posten*: challenge; *Gott usw.*: invoke; *j-s Hilfe,* ⚖ *höhere Instanz*: appeal to; '**~ung** *f* invocation; ⚖ *usw.* appeal (*gen.* to).

'**anrühren** touch; *Brei usw.*: mix.

'**Ansag|e** *f* (15) announcement; '**2en** announce (*a. Radio*); *sein Spiel*: call; *Trumpf* ~ declare trumps; *s. Kampf*; '**~er(in** *f*) *m* (7) announcer (*a. Radio*); *s. a. Conférencier*.

'**ansamm|eln** (*a. sich*) collect; gather, assemble (*a. Personen*); (*anhäufen*) accumulate, amass; *Truppen*: concentrate; '**2lung** *f* gathering; accumulation; assembly; concentration.

ansässig ['~zɛsiç] resident (*in dat.* at *od.* in); *sich* ~ *machen* settle down; **2e** ['~gə] *m, f* resident.

'**Ansatz** *m an e-m Blasinstrument*: embouchure; ⊕ *s.* *~stück*; (*Anfang, Anlauf*) start; *in e-r Rechnung*: rate, charge; ♈ statement; (*Voranschlag*) estimate; (*Anlage*) disposition; *biol.* rudiment; *geol.* deposit; '**~punkt** *m* starting point; '**~stück** ⊕ *n* extension.

'**ansaugen** suck in.

'**anschaff|en** procure, provide; (*kaufen*) buy, purchase (*a. sich et.* ~); '**2ung** *f* procuring, buying *usw.*; purchase; acquisition; '**2ungskosten** *pl.* prime (*od.* purchase) cost; '**2ungspreis** *m* cost price; '**2ungswert** *m* cost value.

'**anschalten** *Licht, Radio*: switch on; ⚡ *mit Draht*: connect.

'**anschau|en** look at, view; '**~lich** graphic(ally *adv.*), clear, vivid.

'**Anschauung** *f* view, opinion; (*Einstellung*) approach, point of view; (*Vorstellung*) conception, idea; '**~smaterial** *n* illustrative material; (*Ton- u. Bildapparate*) audio-visual aids *pl.*; '**~s-unterricht** *m* visual instruction, object-teaching; *fig.* object-lesson; '**~sweise** *f* point of view.

'**Anschein** *m* appearance; *allem ~ nach* to all appearances; *den ~ erwecken* give the impression; *sich den ~ geben* pretend, make believe; *den ~ haben* seem; '**2end** apparent, seeming.

'**anschicken:** *sich ~ (zu)* prepare (for); set about doing *a th.*; *gerade*: be going to.

'**anschießen** wound, shoot, *bsd. Vogel*: wing; *Gewehr*: test, try.

anschirren ['~ʃirən] (25) harness.

'**Anschiß** *sl. m*: *j-m e-n ~ verpassen* give a p. a bollocking.

'**Anschlag** *m* stroke; (*Schätzung*) estimate; (*Berechnung*) calculation; (*Komplott*) plot; (*Attentat*) attempt; ♪, *a. Schwimmen*: touch; ⚔ *des Gewehrs*: aiming (*od.* firing) position; ⊕ stop, detent; *s. ~zettel*; *in ~ bringen* take into account; *Gewehr im ~ halten* level (*auf acc.* at); *e-n ~ verüben auf (acc.)* make an attempt on; '**~brett** *n* notice-board, *Am.* bulletin board, billboard; '**2en** *v/t.* strike (*an acc.* at, against); (*befestigen*) fasten, affix (*an* on); *Plakat*: post up, put up; (*schätzen*) estimate (*hoch* highly), rate; ♪ touch, strike; *Gewehr*: level (*auf acc.* at); *Faß Bier usw.*: tap; *zu hoch ~* overestimate; *zu niedrig ~* underrate; *e-n andern Ton ~* change one's tune; *s. angeschlagen*; *v/i. Glocke*: ring; (*bellen*) give tongue; *Schwimmer*: touch; (*wirken*) take (effect); *Essen*: agree (*bei j-m* with); (*zielen*) take aim (*auf acc.* at); (sn) *mit dem Kopf an die Wand ~* strike one's head against; '**~säule** *f* advertisement (*Am.* advertising) pillar; '**~zettel** *m* bill, placard, poster.

'**anschließen** *v/t.* fix with a lock; (*anketten*) chain; (*anfügen*) add, join, attach, annex; ⊕ join (*an acc.* to), link up (with); ⚡ connect (to), *mit Stecker*: plug in; *sich ~*: *j-m, j-s Bitte, e-r Gesellschaft usw.*: join, *e-r Meinung*: subscribe to, *e-m Beispiel*: follow; *sich ~ an (acc.) Sache*: follow; *v/i. Kleid*: fit close; '**~d** subsequent(ly *adv.*; *an acc.* to).

'**Anschluß** *m* joining; 🚂, ⚡, *teleph.* connection; (*Gas- usw.* 2) supply; *~ an e-n Zug haben* meet a train, have a connection with a train; *im ~ an (acc.)* following; *teleph. ~ bekommen* get through; *fig. ~ finden (suchen)* meet (seek) company; *den ~ verpassen (a. fig.)* miss one's connection, *fig. sl.* miss the bus; '**~-arbeiten** *f/pl.* (*weitere Arbeiten*) follow-up work *sg.*; (*Anschließungsarbeiten*) connection work *sg.*; '**~dose** ⚡ *f* junction box; '**~flug** *m* connecting flight; '**~gebühr** *f* connection fee; '**~klemme** ⚡ *f* terminal; '**~rohr** *n* service-pipe; '**~schnur** ⚡ *f* flex(ible cord); '**~station** 🚂 *f* junction; '**~treffer** *m* goal that leaves one more to level the score; '**~zug** 🚂 *m* connecting train.

'**an|schmiegen** (25): *sich ~ an (acc.)* nestle against; *Kleid*: cling to; '**~schmiegsam** *Kleidung*: soft (and comfortable); *fig.* affectionate; '**~schmieren** (be)smear, daub; grease; F (*betrügen*) cheat; '**~schnallen** (25) buckle on; ✈, *mot. sich ~* fasten one's seat belts.

'**anschnauzen** F (27) blow up, snap at, *Am.* bawl out.

'**an|schneiden** cut (from); *Thema*: broach; '**2schnitt** *m* first cut *od.* slice; '**~schrauben** screw on (*an acc.* to); '**~schreiben 1.** write down; ✝ *j-n*: write to; *Stand e-s Spiels*: score (*a. v/i.*; h.); *Schuld*: charge; *j-m et. ~* put to a p.'s account; *et. ~ lassen* buy on credit; *bei j-m gut (schlecht) angeschrieben sein* be in a p.'s good (bad) books; **2.** 2 *n* cover note; '**~schreien** shout at; '**2schrift** *f* address.

anschuldig|en ['~ʃuldigən] (25) accuse, incriminate; '**2ung** *f* accusation, incrimination.

'**anschwärzen** *fig.* blacken, calumnicate, F sneak against.

'**anschweißen** ⊕ weld on.

'**anschwell|en** *v/i.* (sn) swell; (*zunehmen*) increase, rise; '**2ung** *f* swelling.

'**anschwemmen** wash ashore; [*Land*: deposit.]

'**ansegeln** *Hafen*: make for; *angesegelt kommen* come up (sailing).

'**ansehen 1.** look at; *s. scharf, scheel*; *sich et. ~* take (*od.* have) a look at; (*besichtigen*) view; (*beobachten*) watch; *fig. ~ für od. als* regard as, consider, *fälschlich*: take for; *et.*

mit ~ witness, (*ertragen*) bear; *j-m et.* ~ read a th. in a p.'s face; *man sieht ihm sein Alter nicht an* he does not look his age; **2.** ♀ *n* (6) (*Anschein*) appearance, aspect; (*Geltung*) authority, prestige, standing; (*Achtung*) esteem, reputation; *sich ein* ~ *geben* put on airs; *j-n von* ~ *kennen* know a p. by sight; *ohne* ~ *der Person* without respect of persons.

ansehnlich ['~ze:nliç] considerable; *Person*: fine-looking.

anseilen *mount.* ['~zaɪlən] rope.

'**ansengen** singe.

'**ansetz|en** *v/t.* (*an acc.*) put on (to), apply (to); *Glas, Flöte usw.*: put to one's lips; (*anstücken*) add (to); *Frist*: appoint, fix; (*abschätzen*) rate, assess; *Preis*: fix, quote; (*berechnen*) charge; (*entwickeln*) produce; *Blätter usw.*: put forth; *Fleisch* (*am Körper*), *Speise* (*zum Kochen*), *a. thea. Stück*: put on; *Essig, Likör usw.*: prepare; *Rost*: gather; *die Feder* ~ set pen to the paper; *v/i.* (*versuchen*) try; (*Fett* ~) grow fat; *zu et.* ~ prepare for *od.* to *do*; *zum Sprung* ~ get ready for the jump; '♀**ung** *f e-s Preises*: quotation; *e-s Termins*: appointment.

'**Ansicht** *f* sight, view; *fig.* view, opinion; *meiner* ~ *nach* in my opinion; ✝ *zur* ~ on approval; *der* ~ *sein, daß* be of opinion that; *zu der* ~ *kommen, daß* decide that; *ich bin anderer* ~ I beg to differ; '♀**ig:** *j-s* ~ *werden* catch sight of; '~**s(post)-karte** *f* picture postcard; '~**ssache** *f* matter of opinion.

'**ansied|eln** (29) (*a. sich*) settle, colonize; *fig.* place; '♀**ler** *m* settler; '♀**lung** *f* settlement.

'**Ansinnen** *n* (6) request, demand.

'**anspann|en** stretch; *Muskeln*: flex; *Pferd*: harness; *fig.* tense (*a. sich*); (*anstrengen*) strain; '♀**ung** *fig. f* strain; *unter* ~ *aller Kräfte* by exerting all one's energies.

'**anspeien** spit (up)on *od.* at.

'**anspiel|en** *v/i.* play first, lead; *Sport*: lead off; *Fußball*: kick off; ~ *auf* (*acc.*) allude to, hint at; *v/t. Karte*: lead; *Fußball*: *j-n* ~ pass to; '♀**ung** *f* allusion, hint.

'**anspinnen:** *fig. sich* ~ develop.

'**anspitzen** point, sharpen.

'**Ansporn** *m* spur, encouragement; (*Anreiz*) incentive; '♀**en** spur; *fig. a.* goad (on), encourage.

'**Ansprache** *f* address, speech (*an acc.* to); *e-e* ~ *halten* deliver an address.

'**ansprechen** speak to, address; *fig.* ~ *als* regard as; (*gefallen*) appeal to; (*reagieren, a.* ⊕) respond (*auf acc.* to); '~**d** appealing.

'**anspringen** *v/t.* leap against; *v/i.* (sn) *Motor*: start; *angesprungen kommen* come skipping along.

'**anspritzen** besprinkle, spray.

'**Anspruch** *m* (*auf acc.*) claim, pretension (to); ⚖ title, (*a. Patent*♀) claim (to); *hohe Ansprüche* high demands; *s. aufgeben*; ~ *haben auf* (*acc.*) be entitled to; ~ *machen* (*od. erheben*) *auf* (*acc.*), *in* ~ *nehmen* lay claim to, pretend to; claim to *be*; *j-s Hilfe usw. in* ~ *nehmen* call on, *Vorräte usw.*: draw (up)on; *Zeit, Aufmerksamkeit, Kredit in* ~ *nehmen* take up; *ganz in* ~ *nehmen* engross; *ganz u. gar für sich in* ~ *nehmen* monopolize; (*starke*) *Ansprüche stellen an* (*acc.*) tax severely; '♀**slos** unpretentious; (*schlicht*) unassuming, modest; *Essen*: frugal; (*geistig*) ~ *S.*: undemanding; '~**slosigkeit** *f* unpretentiousness; '♀**svoll** pretentious; (*streng*) exacting; (*wählerisch*) fastidious; *v. Sachen*: ambitious; *geistig*: demanding.

'**anspucken** spit (up)on *od.* at.

'**anspülen** *s. anschwemmen.*

'**anstacheln** goad on, prod, incite.

Anstalt ['~ʃtalt] *f* (16) establishment; institution; *s. Irren(heil)*♀, *Heil*♀, *Lehr*♀; ~ *machen zu* prepare to *inf.*; ~*en treffen zu* make arrangements for.

'**Anstand** *m* (3^3, *o. pl.*) *hunt.* stand; (*Schicklichkeit*) decency, propriety, decorum; (*Einwendung*) objection (*an dat.* to); ~ *nehmen zu* hesitate to.

anständig ['~ʃtɛndiç] *allg.* decent; (*schicklich*) proper; (*achtbar*) respectable; (*beträchtlich*) fair, handsome; *adv.* F (*sehr*) thoroughly; '♀**keit** *f* decency; propriety.

'**Anstands|besuch** *m* formal call; '~**dame** *f* chaperon; '~**formen** *f/pl.* proprieties *pl.*; '~**gefühl** *n* tact; '♀**halber** for decency's sake; '♀**slos** *adv.* unhesitatingly; (*ungehindert*) freely.

'**anstarren** stare at.

anstatt [~'ʃtat] (*gen.*) instead of.
'**anstauen** dam up; *sich* ~ accumulate.
'**anstaunen** gape at.
'**anstechen** prick; *Faß*: broach, tap.
'**ansteck|en** *v/t.* stick on; *mit e-r Nadel*: pin on; *Ring*: slip on; ⚕ infect; (*anzünden*) set on fire; *Feuer*: kindle; *Kerze, Zigarre usw.*: light; *v/i.* be catching; '**~end** ⚕ infectious; contagious; '**2nadel** *f* badge; (*Schmucknadel*) pin; '**2ung** *f* infection; *durch Berührung*: contagion; '**2ungsgefahr** *f* danger of infection; '**2ungsstoff** *m* infectious matter.
'**anstehen** *in e-r Reihe*: queue (up), *Am.* stand in line (*nach* for); *j-m*: suit, become; (*zögern*) hesitate; (*zu erwarten sein*) be due; ~ *lassen* put off, delay.
'**ansteigen** (sn) *Boden usw.*: rise, ascend; *fig.* rise, increase; 2 *n* rising, rise; increase.
'**anstell|en** place (*an acc.* against); *P.*: engage, employ; *Mechanismus*: start; *Licht, Radio usw.*: switch on; *Unfug*: do; *Versuch usw.*: make; *Vergleich*: draw; (*fertigbringen*) manage; *sich* ~ queue on *od.* up, *Am.* line up (*nach* for); *sich* ~ *als ob* act as if; *sich geschickt* (*ungeschickt*) ~ set to work (*od.* act) cleverly (clumsily); *angestellt bei* in the employ of; '**~ig** handy, clever; '**2igkeit** *f* (25) skill; '**2ung** *f* place; employment, job.
'**ansteuern** steer (*od.* head) for.
Anstieg ['anʃti:k] *m* (3) ascent; *fig.* rise, increase.
'**anstieren** (25) stare at.
'**anstift|en** *j-n, et.*: instigate; *et.*: cause, do, stir up; '**2er**(**in** *f*) *m* instigator; '**2ung** *f* instigation.
'**anstimmen** strike up.
'**Anstoß** *m* (*Antrieb*) impulse; (*Ärgernis*) offence, *Am.* offense; *Fußball*: kick-off; *Stein des* ~*es* stumbling-block; ~ *erregen* give offence (*bei* to), scandalize (*a p.*); ~ *nehmen an* (*dat.*) take offence at, be scandalized at; take exception to; *den* ~ *geben zu* start, initiate; '**2en** *v/t.* push, knock, bump (against); *heimlich*: nudge; *v/i. s. angrenzen*; *mit der Zunge* ~ lisp; ~ *bei j-m* offend, shock; *mit den Gläsern* ~ clink glasses; *auf j-s Gesundheit* ~ drink a p.'s health; '**2end** *s. angrenzend.*

anstößig ['~ʃtø:siç] offensive, shocking.
'**anstrahlen** beam on (*fig.* at); ⚡ floodlight.
'**anstreben** aspire to, strive for.
'**anstreich|en** paint, coat; *Textstelle*: mark; *Fehler*: underline; *fig. j-m et.* ~ make a p. pay for; '**2er** *m* (7) house-painter.
anstreng|en ['~ʃtrɛŋən] (25) exert; (~*d sein für*) *Geist, Körper*: tax, try; *j-n*: fatigue; *sich* ~ exert (*Am.* drive) o.s., (*sich bemühen*) endeavo(u)r (*zu tun* to do); *alle Kräfte* ~ strain every nerve; *s. Prozeß, angestrengt*; '**~end** strenuous; trying (*für* to); '**2ung** *f* exertion, effort; strain.
'**Anstrich** *m* paint; (*Überzug*) coat(-ing); *fig.* varnish; (*leiser* ~) tinge; (*Anschein*) air, appearance.
'**An|sturm** *m* assault, charge; ~ *auf e-e Bank usw.* run on; '**2stürmen** (sn) storm, rush (*gegen* against).
'**ansuchen 1.** (*bei j-m*) *um et.* ~ apply (to a p.) for; **2.** 2 *n* (6) request, application; *auf* ~ by request; *auf j-s* ~ at a p.'s request.
Antarkt|is [ant'ʔarktis] *f the* Antarctic (regions *pl.*); **2isch** antarctic.
'**antasten** touch; *fig. a.* attack.
'**Anteil** *m* share (*a.* ✝), portion; (*Quote*) quota; *fig.* interest; ~ *haben an* (*dat.*) share *od.* participate in; ~ *nehmen an* (*dat.*) take an interest in, *mitleidig*: sympathize with; (*sich interessieren für*) take an interest in; '**2mäßig** proportional; '**~nahme** *f* sympathy; interest; '**~schein** *m* share certificate.
'**antelephonieren** ring up.
Antenne [an'tɛnə] *f* (15) *Radio*: aerial, *bsd. Am.* antenna.
Anthrazit *min.* [~tra'tsi:t] *m* (3[1]) anthracite; **2farben** charcoal.
Anti..., anti... [anti-] anti...
Anti-alko'holiker(**in** *f*) *m* teetotaller.
Anti-'Baby-Pille *f the* pill.
Anti-Be'schlagtuch *n* anti-mist cloth.
Antibiotikum ⚕ [antibi'o:tikum] *n* (9[2]) antibiotic.
Anti-Blockier-System *mot. n* anti-brake-locking system.
Antifaschi|smus [antifa'ʃismus] *m* (16, *o. pl.*) antifascism; **~st** *m* (12), **2stisch** *adj.* antifascist.
Anti'haftbeschichtung *f e-r Pfanne*:

non-stick surface; *mit* ~ non-stick.
antik [an'ti:k] antique; **2e** *f* (15) *Kunstwerk*: antique; *Zeitalter*: die ~ the (classical) antiquity.
'**Antikörper** ⚕ *m* anti-body.
Antilope [anti'lo:pə] *f* (15) antelope.
Antipathie [~pa'ti:] *f* antipathy (*gegen* against, to), aversion (to, for).
'**antippen** touch lightly, tap.
Antiqua *typ.* [~'ti:kva] *f inv.* Roman (type).
Antiquar [anti'kva:r] *m* (3[1]) second-hand bookseller; *s. Antiquitätenhändler*; **~iat** [~kvar'ja:t] *n* (3[1]) second-hand bookshop; **2isch** [~'kva:riʃ] second-hand.
Antiquitäten|händler[~kvi'tɛ:tən-] *m* antique dealer; **~laden** *m* antique shop.
Antisemit [~ze'mi:t] *m* (12) anti-Semite; **2isch** anti-Semitic; **~ismus** [~mi'tismus] *m* anti-Semitism.
anti'statisch antistatic.
Antlitz ['antlits] *n* (3[2]) face.
Antrag ['antra:k] *m* (3[3]) (*Angebot*) offer, (*a. Heirats2*) proposal; (*Gesuch*) application, request, *parl.* motion, ⚖ petition; *e-n ~ stellen auf* (*acc.*) *s. beantragen*; **2en** ['~gən] offer; '**~sformular** *n* application form; **~steller(in** *f*) ['~ʃtɛlər] *m* applicant, ⚖ *a.* petitioner; *parl.* mover.
'**antrauen:** *j-m* ~ wed to a p.
'**antreffen** meet (*et.* with), find.
'**antreiben** *v/i.* (sn) drift (*od.* float) ashore; *v/t.* drive (*od.* push) on; *Pferd*: urge on; *Maschine*: drive; *Schiff usw.*: propel; *fig.* impel.
'**antreten** *v/t. Amt, Dienst, Erbschaft*: enter (up)on; *Reise*: set out on; *die Arbeit* (*den Dienst*) ~ report for work (duty); *s. Beweis*; *v/i.* (sn) take one's place; ⚔ fall in, line up.
'**Antrieb** *m* motive, impulse; (*Anreiz*) incentive; ⊕ drive, propulsion; *aus eigenem* ~ of one's own accord; ⊕ *mit* ...~ ...-powered; '**~s-achse** 🚗 *f* propeller shaft; '**~s-schwäche** ⚕ *f* ab(o)ulia; '**~swelle** *f* driving shaft.
'**Antritt** *m fig.* commencement; *e-s Amtes usw.*: entrance upon; *e-r Reise*: setting out on; '**~sbesuch** *m* courtesy call; '**~srede** *f* inaugural speech; *parl.* maiden speech.
'**antun:** *j-m et.* ~ do a th. to a p.; *sich et.* ~ lay hands upon o.s.; *es j-m* ~ bewitch (*od.* charm) a p.; *s. angetan.*
'**Antwort** *f* (16) answer, reply (*auf acc.* to); '**2en** *v/t. u. v/i.* (26) answer, reply (*j-m* a p.; *auf acc.* to); '**~karte** *f* reply postcard; '**2lich** (*gen.*) ✝ in reply to; '**~schein** *m* reply coupon; '**~schreiben** *n* reply.
'**anvertrauen** confide (*a. Geheimnis*), entrust (*beide*: *dat.* to); *j-m et.* ~ *a.* trust a p. with a th.; *fig. sich j-m* ~ confide in a p.
'**anverwandt** related; '**2e** *m, f* relation.
'**anwachsen** (sn) grow on (*an acc.* to); (*Wurzel schlagen*) take root; *fig.* increase; **2** *n fig.* increase.
Anwalt ['~valt] *m* (3[3]) lawyer, *bsd. Am.* attorney(-at-law); *beratender*: solicitor; *plädierender*: barrister, *Am.* counselor-at-law; *vor Gericht*: counsel (*des Angeklagten* for the defence); *fig.* advocate; '**~schaft** *f* the Bar; '**~skammer** *f* Board of Attorneys; '**~skosten** *pl.* legal expenses.
'**anwand|eln** come over, seize; *ihn wandelte die Lust an, zu inf.* the fancy took him to; '**2lung** *f* fit; (*Antrieb*) impulse.
'**anwärmen** warm up; preheat.
'**Anwärter(in** *f*) *m* (*auf acc.*) candidate (for), aspirant (to); ⚖ expectant, claimant (of).
Anwartschaft ['~vartʃaft] *f* (*auf acc.*) candidacy, qualification (for); ⚖ expectancy (of), claim (to).
'**anweis|en** (*zuteilen*) assign; (*belehren*) instruct; (*beauftragen*) direct; *s. angewiesen*; '**2ung** *f* assignment; instruction; direction; ✝ cheque, *Am.* check, draft; *s. Post2.*
anwend|bar ['~vɛntba:r] practicable; applicable (*auf acc.* to); '**2barkeit** *f* applicability; **~en** ['~dən] employ, use; apply (*auf acc.* to); *Vorsicht*: take; *s. angewandt*; '**2er** *m* (7) *a. Computer*: user; '**2ung** *f* application; *zur ~ bringen s. anwenden*; '**2ungsbeispiel** *n* example of use, illustrative example; '**2ungs-programm** *n Computer*: application program.
'**anwerb|en** ⚔ enlist, recruit, *Am.* levy, enrol(l); *Arbeiter*: recruit, engage; '**2estopp** *m* recruitment stop; '**2ung** *f* ⚔ enlistment, recruitment; engagement.

ˈ**Anwesen** *n* property; ✓ farm, (*Gut*) estate.

ˈ**anwesen|d** present (*bei* at); *die* ♀*en* the persons (*od.* those) present; ♀*e ausgenommen* present company excepted; *verehrte* ♀*e!* Ladies and Gentlemen!; ˈ♀**heit** *f* presence; *in* ~ *gen.* in the ~ of; ˈ♀**heitsliste** *f* attendance list.

anwidern [ˈ~viːdərn] (29) *s. anekeln.*

ˈ**Anwohner** *m* neighbo(u)r; *s. Anlieger.*

ˈ**Anwurf** *m* (*Verleumdung*) aspersion.

ˈ**Anzahl** *f* number; quantity.

ˈ**anzahl|en** pay on account, pay a first instal(l)ment; et. ~ (*als Angeld*) pay a deposit; ˈ♀**ung** *f bei Ratenzahlung*: down payment, payment on account, (first) instal(l)ment; *als Sicherheit*: deposit.

ˈ**anzapfen** tap (*a.* ⚡ *teleph.*), broach.

ˈ**Anzeichen** *n* sign, indication, *a.* ⚕ symptom (*für* of).

Anzeig|e [ˈantsaɪgə] *f* (15) notice; (*Zeitungs*♀ *usw.*) advertisement, F ad; (*Ankündigung*) announcement, ✝ advice; ⚖ information; ⊕ signal, (*Ablesung*) reading; *kleine* ~*n pl.* classified ads; *s. erstatten*; *e-e* ~ *aufgeben* place an advertisement in a newspaper; ˈ♀**en** announce, notify, ✝ advise; *in der Zeitung usw.*: advertise; (*deuten auf*) indicate; *j-n*: denounce, inform against, *et.*: report (*bei* to); *es erscheint angezeigt, zu inf.* it seems expedient *od.* indicated to *inf.*; ˈ~**en-annahme** *f* advertising office; ˈ~**en-auftrag** *m* insertion order; ˈ~**enbüro** *n* advertising agency *od.* office; ˈ~**enteil** *m in der Zeitung*: advertisements *pl.*, ads pages *pl.*; ˈ♀**epflichtig** notifiable; ˈ~**er** *m* advertiser (*a.* ˈ~**enblatt** *n*); ⚖ informer; ⊕ indicator; ˈ~**etafel** *f Sport*: scoreboard.

anzetteln [ˈ~tsɛtəln] (29) *fig.* plot.

ˈ**anziehen** *v/t.* draw, pull; *Zügel*: draw in; *Schraube*: tighten; *Kleid*: put on; *j-n*: dress; *fig.* attract; *v/i.* draw; *Preise*: rise; *im Brettspiel*: make the first move; ˈ~**d** attractive.

ˈ**Anziehung** *f* attraction; ˈ~**skraft** *f* attractive power, pull; *der Erde usw.*: gravitation(al pull); *fig.* attraction, appeal.

ˈ**Anzug** *m* (*Kleidung*) dress; (*Herren*♀) suit; ⚔ dress, uniform; *beim Brettspiel*: first move; *im* ~ *sein* be approaching.

anzüglich [ˈ~tsyːkliç] suggestive; (*stichelnd*) personal; ˈ♀**keit** *f* suggestiveness; personal remark.

ˈ**Anzugstoff** *m* suiting.

ˈ**anzünd|en** light, kindle; *Streichholz*: strike; *Haus*: set on fire; ˈ♀**er** *m* (7) lighter.

ˈ**anzweifeln** doubt, (call in) question.

apart [aˈpart] exquisite.

Apath|ie [apaˈtiː] *f* apathy; ♀**isch** [aˈpɑːtiʃ] apathetic.

Apfel [ˈapfəl] *m* (7[1]) apple; *s. sauer*; ˈ~**baum** *m* apple-tree; ˈ~**kompott** *n* stewed apple; ˈ~**mus** *n* apple-sauce; ˈ~**saft** *m* apple-juice; ˈ~**schimmel** *m* dapple-grey horse; ~**sine** [~ˈziːnə] *f* (15) orange; ˈ~**tasche** *f* apple turnover; ˈ~**wein** *m* cider.

Apostel [aˈpɔstəl] *m* (7) apostle; ~**geschichte** *f the* Acts *pl.* of the Apostles.

apostolisch [apɔˈstoːliʃ] apostolical; *das* ♀*e Glaubensbekenntnis* The Apostles' Creed, The Belief.

Apostroph [apɔˈstroːf] *m* (3[1]) apostrophe.

Apotheke [apoˈteːkə] *f* (15) chemist's shop, *Am.* pharmacy.

Apoˈtheker *m* (7) (dispensing) chemist, *Am.* druggist, pharmacist; ~**gewicht** *n* apothecaries' weight.

Apparat [apaˈrɑːt] *m* (3) *allg.* apparatus; instrument; (*Gerät*) appliance; (*Vorrichtung*) device; *phot.* camera; *Radio*: set; *teleph.* telephone; *fig.* apparatus, organization; *teleph. am* ~*!* speaking!; *am* ~ *bleiben* hold the line (*Am.* wire); ~**ur** [~ˈtuːr] *f* apparatus; outfit; (*Zubehör*) fixtures *pl.*

Appartement [apartəˈmɑ̃ː] *n* (11) flat, *bsd. Am.* apartment; ~**haus** *n* block of flats, *Am.* apartment house.

Appell [aˈpɛl] *m* (3[1]) ⚔ roll-call; inspection; parade; *fig.* appeal (*an acc.* to).

appelˈlieren appeal (*an acc.* to).

Appetit [apeˈtiːt] *m* (3) appetite (*auf acc.* for); ~ *machen* give (an) appetite; ♀**lich** appetizing (*a. fig.*); ~**zügler** *m* (7) appetite suppressant.

applaudieren [aplaʊˈdiːrən] cheer, applaud (*j-m* a p.).

Applaus [aˈplaʊs] *m* (4) applause.

apport [aˈpɔrt] go fetch!; ~**ieren** [~ˈtiːrən] fetch, retrieve.

appret|ieren [apreˈtiːrən] dress, finish; *Papier*: glaze; **2ur** [~ˈtuːr] *f* (16) dressing, finish.

approbiert [aproˈbiːrt] *Arzt*: qualified, *Am.* licensed.

Aprikose [apriˈkoːzə] *f* (15) apricot.

April [aˈpril] *m* (3¹) April; *j-n in den ~ schicken* make an April-fool of a p.; **~scherz** *m* April-fool joke; **~wetter** *n* April weather.

Aquaplaning [akvaˈplɑːniŋ] *n* (11¹, *o. pl.*) aquaplaning.

Aquarell [akvaˈrɛl] *n* (3¹) water--colo(u)r; **~farbe** *f* water-colo(u)r; **~maler(in** *f*) *m* aquarellist, water--colo(u)rist.

Äquator [ɛˈkvɑːtɔr] *m* (8, *o. pl.*) equator.

Äquivalent [ɛːkvivaˈlɛnt] *n*, **2** *adj.* equivalent.

Ar [ɑːr] *n* (3¹, *nach Zahlen inv.*) are.

Ära [ˈɛːra] *f* (16²) era.

Arab|er [ˈarabər] *m* Arab; *Pferd*: [aˈrɑːbər] Arab; **ˈ~erin** *f* Arabian (woman); **~eske** [araˈbɛskə] *f* (15) arabesque; **2isch** [aˈrɑːbiʃ] Arabian; Arabic.

Arbeit [ˈarbaɪt] *f* (16) work; (*mühevolle ~*) labo(u)r, toil; (*Beschäftigung*) employment, job; (*Tätigkeit, Geschäft*) business; (*aufgegebene ~, Schul2*) task; (*schriftliche ~*) paper; (*Fabrikat*) make; (*Ausführungsart*) workmanship; *phys.* work; ⚡ energy; ⊕ performance; *e-e gute (schlechte) ~* a good (bad) piece of work; *bei der ~* at work; *sich an die ~ machen, an die ~ gehen* set to work; *(keine) ~ haben* be in (out of) work; *s. antreten, niederlegen*; *et. in ~ geben (nehmen)* put (take) a. th. in hand; *in ~ sein (S.)* be in hand; *bei j-m in ~ stehen* be in the employ of a p.; *gute ~ leisten* make a good job of it; **ˈ2en** *v/i.* (26) work (*a. v/t.*); (*schwer ~*) labo(u)r, toil; *~ an (dat.)* be working at; ⚕ *mit e-r Firma ~* do business with; *Kapital ~ lassen* employ, invest.

ˈArbeiter *m* worker (*a. zo.*); (*Hand2*) workman; *ungelernt*: labo(u)rer, hand; *die ~ s. ~schaft*; **ˈ~in** *f* (female) worker; working woman, workwoman; **ˈ~klasse** *f* working class(es *pl.*); **ˈ~mangel** *m* shortage of workers; **ˈ~partei** *f* Labo(u)r Party; **ˈ~schaft** *f*, **ˈ~stand** *m* working class(es *pl.*), *a. pol.* labo(u)r.

ˈArbeit|geber(in *f*) *m* employer; **~ˈgeber-anteil** *m* employer's contribution; **ˈ~nehmer(in** *f*) *m* employee.

ˈarbeitsam industrious, diligent; **ˈ2keit** *f* industry, diligence.

ˈArbeits... *mst* working ...; **ˈ~-amt** *n* Labo(u)r Exchange; **ˈ~-anzug** *m* working clothes *pl.*; overall; **ˈ~ausschuß** *m* working committee; **ˈ~bedingungen** *f/pl.* working (⊕ operating) conditions; **ˈ~beschaffung** *f* provision of work; **ˈ~beschaffungsprogramm** *n* job creation scheme; **ˈ~bescheinigung** *f* certificate of employment; **ˈ~bogen** *m Schule*: work folder; **ˈ~buch** *n* employment record; **ˈ~dienst** *m* labo(u)r service; ⚔ fatigue; **ˈ~dienstpflicht** *f* industrial conscription; **ˈ~direktor** *m* workers' representative; **ˈ~-einkommen** *n* earned income; **ˈ~-einstellung** *f* stoppage of work; *e-s Betriebs*: closure; (*Streik*) strike; **ˈ~-erlaubnis** *f* work permit; **ˈ~-essen** *n* working lunch; **ˈ2fähig** fit (*od.* able) to work; **ˈ~fähigkeit** *f*: *j-s ~ feststellen* declare a p. fit to work; **ˈ~feld** *n* field (*od.* sphere) of work *od.* activity; **ˈ~fläche** *f* work-surface; **ˈ2freudig** willing to work; **ˈ~frieden** *m* industrial peace; **ˈ~gang** *m* working operation, process; **ˈ~gemeinschaft** *f* study group; ⚕ working pool; *Schule*: seminar group; **ˈ~gericht** *n* industrial court; **ˈ~kleidung** *f* work clothes *pl.*; **ˈ~klima** *n* work climate; **ˈ~konflikt** *m* labo(u)r dispute; **ˈ~kosten** *pl.* work cost; *~anteil* work cost per unit; **ˈ~kraft** *f* capacity for work; (*Arbeiter*) workman, hand; *pl. a.* labo(u)r *sg.*, manpower; **ˈ~lager** *n* labo(u)r camp; **ˈ~leistung** *f* working capacity, efficiency; *a.* ⊕ performance, output; **ˈ~lohn** *m* wages *pl.*, pay; **ˈ2los** out of work, unemployed, jobless; *~ machen* put out of work; **ˈ~lose** *m, f* unemployed person; **ˈ~losenquote** *f* unemployment rate; **ˈ~losenunterstützung** *f* unemployment benefit; *~ beziehen* be on the dole; **ˈ~losenversicherung** *f* unemployment insurance; **ˈ~losigkeit** *f* unemployment; **ˈ~markt** *m* labo(u)r market; **ˈ~methode** *f* working method; **ˈ~minister** *m* Minister of Labour, *Am.* Secretary for Labor; **ˈ~moral** *f* (working) morale; **ˈ~nachweis(stelle** *f*) *m* employment registry office;

ˈ~**niederlegung** *f* strike; ˈ~**platz** *m* place of employment; (*Stelle*) job; *Sicherheit des* ~*es* job security; ˈ~**platzbeschreibung** *f* job description; ˈ~**platzgarantie** *f* job guarantee; ˈ~**platzteilung** *f* job sharing; ˈ~**raum** *m* workroom; ˈ~**recht** *n* industrial law; ˈ2**scheu** work-shy; ˈ~**scheu** *f* aversion to work; ˈ~**soll** *n* target; ˈ2**sparend** labo(u)r-saving; ˈ~**streit**(**igkeit** *f*) *m* labo(u)r dispute; ˈ~**stunde** *f als Maßeinheit*: man-hour; *pl.* working hours; ˈ~**suche** *f* job hunting; *auf* ~ *sein* be job hunting; ˈ~**süchtige** *m, f* workaholic; ˈ~**tag** *m* working day; ˈ~**takt** *mot. m* power stroke; ˈ~**teilung** *f* division of labo(u)r; ˈ~**tier** F *n* demon for work; ˈ2-**unfähig** unfit for work; *dauernd*: disabled; ˈ~-**unfall** *m* industrial accident; ˈ~**vertrag** *m* employment contract; ˈ~**weise** *f* working method; ⊕ (mode of) operation; ˈ~**vermittlung** *f* employment exchange; ˈ~**vorbereitung** *f* operations scheduling; ˈ~**willige** *m* (18) non-striker; ˈ~**zeit** *f* working time; working hours *pl.*; *gleitende* ~ flexible working hours *pl.*; ˈ~**zeitregelung** *f* regulation of working hours; ˈ~**zeitverkürzung** *f* reduction in working hours; ˈ~**zeug** *n* tools *pl.*, kit; ˈ~**zimmer** *n* study.

Archäolog|e [arçεoˈlo:gə] *m* (13) arch(a)eologist; ~**ie** [~loˈgi:] *f* arch(a)eology; 2**isch** [~ˈlo:giʃ] arch(a)eological.

Arche [ˈarçə] *f* (15) ark.

Archipel [arçiˈpe:l] *m* (3[1]) archipelago.

Architekt [arçiˈtεkt] *m* (12) architect; 2**onisch** [~ˈto:niʃ] architectural; ~**ur** [~ˈtu:r] *f* architecture.

Archiv [arˈçi:f] *n* (3[1]) archives *pl.*; record-office; ~**ar** [~çiˈva:r] *m* (3[1]) archivist, registrar; ~-**exemplar** *n* record copy.

Areal [areˈa:l] *n* (3[1]) area.

Arena [aˈre:na] *f* (16[2]) arena.

arg [ark] **1.** (18[2]) *allg.* bad; (*moralisch schlecht*) wicked; *Sünder*: hopeless; *Versehen*: gross; *sein ärgster Feind* his worst enemy; ~ *enttäuscht* badly disappointed; *das ist zu* ~ that is too much; 2*es denken von* think ill of; *im* ~*en liegen* be in a sorry state; **2.** 2 *n* (11, *o. pl.*) malice, harm.

Ärger [ˈεrgər] *m* (7, *o. pl.*) (*Verdruß*) vexation, annoyance, chagrin; (*Zorn*) anger; *j-m* ~ *machen* give a p. trouble; ˈ2**lich** *Sache*: annoying, vexatious; *Person*: angry, vexed, irritated (*auf, über acc. et.* at, *j-n* with); ˈ2**n** (29) make angry, annoy, vex, anger, irritate; *sich* ~ (*über acc.*) feel angry (at, about *a th.*; with *a p.*) *od.* vexed (by); ˈ~**nis** *n* (4[1]) scandal, offen|ce, *Am.* -se; (*Mißstand*) (*öffentliches* public) nuisance; ~ *erregen* cause offence; ~ *an dat. nehmen* be scandalized at.

ˈ**Arg|list** *f* craft(iness), malice; ⚖ fraud; ˈ2**listig** crafty, insidious, deceitful; ⚖ fraudulent; ˈ2**los** guileless, innocent; (*nichtsahnend*) unsuspecting; (*ohne Argwohn*) unsuspicious; ˈ~**losigkeit** *f* guilelessness.

Argumen|t [arguˈmεnt] *n* (3) argument; ~ˈ**tieren** argue, reason.

Arg|wohn [ˈ~vo:n] *m* (3, *o. pl.*) suspicion (*gegen* of); 2**wöhnen** [ˈ~vø:nən] (25) suspect; ˈ2**wöhnisch** suspicious.

Arie ♪ [ˈa:rjə] *f* (15) aria.

Arier [ˈa:rjər] *m* (7), ˈ~**in** *f*, ˈ**arisch** } [Aryan.]

Aristokrat [aristoˈkra:t] *m* (12), ~**in** *f* aristocrat; ~**ie** [~kraˈti:] *f* aristocracy; 2**isch** [~ˈkra:tiʃ] aristocratic(ally *adv.*).

Arithme|tik [aritˈme:tik] *f* (16) arithmetic; 2**tisch** arithmetical.

Arkt|is [ˈarktis] *f the* Arctic (regions *pl.*); ˈ2**isch** arctic.

arm[1] [arm] (18[2]) poor (*an dat.* in); *ein* 2*er* a poor man; *die* 2*en pl.* the poor; *ich* 2*er!* poor me!

Arm[2] *m* (3) arm; *Fluß, Leuchter*: branch; *auf den* ~ *nehmen Kind*: take in one's arms, F *fig. j-n*: pull a p.'s leg; *in die* ~*e schließen* clasp in one's arms; *j-m unter die* ~*e greifen* help a p. (out).

Armatur ⚡ [armaˈtu:r] *f* (16) armature; ~**en** *pl.* fittings; ~**enbrett** *n* instrument panel, dashboard.

ˈ**Arm|band** *n* bracelet; *als Halt od. Schutz*: wristlet; ˈ~**band-uhr** *f* wrist watch; ˈ~**binde** *f* ⚕ (arm-) sling; *als Abzeichen*: armlet; ˈ~**bruch** *m* fracture of the arm; ˈ~**brust** *f* cross-bow.

Armee [arˈme:] *f* (15) army; ~**korps** *n* army corps.

Ärmel [ˈεrməl] *m* (7) sleeve; *fig. aus dem* ~ *schütteln* do offhand; ˈ~-**auf-**

schlag *m* cuff; '**~kanal** *m the* (English) Channel; '**2los** sleeveless.
'**Armen|haus** *n* poorhouse; *neuerdings*: public assistance institution; '**~kasse** *f* relief-fund; *eccl.* poor--box; '**~pflege** *f* poor-relief; '**~pfleger(in** *f*) *m* relieving officer; '**~recht** *n* poor-law; ⚖ *auf ~ klagen* sue in forma pauperis.
Arme'sündergesicht *n* hangdog look.
armieren [ar'mi:rən] ⚔ arm; ⊕ armo(u)r; *Beton*: reinforce.
...armig ...-armed; ...-branched.
'**Arm|lehne** *f* arm; '**~leuchter** *m* chandelier; F *fig.* idiot.
ärmlich ['ɛrmliç] *s. armselig.*
'**Armreif** *m* (3), '**~en** bangle.
'**armselig** poor; (*schäbig*) shabby; *fig. a.* miserable; (*dürftig*) paltry; '**2keit** *f* poorness.
'**Arm|sessel** *m*, '**~stuhl** *m* arm-chair, easy chair.
Armut ['armu:t] *f* (16, *o. pl.*) poverty; '**~szeugnis** *n*: *sich ein ~ ausstellen* give a poor account of o.s.
Aroma [a'ro:ma] *n* (11²) aroma, flavo(u)r; **2tisch** [aro'ma:tiʃ] aromatic.
Arrak ['arak] *m* (3¹) arrack.
arrangieren [arɑ̃'ʒi:rən] arrange.
Arrest [a'rɛst] *m* (3²) (*Haft*) arrest; confinement, (*a. Schul2*) detention; ⚖ (*Beschlagnahme*) attachment; *mit ~ bestrafen* put under arrest; **~ant** [~'tant] *m* (12) prisoner.
arretieren [are'ti:rən] arrest; ⊕ (*sperren*) arrest, lock.
arrogant [aro'gant] arrogant.
Arsch V [arʃ] *m* (3² *u.* ³) arse, bum; *leck mich am ~!* fuck you!; '**~loch** *n* arsehole.
Arsenal [arze'na:l] *n* (3¹) arsenal.
Art [a:rt] *f* (16) (*Gattung*) kind, sort, 🕮 species, *zo. a.* race, breed; (*Typ*) type; (*äußere Form*) style; (*Weise*) manner, way, fashion; (*Natur*) nature; (*Benehmen*) manners *pl.*; *~ und Weise* way, mode; *Fortpflanzung der ~* propagation of the species; *auf die(se) ~* in this way; *das ist keine ~* this is bad form; *aus der ~ schlagen* degenerate.
'**art-eigen** characteristic.
'**arten** (26, sn): *~ nach* take after; *s. geartet.*
'**arten|-arm** with few animal (*od.* plant) species; '**~reich** with a richly varied animal (*od.* plant) population.
Arterie [ar'te:rjə] *f* (15) artery; **~nverkalkung** *f* hardening of the arteries, arteriosclerosis.
'**artfremd** alien.
artig ['a:rtiç] (*hübsch, nett*) nice, pretty; *Kind*: good, well-behaved; (*höflich*) civil, polite; *sei ~!* be (*od.* there's) a good child!; '**2keit** *f* prettiness; good behavio(u)r; politeness, (*a. pl.*) civility.
Artikel [ar'ti:kəl] *m* (7) *allg., a.* ✝ article.
artikulieren [~tiku'li:rən] articulate.
Artiller|ie [artilə'ri:] *f* (15) artillery; **~ist** [~'rist] *m* (12) artilleryman, gunner.
Artischocke [arti'ʃɔkə] *f* (15) artichoke.
Artist [ar'tist] *m* (12), **~in** *f* acrobat, variety artist, circus performer.
Arznei [arts'naɪ] *f* (16) medicine; **~kunde** *f*, **~kunst** *f* pharmaceutics *sg.*; **~mittel** *n* medicine, medicament; drug; **~mittel-abhängigkeit** *f* drug dependence; **~mittellehre** *f* pharmacology; **~mittelmißbrauch** *m* drug abuse; **~schrank** *m* medicine cabinet.
Arzt [a:rtst] *m* (3² *u.* ³) medical practitioner, doctor, F medical man; *Berufsbezeichnung*: physician; *s. praktisch.*
'**Ärztemuster** *n* sample.
'**Arzthelferin** *f* doctor's receptionist.
Ärztin ['ɛ:rtstin] *f* (16¹) woman (*od.* lady) doctor *od.* physician.
'**ärztlich** medical.
As¹ [as] *n* (4¹) *Spiel*: ace (*a. fig. P.*).
As² ♪ *n inv.* A flat; *As-Dur* (*as-Moll*) A flat major (minor).
Asbest [as'bɛst] *m* (3²) asbestos.
'**aschblond** ashy-fair.
Asche ['aʃə] *f* (15) ashes *pl.*
'**Aschen...** *mst* ash...; '**~bahn** *f* cinder track; '**~becher** *m* ash-tray; '**~brödel** *n* (7) Cinderella (*a. fig.*); '**~platz** *m Sport*: cinder pitch.
Ascher'mittwoch *m* Ash Wednesday.
'**asch|fahl** ashen; '**~farben**, '**~farbig** ash-colo(u)red; '**~grau** ash--grey (*Am.* -gray).
äsen ['ɛ:zən] (27) *v/i. u. v/t. hunt.* graze, browse, feed (*et.* on).
Asiat [az'ja:t] *m* (12), **~in** *f*, **2isch** Asiatic.

Askese [as'ke:zə] *f* (15, *o. pl.*) asceticism.
As'ket *m* (12), **~in** *f* (16¹), **2isch** ascetic.
asozial ['azotsja:l] antisocial.
Aspekt [as'pɛkt] *m* (3¹ *u.* ²) aspect.
Asphalt [as'falt] *m* (3) asphalt; **2ieren** [~'ti:rən] asphalt; '**~presse** *f* yellow press.
aß [a:s] *pret. von essen* 1.
Asservat [asɛr'va:t] ⚖ *n* (3) court exhibit.
Assessor [a'sɛsɔr] *m* (8¹) assessor; ⚖ assistant judge.
Assisten|t [asis'tɛnt] *m* (12), **~tin** *f* assistant; **~z-arzt** [~ts-] *m* assistant doctor (*od.* surgeon); *Am. im Krankenhaus*: intern.
assis'tieren assist.
Ast [ast] *m* (3² *u.* ³) bough; *schwacher*: branch; *im Holz*: knot; *s. lachen.*
Aster ['astər] *f* (15) aster.
Asteroid [astero'i:t] *m* (12) asteroid.
Ästhet|ik [ɛ'ste:tik] *f* (16) (a)esthetics *sg.*; **~iker(in** *f*) *m* (a)esthete; **2isch** (a)esthetic(al).
Asthma ['astma] *n* (11, *o. pl.*) asthma.
Asthma|tiker [~'ma:tikər] *m* (7), **~tikerin** *f*, **2tisch** asthmatic.
'**Astloch** *n* knot-hole.
Astro|log(e) [astro'lo:k, ~gə] *m* (12 [13]) astrologer; **~logie** [~lo'gi:] *f* (15, *o. pl.*) astrology; **~naut** [~'naʊt] *m* (12) astronaut; **~nautik** [~'naʊtik] *f* astronautics *sg.*; **~nom** [~'no:m] *m* (12) astronomer; **~nomie** [~no'mi:] *f* (15, *o. pl.*) astronomy; **2nomisch** [~'no:m-] astronomical; **~physik** [~fy'zi:k] *f* astrophysics *sg.*
Asyl [a'zy:l] *n* (3¹) asylum; *fig.* sanctuary; (*politisches*) *~ suchen* seek (political) asylum; **~bewerber(in** *f*) *m* person seeking (political) asylum; **~recht** *n* right of asylum.
Atelier [atɛ'lje:] *n* (11) studio.
Atem ['a:təm] *m* (6, *o. pl.*) breath; *~ holen* pause for breath; *außer ~* (*kommen* get) out of breath *od.* winded; *wieder zu ~ kommen* recover one's breath; *j-n in ~ halten* keep a p. busy (*od. in Spannung*: in suspense); *s. anhalten*; '**~beschwerden** *f/pl.* difficulty *sg.* in breathing; '**~gerät** *n* breathing apparatus; ⚕ respirator; '**~geräusch** *n* respiratory sounds *pl.*; '**~holen** *n* respiration; '**2los** breathless (*a. fig.*); '**~not** *f* shortness of breath; '**~pause** *f* breathing-time, breathing-space, breather; '**2raubend** breath-taking; '**~technik** *f* breathing technique; '**~-übungen** *f/pl.* breathing exercises *pl.*; '**~wege** *m/pl.* respiratory tract *sg.*; '**~zug** *m* breath.
Atheismus [ate'ʔismus] *m* (16, *o. pl.*) atheism.
Atheist [~'ʔist] *m* (12), **~in** *f* (16¹) atheist; **2isch** atheistic(al).
Athen [a'te:n] *n* (17) Athens; *Eulen nach ~ tragen* carry coals to Newcastle.
Äther ['ɛ:tər] *m* (7, *o. pl.*) ether (*a.* ⚗); *Radio*: *über den ~* on the air; *mit ~ betäuben* etherize.
ätherisch [ɛ'te:r-] ethereal; *phys.*, *Radio*: etheric; *~es Öl* essential oil.
'**Äther|krieg** *m* radio war; '**~wellen** *phys. f/pl.* ether waves *pl.*
Athlet [at'le:t] *m* (12), **~in** *f* (16¹) athlete; **~ik** *f* (16) athletics *pl.*; **2isch** athletic.
Atlant [at'lant] *m* (12) *s. Atlas* 1.; **2isch** Atlantic; *der 2e Ozean* the Atlantic (Ocean).
Atlas ['atlas] *m* (4¹, *sg. a. inv.*) **1.** *geogr.* atlas; **2.** *Seiden2*: satin; *Baumwoll2*: sateen.
atmen ['a:tmən] (26) *v/i. u. v/t.* breathe.
Atmosphär|e [atmɔ'sfɛ:rə] *f* (15) atmosphere; **2isch** atmospheric; *~e Störungen f/pl. Radio*: atmospherics, statics *pl.*
'**Atmung** *f* breathing, respiration; '**~s-organ** *n*, '**~swerkzeug** *n* respiratory organ.
Atom [a'to:m] *n* (3¹) atom; **~-antrieb** *m* atomic propulsion; **2ar** [ato'ma:r] atomic, nuclear; **~bombe** *f* atomic (*od.* atom-, *abbr.* A-)bomb, fission bomb; **2bombensicher** atom-bomb-proof; **~bombenversuch** *m* A-bomb test; **~bunker** *m* fall-out shelter; **~-energie** *f* atomic energy; **~forscher** *m* nuclear scientist; **~forschung** *f* nuclear research; **~gemeinschaft** *f* Atomic Community; **~geschoß** *n* atomic shell; **~geschütz** *n* atomic gun; **~gewicht** *n* atomic weight; **~kern** *m* atomic nucleus; **~kraft** *f* atomic power; **~kraftwerk** *n* atomic power plant; **~krieg** *m* nuclear war(fare); **~meiler** *m* atomic pile; **~müll** *m* radioactive waste; **~mülldeponie** *f* radioactive waste

dump; **~pilz** *m* mushroom cloud; **~re-aktor** *m* atomic reactor; **~spaltung** *f* atomic fission, atom-splitting; **~sprengkopf** *m* nuclear warhead; **~staub** *m* atomic dust; **~teilchen** *n* atomic particle; **~-U-Boot** *n* nuclear submarine; **~versuch** *m* atomic test; **~waffe** *f* atomic weapon; **Ωwaffenfrei** nuclear-free; **~waffenlager** *n* atomic weapon depot; **~waffensperrvertrag** *m* non-proliferation treaty; **~wissenschaft** *f* atomics *sg.*, nuclear science; **~zeitalter** *n* atomic age; **~zerfall** *m* atomic decay; **~zertrümmerung** *f* atom-smashing.

Attaché [ata'ʃeː] *m* (11) attaché.

Attack|e [a'takə] *f* (15), **Ωieren** [~'kiːrən] (25) attack.

Attentat [atɛn'taːt] *n* (3) attempt upon a p.'s life, (attempted) assassination; *fig.* outrage.

Atten'täter *m* assassin.

Atte|st [a'tɛst] *n* (3²) (medical) certificate; **Ω'stieren** attest, certify.

Attrak|tion [atrak'tsjoːn] *f* attraction; **Ωtiv** [~'tiːf] attractive.

Attrappe [a'trapə] *f* (15) dummy.

Attribut [atri'buːt] *n* (3) attribute; *gr.* attributive; **Ωiv** *gr.* [~bu'tiːf] attributive.

atz|en ['atsən] (27) feed; **'Ωung** *f* feeding; (*Nahrung*) food.

ätz|en ['ɛtsən] (27) corrode; ⚕ cauterize; *auf Kupfer usw.*: etch; **'~end** corrosive; (*a. fig.*) caustic; **'Ωkalk** *m* caustic lime, quicklime; **'Ωkunst** *f* art of etching; **'Ωmittel** *n*, **'Ωstoff** *m* corrosive; *bsd.* ⚕ caustic; **'Ωung** *f* corrosion; ⚕ cauterization; (*Zeichnung*) etching.

au! [au] oh!, ouch!

auch [aux] also; too; likewise; (*selbst, sogar*) even; *du glaubst es — ich ~!* you believe it — so do I!; *er hat keine Freude — wir ~ nicht* he has no pleasure — nor (*od.* neither) have we; *wenn ~* even if, even though, although; *mag er ~ noch so reich sein* let him be ever so rich; *~ nur ein Mensch* nothing but a human being.

Audienz [au'djɛnts] *f* (16) audience.

audiovisuell [audiovizu'ɛl] audio-visual.

Auditorium [audi'toːrjum] *n* (9) (*Raum*) lecture-hall; (*Zuhörerschaft*) audience.

Aue ['auə] *f* (15) fertile plain; (*Wiese*) meadow, *poet.* mead.

Auer|hahn ['auər-] *m* capercaillie; **'~ochs** *m* aurochs.

auf [auf] **1.** *prp.* **a**) *mit dat.*: on, upon; in; at; of; by; *~ dem Tisch* on *od.* upon; *~ dem Markt* in; *~ der Universität*, *~ einem Ball* at; *~ s-r Seite* at (*od.* on) his side; *~ dem nächsten Wege* by the nearest way; **b**) *mit acc.*: on; in; at; to; towards (*a. ~ ... zu*); up; *~ deutsch* in German; *~ e-e Entfernung von* at a range of; *~ die Post usw. gehen* go to; *~ eine Mark gehen 100 Pfennige* ... go to a mark; *es geht ~ neun* it is getting on to nine; *~ ... hin* on the strength of; *~ Jahre hinaus* for years to come; *~ morgen* for tomorrow; **2.** *adv.* up, upwards; *~ und ab gehen* walk up and down *od.* to and fro; **3.** *cj.* *~ daß* (in order) that; *~ daß nicht* that not, lest; **4.** *int.* *~!* up!, arise!; (*los!*) let's go!

'auf-arbeiten *Rückstand*: work (*od.* clear) off; (*auffrischen*) work (*od.* furbish) up; *Kleid*: F do up.

'auf-atmen draw a deep breath; *fig.* breathe again *od.* freely; recover.

aufbahren ['~baːrən] (25) *Sarg*: put on the bier; *Leiche*: lay out (in state).

'Aufbau *m* building(-up); *a. e-s Dramas usw.*: construction; *e-r Organisation usw.*: structure, *bsd. Am.* setup; *mot.* body; ⚠, ⚓ superstructure; **'Ωen** erect, *a. fig. e-e Theorie, Existenz usw.*: build up; *Drama usw.*: construct; *sich ~ auf dat.* be based (up)on; *sich ~ vor P.*: plant o.s. before; **'Ωend** constructive.

'aufbäumen: *sich ~* rear; *fig.* rebel.

'Aufbauphase *f* development stage.

'aufbauschen puff up; *fig.* exaggerate, magnify, F play up.

'aufbegehren flare up; rebel, revolt (*gegen* against).

'aufbehalten *Hut*: keep on.

'aufbekommen *Tür usw.*: get open; *Knoten*: get undone; *Arbeit*: be given *a task.*

'aufbereit|en prepare, process; *Erz, Häute*: dress; *Kohle*: upgrade; **'Ωung** *f* preparation, processing; dressing; upgrading; **'Ωungs-anlage** *f* (re)processing plant.

'**aufbessern** *Gehalt*: raise.
'**aufbewahr|en** keep; *im Lager*: store (up); (*haltbar machen*) preserve; '**2ungs·ort** *m* depository.
'**aufbiet|en** summon; *Kräfte, Mut, etc.*: *a.* muster; ⚔ raise, levy, (*a. fig.*) mobilize; *Brautpaar*: publish (*od.* put up) the banns of; *alles* ~ move heaven and earth; '**2ung** *f* summoning; exertion; *unter* ~ *aller Kräfte* by supreme effort.
'**aufbinden** tie up; (*lösen*) untie; *fig. j-m et. od. e-n Bären* ~ hoax a p.; *sich etwas* ~ *lassen* be taken in.
'**aufbläh|en** puff up, swell; *a. Währung usw.*: inflate; *sich* ~ *fig.* be puffed up (*vor dat.* with); **2ung** *f* inflation.
'**aufblasen** blow up, inflate.
'**aufbleiben** (sn) (*wachen*) sit (*od.* stay) up; *Tür usw.*: remain open.
'**aufblenden** *mot.* turn (the headlights) on; *Film*: fade in.
'**aufblicken** raise one's eyes; look up (*fig. zu j-m* to a p.).
'**aufblitzen** (sn *u.* h.) flash (up).
'**aufblühen** (sn) (begin to) bloom; *fig.* blossom (out); *wirtschaftlich usw.*: flourish, prosper, thrive.
'**aufbocken** *mot.* jack up.
'**aufbrauchen** use up, consume.
'**aufbrausen** (h. *u.* sn) *Gelächter, Sturm*: roar; ⚗ effervesce; *fig.* fly into a passion; '**~d** effervescent; *fig.* irritable, irascible.
'**aufbrechen** *v/t.* break (*od.* force) open; *v/i.* (sn) burst open; (*weggehen*) start, set out (*beide*: *nach* for).
'**aufbringen** bring up; *Mode*: introduce; *Geld, Truppen usw.*: raise; *Schiff*: capture; *Mut*: summon up; *j-n*: provoke, infuriate, anger.
'**Aufbruch** *m* departure, start, outset (*nach, zu* for); *fig.* awakening.
'**aufbrummen** F: *j-m et.* ~ land a p. with a th.
'**aufbügeln** iron; *Hose*: press; *Kenntnisse*: brush up.
'**aufbürden**: (26) *j-m et.* ~ burden a p. with a th.
'**aufbürsten** brush up.
'**aufdecken** *v/t.* uncover; *fig. a.* expose; (*aufklären*) clear up; *v/i.* lay the table.
'**aufdonnern** F: *sich* ~ get dolled up.
'**aufdrängen** *S. od. P.*: force, obtrude (*j-m* [up]on a p.).
'**aufdrehen** *v/t. Schraube*: loosen; *Hahn, Gas usw.*: turn on; *v/i.* F *mot.* step on the gas; (*loslegen*) open up.
'**aufdringen** *s. aufdrängen.*
'**aufdringlich** obtrusive (*a. S.*); '**2keit** *f* obtrusiveness.
'**Aufdruck** *m* (im)print; *auf Postmarken*: surcharge; '**2en** imprint.
'**aufdrücken** (*öffnen*) press open; *Stempel usw.*: impress (*dat. od. auf acc.* on).
auf·einander [~ʔaɪˈnandər] one after (*od.* upon) another; ~ *böse sein* be cross with one another; **2folge** *f* succession; **~folgen** (sn) succeed (one another); **~folgend** successive, consecutive; *an 3 ~en Tagen* on 3 days running; **~prallen** (sn) collide; *fig. Meinungen, a. P.*: clash.
Aufenthalt [ˈ~ɛnthalt] *m* (3) *vorübergehend*: stay, sojourn; whereabouts (*a.* '**~s·ort** *m*); (*Wohnsitz*) residence, abode, domicile; (*Verzögerung*) delay, hindrance; 🚂 *usw.*: stop; '**~sgenehmigung** *f* residence permit; '**~sraum** *m* lounge; day-room.
'**auf·erlegen**: *j-m als Pflicht* ~ enjoin on a p. (et. a th.; *zu inf.* to *inf.*); *Aufgabe, Bedingung, Pflicht, Steuer, s-n Willen usw.*: impose (*j-m* on a p.); *Strafe*: inflict (*j-m* on a p.); *s. Zwang.*
'**auf·ersteh|en** (sn) rise (from the dead); '**2ung** *f* resurrection.
'**auf·erwecken** raise (from the dead).
'**auf·essen** eat up.
'**auffädeln** (29) thread, string.
'**auffahren** *v/i.* (sn) *Schiff*: run aground, (*auf acc.*) run (up)on; *Wagen*: run *od.* drive (*auf acc.* against); (*vorfahren*) drive up; *P.*: *zornig*: fly out, *erschreckt*: start (up); *v/t. Wagen*: park; *Kanonen*: mount; *Speisen usw.* (*a.* ~ *lassen*) dish up; '**~d** passionate, irritable.
'**Auffahrt** *f* (16) ⚒ ascent; *in e-m Wagen*: driving up; (*Platz vor e-m Haus*) drive; '**~srampe** *f* ramp.
'**Auffahr·unfall** *m* rear-end collision.
'**auffallen** *v/i.* (sn) fall (*auf acc.* upon); *fig.* be conspicuous; *j-m* ~ strike; *es fällt allgemein auf* it is generally noticed; *mit dem Kopf* ~ fall on one's head; '**~d,** '**auffällig** striking; (*sichtbar*) conspicuous;

(*sensationell*; *a. Kleid*) flashy; *b.s.* shocking; ~ *gekleidet* showily dressed.

'**auffang|en** catch (up); *Brief, Funkspruch usw.*: intercept; *Hieb*: parry; *fig. Entwicklung*: absorb; '**ℒlager** *n* reception camp.

'**auffärben** redye.

'**auffassen** *v/t. fig.* conceive; (*begreifen*) understand, comprehend; *Bühnenrolle usw.*: interpret, (*deuten*) *a.* read; *falsch* ~ misconceive; *v/i. leicht* ~ be quick of understanding.

'**Auffassung** *f* conception; (*Deutung*) interpretation; (*Fassungskraft*) apprehension; (*Meinung*) opinion, view; *falsche* ~ misconception; *nach meiner* ~ as I see it, from my point of view; *die* ~ *vertreten, daß* hold that; '**~svermögen** *n* perceptive faculty.

auffind|bar ['~fintbɑ:r] discoverable, traceable; **~en** ['~dən] find out, trace, discover, locate; '**ℒung** *f* discovery, finding.

'**auffischen** fish (up).

'**aufflackern** (sn) flare up (*a. fig.*).

'**aufflammen** (sn) flame up.

'**auffliegen** (sn) fly up(wards); *Vogel*: take wing; *Tür*: fly open; *Mine usw.*: explode, (*a. fig.*) burst; *Verein usw.*: be dissolved.

'**aufforder|n** ask, request; (*einladen*) invite; (*drängen*) urge; *anordnend*: order; *bsd.* ⚖ summon; *j-n* ~, *zu inf.* call (up)on a p. to *inf.*; '**ℒung** *f* request; invitation; order; *bsd.* ⚖ summons *sg.*

aufforsten ['~fɔrstən] afforest.

'**auffressen** eat up; devour.

'**auffrischen** (25) refresh (*a. sich*; *a. Gedächtnis*); *Bild*: touch up; *Kenntnisse*: brush up; (*wieder*) ~ *Andenken, Kummer*: revive.

'**aufführ|en** *Bau*: erect, build; *Schauspiel*: perform, act, *a. Film*: present, show; (*aufzählen*) enumerate; *in e-r Liste*: state, show, list; *Zeugen*: produce; put forward; *einzeln* ~ specify, *Am.* itemize; *sich* ~ behave; '**ℒung** *f* erection; *thea.* performance; *Film*: showing; (*Darbietung*) show; enumeration; entry; specification; (*Benehmen*) conduct; *von Zeugen*: production; '**ℒungsrecht** *n* performing rights *pl.*

'**auffüllen** fill (*od.* top) up, refill; *Vorräte usw.*: replenish.

'**Aufgabe** *f* (*Arbeit*) task, assignment, job; (*Pflicht*) duty, function; (*Sendung*) mission; (*Denk*ℒ) problem; (*Schul*ℒ) lesson, task; *e-s Briefes*: posting, *Am.* mailing; *von Gepäck*: booking, *Am.* checking; *von Telegrammen*: dispatch; ⚕ (*Mitteilung*) advice; *e-s Amtes*: resignation; (*Preisgabe*) abandonment; (*Geschäfts*ℒ) giving up business; *Tennis*: service; *es sich zur* ~ *machen, zu inf.* make it one's business to *inf.*

aufgabeln *fig.* ['~gɑ:bəln] pick up.

'**Aufgabe|nheft** *n* book for homework notes; '**~nkreis** *m* scope of duties, functions *pl.*; '**~schein** *m* certificate of delivery, receipt; '**~zeit** *f* time of dispatch.

'**Aufgang** *m* ascent; *ast.* rising, rise; (*Treppe*) staircase.

'**aufgeben** *Sache, Geschäft, Geist, Gewohnheit, Kranke, im Sport usw.*: give up; *Amt*: resign; *Anspruch*: give up, waive; *Anstellung*: quit; *Brief*: post, *Am.* mail; *Gepäck*: book, register, *Am.* check; *Anzeige*: insert, run; *Telegramm*: dispatch; ⚕ *Bestellung*: give, place; (*mitteilen*) advise; *Preise*: quote; *Aufgabe*: set, assign; *Rätsel*: ask, set; *Tennis*: serve; *j-m e-e Aufgabe* ~ set a p. a task; (*es, den Kampf, das Spiel usw.*) ~ give in (*od.* up).

aufgeblasen ['~gəblɑ:zən] puffed up; *fig.* arrogant; bumptious.

'**Aufgebot** *n* public notice; ⚔ levy, (*Streitmacht*) body (of men); (*Ehe*ℒ) banns *pl.*; (*stattliche Reihe*) array; *das* ~ *bestellen* ask the banns.

aufgebracht ['~gəbraxt] angry (*über et.* at, about; *über j-n* with).

'**aufgedonnert** F dressed up to the nines, dolled up.

aufgedunsen ['~gədunzən] bloated.

'**aufgehen** (sn) (*sich öffnen*) open; *Knoten usw.*: come undone, get loose; *Naht*: come open; ⅍ leave no remainder; *Eis, Geschwür*: break (up); *Teig, Gestirn, Vorhang*: rise; *Pflanze*: come up; *fig.* prove right; ~ *in et. Größerem* be merged in; ~ *in e-r Arbeit, e-m Gedanken* be absorbed (*od.* wrapt up) in; *in Flammen* ~ go up in flames; *in Rauch* ~ end in smoke; *die Augen gehen mir auf, mir geht ein Licht auf* I begin to see daylight; *5 geht nicht*

in 9 auf five will not divide into nine.
aufgeklärt ['~gəklɛ:rt] enlightened; '**⁁heit** *f* enlightenment.
aufgeknöpft ['~gəknœpft] F affable, chatty, expansive.
aufgekratzt ['~gəkratst] F in high spirits, chipper.
aufgelegt ['~gəle:kt] disposed (*zu* for *a th.*; to *do*), inclined (to); *~ sein (zu)* be in the mood (to), feel like (*doing*); *gut (schlecht) ~* in a good (bad) mood; F *~er Schwindel* blatant swindle.
aufgeräumt *fig.* ['~gərɔʏmt] in high spirits, cheerful.
aufgeregt ['~gəre:kt] excited; *als Charaktereigenschaft*: excitable.
aufgeschlossen *fig.* ['~gəʃlɔsən] open-minded; open (*dat.* to); (*mitteilsam*) communicative; '**⁁heit** *f* open-mindedness.
aufgeschmissen F ['~gəʃmisən]: *~ sein* be stuck.
aufgestaut ['~gəʃtaʊt] *Zorn usw.*: pent-up.
aufgeweckt *fig.* ['~gəvɛkt] bright.
aufgeworfen ['~gəvɔrfən] *Lippe*: pouting; *Nase*: turned-up.
'**aufgießen** pour (*auf acc.* upon); *Tee*: infuse, make.
'**aufgliedern** subdivide, break down.
'**aufgraben** dig up.
'**aufgreifen** *et.*: snatch up; *j-n*: pick up, seize; *fig.* take up.
'**Aufguß** *m* infusion; '**~beutel** *m* tea (*Kräuter*: herb) bag.
'**aufhaben** *Hut usw.*: have on; *Tür*: have open; *Aufgabe*: have to do.
'**aufhacken** hoe up; pick.
'**aufhaken** unhook.
'**aufhalten** *Tür usw.*: keep open; (*anhalten*) stop; *j-n*: hold up (*a. Auto, Verkehr*), detain; (*hemmen*) check, stay; (*verzögern*) delay, retard; *sich ~* (*Reise unterbrechen*) stop; (*wohnen, verweilen*) stay, dwell (*fig. bei et.* on); *sich ~ über* (*acc.*) find fault with; *ich kann mich damit nicht ~* I cannot waste any time on it.
'**aufhäng|en** hang (up); ⊕ suspend (*an dat.* from); *fig. j-m et. ~* palm off a th. on a p.; **⁁er** ['~hɛŋər] *m* (7) (*Rock⁁*) tab; *fig.* a peg to hang a th. on; '**⁁ung** *f* suspension.
'**aufhäufen** pile up, heap up, (*a. sich ~*) accumulate.
'**Aufhäufung** *f* accumulation.
'**aufheb|en** (*emporheben*) lift (up), raise, *vom Boden*: pick up; *Belagerung, Blockade, Maßnahme usw.*: raise; (*bewahren*) keep, preserve; *Vertrag usw.*: cancel, annul, abolish, *zeitweilig*: suspend; *Erlaß, Verbot*: cancel, remove; *Gesetz*: repeal, abrogate; *Urteil*: quash; *Verlobung*: break off; *Ehe*: annul; *Versammlung*: break up; *Wirkung*: cancel, neutralize; *sich gegenseitig ~* cancel each other out; *die Tafel ~* rise from the table; *viel ⁁s machen (von)* make a fuss (about); *gut aufgehoben sein* be well taken care of; '**⁁ung** *f e-r Belagerung usw.*: raising; (*Abschaffung*) abolition; *e-s Gesetzes*: repeal; *e-s Vertrages, der Ehe usw.*: annulment; *e-r Versammlung*: breaking up; *der Schwerkraft*: neutralization.
'**aufheitern** (29) cheer (up); *sich ~ Wetter*: clear up, *Gesicht*: brighten.
'**Aufheiterung** *f Wetter*: brighter period, sunny interval.
'**aufhelfen**: *j-m ~* help a p. up.
'**aufhellen** (25) (*a. sich*) brighten, clear (up), lighten; *fig.* clarify.
'**aufhetz|en** *j-n*: incite, instigate, stir up; *~ gegen* set *a p.* against; '**⁁er(in** *f*) *m* instigator; '**⁁ung** *f* instigation, incitement; *pol.* agitation, fomenting.
'**aufheulen** yowl.
'**aufholen** *v/t.* make up (for); *v/i.* pull up; ⚓ haul (*od.* hoist) up.
'**aufhorchen** listen attentively; *fig.* sit up and take notice.
'**aufhören 1.** (*zu Ende gehen*) cease; (*ablassen; a. ~ mit*) cease, stop; leave off, have done (with); *~ zu inf.* cease to *inf. od. ger.*, stop, leave off, *Am.* quit *ger.*; F *da hört doch alles auf!* that's the limit!; *hör auf damit!* stop it!; **2.** ⁁ *n* (6) cessation, stop.
'**aufjauchzen** shout with joy.
'**Aufkauf** *m* buying up; '**⁁en** buy up; *um zu spekulieren*: corner.
'**Aufkäufer** *m* speculative buyer, forestaller.
'**aufklappen** *Buch, Messer*: open; *Sitz*: tip up.
'**aufklär|en** clear up (*a. sich ~*); *j-n*: enlighten (*über acc.* on), (*unterrichten*) inform (about); ⚔ (*a. v/i.*) reconnoit|re, *Am.* -er, scout; *j-n* (se-

xuell) ~ tell a p. about the facts of life (*od.* the birds and the bees); *alles hat sich aufgeklärt* everything has been explained; '2**er** *m* (7) enlightener (*a.* '2**erin** *f*); ⚔ scout; '2**ung** *f* clearing-up; (*Erklärung*) explanation; (*Bildung*) enlightenment; *hist. the* Enlightenment; ⚔ reconnaissance; *sexuelle* ~ sex enlightenment.

'**Aufklärungs|-aktion** *f* educational campaign; '~**flug** *m* reconnaissance flight; '~**flugzeug** *n* scout plane, air scout; '~**satellit** *m* reconnaissance satellite; '~**zeit-alter** *n* Age of Enlightenment.

'**aufkleb|bar** adhesive; '~**en** paste, stick (*auf acc.* to, on); '2**er** *m* sticker.

'**aufklinken** (25) unlatch.

'**aufknacken** crack (open).

'**aufknöpfen** unbutton; *s. aufgeknöpft.*

'**aufknüpfen** (*lösen*) untie; *j-n*: hang.

'**aufkochen** *v/t. u. v/i.* (sn, h.) boil (up); *v/t.* ~ (*lassen*) bring to the boil.

'**aufkommen 1.** (sn) (*aufstehen*) get up, rise; *Wind*: spring up; *Wetter*: come up; (*genesen*) recover (*von* from); *Mode, Brauch*: come into fashion *od.* use; *Gedanke*: arise; *für et.* ~ answer for; *für die Kosten* ~ pay, defray; *für den Schaden*: compensate for, make good; *für Schulden, Verluste*: make o.s. liable for; *gegen j-n* ~ prevail against; *Zweifel* ~ *lassen* give rise to; *j-n nicht* ~ *lassen* give a p. no chance; *keinen* ~ *lassen* admit no rival; **2.** 2 *n* (6) (*Entstehen*) rise; (*Erscheinen*) advent; (*Genesung*) recovery; (*Steuer*2) (tax) yield.

'**aufkrempeln** *Hose, Hutrand*: turn up; *Ärmel*: tuck up.

'**aufkreuzen** F *fig. v/i.* (sn) turn up.

'**aufkriegen** F *s. aufbekommen.*

'**aufkündig|en** *s. kündigen*; *Kapital*: recall; *Freundschaft*: renounce, *s. a. absagen*; *Gehorsam*: refuse; '2**ung** *f* warning, notice.

'**auflachen** burst out laughing.

'**aufladen** load; ⚡ charge; *Motor*: boost, supercharge; *j-m et.* ~ burden (*od.* charge) a p. with a th.; *sich et.* ~ saddle o.s. with a th.

'**Auflader** *m* loader, packer; *e-s Motors*: supercharger, *Am.* booster.

'**Auflage** *f* (*Steuer*) tax, duty; (*amtlicher Befehl*) injunction; (*Bedingung*) condition; *e-s Buches*: edition; *e-r Zeitung* (*a.* '~**nziffer** *f*) circulation, run; (*Schicht*) layer; (*Stütze*) rest, support.

'**auflass|en** leave open; ⚖ convey; '2**ung** ⚖ *f* conveyance.

'**auflauern:** *j-m* ~ lie in wait for a p.

'**Auflauf** *m* gathering of people, crowd; ⚖ unlawful assembly; (*Tumult*) riot; *Speise*: soufflé (*fr.*).

'**auflaufen** *v/i.* (sn) rise, swell; *Summen*: accumulate, run up; *Zinsen usw.*: accumulate, accrue; ⚓ run aground; *v/t. sich die Füße* ~ get footsore.

'**Auflaufform** *f* ovenproof dish.

'**aufleben 1.** *v/i.* (sn): (*wieder*) ~ (*lassen*) revive; **2.** 2 *n* (6) revival.

'**auflegen** put, lay (*auf acc.* on); *Buch*: print, publish; *wieder* ~ reprint; *Schiff, Waren*: lay up; *Zeitung*: lay out; *Last*: impose (*j-m* on a p.); *Strafe*: inflict (*j-m* on a p.); *Feuerung*: put on; *teleph.* (*v/i.*) ring off; *sich* ~ lean (*auf acc.* on); *Schminke* ~ lay on rouge; *teleph.* (*den Hörer*) ~ hang up (the receiver).

'**auflehn|en** (*a. sich*) lean (*auf acc.* on); *fig. sich* ~ (*gegen*) rebel, revolt (against); '2**ung** *f* rebellion.

'**auflesen** gather, pick up (*a.* F *fig.*); *Ähren*: glean.

'**aufleuchten** flash (*od.* light) up.

'**aufliegen** lie *od.* lean (*auf dat.* on); *zur Besichtigung usw.*: be laid out (*zu* for); ⚕ *sich* ~ get bedsore.

'**auflockern** loosen; ⚔, *a.* ✝ disperse.

'**auflodern** (sn) blaze up.

'**auflösbar** solvable; ⚗ soluble.

'**auflösen** *Knoten*: undo, untie; *Versammlung*: break up; *Heer usw.*: disband; *Salz usw., Ehe, Geschäft, Parlament, Verein usw.*: dissolve (*a. sich*); (*sich*) *in s-e Bestandteile* ~ disintegrate; *e-e Verbindung*: sever; *Firma, Geschäft*: wind up, liquidate; *Rätsel*, ⅍ *Gleichung, Klammer*: solve; ⅍ *Bruch*: reduce; *gr.*, ⚗ analyse; *aufgelöst fig.* (*außer Fassung*) upset.

'**Auflösung** *f vgl. auflösen*: (dis-)solution; disbandment; liquidation; disintegration; '~**szeichen** ♪ *n* natural.

'**aufmach|en** open; *Kleid, Paket usw.*: *a.* undo; *Schirm*: put up;

(*zurechtmachen*) get up; *Geschäft*: open; *sich* ~ *Wind*: rise; *Wanderer usw.*: set out (*nach* for); (*die Tür*) ~, *wenn es läutet*: answer the door; ⊕ *Dampf* ~ get up steam; '**2ung** *f* (*Äußeres*) make-up (*a. e-s Buches, e-r Zeitung*), get-up; *fig.* display, splash; *in großer* ~ *herausbringen* highlight.

'**Aufmarsch** *m* marching-up; ⚔ concentration; *zur Gefechtslinie*: deployment; (*Parade*) parade, marchpast; '**2ieren** (sn) draw up; form into line; *zur Gefechtslinie*: deploy (*a.* ~ *lassen*).

'**aufmerken** attend, pay attention (*auf acc.* to); *s. aufhorchen*.

'**aufmerksam** attentive (*auf acc.* to); *fig.* (*zuvorkommend*) kind (*gegen* to); *j-n* ~ *machen auf* (*acc.*) call a p.'s attention to; '**2keit** *f* attention (*a. fig.*); *fig.* (*Höflichkeit*) kindness; (*kleines Geschenk*) small token; *s-e* ~ *richten auf* (*acc.*) focus one's attention on; ~ *schenken* (*dat.*) pay attention to.

'**aufmöbeln** F pep up.

'**aufmunter|n** (29) rouse; *fig.* (*ermutigen*) encourage; (*aufheitern*) cheer up; '**~nd** encouraging; ~*e Worte* pep talk; '**2ung** *f* encouragement.

aufmüpfig ['~mʏpfiç] rebellious.

'**aufnäh|en** sew (*auf acc.* on); (*verkürzen*) tuck; '**2er** *m im Kleid*: tuck.

Aufnahme ['~nɑːmə] *f* (15) *der Arbeit, v. Kapital*: taking up; (*Empfang*; *geistige* ~) reception; (*Zulassung*) admission; (*Einbeziehung*) inclusion; ~ *v. Beziehungen*: establishing; *v. Nahrung*: intake; *v. Schulden*: contraction; *surv.* survey; *geogr.* mapping out; *phot. Vorgang*: taking, *Film*: shooting; *Bild*: photo(graph), *bsd. Film*: shot; (*Ton*2) recording; *e-e* ~ *machen* take a photograph *od.* picture, shoot a film; '**2fähig** capacious; *geistig*: receptive (*für* of); '**~fähigkeit** *f* capacity; *geistige*: receptivity; '**~gebühr** *f* admission (*Am.* initiation) fee; '**~gerät** *n phot., Film*: pick-up unit; (*Ton*2) recorder; '**~land** *n* host country; '**~leiter** *m Film*: production manager; '**~prüfung** *f* entrance examination; '**~studio** *n Film*: (film) studio; (*Tonstudio*) (recording) studio.

'**aufnehmen** take up; *vom Boden*: pick up; *j-n*: take in; *Diktat, Stenogramm*: take (down); *geistig*: take in; *Gast*: receive; *phot.* take (*j-n* a p.'s picture); *Film*: shoot; *auf Tonband usw.*: record; *Geld*: borrow; *Anleihe*: raise; *Verzeichnis, Protokoll*: draw up; *Verbindung*: establish; *in e-e Liste usw.*: enter; ⚗ absorb (*a. fig.*); *surv.* survey; *geogr.* map out; *gut* (*übel*) ~ take well (ill); *in e-n Verein* ~ admit to (*od.* enrol[l] in) a club; *in sich* ~ absorb; *es* ~ *mit* cope with, be a match for; *wieder* ~ *e-e Rede*: resume.

'**aufnötigen:** *j-m et.* ~ force upon a p.

'**auf-opfer|n**, '**2ung** *f* sacrifice.

'**aufpass|en** *v/i.* attend (*auf acc.* to); (*beobachten*) watch; (*aufmerken*) be attentive; *paß auf!*, *aufgepaßt!* attention!, (*Vorsicht!*) look out!; *paß* (*mal*) *auf!* look (*Am.* see) here!; *auf j-n* ~ take care of a p.; '**2er**(**in** *f*) *m* (12) watcher; (*Spion*) spy.

'**aufpeitschen** whip up; *j-n, Nerven*: rouse, stimulate.

'**aufpflanzen** set up; *Seitengewehr*: fix; *sich* ~ plant o.s.

'**aufplatzen** (sn) burst (open).

'**aufpolieren** polish up (*a. fig.*).

'**aufprägen** imprint, stamp (*dat.* on).

aufprallen ['~pralən] (sn) bound, bounce (*auf acc.* against); ~ *auf a.* strike.

'**Aufpreis** *m* extra charge, surcharge.

'**aufprobieren** try on.

'**aufpumpen** pump (*od.* blow) up.

'**aufputschen** (27*) stimulate; (*aufhetzen*) rouse; *sich* ~ pep o.s. up.

'**Aufputsch|mittel** *n* stimulant; '**~tablette** *f* pep pill.

'**Aufputz** *m* attire, get-up; '**2en** dress (*od.* smarten) up.

'**aufraffen** snatch up; *sich* ~ pull o.s. together (*zu* for), brace o.s. up (for); *vom Krankenbett*: recover.

'**aufragen** tower up, loom (up).

'**aufräumen** *v/t.* put in order; *Zimmer*: tidy (up), *Am.* straighten up; (*wegräumen*) clear away; *v/i.* ~ *mit et.* do away with; ~ *unter* (*dat.*) play havoc among.

'**aufrechnen** reckon up; (*gegen*) set off (against).

'**aufrecht** upright (*a. fig.*), erect; '**~-erhalten** maintain, uphold; '**2-erhaltung** *f* maintenance.

'**aufreg|en** excite; (*ärgern*) irritate; *s. aufgeregt*; '**2ung** *f* excitement, agitation.
'**aufreiben** rub sore, gall; (*verschleißen*) wear out; (*vernichten*) wipe out; (*sich*) ~ *fig.* wear (o.s.) out, worry (o.s.) to death; '~**d** exhausting, wearing.
'**aufreihen** thread, string.
'**aufreißen** *v/t.* rip (*od.* tear) open; *Tür*: fling open; *Straße*: take up; *Augen usw.*: open (wide); *sl. Mädchen*: pick up; *v/i.* (sn) split open, burst.
'**aufreiz|en** incite, provoke, stir up; '~**end** provocative; *Rede*: inflammatory; '**2ung** *f* incitement, instigation.
'**aufrichten** set up, erect; (*aufhelfen*) help up; (*trösten*) comfort; *sich* ~ arise, straighten o.s.; *im Bett*: sit up.
'**aufrichtig** sincere; upright; '**2keit** *f* sincerity, uprightness.
'**aufriegeln** unbolt.
'**Aufriß** *m* lay-out; (*äußere Ansicht*) elevation; (*Skizze*) sketch; ⚒ vertical section.
'**aufritzen** slit (*od.* rip) open; *die Haut*: scratch open.
'**aufrollen** roll up; (*entfalten*) unroll.
'**aufrücken** (sn) move up, advance; *im Rang usw.*: be promoted; ⚔ *in Reih und Glied*: close the ranks.
'**Aufruf** *m* call, summons; *an die Bevölkerung*: proclamation; '**2en** call up; *j-n zu et.*: call upon; *einzeln beim Namen*: call over; *Banknoten usw.*: call in; *zum Streik* ~ call a strike.
Aufruhr ['~ru:r] *m* (3) rebellion, revolt; (*Meuterei*) mutiny; (*Tumult*) riot; *fig.* uproar.
'**aufrühren** stir up; *alte Geschichte*: rake up; *Erinnerungen*: revive.
'**Aufrührer** *m* (7), '~**in** *f* rebel, insurgent, mutineer; '**2isch** rebellious; *Rede*: inflammatory.
aufrunden ['~rundən] round off.
'**aufrüst|en** ⚔ (re)arm; '**2ung** *f* (re)armament.
'**aufrütteln** shake up; *aus dem Schlaf usw.*: rouse (up).
'**aufsagen** say, repeat; *Gedicht*: recite; *s. aufkündigen.*
'**aufsammeln** pick up, collect.
aufsässig ['~zɛsiç] restive; (*widerspenstig*) refractory, rebellious.
'**Aufsatz** *m* essay; (*Schul2*) essay, *Grundschule*: composition; (*Zeitungs2*) article; *e-s Schrankes usw.*: top; (*Tafel2*) epergne, cent|re- (*Am.* -er)-piece.
'**aufsaug|en** suck up; ⚗ *u. fig.* absorb; '**2ung** *f* absorption.
'**aufschauen** look up (*zu* to; *a. fig.*).
'**aufscheuchen** scare.
'**aufscheuern** scour; *Haut*: chafe.
'**aufschichten** pile up, stack (up).
'**aufschieben** push open; *fig.* put off; defer, postpone; *zögernd*: delay; *auf kurze Zeit*: adjourn.
'**aufschießen** (sn) shoot up; (*schnell wachsen*) grow tall; *hoch aufgeschossen* lanky, gangling.
'**Aufschlag** *m* striking (*auf acc.* [up]on *a th.*); *e-s Geschosses*: impact; (*Rock2*) lapel; (*Ärmel2*) cuff; (*Hosen2*) turn-up; (*Preis2*) increase, (*Zuschlag*) additional charge; (*Steuer2*) additional duty; *Tennis*: (*a.* '~**ball** *m*) service, (~*art*) serve.
'**aufschlagen** *v/t.* (*öffnen*) break open; *Ei*: crack; *Karte, Hosen, Ärmel usw.*: turn up; (*errichten*) put up; *Zelt*: pitch; *Buch, Augen*: open; *Wohnsitz*: take up; *sein Hauptquartier* ~ *in* (*dat.*) make one's headquarters at; *sich den Kopf usw.* ~ bruise one's head *etc.*; *v/i.* (sn) strike (violently) (*auf acc.* [up]on); ⚕ rise in price; *Tennis*: serve.
'**Aufschläger** *m Tennis*: server.
'**aufschließen** unlock, open (*a. fig.*); ⚗ disintegrate; *fig. sich j-m* ~ open one's heart to.
'**aufschlitzen** slit, rip up.
'**Aufschluß** *m fig.* information; ⚗ disintegration; '**2reich** informative, revealing.
'**aufschlüsseln** subdivide, break down; *Kosten*: allocate.
'**aufschnallen** unbuckle; (*anschnallen*) buckle (*od.* strap) on (*auf acc.* to).
'**aufschnappen** *v/t.* snap up; *fig.* pick up; *v/i.* spring open.
'**aufschneid|en** *v/t.* cut open; *Braten*: cut up, carve; *v/i. fig.* brag, boast, show off; '**2er** *m* (7) braggart, boaster; **2erei** [~'raɪ] *f* (16) brag(ging), boast(ing).
'**Aufschnitt** *m*: *kalter* ~ (slices *pl.* of) cold meat, *Am.* cold cuts *pl.*
'**aufschnüren** untie; *Schuh*: unlace; *Knoten*: undo.

'**aufschrauben** screw (*auf acc.* on); (*losschrauben*) unscrew, loosen.
'**aufschrecken** *v/t.* frighten up; *v/i.* (sn) start up.
'**Aufschrei** *m* cry, yell, scream; *fig.* outcry.
'**aufschreiben** write down, make a note of; *amtlich*: book; *j-n polizeilich* ~ take a p.'s name.
'**aufschreien** cry out, scream.
'**Aufschrift** *f* inscription; (*Überschrift*) heading; *e-s Briefes*: address, direction; *e-r Flasche usw.*: label.
'**Aufschub** *m* deferment; (*Verzögerung*) delay; *beabsichtigter*: adjournment; *gewährter*: respite; ⚖ *der Vollstreckung*: reprieve.
'**aufschürfen** *Haut*: graze, skin.
'**aufschütteln** shake up.
'**aufschütten** pour (*od.* put) on; *Sand usw.*: heap up; *Damm*: raise.
'**aufschwatzen:** *j-m et.* ~ talk a p. into buying a th.; *Ware*: palm off a th. on a p.
'**aufschwellen** (sn) swell (up).
'**aufschwemmen** bloat.
'**aufschwingen:** *sich* ~ soar (up), rise; *fig. sich* ~ *zu* brace o.s. up for.
'**Aufschwung** *m Turnen*: upward circle; *fig.* rise, *Am.* upswing, *bsd.* ⚚ boom; (*Besserung*) improvement; *e-n* ~ *nehmen* receive a fresh impetus, revive.
'**aufsehen 1.** look up (*zu* to; *a. fig.*); **2.** ♀ *n* (6) sensation, stir; ~ *erregen* cause a sensation, make a stir; '**~erregend** startling, sensational.
'**Aufseher** *m* (7), '**~in** *f* (16[1]) overseer, inspector; (*Wächter*) guard, attendant.
'**aufsein** (sn) be up; *Tür usw.*: be open.
'**aufsetzen** (*aufrichten*) set up; *Hut, Kessel, Flicken usw.*, *Miene*: put on; (*schriftlich abfassen*) draw up, compose; *Telegramm, Urkunde*: draft; make out; *s. Horn*; *sich* ~ sit up; *s-n Kopf* ~ be obstinate; *Schneiderei*: *aufgesetzte Taschen pl.* patch pockets; *v/i.* ✈ touch down.
'**Aufsicht** *f* inspection, supervision, control; *im Kaufhaus*: shop- (*Am.* floor-)walker; (*Polizei*♀) surveillance; (*Fürsorge*) care; '**~sbe-amte** *m* supervisor, inspector; '**~sbehörde** *f* board of control, supervising authority; '**~srat** *m* ⚚ supervisory board; '**~sratsvorsitzende** *m, f* chairman (*f* chairwoman) of the board.
'**aufsitzen** sit, rest (*auf dat.* on); *nachts*: sit up; *Reiter*: (sn) mount; *fig.* F (sn) be taken in (*j-m* by); *j-n* ~ *lassen* let a p. down.
'**aufspalt|en** *v/t. u. v/refl.* (sn) split up, cleave; ⚗ disintegrate; '♀**ung** *f biol. e-r Zelle*: fission; ⚗ disintegration.
'**aufspannen** stretch; *Schirm*: put up; *Saite*: put on; *Segel*: spread.
'**aufsparen** save; *fig.* reserve.
'**aufspeicher|n** (29) store up; '♀**ung** *f* storage.
'**aufsperren** open wide; (*aufschließen*) unlock; *fig. s. Mund.*
'**aufspielen** *v/t. u. v/i.* strike up; *sich* ~ put on airs; *sich* ~ *als* pose as, set up for.
'**aufspießen** spit; (*durchbohren*) pierce; *mit den Hörnern*: gore.
'**aufsprengen** burst (*od.* force) open; *mit Pulver*: blow up.
'**aufspringen** (sn) leap up, jump up; (*landen*) land; *Ball*: bounce; *Knospe, Tür usw.*: burst open; (*rissig werden*) crack; *Haut*: chap; (*auf e-n Zug*) ~ jump on (to a train).
'**aufspritzen** splash up.
'**aufsprudeln** bubble up.
'**aufspulen** (25) wind (up), reel.
'**aufspüren** *a. fig.* hunt up, track down; ferret out.
'**aufstacheln** goad (*a. fig.*); *fig.* incite, *bsd. b.s.* instigate.
'**aufstampfen** stamp (one's foot *od.* feet).
'**Aufstand** *m* insurrection, rebellion, uprising, revolt.
aufständisch ['~ʃtɛndiʃ] rebellious; *ein* ♀*er* an insurgent, a rebel.
'**aufstapeln** (29) pile up, stack (up); ⚚ store up.
'**aufstechen** puncture, prick open; *Geschwür*: lance.
'**aufstecken** fix; *mit Nadeln*: pin up; *Haar, Gardine usw.*: put up; F (*aufgeben*) give up (*a. v/i.*); *j-m ein Licht* ~ open a p.'s eyes (*über acc.* to).
'**aufstehen** (sn) stand up; rise, *bsd. aus dem Bett*: get up; *vom Sitz*: rise to one's feet; (*offenstehen*; *mst* h.) stand open; *von e-r Krankheit*: recover; *Volk*: rise, revolt.
'**aufsteigen** (sn) rise, ascend; *Flug-*

zeug: take the air, take off; *Reiter*: mount; *beruflich*: be promoted; *Gefühl*: well up; *ein Gedanke (Verdacht) stieg in mir auf* a thought struck me (I had a suspicion).

'**Aufsteiger** *m in der Gesellschaft*: social climber; *Sport*: league climber.

'**aufstell|en** set up; ⚔ *usw.* line up, *Wachposten*: post, station, *Einheit*: organize; *Behauptung*: make; *Beispiel*: set; *Bildsäule usw.*: erect; *Falle*: set; *als Kandidaten*: nominate; *Leiter*: raise; *Maschine*: set up, mount; *Liste*: make out; *Rechnung*: draw (*od.* make) up; *Kosten*: specify; *Grundsatz*: lay down; *Problem, Regel*: state; *Lehre, Theorie*: propound, advance; *Rekord*: set, establish; *Waren*: expose; *Mannschaft*: compose; *sich ~* take one's stand, place o.s.; *sich ~ lassen für e-n Sitz im Parlament* stand (*Am.* run) for; '**2ung** *f* setting up (*a.* ⊕); (*Anordnung*) formation (*a.* ⚔); *Sport*: team composition; *e-r Behauptung*: assertion; *pol.* nomination; mounting; ✝ statement (of account); (*Liste*) list, schedule.

Aufstieg ['~ʃti:k] *m* (3) ascent, *Am. mst* ascension; *fig.* rise; (*Beförderung*) promotion; '**~s-chancen** *f/pl.* promotion prospects; '**~srunde** *f* league-qualifying round; '**~sspiel** *n* league-qualifying game.

'**aufstöbern** *Wild*: start, rouse; *fig.* ferret out, hunt up.

'**aufstocken** ✝ step up; *Vorräte*: stock up on.

'**aufstören** rouse up, disturb.

'**aufstoßen** *v/t. Tür usw.*: push open; *~ auf (acc.)* knock against; *v/i.* (h. *u.* sn) *Speise*: rise up, repeat; *P.*: belch; ⚓ run aground; *~ auf (acc.)* strike on; *fig. j-m*: meet with *a th.*, come across *a th.*

'**aufstreben** rise, tower up; *fig.* aspire.

'**aufstreichen** *auf Brot*: spread.

'**aufstreuen** strew (*auf acc.* on).

'**Aufstrich** *m beim Schreiben*: upstroke; *auf Brot*: spread.

'**aufstülpen** turn up; *sich den Hut ~* clap on one's hat.

'**aufstützen** (*stützen*) prop up; *sich ~ auf (dat. u. acc.)* lean (up)on *the table etc.*

'**aufsuchen** search for; *in e-m Buche*: look up; *j-n ~* (go to) see a p., look a p. up; *Ort*: visit; *vom Boden*: pick up.

'**auftakeln** rig; *fig. sich ~* rig o.s. up; *aufgetakelt s. aufgedonnert.*

'**Auftakt** *m* ♪ upbeat, pickup; *fig.* prelude (*zu* to).

'**auftanken** fill up.

'**auftauchen** (sn) emerge, appear, turn up; *U-Boot*: surface; *Frage usw.*: crop up; *Gerücht*: get afloat.

'**auftauen** *v/t., v/i.* (sn) *a.fig.* thaw.

'**aufteilen** divide up, partition; *Land*: parcel out, allot; (*verteilen*) distribute.

auftischen ['~tiʃən] (27) dish up (*a. fig.*), serve up.

Auftrag ['~tra:k] *m* (3[1]) commission; (*Befehl, Pflicht*) charge; (*Weisung*) instruction; (*Sendung*) mission; ⚖ mandate; ✝ (*Bestellung*) order; *v. Farbe*: application; *im ~ von* by order of; *abbr. i. A. vor Unterschriften*: on instruction, *im Behördenbrief*: by order; *e-n ~ erteilen* give an order; *im ~ handeln von* act on (*od.* in) behalf of; '**2en** *Speisen*: serve (up); *Farbe*: lay on; *Kleid usw.*: wear out; *j-m et. ~* charge a p. with; *fig. dick ~* lay it on thick; **~geber** ['~tra:k-] *m* employer; (*Besteller*) orderer; (*Kunde*) customer; ⚖ mandator; *Börse*: principal; '**~sbestand** *m* orders in hand; '**~sbestätigung** *f* confirmation of order; '**~sbuch** ✝ *n* order-book; '**~s-eingang** *m* incoming orders *pl.*; '**~s-erteilung** *f* placing of order; *bei Ausschreibung*: award; contract; '**~sformular** *n* order form, *Am.* blank; '**2sgemäß** as ordered; '**~srückgang** *m* drop in orders.

'**auftreffen** strike, hit.

'**auftreiben** drive up; (*aufblähen*) swell up, distend; (*beschaffen*) hunt up, get hold of; *Geld*: raise.

'**auftrennen** rip (up); *Naht*: undo.

'**auftreten 1.** *v/t. Tür usw.*: kick open; *v/i.* (sn) *leise usw.*: tread; *thea., als Zeuge usw.*: appear (*als* as); *als Redner od. Sänger*: take the floor; (*sich benehmen*) act, behave; *fig.* (*eintreten*) occur; *Schwierigkeit usw.*: arise; *plötzlich*: crop up; *~ als (sich brüsten als)* pose as; *~ gegen* rise against, oppose; *energisch ~* F put one's foot down; *thea. zum ersten Mal ~* make one's debut;

2. ≈ *n* (6) (*Erscheinen*) appearance; (*Vorkommen*) occurrence; *bsd. e-r Krankheit*: incidence; (*Benehmen*) behavio(u)r, demeano(u)r, bearing.

ˈ**Auftrieb** *m phys. u. fig.* buoyancy; ✈ lift; (*Anstoß*) impetus; *neuen ~ verleihen* give a fresh impetus (*dat.* to).

ˈ**Auftritt** *m thea.* scene; *e-s Schauspielers*: appearance; *fig. einen ~ mit j-m haben* have a row with a p.; *j-m einen ~ machen* make a p. a scene.

ˈ**auftrumpfen** *fig.* put one's foot down.

ˈ**auftun** open (*a. sich ~*); F *sich ~ Verein usw.*: get started.

ˈ**auftürmen** pile (*od.* heap) up; *sich ~* tower up; *Schwierigkeiten usw.*: mount (up), accumulate.

ˈ**aufwachen** (sn) awake, wake up.

ˈ**aufwachsen** (sn) grow up.

ˈ**aufwallen** (sn) boil up; *See*: rage; *Blut, Leidenschaft*: boil.

Aufwand [ˈ~vant] *m* (3) expense, (*a. fig.*) expenditure (*an dat.* of); (*Prunk*) pomp; *von Worten, Luxus*: display.

ˈ**aufwärmen** warm up; *fig.* bring up again, rake up, rehash.

ˈ**Aufwartefrau** *f* charwoman.

ˈ**aufwarten** *j-m*: wait (up)on, attend on; *bei Tische*: wait; *~ mit* offer, *fig. a.* come up with.

aufwärts [ˈ~vɛrts] upward(s); (*bergan*) uphill; *Fahrstuhl*: going up!; ˈ≈**-entwicklung** *f* upward trend; ˈ≈**-haken** *m Boxen*: uppercut.

ˈ**Aufwartung** *f* attendance, service; (*Besuch*) visit; *j-m s-e ~ machen* pay one's respects to a p.

ˈ**aufwaschen** wash (up).

ˈ**aufwecken** wake up, (*a. fig.*) rouse.

ˈ**aufweichen** *v/t. u. v/i.* (sn) soften; *mit Flüssigkeit*: soak.

ˈ**aufweisen** show, have.

ˈ**aufwend|en** spend, expend; (*anwenden*) use, apply; *Mühe ~* take pains; *viel Geld ~* go to great expense; ˈ**~ig** costly; large-scale; ˈ≈**ungen** *f/pl.* expenditure(s).

ˈ**aufwerfen** *Schanze usw.*: throw up; *Graben*: dig; *Tür usw.*: throw open; *Blasen*: raise; *Frage*: raise, pose; *Kopf*: toss; *sich ~ als* set up for.

aufwert|en [ˈ~veːrtən] revalorize; ˈ≈**ung** *f* revalorization.

ˈ**aufwickeln** (*a. sich ~*) wind (up); *Haar*: curl up, roll up; (*loswickeln*) unwind; *Paket*: unwrap; ⚓ *Tau*: coil.

aufwiegel|n [ˈ~viːgəln] (29) stir up, incite, instigate; ˈ≈**ung** *f* instigation, sedition.

ˈ**aufwiegen** *fig.* outweigh, make up for.

Aufwiegler [ˈ~viːglər] *m* (7), ˈ**~in** *f* (16^1) *s. Aufrührer*; ˈ≈**isch** *s. aufrührerisch.*

ˈ**Aufwind** ✈ *m* upwind.

ˈ**aufwinden** wind up; *mit e-r Winde usw.*: hoist; *Anker*: weigh.

ˈ**aufwirbeln** whirl up (*a. v/i.*); *Staub*: raise; *fig. viel Staub ~* create quite a stir.

ˈ**aufwischen** mop up.

ˈ**aufwühlen** *Erde*: turn up; *von Schweinen*: root up; *Meer*: toss up; *Seele*: stir, agitate; ˈ**~d** *fig.* heart-stirring.

ˈ**aufzähl|en** enumerate, *Am. a.* call off; *einzeln*: specify, *Am.* itemize; *Geld*: count down; ˈ≈**ung** *f* enumeration; specification.

ˈ**aufzäumen** bridle; *s. Pferd.*

ˈ**aufzehren** consume (*a. fig.*), eat up.

ˈ**aufzeichn|en** draw (*auf acc.* upon); (*notieren*) note down; *amtlich*: register, record; *geschichtlich*: chronicle, record; ⊕ *v. Geräten*: record; ˈ≈**ung** *f* drawing; note; record; ⊕ recording.

ˈ**aufzeigen** show, point out.

ˈ**aufziehen** *v/t.* draw (*od.* pull) up; *Flagge usw.*: hoist; *Anker*: weigh; (*öffnen*) (pull) open; *Kind*: bring up, *a. Tier*: rear, breed; *Bild usw.*: mount; *Perlen usw.*: thread; *Pflanze*: cultivate; *Saite*: put on; *Uhr*: wind up; F *j-n*: chaff, tease, F kid; *fig. andere Saiten ~* change one's tune; *v/i.* (sn) ⚔ draw up; *Gewitter*: approach.

ˈ**Aufzucht** *f* breeding.

ˈ**Aufzug** *m* procession, parade; *thea.* act; ⊕ hoist; (*Fahrstuhl*) lift, *Am.* elevator; (*Gewand*) attire, F get-up; (*Pomp*) show, pomp; *Turnen*: pull-up.

ˈ**auf|zwängen** force open; ˈ**~zwingen:** *j-m et.*: force upon a p.

Aug-apfel [ˈaʊk-] *m* (7^1) eyeball; *fig.* apple of the eye.

Auge [ˈaʊgə] *n* (10) eye; (*Sehkraft*) sight; ✿ bud; *auf Karten, Würfeln*: pip, spot; *ganz ~ sein* be all eyes;

fig. ~ *um* ~ an eye for an eye; *in m-n* ~*n* in my view; *nur fürs* ~ just for show; *et. im* ~ *behalten* keep one's eye on, keep in mind; *j-m schöne* ~*n machen* give a p. the glad eye; *aus den* ~*n verlieren* lose sight of; *aus den* ~*n, aus dem Sinn* out of sight, out of mind; *bei et. ein* ~ *zudrücken* wink at, turn a blind eye to; *j-m ins* ~ *fallen od. in die* ~*n stechen* catch (*od.* strike) a p.'s eye; *ins* ~ *fallend* striking, evident, obvious; *große* ~*n machen* gape, stare; *Ziel usw. ins* ~ *fassen* envisage; *j-m ins* ~ *sehen* look a p. full in the face; *e-r Gefahr* (*Tatsache*) *ins* ~ *sehen* look a danger (fact) in the face, envisage a danger (fact); *unter vier* ~*n* face to face, privately; *vor* ~*n führen* demonstrate; *vor* ~*n haben* have in view; *sich vor* ~*n halten* bear in mind; *kein* ~ *zutun* not to get a wink of sleep; *s. blau.*

äugeln [ɔʏgəln] (29) ogle.

'**Augen**|**-arzt** *m* eye specialist; '~**-bank** *f* eye-transplant bank; '~**blick** *m* moment, instant; *alle* ~*e* every now and then; *im* ~ at the moment, at present, (*im Nu*) in the twinkling of an eye; *im ersten* ~ for a moment; *in diesem* ~ at this moment *od.* instant; '≗**blicklich** instantaneous, immediate; (*vorübergehend*) momentary; (*gegenwärtig*) present; *adv.* instantaneously, immediately, instantly; at (*od.* for the) present; '~**braue** *f* eyebrow; '~**brauenstift** *m* eyebrow pencil; '~**-entzündung** *f* inflammation of the eye; '≗**fällig** conspicuous; *s. augenscheinlich*; '~**flimmern** *n* flickering before the eyes; '~**glas** *n* eye-glass; '~**höhle** *f* eye-socket, ⚕ orbit; '~**klappe** *f* eye patch; '~**klinik** *f* ophthalmic hospital, *Am.* eye-clinic; '~**leiden** *n* eye-complaint; '~**licht** *n* eyesight; '~**lid** *n* eyelid; '~**maß** *n* sense of proportion; *ein gutes* ~ a sure eye; *nach dem* ~ by eye; '~**merk** *n* attention; (*Ziel*) aim; *sein* ~ *richten auf* (*acc.*) direct one's attention to; '~**nerv** *m* optic nerve; '~**schein** *m* inspection; (*Anschein*) appearance, evidence; *in* ~ *nehmen* inspect; '≗**scheinlich** evident, obvious, apparent; '~**scheinlichkeit** *f* obviousness; '~**schirm** *m* eye-shade; '~**stern** *m* pupil; '~**täuschung** *f* optical illusion; '~**tropfen** *m/pl.* eyedrops; '~**wasser** *n* eye-lotion; '~**weide** *f* feast for the eyes, sight for sore eyes; '~**wimper** *f* eyelash; '~**winkel** *m* corner of the eye; '~**wischerei** *f fig.* eyewash; '~**zahn** *m* eye-tooth; '~**zeuge** *m* eye-witness; ~*nbericht* eye-witness report; '~**zwinkern** *n* winking.

...äugig [-ɔʏgiç] ...-eyed.

August [au'gust] *m* (3) *Monat*: August; *im* ~ in August.

Auktion [auk'tsjo:n] *f* (16) auction, public sale; ~**ator** [~jo'na:tɔr] *m* (8[1]) auctioneer; ~**slokal** [auk'tsjo:nsloka:l] *n* sale-room.

Aula ['aula] *f* (16[2] *u.* 11[1]) great hall, assembly-hall, *Am.* auditorium.

aus [aus] **1.** *prp.* out of; from; of; by; for; on, upon; in; ~ *Achtung* out of respect; ~ *London kommen* come from London; ~ *diesem Grunde* for this reason; ~ *Ihrem Brief ersehe ich* I see by your letter; *von mir* ~ I don't mind, for all I care; **2.** *adv.* out; over; (*erledigt*) done with, finished; ⊕ (*abgeschaltet*) off; *die Kirche ist* ~ church is over; *auf et.* ~ *sein* be set (*od.* bent, keen) on a th.; *es ist* ~ *mit ihm* it is all over (*od.* up) with him; *das Spiel ist* ~*!* the game is up!; *er weiß weder ein noch* ~ he is at his wits' end.

Aus *n Sport*: *im* ~ out (of play).

'**aus-arbeit**|**en** work out, elaborate; (*entwerfen*) prepare, draw up; '≗**ung** *f* preparation, working out, elaboration.

'**aus-arten** (sn) degenerate (*in acc.* into); *Spiel usw.*: get out of hand.

'**aus-atmen** *v/t.* exhale.

'**ausbaden** *fig.* pay (*od.* suffer) for; *die Sache* ~ face the music.

'**ausbaggern** dredge.

'**ausbalancieren** balance (out).

'**Ausbau** *m* development, extension; (*Festigung*) consolidation; *Haus*: (inside) finish; ⊕ (*Abbau*) removal; '≗**en** (*erweitern*) develop, extend; (*fertigstellen*) finish; (*festigen*) consolidate; ⊕ remove; '~**phase** *f* consolidation (*od.* extension) stage.

'**ausbauch**|**en** (*a. sich*), '≗**ung** *f* bulge.

'**ausbedingen** stipulate; *sich et.* ~ reserve to o.s., (*bestehen auf*) insist on.

'**ausbesser**|**n** mend, repair, fix; *Bild*:

touch up; '≈**ung** *f* mending, repair.
'**ausbeulen** *v/t.* (25) beat out; *Kleidung*: make baggy; *v/i. Kleidung*: go baggy.
'**Ausbeut|e** *f* gain, profit; (*Ertrag*) yield; output (*a.* ⊕, ⚒); '≈**en** (26) exploit (*allg. a. fig. b.s.*); '~**ung** *f* exploitation (*a. b.s.*).
'**ausbiegen** *v/t.* bend out(wards); *v/i.* turn aside; *j-m, e-m Wagen usw.* ~ make way for.
'**ausbieten** offer (*zum Verkauf* for sale).
'**ausbild|en** develop; *Geist usw.*: cultivate; (*schulen*) train; (*lehren*) instruct, educate; ⚔ (*exerzieren*) drill; ⊕ design; *sich* ~ *zu* train (*od.* study) for; *sich im Gesang* ~ train to be a singer; '≈**er** (7) *m* instructor; '≈**ung** *f* development; cultivation; instruction, education; training, ⚔ *a.* drill; '≈**ungsförderung** *f* grant(s *pl.*); '≈**ungsgang** *m* training; '≈**ungslehrgang** *m* training course.
'**ausbitten:** *sich* ~ request; *das bitte ich mir aus* I must insist on this.
'**ausblasen** blow out.
'**ausbleiben 1.** (sn) stay away, fail to appear *od.* come; (*fehlen*) be wanting; (*nicht*) *lange* ~ be (not) long in coming; *es konnte nicht* ~, *daß* it was inevitable that; **2.** ≈ *n* non-appearance, absence; non-arrival.
'**ausbleichen** (25) *s. bleichen.*
'**ausblenden** *Film, Radio*: fade out.
'**Ausblick** *m* outlook, prospect, view (*auf acc.* of); (*a. fig.*) vista (*auf acc.* of); *fig.* outlook (*in die Zukunft* on).
'**ausbluten** *v/i. Wunde*: cease bleeding; *P.*: bleed to death; *Wunde* ~ *lassen* allow to bleed; *v/t.* bleed to death.
'**ausbohren** bore.
'**ausbooten** (26) disembark; *fig.* [oust.]
'**ausborgen:** *sich et.* ~ borrow (*von* from); *j-m et.* ~ lend to a p.
'**ausbrechen** *v/t.* break out; (*erbrechen*) vomit; *v/i.* (sn) break out (*a. fig. Feuer, Krieg usw.*); *fig.* burst out (*in Gelächter* laughing; *in Tränen* crying); *in Beifall* (*Schweiß*) ~ break into applause (a sweat).
'**ausbreit|en** spread (out); *Macht, Geschäft usw.*: expand; *Lehre*: propagate; *sich* ~ spread; (*ausführlich werden*) enlarge (*über acc.* upon); *s. a. verbreiten*; '≈**ung** *f* spread(ing); expansion; propagation.
'**ausbrennen** *v/t.* burn out; ⚕ cauterize; *v/i.* (sn) cease burning; *Haus usw.*: burn out, be gutted; *ausgebrannt* (*Vulkan*) extinct; *Haus*: gutted; *P.*: exhausted.
'**ausbringen** bring out; *j-s Gesundheit* ~ propose a p.'s health.
'**Ausbruch** *m* outbreak; *e-s Vulkans*: eruption; *e-s Gefangenen*: escape; (*Gefühls*≈) outburst; ⚔ break-out; *fig. zum* ~ *kommen* break out.
'**ausbrüten** hatch (*a. fig.*).
'**Ausbuchtung** *f* bulge.
'**ausbuddeln** dig out.
'**ausbügeln** iron out (*a.* F *fig.*).
'**Ausbund** *m* paragon *of beauty etc.*; *ein* ~ *von Bosheit* a regular demon.
'**ausbürgern** (29) deprive of citizenship; (*ausweisen*) expatriate.
'**ausbürsten** brush out.
'**Ausdauer** *f* perseverance; *im Ertragen*: endurance; *bsd. Sport*: stamina, staying power; (*Zähigkeit*) tenacity; '≈**n** hold out, last; *fig.* persevere; '≈**nd** persevering; tenacious; ⚘ perennial.
'**ausdehnbar** extensible; expansible; '≈**keit** *f Länge*: extensibility; *Raum*: expansibility.
'**ausdehnen** (*a. sich*) extend (*auf acc.* to); enlarge; expand; (*strecken*) stretch.
'**Ausdehnung** *f* expansion; *phys.* extension; ⩓ dimension; ⚕ dilatation; (*Umfang*) extent; '~**svermögen** *n* expansive force.
'**ausdenken** (*zu Ende denken*) think out; (*erdenken, a. sich* ~) think out (*Am.* up), contrive, devise, invent, (*vorstellen*) imagine; *nicht auszudenken* inconceivable, (*verheerend*) disastrous.
'**ausdeuten** interpret, explain.
'**ausdienen** serve one's time; *s. ausgedient.*
'**ausdorren** (25) *v/i.* (sn) dry up.
'**ausdörren** *v/t.* dry up, parch; (*versengen*) scorch; *ausgedörrt a.* arid.
'**ausdrehen** *Lampe, Gas*: turn off; *elektr. Licht*: *a.* switch off.
'**Ausdruck**[1] *m* (3^3) expression; *bsd. fachlicher*: term; *das ist gar kein* ~! that's putting it mildly; (3, *o.pl.*) *auf dem Gesicht, in Worten*: expression; *e-m Gefühl usw.* ~ *geben* give utterance (*od.* voice) to; *zum* ~ *bringen*

express, voice; *zum ~ kommen* be expressed.

'**Ausdruck**[2] *m* (3) (*Ausgedrucktes*) *typ.* printing; *Computer*: printout; '**2en** *Computer*: print out.

'**ausdrück|en** press (out); squeeze out; *Zigarette*: stub (out); *fig.* express (*sich* o.s.); *sich kurz ~* be brief; '**~lich** express, explicit.

'**ausdrucks|fähig** expressionable; '**2kraft** *f* expressiveness; '**~los** inexpressive, blank; '**~voll** expressive; '**2weise** *f* style, diction; *weitS.* language.

'**ausdünst|en** *v/i.* (sn) *u. v/t.* (26) evaporate; *Körper*: transpire, perspire; *v/t.* (*ausatmen*) exhale; (*ausschwitzen*) sweat out; '**2ung** *f* evaporation; exhalation; (*Schweiß*) perspiration.

aus·ei'nander apart; separate(d); **~brechen** *v/t.* break in two; *v/i.* (sn) break up; **~bringen** separate; **~fallen** fall apart; **~gehen** (sn) come apart; *Versammlung*: break up; *Menge*: disperse; *Freunde usw.*: part (company); *Meinungen*: differ, be divided; *~d* divergent; **~halten** keep apart; *fig.* distinguish between; **~jagen** scatter; **~leben** *v/refl.* drift apart; **~nehmen** take to pieces; ⊕ strip, dismantle; **~reißen** tear apart; **~setzen** separate; *fig.* explain; *sich mit j-m ~ über Ansichten*: argue with, *gründlich*: have it out with; (*sich einigen*) come to terms with; *über Ansprüche*: arrange with, ✝ compound with; *sich mit e-m Problem ~* get down to a problem; **2setzung** *f* (*Erörterung*) discussion; (*Streit*) argument, dispute; (*kriegerische*) ~ (armed) conflict; (*Übereinkommen*) arrangement, ✝ composition; **~treiben** *v/t.* disperse, scatter; *mit e-m Keil*: cleave asunder; *v/i.* drift apart.

'**aus-erkoren** chosen, selected, elect.

'**aus-erlesen 1.** *s. ausersehen*; **2.** *adj.* choice; picked; select(ed).

'**aus-ersehen** (30) choose, select.

'**aus-erwählen** select, choose; *s-e Auserwählte* the girl of his choice; (*Braut*) his bride elect; *das Auserwählte Volk* the chosen people.

'**aus-essen** eat up; *Schüssel*: clear; *fig.* pay for.

'**ausfahren** *v/t.* *Weg*: wear out, rut; *j-n ~* take out for a drive; ✈ *Fahrgestell*: lower, extend; ⚓ *Sehrohr*: lift; *mot.* run (*the engine*) up to top speed; *Kurve*: round; *ausgefahren Weg*: rutted, rutty; *v/i.* (sn) drive out; 🚂 pull out; ⚓ put to sea; ⚒ ascend.

'**Ausfahrt** *f* drive, excursion; (*Tor*) doorway, gateway; *e-r Autobahn*: turn-off, exit; (*Hafen2*) mouth; (*Abfahrt*) departure (*a.* ⚓).

'**Ausfall** *m* falling out; (*Ergebnis*) result; ⚗ precipitate; (*radioaktiver Niederschlag*) fall-out; (*Verlust*) loss; (*Fehlbetrag*) deficit; ⊕ (*Versagen*) failure, breakdown; *fenc.* pass, lunge; *fig.* attack; ⚔ sally, sortie; ⚔ (*Verlust*) casualty; '**2en** *v/i.* (sn) fall out; (*nicht stattfinden*) not (*od.* fail) to take place, be cancelled (*od.* called off); (*ausgelassen werden*) be omitted; ⊕ (*versagen*) fail, break down; *Sport*: drop out; *fenc.* lunge; ⚔ sally out; *Ergebnis*: turn out, prove; *die Haare fallen ihm aus* he is losing his hair; *die Schule fällt aus* there is no school; *e-e Stunde, Sitzung usw. ~ lassen* drop; '**2end**, '**ausfällig** aggressive; *~ werden* become abusive; '**~s-erscheinung** ⚕ *f* outfall symptom; '**~straße** *f* radial route.

'**ausfasern** (sn) ravel out, fray (out).

'**ausfechten** fight out; et. *mit j-m ~* have it out with a p.

'**ausfegen** sweep (out).

'**ausfeilen** file out; *fig.* file.

'**ausfertig|en** *Schriftstück*: draw up; *Paß*: issue; ⚖ *Urkunde*: execute; *Rechnung*: make out; '**2ung** *f* drawing up; issue; execution; (*Abschrift*) copy; *in doppelter ~* in duplicate.

'**ausfindig:** *~ machen* find out; (*entdecken*) discover; (*örtlich feststellen*) locate; (*aufspüren*) ferret out.

'**ausflicken** patch up.

'**ausfliegen** (sn) fly out; *fig.* leave home; go on a trip.

'**ausfließen** (sn) flow out; *fig.* emanate.

ausflippen *sl.* ['~flipən] (sn) freak out.

'**Ausflucht** *f* evasion, subterfuge; (*Vorwand*) excuse, pretext; *Ausflüchte machen* prevaricate, shuffle, dodge.

'**Ausflug** *m* excursion (*a. fig.*), outing, trip.

Ausflügler ['~fly:glər] *m* excursionist, F tripper, *bsd. Am.* tourist.

ˈ**Ausfluß** *m* flowing out, effluence; ⚕ discharge; (*Mündung*) outfall, issue, outlet; ⚗, *fig.* emanation; *fig.* (*Ergebnis*) result.

ˈ**ausforschen** investigate, inquire into; *j-n*: sound.

ˈ**ausfragen** *j-n*: interrogate, question; *prüfend*: *bsd. Am.* quiz; *neugierig*: sound, pump.

ausfransen [ˈ~franzən] fray (out).

ˈ**ausfressen** *s. ausessen*; ⚗ corrode; F *et.* ~ make mischief.

Ausfuhr [ˈ~fu:r] *f* (16) export (-ation); (*Waren*) exports *pl.*; ˈ~**artikel** *m* export(ed article).

ˈ**ausführbar** practicable, feasible, workable; ✝ exportable; ˈ2**keit** *f* practicability; ✝ exportability.

ˈ**Ausfuhrbewilligung** *f* export permit *od.* licen|ce, *Am.* -se.

ˈ**ausführen** execute, carry out, perform, *Auftrag*: *Am. a.* fill; *Ware*: export; (*darlegen*) explain, point out, state; *j-n*: take out.

ˈ**Ausfuhr|handel** *m* export trade; ˈ~**land** *n* exporting country.

ˈ**ausführlich** full(-length), detailed; (*umfassend*) comprehensive; *adv.* in detail; *sehr* ~ at full (*od.* great) length; *ziemlich* ~ at some length; ~ *schreiben* write fully; ˈ2**keit** *f* (*Genauigkeit*) minuteness of detail; *in Einzelheiten*: particularity; (*Weitschweifigkeit*) copiousness.

ˈ**Ausfuhr|papiere** ✝ *n/pl.* export documents; ˈ~**prämie** ✝ *f* (export) bounty; ˈ~**sperre** *f* embargo on exports.

ˈ**Ausführung** *f* ✝ exportation; *fig.* execution, performance (*a. e-s Vertrags*); *e-s Gesetzes*: implementation; (*Fertigstellung*) completion; ⊕ (*Konstruktion*) design; *handwerklich*: workmanship; (*Type*) type, model; (*Darlegung*) explanation, statement.

ˈ**Ausfuhr|verbot** *n* prohibition of exportation; ˈ~**waren** *f/pl.* exports *pl.*; ˈ~**zoll** *m* export duty.

ˈ**ausfüllen** fill out; *Formular usw.*: fill in *od.* up; *fig.* fill; *j-n*: absorb.

ˈ**ausfüttern** line (*a.* ⊕).

ˈ**Ausgabe** *f von Briefen usw.*: delivery; (*Verteilung*) distribution; *Computer*: output; *e-s Buches*: edition, (*Exemplar*) copy; (*Geld*2) expense, expenditure; *von Aktien, Papiergeld usw.*: issue; (~*stelle*) issuing office; ˈ~**daten** *n/pl.* (computer) output data.

ˈ**Ausgang** *m* (*Ausgehen*) going out, exit; (*Tür usw.*) way out, exit; (*Auslaß*) outlet; (*Ende*) end; (*Ergebnis*) result, upshot; ~ *haben Hauspersonal*: have one's day (*od.* evening) off; ˈ~**sbasis** *f fig.* starting point, working basis; ˈ~**smaterial** *n* source material; ˈ~**s-punkt** *m* starting-point; ˈ~**ssperre** *f* curfew; ˈ~**ssprache** *f* source language.

ˈ**ausgeben** *v/t.* give out; (*verteilen*) distribute; *Befehl, Aktien, Papiergeld, Fahrkarten*: issue; *Briefe, Waren*: deliver; *Spielkarten*: deal; *Geld*: spend; *fig.* extend o.s. (*bei* in); *s. a. verausgaben*; *sich* ~ *für* pass o.s. off for, pose as; *v/i. gut usw.* ~ (*Tee usw.*) yield well *etc.*

ˈ**ausgebeult** *Hose*: baggy.

ausgebombt [ˈ~gəbɔmpt] bombed out.

ausgebufft [ˈ~gəbuft] *sl.* fly, sharp.

ˈ**Ausgeburt** *f* (monstrous) product; *P.*: monster; *der Phantasie*: phantom.

ausgedient [ˈ~gədi:nt] *P.*: pensioned-off; past use, worn-out; ~ (*haben*) *P. u. S.*: (be) superannuated; ~*er Soldat* ex-serviceman, veteran.

ˈ**ausgefallen** *fig.* eccentric, odd.

ˈ**ausgefeilt** *fig.* elaborate.

ˈ**ausgeflippt** *sl.* freaked (*od.* flipped) out.

ausgefranst [ˈ~gəfranst] frayed [(out).]

ausgeglichen [ˈ~gəgliçən] *fig.* well-balanced, well-poised.

ˈ**Ausgeh-anzug** *m* outdoor-dress; ⚔ dress uniform.

ˈ**ausgehen** (sn) go out; (*spazierengehen*) take a walk; (*enden*) end (*auf acc.* in); *Farbe*: fade; *Haar*: fall out; *Geld, Vorrat*: run short, give out; *Feuer, Licht*: go out; *gut usw.* ~ turn out well *etc.*; *frei* ~ get off scot-free; *leer* ~ come away empty-handed; *von et.* ~ start (*od.* proceed) from; *von j-m* ~ *Vorschlag usw.*: come from; *auf et.* (*acc.*) ~ (*suchen*) seek, look for, (*anstreben*) be out to *inf.*, aim at *ger.*; *ihm ging das Geld aus* he ran short of money.

Ausgehverbot [ˈ~ge:-] *n* curfew.

ausgeklügelt [ˈ~gəkly:gəlt] ingenious, clever.

ˈ**ausgekocht** *fig.* hard-boiled; (*erfahren*) seasoned.

ausgelassen ['~gəlasən] frolicsome; wild; '**≗heit** *f* (16) frolicsomeness.
ausgeleiert ['~gəlaɪərt] *a. fig.* worn-out.
ausgemacht ['~gəmaxt] settled; (*sicher*) confirmed, established; *Gauner usw.*: downright, thorough; *~e Sache* foregone conclusion.
ausgenommen ['~gənɔmən] except; *du nicht ~* not excepting you.
ausgerechnet ['~gərɛçnət] *fig.* exact(ly), just; *~ er* he of all people.
ausgeschlossen ['~gəʃlɔsən] impossible, out of the question.
'**ausgeschnitten** *Kleid*: low-cut.
Ausgesiedelte ['~gəzi:dəltə] *m, f* evacuee.
ausgesprochen ['~gəʃprɔxən] decided, pronounced.
'**ausgestalten** *s. gestalten.*
'**ausgesucht** exquisite (*a. Höflichkeit*), choice; *P.*: (hand-)picked; *Worte*: well-chosen.
ausgetreten ['~gətre:tən]: *fig. ~er Weg* beaten (*od.* trodden) path; *Schuh*: trodden-down.
'**ausgewachsen:** *fig. ein ~er Unsinn* utter nonsense.
Ausgewiesene ['~gəvi:zənə] *m, f* expellee.
ausgezeichnet ['~gətsaɪçnət] excellent, first-class; F capital.
ausgiebig ['~gi:biç] *s. reichlich, ergiebig*; *~en Gebrauch machen von* make full use of.
'**ausgießen** pour out.
Ausgleich ['~glaɪç] *m* (3) equalization (*a. Sport*); *Tennis*: deuce; (*Vergleich*) arrangement, compromise; (*Ersatz*) compensation, offset; *s. ~ung*; '**~behälter** *mot. m* expansion tank; '**≗en** equalize; *Verlust*: compensate; ✝ balance; *Streit*: settle; '**~er** *m Sport*: handicapper; '**~stor** *n* equalizer; '**~ung** *f* equalization; compensation; balance.
'**ausgleiten** (30, sn) slip, lose one's footing; *fig.* slip.
'**ausgrab|en** dig out *od.* up (*a. fig.*); excavate; *Leiche*: exhume; '**≗ung** *f* excavation; exhumation.
'**ausgreifen** *Pferd*: step out.
Ausguck ['~guk] *m* (3) look-out.
'**Ausguß** *m* (*~becken*) sink; (*Tülle*) spout; '**~eimer** *m* slop-pail.
'**aushacken** hew (*od.* hack) out; *die Augen*: pick out.
'**aushaken** unhook.
'**aushalten** *v/t.* endure, bear; *Angriff, Hitze, Probe, Vergleich usw.*: stand; *Ton*: hold, sustain; *v/i.* hold out; *fig. a.* persevere; *nicht zum ≗* beyond endurance.
aushändig|en ['~hɛndigən] (25) deliver up, hand over (*dat.* to); '**≗ung** *f* delivery, surrender.
'**Aushang** *m* (3[3]) notice, bulletin.
'**aushänge|n** *v/t.* hang out (*a. v/i.*); *Tür*: unhinge; *Plakat*: post (up); '**≗schild** *n* sign-board, shop sign; *fig.* front; (*Paradestück*) show-piece.
'**ausharren** hold out, persevere.
'**aushauen** hew out, carve; *Wald*: thin.
'**aushebl|en** lift out; *Tür*: unhinge; *Truppen*: levy, *den einzelnen*: enrol(l), enlist, draft; *Erde, Grube*: excavate; *Verbrechernest usw.*: raid, mop up; '**≗ung** ⚔ *f* draft(ing), conscription.
'**aushecken** *fig.* hatch, F cook up.
'**ausheilen** *v/t. u. v/i.* (sn) heal (up).
'**aushelfen** help out (*j-m* a p.); supply *a p.* (*mit* with).
'**Aushilf|e** *f* help (*a. P.*), assistance; (*Notbehelf*) stopgap; '**~skraft** *f* temporary worker, help; **≗sweise** ['~hilfsvaɪzə] as a stopgap; *weitS.* temporarily.
aushöhl|en ['~hø:lən] (25) hollow out, excavate; *fig.* sap, erode; '**≗ung** *f* excavation.
'**ausholen** *v/i.* swing, strike out; *Erzählung*: *weit ~* go far back; *v/t. j-n*: sound, pump.
'**aushorchen** *j-n*: sound, draw.
'**Aushub** *m Erdarbeiten*: digging, excavations *pl.*
'**aushungern** starve (out); *ausgehungert* famished, starved.
'**aushusten** cough up, expectorate.
'**auskämpfen** fight out.
'**auskehren** (25) sweep out.
'**auskennen:** *sich ~ in e-m Ort* know (one's way about) a place; *in e-r S.*: be quite at home in a th., know all about a th.
'**ausklammern** *fig.* leave out of consideration, shelve.
'**Ausklang** *m* end.
'**ausklauben** pick out.
'**auskleiden** (*a. sich*) undress; ⊕ line, coat.
'**ausklingen** fade away; *fig. ~ in* (*acc.*) end in.
'**ausklopfen** beat (out); *Kleid usw.*: dust; *Pfeife*: knock out.

ausklügeln ['~kly:gəln] puzzle out; *s. ausgeklügelt.*
'**auskneifen** F *v/i.* decamp, bolt.
'**ausknipsen** F ⚡ switch off.
'**ausknobeln** F dice (*od.* toss) for; *fig.* puzzle (*od.* figure) out.
'**auskochen** boil (out); *Saft usw.*: decoct; *s. ausgekocht.*
'**auskommen 1.** *v/i.* (sn) come out; *Feuer*: break out; *geldlich*: make both ends meet; *mit* (*ohne*) *et.* ~ do *od.* manage with(out); *mit j-m* ~ get on (*od.* along) with; **2.** ♀ *n* (6) competency; *sein* ~ *haben* make a living, have a competency; *sein gutes* ~ *haben* be well off; *es ist kein* ~ *mit ihm* there is no getting on with him.
auskömmlich ['~kœmliç] sufficient.
'**auskosten** *fig.* enjoy thoroughly, *a. ironisch*: taste fully.
'**auskramen** rummage out; *fig.* bring up; *Wissen*: *co.* trot out.
'**auskratzen** *v/t.* scratch out; ⚕ curette; *v/i.* (sn) F bolt.
'**auskundschaften** explore; ⚔ reconnoit|re, *Am.* -er, scout.
Auskunft ['~kunft] *f* (14[1]) information; (*~schalter*) inquiry-office, *Am.* information desk; **~ei** [~'taɪ] *f* (16) inquiry-agency, *Am.* information bureau; '**~s-pflicht** *f* obligation to give information.
'**auskuppeln** ⊕ disconnect, uncouple; *mot.* declutch.
'**auslachen** laugh at, deride.
'**ausladen** *v/t.* unload, discharge; *Truppen, Passagiere*: disembark; *Gast*: put off; *v/i.* (sn) ⚠ project.
'**Auslage** *f* (*Geld*♀) outlay; *~n pl.* expenses *pl.*; (*Waren*♀) display; *Boxen, fenc.* guard; *die ~n ansehen* go window-shopping.
'**Ausland** *n* foreign country *od.* countries *pl.*; *ins* ~, *im* ~ abroad.
Ausländ|er ['~lɛndər] *m*, '**~erin** *f* foreigner; *im Lande seßhafter, nicht naturalisierter*: alien; '**♀erfeindlich** hostile to foreigners; '**~erfeindlichkeit** *f* hostility to foreigners; '**~erhaß** *m* xenophobia; '**♀isch** foreign; ⚘, *zo.* exotic.
'**Auslands...** *mst* foreign; '**~-aufenthalt** *m* stay abroad; '**~flug** *m* international flight; '**~gespräch** *n teleph.* international call; '**~reise** *f* trip abroad; '**~verschuldung** *f* foreign debts *pl.*

'**auslass|en** let out; *Wort usw.*: leave out, omit, skip; *Fett*: melt (down); *Kleid*: let out; *s-e Wut usw.* ~ *an* (*dat.*) vent ... on; *sich* ~ express o.s. (*über acc.* about), *weitläufig*: enlarge (upon); '**♀ung** *f* omission; (*Äußerung*) utterance.
'**Auslauf** *m für Tiere*: run; *Tennis*: margin; '**♀en** (sn) run out; *Gefäß*: leak; ⚓ put to sea; (*enden*) (come to an) end; *sich* ~ have a good run; *fig.* ~ *lassen* taper off.
'**Ausläufer** *m* errand-boy; ⚘ runner; *pl. e-s Gebirges*: foothills *pl.*; *e-r Stadt*: outskirts *pl.*
'**Auslaufmodell** *n* phase-out model.
'**Auslaut** *m* terminal sound; *im* ~ when final; '**♀en** terminate, end (*auf acc.* in).
'**ausleben** (*sich*) live one's life fully.
'**auslecken** lick out, lick clean.
'**ausleer|en** empty, clear; ⚕ evacuate; '**♀ung** *f* emptying.
'**auslegen** lay out; (*zur Schau stellen*) display; (*deuten*) interpret, construe, read, explain; *Geld*: advance; (*entwerfen*) design; ⊕ line, cover; (*verzieren*) inlay; *falsch* ~ misinterpret.
'**Ausleger** *m* (7), '**~in** *f* expositor, expounder; ⊕ arm; *e-s Krans*: jib; ⚠ cantilever; '**~(boot** *n*) *m* outrigger.
'**Auslegeware** *f* floor coverings *pl.*
'**Auslegung** *f* laying out; (*Deutung*) interpretation, construction.
'**ausleihen** lend (out), *bsd. Am.* loan; *sich et.* ~ borrow.
'**auslernen** complete one's training; *man lernt nie aus* we live and learn.
'**Auslese** *f* (15) choice, selection; *fig.* pick, cream, élite; '**♀n a)** (*sortieren*) pick out, select; **b)** *Buch*: finish.
'**ausliefern** deliver (up); *Gefangenen*: give up; *ausländischen Verbrecher*: extradite; *j-m ausgeliefert sein* be at the mercy of a p.
'**Auslieferung** *f* delivery; *von Verbrechern*: extradition; '**~shaft** *f* custody pending extradition; '**~slager** *n* supply depot; '**~sstelle** *f* distribution cent|re, *Am.* -er; '**~svertrag** *m* extradition treaty.
'**ausliegen** *Ware*: be displayed; *Zeitung*: be kept; (*zur Einsichtnahme*) ~ be open to inspection.
'**auslöffeln** spoon out; *s. Suppe.*
'**auslöschen** *Licht*: put out; *Feuer*

u. fig.: extinguish; *Schrift*: efface; (*auswischen*) wipe out (*a. fig.*).

'**auslos|en** draw lots for; *Staatspapiere*: draw; '**2ung** *f* draw.

'**auslös|en** loosen; *Gefangene*: redeem, ransom; *Pfand, Wechsel*: redeem; ⊕ release, (*betätigen*) *a.* actuate; *fig.* start, trigger; *Wirkung*: produce; *Beifall usw.*: arouse; '**2er** *m* (7) release; *phot.* trigger; '**2ung** *f* redeeming, redemption; (*Trennungsgeld*) severance pay; *s. Auslöser.*

'**auslüften** air, ventilate.

'**ausmachen** *Feuer, Licht*: put out; ⚡ switch off; *Hülsenfrüchte*: husk, shell; (*betragen*) come to, amount to; (*bilden*) make up, constitute; *Streitsache*: settle; (*erkennen*) make out; (*vereinbaren*) agree upon, arrange; *es macht nichts aus* it does not matter; *würde es Ihnen etwas* ~, *wenn ...?* would it make any difference to you if ...?; *wenn es Ihnen nichts ausmacht* if you don't mind; *s. ausgemacht.*

'**ausmalen** paint; (*illustrieren, bunt* ~) illuminate; *sich et.* ~ picture a th. (to o.s.), visualize a th.

'**Ausmarsch** *m* departure; '**2ieren** (sn) march out.

'**Ausmaß** *n* dimension(s *pl.*), measurement(s *pl.*); *fig.* extent; *erschreckende* ~*e* alarming proportions; *in großem* ~ on a large scale, *fig.* to a great extent.

ausmergeln ['~mɛrgəln] emaciate.

ausmerzen ['~mɛrtsən] reject; *Fehler*: expunge; (*ausrotten*) eradicate.

'**ausmess|en** measure; *Grundstück*: survey; *Gefäß*: ga(u)ge; '**2ung** *f* measuring; survey; ga(u)ge.

'**ausmisten** 🌾 clear (of dung); F *fig.* clear up (the mess).

'**ausmustern** ⚔ discharge; *weitS.* discard, reject; *Maschine*: scrap.

Ausnahme ['~nɑːmə] *f* (15) exception; *mit* ~ *von od. gen.* with the exception of; '**~...** *mst* exceptional; '**~zustand** *m* (state of) emergency; ⚔ (state of) martial law.

'**ausnahms|los** without exception; '**~weise** exceptionally, by way of exception; (*für diesmal*) for once.

'**ausnehmen** take out; (*ausschließen*) except, exempt; (*ausweiden*) disembowel, *Fisch*: gut, *Geflügel*: draw; *fig.* fleece; *sich gut* ~ look well; '**~d** *adv.* exceedingly.

'**Ausnüchterungszelle** *f* drying-out cell.

ausnutz|en ['~nutsən] utilize; profit by; *Gelegenheit, b.s. j-n*: take advantage of, *a.* ⚒, ⚔ exploit; '**2ung** *f* utilization; exploitation.

'**auspacken** unpack; F *fig.* talk; *zornig*: speak one's mind.

'**auspeitschen** whip, scourge, flog.

'**auspfänd|en** *j-n*: distrain (up)on a p.('s goods); '**2ung** *f* distraint.

'**aus|pfeifen** boo; *thea.* hiss (off the stage); '**~plaudern** blab (*od.* let) out; '**~plündern** *s. plündern*; '**~polstern** stuff, pad; (*wattieren*) wad; '**~posaunen** (25) trumpet (forth); noise abroad; **~powern** ['~poːvərn] impoverish; '**~prägen** coin, stamp; *ausgeprägt fig.* marked; '**~pressen** squeeze out; '**~probieren** try, test.

Auspuff ['~puf] *m* (3) *mot.* exhaust; '**~gas** *n* exhaust gas; '**~rohr** *n* exhaust pipe; '**~topf** *m* silencer, *Am.* muffler.

'**aus|pumpen** pump out; *Luft*: exhaust; '**~punkten** (26) *Boxen*: beat by points; '**~putzen** (*reinigen*) clean; (*schmücken*) adorn; '**2putzer** *m Fußball*: sweeper; '**~quartieren** dislodge; ⚔ billet out; '**~quetschen** squeeze out; F *fig.* grill; '**~radieren** erase; '**~rangieren** discard; *Schiff usw.*: scrap; '**~rauben** rob; '**~räuchern** fumigate; *Bienen usw., a.* ⚔: smoke out; '**~raufen** tear out; *s. Haar*; '**~räumen** *Zimmer usw.*: clear; *Möbel usw.*: remove.

'**ausrechn|en** calculate; *Am.* figure out; *s. ausgerechnet*; '**2ung** *f* calculation.

'**Ausrede** *f* excuse, pretext; evasion; '**2n** *v/i.* finish speaking; *j-n* ~ *lassen* hear a p. out; *v/t. j-m et.* ~ dissuade a p. from a th., talk a p. out of a th.

'**ausreichen** suffice; *das reicht aus* that will do; '**~d** sufficient; '**2d** *n* (*Schulzensur*) satisfactory.

'**Ausreise** *f* departure, exit; ⚓ voyage out; '**~erlaubnis** *f* exit permit.

'**ausreiß|en** *v/t.* pull (*od.* tear) out; *v/i.* (sn) (*fliehen*) run away, decamp, *a. Pferd*: bolt; '**2er** *m* (7), '**2erin** *f* runaway.

'**aus|reiten** (sn) ride out, go for a ride; **~renken** ['~rɛŋkən] (25) dislocate; '**~richten** straighten; (*fluch-*

ten) align; ⚔ dress; *Karte*: orient; *fig.* orientate, *pol. a.* streamline; *Botschaft*: deliver; (*bewirken*) do, effect; (*vollbringen*) accomplish; (*erlangen*) obtain; *Veranstaltung*: organize; *Benehmen usw.*: ~ *nach* adjust to; *Grüße von j-m* ~ present a p.'s compliments; '**~ringen** *Wäsche*: wring out; '**2ritt** *m* ride; '**~roden** root out, stub up; '**~rollen 1.** *v/t. Teig*: roll out; *v/i.* ✈ (sn) taxi to a standstill; **2.** 2 ✈ *n* landing run.

'**ausrott|en** (26) *Pflanze, a. fig.*: root out; *fig.* eradicate, extirpate; *Volk*: exterminate; '**2ung** *f* eradication, extermination.

'**ausrücken** *v/i.* (sn) march out; F (*weglaufen*) run away, bolt; *v/t.* ⊕ disengage.

'**Ausruf** *m* cry, outcry, *mit Worten*: exclamation; '**2en** *v/i.* cry out, exclaim; *v/t.* proclaim.

'**Ausrufung** *f* proclamation; '**~s-wort** *gr. n* interjection; '**~szeichen** *n* exclamation-mark (*Am.* -point).

'**ausruhen** *v/i.* (*a. sich*) (take a) rest.

'**ausrupfen** pluck out.

'**ausrüst|en** equip; '**2ung** *f* fitting out; (*Sport2 usw.*) outfit, (*a.* ⚔ *u.* ⊕) equipment; *des Soldaten*: kit; (*Zubehör*) accessories *pl.*

'**ausrutschen** *s. ausgleiten.*

'**Aussaat** *f* sowing; *konkret*: seed.

'**aussäen** sow; *fig.* spread, disseminate.

'**Aussage** *f* (15) statement (*a.* ⚖ *u. literarisch*); (*Erklärung*) declaration; ⚖ (*Zeugnis*) testimony; *gr.* predicate; *e-e* ~ *machen s. aussagen*; '**~kraft** *f* (*Beweiskraft*) validity, strength; (*Ausdruckskraft*) expressiveness; '**2n** state, declare; ⚖ testify, give evidence; *gr.* predicate; '**~satz** *m* affirmative proposition.

'**Aussatz** ⚕ *m* (3², *o. pl.*) leprosy.

aussätzig ⚕ ['~zɛtsiç] leprous; **2e** ['~gə] *m, f* leper.

'**aussaugen** suck (out); *fig.* drain, exhaust; *j-n.*: bleed *a p.* white.

'**Ausschabung** ⚕ *f* scrape.

ausschachten ['~ʃaxtən] (26) excavate; ⚒, *Brunnen*: sink.

'**ausschalt|en** *j-n od. et.*: eliminate; ⚡ break, cut out, *Licht, Gerät*: switch (*od.* turn) off; *Kupplung*: throw out; '**2er** ⚡ *m* (7) cut-out, circuit-breaker; '**2ung** *f* elimination.

'**Ausschank** *m* (3¹) retail; (*Schankstätte*) public house, F pub.

'**Ausschau** *f*: ~ *halten* be on the look-out (*nach* for); '**2en** *nach j-m*: look out for; *s. aussehen.*

'**ausscheid|en** *v/t.* eliminate (*a.* 🜄, ⚗); (*wegtun*) discard; *physiol.* secrete; ⚕ excrete; *v/i.* (sn) *aus e-m Amt usw.*: retire, *a. aus e-m Klub usw.*: withdraw (from); *Sport*: drop out, be eliminated; *fig. das scheidet aus* that's out (of the question); '**2ung** *f* (*a. Sport*) elimination; *physiol.* secretion; ⚕ excretion; '**2ungskampf** *m Sport*: eliminating contest, tie; '**2ungs-spiel** *n Sport*: tie.

'**aus|schelten** scold, chide; '**~schenken** pour out; *als Schankwirt*: retail; '**~scheren** veer out; *fig.* step out of line; '**~schicken** send out.

'**ausschiff|en** (*a. sich*) disembark, debark; '**2ung** *f* disembarkation.

'**aus|schimpfen** scold, upbraid; '**~schlachten** cut up; F ⊕ salvage, *Auto usw.*: cannibalize; (*ausnutzen*) exploit; '**~schlafen** *v/i.* sleep one's fill; *v/t. Rausch usw.*: sleep off.

'**Ausschlag** *m* ⚕ eruption, rash; *e-s Zeigers*: deflection; *des Pendels*: swing; *der Waage*: turn of the scale(s); *den* ~ *geben* turn the scale, settle it; '**2en** *v/t.* beat out; knock out; *mit Tuch usw.*: line; (*ablehnen*) refuse, decline; *Erbschaft*: waive; *v/i.* (h., sn) ⚘ sprout, bud; *Bäume*: break into leaf; (*feucht werden*) grow moist; *Pferd*: kick; *Zeiger*: deflect; *Pendel*: swing; *Waage*: turn; *fig.* (*gut, schlecht*) turn out; '**2gebend** decisive; ~*e Stimme* casting vote.

'**ausschließ|en** shut (*od.* lock) out; *fig.* exclude; *v. e-r Schule, e-m Verein usw.*: expel; *Sport*: disqualify, *zeitweilig*: suspend; *sich* ~ exclude o.s. (*von* from); *s. ausgeschlossen*; '**~lich** exclusive; '**2ung** *f*, '**Ausschluß** *m* exclusion; expulsion; disqualification, suspension; *unter* ~ *der Öffentlichkeit* in camera.

'**aus|schlüpfen** (sn) *aus dem Ei*: hatch; '**~schmelzen** melt out; *Erz*: fuse; '**~schmieren** *Fugen*: point.

'**ausschmück|en** adorn, decorate; *Erzählung*: embroider; '**2ung** *f* adornment; *fig.* embellishment.

'**ausschnauben:** *sich die Nase* ~ blow one's nose.

'**ausschneiden** cut out; *tief ausgeschnitten Kleid*: low-necked.

'**Ausschnitt** *m* cut; (*Zeitungs*♀) cutting, *Am.* clipping; *am Kleid*: neck-line; (*Kreis*♀) sector; *fig.* section.

'**ausschöpfen** scoop; ladle out; *Boot*: bale out; *fig. Thema*: exhaust.

'**ausschreib|en** write out; *Brief usw.*: finish; *Heft*: fill; *Wort usw.*: write in full; *Zahl, Abkürzung*: expand; *Kurzschrift*: extend; *Rechnung*: make out; (*abschreiben*) copy; (*ankündigen*) announce; (*zs.-berufen*) convoke; *Steuern*: impose; *Stelle usw.*: advertise; *Wahlen* ~ issue the writs for elections; *e-n Wettbewerb*: invite entries for (*a competition*), ⚕ invite tenders (for); *sich* ~ write o.s. out; '♀**ung** *f* convocation; announcement; advertisement; ⚕ call for tenders; *Sport*: invitation to a competition.

'**ausschreit|en** (sn) step out; '♀**ung** *f* excess, outrage; ~*en pl.* riots *pl.*

'**Ausschuß** *m* refuse, waste; *s.* ~*ware*; ⚕ (~*wunde*) exit wound; (*Vertretung*) committee, board; '~**sitzung** *f* committee meeting; '~**ware** *f* rejects *pl.*

'**aus|schütten** pour (*od.* dump) out; (*verschütten*) spill; *Dividende*: distribute; (*j-m*) *sein Herz* ~ pour out one's heart (to a p.); *sich vor Lachen* ~ split one's sides with laughing; '~**schwärmen** (sn) swarm (out); ⚔ ~ (*lassen*) extend, deploy; '~**schwatzen** blab out; '~**schweben** ✈ *v/i.* (sn) flatten out.

'**ausschweif|end** *Phantasie*: extravagant; (*liederlich*) dissolute, licentious; '♀**ung** *f* extravagance; debauch, excess.

'**ausschweigen:** *sich* ~ be silent (*über acc.* on).

'**ausschwitz|en** exude; '♀**ung** *f* exudation.

'**aussehen 1.** *v/i.* look; *nach j-m* ~ look out for a p.; ~, *als ob* ... look as if ...; *bleich* (*gesund*) ~ look pale (well); *er sieht sehr gut aus* he is very good-looking; *sie sieht nicht übel aus* she is not bad-looking; *wie sieht er aus?* what does he look like?; *wie siehst du nur aus!* what a sight you are!; *es sieht nach Regen aus* it looks like rain; F *damit es nach et. aussieht* just for looks; *es sieht schlimm mit ihm aus* he is in a bad way; **2.** ♀ *n* (6) appearance, look(s *pl.*); *j-n dem* ~ *nach kennen* know a p. by sight; *nach dem* ~ *urteilen* judge by appearances.

außen ['ausən] out; (*außerhalb*) without, (on the) outside; (*im Freien*) out of doors; *von* ~ *her* from (the) outside; *nach* ~ (*hin*) outwards; '♀-**ansicht** *f* outside view; '♀-**anstrich** *m* façade; '♀-**aufnahme** *f Film*: outdoor shot; '♀**bezirk** *m* outlying district; ~*e pl. e-r Stadt* outskirts *pl.*; '♀**bordmotor** ⚓ *m* outboard motor.

'**aussenden** send out.

'**Außen|dienst** ⚕ *m* external duty; '~**dienstmitarbeiter**(**in** *f*) *m* representative; '~**durchmesser** *m* outside diameter; '~**hafen** *m* outport; '~**handel** *m* foreign trade; ~*sbilanz* balance of trade; '~**minister** *m* Foreign Minister; *Brt.* Foreign Secretary; *Am.* Secretary of State; '~**ministerium** *n* Foreign Ministry; *Brt.* Foreign Office; *Am.* Department of State; '~**politik** *f* foreign policy; '♀-**politisch** of (*od.* referring to, *adv.* with regard to) foreign policy; '~**rand** *m* outer margin; '~**seite** *f* outside, surface; '~**seiter** *m* (7) outsider; '~**spiegel** *m* outside mirror; ~**stände** ['~ʃtɛndə] *m/pl.* outstanding debts; '~**stelle** *f* branch office; '~**stürmer** *m* wing; '~**tasche** *f* outer pocket; '~**verteidiger** *m* outside defender; '~**welt** *f* outer (*od.* outside) world; '~**winkel** *m* external angle; '~**wirtschaft** *f* foreign trade.

außer ['ausər] **1.** *prp.* out of; (*neben, hinzukommend zu*) besides, apart from; in addition to; (*ausgenommen*) except; ~ *Zweifel* beyond all doubt; *alle* ~ *e-m* all but one; ~ *sich sein od. geraten* be *od.* get beside o.s. (*vor* with); **2.** *cj.* ~ *daß* except that, save that; ~ *wenn* unless; *s. Betrieb usw.*; '~**beruflich** private; '~**dem** besides.

äußere ['ɔysərə] **1.** *adj.* exterior, outer, external, outward; **2.** ♀ *n* outward appearance, exterior; *Minister des* ~*n s. Außenminister.*

'**außer|-ehelich** *Kind*: illegitimate; *Verkehr*: extramarital; '~**gerichtlich** extrajudicial; '~**gewöhnlich** exceptional, uncommon; *et.* ♀*es* something out of the ordinary; '~**halb** *prp.* outside; out of; (*jenseits*) beyond; *adv.* (on the) outside; '**~-irdisch** extraterrestrial; '**&-irdische** *m*, *f* extraterrestrial being.

äußerlich ['ɔʏsərliç] external, outward; (*oberflächlich*) superficial; (*schon*) *rein ~ betrachtet* on the face of it; '**&keit** *f* superficiality; (*Formalität*) formality; '**&keiten** *pl.* externals; formalities.

'**äußern** (29) utter, express, voice; *sich ~ P.*: express o.s.; *S.*: manifest (*od.* show) itself.

'**außer|-ordentlich** extraordinary; *~er Professor* senior lecturer, *Am.* associate professor; '**~parlamentarisch** *adj.* extra-parliamentary (*opposition*); '**~planmäßig** extraordinary; *Beamte*: supernumerary; *Budget*: extra-budgetary.

äußerst ['ɔʏsərst] outermost; *fig.* utmost, extreme; *adv.* extremely, exceedingly; *sein &es tun* do one's utmost; *auf das &e gefaßt* prepared for the worst; *bis zum &en gehen* go to extremes, *Am.* go the limit; *zum &en entschlossen* desperate; *zum &en treiben* drive to extremes.

außerstande ['~'ʃtandə] unable.

Äußerung ['ɔʏsəruŋ] *f* (16) utterance, declaration, remark; *fig.* manifestation.

aussetz|en ['auszɛtsən] *v/t.* set (*od.* put) out; *Boot*: lower; (*an Land setzen*) put ashore; *Belohnung*: offer; *Rente*: settle (*j-m* on a p.); (*vermachen*) bequeath; (*aufschieben*) defer; *Tätigkeit usw.*: interrupt, stop; *Zahlung*, *Urteil*: suspend; *Verfahren*: stay; *Kind*: expose; *dem Wetter*, *e-r Gefahr usw.*: expose to; et. *~ an* (*dat.*) find fault with, object to; *was ist daran auszusetzen?* what's wrong with it?; *v/i.* intermit, (*versagen*) fail; *Motor*: stall, misfire; *~ mit et.* interrupt; (*sich Ruhe gönnen*) take a rest; *~ müssen im Spiel*: lose a turn; '**&en** *n* (6) intermission, interruption; failure; misfiring; '**&ung** *f* offer; settlement; bequest; stay; suspension; exposure; disembarkation; (*Tadel*) objection, criticism.

'**Aussicht** *f* view (*auf acc.* of); *fig.* prospect, outlook; *nicht die geringste ~* not the slightest chance; *das Zimmer hat ~ nach Süden ...* looks towards the south; *in ~ haben* have in prospect; *in ~ nehmen* consider, plan; et. *in ~ stellen* hold out a prospect of, promise; '**&slos** hopeless; '**~s-punkt** *m* vantage point; '**&sreich**, '**&svoll** promising; '**~s-turm** *m* look-out tower, *Am.* observatory.

'**aussieben** sift out; *fig.* screen.

'**aussied|eln** evacuate; '**&ler(in** *f*) *m* evacuee; '**&lung** *f* compulsory transfer, evacuation.

'**aussinnen** *s. ausdenken.*

aussöhn|en ['~zøːnən] (25) reconcile (*sich* o.s.) (*mit* to, with); '**&ung** *f* reconciliation.

'**aussondern** (*auswählen*) single out; (*trennen*) separate; *s. ausscheiden.*

'**ausspähen** *v/t.* spy out; *v/i.* look out (*nach* for); ⚔ scout.

'**ausspann|en** *v/t.* stretch; extend; *Zugtier*: unharness; ⊕ *Werkstück*: unclamp; *v/i. fig.* relax, (take a) rest; '**&ung** *f fig.* relaxation.

'**ausspeien** spit out; *fig.* vomit.

'**aussperr|en** *j-n*: shut out, *a. Arbeiter*: lock out; *typ.* space out; '**&ung** *f* lock-out.

'**ausspielen** *v/t. Karte*: lead; *Preis*: play for; *gegeneinander ~* play off against each other; *v/i.* finish playing; *wer spielt aus?* whose lead is it?; *ausgespielt haben fig.* be done for.

'**ausspionieren** spy out.

'**Aussprache** *f* pronunciation; accent; (*Erörterung*) discussion, talk; '**~bezeichnung** *f* phonetic transcription.

'**aussprechen** pronounce (*a.* ⚖), *deutlich*: articulate; (*ausdrücken*) express; *gr. nicht ausgesprochen werden* be silent *od.* mute; *sich ~* speak (out) one's mind (*über acc.* about), (*sein Herz ausschütten*) unburden o.s.; (*sich erklären*) declare o.s. (*für* for, *gegen* against); *sich mit j-m über et. ~* talk a th. over with a p.; *v/i.* finish (speaking); *s. ausgesprochen.*

'**aus|sprengen** *Gerücht*: spread; '**~spritzen** squirt out; ⚕ *Ohr*: syringe; '**&spruch** *m* utterance, saying, remark; '**~spülen** rinse; '**~spüren** track down, trace.

'**ausstaffier|en** (25) fit out; (*schmükken*) dress up, rig out; '**&ung** *f* outfit, equipment; trimming.

'**Ausstand** *m* (*Arbeitseinstellung*)

strike, *Am. a.* walkout; *Ausstände pl.* outstanding debts; *in den ~ treten* go on strike, *Am. a.* walk out.

'**ausständig** outstanding; *Arbeiter*: striking, on strike; '**2e** *m* striker.

'**ausstanzen** ⊕ punch out.

ausstatten ['~ʃtatən] (26) fit out, equip; provide, supply (*mit* with); *Buch usw.*: get up; (*möblieren*) furnish; *mit Befugnissen*: vest; *Tochter*: portion (off); *fig.* (*begaben*) endow.

'**Ausstattung** *f* (16) outfit, equipment; supply; get-up; *s. Aussteuer*; furniture, appointments *pl.*; ⊕ fittings *pl.*; *thea.* setting, décor (*fr.*); '**~sstück** *n thea.* spectacular show; (*Gegenstand*) fitment.

'**ausstechen** *Torf usw., fig. Rivalen*: cut out; *Auge*: put out; *Apfel*: core; *fig.* outdo.

'**ausstehen** *v/i.* be overdue; have not yet come; (*noch ~*) *Geld*: be owing; *~de Schulden f/pl.* outstanding debts; *v/t.* (*ertragen*) endure, bear, stand (*a th. or p.*).

'**aussteigen** (sn) get out (*aus* of; *a.* F *fig.*); alight (from); ⚓, ✈ disembark; F ✈ bale (*bsd. Am.* bail) out.

'**Aussteiger** F *m* (7) drop-out.

'**ausstell|en** *zur Schau*: exhibit, display; *Wache*: post; *Quittung usw.*: give, issue; *Wechsel*: draw (*auf j-n* on, upon); *Rechnung, Scheck, Urkunde*: make out; '**2er** *m* (7), '**2erin** *f* (16[1]) exhibitor; issuer; drawer; '**2-fenster** *mot. n* quarterlight.

'**Ausstellung** *f* exhibition, show, *Am. a.* exposition; drawing; issue; '**~s-datum** *n* date of issue; '**~sgelände** *n* exhibition grounds *pl.*; '**~sraum** *m* show-room; '**~sstück** *n* exhibit.

'**ausstempeln** clock out.

'**aussterben** (sn) die out; *ausgestorben* extinct; *Straße usw.*: deserted.

'**Aussteuer** *f* (*Geld*) dowry; (*Wäsche usw.*) trousseau; '**2n** portion (off); *Radio*: modulate; *s. ausstatten.*

'**Ausstieg** *m* (3) exit.

'**ausstopfe|n** stuff; '**2r** *m* taxidermist.

'**Ausstoß** *m* ✝ output; ⊕ ejection.

'**ausstoß|en** thrust out, eject; (*ausschließen*) expel (*aus* from); (*ausscheiden*) eliminate; *gr.* elide; *Verwünschung, Schrei*: utter; *Seufzer*: heave; *phys.* emit, give off; '**2ung** *f* expulsion; elimination; utterance.

'**ausstrahl|en** *v/i.* (sn) *u. v/t.* radiate (*a. fig.*); *Radio*: broadcast; '**2ung** *f* radiation; *fig. e-r P.*: aura, personal magnetism; '**2ungskraft** *f* charisma.

'**ausstrecken** stretch (out).

'**ausstreichen** strike (*od.* cross) out; (*glätten*) smooth down.

'**ausstreuen** scatter; *Gerücht*: spread.

'**ausström|en** *v/t.* pour forth; *Gas usw.*: emit; *phys.* emanate (*a. fig.*); *v/i.* (sn) stream forth; *phys.* emanate; *Gas, Dampf*: escape; '**2ung** *f* emanation; escape.

'**ausstudieren** finish one's studies.

'**aussuchen** choose, select.

'**Austausch** *m* exchange; interchange; *v. Gütern*: *a.* barter; *im ~ gegen* in exchange for; '**2bar** exchangeable; interchangeable; '**2en** exchange (*gegen* for); (*unter-ea.*) interchange; *Güter*: *a.* barter; '**~-motor** *m* replacement engine; '**~-schüler(in** *f*) *m*, '**~student(in** *f*) *m* exchange student.

'**austeil|en** distribute, hand out; *Befehle*: issue, give; *Hiebe*: deal out; (*spenden*) dispense; '**2ung** *f* distribution.

Auster ['aʊstər] *f* (15) oyster; '**~n-bank** *f* oyster-bed; '**~nfischerei** *f* oyster-dredging; '**~ngabel** *f* oyster fork; '**~nschale** *f* oyster-shell; '**~n-zucht** *f* oyster-culture.

'**austilg|en** (25) exterminate; '**2ung** *f* extermination.

'**austoben** *v/i.* cease raging; *v/t. s-e Wut*: give vent to; *v/refl. Jugend*: sow one's wild oats; *weitS.* let off steam; *Sturm*: spend itself.

Austrag ['~tra:k] *m* (3[3]) (*Entscheidung*) decision; **2en** ['~gən] carry out; *Briefe usw.*: deliver; *Klatsch usw.*: retail; *Streit*: settle; *Wettkampf*: hold; *Buchungsposten*: cancel.

'**Austräger(in** *f*) *m* carrier, roundsman; *b.s. fig.* telltale.

'**Austragung** *f Sport*: holding; '**~s-ort** *m* venue.

Austral|ier [au'stra:ljər] *m*, **2isch** Australian.

austreib|en ['aʊstraɪbən] drive out; (*vertreiben*) expel; *Teufel*: exorcize; *fig. j-m et. ~* cure a p. of a th.; '**2ung** *f* expulsion; exorcism.

'**aus|treten** *v/t.* tread out; *Schuh, Treppe*: wear out; *s. ausgetreten*; *v/i.* (sn) come forth; (*überfließen*) overflow; (*sich abmelden*) retire (*aus* from); *aus e-r Partei, Schule usw.*: leave; (*ein Bedürfnis verrichten*) F spend a penny; ˈ**~tricksen** (27) F outwit; ˈ**~trinken** drink up; (*leeren*) empty; ˈ**ℒtritt** *m* retirement, withdrawal, leaving; ˈ**ℒtritts-erklärung** *f* resignation; ˈ**~trocknen** *v/t.* dry up (*a. v/i.*, sn); *Holz*: season; *Kehle, Land*: parch; ˈ**~trommeln** publish by beat of drum; *fig.* noise abroad; ˈ**~trompeten** *s. ausposaunen*; ˈ**~tüfteln** puzzle out.

ˈ**aus-üb|en** *Aufsicht, Macht, Recht usw.*: exercise; *Beruf*: practise; *Druck, Einfluß usw.*: exert; *Gewerbe*: carry on; *Verbrechen*: commit; ˈ**~end** practising; *Gewalt*: executive; ˈ**ℒung** *f* exercise; practise.

ˈ**Ausverkauf** *m* selling off, clearance (*od.* bargain) sale; *fig.* sellout; ˈ**ℒen** sell out; *um den Rest zu räumen*: sell off, clear out (stock); ˈ**ℒt** ✝, *thea.* sold out.

ˈ**auswachsen** *v/i.* (sn) grow up; *v/t. Kleid*: outgrow; *sich ~* grow up; *sich ~ zu* grow (*od.* develop) into; F *zum ℒ* awful.

ˈ**Auswahl** *f* choice, selection; ✝ assortment, collection, range; *Hunderte von Büchern zur ~* hundreds of books to choose from.

ˈ**auswählen** choose, select.

ˈ**Auswahl|mannschaft** *f Sport*: select team; ˈ**~sendung** ✝ *f* samples *pl.* (sent for selection).

ˈ**Auswander|er** *m* (7), ˈ**~in** *f* (16[1]) emigrant; ˈ**ℒn** emigrate; ˈ**~ung** *f* emigration.

auswärt|ig [ˈ~vɛrtiç] (*aus der Provinz*) out-of-town; (*nicht ansässig*) non-resident; (*ausländisch, fremd*) foreign; *das ℒe Amt s. Außenministerium*; *~e Angelegenheiten pl.* foreign affairs; **~s** [ˈ~vɛrts] outward(s); (*außer dem Hause*) not at home, away; (*außer der Stadt*) out of town; (*im Ausland*) abroad; *~ essen usw.*: dine *etc.* out; ˈ**ℒsspiel** *n Sport*: away match.

ˈ**auswaschen** wash out; *geol.* erode.

ˈ**auswechsel|bar** interchangeable, exchangeable; ˈ**~n** exchange, interchange; *Rad, Batterie usw.*: change; (*ersetzen*) replace; ˈ**ℒspieler** *m Sport*: substitute; ˈ**ℒung** *f* exchange, interchange; replacement.

ˈ**Ausweg** *m* way out (*a. fig.*); exit; outlet; *fig.* expedient; *letzter ~* last resort; ˈ**ℒlos** hopeless.

ausweichen (sn; *dat.*) make way (for); *e-m Schlag, Wagen usw., a. fig.* avoid, dodge; *fig.* elude, evade, avoid; *~ auf* switch over to; ˈ**~d** evasive.

ˈ**Ausweich|gleis** 🚂 *n* siding; ˈ**~möglichkeit** *f fig.* alternative.

ˈ**ausweiden** disembowel, eviscerate.

ˈ**ausweinen** *v/i.* cease weeping; *v/t. sich ~* have a good cry; *sich die Augen ~* cry one's eyes out.

Ausweis [ˈ~vaɪs] *m* (4) (*Beleg*) voucher; (*Bankℒ, Rechnungsℒ*) statement; (*Personalℒ*) identity card; ˈ**ℒen** turn out, expel; *aus Besitz*: evict; (*verbannen*) banish; *lästige Ausländer*: deport; (*zeigen*) show, prove; *j-n als USA-Bürger usw. ~* identify a p. as; *sich ~* prove one's identity; *sich ~ über* (*acc.*) give an account of; ˈ**~karte** *f* identity card; (*Zulassungskarte*) (admission) ticket; ˈ**~kontrolle** *f* identity check; ˈ**~ung** *f* expulsion; eviction; deportation; ˈ**~ungsbefehl** *m* deportation order.

ˈ**ausweiten** (*a. sich ~*) widen, stretch; expand (*a. fig.*); *fig.* spread.

ˈ**auswendig** outward, outside; *fig.* by heart, *mechanisch*: by rote.

ˈ**auswerfen** throw out; *Anker*: cast; ⚕ expectorate; ⊕, *Lava usw.*: eject; *Summe*: allow, grant.

ˈ**auswert|en** *Daten*: evaluate; (*ausnützen*) make full use of, *a.* ✝ exploit; *Karte, Luftbild*: interpret; ˈ**ℒung** *f* evaluation; utilization; exploitation; interpretation.

ˈ**aus|wickeln** unwrap; ˈ**~wiegen** weigh out; ˈ**~winden** wring out; ˈ**~wirken** *v/t. fig.* effect, obtain; *sich ~* take effect, operate; *sich ~ auf* (*acc.*) affect; ˈ**ℒwirkung** *f* effect; ˈ**~wischen** wipe out; *sich die Augen ~* wipe one's eyes; F *j-m eins ~* F put one over on a p.; ˈ**~wringen** *Wäsche*: wring out; ˈ**ℒwuchs** *m* (4[2]) outgrowth (*a. der Phantasie*); (*a. fig.*) excrescence; (*Höcker*) protuberance; (*Mißstand*) abuse; ˈ**ℒwurf** *m* ⚕ expectoration; sputum; *v. Lava usw.*: eruption; *fig.* dregs *pl.*, scum.

ˈ**auszacken** jag; ⊕ indent, tooth.

ˈ**auszahlen** pay (out); *j-n*: pay off; *bar ~* pay in cash; *sich ~ fig.* pay.

'**auszählen** *parl. u. Boxen*: count out.
'**Auszahlung** *f* payment.
'**auszanken** scold.
'**auszehr|en** *v/t.* consume; *v/i.* (sn) waste away; '**²ung** *f* consumption.
'**auszeichn|en** mark; *mit Orden*: decorate; *fig.* distinguish (*sich* o.s.); '**²ung** *f* marking; distinction; hono(u)r; (*Orden*) decoration; *mit* ~ *bestehen* take first-class hono(u)rs.
'**auszieh|bar** extensible, telescopic; '**~en** *v/t. Kleid*: take off; (*herausziehen*) draw out, (*a.* ⚕, ⚗ *u. aus Büchern*) extract; *Rechnung*: make out; *Zeichnung*: trace; *Farbe*: fade (*a. v/i.*); *j-n, a. sich*: undress; *v/i.* (sn) set out; (*aus e-r Wohnung*) (re-) move (from); *Farbe*: fade; '**²leiter** *f* extension ladder; '**²platte** *f e-s Tisches*: leaf; '**²tisch** *m* pull-out table; '**²tusche** *f* drawing ink.
'**auszischen** *thea.* hiss (at).
'**Auszubildende** *m, f* trainee.
'**Auszug** *m* departure; *biblisch u. fig.*: exodus; *aus e-m Buch, a.* ⚗: extract; (*Abriß*) epitome; (*Hauptinhalt*) summary; *einzelne Stellen*: excerpt; *aus e-r Rechnung*: abstract; (*Konto²*) statement (of account); *aus e-r Wohnung*: removal; '**²sweise** by (way of) extract, in extracts.
'**auszupfen** pluck out; pick; *Fäden*: unravel.
autark [au'tark] self-supporting, (economically) self-sufficient.
Autarkie [autar'ki:] *f* (15) autarky, self-sufficiency.
authentisch [au'tentiʃ] authentic (-ally *adv.*).
Auto ['auto] *n* (11) (motor-)car, *Am. a.* auto(mobile); ~ *fahren* drive (a car); *sich im* ~ *mitnehmen lassen* hitch-hike; '**~-abstellplatz** *m*: *überdachter* ~ carport; '**~-apotheke** *f* first-aid kit; '**~-atlas** road atlas; '**~-ausstellung** *f* motor-show; '**~bahn** *f* motorway, *Am.* superhighway; '**~-bahn-abschnitt** *m* section; '**~bahn-auffahrt** *f* entrance; '**~bahn-ausfahrt** *f* exit; '**~bahnbe'nützungsgebühr** *f* toll; '**~bahndreieck** *n* motorway junction; '**~bahnkreuz** *n* intersection; **~biogra'phie** *f* autobiography; **~bus** ['~bus] *m* (4[1]) (motor) bus, autobus, motor coach; **~didakt** [~di'dakt] *m* self-educated person; '**~dieb** *m* car thief; '**~fähre** *f* car ferry; '**~fahrer** *m* (7) motorist, (car-)driver; '**~falle** *f* police-trap; '**~friedhof** *m* car dump; **²gen** ⊕ [~'ge:n] autogenous; **~'gramm** *n* autograph; **~'grammjäger** *m* autograph hunter; '**~hof** *m* motor-court, *Am.* auto court; '**~karte** *f* road map; '**~kino** *n* drive-in cinema; **~krat** [~'kra:t] *m* (12) autocrat; **~kratie** [~kra'ti:] *f* (15) autocracy; **~mat** [~'ma:t] *m* (12) automaton; ⊕ automatic machine, robot; ✝ slot-machine; *s. Musik²*; **~'matenrestaurant** *n* self-service restaurant, *Am.* automat; **~matik** [~'ma:tik] *f* (16) automatism; ⊕ automatic; *mot.* automatic transmission; **~'matikgurt** *m* inertia reel seat belt; **~mation** ⊕ [~ma'tsjo:n] *f* (16) automation; **²matisch** [~'ma:tiʃ] automatic(ally); **²matisieren** [~mati'zi:rən] automatize; **~matisierung** [~mati'zi:ruŋ] *f* automation; **~mo'bil** [~mo'bi:l] *n* (3[1]) *s. Auto*; **~mo'bil-industrie** *f* car (*Am.* auto) industry; **²nom** [~'no:m] autonomous; **~nomie** [~no'mi:] *f* (15) autonomy; '**~nummer** *f* registration number.
Autor ['autɔr] *m* (8[1]), **~in** [~'to:rin] *f* (16[1]) author, writer.
'**Autoreisezug** *m* motorail train.
autor|isieren [~tori'zi:rən] authorize; **~itär** [~i'tɛ:r] authoritarian; **²ität** [~i'tɛ:t] *f* authority; **~itativ** [~ita'ti:f] authoritative.
'**Auto|schalter** ✝ *m* drive-in counter; '**~schlosser** *m* car-mechanic; '**~skooter** *m* (7) dodgem; '**~straße** *f* motor-road, *Am.* highway; **~suggesti'on** *f* auto-suggestion; '**~telephon** *n* car telephone; '**~-unfall** *m* car accident; '**~verleih** *m*, '**~vermietung** *f* car-hiring service, rent-a-car (service); '**~veteran** *m* veteran-car; '**~wäsche** *f* car wash.
avantgardistisch [avãgar'distiʃ] avant-garde.
Avers [a'vɛrs] *m* obverse.
Avis [a'vi:] *m* (4) advice.
avisieren [avi'zi:rən] advise.
Axt [akst] *f* (14[1]) axe, *Am.* ax.
Azalee ⚘ [atsa'le:ə] *f* (15) azalea.
Azetatseide [atse'ta:t-] *f* acetate (*od.* cellulose) silk.
Azeton [atse'to:n] *n* (9, *o. pl.*) acetone.
Azetylen ⚗ [atsety'le:n] *n* (3[1]) acetylene.
Azur [a'tsu:r] *m*, **²(e)n** azure.

B

B, b [be:] B, b; ♪ B flat; *B-Dur* B flat major; *b-Moll* B flat minor.
Baby ['be:bi] *n* (11) baby; '**~-ausstattung** *f* layette; '**~bad** *n* baby bath oil; '**~hös-chen** *n* (*pl.*) baby pants; '**~nahrung** *f* baby food; '**~-öl** *n* baby oil; '**~schuhe** *m/pl.* bootees; '**~sitter** *m* (7) baby-sitter; '**~speck** *m* F puppy fat; '**~sprache** *f* baby-talk; '**~tragetasche** *f* carrycot.
Bacchant [ba'xant] *m* (12), **~in** *f* bacchant(e *f*); **⁀isch** bacchanal.
Bach [bax] *m* (3³) brook.
'**Bachstelze** *zo. f* (water) wagtail.
back ⚓ [bak] **1.** aback; **2.** ⁀ *f* forecastle; (*Schüssel*) bowl; (*gemeinsamer Tisch*) mess; '**⁀blech** *n* baking-tin; '**⁀bord** ⚓ *n* port.
Backe ['bakə] *f* (15) cheek; ⊕ **~n** *pl. e-s Schraubstocks:* jaws; (*Schneid⁀*) die; *am Schi*: toe-piece.
backen ['bakən] (30) *v/t. u. v/i.* bake; *in der Pfanne*: fry; *Obst*: dry; *Schnee usw.*: cake, stick.
Backen|bart *m* sideburns *pl.*; '**~knochen** *m* cheek-bone; '**~tasche** *f* cheek-pouch; '**~zahn** *m* molar (tooth), grinder.
Bäcker ['bɛkər] *m* (7) baker; **~ei** [~'raɪ] *f* (16) bakery; '**~laden** *m* bakery, baker's (shop); '**~meister** *m* master baker.
'**Back|fett** *n* shortening; '**~fisch** *m* fried fish; *fig.* † teenage girl; '**~huhn** *n* fried chicken; '**~-obst** *n* dried fruit; '**~-ofen** *m* (baking) oven; '**~pfeife** *f* box on the ear; '**~pflaume** *f* prune; '**~pulver** *n* baking-powder; '**~stein** *m* brick; '**~trog** *m* kneading-trough; '**~waren** *f/pl.* bread and cakes; '**~werk** *n* pastries *pl.*
Bad [bɑ:t] *n* (1²) bath; *im Freien*: bathe; *s. a. Badeanstalt, Badeort, Badezimmer.*
Bade|anstalt ['bɑ:dəˀanʃtalt] *f* public baths *pl.*; '**~-anzug** *m* bathing-costume (*od.* -suit); '**~gast** *m* visitor (at a watering-place); '**~hose** *f* (*eine* ~ a pair of) bathing-trunks *pl.* (*od.* -shorts *pl.*); '**~kappe** *f* bathing-cap; '**~kur** *f* bathing-cure; '**~mantel** *m* bathing-gown, *bsd. Am.* bathrobe; '**~matte** *f* bath-mat; '**~meister** *m* bath attendant; *Schwimmbad*: swimming instructor; '**⁀n** (26) *v/t. Kind, Kranke*: bath; *v/i. im Freien*: bathe; *in der Wanne*: take (*od.* have) a bath; '**~nde** *m, f* bather; '**~-ofen** *m* bath-heater; (*Gas⁀*) geyser, *Am.* hot-water heater; '**~-ort** *m* watering-place; *mit Heilquellen*: spa; '**~salz** *n* bath-salts *pl.*; '**~schuhe** *m/pl.* bathing shoes; '**~strand** *m* bathing-beach; '**~tuch** *n* bath-towel; '**~wanne** *f* bath, (bath-)tub; '**~zeug** *n* swimming things *pl.*; '**~zimmer** *n* bathroom; '**~zimmerschrank** *m* bathroom cabinet.
Bagage [ba'gɑ:ʒə] *f* (15) ⚔ baggage; *fig. contp.* rabble, lot.
Bagatell|e [baga'tɛlə] *f* (15) trifle, bagatelle; **⁀i'sieren** play down.
Bagger ['bagər] *m* (7), '**~maschine** *f* dredge(r), excavator; '**~eimer** *m* bucket; '**~löffel** *m* shovel; '**⁀n** (29) *v/i. u. v/t.* dredge.
Bahn [bɑ:n] *f* (16) course; (*Pfad*) path, road; *Sport*: course, track; *ast.* orbit; *fig.* (*Laufbahn*) career; *Tuch usw.*: breadth, width; (*Flug⁀*) trajectory; (*Eisen⁀*) railway, *bsd. Am.* railroad, (*Strecke*) line; *mot.* (*Fahr⁀*) lane (*a. Sport*: *des Läufers usw.*); *mit der* ~ by train; *j-n zur* ~ *bringen* see a p. off; *zur* ~ *gehen* go to the station; '**~-arbeiter** *m* railwayman, *Am.* railroader; '**~beamte** *m* railway official; '**⁀brechend** pioneer(ing), epoch-making; '**~brecher** *m* pioneer; '**~damm** *m* railway embankment; '**⁀en** (25) *e-n Weg*: open (up), beat; *fig.* pave *the way* (*dat.* for); *sich einen Weg* ~ force one's way; '**~fahrt** *f* train-journey; '**~fracht** ✝ *f* rail carriage (*Am.* freight); '**~gleis** *n* track; '**~hof** *m* (railway) station; '**~hofsmission** *f* travel(l)er's aid; '**~hofsvorsteher** *m* station-master, *Am.* station agent; '**~körper** *m* permanent way; '**⁀lagernd** to be collected from the station; '**~linie** *f* railway line; '**~polizei** *f* railway police; '**~steig** *m* platform; '**~steigkarte** *f* platform ticket; '**~strecke** *f* line, *bsd. Am.* track; '**~übergang** *m* level (*Am.* grade) crossing; '**~verbindung** *f* train connection; '**~wärter** *m* linesman; (*Schrankenwärter*) gatekeeper.
Bahre ['bɑ:re] *f* (15) barrow; (*Kranken⁀*) stretcher; (*Toten⁀*) bier.

Baiser [be'ze:] *n* (11) meringue.

Baisse ✝ ['bɛ:s(ə)] *f* (15) slump (in prices); *auf ~ spekulieren* (sell) bear, *Am.* sell short; '**~spekulation** *f* bear speculation; '**~stimmung** *f* downward tendency.

Bajonett ⚔ [bajo'nɛt] *n* (3) bayonet; **~verschluß** ⊕ *m* bayonet catch.

Bake ⚓ ['bɑ:kə] *f* (15) beacon.

Bakterie [bak'te:rjə] *f* (15) bacterium (*pl.* -ia), germ; **~nbombe** *f* bacteria bomb; **~nkrieg** *m* germ warfare.

Bakteriologe [~terjo'lo:gə] *m* (13) bacteriologist.

Balance [ba'lɑ̃:sə, ba'laŋsə] *f* (15) balance, equilibrium; **~-akt** *m fig.* balancing act.

balancier|en [~'si:rən] *v/t. u. v/i.* balance; **2stange** *f* balancing-pole.

bald [balt] soon; (*in Kürze*) shortly; (*beinahe*) almost, nearly; *so ~ als möglich s. baldigst*; *~ ..., ~ ...* now..., now...

Baldachin ['baldaxi:n] *m* (3[1]) canopy.

baldig ['baldiç] early, speedy; '**~st** as soon as possible.

Baldrian ['baldriɑ:n] *m* (3[1]) valerian.

Balg [balk] *m* (3[3]) skin; F (*Kind*) [*pl. Bälger*] brat, urchin; [*pl. Bälge*] (*Orgel2*) bellows *pl.*; *phot.* (*mst* **~en** ['~gən] *m*) bellows *pl.*; **2en** ['~gən] (25): *sich ~* scuffle, scramble, tussle (*um* for); *Kinder*: romp; **~erei** [~gə'raɪ] *f* scuffle, scramble (*um* for); romp.

Balken ['balkən] *m* (6) beam.

Balkon [bal'kɔ̃, ~'ko:n] *m* (11; 3[1]) balcony; *thea.* dress-circle, *Am.* balcony; **~tür** *f* French window.

Ball *m* (3[3]) **1.** ball; **2.** ball, dance; *auf dem ~* at the ball.

Ballade [ba'lɑ:də] *f* (15) ballad.

Ballast ['balast] *m* (3[2]) ballast; **~stoffe** *m/pl.* roughage *sg.*

ballen[1] ['balən] (25) (*a. sich*) (form into a) ball; *Faust*: clench; **2**[2] *m* (6) bale; *anat.* ball; ⚕ (*entzündeter Fuß2*) bunion; '**~weise** by the bale.

Ballermann ['balər-] *m sl.* shooter.

ballern ['balərn] (29) bang; *j-m e-e ~* F clout a p. one.

Ballett [ba'lɛt] *n* (3) ballet; **~tänzer** (**-in** *f*) *m* ballet-dancer.

'**ball|förmig** ball-shaped; '**2junge** *m* ball-boy; '**2kleid** *n* ball-dress.

Ballon [ba'lɔ̃, ~'lo:n] *m* (11; 3[1]) balloon; (*große Flasche*) carboy; **~sperre** *f* balloon barrage.

'**Ball|saal** *m* ball-room; '**~spiel** *n* ball-game.

'**Ballung** *f* concentration; (*Überfüllung*) overcrowding, congestion; '**~sgebiet** *n* overcrowded region.

Balsam ['balzɑ:m] *m* (3[1]) balsam, (*a. fig.*) balm; **2ieren** [~za'mi:rən] embalm; **2isch** [~'zɑ:miʃ] balmy.

baltisch ['baltiʃ] Baltic.

balzen ['baltsən] (27) mate, pair; (*den Balzruf ausstoßen*) call.

Bambus ['bambus] *m* (*inv. od.* 4[1]), '**~rohr** *n* bamboo (cane).

banal [ba'nɑ:l] commonplace, banal; **2ität** [~nali'tɛ:t] *f* banality.

Banane [ba'nɑ:nə] *f* (15) banana; **~nstecker** ⚡ *m* banana plug.

Banause [ba'nauzə] *m* (13) Philistine, low-brow.

Band [bant] **1.** *m* (3[3]) volume; *dicker*: tome; (*Einband*) binding; **2.** *n* (1[2]) band; (*Farb2*, *Schmuck2*) ribbon; (*Isolier2*, *Meß2*, *Ton2*, *Ziel2*) tape; ⊕ (*Förder2*) (conveyor) belt; (*Montage2*) assembly line; *anat.* ligament; *am laufenden ~* on the assembly line, *fig.* continuously; **3.** *n* (*pl.* '*~e*) *fig.* tie, bond; **4. 2** *pret. v. binden.*

Bandag|e [ban'dɑ:ʒə] *f* (15) bandage; **2ieren** [~da'ʒi:rən] bandage.

'**Band|-aufnahme** *f* tape recording; '**~breite** *f* ⚡ band-width; *fig.* spread.

Bande ['bandə] *f* (15) *Billard*: cushion; *fig.* gang (*a. contp.*); '**~nkrieg** *m* guerilla war(fare).

Band-eisen ['bant-] *n* band iron.

Banderole [~də'ro:lə] *f* (15) *Steuerwesen*: revenue stamp; (*Klebeband*) adhesive tape.

Bänder|riß ['bɛndəris] *m* torn ligament; **~zerrung** ['~tsɛruŋ] *f* pulled ligament.

bändig|en ['bɛndigən] (25) tame; *fig. a.* subdue, restrain, master; '**2ung** *f* taming.

Bandit [ban'di:t] *m* (12) bandit.

'**Band|maß** *n* tape-measure; '**~säge** *f* band-saw; '**~scheibe** *anat. f* (intervertebral) disc; '**~scheibenschaden** ⚕ *m* damaged disc; '**~wurm** *m* tapeworm; '**~zählwerk** *n* tape counter.

bang, ~e ['baŋə] anxious (*um* about); *mir ist ~* I am afraid (*vor dat.* of); *j-m ~ machen* make a p. afraid, frighten a p.; *keine Bange!*

don't worry!; **≈emacher** ['~-maxər] *m* alarmist; '**~en** (25) be afraid (*vor dat.* of); *sich ~ um* be anxious (*od.* worried) about; '**≈igkeit** *f* (16, *o. pl.*) anxiety, fear.

Bank [baŋk] *f* **1.** (14¹) bench; *Schule*: form; *auf die lange ~ schieben* put off; F *durch die ~* without exception, down the line; **2.** (16) ✝ bank; '**~-aktie** *f* bank share (*Am.* stock); '**~-anweisung** *f* cheque, *Am.* check; '**~-ausweis** *m* bank return (*Am.* statement); '**~beamte** *m* bank clerk; '**~direktor** *m* bank manager; '**~diskont** *m* bank discount; (*~satz*) bank-rate.

Bänkelsänger ['bɛŋkəlzɛŋər] *m* ballad-singer.

bank(e)rott [baŋk(ə)'rɔt] **1.** bankrupt; *~ werden* go (*od.* become) bankrupt; **2.** ≈ *m* (3) bankruptcy (*a. fig.*), failure, F crash; *~ machen* go (*od.* become) bankrupt; **≈-erklärung** *f* declaration of bankrupty; *fig.* sell-out; **≈eur** [~rɔ'tø:r] *m* (3¹) bankrupt.

Bankett [baŋ'kɛt] *n* (3) banquet.

'**bankfähig** bankable, negotiable.

'**Bank|gebühren** *f/pl.* banking charges; '**~geheimnis** *n* banker's discretion; '**~geschäft** *n* banking transaction; (*Bankwesen*) banking (business), banking trade; '**~guthaben** *n* bank balance; '**~halter** *m* banker; '**~haus** *n* bank(ing-house).

Bankier [~'je:] *m* (11) banker.

'**Bank|kaufmann** *m* bank clerk; '**~konto** *n* banking-account, *Am.* bank account; '**~leitzahl** *f* bank code number; '**~note** *f* bank-note, *Am.* bill; '**~räuber** *m* bank robber; '**~überfall** *m* bank raid (*od.* holdup); '**~wechsel** *m* bank-bill, draft; '**~wesen** *n* banking.

Bann [ban] *m* (3) ban; *fig.* spell; *eccl.* excommunication; *in den ~ tun* put under the ban, *eccl.* excommunicate; '**≈en** (25) banish (*a. fig. Sorgen usw.*); *Gefahr*: avert; (*fesseln*) spellbind; (*festhalten*) *auf Bild, Papier usw.*: capture, record; *gebannt* spellbound.

Banner ['banər] *n* (7) standard, banner (*a. fig.*); '**~träger** *m* standard-bearer.

'**Bann|fluch** *m* anathema; '**~meile** *f* boundary.

bar¹ [bɑ:r] *e-r S. ~* destitute (*od.* devoid) of; *~es Geld* ready money, cash; *~er Unsinn* sheer nonsense; *~ bezahlen* pay cash (down); *gegen ~* for cash; *s. Münze.*

Bar² [~] *f* (11¹) (*Ausschank*) bar.

Bär [bɛ:r] *m* (12) bear; *der Große ~* the Great(er) Bear; *der Kleine ~* the Little (*od.* Lesser) Bear; *fig. j-m e-n ~en aufbinden* hoax a p.

Baracke [ba'rakə] *f* (15) (wooden) hut, barrack.

Barbar [bar'bɑ:r] *m* (12), **~in** *f* (16¹) barbarian; **~ei** [~ba'raɪ] *f* (16) barbarism; (*Grausamkeit*) barbarity; **≈isch** [~'bɑ:riʃ] barbarian; *contp.* barbarous; *fig.* barbaric.

bärbeißig ['bɛ:rbaɪsiç] gruff.

'**Bar|bestand** *m* cash in hand; '**~betrag** *m* amount in cash.

Barbier [bar'bi:r] *m* (3¹) barber; **≈en** (25) shave; F *fig. j-n über den Löffel ~* do a p. in the eye.

'**Bar|dame** *f* barmaid; '**~einnahme** *f* cash receipts *pl.*

'**Bären|dienst** *m*: *j-m e-n ~ leisten* do a p. a disservice; '**~führer** *m* bear-leader (*a. fig.*); '**~hunger** F *m* ravenous hunger; *e-n ~ haben* be ravenous, be starving.

Barett [ba'rɛt] *n* (3) cap, beret.

bar|fuß ['bɑ:rfu:s] bare-foot(ed); **~füßig** ['~fy:siç] bare-footed.

barg [bark] *pret. v. bergen.*

'**Bar|geld** *n* cash, ready money; '**≈geldlos** cashless; **≈häuptig** ['~hɔʏptiç] bare-headed.

Bärin ['bɛ:rin] *f* (16¹) she-bear.

Bariton ['bɑ:ritɔn] *m* (3¹) baritone.

Barkasse ⚓ [bar'kasə] *f* (15) launch.

'**Barkauf** *m* cash purchase.

Barke ⚓ ['barkə] *f* (15) barque.

'**Barkredit** *m* cash loan.

barmherzig [barm'hɛrtsiç] merciful, charitable; *der ~e Samariter* the good Samaritan; *~e Schwester* sister of charity; **≈keit** *f* mercy, charity.

'**Barmittel** *n/pl.* cash (funds *pl.*).

'**Barmixer** *m* cocktail waiter, barman.

barock [ba'rɔk] **1.** baroque; *fig.* grotesque, odd; **2.** ≈ *n* Baroque.

Barometer [baro'me:tər] *n* (7) barometer (*a. fig.*); **~säule** *f* barometric column; **~stand** *m* barometer reading.

Baron [ba'ro:n] *m* (3¹) baron; **~in** *f* (16¹) baroness.

Barre ['barə] *f* (15) bar; '**~n** *m* (6)

metall. billet; (*Gold*♀, *Silber*♀) bullion, ingot; *Turnen*: parallel bars *pl.*; '**~ngold** *n* gold bullion.
Barriere [bar'jɛːrə] *f* (15) barrier.
Barrikade [bari'kaːdə] *f* (15) barricade.
Barsch[1] [barʃ] *m* (3²) perch.
barsch[2] [~] gruff, brusque.
Bar|schaft ['baːrʃaft] *f* (16) ready money, cash; '**~scheck** ✝ *m* uncrossed cheque (*Am.* check).
'**Barschheit** *f* gruffness.
barst [barst] *pret. v. bersten.*
Bart [baːrt] *m* (3³) beard; (*Schlüssel*♀) bit; *fig. j-m um den ~ gehen* cajole a p.; *sich e-n ~ wachsen* (*od. stehen*) *lassen* grow a beard.
bärtig ['bɛːrtiç] bearded.
'**bartlos** beardless.
'**Bar|verkauf** *m* cash sale; '**~verlust** *m* clear loss; '**~zahlung** *f* cash payment; *gegen ~* cash down.
Basar [ba'zaːr] *m* (3¹) (*a. Wohltätigkeits*♀) bazaar.
Base ['baːzə] *f* (15) **1.** (female) cousin; **2.** ⚗ base.
basieren [ba'ziːrən] *v/t.* base, found (*auf dat.* upon); *v/i. ~ auf* (*dat.*) be based upon.
Basilikum ⚘ [ba'ziːlikum] *n* (11, 9) basil.
Bas|is ['baːzis] *f* (16²) base, *mst fig.* basis; '♀**isch** basic.
'**Basislager** *mount. n* base camp.
Baskenmütze ['baskən-] *f* beret.
Baß [bas] *m* (4²) bass; '**~geige** *f* bass viol; *große*: contrabass; '**~gitarre** *f* bass guitar.
Bassin [ba'sɛ̃] *n* (11) basin; reservoir; (*Schwimm*♀) swimming-pool.
Bassist [~'sist] *m* (12) bass(-singer).
'**Baß|schlüssel** ♪ *m* bass clef; '**~stimme** *f* bass voice.
Bast [bast] *m* (3²) bast.
basta ['basta]: *und damit ~!* so that's that!, so there!
Bastard ['bastart] *m* (3) bastard; *zo.*, ⚘ hybrid.
Bastei [ba'staɪ] *f* (16) bastion, bulwark.
bast|eln ['bastəln] (29) tinker (*an dat.* at); (*bauen*) rig up; '♀**ler** *m* (7) amateur constructor, hobbyist, home-mechanic.
'**Bastseide** *f* raw silk.
bat [baːt] *pret. v. bitten.*
Bataillon [batal'joːn] *n* (3¹) battalion.
Batik ['baːtik] *f* (16) batik.
Batist [ba'tist] *m* (3³) batiste, cambric.
Batterie [batə'riː] *f* (15) battery; ♀**betrieben** battery-operated; **~lader** *mot. m* (7) battery charger.
Bau [baʊ] *m* (3; *pl. a.* '**~ten**) (*Bauen*) building, construction (*a.* ⊕); (*Gebäude*) building, edifice; structure (*a. Gefüge*); (*o. pl.*) ⸙ cultivation; (*Körper*♀) build, frame; (*pl.* '**~e**) (*Tier*♀) burrow, (*a. fig.*) den, earth; *im ~* (*begriffen*) being built, under construction; '**~-amt** *n* Surveyor's Office; '**~-arbeiten** *f/pl.* construction work *sg.*; *an Straßen*: roadworks; '**~-arbeiter** *m* construction worker; '**~-art** *f* structure; build; ⊕ construction, design, (*Typ*) type, model; ♎ (style of) architecture; '**~beginn** *m* start of building.
Bauch [baʊx] *m* (3³) belly (*a. fig.*); *anat.* abdomen; '**~fell** *n* peritoneum; '**~fell-entzündung** *f* peritonitis; '♀**ig** bulgy; ...-bellied; '**~klatscher** ['~klatʃər] *m* (7) belly-flop; '**~landung** *f* belly-landing; '**~muskel** *m* abdominal muscle; '**~nabel** *m* navel, F belly button; '♀**reden** ventriloquize; '**~redner** *m* ventriloquist; '**~redne'rei** *f* ventriloquism; '**~schmerzen** *m/pl.*, '**~weh** *n* stomach-ache; '**~speicheldrüse** *f* pancreas; '**~tanz** *m* belly dance.
'**Bau|denkmal** *n* historical monument; '**~-element** *n Fertigbau*: construction element.
bauen ['baʊən] (25) *v/t.* build; construct; ⸙ cultivate, grow; *Hoffnung usw.*: base (*auf acc.* on); *v/i. ~ auf* (*acc.*) rely (*od.* build) on.
Bauer ['baʊər] **1.** *n* (7) cage; **2.** *m* (7) builder; **3.** *m* (10 *od.* 13) ⸙ farmer, peasant; *fig.* boor; *Schach*: pawn; *Karten*: knave.
Bäuerin ['bɔʏərin] *f* (16¹) countrywoman; *engS.* farmer's wife.
'**bäu(e)risch** *contp.* boorish.
'**Bau-erlaubnis** *f* building permit.
'**bäuerlich** rural, rustic.
'**Bauern|bursche** *m* country lad; '**~fänger** *m* (7) sharper, confidence man; '**~fängerei** *f* confidence trick (*Am.* game); '**~frau** *f s. Bäuerin*; '**~gut** *n* farm; '**~haus** *n* farm-house; '**~hof** *m* farm; '**~regel** *f* weather maxim; '**~schaft** *f*, '**~stand** *m* peasantry.
'**Bau|-erwartungsland** *n* development area; '**~fach** *n* architecture;

building trade; '2**fällig** out of repair, dilapidated, tumble-down; '~**fälligkeit** *f* dilapidation, state of decay; '~**firma** *f*, '~**geschäft** *n* builders and contractors *pl.*; '~**gelände** *n* building land; '~**genehmigung** *f* planning and building permission; '~**gerüst** *n* scaffolding; '~**gewerbe** *n* building trade; '~**grube** *f* excavation; '~**handwerker** *m* craftsman in the building trade; '~**herr** *m* building owner; '~**holz** *n* timber, *Am.* lumber; '~-**ingenieur** *m* constructional engineer; '~**jahr** *n* year of construction; *Auto*: model; '~**kasten** *m* box of bricks; (*Stabil*2) construction set; '~**kastensystem** *n* unit construction system; '~**kunst** *f* architecture; '~**land** *n* building land; '2**lich** architectural; *in gutem ~em Zustand* in good repair.

Baum [baʊm] *m* (3³) tree; (*Hebe*2, *Weber*2 *usw.*) beam; ⚓ boom; '~**bestand** *m* stand (of timber-trees).

'**Baumeister** *m* architect; master-builder.

baumeln ['baʊməln] (29) dangle, swing (*an dat.* from); *mit den Beinen ~* swing one's legs.

bäumen ['bɔʏmən] *v/refl.* (25) rear, prance; *P. vor Schmerzen*: writhe (with).

'**Baum|grenze** *f* timber-line; '2**lang** (as) tall as a lamp-post; '~**schere** *f* (*eine* a pair of) pruning-shears *pl.*; '~**schule** *f* tree-nursery; '~**stamm** *m* trunk; '2**stark** (as) strong as an ox; '~**sterben** *n* (6) death of trees; '~**wolle** *f* cotton; '2**wollen** (made of) cotton; '~**wollsamt** *m* velveteen.

'**Bau|plan** *m* architect's plan; ⊕ blueprint; '~**platz** *m* (building) site (*od.* plot).

Bausch [baʊʃ] *m* (3² *u.* 3³) pad, bolster; *Watte*: wad; *in ~ und Bogen* in the lump; '2**en** (27) swell out (*a. sich*), puff; bag; '2**ig** puffy, swelled; baggy.

'**Bau|schlosser** *m* building fitter, locksmith; '~**schule** *f* school of architecture; '~**sparkasse** *f* building society, *Am.* building and loan association; '~**sparvertrag** *m* building society savings agreement; '~**stein** *m* building-stone, *a. für Kinder*: brick; '~**stelle** *f* (building) site; '~**stil** *m* (architectural) style; '~**stoff** *m* building material; '~**stopp** *m* building freeze; *e-n ~ verhängen* impose a halt on building; '~**techniker** *m* constructional engineer; '~**teil** *n* structural member, component part; '~**ten** *m/pl.* buildings *pl.*, structures *pl.*; *thea.* setting *sg.*, *Film*: *a.* architecture; *öffentliche ~* public works; '~-**unternehmer** *m* building contractor; '~**vorhaben** *n* building project; '~**weise** *f* method of construction; '~**werk** *n* edifice, building; '~**wesen** *n s. Baufach*; '~**zeichnung** *f* construction drawing.

Bayer ['baɪər] *m* (13), '~**in** *f* (16¹), '**bay(e)risch** Bavarian.

Bazill|enträger [ba'tsiləntrɛːgər] *m* carrier; ~**us** [~'tsilus] *m* (16²) bacillus (*pl.* -cilli), germ.

beabsichtigen [bə'ˀapziçtigən] (25) intend, mean, propose (*zu tun* to do, doing).

be'-acht|en (26) note, pay attention to; *j-n*: notice; (*berücksichtigen*) consider; *Vorschrift usw.*: observe; *nicht ~* ignore; ~**enswert** noteworthy, remarkable; ~**lich** noticeable, considerable; 2**ung** *f* notice, attention; consideration; observance.

Beamt|e [bə'ˀamtə] *m* (18), ~**in** *f* (16¹) official; *höherer*: functionary, officer; (*Staats*2) civil (*Am.* public) servant; ~**enschaft** *f* civil servants *pl.*

be'-ängstig|en make anxious, alarm; 2**ung** *f* anxiety, uneasiness.

beanspruch|en [~'ˀanʃpruxən] (25) claim; *Mühe, Platz, Zeit*: require, take; ⊕ stress; 2**ung** *f* claim (*gen.* to); demand (on); ⊕ stress, strain.

beanstand|en [~'ˀanʃtandən] (26) object to; *Wahl*: contest; ✝ complain of; 2**ung** *f* objection (*gen.* to); complaint.

beantragen [~'ˀantraːgən] (25) apply for (*bei j-m* to); (*vorschlagen*) propose; *parl.*, ⚖ move.

be'-antwort|en answer; 2**ung** *f* answer(ing); *in ~ (gen.)* in reply to.

be'-arbeit|en work; *maschinell*: *a.* machine, tool; ✓ cultivate; *thea. usw.* adapt (*nach* from), *bsd.* ♪ arrange; *Thema*: treat; *Buch*: revise; *Antrag usw.*: act upon, deal with, handle; *j-n ~* work on, *a. mit Schlägen*: belabo(u)r; 2**ung** *f* working; cultivation; adaptation, *bsd.* ♪ arrangement; treatment; revision; handling; ²**ungsgebühr** *f* handling charge.

be'-argwöhnen be suspicious of.

Be'-atmung *f*: *künstliche* ~ artificial respiration.

beaufsichtig|en [~'ʔaʊfzɪçtɪgən] (25) supervise, superintend; control; *Kind*: look after; ²**ung** *f* supervision; control.

beauftrag|en [~'ʔaʊftra:gən] commission, charge; (*berufen*) appoint; ²**te** [~tra:ktə] *m*, *f* (18) commissioner; authorized representative, agent, deputy.

be'bau|en build on; ✓ cultivate; ²**ungs-plan** *m* development scheme.

beben ['be:bən] **1.** (25) shake, tremble; (*schaudern*) shiver; *Erde*: quake (*alle*: *vor dat.* with); **2.** ² *n* (6) (*Erd*²) earthquake.

be|bildern [bə'bɪldərn] (29) illustrate; **~brillt** [~'brɪlt] spectacled.

Becher ['bɛçər] *m* (7) cup; *ohne Fuß*: tumbler, mug.

Becken ['bɛkən] *n* (6) basin, *Am. a.* bowl; ♪ cymbal(s *pl.*); *anat.* pelvis; '**~knochen** *m/pl.* pelvic bones.

Bedacht [~'daxt] **1.** *m* (3, *o. pl.*) consideration, care; *mit* ~ deliberately; ~ *nehmen auf* (*acc.*) take *a th.* into consideration; **2.** ²: ~ *auf* (*acc.*) intent on; *darauf* ~ *sein, zu inf.* be careful to *inf.*

bedächtig [~'dɛçtɪç], **bedachtsam** [~'daxtza:m] (*überlegt*) deliberate; (*vorsichtig*) careful; (*langsam*) slow; ²**keit** *f* deliberateness.

Be'dachung *f* roofing.

be'danken: *sich* ~ (*bei j-m*; *für et.*) thank (a p.; for a th.); *ablehnend*: *dafür bedanke ich mich!* thank you for nothing!

Bedarf [bə'darf] *m* (3) need, want (*an dat.* of); ⚕ demand (for); requirements *pl.*; (*Verbrauch*) consumption; *bei* ~ if required; *nach* ~ as required; ~ *haben an* (*dat.*) be in need (*od.* want) of; *s-n* ~ *decken* cover one's requirements; **~s-artikel** *m* (essential) commodity, *pl. a.* supplies *pl.*, requisites *pl.*; **~sfall** *m*: *im* ~ if required; **~shalte-stelle** *f* request stop.

bedauerlich [~'daʊərlɪç] regrettable, deplorable; **~erweise** unfortunately.

be'dauern (29) **1.** *j-n*: be sorry for, pity; *et.*: regret, deplore; *ich bedaure sehr, daß ...* I am very sorry for *ger. od.* that ...; **2.** ² *n* (6) regret (*über acc.* for); (*Mitleid*) pity (*mit* for); **~swert** pitiable.

be'deck|en cover; **~t** *Himmel*: overcast; ²**ung** *f* covering; *bsd.* ⚔ escort; *bsd.* ⚓ convoy.

be'denken **1.** consider; (*beachten*) (bear in) mind; *im Testament*: remember; *j-n mit et.* ~ endow a p. with a th.; *sich* ~ deliberate; *sich anders* ~ change one's mind; **2.** ² *n* (6) (*Erwägung*) consideration; (*Einwand*) objection; (*Zaudern*) hesitation; (*Zweifel*) doubt, scruple; ~ *haben* hesitate; *kein* ~ *tragen zu tun* make no scruple to do; **~los** *adj.* unscrupulous; *adv.* without hesitation.

be'denklich doubtful; *stärker*: critical, serious; (*heikel*) delicate; *Lage usw.*: *a.* precarious; *P.*: doubtful; thoughtful; ²**keit** *f* doubtfulness; critical state; precariousness.

Be'denkzeit *f* time for reflection.

be'deuten mean, signify; stand for; (*in sich schließen*) imply, involve; (*vorbedeuten*) (fore)bode; *j-m* (*od. j-n*) ~ *zu inf.* give a p. a sign to *inf.*, intimate a p. to *inf.*; *es hat nichts zu* ~ it is of no consequence; **~d** important; *Person*: *a.* eminent; (*beträchtlich*) considerable.

be'deutsam significant; ²**keit** *f* significance.

Be'deutung *f* meaning, signification; (*Wichtigkeit*) importance; ²**s-los** insignificant; (*ohne Sinn*) meaningless; ²**svoll** significant.

be'dien|en *v/t.* serve, wait on; ⚕ attend to; *Maschine usw.*: work, attend, operate; *sich* ~ *bei Tisch*: help o.s.; *sich e-r S.* ~ make use of; *v/i. bei Tisch*: wait (at table); *Karten*: follow suit, *nicht* ~ revoke; ²**stete** *m*, *f* (18) employé(e *f*) *m* (*fr.*), employee; ²**te** *m* (18) (man-)servant.

Be'dienung *f* service, ⚕ *a.* attendance; ⊕ working, operation; (*Dienerschaft*) servants *pl.*; (*Kellner*[*in*]) waiter (*f* waitress); (*Bedienungsgeld*) service charge; **~s-anleitung** *f* directions *pl.* for use, operating instructions *pl.*; **~sknopf** *m* control knob; **~skomfort** *m* easy operation.

beding|en [bə'dɪŋən] stipulate; (*in*

sich schließen) imply; (*erfordern*) require; (*bewirken*) cause; **~t** conditional (*durch* on); ~ *sein durch* be conditioned by.

Be'dingung *f* condition; *pl.* *~en* ✝, ⚖ terms *pl.*; *unter der ~, daß* on condition that; *es zur ~ machen, daß* make it a condition that; *unter keiner ~* on no account; **2slos** unconditional.

be'dräng|en press hard; *fig. a.* afflict, beset; *bedrängte Lage* distress; **2nis** [~'drɛŋnis] *f* (14²) distress, trouble, plight.

be'droh|en threaten, menace; **~lich** threatening; **2ung** *f* threat, menace (*gen.* to).

be'drucken print (on).

be'drück|en oppress; *seelisch*: depress; **2er(in** *f*) *m* oppressor; **2ung** *f* oppression; depression.

be'dürfen (*gen.*) need, want, require.

Be'dürfnis *n* (4¹) need, want; necessity, requirement; *(s)ein ~ verrichten* relieve nature; **~-anstalt** *f* (public) lavatory; **2los** frugal.

be'dürftig needy, indigent; *e-r Sache*: in need of; **2keit** *f* indigence, neediness.

Beefsteak ['bi:fste(:)k] *n* (11) (beef-) steak; *deutsches ~ s. Frikadelle.*

be'-ehren hono(u)r; ✝ *mit Aufträgen usw.*: favo(u)r; *ich beehre mich zu* ... I have the hono(u)r to ...

beeid|(ig)en [bə'ˀaɪd(ig)ən] (26 [25]) *et.*: affirm by oath, swear to; *j-n*: swear in; **~igt, ~et** sworn; **2igung** *f* confirmation by oath.

be'-eilen: *sich ~* hurry, make haste; *beeil dich!* hurry up!

beeindrucken [~'ˀaɪndrukən] *v/t.* impress.

beeinfluss|en [~'ˀaɪnflusən] (28) influence; *nachteilig*: affect; **2ung** *f* influence (*gen.* on).

beeinträchtig|en [~'ˀaɪntrɛçtigən] (25) impair, affect (adversely); *Ruf, Schönheit usw.*: detract from; *Recht, Wert*: prejudice; (*behindern*) hamper; **2ung** *f* impairment (*gen.* of); prejudice (to); detraction (from).

be'-end(ig)|en (bring to an) end, finish, conclude, terminate; **2ung** *f* termination, close.

beengen [~'ˀɛŋən] (25) cramp, narrow; *fig. a.* confine.

be'-erben *j-n*: be a p.'s heir.

beerdigen [~'ˀe:rdigən] (25) bury.

Be'-erdigung *f* burial, interment; **~s-institut** *n* undertaker's, funeral directors *pl.*; **~skosten** *pl.* funeral expenses.

Beere ['be:rə] *f* (15) berry.

Beet [be:t] *n* (3) bed.

befähig|en [bə'fɛ:igən] (25) enable (*to do*); qualify (*für, zu* for); **~t** able; **2ung** *f* qualification; (*Fähigkeit*) ability; **2ungsnachweis** *m* certificate of qualification.

befahr|bar [~'fa:rba:r] *Weg*: practicable, negotiable; *Wasser*: navigable; **~en** travel on, pass over; *Fluß, Meer*: navigate, ply; *eine stark ~e Straße* a much frequented road.

be'fallen (30) befall, attack; *Krankheit*: strike; *~ werden von Krankheit, Furcht* be seized with; *von Insekten usw.*: be infested by.

be'fangen embarrassed; (*schüchtern*) shy, self-conscious; (*voreingenommen*) prejudiced, bias(s)ed (*a.* ⚖); *in e-m Irrtum ~ sein* be mistaken; **2heit** *f* embarrassment; shyness, self-consciousness; prejudice.

be'fassen touch, handle; *sich ~ mit* occupy o.s. with; *a. S.*: deal with.

befehden [~'fe:dən] (26) make war upon, (*a. fig.*) fight against.

Befehl [bə'fe:l] *m* (3) order (*a.* ⚖); (*a. Ober2*) command; *auf ~* (*gen.*) by order (of); **2en** (30) order, command; *wie Sie ~* as you wish; **2igen** [~'fe:ligən] (25) command.

Be'fehls|form *gr. f* imperative (mood); **2gemäß** as ordered; **~haber** *m* (7) commander(-in-chief); **2haberisch** imperious, dictatorial.

befestig|en [~'fɛstigən] fasten, fix, attach (*an dat.* to); ⚔, *fig.* fortify; *fig.* strengthen; *sich ~* ✝ *Preise*: stiffen, harden; **2ung** *f* fastening; ⚔ fortification; strengthening.

befeuchten [~'fɔʏçtən] (26) moisten, damp; *stärker*: wet.

be'find|en 1. find, deem; *sich ~* be; *gesundheitlich*: be, feel; **2.** 2 *n* (6) (state of) health; (*Meinung*) opinion; **~lich** [~'fint-] being; *~ in* (*dat.*) (contained) in.

be'flaggen flag.

beflecken [~'flɛkən] (25) spot, stain; (*besudeln*) pollute; *nur fig.* sully, tarnish, defile.

befleißigen [~'flaɪsigən] (25): *sich e-r S. ~* apply o.s. to; take pains to *inf.*, be studious to *inf.*

beflissen [~'flisən] (*gen.*) studious (of); **2heit** *f* studiousness, assiduity.
beflügeln [~'fly:gəln] (29) wing (*a. fig.*); *fig.* lend wings to.
befohlen [~'fo:lən] *p. p. v. befehlen.*
be'folg|en follow, obey, observe; comply with; **2ung** *f* observance (of), compliance (with).
be'förder|n convey; carry; transport, *bsd. Am.* ship; (*spedieren*) *Güter*: forward; *im Amt od. Rang*: promote (*zum Major usw.* [to be] major *etc.*), *a.* prefer (*zu* to); (*fördern*) further, promote; **2ung** *f* conveyance; transport(ation); forwarding; shipment; preferment, promotion; furtherance; **2ungsmittel** *n* (means of) transport(ation *Am.*).
befrachten [~'fraxtən] (26) load; ⚓ freight, charter.
be'fragen question, interrogate; interview; *um Rat*: consult.
be'frei|en (25) free; deliver; liberate (*alle*: *von* from); *von e-r Verpflichtung* ~ release (*od.* exempt) from; **2er(in** *f*) [~'fraɪər(in)] *m* liberator; **2ung** *f* liberation, deliverance; release, exemption; **2ungsfront** *f* liberation front; **2ungskrieg** *m* war of liberation; **2ungsversuch** *m* escape attempt.
befremd|en [~'frɛmdən] (26) **1.** surprise, astonish, shock; **2.** 2 *n* (6) surprise; **~lich** [~'frɛmtliç] strange.
befreunde|n [bə'frɔYndən] (26): *sich ~* become friends; *sich ~ mit* make friends with; *fig.* reconcile o.s. to; **~t** friendly; *~ sein* be on friendly terms, be friends.
befried|en [~'fri:dən] (26) pacify; **2ung** *f* pacification.
be'friedig|en [~digən] (25) satisfy; *Erwartungen, Nachfrage*: meet; *schwer zu ~* hard to please; **~end** satisfactory; **2ung** *f* satisfaction.
befrist|en [~'fristən] limit (in time), set a time-limit on, *Am. a.* deadline; **2ung** *f* (setting a) time-limit.
be'frucht|en (26) fecundate, fertilize, fructify (*alle a. fig.*); (*schwängern*) impregnate; *e-e Blüte*: pollinate; **2ung** *f* fecundation; fertilization; impregnation; ⚕ *künstliche ~* artificial insemination.
Befug|nis [~'fu:knis] (14²) *f* authority, power, *bsd.* ⚖ competence; **~se** *pl.* powers *pl.*; **2t** authorized, empowered, *bsd.* ⚖ competent.
be'fühlen feel, touch, handle.
Be'fund *m* (3) state (*gen.* of *a th.*); *bsd.* ⚖ *u.* ⚕ finding(s *pl.*).
be'fürcht|en fear, apprehend; **2ung** *f* fear, apprehension.
befürwort|en [~'fy:rvɔrtən] (26) plead for, advocate; (*anraten*) recommend; *Antrag*: support; **2er(in** *f*) *m* advocate, supporter; **2ung** *f* recommendation; support.
begab|en [~'ga:bən] (25): *~ mit* endow with; **~t** [~pt] gifted, talented; **2ung** [~buŋ] *f* aptitude; talent(s *pl.*), endowment(s *pl.*).
begann [~'gan] *pret. v. beginnen*[1].
begatt|en [~'gatən] (26) couple *od.* copulate with; **2ung** *f* copulation.
begaunern F [~'gaʊnərn] (29) cheat, swindle, *Am. sl.* gyp.
be'geben (30) *Wechsel*: negotiate; *sich ~ nach* go to, betake o.s. to; *zu j-m*: join a p.; *sich ~* (*sich ereignen*) happen, occur; *sich e-r S. ~* give up, renounce, ⚖ waive; *sich zur Ruhe ~* go to rest; *sich auf die Flucht ~* take to flight; *sich auf die Reise ~* set out (on one's journey); *sich in Gefahr ~* expose o.s. to danger; **2heit** *f* event, occurrence.
begegn|en [~'ge:gnən] (26, sn) (*dat.*) (*treffen*) meet (*a p.*; *zufällig*: with); *dem Feind, Schwierigkeiten*: encounter; (*widerfahren*) happen (to); (*vorbeugen*) prevent; obviate; *e-m Wunsch, der Nachfrage usw.*: meet; *j-m freundlich* (*grob*) *~* treat a p. kindly (rudely); **2ung** *f* meeting; *feindlich*: encounter.
begeh|bar [~'ge:ba:r] *Weg*: passable; **~en** (30) walk (on); *besichtigend*: inspect; *Fehler, Verbrechen*: commit; *Fest*: celebrate.
Begehr [bə'ge:r] *m, n* (3) desire; **2en** (25) desire, crave for; (*fordern*) demand; ☤ (*sehr*) *begehrt* in (great) demand; **2enswert** desirable; **2lich** covetous, greedy; **~lichkeit** *f* covetousness, greed(iness).
Be'gehung *f vgl. begehen*: inspection; celebration; commission.
begeister|n [~'gaɪstərn] (29) inspire, fill with enthusiasm, enthuse, thrill; *sich ~ für* be(come) enthusiastic about; **~t** enthusiastic(ally *adv.*); **2ung** *f* enthusiasm.
Begier *f*, **~de** [bə'gi:r(də)] *f* (16, 15)

desire, appetite, craving (*nach* for); ♀**ig** [~ˈgiːriç] eager (*nach* for; to *do*), desirous (of; to *do*); (*habgierig*) covetous (of); ~ *zu erfahren* anxious to know.

be'gießen water, sprinkle; *Braten*: baste; F (*feiern*) wet, celebrate.

Beginn [bəˈgin] *m* (3) beginning; (*Ursprung*) origin; ♀**en** *v/t. u. v/i.* (30) begin, *förmlich*: commence; (*tun*) do; (*den Anfang machen*) lead off; ~**en** *n* (6) beginning; (*Unternehmen*) enterprise, undertaking.

beglaubig|en [~ˈglaubigən] (25) attest, certify, authenticate; *j-n*: accredit (*bei* to); ~**t** [~biçt] certified; ♀**ung** *f* certification, authentication; ♀**ungsschreiben** *n* credentials *pl.*

be'gleich|en balance; *Rechnung*: pay, settle; ♀**ung** *f* settlement.

Begleit|adresse [bəˈglaɪtˀadrɛsə] *f* declaration form, *Am.* pass-bill; ~**brief** *m* covering letter; ♀**en** (26) accompany (*a.* ♪); *höflich od. zum Schutz, a.* ⚔ escort; *j-n heim-, hinaus-, zur Bahn usw.* ~ see a p. home, out, off *etc.*; ~**er(in** *f*) *m* companion, attendant; ♪ accompanist; ~**-erscheinung** *f* accompaniment, concomitant; ~**-instrument** *n* accompanying instrument; ~**musik** *f* incidental music; ~**schein** ✝ *m* way-bill; (*Zollfreischein*) pass-bill, permit; ~**schiff** *n* escort vessel; ~**schreiben** *n* covering letter; ~**-umstand** *m* attendant circumstance, concomitant; ~**ung** *f* company; (*Gefolge*) attendants *pl.*; retinue; ♪ accompaniment; *bsd.* ⚔ escort.

be'glück|en make happy; bless; ~**wünschen** (27) congratulate (*zu* on); ♀**wünschung** *f* congratulation.

begnadet [~ˈgnɑːdət] inspired, highly gifted; ~ *mit* blessed with.

begnadig|en [~ˈgnɑːdigən] (25) pardon; *pol.* amnesty; ♀**ung** *f* pardon; amnesty; ♀**ungsgesuch** *n* plea for a reprieve (*od.* pardon).

begnügen [~ˈgnyːgən]: (25) *sich* ~ content o.s. (*mit* with), be satisfied (with).

begonnen [~ˈgɔnən] *p.p. v. beginnen.*

be'graben bury (*a. fig.*), inter.

Begräbnis [~ˈgrɛːpnis] *n* (4¹) burial; (*Leichenbegängnis*) funeral, *feierliches*: obsequies *pl.*

begradigen [~ˈgrɑːdigən] (*a.* ⚔ *die Front*) straighten; align.

be'greifen (*verstehen*) comprehend, understand, grasp; *in sich* ~ comprise, include; *s. begriffen.*

be'greiflich understandable, conceivable; *j-m et.* ~ *machen* make a p. understand a th.; ~**er'weise** logically, naturally.

be'grenz|en bound, form the boundary of; *fig.* limit (*auf acc.* to); ♀**theit** *f* limitation; *fig.* narrowness; ♀**ung** *f* bounds *pl.*; limitation; ⊕ stop; ♀**ungsstreifen** *mot. m* white line.

Be'griff *m* (3) idea, notion; (*Vorstellung*) conception; (*Ausdruck*) term; *sich e-n* ~ *machen von* get (*od.* form) an idea of; *das geht über meine* ~*e* that's beyond me; *du machst dir keinen* ~! you have no idea!; *im* ~ *sein zu inf.* be about (*od.* going) to *inf.*, be on the point of *ger.*; F *schwer von* ~ *s. begriffsstutzig*; ♀**en:** ~ *sein in* (*dat.*) be doing (*a th.*); *im Fortgehen* ~ leaving; *s. Bau, Entstehen*; ~**sbestimmung** *f* definition (of terms); ♀**s-stutzig** F slow in the uptake, dense; ~**svermögen** *n* comprehension; ~**sverwirrung** *f* confusion of ideas.

be'gründ|en found; establish, set up; *Behauptung usw.*: give reasons for, prove, substantiate; *Handlung*: motivate, explain; ⚖ *Rechte usw.*: create, vest; ♀**er(in** *f*) *m* founder; ♀**ung** *f* establishment; *fig.* argument(ation), reason(s *pl.*), proof(s *pl.*); substantiation; *mit der* ~, *daß* on the grounds that.

be'grüß|en greet, salute; *freudig*: welcome (*a. fig.*); ♀**ung** *f* greeting, salutation; welcome.

begünstig|en [~ˈgynstigən] (25) favo(u)r; (*fördern*) promote; (*helfen*) aid (*a.* ⚖); ♀**ung** *f* favo(u)r; promotion; aid, patronage; ⚖ acting as an accessory after the fact.

be'gut-achten (26) give an opinion on; (*prüfen*) examine; ~ *lassen* obtain expert opinion on, submit to an expert.

begütert [~ˈgyːtərt] well-to-do.

begütigen [~ˈgyːtigən] (25) soothe, appease, placate.

behaart [bəˈhɑːrt] hairy.

behäbig [~ˈhɛːbiç] sedate; (*Gestalt*) portly.

behaftet [~ˈhaftət] *mit e-r Krank-*

heit: affected with; *mit Haaren usw.*: covered with; *mit Fehlern usw.*: full of; *mit Schulden*: burdened with.

behag|en [~'ha:gən] **1.** (25) (*dat.*) please, suit; **2.** ⚬ *n* (6) ease, comfort; (*Vergnügen*) pleasure; *mit* ~ with relish; **~lich** [~'ha:kliç] comfortable; (*traulich*) cosy, snug; *sich* ~ *fühlen* feel at one's ease; **⚬lichkeit** *f* ease, comfortableness; cosiness.

be'halten retain, keep (*für sich* to o.s.); (*im Gedächtnis* ~) remember, retain; *recht* ~ be right, be confirmed.

Behält|er [bə'hɛltər] *m* (7), **~nis** *n* (4[1]) container; receptacle; (*Kiste*) case, box; (*Kasten*) bin; *für Öl usw.*: tank.

be'hand|eln treat; (*verfahren mit*) *a.* handle, deal with (*alle a. Thema usw.*); ⚕ *Patienten*: treat, attend, *Wunde*: *a.* dress; **⚬lung** *f* treatment; handling; *in* (*ärztlicher*) ~ under medical treatment.

Be'hang *m* (3[3]) (*Wand*⚬) hangings *pl.*; (*Anhängsel*) appendage.

be'hängen hang; (*drapieren*) drape.

beharr|en [~'harən] persevere (*bei* in); continue; *hartnäckig*: persist (*bei, auf dat.* in); ~ *auf e-m Grundsatz usw.*: stick to, *s-r Meinung*: *a.* stand to; **~lich** [~'harliç] persevering, persistent; **⚬lichkeit** *f* perseverance, persistence.

be'hauen hew; ⊕ dress, trim.

behaupt|en [~'hauptən] (26) assert, maintain, hold, claim, contend, say (*daß* that); *Recht usw.*: assert; *Stellung, Ruf, Meinung*: maintain; *das Feld* ~ hold the field; *sich* ~ hold one's ground (*od.* own); *Preise*: remain firm; **⚬ung** *f* assertion; statement, contention (*daß* that); maintaining.

Behausung [~'hauzuŋ] *f* lodging, quarters *pl.*, accommodation.

be'heb|en remedy, repair; **⚬ung** *f* reparation.

beheimatet [~'haɪma:tət] native (*in dat.* of); domiciled (in).

Behelf [bə'hɛlf] *m* (3) expedient, (make)shift; *s. Notbehelf*; **⚬en:** *sich* ~ make do, manage; *sich* ~ *ohne* do without; **~sheim** *n* temporary home; **~s...**, **⚬smäßig** makeshift, improvised, temporary.

behellig|en [~'hɛligən] (25) trouble, bother; importune, molest; **⚬ung** *f* trouble, bother; molestation.

behend, ~e [~'hɛnt, ~də] nimble, agile; (*gewandt*) adroit, dexterous; **⚬igkeit** [~diç-] *f* agility, nimbleness; dexterity.

beherbergen [~'hɛrbɛrgən] (25) lodge, accommodate, shelter, put up.

be'herrsch|en rule, govern (*a. fig.*); *die Lage, Leidenschaft,* ✝ *Markt usw.*: control; (*überragen, v. e-m Berg usw.*) command, dominate; *Sprache, Thema*: master, have (a good) command of; *sich* ~ control o.s.; **⚬er(in** *f*) *m* ruler; master, *f* mistress (*alle*: *gen.* over, of); **⚬ung** *f* rule, domination; command (*a. e-r Sprache*); control; *fig.* mastery; (*Selbst*⚬) self-control.

beherzigen [~'hɛrtsigən] (25) take to heart, (bear in) mind, remember; **~swert** worth remembering.

be'herzt courageous, stout-hearted; **⚬heit** *f* courage; intrepidity.

be'hexen bewitch.

behilflich [~'hilfliç]: *j-m* ~ *sein* help (*od.* assist) a p. (*bei* in); be of service to a p.

be'hinder|n hinder, hamper; *a. Sicht, Verkehr*: obstruct; **~t** handicapped; *körperlich* (*geistig*) ~ physically (mentally) handicapped; **⚬te** *m, f* handicapped person; **⚬tenwerkstatt** *f* sheltered workshop; **⚬ung** *f* hindrance; impediment; obstruction; handicap.

Behörd|e [bə'hø:rdə] *f* (15) authority (*mst pl.*); *engS.* agency, board; **⚬lich** [~'hø:rtliç] official.

Behuf [~'hu:f] *m* (3): *zu diesem* ~ for this purpose; **⚬s** (*gen.*) for the purpose of, with a view to.

be'hüt|en guard, protect, keep (*vor dat.* from); watch over, look after; *behüte!* by no means!; *Gott behüte!* God forbid!

behutsam [~'hu:tza:m] cautious, careful, wary; (*sacht*) gentle; gingerly; **⚬keit** *f* caution, care.

bei [baɪ] by; near; at; with; about; among(st); in; on; of; to; (*wohnhaft bei*) *Anschrift*: care of (*abbr.* c/o); ~ *j-m sitzen usw.* sit *etc.* by a p.; ~ *der Hand usw. nehmen* take by the hand *etc.*; *j-n* ~*m Namen nennen* call a p. by his name; ~ *Gott!* by God!; ~ *der Kirche* near the church; ~ (*trotz*) *aller Gelehrsamkeit* for all his learning; *~m Buchhändler* at the bookseller's; *~ Brauns* at the Browns; *~ Hofe* at court; *~m Essen* at dinner; *~m Spiel* at play; *~ Tagesanbruch* at dawn; *~ uns* with us; *~ offenen Fenstern* with the windows open; *ich habe kein Geld ~ mir* I have no money about me; *~ den Griechen* among (*od.* with) the Greeks; *~ guter Gesundheit* in good health; *ich lese ~ Horaz* in Horace; *man fand e-n Brief ~ ihm* a letter was found on him; *gleich ~ m-r Ankunft* on my arrival; *die Schlacht ~ Waterloo* the battle of Waterloo; *~ sich behalten* keep to o.s.; *Besuch ~* visit to; *~ e-m Glase Wein* over a glass of wine; *~ alledem* for all that; *Stunden nehmen ~* take lessons from *od.* of; *~ günstigem Wetter* weather permitting.

'**beibehalt|en** keep, retain; '**⁀ung** *f* keeping, retention, maintenance.

'**Beiblatt** *n* supplement (*gen.* to).

'**beibringen** furnish, supply, provide; *Zeugen, Beweis*: produce; *j-m eine Niederlage, Wunde ~* inflict on a p.; *j-m et. ~ lehrend*: impart a th. to a p., teach a p. a th.; *erklärend*: explain a th. to a p.; *nachdrücklich*: bring a th. home to a p.; *schonend*: break a th. (gently) to a p.; *j-m ~, daß* make a p. understand that.

Beicht|e ['baɪçtə] *f* (15) confession; *j-m die ~ abnehmen* confess a p.; '**⁀en** (26) *v/t. u. v/i.* confess; '**~geheimnis** *n* confessional secret; '**~kind** *n* penitent; '**~stuhl** *m* confessional; '**~vater** *m* father confessor.

beide ['baɪdə] (18) the two; *betont*: both; (*jeder von zweien*) either (*sg.*); *wir ~* both of us, we two; *alle ~* both of them; *in ~n Fällen* in either case.

beider|lei ['~dərlaɪ] (of) both kinds, (of) either sort; '**~seitig** *adj.* on both sides; (*gegenseitig*) mutual; *adv.* (= '**~seits**) on both sides; mutually.

'**beidrehen** ⚓ heave to.

bei-ei'nander together.

'**Beifahrer** *m* front passenger; *im Lkw, a. beim Rennen*: co-driver; '**~sitz** *m* front-passenger seat.

'**Beifall** *m* (3, *o. pl.*) approval; *durch Händeklatschen*: applause; *durch Zuruf*: acclaim, cheers *pl.*; *~ ernten od. finden* meet with approval, *beim Publikum*: earn applause; *~ klatschen od. spenden* applaud (*j-m* a p.); *stürmischen ~ hervorrufen thea.* bring down the house.

'**beifällig** approving.

'**Beifalls|ruf** *m* acclaim; *pl.* cheers; '**~sturm** *m* thundering applause.

'**Beifilm** *m* supporting film.

'**beifüg|en** add; *e-m Brief*: enclose; '**⁀ung** *f* addition; *gr.* attributive.

'**Beigabe** *f* addition; extra.

'**beigeben** add, join (*dat.* to); *klein ~* knuckle under, eat humble pie.

Beigeordnete ['~gəʔɔrdnətə] *m, f* assistant, deputy.

'**Beigeschmack** *m* (*a. fig.*) smack.

'**beigesellen** join (*dat.* to); *sich j-m ~* join a p.

'**Beihilfe** *f* aid, assistance; (*Geld⁀*) allowance, grant; subsidy; ⚖ aiding and abetting.

'**beikommen** (sn) (*dat.*) get at.

Beil [baɪl] *n* (3) hatchet; (*Hack⁀*) chopper; (*Fleischer⁀*) cleaver; (*Henker⁀*) ax(e).

'**Beilage** *f e-s Briefes*: enclosure (*gen.* to); *e-r Zeitung*: supplement (*gen.* to); (*Reklame⁀*) inset; *zu e-r Speise*: garnishing, vegetables *pl.*

beiläufig ['~lɔʏfiç] incidental; *Bemerkung*: casual; (*übrigens*) by the way.

'**beileg|en** adjoin, add (*dat.* to); *e-m Brief*: enclose (with); (*zuschreiben*) attribute (to); *Titel*: confer (on); *Namen*: give; *Streit*: settle; *Bedeutung, Wert*: attach *importance* (to); *sich e-n Titel usw. ~* assume; '**⁀ung** *f* addition; attribution; conferment; settlement.

beileibe [~'laɪbə]: *~ nicht!* certainly not!, by no means!; *~ kein Narr* certainly no fool.

Beileid ['baɪlaɪt] *n* (3, *o. pl.*) condolence; *weitS.* sympathy; *j-m (sein) ~ bezeigen* offer a p. one's condolences; '**~sbrief** *m* letter of condolence.

'**beiliegen** be enclosed (*e-m Brief* with); '**~d** enclosed; *~ sende ich ...* enclosed please find ...

'**beimengen** *s. beimischen.*

'**beimessen:** *j-m et. ~* attribute (*od.* ascribe) a th. to a p.; *e-r S. Glauben ~* give credence (*od.* credit) to a th.; *e-r S. Bedeutung usw. ~* attach importance *etc.* to a th.

ˈ**beimisch|en:** *e-r S.* et. ~ admix (*od.* add) a th. to, mix with a th.; ˈ**2ung** *f* admixture; *fig.* tinge.

Bein [baɪn] *n* (3) leg; (*Knochen*) bone; *den ganzen Tag auf den ~en* on the trot; *j-m auf die ~e helfen* help a p. up, *fig.* give a p. a leg up; *j-m ein ~ stellen* trip a p. (up); *fig.* et. *auf die ~e stellen* set a th. on foot; F *j-m ~e machen* make a p. find his legs; *sich auf die ~e machen* be (*od.* toddle) off; *die ~e in die Hand nehmen* take to one's heels.

beiˈnah(e) almost; nearly; et. ~ *tun* come near doing a th.; **2-unfall** *m*, **2zusammenstoß** *m* near-miss.

ˈ**Beiname** *m* surname; (*Spitzname*) nickname.

ˈ**Bein|-arbeit** *f Sport*: leg-work; *Boxen*: foot-work; ˈ**~bruch** *m* fracture of the leg; *fig. das ist kein ~!* that's no tragedy!; ˈ**~freiheit** *f* leg-room.

beinhalten [bəˈʔinhaltən] contain; (*ausdrücken*) express, say.

ˈ**bei-ordnen** adjoin; (*an die Seite stellen*) coordinate (*a. gr.*); *j-n*: assign (*dat.* to).

ˈ**Beipackzettel** *m* instructions *pl.*

beipflicht|en [ˈ~pfliçtən] (26) *j-m*: agree with; *e-r Ansicht usw.*: assent to; *e-r Maßregel*: approve of; ˈ**2ung** *f* agreement; approbation.

ˈ**Beiprogramm** *n Film*: supporting program(me).

ˈ**Beirat** *m Person*: adviser; *Körperschaft*: advisory board.

beirren [bəˈʔirən] confuse; (*erschüttern*) disconcert, fluster; (*ablenken*) divert; *er läßt sich nicht ~* F he sticks to his guns.

beisammen [baɪˈzamən] together; **2sein** *n* (6, *o. pl.*) being together; *geselliges ~* (social) gathering.

ˈ**Beischlaf** *m* sexual intercourse, coition; ˈ**2en** (*dat.*) sleep with.

ˈ**beischließen** enclose.

ˈ**Beisein** *n*: *im ~ von* (*od. gen.*) in the presence of.

beiˈseite aside (*a. thea.*), apart; ~ *bringen od. schaffen* remove; ~ *lassen* disregard; ~ *legen* put aside; *Geld*: put by; ~ *schieben fig.* brush aside; ~ *treten* step (*od.* stand) aside.

ˈ**beisetz|en** *Leiche*: inter, bury; (*hinzusetzen*) add; ˈ**2ung** *f s. Bestattung.*

ˈ**Beisitzer** *m* (7) assessor.

ˈ**Beispiel** *n* (*Muster, Vorbild*) example, model; (*Beleg*) example, instance; *zum ~* for example, for instance; *ein ~ geben, mit gutem ~ vorangehen* set an example; *sich ein ~ an j-m nehmen* take example by a p.; ˈ**2haft** exemplary; ˈ**2los** unprecedented, unparalleled, matchless; ˈ**~losigkeit** *f* singularity; matchlessness; ˈ**2sweise** for (*od.* by way of) example.

ˈ**beispringen** (sn) *s. beistehen.*

beißen [ˈbaɪsən] (30) *v/t. u. v/i.* bite (*auf, in* et. [*acc.*] on, into a th.; *nach* at); *Pfeffer usw.*: sting (*auf der Zunge* a p.'s tongue); ˈ**~d** biting, pungent (*beide a. fig.*).

ˈ**Beißerchen** F [ˈbaɪsərçən] *n/pl.* (6) toothy-pegs.

ˈ**Beiß|korb** *m* muzzle; ˈ**~ring** *m für Babys*: teething ring; ˈ**~zange** *f* (eine a pair of) nippers *od.* pincers *pl.*

Beistand [ˈbaɪʃtant] *m* (3[1]) assistance, aid; *Person*: assistant, stand-by; *s. Rechts2*; *j-m ~ leisten* lend assistance to a p.; ⚕ attend a p.; ˈ**~s-pakt** *m* mutual assistance treaty, *Am.* mutual aid pact.

ˈ**beistehen:** *j-m ~* stand by (*od.* assist, aid) a p., come to a p.'s aid.

ˈ**Beistelltisch** *m* side (*od.* occasional) table.

ˈ**Beisteuer** *f* contribution; ˈ**2n** contribute (*zu* to).

ˈ**beistimm|en** *j-m*: agree with; *e-r Meinung usw.*: assent (to), agree (to); ˈ**2ung** *f* agreement; assent.

ˈ**Beistrich** *gr. m* comma.

Beitrag [ˈ~traːk] *m* contribution; (*~santeil*) share; (*Mitglieds2*) (membership) fee (*od.* subscription), *Am.* dues *pl.*; *e-n ~ leisten* make a contribution; **2en** [ˈ~gən] *v/t. u. v/i.* contribute (*zu* to); **2spflichtig** [ˈ~spfliçtiç] liable to subscription.

ˈ**beitreib|en** collect, enforce payment of; *Abgaben*: exact; ˈ**2ung** *f* collection; exaction.

ˈ**bei|treten** (sn) *e-r Meinung usw.*: assent to; *e-m Vertrag*: accede to; *e-r Partei usw.*: join; ˈ**2tritt** *m* accession (*zu* to); joining.

ˈ**Beiwagen** *mot. m* side-car; (*Anhänger*) trailer; *s. a. Motorrad.*

ˈ**Beiwerk** *n* accessories *pl.*

ˈ**beiwohnen** (*dat.*) assist (*od.* be present) at, attend; *geschlechtlich*: cohabit with.

ˈ**Beiwort** *n* epithet; *gr.* adjective.

Beize [ˈbaɪtsə] *f* (15) *Vorgang*: corrosion; *Mittel*: corrosive; mordant; (*Holz*⩍) stain; *Gerberei*: bate; *metall.* pickle; (*Tabak*⩍) sauce; (*Falken*⩍) hawking.

beizeiten [baɪ'tsaɪtən] (*früh*) early; (*rechtzeitig*) in (good) time.

beizen ['baɪtsən] (27) (*ätzen*) corrode; *Holz*: stain; *Häute*: bate; *metall.* pickle; ⚕ cauterize.

bejah|en [bə'jɑːən] (25) answer in the affirmative (*a. v/i.*), affirm; *fig.* say yes to; **~end** affirmative; **⩍ung** *f* affirmation, affirmative answer.

bejahrt [~'jɑːrt] aged, advanced in years.

be'jammern *s. beklagen.*

be'kämpf|en fight (against), combat; *Meinung usw.*: *a.* attack, oppose, resist; **⩍ung** *f* fight(ing), combat (*gen.* against).

bekannt [~'kant] known; (*berühmt*) well-known, noted (*wegen* for); *~ mit e-r P. od. S.* acquainted with; *j-n mit j-m ~ machen* introduce a p. to a p.; *j-n mit e-r S. ~ machen* acquaint a p. with; *als ~ voraussetzen* take for granted; *er ist ~ als ...* he is known to be; **⩍e** *m, f* acquaintance, *mst* friend; **⩍gabe** *f s. Bekanntmachung*; **~geben** *s. bekanntmachen*; **~lich** as everybody knows; **~machen** make known, notify; publish, announce; *in der Zeitung*: *a.* advertise; **⩍machung** *f* publication; proclamation; announcement; notification; advertisement; *durch Anschlag*: public notice, bulletin; **⩍schaft** *f* acquaintance; **⩍schaftsanzeige** *f* lonely hearts advertisement.

be'kehr|en convert; *sich ~* become a convert (*zu* to); *fig. a.* come round to; (*sich bessern*) turn over a new leaf; **⩍er(in** *f*) *m* converter; **⩍te** *m,f* (18) convert, proselyte; **⩍ung** *f* conversion.

be'kenn|en confess, avow; (*zugestehen*) admit; *sich ~ zu* confess, *fig.* declare o.s. for; *eccl.* profess; *sich schuldig ~* plead guilty; *Farbe ~ Karten*: follow suit, *fig.* show one's hand; **⩍er** *m* confessor.

Be'kenntnis *n* (4[1]) confession; (*Glaubens*⩍) creed; **~schule** *f* denominational school.

be'klagen lament, deplore; (*bemitleiden*) pity; *sich ~* complain (*über acc.* of); **~swert** deplorable.

Beklagte [~'klɑːktə] *m, f* (18) *im Zivilprozeß*: defendant.

be'klatschen applaud, clap.

be'kleben paste; *mit Zettel*: label.

be'kleckern, be'klecksen stain, blotch; *mit Tinte*: blot; *allg.* soil, bespatter.

be'kleid|en clothe, dress; *mit Marmor usw.*: line, face; *Amt usw.*: hold, fill; *fig. ~ mit* invest with; **⩍ung** *f* clothing; clothes *pl.*; lining, facing; holding, administration; *mit e-m Amt usw.*: investiture; **⩍ungsindustrie** *f* clothing industry.

be'klemm|en *fig.* oppress; **⩍ung** *f* oppression, anguish, anxiety.

beklommen [~'klɔmən] oppressed, uneasy, anxious; **⩍heit** *f* uneasiness; *s. a. Beklemmung.*

be'klopfen tap; ⚕ percuss.

bekloppt [~'klɔpt] F, **beknackt** [~'knakt] F mad, crazy, *Person*: *a.* round the bend *pred.*

be'kommen *v/t. allg.* get; receive; be given; have; (*erlangen*) obtain; *Krankheit*: get; *Ansteckung*: catch, contract; *Kind, Junge*: have; *e-n Zug usw.*: catch; *das ist nicht zu ~* that is not to be had; *sie bekommt ein Kind* she is going to have a baby; *Zähne ~* cut one's teeth; *wieviel ~ Sie (von mir)?* how much do I owe you?; *v/i.* (sn) *j-m*: agree with; *nicht (od. schlecht) ~* disagree with; *j-m gut ~* do a p. good; *wohl bekomm's!* your health!, cheers!; *fig. es wird ihm schlecht ~* he will pay for it.

bekömmlich [~'kœmliç] wholesome; *Klima, Luft*: salubrious.

beköstig|en [~'kœstigən] (25) board; *sich selbst ~* find o.s.; **⩍ung** *f* board(ing); *Wohnung und ~* board and lodging; *ohne ~* without meals.

be'kräftig|en confirm; **⩍ung** *f* confirmation.

be'kränzen wreathe, festoon.

be'kreuz(ig)en: *sich ~* cross o.s.

be'kriegen make war (up)on.

be'kritteln carp (*od.* cavil) at.

be'kritzeln scribble over.

be'kümmern afflict, grieve, trouble; *sich ~ um* concern o.s. with, take care of; **⩍is** *f* (14[2]) grief, trouble, affliction.

bekunden [~'kundən] (26) state, ⚖ *a.* testify; (*offenbaren*) manifest, show.

be'lächeln smile at.

be'laden load; *fig.* burden.
Belag [bə'la:k] *m* (3³) covering; ⊕ coat(ing) (*Brems*∼ *usw.*) lining; (*Brot*∼) spread; (*Zungen*∼) fur; (*Zahn*∼) film; (*Spiegel*∼) foil.
Belager|er [∼'la:gərər] *m* (7) besieger; ∼**n** besiege, beleaguer (*beide a. fig.*), lay siege to; ∼**ung** *f* siege; ∼**ungszustand** *m* state of siege *od.* of martial law.
Belang [∼'laŋ] *m* (3) importance, relevancy; ∼e *pl.* interests *pl.*; *von (ohne)* ∼ *(für)* of (of no) consequence (to); ∼**en** concern; ⚖ sue, prosecute; *was mich belangt* as for me; ∼**los** irrelevant (*für* to); (*unwichtig*) unimportant; (*gering*) negligible; ∼**losigkeit** *f* irrelevance; insignificance; ∼**reich** important, relevant (*für* to); ∼**ung** *f* prosecution.
belasten [∼'lastən] load, charge (*beide a.* ⊕, ⚡); *fig.* burden; ⚕ charge (*j-n mit e-r Summe* a sum to a p.), debit; ⚖ incriminate; *Grundstück, Haus*: encumber; *erblich belastet* tainted with a hereditary disease; *politisch belastet* politically incriminated.
belästig|en [∼'lɛstigən] (25) molest; (*stören*) trouble, annoy, bother; *unabsichtlich*: inconvenience, incommode; *mit Bitten od. Fragen*: importune, pester; ∼**ung** *f* molestation; trouble; inconvenience.
Be'lastung *f* load (*a.* ⚡, ⊕); ⊕ stress; *fig.* burden, strain; (*Sorge*) worry; ⚕ debit; *e-s Grundstücks*: encumbrance; *erbliche* ∼ hereditary taint; *politische* ∼ political incrimination; ∼**s-probe** *f* load-test; *fig.* (severe) test; ∼**szeuge** *m* witness for the prosecution.
belaubt [∼'laupt] in leaf, covered in leaves.
be'laufen: *sich* ∼ *auf* (*acc.*) amount to, run up to, total.
be'lauschen overhear, listen to.
be'leb|en enliven, animate; *a. Getränk usw.*: stimulate; ∼**t** [∼pt] animated, lively; *Straße usw.*: crowded, busy; ∼**t-heit** *f* animation; liveliness (*a. e-r Straße*); ∼**ung** *f* animation, stimulation; *s. Wieder*∼.
be'lecken lick.
Beleg [bə'le:k] *m* (3) proof; (∼*schein, Unterlage*) voucher; (*Quittung*) receipt; (*Beispiel*) example; ∼**en** [∼gən] overlay, cover; *Platz*: engage, occupy, (*vorherbestellen*) reserve, book; *Sport*: be placed (*first, etc.*); *Stute usw.*: cover; (*beweisen*) prove, verify, substantiate; *Vorlesung*: enter one's name for; ∼ *mit e-m Teppich, Stroh usw.*: lay with; *durch Beispiele* ∼ exemplify; *mit Strafe* ∼ inflict punishment on; *einen Ort mit Truppen* ∼ quarter (*od.* billet) troops in a place; ∼**-exemplar** *n* voucher copy; ∼**schaft** *f* personnel, staff; workers *pl.*; ∼**stelle** *f* reference, quotation; ∼**t** *Platz*: engaged, reserved; *Stimme*: husky; *Zunge*: furred; *teleph.* engaged, *Am.* busy; ∼*es Brot* sandwich.
be'lehr|en inform; instruct; *sich* ∼ *lassen* take advice; *eines Bessern* ∼ set right; ∼**end** instructive; ∼**ung** *f* instruction; (*Rat*) advice.
beleibt [bə'laıpt] corpulent, stout; ∼**heit** *f* corpulence.
beleidig|en [∼'laıdigən] (25) offend (*a. fig.*); *gröblich*: insult; *ich wollte Sie nicht* ∼ no offence (*Am.* offense) (meant); ∼**end** insulting; ∼**ung** *f* offen|ce, *Am.* -se; insult; affront; ⚖ defamation.
be'leihen (grant a) loan on.
be'lesen well-read; ∼**heit** *f* extensive (*od.* wide) reading.
be'leucht|en light (up); *festlich*: illuminate; *fig.* elucidate, illustrate; *näher* ∼ examine more closely; ∼**er** *m thea. usw.*: lighter.
Be'leuchtung *f* lighting; illumination; *fig.* elucidation, illustration; *konkret*: lights *pl.*; ∼**skörper** *m* lighting fixture, lamp.
Belg|ier ['bɛlgjər] *m*, '∼**ierin** *f*, '∼**isch** Belgian.
belicht|en [bə'liçtən] *phot.* expose; ∼**ung** *f* exposure; ∼**ungsdauer** *f*, ∼**ungszeit** *f* time of exposure; ∼**ungsmesser** *m* exposure meter; ∼**ungs-tabelle** *f* exposure table.
be'lieb|en 1. *v/t.* deign, choose; *v/i.* please; *wie es Ihnen beliebt* as you please; **2.** ∼ *n* (6) will, pleasure; *nach (Ihrem)* ∼ at pleasure, at will, as you like; *es steht in Ihrem* ∼ it rests with you; ∼**ig:** *ein* ∼*er usw.* any; *jedes* ∼*e Land* any given country; *adv.* at pleasure; ∼ *viele* as many as you *etc.* like; ∼**t** [∼pt] liked, favo(u)rite; (*allgemein* ∼) popular

(*bei* with); *Ware*: sought-after; *Mode*: ~ *sein* be in vogue; *sich bei j-m* ~ *machen* ingratiate o.s. with a p.; ≗**t-heit** *f* popularity.
be'liefer|n, ≗**ung** *f* supply.
bellen ['bɛlən] (25) bark (*a. fig.*).
Belletrist [bɛle'trist] *m* (12) literary man, belletrist; **~ik** *f* (16) belles-lettres *pl.*; fiction; ≗**isch** belletristic; ~*e Zeitschrift f* literary magazine.
be'lob|en praise, commend; ≗**(ig)ung** *f* praise, commendation.
be'lohn|en, ≗**ung** *f* reward.
be'lügen: *j-n* ~ tell a p. a lie.
belustig|en [~'lustigən] (25) amuse, divert, entertain; *sich* ~ amuse o.s., make merry; ≗**ung** *f* amusement, diversion, entertainment.
bemächtigen [~'mɛçtigən] (25): *sich e-r P. od. S.* ~ seize.
be'mäkeln cavil (*od.* carp) at.
be'malen paint (over).
bemängeln [~'mɛŋəln] (29) find fault with, criticize.
bemann|en [~'manən] (25) man; **~t:** ~*er Raumflug* manned space flight; ≗**ung** *f* manning; (*Mannschaft*) crew.
bemäntel|n [~'mɛntəln] (29) (*verdecken*) cloak; (*beschönigen*) palliate; ≗**ung** *f* cloaking, palliation.
bemerk|bar [~'mɛrkba:r] perceptible, noticeable; *sich* ~ *machen P.*: attract attention, *S.*: make itself felt; **~en** observe, notice, feel, perceive; (*äußern*) remark, observe; **~enswert** remarkable; ≗**ung** *f* remark, observation; *schriftliche*: note.
be'messen measure; (*verhältnismäßig zuteilen*) proportion (*nach* to); *zeitlich*: time; ⊕ dimension; *Leistung*: rate; *meine Zeit ist knapp* ~ I am short of time.
bemitleiden [~'mitlaɪdən] (25) pity, commiserate; **~swert** pitiable.
bemittelt [~'mitəlt] well-off, well-to-do; *pred.* well off.
be'mogeln F cheat, trick.
bemüh|en [~'my:ən] trouble (*j-n um et.* a p. for a th.); *sich* ~ take pains, endeavo(u)r, exert o.s.; *sich für j-n* ~ exert o.s. on behalf of; *sich um et.* ~ exert o.s. for, strive for; *sich um e-n Verletzten usw.* ~ attend to; *sich um j-s Gunst od. um j-n* ~ woo a p.; *sich um e-e Stellung* ~ apply for, seek; *sich zu j-m* ~ betake o.s. to a p.; *bemüht sein zu inf.* be anxious to *inf.*, be endeavo(u)red to *inf.*; ~ *Sie sich nicht!* don't trouble *od.* bother!; ≗**ung** *f* trouble, endeavo(u)r, pains *pl.*; (*Anstrengung*) effort (*um et.* for, toward).
bemüßigt [~'my:siçt]: *sich* ~ *fühlen zu inf.* feel bound to.
bemuttern [~'mutərn] (29) mother.
be'nachbart neighbo(u)ring.
benachrichtig|en [~'na:xriçtigən] (25) inform (*von* of; *daß* that), send *a p.* word (that); *formell*: notify (of; that); ⚕ advise (of); ≗**ung** *f* information; notification; ⚕ advice.
benachteilig|en [~'na:xtaɪligən] (25) place *a p.* at a disadvantage, handicap; discriminate against; (*schädigen*) injure; ≗**ung** *f* disadvantage (*gen.* to); discrimination (against); injury (to).
be'nagen gnaw (at).
benebel|n [~'ne:bəln] (29) (be)fog (*a. fig.*); **~t** *fig. co.* fuddled.
Benediktiner [benedik'ti:nər] *m* Benedictine (*a. Likör*).
Benefiz [bene'fi:ts] *n* (3[3]) benefit; **~spiel** *n Sport*: charity game, benefit (match); **~vorstellung** *f* benefit (-night).
be'nehmen: 1. take away (*j-m den Atem usw.* a p.'s breath *etc.*); *j-m die Hoffnung usw.* ~ deprive a p. of; *sich* ~ behave (o.s.); **2.** ≗ *n* (6) behavio(u)r, conduct; manners *pl.*; *im* ~ *mit* in agreement with; *sich ins* ~ *setzen mit* contact *a p.*, confer (*od.* consult) with (*über acc.* about).
be'neiden envy (*j-n um et.* a p. a th.); **~swert** enviable.
be'nenn|en *j-n, et.*: name; *et.*: *a.* designate, term; *e-n Termin*: fix; *benannt* ⅍ concrete; ≗**ung** *f* naming, name; denomination; (*Fachsprache*) nomenclature.
be'netzen wet, moisten.
Bengel ['bɛŋəl] *m* (7) lout; (*Schelm*) rascal; *kleiner*: urchin; *dummer* ~ silly fool, booby.
benommen [bə'nɔmən] benumbed; (*schwindlig*) dizzy; ≗**heit** *f* numbness; dizziness.
be'nötigen want, need, require.
benutz|en [~'nutsən] use, make use of, utilize; (*sich zunutze machen*) *a.* profit by; *die Gelegenheit* ~ seize the opportunity; ≗**er** *m* user; **~er-**

freundlich user-friendly; ²**ung** *f* use; utilization.

Benzin [bɛnˈtsiːn] *n* (3¹) benzine; *mot.* petrol, *Am.* gas(oline); ~**gutschein** *m* petrol coupon; ~**kanister** *m* (7) petrol (*Am.* gas) container; ~**leitung** *f* fuel pipe; ~**motor** *m* petrol (*Am.* gasoline) engine; ~-**pumpe** *f* fuel pump; *an Tankstelle*: petrol pump; ~**tank** *m* fuel tank; ~-**uhr** *f* fuel gauge; ~**verbrauch** *m* petrol (*Am.* gasoline) consumption.

Benzol [bɛnˈtsoːl] *n* benzene, benzol(e).

beobacht|en [bəˈʔoːbaxtən] (26) observe (*a. fig. Stillschweigen, Vorschrift usw.*); *genau*: watch; ²**er(in** *f*) *m* observer; ✈ navigator; ⚔ *a.* spotter; ²**ung** *f* observation; *fig.* observance (*gen.* of), compliance (with); ²**ungsgabe** *f* (power of) observation; ²**ungsposten** *m* ⚔ observation post; ²**ungsstation** *f* *ast.* observatory; ⚕ observation ward.

beordern [~ˈʔɔrdərn] (29) order.

beˈpacken load, pack.

beˈpflanzen plant.

bequem [bəˈkveːm] convenient; (*behaglich*) comfortable; (*leicht*) easy; *Schuh usw.*: easy; *P.*: easy-going, *b.s.* indolent; *es sich ~ machen* relax, make o.s. at home; ~**en** (25): *sich ~ zu et.* comply with, submit to; *b.s.* condescend to; ²**lichkeit** *f* convenience; comfort, ease; *b.s.* indolence.

berappen F [~ˈrapən] (25) pay up, [fork out.]

beˈrat|en *j-n*: advise, counsel; *et.*: deliberate on; (*sich*) ~, **beˈratschlagen** (25) deliberate (*über acc.* on, about); (*mit j-m*) consult, confer (with); *gut* (*schlecht*) ~ well- (ill-) -advised; ~**end** advisory, consultative; ²**er** *m* adviser; consultant; ²**ung** *f* advice, counsel (*j-s* to a p.); consultation (*a.* ⚕, ⚚); deliberation; (*Konferenz*) conference; ²**ungsfirma** *f* consultancy firm; ²**ungsstelle** *f* advisory board; information cent|re, *Am.* -er; *soziale*: welfare cent|re, *Am.* -er.

beˈraub|en rob, *fig. a.* deprive (*gen.* of); ²**ung** *f* robbing, deprivation.

beˈrauschen intoxicate; *sich ~* get drunk; *fig.* be (*od.* get) intoxicated (*an dat.* with); ~**d** intoxicating (*a. fig.*).

beˈrechn|en calculate, compute; (*schätzen*) estimate (*auf acc.* at); ⚚ charge; *darauf berechnet sein, zu inf.* be calculated to *inf.*; ~**end** calculating; ²**ung** *f* calculation.

berechtig|en [~ˈrɛçtigən] (25) *v/t. j-n*: entitle (*zu* to *a th.*; to *inf.*); (*ermächtigen*) authorize (to *inf.*); (*befähigen*) qualify (to); *v/i. zu et.* ~ justify; *zu Hoffnungen ~* bid fair, promise well; ~**t** entitled, *etc.*, *s. berechtigen*; *attr. Anspruch, Hoffnung usw.*: legitimate; ²**ung** *f* right, title (*zu* to); authorization; justification; ²**ungsschein** *m* permit; ⚚ *für Dividende, Zinsen*: warrant.

beˈred|en (*überreden*) persuade; (*über et. reden*) talk *a th.* over; *sich ~ mit* confer with; ²**samkeit** [~ˈreːt-] *f* eloquence; ~**t** eloquent.

Beˈreich *m, n* (3) reach, area; *fig. a.* compass, scope, (*a.* ⚔) range; (*Gebiet*) field, sphere, domain; ²**ern** (29) enrich; ~**erung** *f* enrichment.

bereif|en[1] [~ˈraɪfən] cover with hoarfrost; ~**en**[2] *Faß*: hoop; *Rad*: tyre, *Am.* tire; ²**ung** *f mot.* tyres, *mst* tires *pl.*

beˈreinig|en settle, straighten out; ²**ung** *f* settlement.

beˈreisen travel, tour; ⚚ *a.* work.

bereit [bəˈraɪt] ready, prepared; *sich ~ erklären od. finden zu* agree to; *sich ~ machen zu* get ready (*od.* prepare o.s.) for; ~**en** (26) prepare, make ready; *Freude, Verdruß usw.*: give; *Niederlage*: inflict (*dat.* upon); ~**halten** keep ready; *fig. für j-n* have in store for; ~**s** already; (*bei Fragen und Verneinungen*) yet; ²**schaft** *f* (16) readiness; (*Polizeimannschaft*) squad; ²**schafts-arzt** *m* duty doctor; ²**schaftsdienst** *m* stand-by service; ²**schafts-polizei** *f* riot police; ~**stehen** be ready; ~**stellen** make available, provide; ²**ung** *f* preparation; ~**willig** ready, willing; ²**willigkeit** *f* readiness, willingness.

beˈreuen repent; (*bedauern*) regret.

Berg [bɛrk] *m* (3) mountain, (*Hügel*) hill; *fig.* ~*e von ...* heaps of ...; ~*e versetzen* move mountains; *hinterm ~ halten mit* hold back, keep *a th.* dark; *die Haare standen mir zu ~e* my hair stood on end; *über alle ~e sein* be off and away; *wir sind noch nicht über den ~* we are not yet out of the wood; ²ˈ-**ab**

downhill (*a. fig.*); ˈ~-**akademie** *f* mining college; ˈ~-**amt** *n* mining office; 2ˈ-**an**, 2ˈ-**auf** uphill (*a. fig.*); ˈ~-**arbeiter** *m s.* ~*mann*; ˈ~**bahn** 🚂 *f* mountain-railway; ˈ~**bau** *m* mining; ˈ~**besteigung** *f* climb; ˈ~-**bewohner**(**in** *f*) *m* highlander.

bergen [ˈbɛrgən] (30) save; ⚓ salv(ag)e; *mot.* recover; (*enthalten*) contain; *fig.* harbo(u)r; (*verbergen*) conceal; *s. geborgen.*

Berg|führer [ˈbɛrk-] *m* mountain guide; 2**ig** [ˈ~giç] mountainous, (*hügelig*) hilly; ˈ~-**ingenieur** *m* mining engineer; ˈ~**kette** *f* mountain range; ˈ~**knappe** *m* miner; ˈ~-**krankheit** *f* mountain sickness; ˈ~**kristall** *m* rock crystal; ˈ~**land** *n* mountainous (*od.* hilly) country; ˈ~**mann** *m* (*pl.* Bergleute) miner; *im Kohlenbergwerk*: pitman, collier; ˈ~**predigt** *f* Sermon on the Mount; ˈ~**recht** *n* mining laws *pl.*; ˈ~**rennen** *n Sport*: mountain race; ˈ~-**rücken** *m* ridge; ˈ~**rutsch** *m* landslip, *Am. od. pol.* landslide; ˈ~**salz** *n* rock salt; ˈ~**schuh** *m* climbing boot; ˈ~**spitze** *f* mountain peak; ˈ~**steigen** *n* mountaineering; ˈ~**steiger**(**in** *f*) *m* mountaineer; ˈ~**stock** *m* alpenstock; ˈ~**sturz** *m s.* Bergrutsch; ˈ**Berg-und-ˈTal-Bahn** *f* switchback (railway), *Am.* roller-coaster; ~**ung** [ˈ~guŋ] *f* saving, ⚓ salvage; *mot.* recovery; *von Menschen*: rescue; ˈ~**ungs-arbeiten** *f/pl.* ⚓ salvage operations; *für Menschen*: rescue work; ˈ~**ungsfahrzeug** *n mot.* recovery vehicle, *Am.* wrecker truck; ⚓ salvage vessel; ✈ crash tender; ˈ~**ungsmannschaft** *f* salvage crew; *für Menschen*: rescue party; ˈ~**werk** *n* mine; (*Kohlengrube*) pit; ˈ~**werksgesellschaft** *f* mining company; ˈ~**wesen** *n* mining.

Bericht [bəˈriçt] *m* (3) report, account; *statistische* ~*e pl.* official returns; ~ *erstatten s. berichten*; 2**en** report (*über acc.* on; *j-m* to a p.); *in der Presse*: *Am. a.* cover (*über et.* a th.); (*erzählen*) relate; *j-m et.* ~ (*melden*) inform a p. of a th.; ~-**erstatter** *m* (7) reporter; *auswärtiger*: correspondent; *Radio*: commentator; *Referent*: reporter, *Am.* referee; ~-**erstattung** *f* reporting, *Am. a.* coverage; (*Bericht*) report.

beˈrichtig|en [~igən] (25) *et.*: rectify; *et.*, *j-n*: correct, set right; *Rechnung usw.*: settle; ⊕ adjust; *Schuld*: settle; 2**ung** *f* rectification; correction; settlement; adjustment.

Beˈrichtsjahr *n* year under review.

beˈriechen smell at.

beˈriesel|n *Land*: irrigate; (*besprengen*) sprinkle; 2**ung** *f* irrigation; sprinkling.

beritten [~ˈritən] mounted.

Berliner [bɛrˈliːnər] **1.** *m* (7), ~**in** *f* Berlinian, Berliner; **2.** *adj.* Berlin.

Bernstein [ˈbɛrnʃtaɪn] *m* amber.

bersten [ˈbɛrstən] (30, sn) burst (*fig. vor dat.* with).

berüchtigt [bəˈryçtiçt] notorious (*wegen* for), ill-famed.

beˈrücken captivate; ~**d** captivating; *Schönheit*: fascinating.

beˈrücksichtig|en [~ziçtigən] (25) *et.*: take into consideration (*od.* account), *a. j-n*: consider; (*an-, abrechnen*) allow for; 2**ung** *f* consideration (*gen.* of), regard (to); *unter* ~ (*gen.*) in consideration of.

Beruf [bəˈruːf] *m* (3) calling; (*Tätigkeit*) occupation, job; (*Geschäft*) business; (*Gewerbe*) trade; (*Amt*) office; (*höherer* ~) profession; (*innerer* ~) vocation, mission; *von* ~ by occupation; by profession; by trade; *freier* ~ liberal profession; 2**en**[1] *v/t.* call; *Versammlung*: convene; *Parlament usw.*: convoke; *j-n zu e-m Amt*: appoint (to); *sich* ~ *auf* (*acc.*) appeal to, *entschuldigend*: plead, (*sich beziehen auf*) refer to; 2**en**[2] *adj.* competent (*zu* for *a th.*; to *inf.*); *sich* ~ *fühlen zu inf.* feel called upon to *inf.*; 2**lich** *s. Berufs...*

Beˈrufs... vocational, occupational, professional; ~-**ausbildung** *f* vocational training; ~**be-amtentum** *n* officialdom; ~**berater**(**in** *f*) *m* careers adviser; ~**beratung** *f* vocational guidance; ~**kleidung** *f* work (-ing) clothes *pl.*; ~**krankheit** *f* occupational disease; ~-**offizier** *m* regular officer; ~**risiko** *n* occupational hazard; ~**schule** *f* vocational school; ~**spieler** *m Sport*: professional; ~-**sport** *m* professional sport(s *pl.*); 2**tätig** working; (gainfully) employed; practising a profession; ~-**verbot** *n* professional ban; ~**verbrecher** *m* professional criminal.

Beˈrufung *f* (16) *s. berufen*: call; convocation; appointment (*zu* to); appeal (*auf acc.*, ⚖ *an acc.* to, *gegen* from); reference (*auf acc.* to); *s. einlegen*; **~sgericht** *n*, **~s-instanz** *f* court of appeal; **~sklage** *f* appeal; **~skläger(in** *f*) *m* appellant; **~s-recht** *n* right of appeal.

beˈruhen: ~ *auf* (*dat.*) rest (*od.* be based *od.* depend) on; et. *auf sich ~ lassen* let a th. rest (*od.* pass).

beruhig|en [~ˈruːigən] (25) quiet, calm, soothe; *Ängstliche*: ease, set at rest; *Erregte*: appease; *P. od. S.*: *sich ~* calm down; **2ung** *f* quieting, calming; appeasement; (*Trost*) consolation; **2ungsmittel** *n*, **2ungs-pille** ⚕ *f* sedative; *fig.* placebo.

berühmt [~ˈryːmt] famous (*wegen* for), celebrated; renowned; **2heit** *f* renown; *Person*: celebrity, star.

beˈrühr|en touch; *fig.* (*erwähnen*) touch (up)on, allude to; (*wirken auf*) affect; *j-s Interessen usw.*: concern; *Hafen*, *Haltestelle*: touch at; *sich* (*od. ea.*) ~ touch, meet; *j-n (un)angenehm ~* (dis)please a p.; *es berührt seltsam, daß* it is strange that; **2ung** *f* touching; touch, contact; *mit j-m in ~ bleiben* keep in touch with; *in ~ kommen mit* come in(to) contact (*od.* touch) with; **2ungsfläche** *f* surface of contact; **2ungslinie** ⩘ *f* tangent; **2ungs-punkt** *m* point of contact.

beˈsä|en sow; **~t** *fig.* studded, dotted; *mit Sternen ~* star-spangled.

beˈsag|en say; (*bedeuten*) mean, signify, imply; *das will wenig ~* it little matters; **~t** [~kt] (afore-)said.

besaiten [~ˈzaɪtən] string; *zart besaitet fig.* very sensitive.

Besan ⚓ [bəˈzɑːn] *m* (3^1) miz(z)en.

besänftig|en [bəˈzɛnftigən] (25) soothe; assuage; appease; *sich ~* calm down; **2ung** *f* soothing; appeasement.

Beˈsatz *m* border; (*Garnierung*) trimming; (*Borte*) braid.

Beˈsatzung *f* garrison; ⚓, ✈ crew; (*Besetzung*) occupation; **~smacht** *f* occupying power; **~sstreitkräfte** *f/pl.* occupation forces; **~szone** *f* occupation zone.

beˈsaufen: F *sich ~* get drunk.

Beˈsäufnis *n* (4^1) F booze-up.

beˈschädig|en *S.*: damage, injure; *P.*: injure, hurt; **2ung** *f* damage, injury (*gen.* to); ⚓ average.

beˈschaff|en 1. *v/t.* procure, make available; **2.** *adj.* constituted; *gut (schlecht) ~* well- (ill-)conditioned; *die Sache ist so ~* the matter stands thus; **2enheit** *f* condition; (*Eigenschaft*) quality; (*Natur*) nature; **2ung** *f* procurement.

beschäftig|en [~ˈʃɛftigən] (25) occupy, engage; *Angestellte*: employ; *geistig*: preoccupy; *sich ~ mit* busy (*od.* occupy) o.s. with, be engaged in, be busy *ger.*; **~t** [~tiçt]: *~ bei* in the employ of, working for; *~ mit* engaged in, occupied with; **2ung** [~guŋ] *f* occupation; employment, job; (*Geschäft*) business; **~ungslos** unemployed, out of work; **2ungs-therapeut** ⚕ *m* occupational therapist; **2ungs-therapie** ⚕ *f* occupational therapy.

beˈschäl|en *Stute*: cover; **2er** *m* (7) stallion, stud(-horse).

beˈschäm|en make ashamed, (put to) shame; (*verlegen machen*) embarrass; **~d** humiliating; **~t** ashamed (*über acc.* of); **2ung** *f* confusion; *Zustand*: shame.

beschatten [~ˈʃatən] (26) shade; (*heimlich verfolgen*) shadow.

beˈschau|en look at; view; *prüfend*: examine; *Fleisch usw.*: inspect; *fig.* contemplate; **~lich** contemplative; (*friedlich*) tranquil; (*behaglich*) leisurely; **2lichkeit** *f* contemplativeness; tranquillity.

Bescheid [bəˈʃaɪt] *m* (3) answer; ⚖ *usw.* decision; (*Mitteilung*, *Auskunft*) information (*über acc.* about); *j-m ~ geben* send a p. word, let a p. know (about); *j-m gehörig ~ sagen* (*abkanzeln*) give a p. a piece of one's mind; *j-m trinkend ~ tun* pledge a p.; *~ wissen* (be in the) know; *~ wissen mit od. in* (*dat.*) *od. über* (*acc.*) know all about, be aware of; *ich weiß hier ~* I know this place.

beˈscheiden 1. *v/t.* (*zuteilen*) allot; *j-n wohin*: direct, order; (*benachrichtigen*) inform; *j-n abschlägig ~* give a p. a refusal; *sich ~* be content; *sich mit et. ~* resign o.s. to; *es war mir nicht beschieden* it was not granted to me; **2.** *adj.* modest; **2-heit** *f* modesty.

beˈscheinen shine (up)on.

bescheinig|en [~'ʃaɪnigən] (25) certify (*j-m* to a p.), (*a. fig.*) attest; *den Empfang* (*gen.*) ~ acknowledge receipt (of *a letter, etc.*); (give a) receipt (for *money paid*); *es wird hiermit bescheinigt, daß* ... this is to certify that ...; **2ung** *f* certificate; receipt.
be'scheißen P cheat.
be'schenken *j-n*: make a p. a present; *j-n mit et.*: present a p. with a th.
be'scher|en: *j-m et.* ~ give a p. a th., bestow a th. (up)on a p.; **2ung** *f* distribution of presents; *fig. eine schöne* ~! a nice mess!; *da haben wir die* ~! there we are! *die ganze* ~ the whole bag of tricks.
bescheuert [~'ʃɔʏərt] F *s. bekloppt.*
be'schick|en *Parlament usw.*: send deputies to; *Ausstellung, Messe*: exhibit at; ⊕ charge; **2ung** *f* (*gen.*) sending of delegates (to); representation (at); ⊕ charging (of).
be'schieß|en fire on; *mit Kanonen*: bombard (*a. phys.*), shell; **2ung** *f* fire; bombardment, shelling.
be'schimpf|en insult, call a p. names; **2ung** *f* insult (*gen.* to).
be'schirm|en (25) protect, shield, shelter (*vor dat.* from).
be'schlafen *et.*: sleep on.
Be'schlag *m* metal (*od.* iron) fittings *pl.*; mounting; (*Huf*2) shoeing, *konkret*: shoes *pl.*; ⚗ efflorescence; ⚖ *s.* ~*nahme*; *in* ~ *nehmen, mit* ~ *belegen* seize, *fig. a.* monopolize; ~ *legen auf* distrain (up)on; ⚓ embargo.
be'schlagen 1. *v/t.* mount; *Pferd*: shoe; *Stock*: tip; *mit Ziernägeln*: stud; *v/i.* (sn) *Eßware*: grow mo(u)ldy; *Fenster*: get covered with damp; **2.** *adj. Glas*: clouded, steamed; *in e-r S. gut* ~ *sein* be well versed (*od.* up) in; **2heit** *f* experience, (profound) knowledge (*in dat.* of).
Be'schlagnahm|e [~kna:mə] *f* (15, *o. pl.*) seizure, confiscation; sequestration; ⚔ requisition; ⚓ embargo; **2en** seize, confiscate; sequestrate; ⚔ requisition.
be'schleichen sneak up to; *Wild, Feind*: stalk; *fig.* steal (*od.* creep) (up)on.
beschleunig|en [bə'ʃlɔʏnigən] (25) accelerate; hasten, speed up; **2er** *mot. phot. m* accelerator (*a. Kernphysik*); **2ung** *f* acceleration (*a. phys.*); speeding up; **2ungsspur** *mot. f* acceleration lane; **2ungsvermögen** *n* acceleration.
be'schließen (*beenden*) close, conclude; (*sich entscheiden*) determine, decide (*beide a.* ⚖), resolve.
Be'schluß *m* (4[2]) (*Entscheidung*) decision, resolution (*a. parl.*), *Am.* resolve; ⚖ (court) order, decree; **2fähig:** *e-e* ~*e Anzahl od. Versammlung* a quorum; *das Haus ist* (*nicht*) ~ there is a (no) quorum; **~fähigkeit** *f* quorum, competence; **~fassung** *f* (passing of a) resolution.
be'schmieren (be)smear; *s. bestreichen.*
be'schmutzen soil (*a. fig.*), dirty.
be'schneid|en clip; cut; *Baum*: lop; *Fingernägel*: pare; ⚕ circumcise; *fig.* cut (down), curtail; **2ung** *f* clipping; circumcision; cut.
be'schneit snowy.
be'schnüffeln, be'schnuppern sniff at.
beschönig|en [~'ʃø:nigən] (25) palliate, extenuate, gloss over; **2ung** *f* palliation, extenuation.
beschränk|en [~'ʃrɛŋkən] (25) confine, limit, restrict, *Am. a.* curb; *sich* ~ *auf* (*acc.*) restrict o.s. to; **~t** [~kt] limited, restricted; *geistig*: narrow(-minded), (*dumm*) obtuse; **2t-heit** *f* narrowness; dul(l)ness; **2ung** *f* limitation, restriction.
be'schreib|en *Blatt*: write (up)on; (*schildern*) describe (*a. Kreis usw.*); **~end** descriptive; **2ung** *f* description; ⊕ specification; *jeder* ~ *spotten* beggar all description.
be'schreiten walk on; *fig. e-n Weg* ~ follow a course; *neue Wege* ~ apply new methods; *s. Rechtsweg.*
beschrift|en [~'ʃriftən] (26) inscribe, letter; *Kiste usw.*: mark; **2ung** *f* lettering; (*Inschrift*) inscription; *erläuternde*: caption, legend.
beschuldig|en [~'ʃuldigən] (25) accuse (*gen.* of), charge (with); **2te** [~diçtə] *m, f* (18) accused; **2ung** [~guŋ] *f* accusation, charge.
beschummeln F [~'ʃuməln] (29) cheat, trick (*um* out of).
Be'schuß *m* (4[2]) fire; bombardment (*a. phys.*), shelling.
be'schütz|en (*vor dat.*) protect

(from), defend (against); **≈er** *m* (7) protector; **≈erin** *f* (16¹) protectress.

be'schwatzen talk *a p.* over; coax (*zu* to *inf.*; into *ger.*); ~ *zu* talk *a p.* into *ger.*

Beschwerde [bə'ʃve:rdə] *f* (15) trouble; (*Klage*) complaint; (~*grund*) grievance; ⚖ appeal (*gegen* from); (*Krankheit*) complaint, trouble; **~buch** *n* complaints book; **~führer(in** *f*) *m* complainant.

beschwer|en [~'ʃve:rən] (25) burden, charge (*a. fig.*); *lose Papiere usw.*: weight; *Magen*: lie heavy on; *sich* ~ complain (*über acc.* about, of; *bei* to); **~lich** troublesome; *j-m* ~ *fallen* give a p. trouble.

beschwichtigen [~'ʃviçtigən] (25) appease; *Gewissen*: silence.

Be'schwichtigungspolitik *f* appeasement policy.

be'schwindeln cheat, swindle (*um et.* out of).

beschwingt [~'ʃviŋt] winged; *fig.* elated, buoyant; *Melodie*: racy.

beschwipst F [~'ʃvipst] tipsy.

be'schwör|en *et.*: confirm by oath, swear (to); *Geister*: conjure, (*bannen*) conjure away; *Gefahr*: banish; *j-n*: (*anflehen*) implore; **≈ung** *f* confirmation by oath, swearing; conjuration; banishment; imploring.

beseel|en [~'ze:lən] (25) animate; **~t** animated; *fig.* soulful.

be'sehen look at; *prüfend*: inspect.

beseitig|en [bə'zaɪtigən] (25) remove; (*abschaffen*) *a.* abolish, do away with (*a. j-n*); **≈ung** *f* removal.

beseligen [~'ze:ligən] (25) make happy, fill with bliss.

Besen ['be:zən] *m* (6) broom; (*Reisig≈*) besom; *kleiner* ~ (hand-) -brush; *fig. mit eisernem* ~ with a rod of iron; *neue* ~ *kehren gut* a new broom sweeps clean; F *ich fresse e-n* ~, *wenn* ... I'll eat my hat if ...; **'~schrank** *m* broom-cupboard; **'~stiel** *m* broom-stick.

besessen [~'zɛsən] obsessed, possessed (*von* by, with); *wie* ~ like mad; **≈e** *m, f* man (woman) possessed, maniac; **≈heit** *f* obsession; (*Raserei*) frenzy.

be'setz|en *Kleid usw.*: trim; *mit Edelsteinen usw.*: set; ⚔ occupy; ⚓ man; *Amt, Stelle*: fill; (*Sitz-*) *Platz*: engage; *thea. Rolle, Stück*: cast; **~t** *Platz, Gebiet*: occupied; *Bus usw.*: full up; *dicht* ~ crowded, packed; *teleph.* engaged, *Am.* busy; *meine Zeit ist* ~ occupied; **≈tzeichen** *n* engaged (*Am.* busy) signal; **≈ung** *f* occupation; filling; *thea.* cast; (*Personal*) staff; *Sport*: team composition.

besichtig|en [~'ziçtigən] (25) view, inspect, survey; *zu* ~ *sein* be on view; **≈ung** *f* inspection (*a.* ⚔); *von Sehenswürdigkeiten*: sightseeing, visit (*gen.* to).

be'siedel|n settle, colonize; **≈ung** *f* settlement, colonization.

be'siegeln seal (*a. fig.*).

be'sieg|en defeat; **≈er(in** *f*) *m* (7) conqueror; **≈te** *m, f* loser; **≈ung** *f* defeat; conquest.

be'singen sing (of).

be'sinn|en 1. *sich* ~ (*überlegen*) reflect, consider; (*sich erinnern*) recollect, remember (*auf* et. a thing); *sich anders* (*od. e-s andern*) ~ change one's mind; *sich e-s Besseren* ~ think better of it; **2.** ≈ *n* (6) reflection; **~lich** contemplative, reflective.

Be'sinnung *f* consciousness; (*Überlegung*) reflection, consideration; *die* ~ *verlieren* lose consciousness, *fig.* lose one's head; *wieder zur* ~ *kommen* recover consciousness, *fig.* come to one's senses; *j-n zur* ~ *bringen* bring a p. to his senses; **~saufsatz** *m* contemplative essay; **≈slos** unconscious; *fig.* senseless, blind; **~slosigkeit** *f* unconsciousness; *fig.* senselessness.

Be'sitz *m* (3²) possession; *s.* ~*tum*; ~ *ergreifen von, in* ~ *nehmen* take possession of, occupy, *Person*: take hold of; *im* ~ *e-r S. sein* be in possession of a th.; *im* ~ *e-r P. sein* be in the possession of a p.; *in den* ~ *e-r S. setzen* put in possession of; **≈-anzeigend** *gr.* possessive; **≈en** possess, have; **≈end** propertied; **~er(in** *f*) *m* possessor; (*Eigentümer* [*-in*]) owner, propriet|or, *f* -ress; *e-s Wertpapiers, Passes usw.*: holder; *den* ~ *wechseln* change hands; **~ergreifung** *f*, **~nahme** *f* taking possession (*von* of), occupation; **≈erlos** abandoned; **≈los** unpropertied; **~stand** *m* ownership; ☤ assets *pl.*; **~störung** *f* trespass; **~titel** *m* possessory title; **~tum** *n* (1²), **~ung** *f*

possession; property, estate; **~-urkunde** *f* title-deed.
besoffen P [bəˈzɔfən] (roaring) drunk.
besohlen [~ˈzoːlən] (25) sole.
besold|en [~ˈzɔldən] (26) pay (a salary); **~et** salaried; **2ung** *f* (16) pay; salary.
beˈsonder particular, special; (*einmalig*) singular; (*eigenartig*) peculiar; (*gesondert*) separate; et. 2es something special; *nichts* 2es nothing out of the way; *im* ~en in particular; **2heit** *f* particularity; peculiarity; special quality (*od.* feature); **~s** especially, particularly; separately, apart.
besonnen [~ˈzɔnən] prudent; (*bedacht*) considerate; (*vernünftig*) sensible, level-headed; **2heit** *f* prudence; considerateness; (*Geistesgegenwart*) presence of mind.
beˈsorgen (*fürchten*) apprehend, fear; (*Sorge tragen für*) take care of; (*erledigen*) attend to; (*beschaffen*) get (*j-m* et. a p. a th., a th. for a p.), procure, provide (a th. for a p.); *Haushalt usw.*: manage; F es *j-m* ~ settle a p.'s hash.
Besorgnis [bəˈzɔrknis] *f* (14²) apprehension, fear, anxiety; **2-erregend** alarming.
beˈsorgt [~kt] (*fürchtend*) alarmed (*um* for); (*ängstlich bemüht*) anxious, solicitous (*um* about, for); **2heit** *f* s. *Besorgnis*; solicitude.
Beˈsorgung [~guŋ] *f* (*Erledigung*) handling, management; (*Beschaffung*) procurement; (*Einkauf*) purchase; (*Auftrag*) errand; ~*en machen* go shopping; **~sgebühr** *f* service charge.
beˈspann|en put (the) horses to; *mit Saiten*: string; *mit Stoff*: cover; **2ung** *f* stringing; covering.
beˈspeien spit on *od.* at.
beˈspiegeln: *sich* ~ look at o.s. (F admire o.s.) in the glass.
beˈspielt *Musik-*, *Videokassette*: prerecorded.
beˈspitzeln (29) spy on *a. p.*
beˈspötteln (29) ridicule.
beˈsprech|en discuss, talk *a th.* over; *Buch usw.*: review; (*vereinbaren*) arrange, agree upon; *Schallplatte usw.*: make a recording on; *sich* ~ *mit* confer with; **2er(in** *f*) *m e-s Buches usw.*: reviewer; **2ung** *f* discussion; review; conference; **2ungs-exemplar** *n e-s Buches*: review copy.
beˈsprengen sprinkle, spray.
beˈspritzen (be)spatter, splash.
beˈspucken spit at *od.* (up)on.
besser [ˈbɛsər] better; (*überlegen*) superior; *es* ~ *haben als ein anderer* be better off than; *es geht* (*wirtschaftlich*) ~ things are looking up; *es geht ihm heute* ~ he is better today; *ich täte* ~ (*daran*) *zu gehen* I had better go; *es* ~ *wissen* know better; ~ *gesagt* or rather; *um so* ~ all the better; *du könntest nichts* 2es *tun* you could not do better; *s. belehren, besinnen, Hälfte*; **ˈ~n** (29) improve; *moralisch*: reform; *sich* ~ (grow) better, improve; *moralisch*: reform, mend one's ways.
ˈBesserung *f* improvement (*a.* ⚕ *u.* †); (*Wendung*) change for the better; *moralisch*: reform; *gute* ~*!* hope you will be better soon; **ˈ~s-anstalt** *f für Jugendliche*: reformatory, *Am. mst* reform school.
ˈBesserverdienende *m/pl.* (18) better earners, higher income bracket *sg.*
ˈBesserwisser *m* know-all.
best [bɛst] best; *der erste* ~*e* the first comer; *am* ~*en* best; *aufs* ~*e*, ~*ens* in the best way; *auf dem* ~*en Wege sein zu inf.* be in a fair way to *inf.*; *zum* ~*en geben Lied*: oblige with, *Geschichte*: tell, relate, entertain with; *j-n zum* ~*en haben* make fun of a p.; *nach* ~*en Kräften* to the best of one's power; *nach meinem* ~*en Wissen* to the best of my knowledge; *sich von der* ~*en Seite zeigen* show o.s. (*od.* be) at one's best; *zu Ihrem* 2*en* in your interest; *zum* 2*en der Armen* for the benefit of the poor; *in den* ~*en Jahren* in the prime of life; *fig. das* 2*e herausholen* make the best of it; *sein* 2*es geben* do one's best; *ich täte am* ~*en zu gehen* I had best go; *empfehlen Sie mich* ~*ens!* remember me most kindly!; *ich danke* ~*ens* thank you very much!, *ablehnend*: I would rather be excused!, *contp.* thank you for nothing!
bestall|en [bəˈʃtalən] (25) appoint (*zu* to); **2ung** *f* appointment; **2ungs-urkunde** *f* certificate of appointment.
Beˈstand *m* (3³) (*Bestehen*) existence;

(*Fortdauer*) continuance, duration; (*Haltbarkeit*) stability, durability; (*Vorrat*) stock; (*Kapital*2) assets *pl.*; (*Aktien*2 *usw.*) holdings *pl.*; (*Kassen*2) cash (*od.* balance) in hand; (*Waren*2) stock on hand; (*Fahrzeug*2) rolling stock, fleet; ⚔ (*Mannschafts*2) strength; (*Rest*2) rest, remainder; *von* ~ *sein*, ~ *haben* be durable (*od.* lasting), endure, last.

be'ständig constant, steady; (*unveränderlich*) invariable; (*dauerhaft*) lasting, permanent, stable; (*andauernd*) continual; (*beharrlich*) persistent; *Wetter*: settled; *Barometerstand*: set fair; **~e** *Valuta* stable currency; **2keit** *f* constancy, steadiness; stability, permanence; continuance.

Be'stand|s-aufnahme ✝ *f* stock-taking (*a. fig.*), *Am.* inventory; **~teil** *m* component (part), constituent (part); element; *e-r Mischung*: ingredient; (*Einzelteil*) part; *s. auflösen*

be'stärken *j-n, e-e Vermutung usw.*: confirm; (*ermutigen*) encourage; (*verstärken*) strengthen.

bestätig|en [~'ʃtɛ:tigən] (25) confirm; *amtlich*: attest; (*erhärten*) corroborate; *Vertrag, Gesetz*: ratify; ⚖ *Urteil*: uphold; *Empfang*: acknowledge; *sich* (*nicht*) ~ (not) to be confirmed, prove true (false); **2ung** *f* confirmation; attestation; corroboration; ratification; acknowledg(e)ment.

bestatt|en [~'ʃtatən] (26) bury, inter; **2ung** *f* funeral; (*Beerdigung*) burial, interment; (*Feuer*2) cremation; **2ungs-institut** *n* (firm of) undertakers *pl.*, *Am.* funeral home.

be'stäub|en dust, spray; ⚘ pollinate; **2ung** *f* dusting, spraying; ⚘ pollination.

be'stechen bribe, corrupt; *fig.* be fascinating, impress; **~d** brilliant, fascinating, impressive; *Wesen*: engaging.

be'stechlich corruptible; **2keit** *f* corruptibility.

Be'stechung *f* bribery, corruption; **~s-affäre** *f* bribery scandal; **~sgeld** *n* bribe.

Besteck [bə'ʃtɛk] *n* (3) ⚕ set of instruments; (*Eß*2) knife, fork and spoon, (set of) cutlery; ⚓ reckoning.

be'stecken stick (*mit* with).

be'stehen 1. *v/t.* overcome, conquer; (*durchmachen*) undergo, endure, go through; *Kampf*: win; *Probe*: stand; *Prüfung*: pass; *e-e Prüfung nicht* ~ fail in an examination; *v/i.* be, exist; subsist; (*fort*~) last, continue; ~ *auf* (*acc.*) insist (up)on; ~ *aus* consist of, be composed of; ~ *in* (*dat.*) consist in; *nicht* ~ *Prüfling*: fail; **2.** 2 *n* existence; *e-r Prüfung*: passing; (*j-s*) ~ *auf* (*acc.*) insistence (by a p.) on; **~d** existing; (*gegenwärtig*) present.

be'stehlen rob, steal from.

be'steig|en ascend (*a. Thron*), climb (on); *Pferd, Fahrrad*: mount; *Schiff*: (go on) board *a ship*; *Wagen usw.*: enter, *bsd. Am.* board; **2ung** *f* ascent.

Be'stell|buch ✝ *n* order-book; **2en** *Ware, Speise usw.*: order; *Zeitung*: subscribe to; *Platz, Zimmer*: book; (*kommen lassen*) ask *a p.* to come; send for; (*ernennen*) appoint (*zum Statthalter usw.* [to be] governor *etc.*); *Brief, Botschaft*: deliver; *Feld*: till, cultivate; *Grüße*: give; *sein Haus* ~ put one's house in order; *es ist schlecht mit ihm* (*od. um ihn*) *bestellt* he is in a bad way; **~er** *m* orderer; *e-r Zeitung*: subscriber; **~karte** *f*, **~schein** *m*, **~zettel** *m* order form (*od.* slip); **~ung** *f* order, commission; subscription (*gen.* to); appointment; ⚒ cultivation; *e-s Briefes*: delivery; *auf* ~ *gemacht* made to order, *Am.* custom-made.

'bestenfalls at best.

be'steuer|n tax; **2ung** *f* taxation.

bestial|isch [bɛst'ja:liʃ] beastly; bestial; **2ität** [~jali'tɛ:t] *f* bestiality.

Bestie ['bɛstjə] *f* (15) beast, brute.

bestimm|en [bə'ʃtimən] (*entscheiden*) determine; decide; *Preis*: fix; *Ort, Zeit usw.*: appoint; *vom Gesetz*: lay down; *v. höherer Gewalt*: ordain; *Begriff*: define; *Daten, Werte*: determine; *j-n zu, für et.* ~ destine (*od.* intend) for; *j-n* ~ *et. zu tun* determine (*od.* induce) a p. to do a th.; ~ *über* (*acc.*) dispose of; **~t** *Zeit*: appointed; *Summe usw.*: fixed; (*entschlossen*) decided, determined; (*sicher*) certain, positive; *Antwort, Begriff, gr.*: definite; ~ *sein für od. zu* be intended for; *sich* ~ *ausdrücken* express o.s. distinctly;

(*ganz*) ~ decidedly; certainly!, *Am.* sure!; et. ~ *wissen* know a th. for certain; ~ *nach* ⚓, ✈ bound for; **ꝛt-heit** *f* exactitude; determination; certainty; *mit* ~ positively; **ꝛung** *f* determination; destination (*a. Ort*); (*Geschick*) destiny; (*Beruf*) vocation; (*Begriffs*ꝛ) definition; (*Vorschrift*) direction, instruction; ⚖ provision; *amtliche* ~*en pl.* regulations; **ꝛungsland** ✝ *n* country of destination; **ꝛungs-ort** *m* (point of) destination.

'Best|leistung *f* record (performance); **'ꝛmöglich** best possible.

be'straf|en punish; **ꝛung** *f* punishment; (*Strafe*) *a.* penalty.

be'strahl|en irradiate; ⚕ ray-treat, *mit Radium*: radio; **ꝛung** *f* irradiation; ⚕ ray-treatment.

be'streb|en 1. *sich* ~ (*od. bestrebt sein*) *zu inf.* endeavo(u)r (*od.* strive) to *inf.*, *begierig*: be anxious to *inf.*; **2.** ꝛ *n* (6) (*Neigung*) tendency; = **ꝛung** *f* effort, endeavo(u)r, attempt.

be'streichen spread; ⚔ *mit Feuer*: rake, sweep; *mit Butter* ~ butter.

be'streiken *Betrieb*: strike; *bestreikt* strikebound, struck.

be'streit|bar contestable, disputable; **~en** (*anfechten*) contest, dispute; (*leugnen*) deny; *Ausgaben*: bear, defray; *Bedürfnisse*: supply; *Unterhaltung*: do (*the talking*); **ꝛung** *f der Kosten*: defrayal.

be'streuen strew; *mit Salz usw.* ~ sprinkle with salt, *etc.*; *mit Kies* ~ gravel; *mit Zucker* ~ sugar.

be'stricken *fig.* ensnare; (*berücken*) charm, bewitch.

Bestseller ['bɛstzɛlər] *m* (7) bestseller; **'~-autor** *m* bestselling author.

be'stück|en ⚔, ⚓ arm (with guns); **ꝛung** *f* armament, guns *pl.*

be'stürm|en storm, assail; *fig. mit Bitten, Fragen usw.*: assail (with); **ꝛung** *f* storming, assault.

bestürz|t [~'ʃtyrtst] dismayed (*über acc.* at); perplexed; **ꝛung** *f* consternation, dismay.

Besuch [~'zu:x] *m* (3) visit (*gen.*; *bei, in dat.* to); *kurzer*: call (*bei* on); (*Besucher*) visitor(s *pl.*), company; *gewohnheitsmäßiger* ~ *e-s Gasthauses usw.*: frequentation; *der Schule usw.*: attendance (*gen.* at); (*Besichtigung*) visit (*gen.* to); *auf* (*od. zu*) ~ on a visit; *e-n* ~ *machen* pay a visit *od.* call; **ꝛen** visit; *P.*: go (*od.* come) to see, call on; *Ort, Gasthaus usw. gewohnheitsgemäß* ~: frequent; *Schule, Versammlung usw.*: attend; *Kino, Theater*: go to; *gut besucht* well attended; **~er**(**in** *f*) *m* visitor (*gen.* to); caller; (*Gast*) guest; (*Zuschauer*) spectator; **~szeit** *f* visiting hours *pl.*; **~szimmer** *n* visitors' room.

be'sudeln soil; *fig. a.* sully; (*bekritzeln*) scribble over.

betagt [~'tɑ:kt] *s. bejahrt.*

be'takel|n ⚓ rig; **ꝛung** *f* rigging.

be'tasten finger, feel, touch.

betätig|en [~'tɛ:tigən] (25) ⊕ manipulate; *Bremse usw.*: actuate, operate; *sich* ~ busy o.s.; *als*: act as; *bei et.*: take an active part in, participate in; **ꝛung** *f* operation, actuation; (*Tätigkeit*) activity.

betäub|en [~'tɔʏbən] (25) *durch Lärm, e-n Schlag usw. od. fig.*: stun, daze; *durch Schlafmittel usw. od. fig.*: drug; ⚕ an(a)esthetize, narcotize; *Schmerz*: deaden, dull; *fig. sich* ~ divert o.s.; **~end** stunning (*a. fig.*); *Lärm*: deafening; ⚕ narcotic; **ꝛung** *f* stunning; stupefaction; ⚕ narcotization, an(a)esthesia, (*Zustand*) narcosis; **ꝛungsmittel** *n* narcotic.

Betbruder ['be:t-] *m* devotee, bigot.

Bete ⚘ ['be:tə] *f* (15) beet(-root).

beteilig|en [bə'taɪligən] (25): *j-n* ~ give a p. a share *od.* interest (*an od. bei dat.* in); *sich* ~ *an od. bei* participate (*od.* take part) in; *beteiligt sein bei* have a share (*od.* interest) in, be interested in, (*verwickelt sein*) be involved in; **ꝛte** [~çtə] *m, f* party (*od.* person) concerned, participant; ⚖ party (*an dat.* to); **ꝛung** [~guŋ] *f* participation; ✝ *a.* (*Teilhaberschaft*) partnership; (*Anteil*) share, interest; (*Teilnehmerzahl*) attendance.

beten ['be:tən] (26) *v/i.* pray (*um* for), say one's prayers; *bei Tische*: say grace; *v/t.* say (*a prayer*).

beteuer|n [bə'tɔʏərn] (29) protest, affirm; **'ꝛung** *f* protestation; affirmation (*a.* ⚖).

betiteln [~'ti:təln] (29) *P., Buch usw.*: entitle; (*nennen*) style, call.

Beton ⊕ [be'tõ, ~'to:n] *m* (11) concrete.

beton|en [bə'to:nən] (25) stress (*a.*

fig.), accent; *fig. nachdrücklich* ~ emphasize; *fig. betont* studied, emphatic(ally); ²**ung** *f* accentuation; (*Silbenton*) accent, stress; emphasis (*alle a. fig.*).

betonieren [beto'ni:rən] concrete.

Be'ton|klotz *m* concrete block; *contp.* (*Haus*) concrete pile; **~mischmaschine** *f* cement mixer; **~wüste** *f contp.* concrete jungle.

betören [bə'tø:rən] (25) befool; (*verliebt machen*) bewitch, infatuate, charm.

Betracht [~'traxt] *m* (3, *o. pl.*): *in ~ ziehen* take into consideration, consider; (*einkalkulieren*) allow (*od.* make allowance) for; *außer ~ lassen* disregard; (*nicht*) *in ~ kommen* (not) to come into question, (not) to be concerned; ²**en** view (*a. fig.*); (*genau*) inspect; *sinnend*: contemplate; *fig. ~ als* consider; **~er(in** *f*) *m* viewer, observer; **~ung** *f* view; contemplation; consideration; **~ungsweise** *f* way of looking at things.

beträchtlich [~'trɛçtliç] considerable.

Betrag [~'tra:k] *m* (3³) amount; (*Gesamt*²) (sum) total; *im ~e von* to the amount of; ²**en** [~gən] **1.** amount to; (*insgesamt ~*) total; *sich ~* behave (o.s.); **2.** ² *n* (6) behavio(u)r, conduct.

be'trauen entrust (*mit* with).

be'trauern mourn (for), deplore.

Betreff [bə'trɛf] *m am Briefanfang*: subject, re; *in* ², ²*s* (*gen.*) with regard to, in respect of, concerning; ²**en** (*befallen*) befall; (*fig. berühren*) affect, touch; (*angehen*) concern; (*sich beziehen auf*) refer (*od.* relate) to; (*behandeln*) deal with; *was mich betrifft* as for me, as far as I am concerned; *was das betrifft* as to that; *betrifft* (*am Briefanfang*) subject, re; ²**end** concerning *a th.*; *die ~e Person* the person concerned *od.* in question; *das ~e* (*erwähnte*) *Buch* the book referred to.

be'treiben 1. *Geschäft*: carry on, run; *Studien, Gewerbe usw.*: pursue; *Eisenbahn usw.*: work, *Am.* operate; (*beschleunigen*) urge *a th.* on, push forward; **2.** ² *n*: *auf ~ von* (*od. gen.*) at the instigation of.

be'treten 1. set foot on *od.* in, step on (to); *Raum*: enter; *Schwelle*: cross; ² *des Rasens usw. verboten!* keep off the grass *etc.*!; **2.** *adj. fig.* embarrassed.

betreu|en [~'trɔʏən] (25) care for; attend (on), look after; ²**ung** *f* care (*gen.* of, for).

Betrieb [bə'tri:p] *m* (3) (*Betreiben*) management, working, running, *bsd. Am.* operation; (*Unternehmen*) enterprise, concern; (*Anlage*) plant; (*Werkstatt*) workshop; (*Fabrikanlage*) works, factory, *Am.* plant; (*Eisenbahn*², *Schiffs*² *usw.*) service; (*Geschäftigkeit*) activity; (*lebhaftes Treiben*) bustle; *öffentlicher ~* public utility; *außer ~* out of operation, (*defekt*) out of order; *in ~* working, operating, in operation; *in ~ setzen* start; *den ~ einstellen* shut down; *den ~ wiederaufnehmen* reopen.

be'triebsam active, industrious; ²**keit** *f* activity, bustle; industry.

Be'triebs|-anleitung *f* operating instructions *pl.*; **~-ausflug** *m* works outing; ²**fähig** serviceable; ²**fertig** ready for service; **~führer** *m s. Betriebsleiter*; **~geheimnis** *n* trade secret; **~-ingenieur** *m* production engineer; **~kapital** *n* working capital; **~klima** *n* working conditions *pl.*; **~kosten** *pl.* running expense(s *pl.*), *Am.* operating cost; **~leiter** *m* (works) manager; **~material** *n* working stock; **~-obmann** *m* shop steward; **~rat** *m* (*P.*: member of the) works council; ²**sicher** safe (to operate); (*zuverlässig*) reliable (in service); **~sicherheit** *f* safety (in operation); reliability; **~stoff** *m mot.* fuel; **~störung** *f* trouble; breakdown, stoppage; **~-unfall** *m* industrial accident; **~wirtschaft(slehre)** *f* management.

betrinken: *sich ~* get drunk.

betroffen [~'trɔfən] *fig.* shocked, startled; *von Krankheit usw. ~* stricken (*od.* afflicted) with; *s. betreffend*; ²**heit** *f* perplexity, shock.

betrüb|en [~'try:bən] grieve, afflict; **~lich** [~'try:p-] sad; ²**nis** *f* (14²) affliction, grief; **~t** sad, grieved (*über acc.* at, about).

Be'trug *m* (3) cheat; ⚖, *a. fig.* fraud, deceit; *bsd. fig.* deception.

be'trüg|en cheat, deceive, defraud; *j-n um et. ~* cheat a p. out of; ²**er** (**-in** *f*) *m* cheat, deceiver, swindler;

Ꙃe'rei *f* cheating, fraud(ulence); **⁓erisch** deceitful, fraudulent.

be'trunken drunken, *pred.* drunk; **Ꙃe** *m* (18) drunken man; **Ꙃheit** *f* drunkenness, intoxication.

Bet|saal ['be:tzɑ:l] *m* chapel, oratory; '**⁓stuhl** *m* praying-desk.

Bett [bɛt] *n* (5) bed (*a. geol.*, ⊕); *am* ⁓ at the bedside; *das* ⁓ *hüten* keep one's bed; *zu* ⁓ *bringen* put to bed; *zu* ⁓ *gehen* go to bed, F turn in; *krank zu* ⁓ *liegen* be laid up; '**⁓couch** ['⁓kautʃ] *f* (16, *pl. inv.* ⁓es) bed-couch, divan bed; '**⁓decke** *f* bedspread, coverlet, counterpane; *wollene* ⁓ blanket; *gesteppte* ⁓ quilt.

Bettel ['bɛtəl] *m* (7, *o. pl.*) (*Plunder*) trash; *der ganze* ⁓ the whole lot; 'Ꙃ'**-arm** desperately poor; '**⁓brief** *m* begging letter; '**⁓brot** *n* bread of charity; **⁓ei** [⁓'laɪ] *f* (16) begging; mendicancy; '**⁓kram** *m s. Bettel*; '**⁓mönch** *m* mendicant friar; 'Ꙃ**n** (29) beg (*um* for); ⁓ *gehen* go begging; '**⁓stab** *m*: *an den* ⁓ *bringen* reduce to beggary, ruin.

'**betten** (26) bed (*a.* ⊕); *fig.* embed; *sich* ⁓ make one's bed; *wie man sich bettet, so liegt man* as you make your bed so you must lie on it.

'**Bett|flasche** *f* hot-water bottle; '**⁓lade** *f* bedstead.

bettlägerig ['⁓lɛ:gəriç] bedridden, confined to bed, *Am. a.* bedfast; 'Ꙃ**keit** *f* confinement to bed.

'**Bettlaken** *n* sheet.

'**Bettler** *m* (7) beggar; '**⁓in** *f* beggar (-woman).

Bett|nässer ['⁓nɛsər] *m* (7) bed-wetter; '**⁓stelle** *f* bedstead; '**⁓tuch** *n* sheet; '**⁓-überzug** *m* pillow-case; '**⁓ung** ⊕ *f* bed(ding), bed-plate; '**⁓vorleger** *m* (7) bedside rug; '**⁓wäsche** *f* bed-linen; '**⁓zeug** *n* bedding.

betucht [⁓'tu:xt] F well-heeled.

betupfen [bə'tupfən] dab.

beug|en ['bɔʏgən] (25) bend, bow (*a. sich* ⁓; *vor dat.* to); *Stolz*: humble; *durch Kummer*: bow down, afflict; *gr.* inflect; *das Recht* ⁓ pervert justice; *vom Alter gebeugt* bowed down by age; 'Ꙃ**ung** *f* bending; *gr.* inflexion, inflection.

Beule ['bɔʏlə] *f* (15) bump, swelling; (*Geschwür*) boil; *in Blech usw.*: dent; '**⁓npest** *f* bubonic plague.

be-unruhig|en [bə'ʔunru:igən] (25) disturb, trouble; *fig. a.* worry, disquiet, alarm; *sich* ⁓ *über* (*acc.*) worry about; Ꙃ**ung** *f* trouble; anxiety, alarm; worry.

be-urkund|en [⁓'ʔu:rkundən] (26) authenticate, certify, legalize; Ꙃ**ung** *f* authentication, legalization.

be-urlaub|en [⁓'ʔu:rlaubən] (25) grant leave (of absence); *vom Amt*: suspend; *sich* ⁓ take (one's) leave; **⁓t** [⁓pt] (absent) on leave; Ꙃ**ung** [⁓buŋ] *f* (granting of a) leave; suspension.

be-urteil|en [⁓'ʔurtaɪlən] judge (*nach* by); Ꙃ**er(in** *f*) *m* (7) judge; critic; Ꙃ**ung** *f* judg(e)ment, opinion (*gen.* of, on).

Beute ['bɔʏtə] *f* (15) booty, spoil; (*a. Diebes*Ꙃ) loot; *e-s Tieres*: prey (*a. fig.*: *gen.* to); *hunt.* bag; *auf* ⁓ *ausgehen* go plundering.

Beutel ['bɔʏtəl] *m* (7) bag; (*zo.*; *Tabaks*Ꙃ) pouch; (*Geld*Ꙃ) purse; *biol.* sac; *beim Billard*: pocket; 'Ꙃ**ig** baggy; 'Ꙃ**n** (29) shake; *Mehl*: bolt; '**⁓schneider** *m s. Betrüger*; '**⁓tier** *n* marsupial.

'**Beutezug** *m* raid.

bevölker|n [bə'fœlkərn] (29) people, populate; Ꙃ**ung** *f* population.

Be'völkerungs|dichte *f* density of population; **⁓-explosion** *f* population explosion; **⁓politik** *f* population policy; **⁓stand** *m* (level of) population; **⁓-überschuß** *m* surplus population.

bevollmächtig|en [⁓'fɔlmɛçtigən] (25) authorize, empower; Ꙃ**te** [⁓tiçtə] *m* (18) authorized agent; proxy, deputy; Ꙃ**ung** [⁓guŋ] *f* authorization; *s. Vollmacht.*

be'vor before.

be'vormund|en (26) keep in tutelage, hold in leading-strings; Ꙃ**ung** *f* tutelage.

be'vorraten (25) stock up.

be'vorrecht(ig)en (26) privilege.

Be'vorschussung *f* advance.

be'vorstehen be near *od.* forthcoming, lie ahead; *Gefahr*: be imminent; *j-m*: be in store for; **⁓d** forthcoming, approaching; *Gefahr*: imminent; (*nächst*) next (*week, etc.*).

bevorzug|en [⁓'fo:rtsu:gən] (25) prefer; favo(u)r; ⚖ privilege; Ꙃ**ung** *f* preference.

be'wach|en guard, watch; *Sport*: mark; Ꙃ**ung** *f* guard; custody.

be'wachsen: ~ *mit* grown (over) with.

be'waffn|en arm; **~et** armed; *Auge*: aided; *mit ~er Hand* by force of arms; **≗ung** *f* armament (*a. e-s Schiffes*); (*Waffen*) arms *pl.*

be'wahren (*erhalten*) keep, preserve; (*behüten*) preserve (*vor dat.* from); (*Gott*) *bewahre!* Heaven forbid!

be'währen prove; *sich* ~ stand the test; prove good *od.* a success; *Grundsatz*: hold good.

Be'wahrer(in *f*) *m* (7) keeper.

bewahrheiten [~'vɑːrhaɪtən] (26) verify; *sich* ~ come (*od.* prove) true.

bewährt [~'vɛːrt] (well) tried, tested, proved; (*zuverlässig*) reliable.

Be'wahrung *f* keeping, preservation (*vor dat.* from).

Be'währung *f* proof, trial, (crucial) test; ⚖ = **~sfrist** *f* probation(ary period); **~shelfer(in** *f*) *m* probation officer; **~s-probe** *f* test; **~szeit** *f s. Bewährungsfrist.*

bewaldet [~'valdət] wooded, woody.

bewältigen [~'vɛltigən] (25) cope with, master, handle.

bewandert [~'vandərt] versed; skilled; experienced (*in dat.* in).

Bewandtnis [~'vantnis] *f* (14[2]): *damit hat es folgende* ~ the case is this; *das hat seine eigene* ~ that is a matter apart, thereby hangs a tale.

bewässer|n [~'vɛsərn] *Garten*: water; *Land*: irrigate; **≗ung** *f* watering; irrigation; **≗ungs-anlage** *f* irrigation plant.

beweg|en [~'veːgən] (30) (*a. sich*) move, stir (*beide a. seelisch*); *sich im Kreise* (*fig. in feinen Kreisen*) ~ move in a circle (in good society); (*sich*) *von der Stelle* ~ budge; *sich* ~ *lassen* be moved (*von, durch* with *pity etc.*); *j-n zu et.* ~ induce, get; *s. bewogen*; **~end** moving (*a. fig.*); *~de Kraft* motive power; **≗grund** [~'veːk-] *m* motive; **~lich** movable; *P., Geist*: versatile; (*behend*) agile, nimble; *Zunge*: voluble; *~e Habe* movables *pl.*; **≗lichkeit** *f* mobility; movableness; versatility; agility; volubility; **~t** *See*: agitated; *fig.* (*gerührt*) moved, touched; *Leben*: eventful; *Zeit*: stirring, turbulent.

Be'wegung [~guŋ] *f* movement (*a. pol. usw.*); *unruhige*: stir; *phys.* motion; (*Gemüts≗*) emotion, *stärker*: agitation; *körperliche* ~ (*Sport usw.*) physical exercises *pl.*; *in* ~ *setzen* set in motion; *sich in* ~ *setzen* start, get going; *sich* ~ *machen* take exercise; *s. Hebel*; **~sfreiheit** *f* freedom of movement; *fig.* liberty of action; **~skrieg** *m* mobile warfare; **≗slos** motionless; **~s-therapie** ⚕ *f* kinesiotherapy; **≗s-unfähig** unable to move.

be'wehren arm (*a. zo.*, ⚘, ⊕); *Beton*: reinforce.

be'weihräuchern cense; *fig.* adulate.

be'weinen deplore, mourn.

Beweis [bə'vaɪs] *m* (4) proof (*für* of); evidence (of); *s. ~grund*; *zum* ~ *e-r S.* in proof of a th.; *den* ~ *für et. antreten* undertake to prove a th.; *den* ~ *für et. erbringen* furnish proof of, prove; **~-aufnahme** *f* taking of evidence; **≗bar** provable, demonstrable; **≗en** [~zən] prove; demonstrate; *Interesse usw.*: show; **~führung** *f* reasoning, argumentation; **~grund** *m* argument; **~kraft** *f* argumentative (*bsd.* ⚖ probative) force; **~material** *n* evidence; **~stück** *n* (piece of) evidence; *vor Gericht*: exhibit.

be'wenden 1. *es* ~ *lassen bei* leave it at; **2.** ≗ *n*: *dabei hat es sein* ~ there the matter rests.

be'werb|en: *sich* ~ *um* apply for (*bei* to); (*kandidieren*) stand for, *Am. a.* run for; *um Stimmen*: canvass; ✝ *um Aufträge*: solicit; *sich* (*mit andern*) ~ (*um e-n Preis*) compete (with *others* for *a prize*); *sich um e-e Dame* ~ court, woo; **≗er** *m um ein Amt*: applicant; candidate; *um e-n Preis*: competitor (*alle a.* **≗erin** *f*; *um* for); (*Freier*) suitor, wooer; **≗ung** *f* application; candidature; competition; courtship (*um* of); **≗ungsformular** *n* application sheet; **≗ungsschreiben** *n* letter of application; **≗ungsverfahren** *n* application procedure.

be'werfen pelt; ⚠ plaster.

bewerkstellig|en [~'vɛrkʃtɛligən] (25) manage, bring about, contrive; **≗ung** *f* effecting, accomplishment.

bewert|en [~'veːrtən] value (*auf acc.* at; *nach* by); (*einschätzen*) rate; **≗ung** *f* valuation; rating.

bewillig|en [~'viligən] (25) grant, allow; **≗ung** *f* grant, allowance.

be'wirken effect; (*verursachen*) cause (*daß j. tut* a p. to do; *daß et. geschieht* a th. to be done); (*hervorrufen*) produce, give rise to.

bewirt|en [~'virtən] (25) entertain; **2ung** *f* entertainment.

be'wirtschaft|en *Betrieb*: manage, run; *Mangelware*: ration, *a. Devisen*: control; **2ung** *f* management, running; rationing, control.

bewog [~'vo:k] *pret. v. fig. bewegen*; **~en** [~'vo:gən] *p.p. v. fig. bewegen*; *sich ~ fühlen zu* feel bound to *inf.*

bewohn|bar [~'vo:nbɑ:r] habitable; **2barkeit** *f* habitableness; **~en** inhabit, live in; occupy; **2er(in** *f*) *m* (7 [16[1]]) inhabitant; *e-s Hauses*: occupant, *bei mehreren*: *a.* inmate.

bewölk|en [~'vœlkən] (25) cloud; *sich ~* cloud over; **~t** cloudy; **2ung** *f* clouding.

Bewunder|er [~'vundərər] *m* (7), **~in** *f* admirer; **2n** admire; **2nswert** [~sve:rt], **2nswürdig** admirable; **~ung** *f* admiration.

bewußt [~'vust] conscious; (*bekannt*) known; (*absichtlich*) deliberate, *adv. a.* knowingly; *sich e-r S. ~ sein* be conscious (*od.* aware) of; *die ~e Sache* the matter in question; **~los** unconscious; *~ werden* lose consciousness; **2losigkeit** *f* unconsciousness; **2sein** *n* consciousness; *in dem ~* conscious (*gen.* of; *daß* that); *bei ~ sein* be conscious; *j-m et. zum ~ bringen* bring a th. home to a p.; *j-m zum ~ kommen* come home to a p.; *wieder zum ~ bringen* (*kommen*) bring *a p.* (come) round *od.* to; **~seins-erweiternd** *Droge*: mind-expanding.

be'zahl|en pay; *Gekauftes*: pay for; *sich bezahlt machen* (*S.*): pay (for itself); **2ung** *f* pay(ment).

be'zähmen tame; *fig.* restrain.

be'zauber|n bewitch, enchant; *fig. a.* charm, fascinate; **~t** *von* enchanted with; **2ung** *f* enchantment.

be'zeichn|en mark; *fig.* (*bedeuten*) denote, signify; (*benennen, a. für ein Amt*) designate (*als* as); call, name; (*zeigen*) point out; (*kennzeichnen*) characterize; **~end** typical, characteristic (*für* of); **~enderweise** typically enough; **2ung** *f* marking, *konkret*: mark; denotation; designation; name, term; sign.

be'zeig|en show, express, manifest; **2ung** *f* expression, manifestation.

be'zeug|en (*a.* ⚖) bear witness to, testify to *od.* that; (*bescheinigen*) certify; **2ung** *f* attestation.

bezichtigen [bə'tsiçtigən] (25) *s. beschuldigen.*

be'zieh|bar *Wohnung*: ready for occupation; *Ware*: obtainable; **~en** *Schirm usw.*: (*neu ~* re)cover; *mit Saiten*: string; *Wohnung*: move into, occupy; *Universität usw.*: enter, go up to; *Ware*: obtain, procure, get; *Zeitung*: take in; *Lohn usw.*: draw, receive; *Bett*: sheet; ⚔ *Stellung*: take up; ⚔ *ein Lager ~* encamp; *~ auf* (*acc.*) apply (*od.* relate) to; *sich ~ Himmel*: become overcast; *sich ~ auf* (*acc.*) refer (*od.* relate) to; *sich auf j-n ~* use a p.'s name as (a) reference; **2er(in** *f*) *m* (7) *e-s Wechsels*: drawer; *e-r Zeitung*: subscriber (*gen.* to); (*Käufer*) buyer, taker.

Be'ziehung *f* relation, reference (*zu* to); *persönliche ~en pl.* connexions, relations (*zu j-m* with); *gute ~en haben* be well connected; *in dieser usw. ~* in this *etc.* respect; *in politischer, wirtschaftlicher usw. ~* politically, economically *etc.*; *in ~ stehen zu* (*S.*) be related to; *in guten usw. ~en stehen* be on good *etc.* terms (*zu j-m* with); **2slos** irrelative, unconnected; **2svoll** suggestive; **2sweise** respectively.

beziffern [~'tsifərn] (29) figure; *~ auf* (*acc.*) figure at; *sich ~ auf* figure (*od.* work) out at, amount to.

Bezirk [bə'tsirk] *m* (3) district; *Am.* (*Polizei2, Wahl2*) precinct; *fig. s. Bereich.*

Bezogene ✝ [~'tso:gənə] *m* (18) drawee.

Be'zug [bə'tsu:k] *m* (3[3]) cover(ing), case; (*Kissen2*) slip; *v. Ware*: purchase, supply; *e-r Zeitung, a. von Aktien*: subscription (*gen.* to); *fig.* relation, reference; *bei ~ von 25 Stück* on orders for; *in 2 auf* (*acc.*) as for, as to; with regard to, in relation to; *~ haben* (*od. nehmen*) refer to.

Bezüg|e [~'tsy:gə] *m/pl.* emoluments, drawings, income *sg.*; (*Gehalt*) pay, salary; (*Lieferungen*) supplies; **2lich** [~'tsy:kliç] *adj.* (*auf acc.*), *prp.* (*gen.*) relative to; *gr. ~es Fürwort* relative pronoun.

Be'zugnahme [~na:mə] *f* (15) reference; *unter ~ auf* (*acc.*) with reference to, referring to.
Bezugs... [~'tsu:ks-]: **~bedingungen** *f/pl.* terms of delivery; **~-person** *f* person to whom one relates most closely; **~-preis** *m* subscription (*od.* issue) price; **~-punkt** *m* reference point; **~quelle** *f* source of supply; **~schein** *m* purchase permit.
bezwecken [~'tsvɛkən] (25) aim at; *et. ~ mit* intend by.
be'zweifeln doubt, question.
be'zwing|en master, overcome; conquer; subdue; *sich ~* restrain o.s.; **2er(in** *f*) *m* (7 [16[1]]) subduer.
Bibel ['bi:bəl] *f* (15) Bible; '**~spruch** *m* verse from the Bible, text; '**~stelle** *f* scriptural passage, text.
Biber ['bi:bər] *m* (7) beaver; '**~pelz** *m* beaver (fur).
Biblio|graph [bi:blio'gra:f] *m* (12) bibliographer; **~graphie** ['~gra'fi:] *f* (15) bibliography; **~thek** [~'te:k] *f* (15) library; **~thekar** [~te'ka:r] *m* (3[1]) librarian.
biblisch ['bi:bliʃ] biblical, scriptural; *~e Geschichte* scripture.
bieder ['bi:dər] honest, upright; *a. ironisch*: worthy; '**2keit** *f* honesty, uprightness; '**2mann** *m* (1[2]) honest (*od.* upright) man; worthy.
bieg|en ['bi:gən] (30) *v/t.* (*a. sich*) bend; *gr.* inflect; *sich vor Lachen ~* be doubled up with laughter; *v/i.* (sn): *um e-e Ecke ~* turn (round) a corner; *auf 2 oder Brechen* by hook or by crook; **~sam** ['~kza:m] flexible, supple; *fig. a.* pliant; '**2samkeit** *f* flexibility, suppleness; pliancy; **2ung** ['~guŋ] *f* bend(ing); *gr.* inflexion; (*Weg2, Fluß2*) bend, turn.
Biene ['bi:nə] *f* (15) bee; F (*Mädel*) [doll.
'**Bienen|fleiß** *m* assiduity; '**~haus** *n* apiary, bee-house; '**~königin** *f* queen bee; '**~korb** *m* bee-hive; '**~schwarm** *m* swarm of bees; '**~stich** *m* bee's sting; '**~stock** *m* bee-hive; '**~wachs** *n* beeswax; '**~zucht** *f* bee-keeping; '**~züchter** *m* bee-keeper.
Bier [bi:r] *n* (3) beer; *helles ~* pale ale; *dunkles ~* dark ale; *~ vom Faß* beer on draught; (*Lager2*) lager; F *das ist dein ~* that's your problem; '**~baß** F *m* beery voice; '**~bauch** *m* beer-belly; '**~brauer** *m* brewer; '**~brauerei** *f* brewery; '**~deckel** *m* beer mat; '**~dose** *f* beer can; '**~-eifer** *m* excessive zeal; '**~fahrer** *m* beer lorry (*Am.* truck) driver; '**~faß** *n* beer-barrel; '**~garten** *m* beer garden; '**~hefe** *f* brewer's yeast, barm; '**~krug** *m* beer-mug, *Am.* stein; '**~kutscher** *m* drayman; '**~reise** F *f* pub-crawl; '**~ruhe** F *f* imperturbable calm; '**2selig** F beery, tiddly; '**~stube** *f*, '**~wirtschaft** *f* public house, F pub, *Am.* beer-saloon.
Biese ['bi:zə] *Schneiderei*: (pin) tuck; ⚔ piping.
Biest [bi:st] *n* (1[1]) beast (*a.* F *fig.*).
bieten ['bi:tən] (30) offer; *e-n guten Morgen*, ✝, *bei Auktion*: bid; *sich ~* (*Gelegenheit*) present (*od.* offer) itself; *das läßt er sich nicht ~* he won't stand that; *s. Stirn.*
Bigamie [bi:ga'mi:] *f* (15) bigamy.
bigott [bi'gɔt] bigoted; **2e'rie** *f* (15) bigotry.
Bilanz [bi'lants] *f* (16) balance; (*Aufstellung*) balance-sheet; *Am. a.* statement; *die ~ ziehen* strike the balance; **2ieren** [~'tsi:rən] balance, show in the balance-sheet.
Bild [bilt] *n* (1) *allg.* picture; (*Ab2, Eben2*) image (*a. opt., TV*); *in e-m Buch*: illustration; (*Bildnis*) portrait; *rhet.* metaphor; (*Vorstellung*) idea; *im ~e sein* be in the picture; *im ~e sein über* (*acc.*) be aware of, know about; *j-n ins ~ setzen* inform a p., put a p. in the picture; *sich ein ~ machen von et.* picture a th. to o.s.; '**~-archiv** *n* photo library; '**~band** *m* illustrated book; '**~bericht** *m Presse*: picture-story.
bilden ['bildən] (26) *allg.* (*a. sich*) form; (*gestalten*) *a.* shape, fashion; *Geist*: cultivate; *Ausschuß, Gruppe*: constitute; *sich geistig ~* educate o.s.; '**~d** (*belehrend*) instructive; *~e Künste f/pl.* fine (*od.* plastic) arts.
'**Bilder|-anbetung** *f* image-worship; '**~bogen** *m* picture-sheet; '**~buch** *n* picture-book; '**~galerie** *f* picture-gallery; '**~rätsel** *n* rebus; '**2reich** rich in pictures; *Sprache*: flowery; '**~schrift** *f* picture-writing; '**~sprache** *f* imagery; '**~stürmer** *m* iconoclast.
Bild|fläche ['bilt-] *f* image area *od.* plane; *Film*: screen; *auf der ~ erscheinen* appear on the scene, turn

up; *von der ~ verschwinden* vanish; '**~funk** *m* (3[1]) radio picture transmission; *TV* television; '**2haft** plastic; '**~hauer(in** *f*) *m* sculptor; **~haue'rei** *f* sculpture; '2'**hübsch** very pretty; '**~karte** *f Karten*: court-card, *Am.* face card; '**2lich** pictorial, graphic; *Ausdruck usw.*: figurative; **~ner** ['~dnər] *m* (7), '**~nerin** *f* sculptor; *fig.* mo(u)lder; **~nis** ['bilt-] *n* (4[1]) portrait, likeness; effigy; '**~platte** *f* videodisc; '**~plattenspieler** *m* videodisc player; '**~qualität** *f* image (*phot.* picture) quality; '**~röhre** *f* picture tube; '**2sam** (*a. fig.*) plastic; '**~säule** *f* statue; '**~schirm** *m* (television) screen; '**~schirmgerät** *n Computer*: (video) display (terminal); '**~schirmtext** *m* videotex; '**~schnitzer** *m* (wood-) carver; '2'**schön** most beautiful; '**~sendung** *f*, '**~-übertragung** *f* picture transmission; '**~streifen** *m* film strip; (*Zeichnung*) strip cartoon; '**~telegraphie** *f* phototelegraphy; '**~telephon** *n* videophone.

Bildung ['bildʊŋ] *f* (16) *allg.* formation; *des Körpers*: form, shape; (*Gründung*) foundation, organization; *e-s Ausschusses usw.*: constitution; (*Aus2*) education; (*Kultur*) culture; (*Kenntnisse*) knowledge, information; (*Gelehrsamkeit*) learning; (*feine Sitte*) refinement, good breeding; '**2sfähig** cultivable; '**~sgang** *m* course of education; '**~sgrad** *m* educational standard; '**~slücke** *f* gap in *a p.'s* education; '**~snotstand** *m* educational crisis; '**~s-politik** *f* educational policy; '**~s-urlaub** *m* educational holiday.

'**Bildwerk** *n* sculpture; imagery; (*Buch*) book of plates.

Billard ['biljart] *n* (3[1] *u.* 11) billiards *sg.*; (*~tisch*) billiard-table; '**~kugel** *f* billiard-ball; '**~stock** *m* cue.

Billett [bil'jɛt] *n* (3) ticket; **~-ausgabe** *f*, **~schalter** *m* ticket-office; *s. Karten...*

Billiarde [bil'jardə] *f* (15) *a* thousand billions, *Am.* quadrillion.

billig ['biliç] (*gerecht*) equitable, fair, just; (*vernünftig, mäßig*) reasonable; (*wohlfeil*) cheap (*a. fig. contp.*); '**2-angebot** *n* cut-price offer; '**~en** (25) approve (of); (*genehmigen*) sanction; '**2keit** *f* equitableness, fairness, justice, *bsd.* ⚖ equity; cheapness; **2ung** ['~gʊŋ] *f* approval; sanction.

Billion [bil'jo:n] *f* (16) billion, *Am.* trillion.

bimbam! ['bim'bam] ding-dong!

bimmeln F ['biməln] (29) tinkle.

Bimsstein ['bimsʃtaɪn] *m* pumice (-stone).

Binde ['bində] *f* (15) band; ⚕ bandage, *für den Arm*: sling; (*Hals2*) (neck)tie; (*Kopf2*) fillet; (*Stirn2*) bandeau; *j-m e-e ~ vor die Augen tun* blindfold a p.; *fig. j-m die ~ von den Augen nehmen* open a p.'s eyes; '**~gewebe** *anat. n* connective tissue; '**~glied** *n* connecting link; '**~haut** *f* conjunctiva; '**~haut-entzündung** *f* conjunctivitis; '**~mittel** *n* binding agent; ⚠ *u. fig.* cement; '**2n** (30) (*a. fig.*) bind, tie (*an acc.* to); *Buch*: bind; *Knoten, Schlips, Schnürband*: tie; *Besen, Strauß*: make; *Faß*: hoop; ♪ slur; *sich ~* bind o.s.; '**2nd** binding (*für* upon); '**~r** *m* (*Schlips*) (neck-)tie; '**~strich** *m* hyphen; *mit ~ schreiben* hyphen (-ate); '**~wort** *n* conjunction.

Bind|faden ['bint-] *m* string; *stärker*: packthread, twine; **~ung** ['~dʊŋ] *f a. Ski*: binding; ⚠, *fig.*: bond; ♪ slur, ligature; *fig., a.* ♪ tie; (*Verpflichtung*) commitment; *fig.* *~en pl.* bonds, ties.

binnen ['binən] (*dat. od. gen.*) within; *~ kurzem* before long.

'**Binnen|gewässer** *n* inland water; '**~hafen** *m* inner harbo(u)r; '**~handel** *m* inland (*od.* home) trade; '**~land** *n* inland, interior; '**~länder (-in** *f*) *m* inlander; '**2ländisch** inland, internal; '**~markt** *m* home market; '**~meer** *n* inland sea; '**~schiffahrt** *f* inland navigation; '**~schiffer** *m* bargee, *Am.* bargeman; '**~verkehr** *m* inland traffic.

Binse ['binzə] *f* (15) rush; F *in die ~n gehen* go to pot; '**~nwahrheit** *f*, '**~nweisheit** *f* truism.

Biochem|ie [bioçe'mi:] *f* biochemistry; **~iker** [~'çe:mikər] *m* biochemist; **2isch** biochemical.

Bio|-Chip ['bi:o-] *m Computer*: bio-chip; '**~gas** *n* biogas; '**~gas-anlage** *f* biogas (heating) system.

Biograph [bio'gra:f] *m* (12), **~in** *f* biographer; **~ie** [~gra'fi:] *f* biography; **2isch** [~'gra:fiʃ] biographical.

'**Bioladen** *m* health food shop.

Biolog|e [bio'lo:gə] *m* (13) biologist; **~ie** [~lo'gi:] *f* biology; **≈isch** [~'lo:giʃ] biological.

'**Bio|masse** *f* biomass; '**~physik** *f* biophysics *sg.*; '**~rhythmus** *m* biorhythm; **~'top** [-'to:p] *n* (3) biotope.

Birke ['birkə] *f* (15) birch(-tree).

'**Birk|hahn** *m* black-cock; '**~henne** *f*, '**~huhn** *n* grey-hen.

'**Birnbaum** *m* (3[1]) pear-tree.

Birne ['birnə] *f* (15) ⚘ pear; (*Glüh≈*) bulb; *sl.* (*Kopf*) pate, *Am.* bean.

birnenförmig ['~fœrmiç] pear-shaped.

bis [bis] **1.** *prp. räumlich*: to; up to; (~ *nach*) as far as; *zeitlich*: till; until; down to; (~ *spätestens*) by; *zwei ~ drei* two or three; ~ *an*, ~ *auf* (*acc.*) to, up to; ~ *auf weiteres* until further notice; ~ *auf* (*acc.*) *s. abgesehen von*; *alle ~ auf drei* all but three; ~ *dahin* so far; ~ *hierher* thus far; ~ *heute* up to this day, *Am.* F todate; ~ *jetzt* till now, up to the present; ~ *jetzt noch nicht* not as yet; ~ *vier zählen* count up to four; **2.** *cj.* till, until.

Bisam ['bi:zam] *m* (3[1]) musk; (*Pelz*) musquash; '**~ratte** *f* musk-rat.

Bischof ['biʃɔf] *m* (3[1] *u.* 3[3]) bishop.

bischöflich ['~ʃø:fliç] episcopal.

'**Bischofs|-amt** *n* episcopate; '**~sitz** *m* (episcopal) see; cathedral town; '**~stab** *m* crosier.

bisher [bis'he:r] hitherto, till (*od.* up to) now, so far, as yet; **~ig** hitherto existing; previous; (*jetzig*) present.

Biskuit [bis'kvi:t] *n* biscuit; **~kuchen** *m* sponge-cake.

Biß[1] [bis] *m* (4) bite (*a. ~wunde*).

biß[2] *pret. v. beißen.*

bißchen ['~çən]: *ein* ~ a little (bit).

Bissen ['bisən] *m* (6) bit, morsel.

'**bissig** biting; *Hund, a. P.*: snappish; *Bemerkung usw.*: cutting; *Vorsicht, ~er Hund!* Beware of the dog!; '**≈keit** *f* snappishness.

Bistum ['bistu:m] *n* (1[2]) bishopric.

bisweilen [bis'vaɪlən] sometimes.

Bit [bit] *n* (11) *Computer*: bit.

Bitte ['bitə] *f* (15) request; (*dringende ~*) entreaty; *auf j-s ~* at a p.'s request; *ich habe e-e ~ an Sie* I have a favo(u)r to ask of you.

'**bitten** (30) *v/t.* ask, request; *dringend*: entreat; (*einladen*) invite; *j-n um Verzeihung ~* beg a p.'s pardon; *sich (lange) ~ lassen* want a lot of asking; *v/i. ~ für j-n* intercede for; *~ um et.* ask for; *bitte* please; *nach danke!*: (you're) welcome, don't mention it; (*wie*) *bitte?* (I beg your) pardon!; *Spiel*: *bitte!* play!; *dürfte ich Sie um ... ~?* may I trouble you for ...?; *Wünschen Sie noch eine Tasse Tee? Bitte (sehr)!* Yes, thank you!

bitter ['bitər] bitter; *fig. a.* severe, sharp; *Schokolade*: plain; *~er Ernst* bitter earnest; '**~'böse** furious; (*schlimm*) very wicked; '**~'ernst** dead serious; '**≈keit** *f* bitterness (*a. fig.*); '**~lich** bitterish; *adv.* bitterly; '**≈salz** ⚗ *n* Epsom salts *pl.*; '**≈wasser** *n* bitter mineral water.

'**Bitt|gang** *m* procession; '**~gesuch** *n*, '**~schrift** *f* petition; '**~steller** (**-in** *f*) *m* petitioner.

Biwak ['bi:vak] *n* (3[1]), **≈ieren** [~'ki:rən] bivouac.

bizarr [bi'tsar] bizarre.

Bizeps ['bi:tsɛps] *m* (3[2]) biceps.

bläh|en ['blɛ:ən] (25) *v/t.* inflate, (*a. sich*) swell (*a. fig.*: *vor dat.* with); *v/i.* ⚕ cause flatulence; '**~end** ⚕ flatulent; '**≈ung** ⚕ *f* flatulence, wind.

Blam|age [bla'mɑ:ʒə] *f* (15) shame, disgrace; **≈ieren** [~'mi:rən] (*bloßstellen*) compromise (*sich* o.s.); (*lächerlich machen*) ridicule; *sich ~* make a fool of o.s.

blank [blaŋk] bright, shining; (~ *geputzt*) polished; *Schuh*: shiny; (*bloß*) naked, bare (*a.* ⊕); (*abgetragen*) shiny; F (*ohne Geld*) broke; *~er Unsinn* sheer nonsense; *~ ziehen* draw (one's sword).

Blankett [blaŋ'kɛt] *n* blank form, *Am. a.* blank; *s. Blankovollmacht.*

blanko † ['blaŋko] (*adv.* in) blank; '**≈...** blank; '**≈vollmacht** *f* full discretionary power, carte blanche (*fr.*).

Bläs-chen ['blɛ:sˀçən] *n* (6) small bubble; ⚕ pustule.

Blase ['blɑ:zə] *f* (15) (*Luft≈*) bubble; (*Harn≈ usw.*) bladder; (*Haut≈*) blister, ⚕ vesicle; *im Glas usw.*: flaw; F *contp.* gang; '**~balg** *m* bellows *pl.*; '**≈n** (30) blow; *Horn usw.*: sound (*zum Angriff usw.* the charge *etc.*); '**~n-entzündung** *f* cystitis; '**~nkrebs** *m* bladder cancer; '**~nleiden** *n* bladder trouble; '**≈nziehend** ⚕ vesicant.

Bläser ['blɛ:zər] *m* (7) blower; ♪ *die* ~ *pl. im Orchester* the wind.
blasiert [bla'zi:rt] blasé (*fr.*).
blasig ['bla:ziç] bubbly; blistery.
'**Blas|-instrument** ♪ *n* wind-instrument; *die* ~*e pl. im Orchester* the wind; '~**kapelle** *f* brass-band; '~**rohr** *n* blowpipe; *zum Schießen*: *a.* pea-shooter.
Blasphemie [blasfe'mi:] (15) *f* blasphemy.
blaß [blas] pale; ~*rot usw.* pale red *etc.*; ~ *werden* (turn) pale, *Farbe*: fade; *blasser Neid* green envy; *keine blasse Ahnung* not the faintest idea.
Blässe ['blɛsə] *f* (15) paleness, pallor.
Blatt [blat] *n* (1², *als Maß im pl. inv.*) *Pflanze*, *Buch*: leaf; *Papier*: sheet; *Schulter*, *Ruder*, *Schwert*: blade; (*Zeitung*) (news)paper; *Karten*: *ein gutes* ~ a good hand; ♪ *vom* ~ *spielen* play at sight; *kein* ~ *vor den Mund nehmen* not to mince matters; *fig. das* ~ *hat sich gewendet* the tables are turned.
Blatter ['blatər] *f* (15) pustule; pock; '~**n** *pl.* smallpox.
blätt(e)rig ['blɛt(ə)riç] leafy, *in Zssgn* ...-leaved; *min.* laminate(d).
blättern ['blɛtərn] (29) turn over the leaves (*in dat.* of).
'**Blatter|narbe** *f* pock-mark; '♀**narbig** pock-marked.
'**Blätterteig** *m* puff-paste.
'**Blatt|gold** *n* gold-leaf; '~**grün** *n* chlorophyll; '~**laus** *f* plant-louse; '~**pflanze** *f* foliage plant; '~**stiel** *m* leaf-stalk; '~**werk** *n* foliage.
blau [blaʊ] **1.** blue; F (*betrunken*) *sl.* tight, plastered; ~*es Auge fig.* black eye; *mit e-m* ~*en Auge davonkommen* get off cheaply; F ~ *machen* take a day off; *s. Blut, Dunst, Wunder*; **2.** ♀ *n* blue; *ins* ~*e hinein* at random; ~**äugig** ['~ˀɔʏgiç] blue-eyed; *fig.* gullible, naive; '♀**beere** *f* bilberry, *Am.* blueberry; '~**blütig** blue-blooded.
Bläue ['blɔʏə] *f* (15, *o. pl.*) blue (-ness).
bläuen ['blɔʏən] (25) (dye) blue.
'**Blau|fuchs** *m* arctic (✝ blue) fox; '♀**grau** bluish grey; '~**kraut** *n* red cabbage.
'**bläulich** bluish.
'**Blau|meise** *f* bluetit; '~**pause** *f* blueprint; '~**säure** *f* prussic acid; '~**stift** *m* blue pencil; '~**strumpf** *fig. m* blue-stocking.
Blech [blɛç] *n* (3) sheet metal; *s. Feinblech usw.*; F (*Unsinn*) rot, bosh, *Am.* blah; '~**büchse** *f* tin (box), *Am.* (tin) can.
'**blechen** F (25) pay (up).
'**blechern** (of) tin; *Klang*: tinny.
'**Blech|geschirr** *n* tin-plate vessels *pl.*; '~**-instrument** ♪ *n* brass instrument; *die* ~*e pl. im Orchester* the brass; '~**musik** *f* (music of a) brass band; '~**schere** *f* plate-shears *pl.*; '~**schmied** *m* tinsmith; '~**verkleidung** *f* sheeting; '~**ware**(**n** *pl.*) *f* tinware.
blecken ['blɛkən] (25): *die Zähne* ~ show one's teeth.
Blei [blaɪ] *n* (3) lead; ⚓ plummet; (~*stift*) (lead) pencil; (*Geschoß*) shot.
bleiben ['blaɪbən] (30, sn) remain, stay; (*übrig*~) be left, remain; *in der Schlacht*: fall; (*andauern*) continue; *treu usw.* ~ remain; *bei et.* ~ keep to, stick to, abide by; *dabei muß es* ~ there the matter must rest; *es bleibt dabei!* agreed!; '~**d** lasting, permanent; '~**lassen** leave (*od.* let) *a th.* alone.
bleich [blaɪç] pale; ~ *werden* turn pale; '♀**e** *f* (15) paleness; *der Wäsche*: bleaching; (*Bleichplatz*) bleaching-ground; '~**en** (25) *v/t. u. v/i.* (sn) bleach, blanch; *Farbe*: fade; '♀**sucht** *f* greensickness, 🕮 chlorosis; ~**süchtig** ['zyçtiç] greensick, 🕮 chlorotic.
bleiern ['blaɪərn] leaden (*a. fig.*).
'**blei|farben** lead-colo(u)red; '~**frei** *Benzin*: unleaded, *Am.* lead-free; '♀**gehalt** *m* lead content; '~**haltig** containing lead, plumbiferous; *Benzin*: leaded; '♀**kugel** *f* (lead-)bullet; '♀**lot** *n* plumb(-line); ⚓ lead, plummet; '♀**rohr** *n* lead pipe; '♀**satz** *typ. m* hot-metal setting; '♀**soldat** *m* tin soldier; '♀**stift** *m* (lead) pencil; '♀**stiftspitzer** *m* pencil-sharpener; '♀**vergiftung** *f* lead poisoning; '♀**weiß** *n* white lead.
Blend|e ['blɛndə] *f* (15) blind; △ blind window *od.* door; ⚒ blend; *phot.* diaphragm, stop; '♀**en** (26) blind; *auf kurze Zeit od. fig.*: dazzle; '~**er** *m fig.* bluffer, F dazzler; '♀**frei** ⊕ dazzle-free; '~**laterne** ['blɛnt-] *f* dark lantern; '~**ling** *zo. m* bastard,

mongrel; '**~rahmen** *m* blind frame; '**~schutzscheibe** *f* anti-dazzle screen, *Am.* (sun) visor; '**~schutzzaun** *m Autobahn*: anti-dazzle barrier; **~ung** ['~duŋ] *f* blinding; dazzling; '**~werk** ['blɛnt-] *n* delusion; (*Betrug*) deception.

Blesse ['blɛsə] *f* (15) blaze, white spot; (*Pferd*) horse with a blaze.

Blick [blik] *m* (3) look; *flüchtiger*: glance; (*Aussicht*) view (*auf acc.* of); *auf den ersten ~* at first sight; *mit einem ~* at a glance; *einen (keinen) ~ für et. haben* have an (no) eye for; *e-n ~ werfen auf* cast a glance (*od.* take a look) at; '**2en** (25) look, glance (*auf acc., nach* at); *sich ~ lassen* show o.s., appear; '**~fang** *m* eye-catcher; '**~feld** *n* field of vision; *fig.* range (of vision); '**~punkt** *m* visual focus; *fig.* focus; *im ~* in the cent|re (*Am.* -ter) of interest; '**~winkel** *m* visual angle; *fig.* point of view.

blieb [bli:p] *pret. v. bleiben.*

blies [bli:s] *pret. v. blasen.*

blind [blint] blind (*a. fig.*: *für, gegen* to); (*trübe*) tarnished, dull; *Patrone*: blank; *Gehorsam, Glaube, Liebe, Wut*: blind; ⚠ blind, sham; *auf e-m Auge ~* blind of (*Am.* in) one eye; *~er Alarm* false alarm; *~er Passagier* deadhead, ⚓ stowaway.

'**Blinddarm** *m* blind gut, 🕮 caecum; (*Wurmfortsatz*) appendix; '**~-entzündung** *f* appendicitis; '**~-operation** *f* appendectomy.

'**Blinde** *m* blind man, *f* blind woman.

'**Blindekuh** *f* blind-man's-buff.

'**Blinden|-anstalt** *f* blind asylum, home for the blind; '**~hund** *m* blind man's dog, guide-dog, *Am.* seeing-eye dog; '**~schrift** *f* braille; '**~stock** *m* blind man's cane.

blind|fliegen ✈ ['blint-] fly blind, fly on instruments; '**2flug** *m* instrument (*od.* blind) flying; **2gänger** ⚔ ['~gɛŋər] *m* (7) blind (shell), *sl.* dud; F *fig.* washout; '**2heit** *f* blindness; *mit ~ geschlagen* struck blind; **~lings** ['~liŋs] blindly; **2schleiche** ['~ʃlaɪçə] *f* (15) slow-worm; '**~schreiben** *Schreibmaschine*: touch-type.

blink|en ['bliŋkən] (25) blink; gleam, *bsd. Sterne*: twinkle; ⚔, ⚓ (*signalisieren*) flash; '**2feuer** *n* intermittent light; '**2licht** *n* ⚔ intermittent light; *mot.*, ✈ indicator; '**2zeichen** *n* flash signal.

blinzeln ['blintsəln] (29) blink; *mit einem Auge, a. lustig*: wink.

Blitz [blits] *m* (3^2) lightning; *fig.* flash; *s. ~strahl*; *phot.* flash(-light); *wie der ~* like a shot; *vom ~ getroffen* struck by lightning; *ein ~ aus heiterem Himmel* a bolt from the blue; **~ableiter** ['~ʔaplaɪtər] *m* (7) lightning-rod; '**~besuch** *m* flying visit; '**2'blank** shining; *pred.* spick and span; '**2en** (27) *v/i.* flash; *es blitzt* there is lightning; '**~gerät** *phot. n* flash gun; '**~gespräch** *teleph. n* special priority call; '**~krieg** *m* blitz; '**~licht** *phot. n* flash-light; '**~schlag** *m* lightning-stroke; '**2schnell** as quick as lightning; *adv. a.* with lightning speed; '**~strahl** *m* thunder-bolt; '**~würfel** *phot. m* flash cube.

Block [blɔk] *m* (3^3) block (*a. von Häusern usw.*); (*Holz2*) log; (*Fahrkarten2*) book; (*Schreib2*) pad, book; *pol.* bloc; **~ade** [~'ka:də] *f* (15) blockade; **~debrecher** *m* blockade-runner; '**~flöte** *f* recorder; '**2frei** *pol.* non-aligned; '**~haus** *n* log-house; ⚔ blockhouse; **2ieren** [~'ki:rən] block (up); ⊕ jam; '**~säge** *f* pit-saw; '**~satz** *typ. m* justified lines *pl.*; '**~schrift** *f* block letters.

blöd|e ['blø:də] (*schwachsinnig*) imbecile; (*dumm*) stupid, dull; (*albern*) silly; (*schüchtern*) shy; (*unangenehm*) awkward, stupid; **2heit** ['blø:t-] *f* imbecility; stupidity, dul(l)ness; silliness; '**2mann** F *m* dimwit, jerk; **2sinn** ['blø:tzin] *m* imbecility, idiocy; (*Unsinn*) nonsense, *sl.* rot; '**~sinnig** silly, idiotic; *adv.* F awfully; **2sinnige** ['~zinigə] *m, f* idiot.

blöken ['blø:kən] (25) bleat; *Kalb*: low.

blond [blɔnt] blond(e *f*), fair; '**~gelockt** blond and curly-haired; **2ine** [~'di:nə] *f* (15) blonde.

bloß [blo:s] **1.** bare, naked; (*nichts als*) mere, simple; *Schwert, Auge*: naked; *mit ~em Kopf* bare-headed; **2.** *adv.* merely, only, simply.

Blöße ['blø:sə] *f* (15) bareness, nakedness; ⚔, *fenc.*, *fig.* weak point *od.* spot, opening; (*Lichtung*) glade; *sich e-e ~ geben* expose o.s.; *sich j-m gegenüber e-e (empfindliche) ~ geben* leave o.s. (wide) open to a p.

'**bloß|legen** lay bare; '**~stellen** expose, show up; *sich* ~ compromise o.s.; '2**stellung** *f* exposure.

blühen ['bly:ən] (25) bloom, blossom; *fig.* flourish; F *j-m* ~ be in store for a p.; '~**d** *Aussehen*: rosy; *Unternehmen*: flourishing.

Blume ['blu:mə] *f* (15) flower; *des Weins*: bouquet; *des Biers*: froth; *hunt.* tail; *durch die* ~ *sagen* say *a th.* under the rose; *laßt* ~*n sprechen!* say it with flowers!

'**Blumen**|-**ausstellung** *f* flower-show; '~**beet** *n* flower-bed; '~**blatt** *n* petal; '~**draht** *m* florist's wire; '~**dünger** *m* plant fertilizer; '~-**erde** *f* garden-mo(u)ld; '~**händler**(**in** *f*) *m* florist; '~**kelch** *m* calyx; '~**kohl** *m* cauliflower; '~**korso** *m* carnival of flowers; '~**krone** ⚘ *f* corolla; '2**reich** flowery (*a. fig.*); '~**strauß** *m* bunch of flowers, bouquet; '~**topf** *m* flower-pot; '~**zucht** *f* floriculture; '~**züchter**(**in** *f*) *m* florist; '~**zwiebel** *f* flower-bulb.

'**blumig** flowery (*a. fig.*).

Bluse ['blu:zə] *f* (15) blouse.

Blut [blu:t] *n* (3, *o. pl.*) blood; *blaues* (*junges*) ~ blue (young) blood; *bis aufs* ~ to the quick; *böses* ~ *machen* breed bad blood; ~ *lecken* (*schwitzen*) taste (sweat) blood; *ruhig* ~*!* keep cool!; '~-**alkohol** *m* blood alcohol; '~-**andrang** *m* rush of blood (to the head), 🕮 congestion; '2-**arm** an(a)emic; *blut'arm* extremely poor, penniless; '~-**armut** *f* an(a)emia; '~**bad** *n* carnage, massacre; '~**bank** ⚕ *f* blood bank; '~**bild** ⚕ *n* blood picture (*od.* count); '~**blase** *f* blood blister; '~**buche** *f* copper-beech; '~**druck** *m* blood-pressure; '~**durst** *m* bloodthirstiness; 2**dürstig** ['~dyrstiç] bloodthirsty.

Blüte ['bly:tə] *f* (15) blossom, bloom; flower (*a. fig. Elite*); *der Jahre*: prime; (*Wohlstand*) prosperity; *s.* ~*zeit*; *e-e neue* ~ *erleben* go through a time of revival.

'**Blut-egel** *m* leech.

'**bluten** (26) *a. fig.* bleed (*aus* from).

'**Blüten**|**knospe** *f* bud; '~**lese** *f* anthology; '~**staub** *m* pollen; '~**stengel** *m* peduncle.

'**Blut**|-**entnahme** *f* (taking of a) blood sample; '~-**erguß** *m* effusion of blood.

'**Blütezeit** *f* (16) flowering time; *fig. a.* heyday.

'**Blut**|**farbstoff** *m* h(a)emoglobin; '~**fleck** *m* blood-stain; '~**gefäß** *n* blood-vessel; '~**gerinnsel** *n* clot of blood; '~**geschwür** *n* boil; '~**gier** *f s. Blutdurst*; '~**gruppe** *f* blood-group; '~**hund** *m* bloodhound; '2**ig** bloody; *Schlacht*: sanguinary; *fig.* cruel; ~*er Anfänger* greenhorn; ~*er Ernst* deadly earnest; '2'**jung** very young; '~**konserve** *f* unit of stored blood; ~**körperchen** ['~kœrpərçən] *n* (6) blood-corpuscle; '~**kreislauf** *m* blood circulation; '2**leer**, '2**los** bloodless; '~**pfropfen** *m* blood clot; '~**plasma** *n* blood plasma; '~**probe** *f* blood test; (*entnommenes Blut*) blood sample; '~**rache** *f* blood revenge, vendetta; '2**reinigend** purifying the blood, depurative; '2'**rot** blood-red; 2**rünstig** ['~rynstiç] bloody; '~**sauger** *m* blood-sucker, vampire; '~**schande** *f* incest; 2**schänderisch** ['~ʃɛndəriʃ] incestuous; '~**schuld** *f* blood-guiltiness; '~**senkung** *f* blood sedimentation; '~**spender**(**in** *f*) *m* blood donor; '2**stillend** blood-sta(u)nching, styptic; '~**s-tropfen** *m* drop of blood; '~**sturz** *m* h(a)emorrhage; '2**sverwandt** related by blood (*mit* to); '~**sverwandte** *m*, *f* blood relation; '~**sverwandtschaft** *f* consanguinity; '~**tat** *f* bloody deed; '2**triefend** dripping with blood; '2-**überströmt** covered with blood; '~**übertragung** *f* blood transfusion; '~**ung** *f* bleeding, h(a)emorrhage; '2-**unterlaufen** bloodshot; '~**vergießen** *n* bloodshed; '~**vergiftung** *f* blood-poisoning; '~**verlust** *m* loss of blood; '2**verschmiert** smeared with blood; '~**wäsche** *f* dialysis; '2**wurst** *f* black pudding; '~**zoll** *m* toll of lives; '~**zucker** *m* blood sugar.

Bö [bø:] *f* (16) gust, squall.

Bob [bɔp] *m* (11) *Sport*: bob(sleigh).

Bock [bɔk] *m* (3^3) buck; (*Widder*) ram; (*Ziegen*2) he-goat; *Gerät*: trestle, (*Turnen*: buck-)horse; (*Kutschersitz*) box; *e-n* ~ *schießen* commit a blunder, *Am.* F pull a boner; *den* ~ *zum Gärtner machen* set the fox to keep the geese; 2**beinig** ['~baɪniç] *fig.* stubborn (as a mule).

bock|**en** ['bɔkən] (25) buck (*a. mot.*); *Mensch*: sulk; '~**ig** obstinate.

'**Bock**|**leder** *n*, '2**ledern** buckskin;

ˈ**~leiter** *f* step-ladder; ˈ**~shorn** *n*: *ins ~ jagen* scare; ˈ**2springen** play (at) leap-frog; ˈ**~sprung** *m* caper, gambol; *Bocksprünge machen* caper, gambol.

Boden [ˈbo:dən] *m* (6[1]) (*Erde*) ground; ↗ *u. fig.* soil; *e-s Gefäßes, des Meeres*: bottom; *e-s Zimmers*: floor; *e-s Hauses*: garret, loft; (*festen*) *~ fassen* get a (firm) footing; *~ gewinnen* (*verlieren*) gain (lose) ground; *zu ~ schlagen* (*gehen*) knock (go) down; ˈ**~-abwehr** ⚔ *f* ground defen|ce, *Am.* -se; ˈ**~belag** *m* floor covering; ˈ**~-erhebung** *f* rise, elevation; ˈ**~-ertrag** *m* crop yield; ˈ**~fläche** *f* acreage; △ *u.* ⊕ floor-space; ˈ**~haftung** *mot. f* road traction; ˈ**~kammer** *f* garret; ˈ**~kreˈdit-anstalt** *f* land mortgage bank; ˈ**~-ˈLuft-Rakete** *f* ground (*od.* surface)-to-air missile; ˈ**2los** bottomless; *fig.* enormous; ˈ**~personal** ✈ *n* ground personnel, *Am.* ground crew; ˈ**~radar** *n* ground-based radar; ˈ**~reform** *f* land reform; ˈ**~satz** *m* grounds, dregs *pl.*, sediment; **~schätze** [ˈ~ʃɛtsə] *m/pl.* treasures of the soil, (mineral) resources; ˈ**2ständig** native; racy of the soil; *mil.* home; ˈ**~station** *f Raumfahrt*: tracking station; ˈ**~streitkräfte** *f/pl.* ground forces; ˈ**~turnen** *n* mat-work.

Bodmerei ⚓ [bo:dməˈraɪ] *f* (16) bottomry.

bog [bo:k] *pret. v. biegen.*

Bogen [ˈbo:gən] *m* (6) bow; *e-s Flusses usw.*: bend, curve; ⅄ arc; △ arch, vault; *v. Papier*: sheet; *e-n großen ~ um j-n machen* give a p. a wide berth; *fig. den ~ überspannen* go too far; ˈ**~fenster** *n* bow window; ˈ**2förmig** arched; ˈ**~führung** ♪ *f* bowing; ˈ**~gang** △ *m* arcade; ˈ**~lampe** ⚡ *f* arc-lamp; ˈ**~schießen** *n* archery; ˈ**~schütze** *m* archer; ˈ**~sehne** *f* bow-string; ˈ**~zirkel** *m* bow compasses *pl.*

Bohle [ˈbo:lə] *f* (15) plank, thick board; ˈ**2n** (25) plank.

Böhm|e [ˈbø:mə] *m* (13), ˈ**~in** *f*, ˈ**2isch** Bohemian; *das sind mir ~e Dörfer* that's all Greek to me.

Bohne [ˈbo:nə] *f* (15) bean; *grüne ~n pl.* French (*Am.* string) beans; *weiße ~n pl.* haricot beans; (*Sau2*) broad bean; *fig. blaue ~* bullet.

ˈ**Bohnen|kaffee** *m* pure coffee; ˈ**~kraut** ⚘ *n* savory; ˈ**~stange** *f* bean-pole (*a.* F *fig.*).

Bohner [ˈbo:nər] *m* (7) (floor-) polisher; ˈ**2n** (29) wax, polish; ˈ**~wachs** *n* floor-wax.

bohr|en [ˈbo:rən] (25) bore, drill; *Brunnen*: sink; *nach Öl ~* prospect (*od.* drill) for oil; *fig.* (*forschen*) bore; (*quälen*) harass; ˈ**2er** *m* (7) borer, drill; ˈ**2-insel** *f* oil rig; ˈ**2loch** *n* drill-hole; ˈ**2maschine** *f* boring (*od.* drilling) machine; ˈ**2turm** *m* derrick; ˈ**2ung** *f* drilling; boring; (*Loch*) (drill)hole; (*Durchmesser*) diameter (of bore); *mot.* bore; (*Kaliber*) cali|bre, *Am.* -ber.

böig [ˈbø:iç] squally.

Boje [ˈbo:jə] *f* (15) buoy.

Böller [ˈbœlər] *m* (7) small mortar.

Bollwerk [ˈbɔlvɛrk] *n* (3) bulwark.

Bolschewis|mus [bɔlʃəˈvismus] *m* (16) Bolshevism; **~t**(**in** *f*) [~ˈvist] *m* (12 [16[1]]) Bolshevist; **2tisch** Bolshevist(ic).

Bolzen [ˈbɔltsən] *m* (6) bolt (*a.* ⊕).

Bombard|ement [bɔmbardəˈmɑ̃] *n* (11) bombardment; **2ieren** [~ˈdi:rən] bombard (*a. fig.*); bomb.

Bombast [bɔmˈbast] *m* (3[2]) bombast; **2isch** bombastic(ally *adv.*).

Bombe [ˈbɔmbə] *f* (15) bomb (*a. mit ~n belegen*); *fig.* bombshell; *Fußball*: cracker; ˈ**~n-alarm** *m* bomb alert; ˈ**~n-angriff** *m* bomb-raid; ˈ**~n-anschlag** *m* bomb attempt; ˈ**~ndrohung** *f* bomb threat; ˈ**~n-erfolg** *m* huge success, *sl.* smash hit; ˈ**2nfest**, ˈ**2nsicher** bomb-proof; *fig.* F dead sure; ˈ**~nflugzeug** *n*, ˈ**~r** *m* bomber; ˈ**~ngeschäft** F *n* roaring trade; ˈ**~nleger** *m* (7) bomber; ˈ**~nräumkommando** *n* bomb disposal squad; ˈ**~nsache** F *f sl.* knockout; ˈ**~nschaden** *m* bomb-damage; ˈ**~ntrichter** *m* bomb-crater.

Bon [bɔ̃] *m* (11) coupon; voucher; (*Gutschein*) credit note.

Bonbon [bɔ̃ˈbɔ̃] *m*, *n* (11) bonbon, sweet(meat), *Am.* (hard) candy.

Bonbonniere [bɔ̃bɔˈnjɛ:rə] *f* (15) sweetmeat-box.

bongen [ˈbɔŋən] (25) F *Registrierkasse*: ring up; *gebongt!* sure!

Bonus ✝ [ˈbo:nus] *m* (14[2] *od. inv.*) bonus.

Bonze F [ˈbɔntsə] *m* (13) bigwig, big bug, big shot, *bsd. pol.* (party-) boss.

Boot [boːt] *n* (3) boat; '**~shaus** *n* boat-house; '**~smann** *m* boatswain; ⚔, ⚓ petty officer.
Bor ⚗ [boːr] *n* (3¹, *o. pl.*) boron; **~ax** ['boːraks] *m* (11¹ *od.* 3², *o. pl.*) borax.
Bord [bɔrt] *m* (3) ⚓, ✈ board; (*Rand*) edge, border, rim; *an ~ e-s Schiffes* on board a ship; *an ~ nehmen* take aboard; *über ~ werfen* throw overboard (*a. fig.*); '**~computer** *mot. m* dashboard computer; '**~-elektronik** ✈ *f* avionics *sg.*
Bordell [bɔr'dɛl] *n* (3¹) brothel.
'**Bord|flugzeug** *n* ship-plane, ship-borne aircraft; '**~funker** ✈ *m* air wireless (*Am.* radio) operator; '**~karte** ✈ *f* boarding card; '**~mechaniker** *m*, '**~monteur** ✈ *m* air mechanic; '**~radar** *n* air-borne radar; '**~schwelle** *f*, '**~stein** *m* kerb(stone), *Am.* curb(stone); '**~wand** *f* ship's side; '**~werkzeug** *mot. n* tool kit.
Bordüre [bɔr'dyːrə] *f* (15) border, braiding.
Borg [bɔrk] *m* (3) borrowing; *auf ~* on credit, F on tick; **2en** ['bɔrgən] borrow; *j-m et.*: lend, *bsd. Am.* loan.
Borke ['bɔrkə] *f* (15) bark, rind; (*Kruste*) crust.
Born [bɔrn] *m* (3) spring, well.
borniert [bɔr'niːrt] narrow-minded.
Bor|salbe ['boːrzalbə] *f* borax ointment; '**~säure** *f* boric acid.
Börse ['bøːrzə] *f* (15) purse; ✝ Exchange, F (')Change; (*Effekten*2) Stock Exchange; *an* (*od. auf*) *der ~* on the Exchange; '**~nbericht** *m* Exchange (*od.* market) report; *in der Zeitung*: City article *od.* news; '**~nblatt** *n* Stock Exchange journal; '**2nfähig** negotiable (*od.* marketable) on the Stock Exchange; '**~ngeschäft** *n* (Stock) Exchange transaction; '**~nkrise** *f* crisis of the (Stock) Exchange; '**~nkurs** *m* Exchange rate; '**~nmakler** *m* stock-broker; '**~nnotierung** *f* (market-) quotation; '**~npapiere** *n/pl.* stocks *pl.*; '**~nschluß** *m* close of the Exchange; '**~nspekulant** *m* stock-jobber; '**~nzeitung** *f* financial paper; '**~nzettel** *m* stock-list, market-report.
Borste ['bɔrstə] *f* (15) bristle.
'**borstig** bristly; *fig.* F surly.
Borte ['bɔrtə] *f* (15) border; (*Besatz*2) braid.
Borwasser ['boːrvasər] *n* boric acid solution.
bös [bøːs] *s. böse*; '**~-artig** ill-natured, malicious, *Am.* F ugly; *Tier*: vicious; ⚕ malignant; '**2-artigkeit** *f* malignity; viciousness; ⚕ malignancy.
Böschung ['bœʃuŋ] *f* slope; (*Fluß*2 *usw.*) embankment; *bsd.* ⚔ scarp.
böse ['bøːzə] *allg.* bad; (*verrucht*) evil; (*boshaft*) malicious, wicked; (*zornig*) angry, cross (*über et.* at, about; *auf j-n, mit j-m*, F *j-m* with), *Am.* mad (at *a p.*); *er meint es nicht ~* he means no harm; *der* 2 (18) the Evil One; '2 *n* (18) evil; '**2wicht** *m* villain (*a. fig. co.*).
bos|haft ['boːs-haft] malicious; (*mutwillig*) mischievous; (*tückisch*) spiteful; '**2heit** *f* malice; malignity; *aus ~* out of spite.
bossieren [bɔ'siːrən] emboss.
'**böswillig** malevolent; *~e Absicht* ⚖ malice prepense; *adv.* ⚖ wilfully; '**2keit** *f* malevolence.
bot [boːt] *pret. v. bieten.*
Botanik [bo'tɑːnik] *f* (16) botany; **~er** *m* (7) botanist.
bo'tanisch botanic(al).
botanisier|en [~ni'ziːrən] botanize; **2trommel** *f* vasculum.
Bot|e ['boːtə] *m* (13), '**~in** *f* (16¹) messenger.
'**Botengang** *m* errand.
'**botmäßig** subject; (*gehorsam*) obedient; '**2keit** *f* dominion, rule, sway.
'**Botschaft** *f* message; *Amt*: embassy; *gute ~* good tidings *pl. od. sg.*; '**~er** *m* (7) ambassador; '**~erin** *f* ambassadress; '**~erkonferenz** *f* ambassadors' conference.
Böttcher ['bœtçər] *m* (7) cooper; **~ei** [~'raɪ] *f* cooper's workshop; *Handwerk*: cooper's trade.
Bottich ['bɔtiç] *m* (3) tub, vat.
Bouillon [bul'jɔ̃] *f* (11¹) broth, clear soup, beef-tea; **~würfel** *m* beef-tea cube.
Boutique [bu'tiːk] *f* (16) boutique.
Bowle ['boːlə] *f* (15) bowl; (*Getränk*) spiced wine, cup.
Box [bɔks] *f* (16) **1.** (*a.* **~e** [15]) *für Pferde*: box; *mot.* pit; **2.** (*~kamera*) box-camera; **3.** (*Lautsprecher*2) speaker.
box|en ['bɔksən] (27) box; '**2er** (7) *m* boxer; '**2handschuh** *m* boxing-glove; '**2kampf** *m* boxing-match;

ˈ≈ring *m* ring; ˈ≈sport *m* boxing.
Boykott [bɔʏˈkɔt] *m* (3), ≈**ieren** [~ˈtiːrən] boycott.
brabbeln F [ˈbrabəln] (29) babble, mutter.
brach[1] [braːx] *pret. v. brechen.*
brach[2] fallow (*a. fig.*); ˈ≈**-acker** *m*, ˈ≈**feld** *n* fallow land.
Brachialgewalt [braxˈjaːlgəvalt] *f* (*mit* ~ by) brute force (*od.* strength).
ˈ**brach|legen** lay fallow; ˈ~**liegen** *v/i.* lie fallow; *fig.* lie idle, be neglected; ˈ≈**schnepfe** *f*, ˈ≈**vogel** *m* curlew.
brachte [ˈbraxtə] *pret. v. bringen.*
Brahman|e [braˈmaːnə] *m* (13), ≈**isch** Brahman, *mst* Brahmin.
Bramsegel ⚓ [ˈbraːm-] *n* topgallant sail.
Branche ✝ [ˈbrãʃə] *f* (15) branch, line, trade; industry; ˈ~**nkenntnis** *f* knowledge of the trade; ˈ≈**n-üblich** customary in the industry concerned; ˈ~**nverzeichnis** *n* classified directory.
Brand [brant] *m* (3² *u.* ³) burning; (*Feuersbrunst*) fire, conflagration; ⚕ gangrene, (*kalter* ~) mortification; ⚘ blight, mildew; ⚒ smut; *in ~ geraten* catch fire; *in ~ stecken* set on fire; ˈ~**-anschlag** *m* arson attack; ˈ~**blase** *f* blister; ˈ~**bombe** *f* incendiary bomb; ˈ~**brief** *m fig.* threatening (*od.* urgent) letter; ≈**en** [ˈ~dən] (26) surge (*a. fig.*); ˈ~**er** *m* (7) fireship; ˈ~**flasche** *f* Molotov cocktail; ˈ~**fleck(en)** *m* burn; ˈ~**geruch** *m* burnt smell; ≈**ig** [ˈ~diç] ⚘ blighted, blasted; ⚕ gangrenous; ~ *riechen* have a burnt smell; ~**mal** [ˈbrant-] *n* brand; *fig.* stigma; ~**maleˈrei** *f* poker-work; ˈ≈**marken** (25) brand; *fig. a.* stigmatize, denounce; ˈ~**markung** *f fig.* stigmatization; ˈ~**mauer** *f* fire-proof wall; ˈ~**rede** *f* incendiary speech; ˈ~**schaden** *m* damage caused by fire; ˈ≈**schatzen** (27) lay under contribution; (*plündern*) sack, pillage; ˈ~**sohle** *f* insole; ˈ~**stätte** *f*, ˈ~**stelle** *f* scene of fire; ˈ~**stifter(in** *f*) *m* incendiary; ˈ~**stiftung** *f* arson.
Brandung [ˈ~duŋ] *f* breakers *pl.*, surf, surge; ˈ~**swelle** *f* breaker.
ˈ**Brand|wache** *f* fire-watch; ˈ~**wunde** *f* burn; ˈ~**zeichen** *n* brand.
brannte [ˈbrantə] *pret. v. brennen.*
Branntwein [ˈbrantvaɪn] *m* brandy, spirits *pl.*; ˈ~**brennerei** *f* distillery.
Brasil [braˈziːl] *f* (*inv.*) Brazil cigar.
Brasilianer [brazilˈjaːnər] *m* (7), ~**in** *f*, **Brasilier** [~ˈziːljər] *m* (7), ~**in** *f*, **brasiliˈanisch**, **braˈsilisch** Brazilian.
brassen ⚓ [ˈbrasən] (28) brace.
ˈ**Brat-apfel** *m* baked apple.
braten[1] [ˈbraːtən] *v/t. u. v/i.* (30) roast; *im Ofen*: bake; *auf dem Roste*: grill, broil; *in der Pfanne*: fry; F (*nur v/i.*) (*in der Sonne* ~) roast (in the sun).
ˈ**Braten**[2] *m* (6) roast, joint; *fig. den ~ riechen* smell a rat; ˈ~**fett** *n* dripping; ˈ~**platte** *f* meat-dish; ˈ~**soße** *f* gravy; ˈ~**topf** *m* roaster.
ˈ**brat|fertig** oven-ready; ˈ≈**fisch** *m* fried fish; ˈ≈**huhn** *n* roaster, broiler; ˈ≈**kartoffeln** *f/pl.* fried potatoes; ˈ≈**ofen** *m* oven; ˈ≈**pfanne** *f* frying-pan; ˈ≈**röhre** *f s. Bratofen.*
Bratsche ♪ [ˈbraːtʃə] *f* (15) viola; ˈ~**r** *m* (7) violist.
ˈ**Brat|spieß** *m* spit; ˈ~**wurst** *f* sausage (for frying); fried sausage.
Bräu [brɔʏ] *n* (3) (*Gebräu*) brew; (*~haus*) brewery.
Brauch [braux] *m* (3³) (*Sitte*) custom; (*Gewohnheit*) use, practice, *bsd.* ✝ *od. sprachlich*: usage; ˈ≈**bar** useful; *P.*: *a.* able; *S.*: *a.* serviceable, handy; ˈ~**barkeit** *f* usefulness; ˈ≈**en** (25) (*nötig haben*) want, need; (*erfordern*) require; *Zeit*: take; *s. gebrauchen, verbrauchen*; *er braucht nicht zu gehen* he need not go; *ich brauche drei Tage dazu* it will take me three days; ˈ~**tum** *n* (1²) customs *pl.*; folklore.
Braue [ˈbrauə] *f* (15) eyebrow.
brau|en [ˈbrauən] (25) brew; ˈ≈**er** *m* (7) brewer; ≈**erei** [~əˈraɪ] *f*, ˈ≈**haus** *n* brewery.
braun [braun] brown; *Pferd*: bay; (*sonngebräunt*) (sun-)tanned; *~e Butter* fried butter; ˈ≈**e** *m* (18) bay (horse).
Bräune [ˈbrɔʏnə] *f* (15) brownness; ⚕ quinsy, angina; *häutige ~* croup; ˈ≈**n** *v/t.* (25) brown; *v. der Sonne*: *a.* tan, bronze; *v/i. od. sich ~* (grow *od.* become) brown; tan.
ˈ**braun|gelb** brownish yellow; ˈ≈**kohle** *f* brown coal, lignite.
bräunlich [ˈbrɔʏnliç] brownish.
ˈ**braunrot** brownish red.
Braus [braus] *m* (4, *o. pl.*) *s. Saus.*
Brause [ˈbrauzə] *f* (15) (*Gießkannen≈*) rose; *s. ~bad*; *s. ~limonade*;

'**~bad** *n* shower-bath; '**~kopf** *m* hothead, hotspur; '**~limonade** *f* fizzy drink, *Am.* soda pop; '**2n** (27) roar, bluster; (*eilen, stürmen*) rush, sweep; *Orgel*: peal; ⚗ effervesce; (*sich ab~*) take a shower(-bath); '**~pulver** *n* sherbet powder; '**~tablette** *f* effervescent tablet.

Braut [braʊt] *f* (14[1]) fiancée, bride-to-be; *lit. a.* betrothed; *am Hochzeitstag*: bride; '**~-ausstattung** *f* trousseau; '**~bett** *n* bridal bed; '**~führer** *m* best man.

Bräutigam ['brɔʏtigam] *m* (3[1]) fiancé; *am Hochzeitstag*: bridegroom, *Am. a.* groom.

'**Braut|jungfer** *f* bridesmaid; '**~kleid** *n* wedding-dress; '**~leute** *pl. s. Brautpaar.*

bräutlich ['brɔʏtliç] bridal.

'**Braut|paar** *n* engaged couple; *am Hochzeitstag*: bride and bridegroom; '**~schau** *f*: *auf ~ gehen* look out for a wife; '**~schleier** *m* bridal veil; '**~zug** *m* bridal procession.

brav [brɑːf] honest, upright; (*tapfer*) brave, gallant; (*artig*) good; *~ gemacht!* well done!; '**2heit** *f* honesty; good behavio(u)r.

bravo! ['brɑːvo] bravo!, well done!

Bravour [bra'vuːr] *f* bravado; *mit ~* brilliantly; **~stück** *n* feat of daring, stunt; ♪ bravura.

Brech|bohnen ['brɛç-] *f/pl.* broken French beans; '**~durchfall** *m* diarrh(o)ea with vomiting, cholerine; '**~-eisen** *n* jemmy, *Am.* jimmy; '**2en** *v/t.* (30) break (*a. fig. Eid, Eis, Gesetz, Rekord, Stille usw.*); *Blume*: pluck, pick; *Lichtstrahl*: refract; *Papier*: fold; *Steine*: quarry; (*er~*) vomit; *die Ehe ~* commit adultery; *sich ~* break; *opt.* be refracted; *sich den Arm ~* break one's arm; *v/i.* (sn) break; (h.) *mit j-m ~* break with; (*er~*) vomit, be sick; '**~er** ⚓ *m* (7) breaker; '**~mittel** *n* emetic, vomitive; F *fig.* pest; '**~nuß** *f* vomit-nut; '**~reiz** *m* nausea, retching; '**~stange** *f* crowbar; '**~ung** *f* breaking; *opt.* refraction; '**~ungswinkel** *m* angle of refraction.

Brei [braɪ] *m* (3) (*bsd. Kinder2*) pap; (*bsd. Hafer2*) porridge; (*~masse*) pulp, squash; (*Mus*) mash; (*Teig*) paste; *s. Katze*; '**2ig** pulpy; pasty.

breit [braɪt] broad (*a. Akzent, Lachen usw.*), (*a.* ⊕) wide; (*weitschweifig*) diffuse; *~es Publikum* wide public; *s. Masse*; '**~beinig** straddle-legged, straddling.

Breite ['~tə] *f* (15) *vgl. breit*: breadth; width; diffuseness; *ast., geogr.* latitude; '**2n** spread; '**~ngrad** *m* degree of latitude; '**~nkreis** *m* parallel (of latitude).

'**breit|machen:** *sich ~* spread o.s.; *fig.* obtrude o.s.; '**~schlagen** F: *j-n ~* talk a p. round, *zu et.*: talk a p. into; '**~schult(e)rig** broad-shouldered; '**2seite** *f* broadside; '**~spurig** 🚂 broad-ga(u)ge; *fig.* F bumptious; '**~treten** *fig.* expatiate on; '**2wandfilm** *m* wide-screen picture.

Bremse[1] *zo.* ['brɛmzə] *f* (15) gad-fly, horse-fly.

'**Bremse**[2] *f* (15) (*Wagen2 usw.*) brake; '**2n** (27) *v/t.* brake; *fig. a.* check; *v/i.* (put on the) brake; *fig.* go slow; '**~r** *m* (7) brake(s)man.

Brems|fußhebel ['brɛms-] *m* brake pedal; '**~klotz** *m* brake-block; '**~leuchte** *f*, '**~licht** *mot. n* stop light; '**~pedal** *n* brake pedal; '**~scheibe** *f* brake disc (*Am.* disk); '**~schuh** *m* brake-shoe; '**~spur** *f* skid mark; '**~vorrichtung** *f* brake-mechanism; '**~weg** *m* braking distance.

brenn|bar ['brɛn-] combustible; '**2-dauer** *f* burning-time; '**2-element** *n Kernreaktor*: fuel element; '**~en** *v/t.* (30) burn; *Branntwein*: distil(l *Am.*); *das Haar*: curl; *Kaffee, Mehl*: roast; ⚕ cauterize; *Ziegel usw.*: bake; F *sich ~* (*täuschen*) be mistaken; *v/i.* burn (*a. fig. Augen, Wunde usw.*); *Nessel*: sting; *Pfeffer usw.*: bite, be hot; *vor Ungeduld ~* burn with impatience; F *darauf ~, zu inf.* be dying (*od.* itching) to *inf.*; *es brennt!* fire!; *~d* burning (*a. fig. Durst, Frage, Leidenschaft usw.*); '**2er** *m* (7) distiller; (*Gas2*) burner; (*Schweiß2*) torch; (*Atom2*) pile; **2erei** [~'raɪ] *f* distillery; '**2glas** *n* burning-glass; '**2holz** *n* firewood; '**2material** *n* fuel; '**2nessel** *f* stinging nettle; '**2-öl** *n* lamp-oil; (*Heiz2*) fuel oil; '**2punkt** *m* focus; *in den ~ rücken* bring into focus (*a. fig.*); '**2schere** *f* (*eine* a pair of) curling tongs *pl.*; '**2spiegel** *m* burning-mirror; '**2spiritus** *m* methylated spirit; '**2stab** *m Kernenergie*: fuel rod; '**2stoff** *m* combustible; *bsd. mot.*, ✈ fuel; '**2weite** *opt. f* focal distance.

brenzlig ['brɛntsliç] *Geruch, Geschmack*: burnt; F *fig.* ticklish.

Bresche ['brɛʃə] *f* (15) breach; *e-e* ~ *schlagen od. schießen* make a breach; *fig. in die* ~ *springen* stand in the breach.

Brett [brɛt] *n* (1) board; *dickes*: plank; (*Regal*) shelf; ~*er pl.* (*Bühne*) boards *pl.*; (*Skier*) woods *pl.*; *Boxen*: *auf die* ~*er schicken* (knock) down; *fig. ein* ~ *vor dem Kopf haben* be very dense; '~**erbude** *f* wooden shed *od.* hut, shack; '~**erzaun** *m* hoarding, *Am.* board fence; '~**spiel** *n* board game.

Brevier [bre'vi:r] *n* (3[1]) breviary.

Brezel ['bre:tsəl] *f* (15) pretzel.

Brief [bri:f] *m* (3) letter; (*Sendschreiben*) epistle; '~**-aufschrift** *f* address; '~**beschwerer** *m* (7) paper-weight; '~**bogen** *m* sheet of note-paper; '~**bombe** *f* letter bomb; '~**fach** *n* pigeon-hole; '~**freund(in** *f*) *m* pen friend; '~**geheimnis** *n* privacy (*od.* secrecy) of letters; '~**kasten** *m* letter-box, pillar-box, *Am.* mailbox; *Zeitungsrubrik*: Question and Answer Column; *den* ~ *leeren* clear the letter-box, *Am.* collect the mail; '~**kastentante** F *f* sob sister; '~**kopf** *m* letter-head; '♀**lich** *adj. u. adv.* by letter; ~*er Verkehr* correspondence; '~**marke** *f* (postage) stamp; '~**markensammler** *m* stamp-collector, philatelist; '~**markensammlung** *f* stamp collection; '~**-öffner** *m* (7) letter-opener, paper knife; '~**-ordner** *m* letter-file; '~**papier** *n* note- (*od.* letter-)paper; '~**porto** *n* postage; '~**post** *f* mail, post, *Am. a.* first--class matter; '~**tasche** *f* wallet; *mit Notizbuch*: pocket-book; '~**taube** *f* carrier pigeon, homing pigeon; '~**-telegramm** *n* letter telegram, *Am.* lettergram; '~**träger** *m* postman, *Am. a.* mailman; '~**-umschlag** *m* envelope; '~**waage** *f* letter-balance; '~**wahl** *f* postal vote, *bsd. Am.* absentee ballot; '~**wähler** *m* postal voter, *bsd. Am.* absentee voter; '~**-wechsel** *m* correspondence.

briet [bri:t] *pret. v. braten*[1].

Brigade [bri'gɑ:də] *f* (15) brigade.

Brigg ⚓ [brik] *f* (11[1]) brig.

Brikett [bri'kɛt] *n* (3 *od.* 11) briquet(te).

Brillant [bril'jant] *m* (12), ♀ *adj.* brilliant; ~**ring** *m* diamond ring.

Brille ['brilə] *f* (15) (*eine* a pair of) spectacles *pl.*, glasses *pl.*, F specs *pl.*; (*Schutz*♀) goggles *pl.*; (*Klosett*♀) seat; '~**nfutteral** *n* spectacle-case; '~**nschlange** *f* cobra; '~**nträger(in** *f*) *m*: ~ *sein* wear glasses.

bringen ['briŋən] (30) (*her*~) bring; (*fort*~) take; (*geleiten*) conduct; *s. begleiten*; *thea. usw.* present, show; *Zeitung*: print, contain; (*ein*~, *verursachen*) bring, cause; *Opfer*: make; *Zinsen*: yield; *an sich* ~ acquire, appropriate; *j-n wieder auf die Beine* (*od. zu sich*) ~ bring a p. round; *auf einen Nenner* ~ reduce to a common denominator; *es bis zum Major usw.* ~ rise to the rank of major *etc.*; *j-n dahin* ~, *daß* induce (*od.* prevail upon) a p. to *inf.*; *es dahin* ~, *daß* manage (*od.* contrive) to *inf.*; *fig. es mit sich* ~ involve; *es weit* ~, *es zu etwas* ~ get on (*od.* succeed) in the world; *es zu nichts* ~ fail (in life); *j-n um et.* ~ deprive (*od.* rob) a p. of a th.; *j-n zum Lachen usw.* ~ make a p. laugh *etc.*

brisan|t [bri'zant] high-explosive; ♀**z** *f* explosive effect; *in Zssgn* high-explosive.

Brise ⚓ ['bri:zə] *f* (15) breeze.

Brit|e ['britə] *m* (13), '~**in** *f* Briton, *Am.* Britisher; *die Briten pl.* the British; '♀**isch** British.

bröck|(e)lig ['brœk(ə)liç] crumbly, *feiner*: friable; '~**eln** *v/t. u. v/i.* (29, sn) crumble.

Brocken ['brɔkən] *m* (6) piece; *Brot*: crumb; (*Bissen*) morsel; (*Teilchen*) bit, scrap; (*Klumpen*) lump; *fig.* ~ *pl. e-r Sprache*: scraps *pl.*, *e-r Unterhaltung*: snatches *pl.*; *harter* ~ hard nut.

brodeln ['bro:dəln] (29) bubble, simmer, seethe (*a. fig.*).

Brokat [bro'kɑ:t] *m* (3) brocade.

Brom ⚗ [bro:m] *n* (3[1]) bromine.

Brombeer|e ['brɔmbe:rə] *f* blackberry; '~**strauch** *m* bramble.

'**Brom|säure** *f* bromic acid; '~**silber** *n* bromide of silver.

Bronch|ialkatarrh [brɔn'çiɑ:lkatar] *m* bronchial catarrh; ~**ien** ['~çiən] *m/pl.* bronchi *pl.*; ~**itis** [~'çi:tis] *f* bronchitis.

Bronze ['brɔ̃sə] *f* (15) bronze; '~**plastik** *f* bronze sculpture.

bronzieren [~'si:rən] bronze.

Brosame ['bro:zamə] *f* (15) crumb.

Brosche [ˈbrɔʃə] *f* (15) brooch.
broschier|en [~ˈʃiːrən] stitch; **~t** in paper cover, stitched.
Broschüre [~ˈʃyːrə] *f* (15) booklet, pamphlet, brochure.
Brot [broːt] *n* (3) bread; *ganzes*: loaf; *fig.* bread, livelihood; *belegtes ~* sandwich; ˈ**~-aufstrich** *m* spread; ˈ**~beutel** *m* haversack.
Brötchen [ˈbrøːtçən] *n* (6) roll; ˈ**~geber** F *m* employer, boss.
ˈ**Brot|-erwerb** *m* bread-winning, (making a) living; ˈ**~korb** *m* bread-basket; *j-m den ~ höher hängen* put a p. on short allowance; ˈ**~krume** *f* bread-crumb; ˈ**2los** unemployed; *Tätigkeit*: unprofitable; ˈ**~neid** *m* trade jealousy, professional envy; ˈ**~rinde** *f* crust (of bread); ˈ**~röster** *m* (7) toaster; ˈ**~schneidemaschine** *f* bread-cutter; ˈ**~schnitte** *f* slice of bread; ˈ**~studium** *n* utilitarian study.
brr! (*halt*) whoa!, wo!; (*pfui*) ugh!
Bruch[1] [bruːx] *m*, *n* (3[2]) bog, fen.
Bruch[2] [brux] *m* (3[3]) breach (*a. fig.*); (*Brechen*) breaking; (*Knochen2*) fracture; (*Unterleibs2*) rupture, 🕮 hernia; *im Papier*: fold; *im Stoff*: crease; ⅍ fraction; *des Eides, des Friedens usw.*: violation; (*~schaden*) breakage; (*Schrott*) scrap; F (*Schund*) trash, rubbish; ⅍ *gewöhnlicher ~* vulgar fraction, *echter ~* proper fraction; *in die Brüche gehen* come to grief, *bsd. Ehe*: go on the rocks; ✈ *~ machen* crash; ˈ**~band** *n* truss; ˈ**~bude** F *f* tumbledown shanty, ramshackle house.
brüchig [ˈbryçiç] brittle, fragile.
ˈ**Bruch|landung** ✈ *f* crash landing; ˈ**~rechnung** *f* fractions *pl.*; ˈ**~schaden** *m* breakage; ˈ**~stein** *m* quarry-stone; ˈ**~stelle** *f* point of fracture; ˈ**~strich** ⅍ *m* fraction stroke; ˈ**~stück** *n* fragment; *pl. fig. a.* scraps, snatches *pl.*; ˈ**2stückhaft** fragmentary; ˈ**2stückweise** in fragments; ˈ**~teil** *m* fraction; *im ~ e-r Sekunde* in a split second; ˈ**~zahl** *f* fractional number.
Brücke [ˈbrykə] *f* (15) bridge (*a.* ⚓, ⚡; *a. beim Ringen u. Zahnprothese*); (*kleiner Teppich*) rug; *Sport*: back-bend; *e-e ~ schlagen über* (*acc.*) throw a bridge across; *fig. s. abbrechen*; ˈ**~nkopf** *m* bridge-head; ˈ**~npfeiler** *m* bridge pier; ˈ**~nwaage** *f* weigh-bridge.
Bruder [ˈbruːdər] *m* (7[1]) brother; (*Mönch*) friar; *lustiger ~* jolly fellow; ˈ**~krieg** *m* fratricidal war.
brüderlich [ˈbryːdərliç] brotherly, fraternal; ˈ**2keit** *f* brotherliness.
ˈ**Bruder|liebe** *f* brotherly love; ˈ**~mord** *m*, ˈ**~mörder**(**in** *f*) *m* fratricide.
ˈ**Brüderschaft** *f* (16) brotherhood, fellowship; *~ trinken* pledge close friendship.
ˈ**Brudervolk** *n* sister nation.
Brüh|e [ˈbryːə] *f* (15) broth; (*Soße*) sauce; (*Fleischsaft*) gravy; *als Suppengrundlage*: stock; *contp.* slop; ˈ**2en** (25) scald; ˈ**2heiß** scalding (hot); ˈ**~kartoffeln** *f/pl.* potatoes *pl.* boiled in broth; ˈ**2warm** *fig.* red hot (*news*); *j-m et. ~ wiedererzählen* take a story straight away to a p.; ˈ**~würfel** *m* beef-cube.
brüllen [ˈbrylən] (25) roar; *Rind*: bellow; (*muhen*) low; *Mensch*: roar, (*a. heulen*); howl, bawl; *vor Lachen usw. ~* roar with laughter *etc.*; F *er* (*es*) *ist zum 2* he (it) is a scream.
ˈ**Brumm|bär** *m* grumbler, growler, *Am.* F grouch; ˈ**~baß** *m* ♪ double-bass; *fig.* rumbling bass; **2en** [ˈbrumən] *v/i. u. v/t.* (25) *Tier*: growl; *Fliege usw.*: buzz; *Mensch*: grumble, *Am.* grouch; F (*im Gefängnis sein*) do time; *in den Bart ~* mutter to o.s.; *mir brummt der Kopf* my head is buzzing; ˈ**~er** *m* (7) (*Fliege*) blowfly, bluebottle; (*Käfer*) dung-beetle; ˈ**2ig** grumbling, *Am.* F grouchy; ˈ**~kreisel** *m* humming-top; ˈ**~schädel** F *m* headache.
brünett [bryˈnɛt] dark(-complexioned); *Frau*: brunette (*a.* **2e** [~ˈnɛtə] *f*).
Brunft [brunft] *f* (14[1]) *hunt.* rut; ˈ**2en** (26) rut; ˈ**2ig** rutting; ˈ**~schrei** *m* bell; ˈ**~zeit** *f* rutting-season.
brünieren [bryˈniːrən] (25) brown.
Brunnen [ˈbrunən] *m* (6) well (*a. fig.*); (*Quelle*) spring; (*Spring2*) fountain; ⚕ (mineral) waters *pl.*; *~ trinken* take the waters; ˈ**~kresse** *f* water-cress; ˈ**~kur** *f* mineral-water cure; ˈ**~vergiftung** *f fig.* vitiating the political atmosphere.
Brunst [brunst] *f* (14[1]) *zo.* rut, *des weiblichen Tieres*: heat; *v. Menschen*: lust; *fig. s. Inbrunst.*
brünstig [ˈbrynstiç] (*vgl.* **Brunst**) *zo.*

rutting, on (*od.* in) heat; lustful; *fig. s. inbrünstig.*

Brust [brust] *f* (14[1]) breast; (*~kasten*) chest; (*Busen*) bosom; *am Braten*: brisket; *sich in die ~ werfen* give o.s. airs, bridle (up); *~ an ~* neck and neck; '**~bein** *n* breastbone; '**~beschwerden** *f/pl.* chest-trouble; '**~bild** *n* half-length portrait *od.* photo; '**~bonbon** *m* pectoral lozenge; '**~drüse** *f* mamma(ry gland).

brüsten ['brystən] (26): *sich ~* give o.s. airs; boast, brag (*mit* with); *sich ~ als* ... pose as.

'**Brustfell** *n* pleura; '**~-entzündung** *f* pleurisy.

...brüstig ...breasted, ...chested.

'**Brust|kasten** *m*, '**~korb** *m* chest; '**~kind** *n* breast-fed child; '**≗krank** suffering from chest-trouble; '**~krebs** *m* breast cancer; '**~schwimmen** *n* breast-stroke; '**~stimme** *f* chest-voice; '**~stück** *n am Braten*: brisket; '**~tasche** *f* breast pocket; '**~tee** *m* pectoral herb-tea; '**~ton** *m* chest-note; *fig. ~ der Überzeugung* true ring of conviction; '**~-umfang** *m s. Brustweite.*

Brüstung ['brystuŋ] *f* balustrade; parapet; (*Fenster≗*) sill.

'**Brust|warze** *f* nipple; '**~wehr** *f* breastwork; '**~weite** *f* chest-measurement; *der Frau*: bust(-measurement).

Brut [bru:t] *f* (16) brood (*a. fig.*); (*Fisch≗*) fry, spawn; *fig. b.s.* scum, lot.

brutal [bru'tɑ:l] brutal; **≗ität** [~tali'tɛ:t] *f* brutality.

'**Brut|-apparat** *m*, '**~-ofen** *m* incubator; '**~-ei** *n* egg for hatching.

brüten ['bry:tən] (26) brood, sit, incubate; *fig.* brood (*über dat.* over, on); *s. Rache.*

'**Brüter** *m* (7) (*Brutreaktor*) *schneller ~* fast breeder (reactor).

'**Brut|henne** *f* sitting hen; '**~kasten** *m* incubator; '**~re-aktor** *m* breeder reactor; '**~stätte** *f* breeding-place; *fig.* hotbed.

brutto ['bruto] gross, in gross; '**≗einkommen** *n* gross income; '**≗gewicht** *n* gross weight; '**≗registertonne** *f* gross register ton; '**≗sozialprodukt** *n* gross national product; '**≗verdienst** *m* gross earnings *pl.*

Bube ['bu:bə] *m* (13) boy, lad; (*Schurke*) rascal; *Karten*: knave, *bsd. Am. a.* jack; '**~nstreich** *m*, '**~nstück** *n* knavish trick.

Bubikopf ['bu:bikɔpf] *m* bobbed hair.

bübisch ['by:biʃ] knavish.

Buch [bu:x] *n* (1[2]) book; *~ Papier* quire; *s. Dreh≗*; '**~besprechung** *f* book review; '**~binder** *m* (book-) binder; **~binde'rei** *f* bookbinder's (work)shop, *Am.* (book)bindery; *Gewerbe*: bookbinding; '**~druck** *m* letterpress printing; '**~drucker** *m* (letterpress) printer; **~drucke'rei** *f* printing-office, *Am. a.* print(ing) shop; *Gewerbe*: printing (of books).

Buch|e ['bu:xə] *f* (15) beech(-tree); **~ecker** ['~ʔɛkər] *f* (15) beech-nut.

buchen ['bu:xən] (25) ✝ enter, post; *e-n Platz usw.*: book; *fig. als Erfolg usw.*: count as.

Bücher|-abschluß ✝ ['by:çər-] *m* balancing of the books; '**~brett** *n* bookshelf; **~ei** [~'raɪ] *f* (16) library; '**~freund** *m* book-lover, bibliophile; '**~gutschein** *m* book token; '**~kunde** *f* bibliography; '**~mappe** *f* satchel; '**~narr** *m* bibliomaniac; '**~regal** *n* bookshelf; '**~revisor** *m* auditor, accountant; '**~schrank** *m* bookcase; '**~stand** *m* bookstall, *Am.* bookstand; '**~stütze** *f* book-end; '**~weisheit** *f* book-learning; '**~wurm** *m* bookworm.

'**Buch|fink** *m* chaffinch; '**~forderungen** ✝ *f/pl.* book claims; '**~führer** *m*, '**~halter** *m* book-keeper; '**~führung** *f*, '**~haltung** *f* book-keeping; *doppelte ~* book-keeping by double entry; '**~gemeinschaft** *f* book club; **~halterei** [~'raɪ] *f* (16) book-keeping department; '**~halterin** *f* (lady) book-keeper; '**~handel** *m* booktrade; '**~händler** *m* bookseller; '**~handlung** *f* bookseller's shop, bookshop, *Am. a.* bookstore; '**~hülle** *f* book wrapper; '**~macher** *m* bookmaker; '**~messe** *f* book fair; '**≗mäßig** according to the books; '**~prüfer** *m* auditor, accountant.

Buchsbaum ['buksbaum] *m* box (-tree).

Buchse ⊕ ['buksə] *f* bush(ing); (*Muffe*) sleeve; (*Fett≗*) cup; ⚡ socket.

Büchse ['byksə] *f* (15) box, case; *aus Blech*: tin (box), *Am.* can; *für Salben*: pot, jar; (*Gewehr*) rifle; '**~nfleisch** *n* tinned (*Am.* canned) meat; '**~nmacher** *m* gunsmith;

'**~n-öffner** *m* (7) tin-opener, *Am.* can opener.
Buchstabe ['bu:xʃtɑ:bə] *m* (13[1]) letter; (*Schriftzug*) character; *typ.* type; *großer* (*kleiner*) ~ capital (small) letter; '**~nrätsel** *n* logogriph; '**~nrechnung** *f* algebra; '**~nschloß** *n* puzzle lock.
buchstabieren [~ʃta'bi:rən] spell; (*mühsam lesen*) spell out.
buchstäblich ['~ʃtɛ:pliç] literal.
Bucht [buxt] *f* (16) inlet, bay; *kleine*: creek.
'**Buch|-umschlag** *m* (book) wrapper *od.* jacket; '**~ung** *f* booking, entry.
'**Buchweizen** *m* buckwheat.
Buckel ['bukəl] *m* **1.** (7) hump (-back); F (*Rücken*) back; *e-n* ~ *machen* stoop, *Katze*: put up its back; **2.** *Verzierung*: boss, stud.
'**buck(e)lig** humpbacked; **≈e** ['~(ə)-ligə] *m, f* (18) hunchback.
bücken ['bykən] (25) (*mst sich*) bend, stoop; *sich vor j-m* ~ bow to, *kriecherisch*: cringe to.
Bück(l)ing[1] ['byk(l)iŋ] *m* (3[1]) bloater, red herring, kipper.
'**Bückling**[2] *m* (3[1]) bow, obeisance.
buddeln F ['budəln] (29) dig.
Bude ['bu:də] *f* (15) stall, booth, F (*Hütte*) shanty, shack; (*Studenten≈*) pad, digs *pl.*; (*Laden*) shop.
Budget [by'dʒe:] *n* (11) budget; *im* ~ *vorsehen* budget for.
Büfett [by'fe:, by'fɛt] *n* (3) buffet, sideboard; (*Schenktisch*) bar, *Am.* counter; *kaltes* ~ cold buffet; **~ier** [byfɛt'je:] *m* barkeeper, barman, *Am.* bartender.
Büffel ['byfəl] *m* (7) buffalo; '**≈n** F *v/i.* (29) grind, *sl.* mug, *Am.* F bone; (*a. v/t.*) cram, *sl.* swot.
Büffler F ['byflər] *m* (7) *sl.* swot.
Bug [bu:k] *m* (3[3]) bow (*a.* ⚓), bend; (*Knie≈*) hock; (*Vorder≈*) shoulder.
Bügel ['by:gəl] *m* (7) bow; *s. Kleider≈*, *Steig≈*; '**~-eisen** *n* flat-iron; '**~falte** *f* crease; '**≈frei** non-iron; '**≈n** (29) *Wäsche*: iron; *Kleid*: press.
Bugsier|dampfer [buk'si:r-] *m* (steam-)tug; **≈en** tow; *fig.* steer, manœuvre, *Am.* maneuver.
Bugspriet ⚓ ['bu:kʃpri:t] *n* (3) bowsprit.
Buhle ['bu:lə] *m* (13), *f* (15) lover; *jetzt mst b.s.* paramour; '**≈n** (25) *um et.*: court, woo; *mit j-m*: sleep (*od.* wanton) with; *um j-s Gunst* ~ curry favo(u)r with a p.
Buhmann ['bu:-] *m fig.* bogeyman.
Buhne ['bu:nə] *f* (15) groyne.
Bühne ['by:nə] *f* (15) scaffold; (*Redner≈*) *od.* ⊕ platform; *thea.* stage; *fig.* scene, arena; *zur* ~ *gehen* go on the stage; '**~n-anweisung** *f* stage direction; '**~n-arbeiter** *m* stage-hand; '**~n-ausstattung** *f*, '**~nbild** *n* scene(ry); '**~nbe-arbeitung** *f* dramatization; '**~nbildner(in** *f*) *m* stage designer; '**~ndichter** *m* playwright, dramatist; '**≈nfähig** stage-worthy; '**~nfassung** *f* stage version; '**~nkünstler(in** *f*) *m* stage actor (*f* actress); '**~nlaufbahn** *f* theatrical career; '**~nleiter** *m* stage manager; '**~nmaler** *m* scene-painter; '**~nrecht** *n* dramatic right; '**~nschriftsteller** *m s. Bühnendichter*; '**~nstück** *n* stageplay.
buk [bu:k] *pret. v. backen.*
Bukett [bu'kɛt] *n* (3) bouquet.
Bulette [bu'lɛtə] *f* (15) meatball, rissole, hamburger.
Bulgar|e [bul'gɑ:rə] *m* (13), **~in** *f* (16[1]) Bulgarian; **≈isch** Bulgarian.
'**Bull|-auge** *n* bull's eye, porthole; '**~dogge** *f* bulldog.
Bulle[1] ['bulə] *m* (13) bull; *sl. die* ~*n* (*Polizei*) the fuzz *pl.*; '~[2] *eccl. f* (15) bull; '**~nbeißer** *m* (7) bulldog.
bullern ['bulərn] (29) rumble; *Feuer im Ofen*: roar.
bum(m)! [bum] boom!, bang!
Bumerang ['bu:məraŋ] *m* (3[1]) boomerang.
Bummel F ['buməl] *m* (7) (*Spaziergang*) stroll; (*Bierreise usw.*) spree, binge; *e-n* ~ *machen* go for a stroll; *auf den* ~ *gehen* go on the spree; **~ei** [~'laɪ] *f* (16) dawdling, loafing; (*Nachlässigkeit*) slackness; '**≈ig** dawdling; careless; '**≈n** (29) (*müßig gehen*) loaf; (*trödeln*) dawdle; (*gemächlich gehen*) stroll, saunter; (*Berufsarbeit aussetzen*) (be) idle; (*sich amüsieren*) be on the spree; '**~streik** *m* go-slow; '**~zug** *m* slow train.
'**Bummler** *m* (7) loafer.
bums! [bums] bang!; **≈** *m* bang; '**~en** bang, bump; V ball, have it off; '**≈lokal** F *n sl.* dive.
Bund [bunt] **1.** *n* (3, *nach Zahlen im pl. inv.*) bundle; *Schlüssel*: bunch; *Heu, Stroh* (*als Maß*): truss; **2.** *m* (3[3]) (*Band*) band, tie; *Schnei-*

derei: waistband; *fig.* union (*a. Ehe*); (*Bündnis*) alliance; *pol. a.* league, federation, confederacy; (*Bundesregierung*) Federal Government; *bsd. eccl.* covenant; *im ~e mit* in league with.

Bündel ['byndəl] *n* (7) bundle; '**⁀n** (29) bundle (up); '**⁀weise** by bundles.

'**Bundes...** *in Zssgn* federal; '**~bahn** *f* Federal Railway(s *pl.*); '**~gebiet** *n* Federal Territory; '**~genosse** *m* confederate, ally; '**~kanzler** *m* Federal Chancellor; '**~liga** *f* National League; '**~präsident** *m* President of the Federal Republic; '**~rat** *m* Federal Council; *parl.* Upper House; '**~regierung** *f* Federal Government; '**~republik** *f* **Deutschland** Federal Republic of Germany; '**~staat** *m einzelner*: federal state; *Gesamtheit der einzelnen*: (con)federation; '**~straße** *f* Federal Highway; '**~tag** *m* Lower House (of the Federal Parliament); '**~trainer** *m* national coach; *der neue ~* Germany's new coach; '**~wehr** ⚔ *f* Federal Armed Forces *pl.*; '**⁀weit** nationwide.

bündig ['byndiç] (*gültig*) binding; (*überzeugend*) conclusive; *Stil, Rede*: concise, terse; *kurz und ~* succinctly; '**⁀keit** *f* conclusiveness; conciseness.

Bündnis ['byntnis] *n* (4[1]) alliance; '**⁀frei** nonaligned; '**~freiheit** *f* nonalignment.

Bungalow ['buŋgalo] *m* (11) bungalow, *Am.* ranch house.

Bunker ['buŋkər] *m* (7) ⚓ (*Kohlenvorratsraum*) bunker; (*Schutzraum*) shelter, refuge, ⚔ bunker, pillbox; ⚓ *für U-Boote*: pen.

bunt [bunt] colo(u)rful (*a. fig.*); (*farbig*) (many)colo(u)red; (*~gefleckt*) variegated; (*scheckig*) motley; (*lebhaft gefärbt*) gay; (*grell*) gaudy; *Glas*: stained; *gewürfelt*: chequered; (*gemischt*) motley, mixed (*crowd etc.*); (*abwechslungsreich*) varied; *~er Abend, ~e Unterhaltung* variety show; *~e Reihe machen* pair off ladies and gentlemen; *er treibt es zu ~* he goes too far; *es ging ~ zu* there were fine goings-on; '**⁀druck** *m* colo(u)r-printing; (*Bild*) chromolithograph; '**~fleckig** spotted, (*a. fig.*) motley; '**⁀metall** *n* nonferrous metal; '**⁀stift** *m* colo(u)red pencil, crayon.

Bürde ['byrdə] *f* (15) burden (*a. fig.*: *für j-n* to), load.

Burg [burk] *f* (16) castle; (*Festung, a. fig.*) citadel, stronghold.

Bürge ['byrgə] *m* (13) bail, surety; guarantor (*a. fig.*); *e-n ~n stellen* give (*od.* offer) bail, *Am. a.* post bond; '**⁀n** (25) *für j-n*: go bail for, stand surety for, *Am.* bond *a p.*; *für et.*: guarantee (*od.* vouch for) a th.

Bürger ['~gər] *m* (7), '**~in** *f* citizen; (*Stadtbewohner*) townsman, *f* townswoman, *pl.* townsfolk; (*Einwohner*) inhabitant; (*~licher*) commoner; '**~initiative** *f* civic action group; '**~krieg** *m* civil war; '**~kunde** *f* civics *sg.*; '**⁀lich** civil; middle-class; (*nichtadlig*) common, untitled; *Küche usw.*: plain; *~e Ehrenrechte n/pl.* civic rights *pl.*; *~es Gesetzbuch* code of civil law; '**~liche** *m, f* (18) commoner; '**~meister** *m* mayor; *in Deutschland*: burgomaster; '**~meister-amt** *n* mayor's office; '**~pflicht** *f* civic duty; '**~recht** *n* civic rights *pl.*; freedom of a city; '**~rechtler**(**in** *f*) *m* civil rights activist; '**~rechtsbewegung** *f* civil rights movement; '**~schaft** *f* (16) citizens *pl.*; '**~sinn** *m* public spirit; '**~stand** *m* middle classes *pl.*; '**~steig** *m* pavement, *Am.* sidewalk; '**~tum** *n* (1[2], *o. pl.*) citizenship; *konkret*: middle classes *pl.*; *contp.* bourgeoisie; '**~wehr** *f* militia.

'**Burg|friede**(**n**) *m* public peace; *pol.* truce; '**~graf** *m* burgrave.

Bürgschaft ['byrkʃaft] *f* (16) (*Sicherheit*) security, surety, guarantee; *im Strafrecht*: bail; *~ leisten od. übernehmen* give (*od.* provide) security, stand surety; *im Strafrecht*: go bail (*Bürge*), give bail (*Angeklagter*).

Burgunder [bur'gundər] *m* (7) Burgundian; *Wein*: burgundy.

'**Burgverlies** *n* (4) keep, dungeon.

burlesk [bur'lɛsk], **⁀e** *f* burlesque.

Büro [by'roː] *n* (11) office; **~-angestellte** *m, f* clerk, office worker; **~-automatisierung** *f* office automation; **~be-amte** *m* clerk; **~bedarf**(**s-artikel** *m/pl.*) *m* office supplies *pl.*; **~chef** *m* head clerk; **~gehilfe** *m*, **~gehilfin** *f* office junior, clerical assistant; **~klammer** *f* (paper)clip; **~krat** [~ro'kraːt] *m* (12) red-tapist, bureaucrat; **~kratie** [~kra'tiː] *f* (15) red-tapism, bureaucracy; ²**kratisch** [~ˈkrɑːtiʃ] bureaucratic; ~**kratismus** [~kraˈtismus] *m* bureaucratism; ~**maschine** [by-ˈroː-] *f* office machine; ~**möbel** *n/pl.* office furniture; ~**personal** *n* office personnel; ~**stunden** *f/pl.* office-hours, *Am. a.* duty hours; ~**technik** *f* office technology; ~**vorsteher** *m s. Bürochef.*

Bursch(e) [ˈburʃə] *m* (13) boy, lad, fellow; (*Kerl*) *a. freundschaftlich*: chap, *Am.* guy; ⚔ orderly, batman; *univ.* senior man, *weitS.* student.

burschikos [~ʃiˈkoːs] pert.

Bürste [ˈbyrstə] *f* (15), ˈ²**n** (26) brush; ˈ~**n-abzug** *typ. m* brush-proof; ˈ~**nbinder** *m* brush-maker; ˈ~**nhaarschnitt** *m* crew cut.

Bürzel [ˈbyrtsəl] *m* (7) rump; *am Brathuhn usw.*: parson's nose.

Bus [bus] F *m* (4¹) bus; ˈ~**haltestelle** *f* bus-stop.

Busch [buʃ] *m* (3² *u.* ³) bush (*a. Urwald*); (*kleines Gehölz*) copse, thicket; *s. Büschel*; *bei j-m auf den ~ klopfen* sound a p.; *sich* (*seitwärts*) *in die Büsche schlagen* slip away.

Büschel [ˈbyʃəl] *n* (7) bunch; *Haare usw.*: tuft, wisp.

ˈ**Busch|hemd** *n* jacket-shirt; ˈ~**holz** *n* underwood; ˈ²**ig** bushy; *Haar*: shaggy; ˈ~**klepper** *m* bush-ranger; ˈ~**werk** *n* bushes *pl.*, *Am.* brush; ˈ~**windrös-chen** *n* wood-anemone.

Busen [ˈbuːzən] *m* (6) bosom, breast; (*Meer*²) bay, gulf; ˈ~**freund** (**-in** *f*) *m* bosom-friend.

Bussard [ˈbusart] *m* (3) buzzard.

Buße [ˈbuːsə] *f* (15) penance; (*Sühne*) atonement; (*Geldstrafe*) fine; ~ *tun s. büßen.*

büßen [ˈbyːsən] (27) do penance (for), atone (for); *Verbrechen*: expiate; *mit Geld*: be fined for; *fig.* pay (*od.* suffer) for.

ˈ**Büßer** *m* (7), ˈ~**in** *f* (16¹) penitent; ˈ~**bank** *f* penitent bench.

ˈ**bußfertig** penitent, repentant; ˈ²**keit** *f* penitence, repentance.

ˈ**Bußgeld** *n* fine; ˈ~**bescheid** *m* notice of fine due; ˈ~**katalog** *m* list of fines.

Bussole [buˈsoːlə] *f* (15) compass.

ˈ**Buß|predigt** *f* penitential sermon; ˈ~**tag** *m* day of repentance.

Büste [ˈbystə] *f* (15) bust; ˈ~**nhalter** *m* brassière, F bra; ˈ~**nhebe** *f* uplift brassière.

Butan ⚗ [buˈtaːn] *n* (11, *o. pl.*) butane.

Butt [but] *m* (3) (*Fisch*) butt.

Butte [ˈbutə] *f*, **Bütte** [ˈbytə] *f* (15) tub, vat.

Büttel [ˈbytəl] *m* (7) beadle, bailiff.

Büttenpapier [ˈbytənpapiːr] *n handgeschöpft*: hand-made paper; (*Werks*²) mo(u)ld paper.

Butter [ˈbutər] *f* (15) butter; F *alles in ~!* everything's okay!; ˈ~**blume** *f* buttercup; ˈ~**brot** *n* (slice of) bread and butter; *fig. für ein ~* for a song; ˈ~**brotpapier** *n* greaseproof paper; ˈ~**dose** *f* butter-dish; ˈ~**faß** *n* churn; ˈ~**milch** *f* butter-milk; ˈ²**n** *v/t. u. v/i.* (29) churn; (*bestreichen*) (spread with) butter.

Button [ˈbatən] *m* (11) badge.

Butzen [ˈbutsən] *m* (6) *im Geschwür, Obst usw.*: core; ˈ~**scheibe** *f* bull's-eye pane.

Byzantin|er [bytsanˈtiːnər] *m* (7), ~**erin** *f*, ²**isch** Byzantine; ~**ismus** [~tiˈnismus] *m* (16, *o. pl.*) *fig.* Byzantinism.

C

C [tseː], **c** *n inv.* C, c; ♪ C.

Café [kaˈfeː] *n* (11) coffee-house, café.

Camping|-ausrüstung [ˈkɛmpiŋ-] *f* camping gear; ˈ~**bus** *m* camper; ˈ~**platz** *m* camping site, campsite; *für Wohnwagen*: caravan site.

Canaille [kaˈnaljə] *f* (15) (*Pöbel*) rabble, mob; (*Schurke*) rascal.

Cape [keːp] *n* (11) cape.

C-Dur ♪ *n* C major.

Cellist [tʃɛˈlist] *m* (12) cellist.

Cello [ˈtʃɛlo] *n* (11) cello.

Cellophan [tsɛloˈfaːn] *n* cellophane.

Celsius [ˈtsɛlzjus] *m* (*inv.*, *o. pl.*)

(degree) centigrade, Celsius (*abbr.* °C).
Cembalo [ˈtʃɛmbalo] *n* (11) harpsichord.
Ces ♪ [tsɛs] *n* C flat.
Chagrinleder [ʃaˈgrɛ̃-] *n* shagreen.
Chaiselongue [ʃɛːz(ə)ˈlɔ̃(g)] *f* (11¹) lounge-chair.
Chamäleon [kaˈmɛːleɔn] *n* (11) chameleon.
Champagner [ʃamˈpanjər] *m* (7) champagne.
Champignon [ˈʃampinjɔ̃] *m* (11) (field) mushroom.
Chance [ˈʃɑ̃sə] *f* (15) chance; *j-m eine ~ geben* give a p. a chance (F a break); *die ~n sind gleich* the odds are even; **ˈ~ngleichheit** *f* equal opportunities *pl.*
changieren [ʃɑ̃ˈʒiːrən] *Seide*: be shot; **~d** shot.
Chaos [ˈkɑːɔs] *n inv.* chaos.
chaotisch [kaˈoːtiʃ] chaotic.
Charakter [kaˈraktər] *m* (3¹, *pl. Charaktere* [~ˈteːrə]) character; **~bild** *n* portrait; **~eigenschaft** *f* characteristic; **2bildend** *adj.*, **~bildung** *f* character-building; **~fehler** *m* defect in *a p.'s* character, weakness; **2fest** of firm character; **2iˈsieren** characterize; **~iˈsierung** *f*, **~istik** [~ˈristik] *f* (16) characterization; ⊕, ⚕ characteristic; **2istisch** [~ˈristiʃ] characteristic (*für* of); **~kopf** *m* fine head; **2lich** (*adv.* in) character; **2los** unprincipled; (*schwach*) weak, spineless; **~losigkeit** *f* want of principles; **~schwäche** *f* weakness of character; **~stärke** *f* strength of character; **2voll** full of personality; **~zug** *m* characteristic, feature, trait.
Charge [ˈʃarʒə] *f* (15) *mil.* post, rank; *P.*: (*bsd.* non-commissioned) officer; *thea.* (small) character part; *metall.* charge.
Charlatan [ˈʃarlatan] *m s. Scharlatan.*
charm|ant [ʃarˈmant] charming; **2e** [ʃarm] *m* (11, *o.pl.*) charm, grace.
Charter [ˈʃartər] *f inv.* charter; **ˈ~flug** *m* charter(ed) flight; **ˈ~flugzeug** *n*, **ˈ~maschine** *f* charter plane; **ˈ2n** (29) charter.
Chassis [ʃaˈsiː] *n* (11) chassis.
Chauff|eur [ʃɔˈføːr] *m* (3¹) chauffeur, driver; **2ieren** [~ˈfiːrən] drive.
Chaussee [ʃoˈseː] *f* (15) high road, *Am.* highway.
Chauvi F [ˈʃoːvi] *m* (11) male chauvinist (pig); **~nismus** [ʃoviˈnismus] *m* (16) chauvinism, *Brt. a.* jingoism; **~ˈnist(in** *f*) *m* chauvinist, *Brt. a.* jingo; **2ˈnistisch** chauvinistic.
Chef [ʃɛf] *m* (11) chief; head; ✝ principal, employer; F governor, *bsd. Am.* boss; **ˈ~-arzt** *m* medical superintendent; **ˈ~dirigent** *m* principal conductor; **ˈ~-etage** *f* executive floor; **ˈ~-ideologe** *m* chief ideologist; **ˈ~pilot** *m* chief pilot; **ˈ~redakteur** *m* chief editor; **ˈ~sekretärin** *f* director's secretary.
Chemie [çeˈmiː] *f* (15) chemistry; **~faser** *f* synthetic fib|re, *Am.* -er; **~müll** *m* chemical waste.
Chemikalien [çemiˈkɑːljən] *f/pl.* (15) chemicals.
Chemiker [ˈçeːmikər] *m* (7) (analytical) chemist.
chemisch [ˈçeːmiʃ] chemical; *~ reinigen* dry-clean.
Chicorée [ˈʃikore] *f*, *m* (11, *o. pl.*) chicory.
Chiffre [ˈʃifrə] *f* (15) cipher, code; **ˈ~-anzeige** *f* box-number advertisement; **ˈ~nummer** *f* box-number; **ˈ~schrift** *f* cryptography.
chiffrieren [ʃiˈfriːrən] (en)cipher, (en)code.
China|kohl [ˈçiːna-] *m* Chinese cabbage; **ˈ~rinde** *f* Peruvian bark.
Chines|e [çiˈneːzə] *m* (13), **~in** *f* (16¹), **2isch** Chinese.
Chinin [çiˈniːn] *n* (11, *o. pl.*) quinine.
Chintz [tʃints] *m* (3) chintz.
Chip [ˈtʃip] *m* (11) (*Kartoffel2*) crisp, *Am.* potato chip; (*Spiel2*), *Computer*: chip.
Chirurg [çiˈrurk] *m* (12) surgeon; **~ie** [~ˈgiː] *f* (15) surgery; (*Station*) surgical ward; **2isch** [~ˈrurgiʃ] surgical.
Chlor [kloːr] *n* (3²) chlorine; **ˈ2en** chlorinate; **~ˈkalium** *n* potassium chloride; **ˈ~kalk** *m*, **~ˈkalzium** *n* chloride of lime, calcium chloride.
Chloroform [kloroˈfɔrm] *n* (11), **2ieren** [~ˈmiːrən] chloroform.
Chlorophyll [kloroˈfyl] *n* (11, *o. pl.*) chlorophyll.
ˈChlorsäuresalz *n* chlorate.
Choke [ˈtʃoːk] *mot. m* (11) choke.
Cholera [ˈkoːləra] *f inv.* cholera.
cholerisch [koˈleːriʃ] choleric.
Cholesterin ⚗ [kolɛsteˈriːn] *n* (11, *o. pl.*) cholesterol; **~spiegel** *m* cholesterol level.

Chor [koːr] *m* (3³) chorus; (*Sänger*≈) choir; ⚠ *m* (*od. n*) chancel, choir; *im ~ a. fig.* in chorus.
Choral [koˈrɑːl] *m* (3¹ *u.* ³) hymn, choral(e).
ˈ**Chor-altar** *m* high altar.
Choreograph [koreoˈgrɑːf] *m* (12), **~in** *f* (16¹) choreographer; **~ie** [~-graˈfiː] *f* (15) choreography.
Chor|gang [ˈkoːr-] *m* aisle; ˈ**~gesang** *m* choral singing (*od.* song); chorus; **~gestühl** [ˈ~gəʃtyːl] *n* (3) choir-stalls *pl.*; ˈ**~hemd** *n* surplice; ˈ**~herr** *m* canon.
Chorist [koˈrist] *m* (12), **~in** *f* (16¹) chorister; *thea.* chorus-singer.
Chor|knabe [ˈkoːr-] *m* choir-boy; ˈ**~sänger** *m* chorus-singer; ˈ**~stuhl** *m* stall.
Christ [krist] **1.** *m* (3¹) Christ; **2.** *m* (12), ˈ**~in** *f* (16¹) Christian.
Christ... *s. Weihnachts...*
ˈ**Christen|heit** *f* (16) Christendom; ˈ**~tum** *n* (1²) Christianity; ˈ**~verfolgung** *f* persecution of Christians.
ˈ**Christkind** *n* Infant Jesus, Christ-child.
ˈ**christlich** Christian.
Chrom [kroːm] *n* (3¹) (*Metall*) chromium; (*Farbe*) chrome.
chromatisch [kroˈmɑːtiʃ] chromatic.
chromgelb [ˈkroːm-] chrome yellow.
Chromosom [kromoˈzoːm] *n* (5²) chromosome.
ˈ**Chromsäure** *f* chromic acid.
Chronik [ˈkroːnik] *f* (16) chronicle.
ˈ**chronisch** chronic.
Chronist [kroˈnist] *m* (12) chronicler.
Chronolog|ie [~noloˈgiː] *f* (15) chronology; ≈**isch** [~ˈloːgiʃ] chronological.
Chronometer [~noˈmeːtər] *n* (7) chronometer.
circa [ˈtsirka] about, circa.
Cis ♪ [tsis] *n* C sharp.
Claque *thea.* [ˈklakə] *f* (15) claque.
Clique [ˈklikə] *f* (15) clique, coterie; ˈ**~nwesen** *n* cliquism.
Clou [kluː] *m* (11) highlight. (*Höhepunkt*) climax; (*Pointe*) point.
Cod|e [koːt] *m* (11) code; ≈**ieren** [koˈdiːrən] (en)code; **~ierung** *f* coding.
Coeur [køːr] *n Karten*: heart(s *pl.*).
Collaborateur *pol.* [kɔlaboraˈtøːr] *m* (3¹) collaborationist.
Computer [kɔmˈpjuːtər] *m* (7) computer; ≈**gesteuert** computer-controlled; ≈**isieren** [~pjutəriˈziːrən] computerize; **~kasse** *f* computerised cash register; **~spiel** *n* computer game.
Conférencier [kõferɑ̃ˈsjeː] *m* compère, *Am.* master of ceremonies (*abbr.* M.C.); *als ~ leiten* compère (*Am.* emcee) *a show.*
Container [kɔnˈteːnər] *m* (7) container; ≈**isieren** containerize; **~schiff** *n* container ship.
Contergan [kɔntɛrˈgɑːn] *n* (11, *o. pl.*) thalidomide; **~kind** *n* thalidomide child.
Couch [kaʊtʃ] *f* (16) couch; ˈ**~garnitur** *f* lounge (*od.* three-piece) suite; ˈ**~tisch** *m* coffee table.
Coupé [kuˈpeː] *n* (11) 🚃 compartment; (*Wagen*) coupé (*a. mot.*).
Couplet [~ˈpleː] *n* (11) comic (*od.* music-hall) song; *politisches usw.*: topical song.
Coupon [kuˈpõ] *m* (11) coupon.
Cour [kuːr] *f bei Hofe*: levee; *j-m die ~ machen* court; **~age** [kuˈrɑːʒə] *f inv.* courage.
Cousin [kuˈzɛ̃] *m* (11), **~e** [~ˈziːnə] *f* (15) cousin.
Creme [ˈkrɛːm(ə)] *f* (11¹) cream (*a. fig.*); ˈ≈**farben** cream-colo(u)red; ˈ**~torte** *f* cream tart.
Cutaway [ˈkatəveː] *m*, F **Cut** *m* (11) morning coat, cutaway.

D

D [deː], **d** *n* D, d; ♪ D.
da [dɑː] **1.** *adv. räumlich*: (*dort*) there; (*hier*) here; *zeitlich*: then; *in der Erzählung*: now; *du ~* you there; *der Mann ~* that man there; *~ drüben* over there; *~ sein* be there (*vgl. dasein*); (*zur Hand*) be at hand; (*angekommen*) have (*od.* be)

arrived; ~ *bin ich* here I am; *dein Vater war* ~ was here; *ist j.* ~*gewesen?* has anybody called?; *wieder* ~ here (*od.* back) again, back once more; ~ *und* ~ at such and such a place; *von* ~ *an od. ab räumlich*: from there; *zeitlich*: from that time on; *was läßt sich* ~ *machen?* what can be done in such a case?; *wer* ~*?* who is (⚔ goes) there?; *nichts* ~*!* nothing of the kind!, on no account!; ~ *haben wir's!* there we are!; **2.** *cj. Zeit*: when; while; *Grund*: as; (*da ja*) since; ~ *nun*, ~ *doch* now since, since indeed.

dabei [daˈbaɪ] near by, close by; (*anwesend*) there, present; (*überdies*) besides, moreover, as well; (*noch dazu*; *trotzdem*) yet, for all that; (*währenddessen*) all the time, in doing so; (*bei diesem Anlaß*) on the occasion, then; ~ *sein bei der Arbeit*: be at it; ~ *sein zu inf.* be about to *inf.*, be on the point of *ger.*; *darf ich mit* ~ *sein?* may I join the party?; *ich bin* ~*!* agreed!, count me in!, F I'm on; *was ist denn* ~*?* what harm is there in it?; ~ *bleiben* persist; *s. a. bleiben*; **~sein** be present (*od.* there), take part; **~stehen** stand by.

ˈ**dableiben** (sn) stay.

da capo [da ˈkɑːpo] da capo, encore; ~ *rufen* encore; *s. Dakapo.*

Dach [dax] *n* (1²) roof; *mot. a.* top; *fig.* shelter, house; *unter* ~ *und Fach* under cover, *fig.* all settled; *fig.* F *eins aufs* ~ *kriegen* cop it; ˈ**~balken** *m* roof-tree; rafter; ˈ**~boden** *m* loft; ˈ**~decker** *m* roofer; (*Ziegeldecker*) tiler; (*Schieferdecker*) slater; ˈ**~fenster** *n* dormer-window; ˈ**~first** *m* ridge (of a roof); ˈ**~garten** *m* roof-garden; ˈ**~gepäckträger** *mot. m* roof rack; ˈ**~geschoß** *n* attic stor(e)y; loft; ˈ**~gesellschaft** ⚕ *f* holding company; ˈ**~himmel** *mot. m* roof lining; ˈ**~kammer** *f* attic, garret; ˈ**~-organisation** *f* umbrella organization; ˈ**~pappe** *f* roofing (felt); ˈ**~pfanne** *f* pantile; ˈ**~reiter** *m* (ridge-)turret; ˈ**~rinne** *f* gutter, eaves *pl.*

Dachs [daks] *m* (4) badger.

ˈ**Dach|schiefer** *m* roofing slate; ˈ**~schindel** *f* roof shingle.

Dachshund *m* dachshund.

ˈ**Dach|sparren** *m* rafter; ˈ**~stube** *f* attic, garret; ˈ**~stuhl** *m* roof-truss.

dachte [ˈdaxtə] *pret. v. denken.*

ˈ**Dach|traufe** *f* eaves *pl.*; ˈ**~werk** *n* roofing; ˈ**~wohnung** *f* attic flat; ˈ**~ziegel** *m* (roofing) tile.

Dackel [ˈdakəl] *m* (7) dachshund.

ˈ**dadurch** *örtlich*: through that *od.* it; *Mittel*: through (*od.* by) it; thereby; by this means, thus; ~ *daß* ... by *ger.*

dafür [daˈfyːr] for that; for it *od.* them; (*als Ersatz*) in return (for it), in exchange; (*statt dessen*) instead of it; *ich kann nichts* ~ it is not my fault; ~ *sein* be in favo(u)r of it; (~ *stimmen*) vote for it; **2halten:** *nach meinem* 2 in my opinion, as I see it.

daˈgegen 1. *adv.* against that; against it; *Vergleich*: in comparison with it; *Tausch, Ersatz*: in return *od.* exchange (for it); (*anderseits*) on the other hand; *ich habe nichts* ~ I have no objection (to it), I don't mind; ~ *sein* be against it; (~ *stimmen*) vote against it; **2.** *cj. Gegensatz*: on the contrary, on the other hand.

daheim [~ˈhaɪm] at home; (*in der Heimat*) in one's own country; 2 *n* home.

daher [ˈdaːheːr, daˈheːr] from there; *Ursache*: hence; therefore; *bei Verben der Bewegung*: along.

daherum [ˈdaːhɛrum] thereabouts.

dahin [ˈdaːhin, daˈhin] there; to that place; (*vergangen*) gone, past, over; (*verloren*) gone, lost; *bei Verben bisweilen* = **weg...**: away; *bei Verben der Bewegung*: along; *j-n* ~ *bringen, daß* make a p. *do a th.*; *es* ~ *bringen, daß j. od. et.* ... cause a p. *od.* a th. to *inf.*; succeed in *ger.*; **~fliegen** [daˈhin-] (sn) fly along; *Zeit*: fly; **~gehen** (sn) walk along; *Zeit*: pass; (*sterben*) pass away; **~gehend** [ˈdaːhin-] to the effect (*that*); **~gestellt** [daˈhin-]: ~ *sein lassen* leave undecided; **~reden** speak thoughtlessly; **~siechen** *v/i.* (sn) waste away; **~stehen** remain to be seen.

daˈhinten back there.

daˈhinter behind it (*a. fig.*); **~kommen** (sn) find out (about it); **~machen** *od.* **~setzen:** *sich* ~ set to work, get down to it; **~stecken** be at the bottom of it.

Dakapo *n* repeat; encore; *s. da capo.*

damal|ig [ˈdaːmaːliç] of that time;

der ~e *Besitzer* the then owner; '~s then, at that time.

Damas|t [da'mast] *m* (3²), **2ten** damask; **2'zieren** *Stoff*: damask; *Stahl*: damascene.

Dambrett ['dɑːm-] *n* draught-bord, *Am.* checkerboard.

Dämchen ['dɛːmçən] *n* (6) damsel.

Dame ['dɑːmə] *f* (15) lady; *beim Tanz usw.*: partner; (*Karte*) queen; *s. ~spiel*; *im Damespiel*: king; *meine ~!* madam!; *meine ~n (und Herren)!* ladies (and gentlemen)!

'**Damen|besuch** *m* lady-visitor(s *pl.*); '**~binde** *f* sanitary towel (*Am.* napkin); '**~'doppel(spiel)** *n Tennis*: *the* women's doubles *pl.*; '**~'-einzel(-spiel)** *n Tennis*: *the* women's singles *pl.*; '**~friseur** *m* ladies' hairdresser; '**2haft** ladylike; '**~kleidung** *f* ladies' wear; '**~konfektion** *f* ladies' ready-made (*Am.* ready-to-wear) clothing; '**~mannschaft** *f Sport*: women's team; '**~schneider** *m* ladies' tailor; '**~toilette** *f* ladies' toilet (*Am.* restroom); '**~-unterwäsche** *f* ladies' underwear; *feine*: lingerie; '**~wahl** *f* ladies' choice; '**~welt** *f the* ladies *pl.*, *the* fair sex.

'**Damespiel** *n* draughts *sg.*, *Am.* checkers *sg.*

Damhirsch ['damhirʃ] *m* (3²) (fallow-)buck.

da'mit **1.** *adv.* with it; with that, by it *od.* this, thereby; **2.** *cj.* (in order) that *od.* to; *~ nicht* lest, (in order) that ... not; for fear that.

dämlich F ['dɛːmliç] stupid, silly.

Damm [dam] *m* (3²) dam; (*Deich*) dike; (*Bahn2, Fluß2*) embankment; (*Hafen2*) mole; (*Straßen2*) bank; (*Fahr2*) roadway; *anat.* perineum; *fig.* barrier; *fig.* F *j-n wieder auf den ~ bringen* set a p. on his feet again; *auf dem ~ sein* be all right, feel up to it; '**~bruch** *m* bursting of a dam; (*Lücke*) break in a dam.

dämmen ['dɛmən] (25) dam (up); *fig.* stem, check.

dämmer|ig ['dɛməriç] dusky; '**2licht** *n* twilight; *morgens*: grey dawn of day; *weitS.* dim light; '**~n** (29) grow dusky; *morgens*: dawn (*a. fig.*); *fig. es dämmert bei ihm* it is beginning to dawn on him; '**2schein** *m s. 2licht*; '**2schoppen** *m* F sundowner; '**2stunde** *f* hour of twilight; *in der ~* in the dusk of the evening; '**2ung** *f* (*Morgen2*) dawn(-ing); (*Abend2, Dämmerlicht*) twilight, dusk.

Dämon ['dɛːmɔn] *m* (8¹) demon; **2isch** [dɛ'moːniʃ] demoniac(al).

Dampf [dampf] *m* (3³) steam; *weitS.* vapo(u)r; (*Rauch*) smoke; '**~bad** *n* steam-bath; '**~boot** *n* steamboat; '**~bügeleisen** *n* steam iron; '**~druck** *m* steam-pressure; '**2en** (25) steam; F (*rauchen*) smoke.

dämpfen ['dɛmpfən] (25) (*abschwächen*) damp; *Farbe, Ton, Licht*: soften (down), subdue; *Feuer*: quench; *Stoß, Schall*: deaden; ✈ stabilize; (*mit Dampf behandeln*; *im Dampfbad kochen*) steam; *mit gedämpfter Stimme* in an undertone.

'**Dampfer** *m* (7) steamer.

'**Dämpfer** *m* (7) damper (*a. am Klavier*); ♪ *bsd. für Geige*: mute; *Radio*: baffle; *Kernphysik*: moderator; *s. Schall2, Stoß2*; *fig. j-m e-n ~ aufsetzen* damp a p.'s enthusiasm.

'**Dampfheizung** *f* steam-heating.

'**dampfig** steamy.

'**dämpfig** (*schwül*) sultry; *vet.* broken-winded.

'**Dampf|kessel** *m* (steam-)boiler; '**~kochtopf** *m* pressure cooker; '**~kraft** *f* steam power; '**~maschine** *f* steam-engine; '**~nudel** *f* yeast dumpling; '**~schiff** *n* steamer, steamship, steamboat; *vor dem Schiffsnamen*: S. S.; '**~schiffahrt** *f* steam navigation.

Dämpfung ['dɛmpfuŋ] *f s. dämpfen*: damping *usw.*; (*a. fig.*) suppression; ✈ stabilization; '**~sflosse** ✈ *f* stabilizer.

'**Dampfwalze** *f* steam-roller.

Damwild ['damvilt] *n* fallow-deer.

da'nach after that *od.* it; (*nachher*) afterwards; (*demgemäß*) accordingly, according to that; *er trägt Verlangen ~* he has a desire for it; *er sieht ganz ~ aus* he looks very much like it; *es ist aber auch ~* don't ask what it is like.

Dän|e ['dɛːnə] *m* (13), '**~in** *f* Dane.

daneben [da'neːbən] beside (*od.* near) it, next to it *od.* that; (*außerdem*) besides; (*gleichzeitig*) at the same time; **~gehen** (sn) miss (the mark); *fig.* go amiss; **~liegen** *fig.* (*sich irren*) be off beam; **~treffen** miss (the mark).

dang [daŋ] *pret. v. dingen.*
daniederliegen [~'niːdərliːgən]: (*krank*) ~ be laid up (*an dat.* with); *Handel usw.*: languish, stagnate.
dänisch ['dɛːniʃ] Danish.
Dank [daŋk] *m* (3) thanks *pl.*; (*~barkeit*) gratitude; (*Lohn*) reward; *j-m ~ sagen* thank a p., return thanks to a p.; *j-m ~ wissen für* be obliged to a p. for; *Gott sei ~!* thank God!; *vielen (od. schönen) ~!* many thanks!, *Am.* F thanks a lot!; *zum ~* by way of thanks, in reward (*für* for); *iro. das ist der (ganze) ~ dafür!* that's all the thanks one gets!; *2 seiner Güte* owing (*od.* [*a. iro.*] thanks) to his kindness; **'~-adresse** *f* vote of thanks.
'dankbar thankful, grateful (*j-m* to a p.; *für* for); (*lohnend*) profitable; (*befriedigend*) *Aufgabe*: rewarding; *ich wäre Ihnen ~ für* I will thank you for; **'2keit** *f* gratitude.
'danken *v/i.* thank (*j-m* a p.), return thanks; *~ für* (*ablehnen*) decline with thanks; *danke!* thank you!, F thanks!; *bei Ablehnung*: no thank you!; *danke schön!* many thanks!; *v/t. j-m et. ~* (*lohnen*) reward a p. for a th.; (*ver~*) owe a th. to a p.; *~d erhalten* received with thanks; **'~swert** meritorious.
'Dank|e-schön *n* (11, *o. pl.*) thank-you; **'~eswort** *n* (3) words *pl.* of thanks.
'Dank|gebet *n* thanksgiving (prayer); **'~gottesdienst** *m* thanksgiving service; **'~-opfer** *n* thank-offering; **~sagung** ['~zaːguŋ] *f* thanks; *eccl.* thanksgiving; **'~schreiben** *n* letter of thanks.
dann [dan] then; *~ und wann* now and then; **'~en: *von ~*** (from) thence; (*weg*) off, away.
daran [da'ran] at (*od.* by, in, on, to) that *od.* it; *sich ~ machen s. ~gehen*; *nahe ~ sein zu inf.* be on the point of *ger.*; *was liegt ~?* what does it matter?; *es ist nichts ~* there is nothing in it; *er ist gut (übel) ~* he is well (badly) off; *er tut gut ~ (zu inf.)* he does well (to *inf.*); *wie ist er mit Kleidern ~?* how is he off for clothes?; *ich bin (od. komme) ~* it is my turn; *Spiel*: *wer ist ~?* whose turn is it?; **~gehen** (sn) go (*od.* set) about it; *~ zu inf.* proceed to *inf.*; **~setzen** stake, risk.
darauf [~'rauf] *räumlich*: on it *od.* them, upon that; *zeitlich*: then, after that; *den Tag ~* the next day; *gleich ~* directly afterwards; *gerade ~ zu* straight towards it; **~folgend** following; **'darauf'hin** thereupon.
daraus [~'raus] from this *od.* that *od.* them; *~ folgt* hence it follows; *es kann nichts ~ werden* nothing can come of it; *~ wird nichts!* F nothing doing!
darben ['darbən] (25) suffer want; *stärker*: starve.
darbiet|en ['daːr-] offer, present; **'2ung** *f thea. usw.* performance; *weitS.* entertainment, event.
'darbringen present, offer, give.
darein [da'raɪn] into that *od.* it; **~finden, ~fügen, ~schicken:** *sich ~* resign o.s. to it, put up with it; **~geben** give into the bargain; **~mischen:** *sich ~* meddle (with it), interfere (with it); *vermittelnd*: intervene; **~reden** *v/i.* interrupt; *fig.* interfere; **~willigen** consent (to it).
darin [~'rin] in that, in it *od.* them; (*in dieser Hinsicht*) in this respect; *~, daß ...* in that ...
darleg|en ['daːr-] lay open, expose; (*auseinandersetzen*) explain, point out; (*ausführen*) state; (*offen ~, anführen*) set forth, show; **'2ung** *f* exposition; explanation; statement, showing.
Darleh(e)n ['daːrleːən] *n* (6) loan; **'~skasse** *f* loan-office, loan bank.
Darm [darm] *m* (3[3]) gut; (*Wursthaut*) skin; *Därme pl.* intestines, bowels; **'~geschwür** *n* intestinal ulcer; **'~-infektion** *f* intestinal infection; **'~krebs** *m* cancer of the intestine; **'~saite** *f* catgut string; **'~verschlingung** *f* twisting of the guts; **'~verschluß** ⚕ *m* ileus.
Darre ['darə] *f* (15) (*Vorgang*) kiln-drying; (*Darrofen*) (drying-)kiln; (*Vogelkrankheit*) roup, pip.
darreichen ['daːr-] offer, present; ⚕ *u. eccl.* administer.
darren ['darən] (25) kiln-dry.
darstell|bar ['daːrʃtɛlbaːr] representable; **'~en** *allg.* represent; (*abbilden*; *graphisch ~*) figure; *thea. Rolle*: (im)personate, do; ⚙ disengage; *sich ~* present itself; *~de Kunst* interpretative art; **'2er(in** *f*) *thea. m* performer; **'2ung** *f* repre-

sentation; (im)personation, acting; ⚙ disengagement; *graphische* ~ diagram, graph.

dartun [ˈdɑːr-] show; demonstrate.

darüber [daˈryːbər] over that, over it *od.* them; (*querüber*) across it; (*was dies anbetrifft*) about that *od.* it, on that point; *zeitlich*: meanwhile; *zwei Pfund* ~ two pounds more; *zwei Jahre und* ~ two years and upward; ~ *hinaus* beyond it, past it, *fig. a.* in addition (to this); *wir sind* ~ *hinweg* we got over it; *es geht nichts* ~ there is nothing like it.

darum [~ˈrum] **1.** *adv.* around that *od.* it *od.* them; about that; *er weiß* ~ he is aware of it; *es ist mir sehr* ~ *zu tun, daß* I set great store by *ger.*; *es ist mir nur* ~ *zu tun* my only object is; **2.** *cj.* [ˈdaːrum] (*deshalb*) therefore, that's why.

darunter [daˈruntər] under that *od.* it *od.* them; *unter e-r Anzahl*: among them; (*einschließlich*) including; (*weniger*) less; *zwei Jahre und* ~ two years and under; *was verstehst du* ~? what do you understand by it?

das [das] *s. der.*

dasein [ˈdɑː-] **1.** (sn) be there; (*anwesend sein*) be present; (*vorhanden sein*) exist; *noch nie dagewesen* unprecedented; *vgl. da*; **2.** ♀ *n* (6) existence, being; life; (*Gegenwart, Anwesenheit*) presence; *ins* ~ *treten* come into being; ˈ♀**sberechtigung** *f* raison d'être (*fr.*); ˈ♀**skampf** *m* struggle for existence.

daˈselbst [da-] there, in that very place.

daß [das] that; ~ *nicht* lest; *bis* ~ till.

dastehen [ˈdɑː-] stand (there).

Daten [ˈdɑːtən] *n/pl.* (9²) data, facts; particulars; ˈ~-**ausgabe** *f* data output; ˈ~**bank** *f* data bank; ˈ~-**eingabe** *f* data input; ˈ~**schreiber** *m* data printer; ˈ~**schutz** *m* data protection; ˈ~**träger** *m* data medium; ˈ~**typist** (-**in** *f*) *m* terminal operator; ˈ~-**übertragung** *f* data transmission; ˈ♀**verarbeitend**, ˈ~**verarbeitung** *f* data processing; ˈ~**verbund** *m* aggregate.

datieren [daˈtiːrən] date.

Dativ [ˈdɑːtiːf] *m* (3¹) dative (case).

dato [ˈdɑːto]: *bis* ~ to date, hitherto; (*nach*) ~ after date.

Dattel [ˈdatəl] *f* (15) date.

Datum [ˈdɑːtum] *n* (9²) date; *welches* ~ *haben wir heute?* which day of the month is it?; ˈ~**stempel** *m* date stamp; (*Gerät*) dater.

Daube [ˈdaubə] *f* (15) stave.

Dauer [ˈdauər] *f* (15) duration; (*Fortdauer*) continuance; (*Ständigkeit*) permanence; *auf die* ~ in the long run; *für die* ~ *von* for a period (*od.* term) of ...; *von kurzer* ~ of short duration; *von* ~ *sein* last; ˈ~-**auftrag** ✝ *m* standing order; ˈ~**betrieb** ⊕ *m* continuous operation; ˈ~**brenner** *m* (*Ofen*) slow-combustion stove; (*Erfolg*) long-running hit; F (*Kuß*) long kiss; ˈ~**feuer** ⚔ *n* sustained fire; ˈ~**flug** *m* endurance flight; non-stop flight; ˈ♀**haft** durable, lasting; ~ *sein Stoff*: wear well; ˈ~**haftigkeit** *f* durability; ˈ~**karte** *f* season-ticket, *Am.* commutation ticket; ˈ~**lauf** *m* endurance run; *leichter*: jog-trot; ˈ~**leistung** *f* continuous output; ˈ~**lutscher** *m* lollipop; ˈ♀**n** (29) **1.** continue, last; *e-e gewisse Zeit* ~ take; ~*d* lasting, permanent, (*ständig*) constant; **2.** *er* (*es*) *dauert mich* I feel sorry for him (it); I pity him (it); ˈ~**stellung** *f* permanent position, permanency; ˈ~**welle** *f im Haar*: permanent wave, F perm; ˈ~**zustand** *m* permanent condition.

Daumen [ˈdaumən] *m* (6) thumb; F *j-m den* ~ *drücken* keep one's fingers crossed for a p.; *die* ~ *drehen* twiddle one's thumbs; ˈ~**breite** *f* thumb's breadth; ˈ~**register** *n* thumb index; ˈ~**schraube** *f* thumbscrew (*a. fig.*).

Daune [ˈdaunə] *f* (15) down; ˈ~**n-decke** *f* eider-down.

davon [daˈfɔn] of that *od.* it *od.* them; by that *od.* it; (*fort, weg*) off; *was habe ich* ~? what does it get me?; ~**kommen** get away *od.* off; *s. Schreck*; ~**laufen** (sn) run away; ~**machen:** *sich* ~ make off; ~**schleichen:** *sich* ~ steal away *od.* off; ~**tragen** carry off; *fig.* incur, get; *s. Sieg.*

daˈvor before that *od.* it *od.* them; of it.

dazu [daˈtsuː] to that *od.* it *od.* them; (*zu dem Zweck*) for that purpose; (*außerdem*) in addition to that; *noch* ~ at that; moreover, into the bargain; ~ *gehört Zeit* that requires time; ~ *kommt* add to this; *wie kommst du* ~? how could you?; *ich kam nie* ~ I never got (a)round to

do it; **~gehören** belong to it *od.* them; **~gehörig** belonging to it; **~kommen** (sn) come along; *unvermutet*: supervene; *s. a. dazu.*
dazumal ['dɑ:tsumɑ:l] at that time.
da'zutun add (to it).
dazwischen [da'tsviʃən] between (them); **~fahren** (sn), **~funken** F interfere; **~kommen** (sn) intervene; **2kunft** *f* (16) intervention; **~liegend** intermediate; **~treten** (sn) intervene.
Dealer *sl.* ['di:lər] *m* (7) (drug) pusher.
Debatte [de'batə] *f* (15) debate; *zur ~ stehen* be under discussion, be at issue.
debat'tieren debate.
Debet ✝ ['de:bɛt] *n* (11) debit.
Debüt [de'by:] *n* (11) first appearance, début (*fr.*); **~ant(in** *f*) *m* [~by'tant(in)] débutant(e *f*) (*fr.*); **2ieren** [~'ti:rən] make one's début.
dechiffrieren [deʃif'ri:rən] decipher, decode.
Deck ⚓ [dɛk] *n* (3) deck; '**~-adresse** *f* cover (address); '**~bett** *n* feather-bed; '**~blatt** *n e-r Zigarre*: wrapper; *zu Büchern usw.*: errata slip.
Decke ['dɛkə] *f* (15) cover; (*Bett2*) coverlet, *wollene*: blanket; *e-s Zimmers*: ceiling; *mot.* (*Reifen2*) casing; *unter e-r ~ stecken* conspire together; *sich nach der ~ strecken* cut one's coat according to one's cloth, make both ends meet.
Deckel ['dɛkəl] *m* (7) lid, (*a. Buch2*) cover; F (*Hut*) lid.
decken ['dɛkən] (25) cover (*a.* ⚔, ✝, *Stute usw.*; *a. Boxen*); *Dach*: (*mit Ziegeln ~*) tile, (*mit Schiefer ~*) slate; *Sport*: mark; *fig. j-n*: shield; *Bedarf*: meet, supply; *den Tisch ~* lay the cloth *od.* table; *für sechs Personen ~* lay covers for six persons; *e-n Wechsel ~* meet a bill; *hinlänglich gedeckt sein* have sufficient security; *a.* ⩕ *sich ~* coincide; *fenc. usw.* guard (*a. fig.*; *gegen* against).
'**Decken|beleuchtung** *f* ceiling lighting; '**~gemälde** *n* ceiling fresco.
'**Deck|farbe** *f* body-colo(u)r; '**~mantel** *m fig.* cloak; '**~name** *m* cover name, pseudonym; '**~ung** *f* covering; ✝ (*Sicherheit*) cover, security, (*Mittel*) funds *pl.*; *des Bedarfs*: supply; (*Zahlung*) payment; *fenc. usw.* guard; (*Schutz*) cover; '**~weiß** *n* (4, 16, *o. pl.*) opaque white.
defekt [de'fɛkt] **1.** defective; **2.** **2** *m* (3) defect.
defensiv [defɛn'zi:f] defensive; **2e** [~'zi:və] *f* (15) defensive; *in der ~* on the defensive.
defilieren [defi'li:rən] (h. *u.* sn) march past, pass in review, parade.
defi'nier|bar definable; **~en** [~'ni:rən] define.
Definition [~ni'tsjo:n] *f* (16) definition.
definitiv [~'ti:f] (*bestimmt*) definite; (*endgültig*) definitive, final.
Defizit ['de:fitsit] *n* (3) deficit, deficiency; *ein ~ decken* make good a deficiency.
Deflation [defla'tsjo:n] *f* deflation.
Degen ['de:gən] *m* (6) sword; *Sport*: épée (*fr.*).
degenerieren [degene'ri:rən] degenerate.
degradier|en [degra'di:rən] degrade, *Am.* demote; **2ung** *f* degradation, *Am.* demotion.
dehn|bar ['de:nbɑ:r] extensible; elastic (*a. fig.*); *fig.* (*vage*) vague; '**2barkeit** *f* extensibility; elasticity; vagueness; '**~en** (25) extend; *elastisch*: stretch (*a. sich*); *phys.* expand (*a. sich*); *die Worte*: drawl; *Vokal*: lengthen; '**2ung** *f* extension; stretch(ing); expansion; lengthening.
dehydrieren [dehy'dri:rən] dehydrate.
Deich [daɪç] *m* (3) dike, dam.
Deichsel ['daɪksəl] *f* (15) pole, shaft; (*Gabel2*) thill; '**2n** F (29) manage, F wangle, engineer.
dein [daɪn] (20) your; *eccl., poet.* thy; *pred. od. der (die, das) dein(ig)e* yours; *eccl., poet.* thine; *die 2en* your family *od.* people; '**~er** (20) **a**) of you; *refl.* of yourself; **b**) yours; **~erseits** ['~ərzaɪts] for (*od.* on) your part; **~esgleichen** ['~əs'glaɪçən] your like(s *pl.*), F the like(s *pl.*) of you; **~ethalben** ['~əthalbən], '**~etwegen**, (*um*) '**~etwillen** for your sake; on your account; **~ige** ['~igə] (18b) *s. dein.*
Dekade [de'kɑ:də] *f* (15) decade; (*zehn Tage*) ten-day period.
dekaden|t [deka'dɛnt] decadent; *biol.* degenerate; **2z** *f* (16) decadence.

Dekan [de'ka:n] *m* (3¹) dean.
dekatieren [deka'ti:rən] decatize.
Deklam|ation [deklama'tsjo:n] *f* declamation; **~ator** [~'ma:tɔr] *m* (8¹) declaimer; **≈atorisch** [~ma'to:riʃ] declamatory; **≈ieren** [~'mi:rən] *v/t.* recite; *mst v/i.* declaim.
deklarieren [~'ri:rən] declare.
Dekli|nation [deklina'tsjo:n] *f* (16) declension; *phys.* declination; **≈'nierbar** declinable; **≈'nieren** decline.
Dekolle|té [dekɔlte:] *n* (low) neckline; **≈'tiert** low-necked, décolleté (*fr.*).
Dekorateur [dekora'tø:r] *m* (3¹) (*Maler*) decorator; (*Tapezierer*) upholsterer; (*Schaufenster≈*) window-dresser; *thea.* scene-painter.
Dekoration [~'tsjo:n] *f* (16) decoration; (*Schaufenster≈*) window-dressing; *thea.* scenery; **~smaler** *m* decorator; *thea.* scene-painter; **~sstoff** *m* furnishing fabric.
dekorativ [dekora'ti:f] decorative.
deko'rieren decorate (*a. j-n mit Orden*); (*behängen*) drape; *Schaufenster*: dress.
Dekret [de'kre:t] *n* (3), **≈ieren** [~kre'ti:rən] decree.
Deleg|ation [delega'tsjo:n] *f* delegation; **≈ieren** [~'gi:rən] delegate; **~ierte** [~'gi:rtə] *m, f* delegate.
delikat [deli'ka:t] delicate (*a. fig.*), dainty; (*köstlich*) delicious.
Delikatesse [~ka'tɛsə] *f* (15) delicacy (*a. fig.*); (*Leckerbissen*) *a.* dainty, titbit (*a. fig.*); *~n pl. bsd. Am.* delicatessen *pl.*; **~nhandlung** *f* delicatessen (store) *sg.*
Delikt [de'likt] *n* (3) delict.
Delirium [de'li:rjum] *n* (9) delirium.
Delle ['dɛlə] *f* (15) dent.
Delphin [dɛl'fi:n] *m* (3¹) dolphin.
Delta ['dɛlta] *n* (11[¹]) delta.
dem [de:m]: *wie ~ auch sei* however that may be; *wenn ~ so ist* if that be true.
Demagog [dema'go:k], **~e** [~gə] *m* (12) demagog(ue); **~ie** [~go'gi:] *f* (15) demagogy; **≈isch** [~'go:giʃ] demagogic.
Demarkationslinie [demarka'tsjo:nsli:njə] *f* line of demarcation.
demaskieren [demas'ki:rən] unmask.
Dement|i [de'mɛnti] *n* (11) (official) denial; **≈ieren** [~'ti:rən] deny.
'**dem|gegen**'**-über** in contrast to this; '**~gemäß** accordingly; '**~nach** therefore, hence; accordingly; '**~**'**nächst** shortly, soon, before long.
Demo ['de:mo] *f* (11¹) F demo.
demobilisier|en [demobili'zi:rən] *v/t. u. v/i.* demobilize; **≈ung** *f* demobilization.
'**Demokassette** F *f* demo (tape).
Demokrat [demo'kra:t] *m* (12), **~in** *f* (16¹) democrat; **~ie** [~kra'ti:] *f* (15) democracy; **≈isch** [~'kra:tiʃ] democratic; **≈isieren** [~krati'zi:rən] democratize.
demolier|en [demo'li:rən] demolish; **≈ung** *f* demolition.
Demonstr|ant [demɔn'strant] *m* (12) demonstrator; **~ation** [~stra'tsjo:n] *f* (16) demonstration; **~ationsmaterial** *n* teaching aids *pl.*; **~ationsrecht** *n* right to demonstrate; **~ationsverbot** *n* ban on demonstrating; **~ationszug** *m* protest march; **≈ieren** [~'stri:rən] *v/t. u. v/i.* demonstrate.
Demont|age [~'ta:ʒə] *f* (15) disassembly; dismantling; **≈ieren** [~'ti:rən] disassemble; *a. Fabrik usw.*: dismantle.
demoralisieren [demorali'zi:rən] demoralize.
Demoskopie [~sko'pi:] *f* (15) opinion poll(ing).
Demut ['de:mu:t] *f* (16) humility.
demütig ['~my:tiç] humble; **~en** ['~gən] (25) humble (*sich* o.s.), humiliate; '**≈ung** *f* humiliation.
'**demzufolge** accordingly.
denaturieren ⚗ [denatu'ri:rən] (25) denature.
'**Denk|-anstoß** *m* a th. to start one thinking; *j-m e-n ~ geben* set a p. thinking about a th.; '**~-art** *f* way of thinking, mentality; '**≈bar** thinkable; (*vorstellbar*) imaginable; (*faßbar*) conceivable; '**≈en** *v/t.* (30) think; (*vermuten*) suppose, *Am.* F guess (*alle a. v/i.*); (*beabsichtigen*) intend; *~ an* (*acc.*) think of; (*sich erinnern*) remember *a p., a th.*; *~ über* (*acc.*) think about; *sich et. ~* think, (*vorstellen*) imagine, fancy; *j-m zu ~ geben* set a p. thinking; *~ Sie nur!* just fancy!; *ich denke nicht daran!* I wouldn't think of it!; '**~er** *m* (7) thinker; '**≈fähig** intelligent; '**≈faul** too lazy to think, mentally inert;

'**~fehler** *m* false reasoning; '**~freiheit** *f* freedom of thought; '**~lehre** *f* logic; '**~mal** *n* (1³ *u.* 3) monument; (*Ehrenmal*) memorial; '**~malschutz** *m*: *unter* ~ listed; '**~modell** *n* (theoretical) model, blueprint; '**~münze** *f* commemorative medal; '**~prozeß** *m* process of reasoning; '**~schrift** *f* memoir; memorial; memorandum; '**~sport** *m* mental exercise; *~aufgabe* problem, brain-twister, *Am.* quiz; '**~spruch** *m* motto, sentence; '**~stein** *m* memorial stone; '**~vermögen** *n* intellectual power; '**~weise** *f s. Denkart*; '**Ωwürdig** memorable; '**~würdigkeit** *f* memorableness; *pl.* memorabilia; '**~zettel** *m fig.* reminder; lesson.

denn [dɛn] for; *nach comp.*: than; (*tonlos = also, schließlich*) then.

'**dennoch** nevertheless, yet, still.

Dentist [dɛn'tist] *m* (12), **~in** *f* (16¹) dentist.

Denun|ziant [denun'tsjant] *m* (12), **~ziantin** *f* (16¹) informer; **~ziation** [~tsja'tsjo:n] *f* (16) denunciation; Ω'**zieren** inform against, denounce.

Deo|dorant [deodo'rant] *n* (3¹, 11) deodorant; '**~-Roller** *m* roll-on (deodorant); '**~spray** *m, n* deodorant spray; '**~stift** *m* deodorant stick.

Depesch|e [de'pɛʃə] *f* (15) dispatch; *telegraphisch*: telegram, wire; *drahtlos*: wireless, radio; (*Kabel*Ω) cable (-gram); Ω**ieren** [~'ʃi:rən] telegraph, wire, cable.

Deponie [depo'ni:] *f* (15) (*Müll*Ω) dump, tip; Ω**ren** [~'ni:rən] deposit.

deportieren [~pɔr'ti:rən] deport.

Depositen [~'zi:tən] *pl.* (9) deposits *pl.*; **~bank** *f* deposit bank; **~kasse** *f* branch-office *of a bank*; **~konto** *n* deposit account.

Depot [de'po:] *n* (11) ✝ deposit; ⚔ (*a. Straßenbahn*Ω) depot; **~-effekt** *pharm. m* controlled sustained release.

Depress|ion [deprɛ'sjo:n] *f* (16) depression (*a.* ✝); Ω**iv** [~'si:f] depressed; *Stimmung etc.*: depressing, gloomy.

deprimieren [depri'mi:rən] depress.

Depu|tation [deputa'tsjo:n] *f* (16) deputation; Ω'**tieren** depute; **~'tierte** *m, f* (18) deputy.

der [de:r], **die** [di:], **das** [das] **1.** *art.* (22) the; **2.** *dem. pron.* (22¹) that, this, he, she, it; *die pl.* these, those, they; *der und der usw.*: *adj.* such-and-such (a); *su.* so-and-so; **3.** *rel. pron.* (23) who, which, that.

'**der-art** in such a manner; to such a degree; '**~ig** such, of such a kind; *nichts* Ω*es* nothing of the kind.

derb [dɛrp] firm, solid; (*kräftig*) robust; (*stämmig*) sturdy; (*scharf*) severe; (*grob*) coarse (*a. zotig*), rough; (*unverblümt*) blunt; 'Ω**heit** *f* robustness; sturdiness; roughness.

der'-einst some day, in (the) future; **~ig** future.

derent|halben ['de:rənthalbən], '**~wegen**, '**~willen** on her (their, whose) account. [*daß* so that.]

'**dergestalt** in such a manner; ~

der'gleichen such; *su.* the like; *und* ~ and the like; *nichts* ~ nothing of the kind.

der-, die-, dasjenige ['~jenigə] (22¹) he *who*, she *who*, that *which*; *pl.* those *who*, *S.*: those *which*.

dermaßen ['~ma:sən] *s. derart.*

der-, die-, dasselbe [~'zɛlbə] (22¹) the same; he, she, it.

'**derzeit** at present; '**~ig** present.

Des ♪ [dɛs] *n* D flat.

desensibilisieren [dezɛnzibili'zi:rən] ⚗, *phot.* desensitize.

Desert|eur [dezɛr'tø:r] *m* (3¹) deserter; Ω**ieren** [~'ti:rən] (sn) desert.

desgleichen [dɛs'glaɪçən] *adv.* likewise.

deshalb ['dɛshalp] therefore, for that reason, that is why.

Desinfektion [dɛsʔinfɛk'tsjo:n] *f* disinfection; **~smittel** *n* disinfectant.

des-infizieren [~fi'tsi:rən] disinfect.

'**Des|-information** *f* disinformation; '**~-interesse** *n* lack of interest.

desodorisieren [dɛsʔodori'zi:rən] deodorize.

Despot [dɛs'po:t] *m* (12), **~in** *f* despot; Ω**isch** despotic; **~ie** [~po'ti:] *f* (16), **~ismus** [~'tismus] *m* (16, *o. pl.*) despotism.

dessenungeachtet ['dɛsən'ʔungeʔaxtət] notwithstanding (that), nevertheless.

Dessert [dɛ'se:r] *n* (11) dessert.

Dessin [dɛ'sɛ̃] *n* (11) design, pattern.

Destill|ation [dɛstila'tsjo:n] *f* (16) distillation; Ω**ieren** [~'li:rən] *v/i. u. v/t.* distil(l); **~ierung** *f* distillation.

desto ['dɛsto] the; ~ *besser* all (*od.* so much) the better; *s. je.*

destruktiv [destruk'ti:f] destructive.
deswegen ['dɛsve:gən] *s. deshalb.*
Detail [de'taj] *n* (11) detail; ✝ retail; **~geschäft** *n* retail business; (*Laden*) retail shop; **~handel** *m* retail trade; **~händler** *m* retail dealer; **≈lieren** [~'ji:rən] specify; **~list** [~'jist] *m* (12) retailer.
Detektiv [detɛk'ti:f] *m* (3¹) detective.
Detektor [de'tɛktɔr] *m* (8¹) *Radio*: detector.
Deto|nation [detona'tsjo:n] *f* (16) detonation; **≈'nieren** detonate.
deuchte ['dɔʏçtə] *pret. v. dünken.*
Deut [dɔʏt] *m*: *keinen ~ wert* not worth a farthing.
deut|eln ['~əln] (29) *v/i.* subtilize; *~ an (dat.)* quibble at; **'~en** *v/i.* (26): *~ auf (acc.)* point to, *fig. a.* signify; *v/t.* interpret, construe, explain; *Traum, Zeichen*: read; *falsch ~* misinterpret; **'~lich** clear, distinct; *fig. ~ werden (mit j-m)* be outspoken (with a p.); **'≈lichkeit** *f* clearness, distinctness.
deutsch [dɔʏtʃ], **≈** *n* German; **'≈e** *m, f* (18) German; **'≈tum** *n* (1²) German character, Germanity; *konkret*: Germans *pl.*
'Deutung *f* (16) interpretation; construction.
Devise [de'vi:zə] *f* (15) device, motto; ✝ (*a. pl.*) foreign exchange *od.* currency; **~nausgleichsfonds** *m* exchange equalization funds; **~nhandel** *m* foreign exchange dealing; **~nkontrollstelle** *f* foreign exchange control office; **~nmarkt** *m* currency market; **~nschmuggel** *m* currency smuggling; **~nsperre** *f* exchange embargo.
devot [de'vo:t] submissive.
Dezember [de'tsɛmbər] *m* (7) December.
dezent [de'tsɛnt] discreet; (*unaufdringlich*) unobtrusive; *Farbe, Licht usw.*: subdued, mellow.
dezentralisieren [detsɛntrali'zi:rən] decentralize.
Dezernat [detsɛr'nɑ:t] *n* (3) department.
dezimal [detsi'mɑ:l] decimal; **≈bruch** *m* decimal fraction; **≈stelle** *f* decimal place; **≈system** *n* decimal system.
dezi'mieren decimate.
Dia ['di:a] *n* (11) *s. Diapositiv.*
Diabe|tiker [dia'be:tikər] *m* (7), **≈tisch** diabetic.
diabolisch [dia'bo:liʃ] diabolic(al).
'Diabetrachter *m* slide viewer.
Diadem [dia'de:m] *n* (3¹) diadem.
Diagnose [~'gno:zə] *f* (15) diagnosis.
diagnostizieren [~gnɔsti'tsi:rən] diagnose.
diagonal [~go'nɑ:l], **≈e** *f* (15) diagonal; **≈reifen** *mot. m* crossply tyre (*Am.* tire).
Diagramm [dia'gram] *n* (3) diagram.
Diakon [dia'ko:n] *m* (3¹ *u.* 8), **Diakonus** [di'ɑ:konus] *m* (14³ *u.* 16²) deacon.
Diako'niss|e [diako'nisə] *f* (15), **~in** (16¹) Protestant (nursing) sister.
Dialekt [dia'lɛkt] *m* (3) dialect; **~ik** *f* (16, *no pl.*) dialectic(s *pl.*); **≈isch** dialectal.
Dialog [~'lo:k] *m* (3¹) dialog(ue).
Dialyse [dia'ly:zə] ⚕ *f* (15) dialysis.
Diamant [~'mant] *m* (12), **≈en** diamond.
diametral [~me'trɑ:l] diametrical.
Dia|positiv [diapozi'ti:f] *n* (3¹) slide, transparency; **~projektor** ['~projɛktɔr] *m* (8¹) slide projector.
Diarrhöe [dia'rø:] *f* (15) diarrh(o)ea.
Diät [di'ɛ:t] *f* (16) (special) diet, regimen; **≈** *leben* diet o.s.; **~-assistent(in** *f*) *m* dietician; **~en** *f/pl.* daily allowance *sg.*; **~kost** *f* dietary food.
dich [diç] you; *refl.* yourself.
dicht [diçt] (*undurchlässig*) tight; (*zusammengedrängt*) compact; *phys., Nebel, Verkehr, Wald, Bevölkerung*: dense; *Haar, Laub, Gedränge*: thick; *Stoff*: thick, close; *~ an (dat.) od. bei* close by; *~ hinter (dat.)* close behind; **'≈e** *f* (15) *a. phys.* density; *s. Dichtheit.*
'dichten 1. (26) make tight; ⊕ seal; *Fuge*: flush; **2.** *v/t.* compose (*a. v/i.*); *v/i.* write poetry.
'Dichter *m* (7) poet; **'~in** *f* poetess; **'~lesung** *f* reading; *e-e ~ halten* give a reading; **'~ling** *m* (3) would-be poet, poetaster; **'≈isch** poetic(al).
'Dicht|heit *f*, **'~igkeit** *f* (16) tightness; compactness; density; thickness; closeness.
'Dichtkunst *f* poetry.
'dichtmachen F *v/i.* shut up shop; *v/t.* shut (up).
'Dichtung *f* (16) **1.** ⊕ sealing; *konkret*: seal; packing; *aus Werg*:

gasket; **2.** poetry; (*Einzel*≈) poem; work of fiction; (*Er*≈) fiction; '**~s-masse** ⊕ *f* sealing compound; '**~s-ring** ⊕ *m*, '**~sscheibe** ⊕ *f* washer.

dick [dik] thick; (*massig*) big; (*umfangreich*) voluminous; (*beleibt*) stout, corpulent; F *das ~e Ende kommt noch* the worst is yet to come; F *sie sind ~e Freunde* as thick as thieves; *~e Milch* curdled milk; F *~e Luft!* trouble's brewing!; *durch ~ und dünn* through thick and thin; F (*sich*) *~ tun* talk big; *mit et.* brag of; *~ auftragen* lay it on thick.

dick|bäuchig ['~bɔʏçiç] big-bellied; '**≈darm** *m* great gut, 🕮 colon; '**≈e** *f* (15, *o. pl.*) thickness; stoutness; '**≈erchen** F *n* (6) fatso; **~fellig** ['~fɛliç] thick-skinned; '**~flüssig** viscous; **≈häuter** ['~hɔʏtər] *m* (7) pachyderm; **≈icht** ['~içt] *n* (3[1]) thicket; '**≈kopf** *m* pig-headed fellow; **~köpfig** ['~kœpfiç] pig-headed; **~leibig** ['~laɪbiç] corpulent; *fig.* bulky; '**≈leibigkeit** *f* corpulency; bulkiness; '**≈milch** *f* sour milk; '**≈wanst** *m* paunch.

Didaktik [di'daktik] *f* (16) didactics *sg.*

die [di:] *s. der.*

Dieb [di:p] *m* (3) thief; **~erei** [~bə'raɪ] *f* (16) thieving, thievery.

Diebes|bande ['di:bəs-] *f* gang of thieves; '**~höhle** *f* nest of thieves; '**≈sicher** theft-proof.

Dieb|in ['di:bin] *f* (16[1]) (female) thief; **≈isch** ['di:biʃ] thievish; F *Freude usw.*: devilish; **~stahl** ['di:pʃta:l] *m* (3[3]) theft, ⚖ larceny; '**~stahlsicherung** *f* theft prevention device; '**~stahlversicherung** *f* insurance against theft.

Diele ['di:lə] *f* (15) (*Brett*) board; (*Fußboden*) floor; (*Vorraum*) hall; '**≈n** board; floor.

dienen ['di:nən] *v/i.* (25) serve (*j-m* a p.; *als* as; *zu* for; *dazu, zu inf.* to *inf.*); *zu nichts ~* be of no use; ✝ *womit kann ich ~?* what can I do for you?, *Am.* may I help you?

'**Diener** *m* (7) (man-)servant; (*Verbeugung*) bow; *stummer ~* (*Nebentischchen*) dumb-waiter; '**~in** *f* (16[1]) maid-servant, maid; *fig.* handmaid; '**~schaft** *f* domestics *pl.*

'**dienlich** useful, helpful, serviceable (*dat.* to).

Dienst [di:nst] *m* (3[2]) service (*a.* ⚔ *u. Einrichtung*); (*Stelle*) post, employment; *im* (*außer*) *~* on (off) duty; *~ am Kunden* prompt service to the customer; *j-m e-n ~ erweisen* do a p. a good turn; *gute ~e leisten* render good services; *j-m zu ~en stehen* be at a p.'s service; *s. stellen.*

Dienstag ['di:nsta:k] *m* (3) Tuesday.

'**Dienst|-alter** *n* seniority; '**≈-ältest** *adj.*, '**~-älteste** *m* senior; '**~-antritt** *m* entering upon service; '**~-anzug** ⚔ *m* service uniform *od.* dress; '**≈bar** subservient (*dat.* to); *~er Geist fig.* factotum; *s-n Zwekken ~ machen* make *a p. od. th.* serve one's purpose; '**~barkeit** *f* servitude, bondage; '**≈beflissen** *s. ~eifrig*; '**≈bereit** ready for service; (*gefällig*) obliging; '**~bote** *m* domestic (servant); '**~-eid** *m* oath of office; '**~-eifer** *m* zeal; obligingness; '**≈-eifrig** zealous, assiduous; obliging; '**≈fähig** *s. ~tauglich*; '**≈fertig** *s. ~eifrig*; '**≈frei:** *~ sein* be off duty; *~er Tag* off day; '**~geheimnis** *n* official secret; '**~gespräch** *n* official call; '**~grad** *m* ⚔ rank; *der Unteroffiziere u. Mannschaften*: *Am.* grade; ⚓ rating; '**≈habend** (on) duty; '**~herr** *m* master, employer; '**~jahre** *n/pl.* years of service; '**~leistung** *f* service; '**~leistungsbetrieb** *m* service company; '**≈lich** official; on business; '**~mädchen** *n* maid-servant, help; '**~mann** *m* porter, commissionaire; '**~-ordnung** *f* official regulations *pl.*; '**~pflicht** *f* official duty; ⚔ compulsory (military) service; '**~plan** *m* roster; '**~reise** *f* official journey; '**~stelle** *f* office, agency; '**~stunden** *f/pl.* duty (*od.* office) hours; '**≈tauglich** fit for (⚔ active) service; **≈tuend** ['~tu:ənt] acting; (*im Dienst*) on duty; '**≈-unfähig**, '**≈-untauglich** unfit for service; '**~vergehen** *n* official misdemeano(u)r; '**~verhältnis** *n* (contract of) employment; '**≈verpflichtet** conscripted for essential service; '**~vertrag** *m* contract of employment; '**~vorschrift** *f* regulations *pl.*; '**~wagen** *m* official car; '**~weg** *m* official channels *pl.*; '**≈willig** *s. ~bereit*; '**~wohnung** *f* official residence; '**~zeit** *f* (period of) service.

'**diesbezüglich** relevant (to this); referring to this.

Dieselmotor ['di:zəlmo:tɔr] *m* Diesel engine.

dies|er ['di:zər], '**~e**, '**~es** *od.* **dies** [di:s] (21) *adj.* this; *su.* this one; '**~e** *pl.* these; **~jährig** ['~jɛ:riç] this year's, of this year; '**~mal** this time; **~seitig** ['~zaɪtiç] on this (*od.* my, our) side; **~seits** ['~zaɪts] on this side (*gen.* of).

diesig ['di:ziç] hazy, misty.

Dietrich ['di:triç] *m* (3) skeleton key; *des Einbrechers*: picklock.

diffamieren [difa'mi:rən] defame.

Differential... [difərɛn'tsja:l] differential.

Diffe'renz *f* (16) difference.

differenzieren [~'tsi:rən] differentiate.

diffe'rieren differ.

Digital|-anzeige [digi'ta:l-] *f* digital display; **~-aufnahme** *f* digital recording; **~rechner** *m* digital computer; **~technik** *f Computer*: digital computing system; **~-uhr** *f* digital clock (*od.* watch).

Diktat [dik'ta:t] *n* (3) dictation; (*Befehl*) dictate; *nach ~ schreiben* write from dictation; **~or** [~tɔr] *m* (8[1]) dictator; **≈orisch** [~ta'to:riʃ] dictatorial; **~ur** [~'tu:r] *f* (16) dictatorship.

dik'tier|en dictate; **≈gerät** *n* dictating machine.

Dilemma [di'lɛma] *n* (11) dilemma.

Dilettant [dilɛ'tant] *m* (12), **~in** *f* amateur, dilettante; **≈isch** amateurish, dilettante.

Dill ⚘ [dil] *m* (3) dill.

Dimension [dimɛn'zjo:n] *f* (16) dimension.

Ding [diŋ] *n* (3) thing; *vor allen ~en* first of all; *das geht nicht mit rechten ~en zu* there's something wrong about it; '**≈en** *v/t.* (30) hire; '**≈fest:** *j-n ~ machen* arrest a p.; '**≈lich** ⚖ real.

dinieren [di'ni:rən] dine.

Diode ⚡ [di'o:də] *f* (15) diode.

Diözese [diø'tse:zə] *f* (15) diocese.

Diphtherie [diftə'ri:] *f* (15, *o. pl.*) diphtheria.

Diphthong [dif'tɔŋ] *m* (3[1] *u.* 12) diphthong; **≈isch** diphthongal.

Diplom [di'plo:m] *n* (3[1]) diploma; **~-arbeit** *f* dissertation.

Diplomat [~plo'ma:t] *m* (12) diplomat; **~enkoffer** *m* executive case; **~ie** [~ma'ti:] *f* (16) diplomacy; **≈isch** [~'ma:tiʃ] diplomatic.

Di'plom-ingenieur *m* graduated engineer.

dir [di:r] (to) you; *refl.* (to) yourself.

direkt [di'rɛkt] direct; *~er Wagen* 🚂 through carriage; **≈-antrieb** ⊕ *m* direct drive; **≈flug** *m* through flight, non-stop flight.

Direktion [dirɛk'tsjo:n] *f* (16) direction; (*Verwaltung*) management; *s. Direktorium*; **~s-etage** *f* executive floor.

Direktive [dirɛk'ti:və] *f* (16) directive, (general) instruction.

Di'rektmandat *pol. n* direct mandate.

Direktor [di'rɛktɔr] *m* (8[1]) manager, director; (*Schul≈*) headmaster, *Am.* principal; **~at** [~'ra:t] *n* (3) directorship; **~ium** [~'to:rium] *n* (9) board of directors.

Direktrice [~'tri:sə] *f* (15) manageress, directress.

Di'rekt-übertragung *f* live broadcast.

Dirig|ent ♪ [diri'gɛnt] *m* (12) conductor, leader; **≈ieren** [~'gi:rən] direct, manage; ♪ conduct; **~ismus** [~'gismus] ✝ *m* (14, *o. pl.*) planned economy.

Dirne ['dirnə] *f* (15) prostitute, whore.

Dis ♪ [dis] *n* D sharp.

Dishar|monie [disharmo'ni:] *f* (15) discord; **≈monisch** [~'mo:niʃ] discordant.

Diskant ♪ [dis'kant] *m* (3) treble, soprano.

Diskette [dis'kɛtə] *f* (15) *Computer*: diskette, disk.

Diskjockey ['diskdʒɔke] *m* (11) disc jockey.

Diskont ✝ [~'kɔnt] *m* (3), **~o** *m* (11), **≈ieren** [~'ti:rən] discount; **~satz** *m* discount rate; bank-rate.

Diskothek [disko'te:k] *f* (15) discotheque.

diskret [dis'kre:t] discreet; **≈ion** [~kre'tsjo:n] *f* (16) discretion.

Diskriminierung [~krimi'ni:ruŋ] *f* discrimination.

Diskussion [~ku'sjo:n] *f* (16) discussion; **~sleiter** *m* chairman; **~sveranstaltung** *f* discussion meeting, *Am.* forum.

Diskuswerfen ['diskusvɛrfən] *n* (6) discus-throwing.

diskutieren [disku'ti:rən] discuss, debate.

Dispens [dis'pɛns] *m* (4) dispensation; **⁀ieren** [⁓'ziːrən] dispense (*von* from), exempt (from).

disponieren [⁓po'niːrən] dispose (*über acc.* of); plan ahead.

Disposition [⁓zi'tsjoːn] *f* (16) disposition; (*Anordnung*) *a.* arrangement; *s-e ⁓en treffen* make one's arrangements; **⁓skredit** *m* overdraft facilities *pl.*

disputieren [dispu'tiːrən] debate.

disqualifizieren [⁓kvalifi'tsiːrən] disqualify.

Dissertation [disɛrta'tsjoːn] *f* (16) dissertation; (*Doktor⁀*) *a.* thesis.

Distanz [di'stants] *f* (16) distance (*a. fig.*); **⁀ieren** [⁓'tsiːrən]: *sich ⁓* keep one's distance; *weitS.* dissociate o.s. (*von* from).

Distel ['distəl] *f* (15) thistle; '**⁓fink** *m* goldfinch.

Distrikt [di'strikt] *m* (3) district.

Disziplin [distsi'pliːn] *f* (16) discipline; (*Sparte*) branch; *Sport*: event; **⁀arisch** [⁓pli'nɑːriʃ] disciplinary; **⁓arstrafe** [⁓'nɑːr-] *f* disciplinary punishment; **⁓arverfahren** *n* disciplinary action; **⁀iert** [⁓'niːrt] disciplined; **⁀los** undisciplined, unruly.

dito ['diːto] ditto.

divers [di'vɛrs] sundry.

Dividend ⚘ [divi'dɛnt] *m* (12) dividend; **⁓e** [⁓də] *f* (15) dividend.

divi'dieren divide.

Division [⁓'zjoːn] *f* (16) division.

Divisor [di'viːzɔr] *m* (8[1]) divisor.

Diwan ['diːvɑːn] *m* (3[1]) divan.

doch [dɔx] (*dennoch*) yet; however; nevertheless; (*je⁓*) but; *auffordernd*: do (*z. B. setz dich ⁓!* do sit down); *nach verneinter Frage*: *siehst du's nicht? ⁓!* yes, I do!; *willst du nicht kommen? ⁓!* O, yes, I will!; *du kommst ⁓?* surely you will come?; *ja ⁓* yes, indeed; *nicht ⁓!* don't!, (*gewiß nicht*) certainly not!

Docht [dɔxt] *m* (3) wick.

Dock [dɔk] *n* (3[1] *u.* 11) dock; '**⁓arbeiter** *m* docker, *Am.* dock laborer.

'**docken** ⚓ (25) dock.

Dogge ['dɔgə] *f* (15): *deutsche ⁓* Great Dane; *englische ⁓* mastiff.

Dogma ['dɔgma] *n* (9[1]) dogma.

Dogma|tiker [⁓'mɑːtikər] *m* (7) dogmatist; **⁀tisch** dogmatic.

Dohle *zo.* ['doːlə] *f* (15) (jack)daw.

Doktor ['dɔktɔr] *m* (8[1]) doctor (*abbr.* Dr.); *den ⁓ machen* take one's (doctor's) degree; **⁓and** [⁓o'rant] *m* (12) doctoral (*od.* PhD, DSc *etc.*) candidate; '**⁓arbeit** *f* doctoral thesis; '**⁓frage** *f fig.* vexed question; '**⁓grad** *m* doctorate; '**⁓prüfung** *f* viva; '**⁓vater** *m* supervisor; '**⁓würde** *f* doctorate.

Doktrin [dɔk'triːn] *f* (16) doctrine.

Dokument [doku'mɛnt] *n* (3) document, ⚖ *a.* deed, instrument; **⁓arfilm** [⁓'tɑːr-] *m* documentary (film); **⁀arisch** [⁓'tɑːriʃ] documentary; **⁀en-echt** waterproof; **⁀ieren** [⁓'tiːrən] document; *fig.* reveal.

Dolch [dɔlç] *m* (3) dagger; '**⁓messer** *n* case-knife, *Am.* bowie-knife; '**⁓stich** *m*, '**⁓stoß** *m* stab with a dagger.

Dolde ['dɔldə] *f* (15) umbel.

Dollar ['dɔlar] *m* (11, *pl. nach Zahlen inv.*) dollar.

Dolle ⚓ ['dɔlə] *f* (15) rowlock.

dolmetsch|en ['dɔlmɛtʃən] *v/i. u. v/t.* (27) interpret; '**⁀(er)** *m* (4 *u.* [7]), '**⁀erin** *f* (16[1]) interpreter; *fig.* mouthpiece.

Dom [doːm] *m* (3) cathedral.

Domäne [do'mɛːnə] *f* (15) domain.

dominieren [domi'niːrən] *v/i.* dominate.

Domino ['doːmino] (11): **a)** *m* (*Kleidung*) domino; **b)** *n* (*Spiel*) (game of) dominoes *sg.*

Domizil [domi'tsiːl] *n* (3[1]) domicile.

'**Dompfaff** *m* bullfinch.

Donner ['dɔnər] *m* (7) thunder; *wie vom ⁓ gerührt* thunder-struck; '**⁀n** (26) thunder (*a. fig.*); '**⁓schlag** *m* clap (*od.* peal) of thunder; *fig.* thunderclap; '**⁓s-tag** *m* Thursday; '**⁓stimme** *f* thundering voice; '**⁓wetter** *n* thunderstorm; (*zum*) *⁓!* hang it (all)!, *staunend*: wow!

doof F [doːf] silly; '**⁀mann** F *m* thickhead.

dop|en ['dɔpən, 'doːpən] (25) *Sport*: dope; '**⁀ing** *n* (11) doping.

Doppel ['dɔpəl] *n* (6) double, duplicate; *s. ⁓spiel 1*; '**⁓-adler** *m* double eagle; '**⁓-agent** *m* double agent; '**⁓belichtung** *phot. f* double exposure; '**⁓bett** *n* double bed; '**⁓decker** *m* (7) biplane; F (*Bus*) double-decker; '**⁓ehe** *f* bigamy; '**⁓fehler** *m* *Tennis*: double fault; '**⁓fenster** *n* double window; **⁓gänger** ['⁓gɛŋər] *m* (7) double; '**⁓haushälfte** *f* semi-detached (house); '**⁓kinn** *n* double chin; '**~laut** *m* diphthong; '**~moral** *f* double standards *pl.*; '**~mord** *m* double murder; '**~punkt** *m* colon; **Ωreihig** ['~raɪiç] *Jackett*: double-breasted; **Ωseitig** ['~zaɪtiç] *Stoff*: double-faced, reversible; '**~sinn** *m* double meaning, ambiguity; '**Ωsinnig** ambiguous, equivocal; '**~sohle** *f* clump sole; '**~spiel** *n* **1.** *Tennis*: double; **2.** *fig.* double game; '**~stecker** ⚡ *m* two-way adapter; '**Ωt** double; *adv.* doubly; ~ *so groß* twice as big; '**~tür** *f* double-door; (*Flügeltür*) folding doors *pl.*; '**~verdiener** *m/pl.* dual-income family *sg.*; '**~verglasung** *f* double glazing; '**~währung** *f* double standard; '**~zentner** *m* quintal; '**~zimmer** *n* double (-bedded) room; **Ωzüngig** ['~tsyŋic], '**~züngigkeit** *f* double-dealing.

Dorf [dɔrf] *n* (1²) village; '**~bewohner(in** *f*) *m* villager; '**~trottel** *m* village idiot.

Dorn [dɔrn] *m* (5) thorn; (*Stachel*) prickle; ⚘ *a.* spine; ⊕ mandrel; *e-r Schnalle*: tongue; *j-m ein ~ im Auge sein* be a thorn in a p.'s side; '**~enhecke** *f* thorn-hedge; '**~enkrone** *f* crown of thorns; '**Ωenvoll,** '**Ωig** thorny (*a. fig.*); **~rös-chen** [~'rø:sçən] *n* Sleeping Beauty; '**~strauch** *m* brier, bramble.

dörr|en ['dœrən] (25) dry; '**Ωfleisch** *n* dried meat; '**Ωgemüse** *n* dried vegetables *pl.*; '**Ω-obst** *n* dried fruit.

Dorsch [dɔrʃ] *m* (3²) cod.

dort [dɔrt] there; (*drüben*) over there; '**~her** from there; '**~hin** there, that way; '**~ig** of that place, there.

Dose ['do:zə] *f* (15) box; (*KonservenΩ*) tin, *Am.* can; '**~n-öffner** *m* (7) tin-opener, *Am.* can opener.

dösen F ['dø:zən] (27) doze.

dosieren [do'zi:rən] dose.

Dosis ['do:zis] *f* (16²) dose; *zu starke ~* overdose.

dotier|en [do'ti:rən] endow; **Ωung** *f* endowment.

Dotter ['dɔtər] *m* (7) yolk; '**~blume** *f* marsh-marigold.

Double ['du:bl] *n* (11) *Film*: double.

Doz|ent [do'tsɛnt] *m* (12) university teacher, lecturer, reader, *Am.* assistant professor, instructor; **Ωieren** [~'tsi:rən] lecture.

Drache ['draxə] *m* (13) dragon; '**~n** *m* (6) (*PapierΩ*) kite; *Sport*: hang-glider; *fig.* (*böses Weib*) termagant, shrew; *e-n ~ steigen lassen* fly a kite; '**~fliegen** *n Sport*: hang-gliding; '**~nflieger(in** *f*) *m Sport*: hang-glider.

Dragée [dra'ʒe:] *n* (11) coated tablet.

Draht [dra:t] *m* (3³) wire; F *auf ~ sein* be in good form, (*wachsam*) be on the ball; *pol. heißer ~* hot line; '**~-anschrift** *f* cable address; '**~-antwort** *f* reply by telegram; '**~bürste** *f* wire brush; '**Ωen** (27) wire; '**~-esel** *m* F bike; '**~gaze** *f* wire gauze; '**~geflecht** *n* wire netting; '**~gitter** *n* wire grating; '**~haarterrier** *m* wire-haired terrier; '**Ωig** wiry; '**Ωlos** wireless, radio-...; '**~nachricht** *f* wire; '**~puppe** *f* puppet; '**~saite** *f* wire string; '**~schere** *f* (*eine* a pair of) wire-shears *pl.*; '**~seil** *n* wire rope; '**~seilbahn** *f* funicular (railway); '**~stift** *m* wire-tack; '**~zange** *f* (*eine* a pair of) wire-pliers *pl.*; **~zieher** ['~tsi:ər] *m* (7) wire-drawer; *fig.* wire-puller.

drakonisch [dra'ko:niʃ] Draconian.

Drall¹ ⊕ [dral] *m* (3) twist; *im Gewehr*: *a.* rifling; *Ball*: spin.

drall² buxom, strapping.

Drama ['dra:ma] *n* (9¹) drama; **~tik** [dra'ma:tik] *f* (16, *o. pl.*) dramatic art; *weitS. u. fig.* drama; **~tiker** *m* (7) dramatist; **Ωtisch** [~'ma:tiʃ] dramatic; **Ωtisieren** [~mati'zi:rən] dramatize (*a. fig.*).

Dramaturg [drama'turk] *m* (12 *u.* 5²) dramatic adviser; **~ie** [~'gi:] *f* dramaturgy.

dran F [dran] *s. daran.*

Dränage [drɛ:'na:ʒə] *f* (15) drainage.

Drang¹ [draŋ] *m* (3) *fig. der Geschäfte*: pressure, rush; (*Antrieb*) impulse, impetus; (*Trieb*) urge; (*Bedrängnis*) distress; (*Eile*) hurry.

drang² *pret. v. dringen.*

dräng|eln F ['drɛŋəln] (29) push, jostle; '**~en** (25) press, push, shove; *sich ~* crowd, throng; *fig.* urge (*auf acc.* a th.); *auf Eile*: urge, hurry; *es drängt mich, zu inf.* I feel moved to *inf.*; *die Zeit drängt* time presses; *s. gedrängt.*

Drangsal ['draŋza:l] *f* (14) affliction, distress; *~e pl.* hardships *pl.*; **Ωieren** [~za'li:rən] persecute.

dränieren [drɛ:'ni:rən] drain.

'**dran|kommen** F (sn) (*erreichen*) be able to reach; (*an e-e S.* a th.); (*an die*

Reihe kommen) have one's turn; *in der Schule*: be called on; '**~nehmen** see; *in der Schule*: ask.

drapieren [dra'pi:rən] drape.

drastisch ['drastiʃ] drastic(ally *adv.*).

drauf F [drauf] *s. darauf*; ~ *und dran sein, zu inf.* be on the point of *ger.*; **2gänger** ['~gɛŋər] *m* (7) daredevil; (*Erfolgsmensch*) go-ahead fellow, *Am.* go-getter; '**2gängertum** *n* pluck; go-aheadedness; '**~gehen** (sn) go, be lost; (*kaputtgehen*) go to pot; (*sterben*) be killed; **~'los** straight ahead; (*wild*) recklessly, blindly.

draußen ['drausən] outside; out of doors; (*in der Fremde*) abroad.

drechseln ['drɛksəln] (29) turn; *gedrechselt fig.* well-turned.

'**Drechsler** *m* (7) turner; '**~-arbeit** *f* turnery; **~ei** [~'raɪ] *f* (16) turnery; turner's shop.

Dreck F [drɛk] *m* (3) dirt; (*Schlamm*) mud; (*Unflat*) filth; *fig. contp.* rubbish; '**2ig** dirty; muddy; filthy; '**~s-kerl** F *m* bastard; '**~spatz** F *m* mucky pup.

Dreh|-arbeit ['dre:-] *f Film*: (*a. pl.*) shooting; '**~bank** *f* (turning-)lathe; '**2bar** revolving; '**~bleistift** *m* propelling pencil; '**~brücke** *f* swing-bridge; '**~buch** *n Film*: scenario, *bsd. Am. a.* script; '**~bühne** *thea. f* revolving stage; '**2en** (25) (*a. sich* ~) turn (*a.* ⊕); *Film*: shoot; *Szene*: take; *Zigarette*: roll; *sich* ~ *um e-n Mittelpunkt, e-e Achse* revolve (*um* round *a centre*, on *an axis*); *fig. Thema*: be about; *es dreht sich darum, daß* the point is whether; *die Frage dreht sich um* the question turns (*od.* hinges) on; *mir dreht sich der Kopf* my head swims; '**~er** ⊕ *m* (7) turner; '**~griff** *m* turning handle; '**~knopf** ⊕ *m* (control) knob; '**~kran** *m* swing crane; '**~kreuz** *n* turnstile; '**~-orgel** *f* barrel-organ; '**~punkt** *m* cent|re (*Am.* -er) of rotation, fulcrum; (*a. fig.*) pivot; '**~schalter** ⚡ *m* turn (*od.* rotary) switch; '**~scheibe** *f* 🚂 turntable; (*Töpfer2*) potter's wheel; '**~strom** ⚡ *m* three-phase current; '**~stuhl** *m* revolving chair; '**~tür** *f* revolving door; '**~ung** *f* turn(ing); *um e-e Achse*: rotation; *um e-n Körper*: revolution; '**~zahl** ⊕ *f* number of revolutions; ~ *per Minute* revolutions *pl.* per minute (*abbr.* r.p.m.); '**~zahlregler** ⊕ *m* speed governor; '**~zapfen** *m* pivot.

drei [draɪ] **1.** three; ~ *Viertel zehn* a quarter to (*Am.* of) ten; *sie waren zu* ~*en* there were three of them; *er sieht aus, als ob er nicht bis* ~ *zählen kann* he looks as if butter would not melt in his mouth; **2.** 2 *f* (16) (number) three; (*Schulzensur*) fair; '**2-akter** *thea. m* three-act play; **~armig** ['~ˀarmiç] three-armed; **~beinig** ['~baɪniç] three-legged; '**2blatt** *n* (*Klee*) trefoil; **~blätterig** ['~blɛtəriç] three-leaved; **~dimensional** ['~dimɛnzjo'nɑ:l] three-dimensional; '**2-eck** *n* (3) triangle; '**~-eckig** three-cornered; ⩓ triangular; **2'-einigkeit** *f* Trinity.

dreierlei ['draɪər'laɪ] of three kinds.

drei|fach ['~fax], **~fältig** ['~fɛltiç] threefold, treble; **2faltigkeit** [~'faltiçkaɪt] *f* Trinity; **2'farben...** three-colo(u)r; '**~farbig** tricolo(u)red; '**2fuß** *m* tripod; '**2gespann** *fig. n* trio; '**~'hundert** three hundred; **2käsehoch** F [~'kɛ:zəho:x] *m* (3) hop-o'-my-thumb, whipper-snapper; '**2klang** ♪ *m* triad; **2'königsfest** *n* Epiphany; '**~mal** three times; **~malig** ['~mɑ:liç] thrice repeated; '**2'meilenzone** ⚓, ⚖ *f* three-mile limit; **~monatig** ['~mo:natiç] three-months, lasting three months; '**~monatlich** three-monthly; *adv.* every three months; **~motorig** ['~moto:riç] three-engine(d).

drein [draɪn] *s. darein*; '**~schlagen** lay about one.

'**Drei|rad** *n* tricycle; '**~satz** ⩓ *m* rule of three; **2seitig** ['~zaɪtiç] three-sided, 🕮 trilateral; **2silbig** ['~zilbiç] trisyllabic; **2sprachig** ['~ʃprɑ:xiç] in three languages, 🕮 trilingual; '**~sprung** *m* triple jump.

dreißig ['draɪsiç] thirty; **2er** ['~gər] *m* (7) man of thirty; **~jährig** ['~jɛ:riç] thirty-year-old; of thirty years; *der* 2*e Krieg* the Thirty Years' War; '**~ste** thirtieth.

dreist [draɪst] bold; (*frech*) impudent.

dreistellig ['~ʃtɛliç] of three places; ~*e Zahl a.* three-figure number.

'**Dreistigkeit** *f* boldness; (*Frechheit*) impudence.

drei|stimmig ['~ʃtimiç] for (*od.* in)

three voices; '**⁀stufenrakete** *f* three-stage rocket; **~tägig** ['~tɛːgiç] three days', three-day; **~teilig** ['~taɪliç] (consisting) of three parts, 🕮 tripartite; *Anzug*: three-piece; ⁀'**vierteltakt** ♪ *m* three-four time; '**⁀zack** *m* (3) trident; '**~zehn**(**te**) thirteen(th).

Dresch|e F ['drɛʃə] *f* (15, *o. pl.*) thrashing; '**⁀en** (30) thresh; (*prügeln*) thrash; '**~er** *m* (7) thresher; '**~flegel** *m* flail; '**~maschine** *f* threshing-machine.

Dress|eur [drɛ'søːr] *m* (3^1) trainer; (*Bändiger*) tamer; **⁀ieren** [drɛ'siːrən] train; *Pferd*: break in; **~man** ['drɛsmən] *m* male model; **~ur** [~'suːr] *f* (16) training; breaking in.

Drill [dril] ⚔ *m* (3, *o. pl.*) drill; '**~bohrer** *m* drill; '**⁀en** ⚔, ⚒ (25) drill; **~ich** ['~iç] *m* drill; denim, canvas; '**~ich-anzug** ⚔ *m* fatigues *pl.*; '**~ing** ['~iŋ] *m* (3^1) (*Kind*) triplet; ⚔ *hunt.* three-barrel(l)ed gun; '**~lings...** ⊕ triple...

drin F [drin] *s. darin.*

dringen ['driŋən] (30): **a**) (sn) *durch et.*: force one's way through, get through; penetrate through; pierce; *aus et.*: break forth from; *in et.* (*acc.*): penetrate into; *in die Öffentlichkeit* ~ leak out; *zum Herzen*: go to; **b**) (h.) ~ *auf* (*acc.*) urge, insist on; ~ *in j-n* urge (*od.* press) a p.; '**~d** urgent(ly *adv.*); *Gefahr*: imminent; *Verdacht*: strong; ~ *verdächtig* highly suspect; ~ *notwendig* imperative; ~ *brauchen* want badly; ~ *bitten* entreat.

'**dringlich** urgent; '**⁀keit** *f* urgency; (*Vor⁀*) priority; '**⁀keits-antrag** *parl. m* motion of urgency; '**⁀keitsstufe** *f* priority; ~ *1* top priority.

drinnen ['drinən] inside, within.

dritte ['dritə], '**⁀l** *n* (7) third; '**~ns** thirdly.

'**dritt|letzt** last but two; '**~rangig** third-rate.

droben ['droːbən] above (there); up there; (*im Himmel*) on high.

Droge ['droːgə] *f* (15) drug; '**⁀nabhängig** addicted to drugs; '**~nabhängige** *m, f* drug addict; '**~nhandel** *m* drug traffic(king); '**~nhändler**(**in** *f*) *m sl.* pusher; '**~nmißbrauch** *m* drug abuse; '**~nszene** *f* drug scene; **~rie** [drogə'riː] *f* (15) chemist's (shop), *Am.* drugstore.

Drogist [~'gist] *m* (12) chemist, *Am.* druggist.

'**Drohbrief** *m* threatening letter.

drohen ['droːən] (25) threaten (*a. fig.*), menace (*j-m* a p.); '**~d** threatening, menacing; (*bevorstehend*) imminent.

Drohne ['droːnə] *f* (15) (*a. fig.*) drone.

dröhnen ['drøːnən] (25) boom, roar; *Raum*: resound (*von* with).

Drohung ['droːuŋ] *f* threat, menace.

drollig ['drɔliç] droll, funny.

Dromedar [drɔme'dɑːr] *n* (3^1) dromedary.

Drops [drɔps] (*m/pl. inv.*) (*saure* acid) drops.

drosch [drɔʃ] *pret. v. dreschen.*

Droschke ['drɔʃkə] *f* (15) cab; (*Auto*) *a.* taxi(-cab).

Drossel *zo.* ['drɔsəl] *f* (15) thrush.

'**Drossel|klappe** ⊕ *f*, '**~ventil** ⊕ *n* throttle (-valve); '**⁀n** ⊕ (29) throttle (*a. fig.*); *Heizung*: turn down; '**~spule** ⚡ *f* choke coil.

drüben ['dryːbən] over there; on the other side.

Druck [druk] *m* **a**) (3^3) pressure; *der Hand*: squeeze; (*Last*) weight, burden; ~ *ausüben auf* (*acc.*) exert pressure on; *j-n unter* ~ *setzen* put pressure on a p.; **b**) *typ.* (3) impression, print; (*~en*) printing; *großer* (*kleiner*) ~ large (small) print *od.* type; *im* ~ *sein* be printing; *in* ~ *geben* (*gehen*) send (go) to the press; '**~bogen** *m* printed sheet; '**~buchstabe** *m* block letter; *in ~n schreiben* print.

Drückeberger F ['drykəbɛrgər] *m* (7) shirker; **~ei** F [~'raɪ] *f* (16) shirking; *im Betrieb*: absenteeism.

'**druck-empfindlich** sensitive to pressure, ⚕ *a.* tender.

drucken ['drukən] (25) print.

drücken ['drykən] (25) press; *Hand*: *a.* squeeze; *fig.* (*nieder~*) oppress; pinch (*Schuh*); *Markt, Preise*: bring (*od.* force) down; *Rekord*: lower, better; *j-n an sich* ~ give a p. a hug; *auf den Knopf* ~ press the button; F *sich* ~ sneak away; *sich in e-e Ecke usw.* ~ dodge into; *sich von e-r Pflicht* ~ shirk, dodge *a duty*; *sich um e-e Antwort, Verpflichtung usw.* ~ evade, dodge; '**~d** heavy, oppressive.

'**Drucker** *m* (7) *a. Computer*: printer.
'**Drücker** *m* (7) push-button; *am Gewehr*: trigger; (*Tür*⌒) door-handle.
Drucke'rei *f* (16) printing-office, *bsd. Am.* printing shop.
'**Druck-erlaubnis** *f* printing licence (*Am.* license); imprimatur.
'**Drucker|presse** *f* printing-press; '**~schwärze** *f* printer's ink.
'**Druck|fahne** *f* (galley-)proof; '**~farbe** *f* printing-ink; '**~fehler** *m* misprint, erratum; '**~fehlerteufel** *m* demon of misprints; '**~fehlerverzeichnis** *n* errata *pl.*; '**⌒fertig** ready for the press; '**⌒frisch** fresh from the press; '**~kammer** *f* pressure chamber; '**~knopf** *m am Kleid*: press-stud, snap-fastener; ⚡ push-button; '**~legung** *f* printing; '**~luft** *f* compressed air; *attr.* compressed-air *cylinder*; pneumatic, air *brake, etc.*; '**~maschine** *f typ.* printing machine; '**~messer** *m* pressure-ga(u)ge; '**~mittel** *n fig.* lever; '**~probe** *f typ.* proof; '**~pumpe** *f* force-pump; '**⌒reif** ready for the press; '**~sache(n** *pl.*) ✉ *f* printed matter, *Am. a.* second-class matter; '**~schalter** ⚡ *m* push- (*od.* press-)button switch; '**~schrift** *f* print, type; (*Abhandlung*) publication; '**~taste** *f* push-button; '**~welle** *f e-r Explosion*: shock wave.
drum [drum] *s. darum*; *das* ⌒ *und Dran* the paraphernalia *pl.*
drunten ['druntən] below (there).
'**drunter und** '**drüber** upside down, topsy-turvy, F higgledy-piggledy.
Drüse ['dry:zə] *f* (15) gland; **~n...** glandular.
Dschungel ['dʒuŋəl] *m, n* (7) jungle.
du [du:] you; *eccl., poet.* thou; *auf ~ und ~ stehen* be on intimate terms.
Dübel ⊕ ['dy:bəl] *m* (7) dowel, peg.
Dublee(gold) [du'ble:-] *n* (11) rolled gold.
Dublette [du'blɛtə] *f* (15) duplicate; *hunt.* right-and-left (shot).
ducken ['dukən] (25) *den Kopf*: duck; *j-n*: *fig.* take *a p.* down a peg or two; *sich ~* crouch, *ausweichend*: duck, *fig.* knuckle under.
Duckmäuser ['~mɔʏzər] *m* (7) sneak; (*Scheinheiliger*) hypocrite; '**⌒ig** sneaking; hypocritical.
dudeln ['du:dəln] (29) tootle.
'**Dudelsack** *m* bagpipe.
Duell [du'ˀɛl] *n* (3[1]) duel (*auf Degen usw.* with); **~ant** [~'lant] *m* (12) duellist; **⌒ieren** [~'li:rən]: *sich ~* (fight a) duel.
Duett [du'ˀɛt] *n* (3) duet.
Duft [duft] *m* (3[3]) scent; fragrance; perfume; '**⌒en** (26) be fragrant, smell (*süß* sweet); '**⌒end** fragrant; '**⌒ig** (*leicht, zart*) flimsy, filmy, dainty; '**~stoff** *m* odorous substance.
duld|en ['duldən] (26) (*ertragen*) bear, endure; (*leiden*) suffer (*a. v/i.*); (*zulassen*) tolerate; '**⌒er(in** *f*) *m* sufferer; **~sam** ['dultza:m] tolerant (*gegen* of); '**⌒samkeit** *f* tolerance, toleration; **⌒ung** ['~duŋ] *f* toleration.
dumm [dum] stupid, dull, *Am.* F dumb; (*einfältig*) silly, foolish; (*unangenehm*; *ungeschickt*) awkward; (*schwindlig*) dizzy (*von, vor dat.* with); *~er Junge* young shaver; *~er Streich* foolish prank; *~es Zeug* nonsense; *der ⌒e sein* be the loser; *die ⌒en werden nicht alle* fools never die out; '**~dreist** impertinent; '**⌒heit** *f* stupidity; (*a. dumme Handlung usw.*) folly; (*Fehler*) blunder; (*Unbesonnenheit*) indiscretion; *~en machen* (play the) clown; *fig.* get into trouble; '**⌒kopf** *m* fool, stupid, *Am. a.* sap(head).
dümmlich ['dymliç] silly, dumb.
dumpf [dumpf] *Schall*: hollow; *Geräusch, Gefühl, Schmerz*: dull; *Donner*: rumbling; (*düster*) gloomy; (*feucht*) damp; *Luft*: heavy, *im Zimmer*: close; '**~ig** (*feucht*) damp; (*modrig*) mo(u)ldy, musty; (*muffig*) fusty; (*stickig*) stuffy, close.
Düne ['dy:nə] *f* (15) sandhill, dune.
Dung [duŋ] *m* (3), **Dünger** ['dyŋər] *m* (7) dung, manure; (*Misch*⌒) compost; *bsd. künstlicher*: fertilizer.
Dünge|mittel ['dyŋə-] *n* fertilizer; '**⌒n** (25) dung, manure, fertilize.
'**Dunggrube** *f* manure pit.
dunkel ['duŋkəl] **1.** *allg.* dark; (*trüb*) dim; (*finster*) gloomy; (*unklar*) obscure; *Erinnerung*: vague; **2.** ⌒ *n* (7) *the* dark; *fig. j-n im* ⌒*n lassen* leave a p. in the dark (*über acc.* about).
Dünkel ['dyŋkəl] *m* (7) conceit.
'**dunkelblau** dark-blue.
'**dünkelhaft** conceited, arrogant.

ˈ**Dunkel|heit** *f* darkness; *fig.* obscurity; *bei anbrechender* ~ at nightfall; ˈ**~kammer** *phot. f* darkroom.
ˈ**dunkeln** (29) grow dark, darken.
ˈ**Dunkelziffer** *f* number of undetected cases.
dünken [ˈdyŋkən] (30) seem; *es dünkt mich* (*a. mir*) it seems to me; *sich* ... ~ imagine (*od.* fancy) o.s. ...
dünn [dyn] *allg.* thin; (*schmächtig*) slim; *Flüssigkeit*: *a.* weak; (*spärlich*) sparse; *Luft*, *phys.* rare; ˈ**2darm** *m* small gut; ˈ**2e** *f* (15, *o. pl.*) *s. Dünnheit*; ˈ**~flüssig** thin, fluid; ˈ**2heit** *f* thinness; *der Luft*, *phys.* rarity.
Dunst [dunst] *m* (3^2 *u.* ^{3}) vapo(u)r; (*Ausdünstung*) exhalation; *in der Luft*: haze; *über e-r Stadt*: F smog; *des Alkohols usw.*: fume; *sl. blauer* ~ hot air; *j-m blauen* ~ *vormachen* humbug a p.
dünsten [ˈdynstən] (26) *Speise*: steam.
ˈ**dunstig** vaporous; (*feucht*) damp; (*nebelig*) hazy.
ˈ**Dunstkreis** *m* atmosphere.
Dünung ⚓ [ˈdy:nuŋ] *f* swell.
düpieren [dyˈpi:rən] dupe.
Duplikat [dupliˈkɑ:t] *n* (3) duplicate.
Duplizität [duplitsiˈtɛ:t] *f* (16) duplicity.
Dur ♪ [du:r] *n inv.* major.
durch [durç] **1.** *prp.* through; (*quer* ~) across; *Mittel*, *Ursache*: through, by; *Zeitdauer*: through(out); **2.** *adv.*: *das ganze Jahr* ~ throughout the year; *die ganze Nacht* ~ all night long; *es ist drei* (*Uhr*) ~ it is past three; ~ *und* ~ through and through, *fig. a.* to the backbone; *ein Schurke* ~ *und* ~ a thorough scoundrel.
ˈ**durch-ackern** *fig.* plough (*Am.* plow) through.
ˈ**durch-arbeiten** work through; *sich* ~ make one's way through.
ˈ**durch**ˈ**-aus** throughout, thoroughly; (*ganz und gar*) out and out; (*geradezu*) downright; (*unbedingt*) absolutely, quite; by all means; ~ *nicht* not at all, by no means.
ˈ**durchbeißen** bite through; *sich* ~ struggle through.
ˈ**durchbilden** educate (*od.* train) thoroughly.
ˈ**durchblättern** leaf (*od.* glance, skim) through.
ˈ**Durchblick** *m* vista; ˈ**2en** *v/i.* look through; *fig.* appear, show; ~ *lassen* give to understand.
durchˈ**bluten** supply with blood.
durchˈ**bohren** *v/t.* pierce; (*durchlöchern*) perforate; *j-n mit* (*den*) *Blicken* ~ look daggers at a p.; *v/i.* ˈ*durchbohren* bore through.
ˈ**durchbraten** roast thoroughly; *durchgebraten* well done; *nicht durchgebraten* underdone, rare.
ˈ**durchbrechen** *v/i.* (sn) break through; *v/t. durch*ˈ*brechen* break through; pierce; penetrate.
ˈ**durchbrennen** (sn) burn through; ⚡ *Sicherung*: fuse, blow; *Radioröhre*: burn out; F *fig.* run away, bolt (*mit et.* with); *Frau*: elope.
ˈ**durchbringen** bring through; *Gesetz*: pass; *Geld*: dissipate; *sich* ~ make both ends meet; *sich ehrlich* ~ get an honest living; *sich kümmerlich* ~ make a poor living; *e-n Kranken*: pull *a p.* through.
ˈ**Durchbruch** *m* breach; *e-s Dammes*, *a.* ⚕ rupture; *der Zähne*: cutting; ⚔ break-through (*a. fig. Erfolg*); *e-r Mauer*: break.
durchdacht [~ˈdaxt]: *gut* ~ *Rede usw.*: well-reasoned; *Plan*: well--devised.
durchˈ**denken** think over (*od.* out).
ˈ**durchdrängen** force through; *sich* ~ force one's way through.
ˈ**durchdrehen** *v/t. Fleisch*: pass through the mincer; ✈ swing; *v/i.* F *P.*: crack up; *mot. Räder*: spin.
ˈ**durchdringen 1.** *v/i.* (sn) get through; penetrate; *Flüssigkeit*: percolate, permeate; *Meinung*: prevail; **2.** *durch*ˈ*dringen v/t.* penetrate; pierce; *durch*ˈ*drungen von e-m Gefühl usw.* imbued with; **~d** [ˈ~driŋənt] penetrating; piercing.
Durchˈ**dringung** *f* penetration.
ˈ**durchdrücken** press through; F *fig. s. durchsetzen.*
durchˈ**-eilen** hasten (*od.* hurry) through.
durch-eiˈ**nander 1.** in confusion; in a jumble; pell-mell; (*wahllos*) promiscuously; *ganz* ~ *sein P.*: be all mixed up, be all upset; **2.** 2 *n* muddle, jumble; confusion; medley *of voices*; **~bringen** muddle up; *j-n*: upset, bewilder; *Begriffe*: mix up; **~geraten** get mixed up; **~werfen** jumble up; *fig.* mix up.
ˈ**durchfahr|en 1.** *v/i.* (sn) pass (*od.*

drive *od.* sail) through; **2.** *durch'fahren v/t.* = ~ 1.; *fig.* rush through; '**2t** *f* passage; (*Tor*) gate (-way); ~ *verboten!* no thoroughfare!

'**Durchfall** *m* ⚕ diarrh(o)ea; (*Mißerfolg*) failure, *Am.* F flunk, *thea. usw. sl.* flop; '**2en** (sn) fall through; *im Examen usw.*: fail, be rejected, *Am.* F flunk; *thea.* (turn out a) flop; ~ *lassen* reject, *Am.* F flunk; *thea.* damn.

'**durchfechten** fight *a th.* through, see *a th.* through.

'**durchfeilen** file through.

'**durchfinden:** *sich* ~ find one's way through.

durch'flechten interweave.

durch'fliegen fly through; *fig. Buch usw.*: run through.

durch'fließen, durch'fluten flow (*od.* run) through (*a. fig.*).

durch'forsch|en search through, investigate; *Land*: explore; **2ung** *f* investigation; exploration.

'**durchfragen:** *sich* ~ ask one's way through.

'**durchfressen** eat through; *geol., ätzend*: corrode.

'**durchfrieren** (sn) freeze (*od.* chill) through.

durchführ|bar ['~fy:rba:r] practicable, feasible; '**~en** lead (*od.* convey) through; *Draht usw.*: pass through; *fig.* carry through *od.* out; *Gesetz usw.*: implement, (*a.* ⚖) enforce; '**2ung** *f* carrying-out; realization; enforcement; '**2ungsbestimmungen** *f/pl.* implementing regulations.

'**Durchgabe** *f* transmission; (*Bekanntgabe*) special announcement, (radio) flash.

'**Durchgang** *m* passage; *v. Waren od. ast.*: transit; *Sport*: heat; ~ *verboten!* no thoroughfare!, no trespassing!

durchgängig ['~gɛŋiç] general(ly *adv.*).

'**Durchgangs|handel** *m* transit trade; '**~lager** *n* transit camp; '**~straße** *f* through road; '**~verkehr** *m* through traffic; ⚕ transit trade; '**~zoll** *m* transit duty; '**~zug** *m* corridor train.

'**durchgeben** pass on; *Nachricht*: transmit; *Radio*: announce.

'**durchgehen** *v/i.* (sn) go (*od.* walk) through, pass (through); (*fliehen*) abscond, *a. Pferd*: bolt, *Liebende*: elope; *Antrag, Gesetz*: pass, be carried; (*geduldet werden*) pass; *et.* ~ *lassen* overlook; *j-m nichts* ~ *lassen* pass a p. nothing; *mit j-m* ~ *Gefühl usw.*: run away with a p.; *v/t.* (*erörtern*; *prüfen*) go through *a th.*; (*durchlesen*) go over *a th.*; '**~d** through; *zeitlich*: continuous; 🚂 ~*er Wagen* (*Zug*) through carriage (train); *adv.* generally; (*durchweg*) throughout; ~ *geöffnet* open throughout.

durch'geistigt spiritual, highly intellectual.

'**durchgreifen** pass one's hand through; *fig.* take drastic measures; '**~d** drastic; radical, sweeping.

'**durchhalte|n** *v/i.* hold out (to the end), see it through; '**2vermögen** *n* staying power, stamina.

'**durchhecheln** *fig.* gossip about *a p.*

'**durchhelfen** (*dat.*) help through; *sich* ~ manage, make shift.

'**durchkämmen** comb (thoroughly); *fig.* comb (out).

'**durchkämpfen** fight out; *sich* ~ fight one's way through.

'**durchkochen** boil thoroughly; '*durchgekocht* well done.

'**durchkommen** (sn) come (*od.* get) through; *durch Krankheit usw.*: pull through; *im Examen*: pass, *knapp*: scrape through; (*auskommen*) get along; *fig.* succeed.

durch'kreuzen cross; *fig. a.* thwart.

Durch|laß ['durçlas] *m* (1²) passage; outlet; '**2lassen** let through, allow to pass; *Licht*: transmit; *im Examen*: pass; '**2lässig** permeable (*für* to).

Durchlaucht ['~lauxt] *f* (16) Serene Highness; **2ig** [~'lauxtiç] serene.

'**durchlaufen** *v/i.* (sn) run through; *s. durchsickern*; *v/t. Schuhe*: wear through; *durch'laufen v/t.* run through (*a. fig. Gefühl*); *Schule*: pass through; *Strecke*: cover.

'**Durchlauf-erhitzer** ⚡ *m* (7) continuous-flow water heater.

durch'leben live (*od.* pass) through.

'**durchlesen** read through *od.* over; *sorgfältig*: peruse; *flüchtig*: skim.

durch'leucht|en (flood with) light, illuminate; ⚕ X-ray, screen; *Ei*: test, *Am.* candle; *fig.* investigate, screen; **2ung** *f* illumination; X-ray examination; screening; **ᵋungsschirm** ⚕ *m* fluorescent screen.

ˈ**durchliegen:** *sich* ~ get bedsore.

durch|lochen [~ˈlɔxən] (25) *Fahrkarte usw.*: punch; **~löchern** [~ˈlœçərn] (29) perforate; (*durchbohren*) pierce; *mit Kugeln*: riddle.

ˈ**durchlüften**, *a.* *durch*ˈ*lüften* air.

ˈ**durchmachen** go (*od.* pass) through; suffer.

ˈ**Durchmarsch** *m* march(ing) through; F ⚕ diarrh(o)ea; ˈ**ᵋieren** (sn) march through.

durchˈ**messen** traverse.

ˈ**Durchmesser** *m* (7) diameter.

ˈ**durchmustern**, *a.* *durch*ˈ*mustern* pass in review, examine carefully, scrutinize.

ˈ**durchnässen**, *a.* *durch*ˈ*nässen* wet through, drench, soak.

ˈ**durchnehmen** *Thema*: go through *od.* over, deal with, treat.

ˈ**durchpausen** trace, calk.

ˈ**durchpeitschen** whip soundly; *fig.* hurry through; *parl.* rush *a bill* through.

ˈ**durchprügeln** beat soundly, thrash.

durchqueren [durçˈkveːrən] (25) pass through, cross, traverse.

ˈ**durchrechnen** count (*od.* calculate, go) over; check.

ˈ**durchreiben** *s.* *durchscheuern*.

Durchreiche [ˈ~raıçə] *f* (15) (service) hatch; ˈ**ᵋn** hand (*od.* pass) through.

ˈ**Durchreise** *f* passage, transit; ˈ**ᵋn** *v/i.* (sn) travel (*od.* pass) through; *durch*ˈ*reisen* *v/t.* travel over; ˈ**~nde** *m*, *f* travel(l)er, *Am.* *a.* transient; 🚂 through passenger.

ˈ**durchreißen** *v/i.* (sn) get torn; *Faden*: break; *a.* *durch*ˈ*reißen* *v/t.* rend, tear.

ˈ**durchreiten** *Pferd*: gall by riding; *sich* ~ chafe o.s. by riding; *durch*ˈ*reiten* ride through.

durchˈ**rieseln** *v/t.* run through; *fig.* *a.* thrill *a p.*; *v/i.* ˈ*durchrieseln* trickle through.

ˈ**durchringen:** *sich* ~ struggle through (*zu* to); *sich zu e-m Entschluß* ~ make up one's mind (after long inner struggles).

ˈ**durchsacken** ✈ *v/i.* (sn) pancake.

ˈ**Durchsage** *f* *s.* *Durchgabe*; ˈ**ᵋn** pass on; *Radio*: announce.

ˈ**durchsägen** saw through.

durchˈ**schaubar** clear; *schwer* ~ inscrutable; ˈ**durchschauen** *v/i.* look through; *fig.* *durch*ˈ*schauen* *v/t.* see through.

ˈ**durchscheinen** shine through; ˈ**~d** translucent, transparent.

ˈ**durchscheuern** rub through, gall, chafe; *Stoff*: wear through; *sich* ~ get chafed.

ˈ**durchschießen** *v/i.* shoot through (*a. fig.*); (*durcheilen*) dash through; *durch*ˈ*schießen* *v/t.* shoot through; *typ.* lead; *mit Papier*: interleave.

ˈ**durchschimmern** shine through.

ˈ**Durchschlag** *m* (*Sieb*) strainer; *v. Maschinenschrift*: (carbon) copy, F carbon; *e-s Geschosses*: penetration; ⚡ disruptive discharge; ⊕ punch; **ᵋen** [ˈ~gən] *v/i.* (ˈ*durchdringen*) get through; (*wirken*) have (*od.* take) effect; *Papier*: blot; *Farbe*: show through; ⚡ break down, spark; *fig.* be dominant; (*sich zeigen*) show; *v/t.* beat through; *Erbsen usw.*: strain; *sich* ~ fight one's way through; *fig.* *s.* *sich durchbringen*; *durch*ˈ*schlagen* beat through; (*durchbohren* pierce; *Geschoß*: penetrate; ˈ**ᵋend** (*wirkungsvoll*) effective, telling; *~er Erfolg* striking (*od.* complete) success; ˈ**~papier** *n* copying paper, flimsy; (*Kohlepapier*) carbon paper; ˈ**~skraft** *f* penetrating power; *fig.* force, impact.

ˈ**durchschlängeln:** *sich* ~ wind through; *fig.* *P.*: wriggle through.

ˈ**durchschleichen:** *sich* ~ sneak through.

ˈ**durchschleusen** pass through (the lock); *fig.* pass (through).

ˈ**durchschlüpfen** (sn) slip through.

ˈ**durchschmelzen** melt, fuse.

ˈ**durchschneiden** cut through; *fig.* intersect; *durch*ˈ*schneiden* (*kreuzen*) cross, traverse.

ˈ**Durchschnitt** *m* cutting through; ⊕ section, profile; ⅍ *u. fig.* average; *über* (*unter*) *dem* ~ above (below) average; *im* ~ *s.* ᵋ*lich adv.*; ˈ**ᵋlich** average; *adv.* on an average; ~ *betragen* (*leisten usw.*) average; ˈ**~s...** average ...

ˈ**Durchschreibe|block** *m* carbon copy pad; ˈ**~buch** *n* transfer copying (*od.* duplicating) book; ˈ**~verfahren** *n* copying process.

durchˈ**schreiten** walk through; pass (through); cross.

ˈ**Durchschrift** *f* (carbon) copy.

'**Durchschuß** *m typ.* lead; *Weberei*: weft; (*a.* '**~blatt** *n*) interleaf; ~ des Armes shot through the arm.

durch'schwimmen swim (through *od.* across).

'**durchschwitzen** soak with sweat.

durch'segeln sail (through).

'**durchsehen** *v/i.* look (*od.* see) through; *v/t.* look *a th.* over; (*prüfen*) examine; *bsd. typ. Korrekturbogen*: read.

'**durchseihen** strain, filter.

'**durchsetzen:** *fig. et.* ~ carry through; (*erzwingen*) enforce; (es) ~, daß et. geschieht cause a th. to be done; s-n Kopf ~ have one's way; sich ~ assert o.s.; win through, prevail, succeed; durch'setzen intersperse (mit with).

'**Durchsicht** *f s.* durchsehen: looking over; examination; inspection; *bsd. typ.* reading; revision; '**2ig** transparent (*a. fig.*); *fig.* perspicuous, lucid; '**~igkeit** *f* transparency (*a. fig.*); *fig.* perspicuity, lucidity.

'**durchsickern** (sn) ooze (*od.* seep) through *od.* out (*a. fig.*); *fig. Nachricht*: leak out.

'**durchsieben** sift, screen (*beide a. fig.*); *mit Kugeln* durch'sieben riddle with.

'**durchsprechen** talk over, discuss.

'**durchstech|en** pierce through; durch'stechen perforate; *mit e-r Nadel*: prick; *Damm*: cut; **2erei** [~'raı] *f* (16) underhand dealing(s *pl.*).

'**durchstecken** pass through.

'**durchstehen** *fig.* see *a th.* through.

'**Durchstich** *m* cut(ting).

durch'stöbern rummage through; *Gebiet*: scour.

'**durchstoßen** push (*od.* thrust) through; durch'stoßen pierce.

'**durchstreichen,** *a.* durch'streichen cross (*od.* strike, score) out, cancel.

durch'streifen roam through; *suchend*: scour.

'**durchströmen** *v/i.* (sn) *u.* durch'strömen *v/t.* run through (*a. fig.*).

durch'such|en search; *Gebiet*: *a.* scour, comb; **2ung** *f* search.

durch'tränken impregnate, soak.

durchtrieben [durç'tri:bən] cunning, sly, tricky; (*schalkhaft*) mischievous; **2heit** *f* cunning, trickiness, slyness.

durch'wachen pass (*od.* spend) *the night* waking.

'**durchwachsen** (sn) grow through; *adj.* durch'wachsen *Fleisch, Speck*: streaky; *fig.* mixed.

'**Durchwahl** *teleph. f* direct dial(l)ing.

'**durchwählen** *teleph.* dial through.

durch'wandern *v/t.* wander through (*a. v/i.* [sn] 'durchwandern); traverse.

durch'wärmen, *a.* 'durchwärmen warm through.

durch'waten *v/t. u.* 'durchwaten *v/i.* (sn) wade (through), ford.

durch'weben interweave.

durchweg ['durç'vɛk] throughout; without exception.

durch'weichen (25) soak through (*a. v/i.* [sn] 'durchweichen), drench.

'**durchwinden:** sich ~ worm (*od.* thread) one's way through.

durch'wühlen *Erde*: rake (*od.* root) up; (*durchsuchen*) search, rummage; (*a. plündern*) ransack.

'**durchwursteln** F: sich ~ muddle through.

'**durchzählen** count over.

'**durchzeichnen** trace.

'**durchziehen** *v/t.* pull through; *Faden*: pass through; sich ~ run through (*a. fig.*); durch'ziehen pass through; *mit Fäden usw.*: interlace; *v/i.* 'durchziehen (sn) pass (*od.* march) through.

durch'zucken flash through.

'**Durchzug** *m* passage; (*Luft*) draught, *Am.* draft; circulation; ⚠ girder; ~ machen let in fresh air.

'**durchzwängen** (25) force through; sich ~ squeeze o.s. through.

dürfen ['dyrfən] (30) be permitted *od.* allowed; (*wagen*) dare; ich darf I may; darf ich? may I?; ich darf nicht I must not; wenn ich bitten darf (if you) please; es dürfte ein leichtes sein it should be easy; er dürfte recht haben he is probably right.

durfte ['durftə] *pret. v.* dürfen.

dürftig ['dyrftiç] (*bedürftig*) needy; (*ungenügend*) poor, inadequate; (*spärlich*) scanty, meag|re (*Am.* -er); (*erbärmlich, gering*) paltry, measly; in ~en Verhältnissen in needy circumstances; '**2keit** *f* neediness; *fig.* poorness, scantiness, paltriness.

dürr [dyr] dry; *Baum usw.*: dead; *Boden*: arid, barren; (*mager*) lean, spindly; *mit ~en Worten* in plain terms, bluntly.

'**Dürre** *f* (15) dryness; aridity; barrenness; leanness; (*Regenmangel*) drought.

Durst [durst] *m* (3²) thirst (*nach* for); ~ *haben* be thirsty; ~ *bekommen* get thirsty.

dürsten ['dyrstən] *v/i.* (26) be thirsty; *fig.* thirst (*nach* for, after).

'**durstig** thirsty (*nach* for); F dry.

'**Durststrecke** *f fig.* hard times *pl.*

Dusch|e ['du:ʃə] *f* (15) douche (*a.* ⚕), shower; (*Brausebad*) shower-bath; '**2en** (27) douche, have (*Am.* take) a shower; **~gel** ['~ge:l] *n* shower foam; '**~kabine** *f* shower cubicle; '**~raum** *m* shower room; '**~vorhang** *m* shower curtain.

Düse ['dy:zə] *f* (15) *allg.* nozzle; (*Spritz2*, *Strahl2*) jet.

Dusel ['du:zəl] *m* (7) dizziness; F luck, fluke; ~ *haben* be lucky.

'**dus(e)lig** dizzy.

'**Düsen|-antrieb** *m* jet propulsion; *mit* ~ jet-powered, jet-propelled; '**~flugzeug** *n* jetplane; '**~jäger** *m* jetfighter; '**~triebwerk** *n* jet engine.

Dussel F ['dusəl] *m* (7) idiot.

düster ['dy:stər] dark, gloomy (*a. fig.*); (*traurig*) sad; '**2heit** *f*, '**2keit** *f* gloom(iness).

Dutzend ['dutsənt] *n* (3¹) dozen; '**~mensch** *m* commonplace man; '**2weise** by the dozen, in dozens.

Duz|bruder ['du:ts-] *m* intimate friend; '**2en** (27) *j-n* ~ be on familiar terms with a p.

Dynam|ik [dy'nɑ:mik] *f* (16) dynamics *sg.*; *fig.* dynamic force; **2isch** dynamic(al); *Rente*: index-linked.

Dynamit [dyna'mi:t] *n* (3) dynamite (*a. v/t. mit* ~ *sprengen*).

Dynamo *m* (11), **~maschine** [dy'nɑ:moma'ʃi:nə] *f* dynamo (machine), generator.

Dynastie [dynas'ti:] *f* (16) dynasty.

D-Zug ['de:tsu:k] *m* corridor-train, *Am. a.* vestibule-train.

E

E [e:], **e** *n inv.* E, e; ♪ E.

Ebbe ['ɛbə] *f* (15) ebb(-tide); low tide, low water; *es ist* ~ the tide is out *od.* down; *es tritt* ~ *ein* the tide is going out; *fig. bei mir ist* ~ I am broke; '**2n** (25) ebb.

eben ['e:bən] **1.** *adj.* even; (*flach*) plain, level; ⩚ plane; *zu ~er Erde* on the ground (*Am.* first) floor; **2.** *adv.* evenly; (*genau*) exactly; (*gerade*) just; (*schließlich*) after all; ~ *tun wollen* be just going to do; ~ *erst* just now; '**2bild** *n* image, (exact) likeness; **~bürtig** ['~byrtiç] of equal birth; *fig. j-m* ~ *sein* be a match for a p., be a p.'s equal; **~der'selbe** the very same; **~'deswegen** for that very reason.

'**Ebene** *f* (15) plain; ⩚ plane; *fig.* level; *s. schief.*

'**eben|falls** likewise; '**2heit** *f* evenness; '**2holz** *n* ebony; '**2maß** *n* symmetry; '**~mäßig** symmetrical; '**~so** just so; just as ...; (*auch*) likewise; '**~sogut** *adv.* just as well; '**~soviel** just as much; '**~sowenig** just as little *od. pl.* few.

Eber ['e:bər] *m* (7) boar; '**~-esche** ⚘ *f* mountain-ash.

ebnen ['e:bnən] (26) even, level; (*glätten*) smooth; *fig. j-m den Weg* ~ smooth the way for a p.

Echo ['ɛço:] *n* (11) echo; '**~lot** *n* ⚓ echo sounder; ✈ sonic altimeter.

echt [ɛçt] genuine; (*wahr*) true; (*rein*) pure; (*wirklich*) real; (*rechtmäßig*) legitimate; *Farbe*: (*haltbar*) fast; *Gold, Silber*: sterling; *Haar*: natural; (*glaubwürdig*) authentic; ⩚ *~er Bruch* proper fraction; '**2heit** *f* genuineness; purity; reality; legitimacy; fastness; authenticity.

Eck|ball ['ɛk-] *m Sport*: corner-kick; '**~e** *f* (15) corner; (*Kante*) edge; (*kurzer Weg*) short distance; *in die* ~ *drängen* (*a. fig.*) corner; F *um die* ~ *bringen* do in; *um die* ~ *gehen* turn (round) the corner, F *fig.*

go west; *an allen ~n und Enden* everywhere; *von allen ~n und Enden* from all parts; '**~ensteher** *m* (7) loafer.
Ecker ⚘ ['ɛkər] *f* (15) acorn.
'**eck|ig** angular (*a. fig.*); ...~ ...-cornered; '**2pfeiler** *m* corner-pillar; '**2platz** *m* corner-seat; '**2stein** *m* corner-stone; '**2zahn** *m* canine tooth, eye-tooth; '**2zins** *m* prime rate.
edel ['e:dəl] noble; *Metall*: precious; *edles Pferd* thorough-bred (horse); *physiol. edle Teile m/pl.* vital parts *pl.*; '**~denkend,** '**~gesinnt** noble-minded; '**2frau** *f* noblewoman; '**2gas** *n* inert gas; '**2hirsch** *m* stag; '**2holz** *n* rare wood; '**2leute** *pl.* noblemen, nobles; '**2mann** *m* nobleman; '**2metall** *n* precious metal; '**2mut** *m* noble-mindedness, generosity; **~mütig** ['~my:tiç] noble-minded, generous; '**2-obst** *n* choice fruit; '**2stahl** *m* high-grade steel; '**2stein** *m* precious stone; *geschliffener*: gem; '**2tanne** *f* silver fir; '**2weiß** ⚘ *n* (3²) edelweiss.
Edikt [e'dikt] *n* (3) edict.
Edition [edi'tsjo:n] *f* critical edition.
EDV-Anlage ['e:'de:'faʊ-] *f* electronic data processing equipment.
Efeu ['e:fɔʏ] *m* (11) ivy; *mit ~ bewachsen* ivy-clad.
Eff-eff F ['ɛf'ʔɛf] *n inv.*: *et. aus dem ~ können* have a th. at one's fingers' ends *od.* finger-tips.
Effekt [ɛ'fɛkt] *m* (3) effect; *nach ~ haschen* strain after effect; **~en** *pl.* effects; ✝ securities; **~enbörse** *f* Stock Exchange; **~enhandel** *m* stock(-exchange) business; **~enhändler** *m* stock-jobber; **~enmakler** *m* stock-broker; **~hasche'rei** *f* (16) claptrap, sensationalism.
effektiv [ɛfɛk'ti:f] effective, actual.
ef'fektvoll effective, striking.
egal [e'gɑ:l] (*gleich*) equal; (*einerlei*) all the same (*mir* to me); *ganz ~ wo* no matter where.
Egel *zo.* ['e:gəl] *m* (7) leech.
Egge ['ɛgə] *f* (15), '**2n** (25) harrow.
Egoismus [ego'ʔismus] *m* (16) egoism.
Ego'-ist *m* (12), **~in** *f* (16¹) egotist; **2isch** egotistic(al), selfish.
egozentrisch [~'tsɛntriʃ] self-centred, *Am.* -centered.
eh' [e:], **ehe¹** ['e:ə] *cj.* before, *lit.* ere.
'**Ehe²** (15) marriage; *s. Ehestand*: wedlock; *Kind aus erster usw. ~* child by the first *etc.* marriage; *die ~ brechen* commit adultery; '**~-anbahnung** *f* match-making; '**~berater** *m* marriage guidance counsellor; '**~bett** *n* nuptial bed; '**2-brechen** (*nur im inf.*) commit adultery; '**~brecher** *m* (7) adulterer; '**~brecherin** *f* (16¹) adulteress; '**2brecherisch** adulterous; '**~bruch** *m* adultery.
ehedem ['~de:m] formerly.
'**Ehe|frau** *f* wife; '**~gatte** *m*, '**~gattin** *f* spouse; '**~glück** *n* wedded bliss; '**~hälfte** *f* better half; '**~leben** *n* married life; '**~leute** *pl.* married couple(s *pl.*); '**2lich** conjugal; matrimonial; *Kind*: legitimate; '**2lichen** (25) marry; '**2los** unmarried, single; '**~losigkeit** *f* celibacy.
ehemal|ig ['~mɑ:liç] (*früher*) former, *bsd. Am.* one-time; (*verstorben*; *pensioniert*) late; ex-... (*z. B. ex-president*); '**~s** formerly.
'**Ehe|mann** *m* husband; '**2mündig** marriageable; '**~paar** *n* married couple; '**~partner** *m* (*Mann*) husband; (*Frau*) wife.
'**eher** sooner, earlier; (*lieber*) rather; (*leichter*) more easily; *je ~, je lieber* the sooner the better.
'**Ehe|recht** *n* marriage law; '**~ring** *m* wedding ring.
ehern ['e:ərn] brazen, of brass; *fig.* iron (*law, etc.*); *mit ~er Stirn* brazen-faced.
'**Ehe|scheidung** *f* divorce; '**~scheidungsklage** *f* divorce-suit; '**~schließung** *f* (contraction of) marriage; '**~stand** *m* married state, matrimony, *gewählt*: wedlock.
ehestens ['e:əstəns] at the earliest; (*möglichst bald*) as soon as possible.
'**Ehe|stifter**(**in** *f*) *m* match-maker; '**~vermittlung** *f s. Eheanbahnung*; '**~versprechen** *n* promise of marriage; '**~vertrag** *m* marriage settlement.
Ehrabschneider(**in** *f*) ['e:rʔapʃnaɪdər] *m* slanderer.
'**ehrbar** hono(u)rable, respectable; *Benehmen*: decent, modest; '**2keit** *f* honesty, respectability; decency.
Ehre ['e:rə] *f* (15) hono(u)r; *zu ~n* (*gen.*) in hono(u)r of; *mit wem habe ich die ~ (zu sprechen)?* whom have I the hono(u)r to address?;

j-m (e-e) ~ antun (erweisen) do (*od.* pay) hono(u)r to a p.; *j-m ~ machen* do a p. credit; *j-n bei s-r ~ packen* put a p. on his hono(u)r; *s. einlegen*; ˈ**2n** (25) hono(u)r.

ˈ**Ehren|·amt** *n* honorary post; ˈ**2amtlich** honorary; ˈ**~bezeigung** *f* mark of respect; ⚔ salute; ˈ**~bürger** *m* honorary citizen, freeman; ˈ**~bürgerrecht** *n* freedom (of a city); ˈ**~doktor** *m* honorary doctor; ˈ**~-erklärung** *f* (full) apology; ˈ**~gast** *m* guest of hono(u)r; ˈ**~gericht** *n* court of hono(u)r; ˈ**2haft** hono(u)rable; honest; **2halber** [ˈ~halbər] for hono(u)r's sake; *Doktor ~* Doctor honoris causa; ˈ**~handel** *m* affair of hono(u)r; ˈ**~kränkung** *f* insult to *a p.'s* hono(u)r, affront; ˈ**~mal** *n* memorial; ˈ**~mann** *m* man of hono(u)r, hono(u)rable man; ˈ**~mitglied** *n* honorary member; ˈ**~pflicht** *f* honorary obligation; *es ist für mich e-e ~* I am in hono(u)r bound; ˈ**~platz** *m* place (*engS.* seat) of hono(u)r; ˈ**~preis** *m* prize; ⚘ speedwell; ˈ**~recht** *n*: *Verlust (od. Aberkennung) der bürgerlichen ~e* loss of civil rights, civic degradation; ˈ**~rettung** *f* vindication (of *a p.'s* hono[u]r); ˈ**2rührig** defamatory; ˈ**~runde** *f Sport*: lap of hono(u)r; ˈ**~sache** *f s. Ehrenhandel*; *es ist für mich ~* it is a point of hono(u)r with me; ˈ**~schuld** *f* debt of hono(u)r; ˈ**~tag** *m* great day; ˈ**~titel** *m* honorary title; ˈ**~tor** *n Sport*: consolation goal; ˈ**2voll** hono(u)rable; ˈ**~vorsitzende** *m* (18) honorary chairman; ˈ**2wert** hono(u)rable; (*achtbar*) respectable; ˈ**~wort** *n* word of hono(u)r; *auf ~ entlassen usw.* on parole; ˈ**~zeichen** *n* decoration.

ehr|erbietig [ˈ~ʔɛrbiːtiç] respectful, deferential; ˈ**2-erbietung** *f*, ˈ**2furcht** *f* respect, deference, reverence; *stärker*: awe (*vor dat.* of); ˈ**~furchtgebietend** awe-inspiring, awesome; **~fürchtig** [ˈ~fyrçtiç], ˈ**~furchtsvoll** respectful, reverential; ˈ**2gefühl** *n* sense of hono(u)r; (*Selbstachtung*) self-respect; ˈ**2geiz** *m* ambition; ˈ**~geizig** ambitious.

ˈ**ehrlich** honest; (*aufrichtig*) sincere; (*echt*) genuine; *Handel, Spiel*: fair; *Meinung*: frank; *Handlungsweise*: plain-dealing; *~ währt am längsten* honesty is the best policy; F *~!* really!, indeed!; ˈ**2keit** *f* honesty; fairness; frankness; plain dealing.

ˈ**ehrlos** dishono(u)rable, infamous; ˈ**2igkeit** *f* dishonesty, infamy.

ˈ**ehrsam** hono(u)rable, respectable; ˈ**2keit** *f* respectability.

ˈ**Ehr|sucht** *f* immoderate ambition; ˈ**2süchtig** (over-)ambitious; ˈ**2ung** *f* hono(u)r (conferred on *a p.*); ˈ**2vergessen** infamous, disgraceful; ˈ**~verlust** ⚖ *m s. Ehrenrecht*; ˈ**~würden:** *Ew. ~* Reverend Sir; ˈ**2würdig** venerable, reverend; ˈ**~würdigkeit** *f* venerableness.

ei[1] [aɪ] ah!, indeed!

Ei[2] *n* (1) egg; 📖 ovum; V *~er pl.* (*Hoden*) balls; (*wie*) *auf ~ern gehen* walk gingerly; *wie ein ~ dem andern gleichen* be as like as two peas; F *wie aus dem ~ gepellt* spick-and-span; *wie ein rohes ~ behandeln* handle with kid-gloves.

Eibe ⚘ [ˈaɪbə] *f* (15) yew(-tree).

Eibisch ⚘ [ˈaɪbiʃ] *m* (4) marsh-mallow.

Eichamt [ˈaɪçʔamt] *n* Office of Weights and Measures, *Am.* Bureau of Standards.

Eiche [ˈaɪçə] *f* (15) oak.

Eichel [ˈaɪçəl] *f* (15) acorn; *anat.* glans; *Karte*: club; **~häher** *zo.* [ˈ~hɛːər] *m* (7) jay.

eichen[1] [ˈaɪçən] (25) *v/t. Gewichte*: ga(u)ge; *Rohre*: calibrate.

ˈ**eichen**[2] *adj.* of oak, oaken.

ˈ**Eichen...**[3] *in Zssgn* oak ...

ˈ**Eich|hörnchen** *n*, ˈ**~kätzchen** *n* squirrel; ˈ**~maß** *n* standard; ga(u)ge; ˈ**~meister** *m* ga(u)ger.

Eid [aɪt] *m* (3) oath; *an ~es Statt* in lieu of oath; *unter ~* on oath.

Eidechse [ˈaɪdɛksə] *f* (15) lizard.

Eider|daunen [ˈaɪdər-] *f/pl.* eider-down; ˈ**~-ente** *f* eider (duck).

eidesstattlich [ˈaɪdəs-] in lieu of (an) oath; *~e Erklärung* affidavit.

Eid|genosse [ˈaɪt-] *m* confederate; ˈ**~genossenschaft** *f* (Swiss) Confederation; **2genössisch** [ˈ~gənœsiʃ] Federal; Swiss; ˈ**2lich** sworn; *adv.* on oath.

Eidotter [ˈaɪdɔtər] *m* (7) yolk.

Eidschwur [ˈaɪt-] *m* oath.

ˈ**Eier|becher** *m* egg-cup; ˈ**~kuchen** *m* omelet, pancake; ˈ**~likör** *m* advocaat; ˈ**~schale** *f* egg-shell; ˈ**~stock** *m* ovary; ˈ**~-uhr** *f* egg-timer.

Eifer [ˈaɪfər] *m* (7, *o. pl.*) zeal; eagerness; *stärker*: ardo(u)r; (*Zorn*) passion; *blinder* ~ rashness; *blinder* ~ *schadet nur* haste is waste; '**~er** *m* (7) zealot, fanatic; '**2n** (29) (*heftig streben*) be eager (*nach* for); (*schmähen*) declaim, inveigh (*gegen* against); *s. wetteifern*; '**~sucht** *f* jealousy (*auf acc.* of); '**2süchtig** jealous (*auf acc.* of).

eifrig ['aɪfrɪç] zealous, eager, keen; *stärker*: ardent.

'**Eigelb** *n* (3) yellow of an egg, yolk.

eigen ['aɪgən] own, proper; (*besonder*; *genau*; *wählerisch*) particular; *j-m* ~ peculiar (to); (*seltsam*) strange, odd; *in Zssgn* ...-owned, *z. B. staats*~ state-owned; *ein* ~*es Zimmer* a room of one's own; *sich e-e Ansicht usw. zu* ~ *machen* adopt; '**2-art** *f* peculiarity; (*Originalität*) originality; '**~-artig** peculiar; original; '**2bedarf** *m* one's own requirements *pl.*; **2brötler** ['~brø:tlər] *m* (7) eccentric; '**2dünkel** *m* self-conceit; '**2fabrikat** *n* self-produced article; '**2gewicht** *n* dead weight; '**~händig** with one's own hand; ~*e Unterschrift* one's own signature, autograph; ~ *übergeben* deliver personally; '**2heim** *n* home of one's own; owner-occupied house.

'**Eigen|heit** *f* peculiarity; (*Seltsamkeit*) oddity; *der Sprache*: idiom; '**~kapital** *n* privately owned capital; capital resources *pl.*; '**~liebe** *f* self-love; '**~lob** *n* self-praise; '**2-mächtig** arbitrary; '**~mächtigkeit** *f* arbitrariness; '**~name** *m* proper name; '**~nutz** *m* (3^2, *o. pl.*) self-interest; '**2nützig** self-interested, selfish; '**2s** expressly, specially, on purpose.

'**Eigenschaft** *f* quality; (*Merkmal*) attribute, *e-r S.*: property; *in s-r* ~ *als* in his capacity as; '**~swort** *n* adjective.

'**Eigen|sinn** *m* wil(l)fulness; (*Hartnäckigkeit*) obstinacy; '**2sinnig** wil(l)ful; obstinate.

'**eigentlich** (*genau*) proper; (*tatsächlich*) actual; (*wirklich*) true, real; (*dem Wesen nach*) virtual; *adv.* properly; actually, really; (*genau gesagt*) properly speaking; *das* ~*e London* London proper; *was wollen Sie* ~? what do you want anyhow?

'**Eigentor** *n Sport*: own goal.

Eigentum ['~tu:m] *n* (1^2) property.

Eigentüm|er ['~ty:mər] *m* (7) owner, proprietor; '**~erin** *f* owner, proprietress; '**2lich** proper; (*eigenartig*) peculiar (*dat.* to); (*seltsam*) queer, odd; '**~lichkeit** *f* peculiarity.

'**Eigentums|recht** *n* proprietary right, title (*an dat.* to); '**~wohnung** *f* freehold flat, *Am.* condominium apartment.

'**Eigen|wechsel** ⚕ *m* promissory note; '**~wille** *m* wil(l)fulness; '**2willig** self-willed, wil(l)ful.

eign|en ['aɪgnən] (29): *sich* ~ (*für j-n*) suit (a p.); (*für et.*) be suitable (for), *P.*: be qualified (for); *j-m* ~ be peculiar to; *s. geeignet*; '**2er** *m* (7) owner; '**2ung** *f* aptitude, qualification; suitability, fitness; '**2ungsprüfung** *f* aptitude test.

Eiland ['aɪlant] *n* (3) island.

'**Eil|-auftrag** ⚕ *m* rush order; '**~bote** *m* express (*od.* special) messenger; *durch* ~*n* by special delivery; '**~brief** *m* express letter, *Am.* special delivery letter.

Eile ['aɪlə] *f* (15) haste, speed; *große*: hurry; ~ *haben P.*: be in a hurry; *S.*: be urgent.

'**eilen** (25, sn *u.* h.) hasten, (*a. sich*) make haste; hurry; *S.*: be urgent; *Aufschrift*: *eilt!* urgent!; *eile mit Weile* more haste, less speed; **~ds** ['~ts] quickly, speedily, in haste.

'**eil|fertig** hasty; rash; '**2fertigkeit** *f* hastiness; rashness; '**2fracht** *f*, '**2gut** *n* express (*od.* dispatch) goods *pl.*, *Am.* fast freight.

'**eilig** hasty, speedy; (*dringend*) pressing, urgent; ~*st* in great haste; *es* ~ *haben* be in a hurry.

'**Eil|marsch** *m* forced march; '**~paket** *n* express parcel; '**~schrift** *f* high-speed shorthand; '**~tempo** *n* (11, *o. pl.*): *im* ~ at top speed; '**~zug** *m* semi-fast train; '**~zustellung** *f* express (*Am.* special) delivery.

Eimer ['aɪmər] *m* (7) bucket (*a.* ⊕), pail; '**2weise** in buckets.

ein [aɪn] (20) **1.** one; **2.** *art.* a, an; **3.** *pron.* one; *s. allemal.*

'**Ein-akter** *thea. m* (7) one-act play.

einander [aɪ'nandər] one another, each other.

'**ein-arbeit|en** work (*od.* break) in; *sich* ~ work o.s. in; *sich* ~ *in* (*acc.*) make o.s. acquainted with; '**2ungszeit** *f* training period.

'**ein-armig** one-armed.

einäscher|n ['~ʔɛʃərn] (29) burn to

ashes; *Leiche*: cremate, incinerate; 'ꭥ**ung** *f* cremation, incineration.
'**ein-atmen** breathe in, inhale.
einäugig ['~ʔɔʏgiç] one-eyed.
'**Einbahnstraße** *f* one-way street.
'**einbalsamier|en** embalm; 'ꭥ**ung** *f* embalming.
'**Einband** *m* (3³) binding; '**~decke** *f* cover.
einbändig ['~bɛndiç] in one volume.
'**einbauen** build in(to *in acc.*); install, fit, fix.
'**Einbau|küche** *f* fitted kitchen; '**~möbel** *n/pl.* built-in furniture; '**~schrank** *m* fitted cupboard; '**~spüle** *f* fitted sink.
einbegriffen ['~bəgrifən] included, inclusive (of).
'**einbehalten** detain, keep back.
'**einberuf|en** convene; *parl.* convoke; ⚔ call up, *Am.* draft, induct; 'ꭥ**ung** *f* convocation; ⚔ call(ing)-up, *Am.* draft, induction; 'ꭥ**ungsbescheid** ⚔ *m* call-up order, *Am.* induction order.
'**Einbett|...** *Zimmer*: single-bed; ⚓ *Kabine*: single-berth; 'ꭥ**en** embed (*a.* ⊕); '**~zimmer** *n* single.
einbeulen ['aɪnbɔʏlən] (25) dent.
'**einbeziehen** comprise, include, embrace, cover.
'**einbiegen** *v/t.* bend inwards; *v/i.* (sn) turn (*in acc.* into).
'**einbilden:** *sich et.* ~ fancy, imagine; *sich et.* ~ *auf* (*acc.*) pride (*od.* pique) o.s. on; *sich viel* ~ be conceited; *darauf kann er sich et.* ~ that is a feather in his cap.
'**Einbildung** *f* imagination, fancy; (*Dünkel*) conceit; '**~skraft** *f* (power of) imagination.
'**einbinden** *Buch*: bind; *neu* ~ rebind.
'**einblasen** blow in; *fig.* prompt (*j-m et.* a th. to a p.).
'**einblend|en** *Film, Radio*: fade in; 'ꭥ**ung** *f Fernsehen*: insert.
'**einbleuen** (25): *j-m et.* ~ pound (*od.* hammer) into a p.'s head.
'**Einblick** *m* insight (*in acc.* into); ~ *gewähren in* afford an insight into; ~ *nehmen in* inspect.
'**einbrech|en** *v/t.* break open *od.* down; *v/i.* (sn) break in, collapse; *Dieb*: break in(to *in ein Haus*), burglarize (*in ein Haus* a house); (*einsetzen*) set in, come suddenly; ⚔ penetrate, breach; *in ein Land*: invade; ~ *bei j-m, in ein Haus*: burgle; 'ꭥ**er** *m* (7) housebreaker; *bei Nacht*: burglar.
Einbrenne ['~brɛnə] *f* (15) (*Mehlschwitze*) roux.
'**einbrennen** burn in(to *in acc.*).
'**einbringen** bring in; *Gewinn*: yield; *et. wieder* ~ retrieve; *verlorene Zeit usw.*: make up for; *eingebrachtes Gut* dowry.
'**einbrocken** (25) crumble (*in acc.* into); *fig. j-m* (*a. sich*) *et.* ~ get into trouble; *das hast du dir selbst eingebrockt* that's your own doing.
'**Einbruch** *m* breaking-in; *in ein Land*: invasion (*in acc.* of); (*Haus*ꭥ) housebreaking, burglary (*a.* '**~sdiebstahl** *m*); ⚔ penetration, breach; *fig.* inroad; ~ *der Nacht* nightfall.
Einbuchtung ['~buxtuŋ] *f* (*Bucht*) inlet; (*Auszackung*) indentation.
einbürger|n ['~byrgərn] (29) naturalize; *sich* ~ become naturalized; 'ꭥ**ung** *f* naturalization.
'**Einbuße** *f* loss, damage.
'**einbüßen** lose, forfeit.
einchecken ['~tʃɛkən] ✈ (25) check in.
eincremen ['~kreːmən] (25) cream.
'**eindämm|en** (25) dam up (*a. fig.*); *Fluß usw.*: embank; 'ꭥ**ung** *f* damming(-up); embankment; 'ꭥ**ungspolitik** *f* policy of containment.
'**eindampfen** evaporate.
'**eindecken** cover; *mit Artilleriefeuer*: straddle; *sich* ~ provide o.s. (*mit* with); stock up (on).
'**Eindecker** ✈ *m* (7) monoplane.
'**eindeutig** unequivocal, definite, clear-cut; clear(ly *adv.*).
'**eindicken** thicken; *durch Eindampfen*: condense, inspissate.
'**eindosen** (27) tin, *Am.* can.
'**eindrängen:** *sich* ~ intrude (*in acc.* into).
'**eindring|en** (sn) enter (*in et.* a th.); *unbefugt*: intrude (into); (*a. fig.*) penetrate (into); '**~lich** urgent; forceful; ꭥ**ling** ['~liŋ] *m* (3¹) intruder; (*Angreifer*) invader.
'**Eindruck** *m* (3¹) impression (*a. fig.*); *den* ~ *haben, daß* be under the impression that; *s. schinden.*
'**eindrücken** press in; (*einprägen*) impress; (*zermalmen*) crush; *Glasscheibe*: break; *Sporen*: dig in.
'**eindrucksvoll** impressive, striking.

'**Ein·ehe** *f* monogamy.
eineiig *biol.* ['~ʔaɪiç] uniovular; ~e *Zwillinge* identical twins.
'**ein·engen** (25) narrow (*a. fig.*).
einer ['aɪnər] **1.** *s. ein*; **2.** ♀ *m* (7) ℞ digit, unit; ⚓ single (sculler).
'**einer'lei 1.** of the same kind; (*unwesentlich*) immaterial; *es ist (mir)* ~ it is all the same (to me); it is all one to me; ~ *wer usw.* whoever *etc.*, no matter who *etc.*; **2.** ♀ *n* (6, *o.pl.*) sameness; (*Eintönigkeit*) monotony, humdrum.
einerseits ['aɪnərzaɪts], **eines·teils** ['aɪnəstaɪls] on the one hand.
einfach ['~fax] simple; (*einzeln*) single; (*schlicht*) plain; *Mahlzeit*: frugal; *Fahrkarte*: single, *Am.* one-way; ⚕ ~e *Buchführung* book-keeping by single entry; *adv.* simply, just (*wonderful*, *etc.*); '♀**heit** *f* simplicity.
'**einfädeln** (29) thread; *fig.* contrive; *mot. sich (in den Verkehr)* ~ filter in, *Am.* merge.
'**einfahr|en** *v/t.* carry in; *Pferd*: break in; *Auto*: run in; ✈ *Fahrgestell*: retract; *v/i.* (sn) drive in; enter (*in den Bahnhof usw.* the station, *etc.*); ⚒ descend; '♀**t** *f* entrance; (*Torweg*) gateway; (*Hafen*♀) mouth; ⚒ descent.
'**Einfall** *m* (3³) ⚔ invasion (*in ein Land* of a country), raid (into); *fig.* idea; *glücklicher* ~ brain-wave; '♀**en** (sn) fall in, collapse; *Hohlraum*: cave in; *feindlich*: invade (*in ein Land* a country); *in die Rede*: break in; ♪ join in; *j-m* ~ occur to a p., come to a p.'s mind; *sich* ~ *lassen* take into one's head; *sich nicht* ~ *lassen* not to dream of; F (*das*) *fällt mir nicht ein!* catch me!; '♀**sreich** imaginative; '~**swinkel** *m* angle of incidence.
Einfalt ['~falt] *f* (16) (*Einfachheit*) simplicity; (*Unschuld*) innocence; (*Dummheit*) silliness.
einfältig ['~fɛltiç] (*dumm*) dull; (*arglos*) simple; (*albern*) silly.
'**Einfalts·pinsel** *m* simpleton.
'**Einfamilienhaus** *n* one-family house.
'**einfangen** catch; (*a. fig.*) capture.
'**einfarbig** one-colo(u)red, unicolo(u)red.
'**einfass|en** border, edge; *mit e-m Zaun usw.*: enclose; *Schneiderei*: trim; *Edelstein*: set, mount (*mit* in); (*einrahmen, a. fig.*) frame; '♀**ung** *f* bordering, edging; enclosure; trimming; setting, mounting; framing.
einfetten ['aɪnfɛtən] (26) grease.
'**einfinden:** *sich* ~ appear, arrive, F turn up.
'**einflechten** interlace; *Haar*: braid; *fig.* put in, insert.
'**einfliegen** ✈ *v/i.* enter (by air); *v/t. Flugzeug*: test, fly in.
'**einfließen** (sn) flow in(to *in acc.*); *fig.* ~ *lassen* drop, mention in passing.
'**einflößen** (27) *j-m et.*: pour into a p.'s mouth; feed; *fig. j-m Mut usw.* ~ inspire a p. with courage; *j-m Angst usw.* ~ fill a p. with fear *etc.*
'**Einflugschneise** *f* approach corridor.
'**Einfluß** *m* influx; *fig.* influence (*auf acc.* on, *bei* with); ~ *haben auf* influence; '~**bereich** *m* sphere of influence; '♀**reich** influential.
'**einflüstern** *j-m*: whisper to; *fig. a.* insinuate (*od.* suggest) to.
'**einfordern** call in.
einförmig ['~fœrmiç] monotonous; '♀**keit** *f* monotony.
einfriedig|en ['~fri:digən] (25) enclose; '♀**ung** *f* enclosure.
'**einfrieren** *v/i.* (sn) freeze in; *v/t. Lebensmittel*: deep-freeze; ⚕ *Guthaben, Löhne etc.*: freeze.
'**einfüg|en** put in; insert (*in acc.* in[to]); (*sich*) ~ fit in; *Person*: *sich* ~ adapt o.s. (*in acc.* to); '♀**ung** *f* insertion; adaptation.
'**einfühl|en:** *sich* ~ project o.s. (*in j-n* into a p.'s mind); *in et.*: get into the spirit of; '♀**ungsvermögen** *n* sympathetic understanding, 🕮 empathy.
Einfuhr ['~fu:r] *f* (16) import (-ation); *konkret*: imports *pl.*; '~**genehmigung** *f* import licence (*Am.* license); '~**handel** *m* import trade; '~**verbot** *n* import ban; '~**waren** *f/pl.* imports; '~**zoll** *m* import duty.
'**einführ|en** *allg., a. j-n, Brauch*: introduce; ⊕ *usw. a.* insert; ⚕ import; (*einweihen*) initiate (*in acc.* into); *in Amt*: install (in); ⚕ (*gut*) *eingeführt sein Firma*: be (well) established; '♀**ung** *f* insertion; importation; introduction; initiation; installation, establishment; '♀**ungs-**

angebot ✝ *n* trial offer; ˈ**≈ungspreis** ✝ *m* introductory price.
ˈ**einfüllen** fill in(to *in acc.*).
ˈ**Eingabe** *f* application (*an acc.* to; *um* for); (*Bittschrift*) petition (to; for); *Computer*: input; ˈ**~daten** *n/pl. Computer*: input data; ˈ**~gerät** *n Computer*: terminal.
ˈ**Eingang** *m Ort*: entrance; (*Eintreten*) entry; (*Anfang*) beginning; *v. Waren*: arrival; *nach* ~ on receipt; *Eingänge m/pl. v. Waren*: goods, *v. Post*: mail *sg.* received, *v. Geld*: receipts; ˈ**≈s** at the beginning; ˈ**~sbuch** *n* book of entries; ˈ**~s-empfindlichkeit** *f Radio*: input sensitivity; ˈ**~sformel** *f* preamble; ˈ**~szoll** *m* import duty.
ˈ**eingeben** *Arznei*: give; *Gedanken usw.*: prompt, suggest (*dat.* to); *Computer*: enter.
eingebildet [ˈ~gəbildət] imaginary; (*dünkelhaft*) conceited (*auf acc.* about).
ˈ**eingeboren** native; *Sohn Gottes*: only begotten; ˈ**≈e** *m, f* native.
Eingebung [ˈ~geːbuŋ] *f* inspiration.
eingedenk [ˈ~gədɛŋk] mindful (*gen.* of); ~ *sein* (*gen.*) remember, bear in mind.
ˈ**eingefallen** *Augen*: sunken; *Wangen*: hollow; (*abgezehrt*) emaciated.
eingefleischt [ˈ~gəflaɪʃt] inveterate, ingrained, confirmed.
ˈ**eingehen** *v/i.* (sn) *Brief, Ware*: come in, arrive; ⚘, *Tier*: die; (*aufhören*) cease, F fizzle out; *Betrieb*: close down; *Zeitung*: perish; *Stoff*: shrink; *j-m* ~ go down with a p.; ~ *auf* (*acc.*) agree to; *auf Einzelheiten*: enter into; ~ *lassen* (*aufgeben*) give up, drop, discontinue; *v/t.* (h., sn) *Beziehungen, Vertrag usw.*: enter into; *Ehe*: contract; *e-n Vergleich* ~ *mit* settle with; *Verpflichtungen* ~ incur liabilities; *e-e Wette* ~ make a bet, lay a wager; *eingegangene Gelder n/pl.* receipts *pl.*; ˈ**~d** detailed; (*gründlich*) thorough; *Prüfung*: close.
Eingemachte [ˈ~gəmaxtə] *n* (18) *in Zucker*: preserves *pl.*; *in Essig*: pickles *pl.*
eingemeind|en [ˈ~gəmaɪndən] (26) incorporate (*dat.* into); ˈ**≈ung** *f* incorporation.
eingenommen [ˈ~gənɔmən] prepossessed (*für* in favo[u]r of), partial (to); prejudiced (*gegen* against); *von sich* ~ self-conceited; ˈ**≈heit** *f* prepossession; prejudice, bias; self-conceit.
eingeschnappt F [ˈ~gəʃnapt] *fig.* [cross, peeved.]
ˈ**eingesessen**, ˈ**≈e** *m, f* resident.
eingestandenermaßen [ˈ~gəʃtandənərˈmaːsen] admittedly.
ˈ**Eingeständnis** *n* confession, avowal, admission.
ˈ**eingestehen** confess, avow.
eingetragen [ˈ~gətraːgən] *amtlich*: registered.
Eingeweide [ˈ~gəvaɪdə] *n/pl.* (7) *allg. anat.* viscera; (*Gedärme*) bowels; *bsd. v. Vieh*: entrails; *anat.* intestines.
Eingeweihte [ˈaɪngəvaɪtə] *m, f* initiate.
ˈ**eingewöhnen** (*a. sich*) acclimatize, *Am.* acclimate (*in dat. u. acc.* to); accustom (to); *sich* ~ get accustomed (to).
eingewurzelt [ˈ~gəvurtsəlt] deep-rooted, engrained.
ˈ**eingießen** pour in(to *in acc.*); (*einschenken*) pour out.
eingleisig [ˈ~glaɪziç] single-track.
ˈ**eingliedern** incorporate, integrate (*in acc.* in[to]); *Gebiet*: annex (to).
ˈ**eingraben** dig in; (*beerdigen*) bury; *in Stein usw., fig. ins Gedächtnis*: engrave (*in acc.* upon); ⚔ *sich* ~ entrench o.s.
ˈ**eingravieren** engrave.
ˈ**eingreifen 1.** ⊕ engage (*in acc.* in *od.* with); *Getriebe usw.*: gear in(to), mesh; *fig.* take action; ⚔ come into action; *vermittelnd*: intervene; *störend*: interfere (*in acc.* with); *fig.* interfere (with); *in die Debatte* ~ join in the debate; **2.** ≈ *n* (6) engagement; meshing; action; intervention; interference.
ˈ**Eingriff** *m s. eingreifen*: gearing; ⚕ operation; *fig. s. Eingreifen.*
ˈ**einhaken** hook in(to *in acc.*); *fig. sich bei j-m* ~ link arms with a p.; *fig.* cut in; *bei et.*: take a th. up.
ˈ**Einhalt** *m*: ~ *gebieten od. tun* (*dat.*) put a stop to; ˈ**≈en** *v/t.* (*hemmen*) stop, check; (*genau beachten*) observe, comply with, keep; *Kurs usw.*: follow; *Versprechen*: keep; *Verpflichtung*: meet; *die Zeit* ~ be punctual; *v/i.* stop, leave off; ˈ**~ung** *f* (*gen.*) observance (of), compliance (with).

'**einhandeln** obtain; trade in.
einhändig|en['~hɛndigən](25)hand over, deliver; '**⁀ung** *f* delivery.
'**einhängen** *v/t.* hang in; (*aufhängen*) hang (up); *Tür*: put on its hinges; *sich bei j-m ~* link arms with a p.; *v/i. teleph.* hang up.
'**einhauen** *v/t.* hew in; (*aufbrechen*) cut open; *v/i. ~ auf* (*acc.*) fall upon; F *beim Essen*: F tuck in.
'**einheften** sew (*od.* stitch) in; *Akten*: file.
'**einhegen** *s. einfriedigen.*
'**einheimisch** native (*in dat.* to), (*a.* ⚘) indigenous (to); domestic (*a.* ⚕); home-made; *Krankheit*: endemic; '**⁀e** *m, f* native; resident.
einheimsen ['~haɪmzən] (27) *Ernte*: reap; *fig. a.* pocket.
'**Einheirat** *f*: ~ *in* (*acc.*) marriage into; '**⁀en** *v/i.*: ~ *in* (*acc.*) marry into.
'**Einheit** *f* unity; (*Gleichheit*) oneness; ⚔, *phys.*, ⊕, ⚔ unit; '**⁀lich** uniform; '**~lichkeit** *f* uniformity; '**~s-partei** *f* united party; '**~s-preis** *m* standard (*od.* flat) price; '**~sschule** *f* comprehensive school; '**~sstaat** *m* centralized state; '**~swert** *m* ⚕ rateable value.
'**einheizen** light a fire; heat; F *fig. j-m ~* make it hot for a p.
einhellig ['aɪnhɛliç] unanimous; '**⁀keit** *f* unanimity.
einher [~'he:r] along.
'**einholen** *v/t.* (*erreichen*) catch up with, overtake; *Versäumtes*: make up for; *Genehmigung*: apply for; *Gutachten usw.*: obtain; *Befehl*: take; *Rat*: seek, take; (*einkaufen*) buy; *Segel*: strike; *Flagge*: haul down; *v/i.* go shopping.
'**Einhorn** *n* unicorn.
Einhufer ['~hu:fər] *m* (7) solid--hoofed animal, soliped.
'**einhüllen** wrap (up); envelop.
einig ['aɪniç] united; (*sich*) ~ *sein* be at one, be agreed, agree; (*sich*) *nicht ~ sein* (*über acc.*) differ (about); (*sich*) ~ *werden* come to an agreement *od.* to terms.
einige ['aɪnigə] some, a few; several; '**~n** (25) (*vereinigen*) unite; *sich ~* come to terms; agree (*mit* with *a p.*; *auf acc.*, *über acc.* [up]on); **~rmaßen** ['~r'ma:sən] to some extent; (*ziemlich*) rather, fairly; '**~s** something, several things.
'**Einigkeit** *f* (16) unity; (*Übereinstimmung*) agreement; (*Eintracht*) concord; (*Einmütigkeit*) unanimity.
'**Einigung** ['~guŋ] *f* union; (*Übereinstimmung*) agreement; (*Vergleich*) settlement; *pol.* unification.
'**ein-impf|en** inoculate (*a. fig. j-m* into a p.); '**⁀ung** *f* inoculation.
'**einjagen:** *j-m Furcht ~* frighten a p.
'**einjährig** (one-)year-old; *Dauer*: of one year, one year's; *bsd.* ⚘ annual.
'**einkalkulieren** take into account; [allow for.]
'**einkassier|en** cash; *Schulden*: collect; '**⁀ung** *f* cashing; collection.
'**Einkauf** *m* purchase; *Einkäufe machen* go shopping; '**⁀en** buy, purchase; *v/i.* ~ (*gehen*) go shopping.
'**Einkäufer** ⚕ *m* buyer.
'**Einkaufs|liste** *f* shopping list; '**~möglichkeit** *f* shopping facility; **~netz** *n* string bag; '**~passage** *f* shopping arcade, *Am.* shopping mall; '**~preis** *m* cost-price, first (*od.* prime) cost; '**~straße** *f* shopping street, *Am.* mall; '**~tasche** *f* shopping bag; '**~wagen** *m* trolley, *Am.* shopping cart; '**~zentrum** *n* shopping cent|re (*Am.* -er).
Einkehr ['~ke:r] *f* (16) putting up (*in dat.*, *bei* at); *fig.* contemplation; *fig. ~ bei sich halten* commune with o.s.; '**⁀en** (25) *in e-m Gasthaus*: stop at *an inn* (for drink, food); (*übernachten*) put up (*in dat.*, *bei* at).
einkeilen ['~kaɪlən] *fig.* wedge in.
einkellern ['~kɛlərn] (29) lay in.
'**einkerb|en** (25), '**⁀ung** *f* notch.
einkerker|n ['~kɛrkərn] (29) imprison, incarcerate; '**⁀ung** *f* imprisonment, incarceration.
'**einklagen** *Schuld*: sue for.
'**einklammern** *Wort usw.*: bracket, put in parentheses.
'**Einklang** *m* unison; harmony; accord; *in ~ bringen* bring into line, harmonize, square (*mit* with); *im ~ stehen* be compatible *od.* in keeping, coincide, square (*mit* with).
'**einkleben** paste in(to *in acc.*).
'**einkleid|en** clothe; (*a. fig.*) invest; '**⁀ung** *f* clothing; investiture.
'**einklemmen** squeeze in; jam (*od.* wedge) in.
'**einklinken** latch; ⊕ engage.
'**einknicken** *v/t. u. v/i.* (sn) bend in, break; *a. Knie*: buckle.

'**einkochen** *v/t. u. v/i.* (sn) (*eindicken*) boil down; (*einmachen*) preserve.

'**einkommen 1.** (sn): *bei j-m*: petition, apply to (*um* for); *s. Abschied*; **2.** ♀ *n* (6) income; *pol.* revenue; '♀**sgefälle** *n* income differential; '~**s-schwach** low-income *attr.*; '~**sstark** high-income *attr.*; '~(**s**)**steuer** *f* income-tax; '~(**s**)**stufe** *f* income class (*Am.* bracket).

'**einkreis|en** encircle; '♀**ung** *f* encirclement.

Einkünfte ['~kynftə] *pl.* (14[1]) proceeds, receipts; (*Einkommen*) income; *pol.* revenue *sg.*

'**einkuppeln** ⊕ clutch, couple, *mot.* (let in *or* engage the) clutch.

'**einlad|en** *et.*: load in; *j-n*: invite; '~**end** inviting; '♀**ung** *f* invitation.

'**Einlage** *f im Brief*: enclosure; ⊕ insert; (*Schicht*) layer; (*Zahn*♀) temporary filling; *Schneiderei*: padding; *Küche*: garnish; (*Schuh*♀) (arch-)support; ✝ investment; (*Bank*♀) deposit; *Spiel*: stake; *thea.* insert(ed piece), extra; (*a. fig.*) interlude.

'**einlagern** lay in; ✝ warehouse, store, put into stock.

Einlaß ['~las] *m* (4) admission, admittance; ⊕ inlet.

'**einlassen** let in, admit; (*einfügen*) put in; *sich in* (*od. auf*) *et.* (*acc.*) ~ engage in, enter into; embark on; *leichtsinnig*: meddle with; *sich mit j-m* ~ have dealings with, *feindselig*: tangle with.

'**Einlauf** ⚕ *m* enema.

'**einlaufen** (sn) come in, arrive; *Schiff*: enter; *Stoff*: shrink; *nicht* ~*d* shrink-proof; *Bad* ~ *lassen* run the bath.

'**einläuten** ring in.

'**einleben:** *sich* ~ accustom o.s. (*in dat. u. acc.* to).

'**Einlege-arbeit** *f* inlaid work.

'**einlegen** lay (*od.* put) in; ⊕ *mit et.*: inlay; *Geld*: deposit; *in Salz*: salt; pickle; *Früchte*: preserve; *Berufung* ~ lodge an appeal (*bei* with); *Ehre* ~ *mit* gain hono(u)r (*od.* credit) by; *ein Wort* ~ *für* intercede for.

'**Einlegesohle** *f* insole, *Brt. a.* sock.

'**einleit|en** introduce; start, launch; *Verhandlungen usw.*: open; ⚖ institute; '~**end** introductory; '♀**ung** *f* introduction; ⚖ institution.

'**einlenken** turn in; *fig.* come round.

'**einlernen:** *sich et.* ~ learn thoroughly; *j-m et.* ~ teach a p. a th.

'**einleuchten** be evident *od.* obvious; *das will mir nicht* ~ I cannot see that; '~**d** evident, obvious, clear.

'**einliefer|n** deliver (up); *e-n Gefangenen*: commit (to prison); *in ein Krankenhaus* ~ take to a hospital, *Am.* hospitalize; '♀**ung** *f* delivery; '♀**ungsschein** *m* receipt of delivery.

'**einliegend** *im Brief*: enclosed.

'**einlochen** F lock up.

'**einlös|en** redeem; *Schuld, Rechnung*: discharge; ✝ *Wechsel*: hono(u)r, take up; *Scheck*: cash; '♀**ung** *f* redemption; discharge, payment; cashing, passing.

einlullen ['~lulən] (25) lull to sleep; *fig.* lull.

'**einmach|en** *Früchte*: preserve, bottle; *Fleisch*: pot; '♀**glas** *n* preserving jar.

'**einmal** once; (*künftig*) one day, some time; *auf* ~ (*plötzlich*) all at once, (*gleichzeitig*) at the same time; *es war* ~ once (upon a time) there was; *nicht* ~ not even, not so much as; *stellen Sie sich* ~ *vor* just fancy; ~ *ist keinmal* one and none is all one.

Einmal'-**eins** *n* (*Tabelle*) multiplication-table; *großes* (*kleines*) ~ compound (simple) multiplication.

'**Einmalhandtuch** *n* disposable towel.

'**einmalig** single, one; *Zahlung usw.*: non-recurring; *fig.* singular; ~*e Gelegenheit* unique opportunity.

'**Einmal|rasierer** *m* (7) disposable razor; '~**spritze** *f* disposable syringe.

'**Einmarsch** *m* marching-in, entry; '♀**ieren** (sn) march in, enter.

'**einmauern** immure, wall in.

'**einmeißeln** chisel in, engrave.

'**einmengen** mix in; *sich* ~ meddle, interfere (*in acc.* with), F *bsd. Am.* butt in.

'**einmieten** take lodgings (*j-n* for a p.; *bei j-m* with a p.); *Kartoffeln usw.*: pit.

'**einmischen** *s. einmengen.*

'**Einmischung** *f* interference.

einmotorig ✈ ['~mo'to:riç] single--engine(d).

'**einmotten** mothball (*a. Schiff usw.*).

'**einmünd|en:** ~ *in* (*acc.*) *Straße*: run into, join; *Fluß*: flow into; '**&ung** *f Straße*: junction; *Fluß*: mouth.

einmütig ['~my:tiç] unanimous; '**&keit** *f* unanimity.

Einnahme ['~na:mə] *f* (15) ⚔ taking, conquest, capture; (*Geld&*) receipt, *mst* ~*n pl.* takings, receipts.

'**einnebeln** (29) smoke-screen.

'**einnehmen** take in; *Geld usw.*: receive; *Steuern*: collect; ⚔ take; *Raum*: take up, occupy; *Arznei, Mahlzeit, s-n Platz*: take; *Haltung*: assume; *Stelle*: hold; *fig.* captivate, charm; *j-n* ~ *für* (*gegen*) prejudice in favo(u)r of (against); '**~d** winning, engaging, charming.

'**einnicken** (sn) doze off.

'**einnisten:** *sich* ~ nestle (down); *fig.* settle (down).

'**Ein·öde** *f* desert, solitude.

'**ein·ölen** oil.

'**ein·ordnen** arrange in (proper) order; *Brief usw.*: file; *in Klassen*: classify; *ins Ganze*: integrate (*in acc.* into); *mot. sich* (*rechts*) ~ get into (the right) lane.

'**einpacken** *v/t.* pack up; (*einwickeln*) wrap up; *v/i.* F *fig.* pack up.

'**einpassen** fit in(to *in acc.*).

'**einpauken** F cram.

'**Einpeitscher** *m* (7) slave-driver.

'**einpendeln:** *sich* ~ *fig.* even out, come right.

'**einpferchen** pen in; *fig.* cram (*od.* pack) together.

'**einpflanzen** plant; *fig.* implant (*j-m* in a p.'s mind).

einphasig ⚡ ['~fa:ziç] single-phase, monophase.

'**einplanen** include, allow for.

'**einpökeln** pickle, salt, corn.

einpolig ⚡ ['~po:liç] unipolar.

'**einpräg|en** imprint; *j-m et.*: impress on a p.'s mind; *sich* ~ sink into the mind *od.* memory; *sich et.* ~ commit a th. to one's memory; **~sam** ['~prɛ:kza:m] impressive.

'**einprogrammieren** *Computer*: feed in.

'**einquartier|en** quarter, billet (*in e-n Ort, bei j-m* on; *in e-e Wohnung* in); '**&ung** *f* billeting; soldiers *pl.* billeted *od.* quartered, billetees.

'**einrahmen** (25) frame.

'**einrammen** ram in(to *in acc.*).

'**einrasten** (sn) engage (*in acc.* in).

'**einräum|en** (*wegpacken*) clear away; *Möbel*: place (*od.* put) in; *Zimmer*: put the furniture in *a room*; (*abtreten*) give up, cede (*j-m* to); (*zugestehen*) grant, concede; † *Frist, Kredit usw.*: grant, allow; '**~end** *gr.* concessive; '**&ung** *f* grant (-ing), concession.

'**einrechnen** include; (*einkalkulieren*) allow for; (*nicht*) *eingerechnet* ... (not) including ...

'**Einrede** *f* objection; ⚖ demurrer, plea; '**&n** *v/t. j-m et.*: make a p. believe *a th.*, talk a p. into; *sich et.* ~ imagine a th.; *v/i. auf j-n* ~ talk (insistently) to a p., *drängend*: urge a p.

'**einreiben** rub in(to *in acc.*); ~ *mit* rub with; *mit Fett* ~ grease.

'**einreichen** hand in; *Gesuch, Rechnung usw.*: submit, file, present; *s-e Entlassung*: hand in, tender (*one's resignation*); *Klage*: file, lodge.

'**einreihen** range (*in acc.* in; *unter acc.* among).

einreihig ['~raiiç] *Jacke*: single--breasted.

'**Einreise** *f* entry (*in acc.* into); '**~erlaubnis** *f* entry permit; '**~verbot** *n*: *j-m* ~ *erteilen* refuse a p. entry; '**~visum** *n* entry visa.

'**einreißen** *v/t.* tear; *Haus*: pull down, demolish; *v/i.* (sn) tear; *fig.* spread, gain ground.

einrenken ['~rɛŋkən] (25) set; *fig.* set right; *sich* ~ come right.

'**einrennen** crash through; *j-m das Haus* ~ pester a p.; *offene Türen* ~ force an open door.

'**einricht|en** *Glied*: set; *Wohnung*: fit up, furnish; ⊕ install; *Geschäft, Schule usw.*: establish; set up; (*ausstatten*) equip; (*errichten*) establish; (*ermöglichen*) arrange (*a.* ♪), manage; *es* (*so*) ~, *daß* arrange (*od.* see to) it that; *sich* ~ establish o.s., settle down; *sparsam*: economize; *sich* ~ *auf* (*acc.*) prepare for; *sich* ~ *mit* manage with; *sich* ~ *nach* adapt o.s. to; *es läßt sich* ~ it can be arranged; '**&ung** *f* (*Ausstattung*) equipment; *e-s Hauses etc.*: furnishings *pl.*, appointments *pl.*; (*Laden&*) fittings *pl.*; ⊕ (*Anlage od. Einbau*) installation; (*bequeme* ~) facility; (*Anordnung*) arrangement; (*Gründung od. Anstalt*) establishment; (*öffentliche* ~ public) institution; '♀**ungsgegenstand** *m* piece of furniture; *mst pl. Einrichtungsgegenstände* fixtures, fittings.

'**einrosten** (sn) get rusty (*a. fig.*).

'**einrücken** *v/i.* (sn) enter, march in; ⚔ *zur Truppe*: be called up; *v/t. in die Zeitung*: insert; *typ. Zeile*: indent; ⊕ *Kupplung usw.*: engage; *Gang*: shift.

'**einrühren** stir, mix in.

eins [aɪns] **1.** one; *es ist mir alles* ~ it is all one (*od.* the same) to me; ~ *ums andere* one after the other, *abwechselnd*: by (*od.* in) turns; ~ *trinken* have a glass; ~ *sein fig.* be at one; *nicht* ~ *sein* differ; **2.** ♀ *f* (16³) one; *auf Würfeln*: ace; (*Schulnote*) alpha, grade one.

einsacken ['aɪnzakən] (25) bag, sack; *fig.* pocket.

'**einsalzen** salt.

'**einsam** lonely, solitary; '♀**keit** *f* loneliness, solitude.

'**einsammeln** gather; *Geld usw.*: collect.

'**Einsatz** *m* ⊕ inset; *am Hemd*: shirt-front; *am Kleid*: insertion; *im Koffer*: tray; (*Gefäß usw.*) insert; (*Spiel*♀) stake, *gemeinsamer*: pool; ♪ striking in, intonation; (*Verwendung*) use, employment; *v. Truppen*: engagement, action; ⚔ (*Auftrag*) mission, operation; *v. Arbeitskräften*: employment; (*Anstrengung*) effort; *im* ~ in action (*a.* ⊕); ⚔, ✈ ~ *fliegen* fly a sortie *od.* mission; *mit vollem* ~ all out; *unter* ~ *s-s Lebens* at the risk of one's life; '♀**bereit** ready for action (⊕ for operation); *fig.* devoted; '♀**fähig** serviceable; (*verfügbar*) available; ⚔ fit for action; '~**gruppe** ⚔ *f* task force.

'**einsäumen** hem in.

'**einschalt|en** insert; ⚡, *Radio*: switch (*od.* turn) on; *Kupplung*: throw in; *mot.* start; *fig.* (*einschieben*) insert; *j-n*: call in; *sich* ~ intervene; '♀**quote** *f* program(me) rating; '♀**ung** *f* insertion; intervention.

'**einschärfen** enjoin (*dat.* upon).

'**einscharren** bury.

'**einschätz|en** estimate, assess (*auf acc.* at); *fig. j-n*: appraise, F size up; '♀**ung** *f* estimation, assessment; appraisal.

'**einschenken** pour out *od.* in(to *in acc.*); *j-m Wein usw.* ~ help a p. to; *s. rein.*

'**einschicken** send in.

'**einschieb|en** push (*od.* slip) in; insert (*a. fig. Worte usw.*); '♀**ung** *f* insertion.

'**einschießen** shoot (*od.* batter) down; *ein Gewehr*: test, try; *Fußball*: score, net; *Geld*: contribute; *sich* ~ *auf ein Ziel* find the range of, bracket.

'**einschiff|en** (*a. sich*) embark (*nach* for); '♀**ung** *f* embarkation.

'**einschlafen** (sn) fall asleep; *Glied*: go to sleep; *fig.* (*sterben*) pass away; *Briefwechsel usw.*: drop, fizzle out; ~ *lassen* drop.

'**einschläf(e)rig** *Bett*: single.

einschläfern ['aɪnʃlɛ:fərn] (29) lull to sleep; *fig.* lull (into security); narcotize; *Tier*: put to sleep; '~**d** soporific, narcotic.

'**Einschlag** *m* (*Hülle*) wrapper, cover, envelope; *Weberei*: woof, weft; *am Kleid*: tuck; *e-s Geschosses*: impact; *fig.* infusion, streak, touch.

'**einschlagen** *v/t. Nagel*: drive in(to *in acc.*); (*zerbrechen*) break (in); *Fenster, Schädel*: smash (in); (*einhüllen*) envelop, wrap up; *Weg*: take; *Laufbahn*: enter upon; (*zs.-falten*) tuck in; *v/i.* shake hands; *Blitz*: strike (*in ein Haus* a house); *Geschoß*: hit; (*Erfolg haben*) be a success *od.* hit; *nicht* ~ fail; ~ *auf* (*acc.*) strike out at.

'**Einschlag(e)papier** *n* wrapping paper.

einschlägig ['~ʃlɛ:giç] pertinent, relevant.

'**einschleichen** (sn) *mst sich* ~ creep (*od.* sneak) in(to *in acc.*); *fig. sich* ~ *Fehler usw.*: creep in; *in j-s Vertrauen usw.* worm o.s. into.

'**einschleppen** drag in; *Krankheit*: import.

'**einschleusen** channel (*od.* let) in; *Spione*: infiltrate.

'**einschließ|en** lock in *od.* up; (*umgeben*; *in e-n Brief* ~) enclose; ⚔ surround, encircle; *fig.* include; '~**lich** (*gen.*) including, inclusive (of); *Seite 1 bis 10* ~ pages 1 to 10 inclusive.

'**einschlummern** (sn) doze off.

'**Einschluß** *m*: *mit* ~ (*gen.*) including, inclusive of.

ˈ**einschmeicheln:** *sich* ~ ingratiate o.s. (*bei* with); ˈ**~d** ingratiating.

ˈ**einschmelzen** melt down.

ˈ**einschmieren** smear; *mit Fett*: grease; *mit Krem*: cream.

ˈ**einschmuggeln** smuggle in.

ˈ**einschnappen** (sn) catch, click; *fig. s. eingeschnappt.*

ˈ**einschneiden** cut in; *Namen usw.*: carve (*in acc.* in); (*einkerben*) notch; (*auszacken*) indent; ˈ**~d** *fig.* incisive.

ˈ**einschneien** snow up *od.* in.

ˈ**Einschnitt** *m* cut, incision; (*Kerbe*) notch; *fig.* cut, turning-point.

ˈ**einschnüren** *Taille*: lace; *Hals*: strangle; *s. schnüren, einengen.*

ˈ**einschränk|en** (25) restrict, confine (*auf acc.* to); *Ausgaben, Produktion, Umfang*: reduce; *Behauptung usw.*: qualify; *sich* ~ economize; ˈ**~end** restrictive; ˈ**ᘓung** *f* restriction; reduction; qualification; *mit* (*ohne*) ~ (*Vorbehalt*) with (without) reservation.

ˈ**einschrauben** screw in(to *in acc.*).

ˈ**Einschreibe|brief** *m* registered (*od.* recorded delivery) letter; ˈ**~gebühr** *f* registration-fee.

ˈ**einschreiben 1.** (*eintragen*) enter; (*buchen*) book; *als Mitglied u.* ⚔: enrol(l); 📯 register; *e-n Brief* ~ *lassen* have a letter registered; *sich* ~ enter one's name; **2.** ᘓ *n* registered (*od.* recorded delivery) letter; *per* ~ by recorded delivery (*od.* registered mail).

ˈ**einschreiten 1.** (sn) *fig.* step in, interfere, intervene; ~ *gegen* proceed against; **2.** ᘓ *n* (6) intervention.

ˈ**einschrumpfen** (sn) shrink.

ˈ**einschüchter|n** (29) intimidate, cow; *durch Gewalttätigkeit*: bully; *durch Drohungen*: browbeat; ˈ**ᘓung** *f* intimidation; ˈ**ᘓungsversuch** *m* attempt at intimidation.

ˈ**einschulen** put to school.

ˈ**Einschuß** *m* bullet-hole; (*Wunde*) entry wound; ⚕ capital invested (*od.* paid in); *Weberei*: woof, weft.

ˈ**einschütten** pour in(to *in acc.*).

ˈ**einschweißen** *Waren*: shrink-wrap.

ˈ**einsegn|en** consecrate; *Kinder*: confirm; ˈ**ᘓung** *f* consecration; confirmation.

ˈ**einsehen 1.** look into *od.* over; (*prüfen*) inspect; (*verstehen*) see, understand; (*erkennen*) realize; (*richtig einschätzen*) appreciate; **2.** ᘓ *n*: *ein* ~ *haben* show consideration.

ˈ**einseifen** soap; *beim Rasieren*: lather; *fig.* F (*betrügen*) take in.

einseitig [ˈaɪnzaɪtɪç] one-sided (*a. fig.*); 📖, *pol.*, ⚖ unilateral; ~*e Lungenentzündung* single pneumonia; ˈ**ᘓkeit** *f* one-sidedness.

ˈ**einsend|en** send in; (*einreichen*) hand in, submit; *Fußball*: net; ˈ**ᘓer(in** *f*) *m* sender; *an e-e Zeitung*: contributor; ˈ**~eschluß** *m* closing date (for entries); ˈ**ᘓung** *f* sending in; (*Zuschrift*) letter.

ˈ**einsetz|en** *v/t.* set (*od.* put) in; *Geld*: stake; (*einfügen*; *inserieren*) insert; (*stiften, gründen*) institute; *in ein Amt*: install (*in acc.* in), appoint (to); (*anwenden*) use, apply, (*a.* ⚔) employ, bring into action; *Leben*: risk, stake; *sich* ~ extend o.s.; *sich* ~ *für* stand up for; (*bitten, plädieren*) plead for, advocate; *v/i.* ♪ strike (*fig.* chime) in; *Fieber, Wetter usw.*: set in; ˈ**ᘓung** *f* insertion; appointment, installation; *s. Einsatz.*

ˈ**Einsicht** *f* (16) inspection; *fig.* insight; judg(e)ment; understanding; ˈ**ᘓig** *s. einsichtsvoll*; **~nahme** [ˈ~naːmə] *f* (15): *zur* ~ for inspection; *nach* ~ on sight; ˈ**ᘓsvoll** judicious; (*verständig*) sensible.

ˈ**einsickern** (sn) infiltrate (*a.* ⚔ *usw.*), ooze (*od.* soak, seep) in(to *in acc.*).

ˈ**Einsiedler** *m* (7), ˈ**~in** *f* (16[1]) hermit; ˈ**ᘓisch** recluse, solitary.

einsilbig [ˈ~zilbiç] monosyllabic; (*wortkarg*) taciturn; ~*es Wort* monosyllable; ˈ**ᘓkeit** *f fig.* taciturnity.

ˈ**einsinken** (sn) sink in(to *in acc.*).

Einsitz|er [ˈ~zitsər] *m* (7) single-seater; ˈ**ᘓig** single-seated.

ˈ**einspannen** stretch (*in e-n Rahmen* in a frame); ⊕ clamp, chuck; *Pferd, a. fig.*: harness (*für, in acc* to); *j-n*: make *a p.* work; *an den Wagen*: put to.

Einspänner [ˈ~ʃpɛnər] *m* (7) one-horse carriage; F *fig.* recluse.

ˈ**einspar|en** economize; *Material, Zeit*: save; ˈ**ᘓung** *f* economization; saving(s *pl.*); economies *pl.*

ˈ**einsperren** lock up.

ˈ**einspielen** *Waage*: (*a. sich*) balance (out); *Geld*: realize, net; *sich* ~ *Sport*: play o.s. in, warm up; *fig.*

S.: get into its stride; *sich aufeinander* ~ become co-ordinated; *sie sind gut aufeinander eingespielt* they are a fine team.

'**Einsprache** *f s. Einspruch.*

'**einsprechen** *v/t.*: *j-m Mut* ~ encourage a p.; *j-m Trost* ~ comfort a p.; *v/i. s. einreden.*

'**einsprengen** *Wäsche*: sprinkle; *geol.* intersperse (*a. fig.*).

'**einspringen** (sn) ⊕ catch, snap; *Stoff*: shrink; (*sich einbiegen*) bend in; *fig.* (*aushelfen*) step in(to the breach), help out; *für j-n* ~ substitute (*Am. a.* pinchhit) for a p.; ~ *auf* (*acc.*) fly at; ~*der Winkel* re--entrant angle.

'**einspritz|en** inject; '**≗motor** *m* fuel injection engine; '**≗ung** *f* injection.

'**Einspruch** *m* objection (*a.* ⚖); protest, veto; (*Berufung*) appeal; ~ *erheben* enter a protest (*gegen* against), take exception (to), veto (*gegen* et. a thing); '**~srecht** *n* veto.

einspurig ['~ʃpuːriç] 🚂 single-track; *Straße*: single-lane.

einst [aɪnst] (*vormals*) once; (*künftig*) one (*od.* some) day.

einstampfen ['aɪnʃtampfən] *Schriften*: pulp.

'**Einstand** *m* (*Antritt*) entrance; *Tennis*: deuce.

'**einstechen** prick, puncture; *Nadel*: stick in.

'**einstecken** put in; *in die Tasche*, *a. Beleidigung*: pocket; *ins Gefängnis*: put in; *Schwert*: sheathe.

'**einstehen** (sn): ~ *für* answer for.

'**Einsteig|dieb** *m* cat burglar; '**~diebstahl** *m* burglary; '**≗en** (sn) get in; 🚂 *alles* ~! all aboard!

'**einstell|bar** ⊕ adjustable; '**~en** put in; ⚔ enrol(l), enlist; *Arbeiter, Hausgehilfin*: engage, *Am.* hire; (*aufgeben*) give up, drop, discontinue; *Zahlung, Feindseligkeiten usw.*: suspend, stop; *Mechanismus, a. fig.*: adjust (*auf acc.* to); *Radio*: tune in (to); *Arbeit*: stop; *Fabrikbetrieb*: shut down; *opt., a. fig. Gedanken usw.*: focus (*auf acc.* on); *Auto*: garage; *Rekord*: tie; ⚔ *das Feuer* ~ cease fire; *sich* ~ appear, turn up, show up; *Wetter usw.*: set in; *fig. sich* ~ *auf* (*acc.*) adjust (*od.* adapt) o.s. to, *vorbereitend*: prepare for; *sozial usw. eingestellt* socially *etc.* minded; *eingestellt auf* (*acc.*) prepared for *a th.*, to *inf.*; *eingestellt gegen* opposed to; '**~ig** *A* of one place *od.* figure; '**≗ung** *f* recruiting, enlistment; engagement; suspension; adjustment; strike; focus; *geistig*: mental attitude, mentality, outlook.

'**einstempeln** clock in.

einstig ['aɪnstiç] (*künftig*) future; (*ehemalig*) former, one-time; (*verstorben*) late.

'**einstimm|en** chime (*od.* join) in; *fig. a.* agree (*in acc.* to); '**~ig** ♪ of (*od.* for) one voice; (*einmütig*) unanimous; '**≗igkeit** *f* unanimity.

einstmals ['aɪnstmaːls] *s. einst.*

einstöckig ['~ʃtœkiç] one-storied.

'**einstöpseln** ⚡ plug in.

'**einstoßen** push (*od.* thrust) in; *Fensterscheibe usw.*: smash in.

'**einstreichen** *Geld*: pocket.

'**einstreuen** strew in(to *in acc.*); *fig.* intersperse.

'**einströmen** (sn) stream (*od.* pour) in.

'**einstudieren** study; *thea. Stück*: rehearse; *Rolle*: get up.

'**einstuf|en** (25) classify; grade, rate; '**≗ung** *f* classification; rating; '**≗ungs-prüfung** *f* placement test.

'**einstürmen** (sn) rush in; *fig. auf j-n* ~ rush at a p., assail a p.

'**Einsturz** *m* falling-in, collapse.

'**einstürzen** *v/i.* (sn) fall in, break (*od.* tumble) down, collapse; *fig. auf j-n*: overwhelm.

einstweil|en ['aɪnstvaɪlən] in the meantime; (*für jetzt*) for the present; '**~ig** temporary; ⚖ ~*e Verfügung* restraining order.

eintägig ['aɪntɛːgiç] one-day.

Eintagsfliege ['~taːks-] *f* ephemera (*a. fig.*).

'**eintasten** *Computer*: key in.

'**eintauchen** *v/t. u. v/i.* (sn) dip in.

'**eintauschen** exchange, barter (*beide*: *gegen* for).

'**einteil|en** divide (*in acc.* into); (*verteilen*) distribute; (*planen*) plan; *in Klassen*: classify; *zeitlich*: time; *zur Arbeit*: assign (to); detail; **~ig** ['~taɪliç] one-piece; '**≗ung** *f* division; distribution; classification.

eintönig ['~tøːniç] monotonous; '**≗keit** *f* monotony.

'**Eintopf**(**gericht** *n*) *m* hot-pot.

'**Eintracht** *f* harmony, concord.

einträchtig ['~trɛçtiç] harmonious; peaceful.

Eintrag ['~tra:k] *m* (3³) *s. Eintragung*; (*Abbruch*) prejudice; (*Schaden*) damage; ~ *tun* (*dat.*) prejudice, injure; **Ձen** ['~tra:gən] *schriftlich*: enter; *amtlich*: register; *als Mitglied*: enrol(l); *Gewinn*: bring in, yield; *sich* ~ (*P.*) enter one's name; register (*bei* with); *fig. j-m Böses*: bring on.

einträglich ['aɪntrɛ:kliç] profitable.

Eintragung ['~tra:guŋ] *f* entry; (*Posten*) item; *amtliche*: registration.

'**eintränken:** *ich werde es dir* ~ I'll make you pay for it.

'**eintreffen** (sn) arrive; (*geschehen*) happen; *Voraussagung*: come true; 'Ձ *n* arrival.

'**eintreiben** drive in *od.* home; *Schulden, Steuern*: collect.

'**eintreten** *v/i.* (sn) enter (*in ein Haus* a house); step in; *in das Heer, ein Geschäft usw.*: join; *in ein Amt*: enter on; *in Verhandlungen*: enter into; (*sich ereignen*) occur (*a. Tod*), happen, take place; *Fall, Umstände*: arise; *Wetter usw.*: set in; *für j-n*: answer (*od.* stand up *od.* intercede) for; *v/t. Tür*: kick in; *sich et.* ~ run a th. into one's foot.

eintrichtern ['~triçtərn] (29) *fig. j-m et.*: drum into a p.'s head.

'**Eintritt** *m* entry, entrance; (*Einlaß*) admittance; (*Anfang*) beginning; *des Winters usw.*: setting in; ~ *frei!* admission free!; ~ *verboten!* no admittance!; '**~sgeld** *n* entrance--fee; '**~skarte** *f* admission ticket.

'**eintrocknen** (sn) dry in *od.* up.

eintunken ['~tuŋkən] (25) dip in; *Brot usw.*: sop, dunk.

'**ein-üben** *et.*: (*a. sich*) practise; *j-n*: train, coach, drill.

einverleib|en ['~fɛrlaɪbən] (25) incorporate (*dat. od. in acc.* in, with); (*aneignen*) annex (to); '**Ձung** *f* incorporation; annexation.

Einver|nehmen ['~fɛrne:mən] *n* (6), '**~ständnis** *n* agreement, understanding; *in gutem* ~ on friendly terms; *sich mit j-m ins* ~ *setzen* come to an understanding with a p.; **Ձstanden** ['~fɛrʃtandən]: ~! agreed!; (*nicht*) ~ *sein* (dis)agree.

Einwand ['~vant] *m* (3³) objection (*gegen* to); ~ *erheben* raise an objection.

'**Einwander|er** *m* (7) immigrant; '**Ձn** (sn) immigrate; '**~ung** *f* immigration.

'**einwandfrei** *adj.* unobjectionable; (*unanfechtbar*) incontestable; (*tadellos*) blameless; ✝ faultless; *~e Führung* irreproachable conduct; *nicht* ~ objectionable; *adv.* absolutely.

einwärts ['~vɛrts] inward(s).

'**einwechseln** change; (*tauschen*) exchange.

'**Einwegflasche** *f* non-returnable bottle.

'**einweichen** (25) steep, soak.

'**einweih|en** *eccl.* consecrate; *Denkmal usw.*: inaugurate; *in* (*acc.*) ~ initiate into, *in ein Geheimnis* ~ *a.* let into; *eingeweiht* (*Mitwisser*) *sein* be in the secret, F be in the know; '**Ձung** *f* consecration; inauguration; initiation; '**Ձungsfeier** *f* (official) opening.

'**einweis|en** install (*in ein Amt* in); assign (*in e-e Wohnung* in[to]); (*lenken*) direct; ✈ *am Boden*: marshal, *in der Luft*: vector; (*unterweisen*) instruct, brief; '**Ձung** *f* installation; assignment; instruction, briefing.

'**einwend|en** object (*gegen* to); ~, *daß ...* argue that ...; '**Ձung** *f* objection.

'**einwerfen** throw in (*a. fig.*); *Fenster*: smash, break; *Bemerkung usw.*: interject; (*einwenden*) object.

'**einwickel|n** wrap (up), envelop (*in acc.* in); F *fig. j-n*: *sl.* bamboozle; '**Ձpapier** *n* wrapping paper.

einwillig|en ['aɪnviligən] consent, agree (*in acc.* to); '**Ձung** *f* consent.

'**einwirk|en:** *fig.* ~ *auf* (*acc*) act (up)on; (*angreifen*) affect; (*beeinflussen*) influence, work (up)on *a p.*; '**Ձung** *f* action; effect; influence.

einwöchig ['aɪnvœçıç] one-week.

Einwohner ['~vo:nər] *m* (7), '**~in** *f* inhabitant, resident; '**~'melde-amt** *n* registration office; '**~schaft** *f* inhabitants *pl.*

'**Einwurf** *m Sport*: throw-in; *fig.* objection; *für Briefe usw.*: opening, slit; *für Münzen*: slot.

'**einwurzeln** (sn) take root; *s. eingewurzelt.*

'**Einzahl** *f* singular (number); '**Ձen** pay in; '**~ung** *f* payment; *Bank*: deposit; '**~ungsschein** *m* paying-in slip, *Am.* deposit slip.

einzäun|en ['~tsɔʏnən] (25) fence in; '**2ung** *f* enclosure; fence.

'**einzeichn|en** draw in; *sich* ~ enter one's name; '**2ung** *f* entry.

Einzel ['aɪntsəl] *n s.* ~*spiel*; '**~-aufhängung** *mot. f* independent suspension; '**~-aufstellung** *f* itemized list; '**~fall** *m* individual case; '**~firma** ⚕ *f* one-man firm; '**~gänger** *m* outsider, F lone wolf; '**~haft** *f* solitary confinement; '**~handel** *m* retail trade; '**~händler** *m* retailer; '**~haus** *n* detached house; '**~heit** *f* particular point, detail, item; ~*en pl.* particulars, details; *bis in alle* ~*en* down to the smallest detail; '**~kampf** *m* single combat *od.* fight; '**2n** single; (*besonder*) particular; (*für sich allein*) individual, isolated; (*abgetrennt*) separate; *Schuh usw.*: odd; *im* ~*en* in detail; ~ *angeben od. aufführen* specify, *bsd. Am.* itemize; *ins* ~*e gehen* go into detail(s); *der* 2*e* the individual; *jeder* ~*e* each man; each (one); '**2nstehend** *s. alleinstehend*; '**~persönlichkeit** *f* individual; '**~spiel** *n Tennis*: single; '**~teil** *m* component (part); '**~verkauf** *m* sale by retail; '**~wesen** *n* individual; '**~zelle** *f* solitary cell; '**~zimmer** *n* single room.

einzieh|bar ✈ ['aɪntsi:ba:r] *Fahrgestell*: retractable; '**~en** *v/t.* draw in; *bsd.* ⊕ retract; *Flagge*: strike; *Segel*: take in; ⚔ call up, *Am.* draft, induct; ⚖ seize, confiscate; *Steuer usw.*: collect; *Geldscheine, Münzen*: withdraw; *Erkundigungen* ~ make inquiries (*über acc.* on, about), gather information (on, about); *v/i.* (sn) enter, march in; *in e-e Wohnung*: move in; *Flüssigkeit*: soak in; '**2ung** *f* ⚔ calling-up, *Am.* drafting, induction; ⚖ confiscation; collection; withdrawal.

einzig ['aɪntsiç] *adj.* only; (*einzeln*) single; (*alleinig*) sole; *s. einzigartig*; *der* ~*e* the only one; *das* ~*e* the only thing; *adv.* ~ *und allein* solely; '**~-artig** unique, singular.

'**Einzimmerwohnung** *f* one-room flat (*Am.* apartment).

'**Einzug** *m* entry, entrance; *in ein Haus usw.*: moving-in(to *in acc.*), occupation (of); *v. Truppen*: marching-in; *s. Einziehung.*

'**einzwängen** squeeze (in).

Eis [aɪs] *n* (4) ice; (*Speise*2) ice-cream; ~ *am Stiel* ice-lolly; *fig. das* ~ *brechen* break the ice; *auf* ~ *legen* put into cold storage (*a. fig.*).

Eis ♪ ['e:ʔis] *n* E sharp.

'**Eis|bahn** *f* skating-rink; '**~bär** *m* polar bear; '**~becher** *m* sundae; '**~bein** *n* pig's knuckles *pl.*; '**~berg** *m* iceberg; '**~beutel** *m* ice-bag; '**~blume** *f am Fenster*: frost-flower; '**~bombe** *f* ice-cream bombe; '**~brecher** *m* (7) ice-breaker; '**~creme** *f* ice-cream; '**~decke** *f* sheet of ice; '**~diele** *f* ice-cream parlo(u)r.

Eisen ['aɪzən] *n* (6) iron; (*Huf*2) horseshoe; *altes* ~ scrap-iron; *zum alten* ~ *werfen* (*a. fig.*) throw on the scrap-heap; *zwei* ~ *im Feuer haben* have two strings to one's bow; (*man muß*) *das* ~ *schmieden, solange es heiß ist* strike the iron while it is hot.

Eisenbahn ['~ba:n] *f* railway, *Am.* railroad; *mit der* ~ by rail, by train; *s. Bahn...*; '**~-abteil** *n* railway compartment; '**~er** *m* (7) railwayman; '**~erstreik** *m* rail strike; '**~knotenpunkt** *m* (railway) junction; '**~netz** *n* railway (*Am.* railroad) network; '**~schwelle** *f* sleeper, *Am.* tie; '**~station** *f* railway (*Am.* railroad) station, *Am. a.* depot; '**~strecke** *f* (railway) line, *Am.* road; '**~-überführung** *f* railway overpass; '**~-unglück** *n* railway accident, train disaster; '**~-unterführung** *f* railway underpass; '**~wagen** *m* railway carriage *od.* coach, *Am.* railroad car.

'**Eisen|bergwerk** *n* iron mine, iron pit; '**~beschlag** *m* iron-mounting; '**~beton** *m* reinforced concrete; '**~blech** *n* sheet-iron; '**~-erz** *n* iron-ore; '**~gießerei** *f* iron-foundry; '**~guß** *m* iron casting; (*Gußeisen*) cast iron; '**2haltig** ferruginous; '**~hammer** *m* iron-works *sg.*; '**2hart** (as) hard as iron; '**~hütte** *f* iron-works *sg.*; '**~-oxyd** *n* ferric oxide; '**~stange** *f* iron rod; '**~träger** *m* iron girder; '**~vitriol** *m, n* green vitriol; '**~waren** *f/pl.* ironware, *bsd. Am.* hardware; '**~warenhändler** *m* ironmonger, *Am.* hardware dealer; '**~warenhandlung** *f* ironmonger's (shop), *Am.* hardware store; '**~werk** *n* iron-work; *Fabrik*: iron-works *pl. od. sg.*

eisern ['aɪzərn] (of) iron (*a. fig.*); *fig. Gesundheit*: cast-iron; ~*e Ra-*

tion iron ration; *~er Bestand* permanent stock; *~er Fleiß* untiring industry; *~er Wille* iron will; *s. Besen, Lunge, Vorhang.*

ˈeis|frei free from ice; **ˈ2gang** *m* ice-drift; **ˈ~gekühlt** iced; **ˈ~grau** hoary; **ˈ2heiligen** *m/pl.* Ice Saints; **ˈ2hockey** *n Sport*: ice-hockey.

eisig [ˈaɪziç] icy, glacial (*a. fig.*).

ˈeis|kalt icy-cold; *fig.* cool; **ˈ2kunstlauf** *m* figure skating; **ˈ2lauf(en** *n*) *m* skating; **ˈ2läufer(in** *f*) *m* skater; **ˈ2maschine** *f* ice-machine; **ˈ2meer** *n* polar sea; *Nördliches ~* Arctic, *Südliches ~* Antarctic Ocean; **ˈ2pickel** *m* ice-ax(e).

ˈEi-sprung *biol. m* ovulation.

ˈEis|revue *f* ice-show; **ˈ~schießen** *n* curling; **ˈ~schnellauf** *m* speed skating; **ˈ~scholle** *f* ice-floe; **ˈ~schrank** *m* refrigerator, icebox; **ˈ~segeln** *n* ice-yachting; **ˈ~stockschießen** *n* curling; **ˈ~verkäufer** *m* ice-cream man; **ˈ~verkäuferin** *f* ice-cream lady; **ˈ~würfel** *m* ice-cube; **ˈ~zapfen** *m* icicle; **ˈ~zeit** *f* ice-age, glacial epoch.

eitel [ˈaɪtəl] vain (*auf acc.* of); *fig.* (*leer*) vain, empty; (*fruchtlos*) vain, futile; (*bloß*) mere; *eitles Gerede* idle talk; *~ Gold* pure gold; *eitle Hoffnung* idle (*od.* vain) hope; **ˈ2keit** *f* vanity.

Eiter [ˈaɪtər] *m* (7) matter, pus; **ˈ~beule** *f* abscess; **ˈ~pfropf** *m* core; **ˈ~pustel** *f* pustule.

eit(e)rig [ˈaɪt(ə)riç] purulent.

ˈeiter|n (29) fester, discharge matter, 🕮 suppurate; **ˈ2ung** *f* suppuration.

ˈEiweiß *n* (3^2) white of egg, 🕮 albumen; **ˈ2-arm** low in protein, low-protein *attr.*; **2haltig** [ˈ~haltiç] albuminous; **ˈ2reich** high in protein, high-protein *attr.*; **ˈ~stoff** *m* albumen.

Ekel [ˈeːkəl] **1.** *m* (7) disgust (*vor dat.* at), nausea; *er ist mir ein ~* he is my aversion; **2.** *n* F *Person*: nasty fellow, pest; **ˈ2haft, ˈek(e)lig** nauseous, disgusting; nasty; **ˈ2n** (29) disgust, sicken; *sich ~ vor* (*dat.*) loathe, be disgusted with *od.* at; be nauseated at.

eklatant [eklaˈtant] spectacular; (*auffällig*) striking.

Eksta|se [ɛkˈstɑːzə] *f* (15) ecstasy; **2tisch** ecstatic(ally *adv.*).

Ekzem ⚕ [ɛkˈtseːm] *n* (3^1) eczema.

Elan [eˈlɑ̃] *m* (11) élan (*fr.*), verve, vim, dash, spirit.

elast|isch [eˈlastiʃ] elastic; **2izität** [~tsiˈtɛːt] *f* elasticity.

Elch *zo.* [ɛlç] *m* (3) elk.

Elefant [eleˈfant] *m* (12) elephant; F *~ im Porzellanladen* bull in a china shop; *s. Mücke*; **~enrüssel** *m* elephant's trunk; **~enzahn** *m* elephant's tusk.

elegan|t [eleˈgant] elegant (*a. fig.*), fashionable; *Kleidung*: *a.* stylish, smart; **2z** *f* (16) elegance.

Elegie [eleˈgiː] *f* (15) elegy.

elegisch [eˈleːgiʃ] elegiac.

elektrifizier|en [elɛktrifiˈtsiːrən] electrify; **2ung** *f* electrification.

Eˈlektriker *m* (7) electrician.

eˈlektrisch electric(al).

elektrisier|en [~ˈziːrən] electrify (*a. fig.*); **2maschine** *f* electrical machine.

Elektrizität [~tsiˈtɛːt] *f* (16) electricity; **~sgesellschaft** *f* electric supply company; **~swerk** *n* (electric) power station; **~szähler** *m* electricity meter.

Elektro|chemie [elɛktroçeˈmiː] *f* electrochemistry; **2chemisch** [~ˈçeːmiʃ] electrochemical.

Elektrode [elɛkˈtroːdə] *f* (15) electrode.

Elektro|dyˈnamik *f* electrodynamics *sg.*; **~geschäft** [eˈlɛktro-] *n* electrical shop; **~herd** *m* electric range; **~-ingenieur** *m* electrical engineer; **~-installateur** *m* electrician; **~lyse** [~ˈlyːzə] *f* electrolysis; **~motor** *m* (electric) motor.

Elektron ⚡ [eˈlɛktrɔn] *n* (8^1) electron; **~enblitz** [~ˈtroːnən-] *phot. m* electronic flash; **~engehirn** *n* electronic brain; **~enmikroskop** *n* electron microscope; **~enröhre** *f* electron valve (*Am.* tube); **~entechnik** *f*, **~ik** [elɛkˈtroːnik] *f* (16, *o. pl.*) electronics *sg.*; **2isch** electronic; *~e Datenverarbeitung* electronic data processing.

Eˈlektro|rasenmäher *m* electric lawn-mower; **~rasierer** *m* electric razor; **~ˈtechnik** *f* electrical engineering; **~ˈtechniker** *m* electrical engineer; **2ˈtechnisch** electrotechnical.

Element [eleˈmɛnt] *n* (3) *allg.* element; ⚡ *a.* cell.

elementar [~'taːr] elementary; ~*e Gewalt* elemental force; **♀klasse** *f* junior form; **♀schule** *f* elementary (*a.* primary, *Am.* grade) school; **♀unterricht** *m* elementary instruction.

Elen ['eːlɛn] *m*, *n* (6), '**~tier** *n* elk.

Elend ['eːlɛnt] **1.** *n* (3, *o.pl.*) misery; (*Not*) need, distress; F *das graue* ~ the blues *sg.*; *s. stürzen*; **2.** ♀ miserable, wretched (*beide a. contp.*); ~ *aussehen* look very poorly; *sich* ~ *fühlen* feel miserable *od.* wretched; '**~sviertel** *n* slums *pl.*

elf [ɛlf] **1.** eleven; **2.** ♀ *f* (16) *Fußball*: eleven, team.

Elf *m* (12), **~e** ['ɛlfə] *f* (15) elf, fairy.

'**Elfenbein** *n*, '**♀ern** ivory.

Elf'meter *m Fußball*: penalty kick; **~marke** *f* penalty spot; **~schießen** *n* sudden-death play-off; **~tor** *n* penalty goal.

'**elfte** eleventh; '**♀l** *n* (6) eleventh (part); '**~ns** in the eleventh place.

Elite [e'liːtə] *f* (15) *the* élite (*fr.*); **~denken** *n* elitism.

Elixier [eli'ksiːr] *n* (3¹) elixir.

'**Ellbogen** *m* elbow; '**~freiheit** *f* elbow-room.

Elle ['ɛlə] *f* (15) yard; *anat.* ulna; '**♀n'lang** *fig.* incredibly long (*Person*: tall); interminable.

Ellip|se [ɛ'lipsə] *f* (15) ⊿ ellipse; *gr.* ellipsis; **♀tisch** elliptic(al).

Elsäss|er ['ɛlzɛsər] *m* (7), '**~erin** *f* (16¹), '**♀isch** Alsatian.

Elster ['ɛlstər] *f* (15) magpie.

elter|lich ['ɛltərliç] parental; '**♀n** *pl. inv.* parents; '**♀n-abend** *m* parent-teacher meeting; '**♀nbeirat** *m* Parents' Council; '**~nlos** parentless, without parents; '**♀nsprechstunde** *f* consultation hour (for parents); '**♀nsprechtag** *m* open day (for parents).

Email [e'maːj] *n* (11), **~le** [*a.* e'maljə] *f* (15), **♀lieren** [ema(l)'jiːrən] enamel.

Emanze [e'mantsə] F *f* (15) women's libber.

Emanzi|pation *f* [emantsipa'tsjoːn] *f* emancipation; **~pationsbewegung** *f* emancipatory movement; **♀patorisch** [~'toːriʃ] emancipatory; **♀'pieren** emancipate.

Embargo [ɛm'bargo] *n* (11) (*Ausfuhrverbot*) embargo.

Embolie ⚕ [ɛmbo'liː] *f* (15) embolism.

Embryo *biol.* ['ɛmbryo] *m* (8¹) embryo; **♀nal** [~'naːl] embryonic.

Emigr|ant [emi'grant] *m* (12) emigrant; **♀ieren** [~'griːrən] emigrate.

Emotion [emo'tsjoːn] *f* emotion; **♀al** [~tsjo'naːl], **♀ell** [~'nɛl] emotional; **♀sgeladen** emotionally charged.

empfahl [ɛm'pfaːl] *pret. v. empfehlen.*

Empfang [ɛm'pfaŋ] *m* (3³) reception (*a. Radio*); *e-s Briefes usw.*: receipt; *nach* (*od. bei*) ~ (*gen.*) on receipt of; *in* ~ *nehmen* receive; **♀en** *v/t.* (30) receive; *freundlich*: *a.* welcome; *v/i.* (*schwanger werden*) conceive.

Empfänger [~'pfɛŋər] *m* (7) *P. u. Gerät*: receiver; *v. Waren*: consignee; *e-s Briefes*: addressee.

em'pfänglich impressionable; susceptible (*für* to); receptive (to, of); **♀keit** *f* susceptibility.

Em'pfängnis *f* (14²) conception; **♀verhütend:** ~*es Mittel* contraceptive; **~verhütung** *f* contraception.

Em'pfangs|bereich *m Radio*: reception area; **~bescheinigung** *f* receipt; **~chef** *m* reception (*Am.* room) clerk; **~dame** *f*, **~herr** *m* receptionist; **~gerät** *n* receiving set; **~schein** *m* receipt; **~station** *f Radio*: receiving station; **~tag** *m* at-home; **~zimmer** *n* reception-room.

empfehlen [ɛm'pfeːlən] (30) (*als geeignet* ~) recommend; (*anvertrauen*) (re)commend; ~ *Sie mich* (*dat.*) please remember me to; *sich j-m* ~ present one's respects (*od.* compliments) to; *sich* ~ (*gehen*) take leave; *S.*: commend itself; *es empfiehlt sich* it is (re)commendable; **~swert** (re)commendable.

Em'pfehlung *f* recommendation; (*Gruß*) compliments *pl.*; **~sschreiben** *n* letter of recommendation.

empfinden [~'pfindən] (30) feel (*als lästig usw.* to be troublesome *etc.*); (*gewahren*) perceive, sense.

empfindlich [~'pfintliç] sensitive (*a. phot.*, ⚗, ⊕; *für, gegen* to); *pred. a.* susceptible (*gegen* to); (*zart*) delicate; (*reizbar*) irritable; (*leicht gekränkt*) touchy; (*fühlbar*) sensible; *Kälte, Strafe, Verlust*: severe; *Kränkung*: grievous; *Schmerz*: acute; *fig. s-e* ~*ste Stelle* his sore spot; **♀keit** *f* sensitiveness; irritability; sensibility; touchiness; delicacy.

empfindsam [~'pfintzɑːm] sensitive; sentimental; **2keit** *f* sensitiveness; sentimentality.

Empfindung [~'pfinduŋ] *f* sensation; (*Wahrnehmung*) perception; *weitS.* feeling; **2slos** insensitive (*für, gegen* to); insensible; *bsd. fig.* unfeeling; **~slosigkeit** *f* insensitiveness (*für, gegen* to); insensibility; **~svermögen** *n* sensitive (*od.* perceptive) faculty.

empfohlen [ɛm'pfoːlən] *p.p. v. empfehlen.*

empor [ɛm'poːr] up, upwards; **~arbeiten:** *sich ~* work one's way up; **~blicken** look up (*zu* to).

Empore ⚠ [ɛm'poːrə] *f* (15) gallery.

empören [ɛm'pøːrən] (*aufbringen*) (rouse to) anger, incense; scandalize, shock; *sich ~* revolt, rebel (*beide a. fig.*; *über acc.* at); (*zornig werden*) grow furious; *empört* indignant, shocked, scandalized (*über acc.* at); **~d** outrageous; shocking.

Em'pörer *m* (7), **~in** *f* insurgent, rebel; **2isch** rebellious, mutinous.

em'por|kommen (sn) rise (in the world); **2kömmling** *m* upstart; **~ragen** (h.) tower (*über acc.* above), rise; **~schießen** (sn) shoot up; *sich* **~schwingen** rise, soar up; **~steigen** (sn) rise, ascend; **~streben** (h.) strive upward(s); *fig.* aspire (*zu* to); **~treiben** force up(wards).

Empörung [ɛm'pøːruŋ] *f* rebellion, revolt; (*Unwille*) indignation.

emsig ['ɛmziç] (*tätig*) busy, active; (*fleißig*) industrious, assiduous; **'2keit** *f* industry, activity; assiduity.

Emulsion [emul'zjoːn] *f* (16) emulsion.

End-abnehmer ['ɛntˀapneːmər] *m*, **~in** *f* ultimate buyer, consumer.

Ende ['ɛndə] *n* (10) *allg.* end; *zeitlich a.* close; (*Ergebnis*) *a.* upshot; *am Geweih*: antler; *am ~* at (*od.* in) the end, (*doch*) after all, (*schließlich*) eventually, at length, (*vielleicht*) perhaps, maybe; *s. dick*; *zu ~ gehen* (come to an) end, (*ablaufen*) expire, (*knapp werden*) run short; *zu ~ sein* be at an end; *s. Weisheit*; *e-r S. ein ~ machen* put an end to; *ein böses ~ nehmen* come to a bad end.

'enden (26) *v/t. s. beend(ig)en*; *v/i.* (h.) end, terminate; (*aufhören*) cease, finish; *nicht ~ wollend* unending.

Endergebnis ['ɛntˀɛrgeːpnis] *n* final result, upshot.

Endes-unterzeichnete ['ɛndəs-] *m, f* (18) *the* undersigned.

'Endfassung *f* final version.

endgültig ['ɛnt-] final, definitive, conclusive.

'Endhaltestelle *f* terminus.

endigen ['ɛndigən] (25) *s. enden*; *gr. ~ auf* (*acc.*) terminate in.

Endivie ⚘ [ɛn'diːvjə] *f* (15) endive.

End|kampf ['ɛntkampf] *m Sport*: final (contest); **'~lagerung** *f* final storage; **'~lauf** *m* final (heat).

'endlich *adj.* final, ultimate; *phls.* finite; *adv.* finally, at last, at length; *~ doch* after all; **'2keit** *f* finiteness.

'end|los endless (*a.* ⊕); **'2losigkeit** *f* endlessness; **'2montage** *f* final assembly; **'2phase** *f* final stage; **'2produkt** *n* end (*od.* final) product; **'2punkt** *m* final point; **'2reim** *m* end-rhyme; **'2resultat** *n* final result, upshot; **'2runde** *f Sport*: final; **'2rundenteilnehmer(in** *f*) *m Sport*: finalist; **'2silbe** *f* final syllable; **'2spiel** *n* final (match); **2spurt** ['~ʃpurt] *m Sport*: final spurt, finish; **'2station** 🚂 *f* terminus, *Am.* terminal; **'2summe** *f* (sum) total.

Endung ['ɛnduŋ] *f* ending.

End|verbraucher ⚕ ['ɛnt-] *m* ultimate consumer; **'~ziel** *n*, **'~zweck** *m* ultimate object.

Energie [enɛr'giː] *f* (15) energy; **~bedarf** *m* energy requirement; **~krise** *f* energy crisis; **2los** lacking (in) energy; **~quelle** *f* source of energy; **~sparen** *n* energy saving; **2sparend** energy-saving; **~sparmaßnahme** *f* energy-saving measure; **~träger** *m* energy source; **~verbrauch** *m* energy consumption; **~verschwendung** *f* waste of energy; **~wirtschaft** *f* power industry; **~zufuhr** *f* energy supply.

e'nergisch energetic(ally *adv.*); *~ werden* put one's foot down.

eng [ɛŋ] narrow; *Kleidung*: tight; (*~ anliegend*) clinging; (*dicht*; *nah*) close; (*innig*) intimate; *~ befreundet sein* be great friends; *~ sitzen* (*od. stehen*) sit (*od.* stand) closely together; *im ~eren Sinne* strictly speaking; *s. Wahl.*

Engag|ement [ɑ̃gaʒ'mɑ̃] *n* (11) engagement; *fig.* commitment; **2ieren** [~'ʒiːrən] engage, *Am. a.* hire; **2iert** *fig.* committed.

Enge [ˈɛŋə] *f* (15) narrowness; *der Kleidung*: tightness; (*Engpaß*) bottle-neck (*a. fig.*); *fig.* straits *pl.*; *in die* ~ *treiben* corner.

Engel [ˈɛŋəl] *m* (7) angel; ˈ**♀haft** angelic; ˈ**~macher(in** *f*) *m* back-street abortionist; ˈ**~sgeduld** *f* angelic patience.

Engerling [ˈɛŋərliŋ] *m* (3[1]) grub of the cockchafer.

ˈ**engherzig** narrow-minded, hidebound.

Engländer [ˈɛŋlɛndər] *m* (7) Englishman, *Am. a.* Britisher; *pl.* (*als Volk*) *the* English; ⊕ *m* (*Schraubenschlüssel*) monkey-wrench; ˈ**~in** *f* (16[1]) Englishwoman.

englisch [ˈɛŋliʃ] English; *weitS.* British; *~e Kirche* Church of England, English (*od.* Anglican) Church; *~e Krankheit* rickets *pl. od. sg.*; *~es Pflaster* court-plaster; ♀ *n*: *ins ~e* into English; *aus dem ~en* from (the) English.

engmaschig [ˈɛŋmaʃiç] close-meshed.

ˈ**Engpaß** *m* defile, narrow pass, *Am. a.* notch; *bsd. fig.* bottle-neck.

en gros [ɑ̃ˈgroː], **Enˈgros...** wholesale.

engstirnig [ˈɛŋʃtirniç] narrow-minded.

Enkel [ˈɛŋkəl] *m* (7) grandchild; (*~sohn*) grandson; *weitS.* (*Nachkomme*) descendant; ˈ**~in** *f* (16[1]) granddaughter.

enorm [eˈnɔrm] enormous; F (*famos*) terrific.

Ensemble *thea.* [ɑ̃ˈsɑ̃ːbl(ə)] *n* (11) ensemble; (*Besetzung*) cast.

entˈ-artlen [ɛnt-] (26) degenerate; **~et** degenerate; decadent; **♀ung** *f* degeneration.

entˈ-äußern: *sich e-r S.* ~ dispose of, part with.

entbehr|en [ɛntˈbeːrən] (25) (*nicht haben, vermissen*) lack, miss, want; (*auskommen ohne*) dispense with, do without; *ich kann ihn nicht ~* I cannot spare him; **~lich** dispensable; **♀ung** *f* want, privation.

entˈbieten: *j-m s-n Gruß ~* present one's compliments to a p.; *j-n zu sich ~* send for, summon.

entˈbinden dispense, release (*von* from); *Frau*: deliver (of).

Entˈbindung *f* dispensation, release (*von* from); *e-r Frau*: delivery; **~s-anstalt** *f*, **~s-heim** *n* maternity hospital (*od.* clinic); **~ssaal** *m* delivery room; **~sstation** *f* delivery ward.

entˈblättern strip of leaves; *sich ~* shed its leaves; F *fig.* strip.

entblöden [ɛntˈbløːdən] (26): *sich nicht ~ zu inf.* not to be ashamed to *inf.*

entblöß|en [~ˈbløːsən] (27) denude, strip (*gen.* of); *das Haupt*: uncover; ⚔ expose; **~t** bare; *fig.* destitute (*gen.* of); **♀ung** *f* denudation; *fig.* destitution.

entˈbrennen (sn) *fig.* be inflamed (*in Liebe zu j-m* with love for a p.); *Zorn*: blaze up; *Kampf usw.*: break out, flare up.

entˈdecken discover; (*herausfinden*) detect; (*aufdecken*) reveal; *sich j-m ~* confide in a p.

Entˈdecker *m* (7), **~in** *f* discoverer.

Entˈdeckung *f* discovery; **~sreise** *f* voyage of discovery, expedition.

Ente [ˈɛntə] *f* (15) duck; *fig.* (*Zeitungs♀*) canard, hoax.

entehr|en [ɛntˈʔeːrən] dishono(u)r; **~end** dishono(u)ring, disgraceful; **♀ung** *f* disgrace; degradation.

enteign|en [~ˈʔaɪgnən] (25) *j-n, et.*: expropriate; *j-n*: dispossess; **♀ung** *f* expropriation; dispossession.

entˈ-eilen (sn) hasten away.

enteis|en [~ˈʔaɪzən] *mot.*, ✈ *usw.* de-ice; **♀ungs-anlage** *f* de-icer.

ˈ**Enten|braten** *m* roast duck; ˈ**~jagd** *f* duck-shooting.

ˈ**Enterbeil** ⚓ *n* boarding-ax(e).

entˈ-erb|en disinherit; **♀ung** *f* disinheritance.

ˈ**Enterhaken** ⚓ *m* grapnel.

Enterich [ˈɛntəriç] *m* (3) drake.

entern [ˈɛntərn] (29) board, grapple.

entfachen [ɛntˈfaxən] (25) kindle.

entˈfahren (sn): *j-m ~* drop from a p.'s *hand etc.*

entˈfallen *v/i.* (sn): *j-m ~* escape a p.; *fig.* slip a p.'s memory; *s. wegfallen*; (*nicht in Frage kommen*) be inapplicable; *auf j-n ~* fall to a p.'s share.

entˈfalt|en (*a. sich*) unfold; *fig.* (*a. sich*) develop (*zu* into); (*zeigen*) display; ⚔ *Truppen*: deploy; **♀ung** *f* display; development.

entˈfärbe|n decolorize; (*bleichen*) bleach; *sich ~ s. verfärben*; **♀r** *m* (7) decolorant.

entfern|en [~ˈfɛrnən] (25) *allg.* remove; *bsd. Fleck*: take out; *sich ~*

withdraw; **~t** distant, remote (*a. fig. Ähnlichkeit usw.*); *weit davon ~ zu inf.* far from *ger.*; *nicht im ~esten* not in the least; **2ung** *f* removal; (*Abstand, Ferne*) distance; (*Reichweite*) range; *in e-r gewissen ~* at a distance; **2ungsmesser** *m* range-finder.

ent'fessel|n unchain; *fig.* unleash; **2ungskünstler** *m* escape artist.

entfetten [~'fɛtən] (26) degrease; *Wolle*: scour.

Entfettungskur [ɛnt'fɛtuŋsku:r] *f* slimming-cure.

ent'flammen inflame.

ent'flecht|en ✝ decartelize; **2ung** *f* decartelization.

ent'fliegen (sn) fly away (*dat.* from).

ent'fliehen (sn) flee, escape (*aus od. dat.* from); *Zeit*: fly.

entfremd|en [~'frɛmdən] (26) estrange, alienate (*j-m* from a p.); **2ung** *f* estrangement, alienation.

entfrosten [~'frɔstən] (26) defrost.

ent'führ|en carry off; *ein Mädchen*: elope with; *mit Gewalt*: abduct, *bsd. Kind*: kidnap; *Flugzeug*: hijack, F skyjack; **2er** *m* (7), **2erin** *f* abductor, kidnap(p)er; (*Flugzeug2*) hijacker, F skyjacker; **2ung** *f* abduction, kidnap(p)ing; elopement; hijacking.

entgasen [ɛnt'ga:zən] (27) degas.

entgegen [ɛnt'ge:gən] **1.** *adv., prp.* (*dat.*) *Gegensatz*: in opposition to, contrary to; *Richtung*: towards; **2.** *adj. s. entgegengesetzt*; **~arbeiten** counteract, work against, oppose (*e-r S.* a th., *j-m* a p.); **~bringen** *j-m et.*: carry towards a p.; *j-m ein Gefühl ~* meet a p. with a feeling; **~eilen** (sn) hasten to meet; **~gehen** (sn) go to meet (*a p.*); *e-r Gefahr, e-r Zukunft*: face, be in for (*a th.*); *dem Ende ~* be drawing to a close; **~gesetzt** opposite; *fig.* contrary, opposed (*dat.* to); **~halten** (*einwenden*) object; *zum Vergleich*: contrast (*e-r S. et. anderes* a th. with another th.); **~handeln** act against; *e-m Gesetz usw.*: contravene (*a th.*) **~kommen** (sn) come to meet (*a p.*); *fig. j-m ~* meet a p.('s wishes) halfway; **2kommen** *n* obligingness; **~kommend** *adj.* obliging, accommodating; **~laufen** (sn) run to meet (*a p.*); **~nehmen** accept, receive; **~sehen** look forward to, expect (*a th.*); *e-r baldigen Antwort ~d* awaiting an early reply; **~setzen** oppose (*dat.* to); *Widerstand*: put up; **~stehen** (h.) be opposed (*dat.* to); (*ausschließen*) bar; **~stellen** oppose (*dat.* to); *fig. sich e-r S. ~* set o.s. against; **~strecken** hold out (*dat.* to); **~treten** (sn) meet (*a p.*), face (*a. e-r Gefahr*); *feindlich*: oppose *a p.*; **~wirken** *s. entgegenarbeiten.*

entgegn|en [~'ge:gnən] (25) reply; return; *schlagfertig*: retort; **2ung** *f* reply; retort.

ent'gehen (sn) escape (*j-m* a p.; *e-r S.* [from] a th.); *fig. j-m ~* escape a p.('s notice); *sich die Gelegenheit ~ lassen* miss one's opportunity.

entgeistert [~'gaɪstərt] aghast.

Entgelt [ɛnt'gɛlt] *n* (3) (*Lohn*) recompense, remuneration; (*vertragliche Gegenleistung*) consideration; (*Ersatz*) compensation; *gegen ~* for a (valuable) consideration; **2en** (*büßen*) atone (*od.* suffer) for.

ent'giften decontaminate (*a. fig.*).

entgleis|en [~'glaɪzən] (27 sn) run off the rails, be derailed; *fig.* (make a) slip; *~ lassen* derail; **2ung** *f* derailment; *fig.* slip, faux pas (*fr.*).

ent'gleiten (sn) slip (*dat.* from).

entgräten [~'grɛ:tən] (26) bone.

ent'haaren (25) depilate.

Ent'haarungsmittel *n* depilatory.

ent'halt|en contain, hold, include; *sich ~* (*gen.*) abstain (*od.* refrain) from; *er konnte sich des Lachens nicht ~* he could not help laughing; **2ung** *f* abstention; **~sam** abstinent; (*keinen Alkohol trinkend*) teetotal; **2samkeit** *f* abstinence; teetotalism.

ent'härten ⊕ soften; *metall.* anneal.

enthaupt|en [ɛnt'hauptən] (26) behead, decapitate; **2ung** *f* beheading, decapitation.

ent'heb|en (*gen.*) relieve of; *e-r Pflicht usw.*: exempt from; *des Amtes*: remove from, *vorläufig*: suspend from; **2ung** *f* relief; exemption; removal.

ent'heilig|en profane, desecrate; **2ung** *f* profanation, desecration.

ent'hemmen: *j-n ~* free a p. from his (*od.* her) inhibitions.

ent'hüll|en uncover; *Gesicht, Denkmal, a. fig.*; unveil; *fig.* reveal, disclose; (*zeigen*) show; (*aufdecken*) expose; **2ung** *f* unveiling; *fig.* revelation, disclosure; exposure.

enthülsen [~'hylzən] (27) husk.

Enthusias|mus [ɛntuzi'asmus] *m* (16²) enthusiasm; **~t** *m* (12), **~tin** *f* enthusiast; *für Film, Sport*: F fan; **ꙭtisch** enthusiastic(ally *adv.*).
ent'jungfer|n (25) deflower; **ꙭung** *f* defloration.
ent'kalken (25) decalcify; *Boiler etc.*: descale.
ent'keimen *v/t.* sterilize; *v/i.* ⚘ germinate, sprout (*dat.* from); *fig.* spring (from).
entkernen [~'kɛrnən] (25) stone; *Äpfel*: core.
ent'kleiden unclothe; (*a. fig.*) strip (*gen.* of); (*a. sich*) undress; *bsd. fig.* divest (*gen.* of).
ent'kommen 1. (sn) escape (*j-m* a p.; *aus* from), get away (*od.* off); **2.** ꙭ *n* escape, getaway.
entkorken [~'kɔrkən] (25) uncork.
entkräft|en [~'krɛftən] (26) enfeeble, debilitate; ⚖ (*ungültig machen*) invalidate; (*widerlegen*) refute; **~et** exhausted; **ꙭung** *f* enfeeblement, debilitation; ⚖ invalidation; refutation.
ent'lad|en unload; (*bsd.* ⚡; *a. sich*) discharge; *sich ~ Wolke usw.*: burst; *Gewehr*: go off; **ꙭerampe** *f* unloading platform; **ꙭung** *f* unloading; discharge; *fig.* explosion; *zur ~ bringen* explode.
ent'lang along; *hier ~!* this way.
entlarv|en [ɛnt'larfən] (25) unmask, *fig. a.* expose; **ꙭung** *f* unmasking; *fig.* exposure.
ent'lass|en dismiss; *bsd.* ⚔, ⚕, ⚖ discharge; *Gefangene*: release; **ꙭung** *f* dismissal; discharge; **ꙭungsgesuch** *n* resignation; **ꙭungspapiere** *n/pl.* discharge papers; **ꙭungszeugnis** *n Schule*: school-leaving certificate.
ent'lasten unburden; (*befreien*) relieve (*von* of); ⚖ clear, exonerate; ⚚ *Vorstand usw.*: discharge; *j-n für et. ~* credit a p. with.
Ent'lastung *f* relief; exoneration; ⚚ discharge; credit (of a p.'s account); **~sstraße** *f* by-pass (road); **~szeuge** *m* witness for the defen|ce, *Am.* -se; **~szug** *m* relief train.
ent'laub|en (25) defoliate; **ꙭung** *f* defoliation.
ent'laufen (sn) run away (*dat.* from).
entlausen [~'lauzən] delouse.
entledig|en [ɛnt'le:digən] (25) release (*gen.* from); *sich j-s, e-r S. ~* rid o.s. (*od.* get rid) of; *e-r Pflicht, e-s Auftrags*: acquit o.s. of; **ꙭung** *f* release; *fig.* discharge.
ent'leeren empty.
ent'legen remote, distant, out-of-the-way; **ꙭheit** *f* remoteness.
ent'lehnen borrow (*dat.* of, from).
entleiben [~'laıbən] (25): *sich ~* commit suicide.
ent'leihen *s. entlehnen.*
ent'lob|en: *sich ~* break off one's engagement; **ꙭung** *f* disengagement.
ent'locken draw, elicit (*dat.* from).
ent'lohn|en pay (off); **ꙭung** *f* pay (-ing off); *s. Entgelt.*
ent'lüften evacuate the air from; (*lüften*) air, ventilate.
entmachten [~'maxtən] (26) deprive *a p.* of *his* power.
entmagneti'sieren demagnetize.
entmann|en [~'manən] (25) castrate; *fig.* emasculate; **ꙭung** *f* castration; emasculation.
entmenscht [~'mɛnʃt] inhuman, brutish.
entmilitarisier|en [~militari'zi:rən] demilitarize; **ꙭung** *f* demilitarization.
entmündigen [~'myndigən] (25) ⚖ incapacitate, put under tutelage *od.* restraint.
entmutig|en [~'mu:tigən] (25) discourage; **ꙭung** *f* discouragement.
Entnahme [~'nɑ:mə] *f* (15) taking; *v. Geld*: drawing, withdraw; ⚚ *bei ~ von* by taking *od.* ordering.
ent'nehmen take (*dat.* from); *Geld*: (with)draw (*aus* from); *e-m Buch usw.*: draw, borrow (*dat.* from); *fig.* (*schließen, erfahren*) gather, learn (*dat. od. aus* from); (*folgern*) infer (from).
entnerven [ɛnt'nɛrfən] (25) enervate, unnerve.
ent'-ölen free from oil.
entpuppen [~'pupən] (25): *sich ~* burst the cocoon; *fig.* reveal o.s.; *sich ~ als* turn out to be.
ent'rahmen skim.
enträtseln [~'rɛ:tsəln] (29) puzzle out, solve; (*entziffern*) decipher.
ent'recht|en: *j-n ~* deprive a p. of his (own) rights; **ꙭung** *f* deprivation of rights.
Entree [ɑ̃'tre:] *n* (11) entrance money.

ent'reißen *j-m et.*: tear *od.* snatch (away) from a p.; *a. fig.* wrench from; *dem Tode usw.*: save from.

ent'richt|en pay; **≈ung** *f* payment.

ent'ringen: *j-m* et. ~ wrest a th. from a p.; *sich j-s Lippen usw.* ~ escape from.

ent'rinnen (sn) escape (*dat.* from).

ent'rollen *v/i.* (sn) roll (down) (*dat.* from); *v/t.* (*a. sich*) unroll; *Fahne, Segel usw.*: unfurl; *ein Bild von et.* ~ unfold a picture of a th.

ent'rücken remove (*dat.* from).

entrümpeln [~'rympəln] (29) clear of lumber.

ent'rüst|en fill with indignation, anger; (*schockieren*) scandalize, shock; *sich* ~ become angry *od.* indignant, be scandalized (*über acc.* at); **≈ung** *f* anger, indignation (*über acc.* at *a th.*; with *a p.*).

ent'saft|en (26) extract the juice (from); **≈er** *m* (7) liquidizer.

ent'sag|en (*dat.*) renounce, resign; *dem Thron* ~ abdicate; **≈ung** *f* renunciation, resignation; abdication.

Ent'satz *m* relief.

ent'schädig|en *j-n*: indemnify, compensate; *für* et. ~ make up (*od.* compensate) for a th.; **≈ung** *f* indemnity, compensation.

ent'schärfen *Bombe usw.*: deactivate.

Entscheid [~'ʃaɪt] *m* ⚖ decree; *s. a. Entscheidung*; **≈en** [~'ʃaɪdən] decide; *sich* ~ *Sache*: be decided, *P.*: decide (*für, gegen, über acc.* for, against, on); **≈end** decisive.

Ent'scheidung *f* decision; *der Geschworenen*: verdict; *e-s Schiedsgerichts*: award; (*gerichtliche Verfügung*) ruling; *eine* ~ *treffen* come to (*od.* take) a decision; **~s...** decisive; **~sspiel** *n Sport*: deciding game, tie; (*Endspiel*) final.

entschieden [ɛnt'ʃiːdən] decided; (*entschlossen*) determined, firm; *adv.* decidedly; firmly; **≈heit** *f* determination.

ent'schlafen (sn) fall asleep; *fig.* die, pass away; *der* (*die*) ≈e the deceased.

entschleiern [~'ʃlaɪərn] (29) unveil.

ent'schließ|en: *sich* ~ decide, determine (*zu et.* on; *zu tun* to do), make up one's mind (to do); **≈ung** *f s. Entschluß.*

entschlossen [~'ʃlɔsən] resolute, determined; **≈heit** *f* determination.

ent'schlüpfen (sn) *s. entfallen, entgehen.*

Ent'schluß *m* resolve, resolution; (*Entscheidung*) decision, determination; *zu e-m* ~ *kommen* come to a decision; *zu dem* ~ *kommen, zu inf.* make up one's mind to *inf.*

ent'schlüsseln decipher, decode.

Ent'schlußkraft *f* determination, strength of purpose, initiative.

ent'schuldbar [~'ʃult-] excusable.

entschuldig|en [~'ʃuldigən] (25) excuse; *sich* ~ *a.* apologize (*bei j-m* to a p.; *für* et. for a th.); *sich* ~ *lassen* beg to be excused; *es läßt sich nicht* ~ it admits (*od.* allows) of no excuse; **≈ung** *f* excuse; apology; *Schule*: excuse note; *ich bitte* (*Sie*) *um* ~ (I am) sorry!; *als* (*od. zur*) ~ *für* in excuse of; **≈ungsgrund** *m* excuse.

Ent'schuldung *f* liquidation of *a p.'s* indebtedness.

ent'schwinden (sn) disappear, vanish (*dat.* from); *j-s Gedächtnis* ~ slip a p.'s memory.

entseelt [~'zeːlt] dead, lifeless.

ent'senden send off; *als Vertreter* ~ delegate, depute.

ent'setz|en 1. *des Amtes*: remove (*gen.* from); *Festung*: relieve; (*erschrecken*) terrify, horrify; shock; *sich* ~ be terrified *od.* shocked (*über acc.* at); **2.** ≈ *n* (6) (*Furcht*) terror, horror, dismay; **~lich** terrible, horrible (F *beide a. fig.*); shocking; **≈lichkeit** *f* frightfulness; (*Greuel*) atrocity; **≈ung** *f* removal (from office); ⚔ relief.

entseuch|en [~'zɔʏçən] decontaminate; **≈ung** *f* decontamination.

ent'sichern ⚔ *Gewehr*: unlock; *v/i.* release the safety catch.

ent'sinken (sn; *dat.*) drop (from); *Mut*: fail (*j-m* a p.).

ent'sinnen: *sich* ~ (*gen.*) remember, recall, recollect.

entsittlich|en [~'zitliçən] demoralize; deprave; **≈ung** *f* demoralization; depravation.

Ent'sorgung *f* disposal of nuclear waste.

ent'spann|en relax (*a. Muskeln, Nerven usw.*), ⊕ relieve, release; *Bogen*: unbend; *sich* ~ *P., Gesicht*: relax; *Lage*: ease; ≈ung *f* relaxation, slackening; unbending; easing; *pol.* détente (*fr.*).

ent'spinnen: *sich* ~ **arise, develop.**

ent'sprech|en (*dat.*) answer, correspond to; meet (*e-m Verlangen* a demand); *Anforderungen*: come (*od.* be) up to; **~end** *adj.* corresponding; (*angemessen*) appropriate; (*gleichwertig*) equivalent; *adv.* accordingly; (*gemäß dat.*) according to; **2ung** *f* equivalent.

ent'sprießen (sn) sprout, spring up (*dat.* from); *s. abstammen.*

ent'springen (sn) escape (*dat., aus* from); *Fluß*: rise, spring; (*Ursprung haben*) *s. entstehen.*

ent'stammen (*dat.*) (*abstammen von*) be descended from; (*herrühren von*) come from *od.* of, originate from.

ent'steh|en (sn) arise, develop, originate (*aus* from, in); grow (out of), result (from); come into being; spring up; *im 2 begriffen* in the making, in process of development; **2ung** *f* origin, rise, formation; **2ungsgeschichte** *f* genesis.

ent'stell|en disfigure; deface, deform; *Tatsachen usw.*: distort; **2ung** *f* disfigurement; defacement; distortion.

ent'stör|en *Radio*: free from interference, clear, dejam; **2er** *m* (7) *Radio*: suppressor; **2ung** *f* interference suppression; **2ungsstelle** *teleph. f* fault-clearing service.

ent'täusch|en disappoint; disillusion; **2ung** *f* disappointment; disillusionment.

ent'thron|en dethrone; **2ung** *f* dethronement.

entvölker|n [~'fœlkərn] (29) depopulate, unpeople; **2ung** *f* depopulation.

ent'wachsen (sn; *dat.*) outgrow.

ent'waffn|en disarm; **2ung** *f* disarming.

entwalden [~'valdən] (26) clear of forests, dis(af)forest, deforest.

ent'warn|en sound the all-clear (signal); **2ung** *f* all-clear signal.

ent'wässer|n drain; **2ung** *f* drainage; **2ungs-anlage** *f* drainage plant.

entweder [ɛnt'veːdər]: *~ ... oder* either ... or; *~ — oder!* take it or leave it!

ent'weichen (sn) escape (*aus* from).

ent'weih|en desecrate, profane; **2ung** *f* desecration, profanation.

ent'wend|en (26) purloin, steal, pilfer; misappropriate; **2ung** *f* purloining, misappropriation.

ent'werf|en *Schriftstück, Vertrag*: draft, draw up; (*skizzieren*) sketch, trace (out), outline (*a. fig.*); *Muster, Konstruktion usw.*: design; *Plan*: make, devise; *Gesetz*: frame; **2er** ⊕ *m* designer.

ent'wert|en depreciate; *Briefmarke*: cancel; *fig.* render valueless; **2er** *m* (ticket) cancel(l)ing machine; **2ung** *f* depreciation; cancellation.

ent'wick|eln (*a. sich*) develop (*a. phot.*) (*zu* into); *Gedanken*: evolve; (*darlegen*) explain, set forth; *Tatkraft usw.*: display; ⚔ deploy; **2ler** *phot. m* (7) developer.

Ent'wicklung *f* development; evolution; ⚔ deployment; display; **2sfähig** capable of development; **~sgeschichte** *f* history of (the) development; *biol.* biogenetics; **~helfer** *m* adviser (in developing countries); **~shilfe** *f* economic aid to developing countries; **~sland** *n* developing country; **~slehre** *f* theory of evolution; **~sstufe** *f* stage of development; **~szeit** *f* period of development.

ent'winden: *j-m et. ~* wrest a th. from a p.

entwirren [~'virən] (25) disentangle, unravel.

ent'wischen (sn) slip away (*dat.* from), escape (*j-m* a p.; *aus* from); *j-m ~* give a p. the slip.

entwöhnen [~'vøːnən] (25) disaccustom (*gen.* to); *Kind, Trinker usw.*: wean (from).

ent'würdig|en degrade, disgrace; **2ung** *f* degradation.

Ent'wurf *m* (*Skizze*) (rough) sketch; (*Gestaltung*) design, *schriftlich*: draft; (*Plan*) plan, project, outline, sketch; **~sstadium** *n* planning (*od.* blueprint) stage.

ent'wurzeln uproot (*a. fig.*).

ent'zerr|en *Radio*: equalize; *phot.* rectify; **2ung** *f* equalization; rectification.

ent'zieh|en: *j-m et. ~* deprive a p. of a th.; withdraw a th. from a p.; (*vorenthalten*) withhold a th. from a p.; *sich e-r Pflicht usw. ~* shirk, evade; *das entzieht sich meiner Kenntnis* that is beyond my knowledge; *s. Wort*; **2ung** *f* deprivation, withdrawal; **2ungskur** ⚕ *f* withdrawal treatment.

entziffer|n [~'tsifərn] (29) decipher,

make out; (*entschlüsseln*) decode; 2**ung** *f* deciphering; decoding.

ent'zück|en 1. charm, enchant, delight; *entzückt über (acc.) od. von* delighted with; **2.** 2 *n s. Entzückung*; **~end** delightful, charming; 2**ung** *f* rapture, transport; (*entzücktes Gebaren*) raptures *pl.*, transports *pl.*; *in ~en geraten* go into raptures.

Ent'zug *m* (3, *o. pl.*) *von Arznei, Droge*: withdrawal; *von Genehmigung*: revocation; **~s-erscheinung** *f* withdrawal symptom.

entzünd|bar [ɛnt'tsyntbɑ:r] (in-)flammable; 2**barkeit** *f* (in)flammability; **~en** [~'tsyndən] inflame (*a.* ⚕), kindle; *sich ~* catch fire; ⚕ become inflamed; 2**ung** *f* kindling; ⚕ inflammation.

ent'zwei asunder, in two, in (*od.* to) pieces; (*zerbrochen*) broken; **~brechen** break in two; **~en** (25) disunite, set at variance; *sich ~* quarrel, fall out (*mit* with); **~gehen** break, go to pieces; 2**ung** *f* disunion, quarrel, split.

Enzian ⚘ ['ɛntsjɑ:n] *m* (5) gentian.

Enzyklopäd|ie [ɛntsyklopɛ:'di:] *f* (15) encyclop(a)edia; 2**isch** [~'pɛ:diʃ] encyclop(a)edic(ally *adv.*).

Enzym *biol.* [ɛn'tsy:m] *n* (3) enzyme.

Epide|mie [epide'mi:] *f* (15) epidemic (disease); 2**misch** [~'de:miʃ] epidemic(ally *adv.*).

Epigone [epi'go:nə] *m* (13) epigone.

Epigramm [~'gram] *n* (3[1]) epigram.

Epik ['e:pik] *f* (16) epic poetry; '**~er** *m* epic poet.

Epilep|sie [epilɛp'si:] *f* (15) epilepsy; **~tiker** [~'lɛptikər] *m* (7), 2**tisch** epileptic.

Epilog [~'lo:k] *m* (3) epilog(ue).

episch ['e:piʃ] epic.

Episode [epi'zo:də] *f* (15) episode.

Epistel [e'pistəl] *f* (15) epistle.

Epoche [e'pɔxə] *f* (15) epoch; 2**machend** epoch-making.

Epos ['e:pɔs] *n* (16[2]) epic (poem).

er [e:r] (19) he; *~ selbst* he himself.

erachten [ɛr'ʔaxtən] **1.** consider, judge, deem, think; **2.** 2 *n* (6) opinion, judg(e)ment; *m-s ~s* to my mind, in my opinion.

er'-arbeiten gain by working; *Wissen usw.*: acquire.

Erb|adel ['ɛrpʔɑ:dəl] *m* hereditary nobility; '**~-anspruch** *m* claim to an inheritance.

erbarmen [ɛr'barmən] **1.** (25) *j-n*: move (to pity); *sich j-s ~* pity (*od.* commiserate) a p.; show mercy to a p.; **2.** 2 *n* (6) pity, compassion, commiseration; mercy; **~swert**, **~swürdig** pitiable.

erbärmlich [~'bɛrmliç] pitiful, pitiable; *contp. a.* miserable; *Verhalten*: mean; (*kläglich*) piteous; 2**keit** *f* pitifulness, pitiableness; meanness.

erbarmungslos [~'barmuŋslo:s] pitiless, merciless, relentless.

er'bau|en build (up), construct, raise; *fig.* edify; *sich ~* be edified (*an dat.* by); *nicht erbaut sein von* not to be pleased with; 2**er** *m* (7) builder; constructor; (*Gründer*) founder; **~lich** edifying; 2**ung** *fig. f* edification, *Am. a.* uplift.

erbberechtigt ['ɛrp-] entitled to the inheritance.

Erbe ['ɛrbə] **1.** *m* (13) heir (*gen.* to *a p. od. th.*); **2.** *n* (10, *o. pl.*) inheritance, (*a. fig.*) heritage.

er'beben (sn) tremble, shake, quake.

erben ['ɛrbən] (25) inherit.

er'betteln get (*od.* obtain) by begging, wheedle (*von j-m* out of).

erbeuten [ɛr'bɔʏtən] (26) capture.

erb|fähig ['ɛrp-] capable of inheriting; '2**faktor** *m* gene; '2**fehler** *m* hereditary defect; '2**feind** *m* traditional enemy; '2**folge** *f* (*gesetzliche* intestate) succession; '2**folgekrieg** *m* war of succession.

er'bieten: *sich ~* offer *to do*.

'**Erbin** *f* (16[1]) heiress.

er'bitten beg (*od.* ask) for, request.

erbitter|n [ɛr'bitərn] (29) embitter, exasperate; **~t** embittered (*über acc.* at); (*heftig*) fierce; *Gegner usw.*: bitter; 2**ung** *f* exasperation.

Erbkrankheit ['ɛrp-] *f* hereditary disease.

erblassen [ɛr'blasən] (28, sn) grow (*od.* turn) pale, blanch.

Erb-lasser ['ɛrplasər] *m* (7) testator; '**~in** *f* (16[1]) testatrix.

er'bleichen (30, sn) *s. erblassen.*

erblich[1] ['ɛrpliç] hereditary; '2**keit** *biol. f* heredity.

erblich[2] [ɛr'bliç] *pret.*, **~en** *p.p. v. erbleichen.*

er'blicken catch sight of, see.

erblind|en [ɛr'blindən] (26, sn) grow blind; 2**ung** *f* loss of sight.

er'blühen *s. aufblühen.*
Erbmasse ['ɛrp-] *f* ⚖ estate; *biol.* idioplasm.
erbosen [ɛr'bo:zən] (27) infuriate; *sich* ~ grow angry (*über acc.* with *a p.*, at, about *a th.*).
erbötig [~'bø:tiç] willing, ready.
Erb|pacht ['ɛrp-] *f* hereditary tenure; '**~pächter** *m* hereditary tenant; '**~prinz** *m* hereditary prince.
erbrechen [ɛr'brɛçən] **1.** break (*od.* force) open; ⚕ (*a. sich*) vomit, puke; **2.** ♀ ⚕ *n* (6) vomiting.
Erb·recht ['ɛrp-] *n* law (*des Erben*: right) of succession.
'**Erbschaft** *f* inheritance; *fig.* heritage; '**~ssteuer** *f* estate duty, *Am.* succession tax.
'**Erbschleicher(in** *f*) *m* legacy hunter.
Erbse ['ɛrpsə] *f* (15) pea; '**~nbrei** *m* pease-pudding; '**~nsuppe** *f* pea-soup.
'**Erb|stück** *n* heirloom; '**~sünde** *f* original sin; '**~teil** *n, m* (portion of) inheritance.
Erd|-achse ['e:rt-] *f* axis of the earth; '**~-antenne** *f* ground aerial (*Am.* antenna); '**~-arbeiten** *f/pl.* earth works *pl.*; '**~-arbeiter** *m* digger, excavator, *Am.* laborer; '**~-atmosphäre** *f* earth's atmosphere; '**~bahn** *f* orbit of the earth; '**~ball** *m* globe; '**~beben** *n* earthquake; '**~beere** *f* strawberry; '**~bestattung** *f* interment, burial; '**~boden** *m* ground, soil; *dem* ~ *gleichmachen* level with the ground, raze.
Erde ['e:rdə] *f* (15) earth; (*Boden*) ground; (*Bodenart*) soil, *a.* dirt; (*Humus*) mo(u)ld; (*Welt*) world; '**♀n** ⚡ (26) earth, *Am.* ground.
er'denk|en think out, devise; (*erdichten*) invent; **~lich** imaginable.
Erd|gas ['e:rt-] *n* natural gas; '**~gasleitung** *f* gas pipeline; '**~geschoß** *n* ground-floor, *Am.* first floor; '**~gürtel** *m* zone; '**~halbkugel** *f* hemisphere; '**~harz** *n* asphalt.
er'dicht|en invent (*a. b.s.*); **~et** fictitious.
erdig ['e:rdiç] earthy.
Erd|kabel ['e:rt-] *n* underground cable; '**~kampf** ⚔ *m* ground fighting; '**~karte** *f* map of the earth; '**~kreis** *m*, '**~kugel** *f* (terrestrial) globe; '**~krume** *f* topsoil; '**~kunde** *f* geography; '**~leitung** ⚡ *f* earth-connexion, earth-wire, *Am.* ground connection *od.* wire; '**~nähe** *ast. f* perigee; '**~nuß** *f* peanut; '**~nußbutter** *f* peanut butter; '**~-öl** *n* mineral oil, petroleum.
erdolchen [ɛr'dɔlçən] (25) stab (with a dagger).
Erd|-ölraffinerie ['e:rt-] *f* oil refinery; '**~pech** *n* mineral pitch, bitumen; '**~pol** *m* pole (of the earth); '**~reich** *n* ground, soil, earth.
erdreisten [ɛr'draɪstən] (26): *sich* ~ dare, presume.
er'dröhnen *s. dröhnen.*
er'drosseln strangle, throttle.
er'drücken crush (to death); *fig.* crush; ⚖ *~des Beweismaterial* damning evidence; *~de Mehrheit* overwhelming majority.
Erd|rutsch ['e:rtrutʃ] *m* landslip, (*a. fig.*) landslide; '**~satellit** *m* earth satellite; '**~schicht** *f* layer of earth, stratum; '**~schluß** ⚡ *m* earth (connexion), *Am.* ground (leakage); '**~scholle** *f* clod; '**~stoß** *m* earth-tremor; '**~strich** *m* region, zone; '**~teil** *m* part of the world; *geogr.* continent.
er'dulden suffer, endure.
Erd·umlaufbahn ['e:rt-] *f* earth orbit.
Erdung ⚡ ['e:rduŋ] *f* earth(ing), *Am.* ground(ing).
Erdwärme ['e:rt-] *f* geothermal energy; '**~kraftwerk** *n* geothermal power station.
er'-eifern: *sich* ~ get excited, fly into a passion.
ereignen [ɛr'ˀaɪgnən]: *sich* ~ happen, come to pass *od.* about, occur.
Ereignis [ɛr'ˀaɪknis] *n* (4[1]) event; (*Vorfall*) occurrence, incident; **♀reich** eventful.
er'-eilen overtake.
Eremit [ere'mi:t] *m* (12) hermit.
er'-erben inherit (*von* from).
er'fahr|en 1. learn, come to know, be told; (*hören*) hear, understand; (*erleben*) experience; **2.** *adj.* experienced, expert; (*geübt*) skilled; **♀ung** *f* experience; (*Praxis*) practice; (*Übung*) skill; (*Fachkenntnis*) know-how; *in ~ bringen* learn, (*herausfinden*) find out, discover; *durch ~ klug werden* learn it the hard way; *s-e ~en machen* gain experience; *aus ~* by (*od.* from) experience; **~ungsgemäß** *adv.* according to (*my, our*) experience; **~ungsmäßig** empiric(ally *adv.*).

er'fass|en seize, catch, grasp (*alle a. geistig*); lay hold of; (*in sich schließen*) cover; *statistisch*: register, record; **2ung** *f* registration, recording.

er'finden invent; *b.s. a.* fabricate, cook up; erfunden *Nachricht usw.*: *a.* fictitious.

Er'finder *m* (7) inventor; **~in** *f* (16[1]) inventress; **2isch** inventive.

Er'findung *f* invention; **~sgabe** *f* inventiveness; **2sreich** inventive; resourceful.

er'flehen implore.

Erfolg [ɛr'fɔlk] *m* (3) success; (*Wirkung*) result; ~ haben succeed, be successful; keinen ~ haben fail, be unsuccessful; **2en** [~gən] (sn) ensue, follow, result (aus from); (*sich ereignen*) happen, take place; *Antwort*: be given; *Zahlung*: be made; **2los** unsuccessful, ineffective; *adv.* (*umsonst*) in vain; **~losigkeit** *f* unsuccessfulness; failure; **2reich** successful; **~s-autor(in** *f*) *m* bestselling author; **~sbeteiligung** *f* profit-sharing; **~s-erlebnis** *n* success experience; **~srechnung** ⚕ *f* profit and loss account; **2versprechend** promising.

er'forderlich requisite, required, necessary; **~enfalls** if need be, if necessary *od.* required.

er'forder|n require, demand; **2nis** *n* (4[1]) requirement, exigency.

er'forsch|en inquire into, investigate; *Land*: explore (*a. fig.*); **2er** *m* (7) investigator; explorer; **2ung** *f* investigation; exploration.

er'fragen ask for, ascertain; zu ~ bei inquire at, apply to.

erfrechen [ɛr'frɛçən] (25): sich ~ zu *inf.* have the impudence to *inf.*

er'freu|en please, delight; sich ~ an (*dat.*) rejoice (*od.* delight) in *od.* at, enjoy *a th.*; sich e-r S. ~ enjoy a th.; **~lich** pleasing, gratifying; glad, welcome (*news, etc.*); **~licher'weise** fortunately; **~t** glad (über *acc.* of; zu to *inf.*); pleased (with; to *inf.*); rejoiced (at; to *inf.*); delighted (with, at; to *inf.*).

er'frier|en (sn) freeze to death, die from (*od.* perish with) cold; sich die Ohren ~ have one's ears frozen; erfroren *Körperteil usw.*: frost-bitten; **2ung** *f e-s Körperteils*: frost-bite.

er'frisch|en (27) refresh; **2ung** *f* refreshment; **2ungsraum** *m* refreshment-room; **2ungs-tuch** *n* refresher tissue.

er'füll|en fill; *Bedingung, Pflicht, Versprechen, Wunsch, Zweck usw.*: fulfil(l); *Aufgabe*: accomplish, perform; *Vertrag*: fulfil(l), perform; *Bitte*: comply with; *Erwartungen*: meet; sich ~ be fulfilled; (*wahr werden*) come true; **2ung** *f* fulfil(l)ment; accomplishment; performance; **2ungs-ort** *m* place of performance.

ergänzen [~'gɛntsən] (27) complete; complement (sich *gegenseitig* one another); *hinzufügend*: supplement; *Summe*: make up; ⚕ *Lager*: replenish; **~d** complementary; supplementary (*beide acc.* to).

Er'gänzung *f* completion; (*das Ergänzte*) supplement; replenishment; *gr.* complement; **~s...** supplementary; complementary; **~s-abgabe** ⚕ *f* supplementary tax.

ergattern [~'gatərn] (29) (manage to) get hold of, grab, secure.

er'geben 1. result in; (*liefern*) yield, give; (*erweisen*) prove; ⚔ sich ~ surrender (*dat.* to); *Schwierigkeit usw.*: arise; sich e-r *S.* ~ devote o.s. to, *e-m Laster*: take to; sich ~ aus result (*od.* follow) from; sich ~ (*in ein Schicksal*) resign o.s. (to); **2.** *adj.* devoted (*dat.* to); *e-m Laster*: addicted to; (*untertänig*) humble; (*gefaßt*) resigned (to); ~st *adv.* respectfully; *Brief*: Yours faithfully; **2heit** *f* devotion; resignation.

Ergebnis [~'ge:pnis] *n* (4[1]) result, outcome; *Sport*: (*Punktzahl*) score; **2los** resultless, negative; without result.

Ergebung [~'ge:buŋ] *f* resignation, submission; ⚔ surrender.

er'gehen 1. (sn) *Gesetz usw.*: come out, be published; ~ lassen issue, publish; ein Urteil ~ lassen pass a sentence; über sich ~ lassen submit to; sich ~ (*spazierengehen*) stroll about; *fig.* sich ~ in (*dat.*) indulge in; es wird ihm schlecht ~ he will come off badly, it will go hard with him; es ist mir gut (schlecht) ergangen I fared well (ill); **2.** 2 *n* (state of) health.

ergiebig [~'gi:biç] productive, rich (an *dat.* in); *s.* einträglich; **2keit** *f* productiveness, richness.

er'gießen pour *od.* gush forth (*a. sich*); *sich ~ in (acc.)* discharge into.

er'glühen (sn) glow; *Gesicht*: *a.* blush, flush (*vor dat.* with).

ergötz|en [~'gœtsən] (27) delight; *sich ~ an (dat.)* (take) delight in; **Ȩen** *n* (6) delight; *zu j-s ~* to a p.'s amusement; **~lich** diverting, delightful; amusing; **Ȩung** *f s. Ergötzen.*

er'grauen *v/i.* (sn) (become) grey, *Am.* gray.

er'greifen seize, grasp, grip; lay hold of; *Beruf*: choose; *die Waffen, Feder*: take up; *Gemüt*: move, touch, stir; *Maßregeln, Besitz*: take; *die Flucht ~* take to flight; *s. Partei usw.*

ergriffen [~'grifən] moved, touched, deeply stirred *od.* affected (*von* with); *vom Fieber usw. ~ werden* be struck with fever *etc.*; **Ȩheit** *f* emotion.

ergrimmen [ɛr'grimən] (25, sn) grow angry, flare up.

er'gründen fathom (*a. fig.*); *fig.* penetrate, get to the bottom of.

Er'guß *m* outpour (*a. fig.*); *physiol. u. fig.* effusion.

er'haben elevated; *fig.* exalted, sublime; *~e Arbeit* embossed work, (*Relief*) relief; *~ sein über (acc.)* be above; **Ȩheit** *f* elevation; relief; *fig.* sublimity; loftiness.

er'halt|en 1. *v/t.* get; *förmlich*: obtain; *Nachricht usw.*: receive; (*bewahren*) conserve; (*dauernd machen*) preserve, keep (*am Leben* alive); (*unterhalten*) support, maintain; *sich ~ von* subsist on; **2.** *adj. gut ~ Haus usw.*: in good repair *od.* condition; *~ bleiben* be preserved; **Ȩer** *m* (7), **Ȩerin** *f* preserver; supporter; **Ȩung** *f* conservation; preservation; maintenance, upkeep.

erhältlich [~'hɛltliç] obtainable.

er'hängen hang.

er'härt|en (*bestätigen*) confirm, corroborate; **Ȩung** *f* corroboration.

er'haschen catch, seize.

er'heben lift, raise (*beide a. Augen, Stimme*); *Anspruch, Einwand, Frage, Geschrei usw.*: raise; (*erhöhen*) elevate; (*preisen*) exalt; *Steuern usw.*: levy, raise, (*einziehen*) collect; *e-e Forderung ~* enter (*od.* put in) a claim; *Geld ~* raise money; *Klage* (*Anklage*) *~* bring an action (accusation); *ins Quadrat ~* square; *s. Adelsstand*; *sich ~* rise, start; *Wind*: spring up; *Frage usw.*: arise; (*sich empören*) rise; **~d** *fig.* elevating.

erheblich [ɛr'he:pliç] considerable; **Ȩkeit** *f* consequence, importance.

Er'hebung *f* elevation; exaltation; *v. Steuern*: levy, collecting; (*Empörung*) revolt; (*BodenȨ*) rise; (*Untersuchung*) inquiry, inquest.

erheiter|n [~'haɪtərn] (29) cheer; amuse, exhilarate; **Ȩung** *f* amusement.

erhell|en [~'hɛlən] (25) *v/t.* light up, illuminate; *fig.* clear up, elucidate; *v/i. fig.* appear, become evident; **Ȩung** *f* illumination.

er'hitzen (27) (*a. sich*) heat (*a. fig.*); *sich ~* grow hot, *fig.* become heated.

er'hoffen hope for.

erhöh|en [~'hø:ən] (25) raise, lift, elevate; *fig.* (*steigern*) *allg.* increase, raise (*auf acc.* to; *um* by); enhance; *im Rang od. rühmend*: exalt; *sich ~* (be) increase(d); **Ȩung** *f* (*Anhöhe*) elevation; exaltation; (*Steigerung*) increase, rise; *der Preise*: *a.* advance.

er'hol|en: *sich ~* recover (*von* from); *nach der Arbeit*: (take a) rest, relax; *Preise*: recover, rally; **~sam** restful; **Ȩung** *f* recovery (*a.* ⚕); (*Entspannung*) recreation, relaxation; (*Ferien*) holiday, *bsd. Am.* vacation; **Ȩungsgebiet** *n* recreational area; **Ȩungsheim** *n* rest home; **Ȩungsurlaub** *m* recreation leave; *nach Krankheit*: convalescence leave; **Ȩungswert** *m* recreational value.

er'hören hear; *Bitte*: grant.

er'-inner|lich present to one's mind; *soviel mir ~ ist* as far as I can remember; **~n** [~'ʔinərn] (29) *v/i. ~ an (acc.)* be reminiscent of, recall; *v/t. j-n an (acc.) ~* remind a p. of, call to a p.'s mind; *j-n daran ~, daß od. wie usw. ...* remind a p. that *od.* how *etc.*; *sich ~* (*gen. od. an acc.*) remember, recollect (*a th. od. a p.*).

Er'-innerung *f* remembrance; (*Gedächtnis*) recollection; (*Mahnung*) reminder; *~en pl.* reminiscences; memoirs; *zur ~ an (acc.)* in memory of; **~sstück** *n* keepsake (*an acc.* from); **~svermögen** *n* memory, power of recollection.

er'jagen hunt down; *fig.* catch.

er'kalten (26, sn) cool down, get cold; *fig.* cool (off).

erkält|en [~'kɛltən] (26): *sich (sehr)* ~ catch (a bad) cold; **2ung** *f* cold.

er'kämpfen obtain by fighting.

er'kaufen purchase, buy; (*bestechen*) bribe, corrupt.

er'kenn|bar recognizable; (*wahrnehmbar*) perceptible; **2barkeit** *f* perceptibility; **~en** recognize (*an dat.* by); (*wahrnehmen*) perceive, discern; (*geistig erfassen*) know (*an dat.* by); (*sich vergegenwärtigen*) realize, see; ⚕ credit (*j-n für* a p. with *a sum*); ⚖ judge, find *a p. guilty etc.*; ~ *lassen, zu ~ geben* indicate, suggest; give to understand; *sich zu ~ geben* disclose one's identity; ⚖ ~ *auf (acc.)* pass a sentence of.

er'kenntlich (*dankbar*) grateful; **2keit** *f* gratitude.

Er'kenntnis *vgl. erkennen*: **1.** *f* (14²) perception; realization; **2.** ⚖ *n* (4¹) judg(e)ment, sentence, finding; **~theorie** *f* theory of cognition; **~vermögen** *n* intellectual power.

Er'kennung *f* recognition; **~sdienst** *m Polizei*: police records department; **~smarke** ⚔ *f* identity disk, *Am.* identification tag; **~smelodie** *f Radio*: signature (tune); **~swort** *n* password; **~szeichen** *n* identification sign; distinctive mark, (*Abzeichen*) badge; ⚕ *u. fig.* symptom.

Erker ['ɛrkər] *m* (7) bay; **'~fenster** *n* bay-window.

er'klär|bar explicable; **~en** explain; (*Rechenschaft ablegen über, Gründe angeben für*) account for; (*aussprechen*) declare, state; *sich ~ für, gegen* declare for, against; **2er** *m* (7) commentator, expounder; **~lich** explicable, accountable; **~t** professed, declared; **2ung** *f* explanation; declaration.

erklecklich [ɛr'klɛkliç] considerable.

er'klettern, er'klimmen climb.

er'klingen (sn) sound; (*widerhallen*) resound; ~ *lassen* sound, *Lied*: strike up.

erkor [~'ko:r] *pret.*, **~en** *p.p. v. erkiesen*: chosen, *adj. a.* (s)elect.

er'krank|en (sn) fall (*od.* be taken) ill (*an dat.* of, with); *Organ*: be affected; **2ung** *f* illness, sickness; *e-s Organs*: affection.

erkühnen [~'ky:nən] (25): *sich ~* venture, presume, make bold.

erkunden [~'kundən] (26) explore; ⚔ reconnoitre, *Am.* reconnoiter.

erkundig|en [~'kundigən]: *sich ~* inquire (*über acc., nach P.*: after, for; *S.*: about); **2ung** *f* inquiry.

Er'kundung ⚔ *f* reconnaissance.

er'künsteln (29) affect.

er'lahmen (sn) *fig.* weary, tire; *Interesse usw.*: wane, flag.

er'langen (25) (*fassen*) reach; *fig. a.* achieve; (*sich verschaffen*) obtain, get, secure.

Erlaß [ɛr'las] *m* (4²) exemption (*gen.* from); *e-r Schuld, Strafe usw.*: remission (of); (*Verordnung*) decree; *e-s Gesetzes*: enactment.

er'lassen *Schuld usw.*: remit; *Verpflichtung*: release, dispense (*j-m et.* a p. from a th.); *Verordnung usw.*: issue, publish; *Gesetz*: enact.

erlauben [ɛr'laubən] (25) allow, permit; *sich et. ~* (*gönnen*) indulge in a th.; *sich ~ zu inf.* ⚕ beg to *inf.*, *s. a. sich erkühnen*; *das kann ich mir nicht ~* I cannot afford that; *was ~ Sie sich!* how dare you!

Erlaubnis [~'laupnis] *f* (14²) permission; (*Ermächtigung*) authority; *a.* = **~schein** *m* permit.

erlaucht [~'lauxt] illustrious, noble.

er'läuter|n explain, illustrate; (*kommentieren*) comment (up)on; **2ung** *f* explanation, illustration.

Erle ⚘ ['ɛrlə] *f* (15) alder.

er'leb|en (live to) see; (*erfahren*) experience; *Schlimmes*: go through; (*mit ansehen*) see, witness; *schöne Tage usw.*: have, spend; **2ensversicherung** *f* pure endowment insurance; **2nis** [~'le:pnis] *n* (4¹) occurrence, event; (*Abenteuer*) adventure; (*Erfahrung*) experience; **~nisreich** eventful.

erledig|en [~'le:digən] (25) finish (*a.* F *fig.*); *Auftrag*: execute; *Streitfall*: settle, adjust; *Geschäft*: deal with, handle; *sich ~* be settled; **~t** finished (*a.* F *fig.*); **2ung** *f* handling; execution; settlement.

er'legen *hunt.* kill, shoot.

erleichter|n [~'laɪçtərn] (29) make easy; *e-e Bürde*: lighten; *Not, Schmerz*: relieve, alleviate; *Aufgabe*: facilitate; *j-n, das Herz*: relieve; **2ung** *f* ease; lightening; relief; facilitation; *~en pl.* (*Vorteile*) facilities.

er'leiden suffer, endure; *Schaden, Verlust*: sustain.
er'lernen learn.
er'lesen *adj.* select, choice.
er'leucht|en light (up), illuminate; *fig.* enlighten; **2ung** *f* illumination; enlightenment.
er'liegen (sn) succumb (*dat.* to).
Erlkönig ['ɛrlkø:niç] *m* erlking; *mot.* mystery model.
erlogen [~'lo:gən] false, untrue.
Erlös [~'lø:s] *m* (4) proceeds *pl.*
erlosch [~'lɔʃ] *pret.*, **~en** *p.p. v.* erlöschen; *adj.* extinct.
er'löschen [~'lœʃən] (30, sn) go out, be extinguished; *fig.* become extinct; *Vertrag, Patent*: expire.
er'lös|en save, redeem; (*frei machen*) deliver; **2er** *m* (7) redeemer, deliverer; *eccl.* Redeemer, Savio(u)r; **2ung** *f* redemption; deliverance.
ermächtig|en [~'mɛçtigən] (25) empower, authorize; **2ung** *f* authorization; (*Befugnis*) authority, power.
er'mahn|en admonish, exhort; **2ung** *f* exhortation, admonition.
er'mangel|n *e-r S.*: be wanting in; ~ *zu tun* fail to do; **2ung** *f*: *in* ~ (*gen.*) in default of, failing.
ermannen [ɛr'manən] (25): *sich* ~ take courage *od.* heart.
er'mäßig|en abate, reduce; **2ung** *f* abatement, reduction.
ermatt|en [~'matən] (26) *v/t.* tire, fatigue; (*erschöpfen*) exhaust; *v/i.* (sn) grow weary *od.* tired; (*nachlassen*) slacken (*in dat.* in); *Interesse usw.*: flag; **2ung** *f* weariness, fatigue, exhaustion, lassitude.
er'messen **1.** judge; **2.** **2** *n* (6) judg(e)ment, opinion; *nach freiem* ~ at one's (free) discretion; **2sfrage** *f* matter of discretion; **2sspielraum** *m* latitude, leeway.
ermitt|eln [~'mitəln] (29) ascertain, determine; find out; ⚖ investigate; **2(e)lung** *f* ascertainment; ⚖ investigation; *~en anstellen* make inquiries; **2lungsverfahren** ⚖ *n* judicial inquiry.
ermöglichen [~'mø:k-] (25) render (*od.* make) possible; *es j-m ~ zu tun* enable (*od.* make it possible for) a p. to do.
er'mord|en, **2ung** *f* murder.
ermüd|en [~'my:dən] (26) *v/t.* tire, fatigue; *v/i.* (sn) get tired *od.* fatigued; **2ung** *f* fatigue, tiredness.
ermunter|n [~'muntərn] (29) rouse; (*anfeuern*) incite, encourage, animate; (*erheitern*) cheer (up); *sich* ~ rouse o.s.; **2ung** *f* encouragement, animation.
ermutig|en [~'mu:tigən] (25) encourage; **2ung** *f* encouragement.
er'nähr|en nourish, feed; (*erhalten*) support; **2er** *m* (7) bread-winner, supporter; **2ung** *f* nourishment; support; ⚕ nutrition; **2ungswissenschaft** *f* nutritional science.
er'nenn|en nominate, appoint (*zum Botschafter usw.* ambassador *etc.*); **2ung** *f* nomination, appointment.
erneu|e(r)n [~'nɔʏə(r)n] (25 [29]) renew; (*wieder aufleben lassen*) revive; **2erung** *f* renewal; revival; **~t** *adj.* renewed; *adv.* once more, anew.
erniedrig|en [~'ni:drigən] (25) lower; *im Rang*: degrade; *fig.* humiliate, humble; **2ung** *f* lowering; degradation; humiliation.
Ernst[1] [ɛrnst] *m* (3[1], *o.pl.*) seriousness, earnest; (*Würdigkeit, Wichtigkeit*) gravity; (*Strenge*) severity; *es im ~ (od. 2) meinen* be in earnest, be serious; *~ machen mit et.* go ahead with a th.; *es ist mein voller ~* I mean it; **'~fall** *m* emergency; *im ~* in case of emergency; ⚔ in case of war.
ernst[2], **'~haft**, **'~lich** serious, earnest; (*würdig*) grave; (*streng*) stern; *es ernst meinen s. Ernst*[1]; *et. ernst nehmen* take a th. seriously; **'2haftigkeit** *f s. Ernst*[1].
Ernte ['ɛrntə] *f* (15) harvest; (*Ertrag*) crop; **~'dankfest** *n* harvest festival, *Am.* Thanksgiving Day; **'~fest** *n* harvest home; **'2n** *v/t. u. v/i.* (26) harvest, gather (in), (*a.fig.*) reap.
ernüchter|n [ɛr'nyçtərn] (28) sober; *fig. a.* disillusion; **2ung** *f* sobering; *fig.* disillusionment.
Er'-ober|er *m* (7) conqueror; **2n** [~'ʔo:bərn] (29) conquer; **~ung** *f* conquest; **~ungskrieg** *m* war of conquest.
er'-öffn|en *allg.* open (*a. Konto, Kredit, Sitzung usw.*); *feierlich*: inaugurate; ⚔ *Feuer*: open; *j-m et.*: disclose, reveal, *förmlich*: notify (to); *ein Geschäft ~ (als)* set up a business (as); *sich ~ Möglichkeit*: present itself; **2ung** *f* opening; in-

auguration; disclosure; notification.
erogen [ero'ge:n] erogenous.
erörter|n [~'ˀœrtərn] (29) discuss; **≈ung** *f* discussion.
Erosion [ero'zjo:n] *geol. f* erosion.
Erot|ik [e'ro:tik] *f* eroticism; **≈isch** erotic.
Erpel ['ɛrpəl] *m* (7) drake.
erpicht [ɛr'piçt]: ~ *auf* (*acc.*) bent (*od.* intent, keen) on; *darauf* ~ *sein zu inf.* be anxious to *inf.*
er'press|en *Geld usw.*: extort; *j-n*: blackmail; **≈er(in** *f*) *m* extortioner; blackmailer; **≈erbrief** *m* blackmail letter; **~erisch** extortionate; **≈ung** *f* extortion; blackmail(ing); **≈ungsversuch** *m* attempted extortion.
er'proben try, (put to the) test.
erquick|en [~'kvikən] (25) refresh; **~lich** refreshing; **≈ung** *f* refreshment.
er'raten guess, divine; find out; ~! you guessed!
er'rechnen calculate, compute, figure out.
erreg|bar [~'re:kba:r] excitable, irritable; **≈barkeit** *f* excitability, irritability; **~en** [~gən] excite (*a.* ⚡); (*erzürnen*) irritate, infuriate; (*verursachen*) cause, call forth; *sich* ~ get excited; **~end** exciting; **≈er** *m* (7), **≈erin** *f* (16[1]) ⚕ germ, virus; **≈erkreis** *m Radio*: exciting circuit; **≈ung** *f* excitation; *Zustand*: excitement.
erreich|bar [ɛr'raiçba:r] get-at-able, within reach *od.* call; *fig.* attainable; (*verfügbar*) available; **~en** reach; *Ziel, Zweck usw.*: achieve, attain; (*erlangen*) obtain; *Zug usw.*: catch; *ein gewisses Maß*: come up to; *j-n telephonisch* ~ get a p. on the phone; *von der Bahn leicht zu* ~ within easy reach of the station; **≈ung** *f* reach(ing).
er'rett|en save, rescue; (*befreien*) deliver; **≈er(in** *f*) *m* rescuer, deliverer; **≈ung** *f* rescue, deliverance; *eccl.* Salvation.
er'richt|en erect, raise (*a.* ⟂ *das Lot*); (*gründen*) establish; *Geschäft*: set up; **≈ung** *f* erection; establishment.
er'ringen obtain; *Erfolg, Ruhm usw.*: achieve, gain; *Preis*: win; *s. Sieg.*
er'röten 1. (sn) blush; **2.** ≈ *n* (6) blush(ing).
Errungenschaft [ɛr'ruŋənʃaft] *f* (16) achievement; (*Erwerbung*) acquisition.
Er'satz *m* (3[2], *o. pl.*) (*Vergütung*) compensation; (*Schadloshaltung*) indemnification; (*Schadens≈*) damages *pl.*; (*Austausch*) replacement, *konkret*: *a.* substitute (für for); ⚔ replacement(s *pl.*); (*Rekruten*) recruits *pl.*, draft(s *pl.*); **~...** ersatz (*z.B.* *~kaffee*); *s. Ersetzung, ~mann, ~mittel, ~teil*; ~ *leisten* make restitution *od.* amends (für for); **~anspruch** *m* claim for compensation; **~befriedigung** *f* compensation; **~dienst** *m s. Wehrersatzdienst*; **~mann** *m* substitute, *Am. a.* alternate; *Sport*: reserve, F spare; ⚔ replacement, filler; **~mine** *f für Bleistift*: refill; **~mittel** *n* substitute; *minderwertig*: ersatz; **~pflicht** *f* liability (to pay damages); **~rad** *mot. n* spare wheel; **~reifen** *mot. m* spare tyre; **~stück** *n*, **~teil** ⊕ *n*, *m* replacement part; *mitgeliefert*: spare (part); *~liste* parts list; **~wahl** *f* by-election.
er'saufen P (sn) be drowned.
ersäufen P [~'zɔyfən] (25) drown.
er'schaff|en create; **≈er(in** *f*) *m* creator; **≈ung** *f* creation.
er'schallen (sn) (re)sound; ring.
er'schein|en (sn) appear (*a. Geist*; *j-m* to a p.); *Buch usw.*: *a.* come out, be published; *ratsam* ~ appear advisable; **≈en** *n* appearance; **≈ung** *f* appearance; (*Geister≈*) apparition; (*Traumbild*) vision; (*Natur≈*) phenomenon; (*Krankheits≈*) symptom; *e-e glänzende* ~ *sein* cut a fine figure; *in* ~ *treten* make one's appearance, *fig.* appear, come to the fore; **≈ungsbild** *n Person*: outward appearance; **≈ungsjahr** *n* year of publication; **≈ungstermin** *m* date of publication.
er'schießen shoot (dead).
erschlaff|en [~'ʃlafən] *v/i.* (25, sn) *Muskel*: go limp; *P.*: tire, wilt; *fig.* flag, slacken; *v/t.* relax; exhaust; **≈ung** *f* relaxation; enervation.
er'schlagen kill, slay.
er'schleichen obtain surreptitiously; *Gunst*: creep into.
er'schließen open (*a. sich*); *Gegend*: open up; *Baugelände*: develop.
er'schöpf|en exhaust; ⚡ *Batterie*:

run down; **~end** *fig.* exhaustive; **2ung** *f* exhaustion.

erschrak [~'ʃrɑːk] *pret. v. erschrecken* 2.

er'schrecken 1. *v/t.* (25) frighten, terrify, scare; 2. *v/i.* (30, sn) (*a. sich* ~) be frightened *od.* startled (*über acc.* at); 3. 2 *n* fright, terror; **~d** alarming, startling.

erschrocken [ɛr'ʃrɔkən] 1. *p.p. v. erschrecken* 2.; 2. *adj.* frightened, terrified, scared; startled.

er'schütter|n (29) shake; *fig.* shock, (*rühren*) move; **2ung** *f* shaking; shock; (*Rührung*) emotion; ⚕ concussion; ⊕ percussion.

erschweren [~'ʃveːrən] (25) render more difficult; *Schuld*: aggravate.

er'schwindeln obtain by trickery; *von j-m* ~ swindle out of a p.

er'schwing|en afford; **~lich** attainable, within *a p.'s* means; *Preis*: reasonable.

er'sehen learn, gather (*aus* from).

er'sehnen long for.

er'setz|bar, ~lich *P.*: replaceable; *Schaden, Verlust*: reparable; **~en** (*wiedergutmachen*) repair; (*entschädigen für*) make up for, compensate (for), make good; *j-m et.*: indemnify a p. for a th.; (*an die Stelle setzen od. treten*) replace, substitute, supersede; *j-m Unkosten* ~ reimburse a p. for his expenditure; *er ersetzt ihn nicht* he is not equal to him; *den Schaden ersetzt bekommen* recover damages; **2ung** *f* compensation; replacement.

er'sichtlich evident, obvious.

er'sinnen contrive, devise.

er'spähen (e)spy, F spot.

er'spar|en *Geld*: save; *j-m Geld, Zeit, Ärger usw.* ~ save a p. money, time, trouble, *etc.*; *j-m e-e Demütigung usw.* ~ spare a p. a humiliation, *etc.*; **2nis** *f* (14^2) saving (*an dat.* of); ~se *pl.* savings.

ersprießlich [~'ʃpriːsliç] useful, profitable, beneficial.

erst [eːrst] 1. (18) *der* (*die*) ~e (*od.* 2e) first; *fig.* first, foremost, leading; ~e *Qualität* prime quality; ~e *Hilfe* first aid; *in ~er Linie, an ~er Stelle* in the first place, primarily; *aus ~er Hand* first-hand (*mit su. nur attr.*); *der, die 2e e-r Klasse* the head (*od.* top) boy *od.* girl; *fig. die ~e Geige spielen* play first fiddle; *fürs ~e* for the time being; *bei Auktionen*: *zum ~en, zum zweiten, zum dritten!* going, going, gone!; 2. *adv.* first; (*anfangs*) at first; (*bloß*) only, but; (*nicht früher als*) not before, not till *od.* until; ~ *als* only when; *jetzt* ~ but now; ~ *recht* more than ever; **'2-angriff** ⚔ *m* first strike.

erstarken [ɛr'ʃtarkən] (25, sn) grow strong(er), gain strength.

er'starr|en (sn) grow stiff, stiffen; *Glieder*: grow numb; *vor Schreck*: freeze (with), be paralysed; *metall.* solidify; *Fett*: congeal; *Zement*: set; *Blut*: coagulate, *fig.* run cold; *erstarrt* stiff, numb; **2ung** *f* torpidity; numbness; solidification; congealment; setting.

erstatt|en [~'ʃtatən] (26) restore, return; *Geld*: (re)pay; *s. a. ersetzen*; ⚖ *Anzeige* ~ file an information; *s. Bericht*; **2ung** *f* restitution, compensation; *e-s Berichts*: delivery.

'Erst|-aufführung *thea. f* first (*od.* opening) night; **'~-auflage** *f* first printing.

er'staunen 1. *v/i.* (sn) be astonished (*über acc.* at); *v/t.* astonish; 2. 2 *n* (6) astonishment; *in ~ setzen* astonish.

er'staunlich astonishing, amazing.

'Erst-ausgabe *f* first edition.

'erst'beste: *der, die, das* ~ the first comer.

er'stechen stab.

er'stehen 1. *v/i.* (sn) arise, rise; 2. *v/t.* buy, purchase.

er'steig|en ascend, climb; **2ung** *f* ascent.

erstens ['eːrstəns] first, firstly.

er'sterben (sn) die (away) (*a. fig.*).

'erstere: *der, die, das* ~ the former.

erstgeboren ['~gəboːrən] first-born.

'Erstgeburtsrecht *n* birthright.

er'stick|en *v/t. u. v/i.* (sn) choke (*an dat.* on; *vor Wut usw.* with), suffocate; stifle; *gewaltsam*: smother; *im Keime* ~ nip in the bud; **2ung** *f* suffocation.

erstklassig ['eːrstklasiç] first-class.

'erstlich firstly, in the first place.

'Erstling *m* (3^1) first-born (child); *Tier*: firstling; **'~s...** first; **'~swerk** *n* first publication.

erstmal|ig ['~mɑːliç] *adj.* first; *adv.* = **~s** ['~mɑːls] (for) the first time.

er'streben [ɛr-] strive after; **~swert** desirable.

er'strecken: *sich* ~ extend (*bis zu* to); *fig. a. sich* ~ *auf* (*acc.*) refer to; *sich* ~ *über* (*acc.*) cover.
'Erstschlag ⚔ *m* first-strike; **~s-potential** *n* first-strike potential; **~swaffe** *f* first-strike weapon.
er'stürmen take (by storm).
'Erstwähler(in *f*) *m* first-time voter.
er'suchen 1. ask, request; **2.** ♀ *n* (6) (*auf j-s* ~ at a p.'s) request.
er'tappen catch, surprise; *s. frisch.*
er'teilen give; *s. Auftrag, Wort.*
er'tönen (sn) (re)sound.
Ertrag [ɛr'trɑ:k] *m* (3[3]) produce, yield; (*Einnahmen*) proceeds, returns *pl.*; ⚒ output.
er'trag|en bear, endure; (*leiden*) suffer; (*vertragen*) support, stand; **♀fähigkeit** [~k-] *f* productiveness.
erträglich [~'trɛ:kliç] bearable, endurable; (*leidlich*) tolerable, passable.
Er'tragslage *f* profit situation.
er'tränken drown.
er'träumen dream of.
er'trinken (sn) drown, be (*od.* get) drowned.
ertüchtig|en [~'tyçtigən] (25) make fit, train; **♀ung** *f*: *körperliche* ~ physical training.
erübrigen [~'ˀy:brigən] (25) save; *Zeit*: spare; *sich* ~ be superfluous.
er'wachen (sn) awake.
er'wachsen 1. *v/i.* (sn) arise; spring; *Vorteil usw.*: accrue (*aus* from); **2.** *adj.* grown-up, adult (*a.* **♀e** *m, f*); **♀enbildung** *f* adult education.
er'wäg|en consider; **♀ung** *f* consideration; *in der* ~, *daß* considering that; *in* ~ *ziehen* take into consideration.
er'wählen choose, elect.
er'wähn|en mention; **~enswert** worth mentioning; **♀ung** *f* mention.
er'wärmen (*a. sich*) warm, heat; *fig. sich* ~ *für* warm to.
er'wart|en expect; await; *ein Kind* ~ be expecting; *et. zu* ~ *haben* be in for; **♀ung** *f* expectation; **~ungsvoll** expectant.
er'weck|en awaken (*a. fig.*); *vom Tode*: resuscitate, *a. fig. Erinnerung, Hoffnung usw.*: raise; *fig.* cause; *Eindruck*: give; *Interesse, Verdacht*: arouse; *s. Anschein*; **♀ung** *f* awakening; resuscitation; revival.
er'wehren: *sich* ~ (*gen.*) ward off; *sich der Tränen* ~ restrain one's tears; *ich konnte mich des Lachens nicht* ~ I could not help laughing.
er'weichen (25) soften; *fig. j-n*: *a.* mollify; (*rühren*) move; **~d**(*es Mittel*) emollient.
er'weis|en prove; *Achtung*: show; *e-n Dienst, Gehorsam*: render; *Ehre*: do, pay; *Gunst*: grant, bestow (*j-m* on a p.); *sich* ~ *als* prove (*od.* turn out) to be; **~lich** [~'vaɪsliç] provable.
erweiter|n [~'vaɪtərn] (29) (*a. sich*) extend (*a. fig.*), expand, widen; **~bar** *a. Computer*: expandable; **♀ung** *f* expansion, (*a. gr.*) extension; ⚕ dila(ta)tion.
Erwerb [ɛr'vɛrp] *m* (3) (*Erwerben*) acquisition; (*Unterhalt*) living; (*Verdienst*) earnings *pl.*; **♀en** [~bən] acquire; gain; *durch Arbeit*: earn; *sich Verdienste* ~ *um* deserve well of.
er'werbs|fähig capable of gainful employment; **♀fähigkeit** *f* earning capacity; **~los** *usw. s. arbeitslos usw.*; **♀quelle** *f* source of income; **♀sinn** *m*, **♀trieb** *m* acquisitiveness; **~tätig** working (for a living), gainfully employed; **♀tätige(r** *m*) *f* person gainfully employed; **♀tätigkeit** *f* occupational activities *pl.*, gainful employment; **~-unfähig** incapable of earning one's living; **♀-unfähigkeit** *f* incapacity of earning one's living; **♀zweig** *m* branch of industry (*od.* trade); line (of business), trade.
Er'werbung [~buŋ] *f* acquisition.
erwider|n [~'vi:dərn] (29) return; *Gefälligkeit, Glückwunsch, Zuneigung usw.*: *a.* reciprocate; (*antworten*) reply (*auf acc.* to), *bsd.* ⚖ rejoin; *Beleidigung usw., scharf* ~: retort; **♀ung** *f* return; answer, reply; reciprocation; *bsd.* ⚖ rejoinder.
erwiesen [~'vi:zən] *p.p. v. erweisen*; **~er'maßen** as has been proved.
er'wirken obtain, procure, effect; *e-n Entscheid usw.*: take out.
er'wischen catch, get.
erwünscht [~'vynʃt] desired; (*wünschenswert*) desirable; (*willkommen*) welcome.
er'würgen strangle, throttle.
Erz [e:rts] *n* (3[2]) ⚒ ore; (*Metall*) brass, bronze; **'~-ader** *f* vein of ore.
er'zähl|en tell; (*berichten*) relate; *bsd. formgerecht*: narrate; *man erzählt sich* people (*od.* they) say;

2er(in *f*) *m* narrator; (*Schriftsteller*) story-teller, writer; **2ung** *f* narration; (*Bericht*) report; (*Geschichte*) tale, story, narrative.

ˈ**Erz|bischof** *m* archbishop; ˈ**2bischöflich** archiepiscopal; ˈ**~bistum** *n* archbishopric; ˈ**~-engel** *m* archangel.

er'zeug|en (*zeugen*) beget; (*hervorbringen, -rufen*) produce; (*fabrizieren*) make, manufacture; *Gefühl*: engender; *phys.*, ⚗ generate; **2er** *m* (7) begetter; producer, manufacturer; generator; **2nis** [~'tsɔʏk-] *n* product; (*Boden2*) *mst pl.* ~se produce; *des Geistes, der Kunst*: production; *eigenes* ~ my *etc.* own make; *deutsches* ~ made in Germany; **2ung** [~guŋ] *f* production; manufacture; *phys.*, ⚗ generation.

ˈ**Erz|feind** *m* arch-enemy; ˈ**~gang** *m* vein of ore; ˈ**~gauner** *m* arrant swindler; ˈ**2haltig** ore-bearing; ˈ**~herzog** *m* archduke; ˈ**~herzogin** *f* archduchess; ˈ**~herzogtum** *n* archduchy; ˈ**~hütte** *f* smelting works *pl. od. sg.*

er'ziehen (*aufziehen*) bring up, [rear; *geistig*: educate.

Er'zieher *m* (7) educator; (*Lehrer*) teacher; **~in** *f* governess; **2isch** educational, pedagogic(al).

Er'ziehung *f* (*Aufziehen*) upbringing; (*geistige* ~) education; (*Lebensart*) breeding; *von guter* ~ well-bred; **~s-anstalt** *f* reformatory; **~sberater** *m* educational adviser; **~sberatung** *f* child guidance; **~s-berechtigte** *m, f* parent or guardian; **~swissenschaft** *f* pedagogics *sg.*

er'zielen obtain, reach; *Preis*: realize, fetch; *Erfolg*: achieve; *Treffer*: score.

er'zittern *s. zittern.*

ˈ**erz'konservativ** ultraconservative.

ˈ**Erz|lager** *n* ore deposit *od.* bed; ˈ**~lügner** *m* arch liar; ˈ**~probe** *f* assay; ˈ**~vater** *m* patriarch.

er'zürn|en *v/t.* make angry, infuriate; *sich* ~ = *v/i.* grow angry; **~t** angry.

er'zwingen force, *bsd. gesetzlich*: enforce; *Gehorsam usw.*: compel; *von j-m*: extort from.

es [ɛs] (19) it; *als Ergänzung des Prädikats*: so; *ich bin's* it is I *od.* F me; *sie sind* ~ it is they; *wer ist der Junge?* — ~ *ist mein Freund* who is the boy? — he is my friend; *er sagt* ~ he says so; *ich hoffe* ~ I hope so; *er sagte, ich sollte gehen, und ich tat* ~ he told me to go, and I did so; *er ist reich, ich bin* ~ *auch* he is rich, so am I; ~ *gibt* there is, there are; ~ *wurde getanzt* there was dancing; *ich will* ~ *versuchen* I will try; *ich weiß* ~ I know; *ich ziehe* ~ *vor zu gehen* I prefer to go; ~ *lebe der König!* long live the King!

Es ♪ *n* E flat.

Esche [ˈɛʃə] *f* (15) ash(-tree); ˈ**2n** ash(en); ˈ**~nholz** *n* ash-wood.

Esel [ˈeːzəl] *m* (7) ass, *mst* donkey; F *fig.* (silly) ass; **~ei** [~ˈlaɪ] *f* stupidity; ˈ**2haft** asinine, stupid; ˈ**~in** *f* (16[1]) she-ass.

ˈ**Esels|brücke** *f Schule*: crib, *Am.* F pony; ˈ**~-ohr** *n im Buch*: dog's ear.

Eskal|ation [ɛskalaˈtsjoːn] *f* escalation; **2ieren** [~ˈliːrən] escalate.

Eskorte [ɛsˈkɔrtə] *f* (15), **eskor'tieren** escort, convoy.

Espe ⚘ [ˈɛspə] *f* (15) asp(en); *wie* ~*nlaub zittern* tremble like an aspen-leaf.

eßbar [ˈɛsbɑːr] eatable, edible.

ˈ**Eßbesteck** *n s. Besteck.*

Esse [ˈɛsə] *f* (15) chimney, flue; (*Schmiede2*) forge.

essen [ˈɛsən] **1.** (30) eat; *zu Mittag* ~ (have) lunch; *zu Abend* ~ have supper (*od.* dinner); *auswärts* (*im Restaurant*) ~ eat (*od.* dine) out; **2.** 2 *n* (6) eating; (*Speise*) food; (*Mahlzeit*) meal; (*Mittag2*) lunch; (*Abend2*) supper, dinner; (*Fest2*) dinner, banquet; ~ *auf Rädern* meals on wheels; ˈ**2sgutschein** *m* luncheon voucher; ˈ**2szeit** *f* meal-time; lunch-hour; *abends*: dinner-time.

Essenz [ɛˈsɛnts] *f* (16) essence.

ˈ**Esser(in** *f*) *m* eater; *schwache(r)* ~ poor eater; *starke(r)* ~ great eater.

ˈ**Eß|geschirr** *n* dinner-service; ⚔ mess-tin, *Am.* mess kit; ˈ**~gewohnheiten** *f/pl.* eating habits.

Essig [ˈɛsiç] *m* (3[1]) vinegar; ˈ**~gurke** *f* pickled cucumber, gherkin; ˈ**2sauer** ⚗ acetic, *in Zssgn*: acetate of; *s. Tonerde*; ˈ**~säure** *f* acetic acid.

ˈ**Eß|kastanie** *f* edible chestnut; ˈ**~löffel** *m* table-spoon; ˈ**~lust** *f* appetite; ˈ**~nische** *f* dinette; ˈ**~tisch** *m* dining-table; ˈ**~waren** *f/pl.* eatables, victuals, food *sg.*; ˈ**~zimmer** *n* dining-room.

Estrade [ɛˈstrɑːdə] *f* (15) estrade.

Estragon ['ɛstragɔn] *m* (3¹ *o. pl.*) tarragon.
Estrich ['ɛstriç] *m* (3¹) cement (*od.* plaster *od.* asphalt) floor(ing).
etabl|ieren [eta'bli:rən] establish; *sich* ~ set up in business; ²**issement** [~blis(ə)'mɑ̃] *n* (11) establishment.
Etage [e'tɑ:ʒə] *f* (15) floor, stor(e)y; ~**nbett** *n* bunk bed; ~**nwohnung** *f* flat, *Am.* apartment.
Etappe [e'tapə] *f* (15) ⚔ base, communications zone; *fig.* (*Teilstrecke*) stage, leg; ²**nweise** by stages.
Etat [e'tɑ:] *m* (11) (*Haushaltplan*) budget, *parl. a. the* Estimates *pl.*; *parl.* (*bewilligter* ~) supplies *pl.*; ²**mäßig** *Beamter usw.*: permanent; ~**sjahr** *n* fiscal year.
Ethik ['e:tik] *f* (16) ethics *pl. od. sg.*
'**ethisch** ethical.
Ethnographie [ɛtnogra'fi:] *f* (15) ethnography.
Ethnologie [~lo'gi:] *f* (15) ethnology.
Etikett [eti'kɛt] *n* (11) label, ticket; *gummiertes*: *Am. a.* sticker; ~**e** *f* (15) etiquette; ²**ieren** [~'ti:rən] label.
etliche ['ɛtliçə] *pl.* some, several.
Etüde ♪ [e'ty:də] *f* (15) study.
Etui [e'tvi:] *n* (11) case.
etwa ['ɛtva] perhaps, by chance; (*ungefähr*) about, say, *Am. a.* around; ~**ig** ['~vaˀiç] possible, eventual, any.
etwas ['ɛtvas] *pron.* something; *verneinend, fragend od. bedingend*: anything; *adj.* some; any; *adv.* somewhat; ² *n*: *ein gewisses* ~ a certain something.
Etymolog|ie [etymolo'gi:] *f* (15) etymology; ²**isch** [~'lo:giʃ] etymological.
euch [ɔʏç] (19) you; to you; *refl.* yourselves.
euer ['ɔʏər] (19) of you; (20) '~, '~**e** your; *pred.* yours.
Eule ['ɔʏlə] *f* (15) owl; ~*n nach Athen tragen* carry coals to Newcastle; '~**nspiegel** *m* Owlglass; '~**nspiegelstreich** *m* roguish trick.
euresgleichen ['ɔʏrəs'glaɪçən] your likes *pl.*, people *pl.* of your kind.
euret|halben ['ɔʏrəthalbən], '~**wegen**, (*um*) ~**willen** ['~vilən] for your sake.
'**eurig** (*od. der, die, das* ~e) yours.
Euro|dollar ['ɔʏro-] *m* eurodollar; '~**kommunismus** *m* Eurocommunism; '~**markt** *m* euromarket.
Europä|er [ɔʏro'pɛ:ər] *m* (7), ~**erin** *f*, ²**isch** European; ²**isieren** [~pɛi'zi:rən] Europeanize.
Europa|meister [ɔʏ'ro:pa-] *m* European champion; ~**meisterschaft** *f* European championship; ~**parlament** *n* European parliament; ~**pokal** *m* European cup; ~**rat** *pol. m* Council of Europe.
Euroscheck ['ɔʏro-] *m* Eurocheque; ~**heft** *n* Eurocheque-book; ~**karte** *f* Eurocheque-card.
Euter ['ɔʏtər] *n* (7) udder.
evakuier|en [evaku'ˀi:rən] evacuate; ²**te** *m, f* evacuee.
evangel|isch [evaŋ'ge:liʃ] evangelic(al); Protestant; ²**ist** [~ge'list] *m* (12) evangelist; ²**ium** [~'ge:ljum] *n* (9) gospel.
Eventu|alität [evɛntuali'tɛ:t] *f* (16) eventuality, contingency; ²**ell** [~'ɛl] possible, contingent, potential; *adv.* possibly; perhaps; if necessary.
Ewer ⚓ ['e:vər] *m* (7) lighter.
ewig ['e:viç] eternal; (*unaufhörlich*) everlasting, perpetual; *auf* ~ for ever; '²**keit** *f* eternity; F *seit einer* ~ for ages; ~**lich** ['e:vikliç] eternally.
ex [ɛks]: ~ (*trinken*)! bottoms up!; '²... ex-...
exakt [ɛ'ksakt] exact; ²**heit** *f* exactitude, exactness.
Exam|en [ɛ'ksɑ:mən] *n* (11; *pl. Examina*) examination, F exam; ~**ens-angst** *f* exam(ination) nerves *pl.*; ~**inator** [ɛksami'nɑ:tɔr] *m* (8) examiner; ²**inieren** [~mi'ni:rən] examine; *fig.* question, quiz.
Exekutive [ɛksəku'ti:və] *f* (15) executive power.
Exempel [ɛ'ksɛmpəl] *n* (7) example; 𝔄 problem; *s. statuieren.*
Exemplar [ɛksɛm'plɑ:r] *n* (3) specimen; *e-s Buches*: copy; ²**isch** exemplary; *j-n* ~ *bestrafen* make an example of a p.
exerzier|en [ɛksɛr'tsi:rən] *v/t. u. v/i.* drill; ²**platz** *m* drillground.
Exil [ɛ'ksi:l] *n* (3¹) exile (*a. fig.*); banishment; *im* ~ in exile.
Existenz [ɛksi'stɛnts] *f* (16) existence; (*wirtschaftliche Grundlage*) livelihood; ~**berechtigung** *f* right to exist; ~**grundlage** *f* basis of subsistence; ~**kampf** *m* struggle for existence; ~**minimum** *n* subsistence level; living wage.

exi'stieren exist; (*bestehen können*) subsist.
exklusiv [ɛksklu'zi:f] exclusive.
exkommunizieren [~kɔmuni'tsi:rən] excommunicate.
exotisch [ɛ'kso:tiʃ] exotic.
Exped|ient [ɛkspe'djɛnt] *m* (12) forwarding agent (*od.* clerk); **2ieren** [~'di:rən] dispatch, forward.
Expedition [~di'tsjo:n] *f* (*Versand*) dispatch, forwarding; (*Kriegszug, Forschungsreise*) expedition; (*Versandstelle*) forwarding department.
Experiment [ɛksperi'mɛnt] *n* (3) experiment; **2ell** [~'tɛl] experimental; **2ieren** [~'ti:rən] experiment.
Experte [ɛks'pɛrtə] *m* (13) expert.
explo|dieren [ɛksplo'di:rən] (sn) explode, burst; **2sion** [~'zjo:n] *f* explosion; **~siv** [~'zi:f], **2'siv...** explosive; **2'sivstoff** *m* explosive.
exponieren [ɛkspo'ni:rən] (25) expose.
Export [ɛks'pɔrt] *m* (3) export (-ation); (*Waren*) exports *pl.*; *in Zssgn mst* export; **~-artikel** *m* export article, *pl. mst* exports *pl.*; **~eur** [~'tø:r] *m* (3^1) exporter; **2ieren** [~'ti:rən] export.
expreß [ɛks'prɛs], **2...** express.
Ex'preß 🚂 *m* (4, *pl.* ~züge) express (train); **~bote** *m*, **~gut** *n s.* *Eilbote usw.*
extra ['ɛkstra] extra; **'2...** extra, special; **'2blatt** *n* supplement; *e-r Zeitung*: special edition, *Am.* extra.
extrahieren [ɛkstra'hi:rən] extract.
Extrakt [ɛks'trakt] *m* (3) extract.
'Extrawurst F *f* something (extra-) special.
Extrem [ɛks'tre:m] **1.** *n* (3) extreme; **2.** 2 *adj.* extreme; **~ist** [~tre'mist] *m* (12) extremist; **~itäten** [~tremi'tɛ:tən] *f/pl.* extremities.
Exzellenz [ɛkstsɛ'lɛnts] *f* (16) Excellency.
exzentrisch [~'tsɛntriʃ] eccentric.
Exzeß [ɛks'tsɛs] *m* (3) excess.

F

F [ɛf], **f** *n inv.* F, f; ♪ F.
Fabel ['fɑ:bəl] *f* (15) fable; *e-s Dramas usw.*: *a.* plot; *fig.* tale; **'~dichter** *m* fabulist; **'2haft** fabulous; *fig. a.* capital, marvellous, stunning; **'2n** (29) *v/i.* tell stories (*von* about); **'~wesen** *n* fabulous creature.
Fabrik [fa'bri:k] *f* (16) factory, mill, works (*pl., oft sg.*); **~-anlage** *f* (manufacturing) plant; **~ant** [~bri'kant] *m* (12) manufacturer, maker; **~-arbeit** *f* work in a factory; *s.* *Fabrikware*; **~-arbeiter(in** *f*) *m* factory worker *od.* hand; **~at** [~bri'kɑ:t] *n* (3) make, manufacture, brand; **~ationsfehler** [~ka'tsjo:ns-] *m* flaw; **~ati'onsnummer** *f* serial number; **~besitzer(in** *f*) *m* factory-owner; **~marke** *f* trade mark; **2-neu** brand-new; **~stadt** *f* manufacturing town; **~ware** *f* manufactured (*od.* factory-made) goods *pl. od.* article.
fabrizieren [fabri'tsi:rən] manufacture, make; *fig.* fabricate.
Facett|e ⊕ [fa'sɛtə] *f* (15) facet; **2iert** [~'ti:rt] faceted.
Fach [fax] *n* (2) compartment; *im Schrank usw.*: partition; *im Schreibtisch*: pigeon-hole; *im Bücherbrett usw.*: shelf; (*Schubfach*) drawer; ⚠ panel; *fig.* department, province, branch, field (of activity), line; (*Geschäft*) business; (*Unterrichts2*) subject; *Musiker usw. von ~* by profession; *s.* *schlagen*; **'~-arbeiter(in** *f*) *m* skilled worker; **'~-arzt** *m* (medical) specialist; **'~(-aus)bildung** *f* specialist training; **'~-ausdruck** *m* technical term; **'~bereich** *univ. m* department.
fächeln ['fɛçəln] (29) fan.
Fächer ['fɛçər] *m* (7) fan; **'2förmig** fan-shaped.
'Fach|gebiet *n* (special) field *od.* subject; **'~gelehrte** *m* specialist; **'2gemäß, '2gerecht** workmanlike, expert; **'~geschäft** *n* (specialized) dealer; **'~kenntnisse** *f/pl.* specialized knowledge; **'~kreis** *m*: *in ~en*

among experts; '2**kundig** competent, expert; '~**lehrer** *m* specialist teacher; '2**lich** technical, specialist; '~**literatur** *f* technical literature; '~**mann** *m* expert, specialist; 2**männisch** ['~mɛniʃ] expert; *Arbeit*: workmanlike; '~**schule** *f* technical school; 2**simpeln** ['~zimpəln] (29) talk shop; '~**sprache** *f* technical terminology; '~**studium** *n* specialized study; '~**welt** *f* experts *pl.*; '~**werk** ⚠ *n* framework, half-timbering; '~**wissenschaft** *f* special branch of science; '~**zeitschrift** *f* technical (*od.* trade) journal.

Fackel ['fakəl] *f* (15) torch; '2**n** F (29) *fig.* hesitate; *ohne lange zu* ~ without further ado; '~**schein** *m* torch-light; '~**träger** *m* torch-bearer; '~**zug** *m* torch-light procession.

fad(**e**) ['fa:d(ə)] (*schal*) stale; (*geschmacklos*) insipid; (*langweilig*) boring, dull.

Faden ['fa:dən] *m* (6[1]) thread (*a. fig.*); ⚡ filament; *opt.* hairline; ⚓ *Maß*: fathom; *an e-m* ~ *hängen* hang by a thread; '~**kreuz** *n* cross wires *pl.*, spider lines *pl.*, retic(u)le; '~**netz** *opt. n* graticule; '~**nudeln** *f/pl.* vermicelli *pl.*; 2**scheinig** ['~ʃaɪniç] threadbare (*a. fig.*).

Fading ['fe:diŋ] *n* (11) *Radio*: fading.

Fagott ♪ [fa'gɔt] *n* (3) bassoon; ~**ist** [~'tist] *m* bassoonist.

fähig ['fɛ:iç] (*zu*) able (to), capable (of), fit (for); *speziell*: qualified; '2**keit** *f* ability, capacity; *bsd. geistige*: faculty.

fahl [fa:l] (*bleich*) pale; *Gesichtsfarbe, Himmel*: livid; (*düster*) lurid.

fahnd|**en** ['fa:ndən] *v/i.* (26) search, look (*nach* for); '2**ung** *f Polizei*: criminal investigation (department); (*Suche*) search.

Fahne ['fa:nə] *f* (15) flag, standard, banner; ⚔, ⚓, *fig.* colo(u)rs *pl.*; *typ.* (galley) proof.

'**Fahnen**|-**eid** *m* oath of allegiance; '~**flucht** *f* desertion; '2**flüchtig**: ~ *werden* desert; '~**flüchtige** *m* (18) deserter; '~**stange** *f* flag-staff, *Am. a.* flagpole; '~**träger** *m* standard-bearer.

Fähnrich ['fɛ:nriç] *m* (3) ⚔ cadet; ⚓ midshipman.

'**Fahr**|**bahn** *f* roadway, *Am. a.* driveway; '2**bar** *Maschine usw.*: portable; movable; *Weg usw.*: practicable; ⚓ navigable; '2**bereit** ready to start, in running order; '~**bereitschaft** *f* car pool; '~**damm** *m*, '~**weg** *m s. Fahrbahn*.

Fähre ['fɛ:rə] *f* (15) ferry(-boat).

fahren ['fa:rən] (30) **1.** *v/i.* (sn) *allg.* go; *selbst lenkend*: drive; *auf e-m Fahrrad od. mit e-m öffentlichen Beförderungsmittel*: ride; ⚓ sail, cruise; *Wagen, Schiff, Zug*: go, run; (*in Fahrt sein*) be moving; *gen Himmel* ~ ascend to heaven; *zur Hölle* ~ descend to hell; *mit der Eisenbahn* ~ go by rail *od.* by train; *über e-n Fluß* ~ cross a river; *aus dem Hafen* ~ clear the port; *s. Haut*; *auf Grund* ~ run aground; *aus dem Bette* ~ start up from one's bed; *in die Kleider* ~ slip on one's clothes; *mit der Hand* ~ *über* (*acc.*) pass one's hand over; ~ *lassen fig.* let go, abandon; *gut* (*schlecht*) ~ *bei et.* fare well (ill) at *od.* with; *fahr*(*e*) *wohl!* farewell!; **2.** *v/t.* drive; ⚓ navigate; (*befördern*) convey; *Boot*: sail, row; '~**d** *adj.* vagrant; ~*er Ritter* knight errant; ~*e Habe* movables *pl.*

'**Fahrer** *m* (7) driver; '~**flucht** *f* hit-and-run offen|ce, *Am.* -se; driving away from an accident.

'**Fahr-erlaubnis** *f s. Führerschein.*

'**Fahrgast** *m* passenger.

'**Fahrgeld** *n* fare; '~**zuschuß** *m* travel allowance.

'**Fahr**|**gelegenheit** *f* conveyance; '~**gemeinschaft** *f* car pool; '~**geschwindigkeit** *f* speed; '~**gestell** *n* ✈ under-carriage, landing gear; *mot.* chassis; '2**ig** fidgety, nervous; '~**karte** *f* ticket; '~**karten-ausgabe** *f*, '~**kartenschalter** *m* booking-office, *Am.* ticket office; '2**lässig** reckless, negligent; ~*e Tötung* manslaughter (in the second degree *Am.*); '~**lässigkeit** *f* (*grobe* gross) negligence; '~**lehrer** *mot. m* driving instructor.

'**Fährmann** *m* (1[2]) ferryman.

'**Fahr**|**plan** *m* time-table (*a. fig.*), *Am.* schedule; '2**planmäßig** regular, *Am.* scheduled; *adv.* on time, according to schedule; '~**preis** *m* fare; '~**preis-anzeiger** *m* taximeter; '~**prüfung** *mot. f* driving test; '~**rad** *n* bicycle, F bike; '~**rinne** ⚓ *f* fairway; '~**schein** *m* ticket; '~**schein-automat** *m* ticket machine; '~**scheinentwerter** *m* ticket cancel(l)ing machine; '~**schule** *mot. f* driving school; '~**schüler** *m* learner; '~**stuhl** *m* lift, *Am.* elevator; '~**stuhlführer** *m* lift-attendant, *Am.* elevator operator; '~**stunde** *f* driving lesson.

Fahrt [fɑːrt] *f* (16) *im Wagen*: ride, drive; (*Reise*) journey; (*See*≗) voyage, passage; (*Ausflug*) trip; ⚓ (*Kurs*) course; ~ *ins Blaue* mystery trip; *in voller* ~ (at) full speed; ~ *aufnehmen* gather speed; *in* ~ *kommen* get under way; *fig.* get into one's stride.

Fährte ['fɛːrtə] *f* (15) track, trace; *hunt.* scent (*alle a. fig.*); *auf falscher* ~ *sein* be on the wrong track.

'**Fahrten|buch** *mot. n* (driver's) log-book; '~**schreiber** *mot. m* tachograph.

'**Fahrt|kosten** *pl.* travel(l)ing expenses; '~**richtungs-anzeiger** *m* direction indicator.

'**fahrtüchtig** fit to drive; *Fahrzeug*: roadworthy; '≗**keit** *f* driving capability; *e-s Fahrzeugs*: roadworthiness.

'**Fahrt|-unterbrechung** *f* break of journey, *Am.* stopover; '~**wind** *m* head wind.

'**Fahr|-unterricht** *m* driving instruction; '~**verbot** *n* driving ban; '~**wasser** *n* navigable water; *s. Fahrrinne*; *fig.* track; '~**weg** *m* carriage-road; '~**werk** ✈ *n s. Fahrgestell*; '~**zeug** *n* vehicle; ⚓ vessel, craft; '~**zeughalter** *m* car-owner; '~**zeugpark** *m* fleet.

Fäkalien [fɛ'kɑːljən] *pl.* (8²) f(a)eces, f(a)ecal matter.

Faksimile [fak'ziːmile] *n* (11) facsimile.

faktisch ['faktiʃ] (f)actual.

Faktor ['faktɔr] *m* (8¹) factor.

Faktotum [~'toːtum] *n* (9²) factotum; *altes* ~ old retainer.

Faktum ['faktum] *n* (9²) fact.

Faktur|(a) [~'tuːr(a)] *f* (16²) invoice; ≗**ieren** [~tu'riːrən] invoice.

Fakultät *univ.* [fakul'tɛːt] *f* (16) faculty, *Am.* department.

fakultativ [~ta'tiːf] optional.

falb [falp] dun; ≗**e** ['~bə] *m* dun (horse).

Falke ['falkə] *m* (13) falcon; '~**n-beize** *f*, '~**njagd** *f* falconry, hawking.

Fall [fal] *m* (3²) fall, drop; (*Vorfall*) case, event; *gr.*, ⚖, ⚕ case; *den* ~ *setzen, a. gesetzt den* ~ suppose; *auf alle Fälle* at all events, by all means; *auf jeden* ~ in any case, at any rate; *auf keinen* ~ on no account; *im* ~*e* (*wenn*) ... in case ...; *im* ~*e e-s Krieges usw.* in the event of a war *etc.*; *von* ~ *zu* ~ in each case, singly; *den* ~ *setzen* put the case; *zu* ~ *bringen* bring down *od.* low, *fig.* ruin, *parl. Gesetz usw.*: defeat; *zu* ~ *kommen* have a fall, *fig.* come to grief; '~**beil** *n* guillotine; '~**brücke** *f* drawbridge.

Falle ['falə] *f* (15) trap; *fig. a.* pitfall; (*Schlinge*) snare; *j-m e-e* ~ *stellen* set a trap for; *in die* ~ *gehen* walk into the trap.

fallen ['falən] **1.** (30, sn) fall, drop (*a. Preise usw.*); ⚔ fall, be killed in action; *Festung usw.*: fall; *Schuß*: be fired *od.* heard; *Bemerkung*: fall; ~ *lassen* drop, let fall; *fig.* dismiss, drop; *es fällt mir schwer* it is difficult for me; *j-m in die Rede* ~ interrupt a p.; ~ *unter ein Gesetz, e-e Kategorie usw.* come under; *s. Auge, Last usw.*; **2.** ≗ *n* (6) fall, drop.

fällen ['fɛlən] (25) fell, cut; *Gegner*: fell; *Urteil*: pronounce, pass; *Bajonett*: lower; ⊿ *das Lot*: draw, drop; ⚗ precipitate.

'**Fallensteller** *m* (7) trapper.

'**Fall|geschwindigkeit** *f* rate of fall; '~**gesetz** *phys. n* law of falling bodies; '~**grube** *f* pitfall.

fallieren ✝ [fa'liːrən] fail.

fällig ['fɛliç] due; *Geld*: *a.* payable; *Wechsel*: *a.* mature; *längst* ~ overdue; ~ (*zahlbar*) *sein* (*od. werden*) fall (*od.* become) due, *Wechsel*: *a.* mature; '≗**keits-termin** *m* maturity, due date.

'**Fall|-obst** *n* windfall; ~**reep** ⚓ ['~reːp] *n* (3) gangway; jack ladder; '~**rohr** ⊕ *n* down-pipe.

falls [fals] in case, if.

'**Fall|schirm** *m* parachute; '~**schirm-absprung** *m* parachute jump; '~**schirmjäger** *m* paratrooper; '~**schirmspringen** *n* parachuting; *Sport*: skydiving; '~**schirmspringer** *m* (7) parachutist; *Sport*: skydiver; '~**schirmtruppen** *f/pl.* paratroops; '~**strick** *m* snare; *fig. a.* trap, pitfall; '~**sucht** *f* falling sickness; ≗**süchtig** ['~zyçtiç] epileptic; '~**tür** *f* trap-door; '~**wind** *m* katabatic wind.

falsch [falʃ] *allg.* false (*a. Eid, Freund, Haar, Name, Scham, Stolz, Zähne*); (*verkehrt*) wrong; (*unecht*) counterfeit, *Am.* F phon(e)y, fake; (*nachgemacht, vorgetäuscht*) mock, sham; *Münze*: base; *Wechsel*: forged; *Mensch*: deceitful; e-e S. ~ *anpacken* do a th. the wrong way; ~ *auffassen* misconceive; ~ *aussprechen* mispronounce; ~ *darstellen* misrepresent; ~ *gehen Uhr*: go (*od.* be) wrong; ~ *singen* sing out of tune; *j-n* ~ *unterrichten* misinform a p.; *ohne* 2 guileless; *s. Kehle, Spiel.*

fälschen ['fɛlʃən] (27) falsify; *Geld*: counterfeit; *Bücher, Rechnung*: fake; *Nahrungsmittel*: adulterate; *Urkunde, Unterschrift*: forge.

'**Fälscher** *m* (7), '**~in** *f* falsifier; faker; adulterator; forger.

'**Falschgeld** *n* counterfeit (*od.* bogus) money.

'**Falschheit** *f* falseness, falsity.

'**fälschlich** (*adv. a.* ~*erweise*) false(ly *adv.*); wrong(ly).

'**Falsch|meldung** *f* false report; '**~münzer** *m* (7) counterfeiter; **~münze'rei** *f* counterfeiting; '**~spieler** *m* card-sharper.

'**Fälschung** *f vgl. fälschen*: falsification; fake; adulteration; forgery.

'**Falt|boot** *n* collapsible boat, folding canoe; '**~dach** *mot. n* folding top.

Falte ['faltə] *f* (15) fold; *am Kleid*: pleat; (*Bügel*2) crease; (*Runzel*) wrinkle; *der Stirn*: furrow.

fältel|n ['fɛltəln] (29) pleat; '**2ung** *f* pleat(ing).

falten ['faltən] (26) fold; *Hände*: fold, clasp, join; '**2rock** *m* pleated skirt; '**2wurf** *m* drapery.

'**Falter** *m* (7) butterfly, moth.

'**faltig** folded; pleated; *Stirn*: wrinkled.

'**Faltkarte** *f* folding (*od.* pull-out) map.

Falz [falts] *m* (3²) fold; *Tischlerei*: rabbet; *Buchbinderei*: guard; '**~bein** *n* folder; paper-knife; '**2en** (27) fold; *Tischlerei*: rabbet.

Fama ['fa:ma] *f* fame; (*Gerücht*) rumo(u)r.

familiär [famil'jɛ:r] familiar.

Familie [fa'mi:ljə] *f* (15) family.

Fa'milien|-ähnlichkeit *f* family likeness; **~-angelegenheit** *f* family affair; **~-anschluß** *m*: ~ *haben* live as one of the family; **~betrieb** *m* family business; **~feier** *f* family celebration (*od.* party); **~gericht** ⚖ *n* Family Court; **~glück** *n* domestic happiness; **~leben** *n* family life; **~nachrichten** *f/pl. in Zeitungen*: births, marriages, and deaths; **~name** *m* family (*Am. a.* last) name, surname; **~planung** *f* family planning; **~stand** *m* family status; (*Ehestand*) marital status; **~vater** *m* father of (a) family, family man; **~zuwachs** *m* addition to the family.

famos [fa'mo:s] excellent, capital, F grand, great.

Fan F [fɛn] *m* (11) fan.

Fanal [fa'nɑ:l] *n* (3¹) *bsd. fig.* beacon.

Fanatiker [fa'nɑ:tikər] *m* (7), **~in** *f* (16¹) fanatic; *für Sport usw.*: F fan.

fa'natisch fanatic(al).

Fanatismus [fana'tismus] *m* (16, *o. pl.*) fanaticism.

fand [fant] *pret. v. finden.*

Fanfare [fan'fɑ:rə] *f* (15) fanfare, flourish of trumpets.

Fang [faŋ] *m* (3³) catch; capture (*beide a. konkret*); (*Zahn*) fang; (*Kralle*) claw, talon; (*Beute*) booty; '**~ball** *m* catch-ball; '**~-eisen** *n* iron trap; '**2en** (30) catch; *engS.* capture; *sich* ~ be caught; *fig.* rally; settle down; '**~frage** *f* trick question; '**~zahn** *m* fang; *des Ebers*: tusk.

Fant [fant] *m* (3) coxcomb, fop.

Farb|band ['farpbant] *n* typewriter ribbon; '**~beilage** *f* colo(u)r supplement; '**~bild** *n* colo(u)r photo; '**~druck** *m* colo(u)r print.

Farbe ['~bə] *f* (15) colo(u)r; (*Farbstoff*) dye; (*Färbung, Farbton*) hue; (*Anstrich*) paint; (*Haut*2) complexion; *Kartenspiel*: suit.

farb-echt ['farp-] colo(u)r-fast.

Färbemittel ['fɛrbə-] *n* dye(-stuff).

färben ['fɛrbən] (25) colo(u)r (*a. sich u. fig.*); *Haar, Stoff*: dye; *Papier, Glas, mit Blut*: stain; (*tönen*) tint, tinge.

'**farben|blind** colo(u)r-blind; '**2druck** *m* colo(u)r-printing; *Bild*: colo(u)r-print; '**~freudig,** '**~froh** colo(u)rful, gaily colo(u)red; '**2lehre** *f* theory of colo(u)rs, 🕮 chromatics *pl. u. sg.*; '**~prächtig,** '**~reich** colo(u)rful; '**2spiel** *n* play of colo(u)rs, 🕮 iridescence; '**2zusammenstellung** *f* colo(u)r scheme.

Färber ['fɛrbər] *m* (7) dyer.
Färberei [~'raɪ] *f* (16) dye-house.
Farb|fernsehen ['farp-] *n* colo(u)r television; '**~film** *m* colo(u)r film; '**~filter** *phot. m* colo(u)r filter.
farbig ['farbiç] colo(u)red; *fig.* colo(u)rful.
Farb|kopierer ['farp-] *m* colo(u)r copier; '**2los** colo(u)rless; '**~photographie** *f Bild*: colo(u)r photo; *Verfahren*: colo(u)r photography; '**~stift** *m* colo(u)red pencil; '**~stoff** *m* pigment (*a. physiol.*), colo(u)ring matter; ⊕ dye(-stuff); '**~ton** *m* tone; *vorherrschender*: hue; *bsd. heller*: tint; (*Schattierung*) shade.
Färbung ['fɛrbuŋ] *f* colo(u)ring; hue; *bsd. leichte*: tinge.
Far|ce ['farsə] *f* (15) farce; *Küche*: forcemeat, stuffing; 2'**cieren** stuff.
Farm [farm] *f* (16) farm; *Am. bsd. zur Viehzucht*: ranch; '**~er** *m* (7) farmer; *Am. a.* rancher.
Farn [farn] *m* (3), '**~kraut** *n* fern.
Fasan [fa'zaːn] *m* (3 *u.* 8) pheasant; **~erie** [~ə'riː] *f* (15) pheasantry.
Fasching ['faʃiŋ] *m* (3[1]) carnival.
Faschis|mus [fa'ʃismus] *m* Fascism; **~t** *m* (12), **~tin** *f* (16[1]) Fascist; **2tisch** Fascist(ic).
Fasel|ei [faːzə'laɪ] *f* drivel, twaddle; '**2n** (29) drivel, babble.
Faser ['faːzər] *f* (15) fib|re, *Am.* -er; *im Holz*: grain; ⚘ string; '**2ig** fibrous; *Fleisch etc.*: stringy; '**2n** *v/t. u. v/i.* (29) (*a. sich*) ravel (out), fray, fuzz.
Faß [fas] *n* (2[1]) cask, barrel; (*Bütte*) vat, tub; (*frisch*) *vom ~ beer* on draught, *wine* from the wood; F *das schlägt dem ~ den Boden aus!* that is the last straw!
Fassade [fa'saːdə] *f* (15) façade, front (*a. fig.*); **~nkletterer** *m* cat burglar.
'**Faßbier** *n* draught beer.
Fäßchen ['fɛsçən] *n* (6) small cask *od.* barrel, keg.
fassen ['fasən] (28) seize, get (*od.* take) hold of; *s. einfassen*; (*fangen*) catch (*a. fig.*); (*begreifen*) grasp; (*enthalten*) hold, contain; *Entschluß*: take; *s. Auge usw.*; *e-n Plan ~* form a plan; *Tritt ~* fall into step; *in Worte ~* word; *sich ~* compose o.s.; *sich schnell wieder ~* rally quickly; *sich kurz ~* be brief, cut it short; *zum Hund*: *faß ihn!* sick him!; *s. gefaßt*.
'**faßlich** conceivable, intelligible.
Fasson [fa'sõ] *f* (11[1]) shape, form, style.
'**Fassung** *f s. Einfassung*; *der Brille*: frame; ⚡ holder, socket; *fig.* composure; *schriftliche*: draft(ing); (*Lesart*) version; (*Wortlaut*) wording; *aus der ~ bringen* disconcert, upset; *die ~ verlieren* lose hold of o.s.
'**Fassungs|gabe** *f*, '**~kraft** *f* power of comprehension, (mental) capacity, grasp; '**2los** shaken, speechless; '**~vermögen** *n* capacity; *fig. s. Fassungsgabe*.
fast [fast] *vor su. u. adj. mst* almost; *vor Zahlen, Maß- u. Zeitangaben mst* nearly; *~ nichts* next to nothing; *~ nie* hardly ever; *ich habe es ~ erwartet* F I kind of expected it.
fasten ['fastən] **1.** (26) fast; **2. 2** *n* (6) fasting; *pl.* fast(ing); *s. ~zeit*; '**2zeit** *f* Lent.
'**Fast|nacht** *f* Shrove Tuesday; (*Fasching*) Shrovetide, carnival; '**~tag** *m* fast(ing)-day.
faszinieren [fastsi'niːrən] fascinate.
fatal [fa'taːl] disastrous; (*peinlich*) awkward, annoying.
Fatalismus [fata'lismus] *m* (16, *o. pl.*) fatalism.
Fatum ['faːtum] *n* (9[2]) fate.
fauchen ['fauxən] (25) hiss (*a. fig. P.*).
faul [faul] (*modrig, verdorben*) rotten, putrid, bad; *Zahn*: carious, decayed; (*stinkend*) foul; (*träge*) idle, lazy; (*verdächtig*) fishy; *~er Kunde* bad customer; *~er Witz* bad (*od.* stale) joke; *~er Zauber* humbug.
Fäule ['fɔʏlə] *f* (15) *s. Fäulnis*.
faulen ['faulən] (25) rot, decay.
faulenz|en ['~lɛntsən] (27) loaf, laze; '**2er(in** *f*) *m* idler, sluggard, do--nothing, F lazy-bones (*sg.*); **2erei** [~'raɪ] *f* loafing, laziness.
'**Faul|heit** *f* laziness; '**2ig** rotten, putrid.
Fäulnis ['fɔʏlnis] *f* (14[2], *o. pl.*) rot, rottenness, decay; *in ~ übergehen* rot, putrefy.
'**Faul|pelz** *m s. Faulenzer*; '**~tier** *n* sloth (*a. fig.*).
Faust [faust] *f* (14[1]) fist; *auf eigene ~* on one's own (account); *s. ballen*; *e-e ~ machen* double up one's hand; *mit der ~ auf den Tisch schlagen fig.* put one's foot down; *wie die*

~ *aufs Auge* like a square peg in a round hole.

Fäustchen ['fɔʏstçən] *n* (6): *sich ins ~ lachen* laugh up one's sleeve.

'**faust|dick** (as) big as a fist; *Lüge*: *sl.* whopping; *es ~ hinter den Ohren haben* be a deep one; '**⁀feuerwaffe** *f* handgun; '**⁀handschuh** *m* mitten; '**⁀kampf** *m* boxing; *einzelner*: boxing-match; '**⁀kämpfer** *m* boxer, pugilist; '**⁀pfand** *n* dead pledge, pawn; '**⁀recht** *n* club-law; '**⁀regel** *f* rule of thumb; '**⁀schlag** *m* punch.

Favorit [favo'ri:t] *m* (12), **~in** *f* (16¹) favo(u)rite.

Faxe ['faksə] *f* (15) foolery, antic; *~n machen* clown; '**~nmacher** *m* clown, buffoon.

Fazit ['fɑ:tsit] *n* (3¹ *u.* 11) result, sum (total); *das ~ ziehen* sum (it) up.

Februar ['fe:bruɑ:r] *m* (3¹), *a.* **Feber** ['fe:bər] *m* (7) February.

Fecht|boden ['fɛçt-] *m* fencing-room; '**⁀en** *v/i.* (30) fight (*a. v/t.*); *fenc.* fence; (*betteln*) cadge; '**~er** *m* (7) fighter; fencer; swordsman; (*Bettler*) cadger; '**~kunst** *f* (art of) fencing; '**~meister** *m* fencing-master; '**~schule** *f* fencing-school.

Feder ['fe:dər] *f* (15) feather; (*Schmuck⁀*) plume; (*Schreib⁀*) pen; ⊕ spring; '**~ball** *m* **1.** shuttlecock; **2.** — '**~ballspiel** *n* badminton; '**~bett** *n* feather-bed; '**~brett** *n* *Sport*: springboard; '**~busch** *m*, '**~büschel** *n* tuft of feathers, plume; **~fuchser** ['~fuksər] *m* (7) quill-driver, scribbler; '**⁀führend** *fig.* responsible, in charge; '**~gewicht** (**-ler** *m*) *n* *Boxen*: featherweight; '**~halter** *m* penholder; '**~kasten** *m* pencil box; '**~kernmatratze** *f* spring-interior mattress; '**~kiel** *m* quill; '**~kraft** *f* resilience; '**~krieg** *m* literary feud; '**⁀leicht** (as) light as a feather; '**~lesen** *n*: *nicht viel ~s machen mit* make short work of; **~mäppchen** ['~mɛpçən] *n* (6) pencil case; '**~messer** *n* penknife; '**⁀n** (29) *v/i.* lose feathers; ⊕ be elastic *od.* resilient; (*schnellen*) jerk, bounce; *v/t.* ⊕ spring; *Holz*: tongue; *gut gefedert* well sprung; '**⁀nd** elastic, resilient; ⊕ springy (*a. fig.*); '**~strich** *m* stroke of the pen; '**~ung** *f* springing; springs *pl.*; *mot.* spring-suspension; '**~vieh** *n* poultry; '**~waage** *f* spring-balance; '**~wild** *n* winged game; '**~wolke** *f* cirrus; '**~zeichnung** *f* pen-and-ink drawing.

Fee [fe:] *f* (15) fairy; *gute ~* fairy godmother; '**⁀nhaft** fairylike; '**~nreigen** *m* fairy-ring.

'**Fegefeuer** *n* purgatory.

fegen ['fe:gən] (25) *v/t.* sweep; *v/i.* (*sausen*) rush, flit.

Fehde ['fe:də] *f* (15) feud; '**~handschuh** *m* gauntlet; *den ~ aufnehmen* take up the gauntlet.

Fehl [fe:l] *m*: *ohne ~ P.*: without fault, *S.*: without blemish, flawless; *⁀ am Platze* out of place; '**~-anzeige** *f a.* ⚔ nil return; '**~ball** *m* *Tennis*: fault; '**⁀bar** fallible; '**~besetzung** *f* wrong choice (*od.* man); *thea.* miscast(ing); '**~bestand** *m* deficiency; '**~betrag** *m* deficit, shortage; '**~bitte** *f*: *eine ~ tun* meet with a refusal; '**~diagnose** ⚕ *f* false diagnosis; '**~-einschätzung** *f* miscalculation.

fehlen ['fe:lən] **1.** (25) (*nicht anwesend sein*) be absent (*in der Schule, bei e-r Feier usw.* from); (*irren*) err; (*fehlschlagen*; *im Stich lassen*) fail; (*sündigen*) do wrong; (*nicht vorhanden sein*) be missing (*od.* lacking, wanting); (*vorbeischießen*) miss (*a. v/t.*); *~ gegen* offend against; *es fehlt* (*an dat.*) et. a th. is wanting *od.* lacking; es *fehlt mir an* (*dat.*) I want *od.* lack *a th.*, I am lacking in; es *~ lassen an* (*dat.*) fail in; *er fehlt mir sehr* I miss him badly; *was fehlt Ihnen?* what ails you?, what is the matter with you?, what is wrong with you?; *es fehlte nicht viel, und ich hätte* ... a little more and I would have ...; *das fehlte gerade noch!* it only wanted that!; *wo fehlt's* (*denn*)? what's wrong?; *weit gefehlt!* far from the mark!; **2.** *⁀ n* absence.

'**Fehl-entscheidung** *f* incorrect (*od.* wrong) decision; mistake.

Fehler ['fe:lər] *m* (7) (*Mangel*) defect, flaw (*a.* ⊕); (*Charakter⁀*; *Verstoß*; *Schuld*; *~ beim Tennis*) fault; (*Mißgriff*, *Versehen*) mistake; (*Irrtum*) error; *grober*: blunder; '**⁀frei**, '**⁀los** faultless, *a.* ⊕ flawless; '**⁀haft** faulty, defective; (*unrichtig*) incorrect; '**~quelle** *f* source of error; '**~quote** *f* error rate.

'**Fehl|farbe** *f* off shade; '**~geburt** *f* miscarriage; '**⁀gehen** (sn) miss one's way, (*a. fig.*) go wrong;

Schuß: miss (its mark); (*mißlingen*) fail; '**⁀greifen** miss one's hold; *fig.* make a mistake; '**~griff** *m fig.* mistake, blunder; '**~kalkulation** *f* miscalculation; '**~leistung** *f* slip, blunder; '**⁀schießen** miss (one's aim *od.* the mark); '**~schlag** *m* miss; *fig.* failure; (*Enttäuschung*) disappointment; '**⁀schlagen** miss; *fig.* (sn) fail; '**~schluß** *m* wrong conclusion, fallacy; '**~schuß** *m* miss; '**~start** *m* false start; '**⁀treten** make a false step; '**~tritt** *m* false step; *fig.* blunder, faux pas (*fr.*); *moralisch*; slip, lapse; '**~-urteil** *n* error of judg(e)ment; ⚖ incorrect sentence; '**~verhalten** *n* abnormal behavio(u)r; '**~zeit** *f bei gleitender Arbeitszeit*: time debit; '**⁀zünden** *v/i.*, '**~zündung** *mot. f* misfire.

Feier ['faɪər] *f* (15) (*Arbeitsruhe*) rest; (*Feiertag*) holiday; *e-s Festes*: celebration; *konkret*: ceremony; (*Festlichkeit*) festival; *zur ~ des Tages* to mark the occasion; '**~abend** *m* closing time; *weitS.* leisure-time; *~ machen* leave off work, F knock off; '**⁀lich** solemn; '**~lichkeit** *f* solemnity; (*Feier*) ceremony; (*Aufwand*) pomp; '**⁀n** (29) *v/t.* celebrate; *v/i.* rest (from work), make holiday; (*faulenzen*) take it easy; *s. streiken*; '**~stunde** *f* festive hour; '**~tag** *m* holiday; *gesetzlicher ~* public (*od.* bank) holiday.

feig(e[1]**)** [faɪk, 'faɪgə] cowardly.

'**Feige**[2] *f* (15) fig; '**~nbaum** *m* fig-tree; '**~nblatt** *n* fig-leaf.

Feig|heit ['faɪkhaɪt] *f* cowardice; '**~ling** *m* (3[1]) coward.

feil [faɪl] for sale, to be sold; *fig.* venal; '**~bieten** offer for sale; *contp.* prostitute.

Feile ['faɪlə] *f* (15) file; '**⁀n** (25) file (*a. fig.*).

'**feilhalten** have on sale.

'**Feilheit** *f* venality.

feilschen ['faɪlʃən] (27) (*um*) bargain (for), haggle (about).

fein [faɪn] *allg.* fine; (*verfeinert*; *gebildet*) refined; *Benehmen*: polite; *Gebäck*: fancy; (*geschmackvoll*) elegant; (*zart*) delicate; (*subtil*) subtle; F (*famos*) excellent, splendid; *~er Ton* good form; '**⁀-abstimmung** *f* fine tuning; '**⁀bäckerei** *f* fancy bakery; '**⁀blech** *n* (thin) sheet.

Feind [faɪnt] **1.** *m* (3), **~in** ['~dɪn] *f* (16[1]) enemy; *rhet.* foe; **2.** ⁀ hostile (*dat.* to).

feindlich ['~tlɪç] hostile (*gegen* to); '**⁀keit** *f* hostility.

'**Feindschaft** *f* enmity; hostility; (*Streit*) feud, quarrel; (*Zwietracht*) discord.

'**feindselig** hostile; '**⁀keit** *f* hostility.

'**fein|fühlend**, '**~fühlig** sensitive; (*zartfühlend*) delicate; tactful; '**⁀gefühl** *n* sensitiveness; delicacy; tact; '**⁀gehalt** *m* standard.

'**Feinheit** *f s. fein*: fineness; refinement; politeness; delicacy; subtlety; elegance; *die ~en pl.* niceties.

fein|hörig ['~hø:rɪç] quick of hearing; '**⁀kost** *f s. Delikatessen*; **~maschig** ['~maʃɪç] fine-meshed; '**⁀mechanik** *f* precision engineering; '**⁀mechaniker** *m* precision-instrument maker; '**~mechanisch** precision ...; '**⁀schmecker** *m* (7) gourmet; '**⁀schnitt** *m* (*Tabak*) fine cut; '**~sinnig** subtle; sensitive; '**⁀wäsche** *f* (dainty) lingerie; (*Waschen*) fine laundering.

feist [faɪst] fat, stout.

Feld [fɛlt] *n* (1) field (*a. fig.* ⚔, ⚡, *Sport*); (*Grund, Boden*) ground; △, ⊕ panel, compartment; *Schach*: square; *aus dem ~e schlagen fig.* defeat, outstrip; *ins ~ führen* advance (*arguments*); *fig. freies ~* a clear field; '**~-arbeit** *f* agricultural work; ⚒ *usw.* field work; '**~bahn** *f* field-railway; '**~bau** *m* agriculture, tillage; '**~bett** *n* camp-bed; '**~bluse** ⚔ *f* service blouse; '**~dienst** *m* field duty; '**~flasche** *f* canteen, water-bottle; '**~frucht** *f* fruit of the earth; '**~geistliche** *m* army chaplain; '**~gendarmerie** *f* (15) military police; '**~herr** *m allg.* general; *als Titel*: commander-in-chief; '**~herrnkunst** *f* strategy, generalship; '**~hüter** *m* field-guard; '**~küche** *f* field-kitchen; '**~lager** *n* bivouac, camp; '**~lazarett** *n* casualty clearing station, *Am.* evacuation hospital; '**~marschall** *m* Field Marshal; '**⁀marschmäßig** in (heavy) marching order; '**~maus** *f* field-mouse; '**~messer** *m* (7) surveyor; '**~mütze** *f* forage-cap; '**~salat** *m* lamb's lettuce; '**~schlacht** *f* battle; **~spat** ['~ʃpɑ:t] *m* fel(d)spar; '**~stecher** *m* field-glasses *pl.*; '**~studie** *f Soziologie etc.*: field study; '**~stuhl** *m* camp-stool; **~we-**

bel ['~ve:bəl] *m* (7) sergeant; '**~weg** *m* field-path; '**~zeichen** *n* ensign, standard; '**~zug** *m* campaign (*a. fig.*), expedition.

Felge ['fɛlgə] *f* (15) felloe, felly, *bsd. mot.* rim; *Turnen*: circle.

Fell [fɛl] *n* (3) (*Haut des lebenden Tieres mit Haaren*) coat; (*abgezogenes* ~) *v. größeren Tieren*: hide, *v. kleineren Tieren*: skin; (*rohes* ~ *v. Pelztieren*) pelt; (*Pelz*) fur; *v. Menschen*: hide, skin; *s. abziehen*; *fig. er hat ein sehr dickes* ~ he is very thick--skinned; *fig.* F *j-m das* ~ *gerben* give a p. a good hiding; *j-m das* ~ *über die Ohren ziehen* fleece a p.; *fig. s-e* ~*e davonschwimmen sehen* see a cake turn into dough.

Fels [fɛls] *m* (12¹), **~en** ['~zən] *m* (6) rock; '**~block** *m* rock, boulder.

'**felsen|fest** rock-like; *Glaube usw.*: unshakeable; ~ *überzeugt* firmly convinced; '**2klippe** *f* cliff; '**2riff** *n* reef.

felsig ['fɛlziç] rocky.

Fem|e ['fe:mə] *f* (15) vehme; '**~gericht** *n* vehmic court.

Femininum *gr.* [femi'ni:num] *n* (9²) feminine noun.

Feminis|mus [femi'nismus] *m* (16) feminism; **~t** *m* (12), **~tin** *f* (16¹) feminist.

Fenchel ['fɛnçəl] *m* (7) fennel.

Fenn [fɛn] *n* (3¹) fen, bog.

Fenster ['fɛnstər] *n* (7) window; '**~brett** *n* window-sill; '**~brüstung** *f* window-ledge; '**~flügel** *m* casement (*od.* wing) of the window; '**~gitter** *n* window-grate; '**~glas** *n* window-glass; '**~kreuz** *n* cross--bar(s *pl.*); '**~laden** *m* window shutter; '**~leder** *n* chamois (leather); '**~pfosten** *m* mullion; '**~platz** *m* seat by the window; '**~rahmen** *m* window-frame; *des Schiebefensters*: sash; '**~rose** △ *f* rose window; '**~scheibe** *f* window-pane; '**~sims** *n* window-sill.

Ferien ['fe:rjən] *pl. inv.* holidays *pl.*; ⚖, *univ. od. Am.* vacation; *parl.* recess; ~ *machen, in die* ~ *gehen* take one's holidays, *Am.* (take a) vacation; '**~dorf** *n* holiday camp; '**~haus** *n* holiday home; '**~reisende** *m, f* holiday-maker; '**~wohnung** *f* holiday flat; '**~zeit** *f* holiday season.

Ferkel ['fɛrkəl] *n* (7) young pig; *fig.* pig; '**2n** (29) farrow, pig.

Fermate ♪ [fɛr'ma:tə] *f* (15) pause.

fern [fɛrn] far (*a. adv.*); distant, remote (*beide a. fig.*); (*weit fort*) far off; *von* ~ from afar; *das sei* ~ *von mir* far be it from me.

'**Fern|-amt** *teleph. n* trunk (*Am.* long--distance *od.* toll) exchange; '**~-aufnahme** *f*, '**~bild** *n* telephoto(graph); '**2bleiben** (sn) keep away (*dat.* from), absent o.s. (from); '**~bleiben** *n* (6) absence; *vom Arbeitsplatz*: absenteeism; '**~e** *f* (15) distance, remoteness; *aus der* ~ from a distance, from afar; *in der* ~ in the (*od.* at a) distance.

ferner ['fɛrnər] farther; *fig.* further (-more), moreover; *Sport*: ~ *liefen* ... also ran ...; '**~hin** for the future; henceforth; *auch* ~ *et. tun* continue to do.

'**Fern|fahrer** *m* long-distance lorry (*Am.* truck) driver; '**~flug** ✈ *m* long--distance flight; **2gelenkt** ['~gəlɛŋkt] remote-controlled; *Geschoß*: guided; '**~gespräch** *teleph. n* trunk call, *Am.* long-distance (*od.* toll) call; '**2gesteuert** *s. ferngelenkt*; '**~glas** *n* binocular(s *pl.*); *s. a. Fernrohr*; '**2halten** (*a. sich*) keep away (*von* from); '**~heizung** *f* district heating; '**~kamera** *f* telecamera; '**~kopie** *teleph. f* facsimile; '**~kopierer** *teleph. m* facsimile machine; '**~kurs(us)** *m* correspondence course; '**~laster** *m*, '**~lastwagen** *m* long-distance lorry, *Am.* long haul truck; '**~leitung** *f teleph.* trunk-line, *Am.* long-distance line; (*Röhren2*) pipeline; '**~lenkung** *f* remote control; '**~licht** *mot. n* full beam; '**2liegen** (*dat.*) be far from; '**~meldetechnik** *f*, '**~meldewesen** *n* telecommunications *pl.*; '**2mündlich** telephonic; *adv.* by telephone; '**~rohr** *n* telescope; '**~ruf** *m* telephone call; *s. Ferngespräch*; '**~schnellzug** *m* long-distance express train; '**~schreiben** *n* teleprint, *Am.* teletype (message); '**~schreiber** *m* teleprinter; '**~sehen** *n* (6) television (*abbr.* TV); *im* ~ on television; '**2sehen** *v/i.* watch television; '**~seher** *m P.*: viewer; *s. Fernsehgerät*; '**~sehfilm** *m* telefilm; '**~sehgebühren** *f/pl.* television licence fee *sg.*; '**~sehgerät** *n* television set, F telly; '**~sehkamera** *f* television camera; '**~sehschirm** *m* television screen; '**~sehsender** *m* television transmitter;

(*Fernsehanstalt*) television station; '**~sehsendung** *f* television program(me), telecast; '**~sehserie** *f* television series; '**~sehspiel** *n* teleplay; '**~sehturm** *m* television tower; '**~sicht** *f* (distant) view; **2sichtig** ['~ziçtiç] long-sighted.

'**Fernsprech|-amt** *n* telephone exchange; '**~-anschluß** *m* telephone connection; '**~-apparat** *m* telephone set; '**~-auskunft** *f* directory enquiries *pl.*; '**~-automat** *m* coin-box telephone, *Am.* pay station; '**~buch** *n* telephone directory; '**~er** *m* (7) telephone; *s. a. Telephon*; '**~stelle** *f* (public) call-office; '**~teilnehmer** *m* telephone subscriber; '**~wesen** *n* telephony; '**~zelle** *f* telephone box (*Am.* booth).

'**fern|stehen** (*dat.*) be a stranger to, not to be close to; '**2steuerung** *f* remote (*od.* distant) control; '**2studium** *n*, '**2-unterricht** *m* correspondence course(s *pl.*); '**2verkehr** *m* long-distance traffic; '**2verkehrsstraße** *f* trunk road, *Am.* highway; '**2waffe** *f* long-range weapon; '**2wahl** *teleph. f* trunk (*Am.* direct distance) dial(l)ing; '**2zug** *m* long-distance train.

Ferse ['fɛrzə] *f* (15) heel; *fig. auf den ~n* (*dat.*) on the heels of; '**~ngeld** *n geben* take to one's heels.

fertig ['fɛrtiç] ready; (*beendet*) finished; (*~gekauft*) *Kleid*: ready-made, F reach-me-down; *fig.* (*vollendet*) accomplished, perfect; F (*erschöpft*) all in, (*ruiniert*) done for, (*verblüfft*) flabbergasted; *~ werden mit*, *~ machen* finish; *mit j-m od. et. ~ werden* deal (*od.* cope) with, manage, handle; *s. fertigmachen*; *mit et. ~ sein* have done; *mit j-m ~ sein* have done (F *bsd. Am.* be through) with a p.; *ohne et. ~ werden* manage (*od.* do) without a th.; '**2bauweise** *f* prefab(ricated) construction; '**~bekommen**, '**~bringen** manage (et. a th.); *es ~, zu inf.* manage to *inf.*; **~en** ['~gən] (25) *s. anfertigen*; '**2fabrikat** *n s. Fertigware*; '**2gericht** *n* instant meal; '**2haus** *n* prefab(ricated house); '**2keit** *f* skill; (*Können*) proficiency; (*Sprech2*) fluency; '**~machen** finish, (*a. sich*) get ready (*zu* for); F *fig.* fix, do for, (*erschöpfen, a. seelisch*) finish, (*abkanzeln*) tick *a p.* off; '**~stellen** complete; '**2stellung** *f* completion; **2ung** ['~guŋ] *f* (16) manufacture, production; '**2ungsstraße** ⊕ *f* production line; '**2ware** *f* finished article *od.* product.

Fes ♪ [fɛs] *n* F flat.

fesch [fɛʃ] smart, chic, stylish; (*schneidig*) dashing.

Fessel ['fɛsəl] *f* (15) (*a. fig.*) fetter, chain; *pl.* (*Hand2n*) handcuffs, manacles; *anat.* ankle; *vet.* fetlock, pastern; '**~ballon** *m* captive balloon; '**~gelenk** *vet. n* pastern-joint.

fesseln ['fɛsəln] (29) fetter, chain; (*binden*) tie, bind; *fig.* (*bezaubern*) captivate, fascinate; *Aufmerksamkeit, Auge usw.*: catch, arrest, rivet; *ans Bett, Zimmer ~* confine to one's bed, room; '**~d** *fig.* captivating, fascinating; (*spannend*) gripping.

fest[1] [fɛst] *allg.* firm (*a.* ✝); (*nicht flüssig*; *festgefügt*) solid; (*unbeweglich*) fixed (*a. Preis*); (*nicht losgehend*) fast; (*festhaltend*) tight; (*unerschütterlich*) firm, steady; ⊕ (*orts~*) stationary; ⚔ *Ort usw.*: fortified; *Schlaf*: sound; *Berufsstellung, Wohnsitz*: permanent; *~ schlafen* sleep fast, be fast asleep; *in e-r Wissenschaft ~ sein* be well versed in; *die Tür ist ~ zu* the door is fast; F *~(e)!* go it!; *~ mit j-m gehen* go steady with a p.

Fest[2] [~] *n* (3[2]) festival; fête, festivity; (*kirchliches ~*; *~mahl*) feast; '**~akt** *m* ceremony; '**2besoldet** salaried; '**2binden** fasten, tie (*an dat.* to); '**~e** *f* (15) stronghold; '**~-essen** *n* feast, banquet; *sich* '**2fahren** get stuck; *sich* '**2fressen** ⊕ seize; '**~gelage** *n* feast, banquet; '**~halle** *f s. Festsaal*; '**2halten** *v/t.* hold fast; (*packen*) seize; *polizeilich*: detain; *in Bild, Wort, Ton*: record, *Stimmung usw.*: capture; *j-n ~* (*auf j-n einreden*) buttonhole a p.; *v/i. ~ an* (*dat.*) keep (*od.* cling, adhere) to; (*a. sich ~ an*) hold fast to.

festig|en ['~igən] (25) (*sichern*) secure; (*stärken*) strengthen; *Macht usw.*: establish (firmly), consolidate; *Währung*: stabilize; *sich ~* grow stronger; **2keit** ['~içkaɪt] *f* firmness; solidity; steadiness (*s. fest*); **2ung** ['~iguŋ] *f s. festigen*: strengthening; establishment; consolidation; stabilization.

'**fest|kleben** *v/i.* adhere, stick (*an dat.* to); *v/t.* fasten (*od.* stick) with glue *od.* gum; '2**kleid** *n* festive dress; '2**körper...** ⚡ solid-state; '2**land** *n* mainland; continent; '~**legen** fix; *Geld*: tie up, freeze; *Regel usw.*: lay down; *j-n auf et.* ~ pin a p. down to a th.; *sich auf et.* ~ commit o.s. to a th.

'**festlich** festive, solemn; '2**keit** *f* festivity, solemnity; *s. Fest*².

'**fest|machen** fix, fasten; *Handel*: close; '2**mahl** *n* feast, banquet; 2**nahme** ['~na:mə] *f* (15) arrest; '~**nehmen** seize, arrest; '2**-ordner** *m* steward; '2**-ordnung** *f* table of events; '2**platte** *f Computer*: hard disk; '2**preis** ✝ *m* fixed price; '2**rede** *f* speech of the day; '2**saal** (banqueting-)hall; ballroom; '~**setzen** fix; *sich* ~ settle (down); '2**spiele** *n/pl.* Festival *sg.*; '~**stecken** pin; '~**stehen** be steady; *fig.* be certain; '~**stehend** stationary, fixed; *Regel, Tatsache*: established; '~**stellen** establish; (*ermitteln*) ascertain, find out; *Ort, Lage*: locate; *Personalien*: identify; (*konstatieren*) state; (*erklären*) declare; '2**stellung** *f* establishment; statement; ascertainment; location; identification; '2**tag** *m* festive day, holiday; (*Glückstag*) red-letter day.

'**Festung** *f* (16) fortress; '~**s-anlagen** *f/pl.* fortifications.

'**fest|verzinslich** ✝ fixed interest bearing; '2**wochen** *f/pl.*: *Berliner usw.* ~ Festival; '~**wurzeln** become firmly rooted; '2**zug** *m* (festive) procession.

fett [fɛt] **1.** fat; *fig.* rich; *Boden*: *a.* fertile; *typ.* extra bold; **2.** 2 *n* (3) fat; (*Schmalz*) lard; (*Schmier*2) grease.

'**Fett|-auge** *n* speck of fat; '~**bauch** *m* paunch; '~**druck** *typ. m* extra bold print, heavy-faced type; '2**en** grease; '~**fleck** *m* spot of grease; '~**gehalt** *m* fat content; '2**ig** fat(ty); (*schmierig*) greasy; '~**kohle** *f* fat coal; 2**leibig** ['~laıbiç] corpulent; '~**näpfchen** *n*: *fig. ins* ~ *treten* drop a brick, put one's foot in it; '~**sack** F *m sl.* fat slob; '~**spritze** *mot. f* grease-gun; '~**sucht** *f* obesity.

Fetzen ['fɛtsən] *m* (6) shred; (*Lumpen*) rag, *Am. a.* frazzle; *ein* ~ *Papier* a scrap of paper; *in* ~ in rags.

feucht [fɔYçt] moist; *bsd. Luft*: humid; (*unangenehm* ~) damp; '~**en** (26) moisten; damp.

'**Feuchtigkeit** *f* moisture; humidity; dampness; '~**screme** *f* moisturizing cream; '~**sgehalt** *m* moisture content; '~**smesser** *m* hygrometer.

feudal [fɔY'da:l] feudal; F (*großartig*) sumptuous, *sl.* ritzy.

Feuer ['fɔYər] *n* (7) fire (*a. fig.*); *fig.* ardo(u)r; (*feuriges Temperament*) mettle; ~ *bekommen* ⚔ be fired at; *j-m* ~ *geben* (*für die Zigarre*) give a p. a light; ~ *machen* make (*Am.* build) a fire; '~**-alarm** *m* fire-alarm; '2**bestatten** cremate; '~**bestattung** *f* cremation; '~**bohne** ⚘ *f* scarlet runner; '~**-eifer** *m* ardent zeal, ardo(u)r; '~**-einstellung** ⚔ *f* cessation of fire; '2**fest** fire-proof, fire-resistant; *Baustoff usw.*: refractory; '~**garbe** ⚔ *f* sheaf (*od.* cone) of fire; '2**gefährlich** inflammable; '~**gefecht** *n* gun-fight; '~**hahn** *m* fire-plug; '~**kraft** ⚔ *f* fire power; '~**leiter** *f* fire-ladder; (*Nottreppe*) fire-escape; '~**löscher** *m* fire-extinguisher; '~**melder** *m* fire-alarm; '2**n** (29) fire (*a. fig. entlassen*); F (*werfen*) hurl; '~**probe** *f fig.* crucial (*od.* acid) test; *die* ~ *bestehen* stand the test; '~**rad** *n* Catherine-wheel; '2**rot** flaming red; '~**sbrunst** *f* (great) fire, conflagration; '~**schaden** *m* damage (caused) by fire; '~**schiff** *n* lightship; '~**sgefahr** *f* danger (*od.* risk) of fire; '~**sglut** *f* burning heat; '~**snot** *f* danger from fire; '2**speiend** vomiting fire; volcanic; ~*er Berg* volcano; '~**spritze** *f* fire-engine; '~**stelle** *f* fireplace, hearth; '~**stein** *m min. u. im Feuerzeug*: flint; '~**stoß** ⚔ *m* burst of fire; '~**strahl** *m* flash of fire; '~**taufe** *f* baptism of fire; '~**teufel** *m* (*Brandstifter*) fire bug; '~**treppe** *f* fire escape.

'**Feuerung** *f* firing; (*Heizung*) heating; (*Ofen*) furnace; (*Brennmaterial*) fuel.

'**Feuer|versicherung**(**sgesellschaft**) *f* fire insurance (company); '2**verzinken** ⊕ hot-galvanize; '~**vorhang** *thea. m* fire-curtain; '~**wache** *f* fire-station; '~**waffe** *f* fire-arm; '~**wehr** *f* fire-brigade, *Am.* fire department; '~**wehrmann** *m* fireman; '~**werk** *n* fireworks *pl.* (*a. fig.*); '~**werker** *m* (7) pyrotechnician; ⚔ artificer, ordnance technician; ~**werke'rei** *f* pyrotechnics *sg.*; '~**werkskörper** *m* fire-

cracker; **'~zange** *f* (*eine* a pair of) fire-tongs *pl.*; **'~zeichen** *n* fire--signal; **'~zeug** *n* (cigarette-, pocket-)lighter.
Feuilleton ['fœj(ə)tõ] *n* (11) feuilleton (*fr.*), features section.
feurig ['fɔʏriç] fiery; *fig. a.* ardent.
Fex [fɛks] *m* faddist; *in Zssgn* ... fan.
Fiaker [fi'akər] *m* (7) cab.
Fiasko [fi'asko] *n* (11) fiasco, failure.
Fibel ['fi:bəl] *f* (15) spelling-book, primer.
Fiber ['fi:bər] *f* (15) fib|re, *Am.* -er.
Fichte ['fiçtə] *f* (15) spruce; **'~nholz** *n* pine-wood; **'~nnadel** *f* pine--needle.
ficken V ['fikən] (25) fuck.
fidel [fi'de:l] merry, jolly.
Fidibus ['fi:dibus] *m* (*inv. od.* 4[1]) spill.
Fieber ['fi:bər] *n* (7) fever (*a. fig.*); *~ haben s. fiebern*; *das ~ messen* take the temperature; **'~-anfall** *m* attack of fever; **'2-artig** febrile; **'~frost** *m* chill; **'2haft** feverish (*a. fig.*), febrile; **'~hitze** *f* fever heat; **'2krank** feverish; **'~kurve** *f* temperature--curve; *s. Fiebertabelle*; **'~mittel** *n* febrifuge; **'2n** (29) be feverish, have (*od.* run) a temperature; *fig. ~ nach* yearn for; (*vor Erwartung*) *~* be in a fever (of expectation); **'~rinde** *f* Peruvian bark; **'~schauer** *m* shivering fit; **'~tabelle** *f* temperature--chart; **'~thermometer** *n* clinical thermometer; **'~traum** *m* feverish dream.
fiebrig ['fi:briç] *s.* fieberhaft.
Fiedel ['fi:dəl] *f* (15) fiddle; **'~bogen** *m* fiddle-stick *od.* -bow; **'2n** *v/t u. v/i.* (29) fiddle.
fiel [fi:l] *pret. v. fallen* 1.
fies F [fi:s] F awful, filthy.
Figur [fi'gu:r] *f* (16) figure (*a. Eislauf, Tanz, a.* ♞, ⊕); *Schach*: chessman; *e-e gute* (*schlechte*) *~ machen* cut a fine (poor) figure; **2bewußt** figure--conscious.
figürlich [~'gy:rliç] figurative.
Fiktion [fik'tsjo:n] *f* (16) fiction.
fiktiv [fik'ti:f] fictitious.
Filet [fi'le:] *n* (11) *Handarbeit*: network; *Kochkunst*: fillet; **~braten** *m* roast fillet.
Filial|e [fil'ja:lə] *f* (15) branch (office *od.* establishment); **~geschäft** *n* multiple shop, chain store; *s. Filiale*; **~leiter** *m* branch manager.
Filigran(**-arbeit** *f*) [fili'gra:n-] *n* (3[1]) filigree.
Film [film] *m* (3[1]) *allg.* film; (*~stück*) *Am. a.* (motion) picture, F movie; *beim* (*od. im*) *~* on the films; *phot. e-n ~ einlegen* load the camera; **'~-atelier** *n* (film)studio; **'~-aufnahme** *f* (film) shot; *Vorgang*: shooting (of a film); **'~band** *n* reel; **'~bauten** *pl.* sets; **~diva** ['~di:va] *f* film star; **'2en** (25) film, screen, shoot; **'~gesellschaft** *f* film company; **'~-industrie** *f* film industry; **'~kamera** *f* film camera; **'~kunst** *f* cinematic art; **'~regisseur** *m* film director; **'~reklame** *f* screen advertising; **~reportage** ['~repɔrta:ʒə] *f* screen record; **'~riß** *m fig.* (mental) black-out; **'~schauspieler**(**in** *f*) *m* film (*od.* screen) actor *m* (actress *f*); **'~spule** *f* (film) reel; **'~star** *m* film (*Am.* F movie) star; **'~streifen** *m* film-strip, reel; **'~theater** *n* cinema; **'~verleih** *m* film distribution; (*Firma*) film distributors *pl.*; **'~vorführer** *m* projectionist; **'~vorschau** *f* (film) trailer; **'~vorstellung** *f* film (*Am.* movie) show(ing); **'~welt** *f* film world.
Filter ['filtər] *m, n* (7), **'2n** (29) filter; **'~kaffee** *m* filtered coffee; **'~tüte** *f* filter bag; **'~zigarette** *f* filter-tipped cigarette.
filtrieren [~'tri:rən] filter, strain.
Filz [filts] *m* (3[2]) felt; *fig.* niggard; **'~hut** *m* felt hat; **'2ig** feltlike; (*geizig*) niggardly, stingy; **'~laus** *f* crab-louse; **'~schreiber** *m*, **'~stift** *m* felt(-tipped) pen.
Fimmel F ['fiməl] *m* craze.
Finale [fi'na:le] *n* (11, *pl. inv.* -*le*) ♪ finale; *Sport*: final(s *pl.*).
Finanz|amt [fi'nantsˀamt] *n* (inland) revenue office; **~en** *f/pl.* (16) finances; **2iell** [~'tsjɛl] financial; **2ieren** [~'tsi:rən] finance; **~jahr** *n* fiscal year; **~lage** *f* financial state *od.* standing; **~mann** *m* financier; **~minister** *m* Minister of Finance; *Brt.* Chancellor of the Exchequer, *Am.* Secretary of the Treasury; **~ministerium** *n* Ministry of Finance; *Brt.* Exchequer, *Am.* Treasury Department; **~wesen** *n* finances *pl.*, financial system.
Findelkind ['findəlkint] *n* foundling.
finden ['findən] (30) find; (*antreffen*) meet with; *sich ~ S.*: be found, *P.*: find o.s.; *sich ~ in* (*acc.*) accom-

modate o.s. to; *wie ~ Sie ...?* how do you like ...? *~ Sie nicht?* don't you think so?; *das wird sich ~* we shall see.

'**Finder** *m*, '**~in** *f* finder; '**~lohn** *m* finder's reward.

'**findig** resourceful; '**2keit** *f* resourcefulness.

Findling ['fintliŋ] *m* (3[1]) foundling; *geol.* erratic block, boulder.

fing [fiŋ] *pret. v. fangen.*

Finger ['fiŋər] *m* (7) finger; *sich die ~ verbrennen* (*a. fig.*) burn one's fingers; *die ~ davon lassen* keep one's hands off; *s. rühren*; '**~abdruck** *m* finger-print; '**~fertigkeit** *f* dexterity; '**~glied** *n* finger-joint; '**~handschuh** *m* (fingered) glove; '**~hut** *m* thimble; ⚘ foxglove; '**~ling** *m* (3[1]) finger-stall; '**2n** (29) finger; F *fig. e-e S. ~* wangle *a th.*; '**~nagel** *m* finger-nail; '**~satz** ♪ *m* fingering; '**~spitze** *f* finger-tip; '**~spitzengefühl** *n fig.* flair, subtle intuition; '**~übung** ♪ *f* fingering-exercise; **~zeig** ['~tsaɪk] *m* hint, cue, tip.

fingieren [fiŋ'giːrən] feign.

Fink [fiŋk] *m* (12) finch.

Finne[1] ['finə] *f* (15) pimple; *pl. der Schweine*: measles *pl.*; (*Flosse*) fin.

'**Finne**[2] *m* (13), '**Finnin** *f* (16[1]) Fin(-lander).

'**finnisch** Finnish.

finster ['finstər] dark; *fig. a.* gloomy; (*grimmig*) grim; *~er Blick* scowl; *j-n ~ ansehen* scowl (*od.* look black) at a p., frown at a p.; '**2nis** *f* (14[2]) darkness, obscurity.

Finte ['fintə] *f* (15) feint (*a. fig.*).

Firlefanz ['firləfants] *m* (3[2]) (*Albernheit*) (tom)foolery, nonsense; (*Flitterkram*) frippery, gew-gaws *pl.*; *~ treiben* play the fool.

Firma ['firma] *f* (16[2]) firm, (commercial) house; company; *Briefanschrift*: *~ Langenscheidt* Messrs. Langenscheidt.

Firmament [firma'mɛnt] *n* (3) firmament.

firm|en ['firmən] (25) confirm; '**2ung** *f* confirmation.

'**Firmen|-inhaber** *m* principal; '**~schild** *n* sign(board), facia; '**~sprecher** *m* company spokesman; '**~sprecherin** *f* company spokeswoman; '**~wagen** *m* company car; '**~wert** *m* goodwill.

Firn [firn] *m* (3), '**~feld** *n* névé.

Firnis ['firnis] *m* (4[1]), '**2sen** (28) varnish.

First [first] *m* (3[2]) ridge.

Fis ♪ [fis] *n* F sharp.

Fisch [fiʃ] *m* (3[2]) fish; *~e pl. ast.* Fishes, Pisces; F *kleine ~e* child's play; '**~-auge** *phot. n* fish-eye lens; '**~bein** *n* whalebone; '**~blase** *f* fish-bladder; '**~dampfer** *m* trawler.

'**fischen** *v/t. u. v/i.* (27) fish; *s. trüb.*

'**Fischer** *m* (7) fisherman; '**~boot** *n* fishing-boat; '**~dorf** *n* fishing-village; **~ei** [~'raɪ] *f* (*Gewerbe*) fishery; (*Fischen*) fishing.

'**Fisch|fang** *m* fishing; '**~gerät** *n* fishing-tackle; '**~gericht** *n* fish dish; '**~geruch** *m* fishy smell; '**~gräte** *f* fish-bone; '**~grätenmuster** *n* herring-bone pattern; '**~händler** *m* fishmonger, *Am.* fishdealer; '**~konserve** *f* tinned (*Am.* canned) fish; '**~kunde** *f* ichthyology; '**~laich** *m* spawn; '**~leim** *m* fish-glue; '**~mehl** *n* fish-meal; '**~milch** *f* milt; '**~-otter** *m* otter; '**2reich** abounding in fish; '**~reiher** *m* heron; '**~rogen** *m* roe; '**~schuppe** *f* scale; **~stäbchen** ['~ʃtɛːpçən] *n* (6) fish finger; '**~teich** *m* fish-pond; '**~tran** *m* train-oil; '**~vergiftung** *f* fish-poisoning; '**~zucht** *f* fish-hatching, 🕮 pisciculture; '**~zug** *m* draught (of fishes), haul.

fiskalisch [fis'kɑːliʃ] fiscal.

Fiskus ['fiskus] *m inv.* Exchequer, *bsd. Am.* Treasury.

Fistel ['fistəl] *f* (15) ⚕ fistula; ♪ (*od.* '**~stimme** *f*) falsetto.

Fitnesscenter ['fitnɛstsɛntər] *n* (7) *Sport*: health cent|re, *Am.* -er.

Fittich ['fitiç] *m* (3) wing.

fix [fiks] quick; *Gehalt, Preise usw.*: fixed; *~e Idee* fixed idea; *~ u. fertig* quite ready; all finished (*a.* F *fig. erledigt, erschöpft*); *ein ~er Bursche* a smart fellow; F *mach (mal) ~!* make it snappy!; '**~en** (27) *an der Börse*: bear; *sl.* (*Drogen spritzen*) fix, shoot; '**2er** *m* (7) bear; *sl.* junkie; **2ierbad** *phot.* [~'ksiːrbɑːt] *n* fixer; **~ieren** [~'ksiːrən] fix; *j-n*: stare at; **2iermittel** [~'ksiːrmitəl] *n* fixative; **2ierung** [~'ksiːruŋ] *f* fixation; '**2stern** *m* fixed star; '**2um** *n* (9[2]) fixed sum *od.* salary.

FKK-|Anhänger(in *f*) *m* [ɛfkɑː'kɑː-] nudist, naturist; **~Strand** *m* nudist beach.

flach [flax] flat; (*eben*) plain; *Wasser, Teller u. fig.*: shallow; *Schuhe*: heelless; *die ~e Hand* the flat of the hand; '**2bahn** ⚔ *f* flat trajectory; '**2dach** *n* flat roof.
Fläche ['flɛçə] *f* (15) (*Ebene*) plain, level; (*Ober2*) surface; (*weite ~*) expanse, tract; (*Wasser2 usw.*) sheet; (*~nraum*) area; ⚒ plane; '**~nblitz** *m* sheet lightning; '**~n-inhalt** *m*, '**~nraum** *m* area, superficies; '**~nmaß** *n* square (*od.* surface) measure.
'**Flachheit** *f* flatness; *Wasser u. fig.*: shallowness.
'**Flachmann** F *m* (*Taschenflasche*) hip-flask.
'**Flachrennen** *n* flat race.
Flachs [flaks] *m* (4) flax; '**2en** F wisecrack; '**2haarig** flaxen-haired; '**~kopf** *m* flaxen-haired person.
'**Flachzange** *f* flat-nose(d) pliers *pl.*
flackern ['flakərn] (29) flare, flicker.
Fladen ['flɑːdən] *m* (6) flat cake.
Flagge ['flagə] *f* (15) flag, colo(u)rs *pl.*; *unter falscher ~* under false colo(u)rs; '**~n...** *mst* flag; '**2n** (25) *v/i.* hoist (the) flag; *v/t.* dress; '**~nstock** *m* flagstaff.
'**Flagg|leine** *f* flag-line; '**~offizier** *m* flag-officer; '**~schiff** *n* flagship.
Flakon [fla'kõ] *n, m* (11) small bottle, flask.
Flam|e ['flɑːmə] *m* (12), **~länder** ['~lɛndər] *m* (7), '**~in** *f* (16[1]) Fleming.
flämisch ['flɛmiʃ] Flemish.
Flamm|e ['flamə] *f* (15) flame (*a.* F *Geliebte*); (*lodernde ~*) blaze; *s. aufgehen*; '**2en** *v/i.* (25) flame; blaze; *v/t. Stoff*: water; '**2end** flaming; *fig. Rede*: *a.* stirring; '**~enmeer** *n* sea of flames; '**~(en)-ofen** ⊕ *m* reverberatory (puddling) furnace; '**~enwerfer** ⚔ *m* flame-thrower.
Flammeri ['flaməri] *m* (11) blancmange, flummery.
'**Flammpunkt** *m* flash point.
Flanell [fla'nɛl] *m* (3[1]) flannel; **~anzug** *m*, **~hose** *f* flannels *pl.*
flanieren [fla'niːrən] (sn) saunter.
Flanke ['flaŋkə] *f* (15) flank (*a.* △, ⚔, *mount.*); '**~n-angriff** *m* flank attack; '**~ndeckung** *f* flank protection.
flan'kieren flank; ✝, *pol.* *~de Maßnahmen* supporting measures.
Flansch ⊕ [flanʃ] *m* (3) flange.
Flaps F [flaps] *m* (4) boor, lout.
Fläschchen ['flɛʃçən] *n* (6) small bottle, flask; *pharm.* phial.
Flasche ['flaʃə] *f* (15) bottle; *kleine*: flask; F *Sport usw.*: dud; '**~nbier** *n* bottled beer; '**~ngärung** *f* fermentation in the bottle; '**~nhals** *m* neck of a bottle; '**~nkind** *n* bottle-fed baby; '**~n-öffner** *m* bottle-opener; '**~npost** *f* message in a bottle; '**~nregal** *n* bottle rack; '**~nzug** *m* block and tackle, pulley(-block).
Flatter|geist ['flatər-] *m* **1.** fickle person; **2.** = '**~sinn** *m* fickleness; '**2haft** fickle, inconstant; '**~haftigkeit** *f* fickleness, inconstancy; '**2n** (29, h. *u.* sn) flutter (*a.* ⊕); *mot. Räder*: shimmy, wobble.
flau [flaʊ] (*schwach*) feeble, faint; *Getränk*: stale, flat; *phot.* weak; ✝ flat, dull; *~e Zeit* slack time; *~er werden Wind*: calm down.
Flaum [flaʊm] *m* (3) fluff; = '**~feder** *f* down; '**2ig** downy, fluffy.
Flausch [flaʊʃ] *m* (3) (*Woll-, Haarbüschel*) tuft; (*dicker Wollstoff*) fleece fabric; **2ig** fluffy.
Flause ['flaʊzə] *f* (15) fib, shift; (*Unsinn*) nonsense; '**~nmacher** (**-in** *f*) *m* shuffler.
Flaute ['flaʊtə] *f* (15) ⚓ dead calm, lull; ✝ slackness.
Flechse ['flɛksə] *f* (15) sinew, tendon.
Flecht|e ['flɛçtə] *f* (15) braid; (*Haar2*) *a.* tress, plait; ⚘ lichen; ⚕ herpes; '**2en** (30) twist; *Korb*: weave; *Kranz*: bind; *Haare*: braid, plait; *sich ~* twine, wind (*um* round); '**~werk** *n* plaiting; (*Weiden2*) wicker-work.
Fleck [flɛk] *m* (3) (*Stelle*) spot; (*Flicken*) patch; (*Stück Land*) patch; (*Schmutz2*) stain, blot, spot; (*Makel*) spot, blemish, blur; (*Kaldaunen*) tripe; (*Schuhabsatz2*) heel (-piece); *schöner ~ Erde* beauty spot; *auf dem ~* on the spot; *wir kommen nicht vom ~* we are not getting on.
'**Flecken**[1] *m* (6) *s. Fleck*; (*Ortschaft*) market-town, borough.
'**flecken**[2] (25) spot, stain; '**~los** spotless; *fig. a.* stainless.
'**Fleck|-entferner** *m* (7) spot (*od.* stain) remover; '**~fieber** *n* spotted fever; '**2ig** spotted; (*befleckt*) stained; '**~typhus** *m* typhus; '**~wasser** *n s. Fleckentferner*.

Fledermaus ['fle:dər-] *f* bat.
Flegel ['fle:gəl] *m* (7) flail; *fig.* lout, boor; '**~alter** *n*, '**~jahre** *n/pl.* awkward age *sg.*; **~ei** [~'laɪ] *f* rudeness, churlish conduct; '**2haft** churlish, rude; *sich* '**2n** sprawl, loll.
flehen ['fle:n] **1.** (25) implore, entreat (*um* et. [for] a th., *zu j-m* a p.); **2.** **2** *n* (6) supplication, entreaty; '**~tlich** suppliant, imploring(ly *adv.*), beseeching(ly).
Fleisch [flaɪʃ] *n* (3²) flesh; (*Schlacht*2) meat; (*Frucht*2) pulp; *fig.* *sich ins eigne ~ schneiden* cut one's own throat; '**~bank** *f* butcher's stall, *Am.* meat-counter; '**~beschauer** ['~bəʃauər] *m* meat inspector; '**~brühe** *f* (meat-)broth; *v. Rindfleisch*: beef tea; '**~er** *m* (7) butcher; **~erei** [~'raɪ] *f*, '**~erladen** *m* butcher's (*Am.* butcher) shop.
'**Fleischeslust** *f* carnal desire.
'**Fleisch|-extrakt** *m* meat extract; '**~farbe** *f* flesh-colo(u)r; '**2farben** flesh-colo(u)red; '**2fressend** carnivorous; '**2ig** fleshy; ⚘ pulpous, pulpy; '**~kloß** *m* meat-ball; '**~konserven** *f/pl.* potted (*od.* tinned, *Am.* canned) meat; '**~kost** *f* meat diet; '**2lich** carnal, fleshly; '**2los** fleshless; *Kost*: meatless; '**~pastete** *f* meat-pie; '**~schnitte** *f* slice of meat; steak; '**~speise** *f* (course of) meat; '**~vergiftung** *f* ptomaine poisoning; **~werdung** ['~ve:rduŋ] *f* incarnation; '**~wolf** *m* meat mincer (*Am.* grinder); '**~wunde** *f* flesh-wound.
Fleiß [flaɪs] *m* (3²) diligence, industry; (*Beharrlichkeit*) application, assiduity; *mit ~* intentionally, on purpose; *viel ~ verwenden auf* (*acc.*) take great pains with; '**2ig** assiduous; diligent, industrious, hard-working; (*sorgfältig*) painstaking; *ein ~er Besucher* a frequent visitor.
flektieren *gr.* [flɛk'ti:rən] inflect.
flennen ['flɛnən] (25) cry.
fletschen ['flɛtʃən] (27): *die Zähne ~* show one's teeth, snarl.
Flexion *gr.* [flɛks'jo:n] *f* inflexion; **~s...** inflexional.
Flick|-arbeit ['flik-] *f* patchwork; '**~en** *m* patch; '**2en** (25) mend, patch (up), repair; *fig.* *j-m et. am Zeug ~* pick holes in a p.; '**~er(in** *f*) *m* patcher, mender; **~erei** [~ə'raɪ] *f* patchwork; '**~schuster** *m* cobbler; '**~werk** *n* patchwork; '**~wort** *n* expletive; '**~zeug** *n* sewing (⊕ repair) kit.
Flieder ['fli:dər] *m* (7) (*spanischer*) lilac; (*Holunder*) elder.
Fliege ['fli:gə] *f* (15) fly; (*Bärtchen*) imperial; F (*Krawatte*) bow-tie; *von ~n beschmutzt* fly-blown; *zwei ~n mit e-r Klappe schlagen* kill two birds with one stone.
'**fliegen** **1.** *v/i.* (sn) *u.* *v/t.* (30) fly; *Fahne usw.*: *a.* stream; (*eilen*) fly, rush; F (*entlassen werden*) get the sack, *Am.* get fired; *Sport*: *~der Start* flying start; **2.** **2** *n* (6) flying; ✈ *a.* aviation.
'**Fliegen|fänger** ['~fɛŋər] *m* fly-paper; '**~fenster** *n* fly-screen; '**~gewicht(ler** *m*) *n* *Boxen*: fly-weight; '**~klappe** *f* '**~klatsche** *f* fly-flap, *Am.* fly swatter; '**~pilz** *m* toadstool; '**~schrank** *m* meat-safe.
'**Flieger** *m* (7) flyer, airman, aviator; *berufsmäßiger*: pilot; *s.* *Flugzeug*; *Rad-*, *Rennsport*: sprinter; '**~abwehr** *f* anti-aircraft defen|ce, *Am.* -se; ~... anti-aircraft ...; '**~alarm** *m* air-raid warning, air alert; '**~bombe** *f* aircraft bomb; '**~dreß** *m* flying suit; '**~horst** *m* air station, *Am.* air base; '**~in** *f* (16¹) airwoman, aviatrix; '**2isch** aeronautic(al), flying; '**~offizier** *m* air-force officer; '**~schule** *f* flying school.
fliehen ['fli:ən] *v/i.* (30, sn) flee (*statt* flee[ing] *mst* fly[ing]) (*vor dat.* from); *v/t.* avoid, shun; '**~d** *Stirn*, *Kinn*: receding.
'**Fliehkraft** *f* centrifugal power.
Fliese ['fli:zə] *f* (15) flag(stone), tile.
Fließ|band ['fli:sbant] *n* assembly line; (*Förderband*) conveyor belt; '**~bandfertigung** *f* assembly-line production; '**2en** (30, sn) flow, run; '**2end** flowing; *Sprache*: fluent; '**~heck** *mot.* *n a.* *Wagen mit ~* fastback; '**~papier** *n* blotting-paper.
Flimmer ['flimər] *m* (7), '**2n** (29) glimmer, glitter; *bsd.* *Film*: flicker; *es flimmert mir vor den Augen* my head swims.
flink [fliŋk] quick, nimble, brisk; '**2heit** *f* quickness, nimbleness.
Flinte ['flintə] *f* (15) (shot)gun; *fig.* *die ~ ins Korn werfen* throw up the sponge.
'**Flinten|kolben** *m* butt-end (of a gun); '**~lauf** *m* gun-barrel; '**~schuß** *m* gunshot.

Flipper ['flipər] *m* (7) (*Spielautomat*) pinball machine.
Flirt [flœrt] *m* (11) flirtation; '**⁀en** (26) flirt.
Flitter ['flitər] *m* (7) tinsel, spangle; '**~gold** *n* tinsel, leaf-brass; '**~kram** *m* cheap finery, tinsel; '**~wochen** *f/pl.* honeymoon *sg.*
Flitzbogen ['flits-] *m* boy's bow.
flitzen ['flitsən] (27, sn) flit, whisk.
flocht [flɔxt] *pret. v. flechten.*
Flock|e ['flɔkə] *f* (15) (*Schnee⁀*) flake; (*Woll⁀*) flock; '**~enblume** *f* centaury; '**⁀ig** flaky; flocky, fluffy.
flog [flo:k] *pret. v. fliegen.*
Floh[1] [flo:] *m* (3[2]) flea; *j-m e-n ~ ins Ohr setzen* put ideas into a p.'s head; '**~stich** *m* flea-bite.
floh[2] *pret. v. fliehen.*
Floppy-Disc ['flɔpidisk] *f* (11[1]) *Computer*: floppy-disk.
Flor [flo:r] *m* (3[1]) **1.** bloom; *fig.* bloom, prime; (*Blumenmenge*) display of flowers; *fig. v. Damen*: bevy; **2.** *auf Samt usw.*: nap, pile; (*dünnes Gewebe*) gauze, crépe; (*Trauer⁀*) crape. [**~seide** *f* floss-silk.]
Florett *fenc.* [flo'rɛt] *n* (3) foil;
florieren [flo'ri:rən] flourish, prosper.
Floskel ['flɔskəl] *f* (15) flourish; *contp.* empty phrase
Floß[1] [flo:s] *n* (3[3]) raft, float; '**~brücke** *f* floating bridge.
floß[2] [flɔs] *pret. v. fließen.*
Flosse ['flɔsə] *f* (15) fin.
flößen ['flø:sɛn] (27) float, raft.
'**Flößer** *m* (7) raftsman.
Flöte ['flø:tə] *f* (15) flute; *Kartenspiel*: flush; '**⁀n** (26) *v/i. u. v/t.* play (on) the flute; *fig.* F *~ gehen* go to the dogs *od.* to pot; '**~nbläser** *m*, '**~nspieler** *m* flute-player, flutist.
flott [flɔt] floating, afloat; (*lustig*) gay; *Bursche*: dashing; *Tänzer usw.*: good; *Tanz*: lively; *Kleidung*: stylish, smart; (*schnell*) quick, snappy; *~ leben* lead a jolly (*od.* gay) life, F go the pace.
Flotte ['flɔtə] *f* (15) fleet; (*Marine*) navy; '**~n-abkommen** *n* naval agreement; '**~nschau** *f* naval review; '**~nstation** *f* naval station; '**~nstützpunkt** *m* naval base.
'**flottgehend** *Geschäft usw.*: brisk, lively, flourishing.
Flottille [flɔ'tiljə] *f* (15) flotilla; **~n-admiral** *m* commodore.
'**flottmachen** ⚓ float, set afloat.
Flöz [flø:ts] *n* (3[2]) seam, layer, stratum.
Fluch [flu:x] *m* (3[3]) curse, malediction; (*Redensart*) (profane) oath, F swear-word; '**⁀beladen** under a curse; '**⁀en** (25) curse (*j-m* a p.), swear (*auf acc.* at); '**~er** *m* curser.
Flucht [fluxt] *f* (16) flight (*vor dat.* from); *e-s Gefangenen*: escape; *wilde*: rout, stampede; (*Reihe*) range, row; *s. Zimmer⁀*; *in die ~ schlagen* (*od. jagen od. treiben*) put to flight; *s. begeben, ergreifen*; '**⁀artig** hasty, headlong.
fluchten ['fluxtən] (26) ⊕ align.
flüchten ['flyçtən] (26, sn) flee; (*a. sich*) *~* take refuge; *Gefangener*: escape.
'**Fluchthelfer** *m* escape agent.
'**flüchtig** fugitive (*a. fig.*); (*vergänglich*) fleeting, transitory; *Lächeln*: fleeting; *Mensch*: flighty; (*unsorgfältig*) careless; (*eilig*) hasty; ⚗ volatile; *~er Bekannter* nodding acquaintance; *~er Blick* (cursory) glance; *~ durchlesen* skim (through); *~ werden* abscond; '**⁀keit** *f* transitoriness; flightiness; carelessness; volatility; '**⁀keitsfehler** *m* slip, oversight.
Flüchtling ['flyçtliŋ] *m* (3[1]) fugitive; *pol.* refugee; '**~slager** *n* refugee camp.
'**Flucht|linie** ⚠ *f* alignment; '**~versuch** *m* attempt to escape; '**~wagen** *m* get-away car; '**~weg** *m* escape route.
fluchwürdig ['flu:x-] execrable.
Flug [flu:k] *m* (3[3]) flight; (*Schar*) flock, swarm; *auf dem* (*od. im*) *~e* on the wing, *fig.* in haste; '**~-abwehr...** anti-aircraft ...; '**~bahn** *f* trajectory; ✈ flight path; '**~ball** *m* *Tennis*: volley; '**~betrieb** *m* flying (operations *pl.*); '**~blatt** *n* leaflet, pamphlet; '**~boot** *n* flying boat; '**~deck** *n* flight deck; '**~dienst** *m* air-service.
Flügel ['fly:gəl] *m* (7) wing (*a.* ✈, ⚠, *pol. u. Sport*); (*Fenster⁀*) casement; (*Tür⁀*) leaf, half; (*Windmühlen⁀*) sail; (*Propeller⁀*) blade; ♪ grand (piano); '**~fenster** *n* casement-window; '**⁀lahm** broken-winged; *fig.* lame; '**⁀los** wingless; '**~mann** ✈ *m* flank man, marker; '**~mutter** ⊕ *f* wing nut; '**~schlag**

m beat of the wings; '**~schraube** ⊕ *f* thumb screw; '**~stürmer** *m Fußball*: winger; '**~tür** *f* folding-door.
Fluggast ['flu:k-] *m* air-passenger.
flügge ['flygə] fledged.
Flug|geschwindigkeit ['flu:k-] *f* flying speed; '**~gesellschaft** *f* airline; '**~hafen** *m* airport; '**~höhe** *f* altitude; '**~kapitän** *m* aircraft captain; '**~karte** *f s. Flugticket*; '**~lehrer** *m* flying instructor; '**~linie** *f* air-route, airway; (*Gesellschaft*) airline; *e-e ~ benutzen* ride an airline; '**~lotse** *m* air-traffic controller; '**~maschine** *f* flying-machine; '**~platz** *m* aerodrome, airfield, *Am. a.* airdrome; '**~post** *f* air-mail; '**~preis** *m* (air) fare.
flugs [flu:ks] quickly, swiftly.
'**Flug|sand** *m* quicksand; '**~schalter** *m* flight desk; '**~schreiber** *m* flight recorder; '**~schrift** *f* pamphlet; '**~sicherung** *f* air traffic control; '**~sport** *m* aviation; '**~strecke** *f* flying distance; air-route; '**~stützpunkt** *m* airbase; '**~ticket** *n* plane ticket; '**~verkehr** *m* air traffic; *planmäßiger*: air service; '**~weg** *m* flight path; '**~wetter** *n* flying weather; '**~zeug** *n* aeroplane, F plane, *bsd. Am.* airplane, (*a. ~e pl.*) aircraft.
'**Flugzeug|bau** *m* aircraft construction; '**~-entführer** *m* hijacker, F skyjacker; '**~-entführung** *f* hijacking, F skyjacking; '**~führer** *m* pilot; '**~halle** *f* hangar; '**~katastrophe** *f* air disaster; '**~motor** *m* aircraft engine; '**~rumpf** *m* fuselage; '**~träger** *m* aircraft carrier.
Fluidum ['flu:idum] *n* (9²) *fig.* aura.
fluktuieren [fluktu'i:rən] fluctuate.
Flunder ['flundər] *f* (15) flounder.
Flunker|ei [fluŋkə'raɪ] *f* fib(bing); '**2n** (29) fib, tell fibs.
Fluor ['flu:ɔr] ⚗ *n* (3¹, *o.pl.*) fluorine; **2eszieren** [~ɛs'tsi:rən] fluoresce.
Flur [flu:r] **1.** *f* (16) field, plain, *poet.* lea; **2.** *m* (3) (*Haus2*) (entrance-)hall; (*Gang*) passage, corridor; '**~bereinigung** *f* consolidation (of farmland); '**~garderobe** *f* hall-stand; '**~schaden** *m* damage to crops.
Fluß [flus] *m* (4²*) river, stream; (*das Fließen*) flow(ing); *metall.* melting, fusion; *der Rede*: fluency, flow; ⊕ (*~mittel*) flux; *in ~ bringen* (*kommen*) *fig.* get going, get under way; **2**-'**abwärts** downstream; **2**'-**aufwärts** upstream; '**~bett** *n* river-bed, channel; '**~diagramm** *n Computer*: flowchart.
flüssig ['flysiç] liquid (*a. Kapital*), fluid; *Geld*: ready; *Stil*: flowing, fluent; *~ machen Geld*: disengage; *Wertpapier*: realize; '**2keit** *f* liquid; *Zustand*: liquidity (*a. fig.*); '**2keitsbremse** *f* hydraulic brake; '**2keitsgetriebe** *n* fluid drive; '**2kristall** *m Computer*: liquid crystal; '**2kristallanzeige** *f* liquid crystal display.
'**Fluß|lauf** *m* course of a river; '**~mündung** *f* river-mouth; '**~pferd** *n* hippopotamus; '**~schiffahrt** *f* river-navigation; '**~stahl** *m* ingot steel.
flüster|n ['flystərn] (29) *v/i. u. v/t.* whisper; '**2propaganda** *f* whispering campaign; '**2ton** *m* whisper.
Flut [flu:t] *f* (16) flood; (*Ggs. Ebbe*) high tide, flood-tide; (*Überschwemmung*) inundation; *fig.* flood, spate, deluge; '**2en** (26, h. *u.* sn) flow; '**~licht** *n* floodlight; '**~lichtspiel** *n Sport*: floodlit match; '**~marke** *f* tidemark; '**~wechsel** *m* turn of the tide; '**~welle** *f* tidal wave; '**~zeit** *f* flood-tide.
focht [fɔxt] *pret. v. fechten.*
Fock|mast ⚓ ['fɔkmast] *m* foremast; '**~segel** *n* foresail.
Födera|lismus [fødera'lismus] *m* (16², *o. pl.*) federalism; **~tion** [~'tsjo:n] *f* (16) federation.
Fohlen ['fo:lən] **1.** *n* (6) foal; *s. Füllen²*; **2.** **2** (25) foal.
Föhn [fø:n] *m* (3) föhn (wind), foehn.
Föhre ['fø:rə] *f* (15) pine.
Folge ['fɔlgə] *f* (15) (*Wirkung, logische ~*) consequence; (*Ergebnis*) result; (*Fortsetzung*) continuation; (*Aufeinander2*) sequence, succession; (*Reihe, Serie*) series; (*~zeit*) future; (*Zs.-gehöriges*) set; *in der ~* in the sequel, subsequently; *die ~ war* the result was; *zur ~ haben* result in, entail, bring about; *~ leisten* (*dat.*) obey; *e-r Bitte, e-r Vorschrift*: comply with; *e-r Einladung*: accept; *die ~n tragen* take the consequences; '**~-erscheinung** *f* consequence.
'**folgen** (25, sn; *dat.*) *allg.* (*a. geistig*) follow; *Nachfolger*: succeed (*j-m* a p.; *auf acc.* to *a th.*); (*sich ergeben*) follow, ensue (*aus* from); (h.) (*ge-*

horchen) obey; *s. befolgen*; *j-m auf Schritt und Tritt* ~ dog a p.'s footsteps, *polizeilich usw.*: shadow a p.; '**~d** following; (*später*) subsequent; (*nächst*) next; ~es the following; **~dermaßen** ['~dərma:sən] as follows; '**~schwer** of great consequence, momentous.

'**folgerichtig** logical, consistent; '**2keit** *f* logic(al consistency).

folger|n ['fɔlgərn] (29) infer, conclude, gather (*aus* from); '**2ung** *f* inference, deduction, conclusion.

'**Folge|satz** *m gr.* consecutive clause; ⩕ corollary; '**2widrig** inconsistent; '**~widrigkeit** *f* inconsistency.

folglich ['fɔlk-] consequently.

'**folgsam** obedient, docile; '**2keit** *f* obedience.

Foliant [fol'jant] *m* (12) folio (-volume); *weit S.* (heavy) tome.

Folie ['fo:ljə] *f* (15) foil; *fig. als* ~ *dienen* serve as a foil (*dat.* to); '**~n-kartoffeln** *f/pl.* baked potatoes.

Folter ['fɔltər] *f* (15) torture; rack; *fig. auf die* ~ *spannen* torture, keep *a p.* in suspense; '**~bank** *f* rack; '**~instrument** *n* instrument of torture; '**~kammer** *f* torture-chamber; '**~knecht** *m* torturer; '**2n** (29) torture, torment; '**~qual** *f* torture; *fig. a.* torment.

Fön [fø:n] *m* (3) hair-dryer.

Fond [fõ] *m* (11) (*Grundlage*) bottom, ground; (*Hintergrund*) background; *mot. usw.* back (of the car).

Fonds [fõ] *m* (11) † funds *pl.*; *fig.* fund; '**~börse** *f* stock-exchange.

fönen ['fø:nən] (25) blow-dry.

Fontäne [fɔn'tɛ:nə] *f* (15) fountain.

fopp|en ['fɔpən] (25) (*necken*) tease; (*täuschen*) fool, hoax; **2erei** [~ə'raɪ] *f* teasing; hoaxing.

forcieren [fɔr'si:rən] force.

'**Förder|-anlage** *f* conveyor equipment; '**~band** *n* conveyor belt; '**~er** *m*, '**~in** *f* sponsor, *bsd. der Künste*: patron; '**~kohle** ⚒ *f* pit-coal; '**~korb** *m* cage; '**2lich** conducive (*dat.* to); (*nützlich*) useful (for), beneficial (to).

fordern ['fɔrdərn] (29) ask, demand, call for; require (*von j-m* of a p.); *vor Gericht*: summon; *als Eigentum, Recht*: claim; *Preis*: charge; (*heraus*~) challenge; *zuviel* ~ overcharge.

fördern ['fœrdərn] (29) further, advance, promote, *a. Verdauung*: aid; ⚒ mine, *bsd. Kohle*: haul.

'**Forderung** *f* demand; claim; requirement; charge; challenge.

'**Förderung** *f* furtherance, promotion, advancement; ⚒ hauling, haulage; mining.

Forelle [fo'rɛlə] *f* (15) trout.

Forke ['fɔrkə] *f* (15) (pitch)fork.

Form [fɔrm] *f* (16) form; (*Gestalt*) figure, shape; *bsd.* ⊕ design; (*Muster*) model; (*Gieß2*) mo(u)ld; *Sport*: condition; *in* ~ *sein* (*kommen, bleiben*) be in (get into, keep in) form; *die* ~ *wahren* observe the proprieties.

formal [fɔr'ma:l] formal; technical; **2ien** [~'ma:ljən] *pl.*, **2itäten** [~mali'tɛ:tən] *f/pl.* (16) formalities.

Format [~'ma:t] *n* (3) size; *fig.* calib|re, *Am.* -er; *von großem* ~ large-sized.

Formation [~a'tsjo:n] *f* (16) formation; ⚔ (*Verband*) *a.* unit.

'**Formblatt** *n s. Formular.*

Formel ['fɔrməl] *f* (15) form, formula; '**~buch** *n* formulary.

formell [fɔr'mɛl] formal.

'**formen** (25) form, shape, model, fashion, (*a.* ⊕) mo(u)ld.

'**Formen|lehre** *gr. f* accidence; '**~mensch** *m* formalist.

'**Form|fehler** *m* informality; ⚖ formal defect; '**~gebung** ⊕ *f*, '**~gestaltung** *f* design(ing).

for'mieren form; ⚔ *sich* ~ fall in.

förmlich ['fœrmlıç] formal; ceremonial; *P.*: ceremonious; *ein* ~*er Aufruhr* a regular uproar; '**2keit** *f* formality, ceremony.

'**form|los** formless, shapeless; *fig.* informal; '**~schön** beautifully shaped; '**2sache** *f* formality; '**2tief** *n Sport*: loss of form; *ein* ~ *haben* be badly off-form.

Formular [fɔrmu'la:r] *n* (3^1) (printed) form, blank (form).

formu'lier|en formulate; **2ung** *f* formulation.

'**formvollendet** perfect, finished.

forsch [fɔrʃ] smart, dashing; (*schwungvoll*) brisk, peppy.

forschen ['fɔrʃən] (27) (*nach*) search (for); inquire (after).

'**Forscher** *m* (7), '**~in** *f* investigator; (*Wissenschaftler*) (research) scientist; researcher; *s. Forschungsreisende.*

'**Forschung** *f* inquiry, investigation;

gelehrte: research; '**~s-arbeit** *f* research work; '**~s-auftrag** *m* research assignment; '**~sreise** *f* exploring expedition; '**~sreisende** *m* (18) explorer; '**~ssatellit** *m* research satellite.

Forst [fɔrst] *m* (3²) forest; '**~-amt** *n* forestry superintendent's office; '**~-aufseher** *m* (forest-)keeper, gamekeeper; '**~be-amte** *m* forest-officer.

Förster ['fœrstər] *m* (7) forester, forest ranger; **~ei** [~'raɪ] *f* forester's house.

'**Forst|frevel** *m* infringement of the forest-laws; '**~haus** *n* forester's house; '**~mann** *m* forester; '**~-meister** *m* forestry superintendent; '**~revier** *n* forest district; '**~wesen** *n*, '**~wirtschaft** *f* forestry.

Fort¹ ⚔ [fo:r] *n* (11) fort.

fort² [fɔrt] (*weg*) away; gone; (*weiter*) on; (*vorwärts*) forward; *in e-m ~* uninterruptedly; *~ und ~* continually; *und so ~* and so forth *od.* on; *sie sind schon ~* they have already left; *ich muß ~* I must be off.

'**fort...** (*vgl. a. die Zssgn mit* **weg...**): **~'-an** henceforth; '**~bestehen** *v/i.* continue, survive; '**~bewegen** move (*a. sich ~*); drive; '**⁀bewegung** *f* locomotion; *sich* '**~bilden** continue one's studies; '**⁀bildungs-anstalt** (*od.* **-schule**) *f* continuation school *od.* classes *pl.*; '**~bleiben** stay away; '**⁀dauer** *f* continuance; '**~dauern** continue, last; '**~dauernd** lasting, permanent; continuous; '**⁀-entwick(e)lung** *f* (further) development; '**~fahren** depart; *fig.* continue, go on; '**⁀fall** *m s. Wegfall*; '**~fallen** *s. wegfallen*; '**~führen** continue, go on with; *Geschäft, Krieg*: carry on; '**⁀führung** *f* continuation; carrying on; '**⁀gang** *m* departure; *s. Fortschritt, Fortdauer*; '**~gehen** (sn) go (away), leave; (*weitergehen*) go on; (*fortschreiten*) proceed; (*fortdauern*) continue; '**~geschritten** *Schüler usw.*: advanced; '**~gesetzt** continual; '**~helfen** (*j-m*) help *a. p.* on; '**~kommen** (sn) *s. wegkommen*; (*weiterkommen*) get on *od.* along; F *mach, daß du fortkommst!* be off!, *sl.* beat it!; '**⁀kommen** *n* getting on, progress; (*Lebensunterhalt*) living; '**~lassen** *s. weglassen*; '**~laufen** (sn) run away ([*vor*] *j-m* from a p.); (*weitergehen*) run on, be continued; '**~laufend** continuous, running; '**~leben** live on; '**~pflanzen** (*a. sich*) propagate; '**⁀pflanzung** *f* propagation; *biol. a.* reproduction; '**⁀pflanzungs-trieb** *m* reproductive instinct; '**~reißen**: *j-n mit sich ~ fig.* carry a p. (away) with o.s.; '**⁀satz** *m* (*Vorsprung*) projection; *anat.*, ⚘ process; '**~schaffen** remove; '**~schreiten** (sn) advance, proceed; '**~schreitend** progressive; '**⁀schritt** *m* progress; *~e machen* make progress *od.* headway; *große ~e machen* make great strides; '**~schrittlich** progressive; '**~setzen** continue (*a. sich*), pursue; '**⁀setzung** *f* continuation, pursuit; *~ folgt* to be continued; *sich* '**~stehlen** steal (*od.* sneak) away; '**~stoßen** push away; '**~während** continual, continuous; (*ewig*) perpetual; '**~ziehen** *v/t.* draw away; *v/i.* (sn) *aus der Wohnung*: remove; ⚔ march off; *Vögel*: migrate.

Forum ['fo:rum] *n* (9²) forum.

fossil [fɔ'si:l], ⁀ *n* (8²) fossil.

Fötus ['fø:tus] *m* (4¹) f(o)etus.

'**Foto...** *s. Photo...*

Foul [faul] *n* (11) *Sport*: foul; '**⁀en** (25) foul.

Foyer [foa'je:] *n* (11) *thea.* foyer, *Am. od. parl.* lobby; *im Hotel*: foyer, lounge.

Fracht [fraxt] *f* (16) (*~ladung*) load, goods *pl.*, freight; ⚓ cargo; (*~beförderung*) carriage, *Am.* freight (-age); *s. ~geld*; '**~brief** *m* way-bill; ⚓ *u. Am.* bill of lading; '**~dampfer** *m* cargo-steamer; '**⁀en** (26) freight, load; '**~er** *m* freighter; '**⁀frei** carriage paid; '**~geld** *n* carriage, freight (-age); '**~gut** *n* goods *pl.*, *Am.* ordinary freight; *als ~* by goods train, *Am.* by freight train; '**~raum** *m* cargo compartment; (*Ladefähigkeit*) freight capacity; '**~satz** *m* freight rate; '**~schiff** *n* cargo-ship, freighter; '**~stück** *n* package; '**~verkehr** *m* goods traffic.

Frack [frak] *m* (11 *u.* 3³) dress- (*od.* tail-)coat; *im ~* in full evening dress; '**~-anzug** *m* dress-suit; '**~hemd** *n* dress-shirt.

Frage ['fra:gə] *f* (15) question (*a. fig. Problem*); *gr., rhet.* interrogation; (*Erkundigung*) inquiry; *e-e ~ tun od. stellen* ask a question; *außer ~ stehen* be beyond question; *in ~*

kommen come into question; *das kommt nicht in* ~ that's out (of the question); *in* ~ *stellen* make dubious *od.* uncertain; *in* ~ *ziehen* (call in) question; *ohne* ~ beyond question; '**~bogen** *m* questionnaire; '**~form** *gr. f* interrogative form; '**~fürwort** *n* interrogative pronoun; '**⁀n** *v/t u. v/i.* (25) ask; (*ausfragen*) question; interrogate; (*j-n*) et. ~ ask (a p.) a question; ~ *nach* ask for; *s. erkundigen*; (*sich kümmern um*) care about; *j-n nach s-m Namen, dem Wege usw.* ~ ask a p. his name, the way *etc.*; *ich frage mich, warum usw.* I wonder why *etc.*; *es fragt sich, ob* it is a question whether; *gefragt* ✝ in demand.

'**Frager** *m* (7), '**~in** *f* questioner.

'**Frage|satz** *m* interrogative sentence; '**~steller** *m* (7) questioner; '**~stunde** *parl. f* question-time; '**~wort** *n* interrogative; '**~zeichen** *n* question-mark, mark of interrogation, *Am. mst* interrogation point.

frag|lich ['frɑ:kliç] (*zweifelhaft*) questionable; (*in Rede stehend*) in question (*hinter su.*); '**~los** unquestionably, beyond (all) question.

Fragment [frag'mɛnt] *n* (3) fragment; **⁀arisch** [~'tɑ:riʃ] fragmentary.

fragwürdig ['frɑ:k-] questionable.

Fraktion *parl.* [frak'tsjo:n] *f* (16) parliamentary party; '**~s-vorsitzende** *m* leader (*od.* chairman) of the (parliamentary) group, *Am.* floor leader.

Fraktur [frak'tu:r] *f* ⚕ fracture; *typ.* (*a.* **~schrift** *f*) German type.

frank[1] [fraŋk] frank, free; ~ *und frei* frankly, plainly.

Frank[2] *m* (12), '**~en** *m* (6) *Münze*: franc.

'**Franke** *m* (13), **Fränkin** *f* (16[1]) [Franconian.]

fran'kier|en stamp, prepay; **⁀maschine** *f* franking machine.

franko ['fraŋko] post-paid, prepaid, post-free; *Paket*: carriage paid.

Franse ['franzə] *f* (15) fringe.

Franz|band ['frants-] *m* calf-binding; **~branntwein** ['~brant-] *m* surgical spirit.

Franziskaner [frantsis'kɑ:nər] *m* (7) Franciscan friar.

Franzose [fran'tso:zə] *m* (13) Frenchman; *die* ~*n pl.* the French.

Franzö|sin [~'tsø:zin] *f* Frenchwoman; **⁀sisch** French.

frappant [fra'pant] striking.

fräsen ['frɛ:zən] (27) *v/t.* mill.

Fräsmaschine ['frɛ:s-] *f* milling machine.

Fraß [frɑ:s] **1.** *m* (3[2]) (*Essen*) *sl.* grub; (*Viehfutter*) feed; ⚕ caries; **2.** ⁀ *pret. v. fressen* 1.

Fratze ['fratsə] *f* (15) grimace; F (*Gesicht*) mug; (*Zerrbild*) caricature; e-e ~ *schneiden* make a grimace; '**⁀nhaft** grotesque.

Frau [frau] *f* (16) woman; (*Herrin*) mistress; (*Edelfrau; Dame*) lady; (*Ehe⁀*) wife; *vor Namen*: Mrs. (*Aussprache*: 'misiz); *gnädige* ~ madam; *m-e* ~ my wife, *förmlich*: *Mrs Brown etc.*; *zur* ~ *begehren, geben, nehmen* ask, give, take in marriage.

'**Frauen|-arzt** *m* gyn(a)ecologist; '**~bewegung** *f* Women's Lib; '**⁀haft** womanly; '**~klinik** *f* hospital for women; '**~kloster** *n* nunnery; '**~krankheit** *f* women's disease; '**~leiden** *n* women's complaint; '**~rechte** *n/pl.* women's rights *pl.*; '**~rechtlerin** *f* suffragette; '**~sport** *m* women's sports *pl.*; '**~stimmrecht** *n* women's suffrage; '**~welt** *f* womankind, women *pl.*; '**~zimmer** *n mst contp.* woman, *sl.* skirt.

Fräulein ['frɔʏlaɪn] *n* (6) young lady; unmarried lady; *Titel*: Miss; (*Kellnerin*) waitress; *Ihr* ~ *Tochter* your daughter; *teleph. das* ~ *vom Amt* the operator.

'**fraulich** womanly.

frech [frɛç] impudent, insolent; F saucy, cheeky, *Am. sl.* fresh; '**⁀heit** *f* impudence, insolence; F sauciness.

Fregatte [fre'gatə] *f* (15) frigate; **~nkapitän** *m* commander.

frei [fraɪ] free (*von* from, of); (*offen*) frank; (*unabhängig*) independent; (*von Lasten*) exempt (*von* from); *Stelle*: vacant; *Feld, Himmel*: open; (*unentgeltlich*) free (of charge); (*porto*~) (pre)paid; ~*er Beruf* liberal (*od.* independent) profession; *Journalist, Künstler*: free-lance; *Straße usw.*: clear; ✝ ~ (*ins*) *Haus* free of charge; ✝ ~ *an Bord* free on board (*abbr.* f.o.b.); ~ *heraus* (*offen*) frankly, plainly; *im* ⁀*en, unter* ~*em Himmel* in the open air; *ich bin so* ~ I take the liberty (*zu inf.* of *ger.*); ~ *umherlaufen* be at large; *im* ⁀*en la-*

gern camp out; *~er Mensch* free agent; *~e Künste f/pl.* liberal arts; *~er Nachmittag* afternoon off, half-holiday; *~er Tag* day off, holiday; *~ sprechen Redner*: speak offhand *od.* extempore; *Straße ~!* road clear!; *s. ausgehen, Fuß, Hand, Stück usw.*

'**Frei|bad** *n* open-air swimming pool; '**2beruflich** free-lance; '**~betrag** *m* allowance; **~beuter** ['~bɔʏtər] *m* (7) freebooter, filibuster; '**~billett** *n s. Freikarte*; '**2bleibend** *Preis*: without engagement; '**~brief** *m* charter, (letters *pl.*) patent; *fig.* warrant; '**~denker** *m* free-thinker; '**~denke'rei** *f*, '**2denkerisch** free-thinking.

freien ['fraɪən] (25) *v/i.*: *~ um* court, woo; *v/t.* marry.

'**Freier** *m* (7) suitor; *rhet.* wooer; *auf* '**~sfüßen** *gehen* go courting.

'**Frei|-exemplar** *n* free copy, presentation copy; '**~fahrschein** 🚌 *m* free (travel) ticket; '**~frau** *f* baroness; '**~gabe** *f* release; *bewirtschafteter Ware*: decontrol; '**2geben** release; *s. freilassen*; *gesperrtes Konto*: deblock; *Schule*: give a holiday; *Straße usw.*: open; *Ware*: decontrol; '**2gebig** liberal, generous; '**~gebigkeit** *f* liberality, generosity; '**~gehege** *n* open-air enclosure; '**~geist** *m* free-thinker; '**~gepäck** *n* allowed (*od.* free) luggage; '**~grenze** ☤ *f* duty exemption limit; '**2haben** *Schule*: have a holiday; *Dienst*: have a day off; '**~hafen** *m* free port; '**2halten** *j-n*: pay for; *e-n Platz*: keep free; ☤ *Angebot*: keep open; '**~handel** *m* free trade; '**2händig** without support; *Zeichnen*: freehand; ⚖ privately; ☤ direct.

'**Freiheit** *f* (16) liberty, freedom (*von* from); *v. Lasten*: exemption (from); *bürgerliche ~* civil liberty; *dichterische ~* poetic licen|ce, *Am.* -se; *sich die ~ nehmen zu tun* take the liberty of doing; *in ~ setzen, j-m die ~ schenken* set at liberty; '**2lich** liberal; '**~sberaubung** *f* deprivation of liberty; '**~s-entzug** ⚖ *m* detention; '**~skampf** *m* struggle for freedom; '**~skrieg** *m* war of independence; '**~sstrafe** *f* prison sentence; imprisonment.

freihe'raus frankly.

'**Frei|herr** *m* baron; '**~in** *f* baroness; '**~karte** *f* free (*thea. a.* complimentary) ticket; '**~körperkultur** *f* nudism, naturism; '**~korps** *n* volunteer corps; '**2lassen** release, liberate, set free; *Sklaven*: emancipate; '**~lassung** *f* release, liberation; emancipation; '**~lauf** *m* free-wheel; '**2legen** lay open; '**2lich** certainly, to be sure; *einräumend*: of course, though; '**~lichtbühne** *f* open-air stage; '**2machen** get free; *Weg usw.*: clear; ✉ prepay, stamp; *sich ~* disengage o.s.; *vom Dienst usw.*: take time off; '**~marke** *f* (postage) stamp; '**~maurer** *m* freemason; '**~maure'rei** *f* freemasonry; '**~maurerloge** *f* freemason's lodge; '**~mut** *m* frankness; **2mütig** ['~myːtiç] frank, candid, open; '**2schaffend:** *~er Künstler* free-lance artist; '**~schar** *f s. Freikorps*; **~schärler** ['~ʃɛːrlər] *m* gue(r)rilla, irregular; '**2schwimmen:** *sich ~* pass one's 15 minute swimming test; '**2setzen** release; *Arbeitnehmer*: make redundant; '**~sinn** *m* liberalism; '**2sinnig** liberal; '**2sprechen** absolve (*von* from), ⚖ acquit (of); *Lehrling*: release from his articles; '**~sprechung** *f* absolutism, acquittal; release *of an apprentice*; '**~spruch** ⚖ *m* acquittal; '**~staat** *m* free state; republic; '**~statt** *f*, '**~stätte** *f* asylum, refuge; '**2stehen:** *es steht dir frei zu tun* you are free (*od.* at liberty) to; '**2stehend** *Haus*: detached; '**~stelle** *f* scholarship; '**2stellen** ⚔ exempt (from military service); *Angestellte*: lay off; *j-m et. ~* leave to a p.('s discretion); '**~stil** *m Sport*: free style; '**~stilringen** *n* free-style wrestling; catch-as-catch-can; '**~stoß** *m Fußball*: free kick; '**~stunde** *f* leisure hour; '**~tag** *m* Friday; '**~tod** *m* voluntary death, suicide; '**2tragend** cantilever, self-supporting; '**~treppe** *f* outside staircase, perron, *Am.* stoop; '**~-übungen** *f/pl.* free excercises; '**~-umschlag** *m* stamped envelope; '**~wild** *n* fair game; '**2willig** free, voluntary, spontaneous; *adv. a.* of one's own free will; *sich ~ erbieten od. melden* volunteer; **~willige** ['~viligə] *m* (18) volunteer; '**~willigkeit** *f* voluntariness, spontaneity; '**~wurf** *m Basketball etc.*: free throw; '**~zeit** *f* free (*od.* spare, leisure, off) time; '**~zeitkleidung** *f* leisure wear; **2zügig** ['~tsyːgiç] free to move; *fig.* unhampered; (*großzügig*) permissive; '~**zügigkeit** *f* freedom of movement; permissiveness.

fremd [frɛmt] strange; (*ausländisch*) foreign; (*nicht dazugehörig*) extraneous; *fig.* (*zuwider*) alien; ~*es Gut* other people's property; *ich bin hier* ~ I am a stranger here.

'**fremd·artig** strange, odd; '**꞉keit** *f* strangeness, oddness.

Fremde[1] ['frɛmdə] *f* (15) foreign country; *in der* (*od. die*) ~ abroad; '~[2] *m, f* (18) stranger; (*Ausländer*) foreigner, *nicht naturalisiert*: alien; (*Gast*) guest, visitor; '~**nbuch** *n* visitors' book; '~**nführer** *m* guide; '~**nheim** *n* boarding house, private hotel; '~**n·industrie** *f* tourist industry; '~**nlegion** ⚔ *f* Foreign Legion; '~**nverkehr** *m* tourist traffic; '~**nzimmer** *n* spare (bed)room, guest room.

'**fremdgehen** F (sn) two-time.

'**Fremd|herrschaft** *f* foreign rule; '~**körper** *m* ⚕ foreign body; *fig.* alien element; **꞉ländisch** ['~lɛndiʃ] foreign; ~**ling** ['~liŋ] *m* (3[1]) *s. Fremde*[2]; '~**sprache** *f*, '**꞉sprachlich** foreign language; '~**sprachenkorrespondent** *m* foreign correspondence clerk; '~**sprachensekretärin** *f* linguist-secretary; '~**wort** *n* foreign word.

frequentieren [frekvɛn'tiːrən] } [frequent.]

Fre'quenz [~ts] *f* (16) *phys.* frequency; (*Besucherzahl*) attendance.

fressen ['frɛsən] **1.** eat, feed; (*a. v/i.*; [30]); *Raubtier*: devour; F *Mensch*: devour, (*a. v/i.*) gorge; ⚗ corrode; *nur v/i.* (h.) ⊕ *Lager usw.*: seize; *fig.* swallow, consume; *e-m Tier* (*Gras usw.*) *zu* ~ *geben* feed an animal (on grass *etc.*); **2.** ꞉ *n* (6) feed, food; *ein gefundenes* ~ *für ihn* just what he wanted.

'**Fresser** *m* (7) voracious eater, glutton; ~**ei** [~'raɪ] *f* gluttony.

'**Freß|gier** *f* gluttony, greediness; '**꞉gierig** gluttonous, greedy; '~**napf** *m* feeding dish.

Frettchen ['frɛtçən] *n* (6) ferret.

Freude ['frɔʏdə] *f* (15) joy, gladness; (*Wonne*) delight; (*Vergnügen*) pleasure; ~ *haben* (*od. finden*) *an* (*dat.*) take pleasure in; *mit* ~*n* gladly, with pleasure.

'**Freuden...** *in Zssgn mst* ... of joy; '~**botschaft** *f* glad tidings *pl.*; '~**feier** *f*, '~**fest** *n* feast, rejoicing; '~**feuer** *n* bonfire; '~**geschrei** *n* shouts *pl.* of joy; '~**haus** *n* brothel, disorderly house; '~**mädchen** *n* prostitute; '~**rausch** *m*, '~**taumel** *m* transports *pl.* of joy; '~**tag** *m* day of rejoicing, red-letter day.

'**freudestrahlend** radiant with joy.

'**freudig** joyful; ~*es Ereignis* happy event; '**꞉keit** *f* joyfulness.

freudlos ['frɔʏtloːs] joyless, cheerless.

'**freuen** (25): *es freut mich, zu inf.* I am glad (*od.* pleased) to ...; *es freut mich, daß du gekommen bist* I am glad (*od.* happy) you have come; *sich* ~ (*über acc., zu inf.*) be glad (of, at; to *inf.*), be pleased (with; to *inf.*), be happy (about; to *inf.*); *sich* ~ *an* (*dat.*) delight in, enjoy; *sich* ~ *auf* (*acc.*) look forward to; *ich freue mich darüber* I am glad of it.

Freund [frɔʏnt] *m* (3) (*engS.* boy) friend; ~**in** ['~din] *f* (16[1]) (*engS.* girl) friend; ~ *der Musik usw.* lover; **꞉lich** ['frɔʏnt-] friendly, kind, genial (*a. Klima*); *Zimmer*: cheerful; '~**lichkeit** *f* kindness; *j-m e-e* ~ *erweisen* do a p. a kindness; '**꞉los** friendless; '~**schaft** *f* friendship; ~ *schließen mit* make friends with; '**꞉schaftlich** friendly; '~**schaftsspiel** *n Sport*: friendly match.

Frevel ['freːfəl] *m* (7) outrage (*an dat., gegen* on); (*Mutwille*) wantonness; '**꞉haft** wicked, outrageous, wanton, impious; '**꞉n** (29) commit a crime; ~ *an dat., gegen* outrage; '~**tat** *f* outrage.

freventlich ['~fəntliç] *s. frevelhaft.*

Frevler ['~flər] *m* (7), '~**in** *f* (16[1]) offender, transgressor.

Friede(n) ['friːdə(n)] *m* (13[1][6]) peace; *im* ~ at peace; ~ *schließen* make peace; *laß mich in* ~*!* leave me alone!

'**Friedens|bewegung** *f* peace movement; '~**bruch** *m* breach of (the) peace; '~**forschung** *f* peace research; '~**gespräche** *n/pl.* peace talks; '~**pfeife** *f* peace-pipe; '~**produktion** *f* peace-time production; '~**schluß** *m* conclusion of peace; '~**stärke** ⚔ *f* peace establishment; '~**stifter(in** *f*) *m* peace-maker; '~**truppe** *f* peace-keeping force; '~**verhandlungen** *f/pl.* peace-negotiations; '~**vertrag** *m* peace-treaty.

fried|fertig ['fri:t-] peaceable, pacific; '**♀fertigkeit** *f* peaceableness; '**♀hof** *m* churchyard, cemetery; '**~lich**, '**~sam** peaceable; (*ungestört*) peaceful; '**~liebend** peace-loving; '**~los** peaceless.
frieren ['fri:rən] *v/t. u. v/i.* (30, h. *u.* sn) freeze; *mich friert* I am (*od.* feel) cold; *mich friert an den Füßen* my feet are cold.
Fries [fri:s] *m* (4) △ frieze (*a. Tuch*).
Fries|e ['fri:zə] *m* (13), '**~in** (16[1]) *f*, '**♀isch**, **~länder** ['fri:slɛndər] *m* (7), '**~länderin** *f* (16[1]) Frisian.
Frikadelle [frika'dɛlə] *f* (15) (meat) rissole.
Frikass|ee [frika'se:] *n* (11), **♀ieren** [~'si:rən] fricassee.
frisch [friʃ] *allg.* fresh; *Brot*: new; *Ei*: new-laid; *Wäsche*: clean; (*kühl*) cool; (*neu*) new; (*kürzlich geschehen*) recent; (*kräftig*) vigorous; (*blühend*) florid; (*munter*) brisk, lively; *von ~em* afresh; *j-n auf ~er Tat ergreifen od. ertappen* take a p. in the very act, take a p. red-handed; *~ gestrichen!* wet paint!; '**♀e** *f* (15) freshness; vigo(u)r; '**~en** (27) *Eisen*: refine; '**♀fleisch** *n* butcher's meat; '**♀haltebeutel** *m* keep-fresh bag.
Friseur [fri'zø:r] *m* (3[1]) hairdresser, *Am.* (*für Herren*) *a.* barber; '**~laden** *m* hairdresser's shop, *Am.* (*für Herren*) barbershop.
Friseuse [~'zø:zə] *f* (15) ladies' hairdresser.
fri'sieren: *j-n ~* dress a p.'s hair; F *fig. Bericht usw.*: cook, doctor; *Motor etc.*: F hype (*od.* soup) up.
Fri'sier|mantel *m* peignoir (*fr.*); **~salon** *m* hairdressing saloon; **~tisch** *m*, **~toilette** *f* dressing-table, *Am.* dresser.
Frist [frist] *f* (16) (space of) time; (*festgesetzter Zeitpunkt*) (appointed *od.* fixed) time, (set) term; time-limit; (*Aufschub*) respite, delay; '**♀en** (26): *sein Leben ~* barely manage to exist; make a bare living; '**♀gerecht** timely; '**♀los** without notice.
Frisur [fri'zu:r] *f* (16) hair-style, coiffure (*fr.*), *Am.* hairdo.
Fri|teuse [fri'tø:zə] *f* (15) deep-frying (*od.* chip) pan; **♀'tieren** deep-fry.
frivol [fri'vo:l] frivolous, flippant; **♀ität** [~i'tɛ:t] *f* frivolity, flippancy.
froh [fro:] glad, cheerful, happy; (*freudig*) joyful; *s-s Lebens nicht ~ werden* have no end of trouble.
fröhlich ['frø:liç] merry, gay, cheerful; '**♀keit** *f* gaiety, cheerfulness.
froh'locken exult (*über acc.* at); (*triumphieren*) triumph (over).
'**Frohsinn** *m* cheerfulness.
fromm [frɔm] (18[2]) pious, religious; *Pferd*: quiet; *~er Betrug* pious fraud; *~er Wunsch* idle wish.
Frömmelei [frœmə'laɪ] *f* (16) affected piety, bigotry.
frömmeln (29) be bigoted.
'**Frömm|igkeit** *f* piety; '**~ler(in** *f*) *m* bigot, sanctimonious person.
Fron [fro:n] *f* (16), '**~arbeit** *f*, '**~dienst** *m* compulsory labo(u)r *od.* service; *fig.* drudgery.
frönen ['frø:nən] (25) (*dat.*) indulge in.
Fron'leichnamsfest *n* (feast of) Corpus Christi.
Front [frɔnt] *f* (16) front (*bsd.* ⚔ *u.* △), △ *a.* face; *an der ~* at the front; *~ machen gegen* turn against; *Sport*: *in ~ gehen* take the lead; **♀al** [frɔn'tɑ:l] frontal; head-on; **~alzusammenstoß** *mot. m* head-on collision; '**~antrieb** *mot. m* front-wheel drive; '**~kämpfer** *m* combatant; *ehemaliger*: ex-serviceman, *Am.* veteran; '**~lader** *m* (7) *Video, Hi-Fi*: frontloader; '**~soldat** *m* front-line soldier; '**~wechsel** *m* change of front, face-about.
fror [fro:r] *pret. v. frieren.*
Frosch [frɔʃ] *m* (3[2] *u.* 3[3]) frog; *Feuerwerk*: squib; '**~perspektive** *f* worm's-eye view.
Frost [frɔst] *m* (3[2] *u.* 3[3]) frost; (*Kältegefühl*) chill, coldness; '**♀beständig** frost-resistant; '**~beule** *f* chilblain.
frösteln ['frœstəln] (29) feel chilly, shiver (with cold).
'**frostig** frosty, chilly (*beide a. fig.*); '**♀keit** *f* frostiness.
'**Frost|salbe** *f* chilblain ointment; '**~schaden** *m* damage done by frost; *am Körper*: frostbite; '**~schutzmittel** *n* anti-freezing agent; anti-freeze; '**~schutzscheibe** *mot. f* anti-frost screen; '**~wetter** *n* frosty weather.
Frottee [frɔ'te:] *n* (11) terry (cloth).
frottier|en [frɔ'ti:rən] rub; **♀(hand)tuch** *n* Turkish (*od.* terry) towel.
Frucht [fruxt] *f* (14[1]) fruit (*a. fig.*); (*Getreide*) corn; *fig.* effect, result.
'**frucht|bar** fruitful (*a. biol.*), fertile

(*beide a. fig.*; *an dat.* in); (*produktiv*) prolific; ~ *machen* fertilize; '**⁓barkeit** *f* fruitfulness, fertility; '**~bringend** fruit-bearing; *fig.* productive; '**~en** (26) be of use, have effect; '**⁓knoten** ⚘ *m* seed-vessel; '**~los** fruitless; '**⁓losigkeit** *f* fruitlessness; '**⁓presse** *f* fruit press; '**⁓saft** *m* fruit-juice.

frugal [fru'gɑ:l] frugal.

früh [fry:] (*zeitig*) early; (*morgens*) in the morning; *von ~ bis spät* from morning till night; *~er* earlier, sooner; (*ehemals*) former; *~er als a.* prior to; *~er oder später* sooner or later; *~er habe ich geraucht* (*jetzt nicht mehr*) I used to smoke; *~est* earliest, soonest; *~estens* at the earliest; *~e Morgenstunden* (*1—4 Uhr*) small hours; '**⁓-aufsteher**(**in** *f*) *m* early riser.

Früh|e ['fry:ə] *f* (15) early hour *od.* morning; *in aller ~* very early; '**~-erkennung** ⚕ *f* early diagnosis; '**~geburt** *f* premature birth; '**~gemüse** *n* early vegetable(s *pl.*); '**~gottesdienst** *m* morning service; '**~jahr** *n*, '**~ling** *m* (3[1]) spring; '**~konzert** *n* morning concert; '**~messe** *f* morning prayer, mat(t)ins *pl.*; ⁓'**morgens** early in the morning; '**~-obst** *n* early fruit; '**⁓reif** early(-ripe); *fig.* precocious; '**~reife** *f* earliness; *fig.* precocity; '**~rentner**(**in** *f*) *m* person who has retired early; '**~schicht** *f* early (morning) shift; '**~schoppen** *m* morning pint; '**~sport** *m* early morning exercises *pl.*; '**~stadium** *n* early stage; '**~stück** *n* breakfast; '**⁓stücken** (25) (have) breakfast; '**~warnsystem** *n* early warning system; '**⁓zeitig** early; *fig.* premature; '**~zeitigkeit** *f* earliness; *fig.* prematurity; '**~zug** 🚂 *m* early train; '**~zündung** *f* pre-ignition, advanced ignition.

frustrieren [frus'tri:rən] frustrate.

Fuchs [fuks] *m* (4[2]) fox (*a. fig.*); *Pferd*: sorrel (horse); *univ.* freshman; '**~bau** *m* fox-earth; '**⁓en** (27) F madden; *sich ~* be furious (*über acc.* at, about); **~ie** ⚘ ['fuksjə] *f* (15) fuchsia; '**⁓ig** foxy; F (*ärgerlich*) furious.

Füchsin ['fyksin] *f* she-fox, vixen.

'**Fuchs|jagd** *f* fox-hunt(ing); '**~pelz** *m* (fur of a) fox; '**⁓rot** fox-colo(u)red; '**~schwanz** *m* foxtail; (*Säge*) pad-saw; ⚘ amarant(h); '**⁓teufels**'**wild** mad with rage.

Fuchtel ['fuxtəl] *f* (15) rod; *unter j-s ~* under a p.'s thumb; '**⁓n** (29) *mit* wave (about), brandish.

Fuder ['fu:dər] *n* (7) cart-load.

fuchtig ['fuxtiç] furious.

Fug [fu:k] *m* (3): *mit ~ und Recht* with full right.

Fuge ['fu:ge] *f* (15) joint, seam; (*Falz*) rabbet; ♪ fugue; *aus den ~n bringen* put out of joint, disjoint; '**⁓n** (25) join; rabbet.

fügen ['fʏ:gən] (25) *s. an~, hinzu~, zusammen~*; (*verfügen*) ordain, dispose; *sich ~* (*dat.*) *od. in* (*acc.*) (*nachgeben*) comply with, resign o.s. to, submit to; (*sich anpassen*) accommodate o.s. to; *es fügt sich* it (so) happens. [justly.]

füglich ['fy:k-] *adv.* conveniently,

'**fügsam** pliant, supple; (*lenksam*) tractable; (*folgsam*) obedient; '**⁓keit** *f* pliancy; obedience.

Fügung ['~guŋ] *f* (*Zs.-treffen*) coincidence; (*in acc.*) resignation (to), submission (to); ~ *Gottes* dispensation (of Providence).

'**fühlbar** sensible, palpable, tangible; *geistig*: perceptible, noticeable; *~er Mangel* felt want; '**⁓keit** *f* sensibility; perceptibility.

fühl|en ['fy:lən] (25) feel; *sich glücklich usw. ~* feel happy *etc.*; '**⁓er** *m* (7), '**⁓horn** *n* feeler; '**⁓ung** *f* touch, contact; ~ *haben* (*verlieren*) *mit* be in (lose) touch with; ~ *nehmen mit j-m* get in(to) touch with a p., contact a p.

fuhr [fu:r] *pret. v. fahren.*

Fuhre ['fu:rə] *f* (15) cart-load.

führen ['fy:rən] (25) lead; *e-m Ziele zu*: conduct, guide; ⚔ (*befehligen*) command; (*weg~*) take; *thea. j-n an seinen Platz*: usher; (*tragen*) carry; *Bücher, Liste*: keep; *Geschäft, Gespräch, Prozeß*: carry on; *Namen*: bear; *Feder, Waffe*: (*handhaben*) wield; *Ware*: keep, carry; *Wagen*: drive; *e-e Sprache*: use; *e-n Schlag*: strike; *e-n Titel*: bear, hold; (*beaufsichtigen, verwalten*) manage; *sich gut usw. ~* conduct o.s.; *Besuch hinein~* show in; *durch das Haus ~* show over the house; *zum Munde ~* raise to one's lips; *die Aufsicht ~ über* (*acc.*) superintend; *den Beweis ~* prove; *ein Geschäft ~* carry on (*od.*

run) a business *od.* shop; (*j-m*) *den Haushalt* (*od. die Wirtschaft*) ~ keep house (for a p.); *Klage* (*od. Beschwerde*) ~ complain (*über acc.* of); *Krieg* (*mit j-m*) ~ wage war (with a p.), make war ([up]on a p.); *ein Leben* ~ live a life; *s. Licht, Schild, Vorsitz, Wort usw.*; *v/i.* lead (*zu* to; *a. fig.*); *Sport*: (hold the) lead; *Sport*: *mit Punkten* ~ be ahead (*z. B. 6 : 2*).

'**führend** leading, (top-)ranking, prominent, top; ~ *sein* (hold the) lead, be at the top.

'**Führer** *m* (7), '**~in** *f* leader; (*Leiter*) conductor; (*Wegweiser*) guide (*a. als Buch u.* ⊕); (*Verwalter*) manager(ess *f*); *e-s Wagens*: driver; ✈ pilot; *Sport*: captain; ⚔ (*Zug*~, *Gruppen*~) leader, (*Kompanie*~) commander; '**~los** guideless; *Wagen*: driverless; ✈ pilotless; '**~raum** ✈ *m* cockpit; '**~schaft** *f* leadership; '**~schein** *m mot.* driving licence, *Am.* driver's license; ✈ pilot's licence, *Am.* pilot's certificate; '**~sitz** *m* driver's seat; ✈ (pilot's) cockpit.

'**Fuhr|geld** *n*, '**~lohn** *m* carriage, cartage; '**~mann** *m* (*pl. Fuhrleute*) carrier; (*Kutscher*) driver; '**~park** *m* park; (*Wagen*) fleet.

'**Führung** *f e-m Ziele zu*: guidance; *Sport u. fig.*: lead; (*Leitung*) conduct, direction, management; leadership, ⚔ command; *in e-m Museum usw.*: showing round; *e-s Titels*: use; (*Benehmen*) conduct; ~ *der Bücher* book-keeping; ⚔ *innere* ~ moral leadership; ⊕ guide; *die* ~ *übernehmen* take the lead (*a. Sport*); *in* ~ *liegen* be in the lead; '**~szeugnis** *n* certificate of conduct; *für Personal*: character.

'**Fuhr|-unternehmen** *n* (firm of) carriers *pl. od.* haul(i)ers *pl.*; '**~unternehmer** *m* carrier, haul(i)er, *Am. a.* teamster; '**~werk** *n* vehicle, cart, wag(g)on.

'**Füllbleistift** *m* propelling pencil.

Fülle ['fylə] *f* (15) ful(l)ness (*a. fig.*); (*reicher Vorrat*) plenty, abundance; (*Körper*~) stoutness; '**~n**[1] (25) fill (*a. sich*); *Braten usw.*: stuff; *Zahn*: stop, fill; *auf Flaschen* ~ bottle.

Füllen[2] ['fylən] *n* (6) foal; (*Hengst*~) colt; (*Stuten*~) filly.

'**Füll|er** F *m* (7) = '**~feder(halter** *m*) *f* fountain-pen; '**~horn** *n* horn of plenty; **~sel** ['~zəl] *n* (7) stuffing; '**~ung** *f* filling (*a. Zahn*~); (*Tür*~) panel; (*Ladung*) charge; *s. Füllsel*; '**~wort** *n* expletive.

fummeln F ['fuməln] (29) fumble; (*knutschen*) pet.

Fund [funt] *m* (3) finding, discovery; (*Gefundenes*) find; *einen* ~ *tun od. machen* have a find.

Fundament [funda'mɛnt] *n* (3) foundation(s *pl.*); **~al** [~mɛn'tɑːl] fundamental; **~ieren** [~'tiːrən] lay the foundation(s) of.

'**Fund|büro** *n* lost property office; '**~grube** *f fig.* mine, storehouse.

fundieren [fun'diːrən] found; *Schuld*: fund, consolidate.

'**Fund|-ort** *m* place where a th. was found; '**~sachen** *f/pl.* lost property *sg.*

fünf [fynf] **1.** five; ~ *gerade sein lassen* stretch a point; **2.** ~ *f* (16) (number) five; *auf Würfeln u. Spielkarten*: *a.* cinque; '**~blätt(e)rig** five-leaved; '**~-eck** *n* pentagon; '**~-eckig** pentagonal; '**~erlei** of five kinds; '**~fach**, **~fältig** ['~fɛltiç] fivefold; '**~hundert** five hundred; **~jährig** ['~jɛːriç] five-year-old; '**~jährlich** every five years; '**~kampf** *m Sport*: pentathlon; '**~linge** *m/pl.* quintuplets *pl.*; '**~mal** five times; '**~malig** done (*od.* occurring) five times; '**~seitig** five-sided; '**~stellig** *Zahl*: of five digits; **~stöckig** ['~ʃtœkiç] five-storied; **~tägig** ['~tɛːgiç] of five days; '**~te** fifth; *fig. das* ~ *Rad am Wagen sein* be the fifth wheel on the coach; '**~tel** *n* (7) fifth (part); '**~tens** fifthly.

'**fünfzehn** fifteen; '**~te** fifteenth.

fünfzig ['~tsiç] fifty; **~er** ['~tsigər] *m* (7), '**~erin** *f* quinquagenarian; '**~ste** fiftieth.

'**Fünfzylinder** *mot. m* five-cylinder car.

fungieren [fuŋ'giːrən] (25): ~ *als* act as.

Funk [fuŋk] *m* (3[1], *o. pl.*) radio, *Brt. a.* wireless; '**~-anlage** *f* wireless (*od.* radio) equipment; '**~-apparat** *m s. Funkgerät*; '**~-ausstellung** *f* radio show; '**~bastler** *m* radio amateur *od.* fan; '**~bild** *n* photoradiogram.

Fünkchen ['fyŋkçən] *n* (6) small spark; *fig.* grain.

'**Funkdienst** *m* radio service.

Funke ['fuŋkə] *m* (13), '**~n** *m* (6) spark (*a. fig.*).
'**Funk-einrichtung** *f* radio equipment.
'**funkeln** (29) sparkle (*a. fig.*), glitter.
'**funkel(nagel)'neu** brand-new.
'**funken** (25) radio.
'**Funker** *m* (7) radio operator.
'**Funk|feuer** ✈ *n* radio beacon; '**~gerät** *n* radio (*od.* wireless) set; '**~haus** *n* broadcasting cent|re, *Am.* -er; '**~-ortung** *f* radio location; '**~peilung** *f* radio bearing; '**~sprechgerät** *n* radiophone; *tragbares*: walkie-talkie; '**~spruch** *m* radio message, radiogram; '**~station** *f* radio (*od.* wireless) station; '**~stille** *f* radio silence; '**~streife(nwagen** *m*) *f* radio patrol (car); '**~technik** *f* radio engineering; '**~telegramm** *n* radio telegram, radiogram.
Funktion [fuŋk'tsjo:n] *f* (16) function; **~är** [~tsjo'nɛ:r] *m* (3[1]) functionary; **≗ieren** [~'ni:rən] function, operate, work; **≗sfähig** functioning; **~sstörung** ⚕ *f* malfunction.
'**Funk|turm** *m* radio tower; '**~verbindung** *f* radio connection; '**~verkehr** *m* wireless (*od.* radio) traffic; '**~wagen** *m* radio car *od.* truck; '**~wesen** *n* radio (telegraphy).
für [fy:r] *allg.* for; (*als Ersatz*) *a.* in exchange for; (*zugunsten von*) *a.* in favo(u)r of; *Jahr ~ Jahr* year by year; *Stück ~ Stück* piece by piece; *Tag ~ Tag* day after day; *ich habe* (*esse usw.*) *es ~ mein Leben gern* I am exceedingly fond of it; *ich ~ meine Person* I for one; *~ sich* (*leise*) in an undertone, *thea.* aside; *~ sich leben* live by o.s.; *an und ~ sich* in itself; *das ≗ und Wider* the pros and cons *pl.*; *was ~* (*ein*) *...?* what (kind of) ...?; *s. was*; *sich ~ sich halten* stand aloof.
'**Fürbitte** *f* intercession; *~ einlegen für* intercede (*od.* plead) for.
Furche ['furçə] *f* (15) furrow; (*Runzel*) wrinkle; (*Wagenspur*) rut; '**≗n** (25) furrow; wrinkle.
Furcht [furçt] *f* (16, *o. pl.*) fear, dread, fright; *aus ~ vor* (*dat.*) for (*od.* from) fear of; *in ~ setzen* frighten; '**≗bar** terrible, *stärker*: dreadful, frightful, formidable, horrible (*alle a.* F *ungemein*); F (*sehr groß usw.*) *a.* awful, tremendous.
fürchten ['fyrçtən] (26) fear, dread; *sich ~* be afraid (*vor dat.* of).
'**fürchterlich** *s. furchtbar.*
'**furcht|-erregend** fearsome; '**~los** fearless; '**≗losigkeit** *f* fearlessness; '**~sam** fearful, timid, timorous; '**≗samkeit** *f* timidity.
Furie ['fu:rjə] *f* (15) fury.
Furier ⚔ [fu'ri:r] *m* (3[1]) ration N.C.O. (= noncommissioned officer).
für'liebnehmen: *~ mit* be content with, put up with.
Furnier [fur'ni:r] *n* (3[1]), **≗en** veneer.
Furore [fu'ro:re] *f* (15, *o. pl.*) *od. n* (10, *o. pl.*): *~ machen* create a sensation.
'**Für|sorge** *f* care; *öffentliche ~* public assistance, welfare work; *s. sozial*; '**~sorge-amt** *n* welfare cent|re, *Am.* -er; '**~sorge-erziehung** *f* trustee (*als Strafe*: correctional) education; '**~sorger(in** *f*) *m* welfare officer *od.* worker; '**≗sorglich** solicitous; '**~sprache** *f* intercession; '**~sprecher** *m* advocate.
Fürst [fyrst] *m* (12) prince; (*Herrscher*) sovereign; '**~engeschlecht** *n* dynasty; '**~enstand** *m* princely rank; '**~entum** *n* (1[2]) principality; '**~enwürde** *f s. Fürstenstand*; '**~in** *f* (16[1]) princess; '**≗lich** princely; '**~lichkeit** *f* princeliness; *~en f/pl.* princely personages.
Furt [furt] *f* (16) ford.
Furunkel [fu'ruŋkəl] *m* (7) boil, furuncle; **Furunkulose** [furuŋku'lo:zə] ⚕ *f* (15) furunculosis.
für|'wahr in truth; '**≗witz** *m s. Vorwitz*; '**≗wort** *n* (1[2]) pronoun.
Furz V [furts] *m* (3[2] *u.* [3]), '**≗en** (27) fart.
Fusel F ['fu:zəl] *m* (7) *sl.* rotgut.
Fusion ✝ [fu'zjo:n] *f* (16) fusion, amalgamation, merger; **≗ieren** [~'ni:rən] merge.
Fuß [fu:s] *m* (3[2] *u.* 3[3]) foot; *e-r Säule*: base; *e-s Stuhls, Tisches usw.*: leg; *s. Münz≗*; *festen ~ fassen* gain a foothold; *auf gutem* (*schlechtem*) *~ stehen mit* be on good (bad) terms with; *auf großem ~e leben* live in grand style; *auf freien ~ setzen* set at liberty; *auf eignen Füßen stehen* stand on one's own legs; *auf schwachen Füßen stehen* rest on a weak foundation; *mit beiden Füßen auf der Erde*

stehen keep both feet on the ground; *stehenden* ~*es* on the spot, forthwith; *zu* ~ on foot; *zu* ~ *gehen* walk; *gut zu* ~ *sein* be a good walker.

'**Fuß**|**-abdruck** *m* (3³) footprint; '**~-abstreicher** *m*, '**~-abtreter** *m* shoe scraper; '**~-angel** *f* man-trap; '**~bad** *n* foot-bath; '**~ball** *m* football; '**~ballmannschaft** *f* football team; '**~ballplatz** *m* football field; '**~ballspiel** *n* (*Sportart*) (association) football, F soccer; (*Kampf*) soccer match; '**~ballspieler** *m* football-player, footballer; '**~ballstadion** *n* football stadium; '**~bank** *f* footstool; '**~bekleidung** *f* footwear; '**~boden** *m* floor(ing); '**~bodenbelag** *m* floor covering; '**~bodenheizung** *f* underfloor heating; '**~bremse** *f* foot brake.

Fussel F ['fusəl] *f* (15) fluff, fuzz.

fußen ['fu:sən] (27) *auf* (*dat.*) *Sache*: be based (*od.* rest) on.

'**Fuß**|**fall** *m* prostration; *e-n* ~ *tun* prostrate o.s.; '**♀fällig** prostrate, on one's knees; **~gänger** ['~gɛŋər] *m* (7) pedestrian; '**~gänger-überweg** *m* pedestrian crossing, *Am.* crosswalk; '**~gängerzone** *f* pedestrian zone (*Am.* precinct); '**~gelenk** *n* ankle-joint; '**~gestell** *n* pedestal; '**~knöchel** *m* ankle(-bone); '**~marsch** *m* walk; '**~matte** *f* doormat; *mot.* floormat; '**~note** *f* footnote; '**~pfad** *m* footpath; '**~pflege** *f* pedicure; '**~pilz** ⚕ *m* athlete's foot; '**~punkt** *m ast.* nadir; ⚔ foot; '**~schemel** *m* footstool; '**~sohle** *f* sole of the foot; '**~spur** *f einzelne*: footprint; *Reihe v.* ~*en*: track; '**~stapfe** *f* footstep; '**~steig** *m* footpath; '**~tour** *f* walking tour; '**~tritt** *m* kick; '**~volk** *n* foot; *fig.* rank and file; '**~wanderung** *f* hike; '**~weg** *m* footpath; '**~wurzel** *f* tarsus.

futsch F [futʃ] lost, gone; (*kaputt*) broken; ~ *gehen* go phut.

Futter ['futər] *n* (7) **1.** (*Nahrung*) food, F grub, *Am.* F chow; *für das Vieh*: feed, (*Trocken*♀) fodder; **2.** (*Rock*♀) lining (*a.* ⊕); ⚠ casing.

Futteral [~'rɑ:l] *n* (3) case; (*Schachtel*) box; (*Scheide*) sheath.

'**Futter**|**beutel** *m* nosebag; '**~kasten** *m* feedbox; '**~krippe** *f* crib, manger; '**~krippensystem** *pol. n Am.* spoils system; '**~mittel** *n* feed(ing) stuff; '**~napf** *m* feeding dish; '**~neid** *m* envy, (professional) jealousy.

fütter|**n** ['fytərn] (29) **1.** feed; **2.** (*innen bekleiden*) line; ⚠ case; *mit Pelz*: fur; (*auspolstern*) stuff; '**♀ung** *f* feeding; lining; casing.

'**Futter**|**stoff** *m* lining (material); '**~trog** *m* feeding-trough.

Futurologie [futurolo'gi:] *f* (15, *o. pl.*) futurology.

Futur(um) *gr.* [fu'tu:r(um)] *n* (9²) future (tense).

G

G [ge:], **g** *n inv.* G, g; ♪ G.

gab [gɑ:p] *pret. v. geben.*

Gabardine [gabar'di:n] *m* (6) gabardine.

Gabe ['gɑ:bə] *f* (15) gift, present; *milde*: alms; (*Schenkung*) donation; ⚕ (*Dosis*) dose; (*Talent*) gift, talent; (*Fähigkeit*) skill.

Gabel ['gɑ:bəl] *f* (15) fork; (*Deichsel*♀) (e-e a pair of) shafts *pl.*; ⚔ bracket; **♀förmig** ['~fœrmiç], '**♀ig** forked, bifurcated; '**~frühstück** *n* early lunch; '**♀n** (*a. sich*) (29) fork, bifurcate; '**~stapler** *m* fork-lift truck; '**~ung** *f* bifurcation.

gackern ['gakərn] (29) cackle.

Gaffel ⚓ ['gafəl] *f* (15) gaff; '**~segel** *n* gaff-sail, trysail.

gaffen ['gafən] (25) gape; (*stieren*) stare.

Gage ['gɑ:ʒə] *f* (15) pay, salary.

gähnen ['gɛ:nən] **1.** (25) yawn; **2.** ♀ *n* (6) yawn(ing).

Gala ['gala] *f inv.* gala; *in* (*großer*) ~ in full dress.

Galan [ga'lɑ:n] *m* gallant, squire.

galant [ga'lant] gallant; (*höflich*) courteous; ~*es Abenteuer* love adventure.

Galanterie [~ə'ri:] *f* (15) gallantry; courtesy.

ˈ**Gala|uniform** *f* full(-dress) uniform; ˈ**~vorstellung** *thea. f* gala performance.
Galaxis [gaˈlaksis] *f* (16², *pl. -ien wie* 15) galaxy.
Galeere [gaˈleːrə] *f* (15) galley; **~n-sklave** *m* galley-slave.
Galerie [galəˈriː] *f* (15) gallery.
Galgen [ˈgalgən] *m* (6) gallows *sg.*, gibbet; ˈ**~frist** *f* respite, short grace; ˈ**~humor** *m* gallows humo(u)r; ˈ**~strick** *m*, ˈ**~vogel** *m* gallows-bird.
Gall-apfel [ˈgal-] *m* gall-nut.
Galle [ˈgalə] *f* (15) bile; *v. niederen Tieren*: gall; ˈ**~nblase** *f* gallbladder; ˈ**~nkolik** *f* bilious colic; ˈ**~nleiden** *n* bilious complaint; ˈ**~nstein** *m* gall-stone.
Gallert [ˈgalərt] *n* (3), **~e** [gaˈlɛrtə] *f* (15) gelatine, jelly; ˈ**≈-artig** gelatinous, jelly-like.
Gallier [ˈgaljər] *m* (7) Gaul.
ˈ**gallig** gall-like; *fig.* bilious.
ˈ**gallisch** Gallic, Gaulish.
Galopp [gaˈlɔp] *m* (3) gallop; *im kurzen ~* at an easy canter; *im gestreckten ~* at full gallop *od.* speed; **≈ieren** [~ˈpiːrən] gallop.
Galosche [gaˈlɔʃə] *f* (15) galosh (*mst pl.*), *pl. Am. a.* rubbers.
galt [galt] *pret. v. gelten.*
galvan|isch [galˈvaːniʃ] galvanic; *~ versilbern* electroplate; *~ vergolden* electrogild; **~isieren** [~vaniˈziːrən] galvanize; **≈ismus** [~ˈnismus] *m* (16, *o. pl.*) galvanism.
Galvano [~ˈvaːno] *n* (11) (*galvanisierter Druckstock*) electro(type); **~ˈplastik** *f* galvanoplastics *sg.*; *typ.* electrotypy.
Gamasche [gaˈmaʃə] *f* (15) gaiter, legging; *kurze*: spat.
gamm|eln F [ˈgaməln] (29*) loaf around; ˈ**≈ler** *m* (7) drop-out.
Gang¹ [gaŋ] *m* (3³) walk; *s. Gangart*; *fig.* (*Bewegung, Tätigkeit*) motion; *e-r Maschine*: movement, running, (*Wirkungsweise*) action; (*Boten≈*) errand; (*Weg*) way; (*Baum≈*) alley; (*Bahn, Lauf*; *Verlauf*; *bei Tafel*) course; ⚓ *beim Lavieren*: tack; (*Röhre*) duct; (*Verbindungsweg*) passage; *im Hause*: corridor; gallery; *zwischen Sitzreihen*: gangway, *bsd. Am.* aisle; 🚂 corridor, *Am.* aisle; *Fechten usw.*: bout; round; *anat.* duct; ⊕ *e-r Schraube*: worm, thread; *mot.* speed; *erster, zweiter, dritter ~* low (*od.* bottom), second, third gear; ⚒ vein; *in ~ bringen od. setzen* set going *od.* in motion; *in ~ kommen* get under way; *in ~ halten* keep going; *im ~ sein* be in motion, *fig.* be (going) on, be in progress, be afoot; *in vollem ~* in full swing.
gang²: *~ und gäbe* [ˈgɛːbə] usual, customary, traditional.
ˈ**Gang-art** *f Mensch*: gait, walk; *Pferd*: pace (*a. weitS. Tempo*).
ˈ**gangbar** *Weg*: practicable (*a. fig.*); *Münze*: current; ⚕ marketable, salable.
Gängel|band [ˈgɛŋəlbant] *n* leading-strings *pl.*; *am ~ führen* keep in leading-strings; *sich am ~ führen lassen* be in leading-strings; ˈ**≈n** (29) *fig.* lead by the nose.
ˈ**Gang|(schalt)hebel** *mot. m* gear (-change) lever; ˈ**~schaltung** *f* gear-change, *Am.* gear-shift.
Gangster [ˈgɛŋstər] *m* (7) gangster; ˈ**~bande** *f* band of criminals; ˈ**~braut** *f* gang moll.
Gans [gans] *f* goose (*pl.* geese).
Gäns-chen [ˈgɛnsçən] *n* (6) gosling.
Gänse|blümchen [ˈgɛnzə-] *n* daisy; ˈ**~braten** *m* roast goose; ˈ**~feder** *f* goose-quill; **~füßchen** [ˈ~fyːsçən] *n/pl.* quotation-marks, inverted commas; ˈ**~haut** *f* goose-skin; *fig. a.* goose-flesh, *Am. a.* goose pimples *pl.*; *ich bekam e-e ~* my flesh began to creep; ˈ**~klein** *n* (goose-)giblets *pl.*; ˈ**~leberpastete** *f* pâté de foie gras (*fr.*); ˈ**~marsch** *m* single (*od.* Indian) file; **~rich** [ˈ~riç] *m* (3) gander; ˈ**~schmalz** *n* goose-dripping.
ganz [gants] **1.** *adj.* all; (*ungeteilt*) entire, whole; (*vollständig*) complete, total, full; *~ Deutschland* all Germany, the whole of Germany; *~e Zahl* 𝔄 integer; *den ~en Tag* all day (long); *das ~e Jahr hindurch* throughout the year; *von ~em Herzen* with all my *etc.* heart; *er ist ein ~er Mann* he is a real man; *~e fünf Stunden* full five hours; *die ~e Zeit* all the time; **2.** *adv.* quite; (*s.* 1.) entirely, wholly; completely; (*sehr*) very; (*ziemlich*) pretty; *nicht ~ 10* less than 10, just under 10; *~ Auge* (*Ohr*) all eyes (ears); *~ und gar* wholly, totally; *~ und gar nicht* not at all, by no means; *~ durch* throughout; *~ gut* quite good, F not

bad; *im ~en* on the whole, generally; ✝ in the lump; *ich bin ~ naß* I am wet all over; '2e *n* (18) whole; (*Gesamtheit*) totality; *aufs ~ gehen* go all out, *bsd. Am.* go the whole hog.

'**Ganz|-aufnahme** *f*, '**~bild** *n* full-length (portrait); '**~fabrikat** *n* finished product; '**~heitsmethode** *f Schule*: 'look and say' method; '**~leder** *n*: *in ~ gebunden* whole-bound.

gänzlich ['gɛntslɪç] complete, total, entire; *adv. a.* wholly, absolutely.

'**ganz|seitig** full-page; '**2tagsbeschäftigung** *f* full-time job *od.* occupation; '**2tagsschule** *f* all-day school.

gar [gɑːr] **1.** *adj. Speise*: done; *Leder*: dressed; *Metall*: refined; *nicht ~ Fleisch*: underdone, rare; **2.** *adv.* quite, entirely, very; (*sogar*) even; *~ nicht* not at all; *~ keiner* not a single one; *warum nicht ~!* and why not, indeed?

Garage [ga'rɑːʒə] *f* (15) garage.

Garant [ga'rant] *m* (12) guarantor.

Garantie [~'tiː] *f* (15) guarantee, warranty; **2ren** guarantee, warrant; **~schein** *m* guarantee.

Garaus ['gɑːrʔaʊs] *m inv.*: *j-m den ~ machen* dispatch (*od.* finish) a p.

Garbe ['garbə] *f* (15) sheaf (*a.* ⚔).

Garde ['gardə] *f* (15) guard; *der britischen Königin*: *the* Guards *pl.*

Garderobe [gardə'roːbə] *f* (15) wardrobe; (*Kleiderablage*) cloak-room, *Am.* checkroom; *e-s Schauspielers*: dressing-room; **~nfrau** *f* (*a. thea.* **Garderobiere** [~ro'bjɛːrə] *f*) cloak-room attendant; **~nmarke** *f* cloak-room ticket, *Am.* check; **~nschrank** *m* wardrobe; **~nständer** *m* hat (*od.* hall) stand.

Gardine [gar'diːnə] *f* (15) curtain; **~npredigt** *f* curtain-lecture; **~nstange** *f* curtain rail.

gären ['gɛːrən] (30) ferment (*a. ~ lassen*).

Garküche ['gɑːr-] *f* cook-shop.

'**Gär|mittel** *n*, '**~stoff** *m* ferment.

Garn [garn] *n* (3) yarn; (*Faden*) thread; (*Baumwoll2*) cotton; (*Netz*) net; *ins ~ gehen* fall into the snare; *ins ~ locken* decoy, trap.

Garnele [gar'neːlə] *f* (15) shrimp.

garnier|en [gar'niːrən] trim; *bsd. Speise*: garnish; **2ung** *f* trimming; *e-r Speise*: trimmings *pl.*, garnish.

Garnison [garni'zoːn] *f* (16), **2ieren** [~zo'niːrən] garrison; **~stadt** [~'zoːn-] *f* garrison-town.

Garnitur [~'tuːr] *f* (16) (*Besatz*) trimming; (*Zubehör*) fittings *pl.*; (*Zs.gehöriges*) set; *fig. die erste ~* the élite.

garstig ['garstɪç] nasty, ugly.

Garten ['gartən] *m* (6^1) garden; '**~arbeit** *f* gardening; '**~-architekt** *m* landscape gardener; '**~bau** *m* horticulture; '**~bau...** horticultural; '**~erde** *f* (garden-)mo(u)ld; '**~fest** *n* garden (*Am. a.* lawn) party; '**~geräte** *n/pl.* gardening-tools; '**~haus** *n* summer-house; '**~laube** *f* arbo(u)r; '**~lokal** *n* open-air café (*od.* restaurant); (*Biergarten*) beer-garden; '**~schau** *f* horticultural show; '**~schere** *f* (*eine* a pair of) pruning-shears *pl.*; '**~stadt** *f* garden city; '**~zaun** *m* garden fence.

Gärtner ['gɛrtnər] *m* (7), '**~in** *f* (16^1) gardener; **~ei** [~'raɪ] *f* gardening, horticulture; (*Betrieb*) nursery, market garden.

Gärung ['gɛːrʊŋ] *f* fermentation; *sich in ~ befinden* (*a. fig.*) be in a state of ferment; '**~s-prozeß** *m* process of fermentation.

Gas [gɑːs] *n* (4) gas; *mot. u. fig. ~ geben* step on the gas; *mot. ~ wegnehmen* throttle down; '**~-angriff** ⚔ *m* gas attack; '**~-anzünder** *m* gas lighter; '**2-artig** gaseous; '**~behälter** *m* gasometer, gas-container; '**~beleuchtung** *f* gas-light(ing); '**~brenner** *m* gas-burner; '**~-explosion** *f* gas explosion; '**~feuerzeug** *n* gas lighter; '**~flasche** *f* gas cylinder; **2förmig** ['~fœrmɪç] gaseous; '**~fußhebel** *m s. Gaspedal*; '**~hahn** *m* gas-cock; '**~hebel** *mot. m* throttle (hand) lever; *s. Gaspedal*; '**~heizung** *f* gas-heating; '**~herd** *m* gas-stove *od.* -range; '**~kammer** *f* gas-chamber; '**~kocher** *m* gas cooker; '**~leitung** *f* gas main; '**~licht** *n* gaslight; '**~-'Luftgemisch** *n* gas-air mixture; '**~mann** *m* gas-man; '**~maske** ⚔ *f* gas-mask; '**~messer** *m* gas-meter; '**~-ofen** *m* gasoven; **~ometer** [gazo'meːtər] *m* (7) gasometer; (*Gasbehälter*) gas-holder; '**~pedal** *mot. n* accelerator (pedal).

Gäßchen [gɛsçən] *n* (6) narrow alley *od.* lane.

Gasse ['gasə] *f* (15) lane (*a. fig.*).

'**Gassen|bube** *m*, '**~junge** *m* street

arab, gutter-snipe, urchin; '**~hauer** *m* popular song.

Gast [gast] *m* (3² *u.* 3³) guest (*a. thea. usw.*); (*Besucher*) visitor; (*Wirtshaus*≈) customer; (*regelmäßiger* ~) frequenter; *s. ungebeten*; *zu* ~*e bitten* invite; *Gäste haben* have company; '**~-arbeiter** *m* foreign worker; '**~bett** *n* spare bed; '**~dirigent** *m* guest conductor; '**~dozent** *m* visiting lecturer.

Gäste|buch ['gɛstə-] *n* visitors' book; '**~haus** *n*, '**~heim** *n* guest-house.

'**gast|frei** hospitable; '**≈freiheit** *f* hospitality; '**~freundlich** *s. gastfrei*; '**≈freundschaft** *f* hospitality; '**≈geber** *m* host; *pl. Sport*: home team *sg.*; '**≈geberin** *f* hostess; '**≈haus** *n*, '**≈hof** *m* restaurant; *mit Unterkunft*: inn, hotel; '**≈hörer** *univ. m* guest (*od.* extramural) student; **~ieren** *thea.* [~'tiːrən] give a guest performance; '**≈land** *n* host country; '**~lich** hospitable; ~ *aufnehmen* receive as guest, entertain; '**≈lichkeit** *f* hospitality; '**≈mahl** *n* feast, banquet; '**≈mannschaft** *f Sport*: visiting team; '**≈recht** *n* right of hospitality.

Gastritis [gas'triːtis] ⚕ *f* (16, *pl. inv.* ~*i'tiden*) gastritis.

'**Gast|redner** *m* guest speaker; '**~rolle** *thea. f* guest part; e-e ~ *geben s. gastieren*; *fig.* show up briefly.

Gastronomie [gastrono'miː] *f* (15) gastronomy; (*Gewerbe*) catering trade.

'**Gast|spiel** *n* guest performance; '**~spielreise** *f* tour; '**~stätte** *f* restaurant; '**~stube** *f* (bar) parlo(u)r; '**~vorlesung** *f* guest lecture; '**~vorstellung** *s. Gastspiel*; '**~wirt** *m* landlord, host, innkeeper; '**~wirtin** *f* landlady, hostess; '**~wirtschaft** *f* inn; '**~zimmer** *n* lounge; *weitS.* spare (bed)room.

'**Gas|-uhr** *f* gas-meter; '**~vergiftung** *f* gas poisoning; '**~vorkommen** *n* gas field; '**~werk** *n* gasworks *pl.*

Gatte ['gatə] *m* (13) husband; spouse.

Gatter ['gatər] *n* (7) railing, grating; '**~säge** *f* frame-saw; '**~tor** *n* lattice gate; '**~werk** *n* lattice-work.

'**Gattin** *f* wife; spouse.

Gattung ['gatuŋ] *f* kind, sort; *biol.* race, species, genus; *Kunst*: genre (*fr.*); '**~sname** *m* generic name; *gr.* appellative.

Gau [gaʊ] *m* (3) district, region.

Gaudi ['gaʊdi] F *f* (11), **Gaudium** ['gaʊdjum] *n* (9, *o. pl.*) (bit of) fun.

Gaukel|bild ['gaʊkəl-] *n* illusion, phantasm; **~ei** [~'laɪ] *f*, '**~spiel** *n*, '**~werk** *n* jugglery; (*Täuschung*) trick(ery), delusion; '**≈n** (29) juggle; (*hin und her flattern*) flutter.

Gaukler ['gaʊklər] *m* (7), '**~in** *f* juggler; (*Spaßmacher*) buffoon.

Gaul [gaʊl] *m* (3³) (farm-)horse, nag; *contp. alter* ~ (old) jade.

Gaumen ['gaʊmən] *m* (6) palate; '**~laut** *m* palatal; '**~platte** *f Zahnheilkunde*: (dental) plate.

Gauner ['gaʊnər] *m* (7), '**~in** *f* (16¹) swindler, crook; *co.* rascal; **~ei** [~'raɪ] *f* swindling, sharp practice, trickery; '**≈n** (29) cheat, swindle; '**~sprache** *f* thieves' cant.

Gaze ['gɑːzə] *f* (15) gauze; *feine* ~ ✝ gossamer; '**≈-artig** gauzy.

Gazelle [ga'tsɛlə] *f* (15) gazelle.

Geächtete [gə'ˀɛçtətə] *m* (18) outlaw.

Geächze [~'ˀɛçtsə] *n* (3) groans *pl.*

ge'-artet: *anders* ~ *sein* be of different nature.

Geäst [gə'ˀɛst] (3, *o. pl.*) *n* branches *pl.*

Gebäck [gə'bɛk] *n* (3) baker's goods *pl.*; *feines*: pastry, fancy cakes *pl.*

ge'backen *p.p. v. backen.*

Gebälk [~'bɛlk] *n* (3) timber-work.

geballt [~'balt] *s. ballen*; ~*e Ladung* concentrated charge.

gebar [gə'bɑːr] *pret. v. gebären.*

Gebärde [~'bɛːrdə] *f* (15) gesture; **≈n** (26): *sich* ~ behave, act; **~nspiel** *n* gesticulation; *bsd. thea.* dumb show; **~nsprache** *f* language of gestures.

gebaren [~'bɑːrən] **1.** (26): *sich* ~ behave, act; **2.** ≈ *n* (6) deportment, behavio(u)r.

gebären [~'bɛːrən] (30) bear, bring forth (*a. fig.*), give birth to; *ich bin am ... geboren* I was born on ...

Ge'bärmutter *f* womb, 🕮 uterus; **~hals** *m* cervix; **~halskrebs** *m* cancer of the cervix; **~krebs** *m* cancer of the uterus.

Gebäude [gə'bɔʏdə] *n* (7) building, edifice (*a. fig.*); **~komplex** *m* complex (of buildings).

gebefreudig ['geːbə-] open-handed.

Gebein(e *pl.*) [gə'baɪn] *n* (3) bones *pl.*

Gebell [gə'bɛl] *n* (3) barking.

geben ['geːbən] **1.** (30) *j-m et.*: give

a p. a th.; (*schenken*) present *a p.* with *a th.*; *Ertrag*: yield; *Karten*: deal; (*veranstalten*) give, hold; *thea.* give, perform; *ge~ werden* be on; *Antwort ~* (give an) answer; *s. Anlaß, Beispiel, Mühe, Pflege usw.*; *von sich ~* give out, emit, *Laut*: utter, *Speise*: bring up; *sein Wort ~* pledge one's word; *et.* (*nichts*) *~ auf* (*acc.*) set great (no) store by; *sich ~* (*nachgeben*) yield, (*nachlassen*) abate, settle (down); *sich gefangen ~* surrender; *s. denken, erkennen usw.*; *Tennis*: serve (*v/i.*); *es gibt* there is, there are; *was gibt es?* what is the matter?; F *was es nicht alles gibt!* F it takes all kinds!; F *ich habe es ihm tüchtig ge~* I gave it him hot; **2. ♀** *n* (6) giving; *Kartenspiel*: *am ~ sein* (have the) deal.

'Geber *m* (7), **'~in** *f* giver, donor, donator.

Gebet [gəˈbeːt] *n* (3) prayer; **~buch** *n* prayer-book.

geˈbeten *p.p. v. bitten.*

Gebiet [~ˈbiːt] *n* (3) territory; (*Bezirk*) district, region; (*Fläche*) area; *fig.* (*Fach♀*) field, domain; province; (*Bereich*) sphere.

geˈbieten (30) *v/t.* order, *a. Achtung usw.*: command; *v/i.* (*herrschen*) rule (*über acc.* over), govern.

Geˈbieter *m* (7) master, lord, ruler; **~in** *f* (16[1]) mistress; **♀isch** imperious, commanding.

Geˈbiets|-anspruch *m* territorial claim; **~hoheit** *f* territorial sovereignty; **~reform** *f* regional reorganization.

Gebilde [gəˈbildə] *n* (7) *oft nur*: thing; (*Schöpfung*) creation; (*Form*) form; (*Bau, Gefüge*) structure; (*Bildung, a. geol.*) formation; **♀t** educated, well-bred, cultivated; well-informed, well-read; *die ♀en pl.* the educated classes.

Gebimmel [gəˈbiməl] *n* (7) (continual) ringing *od.* tinkling.

Gebirg|e [gəˈbirgə] *n* (7) (range of) mountains *pl.*; **♀ig** mountainous.

Gebirgs|bewohner [gəˈbirks-] *m* mountain-dweller; **~gegend** *f* mountainous region; **~kamm** *m*, **~rücken** *m* mountain-ridge; **~kette** *f* chain of mountains; **~zug** *m* mountain-range.

Gebiß [gəˈbis] *n* (4) (set of) teeth *pl.*; *künstliches*: denture, (set of) false teeth *pl.*; *am Zaum*: bit; **~-abdruck** *m* denture impression.

geˈbissen *p.p. v. beißen.*

Gebläse [~ˈblɛːzə] *n* (7) blower, blast; *mot.* supercharger.

geˈblasen *p.p. v. blasen.*

geblieben [~ˈbliːbən] *p.p. v. bleiben.*

geblümt [~ˈblyːmt] flowered, flowery; ⚘ floriated, sprigged.

Geblüt [~ˈblyːt] *n* (3) blood; (*Geschlecht*) lineage, race; *Prinz von ~* prince of the blood.

gebogen [~ˈboːgən] **1.** *p.p. v. biegen*; **2.** *adj.* bent, curved.

geboren [~ˈboːrən] **1.** *p.p. v. gebären*; **2.** *adj.* born; *ein ~er Deutscher* German by birth; *~e Schmidt* née Smith; *~ sein für e-n Beruf* be cut out for; *~er Künstler* born artist.

geborgen [~ˈbɔrgən] **1.** *p.p. v. bergen*; **2.** *adj.* safe, sheltered; **♀heit** *f* safety, security.

geborsten [~ˈbɔrstən] *p.p. v. bersten.*

Gebot [~ˈboːt] *n* (3) order; *stärker*: command; (*Angebot*) bid(ding), offer; *die Zehn ~e pl.* the Ten Commandments; *j-m zu ~e stehen* be at a p.'s disposal; *Not kennt kein ~* necessity knows no law; *das ~ der Vernunft* the dictates *pl.* of reason; *dem ~ der Stunde gehorchen* fit in with the needs of the present; **♀en** **1.** *p.p. v. bieten*; **2.** *adj.* necessary, required; (*gehörig*) due.

gebracht [~ˈbraxt] *p.p. v. bringen.*

gebrannt [~ˈbrant] *p.p. v. brennen.*

geˈbraten *p.p. v. braten*[1].

Gebräu [gəˈbrɔʏ] *n* (3) brew (*a.fig.*).

Gebrauch [~ˈbraux] *m* (3[3]) use; usage (*a. Herkommen*); (*Sitte*) custom; *~ machen von* (make) use (of); *in ~ kommen* come into use; **♀en** use, employ; *er ist zu allem* (*zu nichts*) *zu ~* he can turn his hand to anything (he is good for nothing); *gebraucht Kleidung usw.*: second-hand.

gebräuchlich [~ˈbrɔʏçliç] common (-ly used), in use; current; (*üblich*) usual, customary.

Geˈbrauchs|-anweisung *f* directions *pl.* for use; **~-artikel** *m*, **~gegenstand** *m* article for daily use, utility article; **~fahrzeug** *n* utility vehicle; **♀fertig** ready for use; **~graphik** *f* commercial art; **~graphiker** *m* commercial (*od.* industrial) artist; **~güter** *n/pl.* commodities; **~muster** *n* registered design; **~musterschutz** *m* legal protection for registered designs.

Ge'braucht|wagen *mot. m* used *od.* second-hand car; **~waren** *f/pl.* second-hand articles.

Ge'brechen *n* (6) defect, infirmity.

ge'brechlich fragile; *P.*: frail, feeble; **2keit** *f* fragility; frailty, infirmity.

gebrochen [gə'brɔxən] **1.** *p.p. v. brechen*; **2.** *adj.* broken (*a. fig. Herz, Mensch, Sprache, Stimme*).

Gebrüder [gə'bry:dər] *m/pl.* (7): *~ Schmidt* Smith Brothers (*abbr.* Bros.).

Gebrüll [~'bryl] *n* (3) roaring; *des Rindes*: lowing.

Gebühr [~'by:r] *f* (16) duty, rate; fee, charge; *~en pl.* fee(s *pl.*), dues *pl.*; (*das j-m Zukommende*) due; *nach ~* duly, deservedly; *über ~* unduly, immoderately.

ge'bühren (25) (*dat.*) be due to, belong to; *sich ~* be fit *od.* proper; **~d** (*schuldig*) due; (*geziemend*) becoming; (*entsprechend*) proper; **2-einheit** *teleph. f* unit; **2-erhöhung** *f* increase in charges; **2-erlaß** *m* remission of fees; **~frei** free of charges; **2-ordnung** *f* schedule of fees, tariff; **~pflichtig** chargeable; *~e Autostraße* toll road.

ge'bührlich *s. gebührend.*

gebunden [gə'bundən] **1.** *p.p. v. binden*; **2.** *adj.* bound; *Rede*: metrical; (*gelenkt, a.* ⚕) controlled; *Kapital*: tied.

Geburt [~'bu:rt] *f* (16) birth; **~enbeschränkung** *f*, **~enkontrolle** *f*, **~enregelung** *f* birth-control; **~enrückgang** *m* drop in the birth-rate; **2enschwach:** *~er Jahrgang* cohort with a low birth-rate; **2enstark:** *~er Jahrgang* cohort with a high birth-rate; **~enziffer** *f* birth-rate.

gebürtig [~'byrtiç]: *~ aus* a native of, born in, (*German- usw.*) born.

Ge'burts|-anzeige *f* announcement of (a) birth; **~fehler** *m* congenital defect; **~helfer** *m* obstetrician; **~helferin** *f* midwife; **~hilfe** *f* midwifery, 🕮 obstetrics; **~jahr** *n* year of birth; **~land** *n* native country; **~ort** *m* birthplace; **~schein** *m*, **~-urkunde** *f* birth-certificate; **~stadt** *f* native town; **~tag** *m* birthday; **~wehen** *f/pl.* labo(u)r(-pains *pl.*) *sg.*; throes *pl.*

Gebüsch [gə'byʃ] *n* (3²) bushes *pl.*, underbrush, thicket.

Geck [gɛk] *m* (12) fop, dandy.

'geckenhaft foppish, dandyish.

gedacht [gə'daxt] **1.** *p.p. v. denken*; **2.** *adj.* imaginary, fictitious.

Gedächtnis [gə'dɛçtnis] *n* (4¹) memory; (*Erinnerung*) remembrance, recollection; *im ~ behalten* keep in mind; *ins ~ rufen* call to mind, recall; *zum ~* (*gen.*) in memory of; **~feier** *f* commemoration; **~hilfe** *f*, **~stütze** *f* memory-aid; **~lücke** *f* gap in one's memory; **~rede** *f* commemorative address; **~schwäche** *f* weakness of memory; **~schwund** *m*, **~störung** *f* temporary amnesia, disturbed memory; **~verlust** *m* amnesia, loss of memory.

Gedanke [~'daŋkə] *m* (13¹) thought; idea; *in ~n sein* be absorbed in thought; *j-n auf den ~n bringen, daß* ... make a p. think that, give a p. the idea that; *ich kam auf den ~n* the thought occurred to me, it came to my mind; *sich ~n machen über* (*acc.*) worry about; *sich mit dem ~n tragen zu tun* consider doing.

ge'danken|-arm lacking in ideas; **2-austausch** *m* exchange of ideas; **2blitz** *m* brainwave; **2freiheit** *f* freedom of thought; **2gang** *m* train of thought, reasoning; **2leser(in** *f*) *m* thought-reader; **~los** thoughtless; **2losigkeit** *f* thoughtlessness; **~reich** rich in ideas; **2reichtum** *m* wealth of ideas; **2splitter** *m/pl.* aphorisms; **2strich** *m* dash; **2-übertragung** *f* telepathy; **~voll** thoughtful; **2welt** *f* world of ideas, *weitS.* ideal (*od.* intellectual) world.

ge'danklich intellectual, mental.

Gedärm [gə'dɛrm] *n* (3¹ *u.* 3²), **~e** *n* (7) *mst pl.* entrails, bowels *pl.*

Gedeck [~'dɛk] *n* (3) (*Tischzeug*) cover; (*Speisenfolge*) menu; *ein ~ auflegen* lay a place.

gedeihen [~'daɪən] **1.** (30, sn) thrive, prosper, *fig. a.* flourish; (*gelingen*) succeed; (*vorwärtskommen*) progress, get on (well); **2.** 2 *n* (6) thriving, prosperity; success.

gedeihlich [~'daɪliç] thriving, prosperous; successful; profitable.

ge'denk|en (30; *gen.*) think of; be mindful of; (*sich erinnern*) remember, recollect; (*feiern*) commemorate; (*ehren*) hono(u)r; (*erwähnen*) mention; ~ *zu tun* think of doing, intend to do; 2**en** *n* (6) memory; 2**feier** *f* commemoration; 2**rede** *f* commemorative address; 2**stätte** *f* memorial place; 2**stein** *m* commemorative stone; 2**tafel** *f* commemorative tablet; 2**tag** *m* commemoration (day).

Gedicht [gə'diçt] *n* (3) poem; F *fig.* dream, beauty; **~sammlung** *f* collection of poems; *in Auswahl*: anthology.

gediegen [~'di:gən] solid; (*rein*) pure; (*echt*) genuine, true; 2**heit** *f* solidity; purity.

gedieh [~'di:] *pret.*, **~en** *p.p. v. gedeihen 1.*

Gedränge [~'drɛŋə] *n* (7) press, crowd, throng; (*Not*) trouble.

ge'drängt crowded, packed, crammed; *Sprache*: concise; *~e Übersicht* condensed review; ~ *voll* cramfull; 2**heit** *f* conciseness.

ge'droschen *p.p. v. dreschen.*

gedrückt [~'drykt] *fig.* depressed.

gedrungen [~'druŋən] **1.** *p.p. v. dringen*; **2.** *adj.* compact; *P.*: squat, stocky; *Sprache*: concise; *sich ~ fühlen* feel compelled.

Geduld [~'dult] *f* (*inv. o. pl.*) patience; *die ~ verlieren* lose patience; *sich in ~ fassen s. gedulden*; *j-s ~ auf die Probe stellen* try one's patience; *s. reißen, üben*; 2**en** [~'duldən] (26): *sich ~* have patience, wait (patiently); 2**ig** [~'duldiç] patient; **~spiel** [~'dult-] *n* puzzle; **~s-probe** *f* trial of (a p.'s) patience; ordeal.

gedungen [~'duŋən] *p.p. v. dingen.*

gedunsen [~'dunzən] bloated.

gedurft [~'durft] *p.p. v. dürfen.*

geeignet [~'ʔaɪgnət] fit (*für, zu, als* for *a th., inf*); suited, suitable (to, for), proper (for); qualified (for).

Geest [ge:st] *f* (16), '**~land** *n* sandy heath-land.

Gefahr [gə'fɑ:r] *f* (16) danger, peril; (*Wagnis*) risk, jeopardy; *auf meine ~* at my peril *od.* risk; *s. begeben, schweben*; *~ laufen zu verlieren* run the risk of losing; 2**bringend** dangerous.

gefährden [gə'fɛ:rdən] endanger; (*aufs Spiel setzen*) risk, jeopardize.

ge'fahren *p.p. v. fahren.*

Ge'fahren|zone *f* danger area; **~zulage** *f* danger-money;

gefährlich [~'fɛ:rliç] dangerous (*für* to), perilous, risky; *ein ~es Spiel treiben* skate on thin ice.

ge'fahr|los without risk, safe; 2**losigkeit** *f* safety.

Gefährt [~'fɛ:rt] *n* (3) vehicle.

Ge'fährte *m* (13), **Ge'fährtin** *f* companion, fellow, mate.

ge'fahrvoll perilous, dangerous.

Gefälle [~'fɛlə] *n* (7) fall, descent; gradient, *bsd. Am.* grade; *fig.* (*Unterschiede*) differentials *pl.*

Gefallen [~'falən] **1.** *m* (6) (*Gefälligkeit*) favo(u)r, kindness; *dir zu ~* to please you; **2.** *n* (6): *~ finden an* (*dat.*) take pleasure in, take a fancy to; **3.** 2 *v/i.* (30) please (*j-m* a p.); *er (es) gefällt mir* I like him (it); *wie gefällt es Ihnen in B.?* how do you like B.?; *sich ~ lassen* (*sich in et. fügen*) put up with; *das lasse ich mir nicht ~* I won't stand (*Am.* for) that; *sich in e-r Rolle usw. ~* fancy o.s. in, be pleased with; **4.** 2 *p.p. v. fallen*; **5.** 2 *adj.* fallen (*a. Engel, Mädchen, Soldat*); **~e** *m* (18) fallen person; ⚔ *die ~n pl.* the killed, the fallen.

gefällig [gə'fɛliç] pleasing, agreeable; (*verbindlich*) obliging; (*zuvorkommend*) kind; *~st* (if you) please; *Zigaretten ~?* cigarettes, please?; 2**keit** *f* complaisance, kindness; *Handlung*: favo(u)r; 2**keitswechsel** ⚕ *m* accommodation bill.

Ge'fallsucht *f* desire to please; *weibliche*: coquetry.

ge'fallsüchtig [~zyçtiç] coquettish.

ge'fangen 1. *p.p. v. fangen*; **2.** *adj.* captive, imprisoned; *s. geben*; 2**e** *m* prisoner, captive.

Ge'fangen|en-austausch *m* exchange of prisoners; **~enlager** *n* prison(ers') camp; **~enwagen** *m der Polizei*: prison van, *Am.* patrol wagon; 2**halten** keep *a p.* (a) prisoner; **~haltung** *f* detention, confinement; **~nahme** ['~nɑ:mə] *f* (15) capture, seizure; 2**nehmen** take prisoner; *fig.* captivate; **~schaft** *f mil.* captivity; ⚖ imprisonment, custody; 2**setzen** imprison, jail.

Gefängnis [gə'fɛŋnis] *n* (4[1]) prison, jail, *Brt. a.* gaol; *s. ~strafe*; **~direktor** *m* governor, *Am.* warden; **~strafe** *f* (term of) imprisonment; **~wärter** *m* jailer, *Am. a.* (prison) guard.

Gefasel [~ˈfɑːzəl] *n* (7) twaddle.
Gefäß [~ˈfɛːs] *n* (3²) vessel (*a. anat.*).
gefaßt [~ˈfast] *adj.* calm, composed; ~ *auf* (*acc.*) prepared for; *sich* ~ *machen auf* (*acc.*) prepare (o.s.) for.
Gefecht [~ˈfɛçt] *n* (3) engagement; combat, fight; (*~s-tätigkeit*) action; *außer* ~ *setzen* put out of action; **~sbereit** combat-ready; **~sklar:** ⚓ ~ *machen* clear *a ship* for action; **~skopf** *m* warhead; **~s-schießen** *n* field firing; **~s-stand** *m* command post; *im Flugzeug*: turret; **~s-übung** *f* combat practice.
gefeit [gəˈfaɪt] immune (*gegen* from, against), proof (against).
Gefieder [gəˈfiːdər] *n* (7) plumage, feathers *pl.*; **~t** feathered.
Gefilde *poet.* [~ˈfildə] *n* (7) fields *pl.*, regions *pl.*
Geflecht [~ˈflɛçt] *n* (3) plaited work, plait; (*Weiden~*) wickerwork.
gefleckt [~ˈflɛkt] spotted.
geflissentlich [~ˈflisəntliç] intentional, deliberate, studious.
geflochten [~ˈflɔxtən] *p.p. v. flechten.*
geflogen [~ˈfloːgən] *p.p. v. fliegen.*
geflohen [~ˈfloːən] *p.p. v. fliehen.*
geflossen [~ˈflɔsən] *p.p. v. fließen.*
Geˈflügel *n* (7) poultry, fowl(s *pl.*); **~farm** *f* poultry farm; **~händler** *m* poulterer; **~schere** *f* poultry dissectors *pl.*; **~t** winged; *~e Worte n/pl.* winged words; **~zucht** *f* poultry-farming.
Geflunker [gəˈfluŋkər] *n* (7) fibbing; lies *pl.*, humbug.
Geflüster [~ˈflystər] *n* (7) whisper (-ing), whispers *pl.*
gefochten [~ˈfɔxtən] *p.p. v. fechten.*
Gefolg|e [~ˈfɔlgə] *n* (7) *e-s Fürsten*: suite; (*Geleit*) retinue; *von Bediensteten*: attendance; *im* ~ *von fig.* in the wake of; **~schaft** [~ˈfɔlk-] *f* followers *pl.*, following; *im Betrieb*: staff, employees *pl.*
gefräßig [~ˈfrɛːsiç] greedy, voracious; **~keit** *f* gluttony, voracity.
Gefreite [~ˈfraɪtə] *m* (18) lance-corporal, *Am.* private first class.
geˈfressen *p.p. v. fressen* 1.
Gefrier|-anlage [gəˈfriːr-] *f* freezing plant; **~beutel** *m* freezer bag; **~en** (sn) congeal, freeze (*a.* ~ *lassen*); **~fach** *n* freezing compartment; **~fleisch** *n* frozen meat; **~getrocknet** freeze-dried; **~punkt** *m* freezing-point; *auf dem* ~ *stehen* be at zero; **~schrank** *m* (upright) freezer; **~truhe** *f* freezer, deep-freeze.
gefroren [~ˈfroːrən] *p.p. v. frieren*; **~e** *n* (18) ice(-cream).
Gefüge [gəˈfyːgə] *n* (7) structure (*a. fig.*); (*Gewebe*) texture; (*Schicht*) layer; *fig.* make-up, fabric.
geˈfügig pliable, flexible; *P.*: pliant, docile, obedient.
Gefühl [~ˈfyːl] *n* (3) feeling; (*Tastsinn*) touch; (*Empfänglichkeit*) sense (*für* of); *als Wahrnehmung*: sensation; **~los** *Hand usw.*: numb; *P.*: unfeeling, insensible (*gegen* to); **~losigkeit** *f* unfeelingness; **~sbetont** emotional; **~sduselei** [~duːzəˈlaɪ] *f* (16) sentimentalism; **~sduselig** sentimental; **~smensch** *m* emotional character; **~voll** (full of) feeling; (*zärtlich*) tender; (*rührselig*) sentimental.
gefunden [gəˈfundən] *p.p. v. finden.*
gegangen [gəˈgaŋən] *p.p. v. gehen.*
gegeben [gəˈgəːbən] **1.** *p.p. v. geben*; **2.** *adj.* given (*a.* ⅍); *zu ~er Zeit* at the proper time; *die ~e Methode* the best (*od.* obvious) method; **~enfalls** [~ənˈfals] if need be, should the occasion arise; **~heit** *f* (given) fact, reality.
gegen [ˈgeːgən] *örtlich, zeitlich*: towards; *gegensätzlich*: against, ⚖ versus; (*ungefähr*) about, nearly, *Am.* around; *Zeitpunkt*: by; *Mittel* ~ *e-e Krankheit usw.*: for; *vergleichend*: compared with, as against; (*als Entgelt für*) (in exchange) for; *freundlich, grausam usw.* ~ kind, cruel *etc.* to; ~ *die Vernunft usw.* contrary to reason *etc.*; *hundert* ~ *eins* a hundred to one; ~ *Quittung* on receipt.
ˈ**Gegen|-angriff** *m* counter-attack; ˈ**~-anklage** *f*, ˈ**~beschuldigung** *f* counter-charge; ˈ**~-antrag** *m* counter-motion; ˈ**~-antwort** *f* rejoinder; ˈ**~-argument** *n* counter-argument; ˈ**~befehl** *m* counter-order; ˈ**~besuch** *m* return visit; ˈ**~bewegung** *f* counter-movement; ˈ**~beweis** *m* proof to the contrary; ⚖ counter-evidence; ˈ**~bild** *n* counterpart.
Gegend [ˈgeːgənt] *f* (16) region (*a. anat.*), country; (*Bezirk*) district, area; (*Himmels~*) quarter; (*Um~*) environs *pl.*
Gegen|darstellung [ˈgeːgən-] *f* counter-statement; ˈ**~dienst** *m* re-

turn (*od.* reciprocal) service; *j-m e-n* ~ *erweisen* return a p.'s favo(u)r; '~**druck** *m* counter-pressure; *fig.* reaction; ♀**-einander** ['~aɪ'nandər] against one another *od.* each other; '~**-erklärung** *f* counter-statement; '~**fahrbahn** *f* oncoming carriageway (*Am.* highway); '~**forderung** *f* counter-claim; '~**frage** *f* counter-question; '~**füßler** *m* (7) antipode; '~**gerade** *f Sport*: back straight; '~**geschenk** *n* return gift; '~**gewicht** *n* counterbalance, counterpoise; *das* ~ *halten* (*dat.*) counterbalance; '~**gift** *n* antidote; '~**kandidat** *m* rival candidate; '~**klage** *f* counter-charge; '~**leistung** *f* equivalent; ⚖, ⚕ consideration; *als* ~ in return; '~**licht** *n* back light; '~**licht-aufnahme** *f* contre-jour photograph; '~**lichtblende** *f* lens hood; '~**liebe** *f* return of love; *keine* ~ *finden* not to be reciprocated; '~**maßnahme** *f* counter-measure; '~**mittel** *n* remedy (*gegen* for), antidote (against, for); '~**partei** *f* opposite party; '~**probe** *f* check-test; '~**re-aktion** *f* counter-reaction; '~**rechnung** *f* counter-claim; *zum Ausgleich*: set-off, *Am.* offset; '~**rede** *f* reply, objection; '~**revolution** *f* counter-revolution; '~**satz** *m* contrast, opposite; (*Widerspruch*) opposition; antithesis; *im* ~ *zu* in contrast to *od.* with, in opposition to; unlike (*a th. od. p.*); '♀**sätzlich** contrary, opposite; '~**schlag** ⚔ *m* reprisal; '~**seite** *f* opposite side; '♀**seitig** mutual, reciprocal; '~**seitigkeit** *f* reciprocity, mutuality; *auf* ~ *beruhen* be mutual; *das beruht ganz auf* ~ *a.* same here; '~**spieler** *m* opposite number; *fig.* opponent; '~**spionage** *f* counter-espionage; '~**sprech-anlage** *f* intercom; '~**stand** *m* object; (*Thema*) subject, topic; ~ *des Mitleids usw.* object of pity, *etc.*; ♀**ständlich** ['~ʃtɛntlɪç] objective; (*anschaulich*) graphic(ally *adv.*); ♀**standslos** ['~ʃtantsloːs] abstract; *Kunst*: *a.* non-representational; (*sinnlos*) meaningless, irrelevant; (*zwecklos*) to no purpose; '~**standswort** *gr. n* noun; '~**stimme** *f* vote against; (*Meinung*) objection, opposing voice; '~**stoß** *m* (*a.* ⚔) counter-thrust; '~**strömung** *f* counter-current; '~**stück** *n* counterpart; '~**teil** *n* contrary, reverse; *e-s Begriffes*: opposite; *im* ~ on the contrary; '♀**teilig** contrary, opposite; ♀**'über** (*dat.*) opposite (to) *a th. od. p.*; *P.*: face to face (with); (*im Vergleich zu*) compared with, as against; (*im Gegenteil zu*) contrary to; *j-m* ~ *freundlich usw.* kind *etc.* to a p.; *sich e-r Aufgabe usw.* ~ *sehen* be confronted (*od.* faced) with, be up against; ~**'-über** *n* (7) vis-à-vis; *fig. a.* opposite number; ♀**'-überliegend** (*dat.*) opposite; ♀**'-überstehen** (*dat.*) stand opposite, face; *feindlich*: be opposed to; ♀**'-überstellen** (*dat.*) opose (to); *a.* ⚖ confront (with); *fig.* contrast (with); ~**'-überstellung** *f* opposition; confrontation; comparison; ♀**'-übertreten** (*dat.*) *bsd. fig.* face; '~**verkehr** *m* two-way traffic; oncoming traffic; '~**vorschlag** *m* counter-proposal; ~**wart** ['~vart] *f* (14, *o. pl.*) presence; (*jetzige Zeit*) present time; *gr.* present (tense); ♀**wärtig** ['~vɛrtɪç] (*anwesend*) present; (*jetzig*) present, actual; current (*a.* ⚕); *adv.* at present; '~**wartskunde** *f* current affairs, *Am.* social studies *pl.*; '~**wartsliteratur** *f* contemporary literature; '♀**wartsnah** topical; '~**wehr** *f* opposition; '~**wert** *m* equivalent; '~**wind** *m* head wind; '~**winkel** *m* corresponding angle; '~**wirkung** *f* counter-effect, reaction; '♀**zeichnen** countersign; '~**zeichnung** *f* countersignature; '~**zeuge** *m* counterwitness; '~**zug** *m* countermove; 🚂 opposite train.

gegessen [gə'gɛsən] *p.p. v. essen.*

geglichen [gə'glɪçən] *p.p. v. gleichen.*

gegliedert [gə'gliːdərt] articulate; *fig.* organized.

geglitten [gə'glɪtən] *p.p. v. gleiten.*

ge'glommen *p.p. v. glimmen.*

Gegner ['geːgnər] *m* (7) adversary, opponent; rival; '♀**isch** antagonistic, adverse; ⚖ opposing; (*nach su.*) of the enemy; '~**schaft** *f* opponents *pl.*; (*Widerstand*) antagonism, opposition.

gegolten [gə'gɔltən] *p.p. v. gelten.*

gegoren [gə'goːrən] *p.p. v. gären.*

gegossen [gə'gɔsən] *p.p. v. gießen.*

ge'graben *p.p. v. graben.*

gegriffen [gə'grɪfən] *p.p. v. greifen.*

Gehackte [gə'haktə] *n s. Hackfleisch.*

Gehalt [gə'halt] **1.** *m* (3) content; (*Fassungsvermögen*) capacity; (*Fein*♀ *v. Münzen*) standard; *fig.* content, substance; (*innerer Wert*) merit; **2.** *n*

(1²) salary, pay; **≈en 1.** *p.p. v. halten*; **2.** *adj.*: *~ sein zu tun* be bound (*od.* obliged) to do; **≈los** empty, hollow; **~losigkeit** *f* emptiness; **≈reich, ≈voll** *Nahrung*: substantial (*a. fig. Buch usw.*); *Wein*: full-bodied.

Ge'halts|-abzug *m* salary deduction; **~-empfänger** *m* salaried employee; **~-erhöhung** *f*, **~zulage** *f* increase in salary, *Am.* raise; **~forderung** *f* pay claim; **~gruppe** *f*, **~stufe** *f* salary bracket.

Gehänge [gə'hɛŋə] *n* (7) (*Abhang*) slope, declivity; (*Blumen≈*) festoon; (*Schmuck*) pendants *pl.*

gehangen [gə'haŋən] *p.p. v. hängen.*

geharnischt [~'harniʃt] (clad) in armo(u)r; *~e Antwort* sharp reply.

gehässig [~'hɛsiç] malicious, spiteful; **≈keit** *f* malice, spitefulness.

ge'hauen *p.p. v. hauen.*

Gehäuse [gə'hɔʏzə] *n* (7) case, box; ⊕ casing, housing; *v. Obst*: core; *e-r Schnecke*: shell.

Gehege [gə'he:gə] *n* (7) enclosure; fence; *hunt. u. fig.* preserve; *fig. j-m ins ~ kommen* encroach upon a p.'s preserves, get in a p.'s way.

geheim [~'haɪm] secret; *et. ~halten* keep a th. secret; **≈agent** *m* secret agent; **≈bund** *m* secret society; **≈dienst** *m* secret service; **≈fach** *n* secret drawer; **≈haltung** *f* secrecy; **≈konto** *n* secret account.

Ge'heimnis *n* (4¹) secret; (*Rätselhaftes*) mystery; **~krämer** *m* secret-monger; **~kräme'rei** *f* secret-mongering; **~träger** *m* bearer of secrets; **≈umwittert, ≈umwoben** shrouded in secrecy; **≈voll** mysterious; *~ tun* be secretive (*mit et.* about).

Ge'heim|nummer *f* secret number; *teleph.* ex-directory (*Am.* unlisted) number; **~polizei** *f* secret police; **~polizist** *m* detective, plain-clothes man; **~rat** *m* Privy Councillor; **~sache** *f* secret (*od.* security) matter; **~schrift** *f* secret code; **~treffen** *n* secret meeting; **~tuerei** [~tu:ə'raɪ] *f* (16) secretiveness; **≈tuerisch** secretive, mysterious; **~tür** *f* secret door; **~waffe** *f* secret weapon.

Geheiß [gə'haɪs] *n* (3³) command, order; *auf j-s ~* at a p.'s bidding.

ge'heißen *p.p. v. heißen.*

gehen ['ge:ən] (30, sn) go; *zu Fuß*: walk; (*weg~*) leave; *Maschine*: work; *Uhr*: go; *Ware*: sell; *Wind*: blow; *Teig*: rise; (*reichen*) *bis an* (*acc.*) reach; *wie geht es Ihnen?* how are you?; *es geht mir gut* (*schlecht*) I am well (not well); *es geht mir gerade so* F same here; *es geht* (*ist möglich*) it can be done, (*funktioniert*) it works, (*ganz gut*) fairly well; *das geht nicht* that will not do; *~ lassen* let go; *an die Arbeit usw. ~* set about; *s-e Worte usw. ~ dahin, daß ...* aim at *ger.*; *du mußt jetzt ~* you will have to leave; F *ach, geh doch!* go on!; *mit e-m Mädchen ~* go with a girl; *das Fenster geht auf die Straße* (*hinaus*) the window opens (*od.* gives, looks) into the street; *in sich ~* commune with o.s., *reuig*: repent; *er geht ins zwanzigste Jahr* he is entering upon his twentieth year; *vor sich ~* happen; *wenn es nach mir ginge* if I had my way; *es geht nichts über* (*acc.*) ... there is nothing like ...; *s. Horizont*; *um was geht es?* what is it (all) about?; *es geht um dein Leben* your life is at stake; **≈** *n* walking (*a. sport*); **'~lassen:** *sich ~* take it easy, *b.s.* take leave of one's manners.

geheuer [~'hɔʏər]: *nicht ~* (*riskant*) risky; (*unheimlich*) uncanny, eerie; (*verdächtig*) *sl.* fishy; *hier ist es nicht ~* this place is haunted; *ihm war nicht recht ~ zu Mute* he did not feel quite at his ease.

Geheul [~'hɔʏl] *n* (3) howling.

Gehilf|e [~'hilfə] *m* (13), **~in** *f* (16¹) assistant; *fig.* helpmate.

Gehirn [gə'hirn] *n* (3) brain(s *pl. fig.*); **~blutung** *f* cerebral h(a)emorrhage; **~-erschütterung** *f* concussion (of the brain); **~hälfte** *f* cerebral hemisphere; **~schlag** *m* cerebral apoplexy; **~schwund** *m* atrophy of the brain; **~tumor** *m* cerebral tumo(u)r; **~wäsche** *f* brain-washing; *j-n e-r ~ unterziehen* brainwash a p.

gehoben [~'ho:bən] **1.** *p.p. v. heben*; **2.** *adj. Sprache usw.*: elevated; *Stellung*: high, senior; *in ~er Stimmung* in high spirits.

Gehöft [~'hø:ft] *n* (3) farm(stead).

geholfen [gə'hɔlfən] *p.p. v. helfen.*

Gehölz [~'hœlts] *n* (3²) wood, copse.

Gehör [~'hø:r] *n* (3) hearing; ear; *musikalisches ~* musical ear; *nach dem ~* by (the) ear; *~ haben für* have an ear for; *j-m ~ schenken* lend an ear (*od.* listen) to a p.; *sich ~ ver-*

schaffen make o.s. heard; ♪ *zu ~ bringen* perform.

ge'horchen (25) obey (*j-m* a p.).

ge'hören (25, *dat. od. zu*) belong to; *es gehört sich* it is proper *od.* right *od.* fit; *die Sachen ~ in den Schrank* these things go into the cupboard; *dazu gehört Geld* that requires (*od.* takes) money; *das gehört nicht hierher* that's not to the point.

Ge'hörgang *m* auditory passage.

ge'hörig (*dat. od. zu*) belonging to; (*wie sich's gehört*) fit, proper, right; due; (*tüchtig*) good; *adv.* duly, in due form; (*tüchtig*) thoroughly; *s. Meinung*.

ge'hörlos deaf; **&enschule** *f* school for the deaf.

Gehörn [~'hœrn] *n* (3) horns *pl.*; *hunt.* antlers *pl.*; **&t** horned.

gehorsam [~'ho:rza:m] **1.** *adj.* obedient; **2.** & *m* (3) obedience.

'**Geh|steig** *m* pavement, *Am.* sidewalk; '**~versuch** *m* attempt at walking; '**~weg** *m s. Gehsteig*; '**~werk** ⊕ *n* works *pl.*, clockwork.

Geier ['gaɪər] *m* (7) vulture.

Geifer ['gaɪfər] *m* (7) slaver, drivel; *fig.* venom; '**&n** (29) drivel, slaver; *fig.* foam; *fig.* ~ *gegen* vituperate against.

Geige ['gaɪgə] *f* (15) violin, F fiddle; *s. erst, zweit*; '**&n** (25) play (on) the violin, F fiddle; '**~nbogen** *m* (violin-)bow; '**~nharz** *n* colophony, rosin; '**~nkasten** *m* violin-case; '**~nmacher** *m* violin-maker; '**~r** *m* (7), '**~rin** *f* (16[1]) violinist.

'**Geigerzähler** *phys. m* Geiger counter.

geil [gaɪl] lascivious, wanton, lewd; *sl.* horny, randy; (*üppig*) luxuriant, rank; '**&heit** *f* lewdness, wantonness; rankness, luxuriance.

Geisel ['gaɪzəl] *f* (15) hostage; '**~drama** *n* hostage drama; **~nahme** ['~na:mə] *f* (15) taking of hostages; '**~nehmer** *m* (7) kidnapper.

Geiß [gaɪs] *f* (16) goat; '**~blatt** ⚘ *n* honeysuckle, woodbine; '**~bock** *m* he-goat, billy-goat.

Geißel ['gaɪsəl] *f* (15) whip, lash; *fig.* scourge; '**&n** (27) whip, lash; *fig.* lash, castigate; '**~ung** *f* whipping, lashing; *fig.* castigation.

Geist [gaɪst] *m* (1[1]) spirit; (*Verstand*) mind, intellect; (*Genius*) genius; (*Witz*) wit; *ein großer ~ P.*: a great mind; (*Gespenst*) ghost; (*Kobold*) sprite; *der Heilige ~* the Holy Ghost; *den ~ aufgeben* give up the ghost, *fig. a.* conk out (*sl.*); *im ~e bei j-m sein usw.* in (the) spirit *od.* in mind.

'**Geister|bahn** *f* ghost train; '**~beschwörer** *m* (7) (*Geisteranrufer*) necromancer; (*Austreiber*) exorcist; '**~bilder** *n/pl. Fernsehen*: ghosting *sg.*; '**~-erscheinung** *f* apparition; '**&haft** ghostly; '**~hand** *f*: *wie von ~* as if by magic; '**~stunde** *f* witching hour; '**~welt** *f* world of spirits.

'**geistes|-abwesend** absent-minded; '**&-abwesenheit** *f* absent-mindedness; '**&-arbeit** *f* brain-work; '**&-arbeiter** *m* brain-worker; '**&blitz** *m* flash of genius, brainwave; '**&gabe** *f* talent; '**&gegenwart** *f* presence of mind; '**~gegenwärtig** alert, quick-witted; '**&geschichte** *f* intellectual history; '**~gestört** mentally deranged; '**&größe** *f* greatness of mind; '**&haltung** *f* mental attitude, mentality; '**&kraft** *f* power of mind; '**~krank** insane, mentally ill; '**&kranke** *m, f* lunatic; '**&krankheit** *f* insanity, mental disorder; '**&produkt** *n* brain-child; '**~schwach** imbecile; '**&schwäche** *f* feeble-mindedness, imbecility; '**&störung** *f* mental disorder; '**&verfassung** *f* frame of mind; '**~verwandt** congenial (*mit* to); '**&verwandtschaft** *f* congeniality; '**&verwirrung** *f* mental disturbance; '**&wissenschaften** *f/pl. the* humanities, *the* Arts; '**&zustand** *m* state of mind.

'**geistig** intellectual, mental; (*unkörperlich*) spiritual; *~es Auge* mind's eye; *~es Eigentum* intellectual property; *~e Getränke n/pl.* spirits.

'**geistlich** spiritual; *Orden*: religious; (*&e betreffend*) ecclesiastical, clerical; *Musik usw.*: sacred; *~es Amt* ministry; '**&e** *m* (18) clergyman, cleric; *e-r Sekte*: minister; ⚔, ⚓, ⚖ chaplain; '**&keit** *f* clergy.

'**geist|los** mindless; (*langweilig*) dull; (*dumm*) stupid; '**&losigkeit** *f* mindlessness; dul(l)ness; *Redensart*: platitude; '**~reich**, '**~voll** witty; '**~tötend** soul-destroying.

Geiz [gaɪts] *m* (3[2]) avarice; (*Knauserei*) stinginess; '**&en** (27) be avaricious *od.* stingy; *nach et. ~* covet; *mit et. ~* be sparing with, stint *a th.*;

'**~hals** *m*, '**~kragen** *m* miser; '**⁀ig** avaricious; (*knickerig*) niggardly, stingy, mean.
Gejammer [gə'jamər] *n* (7) (endless) lamentation, wailing.
Gejohle [~'jo:lə] *n* (7) hooting.
gekannt [~'kant] *p.p. v. kennen.*
Gekeife [~'kaɪfə] *n* (3) scolding.
Gekicher [~'kiçər] *n* (7) tittering.
Gekläff [~'klɛf] *n* (3) yelping.
Geklapper [~'klapər] *n* (7) rattling.
Geklatsche [~'klatʃə] *n* (7) clapping; *fig.* gossiping.
Geklimper [~'klimpər] *n* (7) *auf dem Klavier*: strum(ming).
Geklirr(e) [~'klir(ə)] *n* (3) clashing, clanking.
ge'klommen *p.p. v. klimmen.*
geklungen [~'kluŋən] *p.p. v. klingen.*
Geknatter [~'knatər] *n s. Geknister.*
gekniffen [~'knifən] *p.p. v. kneifen.*
Geknister [~'knistər] *n* (7) crackling.
ge'kommen *p.p. v. kommen.*
gekonnt [gə'kɔnt] **1.** *p.p. v. können*; **2.** *adj.* competent, expert(ly *adv.*).
geköpert [gə'køpərt] twilled.
Gekreisch [~'kraɪʃ] *n* (4) screaming, screams *pl.*; shrieking, shrieks *pl.*
Gekritzel [~'kritsəl] *n* (7) scrawl(-ing), scribbling, scribble.
gekrochen [~'krɔxən] *p.p. v. kriechen.*
Gekröse [~'krø:zə] *n* (7) tripe; *anat.* mesentery.
gekünstelt [~'kynstəlt] artificial.
Gel [ge:l] *n* (3) gel.
Gelächter [~'lɛçtər] *n* (7) laughter.
ge'laden *p.p. v. laden*[1].
Gelage [gə'lɑ:gə] *n* (7) feast, banquet; (*Zecherei*) drinking-bout.
Gelände [~'lɛndə] *n* (7) tract of land, area; country; (*Boden*) ground; *bsd.* ⚔ terrain; **~fahrt** *f* cross-country drive; **~fahrzeug** *n* cross-country vehicle; **⁀gängig** [~gɛŋiç] cross-country *car*; **~kunde** *f* topography; **~lauf** *m Sport*: cross-country race.
Geländer [~'lɛndər] *n* (7) railing, balustrade; (*Treppen⁀*) banisters *pl.*; (*~stange*) handrail.
ge'lang *pret. v. gelingen* 1.
ge'langen (25, sn): *~ an (acc.), nach, zu* arrive at, get (*od.* come) to, reach; *zu e-m Ziele (a. gewinnen)*: attain (to), gain, (*bekommen*) obtain; *s. Macht*; *auf die Nachwelt*: come (*od.* be handed) down to; *in j-s Hände ~* get into a p.'s hands.
Gelaß [gə'las] *n* (4) room, space.
ge'lassen 1. *p.p. v. lassen*; **2.** *adj.* calm, composed; **⁀heit** *f* calmness.
Gelatin|e [ʒela'ti:nə] *f* (15) gelatine; **⁀ieren** [~ti'ni:rən] gelatinize.
Gelaufe [gə'laʊfə] *n* (7) running (to and fro).
ge'laufen *p.p. v. laufen.*
ge'läufig fluent, easy; *Zunge*: voluble; (*allgemein bekannt*) current; *das ist ihm ~* that is familiar to him; **⁀keit** *f* fluency, ease.
gelaunt [gə'laʊnt] disposed; *gut ~* good-humo(u)red, in good humo(u)r; *schlecht ~* ill-humo(u)red, out of humo(u)r, bad-tempered.
Geläut(e) [gə'lɔʏt(ə)] *n* (3 [7]) ringing; (*die Glocken*) chime.
gelb [gɛlp] yellow; *Verkehrsampel*: amber; **⁀e** ['gɛlbə] *n im Ei*: yolk; '**⁀filter** *phot. m* yellow filter; '**~grün** yellowish-green; '**~lich** yellowish; '**⁀schnabel** *m fig.* greenhorn, whipper-snapper; '**⁀sucht** *f* jaundice; **~süchtig** ['~zyçtiç] jaundiced.
Geld [gɛlt] *n* (1) money; *s. bar, klein, knapp*; *bei ~e sein* be in cash; *ins ~ laufen* run into money; *zu ~ machen* turn into cash; *nicht für ~ und gute Worte* neither for love nor money.
'**Geld|-angelegenheit** *f* money-matter; '**~-abwertung** *f* devaluation; '**~-anlage** *f* investment; '**~-anleihe** *f* loan (of money); '**~-anweisung** *f* remittance; '**~-aufwertung** *f* revaluation of money; '**~-ausgabe** *f* expense; '**~-automat** ✝ *m* cash dispenser; '**~betrag** *m* amount *od.* sum (of money); '**~beutel** *m* purse; '**~brief** *m* money-letter; '**~buße** *f* fine; '**~-entwertung** *f* depreciation of money; *s. Geldabwertung*; '**~-erwerb** *m* money-making; '**~forderung** *f* monetary claim; ✝ outstanding debt; '**~geber** *m* (7) financial backer, financier, investor; '**~geschäfte** *n/pl.* money transactions; '**~geschenk** *n* gratuity, donation; '**~gier** *f* greed for money, avarice; '**⁀gierig** greedy for money, avaricious; '**~heirat** *f* money-match; '**~klemme** F *f* squeeze; '**~knappheit** *f* shortness (✝ scarcity) of money; '**~krise** *f* monetary crisis; '**⁀lich** pecuniary; '**~makler** *m* money-broker; '**~mangel** *m* lack of money;

'**~mann** *m* financier; '**~markt** *m* money market; '**~mittel** *n/pl.* funds, means, resources; '**~not** *f* financial straits *pl.*; '**~quelle** *f* pecuniary resource; '**~sache** *f* money matter; '**~schein** *m* bank-note, *Am.* bill; '**~schrank** *m* safe, strong-box; '**~schrankknacker** *m* (7) safe-cracker; '**~sendung** *f* (cash) remittance; '**~sorte** *f* denomination; *pl.* coins and notes; '**~spende** *f* donation, contribution; '**~strafe** *f* fine; *mit e-r ~ belegen* fine, mulct; '**~stück** *n* coin; '**~tasche** *f* money-bag, purse; *für Scheine*: note-case, pocketbook, *Am.* billfold; '**~-überhang** *m* surplus money; '**~verlegenheit** *f* pecuniary embarrassment; *in ~ sein* be pressed for money, F be hard up; '**~verlust** *m* pecuniary loss; '**~verschwendung** *f* waste of money; '**~wert** *m* value (of money), value of currency.

Gelee [ʒe'le:] *n* (11) jelly.

ge'legen 1. *p.p. v. liegen*; **2.** *adj.* situated, *Am. a.* located; (*passend*) convenient, suitable; *Zeit*: opportune; *es kommt mir gerade ~* it just suits me, it comes in handy; *s. liegen.*

Gelegenheit [gə'le:gənhaɪt] *f* occasion; *gute*: opportunity; (*Zufall*) chance; (*Wasch*~ *usw.*) facility; *bei ~ s. gelegentlich adv.*; *bei dieser ~* on this occasion; *bei jeder ~* at every turn; *j-m ~ bieten* give a p. an opportunity; *die ~ (beim Schopf) ergreifen* seize the opportunity; *~ nehmen zu inf.* take occasion to; **~s-arbeit** *f* casual (*od.* odd) job; **~s-arbeiter** *m* casual labo(u)rer, odd-job worker; **~sdieb** *m* casual thief; **~skauf** *m* chance purchase, bargain.

gelegentlich [~'le:gəntliç] *adj.* occasional; (*zufällig*) casual; chance; *adv.* some time, at one's convenience; *prp.* (*gen.*) on the occasion of.

gelehrig [~'le:riç] docile; clever; **~keit** *f* docility; cleverness.

Ge'lehrsamkeit *f* erudition, learning.

ge'lehrt learned; F *~es Haus* pundit; **~e** *m, f* learned (wo)man, scholar.

Geleise [gə'laɪzə] *n* (7, *mst pl.*) rut, track; 🚂 rails *pl.*, *Am.* track; *fig. im alten ~* in the same old rut; *auf ein totes ~ geraten* reach a deadlock.

Geleit [~'laɪt] *n* (3) *a.* ⚔ escort; ⚓ convoy; (*Gefolge*) attendance; *j-m das ~ geben* accompany (*schützend*: escort) a p., *zum Abschied*: see a p. off; *freies ~* safe-conduct; **~brief** *m* (letter of) safe-conduct; ✝ letter of consignment; **~en** accompany, conduct; *bsd.* ⚔ escort; ⚓ convoy; **~schiff** *n* convoy (vessel); **~wort** *n* foreword; **~zug** ⚓ *m* convoy.

Gelenk [~'lɛŋk] *n* (3) joint; *anat. a.* (*~fügung*) articulation; ⊕ joint; (*Scharnier*) hinge; (*Bindeglied*) link; **~bus** *m* articulated bus; **~-entzündung** ⚕ *f* arthritis; **~ig** lissom(e), agile, (*a.* ⊕) flexible; **~igkeit** *f* agility; flexibility; **~rheumatismus** ⚕ *m* articular rheumatism.

gelernt [~'lɛrnt] *Arbeit(er)*: skilled.

ge'lesen *p.p. v. lesen.*

Gelichter [~'liçtər] *n* (7) lot, riff-raff, rabble.

Geliebte [gə'li:ptə] (18) *m* lover; *~ f* love(r), sweetheart; (*Mätresse*) mistress.

geliehen [gə'li:ən] *p.p. v. leihen.*

gelieren [ʒe'li:rən] gelatinize.

ge'lind(e) soft, gentle, mild (*alle a. fig.*); *Strafe*: mild, lenient; *gelinde gesagt* to put it mildly.

gelingen [gə'liŋən] **1.** (30, sn) succeed; *es gelingt mir, zu tun* I succeed in doing; *es gelingt mir nicht, zu tun* I fail in doing *od.* to do; **2.** ~ *n* (6) success.

Gelispel [~'lispəl] *n* (7) lisping; (*Geflüster*) whispering.

gelitten [~'litən] *p.p. v. leiden* 1.

gellen ['gɛlən] (25) shrill; (*gellend schreien*) *a.* yell, scream; *Ohr*: tingle; '**~d** shrill, piercing.

ge'loben (25) promise; *feierlich*: vow, pledge; *das Gelobte Land* the Land of Promise.

Gelöbnis [gə'lø:pnis] *n* (4¹) (solemn) promise, pledge; vow.

gelogen [gə'lo:gən] *p.p. v. lügen.*

gelt¹ [gɛlt] giving no milk; (*unfruchtbar*) *Tier*: barren.

gelt² F *int.* F isn't it?

gelt|en ['gɛltən] (30) *v/t.* be worth; *v/i.* be of value; (*gültig sein*) be valid *od.* good; (*zählen*) count; *Gesetz*: be in force; *Grund usw.*: hold (good *od.* true); *Münze*: be current; *fig. etwas ~* carry weight, have influence; *j-m ~* be meant for a p.; *~ für* a) (*od. ~ als*) pass for, be reputed (*od.* thought, supposed) to be, rank as, b) (*sich anwenden lassen*) apply to; be right for, be true of; *~ lassen* let pass; allow; ~ *lassen als* pass off as; *s-n Einfluß ~d machen* bring one's influence to bear; *~d machen* a) assert, b) *als Entschuldigung*: plead, c) (*daß*) maintain (that); *das gilt nicht* that is not allowed, that is not fair *od.* does not count; *es gilt!* done!; *es galt unser Leben* our life was at stake; *es gilt zu inf.* the question is to *inf.*, it is necessary to *inf.*; *s. Wette*; '**②ung** *f* (*Gültigkeit*) validity; *e-r Münze*: currency; *e-r P.*: authority, credit, (*Achtung*) prestige, respect; *zur ~ bringen* bring to bear; *Gesetz usw.*: enforce; *zur ~ kommen* (begin to) tell, take effect, (*herausragen*) stand out; '**②ungsbedürfnis** *n*, '**②ungsdrang** *m* craving for recognition.

Gelübde [gə'lypdə] *n* (7) vow.

gelungen [~'luŋən] **1.** *p.p. v. gelingen*; **2.** *adj.* successful; (*vortrefflich*) capital; *du bist ~!* you are funny!

Gelüst [~'lyst] *n* (3[1]) desire, craving, appetite (*alle*: *nach* for); **②en:** *mich gelüstet nach* I crave (for).

gemach[1] [~'maːx] *int.*: *~!* (*sachte!*) gently!

Ge'mach[2] *n* (1[2], *poet.* 3) room, apartment, chamber.

gemächlich [~'mɛːçliç] *adj. u. adv.* leisurely; **②keit** *f* leisureliness, ease.

Gemahl [gə'maːl] *m* (3) husband, consort; *Ihr Herr ~* Mr. X.; **~in** *f* wife, consort; *Ihre Frau ~* Mrs. X.

gemahnen [~'maːnən]: *~ an* (*acc.*) remind of.

Gemälde [~'mɛːldə] *n* (7) painting, picture; **~-ausstellung** *f* exhibition of pictures; **~galerie** *f* picture--gallery, *Am. a.* museum.

gemäß [~'mɛːs] **1.** *adj.* conformable; **2.** *prp.* (*dat.*) according to, in accordance with; *bsd.* ⚖ pursuant to; **~igt** moderate; *geogr.* temperate.

Gemäuer [gə'mɔʏər] *n* (7): *altes ~* decayed building(s *pl.*); ruins *pl.*

gemein [~'maɪn] common; (*allgemein*) *a.* general; *b.s.* low, mean, dirty; (*pöbelhaft*) vulgar; *~er Kerl* beast of a fellow; *~er Soldat, Gemeine m* private (soldier), *Am.* (basic) private; et. *~ haben mit* have a th. in common with; *sich ~ machen mit* keep company with.

Gemeinde [~'maɪndə] *f* (15) community; (*Kirchen②*) parish, (*Kirchgänger*) congregation; (*Stadt②*) municipality; **~bezirk** *m* district; **~haus** *n* municipal hall; *eccl.* parish hall; **~rat** *m* municipal council (*od. P.*: councillor); **~schwester** *f* district nurse; **~steuer** *f* (local) rate, *Am.* local tax; **~vorstand** *m* local board; **~wahl** *f* communal election; **~zentrum** *n* community cent|re, *Am.* -er.

ge'mein|faßlich *s. gemeinverständlich*; **~gefährlich** dangerous to the public; *~er Mensch* public danger, *Am.* public enemy; **②geist** *m* public spirit; **~gültig** generally accepted; **②gut** *n* common property; **②heit** *f* (*Niedrigkeit*) vulgarity, meanness; (*niedrige Tat*) mean trick; **~hin** commonly; **②kosten** *pl.* overhead (costs); **②nutz** *m* (3[2], *o. pl.*) common good; **~nützig** [~nytsiç] of public utility; *Verein*: non-profit; *~e Betriebe* public utilities *pl.*; **②nützigkeit** *f* public utility; **②platz** *m* commonplace; **~sam** common; joint; *②er Markt m* Common Market; *~ mit* in common with; *~e Sache machen mit* make common cause with; **②samkeit** *f*, **②schaft** *f* (16) community; (*Verkehr*) intercourse; **~schaftlich** common, joint; *v. zweien*: mutual; *adv. a.* in common.

Ge'meinschafts|-anschluß *m* party line; **~-antenne** *f* communal aerial; **~-arbeit** *f* teamwork; **~-erziehung** *f* coeducation; **~geist** *m* esprit de corps (*fr.*), community spirit; **~konto** *n* joint account; **~praxis** *f* joint practice; **~produktion** *f* co-production; **~raum** *m* common room; **~sendung** *f* simultaneous broadcast.

Ge'mein|schuldner *m* bankrupt; **~sinn** *m* public spirit; **②verständlich** intelligible to all, popular; **~wesen** *n* community; polity; **~wohl** *n* public weal.

Gemeng|e [gə'mɛŋə] *n* (7) mixture; (*Hand②*) scuffle; **~sel** [~zəl] *n* (7) medley, hotchpotch.

ge'messen 1. *p.p. v. messen*; **2.** *adj.* measured; (*förmlich*) formal; (*feierlich*) grave; **②heit** *f* measuredness; formality; gravity.

Gemetzel [gə'mɛtsəl] *n* (7) slaughter, carnage, massacre.

gemieden [~'miːdən] *p.p. v. meiden.*

Gemisch [~'miʃ] *n* (3[2]) mixture.

gemischt [~'miʃt] mixed (*a. Tennis*; *a. fig. Gefühl usw.*); **②warenhand-**

lung *f* grocery, *Am.* general (merchandise) store.
Gemme ['gɛmə] *f* (15) gem.
gemocht [gə'mɔxt] *p.p. v. mögen.*
gemolken [gə'mɔlkən] *p.p. v. melken.*
Gemse ['gɛmzə] *f* (15) chamois.
Gemurmel [gə'murməl] *n* (7) murmur(ing), mutter(ing).
Gemüse [~'my:zə] *n* (7) vegetable; greens *pl.*; **~bau** *m* vegetable gardening, *Am.* truck farming; **~beet** *n* vegetable bed; **~garten** *m* kitchen-garden; **~händler**(**in** *f*) *m* greengrocer; **~handlung** *f* greengrocer's shop; **~konserven** *f/pl.* preserved (*od.* tinned, *Am.* canned) vegetables; **~schale** *f im Kühlschrank*: salad drawer.
gemüßigt [~'my:siçt]: *sich ~ sehen, zu inf.* feel (*od.* find o.s.) obliged to *inf.*
gemußt [~'must] *p.p. v. müssen.*
gemustert [~'mustərt] *Stoff*: figured, patterned.
Gemüt [~'my:t] *n* (1) mind; (*Gefühl*) feeling; (*Seele*) soul; (*Herz*) heart; (*~s-art*) disposition, temper; *j-m et. zu ~e führen* bring a th. home to a p.; F *sich e-e Flasche Wein usw. zu ~e führen* discuss.
ge'mütlich (*gutmütig*) good-natured; (*freundlich*) genial; (*behaglich*) comfortable, snug, cosy, restful; *~es Beisammensein* social gathering; *~ werden* unbend; *es sich ~ machen* make o.s. at home, relax; **&keit** *f* good nature; geniality; cosiness, snugness.
Ge'müts|-art *f*, **~beschaffenheit** *f* (mental) disposition, temper, character; **~bewegung** *f* emotion; **&-krank** mentally diseased, emotionally disturbed; (*schwermütig*) melancholy; **~krankheit** *f* mental disorder, melancholia; **~mensch** *m* emotional (*od.* warm-hearted) person; **~ruhe** *f* calmness; composure; **~verfassung** *f*, **~zustand** *m* state of mind, humo(u)r.
ge'mütvoll *P.*: warm(-hearted); *S.*: full of feeling.
gen[1] [gɛn] *prp.* towards.
Gen[2] [ge:n] *biol. n* (3[1]) gene.
genannt [gə'nant] *p.p. v. nennen.*
genas [gə'na:s] *pret. v. genesen.*
genau [gə'naʊ] exact, accurate, precise; (*streng*) strict; (*sorgfältig*) careful, scrupulous; *Bericht usw.*: detailed; *~so gut* just as good (*od.* well); *es ~ nehmen* (*mit*) be particular (about); *&eres* full particulars *pl.*; **~genommen** strictly speaking; **&igkeit** *f* accuracy, exactness; precision; strictness.
Gendarm [ʒɑ̃'darm] *m* (12) country policeman; **~erie** [~mə'ri:] *f* (15) rural constabulary.
Genealogie [genealo'gi:] *f* (16) genealogy.
genehm [gə'ne:m] agreeable, convenient (*dat.* to); **~igen** [~migən] (*bewilligen*) grant; consent to; (*gutheißen*) approve (of), authorize; *behördlich*: *a.* license; **&igung** *f* grant; approval; licen|ce, *Am.* -se, permit; (*Erlaubnis*) permission, authorization; (*Einwilligung*) consent.
geneigt [~'naɪkt] inclined (*fig. zu* to); (*j-m*) well disposed (to[wards] a p.); *ein ~es Ohr* a willing ear; *der ~e Leser* the gentle reader.
General [genə'ra:l] *m* (3[1] *u.* 3[2]) general; **~-agent** *m* agent-general; **~-amnestie** *f* general amnesty; **~-anzeiger** *m* (*Zeitung*) General Gazette; **~baß** ♩ *m* thorough-bass; **~bevollmächtigte** *m* chief representative *od.* agent; **~direktor** *m* general manager; **~'feldmarschall** ⚔ *m* Field Marshal; **~-intendant** *thea. m* director; **~ität** ⚔ [~rali'tɛ:t] *f* (16) (body of) generals *pl.*; **~konsul** [~'ra:l-] *m* consul-general; **~konsulat** *n* consulate-general; **~'leutnant** *m* lieutenant-general; **~major** *m* major-general; **~'oberst** *m* colonel-general; **~probe** *f* dress rehearsal; **~sekretär** *m* secretary general; **~'staatsanwalt** *m* Chief State Counsel; **~stab** *m* General Staff; **~stabskarte** *f* ordnance (survey) map, *Am.* strategic map; **~streik** *m* general strike; **~überholung** *f* complete overhaul; **~versammlung** *f* general meeting; **~vertreter** *m* agent-general; **~vollmacht** ⚖ *f* general power of attorney.
Generation [genəra'tsjo:n] *f* (16) generation; **~skonflikt** *m* generation gap.
Generator [~'ra:tɔr] *m* (8[1]) generator; (*Gas&*) *a.* producer.
generell [~'rɛl] general(ly *adv.*).
gene|sen [gə'ne:zən] **1.** (30, sn) recover (*von* from); **2.** *p.p. v.* 1.; **&sende**

m, f convalescent; **2sung** *f* recovery; convalescence; **2sungsheim** *n* convalescent home.

Genet|ik [ge'ne:tik] *f* (16, *o. pl.*) genetics *sg.*; **2isch** genetic.

Genfer ['gɛnfər]: **~ Abkommen** *n*, **~ Konventi'on** *f* Geneva Convention.

genial [gen'jɑ:l] ingenious, brilliant; **2ität** [~jali'tɛ:t] *f* (16) genius, brilliancy.

Genick [gə'nik] *n* (3) (back of the) neck, nape (of the neck); (*sich*) *das ~ brechen* break one's neck; *fig. das brach ihm das ~* that finished him off, that was the last straw; **~schuß** *m* shot in the neck; **~starre** ⚕ *f* cerebrospinal meningitis.

Genie [ʒe'ni:] *n* (11) genius (*a. P.*).

ge'nieren (25) trouble, disturb; *sich ~* feel embarrassed; *zu tun*: be too timid to do; *sich nicht ~ zu inf.* not to be ashamed to *inf.*; *~ Sie sich nicht* don't be shy.

ge'nieß|bar [gə'ni:s-] *Speise*: eatable; *Getränk*: drinkable; *fig.* agreeable; **~en** (30) enjoy; *Speise*: eat; *Getränk*: drink; et. *~* take some food *od.* some refreshments; *j-s Vertrauen ~* be in a p.'s confidence.

Genitalien [geni'tɑ:ljən] *pl.* genitals.

Genitiv *gr.* ['ge:niti:f] *m* (3^1) genitive (case); possessive (case).

Genius ['ge:nius] *m* (16^2) genius; *guter ~* guardian angel.

'Gen|manipulation *f* genetic engineering; **'~mutation** *f* gene mutation.

genommen [gə'nɔmən] *p.p. v. nehmen.*

genormt [gə'nɔrmt] standardized.

genoß [gə'nɔs] *pret. v. genießen.*

Genoss|e [gə'nɔsə] *m* (13), **~in** *f* companion, mate, (*a. pol.*) comrade; **2en** *p.p. v. genießen*; **~enschaft** ✝ *f* co-operative (society).

Genre|bild ['ʒɑ̃r(ə)-] *n* genre-picture; **'~maler** *m* genre-painter.

genug [gə'nu:k] enough, sufficient(-ly); *~ (davon)!* enough (of that)!; no more of this!; *ich habe ~ davon* I am sick of it.

Genüg|e [~'ny:gə] *f* (15): *j-m ~ tun* satisfy a p.; *e-r S.* come up to a th.; *zur ~* enough, sufficiently; **2en** (25) be enough; *das genügt* that will do; *j-m ~* satisfy a p.; (*nicht*) *~* (not to) give satisfaction; *sich ~ lassen* be satisfied with; **2end** sufficient; **2sam** [~'ny:k-] easily satisfied; (*mäßig*) frugal; **~samkeit** *f* contentedness; frugality.

Genugtu-ung [gə'nu:ktu:uŋ] *f* satisfaction; (*Wiedergutmachung*) reparation.

Genus *gr.* ['genus] *n* (16, *pl.* '*Genera*) gender.

Genuß [gə'nus] *m* (4^2) (*Freude; Besitz*) enjoyment; (*Nutznießung*) use; *v. Speisen usw.*: taking; *fig. ein wahrer ~* a real treat; **~mittel** *n* semi-luxury; *anregendes*: stimulant; **2reich** delightful, enjoyable; **~sucht** *f* thirst for pleasure; **2süchtig** pleasure-seeking.

Geo|däsie [geodɛ'si:] *f* (16) geodesy; **~graph** [~'grɑ:f] *m* (12) geographer; **~graphie** [~gra'fi:] *f* geography; **2graphisch** [~'grɑ:fiʃ] geographical; **~log(e)** [~'lo:k, ~gə] *m* (12 [13]) geologist; **~logie** [~lo'gi:] *f* geology; **2logisch** [~'lo:giʃ] geological; **~meter** [~'me:tər] *m* (7) surveyor; **~metrie** [~me'tri:] *f* geometry; **2metrisch** [~'me:triʃ] geometric(al); **~phy'sik** *f* geophysics *sg.*; **~poli'tik** *f* geopolitics *sg.*; **2po'litisch** geopolitical.

ge-ordnet [gə'ʔɔrdnət] orderly.

Gepäck [gə'pɛk] *n* (3) luggage; ⚔ *od. Am.* baggage; **~-annahme**(**stelle**) *f* luggage (registration) office, *Am.* baggage checking counter; **~-aufbewahrung**(**sstelle**) *f* cloak-room, left-luggage office, *Am.* checkroom; **~-ausgabe**(**stelle**) *f* luggage delivery office, *Am.* baggage room; *am Flughafen*: baggage reclaim; **~netz** *n* luggage (*Am.* baggage) rack; **~raum** *m* luggage (*Am.* baggage) hold, belly-hold; **~schein** *m* luggage-ticket, *Am.* baggage check; **~stück** *n* piece of luggage (*Am.* baggage); **~träger** *m* (railway) porter; *mot.* roof-rack; *am Fahrrad*: carrier; **~wagen** *m* luggage-van, *Am.* baggage car.

gepanzert [gə'pantsərt] armo(u)red, iron-clad.

gepfeffert [~'pfɛfərt] *fig. Rechnung*: steep; *Witz*: fruity.

gepfiffen [~'pfifən] *p.p. v. pfeifen.*

gepflegt [~'pfle:kt] *P.*: well-groomed; *S.*: well cared-for; *Stil usw.*: cultivated, refined.

gepflogen [~'pflo:gən] *p.p. v. pflegen*; **2heit** *f* habit; custom.

Geplänkel [~ˈplɛŋkəl] *n* (7) skirmish.
Geplapper [~ˈplapər] *n* (7) babbling, chattering, prattle.
Geplätscher [~ˈplɛtʃər] *n* (7) splashing.
Geplauder [~ˈplaudər] *n* (7) chatting, small talk.
Gepolter [~ˈpɔltər] *n* (7) rumble, rumbling.
Gepräge [~ˈprɛːgə] *n* (7) impression; (*a. fig.*) stamp; *e-r Münze*: coinage.
Gepränge [~ˈprɛŋə] *n* (7) pomp.
Geprassel [~ˈprasəl] *n* (7) crackling.
gepriesen [~ˈpriːzən] *p.p. v. preisen.*
gequollen [~ˈkvɔlən] *p.p. v. quellen.*
gerade [gəˈrɑːdə] **1.** *adj.* straight (*a. fig.*); (*eben*) even; (*unmittelbar*) direct; (*aufrichtig*) upright, plain, straightforward; *Gang, Haltung*: upright, erect; *Zahl*: even; **2.** *adv. s.* ~ 1.; just; *ich bin ~ gekommen* I have just come; *er schrieb ~* he was (just) writing; *ich war ~ (zufällig) dort* I happened to be there; *~ das Gegenteil* the very opposite; *nun ~* now more than ever; *~ an dem Tage* on that very day; **3.** **2** *f* (18) ⩘ straight line; *Lauf-, Rennsport*: *die ~* the straight; **4.** **2** *f, a.* **2r** *m Boxen*: straight; **~ˈ-aus** straight on *od.* ahead; **~heˈraus** freely, frankly, point-blank; **~(n-)wegs** [~veːks] directly, straight(away); **~stehen** stand erect; *fig. für etwas ~* answer for a th.; **~ˈzu** (*geradeaus*) straight on, directly; (*nichts andres als*) downright *nonsense, etc.*
Geradheit [~ˈrɑːthaɪt] *f* straightness; *fig.* straightforwardness.
geradlinig [~ˈrɑːtliːniç] rectilinear.
gerammelt [~ˈraməlt]: *~ voll* chock-ful, crammed.
Gerangel [~ˈraŋəl] *n* (3[1]) wrangling.
gerannt [~ˈrant] *p.p. v. rennen.*
Gerassel [gəˈrasəl] *n* (7) rattling, rattle; *Kette*: *a.* clanking.
Gerät [~ˈrɛːt] *n* (3) tool, implement, utensil; *technisches*: gear, device; (*Apparat*) appliance, apparatus; *teleph., Radio usw.*: set; ⚔ (*Ausrüstung*) equipment; *s. Angel***2**, *Fisch***2**, *Haushalts***2**, *Turn***2**; *elektrisches ~* electric appliance.
geraten [gəˈrɑːtən] **1.** *v/i.* (30, sn) *örtlich*: come, fall, get (*in acc.* in[to]; *auf acc.* [up]on *etc.*); (*ausfallen*) turn out *well etc.*; *nach j-m ~* take after a p.; *über et.* (*acc.*) *~* come across a th.; *s. Abweg, aneinander, außer, Brand, Konkurs, Stocken, Vergessenheit usw.*; **2.** *adj.* successful; (*ratsam*) advisable; **3.** *p.p. v. raten.*
Geˈräte|stecker ⚡ *m* connector plug; **~turnen** *n* apparatus gymnastics *pl.*
Gerateˈwohl *n*: *aufs ~* at random, on the off-chance.
geraum [gəˈraum]: *~e Zeit* long time.
geräumig [gəˈrɔʏmiç] spacious, roomy; **2keit** *f* spaciousness.
Geräusch [~ˈrɔʏʃ] *n* (3[2]) noise; **~dämpfung** *f* sound damping; **~kulisse** *f* background noise; **2los** noiseless, silent; **~losigkeit** *f* noiselessness; **~pegel** *m* noise level; **2voll** noisy, loud.
gerb|en [ˈgɛrbən] (25) tan (*a. fig.* = *prügeln*); *weiß ~* taw; **ˈ2er** *m* (7) tanner; **2erei** [~ˈraɪ] *f* tannery; **2säure** [ˈgɛrp-] *f* tannic acid.
gerecht [gəˈrɛçt] just; (*rechtschaffen*) righteous; (*billig*) fair; *j-m ~ werden* do justice to a p. (*a. fig.*); *e-r Anforderung, e-m Wunsch usw. ~ werden* meet; *allen Seiten ~ werden* deal with all aspects; **~fertigt** justified, justifiable; **2igkeit** *f* justice; righteousness; fairness; *j-m ~ widerfahren lassen* do a p. justice; **2igkeitssinn** *m* sense of justice.
Gerede [gəˈreːdə] *n* (7) talk; (*Geschwätz*) gossip; (*Gerücht*) rumo(u)r; *ins ~ kommen* get talked about.
geˈregelt regulated, ordered; orderly.
geˈreichen (25): *zu et. ~* (turn out to) be a th.; redound to a th.
gereizt [~ˈraɪtst] irritated, nettled, piqued; **2heit** *f* irritation.
geˈreuen: *es gereut mich* I repent (of) it, I am sorry for it; *sich keine Mühe ~ lassen* spare no trouble.
Gericht [~ˈriçt] *n* (3) **1.** (*Speise*) dish, course; **2.** ⚖ law-court, court (of justice), *mst rhet. u. fig.* tribunal; (*Rechtsspruch*) judg(e)ment; *s. jüngst*; *fig. mit j-m ins ~ gehen* take a p. to task; *vor ~ bringen* bring to trial; *vor ~ fordern* summon; *zu ~ sitzen über* (*acc.*) sit in judg(e)ment over *od.* on; **2lich** judicial, legal; *~ vereidigt* sworn.

Ge'richts|barkeit *f* jurisdiction; **~beschluß** *m* court order; *durch* ~ by order of the court; **~diener** *m* (court) usher; **~gebäude** *n* law-court, court-house; **~hof** *m* law-court, court of justice; *mst rhet. u. fig.* tribunal; **~kosten** *pl.* (law-)costs; **~medizin** *f* forensic medicine; **~mediziner** *m* medical expert (*Am.* examiner); **~saal** *m* court-room; **~schreiber** *m* clerk of the court; **~stand** *m* (legal) venue; ⚓ legal domicile; **~-urteil** *n* judg(e)ment (of the court); **~verfahren** *n* legal proceedings *pl.*; (law-)suit; **~verhandlung** *f* (judicial) hearing; (*Straf*2) trial; **~vollzieher** *m* bailiff, *Am.* marshal; **~weg** *m*: *auf dem* ~ by legal proceedings.

gerieben [gə'ri:bən] **1.** *p.p. v. reiben*; **2.** *adj. fig.* smart, crafty, wily.

Geriesel [gə'ri:zəl] *n* (7) purling; *Regen*: drizzling.

gering [gə'riŋ] little, small; (*unbedeutend*) trifling, slight, negligible; (*niedrig*) mean, low; (*ärmlich*) poor; (*minderwertig*) inferior; *mein* ~*es Verdienst* my humble merit; *mit* ~*en Ausnahmen* with but few exceptions; ~ *denken von* think little of; **~-achten** think little of; disregard, slight; **~er** inferior, less, minor; *kein* 2*er als* no less a person than; **~fügig** [~fy:giç] insignificant, trifling, negligible, slight; **2fügigkeit** *f* littleness, insignificance; **~haltig** [~haltiç] of low standard, low-grade; **~schätzen** *s. geringachten*; **~schätzig** [~ʃɛtsiç] depreciatory, disparaging, slighting; **2schätzung** *f* disdain, contempt; **~st** least; slightest; minimum; *nicht im* ~*en* not in the least; **~wertig** [~ve:rtiç] low-value, low-quality, inferior.

ge'rinn|en (30, sn) curdle, coagulate; *bsd. Blut*: clot; **2sel** [~zəl] *n* (7) clot; **2ung** *f* coagulation.

Geripp|e [gə'ripə] *n* (7) skeleton (*a. fig.*); (*dürrer Mensch*) *a.* scrag; ⊕ framework; **2t** ribbed; *Säule usw.*: fluted; *Stoff*: corded.

gerissen [gə'risən] **1.** *p.p. v. reißen* 1.; **2.** *adj. fig. s. gerieben* 2.

geritten [gə'ritən] *p.p. v. reiten*.

German|e [gɛr'ma:nə] *m* (13) Teuton; **2isch** Germanic, Teutonic; **~ist** [~ma'nist] *m* (12) German scholar, Germanist; **~istik** [~'nistik] *f* (16, *o. pl.*) Germanistics *pl.*, *Am.* Germanics *pl.*

gern(e) ['gɛrn(ə)] willingly, gladly, with pleasure; *als Antwort*: *sehr* ~! I should be delighted!, I should love to!; ~ *haben, mögen od. tun* be fond of, like; F *du kannst mich* ~ *haben!* go to blazes!; *ich möchte* ~ *wissen* I should like to know; ~ *gesehen sein* be welcome; ~ *geschehen!* don't mention it!, (you are) welcome!

'Gernegroß *m* (14) show-off.

gerochen [~'rɔxən] *p.p. v. riechen*.

Geröll [gə'rœl] *n* (3) rubble.

geronnen [~'rɔnən] *p.p. v. gerinnen*.

Gerste ['gɛrstə] *f* (15) barley.

'Gersten|graupen *f/pl.* peeled barley; **'~korn** *n* barleycorn; ⚕ sty.

Gerte ['gɛrtə] *f* (15) switch, twig; **'2nschlank** (slim and) willowy.

Geruch [gə'rux] *m* (3^3) smell, (*a. fig.*) odo(u)r; *angenehmer*: scent; *fig.* odo(u)r, reputation; **2los** odo(u)rless; **~snerv** *m* olfactory nerve; **~(s)sinn** *m* (sense of) smell.

Gerücht [gə'ryçt] *n* (3) rumo(u)r, report; *es geht das* ~ it is rumo(u)red; **~emacher** *m* rumo(u)r-monger.

ge'ruchtilgend [~tilgənt], **~es** [~dəs] **Mittel** *n* deodorant.

ge'rufen *p.p. v. rufen*; *das kommt wie* ~ that comes in handy.

ge'ruhen deign, condescend.

Gerümpel [gə'rympəl] *n* (7) lumber, junk.

Gerundium *gr.* [ge'rundjum] *n* (9) gerund.

gerungen [gə'ruŋən] *p.p. v. ringen*.

Gerüst [gə'ryst] *n* (3^1) (*Bau*2) scaffold(ing); (*Schau*2) stage; (*Tragewerk*) frame; (*Gestell*) trestle; ⚠ (*Hängewerk*) truss; *fig.* frame(work).

Ges ♪ [gɛs] *n* G flat.

gesalzen [gə'zaltsən] salted; *fig.* spicy; *Preise usw.*: exorbitant, F steep.

gesamt [gə'zamt] whole, entire, total, all; **2-ansicht** *f* general view; **2-auflage** *f* total circulation; *e-s Buchs*: total number of copies published; **2-ausgabe** *f e-s Werkes*: complete edition; **2betrag** *m* (sum) total; **2-bild** *fig. n* overall picture; **~deutsch** all-German; **2-eindruck** *m* overall impression; **2-einnahme** *f* total receipts *pl.*; **2-ertrag** *m* total proceeds *pl.*; **2heit** *f* total(ity); *the* whole;

²**konzept** *n* overall plan; ²**länge** *f* overall length; ²**note** *f Schule*: aggregate mark; ²**preis** *m* total (*od.* inclusive) price; ²**schule** *f* comprehensive school; ²**sieger**(**in** *f*) *m* overall winner; ²**summe** *f* (sum) total; ²-**umsatz** *m* total turnover; ²**zahl** *f* total number.

gesandt [gəˈzant] *p.p. v. senden*; ²**e** *m* (18) envoy; ²**schaft** *f* legation.

Gesang [gəˈzaŋ] *m* (3^3) singing; (*Lied*) song; (*Lob*²) hymn; (*Teil e-r Dichtung*) canto; ~**buch** *n* book of songs; *eccl.* hymn-book; ~**lehrer**(**in** *f*) *m* singing teacher; ~**s-einlage** *thea. f* song insert; ~**ver-ein** *m* choral society, *Am.* glee club.

Gesäß [gəˈzɛːs] *n* (3^2) seat, bottom; ~**tasche** *f* hip pocket.

geˈschaffen *p.p. v. schaffen.*

Geschäft [gəˈʃɛft] *n* (3) business; (*Unternehmung*) *a.* transaction, deal; (*Angelegenheit*) affair; (*Beschäftigung*) occupation, trade, job; (*Firma*) business, firm; (*Laden*²) shop, *Am.* store; *ein* ~ *tätigen* do a business; *ein* ~ (*Notdurft*) *verrichten* relieve nature; ~*e machen mit j-m* do business with; *ein gutes* ~ *machen* make a bargain; ~**emacher** *m* profiteer; ²**ig** busy, active; ~**igkeit** *f* activity; ²**lich** commercial, business; *adv.* on business; ~*e Beziehungen* business relations.

Geˈschäfts|-abschluß *m* (business) transaction *od.* deal; ~-**anteil** *m* share *od.* interest (in a company); ~-**aufsicht** *f* legal control; ~**bedingungen** *f/pl.* terms of business; ~**bereich** *m* sphere of activity, scope; *e-s Ministers*: portfolio; ⚖ jurisdiction; ~**bericht** *m* business report; ~**brief** *m* business letter; ~**fähigkeit** *f* legal (*od.* disposing) capacity; ~**frau** *f* businesswoman; ~**freund** *m* business friend; ²**führend** managing, executive; ~**führer** *m* manager; *e-s Vereins usw.*: secretary; ~**führung** *f* management; ~**gang** *m* course of business; routine; ~**gebaren** *n* business methods *pl.*; ~**geheimnis** *n* business secret; ~**geist** *m* business acumen; ~**haus** *n* (*Gebäude*) shop (*od.* office) building; (*Firma*) commercial firm; ~-**inhaber** *m* owner of a business; ~**jahr** *n* business (*parl.* financial, *Am.* fiscal) year; ~**kosten** *pl.*: *auf* ~ on expense account; ²**kundig** experienced *od.* versed in business; ~**lage** *f* business situation; ~**leute** *pl.* businessmen; ~**lokal** *n* business premises *pl.*; (*Laden*) shop, *Am.* store; (*Büro*) office; ~**mann** *m* (1, *pl. Geschäftsleute*) businessman; ²**mäßig** businesslike; ~-**ordnung** *f* rules *pl.* (of procedure); *parl.* standing orders *pl.*; *zur* ~ *sprechen* rise to order; ~**papiere** *n/pl.* business papers; ~**partner**(**in** *f*) *m* (business) partner; ~**räume** *m/pl.* business premises; ~**reise** *f* business trip; *auf einer* ~ *sein* be away on business; ~**reisende** *m* commercial traveller, *Am.* traveling salesman; ²**schädigend** damaging (*od.* detrimental) to business; ~**schluß** *m* closing time; ~**sitz** *m* place of business; ~**stelle** *f* office, agency; ~**straße** *f* shopping street; ~**teilhaber**(**in** *f*) *m* partner; ~**träger** *m* agent, representative; *pol.* chargé d'affaires (*fr.*); ²**tüchtig** smart, efficient (in business); ~-**unkosten** *pl.* business expenses; ~-**unternehmen** *n* business enterprise; ~**verbindung** *f* business connection; ~**viertel** *n* business (*od.* shopping) centre, *Am. a.* downtown; ~**welt** *f* business (world); ~**wert** *m e-r Firma*: goodwill; ⚖ *s. Streitwert*; ~**zeit** *f* business (*od.* office) hours *pl.*; ~**zimmer** *n* office; ~**zweig** *m* branch *od.* line (of business).

geschah [gəˈʃaː] *pret. v. geschehen* 1.

geschehen [gəˈʃeːən] **1.** (30, sn) happen, occur, take place; (*getan werden*) be done; ~ *lassen* allow, suffer; *es geschehe* so be it; *es ist um mich* ~ I am done for; *es geschieht ihm recht* it serves him right; *Dein Wille geschehe* Thy will be done; **2.** *p.p. v.* **1.**; **3.** ² *n* happenings *pl.*, events *pl.*

Geˈschehnis *n* occurrence, event.

gescheit [gəˈʃaɪt] clever, intelligent, smart, brainy, bright; *nicht recht* ~ a bit cracked *od.* touched.

Geschenk [gəˈʃɛŋk] *n* (3) present, gift; *j-m et. zum* ~ *machen* make a p. a present of a th.; ~**packung** *f* gift-box.

Geschichte [gəˈʃɪçtə] *f* (15) story; (*Erzählung*) *a.* narrative; tale; *bsd. als Wissenschaft*: history; *e-e schöne* ~! a nice affair!; *die ganze* ~ the whole business; ~**nbuch** *n* story-book; ~**n-erzähler**(**in** *f*) *m* story-teller.

ge'schichtlich historical; (~ *bedeutsam*) historic.

Ge'schichts|fälschung *f* falsification of history; **~forscher** *m* historian; **~forschung** *f* historical research; **~schreiber** *m* historian.

Geschick [gə'ʃik] *n* (3) **1.** fate, destiny; **2.** = **~lichkeit** *f* skill; (*Gewandtheit*) dexterity, adroitness; (*Befähigung*) aptitude; **~lichkeitsprüfung** *f* test of skill; **⁀t** skil(l)ful (*zu* at; *in dat.* in), clever (at), able; dexterous, adroit.

geschieden [gə'ʃi:dən] *p.p. v. scheiden.*

ge'schienen *p.p. v. scheinen.*

Geschirr [~'ʃir] *n* (3) (*Gefäß*) vessel; (*Tafel⁀*) table-ware; (*Silber⁀*) plate; (*Porzellan*) china; *oft nur*: things *pl.*; *irdenes* ~ earthenware, crockery; (*Pferde⁀*) harness; *das ~ abwaschen* wash up (*od.* do) the dishes; **~spüler** *m*, **~spülmaschine** *f* dish-washer, washing-up machine; **~spülmittel** *n* washing-up liquid; **~tuch** *n* tea towel.

ge'schissen V *p.p. v. scheißen.*

ge'schlafen *p.p. v. schlafen.*

ge'schlagen *p.p. v. schlagen.*

Geschlecht [gə'ʃlɛçt] *n* (1) sex; (*Art*) kind, species; (*Abstammung*) race; (*Familie*) family; (*Menschenalter*) generation; *gr.* gender; *s. schön usw.*; *beiderlei ~s* of both sexes; **⁀lich** sexual.

Ge'schlechts|-akt *m* sexual act; **~bestimmung** *f* sex determination; **~hormon** *n* sex hormone; **⁀krank** suffering from venereal disease; **~krankheit** *f* venereal disease; **~leben** *n* sex life; **⁀los** sexless; *biol.* asexual; **~merkmal** *n* sex characteristic; **~-organ** *n* sexual organ; **~reife** *f* sexual maturity; **⁀spezifisch** sex-specific; **~teil** *n mst. pl.* genitals *pl.*; **~trieb** *m* sexual instinct (*od.* urge); **~-umwandlung** *f* sex change; **~verkehr** *m* sexual intercourse; **~wort** *gr. n* article.

ge'schlichen *p.p. v. schleichen.*

ge'schliffen 1. *p.p. v. schleifen* 1.; **2.** *adj. Glas*: cut; *fig.* polished.

ge'schlissen *p.p. v. schleißen.*

ge'schlossen 1. *p.p. v. schließen*; **2.** *adj.* closed; ⚔, *hunt.*, *gr.* close; (*gemeinsam*) united, *adv.* in a body; ⊕ self-contained; *~e Gesellschaft* private party; *~e Veranstaltung* private meeting.

geschlungen [gə'ʃluŋən] *p.p. v. schlingen.*

Geschmack [~'ʃmak] *m* (3[3]) taste (*a. fig. an dat.* for); (*Aroma*) flavo(u)r; *fig.* (*guter*) ~ (good) taste; *~ finden an* (*dat.*) take a fancy to; **⁀los** tasteless; (*fad*) insipid; *fig.* tasteless; (*pred.*) in bad taste; **~losigkeit** *f* tastelessness; *fig.* bad taste; **~srichtung** *f* trend in taste; **~(s)sache** *f* matter of taste; **~ssinn** *m* (sense of) taste; **~sverirrung** *f* lapse of taste; **⁀voll** tasteful, elegant, *pred.* in good taste.

Geschmeide [gə'ʃmaɪdə] *n* (7) trinkets, jewels *pl.*; jewel(le)ry.

ge'schmeidig supple, pliant; flexible; **⁀keit** *f* suppleness, flexibility.

Geschmeiß [~'ʃmaɪs] *n* (3[2]) vermin; *fig. a.* rabble, scum.

Ge'schmiere *n* (7) smearing; (*Gekritzel*) scrawl, scribbling.

ge'schmissen *p.p. v. schmeißen.*

ge'schmolzen *p.p. v. schmelzen.*

Geschnatter [~'ʃnatər] *n* (7) cackling; *fig. a.* chatter(ing).

ge'schnitten *p.p. v. schneiden.*

geschnoben [gə'ʃno:bən] *p.p. v. schnauben.*

geschoben [~'ʃo:bən] *p.p. v. schieben.*

gescholten [~'ʃɔltən] *p.p. v. schelten.*

Geschöpf [~'ʃœpf] *n* (3) creature.

geschoren [~'ʃo:rən] *p.p. v. scheren.*

Geschoß [gə'ʃɔs] *n* (4) projectile; (*Wurf⁀*) missile; (*Gewehr⁀*, *Pistolen⁀*) bullet; (*Granate*) shell; (*Stockwerk*) stor(e)y, floor; **~bahn** *f* trajectory.

ge'schossen *p.p. v. schießen.*

geschraubt [~'ʃraupt] *Stil*: stilted.

Ge'schrei *n* (3) cries *pl.*; shouting; *fig.* noise, fuss; *viel ~ und wenig Wolle* much ado about nothing.

Geschreibsel [gə'ʃraɪpsəl] *n* (7, *o. pl.*) scribble (*a. fig.*).

geschrieben [~'ʃri:bən] *p.p. v. schreiben* 1.

ge'schrie(e)n *p.p. v. schreien.*

ge'schritten *p.p. v. schreiten.*

geschunden [gə'ʃundən] *p.p. v. schinden.*

Geschütz [gə'ʃyts] *n* (3[2]) gun; **~feuer** *n* gun-fire, shelling; **~turm** *m* turret.

Geschwader [~'ʃva:dər] *n* (7) ⚓ squadron; ✈ group, *Am.* wing.

Geschwafel F [\~ˈʃvaːfəl] *n* waffle.
Geschwätz [\~ˈʃvɛts] *n* (3²) idle talk, twaddle, prattle; (*Klatsch*) gossip.
geˈschwätzig talkative, *Am. a.* gabby; **⁀keit** *f* talkativeness.
geschweige [gəˈʃvaɪgə]: (\~ *denn*) not to mention, let alone, much less.
geschwiegen [gəˈʃviːgən] *p.p. v. schweigen* 1.
geschwind [gəˈʃvint] fast, quick, swift.
Geˈschwindigkeit [\~diç-] *f* speed, *bsd. phys.* velocity; (*Maß der Fortbewegung*) rate; *mit e-r* \~ *von* ... at a speed (*od.* rate) of ...; **\~sbegrenzung** *f* speed limit; **\~smesser** *mot. m* speedometer, tachometer; **\~s-rekord** *m* speed record; **\~s-überschreitung** *f* speeding.
Geschwister [gəˈʃvistər] *pl.* (7) brother(s) and sister(s), siblings; **⁀lich** brotherly; sisterly; **\~paar** *n* brother and sister.
geˈschwollen 1. *p.p. v. schwellen*; **2.** *adj.* swollen; *fig. Sprache*: pompous.
geschwommen [\~ˈʃvɔmən] *p.p. v. schwimmen.*
geˈschworen *p.p. v. schwören*; **⁀e** *m* (18) juror; **⁀en** *pl.* jury (*a.* **⁀engericht** *n*); **⁀enliste** *f* panel.
Geschwulst [\~ˈʃvulst] *f* (14¹) swelling; (*Gewächs*) tumo(u)r.
geschwunden [\~ˈʃvundən] *p.p. v. schwinden.*
geschwungen [\~ˈʃvuŋən] *p.p. v. schwingen.*
Geschwür [\~ˈʃvyːr] *n* (3) abscess, boil; (*Magen⁀ usw.*) ulcer; *fig.* sore.
geˈsehen *p.p. v. sehen.*
Gesell(e) [\~ˈzɛl(ə)] *m* (12[13]) companion, fellow; (*Handwerks⁀*) journeyman.
geˈsellen (25) (*a. sich*) (*zu*) associate (with), join (with, to).
Geˈsellen|jahre *n/pl.*, **\~zeit** *f* journeyman's years *pl.* of service.
geˈsellig gregarious (*a. fig.*); (*umgänglich*) sociable; *\~es Leben usw.* social life *etc.*; *er ist ein \~er Mensch* F he is a good mixer; **⁀keit** *f* sociability; (*Verkehr*) sociality.
Geˈsellschaft *f* (16) society; (*Zs.sein mit anderen*; *Besucher, Gäste*) company; *geladene*: party; *allg.* social gathering; ⚚ company; *fig. iro.* lot, bunch; *Dame der* \~ society lady; \~ *mit beschränkter Haftung* limited (liability) company; *s. geschlossen*; *e-e* \~ *geben* give (*Am. a.* throw) a party; *j-m* \~ *leisten* bear (*od.* keep) a p. company; *in guter (schlechter)* \~ in good (bad) company; *in j-s* \~ in a p.'s company; **\~er** *m* (7) companion; ⚚ partner; **⁀lich** social; *\~e Manieren pl.* company manners.
Geˈsellschafts|-anzug *m* evening dress, dress-suit, ⚔ dress uniform; **\~dame** *f* lady companion; **⁀fähig** presentable (in society); **\~kleid** *n* evening gown; **\~kritik** *f* social criticism; **\~kritisch** socio-critical; **\~-ordnung** *f* social order; **\~recht** ⚖ *n* company law; **\~reise** *f* party tour; **\~schicht** *f* (social) class; **\~spiel** *n* parlo(u)r game; **\~tanz** *m* ballroom dance; **\~vermögen** ⚚ *n* company assets *pl.*; **\~zimmer** *n* reception room.
Gesenk ⊕ [gəˈzɛnk] *n* (3¹) die; (*Flachhammer*) swage.
gesessen [gəˈzɛsən] *p.p. v. sitzen.*
Gesetz [gəˈzɛts] *n* (3²) *allg.* law; *geschriebenes*: statute; *parl.* Act; **\~blatt** *n* law gazette; **\~buch** *n* (legal) code; statute-book; **\~-entwurf** *m* bill; **\~eskraft** *f* legal force; \~ *erhalten* pass into law; **\~eslücke** *f* loophole in the law; **⁀gebend** legislative; **\~geber** *m* legislator; **\~gebung** *f* legislation; **⁀lich** legal, statutory; (*rechtmäßig*) lawful, legitimate; \~ *geschützt* patent(ed), registered, proprietary; **\~lichkeit** *f* lawfulness; legality.
geˈsetz|los lawless; anarchic(al); **⁀losigkeit** *f* lawlessness; anarchy; **\~mäßig** *Macht*: legal; *Rechtsmittel*: lawful; *Anspruch*: legitimate; (*satzungsgemäß*) statutory; *fig.* regular; **⁀mäßigkeit** *f* legality; lawfulness; legitimacy; *fig.* regularity, law.
geˈsetzt (*maßvoll*) sedate, staid; (*zuverlässig*) steady; (*besonnen*) composed, staid; *Sport*: seeded; *von \~em Alter* of mature age; \~ (*den Fall*), *es sei wahr* suppose (*od.* supposing) it were (*od.* it to be) true; **⁀heit** *f* sedateness; steadiness.
Geˈsetz|vorschlag *m* bill; **⁀widrig** unlawful, illegal; **\~widrigkeit** *f* illegality.
Gesicht [gəˈziçt] *n* (1) (*Sehvermögen*) (eye)sight; (*Angesicht*) face; (*Miene*) countenance; (*Aussehen*) look; (3) (*Erscheinung*) apparition, vision; *zweites* \~ second sight; *ein*

saures ~ machen look surly; *~er ziehen od. schneiden* make (*od.* pull) faces; *fig. das ~ wahren* save one's face; *j-m wie aus dem ~ geschnitten be* the spit and image of a p.; *j-m et.* (*Unangenehmes*) *ins ~ schleudern* fling a th. into a p.'s face; *zu ~ bekommen* catch sight of.

Ge'sichts|-ausdruck *m* facial expression; **~creme** *f* face-cream; **~farbe** *f* complexion; **~feld** *opt. n* field of vision; **~kreis** *m* horizon; **~massage** *f* facial massage, F facial; **~muskel** *m* facial muscle; **~pakkung** *f* face-pack, F facial; **~punkt** *m* point of view, viewpoint, perspective, angle; **~wasser** *n* face-lotion; **~winkel** *m anat.* facial angle; *opt.* visual angle; **~zug** *m mst pl.* feature(s), lineament(s).

Gesims [gə'zims] *n* (4) ledge; (*Zierleiste*) mo(u)lding; (*Kranz*≗) cornice.

Gesinde [~'zində] *n* (7) servants *pl.*, domestics *pl.*

Ge'sindel *n* (7) rabble, riff-raff.

gesinnt [gə'zint] *well etc.* disposed; *in Zssgn* ...-minded.

Ge'sinnung *f* mind, sentiment(s *pl.*); (*Überzeugung*) conviction; (*Ansichten*) opinions *pl.*; **~sgenosse** *m*, **~sgenossin** *f* like-minded person; **≗slos** unprincipled; **≗s-treu** loyal; **≗stüchtig** sta(u)nch; **~swechsel** *m* change of mind; *bsd. pol.* volteface.

gesitt|et [~'zitət] civilized; (*wohlerzogen*) well-bred, well-mannered; (*höflich*) polite; **≗ung** *f* civilization.

Gesöff [~'zœf] F *n* (3) (vile) brew.

gesoffen [~'zɔfən] *p.p. v. saufen.*

gesogen [~'zo:gən] *p.p. v. saugen.*

gesonnen [~'zɔnən] **1.** *p.p. v. sinnen*; **2.** *adj.* minded; *~ sein* have a mind (*zu inf.* to).

gesotten [~'zɔtən] *p.p. v. sieden.*

Gespann [~'ʃpan] *n* (3) team, *Am. a.* span; *v. Ochsen*: yoke; *fig.* (*Paar*) pair, couple, duo.

ge'spannt stretched, (*a. fig.*) tense; *Seil*: taut; *fig.* intent; *Aufmerksamkeit*: *a.* close; *Beziehungen*: strained; *Lage, Nerven*: tense; *~ sein auf* (*acc.*) be anxious (*od.* on edge) for; *~ sein, ob usw.* be anxious to know if *etc.*; *auf ~em Fuße mit* on bad terms with; **≗heit** *f* tenseness, tension.

Gespenst [gə'ʃpɛnst] *n* (1[1]) ghost, spect|re, *Am.* -er (*a. fig.*); **≗erhaft** ghostly; **~erstunde** *f* ghostly hour; **≗isch** ghostly; nightmarish (*a. fig.*).

Gespiel|(**e**) [gə'ʃpi:l(ə)] *m* (13), **~in** *f* (16[1]) playmate.

gespien [gə'ʃpi:n] *p.p. v. speien.*

Gespinst [~'ʃpinst] *n* (3[2]) (*Gewebe*) web; (*Gesponnenes*) spun yarn.

gesponnen [~'ʃpɔnən] *p.p. v. spinnen.*

Gespött [~'ʃpœt] *n* (3) mockery, derision; *sich zum ~ machen* make a fool of o.s.; *zum ~ der Leute werden* become the laughing-stock of people.

Gespräch [~'ʃprɛ:ç] *n* (3) talk (*a. pol.*); conversation, *teleph. a.* call; (*Zwie*≗) dialog(ue); **≗ig** talkative, communicative; **~igkeit** *f* talkativeness; **~s-einheit** *teleph. f* unit; **~s-leiter** *m* chairman (of the discussion); **~s-partner** *m* interlocutor; **~srunde** *pol. f* round of talks; **~s-stoff** *m* topic(s *pl.*) of conversation; **≗sweise** in conversation; (*vom Hörensagen*) by hearsay.

gespreizt [gə'ʃpraɪtst] *s. spreizen*; *fig.* affected, stilted; **≗heit** *f* affectation.

gesprochen [gə'ʃprɔxən] *p.p. v. sprechen.*

ge'sprossen *p.p. v. sprießen.*

ge'sprungen *p.p. v. springen.*

Gespür [~'ʃpy:r] *n* (3[1], *o. pl.*) nose (*für* for).

Gestade [gə'ʃtɑ:də] *n* (7) shore.

Gestalt [~'ʃtalt] *f* (16) form, figure, shape; (*Wuchs*) stature; (*Weise*) manner, way; *in ~ von* in the form of; (*feste*) *~ annehmen* take shape; **≗en** (26) form, shape; ⊕ design; (*einrichten, organisieren*) arrange, organize; *schöpferisch*: create, produce; *zu et.*: make, turn into; *sich ~* develop (*zu* into), turn out; **~er** *m* shaper; organizer; creator; ⊕ designer.

Ge'staltung *f* shaping; arrangement, organization; creation; ⊕ design(ing); (*Form*) shape; (*Merkmale*) features *pl.*; (*Zustand*) state.

Gestammel [~'ʃtaməl] *n* (7) stammering.

gestanden [~'ʃtandən] *p.p. v. stehen.*

geständ|ig [~'ʃtɛndiç] confessing; *~ sein* confess; **≗nis** [~'ʃtɛnt-] *n* (4[1]) (*a.* ⚖) confession; admission.

Gestank [gə'ʃtaŋk] *m* (3, *o. pl.*) stench, F stink.

gestatten [gə'ʃtatən] (26) allow, permit.

Geste ['gɛstə] *f* (15) gesture.
ge'stehen confess.
Ge'stehungskosten ✝ *pl.* prime [cost.]
Ge'stein *n* (3) rock, stone.
Gestell [gə'ʃtɛl] *n* (3) stand, rack; (*Rahmen, Gerippe*) frame; (*Bock*∻) trestle, horse.
Ge'stellung ⚔ *f* reporting for service; **~sbefehl** *m* calling-up (*Am.* induction) order.
gestern ['gɛstərn] yesterday; ~ *abend* last night.
ge'stiefelt booted, in boots.
gestiegen [~'ʃti:gən] *p.p. v. steigen.*
gestielt [~'ʃti:lt] helved; ⚘ stalked.
gestikulieren [gɛstiku'li:rən] gesticulate.
Gestirn [gə'ʃtirn] *n* (3) star; (*Sternbild*) constellation; **∻t** starred, starry.
gestoben [~'ʃto:bən] *p.p. v. stieben.*
Gestöber [~'ʃtø:bər] *n* (7) drift(ing), flurry (of snow).
gestochen [~'ʃtɔxən] *p.p. v. stechen.*
gestohlen [~'ʃto:lən] *p.p. v. stehlen.*
gestorben [~'ʃtɔrbən] *p.p. v. sterben.*
ge'stoßen *p.p. v. stoßen.*
Gestotter [~'ʃtɔtər] *n* (7) stuttering.
Gesträuch [~'ʃtrɔʏç] *n* (3) bushes *pl.*, shrubs *pl.*
gestreckt [~'ʃtrɛkt] **1.** *p.p. v. strekken*; **2.** *adj.* ⚔ *Ladung*: elongated (*charge*); *s. Galopp.*
gestreift [~'ʃtraɪft] striped, streaky.
gestreng [gə'ʃtrɛŋ] severe.
ge'strichen *p.p. v. streichen.*
gestritten [~'ʃtritən] *p.p. v. streiten.*
gestrig ['gɛstriç] of yesterday; *die ~e Zeitung* yesterday's paper.
Gestrüpp [gə'ʃtryp] *n* (3) scrub, undergrowth, *Am.* brush; *fig.* jungle.
gestunken [~'ʃtuŋkən] *p.p. v. stinken.*
Gestüt [gə'ʃty:t] *n* (3) stud.
Gesuch [~'zu:x] *n* (3) application, request; (*Bittschrift*) petition; **∻t** wanted (*a.* ⚖); (*begehrt*) (much) sought-after, in (great) demand; (*absichtlich*) studied; (*geziert*) affected; (*weit hergeholt*) far-fetched.
Gesudel [~'zu:dəl] *n* (7) (*Schrift*) scribble, scrawl; *paint.* daubing.
gesund [gə'zunt] healthy (*a. fig.*), sound (*a. Ansicht, Firma usw.*), in good health; (*geistig ~*) sane; (*heilsam*; *a. fig.*) wholesome; *~ und munter* fit as a fiddle; *~ wie ein Fisch im Wasser* sound as a roach; *s. Menschenverstand*; **∻beter(in** *f*) *m* faith-healer; **∻bete'rei** *f* faith-healing; **∻brunnen** *m* mineral spring; **~en** [~'zundən] (26, sn) recover, regain one's health.
Gesundheit [gə'zunt-] *f* (16) health; *fig. a.* soundness; (*geistige ~*) sanity; (*Heilsamkeit*) wholesomeness; *~! beim Niesen*: bless you!; *s. ausbringen*; **∻lich** sanitary, hygienic; *~er Zustand* state of health; *~ geht es ihm gut* he is in good health; **~s-amt** *n* public health office; **~s-apostel** *m* health fanatic; **~s-pflege** *f* (personal) hygiene; **∻sschädlich** unhealthy, bad for one's health; **~swesen** *n öffentliches*: Public Health; **~szeugnis** *n* certificate of health; **~szustand** *m* state of health.
Gesundung [gə'zunduŋ] *f* recovery (*a. fig.* ✝ *usw.*).
gesungen [gə'zuŋən] *p.p. v. singen.*
gesunken [gə'zuŋkən] *p.p. v. sinken.*
Getäfel [gə'tɛ:fəl] *n* (7) wainscot.
getan [gə'tɑ:n] *p.p. v. tun* 1.
Getier [~'ti:r] *n* (3, *o. pl.*) animals *pl.*
Getöse [gə'tø:zə] *n* (7) noise, din.
ge'tragen 1. *p.p. v. tragen*; **2.** *adj. fig.* measured, slow; (*feierlich*) solemn.
Getrampel [gə'trampəl] *n* (7) stamping, trampling.
Getränk [gə'trɛŋk] *n* (3) drink, beverage; ⚕ potion; *s. geistig*; **~eautomat** *m* drinks machine; **~ekarte** *f* list of beverages, *oft* wine list; **~esteuer** *f* alcohol tax.
Getrappel [~'trapəl] *n* (7) pattering; (*Pferde*∻) clatter (of hooves).
Getratsche [~'trɑ:tʃə] *n* (7) gossip.
ge'trauen: *sich ~* dare, venture.
Getreide [gə'traɪdə] *n* (7) corn, grain; **~-arten** *f/pl.* cereals; **~bau** *m* grain-growing; **~feld** *n* grain-field; **~händler** *m* grain-merchant; **~land** *n* grain-growing country; **~pflanze** *f* cereal plant; **~silo** *m*, **~speicher** *m* granary.
ge'treten *p.p. v. treten.*
ge'treu, ~lich faithful, true, loyal.
Getriebe [gə'tri:bə] *n* (7) ⊕ gearing, gear unit; (*~räder*) gears *pl.*; (*Räderwerk*) wheelwork; *fig.* wheels *pl.*; (*reges Leben*) bustle.
getrieben [~'tri:bən] *p.p. v. treiben.*
getroffen [~'trɔfən] *p.p. v. treffen.*
getrogen [~'tro:gən] *p.p. v. trügen.*
getrost [gə'tro:st] confident.
ge'trunken *p.p. v. trinken.*

Getto ['gɛto] *n* (11) ghetto.
Getue [gə'tu:ə] *n* (7) fuss.
Getümmel [~'tyməl] *n* (7) turmoil.
Gevatter [~'fatər] *m* (7 *u.* 13) godfather; ~ *Tod* Goodman Death; **~in** *f* (16[1]) godmother.
geviert [gə'fi:rt] **1.** squared; **2.** ♀ *n* (3) square.
Gewächs [gə'vɛks] *n* (4) (*Pflanze*) plant, vegetable; (*Kraut*) herb; (*Erzeugnis*) growth (*a.* ⚕); (*Weinsorte*) vintage; **~haus** *n* greenhouse.
ge'wachsen **1.** *p.p. v. wachsen*; **2.** *adj. j-m ~ sein* be a p.'s equal, be a match for a p.; *e-r Sache ~ sein* be equal to a th.; *sich der Lage ~ zeigen* rise to the occasion.
gewagt [gə'vɑ:kt] daring (*a. fig.*), risky; *Witz*: risqué (*fr.*), *Am.* off-color.
gewählt [~'vɛ:lt] choice; *Sprache*: selected; *Gesellschaft*: select.
ge'wahr *werden* = **~en** perceive, notice, become aware of (*od. daß* that); (*entdecken*) discover.
Gewähr [~'vɛ:r] *f* (16) warrant(y), guarantee, security; *ohne ~* without guarantee, ✝ *a.* without engagement; *~ bieten für* guarantee; **♀en** (25) grant; (*geben*) give, yield, afford; *~ lassen* let *a p.* have his way; **♀leisten** guarantee; **~leistung** *f* guaranty.
Ge'wahrsam *m, n* (3) custody.
Ge'währsmann *m* authority; *für Nachrichten*: informant.
Gewalt [~'valt] *f* (16) power; *amtliche*: *a.* authority; (*Aufsicht*) control; (*Gewalttätigkeit*) force, violence; *höhere ~* force majeure (*fr.*), act of God; *s. roh*; *j-m ~ antun* do violence to a p.; *~ anwenden* resort to force; *sich in der ~ haben* have o.s. under control; *in j-s ~ sein* be in a p.'s power *od.* grip; *mit ~* by force; *mit aller ~* with might and main; *er verlor die ~ über den Wagen* his car got out of hand; **~-akt** *m* act of violence; **~bremsung** *f*: *e-e ~ machen* slam on the brakes; **~enteilung** *f* separation of powers; **~herrschaft** *f* tyranny; **~herrscher** *m* despot; **♀ig** powerful, mighty; (*heftig*) vehement; (*ungeheuer*) enormous, F tremendous; **~kur** *f* drastic measures *pl.*; **♀los** *pol.* non-violent; **~marsch** *m* forced march; **~maßnahme** *f* violent (*fig.* drastic) measure; **~mensch** *m* brute; **♀sam** violent, forcible; **~samkeit** *f* violence; **~streich** *m* bold stroke; **~tat** *f* act of violence; **♀tätig** violent; brutal; **~tätigkeit** *f* violence; **~verbrechen** *n* violent crime; **~verbrecher** *m* violent criminal; **~verzichtsabkommen** *pol. n* non-aggression treaty.
Gewand [gə'vant] *n* (1[2], *poet.* 1[3]) garment, dress; *wallendes*: robe.
ge'wandt **1.** *p.p. v. wenden*; **2.** *adj. bsd. körperlich*: dexterous, adroit; *bsd. geistig*: clever; **♀heit** *f* adroitness, dexterity; cleverness.
ge'wann *pret. v. gewinnen.*
gewärtig [~'vɛrtiç] (*gen.*) expectant (of); *e-r Sache ~ sein*, *et. od. e-e Sache* **~gen** expect, reckon with; *zu ~ haben* be in for, face.
Gewäsch [gə'vɛʃ] *n* (3[2]) twaddle.
ge'waschen *p.p. v. waschen.*
Gewässer [~'vɛsər] *n* (7) waters *pl.*; **~verschmutzung** *f* pollution of rivers and seas.
Gewebe [gə've:bə] *n* (7) (*Stoff*) (woven) fabric, textile, web (*a. fig.*); (*feines ~*) tissue (*a. anat. u. fig.*); (*Webart*) texture (*a. fig.*); **~probe** ⚕ *f* tissue sample; **♀schonend** kind to fabrics.
Ge'wehr *n* (3) gun; ⚔ rifle; **~feuer** *n* rifle fire; **~kolben** *m* (rifle) butt; **~lauf** *m* (rifle) barrel; **~riemen** *m* rifle sling.
Geweih [~'vaɪ] *n* (3) horns, antlers *pl.*
Gewerbe [gə'vɛrbə] *n* (7) trade, business; (*Beruf*) occupation; (*Industrie*) industry; **~-ausstellung** *f* industrial exhibition; **~betrieb** *m* industrial enterprise; **~freiheit** *f* freedom of trade; **~-ordnung** *f* industrial code; **~schein** *m* trade licen|ce, *Am.* -se; **~schule** *f* vocational school; **~steuer** *f* trade tax; **♀tätig** industrial; **~tätigkeit** *f* industry; **♀treibend** engaged in trade; industrial; **~treibende** *m* person carrying on a trade or business; **~zweig** *m* (branch of) trade or industry.
gewerblich [~'vɛrp-] industrial.
ge'werbsmäßig professional.
Ge'werkschaft *f* trade union, *Am.* labor union; **~ler** *m* (7) trade-unionist; **♀lich** *attr.* trade- (*Am.* labor-) union; *adv. sich ~ organisieren* unionize; *~ nicht organisiert* unorganized, not unionized; **~sbeitrag** *m*

union dues *pl.*; **~sbund** *m* federation of trade (*Am.* labor) unions; *Brt. etwa* Trades Union Congress, *Am. etwa* American Federation of Labor and Congress of Industrial Organizations; **~sfunktionär** *m* trade union (*Am.* labor union) official; **~smitglied** *n* union member; **~swesen** *n* trade-unionism.

gewesen [gəˈveːzən] **1.** *p.p. v. sein*; **2.** *adj.* former, ex-...

gewichen [gəˈviçən] *p.p. v. weichen.*

Gewicht [gəˈviçt] *n* (3) weight (*a. fig.*); ~ *haben* (*bei*) carry weight (with); ~ *legen auf* (*acc.*) attach importance to; *nicht ins* ~ *fallen* be of no consequence; **~heben** *n Sport*: weight-lifting; **2ig** weighty (*a. fig.*); **~s-abnahme** *f*, **~sverlust** *m* loss in weight; ⚕ shortage; **~sklasse** *f* weight(-class); **~szunahme** *f* increase in weight.

Gewieher [~ˈviːər] *n* (7) neighing.

gewiesen [~ˈviːzən] *p.p. v. weisen.*

gewillt [~ˈvilt] willing.

Gewimmel [~ˈviməl] *n* (7) swarming; (*Menge*) swarm, crowd, throng.

Gewimmer [~ˈvimər] *n* (7) whimpering.

Gewinde [~ˈvində] *n* (7) winding; (*Blumen2*) garland, wreath; (*Schrauben2*) thread; **~bohrer** *m* (screw-)-tap.

Gewinn [~ˈvin] *m* (3) winning; (*Gewonnenes*) gain, profit; (*Lotterie2*) prize; (*Spiel2*) winnings *pl.*; (*Vorteil*) advantage; *~- und Verlustkonto od. -rechnung* profit-and-loss account (*Am.* statement); ~ *ziehen aus* profit by; **~-anteil** *m* dividend; **~beteiligung** *f* profit-sharing; **2bringend** profitable, paying; **~chancen** *f/pl.* chances of winning; *beim Wetten*: odds; **2en** (30) *v/t.* win; gain; *Vorteil, Vorsprung*: gain (*a. Zeit*), get; ⚒ *usw.*: win, produce; *an Bedeutung usw.* ~ gain in ...; *j-n für sich* ~ win a p. over; *v/i.* gain; *er hat sehr gewonnen* he has greatly improved; *durch et.* ~ gain by a th.; **2end** winning, engaging; **~er** *m* (7), **~erin** *f* winner; **~(n)ummer** *f* winning number; **~spanne** *f* profit margin; **~sucht** *f* greed; **2süchtig** greedy, profit-seeking; **~ung** *f* winning; production; **~zahl** *f* winning number.

Gewinsel [gəˈvinzəl] *n* (7) whining.

Gewirr [~ˈvir] *n* (3) confusion, entanglement; (*Labyrinth*) maze.

gewiß [~ˈvis] certain, sure; *~!* certainly!, to be sure!, *Am.* sure!; *aber ~!* by all means!; *ein gewisser Herr N.* a certain Mr. N.

Gewissen [gəˈvisən] *n* (6) conscience; *ein reines* (*schlechtes*) ~ a good (bad) conscience; *s. Wissen, reden*; **2haft** conscientious (*in dat.* about); **~haftigkeit** *f* conscientiousness; **2los** unscrupulous; **~losigkeit** *f* unscrupulousness.

Geˈwissens|bisse *m/pl.* remorse *sg.*, pangs *pl.* of conscience; **~frage** *f* matter of conscience; **~freiheit** *f* freedom of conscience; **~konflikt** *m*, **~not** *f* moral dilemma; **~zwang** *m* moral constraint; **~zweifel** *m* scruple.

gewissermaßen [~ˈmaːsən] so to speak, as it were.

Geˈwißheit *f* certainty; *sich ~ verschaffen über* (*acc.*) make certain on.

geˈwißlich certainly, surely.

Gewitter [gəˈvitər] *n* (7) (thunder-)storm; **2n** (29) thunder; **~regen** *m* thunder-shower; **~wolke** *f* thunder-cloud.

gewitzt [gəˈvitst] taught by experience; (*pfiffig*) shrewd, smart.

gewoben [~ˈvoːbən] *p.p. v. weben.*

gewogen [~ˈvoːgən] **1.** *p.p. v. wiegen*[1], *wägen*; **2.** *adj.* (*dat.*) well (*od.* kindly) disposed (to[wards]), favo(u)rable (to); **2heit** *f* goodwill; kindness.

gewöhnen [gəˈvøːnən] (25) accustom, habituate (*an acc.* to); *an Strapazen*: inure (to); *j-n ~ an* (*acc.*) get a p. used to; *sich ~* get accustomed *od.* used (*an acc.* to).

Gewohnheit [gəˈvoːnhaɪt] *f* wont; (*Herkommen*) custom; *persönliche*: habit; *zur ~ werden* grow into a habit; **2smäßig** habitual; **~smensch** *m* creature of habit; **~srecht** *n* common law; *weitS.* established right; **~s-trinker** *m* habitual drunkard; **~sverbrecher** *m* habitual criminal.

gewöhnlich [~ˈvøːnliç] (*allgemein*) common; (*alltäglich*) ordinary; (*üblich*) usual, customary; (*gewohnt*) habitual, wonted; *b.s.* (*gemein*) common, vulgar.

gewohnt [gəˈvoːnt] habitual, wonted; *et. ~ sein* be accustomed *od.* used to, be in the habit of *ger.*

Geˈwöhnung *f* accustoming, habituation (*a.* ⚕); inurement (*alle an acc.* to); *s. Gewohnheit.*

Gewölb|e [gəˈvœlbə] *n* (15) vault; (*Bogen*) arch; **2t** [~pt] vaulted; arched.

Gewölk [~ˈvœlk] *n* (3) clouds *pl.*

gewollt [~ˈvɔlt] **1.** *p.p. v. wollen*; **2.** *adj.* deliberate, conscious.

gewonnen [~ˈvɔnən] *p.p. v. gewinnen.*

geworben [~ˈvɔrbən] *p.p. v. werben.*

geworden [~ˈvɔrdən] *p.p. v. werden.*

geworfen [~ˈvɔrfən] *p.p. v. werfen.*

gewrungen [~ˈvruŋən] *p.p. v. wringen.*

Gewühl [~ˈvy:l] *n* (3) bustle; (*Menge*) milling crowd.

gewunden [~ˈvundən] **1.** *p.p. v. winden*; **2.** *adj.* twisted; *bsd. fig.* tortuous.

Gewürm [~ˈvyrm] *n* (3) worms *pl.*; (*Ungeziefer*) vermin.

Gewürz [~ˈvyrts] *n* (3²) spice; *Kochkunst*: condiment, seasoning; **~bord** *n*, **~ständer** *m* spice rack; **~gurke** *f* pickled gherkin; **~händler** *m* spice dealer; **2ig** spicy, aromatic; **~mischung** *f* mixed herbs *pl.*; **~nelke** *f* clove.

gewußt [gəˈvust] *p.p. v. wissen.*

geˈzahnt toothed; ⚘ dentate.

Gezänk [~ˈtsɛŋk] *n* (3) squabble.

Geˈzeit *f, mst* **~en** *pl. inv.* tide; **~en...** tidal.

Gezeter [gəˈtse:tər] *n* (7) shrill clamo(u)r; hue and cry.

geziehen [gəˈtsi:ən] *p.p. v. zeihen.*

geˈziemen (25, *dat.*) (*a. sich ~* [*für*]) become; **~d** becoming, seemly, fit(ting); (*schuldig*) proper, due.

geziert [~ˈtsi:rt] affected; (*geckenhaft*) foppish; (*förmlich*) prim; **2heit** *f* affectation; primness.

Gezisch [~ˈtsiʃ] *n* (3²) hissing; **~el** *n* (7) whispering.

gezogen [~ˈtso:gən] *p.p. v. ziehen.*

Gezücht [~ˈtsyçt] *n* (7) brood, breed.

Gezwitscher [~ˈtsvitʃər] *n* (7) chirping, twitter.

gezwungen [~ˈtsvuŋən] **1.** *p.p. v. zwingen*; **2.** *adj. fig.* forced, constrained; (*geziert*) affected; *~ lachen* force a laugh; **~erˈmaßen** under compulsion.

Gicht [giçt] *f* (16) gout; **ˈ2brüchig**, **ˈ2isch** gouty; **ˈ~knoten** *m* gout node.

Giebel [ˈgi:bəl] *m* (7) gable(-end).

Gier [gi:r] *f* (16) greed(iness) (*nach* of); **ˈ2ig** greedy (*nach* of).

Gießbach [ˈgi:sbax] *m* torrent.

gieß|en [ˈgi:sən] (30) pour; (*verschütten*) spill; ⊕ cast, found; *Pflanze, Garten*: water; *es gießt* it is pouring (with rain); **ˈ2er** *m* (7) founder; **2erei** [~ˈraɪ] *f* (*Gießhaus*) foundry; *Tätigkeit*: casting; **ˈ2kanne** *f* watering-can.

Gift [gift] *n* (3) poison; (*bsd. Schlangen2, a. fig.*) venom; (*Bosheit*) malice; F *darauf kannst du ~ nehmen!* F you bet your life on it!; **ˈ~gas** *n* poison-gas; **ˈ2haltig** *adj.* toxic.

ˈgiftig (*a. fig.*) poisonous; (*boshaft*) malicious, spiteful.

ˈGift|mischer(in *f*) *m* poisoner; **ˈ~mord** *m* (murder by) poisoning; **ˈ~müll** *m* toxic waste; **ˈ~pfeil** *m* poisoned arrow; **ˈ~pflanze** *f* poisonous plant; **ˈ~pilz** *m* poisonous mushroom, toadstool; **ˈ~schlange** *f* venomous (*od.* poisonous) snake; **ˈ~stoff** *m* toxic substance; **ˈ~zahn** *m* venom-tooth.

Gigant [giˈgant] *m* (12) giant; **~in** *f* giantess; **2isch** gigantic.

Gilde [ˈgildə] *f* (15) guild, corporation.

Gimpel [ˈgimpəl] *m* (7) *zo.* bullfinch; *fig.* simpleton, dupe, fool.

ging [giŋ] *pret. v. gehen.*

Ginster ⚘ [ˈginstər] *m* (7) broom.

Gipfel [ˈgipfəl] *m* (7) summit, top; (*Spitze*) peak; *fig. a.* acme; **ˈ~konferenz** *pol. f* summit conference; **ˈ2n** culminate (*a. fig.*); **ˈ~treffen** *n* summit meeting.

Gips [gips] *m* (4) gypsum; ⊕ plaster (of Paris); **ˈ~-abdruck** *m*, **ˈ~-abguß** *m* plaster-cast; **ˈ~bein** F *n* leg in plaster; **ˈ2en** (27) plaster; **ˈ~er** *m* (7) plasterer; **ˈ~figur** *f* plaster figure; **ˈ~verband** *m* plaster dressing *od.* cast.

Giraffe [giˈrafə] *f* (15) giraffe.

Gir|ant ✝ [ʒiˈrant] *m* (12) endorser; **~at** [~ˈrɑ:t] *m* (12) endorsee; **2ieren** [~ˈri:rən] circulate; *Wechsel*: endorse.

Girlande [girˈlandə] *f* (15) garland.

Giro ✝ [ˈʒi:ro] *n* (11) endorsement; **ˈ~bank** *f* clearing bank; **ˈ~konto** *n* giro (transfer) account; **ˈ~verkehr** *m* giro transfer business; **ˈ~zentrale** *f* (central) clearing-house.

girren ['girən] (25) coo.
Gis ♪ [gis] *n inv.* G sharp.
Gischt [giʃt] *m* (3²) foam, spray.
Gitarre [gi'tarə] *f* (15) guitar.
Gitter ['gitər] *n* (7) grating; lattice; (*Zaun*) fence; (*Geländer*) railing; *Radio, a. Landkarte*: grid; *fig. hinter ~n* behind bars; '**~fenster** *n* lattice-window; '**2förmig** latticed; '**~netz** *n Landkarte*: grid; '**~tor** *n* trellised gate; '**~zaun** *m* lattice-work fence.
Glacéhandschuhe [gla'se:hantʃu:ə] *m/pl.* kid gloves (*a. fig.*).
Glanz [glants] *m* (3²) brightness, lust|re, *Am.* -er; brilliancy; (*Herrlichkeit*) splendo(u)r; '**~bürste** *f* polishing brush.
glänzen ['glɛntsən] (27) glitter, shine (*a. fig. vor dat.* with); *s. Abwesenheit*; '**~d** bright, brilliant; (*a. glatt*) glossy; (*poliert*) polished; *fig.* splendid, brilliant.
'**Glanz|leder** *n* patent leather; '**~leinen** *n* glazed linen; '**~leistung** *f* brilliant performance *od.* feat; '**~lichter** *n/pl.* high lights; '**2los** lustreless; '**~papier** *n* glazed paper; '**~periode** *f* brightest period, glorious days *pl.*; '**~politur** *f* gloss polish; '**~punkt** *m* highlight; (*Höhepunkt*) acme; '**~stück** *n* gem; *weit S.* brilliant feat; '**2voll** splendid, magnificent; '**~zeit** *f* heyday.
Glas [glɑ:s] *n* (2¹; *als Maß im pl. inv.*) glass; '**~-auge** *n* glass eye; '**~bläser** *m* glass-blower.
Glaser ['glɑ:zər] *m* (7) glazier; **~ei** [~'raɪ] *f* glazier's workshop.
gläsern ['glɛ:zərn] of glass; *fig.* glassy.
Glas|faser ['glɑ:s-] *f* fibreglass, *Am.* fiberglass; '**~glocke** *f* bell-glass, (glass) shade; '**~hütte** *f* glass-works.
glasieren [gla'zi:rən] glaze; *Kochkunst*: ice, frost.
glasig ['glɑ:ziç] glassy (*a. fig.*), vitreous.
Glas|kasten ['glɑ:s-] *m* glass case; '**~malerei** *f* glass painting; (*Kunstwerk*) stained glass window; '**~perle** *f* glass bead; '**~platte** *f* glass top; '**~scheibe** *f* pane of glass; '**~scherben** *f/pl.* (pieces *pl.* of) broken glass *sg.*; '**~schneider** *m* glass cutter; '**~schrank** *m* glass cupboard; '**~splitter** *m* splinter of glass.
Glasur [gla'zu:r] *f* (16) glaze; (*Schmelz*) enamel; *auf Backwerk*: icing, frosting.
Glas|veranda ['glɑ:s-] *f* glass veranda(h); '**2weise** in glasses, by glassfuls; '**~wolle** *f* glass wool.
glatt [glat] **1.** *adj.* (18²) *allg.* smooth (*a. fig. gewandt*); (*eben*) even; (*poliert*) polished, glossy; (*gefällig*) smooth; *Absage, Lüge usw.*: flat, blunt, downright; (*schlüpfrig*) slippery; **2.** *adv.* smoothly; (*ganz*) entirely, clean (*through, etc.*); (*ohne weiteres*) without ado; ~ *anliegen* fit close; ~ *rasiert* clean-shaven; et. ~ *ableugnen* deny a th. flatly; ~ *heraussagen* tell frankly *od.* bluntly.
Glätte ['glɛtə] *f* (15) smoothness; (*Politur*) polish; (*Schlüpfrigkeit*) slipperiness.
'**Glatt-eis** *n* black ice; *fig. j-n aufs ~ führen* trip a p. up.
glätten ['glɛtən] (26) smooth; (*polieren*) polish.
'**glatt|streichen** smooth down; **~züngig** ['~tsyŋiç] smooth-tongued.
Glatz|e ['glatsə] *f* (15) bald head; **2köpfig** ['~kœpfiç] bald(-headed).
Glaube ['glaʊbə] (13¹) *m*, '**~n¹** (6) *m* (*a. eccl.*) faith, belief (*an acc.* in); *~n schenken* (*dat.*) give credence to, believe; *auf Treu und ~n* on trust; *in gutem ~n* in good faith; '**2n²** (26) *v/t.* believe; (*meinen, annehmen*) *a.* think, suppose, *Am. a.* guess; *es ist nicht zu ~* it is past belief; *v/i.* believe (*j-m* a p.; *an acc.* in); (*Vertrauen haben zu*) put faith in; F *dran ~ müssen* have to die (*od. Sache*: go).
'**Glaubens|bekenntnis** *n* creed (*a. fig.*), confession of faith; '**~freiheit** *f* religious liberty; '**~genosse** *m* fellow-believer; '**~lehre** *f*, '**~satz** *m* dogma; '**~zeuge** *m* martyr.
glaubhaft ['glaʊphaft] credible; (*verbürgt*) authentic; ⚖ ~ *machen* substantiate; '**2igkeit** *f* credibility; authenticity.
gläubig ['glɔʏbiç] believing, faithful; **2e** ['~bigə] *m, f* (18) believer; '**2er** ✝ *m* (7), '**2erin** *f* (16¹) creditor.
glaub|lich ['glaʊp-] credible, believable; '**~würdig** credible, reliable; *P.*: *a.* trustworthy; '**2würdigkeit** *f* credibility.
gleich [glaɪç] **1.** *adj.* equal (*an dat.* in); (*ebenso beschaffen*) like; (*derselbe*) *the* same; (*eben, auf ~er Höhe*) even, level; (*~bleibend*) constant; (*einheitlich*) uniform; *in ~er Weise*

likewise; *zu ~er Zeit* at the same time; *es ist (mir) ganz ~* it is all the same (to me); *s. Münze*; **2.** *adv.* alike, equally; (*so~*) at once, immediately; *es ist ~ acht Uhr* it is close on eight o'clock; *s.* 2e; **'~-altrig** (of) the same age; **'~-artig** of the same kind; homogeneous; (*ähnlich*) like, similar; **'2-artigkeit** *f* homogeneousness; **'~bedeutend** synonymous (*mit* with); equivalent (to), tantamount (to); **'2behandlung** *f* equal treatment; **'~berechtigt** having equal rights; **'2berechtigung** *f* equality, equal rights *pl.*; **'~bleibend** constant, steady, stable; **'2e¹** *m* peer; **'2e²** *n the* same thing; *(j-m) ~s mit ~m vergelten* give (a p.) tit for tat.

'gleichen (30, *dat.*) equal; (*ähnlich sein*) resemble, be (*od.* look) like.

gleicher|ge'stalt, ~'maßen, ~'weise in like manner, likewise.

'gleich|falls also, likewise; *danke, ~!* thanks, the same to you!; **~förmig** ['~fœrmiç] uniform; (*regelmäßig*) regular; (*eintönig*) monotonous; **'2förmigkeit** *f* uniformity; **'~gesinnt** like-minded; **'~gestellt** on a par (*dat.* with); **~gestimmt** ['~gəʃtimt] ♪ (tuned) in unison; *fig.* congenial; **'2gewicht** *n* (*a. fig.*) balance, equilibrium, equipoise; *politisches ~* balance of power; *seelisches ~* mental balance; *aus dem ~ bringen* unbalance, *fig. a.* upset; *ins ~ bringen, im ~ erhalten* balance; *das ~ verlieren* lose one's balance; **'~gültig** indifferent (*gegen* to); unconcerned; *~, ob usw.* no matter if *etc.*; *es ist mir ~* I don't care; **'2gültigkeit** *f* indifference; **'2heit** *f* equality; *völlige*: identity; (*Ähnlichkeit*) likeness; (*Einheitlichkeit*) uniformity; **'2klang** *m* unison, harmony; **'~kommen** (*dat.*) equal, come up to, match; **'~laufend** parallel; (*zeitlich*) synchronous; **'2laut** *m* consonance; **'~lautend** consonant; *Inhalt*: of the same tenor, identical; *~e Abschrift* duplicate, true copy; **'~machen** make equal (*dat.* to); **2mache'rei** *f* egalitarianism, levelling; **'2maß** *n* symmetry, proportion; **'~mäßig** equal, symmetrical; (*ausgeglichen*) even; *s. gleichförmig*; (*stetig*) steady; **'2mut** *m*, **2mütigkeit** ['~my:tiçkaɪt] *f* equanimity, calmness; **'~mütig** calm, imperturbable; **~namig** ['~na:miç] of the same name; 🕮 homonymous; ⚗ correspondent; **'2nis** *n* (4¹) (*Bild*) image; *rhet.* simile; *biblisch*: parable; **~rangig** ['~raŋiç] of the same rank; equal; **'2richter** ⚡ *m* rectifier; **'~sam** as it were; **'~schalten** coordinate, bring into line; **~schenk(e)lig** ['~ʃɛŋk(ə)liç] isosceles; **'2schritt** ⚔ *m* marching in step, *Am.* cadence; **'~seitig** equilateral; **'~setzen** (*dat.*) equate with; **'~stellen** (*dat.*) equate (with), equalize (to, with); *P.*: put on a par (with), *staatsbürgerlich*: assimilate in status (to); **'2stellung** *f* equalization; **'2strom** ⚡ *m* direct current; **'~tun:** *es j-m ~* equal (*od.* match) a p.; **'2ung** *f* equation; **'~'viel:** *~, ob usw.* no matter if *etc.*; **'~wertig** equivalent (*mit* to), of the same value; **'~'wohl** yet, nevertheless, however, all the same; **'~zeitig** simultaneous; (*zeitgenössisch*) contemporary; *adv.* at the same time; **'2zeitigkeit** *f* simultaneousness; **'~ziehen** *Sport*: (*einholen*) catch up (*mit* with); (*ausgleichen*) equalize.

Gleis [glaɪs] *n* (4) *s. Geleise*; **'~-anschluß** *m* siding; **'~körper** *m* railway embankment.

Gleisner ['glaɪsnər] *m* (7) hypocrite; **'2isch** hypocritical.

Gleit|bahn ['glaɪt-] *f* slide; shoot, chute; ⊕ guide(way); **'~boot** *n* gliding boat, glider; **'2en** (30, sn) glide, slide; **'~fläche** *f* gliding plane *od.* surface; **'~flug** *m* gliding flight, glide, volplane; **'~flugzeug** *n* glider; **'~klausel** ✝ *f* escalator clause; **'~mittel** *n* lubricant; **'~rolle** *f* trolley; **'~zeit** *f* flexible working hours *pl.*; **'~zeitkarte** *f* timecard.

Gletscher ['glɛtʃər] *m* (7) glacier; **'2-artig** glacial; **'~spalte** *f* crevasse.

glich [gliç] *pret. v. gleichen.*

Glied [gli:t] *n* (1) limb; (*a. Mit2*) member; (*Ketten2, Binde2*) link; ⚗, *Logik*: term; ⚔ rank.

'glieder|lahm lame in the limbs; ⚕ paralytic; **'~n** (29) joint, articulate; (*anordnen*) arrange; (*einrichten*) organize; *in Teile*: (sub)divide (*in acc.* into); (*gruppieren*) group; **'2puppe** *f* jointed doll; (*Marionette*) puppet; *für Maler*: lay figure; *für Kleider*: mannequin; **'2reißen** *n*, **'2schmerz** *m* pain(s *pl.*) in the limbs, rheumatism; '2**ung** *f* (*Anordnung*) arrangement; (*Aufbau*) structure; (*Einteilung*) division; formation.

Glied|maßen ['gli:tma:sən] *pl.* limbs, extremities; '**~staat** *m* member state.

glimmen ['glimən] (30) *Feuer*: smo(u)lder (*a. fig.*); (*glühen*) glow; (*schimmern*) glimmer, gleam; *~de Asche* embers *pl.*

'**Glimmer** *min. m* (7) mica.

'**Glimmstengel** F *m* fag.

glimpflich ['glimpfliç] lenient, mild; *~ behandeln* deal gently with; *~ davonkommen* get off lightly.

glitsch|en F ['glitʃən] (27, sn) slide; '**~ig** slippery.

glitt [glit] *pret. v. gleiten.*

glitzern ['glitsərn] (29) glitter.

global [glo'ba:l] global.

Globus ['glo:bus] *m* (16² *u.* 4¹) globe.

Glöckchen ['glœkçən] *n*, '**Glöcklein** *n* (6) small bell.

Glocke ['glɔkə] *f* (15) bell; (*Glas*2) shade; (*Uhr*) clock; *fig. et. an die große ~ hängen* noise a th. abroad, make a fuss about a th.

'**Glocken|blume** *f* bell-flower; 2**förmig** ['~fœrmiç] bell-shaped; '**~geläut** *n* bell-ringing; *abgestimmtes*: chime; '**~gießer** *m* bell-founder; '**~rock** *m* wide flared skirt; '**~schlag** *m* stroke (of the clock); '**~spiel** *n* chime(s *pl.*); '**~stuhl** *m* belfry; '**~turm** *m* bell-tower, belfry.

Glöckner ['glœknər] *m* (7) bell-ringer, sexton.

glomm [glɔm] *pret. v. glimmen.*

Glorie ['glo:rjə] *f* (15) glory; '**~nschein** *m fig.* halo, aureola.

glorreich ['glo:raiç] glorious.

Gloss|ar [glɔ'sa:r] *n* (3) glossary; '**~e** *f* (15) gloss, comment; 2**ieren** [~'si:rən] gloss, comment (up)on.

'**Glotz-auge** *n* goggle-eye, *Am. a.* pop-eye.

Glotze F ['glɔtsə] *f* (15) (*Fernsehgerät*) goggle-box, *Am.* tube; '2**n** (27) goggle, stare.

Glück [glyk] *n* (3) fortune; (*Glücksfall*) good luck; (*Gefühl von ~*) happiness; (*Wohlstand*) prosperity; *auf gut ~* at haphazard; *zu meinem ~* luckily for me; *~ haben* be lucky, succeed; *das ~ haben zu inf.* have the good fortune to *inf.*; *~ wünschen* congratulate (*j-m zu* et. a p. [up]on a th.); *zum Geburtstag*: wish many happy returns (of the day); *da können Sie von ~ sagen* you may call yourself lucky; *viel ~!* good luck!; *zum ~* fortunately.

'**glückbringend** lucky.

Glucke ['glukə] *f* (15) clucking hen; '2**n** (25) cluck.

'**glücken** (25, sn) succeed; *mir glückt* et. I succeed in a th.

'**gluckern** (29) *wie Wasser*: gurgle.

'**glücklich** happy; (*von Glück begünstigt*) lucky, fortunate; (*günstig*) *a.* favo(u)rable, auspicious; '**~er'weise** fortunately, luckily; *s. preisen.*

'**Glücksbringer(in** *f*) *m* mascot; (*Gegenstand*) lucky charm.

'**glück'selig** blissful, very happy; 2**keit** *f* blissfulness.

glucksen ['gluksən] (27) gurgle.

'**Glücks|fall** *m* lucky chance, stroke of luck; *unverhoffter*: windfall; '**~göttin** *f* Fortune; '**~kind** *n* lucky person; '**~klee** *m* four-leaf clover; '**~pfennig** *m* lucky penny; '**~pilz** F *m* lucky dog; '**~ritter** *m* soldier of fortune; '**~sache** *f* (matter of) luck; '**~spiel** *n* game of chance; *fig.* gamble; '**~stern** *m* lucky star; '**~strähne** *f* streak of good luck; '**~tag** *m* lucky (*od.* happy) day.

'**glück|strahlend** radiant with happiness; '2**s-treffer** *m Sport*: fluke, lucky shot; *fig.* stroke of (good) luck, (*Geldgewinn*) windfall; '**~verheißend** auspicious; '2**wunsch** *m* congratulation, good wishes *pl.*; *zum Geburtstag*: *s. Glück*; *pl. zu Neujahr usw.*: (season's) greetings *pl.*; '2**wunsch...** congratulatory; '2**wunschkarte** *f* greetings card; '2**wunschtelegramm** *n* greetings telegram.

Glüh|birne ⚡ ['gly:-] *f* (incandescent) bulb; '2**en** *v/t. u. v/i.* (25) glow; *v/t.* ⊕ anneal; '2**end** glowing (*a. fig.*); *Eisen*: *a.* red-hot; *Kohle*: live; *fig.* ardent, fervid; '**~faden** *m* filament; '2'**heiß** red-hot; '**~lampe** *f*, '**~licht** *n* incandescent lamp; '**~strumpf** *m* incandescent mantle; '**~wein** *m* mulled claret; '**~wurm** *m* glow-worm.

Glut [glu:t] *f* (16) heat; *konkret*: glowing fire; live coal; *fig.* glow, ardo(u)r.

Glyzerin [glytsə'ri:n] *n* (3) glycer[in(e).]

Gnade ['gna:də] *f* (15) grace;

(*Gunst*) favo(u)r; (*Barmherzigkeit*) mercy; (*Milde*) clemency; *ohne* ~ without mercy; *von Gottes* ~*n* by the grace of God; *Euer* ~*n* Your Grace; *auf* ~ *oder Ungnade* at discretion; *s. walten.*

'**Gnaden|-akt** *m* act of grace; '**~bild** *n* miraculous image; '**~brot** *n* bread of charity; '**~frist** *f* reprieve, respite, grace; '**~gesuch** *n* petition for mercy; '**~schuß** *m*, '**~stoß** *m* coup de grâce (*fr.*); '**~weg** *m*: *auf dem* ~ by way of grace.

gnädig ['gnɛdiç] gracious; (*freundlich*) kind; (*barmherzig*) merciful; ~*e Frau* madam.

Gnom [gno:m] *m* (12) gnome, goblin; '**2enhaft** gnomish, gnomelike.

Gobelin [gobə'lɛ̃] *m* (11) Gobelin (tapestry).

Gockel F ['gɔkəl] *m* (7) cock.

Gold [gɔlt] *n* (3) gold; '**~-ader** *f* vein of gold; '**~barren** *m* gold ingot, bullion; '**~barsch** *m* ruff; ✝ redfish; '**~bergwerk** *n* gold-mine.

golden ['~dən] (of) gold; *fig.* golden; (*vergoldet*) gilt; ~*e Hochzeit* golden wedding; ⚹ ~*er Schnitt* medial section.

'**gold|farben** gold-colo(u)red, golden; '**2fasan** *m* golden pheasant; '**2fisch** *m* goldfish; '**~gelb** golden; '**2gewicht** *n* troy (weight); '**2gräber** *m* (7) gold-digger; '**2grube** *f*, '**2mine** *f* gold-mine (*a. fig.*); **~ig** ['~diç] sweet, lovely, *Am. a.* cute; '**2kind** *n* darling; '**2klumpen** *m* lump of gold, nugget; '**2lack** *m* gold-varnish; ⚘ wallflower; '**2medaille** *f* gold medal; '**2münze** *f* gold coin; '**2regen** ⚘ *m* laburnum; '**2reserve** *f* gold reserve; '**2schmied** *m* goldsmith; '**2schnitt** *m* gilt edge(s *pl.*); *mit* ~ *Buch*: gilt-edged; '**2stück** *n* gold coin; '**2waage** *f* gold-balance; *fig. jedes Wort auf die* ~ *legen* weigh every word; '**2währung** *f* gold standard; '**2waren** *f/pl.* gold articles.

Golf[1] *geogr.* [gɔlf] *m* (3) gulf.

Golf[2] *n*, '**~spiel** *n* golf; '**~platz** *m* golf-course, (golf-)links *pl.*; '**~schläger** *m* golf-club; '**~spieler(in** *f*) *m* golfer.

'**Golfstrom** *geogr. m* Gulf Stream.

Gondel ['gɔndəl] *f* (15) gondola; *am Ballon, Luftschiff*: *mst* car; '**~bahn** *f* cable-car; '**2n** F bowl (*od.* tool) along.

gönnen ['gœnən] (25): *j-m et.* ~ allow (*od.* grant *od.* not to grudge) a p. a th.; *j-m et. nicht* ~ grudge a p. a th.; *wir* ~ *es ihm von Herzen* we wish him every joy with it; *sich et.* ~ treat o.s. to (*od.* allow o.s.) a th.; *sich et. nicht* ~ grudge (*od.* not to allow) o.s. a th.

'**Gönner** *m* (7) patron, *Am. a.* sponsor; '**2haft** patronizing; '**~in** *f* patroness; '**~miene** *f* patronizing air; '**~schaft** *f* patronage.

gor [go:r] *pret. v. gären.*

Gör F [gø:r] *n* (5), '**Göre** *contp. f* (15) brat.

Gorilla [go'rila] *m* (11) gorilla.

goß [gɔs] *pret. v. gießen.*

Gosse ['gɔsə] *f* (15) gutter.

Got|e ['go:tə] *m* (13) Goth; '**2isch** Gothic.

Gott [gɔt] *m* (1^1 *u.* ^{2}) God; (*Gottheit*) god, deity; ~ *sei Dank!* thank God!; *leider* ~*es* unfortunately; *s. bewahren, behüten*; '**2-ähnlich** godlike; '**2begnadet** god-gifted, inspired.

Götter|bild ['gœtərbilt] *n* image of a god, idol; '**~dämmerung** *f* twilight of the gods.

'**Götter|speise** *f fig.* ambrosia; '**~trank** *m fig.* nectar.

'**Gottes|-acker** *m* churchyard; '**~dienst** *m* divine service; '**~furcht** *f* fear of God; **2fürchtig** ['~fyrçtiç] godfearing; '**~haus** *n* house of God; '**~lästerer** *m* blasphemer; '**2lästerlich** blasphemous; F unholy; '**~lästerung** *f* blasphemy; '**~leugner** *m* atheist; '**~lohn** *m* God's blessing; '**~-urteil** *n* ordeal.

'**gott|gefällig** pleasing to God; '**~gleich** godlike; '**2heit** *f* deity, divinity, god(dess *f*); (*Gottnatur*) godhead.

Göttin ['gœtin] *f* goddess.

'**göttlich** divine, godlike; F *fig.* divine; *Spaß*: capital.

gott|'lob! thank God!; '**~los** godless; impious; F *fig.* godless, unholy; '**2losigkeit** *f* ungodliness; **2seibeiuns** [~zaɪ'baɪˀuns] *m inv.* Old Nick, *the* Devil; '**~s-erbärmlich** pitiful; '**~vergessen** *s. gottlos*; '**~verlassen** god-forsaken; '**2vertrauen** *n* trust in God; '**~voll** F divine; *Spaß*: capital, very funny.

Götze ['gœtsə] *m* (13) idol.

'**Götzen|bild** *n* idol; '**~diener(in** *f*) *m* idolater; '**~dienst** *m* idolatry; '**~tempel** *m* temple of an idol.

Gouvern|ante [guvɛr'nantə] *f* (15)

governess; **~eur** [~'nø:r] *m* (3¹) governor.

Grab [grɑ:p] *n* (1²) grave, *rhet.* (*u.* *~mal*) tomb; *das Heilige ~* the Holy Sepulchre; *j-n zu ~e geleiten* attend a p.'s funeral; *verschwiegen wie das ~* (as) secret as the grave.

Graben ['grɑ:bən] **1.** *m* (6¹) ditch; *bsd.* ⚔ trench; **2.** ♀ (30) dig; *Tier*: burrow; '**~krieg** *m* trench war(fare).

Gräber ['grɛ:bər] *m* (7) digger.

'**Grabes|ruhe** *f*, ~'**stille** *f* deathly silence; '**~stimme** *f* sepulchral voice.

Grab|geläute ['grɑ:p-] *f* (death-) knell (*a. fig.*); '**~gesang** *m* funeral song; '**~gewölbe** *n* vault, tomb; '**~kammer** *f* burial chamber; '**~legung** *f* interment, burial; '**~mal** *n* tomb, sepulch|re, *Am.* -er; '**~rede** *f* funeral speech; '**~schrift** *f* epitaph; '**~stätte** *f*, '**~stelle** *f* burial-place, tomb; '**~stein** *m* tombstone, gravestone.

Grad [grɑ:t] *m* (3, *als Maß im pl. inv.*) *allg.*, *a. univ. u. fig.* degree; (*Rang*) grade; *in* (*od. bis zu*) *e-m gewissen ~* to a certain degree, up to a point; '**~bogen** ⚗ *m* protractor; '**~einteilung** *f* graduation.

gradieren [~'di:rən] graduate.

grad|linig ['grɑ:t-] *s. geradlinig*; '**♀messer** *m* graduator; *fig.* indicator, barometer; '**♀netz** *n Landkarte*: grid.

Graf [grɑ:f] *m* (12) *englischer*: earl; [*nichtenglischer*: count.]

Gräf|in ['grɛfin] *f* countess; '**♀lich** of an earl *od.* a count(ess).

'**Grafschaft** *f* county.

Gral [grɑ:l] *m* (3, *o. pl.*): *der Heilige ~* the Holy Grail.

Gram [grɑ:m] **1.** *m* (3) grief, sorrow; **2.** *j-m ♀ sein* bear a p. ill-will *od.* a grudge.

grämen ['grɛ:mən] (25) (*a. sich*) grieve; *sich zu Tode ~* die with grief.

'**grämlich** morose, peevish.

Gramm [gram] *n* (3, *im pl. nach Zahlen inv.*) gramme, *Am.* gram.

Grammatik [gra'matik] *f* (16) grammar; **♀alisch** [~'kɑ:liʃ], **gram'matisch** grammatical; **~er** *m* grammarian.

Grammophon [gramo'fo:n] *n* (3¹) gramophone, *Am.* phonograph; **~platte** *f* (gramophone) disk *od.* record.

'**gramvoll** sorrowful, grief-stricken.

Gran [grɑ:n] *n* (3¹, *im pl. nach Zahlen inv.*) grain.

Granat *min.* [gra'nɑ:t] *m* garnet; **~apfel** *m* pomegranate; **~e** *f* (15) (*Geschütz♀*) shell; (*Gewehr♀*, *Hand♀*) grenade; **~splitter** *m* shell-splinter; **~trichter** *m* shell-crater; **~werfer** *m* mortar.

Grande ['grandə] *m* (13) grandee.

grandios [gran'djo:s] *adj.* grand(iose), overwhelming.

Granit [gra'ni:t] *m* (3) granite.

Granne ⚘['granə] *f* (15) awn, beard.

Graph|ik ['grɑ:fik] *f* (16, *o. pl.*) graphic arts *pl.*; (*Darstellung*) *s. graphisch*; '**~iker** *m* (7) commercial artist; '**♀isch** graphic(ally *adv.*); *~e Darstellung* graph(ic representation), diagram, chart.

Graphit [gra'fi:t] *m* (3) black lead, graphite, plumbago.

Grapholog|e [grafo'lo:gə] *m* (13), **~in** *f* (16¹) graphologist; **~ie** [~lo'gi:] *f* graphology.

Gras [grɑ:s] *n* (2¹) grass; *fig.* F *das ~ wachsen hören* hear the grass grow; *fig.* F *ins ~ beißen* bite the dust; '**♀bewachsen** grass-grown.

grasen ['grɑ:zən] (27) graze.

'**gras|fressend** graminivorous; '**~grün** grass-green; '**♀halm** *m* blade of grass; '**♀hüpfer** *m* (7) grasshopper; **~ig** ['~ziç] grassy; '**♀land** *n* grassland; '**♀mücke** *zo. f* warbler; '**♀narbe** *f* turf, sod; '**♀platz** *m* grass-plot, lawn, green.

grassieren [gra'si:rən] rage, be rampant, spread.

gräßlich ['grɛsliç] horrible, ghastly; (*scheußlich*) hideous, atrocious; '**♀keit** *f* horribleness; atrocity.

Grat [grɑ:t] *m* (3) edge; *Berg*: ridge.

Gräte ['grɛ:tə] *f* (15) (fish-)bone.

Gratifikation [gratifika'tsjo:n] *f* (16) gratuity, bonus, extra pay.

gratis ['grɑ:tis] gratis, free (of charge); '**♀-exemplar** *n* presentation copy; '**♀probe** ⚕ *f* free sample.

Grätsche ['grɛ:tʃə] *f* (15) *Turnen*: straddling vault; '**♀n** (27) straddle.

Gratul|ant [gratu'lant] *m* (12) congratulator; **~ation** [~la'tsjo:n] *f* congratulation; **♀ieren** [~'li:rən] congratulate (*j-m zu et.* a p. on a th.); *j-m zum Geburtstag ~* wish a p. many happy returns (of the day); (*ich*) *gratuliere!* (my) congratulations!

'**Gratwanderung** *fig. f* tightrope [walk.]

grau [graʊ] grey, *Am.* gray; *Vorzeit*: remote; *fig.* grey, bleak; *der* ~*e Alltag* the drab monotony of everyday life; *s. Haar*; '**~blau** greyish blue; '**2brot** *n* rye bread; '**~en**[1] (25) *Tag*: dawn.

'**grauen**[2] **1.** *mir graut vor (dat.)* I have a horror of, I shudder at; **2.** 2 *n* (6) horror (*vor dat.* of); '**~haft**, '**~voll** horrible, dreadful.

'**grauhaarig** grey- (*Am.* gray-) haired.

graulen ['graʊlən] (25): *sich* ~ *(vor)* be afraid (of); *s. grauen*[2].

gräulich ['grɔʏliç] greyish, *Am.* grayish.

graumeliert ['~me'li:rt] tinged with grey (*Am.* gray), grey-flecked.

Graupe ['graʊpə] *f* (15) (peeled) barley; '**2lig** sleety; '**~ln 1.** *f/pl.* sleet *sg.*; **2.** 2 (29) sleet; '**~lwetter** *n* sleety weather.

'**Graupensuppe** *f* barley broth.

Graus [graʊs] *m* (4) horror.

'**grausam** cruel; '**2keit** *f* cruelty.

'**Grau|schimmel** *m* grey (*Am.* gray) horse; '**~schleier** *fig. m* greyness, *Am.* grayness.

graus|en ['graʊzən] **1.** (27) *s. grauen*[2] 1.; **2.** 2 *n* (6) horror (*vor dat.* of); '**~ig** horrible.

'**Grau|tier** *n* ass, donkey; '**~zone** *f* grey (*Am.* gray) area.

Graveur [gra'vø:r] *m* (3[1]) engraver.

Gravier|-anstalt [gra'vi:r-] *f* engraving establishment; **2en** engrave; **2end** serious; **~ung** *f* engraving.

Gravitations|gesetz [gravita'tsjo:ns-] *n* law of gravitation; **~kraft** *f* gravitational force.

gravitätisch [~vi'tɛ:tiʃ] grave, solemn; *Gang*: stately.

Grazie ['gra:tsjə] *f* (15) grace; *die drei* ~*n* the three Graces.

graziös [gra'tsjø:s] graceful.

Greif [graɪf] *m* (3 *u.* 12) griffin.

'**Greif|-arm** ⊕ *m* claw arm; '**~bagger** *m* grab dredger; '**2bar** seizable; ✝ available, on hand; (*offenbar*) tangible, palpable, obvious; *fig. nicht* ~ impalpable; *in* ~*er Nähe* near at hand; '**2en** (30) *v/t.* seize; ♪ *Saite*: hold down, *Note*: strike; *fig. man kann es mit Händen* ~ it meets the eye; *v/i. an den Hut* ~ touch; *fig. ans Herz* ~ touch deeply; ~ *in (acc.)* put one's hand(s) in(to); ~ *nach* reach for, grasp at, *hastig*: snatch at; *fig. um sich* ~ gain ground, spread; *zu e-m Mittel* ~ resort to; *zur Feder* ~ take up pen; *zu den Waffen* ~ take up arms; *s. Arm*; '**~er** *m* (7) ⊕ claw; *Kran*: grab; *P.*: (*Spürer*) bloodhound; '**~vogel** *m* bird of prey; '**~zange** *f* tongs *pl.*

greinen ['graɪnən] (25) whine.

Greis [graɪs] *m* (4) old man.

Greisen|-alter ['~zən-] *n* old age, senility; '**2haft** senile; '**~haftigkeit** *f* senility.

'**Greisin** *f* (16[1]) old woman.

grell [grɛl] *Farbe, Licht*: glaring (*a. fig.*); *Farbe*: *a.* loud, flashy; *Ton*: shrill.

Gremium ['gre:mjum] *n* (9) body, group.

Grenadier [grena'di:r] *m* (3[1]) infantryman, rifleman; *Traditionsbezeichnung*: grenadier; **~...** infantry ...

'**Grenz|-abfertigung** *f* border clearance; '**~bereich** *m* border area; *fig.* borderline; '**~bewohner** *m* borderer, frontiersman.

Grenze ['grɛntsə] *f* (15) limit; (*Scheidelinie*) boundary; (*Ländergrenze*) frontier, border(s *pl.*); (*äußerstes Ende*) extreme point; *fig. e-e* ~ *ziehen* draw the line; *in* ~*en* within (certain) limits.

'**grenzen** (27) border (*an acc.* on; *a. fig.*); '**~los** boundless; *adv.* ~ *dumm* infernally stupid; '**2losigkeit** *f* boundlessness.

'**Grenz|fall** *m* borderline case; **~gänger** ['~gɛŋər] *m* (7) (illegal) border crosser; (*Arbeiter*) frontier commuter; '**~konflikt** *m* border dispute; '**~kontrolle** *f* border control; '**~land** *n* borderland; '**~linie** *f* boundary-line; demarcation line; *fig.* borderline; '**~pfahl** *m* boundary-post; '**~posten** *m* border guard; '**~schutz** *m* frontier defen|ce, *Am.* -se; *Truppe*: border police; '**~sperre** *f* closing of the frontier, frontier ban; '**~stadt** *f* frontier town; '**~stein** *m* boundary-stone; '**~-übergang** *m* border crossing(-point); '**~verkehr** *m* border traffic; '**~wert** *m* limiting value; '**~zwischenfall** *m* border incident.

Greuel ['grɔʏəl] *m* (7) horror, abomination; *s. Greueltat*; *er (es) ist mir ein* ~ I loathe him (it); '**~märchen** *n* atrocity tale; '**~propaganda** *f* atrocity propaganda; '**~tat** *f* atrocity.

'**greulich** horrid, dreadful.

Grieben ['gri:bən] *f/pl.* (15) greaves *pl.*
Griebs [gri:ps] *m* (4) core.
Griech|e ['gri:çə] *m* (13), '**~in** *f* (16[1]) Greek; '**≗isch** Greek; ⚠ *paint.* Grecian; *~-römischer Ringkampf* Gr(a)eco-Roman wrestling.
Gries|gram ['gri:sgra:m] *m* (3) grumbler, crab, *Am.* F grouch; **≗grämig** ['~grɛ:miç] morose, grumpy, *Am.* F grouchy.
Grieß [gri:s] *m* (3[2]) gravel (*a.* ⚕), grit; (*Weizen≗*) semolina; '**~brei** *m* semolina pudding; '**~kloß** *m* semolina dumpling.
Griff [grif] **1.** *m* (3) grip, grasp, hold; ♪ touch; ⊕ grip; knob; (*Hebel*) lever; *Schirm, Messer usw.*: handle; *Schwert*: hilt; *v. Stoff*: feel, handle; *Ringen*: hold; ⚔ *~e üben od.* F *kloppen* do rifle drill; *fig. ein guter ~* a hit; *fig.* et. *im ~ haben* have the knack of a th.; **2.** ≗ *pret. v. greifen*; '**≗bereit** handy; '**~brett** *n e-r Geige usw.*: finger-board; '**~el** *m* (7) slate pencil; ⚘ pistil; '**≗ig** affording a firm hold; *Tuch*: of good feel; *Werkzeug*: wieldy; *mot.* non-skid.
Grill [gril] *m* (11) *elektrischer etc.*: grill; (*offener Rost*) grill, barbecue.
Grille ['grilə] *f* (15) *zo.* cricket; *fig.* whim, fancy.
grill|en ['grilən] (25) *elektrisch etc.*: grill; *auf dem Rost*: grill, barbecue; '**≗party** *f* barbecue; '**≗restaurant** *n* grillroom.
Grimasse [gri'masə] *f* (15) grimace; *~n schneiden* pull faces, grimace.
Grimm [grim] *m* (3) rage, wrath; '**~en** ⚕ *n* (6) gripes *pl.*, colic; '**≗ig** grim, fierce (*beide a. fig.*); furious.
Grind [grint] *m* (3) scab, scurf; **≗ig** ['~diç] scabbed, scabby, scurfy.
grinsen ['grinzən] (27), ≗ *n* (6) grin (*über acc.* at); *höhnisch*: sneer (at).
Grippe ['gripə] *f* (15) influenza, F flu; grippe.
Grips [grips] F *m* (3) brains *pl.*
grob [grɔp] (18[2]) coarse; (*unhöflich*) rude; (*rauh*; *roh*; *ungeschliffen*; *ungefähr*) rough; *Fehler, Irrtum, Fahrlässigkeit usw.*: gross (*od.* bad) *mistake*; *~es Geschütz* heavy guns *pl.*; *~ gegen j-n sein* be hard on a p.; *aus dem Gröbsten heraus sein* have broken the back of it.
'**Grob|blech** *n* (heavy) plate; '**~einstellung** ⊕ *f* coarse adjustment; '**~heit** *f* coarseness; grossness; roughness; rudeness; *~en pl.* rude things.
Grobian ['gro:bja:n] *m* (3) rude fellow, boor, ruffian.
grobkörnig ['grɔp-] coarse-grained.
gröblich ['grø:pliç]: *~ beleidigen* insult grossly.
grob|maschig ['grɔpmaʃiç] wide-meshed; '**≗schmied** *m* blacksmith; '**≗schnitt** *m* (*Tabak*) coarse cut.
grölen F ['grø:lən] (25) bawl.
Groll [grɔl] *m* (3) grudge, ill-will, ranco(u)r; '**≗en** (25) *Donner*: rumble; *j-m ~* have a grudge (*od.* spite) against a p.
Gros[1] [grɔs] *n* (4[1], *pl. nach Zahlen inv.*) (*12 Dutzend*) gross.
Gros[2] [gro:] *n inv.* main body.
Groschen ['grɔʃən] *m etwa*: penny; F *der ~ ist gefallen!* the penny has dropped!; '**~-automat** *m* (penny-in-the-)slot machine; '**~roman** *m* penny dreadful, *Am.* dime novel.
groß [gro:s] (18[2]) great, large; (*umfangreich*; *bedeutend*) big; *von Wuchs*: tall; (*ungeheuer*) huge; *fig.* great, (*~artig*) grand; *Hitze*: intense; *Kälte*: severe; *Verlust*: heavy; *die ≗en pl.* the grown-ups; *das ~e Publikum* the general public; *im ~en* ⚚ wholesale, *allg.* on a large scale; *im ~en und ganzen* on the whole, by and large; *~er Buchstabe* capital (letter); *~e Ferien* long vacation; *das ≗e Los* the jackpot; *der ≗e Ozean* the Pacific (Ocean); *Rechtschreibung*: *~ schreiben* capitalize; *ich bin kein ~er Tänzer* I am not much of a dancer; *s. klein, Terz, Tier*; '**≗-abnehmer** *m* bulk purchaser; '**≗-aktionär** ⚚ *m* principal shareholder; '**~-angelegt** large-scale; '**≗-angriff** *m* large-scale attack; '**~-artig** grand, great; splendid, marvellous; enormous; '**≗-aufnahme** *f Film*: close-up; '**≗-auftrag** *m* bulk (*od.* substantial) order; '**≗betrieb** *m* large-scale enterprise; '**≗brand** *m s. Großfeuer*; '**≗buchstabe** *m* capital (letter); '**≗druck-ausgabe** *f* (*Buch*) large-print edition.
Größe ['grø:sə] *f* (15) (*Umfang*) size, largeness; *des Wuchses*: tallness, height; ⚚ *e-s Kleides usw.*: size; (*Menge*; *bsd.* ℞) quantity; *fig.*

greatness; *a. ast.* magnitude; (*Person*) celebrity, notability; *thea., Sport*: star.

'**Groß|-einkauf** ✝ *m* bulk purchase; '**~-einsatz** *m* large-scale operation; '**~-eltern** *pl.* grand-parents; '**~-enkel** *m* great-grandson; '**~-enkelin** *f* great-granddaughter.

'**Größen·ordnung** *f* order.

'**großenteils** to a large (*od.* great) extent, largely.

'**Größen|verhältnisse** *n/pl.* proportions, dimensions; '**~wahn** *m* megalomania; '**2wahnsinnig** megalomaniac.

'**Groß|fahndung** *f* dragnet operation; '**~familie** *f* extended (*od.* kinship) family; '**~feuer** *n* large fire, conflagration; '**~format** *n* large size; '**~fürst** *m* grand duke; '**~fürstentum** *n* grand duchy; '**~grundbesitz** *m* large landed property; '**~handel** *m* wholesale trade; '**~handels·preis** *m* wholesale price; '**~händler** *m* wholesale dealer; '**~handlung** *f* wholesale firm; '**2herzig** magnanimous; '**~herzigkeit** *f* magnanimity; '**~herzog** *m* grand duke; '**~herzogin** *f* grand duchess; '**2herzoglich** grand-ducal; '**~herzogtum** *n* grand duchy; '**~hirn** *n* cerebrum; '**~-industrie** *f* big industry; '**~industrielle** *m* (7) big industrialist.

Grossist [grɔ'sist] *m* (12) wholesaler.

'**groß|jährig** of age; ~ *werden* come of age; '**2jährigkeit** *f* full age, majority; '**2kampfschiff** *n* capital ship; '**2-kapitalist** *m* big capitalist; '**2kaufmann** *m* wholesale merchant; '**2-kraftwerk** ⚡ *n* super power station; '**2kreuz** *n* Grand Cross; '**2küche** *f* canteen kitchen; '**2macht** *f* great power; '**~mächtig** mighty; '**2-mannssucht** *f* megalomania; '**2-maul** *n* bigmouth; **~mäulig** ['~mɔʏliç] big-mouthed; '**2mut** *f* magnanimity, generosity; **~mütig** ['~my:tiç] generous, magnanimous; '**2mutter** *f* grandmother; '**2neffe** *m* grand-nephew; '**2nichte** *f* grand-niece; '**2-onkel** *m* great-uncle, grand-uncle; '**2raumbüro** *n* open-plan office; '**2rechner** *m Computer*: mainframe; **2'reinemachen** *n* (6) wholesale house-cleaning; '**2schreibung** *f* capitalization; '**2sprecher** *m* boaster; **2spreche'rei** *f* big talk; '**~sprecherisch** boastful; '**~spurig** arrogant; '**2stadt** *f* large city, metropolis; '**2städter(in** *f*) *m* inhabitant of a large city, metropolitan; '**~städtisch** (characteristic) of a large city, metropolitan; '**2tante** *f* great-aunt, grand-aunt; '**2tat** *f* great deed *od.* exploit, feat.

größtenteils ['grø:stən'taɪls] for the most part, mostly.

'**Groß|tuer** *m* (7) boaster, show-off; '**2tuerisch** boastful; '**2tun** talk big; *sich mit et.* ~ brag of; '**~-unternehmen** *n* large-scale enterprise; '**~-unternehmer** *m* big industrialist, entrepreneur (*fr.*); '**~vater** *m* grandfather; '**~vaterstuhl** *m* arm-chair; '**~verdiener** *m* (7) big earner; '**~vertrieb** *m* distribution in bulk; '**~wildjagd** *f* big game hunt(ing); '**2ziehen** bring up; **2zügig** ['~tsy:giç] liberal, generous (*beide a. freigebig*), broad-minded; *Plan usw.*: large-scale; '**~zügigkeit** *f* broad-mindedness; liberality; generosity.

grotesk [gro'tɛsk] grotesque.

Grotte ['grɔtə] *f* (15) grotto.

grub [gru:p] *pret. v. graben* 2.

Grübchen ['gry:pçən] *n* (6) dimple.

Grube ['gru:bə] *f* (15) pit; ⚒ *a.* mine.

Grübelei [gry:bə'laɪ] *f* (16) brooding, pondering, rumination.

grübeln ['gry:bəln] (29) brood, ponder, pore (*über dat.* over).

'**Gruben|-arbeiter** *m* miner; '**~-brand** *m* pit fire; '**~gas** *n* fire-damp; '**~holz** ⚒ *n* pit-props *pl.*; '**~lampe** *f* miner's lamp; '**~-unglück** *n* mine disaster.

Grübler ['gry:blər] *m* (7), '**~in** *f* (16[1]) ponderer.

Gruft [gruft] *f* (14[1]) tomb, vault.

Grum(me)t ['grum(ə)t] *n* (3) aftermath, *Am.* rowen.

grün [gry:n] **1.** green (*a. fig. unreif, unerfahren*); *Hering*: green, fresh; *~er Junge* greenhorn; *~es Licht Verkehr u. fig.*: green light; *j-m ~es Licht geben* give s.o. the green light (*od.* the go-ahead); *e-e Entscheidung etc. vom ~en Tisch* an armchair decision *etc.*; *j-n ~ und blau schlagen* beat a p. black and blue; *fig. auf e-n ~en Zweig kommen* get somewhere, make it; **2.** 2 *n* (3[1]) green; *der Natur*: verdure; *dasselbe in ~* practically the same thing.

Grund [grunt] *m* (3[3]) ground; (*Erdboden*) soil; ~ *und Boden s.*

Grundbesitz; (*Meeresboden usw.*) bottom; (*Tal*) valley; (*Fundament*) foundation; (*Kaffeesatz*) grounds *pl.*; (*Ursache*) cause; (*Beweg*≗) motive; (*Vernunft*≗) reason; (*Beweis*≗) argument; *auf ~ von* on grounds of, on the strength of, based on, (*wegen*) because of, due to; *aus gesundheitlichen Gründen* for reasons of health; *aus diesem ~e* for this reason; *im ~e (genommen)* at (the) bottom, fundamentally; strictly speaking; *jeden (keinen) ~ haben zu inf.* have every (no) reason to *inf.*; *e-r Sache auf den ~ gehen od. kommen* get to the bottom of a th.; *von ~ aus* thoroughly, fundamentally, radically; **'~ausbildung** ⚔ *f* basic training; **'~bau** *m* foundation; **'~bedeutung** *f* original meaning; **'~bedingung** *f* basic condition; **'~bedürfnis** *n* basic requirement (*od.* need); **'~begriff** *m* basic idea; *~e pl.* fundamentals *pl.*; **'~besitz** *m* landed property, real estate; **'~besitzer** *m* landed proprietor; **'~bestandteil** *m* basic component; **'~buch** *n* land (title and charges) register; **'~buch-amt** *n* land registry; **'≗-ehrlich** thoroughly honest; **'~-eigentum** *n s. Grundbesitz*; **'~-eis** *n* ground-ice.

gründen ['gryndən] (26) found, establish; *fig.* base, ground (*auf acc.* on); ⚕ promote, float; *sich ~ auf* (*acc.*) be based (*od.* founded) on.

'Gründer *m* (7), **'~in** *f* (16[1]) founder; ⚕ *a.* promoter.

'grund|'falsch absolutely wrong; **'≗farbe** *f* ground-colo(u)r; *phys.* primary colo(u)r; **'≗fehler** *m* basic fault; fundamental mistake; **'≗fläche** *f* base; ⊕ floor-space; **'≗gebühr** *f* basic rate *od.* fee; **'≗gedanke** *m* fundamental (*od.* root) idea; **'≗gehalt** *n* basic salary; **'≗gesetz** *pol. n* basic (constitutional) law; **'≗herr** *m* landlord.

grund|ieren *paint.* [~'di:rən] ground, prime; **≗ierfarbe** *f* primer; **≗ierung** *f* priming; *Kosmetik*: foundation.

'Grund|kapital *n* (original) stock; **'~kenntnisse** *f/pl.* basic knowledge *sg.*; **'~lage** *f* basis, foundation; **'~lagenforschung** *f* pure research; **'≗legend** fundamental, basic(ally *adv.*); **'~legung** *f* laying the foundation.

gründlich ['gryntliç] thorough; (*zuverlässig*) solid; *Wissen*: profound; (*durchgreifend*) radical; **'≗keit** *f* thoroughness.

'Grund|linie *f* base-line; **'~lohn** *m* basic wage(s *pl.*); **'≗los** bottomless; *fig.* groundless; (*unbegründet*) unfounded; *adv.* for no reason (at all); **'~losigkeit** *f* groundlessness; **'~mauer** *f* foundation(-wall); **'~nahrungsmittel** *n* staple food.

Grün'donners-tag *m* (3) Maundy Thursday.

'Grund|pfeiler *m* bottom pillar; *weitS.* main support; **'~platte** ⊕ *f* base-plate; **'~prinzip** *n* basic principle; **'~rechte** *pol. n/pl.* basic rights; **'~regel** *f* fundamental rule; **'~riß** *m* ⚠ ground-plan; (*Lehrbuch*) compendium; *fig.* outline(s *pl.*); **'~satz** *m* principle; *unbestreitbarer*: axiom; (*Lebensregel*) maxim; **'≗sätzlich** fundamental; *adv.* on principle; **'~schuld** *f* mortgage; **'~schule** *f* primary (*od.* elementary) school; **'~schullehrer(in** *f*) *m* primary (*Am.* elementary) school teacher; **'~stein** ⚠ *m* foundation-stone; *fig. den ~ legen zu* lay the foundations of; **'~steinlegung** *f* laying (of) the foundation-stone; **'~steuer** *f* land tax; **'~stock** *m* basis; **'~stoff** *m* element; (*Rohstoff*) raw material; *fig.* basic material; **'~stoff-industrie** *f* basic industry; **'~strich** *m* down-stroke; **'~stück** *n* piece of land; (landed *od.* real) estate; (*Parzelle*) plot, *Am.* lot; (*Haus u. Zubehör*) *the* premises *pl.*; **'~stücksmakler** *m* real estate agent, *Am.* realtor; **'~stücks-preis** *m* land price; **'~text** *m* original text; **'~ton** ♪ *m* keynote; **'~übel** *n* basic evil; **'~umsatz** *m* ⚕ basic turnover; *physiol.* basal metabolic rate.

Gründung ['gryndʊŋ] *f* foundation, establishment, creation; **'~smitglied** *n* founding member.

'grund|ver'kehrt utterly wrong; **'~ver'schieden** entirely different; **'≗wahrheit** *f* fundamental truth; **'≗wasser** *n* (under)ground water; **'≗wasserspiegel** *m* ground water level; **'≗wehrdienst** *m* basic military service; **'≗wortschatz** *m* basic vocabulary; **'≗zahl** *f* cardinal number; **'≗zins** *m* ground-rent; **'≗zug** *m* characteristic (feature); **'≗züge** *m/pl.* fundamentals *pl.*

Grüne ['gry:nə] *m*, *f* (13) *mst. pl. the* Greens *pl.*
grünen ['gry:nən] (25) be (*od.* grow) green; *fig.* flourish.
'**Grün|fläche** *f* green space; '**~futter** *n* green food *od.* fodder; '**~gürtel** *m* green belt; '**~kohl** *m* (curly) kale.
'**grünlich** greenish.
'**Grün|schnabel** *fig. m* greenhorn, whippersnapper; '**~span** *m* verdigris; '**~specht** *m* green woodpecker.
grunzen ['gruntsən] (27) grunt.
'**Grünzeug** *n* greens *pl.*; greenstuff.
Gruppe ['grupə] *f* (15) group (*a.* ⚕); ⚔ section, *Am.* squad; ✈ wing, *Am.* group; '**~n-arbeit** *f* teamwork; *Schule*: working in teams (*od.* groups); '**~nbild** *phot. n* group photograph; '**~ndynamik** *f* group dynamics *sg.*; '**~nreise** *f* organized (group) tour; '**~nsex** *m* group sex; '**~ntherapie** *f* group therapy; '**2nweise** in groups; ⚔ in sections, *etc.*
grup'pier|en group; **2ung** *f* grouping.
Grus [gru:s] *m* (4, *o. pl.*) (coal-)slack.
'**Grusel|film** ['gru:zəl-] *m* horror film; '**~geschichte** *f* horror story; '**2ig** creepy; '**2n 1.** (29) *mir* (*od. mich*) *hat's gegruselt* it made my flesh creep; **2.** ~ *n* (6) *the* creeps *pl.*
Gruß [gru:s] (3[2] *u.* [3]) (*Grüßen*) salutation; *vertraulicher*: greeting; *bsd.* ⚔, ⚓ salute; *mst pl. Grüße im Brief*: regards, *förmlich*: respects, compliments *pl.*
grüßen ['gry:sən] (27) greet, *bsd.* ⚔ salute; (*anrufen*) hail; (*j-n*) ~ *lassen* send one's compliments *od.* regards (to a p.); ~ *Sie ihn von mir* remember me to him.
Grütz|beutel ⚕ ['gryts-] *m* wen; '**~e** *f* (15) (*bsd. Hafer2*) grits *pl.*, groats *pl.*; F (*Verstand*) gumption.
gucken ['gukən] (25) look, peep.
'**Guckloch** *n* peep-hole.
Guerillakrieg [ge'riljakri:k] *m* guerrilla war(fare).
Gulasch ['gulaʃ] *n* (3) goulash; '**~suppe** *f* goulash soup.
Gulden ['guldən] *m* (6) florin.
gültig ['gyltiç] valid; (*in Kraft*) effective, in force; (*gesetzlich*) legal; *Münze*: current, good; *Fahrkarte*: available; *für ~ erklären* validate; '**2keit** *f* validity; currency; availability; '**2keitsdauer** *f* (period of) validity; *Vertrag*: *mst* term.
Gummi ['gumi] *m*, *n* (11) (*Kleb2*) gum; (*Kautschuk*) (India) rubber; **~arabikum** [~a'ra:bikum] *n* gum Arabic; '**2-artig** gummy; '**~ball** *m* rubber ball; '**~band** *n* elastic; **~bärchen** ['~bɛ:rçən] *n* (6) jelly bear; '**~baum** *m* gum (*od.* rubber) tree; (*Zimmerpflanze*) rubber plant; '**~boot** *n* rubber dinghy; '**~druck** *typ. m* offset.
gum'mieren gum; ⊕ rubberize.
'**Gummi|handschuh** *m* rubber glove; '**~knüppel** *m* (rubber) truncheon; *Am.* club, F billy; '**~mantel** *m* mackintosh, plastic mac; '**~paragraph** *m* elastic clause; '**~reifen** *m* (rubber) tyre, *Am.* tire; '**~ring** *m* rubber band; '**~schlauch** *m für Wasser*: rubber hose; *mot. usw.*: rubber tube; '**~schnur** *f* elastic; '**~schuhe** *m/pl.* galoshes, rubber shoes, *Am.* rubbers; '**~schwamm** *m* rubber sponge; '**~sohle** *f* rubber sole; '**~stempel** *m* rubber stamp; '**~strumpf** *m* elastic stocking; '**~zelle** *f* padded cell; '**~zug** *m* elastic.
Gunst [gunst] *f* (16) favo(u)r (*a.* '**~bezeigung** *f*); *s. erweisen*; *in ~ stehen bei j-m* be in a p.'s favo(u)r (*od.* good graces); *zu m-n ~en* (*a.* ⚕) to my favo(u)r (*od.* credit); *s. zugunsten.*
günstig ['gynstiç] favo(u)rable (*für* to); *~e Gelegenheit* opportunity; *im ~sten Fall* at best; ⚕ *zu ~en Bedingungen* on easy terms; *~es Angebot* bargain.
Günstling ['~liŋ] *m* (3[1]) favo(u)rite; *contp.* minion; '**~swirtschaft** *f* favo(u)ritism.
Gurgel ['gurgəl] *f* (15) throat; (*Schlund*) gullet; '**2n** *v/i.* (29) *u. v/t.* gargle; '**~wasser** *n* gargle.
Gurke ['gurkə] *f* (15) cucumber; *s. sauer*; '**~nhobel** *m* cucumber slicer; '**~nsalat** *m* cucumber salad.
gurren ['gurən] coo.
Gurt [gurt] *m* (3) belt (*a.* ⚔ *Patronen2*); ⚠ (*u. Sattel2*) girth; (*Trage2*) strap; ⊕ web(bing); *mot.* seat-belt; '**~band** *n* webbing.
Gürtel ['gyrtəl] *m* (7) belt, girdle (*beide a. fig.*); *geogr.* zone; '**~linie** *f* waistline; *a. fig. unter der* (*od. die*) ~ below the belt; '**~reifen** *m* radial (-ply) tyre, *Am.* tire; '**~rose** ⚕ *f* shingles *pl.*; '**~schnalle** *f* belt-buckle; '**~tier** *n* armadillo.

ˈ**gurten** *mot.* put one's seat-belt on.
ˈ**gürten** (26) gird.
Guß [gus] *m* (4²) (*Gießen*) founding, casting, (*Gegossenes*) cast(ing); *typ.* fount, *Am.* font; (*Regen*) downpour, shower (of rain); *aus einem ~* of a piece; *s. Zucker*♀; ˈ**~beton** *m* cast concrete; ˈ**~-eisen** *n* cast iron; ˈ**♀-eisern** cast-iron; ˈ**~form** *f* casting mo(u)ld; ˈ**~stahl** *m* cast steel; ˈ**~waren** *f/pl.* castings *pl.*
gut¹ [gu:t] good; *adv.* well; *~es Wetter* fine weather; *~er Dinge od. ~en Mutes sein* be of good cheer; *ein ~gehendes Geschäft* a flourishing business; *es ist ~!, schon ~!* never mind!: all right!; F *mach's ~! (als Gruß)* cheerio!; *es ~ haben* be well off; *für ~ finden* think proper; *j-m ~ sein* love (*od.* like) a p.; *laß es ~ sein!* never mind!; *Sie haben ~ lachen* it is very well for you to laugh; *im ~en* in a friendly manner; *~e Miene zum bösen Spiel machen* grin and bear it; *so ~ wie fertig usw.* as good as finished, *etc.*; *s. gehen, kurz, lassen, tun*; *s. a. zugute.*
Gut² *n* (1²) good (thing); (*Besitz*) goods *pl.*, possession, property; (*Land*) (landed) estate; *Güter* ⚓ *n/pl.* goods *pl.*, merchandise, 🚂 goods.
ˈ**Gut|-achten** *n* (6) (*engS.* expert) opinion; *schriftlich*: report; ˈ**~-achter** *m* (7) expert; ˈ**♀-artig** good-natured; ⚕ benign; ˈ**~-artigkeit** *f* good nature; ⚕ benignity; ˈ**♀-aussehend** good-looking, attractive; **♀-beˈtucht** well-heeled; ˈ**♀bürgerlich:** *~e Küche* good home cooking; ˈ**~dünken** *n* (6) opinion, discretion; *nach ~* at pleasure, at (one's own) discretion.
ˈ**Gute** *n* (18) *the* good; *~s tun* do good; *des ~n zuviel tun* overdo it; *alles ~!* all the best!
Güte [ˈgy:tə] *f* (15) goodness, kindness; ⚓ class, quality; (*Reinheit*) purity; *in ~* amicably; *haben Sie die ~, zu* be so kind as; *durch die ~ des Herrn S.* by favo(u)r (*od.* by the kind offices) of Mr. S.; F *meine ~!* good gracious!; ˈ**~klasse** *f* grade, quality.
Guteˈnachtˈgeschichte *f* bedtime story; **~kuß** *m* goodnight kiss.
ˈ**Güter|-abfertigung** *f*, ˈ**~-annahme** *f* goods office; ˈ**~bahnhof** *m* goods station, *Am.* freight depot *od.* yard; ˈ**~gemeinschaft** *f* community of property; ˈ**~kraftverkehr** *m* road haulage; ˈ**~schuppen** *m* goods (*Am.* freight) shed; ˈ**~trennung** *f* separation of property; ˈ**~verkehr** *m* goods (*Am.* freight) traffic; ˈ**~wagen** *m* wag(g)on, *Am.* freight car; *offener*: (goods) truck; *geschlossener*: (goods) van, *Am.* boxcar; ˈ**~zug** *m* goods (*Am.* freight) train.
ˈ**Gütesiegel** *n* seal of quality.
gut|gebaut [ˈ~gəbaʊt] well-built; *P.*: with a good figure; ˈ**~gehend** flourishing, prospering; **~gelaunt** [ˈ~gəlaʊnt] in a good mood; **~gemeint** [ˈ~gəmaɪnt] well-meant; **~gesinnt** [ˈ~gəzint] well-disposed (*dat.* to); ˈ**~gläubig** acting (*od.* done) in good faith, bona fide; *s. leichtgläubig*; ˈ**♀haben** *n* credit (balance); (*Konto*) account; ˈ**♀habenzins** *m* interest; ˈ**~heißen** approve (of), F okay; ˈ**~herzig** kind(-hearted).
gütig [ˈgy:tiç] good, kind.
ˈ**gütlich** amicable, friendly; *~er Vergleich* amicable settlement; *sich ~ tun an* (*dat.*) do o.s. well on.
ˈ**gut|machen:** *wieder~* make good, make up for, compensate, repair; **~mütig** [ˈ~my:tiç] good-natured; ˈ**♀mütigkeit** *f* good nature; ˈ**~sagen** *für* be good for.
ˈ**Gutsbesitzer(in** *f*) *m* landowner, landed proprietor (*f* proprietress).
ˈ**Gut|schein** *m* credit note *od.* slip; *j-m* ˈ**♀schreiben** credit a p. with *an amount*; place to a p.'s credit; ˈ**~schrift** ⚓ *f* credit; ˈ**~schriftsanzeige** *f* credit note.
ˈ**Guts|haus** *n* farm-house; ˈ**~herr(in** *f*) *m* lord (*f* lady) of the manor; ˈ**~hof** *m* farmyard; ˈ**~verwalter** *m* (landowner's) steward.
Guttapercha [gutaˈpɛrça] *f* (11²) gutta-percha.
ˈ**Gut|tat** *f* good action, kindness; ˈ**♀tun** (*j-m*) do *a p.* good.
ˈ**gutwillig** voluntary, willing; ˈ**♀keit** *f* willingness.
Gymnasialbildung [gymnaˈzjɑ:l-] *f* secondary (*engS.* classical) education.
Gymnasiast [~ˈzjast] *m* (12), **~in** *f* (16¹) grammar-school boy (*f* girl).
Gymnasium [~ˈnɑ:zjum] *n* (9) (*humanistisches* classical) secondary school.
Gymnast|ik [~ˈnastik] *f* (16)

gymnastics *pl. u. sg.*, physical exercises *pl.*; **~ik-anzug** *m* leotard; **2isch** gymnastic.

Gynäkolo|ge [gynɛːkoˈloːgə] *m* (13) gyn(a)ecologist; **~gie** [~loˈgiː] *f* gyn(a)ecology.

H

H [hɑː], **h** *n inv.* H, h; ♪ B.

ha! [hɑː] ha!, ah!

Haar [hɑːr] *n* (3) hair; *am Tuch*: nap, pile; *die ~e verlieren* lose one's hair; *sich die ~e machen* do (*od.* dress, *Am.* fix) one's hair; *sich die ~e (aus)raufen* tear one's hair; *sich die ~e schneiden lassen* have one's hair cut; *sich das ~ waschen* shampoo one's hair; *fig. aufs ~* to a hair; *um ein ~* within a hair's breadth; *fig.* F *er fand ein ~ in der Suppe* he found a fly in the ointment; *um kein ~ besser* not a bit better; *~e lassen müssen* be fleeced; *sich in den ~en liegen* be at loggerheads; *laß dir darüber keine grauen ~e wachsen* don't give yourself any grey hair; *j-m kein ~ krümmen* not to touch a hair of a p.'s head; *fig. an den ~en herbeiziehen* drag in (by the head and shoulders); *fig. an den ~en herbeigezogen* far-fetched; *kein gutes ~ an j-m lassen* pull a p. to pieces; *~e auf den Zähnen haben* be a Tartar.

ˈ**Haar...** *mst* hair-...; ˈ**~-ansatz** *m* hair-line; ˈ**~-ausfall** *m* loss of hair; ˈ**~boden** *anat. m* hair bed; ˈ**~bürste** *f* hairbrush; ˈ**~büschel** *n* tuft of hair; ˈ**2en** (25) lose (*od.* shed) one's hair; ˈ**~-entferner** *m* (7) depilatory; ˈ**~-ersatz** *m* hair-piece, wig; ˈ**~esbreite** *fig. f*: *um ~* within a hair's breadth; ˈ**~färbemittel** *n* hair-dye; ˈ**2fein** (as) fine as a hair; *fig.* subtle; ˈ**~festiger** *m* (7) setting lotion; ˈ**~gefäß** *n* capillary vessel; ˈ**2geˈnau** to a T, precise (-ly *adv.*); ˈ**2ig** hairy; *in Zssgn* ...-haired; F (*schwierig*) tough; ˈ**2klein** *adv.* to the last detail; ˈ**~klemme** *f* hair clip, *Am.* bobby pin; ˈ**~künstler** *m* hair stylist; ˈ**2los** hairless; ˈ**~nadel** *f* hairpin; ˈ**~nadelkurve** *mot. f* hairpin bend; ˈ**~netz** *n* hair-net; ˈ**~pflege** *f* hair care; ˈ**2scharf** razor-sharp; *fig.* by a hair's breadth; ˈ**~schnitt** *m* haircut; ˈ**~schwund** *m* loss of hair; ˈ**~sieb** *n* hair sieve; **~spalterei** [ˈ~ʃpaltəˈraɪ] *f* (16) hair-splitting; *~ treiben* split hairs; ˈ**2sträubend** hair-raising; shocking; ˈ**~strich** *m* hair-stroke; ˈ**~teil** *n* hair-piece; ˈ**~tracht** *f* coiffure (*fr.*), hair-style, F hairdo; ˈ**~transplantation** *f*, ˈ**~verpflanzung** *f* hair transplant; ˈ**~trockner** *m* (7) hair-dryer; ˈ**~wäsche** *f*, ˈ**~waschmittel** *n* shampoo; ˈ**~wasser** *n* hair lotion; ˈ**~wickel** *m* (7) curler; ˈ**~wuchs** *m* growth of hair; (*Kopf voller Haar*) head of hair; ˈ**~wuchsmittel** *n* hair-restorer; ˈ**~zange** *f* tweezers *pl.*

Habe [ˈhɑːbə] *f* (15) property, (personal) belongings *pl.*, goods *pl.*; *bewegliche ~* movables *pl.*; *unbewegliche ~* immovables *pl.*, real estate; *Hab und Gut* goods and chattels *pl.*

haben [ˈhɑːbən] **1.** (30) have; *s. gern, gut, recht, unrecht*; *~ wollen* want; *sich ~* make a fuss; *etwas (nichts) auf sich ~* be of (no) consequence; *unter sich ~ fig.* be in control of; (*befehligen*) command; *Ware*: *zu ~* obtainable; *ich hab's!* I have got it; *was hast du?* what is the matter with you?; *da ~ wir's!* there we are!; **2. 2** ✝ *n* (6) credit; *s. Soll.*

ˈ**Habenichts** *m* (4 *od. inv.*) beggar, have-not.

ˈ**Haben|saldo** *m* credit balance; ˈ**~seite** *f* credit side; ˈ**~zinsen** *m/pl.* credit interest.

Habicht [ˈhɑːbiçt] *m* (3) hawk.

Habili|tation *univ.* [habilitaˈtsjoːn] *f* (16) habilitation; *sich* **2ˈtieren** habilitate.

Habgier [ˈhɑːp-] *f* greed, avarice; ˈ**2ig** greedy, avaricious.

ˈ**habhaft:** *~ werden* (*gen.*) get hold of.

Hab|seligkeit [ˈhɑːp-] *f* property; *~en pl.* things, belongings *pl.*; ˈ**~-**

sucht *f*, '**⁓süchtig** *s. Habgier, habgierig.*

Hachse ['haksə] *f* (15) knuckle.

'**Hack|beil** *n* chopper, cleaver; '**⁓block** *m* chopping-block; '**⁓braten** *m* mince loaf; '**⁓brett** *n* chopping-board; ♪ dulcimer.

Hacke ['hakə] *f* **1.** (15) hoe, mattock; **2.** = '**⁓n¹** *m* (6) heel.

hacken² ['hakən] (25) hack, chop; (*klein⁓*) mince; (*picken*) pick.

'**Hack|fleisch** *n* minced (*Am.* ground) meat; '**⁓frucht** *f* root vegetable; '**⁓-ordnung** *zo. f* pecking order (*a. fig.*).

Häcksel ['hɛksəl] *m, n* (7) chaff; '**⁓maschine** *f* chaff-cutter.

Hader ['ha:dər] *m* (7) discord, strife, quarrel; '**⁓n** (29) quarrel.

Hafen ['ha:fən] *m* (7¹) port; *bsd. als Schutz*: harbo(u)r; '**⁓-anlagen** ⚓ *f/pl.* docks *pl.*; '**⁓-arbeiter** *m* docker, *Am.* longshoreman; '**⁓damm** *m* jetty, pier; '**⁓meister** *m* harbo(u)r-master; '**⁓sperre** *f* blockade (of a harbo[u]r), embargo; (*Vorrichtung*) barrage; '**⁓stadt** *f* seaport; '**⁓viertel** *n* dock area, waterfront.

Hafer ['ha:fər] *m* (7) oats *pl.*; *in Zssgn mst* oat-...; '**⁓brei** *m* (oatmeal) porridge; '**⁓flocken** *f/pl.* rolled oats; '**⁓grütze** *f* grits, (oat) groats *pl.*; '**⁓schleim** *m* gruel.

Haff [haf] *n* (3) haff, bay.

Haft [haft] *f* (16) custody, detention; (*Verhaftung*) arrest; '**⁓bar** responsible, answerable, liable (*für* for); '**⁓befehl** *m* warrant of arrest; '**⁓en** (26) stick, adhere (*an dat.* to); *⁓ für* answer for, be liable for.

Häftling ['hɛftliŋ] *m* (3¹) prisoner.

'**Haftpflicht** *f* liability; *mit beschränkter ⁓* limited; '**⁓ig** *s. haftbar*; '**⁓versicherung** *f* liability insurance; *mot.* third-party insurance.

'**Haft|reifen** *mot. m* traction tyre, *Am.* tire; '**⁓richter** *m* committing magistrate; '**⁓schale** *opt. f* contact lens.

'**Haftung** *f* liability.

'**Haft|-urlaub** *m* parole from prison; '**⁓vermögen** ⊕ *n* adhesive power.

Hag [ha:k] *m* (3) enclosure; (*Hain*) grove; (*Wald*) wood.

Hage|butte ['ha:gəbutə] *f* hip; '**⁓dorn** *m* hawthorn.

Hagel ['ha:gəl] *m* (7) hail; (*Schrot*) small shot; *fig.* shower; '**⁓dicht** as thick as hail; '**⁓korn** *n* hailstone; '**⁓n** (29) hail; '**⁓schauer** *m* shower of hail; '**⁓schlag** *m* damage by hail; '**⁓wetter** *n* hailstorm.

hager ['ha:gər] lean, gaunt; '**⁓keit** *f* leanness, gauntness.

'**Hagestolz** *m* (3²) (old) bachelor.

Häher ['hɛ:ər] *m* (7) jay.

Hahn [ha:n] *m* (3²) cock, rooster; ⊕ (stop)cock, tap, *Am.* faucet; *am Gewehr*: cock; *es kräht kein ⁓ danach* nobody cares a fig for that; *s. Korb.*

Hähnchen ['hɛ:nçən] *n* (6) cockerel.

'**Hahnen|fuß** ♀ *m* crowfoot; '**⁓kamm** *m* (*a.* ♀) cockscomb; '**⁓kampf** *m* cock-fight; '**⁓schrei** *m* cock-crow; '**⁓tritt** *m im Ei*: (cock-)tread.

Hahnrei ['ha:nraɪ] *m* (3) cuckold.

Hai [haɪ] *m* (3), '**⁓fisch** *m* shark.

Hain *poet.* [haɪn] *m* (3) grove.

Häkchen ['hɛ:kçən] *n* (6) small hook.

'**Häkel|-arbeit** *f* crochet-work; '**⁓n** *v/i. u. v/t.* (29) crochet; '**⁓nadel** *f* crochet-hook.

Haken ['ha:kən] **1.** *m* (6) hook (*a. beim Boxen*); (*Spange*) clasp; *fig.* (*Hindernis*) snag, hitch; *fig. da(s) ist der ⁓* F there's the rub; *die Sache hat e-n ⁓* there is a catch to it; **2.** ⁓ (2) hook; '**⁓kreuz** *n* swastika; '**⁓wurm** *m* hookworm.

halb [halp] **1.** *adj.* half; *eine ⁓e Stunde* half an hour, *Am.* a half-hour; *⁓ 3 Uhr* half past two; *es schlägt ⁓* the half-hour strikes; ♪ *⁓er Ton* semitone; *j-m auf ⁓em Wege entgegenkommen* meet a p. halfway; **2.** *adv.* by halves, half; *⁓ entschlossen* half determined; *⁓ soviel* half as much; *die Sache ist ⁓ so schlimm* things are not as bad as all that.

'**halb|-amtlich** semi-official; '**⁓bildung** *f* superficial education, smattering; '**⁓blut** *n* half-blood; *v. Volksrassen a.*: half-breed, half-caste; (*Pferd*) half-bred; '**⁓bruder** *m* half-brother; '**⁓dunkel** *n* semi-darkness; dusk, twilight; '**⁓-edelstein** *m* semi-precious stone; **... ⁓er** ['halbər] (*wegen*) on account of, owing to; (*um ... willen*) for the sake of; **⁓fabrikat** ['halp-] *n* semi-manufactured product; '**⁓fertig** half-finished; ✝ semi-manufactured; '**⁓fett** *typ.* semi-bold; '**⁓-**

finale *n Sport*: semi-final; '**♀franzband** *m* half-calf (binding); '**~gar** underdone, *Am.* rare; '**~gebildet** semi-cultured; '**♀geschwister** *pl.* half-brothers and -sisters; '**♀gott** *m* demigod; '**♀heit** *f* (16) half-measure.

halbieren [~'bi:rən] halve; ⩓ bisect.

'**Halb|-insel** *f* peninsula; '**~jahr** *n* half-year, six months *pl.*; '**♀jährig** of six months; '**♀jährlich** half-yearly; '**~kreis** *m* semicircle; '**~kugel** *f* hemisphere; '**♀laut** in an undertone; '**~leder** *n*: *in ~ gebunden* half-bound (*od.* -calf); '**~lederband** *m* half-binding; '**~leinen** *n* half-linen; '**~leiter** ⚡ *m* semiconductor; ~... solid-state; '**♀mast** *od. auf ♀* (at) half-mast; '**~messer** *m* radius; '**♀monatlich**, '**~monats...** fortnightly; '**~mond** *m* half-moon, crescent; '**♀nackt** half-naked; ♀'**-offen** *Tür*: ajar; '**♀part:** *~ machen* go halves, F go fifty-fifty; '**~pension** *f* demi-pension, half board; '**~profil** *n* semi-profile; '**~schlaf** *m* doze; '**~schuh** *m* (*Damen♀* flat) shoe; '**~schwergewicht**(**ler** *m*) *n* light-heavyweight; '**~schwester** *f* half-sister; '**~seide** *f* half silk; '**~starke** *m* (18) hooligan; '**♀starr** ✈ semi-rigid; '**~stiefel** *m* ankle boot; '**♀stündlich** half-hourly; '**~tagsbeschäftigte** *m, f* part-timer; '**~tagsbeschäftigung** *f* part-time job *od.* employment; '**~ton** ♪, *phot. m* half-tone; '**♀'tot** half-dead; '**~vokal** *m* semivowel; **♀wegs** ['~ve:ks] half-way; (*ziemlich*) tolerably; '**~welt** *f* demi-monde; '**~wertszeit** *phys. f* half-life; '**~wissen** *n s. Halbbildung*; **♀wüchsig** ['~vy:ksiç] adolescent, teenage; '**~wüchsige** *m, f* adolescent, teenager; '**~zeit** *f Sport*: half-time; '**~zeug** ⊕ *n* semi-product; *Papier*: half-stuff.

Halde ['haldə] *f* (15) slope, declivity; ⚒ dump.

half [half] *pret. v. helfen.*

Hälfte ['hɛlftə] *f* (15) half; F *m-e bessere ~* my better half; *die ~ der Leute* half the men; *um die ~ mehr* (*weniger*) half as much again (less by half); *zur ~* half.

Halfter ['halftər] *m od. n* (7) halter.

Halle ['halə] *f* (15) hall; (*Vor♀*) porch; *e-s Hotels*: lounge; *Tennis*: covered court; (*Markt♀*) market-hall; ✈ hangar.

hallen ['halən] (25) (re)sound, echo.

'**Hallen|handball** *m* indoor handball (game); '**~(schwimm)bad** *n* indoor swimming-pool.

hallo! [ha'lo:] hallo!, hullo!, hello!; ♀ *n* (11) *fig.* hullabaloo.

Halluzin|ation [halutsina'tsjo:n] *f* hallucination; **♀a'torisch** hallucinatory; **♀o'gen** hallucinogenic.

Halm [halm] *m* (3) blade; (*Getreide♀*) stalk; (*Stroh♀*) straw.

Halogen ⚗ [halo'ge:n] *n* (3[1]) halogen; **~scheinwerfer** *m* halogen headlight.

Hals [hals] *m* (4[2]) neck; (*Kehle*) throat; *~ über Kopf* head over heels, (*hastig*) headlong, helter-skelter; *auf dem ~e haben* have on one's back, be saddled with; *sich vom ~e schaffen* get rid of; *j-m um den ~ fallen* fall on a p.'s neck; *sich j-m an den ~ werfen* throw o.s. at the head of a p.; *aus vollem ~e lachen* have a good laugh; *aus vollem ~e schreien* shout at the top of one's voice; *bis über den ~* over head and ears, up to the eyes; F *es hängt mir zum ~e heraus* I am fed up (to the teeth) with it, I am sick of it; *sich den ~ verrenken aus Neugier* crane one's neck (*nach* for); '**~-abschneider** *m* cut-throat; '**~-ausschnitt** *m* (*tiefer* low) neck; '**~band** *n* necklace; *bsd. für Tiere*: collar; '**~binde** *f* (neck)tie; '**~bräune** *f* quinsy; '**♀brecherisch** breakneck; '**~-entzündung** *f* inflammation of the throat; '**~kette** *f* necklace; '**~kragen** *m* collar; neckband; '**~-'Nasen-'Ohren-Arzt** *m* ear, nose and throat specialist; '**~schlag-ader** *f* carotid artery; '**~schmerzen** *m/pl. s. Halsweh*; '**♀starrig** obstinate, stubborn; '**~starrigkeit** *f* obstinacy; '**~tuch** *n* scarf, neckerchief; '**~weh** *n* sore throat; '**~wirbel** *m* cervical vertebra; '**~wirbelsäule** *f* cervical vertebrae *pl.*

Halt [halt] **1.** *m* (3) hold; (*Innehalten*) halt, stop; (*Stütze*) support (*a. fig.*); *s. haltmachen*; **2.** ♀**!** *int.* stop!, ⚔ *usw.* halt!; **3.** ♀ *adv.* you know; *das ist ~ so* that's how it is, it can't be helped.

'**haltbar** (*dauerhaft*) durable, lasting; *fig.* tenable; es *ist ~* it wears well; '**♀keit** *f* durability; '**♀keitsdatum** *n auf Lebensmitteln*: pull date.

'**Haltebucht** *f für Busse etc.*: bay.

halten ['haltən] (30) *v/t.* (*fest~, auf~, zurück~, an~, ent~*) hold; (*beibe~, fest~, an~, zurück~, feil~, ver~*) keep; *den Körper gerade usw.* ~; *Sitzung, Versammlung*: hold; *Feiertag, Schule, Personal, Tier, Versprechen*: keep; (*stützen*) support; (*enthalten*) contain; *Predigt, Rede*: deliver; *Vorlesung*: give; *Zeitung*: take in; *sich* ~ (*stand~*) hold (out); (*in e-r bestimmten Richtung bleiben, in e-m* [*guten*] *Zustand bleiben*) keep; *sich bereit~* be ready; ~ *für* hold, think, take to be, *irrtümlich*: take for; *es* ~ *mit* side with; *Frieden* ~ keep peace; *s. kurz, Mund, Narr, Ordnung, Schach, Schritt*; *große Stücke od. viel* (*wenig*) ~ *auf* (*acc.*) *od. von* make much (little) of, think highly (little) of; *sich* ~ *an* (*acc.*) keep to; *sich gut* ~ *S.*: keep well, *P.*: stand one's ground; *das kannst du* ~, *wie du willst* you can please yourself; *was* ~ *Sie von ...?* what do you think of ...?; *v/i.* stop; (*ganz bleiben*) last; (*aushalten, dauern*) hold out, endure; (*festsitzen*) hold; *Eis*: bear; *es hält schwer* it is difficult; *dafür* ~, *daß* hold that; *zu j-m* ~ adhere (*od.* stick) to; *auf et.* ~ insist on, set store by.

'**Halte|platz** *m*, '**~punkt** *m*, '**~stelle** *f* stop; (*Droschken*≗) taxi-rank; '**~verbot** *n* no stopping area.

'**halt|los** without support; *Charakter*: unsteady; '**≗losigkeit** *f* unsteadiness; '**~machen** (make a) halt, stop.

'**Haltung** *f* (*Körper*≗) bearing, carriage; (*Benehmen*) deportment; (*Stellung*) posture, (*a. Geistes*≗) attitude; *der Börse*: tone; ~ *bewahren* remain composed, control o.s.; *s-e* ~ *wiedergewinnen* recover one's composure.

'**Haltzeichen** *n im Straßenverkehr*: stop-signal.

Halunke [ha'luŋkə] *m* (13) rascal.

hämisch ['hɛ:miʃ] malicious.

Hammel ['haməl] *m* (7[1]) wether; '**~braten** *m* roast mutton; '**~fleisch** *n* mutton; '**~keule** *f* leg of mutton; '**~sprung** *parl. m* division.

Hammer ['hamər] *m* (7[1]) hammer (*a. Sport*); ~ *des Auktionators usw.*: gavel; *a.* = ~*werk*; *unter den* ~ *kommen* come under the hammer.

'**hämmer|bar** malleable; **~n** ['hɛmərn] *v/t. u. v/i.* (29) hammer; *Motor*: knock; (*stampfen*) pound.

'**Hammer|schlag** *m* stroke with a hammer; (*Abgang vom Eisen*) hammer-scales *pl.*; '**~schmied** *m* blacksmith; '**~werk** *n* forge shop, hammer mill; '**~werfen** *n Sport*: throwing the hammer.

Hämorrhoiden [hɛ:mɔro'i:dən] *f/pl.* (15) h(a)emorrhoids *pl.*, piles *pl.*

Hampelmann ['hampəlman] *m* (1[2]) jumping jack; *fig.* puppet; *contp.* clown.

Hamster ['hamstər] *m* (7) hamster; **~ei** [~'raɪ] *f* hoarding; '**~er** *m* (7) hoarder; '**≗n** *v/i. u. v/t.* (29) hoard.

Hand [hant] *f* (14[1]) hand; *s. flach, hohl*; *j-m die* ~ *drücken* shake hands with a p.; *j-m freie* ~ *lassen* give a p. a free hand; *sich die Hände reichen* join hands; ~ *an j-n legen* lay hands on a p.; ~ *an et. legen* put one's hand to a th.; ~ *ans Werk legen* set to work; *s. letzt*; *an* ~ *von* by means of, guided by; *auf eigene* ~ of one's own accord; *an die* ~ *geben* supply with; *aus der* ~ *geben* part with; *aus erster* ~ at first hand; *bei der* ~, *zur* ~ at hand, handy; *die Hände in den Schoß legen* rest upon one's oars; *in die* ~ *nehmen* take in hand; *j-m et. in die Hände spielen* help a p. to a th.; *mit der* ~ *gemacht usw.* by hand; *von langer* ~ for a long time past; *von der* ~ *in den Mund leben* live from hand to mouth; *von der* ~ *weisen* decline, reject; *unter den Händen haben* have in hand; *unter der* ~ in secret, privately; *auf Brief*: *zu Händen* (*gen.*) care of (*abbr.* c/o), *Am.* attention; *fig.* ~ *und Fuß haben* hold water; *ohne* ~ *und Fuß* without rhyme or reason; *s-e* ~ *im Spiele haben* have a finger in the pie; *s-e* ~ *ins Feuer legen für etwas od. j-n* put one's hand into the fire for a th. *od.* a p.; *eine* ~ *wäscht die andere* one good turn deserves another; *s. öffentlich*; '**~-arbeit** *f* manual labo(u)r; (*Ggs. Maschinenarbeit*) handwork; *weibliche*: needlework; *das ist* ~ it is handmade; '**~-arbeiter** *m* manual labo(u)rer, (handi)craftsman; '**~-aufheben** *n bei Abstimmungen*: show of hands; '**~-ausgabe** *f* concise edition; '**~-**

ball *m* handball; '**~beil** *n* hatchet; '**~bibliothek** *f* reference library; '**²breit** of a hand's breadth; '**~breit(e)** *f* hand's breadth; '**~bremse** *f* hand-brake; '**~buch** *n* manual, handbook; '**~creme** *f* hand cream.

Hände|druck ['hɛndə-] *m* shaking of hands, handshake; '**~klatschen** *n* (6) clapping of hands.

Handel ['handəl] *m* (7[1]) (*geschäftlicher Verkehr*) trade; *in großem Maßstab*: commerce; *weitS.* traffic; (*Geschäft*) transaction, business; (*abgeschlossener* ~) bargain; (*schlimme usw. Sache*) affair; ⚖ lawsuit; ~ *treiben* trade; *im* ~ on the market; *nicht mehr im* ~ off the market; *ein ehrlicher* ~ a square deal.

Händel ['hɛndəl] *m/pl.* quarrel *sg.*; ~ *suchen* pick a quarrel.

handeln ['handəln] (29) act; (*Handel treiben*) trade (*mit* with *a p.*; in *goods*); deal (*nur* in *goods*); (*feilschen*) bargain (*um* for); *in e-r Rede usw.*: ~ *von od. über* (*acc.*) treat of, deal with; *es handelt sich um* it is a question (*od.* matter) of, ... is concerned; *es handelt sich darum, wer usw.* the question is who *etc.*; *worum handelt es sich?* what is the (point in) question?, what is it all about?

'**Handels|-abkommen** *n* trade agreement; '**~-adreßbuch** *n* commercial directory; '**~-artikel** *m* commodity; '**~bank** *f* commercial bank; '**~beziehungen** *f/pl.* trade relations; '**~bilanz** *f* balance of trade; '**~blatt** *n* trade journal; **~bücher** ['~by:çər] *n/pl.* commercial books, account books; '**²-einig** *werden* come to terms; '**~flotte** *f* merchant (*od.* mercantile) fleet; '**~gärtner** *m* market-gardener, *Am.* truck farmer; '**~genossenschaft** *f* traders' co-operative (society); '**~gericht** *n* commercial court; '**~gesellschaft** *f* trading company; *offene* ~ general partnership; '**~gesetzbuch** *n* Commercial Code; '**~hafen** *m* commercial port; '**~haus** *n* commercial house; '**~hochschule** *f* commercial academy; '**~kammer** *f* Chamber of Commerce, *Am. a.* Board of Trade; '**~mann** *m* tradesman; '**~marine** *f* mercantile marine; '**~marke** *f* trade-mark; '**~metropole** *f* cent|re (*Am.* center) of commerce; '**~minister** *m allg.* Minister of Commerce; *Brt.* President of the Board of Trade, *Am.* Secretary of Commerce; '**~ministerium** *n allg.* Ministry of Commerce; *Brt.* Board of Trade, *Am.* Department of Commerce; '**~müll** *m* commercial refuse, trade waste; '**~nation** *f* trading nation; '**~platz** *m* emporium, trading cen|tre, *Am.* -er; '**~politik** *f* trade policy; '**~produkt** *n* commercial product; '**~recht** *n* commercial law; '**~register** *n* commercial register; *im* ~ *eintragen* register, *Am.* incorporate; '**~richter** *m* commercial judge; '**~schiff** *n* trading vessel; '**~schiffahrt** *f* merchant shipping; '**~schule** *f* commercial school, *Am.* business college; '**~spanne** *f* trade margin; '**~sperre** *f* embargo; '**~stadt** *f* commercial town; '**²-üblich** customary in the trade.

händelsüchtig ['hɛndəl-] quarrelsome.

'**Handels|verkehr** *m* traffic, trade; '**~vertrag** *m* commercial treaty; '**~vertreter** *m* commercial representative; '**~ware** *f* commodity; '**~wechsel** *m* commercial bill; '**~weg** *m* trade route; '**~wert** *m* trading value; '**~zeichen** *n* trade-mark; '**~zweig** *m* branch of trade.

'**handeltreibend** trading.

'**Hand|feger** *m* hand-brush; '**~fertigkeit** *f* manual skill; handicraft; '**~fesseln** *f/pl.* handcuffs, manacles; '**²fest** sturdy, robust; *fig.* sound; '**~feuerwaffe** *f* hand gun; *pl.* small arms *pl.*; '**~fläche** *f* flat of the hand, palm; '**²ge-arbeitet** handmade; '**~geld** *n* handsel; † earnest money; ⚔ bounty; '**~gelenk** *n* wrist; *fig. aus dem* ~ offhand, just like that; '**²gemein** *werden* come to blows (*od.* grips); '**~gemenge** *n* fray, mêlée (*fr.*); (*Balgerei*) scuffle; '**~gepäck** *n* hand luggage (*Am.* baggage); '**²gerecht** handy; '**²geschrieben** hand-written, written by hand; '**²gesteuert** manually operated; '**²gestrickt** hand-knitted; F *fig.* home-made; '**~granate** ⚔ *f* hand-grenade; '**²greiflich** palpable; (*offensichtlich*) obvious; ~ *werden* turn violent, F get rough; '**~griff** *m* grasp; grip, manipulation; *konkret*: grip, handle; '**~habe** *f* (15) handle (*a. fig.*); '**≗haben** (25) handle, manipulate; *Maschine*: operate; *Rechtspflege*: administer; *fig.* handle; '**~habung** *f* handling, manipulation; operation.

...händig [hɛndiç] ...-handed.

'**Hand|karren** *m* hand-cart; '**~koffer** *m* (small) suitcase, attaché case, *Am.* valise; '**~korb** *m* hand-basket; '**~kuß** *m* kiss on the hand; F *mit* ~ gladly; '**~langer** *m* (7) handy man, odd-jobber, *Am.* hand; ⚠ hodman; *contp.* underling.

Händler ['hɛndlər] *m* (7), '**~in** *f* (16^1) dealer, trader.

'**Handleser(in** *f*) *m* palmist.

'**Handlesekunst** *f* palmistry.

handlich ['hantliç] handy.

Handlung ['handluŋ] *f* act(ion), deed; *e-s Dramas usw.*: action, *a.* plot; (*Laden*) shop, *Am.* store; *strafbare* ~ punishable act; '**~sbevollmächtigte** *m* authorized agent; '**~sfreiheit** *f* liberty of action, *a* free hand; '**~sgehilfe** *m* (commercial) clerk; (*Verkäufer*) shop-assistant; '**~sreisende** *m* commercial traveller, *bsd. Am.* traveling salesman; '**~sweise** *f* way of acting, conduct; (*Verfahren*) procedure; (*Methoden*) methods *pl.*

'**Hand|pflege** *f* manicure; '**~reichung** *f* help, assistance; '**~rücken** *m* back of the hand; '**~säge** *f* hand-saw; '**~schelle** *f* handcuff; '**~schlag** *m* handshake; '**~schreiben** *n* autograph letter; '**~schrift** *f* handwriting; (*geschriebenes Werk*) manuscript; '**~schriftendeutung** *f* graphology; '**≗schriftlich** *adj.* hand-written, in writing, manuscript; *adv.* in writing; in manuscript; '**~schuh** *m* glove; '**~schuhfach** *mot. n* glove compartment; '**~spiegel** *m* hand-glass; '**~stand** *m* handstand; '**~staubsauger** *m* portable vacuum cleaner; '**~streich** *m* coup de main (*fr.*), surprise raid; '**~tasche** *f* handbag, *Am.* purse; '**~teller** *m* palm (of the hand); '**~tuch** *n* towel; '**~tuchautomat** *m* towel dispenser; '**~tuchhalter** *m* towel-rail *od.* -rack; '**~-umdrehen** *n*: *im* ~ in a jiffy, in no time; '**~voll** *f* handful; '**~waffe** *f* hand weapon; '**~wagen** *m* hand-cart; '**~waschbecken** *n* wash-hand basin; '**~werk** *n* trade, (handi)craft; *j-m das* ~ *legen* put a stop to a p.'s practices; *sein* ~ *verstehen* know one's business; *s. pfuschen*; '**~werker** *m* (7) craftsman, artisan; *weitS.* workman; '**~werksbursche** *m* (travel[l]ing) journeyman; '**~werkskammer** *f* chamber of handicrafts; '**≗werksmäßig** workmanlike; *bsd. fig.* mechanical; '**~werksmeister** *m* master craftsman; '**~werkszeug** *n* (set of) tools *pl.*; '**~wörterbuch** *n* concise dictionary; '**~wurzel** *f* wrist; '**~zeichen** *n* hand signal; *statt Unterschrift*: initials *pl.*; '**~zeichnung** *f* hand drawing; '**~zettel** *m* handbill.

Hanf [hanf] *m* (3) hemp; *in Zssgn mst* hemp-...; '**≗en** hempen.

Hänfling ['hɛnfliŋ] *m* (3^1) linnet.

Hang [haŋ] *m* (3^2) slope; (*Abdachung*) declivity; *fig.* inclination, propensity (*zu* to, for); tendency (to).

Hänge|backe ['hɛŋə-] *f* flabby cheek; '**~bahn** *f* suspension railway (*Am.* railroad); '**~bauch** *m* paunch; '**~boden** *m* loft; '**~brücke** *f* suspension bridge; '**~busen** *m* drooping breasts *pl.*; '**~lampe** *f* hanging-lamp; '**~matte** *f* hammock.

hangeln ['haŋəln] (29) climb (*od.* travel) hand over hand.

hängen ['hɛŋən] *v/t.* (30) hang; suspend; *s. Herz*; *v/i.* hang; be suspended; (*haften*) adhere, stick, cling (*an dat.* to); *fig.* ~ *an* (*dat.*) cling to, be attached to; *den Kopf* ~ *lassen* hang one's head, be down in the mouth; '**~bleiben** (sn) be caught (*an dat.* by), catch (on).

'**Hängeschrank** *m* wall cabinet.

Hansdampf [hans'dampf] *m*: ~ *in allen Gassen* Jack-of-all-trades.

hänseln ['hɛnzəln] (29) tease, chaff.

'**Hansestadt** *f* Hanse town.

Hans|'narr *m* tomfool; **~'wurst** *m* (3^2) clown (*a. contp.*).

Hantel ['hantəl] *f* (15) dumb-bell.

han'tier|en *v/i.*: ~ *mit* work with, operate, handle, wield; (*geschäftig sein*) be busy.

hapern ['ha:pərn] (29): *es hapert mit* there is a problem with; *bei ihm hapert's im Englischen* he is weak in English; *es hapert uns an Geld* we are short of money.

Hap|pen ['hapən] *m* (6) mouthful, morsel, bite; *fetter* ~ juicy morsel, *fig.* fine catch; '**≗ig** F *Preis etc.*: steep, hefty.

Harfe ['harfə] *f* (15) harp.

Harfeˈnist(in *f*) *m* harp-player, harpist.
Harke [ˈharkə] *f* (15) rake; *j-m zeigen, was e-e ~ ist* show a p. what's what; ˈ**2n** *v/t. u. v/i.* (25) rake.
Harm [harm] *m* (3) grief, sorrow; (*Kränkung*) injury, wrong.
härmen [ˈhɛrmən]: *sich ~* grieve (*um* about, over).
ˈ**harmlos** harmless (*a. fig.*).
ˈ**Harmlosigkeit** *f* harmlessness.
Harmon|ie [harmoˈniː] *f* (15) harmony; **2ieren** [~ˈniːrən] harmonize; *fig. a.* agree; **~ika** [~ˈmoːnika] *f* (16[2] *u.* 11) accordion; **2isch** harmonious; **2isieren** [~moniˈziːrən] *v/i. u. v/t.* harmonize; **~ium** ♪ [~ˈmoːnjum] *n* (11[1], 9) harmonium.
Harn [harn] *m* (3) urine; ˈ**~blase** *f* (urinary) bladder.
ˈ**harnen** (25) pass water, urinate.
ˈ**Harn|fluß** *m* incontinence of urine; ˈ**~glas** *n* urinal; ˈ**~grieß** *m* gravel.
Harnisch [ˈharniʃ] *m* (3[2]) armo(u)r; *fig. j-n in ~ bringen* infuriate a p.; *in ~ geraten* fly into a rage.
ˈ**Harn|leiter** *anat. m* ureter; ˈ**~röhre** *f* urethra; ˈ**~säure** *f* uric acid; ˈ**~stoff** *m* urea; ˈ**~untersuchung** *f* uranalysis, *Am.* urinalysis; ˈ**~wege** *m/pl.* urinary tract *sg.*
Harpun|e [harˈpuːnə] *f* (15), **2ieren** [~ˈpuniːrən] harpoon.
harren [ˈharən] (25, *gen. od. auf acc.*) wait (for); *fig.* hope (for).
harsch [harʃ] harsh, rough; ˈ**2schnee** *m* crusted snow.
hart [hart] hard; *fig. a.* severe; *~ werden* harden; *adv. ~ arbeiten* work hard; *es ging ~ auf ~* it was either do or die; *s. Nuß.*
Härte [ˈhɛrtə] *f* (15) hardness; *fig. a.* severity; *unbillige ~* undue hardship; ˈ**~fall** *m* case of hardship.
ˈ**härten** (*a. sich*) harden.
ˈ**Hart|faserplatte** *f* fibreboard, *Am.* fiberboard; ˈ**~geld** *n* coined money, coins *pl.*, specie; ˈ**2gesotten** *fig.* hard-boiled; ˈ**~gummi** *m, n* hard rubber; ⚒ vulcanite, ebonite; ˈ**2herzig** hard-hearted; ˈ**~holz** *n* hard wood; **2leibig** [ˈ~laɪbiç] constipated, costive; ˈ**~leibigkeit** ⚕ *f* constipation, costiveness; ˈ**2löten** braze, hard-solder; **2mäulig** [ˈ~mɔʏliç] hard-mouthed; **2näckig** [ˈ~nɛkiç] obstinate, pertinacious, *bsd. Krankheit*: refractory; ˈ**~näckigkeit** *f* obstinacy, pertinacity; ˈ**~pappe** *f* hardboard; ˈ**~platz** *m Tennis*: hard court; ˈ**~spiritus** *m* solid alcohol; ˈ**~wurst** *f* hard sausage.
Harz [hɑːrts] *n* (3[2]) resin; (*Geigen2*) rosin; ˈ**2en** *v/t.* (27) resin; *Geigenbogen*: rosin; ˈ**2ig** resinous.
Hasardspiel [haˈzartʃpiːl] *n* (3) game of chance; *fig.* gamble.
Häs-chen [ˈhɛːsçən] *n* (6) young hare, leveret.
haschen[1] [ˈhaʃən] (27) *v/t.* snatch, catch; *v/i. ~ nach* snatch at; *fig. a.* aim at; *nach Komplimenten*: fish for.
haschen[2] F [ˈhaʃen] (27) smoke hash.
Häscher [ˈhɛʃər] *m* (7) catchpole.
Haschisch [ˈhaʃiʃ] *n* (*inv., o. pl.*) hashish, F hash.
Hase [ˈhɑːzə] *m* (13) hare; *fig. alter ~* old hand; F *da liegt der ~ im Pfeffer* there's the rub; *sehen, wie der ~ läuft* see which way the cat jumps.
Hasel|huhn [ˈhɑːzəlhuːn] *n* hazel-hen; ˈ**~maus** *f* dormouse; ˈ**~nuß** *f* hazel-nut; ˈ**~strauch** *m* hazel(-tree).
ˈ**Hasen|braten** *m* roast hare; ˈ**~fuß** *m* hare's foot; *fig.* coward; ˈ**~jagd** *f* hare-hunt(ing); ˈ**~klein** *n*, ˈ**~pfeffer** *m* jugged hare; ˈ**~panier** *n*: *das ~ ergreifen* take to one's heels; ˈ**~scharte** *f* harelip.
Häsin [ˈhɛːzin] *f* female hare, doe.
Haspe [ˈhaspə] *f* (15) hasp, hinge.
Haspel [ˈhaspəl] *f* (15) reel; (*Winde*) windlass; ˈ**2n** (29) reel.
Haß [has] *m* (4) hatred.
ˈ**hass|en** (28) hate; ˈ**~enswert** hateful, odious; ˈ**2er(in** *f*) *m* hater.
häßlich [ˈhɛsliç] ugly; *fig. a.* mean, nasty; ˈ**2keit** *f* ugliness; meanness.
ˈ**Haßliebe** *f* love-hate relationship.
Hast [hast] *f* (16) haste, hurry; ˈ**2en** (26, sn) hasten, hurry; ˈ**2ig** hasty, hurried; ˈ**~igkeit** *f* hastiness.
hätscheln [ˈhɛːtʃəln] (29) caress, fondle, cuddle, pet; (*verzärteln*) pamper, coddle.
hatte [ˈhatə] *pret. v. haben* 1.
Haube [ˈhaʊbə] *f* (15) bonnet, cap; (*Schwestern2*) cornet; *zo.* tuft, crest; ⊕ *u. mot.* bonnet, *mot. Am.* hood; *unter die ~ bringen* find a husband for; *unter die ~ kommen* get married.
Hauch [haʊx] *m* (3) breath; (*leiser Luftzug*) breeze, whiff; (*leiser Duft*)

waft; *fig.* (*Spur*) touch, tinge; *gr.* aspiration; '**2'dünn** wafer-thin; '**2en** (25) *v/i.* breathe; *v/t.* exhale; *gr.* aspirate; '**~laut** *m* aspirate.

'**Haudegen** *m* (6) *fig.* (old) blade.

Haue ['hauə] *f* (15) **1.** hoe, mattock; **2.** F (*Prügel*) hiding, spanking.

'**hauen** (30) *v/t.* (*hacken*) hew, chop, *Holz*: *a.* cut; *Loch, Stufen, Weg*: cut; (*schlagen*) strike; F (*prügeln*) thrash, hide; *sich ~* fight; *v/i. ~ nach* strike at; *um sich ~* lay about one.

'**Hauer** *m* (7) hewer (*a.* ⚒); *zo.* tusk.

häufeln ['hɔʏfəln] (29) hill (up).

Haufen ['haufən] *m* (13¹ [6]) heap (F *a. fig.*: *Menge, Zahl*), pile; (*Schwarm*) crowd; F *ein ~ ...* a lot of ...; *e-n ~ (Geld) verdienen* make a pile (of money); *der große ~* the multitude; *über den ~ werfen* overthrow, *bsd. fig.* upset.

häufen ['hɔʏfən] (25) heap (up), (*a. sich*) accumulate.

'**haufen|weise** in heaps; (*scharenweise*) in crowds; '**2wolke** *f* cumulus (cloud).

'**häufig** frequent(ly *adv.*); '**2keit** *f* frequency.

'**Häufung** *f* accumulation.

'**Hauklotz** *m* (3¹ *u.* ³) chopping block.

Haupt [haupt] *n* (1²) head; (*Ober2*) head, chief; '**~...** principal, chief, main; '**~-aktionär** *m* principal shareholder (*Am.* stockholder); '**~-akzent** *m* main stress; '**~-altar** *m* high altar; '**2-amtlich** full-time; *adv.* on a full-time basis; '**~-anliegen** *n* main (*od.* chief) concern; '**~-anschluß** *m teleph.* main station; ⚡ *usw.* mains connection; '**~-anteil** *m* main share; '**~bahnhof** *m* main (*od.* central) station; '**~beruf** *m*, '**~beschäftigung** *f* main occupation; '**2beruflich** full-time; '**~bestandteil** *m* chief ingredient (*od.* component); '**~buch** *n* ledger; '**~darsteller(in** *f*) *thea. m* leading man (*f* lady), lead; '**~-eingang** *m* main entrance; '**~fach** *n Studium*: main subject, *Am.* major; ... *als ~ studieren* take ... as one's main subject, *Am.* major in ...; '**~feldwebel** *m* sergeant major, *Am.* first sergeant; '**~film** *m des Programms*: feature (film); '**~gang** *m* main corridor; *beim Essen*: main course; '**~gebäude** *n* main building; '**~geschäft** *n* main business; '**~geschäftszeit** *f* rush hours *pl.*; '**~gewinn** *m* first prize; '**~haar** *n* hair of the head; '**~hahn** *m* mains tap; '**~leitung** *f* ⚡, *Wasser*: main(s *pl.*); '**~lieferant** *m* main supplier.

Häuptling ['hɔʏptliŋ] *m* (3¹) chief, chieftain.

'**Haupt|mahlzeit** *f* main meal; '**~mann** *m* (1, *pl. Hauptleute*) captain; '**~masse** *f* bulk; '**~merkmal** *n* chief characteristic; '**~nahrung** *f* staple food; '**~nenner** *m* common denominator; '**~person** *f* most important person; *thea. usw.* main character; '**~post-amt** *n* General (*Am.* Main) Post Office; '**~probe** *f* dress rehearsal; '**~punkt** *m* main (*od.* cardinal) point; '**~quartier** *n* headquarters *pl.*; '**~rolle** *f* leading part (*bsd. Film*: rôle), *ein Film mit N. N. in der ~* a film featuring N. N.; '**~sache** *f* main point *od.* thing; *in der ~* mainly; '**2sächlich** chief, main, principal; '**~saison** *f* peak season; '**~satz** *gr. m* main *od.* principal clause; '**~schalter** ⚡ *m* main (*od.* master) switch; '**~schlag-ader** *f* aorta; '**~schlüssel** *m* master-key; '**~schuldige** *m* chief culprit; '**~sendezeit** *f* prime time; '**~spaß** *m* great fun; '**~stadt** *f* capital; '**2städtisch** metropolitan; '**~straße** *f* main street; major road; '**~täter** ⚖ *m* principal offender; '**~ton** *m* principal (*od.* main) stress; '**~treffer** *m* jackpot; '**~verhandlung** ⚖ *f* main hearing, trial; '**~verkehrsstraße** *f* arterial road, thoroughfare, *Am.* highway; '**~verkehrsstunden** *f/pl.*, '**~verkehrszeit** *f* peak (*od.* rush) hour(s *pl.*); '**~versammlung** *f* general meeting; '**~verwaltung** *f* central office; '**~waschgang** *m* main wash; '**~werk** *n* main work; '**~wort** *gr. n* noun, substantive; '**~zeuge** *m*, '**~zeugin** *f* main (*od.* chief) witness.

Haus [haus] *n* (2¹) house; (*Heim*) home; house, firm; *~ und Hof* house and home; *nach ~e* home; *zu ~e* at home; *er ist (nicht) zu ~* F he is (not) in; *fig. in e-r S. zu ~e sein* be at home (*od.* well versed) in a th.; *fig. ein fideles ~* a jolly fellow; *ein großes ~ führen* live in great style; *aus gutem ~ sein* come of a good house (*od.* family); *so tun, als ob man zu ~ wäre* make o.s. at home; '**~-angestellte** *m, f* domestic (servant), household help; '**~-an-**

schluß *m allg.* house connection; *für Wasser*: service pipe; '~-**apotheke** *f* (household) medicine-cabinet *od.* -chest; '~-**arbeit** *f* housework; *Schule*: homework; '~-**arrest** *m* house arrest; '~-**arzt** *m* family doctor; '~-**aufgabe** *f* homework; '2**backen** home-made; *fig.* plain, homely; (*langweilig*) humdrum; '~**bar** *f* cocktail cabinet; '~**bedarf** *m* household requirements *pl.*; *für den ~* for the home; '~**besetzer** *m* squatter; '~**besitzer**(**in** *f*) *m* house-owner; '~**bewohner**(**in** *f*) *m* occupant (of the house); '~**boot** *n* house-boat.

Häus-chen ['hɔʏsçən] *n* (6) small house; *fig. aus dem ~ sein* be beside o.s. (*vor* with); *aus dem ~ geraten* go mad (*vor* with).

'**Haus|detektiv** *m* store detective; '~**diener** *m im Hotel*: boots.

hausen[1] ['haʊzən] (27) live, house, dwell; *arg ~ in* (*dat.*), *mit, unter* (*dat.*) play havoc among, *mit Vorräten*: be heavy on *supplies*.

'**Hausen**[2] *zo.* [~] *m* (6) sturgeon; '~**blase** *f* isinglass.

Häuser|block ['hɔʏzərblɔk] *m* block (of houses); '~**makler** *m* house agent, *Am.* realtor; '~**reihe** *f* row of (terraced) houses.

'**Haus|flur** *m* (entrance-)hall, *Am. a.* hallway; '~**frau** *f* housewife; (*Herrin*) lady of the house; '~**friedensbruch** *m* trespass (in a p.'s house); '~**garten** *m* back garden; '~**gebrauch** *m* domestic use; '~**gehilfin** *f s. Hausangestellte*; '~**genosse** *m* (fellow-)tenant; '~**hahn** *m* domestic cock, rooster; '~**halt** *m* household; *parl.* budget; *fig.* economy; *s. führen*; '2**halten** keep house; *~ mit* husband, economize; ~**hälter** ['~hɛltər] *m* (7), '~**hälterin** *f* (16[1]) housekeeper; '2**hälterisch** economical; '~**halts-artikel** *m* domestic (*od.* household) article; '~**halts-ausschuß** *parl. m* Budget Committee; *Brt.* Estimates Committee, *Am.* Appropriations Committee; '~**haltsdebatte** *parl. f* budget debate; '~**haltsdefizit** *parl. n* budgetary deficit; '~**haltsgeräte** *n/pl.* household appliances; '~**haltsjahr** *n* fiscal (*od.* financial) year; '~**halts-packung** *f* economy pack; '~**halts-plan** *parl. m* budget; '~**halts-politik** *f* budgetary policy; '~**halts**('**vor**)-**anschlag** *parl. m the* Estimates *pl.*; '~**haltung** *f* housekeeping; *s. Haushalt*; '~**haltungskosten** *pl.* household expenses; '~**haltungsvorstand** *m* head of the household; '~**herr** *m* master of the house, head of the family; *als Gastgeber*: host; *als Vermieter*: landlord; '2**hoch** as high as a house; *fig.* vast; *~ überlegen* (*dat.*) head and shoulders above *a p.*, vastly superior (to); '~**huhn** *n* domestic fowl; '~**hund** *m* house-dog.

hausier|en [~'ziːrən] hawk, peddle (*mit et.* a th.); *~ gehen* be a hawker, *a. fig.* peddle (*mit a th.*); 2**er** *m* (7) hawker, pedlar.

'**Haus|katze** *f* domestic cat; '~**kleid** *n* house dress; '~**lehrer** *m*, '~**lehrerin** *f* private tutor.

'**häuslich** domestic; home, *a.* household; (*sparsam*) economical; (*zu Hause bleibend*) home-loving, domesticated; *~e Arbeit s. Hausarbeit*; '2**keit** *f* domesticity; family life; (*Heim*) home.

'**Haus|mädchen** *n* housemaid; '~**mann** *m* house-husband; '~**mannskost** *f* simple (*od.* plain) fare; '~**mantel** *m* house coat; '~**meister** *m s. Hausverwalter*; '~**miete** *f* house-rent; '~**mittel** *n* household medicine; '~**müll** *m* domestic waste; '~**mutter** *f* mother of the family, housewife; (*Heimleiterin*) warden; '~-**ordnung** *f* rules *pl.* of the house; '~**pflege** ⚕ *f* home-nursing; '~**rat** *m* household effects *pl.*; '~**recht** *n* domestic authority; '~**sammlung** *f* house-to-house collection; '~**schlachtung** *f* home slaughtering; '~**schlüssel** *m* latch-key; '~**schuh** *m* slipper; '~**schwamm** *m* dry rot; '~**schwein** *n* domestic pig.

Hausse ✝ ['hoːsə] *f* (15) rise (in prices), boom; *auf ~ spekulieren* speculate for a rise; '~**markt** *m* boom market.

Haussier ✝ [hos'jeː] *m* bull.

'**Haus|stand** *m* household; *e-n ~ gründen* set up house; '~**suchung** ⚖ *f* house search, *Am.* house check; '~**suchungsbefehl** *m* search-warrant; '~**tarif** *m* internal pay scale; '~**tarifvertrag** *m* internal pay agreement; '~**telephon** *n im Geschäftshaus usw.*: intercom(munication system); '~**tier** *n* domestic animal; '~**tochter** *f* lady help; '~**tor** *n* gate; '~**tür** *f* front-

-door; '**~vater** *m* father of the family; (*Heimleiter*) warden; '**~verwalter** *m*, '**~wart** *m* (3) care-taker, janitor, *Am.* superintendent; '**~wirt** *m* landlord; '**~wirtin** *f* landlady; '**~wirtschaft** *f* housekeeping; *weitS.* domestic economy; (*a.* '**~wirtschaftslehre** *f*) domestic science; '**2wirtschaftlich** domestic; household.

Haut [haʊt] *f* (14[1]) skin; (*abgezogene Tier2*) hide; ♀, *anat.*, *zo.* membrane, cuticle; *auf Flüssigkeit*: film; *bis auf die ~* to the skin; *fig. ehrliche ~* honest fellow; *s-e (eigene) ~ retten* F save one's bacon; *aus der ~ fahren* jump out of one's skin; *ich möchte nicht in s-r ~ stecken* I wouldn't like to be in his shoes; *mit ~ und Haar* completely; '**~abschürfung** *f* skin-abrasion, excoriation; '**~arzt** *m* dermatologist; '**~ausschlag** *m* rash.

Häutchen ['hɔʏtçən] *n* (6) membrane, pellicle, film.

'**Hautcreme** *f* skin cream.

'**häuten** (26) skin; *sich ~* cast one's skin; *Schlange usw.*: slough.

'**haut|-eng** *Kleid*: skin-tight; '**2farbe** *f* complexion.

Hautgout [oː'guː] *m* (11, *o. pl.*) high smell; *~ haben* be high.

'**Haut|krankheit** *f* skin disease; '**~krebs** ✠ *m* cancer of the skin; '**~pflege** *f* care of the skin; '**~schere** *f* (*e-e ~* a pair of) cuticle scissors *pl.*; **~transplantation** ['~transplanta'tsjoːn] *f* (16) skin grafting.

'**Häutung** *f* casting of the skin.

'**Hautwunde** *f* skin-wound.

Havanna(zigarre) [ha'vanatsigarə] *f* Havana (cigar).

Havarie [hava'riː] *f* (15) (*große* general, *besondere od. partielle* particular) average.

'**H-Bombe** *f* H-bomb (= hydrogen bomb).

he! [heː] hey!, I say!

Hebamme ['heːpˀamə] *f* midwife.

Hebe|baum ['heːbə-] *m* lever; '**~bock** *m* (lifting-)jack; '**~bühne** *mot. f* lifting ramp; '**~kran** *m* hoist(ing crane).

Hebel ['heːbəl] *m* (7) lever (*a. Ringen*); *fig. alle ~ in Bewegung setzen* move heaven and earth; *fig. am längeren ~ sitzen* have the better leverage; '**~arm** *m* lever-arm; '**~kraft** *f* leverage; '**~schalter** ⚡ *m* lever switch; '**~wirkung** *f* lever action, leverage.

heben ['heːbən] (30) lift, (*a. fig.*) raise; *mit Mühe*: heave; (*hochwinden*) hoist; (*steigern*) increase; (*fördern*) further; *s. Sattel, Taufe*; *sich ~* rise; *s. gehoben*.

'**Heber** *phys. m* (7) siphon; (*Stech2*) pipette.

'**Hebeschiff** *n* salvage ship.

Hebräer [he'brɛːər] *m* (7), **~in** *f* (16[1]), **he'bräisch** Hebrew.

'**Hebung** *f vgl. heben*; raising, lifting; increase; furtherance; *des Bodens*: elevation.

Hechel ['hɛçəl] *f* (15) hatchel. hackle, flax-comb; '**2n** (25) hackle.

Hecht [hɛçt] *m* (3) pike; F *fig.* (*Qualm*) fug; '**2en** *Sport*: dive; *Schwimmen*: do a pike-dive.

Heck [hɛk] *n* (3) ⚓ stern; *mot.* rear; ✈ tail; '**~antrieb** *mot. m* rear (-wheel) drive.

Hecke ['hɛkə] *f* (15) **1.** ⚘ hedge; **2.** *zo.* brood, breed, hatch.

'**hecken** *v/t. u. v/i.* (25) hatch, breed.

'**Hecken|rose** *f* dog-rose; '**~schere** *f* hedge-shears *pl.*; '**~schütze** ⚔ *m* sniper.

'**Heck|klappe** *mot. f* tailgate, hatchback; '**~licht** *n* ⚓ stern-light; ✈, *mot.* tail-light; '**~motor** *m* rear engine; '**~scheibe** *mot. f* rear window (*od.* windscreen, *Am.* windshield); '**~scheibenheizung** *f* rear window heating (*od.* defroster); '**~scheibenwischer** *m* rear windscreen wiper; '**~spoiler** *m* rear spoiler.

heda! ['heːdaː] hey!

Heer [heːr] *n* (3) Army; (*große Schar*) host; '**~es...** *mst* Army ...; '**~esdienst** *m* military service; '**~(es)zug** *m* (military) expedition, campaign; '**~führer** *m* general; commander-in-chief; '**~lager** *n* army camp; *fig.* camp; '**~schar** *f* host; '**~straße** *f* highway.

Hefe ['heːfə] *f* (15) yeast; (*Bodensatz u. fig.*) dregs *pl.*; '**~kuchen** *m* yeast cake.

Heft [hɛft] *n* (3) haft, handle; *e-s Schwertes*: hilt; (*Schreib2*) exercise book, copy-book; *e-r Zeitschrift*: number, issue; (*Broschüre*) booklet, paper book; *das ~ in der Hand haben (behalten)* have (keep) the reins in one's hand.

'heft|en (26) fasten, fix (*an acc.* to; *Augen*: on); *Näherei*: baste, tack; *Buch*: stitch, sew; *sich ~ an* (*acc.*) attach (*od.* cling) to; *geheftet Buch*: in sheets; **'2er** *m für Akten*: folder; *s. Heftmaschine.*

'Heftfaden *m* tacking thread.

'heftig vehement, violent, impetuous; (*reizbar*) irritable; *Kälte*: sharp; *Regen*: heavy; **'2keit** *f* vehemence, violence.

'Heft|klammer *f* paper-clip; *der Heftmaschine*: staple; **'~maschine** *f* stapling machine; **'~nadel** *f* stitching needle; **'~pflaster** *n* sticking plaster, adhesive plaster *od.* tape; **'~stich** *m* tack; **'~zwecke** *f* drawing-pin, *Am.* thumbtack.

Hegemonie [hegəmo'ni:] (15) *f* hegemony, supremacy.

hege|n ['he:gən] (25) cherish; *hunt.* preserve; *Pflanzen usw.*: tend; *Zweifel usw.*: have, entertain; *~ und pflegen* lavish care on; **'2r** *hunt. m* (7) gamekeeper.

Hehl [he:l] *n* (3): *kein ~ machen aus* make no secret of; **'2en** ⚖ (25) *v/i.* receive stolen goods.

'Hehler ⚖ *m* (7), **'~in** *f* receiver (of stolen goods), *sl.* fence; **~ei** ⚖ [~'raɪ] *f* receiving (of stolen goods).

hehr [he:r] noble; lofty, sublime.

Heide[1] ['haɪdə] *m* (13), **'Heidin** *f* heathen, pagan; *biblisch*: Gentile.

Heide[2] [~] *f* (15) heath; **'~kraut** *n* heather; **'~land** *n* moor(land).

'Heidelbeere *f* bilberry *Am.* blueberry, huckleberry.

'Heidelerche *f* woodlark.

'Heiden|-angst F *f* mortal fright, F blue funk; **'~geld** *n* piles *pl.* of money; **'~lärm** *m* tremendous noise; **'2mäßig** enormous, tremendous; **'~spaß** *m* great fun; **'~tum** *n* (1²) paganism.

Heiderös-chen ['~rø:sçən] *n* (6) wild briar, dog-rose.

heidnisch ['haɪdniʃ] heathen, pagan; *biblisch*: Gentile.

heikel ['haɪkəl] delicate; (*wählerisch*) particular, fussy; fastidious, (over-)nice (*mit* about); *S.*: (*schwierig*) delicate, ticklish.

heil [haɪl] **1.** (*ganz*) whole, intact; (*unversehrt*) sound, unhurt; (*geheilt*) healed, restored; **2.** 2 *n* (3) welfare; *eccl.* salvation; *2!* hail!; *Jahr des ~s* year of grace; *sein ~ in der Flucht suchen* seek safety in flight; *sein ~ versuchen* try one's luck.

Heiland ['haɪlant] *m* (3) Savio(u)r.

'Heil|-anstalt *f* sanatorium, *Am.* sanitarium; *für Alkoholiker usw.*: home, (mental) hospital; **'~bad** *n* medicinal bath; (*Kurort*) spa; **'2bar** curable; **'~barkeit** *f* curableness; **'2bringend** salutary, salubrious; **'~butt** *m* (3) halibut; **'2en** (25) *v/t. j-n*: cure (*von* of; *a. fig.*); *Krankheit*: cure; *Wunde*: (*a. v/i.*; sn) heal; **'~gymnastik** *f* physiotherapy.

heilig ['haɪliç] holy, sacred; (*fromm*) saintly; (*feierlich*) solemn; *2er Abend* Christmas Eve; *2e Jungfrau* Blessed Virgin; *2e Nacht* Holy Night; *2er Vater* Holy Father; *fig. ~e Pflicht* sacred duty; *s. Geist, Grab, Gral, Schrift, Stuhl*; **2e** ['~lige] *m, f* saint; **~en** ['~ligən] (25) hallow, (*a. fig.* = *gutheißen*) sanctify; **'2enschein** *m* halo, glory, gloriole; **'2keit** *f* holiness, sanctity; **'~sprechen** canonize; **'2tum** *n* (1²) *Ort*: sanctuary; *Reliquie*: relic.

Heiligung ['~guŋ] *f* sanctification.

'Heil|kraft *f* healing power; **'2kräftig** curative; **'~kraut** *n* officinal herb; **'~kunde** *f* medical science; *praktische*: therapeutics *mst sg.*; **'2los** unholy (F *a. fig.* = *fürchterlich*); F *adv.* hopelessly, frightfully; **'~mittel** *n* remedy (*gegen* for; *a. fig.*), medicament; **'~pädagogik** *f* therapeutic pedagogy; **'~praktiker** *m* healer; **'~quelle** *f* (medicinal) mineral spring.

'heilsam wholesome, salutary; **'2keit** *f* wholesomeness, salutariness.

'Heils-armee *f* Salvation Army.

'Heil|serum *n* antiserum; **'~stätte** *f* sanatorium, *Am.* sanitarium; **'~ung** *f vgl. heilen*; curing, cure; healing; **'~ungs-chancen** *f/pl.* chances of being cured; **'~ungs-prozeß** *m* healing process; **'~ungsquote** *f* cure rate; **'~verfahren** *n* medical treatment, therapy.

heim [haɪm] **1.** *adv.* home; **2.** 2 *n* (3) home (*a. Anstalt*); (*Jugend2*, *Studenten2*) hostel; **'2-arbeit** *f* home-work, outwork; **'2-arbeiter** (**-in** *f*) *m* homeworker.

Heimat ['~a:t] *f* (16) home, native place *od.* country; **'~kunde** *f* local history and geography; **'~land** *n* native country; **'2lich** native; *Ge-*

fühl: homelike; '≈**los** homeless; '~**-ort** *m* native place; '~**stadt** *f* home town; '~**vertriebene** *m, f* (18) expellee.

'**heimbegleiten:** *j-n* ~ see home.

'**Heimbuchung** *f Computer*: home banking.

Heimchen ['~çən] *n* (6) cricket.

'**Heimcomputer** *m* home computer.

heimelig ['haɪməliç] cosy.

'**Heim|fahrt** *f* journey home; '~**fall** ⚖ *m* reversion; '~**gang** *m* going home; *fig*. death; '≈**gehen** go home; '≈**isch** *s. einheimisch*; (*vertraut*) homelike; *sich* ~ *fühlen* feel at home (*a. fig. in dat.* in); ~ *werden* settle down, *S.*: become established; ~**kehr** ['~keːr] *f* (16), ~**kunft** ['~kunft] *f* (14[1]) return (home); '≈**kehren**, '≈**kommen** (sn) return home; '~**kehrer** *m* home-comer, returnee; '~**kind** *n* child in care, institutional child; '≈**leuchten:** *j-m* ~ send a p. packing.

'**heimlich** (*verborgen*) secret; (*verstohlen*) stealthy; *s. heimelig*; '≈**keit** *f* secrecy; (*Geheimnis*) secret; ≈**tuerei** [~'raɪ] *f* secretive behavio(u)r; '~**tun** be secretive (*mit et.* about).

'**Heim|niederlage** *f Sport*: home defeat; '~**reise** *f* homeward journey; journey home; '~**sieg** *m* home win; '~**spiel** *n* home match; '~**stätte** *f* home; (*Siedlung*) home-croft, *Am.* homestead; '≈**suchen** *Geist usw.*: haunt; (*plagen*) afflict, plague; *biblisch*: visit; '~**suchung** *f bibl.* visitation; *fig. a.* affliction; '~**trainer** *m* (*Gerät*) home exerciser; '~**tücke** *f* malice, treachery; '≈**tückisch** malicious; (*a. fig.*) treacherous, insidious; ≈**wärts** ['~vɛrts] homeward; '~**weg** *m* way home; '~**weh** *n* homesickness; ~ *haben* be homesick; '~**werker** *m* hobbyist; *Heimwerker...* do-it-yourself; '≈**zahlen** F: *j-m et.* ~ pay a p. back for a th.

Hein [haɪn] *m*: *Freund* ~ Goodman Death.

Heinzelmännchen ['haɪntsəlmɛnçən] *n* brownie; *pl. a.* little people.

Heirat ['haɪraːt] *f* (16) marriage; '≈**en** *v/t. u. v/i.* (26) marry.

'**Heirats|-antrag** *m* offer (*od.* proposal) of marriage; *e-n* ~ *machen* propose (*dat.* to); '≈**fähig** marriageable; '~**kandidat** *m* suitor; eligible bachelor; '≈**lustig** eager to get married; '~**markt** *m* marriage market; '~**schwindler** *m* marriage impostor; '~**-urkunde** *f* marriage certificate; '~**vermittler(in** *f*) *m* marriage broker; '~**versprechen** *n* promise of marriage.

heischen ['haɪʃən] (27) demand.

heiser ['haɪzər] hoarse; '≈**keit** *f* hoarseness.

heiß [haɪs] hot; *fig. a.* ardent; (*heftig*) fierce; ~*e Zone* torrid zone; *mir ist* ~ I am hot; *s. Hölle*; '~**blütig** hot-blooded.

heißen[1] ['haɪsən] (30) *v/t.* call, name; (*befehlen*) bid, command, order, tell; *j-n willkommen* ~ bid a p. welcome; *v/i.* be called; (*bedeuten*) mean, signify; *das heißt* that is (to say); *es heißt, daß* ... it is said (*od.* reported) that ...; *wie* ~ *Sie?* what is your name?; *wie heißt das auf englisch?* what's that in English?; *was soll das* ~? what is the meaning of this?

heißen[2] ['haɪsən] (27) ⚓ hoist (*the flag, etc.*).

'**Heiß|hunger** *m* ravenous hunger; '≈**hungrig** ravenous; '≈**geliebt** (dearly) beloved; (*sich*) '≈**laufen** ⊕ run hot, overheat; '~**luftherd** *m* convection oven; '~**sporn** *m* hotspur; '≈**-umstritten** highly controversial; '~**wasser...** *s. Warmwasser...*

heiter ['haɪtər] cheerful, merry, serene; *Wetter usw.*: clear, bright; '≈**keit** *f* cheerfulness, mirth; serenity.

Heiz|-anlage ['haɪts-] *f* heating plant; '≈**bar** to be heated; with heating facilities; *Heckscheibe*: defrosting; '~**batterie** *f* filament (*Am.* A-) battery; '~**decke** *f* electric blanket; '≈**en** *v/t. u. v/i.* (27) heat; '~**er** *m* (7) fireman, stoker; (*Gerät*) heater; '~**kessel** *m* boiler; '~**kissen** *n* electric (heating) pad; '~**körper** *m der Zentralheizung*: radiator; ⚡ heater; '~**kosten** *pl.* heating costs; '~**kostenabrechnung** *f* heating bill; '~**lüfter** *m* fan heater; '~**material** *n* fuel; '~**-öl** *n* fuel oil; '~**platte** *f* hot plate; '~**rohr** *n* heating pipe; '~**sonne** *f* bowl-fire; '~**ung** *f* heating.

hektisch ['hɛktiʃ] hectic(ally *adv.*).

Hekto... [hɛkto-] *in Zssgn* hecto...

Held [hɛlt] *m* (12) hero (*a. thea., etc.*).

Helden... ['~dən]: *in Zssgn mst* heroic ...; '~**gedicht** *n* heroic epic;

'**⁲haft** heroic(ally *adv.*); '**~mut** *m* heroism, valo(u)r; **⁲mütig** ['~my:tiç] heroic; '**~tat** *f* heroic deed, exploit; '**~tenor** *m* heroic tenor; '**~tod** *m* heroic death; *den ~ erleiden* die a hero; '**~tum** *n* (1) heroism.

'**Heldin** *f* heroine.

helfen ['hɛlfən] (30, *dat.*) help; (*unterstützen*) aid; (*beistehen*) assist; (*nützen*) avail, profit; *sich zu ~ wissen* be full of resource; *sich nicht zu ~ wissen* be at one's wits' end; *ich kann mir nicht ~* I can't help it; *es hilft (zu) nichts* it is of no use, it is no good.

'**Helfer** *m* (7), '**~in** *f* helper, assistant; *~ in Steuersachen* tax-consultant; '**~s-helfer** *m* accomplice.

hell [hɛl] bright (*a. gescheit*), clear (*a. Klang*); *Haar*: fair; *Bier*: light; *Neid, Unsinn usw.*: sheer; *am ~en Tage* in broad daylight; *es wird ~* it is getting light; '**~blau** light-blue; '**~blond** very fair.

'**Helle** *f* (15) brightness, clearness.

Hellebarde [hɛlə'bardə] *f* (15) halberd.

Hellen|e [hɛ'le:nə] *m* (13) Hellene; **⁲isch** Hellenic.

Heller ['hɛlər] *m* (7) farthing, penny; *auf ~ und Pfennig bezahlen* pay to the last penny; *keinen ~ wert* not worth a penny.

'**hell|glänzend** brightly shining; '**~hörig** quick of hearing; *fig.* perceptive.

Helligkeit ['hɛliçkaıt] *f* brightness.

Helling ['hɛliŋ] *f* (16) ⚓ slip(way).

'**Hell|seher(in** *f*) *m*, '**⁲seherisch** clairvoyant; **~seherei** [~'raı] *f* clairvoyance; **⁲sichtig** ['~ziçtiç] *fig.* clear-sighted; '**⁲'wach** wide awake (*a. fig.*).

Helm [hɛlm] *m* (3) ⚔ helmet; ⚓ helm, rudder; ⚠ dome.

Hemd [hɛmt] *n* (5) (*Männer⁲*) shirt; (*Frauen⁲*) *a.* chemise; *j-n bis aufs ~ ausziehen* strip a p. to the shirt; '**~bluse** *f* shirt(-blouse); '**~blusenkleid** *n* shirt dress; **~hose** ['hɛmt-] *f* (*eine* a pair of) combinations *pl.*, *Am. a.* union suit; (*Damen⁲*) (pair of) cami-knickers *pl.*; '**~knopf** *m* shirt button; '**~(s)-ärmel** *m* shirtsleeve; *in ~n* in one's shirtsleeves.

Hemisphäre [he:mi'sfɛ:rə] *f* (15) hemisphere.

hemmen ['hɛmən] (25) stop, check; (*behindern*) hinder, hamper; impede; (*bremsen*) brake; *seelisch*: inhibit.

'**Hemm|nis** *n* (4[1]) hindrance; '**~schuh** *m* drag (*a. fig. gen.* on); '**~ung** *f* stop(ping), check(ing); obstruction; *Uhr*: escapement; *seelisch*: inhibition; '**⁲ungslos** unrestrained, without restraint.

Hengst [hɛŋst] *m* (3[2]) stallion.

Henkel ['hɛŋkəl] *m* (7) handle; '**~korb** *m* basket with handles.

henken ['hɛŋkən] (25) hang.

'**Henker** *m* (7) hangman, executioner; *zum ~!* the deuce!; *zum ~ mit ...!* hang ...!; '**~sknecht** *m fig.* henchman; '**~smahl(zeit** *f*) *n* last meal.

Henne ['hɛnə] *f* (15) hen.

her [he:r] here; *zeitlich*: *es ist schon ein Jahr ~, daß ...* it is now a year ago since ...; *wie lange ist es ~?* how long is it ago?; *von weit ~* from afar; *s. hin*; *~ sein von* be (*od.* come) from; *hinter (dat.) ~ sein* be after; *~ damit!* out with it!; *s. Alter, hin, weit.*

herab [hɛ'rap] down, downward; *s. oben*; **~drücken** press down; *Preis*: force down, depress; **~lassen** let down; *sich ~ fig.* condescend; **~lassend** condescending; **⁲lassung** *f* condescension; **~sehen** *auf* (*acc.*) look down upon; **~setzen** lower; *im Rang*: degrade, reduce (in rank); (*verächtlich machen*) disparage; *Preis*: reduce, mark (*od.* cut) down; **⁲setzung** *f* lowering; degradation; disparagement; reduction; cut; **~sinken** sink, descend; **~steigen** (sn) climb down, descend; *vom Pferde*: dismount; **~würdigen** degrade; **⁲würdigung** *f* abasement, degradation.

Herald|ik [he'raldik] *f* (16) heraldry; **⁲isch** heraldic.

heran [hɛ'ran] on, near, up; *er ging an sie ~* he went up to them; *nur ~!* come on!; **~bilden** train, educate; **~bringen** bring up; **~gehen** (sn) approach (*an et.* a th.), go up (to); *~ an e-e Arbeit usw.*: set about, tackle; **~kommen** (sn) come on (*od.* near); *~ an (acc.)* come up to (*a. fig.*), (*bekommen*) get at; *die Dinge an sich ~ lassen* wait and see; *sich* **~machen** *an (acc.) et.*: set about, *j-n*: make up to; **~nahen**

(sn) *a. zeitlich*: approach, draw near; *sich* **~pirschen** creep up (*an acc.* to); **~reichen** *an* (*acc.*) reach (up to); *fig.* measure up to; **~schaffen** bring up, move to the spot; supply; **~schleichen:** *sich ~ an* (*acc.*) sneak up to; **~treten** approach (*an j-n* a p.; *a. fig.*); **~wachsen** (sn) grow up; **≈wachsende** *m, f* (18) adolescent; **~ziehen** draw near; *fig. Stelle, Werk*: quote, cite; *j-n*: call *a p.* in; *j-n zu e-r Arbeit usw. ~* call (up)on a p. to *do work, etc.*

herauf [hɛˈrauf] up, upwards; (*hier~*) up here; **~beschwören** conjure up; *fig. a.* bring on; **~kommen** (sn) come up; *Unwetter*: approach; **~setzen** increase, raise; **~steigen** (sn) climb up, ascend; **~ziehen** *v/t.* pull up; *v/i.* (sn) *Unwetter usw.*: approach.

heraus [hɛˈraus] out; *~!* come out!, turn out!; *~ damit!* out with it!; *s. frei*; *die Handhabung von et. ~ haben* have got the knack (*Am.* hang) of *a th.*; *Lösung, Sinn ~ haben* have found out; **~bekommen** get out; *Geld*: get back; *fig.* find out; **~bringen** bring out; (*herausbekommen*) get out; *fig.* find out; *Fabrikat usw.*: launch; *Buch*: *s. herausgeben*; **~finden** find out; **≈forderer** *m* challenger; **~fordern** defy, provoke; *zum Zweikampf*: challenge; **≈forderung** *f* challenge (*a. fig.*); provocation; **~fühlen** feel, sense; **≈gabe** *f* delivery; *e-s Buches usw.*: publication; **~geben** surrender; (*zurückgeben*) give back; *Buch*: publish, *als Bearbeiter*: edit; *Geld*: give ... in change; *Geld ~ auf* (*acc.*) give change for; *Vorschrift usw.*: issue; **≈geber** *m* publisher; (*Redakteur*) editor; **≈geberin** *f* editress; **~greifen** pick out; **~gehen** (sn) *Nagel usw.*: go out; *Fleck*: come out; *fig. aus sich ~* liven up; **~kommen** (sn) come out; (*ruchbar werden*) become known, leak out; *Buch*: be published, appear; (*sich ergeben*) result (*bei* from), come (of); work out; *es kommt auf eins* (*od. dasselbe*) *heraus* it comes to the same thing; *es kommt nichts dabei heraus* it is of no use; *es ist nichts Gutes dabei herausgekommen* nothing good has come (out) of it; **~kriegen** *s. herausbekommen*; **~machen** take out, remove; *fig. sich ~* turn out well; **~nehmen** take out; *sich ~ zu* presume; *sich Freiheiten ~* take liberties (*gegen* with); **~platzen** (sn): *mit et. ~ fig.* blurt a th. out; **~putzen** dress up; **~ragen** *a. fig.* stand out (*aus dat.* from); **~reden:** *frei ~* speak out; *sich ~* make excuses, wriggle out; **~reißen** pull (*od.* tear) out; *fig.* extricate, save; **~rücken** *v/t. u. v/i.* (sn): *~ mit* hand over; *mit Geld*: F shell out; *mit der Wahrheit usw.*: come out with; *mit der Sprache ~* speak out (freely); **~rufen** call out; **~rutschen** (sn) slip out (*a. fig.*); **~schlagen** *fig.* get, *sl.* wangle; *etwas ~ bei* get out of; **~springen** (sn) jump out; *fig.* result, be gained; **~stellen** put out; *Spieler*: turn out; *fig.* give prominence to, feature; *sich ~* appear, turn out, prove (*als* to be), be found (out); **~strecken** put (*od.* stick) out; **~streichen** praise, crack up; **~treten** (sn) step out; ⚕ protrude; *Flüssigkeit usw.*: exude; *sich* **~wagen** venture out; *sich* **~winden** (*aus dat.*) *fig.* extricate o.s. (from), wriggle out (of); **~wirtschaften** obtain; et. ~ make a profit; **~ziehen** *v/t.* draw (*od.* pull) out; extract.

herb [hɛrp] harsh (*a. fig.*); (*sauer*) acid, sour; *Wein usw.*: dry; *Enttäuschung, Worte*: bitter, harsh; *Schönheit, Stil*: austere.

Herbarium [hɛrˈbaːrjum] *n* (9) herbarium.

herbei [hɛrˈbaɪ] hither, *mst* here; *~!* (*komm*[*t*] *her!*) come on *od.* here!; *~ zu mir* up to me; *s. heran...*; **~eilen** (sn) approach in haste; **~führen** *fig.* bring about *od.* on, cause; **~lassen:** *sich ~* condescend; **~rufen** call; **~schaffen** bring on; procure; **~sehnen** long for.

herbemühen [ˈheːrbəmyːən] trouble to come (here); *sich ~* take the trouble of coming.

Herberge [ˈhɛrbɛrgə] *f* (15) shelter, lodging; (*Gasthaus*) inn; (*Jugend≈*) hostel; ˈ**≈n** (25) *v/i.* put up, lodge (*bei* at); *v/t. s. beherbergen.*

Herbergsvater [ˈ~ksfaːtər] *m* warden (of a hostel).

ˈ**her|bestellen** send for, summon; ˈ**~beten** rattle off.

Herbheit [ˈhɛrphaɪt] harshness (*a. fig.*); *fig.* bitterness, severity; austerity; *Wein*: dryness.

ˈ**herbringen** bring here, bring (up).

Herbst [hɛrpst] *m* (3²) autumn, *Am.* fall; ˈ**~-anfang** *m* beginning of autumn; ˈ**2lich** autumnal; ˈ**~tag** *m* autumn day; **~zeitlose** ⚘ [ˈ~tsaɪtloːzə] *f* (15) meadow saffron.

Herd [heːrt] *m* (3) hearth (*a.* = *Heim*); *offener*: fireplace; (*Kochmaschine*) cooking-stove, *großer*: range; *fig.* (*Sitz*) seat.

Herde [ˈheːrdə] *f* (15) *Großvieh*: herd (*contp. a. fig.*); *getriebene*: drove; *Kleinvieh*: flock; *fig.* crowd; ˈ**~ntier** *n* gregarious animal; ˈ**~ntrieb** *m* herd instinct.

herein [hɛˈraɪn] in; *~!* come in!; **~bemühen** trouble to come in; **~bitten** ask (*od.* invite) in; **~brechen** *fig.* (sn) *Nacht*: close in (*über acc.* upon); *Unglück usw.*: *~ über* overtake, befall; **~bringen** bring in; *Verlust wieder ~* make good; **2fall** *m s. Reinfall*; **~fallen** (sn) be taken in (*auf acc.* by); *~ auf Am.* F fall for; **~führen** show (*od.* usher) in; **~kommen** (sn) come in (*a.* ✝); **~lassen** let in, admit; **~legen** F take *a p.* in, fool (*od.* dupe) *a p.*; **~platzen** F (sn) burst in; **~schauen** look in (F *bei j-m* on a p.); **~schneien** *fig.* (sn) blow in.

her|fallen [ˈheːr-] (sn): *über j-n* fall (*od.* set) (up)on; ˈ**2gang** *m* course of events, circumstances *pl.*; *tell me* what happened; ˈ**~geben** deliver, give (away); *fig.* (*gewähren*) yield; *sich* (*s-n Namen*) *~ zu* lend o.s. (one's name) to; ˈ**~gebracht** handed down to us, traditional; (*üblich*) customary; ˈ**~gehören** belong to the matter; ˈ**~gelaufen** *adj.* vagabond; ˈ**~halten** *v/t.* hold out; *v/i.* suffer (*für* for); *~ müssen* F stand the racket; ˈ**~holen** fetch; *weit hergeholt* far-fetched.

Hering [ˈheːrɪŋ] *m* (3¹) herring; (*Zeltpflock*) tent peg; *zusammengedrängt wie die ~e* packed like sardines; *s. grün*; ˈ**~ssalat** *m* pickled-herring salad.

her|kommen [ˈheːr-] (sn): *komm her!* come here!; *~ von* come (*od.* originate) from; *S.*: *a.* be due to; *Wort*: be derived from; ˈ**2kommen** *n* (6) (*Sitte*) convention, custom; (*Abstammung*) origin, extraction; **~kömmlich** [ˈ~kœmlɪç] conventional (*a.* ⚔ *Waffe*); *s. hergebracht*; ˈ**2kunft** *f* (14¹) *P.*: origin, extraction; *S.*: origin, provenance; ˈ**~laufen** (sn): *hinter j-m ~* run after; ˈ**~leiern** F reel off; ˈ**~leiten** (*von*) derive (from); *sich ~ von* (be) derive(d) from; ˈ**2leitung** *f* derivation; *sich* ˈ**~machen** *über* (*acc.*) set about, tackle; *j-n*: set on, attack.

Hermelin [hɛrməˈliːn] *n* (3¹) ermine.

hermetisch [hɛrˈmeːtɪʃ] hermetic (-ally *adv.*).

hernach [hɛrˈnɑːx] after(wards).

hernehmen [ˈheːr-] (*von*) take (from), get (from); *fig. j-n ~* take a p. to task.

hernieder [hɛrˈniːdər] down; *s. herab, herunter.*

Heroin [heroˈiːn] *n* (3¹, *o. pl.*) heroin.

hero|isch [heˈroːɪʃ] heroic(ally *adv.*); **2ismus** [heroˈɪsmus] *m* (16) heroism.

Herold [ˈheːrɔlt] *m* (3) herald.

Heros [ˈheːrɔs] *m* (16²) hero.

herplappern [ˈheːr-] rattle off.

Herr [hɛr] *m* (12²) master; (*bsd. adliger ~*) lord; (*Herrscher*) ruler; (*feiner Mann, a. allg.*) gentleman; (*Gott*) Lord; *Anrede*: Sir, *vor Eigennamen*: Mr.; *mein ~* Sir; *meine ~en* gentlemen; *aus aller ~en Länder(n)* from all over the world; *fig. ~ werden* (*gen.*) master, get under control; *~ der Lage* master of the situation.

ˈ**Herren|-anzug** *m* (gentle)man's suit; ˈ**~-artikel** *m/pl.* gentlemen's outfitting, *Am.* haberdashery *sg.*; ˈ**~bekleidung** *f* (gentle)men's wear; ˈ**~**ˈ**doppel** *n Tennis*: men's doubles *pl.*; ˈ**~**ˈ**-einzel** *n Tennis*: men's singles *pl.*; ˈ**~friseur** *m* (gentle)men's hairdresser, barber; ˈ**~haus** *n* mansion, manor(-house); ˈ**~konfektion** *f* (gentle)men's ready-to-wear clothes; ˈ**2los** ownerless; *Tier*: stray; *~e Güter n/pl.* derelicts; ˈ**~mode** *f* men's fashion; ˈ**~reiter** *m* gentleman rider; ˈ**~schneider** *m* (gentlemen's) tailor; ˈ**~schnitt** *m bei Damen*: Eton crop, shingle; ˈ**~toilette** *f* men's toilet (*Am.* restroom); ˈ**~zimmer** *n* study.

'**Herrgott** *m* (1[1] *u.* [2]) *the* Lord (God), God.

herrichten ['he:rriçtən] arrange, prepare, get *a th.* ready; *Zimmer*: tidy; (*instand setzen*) do up, repair; *sich* ~ smarten o.s. up.

Herrin ['hɛrin] *f* (16[1]) mistress, lady.

'**herrisch** imperious.

herrje! [hɛr'je:] goodness!, dear me!

'**herrlich** marvellous, glorious, magnificent, splendid; '**2keit** *f* magnificence, splendo(u)r, glory.

'**Herrschaft** *f* rule, dominion (*über acc.* of); *a. fig.* mastery, power, control; (*Regierung*) government, *e-s Fürsten*: reign; *der Dienstboten*: master and mistress; *meine* ~*en!* ladies and gentlemen!; *die* ~ *verlieren über* lose control of; '**2lich** belonging (*od.* referring) to a master *od.* lord; (*grundherrlich*) manorial; (*vornehm*) high-class, elegant.

herrschen ['hɛrʃən] (27) rule (*über acc.* over); (*regieren*) govern (*über e-n Staat usw.* a State *etc.*); *als Fürst*: reign (*über* over); (*vor*~) prevail, reign; (*bestehen*) be, exist.

'**Herrscher** *m* (7) ruler, sovereign; '~**haus** *n* dynasty.

'**Herrsch|sucht** *f* thirst for power; F bossiness; '**2süchtig** greedy of power; *weitS.* domineering, F bossy.

her|rufen ['he:r-] call (here); '~**rühren** *s. herkommen*; '~**sagen** recite, say; '~**schreiben:** *sich* ~ *von* come from; '~**sehen** look here *od.* this way; '~**stammen** *s. abstammen*; *s. herkommen*; '~**stellen** place (*od.* put) here; (*erzeugen*) manufacture, produce, make; *fig.* produce, bring about; *Frieden, Ordnung, Verbindungen*: establish; (*wieder*~) restore, repair; *Kranke*: restore to health; '**2steller** *m* (7) manufacturer, maker, producer; '**2stellerfirma** *f* manufacturing firm, manufacturers *pl.*; '**2stellung** *f* manufacture, production; establishment; (*Abteilung*) production department; '**2stellungskosten** ✝ *pl.* production costs; '**2stellungsleiter(in** *f*) *m* production manager; '**2stellungsverfahren** *n* manufacturing method (*od.* process).

Hertz *phys.* [hɛrts] *n inv.* cycles *pl.* per second.

herüber [hɛ'ry:bər] over, across; ~**kommen** (sn) come over (here), come across.

herum [hɛ'rum] *ziellos*: about, *Am. a.* around; (*rings*~) (a)round; (*ungefähr*) about; *hier* ~ hereabout(s); (*vorbei*) over, finished; ~**bekommen** *s. herumkriegen*; ~**bringen** *Zeit*: pass, kill; *j-n*: *s. herumkriegen*; ~**doktern** *an j-m* physic (*od.* doctor) a p.; ~**drehen** turn round; *sich* ~**drücken** *s. herumlungern*; ~**fuchteln** *v/i.* saw the air; *mit et.*: fidget with; ~**führen:** *j-n* ~ (*zur Orientierung*) show a p. round; *j-n* ~ *in* (*dat.*) show a p. over *a house etc.*; *s. Nase*; ~**kommen** (sn) come round; *weit* ~ see much of the world, get about (*Am.* around); *fig.* ~ *um e-e Notwendigkeit usw.* avoid, dodge; ~**kommandieren** order *a p.* about; *j-n* ~**kriegen** win a p. over, talk a p. round; ~**lungern** loaf (*od.* loiter, hang) about; ~**reden:** *um et.* ~ talk (*od.* argue) round a th.; ~**reichen** hand round; ~**reisen** (sn) travel about; ~**reiten** *auf* (*dat.*) *fig.* harp (up)on; ~**scharwenzeln** *um j-n* dance attendance on; *sich* ~**schlagen** *mit* grapple with; ~**spionieren** snoop about; *sich* ~**sprechen** get about; *es hat sich herumgesprochen, daß* it is rumo(u)red that; ~**stehen** stand about; ~ *um* stand (a)round *a th. od. p.*; ~**treiben:** *sich* ~ gad (F knock) about; *s. herumlungern*; ~**ziehen** *v/t.* draw (*od.* pull) (a)round; *v/i.* (sn) wander about; *um et.*: march round.

herunter [hɛ'runtər] *s. herab*; *den Hut* ~*!* off with your hat!; ~**bringen** bring down; *fig. a.* lower, reduce; ~**hauen:** *j-m e-e* ~ F fetch a p. one; ~**kommen** (sn) come down (in the world *fig. v. P.*); (*verfallen*) decay; *heruntergekommen fig.* in reduced circumstances, out-at-elbows, *gesundheitlich*: in poor health; ~**machen** F run (*Am.* F call) down; ~**reißen** pull down; *fig.* (*scharf kritisieren*) pull to pieces; ~**schrauben** *fig.* lower; ~**sein** (sn) *gesundheitlich*: be run down; ~**spielen** ♪ F rattle off; *fig.* play down; ~**wirtschaften** run down.

hervor [hɛr'fo:r] forth, out; ~**bringen** produce; *Worte*: utter; **2brin-**

gung *f* production; **~gehen** (sn) *als Sieger*: come off, emerge (*aus* from); *als Folge*: result *od.* follow (*aus* from); (*ersichtlich sein*) be evident, follow (*aus* from); **~heben** render prominent; *Kunst*: set off; (*herausstreichen*) show off; (*betonen*) emphasize; **~holen** produce; **~ragen** project; stand out, be prominent; *fig. a.* excel; **~ragend** prominent; *nur fig.* excellent, outstanding, eminent; **&ruf** *thea. m* call; **~rufen** call forth; *thea.* call for; *fig.* cause; **~stechen** stick out; *fig.* stand forth; **~stechend** prominent; conspicuous; **~stehen** stand out; *Augen usw.*: protrude; **~treten** (sn) step forth; *s. a. hervorragen, -stechen*; *sich* **~tun** distinguish o.s.; **~ziehen** draw forth, produce.

her|wagen ['he:r-]: *sich ~* venture to come here; '**&weg** *m* way here.

Herz [hɛrts] *n* (12[2]) heart; (*Mut*) *a.* courage, spirit; (*Seele*) *a.* soul; (*Gemüt, Geist*) mind; *Kartenspiel*: hearts *pl.*; *Anrede*: darling, love; *sich ein ~ fassen* take heart; *s. ausschütten, schließen*; *auf ~ und Nieren prüfen* put to the acid-test; *etwas auf dem ~en haben* have something on one's mind; *j-m et. ans ~ legen* enjoin a th. on a p.; *das ~ auf der Zunge haben* wear one's heart on one's sleeve; F *mir ist das ~ in die Hosen gefallen* my heart is in my boots; *s-m ~en Luft machen* give vent to one's feelings; *mit ganzem ~en dabeisein usw.* with one's whole heart; *ich kann es nicht über das ~ bringen* I cannot find it in my heart; *von ganzem ~en danken usw.* with all my *etc.* heart; *sich et. zu ~en nehmen* take a th. to heart; *sein ~ an et. hängen* set one's heart on a th.; *ein ~ und eine Seele sein* be as thick as thieves, be hand in glove; '**~...** ⚕ cardiac (*z. B. cardiac asthma*).

'**Herz|-anfall** *m* heart-attack; '**~-asthma** *n* cardiac asthma; '**~beschwerden** *f/pl.* heart trouble; '**~chen** *n Anrede*: darling.

'**Herzeleid** *n* deep sorrow.

'**herzen** (27) press to one's heart; (*umarmen*) hug, embrace; (*liebkosen*) caress, cuddle.

'**Herzens|-angelegenheit** *f* love-affair; '**~-angst** *f* anguish of mind; '**~brecher** *m* lady-killer; '**&froh** very glad; '**&gut** very kind; '**~güte** *f* kindness of heart; *nach* '**~lust** *f* to one's heart's content, to the top of one's bent; '**~wunsch** *m* heart's desire.

'**herz|-erfrischend** heart-warming; '**~-ergreifend** heart-moving; '**&-erweiterung** *f* dilatation of the heart; '**&fehler** *m* cardiac defect; **~förmig** ['~fœrmiç] heart-shaped; '**&gegend** *f* cardiac region; '**&grube** *f* pit of the stomach; '**~haft** courageous; (*kräftig*) hearty; '**&haftigkeit** *f* courage; heartiness.

herziehen ['he:rtsi:ən]: *~ über j-n* run a p. down.

herzig ['hɛrtsiç] sweet, lovely, *Am.* cute.

'**Herz|-infarkt** *m* coronary (thrombosis), ⚕ cardiac infarction; '**~kammer** *f* ventricle; '**~katheter** ⚕ *m* (*Gerät*) cardiac catheter; (*Untersuchung*) heart (*od.* cardiac) catheter; '**~kirsche** *f* heart cherry; '**~klopfen** *n* beating (*od.* palpitation) of the heart; '**&krank** having heart trouble; '**~leiden** *n* heart complaint.

'**herzlich** heartfelt, warm, sincere; *~ gern* with the greatest of pleasure; *~ wenig* precious little; *im Brief*: *mit ~en Grüßen pl.* yours sincerely, *intimer*: (yours with) love; *~e Grüße an* (*acc.*) kind regards to; '**&keit** *f* heartiness, cordiality, warmth.

herz|los heartless; '**&losigkeit** *f* heartlessness.

Herzog ['hɛrtso:k] *m* (3[3]) duke; **~in** ['~tso:gin] *f* (16[1]) duchess; **&lich** ['~kliç] ducal; '**~tum** *n* (1[2]) dukedom, duchy.

'**Herz|schlag** *m* heartbeat; ⚕ heart attack (*od.* failure); '**~schrittmacher** *m* pace-maker; '**~schwäche** *f* cardiac weakness; '**~spezialist** *m* heart specialist; '**&stärkend** cordial; '**~stillstand** *m* heart stoppage, ⚕ cardiac arrest; '**~tod** *m* cardiac death.

herzu [hɛr'tsu:] = *heran, herbei.*

'**Herzverpflanzung** *f* heart transplant.

'**herzzerreißend** heart-rending.

Hesse ['hɛsə] *m* (13), '**Hessin** *f*, '**hessisch** Hessian.

heterogen [hetero'ge:n] heterogeneous.

Hetze ['hɛtsə] *f* (15) *s. Hetzjagd*;

(*Eile*) hurry, rush; (*Aufreizung*) instigation, agitation (gegen against); '2**n** (27) *v/t. hunt.* course, hunt, chase (*a. fig.*); *fig.* (*umherjagen*) hurry, rush (*a. v/i.*); (*aufreizen*) incite; *e-n Hund auf j-n* ~ set a dog at a p.; *v/i.* cause discord; *gegen j-n* ~ agitate against a p.

'**Hetzer** *m* (7), '~**in** *f fig.* instigator, agitator; '2**isch** inflammatory.

'**Hetz|jagd** *f* coursing, baiting; *fig.* rush, *Am. sl.* rat race; '~**rede** *f* inflammatory speech.

Heu [hɔʏ] *n* (3) hay; F *Geld wie* ~ pots of money; '~**boden** *m* hay-loft.

Heuchel|ei [hɔʏçə'laɪ] *f* (16) hypocrisy; dissimulation; '~**n** (29) *v/t.* simulate, feign; *v/i.* play the hypocrite; dissemble, sham.

'**Heuchler** *m* (7), '~**in** *f* (16[1]) hypocrite; '2**isch** hypocritical.

heuen ['hɔʏən] (25) make hay.

heuer[1] ['hɔʏər] (in) this year.

'**Heuer**[2] *m* haymaker.

'**Heuer**[3] ⚓ *f* (15) wages *pl.*; '2**n** (29) hire.

'**Heu|-ernte** *f* hay-harvest; '~**gabel** *f* hay-fork, pitch-fork.

heul|en ['hɔʏlən] (25) howl; (*weinen*) cry; (*jammern*) wail; *Sirene*: hoot; 2**suse** F ['~zu:zə] *f* cry-baby.

heurig ['hɔʏriç] of this year.

'**Heu|schnupfen** *m* hay fever; '~**schober** *m* haystack, hayrick; '~**schrecke** *f* (15) locust, grasshopper.

heute ['hɔʏtə] today, this day; ~ *abend* this evening, tonight; ~ *früh*, ~ *morgen* this morning; ~ *über* (*vor*) *acht Tage(n)* this day week; ~ *übers Jahr* a year from today; ~ *vor acht Tagen* a week ago (today); *von* ~ *auf morgen fig.* overnight.

'**heutig** of this day, this day's, today's; (*gegenwärtig*) present(-day), modern.

'**heutzutage** nowadays.

Hexe ['hɛksə] *f* (15) witch, sorceress; *fig.* (*altes Weib*) *a.* hag; (*böses Weib*) hell-cat; '2**n** (27) practise witchcraft; *fig.* work miracles.

'**Hexen|jagd** *f fig.* witch-hunt; '~**kessel** *m* inferno; '~**meister** *m* wizard, sorcerer; '~**sabbath** *m* Witches' Sabbath; *fig.* inferno; '~**schuß** ⚕ *m* lumbago.

Hexerei [~'raɪ] *f* (16) witchcraft, (*a. fig.*) magic.

Hieb [hi:p] **1.** *m* (3) stroke, blow; *mit e-m Schwert usw.*: cut; (*Anzüglichkeit*) hit (gegen, *auf acc.* at); ~*e pl.* (*Prügel*) a thrashing *sg.*; **2.** 2 *pret. v. hauen*; '2- **und** '**stichfest** *fig.* watertight, cast-iron.

hielt [hi:lt] *pret. v. halten.*

hienieden [hi:'ni:dən] here below.

hier [hi:r] here; (*am Ort*) in this place; ~ *und da* here and there; ~ *sein* be here *od.* present; *Appell*: ~! present!; ~ *entlang!* this way!; ~, *bitte!* here you are!

hieran ['hi:ran] at (*od.* by, in, on, to) this.

Hierarchie [hi:erar'çi:] *f* (15) hierarchy.

hier|auf ['hi:r-] hereupon, after this *od.* that, next; '~**aus** from (*od.* out of) this; '~**bei** at (*od.* in *od.* with) this; (*inliegend*) enclosed; '~**durch** by this, hereby; '~**für** for this, for it; '~**gegen** against this *od.* it; '~**her** here, hither; this way; *bis* ~ hitherto, so far, till now; '~**herum** hereabout(s); '~**in** herein, in this; '~**mit** herewith, with this; '~**nach** after this; (*dementsprechend*) according to this; '~-**orts** in this place *od.* country; '~**über** over here; (*über dieses Thema*) about this; '~**um** (a)round this; '~**unter** under this; among these; *bei verstehen usw.*: by this; '~**von** of (*od.* from) this; '~**zu** (in addition) to this *od.* it; '~**zulande** in this country.

hiesig ['hi:ziç] of this place *od.* country; local.

hieß [hi:s] *pret. v. heißen.*

Hilfe ['hilfə] *f* (15) help (*a. P.*); (*Beistand*) aid, assistance; (*Rettung*) succour; (*Armen*2) relief (für to); *Erste* ~ first aid; *j-m zu* ~ *kommen* (*eilen*) come (run) to a p.'s assistance (*od.* aid); *j-m* ~ *leisten* help (*od.* assist) a p.; *et. zu* ~ *nehmen* make use of, resort to; *mit* ~ (*gen. od.*) *von* with the help of *a p.*, with (*od.* by) the aid of *a th.*; *ohne* ~ (*selbständig*) unaided, single-handed; '2**flehend** imploring (help), suppliant; '~**leistung** *f* aid, assistance, help; '~**ruf** *m* cry for help; '2**suchend** seeking (for) help.

'**hilf|los** helpless; '2**losigkeit** *f* helplessness; '~**reich** helpful.

'**Hilfs|-aktion** *f* relief action; '~-**arbeiter(in** *f*) *m* unskilled (*od.* auxiliary) worker; '2**bedürftig** needy, indigent; '**~bedürftigkeit** *f* indigence; '**⌂bereit** willing to help, co-operative; '**~geistliche** *m* curate; '**~gelder** *n/pl.* subsidies; '**~kraft** *f* help(er), auxiliary; '**~kreuzer** ⚓ *m* auxiliary cruiser; '**~lehrer** *m* supply teacher; untrained teacher; '**~linie** 🚂 *f* subsidiary line; '**~maschine** *f*, '**~motor** *m* auxiliary engine; '**~mittel** *n* aid; (*Heilmittel*) remedy; *s. Hilfsquelle*; '**~-organisation** *f* relief organization; '**~quelle** *f* resource; '**~schule** *f* school for backward children, *Am.* ungraded classes; '**~truppen** *f/pl.* auxiliaries; '**~werk** *n* relief (work); '**~zeitwort** *n* auxiliary verb.

Himbeere ['himbeːrə] *f* raspberry.

'**Himbeer|saft** *m* raspberry-juice; '**~strauch** *m* raspberry-bush.

Himmel ['himəl] *m* (7) sky, heavens *pl.*; *s. ~sstrich*; *fig.* heaven; (*Trag⌂ usw.*) canopy; *in den ~ heben fig.* praise to the skies; *am ~* in the sky; *fig. im ~* in heaven; *~ auf Erden* heaven on earth; *unter freiem ~* in the open air; *aus heiterem ~* out of a clear sky; *um ~s willen!* goodness!; '**⌂-angst:** F *ihm ist ~* he is scared to death; '**~bett** *n* tester-bed, four-poster; '**⌂blau** sky-blue; '**~fahrt** *f* Ascension; *Mariä ~* Assumption; '**~fahrtsnase** F *f* tip-tilted nose; '**~fahrts-tag** *m* Ascension Day; '**~reich** *n* kingdom of heaven; '**~schlüssel** ⚘ *m* primrose; '**⌂schreiend** outrageous, terrible; *~e Schande* crying shame.

'**Himmels...** *in Zssgn mst* heavenly, celestial; '**~gegend** *f* quarter (of the heavens); *die vier ~en* the four cardinal points of the compass; '**~körper** *m* celestial body; '**~kugel** *f* celestial globe; '**~richtung** *f* cardinal point; *weitS.* direction; '**~strich** *m* climate, zone; '**~zelt** *n* (canopy of) heaven.

himmel|wärts ['~vɛrts] skyward(s); *fig.* heavenward(s); '**~weit** *fig.* vast; *~ verschieden sein* differ widely; *es ist ein ~er Unterschied zwischen ...* there is all the difference in the world between ...

'**himmlisch** celestial, heavenly.

hin [hin] there; (*weg*) gone, lost; (*kaputt*) gone, broken; *an ... ~* along; *~ und her* to and fro, *Am.* back and forth; *~ und zurück* there and back; *~ und wieder* now and then; *er ist ~* (*ruiniert usw.*) he is done for, (*tot*) he is dead; *~ und her überlegen* turn *a th.* over in one's mind.

hinab [hi'nap] down; **~gehen, ~steigen** (sn) go down, descend.

hinan [hi'nan] up; *s. hinauf(...)*.

'**hin-arbeiten** *auf* (*acc.*) aim at.

hinauf [hi'nauf] up; *den Berg ~* up the hill, uphill; *sich* **~-arbeiten** work one's way up; **~gehen** (sn) go up (*a. Preise*); *die Treppe ~* go upstairs; **~setzen** *Preis*: raise; **~steigen** (sn) ascend, mount.

hinaus [~'naus] out; *~ mit euch!* out with you!; *auf (viele) Jahre ~* for many years to come; **~begleiten** *Besuch*: see out; **~gehen** (sn) go (*od.* walk) out; *~ über e-e S.*: go beyond, exceed; *~ auf* (*acc.*) *Fenster usw.*: look out on, face; *Absicht*: aim at; **~kommen** (sn) come out; *fig. auf dasselbe ~* come (down) to the same thing; **~laufen** (sn) run out; *~ auf* (*acc.*) amount to; *Absicht*: aim at; *auf eins* (*od. dasselbe*) *~* come to the same thing; **~schieben** put off, postpone; **~sein:** *fig. über et. hinaussein* be past (*od.* beyond) a th.; **~werfen** throw out, expel; (*zur Tür*) *~* turn *od.* F kick out (of doors); (*entlassen*) *sl.* throw out, *Am.* fire; **~wollen** wish to go out; *hoch ~* aim high; *worauf will er hinaus?* what is he driving at?

'**Hin|blick** *m*: *im ~ auf* (*acc.*) with regard to, in view of; '**⌂bringen** take, carry (*beide*: *zu* to); *Zeit*: spend, pass.

hinder|lich ['hindər-] hindering; troublesome; '**~n** (29) prevent (*an dat.* from *doing*), hinder; *Verkehr*: block, obstruct; '**⌂nis** *n* (4[1]) hindrance; (*Hemmnis*) impediment; *äußerliches*: obstacle; *belastendes*: encumbrance; *Rennsport*: hurdle, obstacle (*beide a. fig.*); '**⌂nisrennen** *n* steeple-chase.

'**hindeuten** *auf* (*acc.*) point to.

hin'durch through(out); across; *s. ganz*; *in Zssgn = durch...*

hinein [hi'naın] in; **~-arbeiten:** *sich in e-e S. ~* get into a matter; **~denken:** *sich ~ in et.* go deeply into; **~gehen** (sn; *in acc.*) go in(to *a th.*), enter (*a th.*); *in den Topf gehen ... hinein* the pot holds ...; *in* *den Saal gehen ... hinein* the hall seats *500 persons*; **~leben:** *in den Tag ~* take it easy; **~legen** put in(to *in acc.*); F *fig. s. hereinlegen*; *sich* **~mischen** *s. einmischen*; **~stecken, ~stellen, ~tun** put in(to *in acc.*); **~ziehen** *a. fig.* drag in(to *in acc.*).

ˈ**Hin|fahrt** *f* journey there; *auf der ~* on the way there; ˈ**2fallen** (sn) fall (down); ˈ**2fällig** (*gebrechlich*) frail, weak, decrepit; *Grund*: futile; (*ungültig*) invalid; *~ machen* invalidate; ˈ**~fälligkeit** *f* frailty, weakness; 2ˈ**fort** henceforth, in (the) future; ˈ**~führen** *a. fig.* lead (*nach, zu* to).

hing [hiŋ] *pret. v. hängen.*

ˈ**Hin|gabe** *f* devotion (*an acc.* to); (*Opfer*) sacrifice; ˈ**~gang** *m* death; ˈ**2geben** give away; (*überlassen*) give up, surrender; (*opfern*) sacrifice; *sich ~* (*dat.*) devote o.s. (*od.* give o.s. up) to; *e-m Laster*: indulge in; ˈ**~gebung** *f* devotion; ˈ**2gebungsvoll** devoted; 2ˈ**gegen** on the other hand; ˈ**2gehen** (sn) go there; (*vergehen*) pass; *~ lassen* let pass; *über et. ~* pass over a th.; ˈ**2geraten** (sn) *zu usw.* get to; ˈ**~gerichtete** *m, f* executed man (*od.* woman); ˈ**2halten** hold out; (*vertrösten*) put off; (*verzögern*) delay; ˈ**2haltend** *Taktik usw.*: delaying; ˈ**2hauen** F *Arbeit*: knock off; *sich ~* flop down, *zum Schlafen*: turn in; *das haut hin!* it works!, that does the trick!; ˈ**2hören** listen.

hinken [ˈhiŋkən] (25, h. *u.* sn) limp, go lame; ˈ**~d** lame, limping.

ˈ**hin|knien** kneel down; ˈ**~länglich** sufficient; ˈ**2länglichkeit** *f* sufficiency; ˈ**~legen** lay down; *sich ~* lie down; ˈ**~nehmen** accept (*a. fig.*), take; (*dulden*) suffer, put up with; (*sich*) ˈ**~neigen** *nach, zu* incline to(wards).

hinnen [ˈhinən]: *von ~* from hence.

ˈ**hin|raffen** snatch away; ˈ**~reichen** *v/t.* reach (out); *v/i.* (*genügen*) suffice, do; ˈ**~reißen** carry away (*a. fig.*); *fig.* (*begeistern*) enrapture, thrill; *sich ~ lassen* let o.s. be carried away; *~d* breath-taking; ˈ**~richten** execute, put to death; ˈ**2richtung** *f* execution; ˈ**2richtungskommando** *n* execution squad; ˈ**~scheiden**[1] (sn) die, pass away; ˈ**2scheiden**[2] *n* (6) decease; ˈ**~schlagen** (sn) fall down heavily; ˈ**~schleppen:** *sich ~* drag on; ˈ**~schreiben** write down; *an j-n*: write to *him, etc.*; ˈ**~schwinden** (sn) vanish *od.* dwindle (away); ˈ**~sehen** *nach, zu* look to(wards) *od.* at; ˈ**~setzen** put down; *j-n*: seat; *sich ~* sit down, take a seat; ˈ**2sicht** *f*: *in ~ auf* (*acc.*) *s. hinsichtlich*; *in anderer ~* in other respects; *in dieser* (*einer, jeder*) *~* in this (one, every) respect; *in gewisser ~* in a way; ˈ**~sichtlich** (*gen.*) with regard to, as to, concerning; ˈ**~siechen** waste away; ˈ**~stellen** place; (*niederstellen*) put down; *~ als* represent as; ˈ**~strecken** stretch out; *j-n*: *a.* fell; *sich ~* stretch o.s. out.

hintan|setzen [hintˈˀan-], **~stellen** *fig.* put last.

hinten [ˈhintən] behind; (*im Hintergrunde*) in the background; (*am Ende*) in the rear; *von ~* from behind; *~ und vorn fig.* everywhere; ˈ**~herum** *fig.* on the quiet; **~**ˈ**-über** backwards.

hinter [ˈhintər] behind, *Am.* F *a.* back of; *~ sich lassen allg.* leave behind; *sich ~ et. machen* get down to (*od.* tackle) *a th.*; ˈ**2-achse** *f* rear-axle; ˈ**2-achsen-antrieb** *mot. m* rear-axle drive; ˈ**2-ansicht** *f* back view; ˈ**2backe** *f* buttock; ˈ**2bänkler** *parl. m* back-bencher; ˈ**2bein** *n* hind leg; **2bliebene(n)** [~ˈbli:bənə(n)] *pl.* surviving dependants; *in Traueranzeigen*: *the* bereaved; **~**ˈ**bringen:** *j-m et. ~* inform a p. of a th.; ˈ**2deck** *n* after-deck; **~drein** [~ˈdraɪn] *s. hinterher*; ˈ**~e** *adj.* back, rear; ˈ**~-ei**ˈ**nander** one after another; successively; ⚡ in series; *fünfmal ~* five times running; ˈ**~-ei**ˈ**nanderschalten** ⚡ connect in series; ˈ**2-eingang** *m* rear (*od.* back) entrance; **~**ˈ**fragen** examine, question in depth; ˈ**2fuß** *m* hind foot; ˈ**2gebäude** *n s. Hinterhaus*; ˈ**2gedanke** *m* ulterior motive, arrière pensée (*fr.*); **~**ˈ**gehen** deceive; 2ˈ**gehung** *f* deception; ˈ**2grund** *m* background; *fig. sich im ~ halten* keep in the background; *in den ~ drängen* thrust into the background; ˈ**~gründig** cryptic; ˈ**2halt** *m* ambush; **~hältig** [ˈ~hɛltiç] *s. hinterlistig*; ˈ**2hand** *f Pferd*: hind quarters *pl.*; *Kartenspiel*: youngest hand; ˈ**2haupt** *n* back of the head, 📖 occiput; ˈ**2haus** *n* back-building, back part (of the house); ~'**her** behind; after; *nur zeitlich*: afterwards; '⁓**hof** *m* backyard; '⁓**kopf** *m s. Hinterhaupt*; '⁓**lader** *m* (7) breech-loader; '⁓**land** *n* hinterland, interior; ~'**lassen 1.** *v/t.* leave (behind); **2.** *adj.* posthumous; ⁓'**lassenschaft** *f* estate; '⁓**lauf** *m* hind leg; ~'**legen** deposit; ⁓'**legung** *f* deposition; '⁓**leib** *zo. m* hind quarters *pl.*; '⁓**list** *f* insidiousness; underhand trick; '~**listig** insidious, deceitful, crafty; '⁓**mann** *m* ⚔ rear-rank man; ✝ subsequent endorser; *fig.* backer; (*Drahtzieher*) wire-puller; '⁓**mannschaft** *f Sport*: defen|ce, *Am.* -se; '⁓**n** F *m* backside, bottom, behind; '⁓**rad** *n* rear wheel; '⁓**rad-antrieb** *mot. m* rear-wheel drive; ~**rücks** ['~ryks] from behind; *fig.* behind *a p.'s* back; '⁓**seite** *f* back; '~**ste** rearmost, backmost; '⁓**teil** *n* back part; ⚓ stern; *zo.* hind quarters *pl.*; *s. Hintern*; '⁓**treffen** *n*: *ins* ~ *geraten* lag (*od.* fall) behind; *weit S.* get the worst of it; ~'**treiben** prevent, thwart; ⁓'**treibung** *f* prevention, frustration; '⁓**treppe** *f* backstairs *pl.*; '⁓**tür** *f* (*a. fig.*) backdoor; ⁓**wäldler** ['~vɛldlər] *m* (7) yokel, *Am. a.* hick; '⁓**wand** *f* back (wall); ~**wärts** ['~vɛrts] backward(s); ~'**ziehen** evade; ⁓'**ziehung** *f* (tax) evasion; '⁓**zimmer** *n* back room.

hinüber [hi'ny:bər] over, across.

'**Hin- und** '**Rückfahrt** *f* journey there and back; *Fahrkarte für* ~ return (*Am.* roundtrip) ticket.

hinunter [hi'nuntər] down; *den Berg* ~ down the hill, downhill; ~**gehen** (sn) go down (*a. Preise*); *die Treppe* ~ go downstairs; ~**schlucken** swallow down; *fig.* swallow.

Hinweg ['~ve:k] *m* way (there).

hinweg [~'vɛk] *adv.* away, off; ~**gehen** *über* (*acc.*) pass over (*a. fig.*); *s. hinwegsetzen*; ~**helfen:** *j-m* ~ *über* (*acc.*) help a p. get (*od.* tide) over; ~**kommen** *über* (*acc.*) get over (*a. fig.*); ~**sehen:** *fig. über* et. ~ overlook a th.; *sich* ~**setzen** *über* (*acc.*) make light of (*od.* disregard) *a th.*; override *a rule, objection, etc.*; *lachend* (*gleichgültig*): laugh (shrug) *a th.* off; ~**täuschen:** *j-n über* et. ~ deceive a p. about a th.

Hin|weis ['~vaɪs] *m* (4) hint, direction, F pointer; ~ *auf* (*acc.*) reference to; '⁓**weisen** *v/t.* direct (*nach, zu* to); *v/i.* ~ *auf* (*acc.*) point to; (*verweisen*) refer to; *darauf* ~, *daß* point out that; '⁓**weisend:** ~*es Fürwort* demonstrative pronoun; '⁓**werfen** throw down; *flüchtig, a. Wort*: drop, *Brief, Zeichnung usw.*: dash off; *fig. Arbeit usw.*: chuck; *j-m* et. ~ throw a th. to a p.; ⁓'**wiederum** again; (*andererseits*) on the other hand; '⁓**wirken** *auf* (*acc.*) work towards; '⁓**ziehen** *v/t.* draw, attract; *räumlich*: extend (*bis* to); *zeitlich*: drag out, protract; *sich* ~ *räumlich*: extend, *Zeit usw.*: drag on; '⁓**zielen** *auf* (*acc.*) aim at.

hin'zu near; there; (*außerdem*) in addition; ~**fügen** add; ⁓**fügung** *f* addition; ~**kommen** (sn) *unvermutet*: supervene; (*noch* ~) be added; *es kommt hinzu, daß* add to this that; ~**setzen** add; ~**treten** (sn) approach; *s. hinzukommen*; ~**tun,** ~**zählen** add; ~**ziehen** *Arzt usw.*: call in, consult.

Hiobs|botschaft *f*, ~**post** ['hi:ɔps-] *f* bad news.

Hirn [hirn] *n* (3) brain; (~*substanz*; *fig. Verstand*) brains *pl.*; '~**gespinst** *n* figment of the mind, (mere) fancy; '~**haut-entzündung** *f* meningitis; '⁓**los** brainless; '~**masse** *f* brain matter; '⁓**rissig** whacky, weird, crazy; '~**schale** *f* brain-pan, cranium; '~**schlag** *m* apoplexy (of the brain); '~**tod** *m* cerebral death; '~**tumor** *m* brain tumo(u)r; '⁓**verbrannt** mad, crazy.

Hirsch [hirʃ] *m* (3^2) stag, hart; *als Gattung*: deer; '~**braten** *m* roast venison; ~**fänger** ['~fɛŋər] *m* hunting-knife; '~**geweih** *n* antlers *pl.*; '~**horn** *n* hartshorn; '~**hornsalz** *n* salt of hartshorn; '~**jagd** *f* stag-hunt(ing); '~**käfer** *m* stag-beetle; '~**kalb** *n* calf of deer; '~**kuh** *f* hind; '~**leder** *n* buckskin; '~**talg** *m* suet (of deer).

Hirse ['hirzə] *f* (15) millet; '~**brei** *m* millet gruel.

Hirt [hirt] *m* (12) herdsman; (*Schaf*⁓) shepherd.

'**Hirten|brief** *eccl. m* pastoral letter; '~**junge** *m*, '~**knabe** *m* shepherd-boy; '~**stab** *m* shepherd's staff; *eccl.* crosier; '~**volk** *n* pastoral tribe.

'**Hirtin** *f* (16) shepherdess.

His ♪ [his] *n* B sharp.
hissen [ˈhisən] (28) hoist.
Historie [hiˈsto:rjə] *f* (15) history; **~nmaler** *m* historical painter.
Hiˈstoriker *m* (7) historian.
hiˈstorisch historical; (*geschichtlich bedeutsam*) historic.
ˈ**Hitzbläs-chen** *n* heat spot (*od.* vesicle); *pl.* heat rash.
Hitze [ˈhitsə] *f* (15) heat; ˈ**~beständig** heat-resistant; ˈ**~grad** *m* degree of heat; ˈ**~welle** *f* heat-wave.
ˈ**hitzig** hot (*a. fig.*); *fig.* heated, fierce *discussion, etc.*; *~ werden* fly into a passion.
ˈ**Hitz|kopf** *m* hothead; **~köpfig** [ˈ~kœpfiç] hot-headed; ˈ**~pickel** *m* *s. Hitzbläschen*; ˈ**~schlag** *m* heat-stroke.
ˈ**H-Milch** *f* long-life milk.
hob [ho:p] *pret. v. heben.*
Hobby [ˈhɔbi] *n* (11) hobby.
Hobel [ˈho:bəl] *m* (7) plane; ˈ**~bank** *f* carpenter's bench; ˈ**~messer** *n* planing knife; ˈ**~n** (29) plane; **~späne** [ˈ~ʃpɛ:nə] *m/pl.* shavings.
hoch [ho:x] **1.** high; (*hochgewachsen*) tall; *fig. a.* noble, sublime; *hohes Alter* great age; *hohe See* open sea; *hohe Strafe* severe punishment, heavy penalty; *hoher Offizier* high (-ranking) officer; *drei Mann ~* three of them; *das ist mir zu ~* that's beyond me; *hohe Ehre* great hono(u)r; *in hoher Fahrt* at full speed; *Hände ~!* hands up!; e-e *hohe Meinung von j-m haben* think highly of a p.; *~ zu stehen kommen* cost dear; *~ lebe die Königin!* long live the queen!; ⅍ 4 ~ 3 (4^3) four in the third (power); **2. ~** *n* (11) (*~ruf*) cheer; (*Trinkspruch*) toast; *barometrisches*: high; *ein ~ auf j-n ausbringen* cheer a p., *bei Tisch*: toast a p.
ˈ**hoch|-achtbar** most respectable; ˈ**~-achten** esteem highly; ˈ**~-achtung** *f* esteem, respect; ˈ**~-achtungsvoll** (most) respectful; *adv. Briefschluß*: Yours very truly; ˈ**~-adel** *m* nobility; ˈ**~-altar** *m* high altar; ˈ**~-amt** *n* high mass; ˈ**~-antenne** *f* overhead (*od.* outdoor) aerial; ˈ**~bahn** *f* overhead railway, *Am.* elevated (railroad); ˈ**~bau** *m* surface engineering; (*Gebäude*) multi-stor(e)y building; ˈ**~beˈgabt** highly gifted; ˈ**~berühmt** very famous; ˈ**~beˈtagt** very aged, well advanced in years; ˈ**~betrieb** *m* intense activity, big rush; ˈ**~bezahlt** highly paid; ˈ**~bringen** *fig.* raise; ˈ**~brisant** *fig. Thema etc.*: explosive; ˈ**~burg** *fig. f* stronghold; ˈ**~deutsch** *n* High German; ˈ**~druck** *m* high pressure; *mit ~* at high pressure; *mit ~ arbeiten* hustle; ˈ**~drükken** push up; ˈ**~druckgebiet** *n* high (-pressure area); ˈ**~-ebene** *f* plateau, tableland; ˈ**~-empfindlich** highly sensitive; ˈ**~-entwickelt** highly developed; ˈ**~-erfreut** delighted; ˈ**~fahrend** high-handed; ˈ**~fein** very refined; ˈ**~finanz** *f* high finance; ˈ**~fliegend** high-flying, lofty; ˈ**~flut** *f* high tide; ˈ**~form** *f*: *in ~* in top form; ˈ**~format** *n* (3) upright format; ˈ**~frequenz** ⚡ *f* high frequency; ˈ**~frisur** *f* upswept hair-style; ˈ**~garage** *f* multi-stor(e)y car park; ˈ**~gebildet** highly educated; ˈ**~gebirge** *n* high mountain region, high mountains *pl.*; ˈ**~gehen** *a. Vorhang, Preise usw.*: go up, rise; *See*: run high; *Bombe, a.* F *Person*: explode; **~gemut** [ˈ~gəmu:t] high-spirited; ˈ**~genuß** *m* great enjoyment, F real treat; *mit ~* with relish; ˈ**~geschwindigkeits...** high-speed; **~gesinnt** [ˈ~gəzint] high-minded; ˈ**~gespannt** *fig. Plan usw.* ambitious; *Erwartung*: great; ˈ**~gestellt** high-ranking; ˈ**~gestochen** jumped-up, sophisticated; ˈ**~glanz** *m* high lustre; high polish; **~gradig** [ˈ~gra:diç] extreme; severe; **~hackig** [ˈ~hakiç] *Schuhe*: high-heeled; ˈ**~halten** hold up; *fig.* hono(u)r, treasure; ˈ**~haus** *n* high-rise flats *pl.*, (*Wolkenkratzer*) skyscraper; ˈ**~heben** lift (up), raise; ˈ**~herzig** generous; ˈ**~herzigkeit** *f* generosity; ˈ**~kant** on edge *od.* end; *~ stellen* upend; ˈ**~karätig** high-carat; *fig.* top-calibre; ˈ**~kommen** (sn) come up; *vom Boden usw.*: get up; *fig.* get on; ˈ**~konjunktur** *f* boom; ˈ**~land** *n* highlands *pl.*; *s. Hochebene*; ˈ**~laufen** run up; ˈ**~leben:** *~ lassen* give *a p.* three cheers; ˈ**~leistung** *f* high performance; ˈ**~leistungs...** high-power(ed); high-speed ...; heavy-duty ...
höchlich [ˈhø:çliç] highly.
ˈ**Hoch|mut** *m* haughtiness, arrogance; **~mütig** [ˈ~my:tiç] haughty, supercilious; **~näsig** F [ˈ~nɛ:ziç] stuck-up; ˈ**~-ofen** *m* blast-furnace;

ˈ**2prozentig** *Alkohol*: high-proof; ˈ**2qualifiziert** highly qualified; ˈ**2ragen** tower up, rise; ˈ**2rappeln:** *sich* ~ struggle to one's feet; ˈ**2rechnen** project, make a computer prediction of; ˈ**~rechnung** *f* projection; ˈ**2rot** flaming red; ˈ**~ruf** *m* cheer; ˈ**~saison** *f* peak season; ˈ**2schätzen** esteem highly; ˈ**2schnellen** leap up (*a. fig.*); ˈ**2schrauben** *Preise*: force up; *Forderungen*: step up; ˈ**~schule** *f* university; (*Akademie*) academy, college; *s. technisch*; ˈ**~schullehrer** *m* university (*od.* college) teacher; ˈ**~schulreife** *f* university entrance qualifications *pl.*; ˈ**2schwanger** far advanced in pregnancy; ˈ**~see** *f* high seas *pl.*; ˈ**~seefischerei** *f* deep-sea fishing; ˈ**~seeflotte** *f* high-seas fleet; ˈ**~seejacht** *f* ocean-going (*od.* sea-going) yacht; ˈ**~sitz** *hunt. m* raised hide; ˈ**~sommer** *m* midsummer; ˈ**~spannung** ⚡ *f* high tension *od.* voltage; ˈ**2spielen** F *fig.* play up; ˈ**~sprache** *f* standard language; *die deutsche* ~ standard German; ˈ**2sprachlich** standard; *nicht* ~ substandard; ˈ**~sprung** *m* high jump.

höchst [hø:çst] *allg.* highest; *fig. a.* greatest, supreme; (*äußerst*) extreme; *s. Zeit*; *adv.* highly; most, extremely; ˈ**2-alter** *n* maximum age.

Hoch|stapelei [~ʃtɑ:pəˈlaɪ] *f* (16) (high-class) swindling, imposture; ˈ**~stapler** *m* (7) impostor, confidence trickster.

ˈ**Höchstbelastung** *f* maximum load.

ˈ**hochstehend** *fig.* high(-ranking); *geistig* ~ of high intellect.

höchstens [ˈhø:çstəns] at (the) most, at best, at the outside (*bei Zahlenangaben alle nachgestellt*).

ˈ**Höchst|fall** *m*: *im* ~ *s. höchstens*; ˈ**~geschwindigkeit** *f* top (*od.* maximum) speed; ˈ**~grenze** *f* maximum limit, ceiling; ˈ**~leistung** *f Sport*: record; *e-r Fabrik*: maximum output, *e-r Maschine usw.*: *a.* maximum efficiency; ˈ**~maß** *n* maximum; ˈ**2-ˈmöglich** highest possible; ˈ**2persönlich** personal(ly); *adv. a.* in person; ˈ**~preis** *m* maximum price, ceiling price; ˈ**~stand** *m* peak (level); ˈ**2wahrscheinlich** most probably; ˈ**~wert** *m* peak (*od.* maximum) value; ˈ**~zahl** *f* maximum (number).

ˈ**Hoch|touren** *f/pl.*: *auf* ~ ⊕ at full speed *od.* pressure, *fig.* in full swing, at full blast; ˈ**2tourig** high-speed; ˈ**2trabend** high-sounding, pompous; ˈ**~- und ˈTiefbau** *m* civil engineering; ˈ**2verdient** highly deserving; ˈ**2ver-ehrt** (highly) esteemed; *~es Publikum!* ladies and gentlemen!; ˈ**~verrat** *m* high treason; ˈ**~verräter** *m* person guilty of high treason, traitor; ˈ**2verräterisch** treasonable; ˈ**~wald** *m* timber(-forest); ˈ**~wasser** *n* high water; (*Überschwemmung*) flood; ˈ**~wasserkatastrophe** *f* flood-disaster; ˈ**~wassermarke** *f* flood mark, high-water mark; ˈ**2wertig** of high value, high-class, high-grade; ˈ**~wild** *n* large game.

Hochzeit [ˈhɔxtsaɪt] *f* wedding; (*Trauung*) marriage; ˈ**2lich** nuptial, bridal; ˈ**~sgeschenk** *n* wedding present; ˈ**~snacht** *f* wedding night; ˈ**~sreise** *f* honeymoon (trip); ˈ**~s-tag** *m* wedding day; (*Jahrestag*) wedding anniversary.

Hocke [ˈhɔkə] *f* (15) ⚒ shock; *Turnen*: crouch, (*Sprung*) squat-vault; ˈ**2n** (25) squat; F (*sitzen*) sit; *sich* ~ squat (*od.* sit) down; ˈ**~r** *m* (7) (*Schemel*) stool.

Höcker [ˈhøkər] *m* (7) *zo. u.* ⚕ hump; *anat.* tubercle; *allg.* bump, knob; ˈ**2ig** bumpy; *Rücken*: hump-backed, hunchbacked.

Hockey|schläger [ˈhɔki-] *m* hockey-stick; ˈ**~spieler** *m* hockey-player.

Hode [ˈho:də] *f* (15) testicle; ˈ**~nsack** *m* scrotum.

Hof [ho:f] *m* (3[3]) court(yard), yard; (*Bauern2*) farm; *e-s Fürsten*: court; *um Sonne, Mond, a.* ⚕: halo, corona; *j-m den* ~ *machen s. hofieren*; ˈ**~dame** *f* lady at court; *im Dienst der Königin usw.*: lady-in-waiting.

Hoffart [ˈhɔfart] *f* (16) haughtiness, arrogance, pride.

hoffärtig [ˈ~fɛrtiç] haughty, proud.

hoffen [ˈhɔfən] *v/t. u. v/i.* (25) hope (*auf acc.* for); ˈ**~tlich** let us hope, I hope (that) ..., *bsd. Am.* hopefully.

Hoffnung [ˈhɔfnuŋ] *f* hope (*auf acc.* for, of); *guter* ~ *sein* be full of hope, *Frau*: be expecting a baby; *j-m* ~(*en*) *machen* raise a p.'s hopes (*auf* of); *sich ~en machen* be hopeful; (*neue*) ~ *schöpfen* gather fresh hope; *s-e* ~ *setzen auf* (*acc.*) pin one's hopes on; *e-e* ~ *zerstören* dash a hope; '≗sfreudig hopeful; '≗slos hopeless (*a. fig.*); '~sstrahl *m* ray of hope; '≗svoll hopeful; (*vielversprechend*) promising.

hofieren [ho'fi:rən] court, pay one's addresses to; *contp.* flatter, fawn (up)on.

höfisch ['hø:fiʃ] courtly.

höflich ['hø:fliç] polite, courteous, civil (*gegen* to); '**≗keit** *f* courtesy, politeness, civility; '**≗keitsbesuch** *m* courtesy call.

Höfling ['hø:fliŋ] *m* (3[1]) courtier.

'**Hof|narr** *m* court jester; '**~staat** *m* royal (*od.* princely) household; (*Gefolge*) retinue; (*Kleid*) court-dress.

Höhe ['hø:ə] *f* (15) height; ✈, *ast.*, *geogr.* altitude; (*Niveau*) level; (*Anhöhe*) hill; (*Gipfel*) summit; ♪ pitch; *e-r Summe*: amount; *e-r Strafe*: degree; ✝ *~ der Preise* level of prices; *Summe in ~ von ...* to the amount of; *auf gleicher ~ mit* on a level with; *fig. auf der ~* up to the mark, *der Zeit*: up to date; ⚓ *auf der ~ von* off; *in die ~* up, upward, aloft; *in die ~ steigen* rise; *Preise in die ~ treiben* force up, *Am.* boost; *aus der ~* from above; F *das ist die ~!* that's the limit!

Hoheit ['ho:haɪt] *f* (16) *pol.* sovereignty; *Titel*: *Seine (Ihre) ~* His (Her) Highness; *fig.* grandeur; '**~s(-ab)zeichen** *n* national emblem; '**~sgebiet** *n* territory; '**~sgewässer** *n/pl.* territorial waters; '**≗svoll** majestic(ally *adv.*).

'**Höhen|flosse** ✈ *f* stabilizer; '**~flug** *m* high-altitude flight; '**~krankheit** *f* altitude sickness; '**~kur-ort** *m* high-altitude health-resort; '**~leitwerk** ✈ *n* elevator unit; '**~linie** *f Karte*: contour line; '**~luft** *f* mountain air; '**~messer** *m* altimeter; '**~regler** *m Radio etc.*: treble control; '**~sonne** *f* Alpine sun; *Gerät*: sun-ray lamp; '**~-unterschied** *m* difference in altitude; '**≗verstellbar** with adjustable height; '**~zug** *m* hill-range.

'**Höhepunkt** *m* highest point; *ast.*, *fig.* culmination; *fig.* climax, peak; height, zenith.

höher ['hø:ər] higher (*a. fig.*); *~er Beruf* (learned) profession; *~e Mathematik* higher mathematics; *~e Schule* secondary school; *s. Gewalt*; '**≗e** *n fig.* higher things *pl.*

hohl [ho:l] hollow (*a. Klang u. fig.*); (*vertieft*) concave; *die ~e Hand* the hollow of the hand; **~äugig** ['~ʔɔʏgiç] hollow-eyed.

Höhle ['hø:lə] *f* (15) cave; (*Tier≗*) den; *bsd.* ⚕ cavity; '**≗n** hollow; '**~nforschung** *f* spel(a)eology; '**~nmensch** *m* cave-man.

'**hohlgeschliffen** hollow-ground.

'**Hohlheit** *f* hollowness.

'**Hohl|kehle** *f* channel, groove; '**~maß** *n* dry measure; '**~raum** *m* hollow (space), cavity; '**~saum** *m* hemstitched hem; '**~schliff** *m* hollow grinding; '**~spiegel** *m* concave mirror.

Höhlung ['hø:luŋ] *f* hollow, cavity.

'**Hohl|weg** *m* (narrow) pass, defile; '**~ziegel** *m* hollow brick.

Hohn [ho:n] *m* (3) scorn, derision; (*~lächeln*; *höhnische Bemerkung*) sneer; *ein ~ auf* (*acc.*) *... sein* be a mockery of; *j-m zum ~* in defiance of a p.

höhnen ['hø:nən] *v/i. u. v/t.* (25) sneer, scoff, jeer (*j-n* at a p.).

'**Hohngelächter** *n* scornful (*od.* mocking) laughter.

'**höhnisch** sneering, scornful.

'**hohn|lächeln**, '**~lachen** sneer; '**~sprechen** (*dat.*) (*trotzen*) defy; (*verspotten*) mock; *fig.* make a mockery of.

Höker ['hø:kər] *m* (7) hawker, huckster; '**≗n** (29) hawk, huckster.

Hokuspokus [ho:kus'po:kus] *m inv.* hocus-pocus; *~! a.* hey presto!

hold [hɔlt] kindly disposed (*dat.* to); (*lieblich*) lovely, sweet; *das Glück war ihm ~* fortune smiled upon him, he was lucky.

'**holdselig** lovely, sweet.

holen ['ho:lən] (25) fetch, get; go for; (*ab~*) come for, pick up; *die Polizei usw.*: call; *~ lassen* send for; *sich ~* (*sich zuziehen*) catch; *s. Atem, Rat.*

holla! ['hɔla] hey!

Holländer ['hɔlɛndər] *m* (7) Dutchman; '**~in** *f* (16[1]) Dutchwoman.

'**holländisch** Dutch.

Hölle ['hœlə] *f* (15) hell; *die ~ ist los* the fat is in the fire; *j-m die ~ heiß machen* make it hot for a p.

'**Höllen|-angst** *f* mortal fright; '**~lärm** *m* infernal noise; '**~maschine** *f* infernal machine, time bomb;

ˈ**~qual** *f* torment of hell; ˈ**~stein** ⚗ *m* lunar caustic.

ˈ**höllisch** (*a.* F *fig.*) hellish, infernal.

Holm [hɔlm] *m* (3^1) beam; (*Barren*♀) bar; ✈ spar.

holper|ig [ˈhɔlpəriç] rough, bumpy; *fig.* stumbling; ˈ**~n** (sn) *Wagen*: jolt, bump; *s. stolpern.*

Holunder [hɔˈlundər] *m* (7) elder.

Holz [hɔlts] *n* (1^1 *u.* ^{2}) wood; (*Nutz*♀) timber, *Am.* lumber; *fig. aus demselben* (*e-m anderen*) ~ *geschnitzt* of the same (of a different) stamp; ˈ**~-apfel** *m* crab-apple; ˈ**~-arbeit(en** *pl.*) *f* woodwork; ˈ♀**artig** ligneous, woody; ˈ**~-axt** *f* (felling-)ax(e); ˈ**~bau** *m* wooden structure, timber-work; ˈ**~be-arbeitung** *f* woodworking; ˈ**~bildhauer** *m* wood-carver; ˈ**~blasinstrument** *n* woodwind instrument; *die* ~*e pl. im Orchester*: the wood(-wind).

ˈ**holzen** (27) fell (*od.* cut) wood; F *Fußball*: play rough.

hölzern [ˈhœltsərn] wooden; *fig.* (*linkisch*) *a.* awkward, clumsy, stiff.

ˈ**Holz|-essig** *m* wood-vinegar; ˈ**~fäller** *m* (7) wood-cutter, *Am.* lumberman; ˈ**~faserplatte** *f* wood-fib|re (*Am.* -fiber) board; ˈ♀**frei** *Papier*: wood-free; ˈ**~hacker** *m*, ˈ**~hauer** *m* (7) wood-cutter; ˈ**~hammer** *m* mallet; F *fig.* sledge-hammer; ˈ**~handel** *m* timber-trade; ˈ**~händler** *m* timber merchant; ˈ**~haus** *n* wooden (*Am.* frame) house; ˈ♀**ig** woody; ˈ**~kohle** *f* charcoal; ˈ**~nagel** *m* wooden peg; ˈ**~platz** *m* timber (*Am.* lumber) yard; ˈ**~schliff** *m* mechanical pulp; ˈ**~schnitt** *m* woodcut; ˈ**~schnitzer** *m* wood-carver; ˈ**~schuh** *m* clog; ˈ**~span** *m* wood-chip; ˈ**~stapel** *m*, ˈ**~stoß** *m* wood-pile; ˈ**~stoff** *m* lignin; ˈ**~taube** *f* wood-pigeon; ˈ**~verkleidung** *f* timber lining; ˈ**~weg** *m* wood-path; *fig. auf dem* ~ *sein* be on the wrong track; ˈ**~werk** *n* woodwork; ˈ**~wolle** *f* wood-wool, *Am.* excelsior; ˈ**~wurm** *m* woodworm.

homogen [homoˈgeːn] homogeneous.

Homöopath [homøoˈpaːt] *m* (12) hom(o)eopathist; **~ie** [~paˈtiː] *f* (16) hom(o)eopathy; **♀isch** [~ˈpaːtiʃ] hom(o)eopathic(ally *adv.*).

Homosex|ualität [homozɛksualiˈtɛːt] *f* homosexuality; ♀**uˈell**, **~uˈelle** *m* homosexual.

Honig [ˈhoːniç] *m* (3^1) honey; ˈ**~biene** *f* honey-bee; ˈ**~kuchen** *m* gingerbread; ˈ♀**süß** honey-sweet; ˈ**~wabe** *f* honeycomb.

Honorar [honoˈraːr] *n* (3^1) fee.

Honoratioren [~raˈtsjoːrən] *m/pl.* notabilities.

honoˈrieren pay a fee (*j-n*: to; *et.*: for); *Wechsel*: hono(u)r; *fig.* show o.s. appreciative of.

Hopfen [ˈhɔpfən] *m* (6) hop; *Brauerei*: hops *pl.*; ˈ**~bau** *m* hop-culture.

hopp! [hɔp] hop!; quick!

hoppla! [ˈhɔpla] whoops!

hops [hɔps]: ~ *gehen* ⚔ *sl.* go west.

hops|a! [ˈhɔpsaː] whoops!; ˈ**~en** (27, sn) hop; ˈ♀**er** *m* (7) hop; (*Tanz*) hop-waltz.

hörbar [ˈhøːrbaːr] audible.

horch|en [ˈhɔrçən] (25) listen (*auf acc.* to); *b.s.* eavesdrop; ˈ♀**er** *m* (7) listener; *b.s.* eavesdropper; ˈ♀**gerät** *n* listening apparatus, sound detector; ˈ♀**posten** ⚔ *m* listening post.

Horde [ˈhɔrdə] *f* (15) horde, gang.

hör|en [ˈhøːrən] *v/t. u. v/i.* (25) hear (*von j-m* from); (*zu*~, *hin*~) listen; (*zufällig mit an*~) overhear; *Radio*: listen (in); *Vorlesung, Messe*: hear, attend; (*erfahren*) hear, learn; ~ *auf* (*acc.*) listen to; *schwer* ~ be hard of hearing; *sich* ~ *lassen als Künstler*: perform; *von sich* ~ *lassen* give news of o.s.; *das läßt sich* ~ there's something in that; *hören Sie mal!* I say!, *Am.* say!, listen!; *auf den Namen …* ~ answer to the name of …; *s. vergehen*; ˈ♀**ensagen** *n*: *vom* ~ by hearsay; ˈ♀**er** *m* (7) hearer; *bsd. Radio*: listener; (*Apparat*) receiver; *e-s Professors*: student; ˈ♀**erbrief** *m* letter from a listener; ˈ♀**erschaft** *f* audience; ˈ♀**frequenz** *f* audio frequency; ˈ♀**funk** *m* radio, sound broadcasting; ˈ♀**gerät** *n* (*für Schwerhörige*) hearing aid; ˈ**~ig**: *j-m* ~ *sein* be enslaved to a p.; ˈ♀**igkeit** *f* bondage.

Horizont [horiˈtsɔnt] *m* (3) horizon; (*~linie*) skyline; *seinen* ~ *erweitern* broaden one's mind; *das geht über m-n* ~ that is beyond me; ♀**al** [~ˈtaːl] horizontal.

Hormon [hɔrˈmoːn] *n* (3) hormone.

ˈ**Hörmuschel** *teleph. f* earpiece.

Horn [hɔrn] *n* (1^2) horn (*a.* ♪);

(*Signal*⌒) bugle; (*Bergspitze*) peak; (*Fühl*⌒) feeler; *fig. sich die Hörner abstoßen* sow one's wild oats; *j-m Hörner aufsetzen* cuckold a p.; '⌒**-artig** like horn, horny; '**~brille** *f* (*eine* a pair of) horn-rimmed glasses.

Hörnchen ['hœrnçən] *n* (6) small horn, cornicle; (*Gebäck*) crescent.

'**Hornhaut** *f* horny skin; *des Auges*: cornea.

Hornisse [hɔr'nisə] *f* (15) hornet.

Hor'nist *m* (12) bugler.

Horn|späne ['~ʃpɛ:nə] *m/pl.* horn parings; '**~vieh** *n* horned cattle.

Horoskop [horɔ'sko:p] *n* (3[1]) horoscope; *j-m das ~ stellen* cast a p.'s horoscope.

horrend [hɔ'rɛnt] enormous.

'**Hör-rohr** *n* ear-trumpet.

Horror ['hɔrɔr] *m* (11, *o. pl.*) horror (*vor dat.* of); '**~film** horror film.

'**Hör|saal** *m* lecture-hall; '**~spiel** *n* radio play.

Horst [hɔrst] *m* (3[2]) eyrie; *s. Flieger*⌒; '⌒**en** (26) build an eyrie.

Hort [hɔrt] *m* (3) hoard, (*sicherer Ort*) sanctuary; (*Schutz*) bulwark, stronghold, refuge; *s. Kinder*⌒; '⌒**en** (26) hoard; '**~ung** *f* hoarding.

'**Hör|verlust** *m* hearing loss; '**~weite** *f*: *in* (*außer*) *~* within (out of) hearing *od.* earshot.

Hös-chen ['hø:sçən] *n* (6) shorts *pl.*, F pants *pl.*; *s. Unterhose, Schlüpfer.*

Hose ['ho:zə] *f* (15) *mst ~n pl.* (*eine* a pair of) trousers, F *od. Am.* pants *pl.*; (*Damen*⌒) slacks *pl.*; (*Knie*⌒) breeches *pl.*; (*kurze ~*) shorts *pl.*; *fig.* F *die ~n anhaben* wear the trousers *od.* pants; *s. Herz, Jacke, kurz.*

'**Hosen|-anzug** *m* trouser suit, pant(s) suit; '**~bein** *n* trouser-leg; '**~boden** *m* (trouser-)seat; '**~rock** *m* (a pair of) culottes *pl.*, pant skirt; '**~rolle** *f* breeches part; '**~schlitz** *m* fly; '**~tasche** *f* trouser pocket; '**~träger** *m* (*a. pl.*) (*ein* a pair of) braces *pl.*, *Am.* suspenders *pl.*

Hospit|al [hɔspi'tɑ:l] *n* (1[2] *u.* 3[1]) hospital; **~ant** [~'tant] *m* (12), **~antin** *f* guest student.

Hospiz [hɔs'pi:ts] *n* (3[2]) hospice.

Hostie ['hɔstjə] *f* (15) host, eucharistic wafer.

Hotel [ho'tɛl] *n* (11) hotel; **~ier** [~'je:] *m* (11), **~besitzer(in** *f*) *m* hotel proprietor; **~boy** *m* (11), **~page** *m* (13) page(-boy), *Am.* bellboy; **~direktor** *m* hotel manager; **~führer** *m* hotel guide; **~gewerbe** *n* hotel industry; **~halle** *f* foyer, lobby.

hott! [hɔt], **hü!** [hy:] gee up!

Hub [hu:p] *m* (3[3]) lift; ⊕ (*Kolben*⌒) stroke.

hüben ['hy:bən] on this side.

'**Hub|pumpe** *f* lifting pump; '**~raum** *m* piston displacement; '**~raumsteuer** *f* tax on engine volume.

hübsch [hypʃ] pretty; (*a.* = *beträchtlich*) handsome; (*nett*) nice; (*anziehend*) attractive, good-looking.

'**Hubschrauber** ✈ *m* helicopter; '**~landeplatz** *m* heliport, helipad.

huckepack ['hukəpak] pick-a-back.

hudeln ['hu:dəln] (29) scamp one's work.

Huf [hu:f] *m* (3) hoof; '**~beschlag** *m* shoeing; *a.* = '**~-eisen** *n* horseshoe; '**~lattich** ⚘ *m* coltsfoot; '**~nagel** *m* hobnail; '**~schlag** *m* horse's kick; (*Geräusch*) hoof-beat; '**~schmied** *m* farrier; '**~tier** *n* hoofed mammal, ungulate.

Hüft|bein ['hyft-] *n* hip-bone; '**~e** *f* (15) hip; '**~gelenk** *n* hip-joint; '**~gürtel** *m* suspender (*Am.* garter) belt; '**~halter** *m* roll-on girdle; '⌒**lahm** hip-shot; '**~-umfang** *m* hip-measurement; '**~weh** *n* sciatica.

Hügel ['hy:gəl] *m* (7) hill, hillock; '⌒**ig** hilly; '**~land** *n* hilly country.

Huhn [hu:n] *n* (1[2]) hen, *a. Küche*: chicken; *junges ~*, **Hühnchen** ['hy:nçən] *n* (6) pullet, chicken; *ein ~ zu rupfen haben mit* have a bone to pick with.

Hühner|-auge ['hy:nər-] *n* corn; '**~brühe** *f* chicken-broth; '**~-ei** *n* hen's egg; '**~habicht** *m* goshawk; '**~hof** *m* chicken-run, *Am.* -yard; '**~hund** *m* pointer; '**~leiter** *f* roost-ladder; '**~schrot** *n* partridge-shot; '**~stall** *m* hen-house; '**~vögel** *m/pl.* gallinaceous birds *pl.*; '**~zucht** *f* chicken-farming.

hui! [hui] whoosh!; (*erstaunt*) ooh!; *in e-m* ⌒ in a trice *od.* flash.

Huld [hult] *f* (16) grace, favo(u)r.

huldig|en ['~digən] (25) pay homage; *fig.* pay tribute to; *e-m Laster usw.*: indulge in.

huld|reich, ~voll ['hult-] gracious.

Hülle ['hylə] *f* (15) cover(ing), wrap, envelope; (*Schleier*) veil; *in ~ und*

Fülle in abundance, plenty of; *die sterbliche* ~ the mortal frame; '⁀n (25) cover, wrap (up); (*kleiden*) clothe; *fig.* shroud; *in Nebel usw.*: envelop.

Hülse ['hylzə] *f* (15) hull, husk; (*Schote*) pod; (*Gehäuse, a.* ⚔) case, shell; ⊕ sleeve; (*Steck*⁀) socket; '**~nfrucht** *f* legume; '**~nfrüchte** *f/pl. a.* pulse.

human [hu'mɑ:n] humane; ⁀**ismus** [huma'nismus] *m* (16, *o. pl.*) humanism; **~istisch** [~'nistiʃ] humanistic, classical; **~itär** [~ni'tɛ:r] humanitarian; ⁀**ität** [~ni'tɛ:t] *f* (16) humanity.

Humbug ['humbuk] *m* (6, *o. pl.*) humbug.

Hummel ['huməl] *f* (17) bumble-bee.

Hummer ['humər] *m* (7) lobster.

Humor [hu'mo:r] *m* (3¹) (sense of) humo(u)r; **~eske** [~mo'rɛskə] *f* (15) humorous sketch; **~ist** [~'rist] *m* (12) humorist; *thea.* comedian; ⁀**istisch** [~'ristiʃ], ⁀**voll** humorous.

humpeln ['humpəln] (29, h. *u.* sn) hobble, limp.

Humpen ['humpən] *m* (6) tankard.

Humus(**erde** *f*) ['hu:mus(ˀe:rdə)] *m* (16, *o. pl.*) vegetable mo(u)ld.

Hund [hunt] *m* (3) dog (*a.* ⚒; *a. fig. v. Menschen*); (*Jagd*⁀) hound; *Schimpfwort*: cur; *da liegt der* ~ *begraben* there's the rub; *fig. auf den* ~ *kommen* reach rock-bottom; *vor die* ~*e gehen* go to the dogs; F *wie* ~ *und Katze leben* lead a cat-and-dog life.

Hunde|**-abteil** 🚂 ['hundə-] *n* dog-box; '**~ausstellung** *f* dog-show; '⁀'**-elend** F: *sich* ~ *fühlen* feel lousy; '**~hütte** *f* dog-kennel; '**~kälte** F *f* biting cold; '**~kuchen** *m* dog-biscuit; '**~leben** F *n* dog's life; '**~leine** *f* (dog-)lead, leash; '**~loch** F *n* dog-hole; '**~marke** *f* dog-tag; '⁀'**müde** dog-tired; '**~peitsche** *f* dog-whip; '**~rasse** *f* dog-breed.

hundert ['hundərt] (a) hundred; *4 vom* ⁀ four per cent (4%); *zu* ⁀*en* by hundreds; '⁀**er** *m* (7) hundred; **~erlei** ['~ər'laɪ] of a hundred different sorts; '**~fach**, **~fältig** ['~fɛltiç] hundredfold; **~gradig** ['~grɑ:diç] centigrade; ⁀'**jahrfeier** *f* centenary, *Am.* centennial; '**~jährig** centenary; '**~mal** a hundred times; ⁀'**markschein** *m* hundred-mark (bank-)note; '**~prozentig** a hundred per cent; *fig. a.* absolute(ly *adv.*); '⁀**satz** *m* percentage; '**~st** hundredth; '⁀**stel** *n* (7) one hundredth (part); '**~weise** by hundreds.

'**Hunde**|**wetter** *n* filthy weather; '**~zucht** *f* dog-breeding; (*~zwinger*) kennel (of dogs).

Hündin ['hyndin] *f* she-dog, bitch.

'**hündisch** *fig.* servile.

Hunds|**fott** ['huntsfɔt] *m* (1²) scoundrel; '⁀**gemein** dirty, mean; '⁀-**mise'rabel** F lousy; **~tage** ['~tɑ:gə] *m/pl.* dog-days.

Hüne ['hy:nə] *m* (13) giant; '**~ngestalt** *f* (person of) Herculean stature; '**~ngrab** *n* megalithic grave; '⁀**nhaft** gigantic.

Hunger ['huŋər] *m* (7) hunger (*fig. nach* for); ~ *bekommen* get hungry; ~ *haben* be hungry; ~*s sterben* starve (to death); '**~kur** *f* fasting cure; '**~leider** *m* (7) starveling; '**~lohn** *m* starvation wage(s *pl.*), *a.* pittance.

'**hungern** (29) hunger (*fig. nach* for), be hungry; (*schlecht leben*) starve; *freiwillig*: starve o.s., fast; *j-n* ~ *lassen* starve a p.

Hunger|**ödem** ⚕ ['~ˀø'de:m] *n* (3¹) hunger (o)edema; '**~snot** *f* famine; '**~streik** *m* hunger-strike; '**~tod** *m* (death from) starvation; '**~tuch** *n*: *am* ~ *nagen* be starving.

'**hungrig** hungry (*fig. nach* for).

Hupe ['hu:pə] *f* (15) horn, hooter; '⁀**n** (25) hoot, honk.

hüpfen ['hypfən] (25, sn) hop, skip.

Hürde ['hyrdə] *f* (15) hurdle; (*Pferch*) fold, pen; '**~nlauf** *m*, '**~nrennen** *n* hurdle-race, hurdles *pl.*; '**~nläufer** *m* hurdler.

Hure ['hu:rə] *f* (15) whore, prostitute; '⁀**n** (25) whore; **~rei** [~'raɪ] *f* (15) whoring; prostitution.

hurra! [hu'rɑ:] hurrah!; ⁀**patriot** *m* patrioteer, jingo(ist); ⁀**patriotismus** *m* patrioteering, jingoism.

hurtig ['hurtiç] quick, swift; (*flink und gewandt*) agile, nimble; '⁀**keit** *f* swiftness, quickness; agility.

Husar [hu'zɑ:r] *m* (12) hussar.

husch! [huʃ] (*plötzlich*) in a flash; *scheuchend*: shoo!; '**~en** (27, sn) scurry, whisk, flit.

hüsteln ['hy:stəln] **1.** (29) cough slightly; **2.** ⁀ *n* (6) slight cough.

husten ['hu:stən] **1.** (26) cough; F *fig.* ~ *auf* (*acc.*) not to care a rap; *ich werde dir was* ~*!* go to hell! **2.** ♀ *m* (6) cough; '♀**-anfall** *m* coughing fit; '♀**bonbon** *m* cough drop; '♀**reiz** *m* urge to cough; '♀**-saft** *m* cough-mixture.

Hut[1] [hu:t] *m* (3[3]) hat; *den* ~ *abnehmen* take off one's hat (*fig. vor j-m* to a p.); ~ *ab!* hat(s) off (*vor* to)!; *fig. unter einen* ~ *bringen* reconcile; F *ihm ging der* ~ *hoch* he blew his top.

Hut[2] *f* (16) (*Obhut, Aufsicht*) care, charge; (*Schutz*) protection; *auf der* ~ *sein s.* (*sich*) *hüten.*

hüten ['hy:tən] (26) (*bewachen*) guard, watch (over); *Vieh*: tend; *s. Bett*; *sich* ~ be on one's guard (*vor dat.* against), look (*Am.* watch) out (for); *sich* ~ *zu tun* be careful not to do; *hüte dich vor ...* beware of ...

'**Hüter** *m* (7), '~**in** *f* keeper, guardian; (*Vieh*♀) herdsman.

'**Hut|futter** *n* hat-lining; '~**geschäft**, *n*, '~**laden** *m* hat shop; '~**krempe** *f* brim (of a hat); '~**macher** *m* hatter; '~**schachtel** *f* hat-box; '~**schnur** *f* hat-string; F *das geht über die* ~ that's (really) too much!

Hütte ['hytə] *f* (15) hut, cabin; (*Bude*) shanty, *Am.* F shack; ⊕ *s. Hüttenwerk.*

'**Hütten|-erz** *n* dressed ore; '~**käse** *m* cottage cheese; '~**kunde** *f* metallurgy; '~**werk** *n* metallurgical plant, smelting-works; '~**wesen** *n* metallurgy.

Hyäne [hy'ɛ:nə] *f* (15) hyena.

Hyazinthe [hya'tsintə] *f* (15) hyacinth.

hybrid [hy'bri:t], ♀**e** [~də] *f*, *m* hybrid.

Hydrant [hy'drant] *m* (12) hydrant, fire-plug.

Hydrauli|k [hy'draulik] *f* (16) hydraulics *pl.*; ♀**sch** hydraulic(ally *adv.*).

hydrieren [hy'dri:rən] hydrogenate.

Hygien|e [hy'gje:nə] *f* (15) hygiene, *a.* hygienics *pl.*; ♀**isch** hygienic(ally *adv.*), sanitary.

Hymne ['hymnə] *f* (15) hymn.

hypermodern ['hypər-] hyper- *od.* ultra-modern.

Hyperbel [hy'pɛrbəl] *f* (15) ⩕ hyperbola; *rhet.* hyperbole.

Hypno|se [hyp'no:zə] *f* (15) hypnosis; ♀**tisch** hypnotic; ~**tiseur** [~noti'zø:r] *m* (3[1]) hypnotist; ♀**ti'sieren** hypnotize.

Hypochon|der [hypo'xɔndər] *m* (7) hypochondriac; ~'**drie** *f* hypochondria; ♀**drisch** hypochondriacal.

Hypotenuse ⩕ [~te'nu:zə] *f* (15) hypotenuse.

Hypothek [~'te:k] *f* (16) mortgage; *e-e* ~ *aufnehmen* raise a mortgage; *mit* ~*en belastet* mortgaged; ♀**arisch** [~te'kɑ:riʃ] hypothecary; *adv.* by (*od.* on) mortgage; ~**enbank** [~'te:kən-] *f* mortgage bank; ~**enbrief** *m* mortgage(-deed); ~**engläubiger** *m* mortgagee; ~**enpfandbrief** *m* mortgage debenture (*od.* bond); ~**enschuldner** *m* mortgagor.

Hypothe|se [hypo'te:zə] *f* (15) hypothesis; ♀**tisch** hypothetic(al).

Hysterie [hyste'ri:] *f* (15) hysteria.

hysterisch [~'ste:riʃ] hysterical.

I

I [i:], **i** *n inv.* I, i.

i! why!; *i nun!* well!; *i freilich!* of course!; *i wo!* certainly not!, not at all!

iah! [i:ɑ:], ♀ *n* (*Eselsschrei*) hee-haw.

Iamb|e ['jambə] *f* (15), ~**us** ['~us] *m* (16[2]) iambus; '♀**isch** iambic.

ich [iç] **1.** (19) I; ~ *bin's!* it is I!, F it's me!; **2.** ♀ *n inv.* self; ego; '~**bezogen** egocentric; *in der* '♀**form** *f* in the first person (singular); '♀**sucht** *f* selfishness.

Ideal [ide'ɑ:l] **1.** *n* (3[1]) ideal; F *fig. a.* dream; **2.** ♀ *adj.* ideal; ~**fall** *m* ideal state of affairs; *im* ~ ideally; ♀**i'sieren** [~ali-] idealize; ~**ismus** [~'lismus] *m*

(16, *o. pl.*) idealism; **~ist** [~'list] *m* (12), **~istin** *f* (16¹), **2istisch** idealist; **~vorstellung** *f* ideal.

Idee [i'de:] *f* (15) idea, notion; *gute ~* good idea!; *ich kam auf die ~ zu inf.* I got the idea to *inf.*, it occurred to me to *inf.*

ideell [ide'ɛl] ideal, imaginary.

I'deen|losigkeit *f* lack of ideas *od.* imagination; **2reich** full of ideas *od.* imagination.

identi|fizieren [idɛntifi'tsi:rən] identify; **2fi'zierung** *f* identification; **~sch** [i'dɛntiʃ] identical; **2tät** [~'tɛ:t] *f* (16) identity; **2'tätsnachweis** *m* proof of identity.

Ideo|logie [ideolo'gi:] *f* (16) ideology; **2logisch** [~'lo:giʃ] ideological.

Idiom [idi'o:m] *n* (3¹) idiom; (*Sprache*) language; **2atisch** [~o-'ma:tiʃ] idiomatic.

Idiot [idi'o:t] *m* (12) idiot; **~en-arbeit** *f* donkey work; **~enhang, ~enhügel** *co. m* nursery slope; **2ensicher** foolproof; **~ie** [~o'ti:] *f* (15) idiocy; **2isch** [~'o:tiʃ] idiotic(al).

Idol [i'do:l] *n* (3¹) idol.

Idyll [i'dyl] *n* (3¹), **~e** *f* (15) idyl(l); **2isch** idyllic(ally *adv.*).

Igel ['i:gəl] *m* (7) hedgehog; ⚔ = **'~stellung** *f* allround defen|ce, *Am.* -se; hedgehog position.

Ignor|ant [igno'rant] *m* (12) ignorant person, ignoramus; **~anz** [~'rants] *f* (16) ignorance; **2ieren** [~'ri:rən] ignore, take no notice of.

ihm [i:m] (to) him; *S.*: (to) it.

ihn [i:n] him; *S.*: it.

'ihnen (to) them; 2 (to) you.

ihr [i:r] **1.** (*dat. von sie sg.*) (to) her; (*nom. pl. von du, im Brief* 2) you; **2.** (20) *besitzanzeigend*: her; *S.* its; *pl.* their; 2 your; **3.** *der* (*die, das*) *~e od. ~ige* ['~igə] hers; *pl.* theirs; *der* (*die, das*) *2e, 2ige* yours.

ihrerseits ['~ərzaɪts] on her (*pl.* their, 2 your) part.

ihresgleichen [~əs'glaɪçən] the like(s) of her *od.* them; their like; her (*od.* their) equals.

ihret|halben ['i:rəthalbən], **'~wegen,** (*um*) **'~willen** for her (*pl.* their, 2 your) sake; on her (their, 2 your) account.

ihrig ['i:riç] *s. ihr* 3.

illegal ['ilega:l] illegal.

illegitim [ilegi'ti:m] illegitimate.

illuminieren [ilumi'ni:rən] illuminate.

Illu|sion [ilu'zjo:n] *f* illusion; **2sorisch** [~'zo:riʃ] illusory.

Illu|stration [ilustra'tsjo:n] *f* illustration; **~strator** [ilu'stra:tɔr] *m* illustrator; **2strieren** [~'stri:rən] illustrate; **~'strierte** *f* (illustrated) magazine.

Iltis ['iltis] *m* (4¹) fitchew, polecat.

im [im] = *in dem* in the.

imaginär [imagi'nɛ:r] imaginary.

Imbiß ['imbis] *m* (4) snack; **'~stube** *f* snack-bar.

Imit|ation [imita'tsjo:n] *f* imitation; **2ieren** [~'ti:rən] imitate.

Imker ['imkər] *m* (7) bee-master; **~ei** [~'raɪ] *f* (7) bee-farming.

Immatrikul|ation [imatrikula-'tsjo:n] *f* registration, enrol(l)ment; **2ieren** [~'li:rən] (*a. sich ~ lassen*) register, enrol(l).

immer ['imər] always; *auf ~, für ~* for ever, for good; *~ mehr* more and more; *~ noch* still; *~ noch nicht* not yet, not even now; *~ weiter* on and on, *reden usw.*: keep *talking, etc.*; *~ wieder* again (*od.* time) and again; **~dar** ['~da:r] always, for ever; **'~fort** always, continually; **'2grün** *n* evergreen; **'~'hin** still, yet; **'~während** everlasting, perpetual; **'~'zu** always.

Immobilien [imo'bi:ljən] *pl. inv.* immovables *pl.*, real estate *sg.*; **~fonds** *m* real estate investment trust; **~makler** *m s. Grundstücksmakler*; **~markt** *m* property market.

immun [i'mu:n] immune (*gegen* from); **~i'sieren** immunize; **2ität** [~'tɛ:t] *f* (16) immunity (from).

Imperativ ['imperati:f] *m* (3¹) imperative (mood); **2isch** [~'ti:viʃ] imperative.

Imperfekt(um) ['impɛrfɛkt(um)] *n* (3 [9²]) imperfect tense.

Imperialis|mus [imperja'lismus] *m* (16, *o. pl.*) imperialism; **2tisch** imperialist(ic).

impertinen|t [impɛrti'nɛnt] impertinent, insolent; **2z** [~'nɛnts] *f* (16) impertinence.

Impf|-arzt ['impf-] *m* vaccinator; **'2en** (25) ⚕ vaccinate, (*a.* ✓) inoculate; **'~ling** *m* (3¹) person due to be vaccinated; **'~paß** *m* vaccination document; **'~pistole** *f* vaccination gun; **'~schein** *m* vaccination certif-

icate; '~**stoff** *m* vaccine; '~**ung** *f* ⚕ vaccination; *a.* ✓ inoculation.
Imponderabilien [impɔndera'bi:ljən] *n/pl. inv.* imponderables.
imponieren [impo'ni:rən]: *j-m* ~ impress a p. strongly; ~**d** imposing.
Import [im'pɔrt] *m* (3) import (-ation); *konkret*: = ~**e** *pl.* imports; ~**beschränkungen** *f/pl.* import restrictions; ~**eur** [~'tø:r] *m* (3[1]) importer; ℒ**ieren** [~'ti:rən] import; ~**ware** *f einzelne*: imported article; *als Sammelbegriff*: imported goods *pl.*
imposant [impo'zant] imposing.
impoten|t ['impotɛnt] impotent; ℒ**z** [~ts] *f* (16) impotence.
imprägnier|en [imprɛ:g'ni:rən] impregnate; (*wasserdicht machen*) (water)proof; ℒ**ung** *f* impregnation.
Impresario [impre'zɑ:rio] *m* (11) impresario, manager.
improvisieren [improvi'zi:rən] improvise.
Impuls [im'puls] *m* (4) impulse; ℒ**iv** [~'zi:f] impulsive; ~ *handeln* act on impulse, act on the spur of the moment.
imstande [im'ʃtandə]: ~ *sein* be able.
in [in] (*acc.*) in, into; (*dat.*) in, at; (*innerhalb*) within.
In'-angriffnahme *f* (15) taking in hand, tackling.
In'-anspruchnahme *f* (15) *e-s Rechts usw.*: laying claim (*gen.* to), assertion (of); (*Benutzung*) utilization; (*Zuhilfenahme*) resort (to); *v. Geldmitteln, Kraft, Material usw.*: strain (*gen.* on); (*Anforderungen*) demands *pl.* (*gen.* on).
'**Inbegriff** *m* essence; (*Verkörperung*) embodiment; (*Muster*) paragon; 'ℒ**en** included, inclusive of.
Inbe'sitznahme *f* taking possession, occupation.
Inbe'triebnahme *f* putting into operation, starting, opening.
'**Inbrunst** *f* (14[1]) ardo(u)r, fervo(u)r.
'**inbrünstig** ardent, fervent.
in'dem whilst, while; (*dadurch, daß*) *mst* by *mit Gerundium*; ~ *er mich ansah, sagte er* looking at me he said.
Inder ['indər] *m* (7), '~**in** *f* (16[1]) Indian.
in'des(sen) **1.** *adv.* meanwhile; **2.** *cj.* while; (*jedoch*) however, yet.
Index ['indɛks] *m* (3[2], *sg. a. inv., pl. a.* '*Indizes*) (*Verzeichnis, a.* ~*ziffer*) index.
Indianer [in'djɑ:nər] *m* (7) Red Indian.
indifferent ['indifərɛnt] indifferent.
indigniert [indi'gni:rt] indignant.
Indigo ['indigo] *m, n* (11) indigo.
Indikation ⚕ [indika'tsjo:n] *f* indication.
Indikativ ['indikati:f] *m* (3[1]) indicative (mood); ℒ**isch** [~'ti:viʃ] indicative.
indirekt ['indirɛkt] indirect; *gr.* ~*e Rede* reported speech.
indisch ['indiʃ] Indian.
indiskret ['indiskre:t] indiscreet; ℒ**ion** [~e'tsjo:n] *f* (16) indiscretion.
indiskutabel ['indiskutɑ:bəl] *pred.* out of the question.
indisponiert ['indisponi:rt] indisposed, unwell.
Individualist [individua'list] *m* individualist; ℒ**isch** individualist(ic).
Individu|alität [~li'tɛ:t] *f* (16) individuality; ℒ'**ell** individual; ~**um** [~'vi:duum] *n* (9) individual.
Indizienbeweis [in'di:tsjənbəvaɪs] *m* circumstantial evidence.
Indoss|ament ⚓ [indɔsa'mɛnt] *n* (3) endorsement; ~**ant** [~'sant] *m* (12) indorser; ~**at** [~'sɑ:t] *m* (12) endorsee; ~**ieren** [~'si:rən] endorse.
Induktion [induk'tsjo:n] *f* induction; ~**sstrom** ⚡ *m* induced current.
industrialisier|en [industriali'zi:rən] industrialize; ℒ**ung** *f* industrialization.
Industrie [~'stri:] *f* (15) industry; ~**-anlage** *f* industrial plant; ~**-arbeiter** *m* industrial worker; ~**ausstellung** *f* industrial exhibition; ~**denkmal** *n* industrial monument; ~**-erzeugnis** *n* industrial product; ~**gebiet** *n* industrial area.
industriell [~stri'ɛl] industrial; ℒ**e** *m* (13) industrialist.
Indu'strie|magnat [~magnɑ:t] *m* (12) business magnate, tycoon; ~**müll** *m* industrial refuse (*od.* waste); ~**nation** *f* industrial nation; ~**roboter** *m* industrial robot; ~**staat** *m* industrial nation; ~**zeit-alter** *n* industrial age; ~**zweig** *m* (branch of) industry.
in-ei'nander into one another; ~**greifen** ⊕ interlock, intermesh; ~**schieben** (*a. sich*) telescope.
infam [in'fɑ:m] shameful; ℒ**ie** [~fa'mi:] *f* (15) infamy.

Infanter|ie [~ə'riː] *f* (15) infantry; **~ist** [~'rist] *m* (12) infantryman.
infantil [infan'tiːl] infantile.
Infarkt [in'farkt] ⚕ *m* (3) infarct.
Infektion [infɛk'tsjoːn] *f* infection; **~sgefahr** *f* danger of infection; **~s-herd** *m* focus of infection; **~skrankheit** *f* infectious disease; **~s-träger** (**-in** *f*) *m* infection agent (*od.* carrier).
Infinitiv ['infinitiːf] *m* (3¹) infinitive (mood); **2isch** [~'tiːviʃ] infinitive.
infizieren [infi'tsiːrən] infect.
Inflation [infla'tsjoːn] *f* (16) inflation; **2är** [~tsjo'nɛːr] inflationary; **2istisch** [~tsjo'nistiʃ] inflationary; **~s-ausgleich** *m* indexation, *Am.* indexing; **~s-politik** *f* inflationary policy (*od.* policies *pl.*); **~srate** *f* rate of inflation.
Influenza [~flu'ɛntsa] *f inv.* influenza, F flu.
infolge [in'fɔlgə] (*gen.*) in consequence of, as a result of, owing to, due to; **~'dessen** consequently, as a result.
Informatik [infɔr'maːtik] *f* (16, *o. pl.*) information (*od.* computer) science; **~er**(**in** *f*) *m* information scientist (*od.* specialist).
Inform|ation [infɔrma'tsjoːn] *f* (16) information; **2ativ** [~'tiːf] informative; **2atorisch** [~'toːriʃ] informatory; **2ieren** [~'miːrən] inform; *falsch* ~ misinform.
infra|rot ['infraroːt] infrared; **2rot-bestrahlung** ⚕ [infra'roːt~] *f* infrared heat treatment; **2rot-Fernbedienung** [infra'roːt~] *f* infrared remote control (unit); **'2schall...** infrasonic; **'2struktur** *f* infrastructure.
Infusorien [infu'zoːrjən] *n/pl.* infusoria.
In'gangsetzung *f* starting.
Ingenieur [inʒe'njøːr] *m* (3¹) engineer; **~schule** *f* engineering college.
'Ingrimm *m* (3) anger, wrath; **'2ig** wrathful, furious.
Ingwer ['iŋvər] *m* (7) ginger.
Inhaber ['inhaːbər] *m* (7), **'~in** *f* (16¹) holder; (*Eigentümer*) owner, proprietor; (*Wohnungs2*) occupant; (*Laden2*) keeper; *e-s Amtes, e-r Aktie, e-s sportlichen Titels od. Preises usw.*: holder; *e-s Wechsels, Schecks*: bearer; **'~aktie** *f* bearer share; **'~scheck** *m* bearer cheque (*Am.* check).
Inhalation [inhala'tsjoːn] *f* (16) inhalation; **~s-apparat** *m* inhaler.
inha'lier|en inhale; **2gerät** *n* inhalator.
'Inhalt *m* (3) contents *pl.* (*a. fig.*); (*Gehalt*) content; (*Raum2*) capacity; (*Körper2*) volume; *e-r Rede, Urkunde usw.*: tenor, content; *des ~s, daß ...* to the effect that; **'~s-angabe** *f* summary; **'2slos** empty; **'2sreich** copious; significant; pregnant; **'2s-schwer** momentous; **'~s-verzeichnis** *n* table of contents, index.
Initiale [ini'tsjaːlə] *f* (15) initial.
Initiative [initsja'tiːvə] *f* (15) initiative; *die ~ ergreifen* take the initiative; *aus eigener ~* of one's own accord, on one's own initiative.
Injektion [injɛk'tsjoːn] *f* injection, F shot.
injizieren [inji'tsiːrən] inject.
Inkasso [in'kaso] *n* (11) encashment, collection.
Inkognito [~'kɔgnito] *n* (11), **2** *adv.* incognito.
inkonsequen|t ['inkɔnzəkvɛnt] inconsistent; **2z** ['~ts] *f* inconsistency.
'inkorrekt incorrect.
In'krafttreten *n* (6) coming into force; *Tag des ~s* effective day.
inkriminieren [inkrimi'niːrən] incriminate.
Inkubationszeit ⚕ [inkuba'tsjoːns-tsaɪt] *f* incubation period.
'Inland *n* (1) inland; (*Ggs. Ausland*) home (*od.* native) country; **'~...** home, domestic, internal.
Inländer ['inlɛndər] *m* (7), **'~in** *f* inlander; (*Ggs. Ausländer*) native.
'Inlandflug *m* domestic flight.
'inländisch native, indigenous; domestic; *Handel*: inland; ✝ *Erzeugnis*: home-made.
'Inlaut *m* (3) medial sound.
Inlett ['inlɛt] *n* (3¹) bedtick; **'~stoff** *m* ticking.
'inliegend enclosed.
in'mitten (*gen.*) in the midst of, amidst, *Am. mst* amid.
inne ['inə] within; **'~haben** *Rekord, Stelle*: hold; *Amt, Wohnung*: occupy; **'~halten** *v/i.* stop, pause; *v/t.* keep to, observe.
innen ['inən] (*innerhalb*) (on the) inside, within; (*im Hause*) within doors; *nach ~* inwards; *von ~* from within, from the inside.

ˈ**Innen|-ansicht** *f* interior view; ˈ**~-antenne** *f* indoor aerial *od.* antenna; ˈ**~-architekt** *m* interior decorator; ˈ**~-architektur** *f* interior decoration; ˈ**~-aufnahme** *phot. f* indoor photograph *od.* shot; ˈ**~-ausstattung** *f* interior equipment; ˈ**~dekoration** *f* interior decoration; ˈ**~leben** *n* inner life; ˈ**~leuchte** *mot. f* courtesy light; ˈ**~minister** *m* Minister of the Interior; *Brt.* Home Secretary; *Am.* Secretary of the Interior; ˈ**~ministerium** *n* Ministry of the Interior; *Brt.* Home Office; *Am.* Department of the Interior; ˈ**~politik** *f* home politics *pl.*; *bestimmte*: domestic policy; ˈ**≗politisch** home affairs ..., domestic (political) ...; *adv.* with regard to home affairs; ˈ**~raum** *m* interior; ˈ**~seite** *f* inner side, inside; ˈ**~spiegel** *mot. m* driver's (*od.* rear-view) mirror; ˈ**~stadt** *f* town (*od.* city) cent|re, *Am.* -er, *Am. a.* downtown.

inner [ˈinər] interior; (*innerlich*) inward, inner; *a.* ⚕, *pol.* internal; ⊕ *a.* inside; *~e Angelegenheit* internal affair; *~e Stimme* inner voice; ˈ**~betrieblich** internal, *Am. a.* in-plant; ˈ**≗e** *n* interior; *fig.* (*Geist*) mind; *Minister(ium) des ~n s. Innenminister(ium)*; **≗eien** [~ˈraɪən] *f/pl.* offal(s); ˈ**~halb** *prp.* (*gen.*) within; *adv.* (on the) inside; ˈ**~lich** *s. inner*; *P.*: introspective, contemplative; ˈ**~parteilich** intra-party; internal.

ˈ**innerst** inmost; ˈ**≗e** *n the* innermost (part); *fig. the* very heart.

ˈ**innewerden** (*gen.*) perceive, become aware of.

ˈ**innewohnen** *v/i.* be inherent (*dat.* in); ˈ**~d** inherent (*dat.* in).

innig [ˈiniç] (*herzlich*) hearty; (*tief empfunden*) heartfelt, profound; (*inbrünstig*) ardent, fervent; (*zärtlich*) tender; *Beziehung*: intimate; ˈ**≗keit** *f* heartiness; fervo(u)r; intimacy.

Innung [ˈinuŋ] *f* (16) guild, corporation.

inoffiziell [ˈinˀɔfitsjɛl] unofficial.

ins [ins] = *in das* into the.

Insasse [ˈinzasə] *m* (13) inmate, occupant; *e-s Wagens usw.*: *a.* passenger.

insbesondere [insbəˈzɔndərə] in particular; especially.

ˈ**Inschrift** *f* inscription; *e-r Münze usw.*: legend.

Insekt [inˈzɛkt] *n* (5) insect; **~enkunde** *f* entomology; **~enpulver** *n* insect-powder.

Insektizid [inzɛktiˈtsiːt] *n* (3) insecticide, pesticide.

Insel [ˈinzəl] *f* (15) island; ˈ**~bewohner(in** *f*) *m* islander; ˈ**~gruppe** *f* archipelago; ˈ**~staat** *m* insular state.

Inser|at [inzəˈrɑːt] *n* (3) advertisement, F ad; *ein ~ aufgeben* put an ad in; **≗ieren** [~ˈriːrən] advertise.

ins|geˈheim secretly; **~geˈmein** generally; **~geˈsamt** altogether.

Insignien [inˈzigniən] *pl.* insignia.

insofern [inˈzoːfɛrn] *adv.* so far; *cj. ~ als* as (*a.* so) far as, in so far as, in that.

insolven|t [ˈinzɔlvɛnt] insolvent; ˈ**≗z** [~ts] *f* (16) insolvency.

Inspekteur [inspɛkˈtøːr] *m* (3[1]) inspector; ⚔ Chief of the Army (*od.* Air Force *od.* Navy) Staff.

Inspektion [inspɛkˈtsjoːn] *f* (16) inspection; (*Amt*) inspectorate; **~sreise** *f* tour of inspection.

Inspektor [~ˈʃpɛktɔr] *m* (8[1]) inspector; (*Aufseher*) overseer.

Inspir|ation [inspiraˈtsjoːn] *f* inspiration; **≗ieren** [~ˈriːrən] inspire.

Inspiz|ient *thea.* [~ˈtsjɛnt] *m* (12) stage-manager; **≗ieren** [~ˈtsiːrən] inspect, superintend.

Install|ateur [instalaˈtøːr] *m* (3[1]) installer, plumber; *für Gas*: gas fitter; **~ation** [~ˈtsjoːn] *f* (15) installation, plumbing; **≗ieren** [~ˈliːrən] install.

instand [inˈʃtant]: *~ halten* maintain, keep up; *~ setzen et.*: repair, restore; (*wieder ~ setzen*) *a.* recondition, *Am.* fix; **≗haltung** *f* maintenance, upkeep.

ˈ**inständig** urgent, instant.

Inˈstandsetzung *f* repair(ing), restoration; reconditioning.

Instanz [inˈstants] *f* (16) instance; ⚖ court of *first etc.* instance; *letzte ~* last resort; **~enweg** *m* stages *pl.* of appeal; *s. Dienstweg.*

Instinkt [inˈstiŋkt] *m* (3) instinct; **≗mäßig**, **≗iv** [~ˈtiːf] instinctive.

Institut [~stiˈtuːt] *n* (3) institute.

Institution [~lstituˈtsjoːn] *f* institution.

instru|ieren [~struˈiːrən] instruct; **≗ktion** [~strukˈtsjoːn] *f* (15) instruction; **~ktiv** [~ˈtiːf] instructive.

Instrument [~stru'mɛnt] *n* (3) instrument; **~almusik** [~'tɑ:l-] *f* instrumental music; **~enbrett** *n* instrument panel, dashboard; **~enflug** instrument flying; **⁓ieren** ♪ [~'ti:rən] instrument, score.

Insulaner [inzu'lɑ:nər] *m* (7) islander.

inszenier|en [instse'ni:rən] (put on the) stage; *fig.* stage; **⁓ung** *f* staging.

intakt [in'takt] intact.

Integralrechnung 𝔄 [inte'grɑ:l-rɛçnuŋ] *f* integral calculus.

Inte|gration [integra'tsjo:n] *f* integration; **⁓grieren** [~'gri:rən] integrate; *~der Bestandteil* integral part.

intellektuell [intɛlɛktu'ɛl], **⁓e** *m, f* (18) intellectual, F highbrow.

intelligen|t [~li'gɛnt] intelligent; **⁓z** [~ts] *f* (16) intelligence; **⁓zbestie** F *f* egghead; **⁓zquotient** *m* intelligence quotient, I. Q.; **⁓ztest** *m* intelligence test.

Intendant [intɛn'dant] *m* (12) superintendent; *thea.* director.

Inten|sität [intɛnzi'tɛ:t] *f* (16, *o. pl.*) intensity; **⁓siv** [~'zi:f] intensive; **~'sivkurs** *m* crash course; **~'sivstation** ⚕ *f* intensive care unit.

Intercity 🚂 [intər'siti] *m* (11) inter--city train.

interessant [intərɛ'sant] interesting.

Interesse [intə'rɛsə] *n* (10) interest (*an dat., für* in); **⁓los** uninterested, indifferent; **~ngebiet** *n* field of interest; **~ngemeinschaft** *f* community of interests; (*Kartell*) pool, combine; **~ngruppe** *pol. f* pressure group, lobby.

Interess|ent [~'sɛnt] *m* (12) interested party; *für e-n Kauf*: prospect; **~envertretung** [~'rɛsən-] *f* representation of interests; **⁓ieren** [~'si:rən] interest (*für* in); *sich ~ für* take an interest in; *interessiert sein an* (*dat.*) be interested in.

'Interims|regierung *f* provisional *od.* interim government; **'~schein** ✝ *m* scrip.

interkontinental [intɛrkɔntinɛn-'tɑ:l] intercontinental; **⁓rakete** *f* intercontinental ballistic missile.

intern [in'tɛrn] internal.

Internat [~'nɑ:t] *n* (3) boarding--school.

inter|national [intɛrnatsjo'nɑ:l] international; **~'nieren** intern; **⁓'nierte** *m* internee; **⁓'nierung** *f* internment; **⁓'nierungslager** *n* internment camp; **⁓'nist** ⚕ *m* (12) internal specialist; **~pellieren** [~pɛ'li:rən] interpellate; **~plane'tarisch** interplanetary; **⁓pretation** [~preta'tsjo:n] *f* interpretation; **~pretieren** [~pre'ti:rən] interpret; **⁓punktion** [~puŋk'tsjo:n] *f* (16) punctuation; **⁓punk'tionszeichen** *n* punctuation mark; **⁓vall** [~'val] *n* (3) interval; **~venieren** [~ve'ni:rən] intervene; **⁓vention** [~vɛn-'tsjo:n] *f* intervention; **⁓view** [~'vju:] *n* (11[1]), **~viewen** (25) interview.

Interzonen|handel [intər'tso:nən-handəl] *m* interzonal trade; **~paß** *m* (inter)zonal pass *od.* permit; **~verkehr** *m* interzonal traffic.

intim [in'ti:m] intimate (*mit* with); **⁓ität** [~timi'tɛ:t] *f* (16) intimacy; **⁓sphäre** *f* privacy.

intoleran|t ['intolərant] intolerant; **'⁓z** [~ts] *f* (16) intolerance.

intransitiv ['intranziti:f] intransitive.

intravenös ⚕ [intrave'nø:s] intravenous.

intrigant [~tri'gant] **1.** intriguing; **2.** ⁓ *m* (13), **⁓in** *f* (16[1]) intriguer.

Intrig|e [in'tri:gə] *f* (15) intrigue; **⁓ieren** [~'gi:rən] intrigue, plot.

introvertiert [introvɛr'ti:rt] introverted.

intus F ['intus]: *et. ~ haben* have got a th. into one's head; (*Essen etc.*) have downed a th.; *e-n ~ haben* have had one too many.

Invalide [inva'li:də] *m* (13) invalid; *engS.* disabled worker *od.* soldier *od.* sailor; **~nrente** *f* disability pension; **~nversicherung** *f* disablement insurance.

Invalidität [invalidi'tɛ:t] *f* disablement, disability.

Invasion [~va'zjo:n] *f* invasion.

Inventar [~vɛn'tɑ:r] *n* (3[1]) inventory, stock; *lebendes und totes ~* live and dead stock; **⁓isieren** [~tari'zi:rən] inventory.

Inventur [~'tu:r] *f* (16) stock--taking; *~ machen* take stock; **~-ausverkauf** *m* stock-taking sale.

investier|en ✝ [~vɛs'ti:rən] invest **⁓ung** *f* investment.

Investition [invɛsti'tsjo:n] *f* investment; **~s-anreiz** *m* investment incentive.

Investment [inˈvɛstmənt] *n* (11) investment; **~fonds** *m* investment fund.
inwärts [ˈinvɛrts] inwards.
ˈ**inwendig** inward.
inwieˈfern, inwieˈweit (in) how far.
ˈ**Inzucht** *f* (16) inbreeding.
inˈzwischen in the meantime, meanwhile; (*seither*) since.
Ion *phys.* [ˈiˀɔn] *n* (8) ion.
ird|en [ˈirdən] earthen; ˈ**~isch** earthly; (*weltlich*) worldly; (*sterblich*) mortal.
Ire [ˈiːrə] *m* (13) *s. Irländer.*
irgend [ˈirgənt] *in Zssgn* some; *allg. u. bei Frage u. Verneinung* any; *so rasch wie ~ möglich* as soon as ever possible; *wenn ich ~ kann* if I possibly can; ˈ**~-ein,** ˈ**~-eine,** ˈ**~-eins** some; any; ˈ**~-einer,** ˈ**~ ˈjemand,** ˈ**~wer** somebody, someone; anybody, anyone; ˈ**~-einmal** some time; ˈ**~ ˈetwas** something; anything; ˈ**~ˈwann** some time (or other); ˈ**~ˈwie** somehow; anyhow; ˈ**~ˈwo** somewhere; anywhere; ˈ**~-woˈher** from somewhere; from anywhere; ˈ**~woˈhin** somewhere; anywhere.
irisch [ˈiːriʃ] Irish.
Irländer [ˈirlɛndər] *m* (7) Irishman; ˈ**~in** *f* (16[1]) Irishwoman.
Iron|ie [iroˈniː] *f* (15) irony; **⁓isch** [iˈroːniʃ] ironic(al).
irrational [ˈiratsjonɑːl] irrational.
irre [ˈirə] **1.** astray; *fig.* wrong; (*verwirrt*) confused; (*verrückt*) lunatic, mad, ⚕ insane; *sl.* (*ausgefallen*) way-out; *~ werden* get confused; *~ werden an* (*dat.*) not to know what to make of, begin to doubt; **2.** ⁓ *m, f* (18) insane person, lunatic; F *wie ein ~r* like mad; **3.** ⁓ *f* (15): *in der* (*od. die*) *~* astray; ˈ**~führen** lead astray; *fig. a.* mislead; ˈ**~gehen** (sn) go astray; ˈ**~machen** puzzle, bewilder; perplex, confound.
irren [ˈirən] (25) err, go astray; (*umherschweifen*) wander; *geistig*: err, make a mistake (*a. sich*); *sich ~* be mistaken (*in dat.* in *a p.*, about *a th.*); be wrong.
ˈ**Irren|-arzt** *m* mental specialist, alienist; ˈ**~haus** *n*, ˈ**~(heil)-anstalt** *f* lunatic asylum, mental home.
ˈ**irrereden** rave.
ˈ**Irr|fahrt** *f* wandering; ˈ**~gang,** ˈ**~garten** *m* labyrinth, maze; ˈ**⁓gläubig** heretical.
ˈ**irrig** erroneous; (*falsch*) false, wrong.
irritieren [iriˈtiːrən] (*ärgern*) irritate; (*be-irren*) puzzle, intrigue.
ˈ**Irr|lehre** *f* false doctrine, heterodoxy; (*Ketzerei*) heresy; ˈ**~licht** *n* will-o'-the-wisp, jack-o'-lantern; ˈ**~pfad** *m* wrong path; ˈ**~sinn** *m* insanity; ˈ**⁓sinnig** insane, mad; ˈ**~tum** *m* (1[2]) error, mistake; *im ~ sein* be mistaken; *in e-m ~ befangen sein* labo(u)r under a mistake; *Irrtümer vorbehalten* errors excepted; **⁓tümlich** [ˈ~tyːm-] erroneous; ˈ**~ung** *f* error, mistake; ˈ**~weg** *m* wrong way; ˈ**~wisch** *m s. Irrlicht*; F *P.*: flibbertigibbet.
Ischias ⚕ [ˈisçias, ˈiʃ-] *f* F *a. n, m inv.* sciatica.
Islam [isˈlɑːm] *m* (11) Islam(ism).
Isländ|er [ˈiːslɛndər] *m* Icelander; ˈ**⁓isch** Icelandic.
Isolation [izolaˈtsjoːn] *f* isolation; *von Häftlingen*: confinement; ⚡ insulation.
Isolator ⚡ [izoˈlɑːtɔr] *m* (8[1]) insulator.
Isolier... ⚡ [~ˈliːr] insulating; **~band** *n* insulating tape; **⁓en** isolate; ⚡ insulate; **~haft** *f* solitary confinement; **~kanne** *f* thermos jug; **~station** ⚕ *f* isolation ward; **~ung** *f* isolation; ⚡ insulation.
isometrisch [izoˈmeːtriʃ] isometric; *~e Übungen* isometrics *pl.*
Isotop ⚗ [izoˈtoːp] *n* (3) isotope.
Israel|i [israˈeːli] *m* (11) Israeli; **~it** [~eˈliːt] *m* (12) Israelite.
Ist|bestand [ˈist-] *m* actual inventory *od.* stock; ˈ**~stärke** *f* effective strength; ˈ**~wert** *m* actual value.
Italien|er [italˈjeːnər] *m* (7) Italian; **~erin** *f* Italian (woman); **⁓isch** Italian.
ˈ**I-Tüpfelchen** *n fig.*: *bis aufs ~* to a T.

J

J [jɔt], **j** *n inv.* J, j.
ja [jaː] yes; ~ *freilich* yes, indeed; to be sure; ~ *sogar*, ~ *selbst* even; *wenn* ~ if so; ~ *sagen* say yes, consent; *er ist* ~ *mein Freund* why, he is my friend; *da ist er* ~! well, there he is!; *ich sagte es Ihnen* ~ I told you so; *tun Sie es* ~ *nicht!* don't you do it!; *vergessen Sie es* ~ *nicht!* be sure not to forget it!
Jacht [jaxt] *f* (16) yacht.
Jäckchen [ˈjɛkçən] *n* (6) (short) jacket, coatee.
Jacke [ˈjakə] *f* (15) jacket; *fig.* F *das ist* ~ *wie Hose* that's six of one and half a dozen of the other; ˈ**~nkleid** *n* lady's suit.
Jackett [ʒaˈkɛt] *n* (11) jacket.
Jagd [jaːkt] *f* (16) hunt(ing); *mit der Flinte*: shooting; (*Verfolgung*) chase, *s. Jagdbezirk*; *fig.* hunt (*nach* for); *weitS.* pursuit (of); *die* ~ *aufnehmen* give chase; *auf* ~ *gehen* go hunting *od.* shooting; ~ *machen auf* (*acc.*) hunt after *od.* for; ˈ**~-aufseher** *m* gamekeeper; ˈ**2bar** fit for hunting, fair; ˈ**~berechtigung** *f* shooting; ˈ**~bezirk** *m* shoot, hunting-ground; ˈ**~bomber** ⚔ *m* fighter-bomber; ˈ**~büchse** *f* sporting rifle; ˈ**~flieger** *m* fighter pilot; ˈ**~flinte** *f* sporting gun; *leichte*: fowling-piece; ˈ**~flugzeug** *n* fighter; ˈ**~geschwader** *n* fighter wing (*Am.* group); ˈ**~gesellschaft** *f* hunting (*od.* shooting) party; ˈ**~haus** *n* shooting (*od.* hunting) lodge; ˈ**~horn** *n* bugle, hunting-horn; ˈ**~hund** *m* hound; ˈ**~hütte** *f* shooting (*od.* hunting) box; ˈ**~messer** *n* hunting knife; ˈ**~pächter** *m* game-tenant; ˈ**~recht** *n* game-laws *pl.*; hunting right(s *pl.*); ˈ**~rennen** *n* steeple-chase; ˈ**~revier** *n s. Jagdbezirk*; ˈ**~schein** *m* shooting-licenc|e, *Am.* -se; ˈ**~schloß** *n* hunting seat.
jagen [ˈjaːgən] *v/i.* (25) hunt; (*rennen usw.*) rush, dash; *fig.* ~ *nach* hunt after; *v/t.* hunt; (*hetzen*) chase, *fig. a.* rush; (*weg*~) drive away, turn out (*aus dem Hause* of doors); *Messer in den Leib usw.*: drive, thrust; *Kugel*: send; *s. Flucht, Luft.*
Jäger [ˈjɛːgər] *m* (7) hunter, sportsman; (*Wildhüter*) gamekeeper; ⚔ rifleman; ✈ fighter; **~ei** [~ˈraɪ] *f* (16) hunting; **~in** [ˈ~rin] *f* huntress; ˈ**~latein** *n* sportsman's slang; (*Aufschneiderei*) huntsman's yarn.
Jaguar [ˈjaːguaːr] *m* (3[1]) jaguar.
jäh [jɛː] abrupt; (*steil*) *a.* precipitous, steep; (*plötzlich*) *a.* sudden; **~lings** [ˈ~liŋs] precipitously; (*plötzlich*) suddenly.
Jahr [jaːr] *n* (3) year; *ein halbes* ~ half a year, six months; *einmal im* ~ once a year; *im* ~ *1900* in 1900; *mit* (*od. im Alter von*) *18* ~*en* at the age of eighteen; *letztes* ~ last year; *bei* ~*en* advanced in years; *das ganze* ~ *hindurch od. über* all the year round; *s. hinaus*; 2ˈ**-aus:** ~, *jahrein* year in, year out; ˈ**~buch** *n* yearbook, annual.
ˈ**jahrelang** for years.
jähren [ˈjɛːrən] (*sich*) (25) be a year ago.
ˈ**Jahres...** *in Zssgn mst* annual, yearly; ˈ**~-abschluß** ✝ *m* annual statement of accounts; ˈ**~bericht** *m* annual report; ˈ**~-einkommen** *n* annual income; ˈ**~-ergebnis** ✝ *n* annual balance; ˈ**~feier** *f* anniversary; ˈ**~gehalt** *n* annual salary; ˈ**~tag** *m* anniversary; ˈ**~wechsel** *m*, ˈ**~wende** *f* turn of the year; ˈ**~zahl** *f* date, year; ˈ**~zeit** *f* season.
ˈ**Jahr|gang** *m e-r Zeitschrift*: annual set; *v. Menschen u. Tieren*: age-class; *v. Wein*: vintage; **~ˈhundert** *n* century; 2ˈ**hunderte-alt** centuries old.
jährig [ˈjɛːriç] a year old; **...~** ...-year-old.
ˈ**jährlich** annual, yearly.
ˈ**Jahr|markt** *m* fair; **~ˈtausend** *n* millennium; **~ˈtausendfeier** *f* millenary; **~ˈzehnt** *n* (3[1]) decade.
Jähzorn [ˈjɛːtsɔrn] *m* (*Ausbruch*) sudden anger; (*Eigenschaft*) irascibility; ˈ**2ig** hot-tempered, irascible.
Jakob [ˈjaːkɔp]: F *der wahre* ~ the real McCoy.
Jalousie [ʒaluˈziː] *f* (15) Venetian blind, *Am. a.* window shade.
ˈ**Jamb|e**, ˈ**~us**, ˈ**2isch** *s.* Iambe *usw.*
Jammer [ˈjamər] *m* (7) lamentation; (*Elend*) misery; *es ist ein* ~ it is a great pity; ˈ**~bild** *n* picture of misery; ˈ**~geschrei** *n* lamentation; ˈ**~gestalt** *f* miserable figure; ˈ**~lappen** *contp. m* F sissy.

jämmerlich ['jɛmərliç] miserable, wretched.
jammern ['jamərn] (29) lament (*um* for; *über acc.* over); (*ächzen, wimmern*) wail, whine; *er jammert mich* I pity him.
'**Jammer...**: *es ist* '**~**'**schade** it is a great pity; '**~tal** *n* vale of tears; '**~voll** *s. jämmerlich.*
Jänner, Januar ['jɛnər, 'janua:r] *m* (3[1]) January.
Japan|er [ja'pa:nər] *m* (7), **~erin** *f* (16[1]), **~isch** Japanese.
jappen ['japən], **japsen** ['japsən] (27) gasp, pant.
Jargon [ʒar'gõ] *m* (11) jargon, slang.
Jasager ['ja:za:gər] *m* (7) yes-man.
Jasmin [jas'mi:n] *m* (3[1]) jasmine.
Jaspis ['jaspis] *m* (4[1]) jasper.
'**Ja-stimme** *parl. f* aye, *Am.* yea.
jäten ['jɛ:tən] *v/t. u. v/i.* (26) weed.
Jauche ['jauxə] *f* (15) liquid manure.
jauchzen ['jauxtsən] **1.** (27) shout with joy, jubilate, exult; **2.** **~** *n* (6) jubilation, exultation.
jaulen ['jaulən] (25) howl.
ja'wohl yes(, indeed).
'**Jawort** *n* (1) consent; *e-m Freier das ~ geben* accept a suitor.
Jazz [jats, dʒɛz] *m* (3[2]) jazz; '**~-kapelle** *f* jazz band.
je [je:] ever, at any time; (*beziehungsweise*) respectively; *~ nachdem* a) *adv.* as the case may be, it depends, b) *cj.* according as; *~ zwei* two at a time, (*zu zweien*) in pairs, by twos; *er gab den drei Knaben ~ zwei Äpfel* he gave the three boys two apples each; *für ~ zehn Wörter* for every ten words; *~ eher, ~ lieber* the sooner the better; *~ mehr, ~ (od. desto) besser* the more the better.
Jeans [dʒi:ns] *pl.* (11) jeans; '**~-anzug** *m* denim suit.
jede ['je:də], '**~r** (*s. a. jedermann*), '**~s** (21) every; *von e-r Gruppe*: each; *von zweien*: either; (*~ beliebige*) any; *jeden zweiten Tag* every other day; '**~nfalls** at all events, in any case; '**~rmann** everyone, everybody; '**~rzeit** always, at any time; '**~s**'**mal** each (*od.* every) time; *~ wenn* whenever.
je'doch however, yet, nevertheless.
jedweder ['je:tve:dər], **jeglicher** ['je:kliçər] *s. jeder.*
jeher ['je:'he:r]: *von ~* at all times.
jemals ['je:ma:ls] ever, at any time.
jemand ['je:mant] (24) somebody, someone; *bei Frage u. Verneinung*: anybody, anyone; *s. sonst.*
jene ['je:nə], '**~r**, '**~s** (21) that; (*Ggs. dieser*) the former.
jenseitig ['jɛnzaɪtiç] opposite.
'**jenseit(s)** **1.** *adv.* on the other side; **2.** *prp.* (*gen.*) on the other side of, beyond; **3.** **~** *n the* other world, *the* beyond.
Jesuit [jezu'ʔi:t] *m* (12) Jesuit; **~isch** Jesuitic(al).
jetzig ['jɛtsiç] present, existing; (*gegenwärtig*) actual, current.
jetzt [jɛtst] now, at present; *für ~* for the present; *von ~ an* from now on; '**~zeit** *f*: *die ~* the present (time), the present day.
jeweil|ig ['je:vaɪliç] respective; *der ~e Präsident usw.* the president *etc.* of the day; '**~s** at a time; respectively, in each case.
Jiu-Jitsu ['dʒi:u'dʒitsu] *n* j(i)u-jitsu.
Joch [jɔx] *n* (3; *im pl. als Maß inv.*) yoke; (*Berg~*) pass; ⚠ bay; '**~bein** *n* cheek-bone.
Jockei ['dʒɔki] *m* (11) jockey.
Jod [jo:t] *n* (3) iodine.
jod|eln ['jo:dəln] (29) yodel; '**~ler** *m* (7) yodel(l)er; (*Jodelruf*) yodel.
Jodoform [jodo'fɔrm] *n* (11) iodoform.
Jodtinktur ['jo:t-] *f* tincture of iodine.
Joga ['jo:ga] *m* (11[1], *o. pl.*) yoga.
Joghurt ['jɔgurt] *m, n* (3[1], *o. pl.*) yog(ho)urt.
Johanni [jo'hani:], **~s** [~is] *n inv.* St. John's Day, Midsummer (Day) (*auch* **~s-tag** *m*, **~sfest** *n*); **~sbeere** *f* (red) currant; **~sbrot** *n* carob.
johlen ['jo:lən] (25) bawl, howl.
Jolle ['jɔlə] *f* (15) jolly(-boat).
Jon|gleur [ʒɔŋ'glø:r] *m* (3[1]) juggler; **~**'**glieren** juggle (*a. fig.*).
Joppe ['jɔpə] *f* (15) jacket.
Journal [ʒur'na:l] *n* (3[1]) journal; **~ismus** [~na'lismus] *m* (16, *o. pl.*) journalism; **~ist** [~na'list] *m* (12), **~istin** *f* (16[1]) journalist.
jovial [jovi'a:l] jovial.
Jubel ['ju:bəl] *m* (7) jubilation, rejoicing; '**~feier** *f*, '**~fest** *n* jubilee; '**~n** (29) shout with joy, rejoice, exult (*alle*: *über acc.* at).
Jubil|ar [ju:bi'la:r] *m* (3[1]), **~arin** *f* person celebrating his (her) jubilee; **~äum** [~'lɛ:um] *n* (9) jubilee; **~äumsband** *m* anniversary edition.

juchhe(i)! [jux'heː, ~'haɪ] hurray!, whoopee!

Juchten ['juxtən] *n*, *m* (6) Russia leather.

jucken ['jukən] (25) itch; *fig.* es juckt mich zu *inf.* I'm itching to *inf.*

Jude ['juːdə] *m* (13) Jew; der ewige ~ the Wandering Jew; '**~ntum** *n* (1[2]) Judaism; *coll.* Jewry; '**~nverfolgung** *f* Jew-baiting.

Jüd|in ['jyːdin] *f* Jewess; '**♀isch** Jewish.

Judo ['juːdo] *n* (11[[1]], *o. pl.*) judo.

Jugend ['juːgənt] *f* (16) youth; '**~-alter** *n* (days *pl.* of) youth; '**~-amt** *n* Youth Welfare Office; '**~buch** *n* book for young people; '**~-erinnerung** *f* reminiscence from one's youth; '**~freund(in** *f*) *m* friend of one's youth; '**~fürsorge** *f* youth welfare; '**~gericht** *n* juvenile court; '**~herberge** *f* youth hostel; '**~jahre** *n/pl.* early years, youth; '**~kraft** *f* youthful strength; **~kriminalität** ['~kriminali'tɛːt] *f* juvenile delinquency; '**♀lich** youthful; juvenile; '**~liche** *m*, *f* (18) juvenile, young person; '**~liebe** *f* first love, *co.* calf-love; '**~schutz** *m* protection of the young; '**~stil** *m* *Kunst*: Art Nouveau (*fr.*); '**~streich** *m* youthful prank; '**~sünde** *f* sin of one's youth; '**~werk** *n* *e-s Autors*: early work; ~e *pl. a.* juvenilia; '**~zeit** *f* youth.

Jugoslaw|e [juːgo'slɑːvə] *m* (13), **~in** *f* (16[1]), **♀isch** Yugoslav.

Juli ['juːli] *m* (11) July.

jung [juŋ] (18[2]) young; (*jugendlich*) youthful; *fig.* young, new, fresh; ~ bleiben stay young; '**♀brunnen** *m* fountain of youth.

'**Junge 1.** *m* (13) boy, lad; *Kartenspiel*: knave; **2.** *n* (18) young; ein ~s a young one; *Hunde♀*: puppy; *Katzen♀*: kitten; *Raubtier♀*: cub; '**♀n** (25) bring forth young; *Katze*: have kittens; '**♀nhaft** boyish; '**~nstreich** *m* boyish prank.

jünger ['jyŋər] **1.** younger; junior; er ist drei Jahre ~ als ich he is three years younger than I, he is my junior by three years; **2.** ♀ *m* (7) disciple (*a. bibl.*), follower.

Jungfer ['juŋfər] *f* (15) virgin, maid(en); (*ledige Frau*) spinster; alte ~ old maid.

jüngferlich ['jyŋfərliç] maidenly.

'**Jungfern|fahrt** *f* maiden voyage; '**~rede** *f* maiden speech; '**~schaft** *f* (16) virginity, maidenhood.

'**Jung|frau** *f* maid; *engS.* virgin; *ast.* Virgin, Virgo; **♀fräulich** ['~frɔʏliç] maiden(ly), virginal; *fig. Boden, Schnee usw.*: virgin; '**~geselle** *m* bachelor; '**~gesellenstand** *m* bachelorhood; '**~gesellin** *f* bachelor girl.

Jüngling ['jyŋliŋ] *m* (3[1]) youth, young man; '**~s-alter** *n* youth.

jüngst [jyŋst] **1.** *adj. sup.* youngest; *Ereignis, Zeit*: recent, latest; ♀er Tag, ♀es Gericht doomsday, Last Judg(e)ment; **2.** *adv.* recently, lately, of late.

'**Jungwähler** *pol. m* young voter.

Juni ['juːni] *m* (11) June.

junior ['juːnjɔr] junior.

Junker ['juŋkər] *m* (7) young nobleman; (*Land♀*) squire.

Jupiterlampe ['juːpitər-] *f* *Film*: Jupiter lamp, *Am. a.* klieg light.

Jura[1] ['juːra] (*pl. v.* Jus): ~ studieren study law.

Jura[2] *geol.* ['juːra] *m* (11, *o. pl.*) Jurassic (period).

Jurist [ju'rist] *m* (12) lawyer, jurist; (*Student*) law-student; **♀isch** legal, juridical, of (the) law; ~e Person legal entity, body corporate.

Jury [ʒy'riː, 'juːri] *f* (11[1], *pl. a.* Juries) jury.

Jus [juːs] *n* law; *s.* Jura.

just [just] just; (*eben erst*) just now; **~ieren** ⊕ [~'tiːrən] adjust; **♀ierung** [~'tiːruŋ] *f* adjustment.

Justiz [ju'stiːts] *f* (16) justice; **~beamte** *m* officer of justice; **~gewalt** *f* judicial power; **~-irrtum** *m* judicial error; **~minister** *m* Minister of Justice, *Brt.* Lord Chancellor, *Am.* Attorney General; **~ministerium** *n* Ministry of Justice, *Brt.* Lord Chancellor's Office(s *pl.*), *Am.* Department of Justice; **~mord** *m* judicial murder; **~rat** *m* *Brt.* King's (*od.* Queen's) Counsel (*abbr.* K.C., Q.C.); **~wesen** *n* judicial system, judiciary.

Jute ['juːtə] *f* (15) jute.

Juwel [ju'veːl] *n* (5[2]) jewel; gem (*a. fig.*); **~en** *n/pl.* jewels, jewel(le)ry *sg.*; **~ier** [juve'liːr] *m* (3[1]) jewel(l)er; **~iergeschäft** [~ve'liːr-] *n* jewel(l)er's shop.

Jux F [juks] *m* (3[2]) joke, prank, F lark.

K

K [ka:], **k** *n inv.* K, k.
Kabale [ka'ba:lə] *f* (15) cabal, intrigue.
Kabarett [kaba'rɛt] *n* (3^1) cabaret; (*~vorführung*) cabaret (show), *Am.* floor show; *satirisches*: (satirical) review; **~ist** [~rɛ'tist] *m* (12) review artiste.
Kabel ['ka:bəl] *n* (7) cable; '**~-anschluß** *m* cable connection; '**~fernsehen** *n* cable television.
Kabeljau ['ka:bəljaʊ] *m* (3^1 *u.* 11) cod(fish).
'**kabel|n** (29) cable; '**2netz** *n* cable network.
Kabine [ka'bi:nə] *f* (15) cabin; (*Abteil*) compartment; (*Fahrstuhl*) cage; ✈ (*Führerraum*) cockpit.
Kabinett [kabi'nɛt] *n* (7) cabinet (*a. pol.*); *als Raum a.* closet; **~ssitzung** *f* cabinet meeting; **~s-umbildung** *f* cabinet reshuffle.
Kabriolett [kabrio'lɛt] *n* (3) cabriolet, *bsd. Am.* convertible.
Kachel ['kaxəl] *f* (15) (Dutch) tile; '**2n** tile; '**~-ofen** *m* tiled stove.
Kadaver [ka'da:vər] *m* (7) carcass; **~gehorsam** *m* blind obedience.
Kader ['ka:dər] ⚔ *m* (7) cadre (*a. fig.*).
Kadett [ka'dɛt] *m* (12) cadet; **~enschiff** *n* cadet ship.
Kadi ['ka:di] F *m* (11) judge, *the* court.
Käfer ['kɛ:fər] *m* (7) beetle, *Am.* bug.
Kaff [kaf] F *n* (11) god-forsaken place.
Kaffee ['kafe] *m* (11) coffee; ~ *verkehrt* milk with a dash; '**~bohne** *f* coffee-bean; '**~gebäck** *n* cakes to serve with coffee; '**~haus** *n* coffee-house; '**~kanne** *f* coffee-pot; '**~klatsch** F *m* hen-party; '**~löffel** *m* tea-spoon, coffee-spoon; '**~maschine** *f* coffee-percolator; '**~mühle** *f* coffee-mill *od.* -grinder; '**~rösterei** *f* coffee-roasting establishment; '**~satz** *m* coffee-grounds *pl.*; '**~tasse** *f* coffee-cup; '**~wärmer** *m* (coffee-pot) cosy.
Käfig ['kɛ:fiç] *m* (3) cage.
kahl [ka:l] bald; *fig. a.* bare, naked; *Baum*: bare; *Landschaft*: barren; '**2heit** *f* baldness; *fig. a.* bareness; barrenness; '**2kopf** *m* bald head; bald-headed person; **~köpfig** ['~kœpfiç] bald-headed; '**2schlag** *m* complete deforestation; (*Lichtung*) clearing.
Kahn [ka:n] *m* (3^3) boat; *kleiner*: skiff; (*Last2*) barge; F (*Gefängnis*) clink, jug.
Kai [kaɪ] *m* (11), '**~-anlage** *f* quay, wharf; '**~gebühr** *f* wharfage; '**~meister** *m* wharfinger.
Kaiser ['kaɪzər] *m* (7) emperor; '**~-adler** *m* imperial eagle; '**~in** *f* (16^1) empress; '**~krone** *f* imperial crown; '**2lich** imperial; *die* '**~lichen** *pl.* the Imperialists; '**~reich** *n*, **~tum** ['~tu:m] *n* (1^2) empire; '**~schnitt** ⚕ *m* Caesarean (section).
Kajak ['ka:jak] ⚓ *m, n* (11) kayak.
Kajüte [ka'jy:tə] *f* (15) cabin.
Kakadu ['kakadu:] *m* (3^1 *u.* 11) cockatoo.
Kakao [ka'ka:o] *m* (11) cocoa; F *j-n durch den ~ ziehen* (*necken*) pull a p.'s leg, (*schlechtmachen*) run a p. down.
Kakerlak ['ka:kərlak] *m* albino; *Insekt*: cockroach.
Kaktee [kak'te:ə] *f* (15), **Kaktus** ['~tus] *m* (14, *pl. Kak'teen* [15]) cactus.
Kalamität [kalami'tɛ:t] *f* (16) calamity.
Kalauer ['ka:laʊər] *m* (7) stale joke *od.* pun, Joe Miller.
Kalb [kalp] *n* (1^2) calf; **2en** ['~bən] (25) calve.
kalbern, kälbern ['kalbərn, 'kɛlbərn] *v/i.* (29) *fig.* frolic.
Kalb|fell ['kalp-] *n* calfskin; '**~fleisch** *n* veal; '**~leder** *n* calf(-leather); *in ~ gebunden* calf-bound.
'**Kalbs|braten** *m* roast veal; **~bries(chen)** ['~bri:s(çən)] *n*, **~bröschen** ['~brø:sçən] *n*, '**~milch** *f* calf's sweetbread; '**~keule** *f* leg of veal; '**~kotelett** *n* veal chop; '**~nierenbraten** *m* loin of veal; '**~schnitzel** *n* veal cutlet.
Kaldaunen [kal'daʊnən] *f/pl.* (15) tripe(s *pl.*) *sg.*
Kalender [ka'lɛndər] *m* (7) calendar, almanac; **~jahr** *n* calendar year; **~methode** *f bei Empfängnisverhütung*: rhythm method.
Kali ['ka:li] *n* (11) potash, potassium carbonate.

Kalib|er [ka'li:bər] *n* (7) cali|bre, *Am.* -ber (*a. fig.*), bore; (*Maß*) ga(u)ge; **²rieren** ⊕ [~li'bri:rən] calibrate, ga(u)ge.

Kalium ['ka:lium] *n* (11) potassium.

Kalk [kalk] *m* (3) lime; (*Tünche*) whitewash; (*~putz*) lime plaster; *physiol.* calcium; (*un*)*gelöschter ~* (un)slaked lime; '**~brenner** *m* lime-burner; '**²en** (25) (*tünchen*) whitewash; ✓ lime; '**~-erde** *f* calcareous earth; '**²ig** limy; '**~mangel** ⚕ *m* calcium deficiency; '**~-ofen** *m* lime-kiln; '**~stein** *m* limestone.

Kalkulation [kalkula'tsjo:n] *f* calculation.

kalkulieren [kalku'li:rən] calculate.

Kalorie *phys.* [kalo'ri:] *f* (15) calorie; **²nreich** [~'ri:ən-] rich in calories; **~nwert** *m* calorific value.

kalt [kalt] (18²) cold (*a. fig.*); *bsd. geogr., a. fig.* frigid; *~er Krieg* cold war; *~e Küche, ~e Platte* cold meats *od.* dishes *pl.*; *mir ist ~* I am (*od.* feel) cold; *j-m die ~e Schulter zeigen* give a p. the cold shoulder; *das läßt mich ~* that leaves me cold.

kaltblütig ['~bly:tiç] cold-blooded (*a. fig.*); *adv.* in cold blood; '**²keit** *f* cold blood, sangfroid (*fr.*).

Kälte ['kɛltə] *f* (15) cold, chill (*a. fig.*); *fig.* coldness; '**²beständig** cold-resistant; '**~-einbruch** *m* sudden cold spell; '**~-erzeuger** *m*, '**~maschine** *f* refrigerator; '**~grad** *m* degree of frost; '**~technik** *f* refrigeration engineering; '**~welle** *f* cold wave, *bsd. Am.* cold snap.

'**kalt|herzig** cold-hearted; '**²leim** *m* cold glue; '**²luft** *f* cold air; '**~machen** F: *j-n ~* (*ermorden*) bump a p. off; '**²schale** *f* cold beer (*od.* fruit *od.* wine) soup; **~schnäuzig** ['~ʃnɔʏtsiç] cool; '**~schweißen** cold-weld; '**²start** *mot. m* cold start; '**~stellen** keep cool, put on ice; *fig.* relegate to the background, shelve.

Kalt'wasserkur *f* coldwater cure.

kalzinieren ⚗ [kaltsi'ni:rən] calcine.

kam [ka:m] *pret. v. kommen.*

Kamel [ka'me:l] *n* (3) camel; **~garn** *n* mohair; **~haar** *n* camel hair (*a.* ✝).

Kamera *phot.* ['kamәra] *f* (11¹) camera.

Kamerad [kamə'ra:t] *m* (12) comrade, companion, fellow, mate; F chum, pal, *Am.* bud(dy); **~schaft** *f* (16) comradeship, companionship; **²schaftlich** comradely; (*gesellig*) companionable; **~schaftlichkeit** *f* comradeliness; **~schafts-ehe** *f* companionate marriage; **~schaftsgeist** *m* esprit de corps (*fr.*).

'**Kameramann** *m* cameraman.

Kamille ⚘ [ka'milə] *f* (15) camomile; **~ntee** *n* camomile tea.

Kamin [ka'mi:n] *m* (3¹) (*Schornstein u. mount.*) chimney; (*offene Feuerstätte im Zimmer*) fire-place, fireside; *fig. et. in den ~ schreiben* write a th. off; **~feger** *m* chimney-sweep.

Kamm [kam] *m* (3³) comb; *zo.* crest; (*Gebirgs²*) ridge; *fig. alle*(*s*) *über 'einen ~ scheren* treat all alike.

kämmen ['kɛmən] (25) comb.

Kammer ['kamər] *f* (15) chamber (*a. anat., zo.,* ⊕), small room, cabinet, closet; *pol. usw.* board, chamber; ⚔ unit stores *pl.*; '**~diener** *m* valet; '**~gericht** *n* supreme court of justice; '**~jäger** *m* vermin exterminator; '**~konzert** *n* chamber concert; '**~musik** *f* chamber music; '**~ton**(**höhe** *f*) ♪ *m* concert pitch; '**~zofe** *f* lady's maid.

'**Kamm|garn** *n* worsted (yarn); '**~rad** *n* cog-wheel.

Kampagne [kam'panjə] *f* (15) campaign.

Kampf [kampf] *m* (3³) fight, combat, battle; *Sport*: contest; *schwerer*: struggle; *der Meinungen usw.*: conflict; *~ ums Dasein* struggle for existence; *j-m* (*den*) *~ ansagen* challenge; *s. stellen*; '**~-ansage** *f* challenge (*an acc.* to); '**~bahn** *f* *Sport*: stadium; arena; '**²bereit** ready for battle (*Sport*: to fight); '**~-einsatz** ⚔ *m* operational mission.

kämpfen ['kɛmpfən] (25) fight; *a. fig.* struggle, battle (*mit* with).

Kampfer ['kampfər] *m* (7) camphor.

Kämpfer ['kɛmpfər] *m* (7), '**~in** *f* **1.** fighter; ⚔ combatant; **2.** △ *m* impost; abutment; '**²isch** fighting; pugnacious.

'**kampf|fähig** fit to fight; ⚔ fit for action; '**²flugzeug** *n* tactical aircraft; '**²geist** *m* fighting spirit; '**²gruppe** *f* brigade (*Am.* combat) group; '**²hahn** *m* fighting-cock; *fig.* quarrelsome fellow; '**²handlung** *f* fighting; action; '**²hubschrauber** *m* gunship; '⁀**lust** *f* pugnacity; '**⁓lustig** pugnacious; '⁀**maßnahme** *f bei Tarifkonflikt*: industrial action; '⁀**platz** *m* battlefield; *Sport u. fig.*: arena; '⁀**preis** *m* prize; '⁀**richter** *m* umpire; '⁀**schwimmer** *m* frogman; '⁀**sport** *m* combatant sport; '⁀**stoff** *m* chemical warfare agent; '⁀**truppe** *f* combat troops *pl.*; '**⁓-unfähig** disabled, out of action; '⁀**verband** *m* fighting (*Am.* combat) unit; '⁀**wagen** *m* combat car, armo(u)red vehicle; tank.

kampieren [kam'pi:rən] camp.

Kanad|ier[1] [ka'nɑ:djər] *m* (7), **⁓ierin** *f* (16[1]), ⁀**isch** Canadian.

Kanadier[2] *m* (7) (*Boot*) Canadian (canoe).

Kanal [ka'nɑ:l] *m* (3[1] *u.* [3]) *künstlicher*: canal; *natürlicher*: channel (*a.* ⊕ *od. fig.*); ⊕ (*Röhre*) duct; (*Abzugs*⁀) sewer, drain; *geogr. the* British Channel; **⁓isation** [⁓naliza'tsjo:n] *f* (15) *e-s Flusses*: canalization; (*Entwässerung*) drainage; *e-r Stadt*: sewerage; (*⁓sanlage*) sewers *pl.*, drains *pl.*; ⁀**isieren** [⁓'zi:rən] *Fluß*: canalize; *Stadt*: sewer; **⁓wähler** *TV m* channel selector.

Kanapee ['kanape:] *n* (11) sofa, settee.

Kanarienvogel [ka'nɑ:rjən-] *m* canary.

Kandare [kan'dɑ:rə] *f* (15) curb (-bit); *fig. j-n an die ⁓ nehmen* put a tight rein on.

Kandelaber [kandə'lɑ:bər] *m* (7) candelabrum.

Kandidat [kandi'dɑ:t] *m* (12) candidate; **⁓enliste** *f* list of candidates; (⁓ *e-r Partei*) *Am.* ticket; **⁓ur** [⁓da'tu:r] *f* candidature, *Am.* candidacy.

kandi'dieren be a candidate, *parl.* contest a seat; *für e-e Wahl ⁓* stand (*Am.* run) for election.

kandieren [kan'di:rən] candy.

Kandis ['kandis] *m inv.*, '**⁓zucker** *m* (sugar-)candy.

Kaneel [ka'ne:l] *m* (3[1]) cinnamon.

Känguruh ['kɛŋguru:] *n* (3[1] *u.* 11) kangaroo.

Kaninchen [ka'ni:nçən] *n* (6) rabbit; **⁓bau** *m* rabbit-burrow; **⁓stall** *m* rabbit-hutch.

Kanister [ka'nistər] *m* (7) container, can.

Kanne ['kanə] *f* (15) can, pot; (*Krug*) jug; (*Bier*⁀) tankard.

kannelieren [⁓'li:rən] channel, flute.

Kannibal|e [kani'bɑ:lə] *m* (13), ⁀**isch** cannibal; *adv. a.* F *fig.* beastly.

kannte ['kantə] *pret. v. kennen.*

Kanon ['kɑ:nɔn] *m* (11) canon.

Kanonade [kano'nɑ:də] *f* (15) bombardment, cannonade.

Kanone [ka'no:nə] *f* (15) cannon, gun; F (*Könner*) wizard, genius; *bsd. Sport*: ace; F *unter aller ⁓* beneath contempt, *sl.* lousy; **⁓nboot** *n* gunboat; **⁓nfutter** F *n* cannon-fodder; **⁓nrohr** *n* gun-barrel; **⁓nschuß** *m* cannon-shot.

Kanonier [⁓no'ni:r] *m* (3[1]) gunner.

Kanon|ikus [ka'no:nikus] *m* (14[2]) canon; ⁀**isch** canonical.

Kante ['kantə] *f* (15) edge; (*Rand*) *a.* brim; *des Tuches*: list, selvage; (*Spitze*) lace; '**⁓l** *m* (7) square ruler; '**⁓n**[1] *m* (6) *des Brotes*: crust; '⁀**n**[2] (26) cant, tilt; *Holz usw.*: square; chamfer.

'**Kantholz** ⊕ *n* square(d) timber.

'**kantig** angular, edged, square.

Kantine [kan'ti:nə] *f* (15) canteen.

Kanton [⁓'to:n] *m* (3[1]) canton; **⁓ist** [⁓to'nist] *m* (12): F *fig. ein unsicherer ⁓* an unreliable fellow.

Kantor ['kantɔr] *m* (8[1]) precentor.

Kanu [ka'nu:] *n* (11) canoe; **⁓te** ['ka'nu:tə] *m* (13) canoeist.

Kanüle ⚕ [⁓'ny:lə] *f* (15) drain tube.

Kanzel ['kantsəl] *f* (15) pulpit; ✈ cockpit; ⚔ turret.

Kanzlei [kants'laɪ] *f* (16) (government-)office, chancellery; (*Büro*) office; chancery.

'**Kanzler** *m* (7) chancellor.

Kap [kap] *n* (3[1] *u.* 11) cape.

Kapaun [ka'paʊn] *m* (3[1]) capon.

Kapazität [kapatsi'tɛ:t] *f* (16) capacity; ⚡ capacitance; *fig.* authority.

Kapell|e [ka'pɛlə] *f* (15) chapel; (*Musik*⁀) band; **⁓meister** *m* conductor; band-master, band leader.

Kaper[1] ⚘ ['kɑ:pər] *f* (15) caper;

'**Kaper**[2] ⚓ *m* (7) privateer, corsair; '**⁓brief** *m* (letters *pl.* of) marque; **⁓ei** [⁓'raɪ] *f* privateering; '⁀**n** (29) capture, seize; '**⁓schiff** *n* privateer.

kapieren F [ka'pi:rən] get (it); *kapiert?* (have you) got it?

Kapillar|gefäß *anat.* [kapi'lɑ:r-] *n* capillary vessel; **⁓röhrchen** [⁓rø:rçən] *n* (6) capillary tube.

Kapital [kapi'tɑ:l] **1.** *n* (3[1] *u.* 8[2]) capital; *fig. a.* asset; *⁓ und Zinsen* principal and interest; *⁓ schlagen* *aus* capitalize on; *s. tot*; **2.** ♀ capital; **~-abwanderung** *f* exodus of capital; **~-anlage** *f* investment; **~-anleger(in** *f*) *m* investor; **~bildung** *f* accumulation of capital; **~-einkommen** *n* investment income; **~-er'tragssteuer** *f* capital yield tax; **~-flucht** *f* flight of capital; **~geber(in** *f*) *m* financier; **~gesellschaft** *f* joint-stock company; **~güter** *n/pl.* capital goods; **♀isieren** [~tali'zi:rən] capitalize; **~ismus** [~'lismus] *m inv.* capitalism; **~ist** [~'list] *m* (12) capitalist; **♀istisch** capitalistic(ally *adv.*); **♀-kräftig** [~'tα:l-] financially sound; **~markt** *m* capital market; **~steuer** *f* tax on capital; **~verbrechen** *n* capital crime; **~zins** *m* interest on capital.

Kapitän [~'tε:n] *m* (3¹) captain (*a. Sport*); ~ *zur See* (naval) captain; **~leutnant** *m* (naval) lieutenant.

Kapitel [ka'pitəl] *n* (7) chapter (*a. eccl.*); *das ist ein ~ für sich* that's another story.

Kapitu|lation [~tula'tsjo:n] *f* (16) capitulation, surrender; (*Dienstverlängerung*) re-enlistment; **♀'lieren** capitulate, surrender (*vor dat.* to); re-enlist.

Kaplan [ka'plα:n] *m* (3¹ *u.* ³) chaplain.

Kappe ['kapə] *f* (15) cap, (*Kapuze*) hood (*beide a.* ⊕); (*oberer Teil*) top-piece; *fig. et. auf s-e ~ nehmen* take the responsibility for; **'♀n** (25) *Tau*: cut; *Baum*: lop, top; *Hahn*: caponize.

Käppi ['kεpi] *n* (11) cap, ⚔ *a.* kepi.

Kapri|ole [kapri'o:lə] *f* (15) caper; *~n machen* cut capers, *fig.* play tricks; **♀'zieren:** *sich ~ auf* (*acc.*) set one's heart on; **♀ziös** [~'tsjø:s] capricious.

Kapsel ['kapsəl] *f* (15) case, box; *anat., pharm.,* ⚘ capsule; *e-r Flasche*: cap; *s. Raumkapsel.*

kaputt [ka'put] broken; out of order; (*verdorben*) spoilt; *fig.* done for; ruined; (*erschöpft*) worn out, all in; (*tot*) dead; **~gehen** (sn) get smashed *od.* ruined, go phut; **~machen** smash, wreck; *fig.* ruin, bust; *P.*: (*sich*) ~ fag (o.s.) out, kill o.s.

Kapuze [ka'pu:tsə] *f* (15) hood; *der Mönche usw.*: cowl.

Kapuziner [kapu'tsi:nər] *m* (7) Capuchin.

Karabiner [kara'bi:nər] *m* (7) car(a)bine; **~haken** *m* spring-hook.

Karaffe [ka'rafə] *f* (15) carafe, decanter.

Karambol|age [karambo'lα:ʒə] *f* (15) collision; *Billard*: cannon, *Am.* carom; **♀ieren** [~'li:rən] *Billard*: cannon, *Am.* carom; *fig.* collide.

Karat [ka'rα:t] *n* (3, *als Maß im pl. inv.*) carat.

Karate [ka'rα:tə] *n* (*inv., o. pl.*) karate; **~schlag** *m* karate-chop.

...karätig [ka'rε:tiç] ... carat.

Karawane [kara'vα:nə] *f* (15) caravan.

Karbid [kar'bi:t] *n* (3¹) carbide.

Karbonade [~bo'nα:də] *f* (15) carbonado.

Karbunkel [kar'buŋkəl] *m* (7) carbuncle.

Kardan|gelenk ⊕ [kar'dα:n-] *n* cardan (*od.* universal) joint; **~welle** ⊕ *f* cardan shaft.

Kardätsche [~'dε:tʃə] *f* (15) (*Woll♀*) card; (*Striegel*) curry-comb; **♀n** (27) card; curry.

Karde ⚘, ⊕ ['kardə] *f* (15) teasel.

Kardinal [kardi'nα:l] *m* (3¹ *u.* ³) cardinal; **~fehler** *m* cardinal fault; **~frage** *f* cardinal question.

Kardiogramm ⚕ [kardio'gram] *n* (3¹) cardiogram.

Karenzzeit [ka'rεntstsaɪt] *f* waiting period.

Kar'freitag [kα:r-] *m* (3) Good Friday.

karg [kark] (18[²]) (*knickerig*) niggardly, stingy; (*dürftig*) scanty, poor; *Boden*: sterile, poor; **~en** ['~gən] (25) be stingy (*mit* with), be sparing (of); **♀heit** ['kark-] *f* stinginess, parsimony.

kärglich ['kεrkliç] scanty, paltry, poor.

kariert [ka'ri:rt] check(ed), chequered, *Am.* checkered.

Karies ['kα:riεs] *f* (16, *o. pl.*) caries.

Karikatur [karika'tu:r] *f* (16) caricature (*a. fig.*), cartoon; **~ist** [~tu'rist] *m* (12) caricaturist, cartoonist.

kari'kieren caricature.

kariös ⚕ [kari'ø:s] decayed, carious.

karitativ [karita'ti:f] charitable.

karmesin [karme'zi:n] crimson.

Karmin [~'mi:n] *n* (3¹) carmine.

Karneval ['karnəval] *m* (3¹) carnival.

Karnickel F [kar'nikəl] *n* (7) rabbit; *fig.* F silly ass.

Karo ['ka:ro] *n* (11) square; *Karte*: diamonds *pl.*; '**~muster** *n* check(ed) pattern.
Karosserie *mot.* [karɔsə'ri:] *f* (15) body.
Karotin ⚗ [karo'ti:n] *n* carotine.
Karotte ⚘ [ka'rɔtə] *f* (15) carrot.
Karpfen ['karpfən] *m* (6) carp.
Karre ['karə] *f* (15) *s. Karren.*
Karree [ka're:] *n* (11) square.
karren ['karən] **1.** (25) wheel, cart; **2.** ♀ *m* (6) cart; (*Hand*♀) (wheel-) barrow; F (*Auto*) car; '**♀gaul** *m* cart-horse.
Karriere [kar'jɛ:rə] *f* (15) gallop; (*Laufbahn*) career; *in voller ~* at full gallop, at a rattling pace; **~macher** *m* careerist.
Kar'samstag [ka:r-] *m* Holy Saturday.
Karte ['kartə] *f* (15) card; (*Land*♀) map; (*See*♀) chart; (*Ausweis*♀, *Fahr*♀, *Zulassungs*♀) ticket; *s. Speisekarte; alles auf eine ~ setzen* put all one's eggs in one basket; *s. legen.*
Kartei [~'taɪ] *f* (16) card-index; **~karte** *f* filing (*od.* index) card; **~kasten** *m* card-index box; **~schrank** *m* card-index (*od.* filing) cabinet.
Kartell [~'tɛl] *n* (3^1) cartel; ✝ *a.* combine, *Am. a.* trust.
'**Karten|brief** *m* letter-card; '**~haus** *n* house of cards; '**~kunststück** *n* card-trick; '**~legerin** *f* fortune-teller; '**~spiel** *n* card-playing; (*Karten*) pack (*Am. a.* deck) of cards; '**~vorverkauf(s-stelle** *f*) *m* advance booking (office); '**~zeichen** *n* conventional sign.
Kartoffel [kar'tɔfəl] *f* (15) potato; **~bau** *m* cultivation of potatoes; **~brei** *m* mashed potatoes *pl.*; **~chips** *m/pl.* potato crisps (*Am.* chips); **~käfer** *m* potato-beetle, *Am.* -bug; **~puffer** *m* potato-pancake; **~salat** *m* potato salad; **~schalen** *f/pl.* potato peelings; **~schäler** *m* (7) potato peeler; **~stampfer** *m* (7) potato masher.
Kartograph [karto'gra:f] *m* (12) cartographer, map-maker; **~ie** [~gra'fi:] *f* (16) cartography.
Karton [kar'tɔ̃] *m* (11) (*~papier*) cardboard; (*Zeichnung*) cartoon; (*Schachtel*) carton, (cardboard) box; *Buchbinderei*: boards *pl.*; **♀ieren** [~to'ni:rən] bind in boards.
Kartothek [~to'te:k] *f* (15) *s. Kartei.*
Kartusche [kar'tuʃə] *f* (16) cartridge.
Karussell [karu'sɛl] *n* (3^1) roundabout, *bsd. Am.* merry-go-round.
Karwoche ['ka:rvɔxə] *f* Passion (*od.* Holy) Week.
Karzer *univ.* ['kartsər] *m* (7) lock-up; (*Strafe*) detention.
Karzinom [kartsi'no:m] ⚕ *n* (3^1) carcinoma.
Käse ['kɛ:zə] *m* (7) cheese; '**~blatt** F *n* rag; '**~gebäck** *n* cheese biscuits *pl.*; '**~glocke** *f* cheese-cover; '**~händler** *m* cheesemonger.
Kasematte [kazə'matə] *f* (15) casemate.
'**Käseplatte** *f* cheeseboard.
Käserei [~'raɪ] *f* (16) cheese-dairy.
Kasern|e [ka'zɛrnə] *f* (15) barracks *pl.*; **~enhof** *m* barrack-yard *od.* -square; **♀ieren** [~'ni:rən] barrack; **♀iert** [~'ni:rt] quartered in barracks.
'**Käsestange** *f* (*Gebäck*) cheese-straw.
'**käsig** cheesy; *Gesicht usw.*: pasty.
Kasino [ka'zi:no] *n* (11) club, casino; (*Offiziers*♀) (officers') mess.
Kaskoversicherung ['kasko-] *mot. f* comprehensive insurance.
Kasperle ['kaspɛrlə] *n* (7) Punch; *fig.* clown; '**~theater** *n* Punch and Judy (show).
Kassa ✝ ['kasa] *f* (16^2): *per ~* in cash; '**~buch** *n* cash-book.
Kasse ['kasə] *f* (15) cash-box; (*Laden*♀) till, cash-register; (*Zahlstelle*) pay-office; (*~nschalter*) cash-desk; (*Theater*♀ *usw.*) ticket-office, booking-office, *thea. a.* box-office; *s. Kranken*♀; (*Bargeld*) cash; ✝ *~ gegen Dokumente* cash against documents; *bei* (*nicht bei*) *~* in (out of) cash; *gut bei ~ sein* F be flush.
'**Kassen|-abschluß** *m* balancing of the cash (accounts); cash-balance; '**~-anweisung** *f* cash order; '**~-arzt** *m* panel doctor; '**~bericht** *m* cash '**~bon** *m* receipt, sales slip; '**~buch** *n* cash-book; '**~-erfolg** *m thea. etc.* box-office success; '**~führer** *m* cashier; '**~patient** *m* panel patient; '**~preis** *m* cash price; '**~prüfung** *f* cash audit; '**~schalter** *m* cash-desk; *e-r Bank*: teller's counter; '**~schein** *m* (*Quittung*) cash voucher; (*Banknote*) treasury note; '**~sturz** *m*: *~ machen* check the cash accounts, F *weit S.* tot up one's cash; '**~wart** *m* treasurer; '**~zettel** *m* sales slip.

Kasserolle [kasə'rɔlə] *f* (15) casserole.
Kassette [ka'sɛtə] *f* (15) casket; *für Bücher*: slip-case; *phot.* cartridge; (*Video*~, *Audio*~) cassette; ⚠ coffer; **~ndeck** *n* cassette deck; **~nrecorder** *m* (7) cassette recorder.
kassier|en [ka'si:rən] *v/i.* cash, collect; (*aufheben*) annul; *Urteil*: quash; (*entlassen*) cashier; **~er** *m* (7), **~erin** *f* cashier; (*Bank*~) *a.* teller.
Kastagnette [kastan'jɛtə] *f* (15) castanet.
Kastanie [ka'sta:njə] *f* (15) chestnut; *fig. die ~n für j-n aus dem Feuer holen* act as a p.'s cat's-paw; **~nbaum** *m* chestnut-tree; **~nbraun** chestnut.
Kästchen ['kɛstçən] *n* (6) little box (*od.* case), casket; *in Zeitungen usw.*: box.
Kaste ['kastə] *f* (15) caste.
kastei|en [ka'staɪən] (25): *sich ~* chasten o.s., mortify the flesh; **~ung** *f* mortification of the flesh.
Kasten ['kastən] *m* (6) chest, box, case; *s. Schrank*; *für Bier usw.*, *a.* F (*Fahrzeug*) crate; F (*Haus*) box; **'~geist** *m* caste-spirit; **'~wesen** *n* caste-system.
Kastr|at [ka'stra:t] *m* (12) eunuch; **~ieren** [~'stri:rən] castrate.
Kasus ['ka:zus] *m inv.* case.
Katalog [~'lo:k] *m* (3[1]), **~isieren** [~logi'zi:rən] catalog(ue).
Katalys|ator [kataly'za:tɔr] *m* (8[1]) ⚗ catalyst; *mot.* catalytic converter; **~ieren** [~'zi:rən] catalyse.
Katapult [~'pult] *m*, *n* (3) catapult (*a.* ✈); **~start** ✈ *m* catapult take-off.
Katarrh [ka'tar] *m* (3[1]) (common) cold, catarrh; **~alisch** [~'ra:liʃ] catarrhal.
Kataster [ka'tastər] *m u. n* (7) land-register.
katastro|phal [katastro'fa:l] catastrophic(ally *adv.*), disastrous; **~phe** [~'stro:fə] *f* (15) catastrophe, disaster; **~phengebiet** *n* disaster area; **~phenhilfe** *f* disaster relief.
Katechismus [kate'çismus] *m* (16[2]) catechism.
Kateg|orie [~go'ri:] *f* (16) category; **~orisch** [~'go:riʃ] categorical.
Kater ['ka:tər] *m* (7) tom cat; F *vom Trinken*: hangover.
Katheder [ka'te:dər] *n*, *m* (7) reading desk; **~blüte** *f* howler.
Kathedrale [kate'dra:lə] *f* (15) cathedral.
Katheter ⚕ [ka'te:tər] *m* (7) catheter.
Kathode ⚡ [ka'to:də] *f* cathode; **~nröhre** *f* cathode ray tube.
Katholik [kato'li:k] *m* (12), **~in** *f* (16[1]), **katholisch** [~'to:liʃ] (Roman) Catholic.
Katholizismus [katoli'tsismus] *m* (16, *o. pl.*) Catholicism.
Kattun [ka'tu:n] *m* (3[1]) calico; *bedruckt*: print; (*Möbel*~) chintz; **~kleid** *n* print-dress.
'katzbuckeln (29) crouch, cringe (*vor dat.* to), bow and scrape.
Kätzchen ['kɛtsçən] *n* (6) kitten; ♀ catkin.
Katze ['katsə] *f* (15) cat; F *das ist für die Katz* that's all for nothing; *die ~ im Sack kaufen* buy a pig in a poke; *die ~ aus dem Sack lassen* let the cat out of the bag; *wie die ~ um den heißen Brei gehen* beat about the bush.
'Katzen|-auge *n a.* ⊕ cat's eye; **'~buckel** *m* cat's (arched) back; **'~freundlich** oversweet; **'~haft** catlike, feline; **'~jammer** F *m* hangover; *moralischer*: *a.* the dumps, the blues *sg.*; **'~klo** *n* cat tray; **'~musik** *f* charivari, *Am.* shivaree; **'~sprung** *m fig.*: *ein ~* a stone's throw; **'~streu** *f* cat litter; **'~wäsche** F *f* cat's lick.
Kauderwelsch ['kaudərvɛlʃ] *n* (3[2]) gibberish, double Dutch; lingo; **'~en** (27) talk gibberish.
kauen ['kauən] *v/t. u. v/i.* (25) chew.
kauern ['kauərn] (29) (*a. sich ~*) cower, squat.
Kauf [kauf] *m* (3[3]) buying, purchase, *Am. a.* buy; (*Handel*) bargain; *in ~ nehmen* take into the bargain, *fig.* put up with; *leichten ~es davonkommen* get off cheaply; **'~-auftrag** *m* buying order; **'~brief** *m* purchase-deed; **'~en** (25) buy (*bei j-m* from a p.), purchase; F (*bestechen*) bribe, buy; F *sich j-n ~* give a p. hell.
Käufer ['kɔʏfər] *m* (7), **'~in** *f* (16[1]) buyer, purchaser.
'Kauf|haus *n* commercial house; (*Warenhaus*) (department) store; **'~kraft** *f* purchasing power; **'~kräftig** able to buy; **'~laden** *m* shop, store.
käuflich ['kɔʏfliç] purchasable; *fig.*

b.s. venal, corrupt; *adv.* by purchase; '**≈keit** *f fig.* venality.
'**Kauf|mann** *m* (*pl. Kaufleute*) merchant; businessman, trader, dealer; *im Laden*: shopkeeper, *Am. a.* storekeeper; (*Angestellter*) commercial clerk; **≈männisch** ['~mɛniʃ] commercial, mercantile; '**~vertrag** *m* contract of purchase; '**~zwang** *m* obligation to buy.
'**Kaugummi** *m* chewing-gum.
Kaulquappe ['kaulkvapə] *f* (15) tadpole.
kaum [kaum] scarcely, hardly; (*nur gerade*) barely; *zeitlich*: ~ ... *als* no sooner ... than, hardly ... when.
kausal [kau'zaːl] causal; **≈zusammenhang** *m* causal connection.
'**Kautabak** *m* chewing-tobacco.
Kaution [kau'tsjoːn] *f* (16) security; *im Strafrecht*: bail.
Kautschuk ['kautʃuk] *m* (3[1]) caoutchouc, India rubber.
'**Kauwerkzeuge** *n/pl.* masticatory organs.
Kauz [kauts] *m* (3[1] *u.* [3]) screech-owl; *fig.* (*a. komischer* ~) (odd) character, queer fish; *alter* ~ old codger.
Kavalier [kava'liːr] *m* (3[1]) cavalier, gentleman; **~sdelikt** *n* peccadillo.
Kavallerie [~lə'riː] *f* (15) cavalry, horse; **~pferd** *n* troop-horse.
Kavalle'rist *m* (12) cavalryman, trooper.
Kaviar ['kaːviar] *m* (3[1]) caviar(e).
keck [kɛk] bold, pert, F saucy; '**≈heit** *f* boldness; F sauciness.
Kegel ['keːgəl] *m* (7) cone; *Spiel*: skittle, pin; *s. Kind*; ~ *schieben s. kegeln*; '**~bahn** *f* skittle- (*Am.* bowling) alley; **≈förmig** ['~fœrmiç] conical, cone-shaped; '**~klub** *m* skittles club; '**~kugel** *f* skittle-ball; '**≈n** (29) play (at) skittles *od.* ninepins; '**~rad** ⊕ *n* bevel gear; '**~schnitt** *m* conic section; '**~spiel** *n*, '**~sport** *m* skittles, ninepin bowling; '**~stumpf** *m* truncated cone.
Kegler ['keːglər] *m* skittle-player.
Kehle ['keːlə] *f* (15) throat; ⊕ groove; *das Messer sitzt ihm an der* ~ he feels the knife at his throat; *etwas in die falsche* ~ *bekommen* swallow a morsel the wrong way, *fig.* take a th. amiss; *das Wort blieb mir in der* ~ *stecken* the word stuck in my throat; *s. zuschnüren.*
'**Kehl|kopf** *m* larynx; '**~kopf-entzündung** ⚕ *f* laryngitis; '**~kopfkrebs** ⚕ *m* cancer of the larynx, F throat cancer; '**~kopfspiegel** *m* laryngoscope; '**~laut** *m* guttural; '**~leiste** *f* ogee, mo(u)lding.
'**Kehr|-aus** *m inv.* last dance; *fig.* clean-out; '**~besen** *m* broom.
Kehre ['keːrə] *f* (15) turn; *Sport*: back-vault; *des Weges*: turn, sharp (*od.* hairpin) bend; '**≈n** (25) sweep; brush; (*um*~) turn; ⚔ *kehrt!* (right) about, turn! (*Am.* face!); *das Oberste zuunterst* ~ turn (everything) upside down; *sich nicht* ~ *an* (*acc.*) ignore, disregard; *fig. j-m den Rücken* ~ turn one's back on a p.; *in sich gekehrt* withdrawn, introverted.
Kehricht ['keːriçt] *m, n* (3[1]) sweepings *pl.*, rubbish; '**~-eimer** *m* dustbin, *Am.* trash-can; '**~schaufel** *f* dust-pan.
'**Kehr|reim** *m* burden, refrain; '**~seite** *f* reverse, back; *fig. a.* seamy side; '**~wert** 𝔄 *m* reciprocal.
'**kehrt|machen** turn round *od.* back; ⚔ face about; '**≈wendung** *f* about-face (*a. fig.*).
keif|en ['kaifən] (25) scold (*mit j-m* a p.); '**≈erin** *f* scold.
Keil [kail] *m* (3) wedge; *typ.* quoin; *Näherei*: gore, gusset; '**~-absatz** *m* wedge heel; '**~e** F *f* thrashing; '**≈en** (25) fasten with wedges; F thrash; '**~er** *hunt. m* (7) wild boar; **~e'rei** F *f* scrap.
keil|förmig ['~fœrmiç] wedge-shaped, cuneiform; '**≈hacke** *f* pick-ax(e); '**≈hosen** *f/pl.* tapered trousers; '**≈riemen** ⊕ *m* V-belt; '**≈schrift** *f* cuneiform characters *pl.*
Keim [kaim] *m* (3) *biol., a. fig.* germ; ♀ *a.* seed, bud; *s. ersticken*; '**~blatt** *n* ♀ cotyledon; *biol.* germ-layer; '**~drüse** *f* genital gland, gonad; '**≈en** (25, h. *u.* sn) germinate; ♀ *a.* sprout.
'**keim|fähig** germinable; '**~frei** sterile; ~ *machen* sterilize; '**≈ling** *m* (3) seed-plant; sprout; '**~tötend** germicidal; '**≈träger** ⚕ *m* (germ-) carrier; '**≈zelle** *f* germ-cell.
kein [kain] (20) *als adj.* no, not any; *als su.* ~*er m*, ~*e f* no one, none, not (any)one, nobody, not anybody; ~(e)s *n* nothing, not anything; ~*er* (*von beiden*) neither; ~ *Ding* nothing.

keinerlei ['~ərlaɪ] of no sort; no ... whatever; *auf ~ Weise* in no way.
'**keines**|'**falls** on no account; **~wegs** ['~'ve:ks] by no means, not at all.
'**keinmal** not once, never.
Keks [ke:ks] *m, n* (4) biscuit, *Am.* cookie, (*knuspriger ~*) cracker.
Kelch [kɛlç] *m* (3) cup; ⚘ calyx; *eccl.* chalice.
Kelle ['kɛlə] *f* (15) ladle; (*Maurer*♀) trowel; (*Signal*♀) signal(l)ing disk.
Keller ['kɛlər] *m* (7) cellar; **~ei** [~'raɪ] *f* (16) (wine-)cellars *pl.*; '**~geschoß** *n* basement; '**~lokal** *n* wine- *od.* beer-cellar; '**~meister** *m* cellarer, cellar man.
Kellner ['kɛlnər] *m* (7) waiter; '**~in** *f* waitress.
Kelte ['kɛltə] *m* (12) Celt.
Kelter ['kɛltər] *f* (15) wine-press; '♀**n** (29) press (out).
'**keltisch** Celtic.
'**kennbar** recognizable.
kennen ['kɛnən] (30) know; '**~lernen** become acquainted with, get (*od.* come) to know, meet.
'**Kenner** *m* (7), '**~in** *f* (16[1]) connoisseur; (*Fachmann*) expert.
'**Kennkarte** *f* identity card.
'**Kennmelodie** *f Radio*: signature tune.
'**kenntlich** recognizable; *~ machen* mark.
'**Kenntnis** *f* (14[2]) knowledge; *~ nehmen von* take note of; *j-n in ~ setzen von* inform a p. of; **~nahme** ['~nɑ:mə] *f inv.*: *zur ~* for your information; '**~se** *pl.* (*Wissen*) knowledge *sg.*; *oberflächliche ~* a smattering.
'**Kennwort** *n* code word; ⚔ *a.* password.
'**Kennzeich**|**en** *n* (distinguishing) mark, sign; characteristic; *fig. a.* criterion; *mot.* registration (*Am.* license) number; *besondere ~ pl.* distinguishing marks; '♀**nen** (26) mark; *fig. a.* characterize, typify.
'**Kennziffer** *f* code number; ✝ reference number.
kentern ⚓ ['kɛntərn] *v/i.* (29, sn) capsize; *a. ~ lassen* overturn.
Keramik [ke'rɑ:mik] *f* (16) ceramics *sg.*; (*Ware*) ceramic article.
Kerbe ['kɛrbə] *f* (15) notch, score.
Kerbel ⚘ ['kɛrbəl] *m* (7) chervil.
'**kerben** (25) notch, score.
Kerb|**holz** ['kɛrp-] *n*: *et. auf dem ~ haben* have done something bad; '**~tier** *n* insect.
Kerker ['kɛrkər] *m* (7) gaol, jail; '**~meister** *m* gaoler, jailer.
Kerl [kɛrl] *m* (3; P *a.* 11) fellow, F bloke, chap, *Am.* guy; *contp.* type; *feiner ~* splendid fellow, *Am.* great guy; *ein lieber od. netter ~* a dear.
Kern [kɛrn] *m* (3) kernel; *v. Apfel usw.*: pip; *v. Steinobst*: stone, *Am.* pit; *fig.* core (*a.* ⊕), nucleus (*a. phys.*); (*Wesen*) essence; *~ der Sache* crux of the matter; *pol. harter ~* hard core; '**~chemie** *f* nuclear chemistry; '**~-energie** *f* nuclear energy; '**~fach** *n Schule, univ.* basic subject; '**~forscher** *m* nuclear scientist; '**~forschung** *f* nuclear research; '**~forschungszentrum** *n* nuclear research cent|re, *Am.*-er; '**~frage** *f* crucial question; '**~frucht** *f* stone-fruit; '**~fusion** *f* nuclear fusion; '**~gehäuse** *n* core; '♀**gesund** thoroughly healthy, F as sound as a bell; '**~holz** *n* heartwood.
'**kernig** full of pips; *fig.* (*markig*) pithy, robust.
'**Kern**|**kraftwerk** *n* nuclear power station (*od.* plant); '**~leder** *n* bend leather; '♀**los** seedless; '**~physik** *f* nuclear physics *sg.*; '**~plasma** *phys. n* (9) nucleoplasm; '**~punkt** *m* central point (*od.* issue); '**~re-aktor** *m* nuclear reactor; '**~seife** *f* curd (*od.* hard) soap; '**~spaltung** *f* nuclear fission; '**~spruch** *m* pithy saying; '**~stück** *n* essential part; '**~truppen** *f/pl.* picked (*od.* elite) troops; '**~waffe** *f* nuclear weapon; '**~zeit** *f* (*Arbeitszeit*) core time.
Kerosin ⚗ [kero'zi:n] *n* (3[1], *o. pl.*) kerosene.
Kerze ['kɛrtsə] *f* (15) candle (*a. phys.*); *s. Zündkerze*; '♀**nge'rade** bolt upright; *auf et. zu*: straight; '**~halter** *m* candlestick, candleholder; '**~licht** *n* (*bei ~* by) candlelight; '**~nstärke** *f* candle-power.
keß F [kɛs] pert, F saucy.
Kessel ['kɛsəl] *m* (7) kettle; *großer*: cauldron, ⊕ vat; (*Dampf*♀) boiler; *geol.* (*Vertiefung*) hollow; (*Becken*) basin; ⚔ pocket; '**~haus** *n* boiler-house; '**~pauke** *f* kettledrum; '**~raum** *m* boiler room; '**~stein** *m* scale, fur; '**~treiben** *hunt. n* battue; *fig.* hunt (*gegen* for); *pol.* witch-hunt.

Kette ['kɛtə] *f* (15) chain (*a. Schmuck*≈; *a.* ⚗, ⚙ *u. fig.*); (*Gebirgs*≈) *a.* range; (*Folge*) series, train; (*Weber*≈) warp; ✈, ✕ flight; ✕ *e-s Panzers*: track; '≈**n** (26) chain (*an acc.* to).
'**Ketten**|**-antrieb** *m* chain-drive; '**~-brief** *m* chain letter; '**~fahrzeug** *n* tracked vehicle; '**~geschäft** *n*, '**~laden** *m* multiple shop, chain store; '**~glied** *n* chain link; '**~hund** *m* watch-dog; '**~raucher** *m* chain-smoker; '**~re-aktion** *phys. f* chain reaction; '**~rechnung** *f*, '**~regel** ⚙ *f* chain rule.
Ketzer ['kɛtsər] *m* (7), '**~in** *f* heretic; **~ei** [~'raɪ] *f* heresy; '≈**isch** heretical.
keuch|**en** ['kɔʏçən] (25) pant, gasp; '≈**husten** *m* (w)hooping-cough.
Keule ['kɔʏlə] *f* (15) club; *Fleisch*: leg; '**~nschlag** *m* blow with a club; *fig.* crushing blow.
keusch [kɔʏʃ] chaste; (*rein*) pure; (*sittsam*) modest; '≈**heit** *f* chastity.
'**Kicher-erbse** *f* chick-pea.
kichern ['kiçərn] (29) titter, giggle.
kicken ['kikən] (25) kick.
Kiebitz ['ki:bits] *m* (3[2]) peewit, lapwing; (*Zugucker*) F kibitzer.
Kiefer[1] ⚘ ['ki:fər] *f* (15) pine.
'**Kiefer**[2] *anat. m* (7) jaw; '**~höhle** *anat. f* maxillary sinus; '**~-orthopäde** *m*, '**~-orthopädin** *f* orthodontist.
Kiel [ki:l] *m* (3) ⚓ keel; (*Feder*≈) quill; '≈**holen** ⚓ careen; ≈'**-oben** keeled over, bottom up; '**~raum** *m* bilge; '**~wasser** *n* wake (*a. fig.*).
Kieme ['ki:mə] *f* (15) gill.
Kien [ki:n] *m* (3) resinous pine-wood; '**~-apfel** *m* pine-cone; '**~-fackel** *f* pine-torch; '**~holz** *n s. Kien*; '**~-öl** *n* pine-oil; '**~ruß** *m* pine-soot; '**~span** *m* chip of pine-wood.
Kiepe ['ki:pə] *f* (15) back-basket.
Kies [ki:s] *m* (4) gravel, grit; *mit ~ bestreuen* gravel.
Kiesel ['ki:zəl] *m* (7) flint, pebble; '≈**-artig** siliceous; '**~-erde** *f* siliceous earth; '**~säure** ⚗ *f* (9, *o.pl.*) silicic acid.
kiesig ['~ziç] gravelly.
'**Kiesweg** *m* gravel walk.
'**kiffen** *sl.* ['kifən] (25) (*Haschisch rauchen*) smoke pot (*od.* hash).
Killer *sl.* ['kilər] *m* (7) hitman; '**~satellit** ✕ *m* killer satellite.
Kilo ['ki:lo] *n* (11[1]), **~'gramm** *n* kilo|gramme, *Am.* -gram; **~hertz** [~'hɛrts] *n* kilo-cycle per second; **~'meter** *n* kilomet|re, *Am.* -er; **~'metergeld** *n* mileage (allowance); **~'meterstand** *m* mileage; **~'meterstein** *m* milestone; **~'metertarif** *m Nahverkehr*: distance fare; ≈'**meterweit** for miles (and miles); **~'meterzähler** *m* mileage indicator, odometer; **~'watt** *n* kilowatt; **~'wattstunde** *f* kilowatt hour (*abbr.* kWh).
Kimme ['kimə] *f* (15) notch (✕ in the backsight).
Kind [kint] *n* (1) child, F kid; (*kleines ~*) baby; *mit ~ und Kegel* (with) bag and baggage; *das ~ beim rechten Namen nennen* call a spade a spade; *wes Geistes ~ ist er?* what sort of a fellow is he?; *s. bekommen, erwarten*; '**~bett** *n* childbed; '**~bettfieber** *n* puerperal fever; '**~chen** *n* (6) little child, baby.
'**Kinder**|**-arzt** ['~dər-] *m*, '**~-ärztin** *f* p(a)ediatrician, p(a)ediatrist; '**~-buch** *n* children's book.
Kinderei [~də'raɪ] *f* (16) childishness; (*dummer Streich*) childish trick; (*Kleinigkeit*) trifle, *Am. a.* chicken feed.
Kinder|**-ermäßigung** ['~dər-] *f* reduction for children; '**~frau** *f* nurse; '**~fräulein** *n* (children's) governess; '**~freund**(**in** *f*) *m*: *ein ~ sein* be fond of children; '**~funk** *m* children's program(me); '**~fürsorge** *f* child welfare; '**~garten** *m* kindergarten; *für 2–5jährige*: nursery-school; *für 5–7jährige*: infant-school; '**~gärtnerin** *f* kindergarten teacher; '**~geld** *n s. Kinderzulage*; '**~gesicht** *n* baby-face; '**~gottesdienst** *m* children's service; '**~hort** *m* day-nursery; '**~kleid** *n* child's dress; '**~kleidung** *f* children's wear; '**~krankheit** *f* children's disease; *fig.* teething troubles *pl.*; '**~lähmung** *f*: (*spinale ~*) infantile paralysis, polio(myelitis); *zerebrale ~* polioencephalitis; '≈'**leicht** dead easy; '≈**lieb** fond of children; '**~lied** *n* nursery-rhyme; '≈**los** childless; '**~mädchen** *n* nurse(maid); '**~märchen** *n* nursery-tale; '**~mord** *m* child-murder; '**~pflege** *f* child care; '**~psychologe** *m*, '**~psychologin** *f* child psychologist; '≈**reich** large (*family*); '**~schreck** *m* bugbear; '≈**sicher** *Schloß etc.*: child-proof; '**~spiel** *n fig.* child's play; '**~sterblichkeit** *f* infant mortality; '**~stube** *fig. f* (*good, bad*) upbringing *od.* manners

pl.; '**~tagesstätte** *f* day nursery, *Am.* day-care center; '**~wagen** *m* perambulator, F pram, *Am.* baby carriage; '**~zeit** *f* childhood; '**~zimmer** *n* nursery, *Am. a.* play-room; '**~zulage** *f* allowance for children.

Kindes|-alter ['~dəs-] *n* infancy; '**~bein:** *von ~en an* from infancy, from a child; '**~-entführung** *f* kidnap(p)ing; '**~kind** *n* grandchild; '**~liebe** *f* filial love; '**~mißhandlung** *f* child abuse; '**~mord** *m* child-murder; '**~mutter** *f* mother (of illegitimate child); '**~tötung** ⚖ *f* infanticide.

Kindheit ['kint-] *f* (16) childhood; *von ~ an* from a child.

kindisch ['~diʃ] childish; *~es Wesen* childishness.

Kindlein ['kintlaɪn] *n s. Kindchen.*

'**kindlich** childlike, childish; *im Verhältnis zu den Eltern*: filial.

'**Kindskopf** F *m* (big) child, silly.

'**Kindtaufe** *f* christening.

Kinet|ik [ki'ne:tik] *f* (16, *o. pl.*) kinetics *sg.*; **2isch** kinetic; *~e Energie* kinetic energy.

Kinkerlitzchen F ['kiŋkərlitsçən] *pl. inv.* gewgaws, knick-knacks *pl.*; *fig.* trivialities *pl.*

Kinn [kin] *n* (3) chin; '**~backen** *m*, '**~lade** *f* jaw(-bone); '**~bart** *m* imperial; '**~haken** *m Boxen*: hook to the chin; uppercut.

Kino ['ki:no] *n* (11) cinema, *the* pictures *od.* F flicks *pl.*, *Am.* motion picture theater, F movies *pl.*; '**~besucher(in** *f*) *m* cinema-goer; '**~reklame** *f s. Filmreklame*; '**~vorstellung** *f* cinema-show.

Kintopp ['ki:ntɔp] F *m* (3¹) *s. Kino.*

Kiosk [ki'ɔsk] *m* (3²) kiosk.

Kipfel ['kipfəl] *n* (7) crescent.

Kippe ['kipə] *f* (15) (*Zigarettenstummel*) F fag-end, stub, *bsd. Am.* butt; *Turnen*: upstart, *Am.* kip; *auf der ~* on the tilt; *fig. es steht auf der ~* it is touch and go; '**2n** (25) *v/t.* tilt, tip; *v/i.* (h. *u.* sn) tip, topple (over).

'**Kipp|fenster** *n* bottom-hung window; '**~frequenz** ⚡ *f* sawtooth (*TV* sweep) frequency; '**~karren** *m* tip-cart; '**~lore** *f* tipping truck, tipper; '**~schalter** ⚡ *m* toggle switch; '**~wagen** *m s. Kipplore.*

Kirche ['kirçə] *f* (15) church.

'**Kirchen|-älteste** *m* churchwarden, elder; '**~bann** *m* excommunication; *in den ~ tun* excommunicate; '**~buch** *n* parochial register; '**~chor** *m* church choir; '**~diener** *m* sexton, sacristan; '**~fürst** *m* prince of the church; '**~gemeinde** *f* parish; '**~geschichte** *f* ecclesiastical history; '**~jahr** *n* ecclesiastical year; '**~konzert** *n* church concert; '**~licht** F *n*: *kein (großes) ~* not very bright; '**~lied** *n* hymn; '**~musik** *f* sacred music; '**~rat** *m* parish council; *P.*: parish councillor; '**~recht** *n* ecclesiastical law; '**~schiff** *n* nave; '**~spaltung** *f* schism; '**~steuer** *f* church rate; '**~stuhl** *m* pew; '**~tag** *m* Church congress; '**~vater** *m* Father of the Church; '**~vorsteher** *m* churchwarden, elder.

'**Kirch|gang** *m* church-going; '**~hof** *m* churchyard; '**2lich** ecclesiastical, church...; '**~spiel** *n*, '**~sprengel** *m* parish; '**~turm** *m* church-tower, steeple; '**~turmpolitik** *f* parish-pump politics *pl.*; '**~turmspitze** *f* spire; **~weih** ['~vaɪ] *f* parish fair.

Kirmes ['kirmɛs] *f* (16³) kermis.

kirre ['kirə] tame; *~ machen* tame.

'**kirren** (25) tame; (*ködern*) bait.

Kirsch *m* [kirʃ] (3²) kirsch; '**~e** *f* (15) cherry; *mit ihm ist nicht gut ~n essen* it's best not to tangle with him; '**~kern** *m* cherry-stone; '**~kuchen** *m* cherry cake; '**~likör** *m* cherry brandy; '**2rot** cherry-red, cherry-colo(u)red, cerise; '**~wasser** *n* kirsch.

Kissen ['kisən] *n* (6) cushion; (*Kopf2*) pillow; '**~bezug** *m* pillow-case.

Kiste ['kistə] *f* (15) chest, box; (*Latten2*) crate; *mot. u.* ✈ *sl.* bus.

Kitsch [kitʃ] *m* (3²) trash, kitsch; '**2ig** trashy.

Kitt [kit] *m* (3) cement; (*Glaser2*) putty.

Kittchen ['kitçən] F *n* (6): *im ~* in clink.

Kittel ['kitəl] *m* (7) smock, frock; (*Arbeits2*) overall; *weißer*: (white) coat; '**~kleid** *n* house frock; '**~schürze** *f* pinafore-type overall.

kitten ['kitən] (26) cement; *Glaserei*: putty; *fig.* patch up.

Kitz(chen) ['kitsçən] *n* (3² [6]) kid; (small) fawn.

Kitzel ['kitsəl] *m* (7) tickling, tickle; *fig.* desire, longing; '**2n** (29) tickle.

'**kitzlig** ticklish (*a. fig.*).

Kladde ['kladə] *f* (15) waste-book, *Am.* blotter.
klaffen ['klafən] (25, h. *u.* sn) gape.
kläff|en ['klɛfən] (25) yap, yelp; '**&er** *m* (7) yelping dog.
Klafter ['klaftər] *f* (15) fathom; *Holz*: cord; '**~holz** *n* cord-wood.
klagbar ['klɑ:kbɑ:r] actionable; ~ *werden (gegen j-n)* sue (a p.).
Klage ['klɑ:gə] *f* (15) *(Beschwerde)* complaint, grievance; *(Wehklage)* lament(ation); ⚖ suit, action (*auf acc.* for); *s. erheben, führen usw.*; '**~grund** *m* cause of action; '**~laut** *m* plaintive sound; '**~lied** *n* lamentation, elegy; '**&n** *v/t.* (25): *j-m et.* ~ complain to a p. of *(od.* about) a th.; *v/i.* lament (*um* for; *über acc.* over); ⚖ sue (*auf acc.* for), bring an action (*gegen* against); ~ *über acc. (leiden an)* complain of.
Kläger ['klɛ:gər] *m* (7), '**~in** *f* (16[1]) plaintiff, complainant; *(Scheidungs-&)* petitioner; '**&isch** of the plaintiff.
'**Klageschrift** *f* statement of claim.
kläglich ['klɛ:kliç] pitiful, piteous (*a. Stimme usw.*), miserable, wretched.
klamm[1] [klam] *(feuchtkalt)* clammy; *(erstarrt)* numb; F ~ *sein (geldlos)* be hard up.
Klamm[2] *f* (16) gorge.
Klammer ['klamər] *f* (15) ⊕ clamp, cramp; *(Büro&, Haar& usw.)* clip; ⚕ *(Zahn&)* brace; *(Wäsche&)* peg; *gr., typ.* bracket (*a.* ⚘), parenthesis; *in ~n setzen* put in parentheses, bracket; '**&n** (29) clamp; clasp; *sich ~ an (acc.)* cling to (*a. fig.*).
Klamotte [kla'mɔtə] F *f* (15): *alte* ~ F oldie; *pl.* *(Kleider, Sachen)* things, rags *pl.*
Klang [klaŋ] **1.** *m* (3[3]) sound; *Glocke*: ringing; *Geld, Stimme usw.*: ring; *(~farbe)* timbre; **2.** & *pret. v. klingen*; '**~fülle** ♪ *f* sonority; '**&lich** tonal; '**&los** toneless; '**~regler** *m Radio etc.*: tone control; '**&reich** sonorous; '**&voll** sonorous; *fig.* illustrious.
'**Klappbett** *n* folding bed.
Klappe ['klapə] *f* (15) *allg.* flap (*a.* ⊕); *(Deckel)* lid; ♪ key, stop; ⊕, *anat.* valve; *(Tisch&, Visier&)* leaf; F mouth, trap; *halt die ~!* shut up!; F *in die ~ gehen* go to bed, F turn in; '**&n** (25) *v/t.*: *in die Höhe ~* tip up; *v/i.* clap, flap (*mit* et. a th.); F *(gutgehen)* work (out well); *zum & kommen (bringen)* come (bring) to a head; *das klappt!* that works!; *s. klappern*; '**~ntext** *m Buch*: blurb.
'**Klapper** *f* (15) rattle; '**&dürr** (as) lean as a rake.
'**klapp(e)rig** F *fig.* shaky, rickety.
'**Klapper|kasten** *m*, '**~kiste** *f*, '**~mühle** F *f* rattletrap.
klappern ['klapərn] (29) clatter, rattle (*mit* et. a th.); *mit den Zähnen ~* chatter one's teeth.
'**Klapper|schlange** *f* rattlesnake; '**~storch** *m* stork.
'**Klapp|horn** ♪ *n* key-bugle; '**~hornvers** *m* nonsense rhyme; '**~hut** *m* opera-hat; '**~messer** *n* jack knife; '**~rad** *n* folding bicycle; '**~sitz** *m* tip-up seat; '**~stuhl** *m* folding chair; '**~tisch** *m* folding table; drop-leaf table; '**~tür** *f* snap-action door.
Klaps [klaps] *m* (4[2]) slap, smack; F *fig. e-n ~ haben* be mad; '**&en** (27) slap, smack; '**~mühle** F *f* F loony bin.
klar [klɑ:r] *allg.* clear (*a. fig.*); *fig. a.* lucid; *(offenbar)* obvious, plain; ⚓, ⚔ clear, ready (*zu* for); *~en Kopf behalten* keep a clear head; *sich über et. ~ sein* realize a th., be aware of a th.; *s. klarmachen usw.*; F *(na) ~!* of course, *Am.* sure!; *das geht (schon) ~!* that will be all right.
'**Klär-anlage** *f* purification plant.
'**klarblickend** clear-sighted.
klären ['klɛ:rən] (25) (*a. sich*) clarify; clear (up) (*beide a. fig.*).
'**Klarheit** *f* clearness, clarity.
Klarinette [klari'nɛtə] *f* (15) clarinet.
'**klar|kommen** (sn) manage, get by; '**~legen**, '**~machen** make *a th.* clear (*dat.* to); '**&schriftbeleg** *m Computer*: hard copy.
'**Klarsicht|folie** *f* transparent film; '**~hülle** *f* transparent cover (*od.* folder); '**~packung** *f* transparent pack.
'**klar|stellen** clear up; *(sagen)* state clearly; '**&text** *m* clear text; *fig. im ~* in (the) clear.
'**Klärung** *f* clarification.
'**klarwerden** become clear (*dat.* to); *sich ~ über (acc.)* realize (*a th.*); get (*a th.*) clear in one's mind.
Klasse ['klasə] *f* (15) *allg.* class; *e-r Schule*: class, form, *Am. bsd. e-r Volksschule*: *a.* grade; F *(ganz große ~)* marvellous, terrific; '**~n-arbeit** *f*

(written) class test; '**~nbeste** *m*, *f* best pupil; '**~nbewußtsein** *n* class-consciousness; '**~ngesellschaft** *f* class society; '**~nhaß** *m* class hatred; '**~nkamerad** *m* classmate; '**~nkampf** *pol.* *m* class war(fare) *od.* struggle; '**~nlehrer** *m* class-teacher, form-master; '**2nlos** classless; '**~nlotterie** *f* class (*od.* Dutch) lottery; '**~nsprecher** *m* class representative; '**~n-unterschied** *m* class distinction; '**~nzimmer** *n* classroom.

klassifizier|en [klasifi'tsi:rən] classify; **2ung** *f* classification.

Klass|iker ['~ikər] *m* (7) classic, classical author; '**2isch** classic(al); *fig.* classic (*mistake, etc.*).

klatsch! [klatʃ] **1.** smack!; (*in*) *Wasser*: splash!; **2. 2** *m* (3²) (*Schlag*) clap; (*Gerede*) gossip; '**2base** *f* gossip; '**2e** *f* (15) fly-flap; F *s.* *Klatschbase*; '**~en** *v/t. u. v/i.* (27) clap (*in die Hände* one's hands); slap; (*in*) *Wasser*: splash; *fig.* gossip; *s. Beifall*; '**2er** *m* (7) clapper; (*Beifall2*) applauder; **2erei** [~ə'raɪ] *f* (16) gossip(ing); '**~haft** gossipy; '**2maul** F *n* gossip, scandalmonger; '**2mohn** ⚘ *m* (corn-)poppy; '**~naß** sopping wet; '**2spalte** *f* gossip column; '**~süchtig** gossip-mongering; '**2tante** *f* gossip.

klauben F ['klaubən] (25) pick.

Klaue ['klauə] *f* (15) claw (*a.* ⊕); (*Pfote*) paw (*a. contp. s. Hand*); *fig.* *b.s.* clutch; F (*schlechte Schrift*) scrawl; '**2n** P (*stehlen*) F pinch, swipe; '**~nfett** *n* neat's-foot oil; '**~nseuche** *f* foot-rot.

Klause ['klauzə] *f* (15) cell, hermitage.

Klausel ['~zəl] *f* (15) clause; (*Vorbehalt*) proviso; stipulation.

Klausner ['klausnər] *m* hermit.

Klausur [klau'zu:r] *f* (16) seclusion; *a.* = **~-arbeit** *f* work written under supervision; **~sitzung** *f* closed session; **~tagung** *f* closed meeting.

Klaviatur [klavja'tu:r] *f* (16) keyboard.

Klavier [kla'vi:r] *n* (3¹) piano(forte); *auf dem* (*am*) ~ on (at) the piano; **~-auszug** ♪ *m* piano-score; **~konzert** *n* piano recital; **~lehrer(in** *f*) *m* piano-teacher; **~schule** *f* (*Buch*) piano tutor; **~sonate** *f* piano sonata; **~spieler(in** *f*) *m* pianist; **~stimmer** *m* (7) tuner; **~stunde** *f* piano lesson.

'**Klebe|band** *n* adhesive tape; '**~folie** *f* self-adhesive plastic sheeting; '**~mittel** *n* adhesive.

klebe|n ['kle:bən] (25) *v/t.* stick, paste; F *j-m eine* ~ paste a p. one; *v/i.* (*a. ~bleiben*) stick, adhere (*an dat.* to); '**2pflaster** *n* adhesive (*od.* sticking) plaster; '**2r** *m* (7) **1.** *s.* *Klebstoff*; **2.** ⚘ gluten; '**2zettel** *m* stick-on label, *Am.* sticker.

'**klebrig** adhesive, sticky; 🕮 viscous; '**2keit** *f* stickiness.

Kleb|stoff ['kle:p-] *m* adhesive; '**~streifen** *m* adhesive tape.

Klecks [klɛks] *m* (4) blot, blotch; (*Masse*) blob; '**2en** (27) blot, make splodges; *Malerei contp.* daub.

Klee [kle:] *m* (3¹) clover, trefoil; '**~blatt** *n* clover-leaf; *fig.* trio.

Kleid [klaɪt] *n* (1) dress, garment; *langes*: robe, *elegantes*: gown; *pl.* clothes; **2en** ['~dən] (26) dress; (*a. fig.*) clothe, dress; *j-n gut usw.* ~ suit, become, look *well etc.* on; *sich* ~ dress.

Kleider|-ablage ['~dər-] *f* cloakroom, *Am.* checkroom; *im Haus*: hall-stand; '**~bügel** *m* coat- *od.* dress-hanger; '**~bürste** *f* clothes-brush; '**~haken** *m* clothes-peg, coat-hook; '**~schrank** *m* wardrobe; '**~schürze** *f* house frock; '**~ständer** *m* (hat and) coat stand; '**~stoff** *m* dress material.

kleidsam ['klaɪt-] becoming.

'**Kleidung** *f* clothing, dress, clothes *pl.*; '**~sstück** *n* article of clothing, garment.

Kleie ['klaɪə] *f* (15) bran.

klein [klaɪn] small, *nur attr.*: little; *fig.* (*unbedeutend*) petty; ~(*er comp.*) (*minder*) minor; *~es Geld* (small) change; *ein ~ wenig* a little (bit); *groß und ~* great and small, (*jung u. alt*) old and young; *von ~ auf* from a child; *s. beigeben*; *im ~en verkaufen* (sell by) retail; *Wort ~ schreiben* write in small letters; *bis ins ~ste* (down) to the last detail; '**2e** *m* little boy; *f* little girl; *n* (*Kind*) little one; *die ~n pl.* the little ones.

'**Klein|-anzeige** *f* classified ad(vertisement); '**~-arbeit** *f* spade-work; '**~auto** *n* small car; '**~bahn** *f* narrow-ga(u)ge railway; '**~bauer** *m* smallholder; '**~betrieb** *m* small(-scale) enterprise; ✓ smallholding; '**~bildkamera** *f* miniature camera; '**~buchstabe** *m* small letter; '**~bürger** *m*, '**2bürgerlich** petty bourgeois; '**~bus** *m* minibus; '**~computer** *m* minicomputer; '**2denkend** small-minded; '**~format** *m* small size; '**~garten** *m* allotment (garden); '**~gärtner** *m* allotment gardener; '**~gebäck** *n* fancy biscuits *pl.*; '**~gedruckte** *n*: *das* ~ the small print; '**~geld** *n* (small) change; '**2gläubig** of little faith, faint-hearted; '**~handel** ⚕ *m* retail trade; '**~händler** *m* retailer; '**~heit** *f* littleness, smallness; '**~hirn** *n* cerebellum; '**~holz** *n* matchwood.

'**Kleinigkeit** *f* trifle; '**~skrämer** *m* pedant, fuss-pot; '**~skrämerei** *f* pedantry.

'**Klein|kaliberbüchse** *f* small-bore (*od.* sub-calibre) rifle; '**2kariert** small-check(ed); *fig.* small-minded; '**~kind** *n* infant; '**~kram** *m* trifles *pl.*; '**~krieg** *m* guer(r)illa warfare; '**~kunstbühne** *f* cabaret; '**2laut** subdued.

'**kleinlich** pedantic; (*engstirnig*) narrow-minded.

'**Klein|mut** *m* pusillanimity, faint-heartedness; **2mütig** ['~my:tiç] pusillanimous, faint-hearted.

Kleinod ['~no:t] *n* (3; *pl. a.* -*ien* [~'no:diən]) jewel, gem; *fig. a.* treasure.

'**Klein|staat** *m* minor state; '**~staaterei** *f* particularism; '**~stadt** *f* small town; '**~städter(in** *f*) *m*, '**2städtisch** provincial; '**~st...** very small, miniature ...; '**~vieh** *n* small cattle; '**~wagen** *m* small car.

Kleister ['klaɪstər] *m* (7), '**2n** (29) paste.

Klemm|e ['klɛmə] *f* (15) ⊕ clamp, (*a. Haar2 usw.*) clip; ⚡ terminal; F *fig. in der* ~ *sein* be in a jam *od.* fix; '**2en** (25) jam (*a.* ⊕), squeeze, pinch; F (*stehlen*) pinch; *sich den Finger* ~ get one's finger jammed; *fig. sich* ~ *hinter* get down to (*work, etc.*); '**~er** *m* (7) pince-nez (*fr.*); '**~schraube** ⊕ *f* setscrew; ⚡ binding screw.

Klempner ['klɛmpnər] *m* (7) tinman, tinsmith; (*Installateur*) plumber; **~ei** [~'raɪ] *f* (16) tinman's trade *od.* workshop; plumbing.

Klepper ['klɛpər] *m* (7) nag, hack.

klerikal [kleri'kɑ:l] clerical.

Kleriker ['kle:-] *m* (7) cleric.

Klerus ['kle:rus] *m* clergy.

Klette ['klɛtə] *f* (15) bur(r) (*a. fig.*), burdock.

Kletter|er ['klɛtərər] *m* (7) climber; '**2n** (29, sn) climb (*auf e-n Baum usw.* [up] a tree, *etc.*); '**~pflanze** *f* climber, creeper; '**~rose** *f* rambler; '**~stange** *f* climbing-pole.

Klient [kli'ɛnt] *m* (12), **~in** *f* client.

Klima ['kli:ma] *n* (11²) climate; *fig. a.* atmosphere; '**~-anlage** *f* air-conditioning (system); **2tisch** [~'mɑ:tiʃ] climatic(ally *adv.*); **~ti'sierung** *f* (15) air conditioning; **~tologe** [~to'lo:gə] *m* (13) climatologist; **~tologie** [~tolo'gi:] *f* (15, *o. pl.*) climatology; '**~wechsel** *m* change of climate.

Klimbim [klim'bim] F *m* (3¹, *o. pl.*) junk; (*Getue*) fuss.

klimm|en ['klimən] (30, sn) climb (*s. klettern*); '**2zug** *m* pull-up.

klimpern ['klimpərn] *v/i.* (29) jingle, tinkle (*beide a.* ~ *mit*); (*a. v/t.*) *auf dem Klavier usw.*: strum.

Klinge ['kliŋə] *f* (15) blade; *mit j-m die* ~*n kreuzen* (*a. fig.*) cross swords with a p.

Klingel ['kliŋəl] *f* (15) (small) bell; (*Tür2*) (door)bell; '**~knopf** *m* bell-push; '**2n** (29) tinkle; *Glocke*: ring; *P.*: ring the bell; *es klingelt* the bell rings; '**~zug** *m* bellpull.

klingen ['kliŋən] (30) sound (*a. fig.*); *Metall*: tinkle; *Glas*: clink; *Glocke*: ring; ~*de Münze* hard cash.

Klin|ik ['kli:nik] *f* (16) hospital (department); (*Privat2*) nursing home, clinic; '**2isch** clinical.

Klinke ['kliŋkə] *f* (15) (*Türgriff*) (door-)handle; *weitS.* latch; ⚡ jack.

'**Klinker** *m* (7) (Dutch) clinker.

klipp [klip]: ~ *und klar* perfectly clear; *adv. say* plainly, straight out.

Klipp|e ['klipə] *f* (15) reef; *weitS.* cliff; *fig.* hurdle; '**2ig** craggy.

'**klipp'klapp** click-clack, flip-flap.

klirren ['kli:rən] (25) *Glas*: clink; *Porzellan usw.*: clatter; *Kette usw.*: clank, clash (*alle a.* ~ *mit*); *Fensterscheibe*: rattle.

Klischee [kli'ʃe:] *n* (11) (stereotype) block *od.* plate, (*a. fig.*) cliché; **~vorstellung** *f* stereotyped idea.

Klistier [kli'sti:r] *n* (3¹) enema; **~spritze** *f* rectal syringe.

klitschig ['klitʃiç] *Brot*: doughy.
klitzeklein ['klitsə-] F tiny little, teeny-weeny.
Klo [klo:] F *n* (11) F loo, *Am.* john.
Kloake [klo'a:kə] *f* (15) sewer; (*Grube*) cesspool (*a. fig.*).
Klob|en ['klo:bən] (6) *m* ⊕ block; (*Holz*) log; '**\~ig** (*massig*) bulky, massy; (*plump*) clumsy.
klomm [klɔm] *pret. v. klimmen.*
klönen ['kløːnən] F chin-wag.
klopf|en ['klɔpfən] *v/t. u. v/i.* (25) knock (*a. mot.*), rap; (*sanft \~*) tap; *Steine*: break; *Teppich*: beat (*v/i. a. Herz*); *es klopft* there's a knock at the door; *s. Busch*; '**\~er** *m* (7) beater; (*Tür\~*) knocker; *tel.* sounder; '**\~fest** *mot.* knockproof.
Klöppel ['klœpəl] *m* (7) *der Glocke*: clapper; (*Spitzen\~*) bobbin; ⚒ swingle; '**\~-arbeit** *f*, **\~ei** [\~'laɪ] *f* bobbin lace work; '**\~kissen** *n* (lace-)-pillow; '**\~n** *v/i.* (29) make lace; '**\~spitzen** *f/pl.* bobbin- (*od.* pillow-)lace *sg.*
Klops [klɔps] *m* (4) meat ball.
Klosett [klo'zɛt] *n* (3) toilet, closet, W.C., lavatory; **\~becken** *n* closet-bowl; **\~papier** *n* toilet-paper.
Kloß [klo:s] *m* (3[2] *u.* [3]) *Küche*: dumpling.
Kloster ['klo:stər] *n* (7[1]) (*Mönchs\~*) monastery; (*Nonnen\~*) convent, nunnery; '**\~bruder** *m* friar; '**\~frau** *f* nun; '**\~leben** *n* monastic life.
klösterlich ['klø:stərliç] monastic; convent(ual).
Klotz [klɔts] *m* (3[2] *u.* [3]) block, (*a. fig.*) log; *fig. contp.* oaf; '**\~ig** (*sehr groß*) mighty; *s. klobig.*
Klub [klup] *m* (11) club; '**\~jacke** *f* blazer; '**\~kamerad** *m* fellow club-member; '**\~sessel** *m* club chair.
Kluft [kluft] *f* (14[1]) gap, cleft; (*grundlose Tiefe*) gulf, abyss, chasm (*alle a. fig.*); F (*Kleidung*) togs *pl.*
klug [klu:k] (*gescheit*) clever, shrewd; (*verständig*) wise, intelligent, judicious, sensible; (*vorsichtig*) prudent; (*schlau*) cunning; *ich kann nicht \~ daraus werden* I can't make head or tail of it; *ich werde aus ihm nicht \~* I cannot make him out; *er hat \~ reden* it is easy for him to say so; *der Klügere gibt nach* the wiser head gives in; '**\~heit** *f* cleverness; intelligence; judiciousness; prudence.
klüglich ['kly:kliç] wisely.
'**Klug|redner** *m*, '**\~schnacker** *m* (7) wiseacre, *Am.* wise guy, smart aleck.
Klump|en ['klumpən] *m* (6) lump, clot; (*Erde*) clod; (*Haufen*) heap; '**\~fuß** *m* club-foot; '**\~ig** lumpy.
Klüngel ['klyŋəl] *m* (7) clique.
Klüver ⚓ ['kly:vər] *m* (7) jib; '**\~baum** ⚓ *m* jib-boom.
knabbern ['knabərn] *v/i. u. v/t.* (29) gnaw, nibble (*an dat.* at).
Knabe ['kna:bə] *m* (13) *allg.* boy; (*Bursche*) lad; F *alter \~* old chap; '**\~n-alter** *n* boyhood; '**\~nchor** *m* boys' choir; '**\~nhaft** boyish.
Knack(s) [knak(s)] *m* (4) crack.
Knäckebrot ['knɛkə-] *n* crispbread.
'**knack|en 1.** *v/t.* (25) crack (*a. fig.*); F *Auto*: break into; *v/i.* crack; snap; *Schloß usw.*: click; **2.** \~ *n* (6) crack; click; '**\~laut** *gr. m* glottal stop; '**\~mandel** *f* shell-almond; '**\~wurst** *f* saveloy.
Knall [knal] *m* (3) bang; (*Schuß*) *a.* report; *bsd. Peitsche*: crack; (*Explosion*) detonation; *\~ und Fall* abruptly; F *e-n \~ haben* be mad (*od.* nuts); '**\~bonbon** *m* (party) cracker; '**\~-effekt** *m* sensation, bang; '**\~en** (25) bang, crack, pop (*alle a. \~ mit*); (*explodieren*) explode, detonate; *\~ gegen* crash against; '**\~-erbse** *f* (toy-)torpedo; '**\~frosch** *m* jumping cracker; '**\~gas** *n* oxyhydrogen gas; '**\~'hart** F tough; *Schuß*: powerful; (*unmißverständlich*) brutal; '**\~ig** F flashy; '**\~kopf** F *m* idiot; '**\~körper** *m* banger; '**\~rot** glaring red.
knapp [knap] (*eng*) *Kleidung*: close, tight; (*spärlich*) scanty, *mst pred.* scarce; *Stil*: concise; *Gewicht*: short; *Mehrheit*: bare; *mit \~er Not* barely, with great difficulty; *mit \~er Not entrinnen od. davonkommen* have (*od.* make) a narrow escape; *\~ an Geld sein* be short of money, be hard up; *\~ werden Vorrat*: run short; *\~ 10 Minuten* just (*od.* barely) ten minutes; '**\~e** *m* (13) *hist.* page, squire; ⚒ miner; '**\~halten** keep *a p.* short; '**\~heit** *f s. knapp*; tightness; scarcity; conciseness; *an Vorräten*: shortage; '**\~schaft** *f* (16) miners' society.
Knarre ['knarə] *f* (15) rattle; F (*Schußwaffe*) gun, F pea-shooter; '**\~n** (25) creak, rattle; *Stimme*: grate.
Knast [knast] *m* (3) (*Holz*) knag;

Brot: crust; F *alter* ~ old fogey; *sl.* (3, *o. pl.*) (*Gefängnis*) clink; *sl.* ~ *schieben* do time.

Knaster ['knastər] *m* (7) canaster; F *contp.* bad tobacco.

knattern ['knatərn] (29) crackle; *Gewehrfeuer*: rattle; *mot.* roar.

Knäuel ['knɔʏəl] *m*, *n* (7) ball; *fig.* tangle; (*Menschen*2) cluster, crowd.

Knauf [knauf] *m* (3³) knob; ⚠ capital; (*Degen*2) pommel.

Knauser ['knauzər] *m* (7) miser; **~ei** [~'raɪ] *f* niggardliness, stinginess; '**2ig** niggardly, stingy; '**2n** (29) be stingy (*mit* with).

knautsch|en F ['knautʃən] (27) crumple; '**2zone** *f* crushable bin.

Knebel ['kne:bəl] *m* (7) ⊕ lever; (*Mund*2) gag; '**~bart** *m* turned-up moustache; '**2n** (29) gag; *fig.* muzzle; (*lähmen*) fetter.

Knecht [knɛçt] *m* (3) servant; ↗ farm-hand; (*Unfreier*) slave; '**2en** (26) enslave; '**2isch** servile, slavish; '**~schaft** *f* servitude, slavery; '**~ung** *f* enslavement.

kneif|en ['knaɪfən] (30) pinch, nip; F *fig.* back (*Am.* chicken) out; ~ *vor* dodge; '**2er** *m* (7) pince-nez (*fr.*); '**2zange** *f* (*eine* a pair of) nippers *pl.*, pincers *pl.*

Kneipe ['knaɪpə] *f* (15) public house, F pub, *Am.* saloon; (*Studenten*2) beer-party, (*Ort*) students' club; '**2n** (*zechen*) tipple, booze; '**~nwirt** *m* publican, *Am.* saloon keeper.

Kneippkur ['knaɪp-] *f* Kneipp('s) cure.

knet|en ['kne:tən] (26) knead; '**2masse** *f* plasticine.

Knick [knik] *m* (3) (*Biegung*) bend; (*Riß*) crack; *in Draht usw.*: kink; *in Papier usw.*: fold, crease; '**2en** *v/i. u. v/t.* (25) bend; crack; crease; *fig.* crush; *geknickt fig.* crestfallen.

Knicker ['knikər] *m* (7), **~ei** [~'raɪ] *f*, '**2ig** *s. Knauser usw.*

'**Knickfuß** *m* pes valgus.

Knicks [kniks] *m* (4) curts(e)y; *e-n* ~ *machen*, '**2en** (27) (drop a) curtsy.

Knie [kni:] *n* (3) knee (*a.* ⊕); (*Biegung*) bend; *et. übers* ~ *brechen* rush a th.; **~beuge** ['~bɔʏgə] *f* (15) *Turnen*: knee-bend; '**~fall** *m* genuflection, prostration; '**2fällig** on one's bended knees; '**~gelenk** *n* knee-joint (*a.* ⊕); '**~hose** *f* (*eine* a pair of) knee-breeches; '**~kehle** *f* hollow of the knee; '**2n** (25) kneel (*vor dat.* to); '**~scheibe** *f* knee-cap, knee-pan; '**~schützer** *m* knee-pad; '**~strumpf** *m* knee-length stocking.

Kniff [knif] **1.** *m* (3) *im Stoff usw.*: crease, fold; *fig.* trick, knack; **2.** 2 *pret. v. kneifen*; '**2(e)lig** tricky; '**2en** (25) fold (down), crease.

knipsen ['knipsən] (27) *v/i.* snap (*mit den Fingern* one's fingers); *v/t.* 🚂 punch; F *phot.* (*a. v/i.*) snap (-shot), take a shot (*v/t.* of).

Knirps [knirps] *m* (4) F hop-o'-my-thumb.

knirschen ['knirʃən] (27) grate, creak; *Kies usw.*: crunch; *mit den Zähnen* ~ gnash one's teeth.

knistern ['knistərn] (29) crackle; *bsd. Seide*: rustle.

knitter|frei ['knitər-] creaseproof, non-creasing, crease-resistant; '**~n** *v/i. u. v/t.* (29) crumple, crease.

knobeln F ['kno:bəln] (29) throw dice (*um* for); (*tüfteln*) puzzle (*an dat.* over).

Knoblauch ['kno:b-] *m* (3) garlic; '**~zehe** *f* clove of garlic.

Knöchel ['knœçəl] *m* (7) knuckle; (*Fuß*2) ankle; '**~bruch** *m* ankle fracture.

Knochen ['knɔxən] *m* (6) bone; '**~bruch** *m* fracture (of a bone); '**~fraß** *m* caries; '**~gerüst** *n* skeleton; '**~mark** *n* (bone) marrow; '**~mehl** *n* bone meal; '**~splitter** *m* bone-splinter.

knöchern ['knœçərn] bone ...; bony, 🕮 osseous.

knochig ['knɔxiç] bony.

Knödel ['knø:dəl] *m* (7) dumpling.

Knolle ['knɔlə] *f* (15) tuber; (*Zwiebel*) bulb; '**~n** *m* (6) lump.

'**knollig** knobby, cloddy; ⚘ tuberous; ⚘ bulbous.

Knopf [knɔpf] *m* (3³) button; (*Degen*2, *Sattel*2, *Turm*2) pommel; (*Griff an der Tür usw.*) knob; (*Nadel*2) head; *s. Hemd*2, *Manschetten*2.

Knöpf|chen ['knœpfçən] *n* (6) small button; '**2en** (25) button.

'**Knopf|druck** *m*: *auf* ~ at the press of a button; '**~loch** *n* buttonhole.

Knorpel ['knɔrpəl] *m* (7) cartilage, gristle; '**2ig** cartilaginous, gristly.

Knorr|en ['knɔrən] *m* (6) knot, knag; '**2ig** knobby, gnarled.

Knosp|e [ˈknɔspə] *f* (15) bud; ˈ**ᘔen** (25) bud.

Knoten [ˈkno:tən] **1.** *m* (6) knot (*a. fig.* = *Schwierigkeit*; ⚓ = *Seemeile*); (*Haarfrisur*) knot, chignon; *e-s Dramas*: plot; **2.** ᘔ (26) knot; ˈ**~punkt** *m* 🚂 junction.

knotig [ˈkno:tiç] knotty (*a. fig.*).

Knuff [knuf] *m* (3³) cuff, thump; ˈ**ᘔen** (25) cuff, poke.

Knülch [knylç] F *m* (3¹) *sl.* bird, [*Am.* guy.]

knüllen [ˈknylən] (25) crumple.

Knüller F [ˈknylər] *m* F (big) hit.

knüpfen [ˈknypfən] (25) tie, knot.

Knüppel [ˈknypəl] *m* (7) cudgel; club, stick; (*Brötchen*) (small) roll; *s. Polizei*ᘔ, *Steuer*ᘔ; ˈ**~damm** *m* log-road, *Am.* corduroy road; ˈ**ᘔn** cudgel, beat; ˈ**~schaltung** *mot. f*: *mit* ~ with floor-mounted gear change.

knurren [ˈknurən] (25) snarl, growl; *fig.* grumble (*alle*: *über acc.* at); *Magen, Eingeweide*: rumble.

ˈ**knurrig** F grumpy.

knusp(e)rig [ˈknusp(ə)riç] crisp.

Knute [ˈknu:tə] *f* (15) knout.

knutsch|en F [ˈknu:tʃən] (27) hug, cuddle, F neck, pet; ˈ**ᘔfleck** *m* love bite.

Knüttel [ˈknytəl] *m* (7) cudgel; ˈ**~vers** *m* doggerel rhyme *od.* verse.

Koalition [ko:ˀaliˈtsjo:n] *pol. f* coalition.

Kobalt *min.* [ˈko:balt] *m* (3) cobalt.

Koben [ˈko:bən] *m* (6) pigsty.

Kobold [ˈko:bɔlt] *m* (3) (hob)goblin, imp (*a. fig.*).

Koch [kɔx] *m* (3³) (man-)cook; ˈ**~birne** *f* cooking pear; ˈ**~buch** *n* cookery-book, *Am.* cookbook; ˈ**ᘔecht** fast to boiling; ˈ**ᘔen** (25) *v/i.* be cooking; *Flüssigkeit*: boil (*a. fig. vor Wut usw.*); *v/t.* cook; boil; ˈ**~er** *m* (7) cooker.

Köcher [ˈkœçər] *m* (7) quiver.

ˈ**Koch|fett** *n* shortening; ˈ**~gelegenheit** *f* cooking facilities *pl.* ˈ**~geschirr** ⚔ *n* mess tin, *Am.* mess kit; ˈ**~herd** *m* (cooking-)range, *Am.* cook stove.

Köchin [ˈkœçin] *f* (16¹) cook.

ˈ**Koch|kiste** *f* haybox; ˈ**~kunst** *f* art of cooking, culinary art; ˈ**~löffel** *m* (wooden) spoon; ˈ**~nische** *f* kitchenette; ˈ**~platte** *f* hot-plate; ˈ**~salz** *n* common salt; ˈ**~topf** *m* cooking-pot.

Köder [ˈkø:dər] *m* (7) (*a. fig.*) bait, lure; ˈ**ᘔn** (29) (*a. fig.*) bait, lure.

Kodex [ˈko:dɛks] *m* (3², *sg. a. inv., pl. a. Kodizes*) code.

Koffein [kɔfeˈˀi:n] *n* (3¹) caffeine; **ᘔfrei** decaffeinated.

Koffer [ˈkɔfər] *m* (7) (*Hand*ᘔ) suitcase, case *Am. a.* grip; *großer*: trunk; ˈ**~-anhänger** *m* address tag; ˈ**~gerät** *n*, ˈ**~radio** *n* portable radio (set); ˈ**~raum** *mot. m* boot, *Am.* trunk.

Kognac [ˈkɔnjak] *m* (3¹ *u.* 11) cognac, (French) brandy.

Kohl [ko:l] *m* (3) cabbage; F *fig.* twaddle, rubbish.

Kohle [ˈko:lə] *f* (15) coal; *s. Holz*ᘔ, *Stein*ᘔ; *zum Zeichnen*, ⚡ *usw.*: carbon; *glühende* ~*n* red-hot (*od.* live) coals; *fig. wie auf* ~*n sitzen* be on tenterhooks; ˈ**~faden(lampe** *f*) *m* carbon filament (lamp); ˈ**~hydrat** ⚗ *n* carbohydrate; ˈ**~kraftwerk** *n* coal power plant (*od.* station); ˈ**ᘔn** *v/i.* (25) (*ver*~, *an*~) char, carbonize; ⚓ coal.

ˈ**Kohlen|becken** *n* brazier; ⚒ *s. Kohlenrevier*; ˈ**~bergwerk** *n* coal-mine, colliery; ˈ**~bunker** *m* (coal)bunker; ˈ**~dioxyd** ⚗ *n* carbon dioxyde; ˈ**~eimer** *m* coal-scuttle; ˈ**~flöz** ⚒ *n* coal seam; ˈ**~gas** *n* coal-gas; ˈ**~händler** *m* coal merchant; ˈ**~-oxyd** *n* carbon monoxide; ˈ**~revier** *n* coal-field *od.* -district; ˈ**ᘔsauer** carbonate of ...; ˈ**~säure** *f* carbonic acid; *weitS.* carbon dioxide; ˈ**~schiff** *n* collier; ˈ**~staub** *m* coal-dust; ˈ**~stoff** *m* carbon; ˈ**~stoffaser** *f* carbon fibre; ˈ**~wasserstoff** *m* hydrocarbon.

ˈ**Kohlepapier** *n* carbon paper.

Köhler [ˈkø:lər] *m* (7) charcoal-burner.

ˈ**Kohle|stift** *m* charcoal pencil; ⚡ carbon-rod; ˈ**~vorkommen** *n* coal field; ˈ**~zeichnung** *f* charcoal-drawing.

ˈ**Kohl|kopf** *m* cabbage; ˈ**ᘔrabenˈschwarz** coal-black; **~rabi** [~ˈra:bi] *m* (11) kohlrabi; ˈ**~rübe** *f* Swedish turnip, swede, *Am. a.* rutabaga; **~weißling** [ˈ~vaɪsliŋ] *m* cabbage-butterfly.

Ko-itus [ˈko:ˀitus] *m* (*inv.*) coition.

Koje ⚓ [ˈko:jə] *f* (15) berth, bunk.

Kokain [kokaˈˀi:n] *n* (3¹) cocaine.

Kokarde [koˈkardə] *f* (15) cockade.

kokett [koˈkɛt] coquettish; **ᘔerie** [~əˈri:] *f* coquetry, coquettishness; **~ieren** [~ˈti:rən] coquet, flirt.

Kokon [ko'kõ] *m* (11) cocoon.

Kokos|baum ['ko:kɔs-] *m* coconut tree; '**~fett** *n* coconut oil; '**~matte** *f* coir mat(ting); '**~nuß** *f* coconut; '**~palme** *f* coconut palm.

Koks [ko:ks] *m* (4) coke (*a. sl. Kokain*); '**2en** *sl.* (27) sniff coke.

Kolben ['kɔlbən] *m* (6) (*Gewehr2*) butt(-end); (*Keule*) mace, club; (*Maschinen2*) piston; ⚘ spike; ⚗ flask; '**~hub** *m* piston stroke; '**~motor** *m* piston engine; '**~ring** *m* piston ring; '**~stange** *f* piston rod.

Kolchose [kɔl'ço:zə] *f* (15) kolkhoz, collective farm.

Kolik ['ko:lik] *f* (16) colic.

Kollaborateur [kɔlabora'tø:r] *m* (3¹) collaborator.

Kollaps ['kɔlaps] *m* (3²) collapse.

Kolleg [kɔ'le:k] *n* (8²) course of lectures; lecture; **~e** [~gə] *m* (13), **~in** *f* (16¹) colleague; **2ial** [~'gja:l] collegial; *weitS.* helpful; **~ium** [~'le:gjum] *n* (9) board, staff; *s. Lehrkörper.*

Kollek|te [kɔ'lɛktə] *f* (15) collection; (*Gebet*) collect; **~tion** ✝ [~'tsjo:n] *f* (16) collection, range; **2tiv** [~'ti:f] **1.** *adj.*, **2.** 2 *n* (3¹) collective; **~'tivvertrag** *m* collective agreement.

Koller ['kɔlər] *m* (7) *vet.* staggers *pl.*; *fig.* rage, tantrum; '**2n** *v/i.* (29, sn; *a. v/t.*) roll; (h.) *Puter*: gobble.

kolli|dieren [kɔli'di:rən] (sn) collide; **2sion** [~'zjo:n] *f* (16) collision.

Kollo ['kɔlo] *n* (11, *pl. a. Kolli* ['~li]) parcel, package.

Kölnischwasser [kœlniʃ'vasər] *n* eau-de-Cologne.

Kolon ['ko:lɔn] *n* (11 *u.* 9²) colon.

Kolonial... [kolo'nja:l-] colonial ...; **~waren** *f/pl.* colonial produce; groceries *pl.*; **~warenhändler** *m* grocer; **~warenhandlung** *f* grocer's shop, grocery.

Kolon|ie [kolo'ni:] *f* (15) colony; **2isieren** [~ni'zi:rən] colonize; **~ist** [~'nist] *m* (12) colonist, settler.

Kolonnade [kolɔ'na:də] *f* (15) colonnade.

Kolonne [ko'lɔnə] *f* (15) column (*a. typ.*); (*Arbeiter2*) gang; **~nspringer** *mot.* F *m* queue-jumper.

Kolophonium [kolo'fo:njum] *n* (9) colophony, rosin.

Koloratur [kolora'tu:r] *f* (16) coloratura; **~sängerin** *f* coloratura singer.

kolor|ieren [~'ri:rən] colo(u)r; **2it** [~'ri:t] *n* (3) colo(u)r(ing).

Koloß [ko'lɔs] *m* (4) colossus.

kolossal [~'sa:l] colossal, huge; *fig. a.* enormous, F terrific.

Kolport|age [kɔlpɔr'ta:ʒə] *f* (15, *o. pl.*) hawking (of books); *fig.* (*Schund*) trash; (*Verbreiten*) spreading; **2ieren** [~'ti:rən] hawk; *fig.* spread.

Kolum|ne [ko'lumnə] *f* (15) column; **~nentitel** *typ. m* running head; **~'nist** [~'nist] *m* (12) columnist.

Kombination [kɔmbina'tsjo:n] *f allg.* combination (*a. Sport*); (*Schutzanzug*) overall, ✈ flying suit; *fig.* (*Folgerung*) deduction; **~sgabe** *f* power of deduction; **~sschloß** *n* combination (*od.* puzzle) lock.

kombinieren [~'ni:rən] combine; (*folgern*) deduce.

Kombiwagen ['kɔmbi-] *m* estate car, *bsd. Am.* station wagon.

Kombüse ⚓ [kɔm'by:zə] *f* (15) galley.

Komet [ko'me:t] *m* (12) comet; **2enhaft** comet-like; **~enschweif** *m* comet's tail.

Komfort [kɔm'fɔ:r, kõ-] *m* (7, *o.pl.*) comfort(s *pl.*); luxury; **2abel** [~fɔr'ta:bəl] comfortable; **~wohnung** *f* luxury flat.

Komik ['ko:mik] *f* (16) comicality, funniness; fun; '**~er** *m* (7) comedian, comic (actor).

'**komisch** comic(al); *fig. a.* funny, queer, odd.

Komitee [komi'te:] *n* (11) committee.

Komma ['kɔma] *n* (11²) comma; *im Dezimalbruch*: decimal point.

Kommand|ant [kɔman'dant] *m* (12), **~eur** [~'dø:r] *m* (3¹) commander, *Am.* commanding officer; **~antur** [~'tu:r] *f* garrison (*od. Am.* post) headquarters *pl.*; **2ieren** [~'di:rən] *v/t. u. v/i.* command; *v/t.* ⚔ (*abstellen*) detach; (*einteilen*) detail; *vorübergehend*: attach; **~itgesellschaft** [~'di:t-] *f* limited partnership; **~itist** [~di'tist] *m* (12) limited partner.

Kommando [~'mando] ⚔ *n* (11) command; (*Abteilung*) detachment; (*~truppe*) commando (unit); **~brücke** ⚓ *f* (navigating) bridge; **~kapsel** *f Raumfahrt*: command module; **~stab** *m* baton; **~turm** *m* ⚓

conning tower; ✈✕ control-tower.

kommen [ˈkɔmən] (30, sn) come; (*gelangen*) get; (*an*~) arrive; (*sich zutragen*) come (to pass); ~ *lassen P.*: send for, *S.*: order; ~ *sehen* foresee; *gegangen* ~ come on foot; *gelaufen* ~ come running; *s. Atem, Fall, Kosten, Reihe, Schluß, Verlegenheit*; *es komme, wie es wolle* come what may; *auf et.* (*acc.*) ~ hit on, find out; *wie kommst du darauf?* what put this idea into your head?; *auf soundsoviel* ~ (*sich belaufen*) amount to; *auf einen Knaben* ~ *zwei Äpfel* there are two apples to one boy; *hinter et.* (*acc.*) ~ find out; *um et.* ~ lose a th.; ~ *von e-r Ursache* be due to; *zu et.* ~ (*bekommen*) come by a th.; *wieder zu sich* ~ come round *od.* to; *drohend*: *wie* ~ *Sie dazu?* how dare you?; *ich komme nie dazu* I can never find time (to do it); *wie kommt es, daß die Tür offen ist?* how come(s it that) the door is open?; *das kommt davon* F that's what comes of it; *s. kurz*; ˈ**~d** coming; ~*es Jahr a.* next year.

Kommen|tar [kɔmɛnˈtɑːr] *m* (3¹) commentary; ~ *überflüssig!*, *kein* ~*!* no comment!; **~ˈtator** [~tɔr] *m* commentator; **2ˈtieren** comment on.

Kommers [kɔˈmɛrs] *m* (4) drinking-bout; **~buch** *n* students' songbook.

kommerz|ialisieren [kɔmɛrtsjaliˈziːrən] commercialize; **~iell** [~ˈtsjɛl] commercial.

Kommilitone [kɔmiliˈtoːnə] *m* (13) fellow student.

Kommis [kɔˈmiː] *m inv.* (*Schreiber*) clerk; (*Verkäufer*) salesman, shopman, *Am.* salesclerk.

Kommiß [kɔˈmis] F *m* (4, *o. pl.*) military service *od.* life, army.

Kommissar [kɔmiˈsɑːr] *m* (3¹) commissioner; *s. Kriminal*2; (*Sowjet*2) commissar; **2isch** deputy; temporary.

Kommission [~ˈsjoːn] *f* commission (*a.* ✝), committee; **~är** ✝ [~ˈnɛːr] *m* (3¹) commission agent; **~sgeschäft** *n* commission business.

Kommode [kɔˈmoːdə] *f* (15) chest of drawers, *Am.* bureau.

Kommunal... [kɔmuˈnɑːl-] local, communal, municipal; **~be-amte** *m* municipal officer; **~politik** *f* local politics *pl.*; **~wahlen** *f/pl.* local elections.

Kommune [kɔˈmuːnə] *f* (15) commune; *weitS. the* Communists *pl.*

Kommunikat|ionsmittel [kɔmunikaˈtsjoːns-] *n* means of communication; *pl. a.* mass media *pl.*; **~ionstechnik** *f* communications technology; **2iv** [~ˈtiːf] communicative.

Kommunion [~ˈnjoːn] *f* (16) (Holy) Communion.

Kommuniqué [kɔmyniˈkeː] *n* (11) communiqué.

Kommunismus [kɔmuˈnismus] *m* (16, *o. pl.*) communism.

Kommuˈnist *m* (12), **~in** *f* (16¹) communist; **2isch** communist(ic).

Komödiant [kɔmøˈdjant] *m* (12) comedian; *contp. a. fig.* play-actor; **~in** *f* (16¹) comedienne.

Komödie [~ˈmøːdjə] *f* (15) comedy; ~ *spielen fig.* play-act.

Kompagnon [ˈkɔmpanjɔ̃] *m* (11) partner.

kompakt [kɔmˈpakt] compact.

Kompanie [kɔmpaˈniː] *f* (15) company; **~chef** *m* company commander; **~geschäft** *n* joint business.

Komparativ *gr.* [ˈkɔmparatiːf] *m* (3¹) comparative (degree).

Kompars|e [kɔmˈparzə] *m* (13), **~in** *f* (16¹) extra, F super.

Kompaß [ˈkɔmpas] *m* (4) compass; **~häus-chen** ⚓ [ˈ~hɔʏsçən] *n* binnacle; ˈ**~nadel** *f* compass-needle; ˈ**~rose** *f* compass-card.

Kompen|sation [kɔmpɛnzaˈtsjoːn] *f* (16) compensation; **~satiˈonsgeschäft** ✝ *n* barter transaction; **~ˈsator** ⚡ *m* potentiometer; **2ˈsieren** compensate for.

kompeten|t [kɔmpeˈtɛnt] competent; **2z** [~ts] *f* (16) competence; **2zstreitigkeit** *f* dispute about competence.

Komplementärfarbe [kɔmplemɛnˈtɛːr-] *f* complementary colo(u)r.

komplett [kɔmˈplɛt] complete.

Komplex [~ˈplɛks] *m* (3²) *allg.* complex (*a. psych*).

Komplikation [kɔmplikaˈtsjoːn] *f* complication.

Kompliment [~pliˈmɛnt] *n* (3) compliment.

Komplize [kɔmˈpliːtsə] *m* (13) accomplice.

komplizieren [~pliˈtsiːrən] complicate; ⚕ *komplizierter Bruch* compound fracture.

Komplott [\~'plɔt] *n* (3) plot; ⁓**ieren** [\~'ti:rən] plot.
Kompo|nente [\~po'nɛntə] *f* (15) component; ⁓**nieren** [\~po'ni:rən] compose; **\~nist** [\~'nist] *m* (12) composer; **\~sition** [\~zi'tsjo:n] *f* (16) composition.
Kompositum *gr.* [kɔm'po:zitum] *n* (9) compound (word).
Kompost ✓ [kɔm'pɔst] *m* (3) compost; **\~haufen** *m* compost-heap.
Kompott [kɔm'pɔt] *n* (3) compote, stewed fruit, *Am.* sauce.
Kompress|e [\~'prɛsə] *f* (15) compress; **\~or** [\~ɔr] *m* (8[1]) ⊕ compressor; *mot.* supercharger.
kompri'mieren [\~pri-] compress.
Komprom|iß [\~pro'mis] *m* (4) compromise; ⁓**ißlos** uncompromising (-ly *adv.*); **\~ißlösung** *f* compromise solution; ⁓**it'tieren** compromise.
Kondens|at [kɔndɛn'za:t] *n* (3) condensate; **\~ator** [\~'za:tɔr] *m* (8[1]) condenser, capacitor; ⁓**ieren** [\~'zi:rən] condense; *kondensierte Milch* = **\~milch** [kɔn'dɛns-] *f* evaporated milk; **\~streifen** *m* vapo(u)r trail; **\~wasser** *n* condensed water.
Kondition [kɔndi'tsjo:n] *f a. Sport*: condition; **\~al** [\~tsjo'na:l] *gr. m* conditional (mood); **\~alsatz** *gr. m* conditional clause; **\~s-training** *n* *Sport*: fitness training.
Konditor [kɔn'di:tɔr] *m* (8[1]) confectioner, pastry-cook; **\~ei** [\~to'raɪ] *f* (16) confectioner's shop, pastry-shop; **\~waren** [\~'di:tɔr-] *f/pl.* confectionery products.
Kondol|enzbrief [kɔndo'lɛnts-] *m* letter of condolence; ⁓**ieren** [\~'li:rən] *v/i.* condole (*j-m* with a p.).
Konfekt [kɔn'fɛkt] *n* (3) chocolates *pl.*; sweets *pl.*, *Am.* (soft) candy.
Konfektion [\~'tsjo:n] *f* manufacture of ready-made clothes; *Ware*: ready-made clothes *pl.*; **\~s-anzug** *m* ready-made suit; **\~sgeschäft** *n* ready-made clothes store; **\~sgröße** *f* size.
Konferenz [\~fe'rɛnts] *f* (16) conference; **\~dolmetscher** *m* conference interpreter; **\~tisch** *m* conference table.
konferieren [\~'ri:rən] confer (*über acc.* on).
Konfession [\~fɛ'sjo:n] *f* confession; creed, denomination; ⁓**ell** [\~jo'nɛl] denominational; ⁓**slos** [\~'sjo:ns-] undenominational; **\~sschule** *f* denominational school.
Konfetti [kɔn'fɛti] *n* (11[1]) confetti.
Konfirm|and [kɔnfir'mant] *m* (12), **\~andin** [\~'mandin] *f* (16[1]) confirmand, confirmee; **\~ation** [\~ma'tsjo:n] *f* confirmation; ⁓**ieren** [\~'mi:rən] confirm.
konfiszieren [\~fis'tsi:rən] confiscate.
Konfitüre [\~fi'ty:rə] *f* (15) jam.
Konflikt [kɔn'flikt] *m* (3) conflict.
Konföderation [kɔnfødəra'tsjo:n] *f* (16) confederation.
konform [\~'fɔrm] concurring (*dat. od. mit* with); *\~ gehen mit* agree with.
Konfront|ation [\~frɔnta'tsjo:n] *f* confrontation; ⁓**ieren** [\~'ti:rən] confront (*mit* with).
konfus [\~'fu:s] (18[1]) confused; muddle-headed, F muddled.
Kongreß [\~'grɛs] *m* (4) congress, *Am. a.* convention; **\~halle** *f* Congress Hall; **\~mitglied** *n Am.* congressman.
kongru|ent [\~gru'ɛnt] congruent; ⁓**'enz** [\~ts] *f* (16) congruity; **\~ieren** [\~gru'i:rən] coincide.
König ['kø:niç] *m* (3) king (*a. Karten, Schach*); **\~in** ['\~gin] *f* queen (*a. zo.*); ⁓**lich** ['\~kliç] royal; (*hoheitsvoll*) kingly; *Insignien u. fig.*: regal; **'\~reich** *n* kingdom; *rhet.* realm; **'\~shaus** *n* (royal) dynasty; **'\~swürde** *f* royal dignity.
konisch ['ko:niʃ] conical.
Konju|gation *gr.* [kɔnjuga'tsjo:n] *f* (16) conjugation; ⁓**'gieren** conjugate.
Konjunkt|ion [kɔnjuŋk'tsjo:n] *f* (16) conjunction; **\~iv** ['\~juŋkti:f] *m* (3[1]) subjunctive (mood).
Konjunktur [\~'tu:r] ⚕ *f* (16) business cycle; (*Hoch*⁓) boom; (*Tendenz*, *Lage*) economic trend (*od.* situation); **\~-aufschwung** *m* economic upswing; **\~barometer** *n* business barometer; ⁓**dämpfend** countercyclical; ⁓**ell** [\~tu'rɛl] cyclical; economic; **\~politik** *f* policy for controlling the trade cycle; **\~rückgang** *m* recession.
konkav [\~'ka:f] concave.
Konkordat [\~kɔr'da:t] *n* (3[1]) concordat.
konkret [\~'kre:t] concrete.
Konkubin|at [\~kubi'na:t] *n* (3)

concubinage; **~e** [~kuˈbi:nə] *f* concubine.

Konkurrent [~kuˈrɛnt] *m* (12), **~in** *f* (16¹) competitor, (✝ *a.* business) rival.

Konkurˈrenz [~ts] *f* competition; (*sportliche Veranstaltung*) event; ✝ competitor(s *pl.*), (business) rival(s *pl.*); *j-m ~ machen* enter into competition with a p.; **≗fähig** able to compete, competitive; **~geschäft** *n* rival firm; **~kampf** *m* competition; **~klausel** *f* restraint clause; **≗los** without competition, unrival(l)ed; **~neid** *m* professional jealousy.

konkurˈrieren compete (*mit* with; *um* for).

Konkurs [~ˈkurs] *m* (4) bankruptcy, failure; *~ anmelden* file a bankruptcy petition; *in ~ gehen* go into bankruptcy; *in ~ geraten* go bankrupt; **~-erklärung** *f* declaration of insolvency; **~masse** *f* bankrupt's estate; **~verfahren** *n* proceedings *pl.* in bankruptcy; **~verwalter** *m* trustee in bankruptcy, (official) receiver.

können [ˈkœnən] **1.** (30) be able; (*verstehen*) know, understand; *ich kann* I can; *er hätte es tun ~* he could have done it; *es kann sein* it may be; *du kannst* (*darfst*) *hingehen* you may go (there); *er kann das* he knows how to do that; *er kann English* he knows English, he can speak English; *was kann ich dafür?* how can I help it?; *s. dafür, umhin*; **2.** ≗ *n* (6) ability; skill, proficiency; (*Wissen*) knowledge; *nach bestem ~* to the best of one's ability.

Könner [ˈkœnər] *m* (7) master, expert.

Konnossement [kɔnɔsəˈmɛnt] *n* (3) bill of lading.

konnte [ˈkɔntə] *pret. v. können.*

konsequen|t [kɔnzeˈkvɛnt] consistent; **≗z** [~ts] *f* (16) consistency; (*Folge*) consequence; *die ~en tragen* bear the consequences; *die ~en ziehen* draw the conclusions (*aus* from), *weitS.* act accordingly.

konservativ [~zɛrvaˈti:f] conservative.

Konservatorium ♪ [~ˈto:rjum] *n* (9) conservatoire (*fr.*), academy of music, *Am.* conservatory.

Konserve [~ˈzɛrvə] *f* (15) preserve; **~n** *pl.* tinned (*bsd. Am.* canned) food; **~nbüchse** *f*, **~ndose** *f* tin, *bsd. Am.* can; **~nfabrik** *f* canning factory, cannery; **~nmusik** F *f* canned music.

konservier|en [~ˈvi:rən] preserve; **≗ung** *f* preservation.

Konsist|enz [~ziˈstɛnts] *f* (16) consistence; **~orium** [~ˈsto:rjum] *n* (9) consistory.

Konsol|e [~ˈzo:lə] *f* (15) console, bracket; **≗iˈdieren** consolidate.

Konsonant [kɔnzoˈnant] *m* (12) consonant.

Konsort|e [~ˈzɔrtə] *m* (13) associate; (*Komplice*) *a.* accomplice; **~ium** [~tsjum] *n* (9) syndicate.

Konspir|ation [~spiraˈtsjo:n] *f* conspiracy; **≗ieren** [~spiˈri:rən] conspire, plot.

konstant [~ˈstant] constant; **≗e** *f* constant (factor).

konstatieren [~staˈti:rən] state; establish; ⚕ diagnose.

Konstellation [~stɛlaˈtsjo:n] *f* constellation.

konsternieren [~stɛrˈni:rən] dismay.

konstitu|ieren [~stituˈi:rən] constitute; *parl. sich ~ als* resolve itself into; **≗tion** [~ˈtsjo:n] *f* constitution; **~tionell** [~tsjoˈnɛl] constitutional.

konstruieren [~struˈi:rən] design, (*a. gr.*) construct.

Konstruk|teur [~kˈtø:r] *m* (3¹) designer, design engineer; **~tion** [~ˈtsjo:n] *f* (16) design(ing), construction; **~tiˈonsfehler** *m* constructional fault *od.* flaw; **≗tiv** [~kˈti:f] constructive.

Konsul [ˈkɔnzul] *m* (10) consul; **~ar…** [~zuˈlɑ:r] consular; **~at** [~ˈlɑ:t] *n* (3) consulate; **~ent** [~ˈlɛnt] *m* (12) legal adviser; **≗ˈtieren** consult.

Konsum **1.** [~ˈzu:m] *m* (3) consumption; **2.** [ˈ~zu:m] *s.* *~geschäft*; **~ent** [~zuˈmɛnt] *m* (12) consumer; **~genossenschaft** [~ˈzu:m-] *f* consumer co-operative; **~geschäft** *n*, **~laden** *m* co-operative store, F co-op; **~gesellschaft** *f* consumer society; **~güter** *n/pl.* consumer goods; **≗ieren** [~zuˈmi:rən] consume; **~verein** [~ˈzu:m-] *m* co-operative society, F co-op; **~verhalten** *n* consumer behavio(u)r.

Kontakt [kɔnˈtakt] *m* (3) contact (*a.* ⚡); *~ aufnehmen* (*od. in ~ stehen*) *mit* *j-m* contact a p.; **~-abzug** *phot. m* contact print; **~-anzeige** *f* contact ad(vertisement); **♀freudig** sociable, being a good mixer; **~gift** *n* contact poison; **~linse** *f*, **~schale** *f* contact lens; **~person** *f bsd.* ⚕ contact.

Konter|admiral [ˈkɔntərˀatmiraːl] *m* rear-admiral; ˈ**~bande** *f* contraband; **~fei** [~ˈfaɪ] *n* (11) portrait; ˈ**♀n** (29*) *Boxen u. fig.*: counter; **~revolution** *f* counter-revolution.

Kontinent [ˈkɔntinɛnt] *m* (3) continent; **♀al** [~nɛnˈtaːl] continental.

Kontingent [~tiŋˈgɛnt] *n* (3) quota; ⚔ contingent; **♀ieren** [~gɛnˈtiːrən] fix a quota on; ration.

kontinu·ierlich [~tinuˈˀiːrliç] continuous.

Konto [ˈkɔnto] *n* (9¹ *u.* 11) account; ˈ**~-auszug** *m* statement of account; ˈ**~buch** *n* account-book; *Bank*: pass-book; **~korrent** [~kɔˈrɛnt] *n* (3), **~...** current account.

Kontor [kɔnˈtoːr] *n* (3¹) office; *fig. Schlag ins ~* (bitter) blow; **~ist** [~toˈrist] *m* (12) clerk; **~istin** *f* (16¹) girl clerk.

kontra [ˈkɔntra] versus; *Kartenspiel*: *♀ geben* double; *s. Pro*; ˈ**♀baß** *m* double-bass; **♀hent** [~ˈhɛnt] *m* (12) ⚖ contracting party; *fig. (Gegner)* opponent.

Kontrakt [kɔnˈtrakt] *m* (3) contract; *s. Vertrag.*

ˈ**Kontrapunkt** ♪ *m* counterpoint.

konträr [kɔnˈtrɛːr] contrary, opposite.

Kontrast [~ˈtrast] *m* (3²) contrast; **♀ieren** [~ˈstiːrən] contrast; **~mittel** ⚕ *n* contrast medium; **♀reich** *phot.* contrasty.

Kontroll|-abschnitt [~ˈtrɔl-] *m* counterfoil, stub; **~be-amte** *m*, **~eur** [~ˈløːr] *m* controller; **~e** *f* (15) control; *(Überwachung)* supervision; *(Prüfung)* check; *unter ~* under control; *außer ~ geraten* get out of control; *die ~ verlieren über* (*acc.*) lose control of; **♀ieren** [~ˈliːrən] *(überwachen)* supervise; *(nachprüfen)* control, verify, check; *(beherrschen)* control; **~kasse** *f* cash register; **~lampe** *f* pilot lamp; **~marke** *f* check; **~-nummer** *f* check number; **~punkt** *m* check point; **~schirm** *m TV etc.* monitor; **~turm** *m* ✈ control tower; **~-uhr** *f* telltale (*od.* check-)clock.

Kontroverse [kɔntroˈvɛrzə] *f* (15) controversy.

Kontur [~ˈtuːr] *f* (16) contour, outline.

Konus [ˈkoːnus] *m* (14²) cone.

Konvention [kɔnvɛnˈtsjoːn] *f* (16) convention; **~alstrafe** [~tsjoˈnaːl-] *f* penalty for non-fulfil(l)ment of a contract; **♀ell** [~ˈnɛl] conventional (*a.* ⚔ *Waffe*).

Konversation [kɔnvɛrzaˈtsjoːn] *f* (16) conversation; **~slexikon** *n* encyclop(a)edia.

konversieren [~ˈziːrən] converse.

konver|tierbar [kɔnvɛrˈtiːrbaːr] convertible; **~ˈtieren** convert.

konvex [~ˈvɛks] convex.

Konvoi [ˈkɔnvɔʏ] *m* (11) convoy.

Konzentr|at [~tsɛnˈtraːt] *n* (3) concentrate; **~ation** [~traˈtsjoːn] *f* concentration; **~ationslager** *n* concentration camp; **♀ieren** [~ˈtriːrən] concentrate; **♀isch** [~ˈtsɛntriʃ] concentric(ally *adv.*).

Konzept [kɔnˈtsɛpt] *n* (3) rough draft *od.* copy; *j-n aus dem ~ bringen* disconcert a p.; **~ion** [~ˈtsjoːn] *f* (16) conception; **~papier** *n* rough paper.

Konzern [~ˈtsɛrn] *m* (3¹) combine, group.

Konzert [~ˈtsɛrt] *n* (3) concert; *(Solovortrag)* recital; **~flügel** *m* concert grand; **♀iert** [~tsɛrˈtiːrt]: *~e Aktion* ✝, *pol.* concerted action; **~saal** *m* concert-hall.

Konzession [kɔntsɛˈsjoːn] *f* (16) *(Zugeständnis)* concession; *(Genehmigung)* licen|ce, *Am.* -se; **♀ieren** [~joˈniːrən] license.

Konzil [kɔnˈtsiːl] *n* (3¹ *u.* 8²) council.

konziliant [~tsilˈjant] conciliatory.

Kooperation [koˀopəraˈtsjoːn] ✝ *f* co-operation.

Koordin|ate [koːˀɔrdiˈnaːtə] *f* (15) co-ordinate; **♀ieren** [~ˈniːrən] co-ordinate.

Köper [ˈkøːpər] *m* (7) twill.

Kopf [kɔpf] *m* (3³) head (*a. von Sachen*); *(oberer Teil)* top; *(Verstand)* brains *pl.*; *(Pfeifen♀)* bowl; *ein fähiger ~* a clever fellow; *~ hoch!* cheer up!; *s. hängen, schlagen, setzen, zerbrechen, zusagen*; *e-n eigensinnigen ~ haben* be obstinate; *Tatsachen auf den ~ stellen* stand facts on their heads; *aus dem ~* by heart; offhand; *mit bloßem ~e* bareheaded;

j-m über den ~ wachsen outgrow a p., *fig. Schwierigkeiten*: get beyond a p.; *von ~ bis Fuß* from head to foot; *j-n vor den ~ stoßen* offend; F *j-m (gehörig) den ~ waschen* give a p. a (good) dressing-down; '**~-arbeit** *f* brain-work; '**~-arbeiter** *m* brain-worker; '**~bahnhof** *m* terminus, terminal; rail head; '**~ball** *m Sport*: header; '**~bedeckung** *f* headgear, hat.

köpfen ['kœpfən] (25) behead, decapitate; *Fußball*: head.

'**Kopf|-ende** *n* head; '**~hörer** *m* headset, headphone; '**~hörer-anschluß** *m* headphone jack; '**~kissen** *n* pillow; '**2lastig** top-heavy; '**2los** headless; *fig.* panicky; *adv.* in panic; '**~nicken** *n* nod; '**~putz** *m* head-dress; '**~rechnen** *n* mental arithmetic; '**~salat** *m* (cabbage-)lettuce; '**2scheu** *Pferd*: restive, skittish; *P.*: nervous, alarmed; '**~schmerz** *m mst pl.* headache; *~en haben* have a headache; '**~sprung** *m* header; '**~stand** *m* head-stand; '**~steinpflaster** *n* cobble-stone pavement; '**~steuer** *f* poll tax; '**~stimme** *f* head-voice, falsetto; '**~stütze** *f* headrest; *mot.* head restraint; '**~tuch** *n* head-scarf, kerchief; **2'-über** head foremost, headlong; '**~zerbrechen** *n*: *j-m ~ machen* puzzle a p.

Kopie [ko'piː] *f* (15) copy; *phot.* print; (*Zweitschrift*) duplicate.

Ko'pier|buch *n* copying-book; **2en** copy (*a. fig.*); *phot.* print; **~er** *m* (7), **~gerät** *n* copier; **~papier** *phot. n* printing-paper; **~stift** *m* copying-pencil.

Kopilot ['koː-] *m* copilot.

Koppel ['kɔpəl] **1.** *f* (15) (*~ Hunde*) leash; couple; (*~ Pferde*) string; (*Gehege*) enclosure, (*Pferde2*) paddock; **2.** ⚔ *n* (7) belt; '**2n** (29) couple (*a.* ⊕, ⚡); *Hunde*: leash; *Pferde*: string together; *Raumfahrt*: link up; '**~ung** *f* coupling; *Raumfahrt*: link-up.

Koproduktion ['koː-] *f* joint production.

Koralle [ko'ralə] *f* (15) coral; **~nbank** *f* coral-reef.

Koran [ko'rɑːn] *m* (3[1]) Koran.

Korb [kɔrp] *m* (3[3]) basket; *fig.* refusal; *fig. Hahn im ~e* cock of the walk; *e-n ~ bekommen* meet with a refusal; *j-m e-n ~ geben* give a p. a refusal; **~ball** *m* netball; '**~flechter** *m*, '**~macher** *m* basket-maker; '**~geflecht** *n* basket-work; '**~möbel** *n/pl.* wicker furniture; '**~wagen** *m* bassinet; '**~waren** *f/pl.* wickerwork *sg.*

Kord ['kɔrt] *m* (3 *u.* 11) corduroy.

Kordel ['kɔrdəl] *f* (15) cord.

Kordon [kɔr'dɔ̃] *m* (11) cordon.

'**Kordsamt** *m* corduroy.

Korinth|e [ko'rintə] *f* (15) currant; **~enkacker** F [~kakər] *m* (7) fusspot, *Am.* cookie pusher; **~er** *m*, **2isch** Corinthian.

Kork [kɔrk] *m* (3) cork; '**2-artig** corky; '**~-eiche** *f* cork-oak; '**2en** (25) cork; '**~(en)zieher** *m* cork-screw.

Korn [kɔrn] **1.** *n* (1[2] *u.* [= *~arten*] 3) *v. Sand, Gold, Weizen usw.*: grain (*a. Getreide*); *am Gewehr*: front sight, bead; *der Münze*: standard, alloy; *aufs ~ nehmen* aim at (*a. fig.*); **2.** *m* (*Schnaps*) rye whisky; '**~-ähre** *f* ear of grain; '**~bau** *m* growing of grain; '**~blume** *f* corn-flower; '**~boden** *m* granary.

Körn|chen ['kœrnçən] *n* (6) grain (*a. fig. of truth, etc.*); '**2en** (25) granulate; *Leder*: grain; '**2ig** granular; *in Zssgn* ...-grained.

'**Korn|feld** *n* grain-field; '**~kammer** *f* granary.

Körper ['kœrpər] *m* (7) body (*a. v. Farbe, Wein*); *phys.*, ⚖ solid; '**~bau** *m* build, physique; '**2behindert** (*schwer* severely) disabled, handicapped; '**~chen** *n* (6) corpuscle, particle; '**~fülle** *f* corpulence; '**~geruch** *m* body odo(u)r; '**~größe** *f* height; '**~haltung** *f* bearing, posture; '**~kontakt** *m* physical contact; '**~kraft** *f* physical strength; '**2lich** bodily, physical; (*stofflich*) corporeal, material; '**~pflege** *f* care of the body, (personal) hygiene; '**~schaft** *f* corporation, corporate body; '**~teil** *m* part (*Glied*: member) of the body; '**~verletzung** *f* (⚖ *schwere* grievous) bodily harm; '**~wärme** *f* body heat.

Korporal ⚔ [kɔrpo'rɑːl] *m* (3[1]) corporal; **~schaft** ⚔ *f* squad.

Korps [koːr] *n inv.* corps; '**~geist** *m* esprit de corps (*fr.*).

Korpulenz [kɔrpu'lɛnts] *f* (16) corpulence, stoutness.

korrekt [kɔ'rɛkt] correct; **2heit** *f* correctness; **2or** [~ɔr] *m* (8[1]) proof-reader.

Korrektur [~'tu:r] *f* (16) correction; *typ.* ~ *lesen* proof-read; **~bogen** *typ. m* page-proof; **~fahne** *typ. f* galley proof; **~zeichen** *n* proof-reader's mark.

Korrespon|dent [kɔrɛspɔn'dɛnt] *m* (12) correspondent; **~'dentenbericht** *m* correspondent's report; **~'denz** [~ts] *f* (16) correspondence; **2'dieren** correspond.

Korridor ['kɔrido:r] *m* (3¹) corridor (*a. pol.*), passage(-way).

korrigieren [kɔri'gi:rən] correct.

korrosionsfest ⊕ [kɔro'zjo:nsfɛst] corrosion-resistant.

kor|rumpieren [kɔrum'pi:rən] corrupt; **~rupt** [~'rupt] corrupt; **2ruption** [~'tsjo:n] *f* (16) corruption.

Kors|e ['kɔrzə] *m* (12), '**2isch** Corsican.

Korsett [kɔr'zɛt] *n* (3) corset.

Korvette ⚓ [kɔr'vɛtə] *f* (15) corvette; **~nkapitän** *m* lieutenant commander.

Koryphäe [kory'fɛ:ə] *f* (15) eminent authority, great expert.

kose|n ['ko:zən] *v/t.* (27) caress, fondle; '**2name** *m* pet name.

Kosmet|ik [kɔs'me:tik] *f* (16) cosmetics *pl.*; **~iker(in** *f*) *m* cosmetician; **2isch** cosmetic (*a.* ⚕).

kosm|isch ['kɔsmiʃ] cosmic(ally *adv.*); **2onaut** [~mo'naut] *m* (12) cosmonaut; **2opolit** [~mopo'li:t] *m* (13) cosmopolitan; **2os** ['~mɔs] *m* (*inv.*, *o. pl.*) cosmos.

Kost [kɔst] *f* (16) food; fare; (*Ernährungsweise*) diet; (*Beköstigung*) board; *schmale* ~ slender fare; ⚕ low diet; *freie* ~ free board; *in* ~ *geben* board out; *in* ~ *sein bei* board with; ~ *und Logis* board and lodging.

'**kostbar** costly, expensive; (*wertvoll*) precious; '**2keit** *f* expensiveness; preciousness; *konkret*: precious thing, *pl. a.* valuables.

'**Kosten 1.** *pl.* cost(s *pl.*), expenses; charges *pl.*; *auf* ~ (*gen.*) at the cost of, at *a p.'s* expense; *auf seine* ~ *kommen* get one's money's worth; **2.** 2 (26) *Geld*: cost; *fig. a.* take, require; **3.** 2 (*schmecken*) taste; '**~anschlag** *m* estimate; '**~anstieg** *m* rise (*od.* increase) in costs; '**~aufwand** *m* expenditure; '**2bewußt** cost-conscious; '**2deckend** cost-covering; '**~erstattung** *f* reimbursement of expenses; '**~frage** *f* question of cost (*od.* what it costs); '**2frei,** '**2los** free (of charge); '**2günstig** cost-effective; '**~-'Nutzen-Analyse** *f* cost-benefit analysis; '**2pflichtig** with costs; '**~preis** *m* cost-price; '**~punkt** *m* (matter of) expense; '**~rechnung** *f* bill of costs; '**~senkung** *f* lowering of costs; '**~stelle** *f* cost cent|re, *Am.* -er; '**~voranschlag** *m* estimate.

Kost|gänger ['~gɛŋər] *m* (7) boarder; '**~geld** *n* board allowance; *der Dienstboten*: board-wages *pl.*

köstlich ['kœstliç] delicious; *fig.* exquisite; (*lustig*) delightful.

'**Kost|probe** *f* taste; *fig.* sample; **2spielig** ['~ʃpi:liç] expensive, costly.

Kostüm [kɔs'ty:m] *n* (3¹) costume, dress; (*Jackenkleid*) (two-piece) suit; **~ball** *m*, **~fest** *n* fancy-dress ball; **2ieren** [~ty'mi:rən] (*a. sich* ~) dress up; **~probe** *thea. f* dress rehearsal.

Kot [ko:t] *m* (3) (*Schmutz*) mud, mire; *physiol.* f(a)eces *pl.*, excrement.

Kotelett [kɔt(ə)'lɛt] *n* (3¹) chop; **~en** *pl.* (*Bart*) side whiskers *pl.*, *Am.* sideburns *pl.*

Köter ['kø:tər] *m* (7) cur, tyke.

'**Kotflügel** *mot. m* mudguard, *Am.* fender.

'**kotig** muddy, miry.

kotzen P ['kɔtsən] (27) vomit, puke, spew; *mot.* splutter.

Krabbe ['krabə] *f* (15) shrimp; (*Taschenkrebs*) crab; *fig.* (*Mädel*) little monkey.

'**krabbeln** *v/i.* (29, sn) crawl; *v/t.* scratch softly.

Krach [krax] *m* (3) crash; (*Lärm*) row, din; (*Streit*) quarrel, F row; ✝ crash, smash; ~ *machen* make (*od.* kick up) a row; '**2en** (25) crash.

krächzen ['krɛçtsən] (27) croak.

Kraft [kraft] **1.** *f* (14¹) strength, (*a. Natur2*) force; (*Macht*; *a.* ⊕ *od. fig.*) power; (*Energie*) energy; (*Rüstigkeit*) vigo(u)r; (*Wirksamkeit*) efficacy; (*Person*) worker; *aus eigner* ~ by o.s.; *in* ~ *sein* (*setzen*, *treten*) be in (put into, come into) operation *od.* force, be (*od.* become) effective; *außer* ~ *setzen* annul, cancel, invalidate; *außer* ~ *treten* lapse, expire; *s. best*, *vereinen*; **2.** 2 (*gen.*) in (*od.* by) virtue of, on the strength of; '**~akt** *m* strong-man act; *fig.* feat; '**~anstrengung** *f*, '**~-**

aufwand *m* (strenuous) effort; '**~ausdruck** *m* swear-word, *pl.* strong language; '**~brühe** *f* beef tea.

Kräfte|gleichgewicht ['krɛftə-] *n* balance of power; '**~verfall** *m* loss of strength.

'**Kraftfahr|er** *m* motorist, (car-)driver; '**~zeug** *n* motor vehicle; '**~zeugbrief** *m* (motor vehicle) registration book; '**~zeugsteuer** *f* motor vehicle tax.

'**Kraft|feld** *n* field of force; '**~futter** *n* concentrated feed.

kräftig ['krɛftiç] strong, robust, sturdy; (*mächtig*) powerful; (*tat~*) vigorous, energetic; (*nahrhaft*) nourishing, substantial; *Farbton*: heavy, deep; *~er Fluch* round oath; **~en** ['~igən] strengthen; *s. a. stärken.*

'**kraft|los** feeble, weak; ⚖ invalid; '**2probe** *f* trial of strength; '**2rad** *n* motor-cycle; '**2stoff** *m* fuel; '**2stoffanzeiger** *m* fuel gauge; '**2stoff-einsparung** *f* fuel-saving; '**2stoff-einspritzung** *f* fuel injection; '**2stoffverbrauch** *m* fuel consumption; '**~strotzend** vigorous; '**2verschwendung** *f* waste of energy; '**~voll** powerful, vigorous; '**2wagen** *m* (motor-) car, *Am. a.* automobile; *allg.* motor vehicle; '**2wagenpark** *m* fleet (of motor vehicles); '**2werk** ⊕ *n* power station *od.* plant; '**2wort** *n s. Kraftausdruck.*

Kragen ['krɑːgən] *m* (6) collar; (*Umhang*) cape; *beim ~ packen* (seize by the) collar; F *ihm platzte der ~* he blew his top; '**~weite** *f* collar size.

Kräh|e ['krɛːə] *f* (15) crow; '**2en** (25) crow.

Krakeel F [kra'keːl] *m* (3[1]) quarrel, brawl; (*Lärm*) row; **2en** (25) brawl; make a row; **~er** *m* brawler.

Kralle ['kralə] *f* (15) claw.

Kram [krɑːm] *m* (3[3]) (*~waren*) small wares *pl.*; *weitS.* things *pl.*; *fig.* stuff; (*Plunder*) rubbish; '**2en** (25) rummage.

Krämer ['krɛːmər] *m* (7) shopkeeper.

'**Kramladen** *m* (small) shop.

Krampe ['krampə] *f* (15) cramp (-iron), clamp; (*Draht2*) staple.

Krampf [krampf] *m* (3[3]) cramp, spasm; *stärker*: convulsion; '**~-ader** *f* varicose vein; '**2haft** convulsive; *fig.* frantic(ally *adv.*).

Kran [krɑːn] *m* (3[3] *u.* 12) crane; '**~führer** *m* crane operator.

Kranich ['krɑːniç] *m* (3) crane.

krank [kraŋk] (18[2]) ill (*nur pred.*); *sonst* sick; *stärker*: diseased (*bsd. Körperteil*); *~ schreiben* give *a p.* a sick-certificate; *sich ~ melden* report (o.s.) sick; *~ werden* fall ill *od.* sick; '**2e** *m, f* (18) sick person, patient.

kränkeln ['krɛŋkəln] (29) be sickly.

kranken ['kraŋkən] (25) suffer (*an dat.* from).

kränken ['krɛŋkən] (25) hurt, wound, offend.

'**Kranken|-anstalt** *f* hospital; '**~auto** *n* (motor) ambulance; '**~bett** *n*, '**~lager** *n* sick-bed; '**~geld** *n* sick-benefit; '**~gymnastik** *f* remedial gymnastics, physiotherapy; '**~haus** *n* hospital; '**~kasse** *f* sick-fund; '**~kost** *f* invalid diet; '**~pflege** *f* nursing; '**~pfleger** *m* male nurse; '**~pflegerin** *f*, '**~schwester** *f* nurse; '**~schein** *m* (*Attest*) medical certificate; *der Krankenkasse*: medical (card); '**~stuhl** *m* invalid-chair; '**~träger** *m* stretcher-bearer; '**~versicherung** *f* health insurance; '**~wagen** *m* (motor) ambulance; '**~wärter** *m* male nurse; '**~zimmer** *n* sick-room.

'**krankhaft** morbid; pathological.

'**Krankheit** *f* illness, sickness, disease; '**~sbild** *n* clinical picture; '**~s-erreger** *m* pathogenic agent; '**~s-erscheinung** *f* symptom; '**sstoff** *m* morbid substance; '**~s-überträger** (**-in** *f*) *m* carrier; '**~s-urlaub** *m* sick-leave.

'**kranklachen:** *sich ~* split one's sides with laughing.

'**kränklich** sickly; '**2keit** *f* sickliness.

'**Kränkung** *f* insult, offen|ce, *Am.* -se.

Kranz [krants] *m* (3[2] *u.* [3]) garland, wreath; ⚠ cornice; *fig.* circle.

Kränz|chen ['krɛntsçən] *n* (6) small wreath; *fig. bsd. v. Damen*: (ladies') circle; '**2en** (27) wreathe, crown.

'**Kranz|gefäß** ⚕ *n* coronary artery; '**~niederlegung** *f* laying of a wreath.

Krapfen ['krapfən] *m* (6) doughnut.

kraß [kras] crass, rank, gross.

Krater ['krɑːtər] *m* (7) crater.

'**Kratz|bürste** *f* scratch-brush; *fig.* crosspatch; '**2bürstig** cross; '**~e** *f* (15) scraper; (*Woll2*, *Hanf2*) card.

Krätze ['krɛtsə] *f* (15) itch, scabies.
'**Kratz-eisen** *n* scraper.
kratz|en ['kratsən] (27) scrape; (*schrammen*) scratch; '**2er** F *m* scratch.
Krätzer ['krɛtsər] *m* (7) rough wine.
krätzig ['krɛtsiç] itchy, scabious.
krau|en ['krauən] (25) tickle, scratch softly; '**~len** (25) *v/t.* = *krauen*; *v/i.* *Schwimmen*: crawl; '**2lschwimmen** *n*, '**2lstil** *m* crawl (-stroke).
kraus [kraus] frizzy, curly; *fig.* muddled; ~ *ziehen s. krausen*; **2e** ['~zə] *f* (15) (*Rüsche*) frill, ruffle; (*Hals2*) ruff.
kräuseln ['krɔʏzəln] *v/t. u. refl.* (29) curl, crimp; (*fälteln*) gather; *Wasser*: ripple, be ruffled; *Rauch*: curl up.
krausen ['krauzən] (27) *Stirn*: knit *one's brow*; *Nase*: wrinkle.
kraus|haarig ['kraus-] curly--haired; '**2kopf** *m* curly head.
Kraut [kraut] *n* (1^2) herb; (*Pflanze*) plant; (*Kohl*) cabbage; *e-r Rübe*: top; F (*Tabak*) weed; *ins ~ schießen* run wild.
Kräuter|butter ['krɔʏtər-] *f* herb butter; '**~käse** *m* green cheese; '**~kunde** *f* herbal lore; '**~tee** *m* herb--tea.
Krawall [kra'val] *m* (3^1) riot, uproar; F rumpus; **~macher** *m* rioter, rowdy.
Krawatte [kra'vatə] *f* (15) (neck-) tie; **~nhalter** *m* tie clip.
kraxeln ['kraksəln] F (29, sn) climb.
kreat|iv [krea'ti:f] creative; **2ivität** [~tivi'tɛ:t] *f* (16) creativity; **~ur** [~'tu:r] *f* (16) creature.
Krebs [kre:ps] *m* (4) crayfish, *Am.* crawfish; *ast.* Crab, Cancer; ⚕ cancer; '**2-artig** cancerous; '**2-erregend** ⚕ carcinogenic; '**~forschung** ⚕ *f* cancer research; '**~geschwulst** ⚕ *f* cancerous tumo(u)r; '**2krank** suffering from cancer; '**~schaden** *m* cancerous affection; *fig.* cancer; '**~schere** *f* crayfish claw; '**~vorsorge** ⚕ *f* cancer prevention; '**~vorsorgeuntersuchung** ⚕ *f* cancer screening; '**~zelle** ⚕ *f* cancer(ous) cell.
kredenz|en [kre'dɛntsən] (27) present, serve.
Kredit 1. [kre'di:t] *m* (3) credit; *auf ~* on credit; **2.** ✝ ['kre:dit] *n* (11) credit; **~bank** [kre'di:t-] *f* credit bank; **~brief** *m* letter of credit; **2fähig** credit-worthy, sound; **~geschäft** *n* credit-business (*od.* transaction); **~gewerbe** *n* banking (business); **~hai** F *m* loan shark.
kredi'tieren [~di-] *v/t. j-m et.*: credit a th. to a p.; *v/i.* (pass to the) credit.
Kre'dit|karte *f* credit card; **~linie** *f* credit limit (*Am.* line); **~markt** *m* loan market; **~nachfrage** *f* credit demand; **~seite** ['kre:dit-] *f* credit--side; **2würdig** [kre'di:t-] *s. kreditfähig*.
Kreide ['kraɪdə] *f* (15) chalk; *bunte*: crayon; '**2n** chalk; '**2'weiß** as white as a sheet; '**~zeichnung** *f* crayon (*od.* chalk) drawing.
kreieren [kre'ʔi:rən] create.
Kreis [kraɪs] *m* (4) circle; (*Wirkungs2*) field, sphere; (*Ideen2*) range; *ast.* orbit; (*Gebiet*) district, *Am.* county; (*Personen2*) circle, *unterrichtete usw.* **~e** quarters *pl.*; ⚡ circuit; *fig.* cycle; *s. bewegen*; '**~-abschnitt** *m* segment; '**~-ausschnitt** *m* sector; '**~bahn** *f* orbit; '**~bogen** *m* arc.
kreischen ['kraɪʃən] (27) scream; *stärker*: shriek (*a. Bremsen usw.*).
Kreisel ['kraɪzəl] *m* (7) (peg)top, whip(ping-)top; ⊕ gyroscope; '**~kompaß** *m* gyrocompass; '**2n** spin (the top); '**~pumpe** *f* rotary pump.
kreisen ['kraɪzən] (27) circle, revolve, rotate; *Blut, Geld usw.*: circulate.
kreis|förmig ['~s-] circular; '**2lauf** *m* circulation (*a.* ⚕); rotation; *der Jahreszeiten usw.*: succession; '**2laufstörung** ⚕ *f* circulatory disturbance; '**2linie** *f* circular line; '**~rund** circular; '**2säge** *f* circular saw.
Kreißsaal ['kraɪs-] ⚕ *m* delivery room.
'**Kreis|stadt** *f* district town, *Am.* county seat; '**~verkehr** *m* roundabout (traffic), *Am.* traffic circle.
Krem [kre:m] *f*, F *m* (3) *s. Creme*.
Krematorium [krema'to:rjum] *n* (9) crematorium, *Am.* crematory.
Kreml ['krɛml] *m the* Kremlin.
Krempe ['krɛmpə] *f* (15) brim.
Krempel ['~pəl] *m* (7) stuff.
krepieren [kre'pi:rən] (sn) *Tier*: perish; *Granate*: burst, explode.
Krepp [krɛp] *m* (11), '**~flor** *m* crêpe; *bsd. für Trauerkleidung*: crape; '**~gummi** *m* crêpe rubber; '**~papier** *n* crêpe paper; '**~sohle** *f* crêpe--rubber sole.

Kresse ⚘ ['krɛsə] *f* (15) cress.
Kreuz [krɔʏts] *n* (3²) cross; *Kartenspiel*: club(s *pl.*); ♪ sharp; *typ.* obelisk; *anat.* (small of the) back, loins *pl.*; *vom Pferd*: crupper, croup; *fig.* cross, affliction; *kreuz und quer* in all directions; *zu* ~*e kriechen* truckle (*vor dat.* to); *über* ~ crosswise; *s. schlagen*; '~**band** *n* (postal) wrapper; *unter* ~ *verschikken* send by book-post.
'**kreuzen** (27) *v/t.* cross; *v/i.* ⚓ cruise.
'**Kreuzer** *m* (7) kreutzer; ⚓ cruiser.
'**Kreuz|fahrer** *m* crusader; '~**fahrt** *f* crusade; ⚓ cruise; '~**feuer** *n* cross-fire; '2**fi'del** as merry as a cricket; '~**gang** *m* cloister; 2**igen** ['~igən] (25) crucify; '~**igung** *f* crucifixion; '2**lahm** broken-backed; *P.*: stiff-backed; '~**-otter** *f* common viper; '~**ritter** *hist. m* Knight of the Cross; '~**schiff** *n der Kirche*: transept; '~**schmerz** *m* lumbago; '~**spinne** *f* cross (*od.* garden) spider; '~**stich** *m* cross-stitch; '~**ung** *f* crossing; *v. Rassen*: cross-breeding; (*Mischrasse*) cross-breed; '~**verhör** *n* cross-examination; *ins* ~ *nehmen* cross-examine; '~**weg** *m* crossroads *pl.*; *eccl.* Way of the Cross; '2**weise** crosswise; '~**worträtsel** *n* crossword puzzle; '~**zeichen** *n* sign of the cross; '~**zug** *m* crusade.
'**kribb(e)lig** (*nervös*) fidgety, edgy.
kribbeln ['kribəln] (29) *v/i. u. v/t.* crawl; (*jucken*) itch.
Kricket ['krikət] *n* (11) cricket.
kriech|en ['kri:çən] (30, sn) creep (*a.* ⚡), crawl; *fig.* cringe (*vor dat.* to), fawn (on, upon); '2**er** *m* (7), '2**erin** *f fig.* toady, crawler; 2**erei** [~'raɪ] *f* (16) toadying; '~**erisch** toadyish; '2**pflanze** *f* creeper; '2**spur** *mot. f* slow lane; '2**tier** *n* reptile.
Krieg [kri:k] *m* (3) war; *im* ~ at war; *s. führen, kalt.*
kriegen ['~gən] F *v/t.* get.
'**Krieg|er** *m* (7) warrior; '~**erdenkmal** *n* war memorial; '2**erisch** (*kriegliebend*) warlike; (*zum Krieg gehörig*) martial; *fig.* belligerent; '~**erwitwe** *f* war widow; 2**führend** ['~k-] belligerent.
Kriegs|-anleihe ['~ks-] *f* war loan; '~**-ausbruch** *m* outbreak of war; '~**beil** *n*: *fig. das* ~ *begraben* bury the hatchet; '~**bericht-erstatter** *m* war correspondent; '2**beschädigt** *P.*: war-disabled; '~**beschädigte** *m* (18) war-disabled person; '~**dienst** *m* war service; '~**dienstverweigerer** *m* (7) conscientious objector; '~**-erklärung** *f* declaration of war; '~**flagge** *f* war-flag; '~**flotte** *f* navy; '~**freiwillige** *m* (18) war volunteer; '~**führung** *f* warfare; '~**fuß** *m*: *mit j-m auf* ~ *stehen* be at daggers drawn with a p.; '~**gebiet** *n* war zone; '~**gefangene** *m* (18) prisoner of war, captive (*a. kriegsgefangen*); '~**gefangenschaft** *f* (war) captivity; '~**gericht** *n* court-martial; ~**gewinnler** ['~gəvinlər] *m* (7) war-profiteer; '~**glück** *n* fortune of war; (*Erfolg*) military success; '~**gott** *m* war-god; '~**gräberfürsorge** *f* war-graves commission; '~**hafen** *m* naval port; '~**held** *m* war hero; '~**hetze** *f* war-mongering; '~**kamerad** *m* fellow soldier; '~**kunst** *f* art of war; '~**list** *f* stratagem; '~**macht** *f* military power, forces *pl.*; '~**marine** *f* navy; '~**-opfer** *n* war victim; '~**pfad** *m*: *auf* (*dem*) ~ on the warpath; '~**rat** *m* council of war; '~**recht** *n* martial law; '~**schaden** *m* war damage; '~**schauplatz** *m* theat|re (*Am.* -er) of war; '~**schiff** *n* man-of-war, warship; '~**schuld** *f* (*Verschulden*) war-guilt; (*Verschuldung*) war debt; '~**teilnehmer** *m* combatant; *ehemaliger*: ex-serviceman, *Am.* veteran; '~**treiber** *m* war-monger; '~**verbrecher** *m* war criminal; '2**versehrt** *s. kriegsbeschädigt*; '~**zug** *m* expedition, campaign; '~**zustand** *m* state of war.
Krimi ['kri:mi] F *m* (11) (crime) thriller.
Kriminal|be-amte [krimi'nɑ:l-] *m* criminal investigator, detective; ~**ist** [~na'list] *m* (12) criminologist; *weitS.* detective; 2**istisch** [~na'listiʃ] criminal investigation ...; *s. kriminell*; ~**ität** [~nali'tɛ:t] *f* criminality, crime; ~**kommissar** [~'nɑ:l-] *m* detective superintendent; ~**polizei** *f* criminal investigation police *od.* departemnt (*abbr.* C.I.D.); ~**polizist** *m s. Kriminalbeamte*; ~**roman** *m* detective (*od.* crime) novel.
kriminell [~'nɛl], 2**e** *m, f* criminal.
krimpen ['krimpən] *v/t. u. v/i.* (sn) (25) ⊕ shrink.

Krimskrams ['krimskrams] *m inv.* junk, rubbish.
Kringel ['kriŋəl] *m* (7) curl; (*Gebäck*) cracknel.
Krinoline [krino'li:nə] *f* (15) crinoline.
Krippe ['kripə] *f* (15) crib, manger; (*Kinderheim*) crèche; (*Weihnachts*≗) (Christmas) crib.
Krise *f*, **Krisis** ['kri:zə, '~zis] *f* (16²) crisis; '**kriseln:** es *kriselt* there is a crisis developing.
'**krisen|fest** stable; '≗**gebiet** *pol. n* crisis area (*od.* spot); '≗**herd** *pol. m* hot (*od.* trouble) spot; '≗**stab** *bsd. pol. m* crisis committee.
Kristall [kri'stal] *m* (3¹) crystal; ✝ crystal(-glass); ≗**i'sieren** *v/t. u. v/i.* (25) crystallize.
Kriterium [kri'te:rium] *n* (9) criterion.
Kritik [kri'ti:k] *f* (16) criticism; (*Besprechung*) critique, review; *unter aller* ~ beneath contempt; ~ *üben an* (*dat.*) criticize.
Krit|iker ['kri:tikər] *m* (7) critic; ≗**iklos** [kri'ti:klo:s] uncritical, undiscriminating; ≗**isch** ['kri:tiʃ] critical (*gegenüber* of); (*entscheidend*) crucial; ≗**isieren** [kriti'zi:rən] criticize; (*besprechen*) review.
Krittel|ei [kritə'laɪ] *f* (16) fault-finding, cavil; '≗**n** (29) find fault (*an dat.* with), cavil (at).
'**Krittler** *m* (7), '~**in** *f* fault-finder.
Kritzel|ei [kritsə'laɪ] *f* (16), '≗**n** (29) *v/i. u. v/t.* scribble, scrawl.
kroch [krɔx] *pret. v. kriechen.*
Krocket ['krɔkɛt] *n* (11) croquet.
Krokant [kro'kant] *m* (6, *o. pl.*) croquant.
Krokodil [kroko'di:l] *n* (3) crocodile.
Krone ['kro:nə] *f* (15) crown (*a.* ⚘, ⊕); (*Adels*≗) coronet.
krönen ['krø:nən] (25) crown (*zum König* king); *fig.* crown, top.
'**Kron|(en)korken** *m* crown cork; '~**leuchter** *m* chandelier, light pendant; *mit Glasbehang*: lust|re, *Am.* -er; *elektrisch*: electrolier; '~**prinz** *m* Crown Prince; *Brt.* Prince of Wales; '~**prinzessin** *f* Crown Princess; *Brt.* Princess Royal.
'**Krönung** *f* coronation; *fig.* culmination.
'**Kronzeuge** *m* chief witness; *Brt.* Queen's (*Am.* state's) evidence.
Kropf [krɔpf] *m* (3³) crop; ⚘ goit|re, *Am.* -er; '≗**ig** goitrous.
Kröte ['krø:tə] *f* (15) toad.
Krücke ['krykə] *f* (15) crutch; *des Croupiers*: rake.
'**Krückstock** *m* crutched stick.
Krug [kru:k] *m* (3³) jug; (*großer Ton*≗) pitcher; (*Trink*≗) mug; (*Bier*≗) tankard; (*Wirtshaus*) inn.
Kruke ['kru:kə] *f* (15) stone jug.
Krüllschnitt ['kryl-] *m* (*Tabak*) crimp cut.
Krume ['kru:mə] *f* (15) crumb; (*Acker*≗) topsoil.
Krüm|chen ['kry:mçən] *n* (6), ~**el** ['~əl] *m* (7) small crumb; '≗**elig** crumbly; '≗**eln** *v/i.* (29) *u. v/t.* crumble.
krumm [krum] crooked (*a. contp. fig.*); bent; (*geschweift*) curved; ~ *gehen* stoop; ~ *sitzen* cower; ~**beinig** ['~baɪniç] bow-legged.
krümm|en ['krymən] (*a. sich*) (25) crook, bend, curve; *sich* ~ grow crooked; *fig.* cringe; *Fluß*: wind; *vor Schmerzen, Verlegenheit*: writhe with; *vor Lachen*: be doubled up with; '≗**er** ⊕ *m* bend, elbow.
'**krummnehmen:** *fig. et.* ~ take a th. amiss.
'**Krümmung** *f* crookedness; curvature; *e-s Baches usw.*: bend, turn, winding.
Kruppe ['krupə] *f* (15) croup, crupper.
Krüppel ['krypəl] *m* (7) cripple; *zum* ~ *machen* cripple; '≗**haft**, '≗**ig** crippled.
Kruste ['krustə] *f* (15) crust; '~**ntier** *n* crustacean.
'**krustig** crusty.
Kruzifix [kru:tsi'fiks] *n* (3²) crucifix.
Krypta ['krypta] *f* (16) crypt.
Kübel ['ky:bəl] *m* (7) bucket, pail.
Kubik|fuß [ku'bi:k-] *m* cubic foot; ~**maß** *n* cubic measure; ~**meter** *n, m* cubic met|re, *Am.* -er; ~**wurzel** *f* cube (*od.* cubic) root.
kubisch ['ku:biʃ] cubic.
Küche ['kyçə] *f* (15) kitchen; (*Kochart*) cuisine, cookery; *s. kalt.*
Kuchen ['ku:xən] *m* (6) cake; '~**blech** *n* baking-tray.
'**Küchenchef** *m* chef (*fr.*).
'**Kuchenform** *f* cake tin.
'**Küchen|gerät** *n*, '~**geschirr** *n* kitchen utensils *pl.*; (*Töpferware*) crockery; '~**herd** *m* (kitchen-)range, cooking stove; '~**kräuter** *n/pl.* pot-herbs;

ˈ~**meister** *m* headcook, chef (*fr.*); ˈ~**personal** *n* kitchen staff; ˈ~**schrank** *m* kitchen cabinet *od.* dresser; ˈ~**wecker** *m* kitchen timer; ˈ~**zettel** *m* menu.
Küchlein [ˈkyːçlaɪn] *n*, **Kü(c)ken** [ˈkyːkən] *n* (6) chick(en).
Kuckuck [ˈkukuk] *m* (3) cuckoo; F *zum* ~! damn it!
Kuddelmuddel F [ˈkudəlˈmudəl] *m*, *n* muddle, jumble.
Kufe [ˈkuːfə] *f* (15) tub, vat; (*Schlitten*≈) runner; ✈ skid.
Küfer [ˈkyːfər] *m* (7) cooper; (*Kellermeister*) cellarman.
Kugel [ˈkuːgəl] *f* (15) ball; (*Gewehr*≈) bullet; ⚔, *geogr.* sphere; *Sport*: weight, *Am.* shot; ˈ~**abschnitt** *m* spherical segment; ˈ≈**fest**, ˈ≈**sicher** bullet-proof; ˈ~**form** *f* spherical form; ˈ≈**förmig** globular, spherical; ˈ~**gelenk** *n anat.* socket-joint; ⊕ ball-and-socket (joint); ˈ~**kopf** *m* golf ball; ˈ~**kopfschreibmaschine** *f* golf-ball typewriter; ˈ~**lager** ⊕ *n* ball bearing; ˈ≈**n** *v/i.* (29, sn) roll (*a. v/t.*); *Spiel*: bowl; ˈ≈**rund** (as) round as a ball; ˈ~**schreiber** *m* ball-point (pen), biro; ˈ≈**sicher** bullet-proof; ˈ~**stoßen** *n* shot-put(ting).
Kuh [kuː] *f* (14[1]) cow; ˈ~**euter** *n* cow's udder; ˈ~**fladen** *m* cow-pat; ˈ~**handel** *m fig.* F *contp.* horse trading; ˈ~**hirt** *m* cowherd.
kühl [kyːl] cool, fresh; *fig.* cool; *j-n* ~ *behandeln* give a p. the cold shoulder; ˈ≈**anlage** *f* cold-storage plant; cooling plant; ˈ≈**apparat** *m* refrigerator; ˈ≈**e** *f* (15) coolness; ˈ~**en** *v/t. u. v/i.* (25) cool, chill.
ˈ**Kühler** *m* (7) cooler; *mot.* radiator; ˈ~**figur** *mot. f* radiator mascot; ˈ~**haube** *mot. f* bonnet, *Am.* hood.
ˈ**Kühl|haus** *n* cold-storage house; ˈ~**mittel** *n* coolant, refrigerant; ˈ~**raum** *m* cold-storage chamber; ˈ~**schlange** *f* cooling pipe; ˈ~**schrank** *m* refrigerator; ˈ~**truhe** *f* (deep) freezer; ˈ~**ung** *f* cooling; ˈ~**wagen** *m* refrigerator truck; ˈ~**wasser** *n* cooling water.
ˈ**Kuh|milch** *f* cow's milk; ˈ~**mist** *m* cow-dung.
kühn [kyːn] bold; (*keck*) daring, audacious; ˈ≈**heit** *f* boldness.
ˈ**Kuh|pocken** *f/pl.* cow-pox; ˈ~**stall** *m* cow-shed.
Küken [ˈkyːkən] *n* (6) chick (*a. fig.*).
kulan|t [kuˈlant] obliging, fair; *Preis*: reasonable; ≈**z** [~ts] *f* (16) fair dealing.
Kuli [ˈkuːli] *m* (11) coolie.
kulinarisch [kuliˈnɑːriʃ] culinary.
Kulisse [kuˈlisə] *f* (15) wing, scenery; *fig.* background; ⊕ link; *hinter den* ~*n* behind the scenes; ~**nmaler** *m* scene-painter; ~**nschieber** *m* scene-shifter.
kullern [ˈkulərn] *v/t. u. v/i.* (sn) (29) roll.
Kulmi|nations-punkt [kulminaˈtsjoːns-] *m* culminating point; ≈ˈ**nieren** culminate.
Kult [kult] *m* (3) cult.
kultivieren [kultiˈviːrən] cultivate.
Kultur [kulˈtuːr] *f* (16) (*Anbau*) cultivation; *fig.* culture (*a.* ⚕), (~*gemeinschaft*, ~*niveau*) *a.* civilization; ~**beutel** *m* toilet bag; ≈**ell** [~tuˈrɛl] cultural; ~**film** [~ˈtuːr-] *m* educational film; ~**geschichte** *f* history of civilization; ~**land** *n bebautes*: cultivated (*od.* tilled) land; *weitS.* civilized nation; ~**schande** *f* insult to good taste; ~**seite** *f e-r Zeitung*: arts page; ~**sprache** *f* civilized language; ~**stufe** *f* stage of civilization; ~**volk** *n* civilized race.
Kultus [ˈkultus] *m* (14[3]) cult, worship; ˈ~**minister** *m* Minister of Education.
Kümmel [ˈkyməl] *m* (7) caraway (-seed); (*Likör*) kümmel; *echter* ~ ⚘ cumin.
Kummer [ˈkumər] *m* (7, *o. pl.*) grief, (*Sorge*) worry; (*Unruhe*) trouble.
kümmer|lich [ˈkymərliç] miserable, wretched; (*wenig*) scant, meag|re, *Am.* -er; *sich* ~ *durchschlagen* eke out a miserable existence; ˈ~**n** *v/t.* (29) (*angehen*) concern; *sich* ~ *um* mind, care about, concern o.s. about *od.* for; (*sorgen für*) see to; ˈ≈**nis** *f* (14[2]) affliction.
ˈ**kummervoll** sorrowful.
Kump|an [kumˈpɑːn] *m* (3[1]) companion, fellow; ~**el** [ˈ~pəl] *m* (7) ⚒ pitman; F (*Freund*) chum, pal.
kund [kunt] known.
künd|bar [ˈkyntbɑːr] *Vertrag usw.*: terminable; *Anstellung*: subject to notice; *Kapital*: at call; *Anleihe*: redeemable; ˈ~**en:** ~ *von* tell of.
Kund|e[1] [ˈkundə] *m* (13), ˈ~**in** *f* (16[1])

customer (*a.* F *fig.*); '**~e²** *f* (15) news; (*Kenntnis*) knowledge; (*Wissenschaft*) science; '**~enberatung** *f* advisory service; '**~endienst** *m* service (to the customer); after-sales service; '**~endienstberater** (**-in** *f*) *m* (customer) service representative; '**~enkreis** *m*, '**~enstamm** *m* clientele, (regular) customers *pl.*; '**~ennummer** *f* client code.

'**kund|geben** make known; '**2gebung** *f* manifestation; (*Erklärung*) declaration; *pol.* meeting, rally; demonstration.

'**kundig** knowing, skil(l)ful; *e-r S.* ~ acquainted with, able to; (*sachverständig*) expert (*gen.* at, in).

kündig|en ['kyndigən] (25) *v/i.* give *a p.* notice *od.* warning (to quit); *v/t. Kapital*: call in; *e-n Vertrag*: give notice to terminate; die Wohnung ~ give notice to vacate; '**2ung** *f* (giving) notice; warning; (*Entlassung*) dismissal; '**2ungsfrist** *f* period of notice; vierteljährliche ~ three months' notice; '**2ungsschutz** *m* protection against unlawful dismissal; *für Mieter*: protection against unwarranted eviction.

kund|machen ['kunt-] make known; '**2machung** *f* publication.

'**Kundschaft** *f* clientele, custom(ers *pl.*); '**2en** (26) reconnoit|re, *Am.* -er, scout; '**~er** *m* (7) ⚔ scout; (*Spion*) spy.

'**kund|tun** make known; '**~werden** (sn) become known.

künftig ['kynftiç] future, next *week*, *year*, *etc.*; in ~en Zeiten in times to come; *adv.* (*a.* '**~hin**) for the (*od.* in) future, henceforth.

Kunst [kunst] *f* (14¹) art; (*Geschicklichkeit*) skill; (*Kniff*) trick; *s.* bildend, frei, schön *usw.*; das ist keine ~! that's easy!; '**~-akademie** *f* academy of arts; '**~-ausstellung** *f* art exhibition; '**~buch** *n* art book; '**~butter** *f* (oleo)margarine; '**~denkmal** *n* monument of art; '**~druck** *m* art print(ing); '**~druckpapier** *n* art paper; '**~dünger** *m* artificial manure (*od.* fertilizer); '**~-eisbahn** *f* artificial ice-rink.

Künstelei [kynstə'laɪ] *f* (16) (*Geziertheit*) affectation.

'**Kunst|fahrer(in** *f*) *m* trick cyclist; '**~faser** *f* synthetic (*od.* man-made) fib|re, *Am.* -er; '**~fehler** ⚕ *m* malpractice; '**2fertig** skil(l)ful, skilled; '**~fertigkeit** *f* skill(fulness); '**~flieger(in** *f*) *m* stunt flyer; '**~flug** *m* aerobatics *pl.*, stunt flying; '**~flug...** aerobatic; '**~freund(in** *f*) *m* lover of the fine arts; '**~gärtner(in** *f*) *m* horticulturist; landscape gardener; '**~gegenstand** *m* objet d'art (*fr.*); '**2gemäß**, '**2gerecht** expert, professional, workmanlike; '**~geschichte** *f* history of art; '**2geschichtlich** art-historical; '**~gewerbe** *n* arts and crafts *pl.*; applied art(s *pl.*); '**~glied** *n* artificial limb; '**~griff** *m* trick, knack, dodge; '**~gummi** *n* synthetic rubber; '**~handel** *m* trade in works of art; '**~händler** *m* art dealer; '**~handlung** *f* art dealer's shop; '**~handwerk** *n s.* Kunstgewerbe; '**~harz** *n* synthetic resin; '**~herz** *n* artificial heart; '**~historiker** *m* art historian; '**~hochschule** *f* art college; '**~kenner(in** *f*) *m* art connoisseur; '**~lauf** *m* *Eissport*: figure-skating; '**~leder** *n* imitation (*od.* artificial) leather.

Künstler ['kynstlər] *m* (7), '**~in** *f* (16¹) artist; ♪, *thea.* performer; '**2isch** artistic(ally *adv.*); '**~name** *m* stage-name; '**~pech** F *n* bad luck; '**~viertel** *n* Latin quarter.

'**künstlich** artificial; *Fasern*: synthetic, man-made; ~er Mond man-made moon.

'**Kunst|liebhaber(in** *f*) *m* art-lover; '**2los** artless; primitive; '**~maler** (**-in** *f*) *m* artist (painter); '**~mappe** *f* art folder; '**~pause** *f* dramatic pause; '**2reich** ingenious; '**~reiter** (**-in** *f*) *m* trick rider; '**~sammlung** *f* art collection; **~schätze** ['~ʃɛtsə] *m/pl.* art treasures *pl.*; '**~schule** *f* school of arts; '**~seide** *f* artificial silk, rayon; '**~sprache** *f* artificial language; '**~springen** *n* fancy diving; '**~sticke'rei** *f* art needlework; '**~stoff** *m* plastic (material); '**~stopfen** *n* invisible mending; '**~stück** *n* trick, feat, *bsd. Am.* F stunt; (das ist kein) ~! anyone can do that!; '**~tischler** *m* cabinet-maker; '**~turnen** *n* gymnastics *pl.*; '**~verlag** *m* art publishers *pl.*; '**~verständige** *m, f* art expert; '**2voll** artistic, elaborate, ingenious; '**~werk** *n* work of art; '**~wolle** *f* artificial wool; '**~wort** *n* coined word.

kunterbunt ['kuntərbunt] *durcheinander*: higgledy-piggledy.
Kupfer ['kupfər] *n* (7) copper; *a.* = *~geld*, *~stich*; '**~barren** *m* copper ingot; '**~blech** *n* sheet copper; '**~draht** *m* copper wire; '**~druck** *m* copperplate(-print[ing]); '**~geld** *n* copper money; '**2haltig** containing copper; '**~hütte** *f* copper-works *pl.*; '**2ig** coppery; '**~münze** *f* copper (coin); '**2n** of copper; copper ...; '**~platte** *f* copperplate; '**2rot** copper-red; '**~schmied** *m* coppersmith; '**~stecher** *m* copperplate engraver; '**~stich** *m* copperplate (engraving); '**~vitriol** *n* blue vitriol.
kupieren [ku'pi:rən] crop, dock.
Kupon [ku'pɔ̃] *m* (11) coupon; ☤ dividend-warrant.
Kuppe ['kupə] *f* (15) top; (*Nagel2*) head.
Kuppel ['~l] *f* (15) cupola, dome; **~ei** [~'laɪ] *f* (16) matchmaking; ⚖ procuring; '**2n** (29) *v/t.* ⊕ couple; *v/i. mot.* (de)clutch; (*Ehe vermitteln*) match-make; *b.s.* pimp, procure.
Kuppler ['kuplər] *m* (7), '**~in** *f* (16¹) matchmaker; *b.s.* procurer, *f* procuress.
Kupplung ['kupluŋ] ⊕ *f* coupling; *mot.* clutch; '**~spedal** *n* clutch pedal; '**~sscheibe** *f* clutch disc.
Kur [ku:r] *f* (16) cure; *e-e ~ machen* take a cure, take a course of treatment.
Kür [ky:r] *f* (16) *Sport*: free exercise (*swimming, etc.*).
Kurat|el [kura'tɛl] *f* (16) guardianship; **~or** [~'rɑ:tɔr] *m* (8¹) guardian, trustee; **~orium** [~ra'to:rjum] *n* (9) board (of trustees).
Kurbel ['kurbəl] *f* (15) crank, handle; '**~gehäuse** ⊕ *n* crankcase; '**2n** (29) crank; *Film*: shoot; '**~welle** *mot. f* crankshaft.
Kürbis ['kyrbis] *m* (4¹) gourd, pumpkin; F (*Kopf*) nut.
küren ['ky:rən] (25) choose; elect.
Kur|fürst ['ku:r-] *m* elector; '**~fürstentum** *n* (1²) electorate; '**~fürstin** *f* (16¹) electoress; '**2fürstlich** electoral; '**~gast** *m* visitor; '**~haus** *n* kurhaus, spa house; '**~hotel** *n* resort hotel.
Kurie ['ku:rjə] *f* (15) Curia.
Kurier [ku'ri:r] *m* (7) courier.
kurieren [ku'ri:rən] cure.
kurios [kur'jo:s] (18¹) curious, odd.
Kuriosität [~jozi'tɛ:t] *f* (16) curiosity; (*Sammlungsstück*) curio(sity).
Kürlauf ['ky:rlauf] *m* (*Eislauf*) free skating.
'**Kur|-ort** *m* health resort, spa; '**~park** *m* spa gardens *pl.*; '**~pfuscher** (**-in** *f*) *m* quack; '**~pfusche'rei** *f* quackery.
Kurrentschrift [ku'rɛntʃrift] *f* running hand.
Kurs [kurs] *m* (4) (*Umlauf*) currency; (*~wert*) rate, price; (*~notierung*) quotation; ⚓, ✈ *u. fig.* course; (*Lehrgang*) course; ⚓ *~ nehmen* (*a. fig.*) head (*auf acc.* for); *außer ~ setzen* withdraw from circulation; *in ~ setzen* circulate; *pol. harter ~* hard line.
Kursaal ['ku:r-] *m* kursaal.
'**Kurs|-anstieg** *m* rise in rates (*od.* prices); '**~bericht** *m* market report; '**~buch** *n* railway (*Am.* railroad) guide.
Kürschner ['kyrʃnər] *m* (7) furrier; **~ei** [~'raɪ] *f* (16) furrier's trade; (*Werkstatt*) furrier's shop; '**~ware** *f* furs and skins *pl.*
'**Kursgewinn** *m* price gain.
kursieren [kur'zi:rən] *Geld*: circulate; *Gerücht*: *a.* go round.
Kursivschrift [~'zi:fʃrift] *f* italics *pl.*
'**Kurs|notierung** *f* quotation; '**~rückgang** *m* fall in rates (*od.* prices); '**~schwankung** *f* price fluctuation.
Kursus ['kurzus] *m* (14³) course.
'**Kurs|verlust** *m* loss on the exchange; '**~wechsel** *pol. m* change of policy; '**~wert** *m* market-value; '**~zettel** *m* exchange list.
Kurtaxe ['ku:r-] *f* visitors' tax.
Kür|turnen ['ky:r-] *n* free gymnastics *pl.*; '**~übung** *f* free exercise.
Kurve ['kurvə] *f* (15) curve, bend; '**2n** curve; *~ um* drive round; '**~nbild** *n*, '**~nblatt** *n* graph; '**2nförmig** curved; '**~nlage** *f* cornering (stability); '**2nreich** full of bends; F curvaceous (*girl*); '**~nschreiber** *m* plotter.
kurz [kurts] (18²) *Raum*: short; *Zeit, Abfassung usw.*: short, brief; *adv.* shortly; (*kurzum*) in short; *~ (und bündig)* concise(ly), brief(ly); *~ angebunden sein* be curt; *~ und gut* in short, in a word; *~e Hose* shorts *pl.*; *~ vor London* short of London; *binnen ~em* before long; *über ~ oder lang* sooner or later; *seit ~em* lately, recently; *vor ~em*

a little while ago; *mit ~en Worten* in a few words; *~ abweisen* be short with *a p.*; *um es ~ zu sagen* to cut a long story short; *s. abfertigen, binnen, fassen, über, Prozeß*; *zu ~ kommen* go short, come off a loser *od.* badly (*bei* in); *den kürzeren ziehen* get worsted; *~ und klein schlagen* smash to bits; '**2-arbeit** *f* short time (work); '**~-arbeiten** be on short time; '**2-arbeiter** *m* short-time worker; **~atmig** ['~ʔaːtmiç] asthmatic, short-winded.

Kürze ['kyrtsə] *f* (15) shortness; brevity; conciseness; *in ~* shortly, before long; *s. Würze*; '**2en** (27) shorten; (*verringern*) cut; *s. a. abkürzen.*

Kürzel ['kyrtsəl] *n* (7) grammalogue.

'**kurz|er'hand** offhand; '**2fassung** *f* abridged version; '**2film** *m* short (film); '**2form** *f* shortened form; '**~fristig** short-term; *adv.* at short notice; '**2geschichte** *f* short story; '**2haar...** short-hair; '**~halten:** *j-n ~* put a p. on short allowance; keep a p. short (*mit* of *money*); **~lebig** ['~leːbiç] short-lived.

kürzlich ['kyrtsliç] recently, not long ago.

'**Kurz|meldung** *f*, '**~nachricht** *f* news flash, brief report; *pl.* news in brief; '**2schließen** ⚡ short-circuit; '**~schluß** ⚡ *m* short circuit; *fig.* (*~handlung*) panic (action); '**~schrift** *f* shorthand(-writing), stenography; '**2sichtig** short- (*Am.* near-)sighted; *fig.* short-sighted; '**~sichtigkeit** *f* short-sightedness (*a. fig.*); '**~streckenflug** *m* short-distance flight; '**~streckenläufer** *m* *Sport*: sprinter; '**2treten** mark time (*a. fig.*); **2'um** in short.

'**Kürzung** *f* shortening; abridg(e)ment; *v. Ausgaben*: cut.

'**Kurz|wahl** *teleph. f* abbreviated address calling; '**~waren** *f/pl.* haberdashery *sg.*, *Am.* notions *pl.*; '**~warenhändler** *m* haberdasher; **2weg** ['~'vek] flatly; '**~weil** *f* (16, *o. pl.*) pastime, amusement; '**2weilig** amusing, funny; '**~welle** ⚡ *f* short wave; '**~wellen...** short-wave ...; '**~zeitgedächtnis** *n* short-term memory; '**~zeitspeicher** *m* *Computer*: short-term storage.

kuschel|ig ['kuʃəliç] cosy, snug; '**~n** (29) *sich ~* snuggle up (*an acc.* to).

kuschen ['kuʃən] (27) *Hund*: lie down; *fig.* knuckle under.

Kusine [ku'ziːnə] *f* (15) (female) cousin.

Kuß [kus] *m* (4¹) kiss; '**2-echt** kiss-proof.

küssen ['kysən] (28) kiss.

'**kuß|fest** kissproof; '**2hand** *f*: *j-m eine ~ zuwerfen* blow a kiss to a p.; *fig. mit ~* with pleasure.

Küste ['kystə] *f* (15) coast, shore.

'**Küsten|gebiet** *n* coastal area; '**~gewässer** *n* coastal waters *pl.*; '**~handel** *m* coasting trade; '**~land** *n*, '**~strich** *m* coastland; '**~schiffahrt** *f* coastal shipping; '**~wache** *f* coast-guard.

Küster ['kystər] *m* (7) sexton; **~ei** [~'raɪ] *f* (16) sexton's office.

Kutsch|e ['kutʃə] *f* (15) coach, carriage; '**~er** *m* (7) coachman, driver; **2ieren** [kut'ʃiːrən] *v/i.* (sn *u.* h.) drive (a coach); '**~pferd** *n* coach-horse.

Kutte ['kutə] *f* (15) cowl.

Kutteln ['kutəln] *f/pl.* tripe(s *pl.*) *sg.*

Kutter ⚓ ['kutər] *m* (7) cutter.

Kuvert [ku'vɛrt] *n* (3) envelope; (*Gedeck*) cover.

Kux ⚒ [kuks] *m* (3²) no-par (value) mining share.

Kybernetik [kybɛr'neːtik] *f* (16, *o. pl.*) cybernetics *sg.*

L

L [ɛl]., **l** *n inv.* L, l.

Lab [laːp] *n* (3) *zo.* rennet; *physiol.* (*Ferment*) rennin.

laben ['laːbən] (25) refresh; *fig. sich an e-m Anblick ~* feast one's eyes on.

labil [la'biːl] unstable (*a.* ⊕, ⚕); *phys.*, ⚗ labile; **2ität** [~bili'tɛːt] *f* (16) instability; *phys.*, ⚗ lability.

Labor [la'boːr] F *n* (11 *od.* 3¹) lab; **~ant** [~bo'rant] *m* (12) laboratory assistant; **~atorium** [~a'to:rjum] *n* (9) laboratory; **≈'ieren** ⚗ experiment; *(leiden)* ~ *an (dat.)* labo(u)r under, suffer from.

Labsal ['la:pza:l] *n* (3), **'Labung** *f* refreshment; *fig.* comfort.

Labyrinth [laby'rint] *n* (3) labyrinth, maze.

Lache¹ F ['laxə] *f* (15) laugh(ter).

'Lache² *f* pool, puddle.

lächeln ['lɛçəln] **1.** *v/i.* (29) smile; *höhnisch* ~ sneer (*beide*: *über acc.* at); **2.** ≈ *n* smile; *höhnisches* ~ sneer.

lachen ['laxən] **1.** *v/i.* (25) laugh (*über acc.* at); *leise vor sich hin* ~ chuckle; *sich e-n Ast* ~ split one's sides with laughing; *du hast gut* ~ F it's all very well for you to laugh; *s. Fäustchen, biegen*; **2.** ≈ *n* (6) laugh, laughter; *das ist (nicht) zum* ~ that's ridiculous (no laughing matter); *s. verbeißen, zumute.*

'Lacher *m* (7), **'~in** *f* (16¹) laugher; *die* ~ *auf s-r Seite haben* have the laugh on one's side.

lächerlich ['lɛçərliç] ridiculous, laughable, absurd; *(unbedeutend)* derisory; ~ *machen* ridicule; *sich* ~ *machen* make a fool (*od.* an ass) of o.s.; **'≈keit** *f* ridiculousness.

lächern ['lɛçərn] (29): *es lächert mich* it makes me laugh.

Lach|fältchen ['~fɛltçən] *n* (6) laughter line; **'~gas** *n* laughing gas.

'lachhaft *s. lächerlich.*

'Lachkrampf *m* convulsive laughter, fit of laughter; *ich krieg 'nen ~!* you'll have me in stitches!

Lachs [laks] *m* (4) salmon; **'~fang** *m*, **'~fischerei** *f* salmon-fishing; **'≈farben** salmon(-pink); **'~schinken** *m* fillet of smoked ham.

Lack [lak] *m* (3) (gum-)lac; *(Firnis)* varnish; *(gefärbter ~)* lacquer, enamel; *mot.* paintwork; **'~-affe** F *m* dandy; **'~-arbeit(en** *pl.*) *f* lacquered work; **'~farbe** *f* *(Klar≈)* varnish; *(Öl≈)* paint; **'~firnis** *m* (lac) varnish; **≈ieren** [~'ki:rən] lacquer, varnish, enamel; paint; F *fig.* dupe; **~ierer** [~'ki:rər] *m* (7) varnisher; **'~leder** *n* patent leather.

Lackmus ⚗ ['~mus] *m inv.* litmus.

'Lackschuh *m* patent (leather) shoe.

Lade ['la:də] *f* (15) case; *für Wäsche usw.*: press; *(Schub≈)* drawer; **'~baum** *m* derrick; **'~fähigkeit** *f* loading capacity; ⚓ tonnage; **'~hemmung** ⚔ *f* jam, stoppage; **'~linie** ⚓ *f* loadline; **'~liste** *f* cargo list; **'~meister** *m* chief-loader.

laden¹ ['la:dən] (30) load, lade; *Schußwaffe*: load, (*a.* ⚡) charge; *als Fracht*: freight; ⚖ cite, summon; *als Gast*: invite, ask; *s. auf~.*

'Laden² *m* (6[¹]) ⚕ shop (*a.* F *fig.*), store; *(Fenster≈)* shutter; *s. schmeißen*; **'~dieb** *m* shop-lifter; **'~diebstahl** *m* shop-lifting; **'~gehilf|e** *m*, **-in** *f* shop assistant, *Am.* sales-clerk; **'~geschäft** *n* shop, store; **'~hüter** *m* drug in (*Am.* on) the market, shelf warmer; **'~-inhaber** (**-in** *f*) *m* shopkeeper, *Am.* storekeeper; **'~kasse** *f* till; **'~kette** *f* chain (of shops); **'~mädchen** *n* shop-girl; **'~preis** *m* selling (*od.* retail) price; **'~schild** *n* shop-sign; **'~schluß** *m* closing time; **'~tisch** *m* counter.

'Lade|platz *m* loading-place; **'~rampe** *f* loading ramp *od.* platform; **'~raum** *m* loading space; ⚓ hold; *Raumfähre*: cargo bay; **'~schein** *m* bill of lading.

lädieren [lɛ'di:rən] damage, injure.

'Ladung *f* (16) loading; *konkr.* load; *Güter*: freight; ⚓ cargo; *e-r Schußwaffe od.* ⚡ charge; ⚖ summons.

Lafette [la'fɛtə] *f* (15) (gun) mount.

Laffe ['lafə] *m* (13) fop, puppy.

lag [la:k] *pret. v. liegen.*

Lage ['la:gə] *f* (15) position, (*a. fig.*) situation; *e-s Hauses usw.*: site, location; *(Zustand)* state, condition; *mißliche*: predicament, plight; *(Haltung)* attitude; *(Schicht)* layer, *geol. a.* stratum; *im Stapel*: tier; ⊕ ply; *(Runde Bier usw.)* round; *(Papier≈)* quire; ⚔ *(Salve)* group, volley; *nach* ~ *der Dinge* as matters stand; *in der* ~ *sein zu tun* be in a position to do; *j-n in die* ~ *versetzen, et. zu tun* enable a p. to do a th.; **'~bericht** *m* situation report; **'~nstaffel** *f* *Schwimmen*: medley relay; **'~plan** *m* site plan.

Lager ['la:gər] *n* (7) couch, bed; *geol.* deposit; *e-s Wildes*: lair; ⊕ bearing; *(Waren≈)* stockroom, warehouse, depot, *(Stapelplatz)* dump; *(Vorrat)* stock(s *pl.*), store; ⚔ *usw.* camp (*a. fig.*); *auf* ~ ⚕ in stock, on hand, *fig.* up one's sleeve; **'~-arbeiter** *m* warehouseman, warehouser; **'~-aufseher** *m* warehouseman; **'~bestellung** *f* stock order; **'~bier** *n* lager (beer);

'**~buch** *n* stock-book; '**~fähigkeit** *f* shelf life; '**~feuer** *n* camp-fire; '**~gebühr** *f*, '**~geld** *n* storage, warehouse-rent; '**~haus** *n* warehouse; '**⁀n** *v/i.* (29, h., sn) lie down, rest (*a. sich ~*); ⚔ (en)camp, be encamped; ✝ be stored; *v/t.* (h.) lay down; *Truppen*: (en)camp; *Waren*: store, warehouse; ⊕ mount in bearings, *Maschine*: seat; '**~platz** *m* ✝ depot, storage place; *s. Lagerstelle*; '**~raum** *m* store-room; '**~schein** *m* warehouse receipt; '**~stätte** *f*, '**~stelle** *f zum Ruhen*: resting-place; *zum Zelten*: camp site; *geol.* deposit; '**~ung** *f von Waren*: storage; *geol.* stratification; ⊕ (mounting in) bearings *pl.*; '**~verwalter** *m s. Lageraufseher*; '**~vorrat** *m* stock; '**~wirtschaft** *f* stockpiling.
'**Lageskizze** *f* sketch map.
Lagune [la'gu:nə] *f* (15) lagoon.
lahm [lɑ:m] lame (*a. fig.*); '**~en** (25) be lame; limp.
lähmen ['lɛ:mən] (25) lame, paralyse (*a. fig.*).
'**lahmlegen** *fig.* paralyse.
'**Lähmung** *f* laming, paralysing; *als Zustand*: paralysis.
Laib [laɪp] *m* (3) loaf.
Laich [laɪç] *m* (3), '**⁀en** (25) spawn.
Laie ['laɪə] *m* (13) layman (*~n pl.* laity); '**~nbruder** *m* lay brother; '**⁀nhaft** amateurish, lay ...; '**~nmaler** *m* amateur painter; '**~npriester** *m* lay priest; '**~nschauspieler** *m* amateur actor.
Lakai [la'kaɪ] *m* (12) lackey, footman; **⁀enhaft** [~ənhaft] servile.
Lake ['lɑ:kə] *f* (15) brine, pickle.
Laken ['lɑ:kən] *n* (6) sheet.
lakonisch [la'ko:niʃ] laconic(ally *adv.*).
Lakritze [la'kritsə] *f* (15) liquorice.
lallen ['lalən] (25) *v/i. u. v/t.* stammer.
Lamelle [la'mɛlə] *f* (15) lamella; ⚡ lamina (*pl.* -ae), bar; ⊕ disc; *der Pilze*: gill.
lament|ieren [~'ti:rən] lament (*um* for; *über acc.* over); **⁀o** [la'mɛnto] *n* (11) lamentations *pl.*
Lametta [la'mɛta] *f inv. od. n* (9, *o. pl.*) silver tinsel.
Lamm [lam] *n* (1²) lamb; '**~braten** *m* roast lamb; '**⁀en** (25) lamb.
Lämm|chen ['lɛmçən] *n* (6) lambkin; **~ergeier** ['lɛmər-] *m* lammergeier; '**~erwolke** *f* cirrus.
'**Lamm|fell** *n* lambskin; '**~fleisch** *n* lamb; '**⁀fromm** (as) gentle as a lamb; meek.
Lampe ['lampə] *f* (15) lamp.
'**Lampen|fieber** *n* stage-fright; '**~licht** *n* lamplight; '**~schirm** *m* lamp-shade.
Lampion [lam'pjõ] *m* (11) Chinese lantern.
lancieren [lɑ̃'si:rən] launch (*a. fig.*).
Land [lant] *n* (1², *poet.* 3) (*Ggs. Wasser*) land; (*Ggs. Stadt*) country; (*Ackerboden*) land, ground, soil; (*Gebiet*) land, territory, country; (*Staat*) country; *pol. in Deutschland*: Land, Federal State; *ans ~* ashore, on shore; *auf dem ~e* in the country; *außer ~es* abroad; *zu ~e* by land; '**~-adel** *m* (landed) gentry; '**~-arbeiter** *m* agricultural labo(u)rer, farm hand; **⁀'aus:** *~ landein* far and wide; '**~besitz** *m* landed property; '**~besitzer** *m* landed proprietor; '**~bewohner** *m* countryman.
Lande|-anflug ✈ ['landə-] *m* landing approach; '**~bahn** *f* runway, landing strip; '**~deck** *n* landing (*od.* flight) deck; '**~-erlaubnis** *f* landing permission; '**~feuer** *n* runway light.
land'-einwärts inland, up-country.
'**landen** *v/i.* (26, sn, h.) *u. v/t. allg.* land; (*ausschiffen*) *a.* disembark.
'**Land-enge** *f* neck of land, isthmus.
Landeplatz ['landə-] *m* quay, wharf; ✈ landing-ground *od.* -field.
Länderei [lɛndə'raɪ] *f* (16) landed property; *pl. a.* lands.
'**Länder|kampf** *m Sport*: international competition *od.* (*Spiel*) match; '**~kunde** *f* geography; '**~spiel** *n Sport*: international match.
'**Landes|beschreibung** *f* topography; '**~farben** *f/pl.* national colo(u)rs; '**~fürst** *m*, '**~herr** *m* sovereign; '**~grenze** *f* frontier, (national) boundary; '**~hoheit** *f* sovereignty; '**~kind** *n* native; '**~kirche** *f* national (*od.* regional) church; '**~meister** *m Sport*: national champion; '**~polizei** *f* state police; '**~regierung** *f* government; *in Deutschland*: Land government; '**~sprache** *f* language of a country, native (*od.* vernacular) language; '**~tracht** *f* national costume; '**~trauer** *f* public mourning; '**⁀-üblich** customary; '**~vater** *m* father of the people, sovereign; '**~verrat** *m* treason; '**~verräter** *m* trai-

tor to his country; '**~verteidigung** *f* national defen|ce, *Am.* -se; '**~verweisung** *f* expatriation; *e-s Landfremden*: deportation; '**⁓weit** nationwide.

'**Landeverbot** *n* landing prohibition.

'**Land|fahrzeug** *n* land vehicle; '**~flucht** *f* rural exodus; '**⁓flüchtig** fugitive; '**~friede**(**nsbruch**) *m* (breach of the) public peace; '**~gang** ⚓ *m* shore leave; '**~gemeinde** *f* rural community; '**~gericht** *n* district (*od.* superior) court; '**~gerichtsrat** *m* district court judge; '**⁓gestützt** ⚔ *Rakete*: land-based; '**~gewinnung** *f* land reclamation; '**~gut** *n* country seat, estate; '**~haus** *n* country house; '**~jäger** *m* rural policeman; '**~junker** *m* (country) squire; '**~karte** *f* map; '**~kreis** *m* (rural) district; '**⁓läufig** current, common; '**~leben** *n* country life; '**~leute** *pl.* country-people.

ländlich ['lɛntliç] rural, country--like; (*bäurisch*) rustic.

'**Land|macht** *f* land power; '**~mann** *m* countryman, farmer; '**~messer** *m* surveyor; '**~partie** *f* outing, picnic; '**~pfarrer** *m* country parson; '**~plage** *f* public calamity; *fig.* (public) nuisance; '**~rat** *m* district president; '**~ratte** ⚓ *f* landlubber; '**~regen** *m* persistent rain; '**~rücken** *m* ridge of land.

'**Landschaft** *f* landscape (*a. paint.*), scenery; (*Bezirk*) region, district; '**⁓lich** provincial; *Schönheit usw.*: scenic; '**~sgärtner** *m* landscape gardener; '**~smaler**(**ei** *f*) *m* landscape-painter (-painting); '**~sschutz** *m* conservation.

Landser ⚔ F ['lantsər] *m* (7) (common) soldier, *Brt.* Tommy (Atkins), *Am.* G.I. (Joe).

'**Landsitz** *m* country seat.

Lands|knecht ['~ts-] *m* mercenary; '**~mann** *m* fellow-countryman, compatriot; *was für ein ~ sind Sie?* what is your native country?; **~männin** ['~mɛnin] *f* fellow--countrywoman; '**~mannschaft** *f* expellee organization.

'**Land|spitze** *f* cape, promontory; '**~stadt** *f* country town; '**~straße** *f* highway; '**~streicher**(**in** *f*) *m* tramp; **~streiche'rei** *f* vagrancy; '**~streitkräfte** *f/pl.* land forces *pl.*; '**~strich** *m* tract of land, region; '**~tag** *m* diet.

Landung ['~duŋ] *f* (16) landing; ✈ *a.* touchdown; (*Ausschiffung*) disembarkation; '**~sbrücke** ⚓ *f schwimmende*: landing-stage; *feste*: jetty, pier.

'**Land-urlaub** ⚓ *m* shore leave.

'**Land|vermessung** *f* land surveying; '**~volk** *n* country-people; '**⁓wärts** landward; '**~wirt** *m* farmer; '**~wirtschaft** *f* agriculture, farming; (*Anwesen*) farm; '**⁓wirtschaftlich**, '**~wirtschafts...** agricultural; '**~zunge** *f* spit (of land).

lang [laŋ] (18²) long; *P.*: *a.* tall; F (*entlang*) along; *drei Fuß ~* three feet long *od.* in length; *e-e Woche ~* for a week; *seit ~em* for a long time (past); *~ und breit* at (full *od.* great) length; *die Zeit wird mir ~* time hangs heavy on my hands; *~ werden Tage*: lengthen; *er machte ein ~es Gesicht* his face fell; *~ entbehrt* (*ersehnt*) long missed (desired); *s. lange, länger, Bank, Hand usw.*; **~atmig** ['~ʔa:tmiç] long-winded; '**~beinig** long-legged.

lange ['laŋə] *adv.* long, a long time; *~ her* long ago; *noch ~ nicht* not for a long time yet, *fig.* not by a long way; *es ist noch ~ nicht fertig* it is not nearly ready; *so ~ bis* till, until.

Länge ['lɛŋə] *f* (15) length (*a. zeitlich*); (*Größe*) tallness; *geogr.*, *ast.* longitude; *fig. in e-m Buch usw.*: tedious passage; *auf die ~* in the long run; *in die ~ ziehen* draw out, protract, *Erzählung*: spin out; *sich in die ~ ziehen* drag on; *der ~ nach* (at) full length, lengthwise.

langen ['laŋən] (25) (*genügen*) suffice, be enough; *~ nach* reach for; F *j-m e-e ~* fetch a p. one; *langt das?* will that do?; *damit lange ich e-e Woche* this will last me a week.

'**Längen|**(**durch**)**schnitt** *m* longitudinal section; '**~grad** *m* degree of longitude; '**~kreis** *m* meridian; '**~maß** *n* long (*od.* linear) measure.

länger ['lɛŋər] longer; (*ziemlich lang*) prolonged; *~e Zeit* (for) some time; *nicht ~* not any longer.

'**Langeweile** *f* (15, *o. pl.*, *gen. u. dat. Lang*[*en*]*weile*) tediousness, boredom, ennui (*fr.*); *~ haben* be bored.

'**Lang|finger** F *m* thief; **⁓fristig** [~'fristiç] long-term; *~ (gesehen)* in the long run; '**⁓haarig** long-haired;

'**⁓jährig** of many years, of long standing; '**⁓lauf** *m* long-distance run(ning); (*Schi⁓*) cross-country skiing; '**⁓läufer** *m* (*Schi⁓*) cross-country skier; **⁓lebig** ['⁓le:biç] long-lived; '**⁓lebigkeit** *f* longevity.

länglich ['lɛŋliç] longish, oblong; '**⁓rund** oval.

'**Lang|mut** *f*, **⁓mütigkeit** ['⁓my:tiçkaɪt] *f* patience, forbearance; '**⁓mütig** patient, forbearing; **⁓ohrig** ['⁓ˀo:riç] long-eared.

längs [lɛŋs] along; *⁓ der Küste* alongshore; '**⁓-achse** *f* longitudinal axis.

langsam ['laŋza:m] slow; '**⁓keit** *f* slowness.

Lang|schäfter ['⁓ʃɛftər] *m/pl.* (7) Wellingtons; '**⁓schiff** *n e-r Kirche*: nave; '**⁓schläfer** *m* late riser; '**⁓spielplatte** *f* long-play(ing) record.

Längs|schnitt ['lɛŋs-] *m* longitudinal section; **⁓seits** ['⁓zaɪts] alongside.

längst [lɛŋst] long ago, long since; *am ⁓en* longest; *⁓ nicht so gut* not nearly as good; '**⁓ens** at the latest.

'**lang|stielig** long-handled; *Blume*: long-stemmed; '**⁓strecken...** long-distance, ⚔ *a.* long-range; '**⁓weile** *s. Langeweile*; '**⁓weilen** bore; *sich ⁓* feel bored; '**⁓weilig** tedious, boring, dull; *⁓e Person* bore; '**⁓welle** *f Radio*: long wave; '**⁓wellen...** long-wave ...; **⁓wierig** ['⁓vi:riç] protracted, lengthy; '**⁓wierigkeit** *f* lengthiness; '**⁓zeitgedächtnis** *n* long-term memory; '**⁓zeitwirkung** *f* long-range (*od.* long-term) effect.

Lanolin [lano'li:n] *n* lanolin.

Lanz|e ['lantsə] *f* (15) lance; *fig.* e-e *⁓ brechen für* stand up for; **⁓ette** [⁓'tsɛtə] *f* (15) lancet.

lapidar [lapi'da:r] lapidary.

Lappalie [la'pa:ljə] *f* (15) trifle.

Lappe ['lapə] *m* (13), '**Lappin** *f* (16[1]) Lapp; *s. a. Lappländer.*

Lappen ['lapən] *m* (6) *anat.*, ⚘ lobe; (*Flicken*) patch; (*Lumpen*) rag; (*Staub⁓*) duster; *s. Putz⁓, Wisch⁓.*

läppern ['lɛpərn] (29): *sich (zusammen)⁓* accumulate.

'**lappig** ragged; *anat.*, ⚘ lobed; (*schlaff*) flabby.

läppisch ['lɛpiʃ] foolish, silly.

Lappländer ['laplɛndər] *m* (7), '**⁓in** *f* (16[1]) Laplander.

Lapsus ['lapsus] *m* (*inv.*) slip.

Lärche ⚘ ['lɛrçə] *f* (15) larch.

Lärm [lɛrm] *m* (3, *o. pl.*) noise; *andauernder*: din; *⁓ machen s. lärmen*; *⁓ schlagen* give the alarm; '**⁓bekämpfung** *f* noise abatement; '**⁓en** (25) make a noise; '**⁓end** noisy; '**⁓pegel** *m* noise level; '**⁓schutz** *m* noise prevention; '**⁓schutzwall** *m* noise barrier.

Larve ['larfə] *f* (15) mask; *zo.* larva.

las [la:s] *pret. v. lesen.*

lasch [laʃ] limp, lax; *Getränk*: insipid, (*abgestanden*) stale.

Lasche ['laʃə] *f* (15) ⊕ strap; *am Schnürschuh*: tongue.

Laser ['le:zər] *m* (7) laser; '**⁓-abtaststrahl** *m* laser scanner; '**⁓drucker** *m typ.* laser-printer; '**⁓platte** *f* laser-disc; '**⁓plattenspieler** *m* laser- (*od.* compact) disc player; '**⁓strahl** *m* laser beam; '**⁓technik** *f* laser technology.

lassen ['lasən] (30) let; leave *open, shut*; (*gestatten*) allow, permit; (*dulden*) suffer; (*veran⁓*) make, cause to, (*befehlen*) order to; (*ver⁓, zurück⁓*) leave; *laßt uns gehen* let us go; *laß (das)!* don't!; *laß das Weinen!* stop crying!; *laß (es) gut sein!* never mind!; *ich kann es nicht ⁓* I cannot help (doing) it; *sein Leben ⁓ für* sacrifice (*od.* give) one's life for; *von et. ⁓* desist from, give up; *drucken ⁓* have ... printed; *gehen ⁓* let ... go; *von sich hören ⁓* send news; *ich habe ihn dieses Buch lesen ⁓* I made him read this book; *sich e-n Zahn ziehen ⁓* have a tooth drawn; *das läßt sich denken* I can imagine; *es läßt sich nicht leugnen* there is no denying (the fact); *der Wein läßt sich trinken* the wine is drinkable; *s. Haar, hören, kommen, machen, Ruhe, sagen, übrig⁓, warten, Wasser, Zeit, zufrieden.*

lässig ['lɛsiç] lazy, indolent; (*träge*) sluggish; (*nach⁓*) negligent; (*unbekümmert*) nonchalant; '**⁓keit** *f* laziness; negligence; nonchalance.

läßlich *eccl.* ['lɛsliç] *Sünde*: venial.

Last [last] *f* (16) load, (*Bürde*) burden, (*Gewicht*) weight (*alle a. fig.*); (*Tragfähigkeit*) tonnage; (*Fracht*) cargo, freight; *fig.* weight, charge, trouble; ⚖ *⁓ der Beweise* weight of the evidence; ✝ *zu ⁓en von* to the debit of; *zu ⁓en gehen von* be chargeable to; *j-m zur ⁓ fallen* be a burden to a p.; *j-m et. zur ~ legen* charge a p. with a th., blame a th. on a p.; '**~-auto** *n s. Lastkraftwagen.*

'**lasten** (26) (*auf dat.*) weigh (upon); '**2-aufzug** *m* goods lift, *Am.* freight elevator; '**2-ausgleich** *m* equalization of burdens; '**~frei** unencumbered; '**2segler** ✈ *m* transport glider.

Laster[1] ['lastər] *n* (7) vice.

'**Laster**[2] *m* (7) *s. Lastkraftwagen.*

'**lasterhaft** depraved, wicked; '**2igkeit** *f* depravity.

'**Lasterhöhle** *f* den of vice.

läster|lich ['lɛstər-] slanderous; (*gottes~*) blasphemous; F (*furchtbar*) F awful; '**2maul** *n* slanderer, backbiter; '**~n** (29) *v/t. Gott*: blaspheme; *v/i. ~ über* (*acc.*) slander, defame; '**2ung** *f* slander, calumny; blasphemy; '**2zunge** *f* slanderous tongue; *s. Lästermaul.*

lästig ['lɛstiç] troublesome, bothersome, annoying; *j-m ~ fallen* (*od. werden*) bother a p.; '**2keit** *f* troublesomeness.

'**Last|kahn** *m* barge; '**~kraftwagen** *m* (motor) lorry, *Am.* truck; '**~pferd** *n* pack-horse; '**~schiff** *n* transport-ship; '**~schrift** ✝ *f* (*Anzeige*) debit note; (*Buchung*) debit item; '**~tier** *n* pack animal; '**~wagen** *m s. Lastkraftwagen*; '**~wagenfahrer** *m* lorry (*Am.* truck) driver; '**~zug** *m* truck trailer.

Lasur [la'zu:r] *f* glaze; **2blau** azure; **~lack** *m* transparent varnish; **~stein** *m* lapis lazuli.

Latein [la'taɪn] *n* (1, *o. pl.*) Latin; *fig. mit s-m ~ am Ende sein* be at one's wits' end; **~er** *m* (7) Latinist; **2isch** Latin.

latent [la'tɛnt] latent.

Laterne [la'tɛrnə] *f* (15) lantern, lamp; **~npfahl** *m* lamp-post.

Latinum [la'ti:num] *n* (9, *o. pl.*): *großes ~* A-level Latin; *kleines ~* O-level Latin.

Latrine [la'tri:nə] *f* (15) latrine.

Latsch|e ['la:tʃə] *f* (15) F (*Pantoffel*) slipper; ⚘ dwarf pine; '**2en** F (27, sn) shuffle (along); '**2ig** shuffling, slouching; *fig.* slovenly.

Latte ['latə] *f* (15) lath; *Hochsprung, Fußball*: (cross-)bar; '**~nkiste** *f* crate; '**~nwerk** *n* lattice; '**~nzaun** *m* paling.

Lattich ['latiç] *m* (3) lettuce.

Latz [lats] *m* (3^2) (*Brust2*) bib; (*Hosen2*) flap.

Lätzchen ['lɛtsçən] *n* (6) *für Kinder*: bib.

'**Latzhose** *f* dungarees *pl.*

lau [laʊ] tepid, (*a. fig.*) lukewarm; *Luft, Wetter*: mild.

Laub [laʊp] *n* (3) foliage, leaves *pl.*; '**~baum** *m* deciduous tree.

Laube ['~bə] *f* (15) arbo(u)r; '**~ngang** *m* arcade; '**~nkolonie** *f* allotment gardens *pl.*

'**Laub|frosch** *m* tree-frog; '**~säge** *f* fretsaw; '**~säge-arbeit** *f* fretwork; '**~wald** *m* deciduous forest; '**~werk** *n* foliage.

Lauch ⚘ [laʊx] *m* (3) leek.

Lauer ['laʊər] *f* (15): *auf der ~* (*liegen*) (lie) in wait; '**2n** (29) lurk (*auf acc.* for); *~ auf e-e Gelegenheit*: watch for; (*j-m auflauern*) lie in wait for; '**2nd** lurking; *Blick usw.*: lowering, (*argwöhnisch*) wary.

Lauf [laʊf] *m* (3) run; *e-s Motors*: running; (*Strömung*) current; (*Fluß2; Verlauf*) course; (*Wett2*) race, (*Kurzstrecken2*) dash; (*Gewehr2*) barrel; *hunt.* leg; ♪ run; *s-n Gefühlen freien ~ lassen* give vent to one's feelings; *in vollem ~* in full career; *im ~e der Zeit* in course of time; *im ~e des Monats* in the course of; '**~bahn** *f* career; '**~bursche** *m* errand-boy.

'**laufen** (30, sn) run (*a.* ⊕); (*zu Fuß gehen*) walk; (*durch~*) *Strecke*: cover, do; (*fließen*) flow; *Zeit*: pass; *fig.* (*ab~*) go; *Gefäß*: leack, (*a. Nase*) run; *Film*: run, be on; *s. Gefahr, Geld, Schi, Sturm usw.*; *die Dinge ~ lassen* let things slide; '**~d** running; *Jahr, Preis, Ausgaben, Konto usw.*: current; *Wartung usw.*: regular; *Nummern*: consecutive, serial; *fig.* (*ständig*) continuous; ✝ *~en Monats* instant (*mst abbr.* inst.); *s. Band*; *auf dem ~en sein* be up to date, be fully informed; *j-n* (*sich*) *auf dem ~en halten* keep a p. (o.s.) informed *od.* F posted; '**~lassen:** *j-n* (*straflos*) *~* let a p. go.

Läufer ['lɔʏfər] *m* (7) runner (*a.* '**~in** *f*); (*Teppich*) runner (*a.* ⚘); (*Treppen2*) stair-carpet; *Schach*: bishop; *Fußball*: half(back); *s. Eis2, Schi2*; ⚡, *a. e-r Turbine*: rotor.

Lauferei [laʊfə'raɪ] *f* running about.

'**Lauf|feuer** *n fig.* wildfire; '**~fläche**

f e-s Radreifens: tread; '**~gewicht** *n* sliding weight.

'**läufig**, '**läufisch** in heat, ruttish.

'**Lauf|junge** *m s. Laufbursche*; '**~kran** ⊕ *m* travel(l)ing crane; '**~kunde** *m* chance customer; '**~masche** *f* ladder, *Am.* run; '**~paß** *m*: F *j-m den ~ geben e-m Freund etc.*: give a p. his marching orders; '**~planke** ⚓ *f* gangway, *Am. a.* gangplank; '**~ruhe** *f* ride quality; '**~schiene** *f* guide rail; '**~schritt** *m* jogtrot; ⚔ double(quick) step; *im ~* at the double; **~ställchen** ['~ʃtɛlçən] *n* (6) playpen; '**~steg** *m für Fußgänger*: foot-bridge; *s. Laufplanke*; '**~werk** ⊕ *n* drive mechanism; *Computer*: disk drive; '**~zeit** *f e-s Vertrags*: term; *e-s Wechsels*: currency; *e-s Films*: run; (*Brunftzeit*) rutting season; '**~zettel** *m* circular (letter); *für Akten*: inter-office slip.

Lauge ['laugə] *f* (15) lye; ⊕ liquor; (*Salz*2) brine; (*Seifen*2) suds *pl.*

'**laugen** (25) ⚗ steep (in lye); '**~artig** alkaline; '**2-asche** *f* alkaline ashes *pl.*

'**Lauheit** *f* lukewarmness (*a. fig.*).

Laune ['launə] *f* (15) humo(u)r; temper; mood; (*Grille*) caprice, fancy, whim; (*nicht*) *bei ~* in (out of) humo(u)r; *guter ~* in (high) spirits; (*nicht*) *in der ~ für* (not) in the mood for.

'**launenhaft** capricious, wayward; '**2igkeit** *f* capriciousness.

'**laun|ig** humorous; '**~isch** ill-humo(u)red; moody; *s. launenhaft.*

Laus [laus] *f* (14¹) louse (*pl.* lice); '**~bub(e)** *m s. Lausejunge*; '**~bubenstreich** *m* boy's prank; *fig.* mischievous trick.

Lausch|-angriff ['lauʃ-] *m* wiretapping (*od.* bugging) operation; '**2en** (27) listen (*dat. od. auf acc.* to); '**~er** *m* (7), '**~erin** *f* (16¹) listener; *b.s.* eavesdropper; '**2ig** snug, cosy; idyllic.

'**Lausejunge** *m* young scamp *od.* rascal.

lausen ['lauzən] (27) louse.

lausig ['lauziç] lousy (*a.* F *fig.*).

laut [laut] **1.** loud (*a. fig.*); (*lärmend*) noisy; (*hörbar*) audible; *so ~ man kann* at the top of one's voice; *~ werden fig.* become public; **2.** *adv.* aloud, loud(ly); **3.** *prp.* according to; ✝ as per; **4.** 2 *m* (3) sound (*a. gr.*); *hunt. ~ geben* give tongue.

Laute ['lautə] *f* (15) lute.

'**lauten** (26) sound; *Inhalt, Worte*: run, read; *~ auf* (*acc.*) *Paß usw.* be issued to, *Urteil*: be.

läuten ['lɔytən] (26) *v/i. u. v/t.* ring; *feierlich*: toll; *es läutet* the bell is ringing.

lauter ['lautər] (*rein*) pure (*a. fig.*); (*klar*) clear; *fig.* (*echt*) genuine; (*aufrichtig*) sincere; (*ehrlich*) honest; (*nichts als*) mere, nothing but; *aus ~ Neid* out of sheer envy; '**2keit** *f* purity; sincerity.

läuter|n ['lɔytərn] (29) purify; *Metall, Zucker*: refine; *Flüssigkeit*: clarify; *fig.* purify, chasten; '**2ung** *f* purification; refining; clarification; *fig.* chastening.

'**Läut(e)werk** *n* alarm.

'**Laut|gesetz** *n* phonetic law; '**~lehre** *f* phonetics *pl.*; phonology; '**2los** soundless, noiseless; (*still*) silent; (*stumm*) mute; *Stille*: hushed; '**~schrift** *f* phonetic transcription; '**~sprecher** *m* loudspeaker; '**~sprecher-anlage** *f*: *öffentliche ~* public-address system; '**~sprecherbox** *f* loudspeaker cabinet; '**~sprecherwagen** *m* loudspeaker van, *Am.* sound truck; '**2stark** vociferous, loud; '**~stärke** *f* sound intensity; loudness; *Radio*: sound-volume; **~stärkeregler** ['~re:glər] *m* volume control; '**~system** *n* phonetic system; '**~verschiebung** *f* shifting of consonants.

'**lauwarm** tepid, lukewarm (*a. fig.*).

Lava ['la:va] *f* (16²) lava.

Lavendel ⚘ [la'vɛndəl] *m* (7) lavender.

lavieren ⚓ [la'vi:rən] (h., sn) tack; *fig.* manœuvre, *Am.* maneuver.

Lawine [la'vi:nə] *f* (15) avalanche; **2n-artig** like an avalanche; *~ anwachsen* snowball; **~ngefahr** *f* danger of avalanches; **2nsicher** avalanche-proof.

lax [laks] lax, loose.

Lazarett [latsa'rɛt] *n* (3) (military) hospital; **~schiff** *n* hospital ship.

leasen ['li:zən] (27) lease.

Leasing ['li:ziŋ] *n* (11) leasing; '**~berater(in** *f*) *m* leasing consultant; '**~vertrag** *m* leasing contract.

Lebe'hoch *n* (11) cheer(s *pl.*).

'**Lebemann** *m* man about town; bon-vivant (*fr.*), playboy.

leben ['le:bən] **1.** (25) live (*a.* =

wohnen); (*am* ♀ *sein*) be alive; ~ *von e-r Nahrung, e-m Einkommen*: live (subsist) on, *von e-m Beruf*: make a living by; *j-n (hoch)*~ *lassen* cheer a p.; *bei Tisch*: drink a p.'s health; *s. wohl*; **2.** ♀ *n* (6) life; (*geschäftiges Treiben*) stir, activity, bustle; *Bild nach dem* ~ to the life; *am* ~ *bleiben* survive; *am* ~ *sein* be alive, live; *am* ~ *erhalten* keep alive; *ein neues* ~ *beginnen* turn over a new leaf; *ins* ~ *rufen* call into being, launch; F ~ *in die Bude bringen* jazz things up a bit; *mit dem* ~ *davonkommen* escape alive; *ums* ~ *kommen* lose one's life, be killed, perish; *sein* ~ *lang* all one's life; *s. lassen, schenken, Spiel*; '**~d** living (*a. Sprache*); live.

lebendig [le'bɛndiç] (*lebend*) living; *pred.* alive; (*flink*) quick; *fig. s. a. lebhaft*; *bei* ~*em Leibe* alive; **♀keit** *f s. Lebhaftigkeit*.

'**Lebens|-abend** *m* evening of life; '**~-ader** *fig. f* life-line; '**~-alter** *n* age; '**~-anschauung** *f* way of looking at life, outlook on life; '**~-arbeitszeit** *f* working life; '**~-art** *f* mode of living; (*Benehmen*) manners *pl.*, behavio(u)r; '**~-auffassung** *f* philosophy (of life); '**~-aufgabe** *f* mission (in life); *allg.* life-task; '**~-bedingungen** *f/pl.* living conditions; '**♀bedrohlich** life-threatening; '**~bedürfnisse** *n/pl.* necessaries of life; '**~bejahung** *f* acceptance of life; '**~beschreibung** *f* life, biography; '**~dauer** *f* duration of life; ⊕ (service) life; '**~-erfahrung** *f* experience of life; '**~erwartung** *f* life expectancy; '**~faden** *m* thread of life; '**♀fähig** ⚕ *u. fig.* viable; '**~fähigkeit** *f* viability; '**~frage** *f* vital question; '**♀fremd** *s. weltfremd*; '**~freude** *f* joy of life, zest (for life); '**~gefahr** *f* danger to life; ~! danger of death!; *in* ~ *Kranker*: in a critical condition; *unter* ~ at the risk of one's life; '**♀gefährlich** dangerous (to life), perilous; '**~gefährt|e** *m*, **~in** *f* life companion; '**~gemeinschaft** *f* community of life; '**~geschichte** *f* life-history, biography; '**♀groß** life-size(d); '**~größe** *f* life-size; *in* ~ life-sized, F *fig.* in the flesh; '**~haltung** *f* living (standard); '**~haltungskosten** *pl.* cost *sg.* of living; '**~-interessen** *n/pl.* vital interests; '**~jahr** *n* year of one's life; *im 20.* ~ at the age of twenty; '**~kraft** *f* vigo(u)r, vitality; '**♀lang**, '**♀länglich** for life (*a.* ⚖), lifelong; ~*e Rente* life annuity; '**~lauf** *m* course of life; *schriftlicher*: personal record, curriculum vitae; '**~licht** *n*: *j-m das* ~ *ausblasen* kill a p.; '**♀lustig** gay; '**~mittel** *n/pl.* food (-stuffs *pl.*) *sg.*, provisions *pl.*; '**~mittel-abteilung** *f* food department; '**~mittelgeschäft** *n* food shop (*bsd. Am.* store); '**~mittelvergiftung** *f* food poisoning; '**♀müde** weary (*od.* tired) of life; '**♀notwendig** vital, essential; '**~qualität** *f* quality of life; '**~raum** *m* living space; '**~regel** *f* rule of life; '**~retter** *m* life-saver; '**~standard** *m* standard of living, living standard; '**~stellung** *f* position in life, social status; *lebenslängliche*: permanent position; '**~stil** *m* life-style; '**♀treu** true to life; '**♀-überdrüssig** *s. lebensmüde*; '**~unterhalt** *m* livelihood, subsistence; *s-n* ~ *verdienen* earn one's living; '**~versicherung** *f* life insurance; '**~wandel** *m* life, conduct; '**~weise** *f* way of life; (*Gewohnheiten*) habits *pl.*; *gesunde* ~ regimen; '**~weisheit** *f* wordly wisdom; '**~werk** *n* life-work; '**♀wichtig** vital, essential; ~*e Organe pl.* vitals; '**~wille** *m* will to live; '**~zeichen** *n* sign of life; '**~zeit** *f* lifetime; *auf* ~ for life; '**~ziel** *n*, '**~zweck** *m* aim in life.

Leber ['le:bər] *f* (15) liver; *fig. frisch* (*od. frei*) *von der* ~ *weg* frankly, bluntly; '**~fleck** *m* mole; **~käs** ['~kɛ:s] *m* liver loaf; '**♀krank**, '**♀leidend** suffering from a liver disease; '**~tran** *m* cod-liver oil; '**~wurst** *f* liver-sausage, *bsd. Am.* liverwurst.

'**Lebewesen** *n* living being, creature; *biol.* organism.

Lebe'wohl *n* farewell.

leb|haft ['le:phaft] *allg.* lively (*a. fig. Nachfrage, Phantasie usw.*); (*munter*) vivacious; (*schwungvoll*) animated, active, brisk (*alle a.* ✝); *Farbe*: gay; *Erinnerung*: vivid; *Interesse*: keen; *Straße*: busy; '**♀haftigkeit** *f* liveliness; vivacity; vividness; briskness; '**♀kuchen** *m* gingerbread (cake); '**~los** lifeless; '**♀losigkeit** *f* lifelessness; '**♀tag** *m*: *mein(e)* ~*(e)* all my life; '**♀zeiten** *f/pl.*: *zu s-n* ~ in his lifetime.

lechzen ['lɛçtsən] (27) (*nach*) thirst, languish, yearn, pant (for).

Leck 1. *n* (3) leak; **2.** ≗ leaky; ⚓ ~ *werden* spring a leak.

lecken¹ ['lɛkən] *v/t.* (25) lick; *Milch usw. auf~*: lap (up); '~² *v/i.* leak; *bsd.* ⚓ have (sprung) a leak.

lecker ['lɛkər] delicious; appetizing; '**≗bissen** *m*, **≗ei** [~'raɪ] *f* (16) titbit (*a. fig.*), dainty; '**≗maul** *n*, '**≗-mäulchen** *n*: *ein ~ sein* have a sweet tooth.

Leder ['le:dər] *n* (7) leather (*a.* F *Fußball*); *in ~ gebunden* calf-bound; '**~band** *m* (*Buch*) calf-binding; '**~-fett** *n* dubbin(g); '**~handel** *m* leather trade; '**~händler** *m* dealer in leather; '**~hose** *f* leather trousers *pl.*; '**≗n** leathern, (of) leather; *fig.* dull; '**~rücken** *m e-s Buches*: leather back; '**~waren** *f/pl.* leather goods *od.* articles; '**~zeug** *n* leathers *pl.*

ledig ['le:diç] (*unverheiratet*) single, unmarried; (*Kind*) illegitimate; (*unbesetzt*) vacant; *e-r S.*: free from, rid of; **~lich** ['~dik-] solely, merely.

Lee ⚓ [le:] *f* (15, *o. pl.*) lee (side).

leer [le:r] *allg.* empty (*a. fig.*); (*unbesetzt*; *a. ausdruckslos*) vacant; (*eitel*) vain; (*unbeschrieben*, *unbespielt*) blank; *~e Drohung* (*~es Versprechen*) empty threat (promise); *~es Gerede* idle talk; *ins ≗e gehen Schlag*: miss; *ins ≗e starren* stare into vacancy; *mit ~en Händen* empty-handed; '**≗e** *f* (15) void, emptiness (*a. fig.*); '**~en** (25) empty, clear; '**≗formel** *f* empty phrase; '**≗gut** ✝ *n* empties *pl.*; '**≗-kassette** *f* blank cassette; '**≗lauf** *m* ✝ idling, idle motion; *mot.* (*Gang*) neutral (gear); *fig.* waste of energy; '**~-laufen** ⊕ (run) idle; '**~stehend** *Wohnung*: unoccupied, vacant; '**≗-taste** *f Schreibmaschine*: space bar; '**≗ung** *f* emptying; clearing; '**≗zeile** *f* white line.

Lefzen ['lɛftsən] *f/pl.* flews *pl.*

legal [le'gɑ:l] legal; **~isieren** [~gali-'zi:rən] legalize; **≗ität** [~gali'tɛt] *f* (16, *o. pl.*) legality.

Legat [le'gɑ:t] **1.** *m* (12) legate; **2.** *n* (3) legacy.

Legation [lega'tsjo:n] *f* legation.

legen ['le:gən] (25) *v/t.* lay, place, put; *Eier*, *Fußboden*, *Teppich*, *Leitung usw.*: lay; *sich (hin)~* lie down, *zu Bett*: *a.* go to bed; *Wind usw.*: calm down, abate; (*nachlassen*) cease, fall; *sich auf e-e S. ~* apply o.s. to, take up; *Karten ~* tell fortunes by the cards; *s. Hand*, *Handwerk*, *Herz*, *Last*, *Mittel*, *Mund*, *Nachdruck*, *Wert 2.*, *Zeug usw.*; *v/i. Huhn usw.*: lay (eggs).

legendär [legɛn'dɛ:r] legendary.

Legende [le'gɛndə] *f* (15) legend.

legier|en [le'gi:rən] alloy; *Kochkunst*: thicken; **≗ung** *f* alloy(ing).

Legion [le'gjo:n] *f* (16) legion; **~är** [~gjo'nɛ:r] *m* (3¹) legionary.

Legisla|tive [le:gisla'ti:və] *f* (15) legislative body *od.* power; **~tur** [~'tu:r] *f* (16) legislature; **~'tur-periode** *f* legislative period.

legitim [legi'ti:m] legitimate; **≗a-tion** [~tima'tsjo:n] *f* (16) legitimation; **≗ati'onspapier** *n* paper of identification; **~ieren** [~'mi:rən] legitimate; *sich ~* prove one's identity; **≗ität** [~mi'tɛ:t] *f* (16) legitimacy.

Leh(e)n ['le:(ə)n] *n* (6) fief, fee; '**~smann** *m* (1², *pl. a. Lehnsleute*) vassal; '**~swesen** *n* feudalism.

Lehm [le:m] *m* (3) loam; (*Ton*) clay; (*Dreck*) mud; '**~boden** *m* loamy soil; '**~grube** *f* loam-pit; '**≗ig** loamy; (*schmutzig*) muddy.

Lehne ['le:nə] *f* (15) support; *e-s Stuhls*: arm, (*Rück≗*) back; (*Abhang*) slope; '**≗n** *v/t.*, *v/i.*, *v/refl.* (25) lean (*an acc.* against).

Lehns... *s. Leh(e)n.*

'**Lehn|sessel** *m*, '**~stuhl** *m* arm- (*od.* easy-)chair; '**~wort** *n* loan-word.

'**Lehr|-amt** *n* teachership; *höheres ~* mastership; *univ.* professorship; '**~-amts-anwärter** *m* trainee teacher; '**~-anstalt** *f* educational establishment, school, academy; *höhere ~* secondary school; '**~beruf** *m* teaching profession; '**~brief** *m* (apprentice's) indenture; '**~buch** *n* textbook.

Lehre ['le:rə] *f* **1.** (15) teaching, doctrine, theory; (*System*) system; (*Wissenschaft*) science; (*Richtschnur*) rule; (*moralische*; *Warnung*) lesson, warning; *e-r Fabel*: moral; (*Unterricht*) system of instruction; *des Lehrlings*: apprenticeship; *e-e ~ ziehen aus* take warning from; *in der ~ sein* be serving one's apprenticeship, *bei j-m* be apprenticed to a p.; *in die ~ geben od. tun* apprentice, article (*bei*, *zu* to); **2.** ⊕ ga(u)ge; (*Schablone*) pattern; △

centering; '**2n** (25) teach, instruct; (*dartun*) show.

Lehrer ['~rər] *m* (7) teacher, master, instructor; *s. Privat2, Klassen2, Hochschul2*; '**~fortbildung** *f* in-service training of teachers; '**~in** *f* (16[1]) (lady) teacher; '**~kollegium** *n*, '**~schaft** *f s. Lehrkörper*; '**~(innen)seminar** *n* teachers' training college; '**~verband** *m* teachers' professional association; '**~zimmer** *n* staff room.

'**Lehr|fach** *n* subject; *s. Lehrberuf*; '**~film** *m* instructional (*od.* training) film; '**~gang** *m* course (of instruction); '**~geld** *n* premium; *fig.* ~ *zahlen* pay dear for one's wisdom; '**2haft** instructive; didactic; '**~herr** *m* master; '**~jahre** *n/pl.* (years *pl.* of) apprenticeship *sg.*; '**~junge** *m* apprentice; '**~körper** *m* teaching staff, (body of) teachers *pl.*; *univ.* professorate, *Am.* faculty; '**~kraft** *m* teacher; '**~ling** *m* (3[1]) apprentice; '**~mädchen** *n* girl apprentice; '**~meister** *m* master; '**~methode** *f* teaching method; '**~mittel** *n/pl.* educational aids *pl. od.* material *sg.*; '**~plan** *m* (school) curriculum; '**2reich** instructive; '**~saal** *m* lecture-room, class-room; '**~satz** *m* ⩓ theorem; *eccl.* dogma; '**~stück** *thea. n* didactic play; '**~stuhl** *m* (professor's) chair, professorship; '**~vertrag** *m* articles *pl.* of apprenticeship; '**~werkstatt** *f* training workshop; '**~zeit** *f* apprenticeship.

Leib [laɪp] *m* (1) body; (*Bauch*) belly; (*Mutter2*) womb; (*Taille*) waist; *am ganzen ~e* all over; *mit ~ und Seele* (with) heart and soul; *zu ~e gehen od. rücken j-m*: attack, *e-r S.*: tackle; *sich j-n vom ~e halten* keep a p. at arm's length; *~ und Leben* life and limb; *s. lebendig*; '**~arzt** *m* physician in ordinary (*j-s* to).

Leibchen ['~çən] *n* (6) bodice; (*Unter2*) vest.

'**leib-eigen** in bondage; '**2e** *m, f* serf, bond(wo)man; '**2schaft** *f* serfdom, bondage.

Leibes|beschaffenheit ['laɪbəs-] *f* constitution; (*Äußeres*) physique; '**~-erbe(n** *pl.*) *m* issue; '**~frucht** *f* fetus; '**~kraft** *f* bodily strength; *aus Leibeskräften* with all one's might; '**~strafe** *f* corporal punishment; '**~-übung** *f* physical exercise; *pl. a.* physical training; '**~visitation** *f* bodily search.

Leib|garde ['laɪp-] *f* body-guard; '**~gericht** *n* favo(u)rite dish.

'**leibhaft**, '**~ig** corporeal, in person; (*wirklich*) real, true; *Ebenbild*: living (*image*); *der ~e Teufel* the devil incarnate.

leiblich ['laɪp-] bodily (*a. adv.*), corporal; *~es Wohl* physical well-being; *~er Bruder* full brother; *~er Vetter* cousin german; *ihr ~er Sohn* her own son.

'**Leib|rente** *f* life-annuity; '**~riemen** *m* belt; '**~schmerzen** *m/pl.* stomach-ache, colic; '**~speise** *f* favo(u)rite dish; '**~wache** *f* body-guard; '**~wäsche** *f* underwear.

Leiche ['laɪçə] *f* (15) (dead) body, corpse; *über ~n gehen* stick at nothing.

'**Leichen|begängnis** *n* (4[1]) funeral; '**~bestatter** *m* undertaker; '**~bittermiene** *f* woeful look *od.* countenance; '**2blaß** deadly pale; '**~feier** *f* obsequies *pl.*; '**~frau** *f* layer-out; '**~geruch** *m* cadaverous smell; '**~gift** *n* ptomaine; '**~halle** *f* mortuary; '**~hemd** *n* shroud; '**~-öffnung** *f* autopsy; '**~rede** *f* funeral oration; '**~schändung** *f* desecration of corpses; *sexuell*: necrophilia; '**~schau** *f* (coroner's) inquest; '**~schauhaus** *n* morgue; '**~starre** *f* rigor mortis; '**~stein** *m* tombstone; '**~träger** *m* (pall) bearer; '**~tuch** *n* shroud (*a. fig.*); '**~verbrennung** *f* cremation; '**~wagen** *m* hearse; '**~zug** *m* funeral procession.

Leichnam ['~na:m] *m* (3) (dead) body, corpse.

leicht [laɪçt] light (*a. fig. Essen, Kleidung, Musik usw.*); ⊕ *a.* light-weight; (*nicht schwierig*) easy; (*gering*) slight; ⚖ petty; *Tabak*: mild; *s. leichtfertig*; *~er Sieg* walk-over; *s. Spiel*; *~ entzündlich* highly inflammable; *~ löslich* readily soluble; *et. auf die ~e Schulter nehmen* make light of a th.; *~en Herzens* with a light heart; *es war ihm ein ~es* it was easy for him; *es ist ~ möglich* it is well possible; *das kann ~ passieren* it may easily happen; '**2athlet** *m* (track and field) athlete; '**2-athletik** *f* (track and field) athletics *sg. u. pl.*, track and field sports *pl.*; '**2bauweise** ⊕ *f* light-weight construction; '**~beschwingt** jaunty; '**~blütig** sanguine.

'**Leichter** ⚓ *m* (7) lighter.

'**leicht|fertig** light, frivolous, flippant; (*unbedacht*) careless; '**2fertigkeit** *f* frivolity, flippancy, levity; carelessness; **~füßig** ['~fy:siç] light-footed; '**2gewicht(ler** *m*) *n Boxen*: light-weight; '**~gläubig** credulous, gullible; '**2gläubigkeit** *f* credulity, gullibility; '**~'hin** airily, casually; **2igkeit** ['~iç-] *f* lightness; *fig. a.* easiness, ease, facility; *mit* ~ easily; **~lebig** ['~le:biç] easy-going; '**2lohngruppe** *f* low-wage unskilled labo(u)r; '**2matrose** *m* ordinary seaman; '**2metall** *n* light metal; '**~nehmen:** es ~ take it easy; '**2sinn** *m s. leichtsinnig*: light-mindedness, frivolity, levity; recklessness; carelessness; '**~sinnig** (*oberflächlich, gedankenlos*) light-minded, frivolous; (*unvorsichtig, fahrlässig*) reckless; (*sorglos*) careless; '**~verdaulich** easy to digest; '**~verderblich(e Waren** *f/pl.*) perishable(s *pl.*); '**~verständlich** easy to understand; '**~verwundet** lightly wounded.

leid [laɪt] **1.** *es tut mir* ~ (*um*) I am sorry (for), I regret; *du tust mir* ~ I am sorry for you; **2.** 2 *n* (3, *o. pl.*) (*Schaden*) harm; (*Unrecht*) injury, wrong; (*Verletzung*) hurt; (*Betrübnis*) grief, sorrow; (*Unglück*) misfortune; *j-m ein ~(s) antun* harm a p., *sich*: lay hands upon o.s.; *j-m sein ~ klagen* pour out one's troubles to a p.

leiden ['laɪdən] **1.** (30) *v/i. u. v/t.* suffer (*an dat.* from); (*nicht*) ~ *mögen* (dis)like; **2.** 2 *n* (6) suffering; ⚕ complaint, disease; *das ~ Christi* The Passion; '**~d** suffering; *gr.* passive.

'**Leidenschaft** *f* passion; '**2lich** passionate; (*glühend*) ardent; (*heftig*) vehement; '**~lichkeit** *f* passionateness; ardo(u)r; vehemence; '**2slos** dispassionate.

'**Leidens|gefährte** *m*, '**~gefährtin** *f* fellow-sufferer; '**~geschichte** *f* tale of woe; *eccl.* Christ's Passion; '**~weg** *m eccl.* way of the cross; *fig.* (life of) suffering.

leid|er ['~dər] unfortunately; *int.* alas!; ~ *muß ich inf.* I'm (so) sorry to *inf.*; *ich muß ~ gehen* I am afraid I have to go; '**~ig** unpleasant; **~lich** ['laɪt-] tolerable; (*halbwegs gut*) passable, fairly well; F (*a. adv.*) middling; '**2tragende** *m, f* (18) mourner; *fig.* sufferer; '**2wesen** *n*: *zu meinem* ~ to my regret.

Leier ['laɪər] *f* (15) lyre; *immer die alte* ~ always the same old story; '**~kasten** *m* barrel-organ; '**~(kasten)mann** *m* organ-grinder; '**2n** (29) grind (out) *a tune*; *fig. s. herleiern.*

Leih|bibliothek ['laɪ-] *f*, '**~bücherei** *f* lending library; '**2en** (30) lend, *Geld a.* loan; (*entlehnen*) borrow (*von* from); *s. Ohr*; '**~gebühr** *f* lending fee(s *pl.*); '**~haus** *n* pawnshop; '**~wagen** *m* hired car; '**2weise** as a loan.

Leim [laɪm] *m* (3) glue; *zum Steifen usw.*: size; (*Vogel2*) bird-lime; F *aus dem ~ gehen* come apart; F *fig. auf den ~ gehen* fall into the trap; '**2en** (25) glue; (*steifen*) size; '**~farbe** *f* glue-colo(u)r; (*Tempera*) distemper; '**2ig** gluey, viscous.

Lein ⚘ [laɪn] *m* (3) flax.

Leine ['laɪnə] *f* (15) line, cord; (*Hunde2*) (dog-)lead, leash.

leinen ['~ən] **1.** linen; **2.** 2 *n* (6) linen; '**2band** *m Buchbinderei*: cloth binding; '**2garn** *n* linen yarn; '**2schuh** *m* canvas shoe; '**2zeug** *n* linen (fabric).

'**Lein|kuchen** *m* linseed cake; '**~öl** *n* linseed-oil; '**~pfad** ⚓ *m* tow(ing)-path; '**~samen** *m* linseed; '**~wand** *f* linen (cloth); *paint.* canvas; *Film*: screen.

leise ['laɪzə] low, soft; (*sanft*) gentle; (*zart*) delicate; (*kaum merklich, gering*) slight, faint (*a. Ahnung, Zweifel usw.*); ~ *schlafen* be a light sleeper; *Radio*: ~ *stellen* tune down; '**2treter** *m* (7) sneak, *Am. sl.* pussyfoot(er).

Leiste ['laɪstə] *f* (15) strip, ledge; △ fillet; *anat.* groin.

'**leisten**[1] (26) do; (*verrichten*) perform (*a.* ⚖ *Vertrag*); (*erfüllen*) fulfil(l); (*vollbringen*) achieve; ⊕ do, perform; *Eid*: take; *Dienst*: render; *ich kann mir das ~* I can afford it; *sich et.* ~ treat o.s. to a th.; *e-n Fehler usw.*: commit; *s. Beitrag, Bürgschaft, Folge, Gesellschaft, Verzicht, Vorschub, Widerstand usw.*

'**Leisten**[2] *m* (6) last; *nur zum Füllen*: shoe-tree; *alles über einen ~ schla-*

gen treat all alike; '~**bruch** ⚕ *m* inguinal hernia.

'**Leistung** *f allg., a. e-s Künstlers od. Sportlers, a.* ⚖, ✝, ⊕: performance; (*Großtat*) achievement; (*Zahlung*) payment; (*Lieferung*) delivery; *e-s Arbeiters*: workmanship, *mengenmäßig*: output (*a. e-r Fabrik usw.*); ⚡ power, *aufgenommene*: input, *abgegebene*: output; piece of work; *e-r Fabrik usw.*: output; ~*en pl. e-s Schülers*: achievements *pl.*; *e-r Versicherung*: benefit *sg.*; *erreichte* ~ result(s obtained); '~**sbewertung** *f* assessment and marking system; '~**sdruck** *m* pressure (to produce results); '2**sfähig** efficient, ⊕ *a.* powerful; *Fabrik usw.*: productive; '~**sfähigkeit** *f* efficiency, ⊕ *a.* power, capacity; '~**sgesellschaft** *f* performance-orientated society, Meritocracy; '~**slohn** *m* efficiency wage(s *pl.*); '2**s-orientiert** efficiency-oriented; '~**s-prinzip** *n* performance principle; '~**s-prüfung** *f* performance test; '2**sschwach** below average; weak (*a.* ✝); ⊕ low-performance; '2**sstark** above average; ⊕ powerful, high-performance; ✝ highly efficient; '2**ssteigernd** increasing efficiency (*od.* performance); '~**ssoll** *n* target; '~**ssport** *m* high-performance sport(s *pl.*); '~**swettbewerb** *m* efficiency contest; '~**szulage** *f* efficiency bonus.

'**Leit|-artikel** *m* leading article, editorial; '~**bild** *n* model; ideal.

leiten ['laɪtən] (26) lead, guide, (*a. phys.*, ⚡, ♪) conduct; ⊕ convey, pass, guide; (*anführen*) head (*a. Staat*); (*beaufsichtigen, verwalten*) direct, run, manage; *Sitzung usw.*: preside over; *Sport*: *das Spiel* ~ referee; *fig. sich von et.* ~ *lassen* be guided by; '~**d** leading; ✝ managerial, executive (*personnel, position*); *phys.* (*nicht*) ~ (non-)conductive.

'**Leiter**[1] *m* (7), '~**in** *f* (16[1]) leader, (*a. phys.*, ♪) conductor (*f* conductress), guide; *e-r Behörde, Abteilung*: head, chief; *e-s Unternehmens*: manager (*f* manageress); *e-r Schule*: head (master, *f* mistress), *bsd. Am.* principal; '~[2] *f* (16) ladder; '~**sprosse** *f* rung of a ladder; '~**wagen** *m* rack-wag(g)on.

'**Leit|faden** *m Buch*: textbook, manual, guide; '~**gedanke** *m* leading idea; '~**hammel** *m* bell-wether (*a. fig.*); '~**motiv** ♪ *n* leitmotiv; *fig.* key-note; '~**planke** *mot. f* guard rail; '~**satz** *m* thesis; '~**schiene** *f* guide rail; '~**spruch** *m* motto; '~**stern** *m* pole-star, lode-star (*a. fig.*); '~**strahl** *m* (guide) beam.

'**Leitung** *f* lead(ing), direction, guidance; (*Beaufsichtigung, Verwaltung*) management; *s.* An2; *phys.* conduction; *konkret*: ⚡ lead; *tel.* line; (*Gas-, Wasser-, Elektrizitäts*2) mains *pl.*; (*Rohr*2) pipeline; *unter s-r* ~ under his direction; *fig.* F *e-e lange* (*kurze*) ~ *haben* be slow (quick) in the uptake; '~**sdraht** *m* conducting wire; '~**srohr** *n* conduit-pipe; *für Gas, Wasser*: main; '~**svermögen** *n* conductivity; '~**swasser** *n* tap water.

'**Leit|währung** *f* reserve currency; '~**werk** ✈ *n* tail unit, control surfaces *pl.*, controls *pl.*

Lektion [lɛk'tsjoːn] *f* (16) lesson; (*a. fig.*) *j-m e-e* ~ *erteilen* teach a p. a lesson.

Lektor ['lɛktɔr] *m* (8[1]) lecturer; (*Verlags*2) editor; ~**at** [~to'rɑːt] *n* (3) editorial office.

Lektüre [lɛk'tyːrə] *f* (15) reading; (*Lesestoff*) reading matter.

Lende ['lɛndə] *f* (15) loin(s *pl.*); (*Hüfte*) haunch, hip.

'**Lenden|braten** *m* roast loin, *vom Rind*: sirloin, *Am.* porterhouse steak; '~**gegend** *f* lumbar region; '2**lahm** hip-shot; '~**schurz** *m* loin--cloth; '~**stück** *n* loin, *Am.* tenderloin.

lenk|bar ['lɛŋkbɑːr] guidable; ⊕ man(o)euvrable; *fig. s. lenksam*; ~*es Luftschiff* dirigible (airship); '~**en** (25) direct, guide; (*wenden*) turn; (*beherrschen*) rule; *Wagen*: drive, *mot. u.* ⚓ *a.* steer; *Staat*: govern; *Aufmerksamkeit auf* (*acc.*) ~ call ... to; '2**er** *m* (7) ruler; *e-s Wagens*: driver; *s. Lenkstange*; '2**rad** *n* steering wheel; '~**sam** tractable, manageable; '2**samkeit** *f* docility, manageableness; '2**stange** *f Fahrrad*: handlebar; '2**ung** *mot. f* steering; '2**waffe** ⚔ *f* guided missile.

Lenz [lɛnts] *m* (3[2]) spring; *fig.* prime (of life).

Leopard [leo'part] *m* (12) leopard.

Lepra ⚕ ['leːpra] *f inv.* leprosy.

Lerche ['lɛrçə] *f* (15) lark.

Lern|begierde ['lɛrn-] *f* desire to learn, studiousness; '**♀begierig** eager to learn, studious; '**~computer** *m* educational computer; '**♀en** (25) learn; (*studieren*) study; *er lernt gut* he is an apt scholar; *s. gelernt*; '**~er** *m* (7) learner; '**~hilfe** *f* learning aid; '**~maschine** *f* teaching machine; '**~mittel** *n/pl.* teaching materials; '**~mittelfreiheit** *f* free supply of teaching materials; '**~prozeß** *psych. m* learning process; '**~spiel** *n* educational game; '**~ziel** *n* educational objective.

Lesart ['le:sˀa:rt] *f* reading, version.

'**lesbar** legible; (*lesenswert*) readable.

Lesbe ['lɛsbə] F *f* (15), **Lesbierin** ['lɛsbiərin] *f* (16[1]) lesbian; *sl.* dike, dyke; **lesbisch** ['lɛsbiʃ] lesbian.

Lese ['le:zə] *f* (15) gathering; (*Ähren*♀) gleaning; (*Wein*♀) vintage; '**~buch** *n* reading-book, reader; '**~exemplar** *n* advance copy; '**~gerät** *n für Mikrofilme*: viewer; '**~halle** *f* public reading-room; '**~lampe** *f* reading-lamp.

'**lesen** (30) **1.** read; *univ.* lecture (*über acc.* on); *die Messe ~* say mass; **2.** (*auflesen*) gather; ✓ glean; (*aussuchen*) pick; '**~swert** worth reading.

'**Lese|probe** *thea. f* reading rehearsal; '**~pult** *n* reading-desk.

'**Leser** *m* (7) reader.

'**Lese·ratte** F *f* bookworm.

'**Leser|brief** *m* reader's letter; *Zeitungsrubrik*: *~e pl.* letters to the editor; '**~kreis** *m*, '**~schaft** *f* (circle of) readers *pl.*; '**♀lich** legible; '**~zuschrift** *f s. Leserbrief.*

'**Lese|stoff** *m* reading (matter); '**~streifen** *m auf Warenpackung*: bar code; '**~zeichen** *n* book-mark.

Lesung *parl.* ['le:zuŋ] *f*: *in dritter ~* on third reading.

Lethargie [letar'gi:] *f* lethargy.

Lett|e ['lɛtə] *m* (13), '**~in** *f* (16[1]), '**♀isch** Latvian.

Letter ['lɛtər] *f* (15) letter; *typ.* type.

letzt [lɛtst] last; (*endgültig*) final; ultimate; *der (die, das) ~ere* (18) the latter; *das ♀e* the end; *zu guter ♀* last but not least, ultimately; *bis ins ~e prüfen* to the last detail; *bis zum ~en* to the last; *~e Nachrichten pl.* latest news; *~e Neuheit* latest novelty; *~en Endes* ultimately, after all; *~e Hand anlegen an (acc.)* put the finishing touches to; *s. Loch, Ölung, Schliff, Schrei*; '**~ens,** '**~hin** lately, the other day; '**~willig** testamentary; *adv.* by will.

Leucht|boje ['lɔyçt-] *f* light buoy; '**~bombe** *f* flare (bomb); '**~di·ode** *f* light-emitting diode; '**~e** *f* (15) light, (*a. fig.*) lamp, (*a. fig., bsd. P.*) luminary; '**♀en**[1] (26) shine; (*strahlen*) *a.* beam; (*glänzen*) gleam, sparkle; *j-m ~* light a p.; '**~en**[2] *n* (6) shining *etc.*; '**♀end** shining (*a. fig. Beispiel*), bright; *a. Uhrziffern usw.*: luminous; '**~er** *m* (7) candlestick; *s. a. Kron♀*; '**~farbe** *f* luminous paint; '**~feuer** *n* beacon; '**~geschoß** *n* star shell; '**~käfer** *m* glow-worm; '**~kugel** *f* (signal) flare; '**~mittel** *n* illuminant; '**~patrone** *f* signal cartridge; '**~pistole** ⚔ *f* Very pistol; '**~rakete** *f* signal rocket; '**~reklame** *f* luminous advertising; '**~röhre** *f* fluorescent tube, luminous discharge lamp; '**~schirm** *m* fluorescent screen; '**~spurgeschoß** *n* tracer bullet; '**~stoffröhre** *f* fluorescent tube; '**~turm** *m* lighthouse; '**~zifferblatt** *n* luminous dial.

leugnen ['lɔygnən] (26) deny; *nicht zu ~* undeniable.

Leukämie [lɔykɛ'mi:] *f* leuk(a)emia.

Leumund ['lɔymunt] *m* reputation; '**~szeugnis** *n* certificate of good conduct.

Leute ['lɔytə] *pl.* (3) people *pl.*; *einzelne*: persons; ⚔ *u. pol.* men *pl.* (*a. Arbeiter*); *die ~ pl.* people *pl.*, the world *sg.*; *meine ~* (*Familie*) my people *pl.*, *Am.* my folks *pl.*; '**~schinder** *m* martinet.

Leutnant ['lɔytnant] *m* (3[1] *u.* 11) ⚔ second lieutenant; ⚓ acting sublieutenant, *Am.* ensign; ✈ pilot officer, *Am.* second lieutenant.

leutselig ['~ze:liç] affable; '**♀keit** *f* affability.

Levkoje ⚘ [lɛf'ko:jə] *f* (15) stock.

lexikalisch [lɛksi'ka:liʃ] lexical.

Lexikograph [~ko'gra:f] *m* (12) lexicographer; **~ie** [~gra'fi:] *f* (16) lexicography; **♀isch** [~'gra:fiʃ] lexicographical.

Lexikon ['lɛksikɔn] *n* (9[1] *u.* [2]) dictionary; *s. a. Konversationslexikon.*

Libelle [li'bɛlə] *f* (15) dragon-fly; ⊕ (water- *od.* spirit-)level.

liberal [libe'ra:l] liberal; **~isieren** [~rali'zi:rən] liberalize; **♀ismus** [~ra'lismus] *m* (16, *o. pl.*) liberalism;

~istisch [~'listiʃ] liberalistic; **ˆität** [~li'tɛ:t] *f* liberality.

Libretto [li'brɛto] ♪ *n* (11, *pl. a.* -*tti*) word-book.

Licht [liçt] **1.** *n* (1 *u.* 3) light; (*leuchtender Körper*) luminary; (*Lampe*) lamp; (*Kerze*) candle; *hunt.* ~*er pl.* eyes; *fig. ans* ~ *bringen* (*kommen*) bring (come) to light; *bei* ~*e arbeiten usw.* by lamp-light; *j-m ein* ~ *aufstecken* open a p.'s eyes (*über acc.* to); *et. bei* ~*e besehen* examine closely, *als Redewendung*: on closer inspection; *das* ~ *der Welt erblicken* be born; *geh mir aus dem* ~*e!* stand out of my light!; ~ *machen* strike a light, ⚡ put on the light; *j-m* (*od. sich selbst*) *im* ~*e stehen* stand in a p.'s (*od.* one's own) light; *ein schlechtes* ~ *werfen auf* (*acc.*) cast a reflection on; *j-n hinter das* ~ *führen* dupe a p.; *jetzt geht mir ein* ~ *auf!* now I see (daylight); *s. Scheffel, schief*; **2.** ˆ light, bright; (*durchsichtig*) clear (*a.* ⊕ *Höhe usw.*); *fig.* lucid; ~*er Augenblick bei Geisteskranken*: lucid interval; ~*er Tag* broad daylight; ⊕ *im* ˆ*en* in the clear; '**~-anlage** *f* lighting system; '**~bad** ⚕ *n* solar bath, insolation; 'ˆ**beständig** fast to light; '**~bild** *n* photograph; '**~bildervortrag** *m* lantern-slide lecture; 'ˆ**blau** light blue; '**~blick** *m* bright spot; '**~bogen** ⚡ *m* arc; 'ˆ**brechend** *opt.* refractive; '**~druck** *m* phototype; 'ˆ**durchlässig** permeable to light, diaphanous; 'ˆ**-echt** fast to light; *Stoff*: non-fading; 'ˆ**-empfindlich** sensitive to light; *phot.* sensitive; ~ *machen* sensitize; '**~-empfindlichkeit** *f* sensitivity; *phot.* speed.

'**lichten** (26) *Wald*: clear; *Reihen, Haar*: (*a. sich*) thin; *s. Anker.*

'**Lichter 1.** ⚓ *m* (7) lighter; **2.** *pl. von Licht*; ˆ**loh** ['~'lo:] blazing, in full blaze; ~ *brennen* be ablaze.

'**Licht|geschwindigkeit** *f* speed of light; '**~griffel** *m Computer*: light pen; '**~hof** *m* glass-roofed court; *phot.* halo; '**~hupe** *mot. f* headlamp flasher; '**~jahr** *n* light year; '**~kegel** *m* cone of light, beam (of light); '**~maschine** *mot. f* generator, dynamo; **~meß** ['~mɛs] *f* Candlemas; '**~-orgel** *f* colo(u)r organ; **~pausapparat** ['~paʊs-] *m* copying apparatus; **~pause** ['~paʊzə] *f* photoprint; '**~pausverfahren** *n* photoprinting; '**~quelle** *f* light source; '**~reklame** *f* luminous advertising; '**~schacht** *m* light-well; '**~schalter** *m* light switch; 'ˆ**scheu** shunning the light; '**~schranke** *f* photoelectric barrier; '**~schutzfaktor** *m* protection factor; '**~seite** *f fig.* bright side; '**~spielhaus** *n*, '**~spieltheater** *n* cinema, *Am.* motion-picture theater; '**~stärke** *f* luminous intensity; *phot.* speed; '**~strahl** *m* ray, beam; 'ˆ**undurchlässig** opaque; '**~ung** *f* clearing.

Lid [li:t] *n* (1) eyelid; '**~schatten** *m* eye-shadow.

lieb [li:p] dear; (*zärtlich geliebt*) beloved; (*nett*) nice, kind; *Kind*: good; *der* ~*e Gott* the good God; *es ist mir* ~, *daß* I am glad that; *das habe ich am* ~*sten* I like that best of all; '**~-äugeln** ogle (*mit j-m od. et.* a p., a th.); flirt (with *an idea*); 'ˆ**chen** *n* (6) love, sweetheart.

Liebe ['li:bə] *f* (15) love (*zu* of, for); *christliche* ~ charity; *aus* ~ for love; *aus* ~ *zu* for the love of; 'ˆ**bedürftig** starved for love; **~dienerei** [~di:nə'raɪ] *f* (16) obsequiousness, toadyism; **~lei** [~'laɪ] *f* (16) flirtation.

liebeln ['li:bəln] (29) flirt, dally.

'**lieben** *v/t.* (25) love (*a. v/i.*); (*gern mögen*) be fond of, like; ~*d gern* gladly; 'ˆ**de** *m, f* (18) lover.

'**liebens|wert** lovable, amiable; '**~würdig** kind, obliging; *s. a. liebenswert*; 'ˆ**würdigkeit** *f* amiability; kindness.

'**lieber** dearer; *adv.* (*eher*) rather, sooner; ~ *haben* prefer, like better.

'**Liebes|-abenteuer** *n*, '**~-affäre** *f* love-adventure, love-affair; '**~brief** *m* love-letter; '**~dienst** *m* favo(u)r, kindness; *j-m e-n* ~ *erweisen* do a p. a good turn; '**~-erklärung** *f* declaration of love; '**~erlebnis** *n* romance; *intimes*: sex adventure; '**~gabe** *f* charitable gift; '**~gedicht** *n* love-poem; '**~geschichte** *f* love-story; '**~heirat** *f* love-match; 'ˆ**krank** love-sick; '**~kummer** *m* lover's grief; '**~leben** *n* love-life; '**~lied** *n* love-song; '**~paar** *n* (pair of) lovers *pl.*, (courting) couple; '**~verhältnis** *n* love-affair; '**~werben** *n* wooing; '**~werk** *n* work of charity.

'**liebevoll** loving, affectionate.

lieb|gewinnen ['li:p-] get (*od.* grow) fond of, take a liking (*od.* fancy) to; '**~haben** love, be fond of; '**≈haber(in** *f*) *m* (7) lover; *Kunst usw.*: amateur; *thea.* erste ~ *m* leading man (*od. f* lady); *thea.* jugendliche ~ *m* juvenile lead; **≈haberei** [~'raɪ] *f* (16) (für) fondness (of), fancy (for, to); *fig.* (*Steckenpferd*) hobby; '**≈haberpreis** *m* fancy price; '**≈haberstück** *n* collector's item; '**≈habertheater** *n* private (*od.* amateur) theat|re, *Am.* -er; '**≈haberwert** *m* collector's value; '**~kosen** caress, fondle; '**≈kosung** *f* caress.

lieblich ['li:pliç] lovely, charming, sweet; *Wein*: mellow; '**≈keit** *f* loveliness.

Liebling ['li:pliŋ] *m* (3^1) darling, favo(u)rite; *bsd. Kind od. Tier*: pet; *bsd. als Anrede*: darling; '**~s...** favo(u)rite.

'**lieb|los** unkind; *weitS.* careless; '**≈losigkeit** *f* unkindness; '**~reich** loving, tender; (*freundlich*) kind; '**≈reiz** *m* charm, grace; '**~reizend** charming, sweet; '**≈schaft** *f* (16) love(-affair); '**≈ste** *m, f* sweetheart, *m a.* lover, *f a.* love; *Anrede*: (my) darling.

Lied [li:t] *n* (1) song; (*Weise*) air, tune; geistliches ~ hymn; es ist das alte ~ it's always the same old story.

Lieder|-abend ['~dər-] *m* lieder recital; '**~buch** *n* song-book; '**~kranz** *m* choral society.

liederlich ['li:dərliç] loose, dissolute; (*unordentlich*) slovenly; '**≈keit** *f* dissoluteness; slovenliness.

'**Liedermacher** *m* (7) singer-songwriter.

lief [li:f] *pret. v. laufen.*

Lieferant [li:fə'rant] *m* (12) supplier; *laut Vertrag*: contractor; *bsd. für Lebensmittel*: caterer, purveyor.

Liefer|-auto ['li:fər-] *n* delivery-van, *Am.* delivery truck; '**≈bar** deliverable; (*vorrätig*) available; '**~frist** *f* term of delivery; '**≈n** (25) deliver; (*beschaffen, a. fig.*) furnish, supply; *Ertrag*: yield; *Schlacht*: give (*battle*); *Kampf*: put up (*a fight*); F ich bin geliefert *sl.* I am sunk; '**~schein** *m* delivery note.

'**Lieferung** *f* delivery, supply, *Am. mst* shipment; (*Buch*) number; '**~sbedingungen** *f/pl.* terms of delivery; '**~swerk** *n* serial.

'**Liefer|wagen** *m s. Lieferauto*; '**~zeit** *f* time (*od.* term) of delivery.

'**Liege** *f* (15) couch; '**~geld** ⚓ *n* demurrage; '**~kur** *f* rest-cure.

liegen ['li:gən] (30) lie; *Stadt, Haus usw.*: be (situated); das Zimmer liegt nach Süden faces south; es liegt mir daran, zu *inf.*, mir ist daran gelegen, daß I am anxious to *inf.*, I am concerned to *inf. od.* that; das (er) liegt mir nicht that (he) is not my cup of tea; es liegt mir nichts daran it does not matter, it is of no importance (to me); es liegt mir viel daran it matters a great deal to me; es liegt an (*od.* bei) ihm, zu *inf.* it is for him to *inf.*; ~ an (*dat.*; *Ursache*) be due to; es liegt daran, daß the reason is that; *Schuld*: an wem liegt es? whose fault is it?; das liegt im Blut (in der Familie) that runs in the blood (family); *s.* Anker, Bett, Luft, Sterben, zugrunde, Zunge *usw.*; '**~bleiben** (sn) keep lying; *im Bett*: stay in bed; *unterwegs, a. mot. usw.*: break down; *Arbeit*: stand over; *Brief usw.*: be left unattended to; *Ware*: remain on hand; '**~lassen** let lie; (*vergessen*) leave behind; (*nicht berühren*) leave (*od.* let) alone; *Arbeit*: leave undone; j-n links ~ ignore (*od.* cut) a p.; '**≈schaften** *f/pl.* real estate *sg.*, (landed) property *sg.*

'**Liege|platz** *m* ⚓ berth; 🚂 couchette; '**~sitz** *mot. m* reclining seat; '**~stuhl** *m* deck-chair; '**~stütz** *m Turnen*: press-up; '**~wagen** 🚂 *m* couchette coach.

lieh [li:] *pret. v. leihen.*

ließ [li:s] *pret. v. lassen.*

Lift [lift] *m* (3) lift, elevator.

Liga ['li:ga] *f* (16^2) league.

Liguster ⚘ [li'gustər] *m* (7) privet.

li-ieren [li'i:rən]: sich ~ mit team up with; liiert sein mit go with *a girl.*

Likör [li'kø:r] *m* (3^1) liqueur.

lila ['li:la] lilac.

Lilie ['li:ljə] *f* (15) lily.

Liliputaner [lilipu'ta:nər] *m* (7), **~in** *f* (16^1) Lilliputian.

Limonade [limo'na:də] *f* (15) fizzy drink, *Am.* soda pop.

Limousine *mot.* [limu'zi:nə] *f* (15) limousine, saloon car, *Am.* sedan.
lind [lint] soft, gentle; (*mild*) mild.
Linde ⚘ ['lində] *f* (15) lime-tree, linden.
lindern ['lindərn] (29) *Übel*: mitigate; (*mildern*) soften; (*erleichtern*) alleviate, soothe; *Schmerzen*: allay.
'**Linderung** *f* alleviation, mitigation; '**~smittel** *n* lenitive, palliative.
Lindwurm ['lintvurm] *m* dragon.
Lineal [line'ɑ:l] *n* (3¹) ruler.
linear [~'ɑ:r] linear; ⚕ *Lohnerhöhung etc.*: across the board.
Linguist [liŋ'guist] *m* (12) linguist.
Linie ['li:njə] *f* (15) line (*a.* ⚓, ✈, ⚔, *u. fig.*); (*Strecke*) route; *auf der ganzen ~* all along (*od.* down) the line; *auf gleicher ~ mit* on a level with; *in erster ~* in the first place.
'**Linien|blatt** *n* (sheet with) guide lines *pl.*; '**~flug** *m* scheduled flight; '**~maschine** ✈ *f* scheduled plane; '**~papier** *n* ruled paper; '**~richter** *m Sport*: linesman; '**2treu:** *~ sein* follow the party line; '**~treue** *m*, *f* (18) party liner.
lin(i)ieren [lin'ji:rən, li'ni:rən] rule.
link [liŋk] (*Ggs. recht*) left; *~e Seite* left(-hand) side, left; *v. Stoff*: reverse side; *mit dem ~en Fuß zuerst aufstehen* get out of bed on the wrong side; '**2e 1.** *f* (18) left hand; *pol. the* Left **2.** *m* (18) *Boxen*: left; '**~isch** awkward, clumsy.
links on (*od.* to) the left; (*nach ~*) (to the) left; (*verkehrt*) inside out; (*~händig*) left-handed; *pol.* leftist; *s. liegenlassen*; '**2...** *pol.* left-wing ...; **2'-außen** *m* (6) outside left; '**2-extremist(in** *f*) *m* left-wing extremist; '**~gerichtet** *pol.* leftist; **2händer** ['~hɛndər] *m* (7) left-hander; '**2kurve** *f* left turn; '**2radikalismus** *pol. m* left-wing radicalism; '**2steuerung** *mot. f* left-hand drive; '**2verkehr** *mot. m*: *in England ist ~* in England people drive on the left.
Linoleum [li'no:leum] *n* (9) linoleum.
Linse ['linzə] *f* (15) lentil; *opt.* lens.
Lippe ['lipə] *f* (15) lip; '**~nbekenntnis** *n*, '**~ndienst** *m* lip-service; '**~nlaut** *m* labial; '**~nstift** *m* lipstick.
Liquid|ation [likvida'tsjo:n] *f* (16) liquidation, winding-up; (*Honorarforderung*) charge; **2ieren** [~'di:rən] liquidate (*a. pol.*), wind up; charge; **~ität** ⚕ [~di'tɛ:t] *f* (16, *o. pl.*) liquidity, solvency.
lispeln ['lispəln] *v/i. u. v/t.* (29) lisp; (*flüstern*) whisper.
List [list] *f* (16) ruse, trick; (*Schlauheit*) cunning.
Liste ['listə] *f* (15) list, roll; *s. schwarz*; '**~npreis** *m* list price.
'**listig** cunning, crafty, sly.
Litanei [lita'naɪ] *f* (16) litany.
Liter ['li:tər] *n*, *m* (7) lit|re, *Am.* -er.
literarisch [litə'rɑ:riʃ] literary.
Literat [~'rɑ:t] *m* (12) man of letters; (*Schriftsteller*) writer.
Literatur [~ra'tu:r] *f* (16) literature; **~geschichte** *f* history of literature; **~kritiker** *m* literary critic; **~preis** *m* literary prize; **~verzeichnis** *n* bibliography; **~wissenschaft** *f* literary studies *pl.*
Litfaßsäule ['litfaszɔʏlə] *f* advertising pillar.
Lithograph [lito'grɑ:f] *m* (12) lithographer; **~ie** [~gra'fi:] *f* (16) lithography; **2ieren** [~'fi:rən] lithograph; **2isch** [~'grɑ:fiʃ] lithographic.
litt [lit] *pret. v. leiden* 1.
Liturgie [litur'gi:] *f* (16) liturgy.
liturgisch [li'turgiʃ] liturgical.
Litze ['litsə] *f* (15) cord, lace, braid; ⚡ strand(ed wire).
Livree [li'vre:] *f* (15) livery.
Lizenz [li'tsɛnts] *f* (16) licen|ce, *Am.* -se; *in ~ herstellen etc.*: under licence; **~geber** *m* licenser; **~gebühr** *f* royalty; **~-inhaber** *m*, **~nehmer** *m* licensee; **~vertrag** *m* licensing (*od.* royalty) agreement.
Lob [lo:p] *n* (3) praise; *zu seinem ~e* in his praise.
loben ['lo:bən] (25) praise; F *da lobe ich mir ...* commend me to ...; '**~swert** laudable.
Lob|gesang ['lo:p-] *m* hymn, song of praise; *fig.* eulogy; **~hude'lei** *f* (16) base flattery; '**2hudeln** give *a p.* fulsome praise.
löblich ['lø:pliç] commendable.
Lob|lied ['lo:p-] *n*: *ein ~ auf j-n singen* sing a p.'s praises; '**2preisen** praise, extol; '**~rede** *f* eulogy; '**~redner** *m* eulogist; '**~spruch** *m* eulogy.
Loch [lɔx] *n* (1²) hole (*a.* F *contp. Wohnung usw.*); F (*Gefängnis*) *sl.* quod; F *auf dem letzten ~ pfeifen* be on one's last legs; '**~-eisen** punch; '**2en** (25) perforate; *Fahr-*

karte, Lochkarte usw.: punch; '**~er** *m* (7) *für Papier, Lochkarten*: punch; (electronic) punch-card machine; *Person*: punch-card operator.

löcherig ['lœçəriç] full of holes.

'**Loch|karte** *f* punch(ed) card; '**~maschine** *f* punching machine; '**~säge** *f* keyhole-saw; '**~streifen** *m* punched tape; '**~ung** *f* perforation; punching; '**~zange** *f* (*eine* a pair of) punch pliers *pl.*; 🚂 ticket punch; '**~ziegel** *m* air-brick.

Locke ['lɔkə] *f* (15) curl, ringlet.

'**locken**[1] (25) (*a. sich*) curl; '~[2] bait, decoy, lure; *fig. a.* allure, attract, entice; tempt.

'**Locken|kopf** *m* curly head; '**~wickler** *m* curler.

locker ['lɔkər] loose (*a. fig. Sitten, Person*); (*schlaff*) slack; *Brot usw.*: spongy; *fig.* lax; *stärker*: dissolute; '**2heit** *f* looseness; sponginess; '**~lassen:** *fig. nicht* ~ stick to one's guns; '**~n** (29) loosen (*a. sich*); *Griff, a. Zwang usw.*: relax; '**2ung** *f* loosening; relaxation.

'**lockig** curly.

'**Lock|mittel** *n*, '**~speise** *f* bait, lure; '**~spitzel** *m* agent provocateur (*fr.*), *bsd. Am.* stool-pigeon; '**~ung** *f* lure, enticement; (*Versuchung*) temptation; '**~vogel** *fig. m* decoy.

Loden ['lo:dən] *m* (6) loden cloth, shag; '**~mantel** *m* lodenmantle.

lodern ['lo:dərn] (29) flame, blaze (*a. fig.*).

Löffel ['lœfəl] *m* (7) spoon; (*Schöpf*2) ladle; ⊕ scoop; *hunt.* ear; *s. barbieren*; '**2n** (29) spoon (out); ladle (out); '**~stiel** *m* spoon-handle; '**~voll** *m* (3[1], *o. pl.*) spoonful.

log[1] [lo:k] *pret. v. lügen.*

Log[2] ⚓ [lɔk] *n* (3[1]) log.

Logarithmus [loga'ritmus] *m* (16[2]) logarithm.

Loge ['lo:ʒə] *f* (15) *thea.* box; (*Freimaurer*2) lodge; '**~nbruder** *m* freemason; '**~nmeister** *m* master of a lodge.

logieren [lo'ʒi:rən] lodge; stay (*bei* with); *Am. a.* room.

Logik ['lo:gik] *f* (16) logic.

Logis [lo'ʒi:] *n inv.* lodging(s *pl.*).

logisch ['lo:giʃ] logical.

Logistik [lo'gistik] ⚔ *f* (16, *o. pl.*) logistics *pl.*

logo *sl.* ['lo:go] sure.

Logopäd|e ⚕ [logo'pɛ:də] *m* (13) logop(a)edist, speech therapist; **~ie** [~pɛ'di:] *f* (16, *o. pl.*) logop(a)edics *sg.*, speech therapy.

Lohe[1] ['lo:ə] *f* (15) (*Flamme*) blaze, flame; '**2n**[1] *v/i.* (25) blaze.

'**Lohe**[2] *f* (15) (*Gerber*2) tan; '**2n**[2] *v/t.* (25) treat with tan.

'**loh|farben** tawny; '**2gerber** *m* tanner; '**2gerbe'rei** *f* tannery.

Lohn [lo:n] *m* (3[3]) (*Arbeits*2) wage(s *pl.*), pay(ment); (*Miet*2) hire; *fig.* reward; '**~-abbau** *m* wage cut(s *pl.*); '**~-abkommen** *n* wage agreement; '**~-arbeiter** *m*, '**~-empfänger** *m* wage-earner, *Am. a.* wage-worker; '**~buchhalter** *m* pay-clerk.

'**lohnen** (25) reward (*j-m et.* a p. for); *Arbeiter*: pay; *sich* ~ pay (*für j-n* a p.), be worth while; '**~d** paying, profitable; worthwhile; *fig. a.* rewarding.

löhnen ['lø:nən] (25) pay.

'**Lohn|-erhöhung** *f* wage increase *od.* rise, *Am.* raise; '**~forderung** *f* wage claim; '**~gruppe** *f* pay bracket; '**2-intensiv** wage-intensive; '**~kampf** *m* wage dispute; '**~kostenanteil** *m* wage factor in cost; '**~liste** *f* pay-roll; '**~skala** *f* wage scale; '**~steuer** *f* wages tax; '**~stopp** *m* pay freeze; '**~streifen** *m* pay (*od.* wage) slip; '**~tarif** *m* wage rate; '**~tüte** *f* pay (*od.* wage) packet.

'**Löhnung** *f* pay; '**~s-tag** *m* pay-day.

Loipe ['lɔʏpə] *f* (15) cross-country (skiing) course.

lokal [lo'kɑ:l] **1.** local; **2.** 2 *n* (3) locality; (*Wirtshaus*) public house, restaurant; *s. a. Geschäfts*2; **2...** local; **~isieren** [lokali'zi:rən] localize; **2-patriotismus** *m* sectional pride; **2-teil** *m e-r Zeitung*: local news *sg.*

Lokomotiv|e [lokomo'ti:və] *f* (15) engine, locomotive; **~führer** [~'ti:f-] *m* engine-driver, *Am.* engineer.

Lokus ['lo:kus] F *m* (14[2] *u. inv.*) *s. Klo.*

Lombardsatz [lɔm'bartzats] ✝ *m* lending rate.

Lorbeer ['lɔrbe:r] *m* (5[2]) laurel, bay; *fig. auf s-n ~en ausruhen* rest on one's laurels.

Lore ⊕ ['lo:rə] *f* (15) lorry.

Los[1] [lo:s] *n* (4) lot; (*Lotterie*2) ticket; (*Schicksal*) fate, destiny; *s. groß*; *das ~ werfen (ziehen) s. losen.*

los[2] (18[1], *s. lose*) loose; (*frei*) *a.* free;

(*ab*) off; *was ist* ~ (*mit ihm*)? what's the matter (with him)?; *was ist heute abend* ~? what's on tonight?; *j-n*, *et.* ~ *sein* be rid of; ~! go ahead!, (*schnell*) let's go!; *Sport*: *Achtung*, *fertig*, ~! are you ready? go!; *mit ihm ist nicht viel* ~ *sl.* he is no great shakes; F *er hat was* ~ *sl.* he is on the ball.

'**los-arbeiten** *v/t.*: *sich* ~ extricate o.s., get loose; *v/i.* (*darauf* ~) work away (*auf acc.* at).

lösbar ['lø:sba:r] soluble.

'**los|binden** untie; '**~brechen** *v/t.* break off; *v/i. fig.* break out.

'**Lösch|blatt** *n*, '**~papier** *n* blotting-paper; '**~-eimer** *m* fire-bucket.

löschen ['lœʃən] (27) *Feuer*, *Licht*: extinguish, put out; *Geschriebenes*: blot out, *a. Bandaufnahme*: erase; (*streichen*) cancel (*a. Schuld*); *Durst*: quench; *Kalk*: slake; ⚓ unload; *Computer*: delete.

'**Löscher** *m* (7) *s. Feuer*2, *Tinten*2.

'**Lösch|kopf** *m Bandgerät*: eraser head; '**~mannschaft** *f* fire-brigade; '**~papier** *n* blotting paper; '**~taste** *f Bandgerät*: erase button.

lose ['lo:zə] loose (*a. fig. Leben*, *Person*, *Zunge usw.*); *s. los*².

'**Lösegeld** *n* ransom.

losen ['lo:zən] (27) cast (*od.* draw) lots (*um* for); *mit Münze*: toss (for).

lösen ['lø:zən] (27) loosen; (*losbinden*) untie; (*wegmachen*) detach; (*lossprechen*) absolve; (*loskaufen*) redeem; *Fahrkarte*: book, take, buy; *Aufgabe*, *Rätsel*, *Zweifel usw.*: solve; *Verbindung*, *Verlobung*: break off; *Ehe*: dissolve (*a.* ⚗ *u. sich*); *Vertrag*: terminate; *sich* ~ get loose, (*sich befreien*) disengage o.s., *Schuß*: ring out, *Spannung*, *Muskeln*, *Griff*: relax; *fig. gelöst* relaxed.

'**los|gehen** (sn) (*sich lockern*) get loose, come off; (*davongehen*; *Schuß*[*waffe*]) go off; (*anfangen*) begin, start; *auf j-n* fly at, go for, attack; *auf ein Ziel usw.* make for; '**~haken** unhook; '**~kaufen** buy off; *Gefangene*: ransom; '**~ketten** unchain; '**~knüpfen** untie; '**~kommen** (sn) get loose *od.* free; *fig. a.* get rid (*von* of); '**~lachen** laugh out; '**~lassen** let loose *od.* off *od.* go, release; *fig.* launch; '**~legen** let go (*mit* with), open up; *leg los!* fire away!; ~ *gegen s. losziehen.*

löslich ⚗ ['lø:sliç] soluble.

'**los|lösen**, '**~machen** *s. lösen*; '**~reißen** tear loose; *sich* ~ break away, *fig.* tear o.s. away; *sich* '**~sagen** *von* dissociate o.s. from, break with; '**~schießen** *v/i. u. v/t.* fire (off); (*sich stürzen*) *auf* (*acc.*) rush at; F *schieß los!* fire away!, shoot!; '**~schlagen** *v/t.* knock off; (*verkaufen*) dispose of; *v/i.* open the attack, strike; ~ *auf j-n* let fly at; '**~schnallen** unbuckle; '**~schrauben** unscrew; loosen; '**~sprechen** absolve; acquit (*von* of); release; '**~springen**, '**~stürzen** (sn) *auf* (*acc.*) pounce upon, fly at; '**~steuern** (sn) *auf* (*acc.*) make for; *fig. a.* be driving at; '**~trennen** detach; *Genähtes*: unstitch; (*a. fig.*) separate.

Losung ['lo:zuŋ] *f des Wildes*: dung; ⚔ password, (*a. fig.*) watchword.

Lösung ['lø:zuŋ] *f* solution (*a.* ⚗, ⚕); '**~sheft** *n* key; '**~smittel** *n* solvent.

'**los|werden** (sn) get rid of; '**~ziehen** (sn) set out, march away; *gegen j-n* ~ inveigh against, let fly at.

Lot [lo:t] *n* (3) (*Blei*2) lead, plummet; (*Lötmetall*) solder; ⚕ perpendicular (line); *ein* ~ *errichten* (*fällen*) raise (drop) a perpendicular; *fig. im* ~ *sein* be in good order; *ins* ~ *bringen* set to rights; '**2en** (26) *v/i. u. v/t.* plumb; ⚓ sound.

löten ['lø:tən] (26) solder.

'**Löt|kolben** *m* soldering-iron; '**~lampe** *f* soldering-lamp, *Am.* blowtorch; '**~metall** *n* solder.

'**lotrecht** perpendicular.

'**Lötrohr** *n* blowpipe.

Lotse ⚓ ['lo:tsə] *m* (13), '**2n** (27) pilot; '**~ndienst** *m* pilotage service.

Lotterie [lɔtə'ri:] *f* (15) lottery; **~los** *n* (lottery) ticket.

Lotterleben ['lɔtər-] *n* dissolute life.

Lotto ['lɔto] *n* (11) numbers pool.

Löwe ['lø:və] *m* (13) lion; *ast.* Leo.

'**Löwen|-anteil** *m* lion's share; '**~bändiger**(**in** *f*) *m* lion-tamer; '**~grube** *f* lion's den; '**~maul** ⚘ *n* snapdragon; '**~zahn** ⚘ *m* dandelion.

'**Löwin** *f* (16[1]) lioness.

loyal [loa'ja:l] loyal; **2ität** [~jali'tɛt] *f* (16) loyalty.

Luchs [luks] *m* (4) lynx; **2äugig** ['~ʔɔʏgiç] lynx-eyed.

Lücke ['lykə] *f* (15) gap; (*Riß, Bruch*) breach; (*offene Stelle*) blank; (*Mangel*) deficiency; '**~nbüßer** *m* stop-gap; '**♀nhaft** defective, incomplete, fragmentary; '**♀nlos** complete; *Beweis*: full, airtight.

Luder ['lu:dər] *n* (7) (*Aas*) carrion; P *fig.* beast; (*Dirne*) hussy; *armes ~* poor wretch.

Luft [luft] *f* (14¹) air; (*Brise*) breeze; *frische ~ schöpfen* draw breath, take the air; *an die ~ gehen* take an airing; *fig. j-n wie ~ behandeln* cut a p. dead; *fig. et. aus der ~ greifen* pull a th. out of thin air; (*völlig*) *aus der ~ gegriffen* totally unfounded; *in freier ~* in the open air; *fig. es liegt et. in der ~* there is something in the wind; *in die ~ fliegen* be blown up; *in die ~ sprengen od. jagen* blow up; F *in die ~ gehen* blow one's top; *s-m Zorn usw. ~ machen* give vent to; *sich ~ machen P.*: unbosom o.s., *Gefühl*: find vent; F *j-n an die ~ setzen* turn a p. out; *s. rein* 1; *schnappen.*

'**Luft|-abwehr** *f* air defen|ce, *Am.* -se; '**~-alarm** *m* air-raid alarm; '**~-angriff** *m* air-raid; '**~-aufklärung** *f* aerial reconnaissance; '**~ballon** *m* (air-)balloon; '**~bild** *n* aerial photo(-graph), aerial view; '**~bildvermessung** *f* aerial survey; '**~blase** *f* air bubble; '**~bremse** *f* air-brake; '**~brücke** ✈ *f* airlift.

Lüftchen ['lyftçən] *n* (6) gentle breeze, breath of air.

'**luft|dicht** airtight; '**♀druck** *m* air (*od.* atmospheric) pressure; *e-r Explosion*: blast; '**♀druckbremse** *f* air (*od.* pneumatic) brake; '**~durchlässig** permeable to air.

lüft|en ['lyftən] (26) air, ventilate; (*heben*) lift, raise; *ein Geheimnis ~* disclose (*od.* reveal) a secret; '**♀er** *m* (7) ventilator; ⊕ (*Ent♀*) air exhauster.

'**Luft|fahrt** *f* aviation; '**~fahrtgesellschaft** *f* airline (company); '**~fahrzeug** *n* aircraft (*a. pl.*); '**~feuchtigkeit** *f* (atmospheric) humidity; air moisture; '**~flotte** *f* air force; '**~fracht** *f* air freight; '**♀gekühlt** air-cooled; '**♀gestützt** ⚔ *Rakete*: air-launched; '**~gewehr** *n* air-gun; '**~hafen** *m* airport; '**~heizung** *f* hot-air heating; '**~herrschaft** *f* air supremacy; '**~hoheit** *f* air sovereignty; '**♀ig** airy; (*windig*) breezy; (*dünn*) flimsy; *P.*: flighty; '**~kampf** *m* aerial combat; '**~kissen** *n* air-cushion; '**~kissenfahrzeug** *n* air-cushion vehicle; '**~klappe** *f* air-valve; '**~korridor** *m* air corridor; '**♀krank** air-sick; '**~krieg** *m* aerial warfare; '**~kühlung** *f* air cooling; '**~kur-ort** *m* climatic health-resort; '**~landetruppen** *f/pl.* airborne troops *pl.*; '**♀leer** void of air, evacuated; *~er Raum* vacuum; '**~linie** *f* air line (distance); *s. a. Luftverkehrslinie*; '**~loch** *n* airhole, vent; ✈ air-pocket; '**~matratze** *f* air mattress; '**~mine** ⚔ *f* aerial mine; '**~pirat** *m* hijacker, skyjacker; '**~pistole** *f* air-pistol; '**~post** *f* air mail; '**~pumpe** *f* air-pump; '**~raum** *m* air space; '**~reifen** *m* pneumatic tyre (*Am.* tire); '**~reklame** *f* sky-line advertising; '**~rettung** *f* air rescue service; '**~röhre** *f* air-tube; *anat.* windpipe, 📖 trachea; '**~sack** *mot. m* airbag; '**~schacht** *m* airshaft; '**~schaukel** *f* swing-boat; '**~schiff** *n* airship; '**~schiffahrt** *f* aviation; '**~schiffer** *m* aeronaut, airman; '**~schlacht** *f* air battle; '**~schlauch** *m* air tube; *Fahrrad, mot.* inner tube; '**~schlösser** *n/pl.* castles in the air; '**~schraube** ✈ *f* air-screw, propeller; '**~schutz** *m* air-raid protection; civil air defence; '**~schutzkeller** *m*, '**~schutzraum** *m* air-raid shelter; '**~schutz-übung** *f* air-raid drill; '**~spiegelung** *f* mirage; '**~sprung** *m* caper; '**~streitkräfte** *f/pl.* air force(s *pl.*); '**~strom** *m* air-stream; '**~stützpunkt** ⚔ *m* air base; '**~taxi** *n* air taxi; '**♀tüchtig** ✈ air-worthy; '**~tüchtigkeit** *f* air-worthiness.

'**Lüftung** ['lyftuŋ] *f* airing; *künstlich*: ventilation; '**~s-anlage** *f* ventilating system.

'**Luft|ver-änderung** *f* change of air; '**~verkehrsgesellschaft** *f* air transport company, airline *od.* airways (company); '**~verkehrslinie** *f* air-line, air-route, airway; '**~verpestung** *f*, '**~verschmutzung** *f* air pollution; '**~verteidigung** *f* air defen|ce, *Am.* -se; '**~waffe** *f* air force; '**~weg** *m* air-route; *anat.* respiratory tract; *auf dem ~e* by air; '**~zufuhr** *f* air supply; '**~zug** *m* draught (*Am.* draft) (of air).

Lug [lu:k] *m* (3): *~ und Trug* falsehood and deceit.

Lüge ['ly:gə] *f* (15) lie, falsehood; *j-n ~n strafen* give a p. the lie.
lugen ['lu:gən] (25) peer.
'**lügen 1.** *v/i.* (30) lie, tell a lie *od.* lies; **2.** ♀ *n* (6) lying; '♀**detektor** *m* lie detector; '**~haft** lying, deceitful, untrue.
Lügner ['ly:gnər] *m* (7), '**~in** *f* (16[1]) liar; '♀**isch** deceitful, lying, false.
Luke ['lu:kə] *f* (15) (*Dachfenster*) dormer-window; ⚓ *usw.* hatch.
lukrativ [lukra'ti:f] lucrative.
lukullisch [lu'kuliʃ] sumptuous.
lullen ['lulən] (25): *in Schlaf ~* lull to sleep.
Lümmel ['lyməl] *m* (7) lout; '♀**haft** loutish; '♀**n** (26) *v/i. u. v/refl.* loll.
Lump [lump] *m* (3 *u.* 12) scoundrel, blackguard, *sl.* louse; '**~en**[1] *m* (6) rag; '♀**en**[2] (25): *sich nicht ~ lassen* come down handsomely.
'**Lumpen|gesindel** *n* riff-raff; (*Schurken*) scoundrels *pl.*; '**~händler** *m* ragman, *Am.* junkman; '**~hund** *m*, '**~kerl** *m s. Lump*; '**~pack** *n s. Lumpengesindel*; '**~papier** *n* rag paper; '**~sammler(in** *f*) *m* ragpicker; '**~wolle** *f* shoddy.
Lumperei [~'raı] *f* (16) shabby trick; (*Kleinigkeit*) trifle.
'**lumpig** ragged; *fig.* paltry (*sum*).
Lunge ['luŋə] *f* (15) lung(s *pl.*); *v. Schlachtvieh*: lights *pl.*; ⚕ *eiserne ~* iron lung; '**~n...** 🕮 pulmonary ...
'**Lungen|-entzündung** *f* inflammation of the lungs, 🕮 pneumonia; '**~flügel** *m* lobe of the lungs; '**~heilstätte** *f* (tuberculosis) sanatorium; '♀**krank**, '**~kranke** *m, f* consumptive; '**~krankheit** *f* lung (*od.* pulmonary) disease; '**~krebs** *m* lung cancer; '**~schwindsucht** *f* pulmonary phthisis.
lungern ['luŋərn] (h. *u.* sn, 29) loiter (about); loll (about).
Lunte ['luntə] *f* (15) slow-match; *fig. ~ riechen* smell a rat.
Lupe ['lu:pə] *f* (15) magnifier; (*Taschen*♀) pocket-lens; *unter die ~ nehmen fig.* scrutinize closely.
Lupine ⚘ [lu'pi:nə] *f* (15) lupine.
Lust [lust] *f* (14[1]) pleasure (*a. psych.*), delight; (*Verlangen*) desire; *mit ~ und Liebe* with a will; *~ bekommen, ~ haben zu inf.* feel like *ger.*; *große (gute) ~ haben zu* have a great (half a) mind to; *die ~ verlieren an* (*dat.*) lose all liking for; *hätten Sie ~ zu inf.?* would you like to *inf.*?; '**~barkeit** *f* diversion; *bsd. öffentliche*: entertainment.
Lüster ['lystər] *m* (7) lust|re, *Am.* -er; '**~klemme** ⚡ *f* strip connector.
lüstern ['lystərn] (*nach*) desirous (of), greedy (of, for); (*fleischlich*) lewd, lascivious; '♀**heit** *f* greediness; lewdness, lasciviousness.
'**Lust|garten** *m* pleasure garden; '**~gefühl** *n* pleasurable sensation; '**~gewinn** *psych. m* pleasure gain.
'**lustig** merry, gay; (*belustigend*) funny; *sich ~ machen über* (*acc.*) make fun of; *~ sein* (*sich festlich vergnügen*) make merry; '♀**keit** *f* gaiety; fun(niness).
Lüstling ['lystliŋ] *m* (3[1]) libertine, rake, debauchee.
'**lust|los** listless, unenthusiastic(al); ⚚ slack; '♀**mord** *m* sex murder; '♀**mörder** *m* sex maniac; '♀**-objekt** *n* sex object; '♀**prinzip** *psych. n* pleasure principle; '♀**schloß** *n* pleasure seat; '♀**seuche** *f* venereal disease, syphilis; '♀**spiel** *n* comedy; '**~wandeln** (sn) walk leisurely along, stroll about.
Lutheraner [lutə'ra:nər] *m* (7), **lutherisch** ['lutəriʃ, lu'te:riʃ] Lutheran.
lutsch|en ['lutʃən] (27) *v/i. u. v/t.* suck; '♀**er** *m für Säuglinge*: comforter, dummy; (*Bonbon*) lollipop.
Luv ⚓ [lu:f] *f* (16, *o. pl.*) luff, weather side; ♀**en** ⚓ ['~vən] (25) luff; **~seite** ['lu:f-] weather side.
luxuriös [luksu'rjø:s] (18[1]) luxurious.
Luxus ['luksus] *m inv.* luxury (*a. fig.*); '**~...** luxury ..., de luxe ...; '**~-artikel** *m* luxury (article); '**~ausgabe** *f* (*Buch*) de luxe edition; '**~dampfer** *m* luxury liner; '**~kabine** ⚓ *f* stateroom; '**~leben** *n* life of luxury; '**~wagen** *mot. m* de luxe model.
Lymph... ['lymf-] lymphatic; '**~drüse** *f* lymph(atic) gland; '**~e** *f* (15) lymph; (*Impfstoff*) vaccine.
lynch|en ['lynçən] (27) lynch; '♀**justiz** *f* lynch law; '♀**mord** *m* lynching.
Lyra ['ly:ra] *f* (16[2]) lyre.
Lyrik ['~rik] *f* (16) lyric poetry; '**~er** *m* (7) lyric poet.
'**lyrisch** lyric; *fig.* lyrical.
Lyzeum [ly'tse:um] *n* (9) secondary school for girls.

M

M [ɛm], **m** *n inv.* M, m.

Maat ⚓ [maːt] *m* (3) mate; ⚔ leading rating, *Am.* petty officer 3rd class.

Mach|-art [ˈmax-] *f* make; ˈ**≈bar** feasible, practicable, possible; ˈ**~e** *f* (15) *fig.* make-believe, F show; *et. in der ~ haben* have in hand; F *j-n in die ~ nehmen* work a p. over.

mach|en [ˈmaxən] (25) (*herstellen*) make; (*tun*) do (*a.* F *thea.*); (*bewirken*) effect, produce; (*verursachen*) cause; (*schaffen*) create; (*erledigen*) deal with, handle, do; *Appetit, Freude usw.*: give; *~ in et.* ✝ deal in, F *fig.* dabble in; *j-n zu et. ~* make a p. a th.; *j-n glücklich usw. ~* make (*od.* render) a p. happy, *etc.*; *was macht die Rechnung?, wieviel macht das?* how much is it?; *das macht 3 Mark* that will be (*od.* comes to) 3 marks; *was macht das (aus)?* what does it matter?; *das macht nichts!* never mind!; *es macht mir nichts (aus)* I don't mind; *nichts zu ~!* nothing doing!; *mach doch (zu)!* hurry up!; *mach, daß ...!* see (to it) that ...!; *mach's gut! (lebwohl)* take care of yourself!; *das macht sich gut* that looks well; *er macht sich jetzt* he is getting on now; *es wird sich ~* it will come right; *dagegen kann man nichts ~* that cannot be helped; *sich ~ an (acc.)* go (*od.* set) about; proceed to *inf.*; *sich an j-n ~* approach a p.; *sich auf den Weg ~* set out; *ich mache mir nichts daraus* I don't care about it; *(sich) et. ~ lassen* have a th. made, order a th.; *das läßt sich (schon) ~* it can be arranged; *laß mich nur ~!* leave it to me!; *gemacht* made (*aus* of), (*unecht*) artificial; F *gemacht!* agreed!, *bsd. Am.* OK!, okay!; *ein gemachter Mann* a made man; *s. Angst, Anspruch, Arbeit, Ausflucht, bekannt, Besuch, Erfahrung, fertig, Feuer usw.*; ˈ**≈enschaften** *f/pl.* machinations; ˈ**≈er** F *m* (7) doer.

Macht [maxt] *f* (14[1]) power (*a. Staat*), might (*beide a. Stärke*); (*Gewalt über acc.*) control (of), sway (over); *gesetzmäßige*: authority; *an der ~* in power; *zur ~ gelangen* come into power; *mit aller ~* with all one's might; *alles, was in m-r ~ steht* everything within my power; ˈ**~befugnis** *f* authority, power; ˈ**~-ergreifung** *f s. Machtübernahme*; ˈ**~haber** *m* (7) ruler; ˈ**≈haberisch** despotic.

mächtig [ˈmɛçtiç] powerful (*a. fig. Körper, Stimme, Schlag usw.*); mighty (*a.* F *adv.*); (*riesig*) huge; ⚒ thick, wide; *e-r S. ~ sein* be master of, *e-r Sprache*: have command of.

ˈ**Macht|kampf** *m* struggle for power; ˈ**≈los** powerless; helpless; ˈ**~mißbrauch** *m* misuse of power; ˈ**~politik** *f* power politics; ˈ**~position** *f* position of power; ˈ**~spruch** *m* authoritative decision; ˈ**~-übernahme** *f* assumption of power, takeover; ˈ**≈voll** powerful, mighty; ˈ**~vollkommenheit** *f* absolute power; *aus eigener ~* of one's own authority; ˈ**~wechsel** *m* changeover of power; ˈ**~wort** *n* (3): *ein ~ sprechen* put one's foot down; ˈ**~zuwachs** *m* increase in power.

ˈ**Machwerk** *n* concoction; *elendes ~* miserable botch.

Macker F [ˈmakər] *m* (7) fellow, guy; (*Freund*) boyfriend.

Mädchen [ˈmɛːtçən] *n* (6) girl; (*Jungfrau*) maid(en); (*Dienst≈*) maid (-servant), servant(-girl); *in Zssgn* girl's ..., girls' ...; *~ für alles* maid-of-all-work (*a. fig.*); ˈ**≈haft** girlish; maidenly; ˈ**~handel** *m* white slavery; ˈ**~name** *m* girl's name; *e-r Frau*: maiden name; ˈ**~pensionat** *n* young ladies' boarding-school; ˈ**~schule** *f* girls' school.

Made [ˈmaːdə] *f* (15) maggot, mite; *in Obst*: worm; *wie die ~ im Speck sitzen* live in clover.

Mädel F [ˈmɛːdəl] *n* (7) girl, lass.

madig [ˈmaːdiç] maggoty; worm-eaten; F *~ machen sl.* knock.

Madonna [maˈdɔna] *f* (16[2]) Holy Virgin, Madonna.

Magazin [magaˈtsiːn] *n* (3[1]) store, warehouse; (⚔; *am Gewehr usw.*; *a. Zeitschrift*) magazine.

Magd [maːkt] *f* (14[1]) maid.

Magen [ˈmaːgən] *m* (6, *a.* 6[1]) stomach; *mit vollem ~* on a full stomach; ˈ**~beschwerden** *f/pl.* stomach (*od.* gastric) trouble, indigestion; ˈ**~bitter** *m* bitters *pl.*; ˈ**~geschwür** *n* gastric ulcer; ˈ**~grube** *f* pit of the stomach; '**~krampf** *m* gastric spasm; '**♀krank** suffering from a gastric complaint; '**~krebs** ⚕ *m* gastric cancer; '**~leiden** *n* gastric complaint; '**~saft** *m* gastric juice; '**~säure** *f* gastric acid; '**~schleimhaut** *f* stomach lining; '**~schmerzen** *m/pl.* stomach-ache; '**♀stärkend** stomachic; '**~verstimmung** *f* indigestion.

mager ['mɑːgər] meag|re, *Am.* -er (*a. fig.*); lean (*a. Fleisch, Treibstoff; fig. Jahre*); (*dürr*) gaunt; *Kost*: slender (*fare*); *Boden*: poor; '**♀keit** *f* meagreness; leanness; '**♀milch** *f* skim milk; '**♀sucht** ⚕ *f* anorexia nervosa.

Magie [ma'giː] *f* (15) magic.

Magier ['mɑːgjər] *m* (7) magician.

'**magisch** magic(al); *Radio*: *~es Auge* magic eye.

Magister [ma'gistər] *m* (7) (school-)master.

Magistrat [magi'strɑːt] *m* (3) municipal (*od.* town *od.* city) council; **~smitglied** *n* town council(l)or.

Magnat [ma'gnɑːt] *m* (12) magnate, *Am. a.* tycoon.

Magnesi|a [ma'gneːzia] *f inv.* magnesia; **~um** [~um] *n* (9, *o. pl.*) magnesium.

Magnet [ma'gneːt] *m* (3, *sg. a.* 12) magnet (*a. fig.*); **~feld** *n* magnetic field; **♀isch** magnetic(ally *adv.*); **~iseur** [~gneti'zøːr] *m* magnetizer; **♀i'sieren** magnetize; **~ismus** [~'tismus] *m* magnetism; **~karte** [~'gneːt-] *f* magnetic (punch)card; **~nadel** *f* magnetic needle.

Mahagoni [maha'goːni] *n* (11) (*a.* **~holz** *n*) mahogany (wood).

Maharadscha [maha'rɑːdʒa] *m* (11) maharaja.

Mahd [mɑːt] *f* (7) mowing; (*Schwaden*) swath.

mähen[1] ['mɛːən] *v/t. u. v/i.* (25) mow (*a. fig.*), cut, reap.

'**mähen**[2] *v/i. Schaf*: bleat.

Mahl [mɑːl] *n* (3 *u.* 1[2]) meal, repast; *festliches*: feast, banquet.

'**mahlen** (25; *p.p.* ge~) grind.

'**Mahlzeit** *f* meal; F *prost ~!* good night!

'**Mähmaschine** *f* reaping-machine, reaper; *für Rasen*: mower.

'**Mahn|bescheid** ⚖ *m* default summons; '**~brief** *m* reminder, dunning letter.

Mähne ['mɛːnə] *f* (15) mane.

mahn|en ['mɑːnən] (25) remind, warn, admonish (*alle*: *an acc.* of); *j-n wegen e-r Schuld ~* press a p. for payment, dun a p.; *zur Geduld usw. ~* urge to be patient *etc.*; '**♀er** *m* (7) admonisher, *um Zahlung*: dun; '**♀ung** *f* admonition, warning; *um Zahlung*: dunning; '**♀mal** *n* (3, *a.* 1[2]) memorial; '**♀schreiben** *n s.* ♀*brief*.

Mähre ['mɛːrə] *f* (15) mare.

Mai [maɪ] *m* (3 *od.* 14) May; *der erste ~* the first of May, May Day; '**~baum** *m* maypole; '**~blume** *f*, '**~glöckchen** *n* lily of the valley.

Maid *poet.* [maɪt] *f* (16) maid(en).

'**Mai|feier** *f* (celebration of) May Day; '**~käfer** *m* cockchafer.

Mais [maɪs] *m* (4) maize, Indian corn, *Am.* corn; '**~flocken** *f/pl. Am.* cornflakes; '**~kolben** *m* (corn) cob.

Maisch|bottich ['maɪʃ-] *m* mash-tub; '**~e** *f* (15), '**♀en** mash.

Maisonettewohnung [mezo'nɛt-] *f* maisonette, *Am.* duplex apartment.

Majestät [majɛ'stɛːt] *f* (16) majesty; **♀isch** majestic; **~sbeleidigung** *f* lese-majesty.

Major [ma'joːr] *m* (3[1]) major.

Majoran ⚘ [~jo'rɑːn] *m* (3) marjoram.

Makel ['mɑːkəl] *m* (7) stain, blot, flaw (*alle a. fig.*); *fig.* blemish.

Mäkelei [mɛːkə'laɪ] *f* (16) fault-finding, carping; *weitS.* fastidiousness.

'**mäkelig** carping; fastidious, *im Essen*: squeamish.

'**makellos** spotless (*a. fig.*), immaculate (*a. Schönheit*); *fig. a.* impeccable.

mäkeln ['mɛːkəln] (29) find fault (*an dat.* with), carp (at).

Makkaroni [maka'roːni] *pl. inv.* macaroni.

Makler ['mɑːklər] *m* (7) broker; '**~gebühr** *f* brokerage; '**~geschäft** *n* broker's business.

'**Mäkler** *m* (7), **~in** *f* fault-finder.

Makrele [ma'kreːlə] *f* (15) mackerel.

Makrone [ma'kroːnə] *f* (15) macaroon.

Makulatur [makula'tuːr] *f* (16) waste paper.

Mal [mɑːl] *n* (3) **1.** (*a.* 1[2]) mark, sign; *beim Spiel*: (*Ablauf*♀) start (-ing-point), (*Ziel*) home, base; (*Fleck*) spot, stain; (*Mutter*♀) mole; *s. Ehren*♀; **2.** time; ✗ times; *dieses ~* this time; *das nächste ~* next time;

zum ersten ~e (for) the first time; *mit e-m* ~e (*plötzlich*) all of a sudden; **3.** ♀ *adv.* F = *einmal.*

Malaria [ma'la:ria] *f* (16²) malaria.

malen ['ma:lən] (25) paint; (*zeichnen*) draw; (*porträtieren*) portray; *fig.* paint, picture; *sich* ~ *lassen* sit for one's portrait.

'**Maler** *m* (7), '**~in** *f* (16¹) painter; *als Künstler oft*: artist; **~ei** [~'raɪ] *f* (16) painting; '**♀isch** picturesque; '**~meister** *m* master (house-) painter.

Malheur [ma'lœr] *n* (3¹ *u.* 11) mishap; trouble.

maliziös [mali'tsjø:s] malicious.

'**Mal|kasten** *m* colo(u)r-box; '**~kreide** *f* crayon.

'**Malkunst** *f* art of painting.

'**malnehmen 1.** multiply; **2.** ♀ *n* (6) multiplication.

Malve ⚘ ['malvə] *f* (15) mallow; '**♀nfarbig** mauve.

Malz [malts] *n* (3²) malt; '**~bier** *n* malt liquor; '**~bonbon** *m, n* cough-lozenge; '**~darre** *f* malt-kiln.

Malzeichen ['ma:ltsaɪçən] *n* multiplication mark.

Mälzer ['mɛltsər] *m* (7) maltster.

'**Malz|-extrakt** *m* malt extract; '**~kaffee** *m* malt-coffee; '**~zucker** *m* malt-sugar.

Mama [ma'ma, F '~] *f* (11¹) mam(m)a, F ma, mum, *Am. a.* mom.

Mammographie [mamogra'fi:] *f* (15) mammography.

Mammon ['mamɔn] *m* (11) mammon, pelf, (filthy) lucre.

Mammut ['mamu:t] *n* (3 *u.* 11) mammoth; '**♀...** *Baum, Firma, usw.*: mammoth; *fig. a.* giant ...

Mamsell [mam'zɛl] *f* (16) miss; (*Wirtschafterin*) housekeeper.

man [man] (*im dat. u. acc. durch* einer *ersetzt*) one, people, we, you, they; ~ *sagte mir* I was told.

manag|en ['mɛnidʒən] manage (*a.* F); '**♀er** *m* (7) manager; '**♀erkrankheit** *f* stress disease.

manch [manç] (21) many a; '**~e** *pl.* some, several; **~erlei** ['~ərlaɪ] *inv.* all sorts of, of several sorts, various; '**~mal** sometimes.

Mandant ⚖ [man'dant] *m* (12) client.

Mandarine [manda'ri:nə] *f* (15) tangerine.

Mandat [~'da:t] *n* (3) mandate; authorization; ⚖ brief; *parl.* seat; **~sgebiet** mandate(d territory).

Mandel ['mandəl] *f* (15) almond; *anat.* tonsil; shock; '**~baum** *m* almond-tree; '**~-entzündung** *f* inflammation of the tonsils, tonsillitis; **♀förmig** ['~fœrmiç] almond-shaped.

Mandoline ♪ [mando'li:nə] *f* (15) mandolin.

Manege [ma'nɛ:ʒə] *f* (15) (circus) ring.

Mangan [maŋ'ga:n] *n* (3¹) manganese; **~säure** *f* manganic acid.

Mange(l¹) ['maŋə(l)] *f* (15) mangle, calender.

'**Mangel²** *m* (7¹) want, lack, deficiency; (*Knappheit*) shortage (*an dat.* of); (*Armut*) penury; (*Fehler*) defect, shortcoming; (*Nachteil*) drawback; *aus* ~ *an* for want of, *s. mangels*; ~ *leiden an* (*dat.*) be short (*od.* in need) of; '**~beruf** *m* critical occupation; '**♀haft** (*fehlerhaft*) defective; (*unzulänglich*) deficient, inadequate; (*unbefriedigend*) unsatisfactory, poor; '**~haftigkeit** *f* defectiveness; deficiency; '**~krankheit** *f* deficiency disease; '**♀n¹** (29) want; be wanting *od.* lacking *od.* deficient (*an dat.* in); *es mangelt mir an* (*dat.*) I am in want of, I want; '**♀n²** mangle, calender; '**♀s** (*gen.*) for lack (*od.* want) of, in the absence of; '**~ware** *f* scarce commodities *pl.*; goods *pl.* in short supply.

Mangold ⚘ ['maŋgɔlt] *m* (3) mangel (-wurzel), mangold.

Manie [ma'ni:] *f* (15) mania.

Manier [~'ni:r] *f* (16) manner.

manieriert [~ni'ri:rt] affected; *Kunst, Literatur*: mannered; **♀heit** *f* affectedness, mannerism.

ma'nierlich mannerly, polite; **♀keit** *f* mannerliness, politeness.

Manifest [mani'fɛst] *n* (3²) manifesto; **~ation** [~fɛsta'tsjo:n] *f* manifestation; **~ieren** [~fɛs'ti:rən] manifest.

Maniküre [~'ky:rə] *f* (15) (*Handpflege*) manicure; (*Handpflegerin*) manicurist; **♀n** (25) manicure.

Manipul|ation [manipula'tsjo:n] *f* manipulation; **♀ieren** [~pu'li:rən] manipulate.

manisch ['ma:niʃ] manic; ~-*depressiv* manic-depressive.

Manko ['maŋko] *n* (11) deficit; deficiency; *fig.* drawback.

Mann [man] *m* (1², *poet.* 5, ⚔ *u.* ⚓ *pl. inv.*) man (*pl.* men); ⚔ enlisted man; (*Gatte*) husband; *der* ~ *auf der Straße* the man in the street; ~*s genug sein für* be man enough for; *an den* ~ *bringen* dispose of; *fig. s-n* ~ *stehen* stand one's ground; make a good job of it; ~ *gegen* ~ hand to hand; F ~ (*Gottes*)! man (alive)!; *s. Wort.*

'**mannbar** marriageable; ~ *werden* reach (wo)manhood; '**≈keit** *f* (wo)manhood; *v. Mädchen a.* marriageable age.

Männchen ['mɛnçən] *n* (6) little man; *zo.* male; *bei Vögeln*: cock; ~ *malen* doodle; ~ *machen Tier*: sit up and beg.

Mannequin ['manəkɛ̃] *n*, *m* (11) mannequin, model.

Männer|gesangver-ein ['mɛnər-] *m* men's singing club; '**~welt** *f* male sex, men *pl.*

'**Mannes|-alter** *n* manhood; *im besten* ~ in the prime of life; '**~kraft** *f* virility.

'**mannhaft** manly, stout; '**≈igkeit** *f* manliness; courage.

mannig|fach ['maniç-], '**~faltig** manifold, various; '**≈faltigkeit** *f* variety, diversity.

männlich ['mɛnliç] male (*a. zo.*, ⊕); masculine (*a. gr. u. fig.*); *fig.* manly; '**≈keit** *f* manhood; manliness; '**≈keitswahn** *m* male chauvinism.

'**Mannsbild** F *n* male, man.

'**Mannschaft** *f* (16) men *pl.*; ⚓, ✈, ⚔ crew; *Sport u. fig.*: team; ⚔ *die* ~*en pl.* the ranks; '**~sführer** *m*, '**~skapitän** *m Sport*: (team) captain; '**~sgeist** *m* team-spirit; '**~skamerad** *m* team mate.

'**manns|hoch** (as) tall as a man; '**≈leute** *pl.* men(folk *sg.*); '**~toll** man-crazy.

'**Mannweib** *n* mannish woman, amazon.

Manometer [mano'me:tər] *n* (7) manometer.

Manö|ver [ma'nø:vər] *n* (7), **≈vrieren** [~nø'vri:rən] manœuvre, *Am. mst* maneuver; **≈'vrierfähig** manœuvrable, *Am. mst* maneuverable; **≈'vrier-unfähig** disabled.

Mansarde [man'zardə] *f* (15) attic; **~nfenster** *n* dormer-window.

mansch|en F ['manʃən] (27) dabble, splash; **≈e'rei** *f* (16) dabbling, mess.

Manschette [man'ʃɛtə] *f* (15) cuff; ⊕ sleeve; F ~*n haben vor* (*dat.*) be afraid of; **~nknopf** *m* cuff-link; *angenäht*: sleeve-button.

Mantel ['mantəl] *m* (7¹) (*Herren≈*) overcoat; (*Damen≈*) coat; *bsd. leichter*: topcoat; *weiter, ärmelloser*: (*a. fig.*) cloak, *für Damen*: mantle (*a.* ⚘, △, *zo.*); ⊕ case, jacket; *mot.*, *Fahrrad*: cover; *fig. den* ~ *nach dem Winde hängen* trim one's sails to the wind; '**~tarif** *m* skeleton (*od.* basic tariff) agreement.

Manu|al ♪ [manu'ɑ:l] *n* (3¹) manual; **≈ell** [~'ɛl] manual.

Manufaktur [~fak'tu:r] *f* manufacture; (*Fabrik*) manufactory; **~waren** *f/pl.* manufactured goods.

Manuskript [~'skript] *n* (3) manuscript (*abbr.* MS.); *typ.* copy.

Mappe ['mapə] *f* (15) portfolio, briefcase; (*Aktendeckel, Schnellhefter*) folder; *s. a. Sammel≈, Schreib≈, Schul≈.*

Mär(**e**) ['mɛ:rə] *f* (15) tale; (*Kunde*) tidings *pl.*

Märchen ['~çən] *n* (6) fairy-tale; *fig.* story; '**~buch** *n* book of fairy-tales; '**≈haft** fabulous.

Marder ['mardər] *m* (7) marten.

Margarine [marga'ri:nə] *f* (15) margarine.

Marien|bild [ma'ri:ən-] *n* image of the Virgin; **~fest** *n* Lady Day; **~käfer** *m* lady-bird, *Am. a.* ladybug; **~kult** *m* Mariolatry.

Marihuana [marihu'ɑ:na] *n* (11, *o. pl.*) marijuana, marihuana.

Marine [ma'ri:nə] *f* (15) marine; (*Kriegs≈*) navy; **≈blau** navy-blue; **~flugzeug** *n* naval aircraft; **~-infanterie** *f*, **~truppen** *f/pl.* marines *pl.*; **~-infanterist** *m* marine; **~-offizier** *m* naval officer.

marinieren [mari'ni:rən] pickle.

Marionette [mario'nɛtə] *f* (15) marionette, puppet (*a. fig.*); **~nregierung** *f* puppet government; **~ntheater** *n* puppet-show.

Mark¹ [mark] *n* (3) marrow; ⚘ *u. fig.* pith; *fig. bis ins* ~ to the core; *j-m durch* ~ *und Bein gehen* set a p.'s teeth on edge; **~²** *f* boundary, border(-country); *die* ~ *Brandenburg* the March of Brandenburg;

~³ (16, *pl. nach Zahlen inv.*) *f* (*Münze*) mark.
markant [~'kant] marked; (*hervorragend*) salient, prominent (*a. fig.*).
Marke ['markə] *f* (15) mark; (*Brief*♀, *Steuer*♀) stamp; (*Lebensmittel*♀) coupon; (*Fabrikat*) make; (*Waren*♀) brand; *s. Garderoben*♀, *Spiel*♀; '**~nartikel** *m* proprietary (*od.* patent *od.* branded) article; '**~nname** *m* trade mark, brand.
'**mark-erschütternd** blood-curdling.
Marketender [~'tɛndər] *m* (7), **~in** *f* (16¹) canteen-(wo)man, sutler.
'**Mark|graf** *m* margrave; '**~gräfin** *f* margravine.
mar'kier|en *v/t.* mark (*a. Sport: den Gegner*); (*vortäuschen*) sham, F put on; *v/i.* sham, F put it on; ♀**ung** *f* mark(ing).
'**markig** marrowy; *fig.* pithy.
Markise [~'ki:zə] *f* (15) blind, (window) awning.
Mark|knochen *m* marrow-bone; '**~stein** *m* boundary-stone; *fig.* landmark, milestone.
Markt [markt] *m* (3³) market (*a. Absatz*♀, *Börse*); *s. ~platz*; (*Jahr*♀) fair; *am ~* in the market; *auf den ~ bringen* (put on the) market; '**~analyse** *f* market analysis; '**~bericht** *m* market report; '**~bude** *f* booth, stall.
'**markten** (26) bargain (*um* for).
'**markt|fähig, ~gängig** ['~gɛŋiç] marketable; '♀**fähigkeit** *f*, '♀**gängigkeit** *f* marketability; '♀**flecken** *m* market town, borough; '♀**forscher** *m* market researcher; '♀**forschung** *f* market research; '♀**führer** *m* market leader; '♀**halle** *f* covered market; '♀**lage** *f* market condition(s *pl.*); '♀**lücke** *f* market gap, opening; '♀**platz** *m* market-place; '♀**schreier** *m* quack; (*Reklamemacher*) puffer; '**~schreierisch** ostentatious, loud; '♀**wert** *m* market value; '♀**wirtschaft** *f* market economy; *freie ~* free enterprise (economy); '**~wirtschaftlich** free-market, market-economy.
Marmelade [marmə'lɑ:də] *f* (15) jam; *v. Apfelsinen*: marmalade.
Marmor ['marmɔr] *m* (3¹) marble; ♀**ieren** [~mo'ri:rən] marble, vein; ♀**n** ['~mɔrn] marble; '**~papier** *n* marbled paper; '**~platte** *f* marble slab.
marod|e [ma'ro:də] tired out; (*krank*) ill, sick; ♀**eur** [~ro'dø:r] *m* (3¹) marauder.
Marone [ma'ro:nə] *f* (15) edible chestnut.
Marotte [ma'rɔtə] *f* (15) caprice, whim; (*Steckenpferd*) hobby, fad.
Mars¹ [mars] *m inv.* Mars; **~²** *m* (3²) ⚓ top.
Marsch¹ [marʃ] *m* (3² *u.* ³) march; (*sich*) *in ~ setzen* march off; *fig.* F *j-m den ~ blasen* give a p. a piece of one's mind; *~!* ⚔ forward, march!, F (*schnell*) let's go!; **~²** *f* (16) marsh.
Marschall ['marʃal] *m* (3¹ *u.* ³) marshal; '**~stab** *m* marshal's baton.
'**Marsch|befehl** *m* marching orders *pl.*; '♀**bereit**, '♀**fertig** ready to march; '**~flugkörper** ⚔ *m* cruise missile; ♀**ieren** [~'ʃi:rən] (25, sn) march; '♀**ig** marshy; '**~kolonne** *f* route column; '**~land** *n* marshy country.
'**Mars|segel** ⚓ *n* topsail; **~stenge** ['~ʃtɛŋə] *f* (15) topmast.
Marstall ['marʃtal] *m* royal stables *pl.*
Marter ['martər] *f* (15) torture; '**~gerät** *n* instrument of torture; '♀**n** (29) torture, torment; '**~pfahl** *m* stake.
Märtyrer ['mɛrtyrər] *m* (7), '**~in** *f* martyr; '**~tod** *m* martyr's death; '**~tum** *n* (1, *o. pl.*) martyrdom.
Marx|ismus [mar'ksismus] *m* (16, *o. pl.*) Marxism; **~ist** [~'ksist] *m* (12), ♀**istisch** [~'ksistiʃ] Marxian.
März [mɛrts] *m* (3² *od.* 14) March.
Marzipan [martsi'pɑ:n] *n*, *m* (3¹) marchpane, marzipan.
Masche ['maʃə] *f* mesh; (*Strick*♀ *usw.*) stitch; F *fig.* trick, line, play; (*leichte, einträgliche Sache*) soft thing; '**~ndraht** *m* wire-mesh; '♀**nfest** *Strumpf*: ladderproof, *Am.* runproof; '**~ngitter** *n* wire-netting; '**~ngitterzaun** *m* wire-netting fence.
'**maschig** meshy, meshed.
Maschine [ma'ʃi:nə] *f* (15) machine (*a. Schreib*♀; *a. weitS. Auto, Flugzeug usw.*); (*Dampf*♀ *usw.*) engine.
maschinell [maʃi'nɛl] mechanical; *~ bearbeiten* machine; *~ hergestellt* machine-made.
Ma'schinen|-antrieb *m* machine drive; *mit ~* machine-driven; **~bau** *m* mechanical engineering; **~garn** *n*

machine-spun yarn; **˜geschrieben** typewritten; **~gewehr** ⚔ *n* machine-gun; **~kode** *m Computer*: machine code; **˜mäßig** mechanical, automatic; **~pistole** *f* submachine gun; **~schaden** *m* engine trouble; **~schlosser** *m* engine (*od.* machine) fitter; **~schreiben** *n* typewriting, typing; **~schrift** *f*: *in* ~ typewritten; **~setzer** *typ. m* keyboard operator.

Maschin|erie [maʃinəˈriː] *f* (15) machinery (*a. fig.*); **~ist** [~ˈnist] *m* machinist, engine operator.

Maser [ˈmaːzər] *f* (15) spot, speck (-le); *im Holz*: vein, streak; **ˈ˜ig** veined, streaky; **ˈ~n** ⚕ *pl.* measles; **ˈ˜n** (29) grain; **ˈ~ung** *f im Holz*: graining.

Maske [ˈmaskə] *f* (15) mask (*a. Schutz˜, Fecht˜; a. P.*); *fig. a.* guise; *thea.* make-up; **ˈ~nball** *m* fancy-dress ball; **ˈ~nbildner** *m* make-up artist; **ˈ~nkostüm** *n* fancy dress; **~rade** [~ˈraːdə] *f* (15) masquerade.

maskier|en [masˈkiːrən] (25), **˜ung** *f* mask, disguise.

Maskulinum [ˈmaskuliːnum] *n* (9²) masculine (word *od.* form).

Maß [maːs] **1.** *n* (3²) measure; (*Verhältnis*) proportion; (*Ausdehnung*) dimension; (*Grad*) degree; (*Mäßigung*) moderation; *~e pl. und Gewichte* weights and measures; *nach ~ gemacht* made to measure, *Am.* custom-made; *j-m ~ nehmen* measure a p. (*zu* for); *in hohem ~e* to a high degree, highly; *in dem ~e wie* in the same measure as; *mit ~ und Ziel* in reason; *ohne ~ und Ziel* excessively; *über alle* (*od. die*) *~n* exceedingly; *das ~ ist voll!* that's the last straw!; **2.** *f* (14, *nach Zahlen inv.*) (~ *Bier*) quart; **3.** ˜ *pret. v. messen*.

Massage [maˈsaːʒə] *f* massage.

massakrieren [masaˈkriːrən] massacre.

ˈMaß|-anzug *m* tailor-made suit, *Am.* custom(-made) suit; **ˈ~-arbeit** *f* bespoke work; *fig.* precision work.

Masse [ˈmasə] *f* (15) mass; (*klebrige usw.* ~) substance; (*Paste*) paste; (*Haupt˜*) bulk; (*Volk*) multitude; (*Erbschafts˜, Konkurs˜*) estate; ⚡ (*Erdung*) earth, *Am.* ground; F *e-e ~ ...* a lot (*od.* lots) of ...; *die breite ~* the masses *pl.*; *in ~n herstellen* mass-produce.

ˈMaß-einheit *f* unit of measurement.

ˈMassekabel ⚡ *n* ground cable.

ˈMassen|-arbeitslosigkeit *f* mass unemployment; **ˈ~-artikel** ⚚ *m* wholesale article, mass-produced article; **ˈ~-entlassung** *f* mass dismissals *pl.*; **ˈ~gesellschaft** *f* mass society; **ˈ~grab** *n* common grave; **ˈ˜haft** plenty (of), abundant; *adv. a.* in coarse numbers; **ˈ~karambolage** *f* pile-up; **ˈ~kundgebung** *f* mass rally; **ˈ~medium** *n* mass medium (*pl.* media); **ˈ~mord** *m* wholesale (*od.* mass) murder; **ˈ~produktion** *f* mass production; **ˈ~psychose** *f* mass psychosis; **ˈ~versammlung** *f* mass meeting, rally; **ˈ˜weise** in masses.

Masseu|r [maˈsøːr] *m* (3) masseur; **~se** [~ˈsøːzə] *f* masseuse.

ˈMaß|gabe *f* measure, proportion; *nach ~* (*gen.*) according to; *mit der ~, daß* provided that; **ˈ˜gebend, ˈ˜geblich** authoritative, standard (*work etc.*); (*entscheidend*) decisive; (*zuständig*) competent; (*führend*) leading; ⚚ *~e Beteiligung* controlling interest; **ˈ˜geschneidert** made-to-measure; **ˈ˜halten** observe moderation.

masˈsieren¹ ⚕ massage; ~² ⚔ mass.

ˈmassig bulky, solid.

mäßig [ˈmɛːsiç] moderate; *im Genuß*: frugal; (*mittel~*) middling; (*ziemlich schlecht*) mediocre, poor; **~en** [ˈ~gən] (25) moderate; (*mildern*) mitigate; *Tempo*: slacken; *sich ~* restrain o.s.; *s. gemäßigt*; **ˈ˜keit** *f* moderation; temperance; frugality; mediocre (*od.* poor) quality; **ˈ˜ung** *f* moderation; mitigation; restraint.

massiv [maˈsiːf] massive (*a. fig.*); ˜ *geol. n* massif; **˜gold** *n* solid gold.

ˈMaß|krug *m* (beer) mug, stein; **~ˈlieb(chen)** ⚘ *n* daisy; **ˈ˜los** (*unmäßig*) immoderate; (*übertrieben*) excessive; (*überspannt*) extravagant; **ˈ~losigkeit** *f* immoderateness; excess; extravagance; **ˈ~nahme** *f*, **ˈ~regel** *f* measure; *~n ergreifen od. treffen* take measures *od.* steps; **ˈ˜regeln** (29) reprimand, inflict disciplinary punishment on; **ˈ~schneider** *m* bespoke tailor, *Am.* custom tailor; **ˈ~stab** *m* measure; *auf Karten usw.*: scale; *fig.* standard; *in großem (kleinem)* ~ on a large (small) scale; e-n ~ *anlegen an (acc.)* apply a standard to; '2**voll** moderate.

Mast[1] [mast] *m* (3[2] *u.* 5[1]), (⚓ *a.* '~**baum** *m*) mast; (*Trage*2) pylon; *tel.* pole.

Mast[2] *f* (16) mast, food; '~**darm** *m* rectum.

mästen ['mɛstən] (26) feed, fatten; *sich* ~ *an (dat.)* batten on.

'**Mast|korb** *m* top, masthead; '~**-ochse** *m* fattened ox; '~**vieh** *n* fattened cattle.

Mater *typ.* ['mɑːtər] *f* (15) matrix.

Material [mater'jɑːl] *n* (8[2]) material (*a. fig.*); ~**disposition** *f* material management; ~**fehler** *m* fault in (the) material; ~**ismus** [~ja'lismus] *m* (16, *o. pl.*) materialism; ~**ist** [~'list] *m* (12) materialist; 2**istisch** [~'listiʃ] materialistic; ~**kosten** *pl.* cost *sg.* of materials; ~**lager** *n* stock of materials.

Mater|ie [~'teːrjə] *f* (15) matter; *fig. a.* subject; 2**iell** [~ter'jɛl] material; (*geldlich*) financial; (~ *eingestellt*) materialistic.

Mathe F ['matə] *f* (16, *o. pl.*) maths, *Am.* math; ~**matik** [matema'tiːk] *f* (16) mathematics *sg.*; ~**matiker** [~'mɑːtikər] *m* (7) mathematician; 2'**matisch** mathematical.

Matinee *thea.* [mati'neː] *f* (15) matinée, morning performance.

Matjeshering ['matjəsheːriŋ] *m* white herring, matie.

Matratze [ma'tratsə] *f* (15) mattress.

Mätresse [mɛ'trɛsə] *f* (15) (kept) mistress.

Matrikel [ma'triːkəl] *f* (15) register, roll.

Matrize [~'triːtsə] *f* (15) matrix, die; (*Schablone u. zum Maschinenschreiben*) stencil.

Matrone [~'troːnə] *f* (15) matron.

Matrose [~'troːzə] *m* (13) sailor, seaman; ~**n-anzug** *m* sailor suit.

Matsch [matʃ] *m* (3[2]) (*Brei*) pulp, squash; (*Schlamm*) mud, slush; '2**ig** pulpy; muddy, slushy.

matt [mat] weak, faint, feeble; (*schlaff*) limp; *Stimme*: faint; *Auge, Licht*: dim; *Farbe, Licht*, ⚕ *Börse, Stil*: dull; *Gold*: dead; *bsd. phot.* mat(t); *Kugel*: spent; *Schach*: mate; ⚡ ~*e Birne* frosted bulb; *Schach*: ~ *setzen* (check)mate.

Matte ['matə] *f* (15) mat; (*Wiese*) meadow.

'**Matt|glas** *n* ground (*od.* frosted) glass; '~**gold** *n* dead gold; '~**heit** *f* faintness; dul(l)ness; 2**ieren** [~'tiːrən] mat; *Glas*: frost; '~**igkeit** *f* (16) exhaustion; '~**scheibe** *f phot.* ground glass; *TV* screen; F *fig.* ~ *haben* be in a daze.

Matur(**um**) [ma'tuːr(um)] *n* (3[1], *o. pl.*) *s. Abitur.*

Mätzchen ['mɛtsçən] F *n/pl.* (6) tricks; (*Unnötiges*) frills; ⊕ gimcracks; ~ *machen* play tricks.

Mauer ['mauər] *f* (15) wall; '~**blümchen** *fig. n* wallflower; '2**n** (29) *v/i.* make a wall, lay bricks; *Sport*: stonewall; *v/t.* build (in stone *od.* brick); '~**segler** *orn. m* (common) swift; '~**stein** *m*, '~**ziegel** *m* brick; '~**werk** *n* masonry.

Mauke *vet.* ['maukə] *f* (15) malanders *pl.*

Maul [maul] *n* mouth; P *das* ~ *halten* hold one's tongue, shut up; *s. a. Mund*; '~**-affe** F *m* gaper; ~*n feilhalten* stand gaping; '~**beere** *f* mulberry.

Mäulchen ['mɔʏlçən] *n* (6) little mouth.

maulen ['maulən] (25) grumble.

'**Maul|-esel** *m* mule; '2**faul** F too lazy to speak; '~**held** *m* braggart; '~**korb** *m* muzzle; '~**schelle** *f* slap; '~**sperre** *f* lock-jaw; '~**tier** *n* mule; '~**- und** '**Klauenseuche** *vet. f* foot-and-mouth disease; '~**werk** F *n* (*gutes* ~ gift of the) gab; '~**wurf** *m* mole; '~**wurfs-haufen** *m* mole-hill.

Maurer ['maurər] *m* (7) bricklayer, mason; '~**kelle** *f* trowel; '~**meister** *m* master mason; '~**polier** *m* bricklayer's foreman.

'**maurisch** Moorish.

Maus [maus] *f* (14[1]) mouse (*pl.* mice).

Mäus-chen ['mɔʏsçən] *n* (6) little mouse; F *fig.* (*Schatz*) darling, pet; '2'**still** stockstill; quite hushed.

mauscheln ['mauʃəln] (29) talk sheeny; *fig.* jabber.

'**Mausefalle** *f* mousetrap; *fig.* death-trap.

mausen ['mauzən] (27) *v/i.* catch mice; *v/t. u. v/i.* F filch, steal.

Mauser ['mauzər] *f* (15) mo(u)lt(-ing); '2**n** (29) (*a. sich*) mo(u)lt.

ˈ**mausetot** quite dead, as dead as mutton.

mausig F [ˈ~ziç]: *sich ~ machen* put on airs.

Maut [maut] *f* (16), ˈ**~gebühr** *f* toll (-charge); ˈ**~stelle** *f* toll-gate; ˈ**~straße** *f* toll-road, *Am.* turnpike.

maximal [maksiˈmɑːl] maximum; *adv.* at the most; *s. a.* *Höchst...*; **2beschleunigung** *f* peak acceleration.

Maxime [maˈksiːmə] *f* (15) maxim.

Maximum [ˈmaksimum] *n* (9[2]) maximum.

Mayonnaise [majɔˈnɛːzə] *f* (15) mayonnaise.

Mäzen [mɛˈtseːn] *m* (3[1]) patron, sponsor.

Mechanik [meˈçɑːnik] *f* (16) mechanics *sg.*; (*Triebwerk*) mechanism; **~er** *m* (7) mechanic(ian).

meˈchan|isch mechanical (*a. fig.*); **~isieren** [~çaniˈziːrən] mechanize; **2ismus** [~ˈnismus] *m* (16[1]) mechanism.

Mecker|er F [ˈmɛkərər] *m* (7) grumbler; ˈ**2n** (29) bleat; F *fig.* grumble, *sl.* grouse, *Am.* F gripe.

Medaill|e [meˈdaljə] *f* (15) medal; **~on** [~ˈjɔ̃] *n* (11) (*~bild usw.*) medallion; (*Schmuckstück*) locket.

Medien [ˈmeːdiən] *n/pl.* (9) media; ˈ**~technologie** *f* media technology; ˈ**~verbund** *m* multi-media system.

Medikament [medikaˈmɛnt] *n* (3) medicament, medicine.

Mediothek [medioˈteːk] *f* (16) media library.

Medium [ˈmeːdium] *n* (9) medium.

Medizin [mediˈtsiːn] *f* (16) *allg.* medicine; (*Arznei*) *a.* medicament; **~er** *m* (7) medical student; (*Arzt*) doctor; **2isch** [~ˈtsiːniʃ] medical; (*arzneilich usw.*) medicinal; *Seife usw.*: medicated.

Meer [meːr] *n* (3) sea, ocean; ˈ**~busen** *m* gulf, bay; ˈ**~-enge** *f* straits *pl.*; ˈ**~esbiologe** *m* marine biologist; ˈ**~esbiologie** *f* marine biology; ˈ**~esfrüchte** *f/pl.* seafood *sg.*; ˈ**~esgrund** *m* sea-bed; ˈ**~eshöhe** *f*, ˈ**~esspiegel** *m* sea level; ˈ**~esstille** *f* calm (at sea); ˈ**~esverschmutzung** *f* pollution of the sea; ˈ**~grün** *n* sea-green; ˈ**~katze** *f* green monkey; ˈ**~rettich** *m* horse-radish; ˈ**~schaum** *m* meerschaum; ˈ**~schwein** *n* porpoise; ˈ**~schweinchen** *n* guinea-pig; ˈ**~-ungeheuer** *n* sea-monster; ˈ**~wasser** *n* sea-water; ˈ**~weib** *n* mermaid.

Mega|hertz [megaˈhɛrts] *n inv.* megacycles *pl.* per second (*abbr.* Mc/s); **~phon** [~ˈfoːn] *n* (3[1]) megaphone.

Mehl [meːl] *n* (3) flour; *grobes*: meal; (*Staub*) dust; ˈ**~brei** *m* pap; ˈ**2ig** mealy, farinaceous; ˈ**~kloß** *m* dumpling; ˈ**~sack** *m* flour-bag; **~schwitze** [ˈ~ʃvitsə] *f* (15) roux; ˈ**~speise** *f* farinaceous food; *süß*: sweet dish, pudding; ˈ**~suppe** *f* gruel; ˈ**~tau** *m* mildew, blight; ˈ**~wurm** *m* meal-worm.

mehr [meːr] **1.** (*comp. v. viel*) more; *nicht ~* no more, *zeitlich a.*: no (*od.* not any) longer; *nie ~* never again; *s. immer*; *~ als* more than, *ein gewisses Maß* in excess of; *~ und ~* more and more; *~ oder weniger* more or less; *nicht ~, nicht minder* neither more nor less; *ich habe niemand* (*nichts*) *~* I have no one (nothing) left; *s. um*; **2.** *n* (*Zuwachs*) increase; (*Überschuß*) (sur)plus; ˈ**2-arbeit** *f* extra work; *im Betrieb*: overtime; ˈ**2-ausgabe** *f* additional expenditure; ˈ**2betrag** *m* surplus; (*Zuschlag*) extra charge; ˈ**~deutig** ambiguous; ˈ**2einnahme** *f* additional receipts.

ˈ**mehr|en** (25) (*a. sich*) augment, increase; ˈ**~ere** several; ˈ**2eres** *n* several things *pl.*; sundries *pl.*; ˈ**~erlei** various, diverse; ˈ**~fach** manifold; (*wiederholt*) repeated; (*a.* ⊕, ⚡) multiple; *adv.* repeatedly, several times; ˈ**2fachbelichtung** *f* multiple exposure; ˈ**2fachsprengkopf** *m* multiple warhead; ˈ**2fahrtenkarte** *f* carnet, multiple-trip ticket; ˈ**2farbendruck** *m* multicolo(u)r print(ing); ˈ**2gebot** *n* higher bid; ˈ**2gewicht** *n* excess weight; ˈ**2heit** *f* (*a. parl.*) majority; ˈ**2heitsbeschluß** *m*: *durch ~* by a majority of votes, *Am.* by a plurality; ˈ**2kosten** *pl.* additional cost *sg.*; (*Zuschlag*) extra charges; **~malig** [ˈ~mɑːliç] repeated; **~mals** [ˈ~mɑːls] several times; **~seitig** [ˈ~zaɪtiç] ⩓ polygonal; *pol.* multilateral; **~silbig** [ˈ~zilbiç] polysyllabic; **~sprachig** [ˈ~ʃprɑːxiç] polyglot; **~stimmig** ♪ [ˈ~ʃtimiç] (arranged) for several voices; *~er Gesang* part-song; **~stöckig** [ˈ~ʃtœkiç] multi-storey; **~stufig** [ˈ~ʃtuːfiç] *Rakete*: multi-stage; ˈ**2ung** *f* increase; **~tägig** [ˈ~tɛːgiç] of several days; ˈ**2-**

verbrauch *m* excess consumption; '**⁓wert** *m* surplus value; '**⁓wertsteuer** *f* value-added tax; '**⁓zahl** *f* majority; *gr.* plural (number); '**⁓zweck...** general-purpose, multi-purpose.

meiden ['maɪdən] (30) avoid, shun.

Meier ['maɪər] *m* (7) dairy-farmer; **⁓ei** [⁓'raɪ] *f*, '**⁓hof** *m* dairy-farm.

Meile ['maɪlə] *f* (15) mile; '**⁓nstein** *m* milestone (*a. fig.*); '**⁓nweit** (extending) for miles; *fig.* very far.

Meiler ['maɪlər] *m* (7) charcoal-pile; (*Atom⁓*) (atomic) pile.

mein [maɪn] (20) my; *der, die, das ⁓e, meinige* mine; *das ⁓ und Dein* mine and thine; *die ⁓en pl.* my people *od.* family *sg.*

Mein-eid ['maɪnʔaɪt] *m* (3) perjury; *e-n ⁓ leisten* commit perjury; **⁓ig** ['⁓diç] perjured; *⁓ werden* perjure o.s.

meinen ['maɪnən] (25) think, believe; (*beabsichtigen; sagen wollen*) mean; (*sagen*) say; *⁓ Sie das ernst?* do you (really) mean it?; *es ehrlich* (*od. gut*) *⁓* mean well.

'**meiner a**) of me; **b**) mine; **⁓seits** ['⁓zaɪts] for my part; *ganz ⁓!* F same here!

meinesgleichen ['⁓əs'glaɪçən] people like me, the like(s) of me.

meinet|halben ['⁓ət'halbən] for my sake, in (*od.* on) my behalf; '**⁓'wegen** *s. meinethalben*; (*ich habe nichts dagegen*) I don't mind.

meinige ['⁓igə] (18b): *der, die, das ⁓* mine; *die ⁓n pl.* my family *sg.*

'**Meinung** *f* opinion, view; *die öffentliche ⁓* (the) public opinion; *meiner ⁓ nach* to my mind, in my opinion; *j-m* (*gehörig*) *die ⁓ sagen* give a p. a piece of one's mind; *mit j-m e-r ⁓ sein* agree with a p.; '**⁓s-äußerung** *f* expression of opinion; '**⁓s-austausch** *m* exchange of views; '**⁓sbefragung** *f*, '**⁓s-umfrage** *f* opinion poll; '**⁓sbildend** opinion-forming; '**⁓sbildner** *m* opinion leader (*od.* maker); '**⁓sforscher** *m* public opinion pollster; '**⁓sforschung** *f* opinion research; '**⁓sfreiheit** *f* freedom of thought; '**⁓sverschiedenheit** *f* difference (of opinion), disagreement.

Meise ['maɪzə] *f* (15) titmouse.

Meißel ['maɪsəl] *m* (7), '**⁓n** (29) chisel.

meist [maɪst] (18, *sup. v. viel*) most; *die ⁓en pl.* most people; *das ⁓e* the most, the greater (*od.* best) part; *am ⁓en* most; *⁓enteils, ⁓ens* mostly, generally; (*gewöhnlich*) usually; '**⁓begünstigungs...** preferential; most favo(u)red nation *clause usw.*; '**⁓bietend** bidding highest; **⁓bietende** ['⁓bi:təndə] *m* (18) highest bidder.

Meister ['maɪstər] *m* (7) master (*a. fig.*); *im Betrieb*: foreman; *Sport*: champion; '**⁓haft**, '**⁓lich** masterly; *adv.* brilliantly; '**⁓in** *f* mistress; master's wife; *Sport*: champion(ess); '**⁓leistung** *f* superb performance; '**⁓n** (29) master (*a. fig. Gefühle, Lage, Sprache usw.*); '**⁓prüfung** *f* trade examination; '**⁓schaft** *f* (16) mastery; *Sport*: championship; '**⁓schaftsspiel** *n* league match; '**⁓schütze** *m* crack shot; '**⁓stück** *n*, '**⁓werk** *n* masterpiece; '**⁓titel** *m Sport*: title.

'**Meistgebot** *n* highest bid.

Melanch|olie [melaŋko'li:] *f* (15), **⁓olisch** [⁓'ko:liʃ] melancholy.

'**Melde|-amt** *n* registration office; '**⁓fahrer** *m* dispatch-rider; **⁓gänger** ⚔ ['⁓gɛŋər] *m* messenger; '**⁓hund** *m* messenger dog; '**⁓liste** *f Sport*: list of entries; '**⁓n** (26) *v/t.* announce; (*berichten*) report; *j-m et. ⁓* inform a p. of a th., *amtlich*: notify a th. to a p.; *dienstlich*: report a th. to a p.; *sich ⁓ dienstlich*: report (*bei* to; *zu* for); *teleph.* answer; *fig.* make itself felt; *sich ⁓ zu* apply for, *freiwillig*: volunteer for; *zum Examen usw.*: enter (one's name) for; *sich ⁓ lassen* send in one's name; *sich auf ein Inserat ⁓* answer an ad(vertisement); *s. krank, Wort*; *v/i. Sport*: enter (*zu* for); '**⁓pflichtig** ⚕ notifiable.

'**Meldung** *f* announcement; (*Nachricht*) advice, information, notification; (*dienstliche ⁓, Zeitungs⁓*) report; (*Funk⁓ usw.*) message; (*Bewerbung*) application; *Sport*: entry.

meliert [me'li:rt] mottled; *Haar*: greying.

Melisse ⚘ [me'lisə] *f* (15) balm-mint; **⁓ngeist** *m* Carmelite water.

melk|en ['mɛlkən] (30) milk; '**⁓maschine** *f* milking machine.

Melod|ie [melo'di:] *f* (15) tune,

melody, air; **♀isch** [~ˈloːdiʃ] melodious.

Melone [meˈloːnə] *f* (15) melon; F (*steifer Hut*) bowler, *Am.* derby.

Meltau [ˈmeːltaʊ] *m* (3) mildew.

Membran(e) [mɛmˈbrɑːn(ə)] *f* (16) membrane; ⊕ diaphragm.

Memme [ˈmɛmə] *f* (15) coward.

Memoiren [memoˈɑːrən] *n/pl.* memoirs.

Memorandum [memoˈrandum] *n* (9[2]) memorandum; (*Notiz*) *mst* memo.

memorieren [memoˈriːrən] memorize.

Menagerie [menaʒəˈriː] *f* (15) menagerie.

Menge [ˈmɛŋə] *f* (15) quantity; amount; ⅍ set; (*Vielheit*) multitude; (*Menschen♀*) crowd; *in großer* ~ in abundance, *v. Menschen u. Tieren*: in crowds; *e-e* ~ *Geld* plenty (*od.* F lots) of money; *e-e* ~ *Bücher* a great many (F a lot of) books; ˈ**♀n** (25) mingle, mix (*a. sich*; *unter acc.* with); *sich* ~ *in* (*acc.*) meddle with; ˈ**~nlehre** ⅍ *f* set theory; ˈ**♀nmäßig** quantitative(ly *adv.*); ˈ**~nrabatt** *m* quantity discount.

Mennig [ˈmɛniç] *m* (3), ˈ**~e** *f* minium, red lead.

Mensch [mɛnʃ] *m* (12) human being, (*a. der* ~ *als Gattung*) man; *einzelner*: person; (*Kerl*) fellow; *die* ~*en pl.* people *pl.*, the world *sg.*, *s.* ~*heit*; *kein* ~ nobody; F ~*!* man!, oh boy!

ˈ**Menschen|-affe** *m* anthropoid ape; ˈ**~-alter** *n* generation, age; ˈ**~feind (-in** *f*) *m* misanthropist; ˈ**~fresser** *m* (7) cannibal; ˈ**~freund(in** *f*) *m* philanthropist, humanitarian; ˈ**♀-freundlich** philanthropic, humanitarian; *seit* ˈ**~gedenken** *n* from time immemorial; within the memory of man; ˈ**~geschlecht** *n* human race, mankind; *in* ˈ**~gestalt** *f* in human shape; ˈ**~handel** *m* slave-trade; ˈ**~haß** *m* misanthropy; ˈ**~jagd** *f* manhunt; ˈ**~kenner(in** *f*) *m* judge of men; ˈ**~kenntnis** *f* knowledge of human nature; ˈ**~kunde** *f* anthropology; ˈ**~leben** *n* (human) life; ˈ**♀leer** deserted; ˈ**~liebe** *f* philanthropy; ˈ**~material** *n* manpower, human stock; ˈ**♀möglich** humanly possible; ˈ**~pflicht** *f* duty of (*od.* as) a human being; ˈ**~raub** *m* kidnap(p)ing; ˈ**~rechte** *n/pl.* human rights; ˈ**~rechtler(in** *f*) *m* human rights activist; ˈ**~rechtsbewegung** *f* human rights movement; ˈ**♀scheu** shy, unsociable; ˈ**~schinder** *m* slave-driver; ˈ**~schlag** *m* race (of men); ˈ**~seele** *f* human soul; *keine* ~ not a living soul; ˈ**~sˈkind!** goodness!, good heavens!; ˈ**~sohn** *m* Son of Man; ˈ**♀ˈ-unwürdig** degrading; ˈ**~verstand** *m*: *gesunder* ~ common sense; ˈ**~würde** *f* man's dignity.

ˈ**Menschheit** *f* mankind, humanity, human race.

ˈ**menschlich** human; (*human*) humane; ˈ**♀keit** *f* human nature; (*Humanität*) humanity, humaneness.

Menschwerdung [ˈ~veːrduŋ] *f* [incarnation.]

Menstru|ation [mɛnstruaˈtsjoːn] *f* menstruation; **♀-ieren** [~ˈiːrən] menstruate.

Mensur [mɛnˈzuːr] *f* (16) ⚗ measure; (*Studenten♀*) students' duel.

Mentalität [mɛntaliˈtɛːt] *f* (16) mentality.

Menthol [mɛnˈtoːl] *n* (3[1]) menthol.

Menü [məˈnyː] *n* (11) set meal, *mittags*: set lunch.

Menuett [menuˈɛt] *n* (3) minuet.

Mergel [ˈmɛrgəl] *m* (7) marl.

Meridi|an [meriˈdjɑːn] *m* (3[1]) meridian; **♀onal** [~djoˈnɑːl] meridional.

Meringe [meˈriŋgə] *f* (15) meringue.

merk|bar [ˈmɛrkbɑːr] perceptible, noticeable; ˈ**♀blatt** *n* (instructional) leaflet; ˈ**♀buch** *n* note-book; ˈ**~en** (25) notice; (*spüren*) feel, sense; (*erkennen*) realize; (*gewahr sein, werden*) be(come) aware of; *sich et.* ~ retain (*od.* remember) a th.; *das werde ich mir* ~ I will bear that in mind; ~ *auf* (*acc.*) pay attention to; ~ *lassen* show, betray; *nichts* ~ *lassen* not to show one's feelings; ˈ**~lich** *s. merkbar*; (*beträchtlich*) considerable; (*deutlich*) marked; ˈ**♀mal** *n* sign, mark; (*Eigentümlichkeit*) characteristic, feature; *besondere* ~*e pl.* peculiarities, *Am.* marks.

ˈ**merkwürdig** (*auffallend*) remarkable, noteworthy; (*seltsam*) odd, curious, strange; **~erweise** [ˈ~igərˈvaɪzə] strange to say, oddly enough; ˈ**♀keit** *f* remarkableness; (*Gegenstand*) curiosity; (*das Seltsame*) oddness.

'**Merk|zeichen** *n* mark; '**~zettel** *m* note, memo.

meschugge [me'ʃugə] F crazy, mad.

Mesner ['mɛsnər] *m* (7) sexton.

meßbar ['mɛsbɑːr] measurable.

'**Meß|becher** *m* measuring cup; ⚗ beaker; '**~buch** *n* missal; '**~diener** *m* acolyte.

Messe ['mɛsə] *f* (15) fair; *eccl.* mass; *s. lesen*; ⚔, ⚓ mess (hall).

messen ['mɛsən] (30) measure (*a. groß usw. sein*; *a. mit Blicken*); *sich ~ mit* compete (*od.* grapple) with, *geistig*: match wits with; *sich nicht ~ können mit P.*: be no match for, *S.*: not to compare with.

Messer[1] ['mɛsər] *n* (7) knife; (*Rasier*≈) razor; ⚕ scalpel; *fig. bis aufs ~* to the knife; *auf des ~s Schneide stehen* be on a razor's edge; *s. Kehle*; **~**[2] *m* (7) (*Gas*≈ *usw.*) meter; '**~held** *m* cut-throat; '**~klinge** *f* knife-blade; '**~rücken** *m* back of a knife; '**≈scharf** razor-sharp (*a. fig.*); '**~schmied** *m* cutler; '**~schneide** *f* edge of a knife; **~stecherei** [~ʃtɛçə'raɪ] knife-battle; '**~stich** *m* thrust (*od.* stab) with a knife.

'**Meßgewand** *n* chasuble.

Messias [mɛ'siːas] *m inv.* Messiah.

Messing ['mɛsiŋ] *n* (3[1]) brass; '**~blech** *n* sheet-brass; '**~draht** *m* brass wire; '**~rohr** *n* brass tube.

'**Meß|-instrument** *n* measuring instrument; '**~latte** *f* surveyor's (*od.* stadia) rod; '**~-opfer** *n* (sacrifice of the) mass; '**~rute** *f* surveyor's rod; '**~tisch** *m* plane table; '**~tischblatt** *n* topographic map.

Messung ['mɛsuŋ] *f* (15) measurement; (*Ablesung*) reading.

Mestize [mɛ'stiːtsə] *m* (12) mestizo.

Met [meːt] *m* (3) mead.

Metall [me'tal] *n* (3[1]) metal; **~arbeiter** *m* metal worker; **~baukasten** *m* meccano; **≈en**, **≈isch** metallic; **~geld** *n* specie, coins *pl.*; **~glanz** *m* metallic lustre; **≈haltig** metalliferous; **≈ic(farben)** [me'talik(-)] metallic; **~-industrie** *f* metal industry; **~säge** *f* hacksaw; **≈verarbeitend** metal-working; **~verbindung** *f* metallic compound; **~vorrat** *m der Bank*: bullion reserve; **~waren** *f/pl.* hardware *sg.*

Metamorphose [metamɔr'foːzə] *f* (15) metamorphosis.

Metapher [me'tafər] *f* (15) metaphor.

Meta|phy'sik *f* metaphysics *pl.*, *oft sg.*; **≈'physisch** metaphysical.

Meteor [mete'ʔoːr] *n*, *m* (3[1]) meteor; **~-eisen** *n* meteoric iron; **~olog(e)** [~ʔoro'loːk, ~gə] *m* (12 [13]) meteorologist; **~ologie** [~lo'giː] *f* (15) meteorology; **≈ologisch** [~'loːgiʃ] meteorologic(al); **~stein** [~'ʔoːr-] *m* meteoric stone, meteorite.

Meter ['meːtər] *n u. m* (7) met|re, *Am.* -er; '**~maß** *n* metre rule; (*Bandmaß*) tape-measure; '**~ware** *f* goods *pl.* sold by the metre.

Method|e [me'toːdə] *f* (15) method; **≈isch** methodical; **~ist** [~to'dist] *m* (12) methodist.

Methan [me'tɑːn] *n* (3[1], *o. pl.*) methane.

Methyl-alkohol [me'tyːlʔalkohol] *m* methyl alcohol.

Metr|ik ['meːtrik] *f* (16) metrics *pl.*, prosody; **≈isch** metrical.

Metronom [metro'noːm] *n* (3[1]) metronome.

Metropole [metro'poːlə] *f* (15) metropolis.

Mette ['mɛtə] *f* (15) matins *pl.*

Mettwurst ['mɛtvurst] *f* Bologna sausage.

Metz|elei [mɛtsə'laɪ] *f* (16) slaughter; '**≈eln** (29) slaughter, butcher; **~ger** ['~gər] *m* (7) butcher.

Meuchel|mord ['mɔʏçəl-] *m* assassination; '**~mörder(in** *f*) *m* assassin; '**≈n** (29) assassinate.

meuch|lerisch ['~ləriʃ] treacherous; **~lings** ['~liŋs] treacherously.

Meute ['mɔʏtə] *f* (15) pack of hounds; *fig.* gang; **~rei** [~'raɪ] *f* (16) mutiny; '**~rer** *m* (7) mutineer; '**≈rn** (29) mutiny; rebel (*a. fig.*); '**≈rnd** mutinous.

Mexikan|er [mɛksi'kɑːnər] *m* (7), **~erin** *f* (16[1]), **≈isch** Mexican.

miau [mi'aʊ], **~en** (25) mew.

mich [miç] (*s. ich* 19) me; *~ selbst* myself.

mied [miːt] *pret. v. meiden.*

Mieder ['miːdər] *n* (7) bodice; '**~höschen** *n* panty girdle; '**~waren** *f/pl.* corsetry *sg.*, *Am.* foundation garments.

Mief F [miːf] *m* (3, *o. pl.*) fug, pong; (*Gestank*) stink, stench; '**≈en** F pong.

Miene ['miːnə] *f* (15) countenance, air; (*Gesicht*) face; *~ machen et. zu tun* offer to do; *e-e ernste ~ auf-*

setzen look stern; *keine ~ verziehen* not to flinch; *s. gut*; '**~nspiel** *n*, '**~nsprache** *f* play of features.

mies [mi:s] F miserable, bad, F awful; **2macher** ['mi:smaxər] *m* alarmist; '**2muschel** *f* mussel.

Miet|-auto ['mi:t-] *n* hired car; '**~e**¹ *f* (15) (*Wohnungs2*) rent; *weitS*. hire; (*Mietsumme*) rental; *in ~ nehmen* hire, rent; *zur ~ wohnen* live in lodgings; **~e**² ⚒ *f* (*Heu2*, *Korn2*) stack, shock, rick; (*Kartoffel2 usw.*) clamp; '**2en** (26) rent; *weitS*. hire; *Schiff usw.*: charter; '**~er** *m* (7), '**~erin** *f* tenant; (*Unter2*) lodger; ⚖ lessee; *v. Sachen*: hirer; '**~erschaft** *f* tenantry; '**~erschutz** *m* (legal) protection of tenants; '**~-ertrag** *m* rental; '**2frei** rent-free; '**~pferd** *n* hired horse; '**~shaus** *n* block of flats, *Am*. apartment house; '**~skaserne** *f* tenement house; '**~spiegel** *m* rent guidelines *pl*.; '**~verhältnis** *n* tenancy; '**~vertrag** *m* lease; '**~wagen** *m* hired car; '**~wagenverleih** *m* car-hire service; '**2weise** on hire; '**~wert** *m* rental value; '**~wohnung** *f* rented flat, *Am*. rental apartment; '**~zins** *m* rent.

Miez(e) F ['mi:ts(ə)] *f* (15) puss, pussy (-cat).

Migräne [mi'grɛ:nə] *f* (15) migraine.

Mikrob|e [mi'kro:bə] *f* (15) microbe; **2isch** microbial.

Mikro|-elektronik ['mi:kro-] *f* microelectronics *sg*.; '**~film** *m* microfilm.

Mikroko'pie [mikro-] *f* microcopy.

Mikrolaufwerk ['mi:kro-] *n Computer*: micro drive.

Mikro'meter [mikro-] *n* micrometer.

Mikro-orga'nismus [mikro-] *m* micro-organism.

Mikrophon [mikro'fo:n] *n* (3¹) microphone, F mike.

Mikroprozessor ['mi:kroprotsɛsɔr] *m* (8¹) microprocessor.

Mikroskop [~'sko:p] *n* (3¹) microscope; **2isch** (*a. ~ klein*) microscopic(ally *adv*.).

Mikrowelle ['mi:kro-] *f* microwave; '**~nherd** *m* microwave oven.

Milbe ['milbə] *f* (15) mite.

Milch [milç] *f* (16) milk; (*Fisch2*) milt, soft roe; '**~bar** *f* milk bar; '**~bart** *m fig*. milksop; '**~brot** *n*, '**~brötchen** *n* (French) roll; '**~bruder** *m* foster-brother; '**~drüse** *f* lacteal gland; '**~er** *m* (7) milter, soft-roe(d) fish; '**~geschäft** *n* dairy, creamery; '**~glas** *n* opalescent (*od*. frosted) glass; '**2ig** milky; '**~kaffee** *m* coffee with milk; '**~kuh** *f* milch cow; '**~kur** *f* milk diet; '**~mädchen** *n* milkmaid; '**~mann** *m* milkman, dairyman; '**~'mixgetränk** *n* milk shake; '**~ner** *m s. Milcher*; '**~pulver** *n* powdered milk; '**~reis** *m* rice-pudding; '**~säure** ⚗ *f* lactic acid; '**~schorf** ⚕ *m* milk crust; '**~speise** *f* milk-food; '**~straße** *ast*. *f* Milky Way, Galaxy; '**~suppe** *f* milk-soup; '**~vieh** *n* dairy cattle; '**~wirtschaft** *f* dairy(-farm); '**~zahn** *m* milk-tooth; '**~zucker** *m* milk sugar, lactose.

mild, **~e**¹ [milt, '~də] *allg*. mild; (*sanft*) gentle, soft; *Wein*: smooth; (*nachsichtig*) indulgent; *Stiftung*: charitable; *Strafe*: mild, lenient; *~e gesagt* to put it mildly.

'**Milde**² *f* (15) mildness *usw*., *s. mild*; *~ walten lassen* be lenient.

milder|n ['~dərn] (29) soften, mitigate; *Schmerz*: soothe, alleviate; (*erleichtern*) relieve; ⚗ correct; *Ausdruck*: qualify; *~de Umstände m/pl*. extenuating circumstances; '**2ung** *f* mitigation; ⚗ correction; '**2ungsgrund** *m* mitigating cause.

'**mild|herzig**, '**~tätig** ['milt-] charitable; '**2herzigkeit** *f* charitableness; '**2tätigkeit** *f* charity.

Milieu [mil'jø:] *n* (11) environment, surroundings *pl*., milieu (*fr*.); **2-bedingt** environmental.

Militär [mili'tɛ:r] (11) **1.** *n* (*o. pl.*) *the* military, soldiery, army; **2.** *m* (11) military man, soldier; *in Zssgn* military; **~-arzt** *m* medical officer, army surgeon; **~-attaché** *m* military attaché; **~bündnis** *n* military alliance; **~dienst** *m* military service; **~diktatur** *f* military dictatorship; **~gericht** *n* military court; **2isch** military; *fig*. martial.

Militarismus [milita'rismus] *m inv*. militarism.

Mili'tär|macht *f* military power; **~musik** *f* military music; **~regierung** *f* military government; **~seelsorge** military religious welfare.

Miliz [mi'li:ts] *f* (16) militia; **~soldat** *m* militiaman.

Milliar|där [miljar'dɛ:r] *m* (3¹) multimillionaire; **~de** [mil'jardə] *f* (15) billion; *in England* † thousand million.

Milli'meter [mili-] *n u. m* millimet|re, *Am.* -er; **~-arbeit** *f* precision work; **~papier** *n* graph paper.

Million [mil'jo:n] *f* (16) million; **~är** [~jo'nɛ:r] *m* (3[1]) millionaire; **2ste(r, s)** [~'jo:nstə] millionth.

Milz [milts] *f* (16) spleen, milt; **'~brand** *m* anthrax; **'~krankheit** *f* splenopathy; **'~stechen** *n* splenalgia.

Mim|e ['mi:mə] *m* (13) mime; **'~ik** *f* (16) mimic art, miming; **'~iker** *m* (7), **'2isch** mimic; **~ikry** ['mimikri] *f* (11[1], *o. pl.*) mimicry.

Mimose [mi'mo:zə] *f* (15) mimosa; **2nhaft** *fig.* oversensitive.

minder ['mindər] (18, *s. gering, wenig*) *adv.* less; *adj.* less(er), smaller; *an Güte*: inferior; (*weniger bedeutend*) minor; *s. mehr*; **'~bemittelt** of moderate means; **'2betrag** *m* deficit, shortage; **'2-einnahme** *f* decrease of receipts; **'2-gewicht** *n* short weight; **'2heit** *f* minority; **'2heitsregierung** *f* minority government; **'~jährig** under age, minor; **2jährige** ['~jɛ:rigə] *m, f* (18) minor; **2jährigkeit** ['~riçkaɪt] *f* minority; **'~n** (29) diminish, lessen; (*herabsetzen*) reduce; **'2ung** *f* diminution; reduction; **'~wertig** inferior; **'2wertigkeitsgefühl** *n* inferiority feeling; **'2wertigkeitskomplex** *m* inferiority complex; **'2zahl** *f* minority.

mindest ['mindəst] (18, *s. minder*) least; (*kleinst*) smallest; *adv.* ~(ens), *zum ~en* at least; *nicht im ~en* not in the least, by no means; **'2...** *mst* minimum; **'2-alter** *n* minimum age; **'2gebot** *n* lowest bid; **'2lohn** *m* minimum wage; **'2maß** *n* minimum; **'2preis** *m* minimum (*od.* bottom *od.* floor) price; **'2zinssatz** *m* minimum interest rate.

Mine ['mi:nə] *f* (15) ⚒ *u.* ⚔ mine; (*Bleistift2*) lead; (*Kugelschreiber2*) cartridge, refill; *auf e-e ~ laufen* hit a mine; *fig. alle ~n springen lassen* set all springs in motion; **'~nleger** ⚓ *m* (7) minelayer; **'~nräumboot** ⚓ *n* minesweeper; **'~nsperre** *f* mine barrier; **'~nsuchgerät** *n* mine detector.

Mineral [minə'ra:l] *n* (3[1] *u.* 8[2]) mineral; **2isch** mineral; **~og(e)** [~ra'lo:k, ~gə] *m* (12 [13]) mineralogist; **~ogie** [~lo'gi:] *f* (15) mineralogy; **~-öl** *n* mineral oil; **~quelle** [~'ra:l-] *f* mineral spring; **~wasser** *n* mineral water, ⚕ *pl.* minerals.

Miniatur [minia'tu:r] *f* (16), **~gemälde** *n* miniature; **~malerei** *f* miniature(-painting).

Mini|golf ['mi:ni-] *n* miniature golf; **'~kleid** *n* mini-dress.

minimal [mini'ma:l] minimal, minimum (*a. in Zssgn*); *fig.* negligible.

Minimum ['mi:nimum] *n* (9[2]) minimum.

Minister [mi'nistər] *m* (7) minister, *Brt.* Secretary of State (*gen.* for), *Am.* Secretary; **~ial...** [~ter'ja:l], **2iell** [~ter'jɛl] ministerial; **~ium** [~'te:rjum] *n* ministry, *Am.* department; **~präsident** *m* Prime Minister; **~rat** *m* Cabinet Council; *beim Europarat usw.*: Council of Ministers.

Ministrant [mini'strant] *m* (12) acolyte, F altar boy.

Minne *poet.* ['minə] *f* (15) love; **'~(ge)sang** *m* minnesong; **'~sänger** *m*, **'~singer** *m* minnesinger.

minor|enn [mino'rɛn] minor; **2ität** [~i'tɛ:t] *f* (16) minority.

minus ['mi:nus] minus.

Minute [mi'nu:tə] *f* (15) minute; *auf die ~* to the minute; *in der ~* per minute; **2nlang** lasting for minutes; *adv.* for (several) minutes; **~nzeiger** *m* minute-hand.

minuziös [minu'tsjø:s] minute.

Minze ⚘ ['mintsə] *f* (15) mint.

mir [mi:r] (*s. ich*, 19) me; to me; *refl.* (to) myself; *s. aus, nichts, schlecht.*

Mirabelle [mira'bɛlə] *f* (15) (small) yellow plum.

Misanthrop [mizan'tro:p] *m* (12) misanthrope.

mischbar ['miʃba:r] miscible; **'2keit** *f* miscibility.

Misch|becher *m* shaker; **'~-ehe** ['miʃ-] *f* mixed marriage; **'2en** (27) mix, mingle; *verschiedene Sorten*: blend; *Karten*: shuffle; *metall.* alloy; *sich ~ in (acc.)* interfere with; *sich ~ unter (acc.)* mix with, join; **'~er** *m* (7) mixer; **'~gemüse** *n* mixed vegetables *pl.*; **'~ling** *m* (3[1]) mongrel; (*Rassen2*) half-breed, half-caste; *zo.*, ⚘ hybrid; **~masch** ['~maʃ] *m* (3[2]) medley, hodge-podge, jumble; **'~-**

pult *n* mixing console, (audio) mixer; '~**rasse** *f* cross(-breed); *von Menschen*: mixed race; '~**sprache** *f* hybrid language.
'**Mischung** *f* mixture; blend; *metall.* alloy; '~**sverhältnis** *n* mixture ratio.
'**Misch|volk** *n* mixed race; '~**wald** *m* mixed forest; '~**wolle** *f* blended wool.
miserabel [mizə'ra:bəl] miserable, *sl.* rotten, lousy.
Misere [mi'ze:rə] *f* (15) calamity.
Mispel ['mispəl] *f* (15) medlar(-tree).
miß|-'achten [mis-] despise; (*vernachlässigen*) disregard, ignore; '**⁀achtung** *f* disdain; disregard; '~**behagen**[1]: *j-m* ~ displease a p.; '**⁀behagen**[2] *n* uneasiness; displeasure; '~**bilden** misshape; '**⁀bildung** *f* deformity; ~'**billigen** disapprove (of); ~'**billigend** disapproving(ly *adv.*); '**⁀billigung** *f* disapproval; '**⁀brauch** *m* abuse; (*unrichtiger Gebrauch*) misuse; ~'**brauchen** abuse (*a. mißhandeln*); (*falsch gebrauchen*) misuse; ~**bräuchlich** ['~brɔʏçliç] improper; ~'**deuten** misinterpret; '**⁀deutung** *f* misinterpretation.
missen ['misən] (28) miss; (*entbehren*) do without.
'**Miß|-erfolg** *m* failure, fiasco; '~**ernte** *f* bad harvest, crop failure.
'**Misse|tat** *f* misdeed; (*Verbrechen*) crime; '~**täter**(**in** *f*) *m* evil-doer.
miß|'fallen[1]: *j-m* ~ displease a p.; '**⁀fallen**[2] *n* (6) displeasure, disgust; '~**fällig** displeasing; (*anstößig*) shocking; (*mißbilligend*) disparaging; '**⁀geburt** *f* monster, freak; '~**gelaunt** *s. mißmutig*; '**⁀geschick** *n* misfortune; (*Unfall*) misadventure, mishap; '**⁀gestalt** *f* deformity; (*Wesen*) monster; '~**gestalt**(**et**) misshapen, deformed; '~**gestimmt** *s. mißmutig*; ~'**glücken** (sn) fail, not to succeed; ~'**gönnen** envy, grudge (*j-m* et. a p. a th.); '**⁀griff** *m* mistake, blunder; '**⁀gunst** *f* ill-will, envy, jealousy; '~**günstig** envious, jealous; ~'**handeln** ill-treat, abuse; (*schlagen*) manhandle; **⁀'handlung** *f* maltreatment, cruelty; '**⁀heirat** *f* misalliance; ~**hellig** ['~hɛliç] discordant, dissentient; '**⁀helligkeit** *f* discord, dissension; unpleasant consequence.
Mission [mis'jo:n] *f* (16) mission (*a. pol. u. fig.*); *Innere* (*Äußere*) ~ home (foreign) mission; ~**ar** [~jo'na:r] *m* (3) missionary.
'**Miß|klang** *m* dissonance; '~**kredit** *m* discredit (*a. in* ~ *bringen*).
mißlang [~'laŋ] *pret. v. mißlingen*[1].
'**mißlich** awkward; (*schwierig*) difficult; (*bedenklich*) critical; '**⁀keit** *f* awkwardness, inconvenience; difficulty.
miß|liebig ['~li:biç] not in favo(u)r; *sich bei j-m* ~ *machen* incur the displeasure of; ~**lingen**[1] [~'liŋən] (sn) fail, miscarry, not to succeed; **⁀'lingen**[2] *n* (6) failure; '**⁀mut** *m* ill-humo(u)r; (*Unzufriedenheit*) discontent; '~**mutig** ill-humo(u)red, cross; (*unzufrieden*) discontented; ~'**raten** *s. mißlingen*; ~*es Kind* wayward child; '**⁀stand** *m* (*Übelstand*) grievance, nuisance; (*Mißbrauch*) abuse; (*Mangel*) defect; '**⁀stimmung** *f* (*Uneinigkeit*) discord(ance), dissonance; *s. Mißmut*; '**⁀ton** *m* discord, dissonance (*a. fig.*); ~**tönig** ['~tø:niç] dissonant; ~'**trauen**[1]: *j-m* ~ distrust a p.; '**⁀trauen**[2] *n* distrust, mistrust, suspicion; '**⁀trauens-antrag** *parl. m* motion of no-confidence; '**⁀trauensvotum** *parl. n* vote of no-confidence; '~**trauisch** distrustful, suspicious; '**⁀vergnügen** *n* displeasure; '~**vergnügt** displeased, discontented; *pol.* malcontent; '**⁀verhältnis** *n* disproportion, incongruity; '**⁀verständnis** *n* misunderstanding, mistake; (*leichter Streit*) disagreement, F tiff; '~**verstehen** misunderstand; '**⁀weisung** *f* (magnetic) declination; '**⁀wirtschaft** *f* mismanagement.
Mist [mist] *m* (3[2]) dung, manure; (*Schmutz*) dirt; F *fig.* rubbish, rot; (*so ein*) ~! damn!; '~**beet** *n* hotbed.
Mistel ♀ ['mistəl] *f* (15) mistletoe.
misten ['mistən] (26) *Acker*: dung; *Stall*: clean; F *fig.* clear.
'**Mist|fink** F *m* pig; '~**gabel** *f* pitchfork; '~**haufen** *n* dung-hill; '~**käfer** *m* dung-beetle; '~**kerl** F *m sl.* bastard.
mit [mit] **1.** *prp.* (*dat.*) with; (*mittels*) *a.* by (means of); ~ *20 Jahren* at the age of twenty; ~ *e-m Schlage* at a blow; ~ *Gewalt* by force; ~ *20 zu 11 Stimmen beschließen* by 20 votes to 11; ~ *e-r Mehrheit* by a majority; ~ *der Bahn, Post usw.*: by; *s. Mal,*

Muße, Wort, Zeit usw.; **2.** *adv.* also, too; ~ *dabei sein* be (one) of the party, be there too, participate.

ˈ**Mit|-angeklagte** *m, f* co-defendant; ♀ˈ**-ansehen** witness; *fig.* tolerate.

ˈ**Mit-arbeit** *f* co-operation, collaboration; ˈ♀**en** collaborate, co-operate (*an dat.* in); contribute (to); *Zeitung usw.*: be on the staff (of); ˈ**~er(in** *f*) *m* co-worker; *wissenschaftlicher*: collaborator; (*Kollege*) colleague; (*Arbeitskamerad*) work-fellow; (*an dat.*) *e-r Zeitung*: contributor (to); *pl. e-s Werkes usw.*: staff (of); ~ *sein bei* be on the staff of; ˈ**~erstab** *m* staff.

ˈ**mitbekommen** be given (along), get; F (*verstehen*) catch, get.

ˈ**mitbenutz|en** use *a th.* jointly; ˈ♀**ung** *f* joint use.

ˈ**Mitbesitz** *m* joint possession; ˈ**~er** (**-in** *f*) *m* joint possessor.

ˈ**Mitbestimmung(srecht** *n*) *f* (right of) co-determination.

mitbewerb|en [ˈ~bəvɛrbən]: *sich um et.* ~ compete for a th.; ˈ♀**er(in** *f*) *m* competitor.

ˈ**Mitbewohner(in** *f*) *m* co-inhabitant; *e-s Hauses*: fellow-lodger.

ˈ**mitbring|en** bring along (with one); ♀**sel** [ˈ~zəl] *n* (7) little present.

ˈ**Mitbürger(in** *f*) *m* fellow-citizen.

ˈ**Mit-eigentümer(in** *f*) *m* joint owner.

mit-eiˈnander together, jointly.

mitˈ-einbeziehen include.

ˈ**mit-empfinden 1.** sympathize (*mit* with), feel (with); **2.** ♀ *n* (6) sympathy.

ˈ**Mit-erb|e** *m*, ˈ**~in** *f* coheir(ess *f*).

ˈ**mit-erleben** *s. erleben.*

ˈ**Mit-esser** ⚕ *m* blackhead, comedo.

ˈ**mitfahren** (sn) ride (*od.* go) with *a p.*; *j-n* ~ *lassen* give a p. a lift.

ˈ**Mitfahrer(in** *f*) *m* (fellow-)passenger; *mot. s. Beifahrer.*

ˈ**mitfühlen** *s. mitempfinden*; ˈ**~d** sympathetic(ally *adv.*).

ˈ**mitführen** carry along (with one).

ˈ**mitgeben** give; *fig. Wissen usw.*: impart (to).

ˈ**Mitgefangene** *m* fellow-prisoner.

ˈ**Mitgefühl** *n* sympathy.

ˈ**mitgehen** (sn) go along (*mit j-m* with a p.), accompany (*mit j-m* a p.); *fig. Publikum*: respond (to); F ~ *lassen* pinch.

ˈ**Mitgift** *f* dowry; ˈ**~jäger** *m* fortune-hunter.

ˈ**Mitglied** *n* member; ˈ**~erversammlung** *f* general meeting; ˈ**~erzahl** *f* membership; ˈ**~sbeitrag** *m* membership subscription, *Am.* dues *pl.*; ˈ**~schaft** *f* membership; ˈ**~skarte** *f* membership card; ˈ**~staat** *m* member state.

ˈ**mithalten** *v/i.* be one of the party; *ich halte mit* I'll join you; (*nicht*) ~ *können* be (not) equal to it.

ˈ**Mit|helfer(in** *f*) *m* helper, assistant; ˈ**~herausgeber** *m* co-editor; ˈ**~hilfe** *f* assistance.

mitˈhin consequently, therefore.

ˈ**mithören** *teleph., Radio*: listen in (*et.* to *od.* on); ⊕ monitor.

ˈ**Mit-inhaber(in** *f*) *m* copartner.

ˈ**mitkämpf|en** join in the fight; ˈ♀**er** *m* (fellow-)combatant.

ˈ**mitkommen** (sn) come along (*mit j-m* with a p.); *fig.* be able to follow; keep up (*od.* pace) (with).

ˈ**mitkriegen** F (*verstehen*) get, catch.

ˈ**Mitläufer** *pol. m* trimmer, hanger-on, fellow-travel(l)er.

ˈ**Mitlaut** *m* (3) consonant.

ˈ**Mitleid** *n* compassion, pity; ~ *haben mit* pity, be sorry for.

ˈ**Mitleidenschaft** *f*: *in* ~ *ziehen* affect, involve; (*beschädigen*) damage.

ˈ**mitleid|ig** compassionate(ly *adv.*); ˈ**~los** pitiless.

ˈ**mitmachen** *v/i.* make one of the party; *Zuhörer*: join in, respond; (*dem Beispiel folgen*) follow suit; *v/t.* take part in, join in; *Veranstaltungen*: go to; *die Mode*: follow; (*erleben*) go through; *ich mache* (*nicht*) *mit!* count me in (out)!

ˈ**Mitmensch** *m* fellow(-man); ˈ♀**lich** human, social.

ˈ**Mitnahmepreis** *m* cash-and-carry price.

ˈ**mitnehmen** take along (with one); *auf der Reise e-n Ort* ~ call at a place; *j-n* (*im Fahrzeug*) ~ give a p. a lift; *fig. j-n arg* ~ treat harshly; (*erschöpfen*) exhaust, wear (out), punish; *seelisch*: hit *a p.* hard; *S.*: (*beschädigen*) damage, batter; *Essen etc.*: *zum* ~ take-away *meal etc.*

mitnichten [~ˈniçtən] by no means, not at all, in no way.

ˈ**mitrechnen** *v/t.* include (in the reckoning); *v/i.* count.

'mitreden join in the conversation; (*mitbestimmen*) have a say (*bei* in).
'mitreisen (sn) travel along (with *a p.*); **'℗de** *m, f* (18) fellow-travel(l)er.
'mitreißen (*h.*) drag along; *fig.* electrify, thrill.
mit'samt together with.
'mit|schneiden *auf Band*: record; **'℗schnitt** *m* recording.
'mitschreiben take down; take notes.
'Mitschuld *f* complicity (*an dat.* in), joint guilt; **℗ig** ['~diç] accessary (to the crime); **~ige** ['~digə] *m* (18) accomplice; **'~ner** *m* (7) joint debtor.
'Mitschüler(in *f*) *m* schoolmate.
'mitsingen join in the song.
'mitspiel|en join in the game, play; *fig. S.*: be involved; *j-m übel ~* use a p. ill, play a p. a nasty trick; **'℗er(in** *f*) *m* partner.
'Mitsprache(recht *n*) *f* (right of) co-determination, *a* say (in the matter).
Mittag ['mita:k] *m* (3) midday, noon; (*Süden*) south; *s.* ~*essen, essen*; *des ~s*, *℗s* at noon.
'Mittag|brot *n*, **'~-essen** *n* lunch.
'mittäglich midday, noonday.
'Mittags|kreis *m*, **'~linie** *f* meridian; **'~pause** *f* lunch hour; **'~ruhe** *f*, **'~schläfchen** *n* (6) after-dinner nap, siesta; **'~sonne** *f* midday-sun; **'~stunde** *f* noon; (*Essensstunde*) lunch hour; **'~tisch** *m* dinner (-table); **'~zeit** *f* noon(tide); (*Essenszeit*) lunch hour.
'mittanzen join in the dance.
'Mittäter ⚖ *m* accomplice.
Mitte ['mitə] *f* (15) middle; (*~lpunkt*) cent|re, *Am.* -er (*a. pol.*); ⩓ mean; *fig. die goldene ~* the happy mean; *aus unserer ~* from our midst, from among us; *~ Dreißig* in one's middle thirties; *~ Juli* in the middle of July; *in die ~ nehmen* take between (*us, them*), *Sport*: sandwich in.
'mitteil|bar communicable; **'~en** communicate (*j-m* to a p.), *amtlich*: *a.* notify (a p.) of; *vertraulich*: intimate (to a p.); *Wissen usw.*: impart (to a p.); *j-m et. ~ od. ~ daß ...* inform a p. of a th. *od.* that ...; *ich werde es dir ~* I shall let you know; *fig. sich ~ Freude, Erregung usw.* communicate (*dat.* to); *die Bewegung teilt sich den Rädern mit* the motion is imparted to the wheels; **'~sam** communicative; **'℗ung** *f* communication (*a. literarisch*); information; *amtliche*: notice, *für die Öffentlichkeit*: communiqué; bulletin; (*Nachricht*) message; (*Bericht*) report.
Mittel ['mitəl] **1.** *n* (7) means *sg. u. pl.*; (*Verfahren*) method; (*Maßnahme*) measure; (*Ausweg*) expedient; (*Heil℗*) remedy (*für, gegen* for), drug; (*Geld℗*) means *pl.*, funds *pl.*; *pl.* (*Reserven, a. geistige ~*) resources *pl.*; (*Durchschnitt*) average; ⩓ mean; *phys.* medium; ⚗ agent; *im ~* on an average; *~ und Wege* ways and means; *mit allen ~n* by every possible means; *sich ins ~ legen* intervene, mediate; *s. Zweck*; **2.** ℗ *adj.* (18; *comp. mittler, sup. mittelst*) middle, central; (*Zwischen...*) intermediate; (*durchschnittlich*) average, medium, ⩓, ⊕, *phys.* mean; (*mittelmäßig*) middling; *mittleren Alters* middle-aged; *von mittlerer Größe* medium-sized; **3. ~..., ℗...** *s. mittel* 2; **'~-alter** *n* Middle Ages *pl.*; **'℗-alterlich** medi(a)eval; **'℗bar** mediate, indirect; **'~ding** *n* intermediate, cross (*zwischen* between); **'~feld** *n Sport*: midfield; **'~feldspieler** *m* midfield player; **'~finger** *m* middle finger; **'℗fristig** medium-term; **'~gebirge** *n* hills, highlands *pl.*; **'~gewicht** (**-ler** *m*) *n Boxen*: middle-weight; **'~größe** *f* medium size; **'℗hochdeutsch** Middle High German; **'℗ländisch** midland; *engS.*: Mediterranean; **'~läufer** *m Sport*: cent|re (*Am.* -er) half; **'℗los** without means, impecunious, destitute; **'℗mäßig** mediocre; (*leidlich*) middling, indifferent; (*durchschnittlich*) average; **'~mäßigkeit** *f* mediocrity; **'~meer** *n* Mediterranean (Sea); **'~-ohr-entzündung** *f* inflammation of the middle ear, 🕮 otitis (media); **'~punkt** *m* cent|re, *Am.* -er; *fig. a.* hub, (*Brennpunkt*) focus (*des Interesses* of attention); **'~scheitel** *m* centre parting, *Am.* center part; *e-n ~ tragen* part one's hair in the middle; **'~schiff** *n e-r Kirche*: nave; **'~schule** *f* lower-grade secondary school; **'~smann** *m*, **'~sperson** *f*

mediator, go-between; ✝ middleman; '**~motor** *mot. m* midengine; '**2s(t)** (*gen.*) by means of, through; '**~stand** *m* middle classes *pl.*; '**~streckenflug** *m* medium-haul flight; '**~streckenlauf** *m Sport*: medium-distance race; '**~streckenrakete** *f* intermediate-range missile; '**~streifen** *mot. m* dividing (*Am.* median) strip; '**~stürmer** *m Fußball*: cent|re (*Am.* -er) forward; '**~weg** *m* (*goldener* golden) mean; middle road; *e-n ~ einschlagen* adopt a middle course; '**~welle** *f Radio*: medium wave; '**~wert** *m* mean (value); '**~wort** *gr. n* participle.

mitten ['mitən]: *~ in (an, auf, unter dat.)* in the midst (*od.* middle) of, *im Gewühl*: in the thick of; *~ aus* from amidst, *aus e-r Menge*: from among; *~ entzwei* right in two; '**~drin** right in the midst; '**~(hin)-'durch** right through.

'**Mitter|nacht** *f* midnight; **2nächtig** ['~nɛçtiç], '**2nächtlich** midnight; '**2nachts** at midnight.

Mittler ['mitlər] **1.** *m* (7), '**~in** *f* mediator; **2.** 2 *adj.* (18) *s. mittel* 2; '**~-amt** *n* mediatorship; **2'weile** in the meantime, meanwhile.

'**mitt|schiffs** ⚓ (a)midships; '**2-sommer** *m* midsummer; **2woch** ['~vɔx] *m* (3) Wednesday.

mit'-unter now and then.

'**Mit|-unterschrift** *f* joint signature; '**~-unterzeichner(in** *f*) *m* co-signatory; '**2verantwortlich** jointly responsible; '**~verschworene** *m* fellow-conspirator; '**~welt** *f* our *etc.* contemporaries *pl.*

'**mitwirk|en** co-operate (*bei* in); *S.*: *a.* concur (with); '**2ende** *m, f thea.* actor, player (*a.* ♪); *pl. the* cast; *s. Mitarbeiter*; '**2ung** *f* co-operation; concurrence.

'**Mitwiss|en** *n* (joint) knowledge; *b.s.* connivance; *ohne j-s ~* without a p.'s knowledge; '**~er(in** *f*) *m* person who is in the secret, confidant; ⚖ accessory.

'**mitzählen** *s. mitrechnen.*

mix|en ['miksən] (28) mix; '**2becher** *m* (cocktail- *etc.*) shaker; **2er** ['miksər] *m* (7), '**2gerät** *n* mixer, liquidizer; '**2getränk** *n* mixed drink; **2tur** [~'tu:r] *f* (15) mixture.

Möbel ['mø:bəl] *n* (7) piece of furniture; *pl.* furniture *sg.*; '**~händler** *m* furniture-dealer; '**~politur** *f* furniture polish; '**~spediteur** *m* furniture-remover; '**~stoff** *m* furniture fabric; '**~stück** *n* piece of furniture; '**~tischler** *m* cabinet-maker; '**~wagen** *m* furniture(-removal) van, *Brt.* pantechnicon, *Am.* furniture truck.

mobil [mo'bi:l] (18) ⚔ mobile; (*flink*) active; *~ machen s. ~isieren*; **2iar** [~bil'ja:r] *n* (3[1]) furniture; **2ien** [~'bi:ljən] *pl. inv.* movables; **~isieren** [~bili'zi:rən] mobilize; **2ität** [~bili'tɛ:t] *f* mobility.

Mobilmachung [mo'bi:lmaxuŋ] *f* mobilization; **~sbefehl** *m* mobilization order.

möblieren [mø'bli:rən] furnish; *neu ~* refurnish; *möbliertes Zimmer* furnished room, bed-sitter.

mochte ['mɔxtə] *pret. v. mögen.*

Modalität [modali'tɛ:t] *f* (16) modality.

Mode ['mo:də] *f* (15) fashion; (*Sitte*) vogue, mode; *contp. neue ~n* newfangled ideas; *in ~* in fashion, in (vogue), fashionable; *aus der ~* out (of fashion); *~ sein* be the fashion; *die große ~ sein* be (all) the rage; *in ~ bringen (kommen)* bring (come) into fashion; *aus der ~ kommen* go out (of fashion); '**~-artikel** *m* fancy article; *pl. a.* novelties *pl.*; '**2bewußt** fashion-conscious, trendy; '**~farbe** *f* fashionable colo(u)r; '**~geschäft** *n* fashion house.

Modell [mo'dɛl] *n* (3[1]) model (*a. paint., Person*); (*Mode2*) model, mannequin; ⊕ (*Typ*) model, type; (*Muster*) pattern; *~ stehen* serve as a model, pose (*j-m* for); **~-eisenbahn** *f* model railway; **~flugzeug** *n* model aircraft; **2ieren** [~'li:rən] model, mo(u)ld, fashion; **~iermasse** [~'li:r-] *f* model(l)ing clay, plasticine; **~kleid** [mo'dɛl-] *n* model (dress); **~macher** *m*, **~tischler** *m* patternmaker; **~studie** *f* pilot study.

modeln ['mo:dəln] (29) *s. modellieren.*

'**Moden|haus** *n* fashion house; '**~schau** *f* fashion show; '**~zeichner (-in** *f*) *m* fashion designer; '**~zeitung** *f* fashion magazine.

Moder ['mo:dər] *m* (7) mo(u)ld; (*Fäulnis*) decay.

Moderator [mode'ra:tɔr] *Radio, TV m* (8[1]) presenter.

'**Modergeruch** *m* musty smell.
moderieren [mode'ri:rən] *Radio, TV Sendung*: present.
'**moder|ig** mo(u)ldy, musty; '**~n** (29) (sn *u.* h.) mo(u)lder, rot.
modern [mo'dɛrn] modern; (*modisch*) fashionable, *a. weitS.* stylish; (*auf dem laufenden*) up-to-date, *pred.* up to date; *das ist ~ (das trägt man heute)* F that's quite the go; **~i'sieren** modernize, bring up to date; **2i'sierung** *f* modernization.
'**Mode|salon** *m* fashion house; '**~schmuck** *m* costume jewel(le)ry; '**~schöpfer** *m* fashion designer, couturier (*fr.*); '**~schriftsteller(in** *f*) *m* fashionable (*od.* popular) writer; '**~waren** *f/pl.* fancy goods; '**~wort** *n* vogue word; '**~zeichner** *s. Modenzeichner.*
modifizieren [modifi'tsi:rən] modify.
modisch ['mo:diʃ] fashionable, stylish.
Modistin [mo'distin] *f* milliner.
modulieren [~du'li:rən] modulate.
Modus ['mo:dus] *m* (16, *pl. Modi*) mode; method; *gr.* mood.
mogeln F ['mo:gəln] (29) cheat.
mögen ['mø:gən] (30) (*gewillt sein*) be willing; (*wollen, wünschen*) want, desire, wish; (*gern haben*) like; *v/aux.* may, might; *ich möchte wissen* I should like to know; *ich mag nicht* I don't want (*od.* like, care) to; *ich mag das nicht* I don't like that; *lieber ~* like better; *ich möchte lieber* I would rather; *was ich auch (immer) tun mag* whatever I may do; *wie dem auch sein mag* be that as it may; *das mag sein* that may be (so); *wo mag er sein?* I wonder where he is; *möge es ihm gelingen* may he succeed; *sie mochte 30 Jahre alt sein* she looked about 30 years old.
möglich ['mø:kliç] possible (*für j-n* for); (*durchführbar*) practicable, feasible; *alle ~en ... s. allerhand*; *nicht ~!* you don't say so!; *es ~ machen, zu inf.* make it possible to *inf.* (*s. ermöglichen*); *~st viel usw.* as much *etc.* as possible; *sein ~stes tun* do one's utmost *od.* best; '**~enfalls, ~er'weise** if possible, possibly; '**2keit** *f* possibility; (*Gelegenheit*) chance; (*Entwicklungs2*) potentiality; *~en (Vorteile) pl.* facilities *pl.*
Mohair [mo'hɛ:r] *m* (3[1]) mohair.
Mohammedan|er [mohame'dɑ:nər] *m* (7), **2isch** Mohammedan.
Mohn ⚘ [mo:n] *m* (3) poppy.
Mohr [mo:r] *m* (12) Moor, negro.
Möhre ⚘ ['mø:rə] *f* (15) carrot.
'**Mohrrübe** ⚘ *f* carrot.
Moi|ré [moa're:] *m, n* (11) moire, watered silk; **2'rieren** water.
mokieren [mɔ'ki:rən]: *sich über (acc.) ~* laugh at.
Mokka ['mɔka] *m* (11) mocha (coffee).
Molch [mɔlç] *m* (3) salamander.
Mole ⚓ ['mo:lə] *f* (15) mole, jetty.
Molekül [mole'ky:l] *n* (3[1]) molecule.
Molekular... [moleku'lɑ:r-] molecular ...
molk [mɔlk] *pret. v. melken.*
Molk|e(n) ['mɔlkə(n)] *f(/pl.)* (15) whey *sg.*; **~e'rei** *f* dairy; '**2ig** wheyish.
Moll ♪ [mɔl] *n inv.* minor.
mollig F ['mɔliç] (*behaglich*) comfy, snug; (*rundlich*) roly-poly.
Molotowcocktail ['mo:lotɔf-] *m* Molotov cocktail, petrol bomb.
Moment [mo'mɛnt] **1.** *m* (3) moment; *s. Augenblick*; **2.** *n* ⊕ momentum; (*Antrieb*) impulse; impetus (*a. fig.*); *fig.* (*Anlaß*) motive; (*Faktor*) fact(or), element; **2an** [~'tɑ:n] momentary; *adv.* at the moment, just now; **~aufnahme** *f* snapshot; (*Bewegungsaufnahme*) action shot.
Monarch [mo'narç] *m* (12), **~in** *f* monarch; **~ie** [~'çi:] *f* (15) monarchy; **2isch** monarchic(al).
Monat ['mo:nat] *m* (3) month; '**2elang** for months; '**2lich** monthly.
'**Monats|binde** *f* sanitary towel *od.* napkin; '**~fluß** ⚕ *m* menses *pl.*, period; '**~gehalt** *n* monthly salary; '**~karte** *f* monthly season-ticket, *Am.* commutation(-ticket); '**~schrift** *f* monthly (magazine); '**~tampon** *m* sanitary tampon.
'**monatweise** *adv.* by the month.
Mönch [mœnç] *m* (3) monk, friar; '**2isch** monkish, monastic.
'**Mönchs|kloster** *n* monastery; '**~kutte** *f* monk's frock; '**~orden** *m* monastic order; '**~tum** *n* (1[2]) monachism; '**~zelle** *f* friar's cell.
mondän [mɔn'dɛ:n] elegant.

Mond [mo:nt] *m* (3) moon (*poet. a. Monat*); '~**-aufgang** *m* moonrise; '~**finsternis** *f* lunar eclipse; '♀**hell** moonlit; '~(**lande**)**fähre** *f* lunar module; '~**landung** *f* landing on the moon; '~**schein** *m* moonlight; '~**scheintarif** F *teleph. m* cheap rate; '~**sichel** *f* crescent; '~**stein** *m* moonstone; '♀**süchtig** moonstruck; '~**wechsel** *m* change of the moon.

Moneten *sl.* [mo'ne:tən] *pl.* dough *sg.*

Mongol|e [mɔŋ'go:lə] *m* (13), ~**in** *f* (16[1]) Mongol; ♀**isch** Mongolian.

monieren [mo'ni:rən] (*rügen*) censure, criticize; (*mahnen*) remind.

Monitor ['mo:nitɔr] *m* (8[1]) *TV usw.*: monitor.

Mono|gamie [monoga'mi:] *f* (15, *o. pl.*) monogamy; ~**gramm** [mono'gram] *n* (3[1]) monogram; *mit* ~ initial(l)ed; ~**graphie** [~gra'fi:] *f* (15) monography.

Monokel [mo'nɔkəl] *n* (7) monocle.

Mono|log [mono'lo:k] *m* (3[1]) (*innerer* ~ interior) monolog(ue); soliloquy; ~**pol** [~'po:l] *n* (3[1]) monopoly (*auf acc.* of, *Am.* on); ♀**polisieren** [~poli'zi:rən] monopolize; ♀**ton** [~'to:n] monotonous; ~**tonie** [~to'ni:] *f* monotony.

Monstranz [mɔn'strants] *f* (16) monstrance.

monströs [mɔn'strø:s] monstrous.

Monstrum ['mɔnstrum] *n* (9[2]) monster.

Monsun [mɔn'zu:n] *m* (3[1]) monsoon.

Montag ['mo:nta:k] *m* (3) Monday; *blauer* ~ blue (*od.* Saint) Monday; '♀**s** on Mondays.

Montage [mɔn'ta:ʒə] *f* (15) ⊕ mounting, fitting; erection; (*Zs.-bau*) assembly; *phot.* montage; ~**band** *n* assembly line; ~**halle** *f* assembly room *od.* shop.

Montan|-industrie [mɔn'ta:n-] *f* coal, iron, and steel industries; ~**union** [~ʔu'nio:n] *f* Coal and Steel Community.

Mont|eur [mɔn'tø:r] *m* (3[1]) fitter; assembly man; *bsd. mot. u.* ✈ mechanic(ian); ~**eur-anzug** *m* overall; ♀**ieren** [~'ti:rən] mount, fit; (*aufstellen*) set up; erect; (*zs.-bauen*) assemble; *typ.* strip; ~**ierung** [~'ti:ruŋ] *f s. Montage*; (*Ausrüstung*) equipment; ~**ur** [~'tu:r] *f* (16) ⚔ uniform; *weitS.* overall.

Monument [monu'mɛnt] *n* (3) monument; ♀**al** [~mɛn'ta:l] monumental.

Moor [mo:r] *n* (3) fen, bog, swamp; '~**bad** *n* mud-bath; '♀**ig** marshy, boggy; '~**land** *n* marshy country; '~**packung** ⚕ *f* mud pack.

Moos [mo:s] *n* (4) moss; *sl.* (*Geld*) dough; ♀**ig** ['~ziç] mossy.

Moped *mot.* ['mo:pe:t] *n* (11) moped.

Mops [mɔps] *m* (4[2]) pug; '♀**en** F (*stehlen*) pinch; *sich* ~ be bored.

Moral [mo'ra:l] *f* (16) (*Sittlichkeit*) morality; morals *pl.*; (*Lehre*) moral; (*Arbeits-, Kampf*♀ *usw.*) morale; ~**-apostel** F *m* moralizer; ♀**isch** moral; ♀**isieren** [~rali'zi:rən] moralize; ~**i'tät** *f* (16) morality; ~**predigt** *f* lecture.

Moräne [mo'rɛ:nə] *f* (15) moraine.

Morast [mo'rast] *m* (3[3] *od.* 3[2]) marsh, slough; (*Schlamm*) mire, mud; ♀**ig** marshy, boggy; muddy.

Mord [mɔrt] *m* (3) murder (*an dat.* of); '~**-anschlag** *m* assassination attempt; ♀**en** ['~dən] *v/t. u. v/i.* (26) murder.

Mörder ['mœrdər] *m* (7) murderer; '~**grube** *f*: *aus s-m Herzen keine* ~ *machen* speak one's mind, be frank (*od.* open); '~**in** *f* murderess; '♀**isch** murderous (*a. fig.*); '♀**lich** terrible, cruel.

'**Mord|gier** *f*, '~**lust** *f* bloodthirstiness; '♀**gierig,** '♀**lustig** bloodthirsty; '~**kommando** *n* death squad; '~**kommission** *f* murder (*Am.* homicide) squad; '~**prozeß** *m* murder trial; '~**s...** F (*enorm*) terrific; '~**s'angst** F *f*: *e-e* ~ *haben* be scared stiff; '~**s'glück** *f* incredible luck; '~**s'kerl** *m* devil of a fellow; '♀**smäßig** awful, terrrific; '~**sspektakel** *m* terrific noise; '~**tat** *f* murder; '~**verdacht** *m* suspicion of murder; '~**versuch** *m* attempt to murder.

Mores ['mo:re:s]: *j-n* ~ *lehren* teach a p. manners.

Morgen ['mɔrgən] **1.** *m* (6) morning; (*Osten*) east; (*Landmaß*) acre; *des* ~*s*, ♀*s*, *am* ~ in the morning; *guten* ~ good morning; **2.** *n the* morrow, *the* future; **3.** ♀ *adv.* tomorrow; ~ *früh* tomorrow morning; ~ *abend* tomorrow evening *od.* night; *s. heute*; '~**-ausgabe** *f* morning edition; '~**blatt** *n* morning paper; '~**dämmerung** *f* dawn; '~-

grauen *n*: *im* ~ at dawn, at daybreak; '**~gymnastik** *f* morning gymnastics *pl.*; '**~land** *n* Orient, East; '**2ländisch** Oriental, Eastern; '**~luft** *f* morning air; *fig.* ~ *wittern* get hopeful; '**~rock** *m e-r Frau*: peignoir (*fr.*), dressing-gown; '**~rot** *n*, '**~röte** *f* dawn; '**2s** *s. Morgen*; '**~stern** *m* morning star; '**~stunde** *f* morning hour; ~ *hat Gold im Munde* the early bird catches the worm; *bis in die frühen ~n* until the small hours; '**~zeitung** *f* morning paper.

'**morgig** of tomorrow, tomorrow's.

Morphium ['mɔrfium] *n* (11) morphine; '**~sucht** *f* morphine addiction.

morsch [mɔrʃ] rotten, decayed; brittle; *fig.* shaky.

Morse|**-alphabet** ['mɔrzə-] *n*, '**~schrift** *f* Morse code; '**2n** morse; '**~zeichen** *n* Morse signal.

Mörser ['mœrzər] *m* (7) mortar (*a.* ⚔); '**~keule** *f* pestle.

Mörtel ['mœrtəl] *m* (7) mortar; (*Putz*) plaster; '**~kelle** *f* trowel.

Mosaik [moza'i:k] *n* (3[1]) mosaic; **~fußboden** *m* tesselated pavement.

Moschee [mɔ'ʃe:] *f* (15) mosque.

Moschus [mɔ'ʃus] *m inv.* musk.

Moskito [mɔs'ki:to] *m* (11) mosquito; **~netz** *n* mosquito-net.

Moslem ['mɔslɛm] *m* (11) Muslim.

Most [mɔst] *m* (3[2]) must; (*Apfel2*) cider.

Mostrich ['mɔstriç] *m* (3) mustard.

Motel [mo'tɛl] *n* (11) motel.

Motiv [mo'ti:f] *n* (3[1]) motive; *paint.*, ♪ motif (*fr.*), theme; **~forschung** *f* motivational research; **2ieren** [~ti'vi:rən] motivate; **~ierung** *f* motivation.

Motor ['mo:tɔr] *m* (8[1]) engine, *bsd.* ⚡ motor; '**~boot** *n* motor boat; '**~fahrzeug** *n* motor vehicle; '**~haube** *f* (engine) bonnet, *Am.* hood; **2isieren** [motori'zi:rən] motorize; ⚔ mechanize; **~i'sierung** *f* motorization; '**~rad** *n* motor-cycle; ~ *mit Beiwagen* motor-cycle combination; '**~radfahrer** *m* motor-cyclist; '**~roller** *m* motor-scooter; '**~säge** *f* power saw; '**~schaden** *m* engine trouble; '**~schlitten** *m* snowmobile; '**~sport** *m* motoring.

Motte ['mɔtə] *f* (15) moth; F *fig.* funny bird; '**2nfest** mothproof; '**~nfraß** *m* damage caused by moths; '**~nkugel** *f* moth-ball; '**2nzerfressen** moth-eaten.

Motto ['mɔto] *n* (11) motto.

motzen F ['mɔtsən] (27) grumble, grouse.

moussieren [mu'si:rən] effervesce, sparkle; **~d** sparkling.

Möwe ['mœ:və] *f* (15) (sea-)gull.

Mucke F ['mukə] *f* (15) whim, caprice; *fig. ~n haben P.*: have one's little moods, *S.*: have its snags, *Motor*: have got the bugs.

Mücke ['mykə] *f* (15) gnat, mosquito; *aus e-r ~ e-n Elefanten machen* make a mountain out of a molehill.

mucken ['mukən] (25) rebel.

'**Mückenstich** *m* gnat-bite.

Mucker ['mukər] *m* (7) bigot, hypocrite.

mucksen ['muksən] (27): *sich* ~ stir, budge.

müd|**e** ['my:də] tired, weary; *e-r S. ~ sein* be tired (*od.* weary *od.* sick) of; '**~igkeit** *f* tiredness, weariness, fatigue.

Muff [muf] *m* (3) **1.** muff; **2.** (*Geruch*) musty smell; '**~e** ⊕ *f* sleeve, socket; '**~el**[1] ⊕ *f* (15) muffle; '**~el**[2] F *fig. m* (7) sourpuss; '**2eln** (29) munch; (*undeutlich reden*) mumble; *a.* = '**2en** F (25) **1.** sulk, grumble; **2.** smell musty; '**2ig** grumbling; *Geruch usw.*: musty; *P.*: sulky, grumbling.

muh! [mu:] moo!; **~en** ['mu:ən] (25) low.

Mühe ['my:ə] *f* (15) trouble, pains *pl.*; (*Anstrengung*) effort, exertion; (*nicht*) *der ~ wert* (not) worth-while; *j-m ~ machen* give a p. trouble; *sich ~ geben mit* et. take pains over (*od.* with) a th.; *sich die ~ machen zu inf.* bother to *inf.*; *mit ~ und Not* barely, with (great) difficulty; '**2los** effortless, easy; '**2n** (25): *sich ~* struggle, toil; '**2voll** troublesome, hard; laborious; **~waltung** ['~valtuŋ] *f* trouble; (*Sorgfalt*) care.

Mühle ['my:lə] *f* (15) mill; F (*Auto usw.*) bus; *s. Wasser.*

'**Mühl(en)**|**rad** *n* mill wheel; '**~stein** *m* millstone.

'**Müh**|**sal** *f* (14) toil, trouble; (*Ungemach*) hardship; (*Strapaze*) strain; '**2sam**, '**2selig** troublesome, difficult, hard; *adv.* with difficulty, laboriously; '~**seligkeit** *f* laboriousness; (great) difficulty.

Mulatt|e [mu'latə] *m* (13), ~**in** *f* (16[1]) mulatto.

Mulde ['muldə] *f* (15) trough; *geogr.* hollow; 2**nförmig** ['~nfœrmiç] trough-shaped.

Mull [mul] *m* (3) mull, gauze; '~**binde** *f* gauze bandage.

Müll [myl] *m* (3) rubbish, refuse, *Am.* garbage; '~-**abfuhr** *f* removal of refuse, *Am.* garbage collection *od.* disposal; '~**beutel** *m* bin liner; '~**deponie** *f* rubbish tip (*od.* dump); '~-**eimer** *m* dustbin, *Am.* garbage pail; '~-**entsorgung** *f* waste disposal.

Müller ['mylər] *m* (7) miller.

'**Müll|fahrer** *m* dustman, *Am.* garbageman; '~**haufen** *m* dust-heap; '~**kasten** *m* dustbin, *Am.* garbage can; '~**schlucker** *m* waste disposal unit, rubbish chute; '~**tonne** *f* dustbin, *Am.* (tr)ashcan; '~**wagen** *m* dustcart, *Am.* garbage truck; '~**wolf** *m* garbage grinder.

mulmig ['mulmiç] mo(u)ldy; F *fig.* (*gefährlich*) ticklish.

multinational ['multi-] multinational.

Multipli|kation [multiplika'tsjo:n] *f* multiplication; ~**kator** [~'ka:tɔr] *m* (8[1]) multiplier; 2**zieren** [~'tsi:rən] multiply (*mit* by).

Mumie ['mu:mjə] *f* (15) mummy.

Mumm [mum] F *m* (3[1], *o. pl.*) spunk, guts *pl.*

Mummelgreis ['muməl-] *m* F old fogey.

Mummenschanz ['mumənʃants] *m* (3[2]) masquerade, mummery.

Mumpitz ['mumpits] F *m* (3[2], *o.pl.*) rubbish, nonsense.

Mumps ⚕ [mumps] *m inv.* mumps.

Mund [munt] *m* (1[2], *rhet. a.* 3) mouth; *den ~ halten* hold one's tongue, F shut up; *reinen ~ halten über* (*acc.*) keep mum about *a th.*; *nicht auf den ~ gefallen sein* have a ready tongue; *j-m über den ~ fahren* cut a p. short; *j-m et. in den ~ legen* suggest a th. to a p.; *den ~ vollnehmen* talk big; *~ und Nase aufsperren* stand gaping, be dumbfounded; *s. Blatt, Hand, spitzen, verbrennen, wässerig usw.*; '~-**art** *f* dialect; '2-**artlich** dialectal.

Mündel ['myndəl] *m, f, n* (7) ward; '~**gelder** *n/pl.* trust-money *sg.*; '2-**sicher:** *~e Papiere pl.* gilt-edged securities.

munden ['mundən] (26) taste good; *es mundet mir* I like it.

münden ['myndən] (26): *~ in* (*acc.*) *Fluß*: flow into; *Straße*: run into.

Mund|fäule ['munt-] ⚕ *f* stomatitis; '2**gerecht** palatable; '~**geruch** *m* (*übler*) bad breath, halitosis; '~-**harmonika** *f* mouth organ; '~-**höhle** *f* cavity of the mouth.

mündig ['myndiç] (*werden* come) of age; *fig. a.* responsible; '2**keit** *f* majority.

mündlich ['myntliç] oral, verbal; *adv. a.* by word of mouth; '2**keit** ⚖ *f* oral proceedings *pl.*

'**Mund|pflege** *f* oral hygiene; '~-**raub** ⚖ *m* theft of food (for immediate consumption); '~**schenk** *m* cup-bearer; '~**sperre** *f* lock-jaw; '~**stück** *n* mouthpiece; *e-r Zigarette*: tip; *mit Kork2* cork-tipped; '2**tot:** *j-n ~ machen* silence (*pol.* gag, muzzle) a p.

Mündung ['mynduŋ] *f* mouth; (*Gezeiten2*) estuary; *anat.* orifice; *e-r Feuerwaffe*: muzzle; '~**sfeuer** *n* muzzle flash.

'**Mund|voll** *m* mouthful; '~**vorrat** *m* provisions *pl.*, victuals *pl.*; '~**wasser** *n* mouth-wash, gargle; '~**werk** *n* mouth; *ein gutes ~ haben* have the gift of the gab; '~**winkel** *m* corner of the mouth; '~-**zu-'Mund-Propaganda** *f* propaganda by word of mouth.

Munition [muni'tsjo:n] *f* ammunition; ~**slager** *n* ammunition depot.

munkeln ['muŋkəln] (29) *v/i. u. v/t.* whisper, rumo(u)r; *man munkelt* it is rumo(u)red.

Münster ['mynstər] *n u. m* (7) cathedral, minster.

munter ['muntər] awake; (*lebhaft*) lively; (*fröhlich*) gay; *s. gesund*; '2**keit** *f* liveliness; merriness; '2**macher** F *m* pick-me-up.

Münz|e ['myntsə] *f* (15) coin; *kleine*: change; (*Denk2*) medal; (*Münzstätte*) mint; *klingende ~* hard cash; *fig. et. für bare ~ nehmen* take a th. for gospel truth; *j-m mit gleicher ~ heimzahlen* pay a p. back in his own coin; '~-**einheit** *f* unit *od.* standard of currency; '2**en** (27) coin; *gemünztes Geld* specie; F *das ist auf ihn gemünzt* that is meant for him; '**~er** *m* (7) coiner; '**~fernsprecher** *m* coin(-box) telephone, public call-office; '**~fuß** *m* standard (of coinage); '**~kunde** *f* numismatics *pl.*; '**~sammlung** *f* numismatic collection; '**~wäscherei** *f* laundrette, *Am.* laundromat; '**~wesen** *n* monetary system.

mürbe ['myrbə] tender; (*sehr reif*) mellow; (*gut durchgekocht*) well-cooked; (*knusperig, bröckelig*) crisp, short; (*brüchig*) brittle; *fig.* weary; *~ machen* wear out, ⚔ soften up; *~ werden* give in, wilt; '**≗kuchen** *m* shortcake; '**≗teig** *m* (short) pastry.

Murmel ['murməl] *f* (15) marble; '**≗n** *v/i. u. v/t.* (29) murmur; '**~tier** *n* marmot, *Am.* woodchuck; *schlafen wie ein ~* sleep like a top.

murren ['murən] (25) grumble (*über acc.* at), *Am.* F grouch.

mürrisch ['myriʃ] surly, sullen.

Mus [mu:s] *n* (4) pap; (*Frucht≗*) stewed fruit, jam; F *fig. j-n zu ~ schlagen* beat to a pulp.

Muschel ['muʃəl] *f* (15) mussel; (*~schale*) shell; *des Telephonhörers*: ear-piece; *s. Ohr≗*; **≗förmig** ['~fœrmiç] mussel-shaped; '**~kalk** *m* shell lime(stone).

Muse ['mu:zə] *f* (15) Muse.

Muselman ['mu:zəlman] *m* (12), '**~n** *m* (1[2]) Mussulman.

Museum [mu'ze:um] *n* (9) museum.

Musical ['mju:zikəl] *n* (11) musical (comedy).

Musik [mu'zi:k] *f* (16) music; (*Musikanten*) (band of) musicians *pl.*; *in ~ setzen* set to music.

Musikalien [~zi'kɑ:ljən] *pl. inv.* (pieces *pl.* of) music *sg.*; **~handlung** *f* music shop.

musik|alisch [muzi'kɑ:liʃ] musical; **≗ant** [~'kant] *m* (12), **≗er** ['mu:zikər] *m* (7) musician; **≗antenknochen** [~'kant-] F *m* funny bone.

Mu'sik|-automat *m*, **~box** ['mu:zikbɔks] *f* musical slot machine, *Am.* F juke-box; **~berieselung** [mu'zi:k-] *f* piped music; **~hochschule** *f* conservatoire (*fr.*), *Am.* conservatory; **~-instrument** *n* musical instrument; **~kapelle** *f*, **~korps** *n* band; **~lehrer** *m* music teacher; **~pavillon** *m* bandstand; **~stunde** *f* music lesson; **~truhe** *f* radiogram, *Am.* radio-phonograph console; **~unterricht** *m* music lessons *pl.*

Musikus ['mu:zikus] *m* musician.

Mu'sikwissenschaft *f* musicology.

musisch ['mu:ziʃ] *P.*: artistically inclined; *Fach usw.*: fine-arts ...

musizieren [muzi'tsi:rən] make music, play; *abends wurde musiziert* they had music in the evening.

Muskat|(nuß *f*) [mus'kɑ:t-] *m* (3) nutmeg; **~blüte** *f* mace.

Muskateller [muska'tɛlər] *m* (7) (*Wein*) muscatel.

Muskel ['muskəl] *m* (10) muscle; '**~kater** *m* muscular ache, *Am.* F charley horse; '**~kraft** *f* muscular strength; '**~protz** F *m* muscle man; '**~riß** *m* torn muscle; '**~schwund** *m* muscular atrophy; '**~zerrung** *f* pulled muscle.

Musket|e [mus'ke:tə] *f* (15) musket; **~ier** [~ke'ti:r] *m* (3[1]) musketeer.

Muskulatur [muskula'tu:r] *f* (16) muscular system, muscles *pl.*

muskulös [~'lø:s] muscular.

Muß [mus] *n inv.* necessity, must.

Muße ['mu:sə] *f* (15) leisure; *mit ~* at (one's) leisure.

Muß-ehe F ['mus-] *f* shotgun wedding.

Musselin [musə'li:n] *m* (3) muslin.

müssen ['mysən] (30): *ich muß* I must, I have to; (*ich bin gezwungen*) I am obliged (*od.* forced *od.* compelled) to; *er muß verrückt sein* he must be mad; *das mußte (einfach) passieren* that was bound to happen; *ich mußte (einfach) lachen* I could not help laughing.

Mußestunde ['mu:sə-] *f* leisure-hour, spare hour.

müßig ['my:siç] idle; (*überflüssig*) superfluous; *~es Geschwätz* useless (*od.* idle) talk; '**≗gang** *m* idleness; **≗gänger** ['~gɛŋər] *m* (7) idler.

mußte ['mustə] *pret. v. müssen.*

Muster ['mustər] *n* (7) model (⊕ *a. Bautyp* type); (*Zeichnung usw.*) pattern, design; (*Probe*) sample, specimen; (*Richtschnur*) standard; (*Vorbild*) model, example; *s. wert* 2.; '**~beispiel** *n* typical example (*für* of); '**~betrieb** *m* model factory *od.* farm; '**~-exemplar** *n* sample copy; '**~gatte** *m* model husband; '**≗gültig**, '**≗haft** exemplary, perfect; (*o. adv.*) model; '**~karte** *f* show (*od.* sample) card; '**~knabe** *m* model boy, paragon; *contp.* prig; '**~koffer** *m* sample-bag; '**~kollektion** ✝ *f* range of samples; '≈n (29) (*prüfen, besehen*) examine, inspect; *neugierig*: eye; *abschätzend*: size *a p.* up; ⚔ *Rekruten*: muster, *Truppe*: inspect; *Stoff*: figure, pattern; '~**prozeß** ⚖ *m* test case; '~**schutz** *m* trade-mark protection; copyright in designs; '~**ung** *f* examination, inspection; ⚔ muster(ing); '~**ungskommission** ⚔ *f* examination (*Am.* draft) board; '~**zeichner(in** *f*) *m* designer.

Mut [mu:t] *m* (3) courage; (*Verwegenheit*) daring; (*Schneid*) pluck; *s. gut*; ~ *fassen* summon up courage, take heart; *j-m* ~ *machen* encourage a p.; *j-m den* ~ *nehmen* discourage a p.; *den* ~ *sinken lassen* lose courage *od.* heart; *nur* ~! cheer up!; *s. zumute*.

Mut|ation [muta'tsjo:n] *f* mutation; ≈**ieren** [~'ti:rən] mutate.

Mütchen ['my:tçən] *n* (6, *o. pl.*): *sein* ~ *kühlen an* (*dat.*) take it out on.

mut|ig ['mu:tiç] courageous, brave; '~**los** discouraged; (*verzagt*) despondent; '≈**losigkeit** *f* discouragement; despondency; ~**maßen** ['~ma:sən] (27) guess, suppose, speculate; '~**maßlich** supposed; presumable; '≈**maßung** *f* conjecture, surmise, speculation.

Mutter ['mutər] *f* (14[1]) mother; *s.* ~*tier*; ⊕ (*Schrauben*≈) (15) nut; *die* ~ *Gottes* the (Blessed *od.* Holy) Virgin; '~**brust** *f* mother's breast.

Mütter|beratungsstelle ['mytər-] *f* maternity cent|re, *Am.* -er; ~**chen** ['~çən] *n* (6) little mother; *altes*: good old woman, F granny.

Mutter|'gottesbild *n* image of the (Blessed *od.* Holy) Virgin; '~**haus** *n fig.* (*Stammhaus*) parent-house; '~**-instinkt** *m* maternal instinct; '~**komplex** *m* mother fixation; '~**korn** *n* ergot; '~**kuchen** *physiol. m* placenta; '~**land** *n* mother country; '~**leib** *m* womb; *vom* ~*e an* from one's birth.

mütterlich ['mytərliç] motherly; (*der Mutter eigen*) maternal; '~**erseits** on one's mother's side.

'**Mutter|liebe** *f* motherly love; '≈**los** motherless; '~**mal** *n* birthmark, mole; '~**milch** *f* mother's milk; '~**pflicht** *f* maternal duty; '~**schaf** *n* ewe; '~**schaft** *f* maternity; motherhood; '~**schaftsgeld** *n* maternity benefit; '~**schafts-urlaub** *m* maternity leave; '~**schiff** *n* mother ship; (*Begleitfahrzeug*) tender; '~**schlüssel** ⊕ *m* (nut) spanner, *Am.* wrench; '~**schraube** *f* female screw; '~**schutz** *m* legal protection for expectant mothers; '~**schwein** *n* sow; '≈**seelen-al'lein** utterly alone; ~**söhnchen** ['~zø:nçən] *n* (6) mother's darling, molly(-coddle), sissy; '~**sprache** *f* mother tongue, native language; ~**sprachler** ['~ʃprɑ:çlər] *m* (7) native speaker; '~**tag** *m* Mother's Day; '~**tier** *n* dam; '~**trompete** *anat. f* fallopian tube; '~**witz** *m* mother-wit, natural wit.

Mutti F ['muti] *f* (11[1]) mum(my).

Mutung ⚒ ['mu:tuŋ] *f* claim.

'**Mut|wille** *m* frolicsomeness; mischievousness; *b.s.* wantonness; '≈**willig** (*ausgelassen*) frolicsome, playful; (*Streiche machend*) mischievous; *b.s.* (*frevlerisch*) wanton; (*bösartig*) malicious; (*vorsätzlich*) wil(l)ful.

Mütze ['mytsə] *f* (15) cap; '~**nschirm** *m* peak.

Myriade [my:r'jɑ:də] *f* (15) myriad.

Myrrhe ['myrə] *f* (15) myrrh.

Myrte ['myrtə] *f* (15) myrtle.

mysteri|ös [myster'jø:s] mysterious; ≈**um** [~'ste:rjum] *n* (9) mystery.

Mystifi|kation [~stifika'tsjo:n] *f* mystification; ≈'**zieren** mystify.

Myst|ik ['mystik] *f* (16) mysticism; '≈**isch** mystical.

Myth|e ['my:tə] *f* (15) myth; '≈**isch** mythic; *bsd. fig.* mythical; ~**ologie** [mytolo'gi:] *f* (15) mythology; ≈**ologisch** [~'lo:giʃ] mythological; ~**os** ['my:tɔs], ~**us** ['~tus] *m* (16[2]) myth.

N

N [ɛn], **n** *n inv.* N, n.
na! [na] well!, why!, *Am. a.* hey!; ~, ~! come, come!; ~ *also!* there you are!; ~ *und?* so what?; ~ *warte!* you just wait!
Nabe ['nɑːbə] *f* (15) hub, nave.
Nabel ['~bəl] *m* (7[1]) navel; '**~binde** *f* umbilical band; '**~bruch** *m* umbilical hernia; '**~schau** F *f* narcissistic introspection; '**~schnur** *f* umbilical cord.
nach [nɑːx] **1.** *prp.* (*dat.*) *Richtung, Streben*: (*a.* ~ ... *hin*) to(wards), for; *Reihenfolge*: after; *Zeit*: after, past; *Art u. Weise, Maß, Vorbild*: according to, in accordance with; *der Zug* ~ *London* the train for London; ~ *dem Gewichte* by the weight; ~ *deutschem Gelde* in German money; *einer* ~ *dem andern* one by one; *fünf Minuten* ~ *eins* five minutes past one; *s. Empfang, Haus, Reihe, schmecken usw.*; **2.** *adv.* after; ~ *und* ~ little by little, gradually; ~ *wie vor* now as before, still; *mir* ~*!* follow me!
'**nach-äffen** (25) *v/t.* ape, mimic; *s. a. nachahmen.*
nach-ahm|en ['~ʔɑːmən] (25) *v/t. u. v/i.* imitate, copy; ape; (*fälschen*) counterfeit; '**~enswert** worth imitating, exemplary; '**2er** *m* (7), '**2erin** *f* imitator; '**2ung** *f* imitation; counterfeit; '**2ungs-trieb** *m* imitative instinct.
'**nach-arbeiten** *v/t.* (*nachahmen*) copy; (*ausbessern*) touch up; *v/i. zeitlich*: make up for lost time.
'**nach-arten:** *j-m* ~ take after a p.
Nachbar ['naxbɑːr] *m* (10 *u.* 13), '**~in** *f* neighbo(u)r; '**~...** neighbo(u)ring, adjacent; '**2lich** neighbo(u)rly; (*benachbart*) neighbo(u)ring; '**~schaft** *f* neighbo(u)rhood (*a. fig.*); '**~staat** *m* neighbo(u)ring state.
'**Nachbau** ⊕ *m* copying; reproduction.
Nachbehandlung ['nɑːx-] *f* ⚕ after-treatment; ⊕ subsequent treatment.
'**nachbestell|en** repeat one's order (et. for a th.); '**2ung** *f* repeat (-order).
'**nachbet|en** *v/i. u. v/t.* repeat mechanically, echo; '**2er** *m* (7), '**2erin** *f* (16[1]) parrot.
'**nachbezahl|en** *v/t. u. v/i.* pay afterwards; *noch et.*: pay the rest (of); *s. a. nachzahlen*; '**2ung** *f* subsequent payment.
'**nachbild|en** copy, imitate; '**2ung** *f* copy, imitation; *genaue*: replica.
'**nachbleiben** (sn) remain (*od.* lag) behind; *Schule*: be kept in.
'**nachblicken** (*dat.*) look after.
'**nachdatieren** (*vorausdatieren*) postdate; (*zurückdatieren*) antedate.
nachdem [~'deːm] *cj. zeitlich*: after, when; *Maß u. Grad*: *s.* je.
'**nachdenk|en 1.** think (*über acc.* over), reflect, meditate (on), *Am.* F mull (over); **2.** 2 *n* (6) reflection, meditation; '**~lich** thoughtful, reflecting, reflective; pensive.
'**Nachdichtung** *f* free version, adaptation.
'**nachdrängen** (sn; *dat.*) press (*od.* crowd) after; pursue closely.
'**nachdringen** (sn; *dat.*) pursue.
'**Nachdruck** *m* **1.** stress, emphasis; (*Tatkraft*) energy; *mit* ~ emphatically; energetically; ~ *legen auf* (*acc.*) stress, emphasize; **2.** *typ.* reprint; (*Raubdruck*) piracy; pirated edition; ~ *verboten* all rights reserved; '**2en** reprint; *ungesetzlich*: pirate.
nachdrücklich ['~drykliç] emphatic (-ally *adv.*); energetic(ally *adv.*), strong(ly *adv.*); ~ *betonen* emphasize.
'**Nachdrucks|recht** *n* copyright; '**2voll** *s. nachdrücklich.*
'**Nach-eifer|er** *m* (7) emulator; '**2n** (*dat.*) emulate; '**~ung** *f* emulation.
'**nach-eilen** (sn; *dat.*) hasten after.
'**nach-ei'nander** one after another, successively; *drei Tage* ~ for three days running.
'**nach-empfinden** *s. nachfühlen.*
Nachen ['naxən] *m* (6) boat, skiff.
'**Nach|-erbe** *m* reversionary heir; '**~-ernte** *f* second crop; *von Heu*: aftermath (*a. fig.*).
'**nach-erzähl|en** (*wiederholen*) repeat; (*wiedererzählen*) retell; *dem Englischen nacherzählt* adapted from the English; '**2ung** *f* repetition; adaption; *Schule*: re-narration.
'**Nachfahr** *m* descendant; '**2en** (sn; *dat.*) follow (in a car, by train, *usw.*).

'**Nachfeier** *f* after-celebration.
'**Nachfolg|e** *f* succession; ~ *Christi* Imitation of Christ; '**~ekonferenz** *f* follow-up conference; '**♀en** (sn; *dat.*) follow, succeed; '**♀end** following; *im ~en* in the following; '**~er(in** *f*) *m* (7 [16¹]) successor.
'**nachforder|n** demand additionally (*od.* subsequently); '**♀ung** *f* subsequent claim.
'**nachforsch|en** (*dat.*) investigate, make inquiries; inquire (*od.* search) for *a p.*, into *a th.*; '**♀ung** *f* investigation, inquiry, search; *~en anstellen s. nachforschen.*
'**Nachfrage** *f* inquiry; ⚕ demand (*nach* for); '**♀n** ask, inquire.
'**nachfühlen:** *j-m et.* ~ (*können*) feel with a p. (for a th.).
'**nachfüllen** fill (*od.* top) up; refill.
'**nachgeben** (*dat.*) give way (to), *S.*: give; *fig.* give in, yield (to), come round.
'**nachgeboren** posthumous.
'**Nachgebühr** ✆ *f* surcharge.
'**Nachgeburt** *f* afterbirth.
'**nachgehen** (sn) *j-m*: follow; *Geschäften*: attend to; (*nachforschen*) trace, follow up; *Uhr*: be slow, lose.
nachgemacht ['~gəmaxt] (*gefälscht*) counterfeit; (*unecht*) fake, phon(e)y; (*künstlich*) artificial, (*nur vor su.*) imitation.
'**nachgenannt** under-mentioned.
nachge-ordnet ['~gəˀɔrdnət] subordinate(d).
'**nachgerade** by now; (*wirklich*) really; (*allmählich*) gradually.
'**Nachgeschmack** *m* aftertaste (*a. fig.*).
nachgiebig ['~giːbiç] yielding (*a.* ⊕ = elastic), compliant; (*nachsichtig*) indulgent; ⚕ *Kurse*: declining; '**♀keit** *f* yieldingness; complaisance; indulgence.
'**nachgießen** add (more).
'**nachgrübeln** (*dat. od. über acc.*) ponder *od.* brood (over).
'**Nachhall** *m* (3¹, *o. pl.*) echo, resonance; '**♀en** (re-)echo, resound.
nachhaltig ['~haltiç] lasting, enduring; (*wirksam*) effective; (*hartnäckig*) persistent.
'**nachhängen** (*dat.*) give o.s. up to *a th.*; *s-n Gedanken* ~ muse; *örtlich*: lag behind.
'**nachhelfen** (*dat.*) help.
nach'her afterwards; (*später*) later (on); *bis ~!* see you later!, so long!; **♀ig** subsequent.
'**Nachhilfe** *f* assistance; *a.* = '**~unterricht** *m* repetitional lessons *pl.*, coaching.
'**nachhinken** lag behind.
'**Nachhol|bedarf** *m* backlog demand; '**♀en** make up for; *Versäumtes* ~ make up leeway.
'**Nachhut** ⚔ *f* rear(-guard).
'**Nach-impfung** ⚕ *f* re-vaccination.
'**nach-industriell** post-industrial.
'**nachjagen** (sn; *dat.*) pursue, chase.
'**Nachklang** *m* resonance; *fig.* reminiscence; (*Wirkung*) after-effect.
'**nachklingen** *s. nachhallen.*
Nachkomme ['~kɔmə] *m* (13) descendant, offspring; '**♀n** (sn; *dat.*) come after, follow; (*Schritt halten*) keep pace (*dat.* with); *fig. e-m Befehl, Wunsch*: comply with; *s-n Verpflichtungen*: meet; *e-m Versprechen*: keep; '**~nschaft** *f* descendants *pl.*, *bsd.* ⚖ issue.
'**Nachkriegs...** post-war.
'**Nachkur** *f* after-treatment.
Nachlaß ['~las] *m* (4[²]) *e-r Strafe usw.*: remission; *am Preis*: reduction; discount; *e-s Verstorbenen*: estate, assets *pl.*; *literarischer*: posthumous works *pl.*
'**nachlassen 1.** *v/t.* leave behind; *Geld*: allow; *et. vom Preise* ~ make a reduction in the price; (*lockern*) relax, let go; *v/i.* (*sich vermindern*) diminish, decrease; *Fieber, Schmerz, Regen, Sturm usw.*: abate; *Tätigkeit, Tempo usw.*: slacken; *Gesundheit*, ⚕ *Preise*: give way; *Interesse*: wane; *P.*: loosen one's grip; **2.** ♀ *n* slackening; decrease; abatement.
'**nachlässig** careless, negligent; '**♀keit** *f* negligence, carelessness.
'**nachlaufen** (sn; *dat.*) run after.
'**nachleben**¹ (*dat.*) (*befolgen*) live up to, observe; '**♀²** *n* after-life.
'**Nachlese** ⚘ *f* gleaning(s *pl.*).
'**nachlesen** *im Buch usw.*: look up.
'**nachliefer|n** *Fehlendes*: deliver subsequently; (*nochmals liefern*) repeat delivery of; '**♀ung** *f* subsequent delivery; repeat delivery.
'**nachlösen:** (*e-e Fahrkarte*) ~ take a supplementary ticket.
'**nachmachen** imitate (*j-m et.* a p. in a th.), copy; (*fälschen*) counterfeit, fake; *s. nachahmen.*
'**nachmalig** subsequent.

'**nachmals** afterwards.
'**nachmessen** check, measure again.
'**Nachmieter** *m* next (*od.* new) tenant.
'**Nachmittag** *m* afternoon; '⁀(s) in the afternoon; '**⁓svorstellung** *thea.* *f* matinée.
Nachnahme ['⁓na:mə] *f* (15) cash (*Am.* collect) on delivery; *gegen* (*od. per*) *⁓* (*schicken*) (send *a th.*) C.O.D.
'**Nachname** *m* last name, surname.
'**nachplappern** parrot.
'**Nachporto** *n* surcharge.
'**nachprüf|en** check; *Richtigkeit*: *a.* verify; (*nochmals prüfen*) re-examine, ⚖ review; '**⁀ung** *f* check (-ing).
'**nachrechnen** reckon over again; (*prüfen*) check.
'**Nachrede** ⚖ *f*: *üble ⁓* defamation, slander; '**⁀n:** *j-m Übles ⁓* slander a p.
Nachricht ['⁓riçt] *f* (16) (e-e a piece of) news; (*Bericht*) report; (*Zeitungs⁀*) news (item); (*Mitteilung*) information, message, notice; *⁓en pl. Radio, TV*: news(cast); *j-m ⁓ geben* let a p. know, inform a p., send a p. word (*über acc., von* of); '**⁓en-agentur** *f* news agency; '**⁓endienst** ⚔ *m* intelligence service; *Radio*: news service; '**⁓ensatellit** *m* communication satellite; '**⁓ensendung** *f* newscast; '**⁓ensperre** *f* news blackout; '**⁓ensprecher** *m* newscaster; '**⁓entechnik** *f* (tele-) communication engineering; communications *pl.*; '**⁓entruppe** ⚔ *f* signal corps; '**⁓enwesen** *n* communications *pl.*
'**nachrücken** (sn) move up.
'**Nachruf** *m* obituary (notice).
'**Nachruhm** *m* posthumous fame.
'**nachrühmen:** *j-m et. ⁓* say (in praise) of a p.
'**nachrüst|en** ⚔ rearm; '**⁀ung** *f* rearmament.
'**nachsagen** repeat; *man sagt ihm nach, daß* ... he is said to *inf.*
'**Nachsaison** *f* after-season.
'**Nachsatz** *gr. m* final clause.
'**nachschauen** have a look.
'**nachschicken:** *j-m et. ⁓* send after a p.; *Brief*: forward.
'**Nachschlage|buch** *n*, '**⁓werk** *n* reference-book.
'**nachschlagen** *in e-m Buch*: refer to, consult; *Wort usw.*: look up; *fig. j-m ⁓* take after a p.
'**nachschleichen** (sn; *dat.*) steal after; (*beschatten*) shadow.
'**nachschleppen** drag after (one).
'**Nachschlüssel** *m* skeleton-key.
'**nachschreiben** write from dictation; (*abschreiben*) copy.
'**Nachschrift** *f im Brief*: postscript (*abbr.* P.S.).
'**Nachschub** *m* supply.
'**nachsehen 1.** *v/i. u. v/t. j-m, e-r S.*: look after; *et.* (*prüfen*) check; (*schauen*) have a look; examine; *s. nachschlagen*; *j-m et. ⁓* (*hingehen lassen*) indulge a p. in a th., overlook (*od.* excuse) a p.'s *mistake etc.*; **2.** ⁀ *n* (6): *das ⁓ haben* be the loser; *Sport*: *dem Gegner das ⁓ geben* dismiss one's opponent.
'**nachsenden** *s. nachschicken.*
'**nachsetzen** *v/t.* place behind; *v/i.* (sn; *dat.*) give chase (to).
'**Nachsicht** *f* indulgence; *⁓ üben* stretch a point, *mit j-m*: have patience with; '**⁀ig**, '**⁀svoll** indulgent, lenient.
'**Nachsilbe** *gr. f* suffix.
'**nachsinnen** meditate, muse (*dat. od. über acc.* [up]on).
'**nachsitzen** *Schule*: be kept in; *⁓ lassen* keep in, detain.
'**Nachsommer** *m* late (*bsd. Am.* Indian) summer.
'**Nachspeise** *f s. Nachtisch.*
'**Nachspiel** *n thea.* afterpiece; ♪ postlude; *fig.* sequel.
'**nachsprechen** repeat (*j-m* a p.'s words).
'**nachspüren** (*dat.*) track, trace; (*nachspionieren*) spy on *a p.*
nächst [nɛ:çst] **1.** *adj.* (18, *s. nahe*) *Reihenfolge, Zeit*: next; *Entfernung, Beziehung, Verwandtschaft*: nearest; *s. Angehörigen, Mal, Zeit*; **2.** *prp.* next to, next after; '**⁓'best** (just) any; '**⁓'dem** soon; '**⁀e** *m* (18) fellow-creature, neighbo(u)r; *jeder ist sich selbst der ⁓* charity begins at home.
'**nachstehen** (*dat.*) be second to; be inferior to; '**⁓d** (*adv.* in the) following.
'**nachstell|en** *v/t.* place behind *od.* after; *Uhr*: put back; *Stellschraube usw.*: readjust; *v/i. j-m ⁓* persecute a p.; '**⁀ung** *f* persecution.
'**Nächst|enliebe** *f* charity; '**⁀ens**

shortly, (very) soon, before long; '2**folgend** next (in order); '2**liegend** nearest; *fig. das* 2*e* the obvious thing. [strive after.]
'**nachstreben** *j-m*: emulate; *e-r S.*:}
'**nachsuch|en** *v/t. u. v/i.* search (for *a th.*); *um et.* ~ apply for; '2**ung** *f* search, inquiry.
Nacht [naxt] *f* (14[1]) night; *fig. a.* darkness; *bei* ~, *des* ~*s s. nachts*; *bei* ~ *und Nebel davongehen* under cover of the night; *bis in die* ~ *hinein arbeiten* burn the midnight oil; *mit einbrechender* ~ at nightfall; F *sich die* ~ *um die Ohren schlagen* make a night of it; *über* ~ overnight (*a. fig.*); *zu* ~ *essen* have supper; *s. heilig*; '~**-arbeit** *f* night-work; '~**blindheit** *f* night-blindness; '~**-dienst** *m* night-duty.
'**Nachteil** *m* disadvantage; (*Mangel*) *a.* drawback; (*Schaden*) detriment, *bsd.* ⚖ prejudice; *im* ~ *sein* be at a disadvantage, be handicapped; *zum* ~ (*gen.*) to the disadvantage *usw.* of; '2**ig** disadvantageous, detrimental, prejudicial; (*abträglich*) derogatory; *sich* ~ *auswirken* (*auf acc.*) affect adversely.
nächtelang ['nɛçtəlaŋ] *adv.* for nights (together), night after night.
'**Nacht|-essen** *n* supper; '~**-eule** *f* night-owl; '~**falter** *m* moth; '~**-frost** *m* night frost; '~**hemd** *n* (*Herren*2) night-shirt; (*Damen*2, *Kinder*2) night-dress, F nightie.
Nachtigall ['naxtigal] *f* (16) nightingale. [night.]
nächtigen ['nɛçtigən] (25) pass the}
'**Nachtisch** *m* dessert, F afters *pl.*; (*Süßspeise*) sweet.
'**Nacht|jäger** ✈ *m* night fighter; '~**klub** *m* night-club; '~**leben** night life.
nächtlich ['nɛçtliç] nightly, nocturnal; '~**er'weile** at night-time.
'**Nacht|lokal** *n* night-club; '~**mahl** *n* supper; '~**musik** *f* serenade; '~**-portier** *m* night-porter; '~**quartier** *n* quarters *pl.* for the night.
Nachtrag ['~tra:k] *m* (3[3]) supplement; *zu e-m Testament*: codicil; *s. Nachschrift*; *Nachträge pl. in e-m Buch*: addenda; '2**en** (*zufügen*) add; ✝ *Bücher*: post up; *Posten*: book; *j-m et.* ~ carry after a p.; *fig. j-m nichts* ~ bear a p. no grudge; '2**end** resentful.
nachträglich ['~trɛ:kliç] (*ergänzend*) additional, supplementary; (*später*) subsequent.
'**Nachtruhe** *f* night rest.
nachts [naxts] at (*od.* by) night.
'**Nacht|schatten** ⚘ *m* nightshade; '~**schicht** *f* night-shift; '2**schlafend**: *zu* ~*er Zeit* in the middle of the night; '~**schwärmer(in** *f*) *m* *fig.* night-revel(l)er; '~**schwester** ⚕ *f* night-sister; '~**speicher-ofen** *m* night storage heater; '~**stuhl** ⚕ *m* night-stool; '~**tisch** *m* bedside table; '~**topf** *m* chamber(-pot).
'**nachtun**: *es j-m* ~ copy (*od.* imitate) a p.; *s. nachmachen.*
'**Nacht|wächter** *m* night-watchman; '2**wandeln** *usw. s. schlafwandeln usw.*; '~**zeug** *n* night-things *pl.*; '~**zug** 🚂 *m* night-train.
'**Nach|-untersuchung** ⚕ *f* follow-up examination; '~**-urlaub** *m* extended leave.
'**nachwachsen** (sn) grow again.
'**Nachwahl** *parl. f* by-election, *Am.* special election.
'**Nachwehen** *f/pl.* after-pains; *fig.* painful consequences, aftermath *sg.*
'**nachweinen** (*dat.*) bewail.
Nachweis ['~vaıs] *m* (4) proof; *s. Arbeits*2; (*Verzeichnis*) record, list; *den* ~ *führen* (*od. erbringen*) prove, show; '2**bar**, '2**lich** demonstrable; traceable; *adv.* as can be proved; 2**en** ['~zən] demonstrate; (*beweisen*) prove, show; (*feststellen*) establish; (*begründen*) substantiate; *j-m et.* ~ *e-e Schuld usw.*: prove that a p. has done a th., *et. Gewünschtes*: inform a p. about a th.
'**Nachwelt** *f* posterity.
'**Nachwinter** *m* second winter.
'**nachwirk|en** produce an after-effect; '2**ung** *f* after-effect; (*Folgen*) consequences *pl.*; ~*en des Krieges* aftermath of war.
'**Nachwort** *n* epilog(ue).
'**Nachwuchs** *m* after-growth; *fig. the* rising generation; '~... junior ...
'**nachzählen** count over, check.
'**nachzahl|en** *v/t. u. v/i.* pay extra *od.* in addition; '2**ung** *f* additional (*od.* extra) payment.
'**nachzeichnen** *v/t. u. v/i.* copy.
'**nachziehen** *v/t.* draw after (one); *den Fuß*: drag; *Strich usw.*: trace; *die Augenbrauen*: pencil; *Schraube usw.*: tighten; *v/i.* (sn; *dat.*) follow.

Nachzügler ['~tsy:glər] *m* (7), '**~in** *f* (16[1]) straggler, late-comer.
Nacken ['nakən] *m* (6) nape (of the neck), neck; *s. steifen*; '**~schlag** *m* rabbit-punch; *fig.* blow.
nackend ['nakənt], **nackt** [nakt] naked, nude; *fig.* bare; *Wahrheit*: naked, plain; *Tatsache*: hard.
'**Nackt|heit** *f* nakedness, nudity; '**~kultur** *f* nudism.
Nadel ['nɑ:dəl] *f* (15) needle (*a.* ⊕); (*Steck*~, *Haar*~) pin; *fig. wie auf ~n sitzen* be on pins and needles; '**~(holz)baum** *m* conifer(ous tree); **~hölzer** ['~hœltsər] *n/pl.* conifers; '**~kopf** *m* pin-head; '**~-öhr** *n* eye of a needle; '**~stich** *m* prick of a needle, stitch; *fig.* pin-prick; '**~streifen** *m/pl. Stoffmuster*: pin stripes *pl.*; '**~wald** *m* conifer(ous) wood.
Nagel ['nɑ:gəl] *m* (7[1]) nail (*a. anat.*); *hölzerner*: peg; (*Zier*~) stud; *langer*: spike; *fig. an den ~ hängen* give up; *den ~ auf den Kopf treffen* hit the nail on the head; *auf den Nägeln brennen* be very urgent; '**~bürste** *f* nail-brush; '**~feile** *f* nail-file; '**~geschwür** *n* whitlow; '**~haut** *f* cuticle; '**~lack** *m* nail-varnish; '~**n** (29) nail (*an, auf acc.* to); '~'**neu** brand-new; '**~pflege** *f* manicure; '**~probe** *f*: *die ~ machen* thumb one's glass; '**~schere** *f* (*eine ~* a pair of) nail-scissors *pl.*
nagen ['nɑ:gən] (25) gnaw, nibble (*an dat.* at); *an e-m Knochen ~* pick a bone; *fig. ~ an* prey upon.
'**Nager** *m*, '**Nagetier** *n* rodent.
nah [nɑ:], **nahe** ['nɑ:ə] (18[2], *sup. nächst*) near, close (*bei* to); *zeitlich*: *a.* impending, forthcoming; *Verwandter*: near; *~ verwandt* closely related; *Gefahr*: imminent; *s. näher, nächst*; *nahe daran sein, et. zu tun* be near doing a th.; *j-m zu nahe treten* hurt a p.'s feelings; *von nah und fern* from far and near.
'**Näh-arbeit** *f* needlework.
'**Nah-aufnahme** *f Film*: close-up.
Nähe ['nɛ:ə] *f* (15) nearness, proximity; *aus der ~* at close range; *in der ~* near at hand, close by; *in s-r ~* near him; *in der ~ der Stadt* near the town.
nahe'bei nearby, close by.
'**nahe|gehen** (sn; *dat.*) affect, grieve; '**~kommen** (sn; *dat.*) (*a. fig.*) come near, approach (to); '**~legen** suggest (*j-m et.* a th. to a p.); '**~liegen** suggest itself, be obvious; '**~liegend** near(by); *fig.* obvious.
nahen ['nɑ:ən] **1.** (25, sn; *a. sich ~*; *dat.*) approach; **2.** ~ *n* approach.
nähen ['nɛ:ən] *v/t. u. v/i.* (25) sew, stitch; ⚕ *a.* suture (up).
näher ['nɛ:ər] (18) nearer *usw.* (*s. nahe*); *~e Einzelheiten* = '~**e(s)** *n* (18) details *pl.*, (further) particulars *pl.*
Näherei [nɛ:ə'raɪ] *f* (15) sewing; [(*Nadelarbeit*) needlework.]
'**Näherin** *f* (16[1]) seamstress.
näher|n ['nɛ:ərn] (25) approach (*sich j-m* a p.); *sich ~* draw near; '**~treten** (*dat.*) *fig.* approach *a p.*, *a th.*; '~**ungswert** *m* approximate value.
'**nahestehend** closely connected [(*dat.* with).]
'**nahezu** *adv.* nearly, almost, next to.
'**Nähgarn** *n* sewing-thread.
'**Nahkampf** ⚔ *m* close combat; *Boxen*: infight(ing).
'**Näh|kästchen** *n* (lady's) work-box; '**~korb** *m* work-basket; '**~maschine** *f* sewing-machine; '**~nadel** *f* (sewing-)needle.
nahm [nɑ:m] *pret. v. nehmen.*
'**Nährboden** *m* fertile soil (*a. fig.*); *für Bazillen*: culture-medium; *des Verbrechens usw.*: hotbed.
nähren ['nɛ:rən] (25) nourish (*a. fig.*); *ein Kind*: nurse; *sich ~ von* live (*od.* feed) on.
'**Nähr|flüssigkeit** *f* nutrient fluid; '**~gehalt** *m* nutrient content.
nahrhaft ['nɑ:rhaft] nutritious, nourishing, nutritive; *Speise*: substantial.
'**Nähr|hefe** *f* nutritive yeast; '**~kraft** *f* nutritive power; '**~krem** *f* skin-food; '**~lösung** ⚕ *f* nutrient solution; '**~mittel** *n(/pl.)* farinacious products, cereal(s); '**~salz** *n* nutritive salt(s *pl.*); '**~stoff** *m* nutrient.
'**Nahrung** *f* food (*a. fig.*), nourishment; (*Kost*) diet; (*Futter*) feed; (*Unterhalt*) support; '**~smangel** *m* food shortage; '**~smittel** *n* (article of) food, foodstuff, *pl.* foodstuffs; '**~smittelchemiker** *m* food chemist; '**~smittelvergiftung** *f* food poisoning; '**~ssorgen** *f/pl.* worries about food; '**~sstoff** *m* nutrient.
'**Nährwert** *m* nutritive value.
'**Nähseide** *f* sewing-silk.
Naht [nɑ:t] *f* (14[1]) seam; ⚕, ♀ suture;

⚔ boundary; ⊕ seam, joint; '≈**los** seamless (*a.* ⊕).

'**Nahverkehr** *m* local (*od.* suburban) traffic; *mot.* short-haul traffic; *teleph.* toll service; '**~smittel** *n/pl.* local transportation *sg.*; '**~szug** *m* commuter train.

'**Nähzeug** *n* sewing-kit.

'**Nahziel** *n* immediate objective.

naiv [na'ʔi:f] naive, ingenuous, simple; ≈**ität** [~ʔivi'tɛ:t] *f* naïveté (*fr.*), ingenuousness, simplicity.

Name ['nɑ:mə] *m* (13[1]) name; *fig.* *im ~n* (*gen.*) on behalf of; (*nur*) *dem ~n nach* nominal, *adv.* in name only; *j-n dem ~ nach kennen* know a p. by name; *ein Ding beim rechten ~n nennen* call a spade a spade; *darf ich um Ihren ~n bitten?* may I ask your name?; *sich e-n ~n machen* make a name for o.s.; *s. namens.*

'**Namen|gebung** *f* naming; '**~liste** *f*, '**~verzeichnis** *n* list (*od.* register) of names; '≈**los** nameless; *fig. a.* unspeakable.

'**namens** named, of the name of; (*gen.*) (*in j-s Namen*) in the name of, on behalf of.

'**Namens|-aktie** ⚕ *f* registered share; '**~-aufruf** *m* roll-call; '**~tag** *m* fête-day, name-day; '**~vetter** *m* namesake; '**~zug** *m* signature, autograph.

'**namentlich** *adj.* nominal; *adv.* by name; (*besonders*) especially; *parl.* *~e Abstimmung* roll-call vote.

namhaft ['nɑ:mhaft] (*berühmt*) notable, renowned; (*bedeutend*) considerable, substantial; *j-n ~ machen* (mention by) name, *weitS.* identify.

nämlich ['nɛ:mliç] **1.** *adj. the* same; **2.** *adv. erläuternd*: namely, that is (to say), (*abbr.* i.e. *od.* viz.); *begründend*: ..., you know.

nannte ['nantə] *pret. v. nennen.*

nanu! [na'nu:] I say!, *Am.* gee!

Napalm ⚗ ['nɑ:palm] *n* (11, *o. pl.*) napalm.

Napf [napf] *m* (3[3]) bowl; '**~kuchen** *m* pound-cake.

Naphtha ['nafta] *n* (11, *o.pl.*) naphtha; **~lin** [~'li:n] *n* (11, *o. pl.*) naphthalene.

Narbe ['narbə] *f* (15) scar; 🕮 cicatrice; (*Leder*≈) grain; ⚘ stigma; '≈**n** (25) scar; cicatrize; *Leder*: grain.

'**narbig** scarred; *Leder*: grained.

Narko|se [nar'ko:zə] *f* (15) narcosis; **~se-arzt** *m* an(a)esthetist; **~tikum** [~'ko:tikum] *n* (9[2]), ≈**tisch** narcotic; ≈**tisieren** [~koti'zi:rən] an(a)esthetize.

Narr [nar] *m* (12) fool; *e-n ~en an j-m gefressen haben* dote (up)on a p., be infatuated with a p.; *zum ~en haben od. halten*, '≈**en** make a fool of, dupe, fool.

'**Narren|freiheit** *f* fool's licen|ce, *Am.* -se; '**~haus** *n* madhouse; '**~kappe** *f* fool's cap; '**~(s)posse(n** *pl.*) *f* foolery *sg.*; '≈**sicher** foolproof; '**~streich** *m* foolish trick.

Narretei [~ə'taɪ] *f* (16), '**Narrheit** *f* folly, tomfoolery.

Närrin ['nɛ:rin] *f* fool(ish woman).

'**närrisch** foolish; (*verrückt*) mad, (F *a. fig.*) crazy; (*sonderbar*) odd.

Narzisse [nar'tsisə] *f* narcissus; *gelbe ~* daffodil.

Narzißmus [~'tsismus] *m* (16, *o.pl.*) narcism.

nasal [na'zɑ:l] nasal; ≈(**laut**) *m* nasal (sound).

naschen ['naʃən] *v/i. u. v/t.* (27) nibble (*an dat.* at); *verstohlen*: eat on the sly; *gern ~* have a sweet tooth.

Nascher ['naʃər] *m* (7), '**~in** *f* (16[1]) sweet-tooth; **~ei** [~'raɪ] *f* (16) sweet(s *pl.*), titbit.

'**nasch|haft** fond of sweet things; '≈**katze** *f* sweet-tooth; '≈**werk** *n* sweets *pl.*; dainties *pl.*

Nase ['nɑ:zə] *f* (15) nose; *zo. a.* snout; *e-r Kanne usw.*: spout; *durch die ~ sprechen s. näseln*; *die ~ hoch tragen* be stuck-up; *j-m e-e lange ~ machen* thumb one's nose at a p.; *fig. e-e* (*gute od. feine*) *~ haben für* have a flair for; *s. putzen, rümpfen*; *j-m auf der ~ herumtanzen* play fast and loose with a p.; *j-n an der ~ herumführen s. nasführen*; *j-m et. auf die ~ binden* tell a p. a th.; *s-e ~ in alles stecken* poke one's nose into other people's business, be a busybody; *immer der ~ nach!* just follow your nose!; F *j-m et. unter die ~ reiben* bring a th. home to a p.; rub it in; *die ~ voll haben von* be fed up with, be sick of.

näseln ['nɛ:zəln] **1.** (29) speak through the nose, nasalize; **2.** ≈ *n* (6) nasal twang; '**~d** *Sprache*: nasal.

'**Nasen|bein** *n* nasal bone; '**~bluten** *n* nose-bleed(ing); '**~flügel** *m* side of the nose; '**⁓länge** *f Rennsport: um e-e ⁓* by a short head; '**⁓loch** *n* nostril; '**⁓schleim** *m* nasal mucus; '**⁓schleimhaut** *f* mucous membrane (of the nose); '**⁓spitze** *f* tip of the nose; '**⁓tropfen** *m/pl.* nose drops.

naseweis ['⁓vaɪs] (18) pert, saucy; '**2heit** *f* sauciness, pertness.

nasführen ['nɑ:sfy:rən] fool.

Nashorn ['nɑ:s-] *n* (1^2) rhinoceros.

naß [nas] **1.** (18^1 [*u.* ^{2}]) wet; (*feucht*) moist; **2.** 2 *n* liquid; water.

Nassauer ['nasaʊər] F *m* (7) sponger; '**2n** sponge (*bei j-m* on).

Nässe ['nɛsə] *f* (15) wet(ness); moisture; *vor ⁓ schützen!* keep dry!; '**2n** (28) wet; moisten.

'**naß|forsch** F brash; '**⁓kalt** damp and cold; clammy.

Nation [na'tsjo:n] *f* (16) nation.

national [⁓jo'nɑ:l] national; **2flagge** *f* national flag; *die britische ⁓* the Union Jack; *die amerikanische ⁓* the Stars and Stripes *pl.*; **2hymne** *f* national anthem; **⁓i'sieren** [⁓nali-] nationalize; **2ismus** [⁓'lismus] *m* nationalism; **2ität** [⁓i'tɛ:t] *f* nationality; **2mannschaft** [⁓'nɑ:l-] *f Sport*: national team; **2-ökono'mie** *f* political economy; **2park** *m* national park; **2sozialismus** *m* National Socialism; **2spieler(in** *f*) *m Sport*: international player.

Natrium ['nɑ:trium] *n* (11) sodium.

Natron ['nɑ:trɔn] *n* (11) natron; (*doppelt*)*kohlensaures ⁓* (bi)carbonate of soda; '**⁓lauge** *f* soda lye.

Natter ['natər] *f* (15) adder, viper.

Natur [na'tu:r] *f* (16) nature; (*Leibesbeschaffenheit*) constitution; (*Gemütsanlage*) *s. Naturell*; *nach der ⁓ zeichnen* draw from nature; *von ⁓* by nature; *j-m zur zweiten ⁓ werden* become second nature with a p.; *in ⁓, in 2a* in kind.

Naturalien [natu'rɑ:ljən] *pl. inv.* natural produce *sg.*; (*Naturalwert*) value in kind; **⁓kabinett** *n*, **⁓sammlung** *f* natural history collection.

natural|i'sieren [⁓rali-] naturalize; **2ismus** [⁓ra'lismus] *m* (16, *o. pl.*) naturalism; **⁓istisch** naturalistic(ally *adv.*).

Natural|leistung [⁓'rɑ:l-] *f* payment in kind; **⁓lohn** *m* wages *pl.* in kind.

Natur|-anlage [na'tu:r-] *f* disposition; **⁓-arzt** *m* nature doctor; **2belassen** natural; **⁓beschreibung** *f* description of nature; **⁓bursche** *m* child of nature.

Naturell [natu'rɛl] *n* (3^1) nature, disposition, temper(ament).

Na'tur|-ereignis *n*, **⁓-erscheinung** *f* phenomenon; **⁓forscher** *m* (natural) scientist; **⁓forschung** *f* natural science; **⁓gabe** *f* gift of nature, talent; **2gemäß** natural(ly *adv.*); **⁓geschichte** *f* natural history; **2geschichtlich** of natural history; **⁓gesetz** *n* natural law; **2getreu** true to nature; life-like; full-scale; **⁓heilkunde** *f* naturopathy, nature cure; **⁓heilkundige** *m* naturopath; **⁓katastrophe** *f* natural disaster; **⁓kraft** *f* natural force; **⁓kunde** *f Schule*: nature study; **⁓lehre** *f* physics *sg.*; **⁓lehrpfad** *m* nature trail.

natürlich [na'ty:rliç] natural (*a.* ⚖, *Kind, Person, Tod*); (*echt*) genuine; (*ungekünstelt*) unaffected, artless; (*einfach*) simple; *adv.* of course, naturally; **2keit** *f* naturalness; simplicity.

Na'tur|mensch *m* man of nature; **⁓notwendigkeit** *f* physical necessity; **⁓recht** *n* natural right; **⁓reich** *n* kingdom of nature; **⁓schutz** *m* conservation; **⁓schützer** *m* (7) conservationist; **⁓schutzgebiet** *n* nature reserve; **⁓seide** *f* natural silk; **⁓trieb** *m* instinct; **⁓volk** *n* primitive race; **⁓wissenschaft** *f* (natural) science; **⁓wissenschaftler** *m* (natural) scientist; **⁓wunder** *n* prodigy.

Naut|ik ['naʊtik] *f* (16) nautical science, nautics *pl.*; '**2isch** nautical.

Navigation [naviga'tsjo:n] *f inv.* navigation.

Nebel ['ne:bəl] *m* (7) fog; *weniger dicht*: mist; ⚔ smoke(-screen); *s. Nacht*; '**⁓bank** *f* fog-bank; '**⁓fleck** *m* nebula; '**2haft** foggy; *fig. a.* nebulous, hazy; '**⁓horn** *n* fog-horn; '**⁓scheinwerfer** *mot. m* fog lamp; '**⁓schleier** *m* veil of mist; '**⁓schlußleuchte** *mot. f* rear fog lamp; '**⁓wetter** *n* foggy weather.

neben ['ne:bən] beside, by the side of; (*unmittelbar ⁓*) next to; (*nahe bei*) close to, near; (*nebst*) apart from, beside; (*verglichen mit*) against, compared with.

'**Neben|-absicht** *f* secondary object; **2'-an** next door; in(to) the next room; '**⁓-anschluß** *teleph. m* extension; '~-**arbeit** *f* extra work; side-line; '~-**ausgaben** *f/pl.* incidental expenses, extras; '~-**ausgang** *m* side-door; '~**bedeutung** *f* secondary meaning, connotation; '~-**begriff** *m* accessory notion; ♀'**bei** close by; (*beiläufig*) by the way, incidentally; (*außerdem*) besides; '~**beruf** *m*, '~**beschäftigung** *f* additional occupation, avocation, side-line; '♀**beruflich** avocational; *nur attr.* spare-time; side-line; '~**buhler** *m* (7), '~**buhlerin** *f* (16¹) rival; '~**buhlerschaft** *f* rivalry; '~-**einander 1.** *n* (7, *o. pl.*) coexistence; **2.** ♀ side by side; (*gleichzeitig*) simultaneously; '~-**ei'nanderschaltung** ⚡ *f* parallel connection; '~-**ein'anderstellen** put side by side; *fig.* (*vergleichen*) compare; '~-**eingang** *m* side-entrance; '~-**einkünfte** *f/pl.*, '~-**einnahmen** *f/pl.* casual emoluments, perquisites *pl.*; '~-**erscheinung** *f* accompaniment; side-effect; '~**fach** *n beim Studium*: subsidiary subject, *Am.* minor; *als ~ studieren* take as subsidiary subject, *Am.* minor in; '~**fluß** *m* tributary; affluent; '~**gasse** *f* by-lane; '~**gebäude** *n* adjoining building; (*Anbau*) annex(e); '~**gedanke** *m* secondary thought; *s. Hintergedanke*; '~**geräusch** *n Radio*: atmospherics, strays *pl.*; '~**gericht** *n* side-dish, entremets (*fr.*); '~**geschmack** *m* smack (*a. fig.*); '~**gewinn** *m* incidental profit; '~**gleis** 🚂 *n* siding, *bsd. Am.* side-track; *auf ein ~ schieben* side-track; '~-**handlung** *f* underplot, episode; '♀'**her**, '♀'**hin** by his (her) side; along with; *s. nebenbei*; '~**höhle** *anat. f* sinus; '~-**interesse** *n* private interest; '~**kläger** ⚖ *m* accessory prosecutor; '~**kosten** *pl.* extras; '~**linie** *f* collateral line; 🚂 branch line; '~-**mann** *m* next man (*a.* ⚔); '~**mensch** *m s. Mitmensch*; '~**niere** *f* adrenal gland; '~**produkt** *n* by-product; *der Raumforschung etc.*: spin-off; '~**rolle** *f* supporting part; '~**sache** *f* matter of secondary importance, minor detail; '♀**sächlich** subordinate, incidental; (*unwichtig*) unimportant; (*abwegig*) irrelevant; '~**saison** *f* off-season; '~-**satz** *gr. m* subordinate clause; '~-**sender** *m Radio*: relay (*lokaler*: regional) station; '♀**stehend** in the margin; '~**stehende** *m, f* by-stander; '~**stelle** *f* branch(-office); *teleph.* extension; '~**straße** *f* side-road (*od.* street); '~**tisch** *m* next table; '~**tür** *f* side-door; '~-**umstand** *m* accessory circumstance; '~**verdienst** *m s. Nebeneinkünfte*; ~**weg** ['~ve:k] *m* by-way; '~**wirkung** *f* side-effect; '~-**zimmer** *n* adjoining room; '~**zweck** *m* subordinate purpose.

'**neblig** foggy, misty.

nebst [ne:pst] (*dat.*) (together) with, besides; in addition to.

Necessaire [nesɛ'sɛ:r] *n* (11) necessaire (*fr.*); toiletry kit.

neck|en ['nɛkən] (25) tease; ♀**erei** [~ə'raɪ] *f* (16) banter; '~**isch** (fond of) teasing; (*mutwillig*) playful; (*drollig*) droll, comical.

Neffe ['nɛfə] *m* (16) nephew.

Negation [nega'tsjo:n] *f* negation.

negativ ['ne:gati:f, ~'ti:f], ♀ *n* (3¹) ⚡, *phys.*, *phot.* negative.

Neger ['ne:gər] *m* (7) negro; '~**in** *f* (16¹) negress.

negieren [ne'gi:rən] answer in the negative; negate.

Negligé [negli'ʒe:] *n* (11) négligé (*fr.*).

nehmen ['ne:mən] (30) *allg.* take (*a. an sich ~*; *a. Beförderungsmittel, Hindernis, Kurve*; *a.* ⚔); (*annehmen*) *a.* accept; (*weg~*) take away (*a. fig. befreien von, rauben*); (*anstellen*) take, engage; *auf sich ~* undertake, *Amt, Bürde*: assume, *Verantwortung*: accept, *Folgen*: bear; *Speise zu sich ~* have, take; (*sich bedienen*) help o.s. (*von* to); *e-n Anfang (ein Ende) ~* begin (end); *j-n zu ~ wissen* have a way with; *ich lasse es mir nicht ~* I insist (*zu inf.* upon *ger.*); *s. Angriff, Anspruch, Beispiel, ernst, Freiheit, genau, Partei, streng usw.*; *wie man's nimmt* that depends!

Neid [naɪt] *m* (3) envy; (*Mißgunst*) jealousy; *aus ~* out of envy; *grün vor ~* green with envy; *das muß ihm der ~ lassen* you have to hand it to him; ♀**en** ['~dən] (26) envy (*j-m et.* a p. a th.); '~**er** *m* (7) envier; ♀**isch** ['~dɪʃ] envious (*auf acc.* of); ♀**los** ['naɪt-] free from envy, ungrudging; '~**hammel** F *m* dog in the manger.

Neige ['naɪgə] *f* (15) slope; *a. fig.* (*Abnahme*) decline; (*Rest*) *im Fasse* *usw.*: dregs *pl.*; *im Glas*: heel-tap; *zur ~ gehen* (be on the) decline, *Vorrat*: run low, *bsd.* ✝ run short; *zeitlich*: draw to an end; *bis zur ~ leeren* drain to the dregs; '**⁓n** (25) *v/t.* bend, incline; (*a. sich ~*) bow; (*kippen*) tilt; *Ebene*: slope; *sich ~ Tag usw.*: draw to a close; *s.* geneigt; *v/i. ~ zu et.* incline to, tend to, be liable (*od.* prone) to.

'**Neigung** *f allg.* inclination; (*Fläche*) slope, incline; 🚂, *Straße*: gradient; ⚒ dip (*a. der Magnetnadel, e-r Straße, e-s Schiffs*); (*Kipplage*) tilt; (*Hang, Vorliebe*) inclination, propensity, bent (*zu* to, for), tendency (towards); (*Zu⁓*) affection (for); (*~ zu Erkrankungen*) liability (to); '**~s-ehe** *f* love match; '**~swinkel** *m* angle of inclination.

nein [naɪn] no; '**⁓stimme** *parl. f* no (*pl.* noes), *Am.* nay.

Nektar ['nɛktaːr] *m* (3¹) nectar.

Nelke ['nɛlkə] *f* (15) carnation, pink; (*Gewürz⁓*) clove.

nennbar ['nɛnbaːr] mentionable.

nennen ['nɛnən] (30) name, call; (*bezeichnen*) *a.* term; *Kandidaten*: nominate; (*erwähnen*) mention; *Sport*: (*sich melden*) enter (*zu* for); *sich ... ~* be called ...; '**~swert** worth mentioning; appreciable.

'**Nenn|er** ⚒ *m* (7) denominator; *s. bringen*; '**~form** *gr. f* infinitive; '**~geld** *n Sport*: entry-fee; '**~kurs** ✝ *m* par value; '**~leistung** ⊕ *f* rated output (*od.* power); '**~ung** *f* naming; *e-s Kandidaten*: nomination; *Sport*: entry; '**~wert** *m* nominal (*od.* face) value; *zum ~* at par.

Neofaschismus *pol.* ['neo-] *m inv.* Neo-Fascism.

Neologismus [neolo'gismus] *m* (16²) neologism.

Neon ⚗ ['neːɔn] *n* (9, *o. pl.*) neon; '**~licht** *n* neon light; '**~röhre** *f* neon tube.

Nerv [nɛrf] *m* (8 *u.* 12) nerve; *j-m auf die ~en fallen od. gehen* get on a p.'s nerves; *die ~en verlieren* lose one's head; '**⁓en** F (25) be a pain in the neck (*j-n* to a p.).

'**Nerven|-arzt** *m* neurologist; '**⁓aufreibend** nerve-racking; '**~bahn** *anat. f* nervous tract; '**~belastung** *f* nerve strain; '**~bündel** *n anat.* nerve bundle; *P.*: bundle of nerves; '**~entzündung** *f* neuritis; '**~gas** *n* nerve gas; '**~heil-anstalt** *f* mental hospital; '**⁓krank,** '**⁓leidend** neurotic; '**~krankheit** *f*, '**~leiden** *n* nervous disease; '**~krieg** *m* war of nerves; '**~sache** *f*: (*eine*) *reine ~* a matter of nerves; '**~schmerz** *m* neuralgia; '**~schock** *m* nervous shock; '**⁓schwach** neurasthenic; '**~schwäche** *f* neurasthenia; *weitS.* bad nerves *pl.*; '**⁓stärkend** tonic; '**~system** *n* nervous system; '**~zelle** *f* nerve cell; '**~zentrum** *n* nerve cent|re, *Am.* -er; '**~zusammenbruch** *m* nervous breakdown.

nerv|ig ['nɛrviç] sinewy; **~ös** [~'vøːs] nervous; *~ machen* (*werden*) make (get) nervous; **⁓osität** [~vozi'tɛːt] *f* (16) nervousness.

Nerz *zo.* [nɛrts] *m* (3²) mink; '**~mantel** *m* mink coat.

Nessel ['nɛsəl] *f* (15) nettle; *fig. sich in die ~n setzen* get into hot water; '**~fieber** *n* nettle-rash; '**~tuch** *n* muslin.

Nest [nɛst] *n* (1¹) nest; *fig.* bed; (*Kleinstadt*) (awful) hole.

nesteln ['nɛstəln] (29): *~ an* (*dat.*) fiddle (*od.* fuss) with.

'**Nest|häkchen** *n*, '**~küken** *n* nestling; *fig.* pet.

nett [nɛt] nice; *~ von dir!* nice of you!; '**⁓igkeit** *f* niceness.

netto ['nɛto] net, clear; '**⁓betrag** *m* net amount; '**⁓-einkommen** *n* net income; '**⁓gewicht** *n* net weight; '**⁓gewinn** *m* net profit; '**⁓lohn** *m* take-home pay; '**⁓preis** *m* net price; '**⁓rendite** *f* net return.

Netz [nɛts] *n* (3²) net; (*Eisenbahn⁓, Fluß⁓*) network; ⚡ mains *pl.*; *Radio*: grid (*a. Kartengitter*), (*Sendebereich*) network; *ins ~ gehen fig.* walk into the trap; '**~-anschluß** *m* mains supply; '**~(-anschluß)-empfänger** *m* mains receiver; '**~-antenne** *f* mains aerial (*Am.* antenna); '**~-auge** *zo. n* compound eye; '**~ball** *m Tennis*: net; '**~betrieb** ⚡ *m*: *mit ~* mains-operated; '**⁓en** (27) moisten; '**~haut** *f des Auges*: retina; '**~hemd** *n* string vest; '**~karte** 🚂 *f* area season ticket; '**~teil** *n e-s Batteriegeräts*: mains-adapter.

neu [nɔʏ] new; (*frisch*) fresh (*a. fig.*); (*~artig*) novel; (*kürzlich geschehen*) recent; (*neuzeitlich*) modern; *aufs ~e, von ~em* anew;

afresh; *~ere Sprachen f/pl.* modern languages; *~e(re) Zeit* modern times *pl.*; *~eren Datums* of recent date; *~estens, in ~ester Zeit* (quite) recently; *2es* something new; *~ste Nachrichten f/pl.* latest news; *was gibt es 2es?* what is the news?, *Am.* what is new?; *das ist mir nichts 2es* that's no news to me; *~ beleben* revive; **'2e** *m* (18) new man; (*Neuling*) novice; *s. Neuankömmling.*

'Neu|-ankömmling *m* newcomer; **'~-anschaffung** *f* recent acquisition; **'2-artig** novel; **'~-auflage** *f*, **'~-ausgabe** *f* new edition, republication; (*Neudruck*) reprint; **'~bau** *m* rebuilding; (*Haus*) new building; **'2be-arbeiten** revise; **'~be-arbeitung** *f* revision; **'~druck** *m* reprint; **'2-entdeckt** recently discovered.

neuer|dings ['~ərdiŋs] of late, recently; **'2er** *m* (7) innovator; **'~lich** *adj.* renewed, fresh; *adv.* lately.

'Neu-erscheinung *typ. f* new publication.

'Neuerung *f* innovation; **'2ssüchtig** bent on innovation(s).

'neu|gebacken fresh; *fig.* newly-fledged; **'~geboren** new-born; *sich wie ~ fühlen* feel a (completely) different person; **'~gestalten** reorganize; *bsd.* ⊕ redesign; **'2gestaltung** *f* reorganization; **2gier(de)** ['~giːr (-də)] *f* curiosity, inquisitiveness; **'~gierig** curious (*auf acc.* about, of), inquisitive, F nosy; *ich bin ~, ob* I wonder whether *od.* if; **'2heit** *f* newness, (*a. Gegenstand*) novelty; **'~hochdeutsch** Modern High German.

'Neuigkeit *f* (e-e a piece of) news; **'~skrämer** *m* newsmonger.

'Neu-inszenierung *f* new staging, new production.

'Neujahr *n* New Year('s Day); **'~s-abend** *m* New Year's Eve; **'~s-wunsch** *m* good wishes *pl.* for the New Year.

'Neu|land *n*: *~ erschließen* break new ground (*a. fig.*); **'2lich** *adv.* the other day, recently; **'~ling** *m* (3[1]) novice, new hand, beginner; *contp.* greenhorn; **'2modisch** fashionable; *contp.* new-fangled; **'~mond** *m* new moon.

neun [nɔʏn] nine; *alle ~(e) werfen* throw all the ninepins; **'2-eck** *n* (3[1]) nonagon; **~erlei** ['~ərlaɪ] of nine (different) sorts; **'~fach, ~fältig** ['~fɛltiç] ninefold; **'~hundert** nine hundred; **'~jährig** nine-year-old; **'~mal** nine times; **'~malklug** *iro.* over-smart; **'2malkluge** *m, f* wiseacre, smart aleck; **'~te** ninth; **'2tel** *n* (7) ninth (part); **'~tens** ninthly; **'~zehn** nineteen; **'~zehnte** nineteenth; **~zig** ['~tsiç] ninety; **'~zigste** ninetieth.

'Neu-ordnung *f* reorganization, reform.

'Neuphilologe *m* student (*od.* teacher) of modern languages.

Neur|algie [nɔʏral'giː] *f* (15) neuralgia; **2algisch** [~'ralgiʃ] neuralgic; **~asthenie** [~asteˈniː] *f* (15) neurasthenia; **~astheniker** [~'steːnikər] *m* (7), **2asthenisch** [~'steːniʃ] neurasthenic.

'Neu|regelung *f* rearrangement, readjustment; **'~reiche** *m* (wealthy) parvenu (*fr.*); *die ~n pl.* the new rich.

Neuro|se ⚕ [nɔʏ'roːzə] *f* (15) neurosis; **~tiker** *m*, **2tisch** neurotic.

'Neu|schnee *m* new-fallen snow; **'~silber** *n* German silver; **'~sprachler** *m s. Neuphilologe*; **'2sprachlich** modern language ...

neutral [nɔʏ'trɑːl] neutral; *~ bleiben* remain neutral; **~i'sieren** [~trali-] neutralize; **2ität** [~'tɛːt] *f* (16) neutrality.

Neutron *phys.* ['nɔʏtrɔn] *n* (8[1]) neutron; **~enbombe** [nɔʏ'troːnən-] *f* neutron bomb.

Neutrum ['nɔʏtrum] *n* (9[2]) neuter (word).

'Neu|verfilmung *f* remake; **'2vermählt** newly married; *die 2en pl.* the newly-weds; **'~wahl** *f* new election; **'2wertig** practically new; **'~wort** *n* neologism; **'~zeit** *f* modern times *pl.*; **'2zeitlich** modern.

nicht [niçt] not; *~ besser* no better; *~ abtrennbar* non-detachable; *~ (doch)!* don't!; *er kam ~* he didn't come, he failed to appear; *s. auch, gar usw.*; *~ wahr?* is it not so?, F isn't that so?; *er ist krank, ~ wahr?* he is ill, isn't he?; *Sie tun es, ~ wahr?* you will do it, won't you?; *du kennst ihn nicht, ~ wahr?* you don't know him, do you?

'**Nicht|-achtung** *f* disregard; want of respect; slight; '**⁀-amtlich** unofficial; '**~'-angriffs-pakt** *m* non-aggression treaty; '**~-annahme** *f* non-acceptance; '**~be-achtung** *f*, '**~befolgung** *f* non-observance; '**~bezahlung** *f* non-payment.

Nichte ['niçtə] *f* (15) niece.

'**nicht|-ehelich** *Kind*: illegitimate; '**⁀-einhaltung** *f* non-observance; '**⁀-einmischung** *f* non-intervention; '**⁀-erfüllung** ⚖ *f* non-performance, default; '**⁀-erscheinen** *n* non-appearance; ⚖ *a.* default.

'**nichtig:** (*null und*) ~ (null and) void, invalid; (*eitel*) vain, futile; *Vorwand*: flimsy; *für* (*null und*) ~ *erklären* declare (null and) void, annul.

'**Nichtigkeit** *f* nullity, invalidity; vanity, nothingness; ~*en pl.* trifles; '**~sklage** ⚖ *f* nullity action.

'**Nicht|leiter** ⚡ *m* non-conductor; '**~mitglied** *n* non-member; '**~raucher** *m* non-smoker; '**⁀rostend** rustproof; *Stahl*: stainless.

nichts [niçts] **1.** nothing, naught, not anything; ~ *als* nothing but; ~ *dergleichen* no such thing; *soviel wie* ~ next to nothing; ~ *weniger als* anything but; *um* ~ for nothing; *um* ~ *spielen* play for love; *mir* ~, *dir* ~ quite cooly; *s. ander, machen, weiter*; **2.** ⁀ *n inv.* nothing(ness); (*a. fig. P.*) nonentity; (*Leere*) void; (*Geringfügigkeit*) trifle, *a* (mere) nothing; *aus dem* ~ from nowhere; *vor dem* ~ *stehen* be faced with utter ruin; '**~-ahnend** unsuspecting.

'**Nichtschwimmer** *m* non-swimmer.

'**nichts|desto'weniger** nevertheless, none the less; '**⁀könner** *m* (7) incapable person, *sl.* washout; **~nutzig** ['~nutsiç] good-for-nothing, useless; '**~sagend** meaningless; (*leer*) empty (*a. Gesicht*); (*farblos*) flat; *Antwort*: vague; **⁀tuer** ['~tu:ər] *m* (7) do-nothing, idler; '**⁀tun** *n* idleness; inaction; '**~wisser** *m* ignoramus; '**~würdig** base, infamous; '**⁀würdigkeit** *f* baseness, infamy.

'**Nicht|vorhandensein** *n* absence; lack; '**~wissen** *n* ignorance; '**~zutreffendes** *streichen* delete which is inapplicable.

Nickel ['nikəl] *n* (7) nickel; '**~brille** *f* steel-rimmed spectacles *pl.*

nick|en ['nikən] (25) nod; '**⁀erchen** F *n* (6): *ein* ~ *machen* have a nap *od.* a snooze.

nie [ni:] never, at no time; *fast* ~ hardly ever; ~ *wieder* never again.

nieder ['ni:dər] **1.** *adj.* low (*a. fig. gemein*); *Wert, Rang*: inferior; *der* ~*e Adel* the gentry; **2.** *adv.* down (*mit* with); '**~brennen** *v/t. u. v/i.* (sn) burn down; '**~brüllen** boo; '**~deutsch** Low German; '**⁀druck** ⊕ *m* low pressure; '**~drücken** press down; *fig.* depress; '**~fallen** (sn) fall down; '**⁀frequenz** ⚡ *f* low frequency; '**⁀gang** *m* decline; '**~gehen** (sn) go down (*a.* ✈); *Gewitter*: burst; *Regen*: fall; '**~geschlagen** *fig.* downcast (*a. Augen*), depressed, down-hearted; '**⁀geschlagenheit** *f* dejection, low spirits *pl.*; '**~halten** *fig.* suppress; '**~hauen** fell; '**~holen** *Flagge*: haul down, lower; '**~kämpfen** overpower; *fig.* overcome; '**~knien** kneel down; '**~knüppeln** bludgeon; '**~kommen** (sn) be confined; **⁀kunft** ['~kunft] *f* (14[1]) confinement; '**⁀lage** *f* defeat; (*Magazin*) depot, warehouse; (*Zweiggeschäft*) branch; '**~lassen** let down; *sich* ~ sit down; *Vogel*: alight; (*sich festsetzen*) establish o.s., settle (down), *Am.* locate; *geschäftlich*: set o.s. up in business; '**⁀lassung** *f* establishment; (*Siedlung*) settlement; ✝ branch, agency; depot; '**~legen** lay down (*a. die Waffen*; *a. fig. Regeln*); *Amt*: resign; *Krone*: abdicate; *sich* ~ lie down (*a. zu Bett*); *die Arbeit* ~ (go on) strike, walk out; *schriftlich* ~ put down in writing; '**⁀legung** *f* laying down; resignation; abdication; '**~machen**, '**~metzeln** kill, slaughter; '**~reißen** pull down; '**~rheinisch** of the Lower Rhine; '**~schießen** *v/t. u. v/i.* shoot down; '**⁀schlag** *m* sediment; ⚗ deposit, precipitate; (*atmosphärischer* ~) precipitation; *Boxen*: knock-down, *bis zehn*: knock-out; *s. radioaktiv*; *fig. s-n* ~ *finden in* (*dat.*) be reflected in; '**~schlagen** knock down, fell; *Augen*: cast down; *Kosten usw.*: cancel; (*unterdrücken*) suppress; *Revolte*: put down, crush; *Forderung*: waive; ⚖

Verfahren: quash; ⚗ precipitate (*a. sich*); *fig.* cast down; *sich ~ in* (*dat.*) be reflected in; '**&schlagung** *f* cancellation; '**~schmettern** dash to the ground; *fig.* crush; '**~schmetternd** *fig.* crushing, shattering; '**~schreiben** write down; '**&schrift** *f* record; (*Protokoll*) minutes *pl.*; '**~setzen** set (*od.* put) down; *sich ~* sit down; '**&spannung** ⚡ *f* low tension; '**~stechen** stab down; '**~strecken** fell; '**~trächtig** base, mean; '**&trächtigkeit** *f* baseness, meanness; '**&ung** *f* lowland; *im Gelände*: depression; '**~werfen** throw down; *Aufstand usw.*: put down, crush; '**&wild** *n* small game.

niedlich ['ni:tliç] nice, sweet, *Am. a.* cute; (*drollig*) droll, funny.

Niednagel ['ni:t-] *m* agnail.

niedrig ['ni:driç] low; *von Stand a.* lowly, humble; (*gemein*) mean, base; *~er hängen fig.* debunk; '**&keit** *f* low(li)ness; humbleness; meanness; '**&preis** *m* low price; '**&stpreis** *m* lowest price; '**&wasser** *n* low water.

niemals ['~ma:ls] *s. nie.*

niemand ['~mant] nobody, no one, not ... anybody; '**&sland** *n* no man's land.

Niere ['ni:rə] *f* (15) kidney; *künstliche ~* kidney machine; '**~nbank** ⚕ *f* kidney transplant bank; '**~nbecken** *n* renal pelvis; '**~nbraten** *m*, '**~nstück** *n* roast loin; '**~n-entzündung** *f* nephritis; '**&nförmig** kidney-shaped; '**~nleiden** *n* kidney trouble; '**~nspender(in** *f*) *m* kidney donor; '**~nstein** ⚕ *m* kidney stone.

nieseln F ['ni:zəln] (29) drizzle.

niesen ['ni:zən] (27) sneeze.

Nießbrauch ['ni:s-] *m* (3) usufruct; '**~er(in** *f*) *m* usufructuary.

Niet [ni:t] *m* (3) rivet; '**~e** *f* (15) *in der Lotterie*: blank; *fig.* F *P. u. S.*: *sl.* flop, washout; '**&en** (26) rivet; '**&- und** '**nagelfest** clinched and riveted.

Nihilismus [nihi'lismus] *m* (16, *o. pl.*) nihilism.

Nikolaus ['ni(:)kolaus] *m* (11[1], *pl.* 3[[3]]) Santa Claus.

Nikotin [niko'ti:n] *n* (3[1]) nicotine; **&frei** nicotine-free; **~vergiftung** *f* nicotine-poisoning.

Nilpferd ['ni:l-] *n* hippopotamus.

Nimbus ['nimbus] *m* (14[2]) nimbus; *fig.* prestige, aura.

nimmer ['nimər] never; '**~mehr** nevermore; (*ganz und gar nicht*) by no means; '**~müde** untiring; '**~satt**[1] insatiable; '**&satt**[2] *m* glutton; '**&**'**wiedersehen** *n*: *auf ~* never to meet again, for good.

Nippel ['nipəl] ⊕ *m* (7) nipple.

nippen ['nipən] (25) sip (*an dat.* at).

'**Nippsachen** *f/pl.* knick-knacks, bric-à-brac *sg.*

nirgend(s) ['nirgənt(s)] nowhere.

Nische ['ni:ʃə] *f* (15) niche, recess.

nisten ['nistən] (26) nest.

Nitrat ⚗ [ni'tra:t] *n* (3) nitrate.

Nitroglyzerin ['ni:troglytsə'ri:n] *n* nitroglycerine.

Niveau [ni'vo:] *n* (11) level; *fig. a.* standard; *unter dem ~* not up to standard.

nivellieren [nivɛ'li:rən] level, grade.

Nix *m* (3[2]), **Nixe** ['niks(ə)] *f* (15) water-sprite; *m a.* nix, merman; *f a.* nixie, mermaid, water-nymph.

nobel ['no:bəl] (*vornehm*) noble; (*großzügig*) generous; (*elegant*) elegant, fashionable.

Nobelpreis [no'bɛl-] *m* Nobel prize; **~träger** *m* Nobel prize winner.

noch [nɔx] still; yet; *~ immer* still; *~ ein* another, one more; *~ einmal* once more *od.* again; *~ einmal so alt wie j.* double a p.'s age; *~ etwas* something more; *~ etwas?* anything else?; *was denn ~ alles?* what next?; *~ nicht* not yet; *~ nie* never before; *~ gestern* only yesterday; *~ heute* this very day; *~ jetzt* even now; *~ im 19. Jahrhundert* as late as the 19th century; *~ so* ever so; *es wird ~ 2 Jahre dauern* it will take two more (*od.* another two) years; *~ und ~* plenty (of); *s. nur, weder usw.*; **~malig** ['~ma:liç] repeated, second, new; **~mals** ['~ma:ls] once more.

Nocke ⊕ ['nɔkə] *f* (15) cam; '**~nwelle** *f* camshaft.

Nomad|e [no'ma:də] *m* (13) nomad; **~en...**, **&isch** nomadic.

Nomin|alwert [nomi'na:lve:rt] *m* nominal value; **~ativ** ['no:minati:f] *m* (3[1]) nominative (case); **&ell** [nomi'nɛl] nominal; **&ieren** [~'ni:rən] nominate.

Nonne ['nɔnə] *f* (15) nun; '**~nkloster** *n* nunnery, convent.

Noppe [ˈnɔpə] *f* (15), ˈ♀**n** burl, nap.

Nord [nɔrt] **1.** north; **2.** *poet. m* (3, *o. pl.*) north (wind); ˈ~**-at**ˈ**lantikpakt** *m* North Atlantic Treaty; ~**en** [ˈ~ən] *m* (6, *o. pl.*) north; ˈ~**hang** *m* north(-ern) slope; ♀**isch** [ˈ~diʃ] northern; (*skandinavisch*) Nordic; ~**länder** [ˈnɔrtlɛndər] *m* (7) inhabitant of the north, northerner.

nördlich [ˈnœrtliç] northern, northerly; ~ *von* (to the) north of.

ˈ**Nord|licht** *n* northern lights *pl.*, aurora borealis; ~ˈ**-ost**(**en**) *m* northeast; ♀ˈ**-östlich** north-east(erly); ˈ~**pol** *m* North Pole; ˈ~**po**ˈ**larkreis** *m* Arctic Circle; ˈ~**-**ˈ**Süd-Konflikt** *m* North-South conflict; ˈ~**see** *f* North Sea; ♀**wärts** [ˈ~vɛrts] northward(s); ˈ~**west**(**en**) *m* north-west; ♀ˈ**westlich** north-west(erly); ˈ~**wind** *m* north wind.

Nörg|elei [nœrgəˈlaɪ] *f* (16) faultfinding, carping; ˈ♀**eln** *v/i.* (29) nag, carp (*an dat.* at), *Am.* F gripe (*od.* kick) (about); ~ *an* (*dat.*) find fault with; ~**ler** [ˈ~glər] *m* (7), ˈ~**lerin** *f* faultfinder, grumbler.

Norm [nɔrm] *f* (16) norm, standard.

normal [~ˈmɑːl] normal; *Maß, Gewicht*: standard; ♀**benzin** *n* regular (petrol, *Am.* gas); ♀**fall** *m* normal case; *im* ~ normally; ♀**geschwindigkeit** *f* normal speed; ♀**gewicht** *n* standard weight; ~**isieren** [~maliˈziːrən] normalize; *sich* ~ return to normal; ~**spurig** 🚂 [~ˈmɑːl-] standard-ga(u)ge; ♀**-uhr** *f* standard clock; ♀**verbraucher** *co. m* man in the street; *geistiger* ~ middlebrow; ♀**zeit** *f* standard time; ♀**zustand** *m* normal condition.

Normanne [nɔrˈmanə] *m* (13) Norman.

Nor|mblatt [ˈnɔrm-] *n* standard sheet; ˈ♀**men** (25), ♀ˈ**mieren** standardize; ~ˈ**mierung** *f* standardization.

Norweg|er [ˈnɔrveːgər] *m* (7), ˈ~**erin** *f* (16¹), ˈ♀**isch** Norwegian.

Not [noːt] *f* (14¹) (*Mangel*) need, want; (*Notlage*) necessity; (*Bedrängtheit*) difficulty, trouble; (*Elend*) misery; (*Gefahr, Unglück*) danger, (*engS.* ⚓) distress; *zur* ~ if need be, at a pinch; ~ *leiden* suffer want; ~ *leiden an* (*dat.*) be short of; *in* ~ *bringen* reduce to want; *s. knapp*; *in Nöten sein* be in trouble; *mir ist* (*od. tut*) ♀ I want; *es tut* ♀, *daß* it is necessary that; ~ *macht erfinderisch* necessity is the mother of invention; *s. Gebot, Teufel*.

Notar [noˈtɑːr] *m* (3¹) notary; ~**iat** [~tarˈjɑːt] *n* notary's office; ♀**iell** [~ˈjɛl] notarial; attested by a notary.

ˈ**Not|-arzt** *m* doctor on call; (*beruflicher* ~) emergency doctor; ˈ~**-aufnahme** *f Krankenhaus*: emergency ward; ˈ~**-ausgang** *m* emergency exit; ˈ~**behelf** *m* makeshift, expedient, stopgap; ˈ~**beleuchtung** *f* emergency lighting; ˈ~**bremse** *f* emergency brake; 🚂 communication cord; ˈ~**brücke** *f* emergency bridge; ˈ~**dienst** *m* emergency service (*od.* duty); ~**durft** [ˈ~durft] *f* (14¹): *s-e* ~ *verrichten* relieve nature; ˈ♀**dürftig** scanty; (*bedürftig*) needy; (*behelfsmäßig*) makeshift; improvised, rough(ly *adv.*).

Note [ˈnoːtə] *f* (15) note (*a. pol.*); (*Banknote*) banknote, *Am.* bill; ♪ note, ~*n pl.* music; *Schule, Sport*: mark; *fig.* (*Ton*) tone; (*Eigenart*) character, feature; *die persönliche* ~ the personal touch; ♪ *ganze* ~ semibreve; *halbe* ~ minim; *nach* ~*n singen* sing at sight; F *fig. nach* ~ properly, thoroughly; ˈ~**n-austausch** *pol. m* exchange of notes; ˈ~**nbank** *f* bank of issue; ˈ~**nblatt** *n* sheet of music; ˈ~**ndurchschnitt** *m* average mark (*Am.* grade); ˈ~**npult** *n* music-stand; ˈ~**nschlüssel** ♪ *m* clef; ˈ~**nschrank** *m* music cabinet; ˈ~**nständer** *m* music-stand; ˈ~**nsystem** *n* ♪ staff; *Schule*: marking (*Am.* grading) system; ˈ~**n-umlauf** *m* circulation of (bank)notes.

ˈ**Not|fall** *m* case of need, emergency; *im* ~, ˈ♀**falls** *s. nötigenfalls*; ˈ~**flagge** *f* flag of distress; ˈ♀**gedrungen** compulsory, forced; *adv.* of necessity, needs; ~ *mußte er* he had no choice but; ˈ~**gemeinschaft** *f* emergency pool; ˈ~**groschen** *m* nest-egg; ˈ~**helfer**(**in** *f*) *m* helper in need; ˈ~**hilfe** *f* help in need; emergency aid; *Technische* ~ Technical Emergency Service.

notier|en [noˈtiːrən] note (down), make a note of; take (*od.* jot) down; ☤ *Preise*: quote (*zu* at); ♀**ung** ☤ *f* quotation.

nötig [ˈnøːtiç] necessary, required;

(*gebührend*) due (*respect etc.*); ~ *haben* want, need, stand in need of, require; *das* ≗e what is necessary; **~en** ['~gən] (25) force, compel; (*drängen*) urge; *e-n Gast*: press; *sich ~ lassen* stand upon ceremony; *sich genötigt sehen, zu inf.* find o.s. compelled to *inf.*; '**~en'falls** in case of need, in an emergency; if necessary, if need be; '**≗ung** *f* coercion, compulsion; pressing (invitation); ⚖ duress, intimidation.

Notiz [no'ti:ts] *f* (16) note, F memo; (*Presse*≗) notice, (news) item; ~ *nehmen von* note, take notice of; *keine ~ nehmen von* ignore; **~block** *m* note block, memo pad; **~buch** *n* notebook.

'**Not|lage** *f* distress, plight, predicament, emergency; '**~lager** *n* shakedown; '**≗landen** ✈ (sn) make a forced landing, force-land; '**~landung** *f* forced landing; '**≗leidend** needy; distressed; ⚕ *Wechsel*: dishono(u)red; '**~lösung** *f* makeshift, expedient; '**~lüge** *f* white lie; '**~maßnahme** *f* emergency measure.

notorisch [no'to:riʃ] notorious.

'**Not|pfennig** *m* savings *pl.*, nest-egg; '**~ruf** *teleph. m* emergency call; (*Nummer*) emergency number; '**~rufsäule** *f* emergency telephone; '**~schlachtung** *f* forced slaughter; '**~schrei** *m* cry of distress; '**~signal** *n* distress signal, SOS; '**~sitz** *m* jump seat, *Am. a.* rumble seat; '**~stand** *m* state of distress, (state of) emergency; ⚖ necessity; '**~standsgebiet** *n* distressed area; '**~standsgesetz** *n* (national) emergency law; '**~standsmaßnahmen** *f/pl.* emergency measures; '**~strom-aggregat** *n* emergency generator; '**~treppe** *f* fire-escape; '**~-unterkunft** *f* provisional accommodation; '**~verband** *m* emergency (*od.* first-aid) dressing; '**~ver-ordnung** *f* emergency decree; '**~wehr** *f* (*aus od. in* in) self-defen|ce, *Am.* -se; '**≗wendig** necessary (*für* to, for; *daß er* for him to *inf.*); '**~wendigkeit** *f* necessity; '**~zeichen** *n* signal of distress; '**~zucht** *f*, '**≗züchtigen** rape.

Nougat ['nu:gat] *m*, *n* (11) nougat.

Novelle [no'vɛlə] *f* (15) short novel; *parl.* amending law.

November [no'vɛmbər] *m* (7) November.

Novität [novi'tɛ:t] *f* (16) novelty.

Novize [no'vi:tsə] *m* (13), *f* (15) novice.

Novum ['no:vum] *n* (9[2]) something new.

Nu [nu:] *m inv.*: *im ~* in no time, F in a trice *od.* jiffy *od.* flash.

Nuan|ce [ny'ɑ̃sə] *f* (15), ≗'**cieren** shade.

nüchtern ['nyçtərn] with an empty stomach, not having eaten (anything); (*Ggs. betrunken*) sober (*a. fig. Urteil, Tatsache usw.*); (*ruhig denkend*) level-headed; (*leidenschaftslos*) cool, unemotional; (*alltäglich, unromantisch, trocken*) prosaic; (*sachlich*) matter-of-fact(ly *adv.*); (*mäßig*) temperate; (*besonnen*) calm; (*geistlos*) jejune; *auf ~en Magen* on an empty stomach; '**≗heit** *f* sobriety; temperance; *fig.* prosiness.

Nudel ['nu:dəl] *f* (15) noodle; '**≗n** (29) stuff.

Nugat ['nu:gat] *m*, *n* (11) *s. Nougat.*

nuklear [nukle'ɑ:r] nuclear.

null [nul] **1.** null; nil (*bsd. bei Fehlanzeige*); *Tennis*: love; *s. nichtig*; **2.** ≗*f* (16) nought, cipher; *Skala*: zero; *fig. P.*: a mere cipher, nonentity; *s. a. Niete*; F *gleich ~* next to nothing, nil; '**≗lösung** *f* zero option; '**≗menge** ⅍ *f* null set; '**≗punkt** *m* zero; ⊕, ⚡ neutral point; *auf dem ~* (*a. fig.*) at zero; '**≗tarif** *m*: *zum ~* free of charge; '**≗wachs-tum** ⚕ *n* zero growth.

numerier|en [numə'ri:rən] number; *numerierter Platz* reserved seat; ≗**ung** *f* numbering.

Nummer ['numər] *f* (15) number (*a. Programm*≗, *Zirkus*≗); *e-r Zeitung*: *a.* copy, issue; ⚕ (*Größe*) size; *Sport*: event; F (*Kauz*) (quite a) character; '**~nkonto** *n* numbered account; '**~nscheibe** *teleph. f* dial; '**~nschild** *mot. n* number-plate.

nun [nu:n] now, at present; *int.* well! *~?* well?; *e-e Rede fortsetzend*: well, why; *cj. ~* (*da*) now that, since; '**~mehr** now; '**~mehrig** present.

Nuntius ['nuntsjus] *m* (16[2]) nuncio.

nur [nu:r] only; solely, merely; (*nichts als*) (nothing) but; (*ausgenommen*) except, but; *nicht ~ … sondern auch …* not only … but also …; *~ noch* still, only; *~ zu!*,

~ *weiter!* go (*od.* carry) on!; *wenn* ~ provided that; *wer* ~ whoever; *wie* ~ how ... ever, how on earth; *das Stück ist* ~ *klein* the piece is but small; *alle*, ~ *er nicht* all except him; *du weißt* ~ *zu gut* you know well enough; *so schwierig es* ~ *sein könnte* as difficult as it could possibly be.

nuscheln F ['nuʃəln] slur, mumble.

Nuß [nus] *f* (14[1]) nut (*a.* ⊕); (*Wal*♀) walnut; *fig.* e-e *harte* ~ a hard nut to crack, a tough job; '**~baum** *m* walnut-tree; '**♀braun** hazel; '**~kern** *m* kernel; '**~knacker** *m* (7) nut-cracker; '**~schale** *f* nut-shell.

Nüster ['ny:stər] *f* (15) nostril.

Nut(**e**) ['nu:tə] *f* (15) groove, *a.* slot.

nutz [nuts], **nütze** ['nytsə] useful; *zu nichts* ~ *sein* be good for nothing; *s. zunutze*; '**♀-anwendung** *f* practical application, utilization; (*Lehre*) moral.

'**nutzbar** useful; *sich et.* ~ *machen* utilize, turn to account; '**♀keit** *f* usefulness; '**♀machung** *f* utilization.

'**nutzbringend** profitable, useful; ~ *anwenden* turn to good account.

'**Nutz-effekt** *m* useful effect, (net) efficiency.

Nutzen ['nutsən] **1.** *m* (6) use; (*Gewinn*) profit; (*Vorteil*) advantage, *a.* ⚖ benefit; *s. Nützlichkeit*; ~ *bringen* bring grist to the mill; ~ *ziehen aus* profit (*od.* benefit) from; *von* ~ *sein s.* 2.; **2.** ♀, **nützen** ['nytsən] *v/i.* (27): be of use *od.* useful (*zu et.* for; *j-m* for a p.); *j-m* ~ *a.* serve a p.; (*vorteilhaft sein*) be of advantage (*j-m* to a p.); *es nützt nichts* it is (of) no use (*zu inf.* to); *was nützt ...?* what is the use of ...?; *v/t.* use, make use of.

'**Nutz|fahrzeug** *n* utility vehicle; '**~fläche** *f* useful area; '**~garten** *m* kitchen-garden; '**~holz** *n* timber; '**~last** *f* payload; '**~leistung** *f* effective capacity, (useful) efficiency; *mot.* brake horsepower.

nützlich ['nytsliç] useful; '**♀keit** *f* usefulness, utility.

'**nutz|los** useless; '**♀losigkeit** *f* uselessness; **♀nießer** ['~ni:sər] *m* (7) usufructuary; *weitS.* beneficiary, *b.s.* profiteer; '**♀nießung** *f* usufruct.

'**Nutzung** *f* using; *s. Nutzbarmachung, Nutznießung*; (*Ausnutzung*) exploitation; (*Ertrag*) yield, produce; (*Einkommen*) revenue; '**~srecht** *n* right of usufruct, right to use; '**~swert** *m* economic value.

Nylon ['naɪlɔn] *n* (11) nylon; '**~strümpfe** *m/pl.* nylons.

Nymph|e ['nymfə] *f* (15) nymph; **~omanie** [~foma'ni:] *f* (15, *o. pl.*) nymphomania.

O

O [o:], **o** *n inv.* O, o.

o! *int.* oh!; ~ *weh!* alas!, oh dear!

Oase [o'ʔɑ:zə] *f* (15) oasis.

ob [ɔp] **1.** *cj.* whether, if; *als* ~ as if, as though; F (*na*) *und* ~! F rather!, *Am.* you bet!; ~ *er wohl kommt?* I wonder if he will come!; **2.** *prp.* **a**) *gen.* (*wegen*) on account of; (*über*) about; **b**) *dat.* (*oberhalb*) above.

Obacht ['o:baxt] *f* (16): ~ *geben* (pay) heed, pay attention (*auf acc.* to), take care (of); ~! look out!, *Am.* watch out!

Obdach ['ɔpdax] *n* (1, *o.pl.*) shelter; (*Wohnstätte*) lodging; '**♀los** homeless; '**~lose** *m, f* casual (pauper).

Obduktion [ɔpduk'tsjo:n] *f* post-mortem (examination), autopsy.

'**O-Beine** *n/pl.* bandy legs, bow legs; '**O-beinig** bandy-legged.

oben ['o:bən] above (*a. im Buch usw.*); (*an der Spitze*) at the top; *im Himmelsraum*: aloft, on high; *im Hause*: upstairs; *hoch* ~ high up; *nach* ~ upwards, *im Hause*: upstairs; *von* ~ from above; *von* ~ *bis unten* from top to bottom; *von* ~ *herab behandeln usw.* haughtily; ~ *ohne* topless; ~'**-an** at the top *od.* head; ~'**-auf** on top, above; uppermost; on the surface; *fig.* F ~ *sein* be going strong; ~'**drein** over and above, into the bargain, on top of it (all); '~-**erwähnt** above(-mentioned); ~'**hin** superficially; *bemerken*: casually.

ober ['oːbər] **1.** (18, *nur attributiv*) upper, higher; *fig. a.* superior, senior, chief; *s. oberst* 1.; **2.** ♀ F *m* (7) (head) waiter.

'**Ober|-arm** *m* upper arm; '~-**arzt** *m* assistant medical director; '~-**aufseher** *m* chief inspector, superintendent; '~-**aufsicht** *f* superintendence; '~**bau** *m* (*pl. Oberbauten*) superstructure (*a. e-r Brücke*); *e-r Straße*: surface; 🚂 permanent way; '~**befehl** *m* supreme command; '~**befehlshaber** *m* commander-in-chief; '~**bekleidung** *f* outer wear; '~**bett** *n* coverlet; '~**bürgermeister** *m* chief burgomaster; *Brt.* Lord Mayor; '~**deck** ⚓ *n* upper deck.

'**Obere** *eccl. m* (Father) Superior.

'**Ober|feldwebel** ⚔ *m* staff sergeant, *Am.* sergeant 1st cl. (= class); ✈ flight (*Am.* technical) sergeant; '~**fläche** *f* (*an der, die* ~ on the) surface; ♀**flächlich** ['~flɛçliç] superficial (*a. fig.*); *Bekanntschaft*: casual; '~**flächlichkeit** *f* superficiality; '~**förster** *m* head forester; '~**gefreite** *m* ⚔ lance corporal, *Am.* private 1st cl. (= class); ✈ leading aircraftman, *Am.* airman 2nd cl. (= class); ⚓ able rating, *Am.* seaman; '♀**halb** above; '~**hand** *f*: *die* ~ *gewinnen* get the upper hand, *über* (*acc.*) get the better of; '~**haupt** *n* head, chief; '~**haus** *n the* Upper House, *Brt. the* (House of) Lords; '~**haut** *f* epidermis; '~**hemd** *n* (day-)shirt; '~**herrschaft** *f* supremacy; '~**hoheit** *f* sovereignty; '~**in** *f eccl.* Mother Superior; ⚕ matron; '~-**ingenieur** *m* chief engineer; '♀-**irdisch** overground; ⚡ ~*e Leitung* overhead line; '~**kellner** *m* head waiter; '~**kiefer** *m* upper jaw; '~**klasse** *f* upper class(es *pl.*); *Schule*: *a.* higher form; '~**kleid** *n* upper garment; '~**kleidung** *s. Oberbekleidung*; '~**kommando** *n* high (*od.* supreme) command; '~**körper** *m* upper part of the body; '~**land** *n* upland; '~'**landesgericht** *n* regional court of appeal; '♀**lastig** top-heavy; '~**lauf** *m e-s Flusses*: upper course; '~**leder** *n* uppers *pl.*; '~**lehrer** *m* senior assistant master; '~**leitung** *f* supervision, direction; ⚡ *s. oberirdisch(e Leitung)*; '~**leutnant** *m* ⚔ (*Am.* first) lieutenant; ⚓ sublieutenant, *Am.* lieutenant (junior grade); ✈ flying officer; '~**licht** *n* skylight; '~**lippe** *f* upper lip; '~'**prima** *f* top grade, *Brt.* Upper Sixth; '~**schenkel** *m* thigh; '~**schicht** *f* top layer; *der Bevölkerung*: upper class(es *pl.*); '~**schule** *f* secondary school; '~**schwester** *f* head nurse, sister; '~**seite** *f* upper side; top (side).

'**oberst 1.** uppermost, top(most); highest (*a. fig.*); *fig.* supreme, chief, principal; *s. kehren, zuoberst*; **2.** ♀ ⚔ *m* (12) colonel.

'**Ober|'staats-anwalt** *m* Senior Public Prosecutor; '~'**stabs-arzt** ⚔ *m* major (medical); '~**steiger** ⚒ *m* foreman of the mine; '~**stimme** ♪ *f* treble, soprano.

'**Oberst'leutnant** *m* lieutenant-colonel.

'**Ober|stübchen** *n* garret, attic; *fig.* F *nicht richtig im* ~ *sein* not to be quite right in the upper stor(e)y; '~'**studiendirektor** *m* head master, *Am.* principal; '~'**studienrat** *m* senior assistant master; '~**tasse** *f* cup; '~**teil** *m, n* upper part, top; '~**wasser** *n e-r Schleuse*: upper water; *Mühle*: overshot water; *fig.* ~ *bekommen* (*od. haben*) get (*od.* have) the upper hand; '~**welt** *f* upper world.

obgleich [ɔp'glaɪç] (al)though.

'**Obhut** *f inv.* care, guard; *in s-e* ~ *nehmen* take care (*od.* charge) of.

obig ['oːbiç] above(-mentioned).

Objekt [ɔp'jɛkt] *n* (3) object; (*Vorhaben*) project; (*Vermögensgegenstand*) property.

objektiv [~'tiːf] **1.** objective; (*unparteiisch*) *a.* impartial, unbiassed; (*tatsächlich*) actual, practical; **2.** ♀ *opt. n* (3[1]) objective, lens; ♀**ität** [~tivi'tɛːt] *f* objectiveness; impartiality.

Ob'jektträger *m des Mikroskops*: [slide.]

Oblate [o'blaːtə] *f* (15) wafer; *eccl.* host.

obliegen ['ɔp-] *e-r Arbeit usw.*: apply o.s. to; *j-m* ~ be incumbent on a p., be a p.'s duty; '♀**heit** *f* duty.

obligat [obli'gaːt] obligatory; (*unerläßlich*) indispensable; *iro.* (*un-*

vermeidlich) inevitable; **⁀ion** [~ga-ˈtsjo:n] ✝ *f* bond, debenture; **~orisch** [~ˈto:riʃ] obligatory (*für* on), compulsory (for).

Obmann [ˈɔpman] *m* (*Vorsitzender*) chairman; (*Schiedsmann*) umpire; (*Betriebs⁀*) spokesman.

Obo|e [oˈbo:ə] *f* (15) hautboy, oboe; **~ist** [oboˈist] *m* (12) oboist.

Obrigkeit [ˈo:briçkaɪt] *f* authorities *pl.*; government; magistracy; ˈ**⁀lich** magisterial; *adv.* by authority; ˈ**~sdenken** *n* (6) authoritarian mentality; ˈ**~sstaat** *m* authoritarian state.

obschon [ɔpˈʃo:n] (al)though.

Observatorium [ɔpzɛrvaˈto:rjum] *n* (9) observatory.

ˈ**obsiegen** be victorious; *weitS.* prevail; ⚖ *~de Partei* successful party.

Obst [o:pst] *n* (3²) fruit; ˈ**~bau** *m* fruit-growing; ˈ**~baum** *m* fruit-tree; ˈ**~-ernte** *f* fruit-gathering; (*Ertrag*) fruit-crop; ˈ**~garten** *m* orchard; ˈ**~händler(in** *f*) *m* fruiterer, *Am.* fruit seller; ˈ**~handlung** *f* fruiterer's (shop), *Am.* fruit store; ˈ**~konserven** *f/pl.* tinned (*bsd. Am.* canned) fruit; ˈ**~messer** *n* fruit-knife.

Obstruktion [ɔpstrukˈtsjo:n] *f* obstruction; *Am. pol. a.* filibuster (*a. v/i. ~ treiben*); *im Betrieb*: ca'canny.

ˈ**Obst|wein** *m* fruit-wine; ˈ**~zucht** *f s. Obstbau*; ˈ**~züchter(in** *f*) *m* fruit-grower, fruit-farmer.

obszön [ɔpsˈtsø:n] obscene; **⁀ität** [~tsøniˈtɛ:t] *f* (16) obscenity.

Obus [ˈo:bus] *m* (4¹) trolley bus.

ˈ**obwalten** exist; *Umstände*: prevail.

obˈwohl (al)though.

Ochse [ˈɔksə] *m* (13) ox (*pl.* oxen); *engS.* bullock; F *P.*: oaf; F *fig. wie der Ochs vorm Berg* stupidly.

ˈ**ochsen** F (27) cram, grind, swot.

ˈ**Ochsen|fleisch** *n* beef; ˈ**~gespann** *n* team of oxen; ˈ**~haut** *f* ox-hide; ˈ**~schwanzsuppe** *f* ox-tail soup.

Ocker [ˈɔkər] *m* (7) och|re, *Am.* -er.

Ode [ˈo:də] *f* (15) ode.

öde [ˈø:də] **1.** deserted, desolate; (*unbebaut*) waste; (*unschön, freudlos*) dreary; (*fad*) dull; **2.** ⁀ *f* (15) desert, solitude.

Ödem ⚕ [øˈde:m] *n* (3¹) edema.

oder [ˈo:dər] or; *~ aber* or else; *~ auch* or rather; (*sonst*) otherwise.

Ödipuskomplex [ˈø:dipus-] *psych. m* Oedipus complex.

Ödland [ˈø:tlant] *n* (5, *pl. Odländereien*) waste (*od.* fallow) land.

Odyssee [odyˈse:] *f* (15) Odyssey.

Ofen [ˈo:fən] *m* (6¹) stove; (*Back⁀*) oven; (*Hoch⁀*) furnace; (*Kalk⁀, Dörr⁀*) kiln; ˈ**~heizung** *f* stove-heating; ˈ**~kachel** *f* Dutch tile; ˈ**~rohr** *n* stove-pipe; ˈ**~röhre** *f* (heating-)oven; ˈ**~setzer** *m* stove-fitter.

offen [ˈɔfən] *allg.* open (*a. Geheimnis, Haß, Markt, Stadt usw.*; *a.* ⚕ *u. gr.*); *Stelle*: *a.* vacant; (*aufrichtig, freimütig*) *a.* frank, sincere, outspoken; (*unentschieden*) open, undecided; *~er Leib* open bowels *pl.*; *~e Rechnung* open account; *~er Wechsel* blank cheque (*Am.* check); *~ gestanden* frankly speaking; *s. Handelsgesellschaft*; *s. a. offenlassen usw.*

offenˈbar evident(ly *adv.*), obvious(-ly); (*anscheinend*) apparent(ly); **~en** (25) disclose, manifest, reveal; **⁀ung** *f* manifestation, (*a. eccl. u. fig.*) revelation; **⁀ungs-eid** *m* affidavit of means.

ˈ**Offenheit** *f* openness; frankness.

ˈ**offen|herzig** open-hearted, candid, frank, sincere; ˈ**⁀herzigkeit** *f* candidness, frankness, sincerity; ˈ**~kundig** well-known, public; *b.s.* notorious; *Lüge usw.*: patent, blatant; ˈ**~lassen** leave open (*a. fig.*); ˈ**~ˈsichtlich** evident(ly *adv.*), obvious(ly).

offensiv [ɔfɛnˈzi:f], **⁀e** [~və] *f* (15) offensive; *die ~ ergreifen* take the offensive.

ˈ**offenstehen** be open (*a. fig. j-m* to); *es steht ihm offen zu inf.* he is free to *inf.*; **~d** ✝ outstanding, open.

öffentlich [ˈœfəntliç] *allg.* public (*a. Dienst, Recht usw.*); *~e Hand* public authorities, *the* Government, ⚖ *in ~er Sitzung* in open court; *~ bekanntmachen* make public; publicise; *~ beglaubigt* authenticated by a notary public; *s. Ärgernis, Betrieb, Fürsorge usw.*; ˈ**⁀keit** *f* publicity; (*das Volk*) *the* (general) public; *an die ~ treten* appear before the public; *in aller ~* in public; *s. Ausschluß*; ˈ**⁀keits-arbeit** *f* public relations *pl.*; ˈ**~-ˈrechtlich** under public law.

offerieren [ɔfəˈri:rən] offer.

Offerte [ɔ'fɛrtə] *f* (15) offer; *auf e-e Ausschreibung*: tender, bid.
offiziell [ɔfi'tsjɛl] official.
Offizier [~'tsiːr] *m* (3[1]) (commissioned) officer; **~korps** *n the* officers *pl.*; **~s-anwärter** *m* officer cadet; **~skasino** *n* officers' mess; **~s-patent** *n* commission.
offiziös [~'tsjøːs] (18[1]) semi-official.
öffn|en ['œfnən] (*a. sich*) (26) open; '**⁀ung** *f* opening, aperture.
oft [ɔft], **oftmals** ['~maːls], **öfters** ['œftərs] often, frequently.
oh! [oː] oh!, o!
Oh(ei)m ['oː(haɪ)m] *m* (3) uncle.
ohne ['oːnə] without; but for; ~ *daß*, ~ *zu inf.* without *ger.*; F ~ *mich!* count me out; F *nicht* ~! not bad!; *s. Frage, weiter usw.*; '**~dem**, ~'**dies**, ~'**hin** anyhow, anyway; **~'gleichen** unequal(l)ed, matchless.
'**Ohn|macht** *f* (*Machtlosigkeit*) impotence, powerlessness; ⚕ (*a.* '**~s-anfall** *m*) faint(ing fit), swoon, (*Bewußtlosigkeit*) unconsciousness; *in* ~ *fallen* faint, swoon; '**⁀mächtig** powerless, impotent; ⚕ unconscious; ~ *werden* faint, swoon.
Ohr [oːr] *n* (5) ear; *ein* ~ *haben für* have an ear for; *j-m sein* ~ *leihen* listen to a p.; *j-m in den* ~*en liegen* pester a p.; *sich aufs* ~ *legen* take a nap; *sich et. hinter die* ~*en schreiben* make a note of a th.; *j-n übers* ~ *hauen* cheat (*od.* fleece) a p.; *die* ~*en hängenlassen* be downcast; *j-m zu* ~*en kommen* come to a p.'s ears; F *halte die* ~*en steif!* keep a stiff upper lip!; *bis über die* ~*en* up to the eyes; *s. faustdick, ganz, spitzen.*
Öhr [øːr] *n* (3) eye.
'**Ohren|-arzt** *m* ear-specialist; '**~beichte** *f* auricular confession; '**⁀betäubend** (ear-)deafening; '**~bläser(in** *f*) *m* talebearer; '**~-entzündung** *f* otitis; '**~leiden** *n* ear complaint; '**~sausen** *n* buzzing in the ear; '**~schmalz** *n* ear-wax; '**~schmaus** *m* (musical) treat; '**~schmerzen** *m/pl.* ear-ache; '**~schützer** *m* earflap, *Am.* earmuff; '**⁀zerreißend** ear-splitting; '**~zeuge** *m* ear-witness.
'**Ohr|feige** *f* slap (in the face; *a. fig.*); '**⁀feigen** (25) *j-n*: box a p.'s ears; '**~gehänge** *n* ear-drops *pl.*, pendants *pl.*; '**~hörer** *m Radio*: earphone; **~läppchen** ['~lɛpçən] *n* ear-lobe; '**~muschel** *anat. f* external ear; '**~ring** *m* ear-ring; '**~wurm** *m* ear-wig; F *fig.* catchy tune.
okkult [ɔ'kult] occult; **⁀ismus** [ɔkul'tismus] *m* (16, *o. pl.*) occultism.
Ökolog|e [øko'loːgə] *m* (13) ecologist; **~ie** [~lo'giː] *f* (15) ecology; **⁀isch** [~'loːgiʃ] ecological; ~*es Gleichgewicht* ecological balance.
Ökonom [øko'noːm] *m* (12) economist; ✓ farmer, agriculturist; (*Verwalter*) manager; **~ie** [~no'miː] *f* (15) economy; agriculture; **⁀isch** [~'noːmiʃ] economical.
Ökosystem ['øːko-] *n* ecosystem.
Oktan(zahl *f*) [ɔk'taːn-] *n* (10, *o.pl.*) octane (number *od.* rating).
Oktav [ɔk'taːf] *n* (3[1]) octavo; **~band** *m* octavo (volume); **~e** ♪ [~və] *f* octave.
Oktober [ɔk'toːbər] *m* (7) October.
Okul|ar *opt.* [oku'laːr] *n* (3[1]) eyepiece, ocular; **⁀ieren** ✓ [~'liːrən] inoculate, graft.
ökumenisch [øku'meːniʃ] *eccl.* (o)ecumenical.
Okzident ['ɔktsidɛnt] *m* (3) occident.
Öl [øːl] *n* (3) oil; *fig.* ~ *ins Feuer gießen* add fuel to the flames; ~ *auf die Wogen gießen* pour oil on troubled waters; '**~baum** *m* olive-tree; '**~berg** *m* Mount of Olives; '**~bild** *n* oil-painting; '**~druck** *m* (*Bild*) oleograph; ⊕ oil pressure; '**~druckbremse** *f* hydraulic brake; '**~-embargo** *n* oil embargo.
ölen ['øːlən] (25) oil, ⊕ *a.* lubricate; (*salben*) anoint; *wie ein geölter Blitz* like (a) greased lightning.
'**Öl|farbe** *f* oil colo(u)r, oil paint; '**~fläschchen** *n* oil-cruet; '**~gemälde** *n* oil-painting; '**~götze** F *m*: *wie ein* ~ like a post; '**~heizung** *f* oil heating; '**⁀ig** oily (*a. fig.*); *fig.* (*salbungsvoll*) unctuous.
Olive [o'liːvə] *f* (15) olive; **~nbaum** *m* olive-tree; **~nfarbe** *f* olive-colo(u)r; **~n-öl** *n* olive oil.
o'livgrün olive-green, *Am. a.* olive drab.
'**Öl|kanne** *f* oil-can, oiler; '**~katastrophe** *f* oil disaster; '**~krise** *f* oil crisis; '**~leitung** ⊕ *f* oil-lead, oil-feed; *über Land*: pipeline; '**~malerei** *f* oil-painting; '**~meßstab** *m* dipstick; '**~-ofen** *m* oil-furnace; '**~papier** *n* oil-paper; '**~pest** *f* oil pol-

lution; '~**produzent** *m* oil producer; '~**quelle** *f erbohrte*: oil-well; *natürliche*: oil-spring, *Am.* gusher; '~**stand** *m* oil level; '~**stand-anzeiger** *m* oil ga(u)ge; '~**tank** *m* oil tank; '~**teppich** *m* oil slick.

'**Ölung** *f* oiling, ⊕ *a.* lubrication; (*Salbung*) anointment; *eccl. letzte* ~ extreme unction.

'**Ölwechsel** *mot. m* oil change.

Olymp|iade [olʏm'pjɑːdə] *f* **a**) Olympiad; **b**) *Sport*: Olympic games *pl.*; ♀**isch** [o'lʏmpɪʃ] Olympian; *Sport*: Olympic; ♀*e Spiele s. Olympiade b*).

'**Öl|zeug** *n* oilskins *pl.*; '~**zweig** *m* olive-branch.

Oma ['oːma] F *f* (11¹) grandma.

Ombudsmann *pol.* ['ɔmbuts-] *m* ombudsman.

Omelett [ɔm(ə)'lɛt] *n* (3), ~**e** [~] *f* (15) omelet(te).

Omen ['oːmən] *n* (6) omen.

ominös [omi'nøːs] ominous.

Omnibus ['ɔmnibus] *m* (4¹ *od. inv.*) omnibus, F bus; (*Überland*♀) coach; '~**haltestelle** *f* bus stop.

Onanie [ona'niː] *f* (15, *o. pl.*) masturbation; ♀**ren** masturbate.

ondulieren [ɔndu'liːrən] *Haar*: wave.

Onkel ['ɔŋkəl] *m* (7) uncle.

Opa ['oːpa] F *m* (11) grandpa.

Opal [o'pɑːl] *m* (3¹) opal; ♀**i'sieren** [opali-] opalesce; ~*d* opalescent.

Oper ['oːpər] *f* (15) opera.

Operateur [opəra'tøːr] *m* (3¹) operator; ⚕ operating surgeon.

Operation [~'tsjoːn] *f* operation; ~**sbasis** ⚔ *f* base of operations; ♀**sfähig** ⚕: (*nicht*) ~ (in)operable; ~**snarbe** *f* postoperative scar; ~**sradius** ⚔ *m* operating radius, range; ~**ssaal** *m* operating theat|re, *Am.* -er; ~**sschwester** *f* theat|re (*Am.* -er) nurse.

operativ [~'tiːf] operative; ⚔ operational.

Operette [opə'rɛtə] *f* (15) operetta, comic opera.

operieren [~'riːrən] (25) *v/i. u. v/t.* operate (⚕ *j-n* on a p.); *sich* ~ *lassen* undergo an operation.

'**Opern|glas** *n* opera-glass(es *pl.*); '~**haus** *n* opera-house; '~**musik** *f* operatic music; '~**sänger(in** *f*) *m* opera-singer, operatic singer; '~**text** *m* libretto.

Opfer ['ɔpfər] *n* (7) sacrifice; (*Gabe*) offering; (*der, das Geopferte*) victim; *ein* ~ *bringen* make a sacrifice; *zum* ~ *fallen* fall a victim of, *e-m Betrüger usw.*: be victimized by; '♀**bereit** *s. opferwillig*; '~**gabe** *f* offering; '~**geld** *n* money-offering; '~**lamm** *n* sacrificial lamb; *eccl. the* Lamb (Jesus); *fig.* victim; '~**mut** *m* spirit of sacrifice; '♀**n** *v/t. u. v/i.* (29) sacrifice (*a. Schach*); '~**stock** *eccl. m* poor-box; '~**tier** *n* victim; '~**tod** *m* sacrifice of one's life; '~**ung** *f* offering, sacrifice; '♀**willig** willing to make sacrifices, self-sacrificing.

Opiat [op'jɑːt] *n* (3) opiate.

Opium ['oːpjum] *n* (11) opium.

Oppon|ent [ɔpo'nɛnt] *m* (12) opponent; ♀**ieren** [ɔpo'niːrən] oppose (*gegen j-n* a p.), resist.

Opportunist [ɔpɔrtu'nist] *m* (12) time-server, opportunist.

Opposition [ɔpozi'tsjoːn] *f* opposition; ~**sführer** *m* opposition leader.

optieren [ɔp'tiːrən] opt (*für* for).

Optik ['ɔptik] *f* (16) optics *sg.*; *phot.* lens system; '~**er** *m* (7) optician.

optim|al [ɔpti'mɑːl] optimal; ~**ieren** [~'miːrən] optimize; ♀**um** ['ɔptimum] *n* (9²) optimum.

Optim|ismus [ɔpti'mismus] *m* (16, *o. pl.*) optimism; ~**ist** *m* (12), ~**istin** *f* optimist; ♀**istisch** optimistic.

Option [ɔp'tsjoːn] *f* (16) option.

'**optisch** optical.

Opus ['oːpus] *n* (*pl. Opera* ['oːpəra]) work; ♪ ~ *12 usw.* opus 12, *etc.*

Orakel [o'rɑːkəl] *n* (7), ~**spruch** *m* oracle; ♀**haft** oracular; ♀**n** (29) speak (*od.* say) oracularly.

Orange [o'raŋʒə] *f* (15) orange; ♀**farben** orange(-colo[u]red); ~**nbaum** *m* orange-tree; ~'**rie** *f* (16) orangery.

Orang-Utan *zo.* ['oːraŋ'ʔuːtan] *m* (11) orang-outang, orang-utan.

Oratorium [ora'toːrjum] *n* (9¹) oratorio.

Orchester [ɔr'kɛstər] *n* (7) orchestra, *als Musikkorps a.* band; ~... orchestral; ~**raum** *thea. m* orchestra pit; ~**sessel** *thea. m* stall, *Am.* orchestra (seat).

orche'strieren orchestrate.

Orchidee [ɔrçi'deː] *f* (15) orchid.

Orden ['ɔrdən] *m* (6) order; (*Ehrenzeichen*) order, decoration, medal.

'**Ordens|band** *n* ribbon (of an

order); '**~bruder** *m* member of an order; *eccl. a.* friar; '**~geistliche** *m* regular; '**~kleid** *n* monastic garb; '**~schnalle** *f* bar, clasp; '**~schwester** *f* sister, nun; '**~verleihung** *f* conferring (of) an order; '**~zeichen** *n* badge of an order.

ordentlich ['ɔrdəntliç] tidy; (*methodisch geordnet; gesittet*) orderly (*a.* ⚖ *Gericht*); (*richtig; sorgfältig*) proper; (*regelrecht*) regular; (*achtbar*) respectable, of orderly habits; (*tüchtig*) good, sound; (*ziemlich gut*) quite good, decent; *adv.* properly; (*sehr*) fairly, thoroughly, downright; *~er Professor* professor in ordinary, *Am.* full professor; '**≗keit** *f* orderliness; respectability.

Order ['ɔrdər] *f* (15) order, command; ✝ *an die ~ von* to the order of.

ordin|är [ɔrdi'nɛ:r] common, ordinary; *b.s.* vulgar, low; **≗arius** [~'nɑ:rjus] *m* (16²) *univ.* professor in ordinary; **≗ation** [~na'tsjo:n] *f* ordination; **~ieren** [~'ni:rən] ordain; *ordiniert* in (holy) orders; *ordiniert werden* take orders.

ordn|en ['ɔrdnən] (26) order, arrange; *Angelegenheit*: arrange, settle, adjust; (*regeln*) regulate; '**≗er** *m* (7) (*Fest≗, Versammlungs≗*) marshal, steward; *Schule*: monitor; *für Akten*: file; (*Brief≗*) letter file.

'**Ordnung** *f* putting in order; (*Zustand, a. Reihenfolge*) order (*a.* ⚗); (*Anordnung*) arrangement; (*Klasse, Stand*) class, rank; (*Vorschrift*) rules *pl.*, regulations *pl.*; *in ~ bringen* put in order, put (*od.* get) straight, *wieder*: repair, *Am.* fix, *fig.* straighten out (*matters*); *~ schaffen* establish order; *in ~ halten* keep in order; *irgend etwas ist nicht in ~* there is something wrong; *ist alles in ~?* is everything all right *od.* O.K. (= okay)?; '**≗sgemäß** *s. ordnungsmäßig*; '**~sliebe** *f* love of order; '**≗sliebend** orderly; '**≗smäßig** orderly, regular; *pred.* in due order; *adv.* duly; '**~sruf** *parl. m* call to order; '**~sstrafe** ⚖ *f* fine; '**≗swidrig** irregular; '**~szahl** *f* ordinal (number).

Ordonnanz ⚔ [ɔrdɔ'nants] *f* (16) orderly; **~-offizier** *m* orderly officer.

Organ [ɔr'gɑ:n] *n* (3¹) *anat.* organ (*weitS. a. Stimme, Zeitung usw.*; *Körperschaft*); (*Behörde*) agency, authority, executive body; **~isation** [ɔrganiza'tsjo:n] *f* organization; **~isati'ons-talent** *n* organizing ability; **~isator** [~'zɑ:tɔr] *m* (8¹) organizer; **≗isatorisch** [~za'to:riʃ] organisational, organizing; **≗isch** [ɔr'gɑ:niʃ] organic(ally *adv.*).

organi'sieren organize; ⚔ *sl.* (*sich beschaffen*) F commandeer; *organisiert(er Arbeiter)* unionist; *nicht organisiert(er Arbeiter)* non-union(ist).

Organ|ismus [~'nismus] *m* (16²) organism; ⚕ system; **~ist** [~'nist] *m* (12) organist.

Or'gan-spende ⚕ *f* donation of an organ; **~r**(**in** *f*) *m* organ donor.

Orgasmus [ɔr'gasmus] *m* (16²) orgasm, climax.

Orgel ['ɔrgəl] *f* (15) organ; '**~bauer** *m* organ-builder; '**~konzert** *n* organ-recital; '**≗n** (29) play (on) an organ; *auf der Drehorgel*: grind a barrel-organ; '**~pfeife** *f* organ-pipe; '**~spieler** *m* organist; '**~stimme** *f* organ-stop, register.

Orgie ['ɔrgjə] *f* (15) orgy (*a. fig.*); *~n feiern* have orgies.

Orien|t... [ori'ɛnt-], **~tale** [~'tɑ:lə] *m* (13), **~'talin** *f* (16¹) oriental; **≗'talisch** oriental.

orientier|en [~'ti:rən] orient(ate); *fig. a.* (*in Kenntnis setzen*) inform (*über acc.* of); *sich ~* orient o.s. (*a. fig.*), take one's bearings (*nach der Sonne usw.* from); *sich nicht (mehr) ~ können* have lost one's bearings; **≗ung** *f* orientation; *fig.* information; **≗ungspunkt** *m* landmark; **≗ungssinn** *m* sense of direction.

Origin|al [origi'nɑ:l] *n* (3¹) (*Text, Person*) original; (*Film, Platte*) master copy; **≗'al** *adj.* original; **~alität** [~nali'tɛ:t] *f* (16) originality; **~alsendung** [~'nɑ:l-] *f Radio, TV*: live broadcast; **~altreue** *f*: *größte ~* high fidelity (*abbr.* hi-fi); **≗ell** [~'nɛl] original; (*spaßhaft*) *a.* funny.

Orkan [ɔr'kɑ:n] *m* (3¹) hurricane; **≗-artig** *Sturm*: violent; *Beifall*: thunderous.

Ornament [ɔrna'mɛnt] *n* (3) ornament.

Ornat [ɔr'nɑ:t] *m* (3) robe(s *pl.*), vestments *pl.*

Ornithologe [ɔrnito'lo:gə] *m* (13) ornithologist.

Ort [ɔrt] *m* (3 *u.* 1²) place; *s. Ortschaft*; (*Fleck, Stelle*) spot; (*Ört-*

lichkeit) locality; ~ *der Handlung* scene (of action); *fig. am* ~ (*angebracht*) appropriate; *an* ~ *und Stelle* on the spot; *höheren* ~*es* at high quarters; '**2en** ⚔ (26) locate, fix the position of.
ortho|dox [ɔrto'dɔks] orthodox; **2do'xie** *f* orthodoxy; **2graphie** [~gra'fiː] *f* orthography; **~graphisch** [~'grɑːfiʃ] orthographic(al); **2päde** [~'pɛːdə] *m* (13) orthop(a)edist; **2pädie** [~pɛ'diː] *f* orthop(a)edics *pl.*; **~pädisch** [~'pɛːdiʃ] orthop(a)edic.
örtlich ['œrtliç] local (*a.* ⚕); '**2keit** *f* locality.
'**Orts|-angabe** *f* statement of place; *auf Brief*: address; '**2-ansässig**, '**~-ansässige** *m, f* resident; '**~behörde** *f* local authorities *pl.*
'**Ortschaft** *f* (16) place; (*Dorf*) village.
'**Orts|-empfang** *m Radio*: local reception; '**2fest** stationary; '**2-fremd** *sein* be a stranger (to the locality); '**~gespräch** *teleph. n* local call; '**~gruppe** *f* local chapter; '**~kenntnis** *f* local knowledge; '**~krankenkasse** *f* local sick-fund; '**2kundig** familiar with the locality; '**~name** *m* place-name; '**~sender** *m* local transmitter; '**~sinn** *m* sense of locality; '**~statut** *n* by(e)-law, *Am.* city ordinance; '**~teil** *m* district; '**2-üblich** locally customary; '**~ver-änderung** *f* change of place; '**~verkehr** *m* local traffic; '**~zeit** *f* local time.
Ortung ['ɔrtuŋ] *f* location, position finding; '**~sgerät** *n* position finder.
Öse ['øːzə] *f* (15) eye, loop.

Ost [ɔst] **1.** east; **2.** *poet. m* (3, *o. pl.*) east (wind); '**~block** *pol. m* Eastern bloc; '**~en** ['~ən] *m* (6, *o. pl.*) east; *geogr., pol.* East; *der Ferne* (*Nahe*) ~ the Far (Near) East.
ostentativ [ɔstɛnta'tiːf] ostentatious.
Oster|-ei ['oːstər-] *n* Easter egg; '**~fest** *n s. Ostern*; '**~glocke** ⚘ *f* (yellow) daffodil; '**~hase** *m* Easter-bunny.
österlich ['øːstərliç] (of) Easter.
Ostern ['oːstərn] *n od. f/pl.* (*inv., mst ohne art.*) Easter.
Österreich|er ['øːstəraɪçər] *m* (7), '**~erin** *f* (16[1]), '**2isch** Austrian.
östlich ['œstliç] eastern, easterly; ~ *von* east of.
'**Ost|hang** *m* east(ern) slope; '**~mark** *f* (*Geld*) East German mark.
Östrogen *biol.* [œstro'geːn] *n* (3) estrogen.
'**Ost|see** *f* Baltic (Sea); **2wärts** ['~vɛrts] eastward; '**~wind** *m* east wind.
Otter ['ɔtər] **1.** *f* (15) (*Schlange*) adder; **2.** *m* (7) (*Fisch2*) otter.
Ouvertüre [uvɛr'tyːrə] *f* (15) overture.
oval [o'vɑːl], **2** *n* (3) oval.
Ovation [ova'tsjoːn] *f* ovation.
Overall ['oːvərɔːl, 'əʊvərɔːl] *m* (11) (*Arbeitsanzug*) overalls *pl.*, boiler suit; *modischer*: catsuit, jumpsuit.
Oxyd [ɔ'ksyːt] *n* (3) oxide; **~ation** [~da'tsjoːn] *f* oxidation; **2ieren** [~'diːrən] *v/t. u. v/i.* (sn) oxidize.
Ozean ['oːtseɑːn] *m* (3[1]) ocean; '**~dampfer** *m* ocean liner; **2isch** [~'ɑːniʃ] oceanic.
Ozon [o'tsoːn] *m, n* (3[1]) ozone; **2haltig** [~haltiç] ozonic, ozoniferous; **~schicht** *f* ozone layer.

P

P [peː], **p** *n inv.* P, p.
Paar [pɑːr] **1.** *n* (3) pair; (*bsd. Mann u. Frau*) couple; *z. B. Rebhühner, Pistolen*: brace; **2.** *ein* **2** a few, some, F a couple of; **3.** **2** even; ~ *oder un*~ odd or even; '**2en** (25) pair, couple, *bsd. Vögel*: mate (*a. sich* ~); *Sport*: pair, match; *sich* ~ *fig.* join (*mit* with); '**2ig** in pairs, paired; '**~laufen** *n Sport*: pair skating; '**2mal**: *ein* ~ several *od.* (a few) times; '**~ung** *f* pairing (*Sport*: *a.* matching); mating, copulation; '**~ungszeit** *f* mating season '**2weise** by pairs, in couples, two and two.
Pacht [paxt] *f* (16) lease, tenure; (~*geld*) rent; *in* ~ *geben* (*nehmen*)

let (take) on lease; '⁓**en** (26) (take on) lease, rent, farm; *fig.* monopolize.

Pächter ['pɛçtər] *m* (7), '⁓**in** *f* (16¹) (*Mieter*) lessee; *von Land*: tenant; *weitS.* farmer; ⚖ leaseholder.

'**Pacht|-ertrag** *m* rental; '⁓**frei** rent-free; '⁓**geld** *n* farm-rent; '⁓**gut** *n* farm; '⁓**ung** *f* taking on lease, farming; (*das Gepachtete*) leasehold; '⁓**vertrag** *m* lease; '⁓**weise** on lease.

Pack [pak] **1.** *m* (3³ *u.* 3) pack; (*Paket*) packet, parcel; (*Ballen*) bale; *s. Sack*; **2.** *n* (3, *o. pl.*) (*Lumpen*⁓) rabble.

Päckchen ['pɛkçən] *n* (6) small parcel; packet, package; *Zigaretten*: pack; F *fig.* burden, worries *pl.*

'**Pack-eis** *n* pack(-ice).

'**packen 1.** (25) pack (up); (*fassen*) seize, grasp, grip; *fig.* grip, thrill; *pack dich! sl.* beat it!; **2.** ⁓ *n* (6) packing; **3.** ⁓ *m* (6) pack; (*Ballen*) bale.

'**Packer** *m* (7), '⁓**in** *f* (16¹) packer.

'**Pack|-esel** *m* sumpter-mule; *fig.* drudge, fag; '⁓**leinwand** *f* pack-cloth; '⁓**material** *n* packing (material); '⁓**papier** *n* wrapping paper; *als Papiersorte*: brown paper; '⁓**pferd** *n* pack-horse; '⁓**sattel** *m* pack-saddle; '⁓**tasche** *f* pannier, saddlebag; '⁓**tier** *n* pack-animal; '⁓**ung** *f* (*Päckchen*) packet, pack (*a.* ⚕); F *fig.* awful beating; '⁓**wagen** *m* *Brt.* (luggage) van, *Am.* baggage car.

Pädagog|e [pɛːda'goːgə] *m* (13), ⁓**in** [⁓gin] *f* education(al)ist; ⁓**ik** [⁓gik] *f* pedagogics *pl.*; ⁓**isch** pedagogic(al).

Paddel ['padəl] *n* (7) paddle; '⁓**boot** *n* canoe; '⁓**n** (29, sn) paddle, canoe.

paff [paf] bang!, pop!; F *ganz* ⁓ *sein* be dumbfounded.

paffen ['pafən] (25) puff (*die Pfeife* at one's pipe).

Page ['pɑːʒə] *m* (13) page; *s. Hotel*⁓; '⁓**nkopf** *m* bob(bed hair).

Pagode [pa'goːdə] *f* (15) pagoda.

pah! [pɑː] pah!; pshaw!

Pak ⚔ [pak] *f* (*sg.* 16, *pl.* 11) anti-tank gun.

Paket [pa'keːt] *n* (3) parcel; *großes*: package (*a. fig. pol. usw.*); *kleines*: packet; ✝ *Wertpapiere*: block; ⁓-**annahme** *f* parcels receiving office; ⁓-**ausgabe** *f* parcel delivery; ⁓**bombe** *f* parcel bomb; ⁓**boot** *n* mail-boat; ⁓**karte** ✉ *f* parcel form; ⁓**post** *f* parcel post.

Pakt [pakt] *m* (3 *u.* 5) pact, agreement; ⁓**ieren** [⁓'tiːrən] make a deal (*mit* with).

Palast [pa'last] *m* (3² *u.* ³) palace; ⁓-**artig** palatial; ⁓**revolution** *fig. f* palace revolution.

Palästinenser [palɛsti'nɛnzər] *m* (7) Palestinian.

Palette [pa'lɛtə] *f* (15) palette.

Palisade [pali'zɑːdə] *f* (15) palisade; ⁓**nzaun** *m* stockade.

Palm|e ['palmə] *f* (15) palm(-tree); F *j-n auf die* ⁓ *bringen* put a p.'s monkey up; '⁓**kätzchen** *n* catkin; '⁓'**sonntag** *m* Palm Sunday.

Pampelmuse ⚘ [pampəl'muːzə] *f* (15) grapefruit.

Pamphlet [pam'fleːt] *n* (3) (*Flugblatt*) pamphlet; (*Schmähschrift*) lampoon; ⁓**ist** [⁓fle'tist] *m* (12) pamphleteer; lampoonist.

Paneel [pa'neːl] *n* (3¹) wainscot, panel.

Panier [pa'niːr] *n* (3¹) banner, standard.

pa'nier|en (25) *Kochkunst*: (bread-) crumb; ⁓**mehl** *n* breadcrumbs *pl.*

Pan|ik ['pɑːnik] *f* (16) panic, scare; '⁓**isch** panic.

Panne ['panə] *f* (15) break-down; (*Motor*⁓) engine failure; (*Reifen*⁓) puncture, blowout; *fig.* mishap, (*Fehler*) F slip-up; e-e ⁓ *haben* break down, have a break-down; '⁓**ndienst** *mot. m* break-down service.

Panoptikum [pa'nɔptikum] *n* (9¹) waxworks *pl.*

Panorama [pano'rɑːma] *n* (9¹) panorama, panoramic view; ⁓**scheibe** *mot. f* panoramic windscreen (*Am.* windshield).

panschen ['panʃən] (27) *s. pantschen.*

Panther ['pantər] *m* (7) panther.

Pantine [pan'tiːnə] *f* (15) clog.

Pantoffel [⁓'tɔfəl] *m* (10 *u.* 7) slipper, mule; *fig. unter dem* ⁓ *stehen* be henpecked; ⁓**held** *m* henpecked husband.

Pantomim|e [panto'miːmə] *f* (15) pantomime, dumb show; ⁓**isch** pantomimic.

pan(t)schen ['pan(t)ʃən] (27) splash (about); (*verfälschen*) adulterate.

Panzer ['pantsər] *m* (7) armo(u)r; (*Kampfwagen*) tank; ⚓ armo(u)r

(-plating); '~**-abwehrgeschütz** *n* anti-tank gun; '~**-abwehrrakete** *f* anti-tank rocket; '**2brechend** armo(u)r-piercing; '~**division** *f* armo(u)red division; '~**faust** ⚔ *f* anti-tank grenade launcher; '~**glas** *n* bullet-proof glass; '~**handschuh** *m* gauntlet; '~**hemd** *n* coat of mail; '~**kreuzer** *m* armo(u)red cruiser; '**2n** (29) armo(u)r; *sich* ~ arm o.s.; *gepanzerte Faust* mailed fist; '~**platte** *f* armo(u)r-plate; '~**schrank** *m* safe; ~**spähwagen** ['~ʃpɛ:-] *m* armo(u)red (reconnaissance) car; '~**sperre** *f* anti-tank obstacle; '~**truppe** *f* tank force *od.* corps; '~**ung** ⚔, ✝ *f* armo(u)r-plating; '~**wagen** *m* armo(u)red car; '~**zug** *m* 🚂 armo(u)red train; ⚔ tank platoon.

Papa [pa'pa, F '~] *m* (11) papa, F dad(dy), *Am.* F pop.

Papagei [papa'gaɪ] *m* (3 *u.* 12) parrot; ~**enkrankheit** *f* psittacosis.

Papier [pa'pi:r] *n* (3[1]) paper; ~**e** *pl.* (*Ausweise*) (identity) papers *pl.*, ✝ (*Wertpapiere*) securities *pl.*, papers *pl.*; (*nur*) *auf dem* ~ on paper (only); *zu* ~ *bringen* commit to paper; ~**bogen** *m* sheet of paper; **2en** (of) paper; ~**fabrik** *f* paper-mill; ~**geld** *n* paper-money; ~**handlung** *f* stationer's (shop), *Am.* stationery (store); ~**handtuch** *n* paper towel; ~**korb** *m* waste-paper basket; ~**krieg** F *m* red tape, paper warfare; ~**maché** [papje:ma'ʃə:] *n* (11[1]) papier mâché; ~**schlange** [pa'pi:r-] *f* paper streamer; ~**schnitzel** *n*, ~**wisch** *m* scrap of paper; ~**taschentuch** *n* tissue; ~**währung** *f* paper-currency; ~**waren** *f/pl.* stationery; ~**warengeschäft** *n s. Papierhandlung*.

Papp [pap] *m* (3) (*Brei*) pap; (*Kleister*) paste; '~**band** *m* pasteboard binding; (book bound in) boards *pl.*; '~**becher** *m* paper cup; '~**deckel** *m* pasteboard.

Pappe ['papə] *f* (15) pasteboard; (*starke* ~) millboard; F *fig. nicht von* ~ quite something.

Pappel ['papəl] *f* (15) poplar.

päppeln ['pɛpəln] (29) feed (with pap); *fig.* coddle, pamper.

'**papp|en** *v/t.* paste; *v/i.* stick; '**2enstiel** F *fig. m* trifle; *für e-n* ~ for a song; ~**erlapapp!** [papərla'pap] fiddlesticks!; '~**ig** sticky; '**2schachtel** *f* cardboard box; '**2schnee** *m* sticky snow; '**2teller** *m* paper plate.

Paprika ['paprika] *m* (11) paprika; ♣ capsicum; '~**schote** *f* pepper.

Papst [pa:pst] *m* (3[2] *u.* [3]) pope.

päpstlich ['pɛ:pstliç] papal.

'**Papsttum** *n* (1, *o. pl.*) papacy.

Parab|el [pa'ra:bəl] *f* (15) (*Gleichnis*) parable; 𝒜 parabola; **2olisch** [para'bo:liʃ] parabolic(ally *adv.*).

Parade [pa'ra:də] *f* (15) parade; (*Prunk*) display; ⚔ review; *fenc.* parry; *Fußball*: save; ~**-anzug** ⚔ *m* dress uniform, F full dress; ~**marsch** ⚔ *m* march in review.

Paradentose ⚕ [paradɛn'to:zə] *f* (15) paradentosis.

Pa'radeplatz ⚔ *m* parade-ground.

paradieren [para'di:rən] parade.

Paradies [~'di:s] *n* (4) paradise.

paradiesisch [~'di:ziʃ] paradisiac (-al); *fig.* heavenly.

Para'diesvogel *m* bird of paradise.

paradox [~'dɔks] paradoxical.

Paraffin [para'fi:n] *n* (3[1]) paraffin; ~**-öl** *n* paraffin oil.

Paragraph [~'gra:f] *m* (12) section, article; (*Absatz*) paragraph; (*das Zeichen* §) section-mark.

parallel [para'le:l] parallel (*mit* to, with); **2e** *f* (15) parallel (line); **2ogramm** [~lelo'gram] *n* (3[1]) parallelogram; **2schaltung** ⚡ *f* parallel connection.

Paraly|se [para'ly:zə] *f* (15) paralysis; **2'sieren** [~ly-] paralyse; **2tisch** [~'ly:tiʃ] paralytic(ally *adv.*).

paranoi|d [parano'i:t] paranoid; **2ker** [~'no:ikər] *m* (7), ~**sch** [~'no:iʃ] paranoiac.

Paranuß ['pa:ra-] *f* Brazil-nut.

Parasit [para'zi:t] *m* (12) parasite; **2isch** parasitic(al).

parat [pa'ra:t] ready; ~ *haben Kenntnisse*: have at one's fingers' ends; *Antwort*: have pat.

Pärchen ['pɛ:rçən] *n* (6) (courting) couple; *a. iro.* twosome.

Pardon [par'dõ] *m* (11) pardon; ⚔ quarter.

Parenthese [parɛn'te:zə] *f* (15) parenthesis.

Parforcejagd [par'fɔrsja:kt] *f* hunt (-ing) on horseback.

Parfüm [par'fy:m] *n* (3[1]) perfume, scent; ~**e'rie** *f*, ~**e'rien** [~fymə'ri:(n)] *pl.* perfumery; ~**fläschchen** (small) scent-bottle; **2ieren** [~fy'mi:rən] perfume, scent.

pari ✝ ['pɑːri] par; *al* ~ at par; *über (unter)* ~ above (below) par.
Paria ['pɑːrja] *m* (11) pariah.
parieren [pa'riːrən] *v/i.* (*dat.*) obey; *v/t. u. v/i. Pferd*: pull up, stop; *Stoß usw.*: parry (*a. fig.*).
Pariser [pa'riːzər] *m* (7) Parisian; F (*Kondom*) rubber.
Parität [pari'tɛːt] *f* (16) parity; **2isch** proportional, pro rata.
Park [park] *m* (3) park; ⚔ *a.* depot; *s. Wagen2*; '**~anlage** *f* park; '**~deck** *mot. n* parking level; '**2en** (25) park; 2 *verboten!* No parking!
Parkett [~'kɛt] *n* (3) parquet; *thea.* stalls *pl.*, *Am.* parquet; **~fußboden** *m* parquet flooring.
'**Park|gebühr** *f* parking fee; '**~haus** *n* multi-storey car park; '**~licht** *n* parking light; '**~lücke** *f* parking space; '**~platz** *m* car park, *Am.* parking lot; (*einzelner Platz*) parking space; '**~scheibe** *f* parking disc; '**~uhr** *f* parking meter; '**~verbot** *n*: *hier ist* ~ there's no parking here; '**~wächter** *mot. m* car park attendant.
Parlament [parla'mɛnt] *n* (3) parliament; **~är** [~'tɛːr] *m* (3[1]) parlementaire (*fr.*); **~arier** [~'tɑːrjər] *m* (7) parliamentarian; **2arisch** [~'tɑːriʃ] parliamentary; **2ieren** [~'tiːrən] parley; **~s-ausschuß** *m* parliamentary committee.
Parmesan [parme'zɑːn] *m* (3, *o. pl.*), **~käse** *m* Parmesan cheese.
Parodie [paro'diː] *f* (15) parody; **2ren** parody.
Parole [pa'roːlə] *f* (15) ⚔ password; *fig.* catchword, slogan.
Paroli [pa'roːli] *fig. n* (11): *j-m* ~ *bieten* stick up to a p.
Partei [par'taɪ] *f* (16) party (*a. pol. u.* ⚖); (*~sektion*) faction; *Sport*: side; *j-s* ~ *ergreifen*, ~ *nehmen für j-n* take the part of a p., side with a p.; *gegen j-n* ~ *ergreifen* take sides against a p.; **~-abzeichen** *n* party badge; **~-apparat** *m* party machine; **~basis** *f* rank and file; **~disziplin** *f* party discipline; *sich der* ~ *beugen* follow the party line; **~führer** *m* party-leader; **~gänger** *m* (7) partisan; **~geist** *m* party spirit; **~genosse** *m* party-member; **2isch, 2lich** partial; **~leitung** *f* party leadership; **~lichkeit** *f* partiality; **2los** impartial, neutral; *pol.* independent, non-party; **~lose** *parl. m* (18) non-party member; **~losigkeit** *f* impartiality, neutrality; **~mitglied** *n* party member; **~nahme** [~nɑːmə] *f* (15) partisanship; **~politik** *f* party politics; **~programm** *n* platform; **~sucht** *f* factious spirit; **~tag** *m* party conference (*Am.* convention); **~ung** *f* division into parties; **~ver-anstaltung** *f* party function; **~versammlung** *f* party meeting; **~zugehörigkeit** *f* party affiliation.
Parterre [par'tɛr] *n* (11) ground floor, *Am.* first floor; *thea.* pit, *Am.* orchestra circle.
Partie [~'tiː] *f* (15) (*Teil*) part; ✝ (*Warenmenge*) lot, parcel; (*Gesellschaft*) party; (*Ausflug*) outing, excursion; *Sport*: match (*a. Heirat*), game; *mit von der* ~ *sein* make one of the party.
partiell [par'tsjɛl] partial.
Partik|el [~'tiːkəl] *f* (15) particle; **~ularismus** [~tikula'rismus] *m* (16) particularism.
Partisan [parti'zɑːn] *m* (12) partisan, guerilla.
Partitur ♪ [~'tuːr] *f* (16) score.
Partizip *gr.* [~'tsiːp] *n* (8[2]) participle.
Partner ['partnər] *m* (7), '**~in** *f* (16[1]) partner; '**~schaft** *f* partnership; '**~stadt** *f* twin town; '**~tausch** *m* wife-swapping.
Party ['pɑːti] *f* (11[1] *u. -ties*) party.
Parvenü [parvə'nyː] *m* (11) upstart, parvenu.
Parze ['partsə] *f* (15): *die* ~*n pl.* [the Fates.]
Parzel|le [par'tsɛlə] *f* (15) plot, allotment, *bsd. Am.* lot; **2'lieren** divide into lots, parcel out.
Pasch [paʃ] *m* (3[2] *u.* [3]) *beim Würfeln*: doublets *pl.*
Pascha ['paʃa] *m* (11) pasha.
Paspel ['paspəl] *m* (7), *f* (15) piping.
Paß [pas] *m* (14[1] *u.* [2]) (*Gebirgs2*) pass; (*Reise2*) passport, *s. Paßgang.*
passabel [pa'sɑːbəl] passable, tolerable, fair(ly good).
Passage [pa'sɑːʒə] *f* (15) passage (*a.* ♪); ⌂ arcade.
Passagier [pasa'ʒiːr] *m* (3[1]) passenger; *im Taxi*: fare; *s. blind*; **~flugzeug** *n* passenger aircraft; **~gut** *n* luggage, *Am.* baggage.
Passah ['pasa] *n* (11, *o. pl.*), *mst* '**~fest** *n* Passover.
'**Paß-amt** *n* pass-port office.
Passant [pa'sant] *m* (12), **~in** *f* (16[1]) passer-by (*pl.* passers-by).

Passat [pa'sa:t] *m* (3), **~wind** *m* trade-wind.

'Paßbild *n* passport photo(graph).

passen ['pasən] (28) fit (*j-m* a p.; *auf acc., für, zu* et. a th.); (*zusagen*) suit (*j-m* a p.); *Spiel*: pass; ~ (*warten*) *auf* (*acc.*) watch (*od.* wait) for; *nicht ~ für* be unfit for; *~ zu e-m Kleid usw.*: go with, *bsd. in der Farbe*: match (with); *sie ~ zueinander* they are well matched; *sich ~* be fit *od.* proper; *das paßt sich nicht* that is not good form; **'~d** fit; suitable; (*kleidsam*) becoming; *bsd. in der Farbe*: to match; (*gelegen*) convenient; *für ~ halten* think proper.

Passepartout [paspar'tu:] *n* (11) masterkey; (*Wechselrahmen*) mount.

'Paß|form *f* fit; **'~gang** *m* amble.

passier|bar [pa'si:rba:r] passable, practicable; **~en** *v/i.* (sn) (*vorbeigehen*) pass; (*sich ereignen*) take place, happen, come to pass; *v/t.* pass (by); *Kochkunst*: strain; **2schein** *m* pass (*bsd.* ⚔); permit.

Passion [pa'sjo:n] *f* (16) passion; (*Liebhaberei*) hobby; **2iert** [~sjo'ni:rt] passionate; **~sspiel** [~'sjo:ns-] *n* Passion play.

passiv ['pasi:f] passive; *~er Widerstand* passive resistance; *~er Wortschatz* recognition vocabulary; **'2** *n* (9, *o. pl.*) *gr.* passive voice; **2a**, *a.* **2en** † [~'si:va, ~vən] *pl.* liabilities; **~ieren** † [~'vi:ren] enter on the liability side; **2ität** [~sivi'tɛ:t] *f* (16) passiveness, passivity; **2posten** † ['pasi:f-] *m* debit item; **'2seite** *f* liability side.

'Paß|kontrolle *f* passport control; **'~stelle** *f* passport office; **'~stück** *n*, **'~teil** ⊕ *n* fitting part.

Paste ['pastə] *f* (15) paste.

Pastell [pa'stɛl] **1.** *n* (3^1) (*Bild, Farbe, Malerei*) pastel; **2.** *m* (*Stift*) crayon; **~farbe** *f*, **~ton** *m* pastel shade; **~maler**(**in** *f*) *m* pastel(l)ist.

Pastete [pa'ste:tə] *f* (15) pie.

pasteurisieren [pastøri'zi:rən] pasteurize.

Pastille [pa'stilə] *f* (15) lozenge.

Pastor ['pastɔr] *m* (8^1) pastor, vicar, minister.

Pate ['pa:tə] *m* (13) godfather; *f* (15) godmother; *m, f* (= **'~nkind** *n*) godchild; *~ stehen bei* stand godfather (*od.* godmother *od. fig.* sponsor) to; **'~nstelle** *f* sponsorship; *~ vertreten bei s. Pate stehen bei.*

Patent [pa'tɛnt] **1.** *n* (3^1) patent; ⚔ commission; *ein ~ anmelden* apply for a patent; (*zum*) *~ angemeldet* patent pending; **2.** 2 F *adj.* clever; *~er Kerl* fine fellow; **~-amt** *n* patent office; **~-anmeldung** *f* patent application; **~-anspruch** *m* patent claim; **~-anwalt** *m* patent attorney; **~beschreibung** *f* patent specification; **2fähig** patentable; **~gebühr** *f* (patent-)fee; **2ieren** [~'ti:rən] patent; *~ lassen* take out a patent for; **~-inhaber** *m* patent-holder, patentee; **~lösung** *f* pat solution; **~recht** *n* patent law; *erworbenes*: patent right; **~schrift** *f* patent specification; **~schutz** *m* protection by patent; **~verletzung** *f* patent infringement; **~verschluß** *m* patent stopper, snap-fastener.

Pater ['pa:tər] *m* (7, *pl. Patres* ['pa:tre:s]) father.

Paternoster [pa:tɛr'nɔstər] *n* (7) paternoster; **~**(**-aufzug**) *m* paternoster lift; **~werk** ⊕ *n* chain-pump; *am Bagger*: (bucket-)elevator.

pathetisch [pa'te:tiʃ] emotional, lofty; *das 2e s. Pathos.*

Pathol|ogie [patolo'gi:] *f* (16) pathology; **2ogisch** [~'lo:giʃ] pathological.

Pathos ['pa:tɔs] *n* (*inv., o. pl.*) emotional (*od.* lofty) speech *od.* style.

Patience [pa'sjã:s] *f* (15) solitaire.

Patient [pa'tsjɛnt] *m* (12), **~in** *f* (16^1) patient.

Patin ['pa:tin] *f* (16^1) godmother.

Patina ['pa:tina] *f* (15, *o.pl.*) patina.

Patriarch [patri'arç] *m* (12) patriarch; **2alisch** [~'ça:liʃ] patriarchal.

Patriot [~tri'o:t] *m* (12), **~in** *f* (16^1) patriot; **2isch** patriotic(ally *adv.*); **~ismus** [~trio'tismus] *m* (16, *o.pl.*) patriotism.

Patriz|e ⊕ [~'tri:tsə] *f* (15) punch(-eon), top die; **~ier** [~tsjər] *m* (7) patrician.

Patron [~'tro:n] *m* (3^1) patron, protector; (*oft b.s.*) fellow; **~at** [~tro'na:t] *n* (3) patronage; **~e** [~'tro:nə] *f* (15) cartridge; **~engurt** *m* cartridge belt; **~enhülse** *f* cartridge case; **~entasche** *f* cartridge pouch; **~in** *f* (16^1) patroness.

Patrouill|e ⚔ [pa'truljə] *f* (15) patrol; ℒ**ieren** ⚔ [~'ji:rən] patrol.

Patsch|e F ['patʃə] *f* (15) **1.** (*auch* '**~hand** *f*) paw; **2.** *in die ~ geraten* get into a scrape (*od.* fix), get into hot water; *in der ~ sitzen* be in a scrape *od.* pickle *od.* in hot water; *j-m aus der ~ helfen* help a p. (out of a scrape); 'ℒ**en** (27, h. *u.* sn) *im Wasser*: splash; (*schlagen*) slap; 'ℒ'**naß** dripping (wet).

Patt [pat] *n* (11), ℒ *adj. Schach*: stalemate.

patz|en ['patsən] F (27) muff (it); 'ℒ**er** F *m* (7) blunder; '**~ig** F snotty.

Pauke ['paukə] *f* (15) kettledrum; F *fig. auf die ~ hauen* go on the racket; *mit ~n und Trompeten* F gloriously, awfully; 'ℒ**n** *v/i.* (25) beat the kettledrum; F *Schule*: (*a. v/t.*) cram, swot, grind; '**~r** *m* (7) kettle-drummer; F (*Lehrer*) crammer, schoolmaster.

pausbäckig ['pausbεkiç] chubby (-faced).

pauschal [pau'ʃa:l] global, overall; *adv. a.* all included; *fig.* in the lump, wholesale; ℒ**-angebot** *n* package deal; ℒ**e** *f*, *n* (9) lump sum; *im Hotel usw.*: all-in price, *Am.* American plan; ℒ**gebühr** *f* flat rate; ℒ**reise** *f* package tour; ℒ**-urteil** *n* sweeping judg(e)ment; ℒ**zahlung** *f* lump-sum (*als Ablösung*: composition) payment.

Pause[1] ['pauze] *f* (15) pause, stop, interval; *Schule, a. Arbeits*ℒ: break, recess; *thea.* interval, *Am.* intermission; ♪ rest; (*Nachlassen*) lull.

'**Pause**[2] [~] *f* (15) (*Pauszeichnung*) tracing, blueprint; 'ℒ**n** (27) trace.

'**pausen|los** uninterrupted; 'ℒ**zeichen** *n Radio*: (station) identification signal.

pau'sieren pause.

Pauspapier ['paus-] *n* tracing-paper.

Pavian ['pa:via:n] *m* (3[1]) baboon.

Pavillon ['paviljɔ̃] *m* (11) pavilion.

Pazifis|mus [patsi'fismus] *m* (16, *o. pl.*) pacifism; **~st** *m* (12) pacifist; ℒ**stisch** pacifist(ic).

Pech [pεç] *n* (3) pitch; *fig.* bad (*Am. a.* hard) luck; *~ haben* be down on one's luck; '**~fackel** *f* torch; '**~kohle** *f* bituminous coal; 'ℒ**schwarz** jet-black; *Nacht*: pitch-dark; '**~strähne** *f* run of bad luck; '**~vogel** *m* unlucky fellow.

Pedal [pe'da:l] *n* (3[1]) pedal.

Pedant [pe'dant] *m* (12) pedant, stickler; **~erie** [~ə'ri:] *f* (16) pedantry; ℒ**isch** [~'dantiʃ] pedantic (-ally *adv.*), punctilious.

Pegel ['pe:gəl] *m* (6) water-ga(u)ge; ⊕ level; '**~stand** *m* (water-)level.

Peil|-antenne ['paɪl-] *f* direction finder (*abbr.* D.F.) aerial; 'ℒ**en** (25) *v/t. Tiefe*: sound; *Land*: take the bearings of; *v/i.* take the bearings; '**~funk** *m Radio*: directional radio; '**~gerät** *n* radio direction finder; '**~ung** *f* sounding; bearing, direction finding.

Pein [paɪn] *f* (16) pain, torture.

peinig|en ['~igən] (25) torment; 'ℒ**er** *m* (7), 'ℒ**erin** *f* (16[1]) tormentor; 'ℒ**ung** *f* torment(ing), torture.

'**peinlich** painful (*dat.* for); (*unangenehm*) embarrassing, awkward; ⚖ capital, penal; (*sehr genau*) precise, scrupulous (*in dat.* about); *j-n ~ berühren* distress a p.; 'ℒ**keit** *f* painfulness; awkwardness; preciseness, scrupulousness.

Peitsche ['paɪtʃə] *f* (15) whip; 'ℒ**n** (27) whip, lash; *parl. s. durchpeitschen*; '**~nhieb** *m* (whip-)lash; '**~nknall** *m* crack of a whip; '**~nschnur** *f* lash.

pekuniär [pekun'jε:r] pecuniary.

Pelerine [pelə'ri:nə] *f* (15) pelerine, cape, (*bsd.* fur) tippet.

Pelikan ['pe:lika:n] *m* (3[1]) pelican.

Pelle ['pεlə] *f* (15) skin, peel; 'ℒ**n** (25) skin, peel; *s. Ei.*

'**Pellkartoffeln** *f/pl.* potatoes in their jackets *od.* skin.

Pelz [pεlts] *m* (3[2]) fur (*als Kleidung mst pl.*); (*Fell*) pelt; *fig.* skin, hide; '**~besatz** *m* fur trimming; 'ℒ**gefüttert** fur-lined; '**~handel** *m* fur-trade; '**~händler** *m* furrier; '**~handschuh** *m* furred glove; 'ℒ**ig** furry; ⚕ *Zunge*: furred; *Glied*: numb; '**~kragen** *m* fur collar *od.* tippet; '**~mantel** *m* fur coat; '**~mütze** *f* fur cap; '**~tiere** *n/pl.* fur-bearing animals, furs; '**~tierfarm** *f* fur-farm; '**~werk** *n* furs *pl.*

Pendel ['pεndəl] *n* (7) pendulum; '**~diplomatie** *f* shuttle diplomacy; 'ℒ**n** (29, h. *u.* sn) oscillate, swing; *Zug usw.*: shuttle, *Am.* commute; *Person*: commute; '**~tür** *f* swing door; '**~-uhr** *f* pendulum clock; '**~-**

verkehr 🚂 *m* shuttle service; '**~zug** *m* shuttle (*Am.* commuter) train.
Pendler ['pɛndlər] *m* (7) commuter.
penetrant [pene'trant] penetrating.
penibel [pe'ni:bəl] fussy, pernickety.
Penis ['pe:nis] *m* (14²) penis.
Penizillin [penitsi'li:n] *n* (9, *o. pl.*) penicillin.
Pennäler [pɛ'nɛ:lər] *m* (7) school-boy.
Pennbruder P ['pɛnbru:dər] *m* tramp, *Am. a.* hobo, *sl.* bum.
'**Penne** F *f* (15) (*Nachtasyl*) doss-house, *Am.* flophouse; (*Schule*) school; '**2n** F (25) snooze.
Pension [pɑ̃'sjo:n] *f* (16) **a**) (old-age) pension; ⚔ retired pay; *in ~ gehen* retire; **b**) (*Kostgeld*) board; (*Fremdenheim*) boarding-house; **~är** [~sjo'nɛ:r] *m* (3) **a**) pensioner; **b**) boarder; **~at** [~'na:t] *n* (3) boarding-school; **2ieren** [~'ni:rən] pension (off); ⚔ put on half-pay; *sich ~ lassen* retire; **~iert** retired, in retirement; **~s-alter** *n* retiring age; **2sberechtigt** pensionable; **~sfonds** *m* superannuation fund.
Pensum ['pɛnzum] *n* (9²) task, lesson; *weitS.* work rate; *großes ~* a great deal of work.
per [pɛr] per, by; *Datum*: as of; *~ Adresse* care of (*abbr.* c/o); *~ Bahn* by train.
perfekt [pɛr'fɛkt] **1.** perfect; *Vertrag usw.*: settled, in the bag; **2.** 2 *gr.* ['pɛrfɛkt] *n* (3) perfect (tense).
perforieren [~fo'ri:rən] perforate.
Pergament [pɛrga'mɛnt] *n* (3) parchment; **~papier** *n* parchment (*od.* vellum) paper; *zum Einwickeln*: greaseproof paper.
Period|e [per'jo:də] *f* (15) period (*a. physiol. der Frau*); ⚡ cycle; **2isch** periodic(al); *~er Dezimalbruch* recurring decimal.
Peripherie [perife'ri:] *f* (16) circumference, periphery; *e-r Stadt*: outskirts *pl.*; **~gerät** *n Computer*: peripheral.
Periskop [peri'sko:p] *n* (3¹) periscope.
perkutan [pɛrku'ta:n] ⚕ percutaneous.
Perle ['pɛrlə] *f* (15) pearl; (*Glas2 usw.*) bead; *fig.* gem; *~n vor die Säue werfen* cast (one's) pearls before swine; '**2n** (25) pearl (*a. Töne*); *Getränk*: sparkle; *Lachen*: ripple; '**~nkette** *f* string of pearls.
'**perl|grau** pearl-grey, *Am.* pearl-gray; '**2huhn** *n* guinea-fowl; '**2muschel** *f* pearl-oyster; **2'mutter** *f inv.* mother-of-pearl, nacre; '**2schrift** *typ. f* pearl.
permanen|t [pɛrma'nɛnt] permanent; **2z** [~ts] *f* (16) permanence.
Perpendikel [pɛrpɛn'di:kəl] *m, n* (7) **1.** pendulum; **2.** perpendicular (line).
perplex [~'plɛks] perplexed, bewildered.
Persenning [pɛr'zɛniŋ] *f* (14) tarpaulin.
Pers|er ['pɛrzər] *m* (7) Persian; '**~erteppich** *m* Persian carpet; **~ianer** [pɛr'zja:nər] *m* (7) Persian lamb(skin); '**2isch** Persian.
Person [pɛr'zo:n] *f* (16) person; *s. juristisch, natürlich*; *thea.* character; *in ~* in person, personally.
Personal [~zo'na:l] *n* (3¹) staff, personnel; **~-abteilung** *f* staff department, *Am.* personnel division; **~-angaben** *f/pl.* personal data; **~-ausweis** *m* identity card; **~chef** *m* personnel manager; **~-Computer** *m* personal computer; **~daten** *n/pl.* personal data; **~fragebogen** *m* application form; **~ien** [~jən] *pl.* particulars, personal data; **~pronomen** *gr. n* personal pronoun.
personell [~zo'nɛl] personal; (*Personal betreffend*) personnel.
Per'sonen|-aufzug *m* (passenger) lift, *bsd. Am.* elevator; **~beförderung** *f* conveyance of passengers; **~kraftwagen** *m* passenger car; **~kreis** *m* circle; **~kult** *m* personality cult; **~schaden** *m* personal injury; **~stand** *m* personal status; **~verzeichnis** *n* list of persons; *thea.* dramatis personae *pl.*; **~wagen** *m* 🚂 passenger-carriage, coach; *mot.* passenger car; **~zug** *m* passenger-train; (*Ggs. Schnellzug*) omnibus (*Am.* accommodation *od.* way) train.
personifizieren [pɛrzonifi'tsi:rən] personify.
persönlich [~'zø:nliç] personal; *adv.* personally, in person; **2keit** *f* personality; (*bedeutender Mensch*) personage.
Perspektiv|e [~spɛk'ti:və] *f* (15) perspective; *fig. a.* prospect; **2isch** perspective; *Figuren ~ zeichnen* foreshorten.

Perücke [pɛˈrykə] *f* (15) wig.
pervers [pɛrˈvɛrs] perverse; **2ität** [~ziˈtɛːt] *f* (16) perversity.
Pessar ⚕ [pɛˈsɑːr] *n* (3[1]) pessary.
Pessi|mismus [pɛsiˈmismus] *m* (16, *o. pl.*) pessimism; ˈ**~mist** *m* (12) pessimist; 2ˈ**mistisch** pessimistic(ally *adv.*).
Pest [pɛst] *f* (16) pestilence, plague; *fig. wie die ~* like poison; ˈ**2-artig** pestilential; ˈ**~beule** *f* plague-boil; *fig.* plague-spot; **~ilenz** [~iˈlɛnts] *f* (16) pestilence.
Petersilie ⚘ [petərˈziːljə] *f* (15) parsley.
Petroleum [peˈtroːleum] *n* (11) petroleum, *Am.* (mineral) oil; (*Leucht2*) paraffin, *bsd. Am.* kerosene; **~lampe** *f* oil (*Am.* kerosene) lamp.
Petschaft [ˈpɛtʃaft] *n* (3) seal, signet.
petto [ˈpɛto]: *et. in ~ haben* have something up one's sleeve.
Petze F [ˈpɛtsə] *f* (15) telltale; *Schul-sl.* sneak; ˈ**2n** F *v/t. u. v/i. sl.* peach (*gegen j-n* on); *Schul-sl.* sneak (against); ~ˈ**rei** F *f* tale-telling.
Pfad [pfɑːt] *m* (3) path, track; **~finder** [ˈ~findər] *m* Boy Scout; ˈ**~finderin** *f* Girl Guide, *Am.* Girl Scout; ˈ**2los** pathless.
Pfaffe *contp.* [ˈpfafə] *m* (13) priest, F parson; ˈ**~ntum** *n* (1, *o. pl.*) clericalism; parsons *pl.*
Pfahl [pfɑːl] *m* (3[3]) stake, pale, pile; (*Pfosten*) post; (*Stange*) pole; *fig. ~ im Fleisch* thorn in one's flesh; ˈ**~bau** ⚠ *m* pile-work; *hist.* lake-dwelling.
pfählen [ˈpfɛːlən] (25) ✓ prop (up); *als Strafe*: impale.
ˈ**Pfahlwurzel** *f* tap-root.
Pfalz [pfalts] *f* (16) imperial palace; *geogr. the* Palatinate.
Pfälzer [ˈpfɛltsər] *m* (7) inhabitant of the Palatinate.
Pfalzgraf [ˈpfaltsgrɑːf] *m* Count Palatine.
Pfand [pfant] *n* (1[2]) pledge; (*Bürgschaft*) security; *im Spiel*: forfeit; *zum ~ geben od. setzen* pawn, mortgage, *fig. Ehre usw.*: pledge, *sein Leben*: stake; ˈ**~brief** *m* mortgage bond.
pfänd|bar [ˈpfɛntbɑːr] distrainable; **~en** [ˈ~dən] (26) *et.*: seize; *j-n od. et.*: distrain (up)on, attach; ˈ**2erspiel** *n* (game of) forfeits *pl.*
ˈ**Pfand|gläubiger** *m* mortgagee; ˈ**~haus** *n*, ˈ**~leihe** *f* pawnshop; ˈ**~leiher** *m* (7) pawnbroker; ˈ**~recht** *n* lien; ˈ**~schein** *m* pawn-ticket; ˈ**~schuldner** *m* mortgagor.
ˈ**Pfändung** *f* seizure, distraint; ˈ**~sbefehl** *m* distress-warrant; ˈ**~sverfahren** *n* attachment proceedings *pl.*
Pfann|e [ˈpfanə] *f* (15) pan; *anat.* socket; ˈ**~enstiel** *m* panhandle; ˈ**~kuchen** *m* pancake; *Berliner ~* doughnut.
Pfarr|amt [ˈpfarʔamt] *n* (*Pflichtbereich*) incumbency; (*Pfarrei*) rectory; (*Pastorat*) pastorate; ˈ**~bezirk** *m* parish; ˈ**~e** *f* (15), **~ei** [~ˈraɪ] *f s. Pfarramt, -bezirk, -gemeinde, -haus, -stelle*; ˈ**~er** *m* (7) parson; *der engl. Staatskirche*: rector, vicar; *bei Dissidenten*: minister; ˈ**~gemeinde** *f* parish; ˈ**~haus** *n* parsonage; *der engl. Staatskirche*: rectory, vicarage; ˈ**~kind** *n* parishioner; ˈ**~kirche** *f* parish-church; ˈ**~stelle** *f* benefice.
Pfau [pfaʊ] *m* (5 *u.* 12) peacock; ˈ**~en-auge** *zo. n* peacock-butterfly; ˈ**~enfeder** *f* peacock's feather.
Pfeffer [ˈpfɛfər] *m* (7) pepper; *fig.* F *j-n hinwünschen, wo der ~ wächst* wish a p. in hell (first); *s. Hase*; ˈ**~büchse** *f* pepper-box; ˈ**~gurke** *f* gherkin; ˈ**~kuchen** *m* gingerbread; ˈ**~minze** ⚘ *f* (15), ˈ**~minzplätzchen** *n* peppermint; ˈ**2n** (29) pepper; *s. gepfeffert*; ˈ**~nuß** *f* ginger-nut, *Am.* -snap; ˈ**~streuer** *m* (7) pepper pot.
Pfeife [ˈpfaɪfə] *f* (15) whistle; ⚓ (*Bootsmanns2*) pipe; (*Orgel2*) (organ-)pipe; (*Quer2*) fife; (*Tabaks2*) (tobacco-)pipe; *nach j-s ~ tanzen* dance to a p.'s tune; ˈ**2n** (30) *v/i. u. v/t.* whistle; *Schiedsrichter*: blow the whistle; *auf e-r Pfeife, a. Radio*: pipe; F *~ auf (acc.)* not to give a hoot about; *s. Loch.*
ˈ**Pfeifen|kopf** *m* pipe-bowl; ˈ**~reiniger** *m* pipe cleaner; ˈ**~stiel** pipe-stem; ˈ**~stopfer** pipe stopper.
ˈ**Pfeif|kessel** *m*, ˈ**~topf** *m* whistling kettle; ˈ**~konzert** *n* (wild) booing.
Pfeil [pfaɪl] *m* (3) arrow (*a. in Zeichnungen usw.*); (*Wurf2, Blas2*) dart.
Pfeiler [ˈpfaɪlər] *m* (7) pillar (*a. fig.*); (*Brücken2 usw.*) pier; ⊕ standard.
ˈ**pfeil|gerade** straight as an arrow; *adv.* straight; ˈ**~schnell** as swift as an arrow; ˈ**2schuß** *m* arrow-shot;

ˈ**~zeichnung** ⊕ *f* functional diagram(me).

Pfennig [ˈpfɛniç] *m* (3, *als Wertangabe im pl. inv.*) pfennig; *fig.* penny, farthing; ˈ**~-absatz** *m* stiletto heel; ˈ**~fuchser** F *m* (7) pinchpenny.

Pferch [pfɛrç] *m* (3) fold, pen; ˈ**2en** (25) pen, fold; *fig.* cram.

Pferd [pfeːrt] *n* (3) horse; (*Turngerät*) vaulting-horse; *zu ~e* on horseback; *fig. das ~ beim Schwanze aufzäumen* put the cart before the horse; *s. a. Roß.*

Pferde|bremse *f*, **~fliege** [ˈpfeːrdə-] *f* horse-fly; ˈ**~fleisch** *n* horse-flesh, horse-meat; ˈ**~fuhrwerk** *n* horse-drawn vehicle; ˈ**~fuß** *m fig.* cloven hoof; ˈ**~futter** *n* horse's fodder; ˈ**~geschirr** *n* harness; ˈ**~händler** *m* horse-dealer; ˈ**~knecht** *m* groom; *im Gasthaus*: (h)ostler; ˈ**~koppel** *f* paddock; ˈ**~kraft** *f s. Pferdestärke*; ˈ**~länge** *f Sport*: *um 3 ~en* by 3 lengths; ˈ**~rennen** *n* horse-race; ˈ**~schwanz** *m* horse's tail; (*Frisur*) pony tail; ˈ**~schwemme** *f* horse-pond; ˈ**~stall** *m* stable; ˈ**~stärke** *f* (*abbr.* PS) horse-power (*abbr.* h.p.); ˈ**~wagen** *m* horse carriage; ˈ**~zucht** *f* horse-breeding.

Pfiff [pfif] **1.** *m* (3) whistle; *fig.* trick; (*Schwung*) ginger; **2.** 2 *pret. v. pfeifen*; **~erling** [ˈ~ərliŋ] *m* (3[1]) ♀ chanterelle; *fig.* trifle, straw; *keinen ~ wert* not worth a rush; ˈ**2ig** sly; **~ikus** [ˈ~ikus] *m* sly dog.

Pfingst|en [ˈpfiŋstən] *n od. f/pl.* (*inv., mst ohne art.*), ˈ**~fest** *n* Whitsuntide; ˈ**~ˈmontag** *m* Whit Monday; ˈ**~rose** *f* peony; ˈ**~ˈsonntag** *m* Whitsunday; ˈ**~woche** *f* Whit(sun) week.

Pfirsich [ˈpfirziç] *m* (3) peach.

Pflanze [ˈpflantsə] *f* (15), ˈ**2n** (27) plant.

ˈ**Pflanzen|faser** *f* vegetable fib|re, *Am.* -er; ˈ**~fett** *n* vegetable fat; *Küche*: vegetable shortening; ˈ**2fressend** herbivorous; ˈ**~kost** *f* vegetable diet; ˈ**~kunde** *f* botany; ˈ**~leben** *n* vegetable life; ˈ**~-öl** *n* vegetable oil; ˈ**~reich** *n*, ˈ**~welt** *f* vegetable kingdom, flora; ˈ**~schutzmittel** *n* pesticide.

ˈ**Pflanz|er** *m* (7), ˈ**~erin** *f* (16[1]) planter; ˈ**~ung** *f* plantation.

Pflaster [ˈpflastər] *n* (7) **1.** (*Straßen2*) pavement; *fig.* (*Ort*) place; **2.** ⚕ (adhesive) plaster; *fig.* salve; ˈ**~er** *m* (7) pavio(u)r, *Am.* paver; ˈ**~maler** *m* pavement artist; ˈ**2n** (29) **1.** *Straße*: pave; **2.** ⚕ plaster (*a.* F *fig. kleben*); ˈ**~stein** *m* paving-stone.

Pflaume [ˈpflaumə] *f* (15) plum; (*Dörr2*) prune; F silly ass; ˈ**~nmus** *n* plum jam.

Pflege [ˈpfleːgə] *f* (15) (*Obhut*) care (*a. der Haut, Zähne usw.*); *e-s Kindes*: (child-)care; *e-s Kranken*: nursing, (medical) care; ⊕ maintenance; *e-s Gartens, der Künste, von Beziehungen*: cultivation; *Kind in ~ geben* put out to nurse; *in ~ nehmen* take charge of; **~befohlene** [ˈ~bəfoːlənə] *m* charge; ˈ**~-eltern** *pl.* foster-parents; ˈ**~heim** *n* charitable home; ⚕ nursing home; ˈ**~kind** *n* foster-child; ˈ**2leicht** wash-and-wear; ˈ**~mutter** *f* foster-mother.

pflegen [ˈpfleːgən] (25, *fig. a.* 30) *v/t.* care for; attend to; *sein Äußeres*: groom; *Kranke*: nurse; *Kranke, Maschine*: tend; (*instand halten*) maintain; *Garten, Künste, Beziehungen*: cultivate; *der Ruhe ~* take rest; *s. gepflegt, Umgang*; *v/i. zu tun ~* be accustomed (*od.* used *od.* wont) to, be in the habit of *ger.*; *nur im pret.* I *etc.* used to.

ˈ**Pflegepersonal** ⚕ *n* nursing staff.

ˈ**Pfleger** *m* (7), ˈ**~in** *f* (16[1]) ⚕ (*m* male) nurse; (*Denkmal2 usw.*) conservator; ⚖ guardian; *für Entmündigte*: curator, (*Verwalter*) *a.* trustee.

ˈ**Pflege|sohn** *m* foster-son; ˈ**~vater** *m* foster-father.

pfleg|lich [ˈ~kliç] careful; *et. ~ behandeln* take good care of; ˈ**2ling** *m* (3[1]) foster-child; (*Pflegebefohlener*) charge; ˈ**2schaft** ⚖ *f* (16) guardianship.

Pflicht [pfliçt] *f* (16) duty; (*Verpflichtung*) obligation; *Sport*: *s. ~übung*; ˈ**2bewußt** responsible; ˈ**~bewußtsein** *n*, ˈ**~gefühl** *n* sense of duty; ˈ**2-eifrig** zealous (in one's duties); ˈ**~-erfüllung** *f* performance of one's duty; ˈ**~fach** *n Schule, univ.*: compulsory subject; ˈ**~gefühl** *n s. Pflichtbewußtsein*; ˈ**2gemäß**, ˈ**2mäßig** dutiful, due; ˈ**~lektüre** *f* required reading, set books *pl.*; ˈ**2schuldig** obligatory; *adv.* duly; ˈ**~teil** *m* compulsory portion; ˈ**2treu** dutiful, loyal; ˈ**~treue** *f* dutifulness, loyalty; ˈ**~-**

übung *f* compulsory (*od.* set) exercise; '**⁓vergessen** disloyal, undutiful; '**⁓vergessenheit** *f* dereliction of duty, disloyalty; '**⁓versäumnis** *f* neglect of duty; '**⁓verteidiger** *m* assigned counsel; '**⁓widrig** undutiful, contrary to (one's) duty.

Pflock [pflɔk] *m* (3[3]) plug, peg.

pflöcken ['pflœkən] (25) peg.

pflog ⚒ [pflo:k] *pret. v. pflegen v/i.*

pflücken ['pflykən] (25) pick, pluck, (*einsammeln*) gather.

Pflug [pflu:k] *m* (3[3]) plough, *Am.* plow; '**⁓-eisen** *n* co(u)lter.

pflüg|en ['pfly:gən] *v/t. u. v/i.* (25) plough, *Am.* plow; '**⁓er** *m* (7) ploughman, *Am.* plowman.

'**Pflugschar** *f* ploughshare.

Pförtchen ['pfœrtçən] *n* (6) little door *od.* gate. [⚓ port.]

Pforte ['pfɔrtə] *f* (15) gate, door;

Pförtner ['pfœrtnər] *m* (7) doorkeeper, porter, *Am.* doorman, (*Hausmeister*) janitor; *anat.* pylorus.

Pfosten ['pfɔstən] *m* (6) post; upright; (*Tür⁓, Fenster⁓*) jamb.

Pfote ['pfo:tə] *f* (15) paw.

Pfriem [pfri:m] *m* (3) awl, bodkin.

Pfropf [pfrɔpf] (3), '**⁓en**[1] (6) *m* stopper; (*Kork⁓*) cork; *weitS.* plug; (*Watte⁓*) wad; *s.* Eiter⁓; '**⁓en**[2] (25) cork; (*stopfen*) cram; ✓ graft; '**⁓messer** *n* grafting-knife; '**⁓reis** ✓ *n* graft.

Pfründe ['pfryndə] *f* (15) *eccl.* prebend; (*Pfarrstelle*) benefice, living; *fig.* sinecure.

Pfuhl [pfu:l] *m* (3) pool, puddle.

Pfühl [pfy:l] *m, n* (3) pillow.

pfui [pfui] fie!, (for) shame!; *Sport usw.*: boo!; *angeekelt*: ugh!, phew!

Pfund [pfunt] *n* (3, *als Mengenangabe im pl. inv.*) pound; (*Geld*) ⁓ (*Sterling*) pound (Sterling); **⁓ig** F ['⁓diç] great, swell, groovy.

Pfund|skerl F ['pfuntskɛrl] *m* brick, *Am.* great guy; '**⁓weise** by the pound.

Pfusch|arbeit ['pfuʃʔarbaɪt] *f s.* *Pfuscherei*; '**⁓en** *v/i. u. v/t.* (27) bungle, botch; *j-m ins Handwerk* ⁓ trespass on a p.'s preserves; '**⁓er** *m* (7) bungler; **⁓erei** [⁓ə'raɪ] *f* (16) bungling; bungle.

Pfütze ['pfytsə] *f* (15) pool, puddle.

Phänomen [fɛno'me:n] *n* (3[1]) phenomenon; **⁓al** [⁓'nɑ:l] phenomenal.

Phantasie [fanta'zi:] *f* (15) fancy; (*schöpferische* ⁓) imagination; (*Traumbild*) vision; ♪ fantasia; **⁓los** unimaginative; **⁓preis** *m* fancy price; **⁓reich** imaginative; **⁓ren** indulge in fancies, (day-)dream; ⚕ rave (*a.* F *fig.*), be delirious; ♪ improvise.

Phantast [⁓'tast] *m* (12), **⁓in** *f* (16[1]) visionary; **⁓erei** [⁓ə'raɪ] *f* (16) fantasy; **⁓isch** [⁓'tastiʃ] fantastic(ally *adv.*) (*a.* F *fig.*); (*großartig*) F great, terrific.

Phantom [⁓'to:m] *n* (3[1]) phantom; **⁓bild** *n* identikit.

Pharisä|er [fari'zɛ:ər] *m* (7) Pharisee; **⁓isch** pharisaic(al).

Pharma-industrie ['farma-] *f* pharmaceutical industry.

Pharmakologie [farmakolo'gi:] *f* (15, *o. pl.*) pharmacology.

Pharmareferent ['farma-] *m* pharmaceutical consultant.

Pharmazeut [farma'tsɔʏt] *m* (12) pharmac(eut)ist; (*Apotheker*) *a.* pharmaceutical chemist, *Am.* druggist; **⁓ik** *f* (16) pharmaceutics *sg.*; **⁓isch** pharmaceutical.

Pharmazie [⁓'tsi:] *f* (15) pharmacy.

Phase ['fɑ:zə] *f* (15) phase (*a.* ⚡).

Philanthrop [filan'tro:p] *m* (12), **⁓in** *f* (16[1]) philanthropist; **⁓isch** philanthropic(ally *adv.*).

Philatel|ie [filate'li:] *f* (15, *o. pl.*) philately; **⁓ist** [⁓'list] *m* (12) philatelist.

Philister [fi'listər] *m* (7), **⁓haft** Philistine; **⁓haftigkeit** *f* philistinism.

Philolog|e [filo'lo:gə] *m* (13), **⁓in** *f* (16[1]) philologist; **⁓ie** [⁓lo'gi:] *f* philology; **⁓isch** [⁓'lo:giʃ] philological.

Philosoph [⁓'zo:f] *m* (12) philosopher; **⁓ie** [⁓zo'fi:] *f* (15) philosophy; **⁓ieren** [⁓'fi:rən] philosophize; **⁓isch** [⁓'zo:fiʃ] philosophic(-al).

Phiole [fi'o:lə] *f* (15) phial, vial.

Phlegma ['flɛgma] *n* (11) phlegm.

Phlegmat|iker [⁓'mɑ:tikər] *m* (7) phlegmatic person; **⁓isch** phlegmatic(ally *adv.*).

Phobie [fo'bi:] *f* (15) phobia.

Phonetik [fo'ne:tik] *f* (16) phonetics *mst sg.*; **⁓er** *m* phonetician.

pho'netisch phonetic(ally *adv.*).

Phonotypistin [fonoty'pistin] *f* (16[1]) audio typist.

Phosphat [fɔs'fɑ:t] *n* (3) phosphate.

Phosphor ['fɔsfɔr] *m* (3¹) phosphorus; '**~...** phosphorous; **~eszenz** [~forɛs'tsɛnts] *f* (16) phosphorescence; **2eszieren** [~'tsi:rən] phosphoresce; *~d* phosphorescent; **2ig** [~'fo:riç] phosphorous.

Photo ['fo:to] *n* (11) photo; '**~-apparat** *m* camera.

photogen [foto'ge:n] photogenic.

Photograph [foto'grɑ:f] *m* (12), **~in** *f* (16¹) photographer; **~ie** [~gra'fi:] *f* (15) *Bild*: photograph, F photo; *Kunst*: photography; **2ieren** [~'fi:rən] *v/t. u. v/i.* photograph, take a picture (of); *sich ~ lassen* have one's photo(graph) taken; **2isch** [~'grɑ:fiʃ] photographic(ally *adv.*).

Photoko'pie *f* photocopy; **2ren** photocopy; **~rgerät** *n* photocopier.

'**Photo|montage** *f* (photo) montage, paste-up; '**~satz** *m typ.* photocomposition.

Photothek [foto'te:k] *f* (16) photo library.

'**Photozelle** *f* photo-electric cell, photocell.

Phrase ['frɑ:zə] *f* (15) phrase; *contp. a.* cliché, *pol.* catchphrase; '**~ndrescher** *m* phrasemonger; '**2nhaft** empty, windy, rhetorical.

Physik [fy'zi:k] *f* (16) physics *sg.*, **2alisch** [~'kɑ:liʃ] physical.

Physik|er ['fy:zikər] *m* (7) physicist, natural philosopher; '**~um** [~kum] *n* preliminary (medical) examination.

Physiognomie [fyzjogno'mi:] *f* physiognomy.

Physiolog|e [~'lo:gə] *m* (13) physiologist; **~ie** [~olo'gi:] *f* physiology; **2isch** [~'lo:giʃ] physiological.

physisch ['fy:ziʃ] physical.

Pian|ino [pia'ni:no] *n* (11) cottage (*od.* upright) piano; **~ist** [~'nist] *m* (12), **~istin** [~'nistin] *f* (16¹) pianist.

Piano [pi'ɑ:no] *n*, **~forte** [piano'fɔrtə] *n* (11) piano(forte).

picheln F ['piçəln] *v/i. u. v/t.* (29) tipple, F booze.

Picke ['pikə] *f* (15) pick(ax[e]).

Pickel ['pikəl] *m* (7) **1.** pimple; **2.** *s. Picke, Eis2*; '**~haube** *f* spiked helmet.

'**pick(e)lig** pimpled, pimply.

picken ['pikən] *v/t. u. v/i.* (25) pick, peck.

Picknick ['~nik] *n* (11) picnic.

pieken F ['pi:kən] (25) prick.

piep|en ['pi:pən] (25) peep; *Maus*: squeak; F *zum 2* a scream; '**2matz** F *m* dicky-bird.

pieps|en ['pi:psən] (25) *s. piepen*; '**2er** F *m* (7) (*Funkrufempfänger*) bleeper.

Pier ⚓ [pi:r] *m* (3¹) jetty, pier.

piesacken F ['pi:zakən] pester, torment, persecute.

Pietät [pie'tɛ:t] *f* (16) piety, reverence; **2los** irreverent; **2voll** reverent.

Pigment [pi'gmɛnt] *n* (3) pigment.

Pik [pi:k] **1.** *m* (11) (*Berg*) peak; **2.** *n* (3¹, *o. pl.*) *Kartenspiel*: spade(s *pl.*); **3.** *m* (11) (*Groll*) grudge.

pikant [pi'kant] *a. fig.* piquant, spicy; *das 2e* (the) piquancy; **2erie** [~tə'ri:] *f* (15) piquant (*od.* spicy) story *od.* remark.

Pike ['pi:kə] *f* (15) pike; *von der ~ auf dienen* rise from the ranks.

pik'fein F tiptop, smart, slap-up.

pikiert [pi'ki:rt] piqued (*über acc.* about).

Pikkolo ['pikolo] *m* (11¹) boy waiter; '**~flöte** *f* piccolo.

Pilger ['pilgər] *m* (7), '**~in** *f* pilgrim; '**~fahrt** *f* pilgrimage; '**2n** (29, sn) make (*od.* go on) a pilgrimage; *weitS.* wander; '**~schaft** *f* pilgrimage; '**~stätte** *f* place of pilgrimage.

Pille ['pilə] *f* (15) pill; F *die ~ nehmen* be on (*od.* take) the pill.

Pilot [pi'lo:t] *m* (12) pilot; **~film** *m* pilot (film); **~projekt** *n* pilot project; **~sendung** *f* pilot broadcast.

Pilz [pilts] *m* (3²) fungus; *eßbarer*: mushroom; *nicht eßbarer*: toadstool; *fig. wie ~e aus der Erde schießen* mushroom (up).

pingelig F ['piŋəliç] mean; pedantic, fussy.

Pinguin ['piŋgui:n] *m* (3) penguin.

Pinie ♀ ['pi:njə] *f* (15) stone-pine.

Pinke F ['piŋkə] *f* (*Geld*) *sl.* dough; '**2ln** P (29) piddle, pee.

Pinscher ['pinʃər] *m* (7) pinscher.

Pinsel ['pinzəl] *m* (7) brush; *feiner*: pencil; *fig.* fool, ass; **~ei** [~'laɪ] *f* (16) daub(ing); '**2n** *v/i.* (29) paint; (*schmieren*) daub; '**~strich** *m* stroke of the brush.

Pinzette [pin'tsɛtə] *f* (15) (*eine* a pair of) tweezers *pl.*

Pionier [pio'ni:r] *m* (3¹) pioneer; ⚔ engineer; *Brt.* (*Dienstgrad*) sapper; **~arbeit** *f fig.* pioneering; **~truppe** *f* engineers *pl.*

Pipett|e [pi'pɛtə] *f* (15), **ꝸieren** [~'ti:rən] pipette.

Pirat [pi'rɑ:t] *m* (12) pirate; **~ensender** *m Radio*: pirate station; **~erie** [~tə'ri:] *f* (15) piracy.

Pirsch [pirʃ] *f* (16) deer-stalking, stalk, *Am.* still hunt; '**ꝸen** (27) still-hunt, stalk (deer); '**~jagd** *f s. Pirsch*; '**~jäger** *m* still-hunter.

Pisse P ['pisə] *f* (15), '**ꝸn** (28) piss.

Pistazie ♀ [pi'stɑ:tsjə] *f* (15) pistachio(-nut).

Piste ['pistə] *f* (15) beaten track; *Rennsport*: course, *Sport*: *a.* ski-run; ✈ runway.

Pistole [pi'sto:lə] *f* (15) pistol; *mit vorgehaltener ~* at pistol-point; *fig. j-m die ~ auf die Brust setzen* hold a pistol to a p.'s head; *wie aus der ~ geschossen* like a shot; **~nschuß** *m*, **~nschütze** *m* pistol-shot; **~ntasche** *f* (pistol) holster.

Pizz|a ['pitsa] *f* (11[1] *u.* 16[2]) pizza; **~eria** [pitse'ri:a] *f* (16[2]) pizzeria.

placier|en [pla'(t)si:rən] place (*a. Sport*, ✝); *sich ~* be placed *second, etc.*; **~t** *Schuß*: well-placed.

plack|en ['plakən] (25) *s. plagen*; **ꝸerei** [~ə'raɪ] *f* (16) drudgery.

plä|dieren [plɛ'di:rən] plead (*auf acc.* et. a th.); *~ für* et. advocate a th.; **ꝸdoyer** [plɛdoa'je:] *n* (11) pleading.

Plage ['plɑ:gə] *f* (15) trouble, vexation, bother, nuisance; *stärker*: torment; *mst biblisch* (*Seuche*): plague; '**~geist** *m* tormentor; '**ꝸn** (25) trouble, bother, worry; torment, F plague; *mit Bitten od. Fragen*: pester; *sich ~* drudge, slave.

Plagiat [plag'jɑ:t] *n* (3) plagiarism; *ein ~ begehen* plagiarize; **~or** [~tɔr] *m* (8[1]) plagiarist.

Plaid [ple:t] *n* (11) plaid; (*Reisedecke*) travel(l)ing rug.

Plakat [pla'kɑ:t] *n* (3) poster, placard, bill; **~farbe** *f* poster colo(u)r; **ꝸieren** [~ka'ti:rən] placard; *v/i.* stick bills; **~maler** *m* poster artist; **~säule** *f* advertisement pillar; **~träger** *m* sandwich-man.

Plakette [~'kɛtə] *f* (15) plaque; (*Abzeichen*) badge.

Plan [plɑ:n] **1.** *m* (3[3]) plan; (*Vorhaben*) *a.* project, scheme; *konkret*: plan; (*Karte*) map; *graphisch*: diagram; (*Blaupause*) blueprint; (*Anlage*) layout; (*Zeitꝸ*) schedule; *s.* Lehrꝸ; *fig. auf den ~ rufen* call up; *auf den ~ treten* enter the lists, *weitS.* make an appearance; **2.** (*Ebene*) plain; **3.** ꝸ *adj.* plain, level; '**~e** *f* (15) awning; *geteerte*: tarpaulin; '**ꝸen** (25) plan, project; map out; *zeitlich*: time.

Pläne|macher *m*, **~schmied** ['plɛ:nə-] *m* schemer, projector.

Planet [pla'ne:t] *m* (12) planet; **ꝸarisch** [~ne'tɑ:riʃ] planetary; **~arium** [~ne'tɑ:rjum] *n* planetarium, orrery; **~en...** planetary.

planier|en ⊕ [pla'ni:rən] level, *Gelände*: *a.* grade; **ꝸmaschine** *f*, **ꝸraupe** *f* bulldozer, grader.

Planimetrie [planime'tri:] *f* (15) plane geometry, planimetry.

Planke ['plaŋkə] *f* (15) plank, board.

Plänk|elei [plɛŋkə'laɪ] *f* (16) skirmishing; '**ꝸeln** (29) skirmish (*a. fig.*).

'**plan|los** aimless, haphazard, unsystematic(ally *adv.*); *adv.* (*aufs Geratewohl*) at random; '**ꝸlosigkeit** *f* aimlessness; '**~mäßig** planned, systematic(ally *adv.*); *Beamtenstelle*: regular; *Verkehr*: scheduled; *adv.* according to plan *od.* (*zeitlich*) to schedule; '**ꝸquadrat** *n* grid square.

Plansch|becken ['planʃ-] *n* paddle-pond; '**ꝸen** (27) splash.

'**Planstelle** *f* permanent post (authorized in the budget).

Plantage [plan'tɑ:ʒə] *f* (15) plantation.

Planung ['plɑ:nuŋ] *f* planning; '**~samt** *n* planning board; '**~sstadium** *n*: *im ~* in the planning (*od.* blueprint) stage.

'**planvoll** methodical.

'**Plan|wagen** *m* covered wag(g)on; '**~wirtschaft** *f* planned economy; '**~ziel** *n* target.

'**Plapper|maul** *n* chatterbox; '**ꝸn** *v/t. u. v/i.* (29) babble, prattle.

plärren F ['plɛ:rən] *v/i. u. v/t.* (25) blare; *singend*: bawl; (*weinen*) blubber, cry.

Plasma *phys.* ['plasma] *n* (16[2]) plasma; '**~physik** *f* plasma physics *sg.*

Plasti|k ['plastik] **1.** *f* (16) plastic art; (*Bildwerk*) sculpture; ⚕ plastic surgery; **2.** *n* (11) plastic; '**~ktüte** *f* polythene bag; '**ꝸsch** plastic(ally *adv.*); *fig.* (*anschaulich*) graphic(ally *adv.*).

Platane [pla'tɑ:nə] *f* (15) plane-tree.

Plateau [pla'to:] *n* (11) plateau.

Platin ['plɑːtiːn] *n* (11, *o. pl.*) platinum.
platonisch [pla'toːniʃ] Platonic(ally *adv.*).
plätschern ['plɛtʃərn] (29) dabble, splash; *Bach usw.*: ripple, murmur.
platt [plat] flat; (*eben*) level; (*nichtssagend*) trite, trivial, commonplace; F *vor Staunen*: dum(b)founded; **ℒ** *n s. Plattdeutsch.*
Plättbrett ['plɛt-] *n* ironing-board.
'**plattdeutsch**, **ℒ(e)** *n* Low German.
Platte ['platə] *f* (15) plate (*a. phot., typ.*); (*Wandℒ usw.*) panel; *Metall, Glas*: sheet; (*Steinℒ*) flag, slab; (*Kachel*) tile; (*Tischℒ*) top, *zum Einlegen*: leaf; (*Präsentierteller*) tray, salver; (*Speise*) dish; *s. kalt*; (*Schallℒ*) disk, record; F *fig.* line; (*Glatze*) F bald pate, (*kahle Stelle*) bald patch; (*Gebißℒ*) dental plate.
Plätt|-eisen ['plɛt-] *n* flat-iron; '**ℒen** (26) iron, press.
'**Platten|sammlung** *f* record collection; '**~spieler** *m* record player; '**~teller** *m* turn-table; **~wechsler** ['~vɛkslər] *m* (7) (automatic) record changer.
platterdings ['platər'diŋs] absolutely, downright.
Plätterin ['plɛtərin] *f* (16¹) ironer.
'**Platt|form** *f* platform (*a. fig. pol.*); '**~fuß** *m* flatfoot; *mot.* F flat; '**~fußeinlage** *f* instep-raiser, arch-support; **ℒfüßig** ['~fyːsiç] flat-footed; '**~heit** *f* flatness; *fig.* triviality, banality, (*nichtssagende Bemerkung*) *a.* platitude; **ℒieren** [~'tiːrən] plate.
'**Plättwäsche** *f* linen to be ironed.
Platz [plats] *m* (3² *u.* ³) place; (*Raum*) space, room; *öffentlicher*: square, *runder*: circus; *zum Sitzen*: seat; *Sport*: field, pitch, *Tennis*: court; *~ machen* (*dat.*) make way *od.* room (for); *~ nehmen* take a seat; *fig.* (*nicht*) *am ~e sein* be in (out of) place; '**~angst** *f* agoraphobia; F claustrophobia; '**~anweiser(in** *f*) *m* usher(ette *f*).
Plätzchen ['plɛtscən] *n* (6) **1.** little place; spot, patch; **2.** (*Süßware*) pastille, drop; (*Gebäck*) biscuit, *Am.* cookie, *knusperig*: cracker.
Platzdeckchen ['~dɛkçən] *n* (6) place mat.
platzen ['platsən] (27, sn) burst; (*Risse bekommen*) crack; *Luftreifen*: blow out; *Granate usw.*: burst, explode; F *Wechsel*: bounce; *ins Zimmer*: burst *into*; *fig. vor Neugier usw. ~* burst with; F *Vorhaben*: not to come off; *fig. ~ lassen* explode; *s. Kragen.*
'**Platz|herren** *m/pl. Sport*: home team; '**~karte** *f* ticket for a reserved seat; '**~patrone** *f* blank cartridge; *mit ~n schießen* fire blank; '**ℒraubend** bulky; '**~regen** *m* cloudburst, downpour; **~wart** ['~vart] *m* (3) *Sport*: groundsman; '**~wechsel** *m* change of place (*Sport*: of ends); ⚕ local bill.
Plauder|ei [plaudə'raɪ] *f* (16) chat; (small-)talk; '**~er** *m* (7), '**~in** *f* (16¹) conversationalist, talker; '**ℒn** (29) (have a) chat; (*aus~*) blab; *s. Schule*; '**~tasche** F *f* chatterbox; '**~ton** *m* conversational tone.
plausibel [plau'ziːbəl] plausible.
pla'zieren [pla'tsiːrən] *s. placieren.*
Plebej|er [ple'beːjər] *m* (6), **~erin** *f* (16¹), **ℒisch** plebeian, vulgar.
Plebiszit [plebis'tsiːt] *n* (3) plebiscite.
Plebs [plɛps] *f* (16) *od. m* (4) mob.
Pleite *sl.* ['plaɪtə] *f* (15) bankruptcy, *sl.* smash; *fig.* flop, washout; *~ machen sl.* go smash (*Am.* bust); *ℒ sein* be broke; '**~geier** F *m the* wolves *pl.*
Plenarsitzung [ple'nɑːrzitsuŋ] *f* plenary meeting.
Plenum *parl.* ['pleːnum] *n* (9, *o.pl.*) plenum.
Pleuelstange ['plɔʏəl-] *f* connecting rod.
Plinse ['plinzə] *f* (15) pancake.
Pliss|ee [pli'seː] *n* (11, *o. pl.*) pleating; **~eerock** *m* pleated skirt; **ℒieren** [~'siːrən] pleat.
Plomb|e ['plɔmbə] *f* (15) (lead) seal; (*Zahnℒ*) stopping, filling, plug; **ℒieren** [~'biːrən] seal (with lead); *Zahn*: plug, stop, fill.
Plötze ['plœtsə] *f* (15) roach.
plötzlich ['plœtsliç] sudden(ly *adv.*), abrupt(ly); *adv. a.* all of a sudden.
plump [plump] plump; (*unbeholfen*) clumsy; (*schwerfällig*) heavy; (*unfein*) coarse; *Lüge usw.*: gross; '**ℒheit** *f* clumsiness; coarseness; **ℒs** *m* thud; *ℒ!* plop!; **~sen** ['~sən] (27, h. *u.* sn) flop, plop, thud.
Plunder ['plundər] *m* (7) lumber, rubbish, trash, *bsd. Am.* junk.
Plünder|er ['plyndərər] *m* (7)

looter; '2**n** *v/t. u. v/i.* (29) plunder (*a. weitS.*), pillage, loot, sack; '**~ung** *f* plundering, pillage, looting, sacking.

Plural ['plu:ra:l] *m* (3[1]) plural (number); **2istisch** [plura'listiʃ] pluralistic.

plus [plus] plus; 2 *n* (*~zeichen*) plus mark; (*Überschuß*) (sur)plus; *fig.* plus, asset.

Plüsch [ply:ʃ] *m* (3[1]) plush.

Plusquamperfekt(um) *gr.* ['~-kvampɛr'fɛkt(um)] *n* (3) pluperfect.

Pneumat|ik [pnɔY'ma:tik] *m* (11) pneumatic tire (*bsd. Brt.* tyre); **2isch** pneumatic(ally *adv.*).

Po [po:] F *m* (11) *s. Popo.*

Pöbel ['pø:bəl] *m* (7) mob, populace, rabble; '**2haft** low, vulgar; '**~haufen** *m* mob; '**~herrschaft** *f* mobrule.

pochen ['pɔxən] *v/i.* (25) knock, rap; *leise*: tap; *Herz*: beat, throb; *fig. auf* (*acc.*) boast of; *auf ein Recht* insist on.

Pocke ['pɔkə] *f* (15) pock; *~n pl.* smallpox; '**~n-impfung** *f* vaccination; '**~nnarbe** *f* pock-mark; '**2n-narbig** pock-marked.

Podagra ['po:dagra] *n* (11) gout.

Podest [po'dɛst] *n, m* (3[2]) pedestal (*a. fig.*); *s. Podium.*

Podium ['po:djum] *n* (9[2]) rostrum, platform; '**~sdiskussion** *f*, '**~sgespräch** *n* panel discussion.

Poesie [poe'zi:] *f* (15) poetry.

Poet [po'e:t] *m* (12) poet; **~ik** *f* (16) poetics *pl.*; **~in** *f* (16[1]) poetess; **2isch** poetic(al).

Point|e ['poɛ̃:tə] *f* (15) point; **2iert** [~ɛ̃'ti:rt] pointed.

Pokal [po'ka:l] *m* (3[1]) goblet; (*Sportpreis*) cup; **~-endspiel** *n Sport*: cup final; **~spiel** *n* cup-tie.

Pökel ['pø:kəl] *m* (7) pickle; '**~fleisch** *n* salt meat; '**~hering** *m* pickled (*od.* red) herring; '**2n** (29) pickle, salt.

Pol [po:l] *m* (3[1]) pole (*a.* ⚡); *fig. der ruhende ~* the one constant factor.

Polar... [po'la:r-] polar.

polari|sieren *phys.* [polari'zi:rən] polarize; **2tät** [~'tɛ:t] *f* (16) polarity.

Po'lar|kreis *m*: *nördlicher ~* Arctic Circle; *südlicher ~* Antarctic Circle; **~luft** *f* polar current; **~stern** *m* Pole star.

Pole ['po:lə] *m* (13), '**Polin** *f* Pole.

Polem|ik [po'le:mik] *f* (16) polemic(s *pl.*); **~iker** *m* polemicist; **2isch** polemic; **2i'sieren** polemize.

polen ⚡ ['po:lən] pole.

Police [po'li:sə] *f* (15) policy.

Polier [po'li:r] *m* (3[1]) foreman; **2en** polish, burnish.

Poliklinik ['po:li-] *f* outpatient clinic *od.* department.

Politbüro [po'li:t-] *n* Politburo.

Politesse [poli'tɛsə] *f* (15) traffic warden, F meter maid.

Polit|ik [poli'ti:k] *f* (16) (*Staats-, Weltklugheit*; *Taktik*; *politische Linie*) policy; (*Wissenschaft, Staatsangelegenheiten*) politics *pl.*; **~iker** [~'li:tikər] *m* (7) politician; *führender*: statesman; **~ikum** [~'li:tikum] *n* (9[2]) political issue; **2isch** [~'li:-tiʃ] political; **2isieren** [~liti'zi:rən] talk politics; *v/t.* politicise; **~ologe** [~to'lo:gə] *m* (13) political scientist; **~ologie** [~tolo'gi:] *f* political science.

Politur [poli'tu:r] *f* (16) polish.

Polizei [~'tsaɪ] *f* (16) police; **~-aktion** *f* police operation; **~-aufsicht** *f*: *unter ~* under police supervision; **~beamte** *m* police officer; **~dienststelle** *f* police station; **~-eskorte** *f* police escort; **~gewalt** *f* police power; **~knüppel** *m* truncheon, *Am.* club; **~kommissar** *m* police inspector; **2lich** (*... der Polizei*) (of the) police; (*von der Polizei*) by the police; **~präsident** *m* Chief Constable, *Am.* Chief of the Police, Police Chief; **~präsidium** *n* police headquarters; **~revier** *n* police station, *Am.* station house; **~schüler** *m* police cadet; **~spion** *m*, **~spitzel** *m* police spy; **~staat** *m* police state; **~streife** *f* police patrol; (*Polizeitrupp*) police squad; (*Razzia*) (police) raid; **~streifenwagen** *m s. Streifenwagen*; **~streitkräfte** *f/pl.* police force *sg.*; **~stunde** *f* closing time (for public houses); **~ver-ordnung** *f* police regulation(s *pl.*); **~wache** *f s. Polizeirevier*; **2widrig** contrary to police regulations; F *fig.* infernally *stupid.*

Polizist [poli'tsist] *m* (12) policeman, constable; **~in** *f* (16[1]) policewoman.

Pollen ⚘ ['pɔlən] *m* (6) pollen.

polnisch ['pɔlniʃ] Polish.

Polo ['po:lo] *n* (11) *Sport*: polo; '**~hemd** *n Mode*: polo shirt.

Polster ['pɔlstər] *n* (7) cushion; *bsd.* ⊕

bolster; (*Füllhaar*) stuffing; (*Wattierung*) pad(ding); '**~gruppe** *f* three-piece suite; '**~möbel** *n/pl.* upholstery *sg.*; '**2n** (29) stuff, upholster; pad; wad; '**~sitz** *m* cushioned seat; '**~stuhl** *m* easy chair; '**~ung** *f* padding, stuffing.

Polter|-abend ['pɔltər-] *m* wedding-eve (party); '**~er** *m* (7) blustering (*od.* noisy) fellow; '**~geist** *m* poltergeist; '**2n** (29) make a row; (*rumpeln*) rumble, lumber; (*schimpfen*) bluster.

Poly|äthylen ⚗ [polyɛty'le:n] *n* (3[1]) polythene; **~gamie** [~ga'mi:] *f* (15, *o. pl.*) polygamy; **2mer** [~'me:r] polymeric.

Polyp [po'ly:p] *m* (12) *zo.* polyp; ⚕ polypus; *~en pl.* (*in der Nase*) adenoids *pl.*; F (*Polizist*) *sl.* bull, cop.

Polytechnikum [poly'tɛçnikum] *n* (9[2]) polytechnic (school).

Pomade [po'ma:də] *f* (15) pomade.

Pomeranze [pomə'rantsə] *f* (15) bitter orange.

Pommes frites (*fr.*) [pɔm'frit] *pl.* (potato) chips, *Am.* French-fried potatoes, French fries.

Pomp [pɔmp] *m* (3) pomp; '**2haft, 2ös** [~'pø:s] pompous.

Ponti|fikat [pɔntifi'ka:t] *n* (3) pontificate; **~us** ['pɔntsjus]: *von ~ zu Pi'latus geschickt werden* F be driven from pillar to post, get the grand run-around.

Ponton [pɔ̃'tɔ̃, pɔn'tɔŋ] *m* (11) pontoon.

Pony ['pɔni] **1.** *n* (11) pony; **2.** *m* (*Frisur*) fringe, *Am.* bangs *pl.*

Popanz ['po:pants] *m* (3[2]) bugbear, *bsd. Am.* bugaboo.

Popelin(e *f*) [popə'li:n] *m* (3) poplin.

Pop|gruppe ['pɔp-] *f* pop group; '**~musik** *f* pop music.

Popo F [po'po:] *m* (11) bottom.

populär [popu'lɛ:r] popular.

populari|sieren [~lari'zi:rən] popularize; **2tät** [~'tɛ:t] *f* (16, *o. pl.*) popularity.

Por|e ['po:rə] *f* (15) pore; **2ös** [po-'rø:s] porous; **~osität** [porozi'tɛ:t] *f* (16) porosity.

Porno F ['pɔrno] *m* (11) (*Pornographie*) porn(o); *s. Pornofilm*; '**~film** *m* porno (film); **~graphie** [~gra'fi:] *f* (15) pornography.

Portal [pɔr'ta:l] *n* (3[1]) portal.

Porte|feuille [pɔrt(ə)'fœj] *n* (11) portfolio (*a. parl.*); **~monnaie** [pɔrtmɔ'nɛ:, ~'ne:] *n* (11) purse.

Portepee [~e'pe:] *n* (11) sword-knot.

Portier [pɔr'tje:] *m* (11) porter, door-keeper, *Am.* doorman, janitor.

Portion [~'tsjo:n] *f* portion; ⚔, ⚓ ration; (*servierte ~*) helping, serving; *zwei ~en Kaffee* coffee for two; F *fig. halbe ~* shrimp, *Am. sl.* punk; *e-e gehörige ~ Frechheit* a good dose of impudence.

Porto ['pɔrto] *n* (11, *pl. a. -ti*) postage; '**2frei** post-free, prepaid, *bsd. Am.* postpaid; '**~gebühren** *f/pl.* postage *sg.*; postal rates; '**~kasse** ☤ *f* petty cash; '**2pflichtig** liable to postage.

Porträt [pɔr'trɛ:] *n* (11) portrait; **2ieren** [~trɛ'ti:rən] portray; **~maler** [~'trɛ:-] *m* portrait-painter, portraitist.

Portugies|e [pɔrtu'gi:zə] *m* (13), **~in** *f* (16[1]), **2isch** Portuguese.

'**Portwein** *m* port(-wine).

Porzellan [pɔrtsə'la:n] *n* (3[1]) china; *fig. unnötig ~ zerschlagen* do a lot of unnecessary damage; *s. Elefant.*

Posaune [po'zaunə] *f* (15) trombone; *fig.* trumpet; **2n** (25) *v/i.* play (on) the trombone; *v/t. fig.* trumpet (forth); **~nbläser** *m*, **Posau'nist** *m* (12) trombonist.

Pose ['po:zə] *f* (15) (*Stellung*) pose, attitude; *fig. a.* air, act.

posieren [po'zi:rən] pose (*als* as).

Position [pozi'tsjo:n] position; *Buchhaltung usw.*: item; *fig. ~ beziehen* take one's stand; **~slicht** *n* position light.

positiv ['po:ziti:f, *a.* pozi'ti:f] positive (*a. phys., phot.,* ⚡); (*bejahend*) affirmative; (*günstig*) favo(u)rable.

Positur [pozi'tu:r] *f* (16) posture; *sich in ~ setzen* strike an attitude.

Posse ['pɔsə] *f* (15) drollery, antic(s *pl.*); *thea. u. fig.* farce; *~n reißen* play the buffoon; *~n treiben* play tricks (*mit* on).

'**Possen** *m* (6) trick, prank; *j-m e-n ~ spielen* play a trick on a p.; '**2haft** droll, farcial; '**~reißer** *m* buffoon, clown; '**~spiel** *thea. n* farce.

pos'sierlich droll, funny.

Post [pɔst] *f* (16) post, *Am.* mail; (*~sachen*) letters *pl.*, mail; *s. ~amt*; *mit der ersten ~* by the first delivery; *mit gewöhnlicher ~* by surface mail; *mit umgehender ~* by return of post; *zur ~ bringen od.*

geben, mit der ~ schicken post, *Am.* mail; **2alisch** [~'tɑ:liʃ] postal.

Postament [pɔsta'mɛnt] *n* (3) pedestal, base.

'**Post|-amt** *n* post office; '**~-anweisung** *f* postal (*od.* money-)order; '**~-auftrag** *m* postal collection order; '**~be-amte** *m* post-office clerk; '**~bote** *m* postman, *Am.* mailman.

Posten ['pɔstən] *m* (6) post, place; (*Anstellung*) post, situation, job; ⚔ sentry, sentinel; *mst* ✝ *in e-r Aufstellung*: item, entry, sum; *Waren*: lot, parcel; *auf dem ~ sein* be on one's toes, *gesundheitlich*: be in good form; *s. verloren*; '**~jäger** *m* place hunter.

'**Post|fach** *n* post-office box (*abbr.* P.O.B.); '**~fachnummer** *f* box-number; '**~gebühr** *f* postage; '**~geheimnis** *n* sanctity of the mails.

posthum [pɔst'hu:m] posthumous.

po'stieren post, place (*sich* o.s.).

Postillion ['pɔstiljo:n] *m* (3[1]) postilion.

'**Post|karte** *f* post (*Am. a.* postal) card; '**~kutsche** *f* stage-coach; '**2lagernd** to be (left till) called for, poste restante (*fr.*), *Am.* (in care of) general delivery; '**~leitzahl** *f Brt.* postcode, *Am.* zip code; '**~meister** *m* postmaster; '**~nachnahme** *f s. Nachnahme*; '**~paket** *n* postal parcel (*Am.* package); '**~sack** *m* mail-bag; '**~scheck** *m* postal cheque (*Am.* check); '**~scheck-amt** *n* postal cheque office; '**~scheckdienst** *m Brt. the* Giro; '**~scheckkonto** *n etwa*: postal cheque account; '**~schiff** *n* mail-boat; '**~schließfach** *n* post-office box; '**~sparbuch** *n* post-office savings book; '**~sparkasse** *f* postal savings bank; '**~station** *f* post station; '**~stempel** *m* postmark; „*Datum des ~s*" date as per postmark.

Postul|at [pɔstu'lɑ:t] *n* (3), **2ieren** [~'li:rən] postulate.

'**Post|versandhaus** *n* mail-order house; '**2wendend** by return (of post); *fig.* directly; '**~wertzeichen** *n* (postage) stamp; '**~wesen** *n* postal system; '**~wurfsendung** *f* mail circular.

Potentat [potɛn'tɑ:t] *m* (12) potentate.

Potenti|al [potɛn'tsjɑ:l] *n* (3[2]), **2ell** [~'tsjɛl] potential.

Potenz [po'tɛnts] *f* (16) (*a. sexual*) potency; ⅍ power; *zweite ~ a.* square; *dritte ~ a.* cube; **2ieren** [~'tsi:rən] raise to a higher power; *fig.* magnify; **~störung** *f* impaired potency.

Potpourri ♪ ['pɔtpuri] *n* (11) potpourri, (musical) selection, medley.

Pott-asche ['pɔt-] *f* potash.

poussieren F [pu'si:rən] flirt.

Präambel [prɛ'ˀambəl] *f* (15) preamble.

Pracht [praxt] *f* (16) splendo(u)r, magnificence; *verschwenderische*: luxury; *feierliche*: pomp; F *e-e wahre ~* just great; '**~-ausgabe** *f* édition de luxe (*fr.*); '**~-exemplar** *n* splendid specimen, beauty.

prächtig ['prɛçtiç] *s. prachtvoll.*

'**Pracht|kerl** F *m* splendid fellow, F brick, *Am. sl.* great guy; '**~straße** *f* boulevard; '**~stück** *n s. Prachtexemplar*; '**2voll** magnificent, splendid (*a. fig.*); gorgeous; (*großartig*) grand, great.

Prädikat [prɛdi'kɑ:t] *n* (3) predicate; *beim Namen*: title; (*Wertung*) attribute; *Schule*: mark; **~snomen** *gr. n* [~'kɑ:tsno:mən] complement.

präge|n ['prɛ:gən] (25) stamp; *Münze, Wort*: coin; *fig. in das Gedächtnis*: engrave on; '**2stanze** *f*, '**2stempel** *m* (stamping) die; *auf Urkunden*: raised seal.

pragmatisch [pra'gmɑ:tiʃ] pragmatic(al).

prägnant [prɛ'gnant] pregnant; (*bündig*) terse, pithy.

'**Prägung** *f* stamping; coining, coinage; *fig.* stamp.

prähistorisch ['prɛ:his'to:riʃ] prehistoric.

prahlen ['prɑ:lən] (25) brag, boast (*mit* of), talk big, bluster; (*angeben*) show off, parade (*mit et.* a th.).

'**Prahler** (*a.* **Prahlhans** ['~hans]) *m* (7), '**~in** *f* (16[1]) boaster, braggart; **~ei** [~'raɪ] *f* (16) boasting, big talk; (*Prunken*) ostentation; '**2isch** bragging, boastful; (*prunkend*) ostentatious.

Prahm ⚓ [prɑ:m] *m* (3) barge.

Prakt|ik ['praktik] *f* (16) practice; *b.s. ~en pl.* (sharp) practices; **~ikant** [~i'kant] *m* (12) probationer, pupil; **~iker** ['~ikər] *m* (7) practical man; expert; **~ikum** ['~ikum] *n* (9[2]) practical course; **~ikus** ['~ikus] *m* (14[2]): *alter ~* old stager *od.* hand;

'2**isch** practical; (*geschickt*) handy (*a. Gerät usw.*); (*tatsächlich*) virtual; *~er Arzt* general practitioner; 2**i-zieren** [~i'tsi:rən] practise.
Prälat [prɛ'lɑ:t] *m* (12) prelate.
Praline [pra'li:nə] *f* (15), **Praliné** ['~line:] *n* (11) chocolate (cream).
prall [pral] **1.** (*straff*) tight, taut; (*feist*) plump (*a. Kissen*); *Backen*: chubby; *Sonne*: blazing; **2.** 2 *m* (3) bound, shock, impact; '**~en** (25, sn) bounce (*auf acc.* against).
Präludium [prɛ'lu:djum] *n* (9) prelude.
Prämie ['prɛ:mjə] *f* (15) *bsd.* ✝ premium; (*Dividende, Leistungs*2) bonus; *zur Förderung der Wirtschaft u.* ⚔ bounty; (*Preis*) award, *bsd. Schule*: prize; (*Belohnung*) reward; '**~nschein** *m* premium-bond.
prämi'ieren award a prize to.
Prämisse [prɛ'misə] *f* (15) premise.
prang|en ['praŋən] (25) be resplendent, shine; '2**er** *m* (7) pillory; *an den ~ stellen* (put in the) pillory.
Pranke ['praŋkə] *f* (15) claw, clutch.
Präpa|rat [prɛpa'rɑ:t] *n* (3) preparation; *Mikroskop*: slide preparation; *anat.* specimen; 2'**rieren** prepare.
Präposition [~pozi'tsjo:n] *f* preposition; 2**al** [~jo'nɑ:l] prepositional.
Prärie [prɛ:'ri:] *f* (15) prairie.
Präsens *gr.* ['prɛ:zɛns] *n inv.* present (tense).
Präsent [prɛ'zɛnt] *n* (3) present; 2**ieren** [~'ti:rən] *v/t.* present; *v/i.* ⚔ present arms; **~ierteller** [~'ti:r-] *m* tray, salver.
Präsenz [prɛ'zɛnts] *f* presence.
Präs|ident [prɛzi'dɛnt] *m* (12) president, chairman; *s. Polizei*2 *usw.*; **~i'dentenwahl** *f* presidential election; 2**i'dieren** preside (*dat. od. bei* over); **~idium** [~'zi:djum] *n* (9), **~i'dentschaft** *f* presidency, chair.
prasseln ['prasəln] (29) *Feuer*: crackle; *Regen*: patter; *Geschosse*: hail; *~der Beifall* thunderous applause.
prass|en ['prasən] (28) feast; *weitS.* live in luxury; '2**er** *m* (7) reveller, spendthrift; 2**erei** [~ə'raɪ] *f* (16) debauchery, luxury, dissipation.
Prätendent [prɛtɛn'dɛnt] *m* (12) pretender (*auf acc.* to).
Präteritum *gr.* [prɛ'te:ritum] *n* (9²) preterite, past tense.
Pratze ['pratsə] *f* (15) paw.
Präventiv|... [prɛvɛn'tif...] preventive, ⚕ *mst* prophylactic; **~-angriff** ⚔ *m*, **~schlag** ⚔ *m* pre-emptive (first) strike; **~krieg** *m* preventive (*od.* pre-emptive) war; **~maßnahme** *f* preventive measure.
Praxis ['praksis] *f* (*sg. inv., pl. Praxen*) practice (*a.* ⚕, ⚖); (*Raum*) consulting room; (*Erfahrung*) experience; *in der ~* in practice; *in die ~ umsetzen* put into practice.
Präzedenzfall [prɛtse'dɛntsfal] *m* precedent, ⚖ *a.* leading case.
präzis [prɛ'tsi:s] precise, exact; **~ieren** [~tsi'zi:rən] define, specify; 2**ion** [~tsi'zjo:n] *f* precision; 2**ions...** *in Zssgn* precision ...
predig|en ['pre:digən] *v/i. u. v/t.* (25) preach; '2**er** *m* preacher; 2**t** ['~diçt] *f* sermon (*a. fig.*).
Preis [praɪs] *m* (4) price; (*Kosten*) cost; (*Kurs; Satz*) rate; (*Fahr*2) fare; *im Wettbewerb*: prize, award; (*Belohnung*) reward; (*Lob*) praise; *um jeden ~* at any price; *um keinen ~* not at any price; *der äußerste ~* the lowest (*od.* keenest) price; *den ~ davontragen* carry off the prize; *im ~ steigen* rise in price, go up; '**~-abbau** *m* reduction of prices; '**~-absprache** *f* prize agreement; '**~-änderung** *f* change in price(s *pl.*); *~en pl. vorbehalten* subject to change; '**~-angabe** *f* quotation (of prices); *ohne ~* not priced, not marked; '**~-anstieg** *m* rise in prices; '**~-aufgabe** *f* (subject for a) prize essay, competition; '**~-aufschlag** *m* extra charge; '**~-ausschreiben** *n* (prize) competition; '**~bildung** *f* price fixing; '**~-boxer** *m* prize-fighter; '**~drücke'rei** *f* price-cutting.
Preiselbeere ['praɪzəlbe:rə] *f* red whortleberry, cranberry.
'**Preis-empfehlung** *f* recommended price.
preisen ['praɪzən] (30) praise; *sich glücklich ~* call o.s. happy.
'**Preis|-entwicklung** *f* trend of prices; '**~-erhöhung** *f* price increase; '**~-ermäßigung** *f* reduction in price(s); '**~festsetzung** *f* price fixing, pricing; '**~frage** *f s. Preisaufgabe*; '**~gabe** *f*, '**~gebung** *f* abandonment; (*Herausgabe*) surrender; *e-s Geheimnisses*: revelation; '2**ge-**

ben abandon; (*herausgeben*) surrender; (*opfern*) sacrifice; *Geheimnis*: reveal; (*sich*) ~ (*dat.*) expose (o.s.) to; '♀**gekrönt** prize-winning; '~**gericht** *n* jury; '~**gestaltung** *f* *s. Preisbildung*; '~**grenze** *f* price limit; '♀**günstig** *s. preiswert*; '~**klasse** *f* price range; '~**lage** *f* price level; *in jeder* ~ in all prices; '~**liste** *f* price-list, list of prices; '~**nachlaß** *m* discount; '~**politik** *f* price policy; '~**rätsel** *n* competition; '~**richter** *m* judge; '~**schießen** *n* rifle competition; '~**schild** *n* price tag (*od.* ticket); '~**schwankung** *f* price fluctuation; '~**senkung** *f* price reduction *od.* cut; '~**spanne** *f* price margin; '~**steigerung** *f* rise in prices; ~**stopp** ['~ʃtɔp] *m* (11) price freeze; '~**sturz** *m* sudden fall of price(s), slump; '~**träger** (-**in** *f*) *m* prize-winner *od.* -holder; ~**treiberei** ['~'raɪ] *f* forcing up of prices; '♀**wert**, '♀**würdig** worth the money; (*billig*) low-priced; ~*es Angebot* bargain; ~ *sein* be good value.

prekär [pre'kɛ:r] precarious.

Prell|bock ['prɛlbɔk] *m* (3[3]) buffer-stop; '♀**en** (25) toss; ⚕ contuse; *fig.* cheat (*um* of); ~**erei** [~ə'raɪ] *f* cheating; '~**stein** *m* kerb-stone, *Am.* curbstone; '~**ung** *f* contusion, bruise.

Premier|e *thea.* [prəm'jɛ:rə] *f* (15) first night; ~**minister** [prəm'je:-ministər] *m* prime minister.

Presse ['prɛsə] *f* (15) ⊕, *typ.* press; *fig. the* Press; *Schule*: cramming-classes *pl.*; *e-e gute* ~ *haben* have a good press; '~-**amt** *n* public relations office; '~**bericht** *m* press report, news item; '~**chef** *m* chief press officer; '~**dienst** *m* news service; '~-**erklärung** *f* press release; '~**feldzug** *m* press campaign; '~**freiheit** *f* freedom of the press; '~**konferenz** *f* press conference; '~**meldung** *f* news item; '~**mitteilung** *f* press release; '♀**n** (28) press; (*formen*) mo(u)ld; '~**photograph** *m* press-photographer; '~**spiegel** *m* press review; '~**sprecher** *m* press spokesman; '~**stimmen** *f/pl.* commentaries of the press; '~**tribüne** *f* press gallery; '~**verlautbarung** *f* press release; '~**vertreter** *m* reporter; '~**zar** *m* press baron (*od.* lord).

'**Preß|glas** *n* mo(u)lded glass; '~**holz** *n* laminar wood.

pressieren [prɛ'si:rən] be urgent; *es pressiert mir* I am in a hurry.

'**Preß|kohle** *f* briquette, compressed fuel; '~**luft** *f* compressed air; '~**luftbohrer** *m* pneumatic (*od.* air) drill; '~**lufthammer** *m* pneumatic hammer; '~**stoff** *m* plastic.

Prestige [prɛs'ti:ʒ(ə)] *n* (11, *o. pl.*) prestige; ~**verlust** *m* loss of prestige.

Preuß|e ['prɔʏsə] *m* (13), '~**in** *f* (16[1]) Prussian; '♀**isch** Prussian.

prickeln ['prikəln] (29) *v/i. u. v/t.* prick(le); *Glieder*: tingle; (*jucken*) itch.

Priem [pri:m] *m* (3) quid, plug.

pries [pri:s] *pret. v. preisen.*

Priester ['pri:stər] *m* (7) priest; '~**amt** *n* priesthood; '~**in** *f* (16[1]) priestess; '♀**lich** priestly; clerical; '~**rock** *m* cassock; '~**schaft** *f*, '~**tum** *n* priesthood; '~**weihe** *f* ordination (of a priest).

prim|a ['pri:ma] **1.** first-class, first-rate, F A 1, A one; ✝ *a.* prime; F swell, super; **2.** ♀ *f* (16) top form; ♀**aner** [pri'mɑ:nər] *m* (7), ♀**anerin** *f* (16[1]) top-form boy (*f* girl); ~**är** [~'mɛ:r] primary; ♀**at** [~'mɑ:t] *m*, *n* (3) primateship; ♀**aten** *biol. m/pl.* (12, *pl.*) primates.

Primel ['pri:məl] *f* (15) primrose.

primitiv [primi'ti:f] primitive.

Primus ['pri:mus] *m* (14[2]) head (*od.* top) boy.

Primzahl ['pri:m-] *f* prime number.

Prinz [prints] *m* (12) prince; ~**essin** [~'tsɛsin] *f* (16[1]) princess; '~**gemahl** *m* Prince Consort.

Prinzip [prin'tsi:p] *n* (3[1] *u.* 8[2]) principle; *im* ~ in principle; *aus* ~ on principle; ~**al** [~tsi'pɑ:l] *m* (3[1]) principal, chief; (*Brotherr*) employer, F boss; ♀**iell** [~tsi'pjɛl] *adv.* on principle; ~**ienreiter** [~'tsi:-pjən-] *m* stickler (for principles).

'**prinzlich** princely.

Prior ['pri:ɔr] *m* (8[1]) prior; ~**in** [pri'o:rin] *f* (16[1]) prioress.

Priorität [~ori'tɛ:t] *f* (16) priority; ~*en setzen* establish priorities; ~**s-aktie** ✝ *f* preference share.

Prise ['pri:zə] *f* (15) **1.** pinch *of salt etc.*; **2.** ⚓ prize.

Prism|a ['prisma] *n* (9[1]) prism; ♀**atisch** [~'mɑ:tiʃ] prismatic(ally *adv.*).

Pritsche ['pritʃə] *f* (15) *des Harle-*

kins: slapstick; *allg.* bat; (*Lagerstatt*) plank-bed.
privat [pri'vaːt] private; personal.
Pri'vat|-adresse *f* home address; **~besitz** *m*, **~-eigentum** *n* private (*od.* personal) property; **~dozent** *m* unsalaried lecturer, *Am.* instructor; **~gespräch** *n* private conversation; *teleph.* private call; **~-initiative** *f* private venture; **~-interesse** *n* private interest; *~n verfolgen bsd. Am.* have an ax(e) to grind; **~leben** *n* private life; **~lehrer** *m* private tutor; **~mann** *m* private gentleman; **~recht** *n* private law; **~schule** *f* private school; **~sphäre** *f* privacy; **~stunde** *f* private lesson; **~-unterricht** *m* private tuition; **~wirtschaft** *f* private enterprise.
privi|legieren [privile'giːrən] privilege; **2leg(ium)** [~'leːk, ~'leːgjum] *n* (8² [9]) privilege.
pro [proː] *prp.* per; **2** *n* (11): *~ und Kontra* pro and con.
probat [pro'baːt] (ap)proved, tested, tried.
Probe ['proːbə] *f* (15) (*Versuch*) experiment; (*Erprobung*) trial, test, *Am.* F tryout; (*Bewährungs2*) probation; (*Beweis*) proof; *iro.* (*Kost2*) taste; *thea.* rehearsal; (*Erprobung e-r P.*) probation; (*Sprech- od. Gesangs2*) audition; (*Prüfstück*) specimen; (*Waren2*) sample; *metall.* assay; *auf ~* on probation, on trial; *Ehe auf ~* trial marriage; *auf die ~ stellen* put to the test; *auf e-e harte ~ stellen* tax, put to a severe test; *e-e ~ seines Mutes ablegen* give proof of one's courage; **'~-abzug** *typ. m* proof-sheet; *phot.* test print; **'~-anwärter(in** *f*) *m* probationer; **'~-aufnahmen** *f/pl. Film*: screen test *sg.*; **'~-auftrag** *m*, **'~bestellung** *f* trial order; **'~bogen** *m s. Probeabzug*; **'~-exemplar** *n* sample copy; **'~fahrt** *f mot.* test drive; ⚓ trial run (*od.* trip); **'2haltig** proof; **'~jahr** *n* trial year; **'~lauf** *m e-r Maschine etc.*: test run; **'2n** (25) *thea. u. weitS.* rehearse; **'~nummer** *f* specimen copy; **'~schuß** *m* trial shot; **'~sendung** *f* sample sent on approval; **'~start** ✈ *m* trial take-off; **'~stück** *n* sample, specimen, test piece; **'2weise** on a trial basis; **'~zeit** *f* trial (*od.* probationary) period.
probier|en [pro'biːrən] try (*a.* = es ~ *mit*), test; *metall.* assay; *Speise usw.*: taste; (*aus~*) sample; **2nadel** *f* touchneedle; **2stein** *m* touchstone.
Problem [pro'bleːm] *n* (3¹) problem; **~atik** [~ble'maːtik] *f* (16, *o. pl.*) problematic nature; problems *pl.*; **2atisch** problematic(al); **~stück** *thea. n* thesis play.
Produkt [~'dukt] *n* (3) product (*a.* ⚗); *des Bodens usw.*: produce; **~enhandel** *m* produce trade; **~enmarkt** *m* produce market.
Produktion [~'tsjoːn] *f* (16) production; (*Fabrikationsmenge*) output; **~s-anlage** *f* production plant(s *pl.*); **~sgüter** *n/pl.* producer goods; **~skosten** *pl.* production cost; **~sleiter** *m* production manager; *Film*: executive producer; **~s-planung** *f* production planning; **~sziel** *n* production target; **~szweig** *m* line of production.
produktiv [~'tiːf] productive; **2ität** [~tivi'tɛːt] *f* (16) productivity.
Produz|ent [produ'tsɛnt] *m* (12) producer; **2ieren** [~'tsiːrən] produce; *contp. sich ~* show off.
profan [pro'faːn], **~ieren** [~fa'niːrən] profane.
Profession [~fɛ'sjoːn] *f* (16) profession; (*Handwerk*) trade; **2ell** [~sjo'nɛl] professional.
Profess|or [~'fɛsɔr] *m* (8¹) professor; *s. ordentlich*; **~ur** [~'suːr] *f* (16) professorship.
Profi F ['proːfi] *m* (11) pro(fessional).
Profil [~'fiːl] *n* (3¹) profile; *mot. Reifen*: tread; *im ~* in profile; **2ieren** [~fi'liːrən] profile; **2iert** [~'liːrt] *fig. P.*: outstanding; **~neurose** *f* image neurosis.
Profit [~'fiːt] *m* (3) profit; **2ieren** [~fi'tiːrən] *v/i. u. v/t.* profit (*von* by).
Proforma|rechnung [proː'fɔrma-] ⚕ *f* pro forma invoice; **~zahlung** *f* token payment.
profund [pro'funt] profound.
Prognose [pro'gnoːzə] *f* (15) forecast, *bsd.* ⚕ prognosis.
Programm [~'gram] *n* (3¹) program(me) (*a. Computer2*); *Rennsport usw.*: card; *Schule*: prospectus; *politisches ~* political programme, *Am.* platform; **~-ausstattung** *f Computer*: software; **2gemäß** according to program(me) (*fig.* to plan); **2ierbar** [~gra'miːr-] programmable; **2ieren**

program(me); **~ierer** *m* programmer; **~musik** [~'gram-] *f* program(me) music; **~punkt** *m* item, *Am. pol.* plank; **~speicher** *m Computer*: program(me) memory; **~speicherplatz** *m Computer*: program(me) storage space; **~vorschau** *f* program(me) preview; *Film*: trailers *pl.*

progressiv [progrɛ'si:f] progressive.

Projekt [~'jɛkt] *n* (3) project; **2ieren** [~'ti:rən] project.

Projektion [~'tsjo:n] *f* (16) projection; **~s-apparat** *m* projector; **~s-schirm** *m* screen.

projizieren [~ji'tsi:rən] project.

Proklam|ation [~klama'tsjo:n] *f* (16) proclamation; **2ieren** [~'mi:rən] proclaim.

Pro-'Kopf-Einkommen *n* per capita income.

Prokur|a [pro'ku:ra] *f inv.* procuration; *per ~* by proxy (*abbr.* per pro., p. p.); **~ist** [~ku'rist] *m* (12) confidential (*od.* signing) clerk.

Prolet *contp.* [~'le:t] *m* cad; **~ariat** [~leta'rja:t] *n* (3) proletariat(e); **~arier** [~'ta:rjər] *m* (7) proletarian; **2arisch** [~'ta:riʃ] proletarian.

Prolog [pro'lo:k] *m* (3[1]) prolog(ue).

prolongier|en ✝ [~lɔŋ'gi:rən] renew, prolong; **2ung** *f* prolongation.

Promenade [~mə'na:də] *f* (15) (*Straße u. Spaziergang*) promenade; **~ndeck** ⚓ *n* promenade deck.

prome'nieren promenade, (take a) stroll.

Promille [pro'milə] *n* (*inv.*) pars pro mille; F *mot.* blood-alcohol concentration; **~grenze** F *mot. f* (blood) alcohol limit.

prominen|t [~mi'nɛnt] prominent; **2te** *m, f* (18) prominent person, celebrity; **2z** [~ts] *f* (16, *o. pl.*) prominence; celebrities *pl.*

Promo|tion *univ.* [promo'tsjo:n] *f* (16) graduation; **2vieren** [~'vi:rən] *v/t.* confer a degree on; *v/i.* graduate, take one's degree.

prompt [prɔmpt] prompt, quick.

Pronom|en [pro'no:mɛn] *n* (6, *pl.* *-mina*) pronoun; **2inal** [~nomi'na:l] pronominal.

Propa|ganda [propa'ganda] *f inv.* propaganda, publicity; **~gan'dist** *m*, **2gan'distisch** propagandist; **2'gieren** propagate.

Propeller [~'pɛlər] *m* (7) propeller.

Prophet [~'fe:t] *m* (12) prophet; **~in** *f* (16[1]) prophetess; **2isch** prophetic(ally *adv.*).

prophezei|en [~fe'tsaɪən] prophesy; **2ung** *f* prophecy.

prophylaktisch [profy'laktiʃ] ⚕ prophylactic(ally *adv.*).

Proportion [~pɔr'tsjo:n] *f* (16) proportion; **2al** [~tsjo'na:l] proportional; **2iert** [~'ni:rt] proportionate.

Propst [pro:pst] *m* (3[2] *u.* [3]) provost.

Prosa ['pro:za] *f inv.* prose.

Prosa|iker [pro'za:ikər] *m* (7) prose writer; **2isch** prosaic(ally *adv.*).

pros(i)t! ['pro:zit, pro:st] your health!, cheers!; *beim Niesen*: bless you!; *~ Neujahr!* a happy New Year to you!

Prospekt [pro'spɛkt] *m* (3) (*Aussicht*) prospect; (*Preisliste*; *Werbeschrift*) prospectus; (*Handels2*) leaflet, brochure, *bsd. Am.* folder.

Prostata *anat.* ['prɔstata] *f* (16, *o. pl.*) prostate (gland).

prostitu|ieren [prostitu'i:rən] prostitute; **2'ierte** *f* (15) prostitute; **2tion** [~'tsjo:n] *f* (16) prostitution.

protegieren [prote'ʒi:rən] patronize.

Protektion [protɛk'tsjo:n] *f* (16) protection, patronage.

Protest [~'tɛst] *m* (3[2]) protest; *als ~ gegen* in protest against; *~ einlegen* enter a protest.

Protestant [~tɛs'tant] *m* (12), **~in** *f* (16[1]), **2isch** Protestant; **~ismus** [~'tismus] *m* (16, *o.pl.*) Protestantism.

protest|ieren [~tɛs'ti:rən] protest (*gegen* against, *Am. a. th.*); **2marsch** [~'tɛst-] *m* protest march; **2versammlung** *f* protest meeting.

Prothese [pro'te:zə] *f* (15) prosthesis, artificial limb; (*Gebiß*) denture.

Protokoll [proto'kɔl] *n* (3[1]) record, minutes *pl.*; *diplomatisches*: protocol; *~ führen* keep the minutes; *zu ~ geben* depose, state (in evidence); *zu ~ nehmen* take down; **2arisch** [~'la:riʃ] recorded, entered in the minutes; *adv.* by the minutes; **~führer** *m* secretary; **2ieren** [~'li:rən] record.

Protz [prɔts] *m* (12) ostentatious person; show-off; **'2en** (27) show off (*mit* [with] *a th.*); **'2ig** ostentatious, showy.

Proviant [pro'vjant] *m* (3) supplies, provisions, victuals *pl.*

Provinz [~'vints] *f* (16) province; **~ial...** [~'tsjɑ:l], **⁲iell** [~'tsjɛl], **~ler** *m* (7), **~lerin** *f* provincial.

Provis|ion [~vi'zjo:n] *f* (16) commission, percentage; **~or** [~'vi:zɔr] *m* (8[1]) chemist's assistant, dispenser; **⁲orisch** [~vi'zo:riʃ] provisional, temporary.

Provo|kation [provoka'tsjo:n] *f* (16) provocation; **⁲'zieren** provoke; *~d* provocative.

Prozedur [protse'du:r] *f* (16) procedure; *iro.* ritual.

Prozent [~'tsɛnt] *n* (3) per cent; (*a.* **~satz** *m*) percentage; **⁲ual** [~u'ɑ:l] percentage, percental; proportional; *~er Anteil* percentage.

Prozeß [~'tsɛs] *m* (3) process; ⚖ lawsuit, action; (*Rechtsfall*) case; (*Rechtsgang*) (legal) proceedings *pl.*; *e-n ~ anstrengen gegen* institute (legal) proceedings against, bring an action against; *kurzen ~ machen mit* make short work of; **~-akten** *f/pl.* minutes *pl. od.* record (of a case); **~führer** *m* litigant; (*Anwalt*) plaintiff's counsel; **~führung** *f* conduct of a lawsuit; **~gegenstand** *m* matter in dispute.

prozes'sieren go to law (*mit* with); carry on a lawsuit (with); litigate.

Prozession [~'jo:n] *f* (16) procession.

Pro'zeß|kosten *pl.* (law) costs; **~ordnung** *f* rule(s *pl.*) of court; **~partei** *f* party to the action; **~recht** *n* adjective law; **~vollmacht** *f* power of attorney.

prüde ['pry:də] prudish; **⁲rie** [prydə'ri:] *f* (15) prudery.

prüf|en ['pry:fən] (25) (*erproben*) try, test; (*nach~*) check, verify; (*examinieren*; *untersuchen*) examine, *stärker*: scrutinize; *Sache*: *a.* investigate, look into; (*erwägen*) consider; ✝ *Bücher usw.*: audit; (*kosten*) taste; (*heimsuchen*) afflict, try; *ein ~der Blick* a searching look; *geprüfter Masseur usw.* licensed; **'⁲er** *m* (7) examiner; tester; checker; auditor; **'⁲feld** ⊕ *n* test bay; **'⁲ling** *m* (3) examinee; **'⁲stand** ⊕ *m* test stand (*od.* bed); **'⁲stein** *m* touchstone, test.

'Prüfung *f* (16) *vgl. prüfen*: trial, test; check, verification; (*mündliche* oral, *schriftliche* written) examination; scrutiny, investigation; ⚖ review; (*Über⁲*, ⊕) inspection; ✝ (*Buch⁲*) audit; *fig.* affliction; *e-e ~ machen* go in for an examination; **'~s-arbeit** *f* examination paper; **'~s-ausschuß** *m*, **'~skommission** *f* board of examiners.

Prügel ['pry:gəl] *m* (7) (*Stock*) cudgel, stick; *pl. fig.* (*a. Tracht ~*) beating, hiding; **~ei** [~'laɪ] *f* (16) fight, brawl; **'~knabe** *m* whipping-boy; (*Sündenbock*) scapegoat; **'⁲n** (29) beat (up), thrash; *sich ~* (have a) fight; **'~strafe** *f* corporal punishment, flogging.

Prunk [pruŋk] *m* (3) pomp, splendo(u)r; *b.s.* ostentation; **'⁲en** (25) make a show (*mit* of), show off (*mit et.* a th.); **'⁲end**, **'⁲haft** ostentatious, showy; **'⁲los** unostentatious, plain; **'~stück** F *n* show piece; **'~sucht** *f* love of display, ostentation; **⁲süchtig** ['~zyçtiç] ostentatious; **'⁲voll** splendid, gorgeous.

prusten ['pru:stən] (26) snort; burst out (*vor Lachen* laughing).

Psalm [psalm] *m* (5[2]) psalm; **~ist** [~'mist] *m* (12) psalmist.

Psalter ['psaltər] *m* (7) psalter.

Pseudo|... ['psɔʏdo-] *in Zssgn* pseudo...; **~nym** [~'ny:m] **1.** *n* (3[1]) assumed name, pseudonym; *e-s Schriftstellers*: pen-name; **2.** ⁲ *adj.* pseudonymous.

pst! [pst] hush!, stop!

Psyche ['psy:çe] *f* (15) psyche.

Psychiat|er [psyçi'ɑ:tər] *m* (7) psychiatrist, alienist; **~rie** [~a'tri:] *f* psychiatry; (*Krankenhausabteilung*) psychiatric ward.

psychisch ['psy:çiʃ] psychic(al).

Psycho-analy|se [psyço'ʔana'ly:zə] *f* psychoanalysis; **~tiker** [~'ly:tikər] *m* (7) psychoanalyst.

Psycholog|e [~o'lo:gə] *m* (13), **~in** *f* (16[1]) psychologist; **~ie** [~lo'gi:] *f* psychology; **⁲isch** [~'lo:giʃ] psychological.

Psychopath [~o'pɑ:t] *m* (12) psychopath; **⁲isch** psychopathic.

Psychopharmaka [~o'farmaka] *n/pl.* (9[2]) psychiatric drugs.

Psychose [psy'ço:zə] *f* (15) psychosis.

psychosomatisch [~oso'mɑ:tiʃ] psychosomatic.

Psychothera'pie *f* psychotherapy; (*Heilmethode*) psychotherapeutics.

Pubertät [pubɛr'tɛ:t] *f* (16) puberty.

publik [pu'bli:k]: *~ machen* make

public; **2ation** [~ka'tsjo:n] *f* publication.

Publikum ['pu:blikum] *n* (9, *o.pl.*) public; (*Zuhörerschaft*) audience; (*Zuschauer*) spectators *pl.*; (*Leser*2) readers *pl.*; (9²) *univ.* (*öffentliche Vorlesung*) open lecture.

publiz|ieren [publi'tsi:rən] publish; **2ist** [~'tsist] *m* (12) writer.

Pudding ['pudiŋ] *m* (3¹) pudding.

Pudel ['pu:dəl] *m* (7) poodle; '**~mütze** *f* fur-cap; '**2'naß** soaked, drenched, sopping (wet).

Puder ['pu:dər] *m* (7) powder; '**~dose** *f* powder-box; *für die Handtasche*: vanity-case, compact; '**2n** (29) powder; '**~quaste** *f* powder-puff; '**~zucker** *m* icing sugar.

Puff [puf] **1.** *m* (3[³]) (*Stoß*) cuff, thump, poke; *leichter*: F dig; (*Knall*) bang, pop; (*Bausch*) puff; P knocking-shop; **2.** *n* (*~spiel*) backgammon; **3.** 2 puff!, bang!; '**-ärmel** *m* puffed sleeve; '**2en** (25) *v/i.* puff; *v/t.* (*schlagen*) cuff, thump; *leicht*: nudge.

Puff|er ['~ər] *m* (7) 🚂 buffer; *s. Kartoffel*2; '**~erlösung** ⚗ *f* buffer solution; '**~erstaat** *m* buffer state; '**~mais** *m* popcorn.

Pulk [pulk] ⚔ *m* (11) group.

Pulle ['pulə] F *f* (15) bottle; '**2n** ⚓ (25) pull, row.

Pull|over [pu'lo:vər] *m* (7) sweater, pullover; **~under** [~'lundər] *m* (7) tank-top.

Puls [puls] *m* (4) pulse; *j-m den ~ fühlen* feel a p.'s pulse (*a. fig.*); '**~-ader** *f* artery; **2ieren** [~'zi:rən] pulsate; '**~schlag** *m* pulsation; '**~zahl** *f* pulse rate.

Pult [pult] *n* (3) desk (*a.* ⊕).

Pulver ['pulfər] *n* (7) powder; (*Schieß*2) gunpowder; F (*Geld*) *sl.* dough; *er hat das ~ nicht erfunden* he is no great light; *s. Schuß*; '**~faß** *n* powder-keg; *fig.* volcano; '**2ig** powdery; **2isieren** [~vəri'zi:rən] pulverize; '**~schnee** *m* powdery snow.

Pump F [pump] *m* (3): *auf ~* on tick; '**~e** *f* (15) pump; '**2en** *v/t. u. v/i.* (25) pump; F (*leihen*) lend, *bsd. Am.* loan; *sich et. ~* borrow; **~ernickel** ['~ərnikəl] *m* (7) pumpernickel; '**~hose** *f* (*eine ~* a pair of) knickerbockers *pl.*, plus-fours *pl.*; '**~werk** *n* pumping-work.

Punkt [puŋkt] *m* (3) point; (*Tüpfelchen*) dot; *typ.*, *gr.* full stop, period; (*Stelle*) spot; *fig.* (*Einzelheit*) point, head, item, detail; (*Gesprächsthema*) topic; *fig. in vielen ~en* on many points; *nach ~en siegen Boxen*: win on points; *~ 10 Uhr* on the stroke of ten, at 10 (o'clock) sharp; *s. tot, wund*; **2ieren** [~'ti:rən] point, dot; *gr.* punctuate; ⚕ puncture, tap; *Kunst*: stipple.

pünktlich ['pyŋktliç] punctual, F sharp; (*genau*) exact, accurate; *sei ~* be on time; *sehr ~* as punctual as clockwork; '**2keit** *f* punctuality; (*Sorgfalt*) diligence.

'**Punkt|richter** *m Sport*: judge; '**~sieg** *m Boxen*: win on points; points decision; '**2um:** (*damit*) *~!* that's flat!; '**~streik** *m* strike at selective sites; '**~zahl** *f Sport*: score.

Punsch [punʃ] *m* (3) punch.

punzen ['puntsən] (27) punch.

Pupille [pu'pilə] *f* (15) pupil.

Puppe ['pupə] *f* (15) doll (*a.* F *Mädchen*); (*Draht*2, *a. fig.*) puppet; *Schneiderei*: dummy; *zo.* chrysalis, pupa; *des Seidenspinners*: cocoon.

'**Puppen|gesicht** *n* doll's face; '**~spiel** *n* puppet-show; '**~stube** *f* doll's house; '**~theater** *n* puppet-show; '**~wagen** *m* doll's pram.

pur [pu:r] pure; (*bloß*) *a.* sheer; *Whisky*: neat, *Am.* straight.

Püree [py're:] *n* (11) purée (*fr.*), mash.

purgier|en [pur'gi:rən] *v/t. u. v/i.* purge; **2mittel** *n* purgative.

Puritaner [puri'ta:nər] *m* (7), **~in** *f* Puritan; **~tum** *n* (1²) Puritanism.

puri'tanisch Puritan.

Purpur ['purpur] *m* (11) purple; '**2farben,** '**2n,** '**2rot** purple.

Purzel|baum ['purtsəlbaum] *m* somersault; *Sport*: roll; *e-n ~ schlagen* turn a somersault; '**2n** (29, sn) tumble.

Pustel ['pustəl] *f* (15) pustule.

puste|n ['pu:stən] *v/i. u. v/t.* (26) puff, (*a. = blasen*) blow; '**2rohr** *n* pea-shooter.

Put|e ['pu:tə] *f* = '**~henne** *f* (15) turkey-hen; *sl. fig. dumme ~* silly goose; '**~er** (7) *m*, '**~hahn** *m* turkey-cock; '**2er-rot** purple, crimson.

Putsch [putʃ] *m* (3²) putsch.

Putz [puts] *m* (3²) dressing, toilet;

(*feine Kleidung*) finery; (*Schmuck*) ornaments *pl.*; (*Mauer*2) rough-cast, plaster(ing); *s.* ~*waren*; '2**en** (27) *Person*: dress, attire; (*schmükken*) adorn; (*reinigen*) clean; (*wischen*) wipe; (*glänzend machen*) polish; *Kerze*: snuff; *Lampe*: trim; *Pferd*: groom; *Schuhe*: polish, *Am.* shine; *Gemüse*: pick; *Zähne*: brush; *sich die Nase* ~ blow (*od.* wipe) one's nose; '~**er** ⚔ *m* (7) batman; '~**fimmel** *m*: *e-n* ~ *haben* be very houseproud; '~**frau** *f* charwoman; '2**ig** funny, droll; '~**lappen** *m* cloth; '~**leder** *n* chamois; ~**macherei** [~maxə'raɪ] *f* millinery; '~**macherin** *f* milliner; '2**süchtig** fond of finery, dressy; '~**waren** *f/pl.* millinery *sg.*; '~**wolle** *f* (cotton) waste; '~**zeug** *n* cleaning things *pl.*

Pygmäe [pyg'mɛːə] *f* pygmy.

Pyjama [py'dʒaːma] *m* (11) (*ein* ~ a suit of) pyjamas, *Am.* pajamas *pl.*

Pyramide [pyra'miːdə] *f* (15) pyramid; ⚔ (*Gewehr*2) stack; 2**nförmig** [~nfœrmiç] pyramidal.

Pyrotechnik [pyro'tɛçnik] *f* pyrotechnics *pl.*; ~**er** *m* pyrotechnist.

pythagoreisch [pytago'reːiʃ] Pythagorean; ~*er Lehrsatz* Pythagorean proposition.

Q

Q [kuː], **q** *n inv.* Q, q.

quabbel|ig ['kvabəliç] flabby; '~**n** (29) wobble.

Quackelei [kvakə'laɪ] *f* foolish talk.

Quacksalber ['kvakzalbər] *m* (7) quack; ~**ei** [~'raɪ] *f* (16) quackery; '2**n** (29) quack.

Quader ['kvaːdər] *m* (7), *f* (15), '~**stein** *m* square stone, ashlar.

Quadrant ⅍ [kva'drant] *m* (12) quadrant.

Quadrat [kva'draːt] *n* (3) square; *2 Fuß im* ~ 2 feet square; 2**isch** square; ⅍ quadratic; ~**meile** *f* square mile; ~**meter** *n* square met|re, *Am.* -er; ~**ur** [~dra'tuːr] *f* (16) quadrature, squaring; ~**wurzel** [~'draːt-] *f* square root.

qua'drieren square.

quadrophon [kvadro'foːn] quadrophonic.

quaken ['kvaːkən] (25) *Ente*: quack; *Frosch*: croak.

quäken ['kvɛːkən] (25) squeak.

Quäker ['kvɛːkər] *m* (7) Quaker.

Qual [kvaːl] *f* (16) pain; *stärker*: torture; *höchster Grad*: agony; *seelisch*: *a.* anguish; (*hartes Los, Nervenprobe*) ordeal; (*Mühsal*) drudgery.

quälen ['kvɛːlən] (25) torment; (*foltern*) torture; *stärker*: agonize; *fig. a.* worry, F bother; *mit Bitten*: pester; (*hänseln*) tease; (*betrüben*) afflict; *sich* ~ (*schwer arbeiten*) drudge.

'**Quäler** *m* (7) tormentor; ~**ei** [~'raɪ] *f* (16) tormenting; *fig.* vexation; '~**in** *f* (16[1]) tormentress.

'**Quälgeist** *m* pest, tormentor.

Qualifikation [kvalifika'tsjoːn] *f* (16) qualification; ~**skampf** *m* *Sport*: qualifying contest, tie.

qualifizieren [~'tsiːrən] (*a. sich*) qualify (*für* for).

Qualität [~'tɛːt] *f* (16) quality.

qualitativ [~ta'tiːf] qualitative.

Quali'täts|-arbeit *f* work of (high) quality; ~**stahl** *m* high-grade steel; ~**ware** *f* high-quality article.

Qualle ['kvalə] *f* (15) jelly-fish.

Qualm [kvalm] *m* (3) smoke; '2**en** (25) *v/i. u. v/t.* smoke; '2**ig** smoky.

'**qualvoll** very painful, agonizing, excruciating.

Quant|enphysik ['kvantən-] *f* quantum physics *sg.*; '~**entheorie** *f* quantum theory; ~**ität** [~ti'tɛːt] *f* (16) quantity; 2**itativ** [~ita'tiːf] quantitative; ~**um** ['~tum] *n* (9) quantum, quantity.

Quappe ['kvapə] *f* (*Fisch*) eel-pout; (*Kaul*2) tadpole.

Quarantäne [karan'tɛːnə] *f* (15) quarantine (*a. v/t. in* ~ *legen*).

Quark [kvark] *m* (3, *o. pl.*) curds

pl.; *fig.* rubbish, tripe; '**~käse** *m* cottage cheese.

Quart [kvart] **1.** *n* (3) quart; *Buch*: quarto; **2.** ~ *f* (15) ♪ fourth; *fenc.* carte, quart(e); **~al** [~'tɑ:l] *n* (3¹) quarter (of a year); (*Schul*2) term; '**~band** *m* quarto volume; '**~e** *f* *s. Quart* 2.; **~ett** ♪ [~'tɛt] *n* (3) quartet(te).

Quartier [kvar'ti:r] *n* (3¹) lodging(s *pl.*); *bsd.* ⚔ quarters *pl.*, billets *pl.*; ~ *beziehen* take up quarters; ~ *machen* prepare quarters; **~macher** ⚔ *m* billeting officer; **~meister** ⚔ *m* quartermaster.

Quarz [kvɑ:rts] *m* (3²) quartz; '**~-uhr** *f* quartz watch.

quasi ['kvɑ:zi] quasi, as it were.

quasseln F ['kvasəln] (29) *s. quatschen.*

Quast [kvast] *m* (3¹) (*Pinsel*) brush; '**~e** *f* (15) (*Troddel*) tassel; *s. Puder*2.

Quatsch F [kvatʃ] *m* (3²) *sl.* rot, bilge, bunk, *Am.* baloney; '2**en** F (27) *v/i.* talk rot, (*a. v/t.*) twaddle, blather; (*plaudern*) chat; '**~kopf** F *m* twaddler; silly ass.

Quecksilb|er ['kvɛkzilbər] *n* quicksilver, mercury; '**~ersäule** *f* mercury column; '2**rig** mercurial; *fig. a.* lively.

Quell [kvɛl] *m* (3) *poet.* = '**~e** *f* (15) source (*a. fig. Ursprung*), spring; (*Spring*2) fountain(-head); (*Brunnen, a. Öl*2) well; *fig.* fount; *literarisch*: authority; (*Gewährsmann*) informant; *aus sicherer* ~ on good authority; '2**en** *v/i.* (30, sn) spring, gush; (*fließen*) flow; (*anschwellen*) swell; *v/t.* (25) cause to swell; (*einweichen*) soak; '**~en-angabe** *f* mention of sources used; '**~enmaterial** *n* source material; '**~enstudium** *n* original research; '**~fluß** *m* source; '**~gebiet** *n e-s Flusses*: headwaters *pl.*; '**~wasser** *n* spring-water.

Quengel|ei [kvɛŋə'laɪ] *f* (16) nagging; '2**ig** nagging, whining; '2**n** (29) nag; whine.

Quentchen ['kvɛntçən] *n* (6) dram; *fig.* grain.

quer [kve:r] cross, transverse; diagonal; (*seitlich*) lateral; *adv.* across, crosswise, athwart; ~ *über* (*acc.*) across; ~ *zu* at right angles to; *s. Kreuz.*

'**Quer...** *in Zssgn mst* cross-...; '**~-achse** *f* lateral axis; '**~balken** *m* cross-beam; '**~e** *f* (15): *der* ~ *nach, in die* ~ crosswise, across; *j-m in die* ~ *kommen* cross a p.'s way *od.* (*fig. a.*) plans; '2**en** *mount.* (25) traverse; '2**feld'-ein** across country; '**~feld'-einlauf** *m* cross-country run *od.* race; '**~flöte** *f* German flute; '**~format** *typ. n* oblong format; '**~frage** *f* cross-question; '2**gestreift** cross-striped; '**~holz** *n* cross-bar; '**~kopf** *m* wrong-headed fellow, crank; 2**köpfig** ['~kœpfiç] wrong-headed, cross-grained, cranky; '**~pfeife** ♪ *f* fife; '**~ruder** ✈ *n* aileron; '**~schiff** ⛪ *n* transept; '**~schläger** *m* ricochet; '**~schnitt** *m* cross-section (*a. fig.*); '2**schnitt**(**s**)**gelähmt**, '**~schnitt**(**s**)**gelähmte** *m, f* paraplegic; '**~schnitt**(**s**)**lähmung** *f* paraplegia; '**~schnittzeichnung** *f* sectional drawing; '**~straße** *f* cross street; *zweite* ~ *rechts* second turning to the right; '**~streifen** *m* cross stripe; '**~strich** *m* cross-line, bar, dash; '**~summe** ⅌ *f* sum of the digits, cross sum; '**~treiber** *m* intriguer; obstructionist; **~treiberei** [~traɪbə'raɪ] *f* intriguing, obstruction(ism).

Querulant [kveru'lant] *m* (12), **~in** *f* (16¹) grumbler, *Am. a.* griper.

'**Quer|verbindung** *f* cross connection; '**~weg** *m* cross road.

quetsch|en ['kvɛtʃən] (27) squeeze; (*kneifen*) pinch; (*zerquetschen*) crush; *Haut*: bruise, contuse; '2**kartoffeln** *f/pl.* mashed potatoes; '2**kommode** F *f* (*Akkordeon*) squeeze-box; '2**ung** *f* crushing; ⚕ (*a.* = '2**wunde** *f*) bruise, contusion.

quieken ['kvi:kən] (25) squeak.

quietsch|en ['kvi:tʃən] (27) squeal, squeak (*a. Tür usw.*); '**~ver'gnügt** F cheerful(ly *adv.*).

Quint|(**e**) ♪ ['kvint(ə)] *f* (16 [15]) fifth; '**~-essenz** *f* (16) quintessence; **~ett** ♪ [~'tɛt] *n* (3) quintet(te).

Quirl [kvirl] *m* (3) twirling-stick; ⚘ whorl; '2**en** (25) twirl; *Eier usw.*: whisk.

quitt [kvit] *pred.* quits, even; '2**e** ⚘ *f* (15) quince; **~ieren** [~'ti:rən] receipt; (*aufgeben*) quit, abandon; '2**ung** *f* receipt.

quoll [kvɔl] *pret. v. quellen v/i.*

Quot|e ['kvo:tə] *f* (15) quota; share; rate; **~ient** [kvo'tsjɛnt] *m* (12) quotient; 2**ieren** ✝ [~'ti:rən] quote.

R

R [ɛr], **r** *inv. n* R, r.
Rabatt [ra'bat] *m* (3) discount, rebate, allowance; **~e** ↙ *f* (15) border; **~marke** *f* discount stamp; **~satz** *m* discount rate.
Rabbiner [ra'bi:nər] *m* (7) rabbi.
Rabe ['rɑ:bə] *m* (13) raven; *fig. weißer ~* rare bird.
'**Raben**|**-eltern** *pl.* unnatural parents; 'ℒ'**schwarz** jet-black; *Nacht*: pitch-dark.
rabiat [ra'bjɑ:t] rabid, furious; (*gefährlich*) desperate.
Rabulist [rabu'list] *m* (12) pettifogger; ℒ**isch** pettifogging.
Rache ['raxə] *f* (15) revenge, vengeance; *~ brüten* (*schwören*) brood (vow) vengeance; *~ nehmen od. üben* take revenge (*an dat.* on); '**~-akt** *m* act of revenge; '**~durst** *m s. Rachgier.*
Rachen ['raxən] *m* (6) throat; (*Tier*ℒ) jaws *pl.* (*a. fig.*).
rächen ['rɛçən] (25) avenge, revenge (*an* [*dat.*] [up]on); *sich ~ an j-m* revenge o.s. (*od.* be revenged) on a p.; *fig. es rächte sich* (*bitter*), *daß er* ... he had to pay dearly for *ger.*
'**Rachen**|**höhle** *f* pharynx; '**~katarrh** *m* cold in the throat.
Rächer ['rɛçər] *m* (7), '**~in** *f* (16[1]) avenger.
'**Rach**|**gier** *f*, '**~sucht** *f* thirst for revenge, revengefulness, vindictiveness; 'ℒ**gierig**, ℒ**süchtig** ['~zyçtiç] revengeful, vindictive.
Rachi|**tis** ⚕ [ra'xi:tis] *f* (15, *o. pl.*) rickets (*sg. od. pl.*), 🕮 rachitis; ℒ**tisch** rickety, 🕮 rachitic.
Racker F ['rakər] *m* (7) rascal, brat; (*Mädchen*) minx; 'ℒ**n** toil.
Rad [rɑ:t] *n* (1[2]) wheel; (*Fahr*ℒ) (bi)cycle, F bike; (*ein*) *~ schlagen Pfau*: spread the tail, *Turnen*: *s. radschlagen*; *unter die Räder kommen* go to the dogs; *s. fünfte*; '**~achse** *f* axle-tree.
Radar [ra'dɑ:r, 'rɑ:dar] *m*, *n* (7, *o. pl.*) radar; **~-anlage** *f* radar unit; **~falle** *f* speed trap; **~gerät** *n* radar set; **~schirm** *m* radar screen; **~suchgerät** *n* radar scanner.
Radau F [ra'daʊ] *m* (3[1]) racket, row; *~ machen* kick up a row, riot.
radebrechen ['rɑ:dəbrɛçən] speak *a language* badly; *französisch usw. ~* speak broken French *etc.*
radeln ['rɑ:dəln] (29, sn) cycle, pedal, F bike.
Rädelsführer ['rɛ:dəls-] *m* ringleader.
räder|**n** ['rɛ:dərn] (29) *Verbrecher*: break (up)on the wheel; *wie gerädert sein* be all in; 'ℒ**werk** *n* wheelwork, gear(ing).
'**rad**|**fahren** (sn) cycle, (ride a) bicycle, F bike; 'ℒ**fahrer(in** *f*) *m* cyclist, *Am.* cycler; 'ℒ**fahrsport** *m* cycling; 'ℒ**fahrweg** *m* cycle track; 'ℒ**felge** *f* wheel rim.
radieren [ra'di:rən] erase, rub out; *Kunst*: etch.
Ra'dier|**gummi** *m* India rubber, *Am.* eraser; **~kunst** *f* (art of) etching; **~messer** *n* eraser, penknife; **~nadel** *f* etching-needle; **~ung** *f* etching.
Radies-chen ♀ [ra'di:sçən] *n* (6) (red) radish.
radikal [radi'kɑ:l] radical; ℒ**e** *pol. m* (18) radical; **~isieren** [~kali'zi:rən] radicalise; ℒ**ismus** [~ka'lismus] *m* (16) radicalism; ℒ**kur** *f* ⚕ drastic (*od.* radical) cure; *fig.* drastic measures *pl.*; (*Diät*) crash diet.
Radio ['rɑ:djo] *n* (11) radio, *Brt. a.* wireless; *im ~ sprechen* speak over the radio; *s. a. Rundfunk*; 'ℒ**-ak'tiv** radio-active; *~er Niederschlag* fall-out; '**~-aktivi'tät** *f* radio-activity; '**~-apparat** *m* radio (set), *Brt. a.* wireless set; **~loge** [~'lo:gə] *m* (13) radiologist; **~logie** [~lo'gi:] *f* (16, *o. pl.*) radiology; ℒ'**logisch** radiological; **~recorder** ['~rekɔrdər] *m* (7) radio cassette recorder; '**~röhre** *f* radio valve (*Am.* tube); '**~sendung** *f*, '**~-übertragung** *f* radio transmission; *Programm*: broadcast; '**~wecker** *m* clock radio.
Radium ['rɑ:djum] *n* (9) radium.
Radius ['rɑ:djus] *m* (16[2]) radius.
'**Rad**|**kappe** *f* hub cap; '**~kranz** *m* rim; '**~nabe** *f* hub, nave; '**~rennbahn** *f* cycling track; '**~rennen** *n* cycle race; '**~schaufel** *f* paddle (-board); 'ℒ**schlagen** *Turnen*: turn cartwheels (*Am.* handsprings); '**~speiche** *f* spoke; '**~sport** *m* cycling; '**~stand** *m* wheel-base; '**~tour** *f* cycle tour; '**~wandern** *n* cycling.

raff|en ['rafən] (25) snatch up; *Kleid*: gather up; *Näherei*: take up; '**2gier** *f* greed.

Raffi|nade [rafi'nɑ:də] *f* (15) refined sugar; **~nerie** [~nə'ri:] *f* (16) refinery; **~nesse** [~'nɛsə] *f* (15) cleverness, *a. künstlerisch usw.*: subtlety; **2'nieren** refine; **2'niert** refined; *fig.* clever, cunning; *a. künstlerisch usw.*: subtle; *Geschmack, Aufmachung*: sophisticated.

ragen ['rɑ:gən] (25) tower, loom.

Ragout [ra'gu:] *n* (11) ragout, stew, hash, (*a. fig.*) hotchpotch.

Rahe ⚓ ['rɑ:ə] *f* (15) yard.

Rahm [rɑ:m] *m* (3) cream; *den ~ abschöpfen* (*a. fig.*) skim off the cream.

Rahmen ['rɑ:mən] **1.** *m* (6) frame (*a.* ⊕, *mot.*); (*Gefüge*) framework; (*Bereich*) scope; *Roman*: (*Ort u. Handlung*) setting; *am Schuh*: welt; *fig. im ~ von* within the scope of; *im ~ des Festes* in the course of the festival; *in bescheidenem ~* on a modest scale; *in engem ~* within a close compass; *aus dem ~ fallen* go off the beaten track; *den ~ e-r S. sprengen* be beyond the scope of; **2.** 2 (25) frame; '**~-abkommen** *n* skeleton agreement; '**~-erzählung** *f* 'link and frame' story; '**~gesetz** *n* skeleton law; '**~kampf** *m Boxen*: supporting bout; '**~ver-anstaltung** *f* fringe event.

'**rahmig** creamy.

Rahsegel ⚓ ['rɑ:-] *n* square sail.

Rain [raɪn] *m* (3) ridge; (*ungepflügter Streifen*) balk.

räkeln ['rɛ:kəln] *s. rekeln*.

Rakete [ra'ke:tə] *f* (15) rocket; **~n-abschußbasis** *f* rocket launching site; **~n-abschußrampe** *f* rocket launcher; **~n-antrieb** ✈ *m* rocket propulsion; *mit ~* rocket-propelled *od.* -powered; **~nfeuer** *n* rocket fire; **~nforschung** *f* rocketry; **~ngeschoß** *n* rocket projectile; **~npotential** *n* missile strength; **~nspitze** *f* nose-cone; **~nstart** *m* blast-off; *e-s Flugzeugs*: rocket-assisted take-off; **~nstellung** *f* missile site; **~nwerfer** *m* rocket launcher.

Rallye ['rali, 'ræli] *mot. f* (11[1]) rally.

Ramm|bär *m*, **~bock** ['ram-] *m* rammer, ram(-block); '**~e** *f* (15) rammer, pile-driver; (*Pflaster*2) beetle; '**2en** (25) ram.

Rampe ['rampə] *f* (15) ramp; 🚂 platform; *thea.* apron; '**~nlicht** *n* footlights *pl.*; *fig. der Öffentlichkeit*: limelight.

ramponiert [rampo'ni:rt] battered, damaged.

Ramsch [ramʃ] *m* (3[2]) job goods *pl.*; *contp.* junk, trash; '**~verkauf** *m* jumble-sale; '**~ware** *f* job lot.

ran! [ran] F *int.* let's go!; *in Zssgn s. heran*; *s. rangehen*.

Rand [rant] *m* (1[2]) edge; (*Saum*) border; *e-s Hutes*: brim; *e-s Tellers*: rim; *e-r Druckseite usw.*: margin; *e-r Wunde*: lip; *am ~e des Verderbens* on the verge of ruin; *außer ~ und Band* wild.

randalieren [randa'li:rən] riot.

'**Rand|-auslöser** *m der Schreibmaschine*: marginal release; '**~bemerkung** *f* marginal note.

ränd|eln ['rɛndəln], '**~ern** (29) rim; ⊕ knurl; *Münze*: mill.

'**Rand|gebiet** *n* borderland; *e-r Stadt*: outskirts *pl.*; '**2los** *Brille*: rimless; '**~gruppe** *f* fringe group; '**~problem** *n* side-issue; '**~staat** *m* border state; '**~stein** *m* kerbstone, *Am.* curbstone; '**~steller** *m der Schreibmaschine*: margin stop; '**2voll** brimful.

Rang[1] [raŋ] *m* (3[3]) rank; grade; (*Stand*) status; (*Stellung*) position; (*Würde*) dignity; *ersten ~es* first-class, first-rate; *thea. erster ~* dress-circle, *Am.* first balcony; *zweiter ~* upper circle, *Am.* second balcony; *j-m den ~ ablaufen* get the start of a p., F steal a march on a p.; *j-m od. e-r S. den ~ streitig machen* compete with; **2**[2] *pret. v. ringen*; '**~-abzeichen** *n* badge of rank.

Range ['raŋə] *m* (13) young scamp, brat; *f* (15) romp, tomboy.

rangehen F ['ran-] *sl.* go it.

'**Rangfolge** *f* order.

Rangier|bahnhof [rɑ̃'ʒi:r-] *m* shunting-station; **2en** *v/t.* arrange; 🚂 shunt, *Am.* switch; *v/i. fig.* rank, be classed; 🚂 shunt; **~gleis** *n* siding; **~maschine** *f* shunting-engine.

'**Rang|liste** *f* ranking list; ⚔ Army (*od.* Navy *od.* Air Force) List, *Am.* Army Register; '**~-ordnung** *f* order (of precedence); '**~stufe** *f* rank, degree, order.

rank [raŋk] slender, slim.
Ranke [ˈraŋkə] *f* (15) tendril, runner; ˈ**2n** (25, *a. sich*) climb, creep.
Ränke [ˈrɛŋkə] *m/pl.* (3³) tricks, intrigues; ~ *schmieden* plot and scheme; ˈ**~schmied** *m* intriguer, plotter, schemer; ˈ**2voll** scheming.
rann [ran] *pret. v. rinnen.*
ˈ**rannte** *pret. v. rennen.*
Ränzel [ˈrɛntsəl] *n* (7), **Ranzen** [ˈrantsən] *m* (6) knapsack; (*Schulmappe*) satchel; F *s. Wanst.*
ranzig [ˈrantsiç] rancid, rank.
rapid(**e**) [raˈpiːt, -də] rapid.
Rapier [raˈpiːr] *n* (3¹) rapier, foil.
Rappe [ˈrapə] *m* (13) black horse.
Rappel F [ˈrapəl] *m* (7) (fit of) madness; *e-n ~ haben* F be cracked; *seinen ~ haben* be in one's tantrums; ˈ**2ig** nervy; cracked; ˈ**2n** F *v/i.* (29) rattle; *es rappelt bei ihm* he is nuts.
Rapport [raˈpɔrt] *m* (3) report.
Raps ⚘ [raps] *m* (4) rape(-seed).
rar [rɑːr] rare, scarce; *sich ~ machen* make o.s. scarce.
Rarität [rariˈtɛːt] *f* (16) rarity, curiosity.
rasan|t [raˈzant] *Geschoßbahn*: flat; *fig.* fast, rapid; **2z** *f* (15. *o. pl.*) flatness; *fig.* rapidity.
rasch [raʃ] quick, swift; (*sofortig*) prompt; (*vorschnell*) rash; (*hastig*) hasty; ~ *machen* be quick; ˈ**~eln** (29) rustle; ˈ**2heit** *f* quickness, swiftness; haste.
rasen¹ [ˈrɑːzən] (27) *vor Zorn*: rage; *vor Begeisterung*: be frantic; (*irre reden*) rave; (sn) *fig.* (*daher~*) race, speed, tear; ˈ**~d** raging; raving; frantic; *Tempo*: tearing, breakneck; *Hunger*: ravenous; *Schmerzen*: agonizing; *j-n ~ machen* drive a p. mad; ~ *werden* go mad, *wütend*: see red.
Rasen² [~] *m* (6) grass; (*~platz*) lawn; (*~decke*) turf; ˈ**~mäher** *m* (7) lawn-mower; ˈ**~platz** *m* lawn, grass-plot; ˈ**~sprenger** *m* lawn-sprinkler.
Raser F [ˈrɑːzər] *mot. m* (7) speeder, reckless driver; **~ei** [~ˈraɪ] *f* (16) *mot.* speeding, reckless driving; (*Wut*) fury; (*Wahnsinn*) frenzy, madness; *in ~ geraten* fly into a rage; *zur ~ bringen* drive *a p.* mad.
Rasier|-apparat [raˈziːr-] *m* safety-razor; *elektrischer*: electric (*od.* dry-)shaver; **~creme** *f* shaving cream; **2en** shave; *sich ~ lassen* get a shave, get shaved; **~klinge** *f* razor-blade; **~messer** *n* razor; **~pinsel** *m* shaving-brush; **~seife** *f* shaving soap; **~wasser** *n* after-shave lotion; **~zeug** *n* shaving things *pl.*
Räson [rɛˈzɔ̃] *f* (16, *o. pl.*) reason; *s. Einsicht, Vernunft*; **2ieren** [~zɔˈniːrən] argue.
Raspel [ˈraspəl] *f* (15) rasp; *Küche*: grater; ˈ**2n** *v/t. u. v/i.* (29) rasp, grate; *s. Süßholz.*
Rasse [ˈrasə] *f* (15) race; *bsd. v. Tieren*: breed; ˈ**~hund** *m* pedigree dog.
Rassel [ˈrasəl] *f* (15) rattle; ˈ**~bande** F *f* (mischievous) gang; ˈ**2n** (29, h. *u.* sn) rattle; F (*im Examen durchfallen*) be ploughed, *Am.* flunk; ~ *lassen* plough, *Am.* flunk.
ˈ**Rassen|diskriminierung** *f* racial discrimination; ˈ**~frage** *f* race problem; ˈ**~gleichheit** *f* racial equality; ˈ**~haß** *m* racial hatred; ˈ**~hygiene** *f* eugenics *pl.*; ˈ**~kampf** *m* racial conflict; ˈ**~kreuzung** *f v. Tieren*: cross-breeding; ˈ**~merkmal** *n* racial characteristic; ˈ**~mischung** *f* mixture of races; (*Tier*) crossbreed; ˈ**~politik** *f* racial policy; ˈ**~schranke** *f* colo(u)r bar; ˈ**~trennung** *f* (racial) segregation.
ˈ**Rasse|pferd** *n* thoroughbred (horse); ˈ**2rein** racially pure; *Tier*: pure-bred, thoroughbred.
ˈ**rass|ig** racy; *bsd. v. Tieren*: thoroughbred; ˈ**~isch** racial.
Rassis|mus [raˈsismus] *m* (16²) racism; **~t** *m* (12), **2tisch** racist.
Rast [rast] *f* (16) rest, repose; ⚔ halt; (*Station*) stage; ⊕ notch, groove; stop; (*e-e*) ~ *machen* take a rest; ˈ**~e** ⊕ *f* stop; (*Fuß2*) foot-rest; ˈ**2en** (26) rest; ⚔ halt.
Raster [ˈrastər] *m* (7) *phot.*, *typ.* screen; *TV*: raster.
ˈ**Rast|haus** *n* road house; ˈ**2los** restless; ˈ**~losigkeit** *f* restlessness; ˈ**~platz** *m* resting place; ˈ**~stätte** *mot. f* service area.
Rasur [raˈzuːr] *f* (16) shave.
Rat [rɑːt] *m* (3³, *pl. mst ~schläge* [ˈ~ʃlɛːgə]) advice, counsel; (*Kollegium*) council, board; (*Person*) council(l)or; (*Beratung*) deliberation; (*Ausweg*) way (out), expedient; ~ *schaffen* find a way (out); ~ *halten s. ratschlagen*; ~ *suchen* (*bei*), *sich* (*bei j-m*) ~ *holen* ask *a p.* for advice; *j-m e-n ~ erteilen* give

a p. a piece of advice; *e-n Arzt usw. zu* ~*e ziehen* consult; *j-s* ~ *befolgen* take a p.'s advice; *j-n um* ~ *fragen* ask a p.'s advice; *mit* ~ *und Tat* with word and deed; (*sich*) *keinen* ~ *wissen* be at one's wits' end; *da ist guter* ~ *teuer!* what are we to do?

Rate ['rɑːtə] *f* (15) instal(l)ment (*a.* ✝); (*Wachstums*2 *usw.*) rate; *in* ~*n* by instal(l)ments.

raten ['rɑːtən] *v/t. u. v/i.* (30) advise, counsel (*j-m* [*zu et.*] a p. [to do a th.]); (*er*~) guess, divine; *Rätsel*: *a.* solve; *sich* (*von j-m*) ~ *lassen* take (a p.'s) advice; F *rate mal!* just guess!

'**raten|weise** by instal(l)ments; '2**zahlung** *f* payment by instal(l)ments; *auf* ~ on the hire-purchase (*Am.* instal[l]ment) plan.

'**Rat|geber(in** *f*) *m* adviser, counsel(l)or; '~**haus** *n* townhall, *Am.* city hall.

Ratifi|kation [ratifika'tsjoːn] *f* (16), ~'**zierung** *f* ratification; 2'**zieren** ratify.

Ration [ra'tsjoːn] *f* (16) ration, allowance; *s. eisern*; 2**al** [~tsjo'nɑːl] rational; 2**alisieren** [~nali'ziːrən] rationalize; ~**ali'sierung** *f* rationalization; ~**ali'sierungsfachmann** *m* efficiency expert, methods study man; ~**alismus** [~'lismus] *m* (16) rationalism; 2**ell** [~'nɛl] rational; (*wirtschaftlich*) efficient, economical; 2**ieren** [~'niːrən] ration; ~**ierung** [~'niːruŋ] *f* rationing.

rätlich ['rɛːtliç] *s. ratsam.*

'**rat|los** helpless, *pred.* at a loss; '2**losigkeit** *f* helplessness.

'**ratsam** advisable; wise; '2**keit** *f* advisability.

'**Rat|schlag** *m* (piece of) advice; '2**schlagen** (25) deliberate, take counsel; '~**schluß** *m* decision; *Gottes* ~ decree of God.

Rätsel ['rɛːtsəl] *n* (7) riddle, puzzle; (*Geheimnis*) *a.* enigma, mystery; *er* (*es*) *ist mir ein* ~ he (it) puzzles me; '2**haft** puzzling; (*geheimnisvoll*) mysterious, enigmatical; '~**raten** *n* solving riddles; *fig.* speculation.

'**Rats|herr** *m* council(l)or; senator; '~**keller** *m* townhall-cellar restaurant, *Am.* rathskeller.

Ratte ['ratə] *f* (15) rat; ~**nfänger** ['~nfɛŋər] *m* rat-catcher; (*Hund*) ratter; *von Hameln, a. fig.*: Pied Piper; '~**ngift** *n* rat-poison.

rattern ['ratərn] (29) rattle; *Motoren*: roar.

Raub [raup] *m* (3) robbery; (*Beute*) loot; *zo. u. fig.* prey; '~**bau** *m* ⚒ ruinous exploitation; ~ *treiben* ⚒ exhaust the soil, ⚒ rob a mine, *mit s-r Gesundheit* undermine one's health; '~**druck** *m* (3) pirate edition.

rauben ['~bən] (25) *v/t.* rob; (*a. fig.*) *j-m et.* ~ rob (*od.* deprive) a p. of a th.; *v/i.* commit robberies.

Räuber ['rɔʏbər] *m* (7) robber; (*Straßen*2) highwayman, brigand; '~**bande** *f* gang of robbers, *Am.* holdup gang; ~**ei** [~'raɪ] *f* (16) robbery; '~**geschichte** F *fig. f* cock-and-bull story; '~'**hauptmann** *m* captain of brigands; '~**höhle** *f* den of robbers; '2**isch** rapacious; ~*er Überfall* holdup.

Raub|fisch ['raup-] *m* fish of prey; '~**gier** *f* rapacity; '2**gierig** rapacious; '~**mord** *m* murder and robbery; '~**mörder** *m* murderer and robber; '~**ritter** *m* robber-knight; '~**tier** *n* beast of prey, predacious animal; '~-**überfall** *m* robbery, holdup; '~**vogel** *m* bird of prey; '~**zug** *m* raid.

Rauch [raux] *m* (3) smoke; *s. aufgehen*; '~**bombe** ⚔ *f* smoke-bomb; '2**en** (25) smoke; 2 *verboten!* No smoking!

'**Raucher** *m* (7), '~**in** *f* (16[1]) smoker; '~-**abteil** *n* smoking compartment.

Räucher|-aal ['rɔʏçər-] *m* smoked eel; '~**faß** *eccl. n* censer; '~**hering** *m* smoked (*od.* red) herring; '~**kammer** *f* smoking-chamber; '~**kerze** *f* fumigating candle; '~**lachs** *m* smoked salmon; '2**n** (29) smoke (-dry); *desinfizierend*: fumigate; (*wohlriechend machen*) perfume; ⊕ *Eichenmöbel*: fume; ~**stäbchen** ['~ʃtɛːpçən] *n* (6) joss stick.

'**Rauch|fahne** *f* trail of smoke; '~**fang** *m* chimney(-hood), flue; '~**fleisch** *n* smoked meat; '2**ig** smoky; '2**los** smokeless; '~**säule** *f* column of smoke; '~**tabak** *m* smoking tobacco; '~**vergiftung** *f* smoke poisoning; '~**verzehrer** *m* smoke consumer; '~**vorhang** ⚔ *m* smoke-screen; '~**waren** *f/pl.* (*Pelzwaren*) furs; (*Tabakwaren*) tobacco products; '~**warenhändler** *m* furrier;

tobacconist; '**~wolke** *f* cloud of smoke.

Räude ['rɔʏdə] *f* (15) mange.

'**räudig** mangy, scabby; *~es Schaf fig.* black sheep.

rauf [rauf] F *adv. s. herauf(...), hinauf(...).*

Rauf|bold ['raufbɔlt] *m* (3) brawler, ruffian, rowdy; '**~e** *f* (15) rack; '**2en** (25) *v/t.* pluck, pull; *s. Haar; sich ~ = v/i.* fight, scuffle (*um* for); **~erei** [~fə'raɪ] *f* scuffle, fight; '**~handel** *m* brawl; '**2lustig** pugnacious.

rauh [rau] *allg.* rough; *Hals*: sore; *Stimme*: hoarse; *Ton, Behandlung*: harsh; (*grob*) coarse, rude; *fig. die ~e Wirklichkeit* the hard facts *pl.*; F *in ~en Mengen* lots of; '**2bein** F *n* rough diamond, *Am.* F roughneck; '**~beinig** *f* rough; **2eit** ['~haɪt] *f* roughness; hoarseness, harshness; rudeness; **~en** ['rauən] (25) roughen; *Tuch*: tease, nap; '**2futter** *n* roughage; '**~haarig** rough-haired, shaggy; '**2reif** *m* hoar-frost.

Raum [raum] *m* (3[1]) room, space; (*Platz*) place; (*Zimmer*) room; (*Bereich*) area, zone; (*Welt2*) space; (*Abteil, Koffer2*) compartment; *s. ~inhalt*; *fig.* scope; *~ geben e-m Gedanken*: give way to, *e-r Hoffnung usw.*: indulge in, *e-r Bitte*: grant.

Räum|boot ['rɔʏm-] *n* mine sweeper; '**2en** (25) clear; (*verlassen*) leave, *bsd.* ⚔ evacuate; *Wohnung*: quit, vacate; ⚓ *Lager*: clear; ⚔ *Minen*: sweep; *s. Weg.*

'**Raum|-ersparnis** *f* space saving; *der ~ wegen* to save room *od.* space; '**~fähre** *f* space shuttle; '**~fahrt** *f* space travel (*od.* flight); astronautics *pl.*; '**~fahrt-industrie** *f* aerospace industry; '**~fahrtzentrum** *n* space cent|re, *Am.*-er; '**~forschung** *f* (aero)space research; '**~-inhalt** *m* volume, capacity; '**~kapsel** *f* space capsule; '**~kreuzer** *m* space cruiser; '**~kunst** *f* interior decoration; '**~labor** *n* space laboratory; '**~lehre** *f* geometry.

'**räumlich** (of) space; (*Ggs. zeitlich*) spatial; *opt.* stereoscopic; '**2keit** *f* spatiality; (*Raum*) space, room; *~en pl. e-s Hauses*: premises.

'**Raum|mangel** *m* lack of space; '**~maß** *n* measure of volume; '**~meter** *n, a. m* cubic met|re, *Am.* -er; '**~patrouille** *f* space patrol; '**~pflegerin** *f* charwoman, cleaner.

'**Räumpflug** *m* bulldozer.

'**Raum|schiff** *n* space-ship; '**~schifffahrt** *f s. Raumfahrt*; '**~sonde** *f* space probe; '**~station** *f* space station.

'**Räumung** *f* (16) clearing; ⚓ clearance; *e-r Stadt*: evacuation; *e-r Wohnung*: quitting, *zwangsweise*: eviction; '**~sbefehl** ⚖ *m* eviction order; '**~sklage** ⚖ *f* action for eviction; '**~sverkauf** *m* clearance sale.

raunen ['raunən] *v/i. u. v/t.* (25) whisper, murmur.

Raupe ['raupə] *f* (15) caterpillar; '**~nfahrzeug** *n* tracked vehicle; '**~nkette** ⊕ *f* track; '**~nschlepper** *m* crawler tractor.

raus [raus] F *s. heraus(...), hinaus (-...)*; *int. ~!* get out!

Rausch [rauʃ] *m* (3[2] *u.* [3]) intoxication, drunkenness; *fig.* transport, ecstasy; *e-n ~ haben* be drunk; *s-n ~ ausschlafen* sleep it off; '**2-arm** low-noise; '**2en** (27, h. *u.* sn) *Blätter, Seide, Wald*: rustle; *Wasser, Wind*: rush; *Brandung, Sturm*: roar; *Beifall*: thunder; *fig.* (*schwungvoll gehen*) sweep; *es rauscht im Radio* there's interference on the radio; '**2end** rustling *usw.*; *Fest*: grand; *Musik*: swelling; '**~filter** *m Radio*: noise filter; '**~gift** *n* narcotic (drug), F dope; '**~giftdezernat** *n* narcotics squad; '**~gifthandel** *m* drug traffic; '**~giftring** *m* drugs ring; '**~giftschieber** F *m* (dope) dealer; '**~giftsucht** *f* drug addiction; '**2giftsüchtig** addicted to drugs; '**~giftsüchtige** *m, f* drug-addict; '**~gold** *n* tinsel.

räuspern ['rɔʏspərn] (29): *sich ~* clear one's throat.

rausschmeiß|en P ['rausʃmaɪsən] kick *a p.* out; '**2er** P *m* chucker-out, *Am.* bouncer.

Raute ['rautə] *f* (15) lozenge; *bsd.* ⟁ rhomb; ⚘ rue; **2nförmig** ['~nfœrmiç] rhombic.

Razzia ['ratsja] *f* (11[1] *u.* 16[2]) (police) raid *od.* round-up.

Reagenz|glas [reˀa'gɛnts-] *n* test tube; **~papier** *n* test paper.

re-a'gieren react (*auf acc.* upon); *fig.* (*u.* ⊕) *a.* respond (to).

Reaktion [reˀak'tsjoːn] *f* (16) reaction (*a. pol.*); *fig. a.* response; **2är** [~tsjo'nɛːr] **1.** reactionary; **2.** 2 *m* (3[1]), **~ärin** *f* (16[1]) reactionary; **~sfähig-**

keit *f* responsiveness; ⚗ reactivity; **2sschnell:** ~ *sein* have fast reactions.
Reaktor *phys.* [re'ʔaktɔr] *m* (8[1]) reactor.
real [re'ʔɑ:l] real; **2gymnasium** *n*, **2schule** *f* non-classical secondary school; **2ien** [~jən] *pl.* real facts; **~isieren** [~ʔali'zi:rən] realize; **2ismus** [~'lismus] *m* (16) realism; **2ist** *m* [~'list] (12), **2istin** *f* realist; **~istisch** [~'listiʃ] realistic(ally *adv.*); **2ität** [~i'tɛ:t] *f* (16) reality; **2lohn** *m* real wages *pl.*
Rebe ['re:bə] *f* (15) vine; (*Ranke*) tendril.
Rebell [re'bɛl] *m* (12), **~in** *f* rebel; **2ieren** [~'li:rən] (*a. fig.*) rebel; **~ion** [~'jo:n] rebellion; **2isch** [~'bɛliʃ] rebellious.
'**Rebensaft** *m* grape-juice, wine.
Reb|huhn ['rɛp-] *n* partridge; **~laus** ['re:p-] *f* vine-louse, 🕮 phylloxera; '**~stock** *m* vine.
Rechen ['reçən] *m* (6) rake; 2 *v/i. u. v/t.* (25) rake.
'**Rechen|-anlage** *f* computer; '**~-aufgabe** *f*, '**~-exempel** *n* (arithmetical) problem; '**~buch** *n* arithmetic-book; '**~fehler** *m* miscalculation, mistake; '**~kunst** *f* arithmetic; '**~künstler** *m* arithmetician; '**~lehrer(in** *f*) *m* teacher of arithmetic; '**~maschine** *f* calculator; computer; '**~schaft** *f*: ~ *ablegen* give (*od.* render) (an) account (*über acc.* of); *zur* ~ *ziehen* call to account (*wegen* for); *j-m* ~ *schuldig sein* be accountable to; '**~schaftsbericht** *m* statement (of accounts), report; '**~schieber** *m* slide rule; '**~tabelle** *f* ready reckoner; '**~zentrum** *n* computer cent|re, *Am.* -er.
Recherche(n *pl.*) [rə'ʃɛrʃə(n)] *f* (15) investigation.
rechn|en[1] ['rɛçnən] *v/t. u. v/i.* (26) reckon; calculate; ~ *auf* (*acc.*) count *od.* rely (up)on, (*erwarten*) expect; ~ *mit et. Zukünftigem* reckon with; ~ *unter* (*acc.*) *od. zu* reckon (*od.* rank) among; (*v/i.*) ~ *zu* rank with; '**2en**[2] *n* arithmetic; calculation; '**2er** *m* (7), '**2erin** *f* calculator, computer (*beide a. Gerät*); *er ist ein guter* ~ he is good at figures; '**~erisch** arithmetic(al).
'**Rechnung** *f* calculation; (*Aufstellung*) bill, account; (*Waren2*) invoice; *im Gasthaus*: bill, *Am.* check; *auf* ~ on account; *laut* ~ as per account; *e-e* ~ *begleichen* balance (*od.* settle) an account; ~ *führen* keep accounts; *auf* ~ *kaufen* buy on credit; ~ *legen* render (an) account (*über acc.* of); *e-r Sache* ~ *tragen* take a th. into account (*bei* in); *es geht auf m-e* ~ it is my treat; *auf s-e* ~ *kommen bei* find one's account in; *j-m in* ~ *stellen* place to a p.'s account; et. *in* ~ *stellen od. ziehen fig.* take into account; *die* ~ *ohne den Wirt machen* reckon without one's host; *s. Strich*; '**~s-abschluß** *m* closing of accounts; '**~sführer** *m* book-keeper, accountant; ⚔ pay sergeant; '**~sführung** *f* accountancy, *Am.* accounting; '**~s-hof** *m* Audit Office; '**~sjahr** *n* financial year; '**~slegung** *f* rendering of the account; '**~sprüfer** *m* auditor; '**~swesen** *n* accounting; accountancy.
recht[1] [rɛçt] (*Ggs. link*) right; (*der Regel, den Wünschen gemäß*) right; (*gerecht*) just; (*schuldig*) due; (*echt, wirklich*) true, real; (*gesetzmäßig*) legitimate; (*richtig*) right, correct; (*geeignet, schicklich*) right, proper; *adv.* right, well; (*sehr*) very; (*ziemlich*) rather; *~e Hand* right hand; *ein ~er Narr* a regular fool; *~er Winkel* right angle; *zur ~en Zeit* at the right moment; *ganz ~!* quite (so)!, exactly!; *erst* ~ all the more; *nun erst* ~ *nicht* now less than ever; *das ist* ~ that is right; *mir ist es* ~ I don't mind, it is all right with me; *mir ist alles* ~ I am pleased with anything; *j-m* ~ *geben* agree with a p.; *es geht nicht mit ~en Dingen zu* there is something funny about it; *es geschieht ihm* ~ it serves him right; ~ *haben* be right; *es j-m* ~ *machen* please a p.; ~ *daran tun, zu inf.* do right to *inf.*; *das kommt mir gerade* ~ that comes in handy; ~ *gut* not bad; ~ *schade* a great pity; *s. behalten.*
Recht[2] [~] *n* (3) right; (*Anspruch; auf acc.*) title (to), claim (on); (*Vor2*) privilege; (*Vollmacht*) power; (*Gesetz*) law; (*Gerechtigkeit*) justice; ~ *sprechen* administer justice; *mit* ~ justly; *von ~s wegen* by rights; *das* ~ *auf s-r Seite haben* be within one's rights; ⚖ *für* ~ *erkennen* adjudge; *zu* ~ *bestehen* be valid *od.*

justified; *(wieder) zu s-m ~ kommen* come into one's own (again).

'**Rechte** 1. *f* (18) right hand; *pol.the* Right; *Boxen*: right; 2. *pol. m, f* (18) rightist, right-winger.

'**Recht·eck** *n* (3) rectangle; '**2ig** rectangular.

'**rechten** (26) dispute, argue; **~s** lawfully, by law; *(gültig)* valid.

'**recht|fertigen** justify; *(verteidigen)* defend; vindicate; '**2fertigung** *f* justification, vindication; '**~gläubig** orthodox; '**2gläubigkeit** *f* orthodoxy; '**2haber(in** *f*) *m* dogmatist; **2haberei** [~hɑːbəˈraɪ] *f* dogmatism; '**~haberisch** dogmatic(ally *adv.*); *(stur)* pigheaded.

'**rechtlich** legal, lawful; *(gerichtlich)* juridical; *(gültig)* valid; *s. redlich*; '**2keit** *f* legality, lawfulness; honesty.

recht|linig [ˈ~liːnɪç] rectilinear; '**~los** having no rights; '**~mäßig** lawful, legitimate; '**2mäßigkeit** *f* lawfulness, legitimacy.

rechts [rɛçts] on the right; *(nach ~)* (to the) right.

'**Rechts|-anspruch** *m* legal claim; '**~-anwalt** *m* lawyer, solicitor; *vor Gericht plädierender*: counsel, *Brt.* barrister-at-law, *Am.* attorney-at-law; '**~'-außen(stürmer)** *m* (6 [7]) *Fußball*: outside right; '**~befugnis** *f* competence; '**~behelf** *m* legal remedy; '**~beistand** *m* legal adviser; '**~belehrung** ⚖ *f* legal instruction; '**~beratungsstelle** *f* legal advisory board; '**~beugung** *f* perversion of justice; '**~bruch** *m* breach of law.

'**rechtschaffen** honest, righteous; '**2heit** *f* honesty, righteousness.

'**Rechtschreibung** *f* orthography.

'**Rechts|drall** ⊕ *m* right-hand twist; '**~-extremist(in** *f*) *m* right-wing extremist; '**2fähig** having legal capacity; '**~fall** *m* (law) case; '**~frage** ⚖ *f* question of law; '**~gelehrte** *m* jurist, lawyer; '**~geschäft** *n* legal transaction; '**~grund** *m* legal argument; '**2gültig** legal(ly valid); *~ machen* validate; '**~gültigkeit** *f* legality; '**~gut·achten** *n* legal opinion; **~händer** [ˈ~hɛndər] *m* (7) right-hander; '**~hilfe** *f* legal aid; '**~kraft** *f* legal force; *~ erlangen* enter into effect; '**2kräftig** legal(ly binding), valid; *Urteil*: final; *Gesetz*: effective; '**~lage** *f* legal position; '**~mittel** *n* legal remedy; (right to) appeal; '**~nachfolger** *m* successor in interest; '**2orientiert** *pol.* right-wing; '**~pflege** *f* administration of justice; '**~pfleger** *m* judicial officer, paralegal.

Rechtsprechung [ˈ~ʃprɛçʊŋ] *f* jurisdiction, administration of justice.

'**Rechts|radikale** *m* rightist; '**~schutz** *m* legal protection; '**~schutzversicherung** *f* legal costs insurance; '**~sprache** *f* legal terminology; '**~spruch** *m* legal decision; *in Zivilsachen*: judg(e)ment; *in Strafsachen*: sentence; '**~staat** *m* constitutional state; '**2staatlich** constitutional; '**~staatlichkeit** *f* rule of law; '**~stellung** *f* legal status; '**~streit** *m* action, lawsuit; '**~titel** *m* legal title; '**2'um!** right face!; '**2-unfähig** (legally) disabled; '**~-unfähigkeit** *f* (legal) disability; '**2'-unwirksam** (legally) ineffective; '**~'-unwirksamkeit** *f* ineffectiveness; '**2verbindlich** (legally) binding *(für* on); '**~verdreher** *m* pettifogging lawyer; '**~verfahren** *n* legal procedure; *(Prozeß)* (legal) proceedings *pl.*; '**~verkehr** *m*: *in Frankreich ist ~* in France they drive on the right; '**~verletzung** *f* infringement; '**~weg** *m* course of law; *den ~ beschreiten* go to law; '**2widrig** illegal; '**~widrigkeit** *f* illegality; '**2wirksam** *s. rechtskräftig*; '**~wissenschaft** *f* jurisprudence.

'**recht|wink(e)lig** right-angled, 🕮 rectangular; '**~zeitig** opportune, timely, well-timed, seasonable; *adv.* in time.

Reck [rɛk] *n* (3) horizontal bar.

Recke [ˈrɛkə] *m* (13) hero, warrior.

recken [ˈ~n] (25) stretch; *mit Geräten*: *a.* rack; *den Hals (nach et.) ~* crane one's neck (to see a th.).

Redakt|eur [redakˈtøːr] *m* (3[1]) editor; **~ion** [~ˈtsjoːn] *f* *Tätigkeit*: editorship; *Personal*: editorial staff; *Büro*: editorial office; *(Fassung)* editing, draft(ing); **2ionell** [~tsjoˈnɛl] editorial.

Rede [ˈreːdə] *f* (15) speech; *(Ansprache) a.* address; *(~weise)* language; *(Gespräch)* conversation, talk; *s. fallen*; *gr. direkte ~* direct speech; *s. halten, schwingen*; *~ (und Antwort) stehen* give an account *(über acc.* of), answer (for); *die in ~ stehende Person* the person in question; *j-n zur ~ stellen* call to account (*über acc.* for), take *a p.* to task (*wegen gen.* for); *wovon ist die ~?* what are you talking about?; *davon kann keine ~ sein!* that's out of the question; (*aber*) *keine ~!* by no means!; *es ist nicht der ~ wert* it is not worth speaking of, (*macht nichts*) never mind!; '**~freiheit** *f* freedom of speech; '**~gabe** *f*, '**~gewandtheit** *f* eloquence; '**≈gewandt** eloquent; '**~kunst** *f* rhetoric; '**≈n** (26) speak, talk (*mit* to); *mit sich ~ lassen* listen to reason; *von sich ~ machen* cause a stir; *j-m ins Gewissen ~* appeal to a p.'s conscience; *du hast gut ~* it is easy for you to talk; *s. Wort.*

'**Redens·art** *f* phrase, expression; (*Spracheigenheit*) idiom; (*sprichwörtliche ~*) saying.

'**Rede|schwall** *m* flood of words; '**~teil** *m* part of speech; '**~wendung** *f s. Redensart.*

redigieren [redi'gi:rən] edit.

redlich ['re:tliç] honest, upright; '**≈keit** *f* honesty, probity, integrity.

Redner ['re:dnər] *m* (7) speaker (*a.* '**~in** *f*); *bsd. geschickter*: orator; '**~bühne** *f* platform; '**≈isch** rhetorical; '**~pult** *n* speaker's desk.

redselig ['re:tze:liç] talkative, garrulous; '**≈keit** *f* talkativeness.

reduzieren [redu'tsi:rən] reduce (*auf acc.* to); *sich ~* be reduced.

Redu'zierstück ⊕ *n* adapter, reducer.

Reede ⚓ ['re:də] *f* (15) roads *pl.*, roadstead; '**~r** *m* (7) shipowner; **~'rei** *f* shipping company.

reell [re'ˀɛl] real; *Firma*: solid, respectable; *Preis, Bedienung*: fair; *~ bedienen* (*bedient werden*) give (get) good value for one's money.

Reep ⚓ [re:p] *n* (3) rope.

Refer|at [refe'rɑ:t] *n* (3) report; *Schule*: essay; (*Dienststelle*) (departmental) section; *ein ~ halten* (*verlesen*) read a paper; **~endar** [~rɛn'dɑ:r] *m* (3[1]) junior barrister *attending the courts and thus qualifying for the title of 'Assessor'*; law clerk; **~ent** [~'rɛnt] *m* (12) official in charge (of a departmental section); (*Berichterstatter*) reporter; *parl. usw.* referee; (*Sachverständiger*) expert; **~enz** [~'rɛnts] *f* (16) reference; **≈ieren** [~'ri:rən] *v/t. u. v/i.* report (*über acc.* on); (give a) lecture (on).

reffen ⚓ ['rɛfən] (25) reef.

reflektieren [reflɛk'ti:rən] *v/t. u. v/i.* reflect; *~ auf* (*acc.*) have *a th.* in view, want (*od.* wish) to have.

Reflektor [re'flɛktɔr] *m* (8[1]) reflector.

Reflex [re'flɛks] *m* (3[2]) reflex; **~bewegung** *f* reflex action; **~ion** [~'ksjo:n] *f* (16) (*Widerschein*) reflex; (*Spiegelbild*) reflection; **≈iv** *gr.* [~'ksi:f] reflexive.

Reform [re'fɔrm] *f* (16) reform; **~ation** [~a'tsjo:n] *f* reformation; **~ator** [~'mɑ:tɔr] *m* (8[1]) reformer; **≈bedürftig** in need of reform; **~bestrebungen** *f/pl.* reformatory efforts; **~haus** *n* health (food) shop (*Am.* store); **≈ieren** [~'mi:rən] reform; **~ierte** [~'mi:rtə] *m* (18) member of the Reformed Church, Calvinist; **~kost** *f* health food(s *pl.*).

Refrain [rə'frɛ̃] *m* (11) refrain, burden.

Regal [re'gɑ:l] *n* (3[1]) shelves *pl.*; **~brett** *n* shelf.

Regatta [re'gata] *f* (16[2]) regatta, boat-race.

rege ['re:gə] active, brisk; lively; *fig. ~ werden* be stirred up, arise.

Regel ['re:gəl] *f* (15) rule; (*Vorschrift*) regulation; ⚕ menses *pl.*; *in der ~* as a rule; '**~getriebe** ⊕ *n* (*stufenloses ~* infinitely) variable speed transmission; '**≈los** irregular; (*unordentlich*) disorderly; '**~losigkeit** *f* irregularity; '**≈mäßig** regular; (*~ wiederkehrend*) periodical; '**~mäßigkeit** *f* regularity; '**≈n** (29) regulate, ⊕ *a.* control; (*ordnen*) arrange, settle; (*steuern*) control; '**≈'recht** regular; '**~ung** *f* regulation, ⊕ *a.* control; arrangement, settlement; control; '**≈widrig** irregular; *Sport*: foul; '**~widrigkeit** *f* irregularity; *Sport*: foul.

regen[1] ['re:gən] (25, *a. sich ~*) move, stir.

Regen[2] [~] *m* (6) rain; *fig. vom ~ in die Traufe kommen* jump out of the frying-pan into the fire; *saurer ~* acid rain; '**≈-arm** with low rainfall; '**~bogen** *m* rainbow; '**~bogenfarben** *f/pl.* colo(u)rs of the rainbow; '**~bogenhaut** *anat. f* iris; '**≈dicht** rainproof.

regenerier|en [regenə'ri:rən] regenerate; **≈ung** *f* regeneration.

ˈ**Regen|guß** *m* downpour; ˈ**~haut** *f* plastic mac; ˈ**~mantel** *m* raincoat; ˈ**~menge** *f* rainfall; ˈ**~pfeifer** *m* *Vogel*: plover; ˈ**&reich** rainy; ˈ**~schauer** *m* shower of rain; ˈ**~schirm** *m* umbrella.

Regent [reˈgɛnt] *m* (12), **~in** *f* (16¹) regent; **~schaft** *f* regency.

ˈ**Regen|tag** *m* rainy day; ˈ**~tropfen** *m* raindrop; ˈ**~wasser** *n* rain-water; ˈ**~wetter** *n* rainy weather; ˈ**~wolke** *f* rainy cloud; ˈ**~wurm** *m* earthworm; ˈ**~zeit** *f* rainy season.

Regie [reˈʒiː] *f* (15) (*a. thea.*) management, (*a. Film*) direction; (*Staatsmonopol*) state monopoly, régie (*fr.*); ~ *führen* (*bei*) direct; **~assistent** *m* assistant director; **~fehler** *m* mistake in the arrangements; **~kosten** *pl.* overhead (expenses); **~pult** *n* *Radio*: mixing desk; *TV*: control desk.

regieren [reˈgiːrən] *v/t.* govern (*a. gr.*), rule; (*leiten*) control, manage; *v/i.* rule, reign (*a. fig.*).

Reˈgierung *f* government, *Am.* (*Präsident u. Kabinett; deren Amtszeit*) administration; (*~szeit*) *e-s Fürsten*: reign; *unter der ~ des ...* under (*od.* in) the reign of ...; **~s...** *mst* governmental; **~s-antritt** *m* accession (to the throne); **~sbeamte** *m* government official; **~s-erklärung** *f* policy statement; **~s-form** *f* form of government, regime; **~sgewalt** *f* governmental power; **~s-lager** *n* government benches *pl.*; **~smannschaft** *f* cabinet; **~s-partei** *f* ruling party; **~ssprecher** *m* government spokesman; **~swechsel** *m* change of government.

Regime [reˈʒiːm] *n* (11) regime; **~kritiker** *m* dissident.

Regiment [regiˈmɛnt] *n* (3) rule; (1) ⚔ regiment; *das ~ haben od. führen* rule, command; **~s...** regimental.

Region [reˈgjoːn] *f* (16) region; **&al** [~gjoˈnaːl] regional; **~alverkehr** *m* regional transport.

Regisseur [reʒiˈsøːr] *m* (3¹) *thea.* stage-manager *od.* -director; *Film*: director.

Regist|er [reˈgistər] *n* (7) register (*a. der Orgel*), record; (*Inhaltsverzeichnis*) index; *ein ~ ziehen* pull a stop; **~rator** [~ˈstraːtɔr] *m* (8¹) recorder, registrar; **~ratur** [~straˈtuːr] *f* (16) registry.

registrier|en [regisˈtriːrən] register (*a. fig.*); *a.* ⊕ record; **&kasse** *f* cash-register; **&ung** *f* registration; recording.

Reglement [regləˈmɑ̃] *n* (11) regulation(s *pl.*).

Regler ⊕ [ˈreːglər] *m* (7) regulator; governor, control(l)er.

reglos [ˈreːkloːs] motionless.

regne|n [ˈregnən] (26) rain; *es regnet in Strömen* it is pouring with rain; ˈ**~risch** rainy.

Regreß [reˈgrɛs] *m* (4) recourse; **&pflichtig** liable to recourse.

regsam [ˈreːkzaːm] active, quick, live; ˈ**&keit** *f* activity.

regulär [reguˈlɛːr] regular.

regulier|bar [~ˈliːrbaːr] adjustable; **~en** regulate, adjust; **&ung** *f* regulation, adjustment.

Regung [ˈreːguŋ] *f* motion; (*Gefühls&*) emotion; (*Anwandlung*) impulse; ˈ**&slos** motionless.

Reh [reː] *n* (3) roe, deer; *weibliches*: doe.

rehabilitier|en [rehabiliˈtiːrən] rehabilitate; **&ung** *f* rehabilitation.

ˈ**Reh|bock** *m* roebuck; ˈ**~braten** *m* roast venison; ˈ**&farben** fawn--colo(u)red; ˈ**~geiß** *f* doe; ˈ**~kalb** *n*, ˈ**~kitz** *n* fawn; ˈ**~keule** *f* leg of venison; ˈ**~posten** *m/pl.* buck-shot; ˈ**~rücken** *m* saddle of venison.

Reibahle [ˈraɪpˀaːlə] *f* reamer.

Reibe [ˈraɪbə] *f* (15), **Reibeisen** [ˈraɪpˀaɪzən] *n* grater.

reib|en [ˈraɪbən] (30) rub; (*zer~*) grate; *Farbe*: grind; (*klein od. fein ~*) pulverize; *sich an j-m ~* quarrel with a p.; *s. Nase, wund*; **&erei** [~əˈraɪ] *f* (constant) friction, squabbling; ˈ**&ung** *f* friction (*a. fig.*); ˈ**&ungsfläche** *f* friction surface; ˈ**~ungslos** frictionless; *fig.* smooth.

reich¹ [raɪç] rich (*an dat.* in); (*vermögend*) wealthy; (*~lich*) copious, ample; ˈ**&e** *m, f* (18) rich man (woman); *die ~n pl.* the rich.

Reich² [~] *n* (3) empire; (*König&; a. Pflanzen&, Tier&*) kingdom; *rhet. od. fig.* realm; *hist. das Deutsche Reich* the (German) Reich.

reichen [ˈraɪçən] (25) *v/t.* reach; *j-m et.*: reach, hand, pass; *s. Hand, Wasser*; *v/i.* reach (*bis* to); (*genügen*) suffice, do, last; *das reicht!* that will do!

reichhaltig [ˈ~haltiç] rich; (*über-*

reich) abundant, copious; '**⁀keit** *f* richness; abundance, copiousness.

'**reichlich** *adj.* ample; abundant, copious, plentiful; *vor su.* plenty of; *adv.* (*ziemlich*) rather, fairly, pretty, F plenty.

'**Reichtum** *m* (1²) riches *pl.*, wealth; (*Überfluß*) opulence, abundance, wealth (*an dat.* of).

'**Reichweite** *f* (15) reach; ⚔, ✈ range; *in* ~ within reach.

reif[1] [raɪf] ripe, mature (*beide a. fig.*).

Reif[2] [~] *m* (3, *o. pl.*) (*Frost*) hoar-frost, white frost.

Reif[3] [~] *m* (3) hoop; ring.

'**Reife** *f* (15) ripeness, maturity.

'**reifen**[1] *v/i.* (25) ripen, mature (*beide a. fig.*); '~[2] *zu Reif*[2]: *es reift* there is a hoar-frost *od.* white frost.

'**Reifen**[3] *m* (6) hoop; ring; (*Rad*⁀) tire, *Brt. a.* tyre; '**~panne** *f*, '**~schaden** *mot. m* puncture, *Am.* blowout; '**~wechsel** *m* change of tire(s *pl.*).

'**Reife|prüfung** *f* leaving-examination, matriculation (examination); '**~zeugnis** *n* (school-)leaving certificate, *Brt.* "A" level G.C.E. (= General Certificate of Education).

'**reiflich** mature, careful; *nach ~er Überlegung* upon mature reflection.

'**Reifrock** *m* crinoline.

Reigen ['raɪgən] *m* (6) round dance; *fig. den ~ eröffnen* open the ball.

Reihe ['raɪə] *f* (15) row; (*Linie*) line; *hintereinander*: file; *nebeneinander*: rank; (*Sitz*⁀) row (of seats), tier; (*Folge*) series, succession; *von Bergen usw.*: range; (*Anzahl*) number; *nach der ~, der ~ nach* in turn, by turns; *ich bin an der ~* it is my turn; *aus der ~ tanzen* have it one's own way; *in Reih' und Glied* in rank and file; *an die ~ kommen* have one's turn; '**⁀n** (25) range, rank; *Perlen usw.*: string; '**~nfertigung** *f* serial production; '**~nfolge** *f* succession, sequence; *alphabetische ~* alphabetical order; '**~nhaus** *n* terrace house, *Am.* row (*od.* attached) house; '**~nschaltung** ⚡ *f* series connection; '**~n-untersuchung** ⚕ *f* mass examination; '**⁀nweise** in rows.

Reiher ['raɪər] *m* (7) heron.

Reim [raɪm] *m* (3) rhyme; '**⁀en** *v/t.*, *v/i.*, *v/refl.* (25) rhyme (*auf acc.* to, with); *nur v/refl. fig.* agree (with); '**⁀los** blank, rhymeless; '**~schmied** *m* rhym(est)er.

rein[1] [raɪn] **1.** *adj.* pure (*a. fig.*); (*sauber*) clean; (*klar*) clear (*a. Haut, Gewissen*); *Gewinn*: net; *Wahrheit*: plain; (*bloß*) mere, sheer; *fig. die Luft ist ~* the coast is clear; *~ machen* clean (up); *fig. ~en Tisch machen* make a clean sweep of it; *fig. j-m ~en Wein einschenken* tell a p. the plain truth; *ins ~e bringen* clear up, settle; *mit j-m ins ~e kommen* come to terms with a p.; *ins ~e schreiben* make a fair copy of; *fig. ~waschen* whitewash; *s. Gewissen, Mund*; **2.** *adv.* (*gänzlich*) quite; *~ gar nichts* nothing at all; *~ unmöglich* quite impossible.

rein[2] [raɪn] F *s. herein(...), hinein(...)*.

Reineclaude [rɛnə'klo:də] ⚘ *f* (15) greengage.

'**Rein|-ertrag** *m* net proceeds *pl.*; '**~fall** F *m* F letdown; F frost, sell, washout; '**~gewicht** *n* net weight; '**~gewinn** *m* net (*od.* clear) profit; '**~heit** *f* purity; cleanness.

'**reinig|en** (25) clean, cleanse (*von* of); *a. fig.* purify; *metall.* refine; *Wolle*: scour; *s. chemisch*; '**⁀ung** *f* clean(s)ing; *a. fig.* purification; *~ und Färberei* cleaners and dyers *pl.*; '**⁀ungs-anstalt** *f* (dry) cleaners *pl.*; '**⁀ungsmittel** *n* detergent, cleansing agent.

'**Reinkultur** *f* pure culture (*a. fig.*); *fig. in ~* unadulterated.

'**reinlegen** *s. hereinlegen.*

'**reinlich** *P.*: cleanly; *S.*: clean; '**⁀keit** *f* cleanliness; neatness.

'**Rein|machefrau** *f* cleaning woman, charwoman; '**⁀rassig** pedigree(d), purebred; *Pferd*: thoroughbred; '**~schrift** *f* fair copy; '**⁀seiden** all-silk; '**⁀waschen** *fig.* whitewash, clear.

Reis[1] [raɪs] *m* (4, *o. pl.*) rice; **~**[2] *n* (2) twig, sprig; (*Pfropf*⁀) scion; '**~-auflauf** *m* rice pudding; '**~brei** *m* rice boiled in milk.

Reise ['raɪzə] *f* (15) journey; ⚓, ✈ voyage; (*längere, bsd. Auslands*⁀) travel; (*Rund*⁀) tour; *mst. kürzere*: trip; (*Überfahrt*) passage; '**~-apotheke** *f* tourist's (*od.* portable) medicine-case; '**~bekanntschaft** *f* travel(l)ing acquaintance; '**~büro** *n* tourist(s') office, travel agency, *Am.* tourist(s') bureau; '**~diplomatie**

pol. f shuttle-diplomacy; '**⁀fertig** ready to start; '**~fieber** *n* travel fever; '**~führer** *m* guide; (*Buch*) guide (-book); '**~gefährte** *m*, '**~gefährtin** *f* fellow-travel(l)er; '**~gepäck** *n* luggage, *Am.* baggage; '**~geschwindigkeit** *f* cruising speed; '**~gesellschaft** *f* tourist party; '**~handbuch** *n* guide(-book); '**~koffer** *m* trunk; *kleiner*: suitcase; '**~kosten** *pl.* travel(l)ing expenses; '**~kostenzuschuß** *m* travel(ling) allowance; '**~leiter** *m* courier; '**⁀lustig** fond of travel(l)ing; **~mobil** ['~mobi:l] *n* (3[1]) camper, *Am.* mobile home; '**⁀müde** travel-weary; '**⁀n** (27, sn) travel, journey; ~ *nach* go to; ~ *über* (*acc.*) go by way of, go via; *wir* ~ *morgen* we (shall) start tomorrow; *fig. auf et.* ~ trade on; ✝ ~ *in* (*dat.*) travel in; '**~nde** *m, f* (18) (✝ commercial) travel(l)er; *in der Bahn usw.*: passenger; (*Vergnügungs*⁀) tourist; '**~paß** *m* passport; '**~prospekt** *m* travel brochure; '**~route** *f* route, itinerary; '**~scheck** *m* traveller's cheque, *Am.* traveler's check; '**~schreibmaschine** *f* portable typewriter; '**~schriftsteller** *m* travel writer; '**~tasche** *f* travel(l)ing (*od.* overnight) bag, holdall; '**~unterlagen** *f/pl.* travel documents; '**~veranstalter** *m* tour operator; '**~verkehr** *m* tourist traffic; '**~wecker** *m* travel(l)ing alarm (clock); '**~zeit** *f* tourist season; '**~ziel** *n* destination.

Reisig ['raɪzɪç] *n* (3) brushwood; '**~besen** *m* birch-broom.

'**Reiß**|'**-aus** *m*: ~ *nehmen* take to one's heels; '**~brett** *n* drawing-board; '**⁀en** **1.** (30) *v/t.* tear; (*zer*~) *a.* rip; (*zerren*) tug; (*ziehen*) pull; (*weg*~) snatch; *an sich* ~ seize, *Macht usw.*: *a.* usurp; *entzwei*~ tear (*od.* rip) in two; *sich* ~ (*ritzen*) scratch o.s. (*an dat.* with); *sich* ~ *um* scramble for; *s. Possen, Witz, Zote*; *v/i.* (sn) tear, burst, split; *Faden usw.*: break, snap; ~ *an* (*dat.*) tear at; *die Geduld riß mir* I lost (all) patience; *es reißt mir in* ... (*dat.*) I have racking pains in ...; **2.** ⁀ *n* (6) bursting, rending; *des Fadens*: break(ing); *in Gliedern*: acute pains *pl.*, *engS.* rheumatism; *Sport*: snatch; '**⁀end** rapid; *Tier*: rapacious; *Schmerz*: acute, violent; *s. Absatz*; '**~er** *m* thriller; box-office success; '**~feder** *f* drawing-pen; '**~festigkeit** *f* tensile strength; '**~leine** *f* rip cord; '**~nagel** *m* drawing-pin, *Am.* thumbtack; '**~schiene** *f* T-square; '**~verschluß** *m* zip fastener, *bsd. Am.* zip(per); '**~wolle** *f* reprocessed wool; '**~zahn** *m* fang, canine tooth; '**~zeug** *n* drawing instruments *pl.*; '**~zwecke** *f s. Reißnagel.*

Reit... *mst* riding-...; '**~-anzug** *m* riding-habit; '**~bahn** *f* riding-ground.

reiten ['raɪtən] (30, sn) ride, go on horseback; '**~d** on horseback.

'**Reiter** *m* (7) rider, horseman; *Polizei*, ⚔ trooper; *Kartei*: tab; **~ei** [~'raɪ] *f* cavalry, horse; '**~in** *f* (16[1]) horsewoman.

'**Reit**|**gerte** *f* riding-whip; '**~hose** *f* (riding-)breeches *pl.*; '**~knecht** *m* groom; '**~kunst** *f* horsemanship; '**~peitsche** *f* riding-whip; '**~pferd** *n* saddle-horse; '**~schule** *f* riding-school; '**~sport** *m* equestrian sport; '**~stiefel** *m/pl.* riding-boots; '**~weg** *m* bridle-path.

Reiz [raɪts] *m* (3[2]) charm, attraction; (*Verlockung*) allurement; (*Erregung*) thrill, *störend*: irritation; *physiol.* stimulus; '**⁀bar** irritable, touchy; '**~barkeit** *f* irritability; '**⁀en** (27) irritate (*a.* ⚕ *entzünden*); (*aufreizen*) provoke; (*ärgern*) nettle; (*lokken*) entice, attract, tempt; (*bezaubern*) charm; *Kartenspiel*: bid; ⚕ (*anregen*) stimulate; *s. a. an*~; '**⁀end** charming, lovely; '**~husten** *m* dry cough; '**⁀los** unattractive; '**~mittel** *n* stimulus, incentive; ⚕ stimulant, *störend*: irritant; '**~stoff** ⚗ *m* irritant; '**~ung** *f* irritation (*a.* ⚕); provocation; (*Anregung*) stimulation; '**⁀voll** charming, attractive; fascinating; '**~wäsche** *f* F flimsies *pl.*, *mit Spitzen*: frillies *pl.*; '**~wort** *n* (1[2]) emotive word.

rekapitulieren [rekapitu'li:rən] recapitulate.

rekeln ['re:kəln]: *sich* ~ loll, lounge.

Reklamation [reklama'tsjo:n] *f* complaint; protest, objection.

Reklame [re'klɑ:mə] *f* (15) advertising; propaganda, publicity; *prahlerische*: puff; (*Schaufenster*⁀ *u. fig.*) window-dressing; ~ *machen* advertise, *lebhaft*: F boost (*beide*: *für et.* a th.); **~-artikel** *m* advertising article; **~büro** *n* advertising agency; **~chef** *m* advertising manager; **~-**

fachmann *m* advertising expert; **~feldzug** *m s. Werbefeldzug*; **~film** *m* advertising film; **~fläche** *f* advertising space; **~rummel** *m sl.* ballyhoo; **~trick** *m* advertising stunt; *s. a. Werbe...*

rekla'mieren *v/t.* claim; *v/i.* complain (*wegen* about).

rekognoszieren [rekɔgnɔs'tsi:rən] reconnoit|re, *Am.* -er.

rekonstru'ieren reconstruct.

Rekonvaleszen|t [rekɔnvalɛs'tsɛnt] *m* (18), **~tin** *f* (16[1]) convalescent; **~z** *f* (16) convalescence.

Rekord [re'kɔrt] *m* (3[1]) record; *s. aufstellen*; **~besuch** *m* record attendance; **~-ernte** *f* bumper crop; **~halter** *m*, **~-inhaber** *m* record holder; **~lauf** *m* record run; **~versuch** *m* record attempt; **~zeit** *f* record time.

Rekrut ⚔ [re'kru:t] *m* (12) recruit; **≗ieren** [~kru'ti:rən] ⚔ recruit; *sich ~ aus* be recruited from; **~ierung** [~'ti:ruŋ] *f* recruitment.

Rektor ['rɛktɔr] *m* (8[1]) headmaster, *Am.* principal; *univ.* rector, vice-chancellor, *Am.* president; **~at** [~to'rɑ:t] *n* (3) headmaster's *etc.* office; headmastership; rectorship.

Relais [rə'lɛ:] *n inv.* relay.

relativ [rela'ti:f] relative; **≗ität** [~tivi'tɛ:t] *f* (16) relativity; **≗satz** *gr.* [~'ti:f-] *m* relative clause.

Releg|ation [relega'tsjo:n] *f* expulsion; **≗ieren** [~'gi:rən] expel, send down.

Relief [rel'jɛf] *n* (11) relief.

Religion [reli'gjo:n] *f* (16) religion; **~sbekenntnis** *n* (religious) profession; **~sfreiheit** *f* freedom of worship, religious liberty; **~sgemeinschaft** *f* religious community; **≗slos** irreligious; **~s-unterricht** *m* scripture.

religi|ös [~'gjø:s] religious; **≗osität** [~gjozi'tɛ:t] *f* religiousness.

Reling ⚓ ['re:liŋ] *f* (16) rail.

Reliquie [re'li:kvjə] *f* (15) relic; **~nschrein** *m* reliquary.

Reminiszenz [reminis'tsɛnts] *f* (16) reminiscence.

Remis [rə'mi:] *n* (*inv. od.* 16) *Schach*: draw.

Remise [re'mi:zə] *f* (15) coach-house.

Remit|tenden [remi'tɛndən] *pl.* returns; **≗'tieren** return, remit.

Remoulade(nsoße) [remu'lɑ:də-] *f* remoulade.

rempeln ['rɛmpəln] (29) jostle, bump (into).

Ren [re:n] *n* (3) reindeer.

Renaissance [rənɛ'sɑ̃s] *f* (15) renaissance.

Rendezvous [rɑ̃de'vu:] *n inv.* rendezvous (*a.* ⚔), date.

Rendite [rɛn'di:tə] ⚕ *f* (15) yield.

reniten|t [reni'tɛnt] refractory; **≗z** *f* (16) refractoriness.

Renn|bahn ['rɛn-] (race-)course, race track; *mot.* speedway; **'~boot** *n* race-boat; **'≗en** (30) *v/i.* (sn) *u. v/t.* run; (*wett~*) race, (*rasen*) *a.* dash, rush; *Messer usw. durch den Leib ~* run *one's knife etc.* through; *s. Verderben*; **'~en** *n* running; (*Wett≗*) race; (*Einzel≗*) heat; *totes ~* dead heat; *das ~ machen* win the race; *fig.* make the running; **'~er** F *m* (*Erfolg*) hit; ⚕ front-runner product; **'~fahrer** *m* racing-driver; **'~lenker** *m am Fahrrad*: dropped handlebars *pl.*; **'~pferd** *n* race-horse; **'~platz** *m s. Rennbahn*; **'~platzbesucher** *m* race-goer; **'~rad** *n* racing bicycle, racer; **'~schi** *m* race ski; **'~schuh** *m* spike(d shoe); **'~sport** *m* racing; *the* turf; **'~stall** *m* racing-stud; **'~strecke** *f* course, (race) track, circuit; **'~tier** *n s. Ren*; **'~wagen** *m* racing-car.

Renom|mee [renɔ'me:] *n* (11) reputation; **≗'mieren** boast, brag (*mit* of); **≗'miert** renowned; **~'mist** *m* (12) braggart, boaster.

renovier|en [reno'vi:rən] do up, renovate; *Innenraum*: redecorate; **≗ung** *f* renovation; redecoration.

rentab|el [rɛn'tɑ:bəl] profitable, paying, lucrative; **≗ilität** [~tabili'tɛ:t] *f* (16) profitability; **≗ilitätsgrenze** *f* breakeven point.

Rent|e ['rɛntə] (15) (*Alters≗*) (old-age) pension; *Versicherung u. Börse*: annuity; (*Zins≗, Pacht≗*) rent; **'~enalter** *n* retirement age; **'~enbrief** *m* annuity bond; **'~en-empfänger(in** *f*) *m s. Rentner*; **'~enversicherung** *f* pension scheme; **~ier** [~'tje:] *m* (11) man of private means; **≗ieren** [~'ti:rən] *v/refl.* pay, be profitable; **'~ner** *m* (7) (old age) pensioner.

Reorganis|ation [reʔɔrganiza'tsjo:n] *f* reorganization; **≗ieren** [~'zi:rən] reorganize.

Reparation [repara'tsjo:n] *f* reparation; *~en leisten* make reparations; **~szahlungen** *f/pl.* reparation payments.

Reparatur [~'tu:r] *f* (16) repair; *in ~* under repair; **2bedürftig** in need of repair; **2fähig** repairable; **~kosten** *pl.* cost of repairs; **~werkstatt** *f* repair-shop.

repa'rieren repair, *Am. a.* fix.

repatriier|en [repatri'ʔi:rən] repatriate; **2ung** *f* repatriation.

Repertoire *thea.* [repɛrto'a:r] *n* (11) repertoire, repertory; **~stück** *n* stock-piece.

repetier|en [repe'ti:rən] repeat; **2-gewehr** *n* magazine rifle, repeater; **2-uhr** *f* repeater.

Replik ⚖ [re'pli:k] *f* (16) reply.

Report [re'pɔrt] *m* (3) report; ✝ contango.

Reportage [repɔr'ta:ʒə] *f* (15) reporting; report, (running) commentary, *Am. a.* coverage.

Reporter [re'pɔrtər] *m* (7) reporter.

Repräsent|ant [reprɛzɛn'tant] *m* (12), **~antin** *f* (16¹) representative; **~ation** [~ta'tsjo:n] *f* representation; **2ieren** [~'ti:rən] represent.

Repressalie [reprɛ'sa:ljə] *f* (15) reprisal; *~n ergreifen* make reprisal(s) (*gegen* on).

repressiv [reprɛ'si:f] repressive.

Reprodu|ktion [reproduk'tsjo:n] *f* reproduction; **2'zieren** reproduce.

Reptil [rɛp'ti:l] *n* (3¹ *u.* 8²) reptile.

Republik [repu'bli:k] *f* (16) republic; **~aner** [~bli'ka:nər] *m* (7), **2anisch** [~'ka:niʃ] republican.

requirieren [rekvi'ri:rən] requisition.

Requisit [~'zi:t] *n* (5) requisite; *thea. ~en pl.* properties *pl.*, F props; **~ion** [~zi'tsjo:n] *f* (16) requisition.

Reservat [rezɛr'va:t] *n* (3) reservation; (*Recht*) prerogative.

Reserve [re'zɛrvə] *f* (15) reserve; **~fonds** *m* reserve-fund; **~-offizier** *m* reserve officer; **~rad** *mot. n* spare wheel; **~speicher** *m Computer*: reserve memory.

reserv|ieren [~'vi:rən] reserve; *~ lassen* book; **~iert** *adj.* reserved (*a. fig.*); **2ist** [~'vist] *m* (12) reservist; **2oir** [~vo'a:r] *n* (11) reservoir.

Resid|enz [rezi'dɛnts] *f* (16) residence; **2ieren** [~'di:rən] reside.

Resign|ation [rezigna'tsjo:n] *f* resignation; **2ieren** [~'gni:rən] resign.

resolut [rezo'lu:t] resolute.

Resonanz [rezo'nants] *f* resonance (*a. fig.*); **~boden** *m* sounding-board.

resozialisier|en [rezotsjali'si:rən] rehabilitate; **2ung** *f* rehabilitation.

Respekt [re'spɛkt] *m* (3), **2ieren** [~'ti:rən] respect; *s. verschaffen*; **2abel** [~'ta:bəl] respectable; **2los** irreverent; **~losigkeit** irreverence; **~s-person** *f* person held in respect; *angesehene*: notability; **2voll** respectful; **2widrig** disrespectful.

Ressentiment [rɛsɑ̃ti'mɑ̃] *n* (11) resentment, grudge; prejudice.

Ressort [rɛ'so:r] *n* (11) department; *das fällt nicht in mein ~* that is not in my province.

Rest [rɛst] *m* (3¹) rest; ✝ balance; (*Über2*) remnant; (*Restbestand*) remainder; *bsd.* ⚗, ⚖ residue; (*Speise2*) left-over; *sterbliche ~e pl.* mortal remains; F *j-m den ~ geben* finish a p.

Restaur|ant [rɛsto'rɑ̃] *n* (11) restaurant; **~ation** *f* [~taʊra'tsjo:n] restoration; [~tora'tsjo:n] (*Lokal*) restaurant; **2ieren** [~taʊ'ri:rən] restore.

'**Rest|bestand** *m* remainder; ⚗ residue; '**2lich** remaining, residual; '**2los** complete, total; *adv. fig. a.* entirely, perfectly; '**~risiko** *n* final risk; '**~zahlung** *f* payment of balance.

Resul|tat [rezul'ta:t] *n* (3) result; *Sport*: score; **2'tieren** result (*aus* from).

Resüm|ee [rezy'me:] *n* (11) résumé (*fr.*), summary; **2ieren** [~'mi:rən] recapitulate.

retirieren [reti'ri:rən] retreat.

Retorte [re'tɔrtə] *f* (15) retort; **~n-baby** *n* test-tube baby.

Retour... [re'tu:r] return.

rett|en ['rɛtən] (26) save, rescue (*aus, vor dat.* from); (*befreien*) deliver; *Güter*: salvage; *j-m das Leben ~* save a p.'s life; *sich ~* save o.s., escape; '**2er** *m* (7) saver, deliverer; (*Heiland*) Savio(u)r.

Rettich ['rɛtiç] *m* (3¹) radish.

Rettung ['rɛtuŋ] *f* rescue; deliverance; (*Entkommen*) escape; (*Bergung*) salvage; *eccl.* salvation; *er ist m-e einzige ~* he is my only hope; '**~s-aktion** *f* rescue operation; '**~s-anker** *m* sheet-anchor; '**~sboje** *f* life-buoy; '**~sboot** *n* life-boat; '**~s-gerät** *n* life-saving equipment *od.*

device; '~**sgürtel** *m* life-belt; '~**sleine** *f* life-line; '♀**slos** past help, irremediable, irretrievable; '~**smannschaft** *f* rescue party; '~**smedaille** *f* life-saving medal; '~**sring** *m* life-belt; '~**sversuch** *m* rescue attempt.

retuschieren [retu'ʃi:rən] retouch.

Reu|e ['rɔʏə] *f* (15) repentance (*über acc.* of), remorse (at); '♀**elos** remorseless; '♀**en** *v/t.* (25): *et. reut mich* I am sorry about (*od.* for) a th.; *vgl. be*~; '♀**evoll,** '♀(**müt**)**ig** repentant, remorseful.

Revanche [re'vɑ̃ʃə] *f* (15) revenge; ~**partie** *f* return match.

revan'chieren: *sich* ~ take one's revenge; reciprocate (*mit e-r Gegengabe* with); *sich für et.* ~ return.

Reverenz [reve'rɛnts] *f* (16) reverence.

Revers [re'vɛrs] *m* (4) bond; (*Erklärung*) declaration; *e-r Münze*: reverse; (*Rockaufschlag*) lapel.

revidieren [revi'di:rən] revise; ✝ audit, check.

Revier [re'vi:r] *n* (3[1]) district; ⚔ dispensary; *s. Jagd*♀; ~**stube** ⚔ *f* sick room.

Revision [revi'zjo:n] *f* revision, revisal; ✝ auditing; ⚖ appeal (on a question of law); ⚖ ~ *einlegen* lodge an appeal.

Revisor [~'vi:zɔr] *m* (8[1]) reviser, ✝ auditor.

Revol|te [re'vɔltə] *f* (15), ♀'**tieren** revolt.

Revolution [revolu'tsjo:n] *f* revolution; ~**är** [~jo'nɛ:r] *m* (3[1]), ♀ *adj.* revolutionary.

Revolver [re'vɔlvər] *m* (7) revolver, *Am. a.* gun.

Revue [rə'vy:] *f* (15) review; *thea.* revue, musical show; ~ *passieren lassen* pass in review.

Rezen|sent [retsɛn'zɛnt] *m* (12) critic, reviewer; ♀'**sieren** review; ~**sion** [~'zjo:n] *f* review; ~**si'onsexemplar** *n* reviewer's copy.

Rezept [re'tsɛpt] *n* (3) ⚕ prescription; (*Koch*♀) recipe (*a. fig.*); ~**gebühr** *f* prescription charge.

Rezeption [retsɛp'tsjo:n] *f im Hotel*: reception, *Am.* check-in desk.

re'zeptpflichtig ⚕: ~*e Medikamente* prescription drugs.

Rezession ✝ [retsɛs'jo:n] *f* (16) recession.

reziprok [retsi'pro:k] reciprocal.

Rezi|tator [retsi'tɑ:tɔr] *m* (8[1]) reciter; ♀'**tieren** *v/t. u. v/i.* recite.

Rhabarber [ra'barbər] *m* (7) rhubarb.

Rhapsodie [rapso'di:] *f* (15) rhapsody.

rhein|isch ['raɪniʃ] of the Rhineland; '♀**wein** *m* Rhine wine, hock.

Rhetor|ik [re'to:rik] *f* (16) rhetoric; ♀**isch** rhetorical.

rheumat|isch [rɔʏ'mɑ:tiʃ] rheumatic(ally *adv.*); ♀**ismus** [~ma'tismus] *m* (16) rheumatism.

Rhinozeros [ri'no:tsərɔs] *n* (4[1] *od.* 14[2]) rhinoceros.

Rhombus ['rɔmbus] *m* (16[2]) rhomb(us).

rhythm|isch ['rytmiʃ] rhythmical; ♀**us** ['~mus] *m* (16[2]) rhythm.

'**Richt|-antenne** *f* directional aerial (*Am.* antenna); '~**beil** *n* executioner's ax(e); '~**blei** *n* plummet; '~**block** *m* executioner's block.

richten ['riçtən] *v/t.* (26) set right, arrange, adjust; *Zimmer*: put in order, tidy; *Segel*: trim; *Uhr*: set; (*zu-, vorbereiten*) prepare; (*zu*~, *a.* ⚔) dress; (*ausbessern*) repair, fix; *Richter*: judge (*a. v/i.*); *Henker*: execute; *s. zugrunde*; ~ *auf* (*acc.*) *Waffe usw.*: level (*od.* point, aim) at, *Augen*: fix on, *Aufmerksamkeit, Bemühungen*: direct to, concentrate on; ~ *an* (*acc.*) *Bitte, Brief usw.*: address to, *Frage*: put to; *in die Höhe* ~ raise, lift up; *sich* ~ *nach* conform to, act according to, (*sich orientieren*) take one's bearings from, *gr.* agree with, (*abhängen von*) depend on, (*bestimmt werden von*) be determined (*od.* governed) by; *ich richte mich nach Ihnen* I leave it to you.

'**Richter** *m* (7), '~**in** *f* judge; '~**-amt** *n* judgeship; '♀**lich** judicial; '~**spruch** *m* judgment, sentence; '~**stand** *m* judicature, *bsd. Am.* judiciary; *the* bench; '~**stuhl** *m* tribunal.

'**Richt|funk** *m* radio relay system; '~**geschwindigkeit** *mot. f* recommended speed.

'**richtig** right; (*einwandfrei*) correct; (*genau*) accurate; (*gehörig*) proper; (*geeignet*) suitable; (*wirklich, echt*) real, true; (*regelrecht*) regular; (*gerecht*) just, fair; ~*e Abschrift* true copy; ~*e Zeit* proper time; ~ *gehen Uhr*: be (*od.* go) right; ~ *rechnen* calculate correctly; *~er gesagt* ... rather; *das ist das ≗e für dich* that's the thing for you; *das ist nicht ganz das ≗e* F that's not quite the ticket; *~!* right (you are)! quite (so)!; F *nicht ganz ~ (im Kopf)* not quite right in the head; **'~gehend** F *fig.* regular, real; **'≗keit** *f* correctness; accuracy; justness; **'~stellen** put right, rectify.

'Richt|linien *f/pl.* guidelines; **'~maß** *n* ga(u)ge, standard; **'~platz** *m s. Richtstätte*; **'~preis** *m* standard price; **'~scheit** *n* level, ruler; **'~schnur** *f* plumb-line; *fig.* guiding principle; **'~schwert** *n* executioner's sword; **'~stätte** *f* place of execution; **'~strahl** *m* (radio) beam; **'~strahlantenne** *f* beam aerial (*Am.* antenna); **'~strahler** *m* (7) beam transmitter; *s. Richtantenne.*

'Richtung *f* direction; (*Weg, Kurs*) course, way; *fig. a.* line, (*Entwicklung*) trend; *in der Wissenschaft usw.*: school of thought; *politische ~* line of policy, (*Ansicht*) political views *pl.*; *in gerader ~* in a straight line; **'~s-anzeiger** *mot. m* direction indicator; **'≗weisend** guiding.

'Richt|waage *f* level; **'~wert** *m* standard value.

Ricke ['rikə] *f* (15) doe.

rieb [ri:p] *pret. v. reiben.*

riechen ['ri:çən] *v/t. u. v/i.* (30) smell(*nach* of; *an dat.* at); (*schnuppern*) sniff; *gut (übel) ~* smell good (bad); F *ich kann ihn nicht ~* I can't stand him; *s. Braten, Lunte.*

Ried [ri:t] *n* (3) reed; (*Moor*) marsh.

rief [ri:f] *pret. v. rufen.*

Riefe ['ri:fə] *f* (15) channel, chamfer; *bsd. an Säulen*: flute; **≗ln** ['~fəln] (29) channel, chamfer; flute.

Riege ['ri:gə] *f* (15) section, squad.

Riegel ['ri:gəl] *m* (7) bar, bolt; (*Kleider≗*) (clothes-)rack; *Seife, Schokolade*: bar; *fig. e-n ~ vorschieben (dat.)* put a stop to; **'≗n** (29) bar, bolt.

Riemen ['ri:mən] *m* (6) strap, thong; (*Leib≗*; ⊕ *Treib≗*) belt; (*Gewehr≗*) sling; ⚓ oar; **'~-antrieb** *m* belt drive; **'~scheibe** ⊕ *f* (belt-) pulley.

Ries [ri:s] *n* (4, *als Maß nach Zahlen inv.*) *Papiermaß*: ream.

Riese ['ri:zə] *m* (13) giant.

rieseln ['ri:zəln] (29, h. *u.* sn) purl, ripple; (*tröpfeln*) trickle; *es rieselt* it drizzles.

'Riesen|-erfolg *m* enormous success; F smash (hit); **'≗groß**, **'≗haft** *s. riesig*; **'~rad** *n* Ferris wheel; **'~schlange** *f* boa constrictor; **'~schritt** *m*: *mit ~en* with giant strides; **'~schwung** *m Turnen*: giant circle; **'~slalom** *m* giant slalom.

'riesig gigantic(ally *adv.*), collossal, huge, enormous; F (*mst adv.*) *fig. a.* immense(ly), tremendous(ly).

'Riesin *f* giantess.

riet [ri:t] *pret. v. raten.*

Riff [rif] *n* (3) reef.

riffeln ['rifəln] (29) *s. riefeln*; *Flachs*: ripple.

Rille ['rilə] *f* (15) groove.

Rind [rint] *n* (1) ox, cow; *pl.* (horned) cattle *sg.*

Rinde ['rində] *f* (15) ⚘ bark; (*Brot≗*) crust; (*Käse≗*) rind; (*Gehirn≗*) cortex.

'Rinder|braten *m* roast beef; **'~pest** *f* cattle-plague; **'~zunge** *f* neat's (*od.* ox) tongue.

'Rind|fleisch *n* beef; **'~(s)leder** *n* neat's leather, cow-hide; **'~vieh** *n* horned cattle; P *fig.* idiot.

Ring [riŋ] *m* (3) ring (*a.* ✝ *u. Boxen*); (*Kreis, a. fig.*) circle; *e-r Kette*: link; ✝ pool, *Am.* combine; **'~bahn** *f* circular railway; **'~buch** *n* ring (*od.* loose-leaf) binder; **'~buch-einlage** *f* loose-leaf pages *pl.*

Ringel ['riŋəl] *m* (7) ringlet, curl; **'~haar** *n* curled hair; **'~locke** *f* ringlet; **'≗n** (29, *a. sich*) curl; **'~natter** *f* grass snake; **'~reihen** *m*, **'~tanz** *m* round dance; **'~taube** *f* ring-dove.

ring|en[1] ['riŋən] (30) *v/i.* wrestle (*a. fig. mit sich, e-m Problem* with); *weitS.* struggle (*um, nach* for); *nach Atem ~* gasp for breath; *s. Tod*; *v/t. die Hände, Wäsche*: wring; **'≗en**[2] *n* wrestling; *fig.* struggle; **'≗er** *m* (7) wrestler.

'Ring|finger *m* ring-finger; **≗förmig** ['~fœrmiç] ring-shaped, annular; **'~kampf** *m* wrestling (match); **'~kämpfer** *m* wrestler; **'~mauer** *f* circular wall; **'~richter** *m Boxen*: referee; **'~sendung** *f Radio*: hook-up.

rings [riŋs] (*a. ~ um prp.*) around; **'~he'rum**, **~'um**, **'~-um'her** round about; (*überall*) everywhere.

Rinn|e ['rinə] *f* (15) (*Rille*) groove; (*Dach*≈) gutter, eaves *pl.*; (*Leitungs*≈) conduit; (*Wasser*≈) gully; (*Kanal*) canal; '≈**en** (30): **a**) (sn) run, flow; (*tröpfeln*) drip, trickle; **b**) (h.) (*lecken*) leak; ~**sal** ['~za:l] *n* streamlet, rill; '~**stein** *m* gutter; *Küche*: sink.

'**Rippchen** *n* (6) rib of pork.

Rippe ['ripə] *f* (15) rib (*a.* ⚘, ✈); ⚠ groin; *mot.*, ✈ fin; *Schokolade*: bar; '≈**n** (25) rib.

'**Rippen|fell** *anat. n* pleura; '~**fellentzündung** *f* pleurisy; '~**stoß** *m* dig in the ribs; *heimlicher*: nudge.

'**Rippe(n)speer** *m* spare rib (of pork).

Rips [rips] *m* (4) *Stoff*: rep.

Risiko ['ri:ziko] *n* (11) risk; *auf eigenes* ~ at one's own risk; *ein* ~ *eingehen* take (*od.* run) a risk; ~**zuschlag** *m* risk allowance.

risk|ant [ris'kant] risky; ~**ieren** [~'ki:rən] risk.

Rispe ⚘ ['rispə] *f* (15) panicle.

Riß [ris] **1.** *m* (4) rent, tear; (*Spalte*) crevice, fissure (*a.* ⊕); (*Sprung*) crack; (*Schramme*) scratch; (*Zeichnung*) draft, plan, sketch; *fig. in der Freundschaft usw.*: rupture; (*Spaltung*) split, schism; *Risse pl. in der Haut*: chaps; **2.** ≈ *pret. v. reißen* 1.

rissig ['risiç] cracked, fissured; *Haut, trockener Boden*: chappy; ~ *werden* crack.

Rist [rist] *m* (3[2]) *des Fußes*: instep; *der Hand*: wrist.

Ritt [rit] **1.** *m* (3) ride; **2.** ≈ *pret. v. reiten.*

'**Ritter** *m* (7) knight; (*Kämpe*) champion; *j-n zum* ~ *schlagen* dub a p. a knight, knight a p.; *arme* ~ *pl.* (*Speise*) fritters; '~**burg** *f* knight's castle; '~**gut** *n* manor; '≈**lich** knightly; *fig.* chivalrous; '~**lichkeit** *f* gallantry, chivalry; '~**-orden** *m* knightly order; '~**schaft** *f* knights *pl.*; (*Eigenschaft*) knighthood; '~**schlag** *m* knighting, dubbing; '~**sporn** ⚘ *m* larkspur; '~**tum** *n* (1, *o. pl.*) chivalry.

rittlings ['~liŋs] astride (*auf dat. a th.*).

'**Rittmeister** *hist. m* captain of horse, (cavalry) captain.

Ritual [ritu'a:l] *n* (3[1]), **rituell** [~'ɛl] ritual.

Ritus ['ri:tus] *m* (16[2] *u. inv.*) rite.

Ritz [rits] *m* (3[2]), '~**e** *f* (15) fissure, crevice, rift; (*Schramme*) scratch; '≈**en** (27) scratch.

Rival|e [ri'va:lə] *m* (13), ~**in** *f* (16[1]) rival; ≈**i'sieren** [~vali-] rival; ~**ität** [~i'tɛ:t] *f* (16) rivalry.

Rizinusöl ['ri:tsinusˀø:l] *n* castor oil.

Robbe ['rɔbə] *f* (15) seal; '≈**n** ⚔ crawl; '~**nfang** *m* sealing.

Robe ['ro:bə] *f* gown; (*Amts*≈) robe.

Roboter ['ro:bɔtər] *m* (7) robot; '~**technik** *f* robot technology.

robust [ro'bust] robust, sturdy.

roch [rɔx] *pret. v. riechen.*

röcheln ['rœçəln] (29) gasp.

Roche(n) ['rɔxə(n)] *m* (6) ray.

rochieren [rɔ'ʃi:rən] *v/i. u. v/t. Schach*: castle (one's king); *v/i. Sport*: switch positions.

Rock [rɔk] *m* (3[3]) coat; (*Jacke*) jacket; (*Damen*~) skirt; '~**en** *m* (6) distaff.

Rodel|bahn ['ro:dəlba:n] *f* toboggan-slide; '≈**n** (29, h. *u.* sn), '~**schlitten** *m* luge, toboggan.

rod|en ['ro:dən] (26) *Wurzeln*: root out, stub up; *Wald, Land*: clear, stub; '≈**ung** *f* clearing.

Rogen ['ro:gən] *m* (6) (hard) roe; '~**er** *m* (*weiblicher Fisch*) spawner.

Roggen ['rɔgən] *m* (6) rye.

roh [ro:] (*unverarbeitet*) raw; *Diamant, Entwurf*: rough; *Öl, Metall* (*a. fig. primitiv*) crude; ✝ (*brutto*) gross; *fig.* rough, rude; brutal; *mit* ~*er Gewalt* with brute force; '≈**bau** *m* carcass; outside finish; '≈**baumwolle** *f* raw cotton; '≈**bilanz** ✝ *f* trial balance; '≈**-eisen** *n* pig-iron.

Roheit ['~haɪt] *f* rawness; (*Rauheit*, *a. fig.*) roughness; *fig.* rudeness, brutality.

'**Roh|-erzeugnis** *n* raw product; '~**faser** *f* crude fib|re, *Am.* -er; '~**fassung** *f* (*Entwurf*) rough draft; '~**gewicht** *n* gross weight; '~**gewinn** *m* gross profit; '~**gummi** *m* crude rubber; '~**kost** *f* raw diet, uncooked (vegetarian) food; '~**köstler(in** *f*) *m* vegetarian, fruitarian; '~**leder** *n* rawhide; '~**ling** *m* (3[1]) brute, ruffian; *metall.* slug; *Gießerei*: blank; '~**material** *n* raw material; '~**metall** *n* crude metal; '~**-öl** *n* crude oil; '~**produkt** *n* raw product.

Rohr [ro:r] *n* (3) (*Schilf*≈) reed; (*Bambus*≈; ~*stock*) cane; ⊕ (*Röhre*) tube, pipe; (*Kanal*) duct; ⚔ barrel; '~**bruch** *m* pipe burst.

Röhrchen ['rø:rçən] *n* (6) *für Alko-*

holtest: breathalyzer; *j-n ins ~ blasen lassen* give a p. a breathalyzer.

Röhre ['rø:rə] *f* (15) tube; (*nur Leitungs*∻) pipe; ⊕ duct; *Radio usw.*: valve, *Am.* tube; (*Brat*∻) oven; '**∻n** *zo.* (25) *Hirsch*: bell; '**∻nförmig** tubular; '**~nhosen** *f/pl.* F drainpipe trousers.

Rohr|krepierer ['~krepi:rər] *m* (7) ⚔ barrel burst; *fig. Idee, Plan*: non-starter; '**~leger** *m* pipe-layer, plumber; '**~leitung** *f* conduit; *im Haus*: plumbing; (*Fernleitung*) pipeline; '**~post** *f* pneumatic post; '**~schelle** *f* pipe clamp; '**~schlange** ⊕ *f* spiral tube, coil; '**~spatz** *m* reed-bunting; F *schimpfen wie ein ~* rant and rave; '**~stock** *m* cane; '**~stuhl** *m* cane(-bottomed) chair; '**~zange** *f* pipe-wrench; '**~zucker** *m* cane-sugar.

'**Roh|seide** *f* raw silk; '**~stahl** *m* crude steel; '**~stoff** *m* raw material; '**~zucker** *m* unrefined sugar.

'**Rolladen** *m* roller blind.

'**Roll|bahn** ✈ *f* runway; '**~brett** *n* skateboard.

Rolle ['rɔlə] *f* (15) roll; (*Walze, Welle*) roller; (*Draht*∻, *Tau*∻) coil; (*Spule*) reel; *am Flaschenzuge*: pulley; *unter Möbeln*: cast|or, *Am.* -er; (*Wäsche*∻) mangle; ~ *Stoff* bolt of cloth; (*Liste*) list, register; *thea. u. fig.* part, rôle; *e-e ~ spielen* play a part (*a. fig. bei, in dat.* in), *fig. a.* figure (in); *das spielt keine ~* that makes no difference; *Geld spielt keine ~* money is no object; *fig. aus der ~ fallen* forget o.s., misbehave.

'**rollen** (25) *v/i.* (h. *u.* sn) *u. v/t.* roll; *auf Rädern*: wheel; ✈ taxi; 🚂 *~des Material* rolling stock; *fig. ins ∻ bringen* (*od. kommen*) get underway.

'**Rollen|besetzung** *thea. f* cast; '**~lager** *n* roller bearing; '**~spiel** *psych. n* role-playing; '**~tausch** *m fig.* exchange of roles.

'**Roller** *m* (7) motor-scooter; *für Kinder*: scooter; *Sport*: daisy-cutter; (*Vogel*) roller.

'**Roll|feld** ✈ *n* taxiway; runway; '**~film** *phot. m* roll-film; '**~kommando** *n* raiding squad; '**~kragen(pullover)** *m* turtle-neck, polo-neck; '**~mops** *m* collared herring; '**~schrank** *m* roll-fronted cabinet; '**~schuh** *m* roller-skate; '**~schuhbahn** *f* skating-rink; '**~schuhläufer** *m* roller-skater; '**~stuhl** *m* wheelchair; '**~treppe** *f* escalator; '**~wagen** *m* truck.

Roman [ro'ma:n] *m* (3[1]) novel, (work of) fiction; (*Ritter*∻ *u. fig.*) romance; **~dichter(in** *f*) *m* novelist; **~en** *pl. the* Romanic peoples; **∻haft** romantic(ally *adv.*), fictitious; **~held** *m* hero of a novel; **∻isch** Romanic; *von Sprachen oft*: Romance; **~ist** [~ma'nist] *m* (12) Romance scholar *od.* student; **~literatur** *f* fiction; **~schriftsteller(in** *f*) *m* novelist.

Romant|ik [~'mantik] *f* (16) romanticism; **~iker** *m* romanticist; **∻isch** romantic(ally *adv.*).

Romanze [~'mantsə] *f* (15) romance (*a. fig.*).

Röm|er ['rø:mər] *m* (7) Roman; (*Pokal*) rummer; '**∻isch** Roman.

Rommé [rɔ'me:] *n* (11) rummy.

röntgen ['rœntgən] (25) ⚕ X-ray; '∻ *n* (*Einheit*) roentgen; '**∻-apparat** *m* X-ray apparatus; '**∻-assistent(in** *f*) *m* radiographer; '**∻-aufnahme** *f*, '**∻bild** *n* X-ray picture, radiograph; '**∻bestrahlung** *f*, '**∻behandlung** *f* X-ray treatment; **∻ologe** [~o'lo:gə] *m* (13) radiologist; **∻ologie** [~olo'gi:] *f* (15, *o. pl.*) radiology; '**∻schirm** *m* (fluorescent) screen; '**∻strahlen** *m/pl.* Roentgen (*od.* X-)rays *pl.*; '**∻-untersuchung** *f* X-ray examination.

rosa ['ro:za] pink; *fig.* rose-colo(u)red.

Rose ['ro:zə] *f* (15) rose; ⚕ *the* rose, erysipelas; *s. Fenster*∻, *Kompaß*∻.

'**Rosen|busch** *m* rose-bush; '**~garten** *m* rosery; '**~kohl** *m* Brussels sprouts *pl.*; '**~kranz** *eccl. m* rosary; **~'montag** *m* monday before Lent; '**~-öl** *n* attar (of roses); '**∻rot** rose-colo(u)red, rosy; '**~stock** *m* rose-tree.

Rosette [ro'zɛtə] *f* (15) rosette.

'**rosig** rosy (*a. fig.*).

Rosine [ro'zi:nə] *f* (15) raisin; *große ~* plum; *kleine ~* currant; F (*große*) *~n im Kopf haben* have high-flown ideas.

Rosmarin ♀ [rɔsma'ri:n] *m* (3[1]) rosemary.

Roß [rɔs] *n* (4) horse; *rhet.* steed; *hoch zu ~* mounted on horseback; *fig. sich aufs hohe ~ setzen* mount the high horse; '**~-arzt** *m* veterinarian.

Rösselsprung ['rœsəlʃpruŋ] *m* *Schach*: knight's move.
Roß|haar *n* horsehair; '**~kastanie** *f* horse-chestnut; '**~kur** *f* drastic cure.
Rost¹ [rɔst] *m* (3) rust; **~**² (*Feuer*♀) grate; (*Brat*♀) gridiron, grill; '♀**-beständig** rust-resistant, rust-proof; '**~braten** *m* roast joint.
'**Röstbrot** *n* toast.
rosten ['rɔstən] (26, h. *u.* sn) rust; *nicht ~d Stahl usw.*: *s. rostfrei.*
rösten ['rø:stən] (26) roast; *Brot*: toast.
'**rost|frei** rustless, rustproof; *bsd. Stahl*: stainless; '**~ig** rusty.
'**Röstkartoffeln** *f/pl.* fried potatoes.
'**Rost|schutzmittel** *n* anticorrosive agent; '**~-umwandler** *m* (7) rust converter.
rot [ro:t] **1.** *adj.* red (*a. pol.*); ♀*es Kreuz* Red Cross; F *~ sehen* see red; (*wie*) *ein ~es Tuch für j-n* a red rag to a p.; *~ werden im Gesicht*: redden, flush, *verlegen*: blush; **2.** ♀ *n* (3) red; (*Schminke*) rouge.
Rotation [rota'tsjo:n] *f* (16) rotation; **~sdruck** *typ. m* rotary printing; **~smaschine** *f* rotary press.
'**rot|blond** sandy; '**~braun** reddish brown; '♀**buche** ⚘ *f* copper-beech; '♀**dorn** ⚘ *m* pink hawthorn; '♀**e** *pol. m* Red.
Röt|e ['rø:tə] *f* (15) redness, red colo(u)r; '**~el** *m* (7) red chalk; '**~eln** ⚕ *pl.* German measles; '♀**en** (26, *a. sich*) redden, flush.
'**Rot|fuchs** *m* (red) fox; (*Pferd*) bay (*od.* sorrel) horse; '♀**gelb** reddish yellow; '♀**glühend** red-hot; '**~glut** *f* red heat; '♀**haarig** red-haired; '**~haut** *f* redskin.
rotieren [ro'ti:rən] rotate.
Rot|käppchen ['~kɛpçən] *n* Red Riding Hood; **~kehlchen** ['~ke:l-çən] *n* (6) robin (redbreast); '**~lauf** ⚕ *m* erysipelas; *vet.* red murrain.
rötlich ['rø:tliç] reddish.
Rot|schwänzchen ['~ʃvɛntsçən] *n* (6) redstart; '**~stift** *m* red pencil; '**~tanne** *f* spruce.
Rotte ['rɔtə] *f* (15) gang (*a. b.s.*); '**~nführer** *m v. Arbeitern*: foreman.
'**Rot|wein** *m* red wine; *französischer*: claret; '**~welsch** *n* thieves' cant; '**~wild** *n* red deer.
Rotz [rɔts] *m* (3²) P snot; *vet.* glanders *pl.*; '♀**ig** P snotty; *vet.* glandered; '**~nase** P *f* snot-nose (*a. als Schimpfwort*).
Rouge [ru:ʒ] *n* (11) rouge, blusher.
Roulade [ru'la:də] *f* (15) *Küche*: meat-roll, *Am.* roulade (*a.* ♪).
Rouleau [ru'lo:] *n* (11) roller-blind.
Roulett(e *f*) [ru'lɛt] *n* (3 *od.* 11) roulette.
Route ['ru:tə] *f* (15) route.
Routin|e [ru'ti:nə] *f* (15), ♀**emäßig** *adj.* routine; ♀**iert** [~ti'ni:rt] experienced.
Rübe ['ry:bə] *f* (15) rape; *weiße ~* white beet, turnip; *rote ~* red beet, beetroot; *gelbe ~* carrot.
Rubel ['ru:bəl] *m* (7) rouble.
'**Rübenzucker** *m* beet sugar.
rüber F ['ry:bər] *s. herüber(...), hinüber(...).*
Rubin [ru'bi:n] *m* (3¹) ruby.
Rubrik [ru'bri:k] *f* (16) heading, rubric; (*Spalte*) column.
'**Rübsamen** *m* rape-seed.
ruch|bar ['ru:xba:r]: *~ werden* become known, get about *od.* abroad; '**~los** wicked, infamous, foul; '♀**-losigkeit** *f* wickedness, profligacy.
Ruck [ruk] *m* (3) jerk, *Am.* F yank; (*Stoß*) shock, jolt (*a. fig.*); *auf einen ~* at one go; *sich e-n ~ geben* pull o.s. together; '♀**-artig** jerky; *adv.* (*plötzlich*) of a sudden.
'**Rück|-ansicht** *f* back view; '**~-anspruch** *m* recourse; '**~-antwort** *f* reply; *Postkarte mit ~* reply post-card; *Telegramm mit bezahlter ~* reply-paid; '♀**bezüglich** *gr.* reflexive; '**~blende** *f*, '**~blendung** *f* *Film*: flashback; '♀**blenden** *Film*: cut back; '**~blick** *m* retrospect(ive view), glance back; '♀**datieren** backdate.
rücken¹ ['rykən] (25) *v/t.* move; (*schieben*) shift; *v/i.* (sn) move; (*Platz machen*) move over; *näher ~* draw near, approach; *im Range höher ~* rise; *an j-s Stelle ~* take a p.'s place; *nicht von der Stelle ~* not to budge (an inch); *s. Leib.*
Rücken² [~] *m* (6) back (*a. Buch*♀, *Hand*♀, *Messer*♀ *usw.*); (*Berg*♀) ridge; (*Nasen*♀) bridge; ⚔ rear; *hinter j-s ~* behind a p.'s back; *j-m in den ~ fallen* attack a p. from the rear, *fig.* stab a p. in the back; *j-m den ~ stärken* stiffen a p.'s back; *s. kehren*; '**~deckung** *f* ⚔

rear cover; *fig.* backing; '**~flug** ✈ *m* inverted flight; '**~lage** *f* supine position; '**~lehne** *f* back(-rest); '**~mark** *n* spinal marrow *od.* cord; '**~schmerzen** *m/pl.* pain in the back, aching back *sg.*; '**~schwimmen** *n* back-stroke; '**~wind** *m* tail wind; '**~wirbel** *anat. m* dorsal vertebra.

'**Rück|-erstattung** *f* restitution; *v. Geld*: refund; *v. Kosten*: reimbursement; '**~fahrkarte** *f* return(-ticket), *Am.* round-trip ticket; '**~fahrt** *f* return (journey *od.* trip); '**~fall** *m* relapse; *e-s Verbrechers*: *a.* recidivism; '**2fällig** relapsing; ⚖ *a.* recidivous; ~ *werden* (have a) relapse; '**~fenster** *n* rear window; '**~flug** ✈ *m* return flight; '**~fracht** *f* return freight; '**~frage** *f* further inquiry, check-back; '**~führung** *f in die Heimat*: repatriation; '**~gabe** *f* return; restitution; '**~gang** *m* (*Rückweg*) return; *fig.* decline, retrogression; ⚕ *der Geschäfte*: recession; *der Produktion*: falling-off; **2gängig** ['~gɛŋiç] retrograde; ⚕ declining; ~ *machen* undo, *Auftrag usw.*: cancel; '**~gewinnung** *f* recovery; '**~grat** *n* spine, (*a. fig.*) backbone; '**2gratlos** *fig.* spineless; '**~griff** *m* recourse (*auf acc.* to); '**~halt** *m* support; '**2haltlos** unreserved, frank; '**~hand**(**schlag** *m*) *f Tennis*: backhand (stroke); '**~kampf** *m Sport*: return match; '**~kauf** *m* repurchase; (*Einlösung*) redemption; '**~kaufswert** *m* surrender value; '**~kehr** *f* (16), **~kunft** ['~kunft] *f* (14[1]) return; '**~kopplung** *f Radio*: feedback; '**~lage** *f* reserve(s *pl.*); '**~lauf** ⚔ *m* recoil; '**2läufig** *s. rückgängig*; '**~licht** *mot. n* rear (*od.* tail) light; '**2lings** backwards; (*von hinten*) from behind; '**~marsch** *m* march back *od.* home; (*Rückzug*) retreat; **~nahme** ['~nɑːmə] *f* taking back; '**~paß** *m Sport*: back pass; '**~porto** *n* return postage; '**~prall** *m* rebound; '**~reise** *f* return journey; '**~ruf** *m* recall.

Rucksack ['rukzak] *m* rucksack, *Am.* backpack; '**~tourismus** *m* backpacking.

'**Rück|schau** *f s. Rückblick*; '**~schlag** *m* backstrike; *fig.* setback, reaction, reverse; *des Gewehrs*: kick; '**~schluß** *m* conclusion, inference; '**~schritt** *m* step back; *fig. a.* retrogression, regress; *pol.* reaction; '**2schrittlich** reactionary; '**~seite** *f* back, reverse; *e-r Münze*: tail; '**~sendung** *f* return; '**~sicht** *f* respect, regard, consideration; ~ *nehmen auf* (*acc.*) have regard for *a p.*, to (*od.* for) *a th.*; (*in Betracht ziehen*) make allowance for; *ohne* ~ *auf* (*acc.*) without regard to *od.* for, without respect to, irrespective of; *mit* ~ *auf* (*acc.*) with regard to, considering; '**~sichtnahme** *f* considerateness, consideration (*auf acc.* of, for); '**2sichtslos** regardless (*gegen* of), inconsiderate; (*unbekümmert*) reckless; (*unbarmherzig*) ruthless; '**~sichtslosigkeit** *f* lack of consideration, inconsiderateness; recklessness; '**2sichtsvoll** regardful (*gegen* of, for); considerate; '**~sitz** *m* back-seat; '**~spiegel** *mot. m* rear-view mirror; '**~spiel** *n Sport*: return match; '**~sprache** *f* consultation; ~ *nehmen mit* consult with; *nach* ~ *mit* … on consultation with; '**~stand** *m* (*Zahlungs2*) arrears *pl.*; (*Arbeits2*) backlog; ⚗ residue; *im* ~ *sein mit* be behind with; '**2ständig** in arrears (*mit* with); *Ansicht*: backward, antiquated; ~*e Miete* arrears *pl.* of rent; '**~ständigkeit** *f* backwardness; '**~stau** *mot. m* tail-back; '**~**(**stell**)**taste** *f* back spacer; '**~stoß** *m* repulsion; *e-r Schußwaffe*: recoil, kick; '**~strahler** *mot. m* (7) rear reflector; '**~strom** ⚡ *m* reverse current; '**~taste** *f* back spacer; '**~tritt** *m* withdrawal, retreat; *vom Amt*: resignation; '**~trittbremse** *f Fahrrad*: backpedalling brake; *Am.* coaster brake; '**~trittsgebühr** *f* cancellation charge (*od.* fee); '**~trittsklausel** *f* cancellation clause; '**~übersetzung** *f* retranslation; '**2vergüten** refund; '**~vergütung** *f* refund, reimbursement; '**~versicherung** *f* reinsurance; **2wärtig** ['~vɛrtiç] rear(ward); '**2wärts** back, backward(s); '**~wärtsgang** *mot. m* reverse (gear); '**~wechsel** ⚕ *m* redraft; '**~weg** *m* way back, return.

'**ruckweise** by jerks, by fits and starts.

'**rück|wirkend** reacting; ⚖ retroactive; ~ *ab* backdated to; '**2wirkung** *f* reaction; (*Auswirkung*) repercussion; '**~zahlbar** repayable;

'**~zahlen** repay; '**2zahlung** *f* repayment; '**2zieher** *m Fußball*: overhead kick; F *fig.* climbdown; *e-n ~ machen* back down; '**2zoll** *m* (customs-) drawback; '**2zollgüter** *n/pl.* debenture goods; '**2zug** *m* retreat; '**2zugsgefecht** *n* running fight.

Rüde[1] ['ry:də] *m* (13) large hound; male dog *od.* fox *od.* wolf; 2[2] rude.

Rudel ['ru:dəl] *n* (7) herd, troop; *Wölfe, U-Boote*: pack.

Ruder ['ru:dər] *n* (7) oar; (*Steuer*2) rudder, helm; ✈ control surface; *fig. am ~* at the helm; *ans ~ kommen* come into power; '**~boot** *n* row(-ing)-boat; '**~er** *m* (7) rower, oarsman; '**~fahrt** *f* row; '**~in** *f* oarswoman; '**~klub** *m* rowing club; '**2n** (29) *v/i.* (h. *u.* sn) *u. v/t.* row; '**~n** *n* (6) rowing; '**~pinne** *f* tiller; '**~regatta** *f* boat race, regatta; '**~sport** *m* rowing (sport).

Ruf [ru:f] *m* (3) call; (*Schrei*) cry, shout; (*Berufung*) summons, *univ.* call; (*Leumund*) reputation, repute; ⚕ standing, credit; (*Ruhm*) fame; *in gutem* (*schlechtem*) *~e stehen* be well (ill) reputed; *im ~e e-s ... stehen* be reputed to be a ...; '**2en** *v/t. u. v/i.* (30) call; (*schreien*) cry, shout (*alle*: *um, nach* for); *den Arzt*: call (in); *~ lassen* send for; *es kommt mir wie gerufen* that comes in handy.

Rüffel F ['ryfəl] *m* (7), '**2n** (29) reprimand.

'**Ruf|mord** *m* character assassination; '**~name** *m* Christian (*od.* first) name; '**~nummer** *teleph. f* call-number; '**~weite** *f*: *in ~* within call *od.* earshot; '**~zeichen** *n Radio usw.*: call-sign(al).

Rüge ['ry:gə] *f* (15) reproof, censure, reprimand; '**2n** (25) reprove; censure, denounce.

Ruhe ['ru:ə] *f* (15) rest, repose; (*Stille, Schweigen*) quiet, silence; (*Frieden*) peace, *innere*: *a.* peace of mind; (*Gelassenheit*) calm(ness), composure; *~ und Ordnung* peace (*od.* law) and order; *~ vor dem Sturm* lull before the storm; *ewige ~* eternal peace; *in aller ~* very calmly, (*gemütlich*) leisurely; *~ bewahren* keep quiet, *nervlich*: keep cool; *sich zur ~ begeben* go to rest; *lassen Sie mich in ~!* let me alone!; *j-m keine ~ lassen* give a p. no rest; *sich zur ~ setzen* retire; *immer mit der ~!* take it easy!; *~!* silence!, be quiet!; '**2bedürftig** in need of rest; '**~bett** *n* couch; '**~gehalt** *n* (retiring) pension; '**~kissen** *n* pillow; '**~lage** ⊕ *f s. Ruhestellung*; '**2los** restless; '**~losigkeit** *f* restlessness; '**2n** *v/i. u. v/t.* (25) rest, *fig. a.* sleep; (*stillstehen*) be at a standstill; ⚖ be in abeyance; *~ auf* (*dat.*) *a. fig.* rest on (*a. Blick*), be based on; *er ruhte nicht, bis* he could not rest till; *hier ruht* here lies; *er ruhe in Frieden!* may he rest in peace!; *laß die Vergangenheit ~!* let bygones be bygones!; '**~pause** *f* break, breather; (*ruhige Zeit*) lull; '**~platz** *m* resting-place; '**~punkt** *m* rest; *bsd.* ♪ pause; ⊕ fulcrum; '**~stand** *m* retirement; *in den ~ versetzen* superannuate, retire, pension off; *im ~* retired; *vorzeitiger ~* early retirement; *in den ~ treten* retire; '**~stätte** *f* place of rest; *letzte ~ fig.* last resting-place; '**~stellung** *f* normal position, ⊕ *a.* neutral (*od.* idle) position; '**~störer(in** *f*) *m* disturber of the peace, peace-breaker, rioter; '**~störung** *f* disturbance, riot; '**~strom** ⚡ *m* closed-circuit current; '**~tag** *m* day of rest; '**~zeit** *f* time of rest.

ruhig ['ru:iç] quiet (*a. Farbe,* ⚕ *Markt*); (*still, schweigend*) silent; (*friedlich*) peaceful, tranquil; calm (*a. See*); (*nervlich ~*) calm, cool; (*beruhigt*) reassured; (*gemächlich*) leisurely (*a. adv.*); *adv.* (*ohne weiteres*) easily, well; ⊕ *~er Gang* smooth running; *~e Sache sl.* soft job; *~ bleiben* keep one's temper; *tu das ~!* go right ahead; *~ verlaufen* be uneventful.

Ruhm [ru:m] *m* (3) glory; (*Berühmtheit*) fame; '**2bedeckt** covered with glory; '**~begier(de)** *f* thirst for glory.

rühmen ['ry:mən] (25) praise, extol; *sich ~* boast (*e-r Sache* of a th.); *sich e-r Sache ~ können* (*besitzen*) boast a th.; '**~swert** praiseworthy.

'**Ruhmesblatt** *n* page of glory.

rühmlich ['ry:mliç] glorious; (*löblich*) laudable.

'**ruhm|los** inglorious; **~redig** ['~re:diç] boastful, vainglorious; '**~voll** glorious.

Ruhr ⚕ [ru:r] *f* (16) dysentery.

Rührei ['ry:rʔaɪ] *n* scrambled eggs.

rühren ['ry:rən] (25, *a. sich ~*) stir,

move; *Kochkunst*: stir, *Eier*: beat; (*innerlich* ~, *ergreifen*) touch, move (*zu Tränen* to tears); ~ *an* (*acc.*) touch; (*her*)~ *von* come from; *fig.* *sich* ~ be active; *sich nicht* ~ not to budge, *fig.* make no move; *keinen Finger* ~, *keine Hand* ~ not to stir a finger; *das rührte ihn wenig* it left him cold; ⚔ *rührt euch!* (stand) at ease!; *s. Donner, Trommel*; '**~d** touching, moving, affecting.

rührig ['ry:riç] active, busy; (*unternehmend*) enterprising; (*flink*) nimble; '**⁲keit** *f* activity; enterprise; nimbleness.

'**Rühr|löffel** *m* (pot-)ladle; '**⁲selig** sentimental; '**~stück** *thea. n* melodrama.

'**Rührung** *f* emotion.

Ruin [ru'ʔi:n] *m* (3) ruin; (*Verfall*) decay; **~e** *f* (15) ruin(s *pl.*); **⁲ieren** [~'ni:rən] *allg.* ruin (*sich* o.s.).

Rülps(**er**) ['rylps(ər)] *m* (4) belch.

'**rülpsen** (27) belch.

Rum [rum] *m* (3^1 *u.* 11) rum.

rum F [rum] *s. herum*(...).

Rumän|e [ru'mɛ:nə] *m* (13), **~in** *f* (16^1), **⁲isch** Ro(u)manian.

Rummel ['ruməl] *m* (7) (*Getöse, Tumult*) hurly-burly, racket; (*Geschäftigkeit*) bustle; (*Aufheben*) stir, F to-do; (*Reklame⁲*) ballyhoo; *s.* ~-*platz*; F *der ganze* ~ the whole bag of tricks; ✝ *im* ~ in the lump; F *den* ~ *kennen* know what's what; '**~platz** *m* amusement park.

rumoren [ru'mo:rən] (25) make a noise; *fig.* rumble

Rumpel|kammer ['rumpəl-] *f* lumber-room; '**⁲n** (29) rumble.

Rumpf [rumpf] *m* (3^3) trunk, body; *e-r Statue u. fig.*: torso; (*Schiffs⁲*) hull; ✈ body, fuselage.

rümpfen ['rympfən] (25): *die Nase* ~ turn up one's nose, sniff (*über acc.* at).

Rumpsteak ['rumpste:k] *n* (11) rumpsteak, *Am.* porterhouse steak.

rund [runt] *allg.* round (*a. fig. Summe usw.*); (*kreisförmig*) circular; (*kugelförmig*) spherical; *Absage usw.*: plain, flat; *adv.* (*etwa*) about, in round figures; ~ *um die Welt* round the world; '**⁲bau** *m* circular building; '**⁲blick** *m* view round, panorama; '**⁲bogen** *m* round arch.

Runde ['rundə] *f* (15) *allg.* round (*a. Boxen*; *a. Bier usw.*); *Renn-, Luftsport*: lap; (*Gesellschaft*) party; *in der* (*od. die*) ~ (a)round; *die* ~ *machen Wächter*: make (*od.* go) one's rounds, *Neuigkeit usw.*: go the round; '**⁲n** (26, *a. sich*) round; *fig.* round off.

'**Rund|-erlaß** *m* circular (notice); '**⁲-erneuern** *Reifen*: retread; '**~fahrt** *f* drive round *a town etc.*; (circular) tour; '**~fahrt-auto** *n* sight-seeing car; '**~flug** ✈ *m* circuit; *um die Welt*: round-the-world flight; '**~frage** *f* inquiry (by questionnaire *od.* circular), poll.

'**Rundfunk** *m* broadcast(ing), radio; *als Einrichtung*: broadcasting system; *durch* ~ *verbreiten* broadcast; *im* (*od. durch*) ~ on (*od.* in) the radio, on (*od.* over) the air; *im* ~ *auftreten od. sprechen* speak over the radio, *Am.* be (*od.* go) on the air; '**~-ansager** *m* (radio) announcer; '**~bericht** *m* radio report; '**~-empfänger** *m*, '**~gerät** *n* (radio) receiver, radio set, *Brt. a.* wireless set; '**~gesellschaft** *f* broadcasting company, *Am.* radio corporation; '**~hörer**(**in** *f*) *m* listener; '**~programm** *n* radio program(me); '**~rechte** *n/pl.* broadcasting rights; '**~sender** *m* broadcast transmitter; *s. a. Rundfunkstation*; '**~sendung** *f* broadcast; program(me); '**~sprecher** *m* broadcaster; '**~station** *f* broadcasting (*od.* radio) station; '**~übertragung** *f* broadcasting, radio transmission; *einzelne*: broadcast.

'**Rund|gang** *m* circuit, tour; (*bsd.* ⚔) round; '**~gesang** *m* roundelay, glee; '**⁲he'raus** plainly, bluntly, point-blank; '**⁲he'rum** round about; '**~holz** *n* round timber; '**~lauf** *m* (*Turngerät*) giant('s) stride; '**⁲lich** round(ish); (*dicklich*) plump, F roly-poly; '**~reise** *f* circular tour *od.* trip, round trip; '**~reisekarte** *f* circular (tour) ticket, tourist ticket, *Am.* round-trip ticket; '**~schau** *f* panorama; (*Zeitung*) review; '**~schreiben** *n* circular (letter); '**~strecke** *f* circuit; **⁲'um** all (a)round; '**~ung** *f* roundness; F curve; '**⁲weg** flatly, plainly; '**~zange** *f* (*eine* a pair of) round-nose(d) pliers *pl.*

Rune ['ru:nə] *f* (15) runic letter, *pl.* runes; '**~nschrift** *f* runic characters *pl.*; '**~nstab** *m* runic wand.

Runge ['ruŋə] *f* (15) stake, stanchion.

Runkel ['ruŋkəl] *f* (15), '**~rübe** *f* beet(root).
Runzel ['runtsəl] *f* (15) wrinkle.
'**runz(e)lig** wrinkled.
'**runzeln** (29) wrinkle; *die Stirn ~* knit one's brows, frown.
Rüpel ['ry:pəl] *m* (7) lout; '**⚬haft** loutish, rude.
rupfen ['rupfən] (25) *Huhn usw.*: pluck (*a. fig. j-n*); (*ausrupfen*) pull up; *fig. j-n*: fleece; *s. Hühnchen.*
ruppig ['rupiç] unkempt, ragged; (*schäbig*) shabby; *fig.* rude, gruff.
Rüsche ['ry:ʃə] *f* (15) ruche, frill, ruffle; '**~nkragen** *m* ruffle collar.
Ruß [ru:s] *m* (3²) soot.
Russ|e ['rusə] *m* (13), '**~in** *f* (16¹), '**⚬isch** Russian.
Rüssel ['rysəl] *m* (7) proboscis; *des Elefanten*: *a.* trunk; *des Schweins*: snout.
ruß|en ['ru:sən] (27) soot, blacken; *v/i.* smoke; '**~ig** sooty.
rüsten ['rystən] (26) *v/t.* prepare (*auf acc., zu* for); *bsd.* ⚔ arm; *s. aus~*; *v/i.* (*a. sich*) prepare, get ready (*zu* for).
Rüster ⚘ ['ry:stər] *f* (15) elm.
rüstig ['rystiç] vigorous, strong, well-preserved; *er ist (für sein Alter) noch recht ~* he bears his years well; '**⚬keit** *f* vigo(u)r.
'**Rüstung** *f* preparation(s *pl.*); (*Bewaffnung*) arming, armament; (*Harnisch*) armo(u)r; '**~s-abbau** *m* arms reduction; '**~s-ausgaben** *f/pl.* defen|ce (*Am.* -se) expenditure *sg.*; '**~s-fabrik** *f* war (*od.* armament) factory; '**~s-industrie** *f* arms industry; '**~s-kontrolle** *f* arms control; '**~sstopp** *m* arms freeze; '**~swettlauf** *m* armament race.
'**Rüstzeug** *n* (set of) tools; *fig.* (*geistiges* mental) equipment.
Rute ['ru:tə] *f* (15) rod; (*Gerte*) switch; *zum Züchtigen*: rod, birch (rod); *anat.* penis; *hunt.* (*Schwanz, bsd. des Fuchses*) brush; *j-m die ~ geben* whip (*od.* flog) a p.
Rutengänger ['~ngɛŋər] *m* (7) dowser, diviner.
Rutsch [rutʃ] *m* (3²) slide, glide; '**~bahn** *f*, '**~e** *f* slide, (*a. Güter⚬, Wasser⚬*) chute; '**⚬en** (27, sn) glide, slide; (*aus~; entgleiten*) slip; *Fahrzeug*: skid; '**⚬fest** *Reifen*: anti-skid; *Sohle*: non-slip; '**⚬ig** slippery.
rütteln ['rytəln] *v/t. u. v/i.* (29) shake, jog; ⊕ vibrate; *Wagen*: jolt; *~ an der Tür* rattle at, *fig.* assail, shake; *daran ist nicht zu ~* that's a fact; *gerüttelt(es) Maß* good measure (of).

S

S [ɛs], **s** *n inv.* S, s.
Saal [za:l] *m* (3³) hall.
Saat [za:t] *f* (16) (*Säen*) sowing; (*Same*) seed; (*sprossende Pflanzen*) standing (*od.* growing) crops *pl.*; '**~gut** *n* seed (-grain); '**~krähe** *f* rook; '**~zeit** *f* seed-time.
Sabbat ['zabat] *m* (3) Sabbath; '**~schändung** *f* Sabbathbreaking.
sabbern ['zabərn] (29) drivel, slaver, *Am.* drool; (*schwatzen*) twaddle.
Säbel ['zɛ:bəl] *m* (7) sab|re, *Am.* -er; *fig. mit dem ~ rasseln* rattle the sabre; '**~beine** *n/pl.* bow-legs; '**⚬beinig** bow-legged; '**~hieb** *m* sword-cut; '**⚬n** (29) sab|re, *Am.* -er.
Sabot|age [zabo'ta:ʒə] *f* (15) sabotage; **~age-akt** *m* act of sabotage; **~eur** [~'tø:r] *m* (3¹) saboteur; **⚬ieren** [~'ti:rən] sabotage.
Sacharin [zaxa'ri:n] *n* (3¹) saccharin(e).
'**Sach|be-arbeiter(in** *f*) *m* referee; *engS.* competent official; *in der Sozialpflege*: case worker; '**~beschädigung** *f* damage to property; '**~beweis** *m* material evidence; '**⚬bezogen** relevant, *pred.* to the point; '**~bezüge** *m/pl.* remuneration *sg.* in kind; '**~bücher** *n/pl.* non-fiction *sg.*; '**~darstellung** ⚖ *f* statement of facts; '**⚬dienlich** relevant, pertinent.
Sache ['zaxə] *f* (15) thing; (*Angelegenheit*) affair, matter, business, concern; (*Thema, Gebiet*) subject;

(*Punkt*) point; (*Streitfrage*) issue; (*Fall*) case; ⚖ case, (*a. weitS.*) cause; *s. gemeinsam*; (*nicht*) *zur* ~ (*gehörig*) (ir)relevant, *pred. a.* to (off) the point; *bei der* ~ *bleiben* stick to the point; *zur* ~ *kommen* come to the point; *er versteht s-e* ~ he knows his job; *ganz bei der* ~ *sn* be all attention; *nicht bei der* ~ *sn* be absent-minded; *s-r* ~ *sicher sein* be sure of one's ground; *das tut nichts zur* ~ that makes no difference; *es ist seine* ~ it is his business (*zu inf.* to *inf.*); *die* ~ *ist die, daß* ... the point is that ...; *s-e* ~ *gut* (*schlecht*) *machen* acquit o.s. well (ill); F *mit 100* ~*n mot.* with sixty (miles per hour); '~**n** *f/pl.* (*Waren, Gepäck usw.*) things, belongings, luggage, clothes, *etc.*

'**Sach|frage** *f* practical issue; '&**fremd** irrelevant; '~**gebiet** *n* subject, field; '&**gemäß**, '&**gerecht** proper(ly *adv.*), appropriate(ly); '~**katalog** *m* subject catalog(ue); '~**kenner** *m*, ~**kundige** ['~kundigə] *m* expert; '~**kenntnis** *f* special (*od.* expert) knowledge, experience; '&**kundig** *s. sachverständig*; '~**lage** *f* state of affairs, position; '~**leistung** *f* performance in kind.

'**sachlich** factual, real; (*zur Sache gehörig*) pertinent, relevant, *pred.* to the point; (*unparteiisch*) unbias(s)ed, impartial; *a.* ⚠ practical; (*Ggs. subjektiv*) objective; (*nüchtern*) matter-of-fact, businesslike, unemotional; *aus* ~*en Gründen* for technical reasons; ~ *richtig* factually correct.

sächlich ['zɛçliç] neuter.

'**Sachlichkeit** *f* objectivity; impartiality; matter-of-factness; realism.

'**Sach|register** *n* (subject) index; '~**schaden** *m* damage to property; *es entstand ein* ~ *von* ... the material damage amounted to ...

Sachse ['zaksə] *m* (13), **Sächsin** ['zɛksin] *f* (16[1]), '**sächsisch** Saxon.

'**Sachspende** *f* gift in kind.

sacht(**e**) ['zaxt(ə)] soft, gentle; (*langsam*) slow; (*vorsichtig*) cautious, gentle; ~! gently!; F (*immer*) ~! take it easy!, come, come!

Sach|verhalt ['~fɛrhalt] *m* (3) facts *pl.* (of the case); *s. a. Sachlage*; '~**vermögen** *n* tangible property; '&**verständig** expert(ly *adv.*), competent(ly); '~**verständige** *m, f* expert; '~**verständigengut-achten** *n* expert opinion; '~**walter** *m* advocate; (*Anwalt*) solicitor; (*Treuhänder*) trustee; (*Vertreter*) agent; '~**wert** *m* real value; *konkret*: ~*e pl.* material assets *pl.*

Sack [zak] *m* (3[3]) sack, bag; *anat., zo.* sac; *mit* ~ *und Pack* with bag and baggage; *s. Katze.*

Säckel ['zɛkəl] *m* (6) purse.

sacken ['zakən] (25) **1.** *v/t.* sack, put into sacks; **2.** *v/i.* (sn) (*sinken*) sink, give way, sag.

'**Sack|gasse** *f* blind alley; *fig.* impasse, deadlock; '~**hüpfen** *n*, '~**laufen** *n* sack-race; '~**leinwand** *f* sacking, burlap; '~**pfeife** *f* bagpipe; '~**tuch** *n* sacking; (*Taschentuch*) pocket-handkerchief.

Sadis|mus [za'dismus] *m inv.* sadism; ~**t** *m* (12) sadist; &**tisch** sadistic.

säen ['zɛːən] *v/t. u. v/i.* (25) sow.

Safari [za'fɑːri] *f* (11[1]) safari; ~**park** *m* safari park, wildlife reserve.

Safe [seːf] *m, n* (11) safe; ~**knacker** ['~knakər] *m* (7) safe-breaker, *sl.* cracksman.

Saffian ['zafjɑːn] *m* (3[1]) morocco (leather).

Safran ['zafrɑːn] *m* (3[1]) saffron; '&**gelb** saffron(-colo[u]red).

Saft [zaft] *m* (3) juice; *bot.* sap (*a. fig.*); *ohne* ~ *und Kraft* wishy-washy; '&**ig** juicy, succulent; (*kraftvoll*) sappy; *fig. Witz usw.*: juicy, spicy; *Niederlage*: crushing; *Ohrfeige*: resounding; '&**los** sapless; juiceless.

Sage ['zɑːgə] *f* (15) legend, myth; (*Überlieferung*) tradition; *es geht die* ~ the story goes.

Säge ['zɛːgə] *f* (15) saw; '~**blatt** *n* saw-blade; '~**bock** *m* saw-horse, *Am. a.* sawbuck; '~**fisch** *m* sawfish; '&**förmig** sawlike, serrate(d); '~**mehl** *n* sawdust.

sagen ['zɑːgən] (25) say; (*mitteilen*) tell; *j-m* ~ *lassen* send a p. word; *ich habe mir* ~ *lassen, daß* I have been told that; *ich muß schon* ~ I dare say; *sich* ~, *daß* ... tell o.s. that ...; *sich nichts* ~ *lassen* take no advice; *er läßt sich nichts* ~ he will not listen to reason; *das will* (*nicht*) ~ ... that is (not) to say ...; *es ist nicht gesagt, daß* ... that doesn't necessarily mean that ...;

unter uns (*gesagt*) between you and me (and the bedpost); *das hat nichts zu* ~ that doesn't matter; ~ *wollen mit* mean by; *j-m gute Nacht* ~ bid a p. good night; *laß dir das gesagt sein* let it be a warning to you; *gesagt, getan* no sooner said than done; *etwas* (*nichts*) *zu* ~ *haben bei* have a (no) say in; *man sagt, er sei krank* they say he is ill; *schwer zu* ~ hard to tell; *sage und schreibe* no less than; ~ *wir* (*mal*) say.

sägen ['zɛːgən] *v/t. u. v/i.* (25) saw.

'**sagen|haft** legendary, mythical; F *fig.* fantastic, fabulous; '**2kreis** *m* legendary cycle.

Säge|späne ['~ʃpɛːnə] *m/pl.* sawdust *sg.*; '**~werk** *n* saw-mill.

Sago ['zɑːgo] *m* (11) sago.

sah [zɑː] *pret. v. sehen.*

Sahne ['zɑːnə] *f* (15) cream; '**~bonbon** *m, n* toffee, toffy, *Am.* taffy; '**~käse** *m* cream cheese; '**~quark** *m* high-fat curd cheese; '**~torte** *f* layer cake.

sahnig ['zɑːniç] creamy.

Saison [sɛ'zɔ̃] *f* (11[1]) season; **~-arbeit**(**er** *m*) *f* seasonal work(er); **~-ausverkauf** *m* seasonal sale; **2bedingt, 2mäßig** seasonal; **~schwankungen** *f/pl.* seasonal fluctuation *sg.*

Saite ['zaɪtə] *f* (15) string, chord; *s. aufziehen*; '**~n-instrument** *n* stringed instrument.

Sakko ['zako] *m* (11) lounge jacket; '**~-anzug** *m* lounge suit.

sakral [za'krɑːl] sacral (*a. anat.*).

Sakrament [zakra'mɛnt] *n* (3) sacrament.

Sakrist|an [zakri'stɑːn] *m* (3[1] *u.* [3]) sexton; **~ei** [~'staɪ] *f* (16) vestry.

Säkular... [zɛːku'lɑːr-] secular; **2isieren** [~lari'ziːrən] secularize.

Salamander [zala'mandər] *m* (7) salamander.

Salami [za'lɑːmi] *f* salami; **~taktik** *fig. f* salami tactics *sg.*

Salat [za'lɑːt] *m* (3) salad; (*Pflanze*) lettuce; **~besteck** *n* salad servers *pl.*; **~-öl** *n* salad oil; **~schüssel** *f* salad bowl; **~soße** *f* salad dressing.

salbadern [zal'bɑːdərn] (29) twaddle.

Salbe ['zalbə] *f* (15) ointment; *mst* [*in Zssgn u. fig.* salve.]

Salbei ⚘ [zal'baɪ] *m* (3[1]), *f* (16) sage.

salben ['zalbən] (25) rub with ointment; *weitS.* anoint (*j-n zum König* a p. king).

'**Salbung** *f* anointing, (*a. fig.*) unction; '**2svoll** unctuous.

saldieren ✝ [zal'diːrən] balance, settle; ~ *mit* set off *a th.* against.

Saldo ['~do] *m* (11; *pl. a.* -*di*) balance; *den* ~ *ziehen* strike the balance; '**~vortrag** *m* balance forward.

Saline [za'liːnə] *f* (15) salt-works.

Salm *zo.* [zalm] *m* (3) salmon.

Salmiak [zal'mjak] *m* (11) sal ammoniac; **~geist** *m* liquid ammonia.

Salmonelle [zalmo'nɛlə] *f* (15) *mst pl.* salmonella; **~n-erkrankung** ⚕ *f* salmonellosis.

Salon [za'lɔ̃] *m* (11) drawing-room, *Am.* parlor; ⚓ saloon; **2fähig** fit for good society; **~held** *m*, **~löwe** *m* carpet-knight, ladies' man; **~wagen** *m* saloon-car, *Am.* Pullman (*od.* parlor) car.

salopp [za'lɔp] sloppy; (*lässig*) nonchalant, casual.

Salpeter [zal'peːtər] *m* (7) saltpet|re, nit|re, *Am.* -er; **~-erde** *f* nitrous earth; **2ig** nitrous; **~säure** *f* nitric acid.

Salto ['zalto] *m* (11) somersault; ~ **mortale** [~ mɔr'tɑːle] *m* breakneck leap.

Salut [za'luːt] *m* (3) salute; ~ *schießen* fire a salute; **2ieren** [~lu'tiːrən] *v/t. u. v/i.* salute.

Salve ['zalvə] *f* (15) (*Gewehr2*; *a. fig.*) volley; (*Geschütz2*) salvo; (*Ehren2*) salute.

Salz [zalts] *n* (3[2]) salt; '**~bergwerk** *n* salt-mine; '**2en** (27) salt; *s. gesalzen*; '**~faß** *n*, '**~fäßchen** *n auf dem Tische*: salt-cellar; '**~fleisch** *n* salt meat; '**~gurke** *f* pickled cucumber; '**~hering** *m* pickled herring; '**2ig** salt(y); (*salzhaltig*) saline; '**~kartoffeln** *f/pl.* boiled potatoes; '**~lake** *f*, '**~lauge** *f* brine, pickle; '**2los** saltless; *Diät*: salt-free; '**~rückstände** *m/pl.* salt residue *sg.*; '**~säule** *f Bibel*: pillar of salt; *fig. zur* ~ *erstarren* freeze; '**~säure** *f* hydrochloric acid; '**~see** *m* salt-lake; **~siederei** ['~ziːdə'raɪ] *f* salt-works, saltern; '**~sole** *f* brine; '**~streuer** *m* (7) salt shaker; '**~wasser** *n* salt-water; '**~werk** *n* salt-works.

Samariter [zama'riːtər] *m* (7) (*barmherziger* good) Samaritan.

Same ['zɑːmə] *m* (13[1]), '**~n** *m* (6) seed (*a. fig.*); *physiol.* sperm; '**~nbehälter** *m*, '**~ngehäuse** *n* seed-case, 🕮 pericarp; '**~n-erguß** *m* ejaculation; '**~n-**

faden *m* spermatozoon; **'~nflüssigkeit** *f* semen; **'~ngang** *m*, **'~nleiter** *m* seminal duct; **'~nkapsel** *f* (seed) capsule; **'~nkorn** *n* grain of seed; **'~nstaub** *m* pollen; **'~nstrang** *m* spermatic cord.

Sämischleder ['zɛːmiʃ-] *n* chamois (leather).

Sammel|-album ['zaməl-] *n* album; **'~band** *m* omnibus volume; **'~becken** *n* reservoir; *geogr.* catchment basin; **'~behälter** *m* collecting tank; **'~bestellung** *f* collective order; **'~bezeichnung** *f* collective name; **'~büchse** *f* collecting-box; **'~güter** *n/pl.* miscellaneous goods *pl.*; **'~ladung** ✝ *f* collective consignment; **'~lager** *n* assembly camp; **'~mappe** *f* file; **'♀n** (29, *a. sich*) gather; *Briefmarken, Geld usw., a.* ⊕: collect; (*anhäufen*) heap up, accumulate, amass; *Kunden, Stimmen*: canvass; (*vereinigen, a.* ⚔) concentrate; (*ver~*) assemble, rally (*beide a. sich*); *fig. sich* (*s-e Gedanken*) ~ concentrate, (*sich fassen*) compose o.s.; ~ *für e-n Zweck* collect money for; **'~name** *gr. m* collective noun; **'~nummer** *f* collective number; **'~-objekt** *n* collectible; **'~platz** *m* place of assembly; ⚔ assembly (*od.* rallying) point; **'~stecker** ⚡ *m* universal adapter plug; **~surium** [~'zuːrjum] *n* jumble, omnium gatherum; **'~taxi** *n* shared taxi; **'~titel** *m* collective title; **'~werk** *n* collected edition; **'~wut** *f* collector's mania.

Sammler ['zamlər] *m* (7) collector (*a.* **'~in** *f* [16[1]]); ⚡ accumulator; **'~batterie** ⚡ *f* storage battery.

'Sammlung *f* collection; *fig.* composure; concentration.

Sams-tag ['zamstaːk] *m* (3) Saturday; **'♀s** on Saturdays.

samt[1] [zamt] together (*od.* along) with; ~ *und sonders* all of them (*etc.*).

Samt[2] [~] *m* (3) velvet; **'♀-artig**, **'♀ig** velvety; **'~handschuh** *m*: *j-n mit ~en anfassen fig.* handle a p. with kid-gloves.

sämtlich ['zɛmtliç] *adj.* all; (*vollständig*) complete; *adv.* all (together *od.* of them).

Sanatorium [zana'toːrjum] *n* (9) sanatorium, *Am.* sanitarium.

Sand [zant] *m* (3) sand; *fig. im ~e verlaufen* come to nothing, peter out; *j-m ~ in die Augen streuen* throw dust in a p.'s eyes; *zahllos wie ~ am Meer* numberless as the sand(s).

Sandale [zan'daːlə] *f* (15) sandal.

'Sand|bahn *f Rennsport*: dirt-track; **'~bank** *f* sandbank; **'~blattnagelfeile** *f* emery board; **'~boden** *m* sandy soil; **'~burg** *f* sandcastle; **'~dorn** ⚘ *m* sea buckthorn.

Sandelholz ['zandəl-] *n* sandalwood.

'Sand|grube *f* sand pit; **♀ig** ['~diç] sandy; **'~kasten** *m* sand-box; *für Kinder*: sand-pit; ⚔ sand-table; **'~korn** *n* grain of sand; **'~mann** *m fig.* sandman; **'~papier** *n* sandpaper; **'~sack** *m* sandbag; *Boxen*: body bag; **'~stein** *m* sandstone; **'~strahlgebläse** ⊕ *n* sandblast unit; **'~sturm** *m* sandstorm.

sandte [zantə] *pret. v. senden.*

'Sand|torte *f* Madeira cake; **'~-uhr** *f* sand-glass; **'~wüste** *f* sandy desert.

sanft [zanft] soft; (*leicht, zart*) *a.* gentle; (*milde*) gentle, mild; (*glatt*) smooth; *Abhang, Tod*: easy.

Sänfte ['zɛnftə] *f* (15) sedan (chair).

'Sanft|heit *f* softness; gentleness; mildness; **'~mut** *f* (16) gentleness; **♀mütig** ['~myːtiç] gentle.

Sang [zaŋ] **1.** *m* (3[3]) song; singing; *ohne ~ und Klang*, *♀- und klanglos fig.* unhono(u)red and unsung; **2. ♀** *pret. v. singen.*

Sänger ['zɛŋər] *m* (7), **'~in** *f* (16[1]) singer; vocalist; (*Dichter*) bard; **'~fest** *n* singing-festival.

Sanguin|iker [zaŋgu'iːnikər] *m* (7) sanguine person; **♀isch** sanguine.

sanier|en [za'niːrən] (*heilen*) cure; (*vorbeugen*) give prophylactic treatment; *Stadtviertel, Haus*: redevelop; ✝ reorganize, (*stabilisieren*) stabilize, rehabilitate; **♀ung** *f* redevelopment; stabilization; rehabilitation; **♀ungsgebiet** *n* redevelopment area.

sanitär [zani'tɛːr] sanitary; *~e Einrichtung* sanitary facility.

Sanitäter [~'tɛːtər] *m* (7) ambulance (*od.* first-aid) man; ⚔ medical orderly.

Sani'täts|-artikel *m/pl.*, **~bedarf** *m* medical supplies *pl.*; **~dienst** *m* medical service; **~flugzeug** *n* air ambulance; **~kasten** *m* first-aid kit; **~raum** *m* first-aid room; **~truppe** *f* medical corps; **~wesen** *n* sanitary

matters *pl.*, ⚔ medical service.
sank [zaŋk] *pret. v. sinken.*
Sankt [zaŋkt], **St.** Saint, St.
Sanktion [zaŋkˈtsjoːn] *f* sanction; **≈ieren** [~tsjoˈniːrən] sanction.
sann [zan] *pret. v. sinnen.*
Saphir [ˈzɑːfir] *m* (3¹) sapphire.
Sard|elle [zarˈdɛlə] *f* (15) anchovy; **~ellenpaste** *f* anchovy paste; **~ine** [~ˈdiːnə] *f* (15) sardine.
Sarg [zark] *m* (3³) coffin, *Am. a.* casket; **ˈ~deckel** *m* coffin-lid; **ˈ~träger** *m* pallbearer.
Sark|asmus [zarˈkasmus] *m* (16²) sarcasm; **≈astisch** [~ˈkastiʃ] sarcastic(ally *adv.*).
Sarkophag [zarkoˈfɑːk] *m* (3¹) sarcophagus.
saß [zɑːs] *pret. v. sitzen.*
Satan [ˈzɑːtan] *m* (3¹) Satan; **≈isch** [zaˈtɑːniʃ] satanic(ally *adv.*).
Satellit [zatɛˈliːt] *m* (12) satellite; **~en-abwehr** ⚔ *f* satellite intelligence; **~enphoto** *n* satellite picture; **~enstaat** *pol. m* satellite state; **~enstadt** *f* satellite town; **~en-übertragung** *f* satellite transmission.
Satin [zaˈtɛ̃] *m* (11) (*Seidenatlas*) satin; (*Baumwoll≈*) sateen; **≈ieren** [zatiˈniːrən] satin, glaze; *Papier*: *a.* calender.
Satir|e [zaˈtiːrə] *f* (15) satire; **~iker** [~rikər] *m* satirist; **≈isch** satiric(al).
Satisfaktion [zatisfakˈtsjoːn] *f* satisfaction.
satt [zat] satisfied, satiate(d), full; *Farbe*: deep, saturated; *ich bin ~* I have enough; *sich ~ essen* eat one's fill; *et. ~ bekommen* (*haben*) get (be) sick of, F get (be) fed up with.
Sattel [ˈzatəl] *m* (7¹) saddle (*a.* = *Gebirgs≈*); *der Nase*: bridge; *aus dem ~ heben* unhorse, (*a. fig.*) unseat; *fest im ~* firmly in the saddle (*a. fig.*); **ˈ~decke** *f* saddle-cloth; **ˈ≈fest** saddle-fast; *fig.* quite firm (*in dat.* in); **ˈ~gurt** *m* girth; **ˈ≈n** *v/t. u. v/i.* (29) saddle; **ˈ~pferd** *n* saddle-horse; **ˈ~platz** *m* paddock; **ˈ~schlepper** *mot. m* articulated lorry; **ˈ~tasche** *f* saddle-bag; **ˈ~zeug** *n* saddle and harness.
ˈSattheit *f* satiety; saturation; *von Farben*: richness.
sättig|en [ˈzɛtigən] (25) satiate, satisfy; *Essen*: be substantial; ⚗ *usw.*: saturate; *j-n* (*sich*) *~* appease a p.'s (one's) hunger; **ˈ≈ung** *f* satiation; ⚗ saturation.
Sattler [ˈzatlər] *m* (7) saddler; **~ei** [~ˈraɪ] *f* (16) saddlery.
ˈsattsam sufficiently; *~ bekannt a.* notorious.
saturieren [zatuˈriːrən] saturate.
Satyr [ˈzɑːtyr] *m* (10 *od.* 13) satyr.
Satz [zats] *m* (3² *u.* ³) sentence (*a. gr.*); *gr.* clause; proposition (*a. phls.*, ♞); (*Boden≈*) sediment, dregs *pl.*; (*Kaffee≈*) grounds *pl.*; *typ.*, ♪ (*Vertonung*) composition; ♪ (*Teil e-s Tonstücks*) movement; (*zs.-gehörige Dinge*) set; ⊕ (*Schub*) batch; *Tennis*: set; (*Sprung*) leap, bound; (*bestimmtes Verhältnis*; *Preis*) rate; **ˈ~-aussage** *gr. f* predicate; **ˈ~ball** *m Tennis*: set point; **ˈ~bau** *m* construction; **ˈ≈fertig** *typ.* ready for composition; **ˈ~gefüge** *gr. n* complex sentence; **ˈ~gegenstand** *gr. m* subject; **ˈ~lehre** *gr. f* syntax; **ˈ~spiegel** *typ. m* type area; **ˈ~teil** *gr. m* part of sentence.
ˈSatzung *f* statute; *e-s Vereins usw.*: (statutes *pl.* and) articles *pl.*, by-laws *pl.*; **ˈ≈smäßig** statutory.
ˈSatzzeichen *n* punctuation mark.
Sau [zaʊ] *f* (14¹) sow; V *fig.* (dirty) pig, (*Frau*) slut; F *unter aller ~* lousy; F *zur ~ machen* let *a p.* have it.
sauber [ˈzaʊbər] clean (*a. fig. moralisch*); *a. fig. Äußeres, Arbeit, Handschrift usw.*: neat; *iro.* fine, nice; **ˈ≈keit** *f* cleanness, neatness; (*Ehrlichkeit*) integrity.
säuberlich [ˈzɔʏbərliç] *s. sauber*; *fig.* proper; (*sorgfältig*) careful.
saubermachen [ˈzaubər-], **säubern** [ˈzɔybərn] (29) clean, cleanse; *Zimmer*: clean up, tidy; (*frei machen*) clear (*von* of); *fig. u. pol.* purge (of, from).
ˈSäuber|ung *f* cleaning, *etc.*; *pol.* = **ˈ≈ungs-aktion** *pol. f* purge.
ˈSaubohne *f* broad (*od.* horse) bean.
Sauce [ˈzoːsə] *f s. Soße.*
Sauciere [zoˈsjɛːrə] *f* (15) sauce-boat.
ˈsauˈdumm F *Person*: (as) thick as two short planks; *Sache*: really stupid.
sauer [ˈzaʊər] (18, *comp. saurer, sup. ~st*) sour, acid (*a.* ⚗); *fig.* hard, painful; (*mürrisch*) cross, sour; *saure Gurke* pickled cucumber; ⚗ *saurer Regen* acid rain; *~ werden* turn sour,

Milch: turn (sour); F *fig.* get cross; *in den sauren Apfel beißen müssen* have to swallow the bitter pill; *j-m das Leben ~ machen* make life miserable for a p.; *~ reagieren auf et.* take *a th.* in bad part; *s. Drops.*

'**Sauer|-ampfer** *m* sorrel; '**~braten** *m* meat soaked in vinegar and stewed; '**~brunnen** *m* acidulous mineral water; **~ei** [zauə'raɪ] F *s. Schweinerei*; '**~kirsche** *f* morello cherry; '**~klee** *m* wood-sorrel; '**~kohl** *m*, '**~kraut** *n* sauerkraut.

säuer|lich ['zɔʏərliç] sourish; ⚗ acidulous; *fig.* wintry (*smile*); '**~n** (29) make sour; ⚗ acidify, acidulate; *Teig*: leaven.

'**Sauer|milch** *f* curdled milk; '**~stoff** *m* oxygen; '**~stoff-apparat** *m* oxygen-respirator; '**~stoffflasche** *f* oxygen cylinder; '**~stoffmangel** ⚕ *m* oxygen deficiency; '**~stoffmaske** *f* oxygen mask; '**~stoffzelt** ⚕ *n* oxygen tent; '**~teig** *m* leaven; **2töpfisch** ['~tœpfiʃ] peevish, sour.

saufen ['zaufən] *v/t. u. v/i.* (30) *Tier*: drink; *P.*: *a.* F booze, guzzle, soak.

Säufer F ['zɔʏfər] *m* (7) drunkard, alcoholic, F boozer.

Sauferei F [zaufə'raɪ] *f* hard drinking; *a.* = '**Saufgelage** *n* drinking-bout, F booze, binge, soak.

saugen ['zaugən] **1.** *v/t. u. v/i.* (30) suck (*an* et. [*dat.*] a th.); **2.** 2 *n* sucking; *mst* ⊕ suction.

säugen ['zɔʏgən] (25) suckle, nurse.

Sauger ['zaugər] *m* (7) sucker; *e-r Flasche*: nipple.

'**Säugetier** *n* mammal.

saug|fähig ['zauk-] absorbent; '**2flasche** *f* feeding-bottle; '**2heber** *m* siphon.

Säugling ['zɔʏkliŋ] *m* (3[1]) baby, infant, suckling; '**~s-ausstattung** *f* (*Wäsche*) layette; '**~sfürsorge** *f* infant welfare; '**~s-heim** *n* crèche (*fr.*); '**~spflege** *f* baby care; '**~s-schwester** *f* baby nurse; '**~ssterblichkeit** *f* infant mortality.

Saug|papier ['zauk-] *n* absorbent paper; '**~pumpe** *f* suction pump; '**~rohr** *n* suction pipe; '**~wirkung** *f* suction effect.

Säule ['zɔʏlə] *f* (15) *allg.* (*a. fig.*) column; (*Pfeiler*) pillar (*a. fig.*); ⚡ pile.

'**Säulen|gang** *m* colonnade, arcade; '**~schaft** *m* shaft of a column.

Saum [zaum] *m* (3[3]) seam, hem; (*Rand*) border, edge; *e-r Stadt*: outskirts *pl.*

'**saumäßig** F beastly, filthy, vile, awful, lousy.

säum|en¹ ['zɔʏmən] (25) *v/t.* hem; (*a. fig.*) border; *fig. die Straßen ~* line the streets; '**~en²** *v/i.* (*zögern, verweilen*) tarry; '**~ig** *s. saumselig.*

'**Saum|pfad** *m* mule-track; '**~pferd** *n* pack-horse; '**~sattel** *m* pack-saddle; '**2selig** tardy, slow; (*trödelnd*) dawdling; (*hinausschiebend*) dilatory; (*nachlässig*) negligent; '**~seligkeit** *f* tardiness; negligence; '**~tier** *n* sumpter-mule.

Sauna ['zauna] *f* (11[1]) sauna.

Säure ['zɔʏrə] *f* (15) sourness, *a.* ⚕ *des Magens*: acidity; ⚗ acid; '**~ballon** *m* carboy; '**2beständig,** '**2fest** acid-proof.

Saure'gurkenzeit *f* silly season.

'**säure|haltig** acidiferous; '**~löslich** acid-soluble.

Saurier ['zaurjər] *m* (7) saurian.

Saus [zaus] *m*: *in ~ und Braus leben* live on the fat of the land, revel and riot.

säuseln ['zɔʏzəln] *v/i. u. v/t.* (29) whisper, rustle; *fig. P.*: purr.

sausen ['zauzən] (27, h. *u.* sn) rush, whiz, flit; *Wind, Geschoß*: whistle.

'**Saustall** *m* pigsty; F *fig. a.* awful mess.

Saxophon ♪ [zakso'fo:n] *n* (3[1]) saxophone.

Schabe ['ʃa:bə] *f* (15) cockroach; '**~fleisch** *n* scraped meat; '**~messer** *n* scraping-knife; '**2n** *v/t. u. v/i.* (25) scrape; *mit Reibeisen usw.*: grate, rasp; '**~r** *m* (7) scraper; **~rnack** ['~nak] *m* (3) practical joke, hoax, prank(s *pl.*); *j-m e-n ~ spielen* play a p. a trick.

schäbig ['ʃɛ:biç] shabby; *fig. a.* mean; '**2keit** *f* shabbiness; *fig. a.* meanness.

Schablone [ʃa'blo:nə] *f* (15) (*Modell*) model; (*Muster*) pattern; (*~nform, Mal2*) stencil; *fig.* (*mechanische Arbeit*) routine; (*Denkweise usw.*) stereotype; **2nhaft, 2nmäßig** stereotyped; (*mechanisch*) mechanical, *nur attr.* routine.

Schach [ʃax] *n* (3) chess; *~ (dem König)! check!*; *~ und matt!* checkmate!; *~ bieten* (give) check, *fig. j-m*: defy a p.; *in ~ halten* keep in check (*a. fig.*), *mit e-r Waffe*: *a.* cover; '**~brett** *n* chessboard; '**2-brett-artig** checkered; '**~computer** *m* chess computer.

Schacher ['ʃaxər] *m* (7) haggling, low trade; *bsd. pol.* jobbery; '**2n** (29) haggle (*um* about, over).

Schächer ['ʃɛçər] *m* (7) *biblisch*: thief; (*Mörder*) murderer; *fig. armer ~* poor wretch.

'**Schach|feld** *n* square; '**~figur** *f* chessman; '**2'matt** (check)mate; *fig.* (*erschöpft*) all in; *~ setzen* checkmate (*a. fig.*); '**~partie** *f*, '**~spiel** *n* game of chess; '**~spieler** *m* chess-player.

Schacht [ʃaxt] *m* (3[3]) shaft, ⚒ *a.* pit; ⚠ (*Licht2 usw.*) well; (*Mannloch*) manhole.

Schachtel ['ʃaxtəl] *f* (15) box; *für Hüte, Putz usw.*: bandbox; *fig.* F *alte ~* old frump; '**~halm** ⚘ *m* shave-grass; '**~satz** *m* involved sentence.

'**Schach|turnier** *n* chess tournament; '**~zug** *m* move (*a. fig.*).

schade ['ʃa:də] **1.** (*es ist [sehr]*) ~ it is a (great) pity (*um* for; *daß* that), F it's too bad (*he couldn't come*); *wie ~!* what a pity!; *zu ~ für ihn* too good for him; **2.** 2 *m* (13[1], *pl. Schäden*) *s. schaden* 2.

Schädel ['ʃɛ:dəl] *m* (7) skull; '**~basis** *f* base of the skull; '**~bruch** *m* fracture of the skull, fractured skull; '**~decke** *f* skullpan.

schaden ['ʃa:dən] **1.** (26) injure, harm, hurt (*j-m* a p.); (*nachteilig sein*) be prejudicial (to a p.); *das schadet nichts* it will do no harm; *das schadet ihm gar nichts* that serves him right; *was schadet es?* what does it matter?; *e-e Aussprache könnte nicht ~* a discussion might not be amiss; **2.** 2 *m* (6[2]) damage (*an dat.* to); (*Mangel*) defect; (*Beschädigung*) injury, harm; (*a.* ⊕) defect; (*Nachteil*) detriment, prejudice; (*Verlust*) loss; *zu meinem ~* to my damage *od.* cost; *j-m ~ zufügen* do a p. harm; *mit ~ verkaufen* sell at a loss; *~ erleiden od. nehmen, zu ~ kommen* be damaged, come to harm; *durch ~ wird man klug* once bitten twice shy; '**2-ersatz** *m* compensation, indemnification; (*Geldsumme*) damages *pl.*; *~ leisten* pay damages (*für* for); *auf ~ verklagen* sue for damages; '**2-ersatzklage** *f* action for damages; '**~-ersatzpflichtig** liable for damage(s); '**2freiheitsrabatt** *mot. m* no-claims bonus; '**2freude** *f* malicious joy, gloating; *voller ~* gloatingly, maliciously; '**~froh** malicious, gloating.

schadhaft ['ʃa:thaft] defective; '**2igkeit** *f* defectiveness.

schädig|en ['ʃɛ:digən] (25) damage, impair; *j-n*: harm, wrong, prejudice; '**2ung** *f* damage, prejudice (*gen.* to).

schädlich ['ʃɛ:tliç] harmful, injurious, hurtful; (*nachteilig*) detrimental, prejudicial; (*gesundheits~*) noxious, unwholesome (*alle*: *dat. od. für* to); '**2keit** *f* harmfulness, injuriousness; noxiousness.

Schädling ['~liŋ] *m* (3[1]) pest; *~e pl.* ✗ *a.* vermin; '**~sbekämpfung** *f* pest control; '**~sbekämpfungsmittel** *n* pesticide.

schadlos ['~lo:s]: *~ halten* indemnify; '**2haltung** *f* indemnification.

'**Schadstoff** *m* pollutant.

Schaf [ʃa:f] *n* (3) sheep; (*Mutter2*) ewe; *fig.* ninny; *schwarzes ~* black sheep; '**~bock** *m* ram.

Schäfchen ['ʃɛ:fçən] *n* (6) little sheep, lamb(kin); *pl.* (*Wolken*) fleecy clouds; *fig. sein ~ ins trockene bringen* feather one's nest.

Schäfer ['~ər] *m* (7), '**~in** *f* shepherd(ess *f*); '**~hund** *m* shepherd('s) dog; *deutscher ~* German shepherd (dog), Alsatian; '**~stündchen** *n* lover's hour.

schaffen ['ʃafən]: **a)** *v/t.* (30) (*er~*) create; (*hervorbringen*) *a.* produce (*a. weitS. Situation usw.*); (*gründen*) organize, set up; *er ist für diesen Posten wie geschaffen* he is cut out for this post; **b)** *v/t. u. v/i.* (25) (*tun, arbeiten*) do, make, work; (*fertig werden mit*) cope with, manage; (*ver~*) provide; (*befördern*) convey, (*weg~*) take, (*her~*) bring; (*bewältigen*) manage, (*erreichen*) *a.* reach, *Am.* make; F *e-e Strecke, e-e Geschwindigkeit, Zeit*: do; F *es ~* suceed, F make it; *viel ~* get a great deal done; *nichts zu ~ haben mit* have nothing to do with; *j-m (viel) zu ~ machen* give a p. (a great deal of) trouble; *sich unbefugt zu ~ machen an* (*dat.*) tamper with; *sich eifrig zu ~ machen mit et.* busy o.s.

(*od.* be busy) with a th.; F *er* (*es*) *schafft mich!* he (it) gets me (down)!; *s. Hals, Rat, Seite, Vergnügen, Weg, Welt.*

ˈ**Schaffens|drang** *m* creative urge; ˈ**~kraft** *f* creative power; *weitS.* vigo(u)r.

ˈ**Schaf-fleisch** *n* mutton.

Schaffner [ˈʃafnər] *m* (7) 🚂 guard, *Am.* conductor; (*Bus*≈ *usw.*) conductor; ˈ**~in** *f* (16[1]) 🚂 conductress.

Schaffung [ˈʃafuŋ] *f* creation; provision; organizing.

ˈ**Schaf|garbe** ⚘ *f* yarrow; ˈ**~herde** *f* flock of sheep; ˈ**~hirt** *m* shepherd; ˈ**~hürde** *f* sheep-pen, -fold; ˈ**~leder** *n* sheepskin; ˈ**~(s)kopf** *m fig.* idiot.

Schafott [ʃaˈfɔt] *n* (3) scaffold.

ˈ**Schaf|pelz** *m*: *Wolf im ~* wolf in sheep's clothing; ˈ**~schur** *f* sheep-shearing; ˈ**~smilch** *f* ewe's milk.

Schaft [ʃaft] *m* (3[3]) shaft; (*Gewehr*≈) stock; *e-s Werkzeugs, Ankers, Schlüssels*: shank; (*Griff*) handle; (*Stiefel*≈) leg.

schäften [ˈʃɛftən] (26) *Gewehr*: stock, mount; *Stiefel*: leg.

ˈ**Schaftstiefel** *m* top boot.

ˈ**Schaf|wolle** *f* sheep's wool; ˈ**~zucht** *f* sheep-breeding.

Schah [ʃɑ:] *m* (11) Shah.

Schakal [ʃaˈkɑ:l] *m* (3[1]) jackal.

Schäker [ˈʃɛ:kər] *m* (7) rogue, wag; (*Hofmacher*) flirt; **~ei** [~ˈraɪ] *f* (16) joking, badinage; (*Liebelei*) flirtation, dalliance; ˈ**≈n** (29) joke, make fun; (*tändeln*) dally; (*liebeln*) flirt.

schal[1] [ʃɑ:l] stale (*a. fig.*).

Schal[2] [~] *m* (3[1] *u.* 11) scarf; (*Schultertuch e-r Frau*) shawl; *wollener*: comforter; ˈ**~brett** *n* slab.

Schale [ˈʃɑ:lə] *f* (15) bowl, basin; *für Früchte usw.*: dish; (*Tasse*) cup; *v. Pellkartoffeln, Obst*: skin; (*Hülse*) shell, husk; (*Schote*) pod; (*Obst*≈) peel; (*abgeschälte ~*) paring, (*bsd. Kartoffel*≈) peeling; (*Eier*≈, *Nuß*≈) shell; (*Muschel*≈) valve; (*Messer*≈; *Waag*≈) scale; *fig.* shell; F *sich in ~ werfen* spruce o.s. up.

schälen [ˈʃɛ:lən] (25) peel, pare; *Hülsenfrüchte*: shell, husk; *Baum*: bark; *sich ~* peel off.

ˈ**Schalheit** *f* staleness.

Schalk [ʃalk] *m* (3[3]) rogue; (*Spaßvogel*) wag; ˈ**≈haft** arch, roguish; (*spaßend*) waggish; ˈ**~haftigkeit** *f* archness, roguery; waggishness.

Schall [ʃal] *m* (3[3]) sound; *schneller als der ~* supersonic; ˈ**~boden** *m* sound(ing)-board; ˈ**≈dämpfend** sound deadening; ˈ**~dämpfer** *m* sound absorber; *mot.* silencer (*a. an Schußwaffen*), *Am.* muffler; ˈ**≈dicht** soundproof; ˈ**≈en** (30, h. *u.* sn) sound, ring; *~des Gelächter* peal of laughter, guffaw; ˈ**~geschwindigkeit** *f* speed of sound, sonic speed; ˈ**~grenze** *f*, ˈ**~mauer** *f* sound (*od.* sonic) barrier; ˈ**~lehre** *f* acoustics; ˈ**~messung** *f* sound ranging; ˈ**~platte** *f* disc, record; ˈ**~platten-aufnahme** *f* disc recording; ˈ**~plattenmusik** *f* recorded music; ˈ**~plattennadel** *f* stylus; ˈ**≈schluckend** sound deadening; ˈ**~schutz** *m* noise control; (*Isolierung*) sound insulation; ˈ**~schutzfenster** *n* soundproof window; ˈ**~trichter** *m* bell-mouth; *des Grammophons*: horn; ˈ**~welle** *f* sound-wave.

Schalmei [ʃalˈmaɪ] *f* (16) shawm.

schalt [ʃalt] *pret. v. schelten.*

ˈ**Schalt|-anlage** *f* switch-gear; ˈ**~bild** *n* wiring (*od.* circuit) diagram; ˈ**~brett** *n* switchboard, control panel; *mot.*, ✈ instrument panel, dashboard.

schalten [ˈʃaltən] (26) ⊕ (*auslösen*) actuate; (*bedienen*) operate; (*steuern*) control; ⚡ (*um~*) switch, (*verbinden*) connect, (*verdrahten*) wire; *mot.* change (*od.* shift) gears; *Kupplung*: engage; *auf den ersten Gang ~* shift (*od.* change) into the bottom gear; *~ und walten* manage, (*hantieren*) potter about; *mit et. ~* deal with; F *fig.* (*schnell*) *~* do some quick thinking.

ˈ**Schalter** *m* (7) 🚂 *usw.*: booking-office; ☏, *Bank*: counter, window, desk; ⚡ switch; ⊕, *mot.* controller; ˈ**~be-amte** *m* counter-clerk; 🚂 *usw.*: booking-clerk; ˈ**~dienst** *m* counter-service.

ˈ**Schalt|getriebe** *n* control gear; *mot.* change-speed gear; ˈ**~hebel** *m* control lever; *mot.* gear(shift) lever; ⚡ switch lever.

Schaltier [ˈʃɑ:lti:r] *n* shellfish, crustacean.

ˈ**Schalt|jahr** *n* leap-year; ˈ**~knopf** *m* (control) button; ˈ**~kreis** *m* circuit; ˈ**~plan** *m*, ˈ**~schema** *n s. Schaltbild*; ˈ**~pult** *n* control desk; ˈ**~tafel** *f* *s. Schaltbrett*; '**~tag** *m* intercalary day; '**~ung** *f* ⊕ control; ⚡ circuit; connection(s *pl.*); (*Verdrahtung*) wiring; (*Umschalten*) switching; *mot.* gear-change, changing, shifting.

Schalung ['ʃa:luŋ] ⚠ *f* form.

Schaluppe ⚓ [ʃa'lupə] *f* (15) sloop.

Scham [ʃa:m] *f* (16, *o. pl.*) shame; (*~haftigkeit*) modesty; *anat.* (*~teile*) private parts *pl.*, genitals *pl.*; (*weibliche*) ~ 🕮 vulva; '**~bein** *n* pubic bone.

schämen ['ʃɛ:mən] (25): *sich* ~ be (*od.* feel) ashamed (*e-r S.* [*wegen*], *über acc.* of).

'**Scham|gefühl** *n* sense of shame; '**~gegend** *f* pubic region; '**~haare** *n/pl.* pubic hair *sg.*; '**2haft** bashful, modest; '**~haftigkeit** *f* bashfulness, modesty; '**2los** shameless; '**~losigkeit** *f* shamelessness.

Schamotte [ʃa'mɔtə] *f* (15) fireclay; **~stein** *m* fire-brick.

'**scham|rot** blushing; ~ *werden* blush; ~ *machen* put to the blush; '**2röte** *f* blush; '**2teile** *m/pl.* private parts, genitals.

schandbar ['ʃantba:r] *s. schändlich.*

Schande ['ʃandə] *f* (15) shame, disgrace; *s. zuschanden.*

schänd|en ['ʃɛndən] (26) dishono(u)r, disgrace; (*entweihen*) desecrate, profane; (*verunstalten*) disfigure; *ein Mädchen*: ravish, rape; '**2er** *m* (7) ravisher; violator.

Schandfleck ['ʃant-] *m* stain, blot; (*häßlicher Anblick*) eyesore.

schändlich ['ʃɛntliç] shameful, infamous; scandalous; '**2keit** *f* infamy; baseness.

'**Schand|mal** *n* stigma, brand; '**~maul** *n* slanderer; '**~pfahl** *m* pillory; '**~tat** *f* infamous action; foul crime.

'**Schändung** *f s. schänden*: violation; desecration; disfigurement; ravishment, rape.

Schank|-erlaubnis ['ʃaŋk-] *f* publican's licence, *Am.* excise license; '**~stätte** *f* licensed premises *pl.*; '**~stube** *f* tap-room, *Am.* bar; '**~wirt** *m* publican, *Am.* saloonkeeper; '**~wirtschaft** *f s. Schenke.*

Schanze ['ʃantsə] *f* (15) entrenchment; ⚓ quarter-deck; *s. Sprungschanze*; *in die* ~ *schlagen* risk, hazard; '**2n** (27) entrench; *fig.* (*schwer arbeiten*) drudge; '**~ntisch** *m Schisport*: ski-jumping platform.

Schar [ʃa:r] *f* (16) **1.** troop, band, group; *v. Gänsen usw.*: flock; (*gedrängte Menge*) crowd; **2.** (*Pflug2*) ploughshare, *Am.* plowshare; '**2en** (25, *a. sich*) assemble, collect, flock (together); *um sich* ~ rally; *sich* ~ *um* (*acc.*) rally round; '**2enweise** in crowds (*od.* droves).

scharf [ʃarf] *allg.* sharp (*a. fig. Blick, Gegensatz, Kurve, Stimme, Verstand, Zunge usw.*); *Schneide, a. fig. Verstand, Beobachter*: keen; (*beißend, brennend*) biting, burning; *Geruch*: pungent; *Pfeffer*: hot; *Brille*: strong; (*streng*) severe, strict; (*schroff*) abrupt, sharp; (*genau*) exact; *phot.* well-focus(s)ed; *Munition*: live; *Mine usw.*: armed; ✝ *Konkurrenz*: stiff; *ein ~es Ohr* a quick ear; *j-n* ~ *ansehen* look hard at a p.; ~ *aufpassen* give close attention; ~ *reiten* ride hard; ~ *schießen* shoot with live ammunition; ~ *sein auf* (*acc.*) be keen on; '**2blick** *m* quick eye; *fig.* penetration.

Schärfe ['ʃɛrfə] *f* (15) sharpness; (*Schneide*) edge.

'**schärfen** (25) sharpen (*a. fig.*).

'**Schärfentiefe** *phot. f* depth of focus.

'**scharf|kantig, ~randig** ['~randiç] sharp-edged; '**~machen** ⚔ arm, activate; *fig.* (*aufhetzen*) instigate; '**2macher** *m fig.* agitator; '**2richter** *m* executioner; '**2schießen** *n* live shooting; '**2schütze** *m* sharp-shooter, marksman; ⚔ sniper; **~sichtig** ['~ziçtiç] sharp-sighted; *fig. a.* penetrating; '**2sinn** *m* sagacity, acumen; '**~sinnig** shrewd, sagacious, penetrating.

Scharlach ['ʃarlax] *m* (3[1]) scarlet; ⚕ = '**~fieber** *n* scarlet fever; '**2rot** scarlet(-red).

Scharlatan ['ʃarlatan] *m* (3[1]) charlatan, quack, mountebank.

Scharm *m usw. s. Charme usw.*

Scharmützel [ʃar'mytsəl] *n* (7) skirmish; **2n** (29) skirmish.

Scharnier [ʃar'ni:r] *n* (3[1]) hinge; joint; **~deckel** *m* hinged lid.

Schärpe ['ʃɛrpə] *f* (15) scarf, sash.

scharren ['ʃarən] *v/t. u. v/i.* (25) scrape, scratch; *Pferd*: paw.

Scharte ['ʃartə] *f* (15) notch; (*Riß*) fissure; (*Lücke*) gap; *s. Schieß2*; *fig.*

die ~ auswetzen wipe out the disgrace, make up for it.
Scharteke [ʃarˈteːkə] *f* (15) old (*od.* trashy) volume.
ˈ**schartig** notchy, jagged.
scharwenzeln F [ʃarˈvɛntsəln] (29) fawn (*um* [up]on).
Schatten [ˈʃatən] *m* (6) (*Schattenbild*) shadow (*a. fig.*); (*Dunkel*) shade; *in den ~ stellen fig.* put in the shade, eclipse; *e-n ~ werfen auf* (*acc.*) *fig.* cast a shadow upon; ˈ**~bild** *n* silhouette; *fig.* phantom; ˈ**~boxen** *n* shadow-boxing; ˈ**~dasein** *n*: *ein ~ führen* live in the shadow; ˈ**2haft** shadowy; ˈ**~kabinett** *pol. n* shadow cabinet; ˈ**~könig** *m* mock king; ˈ**~riß** *m* silhouette; ˈ**~seite** *f* shady side; *fig.* seamy side; ˈ**~spiel** *n* shadow play.
schattier|en [ʃaˈtiːrən] shade, tint; (*schraffieren*) hatch; **2ung** *f* shading; hatching; (*Farbton*) shade, tint.
ˈ**schattig** shady.
Schatulle [ʃaˈtulə] *f* (15) casket; *e-s Fürsten*: privy purse.
Schatz [ʃats] *m* (3² *u.* ³) treasure (*a. fig.*); *als Kosewort*: darling, F deary; F (*Geliebte*[*r*]) sweetheart; ˈ**~-amt** *n* *Brt.* Exchequer, *Am.* Treasury (Department); ˈ**~-anweisung** *f* Treasury bond (*Am.* certificate).
schätzbar [ˈʃɛtsbaːr] estimable.
schätzen [ˈʃɛtsən] (27) estimate; value, assess (*auf acc.* at); (*taxieren*) *a.* rate; (*hoch~*) esteem, *et.*: *a.* treasure; (*würdigen*) appreciate; *sich glücklich ~, zu inf.* be delighted to *inf.*; ˈ**~swert** estimable.
Schätzer [ˈʃɛtsər] *m* (7) valuer; *Versicherung*: appraiser.
ˈ**Schatz|fund** *m* treasure-trove; ˈ**~gräber** *m* treasure-seeker; ˈ**~kammer** *f* treasury; ˈ**~meister** *m* treasurer; ˈ**~suche** *f* treasure hunt.
ˈ**Schätzung** *f* estimate; (*Taxierung*) valuation; assessment; (*Ein2*) rating; (*Würdigung*) estimation; (*Hoch2*) esteem.
Schau [ʃaʊ] *f* (16) (point of) view; (*Ausstellung*) show, exhibition; *zur ~ stellen* exhibit, display; *zur ~ tragen* display, sport, *Miene usw.*: wear; F *e-e ~ abziehen* put on a show; ˈ**~bild** ⊕ *n* chart, graph; diagram; ˈ**~bude** *f* show-booth; ˈ**~budenbesitzer** *m* showman; ˈ**~bühne** *f* stage.
Schauder [ˈʃaʊdər] *m* (7) shudder (-ing), shiver; *fig.* horror; ˈ**2haft** horrible; ˈ**2n** (29, h. *u.* sn) shudder, shiver (*vor dat.* with; *bei* at).
schauen [ˈʃaʊən] (25) *v/t.* see; (*betrachten*) view, behold; *v/i.* look; *~ auf* (*acc.*) look at, *als Vorbild*: look upon.
Schauer [ˈʃaʊər] *m* (7) (*Regen2*, *Hagel2 u. fig.*) shower; (*Schauder*) shudder, shiver; (*Anfall*) attack, fit; (*innere Erregung*) thrill; ˈ**~drama** *n* thriller; ˈ**2lich** horrible, ghastly; ˈ**~mann** ⚓ *m* stevedore, docker, *bsd. Am.* longshoreman; ˈ**2n** (29) *s. schaudern*; *hageln*; ˈ**~roman** *m* F thriller, shocker, *Am.* dime novel.
Schaufel [ˈʃaʊfəl] *f* (15) shovel; *zum Schöpfen*: scoop; (*Rad2*) paddle; (*Geweih2*) palm; ˈ**~geweih** *n* palmed antlers *pl.*; ˈ**2n** *v/t. u. v/i.* (29) shovel; ˈ**~rad** *n* paddle-wheel.
ˈ**Schaufenster** *n* shop-window, *Am.* store window; ˈ**~-auslage** *f* window display; ˈ**~dekoration** *f* window-dressing; ˈ**~reklame** *f* window-display advertising; ˈ**~wettbewerb** *m* window-display competition.
ˈ**Schau|fliegen** *n* stunt (flying), air display; ˈ**~haus** *n* mortuary; ˈ**~kampf** *m* exhibition bout; ˈ**~kasten** *m* showcase, display case.
Schaukel [ˈʃaʊkəl] *f* (15) swing; (*Wipp2*) = ˈ**~brett** *n* seesaw; ˈ**2n** *v/t. u. v/i.* (29) swing; *Wiege, Stuhl, Schiff*: rock; (*wippen*) seesaw; F (*zuwege bringen*) *sl.* swing, wangle; ˈ**~pferd** *n* rocking-horse; ˈ**~politik** *f* seesaw policy; ˈ**~stuhl** *m* rocking-chair.
ˈ**schaulustig** curious; ˈ**2e** *m, f* on-[looker.]
Schaum [ʃaʊm] *m* (3³) foam, (*a. Bier2*) froth; (*Seifen2*) lather; (*Ab2*) scum; *zu ~ schlagen* whip, beat up (*egg*); ˈ**~bad** *n* bubble bath.
schäumen [ˈʃɔʏmən] (25) foam, froth; *Wein usw.*: sparkle; *fig.* (*vor Wut ~*) foam (with rage).
ˈ**Schaum|gebäck** *n* meringue(s *pl.*); ˈ**~gummi** *m* foam rubber; ˈ**2ig** foamy, frothy; ˈ**~löscher** *m* foam fire-extinguisher; ˈ**~schläger** *m* (*Gerät*) whisk, egg-beater; *fig.* (*Prahler*) gas-bag; **~schlägerei** [~ˈraɪ] *f fig.* humbug; ˈ**~teppich** ✈ *m* foam carpet.

ˈ**Schaumünze** *f* medal.
ˈ**Schaumwein** *m* sparkling wine.
ˈ**Schau|nummer** *f fig.* stunt; ˈ**~platz** *m* scene; *s.* Kriegs♀; ˈ**~prozeß** ⚖ *m* show trial.
schaurig [ˈʃaʊriç] horrible, horrid.
ˈ**Schau|spiel** *n* spectacle; *thea.* play; ˈ**~spieler** *m* actor, player; *contp. fig.* play-actor; **~spieleˈrei** *f fig.* play-acting; ˈ**~spielerin** *f* actress; ˈ**♀spielern** (29) *fig.* play-act, sham, F put it on; ˈ**~spielhaus** *n* playhouse, theat|re, *Am.* -er; ˈ**~spielkunst** *f* dramatic art; ˈ**~spielschule** *f* drama school; ˈ**~steller** *m* (7) exhibitor; *auf Jahrmärkten usw.*: showman; ˈ**~stellung** *f* exhibition, show; ˈ**~stück** *n* exhibit.
Scheck [ʃɛk] *m* (11) cheque, *Am.* check; ˈ**~betrug** *m* cheque (*Am.* check) fraud; ˈ**~betrüger(in** *f*) *m* person issuing bad cheques (*Am.* checks); ˈ**~buch** *n*, ˈ**~heft** *n* cheque-book, *Am.* checkbook.
Scheck|e [ˈʃɛkə] *m* (13) piebald (*od.* dappled) horse; ˈ**♀ig** piebald.
ˈ**Scheckkarte** *f* cheque (*Am.* check) card.
scheel [ʃeːl] squint-eyed; *fig.* envious, jealous (*a.* ˈ**~süchtig**); j-n ~ ansehen look askance at a p.
Scheffel [ˈʃɛfəl] *m* (7) bushel; sein Licht unter den ~ stellen hide one's light under a bushel; ˈ**♀n** *Geld*: amass, rake in.
Scheibe [ˈʃaɪbə] *f* (15) disk (*a. der Sonne*); ⊕ *mst* disc, plate; (*Brot*♀ *usw.*) slice; (*Glas*♀) pane; (*Schieß*♀) target; (*Töpfer*♀) potter's wheel; *s. a.* Töpfer♀, Riemen♀, Unterleg♀.
ˈ**Scheiben|bremse** *mot. f* disc brake; ˈ**~honig** *m* honey in the comb; ˈ**~schießen** *n* target practice; ˈ**~stand** *m* butts *pl.*; ˈ**~waschanlage** *mot. f* windscreen (*Am.* windshield) washers *pl.*; ˈ**~wischer** *mot. m* wind-screen (*Am.* windshield) wiper.
Scheich [ʃaɪç] *m* (3^1 *od.* 11) sheik(h).
Scheide [ˈʃaɪdə] *f* (15) (*Säbel*♀) sheath, scabbard; *anat.* vagina; (*Grenze*) borderline; ˈ**~linie** *f* separating line; ˈ**♀n** (30) *v/t.* separate, divide; ⚗ analyse, refine, (*zerlegen*) decompose; *Eheleute*: divorce; *Ehe*: dissolve; sich ~ lassen (seek a) divorce; *v/i.* (sn) separate; (*weggehen*) depart; (*sich trennen*) part; aus dem Dienst ~ retire from service; aus e-r Firma ~ leave a firm; aus dem Leben ~ depart this life; ˈ**♀nd** parting; *Jahr*: closing; ˈ**~wand** *f* partition; *fig.* barrier; ˈ**~wasser** ⚗ *n* aqua fortis; ˈ**~weg** *m* cross-road; *fig.* am ~e at the cross-roads.
ˈ**Scheidung** *f* separation; (*Ehe*♀) divorce; die ~ einreichen file a petition for divorce; ˈ**~s-anwalt** *m* divorce lawyer; ˈ**~sgrund** *m* ground for divorce; ˈ**~sklage** *f* divorce-suit.
Schein [ʃaɪn] *m* (3) shine, light; (*Schimmer*) gleam; (*Strahl*) flash; (*Feuer*♀) blaze; (*Bescheinigung*) certificate; (*Formular*) form; (*Zettel*) slip; (*Fahr*♀) ticket; (*Quittung*) receipt; (*Rechnung usw.*) bill; (*Geld*♀) bank-note, *Am.* bill; (*Ggs. Wirklichkeit*) appearance, *s.* Anschein; (nur) zum ~ just for show; der ~ trügt appearances are deceptive; den ~ wahren keep up appearances; ˈ**~-angriff** *m* feint (attack); ˈ**♀bar** apparent(ly *adv.*), seeming(ly); ˈ**~blüte** ✝ *f* specious prosperity; ˈ**~-ehe** *f* fictitious marriage.
ˈ**scheinen** (30) shine; *fig.* appear, seem; wie es scheint as it seems; es scheint mir it seems to me.
ˈ**Schein|firma** *f* dummy firm; ˈ**~friede** *m* hollow peace; ˈ**~gefecht** *n* sham fight; ˈ**~geschäft** ✝ *n* fictitious transaction; ˈ**~grund** *m* fictitious reason; (*Vorwand*) pretext; ˈ**♀heilig** hypocritical; ˈ**~heilige** *m* (18) hypocrite; ˈ**~heiligkeit** *f* hypocrisy; ˈ**~tod** *m* suspended animation; ˈ**♀tot** seemingly dead; ˈ**~werfer** *m* reflector, projector; ⚔, ⚓ searchlight; *mot.* headlight; *thea.* (*a.* ˈ**~werferlicht** *n*) spotlight.
Scheiß|dreck V [ˈʃaɪs-] *m* crap; (*ärgerliche Situation*) bloody nuisance; sich um jeden ~ kümmern müssen have to see to every bloody little thing; ˈ**~e** V *f* (15) shit; ˈ**♀en** V (30) shit; ˈ**~kerl** V *m* bastard.
Scheit [ʃaɪt] *n* (1 *u.* 3) log.
Scheitel [ˈʃaɪtəl] *m* (7) crown of the head; *von Dingen*: vertex (*bsd.* ⩓), summit, top; (*Haar*♀) parting (of the hair); ˈ**♀n** (29) part; ˈ**~punkt** *m* vertex; *ast.* zenith (*a. fig.*); ˈ**~winkel** *m* (vertically) opposite angle.
ˈ**Scheiterhaufen** *m* (6) (funeral)

pile, pyre; *zur Hinrichtung*: stake.
scheitern ['ʃaɪtərn] (29, sn) (*a. fig.*) be wrecked (*an dat.* on); *fig.* miscarry, fail; *zum* ♀ *bringen* wreck.
Schellack ['ʃɛlak] *m* (3) shellac.
Schelle ['ʃɛlə] *f* (15) (little) bell; ⊕ clamp, clip; *s. Maul*♀; *Kartenspiel*: *~n pl.* diamonds; '**♀n** (25) *s. klingeln.*
'**Schellfisch** *m* haddock.
Schelm [ʃɛlm] *m* (3) rogue; (*Schurke*) knave; *armer* ~ poor wretch; '**~enroman** *m* picaresque novel; '**~enstreich** *m*, **~erei** [~ə-'raɪ] *f* (16) roguish trick; roguery; '**♀isch** roguish, arch.
Schelt|e ['ʃɛltə] *f* (15) scolding; ~ *bekommen* be scolded; '**♀en** (30) *v/t.* scold, chide (*a. v/i.*); (*nennen*) call; '**~wort** *n* (3) abusive word.
Schema ['ʃeːma] *n* (11[²]) scheme; ⊕ *a.* diagram; (*Muster, Anordnung*) pattern; *nach* ~ F by rote; **♀tisch** [ʃe'maːtiʃ] schematic(ally *adv.*); systematic(ally); **♀tisieren** [~mati-'ziːrən] schematize, standardize.
Schemel ['ʃeːməl] *m* (7) (foot)stool.
Schemen ['ʃeːmən] *m* (6) phantom, shadow; '**♀haft** shadowy.
Schenke ['ʃɛŋkə] *f* (15) inn, public (-house), tavern.
Schenkel ['ʃɛŋkəl] *m* (7) (*Ober*♀) thigh; (*Unter*♀) shank; (*Bein*) leg; *e-s Winkels*: side; *e-s Dreiecks, e-r Röhre*: leg; *e-s Zirkels*: foot; '**~bruch** *m* thigh-bone fracture.
schenken ['ʃɛŋkən] (25) give, make a present of; (*stiften*) donate; (*gewähren*) grant; *j-m et.* ~ give a p. a th., present a p. with a th.; *Schuld, Strafe*: remit; *Getränke*: retail, (*ein*~) pour (out); *sich et.* ~ (*weglassen, nicht tun*) skip; *j-m das Leben* ~ spare a *p.'s* life, *e-m Kinde*: give birth to; *s. Aufmerksamkeit, Freiheit, Gehör, Glauben usw.*
'**Schenkung** *f* donation; '**~s-urkunde** *f* deed of gift.
scheppern ['ʃɛpərn] F (29) rattle.
Scherbe ['ʃɛrbə] *f* (15), '**~n** *m* (6) fragment, broken piece *od.* bit; (*Topf*♀) potsherd.
Schere ['ʃeːrə] *f* (15) (*eine* a pair of) scissors *pl.*; (*große* ~) shears *pl.*; (*Krebs*♀) claw; '**♀n** (30, *a.* 25) shear, clip; *Haare*: cut; *Rasen*: mow; ⚓ warp, sheer; *sich* (*weg*)~ F beat it; *sich nicht* ~ *um* not to bother about.
'**Scheren|fernrohr** ⚔ *n* scissor(s)--telescope; '**~schleifer** *m* knife--grinder; '**~schnitt** *m* silhouette.
Schererei [ʃeːrə'raɪ] *f* (16) trouble.
Scherflein ['ʃɛrflaɪn] *n* (6) mite; *sein* ~ *beitragen* give one's mite, *weitS.* do one's bit.
Scherge ['ʃɛrgə] *m* (13) catchpole; *weitS.* myrmidon.
Scherz [ʃɛrts] *m* (3²) jest, joke; ~ *treiben mit* make fun of; *aus* ~ in jest, for fun; ~ *beiseite* joking apart; '**~artikel** *m* novelty; '**♀en** (27) joke, make fun; *damit ist nicht zu* ~ that's not to be trifled with; '**♀haft** joking, jocular; facetious; '**~haftigkeit** *f* facetiousness; '**~wort** *n* (3) jocular word; joke.
scheu [ʃɔʏ] **1.** shy; (*furchtsam*) timid; *Pferd*: skittish; ~ *machen* frighten; **2.** ♀ *f* (16, *o. pl.*) shyness; timidity; (*Ehrfurcht, Angst*) awe (*vor dat.* of).
Scheuche ['ʃɔʏçə] *f* (15) scarecrow; '**♀n** (25) scare, frighten (*Vögel*: shoo) away.
scheuen ['ʃɔʏən] (25) *v/i.* shy *od.* balk (*vor dat.* at); *v/t.* fear; *sich* ~ *vor* (*dat.*) shy at, be afraid of; *sich* ~ *zu inf.* be afraid to *inf.*, shrink from *ger.*
Scheuer ['ʃɔʏər] *f* (15) *s. Scheune*; '**~bürste** *f* scrubbing-brush; '**~lappen** *m*, '**~tuch** *n* scouring-cloth; '**~leiste** *f* skirting-board; '**♀n** (29) scour, scrub; *Haut*: chafe, rub.
'**Scheu|klappe** *f*, '**~leder** *n* blinker (*a. fig.*), *Am.* blinder.
Scheune ['ʃɔʏnə] *f* (15) barn, shed.
Scheusal ['ʃɔʏzaːl] *n* (3) monster; F (*Ekel*) beast; (*häßliche Person*) F fright.
scheußlich ['ʃɔʏsliç] hideous, atrocious, abominable; '**♀keit** *f* hideousness *usw.*; *konkret*: abomination, horror; *Tat*: atrocity.
Schi [ʃiː] *m* (11, *pl.* '~*er*) ski; ~ *laufen* ski; '**~-abfahrt** *f* ski run; '**~-anzug** *m* ski suit.
Schicht [ʃiçt] *f* (16) layer; *geol.* (*a. Gesellschafts*♀) stratum, *pl.* strata; *Holz usw.*: stack, pile; (*Reihe*) tier; *phot.* emulsion; (*Arbeits*♀) shift (*a. die Arbeiter*); (*Pause*) pause, rest; (*Volks*♀) class; *breite* ~*en der Bevölkerung* wide sections; ~ *machen* knock off (work); '**~-arbeit(er** *m*)*f* shift-work(er); '**♀en** (26) put in

layers; stack, pile up; stratify; *nach Klassen*: classify; F (*v/i.*) work in shifts; '**~stoff** *m* laminate(d plastic); '**~ung** *f* stratification; '**~wechsel** *m* change of shift; '**⁓weise** in layers; *bei der Arbeit*: in shifts; '**~zuschlag** *m* shift allowance.

Schick [ʃik] **1.** *m* (3, *o. pl.*) chic, stylishness, elegance; **2.** ⁓ chic, stylish; F swell.

schicken ['ʃikən] (25) send; *nach j-m od. et.* ~ send for; *sich* ~ hurry up; *sich* ~ *für j-n* be becoming to (*od.* befit) a p.; *sich* ~ *in* (*acc.*) put up with, resign o.s. to; *das schickt sich nicht* it isn't done; *s. April, Pontius.*

Schickeria [ʃikə'ri:a] *f* (16, *o. pl.*): *die* ~ the trendies *pl.*

'**schicklich** proper, becoming; (*anständig*) decent; '**⁓keit** *f* propriety, decorum; decency; '**⁓keitsgefühl** *n* sense of propriety.

'**Schicksal** *n* (3) destiny, fate; *j-n s-m* ~ *überlassen* leave a p. to his fate; '**⁓haft** fateful; '**~sfrage** *f* vital question; '**~sgefährte** *m*, '**~sgenosse** *m* companion in misfortune; '**~sglaube** *m* fatalism; '**~sschlag** *m* heavy blow.

'**Schickung** *f* providence, (divine) dispensation.

'**Schiebe|dach** *mot. n* sliding roof; '**~fenster** *n* sash-window.

schieben ['ʃi:bən] *v/t. u. v/i.* (30) push, shove; F *fig.* (*unredlich verfahren*) F wangle; *mit Lebensmitteln usw.*: profiteer, racketeer; *s. Bank, Kegel, Schuh.*

'**Schieber** *m* (7) ⊕ slide; (*Riegel*) bolt, (slide) bar; F *fig.* (*Betrüger*) profiteer, racketeer.

'**Schiebe|sitz** *mot. m* sliding seat; '**~tür** *f* sliding door; '**~vorrichtung** *f* slide, shifter.

'**Schiebung** F *f* swindle, F wangling; profiteering (job), racket; *a. Sport*: put-up job, rigging.

schied [ʃi:t] *pret. v. scheiden.*

Schieds|gericht ['ʃi:ts-] *n* court of arbitration; *Sport usw.*: jury; *sich e-m* ~ *unterwerfen* submit to arbitration; '**~richter** *m* arbitrator; *bei Wettbewerben, Sport*: judge, *pl. a.* jury; *Tennis*: umpire; *Boxen, Fußball*: referee; '**~richterball** *m* throwdown; '**⁓richterlich** arbitral; *adv.* by arbitration; '**~spruch** *m* (arbitral) award; '**~verfahren** *n* arbitration.

schief [ʃi:f] *adj.* (*schräg*) oblique (*a.* ⅍), slanting; (*abfallend*) sloping, inclined; (*nach e-r Seite hängend*) lop-sided; *Mund, Gesicht*: wry; *fig.* (*falsch*) false, wrong; (*schlecht*) bad; (*verdreht*) distorted; *Urteil*: warped; ~*e Lage* false position; ~*e Ebene* inclined plane; *fig. auf die* ~*e Ebene geraten* go astray; *in ein* ~*es Licht setzen* place *a p.* in a bad light; *adv.* obliquely, aslant; at an angle; awry; *j-n* ~ *ansehen* look askance at a p.; '**⁓e** *f* (15) obliquity.

Schiefer ['ʃi:fər] *m* (7) slate; '**~dach** *n* slate roof; '**⁓ig** slaty; '**~tafel** *f* slate.

'**schief|gehen** go wrong; '**~lachen** *s. kranklachen*; '**~wink(e)lig** oblique(-angled).

schielen ['ʃi:lən] **1.** (28) squint; ~ *nach* leer at, *fig. begehrlich*: ogle (at); **2.** ⁓ *n* squint(ing); '**~d** squint(-ing), cross-eyed.

schien [ʃi:n] *pret. v. scheinen.*

Schienbein ['ʃi:nbaɪn] *n* shin-bone.

Schiene ['ʃi:nə] *f* (15) rail; *am Rad*: iron band, rim; ⚕ splint; ⊕ bar, guide rail; '**⁓n** (25) ⚕ splint, put in splints.

'**Schienen|bus** *m* rail bus; '**~fahrzeug** *n* rail vehicle; '**~netz** *n* railway (*Am.* railroad) system; '**~strang** *m* track, railway-line.

schier [ʃi:r] sheer, pure; *adv.* (*beinahe*) almost, nearly.

Schierling ⚘ ['ʃi:rliŋ] *m* (3[1]) hemlock.

'**Schieß|baumwolle** *f* gun-cotton; '**~befehl** *m* firing order; '**~bude** *f* shooting gallery.

schießen ['ʃi:sən] **1.** (30) *v/t.* shoot; (*feuern*) fire; ⚒ blast; *Fußball*: *ein Tor* ~ score (a goal); *sich mit j-m* ~ fight a pistol duel with a p.; *e-e S.* ~ *lassen* let fly *od.* go; F *schieß los!* fire away!; *s. Bock, Zügel*; *v/i.* (h.) shoot (*auf acc.* at); (*das Feuer eröffnen*) open fire; (sn) (*sich schnell bewegen*) shoot, dart, rush; *Wasser, Blut*: gush; *Pflanze usw.*: spring (up); *Gedanke*: flash (*durch den Kopf* through one's mind); *gut* ~ be a good shot; *weit* ~ carry far; *in Samen* ~ go (*od.* run) to seed; *s. Pilz, Kraut*; **2.** ⁓ *n* (6) shooting, firing;

F *er* (*es*) *ist zum* ~! he (it) is a scream!
Schießerei [~'raɪ] *f* (16) shoot-out; (*ständiges Schießen*) shooting.
'**Schieß|hund** *fig. m*: *aufpassen wie ein* ~ watch like a lynx; '**~krieg** *m* shooting war; '**~pulver** *n* gunpowder; '**~scharte** ⚔ *f* loop-hole, embrasure; '**~scheibe** *f* target; '**~stand** *m* shooting-range, ⚔ rifle-range, butts *pl.*; '**~wütig** trigger-happy.
Schiff [ʃif] *n* (3) ship, vessel, *kleineres*: boat, (*a.pl.*) craft; (*Kirchen*~) nave; *typ.* galley.
Schiffahrt *f* navigation.
schiff|bar navigable; '**~bau** *m* shipbuilding; '**~bruch** *m* shipwreck; ~ *erleiden* be shipwrecked, *fig.* be wrecked, fail; '**~brüchig** shipwrecked; '**~brücke** *f* pontoon-bridge; '**~chen** *n* (6) little ship; (*Weber*~) shuttle; ⚔ *sl.* forage cap; '**~en** *v/i.* (25, sn) navigate, sail; F (*harnen*; h.) piss; *v/t.* ship.
Schiffer ['ʃifər] *m* (7) sailor; (*Fluß*~) boatman; (*Schiffsführer*) navigator; (*Handelsschiffskapitän*) skipper; '**~klavier** F *n* accordion.
'**Schiffs·arzt** *m* ship's doctor.
'**Schiffschaukel** *f* swing-boat.
'**Schiffs|eigner** *m* shipowner; '**~fracht** *f* (ship's) freight; '**~frachtbrief** *m* bill of lading; '**~journal** *n* log-book; '**~junge** *m* cabin-boy; '**~kapitän** *m* (sea-)captain; '**~koch** *m* ship's cook; '**~kran** *m* ship's crane; '**~küche** *f* galley, caboose; '**~ladung** *f* shipload; (*Fracht*) cargo, freight; '**~mannschaft** *f* crew; '**~raum** *m* hold; (*Rauminhalt*) tonnage; '**~rumpf** *m* hull; '**~schraube** *f* screw; '**~verkehr** *m* shipping traffic; '**~werft** *f* dockyard; '**~zwieback** *m* ship's biscuit, hard-tack.
'**Schi|gebiet** *n* skiing area; '**~hose** *f* ski pants *pl.*
Schikan|e [ʃi'kɑːnə] *f* (15) chicane (-ry); nasty trick; *pl. a.* persecution; *Rennsport*: hazard; F *fig. mit allen* ~*n* with all the trimmings; **~ieren** [~ka'niːrən] persecute; **~ös** [~'nøːs] vexatious, spiteful.
'**Schi|lauf**(**en** *n*) *m* skiing; '**~läufer** (**-in** *f*) *m* skier.
Schild [ʃilt] **1.** *m* (3) shield (*a.* ⊕); (*Wappen*~) (e)scutcheon, coat-of-arms; *im* ~*e führen* be up to *a th.*; **2.** *n* (1) (*Laden*~) sign(-board), facia; (*Tür*~) door-plate; (*Namens-, Firmen-, Tür*~) name-plate; (*Wegweiser*) sign-post; (*Etikett*) label; (*Mützen*~) peak; '**~bürger** *m* Gothamite; '**~drüse** *f* thyroid gland.
Schilder|haus ['ʃildərhaus] *n* sentry-box; '**~n** (29) *v/t. fig.* describe, depict, *kurz*: outline; '**~ung** *f* description.
'**Schild|knappe** *m* shield-bearer, squire; '**~kröte** *f* (*Land*~) tortoise; (*See*~) turtle; '**~krötensuppe** *f* turtle-soup; **~patt** ['~pat] *n* tortoise-shell; '**~wache** ⚔ *hist. f* sentry.
Schilf [ʃilf] *n* (3) reed; '**~ig** reedy; '**~matte** *f* rush-mat; '**~rohr** *n* reed.
'**Schilift** *m* ski-lift.
schillern ['ʃilərn] (29) play in different colo(u)rs; *in Regenbogenfarben*: iridesce; '**~d** *adj.* iridescent, opalescent; *fig. P.*: dazzling.
Schimär|e [ʃi'mɛːrə] *f* (15) chimera; **~isch** chimerical.
Schimmel ['ʃiməl] *m* (7) **1.** white horse; **2.** (*Pilz*) mo(u)ld, mildew.
'**schimm(e)lig** mo(u)ldy, musty.
'**schimmeln** (29, h. *u.* sn) get mo(ul)dy.
'**Schimmelpilz** *m* mo(u)ld fungus.
Schimmer ['ʃimər] *m* (7) gleam (*a. fig. der Hoffnung*), glimmer; F *keinen* ~ *s. Ahnung*; '**~n** (29) gleam, glisten.
Schimpanse [ʃim'panzə] *m* (13) chimpanzee.
Schimpf [ʃimpf] *m* (3) insult; (*Schande*) disgrace; *mit* ~ *und Schande* ignominiously; '**~en** (25) *v/t.* abuse, revile; *v/i.* be abusive; rail (*über, auf acc.* at, against); '**~lich** ignominious, disgraceful (*für* to); '**~name** *m* abusive name; '**~wort** *n* invective.
Schindel ['ʃindəl] *f* (15) shingle; '**~dach** *n* shingle-roof.
schinden ['ʃindən] (30) flay, skin; (*bedrücken*) oppress, drive hard, *Arbeiter*: sweat; *sich* ~ work hard, slave; F *fig.* (*heraus*~) *sl.* wangle; *Eindruck* ~ show off; *Zeit* ~ play for time.
'**Schinder** *m* (7) knacker; *fig.* oppressor, martinet; sweater; **~ei** [~'raɪ] *fig. f* oppression; sweating; (*schwere Arbeit*) grind, drudgery.

Schindluder F ['ʃintlu:dər] *n*: ~ *treiben mit* play fast and loose with.
Schinken ['ʃiŋkən] *m* (6) ham; F *fig.* (*Bild*) daub; (*Buch*) old *od.* fat book; '**~wurst** *f* spiced ham.
Schipiste ['ʃi:-] *f* ski run.
Schippe ['ʃipə] *f* (15) shovel; *Kartenspiel*: *~n pl.* spades; '**2n** (25) shovel.
Schirm [ʃirm] *m* (3) (*Wand2, Wind2, Projektions2, Bild2*) screen; (*Lampen2*) shade; (*Mützen2*) peak; (*Regen2*) umbrella; (*Schutz2*) shield; *fig. a.* shelter, protection; '**2en** (25) shield, protect; '**~herr(in** *f*) *m* protector, *f* protectress, patron(ess *f*); '**~herrschaft** *f* protectorate; *e-r Veranstaltung*: auspices *pl.*; '**~mütze** *f* peaked cap; '**~ständer** *m* umbrella-stand; '**~wand** *f* screen(ing wall).
Schispringen ['ʃi:-] *n* ski-jumping.
Schiß V [ʃis] **1.** *m* (4) shit(ting); *fig.* (*Angst*) funk; ~ *haben* be in a blue funk (*vor dat.* of); ~ *bekommen* get cold feet; **2.** 2 *pret. v. scheißen.*
'**Schi|stiefel** *m* ski boot; '**~stock** *m* ski stick (*Am.* pole); '**~träger** *mot. m* ski rack.
schizo|phren [ʃitso'fre:n] schizophrenic; **2phrenie** [~fre'ni:] *f* (15) schizophrenia.
Schlacht [ʃlaxt] *f* (16) battle; *e-e* ~ *liefern* give battle (*dat.* to); '**~bank** *f* shambles *pl.*, *oft sg.*; '**~beil** *n* butcher's ax(e); '**2en** (26) kill; slaughter (*a. fig.*); '**~enbummler** *m* camp-follower; *Sport*: fan.
Schlächter ['ʃlɛçtər] *m* (7) butcher; **~ei** [~tə'raɪ] *f* (16) butcher's shop; *fig.* slaughter.
'**Schlacht|feld** *n* battlefield; '**~getümmel** *n* mêlée (*fr.*); '**~haus** *n*, '**~hof** *m* slaughter-house, abattoir (*fr.*); '**~kreuzer** *m* battle-cruiser; '**~messer** *n* butcher's knife; '**~opfer** *n* victim; '**~-ordnung** *f* order of battle; '**~plan** *m* plan of action (*a. fig.*); '**~reihe** *f* line of battle; '**~roß** *hist. n* charger; '**~ruf** *m* war-cry; '**~schiff** *n* battleship; '**~ung** *f* slaughter(ing); '**~vieh** *n* slaughter cattle.
Schlack|e ['ʃlakə] *f* (15) *v. Kohle*: cinder; *metall.* dross, slag, scoria; ⚕ waste product; *~n pl.* (*Diät*) roughage; '**2en** (25) slag; '**2(e)rig** F *Wetter*: slushy; '**2ig** slaggy, drossy; '**~wurst** *f etwa*: German sausage.
Schlaf [ʃla:f] *m* (5, *o. pl.*) sleep; *im* ~ asleep; in one's sleep, *fig.* (*leicht*) blindfold; *e-n festen* (*leichten*) ~ *haben* be a sound (light) sleeper; *in* ~ *sinken* fall asleep; *in tiefem* ~ *liegen* be fast asleep; '**~-abteil** *n* sleeping-compartment; '**~-anzug** *m* pyjamas, *Am.* pajamas *pl.*; **~couch** ['~kaʊtʃ] *f* (11[1], *pl.* -es) daybed.
Schläfchen ['ʃlɛ:fçən] *n* (6) doze, nap; F *ein* ~ *machen* take a nap.
'**Schlafcouch** *f* studio couch.
Schläfe ['ʃlɛ:fə] *f* (15) temple.
schlafen ['ʃla:fən] (30) sleep (*a. fig.*); be asleep; F (*unaufmerksam sein*) be napping; ~ *gehen, sich* ~ *legen* go to bed; *länger* ~ sleep late; ~ *Sie wohl!* good night!, sleep well!; '**2szeit** *f* bedtime.
'**Schlaf-entzug** *m* sleep deprivation.
Schläfer ['ʃlɛ:fər] *m* (7), '**~in** *f* sleeper; '**2n** (29): *mich schläfert* I feel (*od.* I am) sleepy.
schlaff [ʃlaf] slack, loose; (*kraftlos*) limp; *Fleisch, Haut, Charakter*: flabby; *fig. Grundsätze usw.*: lax; (*träge*) indolent; (*nachlässig*; *a.* ✝ *Börse*) slack; (*träge*) sluggish; '**2heit** *f* slackness; limpness; flabbiness; laxity; indolence.
'**Schlaf|gast** *m* overnight guest; '**~gelegenheit** *f* sleeping accommodation; '**~gemach** *n* bedroom.
Schlafittchen [ʃla'fitçən] F *n*: *j-n beim* ~ *nehmen* (seize by the) collar.
'**Schlaf|krankheit** *f* sleeping-sickness; '**~lied** *n* lullaby; '**2los** sleepless; '**~losigkeit** *f* sleeplessness, insomnia; '**~mittel** *n* soporific; '**~mütze** *f* nightcap; F *fig.* slowcoach, sleepyhead.
schläfrig ['ʃlɛ:friç] sleepy, drowsy; '**2keit** *f* drowsiness.
'**Schlaf|rock** *m* dressing-gown; '**~saal** *m* dormitory; '**~sack** *m* sleeping-bag; '**~sofa** *n* bed-couch; '**~stadt** *f* dormitory town; '**~sucht** *f* somnolence; '**~tablette** *f* sleeping-pill; '**~trunk** *m* F nightcap; '**2trunken** drowsy; '**~wagen** 🚃 *m* sleeping-car, *bsd. Am.* sleeper; '**2wandeln** walk in one's sleep; **~wandler** ['~vandlər] *m* sleep-walker; somnambulist; '**2wandlerisch** somnambulistic; *mit ~er Sicherheit* with uncanny sureness, unerringly; '**~zimmer** *n* bedroom.

Schlag [ʃlaːk] *m* (3³) blow (*a. fig.*); *a. der Uhr, des Kolbens, beim Tennis od. Rudern*: stroke; *mit der flachen Hand*: slap; *Boxen* (*a.* *~kraft*): punch; *Pferd, Gewehr*: kick; *mit der Peitsche*: lash; (*Aufprall*) impact; ⚡ shock; *lauter* ~ bang; *dumpfer* ~ thud; (*Krach*) crash; (*Schlagfluß*) apoplexy; (*Puls*≈, *Herz*≈, *Trommel*≈) beat; (*Donner*≈) clap (of thunder); (*Essen, Portion*) helping; (*Vogelsang*) warbling; (*Holz*≈) cut (in the wood); (*Wagen*≈) carriage-door; (*Art*) race, kind, sort, *bsd. vom Tier*: breed; ~ *ins Gesicht* slap in the face (*a. fig.*); *s. Kontor, Wasser; Schläge bekommen* get a beating; ~ *sechs Uhr* on the stroke of six; *mit* ˈ*einem* ~ at a blow, *s. a. schlagartig*; **~-ader** [ˈʃlak-] *f* artery; ˈ**~-anfall** *m* apoplectic fit, stroke; ˈ**≈-artig** abrupt (-ly *adv.*); ˈ**~ball** *m Spiel*: rounders *sg.*; ˈ**~baum** *m* turnpike; ˈ**~bolzen** ⚔ *m* firing-pin; ˈ**~bohrer** *m* percussion drill.

schlagen [ˈʃlaːgən] (30) *v/t.* strike, knock, (*a. verprügeln*) beat; *mit der Faust*: punch, hit; (*besiegen*) defeat, (*a.* = *übertreffen*) beat; *Eier*: beat, whip; *Geld*: coin; *Holz*: fell, hew; *e-e Schlacht*: fight; *ans Kreuz* ~ crucify; *ein Kreuz* ~ make the sign of the cross; *auf den Preis* ~ clap on; *in Papier* ~ wrap up in paper; *s. Alarm, Blindheit, Brücke, Kapital usw.*; *sich* ~ (have a) fight, (*duellieren*) fight a duel; *sich aus dem Kopf od. Sinn* ~ put *a th.* out of one's mind; *sich* ~ *zu j-m* side with; *sich gut* ~ stand one's ground; *sich geschlagen geben* give up, *fig. j-m*: bow to; *fig. geschlagen* (*erschöpft*) all in, (*überrascht*) dum(b)founded, (*entmutigt*) down and out; *e-e geschlagene Stunde* a full (F solid) hour; *v/i.* strike, beat; *Herz, Puls*: beat, *stärker*: throb; *Uhr*: strike; *Pferd, Gewehr usw.*: kick; *Vogel*: warble, sing; *das schlägt nicht in mein Fach* that is not in my line; *um sich* ~ lay about one; *s. Art*; ˈ**~d** *fig.* striking; *Argument, Beweis*: conclusive; *~e Wetter* ⚒ *n/pl.* fire-damp.

Schlager [ˈʃlaːgər] *m* (7) ♪ (song) hit; *thea.* draw, smash hit; ✝ draw-card, (sales) hit; *weitS.* hit.

Schläger [ˈʃlɛːgər] *m* (7) **a**) *Sport*: batsman; (*Raufbold*) rough, *Am.* tough, *sl.* bruiser; (*Pferd*) kicker; **b**) *Gerät, Kricket usw.*: bat; *Golf*: club; *Fechten*: rapier, sword; *Tennis*: racket; *Federball*: battledore; *Hockey*: stick; *Küche*: whisk, (egg-)beater.; **c**) (*Vogel*) warbler; **~ei** [~ˈraɪ] *f* (16) brawl, (free) fight, scuffle.

ˈ**Schlager**|**festival** *n* song festival; ˈ**~musik** *f* pop music; ˈ**~sänger**(**in** *f*) *m* pop singer.

schlag|**fertig** [ˈʃlaːkfɛrtiç] *fig.* ready-witted, quick at repartee; *~e Antwort* repartee; ˈ**≈fertigkeit** *f fig.* ready wit, quickness of repartee; ˈ**≈fluß** *m* apoplexy; ˈ**≈holz** *n Sport*: bat; ˈ**≈-instrument** ♪ *n* percussion instrument; ˈ**≈kraft** *f Boxen u. fig.*: punch; ⚔ combat effectiveness; ˈ**~kräftig** powerful; *Beweis*: conclusive; ˈ**≈licht** *n paint. u. fig.* strong light; ˈ**≈loch** *n* pot-hole; ˈ**≈mann** *m beim Rudern*: stroke; ˈ**≈-obers** *n*, ˈ**≈rahm** *m s. Schlagsahne*; ˈ**≈ring** *m* brass knuckles; ♪ plectrum, quill; ˈ**≈sahne** *f* whipped cream; ˈ**≈schatten** *m* cast shadow; ˈ**≈seite** ⚓ *f* list; ~ *haben* ⚓ list; F (*betrunken sein*) be half-seas-over; ˈ**≈stock** *m der Polizei*: truncheon, baton; ˈ**≈-uhr** *f* striking clock; ˈ**≈wechsel** *m Boxen*: exchange of blows; ˈ**≈werk** *n* striking mechanism; ˈ**≈wort** *n* catchword; *weitS.* slogan; ˈ**≈wortregister** *n* subject index; ˈ**≈zeile** *typ. f* headline; ˈ**≈zeug** ♪ *n* percussion instruments *pl.*, drums *pl.*; ˈ**≈zeuger** ♪ *m* drummer; *im Orchester*: percussionist.

schlaksig F [ˈʃlaːkziç] gangling.

Schlamassel [ʃlaˈmasəl] F *m, n* (7) mess.

Schlamm [ʃlam] *m* (3) mud, mire; ˈ**~bad** *n* mud bath.

schlämmen ⊕ [ˈʃlɛmən] (25) wash.

ˈ**schlammig** muddy, miry.

ˈ**Schlammpackung** *f* mud pack.

Schlamp|**e** [ˈʃlampə] *f* (15) slut, slattern; ˈ**≈en** (25) *v/i.* do a sloppy job; *a. v/t.* botch; ˈ**~er** *m* slouch; **~erei** [~ˈraɪ] slovenliness; (*Nachlässigkeit*) slackness; *konkret*: mess, muddle; sloppy job; ˈ**≈ig** slovenly; *Arbeit*: *a.* sloppy, slipshod.

schlang [ʃlaŋ] *pret. v. schlingen.*

Schlange [ˈʃlaŋə] *f* (15) snake, *bsd. rhet.* serpent; ⊕ coil; *fig.* (*Men-*

schen♀) queue, *Am.* line; *falsche* ~ snake in the grass; ~ *stehen* F stand in queue, queue up, *Am.* stand in line, line up (*nach* for).

schlängeln ['ʃlɛŋəln] (29): *sich* ~ twist, wind; worm o.s. (*durch* through *a crowd etc.*); *hin und her*: wriggle; *bsd. Fluß u. Weg*: meander.

'**Schlangen|beschwörer** *m* snake-charmer; '**~biß** *m* snake-bite; '**~gift** *n* snake-poison; '**~linie** *f* sinuous line; '**~mensch** *m* contortionist; '**~rohr** *n* spiral tube *od.* pipe.

schlank [ʃlaŋk] slender, slim, svelte; *die moderne ~e Linie* the waistline; '**♀heit** *f* slenderness; '**♀heitskur** *f* reducing (*od.* slimming) cure; e-e ~ *machen* reduce, slim; **~weg** ['~'vɛk] flatly.

schlapp [ʃlap] *s. schlaff*; '**♀e** *f* (15) setback, reverse; (*Niederlage*) beating, defeat; '**♀hut** *m* slouch hat; '**~machen** F let down; '**♀macher** *m*, '**♀schwanz** F *m* slacker, F sissy, softy; '**♀schuh** F *m* slipper.

Schlaraffen|land [ʃla'rafənlant] *n* fool's paradise, (land of) Cockaigne; **~leben** *n* idle and luxurious life.

schlau [ʃlaʊ] sly, cunning, crafty, wily; F *fig.* ~*er Posten* soft job; F *ich werde nicht ~ daraus* I can't make head or tail of it; **♀berger** ['~bɛrgər] F *m* (7) slyboots *sg.*, F smartie.

Schlauch [ʃlaʊx] *m* (3[1]) tube, (*biegsamer*: flexible) pipe; *zum Spritzen*: hose; (*Fahrrad*♀, *Auto*♀) inner tube; (*Strapaze*) strain; (*Eselsbrücke*) F crib, *Am.* pony; '**~boot** *n* (air *od.* ⚓ life) raft; (*Gummiboot*) rubber dinghy; '**♀en** F *fig. v/t.* fag *a p.* (out), tell on *a p.*; *seelisch*: go hard with *a p.*; ⚔ give *a p.* hell (*Am. sl.* chicken).

Schläue ['ʃlɔʏə] *f* (15, *o. pl.*) *s. Schlauheit.*

Schlaufe ['ʃlaʊfə] *f* (15) loop.

'**Schlau|heit** *f* slyness, cunning; '**~kopf** *m*, '**~meier** F *m* (7) *s. Schlauberger.*

schlecht [ʃlɛçt] **1.** *adj. allg.* bad; (*boshaft, verworfen*) *a.* wicked; (*böse*) evil; (*gemein*) base, mean; (*armselig, wertlos*) poor; *Ware*: inferior; ~ *sein in* et. be poor at a th.; ~*e Laune haben* be in a bad temper; ~*er Tag leistungsmäßig*: off day; ~*e Zeiten* hard times; *mir ist* ~ I feel sick; ~ *werden* go bad; ~*er werden* get worse, worsen; *s. gehen, stehen, Trost*; **2.** *adv.* badly, ill; ~ *und recht* after a fashion; **~erdings** ['~ər'diŋs] absolutely, downright; '**♀erstellung** *f* discrimination (*gen.* against); **~gelaunt** ['~gə'laʊnt] ill-humo(u)red, in a bad temper; '**~'hin, ~weg** ['~'vɛk] simply; in a word; '**♀igkeit** *f s. schlecht*: badness; baseness; wickedness; '**~machen:** *j-n* ~ run a p. down, backbite a p.; '**♀'wetterfront** *f* bad weather front; '**♀'wetterperiode** *f* spell of bad weather.

schlecken ['ʃlɛkən] *usw. s. lecken.*

Schlegel ['ʃle:gəl] *m* (7) (*Trommel*♀) drumstick; ⊕ mallet, beetle; *vom Kalb usw.*: leg.

Schleh|dorn ⚘ ['ʃle:dɔrn] *m* blackthorn; '**~e** ⚘ *f* (15) sloe, wild plum.

Schlei(**e** *f*) ['ʃlaɪ(ə)] *m* (3 [15]) tench.

schleich|en ['ʃlaɪçən] (30, sn) sneak, slink; (*kriechen, a. Zeit*) creep, crawl; (*sich hinschleppen*) drag; *im Finstern* ~ prowl in the dark; '**~end** sneaking; creeping; (*verstohlen*) furtive; *Fieber, Gift usw.*: slow, lingering; '**♀er** *m* (7) creeper; *fig.* sneak; (*Leisetreter*) *Am.* F pussyfoot(er); **♀erei** [~ə'raɪ] *f* sneaking; '**♀handel** *m* illicit trade; smuggling; (*schwarzer Markt*) black market; **♀weg** ['~ve:k] *m* secret path; *fig.* underhand means *pl.*; *auf ~en* surreptitiously; '**♀werbung** *f* surreptitious advertising, F plugging.

Schleier ['ʃlaɪər] *m* (7) veil (*a. fig.*); (*Dunst*♀, *Nebel*♀) haze; *phot.* fog; *fig. unter dem* ~ (*gen.*) under the veil of; '**~eule** *f* barn-owl; '**~flor** *m* crape; '**♀haft** *fig.* (*verschwommen*) hazy; (*rätselhaft*) mysterious, inexplicable.

Schleif|bahn ['ʃlaɪfba:n] *f* slide; '**~e** *f* (15) (*Schlinge*; *a.* ✈, ⚡) loop; (*gebundene* ~) slip-knot; (*Band*♀) bow, knot; (*Kurve*) loop (*a.* ✈), (horseshoe) bend; (*schlittenartiges Gestell*) sled(ge), drag; *s. Schleifbahn*; '**♀en 1.** (30) *a.* (*schärfen*) grind; (*wetzen*) whet; (*glätten, schmirgeln*) abrade, *feiner*: smooth, polish (*a. fig.*); *Edelstein, Glas*: cut; F ⚔ drill hard, *s. a. schlauchen*; **2.** *v/t. u. v/i.* (25) (*schleppen*) drag; (*rutschen*) skid, slide; *Bauten*: raze, demolish, ⚔ *a.* dismantle; ♪ slur; ˈ**~er** *m* (7) grinder; polisher; (*Edelstein*≈) cutter; F ⚔ martinet; ˈ**~lack** *m* body varnish; ˈ**~maschine** *f* grinding-machine; ˈ**~mittel** *n* abrasive; ˈ**~papier** *n* emery paper; ˈ**~rad** *n* grinding-wheel; ˈ**~ring** ⚡ *m* slip ring; ˈ**~stein** *m* whetstone, hone; *drehbarer*: grindstone.

Schleim [ʃlaɪm] *m* (3) slime; *physiol.*, ⚕ mucus, *bsd. in der Brust*: phlegm; ˈ**~absonderung** *f* mucous secretion; ˈ**~drüse** *f* mucous gland; ˈ**~haut** *f* mucous membrane; ˈ**≈ig** slimy (*a. fig. contp.*); mucous; ˈ**≈lösend** expectorant; ˈ**~suppe** *f* gruel.

schlemm|en [ˈʃlɛmən] (25) feast, gorge, gormandize; *weitS.* revel, live high; ˈ**≈er** *m* (7) (*Feinschmecker*) gourmet; (*Fresser*) glutton; *weitS.* reveller; **≈erei** [~ˈraɪ] *f* feasting, revelry; gormandizing; ˈ**≈erlokal** *n* gourmet restaurant.

schlen|dern [ˈʃlɛndərn] (29, sn) stroll, saunter; **≈drian** [ˈ~driɑːn] *m* (3) (old) jogtrot; (*Bummelei*) dawdling, muddling on.

schlenkern [ˈʃlɛŋkərn] (29) dangle; swing (*mit den Armen usw.* one's arms *etc.*).

Schlepp|dampfer [ˈʃlɛp-] *m* tug (-boat); ˈ**~e** *f* (15) *am Kleid*: train; (*Schweif*) trail; ˈ**≈en** *v/t. u. v/i.* (25) drag (*sich* o.s.), lug; (*schwer tragen*) carry, *Am.* F tote; ⚓, ✈, *mot.* tow, haul, ⚓ tug; ☤ (*Kunden werben*) tout; ˈ**≈end** dragging; (*langsam, a.* ☤) slow, sluggish; *Sprache*: drawling; ˈ**~er** *m* (7) ⚓ tug(-boat); *mot.* tractor; ☤ (*Kundenwerber*) tout; ˈ**~kahn** *m* lighter, barge; ˈ**~lift** *m* ski tow; ˈ**~netz** *n* drag-net; ˈ**~netzfischer(boot** *n*) *m* trawler; ˈ**~schiff** *n* tug(-boat); ˈ**~seil** *n*, ˈ**~tau** *n* tow-rope; *ins Schlepptau nehmen* take in tow (*a. fig.*); ˈ**~zug** *m* train of barges; *mot.* truck train.

Schles|ier [ˈʃleːzjər] *m* (7), ˈ**≈isch** Silesian.

Schleuder [ˈʃlɔʏdər] *f* (15) sling, (*a.* ✈) catapult, *Am.* slingshot; ⊕ *s. ~maschine*; ˈ**~-artikel** ☤ *m* catchpenny article; ˈ**~ball** *m* sling ball; ˈ**~honig** *m* strained honey; ˈ**~maschine** *f* centrifuge; ˈ**≈n** (29) *v/t.* fling, hurl; *mit e-r Schleuder*: sling; ✈ catapult; ⊕ centrifuge; *Honig*: strain; *Wäsche*: spin-dry; *v/i. mot.* skid, side-slip; ˈ**~preis** *m* ruinous (*od.* give-away) price; ˈ**~sitz** ✈ *m* ejector seat; ˈ**~ware** *f* catchpenny article.

schleunig [ˈʃlɔʏniç] quick, speedy; *adv.* (*a.* ˈ**~st**) in all haste; (*sofort*) immediately, forthwith.

Schleuse [ˈʃlɔʏzə] *f* (15) sluice (*a. fig.*); (*Kanal*≈) lock; ˈ**≈n** lock; *fig.* channel; *P.*: direct; *s. ein~*; ˈ**~ntor** *n* flood-gate.

Schlich[1] [ʃliç] *m* (3) trick, dodge; *j-m auf die ~e kommen* find a p. out.

schlich[2] *pret. v. schleichen.*

schlicht [ʃliçt] plain, simple; (*glatt*) smooth, sleek; ˈ**~en** (26) (*glätten*) smooth; *Streit usw.*: settle, adjust; ˈ**≈er** *m* (7), ˈ**≈erin** *f* mediator; *durch Schiedsspruch*: arbitrator; ˈ**≈feile** *f* smooth-cut file; ˈ**≈heit** *f* plainness, simplicity; ˈ**≈ung** *f* settlement; (*Vermittlung*) mediation; *durch Schiedsspruch*: arbitration; ˈ**≈ungs-ausschuß** *m* arbitration committee.

Schlick [ʃlik] *m* (3) mud, slime.

schlief [ʃliːf] *pret. v. schlafen.*

schließ|bar [ˈʃliːsbɑːr] lockable; **≈e** [ˈ~sə] *f* (15) catch, latch; *am Kleid, an der Handtasche usw.*: clasp; ˈ**~en** (30) *v/t.* shut, close (*beide a. sich*; *a.* ⚡ *Stromkreis*); *mit Schlüssel*: lock; *Betrieb*: shut down; *Bündnis, Kreis*: form; *Freundschaft, Ehe*: contract; *Handel*: strike, conclude; *Vertrag, Brief, Rede*: conclude; *Frieden*: conclude, make; (*beenden*) finish, end; *parl. usw. Debatte, Sitzung*: close, *auf Antrag*: closure; *sich ~ Wunde*: close; *sich ~ an* (*acc.*) follow (upon); *in die Arme ~* clasp in one's arms; *j-n ins Herz geschlossen haben fig.* be very fond of a p.; *in sich ~* include, (*unausgesprochen*) imply; *geschlossen für et. sein od. stimmen* go (*od.* be) solid for; *geschlossene Gesellschaft* private party; *v/i.* shut, close; *Läden*: close; *Schule*: break up; *bei e-r Rede usw.*: close (*mit* with); *aus et. ~ auf* (*acc.*) infer (*od.* conclude *od.* gather) *a th.* from a th.; *auf et. ~ lassen* suggest a th.; *dem Aussehen nach zu ~* judging from the appearance; ˈ**≈er** *m* (7) door-keeper; *im Gefängnis*: jailer, turnkey; 2**fach** *n Bank*: safe deposit box; (*Bahnhofs*2) left-luggage locker; *s. Postfach*; '**~lich** final, last, eventual; *adv.* finally, at last; (*am Ende*) eventually; (~ *doch, eigentlich*) after all; '2**muskel** *m* constrictor; '2**ung** *f* closing (*a.* ⚡), conclusion; *e-r Debatte*: closure, *Am.* cloture; *e-s Betriebes*: shut-down, closure.

Schliff [ʃlif] **1.** *m* (3) polish (*a. fig.*); *v. Edelstein, Glas*: cut; *fig. letzter* ~ finishing touch(es); F ⚒ hard drill; **2.** 2 *pret. v. schleifen* 1.

schlimm [ʃlim] *allg.* bad; (*bedenklich*) serious, grave; ~*er* worse; *am* ~*sten, das* 2*ste* the worst; ~*er machen* (*werden*) *s. verschlimmern*; ~ *daran sein* be badly off; '**~sten'falls** at the worst.

Schling|e ['ʃliŋə] *f* (15) sling (*a.* ⚕), loop; *sich zusammenziehende*: noose (*a. fig.*); *gebundene*: (running) knot; *Draht, Tau*: coil; *hunt.* snare (*a. fig.*); *fig. j-m in die* ~ *gehen* walk into a p.'s trap; *sich aus der* ~ *ziehen* wriggle out of it; '**~el** *m* (7) rascal; '2**en** (30) wind, twine; (*gierig schlucken*) gulp, gorge; *sich* ~ *um* wind (*od.* coil) round; '2**ern** ⚓ (29) roll; '**~gewächs** *n*, '**~pflanze** *f* climbing plant, creeper, *bsd. Am.* climber.

Schlips [ʃlips] *m* (4) (neck)tie.

Schlitten ['ʃlitən] *m* (6) sledge, *bsd. Am.* sled; (*bsd. Pferde*2) sleigh; (*Rodel*2) toboggan; ⊕ sliding carriage; *der Schreibmaschine*: carriage; F (*Auto*) car, *sl.* heap; ~ *fahren* sledge, (*rodeln*) toboggan; F *fig. mit j-m* ~ *fahren* F wipe the floor with a p.; '**~bahn** *f* sledge-run; '**~fahrt** *f* sledge-ride; sleigh-ride.

schlittern ['ʃlitərn] (29, h. *u.* sn) slide (*a. fig.*), *a. mot.* skid.

'**Schlittschuh** *m* skate; ~ *laufen* skate; '**~laufen** *n* skating; '**~läufer(in** *f*) *m* skater.

Schlitz [ʃlits] *m* (3^3) slit, *im Kleid*: slash; (*Einwurf*2) slot; '**~-auge** *n* slit eye; '2**-äugig** slit-eyed; '2**en** *v/t. u. v/i.* (27, sn) slit, slash; ⊕ slot.

schlohweiß ['ʃlo:'vaıs] snow-white.

Schloß[1] [ʃlɔs] *n* (2^1) castle; (*Palast*) palace; **~**[2] (*Tür*2, *Schußwaffen*2 *usw.*) lock; (*Gewehr*2) *mst* bolt; (*Buch*2, *Handtaschen*2 *usw.*) clasp; (*Gürtel*2, *Koppel*2) buckle; *hinter* ~ *und Riegel* behind bars; 2[3] *pret. v. schließen.*

Schlößchen ['ʃlœsçən] *n* (6) small castle.

Schloße ['ʃlo:sə] *f* (15) sleet (*a. pl.*).

Schlosser ['ʃlɔsər] *m* (7) locksmith; *weitS.* mechanic, fitter; **~ei** [~'raı] *f* (*a.* '**~werkstatt** *f*) locksmith's workshop; (*a.* '**~handwerk** *n*) locksmith's trade.

Schlot [ʃlo:t] *m* (3[3]) chimney; 🚂, ⚓ funnel; F (*Flegel*) lout.

schlotter|ig ['ʃlɔtəriç] shaky; (*lose*) loose; *fig.* (*schlampig*) slovenly; '**~n** (29) flap; (*zittern*) shake, tremble; (*wackeln*) wobble.

Schlucht [ʃluxt] *f* (16) gorge; (*Hohlweg*) ravine, *Am. a.* gulch.

schluchzen ['ʃluxtən] (27) sob; 2 *n* (6) sobbing, sobs *pl.*

Schluck [ʃluk] *m* (3[3]) gulp; *kleiner* ~ = **Schlückchen** ['ʃlykçən] *n* (6) sip, F drop; '**~-auf** *m* hiccup(s *pl.*); '2**en**[1] (25) *v/t. u. v/i.* swallow (*a. fig. Geld, Tadel usw.*); gulp (down); '**~en**[2] *m* (6) hiccup(s *pl.*); '**~er** *m* (7) *fig. armer* ~ poor wretch; '**~-impfung** ⚕ *f* oral vaccine; '2**weise** in (small) sips.

schluder|ig ['ʃlu:dəriç] sloppy; '**~n** scamp.

schlug [ʃlu:k] *pret. v. schlagen.*

Schlummer ['ʃlumər] *m* (7) slumber; '2**n** (29) slumber; *fig.* lie dormant; '2**nd** *fig.* dormant, latent.

Schlund [ʃlunt] *m* (3^3) throat, gullet; ⚕ pharynx; (*Speiseröhre*) (o)esophagus; (*Abgrund*) abyss.

schlüpf|en ['ʃlypfən] (25, sn) slip, glide; '2**er** *m* (7) (*Unterziehhöschen*) (*ein* a pair of ladies') knickers *pl.*, F panties *pl. od.* briefs *pl.*

Schlupfloch ['ʃlupf-] *n* loop-hole; (*Versteck*) *s. Schlupfwinkel.*

'**schlüpfrig** slippery (*a. fig.*); *fig. Witz usw.*: risqué (*fr.*).

'**Schlupfwinkel** *m* hiding-place, *Am.* hideout; *fig.* recess.

schlurfen ['ʃlurfən] *v/i.* (25, sn) shuffle along, drag one's feet.

schlürfen ['ʃlyrfən] (25) *v/t.* sip.

Schluß [ʃlus] *m* (4^1) close, end; (*Ab*2; *Folgerung*) conclusion; *parl. e-r Debatte*: closing, *auf Antrag*: closure, *Am.* cloture; ~ (*damit*)! stop (it)!; ~ *machen* (*die Arbeit beenden*) call it a day; ~ *machen mit* put an end to *a th.*, have done with *a p.*;

zu dem ~ kommen, daß decide that; *zum ~* finally; **'~-abrechnung** *f* final account; **'~-akt** *thea. m* last act; **'~bemerkung** *f* final observation.

Schlüssel ['ʃlysəl] *m* (7) key (*zu* of; *fig.* to); ♪ *a.* clef; (*Chiffrier*~) code; (*Verteilungsquote*) formula; ⊕ spanner, wrench; **'~bein** *n* collar-bone; **'~blume** *f* cowslip; *blaßgelbe ~* primrose; **'~bund** *m, n* bunch of keys; **'~fertig** ready for occupancy; *~es Haus* turnkey house; **'~-industrie** *f* key industry; **'~kind** *n* latchkey child; **'~loch** *n* key-hole; **'~ring** *m* key-ring; **'~rolle** *f* key role; **'~roman** *m* roman à clef (*fr.*); **'~stellung** *f* key position (*a.* ⚔); **'~wort** *n* key-word; code word.

'Schluß|feier *f Schule*: speech-day, *Am.* commencement; **'~folgerung** *f* conclusion, inference; **'~formel** *f im Brief*: complimentary close.

schlüssig ['ʃlysiç] resolved, determined; *Beweis*: conclusive; *sich ~ werden* make up one's mind.

'Schluß|licht *n* tail-light; F *fig.* tail-ender; *das ~ bilden* bring up the rear; **'~notierung** ✝ *f des Kurses*: closing quotation; **'~pfiff** *m Sport*: final whistle; **'~rechnung** *f* final account; **'~runde** *f Sport*: final; **'~runden-teilnehmer(in** *f*) *m Sport*: finalist; **'~satz** *m* conclusion; ♪ finale; **'~stein** *m* keystone; **'~strich** *m*: *fig. e-n ~ ziehen* draw the line, *unter* (*acc.*) put an end to; **'~szene** *f* final scene; **'~verkauf** *m* (end-of-season) sale; **'~wort** *n* (3) last word; (*Zusammenfassung*) summary.

Schmach [ʃma:x] *f* (16) disgrace; (*Beleidigung*) insult.

schmachten ['ʃmaxtən] (26) languish; *~ nach* yearn for.

schmächtig ['ʃmɛçtiç] slight, thin; *~er Junge* slip of a boy.

schmachvoll ['ʃma:x-] disgraceful.

schmackhaft ['ʃmakhaft] savo(u)ry, tasty; *fig. j-m et. ~ machen* make a th. palatable to a p.; **'~igkeit** *f* savo(u)riness.

schmäh|en ['ʃmɛ:ən] (25) (*schimpfen*) abuse, revile; (*verleumden*) calumniate; **'~lich** ignominious, disgraceful; *adv. fig.* outrageously; **'~rede** *f* abuse, invective; **'~schrift** *f* libel, lampoon; **'~sucht** *f* slanderous disposition; **'~ung** *f* abuse, invective.

schmal [ʃma:l] (18[2]) narrow; (*dünn*) thin; *fig.* small, poor; *~e Kost f* short commons *pl.*

schmäler|n ['ʃmɛ:lərn] (29) curtail, impair; *bsd. fig.* detract from; **'~ung** *f* curtailment, impairment.

'Schmal|film *m* cine film; **'~filmkamera** *f* cine camera; **'~spur** *f*, **'~spurig** narrow-gauge.

Schmalz [ʃmalts] *n* (3[2]) lard; **'~ig** greasy; F *fig.* sentimental, maudlin.

schmarotzen [ʃma'rɔtsən] (27) sponge (*bei* [up]on).

Schma'rotzer *m* (7), **~in** *f* (*a. zo.*, ⚘) parasite; *fig. a.* sponger; **~isch** parasitic; sponging; **~pflanze** *f* parasitic plant; **~tum** [~tu:m] *n* (1[2]) parasitism.

Schmarre ['ʃmarə] *f* (15) cut, slash; (*Narbe*) scar; **'~n** *m* (6) minced pancake; (*Schund*) trash, hokum.

Schmatz F [ʃmats] *m* (3[2]) smack; **'~en** (27) smack (*mit den Lippen* one's lips).

schmauchen ['ʃmauxən] *v/t. u. v/i.* (25) smoke.

Schmaus [ʃmaus] *m* (4[2]) feast, banquet; **~en** ['~zən] (27) feast (*von* upon); eat heartily; **~erei** [~'raɪ] *f* feasting; *s. Schmaus.*

schmecken ['ʃmɛkən] (25) *v/t.* taste; *v/i.* taste (*nach* of); *~ nach a.* smack of (*a. fig.*); *dieser Wein schmeckt mir* I like (*od.* enjoy) this wine.

Schmeichel|ei [ʃmaɪçə'laɪ] *f* (16) *vgl. schmeicheln*: flattery; (flattering) compliment; adulation; cajolery; **'~haft** flattering; **'~katze** *f fig.* cajoler; **'~n** (29) flatter (*j-m* a p.); *kriecherisch*: adulate; *bittend*: coax; *zärtlich*: cajole; (*kosen*) caress; *sich geschmeichelt fühlen* feel flattered; *geschmeichelt Bild*: flattering.

Schmeichler ['ʃmaɪçlər] *m* (7), **'~in** *f* (16[1]) flatterer; **'~isch** flattering.

schmeiß|en F ['ʃmaɪsən] (30) fling, hurl, chuck; *Tür*: slam, bang; F *die Sache* (*od. den Laden*) *~* run the show; **'~fliege** *f* blowfly, blue-bottle.

Schmelz [ʃmɛlts] *m* (3[2]) enamel (*a. Zahn*~); *fig.* bloom; ♪ (melting) sweetness; **'~bar** fusible; **'~draht** *m* fuse wire; **'~e** *f* (15) *des Schnees*: melting; *s. Schmelzhütte*; **'~en** *v/t.* (27, *oft* 30) (*v/i.* [30, sn]) melt (*a. fig.*); *bsd. Metalle*: smelt, fuse;

'**2end** melting; *fig. a.* languishing; ♪ melodious, sweet (*a. Stimme*); **~erei** [~tsə'raɪ] *f*, '**~hütte** *f* smelt-ing-works *pl.*, *oft sg.*; foundry; '**~käse** *m* soft cheese; '**~-ofen** *m* (s)melting furnace; '**~punkt** *m* melt-ing-point; '**~sicherung** ⚡ *f* (safety) fuse; '**~tiegel** *m* melting-pot (*a. fig.*), crucible; '**~wasser** *n* melted snow (*od.* ice).

Schmerbauch ['ʃme:r-] *m* paunch, big (*od.* pot-)belly.

Schmerz [ʃmɛrts] *m* (5[1]) pain, ache; (*Kummer*) grief; (*Qual*) agony; *~en haben* be in pain; '**2en** (27) *v/t. u. v/i.* pain, hurt, (*nur v/i.*) ache; *seelisch*: *a.* grieve.

'**Schmerzens|geld** *n* smart-money; '**~lager** *n* bed of suffering; '**~schrei** *m* cry of pain.

'**schmerz|-erfüllt** grieved; '**~frei** free of pain; '**~haft,** '**~lich** painful; *fig.* grievous; '**~lindernd** soothing; (*a. ~es Mittel*) anodyne, analgesic; '**~los** painless; '**~stillend** *s. schmerzlindernd(es Mittel)*.

Schmetter|ball *m*, **~schlag** ['ʃmɛtər-] *m Tennis*: smash; **~ling** ['~lɪŋ] *m* (3[1]) butterfly; '**~lingsstil** *m Schwimmen*: butterfly (stroke); '**2n** (29) *v/t.* smash; F *Lied*: sing lustily; *v/i. Stimme*: ring (out); *Trompete*: blare; *Vögel*: warble.

Schmied [ʃmi:t] *m* (3) (black)smith; '**2bar** malleable.

Schmiede ['ʃmi:də] *f* (15) forge, smithy; '**~-eisen** *n* wrought iron; '**~hammer** *m* sledge-hammer.

'**schmieden** *v/t. u. v/i.* (26) forge; *fig. a.* form, frame; *s. Eisen, Ränke*; *Pläne*: make, *b.s.* hatch.

schmiegen ['ʃmi:gən] (25, *a. sich*) nestle *od.* snuggle (*an acc.* to).

schmiegsam ['ʃmi:kza:m] pliant, flexible, supple.

Schmier|büchse ['ʃmi:r-] *f* ⊕ grease-box; (*Kanne*) oil-can; '**~e** *f* (15) ooze; (*Fett, Öl*) grease; *thea.* troop of strolling players, *bsd. Am.* barnstormers *pl.*, (*schlechtes Theater*) F penny gaff; P *~e stehen* be look-out man, *sl.* keep cave; '**2en** (25) smear; ⚕ anoint; ⊕ *mit Fett*: grease, *mit Öl*: oil, lubricate; *Brot*: butter; *Butter usw.*: spread; (*schlecht schreiben, kritzeln*) scrawl, scribble; *bsd. paint.* daub; F *j-n ~* (*bestechen*) grease a p.'s palm; F *j-m eine ~* paste a p. one; *wie geschmiert* smoothly, without a hitch; '**~enschauspieler(in** *f*) *m* strolling player, *bsd. Am.* barnstormer, *contp. sl.* ham; '**~er(in** *f*) *m* greaser; (*Sudler*) scribbler; *bsd. paint.* dauber; **~erei** [~'raɪ] *f* (16) *s. schmieren*: smearing; scrawl; daub; '**~esteher** P *m* (7) look-out man; '**~fett** ⊕ *n* grease; '**~fink** *m* dirty fellow; daub(st)er; '**~geld(er** *pl.*) F *n* slush fund; '**2ig** (*fettig*) greasy; (*schmutzig*) grimy; *fig.* sordid; '**~käse** *m* soft cheese; '**~mittel** ⊕ *n* lubricant; '**~-öl** *n* lubricating oil; '**~papier** *n* scribbling-paper; '**~plan** ⊕ *m* lubricating chart; '**~seife** *f* soft soap; '**~stoff** *m* lubricant; '**~ung** ⊕ *f* lubrication.

Schmink|e ['ʃmɪŋkə] *f* (15) (grease) paint, *rote*: rouge; *weitS.* make-up; '**2en** (25, *a. sich*) paint (one's face), make (o.s.) up; *rot*: rouge; *Lippen*: put on lipstick; *fig. Bericht*: colo(u)r; **~täsch-chen** ['~tɛʃçən] *n* (6) make-up bag.

Schmirgel ['ʃmɪrgəl] *m* (7) emery; '**2n** (29) rub with emery, sand; '**~papier** *n* emery paper.

Schmiß[1] [ʃmɪs] *m* (4) gash, cut; (*Narbe*) (duelling) scar; F *fig.* (*Schwung*) verve, go, F pep.

schmiß[2] *pret. v. schmeißen.*

'**schmissig** F racy, F full of pep.

Schmöker ['ʃmø:kər] *m* (7) old book; *s. Schundroman*; '**2n** (29) (29) (*lesen*) browse.

schmoll|en ['ʃmɔlən] (25) pout; *weitS.* sulk; '**2winkel** *m* sulking--corner.

schmolz [ʃmɔlts] *pret. v. schmelzen.*

Schmor|braten ['ʃmo:r-] *m* braised beef; '**2en** *v/t. u. v/i.* (25) stew (*a. fig.*); (*dünsten*) braise; ⚡ scorch.

Schmu F [ʃmu:] *m* (11) swindle, skullduggery.

Schmuck [ʃmʊk] **1.** *m* (3) ornament; (*Putz*) finery; (*Juwelen*) jewels *pl.*, jewel(le)ry; (*Ausschmückung*) decoration; **2.** 2 smart, trim, spruce; (*hübsch*) pretty; '**~blattelegramm** *n* de luxe telegram.

schmücken ['ʃmykən] (25) adorn (*a. fig.*), decorate; *sich ~* dress up.

'**Schmuck|kästchen** *n* jewel-case; *fig.* gem; '**2los** unadorned, plain; '**~sachen** *f/pl.* jewels; '**~stück** *n*

ornament; *engS.* piece of jewel(le)ry; *fig.* gem; '**~waren** *f/pl.* jewel(le)ry *sg.*
Schmuggel ['ʃmugəl] *m* (7), **~ei** [~'laɪ] *f* smuggling; '**2n** *v/t. u. v/i.* (29) smuggle; '**~ware(n** *pl.*) *f* smuggled goods *pl.*, contraband.
Schmuggler ['ʃmuglər] *m* (7) smuggler.
schmunzeln ['ʃmuntsəln] (29) smile, grin; **2** *n* (6*) (amused) smile, grin.
Schmus F [ʃmu:s] *m* (4, *o. pl.*) soft soap; **2en** ['~zən] soft-soap; (*kosen*) pet, F neck.
Schmutz [ʃmuts] *m* (3²) dirt, filth, *fig. b.s. a.* smut; (*Kot, Schlamm*) mud; ~ *und Schund* smut and thrash, ⚖ harmful publications; '**2en** (27) soil, get dirty; '**~fink** F *m* pig, mudlark; '**~fleck** *m* smudge; '**2ig** dirty, filthy, *fig. b.s. a.* smutty; (*beschmutzt*) soiled; *fig.* (*gemein*) dirty, shabby; ~ *machen* dirty, soil; '**~igkeit** *f* dirtiness *etc.*; '**~titel** *m e-s Buches*: half title; '**~zulage** *f* dirty work allowance.
Schnabel ['ʃnɑ:bəl] *m* (7¹) bill, beak; ⊕ nozzle; *e-r Kanne*: spout; F *halt den ~!* shut up; '**2förmig** bill-shaped; '**~tasse** *f* feeding cup; '**~tier** *n* duck-bill, platypus.
schnäbeln ['ʃnɛ:bəln] (29) *v/i. u. sich* ~ bill and coo.
schnacken ['ʃnakən] *v/i. u. v/t.* (25) chatter, chat.
Schnake ['ʃnɑ:kə] *f* (15) crane-fly, *Brt.* daddy-longlegs.
Schnalle ['ʃnalə] *f* (15), '**2n** (25) buckle; '**~nschuh** *m* buckled shoe.
schnalzen ['ʃnaltsən] (27) smack; *mit der Zunge* ~ click one's tongue; *mit den Fingern* ~ snap one's fingers.
'**schnappen** (25) snap; *nach et.* ~ snap at, *a.* snatch at; F (*erwischen*) catch; (*packen*) grab; nab; *nach Luft* ~ gasp for breath; F *Luft* ~ (*gehen*) take an airing.
Schnäpper ['ʃnɛpər] *m* (7) ⊕ snap, catch; (*Blut2*) ⚕ blood lancet.
'**Schnapp|feder** *f* catch-spring; '**~messer** *n* clasp-knife; '**~schloß** *n* spring-lock; '**~schuß** *m* snapshot.
Schnaps ['ʃnaps] *m* (4²) spirit(s *pl.*), strong (*Am.* hard) liquor, schnap(p)s; (*ein Glas* ~) dram; '**~brenne'rei** *f* distillery; '**~flasche** *f* brandy bottle; '**~idee** F *f* crazy idea.
schnarch|en ['ʃnarçən] (25) snore; '**2er** *m* (7) snorer.
Schnarre ['ʃnarə] *f* (15) rattle; '**2n** (25) rattle; (*rauh tönen*) rasp.
schnattern ['ʃnatərn] (29) cackle; *bsd. fig.* chatter; *nur fig.* gabble.
schnauben ['ʃnaubən] *v/i. u. v/t.* (30) pant, puff; *Tier, a. P. verächtlich*: snort; *vor Wut* ~ foam with rage; *Rache* ~ pant for revenge; *sich (die Nase)* ~ blow one's nose.
schnauf|en ['ʃnaufən] (25) breathe heavily; wheeze; (*keuchen*) pant; '**2er** F *m* breath.
Schnauz|bart ['ʃnauts-] *m* (walrus) moustache; '**~e** *f* (15) snout, muzzle; *e-r Kanne usw.*: spout; P *die ~ halten* shut up; '**2en** F (27) jaw, bark; '**~er** *m* (*Hund*) schnauzer.
Schnecke ['ʃnɛkə] *f* (15) snail; (*Nackt2*) slug; *fig.* scroll; *e-r Säule*: *a.* volute; *der Uhr*: fusee; ⊕ worm; (*Förder2*) screw conveyor.
schnecken|förmig ['~fœrmiç] spiral, winding; '**2gang** *m* winding alley; *s. Schneckentempo*; '**2getriebe** *n* worm gear(ing); '**2haus** *n* snail's shell; '**2linie** *f* spiral line; '**2post** *f*: *mit der ~, im* '**2tempo** *n* at a snail's pace.
Schnee [ʃne:] *m* (3¹) snow; (*Ei2*) whipped whites *pl.* of egg, froth; '**~ball** *m* snowball (*a.* ⚘); '**~ballsystem** *n* snowball system; **2bedeckt** ['~bədɛkt] snow-covered; '**~besen** *m Küche*: (egg) whisk, egg-beater; '**2blind** snow-blind; '**~brille** *f* (*eine* a pair of) snow-goggles *pl.*; '**~fall** *m* snowfall; '**~flocke** *f* snow-flake; '**~gestöber** *n* snow-flurry; '**~glöckchen** ⚘ *n* snowdrop; '**~grenze** *f* snow-line; '**~huhn** *n* white grouse; '**~hütte** *f* igloo; '**2ig** snowy; '**~kette** *f* non-skid chain; '**~könig** F *m*: *sich freuen wie ein* ~ be as pleased as Punch; '**~mann** *m* snowman; '**~matsch** *m* slush; **~mobil** ['~mobi:l] *n* (3¹) snowmobile; '**~pflug** *m* snow-plough, *Am.* snowplow; '**~schieber** *m* snow pusher; '**~schläger** *m s. Schneebesen*; '**~schmelze** *f* melting of the snow; '**~schuh** *m* snow-shoe; *s. Schi*; '**~sturm** *m* snowstorm; *heftiger*: blizzard; '**~treiben** *n* snow-flurry; '**~verwehung** *f*, '**~wehe** *f* snow-drift; '**2weiß** snow-white; '**~**

wetter *n* snowy weather; **~wittchen** [~ˈvitçən] *n* (6) Snow-White.

Schneid F [ˈʃnaɪt] *m*, *f* (3) pluck, gut(s); *j-m den ~ abkaufen* discourage a p.; ˈ**~brenner** *m* cutting torch.

Schneide [ˈʃnaɪdə] *f* (15) edge; *s. Messer*; ˈ**~brett** *n* carving-board; ˈ**2n** (30) *allg.* cut (*a. Sport*: *den Ball*); *Fingernägel*: *a.* pare; *Baum be~*: lop, prune; *Hecke*: trim; (*mähen*) mow; *sich ~* ⩕ *Linien*: intersect; *fig.* be mistaken; *s. Grimasse*, *Haar*; ˈ**2nd** cutting, sharp; *Kälte*: biting (*alle a. fig.*).

ˈ**Schneider** *m* (7) tailor; **~ei** [~ˈraɪ] *f* (16) tailoring; ˈ**~in** *f* (16[1]) ladies' tailor, dressmaker; ˈ**~kleid** *n* tailor-made dress; ˈ**~kostüm** *n* tailor-made suit; ˈ**~meister** *m* master tailor; ˈ**2n** (29) *v/i.* do tailoring *od.* dressmaking; *v/t.* make; ˈ**~puppe** *f* dress form, dummy.

ˈ**Schneide|tisch** *m Film*: editing table; ˈ**~werkzeuge** *n/pl.* cutting tools; ˈ**~zahn** *m* incisor, cutter.

ˈ**schneidig** *fig.* (*forsch*) dashing; (*entschlossen*) resolute; (*fesch*) smart; (*mutig*) plucky; *Rede usw.*: terse; ˈ**2keit** *f* dash, smartness; pluck.

schneien [ˈʃnaɪən] (25) snow.

Schneise [ˈʃnaɪzə] *f* (15) (forest-) aisle, vista; ✈ flying lane.

schnell [ʃnɛl] quick, fast; *Handeln*: *a.* speedy, prompt (*a. Erwiderung*); (*~füßig*, *a. Vogel*, *Flug*) swift; *Strömung*, *Wuchs*, ⚔ *Feuer*: rapid; *Rennbahn usw.*: fast; ✝ *Verkauf*: brisk; *Umsatz*: quick; (*plötzlich*) sudden; (*hastig*) hasty; *~!* be quick!; *mach ~!* be quick!, hurry up!, look sharp!; *nicht so ~!* gently!; ˈ**2boot** *n* speedboat; ⚔ motor torpedo boat; ˈ**2bus** *m* express bus; ˈ**~en** (25) *v/t.* jerk; *mit dem Finger*: flick; *v/i.* (sn) jerk, bound, flip; ˈ**2feuer** *n* quick fire; ˈ**2feuergeschütz** *n* quick-firer, automatic gun; **~füßig** [ˈ~fy:siç] swift(-footed); ˈ**2gang** *mot. m* overdrive; ˈ**2gaststätte** *f* fast-food restaurant; ˈ**2gericht** *n* ⚖ summary court; (*Speise*) fast food; ˈ**2hefter** *m* (7) (rapid) letter-file.

ˈ**Schnelligkeit** *f* quickness, fastness; swiftness, rapidity; promptness; (*Tempo*) speed; ⊕ velocity; ˈ**~srekord** *m* speed record.

ˈ**Schnell|-imbiß** *m* snack; ˈ**~-imbißstube** *f* snack bar; ˈ**~kochplatte** *f* high-speed plate; ˈ**~kochtopf** *m* pressure cooker; ˈ**~kraft** *f* elasticity; ˈ**~(l)auf** *m* run, race; (*Eis2*) speed-skating; ˈ**~(l)äufer(in** *f*) *m* sprinter; (*Eis2*) speed-skater; **2(l)ebig** [ˈ~le:biç] *Zeit*: fast-moving; ˈ**~reinigung** *f* express dry-cleaning; ˈ**~schuß** *m* (*rasch produziertes Produkt*) rush job; ˈ**~segler** ⚓ *m* fast sailer; **~stahl** ⊕ *m* high-speed steel; ˈ**~(verkehrs)straße** *f* express roadway, *Am.* speedway; ˈ**~verfahren** *n* ⚖ summary jurisdiction; ⊕ rapid method, short cut; ˈ**~waage** *f* steelyard; ˈ**~zug** *m* fast train, express.

Schnepfe [ˈʃnɛpfə] *f* (15) snipe.

Schneppe [ˈʃnɛpə] *f* (15) spout; *e-r Haube*: peak; ˈ**~r** ⊕ *m* (7) snap.

schneuzen [ˈʃnɔʏtsən] (27): *sich ~* blow one's nose.

schniegeln [ˈʃni:gəln] (29) dress (*od.* spruce *od.* smarten) up.

Schnipp|chen [ˈʃnipçən] *n* (6): *j-m ein ~ schlagen fig.* outwit (*od.* fool) a p.; ˈ**~el** *m*, *n* (7) *s. Schnipsel*; ˈ**2eln** *v/t. u. v/i.* (29) cut, snip; ˈ**2en** *v/t. u. v/i.* (25) snip; (*mit den Fingern*) *~* snap one's fingers; ˈ**2isch** pert, snappish, *Am.* F snippy.

Schnipsel [ˈ~səl] *m*, *n* (7) scrap, shred, snip, bit.

Schnitt [ʃnit] **1.** *m* (3) (*Schneiden*) cutting; *ins Fleisch*: incision; (*Haar2*, *Kleider2*, *~wunde*; *a. Film*) cut; *am Buch*: edge; (*~muster*) pattern; (*Scheibe*) slice; ⩕ (inter)section; (*Längs2*) longitudinal section; (*Durch2*) average; *im ~* on an average; *s. golden*; F (*Gewinn*) profit; **2.** 2 *pret. v. schneiden*; ˈ**~blumen** *f/pl.* cut flowers; ˈ**~bohnen** *f/pl.* sliced French beans; ˈ**~e** *f* (15) cut, slice (of bread *etc.*); *belegte*: sandwich; ˈ**~er** *m* (7), ˈ**~erin** *f* reaper, mower; ˈ**2fest** *Tomaten*: firm; ˈ**~fläche** *f* section(al plane); ˈ**~holz** *n* sawed timber; ˈ**2ig** stylish; *Auto usw.*: streamlined; ˈ**~lauch** ⚘ *m* chive; ˈ**~muster** *n* pattern; ˈ**~punkt** *m Linien*: (point of) intersection; *Winkel*: vertex; ˈ**~stelle** *f* cut; *Computer*: interface; ˈ**~wunde** *f* cut; ˈ**~zeichnung** ⊕ *f* sectional drawing.

Schnitz [ʃnits] *m* (3[2]) cut, slice; ˈ**~arbeit** *f* wood-carving.

Schnitzel[1] [ˈ~əl] *n* (7) (*Fleisch*) esca-

lope, cutlet; *Wiener* ~ (veal) cutlet, Wiener schnitzel.
Schnitzel[2] *n, m* (7) chip, snip; ⊕ ~ *pl.* (*Abfälle*) parings, shavings; (*Papier*~) scraps *pl.*; '**~jagd** *f* paper-chase; '**~n** (29) whittle, chip.
'**schnitzen** (27) carve, cut.
'**Schnitzer** *m* (7) carver, cutter; (*Fehler*) blunder, slip(-up), *Am. sl.* boner; **~ei** [~'raɪ] *f* (16) (wood-) carving; carved work.
'**Schnitz|kunst** *f* (art of) carving; '**~werk** *n* carved work.
schnob [ʃno:p] *pret. v. schnauben.*
schnodd(e)rig F ['ʃnɔd(ə)riç] pert, flippant.
schnöde ['ʃnø:də] (*verächtlich*) scornful; *Undank*: black, base; *Handlungsweise*: vile, shabby; *Profit*: filthy.
Schnorchel ['ʃnɔrçəl] ⚓ *m* (7) snort, snorkel; (*~maske, zum Schwimmen*) snorkel mask.
Schnörkel ['ʃnœrkəl] *m* (7) flourish, squiggle; △ scroll; '**~n** (29) *v/i.* make flourishes; *v/t.* △ (adorn with) scroll(s); '**~haft** full of flourishes.
schnorr|en F ['ʃnɔrən] (25) cadge; '**~er** *m* (7) cadger.
schnüff|eln ['ʃnyfəln] (29) sniff (*an dat.* at), snuffle; nose (*an dat.* at; *nach* after, for); F *fig.* snoop (around); '**~ler** F *fig. m* (7) sniffer; *fig.* spy, F snooper; (*Detektiv*) sleuth.
Schnuller ['ʃnulər] *m* (7) comforter, dummy, *Am.* pacifier.
Schnulze F ['ʃnultsə] *f* (15) *sl.* tear-jerker.
Schnupf|en[1] ['ʃnupfən] *m* (6) cold (in the head), catarrh; *den ~ bekommen* catch (a) cold; '**~en**[2] (25) take snuff; '**~en**[3] *n* (6) taking snuff; '**~tabak** *m* snuff; '**~tuch** *n* (pocket-) handkerchief.
Schnuppe ['ʃnupə] *f* (15) *am Licht*: snuff; (*Stern*~) falling (*od.* shooting) star; F *das ist mir* ~ F I don't care (a damn); '**~rn** (29) *s. schnüffeln.*
Schnur [ʃnu:r] *f* cord; (*Bindfaden*) string; (*Leine*) line; *zum Schnüren*: lace; *fig. über die ~ hauen* kick over the traces, *beim Essen usw.*: over-indulge.
Schnür|boden ['ʃny:r-] *thea. m* gridiron; '**~chen** *n* (6): *das geht wie am ~* it goes like clock-work; *et. wie am ~ können* have a th. at one's finger-tips; '**~en** (25) lace; (*zubinden*) cord, tie up; *sich ~* wear stays.
'**schnurgerade** straight (as an arrow).
Schnurr|bart ['ʃnur-] *m* moustache; '**~e** *fig. f* (15) funny tale; '**~en** (25) hum, buzz; *Rad*: whir(r); *Katze*: purr; F (*schnorren*) cadge.
'**Schnürriemen** *m* lace, strap.
'**schnurrig** droll, funny; (*wunderlich*) odd.
'**Schnür|senkel** *m* shoe-lace, *bsd. Am. a.* shoestring; '**~stiefel** *m* lace-boot.
'**schnurstracks** straight, directly, right away; ~ *zuwider* diametrically opposed; ~ *zugehen auf* (*acc.*) make a bee-line for.
Schnute ['ʃnu:tə] *f* (15) mouth; e-e ~ *ziehen* pout.
schob [ʃo:p] *pret. v. schieben.*
Schober ['ʃo:bər] *m* (7) stack, rick.
Schock[1] [ʃɔk] *n* (3; *nach Zahlen inv.*) threescore; **~**[2] *m* (3[1]) ⚕ *u. fig.* shock; '**~farbe** *f* blaze colo(u)r; **~ieren** [~'ki:rən] shock, scandalize; '**~therapie** *f* shock therapy.
schofel ['ʃo:fəl] mean, shabby.
Schöffe ['ʃœfə] ⚖ *m* (13) lay assessor; '**~ngericht** *n* lay assessors court.
Schokolade [ʃoko'la:də] *f* (15) chocolate; **~ntafel** *f* bar of chocolate.
scholl [ʃɔl] *pret. v. schallen.*
Scholle ['ʃɔlə] *f* (15) clod; (*Eis*~) floe; *Fisch*: plaice; *fig.* soil.
schon [ʃo:n] already; (*jetzt ~*) yet; (*~ einmal, ~ früher*) before; (*sogar*) even; (*natürlich*) of course; (*sicherlich*) sure enough; ~ *damals* even then; ~ *ganz* quite; ~ *deswegen* for that reason alone; ~ *weil* if only because; ~ *immer* all along; ~ *lange* long since, for a long time; ~ *wieder* again; ~ *gut!* all right!; *das ist ~ wahr, aber* ... that is very well (*od.* quite true), but ...; *wenn ~* although; (*na*) *wenn~!* so what?; ~ *der Gedanke* the very idea; ~ *der Name* the bare name; *hast du ~ (ein)mal* ...? have you ever ...?; *er wird ~ kommen* don't worry, he will come; ~ *im 16. Jahrhundert* as early as the 16th century; ~ *um 8 Uhr* as early as 8 o'clock; ~ *seit 50 Jahren*, ~ *50 Jahre* as long as 50 years.
schön [ʃø:n] beautiful; *Frau*: *a.* fair;

bsd. Mann: handsome; (*gut, fein*) good, fine; (*großzügig, ansehnlich*) handsome; (*prächtig*) splendid; (*nett, lieb*) nice, kind (von of); *Wetter*: fair, fine; *das ~e Geschlecht* the fair sex; *die ~en Künste* the fine arts; *~e Literatur* polite letters *pl.*, belles-lettres *pl.*; *~en Dank!* many thanks!; *eines ~en Tages* one day; *~ warm* nice and warm; *es war sehr ~* (*auf dem Fest*) we had a good time; *das wäre noch ~er!* certainly not!; *~ wär's!* some hope!; *das sind mir ~e Sachen!* pretty doings indeed!; *et. ~ bleiben lassen* do nothing of the kind; *aufs ~ste* most beautifully; *~!* all right!, F *od. Am.* okay!; **2e** (18) **1.** *f* belle, beauty; **2.** *das ~* the beautiful.

schonen ['ʃo:nən] (25) spare; (*schonend umgehen mit et.*) be careful with; (*erhalten*) preserve; (*nicht strapazieren*) be easy on; *Augen, Kräfte, Vorrat*: save; *sich ~* take care of o.s., (*a. weitS.*) take it easy; *sich nicht ~* exert (*od.* drive) o.s.; **'~d** careful; (*rücksichtsvoll*) considerate; (*nachsichtig*) indulgent; *s. beibringen.*

Schoner ['ʃo:nər] ⚓ *m* (7) schooner.

'schön|färben *fig.* gloss (over); **'2färber** *m fig.* optimist; **'2geist** *m* (a)esthete, bel esprit (*fr.*); **'~geistig** aesthetical; *Literatur*: belletristic.

'Schönheit *f allg.* beauty; **'~sfehler** *m* corporal defect; *e-s Gegenstandes*: flaw (*a. fig.*); **'~skonkurrenz** *f* beauty contest; **'~s-operation** *f* cosmetic operation; **~s-pflästerchen** ['~pflɛstərçən] *n* (6) beauty spot; **'~s-pflege** *f* beauty culture; **'~ssalon** *m* beauty parlo(u)r; **'~s-wettbewerb** *m* beauty contest.

'Schonkost *f* light food.

'Schön|redner *m contp.* speechifier; (*Schmeichler*) flatterer; **'2tun** *j-m*: (*schmeicheln*) coax, cajole; (*schäkern*) flirt (with).

'Schonung *f* (*Gnade*) mercy; (*Nachsicht*) forbearance; (*pflegliche Behandlung*) careful treatment; (*Erhaltung, Schutz*) protection; (*Baumschule*) tree-nursery; **'2slos** pitiless, relentless.

'Schonzeit *hunt. f* close season, *Am.* closed season.

Schopf [ʃɔpf] *m* (3[3]) (*Haar2*) tuft; *voller*: mop (of hair); *der Vögel*: tuft, crest.

Schöpf|-eimer ['ʃœpf-] *m* pail; **'2en** (25) *v/t.* scoop; draw *water etc.*; *mit e-m Löffel*: ladle; *Atem*: draw, take; *Mut*: take; *s. Hoffnung, Verdacht.*

'Schöpfer *m* (7) creator; (*Gott*) *the* Creator; **'~geist** *m* creative genius; **'~in** *f* (16[1]) creatress; **'2isch** creative.

'Schöpf|kelle *f* scoop, ladle; **'~löffel** *m* ladle; **'~ung** *f* creation.

Schoppen ['ʃɔpən] *m* (6) pint.

schor [ʃo:r] *pret. v. scheren.*

Schorf [ʃɔrf] *m* (3) scurf; (*Wund2*) scab; **'2ig** scurfy, scabby.

Schornstein ['ʃɔrnʃtaɪn] *m* chimney; ⚓, 🚂 funnel; (*Fabrik2*) smokestack; *fig. s. Kamin*; **'~feger** *m* chimney-sweep.

schoß[1] [ʃɔs] *pret. v. schießen.*

Schoß[2] ⚘ [ʃɔs] *m* (3[2]) shoot, sprout.

Schoß[3] [ʃo:s] *m* (4[2]) lap; (*Mutterleib*) womb; (*Rock2*) flap, tail, skirt; *der Kirche, Familie, Partei*: fold; *s. Hand*; **'~hund** *m* lap-dog; **'~kind** *n* darling, pet.

Schößling ⚘ ['ʃœslɪŋ] *m* (3[1]) shoot.

Schote ['ʃo:tə] *f* (15) cod, pod, husk, shell; ⚓ sheet; *~n pl.* green peas.

Schott ⚓ [ʃɔt] *n* (3) bulkhead; **'~e** *m* (13) Scot, Scotsman, Scotchman; *die ~n pl.* the Scots *od.* Scotch; **'~er** *m* (7) metal, gravel; 🚂 ballast; (*Geröll*) rubble; **'~in** *f* (16[1]) Scotswoman, Scotchwoman; **'2isch** Scottish, Scotch.

schraffier|en [ʃra'fi:rən] hatch; **2ung** *f* hatching.

schräg [ʃrɛ:k] oblique, slanting; (*~ abfallend*) sloping; (*~ verlaufend*) diagonal; *~ gegenüber* across (*von* from); **2e** ['~gə] *f* (15) obliquity, slope; **2lage** ['ʃrɛ:k-] *f* sloping position; ✈ bank(ing); **'2strich** *m* oblique, *Am.* slash.

schrak [ʃra:k] *pret. v. schrecken v/i.*

Schramm|e ['ʃramə] *f* (15) scratch; (*Narbe*) scar; **'2en** (25) scratch, scar; *Haut*: *a.* graze; **'2ig** scarred.

Schrank [ʃraŋk] *m* (3[3]) cupboard, *bsd. Am.* closet; (*Kleider2*) wardrobe; (*Spind*) locker; *s. Bücher2, Wäsche2*; **'~bett** *n* fold-away bed.

Schranke ['ʃraŋkə] *f* (15) barrier (*a. fig.*); ⚖ bar; 🚂 gate; **'~n** *pl. des Turnierplatzes*: lists; *fig.* limits, bounds; *in die ~ fordern* challenge;

~n setzen (dat.) set bounds to; *(sich) in ~ halten* keep within bounds; *j-n in s-e ~en weisen* put a p. in his place.

schränken ['ʃrɛŋkən] (25) *Beine*: cross; *Arme*: fold; *Säge*: set.

'**schranken|los** boundless; '**⁀wärter** 🚂 *m* gate-keeper.

'**schrank|fertig** *Wäsche*: washed and ironed; '**⁀koffer** *m* wardrobe trunk; '**⁀wand** *f* wall unit.

Schraubdeckel ['ʃraup-] *m* screw cap.

Schraube ['ʃraubə] *f* (15) screw (*a.* ⚓); ✈ air-screw, *Am.* propeller; *~ und Mutter* bolt and nut; *fig.* F *bei ihm ist e-e ~ locker* he has a screw loose; '**⁀n** *v/t. u. v/i.* (30) screw; (*drehen*) twist, spiral; *fig. niedriger ~* lower, scale down; *s. geschraubt*.

'**Schrauben|dampfer** ⚓ *m* screw steamer; **⁀förmig** ['~fœrmiç] screw-shaped, helical, spiral; '**~gang** *m*, '**~gewinde** *n* screw thread; '**~linie** *f* spiral line; '**~mutter** *f* female screw, nut; '**~schlüssel** *m* wrench, spanner; (*verstellbarer ~*) monkey-wrench; '**~spindel** *f* male screw; **~zieher** ['~tsi:ər] *m* screw-driver.

Schraub|fassung ['ʃraup-] *f* screw fixture; '**~stock** *m* vice, *Am.* vise; '**~verschluß** *m* screw cap.

Schrebergarten ['ʃre:bərgartən] *m* allotment (garden).

Schreck [ʃrɛk] *m* (3), '**~en**[1] *m* (6) fright, terror; shock, panic; *die ~en des Krieges usw.* the horrors of; *in ~en versetzen* frighten, terrify; *mit dem ~en davonkommen* get off with a bad fright; '**⁀en**[2] (*v/t.* [25], *v/i.* 30, sn) = *ab~, auf~, er~*; '**⁀en-erregend** horrific.

'**Schreckens|botschaft** *f* alarming (*od.* terrible) news; '**~herrschaft** *f* reign of terror; '**~ruf** *m* cry of terror; '**~tat** *f* atrocious deed.

'**Schreck|gespenst** *fig. n* bugbear, nightmare; '**⁀haft** easily frightened, nervous; '**⁀lich** frightful, terrible, dreadful; F *fig. a.* awful(ly *adv.*); '**~nis** *n* (4[1]) horror; *s. Schrecken*; '**~schuß** *m* shot in the air; *fig.* false alarm; *e-n ~ abgeben* fire in the air; '**~schußpistole** *f* booby pistol; '**~sekunde** *f* reaction time.

Schrei [ʃraɪ] *m* (3) cry; shout; *gellender*: yell; *spitzer*: scream; (*Brüllen*; *der Menge*) roar; *fig. der letzte ~* the latest rage, the dernier cri (*fr.*).

Schreib|arbeit ['ʃraɪpˀarbaɪt] *f* clerical (*od.* desk) work; *bsd. contp.* paperwork; '**~block** *m* writing-pad; '**~büro** *n* writing office.

schreiben ['ʃraɪbən] **1.** *v/t. u. v/i.* (30) write (*j-m* to a p.; ✝, F a p.; *über ein Thema* on); (*orthographisch ~*) spell; (*mit der*) *Maschine ~* type (-write); *sich* (*od. ea.*) *~* correspond; (*Bücher ~*) be a writer; *wie schreibt er sich?* how does he spell his name?; *s. Ohr, rein* 1, *Zeile*; **2.** **⁀** *n* (6) writing; (*Brief*) letter.

'**Schreiber** *m* (7), '**~in** *f* (16[1]) writer; (*Angestellter*) secretary, clerk; ⊕ *m* recorder; **~ei** [~'raɪ] *f* (endless) writing, scribbling; '**~ling** *contp. m* pen-pusher.

schreib|faul ['ʃraɪpfaul] lazy in writing; '**⁀feder** *f* pen; '**⁀fehler** *m* mistake in spelling *od.* writing, slip of the pen, clerical error; '**⁀gerät** *n* writing utensils *pl.*; ⊕ recorder; '**⁀heft** *n* copy- (*od.* exercise-)book; '**⁀kraft** *f* typist; '**⁀krampf** *m* writer's cramp; '**⁀kunst** *f* art of writing; '**⁀mappe** *f* writing-case; *mit Löschpapier*: blotting-case; '**⁀maschine** *f* typewriter; *~ schreiben* type(write); *mit ~ geschrieben* typewritten; '**⁀maschinenpapier** *n* typing paper; '**⁀material** *n* writing material(s *pl.*), stationery; '**⁀papier** *n* writing-paper; '**⁀pult** *n* (writing-)desk; '**⁀schrift** *f* script; '**⁀stube** ⚔ *f* orderly room, office; '**⁀tisch** *m* desk; writing-table; '**⁀ung** *f* spelling; '**~-unkundig** unable to write; '**⁀-unterlage** *f* writing-pad, blotting-pad; '**⁀waren** *f/pl.* stationery *sg.*; '**⁀warenhändler** *m* stationer; '**⁀warenhandlung** *f* stationer's shop; '**⁀weise** *f* style; *e-s Wortes*: spelling; '**⁀zentrale** *f* typing pool; '**⁀zeug** *n s. Schreibgerät*.

schrei|en ['ʃraɪən] *v/i. u. v/t.* (30) cry (*um, nach* for); *laut*: shout; *gellend*: yell; *spitz*: scream, shriek; (*brüllen*) roar; *nur v/i. Hirsch*: bell; F *zum ⁀* (*komisch*) a scream; '**~end** *fig. Farbe*: loud; *Schande*: crying; *Unrecht*: flagrant; *Gegensatz*: glaring; '**⁀er** *m* (7), '**⁀erin** *f*, '**⁀hals** *m* bawler; (*Lärmmacher*) brawler; *kleiner Schreihals* cry-baby.

Schrein [ʃraɪn] *m* (3) chest; (*Sarg*) coffin; (*Reliquien*≗) shrine; '**~er** *m* (7) joiner; (*Kunst*≗) cabinet-maker.
schreiten ['ʃraɪtən] (30, sn) step, pace, stride; ~ *zu* proceed to.
schrie [ʃriː] *pret. v. schreien.*
schrieb [ʃriːp] *pret. v. schreiben* 1.
Schrift [ʃrift] *f* (16) writing; (*Schreib*≗; *~art*) script; *s. Hand*≗, *In*≗; (*~zeichen*) letter, character; *typ.* typeface; (*~stück*) document, (*a. Abhandlung*) paper; (*Veröffentlichung*) publication; (*Werk*) work; (*Broschüre*) pamphlet; *die Heilige* ~ the Holy Scripture(s *pl.*); '**~art** *f* type; '**~bild** *n* face; '**~deutsch** *n* literary German; '**~enreihe** *f* serial publication; '**~führer(in** *f*) *m* secretary; '**~gelehrte** *m* scribe; '**~gießer** *typ. m* type-founder; '**~leiter** *m* editor; '**~leiterin** *f* editress; '**~leitung** *f* editorship; (*Personal*) editorial staff, editors *pl.*; '≗**lich** written, in writing; (*brieflich*) by letter; *et.* ~ *beantragen* apply for a th. in writing; *wegen e-r S.* ~ *anfragen* write for a th. (*bei j-m* to a p.); ~ *niederlegen* put *a th.* (down) in writing, (put *a th.* on) record; *jetzt haben wir es* ~ now we have it in black and white; '**~muster** *typ. n* type specimen; '**~rolle** *f* scroll; '**~satz** ⚖ *m* memorandum, letter(s *pl.*); '**~setzer** *m* compositor, type-setter; '**~sprache** *f* written (*od.* literary) language; '**~steller** *m* author, writer; **~stellerei** [~'raɪ] *f* writing; '**~stellerin** *f* (16¹) author(ess), writer; '≗**stellerisch** literary; *adv.* as an author; '**~stellerverband** *m* authors' association; '**~stück** *n* document, paper, deed; '**~tum** *n* (1²) literature; '**~wechsel** *m* exchange of letters, correspondence; '**~zeichen** *n* letter, character; '**~zug** *m* character; (*Schnörkel*) flourish.
schrill [ʃril] shrill.
Schrippe ['ʃripə] *f* (15) (French) roll.
Schritt [ʃrit] **1.** *m* (3; *als Maß im pl. inv.*) step (*a. fig. u. pol.*); *a. als Maß*: pace; *langer*: stride; *diplomatischer*: démarche (*fr.*); (*Gangart*) gait, walk; *der Hose*: crotch; *hörbarer*: footstep; ~ *für* ~ step by step (*a. fig.*); ~ *fahren!* dead slow!, drive at walking speed!; ~ *halten* keep step, *fig. a.* keep abreast (*mit* of); *fig.* ~*e tun od. unternehmen* take steps; *auf* ~ *und Tritt* at every turn; *s. folgen*; **2.** ≗ *pret. v. schreiten*; '**~macher** *m Rennsport*: pace-maker (*a. fig.*), pacer; ⚕ (*Herz*≗) pace-maker; *fig. Mode*: trend-setter; '**~macherdienste** *m/pl.* pace-setting *sg.*; '≗**weise** *adj. fig.* gradual; *adv.* step by step (*a. fig.*).
schroff [ʃrɔf] *Berge*: rugged; (*steil*) steep; *fig.* gruff, harsh; (*plötzlich*) abrupt; '≗**heit** *f* steepness; gruffness; abruptness.
schröpfen ['ʃrœpfən] (25) cup, bleed; *fig.* fleece, milk (*um* for).
Schrot [ʃroːt] *m u. n* (3) *zum Schießen*: small shot; (*Korn*) bruised grain, grist; *fig. von echtem* ~ *und Korn* true; '**~brot** *n* whole-meal bread; '≗**en** (26, *p.p.* ⚒ *geschroten*) *Faß usw.*: shoot, lower; ⚓ parbuckle; *Korn*: rough-grind, bruise (*a. Malz*); '**~flinte** *f* shotgun; '**~korn** *n* (grain of) shot; '**~mehl** *n* coarse meal; '**~mühle** *f* bruising mill; '**~säge** *f* crosscut saw.
Schrott [ʃrɔt] *m* (7, *o. pl.*) scrap (iron); '**~händler** *m* scrap-dealer; '**~platz** *m* scrap yard; '≗**reif** ready for the scrap heap; '**~wert** *m* scrap value.
schrubb|en ['ʃrubən] *v/t. u. v/i.* (26) scrub; '≗**er** *m* (7) scrubber.
Schrulle ['ʃrulə] *f* (15) whim, crotchet; (*Frau*) old crone; ~*n haben* F have a kink; '≗**nhaft**, '**schrullig** crotchety, cranky.
schrump(e)lig ['ʃrump(ə)liç] shrivel(l)ed, wrinkled.
schrumpf|en ['ʃrumpfen] (25, sn) shrink (*a.* ⚕, ⊕ *u. fig.*); shrivel; '≗**ung** *f* shrinking, shrinkage.
Schrund|e ['ʃrundə] *f* (15) crack, chap; '≗**ig** cracked, chapped.
Schub [ʃuːp] *m* (3) push; *phys.*, ⊕ thrust; *von Broten usw., a. fig.*: batch; '**~fach** *n*, '**~kasten** *m*, '**~lade** *f* drawer; '**~karren** *m* wheel-barrow, *Am. a.* pushcart; '**~kraft** *f*, '**~leistung** ⊕ *f* thrust.
Schubs F [ʃups] *m* (3) push, shove; '≗**en** push, shove.
schüchtern ['ʃyçtərn] shy, bashful, timid; '≗**heit** *f* shyness, bashfulness, timidity.
schuf [ʃuːf] *pret. v. schaffen.*
Schuft [ʃuft] *m* (3) scoundrel, rascal; '≗**en** (26) drudge, slave; **~erei** [~tə'raɪ] *f* drudgery, F grind; '≗**ig** low, mean.

Schuh [ʃuː] *m* (3) shoe; (*hoher* ~) boot; *fig. j-m et. in die ~e schieben* put the blame for a th. on a p.; '**~-anzieher** *m* (7) shoehorn; '**~band** *n* shoe-lace, *Am. a.* shoe-string; '**~bürste** *f* shoe-brush; '**~creme** *f s. Schuhwichse*; '**~geschäft** *n* shoe-shop; '**~größe** *f* size (of shoes); '**~macher** *m* shoemaker; **~plattler** ['~platlər] *m* (7) Bavarian folk dance; '**~putzer** *m* shoeblack; '**~riemen** *m*, '**~senkel** *m s. Schuhband*; '**~sohle** *f* sole; '**~spanner** *m* shoe-tree; '**~waren** *f/pl.*, '**~werk** *n* footwear, footgear; '**~wichse** *f* shoe-polish, *Am. a.* shoe-shine.

'**Schul|-abgänger** *m* school-leaver; '**~-amt** *n* (*Behörde*) school board, education authority; (*Haupt*∻) Board of Education; '**~-arbeit** *f* **a**) *mst pl.* homework; *~en machen* do one's homework; **b**) = '**~-aufgabe** test (in class), class exercise; '**~-ausgabe** *f* school edition; '**~-ausflug** *m* school outing; '**~bank** *f* desk; *die ~ drücken* go to school; '**~behörde** *f s. Schulamt*; '**~beispiel** *n* test-case, typical example; '**~besuch** *m* attendance at school; '**~bildung** *f* (*höhere* secondary) education; '**~buch** *n* school-book; '**~buchverlag** *m* educational publishers *pl.*

Schuld [ʃult] *f* (16) guilt; (*Veranlassung*; *Fehler*) fault; (*Ursache*) cause; (*Missetat*) wrong; (*Sünde*) sin; (*Geld*∻) debt; (*Verpflichtung*) obligation; *~en machen* incur debts; *in ~en geraten, sich in ~en stürzen* run into debts; *in j-s ~ sein* be indebted to a p.; *er ist* (*od. hat*) ∻ (*daran*), *es ist s-e ~* it is his fault; *j-m* (*od. e-r Sache*) *die ~ geben* blame a p. *od.* a th.; *die schlechten Zeiten sind ∻ daran* the bad times are to blame for it; *j-m die ~* (*an et.*) *zuschieben od. zuschreiben* lay (*od.* put) the blame (for a th.) on a p.; *die ~ auf sich nehmen* take the blame; *ohne m-e ~* through no fault of mine; '**∻beladen** laden with guilt, guilty; '**∻bewußt** conscious of one's guilt; '**~buch** *n* account-book, ledger.

schulden ['ʃuldən] (26): *j-m et. ~* (*a. fig.*) owe a p. a th.; *vgl. schuldig*; '**~frei** free from debt; *Grundbesitz*: unencumbered; '**∻last** *f* burden of debt; *v. Grundbesitz*: encumbrance; '**∻tilgungsfonds** *m* sinking-fund.

'**Schuld|forderung** *f* (active) debt, claim; '**~frage** *f* question of guilt; '**∻haft** culpable.

schuldig ['ʃuldiç] (*strafbar*) guilty (*e-r S.* of a th.), culpable; *Zivilrecht*: responsible; *Geld*: owing, due; (*gebührend*) due; *j-m et. ~ sein od. bleiben* owe a p. *a th.* (*a. fig.*); *j-m et. ~ sein* be indebted to a p. for a th.; *j-m Dank ~ sein* owe gratitude to a p.; *j-m die Antwort ~ bleiben* make no reply; ⚖ *für ~ befinden* find guilty; *j-n ~ sprechen* pronounce a p. guilty; *s. bekennen*; *der, die* **∻e** ['~gə] (18) the culprit; **∻keit** ['~diçkaɪt] *f* duty, obligation.

'**Schuldirektor(in** *f*) *m* headmaster, *f* headmistress, *Am.* principal.

'**schuld|los** guiltless, innocent; '**∻losigkeit** *f* guiltlessness, innocence.

Schuldner ['ʃuldnər] *m* (7), '**~in** *f* (16[1]) debtor.

'**Schuld|recht** ⚖ *n* law of obligation; **~schein** ['ʃultʃaɪn] *m*, '**~verschreibung** *f* promissory note; IOU (= I owe you); *öffentliche*: debenture, bond.

Schule ['ʃuːlə] *f* (15) school (*a. weitS.*); *höhere ~* secondary school, *Am.* high school; *fig. e-e harte ~* a severe school (*od.* test); *Hohe ~ Reiten*: haute école (*fr.*); *auf* (*od. in der*) *~* at school; *in die ~ gehen* go to school; *aus der ~ plaudern* tell tales out of school, blab; *fig. ~ machen* be imitated, spread; *s. schwänzen*; '**∻n** (25) school, train.

Schüler ['ʃyːlər] *m* (7) schoolboy; pupil; *höherer*: student; (*Jünger*) disciple; '**~-austausch** *m* exchange of pupils; '**∻haft** schoolboy-like; **~in** ['~rin] *f* (16[1]) schoolgirl; '**~karte** *f* school season-ticket; '**~lotse** *m* lollipop man; '**~lotsin** *f* lollipop woman.

'**Schul|ferien** *pl.* holidays, *bsd. Am.* vacation(s *pl.*); '**~fernsehen** *n* educational television; '**~flugzeug** *n* training airplane; '**∻frei**: *~ haben* have a holiday; '**~freund(in** *f*) *m* schoolmate; '**~funk** *m* schools' radio; '**~gelände** *n* school-grounds *pl.*, *Am.* campus; '**~geld** *n* school fee(s *pl.*); '**~gelehrsamkeit** *f* book-learning; '**~haus** *n* school(-house), school building; '**~hof** *m* playground, schoolyard; '**~jahr** *n* school year; *~e* *pl.* school-days; '**~jugend** *f* school-children *pl.*; '**~junge** *m* schoolboy; '**~kamerad** *m* schoolmate; '**~kenntnisse** *f/pl.* school knowledge *sg.*; '**~lehrer** *m* schoolmaster, teacher; '**~lehrerin** *f* schoolmistress, (lady) teacher; '**~leiter** *m s. Schuldirektor*; '**~mann** *m* education(al)ist; '**~mappe** *f* school-bag; '**~meister** *contp. m* schoolmaster; '**≈meisterlich** like a schoolmaster, pedantic; '**≈meistern** (29) censure; '**~-ordnung** *f* school regulations *pl.*; '**~pferd** *n* trained horse; '**~pflicht** *f* compulsory education *od.* school attendance; **≈pflichtig** ['~pfliçtiç] schoolable, of school age; *~es Alter* school age; '**~prüfung** *f* school examination; '**~ranzen** *m* satchel; '**~rat** *m* supervisor; '**~raum** *m*, '**~stube** *f* schoolroom; '**~recht** *n* education law; '**~reiten** *n* schooling; '**~schiff** *n* school ship; '**~schluß** *m* break-up; '**~schwänzer** *m* truant; '**~speisung** *f* school lunch; '**~stunde** *f* lesson, period; '**~tasche** *f* school bag *od.* satchel.

Schulter ['ʃultər] *f* (15) shoulder; *~ an ~* (*a. fig.*) shoulder to shoulder; *s. kalt, leicht*; '**~blatt** *n* shoulder-blade; '**≈frei** *Kleid*: off-the-shoulder; (*trägerlos*) strapless; '**~klappe** *f*, '**~stück** ⚔ *n* shoulder strap; '**≈n** (29) shoulder; '**~sieg** *m Ringen*: win by fall.

Schulung ['ʃu:luŋ] *f* training.

'**Schul|-unterricht** *m* school instruction, lessons *pl.*; '**~versuch** *m* education pilot scheme; '**~verwaltung** *f* school administration; '**~weg** *m* way to school; '**~weisheit** *f* book-learning; '**~wesen** *n* education(al system); *öffentliches ~* state education (system); '**~zeit** *f* schooltime; *rückblikkend*: school-days *pl.*; '**~zeugnis** *n* school record *od.* report; '**~zimmer** *n* schoolroom; '**~zwang** *m* compulsory school education.

schummel|n F ['ʃuməln] *v/i.* (29) cheat; '**≈zettel** *m* crib.

schumm(e)rig ['ʃum(ə)riç] dusky.

schund[1] [ʃunt] *pret. v. schinden.*

Schund[2] [ʃunt] *m* (3) trash; ⚖ *~-und-Schmutzgesetz n* Harmful Publications Act; '**~literatur** *f* trashy literature; '**~roman** *m* penny dreadful, *Am.* dime novel.

Schupo F ['ʃu:po] **1.** *f* (*inv. o. pl.*) *abbr. für (Schutz-)Polizei*; **2.** *m* (11) *abbr. für (Schutz-)Polizist*: (police) officer, F bobby, *bsd. Am.* cop.

Schupp|e ['ʃupə] *f* (15) scale; *pl.* (*Kopf≈n*) dandruff *sg.*; *es fiel mir wie ~n von den Augen* the scales fell from my eyes; '**≈en**[1] (25) scale; (*kratzen*) rub, scratch; *sich ~* scale off; '**~en**[2] *m* (6) shed; *mot.* garage; ✈ hangar; '**≈ig** scaly, squamous, flaky.

Schur [ʃu:r] *f* (16) shearing; (*Wolle*) fleece.

Schür|eisen ['ʃy:rˀaɪzən] *n* poker; '**≈en** (25) stir (up *fig.*), poke, rake; *fig.* fan (*the fire*), foment.

schürfen ['ʃyrfən] (25) *v/i. nach Erz*: prospect (*nach* for); *v/t. Haut*: scratch, graze.

schurigeln ['ʃu:ri:gəln] *v/t.* (29) torment, bully, F plague.

Schurk|e ['ʃurkə] *m* (13) scoundrel, villain, knave; '**~enstreich** *m*, **~erei** [~'raɪ] *f* knavish trick, villainy; '**≈isch** rascally, villainous, knavish.

Schurz [ʃurts] *m* (3[2] *u.* [3]) apron.

Schürze ['ʃyrtsə] *f* (15) apron; '**≈n** (27) tuck up; *Knoten*: tie; *Lippen*: purse; '**~nband** *n* apron-string; '**~njäger** *m* philanderer, Casanova; '**~nkleid** overall.

Schuß [ʃus] *m* (4[2]) shot (*a. Sport*); (*Knall*) report; (*Ladung*) charge; (*Munition*) round; *Weberei*: weft, woof; *s. Schußwunde*; (*schießende Bewegung*) rush, dash; *Schisport*: schuss; (*Emporschießen*) shooting; ♀ (*Trieb*) shoot; *ein ~ Wein usw.* (*a. fig.*) a dash of ...; F *fig. gut in* (*od. im*) *~* in good order, *P.*: in good form; *in ~ bringen* get in order, get going; *in ~ kommen* get under way; *keinen ~ Pulver wert P.*: not worth powder and shot, *S.*: no good; '**~bereich** *s. Schußweite*; '**≈bereit** *s. ≈fertig.*

Schussel ['ʃusəl] F *m* (7) fidget; *s. Tolpatsch.*

Schüssel ['ʃysəl] *f* (15) bowl, basin; (*Eß≈ usw.*) dish.

'**Schuß|fahrt** *f Schisport*: schuss; '**≈fertig** ready to fire; *Waffe*: *a.* cocked; '**~linie** *f* line of fire; *fig. in die ~ geraten* come under fire; '**~waffe** *f* fire-arm; '**~wechsel** *m* exchange of fire; '**~weite** *f* range; *in (außer) ~* within (out of) range; '**~wunde** *f* gunshot wound, bullet wound.

Schuster ['ʃustər] *m* (7) shoemaker;

(*Flick*♀; *a. fig.*) cobbler; *auf ~s Rappen* on Shanks's mare *od.* pony; '♀**n** (29) cobble; F *fig.* (*pfuschen*) botch.

Schute ['ʃuːtə] *f* (15) ⚓ barge, lighter; (*Hut*) bonnet.

Schutt [ʃut] *m* (3) rubbish; (*Stein*♀) rubble; *in ~ und Asche legen* lay in ruins; '**~-abladeplatz** *m* dump site.

Schüttel|frost ['ʃytəlfrɔst] *m* shivering fit, *the* shivers *pl.*, chill '♀**n** (29) shake; '**~reim** *m* spoonerism.

schütt|en ['ʃytən] (26) pour; *Korn*: shoot; *es schüttet* it is pouring (with rain).

'**Schutt|halde** *f geol., mount.* scree, talus; '**~haufen** *m* dust-heap, dump; (*Steine*) heap of rubble (*a. fig.*).

Schutz [ʃuts] *m* (3²) protection; (*Verteidigung*) defen|ce, *Am.* -se (*beide*: *vor dat.* from, against); (*Obdach*) shelter; (*Geleit*; *a. fig. Sicherung*) safeguard; (*Deckung*) cover; (*Abschirmung*) screen, shield; *~ suchen* take shelter (*vor dat.* from), take refuge (*bei* with); *in ~ nehmen* defend; '**~-anstrich** *m* protective coat(ing); *zur Tarnung*: ⚔ camouflage paint(ing), ⚓ dazzle-paint (-ing).

Schütz [ʃyts] **1.** ⚡ *n* (3²) contactor; **2.** ⊕ *s.* ~e 2.

'**Schutz|-anzug** *m* overall; '**~befohlene** ['~bəfoːlənə] *m, f* charge, protégé(e *f*); '**~blech** *n* guard-plate; *mot.* mudguard, *Am.* fender; '**~brille** *f* (*eine* a pair of) (safety) goggles *pl.*; glasses *pl.*; '**~bündnis** *n* defensive alliance; '**~dach** *n* protective roof; shelter.

Schütze ['ʃytsə] **1.** *m* (13) marksman, shot; *ast.* Archer, Sagittarius; ⚔ rifleman, (*Dienstgrad*) private; *Ballsport*: scorer; **2.** ⊕ *f* (15) *Wasserbau*: sluice-board; (*Weber*♀) shuttle.

'**schützen** (27) protect, guard; (*verteidigen*) defend (*gegen* against; *vor dat.* from); *gegen Wetter usw.*: shelter *od.* shield (from).

'**Schützen|fest** *n* shooting-match (*a. fig.*); '**~feuer** ⚔ *n* rifle fire; (*selbständiges Schießen*) independent fire.

'**Schutz-engel** *m* guardian angel.

'**Schützen|gilde** *f* rifle-association; '**~graben** *m* trench; '**~hilfe** *fig. f*: *j-m ~ geben* back a p. up; '**~kette** *f*, '**~linie** ⚔ *f* riflemen extended; '**~könig** *m* champion shot; *Sport*: top scorer; '**~loch** ⚔ *n* foxhole, rifle-pit; '**~panzer** ⚔ *m* armo(u)red personnel carrier.

'**Schutz|färbung** *zo. f* protective colo(u)ring; '**~gebiet** *n* protectorate; *s. Natur*♀; '**~geländer** *n* guard rail; '**~geleit** *n* safe-conduct, (*a.* ✈) escort; '**~gitter** *n* guard, protective railing; *Radio*: screen grid; '**~haft** *f* preventive (*od.* protective) custody; '**~haube** *f* (protective) cover *od.* hood; '**~heilige** *m, f* patron saint; '**~helm** *m* safety helmet, *e-s Bauarbeiters*: *a.* F hard hat; '**~herr** *m* patron, protector; '**~herrin** *f* patroness, protectress; '**~herrschaft** *f* protectorate; '**~hülle** *f* protective covering; sheath; *s. Schutzumschlag*; '**~hütte** *f* (shelter) hut, refuge; '**~impfung** *f* protective inoculation; *gegen Pocken*: vaccination; '**~-insel** *f Verkehr*: traffic island.

Schützling ['ʃytsliŋ] *m* (3¹) protégé(e *f*), charge.

'**schutz|los** defenceless, unprotected; '♀**mann** *m* constable, policeman; '♀**marke** *f* trade-mark; '♀**maske** *f* (protective) mask; '♀**maßregel** *f* protective measure, precaution; '♀**mittel** *n* preservative, preventive (*gegen* of); *vorbeugendes*: prophylactic; '♀**patron(in** *f*) *m* patron saint; '♀**polizei** *f* constabulary, police; '♀**polizist** *m s. Schutzmann*; '♀**raum** *m* shelter; '♀**rechte** *n/pl.* patent (*od.* trade-mark) rights; '♀**schild** *m* shield; *der Polizei*: riot shield; '♀**stoff** ⚕ *m* antibody, vaccine; '♀**-umschlag** *m e-s Buches*: (dust) jacket, wrapper; '♀**vorrichtung** *f* protective device; '♀**waffen** *f/pl.* defensive arms; '♀**zoll** *m* protective duty; '♀**zone** *f* protected area; *zur ~ erklären* declare a protected area.

schwabbel|ig ['ʃvabəliç] wobbly; '**~n** F *v/i. u. v/t.* (29) wobble; (*schwatzen*) babble; ⊕ (*polieren*) buff.

Schwabe ['ʃvaːbə] **1.** *m* (13) Swabian; **2.** *f* (15) *Insekt*: cockroach; '**~nstreich** *m* tomfoolery.

Schwäb|in ['ʃvɛːbin] *f* Swabian (woman); '♀**isch** Swabian.

schwach [ʃvax] (18²) *allg.* weak (*a.*

fig.); (*kraftlos*) feeble; (*schlecht*) poor; (*gering*) meag|re (*Am.* -er); *Ähnlichkeit*: remote; *Erinnerung, Hoffnung, Licht, Ton*: faint; *~es Geschlecht the* weaker sex; *~e Seite fig.* weak point; *~e Stunde* scant hour; *fig. a* moment of weakness; *~ werden* weaken.

Schwäche ['ʃvɛçə] *f* (15) weakness (*a. fig.*; für for); *des Charakters*: *a.* foible, weak point; (*Hinfälligkeit*) infirmity; *von Ton, Licht* (*a. ~zustand*) faintness; **'~-anfall** *m* (sudden) feeling of faintness; **'≈n** (25) weaken (*a. fig.*); (*vermindern*) lessen, diminish; **'~zustand** *m* faintness; *allgemeiner*: debility.

'Schwachheit *f* weakness; *moralische*: *a.* frailty.

'schwach|herzig faint-hearted; **'≈-kopf** *m* imbecile; **~köpfig** ['~kœpfiç] brainless.

schwächlich ['ʃvɛçliç] feeble, weakly; (*empfindlich*) delicate; *fig.* weak (-kneed); **'≈keit** *f* feebleness, weakliness; delicacy.

Schwächling ['~liŋ] *m* (3[1]) weakling, F softy.

schwach|sichtig ['~ziçtiç] weak-sighted; **'≈sinn** *m* feeble-mindedness; **'~sinnig** feeble-minded; **'≈-sinnige** *m, f* (*a. contp.*) half-wit, moron; ⚕ mental defective; **'≈-strom** ⚡ *m* weak (*od.* low-voltage) current.

'Schwächung *f* weakening.

Schwaden ['ʃvɑ:dən] *m* (6) **1.** ↗ swath; **2.** (*Rauch≈, Gas≈*) (smoke, gas) cloud; ⚒ fire-damp.

Schwadron [ʃva'dro:n] *f* (16) squadron; **≈ieren** [~dro'ni:rən] swagger, brag.

schwafeln ['ʃvɑ:fəln] F (29) twaddle.

Schwager ['ʃvɑ:gər] *m* (7) brother-in-law.

Schwäger|in ['ʃvɛ:gərin] *f* (16) sister-in-law; **'~schaft** *f* affinity by marriage; *konkret*: in-laws *pl.*

Schwalbe ['ʃvalbə] *f* (15) swallow; **'~nschwanz** *m Tischlerei*: dovetail; F *fig.* (*Frack*) swallow-tail.

Schwall [ʃval] *m* (3[3]) flood (*a. fig.*); *von Worten*: *a.* torrent.

schwamm[1] [ʃvam] *pret. v. schwimmen.*

Schwamm[2] *m* (3[3]) sponge; (*Pilz*) fungus, *eßbarer*: mushroom; (*Feuer≈*) German tinder; (*Haus≈*) dry rot; *~ drüber!* (let's) forget it!; **'≈ig** spongy (*a. fig.*); (*gedunsen*) bloated; **'~taucher(in** *f*) *m* sponge diver.

Schwan [ʃvɑ:n] *m* (3[3]) swan.

schwand [ʃvant] *pret. v. schwinden.*

schwanen ['ʃvɑ:nən] (25): *es schwant mir* (et.) I have a presentiment (of a th.); *ihm schwante nichts Gutes* he had dark forebodings; **'≈gesang** *fig. m* swan song.

schwang [ʃvaŋ] *pret. v. schwingen.*

Schwang [~] *m*: *im ~(e) sein* be a tradition *od.* (*Mode*) the fashion.

schwanger ['ʃvaŋər] pregnant, with child, *feiner*: expectant; **'≈enfürsorge** *f* antenatal care.

schwänger|n ['ʃvɛŋərn] (29) get with child, (*a. fig.*) impregnate; **'≈ung** *f* impregnation.

'Schwangerschaft *f* (16) pregnancy; **'~s-test** *m* pregnancy test; **'~s-unterbrechung** *f* induced abortion; **'~sverhütung** *f* contraception.

Schwank [ʃvaŋk] **1.** *m* (3[3]) merry tale; (*Streich*) prank; *thea.* farce; **2.** ≈ flexible; (*wackelig*) shaky; **'≈en[1]** (25) (*sich wiegen*) wave, swing; (*wanken*) totter, stagger; *Boden usw.*: shake, rock; *Baum usw.*: sway; *Magnetnadel usw.*: oscillate; *fig.* (*zaudern*) waver, falter, vacillate; (*sich ändern*) vary; ☤ *Kurse, Preise*: fluctuate; *~ zwischen ... und P.*: waver between ... and, *S.*: vary (*od.* range) from ... to; *~d* wavering *etc.*; (*unsicher*) unstable; vague; **'~en[2]** *n* (6), **'~ung** *f* waving, staggering *etc.*; ☤ fluctuation; *fig.* vacillation.

Schwanz [ʃvants] *m* (3[2] *u.* [3]) tail.

schwänz|eln ['ʃvɛntsəln] (29) wag one's tail; *contp.* fawn (*um j-n* upon); **'~en** F *v/i. u. v/t.* (27) shirk, miss; (*die Schule*) *~* play truant (*Am. a.* hooky); *geschwänzt* tailed, caudate.

'Schwanz|-ende *n* tip of the tail; *fig.* (*a.* ✈) tail end; **'~feder** *f* tail feather; **'~flosse** *f* tail fin.

schwappen ['ʃvapən] (25, h. *u.* sn) swash, slop.

Schwäre ['ʃvɛ:rə] *f* (15) abscess, boil, festering wound; ulcer; **'≈n** (25, h. *u.* sn) suppurate, fester (*a. fig.*).

Schwarm [ʃvarm] *m* (3[3]) *allg.* swarm; *Vögel*: *a.* flight (*a.* ✈); *Fische*: shoal; (*Menschen≈*) swarm, crowd; *v. Damen, Mädchen*: bevy; F *fig. P.*: idol; (*Angebetete*) flame; *S.*: ideal, F craze.

schwärmen [ˈʃvɛrmən] (25, h. *u.* sn) swarm; ⚔ (*aus*)~ (*lassen*) extend; (*schwelgen*) revel; ~ *für* be enthusiastic (*od.* wild) about *a th.*, have a crush on *a p.*; ~ *von* gush about *a p., a th.*

ˈ**Schwärmer** *m* (7), ˈ**~in** *f* revel(l)er; (*Begeisterter*) enthusiast, *bsd. eccl.* fanatic; (*Träumer*) visionary; *Feuerwerk*: squib; (*Abendfalter*) hawk moth; **~ei** [~ˈraɪ] *f* (16) revel(l)ing; (*für*) enthusiasm (for), *bsd. eccl.* fanaticism, *contp.* gushing; ˈ**⌒isch** enthusiastic(ally *adv.*); fanatical; (*verzückt*) ecstatic(ally *adv.*); (*überspannt*) eccentric.

Schwarte [ˈʃvartə] *f* (15) rind, skin; ⊕ (*Schalbrett*) slab, plank; F (*Buch*) old (*od.* trashy) volume.

schwarz [ʃvarts] **1.** (18²) black; *Teint*: swarthy; *fig.* (*finster*) gloomy, dark, black; (*ungesetzlich*) illicit; ⌒*es Brett für Anschläge* notice (*Am.* bulletin) board; ~*er Erdteil* Black Continent; ~*er Humor* sick humo(u)r, black comedy; ~*e Kunst* art of printing, (*Zauberei*) black art; ~*er Mann* (*Schreckgespenst*) bog(e)y; ~*er Markt* black market; *s. Schaf*; ~ *auf weiß* in black and white; ~ *sehen* be pessimistic; *ich sehe* ~ (*für dich*) things look bad (for you); *auf die* ~*e Liste setzen* blacklist; **2.** ⌒ *n* black; *ins* ~*e treffen* hit the bull's-eye (*a. fig.*).

ˈ**Schwarz|-arbeit** *f* illicit work, F moonlighting; ˈ**~-arbeiter** *m* F moonlighter; ˈ**⌒blau** very dark blue; ˈ**~blech** *n* black sheet-iron; ˈ**~brot** *n* (black) rye bread; ˈ**~drossel** *f* blackbird.

ˈ**Schwarze** *m, f* (18) (*Neger*) black.

Schwärze [ˈʃvɛrtsə] *f* (15) blackness; (*Färbemittel*) blacking; ⊕ *typ.* printer's ink; ˈ**⌒n** (27) blacken.

ˈ**Schwarz|fahrer** *m mot.* joy-rider; (*der kein Fahrgeld zahlt*) fare dodger; ˈ**~fahrt** *mot. f* joy-ride; ˈ**~färber** *m fig.* pessimist; ˈ**~handel** *m* black-market(eering), illicit trade; ˈ**~händler** *m* black-marketeer; ˈ**~hörer** *m* (radio) licen|ce (*Am.* -se) dodger.

schwärzlich [ˈʃvɛrtsliç] blackish.

ˈ**Schwarz|markt** *m* black market; ˈ**~pulver** *n* black powder; ˈ**~schlachtung** *f* illicit slaughtering; ˈ**~seher** (**-in** *f*) *m* pessimist; *TV*: (television) licen|ce (*Am.* -se) dodger; ˈ**~sender** *m* pirate station; ˈ**⌒ˈweiß** black and white; ˈ**~ˈweiß...** *phot. usw.*: black-and-white ...; ˈ**~wild** *n* wild boars *pl.*; ˈ**~wurzel** *f* comfrey.

Schwatz [ʃvats] F *m* (3²) chat; ˈ**~base** F *f s. Schwätzer*; ˈ**⌒en** *v/i. u. v/t.* (27) (*plaudern*) talk, chat; (*schnatternd u. seicht daherreden*) chatter, tattle; (*kindlich plappern*) prattle; (*ausplaudern*) blab.

schwätzen [ˈʃvɛtsən] (27) *s. schwatzen.*

Schwätzer [ˈʃvɛtsər] *m* (7), ˈ**~in** *f* (16¹) chatterbox, babbler; (*Klatschtante*) gossip; (*dummer* ~) blatherskite.

ˈ**schwatzhaft** talkative, garrulous; ˈ**⌒igkeit** *f* talkativeness.

Schwebe [ˈʃveːbə] *f* (15): *in der* ~ in suspense, undecided; ⚖ pending, in abeyance; ˈ**~bahn** *f* suspension railway; ˈ**~balken** *m Sport*: balance beam; ˈ**⌒n** (25, h. *u.* sn) be suspended, float; *Vogel, Hubschrauber usw.*: hover; (*hoch*~) soar; (*unentschieden sein*) be undecided, *Prozeß usw.*: be pending; (*leicht gehen*) glide, swim; *in Gefahr usw.* ~ be in danger *etc.*; *vor Augen* ~ *s. vorschweben*; ˈ**⌒nd** suspended (*a.* ⛏); floating *etc.*; *Frage, Verfahren*: pending.

ˈ**Schwebung** *f Radio*: beat.

Schwed|e [ˈʃveːdə] *m* (13), ˈ**~in** *f* (16¹) Swede; ˈ**⌒isch** Swedish.

Schwefel [ˈʃveːfəl] *m* (7) sulphur; ˈ**~bad** *n* sulphur bath; (*Ort*) sulphur springs *pl.*; ˈ**~blumen** *f/pl.*, ˈ**~blüte** *f* sulphur flowers; ˈ**⌒farbig**, ˈ**⌒gelb** brimstone-colo(u)red.

ˈ**schwef(e)lig** sulphur(e)ous.

ˈ**Schwefel|kies** *m* pyrite(s); ˈ**~kohlenstoff** *m* carbon disulphide; ˈ**⌒n** (29) sulphurate, sulphurize; ˈ**~säure** *f* sulphuric acid; ˈ**~wasserstoff** *m* hydrogen sulphide.

Schweif [ʃvaɪf] *m* (3) tail (*a. ast.*); *fig.* train; ˈ**⌒en** (25) *v/i.* (h. *u.* sn) rove, ramble; *v/t.* curve; ˈ**~ung** *f* curve, bend(ing); ˈ**⌒wedeln** wag one's tail; *fig.* fawn (*vor dat.* upon).

ˈ**Schweige|geld** *n* hush-money; ˈ**~marsch** *m* silent protest march.

schweigen [ˈʃvaɪgən] **1.** (30) be

silent (*a. fig. über acc.* on); say nothing, hold one's tongue; *ganz zu ~ von ...* to say nothing of, let alone; **2.** ♀ *n* (6) silence; *zum ~ bringen* silence (*a.* ⚔); *~ bewahren* keep silence; **'~d** silent; *sich ~ verhalten* keep silent, hold one's peace.

'Schweigepflicht *f* secrecy, professional discretion.

schweigsam ['ʃvaɪkzaːm] silent; (*wortkarg*) taciturn; *s. verschwiegen*; **'♀keit** *f* taciturnity.

Schwein [ʃvaɪn] *n* (3) pig, *bsd. Am.* hog, *zo. u. pl.* swine (*alle a. contp. fig.*); (*~efleisch*) pork; F (*Glück*) luck; F *~ haben* be lucky; F *kein ~* nobody.

'Schweine|braten *m* roast pork; **'~fleisch** *n* pork; **'~hund** P *m contp.* swine, rat; *innerer ~* cowardice; **~rei** [~'raɪ] *f* (16) filthiness; (*Unordnung*) (awful) mess; (*Gemeinheit*) dirty trick; (*Zote*) smut(ty joke), obscenity; (*Schande*) crying shame; **'~stall** *m* pigsty (*a. fig.*); **'~zucht** *f* pig-breeding, *Am.* hog raising; **'~züchter** *m* pig-breeder, *Am.* hog raiser.

Schwein|igel ['ʃvaɪnʔiːgəl] F *m* filthy pig; **~-igelei** [~'laɪ] *f* (16) smut(ty joke), obscenity; **'♀-igeln** F (29) talk smut; **'♀isch** swinish; (*zotig*) smutty.

'Schweins|kotelett *n* pork chop; **'~leder** *n* pigskin.

Schweiß [ʃvaɪs] *m* (3²) sweat, perspiration; *Wolle*: yolk; *hunt.* blood; **'~blatt** *n* dress-shield; **'~brenner** *m* welding torch, blowpipe, oxyacetylene torch; **'~brille** *f* welding goggles *pl.*; **'~drüse** *f* perspiratory gland; **'♀en** (27) *v/t.* ⊕ weld; *v/i. hunt.* bleed; **'~er** *m* (7) welder; **'~fuchs** *m* sorrel horse; **'~fuß** *m* perspiring (*od.* sweaty) foot; **'♀gebadet** bathed in perspiration; **'~hund** *m* bloodhound; **'♀ig** sweaty, perspiring; *hunt.* bloody; **'~naht** ⊕ *f* welding seam; **'~perlen** *f/pl.* beads of perspiration; **'~stelle** ⊕ *f* (point of) weld; **'♀treibend(es Mittel)** sudorific; **'♀triefend** *s. schweißgebadet*; **'~tropfen** *m* drop of sweat.

Schweizer ['ʃvaɪtsər] **1.** *m* (7) Swiss (*a.* **'~in** *f*); (*Melker*) dairyman; **2.** *adj.* Swiss; *~ Käse* Swiss cheese; **'♀isch** Swiss.

schwelen ['ʃveːlən] (25) smo(u)lder.

schwelg|en ['ʃvɛlgən] (25) revel (*in dat.* in); **'♀er** *m* (7), **'♀erin** *f* revel(l)er; **♀erei** [~'raɪ] *f* (16) revelry; (*Ausschweifung*) debauch(ery); **'~erisch** luxurious.

Schwell|e ['ʃvɛlə] *f* (15) doorstep; threshold (*a. fig.*; *a.* ⚕, *phys.*); 🚂 sleeper, *Am. a.* tie; **'♀en** *v/t.* swell; *v/i.* (sn) swell; *Wasser usw.*: rise; (*anwachsen*) increase; **'~körper** *anat. m* erectile tissue; **'~ung** *f* swelling; *des Bodens*: swell.

Schwemm|e ['ʃvɛmə] *f* (15) horse-pond; *für Vieh*: watering-place; *Bierlokal*: tap-room; ✝ glut (*an dat.* of); **'♀n** (25) *Vieh*: water; (*weg~*) wash; *Holz*: float; **'~land** *n* alluvial land.

Schwengel ['ʃvɛŋəl] *m* (7) (*Wagen♀*) swing-bar; (*Glocken♀*) clapper; (*Pumpen♀*) handle.

Schwenk [ʃvɛŋk] *m Film*: panning (shot); **'~-arm** *m* swivel arm; **'♀bar** swivel(ling); **'♀en** *v/t.* (25) swing; *Stock usw.*: flourish, brandish; *Hut, Tuch usw.*: wave; *Film*: pan; ⊕ swivel; (*spülen*) rinse; *v/i.* turn; ⚔, *pol.* wheel (about); (*umkehren*) about-face; **'~kran** *m* slewing crane; **'~ung** *f* swinging *etc.*; ⚔ wheel, pivoting manoeuvre; *fig.* change of mind (about); ⊕ swivel, slew round.

schwer [ʃveːr] *Gewicht u. körperlich*: heavy (*a.* ⚔ *Angriff, Kreuzer usw.*); (*gewichtig*) weighty; (*~fällig*) heavy, ponderous; (*schwierig*) hard, difficult; *Fehler*: bad, gross; *Entscheidung, Kampf, Zeit*: hard; *Krankheit, Unfall, Wunde*: serious; *Strafe*: severe; *Verbrechen usw.*: grave; *Speise*: heavy, rich; *Wein, Zigarre*: strong; *Kleiderstoff*: heavy-weight; *~er Atem* short breath; F *~er Junge* criminal, crook; *~er (gehaltvoller) Kuchen* rich cake; *~ von Begriff* slow (in the uptake), dense; *zwei Pfund ~* weighing two pounds, two pounds in weight; *~ arbeiten* work hard; *~ zu sagen* hard to say; *~ enttäuscht* badly disappointed; **'♀-arbeit** *f* heavy work; **'♀-arbeiter** *m* heavy worker; **'♀-athlet** *m* heavy athlete; **'♀-athletik** *f* heavy athletics *sg. u. pl.*; **'~behindert** severely disabled; **'~beladen** heavily laden; **'♀beschädigte** *m* (18) seriously disabled person; **'~bewaffnet** heavily armed; **'~blütig** grave, heavy; '**≈e** *f* (15) *s. schwer*: heaviness; weight; gravity (*a. phys.*); seriousness; severity; '**~elos** weightless; '**≈elosigkeit** *f* weightlessness; **≈e-nöter** ['~ə'nøːtər] *m* (7) philanderer, gay Lothario; '**~-er'ziehbar** difficult to educate; recalcitrant; '**~fallen** be difficult (*dat.* to); *es fällt mir ~* I find it hard; '**~fällig** heavy, slow; (*unhandlich*) unwieldy, cumbersome; '**≈fälligkeit** *f* heaviness, slowness; unwieldiness, cumbersomeness; '**~flüssig** viscid, viscous; '**≈gewicht** *n* *Boxen*: heavy-weight (*a.* '**≈gewichtler** *m*); *fig.* chief importance, chief stress; '**~halten** be difficult; '**~hörig** hard of hearing; '**≈-industrie** *f* heavy industry; '**≈kraft** *f* (force of) gravity; '**≈'kriegsbeschädigte** *m* (18) seriously disabled war veteran; '**~lich** hardly, scarcely; '**≈mut** *f*, **~mütig** ['~myːtiç] melancholy; '**≈-öl** *n* heavy oil; '**≈punkt** *m* cent|re (*Am.* -er) of gravity; *fig.* focal point; (*Nachdruck*) (chief) stress; '**≈punktstreik** *m* pinpoint strike; **≈spat** ['~ʃpɑːt] *m* barite, heavy spar.

Schwert [ʃveːrt] *n* (1) sword; '**~fisch** *m* sword-fish; '**~lilie** *f* iris.

'**Schwer|transport** *m* transport of heavy goods; '**~transporter** *m* heavy goods vehicle; '**~verbrecher** *m* dangerous criminal, ⚖ felon; '**≈-verdaulich** hard to digest, heavy; '**≈verständlich** difficult to understand; abstruse; '**≈verwundet** seriously wounded; '**≈wiegend** weighty (*a. fig.*); *fig.* grave.

Schwester ['ʃvɛstər] *f* (15) sister; (*Kranken≈*) (hospital) nurse; *s. a. barmherzig*; '**~firma** ⚕ associated company; '**~kind** *n* sister's child; '**≈lich** sisterly; '**~liebe** *f* sisterly love; '**~nhelferin** *f* nursing auxiliary (*Am.* assistant); '**~n-orden** *m*, '**~nschaft** *f* sisterhood, sorority; '**~ntracht** *f* uniform; '**~schiff** *n* sister ship; '**~sohn** *m* sister's son.

schwieg [ʃviːk] *pret. v. schweigen* 1.

Schwieger... ['ʃviːgər-] *mst*: ...-in-law, *z.B.* '**~-eltern** *pl.* parents-in-law; '**~sohn** *m* son-in-law.

Schwiel|e ['ʃviːlə] *f* (15) callosity; (*Strieme*) weal; '**≈ig** callous, horny; full of weals.

schwierig ['ʃviːriç] difficult (*a. P.*), hard; (*verwickelt*) complicated; '**≈keit** *f* difficulty, trouble.

Schwimm|bad ['ʃvim-] *n* swimming bath, swimming pool; '**~blase** *f* (*Fisch≈*) air-bladder; '**~dock** *n* floating dock; '**≈en** (30, h. *u.* sn) swim; *S.*: float; *fig.* (*unsicher sein*; *a. ins ≈ kommen*) flounder; *im Geld ~* be rolling in money; '**~er** *m* (7) swimmer (*a.* '**~erin** *f*); *an Angel, Netz*, ⚓ *u.* ⊕: float; '**~flosse** *f* fin; *Sport*: flipper; '**~flügel** *m/pl.* water-wings; '**~fuß** *m* web-foot; *v. Robben usw.*: flipper; '**~gürtel** *m* swimming-belt; (*Rettungsgürtel*) life-belt; '**~haut** *f* web; '**~lehrer** *m* swimming-master; '**~panzer** *m* amphibious tank; '**~sport** *m* swimming; '**~vogel** *m* web-footed bird; '**~wagen** *m* amphibious car; '**~weste** *f* life-jacket, *Am.* life-preserver (vest).

Schwindel ['ʃvindəl] *m* (7) ⚕ vertigo, giddiness, dizziness; (*Betrug*) swindle, fraud, cheat, *Am.* F flimflam; F *der ganze ~* the whole bag of tricks; '**~-anfall** *m* fit of dizziness; **~ei** [~'laɪ] *f* (16) swindling, cheat; '**≈-erregend** dizzy, giddy; *fig. a.* staggering; '**~firma** ⚕ *f* long firm, *Am.* wildcat (firm); '**≈frei** free from giddiness; *nicht ~* high-shy; '**~gesellschaft** ⚕ *f* bogus company.

'**schwind(e)lig** giddy, dizzy; *fig. a.* staggering; *mir ist ~* I am (*od.* feel) dizzy.

'**schwindeln** (29) *v/i.* (*lügen, betrügen*) cheat, swindle, humbug, *Am. sl.* chisel; *mir schwindelt* I am (*od.* feel) giddy, my head swims; *~ machen fig.* stagger; *~de Höhe* dizzy height.

schwinden ['ʃvindən] (30, sn) dwindle; (*schrumpfen*) shrink; *Ton, Farbe, Licht*: fade; (*ver~*) disappear, vanish.

'**Schwindler** *m* (7), '**~in** *f* swindler, cheat, crook; (*Lügner*) liar.

Schwind|sucht ['ʃvintzuxt] *f* consumption; '**≈süchtig** consumptive.

Schwing|e ['ʃviŋə] *f* (15) wing; (*Getreide≈*) fan; (*Flachs≈*) swingle; '**≈en** *v/t.* swing (*sich* o.s.); (*handhaben*) wield; *Waffe usw.*: brandish; *Flachs*: swingle; F *e-e Rede ~* make a speech; *v/i.* swing; ⊕ (*hin und her ~*) oscillate; *Saite, Ton usw.*: vibrate; '**~er** *m* (7) *Boxen*: swing; '**~ung** *f* swinging; oscillation; vibration; '**≈ungsfrei**

non-oscillating; '**~ungszahl** *f* frequency of oscillations.

Schwips F [ʃvips] *m* (7): *e-n ~ haben* be tipsy.

schwirren ['ʃvirən] (25, h. *u.* sn) whiz(z), whir(r); *Insekt usw.*: buzz.

Schwitz|bad ['ʃvits-] *n* Turkish bath; (*Dampfbad*) steam-bath; '**2en** *v/i. u. v/t.* sweat, *feiner*: perspire; *Fenster*: *s. beschlagen*; '**~kasten** *m Ringen*: headlock; '**~kur** *f* sweating-cure.

schwoll [ʃvɔl] *pret. v. schwellen.*

schwor [ʃvo:r] *pret. v. schwören.*

schwören ['ʃvø:rən] (30) *v/i. u. v/t.* swear (*bei* by), take an oath; *fig. ~ auf (acc.)* F swear by; *s. Rache.*

schwul F [ʃvu:l] queer.

schwül [ʃvy:l] sultry, close, oppressive; *fig.* sultry.

'**Schwule** F *m* (18) queer.

'**Schwüle** *f* (15) sultriness.

Schwulität [ʃvuli'tɛ:t] F *f* (16): *in ~en kommen* get into trouble.

Schwulst [ʃvulst] *m* (3^2 *u.* ^{3}) bombast.

schwülstig ['ʃvylstiç] bombastic (-ally *adv.*).

Schwund [ʃvunt] *m* (3) dwindling; (*Verlust*) loss; *durch Einlaufen*: shrinkage; *durch Aussickern*: leakage, wastage; ⚕ atrophy; *Film, Radio*: fading; *s. a. Haar2*; '**~-ausgleich** *m*, '**~regelung** *f Radio*: automatic volume control.

Schwung [ʃvuŋ] *m* (3^3) swing (*a. Turnen*); *Schisport*: turn; (*Tempo*) speed; *phys.* momentum; *fig.* impetus; (*Energie, Wucht*) energy, drive, F vim; (*Schmiß*) verve, F go, pep; *der Phantasie*: flight; *des Geistes*: buoyancy; (*Menge*) batch; *v. Personen*: F bunch; *in ~ bringen* set *a th.* going; (*richtig*) *in ~ kommen* get into one's stride; '**~feder** *f* pinion; '**2haft** *Geschäft, Handel*: brisk, roaring; '**~kraft** *f* centrifugal force; *fig.* buoyancy, verve; '**2los** spiritless, tired; '**~rad** *n* fly-wheel; '**2voll** full of verve *od.* F go, spirited; *Entwurf*: bold; *Melodie*: racy.

Schwur [ʃvu:r] *m* (3^3) oath; (*Gelübde*) vow; '**~gericht** *n* jury court.

sechs [zɛks] **1.** six; **2.** 2 *f* (16^3) six; '**2-eck** *n* hexagon; '**~-eckig** hexagonal; '**~fach**, **~fältig** ['~fɛltiç] sixfold, sextuple; '**~jährig** six-year(s)-old, 🕮 sexennial; '**~malig** six times repeated; '**~monatig** lasting six months; '**~monatlich** six-monthly; *adv.* every six months; '**~seitig** hexagonal; **~stündig** ['~ʃtyndiç] of six hours; **2'tagerennen** *n* six-day (cycling) race; **~tägig** ['~tɛ:giç] of (*od.* lasting) six days.

sechs|te ['~tə], '**2tel** *n* (7) sixth; '**~tens** sixthly, in the sixth place.

sechzehn ['zɛçtse:n] sixteen; '**~te** sixteenth; '**2tel** *n* (7) sixteenth (part); '**2telnote** ♪ *f* semiquaver; '**~tens** in the sixteenth place.

sechzig ['zɛçtsiç] sixty; **2er** ['~gər] *m* (7), '**2erin** *f* (16^1) sexagenarian.

Sediment [zedi'mɛnt] *n* (3^1) sediment; **2är** [~'tɛ:r] sedimentary.

See [ze:] **1.** *m* (10) lake; **2.** *f* (15) sea; *an die ~ gehen* go to the seaside (*Am.* seashore); *auf ~* at sea; *in ~ gehen od. stechen* put to sea; *zur ~ gehen* go to sea.

'**See|bad** *n* sea-bath; (*Ort*) seaside resort; '**~bär** *m*: *fig. alter ~* F old salt; '**~dienst** *m* naval service; '**2-fahrend** seafaring; '**~fahrer** *m* sailor; '**~fahrt** *f* seafaring; (*Seereise*) voyage, cruise; '**2fest** seaworthy; *P.*: (*nicht*) *~ sein* be a good (bad) sailor; '**~fisch** *m* saltwater fish; '**~fracht** ⚓ *f* sea-freight, *Am.* ocean freight; '**~gang** *m*: *hoher ~* rough sea; *schwerer ~* heavy sea; '**~gefecht** *n* naval action; '**2gestützt** ⚔ sea-based; '**~gras** *n* seaweed; '**~hafen** *m* seaport; '**~handel** *m* maritime trade; '**~held** *m* naval hero; '**~herrschaft** *f* naval supremacy; '**~hund** *m* seal; '**~hundsfell** *n* sealskin; '**~-igel** *m* sea-urchin; '**~kadett** ⚓ *m* naval cadet; '**~karte** *f* (sea-)chart; '**2klar** ready to sail; '**2krank** seasick; *leicht ~ werden* be a bad sailor; '**~krankheit** *f* seasickness; '**~krieg(führung** *f*) *m* naval war(fare); '**~küste** *f* (sea-)coast, seashore; seaboard; '**~lachs** *m* coalfish, pollack.

Seele ['ze:lə] *f* (15) soul (*a. fig.*: *Lebenskraft*; *Kern*; *menschliches Wesen*); (*Geist*) mind; *e-s Herings*: bladder; *e-r Schußwaffe*: bore; *e-s Kabels*: core; e-e *~ von Mensch* a good soul; *fig. keine ~* not a soul; *mit (od. von) ganzer ~* with all one's heart; *er ist die ~ des Ganzen* he is the life and soul of it all; *du sprichst mir aus der ~* you express my sentiments exactly.

Seelen|-amt *n* office for the dead; '**~freund** *m* soul brother; '**~frieden** *m* peace of mind; '**2froh** heartily glad; '**~größe** *f* greatness of mind; '**2gut** kind-hearted, *pred.* a good soul; '**~heil** *n* salvation, spiritual welfare; '**~hirt** *m* pastor; '**~kunde** *f* psychology; '**~leben** *n* inner life; '**~leiden** *n* mental suffering; '**2los** soulless; '**~messe** *f* mass for the dead, requiem; '**~pein** *f*, '**~qual** *f* mental agony; '**~ruhe** *f* peace of mind; *weitS.* calmness; '**2ruhig** *adv.* cooly; '**~stärke** *f* fortitude; '**2vergnügt** (quite) cheerful; '**2verwandt** congenial; ~ *sein* be kindred souls; '**~verwandtschaft** *f* congeniality; '**2voll** soulful; '**~wanderung** *f* transmigration of souls, 🕮 metempsychosis.

'**Seeleute** *pl.* seamen, sailors.

'**seelisch** psychic(al), mental, spiritual.

'**Seelöwe** *m* sea-lion.

'**Seelsorge** *f* religious welfare, care of souls; '**~r** *m* (7) pastor, clergyman.

'**See|luft** *f* sea air; '**~macht** *f* naval (*od.* sea) power; '**~mann** *m* seaman, sailor; **2männisch** ['~mɛnɪʃ] sailor-like, seamanlike; *Fertigkeit usw.*: nautical; '**2mäßig** *Verpackung*: seaworthy; '**~meile** *f* nautical mile; '**~mine** *f* sea-mine; '**~möwe** *f* sea-gull; '**~not** *f* distress at sea; '**~-offizier** *m* naval officer; '**~pferdchen** *n* sea-horse; '**~räuber** *m* pirate; **~räuberei** [~'raɪ] *f* piracy; '**~recht** *n* maritime law; '**~reise** *f* voyage, cruise; '**~rose** *f* water-lily; '**~schaden** *m* sea-damage, average; '**~schiff** *n* sea-going vessel; '**~schlacht** *f* naval battle; '**~schwalbe** *f* tern; '**~sieg** *m* naval victory; '**~stadt** *f* seaside town; '**~stern** *m* starfish; '**~streitkräfte** *f/pl.* naval forces; '**~tier** *n* marine animal; '**~tang** *m* seaweed; '**2tüchtig** seaworthy; '**~-ufer** *n* lakeside, shore; '**~verkehr** *m* ocean traffic; '**~volk** *n* maritime nation; '**~warte** *f* naval observatory; **2wärts** ['~vɛrts] seawards; '**~wasser** *n* sea-water; '**~weg** *m* sea-route; *auf dem* ~ by sea; '**~wind** *m* sea-breeze; '**~zunge** *f Fisch*: sole.

Segel ['ze:gəl] *n* (7) sail; ~ *setzen, unter* ~ *gehen* set sail; ~ *hissen* make sail; *die* ~ *streichen* strike sail, *fig.* give in; '**~boot** *n* sailing-boat, *Am.* sailboat; *Sport*: yacht; '**2fertig** ready to sail; '**~fliegen** *n* (6) gliding, soaring, sailplaning; '**~flieger** *m* glider pilot; *s. Segelflugzeug*; '**~flug** *m* glide; *s. Segelfliegen*; '**~flugzeug** *n* glider, sailplane; '**2klar** *s. segelfertig*; '**~klasse** *f e-s Rennbootes*: rating; '**~klub** *m* yacht-ing club; '**2n** (29, h. *u.* sn) sail (*a. fig.*), *sportlich*: yacht; ✈ glide, soar; '**~regatta** *f* yacht-race, regatta; '**~schiff** *n* sailing-ship; '**~schlitten** *m* ice-yacht; '**~sport** *m* yachting; '**~tuch** *n* sail-cloth, canvas; '**~werk** *n* sails *pl.*

Segen ['ze:gən] *m* (7) blessing (*a. fig. Wohltat, Glück*); (*bsd. eccl.*) benediction; *fig.* (*Fülle*) abundance; F *der ganze* ~ the whole lot; '**2sreich**, '**2svoll** beneficial, blessed; *pred.* a blessing; '**~swunsch** *m* benediction; *pl.* good wishes *pl.*

Segler ['ze:glər] *m* (7) yachtsman; (*Schiff*) sailing-vessel, *good, fast etc.* sailer; '**~in** *f* (16[1]) yachtswoman.

segn|en ['ze:gnən] (26) bless; '**2ung** *f* blessing (*a. fig. der Zivilisation usw.*) (*bsd. eccl.*) benediction.

sehen ['ze:ən] (30) *v/t.* see (*a. v/i.*); (*wahrnehmen*) perceive; (*plötzlich* ~) catch sight of; *fig.* (*ein*~) realize, see; *v/i.* (*hin*~) look; *sieh nur!* just look!; *sieh*(e) *da!* behold!; *sieh mal* look here; *siehe oben* see above; *siehe Seite 14* see page 14; *gut* ~ have good eyes; *auf et.* (*acc.*) ~ look at, *fig.* (*Wert legen auf*) be particular about, *s. a. achten*; *darauf* ~, *daß* see to it that; *nach et.* ~ look for, (*sorgen für*) look (*od.* see) after; ~ *lassen* show; *ich kenne ihn nur vom* 2 I know him only by sight.

'**sehens|wert**, '**~würdig** worth seeing, remarkable; '**2würdigkeit** *f* object of interest, curiosity; *pl. e-r Stadt*: sights *pl.*

Seher ['ze:ər] *m* (7) seer; '**~blick** *m*, '**~gabe** *f* prophetic eye *od.* gift; '**~in** *f* (16[1]) prophetess.

'**Seh|fehler** *m* defective vision; '**~feld** *n* field of vision; '**~kraft** *f* (eye)sight, vision, visual power.

Sehne ['ze:nə] *f* (15) sinew, tendon; *e-s Bogens*: string; ⩓ chord.

sehnen ['ze:nən] **1.** (25) *sich* ~ *nach* long for; *stärker*: yearn for; **2.** 2 *n* (6) longing, yearning.

'**Sehnen|scheiden-entzündung** ⚕ *f* tendovaginitis; '**~zerrung** ⚕ *f* pulled tendon.
'**Sehnerv** *m* optic nerve.
'**sehnig** sinewy; *Fleisch*: stringy.
'**sehn|lich** eager, anxious; (*glühend*) ardent; (*leidenschaftlich*) passionate; '**2sucht** *f* longing, yearning (*nach* for); '**~süchtig** longing, yearning.
'**Sehprüfung** *f* sight test.
sehr [zeːr] *vor adj. u. adv.* very; *beim vb.* (very) much, greatly, highly; F pretty; ~ *vermissen* miss badly; *s. viel, so.*
'**Seh|rohr** *n* periscope; '**~schärfe** *f* visual acuity; '**~schlitz** ⚔ *m* observation slit; '**~störung** *f* defective vision, dysopia; '**~test** *m s. Sehprüfung*; '**~vermögen** *n* (faculty of) vision, sight; '**~weite** *f* range of sight; *in (außer)* ~ (with)in (out of) sight *od.* eyeshot.
seicht [zaɪçt] shallow (*a. fig.*); '**2heit** *f* shallowness.
Seide ['zaɪdə] *f* (15) silk.
Seidel ['zaɪdəl] *n* (7) (*Maß*) pint; (*Trinkgefäß*) mug.
seiden ['zaɪdən] silk(en); '**~-artig** silky; '**2bau** *m* sericulture, silk-culture; '**2faden** *m* silk thread; '**2flor** *m* silk gauze; '**2garn** *n* silk yarn; '**2glanz** *m* silky lustre; '**2papier** *n* tissue-paper; '**2raupe** *f* silkworm; '**2(raupen)zucht** cultivation of silkworms; '**2spinne'rei** *f* silk-spinning mill; '**2stoff** *m* silk cloth *od.* fabric; '**2strümpfe** *m/pl.* silk stockings; '**~weich** (as) soft as silk, silky; '**2zucht** *f s. Seidenbau.*
'**seidig** silky.
Seife ['zaɪfə] *f* (15), '**2n** (25) soap.
'**Seifen|behälter** *m* soap-dish; '**~blase** *f* soap-bubble; '**~kistenrennen** *n* soap-box derby *od.* race; '**~lauge** *f* (soap-)suds *pl.*; '**~pulver** *n* soap-powder; '**~schale** *f* soap-dish; '**~schaum** *m* lather; '**~sieder** *m* soap-boiler; F *fig. ihm ging ein* ~ *auf* the scales fell from his eyes; '**~siede'rei** *f* soap-works; '**~wasser** *n* (soap-)suds *pl.*
'**seifig** soapy.
seih|en ['zaɪən] (25) strain, filter; '**2er** *m* strainer; filter.
Seil [zaɪl] *n* (3) rope; (*Tau*) cable; ~ *springen* skip; '**~bahn** *f* cable (*od.* funicular) railway; '**~er** *m* (7) rope-maker; '**~hüpfen** *n*, '**~springen** *n* (rope-)skipping; '**~schaft** *mount. f* roped party; '**~schwebebahn** *f* suspension railway, (aerial) cable-way; '**~tänzer(in** *f*) *m* rope-dancer.
sein[1] [zaɪn] **1.** (30, sn) be; (*vorhanden* ~) *a.* exist; et. ~ *lassen* leave (*od.* let) a th. alone; *es sei denn, daß* ... unless; *sei es, daß ... oder daß* ... whether ... or ...; *wenn ich nicht gewesen wäre* ... if it had not been for me ...; **2.** 2 *n* (6) being; existence.
sein[2] (20) his; its; *s. seinige.*
seiner|seits ['~ərzaɪts] for his part; '**~zeit** in his (*od.* its) time; (*einst*) then, at that time.
seinesgleichen ['~əs'glaɪçən] his equal(s *pl.*); the likes of him; *nicht* ~ *haben* have no equal *od.* parallel, stand alone.
seinet|halben ['~əthalbən], '**~wegen**, (*um*) '**~willen** for his sake, on his account; (*durch seine Schuld usw.*) because of him.
seinige ['~igə] his; its; *das* 2 (*a. das Seine*) his own; his duty; *die* 2 his wife; *die* 2*n pl.* his family *sg.*
seismisch ['zaɪsmɪʃ] seismic.
Seismo|graph [zaɪsmo'grɑːf] *m* (12) seismograph; **~logie** [~lo'giː] *f* (15, *o. pl.*) seismology.
seit [zaɪt] *prp.* (*von ... an*) since; (*während*) for; ~ *1960* since 1960; ~ *drei Wochen* for (the last) three weeks; ~ *wann* (*welchem Zeitpunkt*)? since when?; ~ *wann* (*wie lange schon*) *sind Sie hier?* how long have you been here?; *s. kurz, lang*; *cj.* since; **~dem** [~'deːm] *adv.* (ever) since, since that time; *cj.* since.
Seite ['zaɪtə] *f* (15) side; (*Flanke, a.* ⚔) flank; (*Richtung*) direction; *im Buch*: page; ⚗ ~ *e-r Gleichung*: member; *fig. e-r Angelegenheit*: side, aspect; *s. schwach, stark*; *an j-s* ~ at (*od.* by) a p.'s side; ~ *an* ~ side by side; *von der* ~ *ansehen* askance; *auf die* ~ *bringen od. schaffen* put aside; *heimlich od. j-n*: make away with; *auf j-s* ~ *sein od. treten od. sich stellen* side with a p.; *in die* ~ *gestemmt Arm*: akimbo; *von* 2*n j-s* on the part of a p., by *od.* from a p.; *j-m zur* ~ *stehen* stand by a p.
'**Seiten|-angriff** *m* flank attack; '**~-ansicht** *f* side-view; '**~blick** *m* side-glance; '**~-eingang** *m* side-entrance; '**~flügel** ⌂ *m* wing; '**~-**

gewehr ⚔ *n* bayonet; *pl. a.* side-arms; '**~gleis** *n* siding; '**~hieb** *fig. m* passing shot, cut (*gegen* at); '**♀lang** pages (and pages) of; '**~lehne** *f* arm; '**~linie** *f e-r Familie*: collateral line; 🚂 branch-line; '**~numerierung** *f* pagination; '**♀s** (*gen.*) on the part of; by (*od.* from) *a p.*; '**~schiff** ⛪ *n* aisle; '**~schwimmen** *n* side-stroke; '**~sprung** *m* side-leap; F *fig.* escapade; '**~stechen** *n* stitch in the side; '**~straße** *f* side road (*od.* street), by-street; '**~stück** *n* side-piece; (*Gegenstück*) counterpart (*zu* of); '**~tasche** *f* side-pocket; '**~tür** *f* side-door; '**♀verkehrt** the wrong way round; '**~wagen** *mot. m* sidecar; '**~wechsel** *m Sport*: change of ends; '**~weg** *m* by-way; '**~wind** *m* cross-wind; '**~zahl** *f* page-number; *insgesamt*: number of pages.

seither [~'he:r] since (that time).

'**seitlich** lateral, side-...

seitwärts ['~vɛrts] sideways, sidewards; aside.

Sekante ⩕ [ze'kantə] *f* (15) secant.

Sekret [ze'kre:t] *n* (3), **~ion** [~kre'tsjo:n] *f* (16) secretion.

Sekret|är [zekre'tɛ:r] *m* (3¹), **~ärin** *f* (16¹) secretary; **~ariat** [~tari'a:t] *n* (3) secretary's office, secretariate.

Sekt [zɛkt] *m* (3) sparkling wine.

Sekte ['zɛktə] *f* (15) sect.

'**Sektfrühstück** *n* champagne breakfast.

Sektierer [~'ti:rər] *m* (7) sectarian.

Sektion [zɛk'tsjo:n] *f* section; *e-r Leiche*: dissection, autopsy.

'**Sektkühler** *m* champagne bucket.

Sektor ['zɛktɔr] *m* (8¹) sector.

'**Sektquirl** *m* swizzle-stick.

Sekun|dant [zekun'dant] *m* (12) second; **♀där** [~'dɛ:r] secondary.

Se'kun|de *f* (15) second; *auf die ~* (*pünktlich*) (punctual) to the second; **♀denlang** for seconds; **~denzeiger** *m* second-hand; **♀'dieren** second (*j-m* a p.).

selb|e ['zɛlbə], **~ig** [~iç] same; '**~er:** *ich ~* I myself.

selbst [zɛlpst] **1.** *pron.* himself (*f* herself, *n* itself), *pl.* themselves; (*ohne fremde Hilfe*) by oneself; *ich ~* I myself; *er ~* he himself; *wir ~* we ourselves; *von ~ entstanden* spontaneous; *von ~* of one's own accord, *S.* of itself, automatically, spontaneously; **2.** *adv.* even; **3.** ♀ *n* (one's own) self; '**♀-achtung** *f* self-respect.

selbständig ['zɛlpʃtɛndiç] *allg.* independent; *beruflich*: *a.* self-employed; *sich ~ machen* set up for o.s.; '**♀keit** *f* independence.

'**Selbst|-anlasser** ⊕ *m* self-starter; '**~-anschluß** *teleph. m* automatic telephone; dial system; '**~-auslöser** *phot. m* self-timer; '**~-ausschaltung** ⚡ *f* automatic cut-out; '**~bedienung(sladen** *m*) *f* self-service (shop); '**~befriedigung** *f* masturbation; '**~behauptung** *f* self-assertion; '**~beherrschung** *f* self-control; *die ~ verlieren* lose one's temper; '**~besinnung** *f* stocktaking of o.s.; '**~bestimmung(srecht** *n*) *f* (right of) self-determination; '**~beteiligung** *f Versicherung*: excess; '**~betrug** *m* self-deception; '**♀bewußt** self-confident; '**~bewußtsein** *n* self-confidence; '**~biographie** *f* autobiography; '**~disziplin** *f* self-discipline; '**~-einschätzung** *f* self-assessment; '**~-entladung** ⚡ *f* self-discharge; '**~-entzündung** *f* spontaneous ignition; '**~-erhaltung** *f* self-preservation; '**~-erhaltungstrieb** *m* instinct of self-preservation; '**~-erkenntnis** *f* self-knowledge; '**~-erniedrigung** *f* self-abasement; '**~fahrer** *m* (*Rollstuhl*) self-propelling chair; *mot.* (*Person*) owner-driver; *Auto für ~* self-drive car; '**♀gebacken** home-made; '**♀gefällig** (self-)complacent; '**~gefälligkeit** *f* (self-)complacency; '**~gefühl** *n* self-esteem, amour-propre (*fr.*); **♀gemacht** ['~gəmaxt] home-made; '**~genügsamkeit** *f* self-sufficiency; '**♀gerecht** self-righteous; '**~gespräch** *n* monologue, soliloquy; '**♀herrlich** high-handed; '**~herrscher** *m* autocrat; '**~hilfe** *f* self-help; '**♀isch** selfish; '**♀klebend** (self-)adhesive; '**~kontrolle** *f* self-control; '**~kosten(preis** *m*) *pl.* prime cost, cost price; '**~kritik** *f* self-criticism; '**~ladepistole** *f* automatic (pistol); '**~laut** *m* vowel; '**♀los** unselfish; self-sacrificing; '**~mitleid** *n* self-pity; '**~mord** *m*, '**~mörder** *m* suicide; '**♀mörderisch** suicidal; '**~mordkommando** *n* suicide squad; '**~porträt** *n* self-portrait; '**♀redend** *s. selbstverständlich*; '**~regierung** *f* self-government; '**♀schmierend** ⊕ self-lubricating; '**~-**

schuß *m* spring-gun; **'~schutz** *m* self-protection; **'2sicher** self-confident; **'~sicherheit** *f* self-confidence, aplomb; **'~sucht** *f* selfishness; **'2süchtig** selfish; **'2tätig** automatic(ally *adv.*), ⊕ *a.* self-acting; **'~täuschung** *f* self-deception; **'~-überschätzung** *f* overestimation of o.s.; **'~-überwindung** *f* self-victory; **'~-unterricht** *m* self-instruction; **'~verachtung** *f* self-contempt; **'2vergessen** lost to the world; **'~verlag** *m*: *im* ~ published by the author; **'~verleugnung** *f* self-denial; **'~vernichtung** *f* self-destruction; **'~verpflegung** *f* self-catering; **'2verschuldet** arising through one's own fault; **~versorger** ['~fɛrzɔːrgər] *m* (7) self-supporter *od.* -supplier; **'~versorgung** *f* self-sufficiency; **'2verständlich** self-evident, obvious; *pred.* a matter of course; *adv.* of course; ~! *a.* by all means!; *es ist* ~, *daß* it goes without saying that ...; *et. als* ~ *betrachten* take a th. for granted; **'~verständlichkeit** *f* matter of course; **'~verteidigung** *f* self-defen|ce, *Am.* -se; **'~vertrauen** *n* self-confidence; **'~verwaltung** *f* self-government; **'~verwirklichung** *f* self-realization; **'~wählbetrieb** *teleph. m* long-distance dialling; **'~wert** *m* self-esteem; **'~zucht** *f* self-discipline; **'2zufrieden** self-satisfied, complacent; **'~zufriedenheit** *f* self-satisfaction, complacency; **'~zündung** *f* self-ignition; **'~zweck** *m* end in itself.

selchen ['zɛlçən] smoke.

Selen ⚗ [ze'leːn] *n* (11) selenium.

selig ['zeːliç] blessed; *fig. a.* blissful, happy; (*verstorben*) late; *die 2en pl.* the blessed; *~en Angedenkens* of blessed memory; **'2keit** *f* happiness, bliss; **'~sprechen** beatify; **'2sprechung** *f* beatification.

Sellerie ['zɛləriː] *m* (11) *u. f* (15) celery; (*Knolle*) celeriac.

selten ['zɛltən] rare (*a. weitS. Schönheit usw.*); (*knapp*) scarce; *adv.* seldom, rarely; **'2heit** *f* rarity (*a. konkret*), scarcity; *nur konkret*: curiosity.

Selterswasser ['zɛltərsvasər] *n* seltzer (water), soda-water.

seltsam ['zɛltzaːm] strange, odd; **'~erweise** strange to say, oddly enough; **'2keit** *f* strangeness, oddness; *konkret*: oddity.

Semester [ze'mɛstər] *univ. n* (7) (half-year) term, semester; **~-abschluß...** end-of-term; **~-ende** *n*, **~-schluß** *m* close of term; **~ferien** *pl.* vacation (between terms).

Semikolon [zemi'koːlɔn] *n* (11, *pl. a.* -*la*) semicolon.

Seminar [~'naːr] *n* (3[1]) *univ.* seminar; (*Lehrer2*) training-college; (*Priester2*) seminary; **~ist** [~na'rist] *m* (12), **~istin** *f* (16[1]) pupil of a training-college; seminarist.

Semit [ze'miːt] *m* (12), **~in** *f* Semite.

Semmel ['zɛməl] *f* (15) roll; *wie warme ~n weggehen* go like hot cakes; *geriebene ~* bread crumbs *pl.*

Senat [ze'naːt] *m* (3) senate; **~or** [~tɔr] *m* (8[1]) senator.

Sendbote ['zɛnt-] *m* emissary.

Sende|-anlage ['zɛndə-] transmitting station; **'~bereich** *m* transmission range; **'~folge** *f* program(me); **'~leiter** *m* producer, production director.

senden ['zɛndən] (30) send (*nach j-m, et.* for); *tel., Radio*: transmit, send, *bsd. Am.* radio; *Radio usw.*: broadcast, *TV a.* telecast; *ein Stück wird gesendet Am.* a show is on the air.

'Sender *m* (7) *tel., Radio*: transmitter; (*Station*) (broadcasting) station.

'Sende|raum *m* studio; **'~reihe** *f* series.

'Sender|gruppe *f*, **'~netz** *n Radio*: network.

'Sende|station *f*, **'~stelle** *f tel., Radio*: transmitting station; **'~zeichen** *n* call-sign; **'~zeit** *f* transmission time; *beste ~* prime time.

'Sendschreiben *n* missive, epistle; circular (letter).

'Sendung *f* sending; *fig.* mission; *v. Waren*: consignment, *Am.* shipment; *tel., Radio*: transmission, (*Programmteil*) broadcast.

Senf [zɛnf] *m* (3) mustard (*a.* ⚘); **'~gas** *n* mustard gas; **'~gurke** *f* cucumber pickled with mustard seeds; **'~korn** *n* (grain of) mustard seed; **'~pflaster** *n* mustard plaster; **'~topf** *m* mustard-pot.

Senge ['zɛŋə] F *f/pl.*: ~ *bekommen* get a beating; **'2n** *v/t. u. v/i.* (25) singe, scorch; ~ *und brennen* lay waste (by fire); *~de Hitze* parching heat.

senil [ze'ni:l] senile; **2ität** [~nili-'tɛ:t] *f* senility.
senior ['ze:njɔr], 2 *m* (8[1]) senior; **2en** [zen'jo:rən] *m/pl.* senior citizens; **2enheim** *n* old people's home.
Senkblei ['zɛŋk-] *n* ⚓ plummet, plumb bob; ⚓ sounding lead.
'**Senke** *geogr. f* (15) depression, hollow.
senk|en ['zɛŋkən] (25) sink (*a.* ⚒); let down, *a. Preis, Stimme*: lower; *Augen*: cast down; *Kopf*: bow; ⚒ lay; *sich* ~ sink, drop, go down; *Mauer*: sag; *Boden(satz)*: settle; *Straße*: dip, fall; *Nacht, Stimmung*: descend; '**2er** ⚒ *m* (7) layer.
'**Senk|fuß** ⚕ *m* flat foot; '**~fußeinlage** *f* arch support, instep raiser; '**~grube** *f* cesspool; '**2recht** vertical, *bsd.* ⚒ perpendicular (*beide a.* '**~rechte** *f* [15]); '**~rechtstarter** *m* ✈ vertical take-off plane; F *fig.* whizz-kid; '**~ung** *f* sinking, *a. der Preise*: lowering; *e-r Mauer usw.*: sag; ⚕ (*Blut2*) sedimentation; (*Vertiefung*) depression, hollow; '**~waage** *f* aerometer.
Senn [zɛn] (3), '**~er** (13) *m* Alpine herdsman; **~erei** [~ə'raɪ] *f* Alpine dairy; '**~erin** *f* (16[1]) Alpine dairy--maid; '**~hütte** *f* chalet.
Sensation [zɛnza'tsjo:n] *f* sensation; **2ell** [~tsjo'nɛl], **~s...** [~-'tsjo:ns-] sensational; **~slust** *f* sensationalism; **2slustig** sensationalist; **~smeldung** *f* sensational report; **~spresse** *f* yellow press.
Sense ['zɛnzə] *f* (15) scythe; '**~nmann** *m* mower; *fig.* Death.
sensi|bel [zɛn'zi:bəl] sensitive; **2bilität** [~zibili'tɛ:t] *f* (16) sensitiveness, sensibility.
Sensor ['zɛnzɔr] *m* (8[1]) sensor; '**~bildschirm** *m Computer*: sensor screen.
Sentenz [zɛn'tɛnts] *f* (16) maxim, aphorism; **2iös** [~'tsjø:s] sententious.
sentimental [zɛntimɛn'ta:l] sentimental; **2ität** [~tali'tɛ:t] *f* (16) sentimentality.
separat [zepa'ra:t] separate; **2ismus** [~ra'tismus] *m* (16, *o. pl.*) separatism.
Sepia ['ze:pja] *f inv. zo.* cuttle-fish; (*Farbe*) sepia.
September [zɛp'tɛmbər] *m* (7) September.
septisch ['zɛptiʃ] septic(ally *adv.*).
Serail [ze'raɪl] *n* (11) seraglio.
Serb|e ['zɛrbə] *m* (13), '**~in** *f* (16[1]) Serb(ian); '**2isch** Serbian.
Serenade [zere'na:də] *f* (15) serenade.
Serie ['ze:rjə] *f* (15) series; (*Satz*) set; *Billard*: break; ✝ *e-e ~ von Waren* a range (*od.* line) of; '**~nausstattung** *f* standard fittings *pl.*; '**~nherstellung** *f*, '**~produktion** *f* serial (*od.* mass) production; '**2nmäßig** standard (type); *adv.* in series; ~ *herstellen* produce in series; '**2nreif** ready for production; '**~nschaltung** *f* series connection; '**~nwagen** *mot. m* stock car.
seriös [ze'rjø:s] serious; (*vertrauenswürdig*) trustworthy.
Serpentine [zɛrpɛn'ti:nə] *f* (15) serpentine (line); (*Straße*) serpentine (road); (*Kurve*) double bend.
Serum ['ze:rum] *n* (9[2]) serum; '**~kunde** *f* serology.
Service [zɛr'vi:s] *n* (7) (*Geschirrsatz*) service, set; ✝, *mot. etc.* ['zørvis] (*a. m*) (*Bedienung, Kundendienst*) service; '**2freundlich** *mot.* easy to service.
Servier|brett [zɛr'vi:r-] *n* tray; **2en** *v/t.* serve; *v/i.* wait (at table); **~erin** *f* (16[1]) waitress; **~tisch** *m* side-table.
Serviette [zɛr'vjɛtə] *f* (15) (table-) napkin; **~nring** *m* napkin-ring.
servil [zɛr'vi:l] servile.
Servo|lenkung ['zɛrvo-] *mot. f* power steering; '**~motor** ⚡ *m* servo-motor.
Sessel ['zɛsəl] *m* (7) arm- (*od.* easy-) chair; '**~lift** *m* chair-lift.
seßhaft ['zɛshaft] settled, established, stationary; (*irgendwo ansässig*) resident; '**2igkeit** *f* settledness, stationariness.
Set [sɛt] *n, m* (11) (*Platzdeckchen*) place mat.
'**Setz-ei** *n* fried egg.
setzen ['zɛtsən] (27) *v/t.* set, place, put; *typ.* set up in type, (*a.* ♪) compose; (*pflanzen*) plant; *Denkmal*: erect, raise; *e-e Frist* ~ fix a term (*j-m* for a p.); *bei Wetten usw.*: stake (*auf acc.* on); *alles daran* ~ do one's utmost; *auf j-s Rechnung* ~ charge to a p.'s account; *es sich in den Kopf* ~, *daß* ... get it into one's head that; *in die Zeitung* ~

insert; *s-e Unterschrift ~ unter* (*acc.*) put (*od.* affix) one's signature to, sign; *sich ~* sit down; *Vogel*: perch; (*sinken*) sink; *Haus, Bodensatz*: settle; *s. Druck, Fall, Freiheit, Gang*[1], *Gefecht, Luft usw.*; *v/i.* (sn) *~ über* (*acc.*) leap (over), clear; *e-n Strom*: cross; (h.) *typ.* set type; *beim Wetten*: *~ auf* (*acc.*) bet on, back.

'**Setzer** *m* (7) compositor, typesetter; **~ei** [~'raɪ] *f* (16) composing room.

'**Setz|kasten** *typ. m* (letter-)case; '**~ling** ⚘ *m* (3[1]) slip, young plant; '**~maschine** *typ. f* composing (*od.* type-setting) machine; '**~reis** ⚘ *n* layer; '**~waage** *f* level.

Seuche ['zɔʏçə] *f* (15) epidemic; '**~nbekämpfung** *f* control of epidemics; '**~nherd** *m* cent|re (*Am.* -er) of an epidemic.

seufz|en ['zɔʏftsən] (27) sigh; '**2er** *m* (7) sigh.

Sex [sɛks] F *m* (3[2], *o. pl.*) sex; **~-Appeal** ['~ə'pi:l] *m* (3[1], *o. pl.*) sex appeal.

Sextett ♩ [zɛks'tɛt] *n* (3) sextet.

sexual, 2... [zɛksu'ɑ:l] sexual.

Sexualität [~ali'tɛ:t] *f* (16) sexuality.

Sexual|kunde [zɛksu'ɑ:l-] *f* sex education; **~verbrechen** *n* sex crime.

sexuell [zɛksu'ɛl] sexual.

Sexus ['zɛksus] *m* (11[1], *o. pl.*) sex.

Sezier|besteck [ze'tsi:r-] *n* dissecting instruments *pl.*; **2en** dissect; **~messer** *n* scalpel.

Showmaster ['ʃo:mɑ:stər, 'ʃəu-] *m* (11) *TV*: compère, host, F emcee.

Sibir|ier [zi'bi:rjər] *m* (7), **2isch** Siberian.

sich [ziç] *allg.*: oneself; *3. P. sg.* himself, herself, itself, *pl.* themselves; *nach prp.* him, her, it, *pl.* them; (*statt*: *einander*) each other, one another.

Sichel ['ziçəl] *f* (15) sickle; (*Mond2*) crescent; **2förmig** ['~fœrmiç] sickle-shaped.

sicher ['ziçər] secure, safe (*beide*: *vor dat.* from); (*gewiß*) certain, sure; (*bestimmt od. zuversichtlich*) positive; (*zuverlässig*) reliable; (*tüchtig*) efficient; *Auge usw.*: sure; *Auftreten*: self-assured; *Ort, Methode*: safe; *Schütze*: sure, dead *shot*; *um ~ zu gehen s. sicherheitshalber*; *s-r S. ~ sein* be quite positive; *sind Sie ~?* are you sure?; *adv. u. int. s. ~lich.*

'**Sicherheit** *f s. sicher*; security (*a.* = *Pfand, Wertpapier*); safety; certainty; positiveness; *des Auftretens*: assurance; *in ~ sein* be safe; *in ~ bringen* place in safety; *sich in ~ bringen* save one's bacon; *~ leisten* ✝ furnish security; ⚖ *~ stellen* give (*od.* offer) bail, *Am. a.* post bond; *s. wiegen*[2]; '**~s-abstand** *m* safe distance; '**~sbe-amte** *m* security agent; '**~sbindung** *f Schi*: safety binding; '**~sfaktor** *m* factor of safety; '**~sglas** *n* safety glass; '**~sgurt** *m* seat belt, *mot. a.* safety belt; '**2shalber** to be on the safe side, to make sure; '**~s-interessen** *n/pl.* security interests; '**~sklausel** *f* safeguard; '**~skontrolle** *f am Flughafen*: security check; '**~smaßnahme** *f* safety measure, precaution; '**~snadel** *f* safety-pin; '**~s-polizei** *f* security police; '**~srat** *m* Security Council; '**~srisiko** *n a. Person*: security risk; '**~sschloß** *n* safety-lock; '**~sventil** *n* safety valve.

'**sicher|lich** surely, certainly; *~! a.* to be sure!, *Am.* F sure!; *~ hat er recht* I am sure he is right; *~ wird er kommen* he is sure to come; '**~n** (29) secure (*a.* ⊕ *u.* ✝), (*schützen*) *a.* (safe)guard (*beide*: *vor dat., gegen* against), protect (from); (*gewährleisten*) ensure; *Waffe*: put at "safe"; *v/i. hunt.* scent; '**~stellen** secure; '**2ung** *f* securing; (*Maßnahme*) safeguard(ing); ⚡ fuse, cut-out; ⊕ safety device; *am Gewehr*: safety(-catch); '**2ungsverwahrung** ⚖ *f* preventive detention.

Sicht [ziçt] *f* (15) sight; (*Aus2*) view (*a. fig.*); (*~verhältnisse*) visibility; ✝ *auf ~, bei ~* at sight; *60 Tage nach ~* 60 days after sight; *fig. auf weite* (*od. lange*) *~* on a long-term basis, (*auf die Dauer*) in the long run; *aus seiner ~* as he sees it; *in ~ kommen* come into sight; *in ~ sein* be in sight; '**2bar** visible; (*auffallend*) conspicuous; *~ machen* (*werden*) show; '**~barkeit** *f* visibleness; '**~beton** *m* fair-faced concrete; '**2en** (26) (*erblicken*) sight; (*sieben*) sift; *fig. a.* screen; (*ordnen*) sort; '**~feld** *n* field of vision; '**~gerät** *n Computer*: visual display terminal; '**2lich** visible; (*offenbar*) evident; '**~**-

tratte ⚕ *f*, '~**wechsel** *m* sight-draft; '~**verhältnisse** *n/pl.* visibility *sg.*; '~**vermerk** *m auf Reisepaß*: visé, visa; *auf Wechsel*: endorsement; '~**weite** *f* range of sight; *in (außer)* ~ in (out of) sight.

sicker|n ['zikərn] (29, sn *u.* h.) trickle, ooze, leak, *bsd. Am.* seep; '2**wasser** *n* water leakage.

sie [zi:] **1.** *pron. sg.* she; *Sache*: it; *pl.* they; *acc. sg.* her; it; *acc. pl.* them; *Sie* you; **2.** 2 *f* she, female.

Sieb [zi:p] *n* (3) sieve; (*grobes* ~) riddle; (*Kies*2 *usw.*) screen.

sieben[1] ['zi:bən] (25) sift, strain; *fig.* (*auslesen*) screen, sift.

sieben[2] [~] **1.** seven; **2.** 2 *f inv.* seven; *böse* ~ vixen, shrew.

'**sieben|fach**, ~**fältig** ['~fɛltiç] sevenfold; '2**gebirge** *n* Seven Mountains *pl.*; '2**gestirn** *n* Pleiades *pl.*; '~**jährig** seven-year(s)-old, of seven years; *der* ~*e Krieg* the Seven Years' War; '~**mal** seven times; '~**malig** seven times repeated; '2'**meilenstiefel** *m/pl.* seven-league boots; '2**sachen** *f/pl.* things, belongings; *seine* ~ *packen* pack up one's traps; '2**schläfer** *m/pl. the* Seven Sleepers; *sg. fig.* = *Langschläfer*; *zo.* dormouse; ~**tägig** ['~tɛ:giç] of (*od.* lasting) seven days.

siebent ['~t] seventh; '2**el** *n* (7) seventh (part); '~**ens** seventhly.

siebzehn ['zi:ptse:n] seventeen; '~**t**, '2**tel** *n* (7) seventeenth.

siebzig ['~tsiç] seventy; 2**er** ['~gər] *m* (7), '2**erin** *f* (16[1]) septuagenarian; '~**ste** seventieth.

siech [zi:ç] sickly, invalid; '~**en** (25) be ailing; languish (*a. fig.*); '2**tum** *n* (1[2]) lingering illness, invalidism.

'**Siede|grad** *m* boiling-point; '~**hitze** *f* boiling heat; '~**kessel** *m* boiler.

siedeln ['zi:dəln] (29) settle.

siede|n ['zi:dən] (30) boil (*a. fig.*); *gelind*: simmer; *nur fig.* seethe; *Zucker*: refine; '2**punkt** *m* boiling-point; '2**r** *m* boiler, refiner.

Siedler ['zi:dlər] *m* (7) (*An*2) settler; (*Arbeiter*2) homecrofter, *Am.* homesteader.

'**Siedlung** *f* settlement; (*Stadt*2) housing estate, suburban colony; '~**sgesellschaft** *f* land-settlement society.

Sieg [zi:k] *m* (3) victory, triumph (*über acc.* over); *Sport*: win; *den* ~ *davontragen od. erringen* gain the victory (*über acc.* over), carry (*od.* win) the day.

Siegel ['zi:gəl] *n* (7) seal; *unter dem* ~ *der Verschwiegenheit* under the seal of secrecy; '~**lack** *m* sealing-wax; '2**n** (29) seal; '~**ring** *m* signet-ring.

sieg|en ['zi:gən] (25) be victorious (*über acc.* over), conquer (*a. p.*); *Sport*: win; '2**er** *m* (7), '2**erin** *f* (16[1]) conqueror, *rhet.* victor; *Sport*: winner; '2**er-ehrung** *f Sport*: presentation ceremony; '2**ermächte** *f/pl.* victorious powers; '2**er-urkunde** *f* (winner's) diploma.

'**Sieges|bogen** *m* triumphal arch; '~**denkmal** *n* victory monument; '2**gewiß** sure of victory; '~**göttin** *f* Victory; '2**trunken** flushed with victory; '~**zeichen** *n* trophy; '~**zug** *m* triumphal procession; *fig.* triumphant advance.

sieg|haft, ~**reich** ['zi:k-] victorious, triumphant.

Siel [zi:l] *n* (3) (*Deichschleuse*) sluice (-way); (*Abwasserleitung*) culvert; '~**e** *f* (15) (*Gurt*) belt; *e-s Pferdes*: breast harness; *fig. in den* ~*n sterben* die in harness.

Sigel ['zi:gəl] *n* (7) *Kurzschrift*: grammalogue.

Signal [zig'nɑ:l] *n* (3[1]) signal; ~**ement** [~nal(ə)'mɑ̃] *n* (11) personal description; ~**flagge** [~'nɑ:l-] *f* signal-flag; ~**horn** *n* signal horn, horn, bugle; 2**i'sieren** *v/t. u. v/i.* signal.

Signatarmächte [zigna'tɑ:rmɛçtə] *pol. f/pl.* signatory powers (*e-s Vertrages* to a treaty).

Sign|atur [~'tu:r] *f* (16) signature; ⚕ mark, brand; *auf Landkarten*: conventional sign; *Bücherei*: call number; 2**ieren** [~'ni:rən] sign; mark, brand.

Silbe ['zilbə] *f* syllable; *fig. keine* ~ not a word; '~**ntrennung** *f* syllabification.

Silber ['zilbər] *n* (7, *o. pl.*) silver; '~**barren** *m* silver ingot; '~**bergwerk** *n* silver mine; '~**gehalt** *m* silver content; '~**geld** *n* silver money; '~**gerät** *n*, '~**geschirr** *n* silver (plate), *Am.* silverware; '2**hell** silvery; '~**medaille** *f Sport*: silver medal; '~**münze** *f* silver coin; '2**n** (of) silver; *Farbe, Klang usw.*: silvery; ~*e Hoch-*

zeit silver wedding; '**~papier** *n* tin foil; '**~pappel** ⚘ *f* white poplar; '**~schmied** *m* silversmith; '**~stahl** *m* silver steel; '**~streifen** *m fig.*: *~ am Horizont* silver lining; '**~währung** *f* silver standard; '**~waren** *f/pl.* silverware *sg.*; '**~zeug** *n s. Silbergeschirr.*

Silhouette [zilu'ɛtə] *f* (15) silhouette.

Silikat [zili'kɑːt] *n* (3) silicate.

Silikon [zili'koːn] *n* (3[1]) silicon; **~zelle** *f* silicon cell.

Silo ['ziːlo] *m* (11) silo; (*Getreide*≈) (grain) elevator; '**~futter** *n* silage.

Silvester [zil'vɛstər] *m, n* (7), **~abend** *m* New Year's Eve; **~ball** *m* New Year's Eve ball.

simpel ['zimpəl] simple, plain; ≈ F *m* blockhead; '**≈fransen** *f/pl.* fringe *sg.*, ponies.

Sims [zims] *m, n* (4) ledge; (*Fenster*≈) sill; (*Wandbrett*) shelf; ⚠ mo(u)lding, cornice.

Simu|lant [zimu'lant] *m* (12), **~'lantin** *f* (16[1]) malingerer; **~lator** [~'lɑːtɔr] ⊕, ⚔ *m* (8[1]) simulator; **≈'lieren** *v/t. u. v/i.* feign, sham; *nur v/t.*: simulate (*a.* ⊕, ⚔, *nachahmen*); *nur v/i.*: (*sich krank stellen*) sham ill, *bsd.* ⚔ *u.* ⚓ malinger.

Simultan... [~'tɑːn] simultaneous; *eccl.*, *Schule*: undenominational; *tel.* composite(d); **~dolmetschen** *n* simultaneous translation; **~dolmetscher(in** *f*) *m* simultaneous translator.

Sinfonie [zinfo'niː] *f* (15) symphony; **~-orchester** *n* symphony orchestra.

Sing... [ziŋ-] *in Zssgn mst* singing ...; '**≈bar** singable; '**~drossel** *f* song thrush; '**≈en** *v/i. u. v/t.* (30) sing; **~sang** ['~zaŋ] *m* singsong; '**~spiel** *n* musical comedy; '**~stimme** *f* singing-voice; ♪ vocal part.

Singular ['ziŋgulɑːr] *m* (3[1]) singular (number).

'**Singvogel** *m* singing bird, songbird, songster.

sinken ['ziŋkən] (30, sn) *allg.* sink; *a. Preise usw.*: drop, go down; *Sonne*: set, sink; *die Stimme ~ lassen* lower one's voice; *fig. tief gesunken* sunk very low; *in Ohnmacht ~* faint, swoon; *s. Mut, Schlaf, Wert.*

Sinn [zin] *m* (3) sense (*für* of); (*Geist, Verstand; Meinung*) mind; (*Vorliebe*) taste (*für* for); (*Instinkt*) flair; (*Wunsch*) wish; (*Bedeutung*) sense, meaning; (*Grundgedanke*) (basic) idea; (*Zweck*) purpose; *~ für Humor* sense of humo(u)r; *der ~ der Sache* the point; *~ haben für* have a taste for, (be able to) appreciate; *anderen ~es werden* change one's mind; *bei* (*von*) *~en sein* be in (out of) one's senses; *im ~e des Gesetzes usw.* within the meaning of; *im ~ haben* have in mind; *in gewissem ~e* in a sense; *ohne ~ und Verstand* without rhyme or reason; *seine fünf ~e beisammen haben* have one's wits about one; *es kam mir in den ~* it occurred to me (*zu inf.* to *inf.*); *das will mir nicht aus dem ~* I can't get it out of my head; *das will mir nicht in den ~* I just can't understand it; *es hat keinen ~* it makes no sense; (*ist zwecklos*) it is no use; *s. schlagen.*

'**Sinnbild** *n* symbol, emblem; '**≈lich** symbolic(al); *~ darstellen* symbolize; *Kunst*: allegorize.

sinnen ['zinən] (30) (*über dat.*) meditate, reflect (*beide*: [up]on), ponder (over); *mit Muße*: muse ([up]on); *~ auf* (*acc.*) meditate, *b.s.* plot, scheme; '**~d** musing, pensive, thoughtful.

'**sinnen|freudig** sensuous; '**≈genuß** *m*, '**≈lust** *f* sensual pleasure, sensuality; '**≈rausch** *m*, '**≈taumel** *m* intoxication of the senses.

'**sinn-entstellend** garbling, distorting.

'**Sinnes|-änderung** *f* change of mind; '**~-art** *f* temper, character; mentality; '**~-organ** *n* sense organ; '**~täuschung** *f* illusion, hallucination; '**~wandel** *m* change of mind.

'**sinn|fällig** obvious, striking; '**≈gedicht** *n* epigram; '**~gemäß** analogous; *adv. a.* accordingly; '**~getreu** faithful; **~ieren** [~'niːrən] ruminate; '**~ig** thoughtful; (*sinnreich*) ingenious; '**~lich** sensual; (*Ggs. geistig*) material, physical; '**≈lichkeit** *f* sensuality; material existence; '**~los** senseless; meaningless; (*unsinnig*) absurd; (*zwecklos*) useless, futile; *~ betrunken* dead drunk; '**≈losigkeit** *f* senselessness; absurdity; futility; '**~reich** ingenious, clever; '**≈spruch** *m* device, motto; '**~verwandt** synonymous; '**~voll** wise; (*zweckvoll*) ingenious, efficient; '**~widrig** absurd.

Sinter ['zintər] *m* (7) ⚒ sinter; *metall.* dross of iron.
Sintflut ['zintflu:t] *f* (great) flood, deluge; *biblisch*: *the* Flood, *the* Deluge.
Sinus ['zi:nus] *m* (*inv. u.* 14²) sine; '**~kurve** *f* sine curve; '**~leistung** *f* *Radio*: sine rating.
Siphon ['zi:fɔn] *m* (11) siphon.
Sipp|e ['zipə] *f* (15), '**~schaft** *f* (16) kin, family, relations *pl.*; *a. zo.*, ♀ tribe; *fig. iro.* clan, clique, gang, lot; '**~enforschung** *f* genealogical research.
Sirene [zi're:nə] *f* (15) *allg.* siren.
Sirup ['zi:rup] *m* (3¹) treacle, *Am.* molasses; (*bsd. Frucht*⁀) syrup, *Am.* sirup.
sistieren [zi'sti:rən] stay, stop; (*verhaften*) arrest.
Sitte ['zitə] *f* (15) custom; (*Gewohnheit*) habit; (*Brauch*) usage; ~*n pl.* manners, (*Moral*) morals.
'**Sitten|bild** *n*, '**~gemälde** *n* picture of manners *od.* morals; '**~gesetz** *n* moral code (*od.* law); '**~lehre** *f* ethics *pl.*, moral philosophy; '**⁀los** immoral; '**~losigkeit** *f* immorality; '**~polizei** *f* Vice Squad; '**~prediger** *m* moralizer; '**~richter** *m* censor; '**⁀streng** austere, puritanical; '**~strolch** F *m* sexual offender; '**~verderbnis** *f* corruption of morals.
Sittich *zo.* ['zitiç] *m* (3) parakeet.
sittig ['~] *s. sittsam.*
sittlich ['zitliç] moral, ethical; '**⁀keit** *f* morality; '**⁀keitsverbrechen** *n* sex crime; '**⁀keitsverbrecher** *m* sex offender.
'**sittsam** (*züchtig*) modest, demure; (*keusch*) chaste, virtuous; (*brav*) well-behaved; (*anständig*) decent; '**⁀keit** *f* modesty; good manners *pl.*; decency.
Situation [zitua'tsjo:n] *f* situation; *die ~ retten* save the situation; **~skomik** *f* comedy of situation, slapstick.
situiert [zitu'i:rt]: *gut ~* well-off, well-to-do, *Am.* F well-fixed.
Sitz [zits] *m* (3²) seat (*a. fig.*); (*Stuhl*) chair; (*Wohnort*) (place of) residence; *e-s Kleides*: fit; '**~bad** *n* sitz-bath.
'**sitzen** (30) sit (*a. fig. tagen*); *Vogel u. fig.* (*hoch oben ~*) be perched; *Firma usw.*: be, have its seat (*in dat.* at); *Kleid*: fit; F *im Gefängnis*: do time; *Hieb*: tell, hit home; F *einen ~ haben* be drunk; *~ bleiben* remain sitting *od.* seated; *bleiben Sie ~!* keep your seat!; '**~bleiben** (sn) *beim Tanz*: be left without partners; *Mädchen*: (*nicht geheiratet werden*) get on the shelf; *in der Schule*: not to get one's remove; '**~d:** *~e Lebensweise* sedentary life; '**~lassen** *fig.* leave, desert, throw *a p.* over; (*im Stich lassen*) let *a p.* down; *e-n Schimpf auf sich ~* pocket an affront.
'**Sitz|fleisch** F *n* perseverance; '**~gelegenheit** *f* seat; '**~gruppe** *f* three-piece suite; '**~ordnung** *f* seating arrangement(s *pl.*); '**~platz** *m* seat; '**~streik** *m* sit-down strike.
'**Sitzung** *f* sitting, ⚖ *a.* hearing; '**~sbericht** *m* minutes *pl.* (of proceedings); '**~s-periode** *f* session; ⚖ term; '**~s-saal** *m* conference room; *parl.* chamber, *Am. a.* floor.
Sizilian|er [zitsil'ja:nər] *m* (7), **~erin** *f* (16¹), **⁀isch** Sicilian.
Skala ['ska:la] *f* (16² *u.* 11¹) scale (*a.* ♪); *in Kreisform*: dial; *bewegliche* (*od. gleitende*) ~ sliding scale.
'**Skalenscheibe** *f* *Radio usw.*: dial.
Skalp [skalp] *m* (3¹), **⁀ieren** [~'pi:rən] scalp.
Skandal [skan'da:l] *m* (3¹) scandal; (*Schande*) disgrace, shame; (*Lärm*) row; **~blatt** *n* scandal-sheet; **⁀ös** [~da'lø:s] scandalous; **~presse** [~'da:l-] *f* gutter press.
skandieren [skan'di:rən] scan.
skandinavisch [skandi'na:viʃ] Scandinavian.
Skat [ska:t] *m* (3) skat.
Skelett [ske'lɛt] *n* (3) skeleton.
Skep|sis ['skɛpsis] *f inv.* scepticism; **~tiker** ['~tikər] *m* (7) sceptic; '**⁀tisch** sceptical.
Sketch [skɛtʃ] *m* (3, *pl. a.* 11) sketch.
Ski [ʃi:] *m usw. s. Schi.*
Skizze ['skitsə] *f* (15) sketch; '**~nbuch** *n* sketch-book; '**⁀nhaft** sketchy, in rough outlines.
skiz'zieren *v/t. u. v/i.* sketch, outline.
Sklav|e ['skla:və] *m* (13), '**~in** *f* slave; '**~enhandel** *m* slave-trade; '**~enhändler** *m* slave-trader; '**~entreiber** *m a. fig.* slave-driver; **~erei** [~ə'raɪ] *f* (16) slavery; '**⁀isch** slavish (*a. fig.*), servile.
Skonto ✝ ['skɔnto] *m, n* (11) discount.

Skorbut [skɔr'bu:t] *m* (3) scurvy.
Skorpion [skɔrp'jo:n] *m* (3[1]) scorpion; *ast.* Scorpio(n).
Skrof|eln ['skro:fəln] *f/pl.* (15) scrofula *sg.*; **&ulös** [skrofu'lø:s] scrofulous; **~ulose** [~'lo:zə] *f* (16) scrofula.
Skrup|el ['skru:pəl] *m* (7) scruple; '**&ellos** unscrupulous; **&ulös** [skrupu'lø:s] scrupulous.
Skulptur [skulp'tu:r] *f* (16) sculpture.
skurril [sku'ri:l] ludicrous.
S-Kurve *mot.* ['ɛs-] *f* double hairpin bend.
Slalom ['slɑ:lɔm] *m, n* (11) *Schi:* [slalom.]
Slaw|e ['slɑ:və] *m* (13), '**~in** *f*, '**&isch** Slav, Slavonian; *adj. a.* Slavic.
Slip [slip] *m* (11) briefs *pl.*; '**~-einlage** *f* panty-liner.
Slowak|e [slo'vɑ:kə] *m* (13) Slovak; **&isch** Slovakian.
Smaragd [sma'rakt] *m* (3), **&en**, **&grün** emerald.
Smoking ['smo:kiŋ] *m* (11) dinner--jacket, *Am.* tuxedo; '**~-anzug** *m* dinner(-jacket) suit.
so [zo:] so, thus; *vergleichend*: as; *cj.* if; ~ *daß* so that; ~ *sehr, daß* so much that; ~ *ein* such a; ~ *etwas* such a thing; F *nein, ~ etwas!* well, I never!; ~ ... *denn* so; ~ ... *wie od. als* as ... as; *nicht ~ ... wie od. als* not so ... as; ~ *oder* ~ one way or another, (*ohnehin*) anyhow; *sie war ~ ... zu inf.* she was ... enough to *inf.*; *wir machen es* ~ we do it this way; ~ *im Nachsatz nicht zu übersetzen, z. B.*: *wenn du Zeit hast, ~ schreibe mir* if you have time, write to me; *s. ach, noch, um, soviel, weit*; **~bald** [zo'balt] (*als*) as soon as.
Söckchen ['zœkçən] *n* (6) anklet.
Socke ['zɔkə] *f* (15) sock; *~n* ✝ *pl. a.* half-hose; '**~l** *m* (7) base, socle, pedestal; '**~nhalter** *m* suspender, *Am.* garter.
Soda ['zo:da] *f, n inv.* soda.
sodann [zo'dan] then.
'**Sodawasser** *n* soda-water.
Sodbrennen ['zo:t-] *n* heartburn.
soeben [zo'ˀe:bən] just (now).
Sofa ['zo:fa] *n* (11) sofa; '**~kissen** *n* sofa-cushion.
so'fern *cj.* so (*od.* as) far as, if; (*wenn nur*) provided that; ~ *nicht* unless.
soff [zɔf] *pret. v. saufen.*
Soffitten *thea.* [zɔ'fitən] *f/pl.* (15) flies; **~lampe** *f* tubular lamp.
sofort [zo'fɔrt] *adv.* at once, directly, instantly, immediately, forthwith, straight (*bsd. Am.* right) away; ✝ ~ *lieferbar od. zahlbar* spot; **&hilfe** *f* emergency (relief) aid; **&hilfeprogramm** *n* emergency aid program(me); **~ig** immediate, prompt, instant; **&maßnahme** *f* immediate action (*a. pl.*), prompt measure.
Software ['zɔftwɛ:ər] *f Computer*: software.
Sog [zo:k] **1.** *m* (3, *o. pl.*) suction; ⚓ (*Kielwasser*), ✈ (*Luftwirbel*) wake (*a. fig.*); **2.** & *pret. v. saugen.*
so|gar [zo'gɑ:r] even; **~genannt** ['zo:gənant] so-called; (*sich für et. ausgebend*) self-styled, would-be; **~gleich** [zo'glaıç] *s. sofort.*
Sohl|e ['zo:lə] *f* (15) sole; *e-s Tals usw.*: bottom; ⚒ floor; '**~(en)leder** *n* sole-leather.
Sohn [zo:n] *m* (3[3]) son; *der verlorene* ~ the prodigal son.
Soiree [soa're:] *f* (15) evening party, soirée.
Sojabohne ['zo:ja-] *f* soya-bean.
so'lange (*als*) so (*od.* as) long as.
Solar|batterie [zo'lɑ:r-] ⚡ *f* solar battery; **~-energie** *f* solar energy.
Solarium [zo'lɑ:rium] *n* (9) solarium.
So'larzelle *f* solar cell.
Solbad ['zo:lbɑ:t] *n* salt-water bath.
solch [zɔlç] (21) such; *als ~er* as such; '**~er-'art**, **~erlei** ['~ər'laı] of such a kind, such; '**~er'maßen**, '**~er'weise** in such a way.
Sold [zɔlt] *m* (3) pay; *fig.* wages *pl.*
Soldat [zɔl'dɑ:t] *m* (12) soldier; serviceman; *aktiver* ~ regular (soldier); *einfacher* ~ private; *gedienter* ~ ex-serviceman; *der Unbekannte* ~ the Unknown Warrior; ~(*en*) *spielen* play at soldiers; **~eska** [~da'tɛska] *f inv. the* soldiery; **&isch** [~'dɑ:tiʃ] soldierlike, military.
'**Soldbuch** ⚔ *n* pay book.
Söld|ling ['zœltliŋ] *m* (3[1]), **~ner** ['~dnər] *m* (7) mercenary.
Sole ['zo:lə] *f* (15) brine.
solidar|isch [zoli'dɑ:riʃ] solidary; ⚖ jointly responsible *od.* liable; *adv.* jointly and severally; *sich ~ erklären mit* declare one's solidarity with; **&ität** [~dari'tɛ:t] *f* solidarity.
solid|(e) [zo'li:t, -də] solid (*a. fig.*); (*kräftig*) robust, rugged; *Grundlage*: sound; *Preise*: reasonable; ✝

Firma: sound, solvent; *fig.* respectable; (*nicht ausschweifend*) steady; **Sität** [~di'tɛ:t] *f* solidity; soundness; *fig.* respectability.
Solist [zo'list] *m* (12), **~in** *f* (16[1]) soloist; solo singer; solo player.
Soll [zɔl] *n* (11 *u. inv.*) debit; (*Lieferungs*S) fixed quota; (*Produktionsziel*) target; ~ *und Haben* debit and credit; '**~bestand** *m* nominal stock; ✝ *a.* calculated assets *pl.*; ⚔ *s.* *Sollstärke.*
'**sollen** (30) *2. u. 3. P.* shall; *sonst*: be to; *angeblich*: be said to; *sollte* should, *stärker*: ought to.
Söller ['zœlər] *m* (7) balcony.
'**Soll|maß** *n* specified size; '**~stärke** ⚔ *f* authorized strength; '**~wert** ⊕ *m* nominal (*od.* rated) value.
Solo ['zo:lo] *n* (11) solo; '**~stimme** *f* solo part; '**~tänzer(in** *f*) *m* dance soloist.
'**Solquelle** *f* salt-spring.
solven|t [zɔl'vɛnt] solvent; **Sz** *f* (16) solvency.
somit [zo'mit] consequently, thus.
Sommer ['zɔmər] *m* (7) summer; '**~-aufenthalt** *m* summer residence *od.* stay; '**~fäden** *m/pl.* gossamer; '**~frische** *f* summer resort; **~-frischler** ['~friʃlər] *m* (7) holiday-maker, *Am.* vacationer; '**~kleidung** *f*, '**~sachen** *f/pl.* summer clothes *pl.*, ✝ summer-wear; '**Slich** summer(l)y; '**~reifen** *mot. m* normal tyre (*Am.* tire); '**~sprosse** *f* freckle; '**Ssprossig** freckled; '**~zeit** *f* summer time, *zur Lichtersparnis*: *a.* daylight-saving time.
sonach [zo'na:x] consequently.
Sonate [zo'na:tə] *f* (15) sonata.
Sonde ['zɔndə] *f* (15) ⚕ sound, (*a. Mond*S *usw.*) probe; ⚓ plummet; *Radar*: sonde.
sonder ['zɔndər] without.
'**Sonder|-abdruck** *m* off-print, separate (print); '**~-anfertigung** *f* special design; '**~-angebot** *n* special (offer); '**~-auftrag** *m* special mission; '**~-ausbildung** *f* special training; '**~-ausgabe** *f* special edition; *geldlich*: extra; '**~-ausschuß** *m* special committee; '**Sbar** strange, odd, peculiar; '**Sbarerweise** oddly enough; '**~barkeit** *f* strangeness, oddity; '**~be-auftragte** *m* special representative; '**~beilage** *f e-r Zeitung*: inset, supplement; '**~berichterstatter** *m* special correspondent; '**~bevollmächtigte** *m* plenipotentiary; '**~druck** *m s. Sonderabdruck*; '**~fall** *m* special (*od.* exceptional) case; '**~frieden** *m* separate peace; **S'gleichen** *adv.* (*im Englischen als adj.*) matchless, unprecedented; '**~interesse** *n* private interest; '**~klasse** *f* special class; *Segelsport*: *Am.* sonderclass; '**~klausel** *f* special clause; '**Slich** special, peculiar, remarkable; *nicht* ~ not particularly, not much (*od.* very); '**~ling** *m* (3[1]) queer fellow, crank; '**~meldung** *f* special announcement; '**Sn 1.** *cj.* but; **2.** *v/t.* (29) separate, sever, segregate; '**~nummer** *f e-r Zeitung usw.*: special edition; '**~recht** *n* privilege; '**~regelung** *f* separate treatment *od.* settlement; '**~sitzung** *f* special session; '**~stellung** *f* exceptional position; '**~ung** *f* separation; '**~-urlaub** *m* special leave; '**~zug** 🚂 *m* special (*od.* extra) train; '**~zulage** *f* special bonus.
sondieren [zɔn'di:rən] *v/t. u. v/i.* ⚕ probe, (*a.* ⚓) sound (*beide a. fig.*); *fig.* (*v/i.*) explore the ground.
Sonett [zo'nɛt] *n* (3) sonnet.
Sonn|-abend ['zɔn-] *m* Saturday; '**~e** *f* (15) sun; '**Sen** (25) sun; *sich* ~ sun o.s., bask in the sun.
'**Sonnen|-aufgang** *m* sunrise, *Am. a.* sunup; '**~bad** *n* sun-bath; '**~blende** *phot. f* lens shade; '**~blume** *f* sunflower; '**~brand** *m* sunburn; '**~brille** *f* (*eine* a pair of) sun-glasses *pl.*; '**~creme** *f* sun(tan) cream; '**~dach** *n vor Fenstern*: sun-blind; *mot.* sunshine roof; '**~-energie** *f* solar energy; '**~finsternis** *f* eclipse of the sun; '**~fleck** *m* sun-spot; '**~jahr** *n* solar year; '**Sklar** as clear as daylight; (quite) obvious; **~kollektor** ['~kɔlɛktɔr] *m* (8[1]) solar panel; '**~kraftwerk** *n* solar power farm; '**~licht** *n* sunlight; '**~-öl** *n* suntan oil; '**~schein** *m* sunshine; '**~schirm** *m* sunshade; *für Damen*: parasol; '**~schutzcreme** *f* sun(tan) cream; '**~segel** *n* awning; '**~seite** *f* sunny side; '**~stich** *m* sunstroke; '**~strahl** *m* sunbeam; '**~system** *n* solar system; '**~-uhr** *f* sun-dial; '**~-untergang** *m* sunset, *Am. a.* sundown; '**Sverbrannt** sunburnt, tanned; '**~wende** *f* solstice; '**~zelt** *n* awning.

ˈ**sonnig** sunny (*a. fig.*).
ˈ**Sonntag** *m* Sunday; 2**s**, *des* ~**s** on Sundays, every Sunday.
ˈ**sonntäglich** Sunday; ~ *gekleidet* dressed in one's Sunday best.
ˈ**Sonntags|-anzug** *m* Sunday best; ˈ~**-ausflügler(in** *f*) *m* week-ender; ˈ~**fahrer** *m mot. contp.* Sunday driver; ˈ~**fahrkarte** *f* week-end ticket; ˈ~**jäger** *m* would-be sportsman; ˈ~**kind** *n* person born on a Sunday; *er ist ein* ~ he was born under a lucky star; ˈ~**maler** *m* Sunday painter; ˈ~**ruhe** *f* Sunday rest; ˈ~**schule** *f* Sunday school; ˈ~**staat** *m* Sunday best.
sonn|verbrannt [ˈzɔn-] sunburnt, tanned; 2**wendfeier** *f* [ˈ~vɛnt-] midsummer festival.
sonor [zoˈnoːr] sonorous.
sonst [zɔnst] else, otherwise; (*ehemals*) formerly; (*außerdem*) besides; (*für gewöhnlich*) as a rule; usually; *drohend*: or else!; ~ (*noch*) et. *od. jemand?* anything (*od.* anybody, anyone) else?; *wer* ~*?* who else?; *wie* ~ as usual; ~ *nichts* nothing else; ~ *nirgends* nowhere else; ˈ~**ig** other; ˈ~**wie** in some other way; ˈ~**wo** elsewhere.
sooft [zoˈʔoft] whenever.
Sophist [zoˈfist] *m* (12), ~**in** *f* sophist; ~**erei** [~əˈraɪ] *f* (16) sophistry; 2**isch** [~ˈfistiʃ] sophistic(al).
Sopran [zoˈprɑːn] *m* (3[1]) soprano, treble; ~**ist** [~praˈnist] *m* (12), ~**istin** *f* (16[1]) sopranist, soprano.
Sorge [ˈzɔrgə] *f* (15) care; (*Kummer*) sorrow; (*Unruhe*) uneasiness, anxiety; (*Angst*) alarm; ⚖ care (and custody) (*für* of); ~ *tragen für* take care of, see to, (*verbürgen*) ensure; *dafür* ~ *tragen, daß* see to it (*od.* ensure) that; *j-m* ~*n machen* worry a p.; *sich* ~*n machen um* be anxious (*od.* worried) about; *sich* ~*e machen, daß* be concerned that; *sei ohne* ~, *mach dir keine* ~*n* don't worry; *lassen Sie das meine* ~ *sein* leave that to me; *ich habe andere* ~*n* F I have other fish to fry.
ˈ**sorgen** (25): **a**) ~ *für* care for, look after (*a.* = *betreuen*), provide for; (*beschaffen*) provide; *für Lebensmittel usw.*: cater for; *für sich selbst* ~ provide for o.s.; *dafür* ~, *daß* ... take care (*od.* see to it) that; *dafür* ~, *daß et. geschieht* see a th. done; **b**) (*in Sorge sein*) *mst sich* ~ be anxious, worry; *sich* ~ *um* be anxious (*od.* worried) about; ˈ2**falten** *f/pl.* worry-lines; ˈ~**frei**, ˈ~**los** free from care, carefree; ˈ2**kind** *n* problem child; F handful; ˈ~**voll** full of cares; *P.*, *Miene*: anxious, worried.
ˈ**Sorgerecht** *n* care and custody.
Sorg|falt [ˈzɔrkfalt] *f* (16) care, carefulness; ˈ2**fältig** careful; ˈ2**lich** careful, anxious; ˈ2**los** (*gedankenlos*) thoughtless; (*nachlässig*) negligent; (*unachtsam*) careless; (*gleichgültig*) unconcerned; (*sorgenfrei*) carefree; ˈ~**losigkeit** *f* thoughtlessness; negligence; carelessness; unconcern; lightheartedness; ˈ2**sam** careful; (*vorsichtig*) cautious.
Sor|te [ˈzɔrtə] *f* (15) sort, kind, type; ✝ (*Qualität*) quality; ~*n pl.* (*Geld*) foreign notes and coins; 2ˈ**tieren** sort (out); assort; *nach Qualität*: grade.
Sortiment [~tiˈmɛnt] *n* (3) assortment, range; *s.* ~*sbuchhandel*; ~**er** *m*, ~**sbuchhändler** *m* (retail) bookseller; ~**sbuchhandel** *m* (retail) book-trade.
Soße [ˈzoːsə] *f* (15) sauce; (*Bratensaft*) gravy; ˈ~**nschüssel** *f* sauceboat.
Souffl|é [suˈfle] *n* (11) soufflé (*fr.*); ~**eur** [~ˈfløːr] *m* (3[1]), ~**euse** [~ˈfløːzə] *f* (15) prompter; ~**eurkasten** [~ˈfløːr-] *m* prompt-box; 2**ieren** [~ˈfliːrən] prompt (*j-m* a p.).
ˈ**so-undso 1.** *adv.* ~ *viel* a certain amount; ~ *viele sl.* umpteen; ~ *oft* over and over again; **2.** 2: *Herr* ~ Mr. What's his name; 2**vielte** *m, f sl.* umpteenth.
Soutane [zuˈtɑːnə] *f* (15) cassock.
Souterrain [zutɛˈrɛ̃] *n* (11) basement; ~**wohnung** *f* basement flat (*Am.* apartment).
Souverän [zuvəˈrɛːn] *m* (3[1]) sovereign; 2 *adj.* sovereign; *fig.* superior; (*a. adv.*) in superior style; ~**ität** [~rɛniˈtɛːt] *f* (16) sovereignty.
soˈviel *adv.* so much; *noch einmal* ~ as much again, twice as much; *conj.* as much as; ~ *ich weiß* as far as I know, for aught I know.
soˈweit *cj.* as (*od.* so) far as; ~ *ich unterrichtet bin* for aught I know.
sowieˈso anyhow, in any case.
Sowjet [zɔvˈjɛt] *m* (11), 2**isch** Soviet.

so'wohl: ~ ... *als* (*auch*) ... as well as ..., both ... and ...
sozial [zo'tsjɑːl] social; ~*e Wohlfahrt* social welfare; ~*e Fürsorge* social welfare work; **≈-abgaben** *f/pl.* social contribution; **≈-amt** *n* social welfare cent|re, *Am.* -er; **≈beitrag** *m* social insurance contribution; **≈demokrat(in** *f*) *m* social democrat; **≈demokratie** *f* social democracy; **~demokratisch** social-democratic; **≈-einrichtungen** *f/pl.* social services; **≈hilfe** *f* social security (*Am.* welfare); *von der ~ leben* be on welfare; **~isieren** [~tsjali'ziːrən] socialize; **≈i'sierung** *f* socialization; **≈ismus** [~'lismus] *m* (16) socialism; **≈ist** [~'list] *m* (12), **≈istin** *f* socialist; **~istisch** [~'listiʃ] socialistic(ally *adv.*); **~kritisch** [~'tsjɑːl-] socio-critical; **≈lasten** *f/pl.* social charges; **≈leistung** *f* social contribution; **≈pädagogik** *f* social p(a)edagogics; **≈politik** *f* social policy; **~politisch** socio-political; **≈-produkt** *n* (gross) national product; **≈-unterstützung** *f* poor (*od.* public) relief; **≈verhalten** *n* social behavio(u)r; **≈versicherung** *f* social insurance; **≈wissenschaft** *f* social science, sociology; **≈wissenschaftler** *m* sociologist; **≈wohnung** *f* council flat, *Am.* publicly financed apartment.
Soziolog|e [zotsjo'loːgə] *m* (13) sociologist; **~ie** [~lo'giː] *f* (15) sociology; **≈isch** [~'loːgiʃ] sociological.
Sozius ['zoːtsjus] *m* (14²) partner; **'~fahrer(in** *f*) *m* pillion-rider; **'~sitz** *mot. m* pillion; *auf dem ~ mitfahren* ride pillion.
sozu'sagen so to speak, as it were.
Spachtel ['ʃpaxtəl] *m* (7) spatula; *a.* = **'~masse** *f* surfacer; **'~messer** *n* putty knife; **'≈n** ⊕ surface.
Spagat [ʃpa'gɑːt] *m u. n* (3): ~ *machen* do the splits *pl.*
Spaghetti [ʃpa'gɛti] *pl.* (*inv.*) spaghetti.
spähen ['ʃpɛːən] (25) look out (*nach* for); (*blicken*) peer; (*spionieren*) spy; ⚔ scout.
'Späher *m* (7), **'~in** *f* spy; ⚔ scout.
'Späh|trupp ⚔ *m* reconnaissance patrol; **'~wagen** ⚔ *m* reconnaissance (*od.* scout) car.
Spalier [ʃpa'liːr] *n* (3¹) espalier, trellis; *fig.* lane; ~ *bilden* form a lane; **~baum** *m* espalier (tree); **~-obst** *n* espalier fruit; *engS.* wall-fruit.
Spalt [ʃpalt] *m* (3), **'~e** *f* (15) crack, split, cleft, crevice, fissure; (*Lücke*) gap; *nur ~e*: *typ.* column; (*Gletscher≈*) crevasse; **'≈bar** cleavable; *phys.* fissile, fissionable; **'≈en** (26; *p.p. mst ge~; a. sich*) split, cleave; chop; rend; (*teilen*) divide; ⚗ decompose; **'≈enlang** covering several columns; **'~pilz** *m* fission fungus, 🕮 schizomycete; **'~ung** *f* splitting, cleavage; *biol., phys.* fission; *fig.* split; cleavage; *e-s Landes, der Meinungen usw.*: division; *eccl.* schism.
Span [ʃpɑːn] *m* (3³) chip, shaving; (*Splitter*) splinter; **'≈-abhebend** ⊕ metal-cutting; **'~ferkel** *n* sucking pig, porkling.
Spange ['ʃpaŋə] *f* (15) clasp; (*Schnalle*) buckle; (*Brosche*) clip; (*Arm≈*) bracelet; (*Haar≈*) slide; (*Ordens≈*) bar; **'~nschuh** *m* strap shoe.
Span|ier ['ʃpɑːnjər] *m* (7), **'~ierin** *f* (16¹) Spaniard; **'≈isch** Spanish.
'Span|korb *m* chip basket; **'≈los** ⊕ non-cutting.
spann¹ [ʃpan] *pret. v. spinnen.*
Spann² *m* (3) instep; **'~beton** *m* pre-stressed concrete; **'~bettuch** *n* fitted sheet; **'~draht** *m* tension wire; **'~e** *f* (15) span; *Zeit*: (short) space; ✝ (*Verdienst≈*) margin; **'≈en** stretch, strain; *Gewehr*: cock; *Bogen*: bend; *Feder, Schraube usw.*: tighten; *Muskeln*: flex; *Neugier usw.*: excite; *s. Folter*; *vor den Wagen ~* put to the carriage; ⊕ *Werkstück*: clamp, chuck; (*v/i.*) *Kleid usw.*: be (too) tight; *s. a. gespannt*; **'≈end** exciting, thrilling, gripping; **'~feder** *f* tension spring; **'~futter** *n* chuck; **'~kraft** *f* elasticity; *fig. a.* energy; **'≈kräftig** elastic(ally *adv.*); **'~ung** *f allg.* tension; ⚡ *a.* voltage; ⊕ *verformende*: strain, *elastische*: stress; △ span; (*Aufmerksamkeit*) close attention; *nervliche*: tension (*a. pol. usw.*), tenseness; (*Ungewißheit*) suspense; *mit* (*od. voll*) ~ with bated breath, intently; *in ~ versetzen* thrill, excite; **'≈ungsgeladen** *Film usw.*: exciting, gripping; **'~ungsprüfer** ⚡ *m* voltage detector; **'~ungsregler** ⚡ *m* voltage regulator; **'~ungsverhältnis** *n* ten-

sion, tense relationship; '**~weite** *f* spread; ⚠, ✈ span; *fig.* range.
'**Spanplatte** *f* chipboard.
Spant [ʃpant] *n* (5) ⚓ rib; ✈ frame.
Spar|brief ['ʃpa:rbri:f] *m* savings certificate; '**~buch** *n* savings account (pass-)book; '**~büchse** *f* money-box; '**~-einlagen** *f/pl.* savings deposits; '**2en** *v/t. u. v/i.* (25) *allg.* save; (*sich einschränken*) economize, (*sparsam umgehen mit*) be sparing of (*a. fig.*); '**~er** *m* (6) saver; *Bank*: depositor.
Spargel ['ʃpargəl] *m* (7) asparagus; '**~spitzen** *f/pl.* asparagus tips.
'**Spar|guthaben** *n* savings balance; (*Konto*) savings account; '**~haushalt** *m* austerity budget; '**~kasse** *f* savings-bank; '**~konto** *n* savings account.
spärlich ['ʃpɛ:rliç] scant(y); (*zerstreut, dünn*) sparse; (*dürftig*) meag|re, *Am.* -er; '**2keit** *f* scantiness; sparseness.
'**Spar|maßnahmen** *f/pl.* austerity measures, economy drive *sg.*; '**~packung** *f* economy size; '**~programm** *n* austerity program(me); *e-r Waschmaschine*: energy-saving cycle.
Sparren ['ʃparən] *m* (6) spar, rafter; *fig.* *e-n ~ zuviel haben* be not quite right in the upper story.
sparsam ['ʃpa:rza:m] saving, economical (*mit* of); *~ umgehen mit* use sparingly, *fig. mit Lob usw.*: *a.* be chary of; '**2keit** *f* economy, thrift; (*strengste Einfachheit*) austerity; (*Knauserigkeit*) parsimony.
spartanisch [ʃpar'ta:niʃ] Spartan (*a. fig.*).
Sparte ['ʃpartə] *f* (15) line.
'**Spar|vertrag** *m* savings agreement; '**~zulage** *f* (tax-free) savings bonus.
Spaß [ʃpa:s] *m* (3² *u.* ³) fun; (*Scherz*) joke, jest; (*Gaudi*) lark; (*Streich*) prank; *aus* (*od. im od. zum*) *~* for (*od.* in) fun; *~ machen* amuse (*j-m* a p.), (*scherzen*) be joking; *s-n ~ treiben mit* make fun of; *das macht* (*keinen*) *~* that's (no) fun; *~ beiseite* joking apart; *viel ~!* have a good time!; *s. verstehen*; '**2en** (27) joke, jest; '**2haft**, '**2ig** facetious, jocose; (*komisch*) funny; '**~macher** *m* wag, joker; *s. a. Hanswurst*; '**~verderber** *m* spoil-sport, kill-joy, F wet blanket; '**~vogel** *m* wag.
spast|isch ⚕ ['spastiʃ], **2iker** ['~ikər] *m* (7), '**2ikerin** *f* (16¹) spastic.
Spat [ʃpa:t] *m* (3) *min.* spar; *vet.* spavin.
spät [ʃpɛ:t] late; *zu ~ kommen* be late (*zu* for); *wie ~ ist es?* what time is it?, what is the time?
Spatel ['ʃpa:təl] *m* (7), *f* (15) ⚕ spatula; *löffelförmig*: scoop.
Spaten ['ʃpa:tən] *m* (6) spade.
'**spät|er** later; (*folgend*) subsequent, posterior (*als* to); *adv. a.* '**~erhin** later on; **~estens** ['~əstəns] at the latest; '**2folgen** ⚕ *f/pl.* late sequelae; '**2herbst** *m* later part of autumn *od. bsd. Am.* fall, late autumn; '**2-obst** *n* late fruit; '**2sommer** *m* late (*od.* Indian) summer.
Spatz [ʃpats] *m* (12) sparrow; *das pfeifen die ~en von den Dächern* it is everybody's secret.
'**Spät|zünder** *m* F: *ein ~ sein* be slow on the uptake; '**~zündung** *mot. f* retarded ignition.
spazieren [ʃpa'tsi:rən] (sn) walk, stroll; **~fahren** *v/i.* (sn) take a drive; *v/t.* (h.) drive out; **~führen** take (out) for a walk; **~gehen** (sn) take (*od.* go for) a walk.
Spa'zier|fahrt *f* drive; *zu Wasser*: sail, row; **~gang** *m* walk, stroll; *fig.* (*leichter Sieg*) walkover; *e-n ~ machen* take a walk; **~gänger** [~gɛŋər] *m* (7) stroller, promenader; **~ritt** *m* ride; **~stock** *m* walking-stick; **~weg** *m* walk.
Specht [ʃpɛçt] *m* (3) woodpecker.
Speck [ʃpɛk] *m* (3) (*Schweine2*) bacon; *weitS.* fat; *s. Made*; '**~bauch** *m* paunch; '**2ig** fat(ty); (*schmierig*) greasy; '**~schnitte** *f* slice of bacon, rasher (of bacon); '**~schwarte** *f* rind (*od.* skin) of bacon; '**~seite** *f* flitch of bacon; '**~stein** *m* soap-stone.
sped|ieren [ʃpe'di:rən] forward, haul; ⚓ *u. Am.* ship; **2iteur** [~di'tø:r] *m* (3¹) forwarding agent, carrier; (*Möbel2*) (furniture) remover.
Spedition [~di'tsjo:n] *f* forwarding, ⚓ *u. Am.* shipping; *a.* = **~sgeschäft** *n* forwarding trade; (*Firma*) forwarding agency, carriers *pl.*
Speer [ʃpe:r] *m* (3) spear; (*Wurf2*) javelin; '**~werfen** *n Sport*: javelin-throw(ing).
Speiche ['ʃpaıçə] *f* (15) spoke; *anat.* radius.
Speichel ['ʃpaıçəl] *m* (7) spittle,

saliva; (*Geifer*) slaver; '**~drüse** *f* salivary gland; '**~fluß** *m* salivation; '**~lecker** *m* toady, sycophant; **~lecke'rei** *f* toadyism.

Speicher ['ʃpaɪçər] *m* (7) (*Getreide*~) granary, *Am.* elevator, (*Möbel-, Waren*~) warehouse, store; (*Wasser*~) reservoir; (*Dachboden*) loft; *Computer*: store, memory; '**~chip** *m Computer*: memory chip; '**~kapazität** *f Computer*: memory (*od.* storage) capacity; '**~modul** *n Computer*: memory module; '**~n** store (up); *Computer*, ⚡: store; '**~ung** *f a.* ⚡ *usw.* storage.

speien ['ʃpaɪən] *v/i. u. v/t.* (30) spit; ([*sich*] *erbrechen*) vomit.

Speise ['ʃpaɪzə] *f* (15) food; (*Mahl*) meal; (*Kost*) fare; (*Gericht*) dish; *s. Süß*~; '**~brei** 🕮 *m* chyme; '**~-eis** *n* ice-cream; '**~fett** *n* edible fat; '**~haus** *n* eating-house; '**~kammer** *f* larder, pantry; '**~karte** *f* menu, bill of fare; '**~leitung** ⊕ *f* feeder (line).

'**speisen** (27) *v/i.* eat, have a meal; *im Gasthaus*: take one's meals; (*zu Mittag* ~) lunch, dine; (*zu Abend* ~) have supper; *v/t.* feed (*a.* ⊕); '~**folge** *f* menu.

'**Speise|-öl** *n* salad-oil; '**~rohr** ⊕ *n* feed pipe; '**~röhre** *anat. f* gullet, 🕮 (o)esophagus; '**~saal** *m* dining-hall; '**~saft** 🕮 *m* chyle; '**~schrank** food-cupboard, (meat-)safe; '**~wagen** 🚃 *m* dining-car, *bsd. Am.* diner; '**~zettel** *m s. Speisekarte*; '**~zimmer** *n* dining-room.

'**Speisung** *f* feeding.

Spektakel [ʃpɛk'tɑːkəl] *m* (7) noise, racket; *s. Lärm.*

Spektr|al-analyse [ʃpɛk'trɑːl-] *f* spectral (*od.* spectrum) analysis; **~um** ['~trum] *n* (9[2]) spectrum.

Speku|lant [ʃpeku'lant] *m* (12) speculator; **~lation** [~la'tsjoːn] *f allg.* speculation; **~lati'onsgeschäft** *n* speculative operation *od.* transaction; ~'**lieren** *allg.* speculate (*auf acc.* on).

Spelunke [ʃpe'luŋkə] *f* (15) den; (*niedere Kneipe*) jerry-shop, *Am.* F dive, *sl.* joint.

Spelz ⚘ [ʃpɛlts] *m* (3[2]) spelt; '**~e** ⚘ *f* (15) beard, 🕮 glume.

Spende ['ʃpɛndə] *f* (15) gift; (*Beitrag*) contribution; (*Almosen*) alms, charity; (*Stiftung*) donation; '~**n** (26) give; *bsd.* ⚕ *Blut usw.*: donate; *Sakrament*: administer; (*austeilen*) deal out, dispense; (*beitragen*) contribute (*zu* to); '**~n-aktion** *f* collection campaign; '**~r** *m* (7), '**~rin** *f* (16[1]) giver; (*bsd.* ⚕ *Blut*~, *Herz*~ *usw.*) donor; contributor; (*Verteiler*) distributor, (*a. Automat*) dispenser; (*Wohltäter*) benefactor.

spen'dieren *v/t.* stand; *j-m et.* ~ treat a p. to a th., stand a p. a th.; *v/i.* stand treat.

Sperber ['ʃpɛrbər] *m* sparrow hawk.

Sperling ['ʃpɛrliŋ] *m* (3[1]) sparrow.

Sperma ['spɛrma] *biol. n* (9[1], *pl. a.* -*ta*) sperm.

'**sperr|-angel'weit** wide open; '~**ballon** ⚔ *m* barrage balloon.

Sperr|e ['ʃpɛrə] *f* (15) shutting, closing; (*Versperrung*) block(ing); ⚓ embargo; (*Blockade*) blockade; (*Gesundheits*~) quarantine; (*Eingang*) gate; 🚃 barrier, *Am.* gate; (*Straßen*~) barricade, road block; (*Sperrbaum*) bar; ⚔ barrage; ⊕ look, stop, detent; (*Verbot*) prohibition, ban; *Sport*: suspension; '~**en** (25) (*auseinander*~) spread open; *die Beine*: straddle; *typ.* space (out); (*ver*~) bar, stop; (*schließen*) close, shut; ⊕ lock, stop, arrest; *Straße*: block, barricade, *amtlich*: close; ⚓, ⚔ *e-n Hafen*: lock; (*blockieren*) blockade; *Warenverkehr*: embargo; *Konto, Löhne, Zahlungen*: stop, freeze; *Gas usw.*: cut off; *Sport*: block, *unfair*: obstruct, *durch Spiel- od. Startverbot*: disqualify, suspend; *ins Gefängnis* ~ put in prison; *sich* ~ (*gegen et.*) oppose (a th.), struggle (against a th.); *gesperrt gedruckt* spaced out; '**~feuer** ⚔ *n* barrage, curtain-fire; '**~gebiet** *n s. Sperrzone*; '**~gut** *n* bulky goods *pl.*, *Am.* bulk freight; '**~hahn** *m* stopcock; '**~haken** *m* click, catch; '**~holz** ⊕ *n* plywood; '~**ig** bulky; '**~kette** *f* drag-chain; '**~konto** *n* blocked account; '**~müll** *m* bulky refuse; '~(**r**)**ad** *n* ratchet-wheel; '**~sitz** *thea. m* stall, reserved seat, *Am.* orchestra (-seat); '**~ung** *f* barring; stoppage; blocking; ⚓ blockade; *s. Sperre*; '**~zoll** *m* prohibitive duty; '**~zone** *f* prohibited area.

Spesen ['ʃpeːzən] *f/pl. inv.* charges, (petty) expenses; '~**frei** free of charges; **'~konto** *n* expense account; **'~rechnung** *f* bill of expenses.

Spezi ['ʃpe:tsi] F *m* (11) crony, *Am.* buddy.

Spezial|-ausbildung [ʃpe'tsja:l-] *f* special training; **~fach** *n* special(i)ty; **~gebiet** *n* special field; **~geschäft** *n* one-line shop; **~i'sieren** [~tsjali-] (*a. sich*) specialize; **~ist(in** *f*) [~'list] *m* (12) specialist; **~ität** [~li'tɛ:t] *f* (16) speciality; (*Sonderfach*) *bsd. Am.* specialty; **~sprunglauf** [ʃpe'tsja:l-] *m* ski-jumping proper.

speziell [ʃpe'tsjɛl] special, specific(ally *adv.*).

Spezies ['spe:tsjɛs] *f inv.* species.

spezifisch [ʃpe'tsi:fiʃ] specific(ally *adv.*); *~es Gewicht* specific gravity.

spezifizieren [ʃpetsifi'tsi:rən] specify, *Am. a.* itemize.

Sphär|e ['sfɛ:rə] *f* (15) sphere; **'~isch** spherical.

spicken ['ʃpikən] (25) lard; *fig. Rede usw.*: interlard; F (*abschreiben*) crib; *gespickt mit* bristling with.

spie [ʃpi:] *pret. v. speien.*

Spiegel ['ʃpi:gəl] *m* (7) mirror, (looking-)glass; *phys.*, ⚕ speculum; ⚓ stern; (*Stand, Höhe, Niveau*) level; *s. Satz~, Meeres~, Wasser~*; **'~bild** *n* mirror image; *fig.* reflection; **'~-blank** shining; **'~-ei** *n* fried egg; **~fechterei** ['~fɛçtə'raɪ] *f* (16) *fig.* humbug, make-believe; **'~glas** *n* plate-glass; **'~glatt** as smooth as a mirror, dead-smooth; **'~n** *v/i.* shine; *v/t.* mirror, reflect (*beide a. fig.*); *sich ~* be mirrored *od.* reflected; (*sich besehen*) look at o.s. in the glass; **'~reflexkamera** *f* reflex camera; **'~-scheibe** *f* (pane of) plate-glass; **'~-schrift** *f* mirror-writing; *typ.* reflected face; **'~teleskop** *n* reflector (telescope); **'~ung** *f* reflection; (*Luft~*) mirage.

Spiel [ʃpi:l] *n* (3) play; (*Karten~, Schach~, Sport~ usw.*) game (*a. Tennis; a. fig. b.s.*); (*Wettkampf*) match; ♪, *thea.* playing, (*Vorführung*) performance, (*Stück*) play; *ein ~ Karten* a pack (*Am.* deck) of cards; ⊕ play, clearance; (*gewagtes ~, Glücks~*) gamble; *leichtes ~ haben* have little trouble; *gewonnenes ~ haben* have made it; *im ~ sein (bei et.)* be involved (in); *ins ~ bringen (kommen)* bring (come) into play; *fig. das ~ verloren geben* throw up the sponge; *auf dem ~ stehen* be at stake; *aufs ~ setzen* stake, jeopardize, *a. sein Leben*: risk; *aus dem ~e lassen* leave out; *sein ~ treiben mit* trifle with; *falsches ~* double-dealing; *ein falsches ~ treiben mit* practise upon; *fig. das ~ ist aus* the game is up; *s. gut, Hand*; **'~-anzug** *m für Kinder*: rompers, play-suit; **'~-art** ⚘, *zo. fig. f* variety; **'~-automat** *m* slot machine; **'~ball** *m* ball; *Tennis*: game ball; *fig.* sport, plaything; *ein ~ der Wellen sein* be at the mercy of the waves; **'~bank** *f* gaming-table; *s. Spielkasino*; **'~dose** *f* musical box; **'~en** *v/i. u. v/t.* (25) *allg.* play (*a. Muskeln, Lächeln usw.*); *Karten, Schach usw.*: play *cards, etc.*; *um Einsatz*: gamble; *thea.* play, act, perform, *e-e Rolle*: *a.* do; *~ mit* (*fingern*) toy with, *mit j-s Gefühlen a.* trifle with; *mit e-m Gedanken ~* toy (*od.* flirt) with an idea; (*vortäuschen*) feign; *den Höflichen ~* do the polite; *Sport*: *A. spielte gegen B.* A. played B.; *ins Blaue ~* have a bluish tint; *fig. ~ lassen* bring into play; *s. Hand, Rolle, Theater*; **'~end** *fig.*: *~ (leicht)* easily, with effortless ease; *~ gewinnen* win hands down; *~ leicht sein* be child's play (*od. Am. sl.* a cinch).

'Spieler *m* (7), **'~in** *f allg.* player; (*Glücks~*) gambler; **~ei** [~'raɪ] *f* (16) play, sport; *fig.* trifle; *s. Spielsachen.*

'Spiel|-ergebnis *n Sport*: score; **'~-feld** *n Sport*: field, ground, pitch; *Tennis*: court; **'~film** *m* feature (film); **'~folge** *f* program(me); **'~-führer** *m* (team) captain; **'~gefährte** *m*, **'~genosse** *m* playmate; **'~geld** *n* play-money; (*Einsatz*) stake, pool; **'~gewinn** *m* gambling profit; **'~halle** *f* amusement arcade; **'~hölle** *f* gambling-den; **'~kamerad** *s. Spielgenosse*; **'~karte** *f* playing-card; **'~kasino** *n* (gambling) casino; **'~leiter** *m thea.* stage-manager; *Film*: director; **'~-mann** *m hist.* minstrel; ⚔ bandsman; **'~marke** *f* counter, chip; **'~-plan** *thea. m* program(me); (*Repertoire*) repertory; **'~platz** *m* playground; **'~raum** *fig. m* free play, elbow-room; (*Frist*) margin, latitude; ⊕ play, clearance; *freien ~ haben* have full scope; **'~regel** *f* rule (of the game); **'~sachen** *f/pl.* playthings, toys; **'~schuld** *f* gambling-debt; **'~schule** *f* pre-school, infant-

-school; '**~tisch** *m* card-table, gaming-table; '**~-uhr** *f* musical clock; '**~verderber(in** *f*) *m* spoil-sport, kill-joy; '**~verlängerung** *f* *Sport*: extra time; '**~waren** *f/pl.* *s.* *Spielsachen*; '**~warenhändler(in** *f*) *m* toy-merchant, F toyman; '**~warenhandlung** *f* toy-shop; '**~wut** *f* passion for gambling; '**~zeit** *f* *thea.*, *Sport*: season; *e-s Kampfes*: time of play; *e-s Films* (*Laufzeit*): run; '**~zeug** *n* toy(s *pl.*), plaything(s *pl.*).

Spieß [ʃpi:s] *m* (3²) spear, pike; (*Brat*~) spit; *typ.* work-up; *am ~ braten* barbecue; *den ~ umdrehen* turn the tables (*gegen* on); *schreien wie am ~* F cry blue murder; '**~bürger** *m* bourgeois, Philistine, *Am.* *a.* Babbitt, *sl.* square; '**~bürgerlich** bourgeois, Philistine, *sl.* square; '**~bürgertum** *n* philistinism, *Am.* *a.* babbittry; '**~en** (27) pierce; spear; spit; '**~er** *m* (7) *s.* *Spießbürger*; '**~ig** *s.* *spießbürgerlich*; '**~geselle** *m* accomplice; '**~ruten** *f/pl.*: *~ laufen* run the ga(u)ntlet (*a. fig.*).

Spill ⚓ [ʃpil] *n* (3) capstan.

spinal [ʃpi'nɑ:l] spinal; *~e Kinderlähmung* infantile paralysis, polio (-myelitis).

Spinat [ʃpi'nɑ:t] *m* (3) spinach.

Spind [ʃpint] *n*, *a.* *m* (3) wardrobe, press; *bsd.* ⚔ locker.

Spindel ['ʃpindəl] *f* (7) spindle; (*Spinnrocken*) distaff; ⊕ *Presse*: screw; (*Dorn*) mandril; (*Leit*~) lead screw; '**~dürr** (as) lean as a rake, spindly.

Spinett [ʃpi'nɛt] ♪ *n* (3) spinet.

Spinn|e ['ʃpinə] *f* (15) spider; '**~e-'feind:** *j-m ~ sein* hate a p. like poison; '**~en** (30) *v/t.* spin; (*ausdenken*) hatch; *v/i.* spin; *Katze*: purr; F (*verrückt sein*) be mad; '**~er** *m* (7), '**~erin** *f* spinner; F (*Narr*) crank; **~erei** [~'raɪ] *f* spinning; (*Fabrik*) spinning-mill; '**~gewebe** *n* cobweb; '**~maschine** *f* spinning-machine; '**~rad** *n* spinning-wheel; '**~rocken** *m* distaff; '**~webe** *f* cobweb.

spintisieren [ʃpinti'zi:rən] muse [(*über acc.* on).

Spion [ʃpi'o:n] *m* (3¹), **~in** *f* spy; **~age** [~o'nɑ:ʒə] *f* (15) espionage, spying; **~age-abwehr** *f* counter-espionage, *Am.* counter-intelligence; **~ieren** [~'ni:rən] spy.

Spiral|e [ʃpi'rɑ:lə] *f* (15) spiral (line); ⊕ worm, helix, coil; ✈ (*Preis*~ *usw.*) spiral; ⚕ *zur Empfängnisverhütung*: coil; **~feder** *f* spiral spring; **~förmig, ~ig** spiral; **~kabel** *n* spiral (spring) cord.

Spiritismus [ʃpiri'tismus] *m* (16) spiritualism, spiritism.

Spiri'tist *m* (12), **~in** *f* spiritualist; **~isch** spiritualistic, spiritist.

Spirituosen [~tu'o:zən] *pl.* spirits, spirituous liquors.

Spiritus ['ʃpi:ritus] *m* (*inv.*, *pl.* *a.* 14²) spirit, alcohol; *gr.* breathing; '**~kocher** *m* spirit stove.

Spital [ʃpi'tɑ:l] *n* (1²) hospital.

Spitz [ʃpits] **1.** *m* (3²) Pomeranian (dog); **2.** ~ pointed; *fig.* *a.* biting; (*kränklich*) peaked; & acute; *~ zulaufen* taper; '**~bart** *m* pointed beard; '**~bauch** *m* paunch; '**~bogen** *m* pointed arch; '**~bube** *m* thief; *weitS.* rogue, rascal; '**~bubenstreich** *m*, **~büberei** [~by:bə'raɪ] *f* roguery, rascality; **~bübisch** ['~by:biʃ] roguish.

Spitz|e ['ʃpitsə] *f* (15) *allg.* point (*a. Kinn*~, *Schuh*~); (*Berg*~) top, summit, peak; (*Baum*~) top; (*Turm*~) spire; (*spitzes Ende*, *a. e-s Körperteils*) tip; (*~engewebe*) lace; ⊕ *Werkzeugmaschine*: cent|re, *Am.* -er; (*~ntempo*) top speed; (*Höchstmaß*, *-wert*) peak; *e-r Kolonne*, *e-s Unternehmens usw.*: head; ⚔ (*Angriffs*~) (spear)head; *Sport*: leading group, (*Führung*) lead; *Fußball*: striker(s *pl.*); (*spitze Bemerkung*) pointed remark, cut; *die ~n der Gesellschaft* the cream of society; *j-m die ~ bieten* make head against, defy; *Sport*: *an der ~ liegen* be in the lead; *an der ~* (*e-r S.*) *stehen* be at the head (of a th.); *auf die ~ treiben* carry to extremes; '**~el** *m* (7) police--spy, informer; *weitS.* spy; '**~en** (27) point, sharpen; *den Mund ~* purse (up) one's lips; *die Ohren ~* prick up one's ears; F (*sich*) *auf et.* (*acc.*) *~* be eager about a th.

'**Spitzen|belastung** ⚡ *f* peak load; '**~drehbank** *f* cent|re (*Am.* -er) lathe; '**~gehalt** *n* top salary; '**~geschwindigkeit** *f* top speed; '**~gruppe** *f* leading group; '**~kandidat** *m* top candidate, front-runner; '**~klasse** *f* champion class, top-rankers *pl.*; élite (*fr.*); '**~kleid** *n* lace dress; '**~leistung** *f* *allg.* peak performance, record; ⊕ peak output; '**~lohn** *m* peak wage(s *pl.*); '**~politiker(in** *f*) *m* top politician; '**~reiter** *m bsd. Sport*: front-runner, leader; '**~tanz** *m* toe-dancing; '**~technologie** *f* leading technology; '**~verdiener(in** *f*) *m* top earner; '**~zeit** *f Sport*: record time; ⚡ *in ~en* (*des Verbrauches*) at peak periods.

'**spitz|findig** subtle; hair-splitting; '**2findigkeit** *f* subtlety, subtleness, sophistry; '**2hacke** *f*, '**2haue** *f* pick (-ax[e]); '**~ig** *s. spitz*; '**~kriegen** F: *et. ~* find a th. out; '**2maus** *f* shrew (-mouse); '**2name** *m* nickname; '**~wink(e)lig** ⊿ acute-angled.

Spleen [spli:n] *m* (3[1]) crotchet, craze; '**2ig** crotchety, eccentric.

Splint ⊕ [ʃplint] *m* (3) cotter.

Splitt [ʃplit] *m* (3[1]) stone chips *pl.*

Splitter ['ʃplitər] *m* (7) splinter; fragment; (*Span*) chip; *biblisch*: mote (*in another's eye*); '**2frei** splinter-proof; *Glas*: non-splintering; '**~gruppe** *pol. f* splinter group; '**2ig** splintery; '**2n** *v/t. u. v/i.* (29, h. *u.* sn) splinter; '**2'nackt** stark naked; '**~partei** *parl. f* splinter party.

Spoiler *mot.* ['spɔʏlər] *m* spoiler.

spontan [ʃpɔn'tɑ:n] spontaneous.

sporadisch [spo'rɑ:diʃ] sporadic (-ally *adv.*).

Spore ⚘ ['ʃpo:rə] *f* (15) spore.

Sporen ['ʃpo:rən] *pl. v. Sporn.*

Sporn [ʃpɔrn] *m* (5[3]) spur; ✈ (tail) skid; *fig.* stimulus; *dem Pferd die Sporen geben* put spurs to; *sich die Sporen verdienen* win one's spurs; '**2en** (25) spur; **~rädchen** ['~rɛ:tçən] *n* rowel; **2streichs** ['~ʃtraɪçs] post-haste, directly.

Sport [ʃpɔrt] *m* (3) sport; athletics *pl.*; *fig.* (*Steckenpferd*) hobby; *~ treiben* go in for sports; '**~-anlage** *f* athletic ground(s *pl.*), sports facilities *pl.*; '**~-anzug** *m* sports suit; '**~art** *f* (form of) sport; (*Disziplin*) event; '**~-artikel** *m/pl.* sports goods; '**~bericht** *m* sporting report; '**~berichterstatter(in** *f*) *m* sports reporter.

Sporteln ['ʃpɔrtəln] **1.** *f/pl.* (15) perquisites, fees; **2.** 2 F (29) *v/i* go in for sports.

'**Sport|fest** *n* sports day; '**~flugzeug** *n* sporting plane; '**~freund(in** *f*) *m* sports enthusiast; '**~geschäft** *n* sporting-goods shop; '**~halle** *f* gymnasium; '**~hemd** *n* sports shirt; '**~herz** ⚕ *n* athlete's heart; '**~hochschule** *f* physical education college; '**~hose** *f* shorts *pl.*; '**~jacke** *f* sports jacket; '**~kleidung** *f* sportswear; '**~klub** *m* sports club; '**~lehrer(in** *f*) *m* sports instructor, trainer; '**~lenkrad** *mot. n* sports steering wheel; '**~ler** *m* (7) sportsman; '**~lerin** *f* (16[1]) sportswoman; '**2lich** sporting, athletic; (*fair*) sportsmanlike; '**~lichkeit** *f* sportsmanship; '**~nachrichten** *f/pl.* sporting news; '**~platz** *m* athletic (*od.* sports) ground *od.* field; '**~schuh** *m* sports shoe; '**~smann** *m* sportsman; '**~tauchen** *n* skin (*od.* scuba) diving; '**2treibend** sporting; '**~ver-anstaltung** *f* sport(ing) event; '**~wagen** *m mot.* sports car; *für Kinder*: pushchair; '**~waren** *f/pl.* sports articles; '**~zeitung** *f* sporting paper.

Spotmarkt ['spɔt-] *m für Erdöl*: spot market.

Spott [ʃpɔt] *m* (3) mockery; *lächerlich machend*: derision; *verächtlich*: scorn; *gutmütig*: banter; (*seinen*) *~ treiben mit* make sport of; '**~bild** *n* caricature; '**2'billig** dirt-cheap.

Spöttel|ei [ʃpœtə'laɪ] *f* (16) mockery, raillery, sarcasm; '**2n** (29) mock, gibe (*über acc.* at).

spotten ['ʃpɔtən] (26) mock, scoff (*über acc.* at), jeer (at), deride; *fig.* (*gen.*) defy; *s. Beschreibung.*

Spötter ['ʃpœtər] *m* (7), '**~in** *f* (16[1]) scoffer, mocker; cynic; **~ei** [~'raɪ] *f* (16) mockery, derision.

'**Spott|gedicht** *n* squib, satirical poem; '**~gelächter** *n* derisive laugh(ter); '**~geld** *n s. Spottpreis*; *für ein ~* for a mere song.

'**spöttisch** mocking; derisive; sarcastic; ironical.

'**Spott|lied** *n* satirical song; '**~lust** *f* mocking spirit; '**~name** *m* nickname; '**~preis** *m* ridiculous price, trifling sum; '**~schrift** *f* satire, lampoon.

sprach [ʃprɑ:x] *pret. v. sprechen.*

'**Sprache** *f* (15) (*Sprachfähigkeit*) speech; (*~ e-s Volkes*) language, *gewählter*: tongue; (*Landes2*) vernacular; (*Ausdrucksweise*) language, parlance; (*Mundart*) idiom; (*Stil*) diction; (*Aussprache*) articulation; *heraus mit der ~!* out with it!, speak out!; *nicht mit der ~ herauswollen* hem and haw; *et. zur ~ bringen* bring up; *zur ~ kommen* come up.

'**Sprach|-eigenheit** *f*, '**~-eigentümlichkeit** *f* idiomatic expression, idiom; '**~endienst** *m* translating service; '**~fehler** *m* grammatical mistake; ⚕ speech defect; '**~forscher** *m* philologist; linguist; '**~forschung** *f* philology; linguistics; '**~führer** *m* phrase-book; '**~gebiet** *n* speech area; '**~gebrauch** *m* usage; '**~gefühl** *n* linguistic instinct; '**~gruppe** *f* speech community; '**~-insel** *f* speech island; '**~kenner** *m* linguist; '**~kundig** versed in languages; '**~labor** *n* language laboratory; '**~lehre** *f* grammar; '**~lehrer(in** *f*) *m* teacher of languages, language-master; '**~lich** of language(s), lingual; (*grammatisch*) grammatical; '**~los** speechless; '**~mittler** *m* interpreter; '**~raum** *m* speech area; '**~regel** *f* rule of grammar; **~reiniger** ['~raɪnigər] *m* purifier of a language; *b.s.* purist; '**~rohr** *n* speaking-tube, megaphone; *fig.* mouthpiece; '**~schatz** *m* vocabulary; '**~störung** *f* speech disorder; '**~studium** *n* study of languages; '**~-unterricht** *m* instruction in languages; *englischer ~* English lessons *pl.*; '**~werkzeug** *n* organ of speech; '**~widrig** incorrect, ungrammatical; '**~wissenschaft** *f* science of language, philology; *engS.* linguistics *pl.*; '**~wissenschaftler** *m* philologist; linguist; '**~wissenschaftlich** philological; linguistic(ally *adv.*).

sprang [ʃpraŋ] *pret. v. springen.*

Spray [ʃpreː; spreː] *n* (11) spray.

Sprech|-anlage ['ʃprɛç-] *f* intercom; *an der Haustür*: entryphone; '**~-art** *f* manner of speaking; '**~blase** *f in Comics*: balloon; '**~chor** *m* speaking chorus; '**~en** *v/i. u. v/t.* (30) speak (*mit* to; *über acc.*, *von* of, about); (*sich unterhalten*) talk (*mit* to, with; *über acc.*, *von* about, of, over); *~ mit* (*konsultieren*) see; *über Politik* (*Geschäfte*) *~* talk politics (business); *er ist nicht zu ~* he is engaged (*od.* busy); *zu ~ kommen auf* (*acc.*) come to speak of; *~ für* speak for *a p.*, *vermittelnd, befürwortend*: plead for; *j-n zu ~ wünschen* wish to see a p.; *von et. anderem ~* change the subject; *s. Recht, schuldig, Urteil, Tischgebet*; *das spricht für j-n od. et.* that speaks well for; *das spricht für sich selbst* this tells its own tale; *laßt Blumen ~!* say it with flowers!; '**~end** *fig. Ähnlichkeit*: speaking; *Augen, Blick*: eloquent; '**~er** *m* (7), '**~erin** *f* speaker; (*Wortführer*) spokesman; *Radio*: (*Ansager*) announcer; '**~frequenz** ⚡ *f* speech frequency; '**~funk** *m* radiotelephony, voice radio; '**~funkgerät** *n* radiotelephone; '**~platte** *f* speech record; '**~stunde** *f ärztliche*: consulting hour; *amtliche*: office hour; '**~stundenhilfe** *f* receptionist; assistant; '**~taste** *f* speaking key; '**~übung** *f* speech practice; '**~weise** *f s. Sprechart*; '**~zimmer** *n* office; *e-s Arztes*: consulting-room.

Spreiz|e ['ʃpraɪtsə] (15) (*Stütze*) stay, prop; (*Strebe*) strut; '**~en** (27) spread; *Beine*: *a.* straddle; *sich ~ fig.* swagger, strut; *gegen*: struggle against; *mit*: boast of; '**~fuß** ⚕ *m* splayfoot.

Spreng|bombe ['ʃprɛŋ-] *f* demolition bomb, high-explosive (*od.* H.E.) bomb; '**~el** *eccl. m* (7) *e-s Bischofs*: diocese; *e-s Pfarrers*: parish; '**~en** (25) *v/t. Flüssigkeit*: sprinkle, spray; *Garten, Pflanze*: water; (*auf~*) burst (*od.* force) open; *Fesseln, Griff*: break; (*in die Luft ~*) blow up, blast; *Mine usw.*: spring; *Versammlung usw.*: break up, disperse; *Bank*: break; *v/i.* (sn) gallop, ride hard; '**~geschoß** *n* high-explosive (*od.* H.E.) shell; '**~kapsel** *f* detonator; '**~kommando** *n* demolition party; *zur Bombenentschärfung*: bomb disposal squad; '**~kopf** ⚔ *m* warhead; '**~körper** *m*, '**~ladung** *f* explosive charge; '**~loch** *n* blast hole; '**~satz** *m* blasting composition; '**~schuß** *m* blast; '**~stoff** *m* explosive; '**~stoffpaket** *n* parcel bomb; '**~ung** *f* sprinkling; blowing-up, blasting; dispersion; breaking; '**~wirkung** *f* explosive effect; '**~wolke** *f* burst cloud; '**~zünder** *m* fuse, detonator.

sprenkeln ['ʃprɛŋkəln] (29) speckle, spot.

Spreu [ʃprɔʏ] *f* (16) chaff; *fig. die ~ vom Weizen sondern* sift the chaff from the wheat.

Sprich|wort ['ʃpriç-] *n* (1^2) proverb, (proverbial) saying; '**~wörtlich** proverbial (*a. fig.*); *~ sein wegen* be a byword for.

sprießen ['ʃpri:sən] (30, h. *u.* sn) sprout.

Spriet ⚓ [ʃpri:t] *n* (3) sprit.

Spring|brunnen ['ʃpriŋ-] *m* fountain; '**2en** (30, sn *u.* h.) jump; *weit*: leap; *lit., a. v. Dingen, bsd. Wasser, Blut*: spring; *elastisch, bsd. Ball*: bound; *beim Schwimmen*: dive; (*zer*~) burst, crack, break; *in die Augen* ~ strike the eye, be obvious; F *et.* ~ *lassen* stand; e-e *Mine* ~ *lassen* spring a mine; *der* ~*de Punkt* the crucial point; *s. Seil*; '~**er** *m* (7) jumper, leaper (*a.* '~**erin** *f*); *Schach*: knight; '~**flut** *f* spring tide; ~**insfeld** ['~ʔinsfɛlt] *m* (3) young whipper-snapper; '~**quell** *m* fountain, spring; '~**seil** *n* skipping--rope.

Sprinkler-anlage ['ʃpriŋklər-] *f* sprinkler system.

Sprint [ʃprint] *m* (3), '**2en** (26) sprint; '~**er** *m* (7) sprinter.

Sprit [ʃprit] *m* (3) spirit, alcohol; F *mot.* fuel, *sl.* juice, *Am.* gas.

Spritz|e ['ʃpritsə] *f* (15) syringe, sprayer; (*Feuer*2) fire-engine; ⚕ syringe, (*Einspritzung*) injection, F shot; *fig.* (*Hilfe*) shot-in-the-arm; '**2en** (27) *v/t.* squirt, syringe; (*be*~) splash; (*sprengen*) sprinkle; *Lack, Parfüm usw.*: spray; ⚕ inject; ⊕ injection-mo(u)ld; *Getränk*: mix with soda-water; *v/i.* throw water, splash; (*heraus*~) spurt; *Feder*: splutter; F (*eilen*) dash, rush; '~**enhaus** *n* fire-station; '~**er** *m* (7) splash; '~**fahrt** F *f* (pleasure-)trip, *mot.* F spin; ~**flakon** ['~flakõ] *n, m* (11) spray bottle; '~**guß** ⊕ *m* die--casting; *Kunststoff*: injection mo(u)lding; '**2ig** *Wein*: sparkling (*a. fig. geistreich*); *fig.* (*behend*) quick; (*lebhaft*) spirited, racy; '**2-lackieren** (paint-)spray; '~**pistole** *f* water-pistol; ⊕ spray gun; '~**tour** *f s. Spritzfahrt.*

spröd|e ['ʃprø:də] brittle (*a. Stimme*); *Haut*: chapped; (*hart*) hard; *fig.* reserved; *Mädchen*: coy, prudish; '**2igkeit** *f* brittleness; reserve; coyness, prudery.

Sproß [ʃprɔs] **1.** *m* (4) shoot, sprout, scion; *fig.* scion, offspring; **2.** 2 *pret. v. sprießen.*

Sprosse ['ʃprɔsə] *f* (15) (*Leiter*2) round, step, rung; *am Geweih*: tine, point; '**2n** (28, h. *u.* sn) sprout.

Sprößling ['ʃprœsliŋ] *m* (3[1]) *s. Sproß*; F (*Sohn*) son, junior.

Sprotte ['ʃprɔtə] *f* (15) sprat.

Spruch [ʃprux] *m* (3[3]) (*Ausspruch*) saying, dictum; (*Weisheits*2) maxim, aphorism; *s. Bibel*2, *Schieds*2, *Urteil*; F (*große*) *Sprüche machen* talk big, brag; '~**band** *n* banner; '**2reif** ripe for decision.

Sprudel ['ʃpru:dəl] *m* (7) bubbling water; (*Mineralwasser*) mineral water; '**2n** (29, sn *u.* h.) bubble (*od.* gush) forth; *Getränk*: effervesce; (*hastig reden*) sputter; *fig.* ~ *vor* bubble with; *in* ~*der Laune* sparkling with humo(u)r.

Sprüh|dose ['ʃpry:-] *f* aerosol, spray (can); '**2en** (25) *v/i.* (sn *u.* h.) *u. v/t. Wasser usw.*: spray; *Funken*: emit, (*v/i.*) fly; *Feuer*: spit; *Regen*: drizzle; *fig. Augen*: flash (*vor Zorn* with anger); *vor Witz* ~ sparkle with wit; '~**farbe** *f* aerosol paint; '~**regen** *m* drizzling rain.

Sprung [ʃpruŋ] *m* (3[3]) jump, bound, leap; *Schwimmen*: dive; (*Riß*) crack, fissure; *auf dem* ~*e sein* be on the alert; *auf dem* ~*e stehen od. sein zu* ... be on the point of *ger.*; *auf e-n* ~ *vorbeikommen* drop in (for a minute); *j-m auf die Sprünge kommen* find a p. out; *j-m auf die Sprünge helfen* help a p. out; *er kann keine großen Sprünge machen* he cannot get far; '~**bein** *n* ankle-bone; '~**brett** *n Schwimmen*: diving-board; *a. Turnen*: spring-board; *fig.* stepping-stone; '~**feder** *f* (elastic) spring; '~**federmatratze** *f* spring mattress; '**2haft** erratic(ally *adv.*); (*plötzlich*) abrupt; ~ *steigen* go up by leaps and bounds; '~**lauf** *m* ski--jumping; '~**schanze** *f* ski-jump; '~**stab** *m* jumping-pole; '~**tuch** *n Feuerwehr*: jumping-sheet; '~**turm** *m* high-diving board; '**2weise** by leaps (and bounds).

Spuck|e ['ʃpukə] *f* (15) spittle, saliva; '**2en** (25) *v/i.* spit; *v/t.* spit out; '~**napf** *m* spittoon, *Am. a.* cuspidor.

Spuk [ʃpu:k] *m* (3) apparition, ghost, spect|re, *Am.* -er; *fig.* nightmare; '**2en** (25) *an e-m Ort* haunt a place; *es spukt in dem Hause* the house is haunted; '~**geschichte** *f* ghost--story; '**2haft** ghostly, weird.

Spule ['ʃpu:lə] *f* (15) spool, reel;

(*Spinn*≙) bobbin; (*Feder*≙) quill; ⚡ coil.

Spüle ['ʃpy:lə] *f* (15) kitchen sink.

spulen ['ʃpu:lən] (25) reel, spool.

spül|en ['ʃpy:lən] (25) rinse; *Geschirr*: wash (up); *Abort*: flush; ⊕, *mot.* scavenge; *an Land* ~ wash ashore; '≙**icht** *n* (3) dish-water, dirty water; '≙**lappen** *m* dish-cloth; '≙**mittel** *n* washing-up liquid; '≙**ung** *f* rinsing; flushing; ⊕, *mot.* scavenging; *Abort*: water flush; '~**wasser** *n* rinsing water; *s. Spülicht.*

'**Spulwurm** *m* mawworm.

Spund [ʃpunt] *m* (3³) bung, plug; *Tischlerei*: tongue; ≙**en** ['~dən] (26) bung; *Tischlerei*: tongue and groove; ~**loch** ['ʃpunt-] *n* bung-hole.

Spur [ʃpu:r] *f* (16) trace (*a.* ⚗, *Leucht*≙ *u. fig.*); (*Fährte, a. fig.*) trail, track; *hunt. a.* scent; (*Abdruck*) print; (*Fuß*≙) footprint; (*Wagen*≙) track, *tiefe*: rut; ⚓ wake; *s.* ~*weite*; (*Fleck, Narbe, Brems*≙, *fig. Merkmal*) mark; (*Anzeichen*) sign; (*Überrest, winzige* ~) vestige; *e-e* ~ *Salz usw.* a touch of salt *etc.*; F *keine* ~! not a bit; *fig. auf die (richtige)* ~ *bringen* give *a p.* a clue; *auf die Spur kommen (dat.)* trace, find out; *auf der falschen* ~ *sein* be on a wrong track.

spür|bar ['ʃpy:rba:r] sensible; *fig.* marked; ~ *sein* be felt; '~**en** (25) track, trace (*a. fig.*); (*empfinden*) feel; *nur innerlich*: sense; (*wahrnehmen*) perceive.

spuren ['ʃpu:rən] F (25) toe the line; '≙**-element** *n* trace element.

'**Spürhund** *m* trackhound; *fig.* (*Detektiv*) sleuth.

'**spurlos**: ~ *verschwinden* disappear without leaving a trace.

'**Spür|nase** *f* scent (*a. fig.*); '~**sinn** *m* flair.

Spurt [ʃpurt] *m* (3), '≙**en** (26) spurt.

'**Spurweite** *f* 🚂 ga(u)ge; *mot.* wheel-track; *Reifen*: tread.

sputen ['ʃpu:tən] (26): *sich* ~ make haste, hurry up.

St. *s. Sankt.*

Staat [ʃta:t] *m* (5) (*Aufwand*) state, pomp; (*Putz*) finery; (~*swesen*) state; (*Regierung*) government; ~ *machen mit* make a show of, parade; '~**enbund** *m* confederation; '≙**enlos** stateless; '≙**lich** state-..., government ..., national, public; political.

'**Staats|-akt** *m* state ceremony; '~**-aktion** F *f* great fuss; '~**-angehörige** *m, f* national, *Brt.* subject, *Am.* citizen; '~**-angehörigkeit** *f* nationality, national status, *Am. mst* citizenship; '~**-angelegenheit** *f* state-affair; '~**-anleihe** *f* government loan; '~**-anwalt** *m* public prosecutor, *Am.* district attorney; '~**-anzeiger** *m* official gazette; '~**-archiv** *n* Public Record Office; '~**be-amte** *m* public (*od. Brt.* civil) servant, government official; '~**begräbnis** *n* state funeral; '~**besuch** *m* state visit; '~**bürger** *m* citizen; '~**bürgerkunde** *f* civics *pl.*; '≙**bürgerlich** civic(ally *adv.*); '~**bürgerschaft** *f* citizenship; '~**chef** *m* head of state; '~**dienst** *m* civil (*Am.* public) service; '≙**-eigen** state-owned; '~**-einkünfte** *f/pl.* public revenue(s *pl.*) *sg.*; '~**feind** *m* public enemy; '≙**feindlich** subversive; '~**form** *f* form of government, polity; '~**gebäude** *n* public building; '~**gefangene** *m* prisoner of state; '~**geheimnis** *n* state (*od. fig.* top) secret; ~**gelder** ['~gɛldər] *n/pl.* public money *sg.*; '~**gewalt** *f* supreme (*od.* executive) power; '~**haushalt** *m* national budget; '~**hoheit** *f* sovereignty; '~**kasse** *f* (public) treasury, *Brt.* exchequer; '~**kirche** *f* state church; *die englische*: Established Church, Church of England; '≙**klug** politic(ally *adv.*), diplomatic (-ally *adv.*); '~**körper** *m* body politic; *auf* '~**kosten** *pl.* at (the) public expense; '~**kunst** *f* statecraft, statesmanship; '~**mann** *m* statesman, politician; ≙**männisch** ['~mɛniʃ] statesmanlike; ~*e Fähigkeiten od. Kunst* statesmanship; '~**minister** *m* Minister of State; '~**oberhaupt** *n* head of state; '~**papiere** *n/pl.* government securities *od.* stocks; '~**prozeß** *m* state-trial; ~**räson** ['~rɛ:zɔ̃] *f* reason of State; '~**rat** *m* Privy Council; (*Person*) Privy Council(l)or; '~**recht** *n* constitutional law; '≙**rechtlich** relating to (*od.* under) constitutional law; '~**regierung** *f* government; '~**schatz** *m s.* ~*kasse*; '~**schuld** *f* national debt; '~**sekretär** *m* State Secretary; '~**sicherheitsdienst** *m* state security service; '**~streich** *m* coup d'état (*fr.*); '**~trauertag** *m* national day of mourning; '**~verbrechen** *n* political crime; '**~verfassung** *f* political constitution; '**~vertrag** *m* (international) treaty; '**~verwaltung** *f* (public) administration; '**~wesen** *n* political system, polity; state; '**~wissenschaft** *f* political science; '**~wohl** *n* public weal; '**~zuschuß** *m* government grant, state subsidy.

Stab [ʃtɑ:p] *m* (3[3]) staff, stick; (*Gitter*♀, *Metall*♀) bar; (*Stange*) rod, pole (*a. Sport*: *Sprung*♀); *Sport*: (*Staffel*♀) baton (*a.* ♪ *Dirigenten*♀, ⚔ *Marschall*♀); *s. Zauber*♀; *fig.* (*Mitarbeiter*♀, *a.* ⚔) staff; ⚔ (*Hauptquartier*) headquarters *pl.*; *den ~ über j-n brechen* condemn a p.; '**~-antenne** *f* rod aerial *od.* antenna; '**~batterie** *f* torch battery; '**~-eisen** *n* bar iron; '**~hochspringer** *m* pole-vaulter; '**~hochsprung** *m* pole-vault(ing).

stabil [sta'bi:l] *allg.* stable; (*fest, robust*) sturdy, rugged; **~i'sieren** [~bili-] stabilize; *sich ~* become stabilized; ♀**i'sierung** *f* stabilization; ♀**ität** *f* [~'tɛ:t] (16) stability.

'**Stabreim** *m* stave rhyme, *weitS.* alliteration.

'**Stabs|-arzt** ⚔ *m* surgeon-major, *Am.* captain (Medical Corps); '**~chef** *m* Chief of Staff; '**~feldwebel** *m Brt.* Warrant Officer Class II, *Am.* master sergeant; '**~-offizier** *m* (*Major bis Oberst*) field (grade) officer; (*Offizier beim Stabe*) staff officer; '**~quartier** *n* headquarters *pl. od. sg.*

stach [ʃtɑ:x] *pret. v. stechen.*

Stachel ['ʃtaxəl] *m* (10) prick; ⚘ *a.* spine (*a. des Igels*); (*Insekten*♀) sting; *am Zaun od. Rennschuh*: spike; *fig.* (*Verletzendes*) sting; (*Ansporn*) goad; '**~beere** *f* gooseberry; '**~draht** *m* barbed wire.

'**stach(e)lig** prickly, (*a. fig.*) thorny.

'**stachel|n** (29) sting, prick; *fig. s. an~*; '♀**schwein** *n* porcupine.

Stadi|on ['ʃtɑ:djɔn] *n* (9[1]) stadium; **~um** ['~um] *n* (9[1]) stage, phase.

Stadt [ʃtat] *f* (14[1]) town; (*Groß*♀) city; '**~-amt** *n* municipal office; '**~-autobahn** *f* urban motorway; '**~bahn** *f* city-railway; '♀**bekannt** known all over the town, notorious; '**~bewohner** *m s. Städter*; '**~bild** *n* townscape.

Städt|chen ['ʃtɛ:t-] *n* (6) small town; '**~ebau** *m* town-planning; urban development; '**~ebauer** *m* town-planner; '**~er** *m* (7) townsman, *pl.* townspeople, city dwellers; '**~erin** *f* (16[1]) townswoman; '**~ezug** *m* interurban (express) train.

'**Stadt|gebiet** *n* urban area; '**~gemeinde** *f* township; '**~gespräch** *n fig. the* talk of the town; **~guerilla** ['~gerilja] *m* (16, *o. pl.*) urban guerilla.

städtisch ['ʃtɛ:tiʃ] town(-)...; municipal; urban.

'**Stadt|kasse** *f* city treasury; '**~köfferchen** *n* attaché case; '**~kommandant** *m* town major; '**~leben** *n* town life, city life; '**~leute** *pl.* townspeople; '**~mauer** *f* town-wall; '**~parlament** *n* city parliament; '**~plan** *m* map of the city; '**~planung** *f s. Städtebau*; '**~rand** *m* outskirts *pl.* of the town *od.* city; '**~randsiedlung** *f* suburban settlement; '**~rat** *m* municipal council; (*Person*) town (*od.* city) council(l)or; '**~recht** *n* freedom of the city; '**~sanierung** *f* urban renewal (*od.* redevelopment); '**~staat** *m* city-state; '**~streicher(in** *f*) *m* city tramp; **~streicherei** ['~ʃtraɪçə'raɪ] *f* urban vagrancy; '**~teil** *m* quarter, district, ward; '**~tor** *n* town-gate; '**~väter** *m/pl.* city fathers; '**~verordnete** *m* (18) town (*od.* city) council(l)or; '**~ver-ordnetenversammlung** *f* town council; '**~verwaltung** *f* municipality; '**~viertel** *n s. Stadtteil*; '**~wappen** *n* city-arms *pl.*

Stafette [ʃta'fɛtə] *f* (15) (mounted) courier; *Sport*: relay; **~nlauf** *m* relay race.

Staffage [ʃta'fɑ:ʒə] *f* (15) accessories *pl.*

Staffel ['ʃtafəl] *f* (15) step; *fig.* degree; *Sport*: relay; (*Teilstrecke*) stage; (*~aufstellung*) echelon (formation); ✈, ⚔ squadron; **~ei** [~'laɪ] *f* (16) easel; ♀**förmig** ['~fœrmiç] in echelons; '**~lauf** *m* relay race; '♀**n** (29) *Steuern usw.*: graduate, differentiate; *Arbeitszeit usw., a.* ⊕, ✈, *Sport*: stagger; '**~ung** *f* graduation, differentiation; staggering.

Stagn|ation [stagna'tsjo:n] stagnation; ♀**ieren** [~'gni:rən] stagnate.

stahl[1] [ʃtɑ:l] *pret. v. stehlen.*

Stahl[2] *m* (3[3]) steel; '**~bad** *n* chalybeate bath (*od. Ort*: spa); '**~bau** *m* steel construction; '**~beton** ⊕ *m* steel concrete; '**♀blau** steel-blue; '**~blech** *n* sheet-steel.

stähl|en ['ʃtɛːlən] (25) temper; *fig.* steel; '**~ern** (of) steel; *fig.* steel(y).

'**Stahl|feder** *f* steel spring; *zum Schreiben*: steel nib; '**~gürtelreifen** *mot. m* belted-bias tyre (*Am.* tire); '**~helm** *m* steel helmet; '**~kammer** *f* strong-room, *Am.* steel-vault; '**~(rohr)möbel** *n/pl.* tubular (steel) furniture *sg.*; **~späne** ['~ʃpɛːnə] *m/pl.*, '**~wolle** *f* steel wool *sg.*; '**~stich** *m* steel engraving; '**~werk** *n* steel works.

stak [ʃtɑːk] *pret. v. stecken*[2].

Staken ['ʃtɑːkən] **1.** *m* (6) stake; **2.** ♀ (25) pole, punt.

Staket [ʃta'kɛt] *n* (3) fence, palisade.

Stall [ʃtal] *m* (3^3) (*Pferde*♀) stable (*a. fig. Renn*♀ *usw.*); (*Kuh*♀) cow-shed; (*Schaf*♀) sheep-pen; *s. Hundehütte, Hühner*♀, *Schweine*♀; (*Schuppen*) shed, *Am. a.* barn; '**~gefährte** *m Sport*: stable companion (*a. fig.*); '**~geld** *n* stable-money, stallage; '**~knecht** *m* groom; '**~meister** *m* equerry; '**~ung** *f* stabling; *~en pl.* stables.

Stamm [ʃtam] *m* (3^3) ⚘ stem (*a. gr.*); (*Stengel*) stalk; (*Baum*♀) trunk (*a. anat.*); (*Volks*♀ *usw.*) race; (*Geschlecht*) stock; (*Familie, Haus*) family, *in Schottland*: clan; (*Eingeborenen*♀) tribe; *von Vieh*: breed; *biol.* phylum; *fig.* (*Bestand*) stock; (*Kern*) core, nucleus; (*Kader*) cadre; *s. Kunden*♀, *Stammpersonal*; '**~-aktie** *f* ordinary share, *Am.* common stock; '**~baum** *m* family (*od.* genealogical) tree; *von Tieren*: pedigree; '**~buch** *n* album; '**~burg** *f* ancestral castle; **~datei** ['~dataɪ] *f Computer*: master file; '**♀eln** *v/i. u. v/t.* (29) stammer; '**~-eltern** *pl.* progenitors, first parents; '**♀en** (25, sn): *~ von P.*: be descended from; (*s-n Ursprung haben in*) originate (*Am. a.* stem) from; *zeitlich*: date from; *gr.* be derived from; *vgl. ab~, her~*; '**~esgeschichte** *f* racial history; *biol.* phylogeny; '**~form** *gr. f* cardinal form; '**~gast** *m* habitué (*fr.*), regular guest; '**~halter** *m* son and heir; '**~haus** ✝ *n* parent house *od.* firm.

stämmig ['ʃtɛmiç] *fig.* (*stark*) sturdy, stalwart, husky, F hefty; (*untersetzt*) stocky.

'**Stamm|kapital** *n* original capital; '**~kunde** *m*, '**~kundin** *f* regular customer; '**~lokal** *n* habitual haunt; '**~personal** *n* permanent staff; (*Mindest*♀) skeleton staff; (*Kader*) cadre personnel; '**~rolle** ⚔, ⚓ *f* personnel roster; '**~silbe** *f* root syllable; '**~sitz** *m* ancestral seat; '**~tafel** *f* genealogical table; '**~tisch** *m* (table reserved for) regular guests; '**~vater** *m* ancestor; '**♀verwandt** kindred, cognate; *pred.* of the same race; '**~volk** *n* aborigines *pl.*, primitive people; '**~wähler** *pol. m* regular voter; '**~wort** *n* (1^2) root word, stem.

Stampfe ['ʃtampfə] *f* (15) tamper; (*Ramme*) rammer; (*Stößel*) pestle; '**♀n** *v/t. u. v/i.* (25) stamp; (*hämmern*) pound; *Schiff*: pitch; (*zer~*) crush; *Kartoffeln usw.*: mash.

Stand [ʃtant] **1.** *m* (3^3) (*Stehen*) stand(ing), upright position; (*Halt für den Fuß*) footing; *s. Standplatz*; (*Niveau*) level; (*Verkaufs*♀, *Pferde*♀) stall; (*Zu*♀) state, condition; (*Lage*) position, state of affairs; (*soziale Stellung*) status, station, rank; (*Klasse*) class; (*Beruf*) profession; (*Gewerbe*) trade; *des Thermometers usw.*: reading; *ast.* position; *Sport*: (*Spiel*♀) score; *pol. die Stände pl.* the estates; *Mann von ~e* man of rank; *Patentrecht*: *~ der Technik* prior art; *j-n in den ~ setzen et. zu tun* enable a p. to do a th.; *Sprung aus dem ~* standing jump; *e-n schweren ~ haben* have a hard time (of it); *auf den neuesten ~ bringen* bring up to date, update; *s. imstande, instand, zustande*; **2.** ♀ *pret. v. stehen.*

Standard ['ʃtandart] *m* (11) standard; **♀i'sieren** [~di-] standardize; **~i'sierung** *f* standardization; **~lösung** ['~dart-] *f* standard solution; '**~werk** *n* standard work.

Standarte [~'dartə] *f* (15) standard.

Standbild ['ʃtant-] *n* statue.

Ständchen ['ʃtɛntçən] *n* (6) serenade; *j-m ein ~ bringen* serenade a p.

Stander ['ʃtandər] *m* (7) pennant.

Ständer ['ʃtɛndər] *m* (7) (*Gestell*) stand; (*Gewehr*♀, *Pfeifen*♀ *usw.*) rack; (*Pfosten*) post, pillar; ⚡ stator.

Standes|amt ['ʃtandəsˀamt] *n* registry office, *Am.* marriage license bureau; '2-**amtlich:** ~e *Trauung* civil marriage; '~**be-amte** *m* registrar; '~**bewußtsein** *n* class-consciousness; '~**dünkel** *m* pride of position, snobbery; '~-**ehre** *f* professional hono(u)r; '2**gemäß**, '2-**mäßig** in accordance with one's rank; '~**person** *f* person of rank *od.* quality; '~-**unterschied** *m* social difference.

'**stand|fest** stable; '2**geld** *n* stall-rent; '2**gericht** ⚔ *n* drumhead court-martial.

'**standhaft** steadfast, steady, firm; '2**igkeit** *f* steadfastness.

'**standhalten** hold one's ground; (*aushalten*) stand; *j-m od. e-r S.* ~ resist a p. *od.* a th.

ständig ['ʃtɛndiç] permanent; (*fortwährend*) constant; *Einkommen*: fixed, regular; *Ausschuß*: standing; ~*er Begleiter* constant companion; *et.* ~ *tun* keep doing a th.

'**Stand|licht** *mot. n* parking light; '~**motor** *m* stationary engine; '~-**ort** *m* (3) station, location, ⚓ *usw.* position (*a. fig.*); ⚔ garrison, *Am.* post; '~**pauke** F *f* severe lecture, harangue; '~**platz** *m* stand(ing-place); '~**punkt** *m* point of view, view(point); *den* ~ *vertreten* take the view (*that*); *j-m den* ~ *klarmachen* give a p. a piece of one's mind; *s. Standort*; '~**quartier** ⚔ *n* fixed quarters *pl.*; '~**recht** ⚔ *n* martial law; '2**rechtlich** according to martial law; '~**spur** *mot. f* hard shoulder; '~-**uhr** *f* grandfather's clock.

Stange ['ʃtaŋə] *f* (15) pole; (*Vogel*2) perch; (*Metall*2) bar, rod; *v. Siegellack usw.*: stick; *v. Zigaretten*: carton; F (*lange Person*) bean-pole; F *e-e* ~ *Geld* F quite a packet; (*Kleid*) *von der* ~ (*fertiggekauft*) F reach- (*Am.* hand-)me-down; *fig. j-m die* ~ *halten* stick up for a p.; F *bei der* ~ *bleiben* stick to it; '~**nbohne** *f* runner bean; '~**nspargel** *m* asparagus spears *pl.*

stank [ʃtaŋk] *pret. v. stinken.*

Stänker F ['ʃtɛŋkər] *m* (7) *fig.* squabbler; ~**ei** [~'raɪ] *f* (16) squabble; '2**n** (29) *fig.* squabble

Stanniol [ʃta'njo:l] *n* (3[1]) tinfoil.

Stanze[1] ['ʃtantsə] *f* (15) (*Strophe*) stanza.

'**Stanze**[2] ⊕ *f* punch; '2**n** punch, [stamp.]

Stapel ['ʃta:pəl] *m* (7) pile, stack; ⚓ slip(way); *der Wolle*: staple; *auf* ~ *legen* lay down; *vom* ~ *lassen* launch (*a. fig.*); *vom* ~ *laufen* be launched (*a. fig.*); '~**güter** *n/pl.* staple commodities; '~**lauf** *m* launch(ing); '2**n** (20) stack, (*a. sich*) pile up; (*lagern*) store; '~**platz** *m* dump; (*Handelsplatz*) emporium.

stapfen ['ʃtapfən] (25) plod, trudge.

Star[1] [ʃta:r] *m* (3[1]) *zo.* starling; ~[2] *m* ⚕ *grauer* ~ cataract, *grüner* ~ glaucoma, *schwarzer* ~ amaurosis; *j-m den* ~ *stechen fig.* open a p.'s eyes; ~[3] [sta:r] *m thea. etc.* star.

Star|allüren ['~ʔaly:rən] *f/pl.* airs and graces; '~-**anwalt** *m* top lawyer (*Am.* attorney).

starb [ʃtarp] *pret. v. sterben.*

'**Starbesetzung** *f thea. etc.* star cast.

stark [ʃtark] (18[2]) **1.** *allg.* strong (*a. Getränk usw., gr. u. fig.*); *P.*: *a.* sturdy; (*a. Maschine, Schlag usw.*) powerful; (*beleibt*) stout, corpulent; ⊕ (*dick*) thick; (*intensiv*) intense; (*heftig*) violent; (*beträchtlich*) large; (*schlimm*) bad; *Fieber*: high; *Frost*: hard; *Familie*: numerous; *Regen, Verkehr*: heavy; ~*e Auflage e-s Buches* large edition; ~*er Band* big volume; ~*e Erkältung* bad cold; ~*er Esser* hearty eater; ~*er Trinker* hard drinker; *pol.* ~*er Mann* strong man; ~*e Meile* (*Stunde*) good mile (hour); ~*e Seite fig.* strong point, forte; F *das ist* (*doch*) *zu* ~! that's a bit thick!; **2.** *adv.* very much; greatly, strongly; hard; badly.

Stärke ['ʃtɛrkə] *f* (15) **1.** *s. stark*: strength (*a. e-s Heeres usw.*); force; stoutness; power (*a.* ⊕ *Leistung*); ⊕ thickness; intensity; violence; largeness; *fig.* forte, strong point; **2.** ⚗ starch; '2**haltig** starchy; '~-**mehl** *n* starch-flour; '2**n** (25) strengthen (*a. fig.*); (*beleben*) invigorate; *Wäsche*: starch; *sich* ~ *fig.* take some refreshment.

'**Starkstrom** ⚡ *m* power (*od.* high-voltage *od.* heavy) current; '~**leitung** *f* power line.

'**Stärkung** *f* strengthening; (*Erfrischung*) refreshment; '~**smittel** *n* restorative, tonic.

starr [ʃtar] rigid (*a. fig. u. Luftschiff*), stiff; *Blick*: staring, fixed; (*unbeugsam*) inflexible; *vor Schreck usw.*: paralysed (with *fear etc.*); *vor Staunen*: dum(b)founded; *vor Kälte*: numb; '~**en** (25) stare (*auf acc.*

at); *von Waffen usw.*: bristle with; *von Schmutz usw.*: be covered with; '**2heit** *f* stiffness, rigidity; numbness; **~köpfig** ['~kœpfiç], '**~sinnig** stubborn, obstinate; '**2krampf** *m* tetanus; '**2sinn** *m* obstinacy, stubbornness; '**2sucht** *f* catalepsy.

Start [ʃtart] *m* (3) start (*a. fig.*); ✈ take-off; (*Raketen2*) lift-off; *Sport*: *fliegender* (*stehender*) ~ flying (standing) start; '**~bahn** ✈ *f* runway; '**2bereit** ready to start; ✈ ready to take off; '**2en** (26, h. *u.* sn) start; *fig. a.* launch; ✈ take off; '**~er** *m* (7) starter; '**~-erlaubnis** *f* permission to start; ✈ clearance for take-off; '**~hilfekabel** *mot. n* jump leads *pl.*; '**~kapital** *n* initial capital; '**2klar** *s. startbereit*; '**~platz** *m* starting-place; '**~schleuder** *f* catapult; '**~schuß** *m Sport*: starting shot; '**~verbot** *n Sport*: suspension; ✈ take-off restriction; ~ *erhalten* be grounded.

Statik ['stɑːtik] *f* (16) statics *sg.*; '**~er** ⚠ *m* stress analyst.

Station [ʃta'tsjoːn] *f allg.* station; (*Kranken2*) ward; (*gegen*) *freie* ~ board and lodging (found); ~ *machen* stop (*in dat.* at); **2är** [~tsjo'nɛːr] stationary; ⚕ in-patient; **2ieren** [~'niːrən] station; **~ierungskosten** [~'niːruŋs-] *pl.* stationing costs; **~s-arzt** [~'tsjoːns-] *m* ward physician; **~s-schwester** *f* ward sister; **~vorsteher** 🚂 *m* station-master, *Am.* station agent.

statisch ['stɑːtiʃ] static(ally *adv.*).

Statist [ʃta'tist] *m* (12), **~in** *f* (16[1]) *thea.* super(numerary); *Film*: extra; **~ik** *f* (16) statistics *pl. u. sg.*; **~iker** *m* (7) statistician; **2isch** statistical.

Stativ [ʃta'tiːf] *n* (3[1]) stand, support; *phot. usw.* tripod.

Statt [ʃtat] **1.** *f* (16, *o. pl.*) place, stead; *an Kindes ~ annehmen* adopt; *s. vonstatten, zustatten*; **2.** 2 *prp.* (*gen., zu mit inf.*) instead of, in lieu of.

Stätte ['ʃtɛtə] *f* (15) place, spot; *e-s Ereignisses*: scene; (*Wohnung*) abode; *keine bleibende ~ haben* have no fixed abode.

'**statt|finden**, '**~haben** take place, happen; come off; *Veranstaltung*: be held; '**~geben** (*dat.*) grant, allow; '**~haft** admissible; (*gesetzlich* ~) legal.

'**Statthalter** *m* (7) governor; *rhet. b.s.* satrap.

'**stattlich** stately; (*ansehnlich*) handsome; (*würdevoll*) portly; (*beträchtlich*) considerable; '**2keit** *f* stateliness *etc.*

Statue ['ʃtɑːtuə] *f* (15) statue; '**2nhaft** statuesque.

statuieren [ʃtatu'iːrən] establish; *ein Exempel* ~ make an example (*an dat.* of).

Statur [ʃta'tuːr] *f* (16) stature, size.

Status ['stɑːtus] *m* (*inv.*) status (*a. fig. Prestige*); state, condition; '**~symbol** *n* status symbol.

Statut [~'tuːt] *n* (5) statute, regulations *pl.*; *~en pl. e-r Handelsgesellschaft usw.*: articles *pl.* of association; **2enmäßig** statutory.

Stau [ʃtau] *m* (3) *s. Stauung.*

Staub [ʃtaup] *m* (3) dust; (*Pulver*) powder; *sich aus dem ~e machen* make off, decamp; *s. aufwirbeln*; '**~beutel** ⚘ *m* anther.

Stäubchen ['ʃtɔʏpçən] *n* (6) particle of dust, mote, atom.

staubdicht ['ʃtaupdiçt] dustproof.

Stau-becken ['ʃtau-] *n* reservoir.

stauben ['~bən] *v/i.* (25, h. *u.* sn) give off dust; *es staubt* it is dusty.

stäuben ['ʃtɔʏbən] *v/t.* dust (*a.* ⚘ *Pflanzen*); *v/i.* = *stauben.*

'**Staub|faden** ⚘ *m* filament; '**~fänger** *m* dust-trap; '**~flocke** *f* fluff; '**2frei** dust-free; '**~gefäß** ⚘ *n* stamen; '**2haltig** dust-laden; **2ig** ['~biç] dusty; '**~korn** *n* dust-particle; '**~lunge** ⚕ *f* pneumoconiosis; '**~mantel** *m* dust--coat; '**~sauger** *m* vacuum cleaner; '**~tuch** *n* duster; '**~wedel** *m* feather duster; '**~wolke** *f* cloud of dust.

stauchen ['ʃtauxən] (25) jolt; *mit dem Fuß*: kick; ⊕ upset.

'**Staudamm** *m* dam.

Staude ['ʃtaudə] *f* (15) shrub, bush.

stauen ['ʃtauən] (25) *Wasser*: dam up; *Güter*: stow (away); *sich ~* be banked up, *weitS.* accumulate.

'**Stauer** ⚓ *m* (7) stevedore.

staunen ['ʃtaunən] **1.** (25) be astonished *od.* amazed (*über acc.* at); **2.** 2 *n* (6) astonishment, amazement; *in ~ versetzen* amaze; '**~swert** astonishing, amazing.

Staupe *vet.* ['ʃtaupə] *f* (15) distemper.

'**Stau|see** *m* storage-lake, reservoir; '**~ung** *f* damming up; (*Stockung*) stoppage; ⚒ (a. *Verkehrs*⁀) congestion; (*Verkehrs*⁀) a. bank-up; (*gestaute Masse*) jam; '~**werk** *n* barrage.

Stearin [ʃtea'ri:n] *n* (3[1]) stearin.

stechen ['ʃtɛçən] **1.** *v/t. u. v/i.* (30) prick; *Insekt*: sting; *Floh, Mücke*: bite; (*durch*~) pierce; *mit e-m Messer usw.*: stab; *Kartenspiel*: trump (*od.* take) *a card*; *Sonne*: burn; *Rasen, Spargel, Torf*: cut; ⊕ *in Kupfer*: cut, engrave; *sich in den Finger* ~ prick one's finger; *s.* Auge, See, Star[2]; **2.** ⁀ *n* (*Schmerz*) stitches *pl.*; *Sport*: jump *od.* shoot *od.* fence *etc.* off; '~**d** *fig. Blick*: piercing; *Geruch, Geschmack*: acrid, pungent; *Schmerz*: stabbing.

'**Stech|fliege** *f* stinging fly; (*Bremse*) gadfly; '~**ginster** *m* furze, gorse; '~**heber** *m* siphon, pipette; '~**karte** *f* clocking-in card; '~**mücke** *f* gnat, mosquito; '~**palme** *f* holly; '~**schritt** ⚔ *m* goose-step; '~**uhr** *f* time-clock; '~**zirkel** *m* dividers *pl.*

'**Steck|brief** *m* warrant of arrest, "wanted" circular; '⁀**brieflich:** *j-n* ~ *verfolgen* take out a warrant against a p.; '~**dose** ⚡ *f* (wall) socket.

Stecken[1] ['ʃtɛkən] *m* (6) stick, staff.

'**stecken**[2] (30) **1.** *v/t.* stick; (*wohin tun*) put; *bsd.* ⊕ insert (*in acc.* into), *Kabel usw.*: plug (into); ⚘ set, plant; (*fest*~) fix; *mit Nadeln*: pin; *fig. Geld in ein Geschäft*: put into; F *j-m et.* ~ tell a p. a th.; *s.* Brand, Decke, Nase, Tasche, Ziel, dahinter~; **2.** *v/i.* (*sich befinden*) be; (*festsitzen*) stick (fast); *in Schulden usw.* ~ be involved in; '~**bleiben** (sn) stick fast, get (*od.* be) stuck, come to a dead stop; *im Sumpf*: bog down (*a. fig. Verhandlungen usw.*); *in e-r Rede*: break down; *s.* Kehle; '~**lassen** leave; '⁀**pferd** *n* hobby-horse; *fig.* hobby.

'**Steck|er** ⚡ *m* (7) plug; '~**kontakt** *m* plug-contact; '~**ling** *m* (3[1]), '~**reis** *n* ⚘ layer, slip, cutting; '~**nadel** *f* pin; *wie e-e* ~ *suchen* hunt for *a p.* (high and low); '~**rübe** ⚘ *f* turnip; '~**schlüssel** ⊕ *m* socket wrench; '~**schuh** *phot. m* accessory shoe; '~**schuß** ⚒ *m* retained missile.

Steg [ʃte:k] *m* (3) path; (*Brücke*) foot-bridge; *typ.* stick; (*Hosen*⁀) strap; (*Brillen*⁀, *Geigen*⁀) bridge; '~**reif** *m*: *aus dem* ~ extempore, off-hand, off the cuff; *aus dem* ~ *sprechen usw.* extemporize, *Am.* F ad-lib.

'**Steh|-auf(männchen** *n*) *m* skip-jack, tumbler; '~**bierhalle** *f* bar.

stehen ['ʃte:ən] **1.** (30, h. *u.* sn) stand (up); (*sein, sich befinden*) be; (*still*~) stand still, *Uhr usw.*: have stopped; (*geschrieben* ~) be written; (*kleiden*) suit, become (*j-m* a p.); ~ *bleiben* remain standing; *es steht bei dir, zu inf.* it is for you to *inf.*; ~ *für* stand (*od.* answer) for; *fig.* ~ *auf* (*acc.*) *Aktien*: be at 75, *Barometer usw.*: point to, stand at; F (*begeistert sein von*) *sl.* dig; *gr. auf ... steht der Akkusativ ...* answers the accusative; *hinter j-m* ~ back a p.; *fig. vor e-m Rätsel, dem Ruin, e-r Schwierigkeit usw.* ~ be faced with; *sich gut* (*schlecht*) ~ be well (badly) off; (*sich*) *gut* (*schlecht*) ~ *mit j-m* be on good (bad) terms with a p.; *es steht schlecht mit ihm* he is in a bad way; *zu j-m* ~ stand by a p.; *zu e-m Versprechen usw.* ~ stand to; *teuer zu* ~ *kommen* cost dear; *was steht in dem Brief?* what does it say in the letter?; *wie steht's mit ...?* what about ...?; *Sport*: *wie steht das Spiel?* what's the score?; *s.* dahinstehen, Debatte, Mann, Modell, Pate, Rede *usw.*; **2.** ⁀ *n* standing; *Mahlzeit im* ~ stand-up meal; *zum* ~ *bringen* (*kommen*) bring (come) to a stop; '~**bleiben** (sn) (*nicht weitergehen*) stand still; stop; *Fehler usw.*: remain, be overlooked; *beim Lesen*: leave off; '~**d** standing (*a. fig. Heer, Regel, Redensart*; *Wasser*); *s.* Fuß; '~**lassen** leave (standing); (*vergessen*) leave (behind); (*nicht anrühren*) let (*od.* leave) *a th.* alone; *s.* Bart.

'**Steher** *m* (7) *Rennsport*: stayer.

'**Stehkragen** *m* stand-up collar.

'**Steh|lampe** *f* standard (lamp); *auf dem Fußboden stehend*: floor-lamp; '~**leiter** *f* stepladder.

stehlen ['ʃte:lən] *v/t. u. v/i.* (30) steal (*j-m Geld usw.* a p.'s money *etc.*).

'**Steh|platz** *m* standing-place *od.* -room; '~**pult** *n* standing-desk, high desk; '~**vermögen** *n Sport usw.*: staying power, stamina.

steif [ʃtaɪf] stiff (*a. fig.*); *bsd. phys.* rigid; *vor Kälte*: numb, benumbed; ~*er Hut* bowler hat, *Am.* derby (hat); *fig.* ~ *und fest* obstinately, categorically; *s. Ohr*; '**~en** (25) stiffen; *Wäsche*: starch; *j-m den Nacken ~* stiffen a p.'s back; '**2heit** *f* stiffness; '**2leinwand** *f* buckram.

Steig [ʃtaɪk] *m* (3) path; '**~bügel** *m* stirrup; **~e** ['~gə] *f* (15) ladder; (*Treppe*) steep stairs *pl.*; (*Zaunübertritt*) stile; (*steiler Pfad*) ascent; (*Kiste*) crate; **~-eisen** ['~k-] *n* climbing-iron; *mount.* crampon; **2en**[1] ['~gən] (30, sn) mount, go up; (*klettern*) climb (up) (*a.* ✈ *u. fig.*); *fig.* (*zunehmen*) increase, *a. Wasser, Temperatur, Barometer, Preis usw.*: rise; *Pferd*: prance, rear; F (*stattfinden*) come off, be staged; *auf e-n Baum ~* climb (up) a tree; *j-m in den Kopf ~* go to a p.'s head; *zu Pferde ~* mount (a horse); *vom Pferde ~* dismount; '**~en**[2] *n* rise; increase; '**2end** *fig.* rising; (*wachsend*) growing; **~er** ⚒ ['~gər] *m* (7) pit-foreman; '**2ern** (29) raise; (*vermehren*) increase; (*verstärken*) enhance; *Produktion*: step up; (*hochtreiben*) force up; *gr.* compare; *sich ~* increase, *Person*: improve, *in Wut*: work o.s. up into a rage.

'**Steigerung** *f* raising; increase, rise; enhancement; *gr.* comparison; '**~sgrad** *gr. m* degree of comparison; '**~srate** *f* rate of increase.

Steigfähigkeit ['~k-] *f* ✈ climbing power; *mot.* hill-climbing ability.

Steigung ['ʃtaɪguŋ] *f* rise, gradient, *Am. a.* grade; (*Hang*) slope; (*Aufstieg*) ascent.

steil [ʃtaɪl] steep; '**2feuer** ⚔ *n* high-angle fire; '**2hang** *m* precipice, steep slope; '**2heit** *f* steepness; '**2paß** *m Fußball*: through ball.

Stein [ʃtaɪn] *m* (3) stone (*a.* ♀, ⚕ *u. Edel2*); (*Fels*) rock; *Uhr*: jewel; *Damespiel*: man; *für Feuerzeuge*: flint; *fig. den ~ ins Rollen bringen* set the ball rolling; *e-n ~ im Brett haben bei j-m* be in a p.'s good books; *ein ~ fällt mir vom Herzen* that takes a load off my mind; *s. Anstoß.*

'**Stein|-adler** *m* golden eagle; '**2'-alt** very old; '**~bock** *m* ibex; *ast.* Capricorn; '**~bruch** *m* quarry; '**~butt** *m* (3) turbot; '**~druck** *m* lithography; (*Bild*) lithograph; '**~drucker** *m* lithographer; '**~-eiche** ♀ *f* holm-oak; '**2ern** stone-..., of stone; *fig.* stony; '**~frucht** *f* stone(-)fruit; '**~garten** *m* rock garden; '**~gut** *n* earthenware, stoneware; '**2'hart** (as) hard as stone.

'**steinig** full of stones, stony, rocky; **~en** ['~igən] (25) stone; '**2ung** *f* stoning.

'**Stein|kohle** *f* mineral (*od.* hard) coal, pit-coal; '**~kohlenbergwerk** *n* colliery; '**~marder** *m* beech marten; '**~metz** *m* (12) stone-mason; '**~-obst** *n* stone-fruit; '**~pilz** *m* (edible) boletus; '**2'reich** *fig.* immensely rich; '**~salz** *n* rock-salt; '**~schlag** *mount. m* rockfall; '**~wurf** *m* stone's throw; '**~zeit** *f* Stone Age.

Steiß [ʃtaɪs] *m* (3[2]) buttocks *pl.*, rump; '**~bein** *anat. n* coccyx.

Stellage [ʃtɛ'lɑːʒə] *f* (15) frame, rack, stand; ✝ *Börse*: put and call; (*~ngeschäft*) dealing in futures.

Stelldichein ['ʃtɛldiçˀaɪn] *n* (*inv. gen. a. ~s*) rendezvous, *bsd. Am.* F date.

Stelle ['ʃtɛlə] *f* (15) place; (*Fleck*) spot; (*wo j. steht*) stand, position; (*Arbeitsstelle*) employment, job, situation, place, post; (*Behörde, Dienststelle*) agency, office; (*Buch2*) passage; *e-r Zahl*: digit, (*Dezimal2*) place; *freie ~* (*freier Arbeitsplatz*) vacancy; *offene ~* (*Öffnung*) opening; *an erster ~* in the first place; *fig. an erster ~ stehen* come first; *an ~ von od. gen.* in place of, instead of; *an deiner ~* in your place; *an j-s ~ treten* take the place of a p.; *auf der ~* on the spot, immediately; *auf der ~ treten* ⚔ *u. fig.* mark time; *nicht von der ~ kommen* not to get ahead; *zur ~ sein* be present *od.* at hand.

'**stellen** (25) put; place, set; stand; (*richtig ein~*) regulate, adjust; *Wecker, Aufgabe*: set; (*aufhalten*) stop; *Verbrecher, Wild*: bring to (*od.* hold at) bay, hunt down; (*herausfordern*) challenge; (*liefern*) furnish, supply; provide; *Zeugen*: produce; *sich wohin ~* place o.s.; ⚔ join up, enlist; (*sich einfinden*) present o.s.; *dem Verfolger*: turn to (*od.* stand at) bay (*a. fig.*); *e-m Gegner*: face up to *an opponent*; *sich ~ gegen et.* oppose; *sich der Polizei ~* give o.s. up to the police; *sich gut mit j-m ~* put o.s. on good terms with a p.; *fig. sich krank usw.*

~ feign (*od.* pretend) to be ill *etc.*; *sich ~, als ob ...* feign (*od.* pretend) to *do*; *sich zum Kampf ~* accept combat; *sich (im Preis) ~ auf* come to, cost; *der Preis stellt sich auf ...* the price is ...; *Bedingungen ~* make conditions; *wie stellt er sich dazu?* what does he say (to it)?; *in Dienst ~* engage, *Schiff*: put into commission; *s. Antrag, Bein, Falle, Frage, Rechnung usw.*; *gestellt Bild usw.*: posed; *gut gestellt sein* be well off; *auf sich selbst gestellt sein* be on one's own.

'**Stellen|-angebot** *n* position offered; *~e pl. in der Zeitung*: vacancies; '**~-ausschreibung** *f* advertising of a post; '**~beschreibung** *f* job description; '**~gesuch** *n* application for a job; *~e pl. in der Zeitung*: jobs wanted; '**~jäger** *m* job-hunter; '**⁓los** unemployed, jobless; '**~markt** *m* job market; '**~nachweis** *m*, '**~vermittlung(sbüro** *n*) *f* employment agency (*Am.* bureau); '**⁓weise** here and there, in places (*od.* spots); '**~wert** *m fig.* rank, rating.

'**Stell|macher** *m* wheelwright; '**~-schraube** *f* adjusting screw.

'**Stellung** *f* position (*a.* ⚔ *u. fig. Einstellung*); (*Berufs⁓*) position, situation, employment, job, place; (*Rang*) (social) position, status, rank; (*Ansehen*) standing; (*Körperhaltung*) posture; (*das Stellen*) furnishing; *~ beziehen, ~ nehmen* declare o.s., give one's opinion, comment (*alle*: *zu* on); *die ~ halten fig.* hold the fort; **~nahme** ['~na:mə] *f* (15) opinion, comment, statement (*zu* on); '**~skrieg** stabilized (*od.* static) warfare; '**⁓slos** *s. stellenlos*; '**~sspiel** *n Sport*: positional play; '**~suchende** *m, f* applicant; '**~s-wechsel** *m* change of position.

'**stell|vertretend** vicarious; *amtlich*: acting, deputy; *~er Vorsitzender* vice-chairman; '**⁓vertreter(in** *f*) *m* representative; *amtlich*: deputy; (*Bevollmächtigter*) proxy; (*Ersatzmann*) substitute; '**⁓vertretung** *f* representation; agency; substitution; '**⁓vorrichtung** *f* adjusting device; '**⁓werk** 🚂 *n* signal box.

Stelze ['ʃtɛltsə] *f* (15) stilt; '**⁓n** (27, sn) stalk.

Stemm|bogen ['ʃtɛm-] *m* stem turn; '**~-eisen** *n* crowbar; (*Meißel*) chisel.

stemmen ['ʃtɛmən] (25) prop, support; (*hochwuchten*) lever up; *Gewicht*: lift; *Loch*: chisel; *sich ~ gegen* press against, *fig.* resist *od.* oppose *a th.*; *die Füße ~ gegen* plant one's feet against.

Stempel ['ʃtɛmpəl] *m* (7) stamp; ⊕ piston; (*Präge⁓*) die; (*Loch⁓*) punch; ⚘ pistil; ⚒ (*Stützholz*) prop; † brand, (*Echtheitszeichen*) hallmark; *fig. den ~ e-r S. tragen* bear the stamp of; '**~bogen** *m* stamped sheet of paper; '**~farbe** *f* stamping-ink; '**~gebühr** *f* stamp-duty; '**~kissen** *n* ink-pad; '**~marke** *f* (duty) stamp; '**⁓n** (29) stamp, mark; *fig. ~ zu* stamp (*od.* label) as; F *~ gehen* be on the dole; '**~-uhr** *f* time-clock.

Stengel ['ʃtɛŋəl] *m* (7) stalk, stem.

Stenogra|mm [ʃteno'gram] *n* (3) shorthand notes *pl.*; **~ph** [~'grɑ:f] *m* (12), **~phin** *f* shorthand writer, stenographer; **~phie** [~gra'fi:] *f* (15) shorthand, stenography; **⁓'phieren** *v/t. u. v/i.* write (in) shorthand; **⁓phisch** [~'grɑ:fiʃ] (*adv.* in) shorthand.

Stenotypist [~ty'pist] *m* (12), **~in** *f* [(16[1]) shorthand typist.

Stentorstimme ['ʃtɛntɔrʃtimə] *f* stentorian voice.

Stepp|decke ['ʃtɛpdɛkə] *f* (continental) quilt; '**~e** *f* (15) steppe; '**⁓en** (25) quilt; '**~naht** *f* quilting-seam.

Steptanz ['ʃtɛptants] *m* tap-dance.

Sterbe|bett ['ʃtɛrbəbɛt] *n* death-bed; '**~fall** *m* (case of) death; '**~fallversicherung** *f* death insurance; '**~geld** *n* death grant; '**~hilfe** ⚕ *f* euthanasia; '**~kasse** *f* burial-fund; '**⁓n 1.** (30, sn) die (*an dat.* of); **2.** ⁓ *n* dying, death; *im ~ liegen* be dying.

'**sterbens|'krank** dangerously ill; '**~'müde** dead tired; '**⁓'wort** *n*, '**⁓-'wörtchen** *n*: *kein ~* not a (single) word.

'**Sterbe|sakramente** *n/pl.* last sacraments; '**~stunde** *f* dying-hour; '**~-urkunde** *f* death-certificate.

sterblich ['ʃtɛrpliç] mortal; *~ verliebt* desperately in love (*in acc.* with); *gewöhnliche ⁓e pl.* ordinary mortals; '**⁓keit** *f* mortality; '**⁓keitsziffer** *f* death-rate, mortality.

Stereo ['ste:reo] *n* stereo; '**~-anlage** *f* stereo set; '**~-aufnahme** *f* stereo recording; *phot.* stereoscopic photo (-graph); **~metrie** [~me'tri:] *f* (15) stereometry, solid geometry; ≈**phon** [~'fo:n] stereophonic; ~**skop** [~'sko:p] *n* (3^1) stereoscope; '~**ton** *m* stereo sound.

stereotyp [~'ty:p] stereotype; *fig.* stereotyped; ≈**e** *f* (15) stereotype; ≈**ie** [~'pi:] *f* (15) stereotype-printing; ~**ieren** [~'pi:rən] stereotype.

steril [ste'ri:l] *allg.* sterile; ~**isieren** [~rili'zi:rən] sterilize; ≈**isation** [~iza'tsjo:n] *f* sterilization; ≈**ität** [~rili'tɛ:t] *f* (16, *o. pl.*) sterility.

Stern [ʃtɛrn] *m* (3) star (*a. fig.*); *(un)glücklicher* ~ (un)lucky star; *typ.* asterisk (*a.* '~**chen** *n* [6]); '~-**bild** *n* constellation; '~**deuter** *m* astrologer; ~**deuterei** [~'raɪ] *f* astrology; '~**enbanner** *n* Star-Spangled Banner, Stars and Stripes *pl.*; '~**fahrt** *mot. f* motor rally; ≈**förmig** ['~fœrmiç] starlike, stellar; *a.* ⊕ radial; '≈**hagelvoll** F dead drunk; '≈**hell**, '≈**klar** starli(gh)t, starry; '~**himmel** *m* firmament, starry sky; '~**kunde** *f* astronomy; '~**licht** *n* starlight; '~**motor** *m* radial engine; '~**schaltung** ⚡ *f* Y-connection; '~**schnuppe** *f* shooting star; '~**stunde** *f* siderial hour; *fig.* fateful hour; '~**warte** *f* observatory.

Sterz [ʃtɛrts] *m* (3^2) tail; (*Pflug*≈) plough-tail, *Am.* plowtail.

stet [ʃte:t] steady, constant; *fig.* ~*er Tropfen höhlt den Stein* little strokes fell big oaks.

'**stetig** continual, constant; (*unerschütterlich*) steady; '≈**keit** *f* steadiness; continuity, constancy.

stets [ʃte:ts] always, constantly.

Steuer ['ʃtɔʏər] **1.** ⚓ *n* (7) rudder, helm; ✈ control(s *pl.*); *mot.* steering wheel; *am* ~ at the helm (*a. fig.*), *mot.* at the wheel; **2.** ~ *f* (15) tax, *bsd. indirekte*: duty; (*Kommunal*≈) rate (*alle*: *auf acc.* on); *von der* ~ *absetzbar* tax-deductible; '~-**abzug** *m* tax deduction; '~-**aufkommen** *n* tax receipts *pl.*, inland (*Am.* internal) revenue; '≈**bar** assessable, taxable; ⊕ *s. lenkbar*; '~**be-amte** *m* revenue-officer; '~**befreiung** *f* tax exemption; '~**behörde** *f* inland-revenue office; '~**berater** *m* tax consultant; '~**bescheid** *m* notice of assessment; '~**bord** ⚓ *n* starboard; '~**delikt** *n* tax offen|ce, *Am.* -se; '~-**einnahmen** *f/pl. s. Steueraufkommen*; '~**erklärung** *f* (income-)tax return; '~-**erlaß** *m* remission of taxes; '~-**erleichterung** *f*, '~-**ermäßigung** *f* tax relief; '~**flosse** ✈ *f* fin; '≈**frei** tax-free, tax-exempt; '~**freibetrag** *m* tax-allowance; '~**freiheit** *f* exemption from taxation; '~**hinterzieher** *m* tax dodger; '~**hinterziehung** *f* tax evasion; '~**klasse** *f* tax bracket; '~**knüppel** ✈ *m* control stick *od.* lever, joystick; '~**last** *f* tax burden; '≈**lich** tax ..., fiscal; '~**mann** ⚓ *m* helmsman; (*Boots*≈) coxswain; (*Titel*) mate; *ohne* ~ (*Bootsrennen*) coxswainless; '~**marke** *f* duty-stamp; '~**mittel** *n/pl.* tax money *sg.*

'**steuern** (h. *u.* sn) steer, *bsd.* ✈ pilot; *mot.* drive; ⊕ control; *e-r S.* ~ check a th., *vorbeugend*: obviate, *abhelfend*: remedy; *der Not* ~ meet need.

'**Steuer**|-**o-ase** *f*, '~**paradies** *n* tax haven; ≈**pflichtig** ['~pfliçtiç] taxable; *S.*: dutiable; '~**politik** *f* fiscal policy; '~**pult** ⊕ *n* control desk; '~**rad** *n* ⚓, *mot.* steering wheel; ✈ control wheel; '≈**rechtlich** fiscal; '~-**rück-erstattung** *f* tax refund; '~-**ruder** *n* ⚓ rudder, helm; ✈ control surface; '~**satz** *m* tax rate; '~**senkung** *f* lowering of taxes; '~**sünder** *m* tax-dodger.

'**Steuerung** *f* steering; piloting; ⊕, ⚡ control; (*Vorrichtung*) steering gear; ✈ controls *pl.*; (*Ventil*≈) valve gear.

'**Steuer**|**ver-anlagung** *f* assessment; '~**zahler** *m Brt. staatlich*: taxpayer, *städtisch*: ratepayer; *Am. allg.* taxpayer.

Steven ⚓ ['ʃte:vən] *m* (6) stem.

Steward ✈, ⚓ ['stju:ərt] *m* (11) steward; ~**eß** ['~dɛs] *f* (16^3) *f* stewardess, air hostess.

stibitzen F [ʃti'bitsən] (27) *sl.* filch.

Stich [ʃtiç] *m* (3) (*Nadel*≈) prick; *e-s Insekts*: sting; (*Dolch*≈, *Messer*≈) stab; (*Näh*≈) stitch; (*Stoß*) thrust; *Karten*: trick; (*Kupfer*≈) engraving; ⚕ (*Schmerz*) stitch, twinge; stitch; ⚓ knot; *fig.* (*Seitenhieb*) cut, gibe; ~ *halten* hold water; *im* ~ *lassen* abandon, desert, *Gefährten*: *a.* forsake, let down, leave in the lurch; *e-n* ~ *haben Bier usw.*: be turning sour, *Fleisch*: be (a bit) high, F *P.*: be touched; *ein* ~ *ins Blaue* a tinge of blue; *es gab ihm e-n* ~ it cut him to the quick.

Stichel ['ʃtiçəl] *m* (7) engraver's

tool; **~ei** [~'laɪ] *f* (16), '**~rede** *f* taunt, sneer, gibe, needling; '**2n** (29) *v/i.* stitch; prick (*beide a. v/t.*); *fig.* taunt, sneer (*gegen* at), needle.

'**stich|fest** proof; '**2flamme** *f* blast flame, flash; '**~haltig** valid, sound; ~ *sein* hold water; '**2haltigkeit** *f* validity, soundness; '**2ler** *m* taunter; '**2ling** *m* (3¹) (*Fisch*) stickleback; '**2probe** *f* spot check; random sample; ✝ sample test; '**2säge** *f* compass saw; '**2tag** *m* fixed day, target-date; deadline; '**2waffe** *f* stabbing (*od.* thrusting) weapon; '**2wahl** *f* second ballot; '**2wort** *n* catchword; *im Wörterbuch*: *a.* entry; *bsd. thea.* cue; '**2wortkatalog** *m* classified catalogue; '**2wortverzeichnis** *n* index; '**2wunde** *f* stab.

sticken ['ʃtikən] (25) embroider.

'**Sticker** *m* (7), '**~in** *f* embroiderer; **~ei** [~'raɪ] *f* (16) embroidery.

'**Stick|garn** *n* embroidery silk; '**2ig** stifling, close, stuffy; '**~luft** *f* close (*od.* stuffy) air; **~oxyd** ⚗ ['~ʔɔksiːt] *n* nitric oxide; '**~rahmen** *m* tambour (-frame); '**~stoff** ⚗ *m* nitrogen; **2stoffhaltig** ['~haltiç] nitrogenous.

stieben ['ʃtiːbən] (30, h. *u.* sn) fly about; *Flüssigkeit*: spray; *Menge*: scatter.

Stiefbruder ['ʃtiːf-] *m* stepbrother.

Stiefel ['ʃtiːfəl] *m* (7) boot, *Am. a.* shoe; F (*Unsinn*) *sl.* rot; '**~hose** *f* (*eine* a pair of) breeches *pl.*; '**~knecht** *m* boot-jack; '**2n** F (29) march; '**~putzer** *m im Hotel*: boots; *auf der Straße*: shoeblack; '**~schaft** *m* leg (of a boot).

'**Stief|geschwister** *pl.* stepbrother(s) and stepsister(s); '**~mutter** *f* stepmother; *b.s.* cruel mother; '**~mütterchen** ⚘ *n* pansy; '**2mütterlich** stepmotherly; *fig.* ~ *behandeln* neglect badly; '**~schwester** *f* stepsister; '**~sohn** *m* stepson; '**~tochter** *f* stepdaughter; '**~vater** *m* stepfather.

stieg [ʃtiːk] *pret. v. steigen*¹.

Stiege ['ʃtiːgə] *f* (15) *s. Steige.*

Stieglitz ['ʃtiːglits] *m* (3²) goldfinch.

Stiel [ʃtiːl] *m* (3) handle; *e-s Glases, e-r Pfeife*: stem; (*Besen2*) stick; ⚘ stalk.

Stier [ʃtiːr] **1.** *m* (3) bull; *ast.* Bull, Taurus; *den ~ bei den Hörnern packen* take the bull by the horns; **2.** 2 *adj.* staring; '**2en** (25) stare (*auf acc., nach* at); (*glotzen*) goggle (at); '**~kampf** *m* bull-fight; '**~kämpfer** *m* bull-fighter; '**2nackig** bull-necked.

stieß [ʃtiːs] *pret. v. stoßen.*

Stift¹ [ʃtift] *m* (3) pin; (*Holz2*) peg; (*Zier2*) stud; (*Zwecke*) tack; (*Zeichen2*) pencil, *farbiger*: crayon; F (*Lehrling*) youngster; **~**² *n* (1 *u.* 3) (charitable) foundation; (*Domkapitel*) chapter(-house); (*Kloster*) convent; (*Altersheim*) home for aged ladies; (*Theologenschule*) seminary; '**2en** (26) found; establish; (*spenden*) give, *Am.* donate; (*verursachen*) cause; *Frieden*: make; *s. Unfriede*; F ~ *gehen* bolt; '**~er** *m* (7), '**~erin** *f* (16¹) founder; donor; (*Urheber*) author.

'**Stifts|dame** *f*, '**~fräulein** *n* canoness; '**~herr** *m* canon, prebendary; '**~kirche** *f* collegiate church.

'**Stiftung** *f* (*Schenkung*) donation, grant; (*Gründung*; *Anstalt*) foundation; *milde* ~ charitable institution, charity; '**~sfest** *n* foundation-festival, founder's day.

'**Stiftzahn** *m* pivot tooth.

Stil [ʃtiːl] *m* (3¹) *allg.* style (*a.* '**~-art** *f*); *im großen* ~ on a large scale, *attr.* large-scale; '**~blüte** F *f* howler; '**2-echt** *s. stilgerecht*; **~ett** [sti'lɛt] *n* (3) stiletto; **~gefühl** ['ʃtiːl-] *n* stilistic sense; '**2gerecht** stylish, true to style; *adv.* in (proper) style; **2i'sieren** stylize; *Text*: compose, word, stylize; **~istik** [~'listik] *f* (16) theory of style; **2istisch** [~'listiʃ] stylistic (-ally *adv.*); **~kunde** ['ʃtiːl-] *f* style.

still [ʃtil] still, quiet; (*schweigend*) *a.* silent; (*ruhig*) calm; (*bewegungslos*) still, motionless; ✝ dull, flat; (*heimlich*) secret (*a. Hoffnung, Liebe, Reserven*); ~! silence!, quiet!; *~es Gebet* silent prayer; *im ~en* silently, (*heimlich*) secretly; *2er Freitag* Good Friday; ✝ *~er Gesellschafter od. Teilhaber* sleeping (*Am.* silent) partner; *der 2e Ozean* the Pacific Ocean; *s. Wasser*; '**2e** *f* (15) stillness, quiet(ness), silence; calm; lull (*vor dem Sturm* before the storm); *in der ~* quietly, (*heimlich*) secretly.

'**Stilleben** *paint. n* (6, *bei Trennung*: *Still-leben*) still life.

'**stilleg|en** (*bei Trennung*: *still-legen*) *Betrieb*: shut (*od.* close) down; *Ver-*

kehr: stop; ˈ2**ung** *f* closure, shut-down; stoppage.

ˈ**stillen** (25) *Schmerz*: still; *Zorn, Hunger*: appease, stay; *Blut*: stop, sta(u)nch; *Durst*: quench; *Kind*: breast-feed, nurse; *Begierde*: gratify.

ˈ**Stillhalte|-abkommen** *n* standstill agreement; ˈ2**n** *v/i.* keep still (*a. v/t.*); *fig.* refrain from action; (*einhalten*) stop.

ˈ**stilliegen** (*bei Trennung*: *still-liegen*; 30) lie still; *fig.* lie dormant; *Betrieb*: lie idle; *Handel usw.*: be at a standstill; *Verkehr*: be suspended.

stillos [ˈʃti:lo:s] without (*od.* in bad) style.

ˈ**still|schweigen** be silent (*zu* about); ˈ2**schweigen** *n* silence; *mit ~ übergehen* pass (over) in silence; ˈ**~schweigend** silent; *fig.* tacit, implied; ˈ2**stand** *m* standstill, stop(page); *v. Verhandlungen usw.*: deadlock; *zum ~ bringen* (*kommen*) bring (come) to a standstill; ˈ**~stehen** stand still; ⚔ stand at attention; ⊕ be idle; *fig.* be at a standstill; ⚔ *stillgestanden!* attention!; *der Verstand stand ihm still* his mind reeled (*bei* at); ˈ2**ung** *f s. stillen*; stilling; appeasing; sta(u)nching; quenching; nursing, suckling; gratification; ˈ**~vergnügt** cheerful(ly *adv.*).

ˈ**Stil|möbel** *n/pl.* period furniture; ˈ**~-übung** *f* stylistic exercise; ˈ2**voll** stylish.

ˈ**Stimm|-abgabe** *f* voting; ˈ**~-aufwand** *m* vocal effort; ˈ**~band** *n* vocal c(h)ord; ˈ2**berechtigt** entitled to vote; ˈ**~bezirk** *m* constituency, electoral district; ˈ**~bruch** *m* change of voice.

Stimme [ˈʃtimə] *f* (15) voice (*a. fig.*); (*Wahl*2) vote; (*Presse*2) comment; ♪ (*Noten*) part; *entscheidende ~* casting vote; (*gut*) *bei ~* in (good) voice; *seine ~ abgeben* (cast *od.* give one's) vote; *mit lauter ~* in a loud voice; ˈ2**n** (25) *v/t.* tune; *fig. günstig usw.*: dispose; *j-n gegen et. ~* prejudice a p. against; *glücklich ~* make (feel) happy; *v/i.* (*zutreffen*) be true; *Summe usw.*: be correct; (*übereinstimmen*) agree, tally; *~ für* (*gegen*) vote for (against); F (*das*) *stimmt* (that's) right; *da stimmt et. nicht* there is something wrong.

ˈ**Stimmen|-einheit** *f* unanimity; ˈ**~fang** *m* vote-getting; ˈ**~gleichheit** *f* parity of votes; *parl.* tie; ˈ**~mehrheit** *f* majority (of votes); *einfache ~* simple majority.

ˈ**Stimm-enthaltung** *f* abstention (from voting).

ˈ**Stimmenzählung** *f* counting of votes.

ˈ**Stimmer** ♪ *m* (7) tuner.

ˈ**stimm|fähig** entitled to vote; ˈ2**gabel** *f* tuning-fork; ˈ**~gewaltig** loud-voiced; ˈ**~haft** *gr.* voiced; ˈ2**lage** *f* pitch; ˈ**~lich** vocal; ˈ**~los** voiceless; *gr. a.* unvoiced; ˈ2**recht** *n* (right to) vote; *nur pol.* franchise, suffrage; ˈ2**ritze** *anat. f* glottis.

ˈ**Stimmung** *f* ♪ tune; *fig.* mood (*a. paint. usw.*), frame of mind; ⚔ *der Truppe*: morale; *der Öffentlichkeit*: sentiment; *allgemeine*: atmosphere; ⚕ *Börse*: tone, tendency; *in guter ~* in good humo(u)r, in high spirits; (*nicht*) *in der ~ zu ...* in the (in no) mood for *a th. od.* to *inf.*; *~ machen für* make propaganda for; ˈ**~skanone** F *f* great joker, life of the party; ˈ**~smache** *f* boom(ing); ˈ**~smensch** *m* moody creature; ˈ**~smusik** *f* mood music; ˈ**~s-umschwung** *m* change of mood (*Börse*: of tone); ˈ2**svoll** atmospheric.

ˈ**Stimm|wechsel** *m* change of voice; ˈ**~zettel** *m* ballot.

Stimul|ans [ˈsti:mulans] *n* (11[1], *pl. -lantia od. -lanzien*) stimulant (*a. fig.*); 2**ieren** [stimuˈli:rən] stimulate.

Stink|bombe [ˈʃtiŋk-] *f* stink-bomb; ˈ2**en** (30) stink (*nach* of; *a. fig.*); ˈ2ˈ**faul** F bone-lazy; ˈ2ˈ**langweilig** F deadly boring; ˈ**~tier** *n* skunk; ˈ**~wut** F *f*: *e-e ~ haben* be furious (*auf* with).

Stipendi|at [ʃtipɛnˈdja:t] *m* (12) scholar; **~um** [~ˈpɛndjum] *n* (9) scholarship.

stipp|en F [ˈʃtipən] (25) steep, dip; ˈ2**visite** F *f* flying visit.

Stirn [ʃtirn] *f* (16) forehead; *fig.* impudence, face; *j-m die ~ bieten* defy; ˈ**~band** *n*, ˈ**~binde** *f* head-band, frontlet; ˈ**~höhle** *f* frontal cavity *od.* 🕮 sinus; ˈ**~höhlenvereiterung** ⚕ *f* frontal sinusitis; ˈ**~locke** *f* forelock; ˈ**~rad** ⊕ *n* spur-gear; ˈ**~runzeln** *n* frown(ing); ˈ**~seite** *f* front (side), face; ˈ**~wand** *f* front wall.

stob [ʃto:p] *pret. v. stieben.*

stöbern [ˈʃtøːbərn] (29) hunt, rummage; *es stöbert* a fine snow (*od.* rain) is falling.

stochern [ˈʃtɔxərn] *v/i.* (29) *im Feuer*: poke, stir; *in den Zähnen*: pick; *im Essen*: pick at.

Stock [ʃtɔk] *m* (3³) stick (*a. Schi*&); (*Rohr*&) cane; ♪ (*Takt*&) baton; *s. Bienen*&, *Billard*& *usw.*; ⚘ stock; (*~werk*) (3, *pl. inv.*) stor(e)y, floor; *im ersten ~* on the first (*Am.* second) floor; *über ~ und Stein* over hedge and ditch; ˈ&ˈ**blind** stone-blind; ˈ**~degen** *m* sword-cane; ˈ&-ˈ**dumm** utterly stupid; ˈ&ˈ**dunkel** pitch-dark.

Stöckelschuh [ˈʃtœkəlʃuː] *m* high-heeled shoe.

stocken [ˈʃtɔkən] (25, h. *u.* sn) stop, come to a standshill; *langsam*: slacken; *Flüssigkeit*, *a. fig.*: stagnate; *Herz*: cease to beat; *mot.* stall; (*zögern*) hesitate; *Stimme*: falter; *Verhandlungen usw.*: reach a deadlock; (*schimmeln*) turn mo(u)ldy *od.* fusty; *Zahn*: decay, rot; *ins & geraten* come to a standstill.

ˈ**Stock**|ˈ**-engländer** *m* thorough (*od.* true-born) Englishman; ˈ**~-ente** *f* mallard; ˈ&ˈ**finster** pitch-dark; ˈ**~fisch** *m* stockfish, dried cod; *fig.* F stick; ˈ**~fleck** *m* damp-stain; *~e pl.* (*a.* ⚘) mildew *sg.*; ˈ&**fleckig** foxed, foxy, (*a.* ⚘) mildewy.

...stöckig [~ʃtœkiç] ...-storeyed, *Am.* ...-storied.

ˈ**stock**|ˈ**konservativ** ultra-conservative; ˈ~ˈ**nüchtern** stone-cold sober; ˈ&**punkt** *m Öl*: solidifying point; ˈ&**schnupfen** *m* chronic cold in the head; ˈ~ˈ**steif** (as) stiff as a poker; ˈ~ˈ**still** stock-still; ˈ~ˈ**taub** stone-deaf; ˈ&**ung** *f s. stocken*; stoppage; stagnation (*a.* ⚕); flagging; standstill; hesitation; *des Verkehrs*: (traffic) jam, congestion (*a.* ⚕ *des Blutes*); *fig.* deadlock; ˈ&**werk** *n* stor(e)y, floor; ˈ&**zahn** *m* molar.

Stoff [ʃtɔf] *m* (3) matter, substance; (*Textil*&) material, fabric; (*Tuch*) cloth; (*Wollzeug*) stuff (*a.* F *Schnaps usw.*); (*Wirk*&) agent; *fig.* subject (-matter); *zu e-m Roman usw.*: material (for); **~el** [ˈ~əl] *m* (7) yokel, boor; ˈ&**lich** material; with regard to the subject-matter; ˈ**~wechsel** *m* metabolism; ~... metabolic.

stöhnen [ˈʃtøːnən] **1.** (25) groan, moan; **2.** & *n* groaning, groans *pl.*

Stoiker [ˈʃtoːˀikər] *m* (7) stoic. ˈ**sto·isch** stoical.

Stola [ˈstoːla] *f* (16²) stole.

Stolle [ˈʃtɔlə] *f* (15) (*Kuchen*) fruit loaf; ˈ**~n** *m* (6) (*Pfosten*) post; ⚒ tunnel, adit, (*a.* ⚔) gallery; *am Hufeisen*; calk; *s. Stolle*.

stolper|**n** [ˈʃtɔlpərn] (29, sn) stumble, trip (*über acc.* over; *beide a. fig.*); ˈ&**stein** *m fig.* stumbling block.

stolz [ʃtɔlts] **1.** *allg.* proud (*auf acc.* of); (*hochmütig*) haughty; *fig.* (*großartig*) proud (*day, ship, etc.*); noble, stately; *~ sein auf* (*acc.*) be proud of, take pride in; **2.** & *m* (3²) pride (*a. fig. Person, Sache*); *s-n ~ setzen in* pride o.s. on.

stolˈ**zieren** (sn) strut, swagger.

stopfen [ˈʃtɔpfən] (25) *v/t.* (*voll*&, *hinein*&) stuff, cram; *Pfeife, Loch*: fill; (*zu~*) stop, plug; ⚕ constipate; *Strümpfe usw.*: darn; ⚔ (*das Feuer*) *~* cease firing; *j-m den Mund ~* stop a p.'s mouth; *gestopft voll* crammed full; ♪ *gestopfte Trompete* muted trumpet; *v/i.* ⚕ cause constipation.

ˈ**Stopf**|**garn** *n* darning-cotton; ˈ**~mittel** ⚕ *n* emplastic; ˈ**~nadel** *f* darning-needle.

Stopp [ʃtɔp] *m* (11) stop; (*Verbot*) prohibition, ban.

Stoppel [ˈʃtɔpəl] *f* (15) stubble; ˈ**~bart** *m* stubbly beard; ˈ**~feld** *n* stubble-field; ˈ&**ig** stubbly; ˈ&**n** *v/t. u. v/i.* (29) glean; *fig.* patch; ˈ**~werk** *n* (literary) patchwork.

stopp|**en** [ˈʃtɔpən] *v/t. u. v/i.* stop; *mit Stoppuhr*: time, clock; ˈ&**licht** *mot. n* stop light; ˈ&**schild** *mot. n* stop sign; ˈ&**-uhr** *f* stop watch.

Stöpsel [ˈʃtœpsəl] *m* (7) stopper, cork, *bsd.* ⚡ plug; F (*kleiner Kerl*) little man, *Am.* F shortie; ˈ&**n** (29) stopper, cork, *bsd.* ⚡ plug.

Stör [ʃtøːr] *m* (3) sturgeon.

Storch [ʃtɔrç] *m* (3³) stork; ˈ**~schnabel** *m* stork's bill; ⊕ pantograph; *bot.* crane's bill.

Store [ʃtoːr] *m* (11) net curtain.

stören [ˈʃtøːrən] (25) disturb, trouble; (*durcheinanderbringen*) upset, disarrange; (*sich einmengen in*) interfere with, *Radio*: *a.* jam; *stört es Sie, wenn ich ...?* do you mind if I ...?; *nur v/i.* be intruding; (*im Wege sein*) be in the way; *das Gesamtbild*: mar the picture; (*unangenehm sein*) be awkward; &**fried**

['~fri:t] *m* (3) intruder; troublemaker.

stornieren [stɔr'ni:rən] *Buchung*: reverse; *Auftrag*: cancel.

störrig ['ʃtœriç], *a.* '**störrisch** stubborn, obstinate; (*stur*) mulish; *bsd. Pferd*: restive; '**2keit** stubbornness, obstinacy; restiveness.

'**Störsender** *m Radio*: jamming station *od.* transmitter, jammer.

'**Störung** *f* disturbance, trouble (*beide a.* ⚕); ⊕ trouble, *völlige*: breakdown; (*Einmischung*) interference, *Radio*: *a.* jamming; (*Eindringen*) intrusion; (*Behinderung*) obstruction; (*Unterbrechung*) interruption; *s. atmosphärisch*; *geistige* ~ mental disorder; '**~sdienst** *m*, '**~sstelle** *teleph. f* fault section; '**2sfrei** undisturbed; ⊕ trouble-free.

Stoß [ʃto:s] *m* (3² *u.* ³) push, shove, (*a. fenc.*; ⚔ *Vor2*; *phys. Schub*) thrust; (*Fuß2*) kick; (*Schlag*) blow; *mit den Hörnern, dem Kopf*: butt; (*Rippen2*) dig, nudge; (*Erschütterung*) shock, jolt; blow; (*Schwimm2*) stroke; *Kugelstoßen*: put; *des Gewehrs*: recoil; (*Anprall*) bump, *phys. u. weitS.* impact; (*Explosions2, Wind2, Trompeten2*) blast; ⊕ (*Ende*) butt joint; (~ *Holz usw.*) pile, stack; (*Brief2*) batch; *fig.* e-n ~ *versetzen* (*dat.*) be a blow to; '**~dämpfer** *mot. m* shock-absorber; '**~degen** *m* rapier, foil.

Stößel ['ʃtø:səl] *m* (7) *Mörser*: pestle; (*Kolben*) plunger; (*Ventil2*) tappet.

stoßen ['ʃto:sən] (30) *v/t.* push, shove; *stärker*: thrust; *mit dem Fuß*: kick; *mit der Faust*: punch; *mit den Hörnern, dem Kopf*: butt; *mit e-m Stock*: poke; *schlagend*: knock, strike; (*rammen*) ram; *Sport*: *die Kugel* ~ put the shot; *Zucker usw.*: pound; ~ *aus dem Hause, e-m Verein usw.*: expel from, turn out of; *j-n in die Rippen* ~ nudge a p.; *von sich* ~ push away, reject; *s. Kopf*; *sich* ~ *an* (*dat.*) strike (*od.* knock *od.* run) against, *fig.* take offen|ce (*Am.* -se) at, stick at, object to; *v/i.* **a**) thrust; kick; butt (*a. v/t.*; *alle*: *nach* at); *Gewehr*: recoil; *Wagen*: jolt, bump; *an et.* (*acc.*) ~ (*grenzen*) adjoin, border (*od.* abut) on; *ins Horn* ~ blow the horn; **b**) (sn) ~ *auf* (*acc.*) (happen to) meet, run into *a p.*, (*entdecken*) come across, stumble on; *auf Ablehnung, Widerstand usw.*: meet with, encounter; *zu j-m* ~ join (up with); **c**) (h. *u.* sn) ~ *gegen od. an* (*acc.*) knock (*od.* strike) against.

'**Stoß|fänger** *m s. Stoßdämpfer*; '**2fest** shockproof; '**~gebet** *n* fast (*od.* ejaculatory) prayer; '**~hobel** ⊕ *m* (cooper's) jointer; '**~kante** *f* hem, edge, lining; '**~keil** ⚔ *m* spearhead; '**~kraft** *f* ⊕ impact (force); *weitS.* impetus, force; '**~kugel** *f Sport*: shot; '**~seufzer** *m* deep sigh, groan; '**2sicher** shockproof; '**~stange** *f mot.* bumper; 🚂 buffer bar; '**~trupp** ⚔ *m* raiding patrol, assault party; '**~truppe** ⚔ *f* shock troops *pl.*; '**~verkehr** *m* rush-hour traffic; '**2weise** intermittently; in waves; '**~zahn** *m* tusk; '**~zeit** *f* rush hour.

Stotter|er ['ʃtɔtərər] *m* (7) stutterer, stammerer; '**2n** *v/i. u. v/t.* (29) stutter, stammer; F *auf 2 kaufen* buy on the never-never.

stracks [ʃtraks] directly.

'**Straf|-anstalt** *f* penal institution, prison; *Am.* (*Zuchthaus*) penitentiary; '**~-antrag** *m* private application (by the injured party); *des Staatsanwaltes*: sentence demanded by the public prosecutor; '**~-anzeige** *f*: ~ *erstatten gegen* bring a (criminal) charge against; '**~-arbeit** *f Schule*: imposition, F lines *pl.*

'**strafbar** punishable; *stärker*: criminal; (*schuldig*) culpable; *sich* ~ *machen* make o.s. liable to prosecution; '**2keit** *f* punishableness.

'**Strafbefehl** ⚖ *m* order of summary punishment.

Strafe ['ʃtra:fə] *f* (15) punishment; ⚖, ✝, *Sport, fig.*: penalty; (*Geld2*) fine; (*Strafurteil*) sentence; *bei* ~ *von* on pain (*od.* penalty) of; ~ *zahlen* ⚖ pay a fine; '**2n** (25) punish; *bsd. Sport, a. fig.* penalize; (*züchtigen*) chastise; *um Geld* ~ fine; *s. Lüge, Verachtung.*

'**Straf|-entlassene** *m* (18) ex-convict; '**~-erlaß** *m* remission of (a) punishment; *allgemeiner*: amnesty; *bedingter* ~ conditional sentence; '**~-expedition** *f* punitive expedition.

straff [ʃtraf] tight; *Seil, Sehne, Muskel*: taut; *Haltung*: erect; *fig.*

rigid, strict; *Stil*: concise; '**2heit** *f* tightness, *etc.*

'**straf|fällig** liable to prosecution; '**~frei** exempt from punishment; ~ *ausgehen* go unpunished; '**2gefangene** *m* convict; '**2gericht** *n* ⚖ criminal court; *fig.* punishment; *göttliches*: judg(e)ment (of God); '**2gesetz** *n* penal law; '**2gesetzbuch** *n* penal code; '**2kammer** *f* criminal division.

sträf|lich ['ʃtrɛ:fliç] punishable, criminal (*a. weitS.*); (*unverzeihlich*) unpardonable; *adv. fig.* badly; '**2ling** ['~liŋ] *m* (3[1]) convict.

'**Straf|liste** *f* police record; '**2los** *s. straffrei*; '**~mandat** ⚖ *n* penalty, *Am.* ticket; '**~maß** *n* degree of punishment; '**2mildernd** extenuating, mitigating; '**~mündigkeit** *f* criminal capacity; '**~porto** *n s. Nachgebühr*; '**~predigt** *f* (severe) lecture; '**~prozeß** *m* criminal case (*od.* proceedings *pl.*), trial; '**~prozeß-ordnung** *f* Code of Criminal Procedure; '**~punkt** *m Sport*: bad point, penalty; '**~raum** *m Fußball*: penalty area; '**~recht** *n* criminal law; '**2rechtlich** criminal, penal; ~ *verfolgen* prosecute; '**~register** *n* penal record; '**~sache** *f* criminal case; '**~stoß** *m Fußball*: penalty kick; '**~tat** *f* (criminal) offen|ce, *Am.* -se; '**~täter** *m* (criminal) offender; '**~verfahren** *n* criminal procedure (*konkret*: proceedings *pl.*); '**2verschärfend** aggravating; '**2versetzen** *v/t.*, '**~versetzung** *f* transfer for disciplinary reasons; '**~verteidiger** *m* trial lawyer; '**~vollstreckung** *f*, '**~vollzug** *m* execution of the sentence; '**~vollzugsbeamte** *m* prison officer; '**2würdig** *s. sträflich*; '**~zettel** *m für falsches Parken*: parking ticket.

Strahl [ʃtrɑ:l] *m* (5) ray (*a. fig. of hope*); (*Licht2*) *a.* beam; (*Blitz2*) flash; (*Wasser2, Luft2, Gas2*) jet; ⩘ radius; '**~-antrieb** ✈ *m* jet propulsion; '**2en** (25) radiate; (*a. fig.*) beam, shine (*vor dat.* with).

'**Strahlen|behandlung** *f* radiotherapy; '**2brechend** refractive; '**~brechung** *f* refraction; '**2d** radiating; *a. fig.* radiant, beaming; **2förmig** ['~fœrmiç] radial; '**~forschung** *phys. f* radiology; '**~heilkunde** *f* radiotherapeutics *pl.*; '**~krone** *f* glory, halo, nimbus; '**~schutz** *m* radiation protection.

'**Strahler** *m* (7) *phys.* emitter; (*Wärme2, Heiz2*) radiator; (*Punktleuchte*) spotlight.

'**strahl|ig** radiate; '**2-ofen** *m* radiator; '**2rohr** ✈ *n* jet pipe; '**2triebwerk** *n* jet (propulsion) engine; '**2turbine** *f* turbo-jet.

'**Strahlung** *f* radiation; '**~s-energie** *f* radiation energy; '**~sschäden** *m/pl.* radiation damage *sg.*; '**2ssicher** radiation-proof.

Strähn|e ['ʃtrɛ:nə] *f* (15) strand; *Garnmaß*: hank, skein; *Haar*: lock; '**2ig** wispy.

stramm [ʃtram] (*straff*) tight; (*kräftig*) strapping, stalwart; (*scharf, streng*) strict, stiff; *Arbeit*: hard; *Soldat, Ehrenbezeigung usw.*: smart; F *adv.* (*schnell, tüchtig*) smartly, briskly; '**~stehen** stand at attention.

Strampel|hös-chen ['ʃtrampəl-] *n* rompers *pl.*; '**2n** (29) kick (about), fidget, struggle; F (*radfahren*) pedal (away); '**~sack** *m* baby's sleeping bag.

Strand [ʃtrant] *m* (3) (sea-)shore, (*a. Bade2*) beach; '**~-anzug** *m* beach suit; '**~bad** *n* bathing-beach, lido; **2en** ['~dən] (26, sn) be stranded; *nur* ⚓ run ashore; *fig.* fail, *Mädchen*: go to the bad; **~gut** ['ʃtrant-] *n* stranded goods *pl.*, jetsam; *fig.* ~ *des Lebens* derelict(s *pl.*); '**~hotel** *n* seaside hotel; '**~korb** *m* (canopied) beach-chair; '**~promenade** *f* promenade, *Am.* boardwalk; '**~räuber** *m* wrecker; '**~schuhe** *m/pl.* beach-shoes; '**~wächter** *m* life-guard.

Strang [ʃtraŋ] *m* (3[3]) cord (*a. anat.*); (*Seil*) rope; *zum Anschirren*: trace; (*Garn2*) skein, hank; 🚂 (*Schienen2*) track; *fig. über die Stränge schlagen* kick over the traces; *an e-m ~ ziehen* pull together; *wenn alle Stränge reißen* as a last resort, if all else fails; '**~presse** ⊕ *f* extrusion press.

strangulieren [ʃtraŋgu'li:rən] strangle.

Strapaz|e [ʃtra'pɑ:tsə] *f* (15) strain; **2ieren** [~pa'tsi:rən] strain (*a. fig.*); exhaust; *sich ~* exert o.s.; *Stoff*: wear hard, F punish; **2ierfähig** [~'tsi:rfɛ:iç] for hard wear; *nur attr.* hard-wearing; **2iös** [~'tsjø:s] exhausting, trying.

Straße [ˈʃtraːsə] *f* (15) road, highway; *e-r Stadt*: street; (*Meerenge*) strait, *bei Namen mst* Straits *pl.*; ⊕ (*Fertigungs*♀ *usw.*) line; *auf der* ~ on the road; *in Städten usw.*: in (*Am.* on) the street; *auf die* ~ *setzen* turn out, sack; *s. Mann.*

ˈ**Straßen|-anzug** *m* lounge suit, *Am.* business suit; ˈ**~-arbeiten** *f/pl.* road works; ˈ**~-arbeiter** *m* roadworker, *Am.* road laborer; ˈ**~bahn** *f* tram; (*~linie*) tram(way), *Am.* trolley line; *s. ~wagen*; ˈ**~bahnführer** *m* tram-driver, *Am.* motorman; ˈ**~bahnwagen** *m* tram(-car), *Am.* streetcar; ˈ**~bau** *m* road construction; ˈ**~belag** *m* road surfacing; ˈ**~beleuchtung** *f* street-lighting; ˈ**~café** *n* pavement (*Am.* sidewalk) café; ˈ**~damm** *m* roadway; ˈ**~dirne** *f* streetwalker; ˈ**~graben** *m* (road) ditch; ˈ**~händler** *m* street-vendor; ˈ**~junge** *m* street urchin; ˈ**~kampf** *m* street-fighting; ˈ**~karte** *f* road map; ˈ**~kehrer** *m*, *a.* ˈ**~kehrmaschine** *f* street-sweeper; ˈ**~kreuzer** *mot. m* road cruiser, *Am. sl.* heap; ˈ**~kreuzung** *f* (street-) crossing; ˈ**~lage** *mot. f* road-holding; ˈ**~laterne** *f* streetlight, streetlamp; ˈ**~mädchen** *n* streetwalker; ˈ**~netz** *n* network of roads; ˈ**~raub** *m* highway robbery; ˈ**~räuber** *m* highwayman; ˈ**~reinigung** *f* street-cleaning, scavenging; ˈ**~rennen** *n Sport*: road race; ˈ**~sammlung** *f* street collection; ˈ**~schild** *n* street (*od.* road) sign; ˈ**~sperre** *f* road block; ˈ**~tunnel** *m* vehicular tunnel; ˈ**~-überführung** *f* overpass; ˈ**~-unterführung** *f* subway, underpass; ˈ**~verkehr** *m* road (*od.* street) traffic; ˈ**~verkehrs-ordnung** *f* Highway Code; ˈ**~walze** *f* road-roller; ˈ**~zustand** *m* road conditions *pl.*

Strateg|e [ʃtraˈteːgə] *m* (13) strategist; **~ie** [~teˈgiː] *f* (15, *o.pl.*) strategy; **♀isch** [~ˈteːgiʃ] strategic(al).

Stratosphäre [stratoˈsfɛːrə] *f* (15) stratosphere; **~nkreuzer** *m* stratocruiser, stratoliner.

sträuben [ˈʃtrɔʏbən] **1.** (25) ruffle; bristle; *sich* ~ *Haar*: stand on end, bristle (up); *fig.* struggle, strive (*gegen* against); **2.** ♀ struggling, resistance.

Strauch [ʃtraux] *m* (1², *pl. Sträucher* [ˈʃtrɔʏçər]) shrub, bush; ˈ**~dieb** *m* footpad.

straucheln [ˈʃtrauxəln] (29, sn) (*a. fig.*) stumble, trip; *fig.* founder, come to grief.

ˈ**Strauchwerk** *n* shrubs *pl.*

Strauß¹ [ʃtraus] *m* (3²) (*Vogel*) ostrich; **~²** *m* (3² *u.* ³) (*Streit*) strife, struggle, (*Zweikampf*) duel, (*Fehde*) feud (*a. fig.*); **~³** *m* (*Blumen*♀) bunch (of flowers), bouquet; ˈ**~enfeder** *f* ostrich-feather.

Strebe ⊕ [ˈʃtreːbə] *f* (15) prop, stay, support; (*Quer*♀) crossbeam; ⊕, ✈ *usw.* (△ *a.* ˈ**~balken** *m*) strut.

ˈ**streben 1.** (25) strive, aspire (*nach* after), struggle (for); (*sich anstrengen*) endeavo(u)r; F *Schule*: *sl.* swot; ~ *nach* (*bezwecken*) aim at, pursue; *zu … hin* ~, *nach e-r Richtung* ~ tend to(wards), *marschierend usw.*: make for; **2.** ♀ *n* (6) striving (*nach* after), aspiration (for, after); pursuit (of); (*Anstrengung*) effort, endeavo(u)r; (*Ehrgeiz*) ambition.

ˈ**Strebepfeiler** *m* buttress.

ˈ**Streber** *m* (7) pusher, careerist, *Am. contp.* place-hunter, *gesellschaftlicher*: tuft-hunter, *Am.* F (social) climber; *Schule*: *sl.* swot; ˈ**~tum** *n* (1¹, *o. pl.*) *contp.* pushing.

strebsam [ˈʃtreːpzaːm] assiduous; aspiring; ambitious; ˈ**♀keit** *f* assiduity; ambition.

ˈ**streckbar** extensible; (*dehnbar*) ductile; (*hämmerbar*) malleable.

Strecke [ˈʃtrɛkə] *f* (15) stretch; (*Gegend*) tract, extent; (*Entfernung*; *a. Sport*) distance; (*Renn*♀) course; Ɐ straight line; 🚂, ⚓, ✈, *teleph.* line; ⚒ roadway; *hunt.* bag; *zur* ~ *bringen* shoot down, bag, *fig.* hunt down; *auf der* ~ *bleiben* break down, *fig. a.* fail, (*sterben*) perish; ˈ**♀n** (25) stretch, extend; *Speise, Vorrat*: eke (*od.* spin) out; *j-n zu Boden* ~ fell; *die Waffen* ~ lay down one's arms; *s. Decke, gestreckt.*

ˈ**Strecken|-arbeiter** 🚂 *m* platelayer; ˈ**~wärter** 🚂 *m* lineman, *Am.* trackman; ˈ**♀weise** here and there.

ˈ**Streck|muskel** *anat. m* extensor (muscle); ˈ**~verband** ⚕ *m* extension bandage; *im* ~ in high traction.

Streich [ʃtraiç] *m* (3) stroke, blow; *fig.* trick, prank; *j-m e-n* ~ *spielen* play a p. a trick; *auf* ˈ*einen* ~ at a blow.

streicheln [ˈʃtraiçəln] (29) stroke, (*a. fig.*) caress.

'**streich|en** (30) *v/t.* stroke, rub gently; *Butter, Pflaster*: spread; (*glätten, a.* ⊕) sleek, smooth; *Messer*: whet; *Rasiermesser*: strop; *Zündhölzchen*: strike (*an acc.* against); (*an*~) paint, *a.* ⊕ coat; *s. frisch*; (*aus*~) strike (*od.* cross) out *od.* off, *bsd. fig.* cancel; *Flagge, Segel*: strike, lower; *Sport*: *Meldung* ~ scratch; *Ziegel*: make; *Wolle*: card; ♪ *Geige usw.*: play; *gestrichen voll* brimful; *drei gestrichene Eßlöffel* three level table-spoons; *v/i.* **a**) (sn) (*sich erstrecken*) extend, sweep, run; (*vorbei*~) pass (*vorbei an j-m* a p.), move, rush (past); (*über, durch, gegen et. hin*~) sweep (over, through, towards (*a. Vogel*); (*wandern*) roam, ramble; *Raubtier, Verbrecher*: prowl; *s. streifen*[2]; **b**) (h.) *mit der Hand über et.* ~ pass one's hand over a th.; '**2er** ♪ *m/pl. the* strings.

'**Streich|holz** *n*, **~hölzchen** ['~-hœltsçən] *n* match, *Am.* F match-stick; '**~holzschachtel** *f* match-box; '**~-instrument** ♪ *n* stringed instrument; *die ~e in e-m Orchester*: the strings; '**~käse** *m* cheese spread; '**~-orchester** ♪ *n* string orchestra; '**~quartett** ♪ *n* string quartet(te); '**~riemen** *m* razor-strop; '**~ung** *f* cancellation (*a. fig.*); *typ.* deletion; (*Kürzung*) cut; '**~wurst** *f etwa* meat paste.

Streif [ʃtraɪf] *m* (3), '**~en**[1] *m* (6) stripe, streak; (*Gelände*2; *Film*2) strip; (*Film*) film; '**~band** *n* (postal) wrapper; *unter* ~ by book-post; '**~blick** *m* (brief) glance; '**~e** *f* (15) (*Polizei*2, *a.* ⚔) patrol; (*Razzia*) raid; '**2en**[2] (25) *v/t.* stripe, streak; (*ab*~) strip off; (*berühren*) graze, brush, *Thema*: touch; *v/i.* (sn) (*wandern*) roam, range (*a. Blick*); (h.) *fig.* ~ *an* (*acc.*) border on; '**~en-polizist** *m bsd. Am.* patrolman; '**~enwagen** *m der Polizei*: patrol (*Am.* squad *od.* prowl, *Brt.* panda) car; '**2ig** striped; '**~licht** *n* side-light; '**~schuß** *m* grazing shot; '**~zug** *m* (roving) expedition, raid.

Streik [ʃtraɪk] *m* (3 *u.* 11) strike, *Am.* F walkout; *in* (*den*) ~ *treten* go on strike; '**~-aufruf** *m* strike call; '**~-brecher** *m* strike-breaker, blackleg, scab; '**2en** (25) (be *od.* go on) strike, *Am.* F walk out; F *fig.* (*sich weigern*) rebel; *Gerät usw.*: refuse to work; '**~ende** *m* (18) striker; '**~geld** *n* strike-pay; '**~kasse** *f* strike-fund; '**~-posten** *m* picket; ~ *stehen* picket; '**~recht** *n* freedom to strike; '**~welle** *f* series of strikes.

Streit [ʃtraɪt] *m* (3) quarrel; (*bsd. Wort*2) dispute, argument; *lauter, handgreiflicher*: brawl, F row; (*Gezänk*) squabble; (*Kampf*) fight; conflict, strife; (*Fehde*) feud; *in* ~ *geraten mit* (have a) quarrel with; *s. suchen*; *e-n* ~ *vom Zaun brechen* pick a quarrel; '**~-axt** *f* battle-ax(e); '**2bar** pugnacious; '**2en** (30) (*a. sich*) *s. Streit*: quarrel; dispute, argue; fight; *darüber läßt sich* ~ that's a moot point (*od.* open to argument); '**~er** *m* (7), '**~erin** *f* quarrel(l)er; combatant; fighter; (*Vorkämpfer*) champion; '**~fall** *m* quarrel; controversy; '**~frage** *f* (point at) issue, (point of) controversy; '**~gegen-stand** ⚖ *m* matter in dispute; '**2ig** (*bestreitbar*) contestable, debatable, disputable, controversial; (*umstritten*) contested, *pred.* in dispute, at issue; *j-m et.* ~ *machen* dispute a p.'s right to; *s. Rang*; '**~igkeit** *f s. Streit*; '**~kräfte** *f/pl.* (armed) forces; '**2lu-stig** belligerent; '**~punkt** *m s. Streitfrage*; '**~sache** *f s. Streitfall*; ⚖ case, litigation; '**~schrift** *f* polemic pamphlet; '**~sucht** *f* quarrelsomeness; **2süchtig** ['~zyçtiç] quarrelsome; '**~-wert** ⚖ *m* value in dispute.

streng [ʃtrɛŋ] (*Ggs. mild*) severe, rigorous (*a. von der Kälte*), stern; (*hart*) harsh (*a. Geschmack*); *Sitte, Stil usw.*: austere; (*scharf, bestimmt*) strict (*gegen j-n* with); ~ *geheim* top secret; ~ *vertraulich* strictly confidential; ~ *verboten* strictly forbidden; '**2e** *f* (15) *s. streng*; severity, rigo(u)r; austerity; strictness; harshness; '**~genommen** strictly speaking; '**~gläubig** orthodox.

Streß [strɛs] ⚕ *m* (3[2]) stress.

Streu [ʃtrɔʏ] *f* (15) litter; *für Menschen*: bed of straw; '**~büchse** *f für Gewürz usw.*: castor; *für Mehl*: dredger; '**2en** (25) *v/t.* strew; (*umher*~) scatter; *v/i. Schußwaffe*: scatter, ⚔ *absichtlich*: sweep; ⚡ stray; *dem Vieh*: litter (down) *the cattle*; *s. Sand.*

streunen ['ʃtrɔʏnən] roam about, rove, stray.

ˈ**Streu|sand** *m* dry sand; *für Tinte*: writing sand; ˈ**~zucker** *m* castor sugar.

Strich [ʃtriç] **1.** *m* (3) stroke; (*Linie*) line; (*Gedanken*~, *Morse*~) dash; (*Streif*) stripe; (*Land*~) region, tract; (*Kompaß*~) point; *der Vögel*: flight; ♪ (*Bogenführung*) bowing; (*Pinsel*~) touch; *des Holzes usw.*: grain; F *j-n auf dem ~ haben* have it in for a p.; F *auf den ~ gehen* walk the streets; *j-m e-n ~ durch die Rechnung machen* cross a p.'s plans; F *fig. das ging mir gegen den ~* it rubbed me the wrong way; *e-n (dicken) ~ unter e-e S. machen* make a clean break with a th.; *nach ~ und Faden* thoroughly; **2.** ~ *pret. v. streichen*; ˈ**~-ätzung** *f* line-plate; ˈ**~-einteilung** *f* graduation; ˈ**~eln** (29) dot; (*schraffieren*) hatch; ˈ**~junge** F *m* male prostitute; ˈ**~mädchen** F *n* streetwalker; ˈ**~punkt** *m* semicolon; ˈ**~regen** *m* local shower; ˈ**~vogel** *m* migratory bird, visitant; ˈ**~weise** by strokes; *s. streckenweise*; ˈ**~zeichnung** *f* line drawing.

Strick [ʃtrik] *m* (3) cord, line; (*Seil*) rope; *s. Strang*; F *fig.* young rascal; *wenn alle ~e reißen* if all else fails; ˈ**~en** *v/t. u. v/i.* (25) knit; ˈ**~er(in** *f*) *m* knitter; ˈ**~garn** *n* knitting-yarn; ˈ**~jacke** *f* cardigan; ˈ**~leiter** *f* rope-ladder; ˈ**~maschine** *f* knitting-machine; ˈ**~nadel** *f* knitting-needle; ˈ**~waren** *f/pl.* knit(ted) goods *pl.*; ˈ**~weste** *f* cardigan (sweater); ˈ**~wolle** *f* knitting wool; ˈ**~zeug** *n* knitting (things *pl.*).

Striegel [ˈʃtri:gəl] *m* (7) curry-comb; ˈ**~n** (29) curry.

Striem|e [ˈʃtri:mə] *f* (15), ˈ**~en** *m* (6) stripe, streak; *in der Haut*: wale, weal; ˈ**~ig** streaked; *Haut*: covered with wales.

strikt [ʃtrikt] strict(ly *adv.*).

Strippe F [ˈʃtripə] *f* (15) strap; (*Schnur*) string; F (tele)phone.

stritt [ʃtrit] *pret. v. streiten.*

strittig [ˈʃtritiç] *s. streitig*; *der ~e Punkt* the point at issue.

Stroh [ʃtro:] *n* (3) straw; (*Dach*~) thatch; *fig. leeres ~ dreschen* talk hot air; ˈ**~dach** *n* thatch(ed roof); ˈ**~farben**, ˈ**~gelb** straw-colo(u)red; ˈ**~feuer** *fig. n* short-lived passion; ˈ**~halm** *m* (blade of) straw; *fig. nach e-m ~ greifen* catch at a straw; ˈ**~hut** *m* straw hat; ˈ**~ig** strawy; ˈ**~kopf** *m* empty head; ˈ**~mann** *m* man of straw; *fig. a.* dummy, front; ˈ**~sack** *m* straw mattress, pallet; ˈ**~matte** *f* straw mat; ˈ**~witwe(r** *m*) *f* F grass-widow(er).

Strolch [ʃtrɔlç] *m* (3) tramp, *Am. sl.* bum; (*Lump*) *a.* blackguard, *Am.* F hoodlum; *a. co.* scamp; ˈ**~en** (h. *u.* sn) roam, ramble, loaf about.

Strom [ʃtro:m] *m* (3³) stream, (large) river; (*Strömung*) current (*a.* ⚡ *u. fig.*), (*a. Menschen*~) stream; ⚡ *a.* power; (*Blut*~, *Verkehrs*~) flow; *v. Tränen, Worten*: flood; ⚡ *unter ~* live; *gegen den ~ schwimmen* (*a. fig.*) swim against the current; *es regnet in Strömen* it is pouring with rain; ˈ**~-abnehmer** ⚡ *m* (current) collector; ~ˈ**-ab(wärts)** downstream; ~ˈ**auf(wärts)** upstream; ˈ**~-ausfall** *m* power failure; ˈ**~bedarf** *m* electricity requirement.

strömen [ˈʃtrø:mən] (25, h. *u.* sn) stream, flow; *Regen*: pour; (*sich drängen*) flock, crowd.

Stromer [ˈʃtro:mər] *m* (7) *s. Strolch.*

ˈ**Strom|-ersparnis** *f* electricity saving; ˈ**~-erzeuger** ⚡ *m* dynamo, generator; (*E-Werk*) power station; ˈ**~erzeugung** *f* power generation; ˈ**~führend** ⚡ live; ˈ**~gebiet** *n* (river-) basin; ˈ**~kreis** ⚡ *m* (electric) circuit; ˈ**~leiter** ⚡ *m* current conductor; ˈ**~linie(nform)** *f* streamline(d design); **~linienförmig** [ˈ~fœrmiç] streamline(d); ˈ**~netz** ⚡ *n* mains supply; ˈ**~schiene** ⚡ *f* contact rail; ˈ**~schnelle** *f* rapid; ˈ**~spannung** ⚡ *f* voltage; ˈ**~sparend** electricity-saving; ˈ**~sperre** *f* power cut; ˈ**~stärke** ⚡ *f* current (intensity); amperage.

ˈ**Strömung** *f* (16) current; *fig. a.* trend.

ˈ**Strom|-unterbrecher** ⚡ *m* circuit-breaker; ˈ**~verbrauch** ⚡ *m* current consumption; ˈ**~versorgung** ⚡ *f* power supply; ˈ**~wandler** ⚡ *m* (7) current transformer; ˈ**~wender** ⚡ *m* (7) commutator; ˈ**~zähler** ⚡ *m* electric meter.

Strophe [ˈʃtro:fə] *f* (15) stanza, verse.

strotzen [ˈʃtrɔtsən] (27) exuberate; *~ von, vor* (*dat.*) abound in; (*wimmeln von*) teem with; *vor Gesundheit usw.* burst with; ˈ**~d** exuberant; *~ von, vor* (*dat.*) abundant in.

strubbelig F [ˈʃtrubəliç] unkempt, dishevel(l)ed; shock-headed.

'**Strudel** *m* (7) **1.** swirl, whirlpool, vortex; **2.** (*Gebäck*) (pastry-)roll; '**2n** (29, h. *u.* sn) swirl, whirl.

Struktur [ʃtruk'tu:r] *f* (16) structure; **2ell** [~tu'rɛl] structural.

Strumpf [ʃtrumpf] *m* (3³) stocking; (*Glüh2*) mantle; ✝ (*lange*) *Strümpfe pl.* hose; '**~band** *n* garter; '**~halter** *m* suspender, *Am.* garter; '**~haltergürtel** *m* suspender (*Am.* garter) belt; '**~hose** *f* tights *pl.*, pantyhose; '**~waren** *f/pl.* hosiery.

Strunk [ʃtruŋk] *m* (3³) stalk; (*Baum2*) stump, trunk.

struppig ['ʃtrupiç] *Haar*: rough; *Bart*: bristly; *Hund*: shaggy.

Struwwel|kopf ['ʃtruvəl-] *m* shock head; '**~peter** *m* shock-headed Peter.

Strychnin [ʃtryç'ni:n] *n* (11) strychnine.

Stube ['ʃtu:bə] *f* (15) room.

'**Stuben|-arrest** *m* confinement to one's room; ⚔ arrest in quarters; '**~fliege** *f* common (house) fly; '**~gelehrsamkeit** *f* book-learning, bookishness; '**~gelehrte** *m* bookworm; '**~hocker** *m*, '**~sitzer** *m* stay-at-home; '**~kamerad** *m* room-mate; '**~mädchen** *n* parlo(u)rmaid; *Hotel*: chambermaid; '**2rein** *Tier*: house-trained, *Am.* housebroken.

Stuck [ʃtuk] *m* (3) stucco.

Stück [ʃtyk] *n* (3; *als Maß nach Zahlen inv.*) piece (*a.* ♪, *paint. usw.*); (*Bißchen*) bit; (*Bissen*) morsel; (*Teil2*) part; (*Bruch2*) fragment; *Vieh*: head; *Zucker*: lump; *thea.* play; (~ *Land*) piece of land, plot; (~ *Weg*) stretch, distance; (*Text*) passage, part; (*Handlung*) act; F (*Person*) type; ~ *Arbeit* job; ~ *für* ~ piece by piece; *aus e-m* ~ all of a piece; *aus freien* ~*en* of one's own free will; *in vielen* ~*en* in many respects; *in* ~*e gehen* go to pieces; *in* ~*e schlagen* smash (to bits); *ein schönes* ~ *Geld* a nice little sum; *große* ~*e halten auf* (*acc.*) think highly of; *das ist ein starkes* ~*!* that's a bit thick!; '**~-arbeit** *f* piece-work; '**~-arbeiter(in** *f*) *m* piece-worker; '**~chen** *n* (6) small piece *etc.* (*s. Stück*); *fig.* (*Streich*) trick; (*Kunst2*) stunt; '**2eln** (29) *s. zerstückeln*; (*flicken*) piece (together); '**~fracht** *f*, '**~gut** *n* mixed cargo; '**~kosten** *pl.* unit cost *sg.*; '**~lohn** *m* piece-wage(s *pl.*); '**~preis** *m* price per unit; '**2weise** piecemeal; ✝ by the piece; '**~werk** *n contp.* patchwork; '**~zahl** *f* number of pieces.

Student [ʃtu'dɛnt] *m* (12), **~in** *f* (16¹) (*f* woman) student, (*f* girl) undergraduate; **~en-ausweis** *m* student card; **~enschaft** *f* (body of) students *pl.*; **~enverbindung** *f* students' club, *Am.* fraternity; **~enwohnheim** *n* student hostel.

Studie ['ʃtu:djə] *f* (15) *paint. usw.*: study; *e-s Schriftstellers*: sketch, essay; ~*n pl. s. Studium*; '**~nberatung** *f* student guidance (service); '**~nbewerber(in** *f*) *m* university applicant; '**~ndirektor(in** *f*) *m* headmaster (headmistress) of a secondary school, *Am.* high-school principal; '**~nfach** *n* subject; '**~ngang** *m*, '**~nplan** *m* course of studies; curriculum; '**~njahr** *n* academic year; ~*e pl. s. Studienzeit*; '**~nplatz** *m* university place; '**~nrat** (**~rätin** ['~rɛ:tin] *f* [16]) *m* (assistant) master (mistress) of a secondary school; '**~nreise** *f* informative trip; '**~nzeit** *f* years *pl.* of study; college days *pl.*

studier|en [ʃtu'di:rən] *v/i. u. v/t.* study (*a. weitS. lesen, betrachten usw.*); (*die Hochschule besuchen*) go to college; ~ *lassen* send to college; **2te** *m* (18) university man; **2zimmer** *n* study.

Studio ['ʃtu:djo] *n* (11) studio.

Studium ['ʃtu:djum] *n* (9) study; (*a. pl. Studien*) studies *pl.*

Stufe ['ʃtu:fə] *f* (15) step; *fig.* (*Entwicklungs2 usw.*; *a.* ⊕, *e-r Rakete*) stage; (*Grad*) degree (*a. gr.*); (*Niveau*) level, standard; (*Rang*) rank; (*Farb2*) shade; *auf gleicher* ~ *mit* on a par with.

'**stufen|-artig**, '**~förmig** step-like; *fig.* graduated, graded; '**2barren** *m Turnen*: asymmetrical bars *pl.*; '**2folge** *f*, '**2gang** *m* gradation, succession; '**2leiter** *f* stepladder; *fig.* scale; '**~los:** ⊕ ~ (*regelbar*) infinitely variable; '**~weise** gradually, by degrees.

Stuhl [ʃtu:l] *m* (3³) chair; seat; (*Kirchen2*) pew; (*Web2*) loom; ⚕ (*Kot*) stool, *s.* ~*gang*; *eccl. der Heilige* ~ the Holy See; *fig. sich zwischen zwei Stühle setzen* fall between two stools; '**~bein** *n* leg of a chair; '**~gang** ⚕ *m* motion, bowel movement; ~ *haben* go to stool, *regelmäßig*: have open bowels; '**~lehne** *f* back of chair.

Stulle F ['ʃtulə] *f* (15) slice of bread (and butter), sandwich.

Stulpe ['ʃtulpə] *f* (15) (*Stiefel*2) top; (*Manschette*) cuff.

stülpen ['ʃtylpən] (25) turn (*hoch*: up); *Hut*: clap (*auf acc.* on), *schief*: cock.

'**Stulp(en)stiefel** *m* top-boot.

'**Stulp(en)handschuh** *m* gauntlet.

'**Stülpnase** *f* turn(ed)-up nose.

stumm [ʃtum] dumb, mute (*beide a. fig.*); (*still*) silent (*a. gr.*); (*sprachlos*) speechless (*vor dat.* with).

Stummel ['ʃtuməl] *m* (7) (*Arm*2, *Baum*2 *usw.*) stump; (*Zigaretten*2) (fag) end, *Am.* butt, stub.

'**Stummfilm** *m* silent film.

Stümper ['ʃtympər] *m* (7), '**~in** *f* bungler; **~ei** [~'raɪ] *f* (16) bungling; '2**haft** bungling, clumsy; '2**n** *v/i. u. v/t.* (29) bungle, botch.

stumpf[1] [ʃtumpf] blunt; *Winkel*: obtuse; *Kegel*: truncate(d); *Geist, Auge usw.*: obtuse, dull; (*teilnahmslos*) apathetic(ally *adv.*).

Stumpf[2] *m* (3³) stump (*a. Arm*2 *usw.*); *mit ~ und Stiel* root and branch; '**~heit** *f* bluntness; *fig.* dullness; '**~sinn** *m* stupidity, dullness; '2**sinnig** stupid, dull; '2**wink(e)lig** obtuse-angled.

Stunde ['ʃtundə] *f* (15) hour; (*Unterricht*) lesson, *Am.* (*Schul*2) period; *fig. in letzter ~* at the eleventh hour; *zur ~* at this hour; *bis zur ~* as yet; *mot. 50 Meilen in der ~* 50 miles per hour; '2**n** (26): (*j-m*) *e-e Zahlung ~* grant (a p.) delay (*od.* a respite) for payment.

'**Stunden|geschwindigkeit** *f* speed per hour; '**~glas** *n* hour-glass; '**~kilometer** *m/pl.* kilomet|res (*Am.* -ers) per hour; '2**lang** *adv.* (*adj.* lasting) for hours; '**~lohn** *m* wage(s *pl.*) per hour; '**~plan** *m* time-table, curriculum, *Am.* schedule; '2**weise** by the hour; '**~zeiger** *m* hour-hand.

Stünd|lein ['ʃtyntlaɪn] *n* (6): *letztes ~* last hour; '2**lich** hourly, every hour, per hour.

'**Stundung** *f* respite, delay.

Stunk [ʃtuŋk] F *m* (3, *o. pl.*): *~ machen sl.* raise a stink.

stupid(e) [ʃtu'pi:t, -də] stupid, idiotic.

stups|en ['ʃtupsən] (27) nudge; '2**nase** *f* snub nose; '**~nasig** snub-nosed.

stur [ʃtu:r] (*störrisch*) stubborn, mulish; (*stumpf*) stolid; (*geisttötend*) dull; *Blick*: fixed.

Sturm [ʃturm] *m* (3³) storm (*a. fig.*); ⚓ gale; ⚔ assault; *Fußball*: forwards *pl.*; *~ und Drang* storm and stress; *~ auf* (*acc.*) ✝ rush for *goods*, run on *a bank*; *~ der Entrüstung* outcry; *~ laufen gegen* assault, assail (*beide a. fig.*); *im ~ erobern* take by storm (*a. fig.*); *~ im Wasserglas* storm in a teacup; '**~boot** ⚔ *n* assault boat.

stürm|en ['ʃtyrmən] (25) *v/t.* storm (*a. fig. u.* ⚔); *v/i.* **a**) (h.) ⚔ assault; *Wind*: rage, roar, storm (*alle a. fig. zürnen*); *es stürmt* it is stormy weather; **b**) (sn) (*rennen*) rush; '2**er** *m* (7) *Fußball*: forward; '2**erreihe** *f Fußball*: forward line.

'**Sturm|flut** *f* storm tide; '**~geschütz** ⚔ *n* (self-propelled) assault gun; '**~glocke** *f* tocsin.

'**stürmisch** stormy; *fig.* (*ungestüm*) impetuous; (*lärmend, tosend*) tumultuous, uproarious; (*leidenschaftlich*) tempestuous; (*schnell*) rapid.

'**sturm|reif**: *~ machen* soften up; '2**schritt** *m*: ⚔ *u. allg. im ~* at the double; '2**spitze** *f Fußball*: spearhead; '2**vogel** *m* (stormy) petrel; '2**warnung** *f* gale warning; '2**wind** *m* heavy gale; '2**wolke** *f* storm cloud.

Sturz [ʃturts] *m* (3² *u.* ³) (sudden) fall, *tiefer*: plunge, *lauter*: crash; (*Untergang*) ruin, (down)fall; *e-r Regierung usw.*: overthrow; *Börse*: slump; (*Ungnade*) disgrace; *s. Temperatursturz*; '**~acker** *m* new-ploughed (*Am.* -plowed) field; '**~bach** *m* torrent.

stürzen ['ʃtyrtsən] (27) *v/i.* (sn) fall, tumble, *krachend*: crash, *tief, ins Wasser, a. Preise*: plunge; (*vorwärts~, eilen*) rush; *Abgrund*: descend precipitously; *v/t.* precipitate; (*tauchen*) plunge; (*werfen*) throw; *Regierung usw.*: overthrow; *nicht ~!* (*Aufschrift auf Kisten*) this side up!; *sich auf j-n ~* rush at, *e-e Arbeit usw.*: throw o.s. into, pounce (up)on; *ins Elend ~* ruin; *in e-n*

Krieg ~ plunge into a war; *sich in Unkosten* ~ put o.s. to expenses; *s. Schuld, Verderben.*

'**Sturz|flug** ✈ *m* (nose-)dive; *e-n* ~ *machen* dive; '**~helm** *m* ✈, *mot.* crash helmet; '**~kampfflugzeug** *n* dive-bomber; '**~see** ⚓ *f* heavy sea; '**~welle** ⚓ *f*: *e-e* ~ *bekommen* ship a sea.

Stuß [ʃtus] F *m* (3², *o. pl.*) *s. Quatsch.*

Stute ['ʃtu:tə] *f* (15) mare; '**~n-füllen** *n* filly.

Stütz [ʃtyts] *f* (3²) *Turnen*: straight-arm rest; '**~balken** *m* supporting beam.

Stütze ['ʃtytsə] *f* (15) (*a. fig.*) support; prop, stay; ~ *der Hausfrau* lady help.

stutzen ['ʃtutsən] **1.** (27) *v/t.* cut (short), curtail (*a. fig.*); *Ohren*: crop; *Flügel, Hecke*: clip; *Bart*: trim; *Schwanz*: dock; *Baum*: lop; *v/i.* (*stutzig werden*) stop short, be startled, start; be puzzled; (*argwöhnisch werden*) become suspicious; **2.** ♀ *m* (6) short rifle, carbine; ⊕ (*Rohransatz*) connecting piece; (*Düse*) nozzle.

stützen ['ʃtytsən] (27) (*a. fig.*) support, uphold; prop, stay; *Behauptung usw.*: ~ *auf* (*acc.*) base (*od.* found) on; *sich* ~ *auf* (*acc.*) lean (*od.* rest) on, *fig.* rely (*od.* base o.s.) on, *Urteil usw.*: be based on.

Stutz|er ['ʃtutsər] *m* (7) fop, dandy, *Am. a.* dude; '**♀erhaft** foppish; '**~flügel** ♪ *m* miniature grand; '**♀ig** startled, taken aback, perplexed; ~ *machen* startle, puzzle, (*Argwohn wecken*) make suspicious; ~ *werden s. stutzen v/i.*

'**Stütz|kurs** *m für schwache Schüler*: remedial instruction; '**~pfeiler** *m* supporting pillar, buttress; '**~punkt** *m* point of support; *fig.* foothold, (*bsd.* ⚔) base; *taktisch*: strong point; (*Hebelpunkt*) fulcrum.

'**Stutz-uhr** *f* mantelpiece clock.

Styropor [ʃtyro'po:r] *n* (3¹, *o. pl.*) polystyrene.

subaltern [zupˀal'tɛrn] subordinate; *bsd.* ⚔ subaltern.

Subjekt [zup'jɛkt] *n* (3) *gr.* subject; F *contp.* (*Person*) fellow, type; **♀iv** [~'ti:f] subjective; **~ivität** [~tivi'tɛ:t] *f* (16) subjectivity.

Subkultur ['zupkultu:r] *f* subculture.

subkutan [zupku'tɑ:n] subcutaneous, hypodermic(ally *adv.*).

Subli|mat [zubli'mɑ:t] *n* (3) sublimate; **♀'mieren** sublimate.

Submission ✝, ⚖ [zupmi'sjo:n] *f* (contract by) tender.

subskribieren [~skri'bi:rən] subscribe (*auf acc.* to).

Subskription [~skrip'tsjo:n] *f* subscription; **~s-preis** *m* prepublication (*od.* subscription) price.

substantiell [zupstan'tsjɛl] substantial.

Substantiv ['~stanti:f] *n* (3¹) substantive, noun; **♀isch** [~'ti:viʃ] substantival.

Substanz [~'stants] *f* (16) substance.

subtil [zup'ti:l] subtle.

subtra|hieren [~tra'hi:rən] subtract; **♀ktion** [~trak'tsjo:n] *f* subtraction.

subtropisch ['zup-] subtropical.

Subvention [~vɛn'tsjo:n] *f* subsidy; **♀ieren** [~tsjo'ni:rən] subsidize.

Such|-aktion ['zu:x-] *f* search; '**~anzeige** *f* want ad(vertisement); '**~dienst** *m* tracing service; '**~e** *f* (15) search, *stärker*: hunt (*nach* for); *auf der* ~ *nach* in search (*od.* quest) of, on the look-out for; '**♀en** (25) *v/t.* (*u. v/i.* ~ *nach*) search for, *bsd. weitS.* seek (*advice, etc.*); *schauend u. weitS.*: look for; *aufgeregt*: hunt for; *Fehler, Vermißte*: trace; *nur v/t.* (*wünschen*) want; ~ *zu inf.* (*sich bemühen*) seek to, try to; *Streit* ~ pick a quarrel; *Sie haben hier nichts zu* ~ you have no business to be here; *s. Rat, Weite, gesucht*; '**~er** *m* (7) seeker (*a. weitS. of truth, etc.*), searcher (*a.* '**~erin** *f*); *opt.* finder; *phot.* view-finder; (*a.* '**~gerät** *n*) detector; '**~kartei** *f* tracing file; '**~mannschaft** *f* search party; '**~scheinwerfer** *m* searchlight.

Sucht [zuxt] *f* (16) mania (*nach* for), *a. Rauschgift usw.*: addiction (to); (*Krankheit*) sickness, disease; '**♀-erzeugend** ⚕ habit-forming, addictive.

süchtig ['zyçtiç] (*e-m Rauschgift usw. verfallen*) addicted, *z. B. morphium*~ addicted to morphine; (*gierend*) craving; (*besessen*) maniac(al); **♀e** ['~igə] *m, f* (18) addict.

'**Suchtmittel** *n* addictive drug.

Suchtrupp ['zu:x-] *m* search party.
Sud [zu:t] *m* (3) decoction.
Süd [zy:t] **1.** south; **2.** *poet. m* (3, *o. pl.*) south (wind); '**2deutsch**, '**~deutsche** *m, f* South German.
Sudel|arbeit ['zu:dəlˀarbaɪt], **~ei** [~'laɪ] *f* (16) dirty (*od. schlampig*: slovenly) work; *paint.* daub; *Geschriebenes*: scrawl, scribble; '**2ig** slovenly, dirty; '**2n** (29) *v/i. u. v/t. malend*: daub; *schreibend*: scribble; (*manschen*) mess about; (*pfuschen*) botch.
Süden ['zy:dən] *m* (6) south; *im ~* in the south, *e-r Stadt usw.*: (to the) south (*gen.* of); *nach ~* south(ward).
Süd|früchte ['zy:tfryçtə] *f/pl.* tropical fruit(s); '**~hang** *m* south(ern) slope; '**~länder** *m* (7), '**~länderin** *f* southerner; '**2ländisch** southern.
Sudler(in *f*) ['zu:dlər] *m s. sudeln*: dauber; scribbler; botcher.
süd|lich ['zy:t-] south (*a. adv.*), southern, southerly; *~ von* south of; **2'-ost(en)** *m* south-east; **~'-östlich** south-east(ern); '**2pol** *m* South Pole; **~wärts** ['~vɛrts] southward(s); '**2wein** *m* sweet wine; **2-'west(en)** *m* southwest; **2'wester** *m* (7) southwester; **~'westlich** south-western; '**2wind** *m* south wind.
Suff [zuf] *m* (3, *o. pl.*) boozing.
süffig ['zyfiç] tasty.
süffisant [syfi'zant] sarcastic(ally) [*adv.*).
suggerieren [zuge'ri:rən] suggest.
Suggestion [zugɛs'tjo:n] *f* suggestion.
suggestiv [~'ti:f] suggestive; **2-frage** *f* leading question.
Suhle *hunt.* ['zu:lə] *f* (15), '**2n**: *sich ~* wallow.
Sühn|e ['zy:nə] *f* (15) expiation, atonement; '**2en** (25) expiate, atone for; '**~etermin** ⚖ *m* conciliation hearing; '**~-opfer** *n* expiatory sacrifice; '**~ung** *f s. Sühne.*
Suite ['svi:tə] *f* (15) suite (*a.* ♪), retinue.
sukzessiv [zuktsɛ'si:f] successive; **~e** [~'si:və] *adv.* gradually.
Sulfonamid *pharm.* [zulfona'mi:t] *n* sulphonamide.
Sultan ['zulta:n] *m* (3¹) sultan; '**~in** *f* sultana; **~ine** [~ta'ni:nə] *f* (15) (*Rosine*) sultana.
Sülze ['zyltsə] *f* (15) aspic; jellied meat; '**2n** (27) jelly.
summarisch [zu'ma:riʃ] summary.
Summ|e ['zumə] *f* (15) sum (*a. fig.*); (*Gesamt2*) (sum) total; (*Betrag*) amount; '**2en** (25) *v/t.* hum; *v/i.* buzz, hum; *Ohr*: tingle; '**~er** ⚡ *m* (7) buzzer; **2ieren** [~'mi:rən] sum (*od.* add); *sich ~* run up.
Sumpf [zumpf] *m* (3³) swamp, bog, marsh; *fig.* morass; *mot.* sump; '**~boden** *m* marshy ground; '**~fieber** *n* malaria; '**~huhn** *n* moorhen; *fig.* rake; (*Säufer*) boozer; '**2ig** boggy, marshy, swampy; '**~land** *n* marshland; '**~pflanze** *f* marsh plant; '**~vogel** *m* wader.
Sums [zums] F *m* (3², *o. pl.*) (great) [fuss.]
Sund [zunt] *m* (3) sound, strait.
Sünde ['zyndə] *f* (15) sin; '**~nbock** *m* scapegoat; '**~n-erlaß** *m* absolution; '**~nfall** *m* fall of man; '**~ngeld** *n* ill-gotten money; (*Riesensumme*) enormous sum; '**~nregister** *n* list of misdeeds.
'**Sünd|er** *m* (7), '**~erin** *f* (16¹) sinner; *armer ~* criminal under sentence of death, *fig.* poor wretch.
sündhaft ['zynt-] sinful; F *~ teuer* awfully expensive.
sündig ['zyndiç] sinful; **~en** ['~digən] (25) sin (*an dat., gegen* against).
Super ['zu:pər] *n* (7, *o. pl.*) *s. Superbenzin*; 2 F *adj.* super, smashing; '**~benzin** *n* super, *Am.* premium gas; '**2klug** overwise; *~er Mensch* wiseacre.
Superlativ ['~lati:f] *m* (3¹) superlative (degree *bsd. gr.*); **2isch** [~'ti:viʃ] superlative.
'**Super|macht** *f* superpower; '**~markt** *m* supermarket.
Suppe ['zupə] *f* (15) soup; *fig.* F *die ~ auslöffeln* face the music; F *j-m die ~ versalzen* give a p. what for.
'**Suppen|fleisch** *n* stock-meat; '**~grün** *n* greens *pl.*; '**~kelle** *f* dipper; '**~kraut** *n* pot-herb; '**~löffel** *m* soup-ladle; *zum Essen*: soup-spoon; '**~schüssel** *f* (soup-)tureen; '**~teller** *m* soup-plate; '**~würfel** *m* soup cube.
Support [zu'pɔrt] ⊕ *m* (3) (slide) rest; (*Schlitten*) carriage.
Surf|brett ['sœrf-] *n* surfboard; '**~er** *m* (7) surfer.
surren ['zurən] (25) whiz(z); *Insekt usw.*: buzz.
Surrogat [zuro'ga:t] *n* (3) substitute, ersatz.
suspekt [zu'spɛkt] suspect.

suspendieren [zuspɛnˈdiːrən] suspend.

süß [zyːs] sweet (*a. allg. fig.*); ˈ**2e** *f* (15) sweetness; *als Kosewort*: sweetie; ˈ**~en** (25) sweeten; ˈ**2holz** *n* liquorice; F ~ *raspeln* flirt; ˈ**2igkeit** *f* sweetness; *~en pl.* sweets, *Am.* candy *sg.*; ˈ**~lich** sweetish; *fig.* honeyed; (*kitschig*) mawkish, treacly; ˈ**2speise** *f* sweet, dessert; ˈ**2stoff** *m* sweetener; ˈ**2waren** *f/pl.* sweets, *Am.* candy *sg.*; ˈ**2warengeschäft** *n* sweet-shop, *Am.* candy store; ˈ**2wasser** *n* fresh water.

Sylphe [ˈzylfə] *f* (15) sylph.

Sylvester [zilˈvɛstər] *s. Silvester.*

Symbol [zymˈboːl] *n* (3¹) symbol; **~ik** *f* (16) symbolism; **2isch** symbolic(al); **2isieren** [~boliˈziːrən] symbolize.

Symmetr|ie [zymeˈtriː] *f* (15) symmetry; **2isch** [~ˈmeːtriʃ] symmetrical.

Sympathie [zympaˈtiː] *f* (15) sympathy; **~streik** *m* sympathetic strike.

Sympath|isant [~patiˈzant] *m* (12) sympathizer; **2isch** [~ˈpaːtiʃ] sympathetic(ally *adv.*); (*gewinnend*) likable, engaging; *er ist mir* ~ I like him; **2iˈsieren** sympathize.

Symphon|ie [zymfoˈniː] *f* (15) symphony; **2isch** [~ˈfoːniʃ] symphonic(ally *adv.*).

Symptom [zympˈtoːm] *n* (3¹) symptom; **2atisch** [~toˈmaːtiʃ] symptomatic (*für* of).

Synagoge [zynaˈgoːgə] *f* (15) synagogue.

synchron [zynˈkroːn] synchronous; *~/nicht~* F in/out of sync(h); **~isieren** [~kroniˈziːrən] synchronize; *Film*: dub; **2getriebe** [~ˈkroːn-] *mot. n* synchromesh gear.

Syndikat [zyndiˈkaːt] *n* (3) syndicate.

Syndikus [ˈzyndikus] *m* (14²) syndic, *Am.* corporation lawyer.

Synkop|e ♪ [zynˈkoːpə] *f* (15) syncope; **2ieren** [~koˈpiːrən] syncopate.

Synode [zyˈnoːdə] *f* (15) synod.

synonym [zynoˈnyːm] **1.** *a.* **~isch** synonymous; **2.** 2 *n* (3¹) synonym.

syntaktisch [zynˈtaktiʃ] syntactic(al).

Syntax [ˈzyntaks] *f* (16) syntax.

Synthe|se [~ˈteːzə] *f* (15) synthesis; **2tisch** [~ˈteːtiʃ] synthetic(ally *adv.*).

Syphil|is [ˈzyːfilis] *f inv.* syphilis; **2itisch** [zyfiˈliːtiʃ] syphilitic.

Syr|(i)er [ˈzyːr(j)ər] *m* (7), ˈ**~(i)erin** *f*, ˈ**2isch** Syrian.

System [zyˈsteːm] *n* (3¹) system; **~atik** [~steˈmaːtik] *f* system(atic manner); **2atisch** systematic(ally *adv.*); **~kritiker(in** *f*) [~ˈsteːm-] *m* dissident; **2los** unmethodical.

Szen|e [ˈstseːnə] *f* (15) scene (*a. fig.*); *Film*: sequence; *in ~ setzen* (put on the) stage, mount, (*sich*) show off; ˈ**~enbild** *n thea, Film*: setting, scenery; **~erie** [~ˈriː] *f* (15) scenery; ˈ**2isch** scenic(ally *adv.*).

T

T [teː], **t** *n inv.* T, t.

Tabak [ˈtaːbak] *m* (3) tobacco; ˈ**~bau** *m* tobacco growing; ˈ**~händler** *m* tobacconist; ˈ**~qualm** *m* tobacco-smoke; ˈ**~sbeutel** *m* tobacco-pouch; ˈ**~sdose** *f* snuff-box; ˈ**~-waren** *f/pl.* tobacco goods, F smokes.

tabellar|isch [tabɛˈlaːriʃ] tabulated, tabular; *adv.* in tabular form; **~isieren** [~lariˈziːrən] tabulate.

Tabelle [taˈbɛlə] *f* (15) table.

Tabernakel [tabɛrˈnaːkəl] *n, m* (7) tabernacle.

Tablett [taˈblɛt] *n* (3) tray; *aus Metall*: salver; **~e** *f* (15) tablet; ⚕ pill.

tabu [taˈbuː] *adj.*, 2 *n* (11) taboo; *ein 2 brechen* break a taboo; *et. für ~ erklären* (put under a) taboo; **~frei:** *~e Gesellschaft* permissive society.

Tabulator [tabuˈlaːtɔr] *m* (8¹) tabulator.

Tachometer ⊕ [taxoˈmeːtər] *n* (7) tachometer; *mot. a.* speedometer.

Tadel [ˈtaːdəl] *m* (7) blame; (*Rüge*) censure; (*Mißbilligung*) reproof; (*Vorwurf*) reproach; (*Makel*) flaw; *ohne ~* = ˈ**2los** faultless, blameless, above reproach; F *fig.* splendid, first-class; '2**n** (29) blame (*wegen* for), censure, criticize; '2**nswert** blameworthy; '2**süchtig** censorious, faultfinding.

Tadler ['tɑːdlər] *m* (7) faultfinder, critic.

Tafel ['tɑːfəl] *f* (15) table (*a. Liste usw.*); (*Platte, a. Bild*2 *im Buch*) plate; (*Stein*2) slab; *Schokolade usw.*: tablet, bar, cake; (*Schreib*2, *a. Gedenk*2) tablet; (*Schiefer*2) slate; (*Wand*2) blackboard; (*Täfelung*) panel; (*das Speisen*) dinner; '2**fertig** ready to serve, instant; '**∼land** *n* table-land, plateau; '2**n** (29) dine, banquet.

täfeln ['tɛːfəln] (29) *Fußboden*: inlay; *Wand*: wainscot, panel.

'**Tafel|-obst** *n* dessert fruit; '**∼runde** *f* (guests *pl.* at) table; '**∼silber** *n* table-plate, *Am.* silverware.

Täfel|ung ['tɛːfəluŋ] *f* inlaying; (*a.* '**∼werk** *n*) wainscot([t]ing).

'**Tafel|wasser** *n* table-water; '**∼wein** *m* table wine.

Taf(**fe**)**t** ['taf(ə)t] *m* (3) taffeta.

Tag [tɑːk] *m* (3) day; *am ∼e* by day; *am ∼e nach* the day after; *bei ∼e* by day, in the day-time, (*bei ∼eslicht*) by daylight; *alle ∼e* every day; *dieser ∼e* (*demnächst*) one of these days, (*jüngst*) the other day; *eines ∼es* some day; *zweimal des ∼es* twice a day; *den ganzen ∼* all day long; *s. frei, heute, Abend*; *∼ für ∼* day by day; *einen ∼ um den andern* every other day; ⚒ *unter ∼e* underground; *guten ∼!* *allg.* how do you do?, *engS.*: good morning!, good afternoon!; F hallo!, *Am.* hello!; *bei Verabschiedung*: good day!, F so long!; *heller ∼* (*∼eslicht*) broad daylight; *es wird ∼* it dawns; *an den ∼ kommen* come to light; *an den ∼ bringen, zu ∼e fördern* bring to light; *an den ∼ legen* exhibit, display; *in den ∼ hinein leben usw.* from hand to mouth, at random; 2'**-aus:** *∼, tag'ein* day in, day out; '**∼**(**e**)**bau** ⚒ *m* open-cast working.

Tage|blatt ['tɑːgə-] *n* daily (paper); '**∼buch** *n* journal, diary; † *a.* daybook; ⚓ logbook; '**∼dieb** *m* idler, loafer; **∼gelder** ['∼gɛldər] *n/pl.* daily allowance *sg.*; '2**lang** for days (together), day after day; '**∼lohn** *m* day's (*od.* daily) wages *pl.*; '**∼löhner** *m* (7) day-labo(u)rer; '**∼marsch** *m* day's march.

tagen ['tɑːgən] (25) dawn; (*beraten*) meet, sit (in conference), ⚖ be in session.

'**Tagereise** *f* day's journey.

'**Tages|-anbruch** *m* (*bei ∼* at) daybreak; '**∼-ausflug** *m* day's excursion; '**∼befehl** *m* order of the day; '**∼creme** *f* day cream; '**∼geld** † *n* call-money; '**∼gespräch** *n* topic of the day; '**∼heim** *n* day-care centre; '**∼heimschule** *f* day school; '**∼kasse** *f thea.* advance-booking office; † receipts of the day; *für kleine Ausgaben*: petty cash; '**∼kurs** *m* † current rate; *e-r Fachschule*: day course; '**∼leistung** *f* day's output; '**∼licht** *n* daylight; *ans ∼ bringen* (*kommen*) bring (come) to light; '**∼mutter** *f* child- (*od.* baby-)minder; '**∼-ordnung** *f* order of the day, *e-r Versammlung*: agenda; *auf der* (*die*) *∼* on the agenda; *zur ∼ übergehen* proceed to the order of the day; *fig. das ist an der ∼* that is the order of the day; '**∼preis** *m* current price; '**∼presse** *f* daily press; '**∼rückfahrkarte** *f* day return (ticket); '**∼tour** *f* day trip; '**∼zeit** *f* time of day; (*Ggs. Nachtzeit*) day-time; *zu jeder ∼* at any time of the day; '**∼zeitung** *f* daily (paper).

'**tage|weise** by the day; '2**werk** *n* day's work; (*Arbeitseinheit*) man-day.

Tagfalter ['tɑːk-] *m* buterfly.

...tägig [-tɛːgiç] of ... days.

täglich ['tɛːkliç] daily; † *∼es Geld* call-money.

tags: *∼ darauf* the day after; *∼ zuvor* the day before; '**∼-über** during the day, in the day-time.

'**tag**|'**täglich** every day; '2**-und-'Nachtdienst** *m* day and night service; '2**-und'nachtgleiche** *f* (15) equinox.

Tagung ['tɑːguŋ] *f* meeting, conference, *Am. a.* convention; '**∼sbericht** *m* proceedings *pl.*

Taifun [taɪ'fuːn] *m* (3[1]) typhoon.

Taill|e ['taljə] *f* (15) waist; (*Mieder*) bodice; 2**iert** [∼'jiːrt] waisted.

Takel ⚓ ['tɑːkəl] *n* (7) tackle; **∼age** [∼'lɑːʒə] *f* (15), '**∼ung** *f*, '**∼werk** *n* rigging, tackle; '2**n** ⚓ (29) rig.

Takt [takt] *m* (3) ♪ time, measure; (*∼strich*) bar; *weitS.* rhythm, cadence; *mot.* cycle; *fig.* tact, delicacy; ~ *halten* keep time; *den ~ schlagen* beat the time; *aus dem ~ kommen* lose the beat, *fig.* be put out; *aus dem ~ bringen fig.* put out; '**⁀fest** steady in keeping time; *fig.* firm; **⁀ieren** [~'ti:rən] beat the time; '**~ik** ⚔ *u. fig. f* tactics *pl. u. sg.*; '**~iker** ⚔ *m* tactician; '**⁀isch** tactical; '**⁀los** tactless; '**~losigkeit** *f* tactlessness, indiscretion; '**~stock** *m* baton; '**~strich** ♪ *m* bar; '**⁀voll** tactful.

Tal [tɑ:l] *n* (1²; *poet. a.* 3) valley; *poet. u. fig.* vale; *zu ~* = **⁀'abwärts** downhill.

Talar [ta'lɑ:r] *m* (3¹) gown, robe.

Talent [ta'lɛnt] *n* (3) talent (*a. Person*; *zu* for); **⁀iert** [~'ti:rt] *s. talentvoll*; **~los** untalented; **~sucher** *m* talent scout; **⁀voll** talented, gifted.

Talg [talk] *m* (3) *roh*: suet; *ausgelassen*: tallow; '**~drüse** *f* sebaceous gland; **⁀ig** ['~giç] suety; tallowy; **~licht** ['talk-] *n* tallow-candle.

Talisman ['tɑ:lisman] *m* (3¹) mascot, (good-luck) charm.

Talk [talk] *m* (3) talc; '**~erde** *f* magnesia; '**~um** *n* (7) talcum.

Talkessel ['tɑ:l-] *m s. Talmulde.*

Talk|master ['tɔ:kmɑ:stər] *m* (7) *im Fernsehen*: host; **~show** ['~ʃo:; '~ʃəu] *f* chat show, *Am.* talk show.

Talmi ['talmi] *n* (11) pinchbeck.

Talmulde ['tɑ:lmuldə] *f* basin (*od.* hollow) of the valley.

Talon ✝ [ta'lɔ̃] *m* (11) talon.

'**Tal|sohle** *f* bottom of the valley; *fig.* ✝ depression; '**~sperre** *f* dam.

Tamburin [tambu'ri:n] *n* (3¹) tambourine.

Tampon ['tampɔn] ⚕ *m* (11) tampon.

Tamtam ['tam'tam] *n inv.* tomtom; *fig.* noise, fuss; (*Reklame*) ballyhoo.

Tand [tant] *m* (3) trumpery, (worthless) trifles *pl.*; (*Flitter*) tinsel; (*Spielzeug*) bauble, gewgaw.

Tändel|ei [tɛndə'laɪ] *f* (16) trifling, dallying; *fig.* flirt(ing), flirtation; '**⁀n** (29) trifle, dally; flirt; (*trödeln*) dawdle.

Tandem ['tandɛm] *n* (11) tandem.

Tang ⚘ [taŋ] *m* (3) seaweed.

Tang|ente ⩘ [taŋ'gɛntə] *f* (15) tangent; **⁀ieren** [~'gi:rən] be tangent to; *fig.* touch, affect.

Tango ['taŋgo:] *m* (11) tango.

Tank [taŋk] *m* (3) tank (*a.* ⚔; *s. Panzer*); '**⁀en** (25) (re)fuel, fill up, take in petrol; '**~er** ⚓ *m* (7), '**~schiff** *n* tanker; '**~er-unglück** *n* (oil) tanker disaster; '**~stelle** *f* filling (*od.* petrol, *Am.* gas) station; '**~verschluß** *m* fuel cap; '**~wagen** *m* tank lorry (*Am.* truck); 🚃 tank car; '**~wart** *m* (3) filling-station attendant.

Tann *poet.* [tan] *m* forest; '**~e** *f*, '**~enbaum** *m* (15) fir(-tree); '**~enholz** *n* fir-wood, deal; '**~ennadel** *f* fir-needle; '**~enzapfen** *m* fir-cone.

Tantalusqualen ['tantalus-] *f/pl.* torments of Tantalus, *weitS. a.* agony, martyrdom.

Tante ['tantə] *f* (15) aunt; **~-'Emma-Laden** F *m* corner shop, *Am.* mom-and-pop store.

Tantieme [tɑ̃'tjɛ:mə] *f* (15) royalty, percentage, share in profits.

Tanz [tants] *m* (3² *u.* ³) dance; '**~abend** *m* dancing-party; '**~bär** *m* dancing bear; '**~bein** *n*: *das ~ schwingen* dance, do the light fantastic.

tänzeln ['tɛntsəln] (29, h. *u.* sn) trip, skip, frisk.

tanzen ['tantsən] *v/t. u. v/i.* (27, h. *u.* sn) dance (*a. fig.*); *s. Reihe.*

Tänzer ['tɛntsər] *m* (7), '**~in** *f* (16¹) dancer; *thea.* (ballet-)dancer, *f a.* danseuse; (*Mit⁀*) partner.

'**Tanz|fläche** *f* dance floor; '**~gesellschaft** *f* dancing-party; '**~kapelle** *f* dance band; '**~lehrer** *m* dancing-master; '**~lokal** *n* dance-hall; '**~musik** *f* dance music; '**~saal** *m* dance-hall, ball-room; '**~schritt** *m* (dancing-)step; '**~schule** *f* dancing-school; '**~stunde** *f* dancing-lesson; '**~turnier** *n* dancing contest.

Tapet [ta'pe:t] *n* (3): *aufs ~ bringen* bring *a subject* up; **~e** *f* (15) wallpaper; **~enwechsel** F *m* change (of scenery).

Tapezier|er [tape'tsi:rər] *m* (7) paperhanger; (*Polsterer*) upholsterer; **⁀en** paper.

tapfer ['tapfər] brave, valiant; '**⁀keit** *f* bravery, valo(u)r.

tappen ['tapən] (25, h. *u.* sn) grope *od.* fumble (about).

täppisch ['tɛpiʃ] awkward, clumsy.

tapsen ['tapsən] walk clumsily.

Tara ✝ ['tɑ:ra] *f inv.* tare.

Tarantel *zo.* [ta'rantəl] *f* (15) tarantula; *fig. wie von der ~ gestochen* like a flash.

tarieren ✝ [ta'ri:rən] tare.

Tarif [ta'ri:f] *m* (3¹) *allg.* rate; (*Lohn⁀*)

(wage) scale; (*Zoll*♀) tariff; **~-abschluß** *m* collective wage agreement; **~-aus-einandersetzungen** *f/pl.* pay disputes; **~-autonomie** *f* free collective bargaining; **~gehalt** *n* agreed-scale salary; **~kündigung** *f* wage reopening; **♀lich, ♀mäßig** standard, contractual, according to scale; **~lohn** *m* standard wage(s *pl.*); **~partner** *m* party to a wage agreement; **~runde** *f* pay round; **~verhandlungen** *f/pl.* collective bargaining, wage negotiations; **~vertrag** *m* (standard) wage agreement, industrial (*Am.* collective) agreement.

tarn|en [ˈtarnən] (25) ⚔, ⚓, *fig.* camouflage; mask; screen; **ˈ♀farbe** *f* camouflage colo(u)r (*od.* paint); **ˈ♀-kappe** *f* magic hood; **ˈ♀-organisation** *f* cover organisation; **ˈ♀ung** *f* camouflage.

Tasche [ˈtaʃə] *f* (15) *in der Kleidung*: pocket; (*Hand*♀, *Reise*♀ *usw.*) bag; (*Etui*) case; (*Beutel*) pouch (*a. anat., zo.*); *s. Akten*♀, *Schul*♀; *in die ~ stecken* (put into one's) pocket, F *j-n*: be head and shoulders above a p.; *j-m auf der ~ liegen* F live off a p.; *tief in die ~ greifen müssen* have to pay through one's nose; *wie s-e ~ kennen* know … like the back of one's hand; F *ich habe es in der ~* it's in the bag.

ˈTaschen|-ausgabe *f* pocket-edition; **ˈ~buch** *n* pocket-book, paperback; **ˈ~computer** *m* hand-held computer; **ˈ~dieb** *m* pickpocket; **ˈ~-feuerzeug** *n* pocket-lighter; **ˈ~flasche** *f* hip flask (*od.* bottle); **ˈ~-format** *n* pocket-size; **ˈ~geld** *n* pocket-money, allowance; **ˈ~kalender** *m* pocket diary; **ˈ~lampe** *f* pocket lamp; (*Stab*♀) (electric) torch, *bsd. Am.* flashlight; **ˈ~messer** *n* pocket-(*od.* clasp-)knife, *Am. a.* jackknife; *kleines*: penknife; **ˈ~rechner** *m* pocket calculator; **ˈ~spieler** *m* juggler; **~spielerei** [ˈ~ʃpiːləˈraɪ] *f* jugglery, sleight of hand; **ˈ~tuch** *n* handkerchief; **ˈ~-uhr** *f* (pocket) watch; **ˈ~wörterbuch** *n* pocket-dictionary.

Tasse [ˈtasə] *f* (15) cup.

Tastatur [tastaˈtuːr] *f* (16) keyboard, keys *pl.*

Tast|e [ˈtastə] *f* (15) key (*a.* ⊕); **ˈ♀en** (26) touch, feel; (*tappen*) grope, fumble (*nach* for; *a. fig.*); *sich ~* (*s-n Weg suchen*) feel one's way; **ˈ♀end** *fig.* groping, tentative; **ˈ~endruck** *m*: *auf ~* at the press of a button; **ˈ~en-(wahl)fernsprecher** *m*, **ˈ~entelephon** *n* digital (*od.* push-button) telephone; **ˈ~er** *m* ⊕, ⚡ probe, feeler (*a. zo.*); (*Druckknopf*) push-button; *Zirkel*: cal(l)iper(s *pl.*); **ˈ~sinn** *m* (sense of) touch.

Tat [tɑːt] **1.** *f* (16) deed, act, action; *große*: feat; ⚖ criminal act, offen|ce (*Am.* -se); *Mann der ~* man of action; *in der ~* indeed, in (point of) fact; *s. frisch, umsetzen*; **2.** ♀ *pret. v. tun* 1.

Tatar [taˈtɑːr] *m* (12) Tartar.

ˈTat|bestand *m* state of affairs; ⚖ facts *pl.* of the case, factual findings *pl.*; **ˈ~-einheit** ⚖ *f*: *in ~ mit* (in coincidence) with.

ˈTaten|drang *m* urge (*od.* zest) for action; **ˈ♀durstig** burning for action; enterprising; **ˈ♀los** inactive.

Täter [ˈtɛːtər] *m* (7), **ˈ~in** *f* (16¹) doer; (*Übeltäter*) perpetrator (*a.* ⚖ = committer); culprit; (*Urheber*) author; **ˈ~schaft** *f* guilt.

ˈtätig active (*a. gr.*); (*geschäftig*) busy; *bei e-r Firma usw. ~ sein* be in the employ of, work for; *~ sein als* act (*od.* work *od.* function) as; **~en** [ˈ~gən] (25) *bsd.* ✝ effect, transact; (*abschließen*) conclude; **ˈ♀keit** *f* activity; *berufliche*: occupation, business; *anat.*, ⊕ *usw.*: action; *in ~ setzen* put in action; *in voller ~* in full swing; **ˈ♀keitsfeld** *n* field of activity; **ˈ♀keitsmerkmale** *n/pl.* job characteristics; **♀ung** [ˈ~guŋ] *f* transaction.

ˈTat|kraft *f* energy; (*Unternehmungsgeist*) enterprise; **ˈ♀kräftig** energetic(ally *adv.*), active.

ˈtätlich violent; *~ werden* resort to violence; *~ werden gegen* assault; ⚖ *~e Beleidigung* assault and battery; **ˈ♀keit** *f* (*mst pl.*) (act of) violence; ⚖ assault (and battery).

ˈTat-ort ⚖ *m* scene of crime.

tätowier|en [tɛtoˈviːrən] tattoo; **♀ung** *f* tattoo(ing).

ˈTat|sache *f* fact; *pl.* (*Unterlagen*) data; *j-n vor vollendete ~n stellen* confront a p. with a fait accompli; **ˈ~sachenbericht** *m* factual (*od.* documentary) report; **ˈ♀sächlich** actual, factual, real; *adv.* actually, in fact (*a.* ⚖), as a matter of fact.

tätscheln ['tɛtʃəln] (29) pat.
'**Tatwerkzeug** *n* (murder) weapon.
Tatze ['tatsə] *f* (15) paw.
Tau[1] [taU] *n* (3) rope; *bsd.* ⚓ cable; ~[2] *m* (3[1], *o. pl.*) dew.
taub [taUp] deaf (*fig.* gegen, für to); *Nuß*: deaf, empty; *Gestein*: dead; *Glieder*: numb; *fig.* auf ~e Ohren stoßen *Mahnungen etc.*: fall on deaf ears.
Taube ['taUbə] *f* (15) pigeon; *rhet.* dove; '**2ngrau** dove-colo(u)red; '**~nschlag** *m* dovecot; '**~nzucht** *f* pigeon-breeding.
'**Tauber** *m* (7), **Täuberich** ['tɔYbəriç] *m* (3) cock pigeon.
Taubheit ['taUphaɪt] *f* deafness; numbness.
'**Taubnessel** ⚘ *f* dead-nettle.
'**taubstumm** deaf and dumb; '**2e** *m, f* (18) deaf-mute; '**2ensprache** *f* deaf-and-dumb language.
tauchen ['taUxən] (25) *v/t.* plunge, dip, duck; *v/i.* (h. *u.* sn) dive (*bsd. Schwimmer*), plunge, dip; *Unterseebot*: submerge.
'**Taucher** *m* (7) diver; '**~-anzug** *m* diving-suit; '**~gerät** *n*, '**~lunge** *f* aqualung; '**~glocke** *f* diving-bell; '**~maske** *f* diving mask.
'**Tauch|sieder** *m* immersion heater; '**~sport** *m* skin-diving.
tauen ['taUən] (25) *v/i.* **a**) (h. *u.* sn) *Eis, Schnee*: thaw, melt; es taut it is thawing; **b**) *Tau*: (h.) es taut dew is falling.
Tauf|-akt ['taUf-] *m* (ceremony of) baptism; '**~becken** *n* baptismal font; '**~buch** *n* parish-register; '**~e** *f* (15) baptism, christening; aus der ~ heben stand godfather (*od.* godmother) to, *fig.* initiate; '**2en** (25) (*a. fig.*) baptize, christen.
Täuf|er ['tɔYfər] *m* (7): Johannes der ~ John the Baptist; '**~ling** *m* (3[1]) child (*od.* person) to be baptized.
'**Tauf|name** *m* Christian name; '**~pate** *m* godfather, *f* (*a.* '**~patin**) godmother; '**~schein** *m* certificate of baptism; '**~stein** *m* baptismal font; '**~zeuge** *m* sponsor.
taugen ['taUgən] (25) be of use, be good *od.* fit (*alle*: zu for); (zu) nichts ~ be good for nothing.
'**Taugenichts** *m* (4; *sg. a. inv.*) good-for-nothing.
tauglich ['taUkliç] fit, good; apt, useful (für, zu for; to *do*); (*fähig*) able; ⚔, ⚓ able-bodied; '**2keit** *f* fitness *etc.*; ability, usefulness.
Taum|el ['taUməl] *m* (7) giddiness; (*Überschwang*) rapture, ecstasy; '**2(e)lig** reeling; (*schwindlig*) giddy; '**2eln** (29, h. *u.* sn) reel, stagger; (*schwindlig sein*) be giddy.
'**Taupunkt** *m* dew-point.
Tausch [taUʃ] *m* (3[2]) exchange; (*~handel*) barter; '**2en** (27) *v/t. u. v/i.* exchange (*a. fig. Blicke, Schläge usw.*); (*ein~*) *a.* barter, F swop (gegen for); ich möchte nicht mit ihm ~ I would not change places with him.
täuschen ['tɔYʃən] (27) *allg.* deceive (*j-n*; *a. Hoffnung*); (*narren*) fool, dupe; (*prellen*) cheat; *Sport*: deceive, *nur v/i.*: feint; sich ~ deceive o.s., (*sich irren*) be mistaken; sich ~ lassen let o.s. be deceived; in *Hoffnungen usw.* getäuscht werden be disappointed in; '**~d** deceptive; *Ähnlichkeit*: striking; ~ nachahmen mimic to perfection.
'**Tausch|geschäft** *n*, '**~handel** *m* barter; '**~mittel** *n* barter-medium; '**~-objekt** *n* bartering object.
'**Täuschung** *f* deception; (*a. Selbst*2) delusion; ⚖ fraud, deceit; optische ~ optical delusion; '**~smanöver** *n* feint, diversion; '**~sversuch** *m* attempted deception.
'**Tauschwert** *m* barter value.
tausend ['taUzənt] (a) thousand; zu 2en by thousands; 2undeine Nacht Arabian Nights *pl.*; **~erlei** ['~dər'laɪ] *adj.* of a thousand different kinds; *als su.* a thousand (different kinds) (of); '**~fach, ~fältig** ['~zəntfɛltiç] thousandfold; '**2fuß** *m*, '**2füß(l)er** *m* millepede, *bsd. Am.* millipede; '**~jährig** of a thousand years; 2es Reich *bibl.* millennium; '**2künstler** *m* wizard; Jack of all trades; '**~mal** a thousand times; **2sasa** ['~sasa] F *m* (11) devil of a fellow; '**2schön(chen)** ⚘ *n* (3[1] [6]) daisy.
'**tausendst,** '**2el** *n* (7) thousandth.
'**Tau|tropfen** *m* dew-drop; '**~werk** *n* ropes *pl.*; '**~wetter** *n* thaw; '**~ziehen** *n* tug of war (*a. fig.*).
Taxameter [taksa'me:tər] *m* (7) (*Fahrpreisanzeiger*) clock, taximeter.
Taxator [ta'ksa:tɔr] *m* (8[1]) appraiser, taxer, valuer.
Taxe ['taksə] *f* (15) rate; (*Steuer*)

tax; (*Gebühr*) fee; (*Schätzung*) estimate, appraisal; (*Autodroschke*) *s. Taxi.*

Taxi ['taksi] *n* (11) taxi(cab), cab.

ta'xieren rate, estimate; *amtlich*: value, tax, appraise, assess.

'Taxi|fahrer *m* taxi-driver; **'~stand** *m* taxi-rank, *Am.* taxi stand.

Technik ['tɛçnik] *f* (16) ⊕ engineering; (*Wissenschaft*) technology; (*Verfahren*) technique (*a. Kunst, Sport*); (*Fertigkeit*) workmanship, skill; *in der Kunst*: technique; **'~er** *m* (7) (technical) engineer; (*Spezialist; a. weitS.*) technician; **~um** ['~um] *n* (9) technical school.

'technisch ⊕ *allg.* engineering (*department, journal, process, etc.*); (*bsd. betriebs~ u. weitS.*) technical; (*mechanisch*) mechanical; *Sport*: *~e Disziplin* field event; *Boxen*: *~er K.o.* technical knock-out; *~es Personal* technical staff; *~e Hochschule* technical college *od.* university; *~e Störung* breakdown.

Technisierung [tɛçni'ziːruŋ] *f* mechanization.

Technolog|ie [tɛçnolo'giː] *f* (15, *o. pl.*) technology; **⁲isch** [~'loːgiʃ] technological.

Techtelmechtel ['tɛçtəl'mɛçtəl] F *n* (7) (love) affair.

Teckel ['tɛkəl] *m* (7) dachshund.

Teddybär ['tɛdibɛːr] *m* Teddy bear.

Tee [teː] *m* (11) tea; **'~beutel** *m* tea-bag; **'~büchse** *f* tea-caddy; **'~-Ei** *n* tea infuser; **'~gebäck** *n* tea-cake; *weiches*: scone; *Am.* biscuit; **'~geschirr** *n* tea-service; **'~kanne** *f* teapot; **'~kessel** *m* tea-kettle; **'~löffel** *m* tea-spoon; **'~löffelvoll** *m* tea-spoonful; **'~maschine** *f* tea-urn; **'~mischung** *f* blend of tea; **'~pause** tea-break.

Teer [teːr] *m* (3) tar; **'⁲en** (25) tar; **'⁲ig** tarry.

'Teerpappe *f* tar-board.

'Tee|sieb *n* tea-strainer; **'~strauch** *m* tea-plant; **'~tasse** *f* teacup; **'~wagen** *m* tea wagon, teacart; **~wärmer** ['~vɛrmər] *m* (7) tea-cosy.

Teich [taɪç] *m* (3) pond, pool; F *der große ~* (*Ozean*) the Pond.

Teig [taɪk] *m* (3) dough, paste; **~ig** ['~giç] doughy, pasty; **'~waren** [taɪk-] *f/pl.* farinaceous products.

Teil [taɪl] *m, n* (3) part (*a.* ⊕); (*Anteil*) portion, share; (*Abschnitt*) section; (*Bestandteil*) component; *edle ~e pl. des Körpers* vital parts; *beide ~e pl.* (*Parteien*) both parties; *ein ~ davon* part of it; *ein großer ~* a great deal; *der größte ~ der Menschen* the greater part (*od.* the majority) of mankind; *zum ~* partly, in part, to some extent; *zum großen ~* largely; *zum größten ~* mostly; *zu gleichen ~en* share and share alike; *sein ~ beitragen* do one's share; *sich sein ~ denken* have one's own thoughts about it; *ich für mein ~* I for my part; **'~-ansicht** *f* partial view; **'⁲bar** divisible; **'~barkeit** *f* divisibility; **'~chen** *n* (6) particle; **'⁲en** (25) divide; (*teilhaben an*) share; **'~er** *m* (7) divider; ♆ divisor; **'~erfolg** *m* partial success; **'⁲haben** participate, share (*beide*: *an dat.* in); **'~haber(in** *f* [16¹]) *m* (7) participator; ✝ partner, associate; **'~haberschaft** *f* partnership; **'⁲haftig** partaking (*gen.* of); *e-r S. ~ werden s. teilhaben.*

...teilig consisting of ... parts, *two-piece ... etc.*

'Teil|kaskoversicherung *f* partial coverage insurance; **~nahme** ['~naːmə] *f* (15) participation (*an dat.* in); *fig.* interest (in); (*Mitgefühl*) sympathy (with); (*Beileid*) condolence(s *pl.*); **'⁲nahmeberechtigt** eligible; **'⁲nahmslos** (*gleichgültig*) indifferent; (*gefühllos*) impassible; (*untätig*) passive; *vor Schwäche*: apathetic(ally *adv.*); **'~nahmslosigkeit** *f* indifference; impassibility; passiveness; apathy; **'⁲nahmsvoll** sympathetic(ally *adv.*); **'⁲nehmen** *an* (*dat.*) take part (*od.* participate) in; *gemeinsam mit anderen*: join in; (*anwesend sn*) be present at, attend; *fig.* take an interest, in, *mitfühlend*: sympathize with; *an e-r Mahlzeit ~* partake of a meal; **'⁲nehmend** *s. teilnahmsvoll*; **'~nehmer(in** *f* [16¹]) *m* (7) participant, participator; *Sport usw.*: competitor, entrant; *teleph.* subscriber; **'~nehmerverzeichnis** *teleph. n* telephone directory.

teils [taɪls] partly.

'Teil|strecke *f* section, fare stage; *weitS.* leg, stage; **'~strich** *m* graduation mark.

'Teilung *f* division; (*Ver⁲*) distribution; (*in Anteile*) sharing; (*Unterteilung*) graduation, scale; **'~s-**

artikel *gr. m* partitive article; '**~s-zahl** *f* dividend.

'**teil|weise** *adv.* partly, partially, in part; '**2zahlung** *f* part-payment, (payment by) instal(l)ment; *auf ~ kaufen* buy on the instal(l)ment-plan; '**2zeit-arbeit** *f* part-time employment; '**2zeit-Arbeitskraft** *f* part-time employee; '**2zeitbeschäftigung** *f* part-time job.

Teint [tɛ̃] *m* (11) complexion.

Tele'fon *usw. s. Telephon.*

Telegramm [tele'gram] *n* (3¹) telegram, wire; (*bsd. Übersee2*) cable; **~-anschrift** *f* cable address; **~formular** *n* telegraph form (*Am.* blank); **~gebühr** *f* telegram charge; **~stil** *m* telegraphic style, telegraphese.

Telegraph [~'grɑːf] *m* (12) telegraph; **~en-amt** *n* telegraph office; **~enmast** *m* telegraph-pole; **~ie** [~gra'fiː] *f* (15) telegraphy; *drahtlose ~* wireless telegraphy; **2ieren** [~'fiːrən] *v/t. u. v/i.* telegraph, wire; *nach Übersee:* cable; **2isch** [~'grɑːfiʃ] telegraphic(ally *adv.*), *adv. mst* by telegram, by wire, by cable; *~e Überweisung* cable transfer; **~ist** [~gra'fist] *m* (12), **~istin** *f* telegraphist, telegraph operator.

Telekommunikation ['teːlekɔmunikatsjoːn] *f* telecommunications *pl.*

Tele-objektiv *phot.* ['teːle-] *f* telephoto lens.

Telepath|ie [~pa'tiː] *f* telepathy; **2isch** [~'pɑːtiʃ] telepathic(ally *adv.*).

Telephon [~'foːn] *n* (3¹) telephone, F phone; *am ~* on the (tele)phone; *ans ~ gehen (wenn es klingelt)* answer the telephone; *~ haben* be on the telephone; **~-anruf** *m* (tele-) phone call; **~-anschluß** *m* telephone connection; *~ haben* be on the telephone *od.* F phone; **~-apparat** *m* telephone set; **~at** [~fo'nɑːt] *n* (3) *s. Telephongespräch*; **~-auskunft** [~'foːn-] *f* directory enquiries *pl.* (*Am.* assistance); **~buch** *n* telephone directory; **~gebühren** *f/pl.* telephone charges; **~gespräch** *n* telephone call *od.* conversation; **~hörer** *m* receiver; **2ieren** [~fo'niːrən] *v/t. u. v/i.* telephone, F phone; **2isch** [~'foːniʃ] telephonic(ally *adv.*); *adv. mst* by telephone; **~ist** [~fo'nist] *m* (12), **~istin** *f* (16¹) telephonist, telephone operator; **~netz** [~'foːn-] *n* telephone network; **~nummer** *f* telephone number; **~verbindung** *f* telephone connection; **~vermittlung** *f*, **~zentrale** *f* (telephone) exchange *od.* (*Am.*) central office; **~zelle** *f* telephone (*od.* call) box.

Teleskop [tele'skoːp] *n* (3¹) telescope; **2isch** telescopic(ally *adv.*).

Television [televi'zjoːn] *f* (16, *o. pl.*) television.

Telex ['teːlɛks] *n* telex.

Teller ['tɛlər] *m* (7) plate; ⊕ disk, disc (*a. Schi2*); '**~mütze** *f* flat cap; (*Baskenmütze*) beret.

Tempel ['tɛmpəl] *m* (7) temple; '**~herr** *m*, '**~ritter** *m* (Knight) Templar; '**~raub** *m*, '**~schändung** *f* sacrilege.

Temperafarbe ['tɛmpera-] *f* dis-temper.

Temperament [tɛmpəra'mɛnt] *n* (3) temper(ament); (*Feuer*) mettle, spirits *pl.*, vivacity; **2los** spiritless; **2voll** vivacious, (high-)spirited, passionate.

Temperatur [~'tuːr] *f* (16) temperature; *~ haben* have (*od.* run) a temperature; *j-s ~ messen* take a p.'s temperature; **~schwankung** *f* variation of temperature.

tempe'rieren temper (*a.* ♪).

Tempo ['tɛmpo] *n* (11) ♪ time, (*a. weitS.*) tempo; (*Gangart*) pace; (*Geschwindigkeit*) speed, rate; *in langsamem ~* at a slow pace; *das ~ angeben* set the pace; **~limit** *mot.* ['~limit] *n* (11) speed limit; **2rär** [~'rɛːr] temporary; *adv.* for the time being.

Tempus *gr.* ['tɛmpus] *n* (*sg. inv.*, *pl. Tempora* ['~pora]) tense.

Tendenz [tɛn'dɛnts] *f* (16) tendency, trend; **2iös** [~'tsjøːs] tendentious; **~roman** *m* tendentious novel, purpose-novel; **~stück** *n* tendentious play, purpose-play.

Tender ['tɛndər] *m* (7) tender.

tendieren [tɛn'diːrən] tend (*nach, zu* to[wards]).

Tenne ['tɛnə] *f* (15) threshing floor.

Tennis ['tɛnis] *n inv.* (lawn-)tennis; '**~ball** *m* tennis-ball; '**~platz** *m* tennis-court; '**~schläger** *m* tennis-racket; '**~spieler**(**in** *f*) *m* tennis-player; '**~turnier** *n* tennis-tournament.

Tenor¹ ['teːnɔr] *bsd.* ⚖ *m* tenor, substance.

Tenor² ♪ [te'noːr] *m* (3¹ *u.* ³) tenor; **~ist** [~no'rist] *m* (12) tenor(-singer).

Teppich ['tɛpiç] *m* (3¹) carpet, *Am. a.*

rug; '**~boden** *m* fitted carpet, wall--to-wall carpeting; '**~kehrmaschine** *f* carpet-sweeper; '**~schaum** *m* carpet foam.

Termin [tɛr'mi:n] *m* (3[1]) (fixed) date *od.* term, (appointed) time, target--date; (*Frist*) time-limit; *äußerster ~* final date, *bsd. Am.* deadline; *Sport*: fixture; ⚖ (*Verhandlung*) hearing; (*Besprechung, Treffen*) appointment; *e-n ~ anberaumen od. stellen* (*absetzen*) fix (rescind) a date.

Terminal ['tœrminəl] *m, n* (11) terminal; *Computer*: (video display) terminal.

Ter'min|geld ⚜ *n* fixed deposit; **⁀gemäß, ⁀gerecht** in due time, on the due date; **~geschäft** ⚜ *n* time--bargain, *pl.* futures; **~kalender** *m* desk diary, appointments calendar; ⚖ cause-list, *Am.* calendar; **~ologie** [~minolo'gi:] *f* (15) terminology; **~plan** *m* schedule.

Termite [tɛr'mi:tə] *f* (15) termite, white ant.

Terpentin [tɛrpən'ti:n] *n, m* (3[1]) turpentine, F turps.

Terrain [tɛ'rɛ̃] *n* (11) ground, terrain; (*Grundstück*) plot of land; (*Bauplatz*) building site.

Terrasse [tɛ'rasə] *f* (15) terrace; **⁀nförmig** [~nfœrmiç] terraced; **~ntür** *f* French window.

Terrine [tɛ'ri:nə] *f* (15) tureen.

terri|torial [tɛritor'ja:l] territorial; **⁀torium** [~'to:rjum] *n* (9[1]) territory.

Terror ['tɛrɔr] *m* (11, *o. pl.*) terror; '**~-akt** *m* act of terrorism; '**~-anschlag** *m* terrorist attack; **⁀isieren** [tɛrori'zi:rən] terrorize; **~ist** [~'rist] *m* (12) terrorist.

Terz [tɛrts] *f* (16) ♩ third; *fenc.* tierce; ♩ *kleine* (*große*) *~* minor (major) third; **~ett** ♩ [~'tsɛt] *n* (3) trio.

Test [tɛst] *m* (3 *u.* 11) test.

Testament [tɛsta'mɛnt] *n* (3) (last) will, ⚖ last will and testament; *eccl.* Testament; *sein ~ machen* make a will; **⁀arisch** [~'ta:riʃ] testamentary; *adv.* by will; **~s-er-öffnung** *f* opening (*od.* probate) of the will; **~svollstrecker** *m* executor; *gerichtlich bestellter*: administrator.

'**Test|bild** *n Fernsehen*: test card; '**⁀en** (26) test; '**~fall** *m* test case.

testieren [tɛ'sti:rən] *v/i.* make a will; *v/t.* (*letztwillig anordnen*) dispose by will; (*bezeugen*) testify.

'**Test|person** *f* subject; '**~pilot** *m* test--pilot; '**~puppe** *f* dummy; '**~stoppabkommen** *n* test-ban treaty; '**~strecke** *mot. f* test track.

teuer ['tɔʏər] dear, costly, expensive; *fig.* dear, beloved; *~e Preise* high prices; *wie ~ ist es?* how much is it?, what does it cost?; *s. Rat, stehen*; '**⁀ung** *f* dearness, high (*od.* rising) prices, high cost of living; '**⁀ungsrate** *f* rate of price increases; '**⁀ungszulage** *f* cost-of-living bonus.

Teufel ['tɔʏfəl] *m* (7) devil; *armer ~* poor devil (*od.* wretch); *pfui ~! angeekelt*: ugh!, *entrüstet*: for shame!, disgusting!; *wer zum ~?* who the devil (*od.* hell); *wie der ~* like mad; *in (des) ~s Küche kommen* get it in the neck; *man soll den ~ nicht an die Wand malen* talk of the devil (and he will appear); *j-n zum ~ jagen* send a p. packing; *in der Not frißt der ~ Fliegen* beggars can't be choosers; *der ~ ist los* the fat is in the fire; *zum ~ gehen* (*Sache*) go to pot; *scher dich zum ~* go to hell; **~ei** [~'laɪ] *f* (16) devilish trick, devil(t)ry; '**~skerl** *m* devil of a fellow; '**~skreis** *fig. m* vicious circle.

'**teuflisch** devilish, diabolic(al).

Text [tɛkst] *m* (3[2]) text; (*Lied⁀*) words *pl.*; (*Opern⁀*) book, libretto; *j-m den ~ lesen* lecture a p.; *aus dem ~ bringen* (*kommen*) (be) put out; '**~buch** *n* play book, libretto.

Textil... [tɛks'ti:l] textile; **~ien** [~jən] *pl. inv.* textiles *pl.*

'**textlich** textual.

'**Text|seite** *f* text page; '**~speicher** *m Computer*: text memory; '**~ver-arbeitung** *f Computer*: word processing; '**~ver-arbeitungs-anlage** *f* word processor.

Theater [te'a:tər] *n* (7) theat|re, *Am.* -er; (*Bühne u. weitS.*) stage; *fig. contp.* farce; (*Aufregung, Getue*) fuss; *fig. ~ spielen* play-act; *zum ~ gehen* go on the stage; **~besucher** (**-in** *f*) *m* play-goer; **~karte** *f* (theat|re, *Am.* -er) ticket; **~kasse** *f* box office; **~kritiker** *m* drama critic; **~stück** *n* (stage-)play; **~vorstellung** *f* theatrical performance; **~zettel** *m* play-bill.

theatralisch [~a'tra:liʃ] theatrical.

Theke ['te:kə] *f* (15) bar, *Am. a.* counter.

Thema [ˈteːma] *n* (9², *pl. a.* ~*ta*) theme (*a.* ♪ *usw.*), subject; (*nur Gesprächs*≈) topic; *beim* ~ *bleiben* stick to the point.

Theolog [teoˈloːk] *m* (12), **~e** [~gə] (13) *m* theologian; **~ie** [~loˈgiː] *f* (15) theology; **≈isch** [~ˈloːgiʃ] theological.

Theoret|iker [teoˈreːtikər] *m* (7) theorist; **≈isch** theoretic(al); **≈iˈsieren** theorize.

Theorie [teoˈriː] *f* (15) theory.

Therap|eut [teraˈpɔʏt] *m* (12) therapist; **~eutik** [~ˈpɔʏtik] *f* (16, *o. pl.*) therapeutics *sg.*; **≈eutisch** therapeutic(ally *adv.*); **~ie** [~ˈpiː] *f* (15) therapy.

Thermal|bad [tɛrˈmaːl-] *n* thermal spa; **~quelle** *f s. Therme.*

Therm|e [ˈtɛrmə] *f* (15) thermal spring; **ˈ≈isch** thermal, thermic.

Thermo|dyˈnamik [tɛrmo-] *f* thermodynamics *sg.*; **ˈ~element** thermocouple.

Thermometer [tɛrmoˈmeːtər] *n* (7) thermometer; **~säule** *f* thermometer column; **~stand** *m* thermometer reading.

thermoˈplastisch thermoplastic(ally *adv.*)

Thermos|flasche [ˈtɛrmɔs-] *f* vacuum (*od.* thermos) flask; **ˈ~kanne** *f* vacuum jug.

Thermostat *phys.* [tɛrmoˈstaːt] *m* (3) thermostat.

These [ˈteːzə] *f* (15) thesis.

Thrombose ⚕ [trɔmˈboːzə] *f* (15) thrombosis.

Thron [troːn] *m* (3) throne; **ˈ~-anwärter** *m* heir apparent; **ˈ~besteigung** *f* accession to the throne; **ˈ~bewerber** *m* pretender to the throne; **ˈ≈en** (25) be enthroned; *fig.* sit, be placed; **ˈ~-erbe** *m* heir to the throne; **ˈ~folge**(**r** *m* [7]) *f* succession (successor) to the throne; **ˈ~himmel** *m* canopy; **ˈ~räuber** *m* usurper; **ˈ~rede** *f Brt. parl.* Queen's (*od.* King's) Speech; **ˈ~wechsel** *m* change of sovereign.

Thunfisch [ˈtuːnfiʃ] *m* tunny, tuna.

Thüring|er [ˈtyːriŋər] *m* (7), **ˈ~erin** *f* (16¹), **ˈ≈isch** Thuringian.

Thymian [ˈtyːmjaːn] *m* (3¹) thyme.

Tick [tik] *m* (3¹ *od.* 11) ⚕ (*mst* **Tic**) tic; (*Schrulle*) fad, kink; **ˈ≈en** (25) tick.

tief [tiːf] **1.** *allg.* deep (*a. fig.*); *Wissen, Geheimnis usw.*: profound; (*niedrig*: *z.B. Tal*) low; *Farbe*: dark; *fig.* (*äußerst*) utter, extreme; *im ~sten Winter* in the depth (*od.* dead) of winter; ~ *in der Nacht* in the dead of night; *bis ~ in die Nacht* far into the night; ~ *enttäuscht* badly disappointed; **2.** ≈ *n* (6) (barometric) depression *od.* low.

ˈTief|-angriff ✈ *m* low-level attack; **ˈ~-atmung** *f* deep breathing; **ˈ~bau** ⊕ *m* (3) underground construction engineering; **ˈ≈beˈtrübt** deeply grieved, very sad; **ˈ≈beˈwegt** deeply moved; **ˈ≈blau** deep blue; **ˈ~blick** *m* keen insight, penetration; **ˈ≈blickend** penetrating; **ˈ~decker** ✈ *m* (7) low-wing monoplane; **ˈ~druck** *print. m* intaglio (printing), roto(gravure); **ˈ~druck(-gebiet** *n*) *m* low-pressure (area); **ˈ~e** *f* (15) depth; *fig. a.* profoundness; profundity; **ˈ~-ebene** *f* (low) plain; **≈empfunden** [ˈ~ʔɛmˈpfundən] heart-felt; **ˈ~enpsychologie** *f* depth psychology; **ˈ~enregler** *m Radio etc.*: bass control; **ˈ~enschärfe** *phot. f* depth of focus; **ˈ~enwirkung** *f* depth effect; *paint.* plastic effect; **ˈ~flug** *m* low-level flight; **ˈ~gang** ⚓ *m* draught; **ˈ~garage** *f* underground car park; **≈gebeugt** [ˈ~gəˈbɔʏkt] *fig.* deeply afflicted; **ˈ≈gefroren** deep-frozen; **≈gefühlt** [ˈ~gəˈfyːlt] heart-felt; **ˈ≈gekühlt** deep-freeze, (fresh-) frozen; **ˈ≈greifend** far-reaching, thorough; radical; **ˈ~kühlfach** *n* freezing compartment; **ˈ~kühlkost** *f*, **ˈ~kühlware** *f* frozen foods *pl.*; **ˈ~kühltruhe** *f* deep-freeze, freezer; **~lader** [ˈ~laːdər] *m* (7) flat-bed car; **ˈ~land** *n* lowland(s *pl.*); **ˈ≈liegend** deep-seated; *Augen*: sunken; **ˈ~punkt** *fig. m* low; **ˈ~schlag** *m Boxen*: low hit, hit below the belt; **ˈ≈schürfend** *fig.* profound; **ˈ≈schwarz** jet-black; **ˈ~see** *f* deep-sea; **ˈ~seeforschung** *f* deep-sea research; **ˈ~sinn** *m* profoundness; (*Schwermut*) melancholy; **ˈ≈sinnig** profound; melancholy; **ˈ~stand** *m* low level; *fig.* low.

Tiegel [ˈtiːgəl] *m* (7) saucepan, stewpan; (*Schmelz*≈) crucible.

Tier [tiːr] *n* (3) animal; *großes*: beast; (*Rohling*) brute; F *fig. großes* (*od. hohes*) ~ bigwig, big shot; **ˈ~-art** *f* (animal) species; **ˈ~-arzt** *m* veterinary (surgeon), *bsd. Am.* veterinarian, F vet; '~**bändiger**(**in** *f*) *m* tamer of wild beasts; '~**freund** *m* animal lover; '~**garten** *m* zoological gardens *pl.*, zoo; '~**handlung** *f* pet shop; '~**heilkunde** *f* veterinary science; '~**heim** *n* animal home (*Am.* shelter); '2**isch** animal; *fig. a.* (*roh*) bestial, brutish; '~**kreis** *ast. m* zodiac; '~**kunde** *f* zoology; '~**leben** *n* animal life; '2**lieb** fond of animals; '~**park** *m* *s. Tiergarten*; '~**pfleger**(**in** *f*) *m* zoo-keeper; ~**präparator** ['~prɛpa'rɑːtɔr] *m* (8[1]) taxidermist; '~**quälerei** *f* cruelty to animals; '~**reich** *n* animal kingdom; '~**schutzver-ein** *m* Society for the Prevention of Cruelty to Animals; '~**versuch** *m* animal test; '~**welt** *f* animal world; '~**zucht** *f* animal (*od.* livestock) breeding.

Tiger ['tiːgər] *m* (7) tiger; '~**fell** *n* tiger skin; '~**in** *f* (16[1]) tigress; '2**n** (29) speckle, spot.

tilgbar ['tilkbɑːr] ✝ redeemable.

tilg|en ['tilgən] (25) extinguish; (*auswischen*) efface, (*a. fig. vernichten*) wipe out; (*streichen*) blot out, obliterate; (*aufheben*) annul, cancel; *Schuld*: pay off, discharge; *Anleihe, Staatsschuld*: redeem; (*amortisieren*) amortize; '2**ung** *f s. tilgen*: extinction; cancel(l)ing; discharge, payment; redemption; '2**ungsfonds** *m* sinking-fund.

Tinktur [tiŋk'tuːr] *f* (16) tincture.

Tinte ['tintə] *f* (15) ink; *fig.* F *in der ~ sitzen* be in a scrape.

'**Tinten|faß** *n* inkpot; *eingelassenes*: ink-well; '~**fisch** *zo. m* cuttle-fish; '~**fleck** *m*, '~**klecks** *m* ink-blot; '~**löscher** *m* (rocker) blotter; '~**stift** *m* copying(-ink) pencil, indelible (ink) pencil.

Tip [tip] *m* (11) tip.

tippeln F ['tipəln] (29) tramp.

tipp|en ['tipən] *v/t. u. v/i.* (25) tap, tip; F (*auf der Maschine schreiben*) type; F (*wetten*) bet; '2**fehler** *m* typing error; 2**se** *contp.* F ['tipsə] *f* (15) typist; ~'**topp** tiptop, first-class; '2**zettel** *m* pools (*od.* lottery) coupon.

Tirol|er [ti'roːlər] *m* (7), ~**erin** *f* (16[1]), 2(**er**)**isch** Tyrolese.

Tisch [tiʃ] *m* (3[2]) table; (*Kost*) board; *bei ~e* at table; *s. decken, grün, rein*; *zu ~ einladen* invite to dinner; *fig. unter den ~ fallen* (*lassen*) fall flat (drop); '~**dame** *f* partner at table; '~**decke** *f* table-cloth; '~**fußball** *m* table football; '~**gerät** *n* table set; '~**gast** *m* guest; '~**gebet** *n*: *das ~ sprechen* say grace; '~**gespräch** *n* table-talk; '~**herr** *m* partner at table; '~**karte** *f* place card; '~**klopfen** *n* table-rapping; '~**lampe** *f* table lamp; (*Schreib*2) desk lamp.

Tischler ['tiʃlər] *m* (7) joiner; (*Kunst*2) cabinet-maker; ~**ei** [~'raɪ] *f* (16) joinery; (*Werkstatt*) joiner's workshop; '~**leim** *m* solid glue; '2**n** (29) *v/i.* do joiner's work; *v/t.* make.

'**Tisch|nachbar**(**in** *f*) *m* neighbo(u)r at table; '~**platte** *f* table-top; *zum Ausziehen*: leaf; '~**rechner** *m* desk calculator; '~**rede** *f* toast, after-dinner speech; '~**rücken** *n* table-turning; '~**telephon** *n* desk-telephone; '~**tennis** *n* table tennis; '~**tuch** *n* table-cloth; '~**wein** *m* table-wine; '~**zeit** *f* dinner-time.

Titan|(**e**) [ti'tɑːn(ə)] *m* (12) Titan; ~**in** *f* (16[1]) Titaness; 2**isch** titanic.

Titel ['tiːtəl] *m* (7) *allg.* title; *Sport*: *e-n ~ innehaben* hold a title; '~**bild** *n* frontispiece; *e-s Magazins usw.*: cover (picture); '~**blatt** *n* title-page; '~**geschichte** *f* cover story; '~**halter** *m Sport*: title-holder; '~**kampf** *m Sport*: title bout; '~**kopf** *m* heading; '~**melodie** *f Film*: theme music; '~**rolle** *f* title-role; '~**seite** *f* front page; '~**verteidiger** *m Sport*: title-holder; '~**zeile** *f* headline.

Titten V ['titən] *f/pl.* (15) tits.

Titul|ar... [titu'lɑːr] titulary, nominal; ~**atur** [~la'tuːr] *f* (16) titles *pl.*; 2**ieren** [~'liːrən] style, call.

Toast [toːst] *m* (3[2]) (*Trinkspruch*) toast (*a. Röstbrot*); *e-n ~ ausbringen* propose a toast; '2**en** (26) (*rösten*) toast; '~**er** *m* (7) toaster.

toben ['toːbən] (25) rage (*a. fig.*); *Kinder*: romp.

Tob|sucht ['toːpzuxt] *f* raving madness, frenzy; '2**süchtig** raving mad, frantic; '~**suchts-anfall** *m* raving fit; *fig.* tantrum.

Tochter ['tɔxtər] *f* (14[1]) daughter; '~**gesellschaft** ✝ *f* subsidiary company.

Tod [toːt] *m* (3) death; *feierlich od.* ⚖ decease; *des ~es sein* be doomed; *den ~ finden* be killed; *sich den ~ holen* (*sich erkälten*) catch one's death (of cold); *mit dem ~e ringen* be in the last agonies; *zu ~e er-*

schrecken, langweilen usw. to death; *für den ~ nicht leiden können* hate like poison; '♀**bringend** deadly, fatal; '♀'-**ernst** deadly serious.

Todes|-ahnung ['~dəs-] *f* presentiment of death; '**~-angst** *f* fear of death; *fig.* mortal dread; '**~-anzeige** *f* obituary (notice); '**~-art** *f* manner of death; '**~-erklärung** *f* declaration of death; '**~fall** *m* (case of) death, decease; '**~gefahr** *f* deadly peril, peril (*od.* danger) of *one's* life; '**~jahr** *n* year of *a p.'s* death; '**~-kampf** *m* death-struggle; '**~kandidat** *m* doomed man; '**~-opfer** *n/pl.* victims *pl.*, casualities *pl.*; '**~-stoß** *m* death-blow; '**~strafe** *f* death penalty, capital punishment; *bei ~* on pain of death; '**~stunde** *f* hour of death; '**~tag** *m* day (*od.* anniversary) of *a p.'s* death; '**~-ursache** *f* cause of *a p.'s* death; '**~-urteil** *n* sentence of death; *fig.* death-warrant; '**~ver-achtung** *f* defiance of death; *mit ~* recklessly; '**~wunde** *f* mortal wound; '**~-wunsch** *m* death-wish; '**~zelle** *f* death cell; *pl. a.* death row *sg.*

'**Tod|feind** *m* deadly enemy; '♀**krank** dangerously ill; '♀'**langweilig** deadly boring.

tödlich ['tøːtliç] deadly, fatal, mortal, lethal.

'**tod|'müde** dead tired, dead-beat; '~'**schick** F dead smart; (*prima*) *a.* F fab(ulous), super; '~'**sicher** cocksure; '♀**sünde** *f* deadly (*od.* mortal) sin.

Tohuwabohu ['toːhuva'boːhu] *n* hubbub, wild confusion.

Toilette [toa'lɛtə] *f* (15) (*Ankleiden, Anzug*) toilet; (*Abort*) lavatory, *bsd. Am.* restroom; *s.* ~*ntisch*; *~ machen* do one's toilet; **~n-artikel** *m* toilet-article; **~nbrille** *f* toilet seat; **~n-frau** *f* toilet attendant; **~ngarnitur** *f* toilet set; **~npapier** *n* toilet-paper; **~nseife** *f* toilet soap; **~ntisch** dressing-table, *Am.* dresser.

tole|rant [tole'rant] tolerant (*gegen* of); ♀'**ranz** *f* (16) tolerance (*a.* ⊕, ⚕); ⊕ *a.* allowance; ~'**rieren** tolerate.

toll [tɔl] mad, crazy, wild (*alle a. fig.*); (*unglaublich*) fantastic; (*großartig*) *a.* F terrific; F *nicht so ~ sl.* not so hot; *wie ~* like mad; ♀**e** F *f* (15) tuft; '**~en**[1] F (25) *Kinder usw.*: romp, frolic; '**~en**[2] (*fälteln*) crimp; '♀**haus** *n* madhouse; *fig.* bedlam; '♀**heit** *f* madness; (*toller Streich*) mad trick; '♀**kirsche** ♀ *f* deadly nightshade; '**~kühn** foolhardy, dare-devil; '♀**kühnheit** *f* foolhardiness; '♀**wut** *f* rabies.

Tolpatsch ['tɔlpatʃ] *m* (3), **Tölpel** ['tœlpəl] *m* (7) awkward (*od.* clumsy) fellow, booby.

Tölpel|ei [~'laɪ] *f* (16) clumsiness; '♀**haft** awkward, clumsy.

Tomate [to'maːtə] *f* (15) tomato; **~n-mark** *n* tomato purée (*Am.* paste).

Tombola ['tɔmbola] *f* (16[1]) raffle.

Ton[1] [toːn] *m* (3[3]) sound; (*Klang, ~fall*) tone (*a. fig.*); ♪ tone, note, (~*art*) key; (*Betonung*) accent, stress; (*Farb*♀) tone (*a. phot.*), *heller*: tint, *dunkler*: shade; *guter ~* good form; *den ~ angeben* give the key-note (*a. fig.*), *fig.* set the tone; *zum guten ~ gehören* be the fashion; F *große Töne reden* talk big; *in höchsten Tönen reden von* rave about; **~**[2] *m* (3) (~*erde*) clay; '**~-abnehmer** *m* pick-up; '♀-**angebend** leading; '**~-arm** *m* tone (*od.* pickup) arm; '**~-art** ♪ *f* key; *fig. e-e andere ~ anschlagen* change one's tune; '**~-aufnahme** *f* sound recording; '**~band** *n* (recording) tape; *auf ~ aufnehmen* tape-record; '**~bandgerät** *n* tape recorder; '**~dichtung** *f* symphonic poem.

'**tonen** *phot.* (25) tone.

tönen ['tøːnən] (25) *v/i.* sound; F *fig.* sound off; *v/t.* (*färben*) tint, tone; shade.

'**Ton-erde** *f* argillaceous earth; *essigsaure ~* alumin(i)um acetate (solution).

tönern ['tøːnərn] (of) clay, earthen.

'**Ton|fall** *m* cadence; *beim Sprechen*: intonation, accent, tone; '**~-film** *m* sound film; '**~frequenz** *f* audio frequency; '**~geschirr** *n* earthenware, pottery; '♀(**halt**)**ig** clayey; '**~höhe** *f* pitch.

Tonika ♪ ['toːnika] *f* (16[2]) tonic.

'**Ton-ingenieur** *m* sound engineer.

'**tonisch** ♪ *u.* ⚕ tonic(ally *adv.*).

'**Ton|kopf** *m von Tonbandgerät etc.*: recording head; *von Plattenspieler*: pick-up; '**~kunst** *f* musical art; '**~-künstler(in** *f*) *m* musician; '**~lage** *f* pitch; '**~leiter** *f* scale, gamut; '♀**los** soundless; *gr.* unstressed; *fig.* toneless; '**~meister** *m* sound engineer.

Tonnage [tɔˈnɑːʒə] *f* (15) tonnage.
Tonne [ˈtɔnə] *f* (15) barrel, cask, tun; ⚓, *Gewicht*: ton; ˈ**~ngehalt** *m* tonnage; ˈ**~ngewölbe** *n* barrel-vault; ˈ**⚬nweise** by (*od.* in) barrels.
ˈ**Ton|pfeife** *f* clay pipe; ˈ**~qualität** *f* sound quality; ˈ**~regler** *m* tone control; ˈ**~silbe** *f* accented syllable; ˈ**~spur** *f*, ˈ**~streifen** *m Film*: sound track.
Tonsur [tɔnˈzuːr] *f* (16) tonsure.
ˈ**Ton|taube** *f Sport*: clay pigeon; ˈ**~taubenschießen** *n* trap shooting; ˈ**~techniker** *m* sound engineer; ˈ**~träger** *m* sound carrier.
Tönung [ˈtøːnuŋ] *f* tint, tinge, shading; *phot.* tone.
ˈ**Tonwaren** *f/pl. s. Töpferware.*
Topas [toˈpɑːs] *m* (4) topaz.
Topf [tɔpf] *m* (3³) pot; *fig. in e-n ~ werfen* lump together; ˈ**~deckel** *m* potlid.
Töpfer [ˈtœpfər] *m* (7) potter; (*Ofensetzer*) stove-fitter; **~ei** [~ˈraɪ] *f* (16) pottery; (*Werkstatt*) potter's shop; ˈ**~scheibe** *f* potter's wheel; ˈ**~ware** *f* earthenware, pottery.
ˈ**Topf|lappen** *m* oven-cloth; ˈ**~pflanze** *f* pot-plant, potted plant.
topographisch [topoˈgrɑːfiʃ] topographic(al).
topp![1] [tɔp] done!, agreed!
Topp[2] ⚓ [~] *m* (3[1] *u.* 11) top, head; ˈ**~mast** *m* topmast; ˈ**~reep** *n* guy; ˈ**~segel** *n* topsail.
Tor[1] [toːr] *n* (3) gate (*a. Slalom*⚬); (*Einfahrt*) gateway (*a. fig.*); *Sport*: goal; *s. schießen.*
Tor[2] [~] *m* (12) fool.
Torf [tɔrf] *m* (3) peat; ˈ**~boden** *m* peat-soil; ˈ**~moor** *n* peat-bog; ˈ**~mull** *m* peat-dust.
Torheit [ˈtoːrhaɪt] *f* folly.
ˈ**Torhüter** *m* gate-keeper; *Sport*: (goal)keeper, F goalie.
töricht [ˈtøːriçt] foolish, silly.
Törin [ˈtøːrin] *f* fool(ish woman).
torkeln [ˈtɔrkəln] (29, h. *u.* sn) reel, stagger, totter.
Tor|latte [ˈtoːr-] *f Fußball*: crossbar; ˈ**~lauf** *m* slalom; ˈ**~linie** *f Sport*: goal-line; ˈ**⚬los** *Sport*: scoreless.
Tornister [tɔrˈnistər] *m* (7) knapsack, ⚔ *a.* pack; (*Schul*⚬) satchel.
torpedieren [tɔrpeˈdiːrən] torpedo.
Torpedo [tɔrˈpeːdo] *m* (11) torpedo; **~boot** *n* torpedo-boat.
ˈ**Tor|pfosten** *m Sport*: goal-post; ˈ**~raum** *m Fußball*: goal area; ˈ**~schlußpanik** *f* last-minute panic; ˈ**~schütze** *m Sport*: scorer; ˈ**~steher** *m Sport*: goal-keeper.
Torso [ˈtɔrzo] *m* (11) torso.
Torte [ˈtɔrtə] *f* (15) gateau; (*Obst*⚬) tart, *Am.* pie; ˈ**~nheber** *m* (7) cake server.
Tortur [tɔrˈtuːr] *f* (16) torture.
ˈ**Torwart** *m* (3) *s. Torhüter.*
tosen [ˈtoːzən] (27, h. *u.* sn) roar, rage, thunder.
tot [toːt] *allg.* dead (*a. fig.*); *~e Zeit* dull (*od.* dead) season; *~er Gang* ⊕ dead travel, lost motion, *e-s Gewindes*: backlash; *⚬e Hand* mortmain; *~es Kapital* unemployed capital; *~er Punkt* ⊕ dead cent|re, *Am.* -er, *fig.* impasse, deadlock, (*Erschöpfung*) exhaustion; *fig. auf dem ~en Punkt ankommen* reach a deadlock, *P.*: be exhausted; *den ~en Punkt überwinden* break the deadlock, *bei Erschöpfung*: get one's second wind; *~er Winkel* blind spot; *~e Zone Radio*: blind spot *od.* area; *s. Geleise, Rennen.*
total [toˈtɑːl] total, complete; (*umfassend*) all-out; **⚬-ausfall** *m* total loss; **⚬-ausverkauf** *m* clearance sale; **⚬isator** [totaliˈzɑːtɔr] *m* (8[1]) totalizator, totalizer.
totalitär [~ˈtɛːr] totalitarian.
Toˈtalschaden *mot. m* write-off.
ˈ**tot-arbeiten:** *sich ~* work o.s. to death.
ˈ**Tote** *m, f* (18) dead (person); *s. Leiche; die ~n pl.* the dead.
töten [ˈtøːtən] (26) kill; *Nerv*: deaden.
ˈ**Toten|bahre** *f* bier; ˈ**~beschwörung** *f* calling up the dead; ˈ**~bett** *n* deathbed; ˈ⚬ˈ**blaß** deadly pale; ˈ**~blässe** *f* deadly pallor; ˈ**~feier** *f* obsequies *pl.*; ˈ**~geläut** *n*, ˈ**~glocke** *f* knell; ˈ**~gräber** *m* (7) grave-digger; ˈ**~hemd** *n* shroud; ˈ**~kopf** *m*, ˈ**~schädel** *m* death's-head (*a. zo. u. Symbol*), skull; ˈ**~liste** *f* list of the dead; *bsd.* ⚔ death-roll; ˈ**~maske** *f* death-mask; ˈ**~messe** *f* mass for the dead, requiem; ˈ**~reich** *n* realm of the dead; ˈ**~schein** *m* death certificate; ˈ**~starre** *f* rigor mortis; ˈ⚬ˈ**still** as still as death; ˈ**~stille** *f* dead(ly) silence; ˈ**~tanz** *m Kunst*: danse macabre (*fr.*); ˈ**~-urne** *f* (funeral) urn; ˈ**~wache** *f* wake.

ˈ**tot|geboren** stillborn; *fig.* abortive; *fig. ein* ~*es Kind Idee, Plan*: a non-starter; ˈ**2geburt** *f* stillbirth; ˈ**~lachen:** *sich* ~ nearly die with laughter; *zum* 2 F a scream; ˈ**2lauf** ⊕ *m* dead travel; ˈ**~laufen:** *sich* ~ *fig.* peter out.

Toto [ˈto:to] *m* (11) (*Totalisator*) tote; (*Fußball*2) (football) pool; *im* ~ *spielen* bet on the pools.

ˈ**tot|schießen** shoot dead; ˈ**2schlag** ⚖ *m* second-degree murder; ˈ**~schlagen** kill, slay; *die Zeit* ~ kill time; ˈ**2schläger** *m* homicide; (*Schlagstock*) life-preserver, *sl.* cosh, *Am.* blackjack; ˈ**~schweigen** hush up; ˈ**~stechen** stab to death; *sich* ˈ**~stellen** feign death.

Tötung [ˈtø:tuŋ] *f* killing.

Toupet [tuˈpe:] *n* (11) toupee.

Tour [tu:r] *f* (16) tour; (*Ausflug*) trip, excursion; ⊕ (*Umdrehung*) revolution, turn; F (*Trick*) dodge, ploy; *auf (der)* ~ on the road; *auf* ~*en bringen mot.* rev (up); *auf* ~*en kommen mot.* pick (*od.* rev) up, *fig.* get going; *fig. auf vollen* ~*en laufen* be in full swing; *in e-r* ~ at a stretch, (*dauernd*) incessantly; ˈ**~enrad** *n* roadster; ˈ**~enschi** *m* touring ski; ˈ**~enwagen** *mot. m* touring car; tourer; ˈ**~enzahl** *f* speed, revolutions *pl.* (per minute) (*abbr.* r.p.m.); ˈ**~enzähler** *m* revolution counter.

Touris|mus [tuˈrismus] *m* (16, *o. pl.*), **~tik** *f* (16, *o. pl.*) tourism; **~t** *m* (12), **~tin** *f* (16[1]) tourist; **~tenattraktion** *f* tourist attraction; **~tenklasse** *f* economy class.

Tournee [turˈne:] *f* (16) tour.

Trab [trɑ:p] *m* (3) trot; *im* ~ at a trot, F *fig.* on the run; *fig. j-n auf (den)* ~ *bringen* make a p. get a move on.

Trabant [traˈbant] *m* (12) satellite; **~enstadt** *f* satellite town.

traben [ˈtrɑ:bən] (25, h. *u.* sn) trot.

ˈ**Traber** *m* (7) trotter.

Trabrennen [ˈtrɑ:p-] *n* trotting race.

Tracht [traxt] *f* (16) **1.** dress, attire, (*a.* traditional) costume; (*Schwestern*2 *usw.*) uniform; (*Mode*) fashion; **2.** (*Last*) load; *der Bienen* (*Ertrag*) yield; *e-e (gehörige)* ~ *Prügel* a sound thrashing.

trachten [ˈtraxtən] **1.** *v/i.* ~ *nach et.* endeavo(u)r after, strive for *od.* after, seek; *(danach)* ~, *zu inf.* endeavo(u)r (*od.* strive, seek, try) to *inf.*; *j-m nach dem Leben* ~ seek a p.'s life; **2.** 2 *n* striving; pursuit (*nach* of).

trächtig [ˈtrɛçtiç] (big) with young, pregnant; ˈ**2keit** *f* pregnancy.

Tradition [tradiˈtsjo:n] *f* (16) tradition; **2ell** [~tsjoˈnɛl] traditional.

traf [trɑ:f] *pret. v. treffen 1.*

Trag|bahre [ˈtrɑ:k-] *f* stretcher, litter; ˈ**~balken** *m* (supporting) beam; (*Längsträger*) girder; (*Querträger*) transom; ˈ**2bar** portable; *Kleid*: wearable; *fig.* bearable; (*annehmbar*) acceptable.

Trage [ˈtrɑ:gə] *f* (15) hand-barrow; *s. Tragbahre.*

träg(e) [trɛ:k, ˈ~gə] lazy, indolent; (*langsam*) sluggish; *phys.* inert.

tragen [ˈtrɑ:gən] (30) *v/t.* carry (*a. v/i. Gewehr, Stimme*); *Kosten, Namen, Verantwortung usw.*: bear; (*ertragen*) bear (*a. v/i. Eis*); (*stützen*) carry; (*hervorbringen*) bear, yield; (*am Körper* ~) wear; *bei sich* ~ have about one; *sich* ~ (*sich kleiden*) dress; *sich gut* ~ (*Stoff*) wear well; ✝ *sich (selbst)* ~ pay its way; *fig. sich mit et.* ~ be thinking of; *von e-r Idee usw. getragen* inspired by, based on; *s. Absicht, Bedenken, Folge, Schau, Sorge, Verlangen, Zins, getragen.*

Träger [ˈtrɛ:gər] *m* (7), ˈ**~in** *f* (16[1]) carrier (*a.* ⚕ *Krankheits*2); (*Gepäck*2) porter; (*Inhaber*) holder, bearer; *e-s Kleides*: wearer; *am Damenhemd usw.*: (shoulder) strap; (*Unterhalts*2) providing body; ⊕ support; △ girder; ⚡ carrier; 🚀 vehicle; ˈ**~lohn** *m* porterage; ˈ**2los** *Kleid*: strapless; ˈ**~rakete** *f Weltraumfahrt*: booster (rocket).

ˈ**Tragetasche** *f* carrier bag.

tragfähig [ˈtrɑ:k-] capable of carrying *od.* bearing; *fig.* sound; *e-e* ~*e Basis für ...* a working basis for ...; ˈ**2keit** *f* carrying (*od.* load) capacity; ⚓ tonnage.

Trag|fläche ✈ [ˈtrɑ:kflɛçə] *f* wing; ˈ**~flächenboot** *n*, ˈ**~flügelboot** *n* hydrofoil (craft).

Trägheit [ˈtrɛ:khaɪt] *f* laziness, indolence, *a. phys.* inertia.

Tragik [ˈtrɑ:gik] *f* (16, *o. pl.*) tragicalness; tragedy; ˈ**~er** *m* (7) tragic poet, tragedian.

tragikom|isch [~giˈko:miʃ] tragicomic(ally *adv.*); ⁀**ödie** [⁀ko'mø:djə] *f* tragicomedy.

'**tragisch** tragic(al *fig.*); *ich nehme es nicht* ⁀ I don't take it hard.

Trag|korb ['trɑ:k-] *m* (back-)basket; '⁀**kraft** *f s. Tragfähigkeit.*

Tragöd|e [tra'gø:də] *m* (13) tragic actor, tragedian; ⁀**ie** [⁀djə] *f* (15) tragedy; ⁀**in** *f* (16¹) tragedienne.

Trag|riemen ['trɑ:kri:mən] *m* (carrying) strap; '⁀**schrauber** *m* gyroplane, autogiro; '⁀**tier** *n* pack animal; '⁀**tüte** *f* carrier bag; '⁀**weite** *f* range; *fig.* import(ance), consequences *pl.*, implications *pl.*; '⁀**werk** ✈ *n* wing unit.

Train|er ['trɛ:nər] *m* (7) trainer, coach; ⁀**ieren** [⁀'ni:rən] *v/t. u. v/i.* train, coach (*zu e-m Sport* for); ⁀**ing** ['⁀niŋ] *n* (11, *o. pl.*) training; '⁀**ings-anzug** *m* training overall, track suit; '⁀**ingslager** *n* training camp.

Trakt|at [trak'tɑ:t] *m*, *n* (3) (*Abhandlung*) treatise; *eccl.* tract; (*Vertrag*) treaty; ⁀**ieren** [⁀'ti:rən] treat.

Traktor ⊕ ['traktɔr] *m* (8¹) tractor.

trällern ['trɛlərn] (29) trill, hum.

trampel|n ['trampəln] (29) trample; '⁀**pfad** *m* beaten path; '⁀**tier** *n* Bactrian camel.

Tran [trɑ:n] *m* (3) train(-oil), whale-oil.

Trance [trɑ̃:ns(ə)] *f* (15) trance.

Tranchier|besteck [trɑ̃'ʃi:r-] *n* (*ein* a pair of) carvers *pl.*; ⁀**brett** *n* carving-board; ⁀**en** carve, cut up; ⁀**messer** *n* carving-knife.

Träne ['trɛ:nə] *f* (15) tear; *den* ⁀*n nahe* on the verge of tears; *unter* ⁀*n* amid tears; *s. ausbrechen.*

'**tränen** (25) water, run with tears; '⁀**drüse** *f* lachrymal gland; '⁀**gas** *n* tear-gas; '⁀**sack** *m* lachrymal sac.

'**tranig** smelling (*od.* tasting) of train-oil; F (*träg*) dull.

Trank [traŋk] **1.** *m* (3³) drink, beverage; ⚕ potion; **2.** ⁀ *pret. v. trinken.*

Tränke ['trɛŋkə] *f* (15) watering-place; '⁀**n** (25) give *a p.* to drink; *Vieh, Boden*: water; (*durchtränken*) soak, steep, ⊕ *a.* impregnate.

trans|atlantisch [trans'ʔat'lantiʃ] transatlantic; ⁀**fer** ✝ [⁀'fe:r] *m* (11), ⁀**ferieren** [⁀fe'ri:rən] transfer; ⁀**formator** ⚡ [⁀fɔr'mɑ:tɔr] *m* transformer; ⁀**formieren** [⁀fɔr'mi:rən] transform.

Transfusion [⁀fu'zjo:n] *f* transfusion.

Transistor [tran'zistɔr] *m* transistor; ⁀**isieren** [⁀tori'zi:rən] transistorize.

Transit|handel [tran'zi:t-] *m* transit-trade; ⁀**iv** ['⁀ziti:f] transitive; ⁀**weg** *m* transit route.

Transkription [transkrip'tsjo:n] *f* transcription.

Transmission ⊕ [transmi'sjo:n] *f* transmission.

transparent [⁀pa'rɛnt] **1.** transparent; **2.** ⁀ *n* (3) transparency; *bei Demonstrationen*: banner.

Transpi|ration [⁀pira'tsjo:n] *f* perspiration; ⁀'**rieren** perspire.

Transplant|ation ⚕ [transplanta'tsjo:n] *f*, ⁀**ieren** [⁀'ti:rən] transplant.

Transport [⁀'pɔrt] *m* (3) transport(-ation), carriage, ⚓ *u. Am. allg.* shipment; (*Straßen*⁀) haulage; ✝ *während des* ⁀*s* in transit; ⁀**abel** [⁀'tɑ:bəl] transportable; (*tragbar*) portable; (*beweglich*) mobile; ⁀-**arbeiter** [⁀'pɔrt-] *m* transport worker; ⁀**er** *m* (7) ⚓ transport; ✈ transport aircraft; *s. Truppen*⁀; ⁀**eur** [⁀'tø:r] *m* (3¹) transporter; 𝔄 protractor; ⁀**fähig** [⁀'pɔrt-] transportable; *Kranke*: transferable; ⁀**flugzeug** *n* transport aircraft *od.* airplane; ⁀**gelegenheit** *f* transport(ation) (facility); ⁀**ieren** [⁀'ti:rən] transport, carry, move, haul; ⁀**mittel** [⁀'pɔrt-] *n* (means of) transport(ation) *od.* conveyance; ⁀**schiff** *n* transport; ⁀-**unternehmen** *n* carriers *pl.*, haulage contractors *pl.*; ⁀**versicherung** *f* transport insurance.

Trapez [tra'pe:ts] *n* (3²) 𝔄 trapezoid; *mit zwei parallelen Seiten*: trapezium; *Turnen*: trapeze; ⁀**künstler**(**in** *f*) *m* trapezist.

trappeln ['trapəln] (29, h. *u.* sn) *Pferd usw.*: clatter; *Kind usw.*: patter.

Tras|sant ✝ [tra'sant] *m* (12) drawer; ⁀**sat** ✝ [⁀'sɑ:t] *m* (12) drawee; '⁀**se** ⊕ *f* (15) line; ⁀'**sieren** ✝ draw; ⊕ lay out, trace (out).

trat [trɑ:t] *pret. v. treten.*

Tratsch [trɑ:tʃ] F *m* (3), '⁀**en** gossip.

Tratte ✝ ['tratə] *f* (15) draft.

'**Trau-altar** *m* marriage-altar.

Traube ['traubə] *f* (15) bunch of

grapes; (*Beere*) grape; *weitS.* cluster; '**~nlese** *f* vintage; '**~nsaft** *m* grape-juice; '**~nzucker** *m* glucose, dextrose.

trauen ['trauən] **1.** *v/t.* marry; *sich (kirchlich) ~ lassen* get married (in church); **2.** *v/i.* trust (*j-m* a p.), have confidence (*dat.* in); *trau, schau, wem!* look before you leap!; *ich traute meinen Ohren nicht* I could not believe my ears; *sich ~ s. getrauen*; *Weg.*

Trauer ['trauər] *f* (15) sorrow, affliction; (*Gram*) grief; (*um e-n Toten*; *~kleidung*, *~zeit*) mourning; '**~-anzeige** *f* obituary (notice); '**~fall** *m* death; '**~feier** *f* obsequies *pl.*; '**~flor** *m* mourning-crape; '**~geleit** *n* funeral train; '**~kleid** *n* mourning(-dress); '**~marsch** *m* funeral march; '**2n** (29) mourn (*um* for); *weitS.* grieve (about); (*äußerlich ~*) be in mourning; '**~rand** *m* mourning-edge; *Briefpapier mit ~* mourning-paper; '**~schleier** *m* mourning-veil, weeper; '**~spiel** *n* tragedy; '**~weide** ⚘ *f* weeping willow; '**~zug** *m* funeral procession.

Traufe ['traufə] *f* (15) eaves *pl.*; *s. Regen.*

träufeln ['trɔʏfəln] (29) drip, trickle.

traulich ['trauliç] (*vertraut*) intimate; (*gemütlich*) cosy, snug; '**2keit** *f* intimacy; cosiness.

Traum [traum] *m* (3³) dream; *das fällt mir nicht im ~e ein* I would not dream of (doing) it; **~a** ['~ma] ⚕ *n* (9¹, *pl. a. ~ta*) (*seelisches ~* psychic) trauma; '**~bild** *n* vision; '**~deuter** *m* (7), '**~deuterin** *f* (16¹) interpreter of dreams.

träum|en ['trɔʏmən] *v/i. u. v/t.* (25) dream (*von* of); '**2er** *m* (7), '**2erin** *f* dreamer; **2erei** [~'raɪ] *f* (16) dreaming; *fig.* reverie, day-dream; '**~erisch** dreamy; (*sinnend*) musing.

'**Traum|fabrik** *f* (*Film*) dream factory; '**~frau** F *f* dream woman; '**~haus** F *n* dream house; '**~land** *n* dreamland; '**~welt** *f* world of dreams.

'**Traurede** *f* marriage sermon.

traurig ['trauriç] sad (*über acc.* at), sorrowful; (*elend*) wretched; (*beklagenswert*) deplorable, sorry; '**2keit** *f* sadness.

'**Trau|ring** *m* wedding-ring; '**~schein** *m* marriage certificate *od.* lines *pl.*

traut [traut] beloved, dear; *s. a. traulich.*

'**Trau|ung** *f* wedding; '**~zeuge** *m* witness to a marriage.

Travestie [travɛ'stiː] *f* (15), **2ren** travesty.

Treber ['treːbər] *pl.* (7) husks of grapes; (*Bier2*) draff *sg.*

Treck [trɛk] *m* (3), '**2en** (25, sn) trek; '**~er** ⊕ *m* (7) tractor.

Treff¹ [trɛf] *n* (11) *Karten*: club(s *pl.*); **~**² *m* F (*Treffen*) rendezvous.

treffen ['trɛfən] **1.** (30) *v/t.* hit; (*befallen*) befall, affect; (*begegnen*) meet; *sich (mit j-m) ~* meet, (*sich versammeln*) *a.* gather, assemble; *sich ~* (*geschehen*) happen; *das trifft sich gut* that's lucky; F *es gut ~* be in luck; *paint.*, *phot. du bist gut getroffen* this is a good likeness of you; *fig. j-n (empfindlich) ~* hit hard, *Kränkung*: cut to the quick; *sich getroffen fühlen* feel hurt; *nicht ~* miss; *das Los traf ihn* the lot fell on him; *s. Anstalt, Blitz, Entscheidung, Maßnahme, Vorkehrung usw.*; *v/i.* hit, go home (*beide a. fig.*); *Boxen*: *a.* land; *nicht ~* miss; *jeder Schuß trifft* every shot tells; *~ auf* (*acc.*) meet with, *zufällig*: come across; *auf den Feind ~* encounter, fall in with; *s. schwarz 2.*; **2.** 2 *n* (6) meeting, *Am. a.* rally; *zwangloses*: gathering; ⚔ encounter; *Gründe ins ~ führen* put forward; '**~d** (*auffallend*) striking; (*angemessen*) appropriate, apt; *Bemerkung*: pertinent, *pred.* to the point.

'**Treffer** *m* (7) hit; *Fußball*: goal; *fig.* (lucky) hit, lucky strike; (*Gewinnlos*) prize.

'**treffgenau** accurate; '**2igkeit** *f* accuracy.

'**trefflich** excellent; '**2keit** *f* excellence.

'**Treff|punkt** *m* meeting point, rendezvous; '**2sicher** accurate; *a. fig. Urteil*: unerring.

Treibeis ['traɪpˀaɪs] *n* drift-ice.

treiben ['~bən] **1.** (30) *v/t. allg.* drive; ⊕ (*an~*) *a.* propel; *Maschine usw.*: *a.* work, operate; *fig.* (*an~*) drive, impel, *stärker*: press, urge; *j-n ~ zu inf.* prompt (*od.* drive) a p. to; (*betreiben*) practise; *Geschäft, Handel usw.*: carry on; *Beruf*: pursue, follow; *e-e Politik*: pursue;

Sprachen: study; *s. Sport*; ⚖ (*verüben*) commit, practise; (*tun*) do; *es toll* ~ carry on like mad; *Metall*: (en)chase, emboss; *Blätter usw.*: put forth; *Pflanze*: force; *die Preise* ~ force up the market; *s. Enge, Flucht, Spitze usw.*; *v/i.* (h. *u.* sn) drive; *im Wasser*: float; drift (*a. v. Schnee usw.*; *in e-n Krieg* into a war); (*keimen*) shoot forth, germinate; ⚓ *vor Anker* ~ drag the anchor; ~*de Kraft* moving power, (*a. fig.*) prime mover; *fig. die Dinge* ~ *lassen* let things drift; *sich* ~ *lassen* float, *fig.* let o.s. drift; **2.** ⁀ *n* (6) driving *etc.*; (*Tun*) doings, activities *pl.*, (*Vorgänge*) *a.* goings-on *pl.*; (*geschäftiges* ~) bustle, stir.

'**Treiber** *m* (7) driver; (*Vieh*⁀) drover; *hunt.* beater.

Treib|gas ['traɪp-] *n* fuel (*od.* propellent) gas; '**~haus** *n* hothouse; '**~hauspflanze** *f* hothouse plant; '**~holz** *n* drift-wood; '**~jagd** *f* battue; *fig.* hunt; '**~kraft** *f*, '**~rad** *n*, '**~sand** *m s. Trieb...*; '**~ladung** *f*, '**~satz** ⚔ *m* propelling charge; '**~mine** *f* floating mine; '**~mittel** ⊕ *n* propell|ant, -ent; '**~-öl** *n* motor (*od.* fuel) oil; '**~riemen** *m* driving belt; '**~stoff** *m* fuel; *s. Benzin(...)*.

treidel|n ⚓ ['traɪdəln] (29) tow; '⁀**pfad** *m* tow(ing)-path.

tremolieren [tremo'liːrən] ♪ quaver, sing with a tremolo.

Trend [trɛnd] *m* (11) trend, tendency (*zu* toward[s]).

'**trennbar** separable.

trenn|en ['trɛnən] (25) separate (*a.* ⊕, ⚗), sever; (*teilen*) divide; *Naht*: rip up; (*loslösen*) detach; (*isolieren*) isolate, segregate; *teleph.*, ⚡ cut off, disconnect; *sich* ~ separate (*von* from), part (*P.*: with; *S.*: from, with); '**~scharf** *Radio*: selective; '⁀**schärfe** *f Radio*: selectivity; '⁀**ung** *f* separation; parting; division (*a. Silben*⁀); segregation; disconnection; ⚖ *eheliche* ~ judicial separation; '⁀**ungslinie** *f* dividing (*od.* parting) line; '⁀**ungsstrich** *m* dash; '⁀(**ungs**)**wand** *f* partition wall.

Trense ['trɛnzə] *f* (15) snaffle.

treppauf [trɛp'ˀauf]: ~, *trepp'-ab* upstairs, downstairs.

Treppe ['trɛpə] *f* (15) staircase, (*eine* a flight of *od.* a pair of) stairs *pl.*; *außerhalb des Hauses*: (*eine* a flight of) steps *pl.*; *2* ~*n hoch* on the second floor; *die* ~ *hinauf* (*hinab*) upstairs (downstairs); '**~n-absatz** *m* landing; '**~nflucht** *f* flight of steps; '**~ngeländer** *n* banisters *pl.*; '**~nhaus** *n* staircase; '**~nläufer** *m* staircarpet; '**~nstufe** *f* stair, step.

Tresor [tre'zoːr] *m* (3[1]) treasury; (*Stahlkammer*) strong-room, *bsd. Am.* vault; *engS.* safe.

Tresse ['trɛsə] *f* (15) galloon, lace; ⚔ stripe.

Trester ['trɛstər] (7) *pl. s. Treber*.

'**Tret|-anlasser** *mot. m* kick-starter; '**~boot** *n* pedal boat; '**~-eimer** *m* pedal-bin.

treten ['treːtən] (30) *v/i.* (h. *u.* sn) tread; (*gehen*) step, walk; *Radfahrer usw.*: treadle, pedal; *ins Haus* ~ enter the house; ~ *Sie näher!* come in!; *j-m zu nahe* ~ offend; *j-m unter die Augen* ~ appear before; *über die Ufer* ~ overflow its banks; *s. Kraft, näher*~, *Verbindung*; *v/t.* tread; (*e-n Fußtritt geben*) kick; *mit Füßen* ~ (*a. fig.*) trample (up)on.

'**Tretmühle** *f* treadmill (*a. fig.*).

treu [trɔʏ] faithful, loyal, true (*dat.* to); *zu* ~*en Händen* in trust; *s. Glauben*.

'**Treu|bruch** *m* breach of faith (*od.* trust); disloyalty; '⁀**brüchig** faithless, disloyal; '**~e** *f* (15) fidelity, faith(fulness), loyalty; *j-m die* ~ *halten* remain loyal to; '**~-eid** *m* oath of allegiance; **~händer** ['~hɛndər] *m* (7) trustee; ⁀**händerisch** ['~hɛndərɪʃ] fiduciary; *adv.* in trust; '**~händerschaft** *f* trusteeship; '**~handgesellschaft** *f* trust-company; '⁀**herzig** guileless; (*offen*) frank; (*naiv*) ingenuous; '⁀**lich** faithfully; (*wahrhaft, aufrichtig*) truly; '⁀**los** faithless, perfidious; '**~losigkeit** *f* faithlessness, perfidy.

Tribun [tri'buːn] *m* (3[1] *u.* 12) tribune; **~al** [~bu'nɑːl] *n* (3[1]) tribunal.

Tribüne [tri'byːnə] *f* (15) (*Redner*⁀) platform, rostrum; (*Zuschauer*⁀) (grand-)stand.

Tribut [~'buːt] *m* (3) tribute; *fig. j-m s-n* ~ *zollen* pay tribute to; ⁀**pflichtig** [~pfliçtiç] tributary.

Trichine [tri'çiːnə] *f* (15) trichina.

Trichter ['triçtər] *m* (7) funnel; ⊕ (*Aufgabe*⁀) feeding hopper; (*Granat*⁀, *Minen*⁀) crater; *des Lautspre-*

chers usw.: horn; **2förmig** ['~fœrmiç] funnel-shaped.

Trick [trik] *m* (11) trick; '**~-aufnahme** *f* trick shot; *auf Tonband*: trick recording; *pl. phot.* trick photography *sg.*; '**~betrüger** *m* trickster; '**~film** *m* trick film; *gezeichneter*: animated cartoon (film).

Trieb [tri:p] **1.** *m* (3) ♀ sprout, young shoot; (*Keimkraft*) germinating power; *fig.* (*treibende Kraft*) driving force; (*Antrieb*) impulse; (*Natur2*) instinct; (*Drang*) urge; (*Geschlechts2*) (sexual) urge; **2.** 2 *pret. v. treiben 1.*; '**~feder** *f* mainspring; *fig. a.* motive; '**2haft** instinctive; animal-like; (*sinnlich*) carnal; '**~kraft** *f* propelling (*od. a. fig.* motive) power, driving power (*od. a. fig.* force); '**~rad** *n* driving-wheel; '**~sand** *m* quicksand; '**~verbrecher** *m* sex maniac; '**~wagen** *m* 🚃 motor coach; *Straßenbahn*: prime mover; '**~werk** *n* drive (mechanism); power plant, ✈ *a.* engine.

trief|äugig ['tri:fʔɔʏgiç] blear-eyed; '**~en** (30) drip (*von* with); *Auge*: run; *Kerze*: gutter; '**~'naß** dripping wet.

triezen F ['tri:tsən] *v/t.* (27) (*quälen*) persecute; (*necken*) tease.

Trift [trift] *f* (15) pasture (land); (*Holz2*) floating; *geol.* drift.

'**triftig** valid; (*gewichtig*) weighty; (*einleuchtend*) conclusive, convincing; (*vernünftig*) sound.

Trigonometr|ie [trigonome'tri:] *f* (15) trigonometry; **2isch** [~'me:triʃ] trigonometrical.

Trikot [tri'ko:] **1.** *m, n* (11) (*Stoff*) tricot; **2.** *n* (11) *der Ballettänzer usw.*: leotard; *der Fußballer usw.*: shirt; **~agen** [~ko'tɑ:ʒən] *pl.* hosiery *sg.*

Triller ['trilər] *m* (7) trill, shake; ♪ quaver; '**2n** *v/i. u. v/t.* (29) trill, shake; ♪ quaver; *Vogel*: warble; '**~pfeife** *f* (alarm) whistle.

Trillion [tril'jo:n] *f* (16) trillion, *Am.* quadrillion.

Trilogie [trilo'gi:] *f* (15) trilogy.

trimm|en ['trimən] (25) *allg.* trim; '**2pfad** *m* fitness trail.

trink|bar ['triŋkbɑ:r] drinkable; '**2becher** *m* drinking-cup; '**2branntwein** *m* potable spirit(s *pl.*); '**~en** (30) *v/t.* drink (*a. v/i.*); *Tee usw.*: take, have; *fig.* (*in sich aufnehmen*) imbibe; ~ *auf j-n od. et.* toast, drink to; '**2er** *m* (7), '**2erin** *f* drinker; *contp.* alcoholic, drunkard; '**2erheil-anstalt** *f* institution for the cure of alcoholics; '**~fest** holding one's liquor well; '**2gelage** *n* drinking-bout; '**2geld** *n* gratuity, *mst* F tip; *j-m (ein) ~ geben* F tip a p.; '**2glas** *n* drinking-glass; '**2halle** *f im Kurort*: pump-room; *auf der Straße*: refreshment kiosk; '**2kur** *f* mineral water cure; '**2lied** *n* drinking-song; '**2spruch** *m* toast; '**2wasser** *n* drinking-water.

Trio ['tri:o] *n* (11) trio.

Triole ♪ [tri'o:lə] *f* (15) triplet.

trippeln ['tripəln] (29, h. *u.* sn) trip.

Tripper ⚕ ['tripər] *m* (7) gonorrh(o)ea, *sl.* clap.

trist [trist] dreary.

Tritt [trit] *m* (3) tread, step; (*Schritt*) pace; (*~spur*) footprint, footstep; (*Geräusch des ~es*) footfall; (*Fuß2*) kick; (*Möbel*) stepstool; ⊕ treadle; *mount.* foothold; *s. ~brett, ~leiter*; *im ~* in step; *in falschem ~* out of step; *~ fassen* fall in step; *~ halten* keep step; *aus dem ~ geraten* break step; *s. Schritt*; '**~brett** *n* foot-board, *mot.* running-board; '**~leiter** *f* step-ladder.

Triumph [tri'umf] *m* (3) triumph; *in Zssgn mst* triumphal, *z.B.* **~bogen** *m* triumphal arch; **2al** [~'fɑ:l] triumphant; **2ieren** [~'fi:rən] triumph (*fig. ~ über j-n* over a p.).

trivial [tri'vjɑ:l] trivial; **2literatur** *f* light fiction.

trocken ['trɔkən] dry (*a. weitS. Husten, Wein*; *fig. Humor usw.*); (*dürr*) arid; *fig.* dull; *im Trockenen* under cover, *fig. im trocknen* in safety; *auf dem trocknen sitzen* be in low water, be on the rocks; *s. Schäfchen.*

'**Trocken|batterie** ⚡ *f* dry (cell) battery; '**~boden** *m* drying-loft; '**~dock** *n* dry dock; '**~-ei** *n* dried (whole) eggs *pl.*; '**~-eis** *n* dry ice; '**~-element** ⚡ *n* dry cell; '**~fäule** *f* dry rot; '**~gemüse** *n* dried (*od.* dehydrated) vegetables *pl.*; '**~gewicht** *n* dry weight; '**~haube** *f* drying hood; '**~hefe** *f* dry yeast; '**~heit** *f* dryness (*a. weitS. u. fig.*); (*Dürre*) drought, aridity; *fig.* dullness; '**2legen** dry up; *Land*: drain; *Säugling*: change *a baby's* nappies (*Am.*

diapers); '**⁓legung** *f* drainage; '**⁓maß** *n* dry measure; '**⁓milch** *f* dried milk; '**⁓rasierer** *m* dry-shaver; '**⁓reinigung** *f* dry-cleaning.

trockn|en ['trɔknən] (26) *v/i.* (sn) *u. v/t.* dry (up); '**ⓢer** *m* drier.

Troddel ['trɔdəl] *f* (15) tassel.

Trödel ['trø:dəl] *m* (7) second-hand articles *pl.*; (*Gerümpel*) lumber, *Am.* junk; (*Schund*) rubbish, trash; **⁓ei** [⁓'laɪ] *f* (16) dawdling; '**⁓kram** *m s. Trödel*; '**⁓markt** *m* rag-fair; '**ⓢn** (29) deal in second-hand goods; *fig.* dawdle.

Trödler ['trø:dlər] *m* (7) second-hand dealer; *fig.* dawdler.

troff [trɔf] *pret. v. triefen.*

Trog¹ [tro:k] *m* (3³) trough.

trog² [⁓] *pret. v. trügen.*

Trojan|er [tro'jɑ:nər] *m* (7), **⁓erin** *f* (16¹), **ⓢisch** Trojan.

trollen ['trɔlən] (25, sn) toddle along; *sich ⁓* toddle off.

Trommel ['trɔməl] *f* (15) drum; ⊕ *a.* cylinder; *die ⁓ rühren* beat the drum, *fig.* advertise; '**⁓fell** *n* drumskin; *anat.* eardrum, 🕮 tympanic membrane; '**⁓fell-entzündung** ⚕ *f* tympanitis; '**⁓feuer** ⚔ *n* drum fire, *a. fig.* barrage; '**ⓢn** *v/i.* (29) drum (*a. v/t.*), beat the drum; *nervös mit den Fingern ⁓* beat the devil's tattoo; '**⁓schlag** *m* beat of the drum; '**⁓schlegel** *m*, '**⁓stock** *m* drumstick; '**⁓wirbel** *m* (drum) roll.

Trommler ['trɔmlər] *m* (7) drummer.

Trompete [trɔm'pe:tə] *f* (15), **ⓢn** (26) trumpet; **⁓r** *m* (7) trumpeter.

Tropen ['tro:pən] *pl.* tropics; '**ⓢfest** tropicalised; '**⁓helm** *m* sun- (*od.* pith-)helmet, topi; '**⁓koller** *m* tropical frenzy.

Tropf¹ [trɔpf] *m* (3³) simpleton; (*Schelm*) rogue; *armer ⁓* poor wretch.

Tropf² ⚕ [⁓] *m* (3, *o. pl.*) drip; *am ⁓ hängen* be on the drip.

tröpfeln ['trœpfəln] *v/i.* (29, h. *u.* sn) drop (*a. v/t.*), drip, trickle; *Wasserhahn*: leak; *Kerze*: gutter.

tropfen ['trɔpfən] **1.** (25) *s. tröpfeln*; **2.** ⓢ *m* (6) drop; (*Schweiß*ⓢ) *a.* bead; ⚕ *pl.* drops; *guter ⁓* splendid wine; *fig. ein ⁓ auf den heißen Stein* a drop in the ocean; *s. stet*; **⁓förmig** ⊕ ['⁓fœrmiç] drop-shaped; '**⁓weise** by drops.

'**tropf|'naß** dripping wet; '**ⓢstein** *m* stalactite, *stehender*: stalagmite.

Trophäe [tro'fɛ:ə] *f* (15) trophy.

tropisch ['tro:piʃ] tropical.

Troß ⚔ [trɔs] *m* (4) train (*a. fig.*), supply lines *pl.*, baggage.

Trosse ['trɔsə *f* (15) cable, ⚓ hawser.

Trost [tro:st] *m* (3²) comfort, consolation; *ein schlechter ⁓* cold comfort; *nicht (recht) bei ⁓e sein* be out of one's mind.

tröst|en ['trø:stən] (26) console, comfort; *sich ⁓* take comfort, console o.s.; '**ⓢer** *m* (7), '**ⓢerin** *f* comforter, consoler; '**⁓lich** *s. trostreich.*

'**trost|los** disconsolate, desolate; *fig.* cheerless; (*öde*) dreary, desolate; (*jämmerlich*) wretched; *v. Dingen*: *a.* hopeless; '**ⓢlosigkeit** *f* desolation; *fig.* dreariness; wretchedness; '**ⓢpreis** *m* consolation prize, F booby-prize; '**⁓reich** comforting.

Tröstung ['trø:stuŋ] *f* consolation.

Trott [trɔt] *m* (3) trot; *fig.* jog-trot, routine; '**⁓el** *m* (7) idiot, F nincompoop, sap; '**ⓢen** (26, h. *u.* sn) trot.

Trottoir [trɔto'ɑ:r] *n* (3¹) pavement, *Am.* sidewalk.

trotz [trɔts] **1.** in spite of, despite; *⁓ alledem* for all that; **2.** ⓢ *m* (3²) defiance; (*Störrigkeit*) obstinacy; *j-m ⁓ bieten* defy; *aus ⁓* out of spite; *mir zum ⁓* to spite me; **⁓dem** [⁓'de:m] *adv.* nevertheless, for all that, notwithstanding, still; *cj.* (al-) though; '**⁓en** (27) defy (*j-m* a p.); *Gefahren*: brave; (*schmollen*) sulk; (*eigensinnig sein*) be obstinate; '**⁓ig**, *a.* **⁓köpfig** ['⁓kœpfiç] defiant; (*widerspenstig*) refractory; (*schmollend*) sulky; (*eigensinnig*) obstinate; '**ⓢkopf** *m* sulky child; *weitS.* pig-headed person; '**ⓢre-aktion** *f* act of defiance.

trüb [try:p], **⁓e** ['⁓bə] *Flüssigkeit*: muddy, turbid, cloudy; (*glanzlos*; *unklar*) dim, dull; *Wetter*: cloudy, *a. fig.*: gloomy, bleak, dreary; *Erfahrung*: sad; *⁓ gestimmt sein* F have the blues; *im ⁓en fischen fig.* fish in troubled waters.

Trubel ['tru:bəl] *m* (7) bustle.

trüben ['try:bən] (25) *s. trüb*: make muddy *etc.*; (*glanzlos, unklar machen*; *a. sich*) dim; *Spiegel usw.*: tarnish; (*dunkel machen*; *a. sich*) darken; *Freude usw.*: spoil; *Sicht, Sinn*: blur; *Beziehungen*: upset, *sich*: become strained; *der Himmel* *trübt sich* the sky is getting overcast.

Trüb|heit ['try:p-] *f s. trüb*: muddiness, turbidness; dimness; *fig.* gloom, dreariness; '**~sal** *f* (14) affliction; (*Elend*) misery; (*Not*) distress; ~ *blasen* F be in the dumps, mope; '**2selig** sad, gloomy, melancholy; (*öde*) bleak, dreary; '**~seligkeit** *f* sadness, gloominess; '**~sinn** *m* melancholy, sadness, gloom, F *the* blues *pl.*; '**2sinnig** melancholy, sad; **~ung** ['~buŋ] *f s. trüben*: making muddy; dimming *etc.*; *Zustand*: *s. Trübheit.*

trudeln ['tru:dəln] (29) *v/i.* (sn) ✈ (go into a) spin.

Trüffel ⚘ ['tryfəl] *f* (15) truffle.

Trug[1] [tru:k] *m* (3, *o. pl.*) deceit, fraud; *der Sinne*: delusion.

trug[2] [~] *pret. v. tragen.*

'**Trugbild** *n* phantom, illusion.

trüg|en ['try:gən] *v/t. u. v/i.* (30) deceive; '**~erisch** deceptive, delusive; (*unzuverlässig*) treacherous.

Trugschluß ['tru:k-] *m* fallacy.

Truhe ['tru:ə] *f* (15) chest.

Trümmer ['trymər] *n/pl.* (7) ruins *pl.*; (*Schutt*) rubble *sg.*, *grober*: debris *sg.*; (*Schiffs2*) wreckage *sg.*; *in ~ legen* lay in ruins; '**~feld** *n* shambles; '**~haufen** *m* heap of ruins *od.* rubble.

Trumpf [trumpf] *m* (3^3) (*a. fig.*) trump(-card); ~ *sein a. fig.* be trumps (*bei* in); *alle Trümpfe in der Hand haben* hold all the trumps (*a. fig.*); '**2en** *v/i. u. v/t.* (25) trump.

Trunk [truŋk] *m* (3^3) drink; (*Schluck*) draught; (*das Trinken*) drinking; *im ~* when drunk *od.* intoxicated.

'**trunken** drunken; *pred.* drunk (*a. fig.*, *von* with); intoxicated; **2bold** ['~bɔlt] *m* (3) drunkard, sot; '**2heit** *f* drunkenness; ~ *am Steuer* drunken driving.

'**Trunksucht** *f* dipsomania, alcoholism.

'**trunksüchtig** addicted to alcohol; **2e** ['~gə] *m* (18) dipsomaniac.

Trupp [trup] *m* (11) troop, band, gang; ⚔ detachment, detail, party.

'**Truppe** *f* (15) ⚔ troop, body; (*Einheit*) unit; *thea.* company, troupe; ⚔ *~n pl.* forces, troops.

'**Truppen|-abzug** ⚔ *m* withdrawal of troops, pull-out; '**~formation** *f* unit, formation; '**~gattung** *f* branch (of service), arm; '**~schau** *f* military review; '**~teil** *m* unit; '**~transporter** *m* (7) ⚓ transport, troopship; ✈ troop-carrier; '**~-übung** *f* (field) exercise; '**~-übungs-platz** *m* training area.

'**Trupp|führer** *m* squad leader; '**2weise** in troops.

Trust [trast] ✝ *m* (3) trust.

Trut|hahn ['tru:thɑ:n] *m* turkey (-cock); '**~henne** *f* turkey-hen.

Trutz *poet.* [truts] *m* (3^2) = *Trotz.*

Tschech|e ['tʃɛçə] *m* (13), '**~in** *f* (16^1), '**2isch** Czech.

tschüs! [tʃYs] F bye-bye, so long.

Tube ['tu:bə] *f* (15) tube; F *auf die ~ drücken* F step on it.

Tuberk|el [tu'bɛrkəl] *f* (15) tubercle; **2ulös** [~ku'lø:s] tubercular, tuberculous; **~ulose** [~'lo:zə] *f* (15) tuberculosis.

Tuch [tu:x] *n*: **a**) (3) (*Stoff*) cloth; **b**) (1^2) (*Kopf2*) kerchief; (*Umhänge2*) shawl; (*Hals2*) scarf, neckerchief; (*Wisch2*) rag; *s. rot*; '**~fabrik** *f* cloth factory; '**~fühlung** *f* close touch; ~ *haben mit fig.* be in close touch with; '**~handel** *m* cloth-trade, drapery; '**~händler** *m* draper; '**~handlung** *f* draper's shop; '**~macher** *m* clothmaker, clothier.

tüchtig ['tyçtiç] able, fit; (*fähig*) (cap)able, competent, clever; (*leistungsfähig*) efficient; (*erfahren*) experienced; (*vortrefflich*) excellent; (*beträchtlich*) good; (*gründlich*) thorough; ~ *arbeiten* work hard; ~ *essen* eat heartily; '**2keit** *f* ability, fitness; cleverness; excellency; efficiency; prowess.

'**Tuchware(n** *pl.*) *f* drapery *sg.*

Tück|e ['tykə] *f* (15) malice; (*Streich*) trick; '**2isch** malicious, insidious; (*böse, gefährlich*) vicious; (*verräterisch*; *a. Eis usw.*) treacherous.

Tuff [tuf] *m* (3^1), '**~stein** *m* tuff.

tüft|eln F ['tyftəln] (29) subtilize; ~ *an* (*dat.*) puzzle over; '**2ler(in** *f*) *m* tinkerer.

Tugend ['tu:gənt] *f* (16) virtue; '**~bold** *m*, '**~held** *m* paragon of virtue; '**2haft**, '**2reich**, '**2sam** virtuous; '**~richter(in** *f*) *m* moralist, censor.

Tüll [tyl] *m* (3^1) (*Stoff*) tulle; '**~e** *f* (15) socket; (*Gießröhre*) spout.

Tulpe ⚘ ['tulpə] *f* (15) tulip.

tummel|n ['tuməln] (29) put in

motion; *Pferd*: work; *sich* ~ disport o.s., bustle about, (*sich beeilen*) hurry, (*sich rühren, arbeiten*) bestir o.s.; *Kind*: romp; '**2platz** *m* playground (*a. fig.*).

Tumor ['tu:mɔr] ⚕ *m* (8[1]) tumo(u)r.

Tümpel ['tympəl] *m* (7) pool.

Tumult [tu'mult] *m* (3) tumult; (*Aufruhr*) riot; **~uant** [~tu'ant] *m* (12) rioter; **2uarisch** [~tu'ɑ:riʃ] tumultuous, riotous.

tun [tu:n] **1.** (30) do; (*ausführen*) perform, make; *Äußerung, Bitte*: make; *Schluck, Schritt, Sprung, Eid*: take; (*wohin* ~) put (*to school, into the bag, etc.*); *so* ~ *als ob* make as if, pretend to *inf.*; *es tut nichts* it doesn't matter; *was tut's?* what does it matter?; *es tut nichts zur Sache* it is irrelevant; *es tut sich etwas* something is going on; *das tut man nicht!* that is not done!; *du tätest besser zu gehen* you had better go; *dazu* ~ (*beitragen*) contribute (*zu* to), (*bewirken*) do in the matter; *ich kann nichts dazu* ~ I cannot help it; *es ist mir darum zu* ~ I am anxious about (it), it is of (great) consequence to me; *ihm ist nur um das Geld zu* ~ he is only interested in the money; *das tut gut!* that does one good!; *das tut nicht gut* no good can come of it; *j-m nicht gut* ~ (*Arznei usw.*) disagree with a p.; *was man zu* ~ *und zu lassen hat* do's and don'ts; *nichts zu* ~ *haben mit* have nothing to do with; *zu* ~ *haben* (*beschäftigt sein*) be busy; *mit den Augen usw. zu* ~ *haben* have trouble with one's eyes *etc.*; *es mit j-m zu* ~ *bekommen* have to deal with a p.; *was ist zu* ~*?* what is to be done?; *s. daran, Haus, leid, vornehm, weh usw.*; **2.** 2 *n* (6) doing(s *pl.*), action; (*Verhalten*) conduct; ~ *und Treiben* doings *pl.*, activities *pl.*

Tünche ['tynçə] *f* (15) whitewash; '**2n** (25) whitewash.

Tunichtgut ['tu:niçtgu:t] *m* (3 *u. inv.*) ne'er-do-well.

Tunke ['tuŋkə] *f* (15) sauce; '**2n** (25) dip, steep.

tunlich ['tu:nliç] feasible, practicable; '**~st** if possible.

Tunnel ['tunəl] *m* (11) tunnel; (*Unterführung*) subway.

Tüpfel ['typfəl] *m, n* (7) dot, spot; '**2n** (29) dot, spot.

tupfen ['tupfən] **1.** (25) touch lightly, dab; *s. tüpfeln*; **2.** 2 *m* (6) dot, spot.

Tupfer ['tupfər] *m* (7) ⚕ tampon, pad, swab; (*Tüpfel*) dot, spot.

Tür [ty:r] *f* (16) door; *in der* ~ in the doorway; *fig. e-r S.* ~ *und Tor öffnen* open a door to; *fig. mit der* ~ *ins Haus fallen* blunder it out; *fig. vor der* ~ *stehen* (*bevorstehen*) be near at hand; *fig. zwischen* ~ *und Angel* while about to leave; '**~-angel** *f* (door-)hinge.

Turban ['turbɑ:n] *m* (3[1]) turban.

Turbine [tur'bi:nə] *f* (15) turbine; **~n-antrieb** *m* turbine drive; **~n-dampfer** *m* turbine steamer; **~n-motor** *m* turbine engine; **~n-strahltriebwerk** *n* turbojet engine.

Turbolader ['turbo-] *mot. m* (7) turbo-charger.

'**Tür|flügel** *m* leaf of a door; '**~füllung** *f* door-panel; '**~griff** *m* door-handle.

Türk|e ['tyrkə] *m* (13) Turk; '**~in** *f* Turk(ish woman); **~is** [~'ki:s] *m* (4) turquoise; '**2isch** Turkish; ~*er Honig* Turkish delight; ~*er Teppich* Turkey (*od.* Turkish) carpet; ⚘ ~*er Weizen* Indian corn.

'**Tür|klinke** *f* door-handle; '**~klopfer** *m* knocker.

Turm [turm] *m* (3[3]) tower; (*Kirch2*) steeple; *Schach*: castle, rook; ⚔ (*Geschütz2*) turret.

Türm|chen ['tyrmçən] *n* (6) turret; '**2en** (25) *v/t.* heap up; *sich* ~ tower (up), *weitS. a.* pile up; *v/i.* F (*sich davonmachen*) F bolt, skedaddle; '**~er** *m* (7) warder (on the tower).

'**Turm|falke** *m* kestrel; '**2hoch:** *j-m* ~ *überlegen sein* be head and shoulders above a p.; '**~spitze** *f* spire; '**~springen** *n* high diving; '**~-uhr** *f* church-clock.

turn|en ['turnən] **1.** (25) practise (*od.* do) gymnastics; **2.** 2 *n* (6) gymnastics *pl.*; '**2er** *m* (7), '**2erin** *f* gymnast; '**~erisch** gymnastic.

'**Turn|gerät**(**e** *pl.*) *n* gymnastic apparatus; '**~halle** *f* gym(nasium); '**~hose**(**n** *pl.*) *f* gym shorts *pl.*

Turnier [tur'ni:r] *n* (3[1]) tournament; *nur hist.* joust(ing); **2en** joust, tilt; **~platz** *m* tiltyard.

'**Turn|lehrer**(**in** *f*) *m* gym instructor; '**~riege** *f* gym squad; '**~schuh** *m* plimsoll, gym shoe; **'~stunde** *f Schule*: gym lesson; **'~-unterricht** *m* instruction in gymnastics.

Turnus ['turnus] *m* (14, *o. pl.*) rotation; *im* ~ in rotation, by turns; **'2mäßig** regular(ly recurring); in rotation.

'Turnver·ein *m* gymnastic club.

'Tür|-öffner *m* (7) *elektrischer*: buzzer; **'~pfosten** *m* door-post; **'~rahmen** *m* door-frame; **'~schild** *n* door-plate; **'~schließer** *m* (*Person*) door-keeper; (*Vorrichtung*) door catch.

Turteltaube ['turtəl-] *f* turtle-dove.

Tusch ♪ [tuʃ] *m* (3³) flourish; **'~e** *f* (15) India(n) ink; *s. Tuschfarbe*; **'2eln** *v/i. u. v/t.* (29) whisper; **'2en** (29) wash; (*aquarellieren*) paint in water-colo(u)rs; *mit schwarzer Tusche*: draw in India(n) ink; **'~farbe** *f* water-colo(u)r; **'~kasten** *m* paint-box; **'~zeichnung** *f* India(n)-ink drawing.

Tüte ['ty:tə] *f* (15) (paper-)bag; F *kommt nicht in die* ~! nothing doing!

tuten ['tu:tən] (26) toot(le); *mot.* honk.

Tüttel ['tytəl] *m* (7), **'~chen** *n* (6) [dot; *fig.* jot.]

Twen [tvɛn] F *m* (11) person in his (*od.* her) twenties; *pl.* under-thirties.

Typ [ty:p] *m* (12), **'~e** *f* (15) type; ⊕ *a.* model; **'~endruck** *m* type printing; **'~enhebel** *m der Schreibmaschine*: typebar; **'~enkopf** *m* type; **'~ennummer** *f* model number; **'~enrad** *n* daisy wheel; **'~enschild** *n* name-plate; **'~ensetzmaschine** *f* typesetting machine.

Typhus ⚕ ['ty:fus] *m inv.* typhoid (fever); **'~kranke** *m, f* typhoid patient.

'typisch typical (*für* of); *das* **'2e** the typical character.

typisieren [typi'zi:rən] typify.

Typograph [ty:po'gra:f] *m* (12) typographer; **2isch** typographic(al).

Typus ['ty:pus] *m* (16²) type.

Tyrann [ty'ran] *m* (12) tyrant; **~ei** [~'naɪ] *f* (16) tyranny; **~in** *f* (female) tyrant; **2isch** tyrannical; **2i'sieren** tyrannize (over) *a p.*, bully *a p.*

U

U [u:], **u** *n inv.* U, u.

U-Bahn ['u:-] *f s. Untergrundbahn.*

übel ['y:bəl] **1.** evil, bad; *adv.* ill; badly; *s. a. schlecht*; (*krank*) sick, *nur pred.* ill; (*stinkend*) foul; (*scheußlich*) vile, nasty; (*katastrophal*) disastrous; *nicht* ~ not bad; *mir ist* ~ I feel sick; *mir wird* ~ I am feeling sick; *dabei kann e-m* ~ *werden* it is enough to make one sick; *sich in e-r üblen Lage befinden* be in a fix; *s. daran, mitspielen, wohl*; **2.** 2 *n* (6) evil; (*Unglück*) mischief, harm; (*Krankheit*) complaint, malady; *s. Übelstand*; *das kleinere* ~ the lesser evil; *vom* ~ no good; **'2befinden** *n* indisposition; **~gelaunt** ['~gəlaunt], **'~launig** ill-humo(u)red, cross; **~gesinnt** ['~gəzint] ill-disposed (*dat.* towards); **'2keit** *f* sickness, nausea; **'~nehmen** take *a th.* ill *od.* amiss, take offen|ce (*Am.* -se) at, resent *a th.*; *es j-m* ~ take it ill of a p.; **'~nehmend**, **'~nehmerisch** easily offended, touchy, huffy; **'~riechend** evil-smelling, malodorous, F smelly; *Atem*: foul, bad; **'2stand** *m* grievance, abuse, nuisance; (*Nachteil*) drawback; **'2tat** *f* misdeed; **'2täter(in** *f*) *m* evil-doer, wrong-doer, malefactor; **'2wollen¹** *n* (6) ill-will, malevolence; **'~wollen²** wish ill (*dat.* to), bear *a p.* a grudge; **'~wollend** malevolent.

üben ['y:bən] *v/t. u. v/i.* (25) (*a. sich* ~ *in dat.*) exercise, (*a.* ♪) practise; *bsd. Sport*: train; *Geduld* ~ have patience; *s. Nachsicht, Rache*; *geübt* (*P.*) practised, experienced.

über ['y:bər] **1.** *prp.* (*wo? dat.*; *wohin? acc.*) over, above; *reisen, gehen usw.* ~: across *a river, the sea*; by way of, via *a town*; *sprechen usw.* ~: about, of; *Vortrag, Buch usw.* ~: on; *nachdenken* ~: *think* about, over; *reflect* (up)on; *schreiben* ~: (up)on; (*nicht*) ~ (not) exceeding; *Fehler* ~

Fehler fault upon fault; *s. heute*; *~s Jahr* next year; ~ ... *(hinaus)* beyond, past; ~ *meine Kräfte* beyond my strength; *s. Maß*; ~ *Nacht* over night; ~ *dem Lesen* while reading; *zehn Minuten* ~ *zwölf* ten minutes past twelve; ~ *hundert* more than a hundred; ~ *kurz oder lang* sooner or later; **2.** *adv.*: ~ *und* ~ over and over, all over; *j-m in et.* (*dat.*) ~ *sein* surpass a p. in a th.; *ich habe es* ~ I am tired (*od.* sick) of it; F *s. übrig, vorüber.*

über'·all everywhere, *Am.* all over; (*in jeder Beziehung*) throughout; **~'hin** everywhere.

überaltert [~'ʔaltərt] superannuated.

'Über|·angebot *n* excessive supply; **'2·ängstlich** over-anxious.

über'·anstreng|en over-exert, overstrain; **2ung** *f* over-exertion, overstrain; ~ *der Augen* eyestrain.

über'·antworten deliver up, give over (*dat.* to).

über'·arbeit|en do over again, retouch; *Buch usw.*: revise; *sich* ~ overwork o.s.; **~et** overworked, overwrought; **2ung** *f* revision; (*zuviel Arbeit*) overwork.

'über'·aus exceedingly, extremely.

'Über|bau *m* superstructure; **'2beanspruchen** ⊕ overload, overstress; *fig.* overtax; **'~bein** ⚕ *n* node, 📖 exostosis; **'2belasten**, **'~belastung** *f* overload; **'2belichten** *phot.* over-expose; **'~belichtung** *f* over-exposure; **'~beschäftigung** *f* overemployment; **'2besetzt** *Betrieb*: overstaffed; **'2betonen** overemphasize; **'2bewerten** overrate.

über'bieten *bsd. Auktion*: outbid; [*fig.* surpass.]

Überbleibsel ['~blaɪpsəl] *n* (7) remainder, remnant, *Am.* holdover; *pl.* remains (*a. fig.*); *e-r Mahlzeit*: leavings, left-overs; *geschichtliches*: survival.

über'blend|en *Film, Radio*: fade over; **2ung** *f* fading.

'Überblick *m* survey (*a. fig. über acc.* of).

über|'blicken survey; **~'bringen** deliver, convey; **2'bringer(in** *f*) *m* bearer; **2'bringung** *f* delivery; **~'brücken** (25) bridge (*a. fig.*), span; **2'brückungsbeihilfe** *f* stopgap relief; **2'brückungsgeld** *n* tide-over allowance; **~'buchen** *Flug, Hotel etc.*: overbook; **~'bürden** (26) overburden; **2'bürdung** *f* overburdening; overpressure; **~dachen** [~'daxən] (25) roof (over); **~'dauern** outlast; **~'decken** cover; **'~denken** think *a th.* over, reflect (up)on *a th.*; **~'dies** besides, moreover.

über|dimensional ['~dimɛnzjonɑːl] outsize, huge; **'2dosis** *f* overdose.

über'drehen *Uhr*: overwind; *Gewinde*: strip.

'Überdruck *m* (*Umdruck*) transfer; 📯 surcharge, overprint; ⊕ overpressure; **2en** [~'drukən] overprint; **'~kabine** *f* pressurized cabin.

Überdruß ['~drus] *m* (4) disgust, (*bis zum* ~ to) satiety.

überdrüssig ['~drysiç] (*gen.*) disgusted with, tired (*od.* sick *od.* weary) of.

'überdurchschnittlich above the average, *attr.* above-average.

'Über·eifer *m* over-zeal; **'2·eifrig** over-zealous.

über'·eign|en transfer, assign (*dat.* to); **2ung** *f* transfer.

über'·eil|en precipitate (*die Sache* matters); *sich* ~ hurry too much; *übereilt* rash, precipitate, overhasty; **2ung** *f* precipitance; *nur keine* ~! take your time!

über·ei'nander one upon another; **~schlagen** *Arme*: fold; *Beine*: cross.

über'·ein|kommen[1] (sn) agree; come to terms; **2kommen**[2] *n* (6), **2kunft** [~kunft] *f* (14[1]) agreement; **~stimmen** *P.*: agree; *S.*: correspond, square, be in keeping (*alle*: *mit* with); **~stimmend** corresponding; (*einstimmig*) unanimous; *adv.* in accordance; **2stimmung** *f* agreement; correspondence, conformity; *in* ~ *bringen* reconcile; *in* ~ *mit* in accordance (*od.* conformity) with.

'über·empfindlich oversensitive.

über'·essen: *sich* ~ overeat o.s.

'überfahren 1. *v/i.* (sn) pass over; **2.** *über'fahren v/t. Person, Hund usw.*: run over; *Signal*: overrun; F *fig. sl.* bulldoze *a p.*; *Sport*: trounce *a team*; *Fluß usw.*: traverse, cross.

'Überfahrt *f* passage; crossing (*über e-n Fluß usw.* a river, *etc.*).

'Überfall *m* sudden attack, surprise (attack), assault; (*Raub2*) hold-up; (*Einfall*) inroad, raid.

über'fallen attack suddenly, surprise, assault; (*einfallen in*) invade, raid; *räuberisch*: hold up; *Nacht, Krankheit usw.*: overtake.
'überfällig overdue.
'Überfallkommando *n der Polizei*: flying (*Am.* riot) squad.
überfeiner|n [~'faɪnərn] (29) over-refine; 2**erung** *f* over-refinement.
über'fliegen fly over; *mit den Augen*: glance over, skim; *den Ozean* ~ fly the ocean.
'überfließen (sn) flow over.
über'flügeln (29) ⚔ outflank; *fig.* surpass, outstrip.
'Überfluß *m* abundance, plenty; (*unnötiger*) superfluity; (*Reichtum, Fülle*) wealth (*alle*: *an dat.* of); ~ *haben an* (*dat.*), *im* ~ *haben* abound in, have plenty of; *zum* ~ unnecessarily; '**~gesellschaft** *f* affluent society.
'überflüssig (*unnötig*) superfluous, unnecessary; (*überschüssig*) surplus, excess.
über'fluten overflow; inundate, flood (*a. fig. u. v. Licht*).
über'fordern *im Preis*: overcharge; *Leistungsfähigkeit usw.*: overtax.
'Über|fracht *f* overweight, excess freight; *Gepäck*: excess luggage; 2**'frachten** overload; *fig. überfrachtet* top-heavy.
Überfremdung [~'frɛmdʊŋ] *f* foreign infiltration *od.* control.
'überführ|en 1. carry *a p.* over, transport; **2.** *über'führen* (*befördern*) transport; ⚖ (*als schuldig erweisen*) convict (*gen.* of); 2**ung** [~'fy:rʊŋ] *f* **1.** transportation; *Straßenbau*, 🚂 road-bridge, fly-over, *Am.* overpass; **2.** ⚖ conviction; 2**ungskosten** [~'fy:rʊŋs-] *pl.* transport costs.
'Überfülle *f* superabundance.
über'füll|en overfill, cram; *mit Menschen*: overcrowd; *Magen*: glut; *den Markt*: overstock, glut; 2**ung** *f* overfilling *etc.*; repletion; *Verkehr*: congestion.
'Überfunktion ⚕ *f* hyperfunction.
über'füttern overfeed.
'Übergabe *f* delivery; handing over; ⚔, *a.* ⚖ surrender.
'Übergang *m* passage; 🚂 crossing; *fig.* transition, change; *zum Feind*: going over (to); ⚖ *v. Rechten*: devolution; '**~sbestimmungen** *f/pl.* transitional regulations; '**~slösung** *f* temporary solution; '**~sregierung** *f* transitional government; '**~sstadium** *n* transition stage; '**~szeit** *f* transition(al) period.
über'geben deliver (up), give up; hand over; ⚔ surrender (*a. sich* ~); *sich* ~ (*erbrechen*) vomit; *dem Verkehr* ~ open for traffic.
'übergehen 1. *v/i.* (sn) pass over (*zu* to); *auf Nachfolger, Stellvertreter* ~ (*Amt usw.*) devolve upon; ~ *in* (*acc.*) pass (*od.* change) into; *s. Fäulnis*; *zu et.* ~ proceed to, switch (over) to; *zu e-m anderen Punkt*: pass on to; *s. Angriff*; *in andre Hände* ~ change hands; **2.** *über'gehen v/t.* (*übersehen*) pass over; ignore; (*auslassen*) omit, skip.
Über'gehung *f* passing over; omission.
'übergenug too much, more than enough.
'überge-ordnet higher, superior.
'Übergewicht *n* overweight; *fig.* preponderance; ~ *haben* be overweight; *das* ~ *bekommen* lose one's balance, *fig.* get the upper hand.
über'gießen pour over; *Braten*: baste; *mit Zuckerguß*: ice.
'überglücklich extremely happy.
'übergreifen overlap; *fig.* ~ *auf od. in* (*acc.*) encroach on; *Feuer, Panik usw.*: spread to.
'Übergriff *m* encroachment.
'übergroß outsize(d); (*riesenhaft*) colossal, immense, huge.
'Übergröße *f* outsize (*a.* ✝), oversize.
über'handnehmen *v/i.*, 2 *n* increase, spread.
'Überhang *m* overhang; (*Geld*2) surplus; (*Auftrags*2 *usw.*) backlog.
'überhängen *v/i.* (30) hang over, overhang; *v/t.* (25) hang over.
über'hastet overhasty, hurried.
über'häufen overwhelm (*od.* swamp) (*mit* with).
über'haupt generally, on the whole; (*eigentlich, tatsächlich*) actually; ~ *nicht* not at all; ~ *kein* ... no ... whatever; *wenn* ~ if at all.
über|'heben exempt (*e-r S.* from); *e-r Mühe usw.* ~ spare *a p.* a trouble *etc.*; *sich* ~ overstrain o.s. (by lifting); *fig.* be overbearing; **~heblich** [~'he:plɪç] overbearing, arrogant; 2**'heblichkeit** *f* arrogance.
überhitzen [~'hitsən] (27) overheat

(*a. fig.*); ⊕ *bsd. Dampf*: superheat.
überhöht [~ˈhøːt] *Kurve*: banked; *Preise*: excessive.
überˈhol|en 1. pass (*a. mot.*), overtake; (*übertreffen*) outdistance, (*a. fig.*) outstrip; ⊕ (*nachsehen u. ausbessern*) overhaul, *bsd. Am.* service; *überholt* (*veraltet*) antiquated, outdated; superseded (*durch* by); **2.** ˈ*überholen* fetch *a p.* over; *v/i.* ⚓ *Schiff*: keel; **2manöver** *n* overtaking manœuvre, *Am.* passing maneuver; **2spur** *mot. f* passing lane.
überˈhören not to hear; *Worte*: miss; *absichtlich*: ignore.
ˈ**über-irdisch** supernatural.
ˈ**Überkapazität** *f* overcapacity.
ˈ**überkippen** tilt (*od.* tip) over.
überˈkleben paste *a th.* over.
ˈ**Überkleidung** *f* (*Ggs. Unterkleidung*) outer wear.
ˈ**überklug** overwise; *~er Mensch* wiseacre.
ˈ**überkochen** (sn) boil over.
überˈkommen *v/t.* receive; *Furcht usw. überkam ihn* he was overcome by fear *etc.*; *v/i.* (sn) *diese Sitte ist uns ~* this custom has been handed down to us.
ˈ**überkonfessionell** interdenominational.
überˈkrusten (*a. sich*) encrust.
ˈ**Überkultur** *f* over-refinement.
überˈladen 1. *v/t.* overload (*a. den Magen*); ⚡, *Bild usw.*: overcharge; *mit Arbeit*: overburden, swamp *with work*; **2.** *adj. Bild, Stil usw.*: florid, too profuse.
überˈlager|n super(im)pose; ⊕ overlay; *Radio*: heterodyne; **2ung** *f* super(im)position; heterodyning.
Überˈland|flug *m* cross-country flight; **~leitung** ⚡ *f* long-distance line.
überˈlass|en: *j-m et. ~* let a p. have a th.; (*anheimstellen*) leave a th. to a p.; (*abtreten*) cede a th. to a p.; (*preisgeben*) abandon a th. to a p.; *sich e-m Gefühl usw. ~* give o.s. up to; *j-n sich selbst ~* leave a p. to himself; **2ung** *f* leaving; ⚖ cession.
ˈ**Überlast** *f* overweight; overload.
überˈlast|en overload, overcharge; *fig.* overburden, overtax; **2ung** *f* overload; *fig.* overstress, overwork.
ˈ**überlaufen 1.** *v/i.* (sn) run (*od.* flow) over; ⚔ desert (*a. fig.*), *weitS.* go over (*zu* to); **2.** *überˈlaufen v/t.* overrun; (*belästigen*) annoy, pester; *Beruf, Gegend ist ~* is overcrowded; *es überlief mich kalt* a cold shudder seized me.
ˈ**Überläufer** *m* deserter; *pol. a.* turncoat.
ˈ**überlaut** too noisy, overloud.
überˈleben survive; *das hat sich überlebt* that has had its day; *die Nacht usw. ~* live the night *etc.* out; **2de** *m, f* (18) survivor; **2s...** survival ...; ˈ**~sgroß** larger than life; **2swille** *m* will to survive.
überlebt [~ˈleːpt] *adj.* antiquated, outdated.
ˈ**überleg|en 1.** lay over; **2.** *überˈlegen* **a**) *v/t.* consider, reflect (up)on; *ich will es mir ~* I will think it over; *es sich wieder* (*od. anders*) *~* (*s-e Meinung ändern*) change one's mind; *wenn ich es mir recht überlege* on second thoughts; *s. zweimal*; **b**) *adj.* superior (*dat.* to; *an dat.* in); *allen anderen weit ~* head and shoulders above the rest; **2enheit** [~ˈleːgənhaɪt] *f* superiority; **~t** [~ˈleːkt] considered; *wohl ~* deliberate; (*klug*) prudent; **2ung** *f* [~ˈleːguŋ] *f* consideration, reflection; (*reifliche ~*) deliberation; *s. reiflich.*
ˈ**überleiten** *v/t.* lead over (*zu* to; *a. v/i.*).
überˈlesen read (*od.* run) *a th.* over, peruse; (*übersehen*) overlook.
überˈliefer|n deliver; *der Nachwelt*: hand down (to); **2ung** *f* delivery; *fig.* tradition.
überˈlisten (26) outwit, fool.
überˈmachen make over (*dat.* to).
ˈ**Übermacht** *f* superiority; *bsd.* ⚔ supremacy (*a. fig.*), superior force; *fig.* predominance.
ˈ**übermächtig** overwhelming, too powerful.
ˈ**übermalen 1.** paint over; **2.** *überˈmalen* paint out (*a.* over).
überˈmannen (25) overcome, overpower.
ˈ**Über|maß** *n* excess; *im ~* in excess; *bis zum ~* to excess; ˈ**2mäßig** excessive; *adv. Am.* F overly.
ˈ**Übermensch** *m* superman; ˈ**2lich** superhuman.
überˈmitt|eln transmit; convey; **2(e)lung** *f* transmission.
ˈ**übermodern** ultra-modern.
ˈ**übermorgen** the day after tomorrow.

über'müd|et overtired; **~ung** *f* overfatigue.

'Über|mut *m* wantonness; (*Ausgelassenheit*) high spirits *pl.*, frolicsomeness; (*Anmaßung*) insolence; **~mütig** ['~my:tiç] wanton; frolicsome, rollicking; insolent.

'übernächst *the* next but one; ~e *Woche* the week after next.

über'nachten (26) pass (*od.* spend) the night, stay over night.

übernächtig ['~nɛçtiç] fatigued (from lack of sleep), blear-eyed.

Über'nachtung *f* passing the night; *im Hotel*: overnight stay; ~ *und Frühstück* bed and breakfast; **~smöglichkeit** *f* overnight accommodation.

Übernahme ['~na:mə] *f s. übernehmen*: taking over; acceptance; undertaking; assumption; (*Inbesitznahme*) taking possession (*gen.* of).

'übernational supra-national.

'übernatürlich supernatural.

über'nehm|en 1. *allg.* take over (*a. v/i.*); *Arbeit, Verantwortung usw.*: undertake; *Amt, Befehl, Pflicht*: assume; *Last, Verantwortung*: take upon o.s.; *Befehl, Führung, Risiko*: take; *Verfahrensweise usw.*: adopt; *Anvertrautes*: take charge of; (*in Besitz nehmen*) take possession of; *Ware, Erbschaft*: accept; *s. Bürgschaft*; *sich* ~ undertake too much, *in e-r S.*: overdo *a th.*; *im Essen*: overeat; *fig.* overreach o.s.; **2.** *'übernehmen*: shoulder; *das Gewehr* ~ slope (*Am.* shoulder) arms.

'über-ordnen: *j-n* (*od.* et.) *j-m* (*od.* e-r S.) ~ place (*od.* set) a p. (*od.* a th.) over a p. (*od.* a th.).

'überparteilich all-party.

'Überproduktion *f* over-production.

über'prüf|en check; ⊕ *a.* test; *genau*: scrutinize; *j-n* (*politisch usw.*): screen; (*bedenken*) (re)consider; (*untersuchen*) investigate, review; *s. nachprüfen*; **~er**(**in** *f*) *m* revisor; **~ung** *f* check(ing); scrutiny, review; consideration; investigation; test(ing).

'überquellen flow over.

überqueren [~'kve:rən] (25) cross.

über'ragen rise above *a th.*, tower above (*a. fig.*); *fig.* excel, surpass; **~d** outstanding, excellent.

über'rasch|en (27) surprise; **~end** surprising; (*unerwartet*) unexpected; **~ung** *f* surprise; **~ungs-angriff** *m* surprise attack; **~ungsmoment** *n* surprise element.

'überre-agieren overreact (*auf acc.* to).

über'red|en persuade (*zu* [in]to); talk *a p.* into (doing) *a th.*; **~ung** *f* persuasion; **~ungskunst** *f* powers *pl.* of persuasion.

'überregional supraregional; *Zeitung*: national; *Sendung*: nationwide.

'überreich abounding (*an dat.* in); superabundant.

über'reichen hand *a th.* over, present, deliver (*alle*: *dat.* to); *schriftlich*: submit; *anliegend*: enclose.

'überreichlich superabundant.

Über'reichung *f* presentation.

'überreif overripe.

über'reizen over-excite.

über'rennen (*umrennen*) run over *od.* down, *bsd.* ⚔ overrun.

'Überrest *m* rest, remainder; (*a.* ~e *pl.*) remains *pl.*; *a. fig.* remnant; (*Rückstand*) residue; *sterbliche* ~ mortal remains.

'Überrollbügel *mot. m* roll-bar.

über'rollen overrun.

über'rumpel|n surprise; ⚔ take by surprise; **~ung** *f* surprise.

über'runden *Sport*: outlap; *fig.* outstrip.

über'sät *fig.* dotted, studded.

'übersatt surfeited (*von* with).

über'sättig|en surfeit; ⚗ oversaturate; **~ung** *f* surfeit; ⚗ oversaturation, supersaturation.

über|'säuert hyperacidic; **~'säuerung** *f* hyperacidity.

'Überschall... *phys.* supersonic; **'~knall** *m* sonic boom.

über'schatten overshadow (*a. fig.*).

über'schätz|en overrate, overestimate; **~ung** *f* overestimation.

über'schau|bar (*leicht verständlich*) easily comprehensible; (*in kleinem Rahmen*) of a manageable size; **~en** overlook, survey.

'überschäumen foam over; *fig.* brim over (*vor Freude usw.* with); **~d** *fig.* exuberant.

'überschießend *Ballast*: shifting; *Betrag*: surplus.

über'schlafen sleep on *a th.*

'Überschlag *m Turnen*: somersault; *Schneiderei*: facing; (*Schätzung*) (rough) estimate; ⚡ flashover.

'überschlagen 1. *v/t. Beine*: cross;

2. *über'schlagen* (*weglassen*) omit, skip, miss *a page*; (*schätzen*) estimate; *sich* ~ go head over, *mot.* overturn, ⚓ capsize, ✈ *beim Kunstflug*: loop, *beim Landen*: nose over; *Stimme*: crack, break; *Ereignisse*: follow hot on the heels of one another; **3.** *über'schlagen adj.* (*lauwarm*) lukewarm, tepid.

'**überschnappen** (sn) *Stimme*: squeak; F (*verrückt werden*) go crazy *od.* mad; *übergeschnappt* F cracked, *sl.* nuts.

über'schneid|en (*a. sich*) overlap (*a. fig.*); *Linien*: *sich* ~ intersect; **⁀ung** *f* overlapping; intersection.

über'schreiben superscribe, entitle; (*übertragen*) transfer, ☤ carry over; (*bezeichnen*) label.

über'schreiten cross, pass over *a th.*, go across *a th.*; *fig.* transgress; *Gesetz*: infringe; *Maß*, *Termin*: exceed; *Kredit*: overdraw.

'**Überschrift** *f* heading, title.

'**Überschuh** *m* overshoe; (*Gummi*⁀) galosh; ~e *pl. Am. a.* rubbers *pl.*

über'schuldet deeply involved in debt; *Grundstück usw.*: heavily encumbered.

'**Überschuß** *m* surplus.

überschüssig ['~ʃysiç] surplus, excess.

über'schütten cover; *fig.* overwhelm; *mit Geschenken*: shower with.

Überschwang ['~ʃvaŋ] *m* (3) exuberance.

über'schwemm|en flood, inundate; *fig.* flood (*od.* swamp) (*mit* with); ☤ *den Markt*: overstock, glut; **⁀ung** *f* flood, inundation; **⁀ungsgebiet** *n* flood area.

überschwenglich ['~ʃvɛŋliç] effusive, gushing; '**⁀keit** *f* effusiveness.

'**Übersee:** *in, nach usw.* ~ oversea(s); '**~...**, '**⁀isch** transoceanic (*steamer*); transmarine (*cable*); oversea (*route*, *trade*, ⚔ *forces*); '**~verkehr** *m* oversea (*od.* transoceanic) traffic.

über'sehbar *s. übersichtlich.*

über'sehen survey; (*nicht bemerken*) overlook, miss; *absichtlich*: disregard, ignore; (*erkennen*) *Lage usw.*: realize, perceive; *s. überblicken.*

über'send|en send, transmit; **⁀ung** *f* transmission; ☤ consignment.

über'setzbar translatable.

'**übersetzen 1.** *v/i.* (sn) pass over, cross; *v/t.* carry *a p.* over; **2.** *über'setzen* translate (*in acc.* into); ⊕ gear, transmit.

Über'setz|er *m* (7), **~erin** *f* (16[1]) translator; **~ung** *f* translation; ⊕ gear ratio, transmission; **~ungsbüro** *n* translating agency; **~ungsrecht** *n* right of translation.

'**Übersicht** *f* survey; *fig. a.* general view; (*Zusammenfassung*) summary, 🕮 synopsis; *die* ~ *verlieren* lose control; '**⁀lich** easy to survey, clear(ly arranged); *Gelände*: open; (*klar gefaßt*) lucid; '**~lichkeit** *f* clearness; lucidity; '**~skarte** *f* general (*Am.* overview) map; '**~s-tabelle** *f* tabular summary.

'**übersied|eln** (29, sn) (re)move; (*auswandern*) emigrate; '**⁀(e)lung** *f* removal; emigration.

'**übersinnlich** transcendental; *Kräfte*: psychic(al).

über'spann|en *mit et.* cover *a th.* over with; (*zu stark spannen*) overstrain; *fig.* exaggerate; *s. Bogen*; **~t** extravagant; eccentric; **⁀t-heit** *f* eccentricity, extravagance.

über'spielen *Sport*: *den Gegner*: outplay; *fig.* outmanœuvre, *Am.* outmaneuver; *Schallplatte usw.*: re-record.

über'spitz|en subtilize; (*übertreiben*) overdo; **~t** over-subtle.

'**überspringen 1.** *v/i.* (sn) leap over; *Funke*: flash over; **2.** *v/t. über'springen* jump (over *od.* across), clear; (*weglassen*) skip.

'**übersprudeln** (sn) bubble (*od.* gush) over (*fig. vor dat.* with).

'**überstaatlich** supernational.

'**überstehen 1.** *v/i.* jut out, project; **2.** *v/t. über'stehen* (*erdulden*) endure, stand; *Krankheit usw.*: get over; (*überleben*) survive.

'**übersteigen 1.** *v/i.* (sn) step over, climb over; **2.** *v/t. über'steigen* cross, pass; *fig.* overcome, surmount; (*hinausgehen über*) exceed, pass.

über'steigern force up; *fig.* overdo.

über'steuern *mot.* oversteer; *Verstärker etc.*: overmodulate.

über'stimmen outvote.

über'strahlen shine upon; (*verdunkeln*) outshine (*a. fig.*).

über'streichen paint *a th.* over.

'**überstreifen** slip *a th.* over.

'**überströmen 1.** *v/i.* (sn) overflow;

2. *v/t.* *über'strömen s. überschwemmen*; '**⁓d** *fig.* gushing.

'**Überstunde** *f*, '**⁓n** *pl.* overtime (hour); *⁓n machen* work overtime.

über'stürz|en hurry, precipitate; *sich ⁓* act rashly; *Ereignisse*: press one another; **⁓t** *adj.* precipitate; **2ung** *f* precipitancy.

Über'tagebau ⚒ *m* surface mining.

übertölpeln [⁓'tœlpəln] (29) dupe.

über'tönen drown (out) *a sound*.

Übertrag ✝ ['⁓tra:k] *m* (3^3) *auf die andere Seite*: carrying forward; (*Posten*) carry-over.

über'trag|bar transferable; ✝ (*begebbar*) negotiable; ⚕ communicable, catching, infectious, *durch Berührung*: contagious; **⁓en** [⁓gən] ✝ carry over, bring forward; (*umbuchen*) transfer; *Besitz*: transfer, make over (*auf j-n* to); (*zedieren*) assign (to); *Blut*: transfuse (*auf acc.* to); *Vollmacht*: delegate (*auf acc.* to); *Amt*: confer (*auf acc.* [up]on); *j-m (die Besorgung von) et. ⁓* charge (*od.* commission) a p. with; *sprachlich*: translate, render, do (*in acc.* into); *Kurzschrift*: transcribe, extend; ⊕, *phys.*, ⚕, *Radio*: transmit; *Radio*: *a.* broadcast, relay; *TV a.* televise; *sich ⁓ Krankheit, Stimmung usw.* communicate itself (*auf acc.* to), be infectious; *⁓e Bedeutung* figurative sense; **2ung** *f* transfer (*a.* ✝); assignment (*of rights, patents, etc.*); *v. Blut*: transfusion; ⊕, *phys.*, ⚕, *Radio*: transmission, (*Sendung*) broadcast, *TV* telecast; *e-s Amtes*: conferring; (*Übersetzung*) translation; *v. Kurzschrift*: transcription; **2ungsfehler** *m Radio, Computer*: transfer error; **2ungswagen** *m Radio*: outside broadcast van; *Fernsehen*: mobile transmission unit.

'**übertrainieren** overtrain.

über'treffen *P.*: excel, outdo; *P. u. S.*: surpass, exceed, beat.

über'treib|en *Tätigkeit*: overdo; carry *a th.* too far; *mit Worten*: exaggerate (*a. v/i.*), overstate; *thea.* overact; *s. übertrieben*; **2ung** *f* exaggeration.

'**übertreten 1.** *v/i.* (sn) pass (*od.* step) over; *fig.* go over (*zu* to); *Fluß*: overflow; *zu e-r andern Partei (Religion) ⁓* change sides (one's religion); *zum Katholizismus ⁓* turn Roman Catholic; **2.** *v/t.* *über'treten Sport*: overstep; *sich den Fuß ⁓* sprain one's ankle; *fig.* trespass against, infringe, violate.

Über'tret|er *m* (7), **⁓erin** *f* transgressor, trespasser, offender; **⁓ung** *f* transgression, trespass; ⚖ infraction, violation; *engS.* petty offen|ce, *Am.* -se.

übertrieben [⁓'tri:bən] exaggerated, excessive.

'**Übertritt** *m* going over (*zu* to); *eccl.* conversion.

über'trumpfen overtrump; *fig.* outdo.

über'tünchen whitewash (*a. fig.*); *fig.* varnish, gloss over.

übervölker|n [⁓'fœlkərn] (29) overpopulate; **2ung** *f* overpopulation.

'**übervoll** brimful; *Raum*: overcrowded.

über'vorteil|en (25) overreach; *beim Kauf*: overcharge, *Brt.* F do (down); (*betrügen*) cheat; **2ung** *f* overreaching *etc.*

über'wach|en watch (over); (*beaufsichtigen*) supervise, superintend, control; *polizeilich*: keep under surveillance, (*beschatten*) shadow; **2ung** *f* supervision, control; *polizeiliche*: surveillance; **2ungs-anlage** *f* monitoring system (*od.* device); **2ungsnetz** *n* monitoring network.

überwältigen [⁓'vɛltigən] (25) overcome, overpower, overwhelm (*alle a. fig.*); **⁓d** *fig.* overwhelming.

über'weis|en assign, transfer; *zur Entscheidung*: refer (*dat. od. an acc.* to); *Geld*: remit; **2ung** *f* assignment, *bsd. v. Besitz*: transfer; *zur Entscheidung*: reference (*an acc.* to); (*Geld2*) remittance.

'**überwerfen 1.** throw over; *Kleid usw.*: fling on; **2.** *über'werfen*: *sich mit j-m ⁓* fall out with a p.

über'wiegen 1. *v/t.* outweigh; *v/i.* preponderate, prevail; (*vorherrschen*) predominate; **2.** 2 *n* (6) preponderance; **⁓d** *adj.* preponderant, prevailing; *Mehrheit*: overwhelming; *⁓er Teil* majority; *adv.* predominantly, mainly.

über'wind|en overcome (*a. fig.*), subdue; (*besiegen*) conquer; *Hindernis*: surmount; *sich ⁓ zu* bring o.s. to (*do*); *ein überwundener Standpunkt* an antiquated view; **2er** *m*

(7) conqueror; **2ung** *f* conquest, overcoming; *s. Selbst2*; ~ *kosten* cost an effort.
überwintern [~ˈvintərn] (29) *v/i.* (pass the) winter; *bsd. Tiere*: hibernate; *v/t.* winter.
überˈwölben arch (over).
überˈwuchern overgrow, overrun.
ˈÜberwurf *m* wrap, shawl; **ˈ~mutter** ⊕ *f* screw cap.
ˈÜberzahl *f* superior number(s) *od.* (*nur* ⚔) forces *pl.*, numerical superiority, odds *pl.*
überˈzahlen overpay.
überˈzählen count *money* over.
ˈüberzählig supernumerary, odd; (*übrig*) surplus, left over.
überˈzeichn|en over-subscribe; **2ung** *f* over-subscription.
überˈzeug|en convince (*von* of); ⚖ satisfy (as to); *weitS. Leistung, Spieler usw.*: be convincing; *sich* ~ (*von*) make sure (of); **~end** convincing (*a. fig.*); **~t** convinced, positive; *Sozialist usw.*: ardent, strong; *Sie dürfen* ~ *sein, daß* you may rest assured that; **2ung** *f* conviction; (*fester Glaube*) persuasion; (*Gewißheit*) assurance; *der* (*festen*) ~ *sein, daß* be (thoroughly) convinced that; **2ungskraft** *f* persuasive power, *bsd. fig.* logic.
überˈziehen 1. cover; (*bestreichen*) coat; (*verkleiden*) line; *Bett*: put fresh linen on; ✝ *Konto*: overdraw; *ein Land mit Krieg* ~ invade a country with war; *sich* ~ *Himmel*: become overcast; **2.** *ˈüberziehen* put (*od.* draw *od.* slip) over; *Kleid usw.*: put on.
ˈÜberzieh|er *m* (7) overcoat; **ˈ~hose** *f* (*eine* a pair of) overalls *pl.*
Überˈziehung ✝ *f* overdraft; **~skredit** *m* overdraft credit; **~szinsen** *m/pl.* interest *sg.* on overdrafts.
überˈzuckern sugar (over).
ˈÜberzug *m* cover, coat(ing); (*Bett2*) case, tick; (*Kissen2*) slip.
üblich [ˈy:pliç] usual, customary.
ˈU-Boot ⚓ *n s. Unterseeboot*; **ˈ~-Jäger** *m* submarine chaser.
übrig [ˈy:briç] left (over), remaining; *die* ~*en pl.* the others, the rest; *im* ~*en*, ~*ens* (as) for the rest, (*beiläufig*) by the way, (*außerdem*) besides; ~ *behalten od. haben* have *a th.* left; *keine Zeit* ~ *haben* have no time to spare; *etwas* (*nichts*) ~ *haben für* (not to) care for; *ein* ~*es tun* make a special effort, go out of one's way (*to do*); *das* ~*e Geld* the rest of the money; **ˈ~bleiben** (sn) be left, remain; *fig. es blieb ihm nichts anderes* ~ (*als*) he had no choice (but); **ˈ~lassen** leave; *viel* (*wenig*) *zu wünschen* ~ leave much (little) to be desired.
Übung [ˈy:buŋ] *f* exercise (*a. Turnen u.* ⚔), practice (*a. praktische Anwendung*); (*Gewohnheit*) practice, use; (*Ausbildung*) training; *nicht mehr in* (*od. aus der*) ~ *sein* be out of practice; **ˈ~s-aufgabe** *f* exercise; **ˈ~sbuch** *n* book of exercises; **ˈ~shang** *m Wintersport*: nursery slope; **ˈ~s-heft** *n* exercise-book, *Am.* composition book; **ˈ~smunition** *f* practice ammunition; **ˈ~s-platz** ⚔ *m* training area *od.* ground.
Ufer [ˈu:fər] *n* (7) (*Meer2, See2*) shore; (*Strand*) beach; (*Fluß2*) bank; *am* (*od. ans*) ~ ashore; **ˈ~damm** *m e-s Flusses*: embankment; **ˈ2los** *fig.* boundless; extravagant; *ins* ~*e führen* lead nowhere; **ˈ~promenade** *f* promenade.
Ufo [ˈu:fo] *n* (11) ufo, unidentified flying object.
Uhr [u:r] *f* (16) (*Turm2 usw.*) clock; (*Taschen2, Armband2*) watch; (*Stunde, Zeit*) hour, time (of the day); *wieviel* ~ *ist es?* what time is it?, F what's the time?; *es ist halb drei* ~ it is half past two; *nach meiner* ~ *ist es vier* by my watch it is four o'clock (*Am. a.* four hours); *um vier* ~ at four o'clock; **ˈ~-armband** *n* watch bracelet; **ˈ~kette** *f* watch-chain; **ˈ~macher** *m* watch-maker, clock-maker; **ˈ~werk** *n* clockwork; works *pl.*; **ˈ~zeiger** *m* hand; **ˈ~zeigersinn** *m*: *im* ~ clockwise; *entgegen dem* ~ anticlockwise; **ˈ~zeit** *f* (clock) time.
Uhu [ˈu:hu:] *m* (3[1]) eagle-owl.
Ukas [ˈu:kas] *m* (3[2]) ukase.
Ulk [ulk] *m* (3) fun, F spree, lark; ~ *treiben* lark, *mit*: make fun of; **ˈ2en** (25) joke, lark; **ˈ2ig** funny.
Ulme [ˈulmə] *f* (15) elm.
Ulster [ˈulstər] *m* (7) ulster.
Ultimatum [ultiˈmɑ:tum] *n* (9) ultimatum; *ein* ~ *stellen* deliver an ultimatum (*dat.* to).
Ultimo [ˈultimo] *m* (11) last day of the month; **ˈ~...** monthly ...
ˈUltra|ˈkurzwelle [ˈultra-] *f Radio*:

ultra high frequency; *phys.* ⚡ ultra-short wave; ˈ~ˈ**kurzwellensender** *m* ultra-short wave transmitter; ˈ2**marˈrin** ultramarine; ˈ2**rot** ultra-red, infra-red; ˈ~**schall** *phys. m* ultra-sound; ˈ~**schall...** ultrasonic, supersonic; ~**schalldiagnostik** [ˈ~diaˈgnɔstik] *f* (16) ultrasonic diagnosis; ˈ~**schallwelle** *f* ultrasonic *od.* supersonic wave; ˈ2**violett** ultra-violet.

um [um] **1.** *prp.* (*acc.*) about; *s. ungefähr*; (~ ... *herum*) (a)round, round about; *Lohn, Preis usw.*: for; *Maß*: by; ~ *vier (Uhr)* at four (o'clock); ~ *die Zeit (herum)* about the time; *einer* ~ *den andern* one by one, (*abwechselnd*) alternately, by turns; ~ *so besser* so much the better; ~ *so mehr* all the more, (so much) the more (*als* as; *weil* because); ~ *so weniger* all the less; ~ *e-r S. od. j-s willen* for the sake (*od.* in behalf) of; ~ *Gottes willen!* for goodness' sake!; *s. Entschuldigung, Leben, Preis, Rat, Tag, Wette, Wort*; **2.** *cj.* ~ *zu* (in order) to; **3.** *adv.* about; ~ *und* ~ round about; ~ (*vorüber*) *sein* be over (*od.* up).

ˈ**um-adressieren** redirect.

ˈ**um-ändern** alter, change.

ˈ**um-arbeit|en** work (*od.* do) over; *Kleid*: make over; *Buch*: revise; *Schriftstück*: rewrite; *für den Film usw.*: readapt; *fig.* ~ *zu et.* make (*od.* turn) into; ˈ2**ung** *f* making over; revision; readaptation.

umarm|en [~ˈʔarmən] (25) embrace, hug; 2**ung** *f* embrace, hug.

ˈ**Umbau** *m* rebuilding; alteration(s *pl.*); reconstruction; conversion; reorganization; ˈ2**en 1.** rebuild; *teilweise*: alter; *Maschine usw.*: reconstruct; *zu e-m neuen Zweck, a. Wohnung*: convert (*in acc.* into); *Verwaltung usw.*: reorganize; **2.** *umˈbauen*: build round; *umbauter Raum* interior space.

ˈ**umbetten** put into a fresh bed.

ˈ**umbiegen** bend (over); *abwärts od. aufwärts*: turn down *od.* up.

ˈ**umbild|en** remodel, reconstruct, transform; reorganize, *bessernd*: reform; *Regierung*: reshuffle; ˈ2**ung** *f* transformation, remodel(l)ing; reorganization; reshuffle.

ˈ**umbinden** tie round; *Schürze usw.*: put on.

ˈ**umblättern** *v/t.* turn over (the leaf *v/i.*).

ˈ**umbrechen 1.** break down *od.* up; **2.** *umˈbrechen typ.* make up (into pages).

ˈ**umbringen** kill.

ˈ**Umbruch** *m typ.* make-up; *am Bildschirm*: page formatting; *fig., bsd. pol.* upheaval; *parl.* landslide.

ˈ**umbuchen** transfer (to another account); *Reise usw.*: book for another date.

ˈ**umdenken** *v/t.* rethink; *v/i.* change one's views.

ˈ**umdirigieren** redirect.

ˈ**umdisponieren** *v/t.* redispose, rearrange; *v/i.* make new arrangements.

ˈ**umdrehen** turn (round, *a. sich*); *j-s Worte, Arm*: twist; *j-m den Hals* ~ wring a p.'s neck; *s. Spieß*.

Umˈdrehung *f* turn(ing round); *phys.* rotation, revolution; ~*en pl. pro Minute* revolutions per minute (*abbr.* r.p.m.); ~**sgeschwindigkeit** *f* speed of rotation.

ˈ**Umdruck** *m* transfer; ˈ2**en** transfer.

ˈ**um-eiˈnander** round each other.

ˈ**Um-erziehung** *f* re-education; ˈ~**s-lager** *n* re-education centre.

ˈ**umfahren** *v/t.* **1.** run down; **2.** *umˈfahren* drive (*od.* sail) round *a th.*

ˈ**umfallen** (sn) fall (down *od.* over); *vor Schwäche*: collapse; *fig.* (*nachgeben*) cave in; *zum* 2 *müde sein* feel ready to drop.

ˈ**Umfang** *m* circumference, circuit; *des Leibes, e-s Baumstammes usw.*: girth; *Schneiderei*: width; (*Ausdehnung, a. fig.*) extent, size (*a. wissenschaftl. Arbeiten*); ♪ compass; (*Bereich*) range; (*Masse, Rauminhalt, Buch*2, *Tonfülle*) volume; *10 Zoll im* ~ 10 inches round; *fig. in vollem* ~*e* in its entirety.

umˈfangen embrace; *fig.* surround.

ˈ**umfangreich** extensive; (*dick*) voluminous; (*geräumig*) wide.

umˈfass|en embrace (*a. fig.*); (*in sich schließen*) comprise, cover; ⚔ envelop, outflank; ~**end** extensive, comprehensive; (*vollständig*) complete; 2**ung** *f* embrace; ⚔ envelopment, outflanking; (*Einfriedigung*) enclosure.

umˈfliegen fly round *a th.*

umflort [umˈfloːrt] *Augen*: dim.

umˈfluten flow round *a th.*

'umform|en transform, remodel; ⚡ transform, convert; **'2er** ⚡ *m* converter, transformer.

'Umfrage *f* (general) inquiry; *s. Meinungs*2; **'~-ergebnis** *n* survey results *pl.*

umfried(ig)|en [~'fri:d(ig)ən] enclose; **2ung** *f* enclosure.

'umfüllen pour into other containers, *etc.*; *Wein*: decant.

'umfunktionieren convert (*in acc.* into).

'Umgang *m* (*Drehung*) rotation; (*Weg*) circular passage; (*Prozession*) procession; (*Verkehr*) (social) intercourse, relations *pl.*; (*Bekanntenkreis*) company, friends *pl.*; (*Art, umzugehen mit*) way how to deal with *a p.*; *~ haben od. pflegen mit* associate with; *wenig ~ haben* not to see many people.

umgänglich ['~gɛŋliç] sociable.

'Umgangs|formen *f/pl.* (social) manners *pl.*; **'~sprache** *f* colloquial language; *englische ~* colloquial English.

umgarnen [um'garnən] (25) *fig.* ensnare.

um'geb|en surround; *~ von* surrounded with *od.* by; **2ung** *f* environs *pl.*, *a. e-r P.*: surroundings *pl.*; *e-r P.* (*a. Milieu*): environment; (*Nachbarschaft*) neighbo(u)rhood, *weitS. a.* vicinity; (*Gesellschaft*) company.

'Umgegend *f* environs *pl.*, vicinity, neighbo(u)rhood.

'umgehen 1. *v/i.* (sn) go round; (*die Runde machen*) circulate; *Geist*: walk, *~ an* (*od. in*) *e-m Ort* haunt a place; *mit j-m ~* keep company with, (*behandeln, a. e-e Sache*) deal with, handle, ⊕ operate, (*vorhaben*) intend, plan, (*beschäftigt sein*) be occupied with; *mit dem Gedanken* (*od. Plan*) *~ zu inf.* be thinking of *ger.*; *mit j-m hart ~* treat a p. harshly; *er weiß mit Frauen* (*Pferden usw.*) *umzugehen* he has a way with women (horses, *etc.*); **2.** *v/t.* *um'gehen* go round (about); (*vermeiden*) avoid, evade, *geschickt*: by--pass (*a. Verkehr*), F dodge; ⚔ outflank; **'~d** *allg.* immediate(ly *adv.*); ✝ *höflich*: at your earliest convenience; *mit ~er Post* by return of post.

Um'gehung *f* by-passing, *Am.* beltway; *fig. a.* evasion; *Verkehr*: *a.* detour(ing); ⚔ outflanking; **~sstraße** *f* bypass (road).

umgekehrt ['~gəke:rt] reverse, inverse; (*dasselbe ~*) vice versa, conversely; (*genauso, mit gleichem Recht usw.*) by the same token; (*entgegengesetzt*) opposite, contrary; (*genau*) *~!* (just) the other way (round)!, quite the contrary!; *das 2e* the reverse (*od.* opposite).

'umgestalten *s. umbilden.*

'umgießen (*umfüllen*) decant; *metall.* refound, recast.

'umgraben dig (*od.* turn) up.

um'grenzen bound; (*umschließen*) encircle; *fig.* circumscribe.

'umgruppier|en regroup; *pol., Sport*: reshuffle; **'2ung** *f* regrouping; reshuffling.

um'gürten gird; *'umgürten* gird on.

'umhaben have on.

'umhacken hoe up; *s. umhauen.*

um'halsen hug, embrace.

'Umhang *m* cape; wrap; (*Umschlagetuch*) shawl.

'umhängen *Mantel usw.*: put on, wrap about one; *Gewehr*: sling; *Bild*: rehang.

'Umhängetasche *f* shoulder-bag.

'umhauen fell, cut down; F *fig.* bowl over.

um'her about, (*Am.* a)round; *s. herum(...)*; **~schweifen, ~streichen, ~streifen, ~ziehen** rove, roam (about), wander (about).

um'hin: *ich kann nicht ~, zu sagen* I cannot help saying.

um'hüll|en wrap up (*mit* in), envelop, cover (*a.* ⊕); ⊕ sheathe; **2ung** *f* wrapping, wrap(per), cover (-ing).

Umkehr ['~ke:r] *f* (16) turning back, return (*zu* to; *a. fig.*); *fig.* (*Änderung*) change; (*Bekehrung*) conversion; **'2en** *v/i.* (sn) turn back, return; *v/t.* turn round *od.* about *od.* the other way round; (*das Unterste zu oberst kehren*) turn upside down; (*umstoßen*) overturn; *Tasche usw.*: turn (inside) out; ♪, ⚗, *gr.* invert; ⚡ reverse; *s. umgekehrt*; **'~ung** *f* reversal; inversion.

'umkippen *v/t.* tip over, upset; *v/i.* (sn) tilt over, be upset; *Fahrzeug*: *a.* overturn, ⚓ capsize; F *s. zusammenklappen v/i.*

um'klammer|n clasp, embrace; *Boxen*: clinch; ⚔ envelop; **2ung** *f* embrace; *Boxen*: clinch; ⚔ envelopment.

ˈ**umklappen** *v/t.* turn down; *e-n Sitz*: tip; *v/i.* F *s. zusammenklappen.*

ˈ**umkleide|n 1.** *j-n* (*sich*) ~ change a p.'s (one's) dress; **2.** *umˈkleiden* clothe, cover; ˈ**♀raum** *m* dressing-room.

ˈ**umknicken** *v/t.* bend (down); snap (off); *v/i.* (sn) *mit dem Fuß* ~ sprain one's foot.

ˈ**umkommen** (sn) perish, die; (*verderben*) spoil.

ˈ**Umkreis** *m* circuit, circumference; (*Nähe*) vicinity; *im* ~ *von* within a radius of, for *three miles* round.

umˈkreisen circle round *a th.*

ˈ**umkrempeln** (29) turn up, tuck up; *völlig*: turn *a th.* inside out; *fig.* turn *a th.* upside down, change radically.

ˈ**umladen** reload; *bsd.* ⚓ transship.

ˈ**Umlage** *f* distribution of cost; *s. Abgabe.*

umˈlagern surround, besiege.

ˈ**Umland** *n* hinterland.

ˈ**Umlauf** *m* circulation (*a. des Geldes*); *phys.* rotation, revolution; (*Zyklus*) cycle; *s.* ~*schreiben*; *in* (*od. im*) ~ in circulation, *ast.* in orbit; *in* ~ *bringen od. setzen od. sein* circulate; *außer* ~ *setzen* withdraw from circulation; ˈ~**bahn** *ast. f* orbit; ˈ**♀en** *v/t.* run down; *v/i.* (sn) revolve; *Blut, Geld, Gerücht*: circulate; ˈ~**geschwindigkeit** *f* rotational speed; *Raumfahrt*: orbital velocity; ˈ~**schreiben** *n* circular (letter).

ˈ**Umlaut** *m* vowel-mutation, umlaut; *Laut*: mutated (*od.* modified) vowel; ˈ**♀en** *v/t.* umlaut.

ˈ**Umlege|kragen** *m* turn-down collar; ˈ**♀n 1.** *Mantel usw.*: put on; (*umkniffen, umdrehen*) turn down; (*zum Liegen bringen*) lay (down); (*anders legen*) place differently, shift; (*kippen*) tilt; ⊕ *Hebel*: throw; *Verkehr*: divert; *fig. Kosten*: apportion; *sl.* (*töten*) bump off; **2.** *umˈlegen*: ~ *mit et.* lay *a th.* round with.

ˈ**umleit|en** *Verkehr*: divert, bypass; ˈ**♀ung** *f* bypass, detour; ˈ**♀ungsschild** *n* diversion (*Am.* detour) sign.

ˈ**umlenken** turn round *od.* back.

ˈ**umlernen** learn anew; *fig.* ~ *müssen* have to change one's views.

ˈ**umliegend** surrounding; ~*e Gegend a.* environs *pl.*

ˈ**ummodeln** change.

ˈ**ummelden:** (*polizeilich*) ~ re-register (with the police).

umˈnacht|et *fig.* clouded; *geistig* ~ mentally deranged; **♀ung** *f*: *geistige* ~ mental derangement.

umˈnebeln (29) *fig.* (be)fog.

ˈ**umnehmen** put on.

ˈ**um-organisieren** reorganize.

ˈ**umpacken** repack.

ˈ**umpflanzen 1.** transplant; **2.** *umˈpflanzen mit* plant *a th.* round with.

ˈ**umpflügen** plough (*Am.* plow) up.

umpol|en ⚡ [ˈ~poːlən] (25) change the polarity; ˈ**♀ung** *f* pole-changing.

ˈ**umquartieren** remove to other quarters; ⚔ rebillet.

umˈrahmen frame.

umrand|en [~ˈrandən] (26) edge, border; **♀ung** *f* edge, border.

umˈranken twine (itself) around *a th.*; ~ *mit et.* entwine with.

ˈ**umräumen** (*umstellen*) move; (*neu ordnen*) rearrange.

ˈ**umrechn|en** convert; ˈ**♀ung** *f* conversion; ˈ**♀ungsfaktor** *m* conversion factor; ˈ**♀ungskurs** *m Börse*: rate of exchange; ˈ**♀ungs-tabelle** *f* conversion table.

ˈ**umreißen 1.** pull down; (*umstoßen*) knock down; **2.** *umˈreißen* outline.

ˈ**umrennen** run down.

umˈringen (25) surround.

ˈ**Umriß** *m* (4) outline (*a. fig.*), contour; ˈ~**zeichnung** *f* sketch.

ˈ**umrühren** stir (up).

ˈ**umsatteln** resaddle; *fig.* change one's occupation *od.* studies; *pol.* change sides; ~ *auf* (*acc.*) switch to.

ˈ**Umsatz** ✝ *m* (3^2 *u.* ^{3}) turnover; (*Absatz*) sales *pl.*; (*Einnahme*) returns *pl.*; ˈ~**beteiligung** *f* commission; ˈ~**steigerung** *f* increase in turnover; ˈ~**steuer** *f* turnover tax.

umˈsäumen hem (round); *fig.* line.

ˈ**umschalt|en** ⚡ switch (over); *mot.* change over (*auf acc.* into), change gears; ˈ**♀er** *m* ⚡ change-over switch, commutator; (*a.* ˈ**♀taste** *f*) *an der Schreibmaschine*: shift-key; ˈ**♀ung** *f* ⚡ switching, commutation.

ˈ**Umschau** *f* look(ing) round; ~ *halten od. sich* ˈ**♀en** look round; *s. a. umsehen.*

ˈ**umschicht|ig** *fig.* by (*od.* in) turns; ˈ**♀ung** *f* regrouping, shifting; *gesellschaftliche* ~ social upheaval.

umˈschiff|en circumnavigate, sail

round; *ein Kap*: double; **2ung** *f* circumnavigation; doubling.

'Umschlag *m* (3[3]) (*Änderung*) (sudden) change; (*Brief*2) envelope; (*Hülle*) cover, wrapper; *bsd. e-s Buches od. Heftes*: jacket; *am Ärmel*: cuff; *an der Hose*: turn-up; ⚕ *feuchter*: compress, (*Brei*2) poultice, cataplasm; (*Umladung*) transfer, transshipment; **'~bild** *n* cover picture; **'2en** *v/i.* (sn) turn over, upset, fall down; ⚓ capsize; (*sich ändern*) turn, change; *Wind*: shift; *Stimme*: break; *v/t.* knock down; *Seite usw.*: turn over; *Saum*: turn up; *Kragen*: turn down; *Ärmel*: tuck up; *Waren*: transship; **'~(e)tuch** *n* shawl; **'~hafen** *m* port of transshipment; **'~platz** *m* reloading (*od.* transfer) point; *weitS.* emporium.

um'schließen surround, enclose; *fig.* encompass.

um'schlingen embrace, clasp.

'umschmelzen remelt, recast.

'umschnallen buckle on.

'umschreib|en 1. (*nochmals schreiben*) rewrite; (*abschreiben*) transcribe; *Besitz*: transfer (*auf acc.* to); **2.** *um'schreiben bsd.* ⩘ circumscribe; *durch Worte*: paraphrase; **'2ung** *f* **1.** transcription; transfer; **2.** *Um'schreibung* paraphrase.

'Umschrift *f e-r Münze*: legend; (*phonetische ~ usw.*) transcription.

'Umschuldungskredit *m* conversion credit.

'umschul|en retrain; **'2ungskurs** *m* course for retraining.

'umschütt|eln shake (up); **'~en** pour out into another vessel; (*umstoßen*) spill.

um'schwärmen swarm round; *fig.* adore.

'Umschweif *m* digression; *ohne ~e* point-blank; **'2ig** roundabout.

'umschwenken (sn) wheel round; *fig.* veer round.

'Umschwung *m* (*Drehung*) revolution; (*Umkehrung*) reversal; (*Änderung*) change; *völliger*: about-face; *der Gefühle*: revulsion.

um'segeln *s. umschiffen.*

'umsehen: *sich ~* look round (*od.* back); *fig.* look out (*nach* for); *an, in e-m Ort usw.* have a look (a)round; *im 2* in a twinkling.

'umseitig overleaf.

'umsetz|bar ⚚ realizable; sal(e)able; **'~en** transpose, shift; ⚘ transplant; ⚚ (*zu Geld machen*) realize, *Ware*: sell; *in die Tat, Musik usw. ~* translate into action, music, *etc.*; *sich ~ in Eiweiß usw.* change into.

'Umsichgreifen *n* spread(ing).

'Umsicht *f* circumspection; **'2ig** circumspect.

'umsied|eln resettle; **'2ler** *m* resettler; **'2lung** *f* resettlement.

'umsinken (sn) sink down.

um'sonst for nothing, gratis, gratuitously, free (of charge); (*vergebens*) in vain; (*zwecklos*) useless, to no purpose; *nicht ~* (*ohne Grund*) not for nothing.

'umspann|en 1. change horses; ⚡ transform; **2.** *um'spannen* span, encompass; *mit der Hand*: clasp; **'2er** ⚡ *m* transformer.

um'spinnen spin (all) round; ⊕ *Draht*: cover.

'umspringen (sn) *Wind*: change, veer; *~ mit* treat, deal with.

'umspulen rewind.

'Umstand *m* circumstance; (*Tatsache*) fact; (*Einzelheit*) detail; *Umstände pl.* (*Lage*) conditions *pl.*, situation *sg.*; *unter Umständen* possibly, (*notfalls*) if need be; *unter allen Umständen* in any case, at all events; *unter keinen Umständen* on no account; F *in andern* (*od. gesegneten*) *Umständen* in the family way; *ohne Umstände* without ceremony; *unter diesen Umständen* in these circumstances, as matters stand; *Umstände machen S.*: cause inconvenience; *P.*: be formal *od.* ceremonious, (make a) fuss; *machen Sie sich keine Umstände* don't (go to) trouble.

umständ|ehalber ['umʃtɛndə-] owing to circumstances; **~lich** ['~ʃtɛntliç] *Erzählung usw.*: circumstantial; (*förmlich*) ceremonious; (*unnötig ~*) fussy; (*verwickelt*) complicated; (*unbequem*) awkward; **'2lichkeit** *f* circumstantiality; formality; fussiness; complicatedness.

'Umstands|kleid *n* maternity dress; **'~krämer** *m* fusspot; **'~wort** *n* adverb.

'umstehend *Seite*: next; *die 2en pl.* the bystanders; (*wie ~* as stated) overleaf.

ˈUmsteige|(fahr)karte *f* tranfer-ticket; **ˈ2n** 🚂 (sn) change (*nach* for).
ˈumstell|en 1. shift, transpose; *Möbel usw.*: rearrange; *Betrieb, Währung*: convert, shift (*auf acc.* to), (*a. sich*) change over (*a.* ⊕); *auf andere Erzeugnisse usw.* switch to; *fig. sich* ~ adapt o.s. (*auf acc.* to), change one's attitude; **2.** *umˈstellen* surround, encircle; **ˈ2ung** *f* transposition; *e-s Betriebes, der Währung*: conversion, change-over; *fig.* adaptation; change.
ˈumsteuern ⊕ reverse.
ˈumstimmen tune to another pitch; *fig. j-n* ~ change a person's mind, bring a p. round.
ˈumstoßen knock down *od.* over, overthrow; *fig.* annul; *Urteil, Entscheid*: set aside, overturn; *Plan*: upset.
umˈstricken *fig.* ensnare.
umstritten [~ˈʃtritən] contested; (*strittig*) controversial.
umstrukturieren [ˈ~ʃtrukturiːrən] restructure. [upheaval.]
ˈUmsturz *m* overthrow, revolution;
ˈumstürz|en *v/t.* upset, overturn; *fig.* overthrow; *v/i.* (sn) fall down *od.* over, overturn; **ˈ2ler** *m* (7), **ˈ2lerin** *f* (16[1]) revolutionist; **ˈ~lerisch** subversive, revolutionary.
ˈumtaufen rebaptize, rename.
ˈUmtausch *m* exchange; *v. Wertpapieren, der Währung*: conversion; **ˈ2en** exchange (*gegen* for); convert; **ˈ~frist** *f* exchange term; **ˈ~recht** *n* right to exchange.
ˈumtreiben *fig.* worry, be on *a p.'s* mind.
Umtriebe [ˈ~triːbə] *m/pl.* machinations, intrigues, activities.
ˈumtun *Tuch usw.*: put on; *sich* ~ *nach* look about for.
ˈumwälz|en roll round; *fig.* revolutionize; **ˈ~end** revolutionary; **ˈ2ung** *f* revolution, upheaval.
ˈumwand|elbar ⚕ convertible; **ˈ~eln** change, (*a. phys.*) transform (*in acc.*, *zu* into); ⚕ *Zinsfuß usw.*: convert; ⚖ *Strafe*: commute (into); **ˈ2lung** *f* change, transformation; ⚕ conversion; ⚖ commutation.
ˈumwechs|eln, ˈ2lung *f* (ex)change.
ˈUmweg *m* detour, roundabout way; *fig. auf* ~*en* indirectly.
ˈUmwelt *f* environment; *weitS.* *the* world around us; **ˈ2bedingt** environmental; **ˈ2bewußt** environment-conscious; **ˈ2feindlich** ecologically harmful; **ˈ~frage** *f*: *die* ~ the environment issue; **ˈ2freundlich** non-polluting; *Stoffe*: *a.* biodegradable; **ˈ~katastrophe** *f* environmental disaster, ecocatastrophe; **ˈ~krise** *f* ecological crisis, ecocrisis; **ˈ~schutz** *m* pollution control; conservation; **ˈ~schutzbewegung** *f* ecology movement; **ˈ~schützer** *m* (7) environmentalist, conservationist; **ˈ~schutz-experte** *m* ecologist; **ˈ~sünder** *m* polluter; **ˈ~verschmutzung** *f* pollution (of the environment); **ˈ~zerstörung** *f* ecocide.
ˈumwenden turn over; *sich* ~ turn round.
umˈwerben court, (*a. fig.*) woo; *umworben a.* sought after.
ˈumwerfen overthrow, overturn, upset; **ˈ~d** *fig.* fabulous.
ˈumwert|en revalue; **ˈ2ung** *f* revaluation.
umˈwickeln wrap up; *a.* ⊕ cover.
umˈwinden wind round, entwine.
ˈUmwohner *m* (7) neighbo(u)r.
umwölken [~ˈvœlkən] (25) (*a. sich*) cloud (over), darken (*beide a. fig.*).
umzäun|en [~ˈtsɔʏnən] (25) fence in, enclose; **2ung** *f* enclosure.
ˈumziehen *v/i.* (sn) (*Wohnung wechseln*) (re)move; *v/t. sich* ~ change (one's clothes).
umzingel|n [~ˈtsiŋəln] (29) surround, encircle; **2ung** *f* encirclement.
ˈUmzug *m* procession; *prächtiger*: pageant; *pol.* demonstration march; (*Wohnungswechsel*) move, removal; *Umzüge besorgen vom Spediteur*: remove furniture.
un-ab|änderlich [ˈunˀapˈˀɛndərliç] unalterable, irrevocable; **~dingbar** [~ˈdiŋbɑːr] unalterable; *Rechte*: inalienable; **~hängig** [ˈ~hɛŋiç] independent (*von* of); ~ *von* (*ohne Rücksicht auf*) irrespective of; **2hängige** *pol.* [ˈ~igə] *m* (18) independent; **ˈ2hängigkeit** *f* independence; **~kömmlich** [ˈ~ˈkœmliç] indispensable; ⚔ in reserved occupation; (*momentan* ~) busy; **ˈ~ˈlässig** incessant, unremitting; **~ˈsehbar** *fig.* not to be foreseen; incalculable; (*ungeheuer*) immense; **~ˈsetzbar** irremovable; **ˈ~sichtlich** unintention-

al; **~weisbar**, **~weislich** [~'vaɪs-] not to be refused; (*dringend*; *gebieterisch*) imperative, peremptory; **~wendbar** [~'vɛntbaːr] inevitable.

'un·achtsam inattentive; careless; **'2keit** *f* carelessness.

'un·ähnlich unlike, dissimilar; **'2keit** *f* unlikeness, dissimilarity.

'un·an|'fechtbar unimpeachable, unchallengeable, incontestable; **~gebaut** ['~ʔangəbaʊt] uncultivated; **'~gebracht** out of place, inappropriate; (*ungelegen*) inopportune; **~gefochten** ['~gəfɔxtən] undisputed; (*unbelästigt*) unmolested; **~gemeldet** ['~gəmɛldət] unannounced; **'~gemessen** unsuitable; (*unschicklich*) improper; (*unangebracht*) inadequate; **'~genehm** disagreeable, unpleasant; (*mißlich*, *peinlich*) awkward; **'~getastet** untouched; **'~greifbar** impregnable (*a. fig.*); **'~nehmbar** unacceptable; **'2nehmlichkeit** *f* unpleasantness; difficulty; (*Übelstand*) inconvenience; trouble (*a. ~en pl.*); *s. zuziehen*; **'~sehnlich** (*unscheinbar*) plain; (*unbedeutend*) insignificant; **'~ständig** indecent (*a. weitS.*); (*unmanierlich*) unmannerly; **'2ständigkeit** *f* indecency; unmannerliness; **'~'tastbar** unimpeachable; *Rechte*: inviolable.

'un·appetitlich unsavo(u)ry, nasty.

'Un·art *f* bad habit *od.* trick; (*Grobheit*) rudeness; ill-breeding; *e-s Kindes*: naughtiness (*a. weitS.*); *vom Pferd*: vice; **'2ig** rude, ill-bred; *Kind*: naughty.

'un·artikuliert inarticulate.

'un·ästhetisch un(a)esthetic(ally *adv.*), offensive; *pred.* not (a)esthetical, in bad taste.

'un·auf|dringlich unobtrusive; **'~fällig** inconspicuous; unobtrusive; **~findbar** ['~'fintbaːr] undiscoverable, *pred.* not to be found; **~gefordert** ['~gəfɔrdərt] unasked; *adv.* spontaneously; **~'haltsam** irresistible; **~'hörlich** incessant; **~'lösbar**, **~'löslich** indissoluble; *a.* ⚗, ⚗ insoluble; **'~merksam** inattentive; **'2merksamkeit** *f* inattention; **'~richtig** insincere; **'2richtigkeit** *f* insincerity; **~schiebbar** ['~'ʃiːpbaːr] not to be delayed; urgent.

un·aus|bleiblich ['~ʔaʊs'blaɪpliç] inevitable; **'~'führbar** impracticable; **'~gefüllt** *Formular usw.*: blank; **~geglichen** ['~gəgliçən] unbalanced; **'2geglichenheit** *f* unbalance; **'~gesetzt** uninterrupted, incessant; **'~'löschlich** indelible (*a. fig.*); **'~'rottbar** ineradicable; **'~'sprechlich** unspeakable, ineffable; **'~'stehlich** insupportable, insufferable, intolerable; (*widerlich*) detestable; **'~'weichlich** inevitable, unavoidable.

unbändig ['unbɛndiç] unruly; F (*ungeheuer*) tremendous.

'unbarmherzig unmerciful, pitiless, relentless; **'2keit** *f* unmercifulness, pitilessness, relentlessness.

'un|be'·absichtigt unintentional; **'~be·achtet** unnoticed; ~ *lassen* disregard; **'~be·anstandet** not objected to, unopposed; **'~be·'antwortet** unanswered; **'~be·arbeitet** (*roh*) raw; ⊕ unfinished, unmachined; *Land*: uncultivated; **'~bebaut** ⚘ untilled; *Gelände*: undeveloped; **'~bedacht(sam)** thoughtless; (*unklug*) imprudent; (*voreilig*) rash; **'~bedenklich** *S.*: unobjectionable; harmless; *P.*: unhesitating; *adv.* without hesitation; **'~bedeutend** insignificant; (*geringfügig*) slight, negligible; **'~bedingt** unconditional, absolute; (*bestimmt*) positive; *Gehorsam*, *Vertrauen*: implicit; *adv.* absolutely; by all means; **'~bedruckt** blank; **'~befahrbar** impassable, impracticable; **'~befangen** (*unparteiisch*) impartial, (*a.* ⚖) unbias(s)ed; (*nicht verlegen*) uninhibited; (*natürlich*) unaffected; **'2befangenheit** *f* impartiality; unaffectedness; **'~befleckt** spotless (*a. fig.*); *fig.*, *a. eccl.* immaculate; **'~befriedigend** unsatisfactory; **'~befriedigt** unsatisfied; **'~befristet** unlimited; **'~befugt** unauthorized; **2en** *ist der Eintritt untersagt* trespassing prohibited, no admittance except on business; **'~begabt** untalented, not gifted; **'~be'greiflich** inconceivable, incomprehensible; **'2be'greiflichkeit** *f* inconceivability; **'~begrenzt** unlimited; **'~begründet** unfounded, groundless; **'2behagen** *n* uneasiness; **'~behaglich** uncomfortable; *fig. a.* uneasy; *pred. a.* ill at ease; **'~behelligt** unmolested; **'~beherrscht** *fig.* lacking self-control; quick-tempered; **'2beherrschtheit**

f lack of self-control; **'~behindert** unhindered, unhampered; **~beholfen** ['~bəhɔlfən] clumsy, awkward; **'2beholfenheit** *f* clumsiness, awkwardness; **'~be-irrbar** imperturbable, unwavering; **~be-irrt** ['~bəʔirt] unswerving, unperturbed; **'~bekannt** unknown; *ich bin hier* ~ I am a stranger here; *die* 2*e* ⩚ *f* (18) the unknown; ~*e Größe* unknown quantity; ⚖ *Anzeige gegen* 2 charge against a person or persons unknown; **'~bekehrbar** inconvertible; *weitS.* inveterate; **'~bekleidet** unclothed, naked; **'~bekömmlich** difficult to digest; **'~bekümmert** careless (*um* of), unconcerned (about); **'~belastet** *P.*: carefree; *Grund*: unencumbered; *pol.* with a clean record; ⚖ uncompromised; **'~belebt** inanimate; *Straße*: unfrequented; **~be'lehrbar** obstinate; ~ *sein* take no advice; **'~belichtet** *phot.* unexposed; **'~beliebt** disliked; unpopular (*bei* with); **'2beliebtheit** *f* unpopularity; **'~bemannt** unmanned; ✈ pilotless; **'~bemerkbar** imperceptible; **'~bemerkt** unnoticed; **'~bemittelt** without means, impecunious; **'~benannt** unnamed; ⩚ abstract; **'~be'nommen:** *es ist* (*od. bleibt*) *Ihnen* ~ *zu* ... you are at liberty to ...; **'~benutzbar** unserviceable; **'~benutzt** unused; *Geld*: idle; **'~be-obachtet** unobserved; **'~bequem** inconvenient, uncomfortable; (*unhandlich*) unwieldy; (*lästig*) troublesome; **'2bequemlichkeit** *f* inconvenience; **~be'rechenbar** incalculable (*a. P.*); (*gefährlich*) dangerous; **'~berechtigt** unauthorized; (*unbillig*) unfair; (*ungerechtfertigt*) unjustified; '~*er'weise* without authority; without reason *od.* justification; **'~bereinigt** unexpurgated; **'~berücksichtigt** not taken into account, disregarded; **'~berufen** *s. unbefugt*; ~! (*mst unbe'rufen*) touch wood!; **'~berühmt** obscure; **'~berührt** untouched; *fig.* ~ *bleiben von* not to be affected by; **~beschadet** ['~bə'ʃɑːdət] (*gen.*) without prejudice to; (*ungeachtet*) irrespective of, notwithstanding; **'~beschädigt** uninjured, (*a.* ⚓) undamaged; **'~beschäftigt** unemployed, non-employed; **'~bescheiden** immodest; *Preis usw.*: unreasonable; **'2bescheidenheit** *f* immodesty; **'~bescholten** blameless, irreproachable; **'2bescholtenheit** *f* blamelessness, integrity; **'~beschränkt** unrestricted; *Macht, Eigentum, Rechte*: absolute; **~beschreiblich** [~be'ʃraɪpliç] indescribable; **~beschrieben** ['~bəʃriːbən] *Papier*: blank; *fig.* ~*es Blatt* unknown quantity; **'~beschwert** *fig.* light-hearted, carefree, free and easy; *Gewissen*: light, easy; **'2beschwertheit** *f* detachment; **'~beseelt** inanimate; **'~be'sehen** unseen; **'~besetzt** unoccupied; *Amt usw.*: vacant; **~besiegbar** [~bə'ziːkbɑːr] invincible; **'~besiegt** undefeated; **'~besoldet** unsalaried; **'~besonnen** thoughtless, reckless, rash; **'2besonnenheit** *f* thoughtlessness, rashness; **'~besorgt** easy, unconcerned; *seien Sie deswegen* ~! don't let it worry you!; **'2bestand** *m s. Unbeständigkeit*; **'~beständig** inconstant, unstable; fickle; (*veränderlich*) changeable; **'2beständigkeit** *f* inconstancy; changeableness; **'~bestätigt** unconfirmed; **~be'stechlich** incorruptible; *fig.* keen, unerring; **2be'stechlichkeit** *f* incorruptibility; **'~bestellbar** 📯 undeliverable; *Brief*: dead; **'~bestimmt** (*undeutlich*) indeterminate; (*a. gr.*) indefinite; vague; (*unsicher*) uncertain; (*unentschieden*) undecided; *auf* ~*e Zeit* for an indefinite time; **'2bestimmtheit** *f* indetermination; indefiniteness; vagueness; uncertainty; **'~bestraft** unpunished; **~be'streitbar** incontestable; **'~be'stritten** uncontested; undisputed; **'~beteiligt** unconcerned, not interested; (*nicht verwickelt*) not involved; (*gleichgültig*) indifferent; **'~betont** unaccented, unstressed; **'~beträchtlich** inconsiderable; **'~beugsam** *fig.* inflexible; uncompromising, rigid; **'~bewacht** unwatched; *fig.* unguarded; **'~bewaffnet** unarmed; *Auge*: naked; **'~bewandert** inexperienced, not versed (*in dat.* in); **'~beweglich** immovable; (*bewegungslos*) motionless; ⊕ fixed, rigid; *s. Habe*; **'2beweglichkeit** *f* immovableness; **~beweibt** ['~bəvaɪpt] unmarried; **'~beweint** unwept (for); **'~bewiesen** unproved; **'~bewohnbar** uninhabitable; **'~bewohnt** uninhabited; *Haus, Raum*: unoccupied; **'~bewußt** unconscious; **~be'zahlbar** priceless (*a. fig.*); '**~bezahlt** unpaid; **~be'zähmbar** untamable; *fig.* indomitable; **~be'zwingbar** invincible.

'**un|biegsam** inflexible; '**2bilden** *pl. der Witterung* inclemency *sg.* of the weather; '**2bildung** *f* lack of education, want of culture, illiteracy; **2bill** ['~bil] *f* (16) injury, wrong; '**~billig** unfair, unjust; '**2billigkeit** *f* unfairness; '**~blutig** bloodless.

'**unbotmäßig** insubordinate, unruly; '**2keit** *f* insubordination.

'**unbrauchbar** useless; (*Abfall...*) waste; ~ *machen* render useless; '**2keit** *f* uselessness.

'**unbrennbar** non-flammable.

'**unchristlich** unchristian.

und [unt] and; F *na ~?* so what? ~ *wenn* (*auch*) even if; ~ *so weiter od. fort* and so on *od.* forth, et cetera (*abbr.* etc., a.s.o.).

'**Undank** *m* ingratitude; ~ *ernten* F get small thanks for it; '**2bar** ungrateful (*gegen* to); *Aufgabe usw.*: thankless; '**~barkeit** *f* ingratitude; thanklessness.

'**un|datiert** undated; '**~defi'nierbar** indefinable; **~'denkbar** unthinkable; '**~denklich:** *seit ~en Zeiten* from times immemorial; '**~deutlich** indistinct; *Laut*: inarticulate; *Bild, Eindruck*: blurred; *fig.* obscure, vague, hazy; '**~deutsch** un-German; '**~dicht** not tight; leaky; '**2ding** *n* absurdity; '**~diszipliniert** undisciplined.

'**unduldsam** intolerant; '**2keit** *f* intolerance.

undurch'dringlich impenetrable (*für* to); *weitS.* impervious; *Gesicht*: inscrutable.

undurch'führbar impracticable.

'**undurchlässig** impervious (*für* to), impermeable; (*wasser~*) watertight, waterproof.

'**undurchsichtig** non-transparent, opaque; *fig.* impenetrable; '**2keit** *f* opacity; *fig.* impenetrability.

'**un-eben** uneven; *fig. nicht ~* not bad; '**2heit** *f* unevenness.

'**un-echt** not genuine, spurious, false; (*gefälscht*) counterfeit(ed), fake(d); (*nachgemacht*) imitation (*nur attr.*), artificial; *Farbe*: fading, not fast; ⚖ improper.

'**un-ehelich** illegitimate.

'**Un-ehr|e** *f* dishono(u)r; '**2enhaft** dishono(u)rable; '**2-erbietig** disrespectful; '**~-erbietigkeit** *f* disrespect(fulness); '**2lich** dishonest; '**~lichkeit** *f* dishonesty.

'**un|-eigennützig** disinterested, unselfish; '**~-eigentlich** not proper; not literal; '**~-eingedenk** unmindful (*gen.* of); **~eingelöst** ['~ˀaɪngəløːst] unredeemed; '**~'-eingeschränkt** unrestricted; '**~-eingeweiht** *P.*: uninitiated; '**2-eingeweihte** *m, f* outsider; *pl. the* uninitiated; '**~-einheitlich** non-uniform; '**~-einig** disagreeing; ~ *sein* be at variance *od.* issue *od.* odds; '**2-einigkeit** *f* disagreement; *stärker*: dissension; **~-ein'nehmbar** impregnable; '**~-eins:** ~ *sein s. uneinig*; '**~-empfänglich** insusceptible (*für* to); '**~-empfindlich** insensible (*gegen* to); ~ *gegen Druck, Licht usw.*: insensitive to; '**2-empfindlichkeit** *f* insensibility; **~'endlich** infinite (*a. fig.*); *phot. auf ~ einstellen* focus for infinity; *adv. fig.* (*sehr*) enormously; ~ *viel* ... immense, no end of; **2'endlichkeit** *f* infinity; (*Raum*) infinite space; '**~-englisch** un-English; **~-ent'behrlich** indispensable; **~-ent'geltlich** gratuitous, free (of charge); *adv. u. adj.* gratis.

'**un-enthaltsam** intemperate; *bsd. geschlechtlich*: incontinent; '**2-enthaltsamkeit** *f* intemperance; incontinence.

unentrinnbar [unˀɛnt'rinbaːr] inescapable.

unentschieden ['unˀɛntʃiːdən] undecided; *s. unentschlossen*; *Sport*: drawn; 2 *n Sport*: draw; ~ *enden* end in a draw; '**2heit** *f* undecidedness; *s. Unentschlossenheit.*

'**un-entschlossen** irresolute; '**2heit** *f* irresolution, indecision.

'**un-entschuldbar** inexcusable.

unentwegt ['~ˀɛnt'veːkt] steadfast, stalwart; *adv.* constantly; '**2e** *pol. m* (18) die-hard, stalwart, *Am.* F standpat(ter); '**2heit** *f* steadfastness; *pol.* die-hardism.

'**un-ent'wirrbar** inextricable.

un|-er'bittlich inexorable; '**~-erfahren** inexperienced; **~erfindlich** ['~ˀɛr'fintliç] mysterious; **~-er'forschlich** inscrutable; '**~-erforscht** unexplored; '**~-erfreulich** unpleasant; '**~-er'füllbar** unrealizable; '**~-erfüllt** unfulfilled; '**~-ergiebig** unproductive; **~ergründlich** ['~ʔɛr'gryntliç] unfathomable; *fig. a.* inscrutable; '**~-erheblich** inconsiderable, insignificant; *bsd.* ⚖ irrelevant (*für* to); '**2-erheblichkeit** *f* inconsiderableness; irrelevance; '**~-erhört 1.** not granted, unheard; **2.** *uner'hört* (*noch nie dagewesen*) unheard-of; (*empörend*) outrageous, scandalous; *~!* F damned cheek!; F (*großartig*) terrific; '**~-erkannt** unrecognized; '**~-erkennbar** unrecognizable; '**~-erklärlich** inexplicable; **~-er'läßlich** indispensable; '**~erlaubt** ['~ʔɛrlaupt] unauthorized; (*ungesetzlich*) illicit; *~e Entfernung von der Truppe* ⚔ absence without leave (A.W.O.L.); ⚖ *~e Handlung* civil wrong; '**~-erledigt** unsettled, not disposed of; '**~-erlöst** unredeemed; **~-er'meßlich** immeasurable, immense; **2-er'meßlichkeit** *f* immeasurableness, immensity; **~ermüdlich** [~ʔɛr'my:tliç] *P.*: indefatigable; *Bemühen*: *a.* untiring, unremitting(ly); **2-er'müdlichkeit** *f* indefatigableness; '**~-er-örtert** undiscussed; '**~-erquicklich** unpleasant; '**~-erreichbar** unattainable; *pred.* out of reach; '**~-erreicht** *fig.* unequal(l)ed, unrival(l)ed; **~ersättlich** [~ʔɛr'zɛtliç] insatiable; '**~-erschlossen** *Gelände, Markt usw.*: undeveloped; **~-er'schöpflich** inexhaustible; '**~-erschrocken** undaunted; intrepid; '**2-erschrockenheit** *f* intrepidity; **~-er'schütterlich** unshakable; *Sinn*: imperturbable, stolid; **~-er'schwinglich** unattainable; *Preis*: exorbitant; *für mich ~* I can't afford it; **~-er'setzlich** irreplaceable; **~-er'sprießlich** unprofitable; unpleasant; **~-er'träglich** intolerable, unbearable; '**~-erwähnt** unmentioned; '**~-erwartet** unexpected; **~-er'weislich** indemonstrable; '**~-erwidert** *Brief*: unanswered; *Liebe*: unrequited; '**~-erwünscht** undesired, undesirable; '**~-erzogen** uneducated; *b.s.* ill-bred.

'**unfähig** incapable (*gen.*, *zu* of *a th.*, of *doing*); (*außerstande*) unable (to *do*); (*untauglich*) unfit (for), incompetent (to *inf.*); (*leistungs~*) inefficient; '**2keit** *f* incapacity (*zu* for [*doing*] *a th.*, to *do*); inability (for); incompetence, unfitness; inefficiency.

'**unfahrplanmäßig** unscheduled.

'**unfair** unfair; *Sport*: *a.* foul.

'**Unfall** *m* accident; *Tod durch ~* accidental death; '**~flucht** ⚖ *f* leaving the scene of an accident; '**~-opfer** *n* casualty; '**~quote** *f* number of accidents; '**~station** *f* first-aid station; *im Krankenhaus*: casualty ward; '**~stelle** *f* scene of (the) accident; '**~tod** *m* accidental death; '**~verhütung** *f* prevention of accidents; '**~versicherung** *f* accident insurance.

un'faßbar incomprehensible.

un'fehlbar (*nie irrend*) infallible (*a. eccl.*); unerring (*a. Schuß, Schütze*); (*nie versagend*) unfailing; *adv.* (*bestimmt*) without fail; (*unvermeidlich*) inevitably; **2keit** *f* infallibility.

'**unfein** indelicate; (*unhöflich*) impolite; (*grob*) coarse; *pred.* not nice, bad form.

'**unfern** not far (off); *prp.* (*gen. od. von*) not far from.

'**unfertig** unfinished; *fig. P.*: immature.

Unflat ['unfla:t] *m* (3) dirt, filth.

unflätig ['~flɛ:tiç] dirty, filthy.

'**unfolgsam** disobedient; '**2keit** *f* disobedience.

unförm|ig ['~fœrmiç] misshapen, monstrous; '**2igkeit** *f* shapelessness; '**~lich** informal, unceremonious.

'**unfrankiert** not prepaid; *Brief*: unstamped.

'**unfrei** unfree, not free; '**~willig** involuntary; *Humor*: unconscious.

'**unfreundlich** unfriendly, unkind (*zu, gegen* to); *Klima, Wetter*: inclement; *Zimmer usw.*: cheerless; '**2keit** *f* unfriendliness; inclemency.

'**Unfriede** *m* discord; *~ stiften* sow discord.

'**unfruchtbar** *a. fig.* barren, sterile; '**2keit** *f* barrenness, sterility.

Unfug ['unfu:k] *m* (3) mischief; nuisance; ⚖ *grober ~* gross misdemeano(u)r; *~ treiben* be up to mischief.

unfügsam intractable.

un'fühlbar intangible, impalpable.

'**ungangbar** impassable; *Münze*: not current; *Ware*: unsal(e)able.

Ungar ['uŋga:r] *m* (13), '**~in** *f* (16[1]), '**2isch** Hungarian.

ˈ**ungastlich** inhospitable.

unge|achtet [ˈ~gəˀaxtət] **1.** *adj.* not esteemed; **2.** *prp.* (*gen.*) regardless of, notwithstanding; ˈ**~-ahndet** unpunished; ˈ**~-ahnt** undreamt-of, unthought-of; (*unerwartet*) unexpected; ˈ**~bahnt** untrodden, unbeaten; **~bärdig** [ˈ~gəbɛːrdiç] unruly; ˈ**~beten** uninvited, unbidden; *~er Gast* intruder; ˈ**~bildet** uneducated; *Benehmen*: ill-bred, unpolished; ˈ**~bräuchlich** unusual; ˈ**~braucht** unused.

ˈ**Ungebühr** *f* impropriety, indecency, unseemliness; ˈ**~lich** improper, indecent, unseemly; *adv.* (*mehr als recht ist*) unduly; ˈ**~lichkeit** *f s. Ungebühr.*

ˈ**ungebunden** unbound; *Buch*: in sheets; *fig.* free, unrestrained; *b.s.* licentious; *~e Rede* prose; ˈ**~heit** *f* freedom; *b.s.* licentiousness.

ˈ**ungedeckt** *allg.* uncovered (*a. Scheck usw.*); *Kredit*: unsecured; *Tisch*: not yet laid.

ˈ**ungedruckt** unprinted.

ˈ**Ungeduld** *f* impatience; **~ig** [ˈ~diç] impatient.

ˈ**unge-eignet** *S.*: unsuitable; *P.*: unfit (*zu* for).

ungefähr [ˈungəfɛːr] approximate, rough; *adv. a.* about, *Am. a.* around; *von ~* by chance; ˈ**~det** unendangered, safe(ly *adv.*), *nur pred.* out of danger; ˈ**~lich** harmless; not dangerous.

ˈ**ungefällig** disobliging, unkind; ˈ**~keit** *f* unkindness.

unge|färbt [ˈ~gəfɛrpt] undyed; ˈ**~fragt** unasked; *adv.* without being asked; ˈ**~füge** unwieldy; ˈ**~fügig** unpliant, unyielding; ˈ**~gerbt** untanned; ˈ**~halten** (*unwillig*) annoyed (*über acc.* at); ˈ**~heilt** uncured; ˈ**~heißen** unbidden; *adv.* of one's own accord; ˈ**~hemmt** unchecked; *adv.* without restraint; ˈ**~heuchelt** unfeigned.

ˈ**ungeheuer** **1.** vast, huge, enormous, immense; monstrous; (*toll*) F tremendous, terrific; **2. ~** *n* (7) monster; ˈ**~lich** monstrous, outrageous; ˈ**~lichkeit** *f* monstrosity.

ungehobelt [ˈ~gəhoːbəlt] *fig.* rude, rough.

ˈ**ungehörig** undue; (*unschicklich*) improper; ˈ**~keit** *f* impropriety.

ˈ**ungehorsam** **1.** disobedient; **2. ~** *m* (3) disobedience.

unge|hört [ˈ~gəhøːrt] unheard; ˈ**~klärt** unsettled; *Abwässer*: untreated, raw; ˈ**~künstelt** unaffected, unstudied; ˈ**~kürzt** *Werk, Recht usw.*: unabridged; ˈ**~laden** *Gast*: uninvited; *Waffe*: unloaded.

ˈ**ungelegen** inopportune, inconvenient, untimely; *j-m ~ kommen* be inconvenient to a p.; ˈ**~heit** *f* inconvenience; *einzelne*: trouble; *j-m ~en machen* give a p. trouble.

ˈ**un|gelehrig** indocile; ˈ**~gelehrt** unlearned; ˈ**~gelenk** awkward, clumsy; ˈ**~gelernt** *Arbeit(er)*: unskilled; ˈ**~gelöscht** *Kalk*: unslaked; ˈ**~gemach** *n* hardship, trouble; ˈ**~gemein** uncommon, extraordinary; *adv.* exceedingly; ˈ**~gemischt** unmixed; ˈ**~gemütlich** uncomfortable; *P.*: unpleasant, nasty; ˈ**~genannt** unnamed; *P.*: anonymous; ˈ**~genau** inaccurate, inexact; ˈ**~genauigkeit** *f* inaccuracy; ˈ**~geniert** [ˈunʒeniːrt] free and easy, nonchalant; (*ungestört*) undisturbed; ˈ**~genießbar** *Speise*: uneatable, inedible; *Getränk*: undrinkable; (*unschmackhaft*; *a. fig.*) unpalatable; F *P.*: in a foul temper.

ˈ**ungenüg|end** insufficient; **~sam** [ˈ~gənyːkzaːm] insatiable; ˈ**~samkeit** *f* insatiability.

ˈ**ungenützt** unused; *~ vorübergehen lassen* let slip.

ˈ**unge|-ordnet** unarranged, unsettled; *b.s.* disorderly; ˈ**~pflastert** unpaved; ˈ**~pflegt** unkempt, neglected; **~rächt** [ˈ~gərɛçt] unavenged; **~rade** [ˈ~raːdə] uneven; *Zahl*: odd; ˈ**~raten** *Kind*: spoilt, undutiful; ˈ**~rechnet** uncounted; (*nicht einbegriffen*) not included.

ˈ**ungerecht** unjust; ˈ**~fertigt** unjustified, unwarranted; ˈ**~igkeit** *f* injustice (*gegen* to).

ungereimt [ˈ~gəraɪmt] unrhymed; *fig.* absurd; ˈ**~heit** *f* absurdity.

ˈ**ungern** unwillingly; (*widerstrebend*) reluctantly; *~ tun a.* hate to do.

ˈ**unge|röstet** unroasted; ˈ**~rührt** *fig.* unmoved, untouched, unaffected; ˈ**~sagt** unsaid; ˈ**~salzen** unsalted; ˈ**~säumt**[1] *Stoff*: seamless; **~**[2] (*sofortig*) prompt; *adv. a.* without delay; ˈ**~schehen** undone; *~ machen* undo; ˈ**~schichtlich** unhistorical.

ˈ**Ungeschick** *n*, ˈ**~lichkeit** *f* awkwardness, clumsiness; ˈ**≈t** awkward, clumsy, maladroit.

unge|schlacht [ˈungəʃlaxt] bulky; (*grob*) uncouth; ˈ**~schliffen** unpolished; *Edelstein*: uncut; *fig.* rude, rough; ˈ**~schmälert** uncurtailed; undiminished; ˈ**~schminkt** unpainted; *fig.* unvarnished, plain; ˈ**~schoren** unshorn; *fig.* unmolested; *~ lassen* leave alone; ˈ**~schrieben:** *~es Gesetz* unwritten law; ˈ**~schützt** unprotected; ˈ**~schwächt** unweakened; *~e Tatkraft* unimpaired energy; ˈ**~sehen** unseen, unnoticed; ˈ**~sellig** unsociable.

ˈ**ungesetzlich** illegal, unlawful, illicit; ˈ**≈keit** *f* illegality.

ˈ**unge|sittet** uncivilized; (*unmanierlich*) unmannerly; ˈ**~stalt(et)** misshapen; ˈ**~stört** undisturbed; ˈ**~straft** unpunished; *adv.* with impunity; *~ davonkommen* go scot-free.

ungestüm [ˈ~gəʃty:m] **1.** impetuous, vehement; **2.** ≈ *m, n* (3, *o. pl.*) impetuosity, vehemence.

ˈ**ungesund** *P.*: unhealthy; *S.*: *a.* unwholesome; *fig.* unsound.

ˈ**unge|teilt** undivided; ˈ**~trübt** unclouded, (*a. fig.*) untroubled; **≈tüm** [ˈ~gəty:m] *n* (3) monster; **~übt** [ˈ~gəˀy:pt] untrained; ˈ**~wandt** unskil(l)ful; awkward.

ˈ**ungewiß** uncertain; *j-n im ungewissen lassen* keep a p. in suspense; ˈ**≈heit** *f* uncertainty; (*spannende ~*) suspense.

ˈ**Ungewitter** *n* thunderstorm.

ˈ**ungewöhnlich** unusual.

ˈ**ungewohnt** *P.*: unaccustomed (*gen.* to); *S.*: unusual; ˈ**≈heit** *f* unwontedness.

ungezählt [ˈ~gətsɛ:lt] numberless, countless.

ungezähmt [ˈ~gətsɛ:mt] untamed.

Ungeziefer [ˈungətsi:fər] *n* (7) vermin.

ˈ**ungeziemend** improper.

ungezogen [ˈ~gətso:gən] ill-bred, rude, uncivil; *Kind*: naughty; ˈ**≈heit** *f* rudeness; naughtiness.

ungezügelt [ˈ~gətsy:gəlt] unbridled; *adv.* unrestrainedly.

ˈ**ungezwungen** un(con)strained; without constraint; (*natürlich*) unaffected, easy; ˈ**≈heit** *f* unconstraint; ease.

ˈ**Unglaube** *m* unbelief.

ˈ**ungläubig** incredulous; *eccl.* unbelieving; (*heidnisch*) infidel; ˈ**≈e** *m, f* (18) unbeliever; infidel.

unglaub|lich [~ˈglauplɪç] incredible; ˈ**~würdig** untrustworthy; *S.*: incredible.

ˈ**ungleich 1.** *adj.* unequal; (*uneben*) uneven; *Zahl*: odd; (*unähnlich*) unlike, dissimilar; **2.** *adv.* (by) far, much (*vor Komparativ*); ˈ**~-artig** heterogeneous, diverse; **~förmig** [ˈ~fœrmɪç] unequal; (*unregelmäßig*) irregular; ˈ**≈gewicht** *n* imbalance; ˈ**≈heit** *f* inequality; irregularity; ˈ**~mäßig** uneven, disproportionate, asymmetrical.

Unglimpf [ˈunglɪmpf] *m* (3) harshness; (*Schimpf*) insult.

ˈ**Unglück** *n* (3, *pl. -sfälle*) misfortune; (*Pech*) ill (*od.* bad) luck; (*Unfall*) accident; (*Katastrophe*) disaster, calamity; (*Elend*) misery; ˈ**≈lich** unfortunate, unlucky; (*a.* = *traurig*) unhappy; (*verhängnisvoll*) fatal; (*elend*) wretched, miserable; *Liebe*: unrequited; ˈ**≈licherˈweise** unfortunately, unluckily; ˈ**~sbringer** *m* voodoo, *Am.* hoodoo, *Am. sl.* jinx; ˈ**≈selig** unfortunate; *S.*: disastrous.

ˈ**Unglücks|fall** *m* misadventure; (*Unfall*) accident; ˈ**~rabe** *fig. m* unlucky fellow *od.* bird; ˈ**~tag** *m* black day.

ˈ**Ungnade** *f* disgrace; *in ~ fallen (bei)* fall into disgrace (with), *bei j-m a.* incur the displeasure of.

ˈ**ungnädig** ungracious, unkind.

ˈ**ungültig** invalid, (null and) void; *Fahrkarte*: not available; *Münze*: not current; *~e (Wahl)Stimme* spoilt vote; *~ machen* cancel, *Scheck*: *usw.* invalidate; ˈ**≈keit** *f* invalidity.

ˈ**Un|gunst** *f* disfavo(u)r; *des Wetters*: inclemency; *zu j-s ~en* in a p.'s disfavo(u)r; ˈ**≈günstig** unfavo(u)rable; (*nachteilig*) disadvantageous; ˈ**≈gut** bad; *~es Gefühl* misgivings *pl.*; *nichts für ~!* no offen|ce, *Am.* -se!, no hard feelings!; ˈ**≈haltbar** untenable; ˈ**≈handlich** unwieldy; ˈ**≈harmonisch** inharmonious.

ˈ**Unheil** *n* mischief, harm; (*Katastrophe*) disaster, calamity; *~ anrichten* cause mischief, *Sturm usw.*: cause havoc; **≈bar** [ˈunhaɪlba:r] incurable; ˈ**≈bringend** fatal, baneful, unlucky; '**~stifter(in)** mischief-maker; '**⁀voll** disastrous, sinister, ominous.

'**unheimlich** uncanny, weird (*beide a. fig.*); (*unheilvoll*) sinister; F *fig.* tremendous, terrific; *adv. a.* awfully.

'**unhöflich** uncivil, impolite; '**⁀keit** *f* incivility, impoliteness.

'**unhold 1.** ungracious; (*abgeneigt*) ill-disposed; **2.** ⁀ *m* (3) monster.

'**unhörbar** inaudible.

'**unhygienisch** insanitary.

Uniform [uni'fɔrm] *f* (16), ⁀ *adj.* uniform; **⁀iert** [~'mi:rt] uniformed.

Unikum ['u:nikum] *n* (11 *u.* 9^2) unique (thing); F *P.*: original, character.

'**un-interess|ant** uninteresting; '**~iert** uninterested (*an dat.* in).

Union [u'njo:n] *f* union.

unisono [uni'zo:no] in unison.

universal [univɛr'zɑ:l] universal; ⁀... ⊕ general-purpose; **⁀-erbe** *m* sole (*od.* universal) heir; **⁀mittel** *n* universal remedy, panacea; **⁀schraubenschlüssel** *m* monkey wrench.

Universität [univɛrzi'tɛ:t] *f* (16) university; **~s-professor** *m* university professor; **~szeit** *f* college years *pl.*

Universum [uni'vɛrzum] *n* (9) universe.

Unke ['uŋkə] *f* (15) toad; '**⁀n** F *fig.* (25) croak.

'**unkennt|lich** unrecognizable; '**⁀lichkeit** *f*: *bis zur ~* past recognition; '**⁀nis** *f* ignorance; *in ~ sein über* (*acc.*) be unaware of; *j-n in ~ lassen* (*über acc.*) keep a p. in the dark (about).

'**unkeusch** unchaste; '**⁀heit** *f* unchastity.

'**unkindlich** unchildlike; *gegen Eltern*: unfilial; (*altklug*) precocious.

'**unklar** not clear; (*trüb*) muddy; (*nebelig*) misty; *fig.* vague, obscure; (*verworren*) muddled; (*undeutlich*) indistinct; *im ~en sein fig.* be in the dark (*über acc.* about); '**⁀heit** *f* want of clearness; vagueness, obscurity.

'**unkleidsam** unbecoming.

'**unklug** unwise, imprudent; '**⁀heit** *f* imprudence.

unkollegial ['unkɔlegjɑ:l] uncooperative.

'**unkompliziert** uncomplicated.

unkontrollierbar ['~kɔntrɔli:rbɑ:r] uncontrollable.

'**unkörperlich** incorporeal, immaterial.

'**Unkosten** *pl.* costs, expenses, charges; *allgemeine od. laufende ~* overhead (*od.* running) expenses, ✝ overhead; *s. stürzen.*

'**Unkraut** *n* weed(s *pl.*); *fig. ~ vergeht nicht* ill weeds grow apace; '**~vertilgungsmittel** *n* weed-killer.

'**un|kultiviert** uncultivated; *P.*: uncultured; '**~kündbar** *Kapital*: non-callable; *Staatspapier*: irredeemable; *Rente*: perpetual; *Stellung*: permanent; '**~kundig** ignorant (*gen.* of), not knowing (*a th. od. how to do a th.*); *des Englischen ~* having no (command of) English; '**~längst** lately, recently; '**~lauter** impure; *Wettbewerb*: unfair; '**~leidlich** intolerable; '**~lenksam** unmanageable, unruly; '**~leserlich** illegible; **~leugbar** [~'lɔʏkbɑ:r] undeniable; '**~lieb** disagreeable; *es ist mir nicht ~* I am rather glad about it; '**~liebsam** disagreeable; '**~liniiert** unruled; '**~logisch** illogical; '**~lösbar** unsolvable; ⚗ = '**~löslich** insoluble.

'**Unlust** *f* listlessness; (*Abneigung*) dislike (*zu* for); '**⁀ig** listless; (*widerstrebend*) reluctant (*zu* to).

'**unmanierlich** unmannerly.

'**unmännlich** unmanly; '**⁀keit** *f* unmanliness.

'**Unmasse** F *f* enormous (*od.* vast) quantity *od.* number; *a.* host *od.* sea (*gen.* of), F lots (of).

'**unmaßgeblich** not authoritative; *nach meiner ~en Meinung* speaking under correction.

'**unmäßig** immoderate, excessive; inordinate; *bsd. im Trinken*: intemperate; '**⁀keit** *f* immoderateness, excess; intemperance.

'**Unmenge** *f s. Unmasse.*

'**Unmensch** *m* monster, brute; '**⁀lich** inhuman; (*menschenunwürdig*) degrading; (*übermenschlich*) superhuman; F *fig.* awful; '**~lichkeit** *f* inhumanity, brutality.

un|merklich [~'mɛrkliç] imperceptible; '**~methodisch** unmethodical; '**~militärisch** unmilitary; '**~mißverständlich** unmistakable; *adv.* (*offen*) plainly, bluntly; '**~mittelbar** immediate, direct;

'**~möbliert** unfurnished; '**~modern** unfashionable, outmoded.
'**unmöglich** impossible; *adv.* not possibly; '**≈keit** *f* impossibility.
'**unmoralisch** immoral.
unmotiviert ['~motivi:rt] unmotivated.
'**unmündig** under age, minor; **≈e** ['~digə] *m, f* minor; '**≈keit** *f* minority.
'**unmusikalisch** unmusical.
'**Unmut** *m* ill humo(u)r, displeasure (*über acc.* about); '**≈ig** annoyed.
un|nachahmlich ['~na:xʔa:mliç] inimitable; '**~nachgiebig** unyielding; '**~nachsichtig** strict, severe, inexorable; **~nahbar** [~'na:ba:r] inaccessible, unapproachable.
'**unnatürlich** unnatural; '**≈keit** *f* unnaturalness; (*Ziererei*) affectation.
un|'nennbar inexpressible; '**~nötig** unnecessary, needless; **~nütz** ['~nyts] useless; *~es Gerede* idle talk; '**~ordentlich** disorderly; *Kleidung, Zimmer usw.*: untidy; '**≈ordnung** *f* disorder, confusion, mess; *in ~* in a mess; *in ~ bringen* mess up; '**~organisch** inorganic; '**~paar** *Zahl*: not even; *Schuhe usw.*: odd; '**~pädagogisch** unpedagogical.
'**unpartei|isch** impartial, unbias(s)ed; '**≈ische** *m* (18) umpire, referee; '**≈lichkeit** *f* impartiality.
'**unpassend** unsuitable; (*unangebracht*) inappropriate, misplaced; (*unschicklich*) improper.
'**unpassierbar** impassable.
unpäßlich ['~pɛsliç] indisposed, unwell, *pred.* poorly, F out of sorts; '**≈keit** *f* indisposition.
'**un|patriotisch** unpatriotic(ally *adv.*); '**~persönlich** impersonal; '**~pfändbar** unseizable; '**~politisch** non-political; *fig.* impolitic; '**~praktisch** unpractical, *Am.* impractical; '**~produktiv** unproductive; '**~qualifiziert** unqualified; '**~pünktlich** unpunctual; '**≈pünktlichkeit** *f* unpunctuality; '**~rasiert** unshaven; '**≈rat** *m* (3, *o. pl.*) rubbish; (*Schmutz*) filth; *~ wittern* F smell a rat; '**~rationell** inefficient, wasteful; **~rätlich** ['~rɛ:tliç], '**~ratsam** unadvisable.
'**unrecht 1.** wrong; (*ungerecht*) unjust; (*ungeeignet*) improper; (*zur ~en Zeit*) inopportune; *an den ≈en kommen* come to the wrong man, catch a Tartar; *fig. am ~en Orte sein* be out of place; *adv. a. zu ~* wrongly; unjustly; **2. ≈** *n* (3, *o. pl.*) wrong; injustice; *j-m ~ tun* do a p. injustice, wrong a p.; *im ~ sein, ≈ haben* be (in the) wrong; *j-m ~ geben* decide against a p.
'**unrechtmäßig** unlawful, illegal; '**≈keit** *f* unlawfulness, illegality.
'**unredlich** dishonest; '**≈keit** *f* dishonesty.
'**unre-ell** dishonest; (*unlauter*) unfair.
'**unregelmäßig** irregular; '**≈keit** *f* irregularity (*a. Verfehlung*).
'**unreif** unripe; *fig.* immature; '**≈e** *f* (15) unripeness; *fig.* immaturity.
'**unrein** impure (*a. fig.*), unclean; '**≈heit** *f* impurity, uncleanness.
'**unreinlich** uncleanly.
unrentabel ['~rɛnta:bəl] unprofitable.
un'rettbar irrecoverable, *pred.* past recovery; *~ verloren* irretrievably lost; *P.*: past help.
'**unrichtig** incorrect, wrong; '**≈keit** *f* incorrectness.
Unruh ['unru:] *f* (16) *der Uhr*: balance; '**~e** *f* (15) restlessness, (*a. fig. im Volk*) unrest; *fig.* uneasiness; (*Störung*) trouble; (*Besorgnis*) alarm, anxiety; (*Bewegung*) commotion, *stärker*: tumult; *~n pl.* (*Aufruhr*) riots, disturbances; '**~estifter** *m* trouble-maker; '**≈ig** restless; (*zappelig*) *a.* fidgety, nervous; *fig.* uneasy (*über acc.* about); (*besorgt*) worried, alarmed (at); (*lärmend*) turbulent; *Zeiten*: troubled.
'**unrühmlich** inglorious.
uns [uns] us; *nur dat.*: to us; *refl.* (to) ourselves; (*einander*) each other; *s. unter.*
'**un|sachgemäß** improper; inexpert, faulty; '**~sachlich** not objective; (*nicht zur S. gehörig*) irrelevant, not pertinent; *pred. od. adv.* off the point; **~sagbar** [~'za:kba:r], **~säglich** [~'zɛ:kliç] unspeakable; ineffable; untold; '**~sanft** ungentle, harsh; '**~sauber** unclean, dirty; (*unlauter*) unfair; '**≈sauberkeit** *f* uncleanliness; '**~schädlich** harmless; *~ machen* render harmless, *Gift*: neutralize, *Verbrecher*: hunt down; '**~scharf** *Bild*: blurred; *opt. ~ eingestellt* dimly focus(s)ed, *pred.* out of focus; **~'schätzbar** in-

estimable, invaluable; ˈ**~scheinbar** insignificant; (*schlicht*) plain, *bsd. Am.* homely; (*unauffällig*) inconspicuous.

ˈ**unschicklich** unbecoming, unseemly, improper; (*unanständig*) indecent; ˈ**2keit** *f* impropriety, unseemliness; indecency.

unˈ**schlagbar** unbeatable.

unschlüssig [ˈ~ʃlysiç] irresolute; ˈ**2keit** *f* irresolution.

ˈ**unschmackhaft** unpalatable, unsavo(u)ry; insipid.

ˈ**unschön** unlovely, unsightly; *fig.* unkind, not nice.

ˈ**Unschuld** *f* innocence; (*Jungfernschaft*) virginity; F ~ *vom Lande* country cousin; *ich wasche m-e Hände in* ~ I am innocent; **2ig** [ˈ~diç] innocent (*an dat.* of); (*keusch*) *a.* chaste; *für* ~ *erklären* declare innocent; ⚖ *sich für* ~ *erklären* plead not guilty; *den 2en spielen* do the innocent.

ˈ**unschwer** not difficult, easy; *adv.* without difficulty.

ˈ**Unsegen** *m* (*Unglück*) adversity; (*Fluch*) curse.

ˈ**unselbständig** dependent (on others); (*unbeholfen*) helpless, resourceless; (*angestellt*) employed; ˈ**2keit** *f* dependence; helplessness.

ˈ**unselig** unfortunate, fatal.

unser [ˈunzər] **1.** *gen. v. wir*: of us; **2.** *besitzanzeigend*: (20) our; *pred.* ours; *der* ~*e od.* **uns(e)rige** [ˈ~igə] (18b) ours; *die Unsrigen pl.* our people; ˈ**~eins** (such as) we; (*a.* **~esgleichen** [ˈ~əsˈglaiçən]) the likes *pl.* of us.

unsert|halben [ˈ~thalbən], ˈ**~wegen** for our sake, on account of us.

ˈ**unsicher** insecure; *Hand usw.*: unsteady, shaky; (*gefährlich*) unsafe; (*ungewiß*) uncertain, precarious; *Gegend* ~ *machen* haunt, *viele Leute*: infest; ˈ**2heit** *f* insecurity; unsteadiness; unsafeness; uncertainty; ˈ**2heitsfaktor** *m* element of uncertainty.

ˈ**unsichtbar** invisible; ˈ**2keit** *f* invisibility.

ˈ**Unsinn** *m* (3, *o. pl.*) nonsense; *s. a. Quatsch*; ~ *machen od. treiben* fool about (*Am.* around); ˈ**2ig** nonsensical; (*närrisch*) foolish; (*sinnlos, maßlos*) mad.

ˈ**Unsitt|e** *f* bad habit; (*Mißbrauch*) abuse; ˈ**2lich** immoral; indecent; ˈ**~lichkeit** *f* immorality.

ˈ**un|solid(e)** not solid; ✝ unreliable; *Charakter, Lebensweise*: loose, dissipated; ˈ**~sozial** unsocial; ˈ**~sportlich** unsportsmanlike; unfair.

unsr(ig)e [ˈunzr(ig)ə] *s. unser* 2.

ˈ**unstatthaft** inadmissible; *pred. a.* not permissible; (*ungesetzlich*) illicit.

ˈ**unsterblich** immortal; F *adv.* awfully; **2keit** [~ˈʃtɛrp-] *f* immortality.

ˈ**Unstern** *m* unlucky star; *fig.* bad luck, misfortune.

ˈ**unstet** unsteady; (*wankelmütig*) inconstant; (*ruhelos*) restless; (*nicht seßhaft*) vagrant; ˈ**2igkeit** *f* unsteadiness; inconstancy; restlessness; vagrancy.

unˈ**stillbar** unappeasable; *Durst*: unquenchable.

Unstimmigkeit [ˈunʃtimiçkaɪt] *f* discrepancy, inconsistency; (*Meinungsverschiedenheit*) dissension.

ˈ**unstreitig** indisputable.

ˈ**Unsumme** *f* vast sum.

ˈ**unsymmetrisch** asymmetrical.

ˈ**unsympathisch** disagreeable, unpleasant; *er (es) ist mir* ~ I don't like him (it).

ˈ**untadel|haft**, ˈ**~ig** blameless, irreproachable; (*einwandfrei*) flawless.

ˈ**Untat** *f* (monstrous) crime, outrage.

ˈ**untätig** inactive; (*müßig, träg*) idle; ˈ**2keit** *f* inactivity; idleness.

ˈ**untauglich** unfit (*a.* ⚔); (*ungeeignet*) unsuitable; (*nutzlos*) useless; (*unfähig*) incompetent; ~ *machen* disqualify, (make) unfit; ˈ**2keit** *f* unfitness; uselessness; disqualification.

unˈ**teilbar** indivisible.

unten [ˈuntən] below; (*a. nach* ~) *im Hause*: downstairs; ~ *am Berge* at the foot of the hill; (*dort*) ~ *am See* down by the lake; ~ *an der Seite* at the bottom (*od.* foot) of the page; *siehe* ~*!* see below!; ~ *im Wasser, Faß* at the bottom of the water, of the cask; *von oben bis* ~ from top to bottom, from head to foot; F *er ist bei mir* ~ *durch* I am through with him; ˈ**~erwähnt**, ˈ**~genannt** undermentioned.

unter [ˈuntər] **1.** *prp.* under, below; (*zwischen*) among; (*während*) during; ~ ... *hervor* from under ...; ~ *Null* below zero; ~ *21 (Jahren)* under 21 (years of age); *einer* ~

hundert one in a hundred; ~ *anderem* among other things; ~ *uns gesagt* between you and me; *wir sind ganz* ~ uns we are quite alone; ~ *10 Mark* for less than 10 marks; ~ *seiner Regierung* under (*od.* in) his reign; ~ *dem 18. 1. 1984* under the date of ...; ~ *Tränen* with tears in one's eyes; ~ *sich haben* be in charge of; *s. Bedingung, Bezugnahme, Hand, Kritik, Tag, Umstand, verstehen, Vorbehalt, Vorwand, Würde usw.*; **2.** *adj.* (18, *sup.* ~*st*) ~(e) low(er), inferior; ~*ste* lowest; **3.** 𝔖 *m* (7) *Karte*: knave.

'**Unter|-abteilung** *f* subdivision; '**~-arm** *m* forearm; '**~-art** *f* subspecies; '**~-ausschuß** *m* subcommittee; '**~bau** ⊕ *m* (3, *pl.* ~*ten*) foundation (*a. fig.*), substructure, base; '**𝔖belichten** *phot.* under-expose; '**~-belichtung** *f* under-exposure; '**~beschäftigung** *f* underemployment; '**𝔖besetzt** understaffed; '**𝔖bewerten** undervalue, understate; '**𝔖bewußt** subsconscious; '**~bewußtsein** *n the* subconscious; *im* ~ subconsciously.

unter'bieten underbid; ✝ *Preis*: undercut; ✝ *Konkurrenz*: undersell; *Rekord*: lower.

'**Unterbilanz** *f* adverse balance, deficit.

'**unterbinden 1.** tie underneath; **2.** *unter'binden* ⚕ tie up, ligature; *fig.* stop; (*verhindern*) forestall.

unter'bleiben (sn) remain undone; not to take place; (*aufhören*) cease; *das muß* ~ that must be stopped.

unter'brech|en interrupt; break; *Fahrt, Reise*: break, (*v/i.*) stop over; ⚡, *teleph.* disconnect; *sich* ~ *P.*: pause; 𝔖**er** ⚡ *m* interrupter, contact-breaker; 𝔖**ung** *f* interruption, break; ⚡, *teleph.* disconnection; 🚂 ~ *der Fahrt* stop-over.

'**unterbreiten 1.** lay (*od.* spread) under; **2.** *unter'breiten*: *j-m* ~ lay before a p., submit to a p.

'**unterbring|en** place (*a p.*; *a.* ✝ *orders, loans, etc.*); (*beherbergen*) lodge, house, accommodate; (*lagern*) store; ✝ (*verkaufen*) sell; ⊕ install, fit (*in dat.* into); '𝔖**ung** *f* placing; accommodation, housing; '𝔖**ungsmöglichkeit(en** *pl.*) *f* accommodation.

'**Unterdeck** ⚓ *n* lower deck.

unterder'hand *adv.* secretly; ✝ privately.

unter|des [~'dɛs], **~dessen** [~'dɛsən] in the meantime, meanwhile.

'**Unterdruck** *m* low pressure.

unter'drück|en *allg.* suppress (*a. Veröffentlichung*); *Fluch, Lachen usw.*: *a.* stifle; (*bedrücken*) oppress; suppress; *Aufstand*: crush, put down, quell; 𝔖**er** *m* (7) oppressor; 𝔖**ung** *f* suppression; oppression.

'**unter-einander 1.** one beneath the other; **2.** *unterein'ander* one (with) another, among one another, mutually.

'**unter-entwickelt** underdeveloped (*a. phot.*); *Kind, Land usw.*: *a.* backward.

'**unter-ernähr|t** underfed, undernourished; '𝔖**ung** *f* malnutrition.

unter'fangen: *sich e-r S.* (*gen.*) ~ attempt, (dare to) undertake *a th.*; *sich* ~ *zu inf.* presume to *inf.*; 𝔖 *n* (6) (bold) attempt *od.* venture, risky enterprise, undertaking.

unter'fertig|en sign; 𝔖**te** *m, f the* undersigned.

Unter'führung *f* subway, *Am.* underpass.

'**Untergang** *m ast.* setting; *fig.* (*Sturz*) (down)fall, ruin; *der Welt*: end; (*Zerstörung*) destruction; ⚓ (ship)wreck.

'**Untergattung** *f* subspecies.

unter'geben: *j-m* ~ *sein* be under a p.'s authority *od.* control; 𝔖**e** *m, f* (18) inferior, subordinate.

'**untergehen** (sn) ⚓ go down *od.* under (*a. fig.*); sink; *ast.* set; *fig.* perish; be ruined; *im Lärm*: be lost in.

untergeordnet ['~gəˀɔrdnət], '𝔖**e** *m, f* (18) subordinate.

'**Untergeschoß** *n* (*Erdgeschoß*) ground-floor, *Am.* first floor.

'**Untergestell** *n* underframe; (*Sockel*) base; *am Wagen*: undercarriage.

'**Untergewicht** *n* underweight.

unter'graben sap, undermine.

'**Untergrund** *m* subsoil; (*Fundament*) foundation; *paint.* ground; *pol. usw.*: underground; '**~bahn** *f* underground (railway), *in London mst* tube, *Am.* subway; '**~bewegung** *f* underground movement; '**~-kämpfer** *m* underground fighter.

'**unterhalb** (*gen.*) below, under (-neath).

'**Unterhalt** *m* (3, *o. pl.*) support;

maintenance, upkeep; (*Lebens*≈) subsistence, livelihood, living.

unter'halt|en *allg.* maintain; (*unterstützen*) support; *Feuer*: feed; (*in Betrieb haben*) operate, have; *Briefwechsel*: keep up, have; (*die Zeit verkürzen*) entertain; (*vergnügen*) amuse; *sich* ~ (*ein Gespräch führen*) converse, talk, (*sich vergnügen*) amuse (*od.* enjoy) o.s.; **~end, ~sam** entertaining, amusing; **≈er** *m* conversationalist; *thea.* entertainer; **'≈s-anspruch** *m* right (*od.* claim) to alimony; **'≈sbeihilfe** *f* subsistence allowance; **'≈skosten** *pl.* maintenance costs; *für Ehepartner u. Kinder*: alimony *sg.*; **'≈s-pflicht** *f* liability to maintain; **'≈s-zahlung** *f* alimony; **≈ung** [~'haltuŋ] *f* (*Vergnügen*) entertainment; (*Gespräch*) conversation, talk; (*Aufrechterhaltung*) maintenance, upkeep; **≈ungs-elektronik** *f* (*Computerspiele*) electronic games; (*Video, Stereo etc.*) video and audio systems *pl.*; **≈ungsfilm** *m* feature film; **≈ungs-industrie** *f* entertainment industry; **≈ungskosten** *pl.* (cost of) upkeep *sg.*; **≈ungslektüre** *f*, **≈ungs-literatur** *f* light reading, fiction; **≈ungsmusik** *f* light music; **≈ungs-programm** *n Radio*: light program(me).

unter'handeln negotiate; ⚔ parley.

'Unterhändler *m* negotiator; ✝ agent; ⚔ parlementaire (*fr.*).

Unter'handlung *f* negotiation; *in ~ stehen* (*treten*) *mit* negotiate (enter into negotiations) with.

'Unterhaus *parl. n* Lower House; *Brt.* House of Commons.

'Unterhemd *n* vest, *Am.* undershirt.

unter'höhlen undermine (*a. fig.*).

'Unterholz *n* underwood, undergrowth, *Am.* underbrush.

'Unterhose(n *pl.*) *f* drawers *pl.*; (*Männer*≈) underpants *pl.*; *lange* ~ F longjohns *pl.*; *s. Schlüpfer*.

'unter-irdisch subterranean, underground.

unterjoch|en [~'jɔxən] (25) subdue, subjugate; **≈ung** *f* subjugation.

unter'kellern provide with a cellar.

'Unter|kiefer *m* lower jaw; **'~kleid** *n* undergarment; *mit Trägern*: slip; **'~kleidung** *f* underwear; **'≈kommen**[1] (sn) find accommodation *od.* (*Anstellung*) employment; **'~kommen**[2] *n* (6) *s. Unterkunft*; (*Anstellung*) place, situation; **'≈kriegen** F bring *a p.* down *od.* to heel; *er läßt sich nicht* ~ he won't give in; **~'kühlung** *f* undercooling; ⚕ hypothermia; **~kunft** ['~kunft] *f* (15) accommodation, lodging(s *pl.*); ⚔ quarters *pl.*; **'~lage** *f* foundation (*a. fig.*); ⊕ base, support; *geol.* substratum; (*Schreib*≈) writing- (*od.* blotting-) pad; (*Beleg*) voucher, proof; *fig.* ~*n pl.* (*Akten*) (supporting) documents, records, material *sg.*, (*Angaben*) data *pl.*; **~lagscheibe** ⊕ ['~lɑːk-] *f* washer; **'~land** *n* lowland, low country; **~laß** ['~las] *m*: *ohne* ~ without intermission, incessantly.

unter'lass|en omit; (*versäumen*) fail (*to do*); *aus Schonung*: forbear; (*sich enthalten*) abstain from; (*aufhören mit*) stop; **≈ung** *f* omission; **≈ungs-sünde** *f* sin of omission, lapse; **≈ungs-urteil** ⚖ *n* restraining order.

'Unterlauf *m* lower course.

unter'laufen 1. (sn) *Fehler usw.*: creep in; *mir ist ein Fehler* ~ I made a mistake; **2.** *p.p. u. adj. mit Blut* ~ bloodshot.

'unterlegen 1. lay (*od.* put) under; *e-n Sinn*: give; **2.** *unter'legen v/t.* underlay; *adj.* inferior (*dat.* to).

Unter'legen|e *m, f* (18[1]) loser; **~heit** *f* inferiority.

'Unterlegscheibe ⊕ ['~leːk-] *f* washer.

'Unterleib *m* abdomen, belly; **'~s...** abdominal; **'~skrebs** *m* cancer of the womb; **'~sschmerzen** *m/pl.* abdominal pains.

unter'liegen (sn) be defeated (*dat.* by; *a. Sport* = lose [to]); succumb; *fig.* be subject to; (*verpflichtet sein*) be liable to; (*zugrunde liegen*) underlie; *es unterliegt keinem Zweifel* there is no doubt about it.

'Unterlippe *f* lower lip.

unter'mal|en *musikalisch*: accompany; **≈ung** *f musikalisch*: background music; *zur ~ dienen* act as a background.

unter'mauern underpin; *fig.* bolster, corroborate.

unter|'mengen, ~'mischen mix.

'Untermensch *m* subman, subhuman creature; *weitS.* brute.

'Untermieter(in *f*) *m* subtenant, lodger, *Am. a.* roomer.

untermi'nieren undermine (*a. fig.*).

unter'nehm|en 1. undertake; (*ver-*

suchen) attempt; *s. Schritt*; **2.** ♀ *n s. Unternehmung*; (*Geschäft*) firm, business, enterprise, company; ⚔ operation; **~end** enterprising; **♀ens-berater** *m* management consultant; **♀ensführung** *f* management; **♀er** *m* (7) enterpreneur (*fr.*); *vertraglicher*: contractor; (*Arbeitgeber*) employer; *weitS.* industrialist; **♀ertum** *n the* industrialists *pl.*, *the* employers *pl.*; *freies* ~ free enterprise; **♀ung** *f* enterprise, undertaking; venture; project; ⚔ operation; **♀ungsgeist** *m* (spirit of) enterprise; **~ungslustig** enterprising; (*verwegen*) adventurous.

'Unter|-offizier *m* non-commissioned officer (*abbr.* NCO); *Dienstgrad*: corporal; **'♀-ordnen** subordinate; *sich* ~ (*dat.*) submit (to); **'~-ordnung** *f* subordination; *biol.* suborder; **'~pfand** *n* pledge.

unter'red|en: *sich* ~ converse, confer; **♀ung** *f* conversation; conference, talk; interview.

Unterricht ['~riçt] *m* (3) instruction; (*Stunden*) lessons *pl.*; *Schule*: classes *pl.*; (*Einzel*♀) tuition.

unter'richten instruct, teach, give lessons; *fig.* inform (*von, über acc.* about).

'Unterrichts|briefe *m/pl.* correspondence-lessons; *Lehrgang in* ~*n* correspondence course; **'~fach** *n*, **'~gegenstand** *m* subject of instruction; **'~film** *m* educational film; **'~plan** *m* syllabus; **'~stunde** *f* lesson, *Am.* period.

Unter'richtung *f* information.

'Unterrock *m* (*mst Halbrock*) petticoat; *mit Trägern*: slip.

unter'sagen forbid (et. a th.; *j-m* et. a p. to do a th.), prohibit (a th.; a p. from doing a th.).

'Untersatz *m* support; (*Gestell*) stand; ⚠ socle; *für Töpfe*: saucer.

'Unterschall... subsonic.

unter'schätz|en underestimate, underrate; **♀ung** *f* undervaluation; underestimate.

unterscheid|bar [~'ʃaɪtbɑːr] distinguishable; discernible; **~en** [~dən] *v/t. u. v/i.* distinguish; *scharfsinnig*: discriminate; (*deutlich wahrnehmen*) discern; *sich* ~ differ; **♀ung** *f* distinction; differentiation; discrimination; **♀ungsmerkmal** *n* distinctive mark; (*a.* ⊕) characteristic; **♀ungsvermögen** *n* power of distinction.

'Unterschenkel *m* shank, lower leg.

'unterschieb|en 1. push under; **2.** *a. unter'schieben als Ersatz*: substitute; *fig.* attribute falsely (*dat.* to), impute (to); **'♀ung** *f* [*a.* ~'ʃiːbuŋ] *f* substitution.

Unterschied ['~ʃiːt] *m* (3) difference, distinction; *zum* ~ *von* ... unlike ..., in contrast to; *ohne* ~ indiscriminately; **'♀lich** different; (*schwankend*) varying; **'♀slos** indiscriminate; undiscriminating.

'unterschlagen cross *one's arms*.

unter'schlag|en *Geld*: embezzle; *Brief*: intercept; *Testament usw.*: suppress; *fig.* (*verheimlichen*) hold back; **♀ung** *f* embezzlement; interception; suppression.

Unterschleif ['~ʃlaɪf] *m* (3) embezzlement.

Unterschlupf ['~ʃlupf] *m* (3[3]) (*Schlupfwinkel*) hiding-place; (*Obdach*) shelter, refuge; *j-m* ~ *gewähren* give a p. shelter, *e-m Verbrecher etc.*: *a.* harbo(u)r a p.

unter'schreiben sign; subscribe (*fig.* to).

unter'schreiten fall short of.

'Unterschrift *f* signature; *s. setzen*; **'~enmappe** *f* signature blotting-book; **'~sstempel** *m* signature stamp.

unterschwellig ['~ʃvɛliç] *psych.* subliminal.

Unterseeboot ['~zeːboːt] *n* submarine (boat); *deutsches*: *a.* U-Boat; **'~krieg** *m* submarine warfare.

unterseeisch ['~zeːiʃ] submarine.

'Unterseite *f* underside, bottom side.

'untersetzen place (*od.* put) under.

unter'setzt stocky, squat.

'untersinken (sn) sink (under).

unter'spülen wash away, hollow out (from below).

unterst ['untərst] lowest, undermost, lowermost, bottommost.

'Unterstand *m* shelter; ⚔ dug-out.

unter'stehen 1. *v/i.*: *j-m* ~ be subordinate to; *j-s Aufsicht* (*od. j-m*) ~ be under a p.'s control; *e-m Gesetz usw.*: be subject to; **2.** *v/refl. sich* ~ (*zu inf.*) dare (to *inf.*); **3.** *'unterstehen v/i.* take shelter.

'unterstell|en 1. place (*od.* put) under; *mot.* garage, park; *sich* ~ *zum Schutz* take shelter; **2.** *unter-*

ˈ*stellen* (*zuschreiben*) impute (*dat.* to); (*vorläufig annehmen*) (pre)suppose, assume; *Truppen usw.*: *j-m* ~ place under a p.'s command *od.* control; ♀**ung** *f zu* 2. imputation.

unterˈstreichen underline (*a. fig.*).

ˈ**Unterstufe** *f* lower grade.

unter|ˈstützen prop, support; *fig.* support, back (up); *beistimmend*: *a.* second; (*helfen*) assist; *Arme*: relieve; ♀ˈ**stützung** *f* support (*a.* ⚔); *fig. a.* aid, assistance; (*Beihilfe durch Geld usw.*) relief; (*staatliche Geld*♀) subsidy; **~ˈsuchen** inquire (*od.* look) into; (*prüfen*) examine (*a.* ⚕); (*erforschen*) explore; *wissenschaftlich u.* ⚖: investigate; ⚗ *u. weitS.* analy|se, *Am.* -ze.

Unterˈsuchung *f* inquiry; examination (*a.* ⚕); investigation (*a.* ⚖); ⚗ analysis (*a. weitS.*); **~s-ausschuß** *m* investigating (*od.* fact-finding) committee; **~sgefangene** *m, f* prisoner at the bar *od.* on trial *od.* on remand; **~shaft** *f* imprisonment on remand, detention pending trial; *die* ~ *anrechnen* compensate the detention; *in* ~ *sein* be on remand; **~srichter** *m* examining magistrate, investigating judge.

Untertagebau [~ˈtɑːgə-] ⚒ *m* underground mining.

Untertan [ˈ~tɑːn] *m* (8) subject; *j-m* ♀ *sein* be subject to a p.

untertänig [ˈ~tɛːniç] subject (*dat.* to); *fig.* submissive, humble; ˈ♀**keit** *f fig.* submission, humility.

ˈ**Untertasse** *f* saucer.

ˈ**untertauchen** *v/i.* (sn) dive, *U-Boot*: submerge, (*a. v/t.*) duck, dip, immerse; *fig. Verbrecher usw.*: go underground, go into hiding.

ˈ**Unterteil** *m, n* lower part; base; ♀**en** [~ˈtaɪlən] subdivide; **~ung** [~ˈtaɪluŋ] *f* subdivision.

ˈ**Untertitel** *m e-s Buches*: subtitle (*a. Film*); *Film, Zeitung*: caption.

ˈ**Unterton** *m* undertone.

Unterˈtreibung *f* understatement.

unterˈtunneln tunnel.

ˈ**untervermieten** sublet.

unterˈwander|n infiltrate; ♀**ung** *f* infiltration.

ˈ**Unterwäsche** *f* underwear.

Unterˈwasser... underwater (*camera, etc.*).

unterwegs [~ˈveːks] on the way, en route (*fr.*) (*nach* for); † in transit.

unterˈweis|en instruct; ♀**ung** *f* instruction.

ˈ**Unterwelt** *f* underworld (*a. fig. Verbrecherwelt*), lower world.

unterˈwerf|en subdue, subjugate; *e-r Herrschaft, e-m Verhör usw.*: subject (*dat.* to); *sich* ~ submit (*dat.* to; *a. fig.*); ♀**ung** *f* subjugation, subjection; *fig.* submission (*unter acc.* to).

unterworfen [~ˈvɔrfən]: *e-r Sache* ~ *sein* be subject to.

unterˈwühlen undermine.

unterwürfig [~ˈvyrfiç] submissive, servile; ♀**keit** *f* submissiveness.

unterˈzeichn|en sign; ♀**er** *m* (7) signer; *e-r Anleihe, Resolution usw.*: subscriber; *e-s Staatsvertrags*: signatory; ♀**ete** *m* (18) undersigned; ♀**ung** *f* signing, signature; *pol.* ratification.

ˈ**Unterzeug** *n* underwear.

ˈ**unterziehen**[1] put on underneath.

unterˈziehen[2] *v/t.* (*dat.*) subject to; *sich e-r Operation usw.* ~ undergo, *e-r Prüfung*: go in for, *e-r Mühe*: take *the trouble*.

ˈ**untief** shallow; ˈ♀**e** *f* shallow, shoal.

ˈ**Untier** *n* monster.

unˈtilgbar indelible; *Anleihe*: irredeemable.

unˈtragbar unbearable, intolerable.

unˈtrennbar inseparable.

ˈ**untreu** unfaithful, disloyal, *bsd. in der Ehe*: untrue (*alle*: *dat.* to); ˈ♀**e** *f* unfaithfulness; disloyalty; infidelity; ⚖ breach of trust.

unˈtröstlich inconsolable, disconsolate.

untrüglich [~ˈtryːkliç] infallible, unfailing; ♀**keit** *f* infallibility.

ˈ**untüchtig** unfit, incapable (*zu* for); incompetent, inefficient.

ˈ**Untugend** *f* vice, bad habit.

un-über|ˈbrückbar unbridgeable; **~legt** [ˈ~ˀyːbərleːkt] ill-considered, unwise; (*übereilt*) rash; **~ˈsehbar** immense, vast, huge; *s. a. unabsehbar*; **~ˈsetzbar** untranslatable; ˈ**~sichtlich** *Anordnung*: badly arranged; difficult to survey; (*verwickelt*) complex, involved; *Kurve*: blind; **~steigbar** [~ˈʃtaɪkbɑːr] insurmountable; **~ˈtrefflich** unsurpassable, matchless; **~windlich** [~ˈvintliç] invincible; *Schwierigkeit*: insurmountable, (*a. Abneigung*) insuperable.

un-um|ˈgänglich unavoidable; ~ (*notwendig*) indispensable, absolutely necessary; **~schränkt** [~umˈʃrɛŋkt] unlimited; *pol.* absolute; autocratic(ally *adv.*); **~stößlich** [~ˈʃtøːsliç] irrefutable; (*unwiderruflich*) irrevocable; **~stritten** [~ˈʃtritən] undisputed, indisputable; **~wunden** [ˈ~vundən] frank(ly *adv.*), plain(ly).

ununterbrochen [ˈ~ˀuntərbrɔxən] uninterrupted, unbroken; (*unaufhörlich*) incessant, continuous.

unver|änderlich [~fɛrˈˀɛndərliç] unchangeable, invariable; **ˈ~-ändert** unchanged; **~ˈ-antwortlich** irresponsible; (*unentschuldbar*) inexcusable; **2ˈ-antwortlichkeit** *f* irresponsibility; **~ˈ-äußerlich** inalienable; **~ˈbesserlich** incorrigible; **~bindlich** [ˈ~fɛrbintliç] not obligatory, *adv.* without obligation; (*zwanglos*) informal; (*unfreundlich*) disobliging; non-committal; **~blümt** [~ˈblyːmt] plain, blunt; **ˈ~braucht** unused; unspent; (*frisch*) fresh; **ˈ~brennbar** incombustible; **~brüchlich** [~ˈbryçliç] inviolable, absolute; *Treue usw.*: unswerving; **~bürgt** [~ˈbyrkt] unwarranted; *Nachricht*: unconfirmed; **ˈ~dächtig** unsuspected; **~daulich** [ˈ~dauliç] indigestible (*a. fig.*); **ˈ2daulichkeit** *f* indigestibility; **ˈ~daut** undigested; **~derbt** [ˈ~dɛrpt], **~dorben** [ˈ~dɔrbən] unspoilt (*a. fig.*); *bsd. fig.* uncorrupted; (*rein*) pure; **ˈ~dient** undeserved; **ˈ~dienterˈmaßen** undeservedly; **ˈ~drossen** indefatigable; (*geduldig*) patient; **ˈ2drossenheit** *f* indefatigability; **ˈ~dünnt** undiluted; **ˈ~-ehelicht** unmarried, single; **ˈ~-eidigt** unsworn; **~ˈ-einbar** incompatible; **ˈ~fälscht** unadulterated, pure; *fig. a.* genuine; **~fänglich** [ˈ~fɛŋliç] harmless; **~froren** [ˈ~froːrən] brazen, impertinent; **ˈ2frorenheit** *f* impertinence, impudence, F cheek; **~gänglich** [ˈ~gɛŋliç] everlasting; immortal; **ˈ~gessen** unforgotten; **~geßlich** [~ˈgɛsliç] unforgettable; **~ˈgleichlich** incomparable; **ˈ~hältnismäßig** disproportionate; **ˈ~heiratet** unmarried, single; **ˈ~hofft** unhoped-for, unexpected; **ˈ~hohlen** unconcealed, open; **ˈ~hüllt** unveiled (*a. fig.*); *fig. s. a.* *unverhohlen*; **ˈ~jährbar** *Recht*: imprescriptible; *Tat*: not subject to the statute of limitations; **ˈ~käuflich** unsal(e)able; (*nicht feil*) not for sale; **ˈ~kauft** unsold; **~ˈkennbar** unmistakable; **ˈ~kürzt** uncurtailed; *Text*: unabridged; *adv.* in full; **~letzbar** [~ˈlɛtsbaːr] invulnerable, (*a. fig.*) inviolable; **ˈ~letzt** uninjured, unhurt; **~ˈlierbar** *fig.* eternal; **ˈ~mählt** unmarried; **~meidlich** [~ˈmaɪtliç] inevitable, unavoidable; *sich ins 2 fügen* bow to the inevitable; **ˈ~mindert** undiminished; **ˈ~mischt** unmixed; **ˈ~mittelt** abrupt.

ˈUnvermögen *n* inability, incapacity; impotence; **ˈ2d** unable (*zu* to), incapable (*zu* of); (*kraftlos*) impotent; (*arm*) impecunious.

ˈunvermutet unexpected(ly *adv.*).

ˈunvernehmlich inaudible.

ˈUnver|nunft *f* lack of reason, unreasonableness; absurdity; **ˈ2nünftig** irrational, unreasonable; absurd.

ˈunver-öffentlicht unpublished.

ˈunverrichtet unperformed; **ˈ~erˈdinge, ˈ~erˈsache** without having achieved one's object, unsuccessfully.

ˈunverschämt impudent, impertinent, shameless; F *Preis, Forderung*: exorbitant; **ˈ2heit** *f* impudence, impertinence, insolence; *die ~ haben zu ...* have the face to ...

ˈunver|schnitten *Getränk*: unadulterated; **ˈ~schuldet** undeserved; (*schuldenfrei*) not in debt; *Grundstück*: unencumbered; **ˈ~sehens** unexpectedly, unawares; **ˈ~sehrt** uninjured, intact; **ˈ~sichert** uninsured; **~siegbar** [~ˈziːkbaːr] inexhaustible; **ˈ~siegelt** unsealed; **ˈ~söhnlich** implacable, irreconcilable; *pol.* intransigent; **ˈ2söhnlichkeit** *f* implacability; *pol.* intransigence; **~sorgt** [ˈ~zɔrkt] unprovided for.

ˈUnverstand *m* lack of judgment, injudiciousness; (*Torheit*) folly.

ˈunver|ständig injudicious, imprudent, foolish; **ˈ~ständlich** unintelligible; **~sucht** [ˈ~zuːxt] untried; *nichts ~ lassen* leave nothing undone, leave no stone unturned (*um zu* to); **ˈ~träglich** quarrelsome; *fig. ~ mit* incompatible with; **ˈ2träglichkeit** *f* unsociableness; incompatibility; **~wandt** [ˈ~vant] *Blick*: fixed, (*a. Bemühungen usw.*) steadfast; **ˈ~wehrt:** *es ist Ihnen ~ zu* you are at liberty to ...; **~weilt** ['~vaılt] without delay; **~welklich** ['~vɛlkliç] unfading; **'~wendbar** unusable; **~wundbar** [~'vuntbɑ:r] invulnerable; **~wüstlich** [~'vy:stliç] indestructible; *fig. Humor usw.*: irrepressible; **~zagt** ['~tsɑ:kt] intrepid, undaunted; **~zeihlich** [~'tsaıliç] unpardonable; **'~zichtbar** *Recht etc.*: inalienable; **~zinslich** [~'tsinsliç] bearing no interest; *~e Wertpapiere* non-interest-bearing securities; *~es Darlehen* free loan; **~züglich** [~'tsy:kliç] immediate; *adv. a.* without delay.

'unvoll-endet unfinished.

'unvollkommen imperfect; **'2heit** *f* imperfection. [*f* incompleteness.]

'unvollständig incomplete; **'2keit**

'unvorbereitet unprepared; *adv. u. adj. Rede usw.*: extempore.

unvordenklich ['~fo:rdɛŋkliç]: *seit ~en Zeiten* from time immemorial.

'unvor-eingenommen unbias(s)ed, unprejudiced.

unvorhergesehen ['unfo:rhe:rgəze:ən] unforeseen.

'unvorschriftsmäßig *adj.* irregular; (*a.* ⊕ *unsachgemäß*) improper; *adv.* contrary to regulations.

'unvorsichtig incautious; (*unklug*) imprudent; (*übereilt*) rash; (*sorglos*) careless; **'2keit** *f* incautiousness; imprudence; carelessness.

'unvorteilhaft unprofitable; *Kleid usw.*: unbecoming.

un'wägbar imponderable.

'unwahr untrue; **'~haftig** untruthful; **'2heit** *f* untruth.

'unwahrscheinlich improbable, unlikely; F *fig.* incredible, fantastic; **'2keit** *f* improbability.

un'wandelbar unchangeable.

unwegsam ['~ve:kzɑ:m] impassable.

'unweiblich unwomanly.

unweigerlich [~'vaıgərliç] unquestionable; *adv.* inevitably; *ich muß ~ tun* I cannot help doing.

'unweise unwise, imprudent.

'unweit *adv.* not far (off); *prp.* (*gen. od. von*) not far from.

'unwert 1. unworthy (*gen.* of); **2. 2** *m* unworthiness.

'Unwesen *n* nuisance; excesses *pl.*; *sein ~ treiben* do one's foul work, F be up to one's tricks; **'2tlich** unessential, immaterial (*für* to); unimportant (*a.* = *geringfügig* negligible).

'Unwetter *n* bad (*od.* stormy) weather; (*Gewitter*) (thunder)storm.

'unwichtig unimportant, insignificant; **'2keit** *f* insignificance.

unwider'leg|bar, ~lich irrefutable; **2barkeit** *f* irrefutability.

unwider'ruflich irrevocable, beyond recall.

unwider'stehlich irresistible; **2keit** *f* irresistibility.

unwieder'bringlich irretrievable.

'Unwill|e *m s. unwillig*: indignation, displeasure, anger; unwillingness; **'2ig** (*ungehalten*) indignant, displeased; (*ärgerlich*) annoyed, angry (*alle*: *über acc.* at); (*widerstrebend*) unwilling; **'2kommen** unwelcome; **'2kürlich** involuntary; instinctive, automatic(ally *adv.*).

'unwirklich unreal.

'unwirksam ineffective, inoperative; ⚗ inactive; **'2keit** *f* inefficacy; inoperativeness; ⚗ inactivity.

unwirsch ['unvirʃ] cross, testy.

'unwirt|lich inhospitable; **'~schaftlich** uneconomic(al); unthrifty; (*unrationell*) inefficient.

'unwissen|d ignorant; **'2heit** *f* ignorance; **'~schaftlich** unscientific(ally *adv.*); **'~tlich** unwitting.

'unwohl unwell (*a. Frau*), indisposed; **'2sein** *n* (6, *o. pl.*) indisposition.

'unwohnlich uncomfortable.

'unwürdig unworthy (*gen.* of); *s. würdelos*; **'2keit** *f* unworthiness.

'Unzahl *f* immense number.

unzählbar, unzählig [~'tsɛ:lbɑ:r, ~'tsɛ:liç] innumerable.

'unzart indelicate; (*rauh*) rough.

Unze ['untsə] *f* (15) ounce.

'Unzeit *f*: *zur ~* at the wrong time, inopportunely; **'2gemäß** unseasonable; (*altmodisch*) old-fashioned; **'2ig** untimely (*a. adv.*), unseasonable; (*ungelegen*) ill-timed.

unzer|'brechlich unbreakable; **~'reißbar** untearable; **~'störbar** indestructible; **~'trennlich** inseparable. [seemly; indecent.]

'unziemend, 'unziemlich un-

'unzivilisiert uncivilized.

'Unzucht *f* lewdness; ⚖ sexual offen|ce, *Am.* -se; (act of) indecency; *außereheliche*: fornication; *gewerbsmäßige*: prostitution. [scene.]

'unzüchtig lewd; indecent; ob-

'**unzufrieden** discontented, dissatisfied, displeased; '**ⴰheit** *f* discontent, dissatisfaction.

'**unzugänglich** inaccessible.

'**unzulänglich** insufficient, inadequate; '**ⴰkeit** *f* insufficiency, inadequacy, deficiency, shortcoming.

'**unzulässig** inadmissible.

'**unzumutbar** unreasonable, unacceptable.

'**unzurechnungsfähig** irresponsible; (*geisteskrank*) insane, ⚖ *a.* non compos (mentis); '**ⴰkeit** *f* irresponsibility; insanity.

'**unzureichend** insufficient.

'**unzusammenhängend** disconnected, incoherent.

'**unzuständig** incompetent, ⚖ *a.* having no jurisdiction; '**ⴰkeit** *f* incompetence.

'**unzuträglich** disadvantageous, prejudicial (*dat.* to), not good (for); (*ungesund*) unwholesome; '**ⴰkeit** *f* unwholesomeness.

'**unzutreffend** incorrect; (*nicht anwendbar*) inapplicable.

'**unzuverlässig** unreliable; (*unsicher*) uncertain; *Eis, Gedächtnis, Wetter*: treacherous; '**ⴰkeit** *f* untrustworthiness; uncertainty; treacherousness.

'**unzweckmäßig** inexpedient, unsuitable; '**ⴰkeit** *f* inexpediency, unsuitableness.

'**unzweideutig** unequivocal, unambiguous.

'**unzweifelhaft** undoubted, indubitable; *adv.* doubtless, without doubt.

üppig ['ypiç] luxurious; ⚘, *Sprache, Gesundheit usw.*: luxuriant, exuberant; *Mahl*: opulent; *Gras, a. Figur, Frau usw.*: lush; (*sinnlich*) voluptuous; (*übermütig*) cocky; (*großzügig*) generous; '**ⴰkeit** *f* luxury; exuberance; opulence; voluptuousness; presumption.

Ur [u:r] *m* (3) aurochs.

Ur... ['u:r-] (*ursprünglich*) original; (*Kern...*) thorough; *als adv. bei adj., z.B. urkomisch*: extremely; '**~-abstimmung** *f* strike ballot; '**~-ahn** *m* great-grandfather; *weitS.* ancestor; '**~-ahne** *f* great-grandmother; *weitS.* ancestress; '**ⴰ-alt** very old, ancient. F old as the hills; '**~-anfang** *m* first beginning; '**ⴰ-anfänglich** original, primeval; '**~-aufführung** *f* first night *od.* performance; *Film*: (world) première.

Uran ⚗ [u'ra:n] *n* (3[1]) uranium; **~brenner** *m* uranium pile; **ⴰhaltig** uraniferous.

urbar ['u:rba:r] arable, cultivated; ~ *machen* cultivate, reclaim; '**ⴰmachung** *f* cultivation; reclamation.

'**Ur|bewohner**, '**~-einwohner** *m/pl.* aborigines; '**~bild** *n* original, prototype; '**ⴰ-eigen** *one's* very own; innate; '**~-eltern** *pl.* ancestors; '**~-enkel** *m* great-grandson; '**~-enkelin** *f* great-granddaughter; '**~form** *f* original form; '**~gebirge** *n* primitive mountains *od.* rocks *pl.*; '**~geschichte** *f* early history; '**ⴰgeschichtlich** prehistoric; '**~großeltern** *pl.* great-grandparents; '**~großmutter** *f* great-grandmother; '**~großvater** *m* great-grandfather.

'**Urheber** *m* author; '**~recht** *n* copyright; '**~schaft** *f* authorship.

Urin [u'ri:n] *m* (3[1]) urine; **ⴰieren** [~ri'ni:rən] urinate; **~-untersuchung** *f* urinalysis.

'**Urknall** *phys. m* big bang.

'**ur'komisch** extremely funny.

'**Ur|kunde** *f* document, deed; (*Protokollⴰ*) record; (*Zeugnis*) diploma; '**~kundenfälschung** *f* forgery of documents; **ⴰkundlich** ['~kuntliç] documentary; (*verbürgt*) authentic (-ally *adv.*); ~ *belegt* documented; '**~kundsbe-amte** *m* Clerk of the Court, registrar; **~laub** ['~laup] *m* (3) leave (of absence); (*Ferien*) vacation, holidays *pl.*; *bsd.* ⚔ furlough; *auf* ~ on vacation, (*a.* ⚔) on leave; **~lauber** ['~laubər] *m* (7) ⚔ man on leave; *Zivilist*: holiday-maker, *Am.* vacationist; '**~lauberverkehr** *m* holiday traffic; '**~laubsanspruch** *m* leave entitlement, *Am.* leave credit; '**~laubsgeld** *n* holiday (*Am.* leave) pay; '**~mensch** *m* primitive man.

Urne ['urnə] *f* (11) urn; (*Wahlⴰ*) ballot-box.

Ur|ochs ['u:rˀɔks] *m* aurochs; 'ⴰ-'**plötzlich** very sudden, abrupt; *adv.* all of a sudden; '**~quell** *m* primary source; '**~sache** *f* cause; (*Anlaß*) occasion; (*Grund*) reason; (*Beweggrund*) motive; *keine* ~! don't mention it!, (you are) welcome!; '**ⴰsächlich** causal; '**~schrift** *f* original (text); '**ⴰschrift-**

lich (*adv.* in the) original; '~**sprache** *f* primitive language; *e-r Übersetzung*: original (language); '~**sprung** *m* source; *fig.* origin; *s-n ~ haben in (dat.)* originate in *od.* from; ♀**sprünglich** ['~ʃpryŋliç] original (*a. fig.*); '~**sprungsland** *n* country of origin; '~**sprungszeugnis** *n* certificate of origin; '~**stoff** *m* primary matter; ⚗ *usw.* element.

Urteil ['urtaɪl] *n* (3) judg(e)ment; (*Ansicht*) opinion; (*Entscheidung*) decision; ⚖ judg(e)ment, (*Strafmaß*) sentence; (~ *der Geschworenen*) verdict; (*Scheidungs*♀) decree; *meinem ~ nach* in my judg(e)ment; *sich ein ~ bilden über (acc.)* form (a) judg(e)ment of *od.* on; *das ~ sprechen (über acc.)* pronounce (*od.* pass) judg(e)ment (on); '♀**en** (25) judge (*über* [of] *a p. od. a th.*; *nach* by *od.* from); *anders darüber ~* take a different view (of it); *nach ... zu ~* judging by ...

'**Urteils**|-**er-öffnung** *f* publication of the judg(e)ment; '♀**fähig** discerning, discriminating; '~**kraft** *f* (power of) judg(e)ment; '~**spruch** *m s. Urteil*; '~**vollstreckung** *f* execution of the sentence.

Ur|**text** ['u:r-] *m* original (text); ♀**tümlich** ['~ty:mliç] original, native; '~-**urgroßvater** *m* great-great-grandfather; '~**väterzeit** *f* olden times *pl.*; '~**volk** *n* primitive people; *s. a. Urbewohner*; '~**wald** *m* primeval (*od.* virgin) forest; jungle; '~**welt** *f* primeval world; '♀**weltlich** primeval, antediluvian; ♀**wüchsig** ['~vy:ksiç] original, native; *Humor, Person*: earthy; '~**zeit** *f* primitive times *pl.*; *fig. vor ~en* ages ago; *seit ~en* for ages; '~**zustand** *m* primitive state.

Usur|**pator** [uzur'pɑ:tɔr] *m* usurper; ♀'**pieren** usurp.

Utensilien [utɛn'zi:ljən] *pl.* utensils.

Utop|**ie** [uto'pi:] *f* (16) Utopia(n idea), chimera; ~**ien** [u'to:pjən] *n* Utopia; ♀**isch**, ~**ist** *m* (12), ~**istin** [uto'pist(in)] *f* (16[1]) Utopian.

uzen F ['u:tsən] (27) tease, chaff.

V

V [faʊ], **v** *n inv.* V, v.

Vagabund [vaga'bunt] *m* (12) vagabond, vagrant, tramp; *Am.* F hobo, bum; ♀**ieren** [~'di:rən] tramp about, vagabondize; ⚡ stray.

vakan|**t** [va'kant] vacant; ♀**z** *f* (16) vacancy.

Vakuum *phys.* ['vɑ:kuum] *n* (9[2]) vacuum; '~**bremse** *f* vacuum brake; '~**pumpe** *f* vacuum pump; '♀**verpackt** vacuum-packed.

Valuta [va'lu:ta] *f* (16[2]) (*Wert*) value; (*Währung*) currency; (*Devisen*) foreign exchange; (*Gelder*) monies *pl.*

Vampir ['vampi:r] *m* (3[1]) vampire.

Vandal|**e** [van'dɑ:lə] *m* (13), ♀**isch** *fig.* Vandal; ~**ismus** [~da'lismus] *m* (16) vandalism.

Vanille [va'niljə] *f* (15) vanilla.

varia|**bel** [vari'ɑ:bəl] variable; ♀**nte** [~'antə] *f* (15) variant; *weitS. a.* version; ♀**tion** [~a'tsjo:n] *f* (16) variation.

Varietät [varie'tɛ:t] *f* (16) variety.

Varieté [varie'te:] *n*, ~**theater** *n* variety theatre, music-hall, *Am.* vaudeville theater; ~**vorstellung** *f* variety show, *Am.* vaudeville.

variieren [vari'ʔi:rən] *v/i. u. v/t.* vary.

Vasall [va'zal] *m* (12) vassal; ~**enstaat** *m* satellite state.

Vase ['vɑ:zə] *f* (15) vase.

Vater ['fɑ:tər] *m* (7[1]) father; *von Tieren*: sire; '~**haus** *n* paternal house; '~**land** *n* native (*od.* one's) country; ♀**ländisch** ['~lɛndiʃ] national; (~ *gesinnt*) patriotic(ally *adv.*); '~**landsliebe** *f* patriotism.

väterlich ['fɛ:tərliç] fatherly; (*dem Vater eigen*) paternal; ~**erseits** ['~ərzaɪts] on one's father's side.

'**Vater**|**liebe** *f* paternal love; '♀**los** fatherless; '~**mord** *m* patricide; '~**mörder** *m* patricide (*a.* '~**mörderin** *f*); (*hoher Kragen*) stand-up collar.

'**Vaterschaft** *f* paternity, fatherhood; '~**sklage** *f* affiliation case.

'**Vater|stadt** *f* native town, home-town; **~'-unser** *n* (7) Lord's Prayer.
Vati F ['fa:ti] *m* (11¹) dad(dy).
Veget|arier [vege'ta:rjər] *m* (7), **ℒarisch** [~'ta:riʃ] vegetarian; **~ation** [~ta'tsjo:n] *f* (16) vegetation; **ℒativ** [~ta'ti:f] vegetative; *~es Nervensystem* autonomic nervous system; **ℒieren** [~'ti:rən] vegetate (*a. fig.*).
Vehikel [ve'hi:kəl] *n* (7) vehicle.
Veilchen ['faılçən] *n* (6) violet; '**ℒ-blau** violet.
Veitstanz ['faıtstants] *m* St. Vitus's dance.
Vene ['ve:nə] *f* (15) vein; '**~n-entzündung** *f* phlebitis.
venerisch [ve'ne:riʃ] venereal.
Venezian|er [vene'tsja:nər] *m* (12), **~erin** *f* (16¹), **ℒisch** Venetian.
Ventil [vɛn'ti:l] *n* (3¹) valve; *fig.* outlet; **~ation** [~tila'tsjo:n] *f* (16) ventilation; **~ator** [~'la:tɔr] *m* (8¹) ventilator, fan; **ℒieren** [~'li:rən] ventilate (*a. fig.*).
verabfolg|en [fɛr'ʔapfɔlgən] give, hand over (*j-m* to); *Speisen, Getränke*: provide, serve; ⚕ administer; *j-m et. ~ lassen* let a p. have a th.; **ℒung** *f* delivery; provision; ⚕ administration.
ver'-abred|en *et.* agree (up)on, arrange; *Zeit, Ort*: appoint, fix; *sich ~* make an appointment; *als Stelldichein*: F (have a) date; *schon anderweitig verabredet sein* have a previous engagement; **ℒung** *f* agreement; appointment, F date.
ver'-abreichen *s. verabfolgen*.
ver'-absäumen neglect, omit.
ver'-abscheuen hate, abhor, detest; **~swert** detestable.
verabschied|en [fɛr'ʔapʃi:dən] dismiss; ⚔ discharge; *Gesetz*: pass; *sich ~* take leave (*von* of); bid farewell, say good-bye (to *a p.*); **ℒung** *f* dismissal; ⚔ discharge; passing.
ver'-achten despise; (*verächtlich abtun; verschmähen*) scorn; *nicht zu ~* F not to be sneezed at.
Verächt|er [fɛr'ʔɛçtər] *m* (7), **~erin** *f* (16¹) despiser; **ℒlich** contemptuous; (*verachtenswert*) despicable, contemptible.
Ver'-achtung *f* contempt, disdain; *mit ~ strafen* ignore.
ver-allge'meiner|n (29) generalize; **ℒung** *f* generalization.
ver'-alte|n (26, sn) become obsolete *od.* antiquated, go out (of date); **~t** antiquated, obsolete, out of date, dated; (*altmodisch*) outmoded.
Veranda [ve'randa] *f* (11¹ *u.* 16²) veranda(h).
veränder|lich [fɛr'ʔɛndərliç] changeable; (*a.* ℞) variable; **ℒlichkeit** *f* changeableness; variability; **~n** (*a. sich*) alter, change; (*abwechseln*) vary; **ℒung** *f* change, alteration; variation.
verängstigt [~'ʔɛŋstiçt] frightened, scared.
ver'-anker|n ⚓ anchor (*a. fig.*); ⊕ stay; ⚠ tie; *fig. in e-m Gesetz usw.*: embody in; **ℒung** *f* ⚓ anchorage; ⊕ staying; ⚠ tying.
ver'-anlag|en (25) *steuerlich*: assess; **~t** *adj.* (*befähigt*) talented; ⚕ predisposed; *methodisch ~ sein* have a methodical turn of mind, be methodical; **ℒung** *f* assessment; *fig.* disposition; (*Neigung*) bent, inclination; (*Begabung*) talent(s *pl.*); ⚕ predisposition.
veranlass|en [~'ʔanlasən] (28) cause, occasion; (*anordnen*) arrange; *j-n zu et. ~* (*a. S.*) induce a p. to do a th., make a p. do a th.; *nur P.*: prevail (up)on a p. to do a th.; **ℒung** *f* occasion, cause; *auf meine ~* at my suggestion; *auf ~ von od. gen.* at the instance of; *zu et. ~ geben* give rise to; *zur (weiteren) ~* for further action.
veranschaulich|en [~'ʔanʃaυliçən] (25) illustrate; *sich et. ~* visualize, picture; **ℒung** *f* illustration.
ver'-anschlag|en (25) rate, value, estimate (*auf acc.* at); **ℒung** *f* valuation, estimate.
ver'-anstalt|en (26) arrange, organize; stage (*a. fig. co.*); *Konzert usw.*: give; **ℒer(in** *f*) *m* (7) organizer; *Sport*: promoter; **ℒung** *f* arrangement, organizing; *konkret*: event; show; *Sport*: event, meeting; **ℒungskalender** *m* calendar of events.
ver'-antwort|en answer for; *sich ~* justify (*od.* defend) o.s.; **~lich** responsible (*a. Stellung usw.*), answerable (*für* for); *~ machen* hold responsible, *weitS.* blame *a p.* (*für* for); **ℒlichkeit** *f* responsibility; **ℒung** *f* responsibility; (*Rechtfertigung*) justification; *auf seine ~* on his own responsibility; *auf eigene ~*

at one's own risk; *j-m die ~ zuschieben* offload the responsibility on a p.; *s. abwälzen*; *die ~ tragen* be responsible; *zur ~ ziehen* call to account; **~ungsbewußt** responsible; **2ungsbewußtsein** *n* sense of responsibility; **~ungslos** irresponsible; **~ungsvoll** responsible.

veräppeln *sl.* [~ˈʔɛpəln] *sl.* kid.

verˈ-arbeit|en work up; ⊕ manufacture, process (*zu* into), *maschinell*: machine; *Speise*, *fig.*: digest; (*abnutzen*) wear (out); *~de Industrie* manufacturing (*od.* finishing) industry; **2ung** *f* working up; manufacturing, processing; digestion; (*Ausführung*) workmanship.

verargen [~ˈʔargən] (25): *j-m et. ~* blame a p. for a th.

verˈ-ärgern annoy, anger.

verarm|en [~ˈʔarmən] (25, sn) become poor; **~t** impoverished; **2ung** *f* impoverishment, pauperization.

verˈ-arzten doctor.

verästel|n [fɛrˈʔɛstəln] (29, *a. sich*) ramify; **2ung** *f* ramification.

verˈ-ausgaben (25) spend, expend; *sich ~* spend (all) one's money; *fig.* spend o.s.

verˈ-auslagen disburse, advance.

verˈ-äußer|lich alienable; *Wertpapier*: negotiable; **~n** alienate; (*verkaufen*) dispose of, sell; **2ung** *f* alienation; disposal, sale; **2ungserlös** *m* sales proceeds *pl.*

Verb [vɛrp] *n* (5[2]) verb; **2al** [~ˈbaːl] verbal.

verballhornen [fɛrˈbalhɔrnən] (26) transmogrify.

Verˈband *m* (3[3]) ⊕ binding; ⚕ dressing, bandage; (*Vereinigung*) federation, union; ⚔ unit, task force, *bsd.* ⚓, ✈ formation; **~kasten** *m* first-aid box; **~stoff** *m*, **~zeug** *n* bandaging material.

verˈbann|en banish, exile; **2ung** *f* banishment, exile; **2te** *m* (18) exile.

verbarrikadieren [~barikaˈdiːrən] barricade.

verˈbauen build up; (*versperren*) obstruct; (*falsch bauen*) build badly; *Geld*, *Material*: spend in building; *fig. j-m* (*a. sich*) *den Weg ~* bar a p.'s (one's) way (*zu* to).

verbauern [~ˈbauərn] (29, sn) become countrified.

verˈbeißen suppress; *sich das Lachen ~* stifle one's laughter; *fig. sich in et. ~* keep grimly at a th.

verˈbergen conceal, hide.

verˈbesser|n (*a. sich*) improve; (*berichtigen*) correct; **2ung** *f* improvement; correction; **2ungsvorschlag** *m* suggestion for improvement.

verˈbeug|en: *sich ~* bow (*vor dat.* to); **2ung** *f* bow.

verbeulen [~ˈbɔʏlən] (25) dent, batter.

verˈbiegen bend, twist, distort.

verˈbieten forbid (*j-m et.* [*zu tun*] a p. [to do] a th.), prohibit (a th.; a p. from doing a th.).

verbilligen [~ˈbiligən] (25) reduce in price, cheapen.

verˈbind|en bind (up); (*vereinigen*; *a. sich*) join, unite, combine (*a.* ⚗) (*mit* with); connect (*a.* ⊕, *teleph.*) (with), link (to); ⚕ bandage, dress (*j-n* a p.'s wounds); † *sich ~ mit* associate with; *sich ehelich ~* (*mit*) marry; *j-m die Augen ~* blindfold; *fig.* (*eng*) *verbunden sein mit* be bound up with; *ich bin Ihnen sehr verbunden* I am greatly obliged to you; *teleph. falsch verbunden!* wrong number!; *mit Gefahr verbunden* dangerous, involving a risk; **~lich** [~ˈbintliç] binding (*für j-n* upon), obligatory; (*höflich*) obliging; *~(st)en Dank!* my best thanks!; **2lichkeit** *f* obligation, liability; (*Höflichkeit*) obligingness, civility, readiness to oblige; (*Schmeichelei*) compliment; † *~en pl.* (*Passiva*) liabilities; *s-n ~en nachkommen* meet one's engagements.

Verˈbindung *f* union (*a. Ehe*); (*Zs.-schluß*; *Vereinigung mehrerer Eigenschaften*) combination; (*Zs.-hang*) connection (*a. teleph.*, 🚂, ⚓, ⊕), junction; (*Personenvereinigung*; *a. Ideen2*) association; *s. Studenten2*; (*Beziehung*) relation; (*Verkehr*) communication; ⚗ compound; ⚔ liaison, *taktisch*: contact; *in ~ bleiben* (*treten*) keep (get) in touch (*mit* with); *in ~ bringen mit* connect with; *sich in ~ setzen mit* get in touch with, contact; *in ~ stehen mit* communicate with, be in touch with, *fig.* be connected with; *teleph. ~ bekommen* (*haben*) get (be) through; *die ~ verlieren mit* lose touch with; **~sgang** *m* connecting passage; **~smann** *m* contact; **~s-offizier** ⚔ *m* liaison officer; **~srohr** *n* connecting tube; **~sschlauch** *m* connecting hose; **~sstelle** *f* junction; ⊕ joint; (*Amt*) liaison office; **~sstraße** *f* feeder road; **~sstück** *n* connecting piece, coupling; *s. Bindeglied*; **~s-tür** *f* connecting door.

verbissen [fɛrˈbisən] grim; (*zäh*) dogged; (*mürrisch*) crabbed; **2heit** *f* sourness of temper; doggedness.

verˈbitten: *sich* ~ (beg to) decline; (*nicht dulden*) not to stand for; *das verbitte ich mir!* I won't have that!

verbitter|n [~ˈbitərn] (29) embitter; *verbittert a.* bitter; **2ung** *f* bitterness (of heart).

verblassen [~ˈblasən] (28, sn) *Stoff usw. u. fig.* fade; *fig.* ~ *gegenüber* (*dat.*) pale beside.

Verbleib [~ˈblaɪp] *m* (3, *o. pl.*) whereabouts; **2en** [~bən] (sn) to be left; remain; (*abmachen*) agree; ~ *bei s-r Meinung usw.* persist in.

verˈblend|en blind, delude; (*närrisch machen*) infatuate; ⊕ face; **2ung** *f* blindness; delusion; infatuation; ⊕ facing.

verblichen [~ˈbliçən] *Farbe usw.*: faded; **2e** *m, f* (18) deceased.

verblöden [~ˈbløːdən] (26, sn) become an idiot; F *fig.* go mad.

verblüff|en [~ˈblyfən] (25) amaze, perplex, puzzle; nonplus, flabbergast; *verblüfft* perplexed; taken aback; **2ung** *f* amazement, perplexity, stupefaction.

verˈblühen (25, sn) fade, wither.

verblümt [~ˈblyːmt] veiled.

verˈbluten (sn) (*a. sich* ~) bleed to death.

verˈbocken F bungle.

verˈbohr|en: *sich* ~ *in* (*acc.*) bend o.s. to, *stärker*: go mad about; **~t** *adj.* cranky; (*stur*) pigheaded.

verˈborgen[1] *v/t.* lend (out).

verˈborgen[2] *adj.* hidden; (*geheim*) secret; *im ~en* secretly; **2heit** *f* concealment; secrecy; (*Zurückgezogenheit*) retirement.

Verbot [fɛrˈboːt] *n* (3) prohibition; *e-r Sache a.* ban (on); **~sschild** *n* prohibitive sign.

verbrämen [~ˈbrɛːmən] (25) border, trim; *fig.* garnish, gloss over.

Verbrauch [~ˈbraʊx] *m* (3, *o. pl.*) consumption; **2en** consume, use up; (*abnutzen*) wear out; (*ausgeben*) spend; (*vergeuden*) waste; *verbraucht Luft*: stale, *P.*: worn out; **~er** *m* (7) consumer; **~ermarkt** *m* hypermarket; **~er-umfrage** *f* consumer survey; **~erverband** *m* consumer association; **~erverhalten** *n* consumer behavio(u)r; **~erwaren** *f/pl.*, **~sgüter** *n/pl.* commodities, consumer goods, articles of consumption; **~ssteuer** *f* excise (duty).

verˈbrech|en 1. (*a.* F *e-n Witz usw.*) perpetrate; *was hat er verbrochen?* what is his offen|ce, *Am.* -se?, what has he done?; **2.** 2 *n* (6) crime; ⚖ *a.* major offen|ce, *Am.* -se; **2er** *m* (7) criminal (*a.* **2erin** *f* [16[1]]); **2er-album** *n* rogues' gallery; **~erisch** criminal; **2ertum** *n* (1[2]) criminality; (*a.* **2erwelt** *f*) underworld; **2ervisage** F *f* criminal face.

verˈbreiten (*a. sich*) spread (*a. Gerücht usw.*); *Licht, Wärme usw.*: *a.* diffuse; *Lehre usw.*: disseminate; *Licht, Frieden*: shed; *sich* ~ spread; *sich ~ über ein Thema* enlarge (up)on, hold forth on; (*weit*) *verbreitet* wide-spread.

verbreitern [~ˈbraɪtərn] (29, *a. sich*) widen, broaden.

Verˈbreitung *f* spread(ing); dissemination.

verˈbrenn|bar combustible; **~en** *v/t. u. v/i.* (sn) burn; *nur v/i. lebend*: be burnt to death; *Leiche*: cremate; (*versengen*) scorch; *fig. sich den Mund* ~ put one's foot in it; *s. Finger.*

Verˈbrennung *f* burning, combustion; (*Leichen2*) cremation; (*Brandwunde*) burn; **~smaschine** *f*, **~smotor** *m* (internal) combustion engine; **~s-ofen** *m* incinerator.

verbriefen [fɛrˈbriːfən] (25) confirm by documents; *verbrieftes Recht* vested right.

verˈbringen spend, pass.

verbrüder|n [~ˈbryːdərn] (29): *sich* ~ fraternize; **2ung** *f* fraternization.

verˈbrüh|en scald; **2ung** *f* scald.

verˈbuchen book; *fig.* secure.

Verbum [ˈvɛrbum] *n* (9[2]) verb.

verˈbummeln [fɛr-] *v/t. Geld*: squander, *sl.* blue; *Zeit*: idle away; F (*versäumen*) neglect, forget; (*verlieren*) lose; *v/i.* (sn) go to seed.

Verbund... [~ˈbunt-] ⊕, ⚡ compound ...; ✝ co-operative, co-ordinate ...; **~bauweise** *f* composite construction.

verbünden [~ˈbyndən] (26) ally (*mit* to); *sich* ~ *a.* form an alliance (with).

Verbundenheit [~'bundənhaɪt] *f* solidarity; bond(s *pl.*), ties *pl.*
Ver'bündete *m*, *f* (18) ally.
verbürg|en [fɛr'byrgən] guarantee; *sich ~ für* vouch for; **~t** established, authentic (*fact*).
ver'büßen: *seine Strafe ~* complete one's sentence, serve one's time.
verchromt [~'kro:mt] chromium-plated.
Verdacht [~'daxt] *m* (3) suspicion; *in ~ haben* suspect; *~ schöpfen* become suspicious, F smell a rat.
verdächtig [~'dɛçtiç] *P.*: suspected, *pred.* suspect (*gen.* of); *P. u. S.*: suspicious; **~en** [~'dɛçtigən] (25) cast suspicion on, suspect (*gen.* of); **2ung** [~tiguŋ] *f* accusation; suspicion.
Ver'dachts|moment *n* suspicious fact; **~person** *f* suspect.
verdamm|en [~'damən] (25) condemn, *a. eccl.* damn; **~enswert, ~lich** damnable; **2nis** *f* (14[2]) damnation; **~t** damned; *~!* damn (it)!; *dazu ~ zu inf. fig.* doomed (*od.* condemned) to *inf.*; **2ung** *f* condemnation; damnation.
ver'dampf|en (sn) evaporate; **2ung** *f* evaporation.
ver'danken: *j-m et. ~* owe a th. to a p., be indebted to a p. for a th.; *es ist diesem Umstand zu ~* it is owing to ...
verdarb [~'darp] *pret v. verderben*[1].
verdattert F [~'datərt] flabbergasted.
verdau|en [~'daʊən] (25) digest (*a. fig.*); **~lich** digestible; **2lichkeit** *f* digestibility; **2ung** *f* digestion.
Ver'dauungs... digestive (*canal, troubles, etc.*); **~-apparat** *m* digestive system; **~spaziergang** *m* constitutional; **~störung** *f* indigestion.
Ver'deck *n* (3) covering; ⚓ deck; *mot.* roof, top; **2en** cover; (*verbergen*) conceal, hide.
ver'denken *s. verargen.*
Verderb [fɛr'dɛrp] *m* (3) ruin; *von Nahrung usw.*: waste; **2en[1]** [~bən] *v/i.* (30, 25, sn) get spoiled, go bad; (*verfaulen*) rot; (*zugrunde gehen*) perish; *es mit j-m ~* get into a p.'s bad books; *v/t.* spoil; *sittlich*: corrupt; (*zugrunde richten*; *a. weitS. Bild, Augen usw.*) ruin; (*verpfuschen*) make a mess of; *sich den Magen ~* upset one's stomach; **~en[2]** *n* (6) corruption; destruction; ruin; *j-n ins ~ stürzen* ruin a p.; *ins ~ rennen* rush (headlong) into destruction; **2lich** [~'dɛrp-] pernicious, fatal; *Ware*: perishable; **~lichkeit** *f* perniciousness; perishableness; **~nis** *f* (14[2]) corruption, depravity; **2t** corrupted, depraved; **~t-heit** *f* corruptness, depravity.
verdeutlichen [~'dɔʏtliçən] (25) make plain, elucidate.
verdeutschen [~'dɔʏtʃən] (25) translate into German.
ver'dicht|en (*a. sich*) condense; **2ung** *f* condensation.
verdicken [fɛr'dikən] (25, *a. sich*) thicken; ⚗ inspissate.
ver'dienen deserve, merit; *Geld*: earn, gain, make; *gut ~* be doing well; *sich verdient machen um* deserve well of.
Ver'dienst 1. *m* (3[2]) earnings *pl.*; (*Lohn*) wages *pl.*; (*Gehalt*) salary; (*Gewinn*) gain, profit; **2.** *fig. n* merit; *es ist sein ~, daß* it is owing to him that; *s. erwerben*; **~-ausfall** loss of earnings; **2lich, 2voll** meritorious, deserving; **~spanne** ⚕ *f* profit margin.
ver'dient *P.*: deserving; *S., a. Strafe*: well-deserved; **~ermaßen** [~ər'ma:sən] deservedly.
ver'dingen (30, 25) *s. vermieten*; *sich ~* go into service (*bei* with).
ver'dolmetschen (27) interpret, translate.
ver'donnern F (*verurteilen*) condemn.
verdoppel|n [fɛr'dɔpəln] (29) double; **2ung** *f* doubling.
verdorben [~'dɔrbən] **1.** *p.p. v. verderben*[1]; **2.** *adj.* spoiled; *Luft*: foul; *sittlich*: corrupt, depraved; *Magen*: disordered.
ver'dorren (25, sn) dry up.
ver'drahten ⚡ wire.
ver'dräng|en push away, thrust aside; *phys. u. fig.* displace; ⚔ dislodge; *fig. a.* supersede, *bsd. durch List*: supplant; *psych.* repress; **2ung** *f* displacement; supersession; repression.
ver'dreh|en distort, twist (*beide a. fig.*); *Glied*: sprain; *Augen*: roll; *Recht*: pervert; *fig. j-m den Kopf ~* turn a p.'s head; **~t** distorted; (*verrückt*) crazy; **2t-heit** *f* craziness; **2ung** *f* distortion, twist(ing).
ver'dreifachen (25) treble.
ver'dreschen F thrash.
verdrieß|en [~'dri:sən] (30) vex, annoy; *sich et. nicht ~ lassen* not

to be discouraged by, not to shrink from; **~lich** vexed, annoyed (*über et. acc.* at); (*schlecht gelaunt*) ill-humo(u)red, peevish, morose; *S.*: annoying, irksome; **2lichkeit** *f* peevishness; *konkret*: vexation, annoyance.

verdroß [~'drɔs] *pret. v. verdrießen.*

verdrossen [~'drɔsən] **1.** *p.p. v. verdrießen*; **2.** *adj.* peevish, sulky; (*unlustig*) listless.

ver'drucken *typ.* misprint.

ver'drücken F (*essen*) polish off; *sich heimlich* ~ slip away.

Verdruß [~'drus] *m* (2) annoyance, vexation; *j-m* ~ *bereiten* vex (*od.* annoy) a p.

ver'duften (sn) F *fig. sl.* beat it.

verdummen [~'dumən] *v/t.* (25) make (*od.* [*v/i.*; sn] become) stupid.

ver'dunkel|n darken (*a. sich*), obscure (*a. fig.*); *durch Wolken, a. fig.* cloud; *Luftschutz*: black out; *ast., fig.* eclipse; **2ung** *f* darkening; obscuration; *Luftschutz*: blackout; *ast.* eclipse; **2ungsgefahr** ⚖ *f* danger of collusion.

verdünn|en [fɛr'dynən] (25) thin; *Gas*: rarefy; *Flüssiges*: dilute; *sich* ~ (*Luft*) thin out; **2ung** *f* thinning; rarefaction; dilution.

verdunst|en [~'dunstən] (26, sn) evaporate; **2er** *m* (7) humidifier; **2ung** *f* evaporation.

verdursten [~'durstən] (24, sn) die with thirst.

verdüstern [~'dy:stərn] (29, *a. sich*) darken.

verdutzen [~'dutsən] (27) startle, nonplus, bewilder.

verebben [~'ʔɛbən] (25), sn) ebb.

veredel|n [~'ʔe:dəln] (29) ennoble; (*verfeinern*) refine; *Güter*: finish; *Boden, Pflanze, Tier*: improve; *Rohstoff*: process, finish; **2ung** *f* refinement; improvement; processing, finishing; **2ungs-industrie** *f* finishing industry.

verehelichen [~'ʔe:əliçən] (25, *sich*) marry.

ver'-ehr|en revere, venerate; (*anbeten*) worship, *fig.* adore; *j-m et.* ~ make a p. a present of a th.; *verehrte Anwesende!* Ladies and Gentlemen!; **2er** *m* (7[1]), **2erin** (16[1]) worship(p)er; (*Bewunderer, Liebhaber*) admirer; *e-s Stars*: fan; **~lich** hono(u)red, estimable (*a.* **~t** *adj.*); **2ung** *f* reverence, veneration; worship, (*a. fig.*) adoration; **~ungswürdig** venerable.

vereid|(ig)en [fɛr'ʔaɪd(ig)ən] (26 [25]) swear *a p.* (in *bei Amtsantritt*), administer an oath to *a p.*; **~igt** *adj.* sworn; **2igung** *f* swearing in.

Verein [fɛr'ʔaɪn] *m* (3) union; *im* ~ *mit* together with; *konkret*: society, association; *geselliger*: club.

ver'-einbar compatible, consistent; **~en** (25) agree (upon *a th.*), arrange; **2keit** *f* compatibility; **2ung** *f* agreement, arrangement.

ver'einen *s. vereinigen*; *Vereinte Nationen* United Nations; *mit vereinten Kräften* with a combined effort, jointly.

vereinfach|en [~'ʔaɪnfaxən] (25) simplify; **2ung** *f* simplification.

vereinheitlich|en [~'ʔaɪnhaɪtliçən] (25) make uniform, standardize; **2ung** *f* standardization.

ver'-einig|en (25) join, unite (*a. sich*); combine (*a. sich u. in sich* ~); (*vergesellschaften*) associate (*a. sich*); (*versammeln*) assemble (*a. sich*); (*in Einklang bringen*) reconcile; *Vereinigte Staaten m/pl. (von Amerika)* United States (of America), U.S.(A.); **2ung** *f* union; combination; *s. Verein.*

ver'-einnahmen (25) receive.

vereinsamen [fɛr'ʔaɪnza:mən] (25, sn) become lonely *od.* isolated.

Ver'-eins|mitglied *n* club member; **'~wesen** *n* clubs and associations *pl.*, club activities *pl.*

ver'-einzel|n isolate; **~t** *adj.* isolated; single; (*verstreut*) sporadic (-ally *adv.*), scattered (*a. Regenschauer*).

vereis|en [fɛr'ʔaɪzən] *v/t. u. v/i.* (27, sn) freeze (*a.* ⚕); *mot.*, ✈ ice (up); **~t** [~'ʔaɪst] ice-coated, iced (over); *geol.* glaciated; **2ung** [~'ʔaɪzuŋ] *f* freezing; icing; ✈ icing-up; *geol.* glaciation.

vereitel|n [~'ʔaɪtəln] (29) thwart, foil, frustrate; defeat; *Hoffnung*: shatter; **2ung** *f* frustration.

ver'-eiter|n (sn) suppurate; **2ung** *f* suppuration.

ver'-ekeln (29): *j-m et.* ~ disgust a p. with a th.

verelend|en [~'ʔe:lɛndən] (26, sn) be reduced to misery; **2ung** *f* reduction to misery, pauperization.

ver'·enden (sn) perish.
vereng|e(r)n [~'ʔɛŋə(r)n] (25[29]) narrow; (*zs.-ziehen*) contract; **2(er)ung** *f* narrowing; contraction.
ver'·erb|en leave (*dat.* to); *biol.* transmit (to); *Brauch usw.*: hand down; *sich* ~ be hereditary; *sich* ~ *auf* (*acc.*) descend (up)on; **~t** *biol.* [~pt] hereditary; **2ung** [~buŋ] *f* leaving, *etc.*; *biol.* (hereditary) transmission, heredity; **2ungsgesetz** *n* Mendelian law; **2ungslehre** *f* genetics *sg.*
verewig|en [fɛr'ʔe:vigən] (25) perpetuate; (*unsterblich machen*) immortalize; **~t** [~viçt] (*verstorben*) deceased, late.
ver'fahren 1. *v/i.* (sn *u.* h.) proceed, act (*nach* on); *mit ...* ~ deal with; *v/t. Geld*: spend on travelling about; *sich* ~ lose one's way, *fig.* blunder; **2.** *adj.* (*verpfuscht*) bungled, muddled; ~ *sein* be in a bad tangle; **3. 2** *n* (6) (*~sweise*) procedure (*a.* ⚖); ⚖ *konkret*: proceedings *pl.*; *a.* ⊕ process, method; (*Schema, Plan*) system; **2s...** procedural; **2s-technik** ⊕ *f* process engineering; **2s-weise** *f s. Verfahren.*
Ver'fall *m* (3, *o. pl.*) decay, ruin, (*a.* ✗) decline; *e-s Hauses*: dilapidation; ⚖ forfeiture; (*Fristablauf*) expiration; *e-s Wechsels*: maturity; *bei* ~ when due, at maturity; *in* ~ *geraten s. verfallen*; **2en 1.** *v/i.* (sn) (fall into) decay; ⊕, *Haus*: dilapidate, fall into disrepair; (*ablaufen*) expire; *Pfand*: become forfeited; *Recht*: lapse; *Wechsel*: fall due; *Kranker*: waste away; *j-m* ~ become a slave to *a p.*, *e-m Laster*: become addicted to; *Karte* ~ *lassen* let go to waste; ~ *auf* (*acc.*) hit upon *an idea, etc.*; ~ *in* (*acc.*) fall (*od.* run) into; *in Strafe* ~ incur; *in e-e Krankheit* ~ fall ill; **2.** *adj.* decayed; *Gebäude*: dilapidated; *Gesichtszüge*: wasted, worn; ⚖ forfeited, lapsed; *Fahrschein usw.*: expired; *e-m Laster*: addicted to; **~tag** *m*, **~zeit** *f* day of payment; due date.
ver'fälsch|en falsify; *Wein usw.*: adulterate; **2er** *m* (7) falsifier; *v. Wein usw.*: adulterator; **2ung** *f* falsification; adulteration.
ver'fangen (*Erfolg haben*) tell (*bei* on); *das verfängt bei mir nicht* that won't take with me; *sich* ~ become entangled, be caught.
verfänglich [fɛr'fɛŋliç] *Frage*: captious, insidious; *Lage*: risky; (*unangenehm*) embarrassing.
ver'färben discolo(u)r; *sich* ~ change colo(u)r.
ver'fass|en compose, write; **2er** *m* (7) author; **2erin** *f* (16[1]) authoress.
Ver'fassung *f* state, condition; (*Staats2*) constitution; (*Gemüts2*) disposition, frame of mind; *in guter* (*körperlicher*) ~ in good form (*od.* shape); **~s·änderung** *f* amendment of the constitution; **~sfeind** *m* enemy of the constitution; **2sfeindlich** anticonstitutional; *Aktivitäten*: directed against the constitution; **~s-gericht** *n* Constitutional Court; **2s-mäßig, 2srechtlich** constitutional; **~srecht** *n* constitutional law; **~s-schutz** *m*: *Bundesamt für* ~ Office for the Protection of the Constitution; **2swidrig** unconstitutional.
ver'faulen (sn) rot, decay.
ver'fecht|en fight for, defend, advocate; **2er** *m* (7) advocate.
ver'fehl|en *allg.* miss; *nicht* ~ *zu ...* not to fail to; *s. Wirkung*; **~t** wrong, false; (*erfolglos*) abortive; **2ung** *f* (*Vergehen*) offen|ce, *Am.* -se.
verfeind|en [fɛr'faɪndən] (26, *a. sich*) make an enemy (*mit* of); **~et** hostile; on bad terms.
verfeiner|n [~'faɪnərn] (29, *a. sich*) refine; **2ung** *f* refinement.
verfemen [~'fe:mən] (25) outlaw; *gesellschaftlich*: ostracize; *et.* ~ ban a th.
ver'fertig|en make, manufacture; **2er** *m* (7[1]) maker, manufacturer; **2ung** *f* making, manufacture.
Verfettung [~'fɛtuŋ] *f* fatty degeneration, 📖 adiposis.
ver'feuern use up for fuel; *Munition*: fire, use up.
ver'film|en film, screen; **2ung** *f* screening; *konkret*: film-version.
verfilzen [~'filtsən] (27) felt; *Haare*: mat.
verfinstern [~'finstərn] (29) *s. verdunkeln.*
verflachen [~'flaxən] (25) *v/t.* flatten; *v/i.* (sn) (*a. sich* ~) flatten, grow flat, (become) shallow (*a. fig.*).
ver'flecht|en interlace; *fig.* ~ *in* (*acc.*) entangle in, involve in; **2ung** *f* entanglement; ⚘ interlocking.
ver'fliegen (sn) *fig.* vanish; *Zeit*: fly; (*sich verflüchtigen*) evaporate,

⚗ volatilize; *sich* ~ *Vogel*: stray, ✈ lose one's bearings.
ver'fließen (sn) flow away; *Zeit*: elapse.
verflixt F [~'flikst] blasted, darned.
ver'flossen *adj. Zeit*: past; *Freund, Minister usw.*: late, ex-...
ver'fluchen curse; *verflucht s. verdammt.*
verflüchtigen [~'flyçtigən] (25) volatilize; *sich* ~ evaporate (*a. fig.*).
verflüssigen [fɛr'flysigən] (25) (*a. sich*) liquefy.
Verfolg [~'fɔlk] *m* (3, *o. pl.*) course, progress; *im* ~ (*gen.*) in pursuance of, (*im Verlauf*) in course of; **⁲en** [~gən] pursue (*a. fig. Laufbahn, Politik usw.*); *ungerecht, grausam*: persecute; (*beschatten*) shadow, trail; *Spur*: trace: *fig. e-e Sache*: follow up; *v. Gedanken, Träumen*: haunt; *e-n Vorgang*: follow, observe; *gerichtlich* ~ prosecute; **~er** *m* (7), **~erin** *f* (16¹) pursuer; *grausamer*: persecutor; **~ung** *f* pursuit; persecution; (*Fortführung*) pursuance; *gerichtliche* ~ prosecution; **~te** [~ktə] *m, f*: *politisch* ~ political persecutee; **~ungswahn** [~guŋs-] *m* persecution mania.
verform|en ⊕ [~'fɔrmən] (de)form, work, shape; **⁲ung** *f* shaping; *b.s.* deformation.
verfracht|en [~'fraxtən] (26) *Schiff*: charter; *Ware usw.*: freight, *Am. od.* ⚓ ship; **⁲er** *m* freighter.
verfranzen ✈ *sl.* [~'frantsən]: *sich* ~ get lost, lose one's bearings.
Ver'fremdung *f* alienation.
verfroren [~'fro:rən] sensitive to cold; (*durchkältet*) chilled through.
verfrüht [~'fry:t] premature.
verfüg|bar [~'fy:kbɑ:r] available; **⁲barkeit** *f* availability; **~en** [~gən] *v/t.* decree, order; *Gesetz*: enact; *sich* ~ betake o.s. (*nach usw.* to); *v/i.* ~ *über* (*acc.*) have at one's disposal, dispose of, *S.*: have, be equipped with; **⁲ung** *f* decree, order; (*~srecht*) disposal; *j-m zur* ~ *stehen* be at a p.'s disposal *od.* command; et. *zur* ~ *haben* have at one's disposal *od.* command; *j-m et. zur* ~ *stellen* make a th. available to a p., place a th. at a p.'s disposal; **⁲ungsfreiheit** *f* discretion; **⁲ungsrecht** *n* right of disposal.
ver'führ|en seduce; **⁲er** *m* (7), **⁲erin** *f* (16¹) seducer; **~erisch** seductive; **⁲ung** *f* seduction.
ver'fünffachen (25) quintuple.
ver'füttern *Hafer usw.*: feed.
Vergabe [~'gɑ:bə] *f* (15) placing *of an order*, award *of a contract*.
ver'gaffen: *sich* ~ fall in love (*in acc.* with).
vergällen [fɛr'gɛlən] (25) embitter; *Spiritus*: methylate, denature.
ver'gammeln F (29, sn) rot; *fig. a. P.*: go to seed.
vergangen [~'gaŋən] gone, past; *im ~en Jahr* last year; **⁲heit** *f* past; *gr.* past tense; (*Vorleben*) past, antecedents *pl.*; *politische* ~ political background; *s. ruhen*; **⁲heitsbewältigung** *f* coming to terms with the past.
vergänglich [~'gɛŋliç] transient; fugitive; **⁲keit** *f* transitoriness.
vergas|en [~'gɑ:zən] (25) gasify; *mot.* carburet; (*durch Gas töten od. vergiften*) gas; **⁲er** *mot. m* (7) carburet(t)or; **⁲ung** *f* gasifying; *mot.* carburetion; gassing.
vergaß [~'gɑ:s] *pret. v. vergessen* 1.
ver'geb|en give away (*an j-n* to); (*übertragen*) confer, bestow (on); ✝ *Auftrag*: place (with); (*verteilen*) give out; *Chance*: let slip, miss; *Karten*: misdeal; (*verzeihen*) forgive; *sich et.* ~ compromise o.s.; **~ens** in vain, vainly; (*nutzlos*) to no purpose; **~lich** [~'ge:pliç] fruitless, futile, vain; *adv.* in vain; **⁲lichkeit** *f* futility; **⁲ung** [~buŋ] *f* giving (away); bestowal, conferment (*an acc.* on); (*Verzeihung*) forgiveness, pardon(ing); ~ *der Sünden* remission of sins; *s. Vergabe.*
vergegenwärtigen [fɛrge:gən'vɛrtigən] (25) represent; *sich et.* ~ picture *od.* visualize a th.
ver'gehen 1. (sn) pass (away); *allmählich*: fade (away); *fig. vor et.* ~ die of; *ihm verging Hören und Sehen* he was quite stunned; *der Appetit ist mir vergangen* I have lost my appetite; *sich* ~ commit an offen|ce, *Am.* -se; *sich* ~ *an j-m tätlich*: assault, *unsittlich*: violate; *sich gegen das Gesetz usw.* ~ violate, offend against; **2.** ⁲ *n* (6) ⚖ minor offen|ce, *Am.* -se.
vergeistig|en [~'gaɪstigən] (25) spiritualize; **⁲ung** *f* spiritualization.
ver'gelt|en repay (*dat.* to), return;

(*belohnen*) reward (*j-m* et. a p. for a th.); *b.s.* retaliate, pay back; **~ung** *f* requital, return; *b.s.* retribution, retaliation, reprisal; ~ *üben* retaliate (*an dat.* on); **~ungs...** *a.* ⚔ retaliatory...; **~ungsmaßnahme** *f* reprisal; **~ungsschlag** ⚔ *m* retaliatory strike.

verge'sellschaft|en (26) socialize; ✝ convert into a company; ⚖ associate; **~ung** *f* socialization; ✝ conversion into a company; ⚖ association.

vergessen [~'gɛsən] (30) **1.** forget; (*liegenlassen*) leave; (*übersehen*) overlook; *sich* ~ forget o.s., lose one's head; **2.** *p.p. v.* ~ 1; **~heit** *f* oblivion; *in* ~ *geraten* fall (*od.* sink) into oblivion.

vergeßlich [~'gɛsliç] forgetful; **~keit** *f* forgetfulness.

vergeud|en [fɛr'gɔʏdən] (26) *Geld, Vermögen*: dissipate, squander; *weitS.* waste; **~er** *m* (7), **~erin** *f* (16[1]) squanderer; waster; **~ung** *f* dissipation; waste.

vergewaltig|en [~gə'valtigən] (25) violate, do violence to; *Frau*: violate, rape, ravish; **~ung** *f* violation; rape; *fig.* outrage (*gen.* upon).

vergewissern [~gə'visərn] (29): *sich* ~ make sure (*e-r S.* of a th.), ascertain (a th.).

ver'gießen spill; *Blut, Tränen*: shed.

vergift|en [~'giftən] (25) poison; (*verseuchen*) contaminate; **~ung** *f* poisoning; contamination.

vergilbt [~'gilpt] yellowed.

Vergißmeinnicht ⚘ [fɛr'gismaɪnniçt] *n* (3) forget-me-not.

vergittern [~'gitərn] (29) bar up, grate; *mit Holz*: lattice.

verglasen [~'glɑːzən] (27) glaze.

Vergleich [~'glaɪç] *m* (3) comparison; *gütlicher*: arrangement, settlement; *mit Gläubigern*: composition; *s. abschließen*; *im* ~ *zu* compared to, in comparison with; *s. ziehen*; **~bar** comparable; **~en** compare (*mit* with; = *gleichstellen*: to); *sich* ~ come to terms, settle (*mit* with), *mit Gläubigern*: compound (with); *verglichen mit* as against, compared to; **~smaßstab** *m* standard of comparison; **~sweise** comparatively, in comparison; **~ung** *f s. Vergleich.*

ver'glimmen (sn) die away.

vergnüg|en [fɛr'gnyːgən] **1.** (25) amuse; *sich* ~ amuse (*od.* enjoy *od.* divert) o.s.; **2.** ~ *n* (16) pleasure, enjoyment; (*Spaß*) fun; *konkret*: entertainment; *mit* ~ with pleasure, gladly; *viel* ~! have a good time!; ~ *finden an, sein* ~ *haben an* (*dat.*) take pleasure in; *j-m* ~ *bereiten od. schaffen* afford a p. pleasure, amuse a p.; **~lich** [~'gnyːkliç] amusing, pleasant; **~t** (*über acc.*) pleased (with), delighted (at); (*froh*) gay, merry, cheerful.

Ver'gnügung [~guŋ] *f* pleasure, amusement; entertainment; **~spark** *m* amusement park, *bsd. Brt.* fun fair; **~sreise** *f* pleasure-trip; **~sreisende** *m, f* (18) tourist; **~ssteuer** *f* entertainment (*Am.* admission) tax; **~ssucht** *f* (inordinate) love of pleasure; **~ssüchtig** pleasure-seeking; **~sviertel** *n* entertainment cent|re, *Am.* -er.

vergold|en [~'gɔldən] (26) gild; **~er** *m* (7) gilder; **~ung** *f* gilding.

ver'gönnen grant, allow.

vergötter|n [~'gœtərn] (29) deify; *fig.* idolize, adore; **~ung** *f* deification; *fig.* adoration.

ver'graben hide in the ground; (*a. fig.*) bury.

ver'gräm|en *hunt.* frighten away; **~t** care-worn, grief-stricken.

vergraulen F [~'graulən] (25) scare off.

ver'greifen: *sich* ~ be mistaken; ♪ touch the wrong note; *sich* ~ *an j-m*: assault *od.* (*a. geschlechtlich*) violate *a p.*, *an Eigentum*: steal.

vergreis|en [~'graɪzən] (27, sn) become senile; **~ung** *f* senescence.

vergriffen [~'grifən] *Ware*: sold out; *Buch*: out(-)of(-)print.

vergrößer|n [fɛr'grøːsərn] (29, *a. sich*) enlarge (*a. phot.*); *Lupe*: magnify (*a. fig.*); (*ausdehnen*; *a. sich*) expand, extend; (*vermehren*) increase, add to; **~ung** *f* enlargement; magnification; expansion; increase; *phot.* blow-up, enlargement; **~ungs-apparat** *phot. m* enlarger; **~ungsglas** *n* magnifying-glass.

Vergünstigung [~'gynstiguŋ] *f* privilege, favo(u)r; benefit.

vergüt|en [~'gyːtən] (26) compensate (*j-m* et. a. p. for a th.); *Auslagen*: reimburse; *Verlust*: compensate for, make good, indemnify for; ⊕ improve, *Stahl*: temper; **2ung** *f* compensation; reimbursement; (*Honorar*) fee; ⊕ improvement; tempering.

verhaft|en arrest, apprehend; **2ung** *f* arrest, apprehension.

ver'hallen (sn) die away.

ver'halten 1. keep back, retain; *den Atem*: hold in; *Lachen usw.*: suppress; *Pferd*: rope; *sich ~ P.*: behave, conduct o.s., act, *S.*: be; *sich ruhig ~* keep quiet; *wenn es sich so verhält* if that is the case; **2.** *p.p. v.* 1. *u. adj.* restrained; *Atem*: bated; *Stimme*: low; *Gefühle, Zorn*: pent-up; *Lachen*: suppressed; **3.** 2 *n* (6) behavio(u)r (*a. zo. usw.*), conduct; (*Haltung*) attitude; ⊕ characteristics *pl.*; **2s...** behavio(u)ral; **2sforschung** *f* behavio(u)ral research; **~sgestört** maladjusted; **2s-psychologie** *f* behavio(u)ral psychology.

Verhältnis [fɛr'hɛltnis] *n* (4[1]) relation; *a.* ⚹ proportion, ratio; *pl.* (*Umstände*) conditions, circumstances *pl.*; (*Mittel*) means *pl.*; (*Beziehung*) relation(s *pl.*) (*zu* with); (*Liebes2*) liaison, love-affair; (*Geliebte*) mistress; *außer jedem ~ stehen* be out of all proportion; *im ~ zu* in proportion to, compared with; *im ~ von 4 : 1* in the ratio of four to one; *im umgekehrten ~ (zu)* at an inverse ratio (to); *in freundschaftlichem ~ mit* on friendly terms with; *über s-e Verhältnisse leben* live beyond one's means; **2mäßig** proportional; comparative; *adv.* in proportion; comparatively (speaking); relatively; **~wahl** *parl. f* proportional representation; **2widrig** disproportionate; **~wort** *gr. n* (1[2]) preposition.

Ver'haltungsmaßregeln *f/pl.* instructions.

ver'hand|eln *v/i. u. v/t.* negotiate, treat (*über acc., wegen* for); ⚖ try ([*über*] et. a th.; *gegen j-n* a p.); (*verkaufen*) sell; (*erörtern*) discuss; **2lung** *f* negotiation; ⚖ hearing, proceedings *pl.*, *Strafrecht*: trial; discussion; **2lungs-partner** *m* negotiating party; opposite number; **2lungsrunde** *f* round of negotiations; **2lungs-tisch** *m* negotiating table.

ver'häng|en (25) cover, hang (*mit* with); *Strafe*: impose; inflict (*über acc.* [up]on), *a. Sport*: award; **2nis** *n* (4[1]) fate, doom; (*Katastrophe*) disaster; *j-m zum ~ werden* be a p 's undoing; **~nisvoll** fateful, fatal; (*unselig*) disastrous; **2ung** *f* infliction.

ver'harmlosen (27) play down.

verhärmt [~'hɛrmt] care-worn.

ver'harren (h. *u.* sn) persevere; (*auf, bei, in dat.*) persist (in), abide (by), F stick (to).

verharschen [~'harʃən] *v/i.* (27, sn) *Schnee*: crust; *Wunde a.*: close.

ver'härt|en (*a. sich*) harden; **2ung** *f* hardening; *fig. a.* induration.

ver'haspeln (29, *a. sich*) tangle; *sich ~ fig.* get muddled.

verhaßt [~'hast] hated; *S.*: hateful.

ver'hätscheln coddle, pamper.

Verhau [~'hau] *m* (3) abatis; F mess; **2en** thrash; *fig. sl.* muff; *sich ~* (make a) blunder.

verheddern F [~'hɛdərn] (*a. sich*) get entangled; *fig.* get muddled.

verheer|en [~'he:rən] (25) devastate, lay waste; **~end** *fig.* disastrous; **2ung** *f* devastation, havoc.

ver'hehl|en, 2ung *f s. verheimlichen.*

ver'heilen heal (up).

verheimlich|en [fɛr'haɪmliçən] (25) hide, conceal (*dat.* from), keep *a th.* a secret (from); *s. vertuschen*; **2ung** *f* concealment.

ver'heirat|en marry (*mit, an acc.* to); *sich ~ a.* get married; **2ung** *f* marriage.

ver'heiß|en, 2ung *f* promise; **~ungsvoll** promising.

ver'helfen: *j-m ~ zu* help a p. to.

verherrlich|en [~'hɛrliçən] (25) glorify; **2ung** *f* glorification.

ver'hetz|en instigate; fanaticize; **2ung** *f* instigation.

ver'hexen bewitch.

verhimmeln [~'himəln] worship.

ver'hinder|n prevent (*j-n an dat.* a p. from); **2ung** *f* prevention.

ver'höhn|en deride, jeer, taunt; **2ung** *f* derision, mockery.

Verhör ⚖ [~'hø:r] *n* (3) interrogation, examination; *weitS.* trial, hearing; *j-n ins ~ nehmen* = **2en** examine; try, hear; *sich ~* hear wrong.

ver'hüll|en cover, veil; **~t** *fig.* veiled; **2ung** *f* veil, disguise, cover.

verhundertfachen [~ˈhundərtfaxən] (25) centuple.
verˈhungern (sn) die of hunger, starve; ~ *lassen* starve to death.
verhunzen [fɛrˈhuntsən] (27) ruin, *sl.* louse up; *Sprache*: murder.
verˈhüten prevent, avert, obviate.
verhütt|en ⚒ [~ˈhytən] (26) *Erz*: smelt; **Ꞩung** *f* smelting.
Verˈhütung *f* prevention; **~smaßnahme** *f* preventive measure; **~smittel** *n* ⚕ prophylactic; (*Empfängnis*Ꞩ) contraceptive.
verhutzelt [~ˈhutsəlt] shrivel(l)ed; *P.*, *Gesicht*: wizened.
verinnerlich|en [~ˈʔinərliçən] (25) spiritualize; **Ꞩung** *f* spiritualization.
verˈ-irr|en (*sich*) lose one's way, go astray; **~t** *Kugel*, *Tier*: stray; **Ꞩung** *f fig.* aberration, error.
verˈjagen drive (*od.* chase) away.
verjähr|bar [~ˈjɛːrbaːr] prescriptible; **~en** (25, sn) become prescriptive; *bsd. Straftat*: come under the statute of limitations; **~t** ⚖ prescriptive, superannuated (*a. fig.*); statute-barred; **Ꞩung** *f* limitation (by lapse of time); (negative) prescription; **Ꞩungsfrist** *f* limitation period.
verˈjubeln F squander, F blue.
verjüng|en [~ˈjyŋən] (25) make (*sich* ~ grow) young again, (*a. sich*) rejuvenate; *Maßstab*: reduce; *sich* ~ (*spitz zulaufen*) taper (off); **Ꞩung** *f* rejuvenescence; tapering; reduction; **Ꞩungskur** *f* rejuvenating cure; **Ꞩungsmittel** *n* rejuvenation tonic.
verkalk|en [~ˈkalkən] (26) (*a. sich* ~) ⚗, *physiol.* calcify; **~t** ⚕ sclerotic, F fossilated; **Ꞩung** *f* calcification; (arterio)sclerosis.
verkalkuˈlieren: *sich* ~ miscalculate, make a mistake.
verˈkappt disguised, … in disguise; crypto- *communist*, *etc.*
verkapsel|n [~ˈkapsəln] (25): *sich* ~ encyst; **Ꞩung** *f* encystment.
Verˈkauf *m* (3³) sale; **Ꞩen** sell (*a. sich*); *zu* ~(*d*) for sale.
Verˈkäuf|er(in *f*) *m* seller; *im kleinen*: retailer; ⚖ vendor (*a. Straßen*Ꞩ, *Zeitungs*Ꞩ); (*Ladengehilfe*) shop-assistant, *Am.* (sales-)clerk (*m u. f*), *m* salesman, *f* saleswoman, shopgirl, *Am. a.* salesgirl; **Ꞩlich** sal(e)able, marketable; *pred.* for sale; **~lichkeit** *f* sal(e)ableness.
Verˈkaufs|-automat *m* vending machine, vendomat; **~bedingungen** *f/pl.* terms of sale; **~förderung** *f* sales promotion; **~leiter** *m* sales manager; **~-organisation** *f* sales organization; **~personal** *n* sales staff; **~preis** *m* selling-price; **~schlager** *m s. Schlager*; **~ständer** *m* display stand.
Verkehr [~ˈkeːr] *m* (3, *o. pl.*) traffic; (*Beförderung v. Gütern u. Personen*) transport(ation *Am.*); (*Verbindung*) communication; ☏, 🚂, ✈ (~*sdienst*) service; (*Handel*) commerce, trade; *freundschaftlich od. geschlechtlich*: intercourse; *aus dem ~ ziehen* withdraw from service (*Geld*: from circulation); **Ꞩen** *v/t.* reverse; (*verwandeln*) turn, convert (*beide*: *in acc.* into); *fig.* pervert; *v/i. Fahrzeug*: run, be operated; (*regelmäßig hin- u. zurückfahren*) ply *od.* run (*zwischen* between); (*Handel treiben*) traffic, trade; ~ *bei j-m* visit (*od.* go to) a p.'s house; ~ *in e-m Lokal usw.* frequent; *mit j-m* ~ associate (*od.* keep company) with, see a great deal of, *mit e-r Gruppe* ~ *a.* mix with, *geschlechtlich*: have (sexual) intercourse with; *sich* ~ *in* (*acc.*) be changed into.
Verˈkehrs|-ader *f* arterial road; **~ampel** *f* traffic lights *pl.*; **~-andrang** *m* rush (of traffic); **~-aufkommen** *n* volume of traffic; **~behinderung** *f* obstruction of traffic; **~betrieb** *m s. Verkehrsunternehmen*; **~dichte** *f* density of traffic; **~disziplin** *f* road discipline; **~flugzeug** *n* commercial aircraft, air-liner; **~hindernis** *n* traffic block; **~-insel** *f* refuge; **~knotenpunkt** *m* traffic junction; **~kontrolle** *f* traffic (spot-) check; **~meldungen** *f/pl.* traffic news *sg.*; **~minister** *m* Minister of Transport; **~mittel** *n Fahrzeuge*: (*öffentliches* public) conveyance, transport(ation *Am.*); **~netz** *n* network of communication; **~-opfer** *n* road casualty; **~-ordnung** *f* traffic regulations *pl.*; **~polizei** traffic police; **~polizist** *m s. Verkehrsschutzmann*; **~regelung** *f* (*durch Ampeln*: automatic) traffic control; **Ꞩreich** frequented, busy, congested; **~schild** *n* traffic sign; **~schutzmann** *m stehender*: traffic constable,

pointsman; *motorisierter*: mobile policeman, *bsd. Am.* F speed cop; ♀**schwach:** ~*e Zeit* off-peak hours *pl.*; ♀**sicher** *Auto*: roadworthy; ~**sicherheit** *f* roadworthiness; ♀**stark:** ~*e Zeit* rush (*od.* peak) hours *pl.*; ~**stauung** *f*, ~**stockung** *f* traffic jam *od.* congestion *od.* bank-up; ~**störung** *f* interruption of traffic; 🚗 *usw.* breakdown; ~**straße** *f* thoroughfare; ~**sünder** *m* traffic-offender; ~**tafel** *f* traffic sign; ~**teilnehmer** *m* road user; ~**-überwachung** *f* traffic monitoring; ~**-unfall** *m* traffic accident; ~**-unternehmen** *n* transport(ation) service (*od.* company), public carrier; ~**ver-ein** *m* (tourist) information cent|re, *Am.* -er; ~**verhältnisse** *n/pl.* traffic conditions; ~**vorschrift** *f* traffic regulation; ~**wert** ✝ *m* market value; ~**wesen** *n* traffic; (system of) communications *pl.*; transport(ation *Am.*); ~**zählung** *f* traffic census; ~**zeichen** *n* traffic sign.

verkehrt [fɛr'ke:rt] inverted, reversed; upside down; inside out; (*falsch*) wrong; (*unsinnig*) absurd; ♀**heit** *f* wrongness; folly, absurdity.

ver'kennen *P.*: mistake; *S.*: misunderstand, misjudge; (*unterschätzen*) underestimate; *e-e Sache nicht* ~ be fully aware of; *nicht zu* ~ unmistakable; *verkanntes Genie* unappreciated genius.

ver'kett|en (26) chain up; *fig.* link together, concatenate; *bsd.* ⚡ interconnect; ♀**ung** *f fig.* concatenation.

verketzern [~'kɛtsərn] (29) brand as a heretic.

verkitten cement (*a. fig.*), putty.

ver'klagen accuse, inform against; ⚖ sue (*auf acc., wegen* for); *s. verpetzen.*

ver'klär|en transfigure; ♀**ung** *f* [transfiguration.]

verklausulieren [~klauzu'li:rən] safeguard (*od.* hedge) by clauses.

ver'kleben paste *a th.* over *od.* up.

ver'kleid|en disguise; ⊕ line, *außen*: (en)case, *a.* ▲ face; (*täfeln*) wainscot; ⚔ *s. tarnen*; ♀**ung** *f* disguise; ⊕ lining, facing; wainscot(t)ing.

verkleiner|n [~'klaınərn] (29) make smaller, reduce (in size); *Maßstab*, ♣ reduce; (*vermindern*) diminish; *fig.* belittle, minimize; detract from; ♀**ung** *f* reduction; diminution; *fig.* belittling, detraction; ♀**ungswort** *n* (1²) diminutive.

ver'kleistern glue, paste up.

ver'klemmt *fig. P.*: repressed, inhibited.

ver'klingen (sn) die away.

ver'knacken F *s. verurteilen.*

ver'knallen F: *sich* ~ (*in j-n*) fall violently in love with; *verknallt sein in j-n* F be gone on, *Am.* have a crush on.

verknapp|en [~'knapən] *v/i.* (25, sn) run short, become scarce; ♀**ung** *f* shortage, scarcity.

ver'kneifen F: *sich et.* ~ deny o.s. a th.; *er konnte sich nicht* ~ *zu sagen* he couldn't help saying.

verknöcher|n [~'knœçərn] *v/t. u. v/i.* (29, sn) ossify; *fig. a.* fossilize; ♀**ung** *f* ossification; fossilization.

ver'knoten knot, tie (up).

ver'knüpf|en knot *od.* tie (together); *fig.* connect, combine; ~**t** *fig.*: ~ *mit* involving, entailing; ♀**ung** *f* connection.

ver'kohlen (25) *v/t.* (sn) carbonize, char; *v/t.* F (*zum besten haben*) kid.

ver'kommen 1. (sn) decay, go to ruin; *P.*: come down in the world, go to seed; **2.** *adj.* decayed; *sittlich*: depraved; ♀**heit** *f* depravity.

ver'koppeln (29) couple.

ver'korken (25) cork (up).

verkorksen [~'kɔrksən] F (27) *s. verpatzen*; *sich den Magen* ~ upset one's stomach.

verkörper|n [~'kœrpərn] (29) personify, embody; *bsd. thea.* impersonate; ♀**ung** *f* personification, embodiment; impersonation.

verköstigen [~'kœstigən] (25) feed, board.

ver'krachen F: *sich* ~ fall out (*mit* with).

verkraften [~'kraftən] (26) cope with, handle, bear.

ver'krampft cramped.

ver'kriechen: *sich* ~ hide.

ver'krümeln F: *sich* ~ F beat it, make off.

ver'krümm|en crook, curve, bend; ~**t** crooked; ♀**ung** *f*: ~ *der Wirbelsäule* curvature of the spine.

verkrüppeln [fɛr'krypəln] (29) *v/t.* cripple; (*verkümmern*) stunt; *v/i.* (sn) become crippled; become stunted (*od.* deformed).

ver'krusten (en)crust.

ver'kühlen: *sich* ~ catch (a) cold.

ver'kümmer|n *v/i.* (sn) become stunted, 🕮 atrophy; (*dahinsiechen*) waste away, pine (away); *aus Mangel an Nahrung*: starve; *v/t. Recht*: curtail; **~t** stunted.

ver'künd(ig)|en (26 [25]) announce; *öffentlich*: publish, proclaim; *Urteil*: pronounce; **°ung** *f* announcement; proclamation; pronouncement; *Mariä ~* Annunciation, Lady Day.

verkupfern [~'kupfərn] (29) copper.

ver'kuppeln pander, sell, procure; ⊕ couple.

ver'kürz|en shorten; (*abkürzen*) abridge; (*beschränken*) curtail; *Zeit*: beguile; *verkürzte Arbeitszeit* short time; **°ung** *f* shortening; abridg(e)ment.

ver'lachen laugh at, deride.

Ver'lade|bahnhof *m* loading station; **~kran** *m* loading crane.

ver'lad|en load, ship; ⚔ entrain, *in Schiffe*: embark, *in Flugzeuge*: emplane, *in Lastwagen*: entruck; **°erampe** *f* loading platform; **°ung** *f* loading, shipping; entraining *etc.*

Verlag [fɛr'lɑ:k] *m* (3) *Tätigkeit*: publication; *Firma*: *the* publishers *pl.*; *s. Verlagsbuchhandlung*; *im ~ von* published by.

ver'lager|n *v/t. allg.* (*a. sich*) shift; (*überführen*) transfer; (*evakuieren*) evacuate; **°ung** *f* shifting; transfer; evacuation; *fig.* shift.

Ver'lags|-anstalt *f* publishing house; **~buchhandel** *m* publishing trade; **~buchhändler** *m* publisher; **~buchhandlung** *f*, **~haus** *n* publishing house; **~katalog** *m* publisher's list; **~leiter(in** *f*) *m* general manager; **~recht** *n* copyright; **~werk** *n* publication.

ver'langen 1. (25) *v/t.* demand, ask for; (*erfordern*) require, call for; (*beanspruchen*) claim; (*wünschen*) desire; *viel ~ an Leistungen* set a high standard; *es verlangt mich zu inf.* I am anxious to *inf.*; *das ist zuviel verlangt* that's asking too much; *was ~ Sie von ihm?* what do you want of him?; *v/i. ~ nach* ask *od.* (*sich sehnen*) long for; **2. °** *n* (6) desire; (*Sehnsucht*) longing (*nach* for), *Am.* F yen; (*Forderung*) demand, request; *auf ~* by request, ✝ on demand; *auf ~ von* at the request of; *~ tragen nach* have a longing for.

verlänger|n [~'lɛŋərn] (29) lengthen; *Frist usw.*: prolong, extend; **°ung** *f* lengthening; prolongation, extension; *Sport*: (*Spiel°*) extra time; (*Vorsprung*) projection; **°ungsschnur** ⚡ *f* extension flex *od. Am.* cord.

verlangsamen [fɛr'laŋzɑ:mən] (25) (*a. sich*) slow down, slacken; (*verzögern*) retard.

Verlaß [~'las] *m* (4) reliance; *es ist kein ~ auf ihn* there is no relying on him, he is unreliable.

ver'lassen 1. leave, *gänzlich a.* quit; (*im Stich lassen*) forsake, abandon, desert; *sich ~ auf* (*acc.*) rely (*od.* count *od.* depend) on; *Sie können sich darauf ~* you may rely on it, you may rest assured!; **2.** *adj.* forsaken, abandoned; deserted (*a.* = *öde*); (*einsam*) lonely, isolated; **°heit** *f* abandonment; loneliness; isolation.

verläßlich [~'lɛsliç] reliable.

ver'lästern malign, slander, defame.

Verlaub [fɛr'laup] *m* (3): *mit ~* with your permission.

Ver'lauf *m* (3, *o. pl.*) *der Zeit*: lapse, course; *e-s Vorgangs*: progress, course, development; (*Tendenz*) trend; *weiterer ~* sequel; *e-n schlimmen ~ nehmen* take a bad turn; **°en 1.** *v/i.* (sn) *Zeit*: pass, elapse; *Vorgang*: take a ... course, come off, go *well, etc.*; *Grenze, Weg usw.*: run, extend; *Farben*: run, bleed; *sich ~* go astray, lose one's way; *Volksmenge*: scatter, disperse; *s. Sand*; **2.** *adj. Tier*: stray; *Kind*: lost.

verlaust [~'laust] lousy.

verlaut|baren [~'lautbɑ:rən] (25) *v/t.* make known, disclose; *v/i.* (h., *a.* sn) = **~en** (26) be reported *od.* disclosed, transpire; *~ lassen* give to understand, hint; *wie verlautet* as reported.

ver'leb|en spend, pass; **~t** [~'le:pt] worn out; (*hinfällig*) decrepit.

ver'leg|en 1. *v/t.* misplace; *anderswohin*: transfer (*a. Truppen*), shift; remove; *Verlagswerk*: publish; ⊕ *Kabel usw.*: lay; *Straße*, 🚂 relocate; *Weg* (*versperren*): bar, cut off; *zeitlich*: put off, postpone (*auf acc.* to); *sich ~ auf* (*acc.*) apply (*od.* devote) o.s. to, take to, *aufs Bitten, Leugnen usw.*: resort to; **2.** *adj.* embarrassed, confused; self-conscious; ~ *um* at a loss for; **Ձenheit** *f* embarrassment; (*Klemme*) difficulty; (*mißliche Lage*) predicament; *in ~ sein* be at a loss (*um* for); *in ~ bringen* embarrass; *in ~ kommen* get embarrassed; **Ձenheitslösung** *f* stop-gap solution; **Ձenheits-pause** *f* awkward silence; **Ձer** *m* (7) publisher; **~erisch** editorial, publishing; **Ձung** *f* transfer, removal; ⊕ laying; *zeitlich*: postponement.

ver'leiden (26): *j-m et. ~* disgust a p. with a th.; spoil a th. for a p.

Ver'leih *m* hire service; *Film*: distribution, (*Gesellschaft*) distributors *pl.*; **Ձen** lend (out), *Am.* loan; *gegen Miete*: hire out, let out; (*gewähren*) *Titel, Recht usw.*: bestow, confer (*j-m* on a p.); *Gunst*: grant; *Auszeichnung, Preis*: award; *e-n Reiz*: give; **~er** *m* (7), **~erin** *f* (16[1]) lender; bestower; **~ung** *f* lending out; grant; bestowal; award; **~ungsurkunde** *f* diploma.

ver'leit|en mislead, lead astray; (*verführen*) seduce; (*veranlassen*) induce, lead (to *inf.*); *sich ~ lassen zu inf.* be induced to *inf.*, be carried away into *ger.*; **Ձung** *f* misleading; seduction.

ver'lernen unlearn, forget.

ver'lesen read out; *Namen usw.*: call over; *Erbsen usw.*: pick; *sich ~* make a mistake (in reading).

verletz|bar [fɛr'lɛtsbaːr], **~lich** damageable; (*verwundbar*) vulnerable; (*leicht gekränkt*) sensitive, touchy; **~en** (27) hurt, injure; *fig. Gefühl*: hurt; (*kränken*) offend; *Eid, Recht usw.*: violate; *Gesetz*: infringe; **~end** offensive; **Ձte** *m, f* (18) injured person; **Ձung** *f* hurt, (*a.* = *Wunde*) injury; violation; infraction, infringement.

ver'leugn|en deny; *Freund, Kind*: disown; *Grundsatz*: renounce, disclaim; *sich ~ lassen* have o.s. denied, not to be at home (*vor j-m* to); **Ձung** *f* denial; disavowal; renunciation.

verleumd|en [~'lɔʏmdən] (26) calumniate, defame; *a.* ⚖ slander, *schriftlich*: libel; **Ձer** *m* (7), **Ձerin** (16[1]) calumniator, slanderer; **~erisch** defamatory; slanderous; libel(l)ous; **Ձung** *f* calumny, defamation; slander, libel; **Ձungskampagne** *f* smear campaign; **Ձungsklage** *f* libel suit.

ver'lieb|en: *sich ~ in* (*acc.*) fall in love with; **~t** [~pt] (*in acc.*) in love (with), enamo(u)red (of); *a. Blick usw.*: amorous; (*liebeskrank*) love-sick; **Ձtheit** *f* amorousness.

verlier|en [~'liːrən] (30) *v/t.* lose (*a. v/i.*); *Blätter, Haar usw.*: shed; *sich ~* lose o.s., (*verschwinden*) disappear, *Volksmenge*: disperse, *Farbe*: fade, *Schmerz*: subside; *s. Nerv, Geduld, Verstand*; **Ձer** *m* (7) loser; *ein schlechter ~* a bad loser; **Ձerseite** *f*: *auf der ~ sein* be on the losing side.

Ver'lies *n* (4) dungeon, keep.

ver'loben: *sich ~* become engaged *od.* betrothed (*mit* to).

Verlöbnis [~'løːpnis] *n* (4[1]) engagement, betrothal.

Verlob|te [~'loːptə] *m, f* (18): *ihr ~r* her fiancé *od.* intended (husband); *s-e ~* his fiancée *od.* intended (wife); *die ~n pl.* the engaged couple *sg.*, the betrothed *pl.*

Verlobung [~'loːbuŋ] *f* engagement, betrothal; **~s-anzeige** *f* announcement of an engagement; **~sring** *m* engagement ring.

ver'lock|en allure, entice; (*versuchen*) tempt; (*verführen*) seduce; **~end** *adj.* tempting; **Ձung** *f* allurement, enticement; temptation.

verlogen [fɛr'loːgən] (given to) lying, mendacious; **Ձheit** *f* untruthfulness, mendacity.

ver'lohnen *v/refl. s.* (*sich*) *lohnen*.

verlor [~'loːr] *pret. v. verlieren*.

ver'loren *p.p. v. verlieren u. adj.* lost; (*einsam, hilflos*) forlorn; *~e Eier* poached eggs; *~er Haufen* forlorn hope; *~e Partie* losing game; *s. Sohn*; *~ geben* give up for lost; *auf ~em Posten stehen* fight a losing battle; *das Spiel ~ geben* throw up the game, *fig.* give in; **~gehen** (sn) get (*od.* be) lost.

ver'löschen *v/t.* extinguish; *Schrift*: efface; *v/i.* (sn) *s. erlöschen*.

ver'los|en dispose of by lot, raffle (off); **Ձung** *f* lottery, raffle.

ver'löten solder (up).

verlotter|n [~'lɔtərn] (29) go to seed; **~t** *P.*: dissolute, rackety; *S.*: ruined.

Verlust [~'lust] *m* (3[2]) loss; *~e pl.* ⚔ casualties; *im Spiel*: losings; *bei*

~ *von* under pain of, with forfeiture of; *in ~ geraten* get lost; *mit ~ arbeiten, verkaufen usw.* at a loss, at a sacrifice; **~-anzeige** *f* notice of (a) loss; **2bringend** involving (a) loss, losing *business*; **2ig** (*gen.*): *j-n e-r S. für ~ erklären* declare a p. to have forfeited a th.; *e-r S. ~ gehen* forfeit a th.; **~liste** ⚔ *f* casualty list.

ver'machen bequeath *od.* leave (*dat.* to).

Vermächtnis [~'mɛçtnis] *n* (4[1]) (last) will; (*das Vermachte*) bequest; *von Geld*: legacy (*a. fig.*); *von Grundeigentum*: devise.

vermähl|en [~'mɛ:lən] (25) (*a. sich*) wed, marry (*mit* to); **2ung** *f* wedding, marriage.

ver'mahnen *s. ermahnen.*

ver'manschen F mess up.

vermarkt|en [~'marktən] (26) commercialize; **2ung** *f* commercialization.

vermasseln F [~'masəln] (29) *s. verpatzen.*

Vermassung [~'masuŋ] *f* de-personalization.

ver'mauern wall up (*od.* in).

ver'mehr|en (*a. sich*) increase (*um* by), augment, *an Zahl*: *a.* multiply; ([*sich*] *fortpflanzen*) propagate, breed; (*beitragen zu*) add to; **2ung** *f* increase; addition (*gen.* to).

ver'meid|en avoid; **~lich** [~'maɪt-] avoidable; **2ung** [~duŋ] *f* avoidance.

ver'mein|en think, suppose; **~tlich** [~'maɪntliç] supposed, pretended.

ver'melden announce, report.

ver'mengen mix (up), mingle; (*verwechseln*) confound, mix up.

ver'menschlichen (25) humanize.

Vermerk [fɛr'mɛrk] *m* (3) note, entry; **2en** note (down), record; (*eintragen*) enter; *geistig*: observe, make a (mental) note of; *übel ~* take amiss.

ver'mess|en 1. *v/t.* measure; *Land*: survey; *sich ~* measure wrong; (*sich erdreisten*) dare; **2.** *adj.* daring; impudent; **2enheit** *f* presumption; **2ung** *f* measurement; *des Landes*: survey; **2ungs-amt** *n* survey-office; **2ungs-ingenieur** *m* land surveyor.

vermiet|bar [~'mi:tbɑ:r] rentable; **~en** let, *bsd. Am.* rent; hire (out); ⚖ lease; *Haus zu ~* house to (be) let; *Möbel usw. zu ~* furniture *etc.* on hire; **2er** *m* (7) letter, ⚖ lessor; hirer (out); **2ung** *f* letting; leasing; hiring (out).

ver'minder|n (*a. sich*) diminish, decrease, lessen; (*beeinträchtigen*) impair; (*beschränken*) reduce; **2ung** *f* diminution, decrease, lessening; impairment; reduction.

verminen [~'mi:nən] (25) mine.

ver'misch|en mix (up), mingle; *Tee usw.*: blend; *sich ~* mix; **~t** *adj.* mixed; *Nachrichten usw.*: miscellaneous; **2ung** *f* mixing, mixture.

ver'missen miss; (*beklagen*) regret; *~ lassen* lack; *vermißt* missing.

Ver'mißte *m* (18) missing person.

vermitt|eln [~'mitəln] (29) *v/t.* mediate; (*zustande bringen*) arrange; *Frieden, Anleihe*: negotiate; (*beschaffen*) procure; *Eindruck, Vorstellung*: give, convey; *Wissen*: impart (*j-m* to); *v/i.* mediate (*bei* in); intercede, interpose (*zwischen* between); **~els(t)** (*gen.*) by means (*od.* dint) of; **2ler** *m* (7), **2lerin** *f* (16[1]) mediator (*f a.* mediatrix); (*oft b.s.*) go-between; ⚕ middleman; agent; **2lung** *f* mediation; arrangement; intercession; procuring; conveying; imparting; *teleph.* switchboard, (*Amt*) *a.* exchange, (*Person*) operator; *durch* (*gütige*) *~ des Herrn X* by the (good) offices of Mr. X.; **2lungs-amt** *teleph. n* exchange; **2lungsgebühr** *f* commission.

vermöbeln F [~'mø:bəln] (29) *s. verprügeln.*

ver'modern (sn) mo(u)lder, rot.

vermöge [~'mø:gə] (*gen.*) in (*od.* by) virtue of, by dint of.

ver'mögen 1. (*können*) be able to do; *~ zu inf.* be able to; *et. ~ bei j-m* have influence with a p.; **2.** **2** *n* (6) ability, power; (*Geld2*) fortune; (*Besitz*) property; ⚕ (*Aktiva*) assets *pl.*; **~d** wealthy, well-to-do; *pred.* well to do, well off; **2s-abgabe** *f* capital levy; **2s-anlage** *f* (productive) investment; **2sbildung** *f* wealth formation; **~srechtlich** proprietary; **2ssteuer** *f* property tax; **2sverhältnisse** *n/pl.* pecuniary circumstances; **2swerte** *m/pl.* assets *pl.*

vermumm|en [fɛr'mumən] (25) disguise, mask; **2ung** *f* disguise.

vermut|en [~'mu:tən] suppose, presume, *Am. a.* guess; (*argwöhnen*) suspect; **~lich** presumable; probable; *adv. oft* I suppose; **2ung** *f* supposition, presumption; *Am. a.* guess; (*Schluß*) conjecture; (*Gedanke*) idea; (*Mutmaßung*) speculation (*a. pl.*).

vernachlässig|en [~'na:xlɛsigən] (25) neglect; **2ung** *f* neglect(ing).

ver'nagel|n nail (up); *mit Brettern ~* board up; **~t** F: *er war wie ~* his mind was a complete blank.

ver'nähen sew up.

vernarben [~'narbən] (25, sn) (*a. sich*) cicatrice, scar (over).

vernarr|en [~'narən] (25): *sich ~ in* (*acc.*) become infatuated with; **~t** *in* infatuated with, F gone on.

ver'naschen spend on sweets; F *fig.* have it away with.

vernebel|n [~'ne:bəln] (29) ⚔ screen; *fig.* obscure; **2ung** *f* smokescreen (*a. fig.*).

vernehm|bar [~'ne:mba:r] audible; **~en**[1] *v/t.* perceive, hear; (*erfahren*) learn, hear; (*verhören*) interrogate, question, ⚖ *a.* examine; *~ lassen* declare; *sich ~ lassen* make o.s. heard; **2en**[2] *n* (6): *dem ~ nach* according to report, from what I (*od.* we) hear; **~lich** audible, distinct; **2ung** *f* interrogation.

ver'neig|en (*sich*), **2ung** *f* bow (*vor dat.* to).

vernein|en [~'naɪnən] (25) say no, answer in the negative (*eine Frage* to a question); (*leugnen*) deny; **~end** negative; **2ung** *f* negation; denial; *gr.* negative.

vernicht|en [~'niçtən] (26) annihilate; (*zerstören*) destroy; *Hoffnung*: dash; (*ausrotten*) exterminate; **~end** *Blick*, *Kritik*: scathing; *Antwort*, *Schlag*, *Niederlage*: crushing; **2ung** *f* annihilation; destruction; **2ungslager** *n* extermination camp; **2ungskrieg** *m* war of annihilation.

ver'nickeln (29) nickel(-plate).

verniedlichen [~'ni:tliçən] (25) play down.

ver'nieten rivet.

Vernunft [~'nunft] *f* (16) reason; *~ annehmen* listen to reason; *j-n zur ~ bringen* bring a p. to his senses; *wieder zur ~ kommen* come back to one's senses; **~-ehe** *f* marriage of convenience.

vernünftig [~'nynftiç] (*vernunftbegabt*) rational; (*verständig*; *vernunftgemäß*, *angemessen*) reasonable; (*verständig*) sensible, level-headed; *~ reden* talk sense.

ver'nunft|los senseless, unreasonable; **~mäßig** rational; **~widrig** irrational, unreasonable.

veröd|en [~'ʔø:dən] (26) *v/t.* make desolate; (*verheeren*) lay waste, devastate; *v/i.* (sn) become desolate; **2ung** *f* desolation; devastation.

veröffentlich|en [fɛr'ʔœfəntliçən] (25) publish; **2ung** *f* publication.

ver'-ordn|en *gesetzlich*: ordain, decree; (*a.* ⚕) order, ⚕ prescribe (*j-m* for a p.); **2ung** *f* order, ordinance, decree; ⚕ prescription.

ver'pachten lease (*dat.* to).

Ver'pächter *m* (7), **~in** *f* (16[1]) lessor.

Ver'pachtung *f* leasing.

ver'pack|en pack (up); ✝ *einzelne Artikel*: *a.* package; (*einwickeln*) wrap up; **2ung** *f* packing; packaging; (*Packmaterial*) packing (material); (*Hülle*) wrapping; **2ungsmaterial** *n* packaging.

ver'passen let slip; *bsd. Zug usw.*: miss, lose; F *j-m e-n Hieb usw.*: give; ⚔ *Uniform usw.*: fit (on).

verpatzen F [~'patsən] bungle, *bsd. Sport*: muff, *sl.* foozle.

verpesten [~'pɛstən] (26) pollute (*the air*); *weitS. die Luft ~* raise a stench.

ver'petzen inform against, F peach (up)on; *bsd. Schule*: sneak against.

ver'pfänd|en pawn, (*a. fig.*) pledge; mortgage; **2ung** *f* pledging; pawning; mortgaging.

ver'pfeifen F squeal on.

ver'pflanz|en transplant; **2ung** *f* transplanting; ⚕ transplantation.

ver'pfleg|en (25) feed, board; (*mit Lebensmitteln beliefern*) cater for; *im Großen*: provision, victual; **2ung** *f* boarding; catering; *konkret*: food, board; provisions *pl.*, ⚔ rations *pl.*

verpflicht|en [~'pfliçtən] (26) oblige; engage; *sich zu et. ~* bind (*od.* engage) o.s. to do a th.; *zu Dank ~* lay *a p.* under an obligation; *gesetzlich verpflichtet sein* be liable; *j-m zu Dank verpflichtet sein* be obliged to a p.; **2ung** *f* obligation, duty; liability; *übernommene*: engagement, commitment.

ver'pfuschen bungle, botch; *sein Leben*: ruin.

ver'plappern (29), **ver'plaudern** (29) prattle away (*time*); *sich verplappern* blab out a secret.
verplempern F [~'plɛmpərn] (29) fritter away, squander; *sich* ~ fritter away one's energies.
verpönt [~'pø:nt] taboo(ed), despised.
ver'prassen dissipate, squander.
verprovian'tieren supply with food *od.* ⚔ rations; provision.
ver'prügeln thrash, beat up.
ver'puffen (sn) detonate, explode; *fig.* fizzle out.
verpulvern F [~'pulfərn] (29) *Brt.* F blue.
ver'pumpen F lend.
verpuppen [~'pupən] (25) (*sich*) change into a chrysalis.
ver'pusten F (*sich*) recover breath.
Ver'putz ⚠ *m* roughcast, plaster; **≗en** ⚠ roughcast, plaster; F (*ganz aufessen*) polish off.
ver'qualmen fill with smoke.
verquicken [fɛr'kvikən] (25) mix up.
verquollen [~'kvɔlən] *Holz*: warped; *Gesicht*: bloated.
ver'rammeln (29) bar(ricade).
verramschen F [~'ramʃən] sell for a mere song; *Bücher*: remainder.
verrannt [~'rant]: *fig.* ~ *sein in* (*acc.*) be stuck in.
Verrat [~'rɑ:t] *m* (3) ⚖ treason (*an dat.* to); betrayal (of); (*Treulosigkeit*) treachery (to); **≗en** betray (*sich* o.s.); F give *a p.*, *a secret* away; *fig.* (*offenbaren*) show, reveal, betray.
Verräter [~'rɛ:tər] *m* (7) traitor (*an dat.* to); *weitS.* betrayer; **~ei** [~'raɪ] *f* treachery; **~in** *f* (16[1]) traitress; **≗isch** treacherous; ⚖ treasonable, traitorous; *fig. Blick, Spur usw.*: telltale.
ver'rauchen *v/i.* (sn) go off in smoke; *Zorn*: pass away; *v/t.* spend on smoking.
ver'räucher|n fill with smoke; **~t** *adj.* smoky.
ver'rechn|en charge (to account); (*gegeneinander aufrechnen*) set off (*mit* against); (*ausgleichen*) balance; *sich* ~ miscalculate, *a. fig.* make a mistake; *sich verrechnet haben* be out in one's reckoning, *fig.* be mistaken; **≗ung** *f* charging (to account); offset; *im Verrechnungsverkehr*: clearing; *nur zur* ~ only for account.
Ver'rechnungs|scheck *m* crossed (*od.* not negotiable) cheque (*Am.* check); **~stelle** *f* clearing-house; **~verkehr** *m* clearing (system).
ver'recken (sn) *Tier*: perish, die; V *Mensch*: *sl.* peg out, croak.
ver'reg|nen spoil by rain(ing); **~net** rainy.
ver'reisen *v/i.* (sn) go on a journey; *verreist oft*: out of town, away.
ver'reißen F *fig.* pull to pieces.
verrenk|en [~'rɛŋkən] (25) contort; ⚕ wrench, sprain; (*ausrenken*) dislocate; **≗ung** *f* contortion; dislocation.
ver'rennen: *fig. sich in e-e Idee* ~ get stuck in.
ver'richt|en do, perform; (*ausführen*) execute; *s-e Andacht od. sein Gebet* ~ say one's prayer; *s. Notdurft*; **≗ung** *f* performance; (*Arbeit*) work; (*Pflicht*) duty; (*Geschäft*) business.
ver'riegel|n (29) bolt, bar.
verringer|n [~'riŋərn] (29), **≗ung** *f s. vermindern usw.*
ver'rinnen (sn) run off *od.* away; *Zeit*: elapse, fly, pass.
verroh|en [~'ro:ən] (25, sn) become brutalized; **≗ung** *f* brutalization.
ver'rosten (sn) rust.
verrotten [~'rɔtən] (26, sn) rot.
verrucht [~'ru:xt] wicked, villainous; **≗heit** *f* wickedness, villainy.
ver'rück|en displace, (re)move; **~t** mad (*fig. nach dat., auf acc.* on), crazy (for, about), *sl.* nuts (on); *j-n* ~ *machen* drive a p. mad *od. sl.* nuts; *~e Idee* crazy idea; ~ *spielen* F act up; *sl. ich werd'* ~*!* I'll be damned!; *wie* ~ like mad; **≗te** *m, f* (18) lunatic, *m* madman, *f* madwoman; **≗theit** *f* madness; (*Handlung*) *a.* folly; (*Modenarrheit*) craze.
Ver'ruf *m* (3): *in* ~ *bringen* (*kommen*) bring (get) into discredit; *in* ~ *sein* be notorious, *weitS.* be under a cloud; *in* ~ *tun* boycott; **≗en 1.** *v/t.* decry; **2.** *adj.* ill-reputed, ill-famed, notorious.
ver'rutschen slip, get out of place.
Vers [fɛrs] *m* (4) verse; (*Strophe*) stanza; *fig. er kann sich keinen* ~ *darauf machen* he can't make head or tail of it.
ver'sachlichen (25) *Diskussion etc.*: de-emotionalize.
ver'sag|en 1. *v/t.* refuse, deny; *den Dienst* ~ fail; *versagt sein* (*verpflichtet sein*) be engaged; *sich et.* ~ deny o.s. a th., forgo a th.; *v/i.* fail (*a.*

j-m, *Stimme usw.*), ⊕ *a.* break down; *Gewehr*: fail to go off, miss fire; **2.** ꝰ *n* failure; ꝰ**er** *m* (7) *beim Schießen*: misfire; *fig.* failure, F flop; ꝰ**ung** *f* refusal, denial. [Suppe.]
ver'salzen oversalt; *fig.* spoil; *s.*
ver'samm|eln assemble; (*einberufen*) convoke, convene; *sich* ~ assemble, meet; ꝰ**lung** *f* assembly, meeting; ꝰ**lungsfreiheit** *f* freedom of assembly.
Versand [fɛr'zant] *m* (3) dispatch; (*Auslieferung*) delivery; ⚓ *od. Am.* shipment; *durch Post*: mailing; ~**-abteilung** *f* forwarding department; ~**-anweisungen** *f/pl.* shipping instructions; ~**-anzeige** *f* advice of dispatch; ꝰ**bereit** ready for delivery; ~**buchhändler** *m* mail-order bookseller.
versanden [~'zandən] (26, sn) silt up; *fig.* bog down.
Versand|geschäft [~'zant-] *n* mail-order business; (*a.* ~**haus** *n*) mail-order house; ~**hauskatalog** *m* mail-order catalog(ue); ~**kosten** *pl.* forwarding costs; ~**papiere** *n/pl.* shipping papers *pl.*
versauen F [~'zauən] (25) ruin, *sl.* louse up.
versauern [~'zauərn] (29, sn) *fig.* go stale (*od.* sour).
ver'saufen P waste on drink.
ver'säumen *Pflicht usw.*: neglect; *Gelegenheit, Schule, Zug usw.*: miss; ~ *zu tun* fail to do.
Versäumnis [~'zɔʏmnis] *f* (14²), *n* (4¹) neglect, omission, failure; (*Zeit*ꝰ) loss of time; ~**-urteil** *n* judg(e)ment by default.
'Versbau *m* (3) versification.
ver'schachern barter away, job off.
ver'schaffen (25) procure, get (*j-m* for a p.; a p. *a th.*), provide, furnish, supply (a p. with *a th.*); *sich et.* ~ obtain, get, secure; *sich Respekt* ~ make o.s. respected; *s. Gewißheit.*
verschal|en [~'ʃa:lən] (25) plank; ⚠ board; ꝰ**ung** *f* planking; boarding. [*f* bashfulness.]
verschämt [~'ʃɛ:mt] bashful; ꝰ**heit**
verschandeln [~'ʃandəln] (29) disfigure, spoil, deface, ruin.
ver'schanzen entrench, fortify; *fig. sich* ~ *hinter* (*dat.*) shelter behind.
ver'schärf|en add to, (*a. sich*) intensify; (*verschlimmern*; *a. sich*) aggravate; ꝰ**ung** *f* intensification; aggravation.
ver'scharren bury (hurriedly).
ver'scheiden 1. (sn) pass away; **2.** ꝰ *n* (6) decease.
ver'schenken give away (*a. fig.*).
ver'scherzen forfeit, throw away.
ver'scheuchen scare (*bsd. Vögel*: shoo) away; *fig.* banish.
ver'schick|en send away, dispatch; *Sträfling*: deport; ꝰ**ung** *f* sending away, dispatch(ing); deportation.
Ver'schieb|ebahnhof *m* marshalling yard; ꝰ**en** shift, displace; 🚂 shunt; (*in Unordnung bringen*) disarrange; *zeitlich*: defer, put off, postpone; ✝ sell underhand, job away; *sich* ~ shift, get out of place; ~**ung** *f* shifting; postponement; ✝ illicit sale.
verschieden [fɛr'ʃi:dən] different, distinct (*von* from); ~*e pl.* various, several, diverse; ꝰ*es* various things *pl., bsd.* ✝ *n* sundries *pl.*; ~**-artig** of a different kind, different, various; ~**erlei** of various kinds, various, diverse; ~**farbig** of different colo(u)rs, varicolo(u)red; ꝰ**heit** *f* difference; (*Mannigfaltigkeit*) diversity, variety; ~**tlich** repeated(ly *adv.*); *adv.* now and then.
ver'schießen *v/t.* (*verbrauchen*) use up; *v/i.* (sn) *Farbe*: fade.
ver'schiff|en ship; ꝰ**ung** *f* shipment.
ver'schimmeln (sn) get mo(u)ldy.
ver'schlacken (25, sn) turn into dross, slag, scorify.
ver'schlafen 1. *v/t.* miss (*od.* lose *od.* neglect) by sleeping; *Zeit*: sleep away; (*die Zeit* ~, *sich* ~) oversleep (o.s.); **2.** *adj.* sleepy, drowsy; ꝰ**heit** *f* sleepiness.
Ver'schlag *m* partition; (*Bretterbude*) shed; (*Lattenkiste*) crate; ꝰ**en** [~gən] **1.** *v/t.*: *mit Brettern* ~ board (up); *e-n Ball*: lose; *e-e Buchseite* ~ lose one's place (in a book); ~ *werden* ⚓ be driven out of one's course; *in e-e Stadt usw.* ~ *werden* be driven to, find o.s. in; *es verschlägt mir die Sprache* it makes me speechless, it dum(b)founds me; *es verschlägt nichts* it does not matter; **2.** *adj.* cunning, crafty, wily; *Wasser*: lukewarm; ~**enheit** *f* cunning, craftiness.
verschlammen [~'ʃlamən] (25, sn) silt up; become muddy.

ver'schlampen *v/t.* lose; *v/i.* get slovenly.

verschlechter|n [~'ʃlɛçtərn] (29) deteriorate, make worse; *sich* ~ deteriorate, get worse, worsen; **2ung** *f* deterioration, worsening; change for the worse.

verschleier|n [~'ʃlaɪərn] (29) veil (*a. fig.* = mask, disguise); ⚔ screen; ⚕ *b.s.* cook, doctor; **2ung** *f* veiling; *in der Bilanz*: window-dressing.

ver'schleifen *Silben usw.*: slur.

ver'schleimen (25, sn) get obstructed with phlegm.

Verschleiß [~'ʃlaɪs] *m* (3^2) ⊕ wear (and tear); **2en** wear out (*a. sich*); **2fest** wear-resistant.

ver'schlepp|en *Menschen*: carry off, *pol.* displace; (*entführen*) abduct; (*verlegen*) misplace; (*in die Länge ziehen*) delay, protract; ⚕ *Ansteckungsstoff*: spread; *Krankheit*: protract, neglect; **2te** *m, f* (18) displaced person; **2ung** *f* abduction; delay(ing); protraction (*a.* ⚕); **2ungs-taktik** *f* obstructionism.

ver'schleudern dissipate, waste; ⚕ sell at a loss *od.* dirt-cheap.

ver'schließ|bar lockable; **~en** shut, close; *mit e-m Schlüssel*: lock (up); *e-n Brief*: seal; *sich e-r Sache* ~ close one's mind to.

verschlimmer|n [fɛr'ʃlimərn] (29) make worse; *fig. a.* aggravate; *sich* ~ get (*od.* grow) worse; **2ung** *f* aggravation, change for the worse.

ver'schlingen devour, (*a. fig. mit den Augen od. Ohren*) swallow (up *fig.*); *gierig*: gobble (up), wolf; (*in-ea.schlingen*; *a. sich*) intertwine, interlace, entangle; *verschlungen fig.* intricate; *Pfad*: tortuous.

verschlossen [~'ʃlɔsən] closed, shut; locked; *fig.* reserved, taciturn; **2heit** *f* reserve.

ver'schlucken swallow; *sich* ~ swallow the wrong way.

Ver'schluß *m* (~*mittel*) fastener, fastening; (*Schloß*) lock; (*Schnapp-2*) catch; *an Taschen usw.*: clasp; ⊕ (*Dichtung, Plombe*) seal; *phot.* shutter; *e-r Flasche*: stopper; *e-s Geschützes*: breech (mechanism); *Ware in* ~ *legen* bond; *unter* ~ under lock and key; **~laut** *gr. m* explosive.

ver'schlüssel|n (en)code; **2ung** *f* (en)coding.

ver'schmachten (sn) languish, pine away; die (*od.* be dying) of thirst.

ver'schmähen disdain, scorn.

ver'schmelz|en *v/t. u. v/i.* (sn) melt into one another; (*a. fig.*) fuse; ⚗ amalgamate (*a. fig.* = merge) (*zu, mit* in[to]); *Farben usw.*: blend; **2ung** *f* fusion, amalgamation, ⚕ *a.* merger.

ver'schmerzen get over (the loss of).

ver'schmieren smear (over).

verschmitzt [~'ʃmitst] sly; arch(ly *adv.*); **2heit** *f* slyness.

ver'schmutz|en *v/t.* soil; *Luft, Wasser*: pollute; *v/i.* (sn) get dirty, soil; **2ung** *f* pollution.

ver'schnappen: F *sich* ~ let the cat out of the bag, blurt it out.

ver'schnauf|en (*a. sich*) have a breather; **2pause** *f* breather.

ver'schneiden cut (up); *Stoff usw.*: cut wrong; *Wein usw.*: blend; (*kastrieren*) geld, castrate.

verschneit [~'ʃnaɪt] covered with snow, snow-covered, snowed up.

Ver'schnitt *m* blend.

verschnörkelt [fɛr'ʃnœrkəlt] ornate (*a. fig.*).

ver'schnupfen *fig.* nettle, pique; ⚕ *verschnupft sein* have a cold.

ver'schnüren tie up, cord (up); (*a. mit Schnüren zieren*) lace.

verschollen [~'ʃɔlən] not heard of (again); missing; ⚖ presumed dead.

ver'schonen spare; *j-n mit et.* ~ spare a p. a th.; *von Steuern usw. verschont* exempt(ed) from.

verschöne|(r)n [~'ʃø:nə(r)n] (29) embellish, beautify; (*verbessern*; *a. sich*) improve; **2rung** *f* embellishment.

verschossen [~'ʃɔsən] *Farbe*: faded; *fig.* F ~ *in* (*acc.*) madly in love with.

verschränken [~'ʃrɛŋkən] (25) *Arme*: cross.

ver'schrauben screw (up).

ver'schreib|en use (in writing); ⚕ prescribe (*j-m* for a p.); ⚖ assign, make over (to); (*falsch schreiben*) write incorrectly; *sich* ~ make a slip of the pen; *fig. sich e-r S.* ~ devote (*od. b.s.* sell) o.s. to a th.; **2ung** *f* order; prescription; bond, assignment; **~ungs-pflichtig** → *rezeptpflichtig.*

verschrien [~'ʃri:(ə)n] *adj.* notorious.

verschroben [~'ʃro:bən] eccentric, odd, cranky; **2heit** *f* eccentricity.

verschrotten [~ˈʃrɔtən] (26) scrap, *Auto*: *a.* junk.
ver'schrump|fen, ~eln *v/t. u. v/i.* (sn) shrink, shrivel (up).
ver'schüchtern intimidate.
ver'schuld|en 1. encumber with debts; (*schuld sein an*) be guilty of, be to blame for; *fig.* be the cause of; **2.** ♀ *n* (6) wrong, fault; (*Schuld*) guilt; **~et** indebted; involved in debts; *Sache*: encumbered; **♀ung** *f* indebtedness.
ver'schütten *Flüssigkeit*: spill; (*versperren*) block (up); *j-n*: bury alive.
verschwägert [~ˈʃvɛːgərt] related by marriage
ver'schweig|en keep secret, conceal (*j-m* from a p.); ♀ *n* (6) *u.* **♀ung** *f* concealment.
verschwend|en [~ˈʃvɛndən] (26) waste, lavish, squander; **♀er** *m* (7), **♀erin** *f* (16[1]) spendthrift, prodigal; **~erisch** prodigal, lavish (*mit* of); extravagant; wasteful; **♀ung** *f* waste, extravagance; **♀ungssucht** *f* prodigality, squandermania.
verschwiegen [fɛrˈʃviːgən] discreet; *Ort*: secret, secluded; **♀heit** *f* discretion, secrecy.
ver'schwimmen (sn) become indistinct *od.* blurred; *fig.* fade (away).
ver'schwinden 1. (sn) disappear, vanish; *j-n* (*od. et.*) *spurlos ~ lassen* spirit a p. (*od.* a th.) away; F *verschwinde!* make yourself scarce!, beat it!; *~d klein* infinitely small; **2.** ♀ *n* (6) disappearance.
verschwistert [~ˈʃvistərt] brother and sister; *fig.* closely united.
ver'schwitzen soak with sweat; F *fig.* forget (completely).
verschwollen [~ˈʃvɔlən] swollen.
verschwommen [~ˈʃvɔmən] vague, indistinct, hazy; *fig. a.* foggy; *Bild*: blurred; **♀heit** *f* indistinctness, vagueness.
ver'schwör|en: *sich ~* conspire, plot (*zu et.* a th.); **♀er** *m* (7) conspirator; **♀erin** *f* (16[1]) conspiratress; **♀ung** *f* conspiracy, plot.
ver'sehen 1. *Pflichten usw.*: perform, discharge; *Amt*: *a.* hold, administer; *Stellung*: fill; *Haushalt*: look after *the house*, keep *house*; (*übersehen*) overlook; *sich ~* make a mistake; *sich e-r S. ~* expect a th., be aware of a th.; *mit et. ~* furnish (*od.* supply *od.* provide *od.* equip) with; **2.** ♀ *n* (6) oversight; mistake; slip; **~tlich** by (a) mistake, inadvertently.
versehr|en [~ˈzeːrən] (25) injure, disable; **♀te** *m* (18) disabled person.
ver'send|en send, dispatch, forward; *auf dem Wasser-*, *Am. a. Landwege*: ship; *ins Ausland ~* export; **♀ung** *f* dispatch, shipment, forwarding; transport.
ver'sengen singe, burn, scorch.
ver'senk|en sink; *Schraubenkopf usw.*: countersink; *sich ~ in* (*acc.*) immerse o.s. into, *fig.* become absorbed in; **♀ung** *f* sinking; *thea.* trap-door.
versessen [~ˈzɛsən]: *~ auf* (*acc.*) bent (*od. sl.* nuts) on, mad after.
ver'setz|en *v/t.* displace, *a. Schüler*: remove; *bsd. Am. Schüler*: promote; *Baum*: transplant; (*staffeln*; *a.* ⊕) stagger; (*mit-ea. vertauschen*) transpose; *Beamte*: transfer; ⚔ post; (*verpfänden*) pawn, pledge; F (*vergebens warten lassen*) let *a p.* down, *Liebhaber usw.*: stand *a p.* up; (*vermischen*) mix, *metall.* alloy; *Schlag*: give, deal; *in e-e Lage, e-n Zustand ~* put into; *in Schwingungen ~* set vibrating; *s. Angst, Ruhestand usw.*; *v/i.* (*antworten*) reply, retort; **♀ung** *f* removal; transplanting; transposition; transfer; *Schule*: remove, *bsd. Am.* promotion; pledging; alloy; **♀ungszeugnis** *n* end-of-year report.
verseuch|en [fɛrˈzɔʏçən] (25) infect; contaminate; **♀ung** *f* infection, contamination.
'Versfuß *m* (metrical) foot.
Versicher|er [fɛrˈziçərər] *m* (7) insurer; **♀n** assure, affirm; *Eigentum usw.*: insure; *j-n e-r Sache ~* assure a p. of; *sich e-r Sache ~* make sure of, ascertain; *seien Sie dessen versichert* you may rest assured of it; **~te** *m*, *f* (18) insurant, *the* insured.
Ver'sicherung *f* affirmation; (*Eigentums♀ usw.*) insurance; **~sbetrug** *m* insurance fraud; **~sgesellschaft** *f* insurance-company; **~snehmer** *m* insurant, *the* insured; **~s-pflicht** *f* compulsory insurance; **♀s-pflichtig** subject to obligatory insurance; **~s-police** *f*, **~sschein** *m* insurance policy; **~s-prämie** *f* insurance premium; **~sschutz** *m* insurance coverage; **~ssumme** *f* sum insured; **~s-träger** *m* underwriter.
versickern [~ˈzikərn] ooze away.

ver'sieben F *s. verpatzen.*
ver'siegeln seal.
ver'siegen (sn) dry up.
versiert [vɛr'ziːrt] versed (*in dat.* in), experienced.
versilbern [fɛr'zilbərn] (29) silver (*a. fig.*); ⊕ silver-plate; *fig.* (*zu Geld machen*) convert into cash, sell.
ver'sinken (sn) sink; *fig.* lapse (*in acc.* into); *s. versunken.*
ver'sinnbildlich|en (25) symbolize; **2ung** *f* symbolization.
Version [vɛr'sjoːn] *f* version.
versippt [~'zipt] related (*mit* to).
versklaven [fɛr'sklaːvən] enslave.
'Vers|kunst *f* versification; **'~maß** *n* metre, *Am.* meter.
ver'soffen P boozy.
versohlen F [~'zoːlən] *fig.* (25) thrash (soundly); *bsd. Kind:* spank.
versöhn|en [~'zøːnən] (25) reconcile (*mit j-m* to, with; *mit e-m Schicksal usw.* to); *sich (wieder)* ~ be(come) reconciled, make it up; **~lich** conciliatory; ~ *stimmen* conciliate, placate; **2ung** *f* reconciliation.
versonnen [~'zɔnən] pensive.
ver'sorg|en provide, supply (*mit* with); *Familie:* provide for; (*betreuen*) take care of, look after; *Wunde:* tend, dress; **2er** *m* (7), **2erin** *f* (16[1]) provider; **2ung** *f* providing, supplying (with); providing (for); (*a.* ⚔) supply, provision; (*Betreuung*) care; (*Existenz*) subsistence, living; **2ungsbetrieb** *m* public supply service, public utility; **2ungs-empfänger(in** *f*) *m* pensioner; **2ungsgüter** *f/pl.* supplies; **2ungsleitung** *f* supply line; **2ungsnetz** *n* supply system; **2ungsschwierigkeiten** *f/pl.* difficulties of supply.
ver'spannen ⊕ brace, stay, guy.
verspät|en [~'ʃpɛːtən] (26): *sich* ~ be (*od.* come too) late; **~et** belated; **2ung** *f* lateness, delay; *Zug usw.*: (*20 Minuten*) ~ *haben* be (20 minutes) late *od.* overdue; *mit 2 Stunden* ~ 2 hours behind schedule; ~ *aufholen* make up lost time.
ver'speisen eat up.
verspeku'lieren: *sich* ~ make a bad speculation, ruin o.s. by speculation; *fig.* make a mistake.
ver'sperren bar, block up, barricade; *a. Aussicht:* obstruct.
ver'spiel|en *v/t.* lose (at play), gamble away; *v/i.* lose (the game); *fig. bei j-m* ~ get into a p.'s bad books; **~t** *adj.* playful.
versponnen [~'ʃpɔnən] meditative; ~ *in* (*dat., acc.*) wrapt (up) in.
ver'spott|en scoff at, mock, deride; **2ung** *f* derision, scoffing.
ver'sprech|en 1. promise (*a. fig.*); *sich* ~ make a slip (of the tongue); *s. sich verloben; sich etwas* ~ *von* expect much of; **2.** 2 *n* (6), **2ung** *f* promise.
ver'sprengen disperse, scatter.
ver'spritzen squirt (away), spray; (*verschütten*) spill; *sein Blut:* shed.
ver'sprühen spray.
ver'spüren feel, perceive, sense.
verstaatlich|en [fɛr'ʃtaːtliçən] (25) nationalize; **2ung** *f* nationalization.
verstädter|n [~'ʃtɛːtərn] *v/t.* (29) urbanize; **2ung** *f* urbanization.
verstadtlichen [~'ʃtatliçən] (25) municipalize.
Verstand [~'ʃtant] *m* (3) (*Denkkraft*) understanding, intelligence, intellect, brains *pl.*; (*Vernunft*) reason; (*Urteilsfähigkeit*) judg(e)ment; (*praktischer* ~) sense; *gesunder* ~ common sense; *klarer* ~ clear head; *den* ~ *verlieren* lose one's mind; *j-n um den* ~ *bringen* drive a p. mad; *s-n* ~ *zusammennehmen* keep one's wits about one; *das geht über m-n* ~ that's beyond me.
Verstandes|kraft [~'ʃtandəs-] *f* intellectual power *od.* faculty; **2mäßig** rational; **~mensch** *m* matter-of-fact person; **~schärfe** *f* sagacity.
verständ|ig [~'ʃtɛndiç] intelligent; (*vernünftig denkend od. gedacht*) reasonable, sensible; (*richtig urteilend*) judicious; **~igen** [~gən] inform, notify (*von* of); *sich* ~ *mit j-m in e-r fremden Sprache:* make o.s. understood to a p.; (*übereinkommen*) come to an understanding with a p.; **2igung** *f* information; (*Übereinkunft*) understanding, agreement; *teleph. usw.* communication; (*Hörbarkeit*) audibility; **2igungsschwierigkeiten** *f/pl.* communication difficulties; **~lich** [~'ʃtɛnt-] intelligible; (*deutlich*) distinct, clear; *fig.* understandable; *j-m et.* ~ *machen* make a th. clear to a p.; *sich* ~ *machen* make o.s. understood (*j-m* by a p.).
Verständnis [~'ʃtɛntnis] *n* (4[1]) (*Ver-*

stehen) comprehension, *a. weitS.* understanding; (*Einsicht*) insight; (*Würdigung*) appreciation (*für* of); (*Mitfühlen*) sympathy; ~ *haben für* appreciate, understand; 2**-innig** knowing; 2**los** uncomprehending; *Blick, Gesicht*: blank; (*nicht würdigend*) unappreciative; ~**losigkeit** *f* lack of understanding; unappreciativeness; 2**voll** intelligent; *weitS.* understanding; (*würdigend*) appreciative; *Blick*: knowing.

ver'stärk|en strengthen, (*a.* ⚔ *u.* ⊕) reinforce; ⚡ boost; *Radio*: amplify; (*steigern*) intensify, strengthen, increase (*alle a. sich*); 2**er** *m* (7) *Radio*: amplifier; 2**erröhre** amplifier valve (*Am.* tube); 2**ung** *f* strengthening, (*a.* ⚔) reinforcement; amplification; intensification.

ver'staub|en get dusty; ~**t** *fig.* antiquated.

ver'stauch|en (25) sprain; 2**ung** *f* sprain(ing).

ver'stauen stow away.

Versteck [fɛr'ʃtɛk] *n* (3) hiding-place; ~ *spielen* play hide-and-seek; 2**en**[1] *v/t.* (*a. versteckt halten*) hide (*a. sich*), conceal; ~**en**[2] *n od.* ~**spiel** *n* hide-and-seek (*a. fig.*); 2**t** hidden (*a. fig.*).

ver'stehen understand, F get; (*einsehen*) see; (*begreifen*) comprehend, grasp, catch; (*erkennen*) realize; (*deuten*) read; (*können*) *Sprache usw.*: know; *es* ~ *zu inf.* manage to, know how to *inf.*; *sich* ~ *auf* (*acc.*) know well; *sich mit j-m gut* ~ get on (*od.* along) well with a p.; *sich* ~ *zu* (*sich entschließen*) bring o.s. to *do*, (*einwilligen*) agree to; (*j-m*) *zu* ~ *geben* intimate (to a p.), give (a p.) to understand; *Spaß* ~ take (*od.* see) a joke; ~ *Sie?* (do) you see?; *ich verstehe!* I see!; *verstanden?* do you understand (*od.* F get) me?; *falsch* ~ misunderstand; *verstehe mich recht!* don't misunderstand me!; (*das*) *versteht sich!* that's understood!; *was* ~ *Sie unter* (*dat.*) ...? what do you mean (*od.* understand) by ...?; *er versteht etwas davon* he knows a thing or two about it; *er versteht gar nichts davon* he doesn't know the first thing about it; *es versteht sich von selbst* it goes without saying.

ver'steif|en ⊕ strut, prop; (*a. sich* ~) stiffen; *fig. sich* ~ *auf* (*acc.*) keep doggedly at; insist on; 2**ung** *f* ⊕ strut(ting) *etc.*

ver'steigen: *sich* ~ lose one's way (in the mountains); *fig. sich* ~ *zu* ... go so far as to.

ver'steiger|n sell by auction; 2**ung** *f* (sale by [*Am.* at]) auction, public sale.

versteiner|n [~'ʃtaɪnərn] *v/t. u. v/i.* (29, sn) (*a. fig.*) turn (in)to stone, (*a. fig.*) petrify; 2**ung** *f* petrifaction, fossil.

verstell|bar [~'ʃtɛlbɑːr] adjustable; ~**en** (*falsch stellen*) misplace; (*versperren*) block; *Handschrift, Stimme usw.*: disguise, dissemble; ⊕ shift, adjust; *sich* ~ play-act, feign, dissemble; 2**ung** *f* dissimulation; disguise.

ver'steuer|n pay duty (*od.* tax) on; *zu* ~ taxable; 2**ung** *f* payment of duty (*e-r S.* on a th.).

verstiegen [~'ʃtiːgən] *adj. fig.* high-flown, eccentric(ally *adv.*); 2**heit** *f* eccentricity.

ver'stimm|en put out of tune; *Radio*: detune; *fig.* put out (of humo[u]r), annoy; ~**t** out of tune; *fig.* cross (*über acc.* with); 2**ung** *f* ill-humo(u)r; *zwischen zweien*: disagreement, tiff, resentment, ill-feeling.

verstockt [~'ʃtɔkt] hardened, callous; impenitent; 2**heit** *f* obduracy; (*a. eccl.*) impenitence.

verstohlen [~'ʃtoːlən] furtive, stealthy; *adv. a.* by stealth; ~ *lachen* laugh in one's sleeve.

ver'stopf|en stop (up); (*versperren*) clog, obstruct; *Straße*: jam; ⚕ constipate; 2**ung** *f* stopping; obstruction; *Verkehr*: jam; ⚕ constipation.

verstorben [fɛr'ʃtɔrbən] late, deceased, defunct; 2**e** *m, f* deceased.

verstört [~'ʃtøːrt] distracted; consternated, wild; 2**heit** *f* distraction, consternation.

Ver'stoß *m* (3^2 *u.* ^{3}) offen|ce, *Am.* -se (*gegen* against); (*Zuwiderhandlung*) *a.* contravention, violation (of); (*Übertretung*) infringement (of); (*Fehler*) blunder, mistake; 2**en** *v/t.* (*austreiben*) expel (*aus* from); cast off (*od.* out); *Kind usw.*: reject; *v/i.* ~ *gegen* offend against, violate, contravene; ~**ung** *f* expulsion; rejection.

ver'streb|en ⊕ strut, brace; 2**ung** [*f* strut(ting), bracing.]

ver'streichen *v/i.* (sn) *Zeit*: pass (away), slip by; *Frist*: expire; *v/t. Fuge*: stop up; *Butter, Salbe*: spread.

ver'streuen disperse, scatter; *fig. a.* dot (about); *über e-e Fläche verstreut sein* dot *a country etc.*

ver'stricken entangle, ensnare; *verstrickt in e-e S.* involved in.

verstümmel|n [~'ʃtyməln] (29) mutilate; **2ung** *f* mutilation.

verstummen [~'ʃtumən] (25, sn) grow dumb *od.* silent.

Versuch [~'zu:x] *m* (3) attempt, trial (*a.* ⊕), F try; *phys. usw.* experiment; (*Probe, a.* ⊕) test; (*Bemühung*) effort; *e-n ~ machen mit* give *a p. od. a th.* a trial; try *a p. od. a th.*, F have a go at *a th.*; **2en** try, attempt; (*kosten*) taste; *j-n*: tempt; *es ~ mit s. Versuch (machen)*; **~er** *m* (7), **~erin** *f* (16[1]) tempter, *f a.* temptress.

Ver'suchs|-anlage *f* experimental (*od.* pilot) plant; **~-anstalt** *f* research institute; **~ballon** *m* trial balloon; *fig. a.* ballon d'essai (*fr.*), kite; **~bohrung** *f* trial drilling; **~gelände** *n* testing ground; **~-ingenieur** *m* research engineer; **~kaninchen** *n fig.* guinea-pig; **~projekt** *n* pilot project; **~reihe** ⚘, ⊕ *f* series of tests; **~stadium** *n* experimental stage; **~-tier** *n* experimental animal; **2weise** by way of trial *od.* (an) experiment; tentatively; **~zwecke** *m/pl.*: *zu ~n* for experimental purposes.

Ver'suchung *f* temptation; *in ~ bringen* tempt; *in ~ sein (od. kommen)* be tempted.

versumpf|en [~'zumpfən] (25, sn) become marshy; F *fig.* get bogged down; **~t** swampy, boggy.

ver'sündig|en: *sich ~* sin (*an dat.* against); **2ung** *f* sin.

versunken [~'zuŋkən] *fig. ~ in (acc.)* absorbed (*od.* lost) in; **2heit** *f fig.* absorption.

ver'süßen sweeten (*a. fig.*).

ver'tag|en (*a. sich*) adjourn (*auf* till); **2ung** *f* adjournment.

vertändeln trifle away.

vertäuen ⚓ [~'tɔʏən] moor.

ver'tausch|en exchange (*gegen* for); *die Rollen*: reverse; *s. verwechseln*; **2ung** *f* exchange.

verteidig|en [~'taɪdigən] (25) defend; **2er** *m* (7), **2erin** *f* (16[1]) defender; *fig. a.* advocate; ⚖ *~ des Angeklagten*: counsel for the defence, *Am.* defense counsel; *Fußball*: back; **2ung** *f* defen|ce, *Am.* -se; **2ungs-ausgaben** *f/pl.* defen|ce (*Am.* -se) expenditure *sg.*; **2ungsbündnis** *n* defensive alliance; **2ungsfall** *m*: *im ~e* in case of defen|ce, *Am.* -se; **2ungskrieg** *m* defensive war; **2ungsminister** *m* Minister of Defence, *Am.* Secretary of Defense; **2ungsministerium** *n* Ministry of Defence, *Am.* Department of Defense; **2ungs-politik** *f* defen|ce (*Am.* -se) policy; **2ungsrede** *f* speech for the defen|ce, *Am.* -se; *weitS.* apology.

ver'teil|en distribute (*auf acc., unter acc.* among); (*teilen*) divide; (*unter sich ~*) share; *s. zuteilen*; *Farbe usw., a. fig.*: spread; *Geschwulst, Nebel*: (*a. sich*) disperse; **2er** *m* (7) distributor (*a.* ⊕ *u.* ✈); (*Einzelhändler*) retailer; **2erkasten** ⚡ *m* distributor box; **2ung** *f* distribution.

verteuern [fɛr'tɔʏərn] (29) raise (*od.* increase) the price of.

verteufel|n [~'tɔʏfəln] (29) demonise; **~t** F devilish, fiendish, hellish.

vertief|en [~'ti:fən] (25) (*a. sich*) deepen (*a. fig.*); (*aushöhlen*) hollow out; *sich ~ in (acc.)* plunge into, *in Gedanken*: become absorbed in; **2ung** *f* deepening (*a. fig.*); (*Höhlung*) hollow, cavity; (*Aussparung*) recess; *fig.* absorption.

vertiert [fɛr'ti:rt] brutish.

vertikal [vɛrti'kɑ:l] vertical; **2e** *f* (15) vertical line.

vertilg|en [fɛr'tilgən] exterminate; *Vorrat*, F *Speise*: consume; **2ung** *f* extermination.

ver'tippen type wrong; *sich ~* make a typing error.

verton|en ♪ [~'to:nən] (25) set to music; **2ung** *f* setting to music.

vertrackt F [~'trakt] confounded.

Vertrag [~'trɑ:k] *m* (3[3]) agreement, contract; *pol.* treaty; (*Pakt*) pact; *e-n ~ schließen* make (*od.* enter into) an agreement; **2en** [~gən] (*aushalten*) endure, (*a. j-n, Widerspruch, Alkohol usw.*) stand; (*dulden, zulassen*) bear (*a. v. Sachen*), tolerate; *diese Speise kann ich nicht ~* this food does not agree with me; *sich ~ Sachen*: be compatible, *Farben* *usw.*, *a. Personen*: agree; *sich wieder* ~ be reconciled (*mit* with *a p.*), make it up (with); *sich* (*gut, schlecht*) *mit-ea.* ~ get on *od.* along (well, ill) together; ♀**lich** [~'trɑːk-] contractual, (*adv.* as) stipulated; *adv.* by contract; *sich* ~ *verpflichten* contract (*zu* to).

verträglich [fɛr'trɛːkliç] sociable, peaceable; *Nahrung usw.*: (easily) digestible; ♀**keit** *f* sociability; digestibility.

Ver'trags|bedingungen *f/pl.* terms of the contract; ~**bruch** *m* breach of contract; ♀**brüchig** defaulting; ~ *werden* commit a breach of contract.

ver'tragschließend contracting.

Ver'trags|-entwurf *m* draft agreement; ♀**gemäß**, ♀**mäßig** (*adv.* as) stipulated; ~**gegenstand** *m* object of the agreement; ~**händler** *m* authorized retailer; ~**partei** *f*, ~**partner** *m* party to an agreement; ~**strafe** *f* (conventional) penalty; ~**verhältnis** *n* contractual relationship; ♀**widrig** contrary to an agreement.

ver'trauen 1. *v/t. s. an*~; *v/i.* trust (*j-m* a p.); ~ *auf* (*acc.*) trust in, rely (up)on; **2.** ♀ *n* (6) confidence, trust (*auf acc.* in); *im* ~ confidentially; *ganz im* ~ F between you and me; *im* ~ *auf* (*acc.*) trusting to, relying on; ~ *haben zu* have confidence in, trust; *j-m sein* ~ *schenken*, ~ *in j-n setzen* place confidence in a p.; *j-n ins* ~ *ziehen* confide in a p.; ~**-erweckend** inspiring trust *od.* confidence.

Ver'trauens|basis *f* basis of mutual trust; ~**bruch** *m* breach (*od.* betrayal) of trust; ~**frage** *f* matter of trust; *pol. die* ~ *stellen* propose a vote of confidence; ~**mann** *m*, ~**person** *f* confidant(e *f*); (*Sprecher*) spokesman; ~**sache** *f* confidential matter; ♀**selig** (too) confiding; gullible; ~**seligkeit** *f* blind confidence; ~**stellung** *f* position of trust; ♀**voll** trustful, trusting; ~**votum** *n* vote of confidence; ♀**würdig** trustworthy, reliable.

ver'trauern pass in mourning.

ver'traulich confidential; *Verkehr*: intimate, familiar; *s. streng*; ♀**keit** *f* confidence; intimacy, familiarity.

ver'träum|en dream away; ~**t** dreamy.

ver'traut intimate, familiar; ~ *mit* well acquainted with, well versed in; (*sich*) ~ *machen mit* acquaint *od.* familiarize (o.s.) with; ♀**e** *m, f* (18) intimate friend, confidant(e *f*); ♀**heit** *f* familiarity (*mit* with); intimate knowledge (of).

ver'treib|en drive away; (*ausstoßen*) expel (*aus* from); *Ware*: sell, distribute; *Sorgen usw.*: banish; *Krankheit*: cure; (*sich*) *die Zeit* ~ while away; ♀**ung** *f* expulsion.

ver'tret|bar justifiable; *Standpunkt*: tenable; ~**en** *j-n*, *Firma usw.*: represent; *im Amt*: act (*od.* substitute *od.* deputize) for; (*für j-n auftreten*, *a.* ⚖) appear (*od.* plead) for *a p.*; ⚖ *u. fig. j-s Sache* ~ plead a p.'s cause, hold a brief for a p.; *j-s Interesse*: attend to, look after; *Ansicht*: hold, take; *als Fürsprecher*: advocate; *parl. Bezirk*: sit for; (*verantworten*) answer for *a th.*; ~ *sein* (*zugegen od. vorhanden sn*) be present; *sich den Fuß* ~ sprain one's foot; *sich die Beine* ~ stretch one's legs; *j-m den Weg* ~ stop a p.; ♀**er** *m* (7), ♀**erin** *f* (16[1]) representative; ☤ *a.* agent; (*Reise*♀) commercial travel(l)er, *Am.* traveling salesmann; (*Bevollmächtigte*) agent, proxy; *im Amt*: substitute, deputy; (*Fürsprecher*) advocate; (*hervorragender od. typischer* ~) exponent; ♀**ung** *f* representation; ☤ agency; *im Amt*: substitution; *in* ~ by proxy, acting for, (signed) for; *in* ~ *j-s* as representative of a p.; *j-s* ~ *übernehmen* deputize for a p.

Vertrieb [fɛr'triːp] *m* (3) sale, distribution, marketing; ~**ene** [~'triːbənə] *m, f* (18) expellee; ~**s-abteilung** *f* sales department; ~**skosten** *pl.* marketing costs; ~**sleiter**(**in** *f*) *m* sales manager; ~**s-organisation** *f* marketing organization; ~**srecht** *n* right of sale; (*Konzession*) licen|ce, *Am.* -se.

ver'trinken spend on drink.

ver'trocknen (sn) dry (up).

ver'trödeln dawdle away.

ver'trösten feed with hopes (*auf acc.* of); (*hinhalten*) put off.

ver'tun waste, squander; *sich* ~ make a mistake.

ver'tusch|en hush up; ♀**ung**(**smanöver** *n*) *f* cover-up.

ver'-übeln (26) *et.*: take amiss; *j-m et.* ~ blame a p. for a th.; *ich hoffe,*

Sie werden mir die Frage nicht ~ I hope you won't mind the question.
ver'-üb|en commit, perpetrate; **≈ung** *f* committing, perpetration.
ver'-ulken F (25) make fun of, F pull *a p.'s* leg, kid.
ver'-un|glimpfen [~glimpfən] (25) disparage, calumniate; **~glücken** [~glykən] (sn) have (*tödlich*: die in) an accident; *S.*: fail, go wrong; **≈glückte** *m, f* (18) casualty.
ver'-unreinig|en soil; dirty (*a. Wunde*); *Luft, Wasser usw.*: pollute; *fig.* defile; **≈ung** *f* soiling; pollution; defilement.
ver'-unsichern F rattle.
ver'-unstalten [~ʃtaltən] (26) deform, disfigure, deface.
ver'-untreuen [~trɔʏən] (25) embezzle; **≈ung** *f* embezzlement.
ver'-unzieren disfigure, mar.
verursachen [~'ʔu:rzaxən] (25) cause, occasion; give rise to, produce; (*nach sich ziehen*) entail.
ver'-urteil|en sentence; condemn (*a. fig.*); **≈ung** *f* condemnation.
vervielfältig|en [~'fi:lfɛltigən] (25) (*a. sich*) multiply; (*nachbilden, a. Schriftsatz*) duplicate; *Text, Bild*: copy; (*hektographieren*) mimeograph; **≈ung** *f* multiplication; duplication, copying; *konkret*: duplicate; **≈ungs-apparat** *m* duplicator, copying machine.
vervollkommn|en [~'fɔlkɔmnən] (26) perfect; **≈ung** *f* perfection.
vervollständig|en [~'fɔlʃtɛndigən] (25) complete; **≈ung** *f* completion.
ver'wachs|en 1. (sn) grow together; ⚕ *Knochen*: unite; *Wunde*: heal up; (*überwachsen*) become overgrown; **2.** *adj.* (*verkrüppelt*) deformed; (*bucklig*) hunchbacked; *fig.* ~ *mit* bound up with; (deeply) rooted in.
ver'wackeln *phot.* blur.
ver'wahren keep; *fig. sich* ~ protest (*gegen* against).
verwahrlos|en [~'va:rlo:zən] *v/t.* neglect; *v/i.* (sn) be neglected, *P.*: be demoralized, go to the bad; **~t** [~st] *adj.* uncared-for, neglected; *P.*: *a.* unkempt, *sittlich*: demoralized, wayward; **≈ung** [~zuŋ] *f* neglect; demoralization.
Ver'wahrung *f* keeping; (*Obhut*) charge, custody; *fig.* protest; *zur* ~ in trust; (*j-m*) *in* ~ *geben* deposit (with a p.), give into (a p.'s) charge; *in* ~ *nehmen* take charge of; *gegen et.* ~ *einlegen* enter a protest against.
verwaisen [~'vaɪzən] (sn) be orphaned; *fig.* be deserted.
ver'walt|en administer, manage; (*führen*) conduct; *Amt*: hold; **≈er** *m* (7) administrator, manager; (*Treuhänder*) trustee, custodian; (*Guts≈*) steward; (*Haus≈*) caretaker; **≈erin** *f* (16[1]) manageress.
Ver'waltung *f* administration (*a.* = *Staats≈*), management; **~(sbehörde)** *f* administrative authority; **~s-apparat** *m* administrative machinery; **~sbe-amte** *m* Civil Servant; **~sbezirk** *m* administrative district; **~sdienst** *m* Civil Service; **~skosten** *pl.* administrative expenses; **~s-personal** *n* administrative staff; **~srat** *m* managing board; **~szweig** *m* administrative department.
ver'wand|eln change (*a. sich*); (*umwandeln*) turn, convert; (*umformen*) transform (*alle*: *in acc.* into); *Strafe*: commute; *Fußball*: score; *sich* ~ be transformed, *etc.*; **≈lung** *f* change; conversion; transformation; **≈lungskünstler** *m* quick-change artist.
verwandt [fɛr'vant] related (*mit* to); *fig. a.* kindred, (*bsd. Wörter*) cognate (to, with); *pred.* (*a. fig.*) (a)kin (to); *~e Seele* congenial (*od.* kindred) soul; **≈e** *m, f* (18) relative, relation; **≈schaft** *f* relationship (*a. fig.*), kinship; (*die Verwandten*) relations *pl.*; *fig.* congeniality; *bsd. durch Heirat od.* ⚖ affinity; **~schaftlich** as (among) relatives; *~e Beziehungen* relations; **≈schaftsgrad** *m* degree of relationship *od.* affinity.
verwanzt [~'vantst] buggy.
ver'warn|en warn (off), admonish; *strafend*: caution (*a. Sport*); **≈ung** *f* warning, admonition; caution.
ver'waschen 1. *v/t.* use up in washing; **2.** *adj.* washed out, faded; *fig. a.* vapid, wishy-washy.
ver'wässern water (down *a. fig.*).
ver'weben interweave.
ver'wechs|eln change by mistake, exchange; (*durch-ea.-bringen*) confound (*mit* with), mix up (with); *j-n mit e-m andern* ~ (mis)take a p. for another; **≈lung** *f* mistake; confusion.
verwegen [~'ve:gən] audacious, dar-

ing, bold; **2heit** *f* audacity, boldness, daredevilry.

ver'weh|en (sn) blow away; *Stimme usw.*: trail away; **2ung** *f* drift.

ver'wehren *et.*: bar; *j-m et.*: keep (*od.* debar) a p. from.

verweichlich|en [~'vaıçliçən] (25) *v/t.* render effeminate (*od.* soft); *v/i.* (sn) grow effeminate (*od.* soft); **~t** *adj.* effeminate, soft, coddled.

ver'weiger|n deny, refuse; **2ung** *f* denial, refusal.

ver'weilen stay, linger; *fig.* ~ *bei et.* dwell on.

verweint [~'vaınt] tear-stained *face*; *eyes* red with tears.

Verweis [~'vaıs] *m* (4) reprimand, reproof, rebuke; (*Hinweis*) reference; **2en** [~zən] (*verbannen*) banish, exile; *Schüler*: expel; *Sport*: warn (*des Feldes* off the field); *j-m et.* ~ reprimand a p. for; ~ *auf od. an* (*acc.*) refer to; **~ung** *f* banishment; expulsion; reference (*auf, an acc.* to); **~ungszeichen** *n* mark of reference.

ver'welken (sn) fade, wither.

verweltlich|en [fɛr'vɛltliçən] (25) secularize; **2ung** *f* secularization.

verwend|bar [fɛr'vɛntbɑːr] applicable, usable; **2barkeit** *f* usability, applicability; **~en** [~dən] apply (*auf acc., für* to), employ, use (in, for); (*nützlich*) ~ utilize; (*aufwenden*) spend, expend; *Mühe, Sorgfalt* ~ *auf* bestow on; *Zeit* ~ *auf* devote to; *sich bei j-m* ~ *für* intercede with a p. for; **2ung** *f* application, use, employment; intercession; *keine* ~ *haben für* have no use for; **~ungsfähig** *s. verwendbar*; **2ungszweck** *m* use, purpose.

ver'werf|en reject; ⚖ dismiss (*a. weitS.*); *sich* ~ *Holz*: warp; *geol.* fault; **~lich** objectionable, blamable, reprehensible; **2ung** *f* rejection; ⚖ dismissal; warping; *geol.* fault.

verwert|bar [~'veːrtbɑːr] usable; ✝ realizable; **~en** turn to account, utilize, use; (*zu Geld machen*) realize; *geschäftlich*: commercialize; *Patent*: exploit; **2ung** *f* utilization; realization; commercialization; exploitation.

verwes|en [~'veːzən] (27) *v/i.* (sn) rot, putrefy; (*sich zersetzen*) decay, decompose; *v/t.* (*verwalten*) administer; **2er** *m* (7) administrator; **~lich** [~'veːsliç] putrefiable; **2ung** [~zuŋ] *f* decay, putrefaction, decomposition; (*Verwaltung*) administration.

ver'wetten bet, stake (*für* on); (*verlieren*) lose by betting.

ver'wickel|n entangle (*in acc.* in); *fig. a.* engage (in), involve (in); *Angelegenheit*: complicate; **~t** *fig.* complicated, intricate; **2ung** *f* entanglement; complication.

ver'wildern ⚘ *u. fig.* (29, sn) run wild.

ver'wind|en get over *a th.*; ⊕ distort, twist; **2ung** *f* ⊕ distortion.

ver'wirken forfeit; *Strafe*: incur.

ver'wirklich|en (25) realize; *sich* ~ be realized, come true; **2ung** *f* realization.

Ver'wirkung *f* forfeiture.

verwirr|en [~'virən] (25) entangle; *fig. j-n*: confound, bewilder, perplex, *a. et.*: confuse; (*verlegen machen*) embarrass; *sich* ~ get entangled; **2ung** *f* entanglement; *fig.* confusion, perplexity; *in* ~ *geraten od. sein* get into (*od.* be in) confusion.

ver'wirtschaften squander away.

ver'wischen wipe (*od.* blot) out; (*a. fig.*) efface; (*undeutlich machen*) blur.

ver'witter|n (sn) weather; **~t** *adj.* weather-beaten, weather-worn.

verwitwet [~'vitvət] widowed.

verwöhn|en [fɛr'vøːnən] (25) spoil; (*verhätscheln*) coddle, pamper; **~t** *adj.* pampered; *Kind*: *a.* spoilt; *Gaumen, Geschmack*: fastidious; **2ung** *f* spoiling; pampering.

verworfen [~'vɔrfən[depraved; **2heit** *f* depravity.

verworren [~'vɔrən] confused, muddled; **2heit** *f* confusion.

verwund|bar [~'vuntbɑːr] vulnerable; **~en** [~dən] (26) wound.

ver'wunder|lich astonishing, odd, strange; **~n** astonish; *sich* ~ wonder, be astonished (*über acc.* at); *verwundert* amazed; **2ung** *f* astonishment, amazement.

Ver'wund|ete *m* (18) wounded person; ⚔ casualty; **~ung** *f* wound.

ver'wünsch|en curse, execrate; *verwünscht!* confound it!; **2ung** *f* curse.

verwurschteln F [~'vurʃtəln] mess up.

ver'wurzelt deeply rooted.

verwüst|en [~'vy:stən] (26) devastate, (*a. fig.*) ravage; **2ung** *f* devastation, ravage(s *pl.*).
ver'zag|en despair (*an dat.* of); **~t** [~'tsa:kt] despondent, disheartened; **2t-heit** *f* despondency.
ver'zählen: *sich* ~ miscount.
verzahnen [~'tsa:nən] *Rad*: tooth, gear, cog; *Balken usw.*: indent; (*mit-ea.*) ~ *fig.* dovetail, mesh.
ver'zapfen *Bier usw.*: sell on draught; ⊕ tenon, mortise; F *fig.* dish out; *Unsinn* ~ talk nonsense.
verzärtel|n [fɛr'tsɛ:rtəln] (29) coddle, pamper; **2ung** *f* pampering; softness.
ver'zaubern bewitch, enchant, charm; ~ *in* (*acc.*) transform into.
verzehnfachen [~'tse:nfaxən] (25) increase tenfold, decuple.
Ver'zehr *m* (3, *o. pl.*) consumption; **2en** consume (*a. fig.*), eat (up); *fig. sich* ~ *vor* (*dat.*) be consumed with.
ver'zeich|nen note down, register; *in e-r Liste*: list; *amtlich*: record; (*schlecht zeichnen*) draw incorrectly; *opt. u. fig.* distort; *fig.* (*erzielen*) register, secure; **~net** *adj. paint.* out of drawing; **2nis** *n* (4[1]) list; catalog(ue); *amtliches*: register; *v. Möbeln usw.*: inventory; *im Buch*: index; (*Tabelle*) table, schedule.
ver'zeih|en pardon, forgive (*beide*: *j-m* [et.] a p. [a th.]); *bsd.* ⚖ condone; ~ *Sie!* pardon me!, excuse me!; (so) sorry!; **~lich** pardonable; **2ung** *f* pardon; *j-n um* ~ *bitten* beg a p.'s pardon; ~! (I beg your) pardon!; (so) sorry!
ver'zerr|en distort (*a. fig.*); **2ung** *f* distortion; *körperlich*: contortion.
verzetteln [~'tsɛtəln] (29) card-index; *fig.* fritter away; *sich* ~ squander one's strength.
Verzicht [fɛr'tsiçt] *m* (*a.* **~leistung** *f*) renunciation (*auf acc.* of); (*Opfer*) sacrifice; ⚖ waiver; ~ *leisten* = **2en** (26) (*auf acc.*) renounce; dispense with; *auf Vergnügen usw.*: for(e)go; ⚖ waive; *ich kann darauf* ~ I can do without it.
ver'ziehen *v/i.* (sn) (re)move; (*zögern*) linger; *v/t. Kind*: spoil; (*verzerren*) distort; *Mund*: screw up; *das Gesicht* ~ (make a) grimace; *s. Miene*; *sich* ~ *Holz*: warp; (*verschwinden, sich entfernen*) disappear, vanish, F beat it; *Volksmenge, Wolken*: disperse.
ver'zier|en adorn, decorate; **2ung** *f* decoration; (*Schmuck*) ornament.
verzinken [~'tsiŋkən] (25) zinc.
verzinnen [~'tsinən] (25) tin.
verzins|en [~'tsinzən] (27) pay interest for; *e-e Summe zu 3%* ~ pay 3 per cent on a sum; *sich* ~ yield interest; **~lich** [~'tsins-] interest-bearing; ~ *mit 4%* bearing interest at 4 per cent; ~ *anlegen* put out at interest; **2ung** [~zuŋ] *f* (payment of) interest; (*Zinssatz*) interest rate; (*Zinsertrag*) interest return.
ver'zöger|n delay, retard; slow down (*a. sich*); *sich* ~ be delayed; **2ung** *f* delay, retardation; *phys.* lag; **2ungs-taktik** *f* delaying tactics *pl.*
ver'zoll|en pay duty on; ⚓ clear; *haben Sie et. zu* ~? have you anything to declare?; **2ung** *f* payment of duty; ⚓ clearance.
ver'zück|en ecstasize, enrapture; **~t** ecstatic(ally *adv*); **2ung** *f* ecstasy, rapture; *in* ~ *geraten* go into ecstasies.
ver'zuckern (29) sugar (*a. fig*).
Ver'zug *m* (3) delay; *es ist Gefahr im* ~ there is imminent danger; ⚖ *in* ~ *geraten* come in default; *im* ~ *sein* default (*mit* with); **~s-tage** *m/pl.* days of grace; **~szinsen** *m/pl.* interest *sg.* on arrears.
ver'zweif|eln (h. *u.* sn) despair (*an dat.* of); *es ist zum* 2 it is enough to drive one to despair; **~elt** *adj.* despairing; (*aussichtslos*; *rücksichtslos*) desperate; **2lung** *f* despair; *zur* ~ *bringen od. treiben* drive to despair.
verzweig|en [fɛr'tsvaɪgən] (25) (*a. sich*) branch out, ramify; **2ung** *f* ramification, branching.
verzwickt [~'tsvikt] intricate, complicated, tricky.
Vesper *eccl.* ['fɛspər] *f* (15) vespers *pl.*; '**~brot** *n* snack; '**2n** (29) have a snack.
Vestibül [vɛsti'by:l] *n* (3) vestibule, [hall.]
Veteran [vete'ra:n] *m* (12) *bsd. Brt.* ex-serviceman, *Am. od. fig.* veteran.
Veterinär [veteri'nɛ:r] *m* (3) veterinary surgeon, veterinarian; **~klinik** *f* veterinary hospital.
Veto ['ve:to] *n* (11) veto; *ein* ~ *einlegen gegen* put a veto on, veto *a th.*; '**~recht** *n* power of veto.
Vettel ['fɛtəl] *f* (16): *alte* ~ old hag.

Vetter ['fɛtər] *m* (10) cousin; '**~nwirtschaft** *f* nepotism, F cronyism.

Vexier|bild [vɛ'ksi:rbilt] *n* picture-puzzle; **2en** vex, tease; **~spiegel** *m* distorting mirror.

Viadukt [via'dukt] *m* (3) viaduct.

Vibration [vibra'tsjo:n] *f* vibration.

vibrieren [vi'bri:rən] vibrate.

Video|-aufnahme ['vi:deo-] *f* video-recording; '**~band** *n* video tape; '**~film** *m* video film; '**~gerät** *n* video recorder; '**~kamera** *f* video camera; '**~kassette** *f* video cassette; **~recorder** ['~rekɔrdər] *m* (7) video recorder; '**~spiel** *n* video game; '**~system** *n* video system; '**~text** *m* teletext; **~thek** [video'te:k] *f* (15) video-tape library; '**~-überwachung** *f* closed-circuit television monitoring.

Vieh [fi:] (3, *o. pl.*) (*Tier*) animal; *agr.* cattle, livestock; *weitS., a. fig.* brute, beast; '**~-ausstellung** *f* cattle-show; '**~bestand** *m* livestock; '**~bremse** *f* gadfly; '**~futter** *n* fodder; '**~händler** *m* cattle-dealer; '**~hof** *m* stockyard.

'**viehisch** bestial, beastly, brutal.

'**Vieh|markt** *m* cattle-market; '**~seuche** *f* cattle-plague, rinderpest; '**~wagen** 🚃 *m* cattle van; '**~weide** *f* pasturage; '**~zucht** *f* stock-farming, cattle-breeding; '**~züchter** *m* stock-farmer, cattle-breeder.

viel [fi:l] (*comp. mehr, sup. meist*) much, *pl.* many; *sehr ~* a great deal; *sehr ~e pl.* a great many; *~ besser* much better; *ziemlich ~* a good deal (of); *ziemlich ~e pl.* a good many; *viel Platz, Zeit usw.* F plenty of room, time, *etc.*; *das ~e Geld* all that money; *seine ~en Geschäfte* his numerous affairs; *s. Spaß*; '**~beschäftigt** very busy; **~deutig** ['~dɔʏtiç] ambiguous; '**2-eck** *n* (3) polygon; **~erlei** ['~ər'laɪ] *adj.* of many kinds, many kinds of, multifarious; **~erorts** ['~ər'ʔɔrts] in many places, widely; '**~fach** multiple; *adv.* in many cases; frequently; **2falt** ['~falt] *f* (16, *o. pl.*) (great) variety, diversity; **~fältig** ['~fɛltiç] manifold, multifarious; '**2fältigkeit** *f s. Vielfalt*; '**~farbig** many-colo(u)red; **2fraß** ['~fra:s] *m* glutton (*a. zo.*); '**~geliebt** well beloved; **~geprüft** ['~gəpry:ft] much tried; **~gereist** ['~gəraɪst] (much) travel(l)ed; **~gestaltig** ['~gəʃtaltiç] multiform; **2götterei** ['~gœtə'raɪ] *f* polytheism; '**2heit** *f* multiplicity, variety; (*Menge*) multitude; '**~jährig** of many years, many years of ...; **~'leicht** perhaps, *bsd. Am.* maybe; *~ haben Sie recht* you may be right; **~malig** ['~ma:liç] often repeated, frequent; **~mals** ['~ma:ls] many times, frequently; *ich danke Ihnen ~* many thanks; '**~mehr** rather; '**~sagend** significant; *Blick: a.* knowing; '**~seitig** many-sided; *P. a.*: all-round, versatile; *~ verwendbar* multi-purpose, versatile; '**~silbig** polysyllabic; '**~stimmig** many-voiced, polyphonic; '**~verheißend**, '**~versprechend** (very) promising, of great promise; *nicht ~* unpromising; **2völker...** multi-racial; **2weiberei** ['~vaɪbə'raɪ] *f* polygamy; '**2zahl** *f* multitude.

vier [fi:r] four; *unter ~ Augen* confidentially; *auf allen ~en* on all fours; **~beinig** ['~baɪniç] four-legged; **~blätt(e)rig** ['~blɛt(ə)riç] four-leaved; **~dimensional** ['~dimɛnzjona:l] four-dimensional; '**2-eck** *n* square, quadrangle; '**~-eckig** square, quadrangular.

'**Vierer** *m* (7) *Rudern*: four; '**2'lei** *adj.* of four different sorts; *als su.* four different things; '**~(spiel** *n*) *m Golf*: foursome; *Bridge*: four.

'**vier|fach**, **~fältig** ['~fɛltiç] fourfold; quadruple; **~füßig** ['~fy:siç] four-footed; *zo.* quadruped; **2füß(l)er** ['~fy:s(l)ər] *m* (7) quadruped; '**2ganggetriebe** *n* four-speed gearbox; '**2gespann** *n* four-in-hand, carriage-and-four; **~händig** ['~hɛndiç] *zo.* quadrumanous; ♪ four-handed; *~ spielen* play a duet; '**~'hundert** four hundred; '**~jährig** four years old, *attr.* four-year-old; *Dauer*: four-year; '**~kantig** square; '**2linge** *pl.* quadruplets, F quads; **2mächtebesprechung** [~'mɛçtə-] *f* four-power talk; '**~mal** four times; '**~malig** four times repeated; **~motorig** ['~moto:riç] four-engined; **~räd(e)rig** ['~rɛ:d(ə)riç] four-wheeled; **~schrötig** ['~ʃrø:tiç] square-built, thick-set; '**~seitig** four-sided; ⩓ quadrilateral; '**~silbig** of four syllables, 📖 tetrasyllabic; '**2sitzer** *m* (7), '**~sitzig** four-seater; **2spänner** ['~ʃpɛnər] *m* (7) carriage-and-four, (*a.* '**~spännig**) four-in-

-hand; '**~spurig** *mot.* four-lane; '**~stellig** *Zahl*: of four digits; **~stöckig** ['~ʃtøkiç] four-storied; **~tägig** ['~tɛ:giç] of four days, four-day; '**⁀taktmotor** *mot. m* four-stroke (*od.* -cycle) engine; '**~te** fourth; '**~teilen** quarter.

Viertel ['firtəl] *n* (7) fourth (part); (*Maß*; *Stadt*⁀; *Mond*⁀) quarter; (*ein*) ~ *fünf*, (*ein*) ~ *nach vier* a quarter past four; *drei* ~ *vier*, (*ein*) ~ *vor vier* a quarter to (*Am.* of) four; '**~finale** *n Sport*: quarter-finals *pl.*; ~'**jahr** *n* three months, quarter (of a year); ~'**jahres...** quarterly ...; '**⁀jährig** of three months; '**⁀jährlich** three months'; quarterly (*a. adv.*); *adv.* every three months; '**~note** ♩ *f* crotchet; '**~pause** ♩ *f* crotchet-rest; '**~pfund** *n* quarter of a pound; ~'**stunde** *f* quarter of an hour; '**⁀stündlich** every quarter of an hour.

viertens ['fi:rtəns] fourthly.

Vier|'vierteltakt ♩ *m* common time; '**⁀zehn** fourteen; ~ *Tage* a fortnight, *Am.* fourteen days; '**⁀zehntägig** fortnightly, two-week; '**⁀zehnte** fourteenth; '**~zehntel** *n* (7) fourteenth (part); '**~zeiler** *m* four-lined stanza.

vierzig ['firtsiç] forty; **⁀er** ['~gər] *m* (7), '**⁀erin** *f* (16[1]) quadragenarian; *in den Vierzigern* in one's forties; F on the wrong side of forty; '**~ste** fortieth.

Vignette [vin'jɛtə] *f* (15) vignette.

Vikar [vi'ka:r] *m* (3[1]) curate.

Viktualien [viktu'a:ljən] *n/pl.* victuals, provisions, eatables.

Vill|a ['vila] *f* (9[1]) villa; '**~enviertel** *n* residential district.

Viola ♩ [vi'o:la] *f* (16[2]) viola.

violett [vio'lɛt] violet.

Violin|e ♩ [~'li:nə] *f* (15) violin; **~ist** ♩ [~li'nist] *m* (12), **~istin** *f* (16[1]) violinist; **~schlüssel** [~'li:n-] *m* G (*od.* treble) clef.

Violoncell(**o**) [violɔn'tʃɛl(o)] *n* (11, *pl. a. -celli*) violoncello.

Viper *zo.* ['vi:pər] *f* (15) viper.

virtuo|s [virtu'o:s] masterly, virtuoso; **⁀se** [~'o:zə] *m* (13), **⁀sin** *f* (16[1]) virtuo|so, *pl.* -si; **⁀sität** [~ozi'tɛ:t] *f* (16) virtuosity, artistic perfection.

virulent [viru'lɛnt] virulent.

Virus ⚕ ['vi:rus] *n*, *m* (16[2]) virus; '**~-infektion** *f* virus (*od.* viral) infection; '**~krankheit** *f* virus disease.

Visage F [vi'za:ʒə] *f* (15) mug.

Visier [vi'zi:r] *n* (3[1]) *am Helm*: visor; *am Gewehr*: sight; **⁀en** *v/t.* ⊕ adjust; (*eichen*) ga(u)ge; *Paß*: visa; *v/i.* (take) aim *od.* sight; **~kimme** *f* rear sight notch; **~korn** *n* foresight; **~linie** *f* sighting-line.

Vision [vi'zjo:n] *f* vision; **⁀är** [~zjo'nɛ:r] visionary.

Visi|tation [vizita'tsjo:n] *f* (*Durchsuchung*) search; (*Besichtigung*) inspection; **~te** [vi'zi:tə] *f* (15) visit (*a.* ⚕), (social) call; **~tenkarte** *f* visiting-card, *Am.* calling card; **⁀'tieren** search; (*besichtigen*) inspect.

visuell [vizu'ˀɛl] visual.

Visum ['vi:zum] *n* (9[2] *u.* 11) visa.

vital [vi'ta:l] vigorous; **⁀ität** [vitali'tɛ:t] *f* vitality.

Vitamin [vita'mi:n] *n* (3[1]) vitamin(e); *mit* ~(*en*) *anreichern s.* ⁀*isieren*; **⁀-arm** poor in vitamins; **⁀haltig** vitamin-containing; **⁀isieren** [~mini'zi:rən] vitaminize; **~mangel** [~'mi:n-] *m* vitamin deficiency; **⁀reich** rich in vitamins.

Vitrine [vi'tri:nə] *f* (15) glass cupboard; ✝ show-case.

Vitriol [vitri'o:l] *n*, *m* (3[1]) vitriol.

vivat ['vi:vat] **1.** long live ...!; three cheers for ...!; **2.** ⁀ *n* (11) cheer.

Vize... ['fi:tsə, 'vi:tsə] *mst* vice..., *z. B.* '**~-admiral** *m* vice-admiral; '**~kanzler** *m* vice-chancellor; '**~könig** *m* viceroy; '**~konsul** *m* vice-counsel.

Vlies [fli:s] *n* (4) fleece.

Vogel ['fo:gəl] *m* (7[1]) bird; F *fig. e-n* ~ *haben* have a bee in one's bonnet, *sl.* be nuts; *fig. den* ~ *abschießen* steal the show, *sl.* take the cake; *loser* ~ wag; '**~bauer** *n* bird-cage; '**~beerbaum** *m* mountain ash, rowan(-tree); '**~beere** *f* rowan-berry; **~fänger** ['~fɛŋər] *m* (7) bird-catcher; '**~flinte** *f* fowling-piece; '**⁀frei** outlawed; '**~futter** *n* bird-seed; '**~haus** *n* aviary; '**~kunde** *f* ornithology; '**~mist** *m* bird-dung.

vögeln V ['fø:gəln] (29) fuck, screw.

'**Vogel|nest** *n* bird's nest; '**~perspektive** *f*, '**~schau** *f* bird's-eye view; '**~scheuche** *f* scarecrow (*a. fig.*); '**~schutzgebiet** *n* bird sanctuary; '**~steller** *m* (7) bird-catcher; **~-'Strauß-Politik** *f* ostrich policy;

'~**warte** *f* ornithological station; '~**zug** *m* migration of birds.
Vöglein ['føːglaɪn] *n* (6) little bird.
Vogt [foːkt] *m* (3^3) overseer; (*Amtmann*) bailiff; (*Statthalter*) governor; *e-s Gutes*: steward.
Vokab|el [vo'kaːbəl] *f* (15) word; ~**elheft** *n* vocabulary book; ~**ular** [vokabu'laːr] *n* (3^1) vocabulary.
Vokal [vo'kaːl] *m* vowel; ~**musik** *f* vocal music.
Volant [vo'lɑ̃] *m* (11) *Schneiderei*: flounce; *mot.* steering-wheel.
Volk [fɔlk] *n* (1^2) people; (*Leute*) people *pl.*; (*Nation*) nation; (*Rasse, Schlag*) race; (*Masse*) populace; *contp.* (*Pöbel*) mob, rabble; (*Bienen*≈) swarm; *hunt.* (*Rebhühner*≈) covey; *der Mann aus dem ~e* the man in the street.
Völker|bund ['fœlkər-] *m* (*von 1919*) League of Nations; '~**kunde** *f* ethnology; '~**mord** *m* genocide; '~**recht** *n* law of nations, international law; '≈**rechtlich** relating to (*adv.* under) international law; '~**schaft** *f* people; (*Stamm*) tribe; '~**schlacht** *f* battle of (the) nations; '~**verständigung** *f* agreement between nations; '~**wanderung** *f* migration of nations.
'**volkreich** populous.
'**Volks|-abstimmung** *f* plebiscite; '~**-aufstand** *m* (popular) uprising, revolt; '~**-ausgabe** *f* popular edition; '~**begehren** *n* (popular) initiative; '~**bibliothek** *f* public library; '~**bildung** *f* national education; '~**charakter** *m* national character; '~**deutsche** *m, f* ethnic German; '~**dichter** *m* popular (*od.* national) poet; '~**-entscheid** *m* (popular) referendum; '~**feind** *m* public enemy; '~**fest** *n* public festival; '~**gunst** *f* popularity; '~**haufe(n)** *m* crowd; (*die große Masse*) populace, mob; '~**herrschaft** *f* democracy; '~**hochschule** *f* University Extension; *in Deutschland*: adult college; '~**justiz** *f* lynch law; '~**kunde** *f* folklore; '~**lied** *n* folk-song; '~**menge** *f* crowd (of people), multitude, *b.s.* mob; '~**partei** *f* people's party; '~**redner** *m* popular speaker; (*Agitator*) mob (*Am.* stump) orator, '~**sage** *f* folk-tale; '~**schicht** *f* class of (the) people, social stratum; '~**schule** *f* elementary (*od.* primary, *Am. a.* grade) school; '~**schullehrer** *m* elementary (*Am.* grade) teacher; '~**sprache** *f* popular (*od.* vulgar) tongue; (*Landessprache*) vernacular (language); '~**stamm** *m* tribe, race; '~**stimme** *f* voice of the people; '~**stimmung** *f* public feeling; '~**stück** *thea. n* folk-play; '~**tanz** *m* folk-dance; '~**tracht** *f* national costume; '~**tum** *n* (1^2) nationality; '≈**tümlich** national; (*einfach od. beliebt*) popular; '~**tümlichkeit** *f* popularity; '~**versammlung** *f* public meeting; '~**vertreter** *m* representative of the people; '~**vertretung** *f* representation of the people; '~**wirt** *m* (political) economist; '~**wirtschaft** *f praktische*: political economics *pl.*; '~**wirtschaftslehre** *f* political economy; '~**zählung** *f* census.
voll [fɔl] *allg.* full; (*gefüllt*) filled; F (*betrunken*) drunk; (*ganz*) whole, complete, entire (*a. Betrag*); (*füllig, prall*) full, round; ⊕ (*massiv*) solid; *mit ~em Recht* with perfect right; *e-e ~e Stunde* a full (*od.* solid) hour; *ein ~es Jahr* a whole year; *~e Beschäftigung* full (*ganztägige*: full-time) employment; *aus ~er Brust* heartily; *s. Hals, Nase*; *aus ~em Herzen* from the bottom of one's heart; *im ~(st)en Sinne des Wortes* in the fullest sense of the word; *j-n für ~ nehmen* take a p. seriously; *~(er) Knospen* full of; *aus dem ~en schöpfen* draw on plentiful resources; *adv. ~ (und ganz)* fully, entirely; '~**-auf** abundantly, amply, perfectly; '~**-automatisch** fully automatic; '≈**bad** *n* full bath; '≈**bart** *m* full beard; '~**berechtigt** fully qualified; '~**beschäftigt** fully employed; '≈**beschäftigung** *f* full employment; '~**besetzt** *Theater usw.*: packed; '≈**besitz** *m* full possession; '≈**blut(pferd)** *n* thoroughbred (horse); ~**blütig** ['~blyːtiç] full-blooded; ~'**bringen** accomplish, achieve; ≈'**bringung** *f* accomplishment, achievement; ~**busig** ['~buːziç] fullbosomed; '≈**dampf** *m* (*mit* at) full steam; *fig. mit ~* at full blast; '~**-elektronisch** fully electronic (*od.* automatic); ~'**enden** (*beenden*) finish; (*vervollständigen*) complete; (*vervollkommnen*)

perfect, accomplish; ~'-**endet** *adj.* perfect, accomplished; *s. Tatsache.*

vollends ['fɔlɛnts] entirely, wholly, altogether; ~ *da* especially since.

Voll'-endung *f* finishing; completion; (*Zustand*) perfection.

Völlerei [fœlə'raɪ] *f* (16) gluttony.

voll|'führen execute, carry out; *Lärm*: make; '**~füllen** fill (up); '**2gas** *mot. n* (*mit* at) full throttle; ~ *geben* open the throttle, F step on it; '**2gefühl** *n*: *im* ~ (*gen.*) fully conscious of; '**2genuß** *m* full enjoyment; '**~gepfropft** crammed (full), F packed; '**~gießen** fill (up); '**~gültig** of full value, valid; '**2-gummi** *m* solid rubber.

völlig ['fœliç] **1.** *adj.* (*ganz*) full, entire; (*vollständig*) complete, total; (*vollkommen*) perfect; (*gründlich*) thorough; **2.** *adv.* fully, entirely, *etc.*; quite.

'**voll|jährig** of (full) age; '**2jährigkeit** *f* full age, majority; '**2kaskoversicherung** *f* comprehensive insurance; ~'**kommen** perfect; (*völlig ausgebildet*) accomplished; *Macht, Recht usw.*: absolute; *s. völlig*; **2-'kommenheit** *f* perfection; '**2kornbrot** *n* whole-meal bread; '**2kraft** *f* full vigo(u)r; *in der* ~ *des Lebens* in the prime of life; '**~machen** fill (up); *fig.* complete; *um das Unglück vollzumachen* to make things worse; (*beschmutzen*) dirty; '**2macht** *f* full power(s *pl.*), authority; (*Urkunde*) proxy; ⚖ power of attorney; *j-m* ~ *erteilen* give a p. authority; ~ *haben* be authorized; '**2matrose** *m* able-bodied seaman; '**2milch** *f* whole (*od.* unskimmed) milk; '**2mond** *m* full moon; **~mundig** ['~mundiç] *Wein*: full-bodied; '**2narkose** *f* general an(a)esthetic; '**~packen** fill (up); '**2-pension** *f* full board (and lodging); '**~pfropfen** stuff, cram; '**~schenken** fill (up); '**~schlank** full-figured, *Frau*: *a.* matronly; '**2sitzung** *f* plenary session; **~spurig** ['~ʃpu:riç], '**2spur...** 🚂 standard-ga(u)ge; '**~ständig** complete, full; whole, entire, total; *s. völlig*; '**2ständigkeit** *f* completeness; entirety; '**~stopfen** stuff, cram; ~'**streckbar** enforceable; ~'**strecken** execute, ⚖ *a.* enforce; *Fußball*: score; 2'**strecker(in** *f*) *m* executor, *f a.* executrix; 2'**streckung** *f* execution; 2'**streckungsbeamte** ⚖ *m* executory officer; 2'**streckungsbefehl** *m* writ of execution; '**~synthetisch**: ~*e Chemiefaser* synthetic fib|re, *Am.* -er; '**~tanken** fill up; '**2treffer** *m* direct hit; *fig.* bull's-eye; '**2versammlung** *f* plenary assembly; '**~wertig** full, of full value; **~zählig** ['~tsɛ:liç] complete; '**2zähligkeit** *f* completeness; '**2zeit...** full-time; '**2zeit-Arbeitskraft** *f* full-time employee; ~'**ziehen** execute, perform; (*ausführen*) effect; *kirchliche Handlung*: solemnize; *die* ~*de Gewalt* the executive; *sich* ~ take place; 2'**ziehung** *f*, 2'**zug** *m* execution; 2'**zugs-anstalt** *f* penal institution.

Volontär [volɔ̃'tɛ:r] *m* (3¹) improver, trainee, unsalaried clerk.

Volt ⚡ [vɔlt] *n* (3 *u. inv.*) volt; '**~meter** *n* (7) voltmeter; '**~zahl** *f* voltage.

Volumen [vo'lu:mən] *n* (6; *pl. mst Volumina*) volume (*a. fig.*).

vom [fɔm] = *von dem*; *s. von.*

von [fɔn] *räumlich u. zeitlich*: from; *für den Genitiv*: of; *beim Passiv*: by; (*über*) about, of; *s. a. an 2.*; *Stoff*: ~ *Holz* (made) of wood; 2 ~ *3 Kindern* 2 in (*od.* out of) 3 children; *ein Gedicht* ~ *Schiller* a poem by Schiller; *Kinder haben* ~ have children by; ~ *selbst*, ~ *sich aus* of oneself; ~ *mir aus* I don't mind (if); *s. Anfang, früh, Kindheit, vornherein usw.*: **~-nöten** [~'nø:tən] necessary; **~statten** [~'ʃtatən]: ~ *gehen* proceed, pass off.

vor [fo:r] *räumlich u. zeitlich*: before; *räumlich*: in front of; (~ *soundso langer Zeit*) ago; (*früher als*) prior to; (*schützen, verstecken, warnen usw.* ~) from, against; (*zittern* ~ *Freude, Kälte usw.*) with; *vor ...* (*in Gegenwart von*) in the presence of; *s. all*; ~ *e-m Hintergrund* against a background; ~ *Hunger sterben* die of hunger; *sich fürchten* ~ be afraid of, fear; (*heute*) ~ *acht Tagen* a week ago (today); ~ *Zeiten* formerly; *5 Minuten* ~ *9* five minutes to (*Am.* of) 9; ~ *allen Dingen* above all; ~ *der Tür sein* be at the door; ~ *sich gehen* take place, happen, pass off, proceed; *et.* ~ *sich haben* be in for a th.

vor'ab in advance; beforehand.

'**Vor-abend** *m* eve; *am* ~ (*gen.*) on the eve of.

ˈ**vor·ahn|en** have a presentiment of; ˈ**ᘔung** *f* presentiment, foreboding.
voran [foˈran] before, at the head (*dat.* of); *nur ~!* go on!, go ahead!; **~gehen** (sn) *räumlich*: lead the way; (*a. fig.*) take the lead; *zeitlich u. räumlich, a. im Rang*: precede (*j-m usw.* a p. *etc.*); *Arbeit*: *gut ~* = **~kommen** make headway (*od.* progress), get ahead.
ˈ**Vor·ankündigung** *f* announcement.
ˈ**Vor·anmeldung** *f*: *teleph. Gespräch mit ~* person-to-person call.
ˈ**Vor·anschlag** *m* estimate.
ˈ**Vor·anzeige** *f* previous notice.
ˈ**Vor·arbeit** *f* preparatory work, preparations *pl.*; ˈ**ᘔen** *v/t.* prepare, do *a th.* in advance; *v/i.* prepare work; *j-m ~* pave the way for a p.; ˈ**~er** *m* foreman; ˈ**~erin** *f* (16[1]) forewoman.
vorauf [foˈrauf] *s. voran.*
voraus [~ˈraus] in front, ahead (*dat.* of); *im ~, zum ~* (*mst* ˈ*voraus*) in advance, beforehand; *danken*: in anticipation; *Kopf ~* head foremost; *s-m Alter ~ sein* be forward (for one's age); **ᘔ-abteilung** ⚔ *f* advance guard, vanguard; **~bedingen** stipulate beforehand; **~bestellen** *s. vorbestellen*; **~bestimmen** predetermine; **~bezahlen** pay in advance, prepay; **ᘔbezahlung** *f* advance payment; **~denken** look ahead; **~-eilen** (sn) hurry on ahead (*dat.* of); **ᘔ-exemplar** *n* advance copy; **~gehen** (sn) walk ahead (*dat.* of); *s. a. vorangehen*; **~gesetzt:** *~, daß* provided (that); **~haben:** *j-m et. ~* have an advantage over a p.; **ᘔplanung** *f* forward planning; **ᘔsage, ᘔsagung** *f* prediction; (*Prophezeiung*) prophecy; (*Wetter*ᘔ) forecast (*a. fig.* ✝); (*Renntip usw.*) tip; **~sagen** foretell, predict; forecast; **ᘔschau** *f* forecast; **~schauend** far-sighted; long-range; **~schicken** send on in advance; *fig.* mention before; **~sehen** foresee, anticipate; **~setzen** presuppose, require; (*annehmen*) assume; *s. vorausgesetzt*; **ᘔsetzung** *f* (pre)supposition, assumption; *s. Vorbedingung*; *unter der ~, daß* on condition that; *zur ~ haben* presuppose; *die ~en erfüllen* meet the requirements, qualify; **ᘔsicht** *f* foresight; *aller ~ nach* in all probability; **~sichtlich** prospective, probable, presumable; expected; *adv.* probably; *er kommt ~ a.* he is likely (*od.* expected) to come; **ᘔzahlung** *f* advance payment.
ˈ**Vorbau** *m* front building; projecting part *of a building*; ˈ**ᘔen** *v/t.* (*vorspringend bauen*) build out; *v/i. e-r S.*: guard against.
ˈ**Vorbedacht** 1. *m*: *mit ~* deliberately, on purpose; 2. ᘔ premeditated.
ˈ**vorbedeut|en** presage; ˈ**ᘔung** *f* foreboding, omen.
ˈ**Vorbedingung** *f* precondition, prerequisite, (basic) requirement.
Vorbehalt [ˈ~bəhalt] *m* (3) reservation, reserve, proviso; *mit dem ~, daß ...* on the proviso that; *ohne ~* without reservation; unconditionally; *unter ~* with reservations; *unter ~ aller Rechte* all rights reserved; ˈ**ᘔen:** *sich ~* reserve to o.s.; *j-m ~ sein* be reserved for a p.; *Änderungen ~* subject to change (without notice); *es bleibt der Zukunft ~* it remains for the future (*to show, etc.*); ˈ**ᘔlich** with reservation (*gen.* as to); *~ gen.* subject to; ˈ**ᘔlos** unreserved(ly *adv.*).
ˈ**Vorbehandlung** *f* preliminary treatment.
vorbei [forˈbaɪ] along, by, past (*alle a.*: *~ an dat.*); *zeitlich*: over, past, gone; **~fahren** drive past; **~gehen** (sn) pass by (*an j-m* a p.); (*aufhören*) pass; (*fehlgehen*) miss the mark; *im* ᘔ in passing; **~kommen** pass by; *an e-m Hindernis usw.*: get past; F (*besuchen*) drop in; **~lassen** let pass; **ᘔmarsch** *m* march(ing) past; **~marschieren** (sn) march past (*an j-m* a p.); **~müssen** have to pass (*an dat.* by); **~reden:** *an-ea. ~* be at cross purposes; **~schießen** miss (*an e-r S.* a th.).
ˈ**Vorbemerkung** *f* preliminary remark *od.* note; preamble.
vorbenannt [ˈ~bənant] (afore)said, aforementioned.
ˈ**vorbereit|en** (*a. sich ~*) prepare (*für, auf acc.* for); *e-e vorbereitete Rede* a set speech; ˈ**~end** *adj.* preparatory; ˈ**ᘔung** *f* preparation (*für, auf acc.* for); ˈ**ᘔungs...** preparatory.
ˈ**Vorbericht** *m* preliminary report.
ˈ**vorberuflich** prevocational.
ˈ**Vorbesprechung** *f* preliminary discussion.

ˈ**vorbestell|en** order in advance; *Platz, Zimmer usw.*: book, *Am. a.* make a reservation for; ˈ**~ung** *f* advance order; booking, *Am. a.* reservation, billing.

ˈ**vorbestraft** previously convicted; ~ *sein* have a police record.

ˈ**vorbeten** *v/t.*: *j-m et.* ~ repeat a th. to a p.

ˈ**Vorbeugehaft** *f* preventive detention.

ˈ**vorbeug|en** *v/i.* (*dat.*) prevent, obviate, guard against; *v/t.* (*a. sich*) bend forward; ˈ**~end** *adj.* preventive, 🕮, ⚕ prophylactic; ˈ**~ung** *f* prevention; ˈ**~ungsmaßnahme** *f* preventive measure; ˈ**~ungsmittel** *n* preventive, 🕮, ⚕ prophylactic.

ˈ**Vorbild** *n* model; (*Beispiel*) *a.* example; (*Urbild*) prototype; ˈ**~lich** exemplary, *attr. a.* model; (*vollkommen*) ideal; (*kennzeichnend*) typical (*für* of); ˈ**~ung** *f* preparatory training; educational background.

ˈ**Vorbote** *m* forerunner (*a.* ⚕); *fig.* harbinger, precursor; early sign.

ˈ**vorbringen** bring forward, *a.* ⚖ *Beweise*: produce; *Meinung, Entschuldigung*: advance; ⚖ *Klage*: prefer, *als Einwand*: plead; (*behaupten, sagen*) state, say.

ˈ**vorbuchstabieren** spell out (*j-m* to a p.).

ˈ**Vorbühne** *f* apron.

ˈ**vordatieren** (= *zurückdatieren*) antedate; (= *vorausdatieren*) postdate.

vordem [ˈfoːrdeːm] formerly.

vorder [ˈfɔrdər] front, fore.

ˈ**Vorder|-achse** *mot. f* front axle; ˈ**~-ansicht** *f* front view; ˈ**~-arm** *m* forearm; ˈ**~bein** *n* foreleg; ˈ**~deck** *n* foredeck; ˈ**~fuß** *m* forefoot; ˈ**~gebäude,** ˈ**~haus** *n* front building; ˈ**~grund** *m* foreground; *fig. im ~ stehen* (*in den ~ rücken*) be in the (place into the) foreground; *in den ~ treten* come to the fore; **~gründig** [ˈ~gryndiç] *fig.* (*adv.* in the) foreground; ˈ**~hand¹** *f des Pferdes*: forehand.

vorderhand² [ˈfoːrderˈhant] for the present, for the time being.

ˈ**Vorder|lader** *m* (7) muzzle-loader; ˈ**~lastig** ✈ nose-heavy; ˈ**~lauf** *hunt. m* foreleg; ˈ**~mann** *m* man in front (*of a p.*); ✝ *bei Wechsel usw.*: prior endorser, *bei Papieren*: previous holder; F *j-n auf ~ bringen* make a p. toe the line; ˈ**~rad** *n* front wheel; ˈ**~rad-antrieb** *m* front-wheel drive; ˈ**~radbremse** *f* front-wheel brake; ˈ**~reihe** *f* front rank (*od.* row); ˈ**~schinken** *m* shoulder ham; ˈ**~seite** *f* front (side); △, ⊕ *a.* face; ˈ**~sitz** *m* front seat.

ˈ**vorderst** foremost.

ˈ**Vorder|steven** ⚓ *m* stem; ˈ**~teil** *m, n* front (part); ⚓ prow; ˈ**~tür** *f* front door; ˈ**~zahn** *m* front tooth.

ˈ**vordrängen** (*a. sich*) press (*od.* push) forward.

ˈ**vordring|en** (sn) push (*od.* press) forward, advance; ˈ**~lich** urgent, priority ...

ˈ**Vordruck** *m* form, *Am.* blank.

ˈ**vor-ehelich** premarital.

ˈ**vor-eilig** hasty, rash, precipitate; *~e Schlüsse ziehen* jump to conclusions; ˈ**~keit** *f* rashness.

ˈ**vor-eingenommen** prejudiced, bias(s)ed; ˈ**~heit** *f* prejudice, bias.

ˈ**Vor-eltern** *pl.* forefathers, ancestors, progenitors.

ˈ**vor-enthalt|en** keep back, withhold (*j-m* from a p.); ˈ**~ung** *f* withholding.

ˈ**Vor-entscheidung** *f* preliminary decision.

ˈ**vor-erst** for the time being.

vorerwähnt [ˈfoːrˀɛrvɛːnt] aforesaid, before- (*od.* afore)mentioned.

ˈ**Vor-examen** *n s. Vorprüfung.*

Vorfahr [ˈ~faːr] *m* (12) ancestor.

ˈ**vorfahr|en** (sn) drive up; (*vorbeifahren*) pass; *den Wagen ~ lassen* order; ˈ**~t(recht** *n*) *f* right of way; ˈ**~tszeichen** *n* give way (*Am.* yield) sign.

ˈ**Vorfall** *m* incident, occurrence; event; ⚕ prolapsus; ˈ**~en** (sn) happen, occur; ⚕ prolapse.

ˈ**Vor|feier** *f* preliminary celebration; ˈ**~feld** *n* ⚔ forefield; ˈ**~fertigung** *f* prefabrication; ˈ**~film** *m* program(me) picture.

ˈ**vorfinden** find.

ˈ**Vorfrage** *f* preliminary question.

ˈ**Vorfreude** *f* anticipated joy.

ˈ**Vorfrühling** *m* early spring.

ˈ**vorfühlen** put out one's feelers; *bei j-m*: sound out.

ˈ**Vorführ|dame** *f* mannequin; ˈ**~en** bring forward, produce; ⊕ demonstrate; (*zeigen*) show, display; ˈ**~er** *m* (7) demonstrator; *Kino*: projectionist, operator; ˈ**~raum** *m* projection room; '~**ung** *f* production; demonstration; showing; (*Aufführung*) performance, F show; '~**wagen** *m* demonstration car.

'**Vorgabe** *f Spiel, Sport*: points (*od.* odds) *pl.* given, handicap.

'**Vorgang** *m s. Vorfall*; (*Hergang*) proceedings *pl.*; *bsd.* ⊕ process; (*Akte*) file, reference.

Vorgänger ['~gɛŋər] *m* (7), '~**in** *f* (16[1]) predecessor.

'**Vorgarten** *m* front garden, *Am.* frontyard.

'**vorgeben 1.** *v/t. Sport*: give, owe; (*behaupten*) allege, pretend; *v/i.* give odds (*j-m* to a p.); **2.** ♀ *n* (6) preten|ce, *Am.* -se, pretext.

'**Vorgebirge** *n* promontory, cape; (*Vorberge*) foot-hills *pl.*

vorgeblich ['~ge:pliç] pretended, ostensible, alleged.

vorgefaßt ['~gəfast] preconceived.

'**Vorgefühl** *n* presentiment, premonition.

'**vorgehen 1.** (sn) advance; *Uhr*: be fast, gain (*fünf Minuten* five minutes); *im Range*: take precedence (*dat.* of), be more important (than); (*handeln*) take action, act; (*verfahren*) proceed (*a. gerichtlich*; *gegen* against); (*sich ereignen*) go on, happen, occur; **2.** ♀ *n* (6) advance; (*Handlungsweise*) action, proceeding.

'**vorgenannt** *s. vorerwähnt.*

'**Vorgericht** *n* entree, *s. a. Vorspeise.*

'**Vorgeschicht|e** *f* prehistory; *e-r S.*: previous (*od.* past) history; *e-r P.*: antecedents *pl.*; ⚕ case history; '♀**lich** prehistoric(ally *adv.*).

'**Vorgeschmack** *m* foretaste.

Vorgesetzte ['fo:rgəzɛtstə] *m, f* (18) superior; (*Chef*) *bsd. Am.* F boss.

'**Vorgespräche** *n/pl.* preliminary talks.

'**vorgest|ern** the day before yesterday; '~**rig** of the day before yesterday.

'**vorgreifen** anticipate (*j-m, e-r S.* a p., a th.).

'**Vorgriff** *m* anticipation.

'**vorgucken** F *Unterkleid usw.*: show.

'**vorhaben 1.** *Schürze usw.*: have *a th.* on; (*beabsichtigen*) intend, purpose, mean; (*beschäftigt sein mit*) be busy with; *haben Sie heute abend etwas vor?* are you doing anything tonight?; **2.** ♀ *n* (6) intention; plan, scheme; (*Projekt*) project.

'**Vorhalle** *f* vestibule, (entrance-) hall; *parl.* lobby; *thea., Hotel*: *a.* lounge.

'**Vorhalt** *m* ⚔ lead; ♪ suspension; ⚖ query; '♀**en** *v/t. j-m et.* ~ hold a th. before a p.; *fig.* reproach a p. with a th.; *v/i.* (*dauern*) last; *beim Schießen*: apply a lead; '~**ung** *f* remonstrance, representation; *j-m ~en machen* remonstrate with a p.

'**Vorhand** *f Kartenspiel u. fig.*: lead.

vorhanden [fo:r'handən] present, at hand; (*verfügbar*) available; ✝ *a.* on hand, in stock; (*bestehend*) extant, existing; ~ *sein* be at hand *etc.*; exist; ♀**sein** *n* presence, existence.

'**Vorhandschlag** *m Tennis*: forehand (stroke).

'**Vorhang** *m* curtain (*a. thea.*), *Am. a.* shade; *pol. Eiserner* ~ Iron Curtain.

'**Vorhängeschloß** *n* padlock.

'**Vorhaut** *f* foreskin, prepuce.

vorher ['fo:rhe:r] before, previously; (*voraus*) in advance, before (-hand).

vorher|bestimmen [~'he:r-] determine beforehand; *eccl.* predestine; ♀**bestimmung** *f* predetermination; *eccl.* predestination; ~**gehen** (sn; *dat.*) precede (*a. th.*); ~**gehend** foregoing, preceding.

vor'herig preceding, previous.

'**Vorherr|schaft** *f* predominance; '♀**schen** predominate, prevail; '♀**schend** *adj.* predominant, prevalent, prevailing.

Vor'her|sage *f*, ~**sagung** *f*, ♀**sagen** *s. Voraussage usw.*; ♀**sehen** foresee; ♀**wissen** foreknow.

vor'hin a little while ago, just now.

'**Vorhof** *m* vestibule, front-court.

'**Vorhut** ⚔ *f* vanguard.

vorig ['fo:riç] former, previous; (*letztvergangen*) last.

'**vor-industriell** pre-industrial.

'**Vor|jahr** *n* previous year; last year; '♀**jährig** of last year.

'**Vorkämpfer**(**in** *f*) *m* champion.

'**vorkauen** *j-m*: chew *a th.* for; *fig.* F spoon-feed *a th.* to.

'**Vorkauf** *m* pre-emption; '~**srecht** *n* right of pre-emption, option right; *das ~ haben a.* have the refusal.

'**Vorkehrung** *f* precaution; *~en treffen* take precautions *od.* measures; make arrangements.

ˈ**Vorkenntnis** *f* (*a.* ~se *pl.*) previous (*od.* basic) knowledge (von of); (er hat gute) ~se *pl.* in (*dat.*) (he is well grounded in the) elements of ...
ˈ**vorknöpfen:** F sich j-n ~ take a p. to task.
ˈ**vorkomm|en¹** (sn) be found, be met (with), occur; (*sich ereignen*) occur, happen; es kommt mir vor it seems to me; so etwas ist mir noch nicht vorgekommen! F well, I never!; das kommt dir nur so vor you are just imagining that; sich dumm *usw.* ~ feel silly, *etc.*; sich klug ~ fancy o.s. clever; er kommt mir bekannt vor he looks familiar; es kommt mir merkwürdig vor I think it (rather) strange; ˈ2en² *n* (6) occurrence; *min. a.* deposit; ˈ2nis *n* (4¹) occurrence, incidence.
ˈ**Vorkosten** *pl.* preliminary cost *sg.*
ˈ**Vorkriegs...** pre-war.
ˈ**vorlad|en** summon, cite; ˈ2ung *f* summons *sg.*, citation.
ˈ**Vorlage** *f* (*Schreib2, Zeichen2*) copy; (*Muster*) pattern, model; (*Unterbreitung*) submission, presentation; *parl.* bill; *Fußball*: pass; *Ski*: vorlage, forward lean.
ˈ**vorlass|en** let *a p.* pass in front *od.* before; (*zulassen*) admit; ˈ2ung *f* admission, admittance.
ˈ**Vorlauf** *m Sport*: eliminating heat.
Vorläuf|er [ˈfoːrlɔʏfər] *m*, ˈ~erin *f* (16¹) forerunner, precursor; ˈ2ig preliminary; provisional, temporary; *adv.* provisionally, *etc.*; (*fürs erste*) for the time being.
ˈ**vorlaut** forward, pert; ~es Wesen pertness.
ˈ**Vorleben** *n* former life, past, antecedents *pl.*
ˈ**Vorlege|besteck** *n* (ein a pair of) carvers *pl.*; ˈ~gabel *f* carving-fork; ˈ~messer *n* carving-knife.
ˈ**vorlegen** *et.*: put forward; (*vorbringen*) produce; *Plan usw.*: propose; *Schloß*: put on; *Rechnung*: present; j-m et. ~ lay (*od.* place *od.* put) a th. before a p.; *bei Tische*: help a p. to a th.; *zur Prüfung usw.*: submit (*od.* present) a th. to a p.; sich ~ lean forward.
ˈ**Vorlege|r** *m* (7) (*Bett2 usw.*) rug; ˈ~schloß *n* padlock.
ˈ**vorles|en** read (j-m to a p.); ˈ2er (-in *f*) *m* reader; (*Vortragender*) lecturer; ˈ2ung *f* lecture (über *acc.* on; vor *dat.* to); e-e ~ halten (give a) lecture; ˈ2ungsverzeichnis *n* (university) calendar, *Am.* catalog(ue).
vorletzt [ˈ~lɛtst] last but one, *Am.* next to the last.
ˈ**Vorliebe** *f* predilection, preference, special liking (für for).
vorliebnehmen [forˈliːpneːmən]: ~ mit put up with; *beim Essen*: (~ mit dem, was da ist) take potluck.
ˈ**vorliegen:** j-m ~ lie before a p.; *fig. Antrag usw.*: be in hand, be submitted, (*behandelt werden*) be under consideration; *weitS. Grund, Irrtum usw.*: be, exist; es liegt heute nichts vor there is nothing to be discussed (*od.* on) today; was liegt gegen ihn vor? what is the charge against him?; ˈ~d *adj.* present, in hand; in question, under consideration.
ˈ**vorlügen:** j-m et. ~ tell a p. lies.
ˈ**vormachen** *Brett usw.*: put before; j-m et. ~ show a p. how to do a th., (*täuschen*) humbug a p.; sich (selbst) et. ~ fool o.s.
ˈ**Vormacht(stellung)** *f* supremacy; hegemony.
vormal|ig [ˈfoːrmaːliç] former; ˈ~s formerly.
ˈ**Vormarsch** *m* advance.
ˈ**vormerken** make a note of; (*reservieren*) reserve; (*bestellen*) book; *für e-n Zweck*: earmark.
ˈ**Vormieter(in** *f*) *m* previous tenant; s-e ~ the tenants before him.
ˈ**vormilitärisch:** ~e Ausbildung premilitary training.
ˈ**Vormittag** *m* morning, forenoon; ˈ2s in the morning (*abbr.* a.m.).
ˈ**Vormund** *m* guardian; ˈ~schaft *f* guardianship; ˈ2schaftlich of (*adv.* as) a guardian, tutelary; ˈ~schaftsgericht *n* guardianship court.
vorn [fɔrn] in front, before, ahead; ganz ~ right in the front; nach ~ forward; nach ~ heraus wohnen live in the front; nach ~ heraus liegen face the front; von ~ from the front; ich sah sie von ~ I saw her face; von ~ anfangen begin at the beginning, (*von neuem*) begin anew *od.* afresh; von ~ bis hinten from front to back, from first to last; noch einmal von ~ all over again.
Vornahme [ˈfoːrnaːmə] *f* (15) effecting, undertaking.
ˈ**Vorname** *m* Christian name, first name.

vornehm ['⁓ne:m] distinguished, refined; aristocratic; (*elegant*) fashionable; (*edel*) noble; (*erstklassig*) high-class; ⁓*e Gesinnung* high mind; ⁓*es Äußere*, ⁓*er Anstrich* distinguished air *od.* appearance; *die* ⁓*e Welt* the rank and fashion, high society; ⁓ *tun* give o.s. airs; ⁓*ste Pflicht usw.* principal; '**⁓en** take before one; *Schürze*: put on; (*beginnen*) undertake; (*behandeln*) deal with, occupy o.s. with; (*durchführen*) effect; *Änderung usw.*: make; *sich j-n* ⁓ take a p. to task; *sich et.* ⁓ resolve (*od.* decide) to do a th.; *sich vorgenommen haben* intend, purpose; '**2heit** *f* rank, distinction; refinement; high-mindedness; distinguished appearance; '**⁓lich** especially, chiefly.

'**vornherein:** *von* ⁓ from the first.

'**vornotieren** *s. vormerken.*

vorn'-über forward; (*Kopf voraus*) head foremost.

'**Vor-ort** *m* suburb; '**⁓(s)...** *in Zssgn* suburban; '**⁓bahn** *f* suburban (*od.* local) railway; '**⁓zug** *m* suburban train.

'**Vorposten** ⚔ *m* outpost.

'**vorprogrammieren** (pre)program(me); *fig. vorprogrammiert* preprogram(m)ed, predetermined.

'**Vorprüfung** *f* preliminary examination.

'**vorragen** project, protrude.

'**Vorrang** *m* pre-eminence, precedence; priority; *den* ⁓ *haben vor* (*dat.*) take precedence of, *S.*: *a.* have priority over; **2ig** (having) priority.

Vorrat ['fo:ra:t] *m* (3³) store, stock, supply, provision (*an dat.* of); reserve; *heimlicher*: hoard; *an Material*: *bsd. Am.* stockpile.

vorrätig ['⁓rɛ:tiç] available, on hand, in stock, in store; *nicht* (*mehr*) ⁓ out of stock.

'**Vorratskammer** *f* store-room; (*Speisekammer*) pantry.

'**Vorraum** *m* anteroom.

'**vorrechnen** reckon up (*j-m* to a p.).

'**Vorrecht** *n* privilege, prerogative.

'**Vorred|e** *f* preface; '**2en** *j-m* et.: tell a p. tales (*über acc.* about); '**⁓ner** *m* previous speaker.

'**vorricht|en** prepare; '**2ung** *f* preparation; (*Gerät usw.*) device, contrivance, appliance; mechanism.

'**vorrücken** *v/t. Stuhl usw.*: move forward, advance; *Uhr*: put on; *v/i.* (sn) advance; *in vorgerücktem Alter* in an advanced age; *zu e-r vorgerückten Stunde* at a late hour.

'**vorrufen** call forth.

'**Vorrunde** *f Sport*: preliminary round.

'**Vorsaal** *m* anteroom.

'**vorsagen** *v/t. j-m et.*: tell a p. a th.; *v/i.* (*zuflüstern*) *j-m*: prompt a p.

'**Vorsaison** *f* early season.

'**Vorsänger(in** *f*) *eccl. m* precentor.

'**Vorsatz** *m* intention, resolution, design, purpose; ⚖ (criminal) intent; *mit* ⁓ designedly, on purpose; ⚖ wil(l)fully; **⁓blatt** *typ. n* fly-leaf.

'**vorsätzlich** intentional, deliberate; ⚖ wil(l)ful, premeditated.

'**Vorsatzlinse** *phot. f* ancillary lens.

'**Vorschau** *f* preview (*auf acc.* of); (*Wetter2*, *Finanz2 usw.*) forecast; *s. Film2*.

'**Vorschein** *m*: *zum* ⁓ *bringen* bring forward *od.* to light, produce; *zum* ⁓ *kommen* come forward *od.* to light, appear, show.

'**vorschieben** push forward *od.* on, advance; *Riegel*: shoot; *als Entschuldigung, Grund usw.*: plead, pretend; *j-n*: use as a front.

'**vorschießen** *Summe*: advance.

'**Vorschlag** *m* proposal; (*Empfehlung*) recommendation; (*Anregung*) suggestion; (*Anerbieten*) offer; *parl.* motion; *e-s Kandidaten*: nomination; ♪ grace(-note); '**2en** propose; offer; suggest; nominate.

'**Vorschlußrunde** *f Sport*: semifinal.

'**Vorschneide|messer** *n* carving-knife; '**2n** carve.

'**vorschnell** hasty, rash, precipitate.

'**vorschreiben** set a copy of *a th. to a p.*; (*anordnen*) prescribe, order.

'**vorschreiten** (sn) advance.

'**Vorschrift** *f* (*bsd.* ⚕) prescription; (*Anweisung*) direction, instruction; (*Befehl*) order; (*Dienst2*) regulation(s *pl.*); *streng nach* ⁓ *arbeiten* work to rule; '**2smäßig** regulation (*nur attr.*); according to regulations; in due form, duly; '**2swidrig** *adj., adv.* contrary to regulations.

'**Vorschub** *m* assistance; ⊕ feed; ⁓ *leisten* (*dat.*) pander to, encourage, abet; ⚖ aid and abet.

'**Vorschul|-alter** *n* pre-school age; '**⁓e** *f* pre-school, nursery school; '**⁓-erziehung** *f* pre-school education.

ˈ**Vorschuß** *m* advance (*auf acc.* against); (*Gehalts*⁀, *Lohn*⁀) advance (on salary, on wages).

ˈ**vorschützen** plead.

ˈ**vorschweben:** *mir schwebt et. vor* I have a th. in mind.

ˈ**vorschwindeln:** *j-m et.* ~ humbug a p. about a th., tell a p. lies.

ˈ**vorseh|en:** ~ *für e-n Zweck* assign (*od.* earmark) for; (*planen*) schedule for; *sich* ~ take care, be on one's guard; *sich* ~ *vor* (*dat.*) guard against, look out for *a th.*; ˈ⁀**ung** *f* Providence.

ˈ**vorsetzen** put forward; (*dat.*) place (*od.* put *od.* set) before; (*auftischen*) serve; *gr. Silbe*: prefix; *fig. j-m* ~ (*überordnen*) set over a p.

Vorsicht [ˈfoːrziçt] *f* caution; (*Behutsamkeit*) care; *als Aufschrift*: caution!, beware!; *auf Kisten*: (handle) with care!; *mit* ~ cautiously; ~, *Stufe!* mind the step!; *s. a. Achtung*; ˈ⁀**ig** cautious, chary (*in dat.* of); (*behutsam*) careful; *Schätzung usw.*: conservative; ~*!* careful!, look (*Am.* watch) out!; ⁀**shalber** [ˈ~shalbər] as a precaution; ˈ~**smaßnahme**, ˈ~**smaßregel** *f* precaution(ary measure).

ˈ**Vorsilbe** *gr. f* prefix.

ˈ**vorsingen** *v/t. j-m et.* ~ sing a th. to a p.; *v/i.* lead (the choir).

ˈ**vorsintflutlich** antediluvian (*a. fig.*).

ˈ**Vorsitz** *m* presidency, chair(manship); *den* ~ *haben od. führen* be in the chair, preside (*bei* over); *unter* ~ *von* ... with ... in the chair; ~**ende** [ˈ~əndə] *m, f* (18) chairman, president; *f* chairwoman; *des Gerichts*: presiding judge.

ˈ**Vorsorg|e** *f* provision, providence; (*Vorsicht*) precaution; ~ *treffen* take precautions, provide (*gegen* against); ˈ⁀**en** provide (*für* for; against); provide for the future; ˈ~**e-untersuchung** ⚕ *f* (preventive) medical check-up; ⁀**lich** [ˈ~zɔrkliç] provident, precautionary; *adv.* as a precaution.

ˈ**Vorspann** *m Film*: cast and credits *pl.*, credit titles *pl.*; introduction; ˈ⁀**en** put *horses etc.* to the cart *etc.*

ˈ**Vorspeise** *f* hors d'œuvre, appetizer.

ˈ**vorspiegel|n** pretend, feign; *j-m et.* ~ deceive a p. with a th., delude a p. (with false hopes); ˈ⁀**ung** *f* preten|ce, *Am.* -se; (*unter*) ~ *falscher Tatsachen* (under) false pretences *pl.*

ˈ**Vorspiel** *n* ♪ prelude (*a. fig.*; *zu* to); *thea.* curtain-raiser (*a. fig.*), introductory piece; *sexuelles*: foreplay; ˈ⁀**en** *j-m*: play *a th.* to.

ˈ**vorsprechen** *v/t. j-m*: pronounce to a p.; *v/i.* (*Besuch machen*) call (*bei* on *a p.*; at *an office*).

ˈ**vorspringen** (sn) jump (*od.* leap) forward; (*hervortreten*) project, jut (out); ˈ~**d** *adj. Winkel*: salient.

ˈ**Vorsprung** *m* ⚠ projection; (*Sims, a. Fels*⁀) ledge; (*Abstand*) (head) start, lead, advantage (*vor dat.* of); *mit großem* ~ by a wide margin.

ˈ**Vorstadt** *f* suburb.

ˈ**Vorstädt|er(in** *f*) *m* (7 [16[1]]) suburban resident; ˈ⁀**isch** suburban.

ˈ**Vorstand** *m* board of directors, managing (*od.* executive) board; *P.*: head, principal; ˈ~**s-etage** *f* executive suite; ˈ~**smitglied** *n* member of the managing board.

ˈ**vorstecken** put before; *mit e-r Nadel usw.*: pin before; *den Kopf*: stick out; *vorgestecktes Ziel* object, target.

ˈ**vorsteh|en** (*hervorragen*) project, protrude, jut out; *e-r Sache usw.*: direct, be at the head (*od.* in charge) of, manage; ~*d* (*vorhergehend*) foregoing, preceding, above; *wie* ~*d* as above; ˈ⁀**er** *m* (7), ˈ⁀**erin** *f* (16[1]) principal, director, manager(ess *f*), superintendent, head; ˈ⁀**erdrüse** *f* prostate gland; ˈ⁀**hund** *m* pointer; *langhaarig*: setter.

ˈ**vorstell|bar** imaginable; ˈ~**en** put forward *od.* in front; *Uhr*: put on; *j-n j-m*: introduce, *seltener*: present *a p. to a p.*; (*bedeuten*) mean, stand for; (*darstellen*) represent; *j-m et.* ~ (*hinweisen auf*) point out a th. to a p., *mahnend*: remonstrate with a p. about a th.; *sich* ~ stand in front, (*sich bekannt machen*) introduce o.s., *bei*: present o.s. at; *sich et.* ~ imagine, fancy, (*abwägend*) envisage, (*sich ein Bild machen von*) visualize, picture; *ich stelle Ihnen hier Herrn X. vor* allow me to introduce Mr. X. to you, *Am.* meet Mr. X.; F *stell dir (nur) vor!* just fancy!; ˈ~**ig:** ~ *werden bei der Behörde* apply to (*protestierend*: lodge a complaint with) the authorities (*wegen* for); ˈ⁀**ung** *f* introduction, presentation;

thea. performance; *s.* F... *griff*) idea, conception; s... *machen von* form (*od.* get) a... of; (*Mahnung*) remonstrance, re... resentation; '≈**ungsgespräch** *n* interview; '≈**ungsvermögen** *n* imagination.

Vorstoß *m* ⚔ thrust, drive (*a. fig.*); *Sport*: rush; '≈**en** thrust (*Sport*: rush) forward, advance.

'**Vorstrafe** *f* previous conviction; '~**n**(**register** *n*) *pl.* police record.

'**vorstrecken** stretch out; *den Kopf*: stick out; *Geld*: advance.

'**Vorstufe** *f* first step (*od.* stage); *e-s Lehrgangs*: primary course; (*Anfangsgründe*) (first) elements *pl.*

'**vorstürmen** rush forward.

'**vortanzen** lead the dance; *j-m*: dance (...) before a p.

'**vortasten** (*sich*) grope one's way (*bis zu* to).

'**vortäuschen** feign, simulate, sham, pretend, fake.

'**Vorteil** *m* (3) advantage; (*Gewinn*) profit, benefit; *Tennis*: (ad)vantage; *die Vor- und Nachteile e-r S.* the pros and cons; *auf s-n ~ bedacht sein* have an ax(e) to grind; *sich im ~ befinden gegenüber* (*dat.*) have an advantage over; *~ ziehen aus* profit by; '≈**haft** advantageous, profitable (*für* to); *~ aussehen* look one's best.

Vortrag ['fo:rtra:k] *m* (3^3) performance; (~*sweise*) delivery, *rhet.* elocution; *e-s Gedichtes*: recitation; ♪ (*Solo*≈) recital; (~*stechnik*) execution; (*Abhandlung, Vorlesung*) lecture; (*Bericht*) report; ⚕ balance carried forward; (*einen*) *~ halten* read a paper, (give a) lecture (*über acc.* on); ≈**en** ['~gən] carry forward; (*berichten*) report (*über acc.* on, *j-m* to); (*hersagen*) recite; (*Vortrag halten*) lecture (on); *Rede*: deliver; *Gedicht*: recite; ♪ perform; *Ansichten*: state; (*vorschlagen*) propose, submit; ⚕ *den Saldo ~* carry forward the balance; '~**ende** *m, f* (18) (*Künstler*) performer; (*Dozent*) lecturer.

'**Vortrags|kunst** *f* art of reciting *od.* lecturing *od.* delivery; '~**künstler**(**in** *f*) *m rhet.* elocutionist; ♪ executant, performer; '~**reihe** *f* series of lectures; '~**reise** *f* lecture tour.

...**lich** excellent; ≈**keit** *f* ex-...

vor... (sn) step (*od.* come) for-... (*zeitlich*...en) project, protrude. ...cedence; *j-m den ~* ...dence to a p. ...**gehen** (sn) ... along, by, past; (*od.* go) by; ... over, past; ~- transitory; (*zeit*... *räumlich*: pass ... ≈**gehende** *m* (18) ...dj. passing, ... passers-by); ~**ziehen** ...mporary; ... pass by; *Gewitter*: pass. ... by (*pl.* ... past,

'**Vor-übung** *f* preliminary ex... (*od.* practice).

'**Vor-untersuchung** *f* preliminary examination (*od. a.* ⚖ investigation).

'**Vor-urteil** *n* prejudice; '≈**sfrei**, '≈**slos** unprejudiced, unbias(s)ed.

Vorväter ['~fɛ:tər] *m/pl.* ancestors.

'**Vorvergangenheit** *gr. f* past perfect, pluperfect.

'**Vorverkauf** *m* advance sale; *thea.* advance booking; '~**skasse** *f*, '~**sstelle** *f* ticket agency, (advance) booking office.

'**vorverlegen** advance.

'**Vorverstärker** *m Radio*: pre-amplifier.

'**vorvorgestern** three days ago *od.* since.

'**vorvorig** last but one.

'**Vorwahl** *f* preliminary election; ⚡ preselection; *teleph.* dialling (*Am.* area) code.

'**vorwaltend** prevailing.

Vorwand ['~vant] *m* (3^3) pretext, preten|ce, *Am.* -se, excuse; *unter dem ~ von od. daß* on the pretext (*od.* plea) of *od.* that.

'**vorwärmen** preheat.

'**vorwarn|en** warn in advance; '≈**ung** *f* (advance) warning.

vorwärts ['fɔrvɛrts] forward, onward, on; *~!* go ahead!; '~**drängen** press on; '≈**gang** *mot. m* forward gear; '~**gehen** go ahead, advance, *fig. a.* progress; '~**kommen** (sn) get on, make headway; *fig. a. im Leben*: get on (in the world), make one's way; '≈**verteidigung** ⚔ *f* forward defen|ce (*Am.* -se).

'**Vorwäsche** *f Waschmaschine*: prewash.

vorweg [for'vɛk] beforehand; ≈**nahme** *f* anticipation; ~**nehmen** anticipate.

'Vorweihnachtszei
(season).
'vorweisen prod, ...ore; *fig.*
'Vorwelt *f* preh...with a th.
'vorwerfen (d...ate; '**~d** pre-
j-m et. ~ re...inant; *adv. a.*
'vorwiegen ...mostly.
ponderan...evious) knowledge;
mainly, ...unknown to me.
'Vorwis... inquisitiveness; (*vorlaute*
ohne ...wardness, pertness; '**⁀ig** in-
'Vor... ...ive; (*vorlaut*) forward, pert.
'...wort *n* (3) *des Autors*: preface;
bsd. v. e-m andern: foreword.
'**Vorwurf** *m* reproach; *eines Dramas usw.*: subject; *e-n* ~ *od. Vorwürfe machen s. vorwerfen*; '**⁀sfrei** irreproachable; '**⁀svoll** reproachful.
'**vorzählen** enumerate, count out.
'**Vorzeichen** *n* omen; ♪ signature, (*Versetzungszeichen*) accidental; ⅍ sign; ⚕ preliminary symptom; *fig. mit umgekehrten* ~ with reversed premises.
'**vorzeichnen** trace out; *j-m et.* ~ show a p. how to draw a th.; *als Richtschnur*: mark (out) *od.* indicate a th. to a p.
'**vorzeig|en** produce, show; *Wechsel*: present; (*darlegen*) exhibit; '**~bar** presentable; '**⁀ung** *f* producing, showing; exhibition.
'**Vorzeit** *f* (remote) antiquity; *in Erzählungen*: olden times *pl.*
vor'zeiten in olden times.
'**vorzeitig** premature.
'**Vorzensur** *f* precensorship; *e-r* ~ *unterwerfen* pre-censor.
'**vorziehen** draw forth; *Truppen*: move up; *fig.* prefer (*et. e-r anderen S.* a th. to another th.); *es* ~ *zu inf. a.* choose to *inf.*
'**Vorzimmer** *n* antechamber, anteroom; *e-s Büros*: outer office; '**~dame** *f* receptionist.
'**Vorzug** *m* preference; (*Vorteil*) advantage; (*gute Eigenschaft*) merit, virtue; (*Vorrang*) priority (*vor dat.* to); (*Vorrecht*) privilege; *den* ~ *geben s. vorziehen*; *den* ~ *haben zu* ... have the distinction of *ger.*
vorzüglich [~'tsy:kliç] excellent, superior, exquisite, first-rate; *adv.* (*vornehmlich*) expecially; **⁀keit** *f* excellence, superiority.
'**Vorzugs|-aktien** *f/pl.* preference shares, *Am.* preferred stock *sg.*; '**~preis** *m* special price, preferential rate; '**⁀weise** preferably, by preference; '**~zoll** *m* preferential tariff.
votieren [vo'ti:rən] vote.
Votiv|bild [vo'ti:fbilt] *n* votive picture; **~tafel** *f* votive tablet.
Votum ['vo:tum] *n* (9[1] *u.* [2]) vote.
vulgär [vul'gɛ:r] vulgar.
Vulkan [vul'ka:n] *m* (3[1]) volcano; **~ausbruch** *m* volcanic eruption; **⁀isch** volcanic(ally *adv.*); **⁀isieren** [~kani'zi:rən] vulcanize; *Autoreifen*: *a.* recap.

W

W [ve:], **w** *n inv.* W, w.
Waage ['va:gə] *f* (15) balance, (pair of) scales *pl.*; (~ *mit Laufgewicht*) steelyard; (*automatische Abfüll⁀*) weigher; (*Brücken-, Tafel⁀*) weighing-machine; *für Wagenlasten*: weighbridge; (*Wasser⁀*) spirit-level; *ast.* Balance, Libra; *die* ~ *halten* (*dat.*) counterbalance; *in der* ~ *halten* hold in equilibrium; '**~balken** *m* (scale-)beam; '**⁀recht** horizontal, level.
Waagschale ['va:k-] *f* scale; *fig. in die* ~ *fallen* be of weight; *in die* ~ *werfen* throw into the scale(s).
wabbelig ['vabəliç] flabby.
Wabe ['va:bə] *f* (15) honeycomb; '**~nhonig** *m* comb honey.
wach [vax] *pred.* awake; *ganz* ~ wide awake; ~ *werden* awake; *attr.* wakeful *state*; *fig.* alert *mind*; wide-awake *person*; '**⁀dienst** *m* guard-duty.
Wache ['vaxə] *f* (15) watch, guard; (*Wachlokal*) guardhouse, guardroom; (*Polizeidienststelle*) police-station; (*Posten*) guard, ⚔ *a.* sentry, sentinel; *auf* ~ on guard; ~

halten keep guard; ~ *stehen* stand sentry; *auf* ~ *ziehen* mount guard; '**2n** be awake; (*achtgeben*) watch (über *acc.* over), guard; *bei j-m* ~ sit up with a p.

'**Wach|habende** *m* guard commander; '**~haus** *n* guardhouse; '**~hund** *m* watchdog; '**~lokal** *n* guardroom; '**~mannschaft** *f* guard detail, sentry squad.

Wacholder [va'xɔldər] *m* (7) juniper; **~beere** *f* juniper berry; **~branntwein** *m* gin.

'**Wach|posten** *m* guard, ⚔ *a.* sentry; '**2rufen** call forth, rouse; *Erinnerung*: *a.* evoke; '**2rütteln** rouse (*a. fig.*).

Wachs [vaks] *n* (4) wax; '**~-abdruck** *m* impression in wax.

'**wach|sam** watchful, vigilant; ~ *sein* be on the alert; '**2samkeit** *f* vigilance; '**2schiff** *n* guard-ship.

wachsen[1] ['vaksən] *v/i.* (30, sn) grow; *fig. a.* increase (*an dat.* in); *s. gewachsen, Bart.*

'**wachsen**[2] *v/t.* (27) wax.

wächsern ['vɛksərn] wax; *fig.* waxen, waxy.

'**Wachs|figur** *f* wax figure, *pl. a.* waxwork *sg.*; '**~figurenkabinett** *n* waxworks (*mst sg.*); '**~kerze** *f*, '**~licht** *n* wax candle; '**~leinwand** *f* oilcloth; '**~matrize** *f* stencil; '**~puppe** *f* wax doll; '**~streichholz** *n* (wax) vesta; '**~tuch** *n* oilcloth.

'**Wachs-tum** *n* (1, *o. pl.*) growth; *fig. a.* increase; *im* ~ *hindern* stunt; '**2s-hemmend** growth-retarding; '**~s-industrie** *f* growth industry; '**~s-potential** *n* growth potential; '**~s-rate** *f* rate of (economic) growth; '**~sstörung** *f* disturbance of growth.

Wacht(...) [vaxt] *f* (16) *s. Wache, Wach...*

Wächte *mount.* ['vɛçtə] *f* cornice.

Wachtel ['vaxtəl] *f* (15) quail; '**~hund** *m* spaniel.

Wächter ['vɛçtər] *m* (7) watcher (*a.* '**~in** *f*), guard(ian); (*bsd. Nacht2*) watchman; (*Parkplatz2*) attendant.

'**Wachtmeister** *m* sergeant.

'**Wachtraum** *m* day-dream.

'**Wachturm** *m* watch-tower.

'**wack(e)lig** shaky (*a. fig.*), tottery; *alte Möbel usw.*: rickety; *Zahn*: loose; (*baufällig*) ramshackle.

'**Wackelkontakt** ⚡ *m* loose contact.

wackeln ['vakəln] (29) shake; (*wanken*) rock, wobble; (*taumeln, a. ~d gehen*) totter; (*locker sein*) be loose; ~ *mit* wag *a th.*

wacker ['vakər] (*bieder*) honest, worthy (*a. iro.*); (*tapfer*) brave; *adv.* (*tüchtig*) heartily, lustily.

Wade ['vɑ:də] *f* (15) calf (of the leg); '**~nkrampf** *m* cramp in the leg; '**~nstrumpf** *m* half-stocking.

Waffe ['vafə] *f* (15) weapon (*a. fig.*); *mst im pl.* arm; *s. greifen, strecken*; *j-n mit s-n eigenen ~n schlagen* beat a p. at his own game; *unter den ~n stehen* be under arms.

Waffel ['vafəl] *f* (15) waffle, wafer; '**~-eisen** *n* waffle-iron.

'**Waffen|-appell** *m* arms inspection; '**~-arsenal** *n* arsenal; '**~bruder** *m* brother in arms; '**~brüderschaft** *f* brotherhood in arms; '**~dienst** *m* military service; '**~fabrik** *f* arms factory; '**~fabrikant** *m* manufacturer of arms; '**2fähig** fit to bear arms; '**~gang** *m* passage of (*od.* at) arms; '**~gattung** *f* arm, branch (of the service); '**~gewalt** *f* force of arms, armed force; '**~handel** *m* arms trade; '**~kammer** *f* armo(u)ry; '**~lager** *n* ordnance depot; '**~lieferungen** *f/pl.* arms supplies; '**2los** weaponless, unarmed; '**~meister** *m* armo(u)rer; '**~rock** ⚔ *m* service coat; '**~ruhe** *f* truce; *kurze*: suspension of hostilities, cease-fire; '**~schein** *m* firearm certificate, *Am.* gun license; '**~schmied** *m* armo(u)rer; '**~schmuggel** *m* gun-running; '**~stillstand** *m* armistice, (*a. fig.*) truce; '**~stillstandslinie** *f* ceasefire-line; '**~system** *n* weapons system; '**~-übung** *f* military exercise.

waffnen ['vafnən] (26) arm.

wägbar ['vɛ:kbɑ:r] weighable; *fig. a.* ponderable.

Wage|hals ['vɑ:gəhals] *m* (4²) daredevil; **2halsig** ['~halziç] foolhardy, daring, *nur attr.* daredevil, breakneck; '**~halsigkeit** *f* foolhardiness, daredevilry; '**~mut** *m* daring.

wagen[1] ['vɑ:gən] (25) venture (*a. sich*); *et. Gefährliches*: risk, hazard; (*sich getrauen*; *a. sich erdreisten*) dare; *es* ~ take the plunge; *es* ~ *mit* try *a th.*; *wer nicht wagt, der nicht gewinnt* nothing venture nothing have; *s. gewagt.*

Wagen[2] [~] *m* (6) carriage (*a.* 🚂,

Am. car); (*Fahrzeug*) vehicle; (*Kutsche*) coach; *für schwere Fracht*: wag(g)on; (*Karren*) cart; (*Kraft*2) car; (*Last*2) lorry, *Am.* truck; (*Möbel*2) van; *der Schreibmaschine*: carriage; *ast.* der *Große* ~ Charles's Wain, the Plough, *Am.* the Plow, the Big Dipper.

wägen ['vɛːgən] (30) weigh (*nur noch fig.*).

'**Wagen|-abteil** 🚃 *n* compartment; '**~heber** *m* (lifting-)jack; '**~kolonne** *f* line of cars; '**~ladung** *f* carload, wag(g)on-load; '**~park** *m* fleet (of cars); '**~pflege** *f* maintenance (of a car); (*Kundendienst*) servicing; '**~rad** *n* wheel; '**~runge** *f* stanchion; '**~schlag** *m* car(riage) door; '**~schmiere** *f* cart-grease; '**~spur** *f* wheel-track, rut; '**~winde** *f* screw-jack.

'**Wag(e)stück** *n* daring deed.

Waggon [va'gɔ̃] *m* (11) railway carriage, wag(g)on, *Am.* (railroad) car.

Wagnis ['vɑːknis] *n* (4[1]) hazard(ous enterprise), venture, risk.

Wahl [vɑːl] *f* (16) choice; (*freie* ~) option; (~ *zwischen zwei Dingen*) alternative; (*Auslese*) selection; *pol.* election; ✝ erste (zweite) ~ choice (second rate) quality; *pol.* ~en abhalten hold elections; *fig.* die ~ haben have one's choice; *fig.* keine ~ haben have no alternative (als but); ich habe keine (andere) ~ I have no choice; in die engere ~ kommen be on the short list; s-e ~ treffen make one's choice; e-e gute ~ treffen choose well; '**~-akt** *m* polling, voting; '**~-alter** *n* voting age.

'**wählbar** eligible; '**2keit** *f* eligibility.

'**wahl|berechtigt** entitled to vote; '**2bericht** *m* election return; '**2beteiligung** *f* voting, turnout; '**2bezirk** *m* electoral district; *städtischer*: ward.

wählen ['vɛːlən] (25) choose; (*auslesen*) select; *pol.* elect; (*Stimme abgeben*) vote; *teleph.* dial; ~ gehen *pol.* go to the polls.

'**Wähler** *m* (7) voter.

'**Wahl-ergebnis** *n* election result *od.* return.

'**Wähler|in** *f* (16[1]) (female) voter; '**~initiative** *f* electors' initiative; '**2isch** particular, nice (*in dat.* about), choosy; *im Essen*: dainty, *a. weitS.* fastidious; '**~liste** *f* register of voters; '**~schaft** *f* constituency; *weitS.* voting population; '**~scheibe** *teleph. f* dial.

'**Wahl|fach** *n Schule, univ.*: optional subject, *Am.* elective; '**2fähig** *aktiv*: having a vote; *passiv*: eligible; '**~fähigkeit** *f s.* Wahlrecht; '**~feldzug** *m* election campaign; '**2frei** *Schule, univ.*: optional, *Am.* elective; '**~gang** *m* ballot; '**~geschenk** *n* pre-election promise; '**~heimat** *f* adopted country; '**~helfer(in** *f*) *m* polling officer; '**~jahr** *n* election year; '**~kabine** *f* polling booth; '**~kampf** *m* election campaign; '**~kreis** *m s.* Wahlbezirk; '**~lokal** *n* polling-station; '**2los** indiscriminate; '**~mann** *m* (1[2]) delegate, constituent, *Am.* elector; '**~plakat** *n* election poster; '**~prüfer** *m* scrutineer; '**~prüfung** *f* scrutiny; '**~recht** *n aktives*: franchise; *passives*: eligibility; allgemeines ~ universal suffrage; '**~rede** *f* election speech; '**~schlacht** *f* election campaign, electoral battle; '**~spruch** *m* device, motto; (*Schlagwort*) slogan; '**~stimme** *f* vote; '**~tag** *m* election-day; '**~-urne** *f* ballot-box; zur ~ schreiten go to the polls; '**~versammlung** *f* election meeting; '**~versprechen** campaign promise; '**~verwandtschaft** *f* elective affinity; *fig. a.* congeniality; '**~vorschlag** *m* election proposal; '**2weise** alternatively; '**~zelle** *f* polling-booth; '**~zettel** *m* voting-paper, ballot.

Wahn [vɑːn] *m* (3) delusion; *s. a.* Wahnsinn; '**~bild** *n* chimera, phantom.

wähnen ['vɛːnən] (25) fancy, imagine; believe, think.

'**Wahn|sinn**, '**~witz** *m* insanity, (*a. fig.*) madness; '**2sinnig**, '**2witzig** insane, (*a. fig.*) mad (vor *dat.* with); *fig.* frantic(ally *adv.*); *Angst, Schmerzen usw.*: horrible, dreadful; F (*toll*) terrific; *s. a.* verrückt; '**~sinnige** (18) *m* madman; *f* madwoman; lunatic; '**~vorstellung** *f* delusion; hallucination.

wahr [vɑːr] true; (*wirklich*) *a.* real; (*echt*) genuine; (*eigentlich*) proper; (*aufrichtig*) sincere; ein ~er Künstler a true artist; *es ist* eine ~e Wohltat quite a comfort; so ~ ich lebe! as sure as I live!; so ~ mir Gott helfe! so help me God!; et. ~ machen go ahead with a th., make a th. come true; ~ werden come true;

sein ~es Gesicht zeigen show the cloven hoof; *das ist nicht das* ꝰe that's not the real McCoy; '**~en** (25) preserve (*vor dat.* from), (*a. ein Geheimnis*) keep; *Interessen*: safeguard, protect; *s. Form, Schein.*

währen ['vɛːrən] (25) continue, last; '**~d 1.** *prp.* (*gen.*) during; ⚖ pending; **2.** *cj.* while, whilst; *Gegensatz*: whereas, while.

'**wahrhaben:** *er will es nicht ~* he will not admit it.

'**wahrhaft, ~ig** [~'haftiç] true; (*wahrheitsliebend, wahrheitsgemäß*) truthful, veracious; (*wirklich*) true, real; *adv.* truly, really; ꝰ**igkeit** [~'haft-] *f* veracity.

'**Wahrheit** *f* truth; *in ~* in truth; F *j-m die ~ sagen* (*schelten*) give a p. a piece of one's mind; *um die ~ zu sagen* to tell the truth, truth to tell; '**~sbeweis** *m*: *den ~ antreten* prove one's case; 'ꝰ**sgemäß**, 'ꝰ**sgetreu** truthful, true; '**~sliebe** *f* veracity; 'ꝰ**sliebend** truthful, veracious; 'ꝰ**swidrig** contrary to the truth.

'**wahrlich** truly; *Bibel*: verily.

'**wahr|nehmbar** perceptible, noticeable; '**~nehmen** perceive, notice; *Gelegenheit*: make use of, seize; *Interesse*: look after, protect; *Amt*: exercise the functions of ...; *Termin*: observe; ꝰ**nehmung** ['~neːmuŋ] *f* perception; observation; (*Sorge für et.*) care (*gen.* of); *der Interessen*: safeguarding; 'ꝰ**nehmungsvermögen** *n* perceptive faculty; '**~sagen** prophesy; *aus Karten usw.*: tell fortunes; *sich ~ lassen* have one's fortune told; 'ꝰ**sager(in** *f*) *m* soothsayer; *aus Karten usw.*: fortune-teller; ꝰ**sagerei** [~'raɪ] *f* (16) fortune-telling; **~'scheinlich** probable, likely; *er wird ~ (nicht) kommen* he is (not) likely to come; ꝰ'**scheinlichkeit** *f* probability, likelihood; *aller ~ nach* in all probability; ꝰ'**scheinlichkeitsgrad** *m* degree of probability; ꝰ'**scheinlichkeitsrechnung** *f* theory of probabilities; 'ꝰ**spruch** *m* verdict.

'**Wahrung** *f* maintenance; *von Interessen*: safeguarding, protection.

Währung ['vɛːruŋ] *f* currency; (*Gold*ꝰ *usw.*) standard; '**~s-ausgleichsfonds** *m* exchange equalization fund; '**~sbank** *f* bank of issue; '**~s-einheit** *f* currency unit; '**~s-fonds** *m*: *Internationaler ~* International Monetary Fund; '**~skrise** *f* monetary crisis; '**~s-politik** *f* monetary policy; '**~sreform** *f* monetary (*od.* currency) reform.

'**Wahrzeichen** *n* distinctive sign *od.* mark, token; *e-r Stadt usw.*: landmark.

'**Waidmann** *m s. Weidmann.*

Waise ['vaɪzə] *f* (15) orphan; '**~nhaus** *n* orphanage; '**~nkind** *n*, '**~nknabe** *m* orphan; *fig. ein Waisenknabe gegen j-n sein* not to be a patch on a p.

Wal [vaːl] *m* (3) whale.

Wald [valt] *m* (1^2) wood, (*a. fig.*) forest; *er sieht den ~ vor Bäumen nicht* he does not see the wood for trees; 'ꝰ**-arm** sparsely wooded; '**~bestand** *m* forest cover; '**~brand** *m* forest-fire; '**~-erdbeere** *f* wood strawberry; '**~frevel** *m* offen|ce (*Am.* -se) against the forest laws; '**~gebirge** *n* woody mountains *pl.*; '**~gegend** *f* woodland; '**~horn** ♪ *n* French horn; '**~hüter** *m* forest-keeper, ranger.

waldig ['~diç] woody, wooded.

'**Wald|land** *n* woodland; '**~lauf** *m* cross-country race; '**~meister** ⚘ *m* woodruff; '**~nymphe** *f* wood-nymph; '**~rand** *m* edge of the forest; 'ꝰ**reich** rich in forests; '**~sterben** *n* dying(-off) of forests.

Waldung ['~duŋ] *f* wood, forest, woodland.

'**Wald|weg** *m* wood-path; '**~wiese** *f* (forest-)glade.

Wal|fänger ['vaːl-] *m* (*Schiff u. Mensch*) whaler; '**~fisch** *m* whale; '**~-öl** *n*, '**~tran** *m* train-oil.

walk|en ['valkən] (25) full, mill; 'ꝰ**er** *m* (7) fuller; 'ꝰ**mühle** *f* fulling-mill.

Walküre [val'kyːrə] *f* (15) Valkyrie.

Wall [val] *m* (3^3) ⚔ rampart; (*Damm*) dam, dike; (*Erdaufschüttung als Schutz*) mound; *fig.* bulwark, dam.

Wallach ['valax] *m* (3 *od.* 12) gelding.

wallen ['valən] (25, sn *u.* h.) wave; *Haar, Gewand usw.*: flow; (*sieden*) simmer; (*brodeln*; *a. fig. v. Blut*) boil; *s. a. wallfahren.*

'**wall|fahren** (25, sn) (go on a) pilgrimage; 'ꝰ**fahrer** *m* (7) pilgrim; 'ꝰ**fahrt** *f* pilgrimage; 'ꝰ**fahrts-ort** *m* place of pilgrimage.

ˈ**Wallung** *f* ebullition (*a. fig.*); ⚕ (*Blut*𝔖) congestion; (*Hitze*) flush; *fig. in ~ bringen* enrage *a p.*; *in ~ kommen* boil (with rage).

Walnuß [ˈval-] *f* (*Am.* English) walnut; ˈ**~baum** *m* walnut-tree.

Walroß [ˈval-] *n* walrus.

Walstatt [ˈval-] *f* battle-field.

walten [ˈvaltən] **1.** *v/i. u. v/t.* (26) govern, rule; (*wirken*) be at work; *s. schalten*; *seines Amtes ~* do one's duty; *Gnade ~ lassen* show mercy; *Sorgfalt ~ lassen* exercise proper care; *das walte Gott!* God grant it!; **2.** 𝔖 *n* (6) rule; working; *the* hand *of God, etc.*

ˈ**Walzblech** *n* rolled plate.

Walze [ˈvaltsə] *f* (15) roller (*a. typ. u. Straßen*𝔖 *usw.*), cylinder (*a. typ.*); ⊕ *a.* roll; *der Schreibmaschine*: platen; *der Drehorgel usw.*: barrel; F *fig. auf der ~* on the tramp.

ˈ**walzen** (27) **1.** *v/t.* ⊕ roll; **2.** *v/i.* (*Walzer tanzen*) waltz.

wälzen [ˈvɛltsən] (27) (*a. sich*) roll; *sich ~ im Wasser usw.*: wallow; *in s-m Blute*: welter; *fig. von sich ~* off-load *a th.*; *sich vor Lachen ~* be convulsed with laughter; *die Schuld auf j-n ~* lay the blame on a p.

walzenförmig [ˈ~fœrmiç] cylindrical.

Walzer ♪ [ˈvaltsər] *m* (7) waltz.

Wälzer [ˈvɛltsər] *m* (7) bulky volume, huge tome.

ˈ**Walzgold** *n* rolled gold.

ˈ**Wälzlager** ⊕ *n* roller bearing.

ˈ**Walz|straße** ⊕ *f* rolling (*od.* mill) train; ˈ**~werk** *n* rolling-mill.

Wamme [ˈvamə] *f* (15) (*Kehlfalte*) dewlap; F (*dicker Bauch*) paunch.

Wams [vams] *n* (2[1]) jacket; *hist.* doublet.

wand[1] [vant] *pret. v. winden.*

Wand[2] [~] *f* (14[1]) wall; (*Scheide*𝔖) partition; *e-s Gefäßes*: side; *fig. an die ~ gedrückt werden* go to the wall; *j-n an die ~ stellen* execute; ˈ**~-arm** *m* (wall-)bracket; ˈ**~behang** *m* wall hanging.

Wandel [ˈvandəl] *m* (7) change; (*Lebenswandel*) way of living; (*Betragen*) behavio(u)r, conduct; *Handel und ~* trade, commerce; *~ schaffen* bring about a change; ˈ𝔖**bar** changeable, variable; ˈ**~barkeit** *f* changeableness; ˈ**~gang** *m*, ˈ**~halle** *f parl., thea.* lobby; ˈ𝔖**n** (29) *v/i.* (sn) *poet.* walk; (*wandern*) wander, travel; *v/t.* change (*a. sich*); *sich ~ in* (*acc.*) turn into; ˈ**~-obligation** ⚕ *f* convertible bond.

Wander|-ausstellung [ˈvandər-] *f* itinerant (*od.* flying) exhibition; ˈ**~bühne** *f* travelling theatre, *Am.* touring company; ˈ**~bursche** *m* travel(l)ing journeyman; ˈ**~düne** *f* shifting sand dune; ˈ**~er** *m* (7), ˈ**~in** *f* (16[1]) wanderer, travel(l)er; *bsd. sportlich*: hiker; ˈ**~gewerbe** *n* itinerant trade; ˈ**~heuschrecke** *f* migratory locust; ˈ**~jahre** *n/pl.* (journeyman's) years of travel; ˈ**~karte** *f* trail map; ˈ**~leben** *n* vagrant life; ˈ𝔖**n** (29, sn) wander (*a. Blick, Gedanken*), travel; (*umherstreifen*) ramble; (*zu Fuß gehen*) walk; *bsd. sportlich*: hike; *Vögel, Völker usw.*: migrate; *Düne*: shift; F *fig.* go; ˈ**~niere** *f* floating kidney; ˈ**~pokal** *m* challenge cup; ˈ**~prediger** *m* itinerant preacher; ˈ**~preis** *m* challenge trophy; ˈ**~ratte** *f* brown (*od.* Norway) rat; ˈ**~schaft** *f* wanderings *pl.*, travel(l)ing, travels *pl.*; *auf der ~* on the tramp; *auf die ~ gehen* take to the road; ˈ**~smann** *m* (1, *pl.* ˈ*Wandersleute*) *s. Wanderer*; ˈ**~stab** *m* (walking-)stick; *den ~ ergreifen* set out on one's travels; ˈ**~trieb** *m* roving spirit; *zo.* migratory instinct; ˈ**~truppe** *f s. Wanderbühne*; ˈ**~ung** *f* walking-tour; *vgl. wandern*: ramble; hike; migration; ˈ**~ver-ein** *m* rambling club; ˈ**~vogel** *m* bird of passage; ˈ**~zirkus** *m* travel(l)ing circus.

ˈ**Wand|gemälde** *n* mural (painting); ˈ**~halter** *m* (7) wall bracket; ˈ**~kalender** *m* tear-off calendar; ˈ**~karte** *f* wall-map; ˈ**~leuchter** *m* bracket (-lamp), sconce.

Wandlung [ˈvandluŋ] *f* change, (*a.* ⚡) transformation; *eccl.* transsubstantiation; ⚖ redhibition.

ˈ**Wand|male**ˈ**rei** *f* mural painting; ˈ**~pfeiler** *m* pilaster; ˈ**~schirm** *m* folding-screen; ˈ**~schrank** *m* closet, wallchest; ˈ**~spiegel** *m* pier-glass; ˈ**~tafel** *f* blackboard; ˈ**~teppich** *m* tapestry; ˈ**~-uhr** *f* wall-clock.

wandte [ˈvantə] *pret. v. wenden.*

Wange [ˈvaŋə] *f* (15) cheek (*a.* ⊕).

...wangig [...vaŋiç] ...-cheeked.

Wankelmotor [ˈvaŋkəl-] *m* Wankel engine, rotary piston engine.

Wankel|mut [ˈvaŋkəlmu:t] *m* fickleness, inconstancy; ♀**mütig** ['~my:tiç] fickle, inconstant.

wanken ['vaŋkən] (25, h. *u.* sn) totter, stagger; *Boden, Haus*: rock; *fig.* waver, falter; *ins* ♀ *bringen od. kommen* shake.

wann [van] when; *s. dann*; *seit ~?* how long?, since what time?

Wanne ['vanə] *f* (15) tub; (*Bade*♀) bath; '**~nbad** *n* tub-bath.

Wanst [vanst] *m* (3^2 *u.* ^{3}) paunch.

Want ⚓ [vant] *f* (16, *mst pl.*) shroud.

Wanz|e ['vantsə] *f* (15) bug, *Am.* bedbug; F (*Abhörgerät*) bug; '♀**ig** buggy.

Wappen ['vapən] *n* (6) (coat of) arms *pl.*; '**~bild** *n* heraldic figure; '**~kunde** *f* heraldry; '**~schild** *m* escutcheon, blazon; '**~spruch** *m* heraldic motto.

wappnen ['vapnən] (26) arm; *fig. gewappnet* forearmed.

war [va:r] *pret. v. sein*[1] 1.

warb [varp] *pret. v. werben.*

Ware ['va:rə] *f* (15) *allg. u. in Zssgn* ware (*z. B.* earthenware); article (of commerce), commodity; *als Sammelwort*: *~ od. ~n pl.* merchandise *sg.*; *~n pl. a.* goods *pl.*

wäre ['vɛ:rə] *s. sein*; *wie ~ es mit ...?* how about ...?; *wie ~ es, wenn ...?* what if ...?

'**Waren|-angebot** *n* range of items (for sale); '**~-aufzug** *m* hoist, *Am.* (freight-)elevator; '**~-ausfuhr** *f* export(ation of goods); '**~bestand** *m* stock (on hand); '**~börse** *f* Commodity Exchange; '**~haus** *n* department store; '**~konto** *n* goods account; '**~kredit** *m* goods credit; '**~lager** *n* (*Vorrat*) stock-in-trade; (*Raum*) warehouse, *Am.* stockroom; '**~probe** *f* sample; *v. Stoff usw.*: pattern; '**~rechnung** *f* invoice; '**~umsatz** *m* goods turnover; '**~zeichen** *n* trade-mark.

warf [varf] *pret. v. werfen.*

warm [varm] warm (*a. fig.*); *stärker* (*a. Speisen u.* ⊕): hot; *mir ist ~* I am (*od.* feel) warm; *~ halten* keep warm; *~ werden* warm up (*a. fig.*); *~ empfehlen* recommend warmly; '♀**bad** *n* warm bath; (*Quelle*) thermal springs *pl.*; ♀**blüter** ['~bly:tər] (7) warm-blooded animal.

Wärme ['vɛrmə] *f* (15, *o. pl.*) warmth (*a. fig.*); *phys.* heat; '**~behandlung** ⚕ *f* heat treatment; '♀**beständig** heat-resistant; '**~dämmung** *f* heat insulation; '**~-einheit** *f* thermal unit, calorie; '**~-energie** *f* thermal energy; '**~grad** *m* degree of heat; '**~kraftwerk** *n* thermo-electric power plant; '**~lehre** *f* theory of heat; '**~leiter** *m* conductor of heat; '**~messer** *m* thermometer; *nach Kalorien*: calorimeter; '♀**n** (25) warm; heat; '**~pumpe** *f* heat pump; '**~technik** *f* heat engineering; '**~verlust** *m* heat loss.

'**Wärmflasche** *f* hot-water bottle.

'**warm|halten** *fig.*: *sich j-n ~* keep in with a p.; '♀**halteplatte** *f* hot plate; '**~herzig** warmhearted; '♀**luft** *f* warm air; '♀**miete** F *f* rent including heating.

Warm'wasser|bereiter *m* electric water heater; **~heizung** *f* hot-water heating; **~speicher** *m* hot-water tank; **~versorgung** *f* hot-water supply.

Warn|blink-anlage *mot.* ['varn-] *f* warning flashers *pl.*; '**~drei-eck** *mot. n* warning triangle; '♀**en** (25) (*vor dat.*) warn (of, against), caution (against); *vor Dieben usw. wird gewarnt!* beware of ...!; *davor ~, zu inf.* warn against *doing a th.*; *Sie sollten gewarnt sein durch* you should take warning from; '**~er** *m* (7) warner; '**~lampe** *f* warning lamp; '**~schuß** *m* warning shot; '**~signal** *n* danger-signal; '**~streik** *m* token strike; '**~tafel** *f* danger notice; '**~ung** *f* warning; *laß dir das zur ~ dienen* let that be a warning (*od.* lesson) to you.

Warte ['vartə] *f* (15) watch-tower, look-out; *fig.* level; standpoint; '**~frau** *f s. Wärterin*; '**~geld** *n* half-pay; '**~liste** *f* waiting list.

warten ['vartən] (26) *v/i.* wait; (*bleiben*) stay; *~ auf* (*acc.*) wait for, (*bevorstehen*) be in store for *a p.*; (*nicht lange*) *auf sich ~ lassen* (not to) be long in coming; *j-n ~ lassen* keep a p. waiting; *s. na*; *v/t. allg.* tend; (*pflegen*) nurse; *weitS.* attend to, look after; ⊕ service, maintain.

Wärter ['vɛrtər] *m* (7) attendant; (*bsd. Irren*♀) keeper; (*Pfleger*) (male) nurse; (*Wächter*) guard; 🚂 signalman; '**~in** *f* (16^1) (female) attendant; (*Pflegerin*) nurse.

Warte|raum *m*, '**~saal** *m*, '**~zim-**

mer *n* waiting-room; '**~zeit** *f* waiting period.
'**Wartung** *f* attendance; tending; (*Pflege*) nursing; ⊕ maintenance, servicing; '**⁲s-arm** ⊕ low-maintenance; '**⁲sfrei** ⊕ maintenance-free.
warum [va'rum] why, for what reason.
Warz|e ['vartsə] *f* (15) wart; (*Brust⁲*) nipple; ⊕ lug, stud; '**~enschwein** *n* warthog; '**⁲ig** warty.
was [vas] **1.** (24) *interr. pron.* what; *rel. pron.* (= *das, was*) what, *a.* that which; *den Inhalt des vorhergehenden Satzes aufnehmend*: which; ~ *auch immer*, ~ *nur* what(so)ever; ~ *für (ein) ...?* what ...? what sort (*od.* kind) of ...?; ~ *für (ein) ...!* what (a) ...!; *was nun?* F so what?; **2.** F = *etwas*; F *ich will dir ~ sagen* I'll tell you what; **3.** = *wieviel*: ~ *kostet das Buch?* how much is?
'**Wasch|-anlage** ['vaʃ-] *f* car-wash; '**~-automat** *m* washing-machine; '**⁲bar** washable; '**~bär** *m* rac(c)oon, *Am.* F coon; '**~becken** *n* wash- (*od.* hand-)basin; '**~beutel** *m* sponge bag; '**~blau** *n* washing-blue; '**~brett** *n* wash-board.
Wäsche ['vɛʃə] *f* (15) (*Waschen*) wash; (*Waschen; Zeug während des Waschens*) washing; (*schmutzige ~*) laundry; (*Leib⁲, Tisch⁲, Bett⁲*) linen; (*Unter⁲*) underwear; ☨ (*Damenunter⁲*) lingerie; *schmutzige* ~ soiled (*fig.* dirty) linen; *in die ~ geben* get *a th.* washed, send *a th.* to the laundry; *in der ~ sein* be at the wash; '**~beutel** *m* laundry bag.
'**wasch-echt** laundry-proof, fast; *fig.* genuine, true-blue.
'**Wäsche|geschäft** *n* lingerie store; '**~klammer** *f* clothes-peg; '**~korb** *m* linen (*od.* laundry) basket; '**~leine** *f* clothes-line.
waschen ['vaʃən] *v/t., v/i., v/refl.* (30) wash; *Wäsche*: *a.* launder; *Haar*: shampoo; *sich gut ~ lassen* wash well; ⁲ *und Legen* shampoo and set; *s. Kopf.*
'**Wäschepuff** *m* linen (*od.* laundry) basket.
Wäscher ['vɛʃər] *m* (7) washer; *in e-r Wäscherei*: laundryman; **~ei** [~'raɪ] *f* (16) laundry; '**~in** *f* (16[1]) wash(er)-woman, laundress.
'**Wäsche|schleuder** *f* spin drier; '**~schrank** *m* linen-press, clothes-press; '**~ständer** *m* clothes horse; '**~tinte** *f* marking-ink; '**~trockner** ⚡ *m* tumble-drier; '**~zeichen** *n* laundry-mark.
'**Wasch|frau** *f s. Wäscherin*; '**~gelegenheit** *f* washing facility; '**~kessel** *m* wash-boiler; '**~korb** *m* clothes-basket; '**~küche** *f* wash-house; F (*Nebel*) *sl.* pea-soup; '**~lappen** *m fürs Gesicht*: face cloth, *Am.* washrag; *für Geschirr*: dish-cloth; F (*Weichling*) *sl.* sissy; '**~lauge** *f* lye; '**~leder** *n*, '**⁲ledern** wash-leather, chamois, shammy; '**~maschine** *f* washing-machine, washer; '**⁲maschinenfest** machine-washable; '**~mittel** *n* washing agent, detergent; '**~pulver** *n* washing powder; '**~raum** *m* lavatory, *Am. a.* washroom; '**~schüssel** *f* wash bowl; '**~seide** *f* washing silk; '**~seife** *f* washing- (*od.* laundry) soap; '**~tag** *m* washing day; '**~tisch** *m*, '**~toilette** *f* wash-stand; '**~trog** *m* washing trough; '**~ung** *f* washing; *bsd.* ⚕, *eccl.* ablution; '**~weib** *contp. n* old gossip; '**~wasser** *n* washwater; '**~zettel** *m* (*Buchanpreisung*) blurb.
Wasser ['vasər] *n* (7) water; *fig. ein stilles ~* (*Person*) a deep one; *Schlag ins ~ sl.* flop; *zu ~ und zu Lande* by sea and land; ~ *lassen* pass water; *unter ~ setzen* flood, submerge; *ins ~ fallen fig.* not to come off; *zu ~ werden fig.* come to naught, end in smoke; *das ist ~ auf seine Mühle* that is grist to his mill; *er kann ihm nicht das ~ reichen* he is not fit to hold a candle to her; *er ist mit allen ~n gewaschen* he knows all the tricks; *mir läuft das ~ im Munde zusammen* my mouth waters; *fig. sich mühsam über ~ halten* keep one's head barely above water; *s. abgraben*; '**⁲-abstoßend** water-repellent; '**⁲-arm** ill supplied with water, arid; '**~ball** *m* beach-ball; *s. Wasserballspiel*; '**~ballspiel** *n Sport*: water polo; '**~bau** *m* hydraulic engineering; '**~behälter** *m* reservoir; ⊕ cistern, tank; '**~bett** *n* water bed; '**~blase** *f* bubble; *auf der Haut*: blister, vesicle; '**~bombe** *f* depth charge; '**~bruch** ⚕ *m* hydrocele.
Wässerchen ['vɛsər-] *n* (6): *fig. er sah aus, als könne er kein ~ trüben* he looked as though butter would not melt in his mouth.
'**Wasser|dampf** *m* water vapo(u)r,

steam; '**≈dicht** waterproof; ⚓ water-tight; ~ *sein a.* hold water; '**~-eimer** *m* pail, bucket; '**~-enthärter** *m* water softener; '**~fahrzeug** *n* watercraft, vessel; '**~fall** *m* waterfall; *kleiner od. künstlicher*: cascade; *großer*: cataract; '**~farbe** *f* water-colo(u)r; '**~fläche** *f* (*Oberfläche*) surface of (the) water; (*weite Strecke*) sheet of water; '**~flasche** *f* water-bottle; '**~floh** *m* water-flea; '**~flugzeug** *n* seaplane, hydroplane; '**~flut** *f* flood; '**~fracht** *f* waterfreight; '**~glas** *n* water-glass (*a.* ⚗); (*Trinkglas ohne Fuß*) tumbler; *s. Sturm*; '**~graben** *m* drain; ⚔ moat; '**~hahn** *m* (water-)tap, *Am. a.* faucet; '**≈haltig** containing water; ⚗ hydrated; '**~haushalt** *m* water economy; ⚕ water equilibrium; '**~heilkunde** *f* hydrotherapy; '**~hose** *f* waterspout; '**~huhn** *n* coot.

wässerig ['vɛsərɪç] watery; ⚗ *Lösung*: aqueous; ⚕ serous; *fig.* washy; *j-m den Mund ~ machen* make a p.'s mouth water.

'**Wasser|kasten** *m* water tank; '**~kessel** *m* kettle; ⊕ boiler; '**~klosett** *n* water-closet (*abbr.* W.C.); '**~kopf** ⚕ *m* hydrocephalus; '**~kraft** *f* waterpower; '**~kraftwerk** *n* hydroelectric power plant; '**~krug** *m* water-jug, pitcher; '**~kühlung** ⊕ *f* water-cooling (system); *mit ~* water-cooled; '**~kunst** *f* artificial fountain; '**~kur** *f* water-cure; '**~lauf** *m* watercourse; '**~leiche** *f* drowned corpse; '**~leitung** *f* water pipes *pl.*, (water-)main; aqueduct; '**~leitungsrohr** *n* water-pipe; '**~lilie** *f* water-lily; '**~linie** ⚓ *f* water-line; '**≈löslich** water-soluble; '**~mangel** *m* water famine (*od.* shortage); '**~mann** *ast. m* Watercarrier, Aquarius, *Am. a.* Water Bearer; '**~mantel** ⊕ *m* water jacket; '**~melone** *f* water-melon; '**~messer** *m* hydrometer, waterga(u)ge; '**~mühle** *f* water-mill.

wassern ✈ ['vasərn] (29) alight on water.

wässern ['vɛsərn] (29) (*be~; ver~*) water; (*be~*) irrigate; (*einweichen*) water-soak; *phot.* wash.

'**Wasser|nymphe** *f* water-nymph, naiad; '**~pflanze** *f* aquatic plant; '**~pistole** *f* water pistol; '**~pocken** *f/pl.* chicken-pox; '**~polizei** *f* river police; '**~rad** *n* water-wheel; '**~ratte** *f* water-rat; F *fig.* enthusiastic swimmer; '**≈reich** abounding in water; '**~reservoir** *n* reservoir, (water) tank; '**~rohr** *n* water-pipe; '**~rutschbahn** *f* water-chute; '**~säule** *f* water column; '**~schaden** *m* damage caused by water; '**~scheide** *f* watershed, *Am. a.* divide; '**≈scheu**[1] afraid of water; '**~scheu**[2] *f* dread of water, F water-funk; '**~schi** *m* water-ski; *~ fahren* go (*od.* do) water-skiing; '**~schlange** *f* water-snake; '**~schlauch** *m* water-hose; '**~schutzpolizei** *f* river police; '**~speier** *m* (7) gargoyle; '**~spiegel** *m* surface of the water; (*Wasserstand*) water level; '**~sport** *m* aquatic sports *pl.*, aquatics *pl.*; '**~spülung** *f* water flushing; '**~stand** *m* water level; '**~stands-anzeiger** *m* water-level ga(u)ge; '**~stiefel** *m/pl.* waterproof boots, waders *pl.*; '**~stoff** ⚗ *m* hydrogen; '**~stoffbombe** *f* hydrogen bomb, hydrobomb, H-bomb; '**≈stoffhaltig** hydrogenous; **~stoffsuperoxyd** ['~'zu:pər?ɔksy:t] *n* hydrogen peroxide; '**~strahl** *m* jet of water; '**~straße** *f* waterway; '**~sucht** *f* dropsy; '**≈süchtig** dropsical; '**~suppe** *f* water-gruel; F *fig.* slops *pl.*; '**~tank** *m* water tank; '**~tier** *n* aquatic animal; '**~turm** *m* water-tower; '**~uhr** *f* water meter.

Wässerung ['vɛsərʊŋ] *f vgl. wässern*: watering; irrigation; soaking, steeping; *phot.* washing.

'**Wasser|verbrauch** *m* water consumption; '**~verdrängung** *f* displacement (of water); '**~verschmutzung** *f* water pollution; '**~versorgung** *f* water supply; '**~vogel** *m* aquatic bird, *pl. a.* water-fowl; '**~waage** *f* spirit-level; '**~weg** *m* water-way; *auf dem ~* by water; '**~welle** *f* (*Frisur*) water-wave; '**~werfer** *m* water cannon; '**~werk**(**e** *pl.*) *n* water works; '**~zähler** *m* water meter; '**~zeichen** *n* watermark.

wäßrig ['vɛsrɪç] *s. wässerig.*

waten ['va:tən] (26, sn) wade.

watschel|ig ['va:tʃəlɪç] waddling; '**~n** (29, h. *u.* sn) waddle.

Watt[1] [vat] *n* (3) *geogr.* banks *pl.* of sand, flats *pl.*; **~**[2] (11, *im pl. mst inv.*) ⚡ watt; '**~e** *f* (15) cotton (wool); (*zum Ausstopfen*) wadding; '**~ebausch** *m* (cotton) swab *od.* pad; '**~epfropf** *m* cotton plug; **~e-stäbchen** ['~ʃtɛ:pçən] *n* (6) cotton-wool tip; **≈ieren**

[~'ti:rən] pad, wad; '**~leistung** ⚡ *f* wattage.

Watvogel ['vɑ:t-] *m* wader.

wauwau ['vaʊ'vaʊ] **1.** bow-wow!; **2.** ♀ *m* (11) *Kindersprache*: bow-wow.

WC ['ve:'tse:] *n* (11) lavatory, *Am.* restroom; **~-Reiniger** *m* toilet cleaner.

weben ['ve:bən] (30) weave.

'**Weber** *m* (7) weaver; '**~baum** *m* loom-beam; **~ei** [~'raɪ] *f* (16) weaving; (*Gebäude*) weaving-mill; '**~knecht** *zo. m* harvestman, *Am.* daddy-longlegs; '**~schiffchen** *n* shuttle.

Web|fehler ['ve:p-] *m* (weaving) flaw; '**~stuhl** *m* loom; '**~waren** *f/pl.* textiles, woven goods.

Wechsel ['vɛksəl] *m* (7) change; (*Aufeinanderfolge*) succession; (*regelmäßiger Personalaustausch*; *a.* ⚘ *Saat*♀) rotation; (*Tausch*) exchange, *v. Geldsorten*: *a.* change; ⚕ bill (of exchange); (*monatliche Geldzuwendung*) allowance; *hunt.* runway, *Am.* trace; *Sport*: (*Stab*♀) (baton) change, (*Seiten*♀) change of ends; ~ *auf Sicht* bill payable at sight; *eigener* (*od. trockener*) ~ promissory note; *gezogener* (*od. trassierter*) ~ draft (*auf zwei Monate* at two months); *offener* ~ letter of credit; ~ *zum Inkasso* bill for collection; ~ *zum Verkauf* bill for negotiation; '**~-agio** *n* bill discount; '**~-akzept** *n* acceptance of a bill; '**~-aussteller** *m* drawer of a bill; '**~bad** ⚕ *n* contrast bath; '**~balg** *m* changeling; '**~bank** *f* discount-house; '**~beziehung** *f* correlation; '**~brief** *m* bill of exchange; '**~bürgschaft** *f* guarantee for a bill of exchange; **~fälle** ['~fɛlə] *m/pl.* vicissitudes, ups and downs *of life etc.*; '**~fieber** *n* intermittent fever; '**~folge** *f* alternation, rotation; '**~frist** *f* days *pl.* of grace; '**~geld** *n* change; '**~gesang** *m* antiphony, glee; '**~gespräch** *n* dialog(ue); '**~getriebe** ⊕ *n* change-gear, variable gear; '**~gläubiger** *m*, '**~-inhaber** *m* holder of a bill of exchange, bill creditor; '♀**haft** changeable; '**~jahre** *physiol. n/pl.* climacteric (period) *sg.*, menopause *sg.*, change *sg.* of life; '**~kurs** *m* rate of exchange.

wechseln ['vɛksəln] *v/t. u. v/i.* (29) change; (*verschieden sein, ab*~) vary; (*austauschen, a. Briefe, Blicke, Schläge, Worte usw.*) exchange; *Szene*: shift; (*ab*~ [*lassen*]) alternate; *hunt.* pass; *die Kleider* ~ change (one's clothes); ~ *mit den Speisen usw.* vary.

'**Wechsel|nehmer** *m* (7) taker of a bill; '**~protest** *m* bill protest; '**~recht** *n* law of exchange; '**~schuld** *f* bill debt; '♀**seitig** mutual, reciprocal; '**~seitigkeit** *f* reciprocity; '**~strom** ⚡ *m* alternating current (*abbr.* AC, a-c); '**~stube** *f* exchange-office; '♀**voll** changeable; eventful; '**~wähler** *m/pl.* floating voters; '♀**weise** alternately, by turns; (*gegenseitig*) mutually; '**~winkel** *m/pl.* alternate angles; '**~wirkung** *f* reciprocal action *od.* effect, interaction.

Weck [vɛk] *m* (3), '**~e** *f* (15), '**~en**[1] *m* (6) roll; '♀**en**[2] (25) (a)wake, waken (*a. fig.*); F call; (*aufstören*) rouse (*a. fig.*); '**~er** *m* (7) (a)wakener; (*Uhr*) alarm-clock; '**~ruf** *m* reveille.

Wedel ['ve:dəl] *m* (7) (*Fächer*) fan; (*Staub*♀) duster; ⚘ frond; '♀**n** *v/t. u. v/i.* (29) fan; wag (*mit dem Schwanz* the tail).

weder ['ve:dər]: ~ ... *noch* neither ... nor.

Weg[1] [ve:k] *m* (3) way; (*Pfad*) path; (*Straße*) road; (*Reise*♀) route; (*Gang*) walk; (*Durchgang*) passage; (*Strecke*) distance (*a. phys.*); ⊕ travel; *fig.* (*Art und Weise*; *Methode*) way; *fig.* (~ *zum Ziel*) course; *e-e Meile* ~*es* a distance of a mile; *am* ~*e* by the wayside; *auf gütlichem* ~*e* amicably; *fig. auf dem richtigen* ~ *sein* be on the right track; *er steht mir im* ~*e* he is in my way; *s-r* ~*e* (*od. s-s* ~*es*) *gehen* go one's way(s); *aus dem* ~*e gehen* get out of the way, stand aside; *fig.* (*dat.*) (*vermeiden*) avoid, steer clear of; *j-m weit aus dem* ~*e gehen* give a p. a wide berth; *aus dem* ~*e räumen od. schaffen* remove (*a. fig. j-n*); *et. in die* ~*e leiten* set on foot, initiate, (*vorbereiten*) prepare; *ich traue ihm nicht über den* ~ I don't trust him round the corner; *s. ebnen, machen, halb.*

weg[2] [vɛk] away, off; (~*gegangen usw.*) gone; (*verloren*) gone, lost; ~ *da!* be off!; ~ *damit!* off with it!, take it away!; *Hände* ~*!* hands off!; F *ich muß* ~ I must be off; F *völlig od. ganz* ~ (*von Sinnen*) (clean) gone, (*erstaunt*) flabbergasted.

'**wegbekommen** get off; (*verstehen*) get the knack of; *e-e Krankheit*: catch.

Wegbereiter ['ve:k-] *m* pioneer.

weg|blasen ['vɛk-] blow away; *fig.* *wie weggeblasen* clean gone; '**~bleiben** (sn) stay away; (*ausgelassen werden*) be omitted; '**~blicken** look away; '**~bringen** take away; *Sache, Fleck*: *a.* remove.

Wege|lagerer ['ve:gəla:gərər] *m* (7) highwayman; '**~meister** *m* road-surveyor.

wegen ['ve:gən] (*gen. od. dat.*) because of, on account of, by reason of; (*um ... willen*) for the sake of, for; *von Amts ~* ex officio, officially; *von Rechts ~* by right; ⚖ *~ Diebstahls* for larceny; F *von ~!* that's what you think!

'**Wegerecht** *n* right of way.

Wegerich ⚘ ['ve:gəriç] *m* (3) plantain.

weg|fahren ['vɛk-] *v/t.* remove; *v/i.* leave; *im Wagen*: drive away; '**♀fall** *m* (*Auslassung*) omission; (*Aufhören*) cessation; (*Abschaffung*; *a. weitS. v. Gründen, Hindernissen*) removal; *in ~ kommen* = '**~fallen** (sn) fall away; (*ausgelassen werden*) be omitted *od.* dropped; (*nicht in Frage kommen*) be inapplicable; (*aufhören*) cease; (*abgeschafft werden*) be abolished; (*ausfallen*) not to take place; *~ lassen* drop, leave out; '**~fangen**, F '**~fischen** snatch away (*j-m et.* a th. from under a p.'s nose); '**~fegen** sweep away (*a. fig.*); '**~führen** lead (*od.* take) away; '**♀gang** *m* departure; '**~geben** give away; '**~gehen** (sn) go away *od.* off; *Ware*: sell; *~ über* (*acc.*) pass over (*a. fig.*); '**~haben** have got *one's share*; *fig.* (*gut verstehen*) have got the hang of; '**~helfen** (*dat.*) help *a p.* to get away; '**~holen** take away; '**~jagen** drive (*od.* chase) away; '**~kommen** (sn) get away *od.* off; (*abhanden kommen*) be lost; *fig. gut usw. ~* come off well *etc.*, get a good *etc.* deal; '**~lassen** let go; *Sache*: leave out, omit; '**♀lassung** *f* omission; '**~laufen** run away; '**~legen** lay (*od.* put) aside; '**~machen** take away, remove; *Fleck*: take out; *sich ~* make off; '**~müssen:** *ich muß weg* I must go; *der Hund usw. muß weg* (*abgeschafft werden*) must go; **♀nahme** ['~na:mə] *f* (15) taking (away) (*a.* ⚖); (*Beschlagnahme*) seizure; ⚔, ⚓ capture; '**~nehmen** take away (*j-m* from a p.); (*beschlagnahmen*) seize; *Raum, Zeit usw.*: take up, occupy; ⚔, ⚓ capture; '**~packen** pack away; *sich ~* pack off; '**~putzen** wipe away; F (*abschießen*) pick off; F (*essen*) polish off; '**~raffen** carry off; '**~räumen** clear away, remove; '**~reisen** (sn) depart, leave; *s. verreisen*; '**~reißen** tear (*od.* snatch) away (*j-m* from a p.); *durch Sturm usw.*: sweep (*od.* carry) away; '**~rücken** move away (*a. v/i.*); '**~schaffen** clear away, remove, do away with; ⚗ eliminate; *sich* '**~scheren** be off; '**~schicken** send away *od.* off, dispatch; (*sich*) '**~schleichen** steal away; '**~schleppen** drag off; '**~schließen** lock up (*od.* away); '**~schmeißen** F throw away; '**~schnappen** snatch away (*j-m et.* a th. from a p.).

Wegschnecke ['ve:k-] *f* slug.

weg|sehen ['vɛk-] look away; *~ über* (*acc.*) shut one's eyes to *a th.*; '**~sein** be away *od.* absent; (*weggegangen usw.*; *a. verloren sein*; F *verzückt sein*) be gone; *~ über* (*acc.*) have got over *a th.*; '**~setzen** *v/t.* put away; *sich ~ über* (*acc.*) *fig.* disregard; *v/i.* (sn) *~ über* (*acc.*) jump (over) *a th.*, clear *a th.*; '**~streben** *von* tend from.

Wegstrecke ['ve:k-] *f* stretch (of road); *zurückgelegte*: distance covered, mileage.

weg|streichen ['vɛk-] strike out, cancel; '**~treten** (sn) step aside; ⚔ break the ranks; '**~tun** put away *od.* aside, remove; (*tu die*) *Hände weg!* (take your) hands off!

Wegweiser ['ve:k-] *m* (7) signpost, guidepost; *im Gebäude*: directory; (*Person, Buch*) guide.

weg|wenden ['vɛk-] (*a. sich*) turn away *od.* off; *bsd. Gesicht*: avert; '**~werfen** throw away; *fig. sich ~* throw o.s. away (*an j-n* on a p.), degrade o.s.; '**~werfend** disparaging; '**♀werfflasche** *f* non-returnable bottle; '**♀werfgesellschaft** *f* throw-away society; '**♀werfpackung** *f* throw-away pack; '**~wischen** wipe off; '**~zaubern** spirit away.

Wegzehrung ['ve:k-] *f* provisions

pl. for the journey; *eccl. letzte*: viaticum.

wegziehen ['vɛk-] *v/t.* pull (*od.* draw) away; *v/i.* (sn) *aus der Wohnung*: (re)move; ⚔ march away.

weh [ve:] **1.** sore, aching; ~! woe!; ~ *mir!* woe is me!; ~*e dir usw.!* woe be to you *etc.*!, *allg.* just you wait!; ~ *tun* ache; *j-m*: pain (*od.* hurt) a p., cause a p. pain; *seelisch*: *a.* grieve a p.; *sich* ~ *tun* hurt o.s.; **2.** ♀ *n* (3, *o. pl.*) pain; *seelisch*: *a.* grief; *s. wohl* 2.

Wehe[1] ['ve:ə] *f* (15) (*Schnee*♀, *Sand*♀) drift; **~**[2]**:** ~*n pl.* labo(u)r (-pains); *fig.* travail; '♀**n** *v/i. u. v/t.* (25) blow; (*fort*~) drift, waft; (*flattern*) flutter, wave; *fig. Geist*: live.

'**Weh|geschrei** *n* woeful cries *pl.*, wail; '**~klage** *f* lament(ation); '♀**klagen** lament (*um* for; *über acc.* over); '♀**leidig** snivel(l)ing; '**~mut** *f inv.* melancholy, sadness; *über Vergangenes*: nostalgia; ♀**mütig** ['~my:tiç] sad, melancholy; nostalgic.

Wehr[1] [ve:r] *f* (16) (*Ab*♀) defen|ce, *Am.* -se, resistance; (*Waffe*) weapon; (*Panzer*) armo(u)r; (*Schutz*♀) bulwark; *sich zur* ~ *setzen* show (*od.* put up a) fight, *gegen*: struggle against, oppose; *s. a.* (*sich*) *wehren*; **~**[2] *n* (3) weir; '**~beauftragte** *m* ombudsman (for the Armed Forces); '**~bereich** *m* military district; '**~bereichskommando** *n* military district headquarters *od.* command; '**~dienst** ⚔ *m* military service; '**~dienstbeschädigung** *f* disability incurred in line of duty; '♀**diensttauglich** fit for military service; '♀**dienst-untauglich** unfit for military service; '**~dienstverweigerer** *m* conscientious objector; '♀**en** (25) (*dat.*) restrain, check; *dem Feuer* ~ arrest (*od.* check) the spread of fire; *sich* ~ defend o.s., offer resistance; '**~-ersatzdienst** *m* alternative service (for conscientious objectors); '♀**fähig** fit for military service, able-bodied; '♀**los** defen|celess, *Am.* -seless; (*waffenlos*) unarmed; (*hilflos*) helpless; ~ *machen* disarm; '**~losigkeit** *f* defen|celessness, *Am.* -selessness; '**~pflicht** *f*: (*allgemeine*) ~ (universal) compulsory military service, (universal) conscription; '♀**pflichtig** liable to military service; '**~sold** *m* (service) pay; '**~stammrolle** *f* service roster; '**~technik** *f* defen|ce (*Am.* -se) technology.

Weib †, P [vaɪp] *n* (1) woman; (*Gattin*) wife; '**~chen** *n* (6) little woman *od.* wife; *v. Tieren*: female.

Weiber... ['~bər] *mst* women's; '**~-art** *f* women's way(s *pl.*); '**~feind** *m* woman-hater, misogynist; '**~geschwätz** *n* female gossip; '**~held** *m* lady-killer, lady's man; '**~herrschaft** *f*, '**~regiment** *n* petticoat-government; '**~volk** F *n* women(folk *sg.*) *pl.*

weib|isch ['~bɪʃ] womanish, effeminate; **~lich** ['vaɪp-] *Geschlecht*: female, *gr.* feminine; *Wesensart*: womanly, feminine; *das ewig* ♀*e* the Eternal Woman; '♀**lichkeit** *f* womanliness; *die holde* ~ the fair sex.

'**Weibsbild** *n* female, *sl.* broad.

weich [vaɪç] soft (*a. fig.*); (*zart*) tender (*a. Fleisch*); (*schwach*) weak; *s. weichherzig*; ~ *werden* soften; *fig.* (*nachgeben*) yield; (*milder werden*) soften, relent; (*gerührt werden*) be moved (*bei* at); '♀**bild** *n* precincts *pl.*, municipal area; (*Außenbezirke*) outskirts *pl.*; '♀**e**[1] *f* (15) *anat.* flank, side; (*Leiste*) groin; '♀**e**[2] *f* 🚂 switch, *Brt. a.* points *pl.*; ~*n stellen* throw the switch, *fig.* set a new course; '**~en**[1] *v/i.* (30, sn) give way, yield; ⚔ retreat; *Preise*: decline, fall; *von j-m* ~ leave, abandon; *j-m nicht von der Seite* ~ not to budge from a p.'s side; '**~en**[2] (25) *s. aufweichen*.

'**Weichensteller** 🚂 *m* (7) pointsman. *bsd. Am.* switchman.

'**weichgekocht:** ~*e Eier* soft-boiled eggs.

'**Weichheit** *f s. weich*: softness; tenderness; weakness.

'**weichherzig** tender-hearted; '♀**keit** *f* tender-heartedness.

'**weich|lich** soft, tender; *Nahrung*, *Empfinden*: sloppy; *fig.* weak, effeminate; soft; '♀**lichkeit** *f* tenderness; sloppiness; effeminacy, softness; '♀**ling** *m* (3[1]) weakling, mollycoddle, F softie; '♀**macher** ⊕ *m* softener, softening agent.

Weichsel|kirsche ['vaɪksəl-] *f* mahaleb-cherry; '**~rohr** *n* cherrywood tube.

Weich|spüler ['~ʃpy:lər] *m* (7) softener; *für Haare*: conditioner; '~**teile** *anat. m/pl.* soft parts; '~**tier** *n* mollusc.

Weide[1] ⚘ ['vaɪdə] *f* (15) willow; (*Korb*≗) osier; '~[2] *f* pasture; *auf der* ~ at grass; *auf die* ~ *gehen* (*schicken*) go (send) to grass; '~**land** *n* pasture-land *od.* -ground.

weiden ['vaɪdən] *v/i. u. v/t.* (26) graze, pasture; *Vieh* ~ (*lassen*) put to pasture *od.* grass; *s-e Augen* (*a. sich*) ~ *an* (*dat.*) feast one's eyes on, *b.s.* gloat over *a th.*

'**Weiden|baum** *m* willow-tree; '~**kätzchen** ⚘ *n* willow-catkin; '~**korb** *m* wicker-basket.

'**Weideplatz** *m* pasture-ground.

weid|gerecht ['vaɪt-] sportsmanlike; '~**lich** *adv.* thoroughly, greatly.

'**Weid|mann** *m* (1[2]) huntsman, sportsman; ≗**männisch** ['~mɛnɪʃ] sportsmanlike; ~**manns'heil** *n*: ~*!* good sport!; '~**werk** *n the* chase, hunting.

weiger|n ['vaɪgərn] (29) (*sich*) refuse; '≗**ung** *f* refusal.

Weih [vaɪ] *m* (12) (*Vogel*) kite.

'**Weihbischof** *m* suffragan (bishop).

Weihe[1] ['vaɪə] *f* (15) consecration; (*Einweihung*) inauguration; *e-s Priesters*: ordination; '~[2] *f s. Weih*; '≗**n** (25) consecrate; *Priester*: ordain; (*widmen*) devote, dedicate (*dat.* to); *dem Tode usw. geweiht* doomed to death *etc.*

Weiher ['vaɪər] *m* (7) (fish-)pond.

'**weihevoll** solemn.

Weihnacht|en ['vaɪnaxtən] *n* (6) *od. f/pl.* (*inv., mst ohne art.*) Christmas, *verkürzt*: Xmas; *Fröhliche* ~*!* Merry Christmas!; ≗**lich** Christmas(sy).

'**Weihnachts|-abend** *m* Christmas Eve; '~**baum** *m* Christmas-tree; '~**bescherung** *f* (giving) Christmas presents *pl.*; '~(**feier**)**tag** *m* Christmas Day; '~**fest** *n* Christmas; '~**geld** *n s. Weihnachtsgratifikation*; '~**geschäft** *n* Christmas business; '~**geschenk** *n* Christmas present; '~**gratifikation** *f* Christmas bonus; '~**lied** *n* Christmas carol; '~**mann** *m* Father Christmas, Santa Claus; '~**markt** *m* Christmas fair; '~**zeit** *f* Christmas-tide, Yuletide.

'**Weih|rauch** *m* incense; '~**rauchfaß** *n* censer; '~**wasser** *n* holy water; '~**wasserbecken** *n* (holy-water) font.

weil [vaɪl] because, since.

weiland † ['~lant] formerly, erstwhile, *bsd. Am.* onetime.

Weil|chen ['vaɪlçən] *n* (6): *ein* ~ a little while; F a spell; *warte ein* ~ wait a bit; '~**e** *f* (15) *a* while, *a* (space of) time; (*Muße*) leisure; *damit hat es gute* ~ there is no hurry (about it); *s. eilen*; '≗**en** (25) stay; *zu lange*: tarry, linger.

Weiler ['vaɪlər] *m* (7) hamlet.

Wein [vaɪn] *m* (3) wine; (~*stock*) vine; *wilder* ~ Virginia creeper; *s. rein* 1; '~**bau** *m* wine-growing, 🕮 viticulture; '~**baugebiet** *n* wine-growing region; '~**bauer** *m* wine-grower; '~**beere** *f* grape; '~**berg** *m* vineyard; '~**bergschnecke** *f* edible snail; '~**blatt** *n* vine leaf; '~**brand** *m* brandy.

wein|en ['vaɪnən] (25) weep (*um*; *vor dat.* for); *laut*: cry; *dem* ≗ *nahe* on the verge of tears; '~**erlich** tearful; *Stimme, Ton*: whining, lachrymose.

'**Wein|-ernte** *f* vintage; '~**-essig** *m* wine-vinegar; '~**faß** *n* wine-cask; '~**flasche** *f* wine-bottle; '~**garten** *m* vineyard; '~**gärtner** *m* vine-dresser; wine-grower; '~**geist** *m* spirit(s *pl.*) of wine; '~**glas** *n* wine-glass; '~**händler** *m* wine-merchant; '~**handlung** *f* wine shop; '~**jahr** *n*: *ein gutes* (*schlechtes*) ~ a good (bad) wine year (*od.* year for wine); '~**karte** *f* wine-list; '~**keller** *m* wine-cellar; '~**kellerei** *f* winery; '~**kelter** *f* winepress; '~**kenner** *m* connoisseur of wine; '~**krampf** *m* crying fit; '~**krug** *m* wine jug; '~**laub** *n* vine leaves *pl.*; '~**laube** *f* vine arbo(u)r; '~**lese** *f* vintage; '~**leser**(**in** *f*) *m* vintager; '~**most** *m* must; '~**presse** *f* winepress; '~**probe** *f* wine-tasting; '~**rebe** *f* (grape-)vine; '≗**rot** ruby (-colo[u]red); '~**säure** *f* acidity of wine; ⚗ tartaric acid; '~**schenke** *f*, '~**stube** *f* wine tavern; '~**sorte** *f* sort of wine; '~**stein** *m* tartar; '~**stock** *m* vine; '~**traube** *f* bunch of grapes; (*Beere*) grape; '~**trester** *pl.* skins (*od.* husks) *pl.* of pressed grapes.

weise[1] ['vaɪzə] **1.** wise; **2.** ≗ *m* (18) wise man, sage; *die* ~*n aus dem Morgenland* the (three) Magi; *Stein der* ~*n* philosophers' stone.

Weise[2] [~] *f* (15) manner, way; ♪ melody, tune; *auf diese* ~ in this way; *auf jede* ~ in every way; *in keiner* ~ in no way; *in der* ~, *daß* in such a way that, so that; *in Zssgn mst durch adv. z.B. natürlicherweise* naturally; '**&n** (30) *v/t.* point out, show; ~ *an* (*acc.*) refer to; *j-n* ~ *nach* direct to; *von sich* ~ refuse, reject; *aus dem Lande* ~ banish, exile; *j-m die Tür* ~ show a p. the door; *das wird sich* ~ we shall see; *v/i.* ~ *auf* (*acc.*) point at *od.* to.

'**Weiser** *m* (7) pointer; indicator; *s.* Weg&.

Weis|heit ['vaɪshaɪt] *f* wisdom; *mit s-r* ~ *zu Ende sein* be at one's wit's end; '**~heitszahn** *m* wisdom-tooth; '**&lich** wisely, prudently; '**&machen:** *j-m et.* ~ make a p. believe a th., tell a p. a yarn; *laß dir nichts* ~*!* don't be fooled!; *mach das anderen weis!* tell that to the marines!

weiß [vaɪs] white; *gebrochen* ~ off-white; *das &e Haus* (*in Washington*) the White House; *der &e Sonntag* the Low Sunday; *das &e im Auge, im Ei* the white; *s. schwarz.*

'**weis|sagen** foretell, predict, prophesy; '**&sager(in** *f*) *m* prophet(ess *f*); '**&sagung** *f* prophecy, prediction.

'**Weiß|bier** *n* wheat beer; '**~blech** *n* tinplate; '**~brot** *n* white bread; '**~buch** *pol. n* white paper, *Am.* white book; '**~buche** ⚘ *f* white beech; '**~dorn** ⚘ *m* whitethorn; '**~e** (18) *m* white man; *f* white woman; '**&en** (27) whiten; (*tünchen*) whitewash; '**~fisch** *m* whiting, dace; *kleinerer*: whitebait; '**&gelb** pale yellow; '**~gerber** *m* tawer; '**&glühend** white-hot; '**~glut** *f* white heat; '**&haarig** white-haired; '**~käse** *m* curds *pl.*; '**~kohl** ⚘ *m* (white-heart) cabbage; '**&lich** whitish; '**~metall** *n* white metal; '**~näherei** *f* plain (needle-) work; '**~näherin** *f* plain seamstress; '**~tanne** ⚘ *f* white fir; '**~waren** *f/pl.* linen goods *pl.*; '**~waschen:** *j-n* ~ white-wash a p.; '**~wein** *m* white wine; hock; '**~zeug** *n* (household-)linen.

Weisung ['vaɪzuŋ] *f* direction, directive; instruction, order; '**~sbefugnis** *f* authority to issue directives; '**&sgebunden** subject to directions; '**&sgemäß** as instructed.

weit [vaɪt] *adj.* (*Ggs. nah*) distant, far; (*ausgedehnt*) extensive; (*breit*) broad; *bsd.* ⊕ wide; (*Ggs. eng*) wide, (*lose*) loose (*a.* ⊕); (*geräumig*) large; *adv.* far; wide(ly); *ein* ~*er Weg* a long way; ~ *entfernt* far away, *fig.* far from it; ~ *und breit* far and wide; ~*es Gewissen* elastic conscience; 5 *Meter* ~ (a distance of) five met|res (*Am.* -ers); *e-e Meile* ~ (*entfernt*) a mile off; *bei* ~*em vor comp. od. sup.* by far; *bei* ~*em nicht so gut* not nearly so good; *von* ~*em* from afar, from a distance; *im* ~*esten Sinne* in the broadest sense; *ich bin so* ~ I am ready; *es ist noch nicht so* ~ things have not come to that point yet; *es ist nicht* ~ *her mit* ... ... is (are) not worth much, *sl.* ... is (are) not so hot; *fig. zu* ~ *gehen* go too far; *s. bringen, fehlen, herholen, Weite, weiter*; '**~'-ab** far away (*von* from); '**~-aus** (by) far; '**&blick** *m* far-sightedness; '**~blikkend** far-sighted.

'**Weite 1.** *f* (15) wideness, width; largeness; (*Ferne*) distance; **2.** *das* ~ *suchen* decamp; '**&n** (26) (*a. sich*) widen, enlarge, expand, *fig. a.* broaden; *Schuhe*: stretch.

'**weiter** wider; (*entfernter*) more distant, farther, (*bsd. fig.*) further; ~*!* go on!; *nichts* ~ nothing more *od.* else; *und so* ~ and so forth *od.* on, et cetera (*abbr.* etc., &c.); *das &e* the rest; *&es* (*Genaueres*) further details, more; *bis auf* ~*es* until further notice; *ohne* ~*es* without further ado, (*mühelos*) easily, (*sofort*) readily, offhand; '**~befördern** forward, send on; '**~beschäftigen** continue to employ; '**&beschäftigung** *f* continued employment; '**&bestand** *m* continued existence, survial; '**~bestehen** continue to exist, survive; '**~bilden** develop; *sich* ~ continue one's studies, develop one's knowledge; '**~bringen** help on; *es* ~ (*im Leben*) get on; *das bringt mich nicht weiter* that's not much help; '**&e** *n s. weiter*; '**~-erzählen** tell others, repeat; '**~führen** carry on; '**~geben** pass on; '**~gehen** (sn) go on, walk on, pass on; (*fortfahren*) continue; *das kann so nicht* ~*!* things cannot go on like this!; '**~hin** in future, further on; (*ferner*) further(more); ~ *tun* continue to do, keep doing; '**~kommen** (sn) get on; *fig. a.* (make) progress, advance; '**~können** be able to go on; '**~leben 1.** live on, survive (*a. fig.*); **2.** ♀ *n* survial; '**~leiten** *Brief usw.*: forward, transmit; *Antrag usw.*: refer (*an acc.* to); '**~lesen** *v/i. u. v/t.* go on (reading), continue reading; '**~machen** carry on, continue; '**~sagen** tell others; '**♀ungen** *f/pl.* complications, (unpleasant) consequences; '**♀ver-arbeitung** *f* processing, finishing; '**~verbreiten** spread, retail.

'**weit|gehend** extensive, large, far-reaching; *Behauptung*: sweeping; *Vollmacht*: wide; *adv.* largely; '**~'her:** *von ~* from afar; '**~herzig** broad-minded; '**~'hin** far off; '**~läufig** (*ausgedehnt*) extensive, vast; (*geräumig*) spacious; (*ausführlich*) detailed; *s. weitschweifig*; *Dorf usw.*: straggling; *Verwandter*: distant; *adv.* at great length; *~ verwandt* distantly related; '**♀läufigkeit** *f* vast extent; *s. Weitschweifigkeit*; *pl. s. Weiterungen*; '**~maschig** wide-meshed; '**~reichend** far-reaching; '**~schweifig** diffuse, lengthy, long-winded; '**♀schweifigkeit** *f* diffuseness, lengthiness, prolixity; '**~sichtig** long-sighted, (*a. fig.*) far-sighted; '**♀sichtigkeit** *f* long-sightedness; '**♀sprung** *m* long (*Am.* broad) jump; '**~tragend** long-range; *fig.* far-reaching; '**~verbreitet** *Ansicht usw.*: wide-spread; '**~verzweigt** widely ramified; '**♀winkel-objektiv** *opt. n* wide-angle lens.

Weizen ['vaɪtsən] *m* (6) wheat; *fig. sein ~ blüht* he is in clover; '**~mehl** *n* wheat(en) flour.

welch [vɛlç] (21[1]) *interr. pron.* what; *auswählend*: which; *rel. pron.* who, which, that; *~er (auch) immer* who(so)ever; *~ ein Mann!* what a man!; *unbestimmtes Fürwort*: some, any, *z.B. haben Sie Geld? ja, ich habe ~es* yes, I have some; *brauchen Sie ~es?* do you want any?; **~erlei** ['~ərlaɪ] *Art usw.* of what kind *etc.*

welk [vɛlk] withered, faded (*a. fig. Reize, Schönheit*); (*schlaff*) flabby; '**~en** (25, sn) fade, wither.

Wellblech ['vɛlblɛç] *n* corrugated sheet iron; '**~baracke** *f* tin hut, *Am.* ⚔ Quonset hut.

Welle ['vɛlə] *f* (15) **1.** wave (*a. im Haar*, ⚡, ⚔ *Angriffs♀*, *fig. der Begeisterung usw.*); *stärkere*: billow; (*Sturz♀*) breaker; *Radio*: wave (-length); *mot. grüne ~* progressive signal system; **2.** ⊕ shaft, axle; '**♀n** (25) *Haar*: (*a. sich*) wave.

'**Wellen|band** *n Radio*: (wave-) band; '**~bereich** *m Radio*: wave-range; '**~bewegung** *f* undulation; '**~brecher** ⚓ *m* breakwater; **♀förmig** ['~fœrmiç] undulatory, wavy; '**~gang** *m* swell; '**~länge** *f Radio*: wave-length; '**~linie** *f* wavy line; '**~reiten** *n* surfing; '**~schlag** *m* wash (*od.* dashing) of the waves; '**~sittich** *m* budgerigar, Australian grass parakeet, love-bird; '**~tal** *n* wave trough; '**~theorie** *f* wave theory.

wellig ['vɛliç] wavy.

'**Wellpappe** *f* corrugated board.

Welpe ['vɛlpə] *m* (13) whelp, puppy.

welsch [vɛlʃ] Roman, Latin, southern (*Italian, French, etc.*).

Welt [vɛlt] *f* (16) world (*a. fig. der Kunst usw.*); *alle ~* all the world; *die ganze ~* the whole world; *auf der ~* in the world; *auf der ganzen ~ bekannt* known all over the world; *was in aller ~ ...?* what in the world (*od.* on earth) ...?; *um alles in der ~!* for goodness sake!; *in die ~ setzen* put into the world; *zur ~ bringen* give birth to; *zur ~ kommen* be born; *aus der ~ schaffen* get rid of, remove.

'**welt|'-abgeschieden** secluded (from the world); '**~'-abgewandt** detached from the world; '**♀-all** *n* universe; '**♀-alter** *n* age; '**~-anschaulich** ideological; '**♀-anschauung** *f* Weltanschauung, philosophy (of life), world-outlook; (*Ideologie*) ideology; '**♀-atlas** *m* world atlas; '**♀-ausstellung** *f* World Fair; '**♀-bank** *f* World Bank; '**~bekannt**, '**~berühmt** world-renowned, world-famed; universally known; '**♀best...** world-best; '**~bewegend:** *nicht ~ iro. sl.* not so hot; '**♀bild** *n* view of life; '**♀bürger** *m* citizen of the world, cosmopolite; '**♀enbummler** *m* globe-trotter; '**♀-ereignis** *n* event of world-wide importance; '**~-erfahren** experienced in the ways of the world, worldly wise; '**♀-erfahrung** *f* experience in the ways of the world.

Weltergewicht(**ler** *m*) *n* ['vɛltər-] *Boxen*: welter-weight.

'**welt|-erschütternd** world-shaking; ˈ~**firma** *f* world-renowned firm; ˈ~**fremd** ignorant of the world; unrealistic; (*idealistisch*) starry-eyed; *Gelehrter usw.*: ivory-towered; ˈ~**friede(n)** *m* universal peace; ˈ~**gefüge** *n* cosmic system; ˈ~**geltung** *f* international reputation; ˈ~**gericht** *n* last judg(e)ment; ˈ~**geschichte** *f* universal history; ˈ~**gewandt** versed in the ways of the world; ˈ~**gewandtheit** *f* savoir faire (*fr.*); ˈ~**geˈwerkschaftsbund** *m* World Federation of Trade Unions; ˈ~**handel** *m* international trade; ˈ~**herrschaft** *f* world supremacy; ˈ~**karte** *f* map of the world; ˈ~**kenntnis** *f* knowledge of the world; ˈ~**kind** *n* worldling, child of this world; ˈ~**klug** worldly-wise, politic(ally *adv.*); ˈ~**klugheit** *f* worldly wisdom; ˈ~**krieg** *m* world war; *der Erste (Zweite)* ~ World War I (World War II); ˈ~**kugel** *f* globe; ˈ~**lage** *f* international situation; ˈ~**lauf** *m* course of the world.

ˈ**weltlich** worldly; (*Ggs. geistlich*) secular, temporal; ~*e Schule* secular school; ~ *gesinnt* worldly-minded.

ˈ**Welt|literatur** *f* universal literature; ˈ~**macht** *f* world power; ˈ~**machtpolitik** *f* imperialist policy, imperialism; ˈ~**mann** *m* man of the world; ˈ~**männisch** gentlemanly, man-of-the-world; ˈ~**markt** *m* world market; ˈ~**meer** *n* ocean; ˈ~**meister(in** *f*) *m* world champion; ˈ~**meisterschaft** *f* world championship; ˈ~-**öffentlichkeit** *f* world public; ˈ~-**ordnung** *f* system of the world; ˈ~**politik** *f* international (*od.* world-)politics *pl.*; ˈ~**postver-ein** *m* (Universal) Postal Union.

ˈ**Weltraum** *m* (outer) space; (*für Zssgn s. Raum...*).

ˈ**Welt|reich** *n* world empire; ˈ~**reise** *f* journey round the world, world tour; ˈ~**reisende** *m, f* globe-trotter; ˈ~**rekord** *m* world('s) record; ~**rekordler** [ˈ~rekɔrtlər] *m*, ˈ~**rekordmann** *m* world-record holder; ˈ~**ruf** *m* world-wide renown; ˈ~**schmerz** *m* world-weariness, Weltschmerz; ˈ~ˈ**sicherheitsrat** *m* U.N. Security Council; ˈ~**sprache** *f* universal language; ˈ~**stadt** *f* metropolis; ˈ~**teil** *m* part of the world, continent; ˈ~-**umfassend** world-wide, global; ˈ~-**umsegler** *m* circumnavigator (of the globe); ˈ~-**umspannend** world-wide; ˈ~-**untergang** *m* end of the world; ˈ~**weise** *m* philosopher; ˈ~**weis-heit** *f* philosophy; ˈ~**weit** world-wide; ˈ~**wirtschaft** *f* world (*od.* international) economy; ˈ~**wirtschaftskrise** *f* world-wide economic crisis; ˈ~**wunder** *n* wonder of the world, prodigy.

wem [veːm] to whom; *von* ~ of whom; by whom.

wen [veːn] whom; F (*jemand*) somebody.

Wend|e[1] [ˈvɛndə] *m* (13), ˈ~**in** *f* (16[1]) Wend; ~[2] *f* (15) turn(ing); (*Wendepunkt*) turning-point (*a. fig.*).

ˈ**Wendekreis** *m geogr.* tropic; ~ *des Krebses* Tropic of Cancer; *mot.* turning circle.

ˈ**Wendel** ⊕ *f* helix; ˈ~**treppe** *f* (*eine* a flight of) winding stairs *pl.*, spiral staircase.

wend|en [ˈvɛndən] *v/t. u. v/i.* (30) (*a. sich*) turn (about *od.* round); *Buchseite usw.*: turn over; *Geld usw.* ~ *an* (*acc.*) spend on; *Mühe, Zeit usw.*: devote to; *bitte* ~! please turn over! (*abbr.* p.t.o.); *mit* ~*der Post* by return of post; *sich* ~ *an j-n* (*ansprechen*) address (o.s. to) a p., *um Auskunft, Erlaubnis usw.*: apply to a p. (*um* for), *um Rat*: consult (*od.* see) a p., *um Hilfe*: turn (*od.* appeal) to a p.; *sich* ~ *gegen* turn against *od.* on; ˈ~**epunkt** *m* turning-point (*a. fig.*); ˈ~**ig** (*behend*) nimble, agile (*a. Geist*); *fig.* flexible; *P.*: versatile; *Auto usw.*: manœuvrable, *Am. a.* maneuverable; ˈ~**ung** *f* turn (-ing); ⚔ facing, turn; *fig.* turn, change (*zum Besseren* for the better); (*Wort*~) *s. Redensart*.

wenig [ˈveːniç] little; *pl.* few; ~*er* less, ℞ *a.* minus; *pl.* fewer; *das* ~*ste* the least; *am* ~*sten* least; *mit* ~*en Worten* in a few words; (*noch*) *ein* ~ a little (more); *nicht* ~*er als* no less than, *pl.* no(t) fewer than; *nichts* ~*er als* anything but; ˈ~**keit** *f* small quantity; (*Kleinigkeit*) little, trifle; *meine* ~ my humble self; ˈ~**stens** at least; *wenn* ~ ... if only.

wenn [vɛn] *zeitlich*: when; *bedingend*: if; ~ *nicht* if not, unless; *s. außer*; (*vorausgesetzt*) provided (that); ~ *nur* if only; ~ *auch* (al-) though, even if *od.* though; ~ *auch* *noch so* ... however ...; ~ ... *nicht gewesen wäre* but for ...; *und* ~ *nun* ...?, *was macht es,* ~ ...? what if ...?; F *(na,)* ~ *schon!* so what?; ~ *man von* ... *spricht* speaking of ...; *wie wäre es,* ~ *wir jetzt heimgingen?* how about going home now?; *ohne* ♀ *und Aber* with no "ifs" or "buts"; ~'**gleich,** ~'**schon** although, though.

wer [veːr] (24) *rel. pron.* who, he who; *interr. pron.* who?; *auswählend*: which?; ~ *auch (immer)* who(so)ever; ⚔ ~ *da?* who goes there?; F *indef. pron. (jemand)* somebody, anybody.

Werbe... ['vɛrbə-] propaganda, *bsd.* ⚚ advertising, publicity; '~-**abteilung** *f* advertising *(od.* publicity) department; '~-**agentur** *f* advertising agency; '~-**aktion** *f s. Werbefeldzug*; '~-**assistent(in** *f) m* advertising assistant; '~**berater** *m* advertising consultant; '~**büro** *n* advertising agency; '~-**etat** *m* advertising budget; '~**fachmann** *m* advertising agent; '~**feldzug** *m* publicity campaign, (advertising) drive; '~**fernsehen** *n* television commercials *pl.*; '~**film** *m* advertising film; '~**funk** *m* radio commercials *pl.*; '~**graphik** *f* commercial art; '~**graphiker** *m* commercial artist; '~**kampagne** *f s. Werbefeldzug*; '~**kosten** *pl.* advertising costs; '~**leiter** *m* advertising *(od.* publicity) manager; '~**mittel** *n* advertising medium *(pl.* media).

werb|en ['vɛrbən] (30) *v/t.* ⚔ enlist, recruit; *Mitglieder usw.*: enlist; *Kunden, Stimmen*: canvass; *j-n für e-e Sache* ~ win a p. over to a cause; *v/i.* make propaganda *(für* for); ⚚ advertise *(a th.)*; ~ *um (acc.)* sue for, *liebend*: court, *rhet.* woo *(beide a. fig.)*; '♀**er** *m* (7) suitor; ⚚ canvasser; ⚔ recruiting officer; '♀**eschrift** *f* advertising pamphlet *(od.* brochure), leaflet; '♀**espruch** *m* (advertising) slogan; '♀**etext** *m* advertisement copy; '♀**etexter** *m* advertising copywriter; '♀**etrommel** *f*: *die* ~ *rühren fig.* make propaganda, advertise; '~**ewirksam** effective; '♀**ung** *f* recruiting; courting, courtship; ⚚ advertising, publicity, canvassing; *weitS.* propaganda; '♀**ungskosten** *pl. steuerlich*: professional expenses *pl.*

'**Werdegang** *m* (3) development; *e-r Person, Partei usw.*: career; ⊕ process of production.

werden ['veːrdən] **1.** (30) *v/i.* (sn) become, get; *allmählich*: grow; *plötzlich*: turn *pale, sour, etc.*; *(entstehen)* come into existence, arise; *(ausfallen)* turn out, prove; *Arzt* ~ become a doctor; *böse* ~ grow angry; *Mohammedaner usw.* ~ turn Mohammedan *etc.*; *es wird kalt usw.* it is getting cold *etc.*; *was soll aus ihm (od. daraus)* ~? what will become of him *(od.* of it)?; *was will er* ~? what is he going to be?; *was soll nun* ~? what are we going to do now?; *es ist nichts daraus geworden* it has come to nothing; *es wird schon* ~ it will be all right; ~*de Mutter* expectant mother; **2.** *v/aux. ich werde fahren* I shall drive; *geliebt* ~ be loved; *sie wird gleich weinen* she is going to cry; **3.** ♀ *n* (6) growing, development; *(Fortschreiten)* progress; *noch im* ~ *sein* be in process of development, be in the making; *große Dinge sind im* ~ great things are preparing.

werf|en ['vɛrfən] (30) *v/t.* throw *(a. v/i.; nach* at); *(schleudern)* fling; *a. Anker, Blick, Licht, Schatten*: cast; *Brief in den Kasten, Bomben, Anker*: drop; *Junge*: bring forth, produce; *Falten* ~ raise folds; *sich* ~ *Holz*: warp; *sich auf e-e Tätigkeit* ~ throw o.s. into; *um sich* ~ *mit Geld usw.* be lavish with; *aufs Papier* ~ jot down; *(sich) hin und her* ~ toss (about); *s. Brust, Hals usw.*; '♀**er** *m Kricket*: bowler; *Baseball*: pitcher; ⚔ *(Granat*♀) mortar; *(Raketen*♀) launcher.

Werft [vɛrft] *f* (16) shipyard, dockyard; '~-**arbeiter** *m* docker.

Werg [vɛrk] *n* (3) tow; *(gezupftes Tauwerk)* oakum.

Werk [~] *n* (3) work *(a. künstlerisch usw.)*; *(Tat)* act, deed; *(Erzeugnis)* work, production; *(Getriebe)* mechanism, works *pl.*; ⚔ work(s *pl.*); *(Fabrik)* works *mst sg.*, factory, plant; *(Unternehmung)* undertaking, enterprise; *ein gutes* ~ *tun* do an act of kindness *(an dat.* to); *ans* ~! let us begin!; *am* ~ *sein* be at work; *im* ~*e sein* be on foot, be in the wind; *ins* ~ *setzen* set on foot, bring about; *ans* ~ *gehen* set to work; *b.s. es war sein* ~ it was his doing; '~**bank** *f* (work-) bench; '~**meister** *m* foreman; '~**schutz** *m* factory security officers *pl.*; '~**spionage** *f* industrial espionage; '~**statt** *f*, '~**stätte** *f* workshop, shop; (*Auto*≈) garage; '~**stoff** *m* material; (*Kunstharz-Preßstoff*) plastic (material); '~**stück** *n* workpiece, work; '~**student** *m* working student; '~**swohnung** *f* company flat (*Am.* apartment); '~**tag** *m* (*Wochentag*) workday, weekday; (*tägliche Arbeitszeit*) working-day; '≈**tags** on weekdays; '≈**tätig** working; *die* ≈*en* the working population; '~**tisch** *m* work--table; '~**vertrag** *m* work contract; '~-**unterricht** *m* handicrafts *pl.*; '~**zeichnung** *f* workshop drawing; '~**zeug** *n* tool (*a. fig.*); *feines*: instrument; (*Gerät*) implement; *physiol.* organ; '~**zeugkasten** *m* tool box (*od.* kit); '~**zeugmacher** *m* toolmaker; '~**zeugmaschine** *f* machine tool; '~**zeugtasche** *f* tool-bag.

Wermut ['ve:rmu:t] *m* (3) ⚘ wormwood; (*Wein*) verm(o)uth; '~**bruder** F *m* wino; '~**s-tropfen** *fig. m* shadow, sorrow.

wert [ve:rt] **1.** worth (e-e *S.* a th.); (*würdig*) worthy (*gen.* of); (*lieb*) dear; (~*geschätzt*) esteemed; *nicht viel* ~ not up to much; *nichts* ~ worth nothing, worthless; *s. Mühe, Rede*; *Ihr* ~*es Schreiben* your letter; **2.** ≈ *m* (3²) value (*a. phys.*, ⚘ *usw.*); worth; (*Gegenwert*) equivalent; (*Vermögens*≈) asset; *phys.*, ⊕ factor, coefficient; ~*e pl. phys.*, ⊕ data; (*Nutzen*) value; *künstlerischer* ~ merit; value; *im* ~*e von ...* of the value of; *von gleichem* ~ tantamount (*wie* to); ✉ (*als*) *Muster ohne* ~ by pattern-post; (*großen*) ~ *legen auf* (*acc.*) set great store by; *im* ~ *sinken* depreciate.

'**Wert**|-**angabe** *f* declaration of value; '~-**arbeit** *f* high-class workmanship; '≈**beständig** of fixed value; *Währung*: stable; '~**beständigkeit** *f* fixed value; stability; '~**brief** *m* insured letter; '≈**en** (26) (*bewerten*) value; (*schätzen*) appraise; (*beurteilen*) judge; *bsd. Sport, Schule*: rate (*nach Leistungen* on performance), (*gelten lassen*) allow; (*auswerten*) evaluate; '~**gegenstand** *m* article of value; *pl.* valuables; '≈**geschätzt** esteemed; '≈**ig** ⚗: 2-~ bivalent, divalent; 3-~ trivalent; '~**igkeit** ⚗ *f* valence; '≈**los** worthless (*a. P.*); valueless; (*nutzlos*) useless; '~**maßstab** *m*, '~**messer** *m* standard (of value); '~**minderung** *f* depreciation; '~**paket** *n* insured parcel; '~**papiere** *n/pl.* securities; '~**sachen** *f/pl.* valuables *pl.*; '≈**schätzen** esteem highly; '~**schätzung** *f* esteem; '~**steigerung** *f* increase in value; '~**ung** *f s. werten*: valuation; appraisal; judging; rating; evaluation; '~**urteil** *n* value judgement; '~**verlust** *m* loss of value; '~**verringerung** *f* depreciation; '≈**voll** valuable; '~**zeichen** ✉ *n* (postage) stamp; '~**zuwachs**(**steuer** *f*) *m* increment-value (tax).

Wesen ['ve:zən] *n* (6) (*Lebe*≈) being, creature; (*inneres Sein, Kern*) essence; (*Natur*) nature, character; (*Betragen*) manners *pl.*, way, air; (*größeres Ganze*) organization; *in Zssgn*: system, *z.B. Sparkassen*≈ savings bank system; (*Getue*) fuss, ado; '~**heit** *f* (*Wesenskern*) essence; (*Wirklichkeit*) substantiality; '≈**los** unsubstantial; unreal; '~**s-art** *f* nature, character; '≈**sfremd** foreign to one's nature; '≈**sgleich** identical in character; '~**szug** *m* characteristic (feature *od.* trait); '≈**tlich** essential, (*a. beträchtlich*) substantial; (*wichtig*) material (*für* to); (*grundlegend*) fundamental; *adv.* ~ *verschieden* very (*od.* vastly) different; *das* ≈*e* the essential; *im* ~*en* essentially, in the main.

weshalb [ves'halp] **1.** *interr. pron.* why; **2.** *cj.* and so, and that's why.

Wespe ['vespə] *f* (15) wasp; '~**n-nest** *n* wasps' nest; *fig. in ein* ~ *stechen* stir up a hornet's nest; '~**n-stich** *m* wasp's sting; '~**ntaille** *f* wasp-waist.

wessen ['vesən] whose.

West [vest] **1.** west; **2.** *poet. m* (3², *o. pl.*) west(wind); '~**en** (6) *m* west; (*Land*) West, (*Abendland a.*) Occident.

Weste ['vestə] *f* (15) waistcoat, ✝ *u. Am.* vest; e-e *reine* ~ *haben fig.* have a clean slate; '~**ntasche** *f* vest-pocket; F *wie s-e* ~ *kennen* know *a p. or th.* inside out; *im* '~**ntaschenformat** *n* pocket-size *car, etc.*

West|fale [vɛst'fɑːlə] *m* (13), **⁓fälisch** [⁓'fɛːliʃ] Westphalian.
'**Westhang** *m* west(ern) slope.
'**westlich** west(ern); westerly; ⁓ *von* (to the) west of.
'**West|mächte** *f/pl.* Western powers; '**⁓mark** *f* (*Geld*) Western mark; **⁓wärts** ['⁓vɛrts] westward; '**⁓wind** *m* west(erly) wind.
weswegen ['vɛs'veːgən] *s. weshalb.*
wett [vɛt] even, equal, F quits; '**⁓bewerb** *m* competition; *Sport*: *a.* (*Einzel⁓*) event; *in ⁓ treten mit* enter into competition with; '**⁓bewerber(in** *f*) *m* competitor; '**⁓bewerbsfähig** competitive; '**⁓büro** *n* betting office.
Wette ['vɛtə] *f* (15) bet, wager; e-e ⁓ *eingehen* make a bet; *was gilt die ⁓?* what do (*od.* will) you bet?; *et. um die ⁓ tun* vie with each other in doing a th.; *um die ⁓ laufen* race each other.
'**Wett-eifer** *m* rivalry; '**⁓n** vie (*mit j-m* with; *in e-r Eigenschaft* in); compete (with; *in e-r Tätigkeit* in; *um et.* for); *mit j-m ⁓ a.* emulate (*od.* rival) a p.
wetten ['vɛtən] *v/i. u. v/t.* (26) bet, wager (*mit j-m* a p.; *um* et. a th.); *Rennsport*: ⁓ *auf* (*acc.*) back; '**⁓de** *m, f* (18) *s. Wetter*².
Wetter¹ ['vɛtər] *n* (7) weather; (*Un⁓*) storm; (*Gewitter*) thunderstorm; ⚒ *böses ⁓* damp; *schlagende ⁓ pl.* firedamp *sg.*; *alle ⁓!* dear me!; '**⁓**² *m* (7) ('**⁓in** *f* [16¹]) better, backer; '**⁓-aussichten** *f/pl.* weather outlook; '**⁓bedingungen** *f/pl.* weather conditions; '**⁓be-obachtung** *f* meteorological observation; '**⁓bericht** *m* weather report; '**⁓beständig** weather-proof; '**⁓dienst** *m* weather service; '**⁓fahne** *f* (weather-)vane; '**⁓fest** weather-proof; '**⁓frosch** F *m* weatherman; '**⁓fühlig** sensitive to changes in the weather; '**⁓hahn** *m* weathercock; '**⁓hart** weather-beaten; '**⁓häus-chen** *n* weather house; '**⁓karte** *f* weather chart (*od.* map); '**⁓kunde** *f* meteorology; '**⁓lage** *f* weather conditions *pl.*; '**⁓leuchten** *n* (6) sheet lightning; '**⁓mantel** *m* trench-coat; '**⁓meldung** *f* weather report; '**⁓n** (29) be stormy; *fig.* storm, thunder; '**⁓prophet** *m* weather-prophet; '**⁓satellit** *m* weather satellite; '**⁓schacht** ⚒ *m* air-shaft; '**⁓schaden** *m* damage caused by the weather; '**⁓seite** *f* weather-side; '**⁓station** *f* weather station; '**⁓sturz** *m* sudden fall of temperature; '**⁓verhältnisse** *n/pl.* weather conditions; '**⁓voraussage** *f* weather-forecast; '**⁓warte** *f* weather-station; '**⁓wechsel** *m* change in the weather; '**⁓wendisch** changeable, fickle; '**⁓wolke** *f* thunder-cloud.
'**Wett|fahrt** *f* race; '**⁓fliegen** *n*, '**⁓flug** *m* air-race; '**⁓gesang** *m* singing-match; '**⁓kampf** *m* contest, match, competition; '**⁓kämpfer(in** *f*) *m* competitor; '**⁓lauf** *m* (foot)race; *fig.* ⁓ *mit der Zeit* race against time; '**⁓läufer(in** *f*) *m* runner; '**⁓machen** make up for, make good; '**⁓rennen** *n* race; '**⁓rudern** *n* boat-race; '**⁓rüsten** *n* arms race; '**⁓schwimmen** *n* swimming match; '**⁓segeln** *n* regatta; '**⁓spiel** *n* match, *Am.* game; '**⁓streit** *m* contest, match; '**⁓zettel** *m* betting-slip.
wetzen ['vɛtsən] (27) whet, sharpen.
'**Wetz|stahl** *m* whet steel; '**⁓stein** *m* whetstone, hone.
Whisky ['wiski] *m* whisk(e)y.
wich [viç] *pret. v. weichen* 1.
Wichs [viks] *m* (4) gala; *in vollem ⁓* in full dress, F in full fig; '**⁓bürste** *f* blacking (*od.* polishing) brush.
Wichse ['viksə] *f* (15) blacking, polish; F (*Prügel*) thrashing; '**⁓n** (27) black, polish, shine; F (*prügeln*) thrash, lick.
Wicht [viçt] *m* (3) wight, creature; *armer ⁓* poor wretch; *kleiner ⁓* whipper-snapper, (*Kind*) urchin, brat.
wichtig ['viçtiç] important (*für* to); ⁓ *tun* give o.s. airs; '**⁓keit** *f* importance; *von ⁓* of importance; **⁓tuer** ['⁓tuːər] *m* (7) pompous fellow; **⁓tuerei** [⁓'raɪ] *f* pomposity.
Wicke ♀ ['vikə] *f* (15) vetch.
Wickel ['vikəl] *m* (7) roll(er); ⚕ (*Umschlag*) pack; *heißer ⁓* fomentation; (*Haar⁓* hair-)curler; '**⁓gamasche** *f* puttee; '**⁓kind** *n* child in swaddling-clothes, baby (in arms); '**⁓kommode** *f* baby's changing unit; '**⁓n** (29) wind, roll, coil (*alle a. sich*); *Haar*: curl; (*ein⁓*) wrap up; *Säugling*: swathe, swaddle; *j-n um den (kleinen) Finger ⁓ fig.* twist s.o. round one's (little) finger; '**⁓rock** *m* wrap-around skirt.

Wick(e)lung ['vik(ə)luŋ] *f* bandaging; ⚡ coil.
Widder ['vidər] *m* (7) ram; *ast.* Ram, Aries.
wider ['vi:dər] (*acc.*) against, contrary to; versus; *s. für, Wille*; '**~borstig** stubborn, cross-grained; **~'fahren** (sn) *j-m*: befall a p., happen to a p.; *s. Gerechtigkeit*; '**~haarig** refractory; '**2haken** *m* barbed hook; *an Pfeil, Angel usw.*: barb; *mit ~ (versehen)* barbed; '**2hall** *m* echo, reverberation, resonance (*alle a. fig.*); *fig. keinen ~ finden* meet with no response; '**~hallen** (re-)echo, resound (*von* with); '**2lager** *n* ⚠ abutment; (*Gegenpfeiler*) counterfort; ⊕ support; **~legbar** [~'le:k-] refutable; **~'legen** refute, disprove; **2'legung** *f* refutation.
widerlich ['vi:dərliç] repulsive, repugnant; (*ekelhaft*) disgusting, loathsome, sickening; '**2keit** *f* repulsiveness.
'**wider|natürlich** unnatural; perverse; '**2part** *m* opponent; *~ halten* (*dat.*) oppose; **~'raten** *j-m et.*: dissuade a p. from; '**~rechtlich** illegal, unlawful; ⚖ *~ betreten* trespass (up)on; '**2rede** *f* contradiction; '**2ruf** *m* revocation; *e-r Erklärung*: recantation, retractation; (*Rückgängigmachen*) cancel(l)ation; (*Abbestellung*) countermand; *gültig bis auf ~* until recalled, unless countermanded; **~'rufen** revoke; *Aussage*: retract; *Gesetz*: repeal; *Auftrag, Befehl, Vertrag*: cancel, countermand; **~'ruflich** revocable; **2sacher** ['~zaxər] *m* (7), '**2sacherin** *f* (16[1]) adversary; (*der Teufel*) *the* Foe; '**2schein** *m* reflection; *sich* **~'setzen** (*dat.*) oppose, resist, struggle against; *e-m Befehl*: disobey; **~'setzlich** refractory; *bsd. im Dienst*: insubordinate; **2'setzlichkeit** *f* refractoriness; insubordination; '**2sinn** *m* nonsense, absurdity; '**~sinnig** absurd, paradoxical, preposterous; **~spenstig** ['~ʃpɛnstiç] refractory, rebellious; obstinate; '**2spenstigkeit** *f* refractoriness, obstinacy; '**~spiegeln** reflect; *sich ~* be reflected (*in dat.* by); **~'sprechen** (*dat.*) contradict (*sich* o.s.); *e-m Vorschlag*: oppose; *sich od. einander ~ Meinungen usw.*: be contradictory; **~'sprechend** contradictory; '**2spruch** *m* contradiction (*in sich selbst* in terms); *gegen e-n Vorschlag*: opposition to; *im ~ zu* in contradiction to; '**~sprüchlich** contradictory, inconsistent; '**2spruchsgeist** *m* spirit of contradiction; '**~spruchslos** uncontradicted; *adv.* without contradiction; (*demütig*) meekly; '**~spruchsvoll** *s. widersprüchlich*; '**2stand** *m* resistance, opposition (*gegen* to); ⚡ resistance, (*Gerät*) resistor; *~ leisten* offer resistance; *den ~ aufgeben* give in; '**2standsbewegung** *f* resistance movement; '**~standsfähig** resistant, robust; '**2standsfähigkeit** *f* (capability of) resistance; '**2standskämpfer** *pol. m* member of the Resistance; '**2standskraft** *f* power of resistance; ⊕ strength; '**~standslos** unresisting; **~'stehen** (*dat.*) resist, withstand; (*zuwider sein*) be repugnant to; **~'streben** **1.** (*dat.*) oppose, resist; (*zuwider sein*) be repugnant to; **2.** **2** *n* resistance; (*Unwilligkeit*) reluctance; *mit ~* = **~'strebend** *adv.* reluctantly; '**2streit** *m* opposition; *fig.* conflict, clash; **~'streiten** (*dat.*) conflict (*od.* clash) with, be contrary to; **~wärtig** ['~vɛrtiç] unpleasant, disagreeable; (*scheußlich*) repulsive; (*ekelhaft*) disgusting, loathsome; (*verhaßt*) hateful, odious; '**2wärtigkeit** *f* unpleasantness, disagreeableness; repulsiveness; (*widriger Zufall*) adversity; '**2wille** *m* aversion (*gegen* to), dislike (for); (*Ekel*) disgust (for); (*Unwilligkeit*) reluctance; '**~willig** unwilling, reluctant.
widm|en ['vitmən] (26) (*zueignen*) dedicate, (*weihen, a. Zeit, Aufmerksamkeit*) devote (*dat.* to); *sich e-r S. ~* devote o.s. (*od.* apply o.s.) to a th.; '**2ung** *f* dedication; '**2ungsexemplar** *n* presentation copy.
widrig ['vi:driç] adverse, untoward; **~enfalls** ['~gən-] failing which, in default of which; '**2keit** *f* contrariety; (*widriger Zufall*) adversity.
wie [vi:] *in Frage u. Ausruf*: how; *im Vergleich*: as; (*gleich e-m ...*) like; *zeitlich*: as; *~ auch (immer)* however; *~ bitte?* (I beg your) pardon!; *s. heißen*; *~ ist (od. war) es mit ...?* what about ...?; *~ wäre es mit ...?* how about ...?; *~ dem auch sei*

be that as it may; ~ *du mir, so ich dir* tit for tat; F *und ~!* and how!

Wiedehopf ['vi:dəhɔpf] *m* (3) hoopoe.

wieder ['vi:dər] again, anew; (*zurück*) back; (*als Vergeltung*) in return; *in Zssgn allg.* re..., re-...; *s. hin, immer*; '**2-abdruck** *m* reprint; '**2-anfang** *m s. Wiederbeginn*; **~'-anknüpfen** *fig.* renew; **~'-anstellen** reappoint, reinstall; **2'-anstellung** *f* reappointment; **2'-aufbau** *m* reconstruction (*a. wirtschaftlicher usw.*); rebuilding; **~'-aufbauen** rebuild, reconstruct; **~'-aufbereiten** reprocess; **2'-aufbereitungs-anlage** *f* reprocessing plant; **~'-aufblühen** (sn) *s. wiederaufleben*; **~'-auf-erstehen** (sn) rise from the dead; **2'-auf-erstehung** *f* resurrection; '**2-aufführung** *thea. f* revival; **~'-aufkommen 1.** (sn) *Mode usw.*: revive, come into fashion again; *Kranker*: recover; **2.** 2 *n e-s Kranken*: recovery; **~'-aufleben 1.** (sn) revive; **2.** 2 *n* revival; **2'-aufnahme** *f* resumption; ⚖ reopening; **2'aufnahmeverfahren** ⚖ *n* new hearing; *Strafrecht*: retrial; **~'-aufnehmen** resume; **2'-aufrüstung** *f* rearmament; **2'-auftreten** *n* reappearance; '**2beginn** *m* recommencement; *Schule usw.*: reopening; '**~bekommen** get back, recover; '**~beleben** resuscitate; *fig.* revive, reanimate; '**2belebung** *f* resuscitation; *fig.* revival; '**2belebungsversuch** *m* attempt at resuscitation; '**~bewaffnen** rearm; '**~bringen** bring back; (*zurückgeben*) restore (*dat.* to); **~'einbringen** make good, recover; *sich* **~'-einfinden** turn up again; **~'einführen** reintroduce; *Gebrauch usw.*: re-establish; ✝ re-import; **2'einführung** *f* reintroduction; re-establishment; **2'-eingliederung** *f* reintegration; **~'-einlösen** redeem; **2'-einlösung** *f* redemption; **2'-einnahme** *f* recapture; **~'-einnehmen** recapture; *e-n Platz*: resume; **2'einschiffung** *f* re-embarkation; **~'-einsetzen** replace; *in ein Amt usw.*: reinstate (*in acc.* in), restore (to); **2'-einsetzung** *f* reinstatement, restoration; **~'-einstellen** *Arbeiter usw.*: re-engage; ⚔ re-enlist; *sich ~* turn up again; **2'-einstellung** *f* re-engagement; re-enlistment; **2'-eintritt** *m*: ~ *in die Erdatmosphäre* re-entry; '**~-ergreifen** *Flüchtling*, '**2-ergreifung** *f* recapture; '**~-erkennen** recognize; *nicht wiederzuerkennen* totally changed, (*verstümmelt usw.*) past recognition; '**2-erkennung** *f* recognition; '**~-erlangen** recover; '**2-erlangung** *f* recovery; '**2-er-öffnung** *f* reopening; '**~-erstatten** restore, return; *Kosten*: refund, reimburse; '**2-erstattung** *f* restitution; *der Kosten*: refund, reimbursement; '**~-erstehen** rise again; be rebuilt; *fig.* (*a. ~ lassen*) revive; '**~-erzählen** retell; '**~finden** find again; '**2gabe** *f* restitution, return; *im Bilde usw.*: reproduction; *e-s Textes od. Musikstücks*: rendering; '**2gabequalität** *f* reproduction quality; '**~geben** give back, return; *Ehre, Gesundheit*: restore; (*übersetzen usw.*) render; (*nachbilden*; *a. Ton usw.*) reproduce; *Musikstück, Rolle*: interpret; (*zitieren*) quote; '**2geburt** *f* rebirth; '**~genesen** (sn) recover; '**2genesung** *f* recovery; '**~gewinnen** regain; ⊕ reclaim; **~'gutmachen** make good, repair; **2'gutmachung** *f* reparation; **~'herstellen** restore; **2'herstellung** *f* restoration; rehabilitation; *e-s Kranken*: recovery; **~'holen** repeat; (*öfter sagen od. tun*) reiterate; '*wiederholen* fetch back; (*zurücknehmen*) take back; **~'holt** repeated(ly *adv.*); **2'holung** *f* repetition; reiteration; *TV*: repeat, rerun, *e-r Szene*: replay; **2'holungsfall** *m*: *im ~e* in case of recurrence; **2'holungsspiel** *n Sport*: replay; **~-in'standsetzen** repair; **2-in'standsetzung** *f* repair; **~käuen** ['~kɔYən] (25) ruminate; *fig.* rehash; '**2käuer** *m* (7) ruminant; '**2kauf** *m* repurchase; **2kehr** ['~ke:r] *f* (16, *no pl.*) return; *periodische*: recurrence; '**~kehren** (sn) return; recur; '**~kehrend** recurrent; '**~kommen** (sn) come again; (*zurückkommen*) come back, return; **2kunft** ['~kunft] *f* (14[1]) return; '**~sagen** repeat; '**~sehen 1.** (*a. sich*) see (*od.* meet) again; **2.** 2 *n* (6) meeting again, reunion; *auf ~!* good-by(e)!, (hope to) see you again!, F so long!; '**2taufe** *f* rebaptism; '**2täufer** *m* anabaptist; '**~tun** do again, repeat; '**~um** again, anew; **~'-umkehren** (sn) turn back, retrace one's steps; '**~ver-einigen** (*a. sich*) reunite; '2-

ver·einigung *f* reunion; *a. pol.* reunification; '**~vergelten** *b.s.* pay back, requite; '**2vergeltung** *f* requital, retaliation; '**~verheiraten** (*a. sich*) remarry; '**2verheiratung** *f* remarriage; '**2verkäufer** *m* reseller; (*Einzelhändler*) retailer, retail dealer; '**2verkaufspreis** *m* trade price; '**2verwendung** *f* re-use; '**2verwertung** *f* recycling; '**2wahl** *f* re-election; '**~wählbar** re-eligible; '**~wählen** re-elect; **~'zulassen** readmit; **2'zulassung** *f* readmission; **~'zustellen, 2'zustellung** *f* return.

Wiege ['vi:gə] *f* (15) cradle; '**~messer** *n* mincing-knife.

wiegen[1] ['vi:gən] *v/t. u. v/i.* (30) weigh.

'**wiegen**[2] *v/t.* (25) **1.** (*schaukeln*) rock; *sich ~* sway; *fig.* (*sich*) *in Sicherheit ~* lull (o.s.) into security; **2.** (*zerkleinern*) mince.

'**Wiegen|fest** *n* birthday; '**~lied** *n* lullaby.

wiehern ['vi:ərn] **1.** (29) neigh; *vor Lachen*: guffaw; *~des Gelächter* horse-laugh; **2.** 2 *n* (6) neighing.

Wiener ['vi:nər] *m* (7), '**~in** *f* (16[1]), '**2isch** Viennese.

wies [vi:s] *pret. v. weisen.*

Wiese ['vi:zə] *f* (15) meadow.

Wiesel *zo.* ['vi:zəl] *n* (7) weasel.

'**Wiesenland** *n* meadow-land.

wie'so? why?

wie'viel how much; *pl.* how many; **~mal** how many times?

wievielte [~'fi:ltə] *m, f, n* which; *den 2n haben wir?* what day of the month is it?

wie'wohl though, although.

wild [vilt] **1.** *allg.* wild; (*unzivilisiert*) savage; (*grausam*) ferocious; (*grimmig*) fierce; (*wütend*) furious; *Kind*: unruly; *Stier*; *fig. Hast*: mad; *~e Ehe* concubinage; *~er Streik* unofficial (*bsd. Am.* wildcat) strike; *s. Wein*; *~ machen* infuriate, *Tier*: frighten; *fig. ~ sein auf* (*acc.*) be mad for *od.* about; *~ wachsen* grow wild; *~ werden* turn wild, *fig.* see red; **2.** 2 *n* (1, *o. pl.*) game; (*Reh*) deer; *s. Wildbret.*

'**Wild|bach** *m* torrent; '**~bad** *n* thermal baths *pl.*, hot springs *pl.*; '**~bahn** *f* hunting-ground; '**~braten** *m* roast venison; **~bret** ['~brɛt] *n* (11) game; *v. Hochwild*: venison; '**~dieb** *m* poacher; **~diebe'rei** *f* poaching; '**~-ente** *f* wild duck.

Wilde ['vildə] *m, f* (18) savage; F *wie ein ~r* like mad.

Wilder|er ['~rər] *m* (7) poacher; '**2n** (29) poach.

'**Wild|fang** *m* madcap; *Mädchen*: *a.* romp, tomboy; '**2'fremd** quite strange; *~er Mensch* complete stranger; '**~heit** *f s. wild* 1: wildness; savageness; fierceness; '**~hüter** *m* gamekeeper; '**~leder** *n*, '**2ledern** buckskin; *bsd. Handschuh*: doeskin, chamois (leather), suède; '**~lederschuhe** *m/pl.* suède shoes *pl.*; '**~ling** *m* (3[1]) ⚘ wild stock *od.* tree, wild(l)ing; *s. Wildfang*; '**~nis** *f* (14[2]) wilderness; '**~park** *m* (game-)preserve, deer-park; '**~sau** *f* wild sow; '**~schaden** *m* damage caused by game; '**~schütz(e)** *m* poacher; '**~schwein** *n* wild boar; '**~stand** *m* stock of game; '**2wachsend** (growing) wild; '**~wasser** *n* torrent; '**~wechsel** *m* game pass; **~'west..., ~'westfilm** *m* Western.

Wille ['vilə] (13[1]), '**~n** *m* (6) will; (*Absicht*) intention; *aus freiem ~n* of one's own free will; *guter ~* good intention; *Letzter ~* (last) will; *s. um*; *wider ~n* unwillingly; *2ns sein* be willing, be ready; *j-m s-n ~n lassen* let a p. have his own way; *j-m zu ~n sein* comply with a p.'s wishes; *ich kann es beim besten ~n nicht tun* I cannot do it, much as I should like to; *es geht beim besten ~n nicht* it just can't be done.

'**willen|los** lacking will-power; (*unentschlossen*) irresolute; (*weich*) spineless; '**2losigkeit** *f* lack of will-power.

'**Willens|-akt** *m* act of volition; '**~-erklärung** ⚖ *f* declaratory act; '**~freiheit** *f* free will; '**~kraft** *f* will-power; '**2schwach** weak-willed; '**~schwäche** *f* weak will; '**2stark** strong-willed; '**~stärke** *f* will-power, strong will.

willfahren [~'fa:rən] (25) (*dat.*) comply with, grant; *j-m ~* humour a p.

willfährig ['~fɛ:riç] compliant, complaisant; *j-s ~es Werkzeug sein* be at a p.'s beck and call; '**2keit** *f* compliance, complaisance.

'**willig** willing, ready; '**2keit** *f* willingness, readiness.

ˈ**Will|komm** *m* (3[1]), ~ˈ**kommen**[1] *n*, *m* (6), 2ˈ**kommen**[2] *adj.* welcome; *s. heißen*; ~**kür** [ˈ~ky:r] *f* (16) arbitrariness; *a.* = ˈ~**kür-akt** *m* arbitrary act; ˈ2**kürlich** arbitrary, high-handed; ˈ~**kürlichkeit** *f s. Willkür.*

wimmeln [ˈviməln] (29) (*a. fig.*) swarm *od.* teem (*von* with).

wimmern [ˈvimərn] (29) whimper.

Wimpel [ˈvimpəl] *m* (7) pennant.

Wimper [ˈvimpər] *f* (15) eyelash; *ohne mit der* ~ *zu zucken* without turning a hair, without wincing; ˈ~**n-tusche** *f* mascara.

Wind [vint] *m* (3) wind; (*Blähung*) flatulence, wind; *guter* ~ fair wind; *sanfter* ~ gentle breeze; *fig.* ~ *bekommen von* get wind of; *fig.* ~ *machen* boast, brag (*mit* of); *bei* ~ *und Wetter* in storm and rain; *fig. in den* ~ *reden* waste one's breath; *in den* ~ *schlagen* ignore, disregard; *fig. j-m den* ~ *aus den Segeln nehmen* take the wind out of a p.'s sails; *den Mantel nach dem* ~ *hängen* trim one's sails to the wind; *in alle* ~*e zerstreuen* scatter to the four winds; *gegen den Wind* into the wind; *wie der* ~ rapidly; ˈ~**beutel** *m* cream puff; F *fig.* windbag.

Winde [ˈvində] *f* (15) ⊕ windlass, winch, hoist; (*Anker*2) capstan; (*Garn*2) reel; ⚘ bindweed.

ˈ**Wind-ei** *n* wind-egg.

Windel [ˈvindəl] *f* (15) diaper, napkin; *pl.* ~*n mst* swaddling-clothes *pl.* (*a. fig.*); ˈ2**n** (29) (*wickeln*) swaddle, swathe; ˈ2ˈ**weich:** ~ *schlagen* beat to a jelly.

winden [ˈvindən] (30) wind; (*hoch*2) hoist; *Garn usw.*: reel; *Kranz*: make, bind; *j-m et. aus den Händen* ~ wrest a th. out of a p.'s hands; *sich* ~ wind; *vor Schmerz*: writhe; *Fluß*: meander.

ˈ**Windes-eile** *f*: *mit* ~ at lightning speed.

ˈ**Wind|fahne** *f* (weather) vane; ˈ2**geschützt** protected against the wind; ˈ~**harfe** *f* Aeolian harp; ˈ~**hose** *f* whirlwind; ˈ~**hund** *m* greyhound; *fig.* fly-by-night.

windig [ˈ~diç] windy; *fig. Person*: giddy; *Sache*: precarious; *Ausrede*: thin, lame.

ˈ**Wind|jacke** *f* windcheater; ˈ~**kanal** *m* wind tunnel; ˈ~**messer** *m* anemometer; ˈ~**mühle** *f* windmill; *fig. gegen* ~*n kämpfen* fight windmills; ˈ~**pocken** *f/pl.* chicken-pox; ˈ~**richtung** *f* direction of the wind; ~**röschen** ⚘ [ˈ~rø:sçən] *n* anemone; ˈ~**rose** ⚓ *f* compass card; ˈ2**schief** (a)skew; *fig.* awry, *sl.* cockeyed; ˈ2**schlüpfig,** ˈ2**schnittig** streamlined; ˈ~**schutzscheibe** ✈, *mot. f* windscreen, *Am.* windshield; ˈ~**spiel** *n* whippet; ˈ~**stärke** *f* wind force *od.* velocity; ˈ2**still** calm; ˈ~**stille** *f* calm; ˈ~**stoß** *m* blast of wind, gust; ˈ~**surfen** *n* wind-surfing.

Windung [ˈvinduŋ] *f* winding, turn, convolution; *e-s Weges, Stromes*: bend; *e-r Taurolle, Schlange*: coil; *e-r Spirale, Muschel*: whorl.

Wink [viŋk] *m* (3) sign; *mit der Hand*: wave; *mit den Augen*: wink; *durch Nicken*: nod; *fig.* hint, tip, F pointer; *j-m e-n* ~ *geben* give (*od.* drop) a p. a hint; *s. Zaunpfahl.*

Winkel [ˈviŋkəl] *m* (7) ⩓ angle; *weitS.* (*Ecke*) corner, nook; ⚔ (*Abzeichen am Ärmel*) chevron; ⊕ square; ˈ~**-advokat** *m* pettifogger, hedge-lawyer; *Am.* F shyster; ˈ~**-eisen** *n* angle iron; 2**förmig** [ˈ~fœrmiç] angular; ˈ~**haken** *typ. m* composing-stick.

ˈ**wink(e)lig** angular; *in Zssgn, bsd.* ⩓ ...-angled; *Straße*: crooked.

ˈ**Winkel|maß** ⊕ *n* square; ˈ~**messer** *m* ⩓ protractor; *surv.* goniometer; ˈ~**zug** *m* dodge, subterfuge, trick; (*Ausflucht*) evasion; *Winkelzüge machen* dodge, shuffle, prevaricate.

wink|en [ˈviŋkən] (25) make a sign, signal (*dat.* to); *mit der Hand*: wave, (*her*~) beckon; *mit den Augen*: wink; ⚔ signal, flag, *mit Winkflagge*: semaphore; *fig. Belohnung usw.*: be in store (*dat.* for); *mit der Hand od. dem Taschentuch* ~ wave one's hand *od.* handkerchief; ˈ2**er** *m* (7) *mot.* direction indicator; ⚔ flagman, signalman; ˈ2**spruch** ⚔ *m* semaphore message.

winseln [ˈvinzəln] (29) whimper, whine.

Winter [ˈvintər] *m* (7) winter; ˈ2**fest** wintertight; ⚘ hardy; ~ *machen* winterize; ˈ~**frucht** *f*, ˈ~**getreide** *n*, ˈ~**korn** *n* winter grain; ˈ~**garten** *m* winter garden; ˈ~**halbjahr** *n* winter half-year; ˈ2**lich** wintry; ˈ~**mantel** *m* winter overcoat; '~**-olympiade** *f*, '~**-spiele** *n/pl.* Olympic Winter Games; '~**reifen** *m* winter tyre (*Am.* tire); '~**saat** *f* winter corn; '~**schlaf** *m* hibernation; ~ *halten* hibernate; '~-'**schlußverkauf** *m* winter clearance sale; '~**sport** *m* winter sport(s *pl.*); '~**sport-ort** *m* winter resort; '~**(s)-zeit** *f* winter time; '~**vorrat** *m* winter stock.

Winzer ['vintsər] *m* (7) vine-dresser; (*Traubenleser*) vintager; (*Weinzüchter*) wine-grower.

winzig ['vintsiç] tiny, minute.

Wipfel ['vipfəl] *m* (7) (tree-)top.

Wippe ['vipə] *f* (15) seesaw; '**2n** (25) seesaw, rock; ~ *mit* wag *a th.*

wir [vi:r] we; ~ *alle* all of us; ~ *drei* we three, the three of us.

Wirbel ['virbəl] *m* (7) (*Drehung*) whirl (*a. fig.*); (*Knochen*2) vertebra; (*Haar*2) crown (of the head); (*Trommel*2) roll; (*Violin*2) peg; (*Wind*2) whirlwind; (*Wasser*2) eddy, *größerer*: whirlpool, vortex; *v. Rauch usw.*: wreath, eddy; *v. Schnee, Staub, Hieben*: flurry; ⊕ (*Drehring*) swivel; F *e-n* ~ *machen* (*Aufhebens*) make a big fuss; '**2ig** whirling; *fig.* giddy; '~**knochen** *m* vertebra; '**2los** invertebrate; '**2n** (20) *v/t.* whirl; eddy; *Trommel*: roll; *Lerche usw.*: warble (*a. v/t.*); *mir wirbelt der Kopf* my head swims; '~**säule** *f* vertebral column, spine; '~**sturm** *m* cyclone, tornado; '~**tier** *n* vertebrate; '~**wind** *m* whirlwind (*a. fig.*).

wirk|en ['virkən] **1.** (25) *v/t.* work, cause; *Strümpfe usw.*: knit, weave; *Teig*: knead; *v/i.* (be at) work; operate; take (effect) (*a.* ⚕); (*treffen*) tell (*alle*: *auf acc.* [up]on); ~ *als* act as, function as (*a.* ⊕); *beruhigend usw.* ~ have a soothing *etc.* effect; *auf die Sinne* ~ affect the senses; *dahin* ~, *daß* ... see that ...; *er wirkt viel jünger* he looks (*od.* seems to be) much younger; **2.** 2 *n* work; effect; functioning; activity; '**2er** ⊕ *m* knitter; '~**lich** real, actual; (*echt*) true; (*wesentlich*) substantial; ~? really?, indeed?; ~*e Leistung* ⊕ effective output, actual power; '**2lichkeit** *f* reality; '~**lichkeitsfremd** unrealistic; '~**lichkeitsnah** realistic; '~**sam** effective, efficacious; efficient; operative; *Hieb usw.*: telling; ~ *werden* take effect (*a. Gesetz*); '**2samkeit** *f* efficacy, effectiveness; '**2stoff** ⚗ *m* active substance.

'**Wirkung** *f* effect; (*Tätigkeit*) operation, action; (*Erfolg*) result; (*Eindruck*) impression; (*starke* ~) impact; *mit* ~ *vom* ... as from ...; *mit sofortiger* ~ effective immediately; ~ *haben* take (*od.* be of) effect; *s-e* ~ *verfehlen* fail to work, prove ineffectual; '~**sbereich** *m* sphere (⚔ radius) of action; *Gesetz*: operation; '~**sgrad** ⊕ *m* efficiency; '~**skraft** *f* efficacy; '~**skreis** *m* sphere (*od.* field) of activity, province, domain; '**2slos** inefficacious, ineffectual; '~**slosigkeit** *f* inefficacy; '**2svoll** *s. wirksam*; '~**sweise** *f* (mode of) operation, working; functioning.

'**Wirkwaren** *f/pl.* knit(ted) goods.

wirr [vir] confused; *Haar*: dishevel(l)ed.

'**Wirren** *f/pl.* disorders, troubles.

'**Wirr|kopf** *m fig.* muddle-headed fellow, scatter-brain; '~**nis** *f* (14²), '~**sal** *n* (3) chaos, confusion; ~**warr** ['~var] *m* (3¹) confusion, chaos, jumble, muddle, mess.

Wirsing(kohl) ['virziŋ(-)] *m* savoy.

Wirt [virt] *m* (3) host (*a. biol.*); (*Haus*2, *Gast*2) landlord; (*Gast*2) innkeeper; *s. Rechnung*; '~**in** *f* hostess; (*Haus*2, *Gast*2) landlady; '**2lich** hospitable.

'**Wirtschaft** *f* (*Haushaltung*) housekeeping; ✝ *e-s Gemeinwesens*: economy; (*gewerbliche* ~) business, trade and industry; *freie* ~ free enterprise; (*Hauswesen*) household; (*Bauernhof*) farm; (*Treiben*) goings--on *pl.*; (*Durcheinander*) mess; *s. Wirtshaus*; '**2en** (26) keep house; *gut* ~ economize, manage well, *schlecht* ~ mismanage; (*geräuschvoll hantieren*) bustle (*od.* potter) about; '~**er** *m* (7) manager; (*Gutsverwalter*) steward; '~**erin** *f* (16¹) manageress; *im Haushalt*: housekeeper; '~**ler** *m* economist; '**2lich** economic(ally *adv.*); ✝ *a.* business..., commercial; financial; (*haushälterisch*) economical; (*rationell*) efficient; (*ertragreich*) profitable; '~**lichkeit** *f* economy; efficiency; '~**s-abkommen** *n* trade agreement; '~**sberater** *m* business consultant; '~**sbeziehungen** *f/pl.* trade relations; '~**sgebäude** *n/pl.* farm-buildings, outhouses; '**\~sgeld** *n* housekeeping money; '**\~sgemeinschaft** *f*: *Europäische \~* European Economic Community; '**\~sgeographie** *f* economic geography; '**\~sgipfel** *m* economic summit; '**\~sgymnasium** *n* commercial high school; '**\~shilfe** *f* economic aid; '**\~sjahr** *n* financial year; '**\~skriminalität** *f* white-collar crime; '**\~skrise** *f* economic crisis; '**\~sminister** *m* Minister of Economics; '**\~sministerium** *n* Ministry of Economics; '**\~spolitik** *f* economic policy; '**2s-politisch** economic(ally *adv.*), pertaining to economic policy; '**\~s-prüfer** *m* chartered accountant, *Am.* certified public accountant; '**\~sverband** *m* trade association; '**\~swachstum** *n* economic growth; '**\~swissenschaft** *f* economics; '**\~swissenschaftler** *m* economist; '**\~swunder** *n* economic miracle; '**\~szweig** *m* sector of the economy, branch of trade.

'**Wirts|haus** *n* public house, F pub, *Am.* saloon; *mst ländlich*: inn; '**\~leute** *pl.* host and hostess.

Wisch [viʃ] *m* (3²) wisp *of straw etc.*; *contp.* (*Papier2*) scrap of paper; '**2en** (27) wipe; '**\~er** *m* (7) wiper (*a. mot.*); *zum Zeichnen*: stump; '**\~erblatt** *mot. n* wiper blade; '**\~lappen** *m für Geschirr*: dish-cloth; *für den Fußboden*: floor-cloth; (*Staubtuch*) duster.

Wisent ['vi:zɛnt] *m* (3) bison, aurochs.

wispern ['vispərn] *v/i. u. v/t.* (29) whisper.

Wiß|begierde ['vis-] *f* thirst for knowledge; (*Neugier*) curiosity; '**2begierig** eager for knowledge *od.* to learn; *weitS.* curious, inquisitive.

wissen ['visən] **1.** (30) know (et. a th.; *um, von* about of); *\~ von a.* be aware of; *\~ zu inf.* know how to *inf.*; *j-n etwas \~ lassen* let a p. know a th.; *ich möchte (gern) \~, ob ..., wie ... usw.* I should like to know (*od.* I wonder) whether *od.* if, how ... *etc.*; *man kann nie \~* you never know *od.* can tell; *nicht daß ich wüßte!* not that I know of!; *weißt du noch?* do you remember?; F *ich will von ihr nichts mehr \~* I am through with her; *s. aus 2., Bescheid, bestimmt usw.*; **2.** 2 *n* (6) knowledge; (*Bildung*) learning; *ohne mein \~* without my knowledge; *meines \~s* to my knowledge, as far as I know; *wider besseres \~* despite one's better knowledge; *nach bestem \~ und Gewissen* to the best of a p.'s knowledge and belief.

'**Wissenschaft** *f* science; (*Wissen*) knowledge; '**\~ler** *m* (7) scholar; (*bsd. Natur2*) scientist, scientific man; '**2lich** scientific(ally *adv.*); *\~ gebildet* academically trained.

'**Wissens|drang**, '**\~durst**, '**\~trieb** *m* urge (*od.* thirst) for knowledge; '**\~gebiet** *n*, '**\~zweig** *m* field of knowledge; '**2wert** worth knowing, interesting; '**\~schatz** *m* store of knowledge.

'**wissentlich** knowing, conscious; (*absichtlich*) wil(l)ful.

wittern ['vitərn] (29) scent, smell; *Gefahr \~* smell a rat.

'**Witterung** *f* weather; (*Geruch*) scent; *bei günstiger \~* weather permitting; '**2sbeständig** weather-resisting; '**\~s-einflüsse** *m/pl.* influence *sg.* of the weather; '**\~s-umschlag** *m* sudden change of the weather; '**\~s-verhältnisse** *n/pl.* atmospheric (*od.* meteorological) conditions.

Witwe ['vitvə] *f* (15) widow; (*\~ von Stande*) dowager, *z.B. Königin2* Queen dowager; '**\~ngeld** *n* widow's allowance; '**\~nkleidung** *f* widow's weeds *pl.*; '**\~nrente** *f* widow's pension; '**\~nstand** *m* widowhood.

'**Witwer** *m* (7) widower.

Witz [vits] *m* (3²) (*Geist*) wit; (*Scherz, Spaß*) joke; (*witzige Bemerkung*) quip, gag; *alter \~* stale joke, F chestnut; *\~e reißen* crack jokes; F *das ist der \~ an der Sache* that's where the fun comes in, *weitS.* that's the point (of it); '**\~blatt** *n* comic paper; **\~bold** ['\~bɔlt] *m* (3) wag, witty fellow, *Am.* F wisecracker; **\~elei** [\~ə'laɪ] *f* (16) witticism(s *pl.*); '**2eln** (29) quip, F wisecrack; '**\~figur** *f* ridiculous figure; '**2ig** witty; (*spaßig*) funny; '**\~igkeit** *f* wittiness.

wo [vo:] where; *\~ nicht* if not, unless; *\~ auch, \~ nur* wherever; F (*irgend\~*) somewhere; *zeitlich*: when; **\~'-anders** elsewhere, somewhere else.

wob [vo:p] *pret. v. weben.*

wobei [\~'baɪ] *interr. adv.* at what?; *rel. adv.* at which; in doing so, in the course of which; (*wodurch*) whereby, through which.

Woche [ˈvɔxə] *f* (15) week; *in e-r* ~ in a week; *heute über* (*od. vor*) *drei* ~*n* this day three weeks; *dreimal die* (*od. in der*) ~ three times a week; *in den* ~*n sein* be lying in; *in die* ~*n kommen* be confined, *mit e-m Kind*: be delivered of.

ˈ**Wochen**|**-arbeitszeit** *f* working week; ˈ~**bett** *n* childbed, confinement; ˈ~**blatt** *n* weekly (paper); ~**end...** [ˈ~ʔɛnt-], ˈ~**-ende** *n* week-end; ˈ♀**lang** for weeks; *nach* ~*em Warten* after many weeks of waiting; ˈ~**lohn** *m* weekly pay *sg. od.* wages *pl.*; ˈ~**markt** *m* weekly market; ˈ~**schau** *f Film*: news-reel; ˈ~**tag** *m* week-day; *bestimmter*: day of the week; ˈ♀**tags** on week-days.

wöchentlich [ˈvœçəntliç] weekly; *adv.* every week, weekly; *einmal* ~ once a week.

ˈ**wochenweise** by the week.

Wöchnerin [ˈvœçnərin] *f* (16[1]) woman in childbed; ˈ~**nen-abteilung** *f* maternity ward; ˈ~**nenheim** *n* maternity home.

wo|ˈ**durch** *interr. adv.* by what?, whereby?, how?; *rel. adv.* by which, whereby; ~ˈ**fern** provided that, if; ~ *nicht* unless; ~ˈ**für** *interr. adv.* for what?, what (...) for?; *rel. adv.* for which.

wog [vo:k] *pret. v. wägen u. wiegen*[1].

Woge [ˈvo:gə] *f* (15) wave (*a. fig.*); *fig. die* ~*n glätten* pour oil on troubled waters.

woˈ**gegen** *interr. adv.* against what?; *rel. adv.* against which; *tauschend*: in exchange for what? *od.* which; *conj.* whereas.

wogen [ˈvo:gən] (25) surge (*a. fig.*), billow; *Getreide*: *a.* wave; *schwellend*: heave; *hin u. her*: fluctuate, *Kampf*: seesaw.

wo|ˈ**her** from where; ~ *kommt er?* where does he come from?; ~ *wissen Sie das?* how do you know?; ~ˈ**hin** *interr. u. rel. adv.* where (... to); *indef. adv.* somewhere; ~**hin**ˈ**gegen** whereas.

wohl [vo:l] **1. a**) well, *Am.* F good; *er ist* ~ he is well; *ihm ist* ~ he is feeling fine; ~ *oder übel* willy-nilly; *leben Sie* ~*!* good-by(e)!, farewell!; *ich habe mich nie so* ~ *gefühlt* I never felt better; *es sich* ~ *sein lassen* enjoy o.s.; ~ *dem, der ...* happy he who ...; *s. bekommen*, ~*tun*; **b**) *vermutend, einräumend*: I presume (*od.* suppose, think); *er wird* ~ *reich sein* he is rich, I suppose; **c**) *fragend*: *ob sie* ~ *...?* I wonder whether (*od.* if) she ...; **2.** ♀ *n* (3) welfare; (*Gedeihen*) well-being, prosperity; (*Nutzen, Vorteil*) benefit, good; *das gemeine* ~ the common weal; *sein* ~ *und Weh* his weal and woe; *auf Ihr* ~*!* your health!, here's to you!

wohl|ˈ**-an** well then!; ˈ~**-angebracht** (very) apt; ˈ~**-anständig** decent; ~ˈ**-auf** well, in good health; *int.* well!, cheer up!; ˈ~**bedacht** well-considered; ˈ♀**befinden** *n* well-being; good health; ˈ~**begründet** well-founded; ˈ♀**behagen** *n* comfort, pleasure; ˈ~**behalten** safe (and sound); ˈ~**bekannt** well-known; ˈ~**beleibt** corpulent; ˈ♀**-ergehen** *n* (6) well-being, welfare, prosperity; ˈ~**-erwogen** well-considered; ~**erworben** [ˈ~ʔɛrvɔrbən] duly acquired; ~*e Rechte n/pl.* vested (*od.* well established) rights; ~**erzogen** [ˈ~ʔɛrtso:gən] well-bred; ˈ♀**fahrt** *f* (16, *o. pl.*) welfare; (*öffentliche*) ~ *a.* (public) relief, public assistance; ˈ♀**fahrtsamt** *n* welfare cen|tre, *Am.* -er; ˈ♀**fahrts-einrichtung** *f* welfare institution; ˈ♀**fahrtspflege** *f* welfare work; ˈ♀**fahrtsstaat** *m* welfare state; ˈ♀**fahrts-unterstützung** *f* public relief; ˈ~**feil** cheap; ˈ♀**gefallen** *n* pleasure, satisfaction; *sein* ~ *haben an* (*dat.*) take pleasure in; *sich in* ~ *auflösen co.* end in smoke, (*verschwinden*) vanish (into thin air); ˈ~**gefällig** pleasant, agreeable; (*selbstzufrieden*) complacent; ˈ♀**gefühl** *n* pleasant sensation; *allgemeines*: sense of well-being; ˈ~**gemeint** well-meant; ˈ~**gemerkt!** mark you!, mind you!, remember!; ˈ~**gemut** cheerful; ˈ~**genährt** well-fed; ˈ~**geraten** *Kind*: good; ˈ♀**geruch** *m* fragrance, perfume; ˈ♀**geschmack** *m* pleasant taste *od.* flavo(u)r; ˈ~**gesinnt** well-meaning; *j-m* ~ well-disposed towards a p.; ˈ~**gesittet** well-mannered; ˈ~**gestaltet** well-shaped, shapely; ˈ~**habend** well-to-do, wealthy, prosperous, well-off (*pred.* well off); ˈ♀**habenheit** *f s. Wohlstand.*

ˈ**wohlig** comfortable.

ˈ**Wohl**|**klang** *m*, ˈ~**laut** *m* melodious

sound, harmony, euphony; '**⁓klingend** harmonious, melodious; '**⁓leben** *n* life of pleasure, good living, luxury; '**⁓meinend** well-meaning; '**⁓riechend** fragrant, sweet-scented; '**⁓schmeckend** savo(u)ry, tasty; '**⁓sein** *n s. Wohlbefinden*; '**⁓stand** *m* prosperity, affluence, wealth; '**⁓standsgesellschaft** *f* affluent society; '**⁓tat** *f* good deed, kindness; (*a.* ⚖) benefit; *fig.* boon, comfort; *s. wahr*; '**⁓täter** *m* benefactor; '**⁓täterin** *f* (16[1]) benefactress; '**⁓tätig** beneficent; (*mildtätig*) charitable; '**⁓tätigkeit** *f* charity; '**⁓tätigkeitsbasar** *m* charity bazaar; '**⁓tätigkeitsver-anstaltung** *f* charity performance; '**⁓tätigkeitsver-ein** *m* charitable society; **⁓tuend** ['⁓tu:ənt] pleasant, beneficial; '**⁓tun:** (*j-m*) ⁓ do (a p.) good; *das tut e-m wohl* it does one good; '**⁓-überlegt** well-considered; '**⁓-unterrichtet** well-informed; '**⁓verdient** well-deserved; '**⁓verstanden** well-understood; ⁓*!* mind you!; '**⁓weislich** very wisely, prudently; '**⁓wollen**[1] *n* (6) goodwill, benevolence; '**⁓wollen**[2] *j-m*: wish a p. well; '**⁓wollend** kind, benevolent; (*günstig*) favo(u)rable.

'**Wohn|-anhänger** *m s. Wohnwagen*; '**⁓-anlage** *f* housing estate (*Am.* development); '**⁓bezirk** *m* residential area; '**⁓block** *m* block of flats; '**⁓-einheit** *f* dwelling unit.

wohnen ['vo:nən] (25) live (*bei j-m* with), *feiner*: dwell, reside (*alle a. fig.*); *amtlich*: reside (*in dat.* at); *vorübergehend*: stay (*bei* with); *als Mieter*: lodge, *Am. a.* room (*in dat.* at, *bei* with).

'**Wohn|gebäude** *n* dwelling-house; (*Etagenhaus*) block of flats, *Am.* apartment house; '**⁓gebiet** *n*, '**⁓gegend** *f* residential area; '**⁓geld** *n* housing subsidy; '**⁓gelegenheit** *f* living accommodation; '**⁓gemeinschaft** *f* flat-sharing community; '**⁓haft** living, resident (*in dat.* at); '**⁓haus** *n s. Wohngebäude*; '**⁓heim** *n* hostel; '**⁓küche** *f* kitchen-living-room; '**⁓lich** comfortable; (*traulich*) cosy; **⁓mobil** ['⁓mobi:l] *n* (3[1]) mobile home, camper; '**⁓-ort** *m* (place of) residence, ⚖ *a.* domicile; '**⁓raum** *m* housing space; '**⁓recht** *n* right of residence; '**⁓schlafzimmer** *n* bed-sitting-room; '**⁓sitz** *m s. Wohnort*; '**⁓stube** *f s. Wohnzimmer*.

'**Wohnung** *f* dwelling, home; *engS.* lodgings, rooms, apartments *pl.*; *im Stockwerk*: flat, *Am.* apartment; '**⁓s-amt** *n* Housing Office; '**⁓sbau** *m* housing construction; '**⁓sbauprojekt** *n* housing scheme; '**⁓s-inhaber** *m* occupant, tenant; '**⁓smangel** *m*, '**⁓snot** *f* housing shortage; '**⁓ssuche** *f* house-hunting; '**⁓s-tür** *f* front-door; '**⁓swechsel** *m* change of residence.

'**Wohn|viertel** *n* residential quarter (*Am.* section); '**⁓wagen** *m* caravan, *Am.* trailer; '**⁓zimmer** *n* sitting-room, *bsd. Am.* living room.

wölb|en ['vœlbən] (25) vault; (*a. sich*) arch; '**⁓ung** *f* vault; (*gewölbte Form*) curvature; ⊕ camber.

Wolf [vɔlf] *m* (3[3]) wolf; *Spinnerei*: willow; *metall.* devil; (*Fleischhackmaschine*) mincer; ⚕ chafe, gall; *fig. man muß mit den Wölfen heulen* when (you are) in Rome do as the Romans do; *s. Schafpelz*.

Wölfin ['vœlfin] *f* (16[1]) she-wolf.

Wolfram ⚗ ['vɔlfram] *n* (6, *o. pl.*) tungsten.

'**Wolfs|hund** *m* wolf-hound, wolf dog; '**⁓hunger** *m* ravenous hunger; '**⁓milch** ⚘ *f* spurge.

Wolke ['vɔlkə] *f* (15) cloud (*a. fig.*); *fig. aus allen* ⁓*n fallen* be thunderstruck.

'**Wolken|bruch** *m* cloud-burst; '**⁓decke** *f* cloud cover; '**⁓himmel** *m* clouded sky; '**⁓kratzer** *m* skyscraper; **⁓'kuckucks-heim** *n* Cloud-Cuckoo-Land; '**⁓los** cloudless; '**⁓schicht** *f* cloud layer; **⁓verhangen** ['⁓fɛrhaŋən] overcast.

'**wolkig** cloudy; *Himmel*: clouded.

Woll|decke ['vɔl-] *f* (wool) blanket; '**⁓e** *f* (15) wool; *fig. in der* ⁓ *sitzen* live in clover; *sich in die* ⁓ *geraten* F have a row; '**⁓en**[1] *adj.* wool(l)en; *Strumpf*: *a.* worsted.

'**wollen**[2] **1.** (30) wish; (*verlangen*) want; (*bereit sein*) be willing; (*beabsichtigen*) intend; (*im Begriff sein zu* ...) be going to, be about to; *lieber* ⁓ prefer; *nicht* ⁓ refuse; *so Gott will!* please God!; *ich will es* (*nicht*) *tun* I will (won't) do it; *ich wollte, ich hätte es getan* I wish I had done it; *was* ⁓ *Sie* (*von mir*)? what do you want (of me)?; *was* ⁓ *Sie damit sagen?* what do you mean by it?; *er mag ~ oder nicht* willy-nilly, whether he likes it or not; *ich will* (*od. wollte*) *lieber* I would (*od.* had) rather, I should prefer; *das will ich meinen* I should think so; *das will überlegt sein* that requires some thinking; *dem sei wie ihm wolle* be that as it may; *er weiß, was er will* he knows his own mind; *mach was du willst!* do what you want!, *ärgerlich*: do your worst!; *wir ~ gehen* let us go; *wie du willst* as you like; **2.** ♀ *n* (6, *o. pl.*) will; *phls.* volition.

'**Woll|fett** *n* wool-grease, yolk; '**~garn** *n* wool(l)en yarn, worsted; '**~handel** *m* wool-trade; '**♀ig** wool(l)y; '**~jacke** *f* cardigan; '**~schur** *f* sheep-shearing; '**~spinne'rei** *f* wool-spinning (mill *Fabrik*); '**~stoff** *m* wool(l)en (fabric).

Wol|lust ['vɔlust] *f* (14[1]) voluptuousness, lust; **♀lüstig** ['~lystiç] voluptuous; *s. a. lüstern*; '**~lüstling** *m* (3[1]) libertine, debauchee.

'**Wollwaren** *f/pl.* wool(l)en goods, wool(l)ens; '**~händler** *m* wool(l)en-draper.

wo|'mit with what?; what ... with?; *rel. adv.* with which; *s. dienen*; **~'möglich** possibly; **~'nach** after what?; *rel. adv.* after which, whereupon; (*gemäß*) according to which.

Wonne ['vɔnə] *f* (15) delight, bliss; F *mit ~* with relish; '**~monat** *m*, '**~mond** *m* month of delight (*od.* of May); '**♀trunken** blissful, enraptured; *pred.* in raptures.

'**wonnig** delightful, blissful; (*herzig*) lovely, sweet.

wo|ran [voː'ran] at what?; *rel. adv.* at (*od.* by) which; *~ denken Sie?* what are you thinking of?; *ich weiß nicht, ~ ich bin* I don't know where I stand; *~ liegt es, daß ...?* how is it that ...?; *~ erkennt man ...?* how (*od.* by what) do you see ...?; **~'rauf** on what?; *~ warten Sie?* what are you waiting for?; *rel. adv.* on which; (*und danach*) whereupon; **~'raus** out of (*od.* from) what?; *~ ist das gemacht?* what is it made of?; *rel. adv.* out of (*od.* from) which, whence; **~'rein** into what?; *rel. adv.* into which.

worfeln ↗ ['vɔrfəln] (29) winnow.

worin [voː'rin] in what?; *rel. adv.* in which, wherein.

Wort [vɔrt] *n* (3, *einzeln*: 1[2]) word; (*Ausdruck*) term, expression; (*Ausspruch*) saying; (*Ehren♀*) word (of hono[u]r); *das ~ Gottes* the Gospel; *bei Zahlenangaben*: *in ~en ...* in letters ...; *ein Mann von ~ sein* be as good as one's word; *ein Mann, ein ~!* word of hono(u)r!, hono(u)r bright!; *auf ein ~!* a word with you!; *aufs ~ gehorchen* obey to the letter; *j-m ins ~ fallen, j-m das ~ abschneiden* cut a p. short; *mit andern ~en* in other words; *mit e-m ~* in a word; *ums ~ bitten, sich zu ~ melden* ask permission to speak; *zu ~e kommen* get a hearing; *nicht zu ~ kommen* not to get a word in edgewise; *das ~ ergreifen* (begin to) speak, *parl.* rise to speak, address the House, *bsd. Am.* take the floor; *j-m das ~ erteilen* give a p. permission to speak; *parl. j-m das ~ entziehen* rule a p. out of order; *das ~ erhalten* be allowed to speak, *parl.* catch the Speaker's eye, *bsd. Am.* get the floor; *das ~ führen* be the spokesman; *das große ~ führen* talk big; (*tonangebend sein*) lay down the law; *~ halten* keep one's word; *parl. das ~ haben* have the ear of the House, *bsd. Am.* have the floor; *ein ~ gab das andere* one word led another; *kein ~ mehr!* not another word!; *j-n beim ~e nehmen* take a p. at his (*od.* her) word; *mit j-m ein ~ reden* have a word with a p.; *e-r S. das ~ reden* hold a brief for; *s. einlegen, geben, Geld, Kehle, kurz, zurücknehmen.*

'**Wort|-akzent** *m* word-stress; '**♀-arm** poor in words; '**~-armut** *f* poverty of words; '**~-art** *gr. f* part of speech, class of word; '**~bedeutungslehre** *f* semantics; '**~bildung** *f* word-formation; '**~bruch** *m* breach of one's word *od.* of faith; '**♀brüchig** false to one's word; *~ werden* break one's word.

'**Wortemacher**(**in** *f*) *m* big talker.

Wörter|buch ['vœrtər-] *n* dictionary; '**~verzeichnis** *n* list of words, vocabulary, word-index.

'**Wort|folge** *f* word-order; '**~fügung** *f* construction; (*a.* '**~fügungslehre** *f*) syntax; '**~führer**(**in** *f*) *m* speaker; *nur m* spokesman; '**~fülle** *f* verbosity; '**~gefecht** *n* dispute;

'⁓**getreu** literal; '⁓**gewandt** eloquent, glib; '⁓**karg** taciturn, silent; '⁓**kargheit** *f* taciturnity; '⁓**klasse** *gr. f s. Wortart*; '⁓**klauber** *m* (7) quibbler, word-splitter; ⁓**klauberei** ['⁓'raɪ] *f* (16) word-splitting; '⁓**laut** *m* wording; (*Inhalt*) text; ⚖ (*genauer* ⁓) tenor; *der Brief usw. hat folgenden* ⁓ runs as follows.

wörtlich ['vœrt-] literal.

'**wort|los** wordless(ly *adv.*); '⁓**reich** abundant in words; *contp.* verbose; '⁓**schatz** *m* stock of words, vocabulary; '⁓**schwall** *m* flood of words, verbiage; '⁓**sinn** *m* literal sense; '⁓**spiel** *n* play on words, pun; '⁓**stamm** *m* stem, root; '⁓**stellung** *f* word-order; '⁓**streit** *m* dispute; '⁓**verdreher**(**in** *f*) *m* distorter of words; '⁓**verdrehung** *f* distortion of words; '⁓**wechsel** *m* dispute, altercation; *e-n* ⁓ *haben* have words.

wo|rüber [voː'ryːbər] over (*od.* upon) what?, what ... about?; *rel. adv.* over (*od.* upon, about) which; *vgl. a. Zeitwörter wie z.B. lachen*; ⁓'**rum** about what?, what ... about?; *rel. adv.* about which; *vgl. a. Zeitwörter wie z.B. trauern*; ⁓'**runter** under (*od.* among) what?; *rel. adv.* under (*od.* among) which.

wo|'selbst where; ⁓'**von** of (*od.* from) what?; what *are you talking* about?; *rel. adv.* of (*od.* from) which; *vgl. a. Zeitwörter wie z.B. leben*; ⁓'**vor** before what?; *rel. adv.* before which; *vgl. a. Zeitwörter wie z.B. sich fürchten*; ⁓'**zu** for what?, F what for?; *rel. adv.* for which; (*warum*) why; ⁓ *noch kommt, daß* to which must be added that.

Wrack ⚓ [vrak] *n* (3) wreck (*a. fig.*); '⁓**gut** *n* wreckage.

wrang [vraŋ] *pret. v. wringen*.

wringen ['vriŋən] (30) wring.

Wucher ['vuːxər] *m* (7) usury; (*Waren*⁓) profiteering; ⁓ *treiben s. wuchern*; '⁓**er** *m* (7) usurer; (*Waren*⁓) profiteer; '⁓**haft**, '⁓**isch** usurious; *mit Waren*: profiteering; '⁓**handel** *m* usurious trade, profiteering; '⁓**miete** *f* rack-rent; '⁓**n** (29) ♀ grow exuberantly, proliferate; (*Wucher treiben*) practise usury; *mit Waren*: profiteer; '⁓**ung** ⚕ *f* excrescence, growth; *bsd. in Nase u. Rachen*: vegetation; '⁓**zins** *m*, '⁓**zinsen** *pl.* usurious interest.

Wuchs[1] [vuːks] *m* (4[2]) growth; (*Gestalt*) figure, stature, build.

wuchs[2] *pret. v. wachsen*[1].

Wucht [vuxt] *f* (16) weight; (*Gewalt*) force; (*Schwung*) impetus; (*Anprall*) impact (*a. fig.*); F *'ne Wucht! (tolle Sache) sl.* a wow!; *mit voller* ⁓ *gegen ... rennen* cannon against; '⁓**en** (26) *v/i.* weigh heavy; *v/t.* lever up, heave; '⁓**ig** weighty, heavy; *Schlag, Gestalt, a. fig. Stil usw.*: powerful.

Wühl|-arbeit ['vyːl-] *f fig.* subversive activity; '⁓**en** (25) dig; *Tier*: burrow; *Schwein*: root; (*wild umhersuchen*) rummage; *fig. mst pol.* agitate; *im Gelde* ⁓ *fig.* wallow (*od.* be rolling) in money; '⁓**er** *m* (7) *fig.* agitator; '⁓**erisch** subversive; '⁓**maus** *f* vole; '⁓**tisch** F *m im Warenhaus*: rummage counter.

Wulst [vulst] *m* (3[2] *u.* [3]) roll; *zum Ausstopfen*: pad; (*Ausbauchung*) bulge; (*Reifen*⁓) bead (of a tyre); '⁓**ig** stuffed, padded; (*bauchig*) bulging; (*aufgedunsen*) puffed up; *Lippen*: protruding, thick.

wund [vunt] (*offen*) sore; (*verwundet*) wounded; ⁓*e Stelle* sore; *fig.* ⁓*er Punkt* tender spot; *sich die Füße* ⁓ *laufen* become footsore; ⁓ *reiben* gall, chafe; '⁓**brand** *m* gangrene; ⁓**e** ['vundə] *f* (15) wound; *die Zeit heilt alle* ⁓*n* time is a great healer; *fig. alte* ⁓*n wieder aufreißen* open old sores.

Wunder ['vundər] *n* (7) miracle; (*a. Sache, Vorgang, Person*) wonder, marvel, prodigy; ⁓ *der Technik* engineering marvel; ⁓ *tun* (*od. vollbringen, wirken*) do (*od.* work) wonders, perform miracles; (*es ist*) *kein* ⁓, *daß* ... small wonder that ...; *es geschehen Zeichen und* ⁓ wonders will never cease; *sein blaues* ⁓ *erleben* get the shock of one's life; ⁓ *was halten von* think a world of; '⁓**bar** wonderful, marvel(l)ous; (*übernatürlich*; *a. fig.*) miraculous; '⁓**bild** *n* miraculous image; '⁓**ding** *n* prodigy; ⁓*e pl. vollbringen* perform miracles; '⁓**doktor** *m* quack; '⁓**droge** *f* miracle drug; '⁓**glaube** *m* belief in miracles; '⁓'**hübsch** lovely; '⁓**kind** *n* infant prodigy; '⁓**knabe** *m* boy-wonder; '⁓**kur** *f* miraculous cure; '⁓**land** *n* Fairyland, wonderland;

'**⁀lich** queer, odd, strange; (*launisch*) whimsical; '**~lichkeit** *f* queerness, oddity, strangeness; '**⁀n** (29): *sich* ~ wonder (*über acc.* at), be surprised (at); be surprised to see *etc.* (*a. th.*); *es wundert mich* I am surprised *od.* astonished; (*ich frage mich*) I wonder (*wo usw.* where *etc.*); *es sollte mich nicht* ~ I shouldn't wonder; '**⁀nehmen:** *es nimmt mich wunder, daß* I am astonished that; '**⁀sam** wondrous; '**⁀'schön** very beautiful, of breathtaking beauty; '**~tat** *f* miracle; '**~täter(in** *f*) *m* miracle-worker; '**⁀tätig** wonder-working, miraculous; '**~tier** *n* monster; *fig.* prodigy; '**⁀voll** wonderful, marvel(l)ous; '**~welt** *f* world of wonders; '**~werk** *n* miracle; *fig. a.* wonder; '**~zeichen** *n* miraculous sign.

'**Wund|fieber** *n* wound-fever; *sich* '**⁀laufen** get footsore; *sich* '**⁀liegen** get bedsore; '**~mal** *n* scar; ~*e pl. eccl.* stigmata; '**~salbe** *f* healing ointment; '**~starrkrampf** *m* tetanus.

Wunsch [vunʃ] *m* (3^2 *u.* ^{3}) wish, desire; *auf* ~ on request; *auf j-s* ~ at a p.'s desire *od.* request; (*je*) *nach* ~ as desired; *mit den besten Wünschen zum Fest* with the compliments of the season; '**~bild** *n* ideal; '**~denken** *n* wishful thinking.

Wünschelrute ['vynʃəl-] *f* divining-rod; **~ngänger** ['~gɛŋər] *m* (7) diviner, dowser.

wünschen ['vynʃən] (27) wish, want, desire; *s. Glück*; *viel zu* ~ *übrig lassen* leave much to be desired; *wie Sie* ~ as you wish; *was* ~ *Sie?* may I help you?; '**~swert** desirable.

'**wunsch|gemäß** as desired; '**⁀kind** *n* planned child; '**⁀konzert** *n* (musical) request program(me); '**~los:** ~ *glücklich* perfectly happy; '**⁀traum** *m* wishdream, wishful thinking, *Am.* F pipe dream; '**⁀zettel** *m* list of things desired.

wurde ['vurdə] *pret. v. werden* 1 *u.* 2.

Würde ['vyrdə] *f* (15) dignity (*a. weitS.*); (*Ehre*) hono(u)r; (*Titel*) title; *akademische*: degree; *unter j-s* ~ beneath one's dignity; *unter aller* ~ beneath contempt; '**⁀los** undignified; '**~nträger** *m* dignitary; '**⁀voll** dignified; (*feierlich*) solemn, grave.

würdig ['~diç] worthy (*gen.* of); (*verdient*) deserving (of); *s. würdevoll*; **~en** ['~gən] (25) appreciate, value; (*erwähnen*) mention hono(u)rably, laud; *j-n e-s Blickes* (*Wortes*) ~ deign to look at (speak to) a p.; **⁀keit** ['~diç-] *f* worthiness; (*Verdienst*) merit; (*würdiges Äußere*) dignified appearance; **⁀ung** ['~guŋ] *f* appreciation; assessment (*a.* ⚖).

Wurf [vurf] *m* (3^3) throw; (~ *Junge*) brood, litter; *fig. großer* ~ great success; *alles auf einen* ~ *setzen* stake all on a single card.

Würfel ['vyrfəl] *m* (7) die; ⅍ cube (*a. Eis⁀ usw.*); *die* ~ *sind gefallen* the die is cast; '**~becher** *m* dice-box; **⁀förmig** ['~fœrmiç] cubic (-al); '**⁀ig** cubical; *Muster*: chequered, *bsd. Am.* check(er)ed; '**⁀n** (29) *v/i.* play (at) dice; ~ *um* throw dice for; *v/t. Stoff*: chequer, *bsd. Am.* check(er); '**~spiel** *n* game of dice; '**~zucker** *m* lump sugar.

'**Wurf|geschoß** *n* missile; '**~kreis** *m Sport*: (throwing) circle; '**~pfeil** *m* dart; '**~scheibe** *f* quoit; (*Diskus*) discus; '**~speer** *m*, '**~spieß** *m* javelin, dart; '**~taube** *f Schießsport*: clay pigeon.

würg|en ['vyrgən] (25) *v/t.* throttle, choke (*beide a.* ⊕); *poet.* (*töten*) slay; *v/i.* choke; *beim Erbrechen*: retch; *beim Essen*: gag on one's food; *fig. an e-r Arbeit*: struggle hard at; **⁀-engel** ['vyrk-] *m* destroying angel; **⁀er** ['~gər] *m* (7) slayer, murderer (*a.* '**⁀erin** *f*); (*Vogel*) butcher-bird.

Wurm [vurm] *m* (1^2) worm (*a. fig.*); (*Made*) maggot, grub; ⚕ *am Finger*: whitlow; F *n* (*bsd. Kind*) little mite; F *j-m die Würmer aus der Nase ziehen* draw a p. out.

Würmchen ['vyrmçən] *n* (6) little worm; *fig.* tiny mite.

wurmen ['vurmən] (25) gall, vex.

wurm|förmig ['~fœrmiç] worm-shaped, vermiform; '**⁀fortsatz** *anat. m* appendix; '**~ig** wormy; maggoty; '**~krank** suffering from worms; '**⁀mittel** *n* vermifuge; '**⁀stich** *m*, '**⁀loch** *n* worm-hole; '**~stichig** worm-eaten; *fig.* unsound, rotten.

Wurst [vurst] *f* (14^1) sausage; F ~

wider ~ tit for tat; F *jetzt geht's um die* ~*!* it's do or die now!; F *es ist mir* ~ I don't care (a rap); '~**blatt** F *n* (*Zeitung*) (lousy) rag.

Würstchen ['vyrstçən] *n* (6): *warme* ~ *pl.* hot sausages, *Am.* hot dogs; F *fig. armes* ~ poor thing.

Wurstel|ei F [vurstə'laɪ] *f* (16) muddling, muddle; '**∼n** F (29) muddle.

wurst|ig *sl.* absolutely indifferent; '**∼vergiftung** *f* sausage-poisoning, 🕮 botulism; '**∼waren** *f/pl.* sausages.

Würze ['vyrtsə] *f* (15) (*Gewürz*) spice, condiment; (*Aroma*) seasoning, flavo(u)r; ⊕ (*Bier∼*) wort; *fig.* zest, flavo(u)r; *in der Kürze liegt die* ~ brevity is the soul of wit.

Wurzel ['vurtsəl] *f* (16) root (*a. gr.*, ℞, *Zahn∼ u. fig.*); ~ *fassen od. schlagen* (*a. fig.*) take (*od.* strike) root; '~**behandlung** ⚕ *f* root-treatment; '~**größe** ℞ *f* radical quantity; '~**knolle** *f* tuber, bulb.

'**wurzeln** (29, h. *u.* sn) (take) root; ~ *in* (*dat.*) be rooted in; '~**d** rooted.

'**Wurzel|schößling** *m* sucker, runner; '~**stock** *m* root-stock; '~**werk** *n* roots *pl.*; '~**wort** *n* radical word, root; '~**zeichen** ℞ *n* radical sign; '~**ziehen** ℞ *n* evolution, root extraction.

würz|en ['vyrtsən] (27) season, flavo(u)r, spice; '~**ig** spicy; aromatic; '**∼mischung** *f* mixed herbs *pl.*

wusch [vu:ʃ] *pret. v. waschen.*

wußte ['vustə] *pret. v. wissen* 1.

Wust [vu:st] *m* (3) tangled mass; (*Kram*) trash; (*Durcheinander*) mess, jumble.

wüst [vy:st] desert, waste; (*wirr*) confused; (*liederlich*) depraved; (*roh*) rude; (*gemein*) vile; F (*arg*) awful; **∼e** ['~ə] *f*, **∼enei** [~'naɪ] *f* (15) desert, waste; '**∼ensand** *m* desert sand; '**∼ling** *m* (3[1]) libertine, rake, lecher.

Wut [vu:t] *f* (16, *o. pl.*) rage, fury; *in* ~ in a rage; *j-n in* ~ *bringen* enrage (*od.* infuriate) a p.; *in* ~ *geraten* fly into a rage; '~**-anfall** *m*, '~**-ausbruch** *m* fit (*od.* outburst) of rage.

wüten ['vy:tən] (26) *allg.* rage; '~**d** furious (*a. fig. heftig*); F *bsd. Am.* mad (*beide*: *auf, über acc.* at; with *a p.*).

'**wut-entbrannt** enraged.

'**wutschäumend** foaming with rage.

'**wutschnaubend** furious.

X, Y

X [iks], **x** *n inv.* X, x; *j-m ein X für ein U vormachen* throw dust in a p.'s eyes.

'**X-Achse** ℞ *f* axis of x.

Xanthippe [ksan'tipə] *f* (15) *fig.* Xanthippe, termagant.

'**X-Beine** *n/pl.* turned-in legs, knock-knees; '**X-beinig** knock-kneed.

x-be'liebig any (... you please); *jede(r, s)* ~*e* ... any (given) ...

'**x-mal** F (ever so) many times, F umpteen times.

x-te ['ikstə]: F *zum* ~*n Male* for the umpteenth (*od.* nth) time.

Xylograph [ksylo'grɑ:f] *m* (12) xylographer; **∼isch** xylographic(al).

Xylophon ♪ [~'fo:n] *n* (3[1]) xylophone.

Y ['ypsilɔn], **y** *n inv.* Y, y.

'**Y-Achse** ℞ *f* axis of y.

Yacht [jaxt] *f* (16) *s. Jacht.*

Yankee ['jɛŋki] *m* (11) Yankee.

Ysop ⚘ ['y:zɔp] *m* (3[1]) hyssop.

Yucca ⚘ ['juka] *f* (11[1]) yucca.

Z

Z [tsɛt], **z** *n inv.* Z, z; *s.* A.

Zacke ['tsakə] *f* (15), '**~n¹** *m* (6) (sharp) point; (*Zinke*) prong; (*Auszackung*) indent(ation); (*Eisenspitze*) spike; (*Fels*2) jag.

'**zacken²** (25) indent; (*zähnen*) tooth; *ungleichmäßig*: jag; *Kleid*: scallop.

'**zackig** indented, notched; *Felsen, Glas usw.*: jagged; ♀ *Blatt*: crenate; *fig. sl.* (*schneidig*) smart.

zag [tsɑ:k] *s. zaghaft*; **~en** ['tsɑ:gən] **1.** (25) quail; (*zurückschrecken*) shrink, flinch; **2.** 2 *n* (6) quailing; shrinking, flinching; **~haft** ['tsɑ:k-haft] timid; '**2haftigkeit** *f* timidity.

zäh|(**e**) ['tsɛ:(ə)] tough, *fig. a.* tenacious; *Energie*: grim, dogged; *Flüssigkeit*: ropy, viscous; *ein ~es Leben haben* be tenacious of life; '**~flüssig** viscous, sticky; *Verkehr*: slow-moving; '**2igkeit** *f* toughness, tenacity; ropiness, viscosity.

Zahl [tsɑ:l] *f* (16) number; (*Ziffer*) figure (*a.* = *Betrag, Wert*), numeral; (*arabische Ziffer*) cipher; (*Stelle*) digit.

'**zahlbar** payable (*bei* at, with; *an acc.* to); *~ sein od. werden* fall due, be(come) payable; *~ machen od. stellen* make payable, *Wechsel*: domiciliate; *~ bei Lieferung* cash on delivery.

'**zählbar** countable, computable.

zählebig ['~le:biç] tenacious of life.

zahlen ['tsɑ:lən] *v/t. u. v/i.* (25) pay; *im Gasthaus*: *~, bitte!* the bill (*Am.* the check), please!

zählen ['tsɛ:lən] *v/t. u. v/i.* (25) count, (*a.* = *sich belaufen auf*) number; *fig.* (*haben*) have, number; *~ auf* (*acc.*) count on; *unter* (*acc.*) *... ~, zu ... ~* number among, rank with; *er (es) zählt nicht* he (it) does not count; *s. drei.*

'**Zahlen**|**lotto** *n s. Lotto*; '**2mäßig** numerical; *j-m ~ überlegen sein* outnumber; '**~material** *n* numerical data *pl.*, figures *pl.*; '**~schloß** *n* combination lock; '**~verhältnis** *n* numerical proportion.

'**Zahler** *m* (7), '**~in** *f* (16¹) payer.

'**Zähler** *m* (7) ⊕ counter; *für Gasverbrauch usw.*: meter; ⚡ numerator; '**~-ablesung** *f* reading.

'**Zahl**|**grenze** *f* fare stage; '**~karte** *f* paying-in form.

'**zahl**|**los** numberless, countless; '**2meister** *m* ⚔ paymaster; ⚓ purser; '**~reich** numerous; '**2stelle** *f* paying-office; '**2tag** *m* pay-day.

'**Zahlung** *f* payment; *~ leisten* make payment; et. *in ~ nehmen* accept a th. in part payment (*od.* part exchange).

'**Zählung** *f* counting; (*a. als Ergebnis, z.B. Blutkörperchen*2) count; (*Volks*2 *usw.*) census.

'**Zahlungs**|**-abkommen** *n* payments agreement; '**~-anweisung** *f* order to pay; (*Überweisung*) money order; '**~-aufforderung** *f* demand for payment; '**~-aufschub** *m* respite; '**~-auftrag** *m e-s Bankkunden*: banker's order; '**~bedingungen** *f/pl.* terms of payment; *zu erleichterten ~* on easy terms; '**~befehl** ⚖ *m s. Mahnbescheid*; '**~bilanz** *f* balance of payments; '**~-einstellung** *f* suspension of payment; '**~-empfänger** *m* payee; '**~-erleichterung**(**en** *pl.*) *f* facilities (of payment), easy terms *pl.*; '**2fähig** solvent; '**~fähigkeit** *f* solvency; '**~frist** *f* term of payment; *s. Zahlungsaufschub*; '**~mittel** *n* currency; *gesetzliches ~* legal tender; '**~-ort** *m* place of payment; '**~-schwierigkeiten** *f/pl.* financial difficulties *pl.*; '**~termin** *m* date of payment; '**2-unfähig** insolvent; '**~-unfähigkeit** *f* insolvency.

'**Zählwerk** *n* counter.

'**Zahl**|**wort** *gr. n* numeral; '**~zeichen** *n* figure, cipher.

zahm [tsɑ:m] tame (*a. fig.*), domestic(ated); (*gefügig*) tractable.

zähm|**bar** ['tsɛ:m-] tamable; '**~en** (25) tame (*a. fig.*), domesticate; *Pferd*: break in; *fig.* restrain.

'**Zahmheit** *f* tameness.

'**Zähmung** *f* taming.

Zahn [tsɑ:n] *m* (3³) tooth (*pl.* teeth); ⊕ *am ~rad*: tooth, cog; *fig.* F (*Tempo*) speed; *sl.* (*Mädel*) doll, chick; *der ~ der Zeit* the ravages *pl.* of time; *die Zähne zeigen* show one's teeth (*a. fig. j-m* to a p.); *j-m auf den ~ fühlen* sound a p.; *bis an die Zähne bewaffnet* armed to the teeth; *s. Haar, zusammenbeißen*;

'**~-arzt** *m* dentist, dental surgeon; '**2-ärztlich** dental; '**~behandlung** *f* dental treatment; '**~belag** *m* (dental) plaque; '**~bürste** *f* tooth-brush; '**~creme** *f* tooth-paste.

Zähne|fletschen ['tsɛ:nə-] *n* bared teeth *pl.*; '**~klappern** *n* (6) chattering of teeth; '**~knirschen** *n*, '**2-knirschend** (6) gritting one's teeth.

zahnen ['tsa:nən] (25) *v/i.* teethe, cut one's teeth; *v/t.* ⊕ tooth.

zähnen ['tsɛ:nən] (25) *v/t.* indent, notch.

'**Zahn|-ersatz** *m* (artificial) denture; **~fäule** ['~fɔʏlə] *f* (dental) caries, tooth decay; '**~fistel** *f* fistula in the gums; '**~fleisch** *n* gums *pl.*; '**~fleischbluten** *n* bleeding of the gums; '**~füllung** *f* filling, stopping; '**~geschwür** *n* gumboil; '**~heilkunde** *f* dentistry; '**~krone** *f* crown; '**~labor** *n* dental laboratory; '**~laut** *m* dental (sound); '**2los** toothless; '**~lücke** *f* gap between two teeth; '**~medizin** *f* dentistry; '**~nerv** *m* nerve of a tooth; '**~pasta** *f* tooth-paste; '**~pflege** *f* oral hygiene; '**~prothese** *f* dental prosthesis, denture; '**~pulver** *n* tooth-powder; '**~rad** ⊕ *n* gear (wheel), cog-wheel, toothed wheel; '**~rad-antrieb** *m* gear drive; '**~radbahn** 🚂 *f* rack-railway; '**~radgetriebe** *n* toothed gear; '**~schmelz** *m* (tooth) enamel; '**~schmerz** *m* toothache; '**~seide** *f* dental floss; '**~stein** *m* tartar, scale; '**~stocher** *m* (7) toothpick; '**~techniker** *m* dental technician; '**~wechsel** *m* second dentition; '**~weh** *n* toothache; '**~werk** ⊕ *n* rack-work; '**~wurzel** *f* root (of a tooth); '**~zange** *f* dental forceps.

Zähre ['tsɛ:rə] *poet. f* (15) tear.

Zange ['tsaŋə] *f* (15) (*eine* a pair of) tongs *pl.*; (*Kneif2*) nippers *pl.*; (*Rund2, Flach2*) pliers *pl.*; (*Pinzette*) tweezers *pl.*; ⚕, *zo.* forceps; *kleinere*: pincers *pl.*; *fig. j-n in die ~ nehmen* press a p. hard; '**~ngeburt** ⚕ *f* forceps delivery.

Zank [tsaŋk] *m* (3) quarrel; '**~-apfel** *m* apple of discord, bone of contention; '**2en** (25) scold; (*a. sich*) quarrel, squabble; *lärmend*: brawl; *sich ~ mit* have words (*od.* a row) with '**2haft, zänkisch** ['tsɛŋkiʃ] quarrelsome, nagging; '**~sucht** *f* quarrelsomeness; '**2süchtig** quarrelsome, contentious.

Zäpfchen ['tsɛpfçən] *n* (6) little peg; *anat.* uvula; ⚕ (*Einführ2*) suppository; '**~...** *anat., gr.* uvular.

Zapfen ['tsapfən] **1.** *m* (6) plug; (*Pflock*) peg, pin; (*Verbindungs2*) tenon; (*Faß2*) tap, bung; (*Dreh2*) pivot; ♣ cone; **2.** 2 (25) tap; '**~bohrer** *m* tap-borer; '**~lager** *n* pivot (*od.* trunnion) bearing; '**~loch** *n* tap-hole; *Tischlerei*: mortise; '**~streich** ⚔ *m* tattoo, taps *pl.*

'**Zapf|hahn** *m* tap, *Am.* faucet; '**~pistole** *f* (petrol) gun, nozzle; '**~säule** *f* petrol pump.

zappel|ig ['tsapəliç] fidgety; '**~n** (29) flounder; *vor Unruhe*: fidget; *sich windend*: wriggle; *kämpfend*: struggle; *fig. j-n ~ lassen* keep a p. in suspense, tantalize a p.; **2philipp** F ['~fi:lip] *m* fidget.

zappenduster F [tsapən'du:stər] pitch-dark; *fig. dann wird's ~* things will look pretty grim.

Zar [tsa:r] *m* (12) czar, tsar.

Zarge ['tsargə] *f* (15) ⊕ border, edge; (*Rahmen*) frame, case; (*Seitenstück der Geige usw.*) side.

Zarin ['tsa:rin] *f* (16[1]) czarina.

zart [tsa:rt] tender; *Haut, Farbe, Ton usw.*: soft; *Gesundheit usw.*: delicate; (*sanft*) gentle; '**~besaitet** *fig.* (very) sensitive; '**~fühlend** delicate; '**2gefühl** *n* delicacy of feeling, tactfulness; '**2heit** *f* tenderness; softness; delicacy; gentleness.

zärtlich ['tsɛ:rtliç] tender; '**2keit** *f* tenderness; (*Liebkosung*) caress.

Zaster F ['tsastər] *m* (7) (*Geld*) *sl.* dough.

Zauber ['tsaubər] *m* (7) spell, charm, magic (*alle a. fig.*); *s. Zauberei*; (*Bezauberung*) enchantment; (*~glanz*) glamo(u)r; *s. faul*; **~ei** [~'raɪ] *f* (16) magic, sorcery; '**~er** *m* (7) sorcerer, magician; *s. ~künstler*; *fig.* enchanter; '**~flöte** *f* magic flute; '**~formel** *f* magic formula; '**2haft,** '**2isch** magical, enchanting, glamorous; '**~in** *f* sorceress; *fig.* enchantress; '**~kraft** *f* magic power; '**~kunst** *f* magic (art); '**~künstler** *m* illusionist, conjurer; *fig.* wizard; '**~kunststück** *n* conjuring trick; '**~land** *n* enchanted land, Fairyland; '**2n** (29) *v/i.* practise magic; *weitS.* do conjuring tricks; *fig.* do wonders; *v/t.* conjure (up); '**~spie-**

gel *m* magic mirror; '**~spruch** *m* (magic) spell; '**~stab** *m* (magic) wand; '**~trank** *m* magic potion, philt|re, *Am.* -er; '**~wort** *n* magic word.

Zauder|er ['tsaudərər] *m* (7) lingerer; (*Zögernder*) waverer; '**2n¹** (29) linger, delay; (*zögern*) waver, hesitate; '**~n²** *n* (6) lingering; hesitation.

Zaum [tsaum] *m* (3³) bridle; *im ~ halten* keep in check, bridle.

zäumen ['tsɔʏmən] (25) bridle.

'**Zaumzeug** *n* headgear, bridle.

Zaun [tsaun] *m* (3³) fence; *fig. vom ~ brechen e-n Streit*: pick *a quarrel, e-n Krieg*: start; '**~gast** *m* deadhead; '**~könig** *zo. m* wren; '**~pfahl** *m* pale; *ein Wink mit dem ~* a broad hint.

zausen ['tsauzən] (27) pull about.

Zebra *zo.* ['tse:bra] *n* (11) zebra; '**~streifen** *m für Fußgänger*: zebra crossing.

Zech|bruder ['tsɛç-] *m* tippler, toper; '**~e** *f* (15) bill, score; ⚒ mine; (*Kohlen2*) coal-pit, colliery; (*Bergwerksgesellschaft*) mining company; *die ~ bezahlen* foot the bill, F pay the piper; '**2en** (25) carouse, tipple; '**~er** *m* (7) (hard) drinker, tippler, toper; '**~gelage** *n* carouse; '**~kumpan** *m* boon-companion; '**~preller** *m* (7) bilk(er); **~prellerei** [~'raɪ] *f* (16) hotel fraud, bilking.

Zecke ['tsɛkə] *f* (15) tick.

Zeder ⚘ ['tse:dər] *f* (15) cedar.

zedieren ⚖ [tse'di:rən] cede, transfer, assign (*dat.* to).

Zeh [tse:] *m* (3 *u.* 12), '**~e** *f* (15) toe; '**~enspitze** *f* point (*od.* tip) of the toe; *auf (den) ~n* on tiptoe.

zehn [tse:n] **1.** ten; **2.** 2 *f* (16) (number) ten; '**2-eck** *n* (3¹) decagon; '**2-ender** *m* (7) ten-point stag.

Zehner ⚗ ['tse:nər] *m* (7) ten; '**2lei** *adj.* ... of ten sorts *od.* kinds; *als su.* ten different things *pl.*

'**zehn|fach**, **~fältig** ['~fɛltiç] tenfold; 2'**fingersystem** *n* touch system; '**~jährig** ten-year(s)-old; of ten years, ten-year; '**2kampf** *m* decathlon; '**~mal** ten times; '**~malig** ten (times repeated); **~tägig** ['~tɛ:giç] of (*od.* lasting) ten days, ten-day; '**~'tausend** ten thousand; *die oberen 2* the upper ten (*od.* crust); *~e von Exemplaren* tens of thousands of copies.

zehnte ['tse:ntə] **1.** (18) tenth; **2.** 2 *m* (13) tenth; (*Abgabe*) tithe; '**2l** *n* (7) tenth (part); '**~ns** tenthly.

zehr|en ['tse:rən] (25) *am Körper*: make thin; *fig.* (*nagen*) gnaw (*an dat.* at); *~ von* live on; live off (*a. e-m Kapital*); *von e-r Erinnerung ~* feed on; '**~end** ⚕ *adj.* consumptive; '**2ung** *f* (expenses *pl.* of) living; (*Weg2*) provisions *pl.*; (*Schwinden*) waste; *eccl. letzte ~* viaticum.

Zeichen ['tsaɪçən] *n* (6) sign (*a. ast., typ.*, ♪, *Wunder2*), token; (*Merk2, Satz2*) mark; (*An2*) indication, sign, *a.* ⚕ symptom; (*Signal*) signal; (*Vor2*) omen; ✝ (*Waren2*) trade-mark, brand; ✝ *unser ~* our reference (*abbr.* Ref.); *ein ~ geben* make a sign (*dat.* to); *s-s ~s ein Bäcker* a baker by trade; *zum ~ (gen.)* in (*od.* as a) sign of; *zum ~, daß* as a proof that; *s. Wunder*; '**~block** *m* sketch-block; '**~brett** *n* drawing-board; '**~drei-eck** ⚗ *n* set-square; '**~-erklärung** *f* signs and symbols *pl.*; '**~feder** *f* drawing-pen; '**~heft** *n* sketch-book; '**~kunst** *f* (art of) drawing; '**~lehrer** *m* art master; '**~papier** *n* drawing-paper; '**~saal** *m* drawing-office; *Schule*: art room; '**~schule** *f* school of drawing; '**~setzung** *gr. f* punctuation; '**~sprache** *f* sign language; '**~stift** *m* crayon; '**~trickfilm** *m* animated cartoon; '**~unterricht** *m* drawing lessons *pl.*; *Schule*: art.

zeichn|en ['tsaɪçnən] (26) *v/t.* (*a. v/i.*) *paint.* draw (*nach* from); (*entwerfen*) design, *flüchtig* (*a. fig.*): sketch; (*be~, kenn~*) mark; (*unter~*) sign; *Spende usw.*: subscribe (*für e-n Fonds* to); *Anleihe, Aktien*: subscribe (for); *Brief*: *ich zeichne hochachtungsvoll* I remain yours truly; '**2er** *m* (7) draughtsman, *bsd. Am.* draftsman, (*a.* '**2erin** *f*) designer; *e-r Spende, Anleihe usw.*: subscriber (*gen.* to; for); '**2erin** *f* (16¹) draughtswoman, *bsd. Am.* draftswoman; '**~erisch** drawing; *Darstellung*: graphic; '**2ung** *f* drawing (*a.* ⊕), sketch, design; illustration; (*erläuternde Figur*) diagram; (*Kenn2*) marking; (*Muster*) pattern; subscription (to; for); '**~ungsberechtigt** authorized to sign.

'**Zeigefinger** *m* forefinger, index.

zeigen ['tsaɪgən] (25) show; (*deuten auf*) point out; ~ *auf* (*acc.*) point at; (*an~*) indicate; *erklärend*: demonstrate; (*zur Schau stellen, a. fig.*) display, exhibit; (*vorführen*) present, show; *sich* ~ appear, show up, *plötzlich*: turn up, *Sache*: show, (*herausstellen*) turn out, prove; *sich prahlend* ~ *wollen, sich* ~ *mit* show off.

'**Zeige|r** *m* (7) (*Uhr*≗; *großer* long, *kleiner* short) hand; *des Barometers usw.*: pointer; '**~stock** *m* pointer.

zeihen ['tsaɪən] (30) accuse (*gen.* of).

Zeile ['tsaɪlə] *f* (15) (*gedruckte* ~ *usw.*) line; (*Reihe*) row; *TV* (scanning) line; *j-m eine* ~ *od. ein paar* ~*n schreiben* drop a p. a line; '**~nhonorar** *n* linage, *Am.* F space rates *pl.*; '**~nraster** *TV m* line-scanning pattern; '**~nschalter** *m Schreibmaschine*: line space lever; '**≗nweise** by the line.

Zeisig ['tsaɪziç] *m* (3) *zo.* siskin; *fig. lockerer* ~ loose fish.

Zeit [tsaɪt] *f* (16) time; (*~raum*) period, space (of time); (*~alter*) age, era; *gr.* tense; (*Jahres*≗, *Saison, a. geeignete* ~) season; *freie* ~ spare time; *s. ganz* 1.; ≗ *meines Lebens* all my life; *schlimme* ~*en* hard times; *der beste Spieler usw. aller* ~*en* of all time; *die ganze* ~ (*über*) all along; ✝ *auf* ~ on account, on credit; *mit der* ~ in the course of time, with time; *von* ~ *zu* ~ from time to time; *vor der* ~ prematurely; *vor* ~*en* in former times; *vor langer* ~ long ago, a long time ago; *zur* ~ (*gen.*) in the time of; (*jetzt*) (*abbr. z. Z.*) at present; *zu* ~*en* (*gen.*) in the time of; *zu meiner* ~ in my time; *zu s-r* ~ in due course (of time); *s. recht*[1]; *das hat* ~ there is plenty of time for that; *es ist* ~ *anzufangen* it is about time to begin; *es ist die höchste* ~ it is high time; *wenn* (*als*) *es an der* ~ *ist* (*war*) in the fullness of time; *mit der* ~ *gehen* keep pace (*od.* go) with the times; *j-m* ~ *lassen* give a p. time; *laß* (*od. nimm*) *dir* ~! take your time!; *die* ~ *nützen* make the most of *one's* time; *s. vertreiben.*

'**Zeit|-abschnitt** *m* epoch, *a. engS.* period; '**~-abstand** *m* interval; '**~-alter** *n* age; '**~-angabe** *f* date; exact time; '**~-ansage** *f* time-check; '**~-arbeit** *f* temp work; '**~-aufnahme** *phot. f* time exposure; '**~-aufwand** *m* time spent (*für* on); '**≗bedingt** entailed by the times; '**~bombe** *f* time bomb; '**~dauer** *f* space of time, period, duration, term; '**~enfolge** *gr. f* sequence of tenses; '**~faktor** *m* time element; '**~folge** *f* chronological order; '**~form** *gr. f* tense; '**~funk** *m* topical talk(s *pl.*); '**~geist** *m* spirit of the age, zeitgeist; '**≗gemäß** seasonable, opportune, timely; (*zur Zeit üblich*) modern, up-to-date; '**~genosse** *m*, '**~genossin** *f*, **≗genössisch** ['~gənœsiʃ] contemporary; '**≗gerecht** timely; *adv.* on time; '**~geschichte** *f* contemporary history; '**~gewinn** *m* time gained; '**~guthaben** *n bei gleitender Arbeitszeit*: time credit.

'**zeitig** early; (*reif*) mature; **~en** ['~igən] (25) mature, ripen; (*hervorbringen*) produce, call forth.

'**Zeit|karte** *f* season-ticket, *Am.* commuter's ticket; *auf~fahren* travel by season-ticket, *Am.* commute; '**≗kritisch** topical; '**~lang** *f*: *eine* ~ for some time, for a while; '**~lauf** *m* course of time, period; *Zeitläuf*(*t*)*e pl.* times; ≗'**lebens** for life, during life; all one's life; '**≗lich** temporal; time (*factor, etc.*); *das* ≗*e segnen* depart this life; *adv.* as to time; ~ *abstimmen od. berechnen* time; '**~lichkeit** *f* temporality; '**≗los** timeless; '**~lupe** *f Film*: slow-motion camera; '**~lupen-aufnahme** *f* slow-motion picture; *im* '**~lupentempo** *n* in slow motion; *fig.* at a snail's pace; '**~mangel** *m* lack of time; '**~maß** *n* measure of time; *poet.* quantity; ♪ time; '**~messer** *m* chronometer; '**≗nah** up-to-date, topical, current; '**~nehmer** *m* (7) *Sport*: time-keeper; '**~plan** *m* time-table, schedule; '**~punkt** *m* (point of) time; moment; date; '**~raffer** *m* (7) *Film*: time-lapse (*od.* quick-motion) camera; '**~raffer-aufnahme** *f* quick-motion picture; '**≗raubend** taking up much time, time-consuming; '**~raum** *m* space (of time), period; '**~rechnung** *f* chronology; *christliche* ~ Christian era; '**~schalter** ⚡ *m* time switch; (electronic) timer; '**~schrift** *f* journal, periodical, magazine; *literarische*: review; '**~spanne** *f* space (of time); '⁀**sparend** time-saving; '~**studie** *f* time-and-motion study; '~**studienbeamte** ✝ *m* time-study man; '~**tafel** *f* chronological table; '~-**umstände** *m/pl.* circumstances of the time(s).

'**Zeitung** *f* (news)paper, journal.

'**Zeitungs|-abonnement** *n* subscription to a paper; '~-**artikel** *m* newspaper article; '~-**ausschnitt** *m* newspaper cutting; '~**beilage** *f* supplement (of *od.* to a newspaper); '~-**ente** *f* hoax, canard; '~**händler** *m* news-agent, *Am.* newsdealer; '~-**inserat** *n* (newspaper) advertisement, F ad; '~**junge** *m* news-boy; '~**kiosk** *m* news-stall, *bsd. Am.* newsstand; '~**meldung**, '~**notiz** *f* press item; '~**papier** *n* newsprint; '~**redakteur** *m* newspaper editor; '~**schreiber(in** *f*) *m* journalist; '~**sprache** *f*, '~**stil** *m* journalese; '~**stand** *m* newsstand; '~**verkäufer(in** *f*) *m auf der Straße*: news-vendor, news-man; '~**verleger** *m* newspaper publisher; '~**wesen** *n* journalism, *the* (daily) press; '~**wissenschaft** *f* journalism.

'**Zeit|verlust** *m* loss of time; '~**verschiebung** *f* time difference; '~**verschwendung** *f* waste of time; ~**vertreib** ['~fɛrtraɪp] *m* pastime, diversion, amusement; *zum* ~ to pass the time; ⁀**weilig** ['~vaɪliç] temporary; *adv.* = '⁀**weise** (*eine Zeitlang*) for a time; (*von Zeit zu Zeit*) from time to time, at times; '~**wort** *n* (1²) verb; '~**zeichen** *n Radio*: time-signal; '~**zünder** *m* time fuse.

zelebrieren [tsele'bri:rən] solemnize.

Zelle ['tsɛlə] *f* (15) *allg.* cell; ✈ air-frame; *teleph.* booth; '⁀**nförmig** cellular.

'**Zell|gewebe** *n* cell tissue; '~**glas** *n* cellophane; '⁀**ig** cellular; '~**kern** *m* nucleus.

Zellophan [tsɛlo'fɑ:n] *n* cellophane.

'**Zellstoff** *m* cellulose; *Papier*: pulp; '⁀**haltig** cellulosic; '~**watte** *f* cellu-cotton.

'**Zellteilung** *biol. f* cell division.

Zellu|loid [tsɛlulo'ʔi:t, ~'lɔʏt] *n* (3) celluloid; ~'**lose** *f* (15) cellulose.

'**Zell|wand** *anat. f* cell wall; '~**wolle** *f* staple fib|re, *Am.* -er.

Zelt [tsɛlt] *n* (3) tent; '~**bahn** *f* tent square; '~**dach** *n* tent-roof; '⁀**en** *v/i.* (26) camp; go camping; '~**lager** *n* (tent) camp; '~**leine** *f* guy line; '~**pflock** *m* tent-peg; '~**platz** *m* camping site; '~**stadt** *f* tent city; '~**stange** *f* tent-pole.

Zement [tse'mɛnt] *m* (3) cement; ⁀**ieren** [~'ti:rən] cement (*a. fig.*); ~**ierung** [~'ti:ruŋ] *f* cementation.

Zenit [tse'ni:t] *m* (3) (*im* at the) zenith.

zensieren [tsɛn'zi:rən] *Buch usw.*: censor; *Schule*: mark, *Am.* grade.

Zensor ['tsɛnzɔr] *m* (8¹) censor.

Zensur [~'zu:r] *f* (16) censorship; (*Zeugnis*) certificate, marks *pl.*; *für Schüler*: (term's) report, *Am. a.* credit, grade; *für eine Leistung*: mark, *Am.* point; *gute* ~ good mark.

Zenti|'gramm [tsɛnti-] *n* centigram(me); ~'**meter** *n, m* centimetre, *Am.* centimeter.

Zentner ['tsɛntnər] *m* (7) (metric) hundredweight (*abbr.* cwt.); '~**last** *f fig.* heavy burden; '⁀**schwer** very heavy.

zentral [tsɛn'trɑ:l] central; ⁀**e** *f* (15) central office *od.* ⚡ station; headquarters *pl.*; ⊕ control room; (telephone) exchange; ⁀**heizung** *f* central heating; ~**i'sieren** [~trali-] centralize; ⁀**i'sierung** *f* centralization; ⁀'**nervensystem** [~'trɑ:l-] *n* central nervous system; ⁀**verriegelung** *mot. f* central locking (system).

zentrifugal [tsɛntrifu'gɑ:l] centrifugal; ⁀**kraft** *f* centrifugal force.

Zentri|'fuge *f* centrifuge; ⁀**petal** [~pe'tɑ:l] centripetal.

'**zentrisch** centric(al).

Zentrum ['tsɛntrum] *n* (9) cent|re, *Am.* -er; *ins* ~ *treffen* hit the bull's-eye.

Zeppelin [tsɛpə'li:n] *m* (3¹) (*Luftschiff*) Zeppelin, F Zepp.

Zepter ['tsɛptər] *n* (7) sceptre, *Am.* scepter.

zer'beißen [tsɛr-] bite to pieces, crunch.

zer'bersten (sn) burst asunder.

zerbombt [~'bɔmt] bomb-wrecked.

zer'brech|en *v/t. u. v/i.* (sn) (*a. fig.*) break (to pieces), crack; *sich den Kopf* ~ rack one's brains (*über acc.* over); ~**lich** breakable, *a. P., Figur*: fragile; (*spröde*) brittle; ⁀**lichkeit** *f* fragility, brittleness.

zer'bröckeln *v/t. u. v/i.* (sn) crumble.

zer'drücken crush; *Kleid*: crease.

Zeremon|ie [tseremo'ni:] *f* (15) ceremony; ⁀**iell** [~'njɛl], ~**iell** *n*

(3[1]) ceremonial; **~ienmeister** [~-ˈmoːnjən-] *m* master of ceremonies; **⁲iös** [~moˈnjøːs] ceremonious.

zerˈfahren 1. ruin (by driving over); **2.** *adj. Weg*: rutted; *P.*: (*faselig*) flighty, harum-scarum; (*konfus*) scatter-brained; *Antwort usw.*: inconsistent; (*zerstreut*) absent-minded; **⁲heit** *f* flightiness; absent-mindedness.

Zerˈfall *m* ruin, decay; ⚗ decomposition; *phys.* disintegration; **⁲en** (sn) fall to pieces *od.* into ruin, decay; collapse, crumble; *in s-e Bestandteile ~* disintegrate (*a. phys.*); *~ in mehrere Teile* fall (*od.* divide) into; *fig. ~ mit* fall out with; *~ sein mit* be at variance with; **~s-produkt** *n* disintegration product.

zerˈfetzen tear in (*od.* to) pieces, rend; *schlitzend*: slash; *in Stückchen*: shred; *s. zerfleischen.*

zerfleischen [~ˈflaɪʃən] (27) mangle; (*zerreißen*) lacerate; *in Stücke ~* tear to pieces.

zerˈfließen (sn) dissolve, melt (*fig. in Tränen* in tears); *Farbe, Tinte*: run; *Hoffnung usw.*: melt away.

zerˈfressen eat away; ⚗ *usw.* corrode.

zerˈgehen (sn) dissolve, melt.

zerˈglieder|n dismember; *anat.* dissect; *fig.* analy|se, *Am.* -ze; **⁲ung** *f* dismemberment; dissection; analysis.

zerˈhacken cut (in)to pieces; *Holz*: chop (up); *ganz fein*: mince.

zerˈhauen cut asunder *od.* to pieces.

zerˈkauen chew.

zerkleinern [~ˈklaɪnərn] (29) reduce to small pieces; *Holz*: chop (up); *Steine*: crush.

zerklüftet [~ˈklyftət] cleft, rugged.

zerknirsch|t [~ˈknirʃt] contrite; **⁲ung** *f* contrition.

zerˈknittern, zerˈknüllen (c)rumple, wrinkle, crease.

zerˈkochen *v/t. u. v/i.* (sn) cook to rags.

zerˈkratzen scratch.

zerˈlassen melt.

zerˈleg|en take apart; ⊕ *a.* dismantle; ⚕ dissect; *Braten*: carve; *fig.* analy|se, *Am.* -ze; ⚗ decompose; *in zwei Teile ~* divide in two; **⁲ung** *f* taking to pieces; carving; analysis; dissection; dismantling; decomposition.

zerˈlesen *adj.* well-thumbed.

zerlumpt [tsɛrˈlumpt] ragged, tattered.

zerˈmahlen grind.

zermalmen [~ˈmalmən] crush.

zerˈmartern torment; *sich den Kopf ~* rack one's brain.

zermürb|en [~ˈmyrbən] wear down *od.* out; **~end** gruelling, punishing; **⁲ung** *f* wearing down, attrition; **⁲ungskrieg** *m* war of attrition.

zerˈnagen gnaw (asunder); ⚗ *usw.* corrode.

zerˈpflücken pluck (*od. fig.* pull) to pieces.

zerˈplatzen (sn) burst.

zerˈquetschen crush, bruise, squash; *bsd. Kartoffeln*: mash.

Zerrbild [ˈtsɛr-] *n* caricature; *fig. a.* distorted picture.

zerˈreiben grind (*od.* rub) to powder, pulverize.

zerreiß|bar [tsɛrˈraɪs-] capable of being torn, tearable; **~en** *v/t.* tear (*a. v/i.*; sn), rend (*in Stücke* to pieces); (*trennen*) disconnect, disrupt; (*zerstückeln*) dismember; (*zerfleischen*) lacerate; *nur v/i. Faden, Nebel, Wolken*: break; **⁲festigkeit** *f* tensile strength; **⁲probe** *f fig.* gruel(l)ing test; **⁲ung** *f* rending, tearing, dismemberment; ⚕ rupture; laceration.

zerren [ˈtsɛrən] (25) tug, pull (*an dat.* at); (*schleppen*) drag; *Muskel, Sehne*: strain.

zerˈrinnen (sn) melt away; *fig. a.* vanish, dissolve.

zerrissen [tsɛrˈrisən] torn (*a. fig.*); **⁲heit** *f* (*Zerlumptheit*) raggedness; (*a. fig.*) disruption; *seelische*: inner strife.

ˈZerrspiegel *m* distorting mirror.

ˈZerrung ⚕ *f* strain.

zerrütt|en [tsɛrˈrytən] (26) disrupt; *e-e Einrichtung*: disorganize; (*ruinieren*) ruin, *Gesundheit, Nerven*: *a.* shatter; *den Geist*: unhinge, derange; *e-e Ehe*: wreck, break down; **⁲ung** *f* disruption; ruin; derangement; breakdown.

zerˈsägen saw up, saw to pieces.

zerˈschellen (25) *v/t.* smash (to pieces), shatter; *v/i.* (sn) be smashed, ⚓ be wrecked; ✈ crash.

zerˈschießen shoot to pieces, batter.

zerˈschlagen 1. *v/t.* smash (to pieces); *fig.* smash; *sich ~ fig.* come

to nothing; **2.** *adj.* battered; (*erschöpft*) knocked up.
zer'schmelzen melt (away).
zer'schmettern smash, shatter.
zer'schneiden cut to pieces.
zer'schrammen scratch.
zer'setz|en (*a. sich*) decompose, disintegrate (*a. fig.*); *fig.* undermine, demoralize; **2ung** *f* decomposition, disintegration; (*Zerfall*) decay; *pol.* subversion.
zer'spalten cleave, split.
zerspanen ⊕ [tsɛr'ʃpa:nən] cut.
zer'splittern *v/t.* split (up), splinter (*alle a. v/i.*; sn); *Truppen*: disperse; *Zeit, Kraft*: fritter away (*sich* one's powers).
zer'sprengen break, burst open; *Menge*: scatter, disperse, ⚔ rout.
zer'springen (sn) burst; *Glas*: crack; *fig. Kopf*: split.
zer'stampfen crush; *im Mörser*: pound; (*zertreten*) trample down.
zer'stäub|en pulverize; *Flüssigkeit*: spray; *fig.* disperse; **2er** *m* (7) *für Flüssigkeit*: sprayer, *bsd.* ⚕ atomizer; *für Parfüm*: scent-spray.
zer'stechen prick *od.* sting (all over); *v. Ungeziefer*: bite.
zer'stieben (sn) be scattered.
zerstör|bar [tsɛr'ʃtø:r-] destructible; **~en** destroy ruin, wreck (*alle a. fig.*); **2er** *m* (7) destroyer (*a.* ⚓); ✈ pursuit interceptor; **2ung** *f* destruction; **2ungs-trieb** *m* impulse to destroy; **2ungswut** *f* vandalism.
zer'stoßen bruise, break; *im Mörser*: pound; *zu Pulver*: powder.
zer'streu|en disperse, scatter (*beide a. sich*); *Bedenken*: dispel, dissipate; (*belustigen*) divert; **~t** scattered, dispersed; *Licht*: diffuse(d); *fig.* absent(-minded); **2t-heit** *f* absent-mindedness; **2ung** *f* dispersion; (*Erholung*) diversion; *s. Zerstreutheit.*
zerstückel|n [~'ʃtykəln] (29) cut up; *Körper*: dismember, *Land a.* (*parzellieren*) parcel out; **2ung** *f* dismemberment.
zer'teil|en (*a. sich*) divide (*in acc.* into); (*zerstreuen*) disperse; ⚗, ⚕ resolve; **2ung** *f* division; dispersion; ⚕, ⚗ resolution.
zer'trampeln trample down, crush underfoot.
zer'treten tread down; *Feuer, a. fig.* tread out; (*zermalmen*) crush.
zertrümmer|n [~'tryməm] (29) wreck, demolish, smash; **2ung** *f* demolition; smashing.
Zervelatwurst [tsɛrvə'la:t-] *f* saveloy.
zer'wühlen *Erdboden*: root up; *Haar*: dishevel; *a. Bett*: rumple.
Zerwürfnis [~'vyrfnis] *n* (4[1]) discord, disunion, quarrel.
zer'zaus|en rumple, tousle; *j-n*: pull about; **~t** *adj.* untidy; *Haar*: tousled.
Zession [tsɛ'sjo:n] *f* (16) assignment, transfer.
Zeter ['tse:tər] *n* (7, *o. pl.*): ~ *schreien* cry murder, raise a hue and cry; '**~geschrei** *n*, **~mordio** [~'mɔrdjo] *n* (11, *o. pl.*) loud outcry, clamo(u)r; '**2n** (29) (*lärmen*) clamo(u)r; (*schelten*) scold, nag.
Zettel ['tsɛtəl] *m* (7) slip (of paper); (*mit Notiz od. kurzer Mitteilung*) note; (*angeklebter od. angehängter ~ mit Angabe der Adresse, des Inhalts usw.*) ticket, label, (*Kleb2*) adhesive label, *Am.* sticker, (*Anhänge2*) tag; *zum Anschlagen*: placard, bill, poster; (*Hand2*) leaflet; '**~kasten**, '**~katalog** *m* card-index.
Zeug [tsɔyk] *n* (3) stuff (*a.* F *Alkohol usw.*), material; (*Tuch*) cloth; (*Handwerks2*) tools *pl.*; (*Sachen*) things *pl.*; (*schlechtes ~*) trash, (*a. dummes ~*) stuff, rubbish; *er hat das ~ zum Arzt* he has the makings of a doctor; F *was das ~ hält* hell for leather; *sich ins ~ legen* put one's back into it; *scharf ins ~ gehen* not to pull one's punches; *s. flicken.*
Zeuge ['tsɔygə] *m* (13) witness; **2n[1]** (25) *v/i.* ⚖ give evidence; *für* (*od. gegen od. von*) et. ~ testify for (*od.* against *od.* of) a th.; '**2n[2]** beget, procreate; *fig.* generate, produce.
'**Zeugen|-aussage** *f* testimony (of a witness), evidence; '**~bank** *f* witness-box, *Am.* witness stand; '**~beweis** *m* evidence; '**~-eid** *m* oath of a witness; '**~verhör** *n*, '**~vernehmung** *f* hearing of witnesses.
'**Zeughaus** ⚔ *n* arsenal.
Zeugin ['~gin] *f* (16[1]) (female) witness.
Zeugnis ['tsɔyknis] *n* (4[1]) ⚖ testimony, evidence; (*Bescheinigung*) certificate, testimonial; (*Schul2*) (term's) report; *zum ~* (*gen.*) in witness of; *~ ablegen od. geben* bear witness (*für* to; *von* of), testify (to).

Zeugung ['~guŋ] *f* generation, procreation; '**~s-akt** *m* reproductive act; '**2sfähig** capable of begetting; '**~s-kraft** *f* procreative capacity; '**~s-organe** *n/pl.* genital (*od.* reproductive) organs; '**2s-unfähig** sterile, impotent.

Zichorie [tsi'ço:rjə] *f* (15) chicory.

Zick|e ['tsikə] *f* (15) *s. Ziege*; '**~en** F *pl.*: *mach keine ~* stop being awkward; **2ig** F bitchy; '**~lein** *n* kid.

Zickzack ['tsiktsak] *m* (3) zigzag; '**~kurs** *m* zigzag course; '**~schere** *f* pinking shears *pl.*

Ziege ['tsi:gə] *f* (15) goat; *engS.* she-goat, nanny-goat; F bitch.

Ziegel ['tsi:gəl] *m* (7) brick; (*Dach2*) tile; **~brennerei** ['~'raɪ] *f*, **~ei** [~'laɪ] *f* (16) brickworks, brickyard; '**~dach** *n* tiled roof; '**~-ofen** *m* brick-kiln; '**2-rot** brick-red; '**~stein** *m* brick.

'**Ziegen|bart** *m* goat's beard; *v. Menschen*: goatee; '**~bock** *m* he-goat; '**~fell** *n* goatskin; '**~hirt** *m* goatherd; '**~käse** *m* goat-cheese; '**~leder** *n* kid(-leather); '**~milch** *f* goat's milk; '**~peter** ⚕ *m* mumps *sg.*

zieh [tsi:] *pret. v. zeihen.*

'**Zieh|bank** ⊕ *f* draw-bench; '**~brunnen** *m* draw-well.

ziehen ['tsi:ən] (30) **1.** *v/t.* pull, draw; *Linie, Los, Folgerung, Schluß, Waffe usw.*: draw (*a.* ✝ *Wechsel auf j-n* on); ⊕ draw; (*zerren*) drag; (*züchten*) ⚘ cultivate, grow, *zo.* breed; *beim Schach usw.*: move; *Gewehrlauf*: rifle; *Hut*: take off (*vor j-m* to); *Mauer*: build, erect; *Graben*: dig; *Zahn*: draw, pull, extract; *Schiff*: tow; *auf Draht ~* wire; *auf Fäden ~* thread; *auf Flaschen ~* bottle; *Blasen ~* raise blisters; *Wasser ~* leak; *e-n Vergleich ~* draw (*od.* make) a comparison; *j-n an den Haaren usw. ~* pull a p.'s hair *etc.*; *an sich ~* draw to one, *fig.* take hold of; *Aufmerksamkeit usw. auf sich ~* attract; *die Wurzel aus e-r Zahl ~* extract the root of a number; *et. nach sich ~* entail, involve; *s. Affäre, Bilanz, Erwägung, Fell Gesicht, kurz, Länge, Nutzen, Rat, Rechenschaft usw.*; **2.** *v/i.* (h. *u.* sn) pull (*an dat.* at); (*sich bewegen*) move, go; (*marschieren*) march; (*durch ein Dorf usw.*) *~* pass (through a village, etc.); (*Wohnung wechseln*) (re)move; *Vögel*: migrate; *Ofen, Pfeife usw.*: draw; *Schmerz*: twinge, ache; *an der Zigarette usw.*: (have a) drag (at); *Tee*: infuse, draw; *Theaterstück*: catch on, draw (large audiences); *Ware*: draw (custom), take; *dieser Grund zieht bei mir nicht* this reason does not weigh with me; *das* (*dieses Verhalten usw.*) *zieht bei mir nicht sl.* that cuts no ice with me; *es zieht* (*im Zimmer*) there is a draught; **3.** *v/refl. sich ~* extend, stretch; *Holz*: warp; *sich in die Länge ~* drag on; **4.** 2 *n* (6) drawing (*a.* ⊕); cultivation; breeding; (*Wandern, bsd. der Vögel*) migration; (*Schmerz*) twinge(s *pl.*).

'**Zieh|harmonika** *f* accordion; '**~kind** *n* foster-child; '**~ung** *f* drawing (*a.* ✝).

Ziel [tsi:l] *n* (3) aim; *fig. a.* end, object, target; ⚔ *taktisches*: objective; (*~punkt*) mark; *der Reise*: destination; *Sport*: finish(ing line); (*~scheibe*) target; *des Spottes*: butt; (*Termin*) term, ✝ credit; *Sport*: *durchs ~ gehen* finish *od.* come in (*als erster* first); *fig. sein ~ erreichen* gain one's end(s); *sich das ~ setzen od. stecken zu* (*inf.*) aim at (*ger. od.* to *inf.*); *über das ~ hinausschießen* overshoot the mark; *zum ~ führen* succeed; '**~band** *n Sport*: tape; '**2bewußt** purposeful, single-minded; systematic(ally *adv.*); '**2en** (25) (take) aim *od.* level (*auf acc.* at); *fig. ~ auf* (*acc.*) aim at; (*tendieren*) tend to; *fig. gezielt Maßnahme*: specific, carefully directed; '**~fernrohr** *n* telescopic sight; '**~gerade** *f Sport*: home stretch; '**~gruppe** *f* target group; '**~kamera** *f Sport*: photo-finish camera; '**~linie** *f* finishing line; '**2los** aimless; '**~punkt** *m* aiming point; *Sport u. fig.* goal; '**~richter** *m Sport*: judge; '**~scheibe** *f* target; *~ des Spottes* butt of derision, laughing-stock; '**~setzung** *f* object, target; '**2sicher** unerring; '**~sprache** *f* target language; **2strebig** ['~ʃtre:biç] *s. zielbewußt*; '**~strebigkeit** *f* single-mindedness.

ziemen ['tsi:mən] (25) (*a. sich*) *s. geziemen.*

Ziemer ['tsi:mər] *m* (7) (*Wildrücken*) saddle (of venison); (*Peitsche*) whip.

'**ziemlich 1.** *adj.* (*leidlich*) passable, tolerable; *e-e ~e Anzahl* a fair (*od.* good) number; *e-e ~e Strecke* a considerable distance, rather a long way; **2.** *adv.* pretty, fairly, tolerably, rather; (*ungefähr*) about; ~ *spät* rather late; *so* ~ *alles* practically everything; *so* ~ *dasselbe* pretty much (*od.* rather) the same thing.

Zier [tsiːr] *f* (16), **Zierat** [ˈtsiːraːt] *m* (3) ornament, decoration.

ˈ**Zier|de** *f* (15) ornament; *fig. a.* hono(u)r, credit (*für* to); ˈ**2en** (25) adorn, grace; (*verschönern*) embellish; (*schmücken*) decorate; *sich* ~ *fig.* be affected, *bsd. Frau*: be coy, (*Umstände machen*) stand on ceremony; (*sich sträuben*) refuse; **~erei** [~rəˈraɪ] *f* (16) affectation; ˈ**~fisch** *m* toy fish; ˈ**~garten** *m* flower garden; ˈ**~leiste** *f* mo(u)lding (*a. mot.*); ˈ**2lich** (*zart*) dainty, delicate; (*dünn*) slight; (*anmutig*) graceful; ˈ**~lichkeit** *f* daintiness, delicacy; gracefulness; ˈ**~pflanze** *f* ornamental plant.

Ziffer [ˈtsifər] *f* (15) figure, numeral; (*Schriftzeichen*) cipher; ˈ**~blatt** *n* dial(-plate), face.

zig F [tsiç] (*sehr viele*) umpteen.

Zigarette [tsigaˈrɛtə] *f* (15) cigarette, *Am. a.* cigaret; **~n-anzünder** *mot. m* (7) cigarette lighter; **~n-automat** *m* cigarette slot-machine; **~n-etui** *n* cigarette-case; **~npapier** *n* cigarette paper; **~nschachtel** *f* cigarette packet; **~nspitze** *f* cigarette-holder; **~n-stummel** *m* cigarette-end, stub.

Zigarillo [~ˈrilo] *m* (11) cigarillo, small cigar.

Zigarre [tsiˈgarə] *f* (15) cigar; **~n-abschneider** *m* cigar-cutter; **~n-händler** *m* tobacconist; **~nkiste** *f* cigar-box; **~nladen** *m* tobacconist's (shop), *Am.* cigar store; **~nspitze** *f* cigar-holder; (*spitzes Ende e-r Zigarre*) cigar-tip; **~nstummel** *m* cigar-end, butt.

Zigeuner [tsiˈgɔʏnər] *m* (7), **~in** *f* (16[1]) gipsy, *bsd. Am.* gypsy.

Zikade [tsiˈkaːdə] *f* (15) cicada.

Zimmer [ˈtsimər] *n* (7) room; ˈ**~-antenne** *f Radio*: indoor aerial (*Am.* antenna); ˈ**~-einrichtung** *f* furnishing; (*Möbel*) furniture; (*Innenausstattung*) interior (decoration); ˈ**~flucht** *f* suite of rooms; ˈ**~-genosse** *m* room-mate; ˈ**~handwerk** *n* carpenter's trade, carpentry.

...zimmerig ...-roomed.

ˈ**Zimmer|mädchen** *n im Hotel*: chamber-maid; ˈ**~mann** *m* carpenter; ˈ**~meister** *m* master carpenter; ˈ**2n** (29) *v/t.* make *od.* build (of wood); *beruflich*: carpenter (*a. v/i.*); *fig.* frame; ˈ**~nachweis** *m* accommodation bureau; ˈ**~pflanze** *f* indoor plant; ˈ**~reservierung** *f* room reservation(s *pl.*); ˈ**~service** *m im Hotel*: room service; ˈ**~temperatur** *f* room temperature; ˈ**~theater** *n* little thea|tre, *Am.* -er; ˈ**~vermittlung** *f s. Zimmernachweis.*

zimperlich [ˈtsimpərliç] prim; (*prüde*) prudish; (*geziert*) affected; (*heikel, bsd. beim Essen*) squeamish; (*empfindlich*) (super-)sensitive, soft; (*allzu sanft, vorsichtig*) dainty; ˈ**2-keit** *f* primness; prudery; affectation; squeamishness; sensitiveness; daintiness.

Zimt [tsimt] *m* (3) cinnamon; F *fig.* [*s. Quatsch.*]

Zink [tsiŋk] *n* (3) zinc; ˈ**~blech** *n* sheet zinc; *grobes*: zinc-plate.

Zinke [ˈtsiŋkə] *f* (15) prong, tine; *e-s Kammes*: tooth; ˈ**~n** *m* (6) *s. Zinke*; F *co.* (*Nase*) beak, snozzle.

...zinkig ...-pronged.

Zinn [tsin] *n* (3) tin; (*Material für Hausgerät*) pewter.

Zinne [ˈtsinə] *f* (15) △ pinnacle; ⚔ (*Mauer2*) battlement.

ˈ**zinne(r)n** tin; pewter.

ˈ**Zinngeschirr** *n* pewter.

Zinnober [tsiˈnoːbər] *m* (7) cinnabar; F *s. Quatsch*; **2rot** vermilion.

Zins [tsins] *m* (5[1] *u.* [3]; *Mieten* 4) (*Miete, Pacht*) rent; (*Abgabe*) tribute; (*Geld2, mst* ~*en* [ˈ~zən] *pl.*) interest; ~*en tragen* yield (*od.* bear) interest; ˈ**2bar,** ˈ**2bringend** bearing interest, interest-bearing; ~ *anlegen* put out at interest; ˈ**~-erhöhung** *f* increase in interest rates; **~eszins** [ˈ~zəs-] *m* compound interest; ˈ**~fuß** *m* rate of interest; ˈ**2los** interest-free; ˈ**2pflichtig** tributary; ˈ**~rechnung** *f* calculation of interest; *konkret*: interest-account; ˈ**~satz** *m* rate of interest; ˈ**~schein** *m* coupon; *für Aktien*: dividend-warrant; ˈ**~-senkung** *f* lowering of interest rates.

Zionis|mus [tsioˈnismus] *m* (16, *o. pl.*) Zionism; **~t** *m* (12), **~tin** *f* (16[1]), **2tisch** Zionist.

Zipfel [ˈtsipfəl] *m* (7) tip, point; (*Taschentuch2 usw.*) corner; (*Rock2*) lappet; ˈ**~mütze** *f* pointed cap.

zirka [ˈtsirka] about, approximately; ˈ**2preis** *m* tentative price.

Zirkel ['tsirkəl] *m* (7) (*Kreis*) circle (*a. fig.*); (*Gerät*) (ein a pair of) compasses *pl.*, (*Stech*≈) dividers *pl.*; '≈**n** (29) measure with compasses.
Zirku|lar [tsirku'la:r] *n* (3[1]) circular; **~lation** [~la'tsjo:n] *f* (16) circulation; ≈'**lieren** circulate (*a.* ~ *lassen*).
Zirkumflex [tsirkum'flɛks] *m* (3[2]) circumflex.
Zirkus ['tsirkus] *m* (*inv.*, *pl. a.* 4[1]) circus; '**~reiter(in** *f*) *m* circus-rider.
zirpen ['~pən] *v/i. u. v/t.* (25) chirp.
zisch|eln[1] ['tsiʃəln] *v/i. u. v/t.* (29) hiss, whisper; '≈**eln[2]** *n* hiss(ing), whisper(ing); '**~en** (27) hiss; (*schwirren*) whiz(z); '≈**laut** *m* hissing sound; *gr.* sibilant.
Ziselier|-arbeit [tsize'li:r-] *f* chased work; ≈**en** chase.
Zisterne [tsi'stɛrnə] *f* (15) cistern.
Zitadelle [tsita'dɛlə] *f* (15) citadel.
Zitat [tsi'ta:t] *n* (3) quotation.
Zither ♪ ['tsitər] *f* (15) zither.
zitieren [tsi'ti:rən] cite, quote; (*vorladen*) summon, cite.
Zitronat [tsitro'na:t] *n* (3) candied (lemon-)peel.
Zitrone [~'tro:nə] *f* (15) lemon; **~nfalter** *m* brimstone; **~nlimonade** *f* lemonade; *mit Sodawasser*: lemon soda; **~npresse** *f* lemon-squeezer; **~nsaft** *m* lemon juice; **~nsäure** *f* citric acid; **~nschale** *f* lemon-peel; **~nwasser** *n s. Zitronenlimonade.*
zitt(e)rig ['tsit(ə)riç] shaky.
zitter|n ['tsitərn] (29) tremble, shake (*vor* [*dat.*] *Kälte, Furcht, Erregung usw.* with); *Laub, Stimme usw.*: quiver; (*schaudern*) shiver; (*vibrieren*) vibrate; '≈**pappel** *f* (quaking) aspen, trembling poplar.
Zitze ['tsitsə] *f* (15) teat, dug.
zivil [tsi'vi:l] **1.** civil; (*Ggs. militärisch*) civilian; *Preise*: moderate, reasonable; **2.** ≈ *n* (3[1], *o. pl.*) (*Ggs. Militär*) civilians *pl.*; (*Ggs. Uniform*) civilian (*od.* plain) clothes *pl.*, *sl.* mufti, civ(v)ies *pl.*; ≈**bevölkerung** *f* civilian population, civilians *pl.*; ≈**courage** *f* (15) courage of one's opinions, moral courage; ≈**dienst** *m* community service; ≈**-ehe** *f* civil marriage; ≈**fahnder** *m* (7) *der Polizei*: plainclothes policeman; ≈**gericht** *n* civil court; ≈**isation** [~viliza'tsjo:n] *f* civilization; **~isatorisch** [~'to:riʃ] civilizing; **~i'sieren** civilize; ≈**ist** [~'list] *m* (12) civilian; ≈**kleidung** [~'vi:l-] *f* civilian (*od.* plain) clothes *pl.*; ≈**luftfahrt** *f* civil aviation; ≈**prozeß** ⚖ *m* civil action *od.* suit *od.* case; ≈**prozeß-ordnung** *f* Code of Civil Procedure; ≈**recht** *n* civil law; **~rechtlich** civil law ...; *adv.* under (*od.* according to) civil law; ≈**regierung** *f* civilian government.
Zobel ['tso:bəl] *m* (7) *zo.* sable; *a.* = '**~fell** *n* sable-skin; '**~pelz** *m* sable-fur.
Zofe ['tso:fə] *f* (15) lady's maid.
zog [tso:k] *pret. v. ziehen* 1., 2., 3.
zöger|n[1] ['tsø:gərn] (29) hesitate; (*sich aufhalten*) linger; (*Zeit verlieren*) delay; ~ *mit* defer, delay; '≈**n[2]** *n* (6), '≈**ung** *f* hesitation; (*Verzögerung*) delay; '**~nd** hesitating; (*langsam*) slow.
Zögling ['tsø:kliŋ] *m* (3[1]) pupil.
Zölibat [tsøli'ba:t] *m*, *n* (3) celibacy.
Zoll [tsɔl] *m* **1.** (*als Maß im pl. nach Zahlen inv.*) inch; **2.** (*Abgabe*) customs *pl.*, duty; *a.* = *~behörde*; (*Brückenzoll usw.*) toll; (*Zins*; *a. fig.*) tribute; '**~-abfertigung** *f* customs clearance; '**~-amt** *n* custom-house; '**~be-amte** *m* customs officer; '**~behörde** *f* Customs *pl.*, customs authorities *pl.*; '≈**en** (25) *fig.* give, pay; '**~-erklärung** *f* customs declaration; '**~fahnder(in** *f*) *m* customs investigator; '≈**frei** duty-free; '**~gebühren** *f/pl.* customs duties; **~grenzbezirk** *m* customs control area; '**~grenze** *f* customs frontier; '**~haus** *n* custom-house; '**~hinterziehung** *f* evasion of customs duties.
...zöllig [-tsœliç] ...-inch.
'**Zoll|kontrolle** *f* customs examination; '**~krieg** *m* tariff war.
Zöllner ['tsœlnər] *m* (7) customs collector; *Bibel*: publican.
'**zoll|pflichtig** dutiable; '≈**plombe** *f* customs seal; '≈**schein** *m* customs receipt, (bill of) clearance; '≈**schranke** *f* customs barrier; '≈**speicher** *m* bonded warehouse; '≈**stock** *m* foot-rule, folding rule, yard-stick; '≈**tarif** *m* customs tariff; ≈**-union** ['~unjo:n] *f* customs (*od.* tariff) union; '≈**verschluß** *m* customs seal, bond; *unter* ~ bonded; *unter* ~ *lassen* leave in bond; '≈**vorschriften** *f/pl.* customs regulations.

Zone [ˈtsoːnə] *f* (15) *allg.* zone; ˈ**~ngrenze** *f* zonal border.

Zoo [tsoː] *m* (*inv. abbr. für Zoologischer Garten*) Zoo, *abbr. für* Zoological Gardens.

Zoolog|e [tsoˀoˈloːgə] *m* (13) zoologist; **~ie** [~loˈgiː] *f* (15) zoology; **≗isch** [~ˈloːgiʃ] zoological.

Zopf [tsɔpf] *m* (3³) plait (of hair), tress; *der Männer*: pigtail; *fig.* (*alter*) ~ antiquated custom; *sie trägt Zöpfe* she wears her hair plaited *od.* in plaits; ˈ**≗ig** *fig.* pedantic(ally *adv.*); (*altmodisch*) old-fashioned; ˈ**~muster** *n* cable stitch.

Zorn [tsɔrn] *m* (3) anger, *rhet.* wrath; (*Wut*) rage; *in ~ geraten* fly into a passion; ˈ**≗-entbrannt** boiling with rage, furious; ˈ**≗ig** angry (*auf et.* at, *j-n* with); furious (at).

Zote [ˈtsoːtə] *f* (15) smutty joke, obscenity; *~n reißen* talk smut; ˈ**≗nhaft**, ˈ**zotig** obscene, smutty; ˈ**~nreißer** *m* obscene talker.

Zott|e [ˈtsɔtə] *f*, ˈ**~el** *f* (15) tuft (of hair); ˈ**≗eln** *v/i.* toddle; ˈ**≗ig** shaggy.

zu [tsuː] **1.** *prp. Bewegung*: to; towards; (*bis ~*) up to; *Ruhe*: at; in; on; *hinzufügend, -tretend*: in addition to; (*zusammen mit*) along with; (*neben*) beside, next to; *Zweckangabe*: for; *~ Berlin* in (*amtlich*: at) Berlin; *~ Beginn* at the beginning *od.* outset; *~ meinem Erstaunen usw.* to my astonishment *etc.*; *~ e-m ... Preise* at a ... price; *Sport*: *mit 2 ~ 3* by 2 points to 3; *zum Schluß möchte ich ...* in conclusion I should like to ...; *der Schlüssel zum Schrank* the key of the cupboard; *j-n ~m Präsidenten wählen* elect a p. President; *sich ~ j-m setzen* sit down by a p.'s side; *~ Weihnachten usw.* at Christmas *etc.*; *~ zweien usw.* by twos *etc.*; *s. Beispiel, Bett, Hand usw.*; **2.** *adv.* **a**) *vor adj. u. adv.*: too; *~ sehr* too much; *gar ~* far too; **b**) *Richtung bezeichnend*: towards, to; *nach Norden ~* towards the north; **c**) (*Ggs. offen*) closed; *Tür ~!* shut the door!; *die Tür ist ~* is to *od.* shut; **d**) *immer* (*od. nur*) *~!* go on!

zualler|erst [~ˀalərˈˀeːrst] first of all; **~ˈletzt** last of all.

ˈ**zubauen** build (*od.* wall) up *od.* in; (*versperren, a. Aussicht*) block.

Zubehör [ˈ~bəhøːr] *n, a. m* (3) appurtenances (*a.* ⚖), fittings, *Am.* F fixings, *bsd.* ⊕ accessories (*alle pl.*); *Sechszimmerwohnung mit ~* six-roomed flat (*Am.* apartment) with all conveniences; ˈ**~teil** *n* accessory (part).

ˈ**zubeißen** bite; *Hund*: snap (at).

ˈ**zubekommen** get in addition; *Tür usw.*: get *a th.* shut.

Zuber [ˈtsuːbər] *m* (7) tub.

ˈ**zubereit|en** *allg.* prepare; *Medizin*: dispense; ⊕, *Salat usw.* dress; *Speise a.* cook; ˈ**≗ung** *f* preparation.

ˈ**zubilligen** grant, concede, allow; (*zusprechen*) award (*dat.* to).

ˈ**zubinden** tie (*od.* bind) up; *j-m die Augen ~* blindfold.

ˈ**zubleiben** (sn) remain closed *od.* shut.

ˈ**zublinzeln** *j-m*: wink at a p.

ˈ**zubring|en** *Zeit*: pass, spend; ⊕ *Material usw.*: feed; ˈ**≗er** ⊕ *m* (7) feeder; ˈ**≗erbus** *m* shuttle bus; ˈ**≗erstraße** *f* feeder road.

Zucchini [tsuˈkiːni] *f* (11¹, *p.* -*i*) courgette.

Zucht [tsuxt] *f* (16) (*Tätigkeit*) breeding, rearing, farming; *von Kleinwesen* (*Bienen usw.*): culture; *von Pflanzen*: cultivation; (*Rasse*) breed, race; (*gezüchtete Bakterien*) culture; (*Erziehung*) education, training; (*harte ~*) drill; (*Mannes≗ usw.*) discipline; (*Züchtigkeit*) propriety, modesty; ˈ**~buch** *n* stud-book; ˈ**~bulle** *m s. Zuchtstier.*

z|ücht|en [ˈtsyçtən] (26) *Tiere*: breed; *Pflanzen*: grow, cultivate; *Bakterien, Perlen*: culture; ˈ**≗er** *m* (7), ˈ**≗erin** *f* (16¹) *von Vieh*: breeder; *von Bienen*: keeper; *von Pflanzen*: grower.

ˈ**Zucht|haus** *n* penitentiary; (*~strafe*) penal servitude; **~häusler** [ˈ~hɔʏslər] *m* (7) convict; ˈ**~hengst** *m* stud-horse, stallion.

züchtig [ˈtsyçtiç] chaste, modest; **~en** [ˈ~gən] (25) correct, punish; *körperlich*: cane, flog, *rhet.* chastise; ˈ**≗keit** *f* chastity, modesty; ˈ**≗ung** *f* correction, punishment; flogging.

ˈ**zucht|los** undisciplined, without discipline; (*liederlich*) disorderly; ˈ**≗losigkeit** *f* want of discipline; disorderly ways *pl.*; ˈ**≗meister** *m* task-master; ˈ**≗mittel** *n* disciplinary measure; ˈ**≗perle** *f* culture pearl; ˈ**≗rute** *f* rod of correction; ˈ**≗sau** *f* brood-sow; ˈ**≗schaf** *n* ewe

(for breeding); '≗**stier** *m* bull (for breeding); '≗**stute** *f* stock mare.
'**Züchtung** *f von Tieren*: breeding; *von Pflanzen*: growing, cultivation.
'**Zucht|vieh** *n* cattle for breeding; '~**wahl** *f* (natural) selection.
zucken ['tsukən] (25) jerk; *krampfhaft*: move convulsively *od.* suddenly, twitch (*alle*: *mit* et. a th.); *vor Schmerzen*: wince; *Blitz*: flash; *s. Achsel, Wimper.*
zücken ['tsykən] (25) draw.
Zucker ['tsukər] *m* (7) sugar; ⚕ *er hat* ~ he is suffering from diabetes; '~**bäcker** *m* confectioner; '~**büchse,** '~**dose** *f* sugar-basin, *Am.* -bowl; '~-**erbse** ⚘ *f* green pea; '~-**fabrik** *f* sugar factory; '~**guß** *m* (sugar-)icing, frosting, sugar-coating; '~**hut** *m* sugar-loaf; '≗**ig** sugary; '≗**krank,** '~**kranke** *m, f* diabetic; '~**krankheit** *f* diabetes; '≗**n** (29) sugar; '~**rohr** *n* sugar-cane; '~-**rübe** *f* sugar-beet; '~**schale** *f s. Zukkerbüchse*; '~**sirup** *m* molasses *pl.*, treacle; '≗'**süß** (as) sweet as sugar; *fig.* honeyed; '~**wasser** *n* sugared water; '~**watte** *f* candy floss; '~**werk** *n* confectionery, sweetmeats *pl.*, *Am.* candy; '~**würfel** *m* sugar lump; '~-**zange** *f* (*eine* a pair of) sugar-tongs *pl.*
'**Zuckung** *f* convulsion, spasm.
'**zudämmen** dam up.
'**zudecken** cover (up).
zudem [tsu'de:m] besides, moreover.
'**zudenken:** *j-m* et. ~ intend a th. *as a present etc.* for a p.
'**zudiktieren** *Strafe*: impose, inflict (*j-m* [up]on a p.).
'**Zudrang** *m* rush; run (*zu* on).
'**zudrehen** *Wasserhahn usw.*: turn off; *j-m den Rücken* ~ turn one's back on a p.
'**zudringlich** importunate, obtrusive; '≗**keit** *f* importunity, obtrusiveness.
'**zudrücken** close, shut; *s. Auge.*
zueign|en ['~ʔaɪgnən] *Buch*: dedicate (*dat.* to); '≗**ung** *f* dedication.
'**zu-eilen** (sn; *dat.*; *auf acc.*) hasten to *od.* towards, run up to.
'**zu-erkenn|en** award, adjudge (*dat.* to); '≗**ung** *f* award.
zu'-erst [tsu-] (*als erste[r, s]*; *zunächst*) first; (*anfangs*) at first; *fig. wer* ~ *kommt, mahlt* ~ first come first served.
'**zu-erteilen** *s. zuteilen, zuerkennen.*
'**zufahr|en** (sn) drive on; *auf et.* ~ drive to(wards).
'**Zufahrt** *f* approach, access; '~**s-straße** *f* approach (road).
'**Zufall** *m* chance, accident; (*Zs.-treffen*) coincidence; *glücklicher* ~ lucky chance, fluke; *unglücklicher* ~ unfortunate accident; *durch* ~ *s. zufällig* (*adv.*); '≗**en** (sn) *Augen*: be closing; *Tür*: slam shut; *j-m* ~ fall to a p.('s share), *Aufgabe*: fall to a p., *a. Erbe*: devolve upon a p.
'**zufällig** accidental; *nur attr.* chance; fortuitous; (*gelegentlich*) casual; *adv.* accidentally, by chance; *er war* ~(*erweise*) *zu Hause* he happened to be at home; '≗**keit** *f* accidentalness; casualness; fortuitousness; contingency.
'**Zufalls|bekanntschaft** *f* chance acquaintance; '~**treffer** *m* fluke; *Sport*: chance goal.
'**zufassen** (make a) grab; *Hund*: snap; *helfend* (*mit*) ~ lend (*od.* give) a hand; *fig.* (*die Gelegenheit wahrnehmen*) seize the opportunity.
'**zufliegen** (sn; *dat.*; *auf acc.*) fly to(wards); *Tür*: slam (shut), bang.
'**zufließen** (sn; *dat.*) flow to(wards); *fig. j-m*: come to; *j-m* ~ *lassen* grant (to), let *a p.* have.
'**Zuflucht** *f* refuge, shelter, resort; *s-e* ~ *zu et. nehmen* take refuge to, have recourse to, resort to; '~**s-ort** *m* place of refuge, asylum.
'**Zufluß** *m* afflux; (*Einströmen*) influx (*a. fig. Kapital usw.*); (*Nebenfluß*) affluent; ⚚ supply.
'**zuflüstern** *j-m*: whisper to.
zu'folge [tsu-] (*gen. u. dat.*) as a result of, owing to; (*kraft*) on the strength of; (*gemäß, laut*) according to.
zu'frieden content(ed), satisfied, pleased; *j-n* ~ *lassen* let a p. alone; *sich* ~**geben** (*mit*) content o.s. (with); ≗**heit** *f* contentment, satisfaction; ~**stellen** satisfy; ~**stellend** satisfactory; ≗**stellung** *f* satisfaction.
'**zufrieren** (sn) freeze up *od.* over.
'**zufügen** add; (*antun*) do, cause; *Böses, Verluste*: *a.* inflict (*j-m* [up]on a p.).
Zufuhr ['~fu:r] *f* (16) *allg.* supply; (*Versorgungsgüter*) supplies *pl.*; *s. a. Zuführung.*
'**zuführ|en** carry, convey, lead,

bring; ⊕ feed; *Versorgungsgüter, Ware, a.* ⊕: supply; (*liefern*) deliver; ⚡ *Draht*: lead in; '**2ung** *f* conveyance; ⊕ feeding, (*Maschinenteil*) feed; *a.* ☤ supply, delivery; ⚡ (*Drahtleitung*) lead.

'**zufüllen** add; *Loch usw.*: fill up.

Zug [tsu:k] *m* (3³) draw(ing); *a. allg. Sport*: pull; (*Ruck*) jerk; ⊕ traction, (*Spannung*) tension; (*Fisch*2) draught; (*Marsch*) march; (*Fest*2, *Um*2) procession; (*Berg*2) range; (*Eisenbahn*2) train; (*Feder*2) stroke, dash; (*Feld*2) expedition (*a. Forschungs*2), campaign; (*Kolonne*) column; (*Gesichts*2) feature; (*Wesens*2) trait, feature, characteristic; (*Neigung, Hang*) bent, tendency, trend; ⚔ platoon; (*Zugluft, a. im Ofen*) draught, *Am. a.* draft; (*Kamin, Heizrohr*) flue; (*Orgel*2) stop, register; (*Schach*2 *usw.*) move; *beim Trinken*: draught; *beim Rauchen*: drag, puff; *der Vögel*: passage, flight, migration; *im Gewehr*: groove, *pl.* Züge rifling; ~ der Zeit trend of the times; ~ des Herzens promptings *pl.* of one's heart; auf einen ~ *beim Trinken*: at one draught; im ~e (*im Gang*) in train, in progress; im ~e der Neugestaltung *usw.* in the course of the reorganization *etc.*; im besten ~ in full swing, *P.*: going strong; in einem ~e at a stretch; in kurzen Zügen in brief outlines; in den letzten Zügen liegen be breathing one's last, *fig. S.*: be fizzling out; in vollen Zügen genießen enjoy thoroughly; *fig.* er kam nicht zum ~e he did not get a chance.

'**Zugabe** *f* addition; extra; *zum Gewicht*: makeweight; *thea.* encore; als ~ into the bargain.

'**Zugang** *m* access (*a. fig.*); (*Tor*) gate(way *a. fig.*); (*Weg*) approach; (*Eingang*) entrance, entry; (*Zunahme*) increase (zu of); ☤ (*Einnahmen*) receipts *pl.*; (*Ware*) arrivals *pl.*; *v. Büchern, Personal usw.*: accession(s *pl.*).

zugänglich ['~gɛŋliç] accessible (für to; *a. fig.* für Gründe *usw.*); *fig. a.* amenable (to); *fig.* (*umgänglich*) approachable, get-at-able.

'**Zugbrücke** *f* drawbridge.

'**zugeben** add; ☤ give into the bargain; (*zulassen*) tolerate; (*eingestehen*) confess; (*einräumen*) concede, admit, grant, allow; zugegeben granted; ♪ ein Lied ~ give a song as an extra (treat.)

zu'gegen [tsu-] present (bei at).

'**zugehen** (sn) (*sich schließen*) close, shut; (*weiter- od. schneller gehen*) move on, walk faster; (*geschehen*) happen; auf j-n ~ go up to, go *od.* walk towards; *Brief, Ware usw.*: j-m ~ come to a p.'s hand, reach a p.; j-m e-e Sendung ~ lassen forward to a p.; wie geht es zu, daß ...? how is it that ...?; *s.* hergehen, Ding.

'**zugehören** (*dat.*) belong to.

'**zugehörig** (*dat.*) belonging to *a p. od. a th.*; appertaining to *a th.*; '**2keit** *f* membership (zu e-m *Verein* of); belonging (to); affiliation (to).

Zügel ['tsy:gəl] *m* (7) rein; *bsd. des Reitpferdes*: bridle; *fig.* bridle, rein, curb; *fig.* die ~ schießen lassen (*dat.*) give the rein(s) to; '**2los** unbridled, *fig. a.* unrestrained; (*ausschweifend*) licentious; '**~losigkeit** *f* licentiousness; '**2n** (29) rein, pull up; *fig.* rein, curb, check.

'**zugesellen** (*a.* sich) associate (*dat.* with), join *a p.*

'**Zuge|ständnis** *n* concession, admission; '**2stehen** concede, admit.

'**zugetan** (*dat.*) attached to, devoted to; fond of.

'**Zug|festigkeit** *f* tensile strength; '**~führer** *m* 🚂 chief guard, *Am.* conductor; ⚔ platoon-leader.

'**zugießen** add.

zugig ['tsu:giç] draughty, *Am.* drafty.

'**Zug|kraft** *f* tractive power, tensile force; *fig.* attraction, draw; '**2kräftig** *fig.* attractive; ~ sein be a draw.

zu'gleich at the same time; together.

'**Zug|luft** *f* draught, *Am. a.* draft; '**~maschine** *f* prime mover; tractor; '**~mittel** *n fig.* draw, attraction; '**~nummer** *thea. f* drawing card; '**~personal** *n* train staff; '**~pferd** *n* draught- (*Am.* draft) horse; '**~pflaster** *n* blistering plaster.

'**zugreifen** *s.* zufassen; *bei Tisch*: help o.s.; *fig.* seize the opportunity; (*stramm arbeiten*) put one's back into it.

'**Zugriff** *m* grip (*a. fig.*); *Computer*: access; '**~szeit** *f Computer*: access time.

zugrunde [tsu'grundə]: ~ gehen *fig.*

go to ruin, perish; ~ *legen* take as a basis (*dat.* for); *e-r Sache ~ liegen* underlie a th., be at the bottom of a th.; *~liegend* underlying; *~ richten* ruin, destroy, wreck.

'**Zug|schalter** *m* pull switch; '**~seil** *n* towing-line; traction-rope; '**~stück** *n* draw, *Am.* hit; '**~tier** *n* draught (*Am.* draft) animal.

'**zugucken** F (25) *s. zuschauen.*

'**Zug-unglück** *n* train accident.

zugunsten [tsu'gunstən] (*gen.*) in favo(u)r of, for the benefit of.

zu'gute: *j-m et. ~ halten* give a p. credit for a th., (*verzeihen*) pardon a p. a th.; *j-m sein Alter ~ halten* make allowance for a p.'s age; *~ kommen* (*dat.*) be an advantage to, stand *a p.* in good stead; *j-m et. ~ kommen lassen* give a p. the benefit of a th.; *sich et. ~ tun auf e-e S.* pride (*od.* preen) o.s. on a th.

zuguter'letzt in the end; (*endlich*) at long last.

'**Zug|verkehr** *m* train service; railway traffic; '**~vieh** *n* draught- (*Am.* draft) cattle; '**~vogel** *m* bird of passage, migrant (bird); '**~wind** *m s. Zugluft.*

'**zuhaben** keep (*od.* have) ... shut *od.* closed *od.* (*Kleid*) buttoned up.

'**zuhalten** *v/t.* keep ... shut; *Ohren*: stop; *v/i. auf et.* (*acc.*) ~ make for a th.

Zuhälter ['~hɛltər] *m* (7) souteneur (*fr.*), *sl.* pimp.

'**zuhängen** hang (*od.* cover) with curtains *etc.*

'**zuhauen** *v/i.* strike; *v/t.* (*behauen*) rough-hew; dress, trim.

Zuhause [tsu'hauzə] *n* (10, *o. pl.*) home.

zuheften ['tsu:-] stitch up.

'**zuheilen** (sn) heal up.

Zuhilfenahme [tsu'hilfənɑ:mə] *f*: *unter ~ von* by (*od.* with) the aid of.

zu'hinterst last of all, at the end.

zuhören ['tsu:-] (*dat.*) listen (to).

'**Zuhörer** *m*, '**~in** *f* listener, hearer; '**~raum** *m* auditorium; '**~schaft** *f* audience.

'**zujauchzen**, '**zujubeln** (*dat.*) shout to, cheer; *a. fig.* hail.

'**zukaufen** buy in addition.

'**zukehren** (*dat.*) turn to(wards); *j-m den Rücken ~ s. zudrehen.*

'**zuklappen** shut; close with a snap.

'**zukleben** paste (*od.* glue) up.

'**zuklinken** (25) latch.

'**zuknallen** *Tür usw.*: bang, slam (to).

'**zuknöpfen** button (up); *fig. er ist sehr zugeknöpft* he is very reserved.

'**zuknüpfen** tie (up).

'**zukommen** (sn) *auf j-n*: come up to a p.; *j-m ~* (*Brief usw.*) reach a p., (*zuteil werden*) fall to a p.'s share, (*gebühren*) be due to a p.; *das kommt ihm nicht zu* he has no right to (do) that; *j-m et. ~ lassen* let a p. have a th.; send a p. a th.

'**zukorken** (25) cork (up).

Zukunft ['tsu:kunft] *f* (16, *o. pl.*) future, *a.* time to come; *gr.* future (tense); *in ~* in future; *was die ~ j-m bringt* what the future has in store for a p.; *der Mann der ~* the coming man.

'**zukünftig** future; *meine ♀e, mein ♀er* my intended; *adv.* in future.

'**Zukunfts|forscher** *m* futurologist; '**~forschung** *f* futurology; '**~musik** *f fig.* dreams *pl.* of the future; '**♀-orientiert** future-oriented; '**~pläne** *m/pl.* plans for the future; '**♀reich** with a great future; promising; '**~roman** *m* science fiction novel.

'**zulächeln** (*dat.*) smile at *od.* (up)on.

'**Zulage** *f* additional allowance; extra pay; (*Gehaltserhöhung*) rise, *Am.* raise.

zulande [tsu'landə]: *bei uns ~* in my *od.* our country.

'**zulangen** *v/i. bei Tisch*: help o.s.; (*genügen*) be enough *od.* sufficient.

zulänglich ['tsu:lɛŋliç] sufficient, adequate; '**♀keit** *f* sufficiency.

'**zulassen** *Tür usw.*: leave shut; *j-n*: admit; *behördlich*: license; (*geschehen lassen*) allow, suffer; *Deutung, Zweifel*: admit of.

'**zulässig** admissible, permissible, allowable; *das ist* (*nicht*) ~ that is (not) allowed; '**♀keit** *f* admissibility.

'**Zulassung** *f* admission; permission; *amtliche*: licen|ce, *Am.* -se; '**~s-nummer** *mot. f* registration number; '**~s-papiere** *n/pl.* registration papers.

'**Zulauf** *m* (*Andrang*) rush (of people); ⊕ feed, supply, intake; *großen ~ haben* be much sought after, *Theaterstück*: be very popular, draw large crowds; '**♀en** (sn) (*weiter od. schneller laufen*) run on *od.* faster; *j-m in Massen*: crowd (*od.* flock) to; *Hund usw.*: stray (to);

auf j-n ~ run up to; *s. spitz*; *zugelaufener Hund* stray dog.

'**zulegen** add (*dat.* to); *e-m Gehalt et.* ~ increase a salary by; *sich et.* ~ get (o.s.), (*kaufen*) buy.

zuleide [tsu'laɪdə]: *j-m et.* ~ *tun* do a p. harm, harm (*od.* hurt) a p.; *was hat er Ihnen* ~ *getan?* what (harm) has he done you?

zuleit|en ['tsu:-] ⊕ supply, feed; (*dat.*) conduct (*od.* lead *od.* direct) to; (*weitergeben*) pass (*od.* forward, transmit) to *a p.*; '**ↇung** *f* supply; transmittal; ⚡ lead; '**ↇungsrohr** *n* supply (*od.* feed) pipe.

zu'letzt [tsu-] finally, at last; (*als letzter*) last; *bis* ~ *bleiben* sit it out.

zu'liebe: *j-m* ~ for a p.'s sake.

'**Zuliefer|ant** *m*, '**~er** *m* (7) supplier.

zulöten ['tsu:-] solder up.

zum [tsum] = *zu dem*; *s. zu, Teil.*

'**zumachen** *v/t.* shut, close; *Loch*: stop up; *Jacke*: button (up), do up; (*fest* ~) fasten; *v/i.* F *mach zu!* hurry up!

zumal [tsu'ma:l] *cj.* ~ (*da od. weil*) *negativ*: the less so since; *positiv*: especially since.

zumauern ['tsu:-] wall up.

zumeist [tsu'maɪst] mostly.

zumessen ['tsu:-] *j-m s-n Teil, e-e Zeit*: apportion, allot.

zumindest [tsu'mindəst] at least.

zu'mute: *mir ist gut od. schlecht od. eigentümlich* ~ I feel well *od.* ill *od.* queer; *mir ist nicht danach* (*nach Lachen*) ~ I am not in the mood for it (for laughing), I don't feel like it (like laughing).

zumut|en ['tsu:mu:tən] (26): *j-m et.* ~ expect a th. of a p.; *sich zuviel* ~ overtask o.s.; '**ↇung** *f* unreasonable demand; (*Unverschämtheit*) impudence; *eine* (*starke*) ~ a bit strong.

zu'nächst [tsu-] *prp.* (*dat.*) next to; *adv.* (*vor allem*) first of all; (*vorläufig*) for the present, for the time being; (*erstens*) to begin with.

zunageln ['tsu:na:gəln] nail up.

'**zunähen** sew up.

Zunahme ['~na:mə] *f* (15) increase, growth.

'**Zuname** *m* surname, last name.

Zünd|-anlage ['tsynt-] *f* ignition system; '**ↇen** ['tsyndən] (26) *v/i.* catch fire; *fig.* arouse enthusiasm; electrify; *v/t. u. v/i.* kindle; *bsd. mot.* ignite; ⚔ fire; *Sprengung*: detonate.

Zunder ['tsundər] *m* (7) tinder, touchwood.

'**Zünder** ⚔ *u.* ⚒ *m* (7) fuse.

'**Zünd|holz** *n*, **~hölzchen** ['tsynthœltsçən] (6) *n* match; **~hütchen** ⊕ ['~hy:tçən] *n* (6) percussion cap; '**~kapsel** *f* detonator; '**~kerze** *mot. f* spark(ing) plug, *Am.* spark plug; '**~punkt** *m* ignition point; '**~satz** *m* primer; '**~schlüssel** *mot. m* ignition key; '**~schnur** *f* (safety) fuse, slow match; '**~stein** *m* flint; '**~stoff** *m* inflammable matter; *fig.* dynamite.

Zündung *mot.* ['tsyndʊŋ] *f* ignition.

'**zunehmen** increase (*an dat.* in); (*anwachsen*) grow (larger, bigger, longer, stronger, stout[er]); *an Gewicht*: put on weight; '**~d** increasing, growing; *Mond*: waxing; *mit ~em Alter* with advancing years; *in ~em Maße* increasingly; *der ~e Mond* the waxing (*od.* crescent) moon.

'**zuneig|en** (*a. sich*) (*dat.*) incline to(wards); *sich dem Ende* ~ draw to a close; '**ↇung** *f* affection (*für, zu* for); ~ *zu j-m fassen* take a liking to a p.

Zunft [tsunft] *f* (14[1]) guild, corporation; *b.s.* clique, gang.

zünftig ['tsynftiç] belonging to a guild; *fig.* (*kunstgerecht*) expert, competent; *bsd. Sport*: scientific, sportsmanlike; F (*tüchtig*) thorough (-ly *adv.*).

Zunge ['tsuŋə] *f* (15) tongue (*a.* = *Sprache*); (*Fisch*) sole; ♪ reed; *e-e lose* (*spitze*) ~ *haben* have a loose (sharp) tongue; *es lag mir auf der* ~ I had it on the tip of my tongue.

züngeln ['tsyŋəln] (29) play with the tongue; *Flamme*: lick.

'**Zungen|brecher** *m* tongue-twister, crack-jaw; '**ↇfertig** glib, voluble; '**~fertigkeit** *f* volubility; '**ↇförmig** tongue-shaped; '**~kuß** *m* French kiss; '**~laut** *gr. m* lingual (sound); '**~spitze** *f* tip of the tongue.

Zünglein ['tsyŋlaɪn] *n* (6) little tongue; *fig. das* ~ *an der Waage bilden* tip the scales.

zunichte [tsu'niçtə]: ~ *machen* bring to nothing; destroy, ruin; *Plan usw.*: frustrate, defeat; ~ *werden* come to nothing, be frustrated.

zunicken ['tsu:-] (*dat.*) nod to.
zunutze [tsu'nutsə]: *sich et.* ~ *machen* turn a th. to account, utilize a th.
zu'·oberst (quite) at the top, uppermost.
'zu·ordnen (*dat.*) attach (to); class (with).
'zupacken *s. zugreifen.*
zu'paß [tsu-]: ~ *kommen* come at the right time, come in handy; *j-m*: suit *a p.* (admirably).
zupf|en ['tsupfən] (25) *v/t.* pull, pluck, twitch, tug (*alle a. v/i.*; *an dat.* at); *Wolle*: pick; *j-n am Ärmel usw.* ~ pull a p. by the ...; **'⁀-instrument** ♪ *n* plucking instrument.
zupfropfen ['tsu:-] (25) cork (up).
zur [tsu:r] = *zu der*; *s. zu.*
'zuraten *j-m*: advise a p. (to do) a th.; *auf sein* ⁀ on his advice.
'zurechn|en add; *zu e-r Klasse usw.*: number among, class with; *fig. j-m*: ascribe to, *Schlechtes*: *a.* impute to; **'⁀ung** *f* addition; inclusion; attribution; imputation; **'~ungsfähig** sane, of sound mind, ⚖ *a.* responsible; **'⁀ungsfähigkeit** *f* sanity, soundness of mind; ⚖ *a.* (penal) responsibility.
zu'recht [tsu-] (a)right, in order; **~basteln** rig up; **~bringen** put to rights, set right; (*bewerkstelligen*) bring about, manage; **~finden:** *sich* ~ find (*fig.* see) one's way; **~kommen** (sn) arrive in time; *fig.* get on well (*mit* with), *mit et.*: *a.* manage; **~legen** put out; (*a. fig.*) arrange; *sich e-e S.* ~ (*erklären*) explain a th. to o.s.; (*vorher überlegen*) prepare (*od.* figure out) a th.; **~machen** get ready, prepare, *Am.* F fix; *für e-n Zweck*: adapt to *od.* for; *sich* ~ get ready, *Dame*: make (o.s.) up; **~setzen** set right; *j-m den Kopf* ~ bring a p. to his senses; **~stellen** set up; put in the right place; **~stutzen** trim (to size); **~weisen** *v/t.*, **⁀weisung** *f* rebuke, reprimand.
zureden ['tsu:-] **1.** *j-m* ~ try to persuade a p.; (*drängen*) urge a p.; (*ermutigen*) encourage a p.; **2.** ⁀ *n* (6) persuasion; encouragement; (*Bitte*) entreaty, urgent request.
'zureichen *v/t.* hand (over), pass (*dat.* to); *v/i.* be sufficient.
'zureit|en *v/t.* break in; *v/i.* (sn) (*weiter od. schneller reiten*) ride on *od.* faster; ~ *auf* (*acc.*) ride up to; **'⁀er** *m* breaker-in, trainer.
'zurichten prepare; *bsd.* ⊕ dress, fit; *Holz, Steine*: cut, trim; *typ.* get (*od.* make) ready; *übel* ~ *j-n*: use badly, (*verletzen*) maul, *a. et.*: batter.
'zuriegeln (29) bolt.
zürnen ['tsyrnən] (25) be angry (*j-m* with a p.; *über acc.* at, about).
Zur'schaustellung *f* exhibition, display; *fig. a.* parading.
zurück [tsu'ryk] back; (*rückwärts*) backward(s); (*hinten*) behind; (*im Rückstand*) in arrears, behind-handed; ~! stand back!; ~ *an den Absender* returned to writer; **~begeben:** *sich* ~ return; **~begleiten** conduct back; **~behalten** keep back, retain; **~bekommen** get back; **~berufen** call back; **~bezahlen** pay back; **~bleiben** (sn) remain (*od.* stay) behind; be left behind (*a.* = *überleben*); *fig.* fall (*od.* lag) behind; *Sport*: drop back; *als Rest*: be left (over); *in der Entwicklung, geistig*: be backward, be retarded; ~ *hinter Erwartungen usw.* fall short of; *geistig zurückgeblieben* backward, (mentally) retarded; **~blicken** look back; **~bringen** bring (*od.* take) back; ⚗ reduce (*auf acc.* to); **~datieren** backdate; **~denken** think back; ~ *an* (*acc.*) recall *a th.* to memory; *sich* ~ cast one's mind back; **~drängen** push back; *fig.* repress; **~dürfen** be allowed to return; **~eilen** (sn) hasten back; **~erbitten** ask back; **~erobern** reconquer; **~erstatten** restore; *Ausgaben, Kosten*: refund, reimburse; **~fahren** *v/t. u. v/i.* (sn) drive back; *v/i. plötzlich*: start back; **~fallen** (sn) fall back; (*zurückbleiben*) fall (*od.* drop) behind; (*rückfällig werden*) relapse (*in acc.* into); ⚖ (*heimfallen*) ~ *an* (*acc.*) revert to; *sich* **~finden** find one's way back; **~fordern** demand back, reclaim; **~führen** lead back; *in die Heimat*: repatriate; *fig.* ~ *auf e-n Nenner, e-e Regel, ein Minimum usw.* reduce to; ~ *auf e-e Ursache usw.* trace (back) to, attribute to; **⁀gabe** *f* giving back, return, restitution; **~geben** give back, return; *Fußball*: pass back; *in der Rede*: retort; **~-**

gehen (sn) go back, return; ⚔ retreat; *fig.* (*sich vermindern*) diminish, decrease, drop; ⚕ *Preis*: fall, drop, go down; *Geschäfte*: fall off; (*nicht zustande kommen*) be broken off; *auf e-e Quelle* ~ trace back to, have its origin in; be due to; *Sendung* ~ *lassen* return; **~geleiten** escort back; **~gezogen** retired, secluded; **♀gezogenheit** *f* retirement, seclusion; **~greifen:** *fig. auf Reserven usw.* ~ fall back (up)on; *weiter* ~ *in der Erzählung usw.* begin (*od.* go) farther back; **~halten** hold back; *Tränen, Gefühl usw.*: restrain; ~ *mit* hold (*od.* keep) back; *sich* ~ be reserved, keep to o.s., *im Zorn usw.*: restrain o.s.; **~haltend** reserved (*a.* ⚕ *Börse*); (*vorsichtig*) guarded, cautious; **♀haltung** *f* retention; *fig.* reserve; **~holen** fetch back; *j-n* (*a. fig.*): call back; **~kaufen** buy back; **~kehren** (sn) return; **~kommen** (sn) come back, return; *mit der Arbeit usw.* ~ get behind with; *auf e-e Sache* ~ return (*od.* revert) to *a th.*, refer to *a letter*; **~können** be able to return *od.* go back; **♀kunft** [~kunft] *f* (16) return; **~lassen** leave (behind *a. Angehörige*); (*überholen*) outstrip, leave (far) behind; (*Rückkehr erlauben*) allow to return; **~legen** *Geld, Ware*: lay aside; *e-m Käufer*: put aside (for); *Geld* (*sparen*): put by; *Jahre*: complete; *Weg*: cover; *sich* ~ lie back; **~liegen** *zeitlich*: date back; **~melden:** *sich* ~ report back; **~müssen** be obliged to return; *das Buch muß zurück* has to be returned; *der Tisch muß zurück* must be moved back; **♀nahme** [~naːmə] *f* (15) *s. zurücknehmen*: taking back; withdrawal; retraction; revocation; **~nehmen** take back (*a. fig. Wort*); *Truppen*: withdraw; *Angebot, Behauptung, Klage, Versprechen usw.*: withdraw, retract; (*widerrufen*) revoke, *Auftrag*: countermand, cancel; **~prallen** (sn) rebound; *vor Schreck*: recoil, start back; **~rechnen** count back; **~reisen** (sn) travel back, return; **~rufen** call back; *ins Gedächtnis* ~ recall to mind; **~schaffen** take back; **~schaudern** (h. *u.* sn) shrink (back) (*vor dat.* from); **~schauen** look back; **~scheuen** shrink (back) (*vor dat.* from); *vor nichts* ~ stick at nothing; **~schicken** send back; **~schlagen** *v/t.* strike back; *Feind, Angriff*: repel, repulse; *Decke*: fold back; *Mantel*: throw open; *Tennisball*: return; *v/i. Flamme*: flash back; **~schrecken** *v/t.* (25) frighten away; *v/i.* (30, sn) shrink (back) (*von, vor dat.* from); **~schreiben** write back; **~sehnen:** *sich* ~ long to return; **~sein** (sn) be back, have come back; *fig.* be behind(handed) (*mit* with); *in Kenntnissen, in der Entwicklung usw.*: be backward; *sehr* ~ (*rückständig sein*) be very much behind the times; **~setzen** place back; *fig.* slight, neglect; *Preis*: reduce, cut (down); **♀setzung** *f* slight, neglect; **~spulen** *Tonband, Film*: rewind; **~stecken** *fig.* ~ *müssen* have to climb down; **~stehen** (h. *u.* sn) stand back; *fig.* be inferior (*hinter dat.* to); ~ (*müssen*) (have to) take a back seat; **~stellen** put back (*a. Uhr*), replace; (*aufschieben*) defer; (*hintansetzen*) postpone; ⚔ defer; **♀stellung** *f* putting back, replacement; deferment; **~stoßen** *v/t.* push back; *fig.* (*abstoßen*) repel; *v/i.* (sn *u.* h.) *mot.* reverse, back up; **~strahlen** *v/t.* reflect; *v/i.* be reflected; **~streifen** *Ärmel*: turn up; **~stufen** (25) *Person*: demote; *Sache*: downgrade; **♀stufung** *f* demotion; downgrading; **~treiben** drive back; **~treten** (sn) step (*od.* stand) back; *fig.* recede (*von* from); *vom Amt*: resign; (*von*) *e-m Unternehmen usw.*: withdraw (from), *von e-m Vertrag*: *a.* terminate; *fig.* take a back seat; **~-übersetzen** translate back (*ins Englische* into); **~verfolgen** *Weg*: retrace; *fig.* trace back (*zu* to); **~verlangen** reclaim, demand back; **~versetzen** restore (*to a former state*); *Schüler*: send back to a lower form, *Am.* demote; *sich in eine frühere Zeit* ~ turn one's mind back to a former period; **~verwandeln** retransform (*in acc.* into); (*a. sich*) change back (into); **~verweisen** refer back (*an acc.* to); **~weichen** (sn) fall back, retreat; (*a. fig.*) recede; (*nachgeben*) yield; **~weisen** *v/t.* turn back; (*ablehnen*) refuse, decline, reject; *Angriff*: repulse; *als unberechtigt* ~ repudiate; (*a. v/i.*) *auf e-e Anmerkung usw.*: refer to; **♀weisung** *f* refusal, rejection; repulse; repudiation; **~werfen** throw back; *Feind*: *a.* repulse; *den Kopf*: toss; *fig. wirtschaftlich usw.*: set back; *phys. Lichtstrahlen usw.*: reflect, reverberate; **~wirken** react (*auf acc.* upon); **~wünschen** wish back; **~zahlen** pay back, repay (*beide a. fig.*); *Auslagen*: refund; **2zahlung** *f* repayment; refund; **~ziehen** *v/t.* draw back; ⚔ *Truppen, a. fig.* withdraw, retire (*beide a. sich*); *sich* ~ ⚔ *a.* retreat; *sich auf et.* (*acc.*) ~ fall back (up)on; *sich* ~ *von* retire from, give up; *v/i.* move (*od.* march) back; **2ziehung** *f* withdrawal.

'**Zuruf** *m* call; (*Beifalls*2) acclamation; *durch* ~ by acclamation; '**2en** *v/i. u. v/t. j-m*: call (out) to; *laut*: shout to; *beifällig*: acclaim.

'**zurüst|en** prepare; (*ausrüsten*) fit out, equip; '**2ung** *f* preparation; fitting-out, equipment.

'**Zusage** *f* (15) promise; (*Zustimmung*) assent; '**2n** *v/t.* promise; *j-m et. auf den Kopf* ~ tell a p. a th. to his face; *v/i.* promise to come; *j-m* ~ *Speise, Klima usw.*: agree with a p.; (*Einladung annehmen*) accept a p.'s invitation; (*gefallen*) suit *od.* please a p.; *~de Antwort* acceptance.

zusammen [tsu'zamən] together; (*gemeinschaftlich*) *a.* jointly; (*gleichzeitig*) at the same time; ~ *mit* along with; ~ *betragen* amount to, total; *alle* (*pl.*) ~ all in a body; *alles* ~ all in all; *wir haben* ~ *5 Mark* we have 5 marks between us; **2-arbeit** *f* co-operation; *bsd. mit dem Feind* collaboration; *e-r Gemeinschaft*: team-work; **~-arbeiten** work together; co-operate, collaborate; **~ballen** (*a. sich*) form into a ball, conglomerate; gather; *a.* ⚔ concentrate, mass; **2ballung** *f* concentration, conglomeration; **2bau** ⊕ *m* assembly; **~bauen** ⊕ assemble; *die Zähne* **~beißen** clench one's teeth; **~bekommen** get together; *Geld*: raise; **~berufen** convoke, call together; **~binden** bind (*od.* tie) together; **~brauen** concoct (*a. fig.*); *fig. sich* ~ be brewing; **~brechen** (sn) break down, collapse; **~bringen** bring together; (*sammeln*) collect, gather; *Geld*: raise; **2bruch** *m* breakdown, collapse; **~drängen** press together; *Menschen, Tiere*: (*a. sich*) crowd (*od.* huddle) together; (*verdichten*) compress; (*kürzen*) condense; **~drücken** compress; **~fahren** (sn) (*aufea.-fahren, -stoßen*) collide (*mit* with); *fig.* start (*bei e-m Anblick usw.* at; *vor Schreck usw.* with); *schmerzhaft*: wince; **~fallen** fall in, collapse; *zeitlich*: coincide; **~falten** fold (up); **~fassen** (*in sich fassen*) comprise; (*sammeln*) collect; (*mitea. verbinden*) combine; *a.* ⚔ concentrate; (*gedrängt darstellen*) summarize, sum up; *Schriftwerk*: condense; **2fassung** *f e-s Inhalts*: summary, résumé; synopsis; **~finden**: *sich* ~ meet; **~flicken** patch up; **~fließen** (sn) flow together, meet; **2fluß** *m* confluence; **~fügen** join (together), unite (*a. sich*); **~gehen** (sn) go together (*a. fig.*); (*schrumpfen*) shrink; **~gehören** belong together; *Schuhe usw.*: *a.* be fellows; **~gehörig** belonging together; *fig. a.* related, allied; **2gehörigkeit** *f* unity; **2gehörigkeitsgefühl** *n* solidarity; *inniges*: togetherness; **~geraten** (sn) *fig.* clash; **~gesetzt** composed (*aus* of); *bsd.* ⚗, *gr., Arznei, Speise*: compound; (*verwickelt*) complex; *gr. ~er Satz* complex (*od.* compound) sentence; *~es Wort* compound (word); **~gewürfelt** motley, *bsd. Mannschaft*: scratch; **2halt** *m* holding together; *v. Freunden*: sticking together, (*Einigkeit*) unity; **~halten** *v/i.* hold together (*a. v/t.*); *Freunde*: stick together; **2hang** *m* coherence, connection; *des Textes*: context; (*Fortlaufendes*) continuity; *in diesem* ~ in this connection; *aus dem* ~ *reißen* divorce from its context; *in* ~ *bringen mit* connect with; *im* ~ *stehen mit* be connected with; **~hängen** hang together (*a. fig.*), cohere; *fig.* be connected; **~hängend** coherent; (*in Beziehung stehend*) connected; (*verwandt*) related; **~hang(s)los** incoherent; **~hauen** smash to pieces; F *j-n*: beat up; **~häufen** heap up, accumulate; **~heften** *Buch*: stitch together; *Schneiderei*: tack; **~heilen** (sn) heal up *od.* over; **~holen** fetch from all sides; **~kaufen** buy up; **~kitten** cement; **2klang** *m* accord, harmony; **~klappbar** folding, collapsible; **~klappen** *v/t.* fold up; *Messer*: shut; *v/i. P.*: break down; **~kleben** *v/t.* glue (*od.* paste) together; *v/i.* stick together; **~knüllen** (25) crumple; **~kommen** (sn) come together, meet, assemble; **⁀kunft** *f* (14[1]) meeting; *sich* **~läppern** F [~lɛpərn] (29) add up; **~laufen** (sn) run (*od.* crowd) together; ⚗ converge; (*gerinnen*) curdle; *s. Wasser*; **~leben** live together; *mit j-m*: live with; **⁀leben** *n* living together; *mit j-m*: life with; **~legen** lay together; *Brief, Wäsche usw.*: fold up; *Geld*: club (together), pool; (*vereinigen*) combine, consolidate, fuse, merge (into one); **⁀legung** *f* consolidation, merger; **~nehmen** gather (up); *Gedanken*: collect; *sich* ~ collect o.s., *im Benehmen*: be on one's good behavio(u)r, *a. bei Anstrengung*: pull o.s. together; **~packen** pack up; **~passen** *v/t.* adjust, match; *v/i.* be (well) matched, harmonize, go well together; **~pferchen** crowd together; **⁀prall** *m* (3) collision, clash (*beide a. fig.*); **~prallen** collide, clash; **~raffen** snatch up; *Vermögen*: amass; *sich* ~ pull o.s. together; **~rechnen** add up, sum up, total; **~reimen** *fig.* make out; *sich* ~ add up; *es sich* ~ put two and two together; *sich* **~reißen** pull o.s. together; **~rollen** coil up; *sich* ~ *a.* roll o.s. up; *sich* **~rotten** (26) gang (*od.* throng) together; *Aufrührer*: riot; **⁀rottung** *f* riot (-ing), *konkret*: riotous mob (*od.* ⚖ assembly); **~rücken** *v/t.* move together (*od. Stühle usw.*: closer); *v/i.* (sn) move up; **~rufen** call together, convoke; *sich* **~scharen** flock together, rally; **~schießen** shoot down; *mit Kanonen*: batter; *Geld*: club together; **~schlagen** *v/t.* beat (*od.* strike) together; (*zerschlagen*) smash to pieces; *j-n*: beat up; *die Hände* ~ clap one's hands (together); *v/i.* (sn) ~ *über* (*dat.*) close over; (*sich*) **~schließen** join (closely); (*vereinigen*) unite; consolidate; (*gemeinschaftliche Sache machen*) combine; **⁀schluß** *m* union; consolidation; (*Bündnis*) alliance; **~schmelzen** (sn) melt away (*a. fig.*); *v/t.* melt down; **~schnüren** cord up; **~schreiben** *Rechtschreibung*: write in one word; (*aus Büchern usw. zs.-stellen*) compile; *contp.* scribble; **~schrumpfen** (sn) shrivel, shrink (up); **~schweißen** (*a. fig.*) weld together (*zu* into); **⁀sein** *n* meeting, gathering; **~setzen** put together; *zu e-m Ganzen*: compose; ⚗ *Arznei, Wort*: compound; ⊕ assemble; *sich* ~ sit down together; *sich* ~ *aus* (*bestehen aus*) consist of; *s. zusammengesetzt*; **⁀setzung** *f* composition; *gr.*, ⚗ compound; ⊕ assembly; (*Bestandteile*) ingredients *pl.*; **~sinken** (sn) sink down; **⁀spiel** *n Sport, thea.* team-work; **~stecken** *v/t.* put together; *v/i. fig.* be very thick (*mit* with *a friend*); **~stehen** stand (*od. fig.* hold *od.* stick) together; **~stellen** put together; *aus Einzelteilen, z. B. Liste, Medizin, Radiosendung, Wörterbuch usw.*: *a.* compile; (*zusammenfassend vereinigen*) combine; *in e-r Liste*: list; **⁀stellung** *f* putting together; combination; compilation; list; (*Übersicht*) synopsis; **~stoppeln** (29) patch up; **⁀stoß** *m* collision (*a. fig.* = clash, conflict); *mot. usw. a.* crash; ⚔ encounter; **~stoßen** *v/t.* strike (*od.* knock) together; *Gläser*: touch, clink; *v/i.* (sn) collide (*a. fig.* = clash); (*anea.-grenzen*) adjoin, meet; ~ *mit a.* run into, crash with; **~streichen** cut down; **~strömen** (sn) flow together; *Menschen*: flock together; **~stürzen** (sn) collapse; **~suchen** gather; *zu e-r Sammlung*: collect; **~tragen** carry together; gather (*a. fig.*); *Notizen usw.*: compile; **~treffen**[1] (sn) meet; (*gleichzeitig geschehen*) coincide; **⁀treffen**[2] *n* (6) meeting; *feindliches*: encounter; *von Umständen*: coincidence; **~treten** (sn) meet; *parl. a.* assemble, convene; **⁀tritt** *m* meeting; **~trommeln** call together; *weitS.* drum up; **~tun** put together; *sich* ~ combine, join forces, team up (*mit* with); **~wachsen** (sn) grow together; **~werfen** throw together; (*verwechseln*) mix up; *unterschiedslos*: lump together; **~wirken**[1] cooperate; *S.*: combine; **⁀wirken**[2] *n* (6) co-operation; interaction; **~zählen** add up, sum up; **~ziehen** draw together (*a. sich*); (*verengern*) contract (*a. sich*); *Truppen*: gather, concentrate (*a. sich*); *sich* ~ *Gewit-*

ter: be gathering; ♀**ziehung** *f* contraction; ⚔ concentration.

'**Zusatz** *m* (3² *u.* ³) addition; *zu Nahrungsmitteln*: additive; (*Beimischung*) admixture, *zu Metallen*: alloy; (*Anhang*) appendix; (*Ergänzung*) supplement; (*Nachschrift*) postscript; *zu e-m Testament*: codicil; '**~-antrag** *parl. m* supplementary motion; '**~-ausbildung** *f* additional training; '**~frage** *f* additional question; '**~gerät** *n* accessory unit; attachment.

'**zusätzlich** additional, supplementary; *adv.* in addition (*zu* to), besides.

'**Zusatz|ver-einbarung** *f* supplementary agreement; '**~versicherung** *f* additional insurance.

zuschanden [tsu'ʃandən]: ~ *hauen* knock to pieces; ~ *machen* ruin, (*a. Hoffnungen*) destroy; *Plan*: frustrate, thwart; ~ *werden* be ruined *etc.*

'**zuschanzen:** *j-m et.* ~ put a p. in the way of a th.

'**zuscharren** cover (*od.* fill) up.

'**zuschau|en** look on (*e-r S.* at a th.), watch (a th.); *j-m* ~ watch a p. (*bei et.* doing a th.); '♀**er** *m* (7), '♀**erin** *f* (16¹) spectator, looker-on, onlooker; '♀**erraum** *thea. m* auditorium; '♀-**tribüne** *f s. Tribüne.*

'**zuschicken** send, forward (*dat.* to); *mit der Post*: *a.* mail (to).

'**zuschieben** close; *j-m*: push towards a p.; *fig. b.s.* impute to a p.; *s. Schuld, Verantwortung.*

'**zuschießen** *v/t.* (*beitragen*) contribute; *ergänzend*: add, supply; *v/i.* (sn) ~ *auf* (*acc.*) rush up to.

'**Zuschlag** *m* addition; (*Preis*♀) extra charge; *zum Fahrpreis*: excess fare; (*Steuer*♀) surtax; *Auktion*: knocking down; † *bei Ausschreibung*: award (of contract); *metall.* flux; ♀**en** ['~gən] *v/i.* (sn) strike; *v/t. Tür usw.*: bang, (*a. v/i.*) slam; *Auktion*: knock down; '♀(**s**)**frei** without surcharge; '~(**s**)**karte** *f* extra ticket.

'**zuschließen** lock (up).

'**zuschmeißen** F *Tür usw.*: bang, slam; *j-m et.*: throw (*od.* fling) to.

'**zuschmieren** smear over.

'**zuschnallen** buckle (up), strap up.

'**zuschnappen** (h.) snap; (sn) *Schloß usw.*: snap to, close with a snap.

'**zuschneid|en** cut up; *Anzug, a. fig.* cut (to size); '♀**er**(**in** *f*) *m* cutter.

'**Zuschnitt** *m* cut; *weitS.* style.

'**zuschnüren** lace up; *Ballen*: cord up; *j-m den Hals od. die Kehle* ~ strangle (*od.* choke) a p.

'**zuschrauben** screw down *od.* tight.

'**zuschreiben** *v/t. j-m od. e-r S. et.* ~ (*beimessen*) ascribe (*od.* attribute *od.* put down) to; *es ist dem Umstand zuzuschreiben, daß* it is due to the fact that; *das hast du dir selbst zuzuschreiben* that's your own doing.

'**zuschreien** *v/t. u. v/i. j-m*: shout (*od.* call out) to a p.

'**Zuschrift** *f* letter.

zu'schulden [tsu-]: *sich et.* ~ *kommen lassen* do something wrong.

Zuschuß ['tsu:-] *m* (4²) contribution; *staatlicher*: subsidy, grant; '**~betrieb** *m* subsidized undertaking.

'**zuschütten** (*hinzutun*) add; *Graben usw.*: fill up.

'**zusehen** *s. zuschauen*; (*sorgen*) ~, *daß* see (to it) that; *da müssen Sie selber* ~ you must see to it yourself; **~ds** ['~ts] visibly, noticeably.

'**zusenden** send *od.* forward (*dat.* to).

'**zusetzen** *v/t.* (*hinzufügen*) add; *Geld, Zeit usw.*: lose; *v/i.* (*Geld einbüßen*) lose (money); *j-m* ~ press a p. hard, give a p. a hard time, (*in j-n dringen*) urge a p., *mit Fragen, Gründen*: ply a p. with, (*belästigen*) pester a p. with, *weitS. Hitze, Mühsal usw.*: be hard on a p., tell on a p.

'**zusicher|n** *j-m et.*: assure a p. of a th., guarantee a p. a th.; (*versprechen*) promise a p. a th.; '♀**ung** *f* promise, assurance, guarantee; pledge.

'**zusiegeln** seal (up).

Zu'spätkommende *m, f* (18) latecomer.

'**zuspielen** *j-m*: play *a th.* into a p.'s hands; (*a. v/i.*) *Sport*: pass to a p.

'**zuspitzen** point; *sich* ~ taper (off); *fig.* come to a point *od.* head.

'**zusprechen** *v/t. j-m Trost* ~ comfort a p.; *j-m Mut* ~ cheer a p. up; (*zubilligen*) adjudge, award (to); *v/i. e-r Speise wacker* ~ eat heartily of; *Getränken*: drink copiously.

'**zuspringen** (sn) *auf j-n*: leap towards, rush at; *Schloß*: snap to.

'**Zuspruch** *m von Mut*: encouragement; *von Trost*: consolation; *von Kunden*: run; (*Kundschaft*) custom.

'**Zustand** *m* condition; state; *in*

gutem ~ in good condition; *Haus usw.*: in good repair; *in betrunkenem* ~ drunk; F *Zustände bekommen* have a fit; *contp. hier herrschen Zustände!* what a mess!

zustande [tsu'ʃtandə]: ~ *bringen* bring about, manage, achieve; realize; ~ *kommen* come about; be realized; *Vertrag*: be reached (*od.* signed); *die Reise wird* ~ *kommen* will take place; *das Gesetz kommt* ~ will pass; *nicht* ~ *kommen* fail, not to come off, come to naught; **℞kommen** *n* realization.

zuständig ['tsu:ʃtɛndiç] (*befugt*) competent; (*verantwortlich*) responsible; (*maßgeblich*) proper; ⚖ having jurisdiction (*für* over); '**℞keit** *f* competence; responsibility; jurisdiction; '**℞keitsbereich** *m* (sphere of) responsibility, scope; jurisdiction.

zustatten [tsu'ʃtatən]: ~ *kommen* come in handy, *j-m* be useful to a p., stand a p. in good stead.

zustecken ['tsu:-] pin (up); *j-m et.* ~ slip a th. into a p.'s hand.

'**zustehen** (*dat.*) *rechtlich*: be due to, belong to; *es* (*das Besitztum, das Recht*) *steht ihm zu* he is entitled to it; *es steht ihm* (*nicht*) *zu, zu* ... he has a (no) right to ...

'**zustell|en** deliver (*dat.* to); ⚖ *j-m*: serve *a writ* on a p.; '**℞gebühr** *f* delivery charge; '**℞ung** *f* delivery; ⚖ service, ~*en pl.* (service of) legal process; '**℞ungsgebühr** *f s. Zustellgebühr*.

'**zustimm|en** (*dat.*) agree (to *a th.*; with *a p.*); consent (to *a th.*), approve (of *a th.*); F *a.* okay; '**~end** affirmative; ~ *nicken* nod one's approval; '**℞ung** *f* consent, agreement.

'**zustopfen** stop up, plug; *Loch im Strumpf usw.*: mend, darn.

'**zustöpseln** stopper, plug (up).

'**zustoßen** *v/t.* push ... to; *v/i. fenc.* lunge, thrust; (sn) *j-m* ~ happen to a p., befall a p.; *ihm ist ein Unfall zugestoßen* he has had (*od.* met with) an accident.

'**Zustrom** *m von Personen*: concourse, throng, stream; *v. Dingen*: influx.

'**zuströmen** (sn; *dat.*) stream towards; *Personen*: throng to(wards).

'**zustürzen** (sn) *auf* (*acc.*) rush up to.

'**zustutzen** trim; (*passend machen*) fit (up), cut to size (*a. fig.*); *Stück für die Bühne, Text für den Unterricht*: adapt (for).

zutage [tsu'tɑ:gə]: ~ *fördern od. bringen* bring to light; ~ *liegen* be evident; ~ *treten od. kommen* come to light; *geol.* outcrop.

Zutaten ['tsu:tɑ:tən] *f/pl.* (16) *e-r Speise*: ingredients *pl.*; *e-s Kleides*: trimmings *pl.*; (*Stoff*℞) material *sg.*

zu'teil [tsu-]: *j-m* ~ *werden* fall to a p.'s share (*fig. a.* lot); *j-m et.* ~ *werden lassen* allot (*od.* grant) a th. to a p., bestow a th. on a p.; *ihm wurde eine freundliche Aufnahme* ~ he met with a kind reception.

'**zuteil|en** allot (*a.* ✝ *Aktien usw.*), allocate, apportion; (*genehmigen*) grant, allow; (*ausgeben*) issue (*dat.* to); ⚔ *od. pol.* attach (to); '**℞ung** *f* allotment, allocation, apportionment; attachment; (*zugeteilte Ration*) ration; (*Kontingent*) quota.

zu'tiefst deeply.

'**zutragen** carry (*dat.* to; *a. fig.*); *Gerücht*: report; *sich* ~ happen, take place, occur.

'**Zuträger|(in** *f*) *m* talebearer, telltale; **~ei** [~'raɪ] *f* (16) talebearing.

zuträglich ['~trɛ:k-] conducive, beneficial (*dat. od. für* to); *Klima*: salubrious; *Nahrung*: wholesome; *j-m* (*nicht*) ~ *sein* (dis)agree with a p.; '**℞keit** *f* conduciveness; salubrity; wholesomeness.

'**zutrau|en** **1.** *j-m et.* ~ believe a p. capable of a th.; *j-m nicht viel* ~ have no high opinion of a p.; *sich zuviel* ~ overrate o.s., (*sich übernehmen*) take too much on o.s.; *ich traue es mir zu* I think I can do it; *iro. ich traue es ihm glatt zu* I would not put it past him; **2.** ℞ *n* (6) confidence (*zu* in); '**~lich** trusting; *Tier*: friendly, tame; '**℞lichkeit** *f* confidingness; tameness.

'**zutreffen** (sn) be right *od.* true, hold true; ~ *auf* (*acc.*) be true of, (*a.* ~ *für*) apply to; '**~d** right, true; (*anwendbar*) applicable; '**~denfalls** if so; *in Formularen*: where applicable.

'**zutrinken** *j-m*: drink to a p.

'**Zutritt** *m* access; (*Einlaß*) admission; ~ *verboten!* no admittance!, no entry!

'**zutun** **1.** (*schließen*) close; (*hinzufügen*) add; *s. Auge, zugetan*; **2.** ℞ *n*

(6): *ohne sein* ~ without his help, (*ohne s-e Schuld*) through no fault of his.
zu'-ungunsten [tsu-] (*gen.*) to the disadvantage of.
zu'-unterst right at the bottom.
zuverlässig ['tsu:fɛrlɛsiç] reliable (*a.* ⊕); *nur P.*: dependable, trustworthy; (*sicher*) safe (*a.* ✝, ⊕); *Nachricht*: sure, certain; *aus* ~*er Quelle* from a reliable source; *von* ~*er Seite erfahren (haben), daß* ... have it on good authority that ...; '**2keit** *f* reliability; trustworthiness; certainty; '**2keits-prüfung** *mot. f* reliability test; '**2keits-überprüfung** *pol. f des Personals*: security clearance, screening.
Zuversicht ['~fɛrziçt] *f* (16) confidence; '**2lich** confident; '**~lichkeit** *f* confidence; assurance.
zu'viel 1. too much; *einer usw.* ~ one *etc.* too many; **2.** 2 *n* excess.
zu'vor before, previously.
zu'vor|kommen (sn) *j-m*: anticipate, forestall, F beat *a p.* to it; *e-r S.*: obviate, anticipate; **~kommend** obliging; **2kommenheit** *f* obligingness; **~tun:** *es j-m* ~ surpass (*od.* outdo) a p.
Zuwachs ['tsu:-] *m* (4) (*Vermehrung*) increase, increment; *s. Familien*2; *auf* ~ *geschneidert* made so as to allow for growing; '**2en** (sn) become overgrown; ⚕ heal up, close; *j-m* ~ accrue to a p. '**~rate** *f* rate of increase, growth rate.
'**zuwandern** (sn) immigrate.
'**zuwarten** wait (and see).
zuwege [tsu've:gə]: ~ *bringen* bring about, accomplish.
zuwehen ['tsu:-] (*dat.*) blow to *od.* towards; *mit Schnee, Sand*: cover.
zu'weilen sometimes, occasionally.
zuweis|en ['tsu:-] assign, allocate; '**2ung** *f* assignment, allocation.
'**zuwend|en** (*dat.*) turn to(wards); *fig. j-m e-e Gabe usw.* ~ let a p. have, present a p. with, give a p. *a th.*; *Gefühl usw.*: bestow on a p.; *Aufmerksamkeit, Bemühungen*: devote to; *sich e-r Tätigkeit* ~ proceed to *do*, apply o.s. to; *sich e-m Beruf* ~ devote o.s. to; '**2ung** *f* allowance, grant, gift; (*Schenkung*) donation; (*Vermächtnis*) bequest; (*Liebe*) love, (loving) care.
zuwenig [tsu've:niç] too little.
zuwerfen ['tsu:-] *Grube*: fill up; *Tür*: slam; *j-m*: throw to a p., *e-n Blick*: cast to a p.
zuwider [tsu'vi:dər] (*dat.*) contrary to, against; (*verhaßt*) repugnant, distasteful (to); *er (es) ist mir* ~ I loathe him (it); **~handeln** (*dat.*) act contrary to, *bsd.* ⚖ contravene, violate; **2handelnde** *m* (18) offender; **2handlung** ⚖ *f* contravention, violation; **~laufen** (sn; *dat.*) run counter (*od.* be contrary) to.
zuwinken ['tsu:-] (*dat.*) wave to; [*weitS.* make a sign to.]
'**zuzahlen** pay extra.
'**zuzählen** add (*dat. od. zu* to).
zuzeiten [tsu'tsaɪtən] at times.
zuzieh|en ['tsu:-] *v/t. Knoten*: draw together; *Schlinge, Schleife*: (*a. sich*) tighten; *Vorhang*: draw; *Arzt, Berater usw.*: consult, call in; *sich e-e Strafe, Tadel usw.* ~ incur; *Krankheit*: contract, catch; *sich Unannehmlichkeiten* ~ get into trouble; *j-n als Zeugen* ~ call a p. as witness; *v/i.* (sn) *Mieter*: move in; (*sich niederlassen*) settle; '**2ung** *f* consultation, calling in.
'**Zuzug** *m* moving in; arrival, immigration; '**~sgenehmigung** *f* residence permit.
zuzüglich ['~tsy:kliç] plus; (*einschließlich*) including.
Zwang[1] [tsvaŋ] *m* (3, *o. pl.*) compulsion, coercion; *moralischer*: constraint, restraint; (*Druck*) pressure (*a.* ⚕); (*Gewalt*) force; *bsd.* ⚖ duress; *sich* ~ *antun od. auferlegen* restrain o.s.; *unter* ~ *stehen (od. handeln)* be (*od.* act) under coercion.
zwang[2] *pret. v. zwingen.*
zwängen ['tsvɛŋən] (25) press, force.
'**zwanglos** unconstrained; *fig. a.* free and easy, unceremonious, informal; '**2igkeit** *f* ease, informality.
'**Zwangs|-anleihe** *f* forced loan; '**~-arbeit** *f* hard labo(u)r; '**2bewirtschaftet** under economic control, control(l)ed; '**~-ent-eignung** *f* compulsory expropriation; '**2-ernähren** force-feed; '**~-ernährung** *f* forcible feeding; '**~haft** *f* coercive detention; '**~handlung** *f* compulsive act; '**~herrschaft** *f* despotism; '**~-idee** *f* compulsive idea; '**~jacke** *f* strait-jacket (*a. fig.*); '**~lage** *f* quandary, embarrassing situation; '**2läu-**

fig ⊕ guided, geared; *mot.* positive; *fig.* necessary; *adv.* inevitably; '**~maßnahme** *f* coercive measure; *zu ~n greifen* resort to coercion; '**~mittel** *n* means of coercion; '**~neurose** ⚕ *f* compulsion neurosis; '**~räumung** *f* compulsory evacuation; '**~verkauf** *m* forced sale; '**2verpflichtet** conscript; '**~versteigerung** *f* forced sale; '**~verwaltung** *f* forced administration, sequestration; '**~vollstreckung** *f* execution; '**~vorstellung** ⚕ *f* compulsive idea, obsession; '**2weise** compulsorily, by force; '**~wirtschaft** *f* Government control; *die ~ für ein Gewerbe usw. aufheben* decontrol; *Aufhebung der ~* decontrol.

zwanzig ['tsvantsiç] twenty; **2er** ['~gər] *m* (7) person of twenty; *in den ~n sein* be between twenty and thirty; '**~er'lei** *adj.* of twenty kinds; *als su.* twenty different things *pl.*; '**~fach**, '**~fältig** twentyfold; '**~st** twentieth; '**2stel** *n* (7) twentieth (part); '**~stens** in the twentieth place.

zwar [tsvaːr] indeed, (it is) true, of course, to be sure; *und ~* and that, (*nämlich*) that is; *er kam ~, aber* ... he did come, but ..., (al-) though he came, he ...

Zweck [tsvɛk] *m* (3) purpose; (*Ziel*) object (*a.* ✝); aim, end; (*Absicht*) intent; (*Verwendung*) use, application; *ein Mittel zum ~* a means to an end; *e-n ~ verfolgen* pursue an object, be after something; *keinen ~ haben* be useless; *s-n ~ erfüllen, dem ~ entsprechen* answer (*od.* serve) the purpose; *zu dem ~* (*gen. od. zu inf.*) for the purpose of; *zu welchem ~?* to what purpose?, what ... for?; F *das ist der ~ der Übung!* that's the idea!; *der ~ heiligt die Mittel* the end justifies the means; '**~bau** △ *m* functional building; '**2bestimmt** functional; '**2dienlich** serviceable, expedient; useful; (*einschlägig*) pertinent; '**~dienlichkeit** *f* serviceableness, expediency, usefulness.

Zwecke ['tsvɛkə] *f* (15) tack; *s. Reißnagel.*

'**zweck|-entfremdet** alienated (from its purpose); '**~-entsprechend** answering the purpose; proper, appropriate; '**~gebunden** *Gelder*: earmarked, appropriated; '**~los** aimless, purposeless; (*unnütz*) useless, pointless, *pred.* of no use; '**2losigkeit** *f* aimlessness; uselessness, futility; '**~mäßig** expedient, suitable, proper; (*ratsam*) advisable; '**2mäßigkeit** *f* expediency, suitableness; '**2pessimismus** *m* calculated pessimism.

zwecks (*gen.*) for the purpose of.

'**Zweck|verband** *m* local administrative union; '**2widrig** inexpedient, inappropriate, unsuitable.

zwei [tsvaɪ] (*gen.* ~er, *dat.* ~en) two; *zu ~en* in twos.

zwei|armig ['~ˀarmiç] two-armed; '**~bändig** two-volume (*attr.*); **~beinig** ['~baɪniç] two-legged; '**2bettzimmer** *n* twin-bedded room; '**2decker** ✈ *m* (7) biplane; **~deutig** ['~dɔʏtiç] ambiguous, equivocal; *b.s.* suggestive, *Witz usw.*: risqué (*fr.*), *Am.* off-color; '**2deutigkeit** *f* ambiguity, equivocality; *b.s.* risqué joke; '**~dimensional** two-dimensional; **2'drittelmehrheit** *f* two-thirds majority; **~-eiig** *biol.* ['~ˀaɪiç] dizygotic; *~e Zwillinge a.* non-identical twins; '**2er** *m* (7) (figure) two; *Rudern*: pair, two; **~erlei** ['~ər'laɪ] *adj.* of two kinds; *als su.* two different things *pl.*; '**~fach**, '**~fältig** double, two-fold; '**2familienhaus** *n* two-family house, *Am.* duplex house; '**~farbig** two-colo(u)red.

Zweifel ['tsvaɪfəl] *m* (7) doubt; *ohne ~* without doubt; *im ~ sein* be doubtful (*über acc.* about); *in ~ ziehen* call in question; '**2haft** doubtful, *stärker*: dubious; '**2los** undoubted; (*a. adv.*) doubtless; '**2n** (29) doubt (*an e-r S.* [of] a th., *an j-m* a p.); '**~sfall** *m* (*im ~* in) case of doubt; '**2s'-ohne** doubtless, without doubt; '**~sucht** *f* scepticism, *Am.* skepticism.

'**Zweifler** *m* (7), '**~in** *f* (16[1]) doubter, sceptic, *Am.* skeptic; '**2isch** doubting, sceptical, *Am.* skeptical.

Zweig [tsvaɪk] *m* (3) branch (*a. fig.*), bough; *kleiner ~* twig; *s. grün*; '**~bahn** *f* branch-line.

'**Zwei|gespann** *n* carriage-and-pair; *fig.* twosome, duo; '**2geteilt** divided.

'**Zweig|geschäft** *n*, '**~niederlassung** *f* branch(-establishment); '**~stelle** *f* branch(-office).

zwei|gleisig ['~glaɪziç] double-

-track(ed); **~händig** ['~hɛndiç] two-handed; ♪ for two hands; '♀**hufer** *m* (7) cloven-footed animal; '**~jährig** two-year(s)-old; *Dauer*: of two years, two-year; *bsd.* ✿ biennial; '**~jährlich** (happening) every two years, biennial; '♀**kampf** *m* duel; ⚔ single combat; '**~mal** twice; *es sich ~ überlegen* think twice (before doing it); *es sich nicht ~ sagen lassen* not to wait to be told twice; '**~malig** done twice, twice (repeated); '♀**master** ⚓ *m* (7) two-master; **~motorig** ['~mo-to:riç] twin- (*od.* two-)engined; '♀**par'teiensystem** *n* two-party system; '♀**rad** *n* bicycle, F bike; **~räd(e)rig** ['~rɛ:d(ə)riç] two-wheeled; **~reihig** ['~raɪiç] having two rows; *Jacke usw.*: double-breasted; '**~schläf(e)rig** *Bett*: double; '**~schneidig** double-edged (*a. fig.*); *fig. ~ sein a.* cut both ways; **~seitig** ['~zaɪtiç] two-sided; *Vertrag usw.*: bilateral; *Stoff*: reversible; **~silbig** ['~zilbiç] dissyllabic; *~es Wort* dissyllable; '♀**sitzer** *m* (7) two-seater; '**~sitzig** two-seated; ♀**spänner** ['~ʃpɛnər] *m* (7) carriage-and-pair; **~sprachig** ['~ʃprɑ:xiç] in two languages, bilingual; '♀**stärkenbrille** *f* bifocals *pl.*; '**~stellig:** *~e Zahl* two-digit (*od.* two-place) number; '**~stimmig** for (*Gesang*: in) two voices; **~stöckig** ['~ʃtœkiç] two-stor|eyed, *Am.* -ied; **~strahlig** ['~ʃtrɑ:liç] *Triebwerk*: twin-jet; '**~stufig** *Rakete*: two-stage; **~stündig** ['~ʃtyndiç] of two hours, two-hour; '**~stündlich** every two hours.

zweit [tsvaɪt] (18) second; *in Zssgn* ... but one (*s. zweitjüngst*); *ein ~er m, eine ~e f, ein ~es n* another; *Sport:* ♀*e m, f* runner-up, second; *ein ~er Churchill* another Churchill; *s. Gesicht; aus ~er Hand* second-hand (*a. adv.*); *zu ~ (paarweise)* by twos; *wir sind zu ~* we are two of us; *zum ~en, ~ens* secondly, in the second place; *fig. die ~e Geige spielen* play second fiddle.

'**zwei|tägig** of two days, two-day; '♀**taktmotor** *m* two-stroke (*od.* two-cycle) engine.

'**zweit|-'älteste** second eldest; '♀**ausfertigung** *f* duplicate; '**~'best** second-best.

'**zweiteilig** two-part; *Anzug usw.*: two-piece; ✿, ⚖ bipartite.

'**zweit|'größt** second largest; '**~jüngst** youngest but one; '**~klassig** second-class *od.* -rate; '**~'letzt** last but one, *Am.* next to the last; '**~rangig** secondary; '♀**schrift** *f* second copy, duplicate; '♀**wagen** *m* second car; '♀**wohnung** *f* second home.

'**Zwei|-und'dreißigstelnote** *f* demisemiquaver; **~'vierteltakt** *m* two-four time; '♀**wöchentlich** biweekly; '♀**zackig** two-pronged; '**~zeiler** *m* couplet; '♀**zeilig** of two lines; **~'zimmerwohnung** *f* two-room flat (*Am.* apartment).

Zwerchfell ['tsvɛrç-] *n* diaphragm; '♀**-erschütternd** side-splitting.

Zwerg [tsvɛrk] *m* (3), **~in** ['gin] *f* (16[1]) dwarf, gnome; ♀**enhaft** ['~g-] dwarfish; '**~huhn** *n* bantam; '**~kiefer** *f* dwarf pine; '**~mensch** *m* pygmy; '**~schule** *f* one-room school; '**~staat** *m* mini-state.

Zwetsch(g)e ['tsvɛtʃ(g)ə] *f* (15) plum.

Zwick|el ['tsvikəl] *m* (7) *am Strumpf*: clock; *Schneiderei*: gore, gusset; ⊕ wedge; '♀**en**[1] (25) pinch, tweak; '**~en**[2] *n* (6) (*Schmerz*) twinge; '**~er** *m* (7) (*Augenglas*) pince-nez (*fr.*); '**~mühle** *f fig.* dilemma, fix, tight squeeze.

Zwieback ['tsvi:bak] *m* (3[3]) rusk, zwieback.

Zwiebel ['tsvi:bəl] *f* (15) onion; (*Blumen*♀) bulb; '♀**förmig** bulb-shaped, bulbous; '**~gewächs** *n* bulbous plant; '**~haube** *f* onion dome; '**~kuchen** *m* onion tart; '♀**n** F (29) give *a p.* hell, make it hot for *a p.*; '**~schale** *f* onion-skin; '**~turm** *m* onion tower.

zwie|fach ['tsvi:-], **~fältig** ['~fɛltiç] double, twofold; '♀**gespräch** *n* dialog(ue); colloquy; '♀**licht** *n* twilight; '**~lichtig** dusky; *fig.* shady.

'**Zwie|spalt** *m* (*Uneinigkeit*) discord; (*innerer ~* inner) conflict; (*Abweichung*) discrepancy; *im ~ sein mit* be at variance with; ♀**spältig** ['~ʃpɛltiç] disunited; discrepant; *Gefühle*: conflicting; '**~tracht** *f* (16, *o. pl.*) discord; (*Fehde*) feud; (*Kampf*) strife; *~ säen* sow the seeds of discord; '♀**trächtig** discordant, hostile; *nur pred.* at variance.

Zwil(li)ch ['tsvil(i)ç] *m* (3) tick(ing).

Zwilling ['tsviliŋ] *m* (3[1]) twin; '**~e**

pl. ast. Gemini, Twins; '**~sbruder** *m* twin brother; '**~s-paar** *n* pair of twins; '**~sschwester** *f* twin sister.

Zwing|burg ['tsviŋ-] *f* (tyrant's) strong castle; '**~e** *f* (15) (*Stock*2) ferrule; ⊕ clamp; '**2en** (30) compel (*j-n et. zu tun* a p. to do a th.), make (a p. do a th.), *bsd. mit Gewalt*: force; (*verpflichten*) oblige; (*fertigwerden mit*) manage, finish; *sich zu et.* ~ force o.s. to *a th. od.* to *do* (*a th.*); *s. bezwingen, gezwungen*; '**2end** *adj.* compelling; *Grund*: cogent; *Notwendigkeit*: imperative; *Beweis*: conclusive; '**~er** *m* (7) tower, dungeon; (*Hof*) outer court-yard; (*Hunde*2) kennel; (*Bären*2) bear-pit; '**~herr** *m* tyrant, despot; '**~herrschaft** *f* despotism, tyranny.

zwinkern ['tsviŋkərn] (29) blink; *lustig, schlau*: wink.

Zwirn [tsvirn] *m* (3) (twisted) thread; *Spinnerei*: twine, twisted yarn; '**2en 1.** *adj.* thread; **2.** *v/t.* (25) twist; '**~sfaden** *m* thread.

zwischen ['tsviʃən] *zweien*: between; *mehreren*: among.

'**Zwischen|-akt** *m* entr'acte (*fr.*); *im* ~ between the two acts; '**~bemerkung** *f* incidental remark; interruption; '**~bescheid** *m* intermediate reply; '**~bilanz** *f* interim financial statement; '**~deck** ⚓ *n* between-decks *pl.*; '**~ding** *n* mixture, cross; 2'**durch** through; (*inmitten*) in the midst; *zeitlich*: at intervals, occasionally, (*eingeschoben*) in between; '**~-ergebnis** *n* *Sport*: provisional result; '**~-erzeugnis** *n* intermediate (product); '**~fall** *m* incident; '**~frage** *f* interpolated question; '**~gericht** *n* entremets *pl.* (*fr.*); '**~handel** *m* intermediate trade; (*Durchfuhrhandel*) transit trade; (*Großhandel*) wholesale trade; '**~händler** *m* middleman, intermediary; commission agent; '**~handlung** *f* episode; '**~kredit** *m* interim credit; '**~landung** ✈ *f* intermediate landing, stop (-over *Am.*); *Flug ohne* ~ non-stop flight; '**2liegend** intermediate; '**~lösung** *f* interim solution; *s. Notbehelf*; '**2menschlich:** *~e Beziehungen* human relations; '**~pause** *f* interval, intermission; '**~produkt** *n* intermediate product; '**~prüfung** *f* intermediate examination; '**~raum** *m* space, (*a. zeitlich*) interval; (*Entfernung*) distance (between); (*Lücke*) interstice; (*Zeilenabstand*) spacing; '**~raumtaste** *f der Schreibmaschine*: space-bar; '**~ruf** *m* (loud) interruption; *mißbilligend*: boo; '**~rufer** *m* interrupter; '**~runde** *f Sport*: semi-final; '**~satz** *m* parenthesis; '**~spiel** *n* intermezzo, interlude; '**2staatlich** international, *Am.* inter-state; '**~stadium** *n* intermediate stage; '**~station** *f* intermediate stop, stopover; ~ *machen* stop (over *od.* off) (*in* at); '**~stecker** *m* ⚡, *Radio*: adapter; '**~stock** *m* entresol (*fr.*), intermediate stor|ey, *Am.* -y; '**~stück** *n* intermediate piece; connection; ⚡ adapter; *thea.* interlude, entr'acte (*fr.*); '**~stufe** *f* intermediate stage; '**~träger(in** *f*) *m s. Zuträger*; '**~-urteil** ⚖ *n* interlocutory decree; '**~verkauf** ⚕ *m*: ~ *vorbehalten* subject to prior sale; '**~vorhang** *m* drop-scene; '**~wand** *f* partition (wall); '**~zeit** *f* interval; *in der* ~ (*a.* '**2zeitlich**) in the meantime.

Zwist [tsvist] *m* (3²) (*Zwietracht*) discord; (*Uneinigkeit*) disunion; (*Streit*) quarrel; '**2ig** *s. zwieträchtig*; '**~igkeit** *f s. Zwist.*

zwitschern ['tsvitʃərn] (29) twitter, chirp.

Zwitter ['tsvitər] *m* (7) hermaphrodite; (*Mischling*) hybrid (*a.* ⚘); '**2haft** hermaphrodite; hybrid.

zwo [tsvo:] *s. zwei.*

zwölf [tsvœlf] twelve; *um* ~ *Uhr* at twelve (o'clock), *mittags*: *a.* at noon, *nachts*: *a.* at midnight; '**2-eck** *n* dodecagon; '**~-eckig** dodecagonal; '**2-ender** *m* twelve-point stag; '**~er'lei** *adj.* of twelve different kinds *od.* sorts; *als su.* twelve different things *pl.*; '**~fach** twelvefold; 2'**fingerdarm** *m* duodenum; '**~jährig** *Kind*: twelve-year(s)-old; *allg.*: of twelve years; **~stündig** ['~ʃtyndiç] of twelve hours, twelve-hour; **~t** twelfth; **~tägig** ['~tɛ:giç] of twelve days; '**2tel** *n* (7) twelfth (part); '**~tens** in the twelfth place; '**2tonmusik** *f* twelve-tone music.

Zyankali [tsyan'kɑ:li] *n* cyanide of potassium.

zyklisch ['tsy:kliʃ] cyclic(al).

Zyklon [tsy'klo:n] *m* (3¹), **~e** *f* (15) cyclone.

Zyklop [~'klo:p] *m* (12) Cyclops, *pl.* Cyclopes; **2isch** Cyclopean.

Zyklotron [~klo'tro:n] *n* (3) *Atomwissenschaft*: cyclotron.
Zyklus ['tsy:klus] *m* (16[2]) cycle; *v. Vorlesungen usw.*: course, set.
Zylinder [tsy'lindər] *m* (7) ⚔, ⊕ cylinder; (*Lampen*2) chimney; *Hut*: silk hat, top-hat; **~block** ⊕ *m* cylinder block; **~bohrung** ⊕ *f* cylinder bore; **~kopf** ⊕ *m* cylinder head; **~kopfdichtung** *f* cylinder head gasket.
zylindrisch [~'lindriʃ] cylindrical.
Zyn|iker ['tsy:nikər] *m* (7) cynic; '**2isch** cynical; **~ismus** [tsy'nismus] *m* cynicism.
Zypresse [tsy'prɛsə] *f* (15) cypress (-tree).
Zyste ⚕ ['tsystə] *f* (15) cyst.

Proper Names

Eigennamen

(For declension of proper names see page 1331)

A

Aachen [ˈaːxən] *n* Aachen, *Fr.* Aix-la-Chapelle.
Aargau [ˈaːrgaʊ] *m* Argovia (*Swiss canton*).
Adenauer [ˈaːdənaʊər] *first chancellor of the Federal Republic of Germany*.
Adler [ˈaːdlər] *Austrian psychologist*.
Adorno [aˈdɔrno] *German philosopher*.
Adria [ˈaːdria] *f*, **Adriatische(s) Meer** [adriˈaːtiʃə(s)] *n* Adriatic Sea.
Afghanistan [afˈgaːnistaːn] *n* Afghanistan.
Afrika [ˈaːfrika] *n* Africa.
Ägäis [ɛˈgɛːis] *f*, **Ägäische(s) Meer** [ɛˈgɛːiʃə(s)] *n* Aegean Sea.
Ägypten [ɛˈgyptən] *n* Egypt.
Albanien [alˈbaːniən] *n* Albania.
Albert [ˈalbɛrt], **Albrecht** [ˈalbrɛçt] *m* Albert.
Albertus Magnus [alˈbɛrtus ˈmagnus] *German philosopher*.
Alexander [alɛˈksandər] *m* Alexander.
Alfons [ˈalfɔns] *m German Christian name*.
Algerien [alˈgeːriən] *n* Algeria.
Algier [ˈalʒiːr] *n* Algiers.
Allgäu [ˈalgɔʏ] *n* Al(l)gäu (*region of Bavaria*).
Alpen [ˈalpən] *pl.* Alps *pl.*
Altdorfer [ˈaltdɔrfər] *German painter*.
Amazonas [amaˈtsoːnas] *m* Amazon (*river in Brazil*).
Amerika [aˈmeːrika] *n* America.
Anden [ˈandən] *pl.* Andes *pl.*
Andorra [anˈdɔra] *n* Andorra.
Andrea [anˈdreːa] *f*, **Andreas** [anˈdreːas] *m* Andrea, Andrew.
Angola [aŋˈgoːla] *n* Angola.
Anna [ˈana], **Anne** [ˈanə] *f* Anna.
Antarktis [antˈˀarktis] *f* Antarctic.
Antillen [anˈtilən] *pl.* Antilles *pl.*
Anton [ˈantoːn] *m* Anthony.
Antwerpen [antˈvɛrpən] *n* Antwerp.
Apenninen [apɛˈniːnən] *pl.* Apennines *pl.*
Appenzell [apənˈtsɛl] *n Swiss canton.*
Arabien [aˈraːbiən] *n* Arabia.
Argentinien [argɛnˈtiːniən] *n* Argentina.
Ärmelkanal [ˈɛrməlkanaːl] *m* English Channel.
Armenien [arˈmeːniən] *n* Armenia.
Art(h)ur [ˈartur] *m* Arthur.
Asien [ˈaːziən] *n* Asia.
Athen [aˈteːn] *n* Athens.
Äthiopien [ɛtiˈoːpiən] *n* Ethiopia.
Atlantik [atˈlantik], **Atlantische(r) Ozean** [atˈlantiʃə(r)] *m* Atlantic, Atlantic Ocean.
Ätna [ˈɛːtna] *m* Etna.
Augsburg [ˈaʊksburk] *n town in Bavaria.*
Australien [aʊsˈtraːliən] *n* Australia.
Azoren [aˈtsoːrən] *pl.* Azores *pl.*

B

Bach [bax] *German composer*.
Baden-Württemberg [ˈbaːdənˈvyrtəmbɛrk] *n Land of the Federal Republic of Germany*.
Bahrain [baˈraɪn] *n* Bahrein.
Balearen [baleˈaːrən] *pl.* Balearic Islands *pl.*
Balkan [ˈbalkaːn] *m* Balkan Peninsula.
Banglades(c)h [baŋglaˈdɛʃ] *n* Bangladesh.
Barbarossa [barbaˈrɔsa] *hist. appellation of the German emperor Friedrich I.*
Barlach [ˈbarlax] *German sculptor*.

Basel ['bɑːzəl] *n* Basel, Basle, *Fr.* Bâle (*Swiss town and canton*).
Baskenland ['baskənlant] *n*, **Baskische(n) Provinzen** ['baskiʃə(n)] *f/pl.* Basque Provinces *pl.*
Baumeister ['baʊmaɪstər] *German painter.*
Bayern ['baɪərn] *n* Bavaria (*Land of the Federal Republic of Germany*).
Bayerische(r) Wald ['baɪəriʃə(r)] *m* Bavarian Forest.
Bebel ['beːbəl] *German socialist.*
Beckmann ['bɛkman] *German painter.*
Beethoven ['beːthoːfən] *German composer.*
Belgien ['bɛlgiən] *n* Belgium.
Belgrad ['bɛlgrɑːt] *n* Belgrade.
Benn [bɛn] *German writer.*
Beringstraße ['beːriŋʃtrɑːsə] *f* Bering Strait.
Berlin [bɛr'liːn] *n* Berlin.
Bermuda-Inseln [bɛr'muːda-] *f/pl.* Bermudas *pl.*
Bern [bɛrn] *n* Bern, *Fr.* Berne (*capital and canton of Switzerland*).
Bernhard ['bɛrnhart] *m* Bernard.
Birma ['birma] *n* Burma.
Biskaya [bis'kɑːja] *f* Biscay, *Golf von ~ m* Bay of Biscay.
Bloch [blɔx] *German philosopher.*
Bodensee ['boːdənzeː] *m* Lake Constance.
Böhmen ['bøːmən] *n* Bohemia, *Böhmer Wald m* Bohemian Forest.
Bolivien [bo'liːviən] *n* Bolivia.
Böll [bœl] *German author.*
Bonn [bɔn] *n capital of the Federal Republic of Germany.*
Borneo ['bɔrneo] *n* Borneo.
Bosporus ['bɔsporus] *m* Bosporus.
Botswana [bɔts'vɑːna] *n* Botswana.
Brahms [brɑːms] *German composer.*
Brandt [brant] *fourth chancellor of the Federal Republic of Germany.*
Brasilien [bra'ziːliən] *n* Brazil.
Brecht [brɛçt] *German dramatist.*
Bremen ['breːmən] *n Land of the Federal Republic of Germany.*
Brigitte [bri'gitə] *f* Bridget.
Bruckner ['bruknər] *Austrian composer.*
Brüssel ['brysəl] *n* Brussels.
Buber ['buːbər] *German philosopher.*
Büchner ['byːçnər] *German dramatist.*
Bukarest ['buːkarɛst] *n* Bucharest.
Bulgarien [bul'gɑːriən] *n* Bulgaria.
Bundesrepublik Deutschland ['bundəsrepubliːk 'dɔʏtʃlant] *f* Federal Republic of Germany.
Bunsen ['bunzən] *German chemist.*
Burgenland ['burgənlant] *n province of Austria.*
Burgund [bur'gunt] *n* Burgundy.
Burma ['burma] *n* → *Birma.*
Busch [buʃ] *German satirist.*
Butenandt ['buːtənant] *German chemist.*

C

Calais [ka'lɛː] *n*: *Straße von ~ f* Straits of Dover.
Calvin [kal'viːn] *Swiss Protestant reformer.*
Carstens ['karstəns] *fifth president of the Federal Republic of Germany.*
Ceylon ['tsaɪlɔn] *n* Ceylon (*heute* → *Sri Lanka*).
Chile ['tʃiːle] *n* Chile.
China ['çiːna] *n* China.
Christoph ['kristɔf] *m* Christopher.
Christus ['kristus] *m* Christ.

D

Daimler ['daɪmlər] *German inventor.*
Dänemark ['dɛːnəmark] *n* Denmark.
Den Haag [den'hɑːk] *n* The Hague.
Delhi ['deːli] *n* Delhi.
Deutsche Demokratische Republik ['dɔʏtʃə demo'krɑːtiʃə repu'bliːk] *f* German Democratic Republic.
Deutschland ['dɔʏtʃlant] *n* Germany.
Diesel ['diːzəl] *German inventor.*
Döblin ['døːbliːn] *German novelist.*
Dolomiten [dolo'miːtən] *pl.* Dolomites *pl.*
Dominikanische Republik [domini'kɑːniʃə repu'bliːk] *f* Dominican Republic.
Donau ['doːnaʊ] *f* Danube.
Dresden ['dreːsdən] *n town and district in the German Democratic Republic.*
Droste-Hülshoff ['drɔstə 'hylshɔf] *German poetess.*
Dünkirchen ['dyːnkirçən] *n* Dunkirk.
Dürer ['dyːrər] *German painter and engraver.*

Dürrenmatt ['dyrənmat] *Swiss dramatist.*
Düsseldorf ['dysəldɔrf] *n capital of North Rhine-Westphalia.*

E

Ebert ['e:bərt] *first president of the Weimar Republic.*
Ecuador [ekua'do:r] *n* Ecuador.
Egk [ɛk] *German composer.*
Eichendorff ['aɪçəndɔrf] *German poet.*
Einstein ['aɪnʃtaɪn] *German physicist.*
Eismeer ['aɪsme:r] *n* Nördliches ~ Arctic Ocean, Südliches ~ Antarctic Ocean.
Elbe ['ɛlbə] *f German river.*
Elfenbeinküste ['ɛlfənbaɪnkystə] *f* Ivory Coast.
El Salvador [ɛl zalva'do:r] *n* El Salvador.
Elsaß ['ɛlzas] *n* Alsace.
Emil ['e:mi:l] *m German Christian name.*
Engadin ['ɛŋgadi:n] *n* Engadine.
Engels ['ɛŋəls] *German socialist philosopher.*
England ['ɛŋlant] *n* England.
Erhardt ['e:rhart] *second chancellor of the Federal Republic of Germany.*
Eritrea [eri'tre:a] *n* Eritrea.
Estland ['e:stlant] *n* Estonia.
Euphrat ['ɔʏfrat] *m* Euphrates.
Eurasien [ɔʏ'ra:ziən] *n* Eurasia.
Europa [ɔʏ'ro:pa] *n* Europe.
Eva ['e:fa, 'e:va] *f* Eve.

F

Feuerbach ['fɔʏərbax] *German philosopher.*
Fichte ['fixtə] *German philosopher.*
Finnland ['finlant] *n* Finland.
Florenz [flo'rɛnts] *n* Florence.
Fontane [fɔn'ta:nə] *German author.*
Franken ['fraŋkən] *n* Franconia.
Frankfurt (am Main) ['fraŋkfurt] *n* Frankfurt (on the Main).
Frankfurt an der Oder ['fraŋkfurt] *n* Frankfurt on the Oder (*town and district in the German Democratic Republic*).
Frankreich ['fraŋkraɪç] *n* France.
Freiburg ['fraɪburk] *n Fr.* Fribourg (*Swiss town and canton*).
Freiburg im Breisgau ['fraɪburk im 'braɪsgaʊ] *n town in West Germany.*
Freud [frɔʏt] *Austrian psychologist.*
Friedrich ['fri:driç] **1.** *German painter*; **2.** ~ der Große Frederik the Great (*king of Prussia*).
Friedrich ['fri:driç] *m* Frederick.
Friesische(n) Inseln ['fri:ziʃə(n)] *f/pl.* Frisian Islands *pl.*
Frisch [friʃ] *Swiss author.*
Fritz [frits] *m shortened form of* → Friedrich.
Fudschijama [fudʒi'ja:ma] *m* Mount Fuji.

G

Gabun [ga'bu:n] *n* Gabon.
Gambia ['gambia] *n* the Gambia.
Ganges ['gaŋgɛs] *m* Ganges.
Garmisch ['garmiʃ] *n health resort in Bavaria.*
Gauss [gaʊs] *German mathematician.*
Genf [gɛnf] *n* Geneva (*Swiss town and canton*).
Genua ['ge:nua] *n* Genoa.
Georg [ge'ʔɔrk, 'ge:ɔrk] *m* George.
Gera ['ge:ra] *n town and district in the German Democratic Republic.*
Ghana ['ga:na] *n* Ghana.
Gibraltar [gi'braltar] *n* Gibraltar.
Goethe ['gø:tə] *German writer.*
Goldküste ['gɔltkystə] *f* Gold Coast.
Grass [gras] *German writer.*
Graubünden [grau'byndən] *n Fr.* Grisons (*Swiss canton*).
Grenada [gre'na:da] *n* Grenada.
Griechenland ['gri:çənlant] *n* Greece.
Grimm [grim]: Gebrüder ~ *German philologists.*
Grönland ['grø:nlant] *n* Greenland.
Großbritannien [gro:sbri'taniən] *n* Great Britain.
Grünewald ['gry:nəvalt] *German painter.*
Guinea [gi'ne:a] *n* Guinea.
Guyana [gu'ja:na] *n* Guyana.

H

Hahn [ha:n] *German chemist.*
Haiti [ha'i:ti] *n* Haiti.
Hamburg ['hamburk] *n seaport and Land of the Federal Republic of Germany.*

Händel ['hɛndəl] Handel (*German composer*).
Hannover [ha'no:fər] *n* Hanover (*capital of Lower Saxony*).
Hauptmann ['haʊptman] *German dramatist*.
Haydn ['haɪdən] *Austrian composer*.
Hebriden [he'bri:dən] *pl.* Hebrides *pl.*
Hegel ['he:gəl] *German philosopher*.
Heidegger ['haɪdɛgər] *German philosopher*.
Heidelberg ['haɪdəlbɛrk] *n town in West Germany*.
Heine ['haɪnə] *German writer*.
Heinemann ['haɪnəman] *third president of the Federal Republic of Germany*.
Heisenberg ['haɪzənbɛrk] *German physicist*.
Helena ['he:lena], **Helene** [he'le:nə] *f* Helen.
Helgoland ['hɛlgolant] *n* Heligoland.
Hermann der Cherusker ['hɛrman der çe'ruskər] *hist.* Arminius.
Hesse ['hɛsə] *German writer*.
Hessen ['hɛsən] *n* Hesse (*Land of the Federal Republic of Germany*).
Hertz [hɛrts] *German physicist*.
Heuss [hɔʏs] *first president of the Federal Republic of Germany*.
Himalaja [hi'ma:laja] *m the* Himalayas *pl.*
Hindemith ['hindəmit] *German composer*.
Hiros(c)hima [hiro'ʃi:ma] *n* Hiroshima.
Hoffmann ['hɔfman] *German writer*.
Holbein ['hɔlbaɪn] *German painters*.
Hölderlin ['hœldərlin] *German poet*.
Holland ['hɔlant] *n* Holland.

I

Indien ['indiən] *n* India.
Indische(r) Ozean ['indiʃə(r)] *m* Indian Ocean.
Indochina ['indo'çi:na] *n* Indochina.
Indonesien [indo'ne:ziən] *n* Indonesia.
Innerasien ['inɛr'ʔa:ziən] *n* Central Asia.
Innsbruck ['insbruk] *n town in Austria*.
Irak [i'ra:k] *m* Iraq.
Iran [i'ra:n] *m* Iran.
Irische Republik ['i:riʃə] *f* Republic of Ireland, Eire.
Irische See ['i:riʃə] *f* Irish Sea.
Irland ['irlant] *n* Ireland.
Island ['i:slant] *n* Iceland.
Israel ['israɛl] *n* Israel.
Italien [i'ta:liən] *n* Italy.

J

Jalta ['jalta] *n* Yalta.
Jamaika [ja'maɪka] *n* Jamaica.
Japan ['ja:pan] *n* Japan.
Jaspers ['jaspərs] *German philosopher*.
Java ['ja:va] *n* Java.
Jean Paul [ʒɑ̃ 'paʊl] *German writer*.
Jemen ['je:mən] *m* Yemen.
Jerusalem [je'ru:zalɛm] *n* Jerusalem.
Jesus ['je:zus] *m* Jesus.
Johann(es) [jo'hanəs, 'jo:han] *m* John.
Jordanien [jɔr'da:niən] *n* Jordan.
Jugoslawien [jugo'sla:viən] *n* Yugoslavia.
Julia ['ju:lia], **Julie** ['ju:liə] *f* Julia.

K

Kafka ['kafka] *German writer*.
Kairo ['kaɪro] *n* Cairo.
Kalifornien [kali'fɔrniən] *n* California.
Kambodscha [kam'bɔdʒa] *n* Kampuchea.
Kamerun [kamə'ru:n] *n* Cameroon.
Kanada ['kanada] *n* Canada.
Kanalinseln [ka'na:linzəln] *f/pl.* Channel Islands *pl.*
Kanarische(n) Inseln [ka'na:riʃə(n)] *f/pl.* Canary Islands *pl.*, Canaries *pl.*
Kanton ['kantɔn] *n* Canton.
Kap der Guten Hoffnung *n* Cape of Good Hope.
Kapstadt ['kapʃtat] *n* Cape Town.
Karibik [ka'ri:bik] *f* Caribbean.
Karin ['ka:ri:n; -in] *f* Karen.
Karl der Große *hist.* Charlemagne (*Holy Roman emperor*).
Karl-Marx-Stadt [karl'marksʃtat] *n* (*formerly Chemnitz*) *town and district in the German Democratic Republic*.
Kärnten ['kɛrntən] *n* Carinthia (*province of Austria*).
Karpaten [kar'pa:tən] *pl.* Carpathian Mountains *pl.*

Kaschmir ['kaʃmir] *n* Kashmir.
Kaspische(s) Meer ['kaspiʃə(s)] *n* Caspian Sea.
Katharina [kata'ri:na] *f* Catherine.
Kaukasus ['kaukazus] *m* Caucasus Mountains *pl.*
Kenia ['ke:nia] *n* Kenya.
Kiesinger ['ki:ziŋər] *third chancellor of the Federal Republic of Germany.*
Kiew ['ki:ɛf] *n* Kiev.
Kilimandscharo [kiliman'dʒɑ:ro] *m* Mount Kilimanjaro.
Kleinasien [klaɪn'ʔɑ:ziən] *n* Asia Minor.
Kohl [ko:l] *sixth chancellor of the Federal Republic of Germany.*
Köln [kœln] *n* Cologne.
Kolumbien [ko'lumbiən] *n* Columbia.
Kongo ['kɔŋgo] *m* Congo.
Konstanz ['kɔnstants] *n* Constance; → *Bodensee.*
Kopenhagen [kopən'hɑ:gən] *n* Copenhagen.
Korea → *Nordkorea, Südkorea.*
Korfu ['kɔrfu] *n* Corfu.
Korsika ['kɔrzika] *n* Corsica.
Kreml ['kre:məl] *m* Kremlin.
Kreta ['kre:ta] *n* Crete.
Krim [krim] *f* Crimea.
Kuba ['ku:ba] *n* Cuba.
Kuwait [ku'vaɪt] *n* Kuwait.

L

Lappland ['laplant] *n* Lapland.
Lateinamerika [la'taɪname:rika] *n* Latin America.
Leipzig ['laɪptsiç] *n town and district in the German Democratic Republic.*
Lenz [lɛnts] *German writer.*
Leonhard ['le:ɔnhart] *m* Leonard.
Lessing ['lesiŋ] *German dramatist.*
Lettland ['lɛtlant] *n* Latvia.
Libanon ['li:banɔn] *m* Lebanon.
Liberia [li'be:ria] *n* Liberia.
Libyen ['li:byən] *n* Libya.
Liebig ['li:biç] *German chemist.*
Liebknecht ['li:pknɛçt] *German socialist.*
Liechtenstein ['liçtənʃtaɪn] *n* Liechtenstein.
Lissabon ['lisabɔn] *n* Lisbon.
Litauen ['li:taʊən] *n* Lithuania.
London ['lɔndɔn] *n* London.
Lothringen ['lo:triŋən] *n Fr.* Lorraine.
Lübeck ['ly:bɛk] *n town in West Germany.*
Lübke ['lypkə] *second president of the Federal Republic of Germany.*
Ludwig ['lu:tviç] *m* Louis.
Luise [lu'i:zə] *f* Louisa.
Lüneburg ['ly:nəburk] *n town in West Germany,* ~*er Heide f* Lüneburg Heath.
Luxemburg ['luksəmburk] **1.** *n* Luxemb(o)urg; **2.** *German female socialist.*
Luzern [lu'tsɛrn] *n Fr.* Lucerne (*Swiss town and canton*).

M

Maas [mɑ:s] *f* Maas, *Fr.* Meuse.
Madagaskar [mada'gaskar] *n* Madagascar.
Madeira [ma'de:ra] *n* Madeira.
Madrid [ma'drit] *n* Madrid.
Magdeburg ['makdəburk] *n town and district in the German Democratic Republic.*
Mailand ['maɪlant] *n* Milan.
Mainz [maɪnts] *n capital of Rhineland-Palatinate.*
Malaysia [ma'laɪzia] *n* Malaysia.
Malediven [male'di:ven] *pl.* Maldives *pl.*
Mali ['mɑ:li] *n* Mali.
Mallorca [ma'lɔrka] *n* Majorca.
Malta ['malta] *n* Malta.
Mandschurei [mandʒu'raɪ] *f* Manchuria.
Mann [man] *German writers.*
Marcuse [mar'ku:zə] *German sociologist.*
Marokko [ma'rɔko] *n* Morocco.
Marx [marks] *German socialist philosopher.*
Mathilde [ma'tildə] *f* Mat(h)ilda.
Matthias [ma'ti:as] *m* Matthias.
Mauretanien [maʊre'tɑ:niən] *n* Mauritania.
Mauritius [maʊ'ri:tsiʊs] *n* Mauritius.
Max(imilian) [maks(i'mi:liɑ:n)] *m* Max(imilian).
Mazedonien [matsə'do:niən] *n* Macedonia.
Mekka ['mɛka] *n* Mecca.
Memel ['me:məl] *f* Niemen (River).
Mexiko ['mɛksiko] *n* Mexico.
Metternich ['mɛtərniç] *Austrian statesman.*

Michael [ˈmiçaɛl], **Michel** [ˈmiçəl] *m* Michael.
Mittelamerika [ˈmitəlaˈmeːrika] *n* Central America.
Mitteldeutschland [ˈmitəldɔʏtʃlant] *n* Central Germany.
Mitteleuropa [ˈmitəlɔʏˈroːpa] *n* Central Europe.
Mittelmeer [ˈmitəlmeːr] *n* Mediterranean (Sea).
Mittlere(r) Osten *m* Middle East.
Moldau [ˈmɔldaʊ] *f* Moldavia.
Mongolei [mɔŋgoˈlaɪ] *f*: *die Innere* ~ Inner Mongolia; *die Äußere* ~ Outer Mongolia.
Monika [ˈmoːnika] *f* Monica.
Mörike [ˈmøːrikə] *German poet.*
Moritz [ˈmoːrits] *m* Maurice.
Mosel [ˈmoːzəl] *f Fr.* Moselle.
Moskau [ˈmɔskaʊ] *n* Moscow.
Mozambique [mozamˈbik] *n* Mozambique.
Mozart [ˈmoːtsart] *Austrian composer.*
München [ˈmynçən] *n* Munich (*capital of Bavaria*).

N

Nahe(r) Osten [ˈnɑːə(r) ˈɔstən] *m* Near East.
Namibia [naˈmiːbia] *n* Namibia.
Neapel [neˈɑːpəl] *n* Naples.
Nepal [ˈneːpal] *n* Nepal.
Neufundland [nɔʏˈfuntlant] *n* Newfoundland.
Neuguinea [nɔʏgiˈneːa] *n* New Guinea.
Neuseeland [nɔʏˈzeːlant] *n* New Zealand.
Niederlande [ˈniːdərlandə] *pl.* Netherlands *pl.*
Niedersachsen [niːdərzaksən] *n* Lower Saxony (*Land of the Federal Republic of Germany*).
Nigeria [niˈgeːria] *n* Nigeria.
Nikaragua [nikaˈrɑːgua] *n* Nicaragua.
Nikolaus [ˈniːkolaʊs] *m* Nicholas.
Nil [niːl] *m* Nile.
Nizza [ˈnitsa] *n Fr.* Nice.
Nordamerika [ˈnɔrtaˈmeːrika] *n* North America.
Nordirland [ˈnɔrtˈʔirlant] *n* Northern Ireland.
Nordkap [ˈnɔrtkap] *n* North Cape.
Nordkorea [ˈnɔrtkoˈreːa] *n* North Korea.
Nordrhein-Westfalen [ˈnɔrtraɪnvɛstˈfɑːlən] *n* North Rhine-Westphalia (*Land of the Federal Republic of Germany*).
Nordsee [ˈnɔrtzeː] *f* North Sea.
Norwegen [ˈnɔrveːgən] *n* Norway.
Nubien [ˈnuːbiən] *n* Nubia.
Nürnberg [ˈnyrnbɛrk] *n* Nuremberg.

O

Obervolta [oːbərˈvɔlta] *n* Upper Volta.
Odenwald [ˈoːdənvalt] *m mountainous region in Hesse.*
Oder [ˈoːdər] *f German river.*
Oslo [ˈɔslo] *n* Oslo.
Osnabrück [ɔsnaˈbryk] *n town in West Germany.*
Ossietzky [ɔsiˈɛtski] *German writer and pacifist.*
Ostasien [ˈɔstˈʔɑːziən] *n* Eastern Asia.
Ost-Berlin [ˈɔstbɛrliːn] *n* East Berlin (*town and district in the German Democratic Republic*).
Ostende [ɔstˈʔɛndə] *n* Ostend.
Osterinsel [ˈoːstərʔinzəl] *f* Easter Island.
Österreich [ˈøːstəraɪç] *n* Austria.
Ostsee [ˈɔstzeː] *f* Baltic (Sea).
Otto der Große *hist.* Otto the Great (*Holy Roman emperor*).
Ozeanien [otseˈɑːniən] *n* Oceania, South Sea Islands *pl.*

P

Pakistan [ˈpɑːkistɑ(ː)n] *n* Pakistan.
Paraguay [paraguˈɑːi] *n* Paraguay.
Paris [paˈriːs] *n* Paris.
Paul [paʊl] *m*, **Paula** [ˈpaʊla] *f* Paul, Paula.
Pazifik [paˈtsiːfik], **Pazifische(r) Ozean** [paˈtsiːfiʃə(r)] *m* Pacific (Ocean).
Peking [ˈpeːkiŋ] *n* Peking.
Persien [ˈpɛrziən] *n* Persia (*heute* → *Iran*).
Persische(r) Golf [ˈpɛrziʃə(r) ˈgɔlf] *m* Persian Gulf.
Peru [peˈruː] *n* Peru.
Peter [ˈpeːtər] *m* Peter.
Pfalz [pfalts] *f* → *Rheinland-Pfalz*.
Philipp [ˈfiːlip] *m* Philip.
Philippinen [filiˈpiːnən] *pl.* Philippine Islands, Philippines *pl.*

Polen ['po:lən] *n* Poland.
Polynesien [poly'ne:ziən] *n* Polynesia.
Pommern ['pɔmərn] *n* Pomerania.
Portugal ['pɔrtugal] *n* Portugal.
Prag [pra:k] *n* Prague.
Preußen ['prɔʏsən] *n hist.* Prussia.
Puerto Rico [pu'ɛrto 'ri:ko] *n* Puerto Rico.
Pyrenäen [pyre'nɛ:ən] *pl.* Pyrenees *pl.*

Q

Qatar ['katar] *n* Qatar.

R

Rhein [raɪn] *m* Rhine.
Rheinland-Pfalz ['raɪnlant'pfalts] *n* Rhineland-Palatinate (*Land of the Federal Republic of Germany*).
Rhodesien [ro'de:ziən] *n* Rhodesia (*heute* → Simbabwe).
Rhodos ['ro(:)dɔs] *n* Rhodes.
Rom [ro:m] *n* Rome.
Rosemarie ['ro:zəmari:] *f* Rosemary.
Rostock ['rɔstɔk] *n town and district in the German Democratic Republic.*
Rote(s) Meer *n* Red Sea.
Ruhr [ru:r] *f German river*; **~gebiet** *n industrial centre of West Germany.*
Rumänien [ru'mɛ:niən] *n* Ro(u)mania.
Rußland ['ruslant] *n* Russia.

S

Saale ['za:lə] *f German river.*
Saar [za:r] *f affluent of the Moselle*; **~brücken** [~'brykən] *n capital of the Saar*; **~land** ['~lant] *n* Saar (*Land of the Federal Republic of Germany*).
Sachsen ['zaksən] *n* Saxony.
Sahara ['za:hara, za'ha:ra] *f* Sahara.
Salzburg ['zaltsburk] *n town and province of Austria.*
Sambia ['zambia] *n* Zambia.
Sardinien [zar'di:niən] *n* Sardinia.
Saudi-Arabien [zaʊdia'ra:biən] *n* Saudi Arabia.
Scheel [ʃe:l] *fourth president of the Federal Republic of Germany.*
Schiller ['ʃilər] *German poet and dramatist.*
Schlesien ['ʃle:ziən] *n* Silesia.
Schleswig-Holstein ['ʃle:sviç'hɔlʃtaɪn] *n Land of the Federal Republic of Germany.*
Schmidt [ʃmit] *fifth chancellor of the Federal Republic of Germany.*
Schopenhauer ['ʃo:pənhaʊər] *German philosopher.*
Schottland ['ʃɔtlant] *n* Scotland.
Schubert ['ʃu:bərt] *Austrian composer.*
Schwaben ['ʃva:bən] *n* Swabia.
Schwarze(s) Meer *n* Black Sea.
Schwarzwald ['ʃvartsvalt] *m* Black Forest.
Schweden ['ʃve:dən] *n* Sweden.
Schweiz [ʃvaɪts] *f*: die ~ Switzerland.
Schwyz [ʃvi:ts] *n Swiss town and canton.*
Senegal ['ze:negal] *n* Senegal.
Serbien ['zɛrbiən] *n* Serbia.
Seychellen [ze'ʃɛlən] *pl.* Seychelles *pl.*
Shetland-Inseln ['ʃɛtlantinzəln] *f/pl.* Shetland Islands *pl.*
Sibirien [zi'bi:riən] *n* Siberia.
Siebengebirge ['zi:bəngəbirgə] *n mountain range along the Rhine.*
Simbabwe [zim'ba:bve] *n* Zimbabwe.
Sinai ['zi:nai] *m* Sinai.
Singapur ['ziŋgapu:r] *n* Singapore.
Sizilien [zi'tsi:liən] *n* Sicily.
Skandinavien [skandi'na:viən] *n* Scandinavia.
Slowakei [slova'kaɪ] *f*: die ~ Slovakia.
Somalia [zo'ma:lia] *n* Somalia.
Sophie [zo'fi:] *f* Sophia.
Sowjetunion [zɔ'vjɛtunio:n] *f* Soviet Union.
Spanien ['ʃpa:niən] *n* Spain.
Spengler ['ʃpɛŋlər] *German philosopher.*
Spitzbergen ['ʃpitsbɛrgən] *n* Spitsbergen.
Spitzweg ['ʃpitsve:k] *German painter.*
Sri Lanka ['sri: 'laŋka] *n* Sri Lanka.
Stefan, Stephan ['ʃtɛfan] *m* Stephen.
Steiermark ['ʃtaɪərmark] *f* Styria (*province of Austria*).
Stille(r) Ozean *m* → Pazifik.
Stockholm ['ʃtɔkhɔlm] *n* Stockholm.
Straßburg ['ʃtra:sburk] *n Fr.* Strasbourg.

Strauss [ʃtraʊs]: *Richard ~ German composer.*
Strauss [ʃtraʊs]: *Johann ~ Austrian composer.*
Stresemann [ˈʃtreːzəman] *German statesman.*
Stuttgart [ˈʃtutgart] *n capital of Baden-Württemberg.*
Südafrika [ˈzyːtˈʔɑːfrika] *n* South Africa.
Südamerika [ˈzyːtaˈmeːrika] *n* South America.
Sudan [zuˈdɑːn] *m* Sudan.
Sudeten [zuˈdeːtən] *pl.* Sudetes, Sudeten Mountains *pl.*
Südjemen [ˈzyːtjeːmen] *m* Southern Yemen.
Südkorea [ˈzyːtkoˈreːa] *n* South Korea.
Südsee [ˈzyːtzeː] *f* South Pacific.
Südwestafrika [zyːtˈvɛstɑːfrika] *n* South West Africa (*heute → Namibia*).
Sueskanal [ˈzuːɛskanɑːl] *m* Suez Canal.
Sumatra [zuˈmɑːtra; ˈzuːmɑtra] *n* Sumatra.
Susanne [zuˈzanə] *f* Susan.
Swasiland [ˈsvɑːzilant] *n* Swaziland.
Syrien [ˈzyːriən] *n* Syria.

T

Taipeh [taɪˈpeː] *n* Taipei.
Taiwan [taɪˈvan; taɪˈvɑːn] *n* Taiwan.
Tanganjika [taŋganˈjiːka] *n* Tanganyika.
Tansania [tanzaˈniːa] *n* Tanzania.
Tasmanien [tasˈmɑːniən] *n* Tasmania.
Tessin [tɛˈsiːn] *n* Ticino (*Swiss canton*).
Thailand [ˈtaɪlant] *n* Thailand.
Themse [ˈtɛmzə] *f* Thames.
Theodor [ˈteːodoːr] *m* Theodore.
Thüringen [ˈtyːriŋən] *n* Thuringia.
Tibet [ˈtiːbɛt] *n* Tibet.
Tigris [ˈtiːgris] *m* Tigris.
Tirol [tiˈroːl] *n* Tyrol (*province of Austria*).
Tokio [ˈtoːkio] *n* Tokyo.
Toskana [tɔsˈkɑːna] *f* Tuscany.
Tote(s) Meer *n* Dead Sea.
Trier [triːr] *n* Trier, *Fr.* Trèves.
Tschad [tʃat; tʃɑːt] *n* Chad.
Tschechoslowakei [tʃɛçoslovaˈkaɪ] *f*: *die ~* Czechoslovakia.
Tunesien [tuˈneːziən] *n* Tunisia.
Tunis [ˈtuːnis] *n* Tunis.
Türkei [tyrˈkaɪ] *f*: *die ~* Turkey.

U

Uganda [uˈganda] *n* Uganda.
Ukraine [ukraˈiːnə, uˈkraɪnə] *f* Ukraine.
Ungarn [ˈuŋgarn] *n* Hungary.
Union der Sozialistischen Sowjetrepubliken *f* Union of Soviet Socialist Republics.
Ural [uˈrɑːl] *m* Ural, Ural Mountains *pl.*
Uruguay [uruguˈɑːi] *n* Uruguay.

V

Vatikan [vatiˈkɑːn] *m* Vatican.
Venedig [veˈneːdiç] *n* Venice.
Venezuela [venetsuˈeːla] *n* Venezuela.
Vereinigte(s) Königreich (von Großbritannien und Nordirland) *n* United Kingdom (of Great Britain and Northern Ireland).
Vereinigte(n) Staaten (von Amerika) *pl.* United States (of America).
Vesuv [veˈzuːf] *m* Vesuvius.
Vietnam [viɛtˈnam] *n* Vietnam, Viet Nam.
Vogesen [voˈgeːzən] *pl. Fr.* Vosges *pl.*
Volksrepublik China [ˈçiːna] *f* People's Republic of China.
Vorderasien [ˈfɔrdərˈʔɑːziən] *n* Near East.

W

Wagner [ˈvɑːgnər] *German composer.*
Walther von der Vogelweide [ˈvaltər fɔn der ˈfoːgəlvaɪdə] *medieval German poet.*
Warschau [ˈvarʃaʊ] *n* Warsaw.
Weichsel [ˈvaɪksəl] *f* Vistula.
Weiße(s) Meer *n* White Sea.
Weißrußland [ˈvaɪsruslant] *n* White Russia, Byelorussia.
Weizsäcker [ˈvaɪtszɛkər]: *Richard von ~ sixth president of the Federal Republic of Germany.*
Weizsäcker [ˈvaɪtszɛkər]: *Carl Friedrich von ~ German physicist.*
Werfel [ˈvɛrfəl] *Austrian writer.*

Westfalen [vɛstˈfaːlən] *n* Westphalia.
Westindische(n) Inseln [ˈvɛstˈʔindiʃə(n) ˈinzəln] *f/pl.* West Indies *pl.*
Wien [viːn] *n* Vienna (*capital and province of Austria*).
Wiesbaden [ˈviːsbaːdən] *n capital of Hesse.*
Wilhelm [ˈvilhɛlm] *m* William.
Wolfram von Eschenbach [ˈvɔlfram fɔn ˈʔɛʃənbax] *medieval German poet.*
Württemberg [ˈvyrtəmbɛrk] *n* → Baden-Württemberg.
Würzburg [ˈvyrtsburk] *n town in West Germany.*

Z

Zaire [zaˈiːr] *n* Zaïre.
Zentralafrikanische Republik [tsɛnˈtraːlafrikaːniʃə repuˈbliːk] *f* Central African Republic.
Zuckmayer [ˈtsukmaɪər] *German dramatist.*
Zugspitze [ˈtsuːkʃpitsə] *f highest mountain of Germany.*
Zürich [ˈtsyːriç] *n* Zurich (*Swiss town and canton*).
Zypern [ˈtsyːpərn] *n* Cyprus.

Current German Abbreviations

Gebräuchliche deutsche Abkürzungen

A

AA *Auswärtiges Amt* Foreign Office.
Abb. *Abbildung* illustration, *abbr.* fig. (= figure).
Abf. *Abfahrt* departure.
Abk. *Abkürzung* abbreviation.
Abo *Abonnement* subscription.
Abs. *Absatz* paragraph; *Absender* sender.
Abschn. *Abschnitt* paragraph, chapter.
Abt. *Abteilung* department.
a. D. *außer Dienst* retired; *an der Donau* on the Danube.
ADAC *Allgemeiner Deutscher Automobil-Club* German automobile association.
ADN *Allgemeiner Deutscher Nachrichtendienst* General German News Service (*in the* → *DDR*).
AG *Aktiengesellschaft* (public) limited company, *Am.* (stock) corporation.
allg. *allgemein* general.
a. M. *am Main* on the Main.
amtl. *amtlich* official.
Ank. *Ankunft* arrival.
Anm. *Anmerkung* note.
AOK *Allgemeine Ortskrankenkasse* general health insurance scheme.
ao. Prof., a. o. Prof. *außerordentlicher Professor etwa* associate professor.
APO *Außerparlamentarische Opposition* extra-parliamentary opposition.
ARD *Arbeitsgemeinschaft der öffentlich-rechtlichen Rundfunkanstalten der Bundesrepublik Deutschland* Association of the Broadcasting Corporations of the Federal Republic of Germany.
a. Rh. *am Rhein* on the Rhine.
Art. *Artikel* article.
Aufl. *Auflage* edition.
Az *Aktenzeichen* file number.

B

b. *bei* at; with; *place*: near; *address*: care of.
Bd. *Band* volume.
beil. *beiliegend* enclosed.
Bem. *Bemerkung* note, comment, observation.
BENELUX *Belgien, Niederlande, Luxemburg* Belgium, Netherlands, Luxemb(o)urg.
bes. *besonders* especially.
Best.Nr. *Bestellnummer* order number.
Betr. *Betreff, betrifft at head of letter*: subject, re.
betr. *betreffend, betrifft, betreffs* concerning, regarding.
bez. *bezahlt* paid; *bezüglich* with reference to.
BFH *Bundesfinanzhof* Federal Finance Court.
BGB *Bürgerliches Gesetzbuch* (German) Civil Code.
BGH *Bundesgerichtshof* Federal Supreme Court.
BGS *Bundesgrenzschutz* Federal Border Police.
Bhf. *Bahnhof* station.
BLZ *Bankleitzahl* bank code number.
BND *Bundesnachrichtendienst* Federal Intelligence Service.
BP *Bundespost* Federal Postal Administration.
BRD *Bundesrepublik Deutschland* Federal Republic of Germany.
BRT *Brutto-Register-Tonnen* gross register tons.
Bw *Bundeswehr* Federal Armed Forces.
b. w. *bitte wenden* please turn over.
bzgl. *bezüglich* with reference to.
bzw. *beziehungsweise* respectively.

C

C *Celsius* Celsius, centigrade.
ca. *circa, ungefähr, etwa* about, approximately.

cand. *candidatus, Kandidat* candidate.
CDU *Christlich-Demokratische Union* Christian Democratic Union.
Co. *Kompagnon* partner; *Kompanie* Company.
CSU *Christlich-Soziale Union* Christian Social Union.
c. t. *cum tempore, mit akademischem Viertel* with a quarter of an hour's allowance.

D

d. Ä. *der Ältere* the Elder.
DAG *Deutsche Angestellten-Gewerkschaft* Trade Union of German Employees.
DB *Deutsche Bundesbahn* German Federal Railway; *Deutsche Bundesbank* German Federal Bank.
DDR *Deutsche Demokratische Republik* German Democratic Republic, *abbr.* G.D.R.
DFB *Deutscher Fußballbund* German Football Association.
DGB *Deutscher Gewerkschaftsbund* Federation of German Trade Unions.
d. Gr. *der Große* the Great.
d. h. *das heißt* that is, *abbr.* i.e.
d. i. *das ist* that is, *abbr.* i.e.
DIN *Deutsche Industrie-Norm(en)* German Industrial Standard(s).
Dipl. *Diplom(...* holding a) diploma.
d. J. *dieses Jahres* of this year; *der Jüngere* the Younger.
DKP *Deutsche Kommunistische Partei* German Communist Party.
DM *Deutsche Mark* German Mark.
d. M. *dieses Monats* instant.
DNA *Deutscher Normenausschuß* German Committee of Standards.
do. *dito* ditto.
d. O. *der (die, das) Obige* the above-mentioned.
Doz. *Dozent* university lecturer.
dpa *Deutsche Presse-Agentur* German Press Agency.
Dr. *Doktor* Doctor; ~ **jur.** *Doktor der Rechte* Doctor of Laws (LL.D.); ~ **med.** *Doktor der Medizin* Doctor of Medicine (M.D.); ~ **phil.** *Doktor der Philosophie* Doctor of Philosophy (Ph.D., D.Phil.); ~ **theol.** (*evangelisch* **D. theol.**) *Doktor der Theologie* Doctor of Divinity (D.D.).
dt(sch.) *deutsch* German.
Dtschld. *Deutschland* Germany.

E

ebd. *ebenda* ibidem, ib(id).
Ed. *Edition, Ausgabe* edition.
EDV *elektronische Datenverarbeitung* electronic data processing.
EG *Europäische Gemeinschaft* European Community.
e.h. *ehrenhalber of degree*: honorary.
ehem., ehm. *ehemals* formerly.
eig., eigtl. *eigentlich* really, strictly speaking.
einschl. *einschließlich* inclusive(ly), including.
EKD *Evangelische Kirche in Deutschland* Protestant Church in Germany.
EKG *Elektrokardiogramm* electrocardiogram.
entspr. *entsprechend* corresponding.
erg. *ergänze* supply, add.
Erl. *Erläuterung* explanation, (explanatory) note.
Euratom *Europäische Atomgemeinschaft* European Atomic Community.
ev. *evangelisch* Protestant.
e. V. *eingetragener Verein* registered society *or* association.
evtl. *eventuell* perhaps, possibly.
exkl. *exklusive* except(ed), not included.
Expl. *Exemplar* sample, copy.

F

F *Fahrenheit* Fahrenheit.
Fa. *Firma* firm; *in letters*: Messrs.
Fam. *Familie* family.
FDGB *Freier Deutscher Gewerkschaftsbund* Free Federation of German Trade Unions (*of the → DDR*).
FDP *Freie Demokratische Partei* Liberal Democratic Party.
fig. *figürlich, bildlich* figurative.
fortl. *fortlaufend* running, successive.
Forts. *Fortsetzung* continuation.
Fr. *Frau* Mrs., Ms.
frdl. *freundlich* kind.
Frl. *Fräulein* Miss.
FU *Freie Universität (Berlin)* Free University of Berlin.

G

g *Gramm* gram(me).
geb. *geboren* born; *geborene* ... née; *gebunden* bound.
Gebr. *Gebrüder* Brothers.
gegr. *gegründet* founded.
gek. *gekürzt* abbreviated.
Ges. *Gesellschaft* association, company; society; *Gesetz* law.
ges. gesch. *gesetzlich geschützt* registered.
gest. *gestorben* deceased.
gez. *gezeichnet* (*in front of signatures*) signed.
GG *Grundgesetz* Basic Constitutional Law.
GmbH, G.m.b.H. *Gesellschaft mit beschränkter Haftung* limited liability company.

H

Hbf. *Hauptbahnhof* central (*or* main) station.
h. c. *honoris causa*, *ehrenhalber* (*of univ. degree*) honorary.
HG *Handelsgesellschaft* trading company.
HGB *Handelsgesetzbuch* Commercial Code.
höfl. *höflich*(*st*) (most) kindly.
hpts. *hauptsächlich* principally, mainly.
Hr., Hrn. *Herr*(*n*) Mr.

I

i. *im*, *in* in.
i. A. *im Auftrag* for, by order, under instruction.
i. allg. *im allgemeinen* in general, generally speaking.
i. b. *im besonderen* in particular.
i. D. *im Durchschnitt* on average.
IG *Industriegewerkschaft* industrial union.
Ing. *Ingenieur* engineer.
Inh. *Inhaber* proprietor; *Inhalt* contents.
inkl. *inklusive*, *einschließlich* inclusive(ly), including.
Interpol *Internationale Kriminalpolizei-Kommission* International Criminal Police Commission.
i. R. *im Ruhestand* retired, *esp. univ.*: emeritus.
IRK *Internationales Rotes Kreuz* International Red Cross.
i. V. *in Vertretung* by proxy, by order, on behalf of.

J

jhrl. *jährlich* annual.
jr., jun. *junior* junior.
jur. *juristisch* legal.

K

Kap. *Kapitel* chapter.
kath. *katholisch* Catholic.
Kfm. *Kaufmann* merchant.
kfm. *kaufmännisch* commercial.
Kfz. *Kraftfahrzeug* motor vehicle.
KG *Kommanditgesellschaft* limited partnership.
Kl. *Klasse* class.
KP *Kommunistische Partei* Communist Party.
KPdSU *Kommunistische Partei der Sowjetunion* Communist Party of the Soviet Union.
Kripo *Kriminalpolizei* Criminal Investigation Department.
Kto. *Konto* account.
KZ *Konzentrationslager* concentration camp.

L

led. *ledig* unmarried.
lfd. *laufend* current, running.
lfd. Nr. *laufende Nummer* current issue.
Lfg., Lfrg. *Lieferung* delivery; instal(l)ment.
LG *Landgericht* District Court.
Lkw, LKW *Lastkraftwagen* lorry, truck.
Lok *Lokomotive* engine, locomotive.
lt. *laut* according to.
ltd. *leitend* managing.
Ltg. *Leitung* direction, management.
luth. *lutherisch* Lutheran.

M

M *Mark* Mark (*in the* → *DDR*).
MAD *Militärischer Abschirmdienst*

German Counter-Intelligence Service.
max. *maximum* maximum.
m. b. H. *mit beschränkter Haftung* with limited liability.
MdB, M. d. B. *Mitglied des Bundestages* Member of the "Bundestag".
MdL, M. d. L. *Mitglied des Landtages* Member of the "Landtag".
mdl. *mündlich* verbal.
m. E. *meines Erachtens* in my opinion.
MEZ *mitteleuropäische Zeit* Central European Time.
MG *Maschinengewehr* machine-gun.
Mill. *Million(en)* million(s).
Min., min. *Minute(n)* minute(s).
min. *minimal* minimum.
möbl. *möbliert* furnished.
mod. *modern* modern.
MP *Militärpolizei* Military Police; *Maschinenpistole* submachine gun.
Mrd. *Milliarde* billion, *Brt. a.* thousand million.
mtl. *monatlich* monthly.
m. W. *meines Wissens* as far as I know.
MWSt *Mehrwertsteuer* value-added tax.

N

N *Norden* north; *Leistung* power.
Nachf. *Nachfolger* successor.
nachm. *nachmittags* in the afternoon, *abbr.* p.m.
N. B. *notabene* note carefully.
n. Chr. *nach Christus* after Christ, *abbr.* A.D.
N.N. *nescio nomen, Name unbekannt* name unknown.
NO *Nordosten* north-east.
NPD *National-Demokratische Partei Deutschlands* National-Democratic Party of Germany.
Nr. *Numero, Nummer* number.
NW *Nordwesten* north-west.

O

O *Osten* east.
o. *oben* above; *oder* or; *ohne* without.
o. ä. *oder ähnlich* or the like.
OB *Oberbürgermeister* Chief Burgomaster.
o. B. ⚕ *ohne Befund* results negative.
Obb. *Oberbayern* Upper Bavaria.
od. *oder* or.
OEZ *osteuropäische Zeit* East European Time.
öff., öffentl. *öffentlich* public.
offiz. *offiziell* official.
OHG *Offene Handelsgesellschaft* general partnership.
OLG *Oberlandesgericht* Higher Regional Court.
o. Prof. *ordentlicher Professor* (full) professor.
Orig. *Original* original.
orth. *orthodox* orthodox.

P

p. A(dr). *per Adresse* care of.
Pf *Pfennig* (*German coin*) pfennig.
Pfd. *Pfund* (*weight*) German pound.
PH *Pädagogische Hochschule* teachers' college.
Pkw, PKW *Personenkraftwagen* (motor) car.
Pl. *Platz* square.
p.p., p.pa., ppa. *per procura* per proxy.
Prof. *Professor* professor.
PS *Pferdestärke(n)* horse-power; *postscriptum, Nachschrift* postscript.

Q

qkm *Quadratkilometer* square kilometre.
qm *Quadratmeter* square metre.

R

R *Réaumur* Réaumur *abbr.* R.
rd. *rund* roughly.
Reg.Bez. *Regierungsbezirk* administrative district.
Rel. *Religion* religion.
Rep. *Republik* republic.
resp. *respektive* respectively.
RIAS *Rundfunk im amerikanischen Sektor (von Berlin)* Radio in the American Sector (of Berlin).
rk. *römisch-katholisch* Roman Catholic.
röm. *römisch* Roman.

S

S *Süden* south.
S. *Seite* page.
s. *siehe* see, *abbr.* v. (= vide).
S-Bahn *Schnellbahn* city-railway.
sec *Sekunde* second.
SED *Sozialistische Einheitspartei Deutschlands* United Socialist Party of Germany (*of the → DDR*).
sen. *senior* senior.
SO *Südosten* south-east.
s. o. *siehe oben* see above.
sog. *sogenannt* so-called.
SOS *internationales Notsignal* international signal of distress.
SPD *Sozialdemokratische Partei Deutschlands* Social Democratic Party of Germany.
SS *Sommersemester* summer term.
St. *Stück* piece; *Sankt* Saint.
Std., Stde. *Stunde* hour.
stdl. *stündlich* every hour.
stellv. *stellvertretend* assistant.
StGB *Strafgesetzbuch* Penal Code.
StPO *Strafprozeßordnung* Code of Criminal Procedure.
Str. *Straße* street, road.
stud. *studiosus, Student* student.
StVO *Straßenverkehrsordnung* Traffic Regulations.
s. t. *sine tempore, ohne akademisches Viertel* sharp, on time.
s. u. *siehe unten* see below.
SW *Südwesten* south-west.
s. Z. *seinerzeit* at that time.

T

tägl. *täglich* daily, per day.
Tel. *Telephon* telephone; *Telegramm* wire, cable.
TH *Technische Hochschule* technical university *or* college.
TU *Technische Universität* technical university.
TÜV *Technischer Überwachungsverein* Association for Technical Inspection.

U

u. *und* and.
u. a. *und andere*(s) and others; *unter anderem or anderen* among other things, inter alia.
u. ä. *und ähnliche*(s) and the like.
U. A. w. g. *Um Antwort wird gebeten* an answer is requested.
u. dgl. (m.) *und dergleichen (mehr)* and the like.
u. d. M. *unter dem Meeresspiegel* below sea level; **ü. d. M.** *über dem Meeresspiegel* above sea level.
UdSSR *Union der Sozialistischen Sowjetrepubliken* Union of Soviet Socialist Republics.
UKW *Ultrakurzwelle* ultra-short wave, very high frequency.
U/min. *Umdrehungen in der Minute* revolutions per minute.
urspr. *ursprünglich* original(ly).
US(A) *Vereinigte Staaten (von Amerika)* United States (of America).
usw. *und so weiter* and so on, *abbr.* etc.
u. U. *unter Umständen* circumstances permitting.
UV *ultraviolett* ultra-violet.
u. v. a. (m.) *und viele*(s) *andere (mehr)* and many others.
u. zw. *und zwar* that is, namely.

V

v. *von, vom* of; from; by.
V *Volt* volt; *Volumen* volume.
V. *Vers* line, verse.
VB *Verhandlungsbasis* or near(est) offer, *abbr.* o.n.o.
v. Chr. *vor Christus* before Christ, *abbr.* B.C.
VEB *Volkseigener Betrieb* People's Enterprise (*in the → DDR*).
Verf., Vf. *Verfasser* author.
verh. *verheiratet* married.
Verl. *Verlag* publishing firm; *Verleger* publisher.
vgl. *vergleiche* compare, *abbr.* cf., cp.
v. g. u. *vorgelesen, genehmigt, unterschrieben* read, approved and signed.
v. H. *vom Hundert* per cent.
v. J. *vorigen Jahres* of last year.
v. M. *vorigen Monats* of last month.
vorm. *vormittags* in the morning, *abbr.* a.m.; *vormals* formerly.
Vors. *Vorsitzender* chairman.
VR *Volksrepublik* People's Republic.
v. T. *vom Tausend* per thousand.
v. u. *von unten* from below.

W

W *Westen* west; *Watt* watt(s).
WE *Wärmeeinheit* thermal unit.
WEU *Westeuropäische Union* Western European Union.
WEZ *westeuropäische Zeit* Western European Time (Greenwich Mean Time).
WGB *Weltgewerkschaftsbund* World Federation of Trade Unions.
WS *Wintersemester* winter term.
Wz. *Warenzeichen* registered trade-mark.

Z

Z. *Zahl* number; *Zeile* line.
z. *zu*, *zum*, *zur* at; to.
z. B. *zum Beispiel* for instance, *abbr.* e.g.
ZDF *Zweites Deutsches Fernsehen* Second Channel of German Television Broadcasting.
z. H(d). *zu Händen* attention of, to be delivered to.
ZPO *Zivilprozeßordnung* Code of Civil Procedure.
z. T. *zum Teil* partly.
Ztg. *Zeitung* newspaper.
Ztschr. *Zeitschrift* periodical.
zus. *zusammen* together.
zw. *zwischen* between; among.
z. Z(t). *zur Zeit* at the time; at present, for the time being.

Numerals — Zahlwörter

Cardinal Numbers — Grundzahlen

0 null *nought, zero, cipher*
1 eins *one*
2 zwei *two*
3 drei *three*
4 vier *four*
5 fünf *five*
6 sechs *six*
7 sieben *seven*
8 acht *eight*
9 neun *nine*
10 zehn *ten*
11 elf *eleven*
12 zwölf *twelve*
13 dreizehn *thirteen*
14 vierzehn *fourteen*
15 fünfzehn *fifteen*
16 sechzehn *sixteen*
17 siebzehn *seventeen*
18 achtzehn *eighteen*
19 neunzehn *nineteen*
20 zwanzig *twenty*
21 einundzwenzig *twenty-one*
22 zweiundzwanzig *twenty-two*
23 dreiundzwanzig *twenty-three*
30 dreißig *thirty*
31 einunddreißig *thirty-one*
40 vierzig *forty*
41 einundvierzig *forty-one*
50 fünfzig *fifty*
51 einundfünfzig *fifty-one*
60 sechzig *sixty*
61 einundsechzig *sixty-one*
70 siebzig *seventy*
71 einundsiebzig *seventy-one*
80 achtzig *eighty*
81 einundachtzig *eighty-one*
90 neunzig *ninety*
91 einundneunzig *ninety-one*
100 hundert *a* (*od. one*) *hundred*
101 hundert(und)eins *hundred and one*
200 zweihundert *two hundred*
300 dreihundert *three hundred*
572 fünfhundert(und)zweiundsiebzig *five hundred and seventy-two*
1000 tausend *a* (*od. one*) *thousand*
2000 zweitausend *two thousand*
1 000 000 eine Million *a* (*od. one*) *million*
2 000 000 zwei Millionen *two million*
1 000 000 000 eine Milliarde *a billion, Brt. a. a thousand million*

Ordinal Numbers — Ordnungszahlen

1. erste *first*
2. zweite *second*
3. dritte *third*
4. vierte *fourth*
5. fünfte *fifth*
6. sechste *sixth*
7. siebente *seventh*
8. achte *eighth*
9. neunte *ninth*
10. zehnte *tenth*
11. elfte *eleventh*
12. zwölfte *twelfth*
13. dreizehnte *thirteenth*
14. vierzehnte *fourteenth*
15. fünfzehnte *fifteenth*
16. sechzehnte *sixteenth*
17. siebzehnte *seventeenth*
18. achtzehnte *eighteenth*
19. neunzehnte *nineteenth*
20. zwanzigste *twentieth*
21. einundzwanzigste *twenty-first*
22. zweiundzwanzigste *twenty-second*
23. dreiundzwanzigste *twenty-third*
30. dreißigste *thirtieth*
31. einunddreißigste *thirty-first*
40. vierzigste *fortieth*
41. einundvierzigste *forty-first*
50. fünfzigste *fiftieth*

51. einundfünfzigste *fifty-first*
60. sechzigste *sixtieth*
61. einundsechzigste *sixty-first*
70. siebzigste *seventieth*
71. einundsiebzigste *seventy-first*
80. achtzigste *eightieth*
81. einundachtzigste *eighty-first*
90. neunzigste *ninetieth*
100. hundertste (*one*) *hundredth*
101. hundertunderste *hundred and first*
200. zweihundertste *two hundredth*
300. dreihundertste *three hundredth*
572. fünfhundert(und)zweiundsiebzigste *five hundred and seventy-second*
1000. tausendste (*one*) *thousandth*
2000. zweitausendste *two thousandth*
1 000 000. millionste *millionth*
2 000 000. zweimillionste *two millionth*

Fractions and other Numerical Values

Bruchzahlen und andere Zahlenwerte

$^1/_2$ ein halb *one* (*od. a*) *half*
$1^1/_2$ anderthalb *one and a half*
$2^1/_2$ zweieinhalb *two and a half*
$^1/_2$ Meile *half a mile*
$^1/_3$ ein Drittel *one* (*od. a*) *third*
$^2/_3$ zwei Drittel *two thirds*
$^1/_4$ ein Viertel *one* (*od. a*) *fourth, one* (*od. a*) *quarter*
$^3/_4$ drei Viertel *three fourths, three quarters*
$1^1/_4$ ein und eine Viertelstunde *one hour and a quarter*
$^1/_5$ ein Fünftel *one* (*od. a*) *fifth*
$3^4/_5$ drei vier Fünftel *three and four fifths*
0,4 Null Komma vier *point four* (.4)
2,5 zwei Komma fünf *two point five* (2.5)

Einfach *single*
zweifach *double*
dreifach *treble, triple, threefold*
vierfach *fourfold, quadruple*
fünffach *fivefold usw.*

Einmal *once*
zweimal *twice*
drei-, vier-, fünfmal *usw. three, four, five times*
zweimal soviel(e) *twice as much* (*many*)
noch einmal *once more*

Erstens, zweitens, drittens *usw. firstly, secondly, thirdly, in the first* (*second, third*) *place*

$2 \times 3 = 6$ zweimal drei ist (*od.* macht) sechs *twice three are* (*od. make*) *six*

$7 + 8 = 15$ sieben und (*od.* plus) acht ist fünfzehn *seven and eight are fifteen*

$10 - 3 = 7$ zehn weniger (*od.* minus) drei ist sieben *ten less three are seven*

$20 : 5 = 4$ zwanzig geteilt (*od.* dividiert) durch fünf ist vier *twenty divided by five make four*

German Weights and Measures

Deutsche Maße und Gewichte

I. Linear Measures

1 mm *Millimeter* millimetre
= $^1/_{1000}$ metre
= 0.001 093 6 yard
= 0.003 280 9 foot
= 0.039 370 79 inch

1 cm *Zentimeter* centimetre
= $^1/_{100}$ metre
= 0.3937 inch

1 dm *Dezimeter* decimetre
= $^1/_{10}$ metre
= 3.9370 inches

1 m *Meter* metre
= 1.0936 yard
= 3.2809 feet
= 39.37079 inches

1 km *Kilometer* kilometre
= 1000 metres
= 1093.637 yards
= 3280.8692 feet
= 39370.79 inches
= 0.621 38 British or Statute Mile

1 sm *Seemeile* nautical mile
= 1852 metres

II. Surface or Square Measures

1 qmm *Quadratmillimeter* square millimetre
= $^1/_{1\,000\,000}$ square metre
= 0.000001196 square yard
= 0.0000107641 square foot
= 0.00 155 square inch

1 qcm *Quadratzentimeter* square centimetre
= $^1/_{10\,000}$ square metre

1 qdm *Quadratdezimeter* square decimetre
= $^1/_{100}$ square metre

1 qm *Quadratmeter* square metre
= 1 × 1 metre
= 1.19599 square yard
= 10.7641 square feet
= 1550 square inches

1 a *Ar* are
= 100 square metres
= 119.5993 square yards
= 1076.4103 square feet

1 ha *Hektar* hectare
= 100 ares
= 10000 square metres
= 11959.90 square yards
= 107641.03 square feet
= 2.4711 acres

1 qkm *Quadratkilometer* square kilometre
= 100 hectares
= 1000000 square metres
= 247.11 acres
= 0.3861 square mile

1 Morgen
= 25.5322 ares
= about $^2/_3$ acre

III. Cubic or Solid Measures

1 ccm *Kubikzentimeter* cubic centimetre
= 1000 cubic millimetres
= 0.061 cubic inch

1 cdm *Kubikdezimeter* cubic decimetre
= 1000 cubic centimetres
= 61.0253 cubic inches

1 cbm *Kubikmeter*
1 rm *Raummeter*
1 fm *Festmeter*
} cubic metre
= 1000 cubic decimetres
= 1.3079 cubic yard
= 35.3156 cubic feet

1 RT *Registertonne* register ton
= 2.832 cbm
= 100 cubic feet

IV. Measures of Capacity

1 l *Liter* litre
= 10 decilitres
= 1.7607 pint (Brit.)
= 7.0431 gills (Brit.)
= 0.8804 quart (Brit.)
= 0.2201 gallon (Brit.)
= 2.1134 pints (U.S.)
= 8.4534 gills (U.S.)
= 1.0567 quart (U.S.)
= 0.2642 gallon (U.S.)

1 hl *Hektoliter* hectolitre
= 100 litres
= 22.009 gallons (Brit.)
= 2.751 bushels (Brit.)
= 26.418 gallons (U.S.)
= 2.84 bushels (U.S.)

V. Weights

1 mg *Milligramm* milligramme
= $^{1}/_{1000}$ gramme
= 0.0154 grain (troy)

1 g *Gramm* gramme
= $^{1}/_{1000}$ kilogramme
= 15.4324 grains (troy)

1 Pfd *Pfund* pound (German)
= $^{1}/_{2}$ kilogramme
= 500 grammes
= 1.1023 pound (avdp.)
= 1.3396 pound (troy)

1 kg *Kilogramm, Kilo* kilogramme
= 1000 grammes
= 2.2046 pounds (avdp.)
= 2.6792 pounds (troy)

1 Ztr. *Zentner* centner
= 100 pounds (German)
= 50 kilogrammes
= 110.23 pounds (avdp.)
= 0.9842 British hundredweight
= 1.1023 U.S. hundredweight

1 dz *Doppelzentner*
= 100 kilogrammes
= 1.9684 British hundredweight
= 2.2046 U.S. hundredweights

1 t *Tonne* ton
= 1000 kilogrammes
= 0.984 British ton
= 1.1023 U. S. ton

Temperature Conversion Tables

Temperatur-Umrechnungstabellen

1. FROM –273 °C TO + 1000 °C

1. VON –273 °C BIS + 1000 °C

Celsius °C	Kelvin K	Fahrenheit °F	Réaumur °R
1000	1273	1832	800
950	1223	1742	760
900	1173	1652	720
850	1123	1562	680
800	1073	1472	640
750	1023	1382	600
700	973	1292	560
650	923	1202	520
600	873	1112	480
550	823	1022	440
500	773	932	400
450	723	842	360
400	673	752	320
350	623	662	280
300	573	572	240
250	523	482	200
200	473	392	160
150	423	302	120
100	373	212	80
95	368	203	76
90	363	194	72
85	358	185	68
80	353	176	64
75	348	167	60
70	343	158	56
65	338	149	52
60	333	140	48
55	328	131	44
50	323	122	40
45	318	113	36
40	313	104	32
35	308	95	28
30	303	86	24
25	298	77	20
20	293	68	16
15	288	59	12
10	283	50	8
+ 5	278	41	+ 4
0	273.15	32	0
— 5.	268	23	— 4
— 10	263	14	— 8

Celsius °C	Kelvin K	Fahrenheit °F	Réaumur °R
— 15	258	+ 5	— 12
— 17.8	255.4	0	— 14.2
— 20	253	— 4	— 16
— 25	248	— 13	— 20
— 30	243	— 22	— 24
— 35	238	— 31	— 28
— 40	233	— 40	— 32
— 45	228	— 49	— 36
— 50	223	— 58	— 40
— 100	173	— 148	— 80
— 150	123	— 238	— 120
— 200	73	— 328	— 160
— 250	23	— 418	— 200
— 273.15	0	— 459.4	— 218.4

2. CLINICAL THERMOMETER
2. FIEBERTHERMOMETER

Celsius °C	Fahrenheit °F	Réaumur °R
42.0	107.6	33.6
41.8	107.2	33.4
41.6	106.9	33.3
41.4	106.5	33.1
41.2	106.2	33.0
41.0	105.8	32.8
40.8	105.4	32.6
40.6	105.1	32.5
40.4	104.7	32.3
40.2	104.4	32.2
40.0	104.0	32.0
39.8	103.6	31.8
39.6	103.3	31.7
39.4	102.9	31.5
39.2	102.6	31.4
39.0	102.2	31.2
38.8	101.8	31.0
38.6	101.5	30.9
38.4	101.1	30.7
38.2	100.8	30.6
38.0	100.4	30.4
37.8	100.0	30.2
37.6	99.7	30.1
37.4	99.3	29.9
37.2	99.0	29.8
37.0	98.6	29.6
36.8	98.2	29.4
36.6	97.9	29.3

3. RULES FOR CONVERTING TEMPERATURES
3. UMRECHNUNGSREGELN

	Celsius	*Kelvin*
x °C	–	$= x + 273.15$ K
x K	$= x - 273.15$ °C	–
x °F	$= \frac{5}{9}(x - 32)$ °C	$= \frac{5}{9}(x - 32) + 273.15$ K
x °R	$= \frac{5}{4}x$ °C	$= \left(\frac{5}{4}x\right) + 273.15$ K
	Fahrenheit	*Réaumur*
x °C	$= \frac{9}{5}x + 32$ °F	$= \left(\frac{4}{5}x\right)$ °R
x K	$= \frac{9}{5}(x - 273.15) + 32$ °F	$= \frac{4}{5}(x - 273.15)$ °R
x °F	–	$= \frac{4}{9}(x - 32)$ °R
x °R	$= \left(\frac{9}{4}x\right) + 32$ °F	–

Examples of German Declension and Conjugation

Muster für die deutsche Deklination und Konjugation

A. Declension

Order of cases: *nom.*, *gen.*, *dat.*, *acc.*, *sg.* and *pl.* – Compound nouns and adjectives (e.g. *Eisbär*, *Ausgang*, *abfällig* etc.) inflect like their last elements (*Bär*, *Gang*, *fällig*). The letters in parentheses may be omitted.

I. Nouns

1 Bild ~(e)s[1] ~(e) ~
Bilder[2] ~ ~n ~

[1] **es** *only*: Geist, Geistes.
[2] **a, o, u > ä, ö, ü:** Rand, Ränder; Haupt, Häupter; Dorf, Dörfer; Wurm, Würmer.

---

2 Reis* ~es ['~zəs] ~(e) ~
Reiser[1] ['~zər] ~ ~n ~

[1] **a, o > ä, ö:** Glas, Gläser ['glɛ:zər]; Haus, Häuser ['hɔʏzər]; Faß, Fässer; Schloß, Schlösser.
* **ß > ss:** Faß, Fasse(s).

---

3 Arm ~(e)s[1,2] ~(e)[1] ~
Arme[3] ~ ~n ~

[1] *without* **e:** Billard, Billard(s).
[2] **es** *only*: Maß, Maßes.
[3] **a, o, u > ä, ö, ü:** Gang, Gänge; Saal, Säle; Gebrauch, Gebräuche [gə'brɔʏçə]; Sohn, Söhne; Hut, Hüte.

---

4 Greis[1]* ~es ['~zəs] ~(e) ~
Greise[2] ['~zə] ~ ~n ~

[1] **s > ss:** Kürbis, Kürbisse(s).
[2] **a, o, u > ä, ö, ü:** Hals, Hälse; Baß, Bässe; Schoß, Schöße; Fuchs, Füchse; Schuß, Schüsse.
* **ß > ss:** Roß, Rosse(s).

---

5 Strahl ~(e)s[1,2] ~(e)[2] ~
Strahlen[3] ~ ~ ~

[1] **es** *only*: Schmerz, Schmerzes.
[2] *without* **e:** Juwel, Juwel(s).
[3] Sporn, Sporen.

---

6 Lappen ~s ~ ~*
Lappen[1] ~ ~ ~

[1] **a, o > ä, ö:** Graben, Gräben; Boden, Böden.
* *Infinitives used as nouns have no pl.*: Geschehen, Befinden etc.

---

7 Maler ~s ~ ~
Maler[1] ~ ~n ~

[1] **a, o, u > ä, ö, ü:** Vater, Väter; Kloster, Klöster; Bruder, Brüder.

---

8 Untertan ~s ~ ~
Untertanen[1,2] ~ ~ ~

[1] *with change of accent*: Pro'fessor, Profes'soren [~'so:rən]; 'Dämon ['dɛ:mɔn], Dä'monen [dɛ'mo:nən].
[2] *pl.* **ien** [~jən]: Kolleg, Kollegien [~'le:gjən]; Mineral, Mineralien.

9

Studium	~s	~	~
Studien[1,2] ['~djən]	~	~	~

[1] **a** *and* **o(n)** > **en:** Drama, Dramen; Stadion, Stadien.

[2] **on** *and* **um** > **a**: Lexikon, Lexika; Faktum, Fakta.

10

Auge	~s	~	~
Augen	~	~	~

11

Genie	~s[1]*	~	~
Genies[2]*	~	~	~

[1] *without inflexion*: Bouillon etc.

[2] *pl.* **s** *or* **ta:** Komma, Kommas *or* Kommata; *but*: 'Klima, Klimate [kli'mɑːtə] (3).

* **s** *is pronounced*: [ʒe'niːs].

12

Bär[1]*	~en[2]	~en[2]	~en[2]
Bären	~	~	~

[1] **ß** > **ss:** Genoß, Genossen.

[2] Herr, *sg. mst* Herrn; Herz, *gen.* Herzens, *acc.* Herz.

* **...'log** *as well as* **...'loge** (13), e. g. Biolog(e).

13

Knabe	~n[1]	~n	~n
Knaben	~	~	~

[1] **ns:** Name, Namens.

14

Trübsal	~	~	~
Trübsale[1,2,3]	~	~n	~

[1] **a, o, u** > **ä, ö, ü:** Hand, Hände; Braut, Bräute; Not, Nöte; Luft, Lüfte; *without* **e:** Tochter, Töchter; Mutter, Mütter; **ß** > **ss:** Nuß, Nüsse.

[2] **s** > **ss:** Kenntnis, Kenntnisse; Nimbus, Nimbusse.

[3] **is** *or* **us** > **e:** Kultus, Kulte; *with change of accent*: Di'akonus, Dia'kone [~'koːnə].

15

Blume	~	~	~
Blumen	~	~	~

...ee: eː, *pl.* eːən, e. g. I'dee, I'deen.

...ie { *stressed syllable*: iː, *pl.* iːən, e. g. Batte'rie(n). *unstressed syllable*: jə, *pl.* jən, e. g. Ar'terie(n).

16

Frau	~	~	~
Frauen[1,2,3]	~	~	~

[1] **in** > **innen:** Freundin, Freundinnen.

[2] **a, is, os** *and* **us** > **en:** Firma, Firmen; Krisis, Krisen; Epos, Epen; Genius, Genien; *with change of accent*: 'Heros, He'roen [he'roːən]; Di'akonus, Dia'konen [~'koːnən].

[3] **s** *and* **ß** > **ss:** Kirmes, Kirmessen.

II. Proper nouns

17 *In general proper nouns have no pl.*

The following form the gen. sg. with **s:**

1. *Proper nouns without a definite article*: Friedrichs, Paulas, (Friedrich von) Schillers, Deutschlands, Berlins;
2. *Proper nouns, masculine and neuter (except the names of countries) with a definite article and an adjective*: des braven Friedrichs Bruder, des jungen Deutschlands (Söhne).

After **s, sch, ß, tz, x,** *and* **z** *the gen. sg. ends in* **-ens** *or* ' (*instead of* ' *it is more advisable to use the definite article or* **von**), e. g. die Werke des [*or* von] Sokrates, Voß *or* Sokrates', Voß' [*not* Sokratessens, *seldom* Vossens] Werke; *but*: die Umgebung von Mainz.

Feminine names ending in a consonant or the vowel **e** *form the gen. sg. with* **(en)s** *or* **(n)s**; *in the dat. and acc. sg. such names may end in* **(e)n** (*pl.* = *a*).

If a proper noun is followed by a title, only the following forms are inflected:

1. *the title when used with a definite article*:
   der Kaiser Karl (der Große)
   des ~**s** ~ (des ~**n**) etc.;
2. *the (last) name when used without an article*:
   Kaiser Karl (der Große)
   ~ ~**s** (des ~**n**) etc.
   (*but*: Herrn Lehmanns Brief).

III. Adjectives und participles (also used as nouns*), pronouns etc.

18

	m	f	n	pl.	
a) gut	er[1],[2]	~e	~es	~e °	*without article, after prepositions, personal pronouns, and invariables*
	en**	~er	~en**	~er	
	em	~er	~em	~en	
	en	~e	~es	~e	
b) gut	e[1],[2]	~e	~e	~en	*with definite article* (22) *or with pronoun* (21)
	en	~en	~en	~en	
	en	~en	~en	~en	
	en	~e	~e	~en	
c) gut	er[1],[2]	~e	~es	~en	*with indefinite article or with pronoun* (20)
	en	~en	~en	~en	
	en	~en	~en	~en	
	en	~e	~es	~en	

[1]**ß** = **ss:** kraß, krasse(r, ~s, ~st etc.).
[2] **a, o, u** > **ä, ö, ü** *when forming the comp. and sup.*: alt, älter(e, ~es etc.), ältest (der ~e, am ~en); grob, gröber(e, ~es etc.), gröbst (der ~e, am ~en); kurz, kürzer(e, ~es etc.), kürzest (der ~e, am ~en).
* *e. g.* Böse(r) *su.*: der (die, eine) Böse, ein Böser; Böse(s) *n*: das Böse, *without article* Böses; *in the same way* Abgesandte(r) *su.*, Angestellte(r) *su.* etc.; *in some cases the use varies.*
** *Sometimes the gen. sg. ends in* **~es** *instead of* **~en:** gutes (*or* gut**en**) Mutes sein.
° *In* böse, böse(r, ~s, ~st etc.) *one* **e** *is dropped.*

The Grades of Comparison

The endings of the comparative and superlative are:

	reich	schön	*inflected according to* (18[2]).
comp.	reicher	schöner	
sup.	reichst	schönst	

After vowels (except **e** [18°]) *and after* d, s, sch, ß, st, t, tz x, y, z *the sup. ends in* **~est,** *but in unstressed syllables after* **d, sch** *and* **t** *generally in* **~st:** blau, 'blau**est**; rund, 'rund**est**; rasch, 'rasch**est** etc.; *but*: 'dringend, 'dringend**st**; 'närrisch, 'närrisch**st**; ge'eignet, ge'eignet**st**.

Note. — The adjectives ending in **~el, ~en** (*except* **~nen**) *and* **~er** (*e. g.* dunk**el,** eb**en,** heit**er**), *and also the possessive adjectives* uns**er** *and* eu**er** *generally drop* **e** (*in this case* **ss** *changes to* **ß:** angemessen, angemeßner).

Inflexion:	**~e**	**~em**	**~en**	**~er**	**~es,** *and*
~el >	~le	~lem*	~len*	~ler	~les
~en >	~(e)ne	~(e)nem	~(e)nen	~(e)ner °	~(e)nes
~er >	~(e)re	~rem*	~ren*	~(e)rer °	~(e)res

* *or* ~elm, ~eln, ~erm, ~ern; *e. g.* **dunk\|el:** ~le, ~lem (*or* ~elm), ~len (*or* ~eln), ~ler, ~les; **eb\|en:** ~(e)ne, ~(e)nem etc.; **heit\|er:** ~(e)re, ~rem (*or* ~erm) etc.

° *The inflected comp. ends in* ~ner *and* ~rer *only*: eben, ebnere(r, ~s etc.); heiter, heitrere(r, ~s etc.); *but sup.* ebenst, heiterst.

19

	1st pers.	2nd pers.	3rd pers.		
	m, f, n	*m, f, n*	*m*	*f*	*n*
sg.	ich	du	er	sie	es
	meiner*	deiner*	seiner*	ihrer	seiner*
	mir	dir	ihm	ihr	ihm°
	mich	dich	ihn	sie	es°
pl.	wir	ihr		sie	(Sie)
	unser	euer		ihrer	(Ihrer)
	uns	euch		ihnen	(Ihnen)°
	uns	euch		sie	(Sie)°

* *In poetry sometimes without inflexion*: gedenke mein!; *also* **es** *instead of* seiner *n* (= *e-r S.*): ich bin es überdrüssig.
° *Reflexive form*: sich.

20

	m	*f*	*n*	*pl.*
mein		~e	~	~e*
dein	es	~er	~es	~er
sein	em	~er	~em	~en
(k)ein	en	~e	~	~e

* *The indefinite article* ein *has no pl. — In poetry* mein, dein, *and* sein *may stand behind the su. without inflexion*: die Mutter (Kinder) mein, *or as predicate*: *der Hut* [*die Tasche, das Buch*] *ist* mein; *without su.*: meiner *m*, meine *f*, mein(e)s *n*, meine *pl.* etc.: *wem gehört der Hut* [*die Tasche, das Buch*]? *es ist* meiner (meine, mein[e]s); *or with definite article*: der (die, das) meine, *pl.* die meinen (18b). *Regarding* unser *and* euer *see note* (18), *p. 1332.*

21

	m	*f*	*n*	*pl.*
dies	er	~e	~es*	~e**
jen	es	~er	~es	~er[1]
manch	em	~er	~em	~en[1]
welch	en	~e	~es*	~e

[1] **welche(r, s)** *as rel. pron.*: *gen. sg.* dessen, deren, *gen. pl.* deren, *dat. pl.* denen (23).
* *Used as su.*, dies *is preferable to* dieses.
** manch, solch, welch *frequently are uninflected*:

manch	guter	(ein	guter)	Mann
solch	~en	(~es	~en)	~es
welch	~em	(~em	~en)	~e

etc. (18)

Similarly all:

all der	(dieser, mein)	Schmerz
~ des	(~es, ~es)	~es

22

m	*f*	*n*	*pl.*	
der	die	das	die[1]	*definite article*
des	der	des	der	
dem	der	dem	den	
den	die	das	die	

[1] derjenige, derselbe—desjenigen, demjenigen, desselben, demselben etc. (18b).

---

23 *Relative pronoun*

m	*f*	*n*	*pl.*
der	die	das	die
dessen*	deren	dessen*	deren[1]
dem	der	dem	denen
den	die	das	die

[1] *also* derer, *when used as dem. pron.*
* *also* des.

24

wer	was	jemand, niemand
wessen*	wessen	~(e)s
wem	—	~(em°)
wen	was	~(en°)

* *also* wes.
° *preferably without inflexion.*

B. Conjugation

General remarks. — In the conjugation tables (25—30) only the simple verbs may be found; in the alphabetic list [p. 1335—1341] compound verbs are only included when no simple verb exists (e. g. **beginnen**; *ginnen* does not exist). In order to find the conjugation of any compound verb (with separable or inseparable prefix, regular or irregular) look up the respective simple verb.

Verbs with separable and stressed prefixes such as **'ab-**, **'an-**, **'auf-**, **'aus-**, **'bei-**, **be'vor-**, **'dar-**, **'ein-**, **em'por-**, **ent'gegen-**, **'fort-**, **'her-**, **he'rab-** etc. and also *'klar-*[*legen*], *'los-*[*schießen*], *'sitzen-*[*bleiben*], *über'hand-*[*nehmen*] etc. (but not the verbs derived from compound nouns as *be'antragen* or *be'ratschlagen* from *Antrag* and *Ratschlag* etc.) take the preposition **zu** (in the *inf.* and the *p.pr.*) and the syllable **ge** (in the *p.p.* and in the passive voice) between the stressed prefix and their root.

Verbs with inseparable and unstressed prefixes such as **be-**, **emp-**, **ent-**, **er-**, **ge-**, **ver-**, **zer-** and generally **miß-** (in spite of its being stressed) take the preposition **zu** before the prefix and drop the syllable **ge** in the *p.p.* and in the passive voice. The prefixes **durch-**, **hinter-**, **über-**, **um-**, **unter-**, **voll-**, **wi**(**e**)**der-** are separable when stressed and inseparable when unstressed, e. g.

geben: *zu geben*, *zu gebend*; *gegeben*; *ich gebe*, *du gibst* etc.;
'abgeben: *'abzugeben*, *'abzugebend*; *'abgegeben*; *ich gebe* (*du gibst* etc.) *ab*;
ver'geben: *zu ver'geben*, *zu ver'gebend*; *ver'geben*; *ich ver'gebe*, *du ver'gibst* etc.;
'umgehen: *'umzugehen*, *'umzugehend*; *'umgegangen*; *ich gehe* (*du gehst* etc.) *um*;
um'gehen: *zu um'gehen*, *zu um'gehend*; *um'gangen*; *ich um'gehe*, *du um'gehst* etc.

The same rules apply to verbs with two prefixes, e. g.
zu'rückbehalten [see *halten*]: *zu'rückzubehalten*, *zu'rückzubehaltend*; *zu'rückbehalten*; *ich behalte* (*du behältst* etc.) *zurück*;
wieder'aufheben [see *heben*]: *wieder'aufzuheben*, *wieder'aufzuhebend*; *wieder'aufgehoben*; *ich hebe* (*du hebst* etc.) *wieder auf*.

The forms in parentheses ( ) follow the same rules.

a) 'Weak' Conjugation

25 **loben**

prs. ind.	lobe	lobst	lobt
	loben	lobt	loben
prs. subj.	lobe	lobest	lobe
	loben	lobet	loben
pret. ind. and *subj.*	lobte	lobtest	lobte
	lobten	lobtet	lobten

imp.sg. lob(e), ***pl.*** lob(e)t, loben Sie; ***inf.prs.*** loben; ***inf.perf.*** gelobt haben; ***p.pr.*** lobend; ***p.p.*** gelobt (18; 29**).

26 **reden**

prs. ind.	rede	redest	redet
	reden	redet	reden
prs. subj.	rede	redest	rede
	reden	redet	reden
pret. ind. and *subj.*	redete	redetest	redete
	redeten	redetet	redeten

imp.sg. rede, ***pl.*** redet, reden Sie; ***inf.prs.*** reden; ***inf.perf.*** geredet haben; ***p.pr.*** redend; ***p.p.*** geredet (18; 29**).

27 **reisen**

prs. ind.	reise	rei(se)st*	reist
	reisen	reist	reisen
prs. subj.	reise	reisest	reise
	reisen	reiset	reisen
pret. ind. and *subj.*	reiste	reistest	reisten
	reisten	reistet	reisten

imp.sg. reise, ***pl.*** reist, reisen Sie; ***inf.prs.*** reisen; ***inf.perf.*** gereist sein *od. now rare* haben; ***p.pr.*** reisend; ***p.p.*** gereist (18; 29**).

* **sch:** naschen, nasch(e)st; **ß:** spaßen, spaßt (spaßest); **tz:** ritzen, ritzt (ritzest); **x:** hexen, hext (hexest); **z:** reizen, reizt (reizest); faulenzen, faulenzt (faulenzest).

28 **fassen**

prs. ind.	fasse	faßt (fassest)	faßt
	fassen	faßt	fassen
prs. subj.	fasse	fassest	fasse
	fassen	fasset	fassen
pret. ind. and *subj.*	faßte	faßtest	faßte
	faßten	faßtet	faßten

imp.sg. fasse (faß), ***pl.*** faßt, fassen Sie; ***inf.prs.*** fassen; ***inf.perf.*** gefaßt haben; ***p.pr.*** fassend; ***p.p.*** gefaßt (18; 29**).

29 **handeln**

prs. ind.

handle*	handelst	handelt
handeln	handelt	handeln

prs. subj.

handle*	handelst	handle*
handeln	handelt	handeln

pret. ind. and *subj.*

handelte	handeltest	handelte
handelten	handeltet	handelten

imp.sg. handle, *pl.* handelt, handeln Sie; *inf.prs.* handeln; *inf. perf.* gehandelt haben; *p.pr.* handelnd; *p.p.* gehandelt (18).

* *Also* handele; wandern, wand(e)re; bessern, bessere (beßre); donnern, donnere.

** *Without* **ge**, *when the first syllable is unstressed*, e. g. be'grüßen, be'grüßt; ent'stehen, ent'standen; stu'dieren, stu'diert (*not* gestudiert); trom'peten, trom'petet (*also when preceded by a stressed prefix*: 'ausposaunen, 'austrompeten, 'austrompetet, *not* 'ausgetrompetet). *In some weak verbs the p.p. ends in* **en** *instead of* **t**, e. g. mahlen — gemahlen. *With the verbs* brauchen, dürfen, heißen, helfen, hören, können, lassen, lehren, lernen, machen, mögen, müssen, sehen, sollen, wollen *the p.p. is replaced by inf.* (*without* ge), *when used in connection with another inf.*, e. g. ich habe ihn singen hören, du hättest es tun können, er hat gehen müssen, ich hätte ihn laufen lassen sollen.

30

b) 'Strong' Conjugation

fahren

prs. ind.	fahre	fährst	fährt
	fahren	fahrt	fahren
prs. subj.	fahre	fahrest	fahre
	fahren	fahret	fahren
pret. ind.	fuhr	fuhr(e)st*	fuhr
	fuhren	fuhrt	fuhren
pret. subj.	führe	führest	führe*
	führen	führet	führen

imp.sg. fahr(e), *pl.* fahr(e)t, fahren Sie; *inf.prs.* fahren; *inf.perf.* gefahren haben *or* sein; *p.pr.* fahrend; *p.p.* gefahren (18; 29**).

* In the following alphabetical list the 2nd person of the *pret. ind.* is only mentioned when there are doubts as to its formation.

Alphabetical List of Strong and Irregular Verbs

Abbreviations see p. 683 and 684; *subj.* = *subjunctive pret.*

backen *prs.* backe, bäckst, bäckt; *pret.* backte (buk, buk[e]st); *subj.* büke; *imp.* back(e); *p.p.* gebacken.

befehlen *prs.* befehle, befiehlst, befiehlt; *pret.* befahl; *subj.* beföhle (befähle); *imp.* befiehl; *p.p.* befohlen.

beginnen *prs.* beginne, beginnst, beginnt; *pret.* begann; *subj.* begönne (begänne); *imp.* beginn(e); *p.p.* begonnen.

beißen *prs.* beiße, beißt, beißt; *pret.* biß, bissest; *subj.* bisse; *imp.* beiß(e); *p.p.* gebissen.

bergen *prs.* berge, birgst, birgt; *pret.* barg; *subj.* bärge; *imp.* birg; *p.p.* geborgen.

bersten *prs.* berste, birst (*rarely*: berstest), birst (*rarely*: berstet); *pret.* barst, barstest; *subj.* bärste; *imp.* birst; *p. p.* geborsten.

bewegen *prs.* bewege, bewegst, bewegt; *pret.* bewegte (*fig.* bewog); *subj.* bewegte (*fig.* bewöge); *imp.* beweg(e); *p.p.* bewegt (*fig.* bewogen).

biegen *prs.* biege, biegst, biegt; *pret.* bog; *subj.* böge; *imp.* bieg(e); *p.p.* gebogen.

bieten *prs.* biete, biet(e)st, bietet; *pret.* bot, bot(e)st; *subj.* böte; *imp.* biet(e); *p.p.* geboten.

binden *prs.* binde, bindest, bindet; *pret.* band, band(e)st; *subj.* bände; *imp.* bind(e); *p.p.* gebunden.
bitten *prs.* bitte, bittest, bittet; *pret.* bat, bat(e)st; *subj.* bäte; *imp.* bitte (bitt'); *p.p.* gebeten.
blasen *prs.* blase, bläst, bläst; *pret.* blies, bliesest; *subj.* bliese; *imp.* blas(e); *p.p.* geblasen.
bleiben *prs.* bleibe, bleibst, bleibt; *pret.* blieb, bliebst; *subj.* blieb *imp.* bleib(e); *p.p.* geblieben.
braten *prs.* brate, brätst, brät; *pret.* briet, briet(e)st; *subj.* briete; *imp.* brat(e); *p.p.* gebraten.
brechen *prs.* breche, brichst, bricht; *pret.* brach; *subj.* bräche; *imp.* brich; *p.p.* gebrochen*).
brennen *prs.* brenne, brennst, brennt; *pret.* brannte; *subj.* brennte; *imp.* brenne; *p.p.* gebrannt.
bringen *prs.* bringe, bringst, bringt; *pret.* brachte; *subj.* brächte; *imp.* bring(e); *p.p.* gebracht.
denken *prs.* denke, denkst, denkt; *pret.* dachte; *subj.* dächte; *imp.* denk(e); *p.p.* gedacht.
dingen *prs.* dinge, dingst, dingt; *pret.* dingte (dang); *subj.* dingte (dänge); *imp.* dinge; *p.p.* gedungen (*rarely*: gedingt).
dreschen *prs.* dresche, drischst, drischt; *pret.* drosch, drosch(e)st; *subj.* drösche; *imp.* drisch; *p.p.* gedroschen.
dringen *prs.* dringe, dringst, dringt; *pret.* drang, drangst; *subj.* dränge; *imp.* dring(e); *p.p.* gedrungen.
dünken *prs.* mich dünkt (deucht); *pret.* dünkte (deuchte); *subj.* —; *imp.* —; *p.p.* gedünkt (gedeucht).
dürfen *prs.* darf, darfst, darf; *wir* dürfen etc.; *pret.* durfte; *subj.* dürfte; *imp.* —; *p.p.* gedurft (*auxiliary verb*: dürfen).
empfehlen *prs.* empfehle, empfiehlst, empfiehlt; *pret.* empfahl; *subj.* empföhle (empfähle); *imp.* empfiehl; *p.p.* empfohlen.
erbleichen *prs.* erbleiche, erbleichst, erbleicht; *pret.* erbleichte (erblich); *subj.* erbliche (erbleichte); *imp.* erbleiche; *p.p.* erbleicht (erblichen = gestorben).
erkiesen *poet. prs.* erkiese, erkie(se)st, erkiest; *pret.* erkor (erkieste); *subj.* erköre; *imp.* erkies(e); *p.p.* erkoren.
erlöschen *pres.* erlösche, erlischst, erlischt; *pret.* erlosch, erloschest; *subj.* erlösche; *imp.* erlisch; *p.p.* erloschen.
essen *prs.* esse, ißt, ißt; *pret.* aß, aßest; *subj.* äße; *imp.* iß; *p.p.* gegessen.
fahren *prs.* fahre, fährst, fährt; *pret.* fuhr, fuhrst; *subj.* führe; *imp.* fahr(e); *p.p.* gefahren.
fallen *prs.* falle, fällst, fällt; *pret.* fiel; *subj.* fiele; *imp.* fall(e); *p.p.* gefallen.
fangen *prs.* fange, fängst, fängt; *pret.* fing; *subj.* finge; *imp.* fang(e); *p.p.* gefangen.
fechten *prs.* fechte, fichtst, ficht; *pret.* focht, fochtest; *subj.* föchte; *imp.* ficht; *p.p.* gefochten.
finden *pres.* finde, findest, findet; *pret.* fand, fand(e)st; *subj.* fände; *imp.* find(e); *p.p.* gefunden.
flechten *prs.* flechte, flichtst, flicht; *pret.* flocht, flochtest; *subj.* flöchte; *imp.* flicht; *p.p.* geflochten.
fliegen *prs.* fliege, fliegst, fliegt; *pret.* flog, flogst; *subj.* flöge; *imp.* flieg(e); *p.p.* geflogen.
flieh(e)n *prs.* fliehe, fliehst, flieht; *pret.* floh, flohst; *subj.* flöhe; *imp.* flieh(e); *p.p.* geflohen.
fließen *prs.* fließe, fließt, fließt; *pret.* floß, flossest; *subj.* flösse; *imp.* fließ(e); *p.p.* geflossen.
fressen *prs.* fresse, frißt, frißt; *pret.* fraß, fraßest; *subj.* fräße; *imp.* friß; *p.p.* gefressen.
frieren *prs.* friere, frierst, friert; *pret.* fror; *subj.* fröre; *imp.* frier(e); *p.p.* gefroren.
gären *prs.* gäre, gärst, gärt; *pret.* gor (*bsd. fig.* gärte); *subj.* göre (gärte); *imp.* gäre; *p.p.* gegoren (gegärt).
gebären *prs.* gebäre, gebierst, gebiert; *pret.* gebar; *subj.* gebäre; *imp.* gebier; *p.p.* geboren.
geben *prs.* gebe, gibst, gibt; *pret.* gab; *subj.* gäbe; *imp.* gib; *p.p.* gegeben.
gedeihen *prs.* gedeihe, gedeihst, gedeiht; *pret.* gedieh; *subj.* gediehe; *imp.* gedeih(e); *p.p.* gediehen.

*) ehebrechen: daß sie ehebrechen (ehebrachen), but: er bricht (brach) die Ehe, er hat die Ehe gebrochen.

gehen *prs.* gehe, gehst, geht; *pret.* ging; *subj.* ginge, gingest; *imp.* geh(e); *p.p.* gegangen.

gelingen *prs.* es gelingt; *pret.* es gelang; *subj.* es gelänge; *imp.* geling(e); *p.p.* gelungen.

gelten *prs.* gelte, giltst, gilt; *pret.* galt, galt(e)st; *subj.* gölte (gälte); *imp.* gilt; *p.p.* gegolten.

genesen *prs.* genese, genest, genest; *pret.* genas, genasest; *subj.* genäse; *imp.* genese; *p.p.* genesen.

genießen *prs.* genieße, genießt, genießt; *pret.* genoß, genossest; *subj.* genösse; *imp.* genieß(e); *p.p.* genossen.

geschehen *prs.* es geschieht; *pret.* es geschah; *subj.* es geschähe; *imp.* —; *p.p.* geschehen.

gewinnen *prs.* gewinne, gewinnst, gewinnt; *pret.* gewann, gewannst; *subj.* gewönne (gewänne); *imp.* gewinn(e); *p.p.* gewonnen.

gießen *prs.* gieße, gießt, gießt; *pret.* goß, gossest; *subj.* gösse; *imp.* gieß(e); *p.p.* gegossen.

gleichen *pres.* gleiche, gleichst, gleicht; *pret.* glich, glichst; *subj.* gliche; *imp.* gleich(e); *p.p.* geglichen.

gleiten *prs.* gleite, gleitest, gleitet; *pret.* glitt (*rarely*: gleitete), glitt(e)st; *subj.* glitte, glitt(e)st (*rarely*: gleitetest); *imp.* gleit(e); *p.p.* geglitten (*rarely*: gegleitet).

glimmen *prs.* glimme, glimmst, glimmt; *pret.* glomm (*rarely*: glimmte); *subj.* glömme, glömmest (*rarely*: glimmte, glimmtest); *imp.* glimm(e); *p.p.* geglimmt (*rarely*: geglommen).

graben *prs.* grabe, gräbst, gräbt; *pret.* grub, grubst; *subj.* grübe; *imp.* grab(e); *p.p.* gegraben.

greifen *prs.* greife, greifst, greift; *pret.* griff, griffst; *subj.* griffe; *imp.* greif(e); *p.p.* gegriffen.

haben *prs.* habe, hast, hat; *pret.* hatte; *subj.* hätte; *imp.* hab(e); *p.p.* gehabt.

halten *prs.* halte, hältst, hält; *pret.* hielt, hielt(e)st; *subj.* hielte; *imp.* halt(e); *p.p.* gehalten.

hangen, *now usually* **hängen** *v/i.*: *prs.* hänge, hängst, hängt; *pret.* hing, hingst; *subj.* hinge; *imp.* häng(e); *p.p.* gehangen.

hauen *prs.* haue, haust, haut; *pret.* hieb, hiebst; *subj.* hiebe; *imp.* hau(e); *p.p.* gehauen.

heben *prs.* hebe, hebst, hebt; *pret.* hob, hobst; *subj.* höbe; *imp.* heb(e); *p.p.* gehoben.

heißen *prs.* heiße, heißt, heißt; *pret.* hieß, hießest; *subj.* hieße; *imp.* heiß(e); *p.p.* geheißen.

helfen *prs.* helfe, hilfst, hilft; *pret.* half, halfst; *subj.* hülfe (hälfe); *imp.* hilf; *p.p.* geholfen.

kennen *prs.* kenne, kennst, kennt; *pret.* kannte; *subj.* kennte; *imp.* kenne; *p.p.* gekannt.

klimmen *prs.* klimme, klimmst, klimmt; *pret.* klomm (klimmte), klommst (klimmtest); *subj.* klömme (klimmte); *imp.* klimm(e); *p.p.* geklommen (geklimmt).

klingen *prs.* klinge, klingst, klingt; *pret.* klang, klangst; *subj.* klänge; *imp.* kling(e); *p.p.* geklungen.

kneifen *prs.* kneife, kneifst, kneift; *pret.* kniff, kniffst; *subj.* kniffe; *imp.* kneif(e); *p.p.* gekniffen.

kommen *prs.* komme, kommst, kommt; *pret.* kam; *subj.* käme; *imp.* komm(e); *p.p.* gekommen.

können *prs.* kann, kannst, kann; *wir* können etc.; *pret.* konnte; *subj.* könnte; *imp.* —; *p.p.* gekonnt (*auxiliary verb*: können).

kriechen *prs.* krieche, kriechst, kriecht; *pret.* kroch; *subj.* kröche; *imp.* kriech(e); *p.p.* gekrochen.

laden *prs.* lade, lädst (F *fig.* ladest), lädt (F *fig.* ladet); *pret.* lud, lud(e)st; *subj.* lüde; *imp.* lad(e); *p.p.* geladen.

lassen *prs.* lasse, läßt, läßt; *pret.* ließ, ließest; *subj.* ließe; *imp.* laß; *p.p.* gelassen (*auxiliary verb*: lassen).

laufen *prs.* laufe, läufst, läuft; *pret.* lief, liefst; *subj.* liefe; *imp.* lauf(e); *p.p.* gelaufen.

leiden *prs.* leide, leidest, leidet; *pret.* litt, litt(e)st; *subj.* litte; *imp.* leid(e); *p.p.* gelitten.

leihen *prs.* leihe, leihst, leiht; *pret.* lieh, liest; *subj.* liehe; *imp.* leih(e); *p.p.* geliehen.

lesen *prs.* lese, liest, liest; *pret.* las, lasest; *subj.* läse; *imp.* lies; *p.p.* gelesen.

liegen *prs.* liege, liegst, liegt; *pret.* lag; *subj.* läge; *imp.* lieg(e); *p.p.* gelegen.

lügen *prs.* lüge, lügst, lügt; *pret.* log, logst; *subj.* löge; *imp.* lüg(e); *p.p.* gelogen.
meiden *prs.* meide, meidest, meidet; *pret.* mied, mied(e)st; *subj.* miede; *imp.* meid(e); *p.p.* gemieden.
melken *prs.* melke, melkst (milkst), melkt (milkt); *pret.* melkte (molk); *subj.* mölke; *imp.* melk(e); *p.p.* gemolken (gemelkt).
messen *prs.* messe, mißt, mißt, *pret.* maß, maßest; *subj.* mäße; *imp.* miß; *p.p.* gemessen.
mißlingen *prs.* es mißlingt; *pret.* es mißlang; *subj.* es mißlänge; *imp.* —; *p.p.* mißlungen.
mögen *prs.* mag, magst, mag; *wir* mögen etc.; *pret.* mochte; *subj.* möchte; *imp.* —; *p.p.* gemocht (*auxiliary verb*: mögen).
müssen *prs.* muß, mußt, muß; *pl.* müssen, müßt, müssen; *pret.* mußte; *subj.* müßte; *imp.* —; *p.p.* gemußt (*auxiliary verb*: müssen).
nehmen *prs.* nehme, nimmst, nimmt; *pret.* nahm, nahmst; *subj.* nähme; *imp.* nimm; *p.p.* genommen.
nennen *prs.* nenne, nennst, nennt; *pret.* nannte; *subj.* nennte; *imp.* nenn(e); *p.p.* genannt.
pfeifen *prs.* pfeife, pfeifst, pfeift; *pret.* pfiff, pfiffst; *subj.* pfiffe; *imp.* pfeif(e); *p.p.* gepfiffen.
pflegen *prs.* pflege, pflegst, pflegt; *pret.* pflegte (*fig. rarely*: pflog, pflog[e]st); *subj.* pflegte (*fig. rarely*: pflöge); *imp.* pfleg(e); *p.p.* gepflegt (*fig. rarely*: gepflogen).
preisen *prs.* preise, preist, preist; *pret.* pries, priesest; *subj.* priese; *imp.* preis(e); *p.p.* gepriesen.
quellen (*v/i.*) *prs.* quelle, quillst, quillt; *pret.* quoll; *subj.* quölle; *imp.* quill; *p.p.* gequollen.
raten *prs.* rate, rätst, rät; *pret.* riet, riet(e)st; *subj.* riete; *imp.* rat(e); *p.p.* geraten.
reiben *prs.* reibe, reibst, reibt; *pret.* rieb, riebst; *subj.* riebe; *imp.* reib(e); *p.p.* gerieben.
reißen *prs.* reiße, reißt, reißt; *pret.* riß, rissest; *subj.* risse; *imp.* reiß(e); *p.p.* gerissen.
reiten *prs.* reite, reit(e)st, reitet; *pret.* ritt, ritt(e)st; *subj.* ritte; *imp.* reit(e); *p.p.* geritten.
rennen *prs.* renne, rennst, rennt; *pret.* rannte; *subj.* rennte; *imp.* renn(e); *p.p.* gerannt.
riechen *prs.* rieche, riechst, riecht; *pret.* roch; *subj.* röche; *imp.* riech(e); *p.p.* gerochen.
ringen *prs.* ringe, ringst, ringt; *pret.* rang; *subj.* ränge; *imp.* ring(e); *p.p.* gerungen.
rinnen *prs.* rinne, rinnst, rinnt; *pret.* rann, rannst; *subj.* ränne; *imp.* rinn(e); *p.p.* geronnen.
rufen *prs.* rufe, rufst, ruft; *pret.* rief, riefst; *subj.* riefe; *imp.* ruf(e); *p.p.* gerufen.
saufen *prs.* saufe, säufst, säuft; *pret.* soff, soffst; *subj.* söffe; *imp.* sauf(e); *p.p.* gesoffen.
saugen *prs.* sauge, saugst, saugt; *pret.* sog (saugte); *subj.* söge; *imp.* saug(e); *p.p.* gesogen (gesaugt).
schaffen (*schöpferisch hervorbringen*) *prs.* schaffe, schaffst, schafft; *pret.* schuf, schufst; *subj.* schüfe; *imp.* schaff(e); *p.p.* geschaffen.
schallen *prs.* schalle, schallst, schallt; *pret.* schallte (scholl); *subj.* schölle; *imp.* schall(e); *p.p.* geschallt.
scheiden *prs.* scheide, scheidest, scheidet; *pret.* schied, schied(e)st; *subj.* schiede; *imp.* scheid(e); *p.p.* geschieden.
scheinen *prs.* scheine, scheinst, scheint; *pret.* schien, schienst; *subj.* schiene; *imp.* schein(e); *p.p.* geschienen.
scheißen V *prs.* scheiße, scheißt, scheißt; *pret.* schiß; *subj.* schisse; *imp.* scheiß(e); *p.p.* geschissen.
schelten *prs.* schelte, schiltst, schilt; *pret.* schalt, schalt(e)st; *subj.* schölte; *imp.* schilt; *p.p.* gescholten.
scheren (*abschneiden*) *prs.* schere, scherst, schert; *pret.* schor (*refl.* scherte), schor(e)st (*refl.* schertest); *subj.* schöre (*refl.* scherte); *imp.* scher(e); *p.p.* geschoren (*refl.* geschert).
schieben *prs.* schiebe, schiebst, schiebt; *pret.* schob, schobst; *subj.* schöbe; *imp.* schieb(e); *p.p.* geschoben.
schießen *prs.* schieße, schießt, schießt; *pret.* schoß, schossest; *subj.* schösse; *imp.* schieß(e); *p.p.* geschossen.

schinden *prs.* schinde, schindest, schindet; *pret.* schund, schund(e)st; *subj.* schünde; *imp.* schind(e); *p.p.* geschunden.

schlafen *prs.* schlafe, schläfst, schläft; *pret.* schlief, schliefst; *subj.* schliefe; *imp.* schlaf(e); *p.p.* geschlafen.

schlagen *prs.* schlage, schlägst, schlägt; *pret.* schlug, schlugst; *subj.* schlüge; *imp.* schlag(e); *p.p.* geschlagen.

schleichen *prs.* schleiche, schleichst, schleicht; *pret.* schlich, schlichst; *subj.* schliche; *imp.* schleich(e); *p.p.* geschlichen.

schleifen (*schärfen*; *glätten*) *prs.* schleife, schleifst, schleift; *pret.* schliff, schliffst; *subj.* schliffe; *imp.* schleif(e); *p.p.* geschliffen.

schleißen *prs.* schleiße, schleißt, schleißt; *pret.* schliß (schleißte), schlissest (schleißtest); *subj.* schlisse; *imp.* schleiß(e); *p.p.* geschlissen (geschleißt).

schließen *prs.* schließe, schließt (schließest), schließt; *pret.* schloß, schlossest; *subj.* schlösse; *imp.* schließ(e); *p.p.* geschlossen.

schlingen *prs.* schlinge, schlingst, schlingt; *pret.* schlang, schlangst; *subj.* schlänge; *imp.* schling(e); *p.p.* geschlungen.

schmeißen F *prs.* schmeiße, schmeißt, schmeißt; *pret.* schmiß, schmissest; *subj.* schmisse; *imp.* schmeiß(e); *p.p.* geschmissen.

schmelzen *prs.* schmelze, schmilzt, schmilzt; *pret.* schmolz, schmolzest; *subj.* schmölze; *imp.* schmilz; *p.p.* geschmolzen.

schnauben *prs.* schnaube, schnaubst, schnaubt; *pret.* schnaubte (*älter*: schnob); *subj.* schnaubte (*älter*: schnöbe); *imp.* schnaub(e); *p.p.* geschnaubt (*älter*: geschnoben).

schneiden *prs.* schneide, schneidest, schneidet; *pret.* schnitt, schnitt(e)st; *subj.* schnitte; *imp.* schneid(e); *p.p.* geschnitten.

schrecken (*v/i.* = er~) *prs.* schrecke, schrickst, schrickt; *pret.* schrak, schrakst; *subj.* schräke; *imp.* schrick; *p.p.* erschrocken.

schreiben *prs.* schreibe, schreibst, schreibt; *pret.* schrieb, schriebst; *subj.* schriebe; *imp.* schreib(e); *p.p.* geschrieben.

schreien *prs.* schreie, schreist, schreit; *pret.* schrie; *subj.* schriee; *imp.* schrei(e); *p.p.* geschrie(e)n.

schreiten *prs.* schreite, schreitest, schreitet; *pret.* schritt, schritt(e)st; *subj.* schritte; *imp.* schreit(e); *p.p.* geschritten.

schweigen *prs.* schweige, schweigst, schweigt; *pret.* schwieg, schwiegst; *subj.* schwiege; *imp.* schweig(e); *p.p.* geschwiegen.

schwellen (*v/i.*) *prs.* schwelle, schwillst, schwillt; *pret.* schwoll, schwollst; *subj.* schwölle, schwöllest; *imp.* schwill; *p.p.* geschwollen.

schwimmen *prs.* schwimme, schwimmst, schwimmt; *pret.* schwamm, schwammst; *subj.* schwömme (schwämme); *imp.* schwimm(e); *p.p.* geschwommen.

schwinden *prs.* schwinde, schwindest, schwindet; *pret.* schwand, schwand(e)st; *subj.* schwände; *imp.* schwind(e); *p.p.* geschwunden.

schwingen *prs.* schwinge, schwingst, schwingt; *pret.* schwang, schwangst; *subj.* schwänge; *imp.* schwing(e); *p.p.* geschwungen.

schwören *prs.* schwöre, schwörst, schwört; *pret.* schwor (schwur), schwor(e)st (schwur[e]st); *subj.* schwüre; *imp.* schwör(e); *p.p.* geschworen.

sehen *prs.* sehe, siehst, sieht; *pret.* sah; *subj.* sähe; *imp.* sieh(e); *p.p.* gesehen.

sein *prs.* bin, bist, ist; sind, seid, sind; *subj. prs.* sei, sei(e)st, sei; seien, seiet, seien; *pret.* war, warst, war; waren; *subj. pret.* wäre; *imp.* sei; seid; *p.p.* gewesen.

senden *prs.* sende, sendest, sendet; *pret.* sandte (*bsd. Radio*: sendete); *subj.* sendete; *imp.* send(e); *p.p.* gesandt (*bsd. Radio*: gesendet).

sieden *prs.* siede, siedest, siedet; *pret.* sott (siedete), sottest; *subj.* sötte (siedete); *imp.* sied(e); *p.p.* gesotten (gesiedet).

singen *prs.* singe, singst, singt; *pret.* sang, sangst; *subj.* sänge; *imp.* sing(e); *p.p.* gesungen.

sinken *prs.* sinke, sinkst, sinkt; *pret.* sank, sankst; *subj.* sänke; *imp.* sink(e); *p.p.* gesunken.

sinnen *prs.* sinne, sinnst, sinnt;

pret. sann, sannst; *subj.* sänne; *imp.* sinn(e); *p.p.* gesonnen.
sitzen *prs.* sitze, sitzt, sitzt; *pret.* saß, saßest; *subj.* säße; *imp.* sitz(e); *p.p.* gesessen.
sollen *prs.* soll, sollst, soll; *pret.* sollte; *subj.* sollte; *imp.* —; *p.p.* gesollt (*auxiliary verb*: sollen).
speien *prs.* speie, speist, speit; *pret.* spie; *subj.* spiee; *imp.* spei(e); *p.p.* gespie(e)n.
spinnen *prs.* spinne, spinnst, spinnt; *pret.* spann, spannst; *subj.* spönne (spänne); *imp.* spinn(e); *p.p.* gesponnen.
sprechen *prs.* spreche, sprichst, spricht; *pret.* sprach, sprachst; *subj.* spräche; *imp.* sprich; *p.p.* gesprochen.
sprießen *prs.* sprieße, sprießt, sprießt; *pret.* sproß, sprossest; *subj.* sprösse; *imp.* sprieß(e); *p.p.* gesprossen.
springen *prs.* springe, springst, springt; *pret.* sprang, sprangst; *subj.* spränge; *imp.* spring(e); *p.p.* gesprungen.
stechen *prs.* steche, stichst, sticht; *pret.* stach, stachst; *subj.* stäche; *imp.* stich; *p.p.* gestochen.
stecken (*v/i.*) *prs.* stecke, steckst, steckt; *pret.* stak (steckte); *subj.* stäke (steckte); *imp.* steck(e); *p.p.* gesteckt.
stehen *prs.* stehe, stehst, steht; *pret.* stand, standst; *subj.* stände (stünde); *imp.* steh(e); *p.p.* gestanden.
stehlen *prs.* stehle, stiehlst, stiehlt; *pret.* stahl, stahlst; *subj.* stähle; *imp.* stiehl; *p.p.* gestohlen.
steigen *prs.* steige, steigst, steigt; *pret.* stieg, stiegst; *subj.* stiege; *imp.* steig(e); *p.p.* gestiegen.
sterben *prs.* sterbe, stirbst, stirbt; *pret.* starb; *subj.* stürbe; *imp.* stirb; *p.p.* gestorben.
stieben *prs.* stiebe, stiebst, stiebt; *pret.* stob (stiebte), stobst; *subj.* stöbe (*rarely*: stiebte); *imp.* stieb(e); *p.p.* gestoben (gestiebt).
stinken *prs.* stinke, stinkst, stinkt; *pret.* stank, stankst; *subj.* stänke; *imp.* stink(e); *p.p.* gestunken.
stoßen *prs.* stoße, stößt, stößt; *pret.* stieß, stießest; *subj.* stieße; *imp.* stoß(e); *p.p.* gestoßen.
streichen *prs.* streiche, streichst, streicht; *pret.* strich, strichst; *subj.* striche; *imp.* streich(e); *p.p.* gestrichen.
streiten *prs.* streite, streitest, streitet; *pret.* stritt, stritt(e)st; *subj.* stritte; *imp.* streit(e); *p.p.* gestritten.
tragen *prs.* trage, trägst, trägt; *pret.* trug; *subj.* trüge; *imp.* trag(e); *p.p.* getragen.
treffen *prs.* treffe, triffst, trifft; *pret.* traf, trafst; *subj.* träfe; *imp.* triff; *p.p.* getroffen.
treiben *prs.* treibe, treibst, treibt; *pret.* trieb; *subj.* triebe; *imp.* treib(e); *p.p.* getrieben.
treten *prs.* trete, trittst, tritt; *pret.* trat, trat(e)st; *subj.* träte; *imp.* tritt; *p.p.* getreten.
triefen *prs.* triefe, triefst, trieft; *pret.* triefte (troff), trieftest (troffst); *subj.* triefte (tröffe) *imp.* trief(e); *p.p.* getrieft.
trinken *prs.* trinke, trinkst, trinkt; *pret.* trank, trankst; *subj.* tränke; *imp.* trink(e); *p.p.* getrunken.
trügen *prs.* trüge, trügst, trügt; *pret.* trog, trogst; *subj.* tröge; *imp.* trüg(e); *p.p.* getrogen.
tun *prs.* tue, tust, tut; *wir* tun etc.; *pret.* tat, tat(e)st; *subj.* täte; *imp.* tu(e); *p.p.* getan.
verderben *prs.* verderbe, verdirbst, verdirbt; *pret.* verdarb; *subj.* verdürbe; *imp.* verdirb; *p.p.* verdorben.
verdrießen *prs.* verdrieße, verdrießt, verdrießt; *pret.* verdroß, verdrossest; *subj.* verdrösse; *imp.* verdrieß(e); *p.p.* verdrossen.
vergessen *prs.* vergesse, vergißt, vergißt; *pret.* vergaß, vergaßest; *subj.* vergäße; *imp.* vergiß; *p.p.* vergessen.
verlieren *prs.* verliere, verlierst, verliert; *pret.* verlor; *subj.* verlöre; *imp.* verlier(e); *p.p.* verloren.
wachsen *prs.* wachse, wächst, wächst; *pret.* wuchs, wuchsest; *subj.* wüchse; *imp.* wachs(e); *p.p.* gewachsen.
wägen (er~) *prs.* wäge, wägst, wägt; *pret.* wog; *subj.* wöge; *imp.* wäg(e); *p.p.* gewogen.
waschen *prs.* wasche, wäschst, wäscht; *pret.* wusch, wuschest; *subj.* wüsche; *imp.* wasch(e); *p.p.* gewaschen.

weben *prs.* webe, webst, webt; *pret.* webte (wob), webtest (wobst); *subj.* webte (wöbe); *imp.* web(e); *p.p.* gewebt (gewoben).
weichen *prs.* weiche, weichst, weicht; *pret.* wich, wichst; *subj.* wiche; *imp.* weich(e); *p.p.* gewichen.
weisen *prs.* weise, weist, weist; *pret.* wies, wiesest; *subj.* wiese; *imp.* weis(e); *p.p.* gewiesen.
wenden *prs.* wende, wendest, wendet; *pret.* wandte (wendete); *subj.* wendete; *imp.* wende; *p.p.* gewandt (gewendet).
werben *prs.* werbe, wirbst, wirbt; *pret.* warb; *subj.* würbe; *imp.* wirb; *p.p.* geworben.
werden *prs.* werde, wirst, wird; *pret.* wurde (*poet.* ward); *subj.* würde; *imp.* werde; *p.p.* geworden (worden)*).
werfen *prs.* werfe, wirfst, wirft; *pret.* warf, warfst; *subj.* würfe; *imp.* wirf; *p.p.* geworfen.
wiegen *prs.* wiege, wiegst, wiegt; *pret.* wog; *subj.* wöge; *imp.* wieg(e); *p.p.* gewogen.
winden *prs.* winde, windest, windet; *pret.* wand, wandest; *subj.* wände; *imp.* winde; *p.p.* gewunden.
wissen *prs.* weiß, weißt, weiß; *pl.* wissen, wißt, wissen; *pret.* wußte; *subj.* wüßte; *imp.* wisse; *p.p.* gewußt.
wollen *prs.* will, willst, will; *pl.* wollen, wollt, wollen; *pret.* wollte; *subj.* wollte; *imp.* wolle; *p.p.* gewollt (*auxiliary verb*: wollen).
wringen *s.* ringen.
zeihen *prs.* zeihe, zeihst, zeiht; *pret.* zieh, ziehst; *subj.* ziehe; *imp.* zeih(e); *p.p.* geziehen.
ziehen *prs.* ziehe, ziehst, zieht; *pret.* zog, zogst; *subj.* zöge; *imp.* zieh(e); *p.p.* gezogen.
zwingen *prs.* zwinge, zwingst, zwingt; *pret.* zwang, zwangst; *subj.* zwänge; *imp.* zwing(e); *p.p.* gezwungen.

*) only in connection with the *p.p.* of other verbs, e.g. er ist gesehen worden.

Phonetic Alphabets
Buchstabieralphabete

	German	*British English*	*American English*	*International*	*ICAO*
A	Anton	Andrew	Abel	Amsterdam	Alfa
Ä	Ärger	—	—	—	—
B	Berta	Benjamin	Baker	Baltimore	Bravo
C	Cäsar	Charlie	Charlie	Casablanca	Charlie
CH	Charlotte	—	—	—	—
D	Dora	David	Dog	Danemark	Delta
E	Emil	Edward	Easy	Edison	Echo
F	Friedrich	Frederick	Fox	Florida	Foxtrot
G	Gustav	George	George	Gallipoli	Golf
H	Heinrich	Harry	How	Havana	Hotel
I	Ida	Isaac	Item	Italia	India
J	Julius	Jack	Jig	Jérusalem	Juliett
K	Kaufmann	King	King	Kilogramme	Kilo
L	Ludwig	Lucy	Love	Liverpool	Lima
M	Martha	Mary	Mike	Madagaskar	Mike
N	Nordpol	Nellie	Nan	New York	November
O	Otto	Oliver	Oboe	Oslo	Oscar
Ö	Ökonom	—	—	—	—
P	Paula	Peter	Peter	Paris	Papa
Q	Quelle	Queenie	Queen	Québec	Quebec
R	Richard	Robert	Roger	Roma	Romeo
S	Samuel	Sugar	Sugar	Santiago	Sierra
Sch	Schule	—	—	—	—
T	Theodor	Tommy	Tare	Tripoli	Tango
U	Ulrich	Uncle	Uncle	Upsala	Uniform
Ü	Übermut	—	—	—	—
V	Viktor	Victor	Victor	Valencia	Victor
W	Wilhelm	William	William	Washington	Whiskey
X	Xanthippe	Xmas	X	Xanthippe	X-Ray
Y	Ypsilon	Yellow	Yoke	Yokohama	Yankee
Z	Zacharias	Zebra	Zebra	Zürich	Zulu